D0190587

Signature 800

Delivering new technology

Floating above the Signature 800's twin driver bass cabinet on their own IsoPath® gel mountings are the mid-range unit and tweeter. The tweeter's tapered tube, packed with absorbent wadding, soaks up rearward energy while refinements to the voice coil and magnet centre pole push the response to new heights, making the most of new formats such as DVD-A and SACD.

Within the rigid moulded Marlan® enclosure of the mid-range unit beats the heart of the Signature 800: a spherical chamber that works in complete harmony with an integrated rear tube, to disperse unwanted resonances and deliver its wide bandwidth with the minimum of effort and interference.

The Signature 800 mid-range driver features B&W's FST™ (Fixed Suspension Transducer) technology. Surround resonances are eliminated and bending waves in the cone are effectively absorbed by the ring beneath the cone's outer edge. This further enhances the driver's delivery of a crisp sound 'image' through the quietest passages and the greatest crescendos.

Twin 10″ Kevlar®/paper bass drivers achieve the same output level as a single professional 15″ unit. Their physical spacing, however, reduces the excitation of any single room resonance which might otherwise ruin the 'slam' generated by the massive magnet/voice coil system.

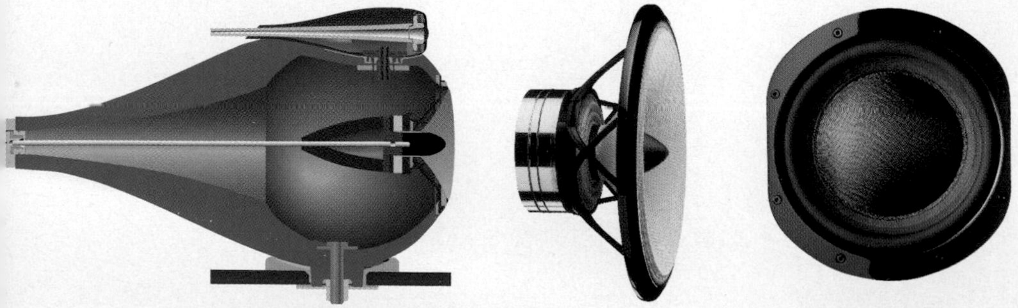

The enigma at the heart of every B&W speaker is its suite of capacitors. In the Signature 800 we opted for high quality polypropylene capacitors which offer an open sound rich in detail. We also use massive inductors in the crossover filter and seriously heavy gauge cable which allows the current to flow freely in time with the music.

Signature 800 bass cabinet boasts B&W's patented system of Matrix™ internal bracing.

Resembling a ship's hull, the strategically placed cross members stiffen the already rigid 35mm thick walls and enable the Signature 800 to go as low as our best studio equipment without the concomitant resonances that would affect the typical domestic speaker.

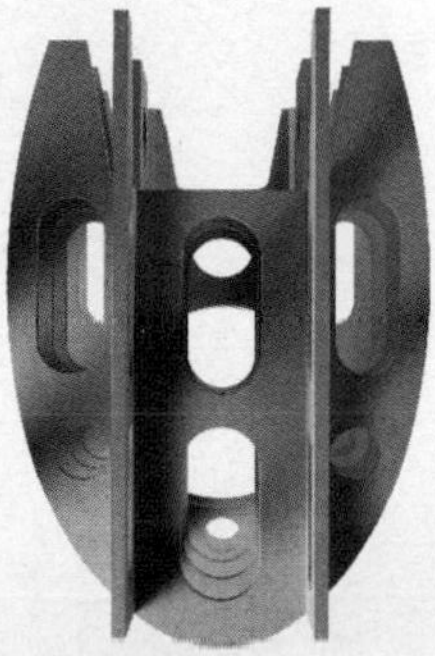

B&W

Signature 800

B&W

Gramophone

Classical GOOD CD GUIDE

2002

Gramophone's *Classical Good CD Guide* is designed to eliminate the confusion of record-buying and unite you, quickly and painlessly, with the best in classical music on disc. Drawing on the expertise of an unequalled panel of critics and on the magazine itself, the *Classical Good CD Guide* will, we are sure, become a trusted friend as you expand your collection of CDs.

Once again we are delighted to be publishing the *Classical Good CD Guide* in association with a fellow British company, B&W Loudspeakers, whose dedication to producing fine audio equipment closely matches the ideals of *Gramophone* itself: the nourishment of expertise based on experience, consistency and an awareness of the needs of the consumer.

Published under licence by Haymarket Magazines Ltd

Gramophone Publications Limited
38-42 Hampton Road
Teddington
Middlesex TW11 0JE
Great Britain

Editor **Kate Bettley**

Sub-editors **Peter McSean**
Daniel Jaffé

Editorial Assistant **Hester Lean**

Production Manager **Darren Jones**

Trade Marketing Manager **Tim Grocutt**

Publisher **Rupert Heseltine**

ISBN 0-860-24987-5

Recording companies reserve the right to withdraw any Compact Disc without giving prior notice, and although every effort is made to obtain the latest information for inclusion in this book, no guarantee can be given that all the discs listed are immediately available. Any difficulties should be referred to the issuing company concerned. When ordering, purchasers are advised to quote all the relevant information in addition to the disc numbers. The publishers cannot accept responsibility for the consequences of any error.

Acknowledgment

Material from GROVE reproduced from The Concise Grove Dictionary of Music under license from Macmillian Publishers Ltd. London, England

Sales and distribution

North America

Music Sales Corporation
257 Park Avenue South
New York, NY 10010 USA
Telephone (212) 254 2100
Fax (212) 254 2013

UK and Rest of World

Gramophone Publications Limited
38-42 Hampton Road
Teddington
Middlesex TW 11 0JE
Great Britain
[illegible] 44 (0)20 8267 5140
Fax +44 (0)20 8267 5866
e-mail gramophonesales@haynet.com

Printed in England by William Clowes Limited,
Beccles, Suffolk NR34 9QE

Contributors

Andrew Achenbach
Nicholas Anderson
Mary Berry
Alan Blyth
Joan Chissell
Robert Cowan
Peter Dickinson
Duncan Druce
John Duarte
Adrian Edwards
Richard T Fairman
David Fallows
David J Fanning
Iain Fenlon
Hilary Finch
Fabrice Fitch
Jonathan Freeman-Attwood
Edward Greenfield
David S Gutman
Martyn Harry
Stephen Johnson
Lindsay Kemp
Tess Knighton
Andrew Lamb
Robert Layton
Ivan March
Ivan Moody
Bryce Morrison
Patrick O'Connor
Michael Oliver
Richard Osborne
Tim Parry
Stephen Plaistow
Nicholas Rast
Guy Rickards
Marc Rochester
Julie-Anne Sadie
Stanley Sadie
Lionel Salter
Alan Sanders
Edward Seckerson
Robert Seeley
John Steane
Michael Stewart
Jonathan Swain
John Warrack
Richard Whitehouse
Arnold Whittall
Richard Wigmore

Contents

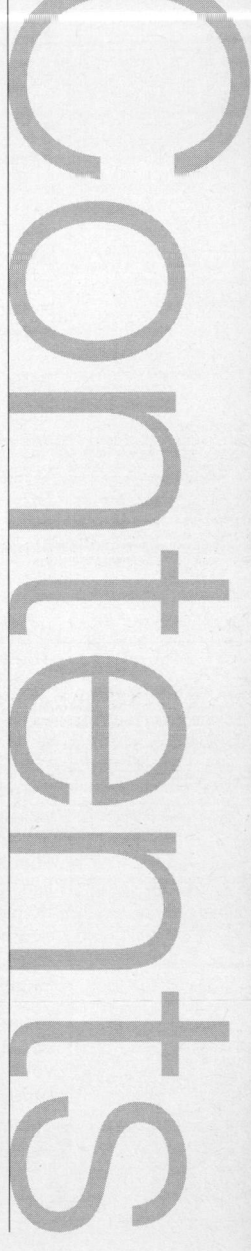

GROVE

Paul Cutts, Gramophone Online Editor, welcomes **www.grovemusic.com**, the ambitious internet arm of the
New Grove Dictionary of Music and Musicians

The world has changed beyond recognition since the first volume of Sir George Grove's authoritative, eponymous music dictionary appeared in 1879. In little more than a century, classical music has moved from late romanticism to new minimalism, from the confines of the concert hall to the anarchic electronic annals of the worldwide web

With its new edition, published last year, *Grove* has grasped the internettle and made all 29 volumes of *The New Grove Dictionary of Music and Musicians, 2nd edition* available online at **www.grovemusic.com**.

What is so impressive about grovemusic.com – relative of the *Grove Concise Dictionary of Music*, from which the *Good CD Guide* has drawn its composer biographies – is not just the depth of its content but its ease of navigation. Simple, uncluttered pages may appear devoid of visual interest but therein lies their strength: with few large picture files to deal with, download times are rapid.

If you want or need to consult a visual image, then you can click on the word 'Illustrations' on the navigation bar from within an article. If there's a picture available, the word 'Illustrations' will appear in white. If not, then it's greyed out and you can't click through. Alternatively, you can visit the Links section of the site and select 'Images' from the drop-down menu, which calls up 500 items from other websites relating to music and musicians.

Search mechanisms on grovemusic.com are straightforward to the user but clearly generated by some sophisticated back-end technology. Sensibly, *Grove* has broken down its searching procedure into three key components: 'Search' (divided into six sub-categories including 'full text', 'biographies' and 'work-lists'); 'Browse' (by articles A-Z, abbreviations, contributors, and index) and 'Explore' to find what you're seeking. A conceptual search on 'Bells', for example, throws up 42 matches – leading with 'bell' (the instrument) and working through Respighi's opera *La campana sommersa* (*The sunken bell*) and English publishing house Stainer and Bell to 'rock gong'.

It's in its speed and interconnectivity that electronic *Grove* has its major advantage over previous editions. Just key in one word from the comfort of your desktop and let cyberspace do the hard work for you. And with tiered subscription rates, everyone can enjoy some or all of **www.grovemusic.com**.

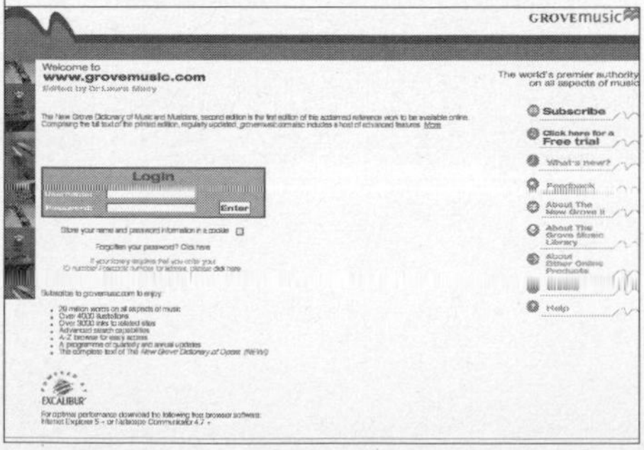

About Gramophone

Gramophone was established in 1923, the idea of novelist and writer Compton Mackenzie and broadcaster Christopher Stone. In the decades since its foundation it has become the world's leading authority on classical recorded music. The finest writers have contributed to the magazine, and while we have spawned numerous imitators none have overthrown *Gramophone*'s trusted position as the pre-eminent guide to classical music on disc.

Gramophone has grown up alongside the record industry. It witnessed the birth of electrical recording, the LP, stereo, digital recording, the CD and DVD. In the 19 years since the release of the first CD, the range of music available has expanded exponentially. Never has there been such baffling choice at such a variety of prices. Hence the *Gramophone Good CD Guide 2002*, which unites the classical music enthusiast with performances of the finest music in the best interpretations.

We have been as diverse in our choice of repertoire as possible – if there are omissions, the chances are there is no entirely recommendable recording of that work available. One guide to our selection of the most outstanding recordings has been the annual *Gramophone* Awards, a celebration of the previous year's finest recordings. Each spring we draw up a vast list of the best recordings in a range of categories which include Orchestral, Concerto, Opera, Vocal, Chamber and Instrumental. After two rounds of voting – the second of which involves all 45 regular contributors to the magazine voting on the final six CDs per category – the Award winners emerge, and one is named Record of the Year (see the previous winners overleaf). All these recordings are flagged in the *Guide*.

The *Classical Good CD Guide* embraces a wealth of great music and great music-making. We trust that our eminent reviewers will lead you to many hours of outstanding musical enjoyment.

Records of the Year

1977 (Opera)
Janáček
*Kát'a Kabanová**
Vienna State Opera Chorus; Vienna Philharmonic Orchestra / Sir Charles Mackerras
Decca ② 421 852-2DH2 (10/89)

1978 (Opera)
Puccini
La Fanciulla del West
Soloists; Royal Opera House Chorus and Orchestra, Covent Garden / Zubin Mehta
DG ② 419 640-2GH2 (11/87)

1979 (Chamber)
Haydn
Piano Trios*
Beaux Arts Trio
Philips ⑨ 432 061-2PM9 (7/92)

1980 (Opera)
Janáček
From the House of the Dead
Soloists; Vienna State Opera Chorus; Vienna Philharmonic Orchestra / Sir Charles Mackerras
Decca ② 430 375-2DH2 (10/91)

1981 (Opera)
Wagner
Parsifal
Soloists; Chorus of the Deutsche Opera Berlin; Berlin Philharmonic Orchestra / Herbert von Karajan
DG ④ 413 347-2GH4 (10/84)

1982-83 (Concerto)
Tippett
Triple Concerto
György Pauk; Nobuko Imai; Ralph Kirshbaum; London Symphony Orchestra / Sir Colin Davis
Philips 420 781-2PH (3/89)

1984 (Orchestral)
Mahler
Symphony No 9
Berlin Philharmonic Orchestra / Herbert von Karajan
DG ② 410 726-2GH2 (7/84)

1985 (Concerto)
Elgar
Violin Concerto
Nigel Kennedy *vn* **London Philharmonic Orchestra / Vernon Handley**
HMV Classics HMV5 72483-2 (12/84)

1986 (Opera)
Rossini
Il viaggio a Reims
Soloists; Prague Philharmonic Chorus; Chamber Orchestra of Europe / Claudio Abbado
DG ② 415 498-2GH2 (1/86)

1987 (Early music)
Josquin Desprez
Masses – *Pange lingua*; *La sol fa re mi**
The Tallis Scholars / Peter Phillips
Gimell CDGIM009 (3/87)

1988 (Orchestral)
Mahler
Symphony No 2, 'Resurrection'
Soloists; City of Birmingham Symphony Orchestra and Chorus / Sir Simon Rattle
EMI ② CDS7 47962-8 (12/87)

1989 (Chamber)
Bartók
String Quartets Nos 1-6
Emerson Quartet
DG ② 423 657-2GH2 (12/88)

1990 (Opera)
Prokofiev
The Love for Three Oranges
Soloists; Chorus and Orchestra of Lyon Opéra / Kent Nagano
Virgin Classics ② VCD7 59566-2 (12/89)

1991 (Choral)
Beethoven
Mass in D, 'Missa solemnis'
Soloists; Monteverdi Choir; English Baroque Soloists / Sir John Eliot Gardiner
Archiv Produktion 429 779-2AH (3/91)

1992 (Orchestral)
Beethoven
Symphonies Nos 1-9
Chamber Orchestra of Europe / Nikolaus Harnoncourt
Teldec ⑤ 2292-46452-2 (11/91)

1993 (Solo vocal)
Grieg
Songs*
Anne Sofie von Otter *mez* **Bengt Forsberg** *pf*
DG Grieg Anniversary Edition 437 521-2GH (6/93)

1994 (Instrumental)
Debussy
*Préludes**
Krystian Zimerman *pf*
DG ② 435 773-2GH2 (3/94)

1995 (Concerto)
Prokofiev Violin Concerto No 1
Shostakovich Violin Concerto No 1
Maxim Vengerov *vn* **London Symphony Orchestra / Mstislav Rostropovich**
Teldec 4509-98143-2 (2/95)

1996 (Concerto)
Sauer and **Scharwenka**
Piano Concertos
Stephen Hough *pf* **City of Birmingham Symphony Orchestra / Lawrence Foster**
Hyperion CDA66790 (11/95)

1997 (Opera)
Puccini
La rondine
Soloists; London Voices; London Symphony Orchestra / Antonio Pappano
EMI ② CDS5 56338-2 (5/97)

1998 (Choral)
Martin
Mass for Double Choir. *Pasacaille*.
Pizzetti *Messa di Requiem. De Profundis*
Westminster Cathedral Choir / James O'Donnell
Hyperion CDA67017 (3/98)

1999 (Opera)
Dvořák
Rusalka
Soloists; Kühn Mixed Choir; Czech Philharmonic Orchestra / Sir Charles Mackerras
Decca ③ 460 568-2DHO3 (11/98)

2000
Mahler (Orchestral)
Symphony No 10 (ed Cooke)
Berlin Philharmonic Orchestra / Sir Simon Rattle
EMI CDC5 56972-2 (5/00)

**denotes a disc listed among the 100 greatest classical recordings of all time – see overleaf*

100 Great Recordings

Bach *Goldberg* Variations
Glenn Gould *pf*
(Sony Classical, r1981)

Bach Cantatas 78 and 106
Felix Prohaska *cond*
(Vanguard, r1954)

Bach Cello Suites
Pablo Casals *vc* (EMI, r1936-39)

Bartók Concerto for Orchestra
Fritz Reiner *cond* (RCA, r1955)

Boulez Répons
Pierre Boulez *cond* (DG, r1996)

Beethoven *Fidelio*
Christa Ludwig *sop* etc
Otto Klemperer *cond* (EMI, r1962)

Beethoven Piano Sonatas
Artur Schnabel *pf* (EMI, r1932-35)

Beethoven Piano Concertos
Nos 1-5 **Wilhelm Kempff** *pf*
Paul van Kempen *cond*
(DG, r1953)

Beethoven
Violin Concerto
Itzhak Perlman *pf* **Carlo Maria Giulini** *cond* (EMI, r1953)

Beethoven Symphony No 3
Otto Klemperer *cond* (EMI, r1954)

Beethoven
Symphonies Nos 5 and 7
Carlos Kleiber *cond*
(DG, r1974, 1976)

Beethoven Symphony No 6
Karl Böhm *cond* (DG, 1971)

Beethoven Symphony No 9
Wilhelm Furtwängler *cond*
(EMI, r1951)

Beethoven String Quartets
Quartetto Italiano
(Philips, 1967-69)

Berlioz *Les Troyens*
Jon Vickers *ten* etc
Colin Davis *cond* (Philips, r1969)

Brahms
Ein deutsches Requiem
Elisabeth Schwarzkopf *sop* etc
Otto Klemperer *cond* (EMI, r1961)

Brahms
Piano Concerto Nos 1 and 2
Emil Gilels *pf*
Eugen Jochum *cond* (DG, r1972)

Brahms Piano Concerto No 1
Clifford Curzon *pf*
George Szell *cond* (Decca, r1955)

Brahms Symphony No 4
Carlos Kleiber *cond* (DG, r1980)

Britten *Peter Grimes*
Peter Pears *ten* etc
Benjamin Britten *cond*
(Decca, r1958)

Britten *War Requiem*
Philip Langridge *ten* etc
Richard Hickox *cond*
(Chandos, r1991)

Bruckner Symphony No 4
Karl Böhm *cond* (Decca, r1973)

Bruckner Symphony No 8
Herbert von Karajan *cond*
(DG, r1988)

Bruckner Masses
Edith Mathis *sop* etc
Eugen Jochum *cond*
(DG, r1962, 1971-72)

Chopin Piano Concerto No 1
Maurizio Pollini *pf*
Paul Kletzki *cond* (EMI, r1960)

Chopin and **Grieg**
Piano Concertos
Dinu Lipatti *pf* **Otto Ackermann, Alceo Galliera** *conds*
(EMI, r1950, 1947)

Chopin
Walzes
Dinu Lipatti *pf*
(EMI, r1947-50)

Debussy Orchestral works
Guido Cantelli *cond*
(Testament, r1954-55)

Debussy and **Ravel**
Orchestral Works
Herbert von Karajan *cond*
(DG, r1964-65)

Debussy Orchestral works
Bernard Haitink *cond*
(Philips, r1957, 1976-77, 79)

Debussy
Pelléas et Mélisande
Irène Joachim *sop* etc **Roger Desormière** *cond* (EMI, r1941)

Debussy *Préludes*
Krystian Zimerman *pf* (DG, r1991)

Delius Orchestral works
Sir Thomas Beecham *cond*
(EMI, r1956-57)

Dvořák Cello Concerto
Mstislav Rostropovich *vc*
Herbert von Karajan *cond*
(DG, r1969)

Dvořák
Symphonies Nos 8 and 9
Rafael Kubelík *cond*
(DG, r1966, 73)

Elgar Cello Concerto
Jacqueline Du Pré *vc*
Sir John Barbirolli *cond*
(EMI, r1965)

Elgar Violin Concerto
Yehudi Menuhin *vn*
Edward Elgar *cond* (EMI, r1932)

Gershwin *Porgy and Bess*
Willard White *bass* etc
Simon Rattle (EMI, r1988)

Grieg Peer Gynt
Sir Thomas Beecham
(DG, r1992)

Grieg Songs
Anne Sofie von Otter *sop*
Bengt Forsberg *pf* (DG, r1992)

Haydn Piano Sonatas
Alfred Brendel *pf*
(Philips, r1979-85)

Haydn Piano Trios
Beaux Arts Trio (Philips, r1970-78)

Hildegard of Bingen
'A Feather on the Breath of God'
Gothic Voices (Hyperion, r1981)

Honegger Symphonies
Herbert von Karajan *cond*
(DG, r1969)

Janáček *Kát'a Kabanová*
Elisabeth Söderström *sop* etc
Charles Mackerras *cond*
(Decca, r1976)

Josquin Desprez Masses
The Tallis Scholars (Gimell, r1986)

Kern *Show Boat*
Frederica von Stade *sop* etc
John McGlinn *cond* (EMI; r1987)

Liszt Piano Concertos
Sviatoslav Richter *pf*
Kyrill Kondrashin *cond*
(Philips, r1961)

Mahler
Das Lied von der Erde
Kathleen Ferrier *contr* **Julius Patzak** *ten* **Bruno Walter** *cond*
(Decca, r1952)

Mahler Symphony No 5
Sir John Barbirolli *cond*
(EMI, r1969)

Mahler Symphony No 6
Herbert von Karajan *cond*
(DG, r1978)

Mahler Symphony No 9
Herbert von Karajan *cond*
(DG, r1982)

Massenet *Werther*
Georges Thill *ten* etc
Elie Cohen *cond* (EMI, r1931)

Mendelssohn
Symphony No 3 etc
Peter Maag *cond* (Decca, r1960)

Mozart Horn Concertos
Dennis Brain *hn* **Herbert von Karajan** *cond* (EMI, r1953)

Mozart Piano Concertos
Murray Perahia *pf/cond*
(Sony Classical, r1975-84)

Mozart String Quintets
Grumiaux Ensemble
(Philips, r1973)

Mozart *Die Zauberflöte*
Tiana Lemnitz *sop* etc
Sir Thomas Beecham *cond*
(Pearl, r1937-38)

Mozart *Don Giovanni*
Joan Sutherland *sop* etc
Carlo Maria Giulini *cond*
(EMI, r1959)

Mozart *Le nozze di Figaro*
Cesare Siepi *bass* etc
Erich Kleiber *cond* (Decca, r1955)

Mussorgsky Songs
Boris Christoff *bass* with various artists (EMI, r1955-57)

Prokofiev
Symphonies Nos 1 and 5
Serge Koussevitzky *cond*
(RCA, r1945-46)

Puccini *La bohème*
Jussi Björling *ten* etc
Sir Thomas Beecham *cond*
(EMI, r1956)

Puccini *Tosca*
Maria Callas *sop* etc **Victor de Sabata** *cond* (EMI, r1953)

Rachmaninov
Piano Concerto No 3
Martha Argerich *pf*
Berlin RSO / Chailly
(Philips, r1982)

Ravel and **Rachmaninov**
Piano Concertos
Arturo Benedetti Michelangeli *pf*
Ettore Gracis *cond* (EMI, r1957)

Ravel
Daphnis et Chloé
Pierre Monteux *cond*
(Decca, r1959)

Rossini
Opera arias
Cecilia Bartoli *sop*
(Decca, r1991)

Schoenberg *Verklärte Nacht*
Herbert von Karajan *cond*
(DG, r1973)

Schubert
Symphonies Nos 3, 5 and 6
Sir Thomas Beecham *cond*
(EMI, r1955-59)

Schubert
String Quartet, D887, 'Death and the Maiden'
Busch Quartet (EMI, r1938)

Schubert *Winterreise*
Dietrich Fischer-Dieskau *bar*
Jörg Demus *pf* (DG, r1965)

Schumann *Fantasie etc*
Sviatoslav Richter *pf*
(EMI, r1961-62)

Shostakovich
String Quartets
Fitzwilliam Quartet
(Decca, r1975-77)

Sibelius
Symphonies Nos 3 and 5
Robert Kajanus *cond*
(Koch, r1932-33)

Sibelius and **Nielsen**
Violin Concertos **Cho-Liang Lin** *vn* **Esa-Pekka Salonen** *cond*
(Sony Classical, r1989)

Smetana *Má vlast*
Václav Talich *cond*
(Supraphon, r1954)

R Strauss Orchestral works
Rudolf Kempe *cond*
(EMI, r1971-74)

R Strauss *Ein Heldenleben. Also sprach Zarathustra*
Fritz Reiner *cond* (RCA, r1954)

R Strauss *Four Last Songs*
Elisabeth Schwarzkopf *sop*
Otto Ackermann *cond* (EMI, r1953)

R Strauss *Salome*
Birgit Nilsson *sop* etc
Sir Georg Solti *cond*
(Decca, r1961)

R Strauss *Der Rosenkavalier*
Elisabeth Schwarzkopf *sop* etc
Herbert von Karajan *cond*
(EMI, r1956)

Stravinsky
Stravinsky Edition
Stravinsky *cond*
(Sony Classical, r1930s-60s)

Tchaikovsky *Francesca da Rimini, Hamlet – excerpt*
Leopold Stokowski *cond*
(dell'Arte, r1958)

Tchaikovsky Symphony No 5
Mariss Jansons *cond*
(Chandos, r1984)

Tchaikovsky
Symphonies Nos 4-6
Evgeny Mravinsky *cond*
(DG, r1960)

Tchaikovsky Symphony No 6
Mikhail Pletnev *cond*
(Virgin Classics, r1991)

Verdi *Aida*
Montserrat Caballé *sop* etc
Riccardo Muti *cond* (EMI, r1974)

Verdi *Otello*
Ramon Vinay *ten* etc
Arturo Toscanini *cond*
(RCA, r1947)

Verdi *Falstaff*
Giuseppe Valdengo *bar* etc
Arturo Toscanini *cond*
(RCA, r1950)

Verdi *Falstaff*
Giuseppe Valdengo *bar* etc
Arturo Toscanini *cond*
(RCA, r1950)

Verdi *La traviata*
Callas *sop* **Chor & Orch La Scala, Milan / Giulini**
(EMI, r1955)

Wagner *Tristan und Isolde*
Kirsten Flagstad *sop* etc
Wilhelm Furtwängler *cond*
(EMI, r1952)

Wagner *Der Ring des Nibelungen* **George London** *bass-bar* **Hans Hotter** *bass-bar* **Régine Crespin** *sop* **Wolfgang Windgassen** *ten* **Birgit Nilsson** *sop* etc **Sir Georg Solti** *cond*
(Decca, r1958-65)

Walton Violin and Viola Concertos **Kennedy** *vn/va* **André Previn** *cond* (EMI, r1987)

Webern Opp 1 and 2
Pierre Boulez *cond*
(Sony Classical, r1969-70)

Martha Argerich *pf*
Début Album (DG, r1960, 71)

David Munrow *var instrs/cond*
The Art of the Netherlands
(EMI, r1975)

Maurizio Pollini *pf*
20th-century piano music
(DG, r1971, 86)

Joan Sutherland *sop*
Art of the Prima Donna
(Decca, r1960)

Suggested Basic Library

Orchestral

Bach Brandenburg Concertos
Bach Concerto for two violins
Bach Orchestral Suites
Barber Adagio for strings
Barber Violin Concerto
Bartók Concerto for Orchestra
Bartók The Miraculous Mandarin
Bartók Violin Concerto No 2
Beethoven Complete symphonies
Beethoven Piano Concertos Nos 4 and 5
Beethoven Violin Concerto
Berg Violin Concerto
Berlioz Symphonie fantastique
Brahms Complete symphonies
Brahms Piano Concerto No 1
Brahms Violin Concerto
Britten Young Person's Guide
Bruch Violin Concerto No 1
Bruckner Symphonies Nos 4 and 9
Chopin Piano Concertos
Copland Appalachian Spring
Copland Fanfare for the Common Man
Corelli 12 Concerti grossi, Op 6
Delibes Coppélia
Debussy Jeux
Debussy La mer
Debussy Prélude à l'après-midi d'un faune
Dvořák Cello Concerto
Dvořák Symphony No 9, New World
Elgar Cello Concerto
Elgar Enigma Variations
Elgar String music
Elgar Symphonies 1-3
Elgar Violin Concerto
Falla Noches en los jardines de España
Gershwin Rhapsody in Blue
Górecki Symphony No 3
Grieg Peer Gynt Suite
Grieg Piano Concerto
Handel Fireworks Music
Handel Water Music
Haydn Cello Concerto in C
Haydn London Symphonies
Haydn Trumpet Concerto
Holst The Planets
Ives Three Places in New England
Mahler Symphonies Nos 5 and 9
Mendelssohn A Midsummer Night's Dream
Mendelssohn Hebrides Overture
Mendelssohn Symphony No 4 , 'Italian'
Mendelssohn Violin Concerto
Messiaen Turangalîla Symphony
Mozart Clarinet Concerto
Mozart Horn Concerto No 4
Mozart Piano Concertos Nos 20-27
Mozart Serenade for 13 Winds
Mozart Symphonies Nos 40 and 41
Mussorgsky Pictures at an Exhibition
Pärt Tabula rasa
Prokofiev Lieutenant Kijé
Prokofiev Peter and the Wolf
Prokofiev Piano Concerto No 3
Prokofiev Romeo and Juliet
Prokofiev Symphony No 1
Prokofiev Symphony No 5
Rachmaninov Paganini Rhapsody
Rachmaninov Piano Concertos Nos 2 and 3
Rachmaninov Symphony No 2
Ravel Boléro
Ravel Daphnis et Chloé
Ravel Piano Concerto in G
Respighi Roman Trilogy
Rimsky-Korsakov Scheherazade
Rodrigo Concierto de Aranjuez
Rossini Overtures
Saint-Saëns Le carnaval des animaux
Saint-Saëns Piano Concerto No 2
Saint-Saëns Symphony No 3
Schoenberg Five Orchestral Pieces, Op 16
Schoenberg Variations for Orchestra, Op 31
Schubert Symphony No 8, Unfinished
Schumann Piano Concerto
Shostakovich Cello Concerto No 1
Shostakovich Piano Concerto No 2
Shostakovich Symphonies Nos 5 and 10
Sibelius Finlandia
Sibelius Symphonies Nos 2 and 5
Sibelius Tapiola
Sibelius Violin Concerto
Smetana Má vlast
Strauss J II Waltzes
Strauss R Alpine Symphony
Strauss R Also sprach Zarathustra
Strauss R Till Eulenspiegel
Stravinsky Agon
Stravinsky Ballets – The Rite of Spring and The Firebird
Tchaikovsky Romeo and Juliet
Tchaikovsky 1812 Overture
Tchaikovsky Ballets – The Nutcracker, Sleeping Beauty and Swan Lake
Tchaikovsky Piano Concerto No 1
Tchaikovsky Symphonies Nos 4-6
Tchaikovsky Violin Concerto
Vaughan Williams Symphony No 2, 'London'
Vaughan Williams Symphony No 5
Vaughan Williams Tallis Fantasia
Vaughan Williams The Lark Ascending
Vivaldi The Four Seasons
Walton Violin and Viola Concertos

Chamber

Bartók String Quartets
Beethoven Piano Trio in B flat, Op 97, 'Archduke'
Beethoven String Quartets [late]
Beethoven Violin Sonatas
Borodin String Quartet No 2
Brahms Clarinet Quintet
Debussy Sonata for Flute, Viola and Harp
Debussy String Quartet
Dvořák String Quartet No 12
Franck Violin Sonata
Haydn String Quartets, Opp 20 and 76
Mendelssohn Octet
Mozart Clarinet Quintet
Mozart String Quartet in C, K465, 'Dissonance'
Mozart String Quintet in G minor, K516
Ravel String Quartet
Reich Different Trains

Schubert Piano Quintet, 'Trout'
Schubert Piano Trios
Schubert Arpeggione Sonata in A minor, D821
Schubert String Quartet No 14
Schubert String Quintet
Shostakovich String Quartet No 8

Instrumental

Bach Cello Suites
Bach Das wohltemperierte Klavier
Bach Goldberg Variations
Bach Solo Violin Sonatas and Partitas
Beethoven Complete piano sonatas
Beethoven Diabelli Variations
Biber Mystery Sonatas
Brahms Variations on a Theme of Paganini
Chopin Nocturnes
Chopin Piano Sonata No 2
Chopin Preludes
Debussy Children's Corner Suite
Debussy Préludes
Grieg Lyric Pieces
Haydn Piano Sonata E flat major, HobXVI/52
Liszt Piano Sonata
Mozart Piano Sonata No 11 in A, K331
Paganini 24 Caprices
Prokofiev Piano Sonata No 7
Ravel Gaspard de la nuit
Satie Piano works
Schubert Impromptus
Schubert Piano Sonata in B flat, D960
Schubert Wandererfantasie
Schumann Carnaval
Schumann Kinderszenen
Schumann Kreiserleriana

Vocal

Allegri Miserere
Bach Cantatas – No 82 'Ich habe genug' and 140 'Wachet auf'
Bach Magnificat
Bach Mass in B minor
Bach St Matthew Passion
Beethoven Missa solemnis
Berlioz Grande messe des morts
Berlioz L'enfance du Christ
Berlioz Les nuits d'été
Bernstein West Side Story
Brahms Ein deutsches Requiem
Britten Serenade
Britten War Requiem
Bruckner Motets
Byrd Masses for 3, 4 and 5 voices
Canteloube Chants d'Auvergne
Duruflé Requiem
Elgar The Dream of Gerontius
Fauré Requiem
Handel Coronation Anthems
Handel Dixit Dominus
Handel Messiah
Haydn Nelson Mass
Haydn The Creation
Howells Hymnus Paradisi
Mahler Das Lied von der Erde
Mahler Kindertotenlieder
Mendelssohn Elijah
Monteverdi 1610 Vespers
Monteverdi Madrigals, Book 8
Mozart Mass in C minor
Mozart Requiem
Orff Carmina burana
Palestrina Missa Papae Marcelli
R Strauss Four Last Songs
Rachmaninov Vespers
Ravel Schéhérazade
Schubert Winterreise
Schumann Dichterliebe
Tallis Spem in alium
Vaughan Williams Serenade to Music
Verdi Requiem
Victoria Requiem
Vivaldi Gloria in D, RV589
Walton Belshazzar's Feast

Opera, Operetta & Stage Works

Bartók Duke Bluebeard's Castle
Beethoven Fidelio
Bellini Norma
Berg Wozzeck
Bizet Carmen
Bizet Les pêcheurs de perles
Britten Peter Grimes
Britten Turn of the Screw
Debussy Pelléas et Mélisande
Gershwin Porgy and Bess
Gluck Orfeo ed Euridice
Handel Alcina
Handel Giulio Cesare
Handel Rinaldo
Janáček The Cunning Little Vixen
Lehár Die lustige Witwe
Leoncavallo Pagliacci
Mascagni Cavalleria rusticana
Monteverdi L'Orfeo
Mozart Die Zauberflöte
Mozart Don Giovanni
Mozart Le nozze di Figaro
Mussorgsky Boris Godunov
Puccini La bohème
Puccini Madama Butterfly
Puccini Tosca
Puccini Turandot
R Strauss Der Rosenkavalier
Rossini Il barbiere di Siviglia
Strauss J II Die Fledermaus
Sullivan The Pirates of Penzance
Tchaikovsky Eugene Onegin
Verdi Aida
Verdi Il trovatore
Verdi La traviata
Verdi Otello
Verdi Rigoletto
Wagner Der Ring des Nibelungen
Wagner Tristan und Isolde
Weber Der Freischütz

PERFORMING AND RECORDING EARLY MUSIC POSES UNIQUE PROBLEMS. **FABRICE FITCH** OUTLINES THE CHALLENGES AND TRACES THE DEVELOPMENT OF WESTERN MUSIC FROM PLAINCHANT TO THE GLORIES OF THE HIGH RENAISSANCE

Music composed before 1600 makes special demands of performer and listener alike. This is because many notions that we take for granted in Western art-music were only established towards the end of this period, or had not yet been fixed by convention. Some of these notions go to the heart of musical performance, of what we mean when we speak of 'a piece of music': the assignment of specific lines to specific instruments; the precise notation of pitches by means of sharps and flats; indications for tempos and tempo relationships; or the use of written and unwritten ornaments. Often, we have lost the inside knowledge (born of practice) that musicians of the period would have taken for granted. These questions therefore devolve to the performer, who must interpret not only the notation, but also the information that gives clues as to possible solutions. So every performance is necessarily conjectural. Of course, what musical notation 'means' is a valid question for any period; but in pre-tonal music it poses itself more starkly, and the diversity of possible answers – or the degree of conjecture informing different interpretations of one and the same piece – is inevitably more startling.

But the challenges facing us when we confront 'early music' do not end with the way the music sounds. The notion of art for art's sake, of absolute music, would probably have seemed quite strange to medieval composers, no matter how experimental their music sometimes appears to us. The perception of composers as individual creative personalities, conscious of their own worth, is difficult to trace until **Guillaume de Machaut**, the first polyphonist to take effective (and successful) steps for the preservation of his work for posterity. Even then, the status of the composer as a skilled craftsman took a long time to take root: although there is ample documentation of patrons' commissions to painters, illuminators or sculptors throughout the medieval period, the first recorded instances of musicians being paid to compose date from the turn of the 16th century. The fact is that music was mostly improvised and rarely written down, while polyphony (that is, composed music involving more than one line simultaneously) was rarer still. Again, in our own time the notion of originality is still central to our ideas about art; but in pre-tonal music, composers often based their works upon pre-existent material, either plainchant or other polyphony. Finally, and perhaps most crucially: performers and scholars are dependent for their interpretations on the pieces and the information that happens to survive; and that must be a tiny fraction of what once existed. Theoretical treatises and letters mention many lost works by the very greatest composers, and countless documents have disappeared which would have given us more precise indications on the manner of their performance. But on the positive side, it only takes the discovery of a new work or a new document – or a fresh look at a well-known one – to reveal unforeseen perspectives, new ways of understanding and performing the music of the past. Many of the recordings in the following pages are the fruit of such discoveries.

Performance in practice

Many questions confront the performer of early repertories, the most basic being the intended performing forces appropriate to a given work. Music carrying a text is obviously meant to be sung, but does not exclude instrumental participation; conversely, the absence of text does not automatically imply the presence of instruments. These were ubiquitous in the medieval and renaissance periods, but most of their music was either improvised or else memorised, and is therefore lost to us. (Another loss concerns the instruments themselves: no original medieval instruments survive, so we rely on copies recreated through descriptions from contemporary documents, illustrations drawn from painting and sculpture, and guesswork.) A distinction was traditionally made between 'high' instruments (typically winds and brass), used in outdoor or ceremonial contexts, and 'low' instruments (plucked or bowed strings and soft winds, such as recorders), used indoors: lutes and plucked keyboards became especially popular in courtly circles when musical proficiency became fashionable. From the late middle ages, instruments were also arranged into 'consorts' or families involving several sizes of the same sort of instrument, or of closely related ones (crumhorns, for example – nowadays the string quartet represents a rare survival of this practice). Although one should be wary of generalisations (since performance traditions undoubtedly varied from place to place, from region to region), it does seem that instrumental families had specific functions and carried distinct associations. Similarly, the mix of voices and instruments, familiar from many recordings of medieval and renaissance music, may not have been as widespread as was once believed.

Even if we assume that a given piece called for exclusively vocal performance, how many singers were involved? Vocal polyphony required specialised singers; until the 15th

Essential listening I

Dufay	Missa San Jacobi etc **The Binchois Consort / Kirkman** Hyperion CDA66997	Ⓕ
Machaut	Messe de Nostre Dame **Oxford Camerata / Summerly** Naxos 8 553833	Ⓢ
Ockeghem	Missa De plus en plus etc **Orlando Consort** Archiv 453 419-2AH	Ⓕ
Perotin	Viderunt omnes etc **Hilliard Ensemble / Hillier** ECM New Series 837 751-2	Ⓕ
Various	'The Marriage of Heaven and Hell' **Gothic Voices / Page** Hyperion CDA66423	Ⓕ
Various	'The Spirits of England and France' Volume 2 **Gothic Voices / Page** Hyperion CDA66773	Ⓕ

century it appears to have been performed by small ensembles, with seldom more than one singer on each line. As regards sacred music, many churches banned the use of instruments within their walls (in some, like Cambrai Cathedral, there is no evidence even of an organ), making all-vocal performance the only option. Gradually these ensembles grew in size according to the wealth of the institutions that supported them. In Italy, wealthy magnates like the Dukes of Ferrara and Milan vied with each other for the best singers in their greatest possible number. As with other forms of artistic patronage, they emulated the more established courts like those of France and Burgundy, whose rosters of singer-composers included the best musicians of the period. The 1400s also saw an increase in the use of boy trebles whose training, education and maintenance was often the direct responsibility of the choirmaster. In England, the two great surviving polyphonic manuscripts of the 15th century (the **Old Hall Manuscript**, copied *c*1415, and the **Eton Choirbook** of *c*1500) show a similar shift from adult male ensembles to those including a substantial number of boys. The role of women in musical performances is by no means clear, though it would have been restricted to the secular field. One of the best known instances dates from 16th-century Ferrara, where composers including **Luca Marenzio** (1553/54-99) and **Luzzascho Luzzaschi** (?1545-1607) wrote for a group of ladies, known as the *Concerto delle donne*, who regularly performed for the duke and his entourage.

But even when the performing forces for a given work can be established as precisely as this, there is no room for dogmatism. A piece might be disseminated hundreds of miles from its place of origin to an area whose performance traditions might be very different. There was no fixed pitch-standard even in the baroque period: each region, town or parish had its own. So the notion of a single authentic manner of performance is a chimera. Besides, contemporary documents tell us very little of sound quality, tone production, and other vital matters. We may be told that the music performed at a given ceremony sounded like the voice of angels, for example, or that singers 'sang very sweetly'; but such descriptions might refer to sounds very different to those with which we might associate them. Medieval representations of singers often show them pulling quite extraordinary faces (think of Van Eyck's singing angels, for instance). Are the artists indulging in caricature, or perhaps mocking singers' vanity? Or did their methods of tone production vary significantly from those of today's singers? Would we have recognised their performances, or they ours?

In order to help readers find their way around the listed recordings, there follows a brief summary of musical developments during the medieval and renaissance periods. Naturally, it is only the briefest of sketches; much detail has been omitted, and not just detail. The insert-notes of individual recordings usually provide sufficient information as to specific works and performances. The aim here is to provide a broader context within which to understand them.

Monody

The earliest notated music in the West is known as plainchant or plainsong. As with literacy in general, musical notation was basically the preserve of the church: even the most powerful lay figures tended to be illiterate. Music notation seems originally to have been devised as an aid to memory: the first examples have no musical staves, and indicate only the relative of pitches' positions (higher or lower). Over time it became more specific, but its interpretation remains a matter of conjecture. Chant traditions proliferated across different parts of Europe, and over the centuries several attempts were made to impose some sort of uniformity across a broad region. The last and most successful of these was the Council of Trent (1545-63), which set down the Roman rite as the standard throughout the Catholic church. By this time polyphony had been established for centuries, but it is important to bear in mind that throughout the middle ages and renaissance periods, plainchant was the norm in church, with polyphony being reserved for special occasions. In the 19th century the monks of Solesmes (France) gathered together and published the corpus of plainchant, and promoted a certain style of performance, which has since been firmly established in the public imagination. More recently, scholars and singers have conducted research into performance traditions based not on the Solesmes style but on historical descriptions from different periods, using original chant manuscripts in preference to modern editions.

Monody was equally important in the secular domain. Certain forms were actually hybrids of the sacred and secular, for example the musical religious dramas devised to make biblical stories come alive for the largely illiterate faithful (a well known example being the **Play of Daniel**). One is set down in a manuscript copied at a Benedictine monastery at Benediktbeuren (Bavaria), a collection that also contains burlesque parodies of scripture (the famous **Carmina Burana**) for use on days when the monks' usually strict rule was relaxed. But perhaps the most famous repertory of secular monody is that of the troubadours (southern French) and trouvères (northern French), who endure in popular lore through the image of the 'wandering minstrel'. Like many such images it is a misleading one, for often these were noblemen who did not wander at all but welcomed musicians and poets into their courts, and practised the arts themselves. Their main theme was the idealised woman whom knights vowed to serve in what has come to be termed 'courtly love' (though we know that such relationships were not always platonic, and that trouvères also sang of physical passion). The tradition of poet-composers reached its apex in the person of **Guillaume de Machaut** (*c*1300-77), who was equally renowned in both fields (and remains so today) and wrote both monophonic and polyphonic songs; and it extended into the next century with the Burgundian court musicians Gilles de Binche (called **Binchois**, *c*1400-60) and **Antoine Busnois** (*c*1430-92).

Sacred polyphony

It is thought that the earliest polyphony arose out of improvisation: singers extemporised new musical parts to existing plainchant. The earliest notated examples date from the 11th century. As with early plainchant, the interpretation of this notation is a matter of conjecture, and is further limited by the small number of surviving sources. The culmination of these early styles is known as the Notre-Dame School which coincided with the foundation of Paris's famous cathedral (1163). Its leading figures are the first named composers of polyphony: **Leoninus** and **Perotinus**. Perotinus was the first composer of four-voice music in the organum style, in which three free voices weave elaborate, repeating patterns around a slow-moving cantus firmus (fragment of plainchant). The idea of basing new works on pre-existing music (usually plainchant, but later polyphony as well) persists, in different forms, throughout sacred music up to and beyond 1600.

Another enduring thread is the mixture of the sacred and the worldly. One of the earliest examples combining both trends is the 13th-century French motet (a term derived from the French for 'word'). Typically this had different texts in each voice: those in the upper voices were in French or Latin and were often related by their subject-matter (the one commenting upon the other – a typical subject being love, requited or otherwise); the lower voice, called tenor (from the french 'tenir', 'to hold', because the long notes hold the music

Repertoire exploration I

Agricola
'A Secret Labyrinth'
Huelgas Ensemble / van Nevel
Sony SK60760 Ⓕ
A superlative recording of one of the early Renaissance's most distinctive voices.

Dufay
Complete Secular Music
Soloists; Medieval Ensemble of London / P & T Davies
L'Oiseau Lyre
⑤ 452 557-2OC5 Ⓑ
Fifteenth-century secular music is hard to come by on disc. But here are all of Dufay's songs together. Pricey perhaps, but indispensable.

Dunstaple
Motets
Hilliard Ensemble / Hillier
Virgin Veritas VER5 61342-2 Ⓜ
A classic recording of one of England's greatest and influential composers.

Machaut
'Dreams in the Pleasure Garden'
Orlando Consort
Archiv 457 618-2AH Ⓕ
A fascinating cross-section of secular song from the 14th-century's greatest composer.

Various
Balades a III chans
Ferrara Ensemble / Young
Arcana A32 Ⓕ
Weird and wonderful secular polyphony from the late 14th century.

Various
'Les premières polyphonies francaises'
Ensemble Gilles Binchois / Vellard
Virgin Veritas VC5 45135-2 Ⓕ
A very impressive recording of pre-Nostre Dame polphony. Out-of-the-way repertory but definately worth seeking out.

Various
'The Art of Courtly Love'
Early Music Consort of London / Munrow
Virgin Veritas
② VED5 61284-2 Ⓑ
A splendid overview of the 14th century, that is still fresh and engaging 25 years on.

together) was either performed by instruments or else vocalised (that is, sung to a single vowel). It consisted of a few notes drawn from plainchant, frequently set to a recurring rhythmic pattern. Most often, the words of the chosen plainchant had some sort of bearing upon the subject matter in the upper parts. The motet continued to flourish in the next century, when the notational system was revised to take account of new rhythmic possibilities. This is the period known as **Ars Nova**, led by **Philippe de Vitry** (1291-1361) and Guillaume de Machaut, one of the outstanding figures of medieval culture. While Machaut was primarily concerned with secular music, he also wrote motets, and his *Messe de Nostre Dame* is famously the first complete setting of the Mass Ordinary in the hand of a single named composer.

Before Machaut's Mass, there appear to have been very few pieces in this genre; but by the turn of the 15th century musicians became interested in relating two or more Mass movements by basing them on the same cantus firmus. Early instances of this stem from the English composers **Leonel Power** (*d*1445) and **John Dunstaple** (*c*1390-1453). Their style, remarkable for its emphasis on triadic sonorities, had a considerable impact on younger continental composers like **Guillaume Dufay** (*c*1397-1474) and his younger contemporary **Johannes Ockeghem** (*c*1420-97). Over the course of the 15th century, the Mass came to replace the motet as the pre-eminent form of sacred composition. It absorbed the idea of cantus firmus, and soon composers began using secular songs as well as plainchant as the basis for Mass compositions. At the same time the motet changed its character: the constructivist principles referred to earlier were jettisoned, and the term itself came to denote a polyphonic sacred piece with a liturgical or paraliturgical text. The first examples of this new breed of motet are found in the **Old Hall Manuscript**. In the 16th century it in turn superseded the Mass as the favoured form of sacred composition, thanks in part to the influence of the late motets of the great **Josquin Desprez** (*c*1455-1521). By the time of Josquin's death, however, motets tended to be freely composed, with no pre-existing material. This marks a general trend through the latter part of the 16th century, which set increasing store in the creation of freely invented pieces: the notion of originality, thereafter one of the hallmarks of creative genius, was coming to the fore. Henceforth the Mass, which persisted in the use of pre-existing material, came to be seen as a rather conservative form. **Orlande de Lassus** (1532-94), perhaps the greatest composer of the high renaissance, wrote over 600 motets but only 50-odd Masses; yet his great Roman contemporary **Giovanni Pierluigi da Palestrina** (1525/26-94) was still able to write over 100 Masses, many of them very elaborate.

Secular polyphony

From its origins, composers of polyphony tended to write music for both sacred and worldly purposes. This is partly because singing (and by extension, composing) polyphony was a skilled craft, and the same lords who kept private chapels also required music for their entertainment; and because in any medieval town, the cathedral, the market square and the dwellings of the wealthy were in close proximity. Traditionally, singers were members of the minor clergy, earning their living from ecclesiastical benefices (often held without the obligation of residency) negotiated for them by the lords who employed them.

The history of secular polyphony is bound up with the poetic forms that were set to music. These forms were highly conventionalised in their organisation. Thus, in the trouvère repertory mentioned above, the *grant chant* had its own rhyme-scheme and verse-structure, its subject matter being the idealised, unattainable Lady; while lighter genres like the *pastourelle* were more simply organised, and involved the more down-to-earth amorous pursuits of shepherds and shepherdesses (the latter sometimes also pursued by knights!). With the Ars nova, polyphony was concentrated on a few poetic forms known collectively as *formes fixes*: the *rondeau*, the *virelai* (sometimes known in its abbreviated form as the *bergerette*) and the most popular and courtly form of the 14th century, the *ballade*. The rhythmic and chromatic sophistication of the Ars nova reached a climax after the death of Machaut in the style known variously as the Avignon school (after the Papal court that was set up there) or **Ars subtilior** ('the subtler art'), whose notational complexity was unsurpassed until the mid 20th century. The next century saw the *rondeau* eclipse the *ballade* in popularity, and the advent of a more direct, tuneful style typified by Guillaume Dufay, though the *formes fixes*' courtly sophistication endured in the songs of Binchois and Busnois at the court of Burgundy, and with Ockeghem at the court of France.

But by 1500 the *formes fixes* were on the wane, replaced in France by simpler verse/refrain and strophic structures, and a lighter melodic style increasingly centered on the top voice. These new songs were widely circulated in print, bringing a host of composers to the fore, including **Claudin de Sermisy** (*c*1490-1562) and **Clément Janequin** (*c*1485-1558), whose descriptive songs enjoyed a wide vogue. At the same time in Italy a new genre came into being which would have far-reaching influences: this was the madrigal. Many of its first great practitioners were not native Italians, but Franco-Flemish (among them **Philippe Verdelot** and **Jacques Arcadelt**, both active in Florence; and **Adrian Willaert**, master of the music at St Mark's in Venice, and his pupil and successor, known by his Italian name **Cipriano da Rore** (1515/16-65). Soon, the madrigal was established as the predominant secular form of its time: it was exported to England, and on the continent the publication of a book of madrigals for one's opus 1 became a rite of passage for aspiring young composers working in Italy. By this time the madrigal had transcended its popular origins and had become an experimental vehicle for every sort of innovation: think of the chromaticism of **Carlo Gesualdo** (*c*1561-1613), or the blending of voices and specific instruments and the introduction of the basso continuo in the fifth madrigal book of **Claudio Monteverdi** (1567-1643). These innovations had far-reaching implications, for instance to do with the rise of opera in Italy; abroad, the solo madrigal (scored for a single voice with bass accompaniment) found its counterparts in the French air de cour and the English lute song. In this sense, the development of the madrigal marks the transition from the renaissance to the baroque.

Instrumental music

In music before 1500 it can be difficult to distinguish between a musical line that happens not to carry a text and one specifically intended for instruments (many variations in performance practice arise from this ambiguity). As mentioned earlier, even when instrumental performance of a given part is possible, it is not always possible to tell whether a specific instrument was intended. Yet a few specifically instrumental forms survive, one of the earliest being the 13th-century *estampie*. And the best instrumentalists achieved renown and made good careers for themselves. Indeed, from the 15th century onwards compositions are increasingly ascribed to named individuals, among them the organist **Conrad Paumann** (*c*1410-73), the lutenists **Francesco Spinacino** (*fl*1507), **Vincenzo Capirola** (1474-after 1548) and **Francesco da Milano** (1497-1543). From the early 15th century come the first manuscripts containing sizeable instrumental repertories: often these were embellished arrangements of pre-existing polyphonic compositions. Typically, specific types of notation called tablature were devised for the different instruments: those for organ, keyboard and lute were the most common. Gradually pieces were written specifically for given instruments: the toccata (from the Italian toccare, 'to touch') was a short, prelude-like piece of an improvisatory, virtuoso character; the fantasia and the ricercar (together with its Spanish counterpart, the *tiento*) were more abstract, polyphonic pieces, forerunners of the fugue; and there were pieces based on ground basses and popular tunes. The lute was the most popular instrument owing to its size and flexibility: it could accompany or play complex polyphony on its own. Music printing (which began at the turn of the 16th century) soon cashed in on this market in a variety of ways; but one has to wait for the early baroque to find examples of what we call 'scoring', that is, the assignment of specific lines to specific instruments.

Essential listening II

Byrd	Masses for 3, 4 and 5 voices **The Cardinall's Musick / Carwood** ASV Gaudeamus ASVGAU206	Ⓕ
Josquin	Missa Pange lingua etc Ensemble Clément Janequin; **Ensemble Organum / Pérès** Harmonia Mundi HMC90 1239	Ⓕ
Lassus	Lagrime di San Pietro etc **Ensemble Vocal Européen / Herreweghe** Harmonia Mundi HMC90 1483	Ⓕ
Palestrina	Missa Assumpta est Maria; Missa Papae Marcelli etc **Pro Cantione Antiqua / Brown** Regis Recordings RRC1025	Ⓑ
Various	'Canciones y Ensaladas' **Ensemble Clément Janequin / Visse** Harmonia Mundi HMC90 1627	Ⓕ
Various	'Music from the Sistine Chapel' **Taverner Consort and Choir / Parrott** HMV Classics HMV5 74371-2	Ⓑ

Old wine, new bottles

It is not only performers and scholars who reinterpret the music of the past: composers of every stripe have sought inspiration in early music, and continue to do so. This is nothing new: Beethoven regarded Handel as the greatest composer ever, and Brahms was a subscriber to the complete edition of Schütz's works. What is surprising today is the breadth of early music's appeal, the way it cuts across aesthetic positions and stylistic boundaries. Figures as diverse as Pärt, Reich, Schnittke, Andriessen, Ligeti, Kagel, Birtwistle, Maxwell Davies and Ferneyhough (to name only these) have engaged with pre-tonal idioms and procedures at various times in their careers. In some cases (for example in the case of minimalist composers) the link between old and new is clearly audible and overt: thus with much of **Pärt**'s vocal and choral music, or in pieces like **Andriessen**'s *Hocketus*; but equally, composers of what used to be called the avant-garde have adopted and adapted procedures derived from the *modus operandi* of pre-tonal musics: examples include the use of canon in certain movements of **Ligeti**'s *Requiem* and in his *Lux aeterna*; of hocket and isorhythm in much of **Birtwistle**'s music. Other examples include the 'transcriptions' by Michael

Finnissy in *Obrecht Motetten* of pieces by the great Flemish composer (*ca*1457-1505); the quotations from Lassus in Schnittke's String Quartet No 3; Kagel's self-explanatorily named *Music for Renaissance Instruments*, in which the soundworld of the period is invoked at its most physical level. Even **Boulez**, that most resolute of modernists, has named some recent works after plainchant forms in recognition of their antiphonal structures: *Répons* and *Anthèmes*.

How can we explain the fascination pre-tonal music holds for present-day composers? It is striking that many of today's tonal composers (for example, Pärt in his *St John Passion*) do not adhere to the tonal system as such, but use elements of its language, most notably its harmonies; similarly, the music of composers like Perotinus or Dunstaple has unmistakable whiffs of tonality, because it uses chords which tonal music subsequently took over and used in a very different way. This mixture of the familiar and the foreign connects Pärt and like-minded composers with earlier music. At the same time, the speculative side of much pre-tonal music – its interest in number, in abstract, speculative compositional procedures, or in the intricacies of notation – can be discerned in music whose connection with early music is not immediately audible. Hence the examples mentioned earlier, of Birtwistle, Finnissy and the like. In this opposition between sound and structure, there is of course an element of over-simplification; one might simplify further by saying that early music offers something for everyone. A related point was made earlier: the amount of interpretation and conjecture that is needed to recreate pre-tonal music in sound. The less we know, the more we have to make up, and the creative licence granted to performers applies also to composers, who focus on whichever aspect of the music happens to suit their turn. Finally, today's composer is faced with a superabundance of riches: the whole of Western art music (and much else besides), immediately accessible in both printed and recorded forms. What this means for the future is anyone's guess, but it is a situation that today's composers are forced to confront one way or another.

Repertoire exploration II

Cornysh Magnificat; Stabat mater; etc
The Tallis Scholars / Phillips
Gimell CDGIM014 Ⓕ
The musical equivalent perpendicular Gothic architecture: dazzling and intricate, and a performance to match.

Gombert Credo. Qui colis Ausoniam; etc
Henry's VIII / Brown
Hyperion CDA66828 Ⓕ
This is dense, rich polyphony for the court of Hapsburg Emperor Charles V.

Josquin Missa L'Homme armé sexti toni; Missa L'Homme armé super voces musicales etc
A Sei Voci / Fabre-Garrus
Astrée Naïve E8809 Ⓕ
A superlative recording of two of Josquin's most consumate Mass settings.

Various 'Consonanze Stravaganti'
Stembridge *org/hpd*
Ars musici AM1207-2 Ⓕ
Keyboard music from late 16th century Naples, which inspired composer such as Frescobaldi.

Various 'The Art of the Netherlands'
Early Music Consort of London / Munrow
Virgin Veritas VED5 61334-2 Ⓜ
An idiosyncratic overview of the 15th century; perhaps David Munrow's finest recording.

THE BAROQUE ERA

THE BAROQUE ERA IS DOMINATED BY THE OUTPUT OF A HANDFUL OF MUSICAL GIANTS. **NICHOLAS ANDERSON**'S WHISTLESTOP TOUR TAKES IN BOTH THE GREAT AND THE FORGOTTEN

The closing decades of the 16th century were crucial to the forming of many styles which affected music, painting, architecture, and literature. It was a period in which ideas were evolved and forms developed to expand musical vocabulary and to accommodate the expression of an ever-widening range of emotions. The enormous variety of these ideas and forms was developed throughout the 17th and early 18th centuries, gradually became governed by a common musical syntax. Yet, in spite of regularisation, the music of this period has preserved a novelty and an unpredictability capable of evincing passionate responses in us. Since the end of the 19th century we have gathered these multifaceted and multicoloured forms under the umbrella-title of 'Baroque' to provide us with the convenience of an all-embracing stylistic concept.

One of the most intense aspirations of the Baroque period was to find new and more powerful means of strengthening the effect of the spoken word. It led to the creation of opera and the development of song. Italy was the fountainhead from which these new ideas emerged, and it was Italian musicians who played a key role in disseminating ideas in other parts of Europe. The leading composers in this early stage of baroque music were **Caccini, Cavalieri, Peri** and, above all **Monteverdi**. Caccini's songs embrace the new monodic style, underpinned by the essence of baroque texture – the basso continuo, whose figured shorthand represents the harmonies and intervals to be played above the bass. Caccini's music has more than mere historic significance, though, and his songs have a simple, melodic appeal which engage our emotional responses, just as the composer intended. Monteverdi's nine collections of madrigals, published between 1585 and 1651, reflect an astonishing range of emotions expressed with intensity and psychological insight. The variety of moods and textual sensibility of which Monteverdi was capable is present in each collection, but is strikingly apparent in the Eighth Book (1638) containing 'Il ballo delle ingrate' and the 'Combattimento di Tancredi e Clorinda'.

Monteverdi's first opera, *Orfeo* (1607) was written and performed at Mantua and followed earlier experimental dramas by Orazio Vecchi, Emilio de' Cavalieri and Jacopo Peri. A conspicuous feature of this work is its ample instrumental requirements signposting a path for the future development of the orchestra. Monteverdi's superior dramatic gifts are even more evident in his two remaining complete operas, *Il ritorno d'Ulisse in patria* (1641), and *L'incoronazione di Poppea* (1642). Here he proves himself a master in handling human relationships and in vivid characterisation. Both operas were written for Venice, where his gifted pupil **Cavalli** produced many successful works during the middle decades of the 17th century. Among these are *Ormindo*, *Giasone* and *Calisto*. Monteverdi's sacred vocal music is collected mainly in two publications, that of 1610 containing the popularly termed Monteverdi *Vespers*, and another of 1641, *Selva morale e spirituale*.

By the middle of the 17th century new forms were beginning to take shape in Italy which were to influence the direction of music during the early 18th century and, in some cases, far beyond. The most important of these were oratorio, cantata, sonata and instrumental concerto. Oratorio, as a musical form, originated in Rome where those of **Carissimi** provide fine examples. His dramatic flair is apparent in Latin oratorios such as *Jephte* where a rich harmonic vocabulary enhances the Old Testament story. Later in the century another Roman composer, **Stradella**, further developed oratorio, introducing an important instrumental dimension. His best-known oratorio is *San Giovanni Battista*, in which the relationships between Herod and John the Baptist and between Herod and his daughter are handled with insight.

After opera and oratorio, the chamber cantata was the most important vocal form in 17th-century Italy. Early pioneers were Luigi Rossi, Cesti and Carissimi but it was **Alessandro Scarlatti** who, more than any composer, standardised an alternating pattern of recitative-aria-recitative-aria which remained more or less in place until the end of the Baroque period. Scarlatti wrote about 600 chamber cantatas as well as longer *serenatas*, which occupy ground somewhere between cantata and opera.

During the later decades of the century the instrumental forms of sonata and concerto were given definition. Sonatas generally fell into two categories, the more serious *sonata da chiesa* (church sonata) in four movements, and the dance-oriented *sonata da camera*, often suite-like and beginning with a prelude. Legrenzi and Vitali were important composers in the early history of the sonata but it was **Corelli** who consolidated forms, drawing on a wealth of ideas for his trio sonatas. These in turn played a significant part in his 12 *Concerti grossi* (Op 6). Here Corelli alternated the trio sonata texture of two violins and cello (*concertino*) with a fuller orchestral sound (*grosso*). But, at the beginning of the 18th century the scene shifted from Rome to Venice for the final development of the baroque concerto.

Alongside new ideas in vocal music, composers were also experimenting with instrumental forms. One of the leading pioneers, above all in keyboard music, was **Frescobaldi**. He introduced a striking virtuosity to his pieces while attaching importance to the emotional involvement entered into by an individual player.

Contributions to the development of the violin and members of the violin family were also to have far-reaching consequences for baroque music. Among the early 17th-century pioneers were composers such as **Marini, Fontana, Merula** and **Uccellini**. They established new forms, expanded instrumental technique and widened expressive possibilities.

The opening of public opera houses in Rome and Venice during the 1630s, quickly followed by others, established the future of sung dramatic entertainment both in Italy and further afield. At the French court of the Bourbons dance and ballet reigned supreme during the early decades of the 17th century; but, in the 1640s Italian opera was introduced to the court of Louis XIV by his Italian prime minister, Cardinal Mazarin. Cavalli's *Egisto* and Luigi Rossi's *Orfeo* were both performed there, followed by others. The French love of dancing was amply catered for by the inclusion of ballets which followed each act.

The arrival of Lully

All this was to change with the rise to fame and influence of Italian-born Lully, one of the most astute operators in the entire history of music. In the early part of his career Lully mainly composed ballets for the court, earning for himself the almost undying approval of Louis XIV, whom he was to serve throughout his life. During the 1660s a partnership with the great comic playwright, Molière, resulted in a succession of highly original *comédies-ballets*, culminating in the greatest of them, *Le bourgeois gentilhomme*. At about the same time experiments were taking place in creating an indigenous French opera, based on Italian models, but using French texts rather than Italian ones. Lully was at first dismissive but then, sensing that he might be upstaged, turned matters to his advantage. By means of politically adroit moves he eventually held a monopoly for performing virtually all kinds of large-scale dramatic music in France. Between 1673 and his death in 1687 Lully produced a steady flow of operas, among them *Alceste* (1674), *Atys* (1676) and *Armide* (1686). Only after Lully's death and a return to the free opera market was another French composer, **Marc-Antoine Charpentier** able to reveal dramatic talents equal to, even superior to those of his rival. His fine tragédie-lyrique *Médée* was staged in Paris in 1693. Some other dramatic pieces by Charpentier such as *Actéon* and *Les Arts Florissants* are on a much smaller scale though another major stage work, *David et Jonathas* (1688), a religious drama, was commissioned for private performance by the Jesuits.

Lully and Charpentier were both skilled in the sphere of sacred vocal music. Lully's *Te Deum* and *Miserere*, strongly contrasting pieces, reveal the composer's sensibility to psalm and canticle texts. These follow the layout and scale of the grand motet, calling for solo voices, choir and instruments. *Petits motets* on the other hand, usually involved two or three voices with basso continuo. Charpentier was a master of both forms, though some of his pieces are better understood as dramatic motets in which Biblical stories are presented both in commentary and in direct speech. *Le reniement de St Pierre* (*St Peter's Denial*) for soloists, chorus and continuo is a masterpiece of the form, whose anguished harmonic progression and grief-stricken inflexions are affecting. Charpentier was unusually gifted in the art of poignant writing, as we can see in his many tenebrae-settings (*Leçons de ténèbres*), but it is in his 11 Masses that he most effectively blends this aspect of his style with more extrovert ceremonial gestures. His last setting of the Mass, *Assumpta est Maria*, is perhaps, the most satisfying of them. It was in the hands of **Lalande**, that the *grand motet* reached one of its high water-marks. Sixty-four of them have survived, of which *De Profundis* provides an outstandingly expressive example.

Essential listening I

Cavalli	Calisto **Concerto Vocale / Jacobs** Harmonia Mundi HMC90 1515/7	Ⓕ
Charpentier	Missa Assumpta Maria **Les Arts Florissants / Christie** Harmonia Mundi HMC90 1298	Ⓕ
Corelli	Concerti grossi, Op 6 **The English Concert / Pinnock** Archiv ② 459 451-2ATA2	Ⓜ
Lully	Le bourgeois gentilhomme **Tolz Boys' Choir; La Petite Bande / Leonhardt** DHM GD77059	Ⓕ
Lully	Te Deum **Concert Spirituel Choir & Orch / Niquet** Naxos 8 554397	Ⓢ
Monteverdi	Madrigals – Book 8 **Concerto Italiano / Alessandrini** Opus 111 OPS30-187	Ⓕ
Monteverdi	1610 Vespers **Taverner Consort; Taverner Choir; Taverner Players / Parrott** Virgin Classics ② VBD5 61662-2	Ⓑ
Purcell	Dido and Aeneas **Soloists; Academy of Ancient Music Chorus & Orchestra / Hogwood** L'Oiseau-Lyre 436 992-2OHO	Ⓕ
Schütz	Musicalisches Exequien **Monteverdi Choir; English Baroque Sols; His Majesty's Sagbutts and Cornetts / Gardiner** Archiv 423 405-2AH	Ⓕ

The Italian influence widens

The influence of Italian music had reached Germany by the early years of the 17th century. But political and religious tensions, and the consequent Thirty Years' War (1618-48) caused such protracted brutality, bitterness and turmoil that artistic endeavour was fragmented. Among the earliest composers to embrace Italian ideas were **Praetorius, Schein** and **Scheidt**. They drew upon newly acquired Italian polychoral techniques in the setting of hymns, Biblical texts and in the deployment of instruments. The leading composer of the early to mid-German Baroque was **Heinrich Schütz** whose rich stylistic vocabulary reflects both a prodigious talent and an unusually long life. Schütz was sent to Venice in 1609 where he studied with Giovanni Gabrieli. He returned to Germany four years later, eventually becoming Kapellmeister at the Dresden court, a post which he held for almost half a century. Schütz visited Venice again in 1628, and this time met Monteverdi while also catching up with new developments in music which had taken place since his previous visit. Schütz's music spans half a century and more and embraces old and evolving compositional styles. By introducing Italian ideas into Germany he laid the foundations of 18th century German sacred music. Among his most impressive achievements are the *Psalms of David*, published in 1619, and *Cantiones sacrae* (1625), both of which reveal Schütz's masterly rapprochement between Italian techniques and Lutheran tradition. The strikingly organised *Musicalisches Exequien* (1636), *Geistliche Chor-Music* (1648), and the emotionally charged *Die sieben Worte unsers lieben Erlösers und Seeligmachers Jesu Christi* (The Seven Last Words of Christ on the Cross) are further examples of Schütz's inspirational gifts in setting sacred texts.

Though Schütz's talent remains unrivalled in early- to mid-17th-century Germany, there were other composers who made enduring contributions to Protestant sacred music. A unique phenomenon was the emergence of a dynasty of musicians, eventually crowned with the genius of its most illustrious member, Johann Sebastian Bach. **Johann Hans Bach**, a younger contemporary of Schütz, contributed a motet of great poignancy, *Unser Leben ist ein Schatten* (Our life is but a shadow), while **Johann Christoph Bach** and **Johann Michael Bach** were also accomplished composers of sacred vocal music. **Franz Tunder, Johann Schelle**, Schütz's pupil **Matthias Weckmann** and, further south, **Johann Erasmus Kindermann** encompassed many of the vocal and instrumental forms of the time and some of these are, at last being explored in recordings.

The leading keyboard composer in Germany during the first half of the 17th century was **Johann Jacob Froberger**. He was influenced by Italian ideas in his toccatas, canzonas and ricercares, while his harpsichord suites incline more toward French idioms. Froberger's puissant and individually expressive powers can be found in his elaborate *Lamentation faite sur la mort très douloureuse de Sa Majesté Impériale, Ferdinand le troisième*.

Among the most important German 17th century composers in the sphere of solo violin and instrumental chamber music were **Rosenmüller, Schmelzer** and **Biber**. Rosenmüller spent much of his active musical life in Italy but returned to Germany towards the end of his life. His compositions provided a fertile channel for the flow of Italian stylistic traits into north and central Germany. Austrian Schmelzer and Bohemian Biber enriched the violin repertoire with music which not only radiated the sounds and colours of central European folk music, but also extended the technique of the instrument itself. Schmelzer's collection, *Sacroprofanus concentus musicus* (1662), his *Fechtschule* and Biber's *Battalia* afford lively examples of their art. But it is Biber's 16 *Mystery Sonatas*, linked to the Catholic devotion of the Rosary, which strike an altogether profounder note, evoking a wide range of emotions, exuberant, contemplative and poignant, in turn.

Though the Low Countries had enjoyed a brilliant indigenous musical culture during the 15th and 16th centuries, the 17th century was less innovative. Musical life continued to thrive but there were fewer leading musicians, apart from Sweelinck whose life embraced the latter decades of the 16th and first two decades of the 17th centuries. **Sweelinck** wrote a small quantity of vocal music but his greater skill lay in instrumental forms, above all those connected with the keyboard. Another gifted composer from the Low Countries at this time was **Jacob van Eyck**, whose recorder music is imaginative and often virtuosic.

English music during the 17th century was receptive to continental developments, the most important stimuli coming from Italy and France. But England was also a favoured destination for foreign musicians, above all Italians, and they in turn may well have responded to stubbornly preserved indigenous musical ideas. In the first quarter of the century madrigals and songs with lute accompaniment were the most popular forms of secular vocal music, with composers such as Dowland, Gibbons, Morley and Weelkes leading a strong and well-populated field. Opera was slow to catch on in England and it was the masque, with its elements of dance, mime and allegory, and plays with music which kept the new Italian entertainment at bay. Masques remained popular up to the mid-century, with composers such as William and Henry Lawes and playwrights like Ben Jonson lending the form real distinction. Among the most gifted composers writing for the Anglican Church were **Thomas Tomkins, Orlando Gibbons** and **Thomas Weelkes**, whose anthems and services are intimately expressive and suitable for wide use. Though instrumental music took second place to music for voices in pre-Restoration England it was a period that none the less sustained a thriving tradition of keyboard and consort music. Among the great keyboard composers were **John Bull** and **Peter Philips**, both of whom were on friendly terms with Sweelinck. Their pieces in variation form are complex and technically brilliant. **Gibbons**, **William Lawes** and **John Jenkins** were all accomplished instrumental composers who made fine, sometimes idiosyncratic contributions to the consort repertoire for viols and/or members of the violin family.

After the Restoration of the monarchy in 1660 musical life in England received a new impetus from the enthusiasm of the king himself. Further experiments were made with opera, the favoured form being semi-opera consisting of music and spoken dialogue. The great master of semi-opera, as of all other musical forms in the last decades of the century was **Purcell**, whose *King Arthur* and *The Fairy Queen* contain music of great originality and charm. Purcell's single true operatic venture, *Dido and Aeneas*, with its wide range of emotions, strikingly imaginative Second Act and its celebrated lament, is musically rewarding at every turn and is one of the great dramatic masterpieces of the Baroque period. A delightful precursor of *Dido and Aeneas* was composed by **John Blow**, whose intimate and fervently expressive *Venus and Adonis* is sung throughout. Purcell was equally at home with instrumental music. As well as trio sonatas he produced a smaller quantity of solo keyboard music – suites and miscellaneous pieces – and 13 subtly expressive fantasias with two *In nomines* for viol consorts. Purcell, along with Pelham Humfrey, Blow and others also enriched Anglican worship with anthems, services, chants and hymns.

The high Baroque

The late Baroque period is dominated by the towering figures of Bach and Handel, yet there were other composers, too, of outstanding and exceptional talent, of whom Vivaldi in Italy, Rameau in France, and Telemann in Germany were the leading lights. The early decades of the 18th century witnessed the crystallisation and stylistic maturity of forms developed in the previous century: opera, oratorio, cantata, sonata, concerto and suite. In Venice, **Albinoni** contributed to the sophistication of the instrumental concerto. His writing for one and two oboes lends distinction to his finest sets of concertos, Opp 7 and 9. But it was another Venetian, **Vivaldi**, whose imagination and organisational skill brought the solo concerto to a definitive peak. Like Albinoni – whose comic intermezzo *Pimpinone* (1708) was one of the earliest of its kind – the Marcello brothers and other Venetians, too, Vivaldi was a skilled composer for the voice. Many of his operas have survived and are receiving growing attention, and it is this sphere of vocal accomplishment that often provided the melodic inspiration for his concertos, especially in slow movements. Sometimes, though, the self-borrowing might occur in reverse. As well as the celebrated printed collections of violin concertos, *L'estro armonico*, *La stravaganza*, *Il cimento dell'armonia e dell'inventione* and *La cetra*, Vivaldi catered generously for the oboe, flute, bassoon and cello and there are few if any dull pieces among them. Vivaldi further demonstrates a lively sense of instrumental colour in concertos for assorted wind and strings while his concertos *a quattro*, for ripieno strings, reveal meticulous craftsmanship, sometimes foreshadowing the idiom of the early symphonists. **Tartini** and **Locatelli** were among the leading composers for the violin in the later years of our period.

Repertoire exploration 1

Monteverdi Madrigals – Book 6
Concerto Italiano / Alessandrini
Arcana A66 Ⓕ
A memorable sense of the text and of its determining power over the notes.

Schütz Seven Last Words
Bach Collegium Japan / Suzuki
BIS-CD831/2 Ⓕ
Aficionados of Schütz will want this recording.

Charpentier Actéon
Les Arts Florissants / Christie
Harmonia Mundi HMA190 1095 Ⓕ
Charpentier's little vignette opera is an astonishingly rich score.

Lully Miserere
Paris Chapelle Royale Chor & Orch Herreweghe
Harmonia Mundi HMC90 1167 Ⓕ
The clear choral sound is a delight; the orchestra achieves a rich sonority.

Desmarest Grands Motets
Les Arts Florissants / Christie
Erato 8573 80223-2 Ⓕ
Such music could not have fallen into better hands than William Christie's.

Purcell Viol Fantasias
Phantasm
Simax PSC1124 Ⓕ
Phantasm emphasise the expressiveness of these extraordinary works.

D'Anglebert Keyboard Works
Rousset *hpd*
L'Oiseau Lyre 458 588-2OH2 Ⓕ
Rousset possesses the refined technique d'Anglebert demands.

Blow Venus and Adonis
Clare College Choir; OAE / Jacobs
Harmonia Mundi HMC90 1684 Ⓕ
This admirable recording puts the work on another footing entirely.

Opera continued to thrive in 18th-century Italy, though important structural changes took place. They were influenced by the ideas and texts of Metastasio (1698-1782). He gradually dispensed with the comic elements and other distractions of 17th-century opera to create texts with well-structured plots which were so widely admired that they were set by virtually all the leading *opera seria* composers of the time. Comedy, instead, was concentrated in the intermezzos performed between the acts of serious opera. Naples fostered a lively intermezzo tradition with **Pergolesi**'s *La serva padrona* providing the most celebrated example. Comic scenes and various types of full-length comic opera (*opera buffa*) were also developed in Naples by **Pergolesi, Leonardo Leo, Leonardo Vinci** and Alessandro Scarlatti.

In Spain and the Iberian peninsula, the rapprochement that existed between foreign and indigenous styles is demonstrated by the prolonged stay of Alessandro Scarlatti's son, **Domenico Scarlatti**, by other foreign, mainly Italian composers and by the great castrato Farinelli. Many of Scarlatti's harpsichord sonatas, of which over 500 are known, evoke the colours, moods and rhythms which we think of as local to Spain and Portugal. The variety which Scarlatti achieves with a single-movement form is as astonishing as the quantity is prodigious. Among the prominent Spanish composers of this period are: **Torrejón y Velasco**, whose opera *La púrpura de la rosa* (1701) was first performed in Peru in 1701; **Antonio Literes** whose zarzuela (music with spoken dialogue) *Azis y Galatea* was first performed at the Spanish court in 1708; **Carlos de Seixas**, who composed mainly for the keyboard, of which he was a virtuoso; and Italian-born **Domenico Zipoli**, who worked in Argentina where he proselytised on behalf of the Jesuits.

After Lully's death, French opera changed little over a period of almost half a century. Features of the Italian style ever-increasingly attracted French composers, among whom **Campra, Marais, Montéclair** and **Destouches** made original contributions to the *tragédie-lyrique* tradition. Campra, moreover, was an effective pioneer of lighter *opéra-ballet*, in which dance and lavish spectacle assumed greater importance. But it was Rameau's début on the operatic scene, at the age of 50, in 1733, that contributed most of all to a rejuvenation and development of music drama in France. His *tragédies-lyriques* include *Hippolyte et Aricie* (1733), *Castor et Pollux* (1737) and *Les Boréades* (1760), while in a lighter vein *Les Indes galantes* (1735), *Les fêtes d'Hébé* (1739) and a comedy, *Platée* (1745), delighted audiences over an extended period of time. **Leclair** and **Mondonville** also wrote operas of distinction.

On a more intimate level, French chamber cantatas enjoyed enormous popularity during the first three decades or so of the 18th century. **Clérambault** was highly esteemed for his skill in this subtly expressive form, but others like **Campra, Nicolas Bernier, Montéclair** and **Rameau** have left us charming examples. Sacred music continued to thrive in the form of the *grand motet*, with Campra, once again providing many effective pieces for voices and instruments. In the mid century the *grand motet* reached a summit in a small number of vividly expressive pieces by Mondonville.

Though French composers were late in taking the Italian forms of the sonata and concerto to heart, more expressively home-grown chamber music flourished. Solo harpsichord music was crowned with the 27 *ordres* (suites) of **Françpis Couperin** and by the much smaller but high quality legacy of Rameau. Rewards can also be found in the harpsichord pieces of **Daquin, Dandrieu, Duphly** and **Balbastre**, while the violin and flute sonatas of Leclair, with their pleasing blend of French delicacy and Italian virtuosity, are among the most sophisticated and technically challenging pieces of their kind in the French baroque repertoire. These fine sonatas may be considered alongside another, more indigenous tradition, that of the bass viol whose music reached unparalleled heights in the masterly suites of **Marais**.

While France had an artistic focal point, first at the Bourbon court then increasingly in Paris, Germany had no centralised culture during the early 18th century. It was both politically fragmented, and also divided in its faith between the Protestant north and Catholic south. North and South were, however, at one in the welcome they gave to French and Italian artists of all kinds. In music this contributed towards an

Essential listening II

JS Bach	Brandenburg Concertos **Vienna Concentus Musicus / Harnoncourt** Teldec Ultima ② 0630-18944-2	Ⓜ
JS Bach	Magnificat **Collegium Musicum 90 Chorus and Orchestra / Hickox** Chandos Chaconne CHAN0518	Ⓕ
Handel	Concerto grossi, Op 6 **Collegium Musicum 90 / Standage** *vn* Chandos Chaconne CHAN0600/16/22	Ⓕ
Handel	Messiah **Gabrieli Consort and Players / McCreesh** Archiv ② 453 464-2AH2	Ⓕ
Handel	Giulio Cesare **Concerto Cologne / Jacobs** Harmonia Mundi ③ HMC90 1385/7	Ⓕ
Vivaldi	L'Estro Armonico, Op 3 **The English Concert / Pinnock** Archiv ⑤ 471 317-2AB5	Ⓑ

unusually rich stylistic blend, influencing the work of Bach, Fux, Telemann and their contemporaries. In church music the multi-sectional cantata began to take precedence over the motet and vocal concerto. Varied cantata techniques before Bach were imaginatively applied by **Buxtehude, Bruhns, Kuhnau, Zachow, Schelle** and others. Bach's cantatas drew upon these to a varying extent but increasingly embraced Italian virtuosity while at the same time preserving with breathtaking originality the Lutheran chorale tradition. **Bach**'s two great *Passions*, the *St John* (1724) and the *St Matthew* (1727) follow an earlier tradition established in Leipzig by his predecessor, **Kuhnau**.

The earliest concertos by German composers were based on the Corellian *concerto grosso* concept. But soon the Venetian concertos, above all those of Vivaldi, with their greater emphasis on solo virtuosity were providing rival models. Bach's concertos owe much to Vivaldian organisation but in his most celebrated collection of *Brandenburgs* the music is sometimes blended with French ingredients. But it is in the *ouverture-suites* of German composers that the French style is most wholeheartedly embraced. Bach, Handel and Telemann excelled in a form that was avidly taken up by **Fasch, Graupner, Stölzel** and others.

The solo instrument, par excellence, in Germany was the organ. Following a tradition established in the 17th century, organ composition and performing virtuosity was brought to a peak by **Buxtehude, Pachelbel, Reincken** and above all Bach, whose music for the instrument has remained unparalleled. Late baroque German solo and trio sonatas abound, Bach's Sonatas and Partitas for Unaccompanied Violin presented performers with new and demanding challenges, while his Sonatas for Violin and Harpsichord were highly rated during and after his lifetime. **Telemann** was a prolific and rewarding composer of trio sonatas but also pioneered the quartet medium for which he was praised both in Germany and in France. Telemann, ever questing for new means of expression left hardly a musical form untried. Some of his late vocal music is of particular interest, the oratorio *Der Tag des Gerichts* (1762) and the dramatic cantata *Ino* (1765) being of especial merit.

Telemann was also a successful opera composer, but it was his compatriot and friend Handel who achieved international renown with a brilliant succession of Italian operas for the London stage. **Handel** left Germany for Italy in his early twenties, arriving in London first in 1710 then, to settle, in 1712. London was a flourishing centre for music during the first half of the century and a veritable honeypot for foreign musicians, several of whom settled there. Italian opera was the mainstay of musical entertainment until the mid 1730s, Handel contributing most of them, including *Rinaldo* (1711), *Giulio Cesare* (1724), *Tamerlano* (1724), *Rodelinda* (1725), *Orlando* (1733), *Ariodante* (1735), and *Alcina* (1735). By the late 1730s Handel was increasingly directing his talents towards English oratorio, a concept of his own which embraced elements of opera and of English sacred choral music. Among these are *Saul* (1739), *Messiah* (1742), *Semele*, which may justly be considered an English opera (1744), and *Belshazzar* (1745). His English masque *Acis and Galatea* (1718), and the English ode, *L'Allegro, il penseroso ed il moderato* (1740) belong on the same creative level. As well as dramatic music Handel wrote anthems, and celebratory canticles for the church, *concerti grossi*, organ concertos and two splendid occasional pieces, the *Water Music* and *Music for the Royal Fireworks*. Among the English composers of vocal and instrumental works who lent distinction to London's musical life were **Thomas Arne** and **William Boyce**, whose eight symphonys have long enjoyed popularity with audiences. **Charles Avison** and **John Stanley** wrote exclusively for instruments, their pleasingly crafted concertos affording proof of the excellent health of indigenous talent at the time.

Repertoire exploration II

F Couperin Trois leçons de ténèbres
Les Arts Florissants / Christie
Erato 0630-17067-2 Ⓕ
All three lessons represent Couperin at his most heart-rendingly intense and William Christie is on fine form.

Leclair Violin Sonatas
Fernandez *vn* **Hantaï** *hpd*
Pierlot *va da gamba*
Auvidis Astrée E8662 Ⓕ
Leclair's technically demanding violin sonatas were hugely popular in his own time and they deserve greater attention from record collectors.

Marais Pièces de viole
Pandolfo *bass viol* **Meyerson** *hpd*
Boysen *theorbo/gtr*
Glossa GCD920404 Ⓕ
Thrilling and individual performances of some of Marais's wonderful viol music.
Don't miss this.

Pergolesi La serva padrona
Soloists; La Petite Bande / Kuijken *vn*
Accent ACC96123D Ⓕ
A lively performance of Pergolesi's influential mini-masterpiece.

Telemann Musique de Table
Orchestra of the Golden Age
Naxos 8 553732 Ⓢ
Recommendable bargain recordings of some of Telemann's finest music.

RICHARD WIGMORE CHARTS THE MUSIC OF THE CLASSICAL ERA AND EXPLAINS HOW THE MAIN CULTURAL DEVELOPMENTS OF THE TIME SHAPED COMPOSERS' CREATIVITY

The period stretching roughly from the death of Bach in 1750 to the death of Beethoven in 1827 is usefully, if rather loosely, termed the Viennese classical age. Though its three chief protagonists, Haydn, Mozart and Beethoven, would not have recognised themselves as 'classicists' – indeed, in Beethoven's lifetime the German writer ETA Hoffmann characterised all three composers as 'romantic' – the word does suggest certain dominant ideals of balance, proportion and reconciliation of contrasts central to the art of the Viennese triumvirate and their lesser contemporaries.

At the heart of the so-called Viennese classical style was the sonata principle (the term 'sonata form' was a fabrication of the later 19th century), which evolved from the binary dance movements of the baroque. But whereas a minuet or *courante* by Bach or Handel typically emphasised continuity of texture, a seamless melodic flow and a single emotion, or *Affekt*, the new sonata structures presented a dynamic, dramatic argument based on the contrast of keys and distinct, sharply articulated events, their working-out and their final resolution in the home key. Such was the power and influence of the sonata style by the 1780s and 1790s, when Haydn and Mozart were at their zenith, that it infiltrated all musical forms and genres. In the Act 3 Sextet from *The Marriage of Figaro*, for instance, the sonata design is a perfect musical equivalent of the stage action as the initial situation spawns confusion, discord and eventual reconciliation.

Compare a movement from a concerto or suite by Handel or Bach with an early example of the new sonata style – say, a symphony by **GB Sammartini** (1700/01-75) **or Johann (Jan) Stamitz** (1717-57), or a sonata by **Galuppi** (1706-85), and you are immediately struck by the radical simplification of texture, phrasing and harmony. Gone are the polyphonic textures and often irregular phrasing of the baroque movements. In their place we have, typically, a series of short, rhythmically defined melodic cells, arranged in two- and four-bar phrases, with frequent cadences. The interest is almost exclusively concentrated on the movement of the top line: accompaniments are thinly textured, with chains of repeated notes, harmonies diatonic and slow-changing. Everything is geared towards elegance, 'naturalness' and easy comprehensibility.

This early classical style, the so-called 'style galant', is a counterpart to rococo (the word comes from the French *rocaille*, meaning shellwork) art – typified by the *scènes galantes* of Watteau – and architecture, with their emphasis on airy lightness, graceful, sinuous lines and delicate wit. The 'style galant' found its finest musical expression in the works of JS Bach's youngest son, **Johann Christian Bach** ('The London Bach', 1735-82), with his rare gift for polished, sensuous melody, and of **Luigi Boccherini** (1743-1805), whose string quartets and quintets (with two cellos) composed for the Spanish court combine colourful, often florid textures with a strain of exoticism and a Mediterranean warmth and *morbidezza*. The 'style galant' also pervades many works of Mozart's boyhood and adolescence: indeed, such pieces as the A major Symphony, No 29, and the last three violin concertos raise it to a supreme level – music that, in the words of Mozart's recent biographer Maynard Solomon, 'transforms loveliness into ecstasy, grace into sublimity'.

The Enlightenment

In its emphasis on simplicity and naturalness, the 'style galant' reflected some of the ideals of the Enlightenment, an intellectual movement which had its origins in the 17th-century English empirical philosophers (Locke and Hume), and the work of Isaac Newton and René Descartes. The crucible of Enlightenment thought was France, where church and monarchy had long held absolute sway. A group of *philosophes*, including men such as Montesquieu, Diderot (editor of the seminal *Encyclopédie*) and Voltaire vigorously – and in Voltaire's case vitriolically – opposed the old superstitions and assumptions, including the divine right of kings and the inherited privileges of the aristocracy. In their place they proposed a view of the world centred on man rather than God, and founded on scientific knowledge, reason, social justice and humanitarianism. Another key figure was Jean-Jacques Rousseau, the champion of the common man, 'primitive' virtues and unaffected feeling whose battle cry was 'Back to Nature'.

The ideals of egalitarianism in Enlightenment thought – and which in France were to have their logical culmination in the Revolution – went hand in hand with a new emphasis on education and moral betterment. This was the period when the rapidly burgeoning middle class began to challenge the social and cultural hegemony of the aristocracy. Aristocratic patronage – witness **Haydn** at Eszterháza and **Mozart** at Salzburg – was still crucial to a musician in the late 18th century. But there was also an ever-growing demand for music from the newly powerful bourgeoisie. This was reflected in the rise of the more 'democratic' genres of *opera buffa* and *Singspiel*, which gradually eclipsed the old aristocratic *opera seria*, and the development of public concerts. Another consequence was the expansion of music publishing. For the first time, domestic music-making created a voracious market for sheet music; and composers, Haydn and Mozart among them, supplied for home consumption reams of sonatas, duos (usually with flute or violin), trios and songs, carefully tailored to limited amateur techniques – Mozart's *galant*, 'easy' C major sonata, K545, is a well-known case in point.

The writings of the *philosophes*, their advocacy of nature and simplicity at the expense of artifice, had a crucial effect on the development of opera, especially in France. Factionalism and pamphleteering were favourite sports in mid-18th-century Paris, as they were in London. And the 1750s saw the celebrated – and much satirised – 'Querelle des Bouffons', with the traditionalist adherents of Lully and Rameau, led by Louis XV, vociferously ranged against those who aligned themselves with Rousseau and the Queen in support of the new Italian *opera buffa*, exemplified by Pergolesi's *La serva padrona*. Rousseau, who fancied himself as a composer, produced an opera of his own dealing with ordinary people, the pastoral intermezzo *Le devin du village* (1752), a work of embarrassing naivety and thinness of invention. But the Rousseau faction, and their propagation of Enlightenment values, did succeed in broadening French operatic taste, and helped pave the way for Gluck's triumphs in Paris in the 1770s.

Gluck and opera reform

In Gluck's famous Viennese reform operas of the 1760s, *Orfeo* and *Alceste*, he had sought to eliminate what he dubbed the 'abuses' of Italian *opera seria* – byzantine, often unmotivated plots, endless repetition of words, the artificial divisions into recitative and aria, vacuous ornamentation in deference to singers' vanity – in favour of dramatic truth, a more continuous texture and simple plots drawn from classical mythology. This use of classical subject matter reflects a new interest in the art of ancient Greece and Rome among historians, painters and architects of the time, crucially influenced by the findings of the German archaeologist Johann Winckelmann, whose *History of the Art of the Ancient World* was published in 1764. In his works written for Paris, culminating in *Iphigénie en Tauride* (1779), Gluck created an individual synthesis of French *tragédie lyrique*, with its lavish use of spectacle, chorus and ballet, and his own brand of 'beautiful simplicity' and emotional directness. *Iphigénie en Tauride* was to leave its mark on Mozart's first operatic masterpiece *Idomeneo*. But if Gluck was the greatest operatic reformer in the 1760s and 1770s, he was by no means alone: the Italians **Nicolò Jommelli** (1714-74) and **Tommaso Traetta** (1727-79) – above all in his masterpiece, *Antigone* (1772) – were equally concerned to put dramatic truth before singers' egos and purge *opera seria* of its superfluous display and its mechanical sequence of *da capo* arias.

Seminal works

CPE Bach	Sinfonias H648, H653 and H654. Harpsichord Concerto, H423. Cello Concerto, H432. **Alpermann** *hpd* **Bruns** *vc* **Akademie für Alte Musick, Berlin** Harmonia Mundi HMC90 1711 Ⓕ
Beethoven	Symphony No 3 in E flat, 'Eroica' **Philharmonia Orch / Klemperer** EMI mono CDM7 63855-2 Ⓜ
	String Quartet, No 14, Op 131 **Végh Quartet** Auvidis Valois V4408 Ⓕ
	Piano Sonata No 32, Op 111 **Brendel** *pf* Philips 446 701-2PH Ⓕ
	Fidelio **Nielsen** Leonore **Winbergh** Florestan **Hungarian Radio Chor; Nicolaus Esterházy Sinf / Halász** Naxos ② 8 660070/1 Ⓢ
Gluck	Orfeo ed Euridice **Ragin** Orfeo **McNair** Euridice **Sieden** Amore; **Monteverdi Choir; English Baroque Soloists / Gardiner** Philips ② 434 093-2PH2 Ⓕ
Haydn	String Quartets, Op 20 **Quatuor Mosaïques** Auvidis Astrée E8785 Ⓕ
	Symphony No 103, 'Drum-Roll' **Concertgebouw / C Davis** Philips Duo ② 442 611-2PM2 Ⓜ
	The Creation **Soloists; Monteverdi Choir; English Baroque Soloists / Gardiner** Archiv ② 449 217-2AH2 Ⓕ
Mozart	Piano Concerto No 25 in C, K503 **Schiff** *pf* **Salzburg Mozarteum Camerata Academica / Végh** Decca 425 791-2DH Ⓕ
	String Quintet in G minor, K516 **Grumiaux, Gérecz** *vns* **Janzer, Lesueur** *vas* **Czako** *vc* Philips ③ 422 511-2PME3 Ⓜ
	Don Giovanni **Waechter** Don Giovanni **Sutherland** Donna Anna **Philharmonia Chor & Orch / Giulini** EMI ② CDS5 56232-2 Ⓕ

The cult of sensibility

Together with the German poet Klopstock and the Irish writer Laurence Sterne, Rousseau was also a key influence on the German aesthetic of *Empfindsamkeit*, or 'heightened sensibility', above all through his novel of unhappy love, jealousy and soulful melancholy, *La nouvelle Héloïse*. In German literature *Empfindsamkeit* manifested itself in such works as the 'bourgeois tragedies' of Lessing and, most famously, Goethe's novel of thwarted love and suicide, *The Sorrows of Young Werther* – later in life Goethe came to disown the novel's 'pitiable self-torment'. In music this aesthetic was cultivated by a group of North German composers, including **CH Graun**, whose cloyingly sentimental oratorio *Tod Jesu* (1755) became a monument to *Empfindsamkeit*. A far more imaginative and enduring figure, though, was JS Bach's second son, **Carl Philipp Emanuel Bach** (1714-88), whose keyboard fantasias, rondos and sonatas reject the elegant frivolities of the 'style galant' and often distil a very personal vein of brooding introspection, with deceptive and *outré* harmonies and strange discontinuities of rhythm and texture.

This aesthetic of 'heightened sensibility', a reaction to the 'rational' strain in Enlightenment thinking, is closely related to the proto-romantic movement commonly known as *Sturm und Drang* (Storm and Stress), after Maximilian Klinger's blood-and-thunder drama on the American Revolution (1776). The literature of *Sturm und Drang*, exemplified by such plays as Goethe's *Götz von Berlichingen* and Schiller's *Die Räuber*, stressed violent, irrational emotion and a defiance of political and social convention. Its musical manifestations – the unbridled symphonies and concertos of CPE Bach, Gluck's revolutionary ballet *Don Juan* and the turbulent minor-keyed symphonies of Haydn, the Bohemian **JB Vaňhal**, the teenage Mozart (the 'little' G minor, K183) and others – actually predate the official literary movement. But the fashion for the sombre, the primitive and the terrifying in European art was already being set in the 1760s by James Macpherson's 'Ossian' poems (the greatest literary fraud of the century), Bishop Percy's *Reliques* and Horace Walpole's Gothic fantasy *The Castle of Otranto*. Such literature was an expression of what the philosopher Edmund Burke termed 'the sublime', which embraced grandeur and terror – inspired by natural phenomena as graveyards, oceans and wild mountains – in contrast to 'the beautiful', which Burke associated with clarity, reason and classical proportion. 'The sublime', as propounded by Burke, became a key concept in late-18th-century aesthetics; and in music it was to be supremely manifested in works such as Mozart's *Don Giovanni*, Haydn's *The Creation* and Beethoven's *Eroica* and Fifth symphonies.

Haydn and the popular style

Goethe renounced the excesses of *Sturm und Drang* with his serene classical drama *Iphigenie auf Tauris* (begun in 1779 – coincidentally the year of Gluck's opera on the same subject), which softens the cruelty of the Euripides original in keeping with the humane values of the Enlightenment. Schiller, too, turned to a loftier, more philosophical manner after the *succès de scandale* of *Die Räuber* in 1782. In Haydn's impassioned, sometimes bizarre symphonies and quartets from around 1770 – in the major as well as the minor mode – intensification of expression does not lead, as it sometimes does in the music of CPE Bach, to the brink of incoherence: a work such as the 'Farewell' symphony (No 45) already shows a formidable power of organisation and cyclic integration. Yet from around 1775 onwards, Haydn tended to abjure violent extremes. Instead he presented an amiable, often jocular face to the world, refining and deepening the language of the comedy of manners, as practised in *opera buffa*, into a supreme vehicle for subtle, civilised discourse. With occasional exceptions, from the mid-1770s onwards Haydn resolves the discordant tensions of the minor key into the major, either in the recapitulation of the opening movement or in the finale: less a question of Haydn's legendary 'cheerfulness' – this was only one aspect of his complex artistic persona – than an acknowledgement of the classical ideal of reconciliation.

In Haydn's hands the sonata style, originally a vehicle for *galant* fripperies, became an infinitely flexible medium, capable of expressing wit, irony, pathos and high drama. In each of his works, whether symphony, string quartet (a genre he evolved almost single-handedly), piano trio or sonata, the material itself dictated the form: and as Tovey pointed out three-quarters of a century ago, no two mature sonata movements by Haydn are identical in design. In his ripest works, from the Op 33 Quartets of 1781 and the 'Paris' symphonies of 1785-86 onwards, Haydn achieved a consummation of the Viennese popular style, in which catchy, folk-like tunes (occasionally, as in the *Drum-Roll* Symphony, No 103, actual folk tunes) formed the basis of immensely complex structures. Haydn's unique combination of intellectual sophistication and popular appeal was infused with 'the sublime' in the two great oratorios and the slow movements of the late quartets and symphonies: indeed, no music of the late 18th century is more exalted or visionary than the 'Chaos' prelude to the *Creation*, whose deeply un-classical effect is, paradoxically, achieved with Haydn's supreme classical control. Both *The Creation* and its equally inspired successor, *The Seasons*, are two of the greatest monuments to the Enlightenment belief in a benign, rationally ordered world and the perfectability of man. More, perhaps, than any music before or since, Haydn's late symphonies, quartets and oratorios appealed to *Kenner* – connoisseurs –

The classical string quartet

Goethe's famous remark that the string quartet is a 'conversation between four intelligent people' neatly characterises an essential aspect of the medium around 1800, the time of Haydn's last and Beethoven's first quartets. The perfection of the string quartet as a subtle, often witty discourse between four nominally equal players was one of the supreme musical achievements of the Age of the Enlightenment, and a reflection of the 18th century's cultivation of the art of civilised conversation.

Mozart contributed his own brand of sensuality and textural richness to the string quartet in his six works dedicated to Haydn, while Beethoven imbued the medium with a new rhetorical force and symphonic amplitude in the three 'Razumovsky' Quartets, Op 59. But it was Haydn who, on his own admission, stumbled on the string quartet 'by accident' in the late 1750s, who played the crucial role in its evolution. Before him there had been spasmodic examples of divertimentos for two solo violins, viola and cello by Viennese composers such as Ignaz Holzbauer and CG Wagenseil. But these older composers showed no interest in exploring the potential of the quartet as a flexible, conversational medium. And it fell to Haydn, in his sets of quartets from Op 20 (1772) to Op 77 (1799), to raise the genre from its humble beginnings in the outdoor serenade to a vehicle for the most sophisticated and challenging musical discussion.

and *Liebhaber* – amateurs – alike. They encapsulated and flattered their listeners' 'taste' (an 18th-century buzzword) and understanding while simultaneously expanding and challenging them.

Mozart: a difficult composer?

Mozart also appealed directly to Viennese popular taste in works such as *Die Entführung aus dem Serail* and *Die Zauberflöte*, two of the greatest successes during his lifetime. We can also see him cultivating a calculatedly popular, *faux-naïf* style, *à la* Haydn, in the romanze-style slow movements of some of the late piano concertos (most famously, the *Larghetto* of the last concerto, in B flat, K595) and the *Andante* of the String Quintet in E flat, K614. But while it would be a gross exaggeration to portray Mozart as a misunderstood (and impoverished) romantic figure, out of step with his age, his mature music was often considered 'difficult' to contemporaries in a way Haydn's was not.

Emperor Joseph II's famous royal critique of *Die Entführung* ('Too many notes, my dear Mozart, and too beautiful for our ears') may be apocryphal, but it does point to a recurrent problem in Mozart's music for 18th-century listeners: his language was simply too rich and intricate. Reviewing the first edition of the string quartets Mozart dedicated to Haydn – among his most 'learned' and esoteric works – one writer complained that they were too 'highly seasoned'. The publisher Hoffmeister rejected Mozart's two piano quartets because of their complexity. Mozart's sensuous, even voluptuous, richness of texture and chromatic harmony, which so delights us today, was bewildering to many listeners in his own time. So was the 'demonic' element in his music, as evinced in such works as the piano concertos in D minor and C minor, the great G minor string quintet and symphony, and *Don Giovanni*, a triumph in Prague but a mixed success in Vienna, which preferred the breezy, undemanding *opere buffe* of such composers as **Paisiello** (1740-1816), **Martín y Soler** (1754-1806) and **Cimarosa** (1749-1801). This demonic strain, first identified as such by ETA Hoffmann, appealed strongly to 19th-century romantics, at a time when most of his music was either patronised for its supposed Dresden-china prettiness, or (by the likes of Tchaikovsky) nostalgically idealised as the emblem of a lost Eden.

Mozart, of course, draws freely on the Italian operatic *lingua franca* of the day; on Viennese popular song, too, in *Die Zauberflöte*. But his mature operas far transcend the elegant frivolities of Soler and Cimarosa, in their musical density and complexity, their long-range structural mastery (shown most obviously in the extended act-finales) and their penetrative human understanding. All of his operatic masterpieces, from *Idomeneo* to *La clemenza di Tito* – a late example of Enlightenment *opera seria* – and the uniquely heterogeneous *Zauberflöte*, are touched by a Shakespearean wisdom, compassion and tolerance; in true Enlightenment spirit, forgiveness and reconciliation lie at the heart of each of these works, sometimes expressed in music of transfigured stillness: the reflections on forgiveness in the two finales of *Die Entführung*; the Countess's pardon of her errant husband near the end of *Figaro*; or the final union of Tamino and Pamina in the second finale of *Die Zauberflöte*. Even in the outwardly cynical, worldly *Così fan tutte*, such numbers as the 'farewell' Quintet and Trio in Act 1 transform the ridiculous into moments of transcendent beauty. The characters may seem self-centred and absurd, but through Mozart's music they are ennobled and redeemed.

Unlike Haydn, Mozart was both a born theatre animal and a supreme keyboard virtuoso. In the first part of the 18th century star performers were almost invariably singers. But with the growing prestige of instrumental music and the rise of public concerts, from the mid-century onwards a new breed of instrumental virtuosos touted their wares around the salons and concert halls of Europe. In Mozart's generation the composer-pianists

Muzio Clementi (1752-1832) and **JL Dussek** (1760-1812) were influential in the development of the keyboard, both through their flamboyant playing and through their taxing and often prophetic piano sonatas. Their most gifted successors in the next generation were **JN Hummel** (1778-1837) and **John Field** (1782-1837), both of whom had a crucial influence on Chopin. Outside the opera house, Mozart had his greatest professional and financial successes performing his piano concertos at his own Viennese subscription concerts. And the great series of concertos he wrote between 1782 and 1786 represent a unique amalgam of operatic characterisation, chamber musical refinement (above all in the miraculous wind writing), virtuoso display and elaborate symphonic organisation.

Beethoven: firebrand and visionary

It was as a keyboard lion that the young Ludwig van Beethoven announced himself in Vienna in the early 1790s. And within a few years the *sans culotte* from provincial Bonn had improbably become the darling of Viennese salons, admired by aristocratic connoisseurs both for his playing and his brilliant, daring keyboard compositions. Some of Beethoven's early works – the Quintet for Piano and Wind, Op 16, is a case in point – are deliberately cautious, paying homage to Mozart, whose stock was rapidly rising in the years after his death. But in the Op 1 piano trios and many of the early piano sonatas, a new sense of dialectical urgency often goes hand in hand with a subversive vehemence. The classical proportions of Haydn and Mozart are observed. But works like the *Pathétique* Sonata and the finale of the *Moonlight* reveal a composer hell-bent on confronting his audience and imposing his will on them. The language of the classical comedy of manners as perfected by Haydn and Mozart has become trenchant and strenuous, even melodramatic. And already, in pieces such as the C minor Trio from Op 1 or the F major String Quartet Op 18 No 1, Beethoven conceives the recapitulation in a sonata-form movement not merely as a homecoming but as a triumphant apotheosis.

After the turn of the new century, the trauma of encroaching deafness and the artistic credo expounded in the Heiligenstadt Testament unleashed a spate of compositions inspired by the notion of heroic struggle. 'I shall seize Fate by the throat; it shall never wholly subdue me', he wrote – words unthinkable from the pen of Haydn or Mozart. For Beethoven heroism was associated with an ethical idealism, inspired by the theory, if not the reality, of the French Revolution – a striving for liberty, fraternity and a just, enlightened social order. It was this sense of growth through mighty, heroic endeavour to ultimate triumph that lay behind works like the unprecedentedly vast *Eroica* – a tribute less to Napoleon, the original dedicatee,

Repertoire exploration

Boccherini String Quintets
Europa Galante
Virgin Veritas VC5 45421-2
Irresistible music performed by players of the highest calibre and sensitivity. An absolute must.

Cherubini Medea
Sass Medea **Luchetti** Jason
Budapest SO; Hungarian Radio and Television Chor / Gardelli
Hungaraton ② HCD11904/5 Ⓕ
A moving, strongly concentrated opera, akin in spirit and inventiveness to Beethoven and Berlioz.

Clementi Keyboard sonatas
Staier *fp*
Teldec 3984 26731-2 Ⓕ
Expressive and often powerful music in superlative performances. A wonderful disc.

Dussek Keyboard sonatas – Op 4, No 3 (C39); Op 10 No 2 (C61); Op 35 No 3 (C151); Op 61 (C211)
Marvin *pf*
Dorian Discovery DIS80125 Ⓕ
Op 4 No 3's second-movement Minuet anticipates Schubert with its gentle, reflective mood and subtly coloured major/minor opposition, while Op 35 No 3's opening movement can stand comparison with Beethoven's *Pathétique*.

Hummel Piano Concertos Nos 2 and 3
Hough *pf*
Chandos CHAN8507 Ⓕ
Exciting and inventive music and superb performances. This disc makes strong demands to be heard.

Traetta Antigona
Bayo Antigona **Anna Maria Panzarella** Ismene; **Accentus Chamber Chor; Les Talens Lyriques / Rousset**
L'Oiseau-Lyre
② 460 204-2OH02 Ⓕ
Compelling performance of a seminal 18th-century opera worthy to be ranked alongside Gluck's reform operas.

Vaňhal Symphonies
Various artists
Teldec 0630 13141-2
High-voltage readings of four inventive, often impassioned symphonies by one of Haydn's most gifted contemporaries.

than to Beethoven-as-hero – and the fanatically concentrated Fifth Symphony. Not surprisingly, many found such works initially disturbing, even repellent. But for an ever-growing number of listeners, Beethoven's dynamic, ethically charged vision communicated itself with an unprecedented directness and force.

Beyond the ideals of the Revolution itself, the grandiose, massively scored Revolutionary music of composers like **Méhul** (1763-1817) and **Gossec** (1734-1829) was certainly an influence on Beethoven's famously 'noisy' orchestral style, though in Beethoven's hands the overtly political is transcended and personalised. Similarly, his only opera *Fidelio* transcends the genre of the Revolutionary rescue opera – and the tradition of French *opéra comique* embodied most powerfully by the works of **Cherubini** (1760-1842) – and becomes a universal hymn to freedom from tyranny and to ideal womanhood: a sort of post-Revolutionary *Zauberflöte* minus the magic and the Freemasonry.

The revised version of *Fidelio*, premièred in 1814, marked the zenith of Beethoven's popular acclaim. With a few notable exceptions, like the titanic *Hammerklavier* Sonata, the *Missa solemnis* and the Ninth Symphony, that mighty late affirmation of Enlightenment ideals, his music now abandons the monumental, heroic vision for a more private, introspective questing – though it should be emphasised that Beethoven did not withdraw from the world to compose his last quartets: they were written to order, like so much of Haydn's and Mozart's music. For all their structural and harmonic innovations, the late piano sonatas and quartets still depend on the classical sonata principle he had used with such far-seeing mastery all his life. And it is this, together with his magnificent sanity and control, even *in extremis*, that confirms Beethoven as an essentially classical artist in an age of burgeoning subjective romanticism. Yet in these sublime late works the sonata ideal is imbued with a new concentration and clarity, while being expanded as never before to embrace fugue, variations, operatic aria (in, for instance, the A flat Sonata, Op 110) and a serene, rarefied lyricism. The lyrical intimacy of much of Beethoven's middle-period music – in, say, the F sharp major Sonata, Op 78, or the E flat Trio Op 70 No 2 – has tended to be overshadowed by the more public, heroic works. But such movements as the final variations of the E major Sonata, Op 109, and the C minor, Op 111, attain a visionary ecstasy that had never been heard in music before. Beethoven's spiritual struggles here find their consummation in music of timeless, transcendental peace.

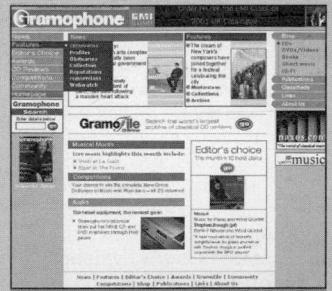

THE ROMANTIC ERA

ROMANTICISM WAS NOT MERELY A MATTER OF EXPRESSION OR SENTIMENT, BUT GAVE A NEW PRIMACY TO THE INDIVIDUAL VOICE, AS **SIMON TREZISE** EXPLAINS

Before we can talk about romanticism in music and its approximate temporal boundaries, the expression has to be defined. The word itself came from the French *lingua romana* and from related literatures, especially romances. As time went on the freedom of the medieval romance was compared unfavourably with the perceived strait-jacket of classical tradition, which was thought to be besotted with rules and formalism. So it was that a breach between spontaneous and hidebound art came under philosophical scrutiny towards the end of the 18th century through the writings of Friedrich and August Schlegel and others. In shifting awareness, the influence of Rousseau was immense, for it was he who declared that 'man is born free and everywhere he is in chains'. He proclaimed the nobility of the savage and adumbrated the romantics' acute interest in the countryside and untrammelled nature, which often found expression in the cultivation of folksong (as in many works of Haydn). Goethe in *The Sorrows of Young Werther* gave birth to the archetypal romantic hero and set the scene for the individualism of much romantic literature and music.

Add to this already extremely rich mixture the French Revolution and all the attendant upheaval in society, which overset the old orders of the Age of Enlightenment, destroyed many of the symbols of faith (in the destruction of windows, statues, etc in French churches), and new forces were released into society that were more questioning and more likely to spur deeper emotions than had hitherto been encouraged in individual expression. Whereas baroque composers had access to a range of musical 'topics' (or 'affects') to express generalised emotions according to a well-sorted set of criteria, Mozart, Beethoven, and their successors could depict complex and often contradictory emotions within a short time span, as in Mozart's Symphony No 40.

All of which raises the question of when musical romanticism actually started. While some would have it in the late 1790s, exemplified by fascinating figures like **Grétry**, others choose to see Beethoven as the last great exponent of the old classical order (challenging and setting many romantic agendas as he went) and therefore place the start in the 1820s or so. It continued, some would argue, into the early 20th century when it was supplanted by realism, symbolism (Debussy) and modernism (Schoenberg). The musicologist Carl Dahlhaus, however, sees the 1860s onwards as neo-romanticism, a period in which the ideals and spontaneity of the early period became stereotyped.

Another, rather attractive possibility is to see classicism and romanticism in music as conjoined streams that needed to coexist, so one finds in Beethoven the formalist Fourth Symphony composed alongside the extremely dramatic, and to many ears, romantic Fifth. To make romanticism depend on expression alone is a nonsense, however, for music of all centuries can be highly expressive: witness Bach's chorale preludes, Haydn's *Sturm und Drang* symphonies and so on. Some of Mozart's later works are surely romantic in every sense in which we have defined the term, and they were claimed as such by the 19th century, especially the minor-key works and *Don Giovanni* (suitably shorn of its thoroughly classical concluding sextet!).

The early Romantics

Allowing for two streams running right through the 19th century, we can at last start to understand **Schubert**, whose early symphonies obediently imitate Mozart and Haydn. While he was writing them he also brought an old form to a new level of expressiveness and versatility, the Lied. His songs among the earliest distinctive fruits of a new spirit in music, and songs such as *Erlkönig* and *Gretchen am Spinnrade* influenced generations of composers from Schumann, through Wagner and beyond. They created a new tonal style strongly contrasted with the structures of the 18th century, and their 'rhetoric' stocked the expressive resources of the new age. Schubert incorporated many of his discoveries into piano sonatas, symphonies, and chamber music, of which his String Quintet is perhaps the most striking fusion of classical forms and romantic expression.

At the same time as Schubert was bringing his all-too-short career to a climax, **Weber** was creating his own revolution in Dresden. His *Singspiel Der Freischütz* is the first unequivocal operatic masterpiece of German romanticism; it became the bread and butter of every aspiring German composer, performer, conductor and music lover for the rest of the century and beyond. Its mixture of diabolical magical elements (the 'guided' bullets), the redemptive powers of womanly love, folklore and countryside were an irresistible cocktail for the romantics and led straight to Wagner's early works.

The first generation after these giants – the one that best represents German romanticism – comprises **Mendelssohn** and **Schumann**, plus a highly distinguished 'guest' from Poland, Chopin. Schumann's piano cycles, including *Carnaval*, display the public and private faces of the composer, represented by the colourful

Seminal works

Beethoven	Symphony No 9, 'Choral' **Berlin Philharmonic Orchestra / Karajan** DG Galleria 415 832-2GGA Ⓜ
Berlioz	Symphonie fantastique **London Symphony Orchestra / C Davis** LSO Live LSO0007CD Ⓢ
Chopin	Nocturnes, Op 27 **Pires** *pf* DG 447 096-2GH2 Ⓕ
Glinka	A Life for the Tsar **Sofia National Op Chor; Sofia Festival Orch / Tchakarov** Sony ③ S3K46487 Ⓕ
Liszt	Piano Sonata in B minor **Argerich** *pf* DG The Originals 447 430-2GOR Ⓜ
Mendelssohn	A Midsummer Night's Dream **London Philharmonic Orchestra / Litton** Classics for Pleasure CD-CFP4593 Ⓑ
Mussorgsky	Boris Godunov (two versions) **Vaneyev, Putilin** Boris **Kirov Chorus & Orchestra / Gergiev** Philips ⑤ 462 230-2PH5 Ⓜ
Schubert	Erlkönig **Schäfer** *sop* **Ainsley** *ten* **George** *bass* **Johnson** *pf* Hyperion CDJ33024 Ⓕ
Schumann	Carnaval **Hess** *pf* Naxos Historical mono 8 110604 Ⓢ
Verdi	La traviata **Callas** Violetta **Kraus** Germont **Lisbon San Carlos National Theatre Orchestra / Ghione** EMI ② CDS5 56330-2
Wagner	Tristan und Isolde **Windgassen** Tristan **Nilsson** Isolde **Bayreuth Festival Chorus & Orchestra / Böhm** DG The Originals ③ 449 772-2GOR3 Ⓜ
Weber	Der Freischütz **Schreier** Max **Janowitz** Agathe **Leipzig Radio Chor; Staatskapelle Dresden / C Kleiber** DG The Originals ② 457 736-2GOR2 Ⓕ

literary tags Florestan and Eusebius. In addition, numerous allusions are delicately encoded into the music by means of musical ciphers, many of which refer to his initially forbidden love for Clara Wieck. In *Davidsbündlertänze* Schumann invites us to a masked ball, where fleeting meetings, intimacies and dances pass in quick succession, influenced by the important novelist Jean Paul. The musical language is highly expressive and the forms are often radical in their epigrammatic style. On the other hand, this most romantic of romantic masters also wrote sonatas and, later, symphonies, which build on the example of Beethoven. After his marriage to Clara he took the Lied further in several magnificent song cycles, including *Dichterliebe*, which perfectly enshrines the agony of romantic love.

Although closely identified with Schumann through geography, shared interests, and friendship, Mendelssohn was quite a different composer. He was less personal in his expressive aims and spent many of his early years pursuing musical studies that would have been perfectly comprehensible to Mozart (similarly Schumann later made an intense study of counterpoint). No surprise then that the early symphonies, mainly written for strings and played at domestic gatherings of his wealthy family, are closely related to those of Haydn. On the other hand, the exquisite *Scottish* breathes the air of high romanticism as it celebrates a strange and distant land and whips up a storm in the first movement. His Fifth Symphony, 'Reformation', celebrates Germany's distant past and looks forward to the nostalgia coursing through the veins of Wagner's *Die Meistersinger*.

Mendelssohn and Schumann set definitive examples for the romantic concerto in their respective Violin Concerto and Piano Concerto. Gone was the long classical orchestral opening (*tutti* or ritornello), to be replaced by a reciprocal exchange of ideas between soloist and orchestra. Both concertos were much imitated. Their symphonies were similarly adaptive of classical forms: Mendelssohn joined up movements in the *Scottish*, and Schumann not only makes his Fourth Symphony (in its second version) flow without a break, he also produces one of the most striking modifications of sonata form in the first movement by basing the recapitulation on a new motive introduced in the development. Sonata form itself, as we also discover in Chopin's sonatas, became less concerned with the contrast of keys in the exposition than with the contrast of themes, so reflecting prevailing dualist ideas in philosophy derived from Hegel. From now on the assertive first subject and more delicate, 'feminine' second subject became commonplace, though not ubiquitous, as Schumann demonstrates.

The greatest instrumental composer of the time alongside Schumann was **Chopin**, whose experiments with form (inspired by Field and others) runs counter to many classical trends. Even so, his works are revered for their classical poise. In Chopin, as in Schubert, Schumann and Mendelssohn, the short character piece became a major purveyor of ideas. He also cultivated national and international dance forms to an astonishing degree in his mazurkas, polonaises and waltzes. In longer works he favoured an episodic solution, like Schumann in his *Fantasie* for piano, Op 17, and the Nocturnes, which lie at the heart of his output, use operatic coloratura (rapid, ornamental passages) to add freedom and eloquence to the singing piano. For many writers trying to sum up the romantic period in music the mixture of melancholy and flights of free fantasy in Chopin are the kernel. They also did much to enhance the status of the pianist as exponent of romantic alienation from society (the piano was the adored instrument of the century). Curiously, Chopin's magnificent *Etudes* display a classical preoccupation with solving single technical problems (for the keyboard), but their tonal structures build ingeniously upon the foundations laid by Schubert.

Berlioz and Liszt

None of this magical trinity was overly concerned with the demonic or more desperate flights of romanticism such as we encounter in that quintessential romantic poet Byron. The adventures of Childe Harold and Don Juan were as congenial to the romantic palette as the plays of Shakespeare; they figure prominently in the next pair of composers to enter the story, **Berlioz** and **Liszt**. Berlioz's *Symphonie fantastique* is a wonderfully grotesque emanation from post-Revolutionary France with its 'March to the Scaffold' and 'Witches' Sabbath'. The symphony is programmatic throughout, depicting the tragic decline of the composer's imagined self as, rejected in love, he takes opium and imagines he has murdered his beloved, hence the scaffold; and then in the finale he enters a gothic world in which reality is supplanted by ghosts, sorcerers and monsters at the Sabbath. This is the very stuff of romanticism, and yet the symphony wasn't conceived in a romantic surge of spontaneous creativity: much of it is a compilation of music written for other works – in other words, it is inspired recycling.

The *Symphonie fantastique* was arranged for piano by Liszt and began its triumphant and controversial tour of the world in this form. This was how Schumann encountered it when he was moved to write a famous essay in its defence. Berlioz went on to write more symphonies, including one based on Byron's *Harold* (*Harold en Italie* has a prominent viola part depicting the hero) and operas, not least the imposing grand opera *Les Troyens* in which the classical influence of Gluck is as strong as contemporary romantic impulses. Goethe enters Berlioz's volcanic output on several

Romantic forms and techniques

Character piece (lyric piano piece)

Thousands of examples of short, often self-contained pieces, mainly for piano, with names such as *Intermezzo*, *Song without words*, etc, often in simple ternary form (ABA). From Beethoven through Schubert, Brahms, Liszt and Grieg into the 20th century such pieces continued to be written. They epitomise romantic sensibility.

Cyclic form

The use of a motive or theme (eg *idée fixe*) in all or some movements of a multi-movement work such as the symphony and concerto. ETA Hoffmann detected it in Beethoven's Fifth Symphony, in which the opening 'da-da-da-dum' returns in varied forms in all movements. Berlioz, Saint-Saëns, Tchaikovsky, Elgar and many others employed it in symphonies and chamber music. It generally entailed bringing back an idea from the first movement in subsequent movements, often in an altered form (such as the twisted 'Witches' Sabbath' version of the *idée fixe* in the finale of Berlioz's *Symphonie fantastique*). It satisfied the romantic desire for explicit unity on the surface, and is closely related to the Lisztian technique of thematic metamorphosis by which an idea changes character but retains its original melodic contour.

Lied

Songs for voice and accompaniment, but differentiated from the 18th century by the independence of the piano part and extensive use of lyric verse inspired and in many instances written by Goethe and his numerous imitators. When groups of songs are brought together through a shared narrative or, more often, poetic source, the distinctive romantic form of the song cycle came into being, as in Schubert's *Winterreise*.

Leitmotif

Found in operas of 18th- and early 19th-century operas and oratorios, but used most extensively by Wagner in the *Ring*, a musical motive or theme (sometimes just a rhythm or chord) used to depict a person, event, mood, or object – Siegmund's sword in *Die Walküre* is represented by a rising arpeggio figure, usually associated with a trumpet.

Symphonic (tone) poem

Liszt invented this genre, which usually comprises a single-movement orchestral piece with a programme of some sort. Sometimes a symphonic poem is more about feelings or impressions than actual events (eg Liszt's *Les préludes*), though in *Don Juan* Richard Strauss graphically depicts the erotic exploits of the old libertine, including an extended wooing sequence that leaves one in no doubt of the outcome.

occasions, most stirringly in his superb *La damnation de Faust*, a secular oratorio – a genre much favoured in the 19th century.

Liszt was a prolific composer and the most famous pianist of his time. His famous *tempo rubato* contrasted with the *bel canto* style of Chopin, which leant towards a more metronomic way of playing. He left hundreds of piano works, many of which encapsulate the erotic and spiritual longings of their charismatic creator. The *Liebesträume* are typical, and romantic interest in exoticism led to the *Hungarian Rhapsodies*, which Liszt mistakenly believed to be based on real Hungarian folksongs (not gypsy melodies based on popular songs as we now know). Even as Liszt wrote character pieces in a single movement in a variety of classical and rhapsodic forms, his classicism burst forth in the one-movement Piano Sonata in B minor. This amazing piece takes over the movements of a classical sonata and fuses them into one movement following the example of Schubert in his *Wandererfantasie*.

Liszt made another major contribution to 19th-century form when he invented the symphonic poem inspired by Beethoven's overtures and Rossini's one-off *William Tell* Overture. Here was a free, usually single-movement form that could satisfy the romantic preoccupation with literature by basing a musical work on some extra-musical source such as a poem, novel, myth or other source. Dvořák in some of his symphonic poems went as far as basing the very melodies themselves on the rhythm of a specific poem, most famously in *The Golden Spinning-Wheel*. Liszt covered a wide range of topics. *Héroïde funèbre* (1850) responds to revolutionary events in 1848 by recalling the savage quelling of Kossuth's revolt from Hungary's more ancient past. *Hamlet* depicts moods and people rather than narratives from Shakespeare's play. Reflecting the origins of the symphonic poem, *Hamlet* was conceived as an overture to the play before taking on its definitive form. Liszt expanded the horizons of the programmatic symphony and gave vent to his lifelong passion for Goethe's *Faust* by basing a three-movement symphony on it. In this substantial work he followed Berlioz in using a 'cyclic' theme, which depicts the eponymous hero and helps integrate the movements. The use of a cyclic theme or, as in Berlioz, *idée fixe*, was widely imitated and is found in symphonies by Franck, Saint-Saëns, Tchaikovsky and Elgar among many others (it is hinted at in Brahms).

Wagner

Liszt's legacy went beyond formal novelty. He innovated tirelessly in harmony, and his highly chromatic music language – which led to atonality in some late works – found its greatest exponent in one of the really gargantuan figures of the century, **Wagner**. Between Weber and Wagner German opera was active but rarely left a great imprint. With Wagner German opera came to dominate the world and influence virtually every major artistic movement thereafter. Wagner came to opera through diverse French, Italian and German examples, all of which can be heard in the romantic operas *Der fliegende Holländer*, *Tannhäuser* and *Lohengrin*. In the first two one finds a favourite Wagner theme of a sinning man redeemed through the self-sacrificing love of a woman. These operas still owe something to traditional operatic forms with their use of closed numbers (arias, etc.). From *Der Ring* onwards, starting with *Das Rhinegold*, Wagner embarked on a new chapter in musical expression and based his operatic forms on open-ended structures held together by leitmotifs – musical figures of any length depicting a character, object, emotion or other dramatic event. Wagner called his operas 'music dramas' and held them up as revolutionary *Gesamtkunstwerke* (total works of art – a pompous term for 'theatre' one suspects). *Der Ring*, arguably the most ambitious single work in the history of Western music, comprises four operas lasting in total some 15 hours which present nothing less than the rise and fall of civilisation in a mythical setting, all painted in the most vivid orchestral colours. *Tristan und Isolde* brought the subject of romantic love to a sumptuous epiphany and erotic explicitness that swept all before it. At around the same time he wrote his loving, nostalgic cry for the artistic soul of the 'old' German nation in the comic opera *Die Meistersinger von Nürnberg*. His last work, *Parsifal*, is also his most difficult. Its religious subject is encrusted with layers of symbolism, and some writers have detected racist overtones, all of which seem transcended by the breathtakingly lovely music so admired by Debussy and countless others.

The age that produced Wagner also produced **Brahms**. A devout classicist, he knew the past as well as he knew the present. His works abound in references to the Renaissance, baroque, classical as well as to the present, including Wagner. He was a friend and disciple of Schumann, and his early works are full of the hot-blooded passion of the romantic movement. As he matured he became more and more entrenched in the classical style. His four concertos even use the Mozartian opening *tutti* (or ritornello) prior to the soloist's entry, long since rejected by the romantics. And yet commingling with his classicism is a poetic soul and a profound identification with nature and other romantic ideals. In 1854 this romantic soul was explicitly bared in the first version of the First Piano Trio, which contains Schumann's Clara themes, but late in life he revised the trio and hid the 'programme'. His symphonies, chamber music, songs, choruses, etc are among the most perfectly formed of all 19th-century works, but it is hardly reasonable that his works should be exalted as emblems of so-called 'absolute' music, which is music with no subject other than music itself.

Italian opera

Crossing the Alps we find a land dominated by opera. Italy was in love with theatre and the human voice. Its classical period had Rossini and its early romantic composers were **Donizetti** and **Bellini**. *Lucia di Lammermoor*, one of Donizetti's finest operas, represents much of Italian romanticism. The orchestral sound is fuller, more horn-dominated than Rossini; the harmony has become chromatic, and the subject matter, with its gloomy churchyards and ruins, is taken from one of the most popular literary figures of romanticism, Sir Walter Scott (*The Bride of Lammermoor*). Donizetti relaxes Rossini's geometric forms, often varying the second verse in the slow part of an aria, and using long scenas with highly varied recitatives now forming a more integrated part of the operatic fabric. The aria in which Lucia loses her reason after murdering her unwanted husband – the Mad scene – is a classic instance of the triumph of the irrational, in this case triggered by tragic events founded, as is so often the way, on thwarted love.

Bellini's poignant melodies and rich orchestration added another layer to Italian romantic opera, best heard in *Norma* and *I puritani*, but it was **Verdi** who set the seal on the Italian century. His works blended nationalism and realism with subjects inherited from romantic poets and novelists to create operas of consummate dramatic power and musical substance. *La traviata* takes the theme of the consumptive courtesan who becomes romantically involved with a man of good birth (after Dumas's *La dame aux camélias*). Family duty intervenes and she is forced to renounce the love of her life, with heartbreaking consequences. Verdi gradually loosens traditional Italian operatic forms, still using arias and ensembles, but often diluting their formal integrity so that whole scenes or even acts are built in a chain-like way. It is a halfway house between Rossini's closed forms and Wagner's endless melody, and it triumphs in the works of Verdi's old age, especially *Otello* and *Falstaff*. *Don Carlos* is a superlative example of grand historical opera; it uses a vast range of musical devices from conventional arias to vast set pieces; and the orchestra is as important as the voice as a carrier of dramatic truth.

Opera was also the staple diet of Paris, where much of France's musical life flourished. The French liked grand opera *à la* **Meyerbeer**, whose *Les Huguenots* satisfied the taste for grand scenes, vocal acrobatics and long ensembles. Berlioz was hard-pressed to compete, as was Wagner on his catastrophic trips to Paris. One composer who did finally succeed in the opera house (albeit in the Opéra-Comique) was **Bizet**, who did not live to see his *Carmen* become one of the favoured vehicles of the new operatic realism (in some ways a post-romantic phenomenon). As the century wore on the concert life of the salons, the setting for France's instrumental life, extended into newly built concert halls where more and more orchestras sprang up. For most of them Liszt was a hallowed model for form, harmony and motivic development. Inspired by **César Franck** many composers started to write quartets, symphonies, etc: classicism returned to France. The apparently cerebral Franck wrote works of great passion, including a Piano Quintet which takes the Belgian composer out of his beloved organ loft and into the scalding embrace of erotic passion.

Key cultural figures

Goethe, Johann Wolfgang von (1749-1832)
He offered a new, individualistic view of humanity in his poetry, novels, plays and scientific writings which had a profound influence on the romantic period as well as providing source material for countless operas, symphonic poems, etc, most notably *Faust*.

Hegel, Georg Wilhelm Friedrich (1770-1831)
The most influential philosopher of the time, he produced a philosophy based on the belief that argument, processes, and so on were based upon the opposition of ideas or the conflict of opposites.

Hoffmann, Ernst Theodor Amadeus (1776-1822)
A novelist, critic, composer, Hoffmann did much to establish the beliefs and aspirations of early romanticism. In particular he was instrumental in establishing Beethoven as the first romantic composer. One of his greatest works was brought back to life by Offenbach in the opera *The Tales of Hoffmann*.

Nietzsche, Friedrich Wilhelm (1844-1900)
A radical atheistic philosopher who argued that man's great mission is to foster the superman, an individual who can find meaning in a meaningless world and who rejects contemporary materialist aspirations.

Richter, Johann Paul Friedrich (1763-1825)
Pen name Jean Paul, his highly eccentric novels inspired piano works by Schumann, who was doubtless attracted by their quirky, incident-rich content.

Rousseau, Jean-Jacques (1712–78)
He advocated more permissive education for children and voice, more extreme emotions than other writers of his time; idealised nature and the native.

Schlegel, Friedrich von (1772-1829)
A philosopher and writer on Classical antiquity, he wrote of the inherent dichotomy of classical and romantic art.

Schopenhauer, Arthur (1788-1860)
A vital influence on Wagner, he described the Will as a destructive impulse in humanity, which leads inevitably to suffering.

Nationalism

It took a while for music in Spain, England, Bohemia, Poland, Hungary, Russia and other countries to develop an individual voice and come forward with major composers. Russia woke up first, in the works of **Glinka**, whose operas used Russian folk music. His example was followed by the 'Five', which comprised Balakirev, Rimsky-Korsakov, Cui, Borodin and **Mussorgsky**. All discovered their roots in Russian folklore and were inspired to base whole works on folksong. Mussorgsky's *Boris Godunov* is probably the greatest product of this movement, but its realism takes us beyond the scope of romanticism. Alongside these overtly nationalistic composers **Tchaikovsky** was more cosmopolitan. He loved French ballet, hated Wagner, and evidently knew Berlioz and Liszt's music very well (as did the 'Five'). Tchaikovsky's classicism manifested itself in seven symphonies, the later examples of which are among the most original and striking adaptions of the classical, four-movement model. True to the romantic movement he identified so closely with, his unnumbered symphony is based on Byron's *Manfred* and uses a Berlioz-like *idée fixe*. Tchaikovsky's ballets are considered his greatest achievement, especially *The Sleeping Beauty*; they combine symphonic development in set pieces with strongly characterised shorter numbers, all underpinned by a visceral excitement unique to this composer.

Many countries found themselves awakening to refreshing romantic air in the nationalist movement. Bohemia boasted Smetana and, later, **Dvořák**, who worked fluently in both the classical Brahms manner and romantic prototypes of Liszt (as in his symphonic poems). Dvořák's individuality is best demonstrated in his symphonies, especially the last three, the Cello Concerto, and his highly varied chamber music. His operas are becoming better known thanks to recordings.

Britain and Ireland were less fortunate in the 19th century, though recent excavation, much of it via CD, has started to uncover some fine Romantic music from Bantock, Parry, Sullivan, Stanford and others. Perhaps the famous renaissance, which started with **Elgar** and **Vaughan Williams**, was not quite so sudden as it sometimes assumed.

The 19th century was a rich, diffuse, multi-layered time for music – far more so than the 18th. Many strands make up the movement loosely referred to as romanticism. However one seeks to define it, by 1900 it had largely run its course. Symbolism, modernism, realism and other movements had taken over, in spite of which romanticism in one form or another continues to play a part in composers as disparate as Barber and Elgar, and a neo-romantic movement is certainly with us today.

Repertoire exploration

Albéniz Iberia
De Larrocha *pf*
Decca ② 417 887-2DH2 Ⓕ
Albéniz's masterpiece is a treasure trove of Spanish nationalism expressed in glowing keyboard writing.

Alkan Grande Sonate
'Les Quatre Ages', Op 33
Hamelin *pf*
Hyperion CDA66794 Ⓕ
Alkan's keyboard virtuosity is staggering, as is his fecundity of invention and resourceful formal structures.

Brüll Piano Concertos No 2, Op 24
Coupling: Piano Concerto No 1, Op 10
Roscoe *pf* **BBC Scottish Symphony Orchestra / Brabbins**
Hyperion CDA67069 Ⓕ
Little-known riches surface in this brilliantly conceived concerto – a reminder of many hidden romantic treasures.

Litolff Concerto symphonique No 4, Op 102
Coupling: Concerto symphonique No 2, Op 22
Donohoe *pf* **Bournemouth Symphony Orchestra / Litton**
Hyperion CDA66889 Ⓕ
A concerto in the grand tradition with a miraculous *Scherzo* and much to relish in other movements.

Lalo Namouna – Suites Nos 1 and 2 plus Allegro vivace; Tambourin; La Gitane; Bacchanale
Monte-Carlo Philharmonic Orchestra / Robertson
Auvidis Valois V4677 Ⓕ
Vivid orchestral writing and rhythmic ideas in this ballet so excited the young Debussy he was evicted from the theatre.

Spohr Nonet, Op 31 and Octet, Op 32
Gaudier Ensemble
Hyperion CDA66699 Ⓕ
Spohr is an archetypal early romantic composer, much better known in his own time than ours, but now back in favour.

OPENING DOORS TO MODERN MUSIC

THE PAST CENTURY PRODUCED A BEWILDERING VARIETY OF MUSICAL LANGUAGES, INCLUDING PLENTY OF TREASURES FOR THE ADVENTUROUS. **MICHAEL OLIVER** OFFERS GUIDANCE

Some of us really looked forward to the end of the 20th century in the hope that we would at long last understand its musical history. Earlier centuries were so much easier, when one could reasonably say that Haydn begat Mozart, who begat Beethoven who begat Schubert and so on. It got a little more complex later on in the 19th century, but by including, so to speak, musical uncles as well as fathers in the chain of heredity we could understand how Wagner and Brahms were if not brothers then fairly close cousins. In the early 20th century it looked as though this pattern might continue, with Richard Strauss audibly the heir of Wagner, and Stravinsky at least for a while audibly the son of Rimsky-Korsakov. But then arrived Schoenberg, and although his descent from Mahler was obvious at first, some other gene soon became dominant. And if there was, even so, a hidden but orderly pattern of descent and influence how on earth did Bartók fit into it? And Hindemith, and Varèse, and Debussy?

There were of course attempts to demonstrate that the 20th century, like the 17th and the 18th, had a central *lingua franca*, and battle lines were drawn between those who thought that it was best represented by Schoenberg and his followers and those who on the contrary saw Stravinsky as the century's crucial figure. Amid the dust of combat faint cries could be heard of 'What about Sibelius, though?', or 'Haven't you forgotten Shostakovich?' or even 'Why do we have to choose one or the other?', but these were on the whole ignored and the controversy degenerated into a war of rival orthodoxies. Partisans of the former camp tended to suggest that the only possible path forward for the art of music was on a line drawn from Wagner through Schoenberg and especially his pupil Anton Webern, and that any composer pursuing any other route was at best an interesting irrelevance, at worst a dangerous saboteur of necessary progress. The followers of Stravinsky were on the whole more tolerant of heterodoxy but most of them were united (since this is why they'd hitched themselves to Stravinsky's bandwagon in the first place) in condemning the serialist tendency.

It is still possible to arouse violent wrath by suggesting that in fact both parties were barking up the wrong tree, but the damage has long since been done. The language of the controversy, and of the attempts to prove either Arnold Schoenberg or Igor Stravinsky the Chosen One was often intemperate and no less frequently phrased in language that most music-lovers found incomprehensible (even those who had taken the trouble to find out what 'sonata form' and 'dominant' and 'canon' meant in the hope of appreciating Beethoven and Haydn the better). The message was unmistakable: most modern music is nasty and difficult, most writing about it is opaque and unhelpful.

Once bitten, twice shy: we have a larger musical public now than at any previous period in history, and the vast majority of them would no sooner go to a concert of contemporary music than they would volunteer for an interesting research project into whether the Black Death was really all that infectious. It isn't so much that they know in advance that the music will be horrid; it's because they know in advance that they won't understand it. Which would be no problem at all if this were true. After all there's no law compelling anyone to like modern music; and the contemporary music public, minority though it is, is capable with a bit of help from the Arts Council of keeping at least a few living composers above the poverty line. And have not eminent composers themselves suggested (like Elliott Carter) that new music should be subsidised as though it were an educational project, not a form of entertainment, or (like Milton Babbitt) that advanced music inevitably appeals at first only to a few and should be treated therefore as an academic discipline, new works being heard and discussed at closed seminars, not profane concerts?

But it is not true. A great deal of the century's music is exciting, colourful, dramatic, immediately attractive and approachable; a lot of it is tuneful; and you no more need to 'understand' it than you need degrees in geology and botany to enjoy a fine landscape. The trouble is... No: there are two troubles, or rather three. The first is that people have been listening to new music with the wrong expectations, and have inevitably been disappointed. If what you want (at the moment, or in general terms) is a simple melody, simply accompanied, then a Bach fugue will disappoint you just as much as a symphony by Sir Peter Maxwell Davies, and for much the same reason. The second problem is that discussion of modern music has concentrated so much on technicalities that listeners have assumed that if they can't hear those technicalities then the music is above their heads and isn't for them. The most important thing about any piece of music is the way it sounds. If it can only be appreciated by understanding how it was constructed then that piece of music has failed. I think I'd better leave the third problem until later.

Seminal works

Bartók	Piano Concerto No 2 **Donohoe** *pf* **CBSO / Rattle** EMI CDC7 54871-2	Ⓕ
Berg	Violin Concerto **Perlman** *vn* **Boston SO / Ozawa** DG 447 445-2GOR	Ⓜ
Boulez	Le marteau sans maître **O de la Martinez** Lorelt LNT108	Ⓕ
Britten	The Turn of the Screw **Pears** *ten* **Cross / Britten** Decca 425 672-2LH2	Ⓕ
Copland	Piano Variations **Hough** *pf* Hyperion CDA67005	Ⓕ
Debussy	La mer **BPO / Karajan** DG 447 426-2GOR	Ⓜ
Harvey	Mortuos Plango, Vivos Voco **Harvey** Sargasso Records SCD28029	Ⓕ
Ives	Three Places in New England **Boston SO / Tilson Thomas** DG 423 243-2GC	Ⓜ
Janáček	Sinfonietta **VPO / Mackerras** Decca 448 255-2DF2	Ⓜ
Ligeti	Atmosphères **Bour** Wergo WER60162-50	Ⓕ
Messiaen	Turangalîla-symphonie **LSO / Previn** EMI CZS5 69752-2	Ⓜ
Schoenberg	Orchestral Variations, Op 31 **Chicago SO / Boulez** Erato 2292 45827-2	Ⓕ
	Five Orchestral Pieces, Op 16 **Chicago SO / Barenboim** Teldec 4509 98256-2	Ⓕ
Shostakovich	Symphony No 10 **Philadelphia Orch / Jansons** EMI CDC5 55232-2	Ⓕ
Stravinsky	Agon **Stravinsky** Sony Classical SM3K46292	Ⓜ
	Rite of Spring **Philharmonia / Markevitch** Testament SBT1076	Ⓕ
Xenakis	Metastasis **FRNO / M Le Roux** Le Chant du Monde LDC278 368	Ⓕ
Varèse	Ionisation and Déserts **Chailly** Decca 460 208-2DH2	Ⓕ

The language expands

Musical language expanded during the 20th century. It had done in every previous century, of course, but between 1900 and 2000 the expansion was much more rapid than ever before, and it affected every single aspect of music. Of course people got confused.

Western music, at least since the classical period, has laid great stress on the related areas of harmonic subtlety (which we all hear, whether or not we can describe what we're hearing) and a strong sense of tension between keys (we can all hear that, too); this latter is also important for giving a piece of music a perceived structure or dramatic scenario. In concentrating on these elements Western music rather neglected melodic refinement. We divide the octave into 12 steps, whereas in various non-European musics there are twice as many or more. Most melodies of the classical and romantic periods are either relatively short, spanning an even number of bars (often eight) or, when longer, proceed in closely inter-related phrases, again relatively short and usually of an even number of bars. These successive phrases often aid memorability by repeating a few notes from an earlier phrase. Some modern composers (not all that many) have used divisions of the octave greater than 12 – microtones. Many have written melodies of irregular phrase-length, with few repeated elements or none.

What we take to be a 'tuneless' melody may in fact be amply tuneful, but because it doesn't proceed in eight-bar phrases but is asymmetrical, because its rises and descents aren't those that we half expect and it doesn't repeat itself, it takes a little effort to grasp. The theme of **Schoenberg**'s *Orchestral Variations*, Op 31, is often described, accurately but off-puttingly and irrelevantly, as consisting of all four basic versions of a 12-note row (the row itself, the same played backwards, played upside-down and then backwards *and* upside-down). What that description misses, what all such descriptions must miss, is that the theme is unusually long, involving numerous wide leaps of a kind you won't hear in Mozart, but that once you get used to these features it is a melody of great, even romantic beauty and expressiveness. And when you realise that, of course, the variations on that theme are almost as easy to grasp as Brahms. Yet analyses of the piece still tend to concentrate on the technicalities of how it was put together. Remember Bernard Shaw's 'analysis' of Hamlet's 'To be, or not to be' soliloquy?:
'Shakespear, dispensing with the customary exordium, announces his subject at once in the infinitive, in which mood it is presently repeated after a short connecting passage in which, brief as it is, we recognize the alternative and negative forms on which so much of the significance of repetition depends. Here we reach a colon; and a pointed pository phrase, in which the accent falls decisively on the relative

pronoun, brings us to the first full stop.'

A good many composers in the 20th century have expanded their language beyond the conventional perception that music consists of melody, harmony, counterpoint and rhythm. Schoenberg once suggested that it should be possible to make a 'melody' not from notes of different pitches but of different tone-colours, and in the third of his *Five Orchestral Pieces* , Op 16, he provided an example. It was originally entitled 'Colours', but he later renamed it 'Summer Morning by a Lake'. It is, in any normal sense, tuneless; to hunt for a melody would be frustrating and pointless. It is a study in shifting and evanescent colour, of the harmonic and instrumental equivalent of sun falling through leaves on to calm water. Provided that you're not vainly searching for a tune it's rather beautiful. And since a lot of modern music explores areas other than melody, harmony, counterpoint and rhythm (though probably including all of those as well), Schoenberg's piece is a useful listening exercise, just as his *Variations* are for exploring what one might call the 20th-century's 'expanded melody'.

Edgard Varèse's *Ionisation* is another piece, entertaining and striking in itself, which is also valuable for stretching the ears. It's scored for 41 percussion instruments, none of them (until a siren appears towards the end) having a precise pitch. It, too, therefore contains no melody nor harmony in any normal sense. Rhythm, yes, and a rich counterpoint of cross-rhythms. But the palette of tone colours – colours unobtainable from wind, string or keyboard instruments – is still richer, and so is what one can only call the piece's repertoire of textures. You could compare them to passing your fingers over velvet, gravel, brocade, a brush and so on, or to the subtle or dense pen-strokes of an artist, his cross-hatchings and stipplings. Texture is also an area that has been much explored by 20th century composers, and Varèse's piece will open many doors – to the music, to take a single example, of György Ligeti.

Varèse wanted to write a music specifically of the 20th century, responding to and using its technological advances. He had, so to speak, an ambition to write electronic music before anyone got round to inventing the means of doing so. He lived long enough to use the tape recorder, in his astonishing *Déserts*, where an instrumental ensemble alternates with pre-recorded industrial sounds on tape (the 'deserts' of his title include not only wastes of sand and ice, but the inhabited deserts of big cities), and in his last completed work, *Poème électronique*, for stereophonic tape alone.

Younger composers, too, have been excited by the ability of electronic sources to produce either sounds that have never been heard before – and to the composer's precise specification – or to 'play' music with a precision no human performer can match. A classic in this field, and again a work that can open many doors, is **Jonathan Harvey**'s *Mortuos Plango, Vivos Voco*, in which all the sounds are derived, with prodigious technical resource but more importantly with prodigious imagination, from the sounds of a bell (bearing the inscription that gives the work its title: 'I lament the dead, I call the living') and the voice of a child (Harvey's son, then a choirboy). But again it's the sounds that matter, not the process that brought them about. You don't need to be a qualified structural engineer to be moved by the soaring arches of a great cathedral.

Serialism

A 19th-century tendency to use notes outside the ostensible key for expressive ends culminated in the *Prelude* to *Tristan und Isolde* in which, to evoke unassuageable yearning, Wagner wrote music that can hardly be said to be in a key at all: you cannot sense where the 'Doh' of his scale might be. But the whole Austro-German symphonic tradition depended on a perceptible sense of key and of conflict between keys – this is what gives the great symphonies from Mozart to Mahler their form, their forward movement and their drama. Schoenberg thought that a music with no sense of key ('atonal' music) was inevitable, but he found that it could only be given structure by sheer imaginative force or by a literary text or programme. He therefore devised a system which would impose a discipline as firm as that governing music under the key system and at the same time guarantee that it would remain atonal. All 12 notes of the Western scale were arranged in a particular order (a 'note-row' or 'tone-row'), which could be played backwards ('retrograde'), upside-down ('inversion') or in retrograde inversion. Any of these could be played at any pitch; any note could be transposed by one or more octaves; parts of the row could be contracted by playing consecutive notes together, as chords; but no note was to be repeated until the other 11 had been heard. The system thus provided an almost limitless range of possibilities, but ensured maximum economy and rigour.

Enjoying dissonance

Rhythm took prodigious steps during the 20th century, and it took most of them in a single work, **Stravinsky**'s *The Rite of Spring*. Because of the popularity of that piece, and because most people have heard enough jazz to be familiar with off-the-beat syncopation, the rhythmic advances of the century have been easier to absorb than some of the others. The other great advance of *The Rite of Spring* however is its unprecedented level of dissonance. In many other works of the last hundred or so years dissonance can unsettle the listener, who in hearing the music of previous centuries has got used to a good deal of dissonance but always with the expectation that it will eventually resolve to a more 'comfortable' harmony – indeed composers have used the device of teasing the ear with dissonance but sooner or later resolving it as a means of giving a sense of forward movement, structure and drama to their music. Twentieth-century composers have used dissonance as a much more 'normal' element in their music; dissonance has become a sort of expansion of the language of harmony.

Listening to **Charles Ives**'s music is useful here, because it soon becomes obvious that he isn't using dissonance out of the demands of some system or theory, but because he enjoys it. It's fun: in his *Country Band March* you can hear him quite accurately recording how a village bandsman will play a wrong note for the hell of it, or see if a quite different tune will 'go with' the one his colleagues are playing (Ives loved the idea of different musics colliding), and how everyone grins when old George comes in a bar too early. But Ives also relished dissonance as an expressive, almost a pictorial resource. How on earth, he might well have asked, referring to his orchestral *Three Places in New England*, can I describe the varied and simultaneous emotions, sights and sounds of a Sunday morning walk with my wife, not long after our wedding, with 'nice' harmonies? How can I portray a regiment of black soldiers, marching to their deaths in the American Civil War, filled with despair but also with heroic resolve, with only the harmonies that text-books approve of? With Ives it often helps, not to know or understand the techniques and processes he was using, but to understand what he was using them for.

Indeed a major reason for the expansion of musical language in the 20th century was the desire of composers to express or to discuss things that had never been expressed or discussed before; it is one of the prime reasons for any advance in art at any period. Too much has been said of Schoenberg's advances having been made 'necessary' by the threat posed to the conventional major-and-minor key system by Wagner's expressive expansions of that system. The threat was perceived as worrying only by those, like Schoenberg, who felt especially close to that system's Viennese mainstream (Russian composers, who'd been struggling for years to establish a symphonic tradition of their own, independent from the Viennese, weren't bothered by it at all). And although Schoenberg devised his *system* to cope with that situation no composer worthy of the name writes *music* in order to counter a threat to the key system. Schoenberg, like Beethoven, like Wagner, had such powerfully original things to say that he needed to stretch the language of music in order to express them.

After Schoenberg

The idea of the 12-note row, and the techniques that Schoenberg devised for manipulating it, had a powerful influence on many of his juniors, but for a variety of reasons, not just because it offered a way forward from what some saw as a post-Wagnerian impasse. Serialism appealed to many because of its rigorous economy: it provided a means whereby every note in a composition earned its place, and was logically related to all the others. There is, for some people, a positive pleasure to be gained from a music of immaculate precision. Stravinsky, for long regarded as Schoenberg's opponent, eventually adopted and adapted his system because in a sense he had been using its essence all along,

Key terms

Aleatory	(From Latin alea, 'dice'). Music which allows an element of chance or free improvisation in performance.
Atonal	Music in which little or no sense of key is perceptible.
Bitonal	See 'Polytonal', below.
Cluster	A group of notes, often adjacent ones, played together but which cannot be heard as a chord.
Dodecaphonic	Music using all 12 notes of the chromatic scale; usually used as though synonymous with 'serial'.
Electroacoustic	Music combining electronic and live performance, the former often modifying the latter.
Mode	A scale. Traditional Western music uses two, the major and minor modes, but numerous others exist, found in folk, early or Eastern music, and others still can be devised.
Musique concrète	Music produced by modifying recordings of natural or industrial sounds.
Neoclassical	Literally music which adopts features of the classical style of Haydn and Mozart; Stravinsky, to whom the term is often applied, objected to it, and many of his works in fact refer to such non-classsical composers as Handel and Verdi.
Polytonal	Music in which two or more keys are used simultaneously.
Total serialism	Music in which not only pitch but rhythm, duration, loudness and other factors are determined by the rules of serialism.

exhaustively permutating short groups of notes ('mini-tone-rows', one might call them) since *The Rite of Spring*. For many of the post-Second World War generation, especially those from the German-speaking countries, serialism provided a language that was unsullied by a shameful past that they needed to reject. Schoenberg's method also attracted pedants, of course, and their music was aridly academic and soon forgotten, but other and fiercely independent composers have found aspects of his system invaluable in forming their own styles.

It is unlikely, for example, that either **Elliott Carter** or **Sir Harrison Birtwistle** would have written the sort of music that they have without Schoenberg's example and impetus. But you might find it much more useful to approach each of them with an image in mind rather than a detailed analysis of how their music is put together. With Carter the image might be of a music that can convey an extraordinary effect of space because it is proceeding at several speeds at once – as different elements of the landscape seem to move at different speeds as you rush past them in a train or an aircraft. Something similar happens also in Birtwistle, but here a more useful image might be that of a music on several levels or strata, with a vast something moving at the lowest of them.

Many other composers have stretched musical language, for their own expressive ends, without needing to adopt Schoenberg's system, which was so well adapted to his own needs. **Olivier Messiaen** respected Schoenberg greatly, used his method briefly (and in so doing mastered it so completely that a high proportion of the post-war avant-garde sought him out as a teacher) but what he and Schoenberg wanted to do were vastly different. 'Ornithologist-musician' as he called himself, mystic-musician as he in fact was, he could not transcribe his beloved bird-song into melodies of the major or minor scales because birds seldom use them. This and other considerations led him to explore other scales that had either never been used in Western 'classical' music or had not been used for centuries and which he found invaluable for writing music that expressed his devout religious faith.

Messiaen was the most thorough explorer of this field, but by no means the first. **Debussy** said that he wanted to write music that was 'neither major nor minor' and was excited to discover the quite different scales used in oriental music. **Béla Bartók**, researching the folk music of Hungary, was overwhelmed by the quality of the melodies that he found, and astonished to discover that some of them used a scale, 'neither major nor minor', that Debussy and other 'advanced' modernists were using. Another expansion: no longer only two permissible scales but a range of possibilities. But also: no longer only two permissible father-figures for modern music (Schoenberg or Stravinsky). Composers of the present generation find exciting unfinished business and pointers to their own development in Bartók, in Debussy, in Carl Nielsen, Sibelius and others.

And the 20th century, particularly the latter part of it, was also particularly rich in independent figures, who accepted no orthodoxy or party-line but who, from a variety of influences or from none, forged an

Repertoire exploration

Cage, John
4'33"
Wayne Marshall
Floating Earth FCD004 Ⓕ
Get hold of a kitchen timer, set it to ring after four minutes and 33 seconds; during that time listen to and think about every sound. You have now performed John Cage's 4'33", a 'composition' that contains no 'music'. Or does it?

Cardew, Cornelius
The Great Learning
Scratch Orchestra
Cortical Foundation CORTI21 Ⓕ
Leader of the British avant-garde who writes 'democratic' music for amateurs and non-musicians: an oddly impressive, timeless ritual.

Eisler, Hanns
Hollywood Songbook
Matthias Görne, Eric Schneider
Decca 460 582-2 Ⓕ
A rebellious Schoenberg pupil, already skilled at cabaret-style political propaganda, masters every style from neo-Schubert to atonality in nostalgic exile's protest at Nazism.

Harrison, Lou
Symphony No 4
California SO / B Jekowsky
Argo 455 590-2ZH Ⓕ
A composer who believes that 'melody is the audience's take-home pay' and who sees no reason why a symphony shouldn't end with someone telling stories.

Nancarrow, Conlon
Studies for Player Piano
C Nancarrow
Wergo WER6907-2 Ⓕ
Single-minded American pioneer investigates music of superhuman velocity, precision and attack.

Thomson, Virgil
Four Saints in Three Acts
Leonard Bernstein
New York Philharmonic NYP9904 Ⓕ
A deceptively simple style rooted in American vernacular – hymn tunes, parlour ballads – reveals radiant lucidity in apparently meaningless text by Gertrude Stein.

immediately recognisable personal language. **Benjamin Britten** is an obvious example, in his youth distrusted by the establishment as a too-clever-by-half modernist, in his latter years dismissed by some of his juniors as hopelessly old-fashioned, but now recognised as a major composer, perhaps the greatest of the century's 'one-offs'. And there have been many of them, writing music in a mind-boggling variety of styles. **John Cage**, for many people not a composer at all, in fact a man who listened entranced to the whole world of sound and wanted every musical event to be an unpredictable voyage of discovery. **Iannis Xenakis**, whose work is very often discussed in terms of the mathematical principles which govern it, but whose very first mature composition, *Metastasis*, had its origin in a terrible memory: of how crowds move when threatened by gunfire, of how ordered movement and disciplined chanting becomes disorder. **György Ligeti**, like Xenakis an explorer of fantastically complex textures, but who is open-eared enough to have been interested and influenced by the minimalists, African drumming, that weird but inspired virtuoso of the player-piano Conlon Nancarrow, even Brahms…

And now, of course, comes the third problem that I mentioned earlier. There are so many composers now, writing so many different sorts of music. Even specialists can't keep up with them all; how can the ordinary music-lover manage (who doesn't want to give up Bach, Beethoven and all the others while he or she devotes a year or two to dolefully and dutifully sampling who knows how many living and recent composers)? 'For heaven's sake don't even try' would be my advice. Start with two or three pieces, say one that intrigues but perplexes you (one of those I've mentioned, perhaps), one that lots of people speak highly of and a third that's as different from the other two as possible, perhaps by a young composer. Listen to them with real concentration several times (the way you used to listen to Beethoven when you first discovered him). Maybe one of them will be as perplexing at the end of this process as it was at the beginning – put it aside and forget about it, at least for the time being. But my bet would be that at least one of the others will be starting to make sense, perhaps much more quickly than you expected. More than that: you may well find that the experience of concentratedly listening to that one will unexpectedly open doors to others. And in music the old saying ('When one door opens another shuts') is most certainly not true. One door opens on a corridor of others, all invitingly open.

Using the Guide

The presentation and design of this Guide is similar to that of its parent publication, *Gramophone*. Reviews of works generally appear in the following sequence: Orchestral, Chamber, Instrumental, Choral and Operatic (for ease of use, operas appear in alphabetical, as opposed to chronological, order). The Guide is now in a new two-column layout, with each recording reviewed under a genre or work heading.

The title for each review contains the following information: Composer(s), work(s), artist(s), record company or label, price range, disc number and recording date, where available. *Gramophone* Award-winning discs from 1977 to 1999 are clearly indicated. The circled numeral before the catalogue number indicates the number of discs (if more than one), while the timing and mode of recording are given in brackets afterwards. (The abbreviations AAD/ADD/DDD denote analogue or digital stages in the recording/editing or mixing/mastering or transcription processes in CD manufacture. Other abbreviations used in this guide are given opposite.)

Generally, where more than three composers are represented on a single disc, the review appears in the Collections section which starts on page 1111. At the end you will also find a new DVD section (plus a few videos), which we hope to expand as more releases become available.

Also new this year is the Index to Couplings – an index of works reviewed under other composers. For example, Franck's *Prélude, choral et fugue* with Evgeni Kissin, is reviewed under its Beethoven *Moonlight* Sonata coupling, and you will find the page reference by looking in the couplings index under Beethoven.

All of the recordings recommended herein are flagged with one or more of the symbols explained below. This year we have also introduced a rating system to help novice collectors in their decision-making, as clearly all the performances in this Guide are recommendable in some way or other.

Key to symbols

Ⓕ Full price £10 and over
Ⓜ Medium price £7-£9·99
Ⓑ Bargain price £5-£6·99
Ⓢ Super bargain price £4·99 and below

H Denotes a Historic recording and generally applies to pre-1960 recordings. It can also be an indication that the recording quality may not be up to the highest standards.

P Denotes recordings where period instruments are used.

Key to ratings

OOO *Gramophone* Award winners and recordings that have acquired legendary status.
OO Outstanding performances and exceptionally fine sound/transfer.
O Strongly recommended.
NO DISC: recommended with perhaps an odd reservation.
$ Outstanding value for money. This symbol is awarded to a very few releases that contain superlative performances and are at bargain price or below.

Although every effort is made to obtain the latest information for inclusion in this book, no guarantee can be given that all the discs listed are immediately available. Any queries concerning availability should be referred to the issuing company concerned. When ordering, purchasers are advised to quote all the relevant information in addition to the disc numbers.

Abbreviations

aas all available separately
alto countertenor/male alto
anon anonymous
arr arranged
attrib attributed
b born
bar baritone
bass-bar bass-baritone
bn bassoon
c circa (about)
cl clarinet
clav clavichord
compl completed
cont continuo
contr contralto
cor ang cor anglais
cpsr composer
cpte(d) complete(d)
d died
db double bass
dig pf digital piano
dir director
ed edited (by)/edition
exc excerpt
fl flute
fl flourished
fp fortepiano
gtr guitar
harm harmonium
hn horn
hp harp
hpd harpsichord
keybd keyboard
lte lute
mez mezzo-soprano
mndl mandolin
narr narrator
oas only available separately
ob oboe
Op opus
orig original
org organ
perc percussion
pf piano
picc piccolo
pub publisher/published
rec recorder
recons reconstructed
rev revised
sax saxophone
sngr singer
sop soprano
spkr speaker
stg string
synth synthesizer
tbn trombone
ten tenor
timp timpani
tpt trumpet
trad traditional
trans transcribed
treb treble
va viola
va da gamba viola da gamba
vars variations
vc cello
vib vibraphone
vn violin
voc vocal/vocalist
wds words

CD Reviews

Adolphe Adam

French 1803-1856

GROVE *Adam studied at the Paris Conservatoire with Reicha (counterpoint) and Boieldieu (composition). A prolific composer, he wrote more than 80 stage works, some of which, especially those produced for the Opéra-Comique such as Le châlet (1834) and Le postillon de Longjumeau (1836), had considerable and lasting success. Other notable works, showing a natural sense of theatre, fresh invention and graceful melody. include the opera Si j'étais roi (1852) and the well known ballet Giselle (1841).*

Le corsaire

English Chamber Orchestra / Richard Bonynge
Decca ② 430 286-2DH2 (131 minutes: DDD) Ⓕ
Recorded 1990

Adam's *Le corsaire* was first heard in Paris during 1856 and was his last ballet score. Although eclipsed by the popularity of *Giselle*, it is superbly crafted and deserves to be more widely recognised. Predictably, the plot is convoluted, and occasionally absurd, but the approval of Parisian audiences secured 43 performances during 1856 alone. Richard Bonynge's realisation is excellent in every respect, and includes later additions by Léo Delibes for the revival of 1867. Stylistically, his 'Pas de fleurs' *divertissement*, interpolated into the final act, hardly reveals an alien hand at work, and could easily pass as part of Adam's original score. The highlights are the splendid bacchanal of the pirate Conrad and his crew, and the 'Pas des éventails' from Scene 2. The Second Act takes place at the Pasha's palace in Adrianople, as Conrad and his men, now disguised as pilgrims, plan to rescue the beautiful Medora from the harem. Due to the treachery of Conrad's henchman Birbanto, he is taken prisoner, and the final act recounts his efforts to escape, returning to his ship with Medora. Arguably the finest music is that portraying the lovers' premature rejoicing at their freedom, and the depiction of the storm which leaves them stranded together upon a rock following the destruction of the ship, reaching safety just as the final curtain falls.

Bonynge draws the diverse threads of the score together with a degree of expertise acquired from a lifetime of involvement with music of this nature, enabling the listener to follow the plot without difficulty. He obtains notably superior playing throughout from the ECO.

Giselle (complete)

Royal Opera House Orchestra, Covent Garden / Richard Bonynge
Double Decca ② 452 185-2DF2 (126 minutes: DDD) Ⓜ
Recorded 1986

Adam's celebrated score has educed harsh words from the more superior music critics, but the public has rightly taken it to heart for its atmospheric writing and tender and haunting themes. The text used for this recording is Adam's complete original score, and Bonynge's desire to re-record it lies in matters of performance and interpretation. (His previous recording, also for Decca, was made with the Monte Carlo Opera Orchestra in 1970.) Reviews of the previous version, on its original appearance and reissue, spoke of the limitations of the woodwind and brass, and suggested that a little more rehearsal time might have brought benefits. Here the musicians of the Royal Opera House bring both a confidence of attack and a refinement that are not quite achieved by the Monte Carlo players. Moreover, that same extra confidence of attack is displayed by Bonynge himself. Each of the discs of this issue is between one-and-a-half and two minutes longer than the older recording, but the dramatic moments are more vigorously attacked and the slower ones more lovingly caressed – always to considerable effect. Add recorded sound that is warmer and more spacious, and there is no hesitation in acknowledging the superiority of this version over the old. Without a doubt, this represents the first-choice version of Adam's complete score.

Slovak Radio Symphony Orchestra / Andrew Mogrelia
Naxos ② 8 550755/6 (114 minutes: DDD) Ⓢ
Recorded 1994

Naxos also offers the complete version of *Giselle* to challenge comparison with Bonynge's recording. Give or take some slight variances in the Act finales, both offer essentially the same text, complete with traditional interpolations. In the ultimate comparison there can be little doubt that Bonynge gives more point to the contrasts in the score, and that the playing of the Covent Garden orchestra and Decca's recorded sound give just the edge over this set. Yet this is a highly enjoyable alternative, with some especially rewarding passages such as the Act 1 'Pas seul'; many collectors will be more than happy to settle for it as a record of the complete text, and at super-bargain price.

Additional recommendation
Giselle
Royal Opera House Orchestra, Covent Garden / Ermler
Royal Opera House Records ROH007
(74 minutes: DDD: 4/94) Ⓕ

A stylish full-price alternative in the hands of a true man of the theatre. Good sound and fine playing.

Le toréado

Michel Trempont *bar* Don Belflor; **Sumi Jo** *sop* Coraline; **John Aler** *ten* Tracolin; **Welsh National Opera Orchestra / Richard Bonynge**
Decca 455 664-2DHO (77 minutes: DDD) Ⓕ
Notes, text and translation included.
Recorded 1996

Richard Bonynge's ability to persuade Decca to record out-of-the-way, 19th-century, French stage works has been to our repeated benefit over the past 40 years. Yet few results have been more welcome than this delightful operatic soufflé. Despite the title, there is little specifically Spanish about the piece beyond the Barcelona setting and the cuckolded elderly husband, who just happens to have been a toreador. The love interest is between the former opera-singer wife and her flautist admirer, and it is the important contribution of the flute that accounts for much of the incidental music. The admirer identifies himself by assorted operatic airs and grades the seriousness of the husband's infidelities by whether he plays a fandango or a cachucha. The score's most familiar number is a set of variations on *Ah, vous dirai-je, maman*; but there is much else that brings out Sumi Jo's crystal-clear, effortless coloratura to marvellous effect, as well as showing off John Aler's ardent, elegant tenor and Michel Trempont's well-practised comic baritone. A delightful recording.

Further listening
Le Positillon de Lonjumeau
Stuttgart Choristers; Kaiserslautern Radio Symphony Orchestra / Arp
Capriccio ② 60 040-2 (97 minutes: DDD) Ⓕ

Celebrated for the fiendishly difficult tenor solo 'Mes amis, écoutez l'histoire', Adam's opera has a lot of charm. This German language recording must be considered a stop-gap until a French version returns to the catalogue.

John Adams

American 1947

GROVE *Adams studied at Harvard with Kirchner, Kim, Del Tredici and Sessions, and in 1972 began teaching at the San Francisco Conservatory. He became interested in electronics (Onyx, 1976), then, influenced by Reich, turned to minimalism. His works, in an elegant minimalist style, include Shaker Loops for strings (1978), Harmonium for orchestra with choir (1981), the exuberant, parodistic Grand Pianola Music (1982), the opera Nixon in China (1987) – summary of his musical languages over 10 years – and a violin concerto (1994). His second opera, The Death of Klinghoffer (1991), is again based on recent events; the story unfolds in meditations and narratives, punctuated by choruses, rather than in action.*

Violin Concerto

Violin Concerto[a]. Shaker Loops[b]
Gidon Kremer *vn*
[a]**London Symphony Orchestra / Kent Nagano;**
[b]**Orchestra of St Luke's / John Adams**
Nonesuch 7559-79360-2 (59 minutes: DDD) Ⓕ
Recorded 1995 ●

This superb CD displays two very different aspects of Adams's evolving art: *Shaker Loops* dancing to a minimalist pulse, lean, fidgety and cleverly designed; and the altogether deeper, more intimate Violin Concerto. The concerto brings Berg to mind – not his Violin Concerto, but *Wozzeck*, Act 3 Scene 4, where an eerie 'drainage' effect symbolises Wozzeck's drowning beneath a blood-red moon. This aural fluidity is common to both works (the scoring is similar, too), although Adams keeps up the momentum for the entire duration of his long first movement, shifting colours constantly until a brief solo passage marks a slowing down in preparation for the ensuing Chaconne. Adams floats his mysterious textures above a quietly undulating accompaniment. The Sibelius of *Tapiola* seems to hover somewhere around five minutes into the first movement (just as parts of *Shaker Loops* suggest an up-tempo *Lemminkäinen*) and the concerto ends with a fast, dancing toccata. In the hands of Gidon Kremer – whose sinewy, lightly bowed tone suits the piece perfectly – it is a compelling monologue.

Shaker Loops is earlier, easier and rather less durable than the Violin Concerto. It started life as a string quartet (*Wavemaker*), then – beyond drastic recomposition – filled out to a septet which, suitably augmented, is how we hear it here. The term 'Shaker' refers to the frenzied dancing of a religious sect and Adams's four-part structure sets up a varied roster of tempos and textures. There have been other recordings of it, but this is surely the best – agile, precise and extremely well balanced. The sound is excellent.

Chamber Symphony

Chamber Symphony. Grand Pianola Music
London Sinfonietta / John Adams
Nonesuch 7559-79219-2 (53 minutes: DDD) Ⓕ
Recorded 1993 ●

A loud bash on an old tin can, and they're off – yelping, tapping, chattering, chasing to and fro, like a barn-yard full of loopy professors. And to think that the prime mover for John Adams's madcap Chamber Symphony (1992) was its 'eponymous predecessor', Schoenberg's Op 9. Even the instrumentation is similar, save that Adams has added synthesizer, jazz-style percussion, trumpet and trombone. It's a raw piece (Adams's minimal directions include 'coarse', 'intense', '*staccatissimo!*'), with the merest suggestion of repose in the central 'Aria with Walking Brass' and a 'Roadrunner' finale that includes a manic violin cadenza followed by an ingenious passage where synthesizer, bass clarinet, bassoon and horn crank up for the panic-stricken home straight. Granted, it might not be exactly rich in tunes, but it is maddeningly moreish, a dazzling, high-speed comedy where all the characters are temporarily on holiday from their more serious selves.

In complete contrast, the far gentler *Grand Pianola Music* (1971) provides a relatively 'easy' listen, what with its smooth-driving motor rhythms, sensual female voices, warming waves of brass tone and occasional bouts of thumping excitement. Clichés there certainly are, especially the 'big tune' that crowns the third section, 'On the Dominant Divide', and which is probably most effective when, towards the end of the work, it slims down to basic harmonic constituents. *Grand Pianola Music* is a sort of aural truck ride, with smooth tarmac, plenty of scenic incident, a glowing sunset on the far horizon and a closing cadence that recalls – rather unexpectedly – Sibelius. Both performances are fine and the recordings are superb.

El Dorado

Adams El Dorado
Busoni Berceuse élégiaque, Op 42 (arr Adams)[a]
Liszt La lugubre gondola, S200 No 1 (arr Adams)[a]
Halló Orchestra / Kent Nagano; [a]London Sinfonietta / John Adams
Nonesuch 7559-79359-2 (47 minutes: DDD) Ⓕ
Recorded 1993

El Dorado is a dramatic commentary on irreconcilable opposites: chromaticism versus pure modalities, malignancy versus rude health, and man's destructive impulses versus the unspoiled glory of unpopulated landscapes. Adams claims to have composed the second movement, 'Soledades' – the one 'without man' – in seven days. Indeed, the whole work appeared to him as a sort of apparition, 'alarmingly complete in its details, even before I wrote down a single sketch'. The first movement, 'A Dream of Gold', opens to sinister held chords, pensive shufflings and rising clouds of string tone. The last section charges forth like some maniacal spectre, racing out of control then stopping dead. By contrast, 'Soledades' weaves a delicate web of sound, at least initially, with unmistakably Sibelian undertones. While 'A Dream of Gold' suggests destructive intervention, 'Soledades' is freer, brighter and lighter in tone. The ending, however, suggests a tranquil death. Overall, the recording of *El Dorado* reproduces a dynamic sound curve. The performance itself is deft and well paced, very much on a par with Adams's own performances of his Busoni and Liszt arrangements.

The *Berceuse élégiaque* is beautifully realised, with woodwinds breaking through the predominantly dark texture like rays of dying sunlight through a bank of cloud. The richly coloured orchestration of Liszt's late *La lugubre gondola* is in total contrast to other, more austere, readings. Adams rows Liszt's funeral gondola slowly and lovingly, using cellos and basses for oars. Winds and solo strings are used to sensitive effect and the playing is uniformly excellent.

Gnarly Buttons

Gnarly Buttons. John's Book of Alleged Dances
Michael Collins *cl*
Kronos Quartet (David Harrington, John Sherba *vns* Hank Dutt *va* Joan Jeanrenaud *vc*)
London Sinfonietta / John Adams
Nonesuch 7559-79465-2 (61 minutes: DDD) Ⓕ
Recorded 1997

It is fascinating to hear the way John Adams works the prepared piano into his *Book of Alleged Dances*. The original idea was to make a digitally sampled loop of the piano part which would then be triggered by one of the quartet members. However, practical considerations necessitated recording the loops, which the quartet now perform live. *John's Book of Alleged Dances* (the equivocation in the title refers to dance steps that have yet to be invented) is prime-cut Adams – fidgety, tuneful, teeming with invention and all-but tactile in its aural variety.

We start by following a streetcar from town to coast and back again, then visit 'Toot Nipple' with 'chainsaw triads on the cello'. There's a raw-edged 'Hoe-Down' for leader David Harrington, a 'Pavane' for cellist Joan Jeanrenaud and a doleful Habanera, 'a lament for a season without baseball' as Adams himself puts it. 'Hammer & Chisel' are contractor friends who construct to a knotty toccata; a slithery 'Alligator Escalator' employs reptilian harmonics and a chirpy 'Serenade' pays subtle homage to Beethoven and Schubert. These and more are kept on a high flame by the Kronos Quartet, whereas *Gnarly Buttons* (with oblique reference to walking sticks and Gertrude Stein) calls on the combined talents of Michael Collins and the London Sinfonietta. A more intense piece by far (rather less memorably, too), its dry but colourful demeanour occasionally recalls Schoenberg's similarly spice-flavoured Serenade. The first movement is based on a Protestant shape-note hymn; the second is a 'Mad-Cow' hoe-down (written for Adams's British friends and the principal point of speculative contact with the Schoenberg); and the third is a warming song of sure-fire hit potential. Collins does Adams proud, and so does the London Sinfonietta. The recordings are first-rate.

Harmonielehre

Harmonielehre. The Chairman Dances. Two Fanfares – Tromba lontana; Short Ride in a Fast Machine
City of Birmingham Symphony Orchestra / Sir Simon Rattle
EMI CDC5 55051-2 (62 minutes: DDD) Ⓕ
Recorded 1993
The Chairman Dances and Short Ride in a Fast Machine are also available on HMV Classics HMV5 73040-2 Ⓑ

Harmonielehre was inspired by a dream vision of a massive tanker that suddenly took flight, displaying a 'beautiful brownish-orange oxide on the bottom part of its hull'; the setting was just off San Francisco Bay Bridge. 'Those pounding E minor chords are like a grinding of gears,' says John Adams of its violent, gunshot opening. Scored for a huge orchestra and structured in three contrasted sections, *Harmonielehre* is probably the nearest thing on offer to a minimalist symphony, and for that reason alone it could well appeal beyond the élite coterie of minimalist-fanciers. Rattle's recording has great heft and dynamic range, an informative balance and a vivid sense of aural perspective. The brass components of those opening chords have enormous weight and presence, and the ringing marimbas thereafter a bright complexion. Adams's frequent requests for subtle tempo transitions are subtly honoured by the conductor. In short, Rattle's view of Adams is recommended particularly to those mainstream collectors who aren't yet sold on minimalism.

The Death of Klinghoffer

Sanford Sylvan *bar* Leon Klinghoffer; **Stephanie Friedman** *mez* Omar; **James Maddalena** *bar* First Officer; **Thomas Hammons** *bar* First Officer; **Thomas Young** *sngr* Molqui; **Eugene Perry** *bar* Mamoud; **Sheila Nadler** *mez* Marilyn Klinghoffer
London Opera Orchestra Chorus; Lyon Opera Orchestra / Kent Nagano
Nonesuch ② 7559-79281-2 (135 minutes: DDD) Ⓕ
Notes and text included. Recorded 1991

One wonders how many living composers would happily watch their scores lead a short life, relevant but finite. Not many; but John Adams might be one of them. First *Nixon in China*, then *The Death of Klinghoffer*: rarely before has a composer snatched subjects from yesterday's news and made operas out of them. They are works for instant consumption. Admittedly, themes of lasting significance lurk beneath this work's immediate surface: conflict between cultures and ideologies, rival claims to ancestral lands, human rights in general. Specifically, however, it takes us back no further than October 1985, when Palestinian terrorists hijacked the Italian cruise liner *Achille Lauro* and murdered wheelchair-bound passenger Leon Klinghoffer. The opera guides us through those events, albeit in an oblique fashion.

Whatever the long-term fate of the opera, Alice Goodman's libretto certainly deserves to be spared from oblivion. It is eloquent and beautiful, compassionate and humanitarian, rich in imagery and spacious in its sentence-structure. Dialogue is virtually absent; it must surely rank as one of the least dramatic librettos ever devised. If *The Death of Klinghoffer* finally disappoints, it is because the marriage of words and music is so fragile. For all that, the opera's musical language is firmly rooted in tradition, but it is doubtful if anyone will come away from *The Death of Klinghoffer* with a memorable lyric moment lodged in the mind.

The recording uses the cast of the original production, and it contains no weak links. As one expects from Adams, the score has been superbly orchestrated, and it is done full justice by the Lyon Opera Orchestra. Least satisfactory is the chorus: Goodman entrusts it with her most purple passages, but little colour emerges from singing that is so carefully accurate and lifeless.

Nixon in China

Sanford Sylvan *bar* Chou en-Lai; **James Maddalena** *bar* Richard Nixon; **Thomas Hammons** *bar* Henry Kissinger; **Mari Opatz** *mez* **Nancy T'ang** First Secretary to Mao; **Stephanie Friedman** *mez* Second Secretary to Mao; **Marion Dry** *mez* Third Secretary to Mao; **John Duykers** *ten* Mao Tse-Tung; **Carolann Page** *sop* Pat Nixon; **Trudy Ellen Craney** *sop* Chiang Ch'ing **St Luke's Chorus and Orchestra / Edo de Waart**
Nonesuch ② 7559-79177-2 (144 minutes: DDD) Ⓕ
Notes and text included
Recorded 1987

Whatever its weaknesses, there's no denying that *Nixon in China* is striking. Structured curiously, its three acts reduce from three scenes to two, and then to one, and they diminish proportionally in duration from more than an hour in Act 1 to the unbroken 30-minute span of Act 3. This last act played out in the statesmen's bedrooms, is a weary sequence of dialogues and soliloquies, ending in a curious but calculated state of anticlimax. Preceding this, though, is a run of colourful scenes that symbolise the main events without imposing any artificial sense of dramatic shape. By the end of the work, the public faces have given way to private lives; even Nixon and Chairman Mao emerge as mere mortals rather than mythical demi-gods. Alice Goodman's poetry reads well, speaks well, and in the hands of another composer might have sung well, but in Adams's setting it does not always register its message.

The music serves the libretto deftly in fast-moving dialogue but the reflective and rhapsodic portions of text seem to leave Adams baffled, the melodic lines wandering aimlessly (if scrupulously matching the rhythm of the words), short on intrinsic musical interest and rarely moving the singers to expressive performances. In the handling of spectacle and scene-setting, by contrast, Adams is in his element. He freely avails himself of any idiom, any oblique references or musical quotation that serves as a means to an end. Some passages would be unthinkable without the operas of Philip Glass; elsewhere lie uncanny ghosts of 1930s Stravinsky. Magpie just about sums this score up. The singing is sympathetic, with James Maddalena as an aptly volatile Nixon and Trudy Ellen Craney coping admirably with the coloratura lines of Madam Mao.

Further listening
The Wound-dresser
Coupling: Fearful symmetries
Sylvan *bar* **Orchestra of St Luke's / Adams**
Nonesuch 7559-79218-2 (47 minutes: DDD: 6/90) Ⓕ
Adams's tender and powerful meditation, to words by Walt Whitman, on the subject of those lost to AIDS. Touchingly performed by Sanford Sylvan.

Richard Addinsell British 1904-1977

GROVE *After study at the Royal College of Music, London, and in Vienna, Addinsell visited the USA (1933), where he wrote for films. Most of his music was for the theatre and cinema; his popular Warsaw Concerto, in the style of Rachmaninov, was used in the film Dangerous Moonlight (1941).*

Film Music

Blithe Spirit – Prelude; Waltz. Encore – Miniature Overture. Gaslight – Prelude. Parisienne – 1885. Southern Rhapsody. Waltz of the Toreadors – March; The General on Parade; Waltz (all arr. Lane). Fire over England – Suite (arr. Zalva). Passionate Friends – Lover's Moon. South Riding – Prelude (both arr Isaacs). A Christmas Carol – Suite (arr S Bernstein). WRNS March (arr Douglas)
Robert Gibbs *vn* **Peter Lawson** *pf* **Royal Ballet Sinfonia / Kenneth Alwyn**
ASV White Line CDWHL2115 (68 minutes: DDD) Ⓜ
Recorded 1998 ●

What delights this disc contains! Nobody should imagine that the *Warsaw Concerto* is all that is worth hearing from this fine composer. Addinsell had an utterly natural feel for richly tuneful, romantic music in the very best tradition of British light music. The diverse subjects for which he was commissioned served to turn these gifts to contrasted musical styles, which together provide a rewardingly varied programme. The most familiar music here for some readers will probably be the swaggering march and haunting waltz from the *Waltz of the Toreadors*. For others it may be the prelude and waltz from David Lean's film of *Blithe Spirit* or the suite from *A Christmas Carol*.

Perennial favourites in this collection are the invigorating *WRNS March* (rewarding material for any military band), the delightfully mysterious prelude to the 1939 film of *Gaslight* and the waltz from the stage play *Parisienne*. This last has been given a splendid Glazunovian orchestration by compiler, producer, arranger and annotator Philip Lane, who again leaves us in his debt, no less than conductor Kenneth Alwyn and the admirable Royal Ballet Sinfonia.

Additional recommendation
Film music
Goodbye Mr Chips – exc. Ring around the moon – exc. Smokey Mountains Concerto. The Isle of Apples. The Prince and the Showgirl – exc. Tune in G. Tom Brown's Schooldays – exc. Festival. Journey to Romance. Fire over England – exc. A Tale of Two Cities – exc
Martin, Elms *pfs* **BBC Concert Orchestra / Alwyn**
Marco Polo 8 223732 (68 minutes: DDD: 4/95) Ⓕ
A most attractive release. Much of the orchestral material for this recording was prepared by Philip Lane, who also provides the informative notes. Fine performances, too.

Further listening
Warsaw Concerto
Coupled with: Rachmaninov Piano Concerto No 2. Gershwin *Rhapsody in Blue*. Gottschalk, Liszt and Litolff
Ortiz *pf* **Royal Philharmonic Orchestra / Atzmon**
Decca 430 726-2DM (56 minutes:DDD: 5/86R) Ⓜ
Addinsell's evergreen piano concerto played with suitably heart-on-sleeve passion by Cristina Ortiz. See Collections.

'Piano Concertos from The Movies'
Warsaw Concerto
Couplings: **Beaver** Portrait of Isla **Rozsa** Spellbound Concerto. **Rota** The Legend of the Glass Mountain **R R Bennett** Murder on the Orient Express – excs. **Bath** Cornish Rhapsody. **Herrmann** Concerto Macabre. **Williams** The Dream of Olwen. **Pennario** Midnight on the Cliffs
Philip Fowke *pf* **RTE Concert Orchestra / O'Duinn**
Naxos 8 554323 (74 minutes: DDD: 7/98) Ⓢ
Philip Fowke plays all the pieces with affection and panache. If you've always wished that the *Warsaw Concerto* were longer, this is the very disc for you.

Thomas Adès

British 1971

One of the leading lights in contemporary classical music, pianist/conductor/composer Adès's meteoric rise to international musical prominence has been phenomenonal. He gained early success as a pianist, winning Second Prize in the 1989 BBC Young Musician of the Year, then read music at King's College, Cambridge (1989-92). Among the works from his student years are his first opus, Five Eliot Landscapes (1990) and the Chamber Symphony (1990) – his first work to receive a professional performance. In 1993 he became Composer in Association to the Hallé Orchestra for whom he wrote The Origin of the Harp (1994) and These Premises Are Alarmed (1996). His most performed work, Living Toys (1993), brought him widespread critical acclaim, though it was the chamber opera Powder Her Face (1995) that earned him an international reputation. In 1998 he became artistic director of the Birmingham Contemporary Music Group and the following year, for his first large-scale orchestral work, Asyla (1997), he received the Ernst von Siemens Prize and the Grawemeyer Award. Also in 1999 he became joint artistic director of the Aldeburgh Festival. Forthcoming commissions include operas for the Royal Opera House, Covent Garden, and Glyndebourne and a Piano Quintet for the Melbourne Festival.

Adès's compositions showed exceptional assurance of style and technique from the start, and his success had much to do with the umistakable presence of a personal accent in music which blends vividness of detail with a clear sense of compelling overall design. Employing well-established compositional genres, from chamber opera to string quartet to symphonic form, his music often alludes to specific models while nevertheless keeping its distance from them.

Asyla

Asyla[bc]. … but all shall be well[bd]. Chamber Symphony[ad]. Concerto conciso[ae]. These Premises are Alarmed[bd]
[a]**Birmingham Contemporary Music Group;** [b]**City of Birmingham Symphony Orchestra /** [c]**Sir Simon Rattle,** [d]**Thomas Adès** [e]*pf*
EMI CDC5 56818-2 (61 minutes: DDD) Ⓕ
Recorded 1998 ●

This CD includes the *Chamber Symphony*, the work that first aroused interest in Adès's work when he was 18, set alongside *Asyla*, a recent un-chamber symphony and his first work for full orchestra. The progression between them is remarkable: the *Chamber Symphony* has both real invention and real economy, and its use of jazz elements is neither patronising nor culinary. Maybe its last movement adds little of consequence to the preceding three, but *Asyla* genuinely grows from the grave, rather Britten-ish horn line that sets it going through the strong drama of the central movements to the almost Sibelian climax of the finale. Despite intimations of the aforementioned composers, Adès's own voice is clearly audible throughout, elegant, coolly intelligent but urgent.

These Premises are Alarmed, a sinewy toccata of bright colour and urgent energy, was written for the opening of the Bridgewater Hall in Manchester. At four minutes it makes rather less impact than it should in the middle of a CD (play it first). In the *Concerto conciso* Adès perhaps takes his pleasure in simple intervals and brief motives a little too far. However, *... but all shall be well* is something else again. It develops abundant, earnest melody from a pair of simple phrases in an impressively sustained argument that reaches a powerful and satisfying climax. Fine performances, admirably recorded.

Living Toys

Arcadiana, Op 12[a]. The Origin of the Harp, Op 13[b]. Sonata da caccia, Op 11[c]. Living Toys, Op 9[d]. Gefriolsae me, Op 3*b*[e]
[c]**Michael Neisemann** *ob* [c]**Andrew Clark** *hn* [c]**Thomas Adès** *hpd* [a]**Endellion Quartet** (Andrew Watkinson, Ralph de Souza *vns* Garfield Jackson *va* David Waterman *vc*); [e]**King's College Choir, Cambridge / Stephen Cleobury;** [b]**instrumental ensemble / Thomas Adès;** [d]**London Sinfonietta / Markus Stenz**
EMI Debut CDZ5 72271-2 (64 minutes: DDD) Ⓑ
Text and translation included. Recorded 1997. ●●●

This collection fully lives up to the excited expectations aroused by the first disc of Adès's music but does not imply that he is at all ready to settle down into a predictable style. The five pieces here suggest a composer as delightedly surprised by his prodigal inventiveness as we are. *Arcadiana*, for example, is a seven-movement string quartet whose central and longest movement (four minutes) contains an extraordinary range of precisely imagined, highly original textures and yet in its penultimate section can settle to a serene and wonderfully beautiful *adagio* whose sound and mood be conveyed only by the adjective 'Beethovenian'.

Far more overtly, the engaging *Sonata da caccia* uses elements that are very directly derived from Couperin, but the sensibility is entirely modern, even when you strongly suspect that this or that phrase is a note-for-note quotation. However, as with Adès's first collection, his is an imagination that you can trust. *Living Toys* has a quite Birtwistle-like sense of ritual to it, although more lyrical, quite frequently with a tangible jazz element. *The Origin of the Harp* is a dark, dramatic chamber tone-poem. *Gefriolsae me*, for male voices and organ, is a brief but impressive motet to Middle English words.

All five pieces are finely performed, all are further evidence of a rich, still developing but clearly exceptional talent. *Arcadiana*, with its exquisite textures and sheer melodic richness, is perhaps Adès's finest achievement so far, a work constantly aware of the musical past (including the string quartet's past) but renewing that past with astonishing freshness.

Life story

Catch, Op 4. Darknesse visible. Still sorrowing, Op 7. Under Hamelin Hill, Op 6. Five Eliot Landscapes, Op 1. Traced overhead, Op 15. Life story, Op 8*b*
Valdine Anderson, Mary Carewe *sops* **Lynsey Marsh** *cl* **Anthony Marwood** *vn* **Louise Hopkins** *vc* **Thomas Adès** *pf/org* **David Goode, Stephen Farr** *orgs*
EMI Debut CDZ5 69699-2 (77 minutes: DDD) Ⓑ
Texts included. Recorded 1996 ●●

Adès has the gift of seizing your attention with strange but ravishingly beautiful sonorities and then holding it with entrancingly mysterious inventions that allure the ear. Yet he also has the much rarer quality of inspiring utter confidence. His style cannot be defined by simply describing any one of these pieces. Each solves a new problem or investigates a new scenario with such adroitness and completeness that each work seems a quite new and delightful adventure. In *Still sorrowing* the starting point is a piano whose central register is muted with a strip of plastic adhesive. The effect on those pitches is obvious: they are dulled to a sort of subdued drumming, but by observing the new light that this casts on the undamped upper and lower registers it is not too much of an exaggeration to say that Adès invents an entirely new and alluring instrument, or rather three of them – a glittering, coruscating 'treble piano', a tolling, gently pounding 'bass piano' and in the middle a subtle sort of muted gamelan. And he plays all three (he is a pretty formidable pianist) with poetry and wonder.

Catch is a game, in which a piano trio tempt and tease an off-stage clarinet; he eventually joins them in sober homophony, for this is a game with serious and lyrical substance as well as a jest. A similar but more ambiguous game is played in *Under Hamelin Hill*, where the piping toccata of one organist attracts two others to join him in co-operative apparent improvisation, but he is left alone for a shadowy soliloquy filled with shudders. *Darknesse visible* is a haunting meditation in which the presence of John Dowland is clearest where the music seems least like him; a magical illusion as well as a moving homage. In *Life story* the soprano is asked to imitate the manner of Billie Holiday in her wry reflection on a casual one-night encounter; it is the dark, searching piano that adds pity and bleakness to turn this into a riveting miniature opera. *Traced overhead* is filled with mysterious, glancing references to remembered piano music, but is grippingly coherent. And as if this were not enough, in the Eliot settings, Op 1, the 17-year-old Adès already proved himself a song-writer of rare talent. The performances are first-rate.

Powder Her Face

Jill Gomez *sop* Duchess; **Valdine Anderson** *sop* Maid, Confidante, Waitress, Mistress, Society Journalist, First Rubbernecker; **Niall Morris** *ten* Electrician, Lounge Lizard, Waiter, Delivery Boy, Second Rubbernecker; **Roger Bryson** *bar* Hotel Manager, Duke, Guest, Laundryman, Judge; **Almeida Ensemble / Thomas Adès**
EMI ② CDS5 56649-2 (116 minutes: DDD) Ⓜ
Text included. Recorded 1996

Powder Her Face was written and had its first performances in 1995, when Thomas Adès was 24. It would be pretty remarkable, as the first opera by a composer of that age, if it demonstrated the fertility of invention and imaginative resource that erupted from the two discs of his shorter pieces (on EMI), combined with a promising but as yet understandably tentative gift for the stage. It does much more than that. The central character, though referred to in the cast-list simply as 'Duchess', is in fact Margaret, Duchess of Argyll, for many years a prominent figure in London society, who in 1963 was at the centre of a protracted and luridly sensational divorce case: the judge, in a verdict running to 65,000 words, described her sexual activities as 'disgusting' and her sexual appetite as 'debased'. Even after the divorce she counted the rich, the famous and the royal among her friends but died, penniless, in 1993.

Adès and librettist Philip Hensher imagine her as 'all cladding – powder, scent, painting, furs – nothing inside', and the risk of course is that she will appear either as an empty monster for whom we can feel little sympathy or as a glittering caricature whom we pity as the subject of the composer's and the librettist's mockery. Their wit is indeed dazzling. Hensher's libretto (*his* first work for the stage, too) is outstandingly good – economical, vivid, filled with the most adroit spurs to the composer's invention – and Adès's score is as satisfyingly rich, surprising and bizarre as his other works would lead one to hope and expect. He takes great risks – an aria and a duet that are sung simultaneously, a musical equivalent of the judge's interminable concluding speech – and they come off brilliantly. He cannot resist alluding to the music that would have furnished the Duchess's glamorous life – the score is pervaded with tangos – but he can use it to convey menace and desolation as well as picturesque period evocation. He uses chamber forces – an orchestra of 15 and four singers enacting 16 roles – but draws astonishingly varied sounds and vivid dramaturgy from them. His highest achievement is his portrayal of the Duchess. From her first appearance, surprising a maid and an electrician sniggering at her grotesque reputation, she has iconic glamour and something like dignity. Although often off-stage – the 'second soprano' probably has more to sing – she dominates the opera effortlessly, and in the long final scene she achieves ... not tragic stature, perhaps, but deep and genuine patho. She is alone 'and there's no one to dress me, and no one to talk to me, and the only people who were ever good to me were paid for it'.

The opera gains enormously from a central performance as alluring and attention-riveting as Jill Gomez's, although all the other singers are very accomplished, Valdine Anderson standing out in a role like Zerbinetta with knobs on: composer and librettist envisaged her multiple roles for a 'Helden-soubrette'. The score also makes huge demands of the orchestral players, many of them required to be virtuoso soloists, and they are very properly all named in the accompanying booklet. The recording is as vivid as it needs to be. A hugely enjoyable opera.

Further listening
Piazzolla María de Buenos Aires
Soloists; Kremerata Musica
Teldec ② 3984-20632-2 (94 minutes: DDD: 11/98) Ⓕ
A flavoursome tango opera, superbly realised.

Alexander Agricola

Franco-Flemish 1446-1506

GROVE *Agricola's career centred mainly on Italian courts (Milan, Florence, Naples) and the French court – from 1498 until his death he served Philip the Handsome of Burgundy at home and abroad. His travels brought him renown as a singer and composer. His works include eight masses, over 20 motets and other sacred pieces, nearly 50 chansons and c25 instrumental works. His style is predominantly northern, akin to Ockeghem's, using long, rhythmically complex contrapuntal lines built from short, decorative motifs and linked with frequent yet unobtrusive cadences.*

Fortuna desperata

A la mignonne de fortune. Adieu m'amour. Adieu m'amour II. Allez, regretz. Ay je rien fait. Cecsus non iudicat de coloribus. De tous biens plaine. De tous biens plaine II. De tous biens plaine III. Et qui la dira. Fortuna desperata. Guarde vostre visage. Guarde vostre visage II. Guarde vostre visage III. J'ay beau huer. S'il vous plaist. Soit loing ou pres. Sonnes muses melodieusement
Ensemble Unicorn (Bernhard Landauer *counterten* Johannes Chum *ten* Colin Mason *bass-bar* Marco Ambrosini *fiddle* Nora Kallai *vihuela d'arco* Thomas Wimmer *vihuela d'arco/lte* Riccardo Delfino *hp/snare hp*) **/ Michael Posch** *rec*
Naxos 8 553840 (65 minutes: DDD) Ⓢ
Recorded 1995

De tous biens plaine. Dung aultre amer. Fortuna desperata. Gaudeamus omnes in Domino. Je n'ay dueil. Missa Je ne demande – Kyrie. Missa secundi toni – Gloria. Missa Le serviteur – Credo. Missa Re fa mi re fa – Sanctus. Missa In myne zyn – Agnus Dei. Salve regina. Se mieulx ne vient d'amours. Virgo sub ethereis à 3
Huelgas Ensemble / Paul van Nevel
Sony Classical SK60760 (67 minutes: DDD) Ⓕ
Texts and translations included. Recorded 1998

Agricola was praised by his contemporaries for the bizarre turn of his inspiration, and his music likened to quicksilver. By the standards of the period this is a highly unusual turn of phrase, but it was, and remains, spot-on. Crawford Young's Ferrara Ensemble anthology, the first ever devoted to the composer, focused on the secular music, both instrumental and vocal; precisely the area covered by Michael Posch and Ensemble Unicorn in this most satisfying disc. Where there is duplication (surprisingly little, in fact) the performances compare with those of the Ferrara Ensemble, although the style of singing is very different. The voices are more upfront and less inflected, perhaps the better to match the high instruments with which they are sometimes doubled (the Ferrara Ensemble used string instruments only). But the tensile quality of Agricola's lines comes through none the less (the opening *A la mignonne* makes for an interesting comparison), as does the miraculous inventiveness and charm of his music. Further, much of what is new to the catalogue really is indispensible, for example Agricola's most famous song, *Allez, regretz*. Unicorn keeps its improvisations and excursions to a minimum, and the music is the better for it. This disc would be indispensable at full price, let alone super-budget. It really is a must-have.

Paul van Nevel's recording is the first ever to include Agricola's Mass music. Under the invented title *Missa Guazzabuglio* (a word meaning hotchpotch or mishmash) van Nevel has assembled individual movements from different Masses, after the fashion of his 'La Dissection d'un Homme Armé' (Sony). It allows us to sample different Masses, but leaves one a little frustrated when an individual piece augurs so well for the rest of the cycle, as does, for example, the sprawling but deliciously profligate *Agnus Dei* on *In myne zyn*. Van Nevel is easily as eccentric as Agricola ever was, and while the singers of the Huelgas Ensemble cope admirably with even his most bizarre directions, some ideas seem to be almost beyond the pale. He claims that fully vocal performance of the instrumental music is at least plausible. In the case of the six-voice *Fortuna desperata* one can hardly disagree with that assertion, but to hear the soprano clambering up two-and-a-half octaves in semiquavers (*Dung aultre amet*) forces admiration and disbelief in equal measure. Rather more problematic is the assertion that such counterpoint represents instances of *chant sur le livre*, a technique of extemporisation on plainsong: there is no basis for this. Equally dubious is van Nevel's performance of the 'Osanna' of the Mass *Re fa mi re fa* according to two different 'legitimate solutions' of the notation, his implication being that both were intended by the composer: the musical result is intriguing, but the claim itself is merely fanciful. Yet the amazing thing is that the singers' sheer athleticism and musicality lends even such dotty notions an air of plausibility. More than that, they confirm the growing perception of Agricola as a composer of the very first rank.

Jehan Alain French 1911-1940

GROVE *Alain studied with Dupré and Dukas at the Paris Conservatoire (1927-39) and was organist of St Nicolas de Maisons Lafitte in Paris (1935-39); he was killed in action. He shared Messiaen's enthusiasms for Debussy and Asian music, reflected in the modalities, rhythmic irregularities and ecstatic ostinatos of his works, which are mostly for the organ or the Catholic Mass. His organ works include Deux danses à Agni Yavishtra (1934), two Fantaisies (1934, 1936), Litanies (1937) and Trois danses (1937-39).*

Organ Works

Suite. Climat. Prélude et Fugue. Choral dorien. Choral phrygien. Aria. Variations sur 'Lucis créator'. Berceuse sur deux notes qui cornent. Deux préludes profanes. Monodie. Ballade en mode phrygien. Choral cistercian pour une élévation. Variations sur un thème de Clément Janequin. Le jardin suspendu. Litanies. Fantasmagorie. Trois danses. Quatre pièces. Grave. Petite pièce. Intermezzo. Lamento. Première fantaisie. Deuxième fantaisie. Deux dances à Agni Yavishta. Cinque pièces faciles – Complainte à la mode ancienne; Fugue en mode de Fa; Verset-Choral; Berceuse. Postlude pour l'office de Complies. Page 21 du huitième cahier de notes de Jehan Alain

Kevin Bowyer *org*

Nimbus ② NI5551/2 (146 minutes: DDD) Ⓕ

Recorded on the Marcussen Organ, Chapel of St Augustine, Tonbridge School, Kent in 1997 ●●●

This is the most comprehensive and most impressive recording yet of Alain's organ music. Bowyer offers nine pieces not included on Eric Lebrun's two-disc survey from Naxos. These may not be among the composer's most substantial creations, but Alain enthusiasts would not like to be without any of them, least of all the intensely moving page from one of Alain's notebooks setting out his musical reactions to the death, in a mountaineering accident, of his sister, Marie-Odile. Bowyer's performances are thought-provoking, stimulating and often inspired. His tempos are not especially quick although he does turn out the fastest performance ever recorded of the *Intermezzo*. Yet even here the choice of speed is symptomatic of Bowyer's whole approach; nobody could deny that when played so rapidly the work takes on a new dimension.

Nimbus achieves a near-perfect balance between clarity and atmosphere on the new Marcussen in Tonbridge School's rebuilt Chapel. When the disarming dialogue between a single reed and the flutes of the charming *Petite pièce* can be revealed in such detail nobody could realistically ask for a better setting for this magical music. Bowyer proves to be an unusually perceptive and persuasive advocate of Alain's music. One suspects it will be a long time before a serious contender to this outstanding release comes along.

Litanies. Petite pièce. Le jardin suspendu. Deuxième fantaisie. Variations sur un thème de Clément Janequin. Deux dances à Agni Yavishta. Deux préludes profanes. Choral cistercian pour une élévation. Climat. Monodie. Ballade en mode phrygien. Choral phrygien. Suite
Eric Lebrun *org*
Naxos 8 553632 (64 minutes: DDD) Ⓢ
Recorded on the organ of the Church of Saint-Antoine des Quinze-Vingts, Paris in 1995

Trois danses. Intermezzo. Variations sur 'Lucis créator'. Berceuse. Grave. Lamento. Première fantaisie. Prélude et Fugue. Choral dorien. Aria. Postlude pour l'office de Complies
Eric Lebrun *org*
Naxos 8 553633 (66 minutes: DDD) Ⓢ
Recorded on the organ of the Church of Saint-Antoine des Quinze-Vingts, Paris in 1995

Whether it's the weirdly sombre *Lamento*, the captivating *Intermezzo*, the pseudo-archaic *Variations sur un thème de Clément Janequin* or the dramatically fervent *Litanies*, to have it all brought together under one roof allows us to revel in that magical mix of mysticism, melancholy and modality which makes Alain's voice so distinctive. This splendid Cavaillé-Coll organ, set in a richly atmospheric acoustic, seems the perfect vehicle for Alain's music, with its kaleidoscopic use of subtle colours and effects. It possesses glorious stops and seems fully equipped to deal with everything Alain's music demands of it. What a shame, then, that the recording itself misses the mark. An indistinct focus blurs much of the detail, while there just isn't enough of the church's ambience to compensate for this lack of clarity. There again, Eric Lebrun is guilty of some pretty indistinct articulation himself, not least in a dreadful account of *Litanies* taken at breakneck speed and with heart-stopping lurches from section to section. That said, much of his playing is outstanding. The best-known works verge on the controversial (*Le jardin suspendu*, for example, is superficial), but in the rarely heard *Suite* he produces playing of conviction and magnetism. And with a deeply moving account of the *Postlude pour l'office de Complies*, he more than justifies Naxos's faith in him. This deserves a place on the shelves of all organ music devotees.

Isaac Albéniz

Spanish 1860-1909

GROVE *Albéniz is one of the most important figures in Spanish musical history; he helped create a national idiom and an indigenous school of piano music. He studied at the Brussels Conservatory and with Liszt, Dukas and d'Indy; other important influences were Felipe Pedrell (who inspired him to turn to Spanish folk music), 19th-century salon piano music and impressionist harmony. But he was not simply a follower of the French school and exchanged ideas with Debussy and Ravel in Paris. Most of his many works are for piano solo, the best known being the suite Iberia (1906-8), distinguished by its complex technique, bold harmony and evocative instrumental effects. He also wrote a notable opera, Pepita Jiménez (1896). Albéniz was also a virtuoso pianist with a highly personal style.*

Iberia

Albéniz Iberia (arr Gray) – El Albaicín; Triana; Rondeña
Granados Valses poéticos (trans Williams)
Rodrigo Invocación y Danza. En los trigales
Anonymous (arr Llobet). Ten Catalan Folksongs
John Williams *gtr* **London Symphony Orchestra / Paul Daniels**
Sony Classical SK48480 (71 minutes: DDD) Ⓕ
Recorded 1989-91

The amalgam of technical guitaristic perfection in the face of daunting demands, fluid musicality and exemplary tone-production, caught in this exceptionally lifelike recording, represents a landmark in the instrument's march towards true parity with other instruments. Granados's *Valses* are unabridged, Rodrigo's moody *Invocación y Danza* comes in its original and more effective form, and two of the charming settings of Catalan folk-songs arranged by Llobet have no other recording. Nothing in Albéniz's virtuosic *Iberia* is accessible to the solo guitar, but with the aid of the London Symphony Orchestra and Gray's enchantingly evocative arrangements, Williams shows three of its movements in a new and colourful light. To anyone with the slightest interest in the guitar or Spanish romantic music, this disc is a required purchase.

Suite española, Op 47. Cantos de España, Op 232 – Córdoba (both orch Frühbeck). Iberia – Evocación; El Corpus en Sevilla; Triana (orch Arbós)
Spanish National Orchestra / Rafael Frühbeck de Burgos
Conifer Classics 75605 51326-2 (61 minutes: DDD) Ⓕ
Recorded 1997

Despite going, at the age of 30, to study with Dukas and d'Indy, Albéniz was ill at ease in writing for the orchestra. His few works for that medium – the *Rapsodia cubana*, the *Rapsodia española* and the Piano Concerto – were all orchestrated by other hands from piano originals, and Dukas has always been suspected of having lent his assistance with *Catalonia*. But Albéniz's piano works are intrinsically so full of colour (and in the case of *Iberia* so bristling with pianistic technical demands) that it is not surprising that they have tempted others to clothe them in orchestral garb. Most expertly as this is done here by the two conductors responsible a certain modification of character from the originals was inevitable. Pianists will continue to cherish Albéniz's Lisztian writing, yet cannot but admire the ingenuity with which black-and-white has been transformed into Technicolor (which is likely to be of greater appeal to the public at large). Frühbeck takes 'Granada' extremely slowly, underlining the emotionalism (logically enough for a serenade); 'Sevilla' emerges very robustly, as does the final section of 'Asturias' (which Albéniz made more Moorish than Asturian); the *jota* of 'Aragon' is brilliantly vivid; and everywhere he adds interesting counterpoints and imitations. Only in 'Castille' and 'Cuba' do you feel that his orchestration over-eggs the pudding. The Spanish National Orchestra responds warmly to all these arrangements. and the recording is first-class.

Iberia. Navarra (compl de Séverac).
Suite española, Op 47
Alicia de Larrocha *pf*
Decca ② 417 887-2DH2 (126 minutes: DDD) Ⓕ
Recorded 1986 **OO**

Written during Albéniz's last three years, *Iberia* is his masterwork for the piano. The full extent of the journey he travelled in his all-too-brief life span of 49 years can't be fully appreciated by comparing these 12 richly colourful 'impressions' with the *Suite española*, generally accepted as his earliest serious foray into the nationalist field. Larrocha also gives us the bonus of the exuberant *Navarra* originally intended by the composer (before he rejected it as 'too plebeian') to end *Iberia*. Coming from such a distinguished specialist in the Spanish field, the album is as musically enjoyable as it is musicologically stimulating. Her playing has immediacy, subtlety and charm besides revealing fingers so magically able to conceal Albéniz's sometimes cruel technical demands. Compared to the old LP recording the clarity of colouring is like an old painting newly cleaned. But it's not just the recording that allows Larrocha's most recent *Iberia* to make a more vivid impact. Everything here carries just that little extra conviction. Every tiny detail in Albéniz's multi-layered textures, every counter-strand, every fleck of colour, is always crystal-clear. As for Larrocha's range of colour, and the sheer sensuous beauty of her tone, that can only be described as a feast for the ear. She plays the *Suite española* with a spontaneous delight in their tunes, textures and rhythms; she enjoys them as the engaging *morceaux de salon* that, in comparison with what follows in *Iberia*, they undoubtedly are.

Additional recommendation
de Larrocha *pf*
Coupling: **Granados** Goyescas
Decca Double ② 448 191-2DF2 (141 minutes: ADD: 4/96) Ⓑ

Alicia de Larrocha's 1972 Decca recording: though not as finely recorded as her digital remake (above), it is still worth considering if you are on a tight budget.

Mallorca

Albéniz Mallorca, Op 202. Suite española, Op 47. Cantos de España, Op 232 – Córdoba **Granados** Cuentos de la juventud – Dedicatoria. 15 Tonadillas – El majo olvidado. 12 Danzas españolas, Op 37 – Villanesca; Andaluza (Playera). 7 Valses poéticos **Rodrigo** Tres Piezas españolas
Julian Bream *gtr*
RCA Navigator 74321 17903-2 Ⓢ
(77 minutes: DDD). Recorded 1982-83 **OO**

In 1982 Julian Bream recorded a solo recital of music by Albéniz and Granados in his favourite recording venue, Wardour Chapel in Wiltshire. It offers playing of extraordinary magnetism and an almost total illusion of the great guitarist seated in the room making music just beyond one's loudspeakers; this effect is particularly striking in Albéniz's *Córdoba* and the *pianissimo* reprise of the central section of the Granados *Danza española* No 5, which is quite magical. The other works included are all played with comparable spontaneity. RCA here reissue this disc at super-bargain price on their enterprising Navigator label; moreover, they have added Rodrigo's *Tres Piezas españolas*, recorded a year later. The second of these, a seven-minute 'Passacaglia', is quite masterly, while the final 'Zapateado' brings characteristically chimerical virtuosity from the soloist. It is difficult to identify another recital of Spanish guitar music that surpasses this, and it is now one of the great bargains in the Navigator catalogue.

Merlin

Carlos Alvarez *bar* Merlin; **Plácido Domingo** *ten* King Arthur; **Jane Henschel** *sop* Morgan le Fay; **Ana María Martínez** *sop* Nivian; **Carlos Chausson** *bass* Archbishop of Canterbury; **Christopher Maltman** *bar* Mordred; **Javier Franco** *bar* Sir Pellinore; **Felipe Bou** *bass* Sir Ector de Maris; **José López Ferrero** *ten* Kay; **Javier Roldán** *bass* King Lot of Orkney; **Angel Rodríguez** *ten* Gawain; **Alfonso X 'El Sabio'; Spanish National Choir; Madrid Community Choir; Madrid Symphony Orchestra / José de Eusebio**
Decca ② 467 096-2DHO2 (136 minutes: DDD) Ⓕ
Recorded 1999 **OO**

This set is a revelation, and hugely enjoyable. While Albéniz has long been celebrated as an inspired composer of colourful piano music with a marked Spanish flavour, here in *Merlin* he emerges as a formidable opera composer, setting out to write his equivalent of Wagner's *Ring* cycle using a libretto (in English) based on the Arthurian legends. Albéniz completed the piano score in 1898, but did not finish the orchestral version until 1902. All plans for performance in the composer's lifetime fell through, and the only staging ever, incomplete, was a one-off event in Barcelona in 1960. Until recently, the full score was thought to be lost, but, encouraged by Spanish scholars José de Eusebio painstakingly collated material from various sources to produce a complete score, as recorded here.

The opening prelude, as dawn breaks on Christmas morning outside St Paul's Church in London, brings echoes of the opening of Wagner's *Rheingold*, while an offstage chorus of monks chanting at the start of the first scene clearly owes something to *Parsifal*, even though it sounds very different, with Albéniz generally adopting a less chromatic, more straightforwardly diatonic idiom than Wagner. In fact, listening to almost any passage of this luxuriant score, it would be hard to identify the composer.

One might just possibly guess Stanford, thanks to the occasional English-sounding motif, or maybe Humperdinck, who is similarly more straightforward than Wagner, or maybe Paul Dukas, one of Albéniz's teachers.

That is all to Albéniz's credit, for even if there are one or two banal moments, the score consistently compels attention with its rich presentation of the Arthurian story. Weaknesses centre on the libretto, written by the composer's English friend and patron, the rich banker Francis Burdett Money-Coutts, who planned *Merlin* as the first part of a trilogy, leading on to *Lancelot* and *Guenevere*. The poetic language is extraordinarily contorted (Arthur's big monologue in Act 2 includes the prize line 'mercy him that asketh give'), using archaic words in the most ham-fisted way, while the plot, admirably direct though it is, with many effective moments, is seriously flawed.

Maybe because this was planned as the first of a trilogy, it leaves you at the end in mid-air, with Merlin imprisoned in a cave through the machinations of Morgan le Fay and with Arthur nowhere to hand. Oddly, instead of illustrating that downbeat close with sinister music, Albéniz makes it surprisingly cheerful, maybe seeking to reflect the emotions of Morgan le Fay and her accomplice, Merlin's Saracen slave-girl Nivian, the only two women characters, both on the side of evil. Overall this is a warm, colourful score, with the major mode dominant. That may limit the emotional and dramatic range, but the purposefulness of the writing consistently leaves one wanting to hear more.

The recorded performance could hardly be finer. Plácido Domingo, as Arthur, sings nobly and with passion, even though he is disappointingly absent from the last half of Act 3. Carlos Alvarez as Merlin is equally fine, using his firm, dark baritone with an incisiveness and expressive range worthy of a Wotan. And though the timbres of the American sopranos, Jane Henschel as Morgan le Fay and Ana María Martínez as Nivian are similar enough to confuse one in places, they both characterise well, singing with consistently rich, warm tone. Christopher Maltman is a suitably evil-sounding Mordred, and outstanding among the others is the young tenor Angel Rodríguez, as Gawain.

The chorus, in colourful contributions, sings with clear, incandescent tone, regularly adding to the thrill of climaxes; and under the dedicated direction of Eusebio the orchestra plays brilliantly, helped by a recording that's exceptionally full, atmospheric and well balanced to give full weight to the orchestra while letting one hear the voices clearly.

Tomaso Albinoni

Italian 1671-1751

GROVE *Born of wealthy parents, Albinoni was a dilettante musician, never seeking a church or court post, though he had contact with noble patrons. He concentrated on instrumental and secular vocal music and had early successes with his opera Zenobia (1694, Venice) and 12 trio sonatas Op 1 (1694). His reputation grew, with operas staged in other cities, beginning with Rodrigo in Algeri (1702, Naples); later operas, such as I veri amici (1722, Munich), were staged abroad. In all he wrote over 50 operas, several other stage works and over 40 solo cantatas; few works date from after 1730.*

Albinoni's instrumental works, mostly for strings, were especially popular; 10 sets were published in his lifetime. Bach based four keyboard fugues on subjects from the Op 1 sonatas. While Albinoni's concertos were less adventurous and soloistic than Vivaldi's, they were probably the earliest consistently in three movements, and his oboe concertos Op 7 (1715) were the first by an Italian to be published. The sonatas (for one to six instruments with continuo) are mostly in four movements. His music is individual, with a strong melodic character and, especially in the early works, formally well balanced.

12 Concerti a cinque, Op 5

Collegium Musicum 90 / Simon Standage *vn* P
Chandos Chaconne CHAN0663 (76 minutes: DDD) Ⓕ
Recorded 2000 OO

Albinoni might be described as a specialist in the medium of the Concerto a cinque, of which he composed 54 under five opus numbers, published at intervals during almost half of his productive life. The first six appeared in his Op 2 (1700), together with six sonatas from which they inherited some structural features, and were followed in 1707 by the 12 of Op 5. They were 'halfway houses' on the road to the violin concerto *per se* as we know it – and as Vivaldi established it four years later. Virtuosic passages for a solo violin appear only *en passant* in flanking movements and 'symmetrically' in the *Adagios* of Nos 3, 6, 9 and 12. Each Concerto is in three-movement form and all the finales are fugal, as they are in the Op 2, though in their simplicity they sound rather like rondos.

There was little by way of innovation in Albinoni's concertos, which leant on past examples and stressed some of their most durable features, but the lyricism of the *Adagios* of No 2, 5, 8 and 11 (again symmetrically placed) was indeed new. Their strength is in his gift of melodic invention, their clearly defined form and thematic material, their conciseness – a virtue that did not survive in some of his later concertos – and their vitality and freshness. The recording and annotation are of the highest standard, and of the performances it might be said that if they are ever bettered in any respect, we and Albinoni will indeed be fortunate.

Concerti a cinque, Opp 7 and 9

Op 7 – No 1 in D; **No 2** in C; **No 3** in B flat; **No 4** in G; **No 5** in C; **No 6** in D; **No 7** in A; **No 8** in D; **No 9** in F; **No 10** in B flat; **No 11** in C; **No 12** in C
Op 9 – No 1 in B flat; **No 2** in D minor; **No 3** in F; **No 4** in A; **No 5** in C; **No 6** in G. **No 7** in D; **No 8** in G minor; **No 9** in C; **No 10** in F; **No 11** in B flat; **No 12** in D

CHAN0579 – Op 7 Nos 3, 6, 9 and 12. Op 9 Nos 2, 5, 8 and 11 **P**
CHAN0602 – Op 7 Nos 1, 2, 4 and 5. Op 9 Nos 1, 3, 4 and 6. Sinfonia in G minor
CHAN0610 – Op 7 Nos 7, 8, 10 and 11. Op 9 Nos 7, 9, 10 and 12
Chandos Chaconne CHAN0579/0602/0610 Ⓕ
(oas: 72, 63 and 65 minutes: DDD)
Anthony Robson, Catherine Latham *obs*
Collegium Musicum 90 / Simon Standage *vn*
Recorded 1993 and 1996

Albinoni's Op 7 and Op 9 consist of four concertos *with* (rather than *for*, as the composer insisted) one oboe, four with two oboes and four for strings only. Overall, the last show a strong family resemblance, with vivacious outer movements and suave slow movements that tend to be more chromatic; but the Op 9 string concertos include a solo violin part, at times very elaborate. The first volume contains the works for solo oboe and strings. Albinoni treats the oboe like a voice and the slow movements have tunes that stay in the mind. The second volume contains the string and double-oboe concertos. All are three-movement *da chiesa* works, with cheerful outer movements and slow ones that often remind you that Albinoni wrote a good deal of vocal music. The two oboes 'sing' together for the most part, either in thirds or in unison. The concertos on Vol 3 for two oboes display rather more individuality – the joyous finale of Op 7 No 11 intriguingly sharpens the fourth of the scale, Op 9 No 9 allows the oboes more independence of each other, while in the outer movements of Op 9 No 12 the oboes put up a good pretence at being trumpets.

Anthony Robson and Catherine Latham contribute deftly to the spirit of enjoyment that emanates from the whole of this disc. Collegium Musicum 90 is one of the very best baroque bands around and here the players are in their element. The recorded balance is just right, keeping soloists and strings in equal perspective. These discs bid strongly for a place on every shelf.

---

12 Concerti a cinque, Op 9 **P**
Andrew Manze *vn* **Frank de Bruine, Alfredo Bernardini** *obs* **Academy of Ancient Music / Christopher Hogwood**
Decca ② 458 129-2OH2 Ⓕ
(117 minutes: DDD)

For consistently amiable, if undemanding entertainment, Albinoni's concertos are hard to beat. Christopher Hogwood and the Academy of Ancient Music here perform the 12 concertos contained in the collection published in 1722 as the composer's Op 9. Neither the formal content nor the musical style differs significantly from Albinoni's earlier collection, Op 7 (1715); each set includes four concertos for strings, four for strings with oboe and four for strings with two oboes. In the Op 9 set, though, greater emphasis is placed on solo violin in the all-string pieces. This set contains perhaps Albinoni's crowning achievement in the concerto sphere, a lyrical *Adagio* for solo oboe with a simple string arpeggio accompaniment belonging to the Second Concerto. Its wistful, undulating melody lingers forever in the memory, outclassing in every respect the spurious G minor *Adagio* upon which, paradoxically, Albinoni's reputation today has largely been established. There are many delightful slow movements in this set, but also some irresistibly sprightly ones. These belong mainly to the pieces for two oboes, the Third and Sixth Concertos of the set providing spirited examples. None of this is lost either on the three accomplished soloists – Andrew Manze, Frank de Bruine and Alfredo Bernardini – or the strings of the Academy of Ancient Music, which provide lively and sensitive support. In short, the set affords uninterrupted pleasure from start to finish.

---

8 550739 12 Concerti a cinque – Op 9 Nos 2, 3, 5, 8, 9 and 11
8 553002 Sinfonia in G (arr Camden). 12 Concerti a cinque – Op 7 Nos 1, 2, 3, 8 and 9. Op 9 No 6.
8 553035 12 Concerti a cinque – Op 7 Nos 4, 5, 6, 11 and 12. Op 9 No 12
Anthony Camden, Julia Girdwood, Alison Alty *obs*
The London Virtuosi / John Georgiadis
Naxos 8 550739/3002/3035 Ⓢ
(64, 58 and 52 minutes: DDD)
Recorded 1992 and 1994

The oboe participates in, rather than dominates, these works in a chamber-music-like fashion. Albinoni had already experimented seven years earlier with the genre in his pioneering Concerti a cinque, Op 7, the weaknesses in which were rectified in those of the more mature Op 9. He was not in the business of springing harmonic surprises, but was a fluent writer of engaging tunes, particularly those in the *Adagios* – each of these works has one – and of elegant discourses between the soloist and the upper strings. Anthony Camden and Julia Girdwood produce liquid sounds from their modern instruments and are as meltingly expressive in the slow movements as they are light on their feet in the flanking ones. The London Virtuosi, also using modern strings, has a nice, clean air about it and gives the music neither more nor less than its due. The recording is bright and well balanced.

Volume 2 begins with a strings-only Sinfonia in G, to which Anthony Camden has added oboe parts; it is thematically related to the Concerto, Op 7 No 4 (given in its original form), but to appreciate this bit of auto-plagiary you will need Vol 3. The three discs are better sampled than listened to from start to finish – unless you are an oboist or an insatiable 'baroque person'; there are some delectable pickings to be had, particularly among the slow movements.

The performances and recording quality are of the same order as those of Vol 1, 'couth, kempt and shevelled' – as is the graceful and amiable music itself. As an archive, the complete set is hard to resist at super-bargain price.

Sonate da chiesa, Op 4

Six Sonate da chiesa, Op 4. 12 Trattenimenti armonici per camera, Op 6 **P**
Locatelli Trio (Elizabeth Wallfisch *vn* Richard Tunnicliffe *vc* Paul Nicholson *hpd/org*)
Hyperion ② CDA66831/2 (159 minutes: DDD) Ⓕ
Recorded 1992

While Albinoni's concertos, and especially those for one and two oboes, have been reasonably well catered for by record companies, his chamber music has been largely overlooked. All the pieces on these discs are violin sonatas rather than trio sonatas but, sensibly, Paul Nicholson uses harpsichord for Op 6 and organ for Op 4, thereby providing the listener with variety in colour. This variety is maximised by a decision to intermingle the two sets. Each sonata is cast in the four movement slow-fast-slow-fast *da chiesa* pattern although, as with Corelli but to an even greater extent, Albinoni far from keeps to the *da chiesa* spirit, introducing instead a wealth of dance measures. Almost invariably the music is graceful in character, melodically appealing – above all, as is so often the case with Albinoni – in the slow movements such as the *Adagio* of Op 4 No 6, and expressively restrained.

These qualities are certainly not lost on Elizabeth Wallfisch, who affectingly captures the limpid, reflective content of slow movements, on the one hand, and the brilliance of the faster ones on the other. Richard Tunnicliffe gives her discreet and sensitive support throughout. Possibly a little more in the way of caprice during the sparkling *Allegros* would be nice. It is not that the playing lacks vitality but that a certain worthiness of approach is sensed; a dimension of playful virtuosity has not perhaps been fully realised. In all essentials, though, this is an enjoyable and very worthwhile release, illuminating less familiar aspects of Albinoni's music.

Hugo Alfvén

Swedish 1872-1960

GROVE *Alfvén studied at the Stockholm Conservatory (1887-91) and privately with Lindegren, also training as a painter. Thereafter he worked as a choirmaster and Director Musices at Uppsala University (1910-39). His music is distinguished by orchestral subtlety and a painterly exploitation of harmony and timbre. It is almost all programmatic, often seeking to evoke the landscapes and seascapes of southern Sweden (eg Midsummer Vigil, 1903; Shepherd-girl's Dance, 1923). His main works include five symphonies, much choral music and songs.*

Swedish Rhapsodies

Swedish Rhapsodies – No 1, Op 19, 'Midsummer Vigil'; No 2, Op 24, 'Upsala-rapsodi'; No 3, 'Dalarapsodi'. A Legend of the Skerries, Op 20. Gustav Adolf II, Op 49 – Elegy
Iceland Symphony Orchestra / Petri Sakari
Chandos CHAN9313 (70 minutes: DDD) Ⓕ
Recorded 1993

Petri Sakari gives us the most natural, unaffected and satisfying *Midsummer Vigil* to be heard on disc. He is light in touch, responsive to each passing mood and every dynamic nuance, self-effacing and completely at the service of the composer. Moreover, in the *Upsala-rapsodi* and its later companion he is fresher and more persuasive than any of his rivals on record. Even the Wagnerian-Straussian echoes from the skerries sound convincing. The only reservation concerns the *Elegy* from the incidental music to Ludwig Nordström's play about Gustav Adolf II, which might have benefited from greater reticence. Unusually for Sakari, he does not tell the tale simply or let the music speak for itself. The recorded sound is refreshingly free from analytical point-making; everything is there in the right perspective, although listeners whose first response is to find the recording recessed will find that a higher level of playback than usual will produce impressively natural results on high-grade equipment.

Cantatas

Cantata, 'At the Turn of the Century', Op 12[ac]. Cantata for the 1917 Reformation Festivities in Uppsala, Op 36[bc]. The Bells, Op 13[b]
[a]**Lena Hoel** *sop* [b]**Karl-Magnus Fredriksson** *bar* [c]**Royal Stockholm Philharmonic Choir; Gävle Symphony Orchestra / Stefan Parkman**
Sterling CDS1036-2 (60 minutes: DDD) Ⓕ
Texts and translations included. Recorded 1999 ●

Cantatas for ceremonial or anniversary occasions have a distinguished tradition in the Nordic countries, as can be seen in the catalogues of Sibelius, Grieg, Nielsen and Holmboe, among others. Hugo Alfvén was as accomplished as any – indeed, comparing the two main works on this new release with Sibelius's 'Conferment' and *Coronation* cantatas (the latter for Tsar Nicholas II – Ondine, 1999), Alfvén was the finer exponent. Listen to the opening movement, 'Life's Empire', of *Vid sekelskiftet* ('At the Turn of the Century'), which has real nobility about it; and if the second and fourth are emptily high-spirited, they still sound fun. Alfvén's style may seem archaic for 1899, but there are sufficient passages – especially in the third movement, 'Väldarnas offer' ('The world's offering', a solo for soprano which can be performed separately) – that reveal the anachronisms to be more calculated than might at first appear. Alfvén's next numbered opus, the ballad *Klockorna* ('The Bells', 1900), was more consistently adventurous in harmony and orchestration (including two pianos), and is an absolute gem, sung beautifully by Karl-Magnus Fredriksson.

Fredriksson also features in the 1917 cantata commemorating the 400th anniversary of Luther nailing his 95 Theses to the chapel door in Wittenberg, thereby setting in motion the Protestant Reformation. The music (built around three Lutheran chorales) is magnificent, particularly in the first two movements, with their deeply affecting nobility of utterance. The final movement does burn at a lower level, slowly building towards the chorale *Ein' feste Burg ist unser Gott*, as if Luther's great hymn cramped Alfvén's compositional style.

Stefan Parkman, who directed several wonderful discs with the Danish National Radio Choir, secures wonderfully full and committed performances from all concerned, and Sterling's recording is warm and clear. A thoroughly estimable project, warmly recommended.

Charles-Valentin Alkan

French 1813-1888

GROVE *Alkan was a leading piano virtuoso and an unusual composer, remarkable in technique and imagination yet largely ignored by his own and succeeding generations. A child prodigy, he studied at the Paris Conservatoire. Although he held no official appointment and rarely played publicly, he was known for the brilliance of his playing, his wide repertory of earlier music and as a champion of the pedal piano (for which he composed). His complex works include extra-musical elements; he favoured obscure titles and subject matter (often with a satanic, childish or mystical tone), bold tonal structures and unusual metres. He exploited brilliantly the keyboard's resources, often making great demands of technique and stamina, and used scrupulously exact notation. Many of his some 70 opus numbers are organised in long schemes of harmonic studies, such as the 25 Préludes in all the major and minor keys Op 31 (1847) and the 12 Études Op 39 (1857); his most famous and demanding works are his Grande Sonate, Op 33 and the Concerto (for piano solo) from Op 39. He was greatly admired by Liszt and Busoni.*

Grand duo concertante, Op 21

Grand duo concertante in F sharp minor, Op 21. Sonate de concert in E, Op 47. Trio in G minor, Op 30
Trio Alkan (Kolja Lessing *vn* Bernhard Schwarz *vc* Rainer Klaas *pf*)
Naxos 8 555352 (75 minutes: DDD) Ⓢ
Recorded 1991

As this disc so persuasively reveals, there are a number of Alkan's chamber works that are long overdue for serious consideration. His violin sonata, the *Grand duo concertante*, for instance, is so thoroughly original and masterly in invention that it should have acquired for itself a prominent place in the French violin sonata repertoire. The somewhat unconventional tonal layout of the bold and memorable first movement suggests, at times, the harmonic world of Berlioz, but perhaps more strikingly looks forward, both here and in the final movement, to the melodic, Gallic charm of the Fauré sonatas.

The *Sonate de concert* for cello and piano is perhaps Alkan's finest and most important contribution to chamber music. It's an expansive work of some 32 minutes. Although clearly rooted in the classical tradition, it shouts Alkan from every page. The second movement, in *siciliano* style, is a fine example of Alkan whimsy; in the slow movement, Alkan draws musical inspiration from his Jewish faith to create a serene and somewhat mystical oasis of calm before launching into the helter-skelter activity of the finale. The earlier Piano Trio of 1841 is perhaps even more classical in design and utterance, and is certainly more terse and economical in its use of material. However, it's no easy ride for the performers. The *Scherzo* is strangely prophetic of Tchaikovsky in places and is graced with a fiendishly difficult finale. The performances are quite superb. Klaas copes admirably with all the keyboard pyrotechnics thrown at him, and Lessing and Schwarz provide performances of dedication and great understanding. Recording is full-bodied and close, although not uncomfortably so.

25 Préludes, Op 31

Awards 1992

Alkan 25 Préludes dans les tons majeurs et mineurs, Op 31 **Shostakovich** 24 Preludes, Op 34
Olli Mustonen *pf* Decca 433 055-2DH Ⓕ
(76 minutes: DDD)
Recorded 1990 OOO

It was brave of Decca to launch the career of its (then) newly signed pianist with a disc of miniatures known to a few people only, since Alkan's *oeuvre* is usually confined to specialist labels and second-rate executants. The 25 Préludes are a reasonably benign introduction to Alkan's idiosyncratic world – elusive and quirky to be sure but less ruthlessly barnstorming than much of his output. They are by no means easy pieces to bring off, but you wouldn't know it from Mustonen's exceptionally assured, brilliantly poised readings. Where rival versions are content to offer the 25 Préludes without coupling, Mustonen adds deft and sparkling performances of Shostakovich's not exactly insubstantial Op 34 Preludes. Exceptional pianism, excellent, bright recording and helpful notes.

Three Etudes, Op 76

Alkan Transcription de concert (Beethoven's Piano Concerto No 3 in C minor, Op 37 – first movement). Three Etudes, Op 76 **Busoni** Sonatina No 6 super Carmen (Kammerfantasie) **Chopin/Alkan** Piano Concerto No 1 in E minor, Op 11 – Romanza **Medtner** Danza festiva, Op 38 No 3
Marc-André Hamelin *pf* Hyperion CDA66765 Ⓕ
(72 minutes: DDD). Recorded live in 1994 OO

The solo transcriptions on the first half of this disc are not intended as substitutes for the real thing – at least not in the context of this disc – but they are presented here as supreme examples of the art of piano transcription in the late 19th century. In addition, they are superb display pieces, revealing not only the subtleties of the transcriber's art and, in this case, the pianist's ability to render them audible, but also Hamelin's extraordinary ability to make the pieces sound like originals rather than transcriptions. Indeed, in the Alkan transcription of the first movement of Beethoven's Third Piano Concerto, the absence of the orchestra never becomes a concern. The principal glory of the disc, however, is Hamelin's account of Alkan's *Etudes*, Op 76, for the hands separately and reunited, an exceptionally formidable opus which here receives a formidable and awe-inspiring performance. We also have the added *frisson* of knowing that what we hear is a single take before a live audience; listen to the hair-raising final study, a blistering, unbroken five-minute salvo of *prestissimo* semiquavers. The remaining items – a scintillating account of Busoni's *Sonatina* No 6 and Medtner's ebullient *Danza festiva* from Op 38 – provide further evidence of Hamelin's undoubted skill. The recorded sound varies a little from piece to piece but all are excellent in quality.

12 Etudes, Op 39

12 Etudes dans les tons mineurs, Op 39. Nocturne, Op 22. Etude in F, Op 35 No 5. Assez vivement, Op 38 No 1. Préludes, Op 31 – No 8, La chanson de la folle au bord de la mer; No 12, Le temps qui n'est plus; No 13, J'étais endormie, mais mon coeur veillait. Esquisses, Op 63 – No 2, La staccatissimo; No 4, Les cloches; No 11, Les soupirs; No 48, En songe. Gros temps, Op 74 No 10. First Suite No 2. Barcarolle, Op 65 No 6.
Jack Gibbons *pf*
ASV ② CDDCS227 (155 minutes: DDD) Ⓕ
Recorded 1995 ●●

'Comme le vent' ('Like the wind'), the opening *Etude* from Op 39, is a real baptism of fire for the pianist. Marked *prestissimamente*, it is an unrelenting deluge of notes which, if played at Alkan's specified metronome marking, travels at the rate of 160 bars per minute, or to put it another way, traverses 20 densely packed pages in just 4'30". Gibbons throws caution to the wind and completes the whirlwind in a staggering 4'38". Despite the odd occasion when he comes perilously close to tumbling into the abyss, this ranks among the most exhilarating feats of pianism to be heard on disc. If Gibbons's credentials as an Alkan pianist are not sealed in his performance of the first *Etude* then his reading of the following two *Etudes*, 'En rythme molossique' and 'Scherzo diabolico', surely confirm him as an Alkan interpreter of exceptional authority. Listening to these commanding and exceedingly sure-footed performances one is left with the feeling that Gibbons has grown with and nurtured these pieces for some time. The following four *Etudes* make up the *Symphony for Solo Piano* and, if anything, Gibbons is even more impressive in his reading of this striking work.

Moving on to the *Concerto for Solo Piano, Etudes* Nos 8-10, Gibbons gives a wildly romantic reading. More extraordinary feats of virtuosity await the listener in the 12th *Etude* ('Le festin d'Esope') and the *Allegro barbaro* from the Op 35 *Etudes*, but the delightful selection of miscellaneous pieces with which Gibbons fills the remainder of the set shows not only the more introverted side of Alkan's creativity but also allows Gibbons to display a less ostentatious and more directly poetic aspect of his playing. The simple *Nocturne* in B major, with its Chopinesque heartbeat, is beautifully rendered as are the 'Les soupirs' and 'En songe' from the *Esquisses*, Op 63 and the *Barcarolle*, Op 65 No 6. However, the highlight of these miniatures comes with Gibbons's sensitive and effective delivery of the potently atmospheric 'La chanson de la folle au bord de la mer' ('Song of the mad woman on the seashore'), surely one of the most curious piano pieces to emerge from the 19th century.

All in all, an exceptionally impressive issue that can be highly recommended to both Alkan devotees and newcomers alike. The recorded sound is excellent.

Grande sonate, Op 33

Grande sonate, Op 33, 'Les quatre âges'. Sonatine, Op 61. Barcarolle, Op 65 No 6. Etudes dans les tons mineurs, Op 39 – No 12, 'Le festin d'Esope'.
Marc-André Hamelin *pf*
Hyperion CDA66794 (70 minutes: DDD) Ⓕ
Recorded 1994 ●●

Les quatre âges is an extraordinary piece in many respects, not least in its rather unconventional layout of four movements, each employing progressively slower tempos. Perhaps for this reason it has never attained a place in the repertoire – the extremely slow finale is hardly the sort of movement to ignite an overwhelming response from an audience at the close of the sonata, despite the feats of hair-raising bravura required in the first two movements. Hamelin's performance is everything one could wish for. The crispness and precision of his finger-work in the dazzling first movement is quite breathtaking and the sometimes superhuman feats of pianism demanded in the Faust-inspired second movement are executed with astounding ease. His reading of the third movement is beautifully poised and charmingly rendered while the tragic, Promethean finale is most effectively and powerfully projected.

The *Sonatine*, Op 61 is an entirely different matter, concise and concentrated in the extreme. Hamelin's direct, finely articulated no-nonsense reading brings out the clarity and economy of the writing, and he is also quick to underscore the work's more classical stance. A beautifully serene and hypnotic account of the seductive 'Barcarolle' follows, and the disc closes with a stunning display of pianistic gymnastics in the shape of 'Le festin d'Esope' from the Op 39 *Etudes*. Recorded sound is excellent.

Further listening

Lyapunov 12 Studies, Etudes d'éxecution transcendante
Scherbakov *pf*
Marco Polo 8 223491 (71 minutes: DDD: 4/94) Ⓕ

Fiendishly challenging studies for pianists who like to live dangerously. Awe-inspiring listening for non-pianists!

Gregorio Allegri

Italian *c*1582-1652

Allegri was a singer and composer at the cathedrals of Fermo and Tivoli and later maestro di cappella of Spirito in Sassia, Rome, and a singer in the papal choir. He composed many of his works for this choir and that of S Maria in Vallicella. His reputation rests on his Miserere, a psalm setting traditionally sung every Holy Week by the papal choir: it is basically a simple five-part chant, transformed by interpolated ornamented passages for a four-part solo choir which reaches top C (rare at that time). These passages were a closely guarded secret for many years; Mozart wrote out the work from memory when he was 14. Allegri was at his best in the a cappella style, as in his five masses; he also published three books of more up-to-date small-scale concertato church music.

Miserere mei

Allegri Miserere mei
Palestrina Motets – Stabat mater a 8. Hodie beata virgo. Senex puerem portabat. Magnificat a 8. Litanie de Beata Virgine Maria I
Roy Goodman *treb* **King's College Choir, Cambridge / Sir David Willcocks**
Decca Legends 466 373-2DM (56 minutes: ADD) Ⓜ
Recorded 1963-64 ooo

It is doubtful if any recording made by the choir of King's College, Cambridge, in the fertile Willcocks era, will prove more enduring than this celebrated performance of Allegri's *Miserere*. Admittedly there are more authentic versions in the catalogue, authentic not only in that they use the original Latin words where Willcocks opts for an English translation, but also in the sense that they search for a style less obviously redolent of choral evensong and the Anglican tradition. At the farthest extreme from King's, other versions strip Allegri's score of its various 18th- and 19th-century accretions – a nice piece of musical archaeology which, ironically, reveals the utter plainness of the *Miserere* when denied its familiar jewels, and sounds like an imposter when dressed up in even more garish baubles. For once, musicology seems doomed to failure; the richly communicative singing of King's remains for many an ideal impression of the piece, however far removed it may be from the orginal intentions of Allegri.

The *Miserere* is accompanied here by some classic Palestrina performances, which are still as fresh as when they were recorded in 1964. Some tape hiss intrudes, but otherwise the sound is excellent. 'Fabulous' is the only descriptive word that does justice to this disc.

Miserere mei (two versions). Missa Vidi turbam magnam. De ore prudentis. Repleti sunt omnes. Cantate domino
A Sei Voci / Bernard Fabre-Garrus with **Dominique Ferran** *org*
Auvidis Astrée E8524 (62 minutes: DDD) Ⓕ
Texts and translations included. Recorded 1994

Allegri's setting of the psalm *Miserere mei* is presented in two versions. The first is sung with ornamentation added by the French musicologist, Jean Lionnet following 17th-century models, while the second presents the Burney-Alfieri version familiar from the classic 1963 Willcocks recording above. The curiously named group A Sei Voci (in fact there are 10 of them) produce a rather varied sound, which is at times somewhat flat and white but at its best is embued with an appropriate Italianate edge. For the most part the embellishments are negotiated with style and verve; just occasionally (in the first *Miserere*) they are fuzzy or insecure. *Miserere mei* apart, hardly any of Allegri's music is heard either liturgically or in the concert hall. By training a pupil of Nanino, a distinguished follower of Palestrina, his best music is written confidently in the High Renaissance contrapuntal manner. The six-voice *Missa Vidi turbam magnam*, composed on one of his own motets, is a fine work, and shows that the *stile antico*, far from being a mere academic exercise, could still be vividly sonorous and dramatic, qualities which are brought out in this reading. The record is nicely rounded out with a selection of short continuo motets in the popular new manner, well established in Northern Italy, which was then becoming fashionable in Rome.

Additional recommendation

Miserere mei
Couplings: **Lotti** Crucifixus – a 6; a 8; a 10. **Gesualdo** Responsoria et alia ad Officum Hebdonadae Sanctae spectantia – Tenebrae factae sunt; Caligaverunt oculi mei. **G Gabrieli** Symphoniae sacrae – O domine Jesu Christe. **Monteverdi** Adoramus te, Christe. **Bai/Allegri** Miserere mei[a]. **John IV** Crux fidelis
Westminster Abbey Choir; [a]Abbey Consort / Neary
Sony Classical SK66615 (77 minutes: DDD: 7/96) Ⓕ

A fascinating collection of polyphony which puts Allegri's famous work in the context of contemporary settings.

William Alwyn

British 1905-1985

Alwyn studied with McEwen at the Royal Academy of Music (1920-23) and later taught there (1926-55); in 1961 he retired to Suffolk to compose. He disowned everything he wrote before the Divertimento for flute (1939), which opened a neo-classical phase, followed in the 1950 by a personal vein of English Romanticism. His music is characterised by precise workmanship. It includes five symphonies (1949, 1953, 1956, 1959, 1973) and two string quartets, opera (Miss Julie, 1976) and songs (often to his own words: he also published poems and essays); he wrote over 60 film scores, too.

Symphony No 3

Violin Concerto. Symphony No 3
Lydia Mordkovitch *vn*
London Symphony Orchestra / Richard Hickox
Chandos CHAN9187 (75 minutes: DDD) Ⓕ
Recorded 1993

The Violin Concerto, although essentially threnodic and lyrical, opens confidently and the orchestra returns with regular bursts of energy. The end of the movement (the rapt *pianissimo* closing section) is exquisite: one is reminded here of Vaughan Williams' *The lark ascending*, although as the second movement *Allegretto* opens, the melodic writing also brings hints of Elgar. The finale is fairly vigorous, but again the lyrical impulse is all important. The work is discursive, yet has moments of great intensity. The performance could not be bettered and Mordkovitch's *pianissimo* playing is touchingly beautiful.

The Third Symphony is an outstanding example of Alwyn's earlier symphonic manner and is in three movements. The first combines driving rhythmic agitation with a powerful lyrical thrust. The *Adagio*, introduced by a peaceful horn theme, has an animated, brassy development, then ethereal strings restore the sense of repose, the horns returning glowingly. The finale restores the forward momentum with its rhythmic zest and has a powerful and satisfying resolution. Hickox's reading is truly convincing and the LSO responds committedly to a work that must be rewarding to play.

Additional recommendation
Symphony No 3
Couplings: Symphonies Nos 2 and 5
London Philharmonic Orchestra / Alwyn
Lyrita SRCD228 (77 minutes: ADD: 10/92) Ⓕ
Passionate, authoritative performances from Alwyn himself.

Symphony No 4

Symphonies – No 1 in D; No 4
London Philharmonic Orchestra / William Alwyn
Lyrita SRCD227 (77 minutes: ADD) Ⓕ
Recorded 1970s

Symphony No 4. Elizabethan Dances. Festival March
London Symphony Orchestra / Richard Hickox
Chandos CHAN8902 (65 minutes: DDD) Ⓕ
Recorded 1992

It is interesting to compare Alwyn's own recording with Hickox's version of No 4, an extraordinarily fine work, as the two accounts are remarkably alike. Indeed, when one compares the composer's phrasing of the long and beautiful string cantilena which opens the *Adagio e molto calmato* of the Passacaglia finale, its ebb and flow and dynamic gradations suggest that either Hickox has listened to the composer's LP or has a remarkable, instinctive feeling for the music (probably both). The *Scherzo* may have a bit more bite with Alwyn, but this is at least partly caused by the more leonine Lyrita sound. The centrepiece of the *Scherzo* brings a glorious blossoming from the violins which is equally thrilling in both performances, while at the very end of the symphony the final brass peroration has great forceful thrust from the composer. However, with the LSO and Hickox the slightly richer, more spacious Chandos recording adds to the weight of sonority. In short, these are both highly compelling performances of a remarkably diverse and well-argued symphony, bursting with lyrical ideas and melodic in the way traditional music is communicative, without being old-fashioned. As to the couplings on Chandos, they are relatively slight. *The Elizabethan Dances* aren't very early Elizabethan, but the languid 'Waltz' (No 2) is rather charming and the 'Poco Allegretto' (No 5) is even more so; the vigorous numbers are more conventional. *The Festival March*, written for the 1951 Festival of Britain, is an agreeable occasional piece, although its big tune isn't as memorable as those of Walton or Elgar. Yet if you want a modern recording of the Fourth Symphony, these are acceptable makeweights. On the other hand, Lyrita offers the Symphony No 1. It is a work teeming with ideas, and quite often reminds one of Alwyn's film music. With its ample scoring, the composer does go over the top a bit at times and this is not nearly so cogently argued a piece as the Fourth, although it has a rather appealing *Adagio*. It is splendidly played and the Lyrita recordings have been remastered most skilfully.

Additional recommendation
Symphony No 1
Coupling: Piano Concerto No 1
Shelley *pf* **London Symphony Orchestra / Hickox**
Chandos CHAN9155 (56 minutes: DDD: 5/93) Ⓕ
A fine modern version of the First Symphony coupled with the eventful First Piano Concerto of 1930.

Further listening
Symphony No 2 Couplings: Overture to a Masque.The Magic Island – symphonic prelude. Overture 'Derby Day'. Fanfare for a Joyful Occasion
London Symphony Orchestra / Hickox
Chandos CHAN9093 (62 minutes: DDD: 2/93)
Hickox's reading of Symphony No 2 has every bit as much power and grip as the composer's own (see above).

Symphony No 5

Piano Concerto No 2. Symphony No 5, 'Hydriotaphia'. Sinfonietta for Strings
Howard Shelley *pf*
London Symphony Orchestra / Richard Hickox
Chandos CHAN9196 (74 minutes: DDD) Ⓕ
Recorded 1993

Piano Concerto No 2 opens heroically and contains a good deal of rhetoric, yet the string writing has a romantic sweep and the *Andante* proves to be the highlight of the piece. Howard Shelley plays with much bravura and an appealing sensitivity.

The powerful Fifth Symphony is a cogent argument distilled into one movement with four sub-sections. The energetically kaleidoscopic first movement is sharply contrasted by a melancholy *Andante*. The violent *Scherzo* is followed by a curiously ambivalent finale which provides a moving and compelling, if equivocal, apotheosis for a succinctly argued work. The richly expansive *Sinfonietta for Strings*, almost twice as long as the symphony, is very much in the English tradition of string writing. It is vigorous in the first movement and hauntingly atmospheric in the beautiful but disconsolate *Adagio*. The unpredictable finale begins impulsively before the mood changes completely and becomes altogether more subdued and muted in feeling. The obviously dedicated LSO is particularly responsive in the masterly *Sinfonietta*.

Additional recommendation
Symphony No 5
Couplings: Symphonies Nos 2 and 3
London Philharmonic Orchestra / Alwyn
Lyrita SRCD228 (77 minutes: ADD: 10/92) Ⓕ
A must if you've caught the Alwyn bug: three very different symphonies, given superb performances.

Lyra Angelica

Lyra Angelica. Autumn Legend. Pastoral Fantasia. Tragic Interlude
Rachel Masters *hp* **Nicholas Daniel** *cor ang*
Stephen Tees *va*
City of London Sinfonia / Richard Hickox
Chandos CHAN9065 (64 minutes: DDD) Ⓕ
Recorded 1991

Alwyn valued his *Lyra Angelica* concerto for harp above all his other music, and it is indeed very beautiful. It received its première at the first night of the 1954 Proms and, unsurprisingly, made an immediate impression. Alwyn is a master of texture as well as form and the textures here, delicately embroidered by the solo harp, are harmonically rich, and the effect on the listener is very moving. The concerto is played with a real feeling for the music's rapture, and the expansive recorded sound, with rich string timbres and a perfect balance with the solo harp is very fine indeed. The *Pastoral Fantasia* was written in 1939 and looks back nostalgically to a more peaceful England. The music opens like Delius, but the entry of the viola brings an immediate affinity with Vaughan Williams as the solo viola begins in rhapsodic soliloquy. The *Tragic Interlude* dates from 1936, when the composer's foreboding of the imminence of the war brought an eloquent protest at the waste of life. The piece opens passionately and gathers momentum, but after its climax, dissolves into a moving elegiac threnody. *Autumn Legend* is much later (1954). It has a particularly lovely opening, with shafts of sunlight on the strings piercing the clouds, and the music's disconsolate manner has an underlying romantic feeling, rather than conveying pessimism. Yet the dark-hued cor anglais line has a pervading melancholy. It is a fine if ambivalent piece, and Nicholas Daniel, the soloist, captures its mood persuasively, while Richard Hickox shows himself in complete affinity with Alwyn's world. The Chandos recording is outstandingly fine.

Additional recommendation
Lyra Angelica
Couplings: Concerto Grosso No 2. Autumn Legend
Browne *cor ang* **Ellis** *hp*
London Philharmonic Orchestra / Alwyn
Lyrita SRCD230 (56 minutes: ADD: 12/92) Ⓕ
A disc of three of Alwyn's most beautiful works.

Miss Julie

Jill Gomez *sop* Miss Julie; **Benjamin Luxon** *bar* Jean; **Della Jones** *mez* Kristin; **John Mitchinson** *ten* Ulrik; **Philharmonia Orchestra / Vilem Tausky**
Lyrita ② SRCD2218 (118 minutes: ADD) Ⓕ
Notes and text included. Recorded 1983

In his colourful and confident adaptation of Strindberg's play, Alwyn consistently demonstrates his mastery of atmosphere and timing, bringing out the chilling intensity of this story of Miss Julie's sudden infatuation for her father's man-servant. He adapted the play himself, and understood far more than most librettists the need for economy over text. His principal modification of Strindberg is that to the play's three characters – Miss Julie, Jean the manservant and Kristin the cook – he adds the gamekeeper, Ulrik, who acts as a commentator. So in his drunken scene of Act 1 he makes explicit what is happening, to the embarrassment of both Miss Julie and Jean. He also shoots (off-stage) the lap-dog which Miss Julie wants to take away with her on her elopement, a convenient but less horrific alternative to the slaughter of the pet finch in the original Strindberg.

The idiom, harmonically rich and warmly lyrical, brings occasional Puccinian echoes which, along with reminiscences of other composers, add to the music's impact. By any reckoning this is a confidently red-blooded opera. Tausky's conducting is strong and forceful, with superb singing from all the principals. Jill Gomez is magnificent in the title-role, producing ravishing sounds. Benjamin Luxon gives a wonderfully swaggering portrait of the unscrupulous manservant, vocally firmer than on almost any of his other recordings. Della Jones is splendidly characterful, relishing her venomous cry of 'Bitch!' when, at the very end of Scene 1, she realises Julie and Jean have gone off together. John Mitchinson is characterful too, in his drunken scene. The recording is excellent.

Louis Andriessen

Dutch 1939

After early training with his father, the composer Hendrik Andriessen, he studied with Kees van Baaren at the Royal Conservatory at The Hague and later with Berio in Milan (1962-63) and Berlin (1964-65). Returning to the Netherlands he established himself as a leading musical figure both through his own compositions and as a performer of his own and others' work. Since 1973 he has taught composition at the Royal Conservatory and since the mid-1980s has been in great demand as a guest lecturer.

After a few youthful works influenced by neo-classicism and serialism Andriessen moved away from the postwar European avant garde toward American minimalism, jazz and Stravinsky, developing a musical language that is marked by extremes of ritual and masquerade, of monumentality and intimacy, of formal rigour and intuitive empiricism. The epitome of the Hague School, he is regarded as the most influential Dutch composer of his generation. His most important works include De volharding (1972) De staat (1972-76) De tijd (1980-81) and De materie (1984-89). In the 1990s he collaborated with film director Peter Greenaway on the video M is for Man, Music, Mozart (1991) and the stage works Rosa, A Horse Drama (1994) and Writing to Vermeer (1997-99).

Rosa: The Death of a Composer

Lyndon Terracini *bar* Juan Manuel de Rosa; **Miranda van Kralingen** *sop* First Singer; Madame de Vries; The Texan Whore; The Investigatrix; **Marie Angel** *sop* Second Singer; The Blonde Woman; Esmeralda; **Christopher Gillett** *ten* / **Roger Smeets** *bar* Alkan; Lully (The Gigolos); The Cowboys; **Phyllis Blanford** *spkr* The Index Singer; **Schönberg Ensemble; Asko Ensemble / Reinbert de Leeuw**
Nonesuch ② 7559-79559-2 (112 minutes: DDD) Ⓕ
Notes and text included. Recorded 1998

Rosa: The Death of a Composer, or 'A Horse Drama', gives us blood on the stable floor, dried, ominous and darkly crusted with sexual symbolism. Louis Andriessen's pile-driving score is a musical enactment related by birth to Stravinsky, though it's probably nearer in spirit to rock, jazz and Broadway. *Rosa* has a wonderful lack of compromise, a snorting aggression – especially at 8'45" into the Seventh Scene where angular rhythms suddenly transform to a wild canter. The mythical Uruguayan composer Juan Manuel de Rosa rides bareback as his hapless fiancée moans, in one of her various guises, of how Juan loves horses more than he loves her. She has already confessed that she 'pretends to be a horse to amuse his [Juan's] lechery' – and if that shocks you, then brace yourself for a feast of debauchery, violence and black humour.

Andriessen's band comprises woodwinds, brass, synthesizers, percussion and a few amplified strings. The style recalls the bold contrasts in, say, *De materie*, with tough-fisted rhythms (mostly jagged and irregular) and stark *fortissimo* chords. The overture is typically confrontational but some of the most powerful music in the score occurs at the end of scene 4 (from around 9'48" on track 5, disc 1) where, in true murder-mystery fashion, a missing clue thwarts the drama's successful resolution. Heavy Blues settle among the opening pages of the fifth scene, and the eleventh opens to a Morricone-style solo harmonica, where the hub of the theme reflects another of Andriessen's obsessions. It's a certain Brahms Waltz (from Op 39, as it happens) that his sister used to hum in their childhood bedroom and that also crops up earlier on in the piece. Who would have thought sentimentality would figure in such a blatantly bestial context, but there you have it! The last scene is trailed by a raunchy, rock-style 'Index Singer' who opens by defining Abattoir ('The location of the opera...A slaughterhouse', etc) and gets as far as Gas, via the likes of Dump and Envy. She eventually makes an exit, but the printed text takes us all the way from Glass-Haired to Zig-Zag.

Rosa was premièred at the Netherlands Opera in 1994 and the performance under review is superb, though special mention should be made of soprano Marie Angel, a marvellous singer and a formidable vocal actress. Film Director Peter Greenaway's libretto is erotic, often lyrical and profoundly ambiguous. Unusually, the words and synopsis complement each other: you read one, then study the other for further elucidation. But the music is pure Andriessen, blanched in the quieter music, and punch-drunk when the going gets hot. It's a music of extremes. If you're unsure, play a minute or so of the overture and the whole of scene 4. That'll tell you all you need to know...more or less.

George Antheil American 1900-1959

GROVE *Antheil studied privately with Sternberg and with Bloch (1920) before moving to Berlin in 1922 to make his name as a modernist. Jazz, noise and ostinato were the means, worked into brutally simple designs in the Airplane Sonata (1922) and Sonata sauvage (1923), these last written after his move from Berlin to Paris. There he wrote the Ballet mécanique (1925) for an ensemble of pianos and percussion including electric bells and propellers. In 1926 he turned to neo-classicism, then to opera: Transatlantic (1930, Frankfurt) was a satire on American political life. In 1936 he settled in Los Angeles, where he wrote symphonies, operas vocal, chamber and piano music along more conventional lines.*

Symphonies Nos 1 and 6

Symphonies – No 1, 'Zingareska'; No 6, 'after Delacroix'. Archipelago
Frankfurt Radio Symphony Orchestra / Hugh Wolff
CPO999 604-2 (63 minutes: DDD) Ⓕ
Recorded 1999

In 1923 Antheil gave a piano recital of his own music at the Théâtre des Champs-Elysées in Paris which created the kind of sensation not seen since *The Rite of Spring* 10 years earlier. Erik Satie was there and applauded vigorously, refusing to be deterred by Milhaud. One can see why. Antheil's *Ballet mécanique* (1926) took the unusual orchestra of Satie's *Parade* (1917) to the limit. But forget the scandals. Antheil is a quirky individual figure in his own right, as centenary activity is abundantly showing.

His Symphony No 1, Zingareska (*Gypsy Song*), comes from the same year as that spectacular piano recital and Antheil was uncertain about it. Odd to think of such a brash larger-than-life character being at all insecure. The gypsy element perhaps covers his own unsettled existence between the USA, Berlin and Paris, but it also symbolises his own kind of style-modulation long before he could have heard anything by Ives. We're now starting to enjoy Antheil's bare-faced kleptomania on his terms. Indeed, there are some lovely things in this young man's music, often beautifully scored and hovering hazardously between *Petrushka* and *Parade*; you never quite know what's going to happen next. In spite of his bravado Antheil had soul – take the delicious opening of the *Doloroso* third movement with celesta background to the oboe or the melodies over ostinato patterns in the middle of the final ragtime – the one which starts at 1'26" gets so close to the first of Stravinsky's *Five Easy Pieces* for piano duet as to be actionable.

It's a pity that Symphony No 6 (partly based on Delacroix's picture *Liberty leading the people*) duplicates the National Symphony Orchestra of the Ukraine under Kuchar on Naxos, since both are strong performances of this substantial piece from 1948. Antheil pays another debt to Satie since the *Larghetto* is a slow *Gymnopédie*, an oasis of calm between patriotic war music. The riotous *Archipelago*, subtitled 'Rhumba', is in the tradition of Gottschalk but, via Gershwin's *Cuban Overture*, is pure 1930s and ends a most impressive and enjoyable case for orchestral Antheil from three different decades.

Symphony No 5, 'Joyous'

Symphonies – No 4, '1942'; No 5, 'Joyous'. Decatur at Algiers
Frankfurt Radio Symphony Orchestra / Hugh Wolff
CPO CPO999 706-2 Ⓕ
(63 minutes: DDD)

The Antheil centenary boom goes on with further convincing advocacy from Hugh Wolff and his Frankfurt team. No 4, written in the worst years of the war, gets an ebullient performance which has the edge over the Ukranians since the recorded sound is richer. The music employs juxtapositions, exactly like cinematic cuts, that have little to do with symphonic development and are less dominated by Stravinsky than some of Antheil's earlier works. The tunes are memorable.

The novelty here is *Decatur at Algiers*, called a nocturne although it's based on Stephen Decatur conquering the Barbary pirates in the early 1800s. There's an attractive Arabic flavour about the spooky principal theme on the oboe. This release also brings the Fifth Symphony – first recorded by the Vienna Philharmonia under Herbert Haefner in 1952 – back into the catalogue. This is a war symphony too. Antheil lost his brother in the conflict and dedicated the symphony to 'the young dead of all countries who sacrificed everything'.

The first movement is continuously bustling in an idiom which crosses Stravinsky with jazz: it works. The *Adagio molto* is an elegiac siciliano, and the finale is a pot-pourri which raises constant echoes – that's how musical kleptomania operates. Almost at the start Antheil recalls the opening of Shostakovich's Fifth in homage to America's wartime ally. These are all fine performances, well recorded too – another impressive case for later Antheil on his own terms.

Thomas Arne British 1710-1778

GROVE *Arne, the son of an upholsterer, was probably encouraged in his musical career by his violin teacher Michael Festing. In 1732-33 he and his sister Susanna (later Mrs Cibber) were associated with musicians who aimed to establish an Italian-style English opera. After the success of his masque Dido and Aeneas (1734), Arne was engaged at Drury Lane Theatre, where he was to produce his works until 1775. In 1737 he married the singer Cecilia Young, who appeared in his next production, Comus (1738); influenced by Handel's Acis and Galatea, it was his most individual and successful work. Also popular was the masque Alfred (1740) (including 'Rule, Britannia'). While in Dublin in 1742-44 Arne produced his oratorio The Death of Abel (1744) and music by Handel. His dialogue Colin and Phoebe established him as a leading composer at the London pleasure gardens; during the next 20 years he published annual song collections. Among his next major works were a miniature English opera buffa, Thomas and Sally (1760), the oratorio Judith (1761) and an English opera seria to a metastasio libretto, Artaxerxes (1762), the first and only such work to achieve lasting fame. After his masque The Arcadian Nuptials (1764) Arne's career declined; L'Olimpiade (1765; now lost), his only Italian opera, was a failure. But his last years saw the production of many of his best works, notably Shakespeare Ode (1769), the masque The Fairy Prince (1771) and the afterpiece May-day (1775); he also wrote catches and glees for concerts at Ranelagh House.*

One of the most significant English composers of his century, Arne wrote over 80 stage works and contributed to some 20 others. His essentially lyrical genius is obvious also in his instrumental music.

Alfred

Jennifer Smith, Christine Brandes *sops* **P**
David Daniels *counterten* **Jamie MacDougall** *ten*
Philharmonia Baroque Chorale and Orchestra / Nicholas McGegan
Conifer Classics 75605 51314-2 (77 minutes: DDD) Ⓕ
Recorded 1998

'Rule, Britannia' was originally composed as a 'Grand Ode' to serve as finale to Arne's *Alfred*, a masque designed as a theatre entertainment but first performed for the Prince of Wales at Cliveden in 1740. *Alfred* is a patriotic tale, thinly based on history: King Alfred (of culinary notoriety) turns up in the countryside, apparently after defeat by the Danes, is reunited with his family, and plans and executes victory over the enemy. This recording omits the original spoken dialogue, but offers the overture and 18 songs, as well as a couple of ensembles. Arne was a gifted theatre composer and many of the songs happily catch the mood and situation, the sad ones in particular. There is Queen Eltruda's mournful little opening air, with its pathetic flute echoes; Prince Edward's touching 'Why beats my heart', with its graceful lines and hints of the minor key, when he is reunited with his father; Edith's lament for her 'youth adorn'd with ev'ry art', with its switch from E major to E minor as she relates the death of her beloved's death; and the extraordinary airs for the Spirits, one a solemn prayer and the other using oboes to imitate weeping.

Nicholas McGegan is adept at capturing the character of these pieces. His tempos are well chosen and he brings out the distinctive orchestration in those items which use wind instruments (chiefly oboes and horns, but also trumpets on occasion). David Daniels sings Edward's music in his pleasantly even and fluid countertenor, and Jamie MacDougall, an admirable stylist, phrases gracefully and projects the words clearly as Alfred – and his *pianissimo* singing is finely controlled in Alfred's big central number, 'From the dawn'. Of the two sopranos, Christine Brandes is bright and direct in manner in the music for the shepherdess Emma and in the first of the Spirit airs; Jennifer Smith's Eltruda is done with finesse and warmth. 'Rule Britannia' is shared between MacDougall and Smith, with trumpets and horns; the tune as Arne wrote it – not to say the harmony and the orchestration – is slightly different from that which one has become accustomed to, and better.

Artaxerxes

Christopher Robson *counterten* Artaxerxes; **Ian Partridge** *ten* Artabanes; **Patricia Spence** *mez* Arbaces; **Richard Edgar-Wilson** *ten* Rimenes; **Catherine Bott** *sop* Mandane; **Philippa Hyde** *sop* Semira; **The Parley of Instruments / Roy Goodman** P
Hyperion ② CDA67051/2 (140 minutes: DDD) Ⓕ
Notes and text included. Recorded 1995 ●

This is a work of great historical importance and musically fascinating. Arne, the leading English composer of his time for the theatre, wanted to write serious as well as comic English operas, and decided that Italian *opera seria* should serve, on the literary side, as his model; he chose the most famous of all the Metastasio librettos, *Artaserse*, as the basis for his first (and last) attempt at the genre. It is generally supposed that the translation was his own work. He performed the opera at Covent Garden in 1762 with considerable success and it remained a favourite for many years. He never followed up that success, and nor, regrettably, did anyone else. English vocal music of this period has quite a distinctive manner, being tuneful, rather short-breathed, often with a faintly 'folky' flavour. It does not naturally reflect the exalted emotional manner of an *opera seria* text. Nevertheless, the music is enormously enjoyable, full of good melodies, richly orchestrated, never (unlike Italian operas of the time) long-winded. Several of its numbers became popular favourites in Arne's time, and for long after.

The story of *Artaxerxes* is a typical Metastasian one, with 'treasonous designs' and misunderstandings, and plenty of opportunity for the expression of strong and varied emotion. Much of the best and most deeply felt music goes to Arbaces, very finely and expressively sung by Patricia Spence. She uses more vibrato than anyone else in the cast but her warmth of tone and expressive power are ample justification. Mandane, Arbaces's beloved, composed for Arne's mistress Charlotte Brent, is another rewarding part and is finely sung here by Catherine Bott, bright in tone and true in pitch and scrupulous in her verbal articulation, who can encompass both the charming English ditties and the more Italianate virtuoso pieces.

The opera begins with a duet for these two. Philippa Hyde sings very gracefully and charmingly in the role of Semira but does not always bring sufficient clarity to the words. As the conspiring Artabanes, Ian Partridge sings as clearly and intelligently as always. The role of Artaxerxes, the king, is taken by Christopher Robson, an excellent stylist, although this castrato part is bound to be testing for a countertenor and he is often covered by the orchestra. The smaller part of Rimenes, an insinuating traitor, is neatly sung and characterised by Richard Edgar-Wilson. Arne's orchestral style here is very rich, with much prominent wind writing; sometimes the singers – given less prominence by the engineers than one might expect – do not ride the full textures very comfortably. Roy Goodman's accompaniments are not generally very subtle or carefully shaded. The original score does not survive complete, a victim (like so many) of the frequent theatre fires of the time; Peter Holman has done a predictably unobtrusive and stylish job of reconstructing some of the lost recitatives for this recording. Recommended warmly to anyone curious about this byway of 18th century opera, and to anyone who is drawn to Arne's very individual and appealing melodic style.

Sir Malcolm Arnold

British 1921

GROVE *Arnold studied with Jacob at the Royal College of Music, London, and in 1941 joined the LPO as a trumpeter, leaving in 1948 to devote himself to composition. His most important works are orchestral (nine symphonies, 1951-82; numerous light and serious pieces). His language is diatonic, owing something to Walton and Sibelius, and the scoring is dramatically brilliant, Berlioz being his acknowledged model. A fluent, versatile composer, he has written scores for nearly 100 films.*

Clarinet Concerto No 2

Arnold Clarinet Concerto No 2, Op 115
Copland Concerto for Clarinet and String Orchestra with Harp and Piano **Hindemith** Clarinet Concerto
Martin Fröst *cl* **Malmö Symphony Orchestra / Lan Shui**
BIS CD893 (57 minutes: DDD) Ⓕ
Recorded 1997 ○○

All three of these concertos were written for Benny Goodman, but, not surprisingly, it is the Arnold work which most fully exploits his dedicatee's jazz background. The first movement is a typical Arnoldian *scherzando*, with an irrepressible *Tam O'Shanter/Beckus the Dandipratt* audacity. Fröst and Lan Shui clearly relish its verve and energy, and then bring a seductive richness to the main theme of the slow movement. Yet they do not miss the plangent emotional ambivalence later – for there are characteristic moments of Arnold-like darkness here too. The outrageous show-stopper finale, with its rooty-tooty clarinet tune and orchestral whoops, also has a surprise up its sleeve in its sudden lyrical interlude; but one and all let their hair down for the boisterous reprise.

At the haunting opening of the Copland concerto, Martin Fröst's clarinet steals in magically on a half-tone. Lan Shui's sympathetic and flexible support contributes to a memorable performance of Copland's masterly first movement, with the coda gently fading into the cadenza. The Hindemith concerto which follows produces a characteristic sinewy lyricism in the first of its four movements, with some nicely touched-in brass and woodwind comments. Again Fröst cajoles the ear with his pliable line and the effect is unexpectedly mellow. With extremely fine recording and marvellous solo playing, this triptych will be hard to surpass.

Flute Concertos

Flute Concertos – No 1, Op 45; No 2, Op 111. Three Shanties, Op 4. Sonatina for Flute and Piano, Op 19. Fantasia, Op 89. Divertimento, Op 37. Flute Sonata, Op 121
James Galway *fl* **James Galway Wind Quintet** (Gareth Hulse *ob* Antony Pay *cl* Rachel Gough *bn* Philip Eastop *hn*); **Philip Moll** *pf* **Academy of St Martin in the Fields / Sir Neville Marriner**
RCA Victor Red Seal 09026 68860-2 Ⓕ
(69 minutes: DDD). Recorded 1995 ○

In this expert, sweet-toned and affectionate music-making, these fine artists audibly enjoy themselves hugely, responding to Arnold's idiomatic and resourceful writing as to the manner born. Galway and friends are particularly enjoyable in the sparkling early *Three Shanties* for wind quintet and the delicious *Divertimento* for flute, oboe and clarinet. Cast in six pithy movements (and masterfully played here), the latter piece contains invention of great freshness and charm, with definite echoes of the *English Dances* from the same period. In the wistful central *Andante* of the First Flute Concerto, Neville Marriner and his beautifully prepared Academy strings provide a poignant backdrop to Galway's ravishing playing, and this music's kinship with the great slow movement of Arnold's Second Symphony is most perceptively brought out. In fact, the performances of both concertos are probably the best yet. Galway himself was the lucky recipient of the Flute Sonata (he gave the première at the 1977 Cardiff Festival), and he and Philip Moll do full justice to this work's entrancing mix of lyricism (the lilting *Andantino* centrepiece boasts a particularly indelible main idea) and exhilarating virtuosity. Recording quality is nicely integrated, too, with Galway never overprominently balanced, although Moll's piano can sound just a touch rough in its lowest reaches. A delightful anthology all the same.

Guitar Concerto, Op 67

Arnold Guitar Concerto, Op 67
Rodrigo Concierto de Aranjuez
Takemitsu To the Edge of Dream
Julian Bream *gtr* **City of Birmingham Symphony Orchestra / Sir Simon Rattle**
EMI CDC7 54661-2 (58 minutes: DDD) Ⓕ
Recorded 1991 ○○

This is Bream's fourth recording of the Rodrigo, and his second version of the Arnold Concerto (his first, recorded in 1959, is available on various RCA reissues). His tempos in the outer movements are a mite slower than of yore but the differences are small and the energy, sparkle and clean delivery are undiminished. What differentiates these performances from others, including Bream's earlier ones, is the extraordinary accounts of their slow movements. Bream's views of the *sardana* and the smoky night club (respectively) come from within, to an extent that makes even the most expressive of others seem 'external', and they are conveyed with such wonderful fluidity of tone and phrasing that one might almost believe the feeling that one is hearing them for the first time. Takemitsu said of *To the Edge of Dream* 'melodic fragments float in a transparent space like so many splinters of dream'; although they never quite coalesce into a stable, protracted melody, they give cohesion to the music. The work is scored for an unusually large orchestra but, as it most often alternates with, rather than opposes, the guitar or is held to a breathless *pianissimo*, the guitar is always audible. It is a work of haunting beauty. And these are desert-island versions of the concertos, adding maturity to virtuosity.

Dances

Four Cornish Dances, Op 91. English Dances, Op 27; Op 33. Irish Dances, Op 126. Four Scottish Dances, Op 59. Solitaire – Sarabande; Polka
London Philharmonic Orchestra / Sir Malcolm Arnold
Lyrita SRCD201 (61 minutes: ADD/DDD) Ⓕ
Recorded 1979-90 ○○

A warm and well-deserved welcome was given to the *English*, *Scottish* and *Cornish Dances*, when these recordings, conducted by the composer, first appeared. Here, with the *Irish Dances* added, as well as the two movements which were written to go with the two sets of *English Dances* as the ballet, *Solitaire*, it is even more of a winner. The analogue sound is given a splendid transfer with plenty of presence and is full and brilliant. The newer items, in digital sound, very well recorded too, bring no feeling of inconsistency. Best known of all is the first of the second set of *English Dances* with its jaunty piccolo theme, but one after another these little jewels first grab and then delight the ear with their brilliant pastiche of folk melodies.

The first of the *Irish Dances*, written in 1986, opens with a rumbustious movement very much in the style of the earlier sets, with characteristic and attractive syncopations, but the other three dances are both sparer in instrumentation and darker in tone, effectively so. The two movements from *Solitaire* are equally valuable, particularly the superb, coolly atmospheric 'Sarabande', the longest and most ambitious movement of any here, again made weightier by Arnold's slow speed. Even if you don't want to play all 22 items at one go – and that is no penance at all – this is a wonderful box of delights.

English Dances – Set 1, Op 27; Set 2, Op 33. Four Scottish Dances, Op 59. Four Cornish Dances, Op 91. Four Irish Dances, Op 126. Four Welsh Dances, Op 138
Queensland Symphony Orchestra / Andrew Penny
Naxos 8 553526 (55 minutes: DDD) Ⓢ
Recorded 1995

This Naxos set of the Arnold Dances from the Queensland Symphony Orchestra under Andrew Penny has the advantage of including the *Four Welsh Dances*, not otherwise available on CD. These were the last to be written, and their mood follows on naturally from the ambivalence of the *Irish Dances*. With the composer working with Penny prior to the recording in Australia, it is not surprising that the tempos are very like Arnold's own in his superb set of performances made with the LPO for Lyrita. Where there is a difference, Penny is slightly faster, but the effect is marginal. The greater character of the LPO under Arnold shows in the very first of the *English Dances*, notably at the reprise, which is more warmly positive, capped with a superb cymbal crash (backwardly balanced and less effective on Naxos). The Queensland Hall is noticeably reverberant and detail is generally less well focused than on the Lyrita disc; yet so vivid is Arnold's scoring that not much is missed. The lovely Mesto third *English Dance* is certainly beautifully done in Queensland and in the second set of *English Dances*, the *Con brio* and *Giubiloso* have all the necessary colour and flair.

The Australian orchestra have obviously warmed up for the Scottish set and the inebriated Glaswegian is nicely observed. For some the lyrical third *Scottish Dance* is one of the most beautiful and memorable of all Arnold's many fine tunes. Penny treats it gently; his coda is particularly delicate, but at its appearance on the full strings the composer is that little bit more romantic. However, Penny's closing dance, a Highland fling, is superb in its drunken abandon. In the opening *Cornish Dance* that follows, Penny captures the mysterious evocation of deserted copper mines well, and in the *Irish Dances*, written some 20 years later, he captures the fragile mood of the central *Commodo* and *Piacevole* tenderly. This is altogether an excellent and inexpensive collection.

Additional recommendation
English Dances
Couplings: Guitar Concerto, Op 67. Symphony for Brass Instruments, Op 123. Quintet for Brass, Op 73
Various artists; London Philharmonic Orchestra / Boult
Decca 468 803-2 (74 minutes: ADD: 9/90[R]) Ⓜ
Boult is masterly in the delightful *English Dances*.

Film Music

Trapeze – Suite. No Love for Johnnie – Suite. David Copperfield – Suite. Stolen Face – Ballade or Piano and Orchestra[b]. The Belles of St Trinian's – Comedy Suite[c]. The Captain's Paradise – Postcard from the Med (all arr Lane). You Know What Sailors Are – Scherzetto[a]. The Holly and The Ivy – Fantasy on Christmas Carols (both arr Palmer). The Roots of Heaven – Overture. Symphonic Study,'Machines', Op 30
[a]John Bradbury *cl* **[b]Phillip Dyson, [c]Paul Janes** *pfs*
BBC Philharmonic Orchestra / Rumon Gamba
Chandos CHAN9851 (79 minutes: DDD) Ⓕ
Recorded 2000

Almost all the film music here comes from the 1950s, when memorable ideas were pouring out of Arnold, and his unique orchestral palette was already glowing luminously.

The suite arranged by Philip Lane from *Trapeze* is quite outstanding in the quality of its invention, including a swinging tune for the horns in the Prelude, an engaging blues for saxophone and guitar to follow, an ebullient circus march, and a deliciously lugubrious 'Elephant waltz' for tuba duet, while the closing sequence opens hauntingly and then introduces an accordion to remind us we are in Paris. The suite from *David Copperfield* has a fine lyrical opening sweep, then introduces a delightfully quirky, syncopated *moto perpetuo* representing 'The Micawbers'. This features a solo clarinet, and Christopher Palmer has arranged another witty clarinet *Scherzetto* from an equally winning theme used in *You Know What Sailors Are*.

The *concertante* Ballade for Piano and Orchestra adeptly arranged by Lane from *Stolen Face* is less memorable, but the overture from *The Roots of Heaven* (provided for the film's New York prèmiere) opens with a splendid Hollywoodian/Waltonian flourish, then follows with more catchy syncopation and a lilting waltz tune. Perhaps the most tender, romantic writing comes in *No Love for Johnnie* (after another rousing march). The irrepressible score for *The Belles of St Trinian's* (the composer's favourite film) has something of the audacious sparkle of Ibert's *Divertissement*, and if *The Holly and the Ivy* brings a rather predictable collection of familiar carols, for the most part fully scored and not particularly individual, Arnold's jaunty samba from *The Captain's Paradise*, which memorably had Alec Guinness in the bigamous title-role, makes a splendid finale. The performances have plenty of zest, and the flow of bittersweet lyrical writing is poignantly caught by Rumon Gamba and the excellent BBC Philharmonic in a recording of top Chandos quality. If you enjoy film music, it doesn't come any better than this.

Additional recommendation
Bridge on the River Kwai. Inn of the Sixth Happiness. Hobson's Choice. Whistle down the Wind. Sound Barrier
London Symphony Orchestra / Hickox
Chandos CHAN9100 (78 minutes: DDD: 2/93) Ⓕ
A well-chosen collection of Arnold film scores, arranged by Christopher Palmer and played with infectious gusto by the LSO and Richard Hickox.

Symphonies Nos 1 and 2

Symphonies – No 1, Op 22; No 2, Op 40
London Symphony Orchestra / Richard Hickox
Chandos CHAN9335 (61 minutes: DDD) Ⓕ
Recorded 1994 ●

Here is an entirely appropriate coupling of the first two symphonies, superbly played by the LSO and given demonstration sound in what is surely an ideal acoustic for this music, with striking depth and amplitude and a wholly natural brilliance. The dynamic range is wide but the moments of spectacle – and there are quite a few – bring no discomfort. Richard Hickox shows himself to be thoroughly at home in both symphonies and the readings have a natural flow and urgency, with the two slow movements bringing haunting, atmospheric feeling.

The First Symphony opens with thrusting confidence on strings and horns, and at its climax, where the strings soar against angry brass ostinatos, the playing generates great intensity; then at the start of the slow movement the purity of the flute solo brings a calm serenity, which returns at the close. There are only three movements and the plangent lyrical melancholia of the expansive march theme of the finale is filled out by some superb horn playing, which is enormously compelling. The first movement of Symphony No 2 brings a most winning clarinet solo (Arnold's fund of melodic ideas seems to be inexhaustible). There is an energetic, bustling *Scherzo* to follow, but again it is the slow movement which one remembers, for its elegiac opening, its arresting climax and its lovely epilogue-like close. Above all, these are real performances without any of the inhibitions of 'studio' recording.

Additional recommendations
Symphonies Nos 1 and 2
National Symphony Orchestra of Ireland / Penny
Naxos 8 553406 (56 minutes: DDD: 5/96) Ⓢ
A bargain coupling without quite the finesse of the Hickox/LSO recordings for Chandos (see above).

Symphony No 2
Couplings: Symphony No 5. Peterloo
Bournemouth Symphony Orchestra / Groves;
City of Birmingham Symphony Orchestra / Arnold
EMI CDM5 66324-2 (77 minutes: ADD) Ⓕ
Arnold conducts his own music with great verve, and the highly accessible Fifth Symphony is a delight.

Symphonies Nos 3 and 4

Symphonies – No 3, Op 63; No 4, Op 71
National Symphony Orchestra of Ireland / Andrew Penny
Naxos 8 553739 (69 minutes: DDD) Ⓢ
Recorded 1996 ●

These recordings of two of Arnold's finest symphonies carry the composer's imprimatur (he attended the sessions). Andrew Penny is clearly right inside every bar of the music and the orchestra plays with impressive ensemble and feeling, and above all great freshness and spontaneity. The Naxos recording's concert-hall ambience has been beautifully caught by Chris Craker, who both produced and engineered this disc. One of the finest players in Dublin is the principal oboe and his solos often bring a specially plangent quality, particularly in the slow movement of No 3 (at 4'55") where there is a real sense of desolation. The finale then lightens the mood with its kaleidoscope of wind and brass and a wispy string melody that soon becomes more fulsome. Penny's momentum and characterisation here are superb, as is the orchestral response. Similarly the winningly scored opening of the Fourth Symphony flashes with colour: that marvellous tune (2'44") is played with captivating delicacy by the violins. The exquisitely fragile *Scherzo* is etched with gossamer lightness and the slow movement is shaped by Penny with fine lyrical feeling and the most subtle use of light and shade. Its romanticism is heart-warming, yet is also balanced by Arnold's underlying unease. The boisterous fugal finale has some of the best playing of all.

Additional recommendation
Symphonies Nos 3 and 4
London Symphony Orchestra / Hickox
Chandos CHAN9290 (74 minutes: DDD) Ⓕ
Richard Hickox has the full measure of both symphonies and the Chandos recording is superb, full of colour and atmosphere.

Symphonies Nos 5 and 6

Symphonies – No 5, Op 74; No 6, Op 95
London Symphony Orchestra / Richard Hickox
Chandos CHAN9385 (58 minutes: DDD) Ⓕ
Recorded 1995 ●

Arnold's Fifth Symphony is one of his most accessible and rewarding works. The inspiration for the symphony was the early deaths of several of the composer's friends and colleagues: Dennis Brain, Frederick Thurston, David Paltenghi and Gerard Hoffnung. They are all remembered in the first movement and Hoffnung's spirit pops up in the third and fourth. The Chandos recording is richly resonant and reinforces the impression that in Hickox's hands the *Andante* has an added degree of acceptance in its elegiac close, while the last two movements are colourfully expansive. The Sixth Symphony is nothing like as comfortable as the Fifth, with a bleak unease in the unrelenting energy of the first movement, which becomes even more discomfiting in the desolate start to the *Lento*. This leads to a forlorn suggestion of a funeral march, which then ironically quickens in pace but is suddenly cut down; the drum strokes become menacingly powerful and the despairing mood of the movement's opening returns. Hickox handles this quite superbly and grips the listener in the music's pessimism, which then lifts completely with the energetic syncopated trumpet theme of the rondo finale. Although later there are moments of ambiguity, and dissonant reminders of the earlier music, these are eclipsed by the thrilling life-asserting coda.

Additional recommendation
Symphonies Nos 5 and 6
National Symphony Orchestra of Ireland / Penny
Naxos 8 552000 (57 minutes: DDD: 6/01) Ⓢ
A good bargain alternative that is well worth considering.

Symphony No 5
Couplings: Symphony No 2. Peterloo.
Bournemouth Symphony Orchestra / Groves;
City of Birmingham Symphony Orchestra / Arnold
EMI CDM5 66324-2 (77 minutes: ADD) Ⓕ
Arnold conducts his touching tribute to lost musical friends with great feeling and skill.

Symphony No 9

Symphony No 9, Op 128
National Symphony Orchestra of Ireland / Andrew Penny
Naxos 8 553540 (57 minutes: DDD) Ⓢ
Includes an interview between the composer and the conductor. Recorded 1995 ●

This culmination to Arnold's symphonic series is both characteristic and distinctive. If at the start and elsewhere one is reminded of Shostakovich, the instrumentation is quite distinctive. The ear is regularly tweaked by the terracing of sounds, at extremes of register as well as of dynamic, culminating in the long slow finale, almost as long as the other three movements combined. With two poignant themes, the mood of tragedy and disillusion is clear. The parallel with the final *Adagio* of Mahler's Ninth Symphony comes obviously to mind. Yet unlike Mahler the music conveys no hint of neurosis or self-pity. The other three movements are just as direct, bald in their arguments but ever pointful, not facile, built on instantly memorable material. Andrew Penny draws not just a concentrated, consistently committed performance from the Irish players, but a warmly resonant one, with the strings sounding glorious and the woodwind and brass consistently brilliant. The recording is rich and full.

Georges Auric French 1899-1983

GROVE *Auric studied at the Paris Conservatoire and with d'Indy at the Schola Cantorum (1914-16), becoming acquainted with Satie, Milhaud and Honegger. He was a member of Les Six, wrote ballets for Dhiagilev (Les fâcheux, 1923) and film scores for Cocteau and was also a music critic. In the 1950s and '60s he held administrative posts while maintaining his musical curiosity: some of his later pieces are serial.*

Film Music (recons Lane)

Suites – Caesar and Cleopatra; Dead of night; Father Brown; The Innocents[a]; It always rains on a Sunday; The Lavender Hill Mob; Moulin Rouge[b]; Passport to Pimlico; The Titfield Thunderbolt; Hue and Cry – Overture
BBC Philharmonic Orchestra / Rumon Gamba with [a]**Anthea Kempston,** [b]**Mary Carewe** *sops*
Chandos CHAN9774 (74 minutes: DDD) Ⓕ
Recorded 1999 ●

All the scores here (expertly reconstructed by Philip Lane) are from British films, for which Auric wrote some 30; but he also wrote another 100 or so for French, German, Italian and American movies. It was in fact by a French film – René Clair's delightful satire *A nous la liberté* – that he first won our hearts in 1932; it wasn't until the end of the war that he was taken up by Denham and Ealing. Auric, not one for the 'hit tune' score beloved by commercial exploiters, nevertheless showed in his *Moulin Rouge* waltz that he could command the popular style with the best. On this disc he is heard running the gamut through the grandiose or the dramatic (*It always rains on a Sunday*, one of his finest pieces of writing), the menacing (the unforgettably scary *Dead of night*) and the atmospheric ('At the Sphinx' in *Caesar and Cleopatra*) to the swirling gaiety of *The Titfield Thunderbolt*, the perky *Passport to Pimlico* and the ebullient high spirits of *Hue and Cry*. From the gusto of the playing throughout, it seems clear that the BBC Philharmonic enjoyed making this disc: understandably so.

Further listening
La belle et la bête
Moscow Symphony Orchestra / Adriano
Marco Polo 8 223765 (62 minutes: DDD: 7/96) Ⓕ
Auric's Ravellian score for Cocteau's 1946 film with Jean Marais, performed with an idiomatic feel for the otherworldliness of this alluring film.

The Ladykillers
Royal Ballet Sinfonia / Alwyn
Silva Screen FILMCD177 (61 minutes: DDD: 7/97)
A splendid collection of scores for Ealing comedies splayed with lashings of gusto and a great feeling for this now sadly lost idiom. A 1997 *Gramophone* Award winner.

Carl Philipp Emanuel Bach

German 1714-1788

GROVE *Carl Philipp Emanuel Bach, second son of Johann Sebastian Bach, studied music under his father at the Leipzig Thomasschule and law at university. In 1738 he became harpsichordist to the Prussian crown prince, moving to Berlin when his employer became King Frederick in 1740. There he was accompanist to the royal chamber music, and had the particular task of accompanying the king's flute solos. His most important compositions of this period were his keyboard sonatas; he also wrote his famous Essay on the True Art of Keyboard Playing (1753-62), which established him as the leading keyboard teacher and theorist of his time. He was however discontented in Berlin, because of the poor salary, the want of opportunity and the narrow scope of his duties. In 1767 Frederick reluctantly released him and he then succeeded Telemann as Kantor and music director in Hamburg, with responsibility for teaching, for some 200 performances of music each year at five churches and for ceremonial music on civic occasions. At this time he produced much church music as well as keyboard music, sets of symphonies and concertos.*

CPE Bach, the best-known member of his family in his lifetime, was greatly respected for his treatise – which summarised the musical philosophy and the musical practices in north Germany at the middle of the 18th century – as well as for his music. His keyboard sonatas (he composed c150 as well as countless miscellaneous pieces) above all break new ground in their treatment of form and material; he also wrote improvisatory fantasias of intense expressiveness. His symphonies – he wrote c20– are in the fiery, energetic manner favoured in north Germany, with dramatic breaks, modulations and changes of mood or texture; usually the movements run continuously. There are twice as many concertos (and more concerto-like sonatinas), also vigorous in style; all were written for harpsichord and some were adapted for other instruments. His chamber works are numerous; there are many songs, as well as choral works from his late years, including two fine oratorios (Die Israeliten in der Wüste, Die Auferstehung und Himmelfahrt Jesu), Passion settings and other church works which often include adaptations of his own and other composers' music.

Cello Concertos

Cello Concertos – A minor, H432; B flat, H436; A, H439 Ⓟ
Bach Collegium Japan / Hidemi Suzuki *vc*
BIS CD807 (68 minutes: DDD) Ⓕ
Recorded 1996

Writing in the booklet for this release, Hidemi Suzuki wonders why it is that cellists who bemoan their lack of concerto repertory continue to neglect CPE Bach's three essays in the genre. One can only agree with him that it is indeed a mystery, for these are excellent pieces, full of infectious nervous energy in their outer movements and tender lyricism in central ones. The Bach concertos are not unknown to the recording catalogues, however, not least because they also exist in alternative versions which the composer made for flute and harpsichord respectively. As Suzuki points out, there are times when the low-lying cello has difficulty making itself heard properly against the orchestra. Having said this, he proceeds to make light of the matter with performances whose agility, lightness and textural clarity make those of Bylsma and the larger-sounding OAE sound heavy-handed. But while Suzuki – thanks to a generally thinner sound – is the more successful in the way he transmits the surface excitement and energy of the quick movements, he cannot match Bylsma's vocal inspiration in the eloquent poetry of the slow movement. Suzuki's, nevertheless, are refreshing and enlivening performances of attractive and substantial music.

Cello Concertos – A minor, H432; B flat, H436; A, H439 Ⓟ
Anner Bylsma *vc* **Orchestra of the Age of Enlightenment / Gustav Leonhardt**
Virgin Classics Veritas VM5 61401-2 Ⓜ
(70 minutes: DDD). Recorded 1998

However unlikely, circumstantially, that the cello versions came first, it is nevertheless that instrument which often seems to bring out the expressive qualities in this music most eloquently. This is, above all, the case in the slow movements, where the cello captures that darkly shaded intensity of expression at which Bach excelled. The most striking of the three is the muted *Largo mesto* of the A major Concerto, which plunges the listener into a shadowy world whose wide-ranging imaginative content presages early German romanticism. None of this is lost on Anner Bylsma, who is quite the most ardently persuasive advocate. His playing of all three slow movements is suffused with an intensity and rapt contemplation. Fast outer movements, in contrast, dance along happily with lightly articulated solo passages, warm tone and eloquent projection. There are, admittedly, a few passages of shaky intonation, but overall they are insignificant. Bylsma brings enormous warmth of spirit to the music, sometimes tender, sometimes quite fiercely passionate and always with sympathetic understanding of Bach's individual gestures. The cadenzas are Bylsma's own and very convincing they are too. The OAE provides strong support, Gustav Leonhardt's direction – from the podium rather than the harpsichord on this occasion – being characteristically sympathetic, bringing many insights to an elusive style. The recorded sound is admirably clear and ideally resonant.

Cello Concertos – A minor, H432;
B flat, H436; A, H439
Timothy Hugh *vc* **Bournemouth Sinfonietta / Richard Studt**
Naxos 8 553298 (71 minutes: DDD) Ⓢ
Recorded 1995

Timothy Hugh's bow dances in the flanking movements and is matched by those of the Bournemouth Sinfonietta, alert to every nuance and disposed to throw their weight around only as much as is fitting. It is, however, the slow movements that are the heart of these works. They are all tinged with sadness but none more than the *Largo* of the A major Concerto, where Hugh's abated vibrato, attenuated lines and resistance to the excessive squeezing of *appoggiaturas* express a sadness that is held within, not spilt in salt tears. This is a recording to set alongside the two reviewed above.

Harpsichord Concertos

Harpsichord Concertos – G minor, H409; Ⓟ
A, H411; D, H421
Miklós Spányi *hpd* **Concerto Armonico / Péter Szüts**
BIS CD767 (68 minutes: DDD) Ⓕ
Recorded 1995

While these particular concertos are not consistently engaging, they demonstrate the emerging inventiveness of CPE's musical personality within a growing trend towards public concerts in the mid-18th century. In fits and starts there are those sparsely etched landscapes, complete with an unsettled weather front, which at their best can captivate us. If decorum is sometimes overworked, Bach's originality is even more remarkable given that the ritornello structure inherited from his father's generation, with its alternating solo and string sections, is less easy to sustain in a relatively uncontrapuntal style. Contrast is therefore a key element and Bach needs a soloist who can discern how the relationship between the harpsichord and the orchestra can be manipulated to good effect. Miklós Spányi and Concerto Armonico, led by Péter Szüts, give wonderfully lucid, flexible and clearly articulated readings. Moreover, Spányi's cultivated asides are matched by a string ensemble which graciously respond to the soloist's discretion. The shading in the finale of the G minor and middle movement of the D major Concertos is also energised by a naturally discursive balance, a deft textural palette for which artist and engineer can take equal credit. With such eloquent and fresh playing, this volume of world première recordings will give the listener more than just an opportunity to refine his perspective on Bach's achievements. It deserves a welcoming audience.

Keyboard Concertos

Keyboard Concertos – D, H414; E, H417; A, H422 Ⓟ
Concerto Armonico / Miklós Spányi *fp*
BIS CD785 (74 minutes: DDD) Ⓕ
Recorded 1996

With his fifth volume of CPE Bach's complete keyboard concertos, Miklós Spányi comes to three works composed in the mid-1740s, which he plays on a copy of a Silbermann fortepiano of that period. The choice is not only determined by the existence of such instruments at Frederick the Great's court, where Carl Philipp was employed, but also because the keyboard layout is more suited to the fortepiano than the harpsichord, and because the A major work here – a first recording, like that of the D major – includes the marking *pianissimo*. The present instrument is light and silvery in tone, which makes for some difficulties of proportion in the D major, performed with additional manuscript parts found in Brussels for trumpets and drums. The more embellished version of the A major Concerto is adopted here. The first movement displays some particularly athletic passagework for the piano. The second movement is striking in starting with a long unison melodic line over a rudimentary bass, with no internal harmonic filling: the attractive finale is characterised by a happy freshness. In the E major Concerto the instrumentation is augmented by horn parts found in a Berlin manuscript. Musically it is the most inventive and unusual, harmonically certainly the most adventurous, of the present three works – a splendid concerto that deserves to be better known. The recording has occasional problems with balance but the performances are praiseworthy.

Keyboard Concertos – E minor, H418; Ⓟ
B flat, H429; G minor, H442
Miklós Spányi *fp* **Concerto Armonico / Péter Szüts** *vn*
BIS CD786 (73 minutes: DDD) Ⓕ
Recorded 1996

On this recording Miklós Spányi has exchanged his previous harpsichord or fortepiano for a tangent piano: this was like a fortepiano but had the strings struck vertically by tangents (as in the clavichord) rather than at an angle by hammers. Its tone could also be modified by raising the dampers completely or only in the treble, employing only one of each note's two strings (*una corda*), inserting a leather strip ('moderator') between tangents and strings, or creating a harp-like effect by damping the strings with small pieces of cloth. The boldness and unusual style of Emanuel's concertos took his contemporaries aback, and even now they can surprise. The extrovert E minor work, for example, begins with dramatic energy but is interrupted by extraordinary, tentative-sounding broken phrases at the soloist's first entry before being allowed to continue on its way: the *Adagio*, which includes striking chromatic progressions, has imitative interplay between the solo instrument and the violins. The finale of the otherwise more 'normal' *galant* G minor Concerto (in whose central movement two flutes join the strings) generates very vehement chordal attacks – or are these being overdone here? Spányi's playing throughout has vitality and neatness, although his lifting of the dampers in running passages inevitably causes them to become blurred.

Sinfonias

C P E Bach Sinfonias, H663-6 – No 1 in D; No 2 in E flat; No 3 in F; No 4 in G
W F Bach Sinfonia in F
Salzburg Chamber Philharmonic Orchestra / Yoon K Lee
Naxos 8 553289 (52 minutes: DDD) Ⓢ
Recorded 1994

The exhilarating CPE Bach symphonies presented here are not the more frequently recorded, surprise-filled string symphonies of 1773 (H657-62), but the set of four for strings, flutes, oboes, bassoons and horns which Bach wrote a couple of years later. They are no less astonishing. Bewildering changes of direction, disorientating rhythmic games and unexpected solos all turn up in this nervous, excitable music, which for originality and sheer life-force could surely only have been matched in its day by that of Haydn. The Salzburg Chamber Philharmonic, under its founder Yoon K Lee, turns in crisp, spirited and (the odd moment of slack tuning apart) disciplined performances which do the music full justice. They are not timid about making the most of Bach's strong contrasts, although they produce them more by the release of some thunderous *forte* passages than by the pursuit of too many unearthly *pianissimos*. The overall effect is wholly convincing, and only in the symphony by Emanuel's older brother Wilhelm Friedemann – more old-fashioned and less successful as a piece, but in its way just as determinedly unorthodox – does the use of modern instruments begin to get in the way of the spirit of music. An undeniably good buy.

Chamber works

Quartet for Keyboard, Flute, Viola and Continuo in D, H538. Viola da gamba Sonata in G minor, Wq88 – Larghetto. Trio Sonatas – Two Violins and Continuo in C minor, H579; Flute, Violin and Continuo in C, H571. Solo Flute Sonata in A minor, H562 **P**
Florilegium (Ashley Solomon *fl* Rachel Podger *vn/va* Lucy Russell *vn* Daniel Yeadon *vc/va da gamba* Neal Peres da Costa *hpd/fp*)
Channel Classics CCS11197 (59 minutes: DDD) Ⓕ
Recorded 1997 ●

More than half a century separates the earliest and the latest of the works here. The C major Trio Sonata was one of Bach's earliest compositions, written at the age of 17 more or less under his father's supervision and the D major Quartet was composed in the last year of his life, while he was Music Director in Hamburg. The remaining items on this disc date from his time at the court of Frederick the Great. The youthful work is distinguished by a sprightly finale and a remarkably fine, harmonically chromatic *Adagio*.

The C minor Sonata is extraordinary, a programmatic work 'portraying a conversation between a Sanguineus and a Melancholicus' who disagree throughout the first two movements, but the former's outlook prevails in the finale. So for much of the sonata the musical phrases alternate expressively between *lamentoso* or melancholy and high spirits. The talented Florilegium players bring out to the full the bewilderingly diverse character of this sonata, which is outstanding even for so strongly individual a composer as Carl Philipp.

If the Sonata for unaccompanied flute was written for Frederick, as seems likely, he must have been quite skilled, able to cope not only with contrasting dynamics and the differentiation of the melodic line from suggestions of the bass and harmony, but also with some fairly virtuosic passagework. Ashley Solomon's performance is most persuasive. How far Carl Philipp developed is shown by the late quartet, an attractive composition which, besides promoting the keyboard (fortepiano here) from a mere continuo to prominent solo status, is already in the style of the Viennese classics in form, and links the first two movements. The whole disc is strongly recommended.

Organ Sonatas

Organ Sonatas – F, H84; A minor, H85; D, H86; G minor, H87; A, H133; B flat, H134 **P**
Marie-Claire Alain *org*
Erato 0630-14777-2 (70 minutes: DDD) Ⓕ
Recorded on the organ of the Karlhorst-Kirche, Berlin in 1996

Bach's sonatas for organ were originally written for Princess Anna Amalia, 'a princess who could not play the pedal or cope with difficulties, even though she had built for herself a beautiful organ with two manuals and pedal and liked to play on it'. It is on that very organ that these sonatas have here been recorded. The organ, built in 1755, makes a simply magical sound, beautifully captured in Erato's intimate, crystal-clear recording. The music may avoid the kind of technical demands with which Princess Anna could not cope and certainly does not require the kind of vast registration resource on which Alain seems to thrive, but as usual we can only marvel at the unending variety of sounds she has been able to conjure up from just 22 speaking stops.

These are endearing performances of undeniably charming music. Little hints of Mozart, maybe even of Bach *père* appear momentarily. For the most part, though, it is Bach's distinctive individual voice which comes through with an approach to the organ which owes nothing to his father other than the skill in writing music which suits the instrument to perfection.

Vocal works

Die Auferstehung und Himmelfahrt Jesu, H777 **P**
Hillevi Martinpelto *sop* **Christoph Prégardien** *ten*
Peter Harvey *bass*

Ghent Collegium Vocale Choir; Orchestra of the Age of Enlightenment / Philippe Herreweghe
Virgin Classics Veritas VC7 59069-2 Ⓕ
(76 minutes: DDD). Text and translation included.
Recorded 1991

Although frequently classified as an oratorio, *Die Auferstehung und Himmelfahrt Jesu* is really a cantata. CPE considered it, in his own words as 'pre-eminent among all my vocal works in expression and in the composition'. The author of the text was Karl Wilhelm Ramler, an important poet of the German Enlightenment whose texts had earlier attracted Telemann. Ramler and Bach engaged in a close collaboration over the *Auferstehung*, entering into a lively correspondence over the details and shape of the cantata. The first performance took place in Hamburg in 1778, when it was warmly received. Many subsequent performances were given, culminating in three directed by Mozart in Vienna. There is a fine trio of soloists and The OAE is notable for its warmth and refinement of sound. The recording is spacious and pleasing and the booklet includes Ramler's German text with English and French translations.

Johann Christian Bach

German 1735-1782

GROVE *Johann Christian Bach, the youngest son of JS Bach, probably studied first under his father, then on his death with his half-brother Carl Philipp Emanuel. in Berlin. In 1754 he left for Italy, where he became Roman Catholic and organist at Milan Cathedral. He also embarked on an operatic career, with operas staged in Turin and Naples. He was then invited to compose for the King's Theatre in London, where he settled in 1762; his operatic career was patchy, but he was soon appointed royal music master and was successful as a teacher. He also promoted and played in a prominent concert series with his friend CF Abel, bringing the newest and best European music to Londoners' notice. (He befriended the boy Mozart on his London visit, 1764-65.) Many of his works were published, including songs written for Vauxhall Pleasure Gardens. In 1772 and 1774 he visited Mannheim for performances of his operas Temistocle and Lucio Silla and in 1779 he wrote Amadis de Gaule for the Paris Opéra, but the success of these works, like that of his London operas, was limited. His popularity faded in the late 1770s, and after financial troubles his health declined; he died at the beginning of 1782, and was soon forgotten.*

JC Bach's music blends sound German technique with Italian fluency and grace; hence its appeal to, and influence upon, the young Mozart. His symphonies follow the Italian three-movement pattern: the light, Italian manner of his earlier ones gave way to richer-textured and more fully developed writing by the mid-1760s. The peak of his output comes in the six symphonies of his Op 18, three for double orchestra and exploiting contrasts of space and timbre. His interest in orchestral colour gave rise to several symphonies concertantes, for various soloists and orchestra, suitable material for his London concerts. At these he also played his piano concertos, attractive for their well-developed solo-tutti relationship though still modest in scale. Of his chamber music, the Op 11 quintets (flute, oboe, strings and continuo) are particularly appealing for their charming conversational style and their use of colour. He also composed keyboard sonatas, with and without violin accompaniment, in a style accessible to his pupils and players of modest ability. His music is often leisurely in manner, and this must have militated against the operas success as dramatic music. He also composed a quantity of Latin sacred music during his time in Italy. Though sometimes regarded as a decadently hedonistic composer by comparison with his brother CPE, Johann Christian stands firmly as the chief master of the galant, who produced music elegant and apt to its social purpose, infusing it with vigour and refined sensibility.

Keyboard concertos

Six Concertos for Keyboard and Strings, Op 7 – No 1 in C; No 2 in F; No 3 in D; No 4 in B flat; No 5 in E flat; No 6 in G
Members of the **Hanover Band** (Graham Cracknell, Anna McDonald *vns* Sebastian Comberti *vc*) / **Anthony Halstead** *fp*
CPO CPO999 600-2 (73 minutes: DDD) Ⓕ
Recorded 1998

On Halstead's previous disc of JC Bach's keyboard concertos, he employed nine strings from the Hanover Band; but the present Op 7 concertos, like those of Op 1, call for only two violins and cello. He played the Op 1 work on the harpsichord, as specified on the title-page of the original edition: here he plays a fortepiano on the grounds that not only does the title-page of Op 7 designate 'Harpsichord or Piano Forte', but also that the fortepiano had made considerable headway in London in the seven years since the Op 1 appeared in 1763. The most interesting of these concertos are the last two of the set, each in three movements. No 5 is particularly fine, not merely because of its brilliant keyboard writing (notably in its finale) but because the sturdy initial *Allegro di molto* is more mature in style, with fresh material appearing in the development, and because of its deeply expressive, almost Mozartian, *Andante*. No 6 is distinguished by its central movement's long cantilena lines and for an extraordinary key-move near the end of the finale. There is a confusion in the booklet-note as to whether the work is played according to the published version or in the longer revision with a more prominent solo part: the former appears to be the case. Halstead's playing is a model of neatness and crisp rhythmicality: his decorations are in good taste, and in No 5 he adopts the composer's own cadenzas. His string colleagues are excellent. In short, this is a very pleasing disc.

Harpsichord Concertos – D minor; B flat; F minor
Hanover Band / Anthony Halstead *hpd*
CPO CPO999 393-2 (57 minutes: DDD) Ⓕ
Recorded 1995

The works of JC Bach's Berlin years are almost indistinguishable from those of his brother, CPE, and anyone putting on this disc could be excused for thinking the first movement of the D minor Concerto – with its purposeful, energetic scales, its stark textures, its heavily used motifs, its rushing harpsichord writing, its sombre minor key and its total lack of lyricism – to be wholly CPE's work. It is in fact a very accomplished piece for a composer less than 20 years old and there are glimmerings of JC's own voice in the *Adagio affettuoso* that follows; it still sounds like North German music, untouched by Italian softness and sunshine, but the harpsichord cantilena certainly has a more personal expressive character and so does some of the string writing in the ritornellos and accompaniment. The slow movements throughout seem individual and appealing in a sense that CPE's are not. The quick movements, especially in the B flat Concerto, contain gestures of the abrupt and musically violent kind that CPE so often used. The finale of the D minor has a curious element of fantasy and an imaginative use of *pizzicato* behind the first solo entry.

Halstead uses a small orchestra, strings only, 3 3 1 1 1, which is quite sufficient and very alert. The solo playing is extremely fluent and indeed brilliant; Halstead plays with ample energy and rhythmic precision and realises the elaborate melodic lines effectively. Some of his cadenzas seem to go harmonically too far afield too quickly and are not entirely convincing, but this is a small blemish in an admirable disc.

Symphonies concertantes

Symphonies concertantes – F, T287 No 2; B flat, T287 No 7; D **P**
Anthony Robson *ob* **Jeremy Ward** *bn* **Graham Cracknell, Anna McDonald** *vns* **Sebastian Comberti** *vc* **Hanover Band / Anthony Halstead**
CPO CPO999 537-2 (52 minutes: DDD) Ⓕ
Recorded 1997 ●

In the notes Ernest Warburton, the leading JC Bach scholar, draws a distinction between the baroque *concerto grosso* and the *symphonie concertante* form that became popular in the last three or four decades of the 18th century. The *symphonie concertante*, predominantly light-hearted, allotted a more prominent role to the solo instruments. The earliest of the present three works is that in F, and Warburton speculates that the choice of a solo oboe and bassoon suggests that it may have been written in 1761 for Naples, where Bach's opera *Catone in Utica* called for outstanding players of just these instruments. It is a cheerfully engaging two-movement work that takes the bassoon up into the tenor register: its first movement is unorthodox in shape. The D major work, in three movements, likewise ends in a minuet, with a trio in the minor for a change. Overall, the writing places more emphasis on virtuosity for the two soloists, and both in the energetic first movement and the more formal second there is a lengthy cadenza (found in the manuscript). The most notable *symphonie concertante* here, however, is that in B flat, long considered lost and rediscovered only in 1996: this is, consequently, its first recording. Probably composed for JC's London concerts in the late 1770s, it allows the orchestra greater say; the initial ritornellos in the first two movements are unusually long. In the *Larghetto* the solo cello drops out, leaving the violin long, sweetly pungent cantilenas – a strikingly fine movement.

Halstead secures neat performances of finesse of all three works, which also benefit from skilful soloists and well-balanced recording. Delightful.

Symphonies

Six Symphonies, Op 6 – No 1 in G; No 2 in D; No 3 in E flat; No 4 in B flat; No 5 in E flat; No 6 in G minor **P**
Hanover Band / Anthony Halstead
CPO CPO999 298-2 (56 minutes: DDD) Ⓕ
Recorded 1994

In the Op 6 Symphonies, the frothy Italianate music of the composer's Italian and early London years was behind him; these pieces, dating from the late 1760s, while still Italian-influenced in their formal clarity and melodic style, are sturdier music, more carefully composed, more symphonic. Both the E flat works in this set have something of the solidity and warmth associated with that key, and each has a C minor *Andante*. The G major's first movement has the confident ring and thematic contrasts of his mature music, and the D major contains Mannheim *crescendos* and some delightful textures, with flutes and divided violas, in its charming and slightly playful middle movement.

The set ends with Bach's single minor-key symphony in G minor, very similar in spirit to Mozart's No 25; this piece, often recorded before, shows an unfamiliar side to his musical personality. Anthony Halstead and his players convey the music's strength and spirit convincingly. The lively finales all go with a swing, and the opening movements have plenty of energy. The slow movements are not always quite so persuasive: the third C minor slow movement of the G minor Symphony is a little overly deliberate and becomes detached and modest in expressive impact. But generally these are strong and appealing performances of some attractive and unfamiliar music, clearly, slightly drily recorded, and admirers of the London Bach and his music need not hesitate.

Symphonies – Op 9: No 1 in B flat; No 2 in E flat; No 3 in B flat; B flat, Sieber No 1; E flat, Sieber No 2; E flat (ed Warburton) **P**
Hanover Band / Anthony Halstead
CPO CPO999 487-2 (60 minutes: DDD) Ⓕ
Recorded 1996 ●

This disc offers the Op 9 Symphonies published in The Hague in 1773, two of them in two versions, along with a little-known symphony. Ernest Warburton explains in his notes that the usual texts for these works, with oboes and horns, are in his view arrangements of originals calling for clarinets – still rarities in most European orchestras at the time – and bassoon, in which form one of them was published in Paris. Here, then, Op 9 Nos 1 and 2 are done twice over to allow comparison; and certainly the versions differ markedly in flavour with clarinets and bassoon. The E flat work, No 2, one of Bach's finest and most vigorously argued symphonies, comes out particularly well, with quite a different ring to its tuttis.

The other work here, an E flat Symphony, also has clarinets, although their parts lie in a lower-middle register. It is an attractive work, with an eloquent violin line in the *Andante*, and a charming final gavotte. Of the works played twice, the B flat is lightish, probably originally an opera overture; the E flat has more substance and notably a C minor slow movement with a melody of a haunting, graceful beauty. The third Op 9 Symphony is a brisk little piece which again started life as an overture. Halstead directs with his usual style and shapeliness.

Adriano in Siria – Overture. Six Grand Overtures, Op 18 – No 1 in E flat; No 4 in D. Symphony in G minor, Op 6 No 6. Sinfonia concertante in C, T289 No 4 (ed Maunder) **P**
Academy of Ancient Music / Simon Standage *vn*
Chandos Chaconne CHAN0540 (65 minutes: DDD) Ⓕ
Recorded 1993 ●

The G minor Symphony is a magnificently fiery piece, similar in manner to Haydn's No 39 and Mozart's No 25; it is done here with plenty of *Sturm und Drang*, notably in the very forceful finale, and the noble ideas of the slow movement are well caught. The opening item is a three-movement D major Symphony, in effect, with a well-worked first movement and an *Andante* with rich wind writing. No other composer, besides Mozart, seems to have had as keen a feeling as JC Bach for the sensuous beauty of wind textures. The *Sinfonia concertante* isn't quite as successful a piece (it's rather repetitive), but it is never less than charming and enjoyable, again with some beautiful wind textures in the *Larghetto* and a delightful 'Two lovely black eyes' theme in the rondo. The solo playing is admirable. Recommended to anyone sympathetic to JC Bach's music.

Overtures

Overtures – Gioas, re di Giuda; Adriano in Siria; Zanaida; Orione. La clemenza di Scipione – Overture; No 5, March in G; No 22, March in E flat. Carattaco – Overture; No 20, March in B flat; No 26, March in G. Symphony in D, Schmitt Op 18 No 1 **P**
Hanover Band / Anthony Halstead
CPO CPO999 488-2 (58 minutes: DDD) Ⓕ
Recorded 1996 ●

Small-scale but elegantly fashioned, melodious and pleasurable music: it is no wonder that the London public in the 1760s and 1770s took JC to their hearts. Here we have the overtures to six works of his that were performed at the King's Theatre in the Haymarket – from his first opera there, *Orione* in 1763, to his last, *La clemenza di Scipione* in 1778, and the 1770 oratorio, *Gioas*, plus a symphony which is a *pasticcio* of the *Clemenza* overture with additional trumpets and drums and a revised version of the *Andante* from the overture to his only completed French opera, the 1779 *Amadis de Gaule*. With the exception of this last and of *Adriano in Siria*, all are either first recordings or the first in their original versions. The most striking feature about all these works, apart from their vigorous openings, is the freedom in the use of wind instruments: *Zanaida* has *soli* clarinets, and the trio of *Orione*'s minuet is for wind band only, as are passages in *Adriano*, the E flat March in *Clemenza* and the brilliant final *Presto* of *Carattaco*. The Hanover Band's playing is vital and fresh, rhythmically crisp and tonally clean-cut; the recording is first-rate.

Endimione

Jörg Hering *ten* Endimione; **Vasiljka Jezovšek** *sop* Diana; **Ann Monoyios** *sop* Nice; **Jörg Waschinski** *alto* Amore
Cologne Vocal Ensemble, Cappella Coloniensis / Bruno Weil
Deutsche Harmonia Mundi ② 05472 77525-2 Ⓕ
(106 minutes: DDD). Notes, text and translation included. Recorded 1999

Endimione is a serenata or *azione drammatica*; JC Bach composed it in 1772 for concert performance at the King's Theatre, the main London opera house. It is a setting of a libretto by Metastasio, telling the tale of Diana's jealousy and her love for Endymion, through Cupid's triumph over the scruples of the chaste huntress and the dedicated hunter. It is a wholly delightful work. The score moves at a fairly leisurely pace; there are some half-dozen lyrical numbers in each act, separated by recitative (a good deal of it orchestrally accompanied); and some arias have ritornellos long enough to make Mozart's to 'Martern aller Arten' seem almost epigrammatic. The music shows Bach at his best – melodically graceful, texturally rich, spacious but always clear in design. If dramatic vitality is not especially abundant, that is partly because this text hardly calls for it.

The performance starts a shade unpromisingly, with an over-vigorous account of the first movement of the overture (which is familiar as the double orchestra symphony, Op 18 No 3), and an *Andante* too speedy to catch the music's expressive character. Thereafter all is well. Ann Monoyios, the singer of Nice, one of Diana's nymphs and her rival for Endymion's hand, shows a light, clearly defined soprano, well fitted to the high-lying music, and shows some nice touches of wit and timing. The Diana herself, Vasiljka Jezovšek, is also quite light of voice for this role, but it is a full and warm sound, and there is sensitive phrasing and precision in the decorative music of her final aria. Jörg Waschinski does well in the two big arias assigned to Cupid (or Amore), and produces some delightfully polished and brilliant singing, especially in the top register. Jörg Hering, although even in voice and sure in style, is a little less interesting, and sometimes constricted in tone, giving the impression that he might flatten. In all, however, this is an impressive account of a beguiling score.

Johann Sebastian Bach

German 1685-1750

Johann Sebastian was the youngest son of Johann Ambrosius Bach, a town musician, from whom he probably learnt the violin and the rudiments of musical theory. When he was 10 he was orphaned and went to live with his elder brother Johann Christoph, organist at St Michael's Church, Ohrdruf, who gave him lessons in keyboard playing. From 1700-02 he attended St Michael's School in Lüneburg, where he sang in the church choir and probably came into contact with organist and composer Georg Böhm. He also visited Hamburg to hear JA Reincken at the organ of St Catherine's Church.

After competing unsuccessfully for an organist's post in Sangerhausen in 1702, Bach spent the spring and summer of 1703 as 'lackey' and violinist at the court of Weimar and then took up the post of organist at the Neukirche in Arnstadt. In June 1707 he moved to St Blasius, Mühlhausen, and four months later married his cousin Maria Barbara Bach in nearby Domheim. Bach was appointed organist and chamber musician to the Duke of Saxe-Weimar in 1708, and in the next nine years he became known as a leading organist and composed many of his finest works for the instrument. During this time he fathered seven children, including Wilhelm Friedemann and Carl Philipp Emanuel. When, in 1717, Bach was appointed Kapellmeister at Cöthen he was at first refused permission to leave Weimar and was allowed to do so only after being held prisoner by the duke for almost a month.

Bach's new employer, Prince Leopold, was a talented musician who loved and understood the art. Since the court was Calvinist, Bach had no chapel duties and instead concentrated on instrumental composition. From this period date his violin concertos and the six Brandenburg Concertos, as well as numerous sonatas, suites and keyboard works, including several (eg the Inventions and Book I of the '48') intended for instruction. In 1720 Maria Barbara died while Bach was visiting Karlsbad with the prince; in December of the following year Bach married Anna Magdalena Wilcke, daughter of a court trumpeter at Weissenfels. A week later Prince Leopold also married, and his bride's lack of interest in the arts led to a decline in the support given to music at the Cöthen court. In 1722 Bach entered his candidature for the prestigious post of Director musices at Leipzig and Kantor of the Thomasschule there. In April 1723 after the preferred candidates, Telemann and Graupner, had withdrawn, he was offered the post and accepted it.

Bach remained as Thomaskantor in Leipzig for the rest of his life, often in conflict with the authorities, but a happy family man and a proud and caring parent. His duties centred on the Sunday and feastday services at the city's two main churches, and during his early years in Leipzig he composed prodigious quantities of church music, including four or five cantata cycles, the Magnificat and the St John and St Matthew Passions. He was by this time renowned as a virtuoso organist and in constant demand as a teacher and an expert in organ construction and design. His fame as a composer gradually spread more widely when, from 1726 onwards, he began to bring out published editions of some of his keyboard and organ music.

From about 1729 Bach's interest in composing church music sharply declined, and most of his sacred works after that date including the B minor Mass and the Christmas Oratorio consist mainly of 'parodies' or arrangements of earlier music. At the same time he took over the direction of the collegium musicum that Telemann had founded in Leipzig in 1702 – a mainly amateur society which gave regular public concerts. For these Bach arranged harpsichord concertos and composed several large-scale cantatas, or serenatas, to impress the Elector of Saxony, by whom he was granted the courtesy title of Hofcompositeur in 1736.

Among the 13 children born to Anna Magdalena at Leipzig was Johann Christian, in 1735. In 1744 Bach's second son, Emanuel, was married and in 1747 Bach visited the couple at Potsdam, where Emanuel was employed as harpsichordist by Frederick the Great. At Potsdam Bach improvised on a theme given to him by the king, and this led to the composition of the Musical Offering, a compendium of fugue, canon and sonata based on the royal theme. Contrapuntal artifice predominates in the work of Bach's last decade, during which his membership (from 1747) of Lorenz Mizler's learned Society of Musical Sciences profoundly affected his musical thinking. The Canonic Variations for organ was one of the works Bach presented to the society; the unfinished Art of Fugue may also have been intended for distribution among its members.

Bach's eyesight began to deteriorate during his last year, and in March and April 1750 he was twice operated on by the itinerant English oculist John Taylor. The operations and the treatment that followed them may have hastened Bach's death. He took final communion on July 22 and died six days later. On July 31 he was buried at St John's cemetery. His widow survived him for 10 years, dying in poverty in 1760.

Bach's output embraces practically every musical genre of his time except for the dramatic ones of opera and oratorio (his three 'oratorios' being oratorios only in a special sense). He opened up new dimensions in virtually every department of creative work to which he turned, in format, musical quality and technical demands. As was normal at the time, his creative production was mostly bound up with the external factors of his places of work and his employers, but the density and complexity of his music are such that analysts and commentators have uncovered in it layers of religious and numerological significance rarely to be found in the music of other composers. Many of his contemporaries, notably the critic JA Scheibe, found his music too involved and lacking in immediate melodic appeal, but his chorale harmonisations and fugal works were soon adopted as models for new generations of musicians. The course of Bach's musical development was undeflected (though not entirely uninfluenced) by the changes in musical style taking place around him. Together with his great contemporary Handel (whom chance prevented his ever meeting), Bach was the last great representative of the Baroque era in an age which was already rejecting the Baroque aesthetic in favour of a new, 'enlightened' one.

Harpsichord Concertos

Harpsichord Concertos – D minor, BWV1052; D, BWV1054. Concerto for Flute, Violin, Harpsichord and Strings in A minor, BWV1044. Das wohltemperierte Klavier, BWV846-93 – Preludes and Fugues: F, BWV880; B, BWV892 P

Le Concert Français / Pierre Hantaï *hpd*

Auvidis Astrée AS128523 (70 minutes: DDD) Ⓜ

Recorded 1993 OO

The concertos come over well. Ensemble are tautly controlled and the string playing effectively articulated, although on occasion the first violin is a little too favoured in the recorded balance. However, the string playing is so unanimous in sound and purpose that there is little to worry about in this department. Hantaï himself is impressive for his wonderfully rhythmic playing, the clarity with which he interprets both his own keyboard textures and those which support and punctuate it, and not least for his supple, muscular concept of the music.

These are extraordinarily invigorating performances, which draw the listener deep into the harmonic and contrapuntal complexities and conceits of Bach's art. Take for instance the elusive *Adagio* of BWV1052, where careful punctuation and sensitive interaction between solo and tutti make for a rewarding coherence. In the A minor Triple Concerto, Hantaï is joined by his flautist brother, Marc, and François Fernandez (violin), the leader of the ensemble. The work is a Leipzig arrangement of movements from earlier pieces not in concerto form, whose extent sources were almost certainly copied after Bach's death. The opening *Allegro* is a little too heavy, but the essentially three-part texture of the middle movement is realised with affection. Altogether a stimulating disc.

Keyboard Concertos – D minor, BWV1052; E, BWV1053; A, BWV1055

Academy of St Martin in the Fields / Murray Perahia *pf*

Sony Classical SK89245 (53 minutes: DDD) Ⓕ

Recorded 2000 OO

Soloist-conducted piano concertos can sometimes mean compromise, even chaos...but not in this case. Indeed, the playing of the Academy of St Martin in the Fields under Murray Perahia is even sprightlier than on a rival EMI recording of the same repertoire where Sir Neville Marriner conducts and Andrei Gavrilov plays the keyboard part. As soloist, Perahia is his usual stylish, discreet and pianistically refined self. He takes the D minor Concerto's opening at a fair lick, a hot-foot sprinter embellishing the line with taste and affecting a little *ritardando* at 3'21" (just as the mood momentarily brightens) *à la* Edwin Fischer.

Elsewhere, he is very much his own man, intensifying his tone for rising sequences (at around 5'06") or softening it to the most rarefied murmur (as from 4'54" into the third movement). His command of colour is as striking here as it was on his recent CD of the *Goldberg* Variations, especially in the *Adagio*, which approaches cantorial heights of intensity. When it comes to the treacherous chordal cadenza at 6'11" into the finale, Perahia keeps up the momentum without either flagging or straining his tone.

As for the E major and A major Concertos, elegance is more of the essence than fire, but there too Perahia delivers. He has a way of accenting without jabbing the keys, tracing counterpoint while keeping the top line well to the fore. And how nice to hear the warming tone of a theorbo (bass lute) in the E major Concerto's central Siciliano, a beautiful performance, more ornamental than cantorial, in keeping with the more decorative nature of the music. Tracks 6 and 7 (the E major's finale and the A major's opening *Allegro*) provide cheering examples of Perahia's buoyant way with Bach's faster music.

Rivals are plentiful, but credible contenders at this level of interpretation are rare. Andrei Gavrilov 'out-Goulds' Gould with his dry *staccatissimo*, and Gould himself was a good deal livelier in concert than on his rather sober commercial recording under Leonard Bernstein. Sviatoslav Richter plays with incredible control while keeping every note alive, but some might find his manner too austere. And while Edwin Fischer is consistently spontaneous, he is rather less elegant than Perahia – and his version of the A major Concerto sounds as if it's 'Busonified' (or something very similar). András Schiff, like Perahia, commands a wide range of colours, though the binding force of Perahia's concentration – always a boon in his latest recordings – leaves the stronger impression. The carefully balanced Sony recordings keep the sound frame tight and lively.

Oboe Concertos

Oboe Concertos – F, BWV1053; A, BWV1055; D minor, BWV1059

Chamber Orchestra of Europe / Douglas Boyd *ob/ob d'amore*

DG 429 225-2GH (46 minutes: DDD) Ⓕ

Recorded 1989 O

Although Bach is not known to have written any concertos for the oboe, he did entrust it with some beautiful *obbligato* parts, so he clearly did not underrate its expressive capacities. He did, however, rearrange many of his works for different instrumental media and there is musicological evidence that original oboe concertos were the (lost) sources from which other works were derived. The Harpsichord Concerto, BWV1055, is believed originally to have been written for the oboe d'amore, while the other two Oboe Concertos have been reassembled from movements found in various cantatas. Whatever the academic reasoning, the results sound very convincing.

Douglas Boyd is a superb oboist, with a clear sound, and a fluency that belies the instrument's technical difficulty. He plays the faster, outer movements with winsome lightness, and with alertness to dynamic nuance; the slow ones, the hearts of these works, are given with sensitivity but without sentimentality – which can easily invade that of BWV1059, taken from Cantata No 156, *Ich steh mit einem Fuss im Grabe*. The Chamber Orchestra of Europe partners him to perfection in this crisp recording.

J S Bach Oboe d'amore Concerto in D, BWV1053*a* (arr Mehl). Cantata No 156, 'Ich steh mit einem Fuss im Grabe' – Sinfonia. Trio in F, BWV1040
C P E Bach Oboe Concertos – B flat, H466; E flat, H468
Heinz Holliger *ob/ob d'amore* **Massimo Polidori** *vc* **Andreas Erisman** *hpd* **Berne Camerata / Thomas Zehetmair** *vn*
Philips 454 450-2PH (63 minutes: DDD) Ⓕ
Recorded 1996

It's nice to see JS's music coupled with that of his second son, Carl Philipp Emanuel. The JS pieces are the Oboe d'amore Concerto reconstructed from the E major Harpsichord Concerto (and very convincingly so); the Sinfonia from Cantata No 156, a sweetly lyrical piece for oboe and strings which also turns up as the slow movement of the F minor Harpsichord Concerto; and a tiny Trio which, in typical Bach fashion, makes light of the fact that it is canonic. The two CPE concertos are both works of his late years in Berlin, expansive and varied as ever, and mixing polite *galanteries* with a more deeply felt, brooding changeableness, especially evident in the slow movements.

The JS pieces receive the more convincing performance: Holliger's playing shows superb technical control; he demonstrates a pleasing variety of articulation in the Concerto and the Trio, while the Sinfonia just oozes with all the gentle flow it demands. How odd then that, by comparison, the CPE Bach performances should sound so old-fashioned, with more vibrato from the strings and a resultant slight loss of clarity and incisiveness. This is music which benefits more from the use of period instruments, but undoubtedly there are plenty who would disagree, and Holliger's musicianship cannot be faulted; there are few baroque oboists who could play with such fluidity. So unless you have an aversion to modern instruments, you can buy with confidence.

Violin Concertos

A minor, **BWV1041**; E, **BWV1042**. Double Concertos – Two Violins and Strings in D minor, **BWV1043**; Oboe, Violin and Strings in C minor, **BWV1060**

Violin Concertos, BWV1041-42.
Double Concertos, BWV1060[a]; BWV1043
Arthur Grumiaux, Herman Krebbers *vns* **Heinz Holliger** *ob* **Les Solistes Romands; New Philharmonia Orchestra / Arpad Gerecz, [a]Edo de Waart**
Philips Silver Line 420 700-2PSL (61 minutes: ADD) Ⓜ
Recorded 1970-78 ●●

In the old days, records of Bach violin concertos were adequately filled by the Concertos in A minor and E major, plus the Double Violin Concerto. On this disc these three works are played strongly by Arthur Grumiaux, who is joined in the Double Concerto by Herman Krebbers. Arpad Gerecz directs Les Solistes Romands and the 1970s recordings are vivid; some may even find it slightly strident. The fourth work (to fill the longer playing time available) is the Concerto for oboe and violin, BWV1060. Heinz Holliger plays beautifully, and Grumiaux is utterly relaxed with the New Philharmonia Orchestra under Edo de Waart in a noticeably warm recording.

Violin Concertos, BWV1041-42. Double Concertos, BWV1043[b]; BWV1060[a]
[a]Albrecht Mayer *ob* **[b]Daniel Stabrawa** *vn* **Berlin Philharmonic Orchestra / Kennedy** *vn*
EMI CDC5 57016-2 (59 minutes: DDD) Ⓕ
Recorded 2000 ●

Though Bach is not a composer one generally associates with Kennedy, this recording of the four most popular concertos is far more than just a dutiful 250th anniversary offering. Kennedy is nothing if not characterful, taking a positive, often robust view of Bach. It is not just his breathtakingly fast speeds in finales and in some first movements, too, that will have listeners pricking up their ears (after all, period performance has accustomed us to that), but often a fierceness of manner which can initially take one aback.

With brilliant playing not just from the soloist but from the strings of the Berlin Philharmonic, the results are certainly exciting. The power of Bach's writing is reinforced thanks also to the rather close recorded balance in the Jesus-Christus Kirche.

However fast Kennedy's speeds in *Allegros*, he counters any feeling of breathlessness not just in his clean articulation, but in his fine detailing. The Berlin players respond very sympathetically, but are not always quite so adept at springing rhythms at such fast speeds, and in the finale of the E major, the slurred phrasing of each duplet is in danger of sounding exaggerated – a very literal reading of the markings in the score.

By contrast, slow movements tend to be taken

broadly, but there again Kennedy has thought through his expressive phrasing in detail, consciously pointing rhythms, shading dynamics and colouring tone. He also adds the occasional cadential flourish, as on the pause at bar 22 of the slow movement of the E major (track 2, 2'20"). His natural magnetism carries one on unerringly, though even more enjoyable is the freshly spontaneous, more songful if less detailed approach of both Grumiaux (Philips) and Joji Hattori (Classic fM), particularly the Hattori, where the joy of Bach's inspiration is more evident, not just in lyrical slow movements but in bouncy *Allegros*.

Yet any reservations over the Kennedy detract not at all from the positive strength of his readings. In the slow movement of the A minor Concerto, for example, the orchestral chords on violins and violas marking each beat of the bar are weightier than usual, again following detailed indications in the score. That helps to set in relief such magic moments as Kennedy's ethereally sustained *pianissimo* entry on a high B flat at bar 17 (track 8, 2'19"), emerging as from afar.

In the Double Concerto Daniel Stabrawa makes a perfectly matched partner for Kennedy, and in the Concerto for oboe and violin there is no question of his seeking to overshadow the fine artistry of the warm-toned Berlin oboist Albrecht Mayer. After all, this reconstruction from the C minor Double Keyboard Concerto, BWV1060, tends to favour the wind instrument rather than the violin. Even though the two rival versions of this ideal coupling make safer recommendations, with such characterful readings this new issue finds its very distinctive place – these are the visions of an exceptional artist, helped by warm, full sound.

Violin Concertos, BWV1041-42[a]. **P**
Double Concertos, BWV1043[b]; BWV1060 (arr Fischer)[c]
[abc]**Ryo Terakado,** [b]**Natsumi Wakamatsu** *vns*
[c]**Marcel Ponseele** *ob* **Bach Collegium Japan / Masaaki Suzuki**
BIS CD961 (59 minutes: DDD) Ⓕ
Recorded 1999 ●

Pigeon-hole these as 'authentic' performances on original or reproduction instruments and at period pitch, then consider the purely musical virtues of the products. There is happy animation in the flanking movements – bows are lifted from or stopped on the strings to ensure the cleanest of textures – and a warmth of expression in the slow ones which comes from a deeper source than mere academic study.

The admirable soloist in the A minor and E major Concertos, Ryo Terakado, and his partner in the Double Concerto, Natsumi Wakamatsu, both studied with Sigiswald Kuijken in The Hague and served with various baroque ensembles in Europe before returning to Japan. It shows in the beautifully 'vocalised' shaping of their lines, the product of emotional osmosis into their bloodstreams. Not once do they or their ripieno colleagues jar the ear with acidic sounds, and in the *Andante* of the A minor Concerto Terakado achieves a *pianissimo* that is near- miraculous in its quality. Marcel Ponseele, the only European on parade, has a comparably distinguished pedigree. In the reconstructed Concerto BWV1060 his fluency, rounded tone and clean articulation are second to none, and he makes the *Adagio* one of the serenely lovely high spots of the entire programme. As for the ripieno, one could not ask for better, and they are recorded in excellent balance with the soloists. Suzuki directs the whole with sure hands.

Additional recommendation
Violin Concertos, BWV1041-43, 1060
Podger *vn* **Academy of Ancient Music / Manze** *vn* **P**
Harmonia Mundi HMU90 7155 (57 minutes: DDD; 4/07) Ⓕ
Manze projects a highly developed sense of fantasy in his interpretations and, mostly, it proves immensely effective.

Brandenburg Concertos

No 1 in F, BWV1046; **No 2** in F, BWV1047;
No 3 in G, BWV1048; **No 4** in G, BWV1049;
No 5 in D, BWV1050; **No 6** in B flat, BWV1051

Vienna Concentus Musicus / Nikolaus Harnoncourt **P**
Teldec Ultima ② 0630-18944-2 (148 minutes: DDD) Ⓜ
Recorded 1981-83 ●●

This is the second set of *Brandenburgs* directed by Nikolaus Harnoncourt, following his pioneering accounts of the 1960s. The later performances, in particular, have been favourites for reissue since their original release in 1982; this is their second reissue. A strong sense of reappraisal lies at the heart of these challenging performances of the *Brandenburgs*, plainly evident in the level of refinement and attention to detail, traits that have now become Harnoncourt's hallmark in later repertoire; the technical limitations of period instrumentalists from the first set are definitely a ghost laid to rest. Concerto No 2, for instance, has a considered nonchalance and the trumpet playing is of a different order here: this is one of the most aristocratic and rounded performances on disc. While perhaps never totally succeeding in displacing the older (1967) version in many people's affections, the present one does have several strong points, not least the extraordinarily high quality of the recording. Where this set scores over the older one is in respect of the brass and woodwind playing. Great advances were made between the 1960s and the 1980s in rediscovering and developing techniques required to bring period horns, trumpets, oboes and flutes to life in a convincing way. The playing at its best is very good indeed. Such is the case with Alice Harnoncourt's solo violin playing in the Fourth Concerto of the set which, from a technical and an interpretative viewpoint, is an outstanding feature of the set. The two string concertos (Nos 3 and 6) also come over well. In summary, nothing here is remotely dull and the level of execution is consistently high. Well worth becoming acquainted with.

Brandenburg Concertos Nos 1-6 **P**
Tafelmusik / Jeanne Lamon *vn*
Sony Classical Vivarte ② S2K66289 Ⓕ
(93 minutes: DDD). Recorded 1993-94 **OO**

Tafelmusik's *Brandenburgs* come straight from the heart and as such they are performances which invite repeated listening and are furthermore both easy and enjoyable to live with. There are no startling novelties here and nothing which attempts to impede the natural course of musical flow. Tempos are sensibly chosen and, once chosen, consistently adhered to. That is not to say that there is an absence of affective gesture or a lack of rhetorical awareness. Everything in fact is punctuated in a way that allows the listener to follow the subtly shaded nuances of Bach's dialogue. Some readers may feel that these interpretations lack the stamp of a strong personality at the helm but any such fears of interpretative neutrality are largely dispelled by the sensibility of the players and their hitherto proven skill at reaching the heart of the music without the assistance either of pretension or muddled intellectual clutter.

Reservations chiefly concern minutiae of tuning and to a much lesser extent, ensemble. Neither these weaknesses, nor the occasional blip or thwack, hindering the production of clean notes from oboe, horns or trumpet, spoil enjoyment of Nos 1 and 2. It is a pity that the first movement of No 3 is marred by indifferent tuning and, more disturbingly, by a marked acceleration in speed beginning at bar 84 (3'26"); but the second *Allegro* of the work is so well done that you are inclined to forgive them. Tafelmusik's account of this brilliant binary movement is not to be missed.

CD80368 Brandenburg Concertos Nos 1-3 **P**
CD80354 Brandenburg Concertos Nos 4-6
Boston Baroque / Martin Pearlman *hpd* Telarc
CD80368/54 (52 and 41 minutes: DDD) Ⓕ
Recorded 1994

Boston Baroque is a close-knit group of highly accomplished and stylish instrumentalists. On their discs their enthusiasm is clear in the bustling outer movements; it's a wise leader who knows his team, in this case Martin Pearlman, who no doubt set the tempos. In the slow movements there is the breathing-space which is often found lacking. The soloists are first-class (though Friedemann Immer's trumpet trills in Concerto No 2 sound a mite uncomfortable) and the multi-talented Daniel Stepner (violone piccolo in No 2, violin soloist in Nos 4 and 5, and viola soloist in No 6) and Pearlman himself (harpsichord) are especially impressive. It is, however, the ensemble, supported by a finely balanced recording, that makes these accounts so outstanding, and those who are allergic to thin or nasal string sounds will find nothing to cringe from in the warmth of tone that characterises these performances. The annotation states (but without explanation) that Concerto No 6 'must remain a chamber piece with one player to a part': whether it must or not, the recording shows it to be wholly effective played in that way. We are also told that 'it includes the transparent sounds of gambas' and so it does, but we are left to guess who their players might be. There can be no clear 'best' in the *Brandenburgs*, but this set is likely to remain among those which will prove to be enduring.

Brandenburg Concertos Nos 1-6 **P**
The English Concert / Trevor Pinnock *hpd*
Archiv Produktion 410 500/1-2AH Ⓕ
(43 and 53 minutes: DDD) Recorded 1978-82

The chief merits here are the overall zest of the performances, the expressive shaping of slow movements, and the individual contributions of some of the soloists – Pinnock himself brilliant in No 5, Philip Pickett, Lisa Beznosiuk and David Reichenberg admirable on recorder, transverse flute and oboe respectively, and Simon Standage in the violin parts performing prodigies, especially at the breakneck speeds adopted for some of the fast movements (the finale of No 4, for example). This tendency to force the pace makes things uncomfortable for the horns in No 1, and also leads elsewhere to some feelings of instability. Obviously several sessions were needed to record all six concertos, and there are some rather disturbing differences of balance and of ambiance between them. In No 2 the recorder, except when in its high octave, has difficulty in making its part heard, even against only the violin, let alone the oboe and trumpet (though it seems to have been brought in slightly closer for the finale); but in No 4 the internal balance between recorders and violin is quite satisfactory. No 1 is the most cramped acoustically, its larger sonorities needing room to expand; at the other extreme is No 3, which seems too resonant for real clarity; much the best and cleanest sound is achieved in Nos 4 and 5. A somewhat variable level of success, then, though at their best the recordings are highly recommendable.

Further listening
Stravinsky Concerto in E flat, Dumbarton Oaks
Couplings: Pulcinella Suite. **Bartók** Romanian Dances. Divertimento
Orpheus Chamber Orchestra
DG 445 541-2GMA (71 minutes: DDD: 4/86 & 6/87R)
Stravinsky's witty take on Bach's *Brandenburg* Concertos, played with precision and finesse by the Orpheus CO.

Orchestral Suites

No 1 in C, BWV1066; **No 2** in B minor, BWV1067; **No 3** in D, BWV1068; **No 4** in D, BWV1069

Orchestral Suites Nos 1-4; **P**
No 5 in G minor, BWV1070 (attrib)
Musica Antiqua Köln / Reinhard Goebel
Archiv Produktion ② 415 671-2AH2 Ⓕ
(111 minutes: DDD). Recorded 1982-85

The Suite in G minor was once in the possession of Bach's eldest son, Wilhelm Friedemann, who might also have been its composer. In an interesting insert-note, Reinhard Goebel explains that between 1982 and the completion of the recordings in 1985, his ideas changed about how to perform the music. Taking an extreme view he considers the earlier essay in style as among the sins of his youth. Much of Goebel's newer thinking is influenced by the writings of the American musicologist, Frederick Neumann. Some of the points are not presented clearly and these are truisms concerning 'authenticity', but his essay comes over as thoughtful and constructive. All this might suggest that there are sweeping and irreconcilable differences between MAK's performances and others of recent years. Not so, for while Goebel does largely put his ideas into practice it is in details of phrase and of articulation that his readings provide the most interesting comparisons. In the B minor Suite, the phrases are beautifully shaped, the tempos nicely judged and the instrumental textures effectively clear. In the remaining three suites the string forces of the ensemble are considerably augmented with four first and four second violins, three violas, two cellos, a violone and two harpsichords. The solo and *ripieno* playing is of a very high order; and it needs to be since some of Goebel's tempos make what occasionally sound like ultimate demands on his wind players.

In its shaping of individual notes and of phrases, these performances are probably more immaculate than any, yet that alone may not prove enough for you to switch your allegiance. Lively, brisk, stylish and highly polished these readings certainly are; they afford many delightful and convincing views of Bach's music, notably in the first two suites and lyrical account of the Air from the Third Suite. Nevertheless, at times you are conscious of a severity of outlook, a rigidity of temperament if not of interpretation which does not accord with the 'occasional' and often jubilant spirit of the music. Without wishing to dilute the considerable virtues of this issue, we would sound a warning bell to anyone tempted to regard it as preferable to others based on comparable tenets of performing style merely on the grounds of its polished executancy. The recorded sound is clear and pleasantly resonant. All Bach's repeats are observed throughout this fascinating and stimulating release.

Orchestral Suites Nos 1-4 **P**
Orchestra of the Age of Enlightenment / Frans Brüggen
Philips ② 442 151-2PH2 (81 minutes: DDD) Ⓕ
Recorded 1994 ○

In Bach's hands the orchestral suite reached a peak of expressive refinement and it is this aspect of the music that Brüggen so effectively highlights, with discerningly applied *appoggiaturas*, gently swung rhythms and concern for eloquent turns of phrase. The Orchestra of the Age of Enlightenment responds well to his ideas and gives an alluringly intimate and relaxed performance of the First Suite in C major. The Second Suite, in B minor, is treated as pure chamber music, with single strings and a continuo of two lutes. This last-mentioned feature is a pleasing touch, and an effective one, too. The Third and Fourth Suites, both in D major, are of an entirely different character from the first two. Enter trumpets and drums to enrich the woodwind and string textures with a splendid sense of occasion. The Third Suite has long been the most popular of the four, chiefly on account of its celebrated 'Air on the G string', and the ebullient Gavottes which follow it. But the real jewel here is the Overture to the Fourth Suite. Its rich and subtle harmonies all contribute towards an exotic flavour which comes over well. The only complaint is that in none of the Suites does Brüggen observe the second half repeats of the overtures themselves. This is something of a pity, because they are supreme examples of the form. However, these performances are lightly delivered, with spirit, subtly shaded dynamics and, in general, a loving attention to every detail in the music. That's what it deserves and it has paid off, handsomely. A satisfying release, superbly recorded.

Bach Orchestral Suite No 2. Brandenburg Concerto No 1 in F, BWV1046. Concerto for Flute, Violin, Harpsichord and Strings in A minor, BWV1044*a*
Telemann Suite in A minor, TWV55:a2
Michala Petri *rec* **Rainer Kussmaul** *vn* **Raphael Alpermann** *hpd* **Berlin Baroque Soloists**
RCA Red Seal 74321 57130-2 (71 minutes: DDD) Ⓕ
Recorded 1998 ○

Michala Petri displays a mastery of her instrument which is breathtaking. Every line she plays is beautifully even, nimble and crisp. Other recorder players might bring out a little more of the playful side of the Telemann perhaps, and in the two Bach flute pieces – the Triple Concerto and Second Orchestral Suite – some of the warmth of the baroque flute is undoubtedly missing, but on the other hand there is an extra clarity of texture to be enjoyed here instead. The support Petri gains from the Berlin Baroque Soloists is first-class. There are times when even an experienced ear would have trouble detecting that these are modern strings: in his solos, Kussmaul draws from his violin a delicacy and flexibility of bowing and phrasing which one normally associates with a baroque instrument, and the string ensemble as a whole brings a consistent lightness and liveliness of touch. In short this is exemplary baroque-playing on modern instruments.

The Art of Fugue, BWV1080

Awards 1986

Davitt Moroney *hpd* **P**
Harmonia Mundi Musique d'Abord
② HMA195 1169/70
(99 minutes: DDD) Ⓑ
Recorded 1986 ○○○

Bach died before the process of engraving his last great work had been completed, thus leaving a number of performance issues in doubt. However, Davitt Moroney is a performer-scholar with a mature understanding of the complexity of Bach's work; in a lucid essay in the booklet, he discusses the problems of presenting *The Art of Fugue* whilst explaining his approach to performing it. Certain aspects of this version will be of particular importance to prospective buyers: Moroney himself has completed Contrapunctus 14 but he also plays the same Contrapunctus in its unfinished state as a fugue on three subjects. He omits Bach's own reworkings for two harpsichords of Contrapunctus 13 on the grounds that they do not play a part in the composer's logically constructed fugue cycle; and he omits the Chorale Prelude in G major (BWV668*a*) which certainly had nothing to do with Bach's scheme but was added in the edition of 1751 so that the work should not end in an incomplete state. Moroney's performing technique is of a high order, placing emphasis on the beauty of the music which he reveals with passionate conviction. Exemplary presentation and an appropriate recorded sound enhance this fine achievement.

Evgeni Koroliov, with **Lyupka Haždigeorgieva** *pfs*
Tacet ② TACET13 (84 minutes: DDD) Ⓜ
Recorded 1990 ○○

Consideration of recordings of *The Art of Fugue* often raises such issues as whether it was intended as a theoretical work or for practical performance, what instrument or instruments it should be played on, and in what order the movements are played. For those obsessed with the last question, the order favoured here is, after the sixth (French) Contrapunctus, to intersperse the canons with the remainder. Evgeni Koroliov approaches the first Fugue very slowly and tranquilly, starting and ending quietly but with increases of tension here and there. Any fears that this is going to be a bland reading of the whole are immediately dispelled by the characterful treatment of the ensuing movements. Contrapunctus 2 (in dotted rhythm) becomes almost pugnacious, Contrapunctus 4 is taken *presto*, and both it and its immediate successor are played *staccato* without sounding in the least gimmicky. Elsewhere Koroliov employs a judicious variety of dynamics and of articulation – *staccato*, *staccatissimo*, *legato* and *détaché* – to convey his unfailingly clear linear thinking. The one weakness in this excellent issue is the inadequate presentation material, which doesn't mention, among everything else. *The Art of Fugue* is often made to sound dull and didactic: this performance is absolutely riveting.

The Art of Fugue. A Musical Offering, BWV1079. Canons, BWV1072-78; 1086-87 **P**
Musica Antiqua Köln / Reinhard Goebel
Archiv Produktion ③ 413 642-2AH3
(140 minutes: ADD) Ⓜ
Recorded 1984 ○

It goes without saying that period instruments or modern replicas are used. The intellectually staggering *Art of Fugue* is a kind of testament to Bach's art and for this recording the instrumentation, unspecified by the composer, has been well chosen. The 14 miniature Canons which close this issue are for the most part a recent discovery and were written on a page of Bach's own copy of the *Goldberg* Variations; of curiosity value certainly but not much more than that. Excellent recording.

Bach The Art of Fugue – Contrapuncti 1-11; Fuga **Mozart** Five Fugues, K405. Fugue in G minor, K401/K375*e* **P**
Phantasm (Laurence Dreyfus, Wendy Gillespie, Jonathan Manson, Markku Luolajan-Mikkola *viols*)
Simax PSC1135 (65 minutes: DDD) Ⓕ
Recorded 1997 ○

Seeing that we enjoy Bach and Mozart on a modern piano – an instrument of course outside their time-frame – should we demur at their music being played on an equally anachronistic consort of viols? Leaving aside the argument advanced in Laurence Dreyfus's booklet-note that much viol consort music was fugal in texture anyway, the fact is that the contrapuntal lines here emerge with great clarity and with a subtlety of timbre, articulation and dynamics beyond even the ablest keyboard player, thanks to Phantasm's accomplished and expressive performances. The group offers the first 11 *contrapuncti*, without the canons or mirror fugues, but plus the final uncompleted *chef d'oeuvre* that was to have crowned the awesome project; Phantasm's playing offers new insights into Bach's prodigious mind. In his transcriptions for string quartet of fugues from the *48* (putting one a semitone down for convenience), Mozart – who, it is reported, constantly had Bach's volume lying open on his piano – made a few small adjustments to details of rhythm and part-writing; and the process also fired him to write several fugues of his own, including the one in G minor (for piano solo or duet) here. The Phantasm ensemble, despite a slight tendency to hurry, brings a smile to one's lips by its intonation, precision and, above all, musicality.

Flute Sonatas, BWV1030-35

No 1 in B minor; **No 2** in E flat; **No 3** in A; **No 4** in C; **No 5** in E minor; **No 6** in E

Flute Sonatas Nos 1, 2 and 4-6
Violin Sonata in G minor, BWV1020 (arr fl)
James Galway *fl* **Sarah Cunningham** *va da gamba*
Philip Moll *hpd*
RCA Victor Red Seal 09026 62555-2 Ⓕ
(75 minutes: DDD). Recorded 1993 ○

The basic six flute sonatas, BWV1030-35, can be accommodated on a single disc but Galway plays safe by keeping to what Bach (or someone else) actually wrote, omitting the unfinished A major Sonata, BWV1032, which other players have chosen to present in variously completed forms. There is, from the purist's point of view, still a 'risk' since it remains unproven that Bach was the composer of BWV1031, 1033 and 1020. However, their quality justifies their inclusion – if Bach didn't write them one doubts that he would have disowned them.

Galway is at his warm, velvet-toned best, phrasing immaculately, caressing the slow movements and fleet of tongue in the quicker ones. His tempos are well chosen and he never allows virtuosity to get the better of his judgement. The 'supporting cast' are no less beyond reproach, but whilst the flute and viola da gamba are well balanced the harpsichord might profitably have been allowed a rather more equal say in BWV1030 and BWV1031, in which it has an obbligato role.

Flute Sonatas Nos 1-6; C, BWV1033 (solo version); Partita in A minor, BWV1013 **P**
Janet See *fl* **Davitt Moroney** *hpd* **Mary Springfels** *va da gamba*
Harmonia Mundi ② HMU90 7024/5
(114 minutes: DDD) Ⓕ
Recorded 1990

The C major Sonata, BWV1033, originally a flute solo, to which Carl Philip Emanuel (the copyist) added a bass line, is presented here in both forms, solo and with continuo. The flute lines seem, when compared with those of BWV1013, less self-sufficient, and See's solo version does not quite convince you that they were originally meant to be unsupported. The mystery remains unsolved, but See/Moroney give everyone the chance to come to his/her own conclusion – if any. Bach's long lines are never more difficult than when they ride on the wind: See's long pauses for breath, some of them in curious places, interrupt the flow of the music in both solo works.

No such intrusions disturb the flow in the accompanied sonatas, of which See gives excellent accounts. She has the style in her bloodstream. In the matter of ornamentation she is extremely cautious when it comes to adding any but the most clearly implied trills. She is splendidly supported by Moroney who is inventive in the with-continuo works. There are no complaints, either, regarding Springfels's gamba playing or the degree of its prominence. For period-instrument performances, See *et al* are a good choice, for their spontaneous expressiveness, the overall balance of the with-continuo sonatas, and for the provocative bonus of the solo version of BWV1033.

Flute Sonatas Nos 1-6 $
William Bennett *fl* **George Malcolm** *hpd*
Michael Evans *vc*
ASV Quicksilva CDQS6108 (77 minutes: ADD) Ⓢ
Recorded 1978 ●●

There is something rather special about the Flute Sonatas and the more so when they are as well played as they are by William Bennett and George Malcolm. They were obviously written during a happy period in Bach's life for they are amiably inventive pieces, which is not to imply that they are slight, just very appealing. What matter if the E flat, BWV1031 (which has an engaging *Siciliano* slow movement), and the C major, BWV1033, are probably spurious – they still offer thoroughly worthwhile music. On this reissue, the first three sonatas (BWV1030-32) are played as a simple duet for flute and harpsichord; in the last three (BWV1033-35), written for flute and bass continuo, Michael Evans joins the ensemble and the balance – especially since his is not a baroque instrument – is quite perfect. As for that superb flautist Bennett, he too uses a modern instrument, yet is the soul of finesse as well as playing creatively and with consistently beautiful tone. The sound is forward but very convincing; and Malcolm's harpsichord is not over-amplified but admirably lifesize. This is a fine recording indeed and at super-bargain price should not be missed.

Solo Flute Sonata in A minor, BWV1013. **P**
Flute Sonatas[a] – B minor, BWV1030; C, BWV1033; E minor, BWV1034; E, BWV1035
Ashley Solomon *fl* [a]**Terence Charlston** *hpd*
Channel Classics CCS15798 (71 minutes: DDD) Ⓕ
Recorded 1999 ●●

This is an impressive and enjoyable CD that easily bears repeated listening. There is a soothing quality to the baroque flute, and its gentle, slightly reedy tone is captured very well here. It is closely recorded in a church acoustic to give a brilliant tone with added depth. Today's makers of the baroque flute are producing highly refined instruments, exemplified here by the Rod Cameron copy of a Denner, which has a strong, even tone and good balance of register, allowing highly accomplished performers like Ashley Solomon complete technical freedom.

This recording is not merely music therapy, however, but a genuine musical experience. His performance of the unaccompanied A minor Partita, for example, is nothing short of commanding: the control in articulation and breathing allows the phrasing to be flexible and unfussy. Indeed, it is the directness of his interpretations that is so telling; there is almost none of that slightly coy *rubato* that some other flautists use to disguise the need to breathe. Rather, Solomon ensures that the phrases are neither choppy nor fragmented. He has an excellent sense of the longer line and the harmonic pull beneath Bach's wonderfully melodic writing. The faster movements are perhaps the most successful, full of buoyancy and energy without seeming rushed or pushed. Try the second movement of the E minor Sonata, for example, or that of the C major. Slow movements are far from inexpressive, but again refreshingly direct: he never wallows (a good example is the introductory movement of the E major Sonata).

Solomon is well partnered by Terence Charlston on a rich-toned Ruckers-copy harpsichord.

Even if you already have a version of Bach's flute works on CD this can be strongly recommended, and it makes an equally good first-time buy too. Prepare to be uplifted.

Trio Sonatas

Trio Sonatas – D minor, BWV527; G, BWV530; A minor, BWV1029; G minor,BWV1030; C, BWV1037 Ⓟ
The Rare Fruits Council (Manfredo Kramer *vn* Pablo Valetti *vn/va* Balàzs Máté *vc* Dirk Boerner *hpd* Alessandro de Marchi *org*)
Astrée Naïve E8804 (67 minutes: DDD) Ⓕ
Recorded 2000 ●●

Following recent recordings of, among others, the complete 'true' trio sonatas from Florilegium and the complete organ trios adapted for strings and continuo from the Purcell Quartet, as well as numerous one-off arrangements dropped as fillers into other Bach chamber releases, this one offers a mixed bag of solutions to the irritating little anomaly that the greatest of baroque instrumental composers wrote hardly any music in one of the baroque period's most ubiquitous instrumental forms. So, here we get convincing arrangements for various combinations of violins, viola, cello, organ and harpsichord of two of the organ trios, the B minor Sonata for flute and obbligato harpsichord, the C major Sonata genuinely written for two violins and continuo – though not, it seems, by Bach (Goldberg is thought to be the man), and the G minor Sonata for gamba and obbligato harpsichord.

That Bach's music can withstand transcription like no one else's has been remarked on countless times, but it is nice to be reminded from time to time of another old truth, namely that there is always something new to be found in this music by those with the wit to look for it. That is exactly what the Rare Fruits Council demonstrate here in performances of uncommon energy and imagination that will surely win over the most resistant of transcription sceptics. Genteel and polite they are not; rather, they embrace the music with an inspiriting boisterousness and wholeheartedness which completely involves the listener. This is music-making simply bursting with life – just try the first movement of BWV530, the quick movements of BWV1037, or any movement from BWV1029, sounding more like a seventh *Brandenburg* than ever.

Most exciting of all, the players revel in Bach's life-enhancing contrapuntal interplay with a joyousness that is almost jazz-like in its freedom and exhilarating spontaneity. Their sound could be described as bold, up-front, occasionally a little coarse, but above all, well, fruity. If you are suffering from Bachian cobwebs, this thoroughly enjoyable release will blow them away.

Additional recommendation

Trio Sonatas, BWV525-30

Nos 1, 3, 5 and 6. Coupling: Four Duets, BWV802-05 14 Verschiedene Canones, BWV1087 Ⓟ
Palladian Ensemble
Linn Records CKD036 (75 minutes: DDD: 8/95) Ⓕ
Refreshingly committed performances which stray from old paths in stimulating and revealing ways and show off the corporate style of the Palladian Ensemble.

Violin and Harpsichord Sonatas

No 1 in B minor, BWV1014; **No 2** in A, BWV1015; **No 3** in E, BWV1016; **No 4** in C minor, BWV1017; **No 5** in F, BWV1018; **No 6** in G, BWV1019

Violin Sonatas Nos 1-6. Sonata for Violin and Continuo in G, BWV1019a[a]. Cantabile, BWV1019a/2. Sonatas for Violin and Continuo[a] – No 2 in G, BWV1021; No 4 in E minor, BWV1023 Ⓟ
Rachel Podger *vn* [a]**Jonathan Manson** *va da gamba* **Trevor Pinnock** *hpd*
Channel Classics ② CCS14798 (139 minutes: DDD) Ⓜ
Recorded 2000 ●●

Another recording of Bach's violin sonatas, and at last one that really hits the spot. Rachel Podger has already attracted much praise for her recordings of the solo violin music, but is heard here to even better advantage in the Six Sonatas for Violin and Obbligato Harpsichord, BWV1014-19, for which she is joined by Trevor Pinnock (of whose English Concert she is now the leader).

The two make a fine match. Both are uncomplicated, utterly instinctive musicians with a sure technical command and sound stylistic sense, and in works as robust and complete as these, that is most of the battle already won. But this is also music of great poetry, and, without straining unduly to make their points, Podger and Pinnock bring this out superbly; Pinnock's harpsichord is gently resonant and softly voiced, and Podger coaxes a lyrical flexibility out of her violin, its singing qualities enhanced thanks to a restrained but tellingly sweetening use of vibrato – one which also enables her to play more consistently and blessedly in tune than almost any other baroque fiddler currently in business.

It is difficult to single out details of this recording for comment; there just seems to be such a tremendous feeling of overall 'rightness' to it. Maybe the finale of Sonata No 2 seems rather frantic and the wonderful *Adagio ma non tanto* of No 3 a touch lumpy, but there really is not much else to criticise. And there are true gems to be enjoyed in the opening movement of BWV1014, where the violin makes an almost imperceptible initial entry, or the warm embrace of BWV1017's *Adagio*, or practically any of the sparkling fast movements, played with invigorating rhythmic drive and clarity, into which Podger's elegant but firmly controlled, willowy bowing tosses myriad subtle impulses and articulations.

This recording's most recent period rival, that of Andrew Manze and Richard Egarr, shows a typical wealth of new ideas and inspired moves but is less satisfying as a whole, and suffers from some intonationally hairy moments and a less precisely pointed sound. The only period recording to touch Podger and Pinnock for technical assurance is that of Fabio Biondi and Rinaldo Alessandrini, but in both sound and interpretation it is heavy-handed compared with the spontaneous musicianship and airy texture on display here, and rather meanly it gives the six obbligato sonatas only.

Though all the recent recordings of these sonatas have had their merits, this – two discs for the price of one – is, quite simply, the best yet.

Additional recommendation

Violin Sonatas Nos 1-6

Biondi *vn* **Alessandrini** *hpd* Ⓟ

Opus ② 111 OPS30-127/8 (90 minutes: DDD: 7/96) Ⓕ

These top period performers bring a moving lyricism to slow movements and a bold, biting energy to faster ones.

Viola da gamba sonatas

Sonatas for Viola da gamba and Harpsichord, BWV1027-29[a] – No 1 in G; No 2 in D; No 3 in G minor[a]. Capriccios – in B flat, BWV992; in E, BWV993 Ⓟ

[a]**Jaap ter Linden** *va da gamba* **Richard Egarr** *hpd*

Harmonia Mundi HMU90 7268 (61 minutes: DDD) Ⓕ

Recorded 1999 ●

Forced to choose just one CD to represent Bach's instrumental chamber music, then among the plethora of transcriptions and double albums there would perhaps be no better group of works to pick than these.

Jaap ter Linden and Richard Egarr enter a largish field which includes a number of modern cellists unable to resist this superb music, but they emerge as serious contenders for a placing. Linden's sound has the smoothness and rich lyricism that one tends to associate with the baroque cello, while at the same time retaining something of the gamba's pleasing incisiveness of line. Egarr's harpsichord is splendidly sonorous, and while his tautly controlled playing is in many ways the opposite of Linden's, the meeting of instruments and minds is nevertheless a happy one. Egarr, playing an obbligato part, has less opportunity to show off his individualism than he would in an improvised continuo accompaniment, but, even if he could have been favoured a little more in the balance, his ability to orchestrate an impressive range of sounds from his instrument is still in evidence, especially in the concerto-like Sonata in G minor. He also dispatches the disc's filler items – two of Bach's early, somewhat old-fashioned solo harpsichord pieces – with vigorous and virtuosic aplomb.

Compared with their recent rivals, then, these are lively performances which steer a comfortable middle course between those of the rich-toned but slightly unimaginative Markku Luolajan-Mikkola and Miklós Spányi and the more intense and inspired but sloppily recorded Jordi Savall and Ton Koopman. Alison Crum and Laurence Cummings suffer too much from a balance unkind to the gamba. It all comes down to taste, of course, but this new recording may just be the one to live with.

Additional recommendation

Viola da Gamba Sonatas, BWV1027-29

Coupled with: Trio Sonata in C, BWV529 Ⓟ

Savall *va da gamba* **Koopman** *hpd*

Alia Vox AV9812 (59 minutes: DDD: 6/00) Ⓕ

A significant Bach gamba release. Savall and Koopman conjure performances whose sheer rightness and creative warmth make the music sound invigoratingly fresh.

Sonatas and Partitas for Solo Violin

Sonatas – No 1 in G minor, BWV1001;
No 2 in A minor, BWV1003, BWV1005; **No 3** in C.
Partitas – No 1 in B minor, BWV1002;
No 2 in D minor, BWV1004; **No 3** in E, BWV1006

Sonatas Nos 1-3. Partitas Nos 1-3. Violin Sonatas[a] – No 3 in E, BWV1016; No 4 in C minor, BWV1017

Arthur Grumiaux *vn* [a]**Egida Giordani Sartori** *hpd*

Philips 50 Great Recordings ② 464 673-2PM2 Ⓜ

(146 minutes: ADD). Recorded 1960-61 ●

Also available without the sonatas on Philips Duo ② 438 736-2PM2 Ⓜ

The totally innocent ear, deprived of any comparison, could be forgiven for judging Grumiaux's to be definitive performances of Bach's Partitas and Sonatas. There is little of the sweetness of a Heifetz, the passing whimsy of a Shumsky here. And yet they define, indeed, as few other performances do, the structural frame and rhythmic working-out of each movement with extraordinary determination and authority. The purity of intonation is absolute; the energy locked into the sheer sound of the instrument startling. *And* two discs, as they say, for the price of one! Those who know and love the artistry of Grumiaux will be thrilled to rediscover these Berlin recordings of the early 1960s, sharply remastered and sounding out in a roomy acoustic. The platinum gleam glancing off every moment of double-stopping, and the flinty brightness struck where contrapuntal voices meet ring out as never before. The arpeggios of the *Presto* of the G minor Sonata flash like light from a prism; and the same mesmeric steadiness of *moto perpetuo* makes for a heady finish to the C major Sonata. What dominates, though, is the rhythmic rigour of Grumiaux's playing. His perfectionism, fused with a real sense of struggle, brings sheer might to the fugues of the Sonatas: it is rather like watching a climber scaling a vast rock face, securing himself with a pick and leaping across the next crevasse.

CCS12198: Sonata No 1. Partitas Nos 1 and 2 Ⓟ

CCS14498: Sonatas Nos 2 and 3. Partita No 3

Rachel Podger *vn*

Channel Classics CCS12198/14498 Ⓕ

(76 and 66 minutes: DDD). Recorded 1997-99 ●●●

Hitherto we have heard Rachel Podger only in early chamber works and as Andrew Manze's partner in Bach double concertos: here now, at last, is an opportunity to hear her on her own. And you couldn't be more on your own than in

Bach's mercilessly revealing Solo Sonatas and Partitas, perhaps the ultimate test of technical mastery, expressiveness, structural phrasing and deep musical perception for a violinist. Playing a baroque instrument, Podger challenges comparison with the much praised and individual reading by Monica Huggett: she has many of the same virtues – flawless intonation, warm tone, expressive nuances, clear understanding of the proper balance of internal strands – but her approach is sometimes markedly different. This is most obvious in the great D minor Chaconne, in which Huggett's rhythmical flexibility worried some people, but in which Podger, here as elsewhere, while fully characterizing the varied repetitions of the ground, is intent on building up the cumulative effect. One pleasing general feature of her playing, indeed, is her firm but unassertive rhythmic sense; others are the absence of any suspicion that technical difficulties exist (instead a calm control, as in the G minor's Siciliano), her subtle phrasing (as in the B minor Corrente, with the fleetest of *doubles*), the cross-rhythms of her G minor *Presto* and, most strikingly, the sheer poetic feeling with which she imbues the initial *Adagio* of the G minor Sonata. She touches in chords lightly: though some might have been split downwards rather than upwards so as to preserve the continuity of a lower part (for example, in bar 5 of the B minor Allemande, bar 10 of the Chaconne and in the 18th and 19th bars of its major section). Her D minor Giga is stunning. Altogether a most impressive and rewarding disc.

As a matter of tactics disregarding the printed order of the works, the second disc opens in the most effective way with a joyous performance of the ever-invigorating E major *Preludio*. At once we can recognise Podger's splendid rhythmic and tonal vitality (not merely Bach's marked terraced dynamics but pulsatingly alive gradations within phrases), her extremely subtle accentuations and harmonic awareness (note her change of colour at the move from E to C sharp major in bar 33), are all within total technical assurances. The *Gavotte en Rondeau* is buoyantly dance-like, and in the most natural way she elaborates its final statement (her stylish ornamentation throughout the Partita is utterly convincing). She takes the *Giga* at a restrained pace that allows of all kinds of tiny rhythmic nuances. Only a rather cut-up performance of the *Loure* stops this being one of the most enjoyable E major Partitas on disc. In the sonatas she shows other sterling qualities. She preserves the shape in the A minor *Grave*'s ornate tangle of notes; she judges to a nicety the balance of the melodic line against the plodding accompanimental quavers of the *Andante*; she imbues the C major's *Adagio* with a hauntingly poetic musing atmosphere, and her lucid part-playing of its *Fuga* could scarcely be bettered. In the *Fuga* of the A minor Sonata, however, she unexpectedly allows herself considerable rhythmic freedom in order to point the structure. The final track is a stunning performance of the C major's closing *Allegro assai* which would bring any audience to its feet.

Sonatas Nos 1-3. Partitas Nos 1-3
Benjamin Schmid *vn*
Arte Nova Classics ② 74321 72113-2 Ⓢ
(133 minutes: DDD). Recorded 1999 ●●

Benjamin Schmid counts Harnoncourt, Végh and Heinrich Schiff as significant musical influences. His Bach, like theirs, uses scholarship to fly. Schmid himself writes of 'telling the story of Bach's harmonic voyage', a priority that registers whenever he allows a harmonic progression to dictate the precise manner of musical gesture (which is most of the time). In the G minor Sonata's opening *Adagio* his sound ranges from a blanched, unwavering line to judiciously gauged vibrato. His chords are tonally generous (he clearly relishes every note) and his 'softly rolled' *arpeggios* allow the music's rich harmonic drift to register. Articulation is exceptionally clean and the Third Partita's dance movements display a winning rhythmic lilt.

Although the D minor Partita's Chaconne clocks up a fairly swift 12'39" (Végh, for one, is slower by two-and-a-half minutes), Schmid balances courtliness and architecture in ideal proportions. The three sonata fugues work extremely well, the C minor being their crowning glory. Schmid alternates sonorous chords with a chirpy approach to shorter, single note-values, always consistently and with a mastery of tonal colouring. Tempos are generally swifter than the 'traditional' norm (though not dissimilar to various period performances), repeats are played and although some might question the odd slowing here or speeding there, most listeners will find Schmid's readings singularly stimulating and imaginative.

This is remarkable music-making and the silly asking price makes purchase truly mandatory – whether for comparison with better-known alternatives or for a first-time encounter with these magnificent works.

Sonatas Nos 1-3. Partitas Nos 1-3 H
Nathan Milstein *vn*
EMI mono ② ZMS7 64793-2 (114 minutes: AAD). Ⓜ
Recorded 1950s ●●

Nathan Milstein was an assured, craftsman-like player with a silken tone, a superb technique and a stylish turn-of-phrase. His recording career began in the 1930s and spanned six decades. Technically and musically, Milstein always remained the stylish aristocrat, and to witness his traversal of Bach's Sonatas and Partitas is breathtaking. His natural brilliance, intelligence, sensitivity to inflexion and feeling for structure mark these mid-1950s solo Bach recordings as truly exceptional – and rather more assured than his 1971 re-makes for DG. Perhaps the high points are the B minor Partita and C major Sonata, the former with its judiciously phrased dance movements, the latter with a dazzlingly resilient fugue and a *Largo* that represents Milstein at his most deeply poetic. The transfers are excellent, and the annotation is informative and well written.

Sonatas Nos 1-3. Partitas Nos 1-3
Itzhak Perlman *vn*
EMI ② CDS7 49483-2 (143 minutes: DDD) Ⓕ
Recorded 1986-87 ●●

These works are brutally difficult to play, not least in securing accurate intonation and in minimising the disruptive effect of hacking out the three- and four-note chords but, given today's Olympian standards, technical shortcomings may be tolerated only in performances that are musically relevatory. Technically Perlman is beyond reproach; chords are traversed deftly and in the *Adagio* of Sonata No 3 skilfully subjugated to the melodic line, and his differentiation between marked *pianos* and *fortes* is very clear. There is brilliance in the faster movements, delicacy in the *galanteries*, and except perhaps for the Allemande of Partita No 2, grave expressiveness in the slower ones; stylistic misfits are far fewer than those of, say, Sándor Végh or Nathan Milstein (1971), and all repeats are offered – usually with some changes of dynamics. Bach with a fair degree of gloss maybe, but a version by one of today's greatest violinists that is justly popular.

Additional recommendations

Sonatas Nos 1-3. Partitas Nos 1-3 (arr Galbraith)
Galbraith *gtr*
Delos ② DE3232 (119 minutes: DDD: 12/98). Ⓕ

Paul Galbraith's embellishments are impeccable. In sum, these thoughtful and majestic performances are strongly recommended, and not only to lovers of the guitar.

Partita No 2 – Chaconne in D minor (arr Busoni)
Couplings: **Schumann** Kreisleriana **Beethoven** Rondos
Kissin *pf*
RCA Victor 09026 68911-2 (63 minutes: DDD: 12/98) Ⓕ

Evgeni Kissin's Bach/Busoni Chaconne is grand and thrilling in its allure; the instrument is taken to its limits.

Solo Cello Suites

No 1 in G, BWV1007; **No 2** in D minor, BWV1008; **No 3** in C, BWV1009; **No 4** in E flat, BWV1010; **No 5** in C minor, BWV1011; **No 6** in D, BWV1012

Solo Cello Suites Nos 1-6
Pierre Fournier *vc*
DG The Originals ② 449 711-2GOR2 Ⓜ
(139 minutes: ADD). Recorded 1961-63 ●●●

Of all the great cellists, Pierre Fournier came closer to the heart of the music than almost any other. He seems to have possessed all the virtues of his fellow cellists without yielding to any of their self-indulgences. He could be brilliant in execution – his technique was second to none, as he proves throughout this set – profound in utterance, aristocratic in poise and wonderfully coherent in his understanding of Bach's articulation and phrases.

We need look no further than the *Prelude* of the First Suite in G major to find the supreme artistry which characterises each and every moment of these performances. There are very occasionally notes which fail to reach their centre but they are few and far between and Fournier's intonation compares favourably with that of some of his virtuoso companions. Fournier's rubato is held tightly in rein and when he does apply it, it is in the interests of enlivening aspects of Bach's formal writing. He can sparkle too, as he does in many of the faster dance-orientated movements such as courantes, gavottes and bourrées; in the sarabandes, he invariably strikes a note of grandeur coupled with a concentration amounting at times almost to abstraction. Above all, his Bach playing is crowned with an eloquence, a lyricism and a grasp of the music's formal and stylistic content which will not easily be matched.

It is hardly surprising that these readings seem as fresh and as valid today as they did in the 1960s. Out and out purists, poor devils, may not be able to adjust to modern pitch, modern instrument and, in the case of Suites Nos 5 and 6, the wrong instrument, but if that is so they are deserving more of compassion than censure. Fine recorded sound and strongly commended on virtually all counts.

Cello Suites Nos 1-6. Ⓗ
English Suite No 6 in D, BWV811 – Gavotte I; Gavotte II (arr Pollain). Musicalisches Gesangbuch – Komm, süsser Tod, BWV478 (arr Siloti). Violin Sonata, BWV1003 – Andante (arr Siloti). Orchestral Suite No 3 in D, BWV1068 – Air (arr Siloti). Toccata, Adagio and Fugue in C, BWV564 – Adagio
Pablo Casals *vc* with **Nikolai Mednikoff, Blas-Net, Otto Schulf** *pfs*
Naxos Historical mono ② 8 110915/6 Ⓢ
(149 minutes: ADD)
Recorded 1927-39 ●

When these recordings first appeared back in the 1930s and '40s, Bach for solo cello was a singular and esoteric concept. Casals had rediscovered the Suites for modern ears and his probing, albeit highly idiosyncratic, playing was a mandatory recommendation. Indeed, in those days it was the only recommendation. You didn't question it, just as you didn't question Albert Schweitzer's organ Preludes or Edwin Fischer's *48*. Nowadays, with countless period-conscious rivals vying for prominence, Casals the pioneer is viewed as a venerable – if somewhat anachronistic – elder statesman. His achievement is still beyond question, but there will be some listeners who won't like what they hear.

After, say, the elegantly tapered playing of János Starker, Casals can initially sound wilful and ungainly. His bow seems to slice through chords like a meat cleaver. His intonation wanders, and his fingers press down on the strings so forcefully that a note 'pings' even before the bow is drawn. After Starker's rhythmic projection Casals reels and rhapsodises as if blind drunk on expressive freedom.

However, this impression is only transitory. What at first sounds gruff, even off-hand soon registers as boldly assertive. The intonation is not so much 'faulty' as expressively employed (at least for most of the time), and as for those pre-echoing 'pings', they soon cease to matter – much as Glenn Gould's mumbling did years later (Casals's own grunts are rarely audible). Time teaches you that the speaking tone, the poetic *tenutos*, the irresistible lilt in faster dance movements and the varied approach to vibrato were part of a grand musical plan, one that is now cherishable.

Casals makes a singular musical experience out of every movement. There is no formula at work save of the dictates of the precise musical moment, of modulation, phrase connections and pure sound. Try the Courante and Sarabande of the Fifth Suite – muscular resolve followed by profound self-communing. These are the dramatic extremes in Casals's playing, but there are as many nourishing ingredients in between.

Transfer-wise, things could hardly have gone better. True, there is some surface noise, but the sound has considerable realism and the broad contours of Casals's tone are untroubled by excessive filtering. A rival package from Pearl (identical couplings plus a transcription from a Bach-Vivaldi Concerto) reports a fatter cello sound with less well-focused contours. EMI's set offers only the Suites in transfers that, while admirably clear, are rather less natural than Ward Marston's for Naxos.

Solo Cello Suites Nos 1-6
Boris Pergamenschikov *vc*
Hänssler Edition Bachakademie ② 92 120 Ⓕ
(128 minutes: DDD)
Recorded 1998 **OO**

Any worthy recording of Bach's solo cello compositions celebrates the balance of mind and body, prayer and dance, scholarship and unspoiled intuition. One of the most striking features of this set is the lavish way Pergamenschikov ornaments the musical line, usually in a repeat, but always with a convincing sense of style. He is equally adept at charting the precise mood of each movement, making free with the various preludes (usually at a fairly fast tempo), pointing courantes with a lively *staccato*, drawing expressive weight from the sarabandes without obscuring their rhythmic profile and dancing through the various minuets and gigues. His phrasing is supple, flexible and musically varied, his use of vibrato subtly expressive within the parameters of period style. There is a noticeable lilt to much of the phrasing, and an expressive *legato* that is unhampered by excessive vibrato. Pergamenschikov indulges a genuine sense of play and knows intuitively where to hold back, where to insert a tiny pause, and where to lean on the beginning of the bar. The recordings are excellent. Pergamenschikov should henceforth take his rightful place among the top modern recommendations of this exalted repertoire.

Solo Cello Suites Nos 1-6
Mstislav Rostropovich *vc*
EMI ② CDS5 55363-2 (147 minutes: DDD) Ⓕ
Recorded 1991

'No thing in the world is more precious to me than these Suites.' Rostropovich even sought out the church of Vézélay in which to record them at last, and he certainly makes a highly personal testament of them. He values the church for its Bach-like 'severity of line and rhythm', and the playing of Casals for its rhapsody. The latter object of reverence seems to exert the stronger pull on his own interpretations. Those in tune with Rostropovich's own idiosyncrasies and generosity of spirit will find much to delight them here: the subtly shifting gradations of tone in the Sarabande of the Fifth Suite, as its even tread makes light of its large melodic leaps; or the fine tracery, scarcely ballasted by resonance, in the Prelude of the First. Viewed in comparison with two other rhapsodically-inclined readings – the earlier, wide-eyed mellifluous Yo-Yo Ma and the rhetorical, granite-hewn Mischa Maisky – Rostropovich's performances seem as volatile and quick-changing as the English weather. Following a beautifully controlled Sarabande in the Second Suite, each note held back, though never held down in sorrow, and the melody modulating subtly in and out of half *voce*, comes a most ungainly Minuet, in which Rostropovich becomes bogged down, and his lack of rhythmic incisiveness makes for a laboured Gigue.

He writes copiously in the accompanying notes on his responses to the Suites, viewing each one, it seems, as a mood-poem. The first, he feels, epitomises 'Lightness', the second 'Sorrow and intensity', the third 'Brilliance' – and so on. This at times seems to create circumscribed expectations and to blunt the sharp strength of the music's abstraction. Having dubbed the Fourth Suite 'Majestic', Rostropovich makes its Prelude seem effortful, with huge steps between each interval. Similarly, in the Fifth Suite, Rostropovich concentrates entirely on its C minor 'Darkness' of pitch and tone, overlooking the high stylised Frenchified dotted rhythms which pervade it and give it shape and contour as well as density. From 'Darkness' to 'Sunlight' in the Sixth Suite. Again, the image seems to drive Rostropovich to a somewhat fractious perpetuum mobile of a Prelude, neither as lithe nor as true of intonation as Ma's, and with a lot of huffing and puffing to sustain any sense of legato between the multiple stops of the Sarabande. A great devotion, a great commitment, and not a little fear, too, rises out of these performances. For some the presence of Rostropovich – rather like that of Maisky too – may begin to smother that of Bach, whereas Ma, within the same stylistic parameters, achieves a happier equipoise.

Solo Cello Suites Nos 1-6 **P**
Pieter Wispelwey *vc*
Channel Classics ② CCS12298 (140 minutes: DDD) Ⓕ
Recorded 1998 **OO**

Netherlands-born cellist, Pieter Wispelwey, is equally at home on baroque and modern instruments. These performances are carefully prepared, beautifully executed and most eloquently expressed. The instruments, too, sound well, Wispelwey having chosen an early 18th-century cello by Barak Norman for the first five Suites, and a five-stringed violoncello piccolo by an unidentified craftsman for the special requirements of the Sixth.

Wispelwey is an imaginative player with a highly developed sense of fantasy. These qualities are as welcome in his performances of Bach as they are to be treated with circumspection in his almost entirely fanciful written introduction to the music. Preludes come across especially well since it is in these wonderfully varied opening movements, with their rhetorical diversity, that the performer can give rein most freely to his or her most natural conversational inflexions. And he makes the most of that thrilling climax at the peak of a chromatic accent through a full scale and a half. Sarabandes are profound and reflective without being weighty, and allemandes graceful and substantial. The *galanteries*, by contrast, are lightly bowed and redolent of playful and demonstrative gestures. That, to an extent, is true also of the courantes, while the gigues are firmly projected, full-toned and splendidly robust.

Wispelwey's set of Bach's Cello Suites, then, is deserving of praise. If you are familiar with the gruff grandeur of Pablo Casals, or the aristocratic nobility of Fournier, then these performances will throw an entirely different light on the music, more conversational and with airier discourse. You may never want to be without the two earlier sets, but Wispelwey's version sits comfortably on the uppermost range of the period-instrument performance ladder.

Lute Suites

Lute Suites – G minor, BWV995; E minor, BWV996; C minor, BWV997; E, BWV1006a. Prelude, Fugue and Allegro in E flat, BWV998. Prelude in C minor, BWV999. Fugue in G minor, BWV1000

Stephan Schmidt *gtr*

Naïve Classique ② V4861 (98 minutes: DDD) Ⓕ

Recorded 1999 ●●●

Whether or not the description of these as 'lute' works is justified has long been a matter for debate, and in their annotation Stephan Schmidt and Claude Chauvel inevitably fail to resolve the matter, though they lean more in the direction of 'yes' than most. In a sense it matters little, for the works have been performed and recorded on a variety of other plucked-string instruments – harpsichord and lute-harpsichord as well as guitar – in exemplary fashion. The 'standard' six-string guitar is a baritone instrument, but its lowest register is not extended enough to avoid the need for compromises; accordingly guitars with more strings (the extra ones at the bass end) have been in use for over 30 years. Göran Söllscher's DG recordings on an 11-string alto guitar (1983 and 1981/84) remain as fresh as they were then. Now Schmidt, using 10 strings, sets a new benchmark with this magnificent set. The extra four strings give firmer bass and more resonant bass lines, as did Söllscher's five, and free the player's left hand from the restriction of having to hold many of them down.

Schmidt's touch is happily light in the *galanteries* and in the Loure of BWV1006*a*, but there is gravity in the unhurried sarabandes – such variations apply not only to pace but to spirit, too. He knows when to embellish (which he does with elegance) and when not. His *rubato* 'bends' a little more than Söllscher's and he is less conservative in his approach to embellishment – but attitudes to such matters have since eased. If there is a better version of these works on any kind of guitar in terms of content and recording quality we have yet to hear it.

Italian Concerto

Italian Concerto in F, BWV971. Capriccios – sopra la lontananza del suo fratello dilettissimo in B flat, BWV992; in E, BWV993. Duets, BWV802-805. French Overture in B minor, BWV831

Angela Hewitt *pf*

Hyperion CDA67306 (69 minutes: DDD) Ⓕ

Recorded 2000 ●●

If you enjoy Bach on the piano, and may merciful heavens grant you enlightenment if you don't, here is an attractive recital of five varied pieces or suites of pieces, familiar and not so familiar, played with her expected intelligence and finish and not a little verve. In her very readable introduction, Hewitt quotes a contemporary review of the *Italian* Concerto describing Bach not only as a great master but as someone 'who has almost alone taken possession of the clavier', and whose compositions are exceedingly difficult to play 'because the efficiency of his own limbs sets his standards'.

They still are, and Hewitt conveys the feeling that the challenges are not just to be met but should be sensed as integral to successful performance. By giving the quick numbers plenty of pace she makes the music sound difficult in the right way. No question of hustling them along, of course not, but rather of touching the core of the rhythmic energy and of making all the lines, throughout the texture, directional and lively. Hewitt's is not a monumental Bach, rooted to the spot, but one which makes us curious as to what lies around the next corner. The brilliant outer movements of the *Italian* Concerto, the long fugal section of the *French* Overture, the second and fourth of the Duets (those extraordinary studies in two-part writing) are all successes of her musical dynamic and high-stepping style. And the Echo movement of the *French* Overture (track 28) has a positively theatrical allure, like something out of Rameau – wonderful!

She cannot disguise the fact, however, that some of the movements in this great suite 'in the French style' lie uneasily on the piano, especially when the sonorities characteristic of a two-manual harpsichord are transcribed as if for a piano without sustaining pedal. If only she would allow herself a dab of it now and then;

the music needs to hang in the air a bit, and the 18th-century harpsichord was, after all, an instrument of mass as well as point, richer in colour and weight of sound than Hewitt's pencil-lines and sometimes rather brittle and over-articulated manner suggest.

On the other hand, her characterisation of the two early Capriccios in terms of the modern piano is a tour de force – sparky, fresh, as if improvised. The greatness of the rest of the music here may put them in the shade, a little, but they are delightful. Bach aged 17, trying his hand at programme music? Well, the Capriccio 'on the departure of his beloved brother' remained his only example of it, but it is a reminder too that there was nothing he couldn't do. A stimulating disc, and beautiful sound.

Keyboard Partitas

No 1 in B flat, BWV825; **No 2** in C minor, BWV826; **No 3** in A minor, BWV827; **No 4** in D, BWV828; **No 5** in G, BWV829; **No 6** in E minor, BWV830

Keyboard Partitas Nos 1-6
Angela Hewitt *pf*
Hyperion ② CDA67191/2 (143 minutes: DDD) Ⓕ
Recorded 1996-97 ●

After ages without any recordings of the Partitas on the piano, along comes Angela Hewitt and saves the situation, effortlessly eclipsing all competitors. If Bach is to be played on the piano, this is the kind of way to do it. Inherent in all her playing is a rhythmic vitality, always under control, that sweeps one along with its momentum, subtly varied articulation, dynamics that follow the natural rise or fall of phrases without exaggerations, an appreciation of Bach's harmonic tensions, an ability to differentiate between the strength of contrapuntal lines, and an unfailing clarity of texture. This is a sane and sensible interpretation, deeply musicianly and devoid of eccentricity. Her attitude, rather like Toscanini's, is to accept the text *com' è scritto* and then to make legitimate adjustments, so we get double-dotting and assimilation of rhythms. Technically she is immaculate, with the cleanest possible ornaments. In the great E minor Sarabande Hewitt is justifiably emotional, without becoming soggy: only in the first half of the A minor Allemande is there a hint of coyness. No, the whole disc gives unalloyed pleasure.

Keyboard Partitas – Nos 2, 4 and 5
Richard Goode *pf*
Nonesuch 7559-79483-2 (72 minutes: DDD) Ⓕ
Recorded 1998 ●

Richard Goode approaches this music with the insights of a performer steeped in Mozart, Beethoven and classical culture in general. His Bach has a profound, self-communing quality, though his technical command of the notes – his sense of contrapuntal perspective – is second to none. He occasionally de-synchronizes chords to heighten a harmonic effect, but his pedalling is judicious and his employment of dynamics reveals a total understanding of phrasal and contrapuntal relationships.

He creates an objective, orderly space in these Partitas, a space pervaded with light and intelligence. The overture to the Fourth Partita, placed first on the recording, announces the artist's intentions: this is grand music for small rooms, music in which larger baroque gestures have been refined and simplified into a more intimate rhetoric. He grabs the listener's attention with a wonderful sleight of hand, by maintaining the overture's formal sweep, yet keeping it small and direct. These intimacies are sustained throughout the recording, which is deeply private yet never agonisingly introspective. The emotional gravity is in the Sarabandes, and the Aria of the Partita No 4, which all share a sweetly lyrical, *bel canto* sense of line, and a haunting vulnerability.

There is something strikingly courteous about Goode's approach, the courtesy of honest, spontaneous expression tempered by textual fidelity and an impulse to underscore Bach's beauties without pedantry. This recording presents a single and thoroughgoing vision of Bach's music; it has a robust honesty and it breathes clean, fresh air and that's enough to make it highly recommended.

Keyboard Preludes

Keyboard Partita No 1 in B flat, BWV825. Five Preludes, BWV939-43. Prelude in C minor, BWV999. Fugue in C, BWV953. Three Minuets, BWV841-43. French Suite No 5 in G, BWV816. Fughetta in C minor, BWV961. Clavier-Büchlein for W F Bach – Preludes: C, BWV924; D, BWV925; D minor, BWV926; F, BWV927; F, BWV928; G minor, BWV930. Concerto in F, BWV971, 'Italian Concerto'. Anna Magdalena Notenbuch – Minuets: G, BWVAnh114; G minor, BWVAnh115 Ⓟ
Richard Egarr *hpd*
EMI Debut CDZ5 69700-2 (78 minutes: DDD) Ⓑ
Recorded 1995 ●●

Richard Egarr's programme is an attractive one in which three major solo harpsichord works – the Partita (BWV825), the *French Suite* (BWV816), and the *Italian Concerto* (BWV971) – are interspersed with Preludes, Minuets and two Fugues from the Kellner Collection, the *Clavier-Büchlein* for Wilhelm Friedemann Bach, 'the son I love, the one who fills me with joy', and the *Notenbuch* for Bach's second wife, Anna Magdalena. The character of Egarr's instrument, a copy by Joel Katzman of a 1638 Ruckers, has been effectively recorded, capturing its warm timbre in an intimate, domestic-sounding ambience.

Egarr's B flat Partita is an unhurried affair, reflective in its Prelude and Allemande and rhythmically supple. Some readers may not at once respond to the extent to which he leans on notes, thereby breaking up that strict regularity of pulse that used to be the order of the day. His articulation and rhythmic flexibility are both illuminating and communicative. The music breathes, and with each breath comes a natural pause in the declamation allowing for rhetorical gesture and a feeling for scansion. Just occasionally in the Sarabande phrases are a little too clipped and skimped over, but such instances, both here and in the *French Suite*, are both few and far between. Each of the little Preludes and Minuets is lovingly shaped and played with a sense of affection for, and understanding of, the music's poetry. In short this is an outstanding disc, both for Egarr's technically accomplished playing and for his delicacy of feeling.

Keyboard Sonatas

Keyboard Sonatas – D minor, BWV964; A minor, BWV965; C, BWV966; G, BWV968. Fugue in B flat, BWV954 P
Andreas Staier *hpd*
Teldec 3984-21461-2 (77 minutes: DDD) Ⓕ
Recorded 1997 ●●

Some readers may be surprised to hear that Bach ever composed sonatas – not suites, but *sonatas* – for harpsichord. Well, actually he didn't. What he did do – if indeed it was he and not his eldest son – was transcribe his BWV1003 A minor Solo Violin Sonata (transposing it down a fifth) and the first movement of the BWV1005 C major (putting it down to G); and, more certainly, he himself adapted a number of movements from the *Hortus musicus* suites (for two violins, gamba and continuo) by Johann Adam Reincken, the aged master to whom, as a teenager, he had journeyed to Hamburg to hear. Taking his cue from Bach, Andreas Staier has transcribed the remaining movements of the C major Violin Sonata and added three movements to the C major Reincken adaptation – a suite, be it noted, not a sonata.

Before purists throw up their hands in horror at Staier's temerity, let them listen to Bach's own startlingly audacious harpsichord version of BWV1005, with offbeat chords, surprising chromaticism and rolling left-hand arpeggios. In his own treatment of that work's Fuga, Staier is very free but most convincingly idiomatic: one would never guess that it was a transcription. Bach's arrangements of Reincken largely adhere to the originals but amplify the fugues by adding episodes, as is also the case in the A minor Gigue. Staier's playing is notable for the crispness and variety of his articulation and – improvisatory Reincken preludes apart – the vitality of his rhythmic drive. A splendid disc.

Das wohltemperierte Klavier

48 Preludes and Fugues – **Book 1** BWV846-69; **Book 2** BWV870-93

Das wohltemperierte Klavier, Books 1 and 2 P
Kenneth Gilbert *hpd*
Archiv Produktion ④ 413 439-2AH4 Ⓕ
(256 minutes: DDD). Recorded 1983

In Book 1 there are virtually no markings and so the performer carries heavy responsibility for phrasing and articulation. Gilbert's blend of scholarship and technique with artistic sensibility makes for notably convincing, often poetic playing. The D minor Prelude is one of many instances where his interpretation haunts the memory. Gilbert's vital rhythmic sense and love of refinement are qualities in his artistry which can be strongly felt throughout this vast project. Some readers may feel that he is comparatively unadventurous in his registration – others, for example, make a greater point of differentiation through instrumental colour – but it is one of the features of Gilbert's performance that is particularly praiseworthy, since he clearly and effectively achieves his contrasts through interpretation, renouncing the facility to emphasise them by more artificial means. In textural clarity he yields nothing to his competitors in this repertoire and, in short, arrives at a solution which is refined, lyrical and sometimes dazzlingly virtuosic, as in the Prelude in B flat, BWV866.

The acoustic of the Musée de Chartres, where the *48* were recorded, is pleasantly resonant. Gilbert plays a 17th-century Flemish harpsichord enlarged first by Blanchet and then by Taskin in the following century. A satisfying achievement and an important issue.

Das wohltemperierte Klavier, Books 1 and 2 H
Rosalyn Tureck *pf*
DG mono ④ 463 305-2GH4 (296 minutes: DDD) Ⓕ
Recorded 1954 ●●●

Here is a performance of a matchless wit, musical grace and eloquence; playing as vivid and life-affirming as any on record, a magical interaction of scholarship and imaginative brio. Tureck can conjure a mystical stillness or a corruscating play of light and shade, of *crescendos* and *decrescendos* that can make the plain-sailing of others seem tentative and inadequate, and much time-honoured wisdom and tradition stale and archaic (try the Third Prelude from Book 1). Here is no 'old wig' but a voice of timeless richness and vitality, one that made Schoenberg declare Bach to be 'the first 12-tone composer'. The devotional flow of the 22nd Prelude in B flat minor is offered with an immaculate and indeed phenomenal pianistic authority and a mastery that allows for a total artistic liberation and unimpeded way to the music's very heart or poetic essence. In each unfailing instance the precise weight and timbre of every polyphonic strand seems to have been sifted and defined a hundred times only to be resolved into a dialogue or continuum as natural as it is piquant and thought-provoking. Early in her career Tureck replaced a highly successful, if more conventional, concert career with a single-minded devotion to a composer who for her makes all others dispensable. Skilfully remastered, lavishly illustrated and annotated, such work is beyond price, deserving, in the words of that most august publication *The Record Guide*, 'a heavenful of stars'.

Das wohltemperierte Klavier H
8 110651/2: Book 1
8 110653/4: Book 2
Edwin Fischer *pf*
Naxos Historical mono ② 8 110651/2 and 8 110653/4
(107 and 126 minutes: ADD) Ⓢ
Recorded 1933-36 ●●

Edwin Fischer's 1933-36 HMV set of Bach's *48* was the first recording by a pianist of the set, and it remains the finest of all. Fischer might well have agreed with András Schiff that Bach is the 'most romantic of all composers', for his superfine musicianship seems to live and breathe in another world, ether or ambience. His sonority is as ravishing as it is apt, never beautiful for its own sake, and graced with a pedal technique so subtle that it results in a light and shade, a subdued sparkle or pointed sense of repartee that eludes lesser artists. Again, no matter what complexity Bach throws at him, Fischer resolves it with a disarming poise and limpidity, qualities as natural as they are profound.

All this is a far cry from, say, Glenn Gould's egotism in the *48*, or the sort of performances that can make genius a pejorative term. Fischer – a blessedly naive artist who told his students to forget 'the material, working world and be on intimate terms with trees, clouds and winds' – showed a deep humility before great art, making the singling out of one or another of his performances an impertinence. Impossible, however, not to mention in passing his ethereal start to the set (that light, bouncing *staccato* above a singing bass-line in No 1), or the disconsolate, phantom yet ordered voice he achieves in No 4. The contrapuntal flow of No 7 – initially grand, then reflective and finally free-wheeling – is realised to perfection, and what a virtuoso play of the elements he recreates in No 15!

In Book 2, you could hardly imagine a more seraphic utterance in No 3, later contrasted with the most skittish *allegro* reply. The list goes on indefinitely, dissolving the supposed barriers between one form of music and another: 'baroque', 'classical', 'romantic', even 'impressionist', become terms of convenience rather than accuracy once you have heard Fischer's Bach. He did, indeed, possess a touch with 'the strength and softness of a lion's velvet paw', and there are few recordings from which today's generation of pianists could learn so much; could absorb by osmosis, so to speak, his way of transforming a supposedly learned tome into a fountain of limitless magic and resource. Here, then, is Fischer at his most sublimely poised and unruffled, at bargain price in beautifully restored sound.

Das wohltemperierte Klavier
CDA67301/2: Book 1
CDA67303/4: Book 2
Angela Hewitt *pf*
Hyperion ② CDA67301/2 and CDA67303/4 Ⓕ
(117 and 148 minutes: DDD). Recorded 1997-99 ●●

Admirers of Canadian pianist Angela Hewitt's lightly articulated and elegantly phrased Bach playing will not be disappointed by this recording. These qualities characterise the playing of each and every one of these profoundly didactic yet sublimely poetic pieces. In respect of her restrained use of the sustaining pedal, her consequently clearly spoken articulation, and the resultant lucidity of musical thought, Hewitt brings to mind those still controversial recorded performances of Edwin Fischer. Hewitt certainly sounds more comfortable in a studio than Fischer ever did, and her technique is more consistently disciplined than Fischer's was under these circumstances. Her reflective view of the more inwardly-looking Fugues, such as the lyrical one in E flat minor, is most attractive. Taut, but with a suppleness that is entirely devoid of stiffness, this is indeed cogent and gracefully beautiful playing of a high order. Some readers may sense, from time to time, an overtly intense element of subjective thought in her understanding of the music, a quality which seems to be endorsed by occasional references in her lively, illuminating and detailed introduction, to Bach's 'sense of inner peace', and so on. However, to conclude on a thoroughly positive and enthusiastic note, these are performances of Book 1 that you will want to hear many times over. The recording and instrument sound well, too.

Hewitt's Book 2 of the *48* is a delight to both ear and mind. While there is nothing in the least Technicolored about her interpretations – everything is in the best of taste and free from all exhibitionism – they are conceived in consciously pianistic terms. There are subtle tonal nuances, natural rises and falls of dynamics, well-defined differentiation of contrapuntal lines and appreciation of the expressive implications of Bach's chromaticisms. All this is at once apparent in the very first C major Prelude, which is also sensitively phrased with flexibility; but it is when she comes to the Fugue – light, airy and positively playful – that her vitality and freshness of approach are so striking. Throughout her playing of these preludes and fugues – several longer, more mature and more demanding than those of Book 1 – there is a sense of unhurried poise, with rhythm that flows. The air of tranquillity she can produce is underlined by her frequent adoption of very quiet openings, many of which then take on a warmer tone towards the end – even the E major Fugue, which Landowska labelled 'combative', is handled quietly, yet she is able to sound contemplative (as in the E major Fugue) without lapsing into Tureckian reverentiality. When brio is called for, as in the C sharp or F major Gigue Fugues, this is buoyantly forthcoming. Her varied articulation maintains interest at all times, and the springiness she brings to the E flat and F sharp minor Fugues is most engaging. Just occasionally Bach's more intense movements tempt her into emotional rubatos which, though musically affecting, take Bach out of his century, and not everyone will care for the big *allargandos* she makes at the ends of some of the earlier movements. Otherwise these are musicianly and imaginative performances.

Das wohltemperierte Klavier – Book 1
Evgeni Koroliov *pf*
Tacet ② TACET93 Ⓕ
(129 minutes: DDD) ⭘

No music is more impervious to the vagaries of interpretation than Bach's. Play his keyboard music on a piano and it remains obstinately in character. Proponents of the harpsichord may disagree, but musicologist Eva Badura-Skoda has thrown a spanner in the works by arguing strongly that Bach, in his Leipzig years, extensively used fortepianos in an effort to help Silbermann perfect these instruments. So a pianoforte was the next step, after all. Edwin Fischer used it in the first recording of the *48*, but his approach and emendations have their detractors. Koroliov's only audible emendation is an extra note in the bass at bar 28 of the C minor Prelude. Otherwise he sticks to the text and his decorations at the endings of a couple of pieces are well within current knowledge of authentic practice.

What intrigues and impresses is that, unlike most pianists, Koroliov largely ignores the sustaining pedal. He often prefers to let fingers, rather than feet, dictate colour; and his fingers are capable of a variety of touch. They can also project the notes with pinpoint velocity which, when wrongly applied, turns the G major Fugue into a mechanical exercise. This is a serious miscalculation, but it is the only one. The instrument is closely miked, which can lead to moments of discomfort, for instance in the A minor Fugue which is starkly presented. But Koroliov isn't always uncompromising, and the B flat minor Prelude offers an example of his sensitivity to the changes within a single work, from rigorous beginnings to a resigned ending. The composer's intention, to prepare the listener for the sepulchral quality of the companion Fugue, is respected.

Koroliov reserves his best for the last pair for which, unusually, Bach added markings, *Andante* and *Largo* respectively. Unusually, too, the Prelude is in binary form, although Koroliov repeats only the first half. But his performance of the Fugue marries tension to an inexorable flow that portrays the structure as an imposing edifice. Purists may quibble at the very slow tempo but this is a tour de force.

English Suites, BWV806-11

Six English Suites, BWV806-11
Glenn Gould *pf*
Sony Classical Glenn Gould Edition ② SM2K52606 Ⓜ
(112 minutes: ADD). Recorded 1971-73 ⭘

No more original genius of the keyboard has existed than Glenn Gould, but this can lead to drawbacks as well as thrilling advantages. You may, for instance, sense how Gould can sacrifice depth of feeling for a relentless and quixotic sense of adventure. Yet love it or deride it, every bar of these lovingly remastered discs (the hiatus is explained in some riveting accompanying notes) tingles with *joie de vivre* and an unequalled force and vitality.

Try the opening of the First Suite. Is such freedom glorious or maddening, or is the way the odd note is nonchalantly flicked in the following sustained argument a naughty alternative to Bach's intention? The pizzicato bass in the second Double from the same Suite is perhaps another instance of an idiosyncrasy bordering on whimsy, an enlivenment or rejuvenation that at least remains open to question. But listen to him in virtually any of the sarabandes from the Suites and you will find a tranquillity and equilibrium that can silence such criticism and even at his most piquant and outrageous his playing remains, mysteriously, all of a piece. The Gigue from the Second Suite is taken at a spanking *Presto* and the Prelude from the Third Suite is a gloriously true *vivace*, never rigid or merely metronomic. The fiercely chromatic, labyrinthine argument concluding the Fifth Suite is thrown off with a unique brio, one of those moments when you realise how Gould can lift Bach out of all possible time-warps and make him one of music's truest modernists.

Toccata in C minor, BWV911. Partita No 2 in C minor, BWV826. English Suite No 2 in A minor, BWV807
Martha Argerich *pf*
DG The Originals 463 604-2GOR (50 minutes: ADD) Ⓜ
Recorded 1979 ⭘

The reissue of Martha Argerich's recordings, their reappearance in this or that format, testifies to the unique and enduring nature of her magisterial temperament and musicianship. This Bach recital, first issued in 1980, is now revived on DG's The Originals. Admirers will of course have heard Argerich in the Second Partita, on the wing, so to speak, in a superlative live performance dating from 1978-79 (and with the Bourée from the Second *English* Suite for an encore) on EMI. Yet even they will surely admit that these slightly later studio recordings carry an extraordinary authority and panache.

Argerich's attack in the C minor Toccata could hardly be bolder or more incisive, a classic instance of virtuosity all the more clear and potent for being so firmly but never rigidly controlled. Here, as elsewhere, her discipline is no less remarkable than her unflagging brio and relish of Bach's glory. Again, in the Second Partita, her playing is quite without those excesses or mannerisms that too often pass for authenticity, and at 2'14" in the *Andante* immediately following the Sinfonie she is expressive yet clear and precise, her following *Allegro* a marvel of high-speed yet always musical bravura. True, some may question her way with the Courante from the Second *English* Suite, finding it hard-driven, even overbearing, yet Argerich's eloquence in the following sublime Sarabande creates its own hypnotic authority. Her final Gigue is a triumph of irrepressible vitality yet, throughout, you are reminded of the comprehensiveness of Argerich's Bach, the way his alternations of robust and interior musical thinking are so tellingly and vividly characterised.

It only remains to add that the dynamic range of these towering, intensely musical performances has been excellently captured by DG.

French Suites, BWV812-17

Six French Suites, BWV812-17
Andrei Gavrilov *pf*
DG ② 445 840-2GH2 (93 minutes: DDD) Ⓕ
Recorded 1993

Bach compiled his *French Suites*, so-called – the composer did not give them this title – towards the end of his Cöthen period and at the beginning of his final appointment at Leipzig. Like others before him, Andrei Gavrilov acknowledges his debt to Glenn Gould, sensing a fellow spirit throwing down the gauntlet and challenging convention at every turn with his fearless mix of directness and idiosyncrasy. Yet as his performances so eloquently convey, there are depths and subtleties in these cosmopolitan Suites which are often erased by Gould's manic determination to redefine the parameters of Bach interpretation. Gavrilov has a way, for instance, of casting light on even the simplest, least polyphonic of the composer's arguments. He may retain some of his former headstrong pugnacity yet in the sarabandes, which like pools of reflection form the nodal and expressive centre of each Suite, he finds an often glorious ease, repose and gently luminous sense of texture. Even those for whom such open-hearted espousal of the modern piano's resources is anachronistic will surely be touched and convinced. The DG sound quality is exemplary.

Six French Suites, BWV812-17. Sonata in D minor, BWV964. Five Preludes, BWV924-28. Prelude in G minor, BWV930. Six Preludes, BWV933-38. Five Preludes, BWV939-43. Prelude in C minor, BWV999. Prelude and Fugue in A minor, BWV894
Angela Hewitt *pf*
Hyperion ② CDA67121/2 (151 minutes: DDD) Ⓕ
Recorded 1995 ●

Even the most out-and-out purists who blench at the thought of Bach on so alien an instrument as the piano (as if Bach himself ever showed any reluctance at transferring his work from one instrument to another!) will find it hard not to be won over by Angela Hewitt's artistry. Eschewing all hieratic pretentiousness on the one hand and self-regarding eccentricities on the other, she gives us Bach performances that are not only admirable in style but marked by poise and what used to be called a 'quiet hand': 'chaste' might not be too fanciful a term, so long as that does not suggest any lack of vitality. There is intelligence in her carefully thought-out phrasing and subtle variety of articulation: gradations of sound are always alive without their becoming precious.

The bulk of this recording is devoted to the *French Suites*. Particularly enjoyable is the lightness of her treatment of the Airs of Nos 2 and 4, the vigour of No 5's Bourrée and the freshness of No 6's Allemande; the extra decorations she adds in repeats everywhere sound properly spontaneous and are in the best of taste; ornaments are always cleanly played and matched up in imitative voices.

Chromatic Fantasia and Fugue, BWV903

Prelude and Fugue in A minor, BWV894. **P**
Chromatic Fantasia and Fugue in D minor, BWV903. Toccatas – C minor, BWV911; D, BWV912. Prelude and Fugue in B minor on a theme of Albinoni, BWV923/951. Fantasia and Fugue in A minor, BWV944. Prelude in C minor, BWV999
Pierre Hantaï *hpd*
Virgin Classics Veritas VC5 45322-2 Ⓕ
(64 minutes: DDD). Recorded 1997 ●●

What connects this miscellany of pieces is that they are all early works of Bach's (although he later revised the *Chromatic Fantasia and Fugue*), none of which was published in his lifetime and of which no autograph manuscripts survive. The vitality and exuberant invention that bubble out of them go far to explain the bewilderment and shock felt by the burghers of Arnstadt and elsewhere at this headstrong and musically daring young man.

It is difficult to imagine the effect on its first hearers of that *Chromatic Fantasia*, with its still astonishing key-shifts. Italian influence on Bach and his interest in his predecessors is exemplified in the B minor Fugue he borrowed from an Albinoni trio sonata, in the process extending it to nearly three times its original length; the multi-sectional Toccata in D curiously combines the improvisational with the fugal; and two of the present works were drawn upon for later compositions – the A minor Fugue, BWV944, became the basis for the BWV543 Fugue for organ, and the BWV894 Prelude and Fugue were lifted wholesale for the Triple Concerto for flute, violin and harpsichord. The fugue in this last is excitingly taken by Hantaï (playing on a copy of a Ruckers) at a breakneck pace, and elsewhere he underlines the young Bach's dashing style by the vigour and thrust of his rhythm. His dazzling runs, and the ferocious energy with which he attacks the *Chromatic Fantasia*, are absolutely electrifying: a performance to put nearly all others in the shade.

Fantasia in C minor, BWV906. 15 Two-Part Inventions, BWV772-86. 15 Three-Part Inventions, BWV787-801. Chromatic Fantasia and Fugue in D minor, BWV903
Angela Hewitt *pf*
Hyperion CDA66746 (63 minutes: DDD) Ⓕ
Recorded 1994 ●

Angela Hewitt's approach may be gleaned from her refreshingly lucid annotation, or simply by listening to what she does. 'A skilful player can [bring out the different voices] with different colours' and 'To be capable of producing a true *legato* without using the pedal will serve a pianist well in any repertoire': Hewitt puts her fingers where her thoughts are. She never upsets the balance of the lines that it is in the nature of the harpsichord to yield, and her economy with the sustaining pedal helps to preserve their clarity.

The two- and three-part *Inventions* are treated as music in their own right, not simply as invaluable exercises; each is given its distinctive character, with a wonderful variety of sensitive touch and shapely rubato that never once threatens to become anachronistic. Her readings of the C minor *Fantasia* and the *Chromatic Fantasia and Fugue* are as eloquent and stimulating as any yet recorded by a harpsichordist.

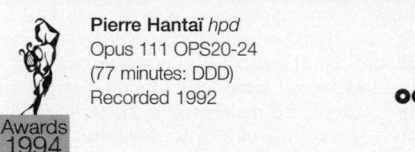

Goldberg Variations, BWV988

Pierre Hantaï *hpd* (P)
Opus 111 OPS20-24
(77 minutes: DDD) (M)
Recorded 1992 ○○○

Awards 1994

Pierre Hantaï's approach to the *Goldberg Variations* is tremendously spirited and energetic but it also exhibits discipline. What is most appealing about this playing, though, is that Hantaï clearly finds the music great fun to perform; some players have been too inclined to make heavy weather over this music. He makes each canon a piece of entertainment while in no sense glossing over Bach's consummate formal mastery. Other movements, such as Var 7 (gigue) and Var 11, effervesce with energy and good humour and he is careful to avoid any display of superficiality. Not for a moment is the listener given the impression that his view of the music is merely skin deep. Indeed, there is a marked concentration of thought in canons such as that at the fourth interval (Var 12). Elsewhere his feeling for the fantasy and poetry of Bach's music is effective and well placed (such as in Var 13). The character of Bruce Kennedy's copy of an early 18th-century instrument by the Berlin craftsman, Michael Mietke is admirably captured by the effectively resonant recorded sound.

Goldberg Variations, BWV988
Murray Perahia *pf*
Sony Classical SK89243 (73 minutes: DDD) (F)
Recorded 2000 ○○○

Murray Perahia's *Goldberg* Variations aren't just colourful, or virtuosic, or thorough in terms of repeats, but profoundly moving as well. Here one senses that what is being played isn't so much 'Bach' as an inevitable musical sequence with a life of its own, music where the themes, harmonies and contrapuntal strands await a mind strong enough to connect them. This Perahia does with sovereign command, and his perceptive programme notes help illuminate the complexion of his thinking.

Rosalyn Tureck was the first recorded Goldbergian to take the structural route and her EMI/Philips set remains among the most cogent of older alternatives. And while Glenn Gould achieves formidable levels of concentration (especially in the second of his two commercial recordings for CBS/Sony), his gargantuan personality – utterly absorbing though it is – does occasionally intrude. Perahia brooks neither distraction nor unwanted mannerism. He invests the *Goldbergs* with the sort of humbling gravitas that Schnabel brings to, say, Schubert's B flat Sonata. Yes, there are fine-tipped details and prominent emphases, but the way themes are traced and followed through suggests a performance where the shape of a phrase is dictated mostly by its place in the larger scheme of things.

The opening Aria is crystalline, lively in tone and with a distinctly singing bass-line. The first repeat is rather softer, whereas the first repeat of the first variation incorporates various added ornaments, a trend that registers time and again through the course of the performance. Middle voices are brought to the fore in Variation 3 and where, in Variation 4, Angela Hewitt (Hyperion) opens boldly and softens for the first repeat, Perahia reverses the process. Variation 7 is crisp and tripping, 16 opens to firmly brushed arpeggios, and Perahia's pianistic gambolling in the snakes and ladders of Variation 23 is delightful. Hewitt is amazingly skilful in the contrary motions of 21 but Perahia keeps a firmer hold on the principal theme and in Variation 25 his classic, sculpted lines conjure a level of purity reminiscent of Lipatti (in Bach generally, that is – not the *Goldbergs* in particular, which Lipatti never recorded).

Perahia never strikes a brittle note and yet his control and projection of rhythm are impeccable. He can trace the most exquisite *cantabile*, even while attending to salient counterpoint, and although clear voicing is a consistent attribute of his performance, so is flexibility. He makes points without labouring them, which is not to deny either the brilliance or the character of his playing. Like Hewitt, he surpasses himself. It's just that in his case the act of surpassing takes him that little bit further. A quite wonderful CD.

Goldberg Variations
Angela Hewitt *pf*
Hyperion CDA67305 (72 minutes: DDD) (F)
Recorded 1999 ○○

Name your leading interpretative preferences in the *Goldberg Variations*, and there's bound to be someone on disc who expresses them. Leaving aside numerous harpsichord versions, the current catalogue is notably rich in colourful piano alternatives. Of the best available options, Rosalyn Tureck holds structure as paramount; Glenn Gould (in his 1981 recording) is strong on rhythmic continuity and contrapuntal clarity and (recently for Hänssler Classic) Evgeni Koroliov is distinctive above all for his imaginative handling of repeats. Hewitt's chosen course is not dissimilar to Koroliov's, at least in principle (both pianists play all the repeats), but her manner of playing is entirely different. Two things strike you more or less from the start: first, that she can summon many dynamic grades simultaneously; and second, that her variations between repeats are not restricted to matters of voicing. For example, in Variation 13, she accelerates her phrases as if caught on a spontaneous impulse, then relaxes for the response (0'32"). When she plays the variation's first half again (1'08") she significantly modifies her tone and *rubato*, then opts for a more formal approach to the second half. All this in just over four and a half minutes!

Her mastery of the keyboard is exemplary. She can launch an elegant *staccato* or allow one voice to weave an ivy-like thread, while others argue above it. Beyond a seamless account of the pivotal 25th variation, Hewitt rattles off manic trills in 23 and favours a grand, free-wheeling approach for 29. Koroliov treats the same sequence (Vars 26-30) as a sort of exultant catharsis after the emotional rigours of the 'Black Pearl'. Both performances are pianistically imposing, but Hewitt is the subtler colourist and her recording is superior. She has never made a better CD. Strongly recommended.

Goldberg Variations
Glenn Gould *pf*
Sony Classical Glenn Gould Edition SMK52619 Ⓜ
(51 minutes: DDD). Recorded 1981 ●●●

This truly astonishing performance was recorded 26 years after Gould's legendary 1955 disc (see below). Gould was not in the habit of re-recording but a growing unease with that earlier performance made him turn once again to a timeless masterpiece and try, via a radically altered outlook, for a more definitive account.

By his own admission he had, during those intervening years, discovered 'slowness' or a meditative quality far removed from flashing fingers and pianistic glory. And it is this 'autumnal repose' that adds such a deeply imaginative dimension to Gould's unimpeded clarity and pin-point definition. The Aria is now mesmerically slow.

The tremulous confidences of Variation 13 in the 1955 performance give way to something more forthright, more trenchantly and determinedly voiced, while Var 19's previously light and dancing measures are humorously slow and precise. Var 21 is painted in the boldest of oils, so to speak, and most importantly of all, Landowska's 'black pearl' (Var 25) is far less romantically susceptible than before, has an almost confrontational assurance.

The Aria's return, too, is overwhelming in its profound sense of solace and resolution. This is surely the finest of Gould's recordings.

Goldberg Variations[a]. 🄷
Das wohltemperierte Klavier, Book 2 – No 33 in E; No 38 in F sharp minor
Glenn Gould *pf*
Sony Glenn Gould Edition mono SMK52594 Ⓜ
(46 minutes: ADD). Item marked [a] recorded 1955 ●

Gould's pianistic skills have been universally and freely acknowledged, but his musical vision has elicited a range of critical response that has few parallels in this century. The view that Bach was a mere mathematical genius and little more has long passed, but it has its echoes in Gould's approach; he was fascinated by the structure of the music and was supremely skilful in showing the Jacquard-loom patterns woven by its contrapuntal threads.

Every structural detail is exposed with crystal clarity but, switching metaphors, what is revealed is a marvellously designed and executed building, inhabited only by a caretaker. An overall time of 38 minutes does not seem unreasonable for the *Goldberg Variations* (here shorn of every repeat) but the statistic is misleading: many variations pass at breakneck speeds. As an exposition of the music's mechanism this is a remarkable performance but, despite occasional intrusions of sing-along and sparing use of the pedals (music first, pianism second), it says little of Bach's humanity.

Two Fugues from the *48* extend the playing time to the lower limit of respectability. Neither is hurried and No. 33 proceeds with the solemnity that some others perceived to be its due. The sound quality of the recordings (the 'youngest' is 45 years old) is impressive, but overall this is probably of archival rather than definitive interest.

Organ Fantasias and Fugues

Fantasias and Fugues – C minor, BWV537; G minor, BWV542; C minor, BWV562; G, BWV572. Preludes and Fugues – D, BWV532; F minor, BWV534; A, BWV536; G, BWV541; A minor, BWV543; B minor, BWV544; C, BWV545; C minor, BWV546; C, BWV547; E minor, BWV548, 'Wedge'; E flat, BWV552, 'St Anne'
Christopher Herrick *org*
Hyperion ② CDA66791/2. (150 minutes: DDD) Ⓕ
Recorded on the organ of the Jesuitenkirche, Lucerne, Switzerland in 1993 ●●

These 15 works constitute some of the finest and most important music ever written for the organ. They are such mainstays of the repertory that no serious lover of organ music could consider a world without them. Herrick's performances are authoritative, scholarly and perceptive, but if that were all it would merely be putting Bach on a pedestal, making him accessible only to those who already possess the key to the door. Herrick's genius is in bringing the music vividly to life, injecting it with a sense of fun and a directness of appeal without for a moment compromising artistic integrity. Few could fail to be captivated by the wonderfully vibrant and smiling countenance of the great E flat Prelude while those of us who have laboured long and hard just to get our feet round that most ankle-twisting of all fugue subjects must surely surrender in the face of Herrick's effortless fluency in BWV542. The glorious Swiss instrument has been brilliantly recorded, portraying not just the instrument itself but its sumptuous aural setting.

Allabreve in D, BWV589. Aria in F, BWV587. Canzona in D minor, BWV588. Four Duets, BWV802-05. Fantasias – A minor, BWV561; C, BWV570. Fantasia con imitazione in B minor, BWV563. Fugues – C minor, BWV575; G, BWV576; G, BWV577, 'Jig Fugue'; G minor, BWV578. Pastorale in F, BWV590. Preludes – A minor, BWV551; G, BWV568; A minor, BWV569. Preludes and Fugues – E minor, BWV533; G minor, BWV535; D minor, BWV539; D minor, BWV549*a*; G, BWV550. Toccata and Fugue in E, BWV566. Trios – D minor, BWV583; C minor, BWV585; G, BWV586. Trio Sonata in G, BWV1027*a* (arr cper). Musikalisches Opfer, BWV1079 – Ricercar a 3; Ricercar a 6

Christopher Herrick *org*

Hyperion ② CDA67211/2 (156 minutes: DDD) Ⓕ

Recorded on the organ of the Stadtkirche, Rheinfelden, Switzerland in 1996

Some might be tempted to describe what we have here as the 'scrapings from the barrel', for when you've taken out the chorale-based works, the trio sonatas, the concertos and the big preludes, fantasias, toccatas, passacaglias and fugues this is what's left. One could, however, be tempted almost to prefer these crumbs from the table of great genius to those stupendous musical feasts which are everybody's idea of the real J S Bach. And when you have those crumbs seasoned with such loving care, such elegance and such finesse as Christopher Herrick gives to, say, the G minor fugue (BWV578) or the enchanting Trio Sonata (BWV1027*a*), you realise that here is music every bit as worthy of close attention as anything Bach wrote for the organ. In matters of registration, tempo, articulation and phrasing, Herrick displays immaculate taste. This is playing of the very highest order. The modest two-manual Metzler, built in 1992, makes an enchanting sound, and the recording fully supports the superlative artistry of the playing.

Chorale Preludes, BWV1090-120

Chorale Preludes – Neumeister Collection, BWV1090-120; Ach Gott und Herr, BWV714; Der Tag, der ist freudenreich, BWV719; Vater unser im Himmelreich, BWV737; Ach Herr, mich armen Sünder, BWV742; Machs mit mir, Gott, nach deiner Güt, BWV957

Christopher Herrick *org*

Hyperion CDA67215 (80 minutes: DDD) Ⓕ

Recorded 1999

These 38 chorale preludes come from a collection of 83 pieces compiled in the 18th century by Johann Gottfried Neumeister. The collection eventually made its way to Yale University, where it was discovered by the Bach scholar Christoph Wolff. Bach's preludes are early works, and as Wolff so aptly wrote: 'Already there is innovation. There is a degree of originality and sophistication that is really quite remarkable.'

Herrick gives clear, attractive performances with rhythmic articulation and lively ornamentation. Some listeners may find his playing too calculated and self-conscious; however, these are sprightly readings, free of excessive mannerisms. The most enjoyable aspect of the CD is the way Herrick gives each chorale prelude its own distinct sound world, despite having only a nine-stop, one-manual Metzler organ. This instrument is one of the most beautiful organs imaginable, and Herrick exploits every conceivable combination of stops to achieve a pleasing variety of colour. The organ is well recorded, too, though some may find it a little too closely miked.

The informative booklet includes a list of the stops which Herrick uses for each prelude. To quote from the booklet: 'There is tremendous variety and imagination in this collection, and these little-known pieces surely deserve to be more widely appreciated ...'.

Schübler Chorales, BWV645-50

Preludes and Fugues – C, BWV545; E flat, BWV552, 'St Anne'. Trio Sonata in E minor, BWV528. Largo in A minor, BWV529. Fantasia in C minor, BWV562. Schübler Chorales, BWV645-50

Piet Kee *org*

Chandos Chaconne CHAN0590 (66 minutes: DDD) Ⓕ

Recorded on the Schnitger organ of the Martinikerk, Groningen, The Netherlands in 1995

This is playing of heart-warming humanity and spiritual equilibrium, combining deep thought with complete spontaneity. Kee's control of the long, singing line goes hand in hand with a poetic command of baroque instrumental articulation. Dip anywhere into the Schübler Chorales or to either of the Trio Sonata slow movements and you can hear the separate melodic lines not only given individual character, shape and direction but also combined with ease and gentle authority. Tempos in extrovert movements are unusually moderate, Bach's markings of *Vivace* and *Allegro* being taken by Kee as indications of mood rather than velocity, and yet the musical discourse is involving and full of wit, helped by registrations that are both simple and wise. The disc is crowned by a magnificent performance of the Prelude and Fugue in E flat, one that fully exploits the vivid contrasts of theme and texture and yet binds the work into a structural unity without a hint of haste or stiffness. Rightly, the recording presents this refined, robust organ as heard within its natural acoustic habitat and Kee has subtly absorbed the church's acoustic into his interpretations.

Schübler Chorales, BWV645-50. Leipzig Chorales, BWV651-68. Chorales from Cantatas Nos 36, 59, 62 and 180. Wenn wir in höchsten Nöten sein, BWV431. Du heiliger Brunst, süsser Trost, BWV226 No 2. An Wasserflüssen Babylon, BWV267. Herr Jesus Christ, dich zu uns wend', BWV332. O Lamm Gottes, unschuldig, BWV401. Nun danket alle Gott, BWV386. Von Gott will ich nicht lassen, BWV418. Allein Gott in

der Höh' sei Ehr', BWV260. Jesus Christus, unser Heiland, BWV363. Komm, Gott Schöpfer, heiliger Geist, BWV370
Amsterdam Baroque Choir / Ton Koopman *org*
Teldec Das Alte Werk ② 4509-94459-2 Ⓕ
(142 minutes: DDD). Texts and translations included. Organ works recorded on the organ of the Grote Kerk, Leeuwarden in 1994 ●●

Koopman's performances have a glorious sense of spontaneity born of the understanding that, with a cantata and a fistful of chorale preludes to compose and perform every week, Bach was hardly involved here in deep, painstaking creativity. Koopman seems totally attuned to the essential practicality of this music. As a result he can indulge in outrageously ebullient ornamentation, which from any other organist might seem merely bad taste, and maintain his light, dispassionate approach even through those Preludes usually afforded particular emotional significance, yet make it all sound stylistically convincing. A link between organ and cantata cycles is forged here by pairing each prelude with its chorale. The complete unity of approach between organist and singers is ingeniously underpinned by the use of organ accompaniment where unaccompanied singing might create a sense of dissociation. There is occasional variation but throughout, the singing of the Amsterdam Baroque Choir is a complete, unalloyed joy. Koopman isn't going to be everybody's cup of tea, but with this beautifully recorded pair of discs any reservations are completely outweighed by the sheer musical integrity of what are truly wonderful performances.

Schübler Chorales. Leipzig Chorales. Kirnberger Chorales, BWV690-91 and BWV694-713
Christopher Herrick *org*
Hyperion ② CDA67071/2 (147 minutes: DDD) Ⓕ
Recorded on the Metzler organ of the Jesuitenkirche, Lucerne, Switzerland in 1995

The Schübler Chorales are mostly drawn from cantata movements, the Leipzig, sometimes known as the '18' and sometimes as the 'great' due to their large stature (including in BWV652 the longest chorale prelude Bach wrote), and some miscellaneous chorale preludes which have nothing in common beyond the fact that Johann Philipp Kirnberger, a pupil and admirer of Bach, bundled them all together. Keenly aware of the artificiality of the situation – obviously no organist in Bach's day would have dreamt of playing 44 chorale preludes in one go – Herrick has approached the task with businesslike vigour. *Wachet auf* fizzes like champagne at a wedding – no wonder the sleepers seem so eager to waken with such a riotous wedding feast clearly already in full swing. But such unrelenting bubbliness can also seem misplaced: Schumann's description of *Schmücke dich, o liebe Seele* (BWV654) as 'priceless, deep and full of soul' hardly fits this dancing performance. Perhaps, then, not a recording from which to extract single preludes, but certainly one which can withstand repeated bouts of continuous listening. As ever, not only has Herrick found a simply ravishing Swiss organ which he uses with impeccable good taste (and his invariably sensitive registrations are all detailed in the booklet) but the Hyperion team have come up with a top-notch recording.

Clavier-Übung III, BWV669-89

Clavier-Übung III, BWV669-89. Prelude and Fugue in E flat, BWV552, 'St Anne'. Fugue in G minor, BWV578. Passacaglia and Fugue in C minor, BWV582. Four Duets, BWV802-05. Concerto in G, BWV973
Kevin Bowyer *org*
Nimbus ② NI5561/2 (119 minutes: DDD) Ⓕ
Recorded on the Marcussen organ, St Hans Kirke, Odense, Denmark in 1997

The music on this pair of discs encompasses almost every style in which Bach wrote for the organ. From the simple two-part *Duets* to the transcribed orchestral textures of a Vivaldi concerto; from the simple chorale prelude played by hands alone on a single four-foot stop (BWV677) to the complex double canon on two manuals and pedals of BWV678; from the transparent polyphony of a Trio (BWV676) to the immense contrapuntal complexity of the *Passacaglia*. Its value as a compact comprehensive compendium of Bach's organ writing is compounded by such uniformly good performances. Kevin Bowyer may not be at the cutting edge of Bach interpretation – but he does present unashamedly English performances. These are solid, reliable performances supported by a more than acceptable recording. Part 3 of the *Clavier-Übung* was never intended to be performed in one sitting by one organist on one organ so recordings such as this inevitably have about them an air of artificiality. Other organists have other approaches but Bowyer takes the broad view, treating it as one homogeneous whole. Bowyer's registrations can best be described as sparing, even in the great C minor *Passacaglia and Fugue*. All in all, a most satisfactory release except for the largely unfathomable booklet-essay. Fledgling note writers would do well to study this booklet as an object-lesson in how to make the accessible inaccessible.

Clavier-Übung III, BWV669-89. Duets, BWV802-5. Fugue in E flat, BWV552 No 2
Kay Johannsen *org*
Hänssler Edition Bachakademie ② 92 101 Ⓕ
(100 minutes: DDD). Recorded on the Erasmus-Bielfeldt organ, St Wilhadi, Stade in 1998 ●

These discs transport the listener back to 1736, the date of the Erasmus-Bielfeldt organ recorded here. Three years later Bach published the third part of his *Clavier-Übung*, an academically austere title which disguises one of his most symbolic and liturgically important cycles. He had high hopes for the commercial success of the volume and its successor, the *Goldberg* Variations. The *Clavier-Übung* features the so-called Organ Mass. A Hymn Mass, it uses Lutheran texts and melodies in one major and several minor arrangements.

The two discs open and close with the Prelude and Fugue in E flat, BWV552. From the Prelude's first notes it is clear that Johannsen's playing is of the highest calibre. There is emotional involvement without a superfluity of ornamentation and *rubato*. Here, too, is tenderness, flamboyance, attack and rhythmic drive. In Johannsen's hands the listener is subtly drawn to the core of the music, its complexity simplified through his beautifully balanced registrations. Highlights include the extended prelude on *Vater unser im Himmelreich*, BWV682 and those on *Aus tiefer Not*, BWV686/687. The Four Duets are stylistically related and unified through an ascending key sequence which, as the notes mention, represent the Passion, Easter, Ascension and Pentecost. The superb booklet includes notes on the individual registrations employed. First-rate recording quality .

Prelude and Fugue in E flat, BWV552, 'St Anne'. Clavier-Übung III, BWV669-89. Four Duets, BWV802-05. Canonic variations on 'Vom Himmel hoch', BWV769*a*
Ton Koopman *org*
Teldec ② 4509-98464-2 (125 minutes: DDD) Ⓕ
Recorded on the Silbermann organ of Freiburg Cathedral, Germany in 1996 ●

Three great joys await on this pair of discs. First there is the sublime collection of chorale preludes, framed by one of the most majestic of all Bach's Preludes and Fugues, which forms the *Clavier-Übung III*. Then there is the glorious instrument, its beautiful flutes, its delicate and subtle reeds, its invigorating full organ all captured magnificently in this vivid Teldec recording. And third there is the playing of Ton Koopman, who brings a wealth of authority and perception flavoured with unflagging enthusiasm. He soothes those jagged double-dotted rhythms of the Prelude without losing one iota of the work's great stature. He imbues the 21 chorale preludes with an almost prayerful atmosphere, and to the four Duets he brings a lighter, more joyful nature, as if to relax the mood before the final, supremely celebratory Fugue. The overall effect is to re-create in musical terms the celebration of the Mass itself. Throughout, ornamentation is not so much discreet as rare. His unusual reticence in this respect extends to a magnificent account of the *Canonic variations* where the clarity of the canonic lines is remarkably vivid. An immensely worthwhile issue.

Orgel-Büchlein, BWV599-644

Orgel-Büchlein, BWV599-644
Christopher Herrick *org* Hyperion CDA66756 Ⓕ
(72 minutes: DDD). Recorded on the Metzler organ in the Stadtkirche, Rheinfelden, Switzerland in 1994

With just two manuals and 32 speaking stops, this wonderful organ is relatively small but still offers sufficient scope for Herrick to find a different registration for each of these 45 Preludes. The softer sounds used for *Herr Jesu Christ, dich zu uns wend* are preferable to the rather coarse *pleno* (*In dir ist Freude*) but it makes an undeniably ravishing sound. The *Orgel-Büchlein*'s 46 Chorale Preludes (here the almost identical pair on *Liebster Jesu* are merged, accounting for the disc's 45 tracks) are so brief that listening to them all in one sitting is the musical equivalent of eating salted peanuts one at a time in quick succession. In an attempt to make it all more palatable Herrick tries two tricks. First, he plays remarkably fast, which some people may not find particularly rewarding. Secondly, he revises the playing order, interspersing those Preludes based on 'general' themes between those for particular times in the church's year, and even mixing up the ones within each group. The booklet deserves paeans of praise. Robin Langley's notes are the perfect match for Herrick's playing: scholarly, erudite, infinitely rewarding and so easily communicative.

Orgel-Büchlein, BWV599-644
Ton Koopman *org*
Teldec Das Alte Werk 3984-21466-2 Ⓕ
(70 minutes: DDD). Recorded in Ottobeuren Abbey, Bavaria in 1998 ●

These are short pieces, but brevity does not necessarily imply inconsequentiality. Koopman is very impressive here, with sensitive, authoritative and perfectly gauged performances, imaginatively registered and stunningly recorded on the 1766 Riepp organ of Ottobeuren Abbey. He never lets the preludes sound short, treating each one as a gem to be lovingly nurtured so that, even when it survives barely 40 seconds, we feel we have lost an old friend as it dies away in the Abbey's ambience. His sense of proportion is flawless, avoiding excessive sentimentality in *O Mensch, bewein' dein' Sünde gross* and creating the perfect balance between liveliness and majesty for *Komm, Gott Schöpfer, Heiliger Geist*. These are distinguished performances indeed, and if in places we hear signs of the instrument's great age, or its action impinges a little heavily on the ear, that serves only to enhance the sense of authority and stature this admirable release lends to some of Bach's briefest creations.

Organ Toccatas

Toccatas – G minor, BWV915; G, BWV916. Fugues on themes of Albinoni – A, BWV950; B minor, BWV951. Fugue in C minor, BWV575. Preludes and Fugues – C, BWV553; D minor, BWV554; E minor, BWV555; F, BWV556; G, BWV557; G minor, BWV558; A minor, BWV559; B flat, BWV560. Fantasia con imitazione in B minor, BWV563
Kevin Bowyer *org*
Nimbus NI5377 (74 minutes: DDD) Ⓕ
Recorded on the Marcussen organ of St Hans Kirke, Odense, Denmark in 1992

While critical opinion and academic argument may deter others, Bowyer is content to let the music speak for itself, whether it is 'by J S Bach, J L Krebs or A N Other'. On this disc the music speaks with absolute conviction. One thinks of the gloriously dramatic rhetoric Bowyer brings to the two Toccatas (BWV915 and 916). Harpsichordists may claim these as their own but who could deny this lovely Odense organ the opportunity to glitter with such flamboyant music? The eight 'short' Preludes and Fugues have a muscular, clean-shaven feel to them underlined by plain and simple registrations. While other recordings of such indefinable pieces seem like scraps from the cutting-room floor, Bowyer sets them firmly in the mainstream of high baroque organ music.

Fantasia and Fugue in G minor, BWV542. Trio Sonata No 1 in E flat, BWV525. Toccata and Fugue in D minor, BWV565. Pastorale in F, BWV590. Organ Concerto No 1 in G, BWV592. Chorale Prelude – Erbarm' dich mein, O Herre Gott, BWV721. Organ Chorale – Aus tiefer Not schrei ich zu dir, BWV1099
Kevin Bowyer *org*
Nimbus NI5280 (67 minutes: DDD) Ⓕ
Recorded on the Marcussen organ of St Hans Kirke, Odense, Denmark in 1991

This disc includes the best-known of all Bach's organ pieces – although some would dispute that it is an organ piece or even that Bach wrote it; Bowyer's account of the *Toccata and Fugue* in D minor is invigorating, exciting and very fast. It sets the scene for a CD of virtuoso performances and sound musicianship. The whole is a well-chosen, self-contained programme which also includes an indisputably 'great' organ work, a Trio Sonata, a transcription Bach made of an effervescent concerto by Ernst, a youthful chorale prelude as well as one from a collection only discovered in 1985 and one real oddity. Much thought has gone into the choice of organ and this instrument serves its purpose admirably; roaring magnificently in the *Fantasia* and emulating the tranquil sounds so characteristic of the *Pastorale*.

Toccata and Fugue in D minor, BWV565. Herzlich tut mich verlangen, BWV727. Fugue in G, BWV577. Erbarm' dich mein, O Herre Gott, BWV721. Fugue on a theme by Corelli in B minor, BWV579. Prelude and Fugue in G, BWV541. Pastorale in F, BWV590. Clavier-Übung III, BWV669-89 – Wir glauben all' an einen Gott, BWV680. Orgel-Büchlein, BWV599-644 – O Mensch, bewein' dein' Sünde gross, BWV622. Passacaglia and Fugue in C minor, BWV582
Peter Hurford *org*
EMI Eminence CD-EMX2218 (73 minutes: DDD) Ⓜ
Recorded on the Schnitger organ of the Martinikerk, Groningen, The Netherlands in 1993 **OO**

'Peter Hurford playing organs of Bach's Time.' While Bach on 'authentic' instruments is no novelty, we certainly don't hear enough of the wondrous Ahrend organ, which begins this series in such style. Ahrend? Builders of Bach's time? Well, we're obviously going to have to take the title with a hefty pinch of salt. Although it dates back more than 500 years, in its present form the organ dates from only 1984. Bach never played it, and even if he had he certainly wouldn't recognise it now, but it sounds quite wonderful; Henry Mitton and Mark Nations have recorded it magnificently, closely focusing the sound within an aura of spaciousness. Splendid playing by Hurford too, of course. He begins with the ubiquitous Toccata and Fugue in D minor. But what a performance! Everything else is given warmly communicative, unpretentious and immensely appealing performances.

Miscellaneous Recitals

Allein Gott in der Höh sei Ehr: BWV715; BWV717; BWV711; BWV260. Christ lag in Todesbanden: BWV4[a]; BWV695. Fugue on a theme by Corelli in B minor, BWV579. Herr Jesu Christ, dich zu uns wend: BWV332[a]; BWV655. Jesus Christus unser Heiland: BWV363[a]; BWV688. Preludes and Fugues – C minor, BWV549; G, BWV550; E flat, BWV552. Prelude in A minor, BWV569. O Lamm Gottes, unschuldig: BWV401[a]; BWV618. Schmücke dich, o liebe Seele: BWV180[a]; BWV654. Trio Sonata No 1 in E flat, BWV525. Valet will ich dir geben: BWV415[a]; BWV736
[a]**Caroline Magalhaes** *mez* [a]**Philippe Froeliger** *ten*
Francis Jacob *org*
Zig-Zag Territoires ② ZZT001001 (90 minutes: DDD) Ⓕ
Played on the Aubertin organ of the Parish Church, Saessolsheim, Alsace. Recorded 2000 **O**

This might look like just another organ recital, but in reality it celebrates the remarkable philanthropy of a small Alsatian community who have collectively funded, over nine years, a beautiful organ in Saessolsheim in the north of Alsace. Here it is played by a local son, Francis Jacob, an accomplished young player whose programme is an imaginative cross-section of Bach's organ works. He is not afraid to play a fugue without a prelude if he feels it serves the greater architectural good of the programme. Indeed, his ideals of passing through carefully ordered genres, keys and colourific possibilities are engaging and perceptive.

As for the performances, one is struck by the ebullience and vitality of Jacob's fast playing, rhythmically assured and with a strong feel for instrumental timbre, not just organ sound – the key to discovering allusions and subtexts as the Bach player must. Lift and immediacy of articulation prevail over endless swathes of *legato*. How refreshing it is to hear such glowing colours in the opening chorale prelude, *Valet will ich dir geben* (a work with some striking formal similarities to *Komm, heiliger Geist* which opens the '18' Leipzig chorale-prelude set).

However invigorating Jacob's playing though, there is a tendency to resist the poetic instinct, as if he is mistaking it for indulgence. *Schmücke dich* sounds unyielding, calculated and even wearing. He produces an idiosyncratic equivalent in the middle movement of the Trio Sonata in C major (what possessed him to break this restful melody up into little squares?), and yet all is forgiven in a deeply touching *O Lamm Gottes*, a chorale marvellously disguised as a taut canonic web irradiating ethereal harmonic consequences – this is where the expressive effect of dissonance is more at consonance with the underlying conceit than consonance could ever be! Jacob rattles off *Allein Gott* with supreme dexterity, and the dazzling upper partials are further evident in a compellingly neurotic reading of the A minor Prelude. The programme of two short CDs ends with the E flat *St Anne* Fugue, not as grand or mature in conception as some, but carefully considered and, like most of this recording, it conveys a notably immediate, 'one-off' and animated musical presence.

Trio Sonatas, BWV525-30

No 1 in E flat; **No 2** in C minor; **No 3** in D minor; **No 4** in E minor; **No 5** in C; **No 6** in G

Trio Sonatas Nos 1-6
Christopher Herrick *org*
Hyperion CDA66390 (72 minutes: DDD) Ⓕ
Recorded on the Metzler organ of the Parish Church of St Nikolaus, Bremgarten, Switzerland in 1989 OO

The common assumption is that Bach wrote his Six Trio Sonatas as training studies for his son Wilhelm Friedmann, and young organists still regard the ability to play them as a prerequisite in establishing proper organ technique. But if ever the notion that this is music 'first to practise and secondly to admire' was shown to be false, this stunning disc presents an unanswerable argument. Herrick's performances are immense fun, brimming over with real affection for the music. He allows himself occasional displays of enthusiasm (adding a few exuberant *glissandos* in the last movement of the E flat major Sonata, for example) and he chooses his stops both to enhance the vitality of the quick movements and to underline the sheer beauty of the slower ones. The recording makes this disc a worthwhile buy if only for the glorious sound; the organ speaks into a rich, opulent acoustic which treats each note as a priceless jewel, to be enhanced by its setting but not in any way to be obscured. A disc of rare beauty and a real gem in any collection.

Trio Sonatas Nos 1-6
Kay Johannsen *org*
Hänssler Classic 92 099 (78 minutes: DDD) Ⓕ
Recorded on the Metzler organ of the Stadtkirche, Stein am Rhein, Germany in 1997 OO

Kay Johannsen is not a particularly familiar name outside his native Germany, but he has something distinctive to say in his Bach interpretations. His performance is distinguished by uniformly stylish, immaculately tailored readings of the Trio Sonatas. At the beginning of the 1990s Herrick's Hyperion recording was perceived as the most persuasive, vivid and compelling performances ever of these sonatas. He has, at last, met his match. Johannsen has every bit as much verve, spirit and musical persuasiveness, the organ is ideal both for these sparkling performances and the transparency of the musical textures (like Herrick, Johannsen has chosen a glorious Swiss Metzler – this time the 1992 instrument in the municipal church of Stein am Rhein), and Hänssler Classic's recording has exceptional presence and clarity. What many may prefer is Johannsen's avoidance of those *glissandos* and exuberant over-the-top gestures which Herrick favours.

Complete Cantatas

Volume 1 – Nos 16, 33, 37, 42, 56, 61, 72, 80, 82, 97, 113, 132, 133, 170. **Volume 2** – Nos 22, 23, 44, 54, 57, 85, 86, 92, 98, 111, 114, 135, 155, 159, 165, 167, 188. **Volume 3** – Nos 17, 35, 87, 90, 99, 106, 117, 123, 153, 161, 168, 172, 173, 182, 199. **Volume 4** – Nos 7, 13, 45, 69, 81, 102, 116, 122, 130, 138, 144, 149, 150, 169, 196. **Volume 5** – Nos 6, 26, 27, 46, 55, 94, 96, 107, 115, 139, 156, 163, 164, 178, 179. **Volume 6** – Nos 2, 3, 8, 60, 62, 78, 93, 103, 128, 145, 151, 154, 171, 185, 186, 192. **Volume 7** – Nos 9, 36, 47, 73, 91, 110, 121, 125, 129, 152, 157, 166, 184, 198. **Volume 8** – Nos 18, 30, 40, 49, 79, 84, 88, 89, 100, 108, 136, 140, 176, 187, 194. **Volume 9** – Nos 1, 5, 14, 20, 32, 38, 50, 51, 58, 63, 83, 104, 109, 162, 183, 195. **Volume 10** – Nos 21, 25, 28, 39, 43, 48, 52, 59, 65, 75, 119, 137, 143, 146, 175, 180, 197. **Volume 11** – Nos 4, 10, 12, 64, 70, 71, 74, 76, 95, 101, 105, 124, 127, 131, 134, 158, 177. **Volume 12** – Nos 19, 24, 29, 31, 34, 41, 66, 67, 68, 77, 112, 120, 126, 147, 148, 174, 181 P
Ruth Holton, Marjon Strijk *sops* **Sytse Buwalda** *counterten* **Marcel Beekman, Martinus Leusink, Nico van der Meel, Knut Schoch** *tens* **Bas Ramselaar** *bass* **Holland Boys Choir; Netherlands Bach Collegium / Pieter Jan Leusink**
Brilliant Boxes ⑤ (12 five-disc sets) 99363/99364/99367/99368/99370/99371/99373/99374/99377-80 (3691 minutes: DDD). Texts included Ⓢ O

Brilliant Classics has, through licensing and creative plundering of old catalogues, has contrived its own Bach Edition. Rather more surprising is that within this patchwork of miscellaneous performances comes a brand new set of the complete cantatas. How on earth can such a project be viable as a realistic competitor to the meticulously prepared work of leading exponents, or even prudent financially? The answer lies in the spirit of the task, one clearly designed to provide a large audience with the opportunity to experience all these masterworks on period instruments, at an affordable price. A ridiculous price actually. The practice of speed-recording represents quite an art in itself, attempting to engender inspiration while also ensuring acceptable standards of performance and recording – all within an intensive low-budget schedule. Unsurprisingly then, Pieter Jan Leusink's standard-sized Holland Boys Choir and Netherlands Bach Collegium deliver a rather uneven collection of performances with highs and lows in close proximity.

Volumes 1-8: Some readings are simply too indistinct to warrant comparison with more considered and glamorous competition, doubtless in those cases where not enough time has been allowed for the performers to find their interpretative feet beyond merely 'getting it together'. Some, like that of the 'Trauer Ode', miss the point with overt force dispatching fragrant delicacy, while a healthy number constitute refreshing accounts disarmingly caught at the point of discovery. You take the rough with the smooth in this roller-coaster enterprise.

If there is one overriding Achilles heel, it is the unreliability of the solo singing. The tenor contributions, in particular, too often undermine Leusink's generally bright and well-judged conceptions. Volume 5 is a case in point, where Knut Schoch, in the solo tenor cantata, No 55, is simply not up to the task. Judging by the qualities the less ubiquitous Marcel Beekman demonstrates in a beautifully executed No 164, he would have been a better first choice throughout. The most seasoned of the tenors, Nico van der Meel, becomes more authoritative as the set progresses. Soprano Marjon Strijk often finds Bach's taxing melisma a squiggle too far, in marked contrast to the expert if somewhat recessed singing of Ruth Holton and the excellent bass contributions of Bas Ramselaar (they also combine well in their many duets, such as the rollicking No 49). Ramselaar is the best singer on the set and would, for the most part, grace any of the current series; he has the grainy intimacy of Klaus Mertens, and also a burly resonance when it suits him. His reading of 'Ich will den Kreuzstab', No 56, is a commendable achievement by any standards, and there are fine arias in the splendid Ascension works, Nos 37 and 128, as well as in 36, 100 and 108.

Further on the credit side, the boy-led choruses can irradiate a compellingly sure-footed and unmannered perspective of Bach, as in Nos 33 and 97 and in the refreshing and unselfconscious clarity of intent sweetly imparted in Nos 94, 6 and 117; the chorales are also luminously immediate and affecting.

Other cantatas are rather down-played, such as Nos 139 and 62, but are still worthy and enjoyable as honest performances in an unpretentious Kappellmeister mould. If there is a shortage of refinement and blend in No 133 or spit and polish in the rhythmically exacting Nos 26 and 33, bright and energetic declamation is agreeably more the rule than the exception in Leusink's no-airs-and-graces approach. In the general firmament of new cantata recordings, these spontaneous performances stand comparison more in terms of individual movements (many, including several mentioned above, of real conviction and distinction) than complete pieces. Of the handful of cantatas where a special vision of the whole work is unanimously conveyed, with the performers firing on all cylinders, one should highlight (in no particular order) Nos 57, 87, 33, 42, 192, 45, 88, 176, 125 and 129. If the choral movements are the best things in these sets, there are still some memorable arias (to counter an abundance of ropey ones) with which Volumes 1, 2, 4, 6, and 8 are particularly well-endowed.

Volumes 9-12: Here, Leusink traverses the final peak with far more consistently enduring accounts than the comparative 'hit or miss' of the earlier readings, though unsurprisingly for an enterprise designed around tight rehearse-record schedules, there will always be scrappy moments.

More encouragingly, there is also a striking and rare quality here which shines through more strongly than in the majority of the earlier volumes and gives Leusink and his Dutch colleagues genuine credentials. It is the unmannered and straightforward approach to delivering the essence of the work in question, the honesty and means to get directly to its heart through real 'performance', often at the point of discovery. In this respect one is reminded of the earlier recordings from Leonhardt/Harnoncourt, a set which one suspects will be increasingly revisited for that very reason. For all the 'al dente' movements here, there are as many refreshingly uninhibited and distinguished readings, notably Nos 119, 43, 74, 197, 127, 104 and 148. There is a keen ear for the fundamental 'conceit' of the music upon which spontaneous music-making happens 'as if live'; unassuming, common sensical and unegotistical, the earthy Kapellmeister approach reminds one of the unspectacular (and occasionally a touch unimaginative) but free-breathing performances by the likes of Karl Ristenpart, Wolfgang Gönnenwein, Fritz Lehmann, Felix Prohaska and Fritz Werner in the 1950s and 60s.

Ears attuned to the refined and homogeneous textures of the top baroque orchestras will find the grainy and sometimes rather thin violins altogether too disturbing. Others may find this more acceptable and, at times, even liberating, especially when joined by the wonderfully colourful wind playing and robust brass playing; the oboe of Peter Frankenberg, in particular, is one of the set's greatest qualities, though not far behind is the trumpet consort, led by Susan Williams. Notable again is the outstanding bass singing of Bas Ramselaar, whose resonant warmth and musicianly response to text is the most significant vocal strength in the set. Also to be admired are the two main sopranos, Ruth Holton and Marjon Strijk. Both have a vocal timbre of the effervescent and light variety though they bring much radiance and projection to their music-making, and far more accuracy in matters of tuning than in the earlier boxes. Holton sings splendidly in the two demanding arias in No 75, with breeziness in No 52 and loving understanding in the stunning *cantabile* of No 120 (which Bach used in a later version of the G major Violin Sonata), and with great cultivation in BWV31. She sails through the treacherous No 51 with great élan. Strijk brings considerable fluency to her arias in both Nos 25 and 28.

The alto part is less appealingly taken. Sytse Buwalda should not have been lumbered with the responsibility for all the alto arias, several movements of which represent some of Bach's most treasured examples of reflective ardour (why not use mezzos, contraltos and even boy altos for these parts, rather than the often excellent but over-used countertenor?). Despite Buwalda's unsteadiness, he occasionally delivers something reasonable though, such as in Nos 148 and 83. Exactly the same complaint can be levelled at Knut Schoch, a courageous tenor but one without the capacity for variation of colour in his sound, as one hears and expects from both Paul Agnew for Koopman (Erato) or Gerd Türk for Suzuki on BIS. Too often, the upper tessitura just isn't there or else he cannot control it. Luckily, Nico van der Meel is wheeled out for the big ones and he is splendid in both 'Ja, tausendmal tausend' in No 43, as well as No 74. In No 31, he is redolent of the deeply touching singing of Helmut Krebs for Werner (nla). Also used is Marcel Beekman, who shines in No 48 and projects a palpable joie de vivre with Ramselaar in the fine duet, 'Wie will ich mich freuen' from No 146, as does Holton with Ramselaar in the duet of No 32.

The boy-led Holland Choir and 'period' band, Netherlands Bach Collegium, are again central to the success and distinctive essence of this series. The teamwork in the choir is admirably demonstrated in some of the most difficult pieces, such as the large 'da capo' chorus of No 34, the fervent No 197 and infectiously crackling No 70, resulting in white-hot expositions of thrilling proportions. Leusink's success elsewhere comes largely through his admirably well-judged feeling for tempos and a means of accentuation which drives the music forward inexorably. There is, however, a fine line here between luminous vitality and sheer panic; the latter afflicts control in some choruses where Bach just cannot be learnt in a rush: Nos 65, 48 and 137 are examples where phrases are snatched, or over-sung, to the detriment of both textural cohesion and intonation, as well as general quality of sound.

In sum, these readings deserve to be recognised, primarily for their attractive and well-measured strides, but also for a lack of dogma or self-importance. Hard-driven and intermittently rough in places (especially string intonation), they are nevertheless consistently honest, rarely disastrous, and occasionally illuminating statements. Bachians, old and new, should investigate the series with an eager circumspection, taking the rough with the smooth but relishing the open-hearted spirit of the enterprise. The best performances will bring the listener close to the solar plexus of Bach's 'Kantatenwelt'.

Miscellaneous Cantata Discs

No 18 Gleich wie der Regen und Schnee
No 21 Ich hatte viel Bekümmernis
No 22 Jesus nahm zu sich die Zwölfe
No 23 Du wahrer Gott und Davids Sohn
No 24 Ein ungefärbt Gemüte
No 25 Es ist nich Gesundes an meinem Liebe
No 27 Wer weiss, wie nahe mir mein Ende!
No 31 Der Himmel lacht! die Erde jubilieret
No 35 Geist und Seele wird verwirret
No 49 Ich gehe und suche mist Verlangen
No 50 Nun ist das Heil und die Kraft
No 51 Jauchzet Gott in allen Landen!
No 54 Widerstehe doch der Sünde
No 56 Ich will den Kreuzstab gerne tragen
No 59 Wer mich liebet, der wird mein Wort halten
No 61 Nun komm, der Heiden Heiland
No 65 Sie werden aus Saba alle kommen
No 67 Halt im Gedächtnis Jesum Christ
No 69 Lobe den Herrn, meine Seele
No 71 Gott ist mein König
No 75 Die Elenden sollen essen
No 76 Die Himmel erzählen die Ehre Gottes
No 78 Jesu, der du meine Seele
No 80 Ein feste Burg ist unser Gott
No 82 Ich habe genug
No 95 Christus, der ist mein Leben
No 104 Du Hirte Israel, höre
No 105 Herr, gehe nicht ins Gericht mit deinem Knecht
No 106 Gottes Zeit ist die allerbeste Zeit
No 115 Mache dich, mein Geist bereit
No 131 Aus der Tiefen rufe ich, Herr, zu dir
No 136 Erforsche mich, Gott, und erfahre mein Herz
No 143 Lobe den Herr, meine Seele
No 144 Nimm, was dein ist, und gehe hin
No 147 Herz und Mund und Tat und Leben
No 148 Bringet dem Herrn Ehre seines Namens
No 152 Tritt auf die Glaubensbahn
No 155 Mein Gott, wie lang, ache lange
No 158 Der Friede sei mit dir
No 161 Komm, du süsse Todesstunde
No 170 Vergnügte Ruh', beliebte Seelenlust
No 173 Erhöhtes Fleisch und Blut
No 179 Siehe zu, dass deine Gottesfurcht
No 180 Schmücke dich, o liebe Seele
No 181 Leichtgesinnte Flattergeister
No 184 Erwünschtes Freudenlicht
No 186 Ärgre dich, o Seele, nicht
No 190 Singet dem Herrn ein neues Lied!
No 198 Lass, Fürstin, lass noch einen Strahl (Trauer Ode)
No 202 Weichet nur, betrübte Schatten
No 208 Was mir behagt, ist nur die muntre Jagd, 'Hunt'
No 209 Non sa che sia dolore
No 210 O holder Tag, erwünschte Zeit
No 211 Schweigt stille, plaudert nicht, 'Coffee'
No 212 Mer hahn en neue Oberkeet, 'Peasant'

Cantatas Nos 18, 143, 152, 155 and 161 **P**
Midori Suzuki, Ingrid Schmithüsen *sops* **Yoshikazu Mera** *counterten* **Makoto Sakurada** *ten* **Peter Kooy** *bass* **Bach Collegium Japan / Masaaki Suzuki** *org*
BIS CD841 (78 minutes: DDD) Ⓕ
Texts and translations included. Recorded 1997 **OO**

The fifth volume of Bach's sacred cantatas performed by the Bach Collegium Japan continues their Weimar survey with five pieces written between *c*1713 and 1716. It begins with No 18, performed in its Weimar version – Bach later revived it for Leipzig, adding two treble recorders to the purely string texture of the upper parts of the earlier composition. The scoring of No 152 is more diverse, featuring in its opening Sinfonia a viola d'amore, viola da gamba, oboe and recorder.

A conspicuous feature of No 155 is its melancholy duet for alto and tenor with bassoon obbligato. While the vocal writing sustains something of the character of a lament the wonderfully athletic, arpeggiated bassoon solo provides a magical third voice. The accompanying essay is confused here, emphasizing the importance of a solo oboe which in fact has no place at all in this work. No 161 is a piece of sustained beauty, scored for a pair of treble recorders, obbligato organ, strings and continuo. Bach's authorship of No 143 has sometimes been questioned. Much of it is un-Bach-like, yet at times it is hard to envisage another composer's hand.

The performances are of unmatched excellence. Suzuki's direction never falters and his solo vocalists go from strength to strength as the series progresses. Suzuki makes a richly rewarding contribution with beautifully poised singing, a crystal-clear voice and an upper range that only very occasionally sounds at all threatened. Mera and Sakurada sustain a delicately balanced partnership in the elegiac duet of No 155, the limpid bassoon-playing completing this trio of outstanding beauty. Kooy is a tower of strength, a sympathetic partner to Suzuki in the dance-like duet between Jesus and the Soul (No 152), and resonantly affirmative in his aria from the same cantata. But the highest praise should go to Mera and Sakurada for their affecting performance in No 161. All the elements of this superb cantata are understood and deeply felt by all concerned. The disc is admirably recorded and, apart from the aforementioned confusion, painstakingly and informatively documented.

Cantatas Nos 21 and 31 **P**

Monika Frimmer *sop* **Gerd Türk** *ten* **Peter Kooy** *bass* **Bach Collegium Japan / Masaaki Suzuki**

BIS CD851 (68 minutes: DDD) Ⓕ

Texts and translations included. Recorded 1997

Both of these are Weimar compositions, dating from *c*1713 and 1715 respectively, and both were later sung at Leipzig. Where No 21 is concerned, the performance history is complex since Bach, who clearly and understandably set great store by this extended and profoundly expressive piece, made no fewer than four versions of it. Following what was probably its second Weimar performance, in 1714, Bach produced a new version which he used as a test-piece in Hamburg's Jacobikirche, when applying for an organist's post there in 1720. It is this version, for soprano and bass soloists only, in which the parts are transposed from C minor to D minor that forms the basis of the present recording.

Suzuki offers listeners an opportunity, by way of an appendix, of hearing Bach's alternative thoughts on certain sections of the cantata. These are meticulously prepared and affectingly declaimed performances. Listen, for instance, to the beautifully articulated and delicately placed bassoon quavers in the poignant opening Sinfonia of No 21. This is most sensitively done and an auspicious beginning to the work. String playing is not always quite as clean as it could be but the instrumental expertise is impressive. The solo line-up is strong, with Monika Frimmer sustaining several demanding soprano arias with eloquence and tonal warmth. Gerd Türk and Peter Kooy are secure and expressive, and the singing of the 18-voice choir of women's and men's voices is impressive, though tenors sound strained in the first chorus of No 21.

Cantatas Nos 22, 23 and 75 **P**

Midori Suzuki *sop* **Yoshikazu Mera** *counterten* **Gerd Türk** *ten* **Peter Kooy** *bass* **Bach Collegium Japan / Masaaki Suzuki** *org*

BIS CD901 (64 minutes: DDD) Ⓕ

Texts and translations included. Recorded 1998 **OO**

This eighth volume of Bach Collegium Japan's Bach cantata series bridges the period between Bach's departure from Cöthen and his arrival at Leipzig, early in 1723. *Du wahrer Gott und Davids Sohn* (No 23) was mainly written at Cöthen, while *Jesus nahm zu sich die Zwölfe* (No 22) must have been composed almost immediately on Bach's reaching Leipzig. The remaining cantata, *Die Elenden sollen essen* is on an altogether grander scale, in two parts, each of seven movements. The performances maintain the high standards of singing, playing and scholarship set by the previous issues in this series. There are little insecurities here and there – the oboes, which play a prominent role in each of the three pieces, are not always perfectly in agreement over tuning – but the careful thought given to the words, their significance and declamation, and the skill with which they are enlivened by the realization of Bach's expressive musical vocabulary, remain immensely satisfying. The disciplined, perceptively phrased and beautifully sustained singing of the two choral numbers of No 23 illuminate the words at every turn, savouring the seemingly infinite expressive nuances of the music. As for No 75, we can only imagine the astonishment with which Leipzig ears must have attuned to its music. In this absolutely superb piece Bach entertains us with a stylistic diversity that is breathtaking. Polyphony, fugue, chorale fantasia, *da capo* aria, instrumental sinfonia, varied recitative, wonderful oboe writing and a rhythmic *richesse* all contribute to the special distinction both of this cantata and No 76. Lose no time in becoming acquainted with this one. It reaches, one might say, those parts which other performances do not.

Cantatas Nos 24, 25, 67, 95, 105, 136, 144, 147, 148, 173, 181 and 184 **P**

Lisa Larsson *sop* **Bogna Bartosz, Elisabeth von Magnus** *mezzos* **Gerd Türk** *ten* **Klaus Mertens** *bass* **Amsterdam Baroque Choir and Orchestra / Ton Koopman** *hpd/org*

Erato ③ 3984-23141-2 (214 minutes: DDD) Ⓕ

Texts and translations included. Recorded 1997

The seventh volume of Ton Koopman's projected complete cantata survey contains pieces which Bach performed at Leipzig in 1723 and 1724. Koopman's line-up of soloists has been taking a while to settle down and, in this volume, the alto solos are shared between Elisabeth von Magnus, one of the greatest strengths of the series so far, and Bogna Bartosz. All the tenor arias are sung by Gerd Türk, and Lisa Larsson and Klaus Mertens provide their stylish and warm-hearted performances as soprano and bass soloists respectively.

As well as containing three superb examples of Bach's genius in the cantata medium – Nos 67, 105 and 147 – Vol 7 contains a handful of rarely heard pieces, of which No 136, with its colourfully brilliant opening chorus, is perhaps the most immediately striking. This highly imaginative movement in A major was later to provide Bach with the 'In gloria Dei patris' of his Lutheran Mass in the same key. At the opposite end of the affective scale is the sombre, penitential chorus which determines the prevalent character of No 25. This technically ingenious double fugue in E minor is difficult to carry off convincingly in performance but Koopman, with his clearly defined contrapuntal strands and responsive choir, succeeds better than any rival version. The gracefulness and fluency in his direction come together rewardingly in No 95. This highly original cantata, with its syncopations, dissonances, bold key changes, and references to four hymns with their associated melodies, all in the opening chorus, is, quite simply, breathtaking. The music commands our attention at every turn, disturbing and pleasing our senses in equal measure. But perhaps it is the following two movements which most readily capture our imagination and win our hearts. Lisa Larsson sings the former with ingenuous charm while Gerd Türk, in the latter, seems to sustain Bach's mercilessly high vocal range with the greatest of ease.

With 12 cantatas under scrutiny it is impossible to discuss them all. But the overall picture of this set is mainly convincing, with some very fine playing and singing – only the occasionally over-assertive projection of countertenor voices from the choir fails to please. Any disappointment here, though, seems relatively slight beside the many excellent contributions of Koopman's artists. If, on balance, No 105 is a shade lacking in strength of purpose, then such feelings are ameliorated by the wellnigh perfect partnership of Larsson and oboist, Marcel Ponseele, in its poignant soprano aria, certainly one of the highest peaks in a stimulating issue.

Cantatas Nos 27, 158 and 198 **P**

Rotraud Hansmann *sop* **Helen Watts** *contr* **Kurt Equiluz** *ten* **Max van Egmond** *bass* **Monteverdi Choir; Concerto Amsterdam / Jürgen Jürgens**

Teldec Das Alte Werk 4509-93687-2 Ⓜ

(67 minutes: ADD). Texts and translations included.

Recorded 1966-67 **OO**

This is a skilfully transferred account of Jürgen Jürgens's classic recording of the *Trauer Ode* (No 198). Unlike many releases from yesteryear, this stands out as a beacon in early 'period performance' awareness of Bach's vocal music (the orchestra comprises Gustav Leonhardt as the continuo player, joined in the appropriate places by Anner Bylsma, Jaap Schröder and Wieland Kuijken), though its lasting qualities come from the same creative vessel as Richter's most successful recordings: incisive and perceptive response to texts and true musical conviction.

Jürgens could hardly have chosen a more carefully assembled or densely argued work for his delectation than the *Trauer Ode*. This beautiful masterpiece was completed late in 1727 for the memorial ceremony of the Electress of Saxony, Queen Christiane Eberhardine. Heavily involved in the *St Matthew Passion* at the time (the 'mourning' *Affekt* in both pieces is strikingly similar), Bach appears to have been acutely aware of the atmospheric potential of 'soft' scorings, in this case with gambas, flutes, lutes and oboe d'amores depicting the bittersweet concoction of pain and consolation. The comprehension of how these unique figures find a meaningful context alongside all the other myriad interpretative considerations is where Jürgens succeeds whilst others fail, succeeding totally in creating sustained poignancy. He attends with typical thoughtfulness to two other cantatas, both of which maintain the theme of death and the hope of eternal life, No 27 being the most substantial. Recommended to Bachians of all persuasions.

Cantatas Nos 35, 54 and 170 **P**

Andreas Scholl *counterten* **Collegium Vocale Orchestra / Philippe Herreweghe**

Harmonia Mundi HMC90 1644 (59 minutes: DDD) Ⓕ

Texts and translations included. Recorded 1997 **OO**

Some 12 years separate the composition of the Weimar cantata, *Widerstehe doch der Sünde* (No 54), from the Leipzig cantatas *Vergnügte Ruh'* (No 170) and *Geist und Seele wird verwirret* (No 35, written in 1726). All three are scored for a solo alto voice with strings and, in the case of the Leipzig pieces, various members of the oboe family and obbligato organ. Andreas Scholl is on top form in *Widerstehe doch der Sünde*, paying close attention to the relationship between text and music. *Vergnügte Ruh'* has long been a favourite piece with singers and audiences alike. Scholl sets an effectively contemplative tempo in the tender introductory aria and sounds comfortable with Bach's broadly spun melody. The remaining work, in two parts, is conceived on an ambitious scale, opening with an extended concerto movement for organ obbligato, oboe d'amore and strings, and containing another, similarly scored piece which serves as an introduction to Part Two. Organist Markus Märkl, with lively support from the orchestral players of the Collegium Vocale, gives a pleasingly jaunty, animated performance of these movements which together with the first aria may have belonged to a lost concerto. Scholl sings his music with warmth and technical fluency, generating a high level of interest for heart and mind alike.

Cantatas – Nos 35: Sinfonias; 56[a]; 82[a] and 158[a]

[a]**Matthias Goerne** *bar*

[a]**Salzburg Bach Choir; Salzburg Camerata Academica / Sir Roger Norrington**

Decca 466 570-2DH (60 minutes: DDD) Ⓕ

Texts and translations included. Recorded 1999 **OOO**

This is an extraordinarily fine recital from Matthias Goerne of the solo bass cantatas. His is the sort of mature, sophisticated, assured and boundless Bach singing which one hears so rarely these days. With the beguiling and cultivated oboe playing of Albrecht Mayer, Goerne takes a refreshingly underivative view of *Ich habe genug* (No 82), involved yet unobtrusively engaged. This, and the famous lullaby 'Schlummert ein', is fragrant, even and soft-spoken.

Norrington's hold on the modern-instrument Salzburg Camerata Academica provides an almost ideal palette for the Lieder-inspired communicative range of Goerne. The strings purr in a gentle if slightly old-fashioned way, yet the orchestra is also receptive to period gesture (including minimal vibrato); just occasionally they rather fall between two stools and seem reticent (a pity about a peculiar glitch in track 3, 2'06", where nearly a beat is skipped). But this pales into insignificance alongside the opening melisma and subsequent translucent illumination of *Ich will den Kreuzstab* (No 56). The heavy cross and its heart-breaking allusions are wonderfully inflected in one of Bach's most revelatory through-composed arias; the build-up and chromatic descent on 'it leads me after all my trials to God and to the promised land' is quite irresistible, as is his radiantly poetic response to the symbol-rich music that follows (the final accompanied recitative is a jewel).

The brief No 158 is also a joy, especially the 'Welt' farewell in the central aria with its glistening violin obbligato and chorale. Another shiveringly beautiful and ethereal world opened up by a singer who, apart from his obvious vocal distinction, brings his own uncircumscribed world of experience to bear on the music. A great Bach recording.

Cantatas Nos 49, 58 and 82 **P**
Nancy Argenta *sop* **Klaus Mertens** *bass*
La Petite Bande / Sigiswald Kuijken *vn*
Accent ACC9395 (63 minutes: DDD) Ⓕ
Texts and translations included. Recorded 1993 ●●

Few readers will be disappointed either by the music or the performances on this disc. It features one of Bach's very finest cantatas, *Ich habe genug* (No 82) for solo baritone, and two 'Dialogue' cantatas for soprano and bass. Leaving out for the moment such issues as instrumental timbre, Sigiswald Kuijken is among the most thoughtful of present-day practitioners of baroque music. That is not to say that you will always like what he does but that he always has a good reason for doing it and is prepared to defend it to the end. Here, there are no complaints whatsoever: tempos are beautifully judged, the string sound is warmer than usual and the overall approach to the music expressive and eloquently shaped. Mertens gives a fine performance of *Ich habe genug*, clearly articulated and resonantly declaimed. Kuijken has opted for the first of several versions of this cantata which Bach made subsequently for various voice pitches and with small instrumental adjustments.

In the two 'Dialogue' cantatas Mertens is joined by Nancy Argenta, an effective piece of casting. Both voices are tonally well focused and project the music in a manner admirably free from needless affectation or contrivance. An expressive peak is reached in Argenta's aria, 'Ich bin herrlich, ich bin schön' (No 49), a ravishing quartet movement with oboe d'amore and a violoncello piccolo beautifully played by Hidemi Suzuki. Add to this a first-rate performance of the organ obbligatos in the opening Sinfonia and final duo of the same cantata and you have a performance of distinction. An outstanding achievement.

Cantatas Nos 49, 115 and 180 **P**
Barbara Schlick *sop* **Andreas Scholl** *counterten*
Christoph Prégardien *ten* **Gotthold Schwarz** *bass*
Concerto Vocale; Limoges Baroque Ensemble / Christophe Coin *vc*
Auvidis Astrée E8530 (71 minutes: DDD) Ⓕ
Texts and translations included. Recorded 1993 ●

Three of Bach's Leipzig church cantatas form a characteristically well-thought-out programme from the French gamba player, cellist and director, Christophe Coin. *Schmücke dich, o liebe Seele* (No 180) and *Mache dich, mein Geist, bereit* (No 115) are among the most overlooked of the cantatas, outside 'complete editions'; but they are towering masterpieces which deserve to be as popular as, for instance, *Wachet auf!* (No 140) or any of the others which find their way, albeit infrequently, into concert programming. There is a more particular reason, however, beyond that of sheer musical excellence, why Coin has chosen to perform these works: it is that in each of them Bach has included a movement calling for the obbligato presence of a small, five-stringed cello, the violoncello piccolo. Nine of Bach's cantatas contain a part for this distinctive-sounding instrument, in each of which the composer employs it with telling effect.

No 180 is a delicately scored piece for two recorders, oboe, oboe da caccia and strings, with an affecting undercurrent of elegy. Coin's direction, his overall grasp of the musical idiom and his evident care over textual detail lead to the heart of the piece. Not everything is refined – there are, for example, some rough moments in the instrumental tuttis – but the spirit of the performance carries everything along with it. This much is true for the remaining cantatas, too.

No 115 contains music of quite extraordinary inventive richness and nowhere more so than in its two *da capo* arias for alto and soprano, respectively: the second, in B minor, seems to lead us into almost uncharted emotional territory in its contemplative profundity. This heart-rending trio for soprano, flute, violoncello piccolo and continuo is one of the most astounding achievements in the entire canon; and it is beautifully sung by Barbara Schlick. The Leipzig Concerto Vocale (a mixed choir of men's and women's voices), and the Limoges Baroque Ensemble have gathered under Coin's direction in performances which probe far beyond musical superficialities.

Cantatas Nos 50, 50 (recons Kleinbussink), 59, 69, 69*a*, 75, 76, 104, 179, 186, and 190 **P**
Ruth Ziesak *sop* **Elisabeth von Magnus** *mez* **Paul Agnew** *ten* **Klaus Mertens** *bass*
Amsterdam Baroque Choir and Orchestra / Ton Koopman *org* Erato Ⓓ 0004 21029-2 Ⓕ
(195 minutes: DDD). Texts and translations included.
Recorded 1997 ●

In his sixth volume of Bach's complete cantatas, Koopman is engaged in the great Leipzig period from 1723. Bach's inaugural offering was a pair of substantial bipartite cantatas, Nos 75 and 76. Koopman gives us the second one initially, *Die Himmel erzählen die Ehre Gottes*, in a muscular and assertive performance. The fine opening chorus, with its swaggering trumpet obbligato, is zestfully negotiated and appropriately full-blooded. The same commitment and character are plentiful in the formidably worked-out contrapuntal edifice of No 75 – a movement passionately declaiming the rewards of seeking God – and the wonderfully evocative imagery in No 104, *Du Hirte Israel, höre*. Memorable for different reasons is *Singet dem Herrn*, No 190, a cantata whose opening two movements require major reconstruction. Koopman has completed the task with a dynamic scoring around the existing vocal parts. If a somewhat over-elaborate setting, it is nevertheless thrilling, and employs the sort of fervent Reformation-like unisons and belting brass which cannot fail to stir.

Koopman has found in Ruth Ziesak a soprano who can get round the notes, sing consistently in tune (despite one under-par aria in No 186) and express the meaning of the music with rhetorical personality. She dances around the lithe 'Ich nehme mein Leiden' from No 75. This latter cantata abounds in arresting arias, none more so than the delicious 'Mein Jesus soll', a creation of such ingenious and agreeable melodic inflexion that Paul Agnew can but relish it devotedly. Both Agnew's and Klaus Mertens's singing throughout is a joy, a happy blend of technical security, musicianly shaping and tonal elegance. Elisabeth von Magnus is, in truth, the weak link. Her contribution to the stirring Part 2 of No 76 is not especially undistinguished but her languid sound is repeatedly enervating, and too often the pitch dips unacceptably. In all other respects this is quite a turn-up for the books after the hits and misses of previous volumes. Bach was clearly intent on impressing his new employers with the most accomplished work he could produce; one only has to hear the richness of these scores (a bonanza here for those who like trumpets, and brilliantly played too) to suppose that Koopman has found similar inspiration at exactly the right time.

Cantatas Nos 51, 202 and 209 **P**
Agnes Giebel *sop* **Concerto Amsterdam / Jaap Schröder** *vn* **Leonhardt Consort / Gustav Leonhardt** *hpd*
Teldec Das Alte Werk 3984-21711-2 Ⓜ
(65 minutes: ADD). Texts and translations included.
Recorded 1966 ●

Followers of historical recordings of Bach's music admire Agnes Giebel for her impeccable delivery and shimmering control of line. She is a worthy mentor to current practitioners in that she communicates an utterly enraptured love of Bach and its expressive world. Whilst her voice may sound old-fashioned in its dignified restraint, that is merely the 'front'; as one can hear in the recitative and *arioso* of *Jauchzet Gott* (No 51), she manipulates her heady control of the phrase with mesmerizing intensity. There is much consistently vintage Giebel in this welcome reissue. Stylish accompaniments from the early Dutch pioneers, Jaap Schröder and the Leonhardts, provide a tantalizing glimpse of how Giebel, had she been a generation younger, would have so ideally suited and relished the exciting possibilities of period instruments; the chamber-like *Non sa che sia dolore* (No 209) has all the refinement and instinct for discerning gesture to render it a remarkably prescient document of its time: the aria, 'Partipur e con dolore' is a case in point and this really is vintage Giebel. No 51 has been a favourite with technically capable sopranos in the post-war period. The opening is a touch pedestrian in the paucity of shaping in the ritornello arpeggios but Giebel's beady encirclement of the fiendish passagework as the piece unfolds is sheer joy. A precious disc of a great Bach singer.

Cantatas Nos 51 (arr W F Bach), 202 and 210 **P**
Christine Schäfer *sop* **Musica Antiqua Köln / Reinhard Goebel** *vn*
DG 459 621-2GH (62 minutes: DDD) Ⓕ
Texts and translations included ●

Of the two wedding cantatas, *Weichet nur, betrübte Schatten* (202) ranks among Bach's best-loved, but the other, *O holder Tag, erwünschte Zeit* (No 210), is much less heard. To these, Christine Schäfer adds another Bach favourite, *Jauchzet Gott in allen Landen!* (No 51) which, although not specifically for a wedding, confirms propriety in a nuptial context. An interesting feature of this reading is its use of a version of the piece arranged by Bach's eldest son, Wilhelm Friedemann, who added a second trumpet and timpani to his father's original scoring for trumpet, strings and continuo. The partnership of Schäfer and Reinhard Goebel with his Musica Antiqua Köln is an interesting one, and rewarding more often than not. Schäfer is a spirited singer with a bright tone and an agile technique. Her clearly articulated phrases accord well with Goebel's well-defined instrumental contours and colourfully characterised rhythms – the fourth aria of No 210, in the rhythm of a polonaise, is admirably enlivened in these respects – and her well-controlled vibrato is a pleasure throughout.

If Emma Kirkby's performance of this piece and No 202 is more understated than the present one there is, none the less, an underlying expressive subtlety and a warmth of vocal timbre in her singing which may prove the more rewarding and enduring. The opening aria of No 202, a sublime piece of musical imagery, points up some of the essential differences between the two approaches: Schäfer declamatory, demonstrative and bright toned, with an edge to the voice, Kirkby, warm toned, alluring and exercising superb control throughout. On the other hand Schäfer's even technique, with its easier access to the highest notes of the range, often has the edge over Kirkby in more virtuosic movements. And in No 210 Schäfer's vocal brilliance and unfailing security, together with Goebel's lively if on occasion provocative gestures, make one of the most alert and interesting performances of the piece. Schäfer also rises brilliantly to the occasion in No 51. A stimulating and often satisfying release.

Bach[a] Cantatas Nos 54 and 170. **P H**
Mass in B minor BWV232 – Agnus Dei
Handel[b] Orlando Ah Stigie larve!. Jephtha, HWV70 – 'Tis Heaven's all-ruling pow'r. Theodora, HWV68 – Kind Heav'n, if Virtue be thy care, Sweet Rose, and Lilly, flow'ry Form
Alfred Deller *counterten* [a]**Leonhardt Baroque Ensemble / Gustav Leonhardt** *org* [b]**Handel Festival Orchestra / Sir Anthony Lewis**
Vanguard Classics Alfred Deller Edition 08.5069.71 Ⓜ
(59 minutes: ADD). Texts and translations included.
Recorded [a]1953, [b]1960 **oo**

Of the many Vanguard reissues this one is, both musically and historically, perhaps the most remarkable. Not only does it contain in the two Bach cantatas and the *Agnus Dei* from the B minor Mass superlative performances by Alfred Deller, then at the height of his powers, but it also must be ranked among the earliest significant recordings to adopt period instruments. Made in 1953 this is probably one of the first appearances on disc of the Leonhardt Baroque Ensemble, later to become the Leonhardt Consort. Many of its members have since played a leading role in the period-instrument revival and many are still going strong today. It's a redoubtable line-up on this recording, but it is Deller himself who immortalises the performances with his unique voice and extraordinary musical sensibility.

The two cantatas are both for solo alto voice. They begin with arias of outstanding beauty to whose deeply contemplative, lyrical spirit Deller contributes his own, distinctively melancholic timbre. This conjunction of voice and music creates an atmosphere of sustained elegy which has not been equalled by any other performance. Of course, as we should expect, the period-instrumental playing then, as Purcell might have said, in its nonage, is still far from refined in all matters concerning tuning and ensemble. But it is so attentive to the contours of the voice and music that the issue pales into relative insignificance beside Deller's supreme artistry. All is stylishly performed. The *Agnus Dei* is on a comparable level with the cantatas in respect of performance, and the Handel pieces are also most enjoyable, though these were recorded several years later and accompanied by a modern instrumental ensemble conducted by Anthony Lewis, a fine Handel exponent but one without much affection for the period-instrument revival. Hamor's ''Tis Heaven's all-ruling pow'r' from Handel's last oratorio, *Jephtha*, is particularly affecting. This is a release which must not be overlooked.

Cantatas Nos 71, 106 and 131 **P**
Midori Suzuki, Aki Yanagisawa *sops* **Yoshikazu Mera** *counterten* **Gerd Türk** *ten* **Peter Kooy** *bass*
Bach Collegium Japan / Masaaki Suzuki
BIS CD781 (63 minutes: DDD) Ⓕ
Texts and translations included. Recorded 1995

Here these artists are abreast of current thinking concerning baroque style, yet sometimes you find yourself longing for a little more expression and a little less fashionable orthodoxy. The three cantatas included here are among Bach's earliest essays in the form. Nos 106 and 131 (*c*1707) belong to the Mühlhausen period, while No 71 was written in 1708. By and large, Suzuki has chosen effective tempos, though there are notable exceptions. One of these affects the beautiful Sonatina for recorders and viola da gamba that introduces the *Actus tragicus* (No 106), a funeral piece of startling intensity. Suzuki feels too slow here, adding a full 40 seconds on to performances by virtually all of his rivals. Elsewhere, and above all in his choice of soloists, Suzuki fields an exceptional team. We can feel this especially in the effortlessly projected singing of Midori Suzuki (Nos 71 and 131) and Aki Yanagisawa (No 106), the uncluttered declamation of Gerd Türk, and the resonant contributions by Peter Kooy. The countertenor here lacks either conviction or consistent aural charm. The Choir is well drilled and, as with the solo element, the voices respond urgently to the spirit of the text. Listen to the thrice supplicatory 'Israel' in the concluding chorus of No 131 for one such example. The recorded sound is splendid.

Cantatas Nos 80 and 147
Ingrid Kertesi *sops* **Judit Nemeth** *mez* **Jozsef Mukk** *ten* **István Gáti** *bar* **Hungarian Radio Chorus; Failoni Chamber Orchestra, Budapest / Mátyás Antál**
Naxos 8 550642 (54 minutes: DDD) Ⓢ
Recorded 1992

Cantatas Nos 51 and 208
Ingrid Kertesi, Julia Pászthy *sops* **Judit Nemeth** *mez* **Jozsef Mukk** *ten* **István Gáti** *bar*
Hungarian Radio Chorus; Failoni Chamber Orchestra, Budapest / Mátyás Antál
Naxos 8 550643 (60 minutes: DDD) Ⓢ
Recorded 1992

On these two discs Naxos have included four of Bach's most celebrated and accessible cantatas. The performances are far removed in character from the complete Harnoncourt and Leonhardt edition on Teldec; women rather than boys sing all the soprano and alto solos, the Hungarian Radio Chorus is a mixed male and female ensemble and the Failoni Chamber Orchestra of

Budapest plays modern rather than period instruments. However, for much of the time this is enjoyable spirited music-making which, in its choice of tempos, its understanding of recitative and its feeling for the lyricism of Bach's writing compares favourably with rival modern instrument versions. The disappointment lies partly in the choice of edition and solution to instrumentation. *Sheep may safely graze* (No 208) is without the treble recorders which Bach specifically asked for and which intensify the pastoral idyll. Here, furthermore the flutes are rather distantly balanced giving them a somewhat irrelevant role which is far from Bach's intention.

More serious is the decision to follow the inflated version of the first and fifth movements of *Ein feste Burg* (No 80) penned by Bach's eldest son, Wilhelm Friedemann shortly after his father's death. Here Friedemann added three trumpets and a kettledrum to the original texture of oboes and strings, and though some may prefer the more overt sense of occasion and the emphasis of the church militant, that this achieves, the scoring of the original is unquestionably effective and in keeping with the piece as a whole. Much else here is sensitively and unsentimentally performed. 'Jesu, joy of man's desiring' (from No 147) is perhaps a shade on the slow side. Most affecting of all though, is the canonic alto/tenor duet from No 80 whose tender writing for oboe da caccia and violin has long been for some one of the purplest of all passages in the entire Bach cantata canon. The soprano Ingrid Kertesi negotiates the many difficulties of *Jauchzet Gott in allen Landen!* fluently and with a youthful zeal and few will be disappointed by her spirited artistry. To sum up, these are two mainly very enjoyable discs which can be confidently recommended. Clear recorded sound.

Cantatas Nos 105[a]; 179 and 186[b]
Miah Persson *sop* [ab]**Robin Blaze** *counterten*
Makoto Sakurada *ten* **Peter Kooy** *bass*
Bach Collegium Japan / Masaaki Suzuki
BIS CD951 (63 minutes: DDD) Ⓕ
Texts and translations included. Recorded 1999 ⭘

Bach Collegium Japan's eloquent advance into the rich repository of cantatas composed during Bach's first year at Leipzig is distinguished in Vol 10 by Masaaki Suzuki's remarkable instinct for the emotional core of each of these three works. Experiencing *Herr, gehe nicht ins Gericht* (No 105) reveals a sense of open-hearted fervour and contemplation, never for a minute cloying or self-regarding at the expense of vibrant expression. This is a work embued with a rich discography, yet what Suzuki uniquely achieves, compelling in the opening chorus, is an intensity born of subtle contrast in vocal and instrumental articulation, underpinned by his uncanny ability to choose a tempo which provides for lyrical intimacy and organic gesture, as the respective texts demand. Suzuki grasps the magnificent nobility of the composer's inspired musical commentary on the human soul in No 105. Miah Persson exhibits sustained control and delectable purity of tone in the continuo-less 'Wie zittern und wanken' and 'Liebster Gott' from No 179. With Peter Kooy's cathartic recitative singing (preparing the spirit of salvation) and the beautifully balanced tenor aria and final chorale, Herreweghe's elegant and fragrant 1990 account, a clear leader until now, has a companion on the top rung.

The bipartite Trinity cantata, *Ärgre dich, o Seele, nicht* (No 186), revised from a Weimar version of 1716, conveys equally Suzuki's assurance and vision. Perhaps the choruses which frame Part 1 are a touch short on gravitas (and tuning is intermittently awry in the first) but here, and in the formidable opening movement of No 179 rhythmic incision is the order of the day and the jorchestral playing as fine as any from Collegium Japan. This is another first-rate achievement (the soloists are slightly recessed but the recorded sound is excellent). Arguably the most complete and mature offering in the series so far.

Cantatas Nos 211 and 212 🅿
Emma Kirkby *sop* **Rogers Covey-Crump** *ten*
David Thomas *bass* **Academy of Ancient Music / Christopher Hogwood**
L'Oiseau-Lyre 417 621-2OH (52 minutes: DDD) Ⓕ
Texts and translations included ⭘
Recorded 1984

These two most delightful of Bach's secular cantatas here receive sparkling performances fully alive to the humour and invention of the music. The *Coffee* Cantata illustrates a family altercation over a current enthusiasm, the drinking of coffee. A narrator tells the story whilst the soprano and bass soloists confront each other in a series of delightful arias. Thomas brings out the crabby dyspeptic side of Schlendrian's character imaginatively and Kirkby makes a charming minx-like Lieschen. Covey-Crump's sweet light tenor acts as a good foil. The *Peasant* Cantata also takes the form of a dialogue, here between a somewhat dull and simple young man and his sweetheart Mieke, a girl who intends to better herself. Through the 24 short movements Bach conjures up a wonderfully rustic picture with some vivid dance numbers and rumbustious ritornellos. The soloists' nicely rounded characterizations emerge with great humour and Hogwood directs with vitality and sprightly rhythmic control. The recording is excellent.

Additional recommendations
Cantatas
Nos 51 and 61
Couplings: St Matthew Passion – excerpts. Chorale Prelude, BWV639. Italian Concerto, BWV971. Double Violin Concerto, BWV1043. Overtures Nos 2 and 3, BWV1067-68
Various artists; Monteverdi Choir; English Baroque Soloists / Gardiner
DG Panorama 469 106-2GP2 Ⓜ
(149 minutes: DDD: 4/85[R] and 2/93[R])

A fine performance of No 51, in which soloist Emma Kirkby captures well the spirit of rejoicing, and an outstandingly successful performance of No 61.

Nos 78 and 106 H
Stich-Randall *sop* **Hermann** *mez* **Dermota** *ten* **Braun** *bar*
Vienna Bach Guild Choir and Orchestra / Prohaska
Omega Records mono/stereo OVC2009 Ⓜ
(49 minutes: ADD). Texts and translations included
Not available in the UK at present but try the internet.

One of the great recordings of the 20th century. Prohaska's No 78 remains unrivalled for its cohesive overall concept and for the great distinction of its soloists. A performance which no lover of Bach's music should be without.

Motets

Motets – Singet dem Herren, BWV225; P
Der Geist hilft unsrer Schwachheit auf, BWV226;
Jesu meine Freude, BWV227; Fürchte dich nicht, BWV228; Komm, Jesu, komm, BWV229;
Lobet den Herren, BWV230
Greta de Reyghere, Katelijne van Laetham *sops* **Martin van der Zeijst, Sytse Buwalda** *countertens* **Hans Hermann Jansen** *tens* **Johannes-Christoph Happel** *bar* **La Petite Bande Choir; La Petite Bande / Sigiswald Kuijken**
Accent ACC9287 (65 minutes: DDD) Ⓕ
Texts and translations included. Recorded 1992

Motets, BWV225-30
Netherlands Chamber Choir / Ton Koopman
Philips 434 165-2PH (63 minutes: DDD) Ⓕ
Texts and translations included. Recorded 1986-87

These two approaches to Bach's Motets differ strongly from one another. Kuijken directs performances with *colla parte* instrumental support, that is to say with instruments doubling each of the vocal strands. Koopman, on the other hand, prefers the vocal strands *a cappella* with instruments providing only the basso continuo. The choir in each version is made up of women sopranos and countertenors with the men's voices. Choosing between the versions is difficult and to a large extent must be a matter of which approach you prefer. Kuijken's performances are more relaxed than those of Koopman. He avoids anything in the nature of overdirection and, while neither singing nor playing is always quite as tidy as it might be, there is a lively spontaneity, especially rewarding in the radiant performance of *Singet dem Herren*. Koopman draws more sharply articulated singing than Kuijken from the Netherlands Chamber Choir though sometimes at the expense of natural declamation and spontaneity. But there is greater linear clarity here than in the other and it pays off handsomely in *Komm, Jesu, komm*. It is a pity that Koopman does not avail himself of the surviving instrumental parts for *Der Geist hilft* but, in other respects, the strengths and weaknesses of the two performances are fairly evenly distributed and both are highly recommended.

Magnificat, BWV243

Bach Magnificat in D, BWV243 P
Vivaldi Ostro picta, RV642. Gloria in D, RV589
Emma Kirkby, Tessa Bonner *sops* **Michael Chance** *counterten* **John Mark Ainsley** *ten* **Stephen Varcoe** *bar* **Collegium Musicum 90 Chorus and Orchestra / Richard Hickox**
Chandos Chaconne CHAN0518 Ⓕ
(64 minutes: DDD). Texts and translations included.
Recorded 1990 ⊙

This issue was the first CD release featuring the then newly founded Collegium Musicum 90 under its directors Richard Hickox and Simon Standage. The Collegium embraces both choir and orchestra who are joined in this programme of Bach and Vivaldi by a comparably fine team of soloists. Hickox sets effective tempos in Bach's *Magnificat* and points up the many striking contrasts in colour and texture with which the piece abounds. From among the many successful features of the recording Stephen Varcoe's 'Quia fecit mihi magna' and the 'Et misericordia' sung by Michael Chance and John Mark Ainsley stand out. Vivaldi's *Gloria*, RV589 is the better known of two settings by the composer in D major. In this programme it is prefaced by an introductory motet *Ostro picta*, which may well in fact belong to the *Gloria* and is here sung with warmth and radiance by Emma Kirkby. Hickox's performance of this evergreen vocal masterpiece comes over with conviction. It is gracefully phrased, sensitively sung and affectingly paced with an admirable rapport between vocalists and instrumentalists. The sound is first-rate.

Bach Magnificat[ab] **Kuhnau** Magnificat in C[a] **Zelenka** Magnificat in C, ZWV107[b]. Magnificat in D, ZWV108[a]
[a]**Miah Persson,** [b]**Yukari Nonoshita** *sops* **Akira Tachikawa** *counterten* **Gerd Türk** *ten* **Chiyuki Urano** *bass* **Bach Collegium Japan / Masaaki Suzuki**
BIS CD1011 (72 minutes: DDD) Ⓕ
Texts and translations included. Recorded 1998

The four settings of the *Magnificat* featured here sit comfortably together. Two of them, by Bach's predecessor at Leipzig, Johann Kuhnau, and by Bach himself, are 'Leipzig-born'. The others, by Bach's contemporary Zelenka, were composed for the court chapel at Dresden. What a pity that so much of Kuhnau's sacred vocal music has been lost. Readers acquainted with his cantata *Wie schön leuchtet der Morgenstern* will not be surprised to learn that his *Magnificat* is full of colourfully effective gestures, textural contrasts and suppleness of form. These instrumentalists bring out the rhythmically buoyant character of the opening chorus wonderfully well. The movement is richly scored for three trumpets, drums, oboe, strings and continuo. With this talented ensemble of voices and instruments there is an unusually highly developed sense of phrase contour and rhythm. Be it recitative, aria, chorus, continuo accompaniment or tutti, the component parts are all carefully and most beautifully shaped. Vocal declamation is fresh and incisive and solo contributions are of uniform excellence. These remarks apply equally to the Zelenka and Bach settings. Zelenka's pieces are much the shortest here, yet he does accommodate the entire canticle within a three- and four-movement scheme, each with an appended 'Amen' chorus. Both settings date from the mid-1720s, the D major work, with trumpets and drums, containing some vividly depictive word-painting.

The performance of Bach's *Magnificat* is spirited and, by and large, excellent, though expressively rather cool; but where Kuhnau and Zelenka present few problems for the brass and woodwind, Bach, as nearly always, puts everyone on his and her metal, and chinks in this formidable armour are occasionally revealed. Nevertheless, it is a fine release, above all for the Kuhnau, which should delight many listeners.

Magnificat. Cantata No 51 Ⓟ

Nancy Argenta, Patrizia Kwella, Emma Kirkby *sops* **Charles Brett** *counterten* **Anthony Rolfe Johnson** *ten* **David Thomas** *bass* **English Baroque Soloists / Sir John Eliot Gardiner**

Philips 50 Great Recordings 464 672-2PM Ⓜ

(41 minutes: DDD). Texts and translations included ●

Bach's *Magnificat* is a work full of contrasts – contrasts of texture, of colour and of temperament – few of which escape the attention of Gardiner, his choir, orchestra and fine group of soloists. The choruses are sung with great vigour and precision; articulation is crisp and diction excellent. The solo singing is of a uniformly high standard with some outstanding contributions from Charles Brett, Anthony Rolfe Johnson and David Thomas. One thinks in particular of the 'Quia fecit', in which Thomas is admirably accompanied by a perfectly balanced continuo texture, and the 'Et misericordia' duet for alto and tenor, which is sung with great tenderness and restraint by these artists. Among the obbligato contributions we must single out that of the oboe d'amore in the 'Quia respexit' which is sensitively played and hauntingly beautiful.

The cantata *Jauchzet Gott in allen Landen!* is one of three for solo soprano which Bach wrote at Leipzig during the 1730s. The spirit of the text, as its title implies, is one of rejoicing. It's a spirit which the soloist, Emma Kirkby, captures well. Her solo partner in the colourful opening movement and in the fugal 'Alleluia' at the close is Crispian Steele-Perkins who manages Bach's exacting trumpet parts with precision. Less enjoyable is the exaggerated acceleration in tempo for the 'Alleluia' section of the final movement, but it's a dazzling display without any doubt. These are fine performances of two of Bach's best-known church compositions, with admirably clear recordings.

Magnificat in D, BWV243

Cantata No 21

Greta de Reyghere *sop* **René Jacobs** *counterten* **Christoph Prégardien** *ten* **Peter Lika** *bass* **Netherlands Chamber Choir; La Petite Bande / Sigiswald Kuijken**

Virgin Classics The Classics VM5 61833-2 Ⓑ

(73 minutes: DDD). Notes, texts and translations included. Recorded 1988 ●

The first of this batch of The Classics, coupling performances of Bach's *Magnificat* with Cantata No 21, is in every way recommendable. Indeed Nicholas Anderson's original review commented that in the *Magnificat* Sigiswald Kuijken and La Petite Bande 'reach the heart of Bach's music more convincingly than almost any other [version] currently available'. He went on to comment that he found Kuijken's performance of *Ich hatte viel Bekümmernis* 'profoundly affecting', although he also noticed some instrumental insecurity. Certainly the lovely solo and choral singing in both works, coupled to a superbly atmospheric recording, make this a Bach CD to treasure.

Mass in B minor, BWV232

Monteverdi Choir; English Baroque Soloists / Sir John Eliot Gardiner Ⓟ

Archiv Produktion ② 415 514-2AH2 Ⓕ

(112 minutes: DDD). Notes, text and translation included. Recorded 1985 ●●

There is much to be said for becoming acquainted with more than one version of Bach's B minor Mass. No single performance of a work of this distinction and stature can embrace all its aspects. The argument for one singer to each vocal part has encouraged performers and audiences alike to think afresh about the forces best suited to the work's vocal element. Gardiner opts for differentiation between soloists and a ripieno chorus. He bases his forces on the famous memorandum which Bach handed to the Leipzig town council in 1730 outlining the vocal and instrumental requirements for performances of his church music.

This is a fine achievement. Some listeners may feel the results would have been more satisfying if Gardiner had let the music unfold with greater natural freedom and not felt the need to tweak rhythms and tempos. Some may like that additional degree of excitement engendered by such methods but Bach, above all composers, perhaps, does not require 'whipping up' any more than his profound utterances benefit from exaggerated tempos in either direction in order to underline a point. The many strong points of Gardiner's direction, among which should be singled out a vital rhythmic understanding, a clear and positive sense of purpose, and a naturally affective response to Bach's music, combine in forming a concept of the work which not only explores its ineffable mysteries but also savours the magnificence of its architecture.

The solo vocal line-up is a strong one and there are few weak moments. If we say that the crowning achievement of Gardiner's recording lies in the vitality, accuracy and homogeneity of the ripieno singing it is in no sense intended to underplay the considerable virtues of the soloists and the orchestra. The ripieno singing at its very best – as it is for example, in the 'Et resurrexit' – is thrilling and gives a fervent imprint to the entire work. There is a spontaneity about this singing to which few listeners could remain indifferent. Gardiner's choruses are immediately striking and handled with such skill and rigorous discipline that repeated hearing in no sense diminishes their impact.

Lutheran Masses

Masses[a] – F, BWV233; G, BWV236. **P**
Trio Sonata in C, BWV529 (arr Boothby)
[a]**Nancy Argenta** *sop* [a]**Michael Chance** *counterten* [a]**Mark Padmore** *ten* [a]**Peter Harvey** *bass* **Purcell Quartet** (Catherine Mackintosh, Catherine Weiss *vns* Richard Boothby *vc* Robert Woolley *org*)
Chandos Chaconne CHAN0653 (65 minutes: DDD) Ⓕ
Text and translation included ●

Thank goodness the absurd prejudice that has long deprived us of adequate recordings of Bach's four Lutheran Masses (or short Masses, as they are also known because, in accordance with Lutheran usage, they set only the *Kyrie* and *Gloria*) seems finally to have died a death. The Masses' crime has been to be made up almost entirely of paraphrases of cantata movements from the 1720s, yet Bach is Bach, whatever the circumstances, and this is wonderful music which, like the B minor Mass, offers sober old-style polyphonic choral movements of impressive cumulative power alongside choruses of almost physical excitement and clamour and some first-rate arias with instrumental obbligato.

As with volume 1 the Purcell Quartet adopt a one-to-a-part approach, with the four vocal soloists also forming the choir and the Purcell Quartet being augmented by whatever extra instruments are needed. The result sounds not in the least underpowered, and gains considerably over Herreweghe's typically well-turned but more traditional choral approach in vividness of texture and harmony, crispness of attack and a madrigalian litheness of expressive response.

The rather dry recording which sometimes caused discomfort in the first volume has here been replaced by a more generous one which allows just the right amount of bloom without becoming washy. There are times when the two higher voices sound further forward than the others, and Michael Chance occasionally disappears a bit towards the bottom of his range, but in general this release brings nothing but pleasure both in the music and in the stylish and lively performances.

Mass in F, BWV233*a*. Cantatas Nos 65 and 180. **P**
Sanctus in D, BWV238
Ann Monoyios *sop* **Angus Davidson** *counterten* **Charles Daniels** *ten* **Peter Harvey** *bar* **Gabrieli Consort and Players / Paul McCreesh**
Archiv Produktion ② 457 631-2AH2 Ⓕ
(160 minutes: DDD). Texts and translations included. Includes readings, congregational hymns and organ works by Bach and Pachelbel. Recorded 1997 ●

This two-disc set contains four vocal works by Bach, set in the context of an Epiphany Mass 'as it might have been celebrated in St Thomas, Leipzig *c*1740'. Though several attempts have been made in the past to re-create the sequence of events at the two main services where Bach's cantatas were sung, the *Hauptgottesdienst*, in the morning, and the Vesper, in the afternoon, this is the first time that such a project has been committed to disc. You are very likely to be captivated by much of what Paul McCreesh and his musicians, with help in liturgical canon from the scholar, Robin A Leaver, have achieved.

The sacred vocal works which have been chosen for this reconstruction of a *Hauptgottesdienst* for the *Dreikönigsfest* ('Feast of the Three Kings') are the F major Lutheran Mass, the *Sanctus* and two cantatas, *Sie werden aus Saba alle kommen*, a true Epiphany piece, and *Schmücke dich, o liebe Seele* which is foremost a Trinity piece but one which Bach may well have used on other occasions. McCreesh did well in securing the services of Ann Monoyios and Peter Harvey, but all involved make an impressive showing. The *Missa* comes over very well, Monoyios's 'Qui tollis peccata mundi' outstanding for its warmth of colour. An interesting experiment is carried out in the resonant Epiphany cantata, No 65. Here the horns are played an octave higher than usual, at trumpet pitch, with striking results. McCreesh emphasises the lyrical character of this glorious movement, rather than its more readily captured processional grandeur.

The brisk tempo chosen for the superb chorale fantasy with which No 180 begins is less convincing. The brilliant tenor aria with virtuoso flute obbligato which follows is, on the other hand, well considered in respect of tempo, and is beautifully articulated by flautist Jed Wentz. But it is Monoyios who, once more, steals the show with her affecting account of the lyrical elaboration with violoncello piccolo of a verse from the Communion hymn on which the cantata is based. And her subsequent aria is comparably fluent and secure.

Much thought has gone into the solo organ elements of the Mass, not least by keyboard players James Johnstone, Timothy Roberts and James O'Donnell. Overall, this project is likely to interest all lovers of Bach's music. The recorded sound, from Freiburg Cathedral and Brand-Erbisdorf in Saxony, is excellent.

Additional recommendation
Lutheran Masses, BWV233-236
Couplings: Cantata Nos 39, 73, 93, 105, 107, 131 and Santus in D, BWV238
Various soloists; Collegium Vocale / Herreweghe
Virgin Classics ④ VBD5 61721-2 (239 minutes: DDD) Ⓢ
Attractive accounts of the Masses (though textural clarity in the choral movements suffers in the reverberant acoustic) and well paced and at times deeply felt accounts of the cantatas, some scrappy ensemble playing aside.

St John Passion, BWV245

Gerd Türk *ten* Evangelist; **Chiyuki Urano** *bass* Jesus; **Ingrid Schmidthüsen, Yoshie Hida** *sops* **Yoshikazu Mera** *counterten* **Makoto Sakurada** *ten* **Peter Kooy** *bass* **P**

Bach Collegium Japan / Masaaki Suzuki
BIS ② CD921/2 (110 minutes: DDD) Ⓕ
Text and translation included. Recorded 1998 **OO**

Bach seems to have performed his *St John Passion* on four Good Fridays during his tenure as Thomaskantor at Leipzig. However, he continued to make significant revisions right up to the last performance under his direction, on April 4, 1749. Of the four versions, the second, dating from 1725, contains the most distinctive revisions, the first version (1724) and the last bearing close affinity with one another. Masaaki Suzuki and his talented Bach Collegium Japan have chosen Bach's latest version. All has evidently been carefully prepared and deeply considered: what is refreshing about their approach is the importance afforded to the relationship between text and music, to the theological source of Bach's inspiration, and the emotional impact of the story and music on its audience. Some of their thoughts may strike readers as simplistic, even perhaps a shade sentimental, but on the strength of this fervent performance we can hardly question their sincerity.

The role of the Evangelist, crucial to the lyrical unfolding of the story, and traditionally a tenor role, is sung with clarity and lightness of inflexion by Gerd Türk. His performance is eloquently measured, his phrasing well shaped and his articulation engagingly varied. All of which makes him a riveting story-teller. The role of Jesus is taken by Chiyuki Urano, an artist with a warm-toned and resonant voice. From among the remaining soloists, Ingrid Schmidthüsen and Yoshikazu Mera make strongly appealing contributions and Peter Kooy is satisfying and affecting. Excellent, too, are the contributions of the Collegium's choir of women's and men's voices. There is great textural clarity here, well balanced, furthermore, with the comparably lucid instrumental textures. Choral and instrumental articulation is incisive, propelling the rhythms with energy. The performance draws you in from the start. This is a major recording event, and an eminently satisfying one.

St John Passion, BWV245 (sung in English)
Sir Peter Pears *ten* Evangelist; **Gwynne Howell** *bass* Jesus; **Heather Harper, Jenny Hill** *sops* **Alfreda Hodgson** *contr* **Robert Tear, Russell Burgess, John Tobin, Adrian Thompson** *tens* **John Shirley-Quirk** *bar* **Wandsworth School Boys' Choir; English Chamber Orchestra / Benjamin Britten**
Double Decca ② 443 859-2DF2 Ⓜ
(130 minutes: ADD). Recorded 1971 **OO**

Britten's recording of the *St John Passion* is very special indeed. He apparently preferred to perform this Bach choral work because of its natural potential for drama. With Peter Pears a superb Evangelist this account takes over the listener completely. The soloists are all splendid, though one must single out Heather Harper, and the choral response is inspirational in its moments of sheer fervour.

Britten's direction is urgent and volatile, the Wandsworth School Boys' Choir sings out full-throatedly and the English Chamber Orchestra underpins the whole performance with gloriously rich string textures. Then there is the analogue recording itself which offers a demonstration of ambient fullness, vividness of detail and natural balance. In fact, one gets the impression that a live performance at The Maltings, Snape has been transported to the area just beyond one's speakers!

St John Passion, BWV245
Ruth Holton *sop* **Bogna Bartosz** *contr* **Markus Brutscher** *ten* **Thomas Laske** *bar* **Tom Sol** *bass* **Cologne Chamber Choir; Collegium Cartusianum / Peter Neumann**
Dabringhaus und Grimm ② MDG332 0983-2 Ⓕ
(114 minutes: DDD) Text and translations included.
Recorded 1999 **O**

Bach never entirely settled on a single view of the *St John* and there are at least four known versions, from Good Friday 1724 (Bach's first Easter in Leipzig) to a performance the year before he died. Peter Neumann expounds here on the virtues of the second, dating from a year after the first. The differences are neither extensive nor merely cosmetic; such is Bach's skilful pacing of the narrative that the original conception can shift markedly with an ever-so-slight nudge. The most immediate difference is the replacement of the austere, imagery-laden opening chorus, 'Herr, unser Herrscher', with the chorale fantasy 'O Mensch, bewein', later employed to conclude Part 1 of the *St Matthew*.

To the unsuspecting, this is the *St John Passion* that can have you thinking you're playing the beginning of the second disc of the *St Matthew*; this and two further movements demonstrate Bach's obsession – as with the cantatas of the period – with employing chorales as integral raw material. Yet perhaps more striking still is the interpolation of new arias, possibly derived from an earlier Passion setting conceived in Weimar. These arias, 'Himmel reisse' and 'Zerschmettert mich', are far more animated and graphic than anything in the earlier version; guilt and allusion to self-flagellation abound ('on the way to the cross, I shall graze on thy thorns') in the former, with its stinging chromaticism and the tenuous adhesive of a chorale alongside. More remarkable still is 'Zerschmettert', performed with dazzling immediacy by Evangelist and tenor soloist Markus Brutscher. This is a superb piece of theatrical posturing of the sort that Handel and Telemann would have filched for their opera, had they only known. The one casualty in this version is 'Erwage', a perennial favourite, though it is easy to see how Bach struggled to prefer the organic unfolding of the first version to the more extravagant gestures of the second.

Given that the majority of the work remains common to all, this account should not be judged merely on its special properties. Neumann conveys strong musical ideas throughout the *Passion*: the choruses are wonderfully attentive to contrapuntal detail, well enunciated by the Collegium Cartusianum, and mesmerisingly varied in articulation. One forgets how beautifully crafted and selected the chorale tunes are in this work, and Neumann allows the music to breathe so that they represent a kind of caesura in the otherwise intense narrative. This is largely achieved through a richly conceived textural palette and an enduring bass-line. So, too, the crowd scenes, which can easily become an unfortunate parody of *Monty Python* if the quicksilver diction leads to prittle-prattle. Neumann makes his crowd an excitable rabble, clearly an organised outfit: 'if he were not a criminal, we would not have brought him before you' is given sinister inevitability with the emphasis on 'nicht'.

Brutscher is an utterly reliable, if somewhat monochrome Evangelist. His technical ease and superb intonation are noteworthy, but often he chooses to remain studiously uninvolved. Ruth Holton is made for the bright-eyed discipleship of 'Ich folge' (as we recall her for Gardiner), but there's more to her Bach than youthful-sounding piping, as we can hear in her sensitive and alert rendering of 'Zerfliesse, mein Herze'. The soloists individually are not, however, what marks out this recording; rather it's Neumann's corporate, controlled and intimate concept. He moves skilfully between incandescence and (when required) emotionally charged intensity. This is, then, a persuasive testament to Bach's most radically different version of the *St John*.

St Luke Passion, BWV246 (attrib)

Mona Spägele *sop* **Christiane Iven** *contr* **Rufus Müller, Harry van Berne** *tens* **Stephan Schreckenberger, Marcus Sandmann** *basses* **Alsfeld Vocal Ensemble; Bremen Baroque Orchestra / Wolfgang Helbich** Ⓟ
CPO ② CPO999 293-2 (106 minutes: DDD) Ⓕ
Text and translation included. Recorded 1996 ●

Those who love Bach will want to investigate the *St Luke Passion*; we know that Bach performed it at Leipzig at least twice, and evidently admired it for what it is: a succinct and highly competent blend of Lutheran *Kapellmeister* craft and a few fashionable *galant* nuances. In terms of scale, rhetorical intensity, structural and stylistic sophistication, musical invention and artistic ambition generally, this work finds no common ground with Bach's two extant passions. That said, Bach judged that a simple juxtaposition of chorus-(chorale)-recitative-chorus, with the occasional aria, could hold its own in the traditional deliberations of Leipzig's Holy Week. The modern listener will find much that is intimate and touching about this Passion setting. The meditative element comes less from contemplative arias than from a continuous and freshly fashioned narrative, although the arias, with their favoured wind obbligato parts, are often skilled and affecting.

Wolfgang Helbich and his Bremen forces pitch the dramatic climate just about right throughout. Smoothly articulated, unmannered and technically accomplished, the chorales and *turba* scenes are especially well judged. The Evangelist, Rufus Müller, conveys the Gospel with soft-grained clarity and understated dignity and the other soloists do more than justice to the six arias. Indeed, for all the many qualities of the performance, especially the affectionate contribution of the Alsfeld Vocal Ensemble, this enterprising recording ever sharpens the distinction of Bach and his relatively functional role as Kantor with the parallel workings of his compositional mind. Whether this is Wolfgang Helbich's tacit intention, Bach's genius glows ever brighter.

St Mark Passion, BWV247

(reconstr Koopman)
Sibylla Rubens *sop* **Bernhard Landauer** *counterten* **Christoph Prégardien, Paul Agnew** *tens* **Peter Kooy, Klaus Mertens** *basses* **Breda Sacraments Choir; Amsterdam Baroque Choir and Orchestra / Ton Koopman**
Erato ② 8573-80221-2 (118 minutes: DDD) Ⓕ
Recorded 1999 ●

Not a note of Bach's *St Mark Passion* exists, but we know it existed once and that it was a parody work. Koopman makes no bones about the purely speculative nature of this project. He pretends he's a Bach student: 'Here is a libretto; set it to music using anything you find in the works I have written up to now (1731). What you do not find, compose yourself.' And how he revels in the opportunity to draw on his vast knowledge of Bach's choral music as he matches cantata choruses and quasi-*turbae* to Picander's extant text of Bach's lost Passion. This has been done before, most recently by Andor Gomme and Simon Heighes but using, as the accepted basis of the contemplative texts, the contemporaneous *Trauer* Ode (BWV196) as well as recitatives and choruses from Keiser's *St Mark Passion*. Koopman feels this is not a satisfying parody, and similarly refuses to raid equivalent music from the *St John Passion* (although he uses 'Zerschmettert mich' from the second version of 1725).

In fact, the *St Mark*, as Bach would have recognised, was a different type of proposition to the *St John* or *St Matthew Passions* and he would have made no attempt to model it on his two previous settings; the libretto here draws more on the austerity of the narrative than the luxuriance of the commentary. Hence, there are fewer arias, fewer moments of poetic reflection and a more concentrated gospel narrative.

Koopman's deft sense of the appropriate idiom is reflected in his choice of the opening chorus, taken from BWV25, luminously sung with its well-disguised Passion chorale intensifying the harmonic direction. The arias witness seasoned Bachians in full flow. Paul Agnew conveys 'Falsche Welt' as a graphic declamation, confirming a brilliantly effective transformation taken from BWV179, 'Hypocrites who thus ignore' becoming 'treacherous world, thy flattering kisses are but poison'. This has a more Passion-like bearing than the music from BWV54 used in Gomme and Heighes's reworking.

As for the recitatives, Koopman 'knows what he is talking about', to quote him. His construction of the recitatives is not entirely unlike the striking Mozartian pastiches of Robert Levin, though there is a tendency for formulas to lead to an imbalance of concentration on a particular pivotal chord; it therefore just misses being idiomatic. It isn't Bach, and how reassuring that is! Yet Koopman's more self-conscious recitatives – and they are few and far between – make for a slightly restless start and not the organic unfolding of Bach's extant Passions, though this is partly caused by injudicious spacing between tracks.

As for the delivery, Christoph Prégardien reveals his best ringing expressivity. This is a voice in fine fettle at present. The cast is indeed strong when you've got two basses such as the poised Klaus Mertens and the authoritative Christus of Peter Kooy. The chorus and orchestra are uniformly fine throughout.

Koopman's version of the *St Mark* – which shuns some of the most historically likely parody movements used by Bach – is inclined to make the piece a rather more sophisticated compilation than it probably was. But as there is no evidence, Koopman is ever the idealist and gives us something of real musical substance, in certain respects more a spiritual parody of the *St John* and *St Matthew*.

Apart from being the most satisfying account to date, it is a performance which best serves the mystery of the Passion, differently told, as a wonderful narrative for musico-poetic dramatic contours. The only gripe is that Koopman does not list the cantata sources in the booklet.

St Matthew Passion, BWV244

Awards 1990

Anthony Rolfe Johnson *ten* Evangelist; **Andreas Schmidt** *bar* Jesus; **Barbara Bonney, Ann Monoyios** *sops* **Anne Sofie von Otter** *mez* **Michael Chance** *counterten* **Howard Crook** *ten* **Olaf Bär** *bar* **Cornelius Hauptmann** *bass* **London Oratory Junior Choir; Monteverdi Choir; English Baroque Soloists / Sir John Eliot Gardiner** P

Archiv Produktion ③ 427 648-2AH3 (167 minutes: DDD). Text and translation included. Recorded 1989 Ⓕ ooo

What makes John Eliot Gardiner's *St Matthew Passion* stand out in the face of stiff competition is perhaps more than anything his vivid sense of theatre. Bach's score is, after all, a sacred drama and Gardiner interprets this aspect of the work with lively and colourful conviction. That in itself, of course, is not sufficient to ensure a fine performance but here we have a first-rate group of solo voices, immediately responsive choral groups in the Monteverdi Choir and the London Oratory Junior Choir – a distinctive element this and refined obbligato and orchestral playing from the English Baroque Soloists. Anthony Rolfe Johnson declaims the Evangelist's role with clarity, authority and the subtle inflexion of an accomplished story-teller. Ann Monoyios, Howard Crook and Olaf Bär also make strong contributions but it is Michael Chance's 'Erbarme dich', tenderly accompanied by the violin obbligato, which sets the seal of distinction on the performance. Singing and playing of this calibre deserve to win many friends and Gardiner's deeply felt account of Bach's great Passion does the music considerable justice. Clear recorded sound.

St Matthew Passion, BWV244 P

Christoph Prégardien *ten* Evangelist; **Matthias Goerne** *bar* Christus; **Christine Schäfer, Dorothea Röschmann** *sops* **Bernarda Fink, Elisabeth von Magnus** *contrs* **Michael Schade, Markus Schäfer** *tens* **Dietrich Henschel, Oliver Widmer** *basses* **Vienna Boys' Choir; Arnold Schoenberg Choir; Concentus Musicus Wien / Nikolaus Harnoncourt**

Teldec ③ 8573 81036-2 (163 minutes: DDD) Ⓕ

Includes enhanced CD with full autograph score. Recorded 2000 oo

Harnoncourt has waited over 30 years to return with his Concentus Musicus Wien to the 'Great Passion', which, but for his live Concertgebouw recording (Teldec – nla), he last recorded in 1970 when he had completed only a handful of cantatas in Teldec's defining series. Harnoncourt's re-visitation presents a unique statement, one which cannot fail to make an impression. Recorded in the sumptuous acoustic of the Jesuitenkirche in Vienna, one can detect the flavour of southern European oratorio, ebulliently theatrical, immediate and free-breathing, and without the austerity of North German rhetoric. What is recognisably perceived as 'spiritual' in the carefully coiffured renderings of Suzuki (BIS) and Herreweghe (Harmonia Mundi) has no place here. Harnoncourt's religiosity is not imposed but stands rather in a lifetime of musical distillation. This is instantly obvious in the opening chorus, where bridal imagery (in the music's secular, balletic lift) is juxtaposed with the physical imagery of what is at stake (in the broad, enduring bow strokes). While Suzuki's visceral chorale is more spine-tingling, the refinement here of 'Sehet, Wohin?' amidst inexorable, paradoxically unquestioning direction, is masterful.

Pacing Part 1 is no easy task, and many a tank has been emptied before reaching what the great Bach scholar Friederich Smend called 'the central message of the work' (encompasssing Nos 46-49). Harnoncourt neither dallies unduly with the chorales nor charges through them; they skilfully counterbalance the remarkably incandescent narrative of Christoph Prégardien's Evangelist. The tenor shows a supreme attention to detail (even if his singing is sometimes effortful), and his dialogue with Matthias Goerne's vital Christus is especially compelling. At such moments, a large liturgical space gives the work a dramatic energy which is matched in the sharply etched arias, each carefully withdrawn from the marketplace of the action to stand on its own merits. Harnoncourt gives 'Blute nur' a touch of characteristic melodrama, but none can doubt how Dorothea Röschmann and the orchestra, between them, project its expressive core.

The well-drilled, medium-sised Arnold Schoenberg Choir's strikingly cultivated crowd scenes make a strong contrast with the relatively brazen chorus in Harnoncourt's 1970 version. 'Lasst ihn, haltet, bindet nicht!' is surprisingly but affectingly understated, yet one might wish for more incision (in No 60, for example) and dynamic contrast elsewhere without the slick physicality of the Monteverdi Choir. Unlike the specialists of the pioneering years, Harnoncourt hand-picks his soloists from the widest possible pool. Apart from the excellent Röschmann, Christine Schäfer impresses here far more than in her rather harried solo Bach disc (DG). More relaxed and controlled, she sings with acute coloration and stillness in 'Aus Liebe'. With Bernarda Fink's beguiling 'Erbarme dich' and Michael Schade's resplendent 'Geduld', only Oliver Widmer (who sings 'Gebt mir') gives less than unalloyed pleasure. The pick of the crop is Dietrich Henschel, who sings with great warmth and penetration with a 'Mache dich' to stand alongside (if not to rival) Fischer-Dieskau for Karl Richter. But with even these wonderful contributions, it still takes clarity of vision to graphically propel the drama yet also ponder it reverentially. Again, Harnoncourt leaves his mark with his unerring compassion at most of the critical points. 'O Schmerz' is dynamic in the juxtaposition of the panicking Zion and the unfazed faithful. The austerity is palpable where Christ gives up the ghost. From that point on, we must return to Richter's 1958 recording for the benchmark. Harnoncourt projects a more resigned and objective set of emotional 'tableaux' compared to Richter's long-breathed and ethereal ritual in the final cadence. Given the way Bach builds the tension at the mid-point from 'O Mensch bewein', there is a degree of anti-climax as Harnoncourt (or his producer) sacrifices momentum by creating large gaps between sections. Are these really intended?

Finally, one should mention Concentus Musicus, grainy and luminous in ensemble, the obbligato wind a far cry from the softer-edged and rounded tonal world of almost all other 'period' groups (though some occasional brittle intonation is slightly disorienting). In short, this is the most culturally alert reading in years. A truly original and illuminating experience (not least, the bonus CD-Rom of the autograph score) blemished only by the shoddy editing of 'silence' between numbers in the last disc.

Additional recommendation

St Matthew Passion, BWV244

Orchestra of the Eighteenth Century / Brüggen Ⓟ

Philips ③ 454 434-2PH3 (160 minutes: DDD) Ⓕ

This is a *St Matthew Passion* which should please many. Frans Brüggen's live interpretation is eloquent, thoughtful in matters of style and expressive content, and has a textural clarity which few competitors can rival.

Christmas Oratorio, BWV248

Monika Frimmer *sop* **Yoshikazu Mera** *counterten* **Gerd Türk** *ten* **Peter Kooy** *bass* **Bach Collegium Japan / Masaaki Suzuki** Ⓟ

BIS ② CD941/2 (145 minutes: DDD) Ⓕ

Text and translation included. Recorded 1998 ●●

The six cantatas that make up Bach's *Christmas Oratorio* are part of a unified work celebrating not just Christmas itself but also the New Year and Epiphany. Masaaki Suzuki faces plentiful if not invariably stiff competition in this work. In fact, it outstrips most of its rivals, in respect both of vocal and instrumental considerations. A notable quality in Masaaki Suzuki's direction is his feeling for naturally expressive contours, allowing the music to breathe freely. Best of all, perhaps, is his refusal to pay even lip service to the upheld beliefs concerning Bach's supposed predilection for fast tempos. Everything here seems to be exceptionally well judged, which is not to say that the pace of individual movements is necessarily slower than those in some competing versions, but rather that it is more interrelated with a concept of each section as a whole, and perhaps more textually conscious than some. In these respects the *Oratorio*'s underlying strength and unity of purpose is wonderfully well served.

The soloists are generally very good indeed. Yoshikazu Mera makes a distinctive contribution and Gerd Türk is a communicative singer whose light articulation well suits his partly narrative role. Peter Kooy never puts a foot wrong, while Monika Frimmer makes a favourable impression in her duet with Kooy, 'Herr, dein Mitleid, dein Erbarmen' (Part 3). Elsewhere, her freshly complexioned voice is seldom other than pleasing. A small, well-balanced choir of technical agility and an accomplished quorum of instrumentalists set the seal on an outstanding achievement. The finest all-round performance of the *Christmas Oratorio* on disc.

Christmas Oratorio, BWV248

Sibylla Rubens *sop* **Ingeborg Danz** *contr* **James Taylor, Marcus Ullmann** *tens* **Hanno Müller-Brachmann** *bass* **Gächinger Kantorei; Stuttgart Bach Collegium / Helmuth Rilling**

Hänssler Classic ③ 92 076 (144 minutes: DDD) Ⓜ

Texts and translations included. Recorded 1999 ●

Here, in Bach's longest oratorio, energetic director Helmut Rilling is more fired up than ever. The choruses crackle with thrilling fervour and – dare one say it – a blistering attack and shine to notes which, alongside a forthright Gächinger Kantorei, carry the day persuasively on modern instruments. There will always be those for whom Rilling represents an inflexibility of phrasing and unyielding articulation in Bach, paradoxically more reminiscent of the least alluring elements of period performance than the 'ebb and flow' of mainstream consciousness. This recording doubtless reinforces the odd prejudice, though the habitually hard-edged orchestral textures of the Bach Collegium Stuttgart seem more mollifying and warm-hearted in movements such as the pastoral Sinfonia at the beginning of Part 2 and the divinely inspired 'Schlafe, mein Liebster' later in the same cantata (it must be said now, flawed by a tiresomely repeated pull-up before the second phrase).

One of the more unusual challenges of performing Bach's *Christmas Oratorio* is to identify salient elements in the six sections which can interconnect the narrative as cohesively as possible – beyond chorale links – and restore momentum after long, self-contained arias: six cantatas, one after another, can make for a long evening. This task falls largely to the Evangelist, though neither he, nor the aria singers, are consistently employed as dramatis personae in either a Handelian manner or, indeed, as Bach conceived for the Passions.

James Taylor is a natural front-bench spokesman: articulate, discriminating, exacting if not emotionally candid. He also retains focus throughout the respective events of each tableau and gives clearly etched readings. Yet much of the credit must also go to the outstanding solo singing. Whatever one feels about Rilling's overall vision, no one can deny that he is one of very few Bachians these days who repeatedly books fine Bach singers and realises their potential. This is evident in the incandescence of Sibylla Rubens and Hanno Müller-Brachmann in the pivotal duet of Part 3, 'Herr, dein Mitleid' and the scene-setting 'Bereite dich, Zion' which Ingeborg Danz sings with such exquisite and gentle poise. If her 'Schlafe' is a touch disappointing, then that reflects the weight of expectation which surrounds this central aria. If you prefer a mezzo to a countertenor, then only Anne Sofie von Otter for Gardiner or Christa Ludwig for Richter can better her largely satisfying contribution. Müller-Brachmann is a fine bass soloist in 'Grosser Herr' and as movingly intimate as Michael George for Philip Pickett in the recitative with chorale, 'Immanuel, O süsses Wort'. Rubens is on really terrific form throughout and her 'Nur in Wink' in Part 6 is a model of outstanding Bach singing.

In a piece that so skilfully parodies the works he had written around 1735, there is always the sense that he was moving towards an increasingly conceptual vision of an oratorio, a statement for posterity much in the same vein as the Mass in B minor. Rilling's strength is that he balances pragmatic concerns with a sense of dignified place in the greater scheme (especially well handled in Part 5 with the wise men's arrival from the East) and the maturity of Bach's comprehensive display of festive spirit leading to the inexorable brilliance of Part 6. There is, then, a spiritual containment which serves its purpose here – there's absolutely no sentimental guff – and yet it perhaps trespasses into the clinical too readily. Rilling, as ever, raises one's hopes and only intermittently fulfils them, but this is still a distinguished reading on many counts.

Easter Oratorio, BWV249

Easter Oratorio. Cantata No 11 **P**
Monika Frimmer *sop* **Ralf Popken** *counterten* **Christoph Prégardien** *ten* **David Wilson-Johnson** *bar* **Choir and Orchestra of the Age of Enlightenment / Gustav Leonhardt**
Philips 442 119-2PH (73 minutes: DDD) Ⓕ
Texts and translations included. Recorded 1993

Of the two Bach oratorios on this generously filled disc, it is the *Easter Oratorio* which is the least performed today. It is a work of customary Bachian brilliance in the quality of individual movements, even if the whole is not entirely satisfying. It does, however, carry a unique flavour and one with which Leonhardt clearly feels a close affinity. This is evident in the way he handles the exuberant Sinfonia with knowing and stately bravura, also providing copious insights into the phrasing of the wonderful wind dialogues – all played with fastidious clarity and *élan* by the OAE. Whilst this movement sparkles, Leonhardt (or rather the oboist, Anthony Robson) gives more flesh to the subsequent *Adagio*; this is splendidly vocalised playing. Both here and in the *Ascension* Oratorio the chorus is fairly streamlined and although the quality of singing goes without saying, greater breadth to Bach's choruses in the second work would have been preferable. The soloists on the latter are variable. Only Ralf Popken in 'Saget, saget mir' is ideal. Despite some misgivings, Leonhardt's perceptive performances will always win friends and his recording of the *Easter Oratorio* still appeals more than its competitors. As for the *Ascension* Oratorio, although not a front-runner, this recording certainly has its revelatory moments.

Wilhelm Friedemann Bach

German 1710-1784

GROVE *Wilhelm Friedemann, the eldest son of JS Bach, studied under his father at the Leipzig Thomasschule; his father put together a 'Clavier-Büchlein' for him and may have written book 1 of the '48' with him in mind. Friedemann also studied the violin with JG Graun. After university study, he became organist at the Dresden Sophienkirche in 1733; he moved to the Liebfrauenkirche, Halle, in 1746 but his years there were turbulent and he left in 1764. He later lived in Brunswick and then in Berlin, but with his difficult temperament and perhaps dissolute character found no regular employment though his organ playing was admired.*

The volatility of his musical style is of a piece with his life. In his early years he wrote mainly for keyboard; at Dresden, for instruments; at Halle, church cantatas and some instrumental music; and in his late years, chiefly chamber and keyboard works. He vacillated in style between old and new, with galant elements alongside conservative Baroque ones, intense north German expressiveness alongside more formal writing. His keyboard music includes fugues and deeply felt polonaises. His gifts are unmistakable here and in such works as the Concerto for two solo harpsichords or the often suite-like Sinfonia in F, but the final impression is of a composer whose potential was never fully realised.

Cantatas

Cantatas – Lasset uns ablegen die Werke der Finsternis, F80. Es ist eine Stimme eines Predigers in der Wüste, F89
Barbara Schlick *sop* **Claudia Schubert** *contr* **Wilfried Jochens** *ten* **Stephan Schreckenberger** *bass* **Rheinische Kantorei; Das Kleine Konzert / Hermann Max**
Capriccio 10 425 (54 minutes: DDD)
Texts and translations included. Recorded 1991

Cantatas – Sinfonia in D, F64.
Dies ist der Tag, F85. Erzittert und fallet, F83
Barbara Schlick *sop* **Claudia Schubert** *contr* **Wilfried Jochens** *ten* **Stephan Schreckenberger** *bass* **Rheinische Kantorei; Das Kleine Konzert / Hermann Max**
Capriccio 10 426 (60 minutes: DDD)
Texts and translations included. Recorded 1991

These two discs of sacred cantatas make a valuable contribution towards a fuller understanding of this highly gifted but complex member of the Bach clan. In the mid-1740s Wilhelm Friedemann was appointed Director of Music and organist at the Marienkirche at Halle. He remained in the post for almost 20 years, a period which witnessed the composition and performance of all the cantatas represented here. Among the many delights to be found in this music are those occasioned by Friedemann's disparate, even opposing terms of reference. In other words the stylistic vocabulary is both rich and varied, often harking back to a strong paternal influence – what better one has there ever been? JS Bach's idiom, for instance, is startlingly apparent in the opening chorus of the Advent cantata, F80 ('Let us cast off the works of darkness'). Both the arias of this fine cantata are of high quality, the first, for soprano with obbligato flute ably demonstrating how carefully Friedemann thought out his declamation. This is a movement of real distinction, lyrical, poignant and admirably well sustained. The remaining three cantatas are rich in points of interest. The athletic trumpet and vocal writing of the opening chorus of the St John's Day cantata, F89 ('The voice of him that crieth in the wilderness') are immediately arresting; so too, is the wonderfully rhapsodic organ obbligato which accompanies the *galant*, virtuoso soprano aria of that work.

The cantatas, F64 ('This is the day') and F83 ('Tremble and fall') probably date from the late-1750s and are less Janus-like in their musical stance. The Whitsun cantata, F85 is a particularly festive piece which is prefaced by a three-movement Sinfonia scored for horns, flutes, oboes, bassoon and strings. This in fact replaces the more usual elaborate choral movement, choral writing being confined to a simple concluding hymn verse. The two arias, one with limpid writing for two flutes, the other with horns, are beguiling and thoroughly in keeping with the developing style of early classicism. For the most part the performances are excellent, discovering with eloquence and stylistic assurance the multifarious details and subtleties of Friedemann Bach's skill in this medium.

The four soloists are first-rate, Barbara Schlick and Wilfried Jochens qualifying for special mention; and the singing of the Rheinische Kantorei is effective, though just occasionally its component 16 voices sound under threat from Bach'ssometimes exacting requirements. Das Kleine Konzert under Hermann Max is strongly supportive and its obbligato players sensitive to the needs of its vocal partners. Imaginative programming and sympathetic performances add to this musical revelation. Full texts and informative notes set the seal on recordings of distinction.

Simon Bainbridge

English 1952

GROVE *Bainbridge studied at the Royal College of Music, London, and Tanglewood; American music, in particular Ives and Reich, has been a formative influence. There is a spatial element in some of his music, which is largely instrumental. Among his most characteristic pieces are the Viola Concerto (1976), Concertante in moto perpetuo (1983) and Fantasia for two orchestras (1984).*

Ad ora incerta

Ad ora incerta (Four orchestral songs from Primo Levi)[a]. Four Primo Levi Settings[b]
Susan Bickley *mez* [a]**Kim Walker** *bn* [b]**Nash Ensemble;** [a]**BBC Symphony Orchestra / Martyn Brabbins**
NMC NMCD059 (54 minutes: DDD). Texts and translations included. Recorded 1997-98

At the beginning of the fourth Primo Levi setting in *Ad ora incerta* (a depiction of the ghastly chemical factory attached to Auschwitz that Levi miraculously survived) there is a slow orchestral *crescendo*, like the panning of a camera to reveal the full horror of the scene. What follows is not a shout of protest but sober lyricism, and when that *crescendo* returns it introduces an eloquently poignant melody. Simon Bainbridge is an uncommonly fine musical dramatist. He lets the words speak, and distils his music so as to clarify them. In *Ad ora incerta* the vocalist has a companion, a solo bassoon. Because that fourth poem repeatedly speaks of a dead companion, of course, but also in the way the bassoon shadows or reflects the voice, there is also a subtle and moving suggestion that after Auschwitz Levi lacked and longed for a companion, a fellow survivor who would understand his memories in ways that none of us can. One can scarcely believe that these beautiful but painful poems could be set to music; certainly not with the delicate and imaginative sympathy that Bainbridge shows here.

The four chamber settings are still sparer but no less gravely beautiful. In the seven brief lines of the first of them Levi distils the impossibility of communicating his experiences yet the imperative need to try. Bainbridge's setting conveys that, but adds the most restrained and loving pity. It is a remarkable and a deeply moving achievement. Both performances are fine, that of the chamber settings beyond praise in its quiet intimacy.

Sir Granville Bantock

British 1868-1946

GROVE *Bantock studied with Corder at the Royal Academy of Music (1889-93), then worked as a conductor and teacher (professor at Birmingham, 1908-34). He did much to promote the music of his English contemporaries and produced a large output of orchestral and large-scale choral works, influenced by early Wagner, a taste for the exotic, and Hebridean folksong. Though much performed at the beginning of the century, when he was at his most productive and a prominent figure in the English musical renaissance, his music has all but disappeared from the repertory; the oratorio Omar Khayyám (1906-09), the overture The Pierrot of the Minute (1908), the Hebridean Symphony (1915) and the Pagan Symphony (1928) have been admired for their undemanding lyricism.*

Pagan Symphony

Pagan Symphony. Fifine at the Fair. Two Heroic Ballads
Royal Philharmonic Orchestra / Vernon Handley
Hyperion CDA66630 (80 minutes: DDD) Ⓕ
Recorded 1992 ●

This collection confirms Bantock as a composer of real achievement whose music has been undeservedly neglected. He was a superb technician, and his impressively large-scale structures (both of the principal works here are single movements lasting over half an hour) have a real urgency. Or perhaps we should say a real enjoyment. Despite the potentially tragic undertones of *Fifine at the Fair*, both works are almost untroubled, filled instead with the geniality of a craftsman joyfully exercising a craft of which he has become master. The cleverness of Bantock's thematic transformations can make you smile with pleasure once you've worked out what he's doing – and then smile again at the realization that the result of the transformation isn't an arid piece of technique for technique's sake, but another jolly good tune. And it is all very beautifully scored. Bantock was a master of the orchestra. Is there anything lacking? Is he just a bit too clever, for ever finding yet another ingenious and delightful thing that can be done with a scale-figure? Possibly, but then he is never dull. Is real emotional depth lacking, despite hints of it whenever the wronged wife appears in Fifine? Maybe; possibly he was more given to enjoying than to pondering. Horses for courses, Bantock for enjoyment. The performances are stunning, the recordings most sumptuous. Oh, and the two *Heroic Ballads*, for all that they're concerned with Cuchullan and his ilk, have not a shred of Irish Sea mist hanging around them: they are bold, colourful and stirring.

Further listening
Hebridean Symphony
Royal Philharmonic Orchestra / Handley
Hyperion CDA66450 (73 minutes: DDD: 5/91) Ⓕ
A rich, romantic score from 1915 with echoes of Janáček and some particularly fine writing for the brass.

Alfvén Symphony No 4
Coupling: A tale from the archipelago
Stockholm Philharmonic Orchestra / N Järvi
BIS CD505 (74 minutes: DDD: 8/92) Ⓕ
Alfvén's Symphony No 4 uses a huge orchestra and employs an overtly romantic language – complete with two soloists. The nearest analogy is Strauss's *Alpine* Symphony, but the mood and reach would appeal to anyone drawn to Bantock's symphonic language.

Cello Sonatas

Cello Sonatas[a] – No 1 in B minor; No 2 in F sharp minor. Solo Cello Sonata in G minor. Hamabdil[b]. Pibroch[b]. Elegiac Poem[a]
Andrew Fuller *vc* with [a]**Michael Dussek** *pf* [b]**Lucy Wakeford** *hp*
Dutton Laboratories Epoch CDLX7107 Ⓜ
(75 minutes: DDD). Recorded 2000

There are some rewarding discoveries to be had here, not least the two sonatas for cello and piano. Both were penned during the first half of the 1940s (towards the end of Bantock's life), though the sketches for the B minor Sonata originally date back to 1900. The latter is a finely sculpted, generously lyrical creation, boasting a particularly lovely slow movement. For the *scherzo* Bantock pressed into service his earlier *Fantastic Poem* of 1925, and the whole work ends in a mood of autumnal nostalgia. Annotator Lewis Foreman informs us that the piece was first heard in 1948 (two years after Bantock's death), whereas its F sharp minor partner is receiving its first performance here. It was conceived over a seven-month period and finally completed in January 1945. Again, one is struck by the sweep, fluency and idiomatic craft of Bantock's inspiration, though melodically it is perhaps not quite up to the standard of its predecessor.

It would appear that the initial impulse behind the unaccompanied G minor Sonata stems from Kodály's magnificent example in the genre (of which Bantock had heard Beatrice Harrison give the British première in 1924). Cast in four compact movements, it's an uncommonly well-knit essay and a demanding workout for any aspiring virtuoso (as the giddy *moto perpetuo* of the finale attests). We also get two offerings for cello and harp: the plaintive 'Hebrew melody', *Hamabdil*, started out as a number from Bantock's incidental music for Arnold Bennett's drama, *Judith*, but even more striking is *Pibroch*, a wonderfully affecting 'Highland lament' from 1915 (a period when Bantock was infatuated with all things Scottish). Lastly, there's the *Elegiac Poem*, a salon morsel that Bantock wrote in 1898 for the Dutch cellist, Marix Loevensohn.

Andrew Fuller is an accomplished artist, mellow of tone and technically secure, and he enjoys sympathetic support from pianist Michael Dussek. Harpist Lucy Wakeford, too, contributes most beautifully in *Hamabdil* and *Pibroch*. With eminently truthful sound and balance throughout, this enterprising collection deserves a warm welcome.

Vocal works

Atalanta in Calydon. Vanity of vanities
BBC Singers / Simon Joly
Albany TROY180 (66 minutes: DDD) Ⓕ
Texts included. Recorded 1995

In 1911 Bantock embarked on the first of his two unaccompanied 'choral symphonies', a half-hour setting of texts from Swinburne's 1865 verse drama, *Atalanta in Calydon*. Written for the amateur Hallé Choir, it is an extraordinarily ambitious offering. Bantock's luxuriant 20-part writing (the composer envisaged 'not less than 10 voices to each part') exhibits a prodigious technical facility allied to a remarkable fluency and poetic sensibility. By comparison, the 35-minute *Vanity of vanities* (based on Bantock's own selection of verses from the Book of Ecclesiastes) is a model of restraint, being laid out for a mere 12 parts. It was completed in September 1913. Again, the sounds created exhibit a ravishing variety of texture, colour and harmony, further testament to Bantock's fantastically vivid aural imagination. Both works impose great technical demands which are easily surmounted in these incisive, dedicated performances, admirably captured by the recording team.

Samuel Barber

American 1910-1981

GROVE *Barber studied as a baritone and composer (with Scalero) at the Curtis Institute (1924-32) and while there began to win acclaim with such works as Dover Beach (1931), written for himself to sing with string quartet. His opulent yet unforced Romanticism struck a chord and during the 1930s he was much in demand: his overture The School for Scandal (1933), First Symphony (1936), First Essay (1937) and Adagio (originally the second movement of his String Quartet, 1936) were widely performed, the lyrical, elegiac Adagio remaining a popular classic. In the 1940s he began to include more 'modern' features of harmony and scoring. Of his operas, Vanessa (1958), praised as 'highly charged with emotional meaning', was more successful than Antony and Cleopatra (1966, for the opening of the new Met).*

Violin Concerto, Op 14

Violin Concerto. Cello Concerto, Op 22. Capricorn Concerto, Op 21
Kyoko Takezawa *vn* **Steven Isserlis** *vc* **Jacob Berg** *fl* **Peter Bowman** *ob* **Susan Slaughter** *tpt*
St Louis Symphony Orchestra / Leonard Slatkin
RCA Victor Red Seal 09026 68283-2 Ⓕ
(65 minutes: DDD). Recorded 1994-95

The Cello Concerto is a restless work touched through and through by the shock, uncertainty and fragile optimism of a world just coming out of war. Steven Isserlis is in many respects just the player for the piece. His agility is a boon in ensuring that it never becomes overly strenuous, that its capriciousness, its touches of irony (all those quizzical pizzicato *glissandos* and harmonics) are not lost in the shadows. The slow movement's cantilena really does warm to his personal touch, his long, canonic duet with oboe for once not a mismatch. Isserlis's cello is the lightest of Lieder baritones with the flexibility and imagination to fine-spin phrases as very few can and do. Listen to his withdrawal into the heart of the slow movement. Isserlis reflecting, Isserlis lost in thought, is always special.

Kyoko Takezawa is not a player to keep much to herself. The casual opening page of the Violin Concerto, starting as it does mid-sentence through a shared confidence, is soon impatient to go public. Her sound – intense and focused – seems to reach way beyond the length of each phrase. She is mindful, too, of the fiercer contrasts, seeking always to maximise them. It's a very 'operatic' performance, the lyric and dramatic elements grippingly interacted. The big 'aria' – in which the first oboe gets to be the envy of all the surrounding players – comes, of course, with that ravishing principal subject of the slow movement, and when Takezawa does finally come to embrace it, the feeling of release, of fulfilment, is worth the wait. Slatkin responds with a full-throated tutti in the strings. All of which is wickedly offset by that mad highland fling of a finale, twirling woodwinds and fractured trumpet fanfares.

Between the two main courses comes the sorbet. Barber's *Capricorn Concerto* (for flute, oboe, trumpet and strings) is a playful *concerto grosso* for the New World, a sharp take on baroque procedures, a streetwise *Brandenburg* No 2.

Awards 1998

Barber Violin Concerto **Bloch** Baal Shem
Walton Violin Concerto in B minor
Joshua Bell *vn* **Baltimore Symphony Orchestra / David Zinman**
Decca 452 851-2DH
(68 minutes: DDD) Ⓕ
Recorded 1996 ooo

Bell's coupling of the Barber Violin Concerto with Walton and Bloch brings together three highly romantic *concertante* works. In the Barber, Bell is placed less forward than in the rich-sounding recordings of Gil Shaham and Itzhak Perlman, but if anything the results are even more intense. In the central slow movement the opening oboe solo leads to a magically hushed first entry for the violin, and the balance of the soloist also allows a quicksilver lightness for the rushing triplets in the *moto perpetuo* finale. Shaham may find more humour in that brief movement, but Bell's view is equally valid.

From an American perspective, Walton can well be seen as Barber's British counterpart. The playing of this American orchestra is warmly idiomatic, defying the idea that non-British orchestras find Walton difficult. Bell gives a commanding account of the solo part – his expansive treatment of the central cadenza of the first movement, making it more deeply reflective – is most appealing. Not just there but in many gentle moments the rapt intensity of his playing is magnetic. Bell's is among the finest versions ever, with Bloch's own 1939 orchestration of *Baal Shem* offering a fine, unusual makeweight.

Barber Violin Concerto, Op 14
E Meyer Violin Concerto
Hilary Hahn *vn* **Saint Paul Chamber Orchestra / Hugh Wolff**
Sony Classical SK89029 (50 minutes: DDD) Ⓕ
Recorded 1999 **OO**

The 19-year-old Hilary Hahn, following up the success of her first Sony disc, once again shows her natural feeling for the American brand of late romanticism, bringing out heartfelt emotion without overplaying it. There have been a number of outstanding versions of the Barber Concerto in recent years and Hahn's is among the finest ever. She stands between the urgently, fullbloodedly romantic Shaham and the more meditative Bell. It is partly a question of recording balances. The latter has the advantage of a recording which, setting him a little further back, allows *pianissimos* to be registered in a genuine hush. Hahn, like Shaham, is placed well forward, and it is hardly her fault that dynamic contrasts are reduced. She certainly plays softly, but the sound that emerges is still fairly robust. The use of a chamber orchestra also affects the balance. The extra weight in the orchestral sound on the DG and Decca discs is here compensated to a degree by the incisiveness of the St Paul Chamber Orchestra under Hugh Wolff, with textures a fraction clearer in detail. Even so, in the long introduction to the *Andante* a smaller body of strings, however refined, cannot quite match in ear-catching beauty the bigger string sections of the LSO and Baltimore Symphony. What Hahn and Wolff nicely achieve between them, though, is a distinction between the first two movements, both of them predominantly lyrical. Deceptively, the first is marked *Allegro* (hardly sounding it), but here one registers it as a taut first movement leading to a powerful climax. Speeds in both the first two movements are a fraction broader than with either rival, but Hahn reserves her big coup for the *Presto* finale which is noticeably faster than either rival's, offering quicksilver brilliance and pinpoint articulation.

Meyer's Concerto makes an apt coupling. Unashamedly tonal and freely lyrical, it opens with a yearning folk-like melody that echoes Vaughan Williams, and there is also a folk-like, pentatonic cut to some of the writing in both of the two substantial movements. The composer's own note is disappointingly vague, but the music itself presents no problem, a free set of variations in clearly contrasted sections leading to a virtuoso exercise in using a persistent pedal note. It is amazing what variety Meyer achieves (a string player himself), considering that conscious limitation of having a sustained drone underlying his argument. The last movement, in clearly defined sections, easily erupts at times into a rustic dance, and ends on a dazzling coda. Hahn plays with passionate commitment, amply justifying her choice of so approachable a new piece for this important issue.

Barber Violin Concerto
Korngold Violin Concerto, Op 35. Much ado about nothing, Op 11 – The maiden in the bridal chamber; Dogberry and Verges; Intermezzo; Hornpipe
Gil Shaham *vn* **London Symphony Orchestra / André Previn** *pf*
DG 439 886-2GH (71 minutes: DDD) Ⓕ
Recorded 1993 **O**

This performance of the Barber, warm and rich with the sound close and immediate, brings out above all the work's bolder side, allowing moments that are not too distant from the world of Hollywood music (no disparagement there) and aptly the Korngold emerges as a central work in that genre. There have been subtler readings of Barber's lovely concerto, with the soloist not always helped by the close balance, but it is good to have a sharp distinction drawn between the purposeful lyricism of the first movement, marked *Allegro*, and the tender lyricism of the heavenly *Andante*. In the finale Shaham brings out the fun behind the movement's manic energy, with Previn pointing the Waltonian wit.

In the Korngold, Gil Shaham may not have quite the flair and panache of the dedicatee, Jascha Heifetz, in his incomparable reading (reviewed under Korngold), but he is warm and committed. What emerges again and again here is how electric the playing of the LSO is under Previn, rich and full as well as committed, echoing vintage Previn/LSO recordings of the 1970s. The recording helps, clear and immediate. The suite from Korngold's incidental music to *Much ado about nothing*, dating from his early precocious period in Vienna, provides a delightful and apt filler, with Previn, as pianist, just as understanding and imaginative an accompanist, and Shaham yearningly warm without sentimentality, clean and precise in attack.

Violin Concerto[a]. Piano Concerto, Op 38[b]. **H**
Adagio for Strings, Op 11[c]. Essay for Orchestra No 2, Op 17[d]. The School for Scandal Overture, Op 5[d]
Isaac Stern *vn* **John Browning** *pt*
New York Philharmonic Orchestra /

[a]Leonard Bernstein, [d]Thomas Schippers; [b]Cleveland Orchestra / George Szell; [c]Philadelphia Orchestra / Eugene Ormandy

Sony Classical SMK60004 (74 minutes: ADD) Ⓜ
Recorded 1964-65, item marked [c]1958

Isaac Stern's 1964 recording of the Barber Violin Concerto with Bernstein and the New York Philharmonic was the recording which belatedly gave this warmly expressive masterpiece the international currency it plainly deserved. It was written at very much the same period, just as the Second World War was beginning, as two British works with which it has clear links, the violin concertos of Walton and Britten, both also dating from 1939. The superb performance from Stern and Bernstein can stand comparison with any version since, easily fluent in the two lyrical movements, demonically intense in the *moto perpetuo* finale. That movement, initially disappointing as a resolution to the first two, may not match the finales of the Walton and Britten in weight, but it certainly makes a powerful conclusion here. The only reservation is that with close-up CBS sound for the soloist you rarely get a true *pianissimo*.

Even more welcome is John Browning's première recording of the Piano Concerto. This is an interpretation of the highest voltage, the more daring and bitingly intense for having been recorded after a long series of performances on tour, full of bravura, with recorded sound rather fuller and more clean than that of the Violin Concerto. Ormandy's resonant recording of the *Adagio*, taken at a flowing speed, and Schippers's dazzling, tautly controlled accounts of the *Essay* No 2 and the Overture, also well transferred, make this an ideal disc for anyone wanting to investigate Barber at his finest.

Additional recommendations

Violin Concerto Couplings: **Bernstein** Serenade. **Foss** Three American Pieces
Perlman *vn* **Boston Symphony Orchestra / Ozawa**
EMI CDC5 55360-2 (67 minutes: DDD: 6/95) Ⓕ

A super disc. The extra weight of Perlman's sound brings dividends in this sumptuously romantic concerto.

Cello Concerto
Couplings: Britten Symphony for Cello and Orchestra.
Ma *vc* **Baltimore Symphony Orchestra / Zinman**
CBS Masterworks MK44900 (62 minutes: DDD: 6/89) Ⓕ

Admirable performances from Yo-Yo Ma and Zinman.

Couplings: Adagio for Strings. Medea
Warner *vc* **Royal Scottish National Orchestra / Alsop**
Naxos 8 559088 (66 minutes: DDD: 3/01) Ⓢ

A good performance; the interesting coupling, *Medea*, makes this disc worth investigating at Naxos price.

Further listening

Korngold Violin Concerto
Shaham *vn* **London Symphony Orchestra / Previn**
DG 439 886-2GH (71 minutes: DDD: 9/94).

Higher in both cholesterol and sugar, Korngold's sole violin concerto makes a wonderful complement to Barber's lyrical work.

Adagio for Strings, Op 11

Barber Adagio for Strings
Bernstein Candide – Overture **Copland** Appalachian Spring – ballet **W Schuman** American Festival Overture
Los Angeles Philharmonic Orchestra / Leonard Bernstein
DG Galleria 439 528-2GGA (54 minutes: DDD) Ⓜ
Recorded live in 1982

This is a beautiful collection of American music, lovingly and brilliantly performed. With Barber's lovely *Adagio* you might fear that Bernstein would 'do a Nimrod' and present it with exaggerated expressiveness. Although the tempo is very slow indeed, the extra hesitations are not excessive and the Los Angeles strings play with angelic refinement and sweetness, as they do also in the many hushed sequences of the Copland ballet. There the live recording made in San Francisco in a dryish acoustic brings a degree of constriction at heavy tuttis, but the advantages of digital recording in this beautiful score are obvious, not least at the climax of the haunting variations on the Shaker hymn, *Simple Gifts*. To the three favourite works here is added William Schuman's brazenly extrovert overture with its virtuoso opening section, its quiet *fugato*, ominously introduced, and a brazen conclusion to match the opening. It is a splendid work, almost as joyously inspired as Bernstein's *Candide* Overture, with the composer here adopting a fairly relaxed speed, though with a wild coda.

Adagio for Strings. Symphony No 1, Op 9. First Essay, Op 12. Second Essay, Op 17. Music for a Scene from Shelley, Op 7. The School for Scandal Overture, Op 5
Baltimore Symphony Orchestra / David Zinman
Argo 436 288-2ZH (64 minutes: DDD) Ⓕ
Recorded 1991

Zinman begins this striking set in quiet understatement with this most challenging of all sustained *legatos* – the *Adagio for Strings*. He and his Baltimore strings are calm, collected, resigned; the grief is contained; no wringing of hands at the climax, rather an intense transfiguration. The first of Barber's bite-size symphonies is rather more demonstrative in its tragedy, working up from the deep-set bass lines of an imposing *Andante sostenuto* to the most public of displays. And then there is the *Second Essay*, Barber rhetoric at its most biblical. The engineering throughout this disc is exceptionally vivid, but nowhere more so than here: the impact of timpani and bass drum is unnervingly realistic, the brass and tam-tam-laden climax comes at you full on. Add to that a pugnacious fugue with Baltimore woodwinds devilishly incisive, and you've an absolute winner.

Zinman's account of the First Symphony is laudably coherent – whole. There is sweep and a strong sense of evolution about its development. The solo oboe and cellos are heart-breakers in the slow movement, the impassioned climax – like everything else here – magnificently inevitable.

The *Music for a Scene from Shelley* is an early piece, but a highly accomplished one. It is an especially beguiling example of Barber's precocious lyric gifts. A sunburst of sound brings on one of Barber's most rapturous melodies, voluptuously scored, and there is an exquisite postlude where two horns briefly ruminate on what has been heard and scented, while the nocturnal murmurings of string and harp quickly evaporate to the barely audible.

Symphonies Nos 1 and 2

Symphonies – No 1, Op 9; No 2, Op 19. First Essay for Orchestra, Op 12. The School for Scandal Overture, Op 5
Royal Scottish National Orchestra / Marin Alsop
Naxos 8 559024 Ⓢ
(70 minutes: DDD)

A protégé of Leonard Bernstein and Seiji Ozawa, and winner of the 1989 Koussevitzky Conducting Prize at Tanglewood, Marin Alsop has won golden plaudits for her pioneering work on behalf of Christopher Rouse (RCA) and Joan Tower (Koch International). That she is a musician of outstanding gifts is amply reinforced by this all-Barber anthology. In her red-blooded rendering of the wartime Second Symphony, Alsop shows just what a powerfully inspired creation it is, extracting every ounce of sinewy logic from its fraught outer movements, while distilling plenty of wonder and atmosphere in the haunting central *Andante, un poco mosso*.

No less convincing is Alsop's reading of the magnificent First Symphony, always acutely responsive to the music's daring expressive scope and building climaxes of riveting cumulative intensity. In its unhurried authority, big heart and epic thrust, it's the kind of interpretation one could have imagined from Bernstein in his NYPO heyday.

Elsewhere, Alsop brings an aptly bardic quality to the outer portions of the *First Essay*, while few could fail to respond to the twinkling affection and gentle wit she lavishes on the irresistible *School for Scandal* Overture. Were the orchestral contribution just a fraction more polished, this would be a world-beater. Zinman's stylish 1991 anthology with the Baltimore SO tends to throw into sharper relief the relative shortcomings of Alsop's hard-working Scots (their fiddles especially lack something in silk-spun refinement and tone when playing above the stave). Moreover, the expert engineering can't quite disguise the acoustical shortcomings of Glasgow's Henry Wood Hall, but the finished article is tonally truthful and conveys plenty of impact when required.

Piano Sonata, Op 26

Ballade, Op 46. Excursions, Op 20. Nocturne, Op 33. Piano Sonata, Op 26. Souvenirs, Op 28
Eric Parkin *pf*
Chandos CHAN9177 (63 minutes: DDD) Ⓕ
Recorded 1992

This is the complete published piano music, apart from *Three Sketches*, but there are quite a lot of unpublished pieces. None of this matters when the playing is as polished and sympathetic as Parkin's. He responds wonderfully to the nostalgic melancholia of Barber. The ballet score, *Souvenirs*, is available in the orchestral and piano-duet versions, but this solo piano treatment is just as engaging. Parkin knows exactly how to present this side of Barber and his treatment of the *Four Excursions* based on different popular idioms is equally convincing. A performer as well versed as Parkin in British post-romantics such as Ireland and Bax finds home ground again in Barber's *Nocturne* and the late *Ballade*. In Barber's classic, the Sonata, Parkin treats the work lyrically and never forces us to regard the finale, especially, as a hard-hitting block-buster in the way that so many young pianists do. He is transparent in the *Scherzo*, sings in the *Adagio*, and the final fugue subject has exactly the catchy, swinging quality that many players miss. At times there is a lack of brilliance, which the rather dull recording emphasises, but this is a winning anthology of this major American romantic.

Piano Sonata, Op 26. Excursions, Op 20. Nocturne, Op 33, 'Homage to John Field'. Three Sketches. Ballade, Op 46. Interludes – No 1, Intermezzo. Souvenirs, Op 28
Daniel Pollack *pf*
Naxos 8 550992 (72 minutes: DDD) Ⓢ
Recorded 1995

Daniel Pollack studied with (among others) Rosina Lhévinne and Wilhelm Kempf. His playing exudes confidence, especially in the more rhythmic and forthright passages. In his hands the Sonata is powerfully driven and crisply articulated, creating a palpable sense of raw energy and excitement. His full sonorities and sense of shape in the *Interlude* and the *Ballade* are also impressive, and while his tempo in the latter may seem a shade fast, it adds to the essential restlessness of the piece. In the more lyrical works, notably the *Nocturne*, however, Pollack's handling is too brusque, trampling roughshod over the contrast between passion and delicacy. The dance pieces of the *Excursions* and *Souvenirs* are generally more sensitive, and he effectively captures the diversity of distinctive flavours, from the slow blues (*Excursions*) to the Schottische (*Souvenirs*). Horowitz inevitably remains the benchmark in the Sonata, and his virtuosic fire is in a class of its own. Nevertheless, despite the poor recorded sound from Naxos's problematic Santa Rosa studio, this is an enjoyable disc and quite a bargain.

Knoxville: Summer of 1915, Op 24

Hermit Songs, Op 29[a]. Sleep now, Op 10 No 2[a]. The Daisies, Op 2 No 1[a]. Nocturne, Op 13 No 4[a]. Nuvoletta, Op 25[a]. Knoxville: Summer of 1915, Op 24[b]. Antony and Cleopatra[b] – Give me some music; Give me my robe Ⓗ

Leontyne Price *sop* **Samuel Barber** *pf*
[b]**New Philharmonia Orchestra / Thomas Schippers**
RCA Victor Gold Seal 09026 61983-2 Ⓜ
(63 minutes: ADD). Texts included. Items marked [a] recorded live in mono in 1953, [b]1968

Leontyne Price's radiant performance of *Knoxville*, that hauntingly evocative cantata to words by James Agee, comes in a coupling with the heroine's arias from the opera, *Antony and Cleopatra*, the role she created at the Met in New York. More than ever it seems cruelly unjust that an over-involved stage production should have so undermined a fine opera, one that certainly didn't deserve to be counted a failure. Sadly, it affected Barber's creative confidence for far too long. In this collection of all Price's Barber recordings those items are splendidly rounded out by the private recordings made at the Library of Congress at the time of the very first performance in October 1953 of the *Hermit Songs*, also specifically written for her. Accompanied by the composer, she is rugged and intense; Barber, though a good pianist, is quite rough. That comes out even more clearly in the four separate songs, which include Barber's longest individual song, *Nuvoletta*, setting a passage, characteristically full of word-play, taken from James Joyce's *Finnegans Wake*.

The other songs are taken quite fast, a typical sign of a composer's impatience in performing his own music – with the charming little setting of James Stephens's *The Daisies* made quite different in character, almost like an Irish folk-song at a speed half as fast again. The mono sound of 1953 is very limited, but conveys the atmosphere of a historic occasion. As on LP the 1968 stereo sound given to the orchestral items (recorded in London) is full and well focused, with the strings of the New Philharmonia under Thomas Schippers sounding pure and sweet.

Barber Knoxville: Summer of 1915, Op 24[a]. Hermit Songs, Op 29[b] **Copland** Old American Songs – Set 1[c]; Set 2d **Thomson** Stabat matere. Capital Capitals[f] Ⓗ
[a]**Eleanor Steber,** [b]**Leontyne Price** *sops* [e]**Jennie Tourel** *mez* [f]**Joseph Crawford** [f]**Clyde S Turner** *tens* [cd]**William Warfield** [f]**Joseph James** *bars* [f]**William C Smith** *bass* [b]**Samuel Barber** [cd]**Aaron Copland** [f]**Virgil Thomson** *pfs* [e]**New Music Quartet** (Broadus Erle, Matthew Raimondi *vns* Walter Trampler *va* Claus Adam *vc*) [a]**Dumbarton Oaks Chamber Orchestra / William Strickland**
Sony Classical Masterworks Heritage mono MHK60899 (80 minutes: ADD) Ⓜ
Recorded 1950-54

In his affectionate memoir to accompany this CD, Ned Rorem recalls the occasion when Barber accompanied Leontyne Price in the European première of his *Hermit Songs* in 1954 for an audience of what Rorem calls 'serial killer' composers. They hissed 'The monk and his cat' and booed at the end. Today no one can remember any of the other music that was presented in the series, and here are Barber and Price recorded later that year. *Knoxville: Summer of 1915* has been recorded by at least half-a-dozen other sopranos since Eleanor Steber's recording, but this is still essential listening. The voice is lovely but the manner somewhat more formal and actressy than later interpreters.

William Warfield's recording of Copland's *Old American Songs* with the nostalgic 'Long time ago', the reverent 'Simple gifts' and the nowadays politically incorrect 'I bought me a cat', was such a success that the composer came up with a second set which has become almost as well-known, with 'Zion's wall' and 'At the river'. In Warfield's account of this second set, never issued before, he has a delightful way of speaking the lyrics without hindering his firm bass-baritone line.

Virgil Thomson's setting of Max Jacob's poem *Stabat mater* is sung with declamatory fervour by Jennie Tourel. *Capital Capitals* is one of Thomson's earliest settings of Gertrude Stein's cubist poetry. All 3000 words of this dialogue are used by Thomson; it has something of the feel of an early try-out for what would become *Four Saints in Three Acts*. The four male soloists have beautifully clear diction. The rhythm of her repetitions and alliteration all makes sense so long as you don't try to make a story out of it. The sound of these recordings, despite their age, is magnificent and the performances definitive.

Additional recomendation
Knoxville: Summer of 1915
Couplings: works by Menotti, Harbison and Stravinsky
Upshaw *sop* **Orchestra of St Luke's / Zinman**
Nonesuch 7559-79187-2 (44 minutes: DDD: 9/89[R]) Ⓕ
Dawn Upshaw captures the childish innocence of Barber's gorgeous scena in a programme of comparable vocal treats.

Agnus Dei, Op 11

Barber Twelfth Night, Op 42 No 1. To be sung on the water, Op 42 No 2. Reincarnations, Op 16. Agnus Dei, Op 11. Heaven-Haven. Sure on this shining night. The monk and his cat. The Virgin Martyrs, Op 8 No 1. Let down the bars, O Death, Op 8 No 2. God's Grandeur **Schuman** Perceptions. Mail Order Madrigals
Anthony Saunders *pf* **The Joyful Company of Singers / Peter Broadbent**
ASV CDDCA939 (66 minutes: DDD) Ⓕ
Texts included. Recorded 1995

Newcomers should make haste to track 6 for a pleasant surprise. Here they will encounter Samuel Barber's indestructible *Adagio* in its alternative and mellifluous 1967 vocal guise, set to the text of the *Agnus Dei*. Peter Broadbent's Joyful Company of Singers acquit themselves extremely well. Elsewhere, one particularly relishes the exquisite Op 42 pairing of *Twelfth Night* and *To be sung on the water*, the carefree lilt of *The monk and his cat* and, above all, the majestic, strikingly ambitious 1938 setting of Gerald Manley Hopkins's sonnet, *God's Grandeur* (perhaps the single most impressive achievement on the disc). Further delights are provided by Barber's countryman and contemporary,

William Schuman. The concise, beautifully sculpted *Perceptions* (1982) are settings of choice aphorisms from the pen of Walt Whitman, while the *Mail Order Madrigals* (1972) wittily utilise the flowery prose drawn from advertisements contained within a Sears and Roebuck catalogue of 1897. A most attractive issue, in short, excellently produced and engineered.

Béla Bartók

Hungarian 1881-1945

GROVE *Bartók began lessons with his mother, who brought up the family after his father's death in 1888. In 1894 they settled in Bratislava, where he attended the Gymnasium (Dohnányi was an elder schoolfellow), studied the piano with László Erkel and Anton Hyrtl, and composed sonatas and quartets. In 1898 he was accepted by the Vienna Conservatory, but following Dohnányi he went to the Budapest Academy (1899-1903), where he studied the piano with Liszt's pupil Istvan Thoman and composition with Janos Koessler. There he deepened his acquaintance with Wagner, though it was the music of Strauss, which he met at the Budapest première of Also sprach Zarathustra in 1902, that had most influence. He wrote a symphonic poem, Kossuth (1903), using Strauss's methods with Hungarian elements in Liszt's manner.*

In 1904 Kossuth was performed in Budapest and Manchester; at the same time Bartók began to make a career as a pianist, writing a Piano Quintet and two Lisztian virtuoso showpieces (Rhapsody Op 1, Scherzo Op 2). Also in 1904 he made his first Hungarian folksong transcription. In 1905 he collected more songs and began his collaboration with Kodály: their first arrangements were published in 1906. The next year he was appointed Thoman's successor at the Budapest Academy, which enabled him to settle in Hungary and continue his folksong collecting, notably in Transylvania. Meanwhile his music was beginning to be influenced by this activity and by the music of Debussy that Kodály had brought back from Paris: both opened the way to new, modal kinds of harmony and irregular metre. The 1908 Violin Concerto is still within the symphonic tradition, but the many small piano pieces of this period show a new, authentically Hungarian Bartók emerging, with the 4ths of Magyar folksong, the rhythms of peasant dance and the scales he had discovered among Hungarian, Romanian and Slovak peoples. The arrival of this new voice is documented in his String Quartet No 1 (1908), introduced at a Budapest concert of his music in 1910.

There followed orchestral pieces and a one-act opera, Bluebeard's Castle, dedicated to his young wife. Influenced by Mussorgsky and Debussy but most directly by Hungarian peasant music (and Strauss, still, in its orchestral pictures), the work, a grim fable of human isolation, failed to win the competition in which it was entered. For two years (1912-14) Bartók practically gave up composition and devoted himself to the collection, arrangement and study of folk music, until World War I put an end to his expeditions. He returned to creative activity with the String Quartet No 2 (1917) and the fairytale ballet The Wooden Prince, whose production in Budapest in 1917 restored him to public favour. The next year Bluebeard's Castle was staged and he began a second ballet, The Miraculous Mandarin, which was not performed until 1926 (there were problems over the subject, the thwarting and consummation of sexual passion). Rich and graphic in invention, the score is practically an opera without words.

While composing The Miraculous Mandarin Bartók came under the influence of Stravinsky and Schoenberg, and produced some of his most complex music in the two violin sonatas of 1921-22. At the same time he was gaining international esteem: his works were published by Universal Edition and he was invited to play them all over Europe. He was now well established at home, too. He wrote the confident Dance Suite (1923); there was then another lull until the sudden rush of works in 1926 designed for himself to play, including the Piano Concerto No 1, the Piano Sonata and the suite Out of Doors. These exploit the piano as a percussion instrument, using its resonances as well as its xylophonic hardness. The search for new sonorities and driving rhythms was continued in the next two string quartets (1927-28), of which No 4, like the concerto, is in a five-section palindromic pattern (ABCBA).

Similar formal schemes, with intensively worked counterpoint, were used in the Piano Concerto No 2 (1931) and String Quartet No 5 (1934), though now Bartók's harmony was becoming more diatonic. The move from inward chromaticism to a glowing major (though modally tinged) tonality is basic to the Music for Strings, Percussion and Celesta (1936) and the Sonata for Two Pianos and Percussion (1937), both written for performance in Switzerland at a time when the political situation in Hungary was growing unsympathetic.

In 1940 Bartók and his second wife (he had divorced and remarried in 1923) left war-torn Europe to live in New York, which he found alien. They gave concerts and for a while he had a research grant to work on a collection of Yugoslav folksong, but their finances were precarious, as increasingly was his health. It seemed that his last European work, the String Quartet No 6 (1939), might be his pessimistic swansong, but then came the exuberant Concerto for Orchestra (1943) and the involuted Sonata for Solo Violin (1944). Piano Concerto No 3, written to provide his widow with an income, was almost finished when he died, a Viola Concerto left in sketch.

Piano Concertos

No 1, Sz83; **No 2**, Sz95; **No 3**, Sz119

Piano Concertos Nos 1-3
Peter Donohoe *pf* **City of Birmingham Symphony Orchestra / Sir Simon Rattle**
EMI CDC7 54871-2 (77 minutes: DDD) Ⓕ
Recorded 1990-92 ●

Piano Concertos Nos 1-3
András Schiff *pf* **Budapest Festival Orchestra / Iván Fischer**
Teldec 0630-13158-2 (76 minutes: DDD) Ⓕ
Recorded 1996 ●●

Making Bartók's First Piano Concerto sound fun must have taken some doing, but Donohoe and Rattle have certainly managed it. The recording blends the instrument in among the orchestra, so that Rattle's sensitivity to nuance, Donohoe's lightness of touch and the accommodating acoustic of Birmingham's Symphony Hall transform what we frequently hear as an angular confrontation into something genuinely palatable. The Second Concerto, in this impressively urgent account, could hold its own in any company, even though there are one or two passages where articulation momentarily falters. The rest is either pungent or evocative: the second movement's 'night music' *Adagio* sections are beautifully sustained and the finale has terrific *élan*. Taken overall, this is a marvellous trio of performances and serves as a fresh reminder of just how great these works are.

Although Schiff's free-flowing renditions are never too far from the written page, they rarely stick rigidly to the letter. The first solo statement in the Second Concerto, for example, is lilting and capricious, quite unlike the earnest pronouncements of Anda, Donohoe or Kocsis. True, his *Presto* isn't quite as nimble as Anda's but most readers will rejoice in the many subtle shifts in pace and dynamics that colour Schiff's performances.

Fischer's Budapest Festival Orchestra are on great form; woodwind solos are characterful, brass choirs have immense force and the juggernaut big drums thrash thunder into the last movement of the Second Concerto. The First Concerto suggests a sense of play that rivals Donohoe and Rattle, especially in the first movement – although never letting you forget Donohoe's mesmerizing account of the *Andante*.

The Third Concerto suits Schiff best of all: his tone is nicely rounded, his chords perfectly weighted and there's some delightfully nifty fingerwork. He virtually sings these concertos, which makes for a near-ideal Third but, in the case of the Second, prompts something of an uneven confrontation. Schiff's contribution to the Second is consistently bright, nimble, even a little coquettish, while Fischer's response is brazen and athletic. The same might also be said of the First Concerto, except that there the sound is so astonishingly lifelike that it virtually amounts to an aural drama on its own terms.

Piano Concertos Nos 1-3 Ⓗ
Géza Anda *pf* **Berlin Radio Symphony Orchestra / Ferenc Fricsay**
DG The Originals 447 399-2GOR Ⓜ
(78 minutes: ADD). Recorded 1959-60 ◉

Much as one would like to tout the new as the best, there are some older recordings where a very special chemistry spells 'definitive', and that pose an almost impossible challenge to subsequent rivals. Such is this 1959 recording of Bartók's Second Piano Concerto, a tough, playful, pianistically aristocratic performance where dialogue is consistently keen and spontaneity is captured on the wing (even throughout numerous sessions). The first movement is relentless but never tires the ear; the second displays two very different levels of tension, one slow and mysterious, the other hectic but controlled; and although others might have thrown off the finale's octaves with even greater abandon, Anda's performance is the most successful in suggesting savage aggression barely held in check.

The Third Concerto is again beautifully moulded and carefully thought-through. Moments such as the loving return from the second movement's chirpy central episode are quite unforgettable, while the finale is both nimble and full-toned. The First Concerto was the last to be recorded and is perhaps the least successful of the three: here ensemble is occasionally loose, and characterization less vivid than with, say, Donohoe and Rattle. Still, it is a fine performance and the current transfer has been lovingly effected.

Bartók Piano Concerto No 3
Prokofiev Piano Concertos – No 1 in D flat, Op 10; No 3 in C, Op 26
Martha Argerich *pf* **Montreal Symphony Orchestra / Charles Dutoit**
EMI CDC5 56654-2 (70 minutes: DDD) Ⓕ
Recorded 1998 ◉

As always with this most mercurial of virtuosos, Martha Argerich's playing is generated by the mood of the moment and many listeners may well be surprised at her relative geniality with Dutoit. Personal and vivacious throughout, she always allows the composer his own voice. This is particularly true in Bartók's Third Concerto where her rich experience in chamber music makes her often *primus inter pares*, a virtuoso who listens to her partners with the greatest care. In the *Adagio religioso* she achieves a poise that has sometimes eluded her in the past and her finale is specially characterful, her stealthy start to the concluding *Presto* allowing the final pages their full glory. Dutoit and the Montreal Symphony achieve a fine unity throughout, a sense of like-minded musicians at work.

All true musicians will recognise performances of a special magic and integrity. In the Prokofiev First Concerto, her opening is arguably more authentically *brioso* than ferocious, her overall view a refreshingly fanciful view of Prokofiev's youthful iconoclasm. The central *Andante assai* is inflected with an improvisatory freedom she would probably not have risked earlier in her career and in the *Allegro scherzando* she trips the light fantastic, reserving a suitably tigerish attack for the final octave bravura display. Her performance of the Third Concerto is less fleet or nimble-fingered than in her early days but is more delectably alive to passing caprice. Once more she is unusually sensitive in the central *Andantino*, to the fourth variation's plunge into Slavic melancholy and introspection. The recordings are clear and naturally balanced and only those in search of metallic thrills and rushes of blood to the head will feel disappointed.

Viola Concerto, Sz120

Bartók Viola Concerto
Eötvös Replica
Kurtág Movement for Viola and Orchestra
Kim Kashkashian *va*
Netherlands Radio Chamber Orchestra / Peter Eötvös
ECM New Series 465 420-2 (50 minutes: DDD) Ⓕ
Recorded 1999

Kashkashian's superbly engineered recording of the Bartók Viola Concerto bears witness to a total identification between performer and composer. Even the tiny pause (00'43") bridging the opening and the secondary idea growing out of it, is perfectly judged. Kashkashian makes this music dance, not just in the finale (where racy rhythms hold sway) but also in the way that she phrases and articulates the entire piece. Peter Eötvös's conducting offers many parallel insights, not least towards the end of the first movement where a growing sense of agitation throws the succeeding *Adagio religioso* into a particularly favourable light. Eötvös employs Tibor Serly's completion, revising odd details and accommodating a few articulations and phrasings that Kashkashian has herself instigated. If you need convincing that Bartók's Viola Concerto is a great work, then Kashkashian and Eötvos should, between them, do the trick.

Of the other pieces, Peter Eötvös's Replica for viola and orchestra is astonishing music where foggy harmonies hover between startled highs and raucous lows, then mutate into a strange, sickly pulsing. Think of a malignant outgrowth of Wozzeck, of a troubled unconscious that can trigger violence at any moment and one has part of the picture. Replica was composed for – and is dedicated to – Kim Kashkashian, who plays it magnificently. By contrast, György Kurtág's early, post-Bartókian Movement for Viola and Orchestra is relatively conventional, with plenty of virtuoso viola writing and the expected alternations between busy solo work and bold orchestral tutti. It's roughly two-thirds of a concerto that Kurtág had completed in 1953-54 and it wears its traditional influences lightly.

Additional recommendation
Bartók Viola Concerto, Sz120
Couplings: **S Albert** Cello Concerto. **Bloch** Schelomo
Yo-Yo Ma *vc/alto vn* **Baltimore Symphony Orchestra / Zinman**
Sony Classical SK57961 (78 minutes: DDD: 3/95). Ⓕ
An enjoyable alto violin version of the score, performed at the work's original pitch, plus the imaginative Albert coupling make this disc an attractive proposition.

Violin Concerto No 2, Sz112

Bartók Violin Concerto No 2
Stravinsky Concerto for Violin and Orchestra in D
Viktoria Mulova *vn* **Los Angeles Philharmonic Orchestra / Esa-Pekka Salonen**
Philips 456 542-2PH (57 minutes: DDD) Ⓕ
Recorded 1997

As strong a contender as any for top digital rating in this most communicative of 20th-century concerto masterpieces, forthright and confident, with energetic support from Salonen and his orchestra. Philips's engineering sounds like a digital upgrade of Mercury's Living Presence technique: instrumental imaging is startlingly immediate, the sound stage is very well defined and the bottom end of the spectrum has enormous power, the bass drum especially. Mullova's playing is committed and intense, with a ripe tone (evident from her first entry) and some filigree passagework in the second-movement variations, where Salonen is careful to clarify every bejewelled strand in Bartók's scoring. The first movement is well thought through, though the timing exceeds Bartók's own (as printed in the score) by some three minutes. Still, most rivals are similarly expansive, and the second movement is actually a few seconds faster than prescribed, which is perhaps one of the reasons why it works so well. The finale is again clearly focused, but the big surprise comes with the inclusion – or, rather, the substitution – of Bartók's rarely heard original ending, where the soloist retires and the orchestra alone shoulder the whole of the coda. The notes makes no specific reference to this 'surprise' finale.

The Stravinsky concerto is another winner, with pert outer movements (the LAPO brass are alert but refreshingly unaggressive) and a ravishing account of the second 'Aria'. Tempos are well chosen, the sound is again first-rate and this performance of the Stravinsky can be ranked higher than any digital rival. As to the Bartók concerto, Thomas Zehetmair and Iván Fischer (Berlin Classics) offer less tonal lustre but more in the way of interpretative daring, while Kyung-Wha Chung (with Rattle – EMI) is marginally more attentive to instrumental minutiae – both, however, are currently unavailable. In sum, Mullova is on a par with the best and Philips's demonstration-worthy soundframe may well persuade readers to make her recording a first choice.

Violin Concerto No 2. Rhapsodies for Violin and Orchestra – No 1, Sz87; No 2, Sz90
Gil Shaham *vn*
Chicago Symphony Orchestra / Pierre Boulez
DG 459 639-2GH (65 minutes: DDD) Ⓕ
Recorded 1998

The constituent parts of this carefully considered production include a velvet-toned solo line, fastidious instrumental balancing, fine orchestral playing and considered articulation from all concerned. Wherever the score quietens, the musical tension is well sustained and so is the rarefied atmosphere created by Bartók's exquisite scoring. The playful banter between soloist and orchestra works especially well. There are odd flashes of drama and also some magical details, a particular favourite being at 5'41" into the second movement, where Shaham's passagework flutters within a dark aural environment like a captive butterfly circulating Bluebeard's castle.

The one reservation about this performance is a certain lack of temperament. Shaham's first entry is too urbane, too carefully calculated. Sometimes his attack is strong, sometimes underpowered. Shaham, although an extremely accomplished player, emerges as overly cool, excessively laid-back. He and Boulez present a workable – and enjoyable – overview of the concerto, but sometimes fail to engage the spirit. In the *Rhapsodies*, No 2's first movement's entrancing recipe of solo violin, woodwinds and gentle percussion make an unforgettable effect.

Additional recommendation

Bartók Violin Concertos Nos [a]1 and [b]2

Chung *vn* **[a]Chicago Symphony Orchestra, [b]London Philharmonic Orchestra / Solti**

Decca Ovation 425 015-2DM Ⓜ

(59 minutes: ADD/DDD: 2/91)

Highly extrovert, primary-coloured performances from Kyung-Wha Chung. She uses Bartók's huge palette of pyrotechnics to generate enormous emotional energy and Solti is a like-minded, like-spirited collaborator.

Concerto for Orchestra, Sz116

Concerto for Orchestra. Kossuth, Sz21. Village Scenes, Sz79

Slovak Folk Ensemble Chorus; Budapest Festival Orchestra / Iván Fischer

Philips 456 575-2PH (67 minutes: DDD) Ⓕ

Recorded 1997 ●●

Bartók's youthful *Kossuth* is as enjoyable a tone-poem as any save for Strauss's or Liszt's best, lyrical and dramatic, especially in the eighth section, where perky bassoons prompt a head-on confrontation by poking fun at the Austrian national anthem. Fischer and his orchestra here steal a lead on all the recorded rivals, at virtually every juncture. Solos in all departments are highly distinctive, while tutti passages have an earthy, upfront quality that lends extra fibre to Bartók's textures. *Kossuth*'s musical effect relies on the conviction of its interpreters, and in that respect alone Fischer wins hands down. Bartók completed his five *Village Scenes* (originally for voice and piano) in 1924, orchestrating three of them two years later at Koussevitzky's suggestion. Bartók places a doleful, slightly unsettling 'Lullaby' between a frisky 'Wedding' and a hyperactive 'Lad's Dance'. The Slovak Folk Ensemble Chorus (all ladies) squeal their hearts out for the wedding and Fischer keeps Bartók's hot-foot syncopations alive and kicking. A pity there are no texts and translations.

As to the *Concerto for Orchestra*, again it is the flavour of the performance that wins the day. Fischer is a dab hand at shaping and inflecting the musical line. He sails into the movement's 'brass chorale' trio without a hint of a pause and invests the 'Elegia' with the maximum respectable quota of passion. The finale is a riot of sunshine and swirling skirts, except for the mysterious – and notoriously tricky – *più presto* coda, with its rushing *sul ponticello* string choirs, which Fischer articulates with great care. One senses that the players are being driven to the very limits of their abilities, which only serves to intensify the excitement. Philips's dynamic sound frame works best in *Kossuth* and the *Village Scenes*, though most of the *Concerto* also sounds excellent. The only complaint is of a marginally flat brass chord in the finale and a quiet, short-lived low electronic hum in the same movement. Otherwise, a clear front runner at full-price.

Concerto for Orchestra. The Miraculous Mandarin

City of Birmingham Symphony Chorus and Orchestra / Sir Simon Rattle

EMI CDC5 55094-2 (70 minutes: DDD) Ⓕ

Recorded 1992-93 ●●

Simon Rattle's Bartókian credentials have never been better displayed on disc, with this particular version of *The Miraculous Mandarin* ballet. Tone and texture are securely on target, and those oddly elusive second and third trumpets at fig 21 (which are curiously absent from many rivals) are here properly reinstated. The strings and winds project with impressive confidence throughout, the trumpets prior to 'The Chase' are more rhythmically secure than most, and the various dramatic incidents that succeed the closing pages of the Suite (and which include some of Bartók's most powerful music for the stage) are given with a genuine sense of pathos. The chorus is well balanced, the percussion too, while Rattle himself drives all with a combination of animal vigour and teeming imagination.

This live recording of the *Concerto for Orchestra*, for sheer character and communicative power, must rank among the top digital recomendations. Right from the opening *Andante non troppo*, it is clear that everyone is wholly engaged in the task in hand. The flight into *Allegro vivace* is especially exciting and the 'Elegia' is especially intense, with a positively outraged return of the first movement's initial *forte* idea – the dotted trumpet lending a genuinely Magyar tang to the proceedings. The closing minute or so of the 'Intermezzo' is more tender than any other in recent years, while the finale is full of witty incident – every little variation played for all its worth and the whole brimming over with life and energy. However, Rattle's most telling interpretative stroke occurs at 7'23", that mysterious, curiously elusive passage that most other conductors treat like some sort of hybrid interpolation marking time until the final pages arrive. Rattle, though, has none of it: his reading betrays pin-point focusing, with intelligent phrasing, careful articulation and a sense of dramatic inevitability that lends the passage a new-found musical logic. The closing moments are thrilling, with a lacerating final chord tailed by a grateful volley of applause.

Concerto for Orchestra. Music for Strings, Percussion and Celesta, Sz106. Hungarian Sketches, Sz97 H

Chicago Symphony Orchestra / Fritz Reiner

RCA Victor Living Stereo 09026 61504-2 Ⓜ

(76 minutes: ADD). Recorded 1955 ●

Reiner's recordings were made in Chicago's Orchestra Hall in October 1955 (not that sampling reveals their age – quite the contrary). RCA's sound reportage of the *Concerto for Orchestra*'s quieter moments has uncanny realism and if the climaxes are occasionally reined in, the sheer fervour of Reiner's direction more than compensates. The 'Pair Play' is a very brisk 6'26", the finale taut and agile: compare the movement's opening with, say, Boulez's version, and Reiner's greater precision and control is immediately apparent. His couplings are excellent: a *Music for Strings, Percussion and Celesta* that goes all out for smooth transitions and fleet execution, and a stylishly turned set of *Hungarian Sketches* – with a substantially augmented percussion line in 'Bear Dance'. These too sound better than ever.

Concerto for Orchestra[a]. Dance Suite, Sz77. Ⓗ
Two Portraits, Sz37. Mikrokosmos, Sz107 (orch Serly): Book 4 – Bourrée; Book 6 – From the diary of a fly[a]
London Symphony Orchestra; Philharmonia Hungarica / Antál Dorati
Mercury Living Presence 432 017-2MM Ⓜ
(72 minutes: ADD). Recorded [a]1962, 1958 ●

Dorati's recording of *Concerto for Orchestra* is probably the finest of all on this label from the early 1960s. It certainly emerges with remarkable vividness and clarity on CD. For bite, intensity and vibrant idiomatic feeling the performance has not been surpassed, and the wit of 'Giuoco delle coppie' and the touching poise of the 'Elegia' match up attractively to the bravura thrills of the outer movements. Here there is tremendous attack from strings and brass alike. The sound is characteristically clean in definition, boldly coloured and firmly placed, but there is a touch of shrillness on top.

On the rest of the disc Dorati conducts the Philharmonia Hungarica and we are offered equally distinguished and vital accounts of the *Dance Suite*, the *Two Portraits* (with Erwin Ramor, the glowingly ardent violin soloist in the first) and as an encore, two engaging excerpts from Tibor Serly's free orchestrations of *Mikrokosmos*. The second, 'From the diary of a fly', energetically buzzes around with sharply focused precision of orchestral detail, until the poor thing is swotted!

The Miraculous Mandarin, Sz73

Awards 1998

The Miraculous Mandarin. Hungarian Peasant Songs, Sz100. Hungarian Sketches, Sz97. Romanian Folkdances, Sz68. Transylvanian Dances, Sz96. Romanian Dance, Sz47
Hungarian Radio Chorus; Budapest Festival Orchestra / Iván Fischer
Philips 454 430-2PH (67 minutes: DDD) Ⓕ
Recorded 1996 ●●●

As *Mandarins* go, they don't come more miraculous than this – a vivid, no-holds-barred performance. Everything tells – the flavour is right, the pacing too and the sound has a toughened, raw-edged quality that is an essential constituent of Bartók's tonal language. Although lurid – even seedy – in narrative detail, *The Miraculous Mandarin* is ultimately a tale of compassion, and Fischer never forgets that fact. Observable detail – all of it musically significant – occurs virtually by the minute. Delicacy trails bullish aggression, forcefulness alternates with an almost graphic suggestiveness – and it's all there in the full score. Fischer never vulgarises, brutalises or overstates the case and, what is most important, he underlines the quickly flickering, folkish elements in Bartók's musical language that other, less intuitive conductors barely acknowledge.

The strongly individual character of the Budapest Festival Orchestra is delightful. The strings have a biting edge, the woodwinds a gipsy-style reediness, while brass and percussion are forceful and incisive but never raucous. All these qualities also come into their own in the five folk-music-inspired works. This is Hungarian-grown Bartók that actually *sounds* Hungarian; it makes one wish that other European orchestras would reclaim parallel levels of individuality.

Additional recommendations

The Miraculous Mandarin
Coupling: Two portraits, Op 5
London Symphony Orchestra / Abbado
DG Masters 445 501-2GMA (minutes: DDD: 9/83[R]) Ⓜ
Abbado directs an imaginative and atmospheric performance: the climaxes, such as that at the mandarin's entrance, are positively awe-inspiring.

Coupling: Concerto for Orchestra
City of Birmingham Symphony Orchestra / Rattle
EMI CDC5 55094-2 (70 minutes: DDD: 1/95) Ⓕ
See the review above.

The Wooden Prince, Sz60

The Wooden Prince, Sz60. Cantata profana, Sz94
John Aler *ten* **John Tomlinson** *bass* **Chicago Symphony Chorus and Orchestra / Pierre Boulez**
DG 435 863-2GH (73 minutes: DDD) Ⓕ
Recorded 1991 ●

Bartók's parable of fathers, sons and fleeing the nest, his 1930 *Cantata profana*, is a mesmerizing, symmetrically designed masterpiece, where words and music are forged into an action-packed 18 minutes. Boulez provides what is by far the best studio recording the work has ever had (also the first to be digitally recorded), and truly state-of-the-art in terms of sound. Boulez is able to command a shimmering, hushed *pp* yet the battle-hardy *Allegro molto* with its hectoring syncopations and warlike percussion is full of grit and muscle. John Aler is wonderfully adroit with Bartók's high-flying solo tenor line, John Tomlinson sounds like an authentic Magyar, and the Chicago Symphony Chorus eggs the proceedings on with tireless zeal.

Turn then to *The Wooden Prince* and you confront the final flowering of Bartók's post-romantic phase; it's an effulgent, exotic piece, full of wistful, melancholy wind solos (clarinet and saxophone figure prominently) and billowing, heavily-scored climaxes. How astonishing to reflect that it was written *after* the composer's trail-blazing opera, *Bluebeard's Castle*. Again, the soft music is wonderfully atmospheric: the *ppp* muted violins in the Prelude have a ghostly pallor that is so typical of this orchestra's quiet string playing, yet when all are engaged at full throttle, the effect is shattering. Detail is legion throughout: the basses, brass and drums have immense presence.

Complete String Quartets

No 1, Sz40; **No 2**, Sz67; **No 3**, Sz85; **No 4**, Sz91; **No 5**, Sz102; **No 6**, Sz114

Hagen Quartet (Lukas Hagen, Rainer Schmidt *vns* Veronika Hagen *va* Clemens Hagen *vc*)
DG ② 463 576-2GH2 (154 minutes: DDD) Ⓕ
Recorded 1995 and 1998 ○○

Of the fine rival versions of Bartók's string quartets three obstinately remain in the front rank – this set by the Hagen Quartet being one. The sound is surprisingly consistent, and the performances consistently adventurous. Though never over-literal, the Hagens take careful heed of Bartók's expressive markings. For example, in the predominantly romantic First Quartet, violist Veronika Hagen stresses the accents in her *molto appassionato rubato* passage at 4'49" more forcefully than most of her rivals. At the other end of the dynamic scale, those infinitely mysterious chords at 6'43" are truly *pp possibile* while darting inflections that are so characteristic of the group as a whole come into recreative play at around 1'35" into the third movement.

Wherever Bartók looks forward, the Hagens take his cue. Theirs is a keen, stylised, animated view of the music, leaner than most and especially strong on colour. The Second Quartet's *leggiero* writing (first movement, at 1'02"), the lightning muted *prestissimo* that closes the second movement (from 6'30") or the veiled, *sotto voce* writing at 5'19" into the finale, all register with extraordinary vividness.

The Third Quartet inspires a highly individual response, though the *sul ponticello* semiquavers that launch the coda seem so single-mindedly intent on making a ghostly effect that they tend to lose rhythmic focus. A little later, when the bows shift 'back from the bridge', the Hagens over-emphasise a crucial chord that falls one bar after fig 3 (00'16" – they do the same sort of thing five bars later), rather disrupting the flow. Turn to the Hungarian Quartet and the same passage reclaims its musical sense. By comparison, the Hagens' Third seems just a little unsure of its ground, particularly in the coda.

The Fourth's opening *Allegro* is unusually expressive (some groups force the music's angularity to virtual ugliness), and the two *Scherzos* – one fast and muted, the other a spidery *pizzicato* – are superbly played. The motor-driven finale takes on some lunging *fortissimos* that punctuate (but never disrupt) the momentum.

On hearing the Fifth Quartet's first movement, one wonders whether the Hagens are trying to mirror Bartók's almost impossible timings (a total of seven-and-a-half minutes painstakingly sub-divided into 12 sections). Indeed, sections one, 10, 11 and 12 are spot-on virtually to the second, though the intervening episodes allow for more leeway in tempo. Not that it matters (or that other groups treat these timings as a priority). The half-crazed 'Tempo 1' dance motive that raises a riot at letter E (2'55") is given with tremendous panache, and the syncopated *Scherzo* has a bright, throw-away feel that never precludes executive precision.

Both the Fifth and Sixth Quartets are packed full of the most delicate ideas, shimmering, self-communing music with occasional bursts of unchecked passion (No 6's *Marcia*) or humour (the close of No 5's finale and 6's *Burletta*). This is truly home territory for the Hagens, though for sheer warmth and intimacy the Tokyo Quartet's DG recording of the Sixth – unfortunately deleted – is hard to beat. Which, of course, begs the inevitable question of comparisons.

To be honest, it's almost impossible to nail a truly definitive first choice. The Takács are supremely natural, always insightful and full of zest, though the DG recording is better focused. The earlier Tokyos (DG – nla) offer a precision-tooled cycle, emotive but meticulous, less energetic perhaps than the Emersons – another excellent set (DG) – and less idiomatic than the wonderfully spontaneous but technically fallible Végh Quartet (Auvidis). The Juilliard Quartet's second, analogue set (nla) is essential listening and stands alongside the Takács, the Hagens, the Véghs and the Emersons as being among the most compelling Bartók quartet cycles ever recorded.

Awards 1998

Takács Quartet (Edward Dusinberre, Károly Schranz *vns* Roger Tapping *va* András Fejér *vc*)
Decca ② 455 297-2DH2
(152 minutes: DDD) Ⓕ
Recorded 1996. ○○○

These performances provide more impressive sampling points than one could hope to enumerate in a single review. The First Quartet's oscillating tempo-shifts work wonderfully well, all with total naturalness. Characterization is equally strong elsewhere, not least the first movement of the Debussian arpeggios of the Second Quartet, and the second movement where Fejér races back into the rustic opening subject. The nightmare climax in the last movement has rarely sounded more prophetic of the great *Divertimento*'s central movement. The middle quartets work very well, with prominent inner voices in the Third and plenty of swagger in the Fourth. The high spots of No 4 are Fejér's improvisational cello solo in the third movement and a finale where the violent opening is a hefty *legato* to compare with the sharper, more Stravinskian attack of, say, the Tokyo Quartet. Likewise, the sudden dance-like episode in the first movement of the Fifth Quartet, savage music played from the pit of the stomach, while the third movement's bleary-eyed viola melody over teeming violin triplets suggests peasants in caricature.

The Takács are responsive to Bartók's sardonic humour – the 'barrel-organ' episode at the end of the Fifth Quartet, and the corny 'Burletta' in the third movement of the Sixth. The Sixth itself has some of the saddest, wildest and wisest music written in the last 100 years: the opening viola solo recalls Mahler's Tenth and the close fades to a mysterious question. Throughout the cycle, Bartók's metronome markings are treated more as guidelines than literal commands. The playing imparts Bartók's all-embracing humanity, and if the greatest string quartets after Beethoven are still unknown to you, this Takács set may well prove the musical journey of a lifetime. The recording here has ambient, full-bodied sound that is more reminiscent of the concert hall than of the studio.

Awards 1989

Emerson Quartet (Eugene Drucker, Philip Setzer *vns* Lawrence Dutton *va* David Finckel *vc*)
DG ② 423 657-2GH2
(149 minutes: DDD) Ⓕ
Recorded 1988 ooo

Any cycle of Bartók quartets has to be pretty special to stand out against the competition. The Emerson Quartet's is, and it does: powerful and refined, paying close attention to the letter of the score, and excelling in virtuoso teamwork. The impression from these recordings is of massive tonal projection and superlative clarity, each textural strand coloured and made audible to a degree possibly unrivalled in the recorded history of these works. DG's close, brightly lit recording quality must share some of the credit for that, of course. Combine this with controlled vehemence, headlong velocity and razor-sharp unanimity (any fast movement from quartets two to five can serve as illustration) and you have a formidable alliance of virtues. Well recorded, when this set first appeared it was hailed as one of the most exciting chamber music recordings for many years.

Additional recommendations

Complete String Quartets

Végh Quartet

Auvidis Valois ③ V4809 (155 minutes: ADD: 9/83ᴿ) Ⓜ

The second Bartók cycle of this great Hungarian quartet: their performances are insightful and compelling and, technical fallibilities notwithstanding, remain a top choice.

Novák Quartet

Philips Duo ② 442 284-2PM2 (158 minutes: ADD: 10/94) Ⓜ

Mixed performances but good value for money: the Novák's mellow reserve can sometimes dull the cutting edge of Bartók's more acerbic writing, though in the last two quartets the Novák's are wonderfully communicative.

Violin Sonatas

Violin Sonatas – No 1,Sz75; No 2, Sz76.
Contrasts, Sz111
Kálmán Berkes *cl* **György Pauk** *vn* **Jenö Jandó** *pf*
Naxos 8 550749 (75 minutes: DDD) Ⓢ
Recorded 1993

Readers who habitually fight shy of Bartók's provocatively astringent piano writing might initially find these endlessly fascinating works rather unpalatable, the First Sonata especially. But careful scrutiny reveals manifold beauties which, once absorbed, tend to haunt one's memory and prompt repeated listening. Jenö Jandó's piano playing is fairly forthright yet without the naked agression of, say, Sviatoslav Richter. Furthermore, it provides an effective foil for György Pauk's warm tone and fluid solo line, especially in the First Sonata, where ungainly tone production could so easily compound one's discomfort. Here, however, the interpretation is at once thoughtful and well shaped, and fully appreciative of the mysterious 'night music' that sits at the heart of the *Adagio*.

The Second Sonata is both gentler and more improvisatory, its language and structure – although still pretty formidable – somewhat in the manner of a rhapsody. Pauk and Jandó again hit the target, and the full-bodied recording makes for a homogeneous sound picture. To have a spirited performance of the multi-faceted *Contrasts* (with Kálmán Berkes on clarinet) as a bonus certainly helps promote this well-annotated CD to the front line of competition. A confident mainstream recommendation, then, and superb value for money.

Awards 1997

Violin Sonata No 1, Sz75. Solo Violin Sonata, Sz117
Isabelle Faust *vn* **Ewa Kupiec** *pf*
Harmonia Mundi Les Nouveaux Interprètes
HMN91 1623 (69 minutes: DDD) Ⓑ
Recorded 1996 ooo

Bartók's First Violin Sonata is notoriously reluctant to yield its secrets yet none is more comprehensively perceptive than this recording by the young violinist Isabelle Faust. Harmonia Mundi counts Faust among the 'cream of the new generation of musicians' and, on this evidence, no one could rightly disagree. Ewa Kupiec provides Faust with motivated support. Faust favours a sensual approach that draws active parallels with the music of Berg. She ventures deep among the first movement's more mysterious episodes. This is empathetic playing, candid, full of temperament and always focused securely on the note's centre. The *crescendo*ing processional that sits at the heart of the second movement is charged with suspense and the steely finale suggests a savage resolve. Faust and Kupiec visit corners in this score that others gloss over, and the recording supports them all the way. The Solo Sonata is virtually as impressive. Here Faust approaches the music from a Bachian axis: her tone is pure, double-stopping immaculate and sense of timing acute. Faust is a persuasive narrator; she and her piano partner break down barriers in the First Sonata that, for some, will mean the difference between approachability and continuing bafflement. Do give them a try.

Violin Sonata No 2, Sz76. Rhapsodies – No 1, Sz86; No 2, Sz89. Six Romanian Folkdances, Sz56
Isabelle Faust *vn* **Florent Boffard** *pf*
Harmonia Mundi Les Nouveaux Interprètes
HMN91 1702 (46 minutes: DDD) Ⓑ
Recorded 1999

The most striking features of Isabelle Faust's first Bartók CD for Harmonia Mundi (see above), which featured the earthen First Sonata, were an empathetic spirit and a fiery temperament. Here, as there, Faust exhibits a defining use of nuance and inflection.

The two contrasting movements of the tauter, folk-music-derived Second Sonata call for a near-schizoid adaptability to changing moods. In the restless *Molto moderato* first movement Faust suggests feelings of sensual insinuation, though the lacerating attack of her bow at 3'50" has real grit. As the music grows more agitated, she follows suit and her pianist-partner Florent Boffard brooks no compromise in his handling of Bartók's dissonant chordal writing.

The *Allegretto* second movement approximates the 'friss' faster section of a Hungarian rhapsody. Faust lands the transition from the first movement on a racy *glissando*, makes great play with the dancing accelerations from 3'58" and calms from orgasmic thrashing at 9'59" to the sky-borne *diminuendo* of the closing bars. The Sonata's musical contours have rarely sounded better focused.

Rivals are unexpectedly plentiful. Anne-Sophie Mutter (DG) is honey and cream next to Faust's chilli and paprika, the Stanzeleit/Fenyö (ASV) and Pauk/Jandó (Naxos – see above) partnerships provide idiomatic though rather less striking options, and while Gidon Kremer (in his second recording, the one with Oleg Maisenberg) comes nearest to Faust in spirit, not everyone will gravitate to his chosen couplings (Enesco, Schulhoff, etc).

Faust offers feisty, high-kicking accounts of the two 1928 *Rhapsodies*, the Second being both the more exotic of the two and the more responsive to interpretative innovation. The stamping 'second part' recalls the orchestral *Dance Suite* of five years earlier and Faust invests it both with delicacy and a palpably rustic 'edge' (she all but 'swings it' from 1'27"). The popular *Romanian Folkdances* provide a tuneful encore sequence (again, beautifully played), though hardly a generous one given that the disc's total timing adds up to a mere 46 minutes. This is a marvellous CD, competitively priced, and a worthy follow-up to its widely celebrated predecessor.

Violin Sonata in E minor, Op posth. Andante. Slovak Folk Songs (arr Móži). Burlesques, Sz47 – A Bit Tipsy (arr Urai). For Children, Sz42 – Ten Pieces (arr Zathureczky). Contrasts, Sz111
Susanne Stanzeleit *vn* **Michael Collins** *cl*
Gusztáv Fenyö *pf*
ASV CDDCA982 (65 minutes: DDD) Ⓕ
Recorded 1995

An interesting case of 'before and after', with the early E minor Sonata representing Bartók in 'czardas' mode and the late *Contrasts* echoing the earthy tang of genuine Hungarian folk music. Susanne Stanzeleit brings a wide range of gipsy-style inflexions to the various short pieces and the tipsy *Burlesque* finds her wisely avoiding a sober straight line. A touch of ruggedness suits the *Contrasts*, though there the real star of the show is clarinettist Michael Collins. True, Fenyö and Stanzeleit set the scene, but Collins's witty, lightly inflected solo has immense colour and personality. The little *Andante* for violin and piano (it lasts for just 3'18" in this performance) was written for Adila Arányi as a 'thank you' for a house party, but wasn't actually premièred until 1955. It's a pleasant but fairly uncharacteristic piece, whereas the half-hour Sonata of 1903 that precedes it contains many auguries of the mature Bartók. Strauss is an audible influence and so is Wagner: the very opening rises out of post-romantic mists, gently brushed by arpeggiated pizzicatos. Although not a masterpiece to compare with the two mature violin sonatas, the E minor Sonata is attractive, memorable and well worth bringing into the repertoire. ASV's recordings are very nicely balanced.

Contrasts, Sz111. Rhapsodies – No 1, Sz86; No 2, Sz89. Six Romanian Folk Dances, Sz56 (arr Székely). Solo Violin Sonata, Sz117
Michael Collins *cl* **Krysia Osostowicz** *vn*
Susan Tomes *pf*
Hyperion CDA66415 (72 minutes: DDD) Ⓕ
Recorded 1990

Unusually for a composer who wrote so much fine chamber music Bartók was not himself a string player. But he did enjoy close artistic understanding with a succession of prominent violin virtuosos, including the Hungarians Jelly d'Arányi, Joseph Szigeti and Zoltán Székely, and, towards the end of his life, Yehudi Menuhin. It was Menuhin who commissioned the Sonata for solo violin, but Bartók died before he could hear him play it – Menuhin was unhappy with the occasional passages in quarter-tones and the composer had reserved judgement on his proposal to omit them. It was Menuhin's edition which was later printed and which has been most often played and recorded; but Krysia Osostowicz returns to the original and, more importantly, plays the whole work with intelligence, imaginative flair and consummate skill.

The Sonata is the most substantial work on this disc, but the rest of the programme is no less thoughtfully prepared or idiomatically delivered. There is the additional attraction of an extremely well balanced and natural-sounding recording. As a complement to the string quartets, which are at the very heart of Bartók's output, this is a most recommendable disc.

Additional recommendation

Bartók Violin Sonata No 2, Sz76

Couplings: **Enescu** Impressions d'enfance. **Schulhoff** Second Violin Sonata. **Plakidis** Two Grasshopper Dances

Kremer *vn* **Oleg Maisenberg** *pf*

Teldec 0630-13597-2 (63 minutes: DDD: 7/97) Ⓕ

See the Collections section (Instrumental).

Violin Duos

44 Duos for Two Violins, Sz98

Sándor Végh, Albert Lysy *vns*

Auvidis Astrée E7720 (50 minutes: ADD) Ⓕ

Recorded 1971 ●

Bartók's violin duos are accessible to virtually all levels of technical accomplishment yet conceal meanings which only the finest artists can bring out. Végh and Lysy are certainly in this category, and listening to all 44 pieces in one go is no hardship when the playing is of this order. This is partly a tribute to their care in devising a satisfying sequence of pieces, with variety of pace, dynamic and technical difficulty, but avoiding constant arbitrary fluctuation (Bartók stated that the published order was for pedagogic purposes only and not to be followed in performance).

One particularly revealing conjunction is of Nos 43, 22 and 36, which might all be taken as studies for the Fourth or Fifth String Quartets (the composition of the Duos falls between those two masterpieces). Intelligent planning is actually less important to the success of the disc than the sheer pungency of the violin playing. The resiny attack, the physical contact of horsehair on gut and steel, is vividly captured in a close-miked recording, and it lends an unmistakably idiomatic quality to the varied moods. Végh and Lysy sound ideally matched in temperament – no trace of the compromise or struggle for supremacy which such enterprises can produce. If you buy this CD to fill a gap or out of curiosity you will probably get a far richer experience than you bargained for.

Solo piano works

For Children, Sz42. The First Term at the Piano, Sz53. 15 Hungarian Peasant Songs, Sz71. Three Hungarian Folksongs from the Csík District, Sz35*a*. Hungarian Folktunes, Sz66. Eight Improvisations on Hungarian Peasant Songs, Sz74. Three Rondos on (Slovak) Folktunes, Sz84. Romanian Christmas Carols, Sz57. Six Romanian Folkdances, Sz56. Two Romanian Dances, Sz43. Suite, Sz62, with original Andante. Piano Sonata, Sz80. Sonatina, Sz55. 14 Bagatelles, Sz38. Four Dirges, Sz45. Petite Suite, Sz105. Violin Duos, Sz98 (arr Sándor) – No 1, Teasing Song; No 17, Marching Song; No 35, Ruthenian kolomejka; No 42, Arabian Song; No 44, Transylvanian Dance. 10 Easy Pieces, Sz39. Allegro barbaro, Sz49. Out of doors, Sz81. Seven Sketches, Sz44. Two Elegies, Sz41. Three Burlesques, Sz47. Nine Little Pieces, Sz82. Three Studies, Sz72

György Sándor *pf* Sony Classical ④ SX4K68275 Ⓜ

(287 minutes: DDD). Recorded 1993-95 ●

There can't be many pianists on the current circuit whose fund of experience extends to working with a major 20th-century master; but of those still recording, György Sándor must surely take pride of place. Sándor prepared Bartók's first two piano concertos under the composer's guidance and gave the world premières of the Third Concerto and the piano version of the *Dance Suite*. The present collection is Sándor's second survey of Bartók's piano music and contains all the major works apart from *Mikrokosmos*.

Many of these performances are exceptionally fine, even though the passage of time has witnessed something of a reduction in Sándor's pianistic powers, mostly where maximum stamina and high velocity fingerwork are required (as in the first *Burlesque*). However, you may be astonished at the heft, energy and puckish humour of Sándor's 1994 recording of the Piano Sonata, a more characterful rendition than its predecessor, with a particularly brilliant account of the folkish *Allegro molto* finale. The *Allegro barbaro* is similarly 'on the beam', while Sándor brings a cordial warmth to the various collections of ethnic pieces, the *Romanian Christmas Carols* especially.

His phrasing, rubato, expressive nuancing, attention to counterpoint and command of tone suggest the touch of a master, while his imagination relishes the exploratory nature of the *Improvisations*, *Bagatelles* and *Miraculous Mandarin*-style *Studies*. Sándor connects with all the music's abundant qualities: harmonic or rhythmic innovation, powerful emotion, humour, introspection, ethnic variety and the sheer scope and complexity of Bartók's piano writing in general. Intuitive interpreters, especially those who knew and understand the composers they perform, are becoming a rare breed. In that respect alone, György Sándor's Bartók deserves an honoured place in every serious CD collection of 20th-century piano music.

---

14 Bagatelles, Sz38. Two Elegies, Sz41. Sonatine, Sz55. Six Romanian Folk Dances, Sz56. Three Hungarian Folktunes, Sz66

Zoltán Kocsis *pf* Philips 434 104-2PH Ⓕ

(54 minutes: DDD). Recorded 1991 ●

The *Bagatelles* and *Sonatine* are also available on Philips 50 Great Recordings 464 676-2PM Ⓜ

Bartók himself admitted that his *Bagatelles* (1908) were largely experimental, and at least half-a-dozen could have fallen from a jazz-pianist's copybook (Nos 7, 11 and 12, particularly). Debussy, too, is much in evidence (No 3), as is Bartók's love of folk-song (Nos 4 and 5). The *Elegies* would sit nicely among the shorter works of Busoni. These virtuosic effusions recall the moon-flecked world of late Liszt, albeit flushed with a Hungarian rather than a gipsy complexion. Folk-song proper informs Kocsis's last three selections: the familiar *Six Romanian Folk Dances*, the cheerful and ingenious *Sonatine* and the relatively dense *Hungarian Folktunes*, Sz66 – the last bringing us to the far edge of the Great War. It's a cliffhanger of a finale, and has us eager for more. Kocsis's readings are absolutely on target. A peach of a disc.

Two Romanian Dances, Sz43. Three Hungarian folksongs from the Csík district, Sz35*a*. Allegro barbaro, Sz49. Four Dirges, Sz45. Suite, Sz62. Romanian Christmas Carols, Sz57. Three Studies, Sz72. Three Rondos on Folktunes, Sz84. The first term at the piano, Sz53
Zoltán Kocsis *pf*
Philips 442 016-2PH (71 minutes: DDD) Ⓕ
Recorded 1993

The Romanian Dances, Hungarian folksongs and Romanian Christmas Carols are also available on Philips 50 Great Recordings 464 676-2PM Ⓜ

Kocsis's Bartók series is the first major interpretative project to call on the substantial evidence of Bartók's own recordings. There was a spontaneity in Bartók's recorded performances, a quality that Kocsis achieves in his own playing. He also displays an ecstatic involvement in Bartók's harmonic writing, most particularly in the delicious, eloquently voiced *Three Hungarian folksongs from the Csík district* (how the second song seems a natural continuation of the first) and the exploratory *Three Studies*, the first as violent as the Miraculous Mandarin's murder, the third, a shifting sequence of computations that anticipates the player-piano studies of Conlon Nancarrow. Kocsis tackles all three *Studies* with absolute confidence. In any case, Kocsis's performances are never mere replications of Bartók's own; rather, they take the composer's lead in generating energy without aggression, poetry without indulgence, accuracy without pedantry.

The rest of the programme is as varied as the incidents within each individual opus. The *Two Romanian Dances*, both of them rich in novel variation, are thrust forwards in heady excitement, the first breaking half-way for a darkly rhapsodic central section, the second, a sort of mad-cap burlesque. The *Allegro barbaro* discards its customary metallic sheen and, instead, assumes more authentically Hungarian characteristics. Then there are the deeply expressive *Four Dirges*, the varied and instantly memorable *Romanian Christmas Carols*, the masterly Suite, Op 14 and, to end on a simplistic note, *The first term at the piano* – attractive teaching material, similar in concept to the first books of *Mikrokosmos*, but strictly for completists. This is a superb CD. The music itself is of exceptionally high quality, the disc contents are imaginatively varied, the interpretations beyond criticism, the recordings superb (warm, close and lifelike) and the documentation highly informative.

Piano Sonata, Sz80. Out of doors, Sz81. Nine Little Pieces, Sz82. Petite Suite, Sz105
Zoltán Kocsis *pf*
Philips 446 369-2PH (49 minutes: DDD) Ⓕ
Recorded 1996

The Piano Sonata and Out of doors are also available coupled with: Two Romanian Dances, Sz43; Three Hungarian Folksongs, Sz35a; Romanian Christmas Carols, Sz57; 14 Bagatelles, Sz38; and Sonatina, Sz55: Philips 50 Great Recordings 464 676-2PM Ⓜ

Kocsis's mastery of tone, rhythm and articulation, allied to his painstaking attention to important source material, make for a level of pianistic distinction that is fairly unique in this repertory. The first movements of the Sonata and *Out of doors* hit hard without hammering, the former displaying a multitude of tiny inflexional gestures and pulse changes, the latter, a quick-boiling final chase of great intensity. Playing of this calibre takes us back to the days of 78s – where so much rhythmic flexibility is achieved within such a disciplined interpretative framework. In *Out of doors*, Kocsis's ability to command differing colours simultaneously heightens the musical effect, especially in the 'Barcarolla' and what is surely the most exquisitely tooled performance of 'The Night's Music' ever recorded. 'The Chase' is pin-sharp, its every gear-change expertly negotiated, while Kocsis makes maximum capital out of the rich harmonic world in 'Musettes'. The *Nine Little Pieces* transcend their brevity, 'Menuetto' recalling the second movement of the First Piano Concerto, the closing 'Preludio – All'Ungherese' providing a little mini-suite all on its own. The disc closes with the *Petite Suite*, a tuneful half-dozen ingeniously refashioned from the *44 Duos* for two violins. This production is of superb quality. This is one of the great piano records of the post-war period.

---

10 Easy Pieces, Sz39. Seven Sketches, Sz44. Three Burlesques, Sz47. 15 Hungarian Peasant Songs, Sz71. Eight Improvisations on Hungarian Peasant Songs, Sz74
Zoltán Kocsis *pf*
Philips 462 902-2PH (62 minutes: ADD/DDD) Ⓕ
Recorded 1980-98

Kocsis's solo Bartók Volume 6 reveals the versicoloured fundamentals of the composer's harmonic language, from the smoky near-Impressionism of the *Seven Sketches* to the *Miraculous Mandarin* sound-alikes squatting at the centre of the *Improvisations on Hungarian Peasant Songs* (Nos 5 and 6). The *15 Hungarian Peasant Songs* are filled with longing or playfulness, the *10 Easy Pieces* with the simplest ideas, strategically employed.

Most of these pieces call for profoundly centred thinking, minutely calculated *rubato* and judicious timing. Kocsis scores on all fronts, even though the *Sketches*, *Peasant Songs* and *Improvisations* were recorded as long ago as 1980. Although there is just a touch more interpretative freedom on the later sessions, the sheer consistency of the playing is remarkable. The sound also matches well, although the later piano image is decidedly richer in texture. The *Seven Sketches* are in no way related to the orchestral *Hungarian Sketches*, although three other pieces on the disc are: 'Slightly Tipsy' (the second *Burlesque*), 'Evening in Transylvania' and 'Bear Dance' (the fifth and tenth of the *10 Easy Pieces*). Kocsis's Bartók legacy stands out as one of the true pinnacles of the recorded piano repertoire – from any period.

Additional recommendation

Solo piano works etc **H**

Bartók *pf*

Pearl mono GEMMCD9166 (69 minutes: ADD: 6/96) Ⓜ

This Bartók plays Bartók compilation offers full-bodied transfers of some fascinating commercial recordings, including the first *Romanian Dance*, *Allegro barbaro* and Liszt's 'Sursum corda'. A must for all Bartókians.

Vocal works

Five Songs, Sz61. Five Songs, Sz63. Hungarian Folksongs, Sz64 – Black is the earth; My God, my God; Wives, let me be one of your company; So much sorrow; If I climb the rocky mountains. Five Songs, Sz61 (orch Kodály). Five Hungarian Folksongs, Sz101

Júlia Hamari *contr* **Ilona Prunyi** *pf*

Hungarian State Orchestra / János Kovács

Hungaroton HCD31535 (67 minutes: DDD) Ⓕ

Texts and translations included. Recorded 1992

Kodály's rose-tinted orchestrations of Bartók's uncompromisingly erotic Op 15 (Sz61) make for pleasant listening, but they sidetrack the real heart of the matter. Bartók had a year-long relationship with the 15-year-old Klára Gombossy, and three of the songs are based on her poetry; the fourth sets a poem by the daughter of Klára's piano teacher, while the remaining 'In Vivid Dreams' is a re-working of another poem by Klára, added later. Heard in its original form for voice and piano, Op 15 is a bold, harmonically far-reaching cycle (countless passages anticipate the harsher Bartók of the 1920s), often angular in design but, within its tough framework, passionately suggestive. Kodály's orchestrations date from 1961 and soften the music's contours in a way that Bartók himself would not have countenanced – at least not in 1915, the year in which the songs were composed. The *Five Songs*, Op 16 consolidate the dark, introspective language of Op 15, while the 10 folk-song settings – Bartók's clearly focused orchestrations (Sz101) and the five for voice and piano (Sz64) – are rather more outgoing and varied.

All this music is so absorbing that one tends temporarily to forget the performers – which wouldn't be possible were they less than good. Júlia Hamari projects a secure, strong body of tone and fully comprehends the potent love images of Op 15, while her accompanist, Ilona Prunyi, etches Bartók's vivid piano writing with a sure hand and much imagination. The orchestral items are patchily dealt with (winds are good, strings not), but the impressionistic nature of the writing (Kodály's especially) responds better to Kovács's soft-centred approach than, say, the *Village Scenes* would have done. The recordings are perfectly adequate. Recommended to all Bartókians and Lieder *aficionados*.

Duke Bluebeard's Castle

Walter Berry *bass-bar* Bluebeard;

Christa Ludwig *mez* Judith

London Symphony Orchestra / István Kertész

Decca Legends 466 377-2DM Ⓜ

(59 minutes: ADD). Notes, text and translation included. Recorded 1965 **OO**

John Tomlinson *bass* Bluebeard; **Anne Sofie von Otter** *mez* Judith; **Sandor Elès** *spkr*

Berlin Philharmonic Orchestra / Bernard Haitink

EMI CDC5 56162-2 (63 minutes: DDD) Ⓕ

Notes, text and translation included.

Recorded live in 1995 **O**

Bernard Haitink's poetic axis is vividly anticipated in the rarely recorded spoken prologue where Sandor Elès bids us search beneath the story's surface. Elès's timing and his sensitivity to word-colouring and the rhythmic inflexions of his native language greet the Gothic imagery of Bartók's solemn opening bars. The main protagonists soon establish very definite personalities, Bluebeard/Tomlinson as commanding, inscrutable and just a little arrogant, von Otter/Judith as profoundly frightened but filled with curiosity. Haitink and the Berlin Philharmonic paint a rich aural backdrop that is neither too slow nor overly lugubrious and that shows due appreciation of Bartók's seamless scoring, especially in terms of the woodwind. The disembodied sighs that greet Judith's violent hammering on the first door mark a momentary retreat from the Philharmonie's ambient acoustic (or so it seems) and in so doing suggest – quite appropriately – a chilling 'world beyond'. Judith's shock as she recoils in horror is conveyed in clipped, halting tones by von Otter (note too how seductively she manipulates Bluebeard into opening the first door).

Beyond the expansive introduction come the doors themselves, and here too Haitink balances the 'outer' and 'inner' aspects of Bartók's score to perfection – whether in the torture chamber, the glowing textures of 'The Secret Garden' or the Brucknerian expanses of the fifth door, 'Bluebeard's Kingdom' (the opera's structural apex), launched here on a series of epic *crescendos*. Von Otter's stunned responses suggest lonely disorientation within a vast space, whereas the sullenness of the 'Lake of Tears' prompts an exquisite blending of instrumental timbres, most particularly between brass and woodwind. Haitink draws an aching curve to the string writing, but when Judith rushes panic-stricken towards the seventh door, fearful of Bluebeard's secret murders, he effects a gradual but cumulatively thrilling *accelerando*. The internment itself is devastating, while Bluebeard's helpless retreat marks a slow journey back to the questioning void. Recording live can have its pitfalls, but here the atmosphere is electric, the grasp of Bartók's sombre tone-painting – whether sung or played – absolute.

EMI's engineering favours a full sound stage rather than picking out specific instrumental details, but the overall effect remains comprehensively satisfying. Kertész, on the other hand, favours a far richer sound stage, with softer contours (his armoury suggests more weight than glinting steel, his torture chamber, anxiety rather than cruelty) and a passionate swell to the string writing. Kertész represents the opera's compassionate core.

When it comes to the husband-and-wife team of Walter Berry and Christa Ludwig, one senses more a woman discovering sinister aspects of the man she loves than an inquisitive shrew intent on plundering Bluebeard's every secret. Here, Judith seems perpetually poised to take Bluebeard's arm and linger lovingly about him, while Berry's assumption of the title-role – which is beautifully, if not terribly idiomatically, sung – suggests neither *Angst* nor impatience. Ludwig, too, was in wonderful voice at the time of this recording, and instances of her eloquence are far too numerous to list individually. The transfer is superb, with a thunderous organ beyond the fifth door and merely the odd rogue edit or spot of tape hiss to betray the passing years.

Additional recommendations

Duke Bluebeard's Castle

Troyanos Judith **Nimsgern** Bluebeard

BBC Symphony Orchestra / Boulez

Sony Classical SMK64110 (61 minutes: ADD: 3/95) Ⓜ

This is the more forceful of Pierre Boulez's two readings (Jessye Norman's souless Judith mars his later DG set). Tatiana Troyanos's vocally winning Judith and Boulez's ideal pacing make this set a top recommendations.

Töpper Judith **Fischer-Dieskau** Bluebeard

Berlin Radio Symphony Orchestra / Fricsay

DG The Originals mono 457 756-2GOR (ADD: 4/60[R]) Ⓜ

A wonderful performance, with Hertha Töpper as an intensely moving Judith and Dietrich Fischer-Dieskau (in his first recording of the work) a compelling Bluebeard. But, the German translation and a few cuts make it a choice for *Bluebeard* devotees only.

Sir Arnold Bax British 1883-1953

GROVE *Bax studied at the Royal College of Music, London, (1900-05). After discovering the poetry of Yeats, with which he was deeply impressed, he strongly identified with Irish Celtic culture. Drawing on many sources (Strauss, Debussy, Ravel, Elgar) he created a style of luxuriant chromatic harmony, rich ornament and broad melody, notably deployed in his tone poems The Garden of Fand (1916), November Woods (1917) and Tintagel (1919). Other important works of this period include his First Quartet (1918) and Second Piano Sonata (1919). In the 1920s his music became clearer in outline and more contrapuntal, though without losing its wide range of harmonic resource: Sibelius became an influence. His main works were now symphonies, seven written 1922-39, though he remained a prolific composer in all non-theatrical genres. In 1942 he was made Master of the King's Music, after which he composed little.*

Tone Poems

Festival Overture. Christmas Eve on the Mountains. Dance of Wild Irravel. Paean. Nympholept. Tintagel[a]

London Philharmonic Orchestra; [a]Ulster Orchestra / Bryden Thomson

Chandos CHAN9168 (76 minutes: DDD) Ⓕ

Recorded 1983-88

These pieces first appeared mostly as fillers to Bryden Thomson's complete recording of the Bax symphonies. Those who are beginning to explore this composer but would rather not start with a symphony will find the purest Bax, of course, in *Tintagel*, and a sumptuous reading it receives, but also in *Nympholept* – alluring wood magic of a kind Bax made peculiarly his own, here ravishingly scored. *Christmas Eve* is a less expected side of him, a moving vision of radiant peace descending upon a troubled Ireland. It just occasionally stumbles into his two besetting sins: sheer density of sound and a certain repetitiveness of rhythm – but Bax's Irish vein is strong within it, so is a powerful solemnity.

Dance of Wild Irravel is Bax's *La valse*; altogether too close to its model, you might think, until you realise that Bax's delirious waltz fantasy precedes Ravel's by a good few years. *Paean* is a deafening piece of pomp and circumstance for an enormous orchestra, redeemed by its exuberance and its brevity. The *Festival Overture* is exactly what its name suggests, but just when you think festivity is wearing a touch thin, a moment of truly Baxian wildness or a vintage Bax tune will lift it from among his occasional works into one of his characteristic ones. Thomson had a pretty well unerring instinct for Bax's elusive, glintingly changing moods – both playing and recorded sound are first-class.

In Memoriam. Concertante for Piano (Left-Hand) and Orchestra[a]. The Bard of the Dimbovitza[b]

[b]Jean Rigby *mez* **[a]Margaret Fingerhut** *pf*

BBC Philharmonic Orchestra / Vernon Handley

Chandos CHAN9715 (77 minutes: DDD) Ⓕ

Recorded 1998

The glorious tune that dominates the 1916 tone-poem *In Memoriam* will be familiar to many Bax enthusiasts from its use in his 1948 film score for David Lean's *Oliver Twist*, and to hear it in its original surroundings is both a moving and thrilling experience. It had long been assumed that the 32-year-old composer never got round to scoring this deeply felt elegy (originally entitled *In Memoriam Pádraig Pearse*), so it's pleasing to find that Vernon Handley and the BBC Philharmonic do full justice to its opulent yet iridescent sound world, with its strong echoes of *The Garden of Fand* and *Nympholept*.

The *Concertante* for left-hand piano and orchestra, written for Harriet Cohen after a domestic accident had left her right hand disabled, is not top-drawer Bax but remains an immensely appealing creation, boasting a central *Moderato tranquillo* in the composer's sweetest lyrical vein. Margaret Fingerhut is the deftest and most sympathetic of soloists.

The five orchestral songs that make up *The Bard of the Dimbovitza*, setting poems allegedly based on Romanian folk-songs, contain not a hint of local colour but are purest Bax, the harmonic idiom and overall mood strikingly similar to his *Enchanted Summer*. Jean Rigby vividly characterises the dialogue in the last two songs ('My girdle I hung on a tree-top tall' and 'Spinning Song'), while bringing plenty of drama to the almost operatic scena that is 'The Well of Tears'. Some typically lustrous Chandos engineering adorns this valuable triptych of recorded premières, and the issue as a whole deserves the heartiest of welcomes.

Additional recommendation

Tintagel

Coupling: **Vaughan Williams** Symphony No 5

Philharmonia Orchestra; London Symphony Orchestra / Barbirolli

EMI British Composers CDM5 652110-2 Ⓜ (54 minutes: ADD: 3/95)

Bax's rugged, wind-swept seascape finds Barbirolli in his element, and his reading is on the whole more passionately involving than either Boult's or Thomson's.

Symphonies Nos 1 and 7

Symphonies – No 1 in E flat[a]; No 7[b]

London Philharmonic Orchestra / [a]Myer Fredman, [b]Raymond Leppard

Lyrita SRCD232 (78 minutes: ADD) Ⓕ

Recorded [a]1970, [b]1974 ●●

Few English composers have expressed such intense and fiercely passionate emotions as Bax has in the first two movements of his First Symphony. Such rage and grief as can be found there seem to suggest a psycho-drama being played out, and when we learn that at the time of its composition (1921) Bax may still have been coming to terms with the aftermath of the First World War, the loss of friends in the Easter Rising in Ireland and the irretrievable breakdown of his marriage, it is tempting to imagine that the symphony is indeed exercising some kind of personal exorcism on these events. Bax himself, however, was always reluctant to admit the existence of such a 'programme' behind the symphony, and in many ways he was probably right to do so. Whatever personal experiences Bax had poured into it, the end result is unquestionably a powerful, cogent symphony of universal appeal.

The Seventh and last of Bax's symphonies makes an intelligent and well-contrasted coupling. The first movement, though not without tension and some storm-tossed passages (very much a Baxian seascape this), has a prevailing mood of hope and expectation – as though embarking on some adventurous seaward journey to new lands, whilst the second movement finds Bax in wistful 'legendary' mood so evocative of the early tone-poems. The last movement begins by echoing the optimism of the first movement, but finally gives way, in the long and beautiful epilogue, to a mood of autumnal nostalgia and sad farewell. These are classic Lyrita recordings, with exceptionally fine performances and superb digital transfers.

Additional recommendation

Symphony No 7

Couplings: Four Songs.

Hill *ten* **London Philharmonic Orchestra / Thomson**

Chandos CHAN8628 (70 minutes: DDD: 12/98) Ⓕ

An admirable performance in superb Chandos sound.

Symphony No 2

Symphony No 2 in E minor/C. November Woods

Royal Scottish National Orchestra / David Lloyd-Jones

Naxos 8 554093 (57 minutes: DDD) Ⓢ

Recorded 1995 ●

From the grinding dissonances at the outset through to the inconsolable coda, Lloyd-Jones and his orchestra bring out the unremitting toughness of Bax's uncompromising, breathtakingly scored Second Symphony; even the gorgeous secondary material in the first movement offers an occasional shaft of pale, wintry sunlight. It helps, too, that Lloyd-Jones has clearly thought hard about the task in hand. How lucidly, for example, he expounds the arresting introduction, where the symphony's main building-blocks are laid out before us, and how well he brings out the distinctive tenor of Bax's highly imaginative writing for low wind and brass. The Scottish brass have a field-day.

Lloyd-Jones proves an equally clear-sighted navigator through the storm-buffeted landscape of *November Woods*, for many people, Bax's greatest tone-poem. Thoroughly refreshing in its enthusiasm and exhilarating sense of orchestral spectacle, this recording has a physical impact and emotional involvement that genuinely compel. A veritable blockbuster.

Additional recommendation

November Woods

Couplings: Northern Ballad No 1. Mediterranean. The Garden of Fand. Tintagel

London Philharmonic Orchestra / Boult

Lyrita SRCD231 (62 minutes: ADD: 9/92) Ⓕ

Boult's performance of this tone-poem is masterly and he generates a great deal of tension, atmosphere and drama. Bryden Thomson's account seems pedestrian and prosaic in comparison. Fine performances of the couplings, too.

Symphony No 3

Symphony No 3. The Happy Forest

Royal Scottish National Orchestra / David Lloyd-Jones

Naxos 8 553608 (54 minutes: DDD) Ⓢ

Recorded 1996 ●

Dedicated to Sir Henry Wood, Bax's Symphony No 3 boasts arguably the richest store of memorable melodic invention to be found in any of the composer's cycle of seven, culminating in an inspired epilogue of wondrous, jaw-dropping beauty. David Lloyd-Jones's clear-headed, purposeful conducting of this intoxicating repertoire is the most judiciously paced and satisfyingly cogent Bax Third we've had since Barbirolli's pioneering 1943-44 Hallé account (nla). Moreover, not only does Lloyd-Jones keep a firm hand on the tiller, he also draws some enthusiastic playing from the RSNO, which responds throughout with commendable polish and keen application. Some Baxians may feel that the brakes are applied too steeply at that tricky *Poco meno mosso* marking at three bars before fig 49 (15'48"), but the exhilarating coda certainly goes with terrific zest and gallumphing swagger.

Finely poised, affectingly full-throated solo work from principal horn and trumpet illuminates the progress of the ensuing *Lento*, whose ravishing landscape Lloyd-Jones surveys in less lingering fashion than either Barbirolli or Thomson. The first half of the finale, too, is a great success, Lloyd-Jones negotiating the fiendish twists and turns dictated by Bax's copious tempo markings with impressive aplomb. Only in the epilogue do you feel a need for a touch more rapt poetry. Tim Handley's excellently balanced recording is rich and refined, though the perspective is perhaps fractionally closer than ideal for *The Happy Forest*, which receives a performance of bounding vigour, gleeful mischief and muscular fibre; just that last, crucial drop of enchantment remains elusive. No matter, a disc not to be missed.

Further listening

Bainton Symphony No 2 in D minor

Couplings: **Clifford** Symphony 1940. **Gough** Serenade

BBC Philharmonic Orchestra / Handley

Chandos CHAN9757 (73 minutes: DDD: 12/99) Ⓕ

A most enjoyable release of enticingly off-the-beaten-track repertoire, including a glowing account of Edgar Bainton's imposing and powerfully communicative Third Symphony.

Symphony No 5

Symphony No 5 in C sharp minor. The Tale the Pine Trees Knew

Royal Scottish National Orchestra / David Lloyd-Jones

Naxos 8 554509 (58 minutes: DDD) Ⓢ

Recorded 1996

The Fifth is perhaps the most characteristic of Bax's cycle of seven symphonies. For all the music's powerful range of emotion and its seemingly bewildering profusion of material and countless moments of bewitching beauty, its resourceful symphonic processes are not easy to assimilate on first hearing. Lloyd-Jones's intelligent, meticulously observant and purposeful direction pays handsome dividends, and a well-drilled RSNO responds with sensitivity and enthusiasm. Lloyd-Jones excels in the opening movement's tightly knit canvas, its epic ambition matched by a compelling sense of momentum, architectural grandeur and organic 'wholeness': he judiciously resists the temptation to dwell too lovingly over Bax's gorgeously lyrical secondary material, and is also successful at bringing out the muscular toughness of the *Allegro con fuoco* main theme.

In the slow movement Lloyd-Jones paints a chillier, more troubled landscape than does Bryden Thomson (Chandos). The finale's main *Allegro* sets out with gleeful dash and a fine rhythmic snap to its heels. Lloyd-Jones judges that tricky, crisis-ridden transition into the epilogue well, and the apotheosis is a hard-won, grudging victory. The 1931 tone-poem *The Tale the Pine Trees Knew* makes an ideal bedfellow, foreshadowing as it does the bracingly 'northern' (to quote the composer) demeanour of the Fifth. Lloyd-Jones's comparatively extrovert treatment of the work's exultant final climax works perfectly convincingly within the context of his overall conception. Another eminently truthful, judiciously balanced sound picture from producer/engineer Tim Handley.

Further listening

Tubin Symphony No 2, 'The Legendary'

Coupling: Symphony No 6

Swedish Radio Symphony Orchestra / N Järvi

BIS CD304 (DDD: 4/86) Ⓕ

Estonian composer Eduard Tubin's Second Symhony, has a luminous beauty and wonderfully organic power that repays acquaintance, especially in so convincing a performance as this from Neeme Järvi.

Chamber works

Octet. String Quintet. Concerto. Threnody and Scherzo. In Memoriam

Margaret Fingerhut *pf*

Academy of St Martin in the Fields Chamber Ensemble

Chandos CHAN9602 (72 minutes: DDD) Ⓕ

Recorded 1997

This is a beautiful and enterprising collection of works by Bax. *In Memoriam* for cor anglais, harp and string quartet probably dates from 1917. Subtitled 'An Irish Elegy', and like the *Elegiac Trio* from the same period, its poignant mood reflects Bax's despair at the tragic events of the Easter Rising. In the single-movement String Quintet (completed in January 1933) Bax draws some luscious, almost orchestral sonorities from his chosen forces. Scored for horn, piano and string sextet, the 1934 Octet (labelled 'Serenade' on the short score) is a two-movement work of strong appeal and engaging charm: the magically evocative opening brings with it echoes of those unforgettable horn solos in the Third Symphony's central *Lento*, while the icy glitter of the piano part from 1'53" in the second-movement *Scherzo* momentarily conjures up the far-Northern landscape of *Winter Legends*.

The *Threnody and Scherzo* for bassoon, harp and string sextet of 1936 is perhaps less immediately striking. The writing is as fluent and accomplished as ever but the melodic material isn't quite as fresh as one might have wished. By contrast, the Concerto for flute, oboe, harp and string quartet now stands revealed as one of Bax's most likeable chamber offerings. This is a captivating transcription for septet of a Sonata for flute and harp from 1928 and proves to be an exquisite gem, its deft and joyous outer movements framing a lovely central 'Cavatina'. The dedicated, sensitive performances have been accorded warm, transparent sound.

Nonet. Oboe Quintet. Elegiac Trio. Clarinet Sonata. Harp Quintet
Nash Ensemble (Philippa Davies *fl* Gareth Hulse *ob* Michael Collins *cl* Marcia Crayford, Iris Juda, Elizabeth Wexler *vns* Roger Chase *va* Christopher van Kampen *vc* Duncan MoTier *db* Skaila Kanga *hp* Ian Brown *pf*)
Hyperion CDA66807 (73 minutes: DDD)   Ⓕ
Recorded 1995   ○○

A truly first-rate modern recording of Bax's Nonet. What a bewitching creation it is, overflowing with beguiling invention and breathtakingly imaginative in its instrumental resource (the sounds created are often almost orchestral). Bax worked on the Nonet at the same time (1929-30) as he was composing his Third Symphony and there are striking similarities between the two works. The Nash Ensemble (under the direction of Ian Brown) gives a masterly, infinitely subtle reading.

The remainder of the disc brings comparable pleasure. The delightful Oboe Quintet (written for Leon Goossens in 1922) receives immensely characterful treatment, especially the jaunty, Irish-jig finale (such sparkling, richly communicative playing). The same is true of the lovely Harp Quintet, which is essayed here with a rapt intensity and delicious poise. In the hands of these stylish artists, the *Elegiac Trio* possesses a delicacy and gentle poignancy that are really quite captivating. That just leaves the engaging Clarinet Sonata, a work that has fared well in the recording studio over the last few years. Suffice to report, Michael Collins and Ian Brown are compelling advocates, and theirs is a performance to set beside (if not supersede) all rivals. Beautiful sound throughout.

Elegiac Trio[a]. Fantasy Sonata[b]. Quintet for Harp   💰
and Strings[c]. Sonata for Flute and Harp[d]
Mobius ([ad]Lorna McGhee *fl* [c]Kanako Ito, [c]Philippe Honoré *vns* [abc]Ashan Pillai *va* [c]Martin Storey *vc* Alison Nicholls *hp*)
Naxos 8 554507 (65 minutes: DDD)   Ⓢ
Recorded 1999   ○○

Mobius is a gifted young London-based ensemble comprising seven prize-winning instrumentalists from four different countries, and their scrupulously shaded, fervent playing betokens a very real empathy with this gorgeous repertoire. In both the *Elegiac Trio* and Harp Quintet these artists favour a more boldly etched, less delicately evanescent approach than that of the Nash Ensemble (which is perhaps marginally more successful in distilling the poignant heartache of two works indissolubly

associated with the tragic events of the 1916 Easter Rising). Especially valuable here is the impassioned rendering of the marvellous *Fantasy Sonata* for harp and viola of 1927. Certainly, harpist Alison Nicholls (such a beguiling presence throughout) copes heroically with the daunting technical and physical demands of Bax's giddily accomplished writing (tailored for the virtuosity of the great Russian harpist, Maria Korchinska); moreover, she is splendidly partnered by violist Ashan Pillai. Likewise, the engagingly relaxed Sonata for Flute and Harp that Bax subsequently reworked into his *Concerto for Seven Instruments* (Chandos) emerges with delightful freshness, its plangent central 'Cavatina' as haunting as ever.

Sound and balance are just fine, and the booklet-essay is excellent too. Terrific value and strongly recommended.

Additional recommendation
Nonet
Couplings: **Delius** Violin Sonata No 3.   Ⓗ
Ferguson Octet **Moeran** String Trio in G
Goossens *ob* various artists; **Griller Quartet**
Dutton CDAX8014 (72 minutes: ADD: 12/95)   Ⓜ
    Superb performances from a constellation of top artists.

Ludwig van Beethoven
German 1770-1827

♫ *Beethoven studied first with his father,* GROVE *Johann, a singer and instrumentalist in the service of the Elector of Cologne at Bonn, but mainly with CG Neefe, court organist. At 11 he was able to deputise for Neefe; at 12 he had some music published. In 1787 he went to Vienna, but quickly returned on hearing that his mother was dying. Five years later he went back to Vienna, where he settled.*

He studied first with Haydn, though there was some clash of temperaments, and also with Schenk, Albrechtsberger and Salieri. Until 1794 he was supported by the Elector at Bonn, but he found patrons among the music-loving Viennese aristocracy and soon enjoyed success as a piano virtuoso, playing at private houses or palaces rather than in public. His public début was in 1795; about the same time his first important publications appeared, three piano trios Op 1 and three piano sonatas Op 2. As a pianist, it was reported he had fire, brilliance and fantasy as well as depth of feeling. It is naturally in the piano sonatas, writing for his own instrument, that he is at his most original in this period; the Pathétique belongs to 1799, the Moonlight ('Sonata quasi una fantasia') to 1801, and these represent only the most obvious innovations in style and emotional content. These years also saw the composition of his first three piano concertos, first two symphonies and a set of six string quartets Op 18.

1802, however, was a year of crisis for Beethoven, with his realisation that the impaired hearing he had noticed for some time was incurable and sure to worsen. That autumn, at a village outside Vienna, Heiligenstadt, he wrote a will-like document, addressed to his two brothers, describing his bitter unhappiness over his affliction in terms suggesting that he thought death was near. But he came through with his determination strengthened and entered a new creative phase, generally called his 'middle period'. It is characterised by a heroic tone, evident in the 'Eroica' Symphony (No 3, originally to have been dedicated not to a noble patron but to Napoleon), in Symphony No 5, where the sombre mood of the C minor first movement ('Fate knocking on the door') ultimately yields to a triumphant C major finale with piccolo, trombones and percussion added to the orchestra, and in his opera Fidelio. Here the heroic theme is made explicit by the story, in which (in the post-French Revolution 'rescue opera' tradition) a wife saves her imprisoned husband from murder at the hands of his oppressive political enemy. The three string quartets of this period – Op 59, are similarly heroic in scale: the first, lasting some 45 minutes, is conceived with great breadth, and it too embodies a sense of triumph as the intense F minor Adagio gives way to a jubilant finale in the major, embodying (at the request of the dedicatee, Count Razumovsky) a Russian folk melody.

Fidelio, unsuccessful at its première, was twice revised by Beethoven and his librettists and successful in its final version of 1814. Here there is more emphasis on the moral force of the story. It deals not only with freedom and justice, and heroism, but also with married love, and in the character of the heroine Leonore, Beethoven's lofty, idealised image of womanhood is to be seen. He did not find it in real life: he fell in love several times, usually with aristocratic pupils (some of them married), and each time was either rejected or saw that the woman did not match his ideals.

With his powerful and expansive middle-period works, which include the Pastoral Symphony (No 6, conjuring up his feelings about the countryside, which he loved), Symphonies Nos 7 and 8, Piano Concertos Nos 4 (a lyrical work) and 5 (the noble and brilliant 'Emperor') and the Violin Concerto, as well as more chamber works and piano sonatas (such as the 'Waldstein' and the 'Appassionata') Beethoven was firmly established as the greatest composer of his time. His piano-playing career had finished in 1808 (a charity appearance in 1814 was a disaster because of his deafness). That year he had considered leaving Vienna for a secure post in Germany, but three Viennese noblemen had banded together to provide him with a steady income and he remained there, although the plan foundered in the ensuing Napoleonic wars in which his patrons suffered and the value of Austrian money declined.

The years after 1812 were relatively unproductive. He seems to have been seriously depressed, by his deafness and the resulting isolation, by the failure of his marital hopes and (from 1815) by anxieties over the custodianship of the son of his late brother, which involved him in legal actions. But he came out of these trials to write his profoundest music. There are seven piano sonatas in this, his 'late period', including the turbulent 'Hammerklavier' Op 106, with its dynamic writing and its harsh, rebarbative fugue, and Op 110, which also has fugues and much eccentric writing at the instrument's extremes of compass; there is a great Mass and a Choral Symphony, No 9 in D minor, where the extended variation-finale is a setting for soloists and chorus of Schiller's Ode to Joy; and there is a group of string quartets, music on a new plane of spiritual depth, with their exalted ideas, abrupt contrasts and emotional intensity. The traditional four-movement scheme and conventional forms are discarded in favour of designs of six or seven movements, some fugal, some akin to variations (these forms especially attracted him in his late years), some song-like, some martial, one even like a chorale prelude. For Beethoven, the act of composition had always been a struggle, as the tortuous scrawls of his sketchbooks show; in these late works the sense of agonising effort is a part of the music.

Musical taste in Vienna had changed during the first decades of the 19th century; the public were chiefly interested in light Italian opera (especially Rossini) and easygoing chamber music and songs, to suit the prevalent bourgeois taste. Yet the Viennese were conscious of Beethoven's greatness: they applauded the Choral Symphony, even though, understandably, they found it difficult, and though baffled by the late quartets they sensed their extraordinary visionary qualities. His reputation went far beyond Vienna: the late Mass was first heard in St Petersburg, and the initial commission that produced the Choral Symphony had come from the Philharmonic Society of London. When he died 10,000 are said to have attended the funeral. He had become a public figure, as no composer had done before. Unlike composers of the preceding generation, he had never been a purveyor of music to the nobility: he had lived into the age, indeed helped create it, of the artist as hero and the property of mankind at large.

Complete Piano Concertos

No 1 in C, Op 15; **No 2** in B flat, Op 19;
No 3 in C minor, Op 37; **No 4** in G, Op 58;
No 5 in E flat, Op 73, 'Emperor'

Piano Concertos Nos 1-5.
Piano Sonata in C minor, Op 111
Wilhelm Kempff *pf*
Berlin Philharmonic Orchestra / Ferdinand Leitner
DG ③ 427 237-2GX3 (195 minutes: ADD) Ⓜ
Recorded 1960s **OO**

Kempff was never a heavyweight among Beethoven pianists. What he had was intellect and imagination in perfect balance, a fabulous touch, great rhythmic *élan*, and a kind of improvisatory zeal that – translated into other terms – can best be described as a true and abiding sense of wonder. And how beautifully Leitner and the Berlin Philharmonic accompany Kempff. This was the new young Berlin Philharmonic of the early 1960s, poet-musicians to a man, trained to listen and respond and then, in performance, take wing into precisely those areas of mind and imagination that were Kempff's own natural habitat.

Kempff's recording of the first two concertos dates from the early 1960s, but the sound quality is pleasingly open and full-bodied, so that the soloist's pearly, immaculate tone quality is heard to good effect. Kempff and Leitner enjoy what is obviously a close rapport and their aristocratic,

Olympian but poetic music-making suits both works admirably. His cadenzas, his own in the first four concertos, will infuriate some as much as they will delight those of us – people who like steam trains and still refer to the wireless – who occasionally tire of all the regimentation and ratiocination of modern music-making.

His account of the *Emperor* remains a classic recording that sounds very well in DG's remastering of the 1962 originals which often bring out previously unnoticed orchestral details with remarkable immediacy. This applies to the set as a whole, which is a very tempting proposition, quirky cadenzas and all. In the Fourth Piano Concerto (1961) you may be less than happy with his decision to use his own cadenzas, but the performance as a whole is such a joy, so light-filled, that even that qualification tends to fade into insignificance. It sounds especially radiant in these transfers. Despite a touch of gruffness in some of the orchestral tuttis in the *Emperor* it, too, generally comes up with glistening clarity. In many ways these are the liveliest performances of all the complete sets available, physically and intellectually, since Schnabel's pre-war set.

Piano Concertos Nos 1-5
Claudio Arrau *pf*
Staatskapelle Dresden / Sir Colin Davis
Philips ③ 422 149-2PH3 (189 minutes: DDD) Ⓕ
Recorded 1986-88

With its sometimes diffuse structuring and recurrent strain of fantasy, Beethoven's C minor Piano Concerto is tricky to bring off, though in a good performance a larger coherence will generally emerge, not least because of Beethoven's long-term exploitation of a pun on the schizoid G sharp/A flat. Initially, the *Largo*'s E major tonality seems merely bleakly to confront the prevailing C minor and E flat major; but all is revealed at the point of transition into the finale when the violins' G sharp in the *Largo*'s final chord is swiftly contradicted and reaffirmed by the piano at the start of the *Rondo*. After that it's a case of 'watch this space'.

This seemingly abstruse detail is mentioned because the moment implies the kind of segue that Beethoven will make mandatory in the lead to the finales of his last two piano concertos. You may well experience horror, then, when you find that Philips has split the C minor Concerto across two discs, with the break coming, believe it or not, between the Concerto's slow movement and finale. This was Arrau's fourth recording of the C minor Concerto and it is far removed in style from the rather more extrovert and brilliant 1947 recording with the Philadelphia Orchestra under Ormandy (once available on Columbia), the accompaniment bright but sometimes slovenly in rhythm. This performance is far better accompanied and is touched with a host of fresh insights conveyed in phrasing and tone-colouring of a rare and settled beauty. Arrau, at best, gives us music-making of rare depth and breeding, but the performances are perhaps best taken singly, the *Emperor* first, followed by the readings of the G major and C major Concertos.

Piano Concertos Nos 1-5.
Choral Fantasia C minor, Op 80
Daniel Barenboim *pf* **John Alldis Choir;**
New Philharmonia Orchestra / Otto Klemperer
EMI ③ CMS7 63360-2 (211 minutes: ADD) Ⓜ
Recorded 1967

Klemperer had done concert cycles, perhaps most memorably in London in the 1950s with Claudio Arrau but his decision to record the piano concertos at the age of 82 came as a result of his admiration for the most precociously talented of all young Beethoven pianists at the time, Daniel Barenboim. Barenboim was 25 and about to embark on what was to be an exceptionally fine cycle of the Beethoven piano sonatas. He was steeped in Beethoven and perhaps peculiarly well suited to the concertos which, we should not forget, are essentially a young man's music. It was a fascinating pairing, Klemperer and Barenboim contrasted in age and to some extent in temperament but at the same time symbiotically at one musically. Had this not been the case, Barenboim would have been swamped, lost in the wash of Klemperer's accompaniments which deliver the orchestral argument and the orchestral detail with an articulacy and authority unique in the history of these works on record.

The performance of the B flat Concerto, the first historically if not numerically, is a typical joy, full of fire and grace and unstoppably vital. Given Klemperer's propensity for taking slow tempos in Beethoven, you might imagine him being taken for a ride by the young Barenboim in the B flat and C major finales. But not a bit of it. It is Klemperer, as much as his youthful soloist, who seems to be the driving force here. Rarely on record has the slow movement of the C major Concerto been played with so natural a sense of concentrated calm, the whole thing profoundly collected on the spiritual plane. One of the joys of the Barenboim/Klemperer cycle is its occasional unpredictability: rock-solid readings that none the less incorporate a sense of 'today we try it this way'.

Ensemble is mostly first-rate during the cycle. The tricky coda of the first movement of the C minor Concerto is both rapt and dramatic. But in the coda of the first movement of the G major there is little doubt that Klemperer drags the pulse. And elsewhere there are some occasionally awkward adjustments to be made between soloist and orchestra. At the time of its initial appearance, the *Emperor* performance was generally adjudged a success. It is again broadly conceived. At first the finale seems a little staid; but later the 6/8 rhythms are made to dance and the performance has a burning energy by the end. So does the account of the *Choral Fantasia*. Barenboim manages to be both imposing and playful in the piano preface.

Given Klemperer's magisterial style and authority, this set could have emerged as five symphonies with piano obbligato. In fact, it is a set of rare authority and spontaneity, and given the slightly unconventional idea of the soloist as *primus inter pares*, it is probably unique.

Piano Concertos Nos 1-5
Murray Perahia *pf* **Concertgebouw Orchestra / Bernard Haitink**
Sony Classical ③ S3K44575 (178 minutes: DDD) Ⓕ
Recorded 1983-86 ○○

Perahia's account of the C minor Concerto (No 3) is a joy from start to finish, wonderfully conceived, executed conducted and recorded. The single issue, coupled with this account of the G major Concerto (No 4), began life by winning the 1986 *Gramophone* Concerto Award. In these two concertos, and in the two earlier ones, Perahia and Haitink are difficult to fault. The First Concerto is especially well done with a quick first movement and the apt and delightful inclusion in the finale of a cadenza that Beethoven sketched in 1800. If Perahia is anywhere slightly below par it is in the *Emperor* Concerto. The reading gives us an emergent view of the work, undiscursive but perhaps at times lacking in a certain largeness of vision and purpose. For that we must return to Kempff or Arrau, which only confirms the pitfalls of buying cycles rather than separate performances. However, the Perahia cycle is one of the most consistently accomplished of those currently available; the recordings are a joy to listen to.

Piano Concertos Nos 1-5
Alfred Brendel *pf*
Vienna Philharmonic Orchestra / Sir Simon Rattle
Philips ③ 462 781-2PH3 (178 minutes: DDD) Ⓕ
Recorded 1998 ○

Happily, Alfred Brendel's fourth recorded cycle of the Beethoven piano concertos shares with the previous three qualities of energy, sensibility, intellectual rigour and high pianistic finish which made the earlier recordings so interesting to contemplate. There has never been anything less than first-rate about the recording partners he has worked with in these concertos and all the cycles have their moments of inspired togetherness. For example, Brendel has always played all five slow movements supremely well, drawing the orchestra around him like a celebrant at the communion table (here we have even finer performances than we have previously had).

In the two early concertos the Vienna Philharmonic's playing has a sweetness and allure, in the grander, later works a black-browed power, that is specially its own. Brendel's playing in the early concertos recalls his fine recordings of the early sonatas and the early and late *Bagatelles*, but it is as a private person impatient with the conventions and frock-coated formalities of the concertos as 'public' works. (It is not for nothing that the cadenzas shine so brightly out, particularly the astonishing and anachronistically late third cadenza Brendel uses in the first movement of the First Concerto.) With the Third Concerto we move into a different world. This is a marvellous performance from all three partners, purposeful and robust, the tonic C minor the cue for a reading which is full of darkness and menace, basses to the fore, drums at the ready. The finale is particularly ominous (relieved only by a gloriously lustrous clarinet solo) after an account of the slow movement, full-toned yet deeply quiet, the like of which one might dream of but rarely hope to hear. The C minor Concerto's heroic antitype, the *Emperor* in E flat, fares less well. Not the slow movement or finale, but the first movement which is slower than heretofore, to no very good effect. Perhaps it is that interpreters nowadays are less happy than their predecessors were with Beethoven's heroic persona.

Back in the private world of the Fourth Concerto, where charmed magic casements open on the foam of perilous seas in faerie lands forlorn, soloist, orchestra and conductor are at their inspired best. Brendel's glittering, wonderfully propelled account of the solo part is superbly backed by playing of real fire and sensitivity. It is a powerful performance, too. The recordings are first-rate.

Piano Concertos Nos 1-5. Rondos, Op 51 H
Wilhelm Kempff *pf*
Berlin Philharmonic Orchestra / Paul van Kempen
DG Dokumente mono ③ 435 744-2GDO3 Ⓜ
(189 minutes: ADD). Recorded 1953 ○

Kempff's Berlin cycle with Paul van Kempen has long been a collectors' item, often preferred to the Leitner set (see above). Apart from Kempff's whimsical though not ineffective line in home-grown cadenzas, these are exemplary performances in matters of style and execution. Yet they are something more. The cycle gives an extraordinary sense of the imaginative dimension of the first four concertos. As the 18th century turned into the 19th so the mists of romanticism began to drift across the landscape. The 1960s stereo set has an equally fine First Concerto and a better recorded *Emperor*. There is generally more glitter and dash. But the Second, Third and Fourth Concertos are all more revealingly realised in 1953.

The mono recordings have been strikingly refocused. What on LP sounded recessed here takes on a startlingly physical immediacy. Whether this is an advance is debatable. At first it seems to be all gain: the slightly dim sounding ritornellos given a new weight and presence. On the other hand, the recordings are now rather more wearing on the ear. In the *Emperor* Concerto, for example, the mono recording sounds – and makes the piano sound – much coarser than one had remembered. However, with suitable doctoring of filters you will be able to come up with a tolerable mix of new-found immediacy and old-fashioned clarity and warmth. A marvellous set, none the less.

Piano Concertos Nos 1-5
Maurizio Pollini *pf* **Berlin Philharmonic Orchestra / Claudio Abbado** DG ③ 439 770-2GH3 Ⓕ
(174 minutes: DDD). Recorded live in 1992-93

There may be more individual and idiosyncratic interpreters of the music than Maurizio Pollini but there is none whose command, at best, is sovereign. The Fourth Concerto has a keenly felt sense of the evolving drama, and a slow movement where the dialogue between piano and orchestra is spellbinding in its intensity. Maybe Pollini is not yet entirely reconciled to Beethoven's prankish first concerto, the Concerto No 2 in B flat. In the outer movements, he can seem brusque: ill-at-ease with Beethoven in his rumbustious, amorous, Hooray Henry mood. By contrast, the performance of the Third is a joy from start to finish. Abbado and Pollini are hand-in-glove, which gives this cycle a cohesiveness which Pollini's previous set with Jochum and Böhm (for DG) rather obviously lacked, though the Berliners don't play the first movement of the *Emperor* Concerto as commandingly as Böhm and the VPO on the earlier recording. But the slow movement goes well, and the finale is more jovial than before. Musically, though, there are evident gains – in these live recordings – moments where the tension is palpable in a way that it rarely is in the recording studio. The sound is full-bodied and immediate, with applause, a few squeaks and ill-timed coughs.

Piano Concertos Nos 1-4

Piano Concertos Nos 1-4[a]. Two Romances – No 1 in G, Op 40; No 2 in F, Op 50[b]
Stephen Kovacevich *pf* **Arthur Grumiaux** *vn*
[a]**BBC Symphony Orchestra / Sir Colin Davis;**
[b]**Concertgebouw Orchestra / Bernard Haitink**
Philips Duo ② 442 577-2PM2 (152 minutes: ADD) Ⓜ
Recorded 1970-74

The Beethoven concerto cycle that Stephen Bishop-Kovacevich (as he then was) and Colin Davis recorded for Philips in London in the early 1970s blazed across the sky like a meteor. Kovacevich's own playing, and the orchestral work, individually and collectively, was fiery and refined. They were serious readings, intellectually rigorous; but they were also readings which left us in no doubt that the music in question is combustible stuff. You could say they are young men's readings, an emanation of the excited mood of the late 1960s: 'Bliss was it in that dawn to be alive/But to be young was very heaven!' Davis conducted a very different cycle for Arrau in the 1980s (see above), more profound, more inward-looking; Davis the Sage of Highbury rather than the white-jacketed whizz-kid of the Promenade. But this earlier set still sounds extraordinarily vivid, musically as well as technically.

Piano Concertos Nos 1 and 2

Lars Vogt *pf*
City of Birmingham Symphony Orchestra / Sir Simon Rattle
EMI CDC5 56266-2 (66 minutes: DDD) Ⓕ
Includes a bonus disc of Piano Concerto No 1 with Glenn Gould's cadenzas. Recorded 1995 ●

This is a remarkable disc, as fine a recorded account of these two concertos as we've had in the 1990s. Alongside these performances, most rivals sound unduly one-dimensional. Vogt's playing in the two slow movements is wonderfully pellucid, but deep too. One thinks of Kempff, here and in the exquisite shaping of the lyric meditation midway through the Second Concerto's first movement. The CBSO's playing is also a miracle of finely wrought colours and despite the fact that these performances have evidently been worked out with great care, they remain spontaneously alive in a way that is rare on record.

In the B flat Concerto, the dialogue between soloist and orchestra in the first movement has a Haydnesque alertness. The slow movement is exquisitely done; the finale is an almost perfect re-enactment of Beethoven's impish game of musical hide-and-seek. Vogt is a great admirer of Glenn Gould. So much so that we have here a rather strange 'bonus'. The performance of the First Concerto is reprinted on a separate CD not with Beethoven's cadenzas (Vogt uses the big third cadenza in the first movement of the main performance) but with Gould's. Although it would probably not sway you one way or another in deciding whether or not to buy this disc, who needs further persuasion when faced with performances of this order of delight?

Piano Concertos Nos 1 and 2
Murray Perahia *pf*
Concertgebouw Orchestra / Bernard Haitink
Sony Classical SK42177 (70 minutes: DDD) Ⓕ
Recorded 1986 ●

It is a pleasure here to salute such all-round excellence: a very remarkable soloist, superb orchestral playing and direction, and a recording which gets everything right, offering the kind of sound picture and natural perspective of solo piano with orchestra as we might experience them from a good seat in the Concertgebouw itself where these performances were recorded.

Precision, clarity of expression, variety of character, beauty of sound: these are the qualities which Haitink and Perahia sustain and through which their readings gain an illuminating force. And it's perhaps in the slow movements that the illumination brings the most distinguished results. Their raptness and distinctive colouring are established from the first notes, and the inward quality of the expression takes breath as if there was nothing to the business of delineating these great set-pieces, so special among the achievements of Beethoven's first maturity, except to sing them through. Perahia has the gift of reducing his voice to the quietest level and still remaining eloquent. The poise of the playing is classical, his authority unblemished by any hint of exaggeration or false emphasis.

Piano Concertos Nos 1 and 2
Martha Argerich *pf*
Philharmonia Orchestra / Giuseppe Sinopoli
DG Masters Series 445 504-2GMA Ⓜ
(65 minutes: DDD) Recorded 1985

Argerich is an exceptionally brilliant pianist, but she needs to be if she is to master a world in which great issues are often rumbustiously addressed. Some works in the Beethoven canon have been tellingly illuminated by pianists like Clara Haskil and Dame Myra Hess but women who can take on Beethoven in his most bullish mood are few and far between. Argerich has something of the necessary dauntlessness; she has also studied with some of the most distinguished as well as the most radical of post-war Beethoven pianists, including Gulda, Michelangeli, and Kempff who as long ago as 1970 singled out Argerich for special praise. She is, of course, a brilliant technician; but there is also a fantastic streak in her make-up, a capacity for creative fantasy, which is needed if areas of these remarkable works are to be brought fully and vividly to life. In both these early concertos, her touch is light and expert. It is difficult to fault Argerich although her performance will unsettle the concentration of some collectors who may be happier with Kempff's performances with Leitner (reviewed above).

Sinopoli is at once attentive and unobtrusive in the C major Concerto, a perfect foil to Argerich. In the B flat Concerto, both Argerich and Sinopoli seem intent on personal point-making. There is room for private improvisation in this concerto as Kempff has amply demonstrated, but it is the pianist who must give the lead here. DG's recording is very agreeable, the ampleness of the orchestral acoustic offset by a certain distance and depth of perspective.

Piano Concertos Nos 2 and 5

Evgeni Kissin *pf*
Philharmonia Orchestra / James Levine
Sony Classical SK62926 (69 minutes: DDD) Ⓕ
Recorded 1996

From his very first entry, in the B flat Concerto, Kissin is revealed as a Beethoven player of great articulacy, brilliance and sensitivity after the manner of such pianists as Kempff, Solomon, and Gilels. The playing is vital and fluent, the technique awesome, not least in the way Kissin is able to refine his tone and taper dynamics in the high-lying coloratura passages where Beethoven's writing is at its most inspired and rarefied. The recitative at the end of the slow movement is predictably beautiful: intense and otherworldly. Levine draws from the Philharmonia playing that is both spirited and engaged. The recorded sound is admirable, too: strong and clean yet appropriately intimate.

The performance of the *Emperor* Concerto is also very fine. If you take the view that this is essentially a symphony with piano obbligato, you may hanker after a grander kind of musical theatre than that provided by Levine. He directs with decision and accompanies superbly. Kissin, too, plays with great flair and technical security. If there is a problem here it is with the articulation of the simple-seeming lyric statements where a degree of self-consciousness occasionally creeps in: where the flow is arrested and music suddenly seems to be walking on stilts. There is an element of this in the slow movement, though Kissin's playing of the bleak, trailing 24-bar-long *diminuendo* close is masterly. Kissin takes a rather dashing view of the finale. This is very much a young man's view of the music, but weighty too, such is the power of his technique.

Piano Concertos Nos 3 and 4

Awards 1986

Murray Perahia *pf*
Concertgebouw Orchestra / Bernard Haitink
Sony Classical SK39814
(70 minutes: DDD) Ⓕ
Recorded 1986 ○○○

These performances have rightly been described as exceptional. They were directly compared to Alfred Brendel's accounts with James Levine (on Philips) but in the event, there is little to choose between these two distinguished soloists. The first movements are brilliantly and sensitively etched (Perahia uses Beethoven's bigger first cadenza in the first movement of the G major Concerto). Tempos are steady but with a fine degree of forward projection. Once past the daunting opening solo, Perahia plays the C minor's slow movement with great sureness and subtlety of touch; and with Haitink as his partner the exchanges in the G major's slow movement are memorably brought off. Note the superior quality of the Sony recordings and the wonderfully judicious accompaniments prepared for Perahia by the Concertgebouw Orchestra under Haitink. If there is little to choose between Perahia and Brendel as soloists, there is a great gulf between Haitink, who is exemplary, and Levine who is unexceptional.

Piano Concertos Nos 3[a] and 4
Mitsuko Uchida *pf*
Royal Concertgebouw Orchestra / Kurt Sanderling
Philips 446 082-2PH (72 minutes: DDD) Ⓕ
Recorded ([a]live) 1994 ○

The playing on this formidable pairing of works is at once brilliant and sensitive, rigorous and free-spirited. Of the two performances, that of the Fourth Concerto is perhaps the more memorable. Uchida re-creates the solo part with flair and imagination, and dazzling technique. And what a wonderful voyage of discovery the slow movement is here. If the performance seems a touch mellower and more confiding than that of the C minor Concerto, it is perhaps because it was being played live to an audience in the Concertgebouw, a hall whose famous acoustic can be a shade severe when empty. What we have here in the Fourth Concerto is a first-rate concert-hall perspective (with the applause edited out).

Some might argue that the C minor Concerto is a severe piece. Certainly, this generally appears to be Sanderling's and Uchida's view of the first movement. The performance is wonderfully alive, which is more than can be said for 75 per cent of extant recordings of this music, but there are pianists – Kempff for example – who have made the music of the first movement move a shade more gracefully and songfully than Uchida does here. The slow movement, by contrast, emerges as a wonderfully rapt soliloquy for the solo pianist, the orchestra doing little more than make simple acts of obeisance before the soloist. (Rather stiff acts of obeisance: throughout the C minor Concerto Sanderling is inclined to make the orchestra sit rather heavily on down-beats and *sforzandos*.) The recording of the C minor Concerto is best heard at a safe distance. Played too loud or heard too close it can seem unduly fierce and odd blemishes show up.

Beethoven Piano Concerto No 4[a] H
Saint-Saëns Piano Concerto No 2 in G minor, Op 22[b]
Artur Rubinstein *pf* [a]**Royal Philharmonic Orchestra / Sir Thomas Beecham;** [b]**Paris Conservatoire Orchestra / Philippe Gaubert**
Testament mono SBT1154 (53 minutes: ADD) Ⓕ
Recorded 1947 and 1939

Rubinstein was unhappy with Gaubert's partnership and the recorded sound in this performance of Saint-Saëns's Second Concerto and he withdrew his permission for release, with the result that this corruscating performance lay entombed and forgotten in the EMI archives. True, Gaubert finds it hard to keep pace with Rubinstein's exuberance which takes virtuosity to the very edge. The closing pages in particular degenerate into an approximate rough-and-tumble. Although Saint-Saëns marks the first-movement development *Un poco animato*, Rubinstein is off like the proverbial hare, scattering all before him. Yet listen to his magically inflected opening or the instantly recognizable depth of his *cantabile* in the elegantly side-stepping second subject and you are in the presence of a master. His *Scherzo* is a riot of high-jinks; a ripple of laughter here, a sly wink there (Saint-Saëns's Second was always among Rubinstein's popular successes).

Beethoven's Fourth may seem an odd bed-fellow for the Saint-Saëns, a linking of Teutonic poetry with Gallic levity. And yet, with both in Rubinstein's hands, you are made to sense a spiritual kinship and never more so than when he chooses Saint-Saëns's gloriously anachronistic cadenzas, spun off with all of his unique virtuoso relish. Elsewhere it is very much a case of full steam ahead. The central climax's anguish is played down and there are times in the finale where Rubinstein's outgoing nature makes the music fall into predictable pattern-making rather than express musical significance. The partnership with Beecham is, however, infinitely superior to Gaubert's in the Saint-Saëns and the 1947 recording is a clear advance on 1939. Whether you prefer this or that pianist in either of these concertos is oddly beside the point. Rubinstein is, after all, Rubinstein, and both these performances tell you that with a mere flick of his wrist he could play most other pianists under the table.

Piano Concertos Nos 4 and 5

Emil Gilels *pf* H
Philharmonia Orchestra / Leopold Ludwig
Testament SBT1095 (73 minutes: ADD) Ⓕ
Recorded 1957 OO

This is one of the – perhaps *the* most – perfect accounts of the Fourth Concerto recorded. Poetry and virtuosity are held in perfect poise, with Ludwig and the Philharmonia providing a near-ideal accompaniment. The recording is also very fine, though be sure to gauge the levels correctly by first sampling one of the tuttis. If the volume is set too high at the start, you will miss the stealing magic of Gilels's and the orchestra's initial entries and you will be further discomfited by tape hiss that, with the disc played at a properly judged level, is more or less inaudible.

The recording of the *Emperor* Concerto is also pretty good, not quite on a par with that of the Fourth. Ludwig and the orchestra tend to follow Gilels rather than always integrate with him and there are times, too, especially in the slow movement, when Gilels's playing borders on the self-indulgent. This is not, however, sufficient reason for overlooking this fine and important Testament reissue.

Piano Concertos Nos 4 and 5
Maurizio Pollini *pf*
Vienna Philharmonic Orchestra / Karl Böhm
DG Classikon 439 483-2GCL (71 minutes: ADD) Ⓑ
Recorded 1976

This is an outstanding coupling of Pollini's earlier recordings of these works (the complete set of his later recordings with Abbado is reviewed above). The present performances are, arguably, more spontaneous and the recording (especially of the piano) more natural, with the VPO expanding warmly within the ambience of the Grosser Saal of the Vienna Musikverein. These readings are freshly individual, with poise and poetry nicely balanced in both works, and with Böhm providing admirable accompaniments (the interchange in the slow movement of the G major is memorable). And Pollini is suitably magisterial in the *Emperor*. Most enjoyable, and stimulating too.

Piano Concerto No 5

Murray Perahia *pf*
Concertgebouw Orchestra / Bernard Haitink
Sony Classical Masterworks SK42330 Ⓕ
(39 minutes: DDD) Recorded 1986 O

This is an excellent *Emperor*, on a level with the best. Comparisons with other pianists, at this level, can be rather futile. It is a splendidly engineered recording, with a natural concert-hall type of balance, and there is good presence to the sound and depth to the perspective. The presentation of the orchestral detail allows one to delight in it, and perhaps to discover new subtleties, without a moment of unease as to whether anything has been forced into the wrong kind of relief. Perahia's performance has the freshness and natural authority one has now come to expect of him in Beethoven. His reading might be described as uncomplicated if that didn't risk implying that it is in some way lightweight, or that he plays like a child of nature. The weight is certainly there, in sound (when he wants it) as in expression.

Perahia himself has spoken of the happy experience of making this Beethoven cycle with Haitink (the other concertos including the complete set are reviewed above). It has indeed been a successful collaboration, and a joyous quality about the music-making communicates itself quite strongly from the beginning.

Piano Concerto No 5
Arturo Benedetti Michelangeli *pf*
Vienna Symphony Orchestra / Carlo Maria Giulini
DG 419 249-2GH (42 minutes: ADD) Ⓕ
Recorded live in 1979 ●

There has, over the years, been mixed reactions to Michelangeli's Beethoven. He was a most perplexing artist, perplexing because he liked to keep his musical personality well hidden – or at any rate mysterious – behind the armour-plated magnificence of his playing; disconcerting too because it is hard to arrive at a reasoned assessment of readings of classical music by someone who is evidently not a man of balance. To interpret texts of the classical masters in a way which will give them the most vivid life does not seem to be his principal concern. There could be an intellectual *froideur* about his playing of Beethoven which verges on the disdainful and which was sometimes more than off-putting.

Not here though. This performance was recorded at a public performance in the Musikverein. He drives the opening flourishes hard, and thereafter responds keenly to Giulini's exposition, grand but always moving forward, matching it with a purpose that seems to derive from just that long-range musical thinking which is so often missing in his accounts of the other concertos. There is spaciousness, and time for everything, and always that rock-like strength of rhythm. The detailing could hardly be bettered but isn't allowed to deflect attention from our perception of the form. The security of the technique is enough to make most other pianists attempting an Olympian view of the concerto seem clumsy; but it does not draw attention to itself. Since the depth of his sonority is perfectly matched to the orchestra's, it makes for some especially exciting listening in the finale. Great playing by a great pianist.

Piano Concerto No 5. Triple Concerto in C, Op 56[a]
Leon Fleisher, Eugene Istomin *pfs* **Isaac Stern** *vn*
Leonard Rose *vc*
Cleveland Orchestra / George Szell; [a]Philadelphia Orchestra / Eugene Ormandy
Sony Classical Essential Classics SBK46549 Ⓑ
(74 minutes: ADD) Recorded 1961, [a]1964 ●

Leon Fleisher's recording of the *Emperor* is very powerful indeed. He was relatively young at the time and obviously George Szell had a considerable influence on the reading, but the solo playing is remarkably fresh and its pianistic authority is striking. That great octave passage in the first movement, just before the recapitulation, is enormously commanding, and Fleisher's lyrical playing, in the slow movement especially, has striking poise. Szell keeps the voltage high throughout, but for all its excitement this is by no means a hard-driven, unfeeling interpretation. The Cleveland Orchestra plays with fervour and there is a joyously buoyant rhythmic lift in the main theme of the finale. The recording is bright, bold and forward in the CBS 1960s manner, and the Severance Hall acoustic prevents any ugliness.

A splendid *Emperor*, then, but what makes this disc even more enticing is the inclusion of an equally distinguished version of the Triple Concerto, recorded in Philadelphia Town Hall (a much more successful venue than many used over the years for this great orchestra). The very gentle opening by the orchestra is full of anticipatory tension, and at the beginning of the slow movement Ormandy's preparation for Rose's glorious cello solo demonstrates what a superb accompanist he is. Indeed, this is no mere accompaniment, but a complete partnership. Although Stern's personality dominates marginally, the three soloists play together like a chamber-music team, without in any way submerging their individuality. The sound is very good for its time. This entire disc is a prime example where Sony's sobriquet 'Essential Classics' is justly appended.

Piano Concerto No 5. **P**
Choral Fantasia in C minor, Op 80
Robert Levin *fp*
Monteverdi Choir; Orchestre Révolutionnaire et Romantique / Sir John Eliot Gardiner
Archiv Produktion 447 771-2AH (60 minutes: DDD) Ⓕ
Text and translation included. Recorded 1995 ●

You may find the very opening of the *Emperor* more disconcerting than Tan's rival period version, not only because Gardiner's orchestra is fuller-bodied, underlining the discrepancy of scale, but because of the instrument Robert Levin has chosen. This 1812 fortepiano by Salvatore Lagrassa has body enough in the lower registers, but at the top there is a disconcertingly twangy, almost harp-like area leading at the very top to notes so unresonant that they sound like a xylophone. However, quickly enough your ears will adjust to the idiosyncrasies of the solo instrument, and you will appreciate the fine, positive qualities of a reading in which the soloist, matching Gardiner himself, takes a more freely expressive view than Tan, playing with a greater element of bravura.

It would have been better if the disc had started with the *Choral Fantasia*, for there with the opening improvisation one has ample time to adjust to the scale and the individual sound of the fortepiano before the orchestra enters. The whole performance, too, has tremendous panache. Gardiner crowns the performance with a superb choral section, in which soloists and full chorus are cleanly contrasted.

As a supplement Levin offers on separate tracks two alternative improvisations of his own, easily interchangeable with the one Beethoven published years after the first performance. There is similar exuberance to that of the *Fantasia* in the finale of the *Emperor*, with crystal-clear passagework from the soloist. In the two earlier movements Levin's speeds are slower than those of Tan. It may help to play the disc at a relatively high volume, when the oddities of the fortepiano are less distracting. Though interpretatively this is probably the first choice for a period-performance *Emperor*, would-be purchasers should sample both discs first.

Piano Concerto No 5. Choral Fantasia in C minor, Op 80
Alfred Brendel *pf*
London Philharmonic Choir and Orchestra / Bernard Haitink
Philips Insignia 434 148-2PM (61 minutes: ADD) Ⓜ
Recorded 1976-77

Philips Insignia has an impressive back catalogue to drawn upon. Philips achieves consistent success with digital remastering, adding a presence and firmness of focus that seldom produce unwanted edginess. This certainly applies to Alfred Brendel's recording of the Fifth Concerto, coupled with his even more impressive *Choral Fantasia*. This latter is unforgettable, he and Haitink making something especially dazzling of this work. No one plays the big opening cadenza with more power and authority than Brendel and a similar magisterial breadth informs the *Emperor*; even though the first movement perhaps sounds a little too controlled, this is still a very satisfying performance. The choral contribution to the *Fantasia* is quite splendid. The recording combines orchestral weight with brilliance, and a most believable piano image.

Violin Concerto in D, Op 61

Beethoven Violin Concerto
Bernstein Serenade
Hilary Hahn *vn* **Baltimore Symphony Orchestra / David Zinman**
Sony Classical SK60584 (75 minutes: DDD) Ⓕ
Recorded 1998

At first glance, this would seem a pretty strange coupling, yet by trailing the most Olympian of classical violin concertos with a semi-concerto based on a Platonic dialogue Hilary Hahn and Sony suggest their own quaint form of programming logic. Hahn employs her sweet-centred tone with utmost finesse and David Zinman's Baltimore accompaniment is smooth, unhurried and clear-sighted. Hahn opts for Kreisler's cadenza and makes a special feature of the simultaneous projection of themes, broadening the pace then re-entering into the movement, as if caught in a trance. Her approach is lyrical and unindulgent, though most definitely post-romantic. She is an immaculate technician who favours a calculated though richly expressive approach to phrasing. She breathes considerable warmth into the *Larghetto* and offers a crisp account of the finale. Of its kind, this performance looks unbeatable.

One of Bernstein's most enduring works, the lovable 1954 *Serenade*, draws on ideas from Plato's *The Symposium*, principally those concerning love, and includes a gorgeous three-part song and a finale that looks sideways at *On the Waterfront* and forwards to *West Side Story*. Hahn's tender-hearted rendition lays claim to being the finest interpretation ever, aided and abetted by Zinman's firmly focused conducting. Both works are beautifully recorded.

Violin Concerto. Romances – No 1 in G, Op 40; No 2 in F, Op 50
Gidon Kremer *vn* **Chamber Orchestra of Europe / Nikolaus Harnoncourt**
Teldec 9031-74881-2 (57 minutes: DDD) Ⓕ
Recorded live in 1992

Gidon Kremer offers one of his most commanding performances, both polished and full of flair, magnetically spontaneous from first to last. Rarely do you hear such consistently pure tone in this work and the orchestral writing too is superbly realised. It has become customary to treat the long first movement as expansively as possible but Kremer takes a more urgent view, and after his thoughtful and dedicated, slightly understated reading of the slow movement, he and Harnoncourt round the performance off magically with a finale that skips along the more infectiously thanks to light, clean articulation and textures. Traditional performances seem heavyweight by comparison. The controversial point for some will be the cadenza in the first movement where he uses a transcription of the big cadenza which Beethoven wrote for his piano arrangement of the work. However, this is altogether one of the most refreshing versions of the concerto ever committed to record, backed up by crisp, unsentimental readings of the two *Romances*.

Violin Concerto. Romance No 2
Oscar Shumsky *vn* **Philharmonia Orchestra / Sir Andrew Davis**
ASV Quicksilva CDQS6080 (54 minutes: DDD) Ⓑ
Recorded 1988

Oscar Shumsky's recording of the Violin Concerto is one of the finest in the catalogue and was strongly recommended at premium price. In this reissue it is a bargain *par excellence*. The reading is relaxed and assured and has a serene purity of line, notably so in the memorable *Larghetto*, which is quite beautifully played. Andrew Davis provides his soloist with admirable support and the orchestral contribution is highly sympathetic. The sound balance favours the soloist with something of a spotlight, but otherwise the recording is very good: those wanting a bargain-price version of this work could hardly better this, especially as the *Romance* in F major is given as an encore.

Awards 1981

Violin Concerto
Itzhak Perlman *vn* **Philharmonia Orchestra / Carlo Maria Giulini**
EMI Great Recordings of the Century
CDM5 66900-2
(44 minutes: DDD) Ⓜ
Recorded 1980

This is a very distinguished performance indeed, as much from Giulini as from Perlman. Early on Guilini makes clear the importance of recognizing the difference between *forte* and *fortissimo* in Beethoven – for example the *ff* of bars 73 and 74 and the *f* which surrounds them; and the marvellous way he gets the Philharmonia to play *sfp* is a pleasure in itself. The liquid smoothness of the wind playing is another joy.

The slow movement has the utmost calm beauty from both soloist and orchestra, while Perlman plays the finale at an admirably swift speed, yet with all the flexibility it needs, so that it really dances lightly. Contrast Chung on Decca whose finale is almost lethargic in comparison, and Kremer for Philips who takes it at a terrible lick but puts it firmly into a strait-jacket. The clarity of the orchestral texture is outstanding too. The bassoon, for example, sings its solos in the finale easily and without the least forcing, whereas on the Chung recording it sounds more consciously brought forward. The Decca is no match in general sound either.

Violin Concerto. Romances Nos 1 and 2 **P**
Thomas Zehetmair *vn***Orchestra of the Eighteenth Century / Frans Brüggen**
Philips 462 123-2PH (54 minutes: DDD) Ⓕ
Recorded live in 1997

This is a great performance, one that simply has to be heard. The first movement is built on a tug of war between dynamic extremes and, for once, it actually sounds like a concerto, and a brilliant one at that. The more familiar average playing time of around 25 minutes (Zehetmair's lasts a mere 22) tends, for all its beautiful effect, to compromise on forward momentum. Here, the use of period instruments adds extra fibre to the aural mix, and Brüggen's conducting has a pressing urgency about it that, again, intensifies the drama. The *Larghetto* is full of subtle nuances and telling inflexions, and the Rondo has great rhythmic verve.

Two recording venues are used, the excellent Muziekcentrum at Enschede for the two *Romances* and the rather cavernous Vredenburg, Utrecht for the concerto. The former yields the more sympathetic acoustic (Zehetmair and Brüggen offer limpidly flowing performances of both pieces), but it is unlikely that the slightly rougher-edged concerto recording will give much cause for complaint. This is one of *the* recordings of Beethoven's Violin Concerto, and is to be strongly recommended.

Beethoven Violin Concerto[a] **H**
Mendelssohn Violin Concerto in E minor, Op 64[b]
Yehudi Menuhin *vn*
[a]**Philharmonia Orchestra,** [b]**Berlin Philharmonic Orchestra / Wilhelm Furtwängler**
EMI Great Recordings of the Century mono
CDM5 66975-2 (71 minutes: ADD) Ⓜ
Recorded 1952-53

Furtwängler and Menuhin enjoyed a long artistic partnership, and Menuhin's support for his older colleague was no small factor in Furtwängler's musical rehabilitation during the late 1940s after he had remained active in Nazi Germany. They recorded the Beethoven Concerto on two occasions, and this second version has an extraordinary quality of spirituality and profundity. Furtwängler's conducting of the opening tutti has a magnificently arresting, weighty quality, and Menuhin's response, profound and rich in re-creative imagination shows the two great artists in perfect accord. Their account of this movement is on the largest scale, yet they convey Beethoven's vision in a humane, approachable fashion. The slow movement has a highly concentrated yet serene character, with Menuhin's rapt, singing tone achieving rare eloquence, and the finale is superbly balanced, with an affecting sense of a shared, joyful experience. The recording sounds quite similar to the original LP issue, but the quality is quite acceptable.

The Mendelssohn was recorded a year earlier, and here remastering has brought a slight roughening in an orchestral sound which was never very ingratiating, though the defect is not serious. Menuhin and Furtwängler float the first movement in an unhurriedly serene, elegantly shaped fashion. In the slow movement they achieve a touchingly tender, almost innocent quality and the finale, taken at a moderate tempo, has lightness and an appealingly eager character. Two very different works are here illuminated by two great artists.

Beethoven Violin Concerto[a] **H** $
Brahms Violin Concerto in D, Op 77[b]
Jascha Heifetz *vn* [a]**NBC Symphony Orchestra / Arturo Toscanini;** [b]**Boston Symphony Orchestra / Serge Koussevitzky**
Naxos Historical mono 8 110936 (77 minutes: AAD). Ⓢ
Recorded [a]1939 and [b]1940

'An old diamond in the rough' is how Robert C Marsh (*Toscanini and the Art of Orchestra Performance*; London: 1956) recalled the original Victor 78s of this 1940 Heifetz Studio 8-H recording of the Beethoven. Of the LP reissue he wrote: 'On the whole, the recording is so dead and artificial that at times the thin line of violin sound reminds one of something from the golden age of Thomas Edison's tinfoil cylinder rather than 1940.' Early CD transfers suggested that all was not lost but even they barely anticipated the extraordinary fineness of the sound we now have on this transfer by archivist and restorer Mark Obert-Thorn.

The performance itself is one of the most remarkable the gramophone has ever given us. The visionary, high *tessitura* violin writing is realised by Heifetz with a technical surety which is indistinguishable, in the final analysis, from his sense of the work as one of Beethoven's most sublime explorations of that world (in Schiller's phrase) 'above the stars where He must dwell'. Those who would query the 'depth' of Heifetz's reading miss this point entirely. To adapt Oscar Wilde, it is they who are in the gutter, Heifetz who is looking at the stars.

As for Toscanini's contribution – another cue for rancorous comment in the past – it, too, is masterly. Now that we can actually hear the performance, the orchestral *tuttis* ('wooden grunts' says Marsh) seem beautifully balanced both within themselves and *vis-à-vis* the soloist. As for the actual accompaniment, it is discreet and self-effacing, fiery yet refined, and always wondrously subtle. Under Toscanini, the fabulously responsive NBC strings match Heifetz every inch of the way in their mastery of the long rhythmically buoyant, subtly inflected, lyric line.

In the case of the Brahms, it is more reasonable to argue that there are other ways of playing the concerto: Kreisler's way, for instance, or that of Kreisler's colleague, Efrem Zimbalist, whose live 1946 recording of the Brahms, also with Koussevitzky and the Boston SO, makes an interesting comparison with this 1939 Heifetz recording. Heifetz's is not a romantic reading. It is lean, athletic, classical, aristocratic, finely drawn, an approach which wears exceptionally well on record – witness his widely collected 1955 remake with Reiner and the Chicago SO.

The Brahms enjoys another impeccable transfer by Mark Obert-Thorn. Musically and technically, this is a real thoroughbred of a release, unignorable at any price, let alone the one Naxos so modestly asks.

Beethoven Violin Concerto[a]
Tchaikovsky Violin Concerto in D, Op 35[b]
Bronislaw Huberman *vn* [a]**Vienna Philharmonic Orchestra / George Szell;** [b]**Staatskapelle Berlin / William Steinberg**
Naxos Historical mono 8 110903 (67 minutes: AAD). Ⓢ
Recorded [a]1934 and [b]1928

Virtuoso violinist Bronislaw Huberman was an idealist, an ardent Pan-European and co-founder (with William Steinberg) of the Israel Philharmonic. He was, in a sense, the prototype for such present-day fiddling mavericks as Kremer, Zehetmair, Tetzlaff and Kennedy. Huberman's open letter to the conductor Wilhelm Furtwängler, in which he pledged support of the persecuted and refused to perform in Nazi Germany, has become famous, and his astringent though frequently dazzling playing translates that steely resolve into musical terms.

This Naxos coupling should have been the answer to a prayer. Indeed, it very nearly is, save for a less-than-perfect transfer of the Beethoven Violin Concerto. But more of that in a moment. The 1929 Tchaikovsky recording is peerless. Huberman's first entry reveals all: elastic phrasing, sweeping *portamentos* and generous *rubato* stamp a giant personality. Thereafter, quicksilver bowing and a steely *spiccato* level with the best of the period.

Brahms loved Huberman's playing (he promised the budding youngster a *Fantasy* but never lived to compose it) and no wonder, given the veiled beauty of Huberman's tone (*Canzonetta*) and the uninhibited swagger of his bravura style (finale). Who could resist the finale's swinging second subject, or stay seated for the lightning pyrotechnics that set the Concerto's closing pages alight?

The Beethoven Concerto is no less striking, being more in line with, say, Zehetmair and Brüggen than with the stately readings of Kreisler, Szigeti, Menuhin or David Oistrakh. Huberman's lively speeds and darting inflections spin silver beams where others opt for (for some misplaced) 'Olympian' heights. The sheer luminosity of the reading, its radiance and refusal to dawdle, run counter to the languid sweetness favoured by various of Huberman's peers and successors.

You simply have to hear Huberman's recording, and Naxos's give-away price makes their coupling a mandatory purchase. Unless you're fussy about transfers, in which case, read on. The Tchaikovsky presents some tricky problems. For one, there's a horrible side-join in the *Canzonetta*, where the clarinet and solo violin need to be skilfully overlaid. Mark Obert-Thorn hits target every time while the actual sound quality is warmer than EMI's (currently unavailable) alternative.

David Lennick's transfer of the Beethoven, although perfectly adequate, is also rather spoiled by excessive digital noise reduction. The intrusion is especially noticeable at the beginning of the slow movement. On one occasion, at 4'57" into Naxos's first movement, the violinist momentarily disappears while in the second movement, two chords have inadvertently become one (an easily misjudged 78 side-join, at 4'08"). Still, these technical reservations will likely prove trifling for anyone who has never heard Huberman before. There are no greater violin recordings in existence, and we urge you to buy them.

Triple Concerto in C, Op 56

Beethoven Triple Concerto[a]
Brahms Double Concerto in A minor, Op 102[b]
David Oistrakh *vn* **Mstislav Rostropovich** *vc*
Sviatoslav Richter *pf*
[a]**Berlin Philharmonic Orchestra / Herbert von Karajan;** [b]**Cleveland Orchestra / George Szell**
EMI Great Recordings of the Century mono
CDM5 66902-2 (70 minutes: ADD) Ⓜ
Recorded 1969

These are illustrious performances and make a splendid coupling. EMI planned for a long time to assemble this starry line-up of soloists, conductor and orchestra for Beethoven's Triple Concerto, and the artists do not disappoint, bringing sweetness as well as strength to a work which in lesser hands can sound clumsy and long-winded. The recording, made in a Berlin church in 1969, is warm, spacious and well balanced, placing the soloists in a gentle spotlight. The account of Brahms's Double Concerto is perhaps the most powerful recorded performance since the days of Heifetz and Feuermann or Thibaud and Casals. The recording has come up extremely well in this remastering: although one cannot deny that the sound is not as smooth as can be achieved nowadays, one soon forgets that and is caught up in the magnificent music-making.

Triple Concerto. Choral Fantasia in C minor, Op 80
Beaux Arts Trio (Ida Kavafian *vn* Peter Wiley *vc* Menahem Pressler *pf*)
Mid-German Radio Chorus; Leipzig Gewandhaus Orchestra / Kurt Masur
Philips 438 005-2PH (52 minutes: DDD) Ⓕ
Recorded 1992-93

Kurt Masur has rarely conducted more electrifying Beethoven performances on disc. The opening tutti of the concerto establishes a speed markedly faster than usual, and if the three soloists modify it slightly, the characteristic which marks this performance is its urgency. But there is no feeling of breathlessness, simply exhilaration. The evenness and clarity of Pressler's articulation in scales and passagework is a delight. As for the brief central meditation, led by the cello, it flows very warmly and naturally, with Peter Wiley just as rich and positive an artist as Pressler. This now stands as one of the very finest versions of a work which at last looks like being appreciated, not as a rarity, but as a pillar of the Beethoven canon.

The *Choral Fantasia* is hardly likely to establish itself in a comparable niche, but this performance is most persuasive. The variations on the corny main theme are regularly pointed with engaging wit, not just by Pressler but by the wind soloists, and the brass sound is glorious. It is rather like having the choral finale of the Ninth anticipated with tongue-in-cheek. Balances are always difficult, not just in this work but notoriously in the Triple Concerto. The soloists are well focused and the orchestral sound is warm and full.

Additional recommendation
Triple Concerto
Coupling: Choral Fantasia in C minor, Op 80
Itzhak Perlman *vn* **Yo-Yo Ma** *vc*
Chorus of the Deutsche Oper, Berlin; Berlin Philharmonic Orchestra / Daniel Barenboim *pf*
EMI CDC5 55516-2 (55 minutes: DDD: 12/95). Ⓕ
Superb live performances which grab you with their refreshing spontaneity. Choice between this and Masur's (see above) might well be left to a preference between crisp co-ordination and the inspiration of the moment.

Overtures

Overtures – Coriolan, Op 62; Die Geschöpfe des Prometheus, Op 43; Die Ruinen von Athen, Op 113; Fidelio, Op 72; Leonore No 1, Op 138; No 2, Op 72; No 3, Op 72; Egmont, Op 84
Chamber Orchestra of Europe / Nikolaus Harnoncourt
Teldec 0630-13140-2 (76 minutes: DDD) Ⓜ
Recorded live (except Op 62) in 1993-96

Harnoncourt's Beethoven overtures are highly eventful affairs that will have your critical faculties working overtime. Surprises emerge virtually by the bar. For example, the orchestral sonority is 'heated' not by the strings, but by the woodwind section. Here, the COE's string tone is sinewy and chaste, with lightly brushed bowing and agile phrasing, while the woodwinds sound far mellower than on most rival discs. Harnoncourt's preference for limpid, baleful woodwind phrasing is familiar from his recordings of baroque music and the option works well in this context. *Coriolan* features a mobile though never over-prominent cello line, the coda more suggesting recollected tragedy than the torture of Coriolan's plight. *Prometheus* opens to thunderclap chords, then busies along excitedly with much animated banter between woodwinds. *Die Ruinen von Athen* is neon-lit and keenly attenuated and the *Fidelio* 'foursome' – the opera's overture plus the three *Leonores* – is delivered with a dramatic impetus that occasionally borders on abruptness. *Fidelio* itself features a majestic introduction and a leisurely, open-plan *Allegro* where individual voices take the lead and where the opening motive gallops back with tremendous vigour. *Leonore* No 1 goes with a swing, the introduction to *Leonore* No 2 suggests intimations of Berlioz and the way Harnoncourt tiers the accumulating woodwind lines is very impressive. A natural ebb and flow is common to both of these 'bigger' *Leonore* overtures; both feature a first-rate off-stage trumpet, and both have fiery codas (*Leonore* No 3's 'last blast' climaxes with colossal power). The disc ends with a fairly forceful *Egmont* overture. These mostly live recordings convey a luminous, dynamic and realistically three-dimensional sound stage. A mandatory purchase for those without preconceptions.

Complete Symphonies

Awards 1992

Charlotte Margiono *sop* **Birgit Remmert** *mez* **Rudolf Schasching** *ten* **Robert Holl** *bass* **Arnold Schoenberg Choir; Chamber Orchestra of Europe / Nikolaus Harnoncourt**
Teldec ⑤ 2292-46452-2 (358 minutes: DDD). Recorded live in 1990-91 Ⓜ
Also available as part of a 10-disc anniversary box which includes the Violin Concerto, Overtures and Missa solemnis – Teldec ⑩ 3984 28144-2 Ⓜ

Brimful of intrepid character and interpretative incident, this is surely one of the most stimulating

Beethoven symphony cycles of recent times. As Harnoncourt himself states in the booklet: 'It has always been my conviction that music is not there to soothe people's nerves...but rather to open their eyes, to give them a good shaking, even to frighten them.' So it transpires that there's a re-creative daring about Harnoncourt's conducting – in essence an embracement of recent scholarly developments and his own pungent sense of characterisation – which is consistently illuminating, thus leaving the listener with the uncanny sensation that he or she is encountering this great music for the first time. In all of this Harnoncourt is backed to the hilt by some superbly responsive, miraculously assured playing from the COE: their personable, unforced assimilation of his specific demands, allied to his intimate knowledge of the inner workings of these scores, make for wonderfully fresh, punchy results. In this respect Nos 6-8 in particular prove immensely rewarding, but the *Eroica* and the Fourth, too, are little short of superb. In sum, a cycle which excitingly reaffirms the life-enhancing mastery of Beethoven's vision for many years to come.

Symphonies Nos 1-9
Gundula Janowitz *sop* **Hilde Rössel-Majdan** *contr*
Waldemar Kmentt *ten* **Walter Berry** *bass*
Vienna Singverein; Berlin Philharmonic Orchestra / Herbert von Karajan
DG Complete Beethoven Edition
⑤ 453 701-2GCB5 (332 minutes: ADD) Ⓜ
Text and translation included. Recorded 1961-2

This was the first set of the Nine to be planned, recorded and sold as an integral cycle. It was also a set that had been extremely carefully positioned from the interpretative point of view. Where Karajan's 1950s Philharmonia cycle had elements in it that owed a certain amount to the old German school of Beethoven interpretation, the new-found virtuosity of the Berliners allowed him to approach more nearly the fierce beauty and lean-toned fiery manner of Toscanini's Beethoven style as Karajan had first encountered it in its halcyon age in the mid-1930s. Nothing demonstrates this better than the 1962 recording of the Fourth Symphony, fiery and radiant as Karajan's reading had not previously been, and never would be again. The old shibboleth among writers and musicians that the even-numbered symphonies were somehow less dramatic than the odd-numbered ones meant nothing to Karajan. His accounts of the Second, Fourth, Sixth and Eighth Symphonies were every bit as intense as their allegedly sturdier neighbours. Only in the Seventh Symphony's third movement Trio and the Menuetto of the Eighth Symphony – where he continued to follow Wagner's idea of this as an essentially stately dance, a kind of surrogate slow movement – did he deviate significantly from the Toscanini model. And it worked. True, the first movement of the *Pastoral* Symphony was a touch airless, lacking some of the easy wonderment of Karajan's old Philharmonia recording. But, then, Toscanini himself had never managed to replicate the unique charm of his pre-war English recording with the BBC SO.

The original review of the cycle entered a number of caveats, some of which still pertain, though it is the lack of certain repeats and the non-antiphonal dispensation of the violins that may worry some most nowadays. What so enthused us back then was the urgency of the music-making, its vitality and, ultimately, a fierce sense of joy that had its natural point of culmination in a thrillingly played and eloquently sung account of the finale of the Ninth. The playing of the new rejuvenated BPO dazzled throughout (it still does), as did Günther Hermanns recordings: clean and clear, and daringly 'lit' with a bright shimmer of reverberation. The recordings have always transferred effortlessly to CD and the present reissue is no exception. It has been finely annotated too, with essays by H C Robbins Landon and Robert Simpson.

Symphonies Nos 1-9 P
Luba Orgonasova *sop* **Anne Sofie von Otter** *mez*
Anthony Rolfe Johnson *ten* **Gilles Cachemaille** *bar*
Monteverdi Choir; Orchestre Révolutionnaire et Romantique / Sir John Eliot Gardiner
Archiv Produktion ⑤ 439 900-2AH5 Ⓕ
(328 minutes: DDD). Recorded 1993-94 OO

This set is remarkable and many will rate it as Mr Knightley rates Emma Woodhouse 'faultless in spite of her faults'. In his booklet essay, Peter Czorny tells us that the recordings are offered in the hope of transporting the listener back 'to that moment when this music burst forth into a world of heroes, wars and revolution, creating its own world of the sublime and ineffable'. This theme is developed by Gardiner in a robust, contentious 20-minute talk on the project that comes free on a sixth CD. Gardiner's opinion that Beethoven wanted his musicians to live dangerously has some peculiar consequences.

Symphony No 1: The opening is superbly judged. Gardiner doesn't overplay the *Adagio molto*, and the *Allegro con brio*, often played with a fatal languor by members of the old German School, is pretty quick. After his absurdly brisk reading of the second movement, Gardiner goes on to conduct dazzlingly successful accounts of the *Scherzo* and finale. Symphony No 2: This is very fine throughout. By following the written tempo markings and his own musical instincts Gardiner produces a perfomance of the first movement that opens out the drama most compellingly. Symphony No 3: More *révolutionnaire* than *romantique*. A very fast first movement gets within spitting distance of an impossible metronome mark. That and keen texturing make for tremendous dramatic urgency. Unfortunately, there is also too little accommodation *en route* of the rich cargo of ideas that Beethoven has shipped into this movement. In their haste to get to the recapitulation itself, Gardiner and his players are decidedly unpoised. He is superb in the last two movements; but these are considerably less than half the story where the *Eroica* is concerned. Symphony No 4: An unusually quick introductory and brisk *Allegro vivace*. Gardiner treats the pivotal drum entry before the recapitulation atmospherically. Glorious slow movement, impossibly quick finale.

Symphony No 5: Here is the stuff of which revolutions are made. Gardiner plays the piece pretty straight, and at white heat. The orchestra is superb, helped by the Francophone bias of its sound base. That said, the *Scherzo* (with repeat) is surely too fast. It starts briskly and not especially quietly. The pace drops back for the Trio, which is just as well since the strings are hard-pressed to articulate clearly. The finale is also very fast, again ahead of what is generally regarded as a good metronome. There is a grandeur to the Scherzo-cum-finale that could be seen to reflect a vision (Hegelian, to be precise) that transcends the politics of revolution. Still, for its *éclat terrible*, this is unbeatable. The slow movement is also superbly shaped and directed. Symphony No 6: Despite some lovely playing in the slow movement and an air of brisk efficiency, this is a rather joyless *Pastoral*. Nor is it a spiritually uplifting one. The *Scherzo* – 'A merry gathering of country folk' – is a very high-speed affair. At such a pace the various amusing false entries rather lose their point; to play in this village band you would need to be a virtuoso, and teetotal to boot.

Symphony No 7: A glorious performance. The introduction sets the scene with an ideal blend of weight and anticipation. The *Vivace* has a splendid dance feel and a power that is utterly unforced. *Scherzo* and finale are also superbly paced. The *Allegretto* is eloquent with a sense of barely sublimated grieving. The recording is magnificent. Symphony No 8: In general, the symphony thrives on the Gardiner approach, though in the finale the emphasis is again on high-speed locomotion. Symphony No 9: The first movement has never been dispatched as rapidly as here. In fact, Gardiner doesn't get the bit between the teeth until bar 51, so the celebrated introduction has room to breathe. Of course, he isn't entirely inflexible and he and his players show remarkable skill in making busy detail 'tell'. Yet a lot does go by the board. The slow movement is also played very quickly. However, Gardiner's finale is superb. Tempos are unerringly chosen, the choral singing is beyond criticism, and there is a rare expressive quality to the singing of the solo quartet.

High quality playing from the orchestra and often exceptional Archiv sound. At best, the physical and intellectual vitality of this music-making brings us close to the *Ding an sich*'. It is a best that occurs only intermittently. That it occurs at all is perhaps a sufficient miracle.

Symphonies Nos 1-9 💰

Ruth Ziesak *sop* **Birgit Remmert** *contr*
Steve Davislim *ten* **Detlef Roth** *bar*
Swiss Chamber Choir; Zurich Tonhalle Orchestra / David Zinman

Arte Nova Classics ⑤ 74321 65410-2 Ⓢ
(336 minutes: DDD). Recorded 1997-99 OO

Also available separately – *74321 63645-2*: Nos 1 and 2 (54 minutes). *74321 59214-2*: Nos 3 and 4 (75 minutes). *74321 49695-2*: Nos 5 and 6 (74 minutes). *74321 56341-2*: Nos 7 and 8 (61 minutes). *74321 65411-2*: No 9 (73 minutes)

Viewed overall, the performances of Nos 1, 4, 6 and 8 are the best in this set, though there is a certain levelling of dynamics in the Eighth. And then in the Seventh and the Fifth, the finales might have benefited from a wider curve of dynamics and a little more in the way of tonal weight. On the other hand, Zinman's fleet-footed *Eroica* grows on you, and the Fourth is among the most vivacious accounts available. As to the Ninth, the *Scherzo*'s super-fast Trio makes particular sense at the very end of the movement where Trio and outer section engage in a brief comic tussle. The fast first movement is suitably dangerous and while the finale will no doubt court controversy (primarily for some unusual tempo relations), the *Adagio* sounds matter-of-fact, even a little impatient. Indeed, it is the one movement in this cycle that seems to misfire.

Zinman has used Barenreiter's new edition of Beethoven's texts, although the extra appoggiaturas and ornaments, invariably sewn along the woodwind lines – were inserted by the conductor, based on sound musicological principles. All repeats are observed, and so are the majority of Beethoven's metronome markings. What matters most is the overall character of Zinman's Beethoven which is swift, lean, exhilarating and transparent. The Tonhalle copes bravely, often with exceptional skill, and the recordings easily compare with their best full-price rivals. Indeed, although Zinman places his violin desks next to each other, the recording is so good that you often hear them as spatially separated.

And the best bargain alternatives? Gunter Wand's sense of structure (RCA) draws a sympathetic response, while Leinsdorf's solid, strong-arm Beethoven also has much to commend it (RCA). Karajan's 1962 cycle is surely the best of four (see above) and although Mackerras (Classics for Pleasure), like Zinman, sheds revealing beams of light here and there, this Zurich set has the greater impact. Those who favour the darker, weightier, more obviously 'heroic' Beethoven known (wrongly, perhaps) as 'old school' will probably not respond quite so readily, but they should still give Zinman a try. On balance, his cycle remains the best bargain digital option. Besides, Arte Nova's asking price is so ludicrously cheap that it is worth buying on impulse, if only for the sake of a refreshing change. Just try to have someone else's *Choral* in reserve.

Additional recommendations

Complete Symphonies

Wiens *sop* **Hartwig** *contr* **Lewis** *ten* **Hermann** *bar*
Hamburg State Opera Chorus; North German Radio Chorus; North German RSO / Wand

RCA Victor Symphony Edition ⑤ 74321 20277-2 Ⓑ
(356 minutes: DDD: 5/95)

Günter Wand's performances are consistently inspired. His tempos are superbly judged, the orchestral balance is ideal, and in the Ninth the soloists make a first-rate team.

NBC Symphony Orchestra / Toscanini Ⓗ
RCA Red Seal ⑦ 74321 666562/7 Ⓢ
Also available separately: ② 74321 55835-2: Symphonies Nos 1-4; Egmont Overture. ② 74321 55836-2: Symphonies Nos 5-8. ② 74321 55837-2: Symphony No 9; Missa solemnis (136, 129 and 139 minutes: ADD: 5/90[R]) Ⓜ

Recorded from 1949 to 1952, these recordings constitute Toscanini's only complete cycle. Strong, lean and direct performances, there isn't a single bar which is unconsidered or routine. Harsh sound but the transfers seem faithful.

Symphonies Nos 1 and 4

Symphonies Nos 1 and 4. Egmont Overture, Op 84[a]
Berlin Philharmonic Orchestra / Herbert von Karajan
DG Galleria 419 048-2GGA (64 minutes: ADD) Ⓜ
Recorded [a]1969, 1975-76 ●

The opening of the First, perfectly timed and chorded, announces playing of rare pedigree, though the *Allegro* itself, taken at a gently ruminative pace, is a surprise. The autumnal side of Karajan's make-up is one we don't often see. It is a beautifully shaped reading, with glorious wind playing and a nobly sustained through-rhythm. The mellow *Andante*, like the Minuet and Trio, emerges as a miracle of instrumental ensemble, reminding one how summer by summer Karajan encouraged his players to make chamber music together on vacation. After so gentle a start, the finale seems strangely quick. Orchestrally, it is the finest quick Beethoven playing imaginable and for all the aerial excitement the final *ff* peaks are compelling placed.

Karajan's instinctively dynamic approach to Beethoven is modified in the Fourth by a contrasted but equally strong feel for the German symphonic tradition. The performance strikes deepest at the points of stasis midway through each of the first three movements. Indeed, the sonority of the performance is remarkable throughout, with great use made of bass and cello colourings (something which the BPO had perfected by this time) and a huge dynamic range – implicit in the score from massive tutti chords down to the most perfectly regulated quiet drum rolls. Thus it is, in playing as subtle as it is creatively alive, that the flame of Beethoven's genius can be seen to burn brightly on. The *Egmont* Overture, played superbly and surprisingly swiftly, makes a welcome filler.

Symphonies Nos 1 and 6

Symphonies Nos 1 and 6. Die Geschöpfe des Prometheus, Op 43 Ⓟ
London Classical Players / Sir Roger Norrington
Virgin Veritas VM5 61374-2 (75 minutes: DDD) Ⓜ
Recorded 1987 ●

Norrington's reading of the finale of the First Symphony is as lithe and witty as you could wish for. The first movement is more difficult to bring off and it is a measure of the competence and confidence of the London Classical Players that the difficult slow introduction is brought off with superb aplomb and that the *Allegro con brio* is reasonably quick but with space in the lyrical subjects and the most ferocious account of the coda on record, the period brass snarling viciously in the tuttis and the timpani roaring menacingly on the final page. Other conductors have played the *Andante cantabile con moto* reasonably swiftly but Norrington is very brisk, the tone nicely set, the whole thing playful and witty in a delightfully brittle way. Again, the articulation of the players is first-rate, giving the performance real presence, style and individuality. This is one of the best accounts of the First.

The *Pastoral* is also a revelation. Norrington adopts a swift tempo in the joyous first movement but there's no hint of that relentless, driven quality which we have sometimes had on record. He is fully up to tempo in the vibrant tuttis; elsewhere he's most careful to allow the music to expand and dance and breathe, the transitions always most sensitively moulded. It is also a joy to hear this symphony on period instruments. The instrumental timbres will come as a revelation to many listeners; equally, they are obviously a source of real joy and fascination to the players. This *Pastoral* is a real voyage of aural discovery. Sometimes the wind tuning is not 100 per cent true, at others it is simply a matter of Norrington teasing us with the timing of a trill's release or pointing up dissonances that usually get smoothed over. The sound is wonderfully clear and trenchant. How marvellous it is at the start of the last movement of the *Pastoral* to have such clean, honest string sound and to have it spread right across the orchestral spectrum as the first and second violins answer one another antiphonally across the landscape.

Symphonies Nos 2 and 8

Awards 1987

Symphonies Nos 2 and 8. Ⓟ
Overtures – Coriolan, Op 62; Egmont, Op 84
London Classical Players / Sir Roger Norrington
Virgin Veritas VM5 61375-2 Ⓜ
(73 minutes: DDD). Recorded 1986 ●●●

Norrington's way with Beethoven – which is recognizably Toscaninian in some of its aspects – is, in his own words, his aim of recapturing much of 'the exhilaration and sheer disturbance that his music certainly generated in his day'. Like Toscanini, Erich Kleiber, and others before him, Norrington achieves this not by the imposition on the music of some world view but by taking up its immediate intellectual and physical challenges. Norrington is not unduly preoccupied by matters of orchestral size but sound interests him a good deal. Throughout, the contributions of horns, trumpets and drums most rivet the attention (the introduction to the Second Symphony's first movement is glorious).

What really fascinates Norrington, though, is

rhythm and pulse and their determining agencies: 18th-century performing styles, instrumental articulacy (most notably, bowing methods), and Beethoven's own metronome markings. In the Second Symphony Norrington makes the music smile and dance without any significant loss of forward momentum, and he treats the metronome marks more consistently than Karajan (who spins out the symphony's introduction), while sharing with him a belief in a really forward-moving pulse in the *Larghetto* (again an approach to the printed metronome if not the thing itself). The recordings are warm and vivid and generally well balanced.

The *fff* climax of the development of the Eighth Symphony's first movement is slightly underpowered, which is odd when the horns and trumpets are elsewhere so thrillingly caught; perhaps, in the Eighth, the recording could have been a shade tighter and drier in order better to define the playing of the London Classical Players. None the less, when it first appeared, it was hailed as the most interesting and enjoyable new record of a Beethoven symphony recorded for some considerable time. This reissue also includes vigorous accounts of the *Coriolan* and *Egmont* Overtures.

Symphony No 3

Symphony No 3. Overtures – Leonore Nos 2 and 3 **H**
Philharmonia Orchestra / Otto Klemperer
EMI mono CDM7 63855-2 (76 minutes: ADD) Ⓜ
Recorded 1954-55 ●●

In 1955 the Philharmonia Orchestra was at the peak of its powers. And what cogency there is sustaining and feeding the drama. Where other orchestras and conductors whip themselves into a terrible lather at the start of the finale, Klemperer and the Philharmonia sail majestically on. This is a great performance, steady yet purposeful, with textures that seem hewn out of granite. There is no exposition repeat, and the trumpets blaze out illicitly in the first movement coda, but this is still one of the great *Eroicas* on record. As Karajan announced to Klemperer after flying in to a concert performance around this time: 'I have come only to thank you, and say that I hope I shall live to conduct the Funeral March as well as you have done'. In the *Leonore* Overtures, recorded in 1954, the playing is a bit more rough-edged.

Symphony No 3. Overture – Coriolan, Op 62 **P**
Le Concert des Nations / Jordi Savall
Auvidis Fontalis ES9959 (52 minutes: DDD) Ⓜ
Recorded 1994

There is a real sense of burgeoning excitement at the start of Savall's performance; and the sound of the orchestra really does conjure up the sense of one being transported back to some dusky Viennese concert room *c*1805 where the musicians are as dangerous a crew as the militias roaming the mud-filled streets outside. Yet as the musical arguments begin to multiply and deepen, so the performance gets slightly garbled. For all Savall's skill in moulding and modifying the pulse, there's a jauntiness about parts of the first movement development section which muddles and trivialises the music.

In the *Marcia funèbre*, the performance is astonishing for the mood it conjures. The drum (calf skin head, hard sticks) is fierce and seductive, an instrument of war that suggests also the soft thud of death. Savall's brass are similarly remarkable, at once brazen and mellow-sounding. The horn section alone – Thomas Muller, Raul Diaz and Javier Bonet – deserves an award for the way the players colour and characterise this astonishing music. There is no disguising the fact that Savall's thinking about tempo is controversial. It is all very modern: post-modern, even. (After Savall, conductors like Norrington sound distressingly 'safe'.) It is typical of Savall that though he conducts very quick, very earthy, very exciting accounts of the *Eroica*'s *Scherzo* (those horns again!) and finale, he still slows up pretty massively for the finale's oboe-led *Poco andante* at bar 348. It is a performance, none the less, that you will want for the sonic profile alone. The Auvidis recording is first-rate: warm and immediate.

Symphonies Nos 1 and 3. Fidelio – Overture **H**
NBC Symphony Orchestra / Arturo Toscanini
Naxos Historical mono ② 8 110802/3 Ⓢ
(91 minutes: ADD). Recorded live in 1939 ●

Symphony No 3 **H**
Vienna Philharmonic Orchestra / Wilhelm Furtwängler
Tahra mono FURT1031 (53 minutes: ADD) Ⓕ
Recorded 1944 ●●

These two *Eroicas* confound critical clichés about their respective conductor. Furtwängler's recording is swifter than you might imagine, certainly in the first movement and Toscanini's forceful 1939 radio broadcast is among the most songful, most flexibly phrased interpretations on disc. They both lay claim to being the best of various alternatives under the same conductors, and both have been reissued many times before; but while Naxos's transfer is only moderately successful, Tahra's is among the finest around. There have been various unofficial transfers – both on CD and LP – in better-focused sound, that run this rather rough-edged Naxos transfer pretty close. Furtwängler's first movement is distinguished above all by warmly arched string phrasing. The second subject slows less perceptibly than in Toscanini's performance. Toscanini keeps the same passage very much in tempo and while his handling of the coda is incandescently intense, Furtwängler draws greater attention to the *crescendo*ing repeated string figures that lead up to it. In the *Marcia funèbre*, Furtwängler is broadly paced and loose-jointed, with mellow lower strings and impressive weight of tone, while Toscanini is anxious, candid and desperately expressive. Furtwängler slows the closing bars so dramatically that the fragmented theme all but disintegrates. Toscanini, however, holds fast to the lyrical line, and the effect is hardly less devastating. His *Scherzo* is fleet and furious, whereas Furtwängler's gentler manner breaks the *Marcia*'s spell like a lone dove fluttering against a stormy sky. Both finales work well, though Toscanini 'holds the plot' with a firmer grip.

You end up being equally well disposed towards both Toscanini and Furtwängler, although not everyone will want Toscanini's hard-driven account, let alone the ephemeral spoken commentaries that surround it. Still, in the *Eroica*, both conductors offer a singular musical experience: gripping, inspired and always worth the effort needed to 'listen through' old sound. The further we journey from these venerable old masters, the more we treasure their individuality and commitment. True, opposing camps will lock horns over who best realises the composer's intentions (as if we could ever know), but those listeners sensible enough to keep an open mind on the matter cannot fail to perceive that both routes lead to the same life-enhancing destination. Which is surely what great music-making is all about.

Symphonies Nos 4 and 7

Symphonies Nos 4 and 7 **P**
London Classical Players / Sir Roger Norrington
Virgin Veritas VM5 61376-2 (69 minutes: DDD) Ⓜ
Recorded 1988

Norrington's opening to the Fourth is subdued, but the tension lies beneath the surface and facilitates a striking contrast with the *allegro*, which is light in feeling, with a very brisk tempo indeed. Norrington presses the *Adagio* forward but it is light and songful. His briskness continues in the *Scherzo* but is slightly tempered by the relatively mellow acoustic. The London Classical Players articulate the bustling finale with great panache.

In this splendid version of the Seventh, Norrington's allegiance to Beethoven's metronome markings is particularly convincing, and not only in the second movement *Allegretto*. His sharp pointing of the accents of the introduction is immediately arresting, and the dance rhythms in the main theme of the first movement and again in the finale bring joyously buoyant articulation to match the sparkle of the *Scherzo* (the swiftly rippling low-register pedal duplets from the second horn which build up to the bold restatement of the Trio are a memorable touch). In the finale the hammering of the timpani is unforgettable and at the close the horns sing out as they do at the triumphant ending of the first movement. Like the pairing of Nos 2 and 8, Norrington's coupling of Nos 4 and 7 is well worth seeking out.

Symphonies Nos 5 and 7

Symphonies Nos 5 and 7
Vienna Philharmonic Orchestra / Carlos Kleiber
DG The Originals 447 400-2GOR (72 minutes: ADD) Ⓜ
Recorded 1974 **OOO**

The recording of the Fifth, always very fine, comes up superbly in this transfer. What, though, of the Seventh, an equally distinguished performance though always perceptibly greyer-sounding on LP, and on CD? Well, it too is superb. What the Original-Image Bit-Processing has done to it, heaven only knows, but the result is a performance of genius that now speaks to us freely and openly for the first time. In some ways this is a more important document than the famous Fifth. Great recordings of the Seventh, greatly played and conducted, but with first and second violins divided left and right, are as rare as gold-dust. Freshly refurbished, this Kleiber Seventh would go right to the top of any short list of recommendable Sevenths. It is wonderful to have these two legendary performances so expertly restored.

Symphonies Nos 5 and 6

Symphonies Nos 5 and 6 **P**
London Classical Players / Sir Roger Norrington
Virgin Veritas VM5 61377-2 (74 minutes: DDD) Ⓜ
Recorded 1988

Norrington conducts an enjoyable, memorable account of the Fifth. He throws off the introduction to the first movement with crisp brilliance, and the *Allegro* conveys enormous underlying energy. His *Andante* is beautifully phrased and flows most delicately; in the bustling double-bass theme at the centre of the *Scherzo* the bowing is light, the effect refined and offering easy virtuosity. Norrington's finale is strongly accented, his horns in the secondary idea broadly sonorous, partly as a result of the resonant EMI sound. The *Pastoral* brings a similarly fast pace in the opening movement, but with subtle shading of dynamics. The contributions of horns and woodwinds produce an attractive exuberance. The slow movement, however, is less convincing, the phrasing curiously choppy. Many will like the warm Abbey Road acoustic, but (apart from the braying horns) the *Scherzo* lacks refined detail. The extra resonance means that the timpani thunderbolts are less effective than they might be. The finale seldom fails, and here the expansive EMI sound adds to the fullness: the lower strings resonate richly and the climax is radiant.

Beethoven Symphony No 6
Schubert Symphony No 5 in B flat, D485
Vienna Philharmonic Orchestra / Karl Böhm
DG The Originals 447 433-2GOR (74 minutes: ADD) Ⓜ
Recorded 1971 and 1979 **OOO**

Karl Böhm's Beethoven is a compound of earth and fire. His VPO recording of Beethoven's Sixth of 1971 dominated the LP catalogue for over a decade, and has done pretty well on CD on its various appearances. His reading is generally glorious and it remains one of the finest accounts of the work ever recorded. It still sounds well (perhaps the bass is a bit lighter than on LP) and the performance (with the first movement exposition repeat included) has an unfolding naturalness and a balance between form and lyrical impulse that is totally satisfying. The brook flows untroubled and the finale is quite lovely, with a wonderfully expansive climax. The Schubert dates from the end of Böhm's recording career. It is a superb version of this lovely symphony, another work that suited Böhm especially well. The reading is weighty but graceful, with a most beautifully phrased *Andante* (worthy of a Furtwängler), a bold Minuet and a thrilling finale. The recording is splendid. If you admire Böhm this is a worthy way to remember his special gifts.

Symphony No 9

Anna Tomowa-Sintow *sop* **Agnes Baltsa** *mez* **Peter Schreier** *ten* **José van Dam** *bass-bar* **Vienna Singverein; Berlin Philharmonic Orchestra / Herbert von Karajan**
DG Galleria 415 832-2GGA (67 minutes: ADD) Ⓜ
Text and translation included
Recorded 1976 OO

All collections need Beethoven's *Choral* Symphony as one of the works at the very core of the 19th-century romantic movement. Within its remarkable span, Beethoven celebrates both the breadth and power of man's conception of his position in relation to the Universe; his sense of spirituality – especially in the great slow movement – and in the finale the essential life-enhancing optimism emerges, which makes human existence philosophically possible against all odds. Karajan lived alongside the Beethoven symphonies throughout his long and very distinguished recording career, and he recorded the Ninth three times in stereo. His 1976 version is the best of the three. The slow movement has great intensity, and the finale brings a surge of incandescent energy and exuberance which is hard to resist. All four soloists are excellent individually and they also make a good team. The reading as a whole has the inevitability of greatness and the recording is vivid, full and clear. At mid-price this is very recommendable indeed.

Symphony No 9 H
Aase Nordmo-Løvberg *sop* **Christa Ludwig** *mez* **Waldemar Kmentt** *ten* **Hans Hotter** *bass-bar* **Philharmonia Chorus and Orchestra / Otto Klemperer**
Testament SBT1177 (71 minutes: ADD) Ⓕ
Recorded live in 1957 OO

This is a revelatory live recording by EMI's engineers of Klemperer's performance of the Ninth Symphony at the Royal Festival Hall, immediately before his 1957 EMI recording. Where the studio recording gives us a frontal, ground-level view of the players spread out across the spaces of the Kingsway Hall, this live Festival Hall recording offers us that special Klemperer balance which gave particular prominence to the winds and the timpani. Strings, and in the finale the chorus, are nicely focused; but from where we are sat, somewhere above the first oboe, it is winds and timpani which are the centre of interest. No one would have dared balance a studio recording this way, yet this is far closer to what a Klemperer performance really sounded like.

There are a couple of oddities in the finale. In the preliminary orchestral statement of the 'joy' theme, the bassoon descant drowns out the violas and cellos; then, later on, we get a less than clear view of the tenor. (A blessed relief, perhaps, given Kmentt's thin, dried-out sound. Kmentt is more at ease in the studio recording.) Interpretatively, the two performances are identical, though the live performance is just that bit more intense, with hair's-breadth tightenings where the studio performance merely trundles reliably on. The first movement does not benefit greatly but the Scherzo is transformed; what rather lumbers in the studio is here a thrilling dance of the Titans. The slow movement also takes on a more numinous quality, with sublimely simple string playing, a nice 'lift' to the tricky 12/8 section, and awe-inspiringly solemn brass annunciations towards the end. The finale is wonderfully performed, thrillingly articulated by the newly-founded Philharmonia Chorus and by the Philharmonia players. Detail after detail shines out, etched into one's imagination by the playing and the persistently enquiring recording.

Symphony No 9 H
Elisabeth Schwarzkopf *sop* **Elisabeth Höngen** *mez* **Hans Hopf** *ten* **Otto Edelmann** *bass* **Bayreuth Festival Chorus and Orchestra / Wilhelm Furtwängler**
EMI Great Recordings of the Century mono
CDM5 66901-2 (75 minutes: ADD) Ⓜ
Recorded live in 1951 OO

This performance has become a legendary one, as much for the occasion of its happening as for the music-making itself. The reopening of Wagner's Festival Theatre in Bayreuth in 1951 after the catastrophe of war was nothing if not symbolic. If anything could lay the ghost of Bayreuth's immediate past, the years from 1930 to 1944 when the theatre was run by the English-born, Nazi-worshipping Winifred Wagner, it might be a performance of the Ninth Symphony under the most celebrated of the German conductors who had lived through Nazi rule without being, in any real sense, morally or artistically party to it. Certainly, it is not difficult to think of the slow movement's second subject, unfolded here in a way that has never been bettered, as an atonement and a benediction.

However, not everyone will respond to this vision of the Ninth: as an interpretation it is broadly based, with some slow tempos and some quirky adjustments of pace; though beneath everything – beneath the gear changes and failures in ensemble – a great current massively flows. The solo vocal and choral work in the finale is electric after the *fugato* but is breezily, bumpily Teutonic before that; Hans Hopf is his usual restless, hectic self. The CD transfer provides some added clarity of image for the generally excellent mono recording; and it also provides an all-important continuity. Instrumental bass frequencies are rather wooden but the recording reproduces higher frequency string, wind, and vocal sound more smoothly than was often the case at this time. Many collectors will be looking to a stereo, digital recording of the Ninth as a CD library acquisition; yet we would be prepared to argue that this performance has a prior, if not absolute, claim on collectors' attention.

Awards 1995

Symphony No 9 **H**
Elisabeth Schwarzkopf *sop* **Elsa Cavelti** *mez* **Ernst Haefliger** *ten* **Otto Edelmann** *bass* **Lucerne Festival Chorus; Philharmonia Orchestra / Wilhelm Furtwängler**
Tahra mono FURT1054/7 Ⓕ
(78 minutes: ADD). Recorded live in 1954 OOO

The 40th anniversary of Furtwängler's death on November 30, 1954 brought forth a rich crop of reissues and remasterings, most notably on the French label Tahra, which secured the rights to publish limited editions of some of Furtwängler's most important (and, it must be said, most frequently pirated) live recordings. Some of Furtwängler's finest performances of Beethoven's music were given in the last months of his life, an odd paradox given his failing health and, by November, the apparent extinction of his will to live. Yet this Lucerne Ninth is a seismic utterance, the final heroic regrouping of musical and psychic powers that in certain works of the repertory have this gangling figure towering over all his rivals. This is arguably the greatest of all Furtwängler's recordings of the symphony. Walter Legge wanted to acquire the performance as EMI's official replacement for the momentous 1951 Bayreuth account, but it wasn't to be. Since then, there have been various 'unofficial' editions. The Tahra differs in being 'official', well transferred, and further enhanced by a few introductory remarks made by Furtwängler himself.

Here, the most significant section is that in which Furtwängler sees the problem of interpreting the Ninth as one that effectively post-dates the performing culture into which it was born. Furtwängler understood the Ninth as well as any conductor in the 20th century. You can argue this way or that over the pacing of the slow movement (though we defy anyone to say that his performance is anything other than deeply eloquent) or the leisurely speed of the second movement Trio. In the all-important first movement, though, there is no doubt that Beethoven's written tempo markings and frequent subsequent modifications clearly presuppose the kind of uniquely singing, flexible, harmonically searching (but by no means over-slow) reading Furtwängler invariably gave us.

Piano Quintet, Op 16

Beethoven Piano Quintet in E flat, Op 16 **H**
Mozart Piano Quintet in E flat, K452. Sinfonia concertante in E flat, K297*b*
Walter Gieseking *pf* **Philharmonia Wind Quartet** (Sidney Sutcliffe *ob* Bernard Walton *cl* Dennis Brain *hn* Cecil James *bn*); **Philharmonia Orchestra / Herbert von Karajan**
Testament mono SBT1091 (80 minutes: ADD) Ⓕ
Recorded 1955 OO

There have never been any doubts about these performances. The horn playing in the *Sinfonia concertante* is unsurpassable and in the quintets Gieseking's lightness and his clarity and sense of style is simply beyond praise. The tempos are on the slow side in the first movement of the Mozart and the finale of the Beethoven but somehow with Gieseking, slow tempos have a way of seeming to be just about right. Richard Osborne's excellent notes quote a letter from Sidney Sutcliffe of touching modesty. Speaking of their run-through of the Mozart, he says, 'On reaching the *Allegro moderato*, the great man played two bars at an absolutely perfect tempo and then stopped and asked in the most gentle and hesitant manner, "Will that be all right for you?" So it was a most happy occasion although I found it a grave responsibility matching the artistry of my colleagues when Bernard [Walton], Cecil [James] and Dennis [Brain] were producing sounds of breath-taking beauty'. Breathtaking is just the right word for all concerned here on what is, after all, one of the great chamber music records of the LP era. Considerable pains have been taken with the transfers, which now sound fresh and full-bodied.

Beethoven Piano Quintet. Horn Sonata in F, Op 17 **P**
Mozart Piano Quintet in E flat, K452
Robert Levin *fp* **Academy of Ancient Music Chamber Ensemble** (Frank de Bruine *ob* Antony Pay *cl* Danny Bond *bn* Anthony Halstead *hn*)
Decca L'Oiseau-Lyre 455 994-2OH Ⓕ
(67 minutes: DDD). Recorded 1996 O

A captivating record. If you like the Viennese classics to sound suave and demure, it may not be for you: there's plenty of mellifluous playing, but the dominant impression is one of rhythmic energy, drama and colour – with the characters of all five instruments vividly projected. Robert Levin is an unusually creative performer – not just in the way that he searches for the right sound and style for every passage, but also in his ability to add happily conceived extra ornamentation and short cadenzas, in the Mozart especially, where he starts to elaborate the text as early as the third bar. The wind players catch the mood and make appropriate decorations, too, particularly during repeated sections. Some may feel that this sort of thing has no place on a recording which may be played many times. The counter-argument is that a recording can never be more than one performance, that the ornamentation, wonderfully stylish, really does add something to the music, and that it's impossible to imagine that Mozart himself would have always stuck to the written text. And the disc would be well worth acquiring just for the Horn Sonata; Levin and Halstead give it a touch of extravagance and bravado that seems to capture the essence of early Beethoven. The recording is clear, with a pleasingly intimate quality.

Septet, Op 20

Beethoven Septet in E flat, Op 20 H
Mendelssohn Octet in E flat, Op 20
Members of the **Vienna Octet**
Decca 421 093-2DM (74 minutes: ADD) Ⓕ
Recorded 1959 and 1972 ⊙

After its triumphant first performance in 1800, Beethoven's Septet went on to become not only one of the most popular but also one of the most influential chamber works of the period. The composer himself grew to dislike the piece, but it remains one of the most treasured products of the classical era. There are many fine performances of the Septet available. Curiously, compared to the 1972 Mendelssohn coupling, the 1959 sound in the Septet seems sweeter and more natural, to complement a performance which is an utter delight. Here is that old-fashioned, spontaneous yet relaxed Viennese style, with ample, beautifully-shaped phrasing and an engaging, slightly rustic quality in the clarinet tone which, alas, seems to have gone out of fashion.

In the Mendelssohn Octet, the playing has a delicious buoyancy of spirit and an abundance of charm. The *Andante*, in particular, has an affecting, wistful delicacy and there is total clarity in the *fugato* which launches a strongly-played finale. The recording is clean and well balanced.

Septet in E flat, Op 20. Piano Quintet in E flat, Op 16. Sextet in E flat, Op 81*b*
Ottó Rácz *ob* **József Balogh** *cl* **József Vajda** *bn*
Jenö Keveházi, János Keveházi, Sándor Berki *hns*
Ildikó Hegyi, Péter Popa *vns* **Gyözö Máthé** *va*
Peter Szabó *vc* **István Toth** *db*
Naxos 8 553090 (74 minutes: DDD) Ⓢ
Recorded 1994

These talented Hungarian players offer a fluent, responsive account of the Septet that highlights the music's intimate chamber character – delight in the music's elegance and perfect balance of instrumental forces. In the present instance, vivid recording creates a clear, natural ambience for this alert, sensitively blended ensemble. In the Sextet, horn players, Jenö and János Keveházi play with subtlety and panache as required, their tone spontaneous and free. This excellent, value-for-money Naxos disc also offers an elegant, well-turned performance of Beethoven's E flat Quintet.

Piano Quartets

WoO36 – No 1 in E flat; **No 2** in D; **No 3** in C.
Op 16 in E flat

Beethoven Piano Quartet in E flat, Op 16
Schumann Piano Quartet in E flat, Op 47
Isaac Stern *vn* **Jaime Laredo** *va* **Yo-Yo Ma** *vc*
Emanuel Ax *pf*
Sony Classical SK53339 (65 minutes: DDD) Ⓕ
Recorded 1992 ⊙

There are numerous recordings of Beethoven's Op 16 in its original Mozart-inspired quintet version for piano and wind against only a few for the piano quartet arrangement in which it rapidly re-emerged. But this 1992 performance of the quartet from Isaac Stern and his eminent younger colleagues makes it hard to believe that it was conceived for any other combination than theirs – and what higher praise than that? The *Andante cantabile*, with its delicately embellished melodic strands, surely gains in expressive eloquence from the more personal inflexions of caressing strings. And with their bold dynamic contrasts and piquant accentuation, what drama all four players draw from the opening movement. As a brilliant pianist himself, Beethoven entrusted the pianist with a great degree of responsibility, at once arrestingly and effortlessly discharged here by Emanuel Ax.

As for Schumann's Piano Quartet, no longer is it dwarfed in popularity by its immediate predecessor in the same key, the Piano Quintet. This recording will surely win new friends – and not only for the mercurial lightness and grace of the Mendelssohnian sprites in the *Scherzo* and the glowing but essentially unsentimentalised intimacy of the *Andante cantabile* (as dedicated a love-song as Schumann ever wrote). The performers' impulse in the two flanking movements is unflagging and the overall impression is of spontaneous enjoyment – friends making music together for their own delight rather than as just another professional engagement. The sound is as vibrant as the playing.

Piano Quartets, WoO36 – Nos 1-3.
E flat, Op 16 (arr Beethoven)
Raphael Oleg *vn* **Miguel da Silva** *va* **Marc Coppey** *vc*
Philippe Cassard *pf*
Auvidis Valois ② V4715 (88 minutes: DDD) Ⓕ
Recorded 1994

This issue of the three piano quartets Beethoven completed at the age of 15 but subsequently suppressed, in double harness with the 26-year-old composer's piano quartet arrangement of his Op 16 Quintet for piano and wind, is more than welcome – despite its shortish playing time. Indebted to the still youthful Mozart the teenage Beethoven may well (and should) have been, as also tempted to entrust too much to the piano But the unpredictability of even immature genius is striking. Never can you for a second foretell what surprise, whether of key, harmony, rhythm or scoring, lies just around the corner. His fluent, confident craftsmanship makes you marvel no less. Even when borrowing the three-movement sequence of Mozart's G major Violin Sonata (K397) for his own E flat major work,

Beethoven gives his chromatically intensified opening *Adagio assai*, his stormy minor-key *Allegro* and even the beguiling variations, an unmistakable stamp of his own.

The playing itself of course contributes to the pleasure, with first praise to Philippe Cassard for never allowing the keyboard to dominate. But all four Paris Conservatoire-trained colleagues are artists of taste and finesse. Their characterization is most sensitively attuned to the music's own true scale. Never does point-making sound self-consciously inflated. The recording itself has a pleasingly soft-grained intimacy.

Complete String Quartets

No 1 in F, Op 18 No 1; **No 2** in G, Op 18 No 2; **No 3** in D, Op 18 No 3; **No 4** in C minor, Op 18 No 4; **No 5** in A, Op 18 No 5; **No 6** in B flat, Op 18 No 6; **No 7** in F, Op 59 No 1, 'Rasumovsky'; **No 8** in E minor, Op 59 No 2, 'Rasumovsky'; **No 9** in C, Op 59 No 3, 'Rasumovsky'; **No 10** in E flat, Op 74, 'Harp'; **No 11** in F minor, Op 95, 'Serioso'; **No 12** in E flat, Op 127; **No 13** in B flat, Op 130; **No 14** in C sharp minor; Op 131; **No 15** in A minor, Op 132; **No 16** in F, Op 135

String Quartets Nos 1-16. Grosse Fuge in B flat, Op 133
Quartetto Italiano (Paolo Borciani, Elisa Pegreffi *vns* Piero Farulli *va* Franco Rossi *vc*)
Philips ⑩ 454 062-2PB10 (544 minutes: ADD) Ⓑ
Recorded 1967-75 **OO**

The early and middle quartets are also available on Philips Duo: *426 046-2PM* (Nos 1-6) and *420 797-2PM3* (Nos 7-11) Ⓑ

The late quartets are also available on Philips Duo: *454 711-2PM2* (Nos 12, 13, 16; Grosse Fuge) and *454 712-2PM2* (Nos 14, 15) Ⓑ
They have also been remastered on a three-disc set: Philips 50 Great recordings ③ 464 684-2PM3 Ⓜ

It goes without saying that no one ensemble can unlock all the secrets contained in these quartets. The Quartetto Italiano recordings have assumed a variety of formats since their first appearance. The quartets now comprise 10 CDs but Philips wisely offers the performances at a highly competitive price in three separate sets and it is as separate entities they should be considered. Their claims are strongest in the Op 18 Quartets. The Quartetto Italiano offers eminently civilised, thoughtful and aristocratic readings. Their approach is reticent but they also convey a strong sense of making music in domestic surroundings. Quite frankly, one could not do very much better than this set. Turning to the middle-period quartets the Italians are hardly less distinguished, even though there are times when the Végh offers even deeper insights: one thinks in particular of the slow movement of Op 59 No 1, which means more in their hands. Taken in isolation, however, the Quartetto Italiano remains eminently satisfying both musically and as recorded sound. As far as sound quality is concerned, it is rich and warm. In Opp 74 and 95, the Quartetto Italiano more than holds its own against all comers. These are finely proportioned readings, poised and articulate.

The gain in clarity because of the remastering entails a very slight loss of warmth in the middle register, but as recordings the late quartets made between 1967 and 1969, can hold their own against their modern rivals. Take care of the sense and the sound takes care of itself: the sonority that the Quartetto Italiano produces is well blended and has a great variety of tone colour and generally speaking, they give each musical point more time to register. Not all of these received universal acclaim at the time of their first release. The opening fugue of No 14 is too slow at four-in-the-bar and far more *espressivo* than it should be but, overall, these performances still strike a finely judged balance between beauty and truth, and are ultimately more satisfying and searching than most of their rivals.

String Quartets Nos 1-9

String Quartets Nos 1-9
Végh Quartet (Sándor Végh, Sándor Zöldy *vns* Georges Janzer *va* Paul Szábo *vc*)
Auvidis Valois ④ V4401/4 Ⓕ
(oas: 57, 71, 66, 71 minutes). Recorded 1974 **OO**

V4401 – Nos 1 and 5. V4402 – Nos 2, 3 and 4. V4403 – Nos 6 and 7. V4404 – Nos 8 and 9

The Végh's classic accounts of the String Quartets are in a completely different league from any of their rivals: there is no cultivation of surface polish but there is no lack of elegance and finesse. Above all, there is no attempt to glamorise their sound. In No 1 they find the *tempo giusto* right at the beginning and they find more depth in the slow movement than anyone else on record. Végh himself floats the melodic line in this movement in a most imaginative way and is wonderfully supported. In the civilised exchanges that open No 2 the Végh brings an altogether light touch to bear and has an elegance and wit that is almost unmatched and, of course, great refinement of tone. There were complaints of the bottom-heavy recording when is appeared on LP, and it is less transparent and lifelike than more modern recordings.

The *Rasumovsky* set is admirable for its alertness of articulation, rhythmic grasp and flexibility and its subtle range of tone-colour. The effortlessness with which the dialogue proceeds silences criticism. The Végh brings special insights to this inexhaustible music. The style and the quality of perception seem so remarkable and so well sustained here that any deficiencies can be overlooked. There are lapses in tone and intonation, most of them on the part of the leader, yet what a musician he is, and what a remarkable guide to the visionary content of these quartets. Where the music demands most in such matters he is never wanting. In sum, these are neither the most 'perfect' nor the most sumptuously recorded accounts available, yet they are the deepest and most searching. When listening to them you are conscious only of Beethoven's own voice. The transfers give a slightly firmer focus and sharper detail though that slight bottom-heaviness still remains.

CDDCA1111: String Quartets Nos 1-3
CDDCA1112: String Quartets Nos 4 and 5.
String Quartet in F, H34
CDDCA1113: String Quartet No 6.
String Quintet in C, Op 29[a]
The Lindsays (Peter Cropper, Ronald Birks *vns* Roger Bigley *va* Bernard Gregor-Smith *vc*)
[a]**Louise Williams** *va*
ASV CDDCA1111-3 Ⓕ
(oas: 78, 66 and 58 minutes: DDD). Recorded 2000

It's wonderful how the Lindsays, after a career of more than 30 years, can still sound so fresh and spontaneous. From the start of Op 18 No 1 we feel that every phrase is shaped individually, the music felt as it's being played. The dynamics are beautifully differentiated; *pianissimo* always has an altered sound compared with *piano*. Presenting the sense of the music and its emotions is always a priority, which leads to some daring interpretative decisions. The fast and fantastical finale of the Op 29 Quintet, with its scary *tremolos* and wild-sounding *rubato* in the first violin arpeggios is one example of a no-holds-barred approach that gets into the character of the music in a way that a more measured style couldn't. It's a splendid idea to include this neglected quintet as well as Beethoven's brilliant arrangement of the Op 14 No 1 Piano Sonata; the Quintet's rich, often complex, textures are relished, helping us to hear this work as a halfway house between the C major Quintets of Mozart and Schubert.

Despite the air of spontaneity, the Lindsays' interpretations of Op 18 have remained very similar to those they offered us 20 years ago. The new recordings are certainly more crisp, immediate than their analogue predecessors, yet the sound has a warmth that enhances the often very atmospheric playing; the mysterious *pianissimo* passages at the ends of the slow movements of Nos 3 and 6, for instance. The main difference in the playing is that the new performances are generally faster, brighter and rhythmically lighter, tending towards clearer articulation. The earlier version of No 2's highly ornamented *Adagio* has a beautiful sustained sound; in this recording Peter Cropper plays the melody with more fantasy, giving a powerful, rhetorical expression to each phrase. The slight increase in speed of most of the *allegros* brings them more into line with Beethoven's often challenging metronome marks – as a result there's more sparkle and excitement, and the light touch means there's rarely any sense of strain. The two Minuets, in Nos 4 and 5, benefit, too, from being played faster; the passionate C minor character in No 4 is brought out most persuasively. For the *Adagio* of No 6 the Lindsays, in common with most other groups, adopt a more flowing speed than Beethoven's very slow suggestion, and their new recording is noticeably faster than the old. Yet, this is one of the most finely played movements in the set, with soft, sensuous tone, delicate ornamentation, and mysterious, tenuous unisons.

For the *Adagio* of No 1, on the other hand, Beethoven provides what seems to be a very fast tempo (138 quavers to the minute). The Lindsays play it a good deal slower – their earlier version has a particularly impressive, concentrated atmosphere. The 1933 Busch Quartet recording, however, shows how it's possible for the movement to sound even more impressive at a speed close to Beethoven's mark; the fiercely dramatic interruptions lose the somewhat ponderous effect they have when taken more slowly.

With these much-recorded quartets – in their way just as challenging to the performers as the later works – it's impossible to have a single favourite version. The Alban Berg Quartet, as daring in their expressive range as The Lindsays, give an unrivalled spring to the more dance-like movements – No 5's Minuet, the *allegretto* section of No 6's finale. The Emerson Quartet, extraordinarily nimble and precise in the quicker music, impart a fizzy, *opera buffa* quality to No 3's finale. The Quartetto Italiano's 1970s recordings still sound amazingly fine – no daringly fast speeds here, but the most finely blended sound and nobility of expression. Into this Pantheon The Lindsays fit very easily. No group that brings out better the startling range of the youthful Beethoven's imagination.

String Quartets Nos 3 and 7
Orpheus Quartet (Charles-André Linale, Emilian Piedicuta *vns* Emile Cantor *va* Laurentiu Sbarcea *vc*)
Channel Classics CCS6094 (68 minutes: DDD) Ⓕ
Recorded 1993

The Orpheus Quartet does not use this music as a vehicle for its virtuosity or prowess; and they do not draw attention to their spot-on ensemble, immaculate intonation and tonal finesse, though they possess all these qualities in no small measure. Take the *Presto* finale of the D major. The sense of pace is in harmony with the horse-drawn rather than the jet-driven; every note speaks, every phrase tells and the overall effect is all the more exhilarating. Generally speaking, the Orpheus find the *tempo giusto* throughout. They remain attuned to the sensibility of the period and relate their pace to a dance movement in a manner that their rivals have lost. There is something very natural about the players' music-making. They are inside these scores and convey their involvement; no auto pilot, no *ersatz* feeling, no exaggerated or mechanised *sforzatos*. What a relief! The recording is bright and clean.

String Quartets Nos 7-9
The Lindsays (Peter Cropper, Ronald Birks *vns* Roger Bigley *va* Bernard Gregor-Smith *vc*)
ASV ② CDDCS207 (115 minutes: DDD) Ⓜ
Recorded 1984

In the few years that separate the Op 18 fromthe Op 59 quartets, Beethoven's world was shattered by the oncoming approach of deafness and the threat of growing isolation. The Op 59 consequently inhabit a totally different plane, one in which the boundaries of sensibility had been extended in much the same way as the map of Europe was being redrawn. Each of the three quartets alludes to a Russian theme by way of compliment to Count Rasumovsky, who had commissioned the set. The immediate impression the F major Quartet conveys is of great space, breadth and vision; this is to the quartet what the *Eroica* is to the symphony. Although The Lindsays may be rivalled (and even surpassed) in some of their insights by the Végh, taken by and large, they are second to none and superior to most. In each movement of the E minor they find the *tempo giusto* and all that they do as a result has the ring of complete conviction. The development and reprise of the first movement are repeated as well as the exposition and how imaginatively they play it too! The C major is not quite in the same class though the opening has real mystery and awe and some listeners might legitimately feel that the whole movement could do with a little more momentum. On the other hand, they move the second movement on rather too smartly. Yet how splendidly they convey the pent-up torrent of energy unleashed in this fugal onrush. Even if it does not command quite the same elevation of feeling or quality of inspiration that distinguishes their F major and E minor quartets, it is still pretty impressive.

The 'Late' String Quartets: Nos 12-16

String Quartets Nos 8 and 13
Talich Quartet (Petr Messiereur, Jan Kvapil *vns* Jan Talich *va* Evzen Rattai *vc*)
Calliope CAL9637 (73 minutes: ADD) Ⓕ
Recorded 1977-80

The advantage of this Talich recording is that it couples a masterpiece from Beethoven's middle period, the great E minor Quartet, with one of the greatest of his last years. The B flat was the third of the late quartets to be composed and at its first performance in 1826 its last movement, the *Grosse Fuge*, baffled his contemporaries. Later that same year, he substituted the present finale. The Talich Quartet has a no less impressive technical command than other ensembles but theirs are essentially private performances, which one is privileged to overhear rather than the overprojected 'public' accounts we so often hear on record nowadays.

String Quartets Nos 11 and 15
Végh Quartet (Sándor Végh, Sándor Zöldy *vns* Georges Janzer va Paul Szabó vc)
Auvidis Valois V4406 (68 minutes: ADD) Ⓕ
Recorded 1972-73 **OO**

String Quartets Nos 15 and 16
Talich Quartet (Petr Messiereur, Jan Kvapil *vns* Jan Talich *va* Evzen Rattai *vc*)
Calliope CAL9639 (68 minutes: ADD) Ⓕ
Recorded 1977-79 **O**

After the expansive canvas of the Op 59 Quartets and the *Eroica*, Beethoven's F minor Quartet, Op 95, displays musical thinking of the utmost compression. The first movement is a highly concentrated sonata design, which encompasses in its four minutes almost as much drama as a full-scale opera. With it comes one of the greatest masterpieces of his last years, the A minor, Op 132. The isolation wrought first by his deafness and secondly, by the change in fashion of which he complained in the early 1820s, forced Beethoven in on himself. Op 132 with its other-worldly *Heiliger Dankgesang*, written on his recovery from an illness, is music neither of the 1820s nor of Vienna, it belongs to that art which transcends time and place. Though other performances may be technically more perfect, these are interpretations that come closer to the spirit of this great music than any other on CD. The Talich Quartet's readings bring a total dedication to this music: their performances are innocent of artifice and completely selfless. There is no attempt to impress with their own virtuosity or to draw attention to themselves. The recordings are eminently faithful and natural, not overbright but the effect is thoroughly pleasing.

Beethoven String Quartet No 11
Schubert String Quartet No 15 in G, D887
Hagen Quartet (Lukas Hagen, Rainer Schmidt *vns* Veronika Hagen *va* Clemens Hagen *vc*)
DG 457 615-2GH (68 minutes: DDD) Ⓕ
Recorded 1996-98 **O**

This disc provides inspiring confirmation of how great music constantly renews itself. That 'perennial newness' is evident from the ferocious opening bars of Op 95 (more *furioso* than *serioso*), through the concise arguments that follow, to the *Allegretto*'s contrapuntal purity, the startled *Scherzo* and the nervously lilting finale. Virtually every bar carries its own neon light, whether read off the page or, as presented here, with maximum drama and inflexional expression. Schubert's glacial G major is given an even more remarkable reading. The Hagen's fine-tipped tone production accentuates the feeling of epic chill, as does the repeated six-minute exposition. That wonderful moment at 15'08" when the recapitulation summons a beam or two of sunlight comes off especially well, and so does the clipped return of the second set. The *Andante*'s opening melody is chaste and a little distracted, rather like a chamber-music equivalent of *Winterreise*'s hurdy-gurdy. The savage interjections at 2'54" have rarely sounded angrier (they gain a further notch of intensity for their second appearance at 6'27"), and the *Scherzo*'s tart outer sections are offset by a soft-textured Trio. The uneasy finale sounds like an inebriated half-brother to the parallel movement from *Death and the Maiden*, full of quiet point-making and ghostly half-lights. Attentive listening locates a wealth of colour in both performances and the recordings have impressive clarity.

String Quartets Nos 4 and 15
Petersen Quartet (Conrad Muck, Gernot Süssmuth *vns* Friedemann Weigle *va* Hans-Jakob Eschenburg *vc*)
Capriccio 10 722 (63 minutes: DDD) Ⓕ
Recorded 1995

The Petersen Quartet possesses impeccable technical address, immaculate ensemble, flawless intonation and tonal finesse. Tempos are judged with real musicianship, and dynamic markings are observed without being exaggerated. The C minor Quartet, Op 18 No 4, has dramatic tension without loss of lyrical fervour and the *Scherzo* has wit. When we move to the first movement of the A minor Quartet the sound world changes as if youth has given way to wisdom and experience. They hardly put a foot wrong here and their *Heiliger Dankgesang* is rapt and inward-looking. They press ahead fractionally in one or two places – on the reprise of the main section in the second movement and when the main theme returns in the finale. But one or two minor reservations apart, theirs is quite simply the most satisfying late Beethoven to have appeared in recent years. Above all the Petersen do not invite you to admire their prowess. They appear to be untouched by the three 'g's (Gloss, Glamour and Glitz) and their concern is with truth rather than beauty.

String Quartets Nos 10 and 12
Végh Quartet (Sándor Végh, Sándor Zöldy *vns* Georges Janzer *va* Paul Szabó *vc*)
Auvidis Valois V4405 (71 minutes: ADD) Ⓕ
Recorded 1973

String Quartets Nos 14 and 16
Végh Quartet
Auvidis Valois V4408 (66 minutes: ADD) Ⓕ
Recorded 1973

Beethoven stepped outside and beyond his period nowhere more so than in the late quartets and the last five piano sonatas. The Op 127 has been called Beethoven's 'crowning monument to lyricism', whilst the Op 131 is more inward-looking. Every ensemble brings a different set of insights to this great music so that it is not possible to hail any single quartet as offering the whole truth – yet these are as near to the whole truth as we are ever likely to come. The Végh give us music-making that has a profundity and spirituality that completely outweigh any tiny blemishes of intonation or ensemble. One does not get the feeling of four professional quartet players performing publicly for an audience but four thoughtful musicians sharing their thoughts about this music in the privacy of their own home. They bring us closer to this music than do any of their high-powered rivals.

String Quartets Nos 13 and 16.
Grosse Fuge in B flat, Op 133
Juilliard Quartet (Robert Mann, Joel Smirnoff *vns* Samuel Rhodes *va* Joel Krosnick *vc*)
Sony Classical SK62792 (76 minutes: DDD) Ⓕ
Recorded 1996

The Juilliard take Op 130's long first-movement repeat then play the *Grosse Fuge* as its rightful finale, relegating the lighter-hearted 'rewrite' to encore status at the very end of the piece. Hearing the fugue as a structural summation rather than a disembodied torso makes good musical sense (its replacement turns most of Op 130 into a sort of elevated divertimento), and the Juilliard's concentration more than justifies their decision. The performance itself is full of subtle beauties, not least in the first movement, at the point near the onset of the development (around 8'29") where *Allegro* fragments prompt *espressivo Adagio* responses and where the players gauge the music's oscillating moods with characteristic perception. Similarly, there is a sense of infinite sadness at 5'16" into the *Andante con moto* third movement, whereas the *Presto* and *Alla danza tedesca* are, by turns, fleeting and elegant; the *Grosse Fuge* struts, sings and swings, and the 'second' finale dances to a pointed *staccato*. This is profound, deeply pondered music-making, the sort that would be impossible to achieve in less than half a lifetime. Op 135 is similarly persuasive, with a playfully disruptive *Vivace*, a heart-rending *Lento assai* and, most significantly, an account of the finale that includes the important second repeat.

String Quartets Nos 15 and 16
Cleveland Quartet (William Preucil, Peter Salaff *vns* James Dunham *va* Paul Katz *vc*)
Telarc CD80427 (69 minutes: DDD) Ⓕ
Recorded 1995

The Cleveland Quartet are upholders of tradition, rather than seekers after new truths. One of this ensemble's most notable characteristics is its rich, warm tone, well captured here. The first movement of the A minor Quartet has a level of emotional commitment that's quite compelling – all the details of this complex music fall into place and contribute to the overall effect. If the rest isn't quite so outstanding it's still very good, with a lovely swinging rhythm to the second movement, and delightfully sprightly accounts of the *Andante* episodes in the slow movement – absolutely 'feeling new strength', as Beethoven's caption puts it. Their Op 135 is also very impressive. The *Lento* is deeply felt, their rich sound coming into its own. And the finale must be one of the best versions on record – spirited, touching, playful, as the music's mood demands.

Piano Trios

Piano Trios – E flat, Op 1 No 1; G, Op 1 No 2; C minor, Op 1 No 3; B flat, Op 11; D, Op 70 No 1, 'Ghost'; E flat, Op 70 No 2; B flat, Op 97, 'Archduke'; B flat, WoO39; E flat, WoO38; E flat, Op 44; G, Op 121*a*
Beaux Arts Trio (Daniel Guilet *vn* Bernard Greenhouse *vc* Menahem Pressler *pf*)
Philips The Early Years ③ 438 948-2PM3 Ⓜ
(235 minutes: ADD). Recorded 1965

The 'Ghost', the 'Archduke' and Op 11 are also available, remastered, on
Philips 50 Great Recordings 464 683-2PM Ⓜ

It's the immediacy and freshness, the wholehearted commitment of the playing by the Beaux Arts Trio that holds you spellbound. In the *joie de vivre* of the E flat and G major Op 1 Trios, it's so good to be reminded that a colossus like Beethoven was once so young at heart – in the persuasive lyricism of slower tempos no less than the teasing, devil-may-care sparkle and wit of their finales (taken at a breathless pace without for a moment sounding gabbled). The crowning performance is the *Archduke*. The players' expansive yet warmly human nobility in the opening *Allegro moderato*, their urgent, mercurial response to the undertones of the *Scherzo*, their raptness in the visionary serenity of the slow movement and their pungency in the finale convince you that no greater piano trio has ever been written. Here, too, you're given the fullest chance to enjoy the silken beauty of Guilet's violin and the velvet richness of Greenhouse's now legendary 1707 Stradivari cello; also the wonderful blend of tone achieved by all three in contexts like the *pizzicato/staccato* of the first movement's development, or the eerie chromatic start to the trio of the *Scherzo*. Hailed in the booklet as 'the soul of the entire ensemble', Pressler achieves many miracles of delicacy and fleetness.

String Trios, Op 9

No 1 in G, **No 2** in D, **No 3** in C minor

String Trio in E flat, Op 3; Serenade in D, Op 8
Leopold String Trio (Marianne Thorsen *vn* Sarah-Jane Bradley *va* Kate Gould *vc*)
Hyperion CDA67253 (73 minutes: DDD) Ⓕ
Recorded 1998 ●

String Trios, Op 9 Nos 1-3
Leopold String Trio
Hyperion CDA67254 (77 minutes: DDD) Ⓕ
Recorded 1998 ●

The Leopold String Trio have the kind of virtues that come from long study together: polished ensemble, excellent intonation and notably consistent and well-conceived interpretations. Just occasionally the viola is swamped by the outer voices, but this is only an infrequent problem; overall it's a particularly well-balanced and recorded set. They show that a restrained style can bring out the inward aspect to the music. On the fourth track of Op 8, where Beethoven alternates a sombre *Adagio* with a facetiously jolly *Scherzo*, the stark yet gentle Leopold playing of the slow music expresses more pathos and melancholy than the intensity of other versions. And the Leopold's care and respect for the text also tips the balance in its favour – in Op 3's second Minuet, for example, Marianne Thorsen's beautiful and exact interpretation is utterly winning. In Op 9 No 1's Scherzo, another splendidly poised and spirited reading, there's a special bonus – a second Trio, omitted from most editions. It's an attractive bit of music and gives the movement a new dimension.

Cello Sonatas

No 1 in F, Op 5 No 1; **No 2** in G minor, Op 5 No 2; **No 3** in A, Op 69; **No 4** in C, Op 102 No 1; **No 5** in D, Op 105 No 2

Beethoven Cello Sonatas Nos 1-5 **H**
Brahms Cello Sonata No 2 in F, Op 99
Pablo Casals *vc* **Mieczyslaw Horszowski, Otto Schulhof** *pfs*
EMI Références mono ② CHS5 65185-2 Ⓜ
(136 minutes: ADD). Recorded 1930-39 ●●

Sensitive phrasing was the very hub of Pablo Casals's art, and these CDs are more revealing than many of how this most communicative of cellists could mould and energise a musical line, reducing his tone to a soulful tenor then thrusting a powerful *sforzando* for maximum dynamic contrast. The Beethoven sonatas are endlessly rewarding in this respect, but even they must bow to the marginal supremacy of Casals's 1936 account of the Brahms F major Sonata. No one since has projected the work's heroic opening with as much confidence (the repeat is observed, by the way), nor brought greater suppleness or tonal variety to the *Adagio affettuoso*. Note, too, how both Casals and Horszowski explore the winding musical thickets of the *Allegro passionato* and make play with the closing *Allegro molto*.

The Beethoven sonatas are equally indelible, the Op 5 works sounding very much their innovatory selves, and those of Op 102 more probing and explosive than most. Both players invest Op 102 No 2's searching *Adagio con molto sentimento d'affetto* with an intriguing sense of the numinous, then dig deep into the succeeding *Allegro fugato* – a gritty debate on the preceding mystery.

Casals recorded the Op 69 Sonata some nine years before Opp 5 and 102, not with Horszowski, but with the stylish and facilitating Otto Schulhof. It differs from its companions in being more songful than soulful and with a *bel canto* solo line that extends to the charming Menuet makeweight. Recordings of this unique quality deserve painstaking restoration, and Andrew Walters's transfers are excellent.

Cello Sonatas Nos 2, 3 and 5 **P**
David Watkin *vc* **Howard Moody** *fp*
Chandos Chaconne CHAN0561 (70 minutes: DDD) Ⓕ
Recorded 1994 ●

If you're not sure about the advantages of original-instrument performance of classical chamber music, try this disc! Watkin and Moody demonstrate that 'authentic' Beethoven need not diminish the music's grandeur and emotional depth. David Watkin, very correctly, uses vibrato discreetly and selectively, and is most imaginative in finding just the right bowstroke for each musical nuance – his urgent phrasing of the G minor Sonata's first *Allegro*, and the way he breathes the phrases at the start of the D major's slow movement are two examples of many memorable details.

Howard Moody plays two original period instruments – a Rosenberger fortepiano of *c*1800 for the G minor Sonata, and an 1826 Graf for the two later works – and seems always able to find reserves of sonority to encompass Beethoven's most dramatic moments. The climactic codas of the A major Sonata's outer movements are especially exciting.

The 'big' feeling of these performances is partly due to the lively, intimate recording – the sound is not diluted in any large spaces and we can also hear quite a bit of mechanical noise from the piano, and sniffs from the players.

Complete Works for Cello and Piano

Cello Sonatas Nos 1-5.
12 Variations on Mozart's 'Ein Mädchen oder Weibchen', Op 66. 12 Variations on Handel's 'See the conqu'ring hero comes', WoO45. Seven Variations on Mozart's 'Bei Männern, welche Liebe fühlen', WoO46
Heinrich Schiff *vc* **Till Fellner** *pf*
Philips ② 462 601-2PH2 (140 minutes: DDD) Ⓕ
Recorded 1998

Schiff and Fellner for the most part give a suave, civilised impression of Beethoven; there are moments of profound contemplation, but fewer rough edges, fewer uncontrollable flights of passion than usual. Fellner's smooth, expressive touch and Schiff's warm, well-rounded tone make for particularly memorable interpretations of the more *cantabile* music: the opening *Allegro* of Op 69 doesn't want for energy, but the emphasis is on the beautifully shaped melodic lines. In one or two of the quicker movements, the playing is perhaps just *too* civilised – the first *Allegro* of Op 5 No 2 could have had more urgency and intensity (incidentally they omit all the long repeats in both Op 5 sonatas). The fugal finale of Op 102 No 2 sounds extraordinarily smooth and poised for such a notoriously knotty piece. That something is lost by such an approach is clear from a comparison with Maisky and Argerich's high-speed, explosively dynamic performance.

In lively movements Schiff sometimes plays the medium-fast detached notes very short and strongly accented, and fast passagework with a rather fierce off-the-string bow-stroke. His desire may be to achieve maximum clarity, but Fellner is so sensitive to balance that (on this very clear recording) the cello has no difficulty being heard and these very unclassical bowings can seem intrusive. What you remember most, though, are the beautifully realised introspective moments. All three variation sets are very fine – the brilliant piano passages in the two earlier works (WoO45 and Op 66) tossed off with unostentatious virtuosity, the dialogue between the instruments both playful and expressive.

Variations for Cello

12 Variations on Handel's 'See the conqu'ring hero comes', WoO45. 12 Variations on Mozart's 'Ein Mädchen oder Weibchen', Op 66. Seven Variations on Mozart's 'Bei Männern, welche Liebe fühlen', WoO46. Horn Sonata, Op 17 (arr vc) **P**

Pieter Wispelwey *vc* **Lois Shapiro** *fp*
Channel Classics CCS6494 (45 minutes: DDD) Ⓕ
Recorded 1994 ●

There are only 45 minutes of it, but this recital of Beethoven variations teems with fresh insights in the irresistible serendipity of its playing. Lois Shapiro partners Pieter Wispelwey's 1701 cello on a 1780 Viennese fortepiano whose wiry energies she unleashes without more ado in an attention-grabbing opening theme for Handel's *See the conqu'ring hero comes*. Her bright-eyed first variation glints as phrases dart from dynamic shadow to light and back again. Then the cello's lean, slightly astringent voice makes itself felt in no uncertain terms before the keyboard gets its own back in mercurial scale passages.

The players' delight in teasing, sparring and debating with each other comes into its own in the variations on *Ein Mädchen oder Weibchen*. The theme itself struts forward cheekily, only to peck its way through the first variation, before the cello makes the most of the wry harmonic subtext of the second. In the seventh, one half of a shared phrase caresses and preens the other; the 10th casts the shadow of Papageno's noose. Each player's imagination and technique is tested to the full in an absorbing account of the more abstracted *Bei Männern* variations. The world of *Singspiel* is not far away, either, in this performance of the Sonata in F major, Op 17: Wispelwey and Shapiro summon up the nascent world of Marzelline and Jacquino in their quick, ardent responses to the music and to each other.

Complete Violin Sonatas

No 1 in D, Op 12 No 1; **No 2** in A, Op 12 No 2; **No 3** in E flat, Op 12 No 3; **No 4** in A minor, Op 23; **No 5** in F, Op 24, 'Spring'; **No 6** in A, Op 30 No 1; **No 7** in C minor, Op 30 No 2; **No 8** in G, Op 30 No 3; **No 9** in A, Op 47, 'Kreutzer'; **No 10** in G, Op 96

Violin Sonatas Nos 1-10
Itzhak Perlman *vn* **Vladimir Ashkenazy** *pf*
Decca Ovation ④ 421 453-2DM4 Ⓜ
(239 minutes: ADD). Recorded 1973-75 ●●

Although Beethoven designated these works as 'for piano and violin', following Mozart's example, it is unlikely that he thought of the piano as leading the proceedings, or the violin either, for that matter: both instruments are equal partners and in that sense this is true chamber music. Perlman and Ashkenazy are artists of the first rank and there is much pleasure to be derived from their set. Such an imaginative musician as Ashkenazy brings great subtlety to these works composed by a supreme pianist-composer. And the better the pianist is in this music, the better does the violinist play. Discernment is matched by spontaneity and the whole series is remarkably fine, while their celebrated performance of the *Kreutzer* Sonata has quite superb eloquence and vitality. The recording boasts unusually truthful violin sound capturing all the colour of Perlman's playing.

Violin Sonatas Nos 1-10 **H**
Wolfgang Schneiderhan *vn* **Wilhelm Kempff** *pf*
DG The Originals ③ 463 605-2GOR3 Ⓜ
(236 minutes: ADD). Recorded 1952

In the 1950s these recordings would have probably given a very up-to-date impression; the playing is extremely clean – there's never a hint of sentimental violin slides or over use of the sustaining pedal. But nearly half a century later, perhaps we're more conscious of the old-world virtues – Schneiderhan's beautiful *legato* bowing and gentle vibrato, Kempff's full, unforced tone, and a flexible approach from both artists, with finely graded *ritardandos* and subtle variations of tempo. The first movement of Op 96 offers one of the best illustrations of their style; moments of intense passion and sudden bursts of energy providing vivid contrast to the tranquil overall mood.

Though not regular sonata partners, Kempff and Schneiderhan have an admirable collective sense of rhythm. They favour moderate, poised speeds, and so tend to miss something of the impulsive quality of early Beethoven. And, in the same way, their dedication to pure, well-balanced, unforced tone means that the grotesque element in such a movement as the finale of Op 30 No 2 is underplayed. It is a delight to hear them find so many ways of interpreting Beethoven's frequent *sforzando* markings, from sharp accents to the expressive melodic emphasis they give to the theme of the *Kreutzer* Sonata's variations. But quite often Kempff downgrades or ignores these accents, smoothing away any angular corners, and this tendency towards blandness occasionally leads to disappointingly inexpressive playing, at the start of the *Spring* Sonata, for instance, where Schneiderhan's beautifully lyrical opening doesn't elicit a comparable response from the piano.

If there are a few let-downs, however, there are far more moments where the characteristically moderate, unexaggerated approach bears rich dividends: at the beginning of Op 47, where the meticulous slow introduction generates a strong feeling of suspense, or the gentle *allegretto con variazioni* finales of Op 30 No 1 and Op 96, whose memorable melodic qualities, plus many fascinating details of harmony and texture, are brought into sharp relief.

Schneiderhan's beautiful singing tone is a constant delight; witness the intensely vocal style of Op 24's finale and the luminous sound of his high register in the last of the *Kreutzer* variations. Similarly, Kempff's continual care for clear textures and his finely balanced chordal playing seem to offer glimpses into the essence of Beethoven's thought. The mono sound is beautifully clear and well balanced; squeezed onto three discs (some repeats are omitted), this distinguished set is quite a bargain.

Violin Sonatas

Violin Sonatas Nos 6-8
Gidon Kremer *vn* **Martha Argerich** *pf*
DG 445 652-2GH (64 minutes: DDD) Ⓕ
Recorded [illegible] ●

Beethoven's Op 30 Violin Sonatas are three irresistibly lively and individual spirits in the hands and imaginations of Martha Argerich and Gidon Kremer. The first, in A major, has that particular quality of blithe and elusive joy reminiscent of the *Spring* Sonata, and created here by the lightest and truest touch on string and key, fused with bright rhythmic clarity. The slow movement is a tremulous song of long-forgotten, far-off things, in which violin and piano find an intimate balance of tone.

The second sonata of the group is here less an heroically clenched C minor fist, more the unfolding of a gripping and tense *Märchen*: a dark children's fairy-tale told through the rapid tapering of a phrase-ending on the violin, the gutsy ebb and flow of a piano *crescendo*, the sudden *pianissimo* picking up after the loud chords of a second theme. At the start of the development, Argerich even seems to be asking if her listeners are sitting comfortably – and rather hoping they are not.

The G major Sonata's centrepiece is its Minuet and Trio, which Argerich and Kremer cunningly tease and charm into revealing its archaic qualities: a dance glimpsed through a lace veil. It is framed by two fast movements that would identify their performers anywhere, with their high-voltage velocity and wittily imaginative anticipation of each other's every move.

Andante favori

Beethoven Andante favori in F, WoO57
Chopin Waltzes, Op 34 – No 2 in A flat; No 3 in A minor; No 4 in F. Scherzo No 2 in B flat minor, Op 31. Barcarolle in F sharp, Op 60
Debussy Suite bergamasque. Estampes
Sviatoslav Richter *pf*
Orfeo d'Or C491981B (75 minutes: ADD) Ⓜ
Recorded live in 1977 **OO**

This live Richter recital from Salzburg must go close to the top of the priority list. Unlike some of his other live recordings, it's superbly recorded, with plenty of air in the sound and an instrument capable of withstanding fairly imperious *fortissimos* without losing its tonal bloom or firmness of tuning. The *Andante favori* is a gem of a performance, tonally ravishing yet unerringly responsive to the structural flow. In the Chopin group Richter not only displays his customary authority but revels in the music and the occasion. Abandon without indiscipline is the key, and the result is a tremendous sense of *élan*, bordering on exaltation; the applause and bravos between each piece seem only fitting. Debussy's *Suite bergamasque* goes like a dream, with a 'Clair de lune' hypnotically slow yet never in danger of becoming merely prosaic, thanks to sheer beauty of sonority and hypersensitive weighting of harmony. Richter's concentration wavers a little more in *Estampes*, but what a treasurable recital this is otherwise.

Bagatelles

Bagatelles – Op 33; Op 119; Op 126; A minor, WoO59, 'Für Elise'[a]; B flat, WoO60. Rondo in C, Op 51 No 1. Allegretto in C minor, WoO53
Alfred Brendel *pf*
Philips 456 031-2PH (77 minutes: DDD) Ⓕ
Recorded 1996, item marked [a]1984

Listening to Beethoven's *Bagatelles* can be like looking over the composer's shoulder as he works. A scrap of a theme, a repeated chord, a formulaic accompanying figure – suddenly blossoms into something rich and strange; the one-dimensional turns magically into the three-dimensional. An unassuming little *Andante con moto* tune dissolves into a cadenza, then emerges transfigured in ecstatic counterpoint (Op 126 No 1); an innocent, almost plain folk-melody reappears floating on high, a voice from another world (Op 119 No 11). And so often in the *Bagatelles* humour is at the core. If there's such a thing as profound levity, this is it. Brendel, who has written so effectively about humour in Beethoven, plainly revels in this aspect of the *Bagatelles*. The quirkiness, the delight in pulling the rug from under the listener's feet – he seems to have made it all his own. One could argue with the approach here or there – Op 119 No 5 strikes one as more laboured than *Risoluto*; the strange half-pedal at the end of Op 119 No 3 produces a momentarily metallic aura around the notes – but much more often, character and texture are calculated to a nicety. He also conveys a sense of Op 126 as – in Beethoven's own words – a 'cycle of *Bagatelles*', the extraordinary No 11 (a gorgeous *Andante amabile*) making a very thought-provoking finale.

Bagatelles – Op 33; Op 119; C minor, WoO52; C, WoO56. Rondos – Op 51: No 1 in C; No 2 in G; C, WoO48; A, WoO49. Six Minuets, WoO10. Polonaise in C, Op 89. Andante favori in F, WoO57. Variations – Six in F on an Original Theme, Op 34; Nine in C minor on a March by Dressler, WoO63; Six in F on a Swiss Song, WoO64; 24 in D on Righini's 'Venni amore', WoO65; 12 in C on Haibel's 'Menuet à la Viganò', WoO68; Six in G on Paisiello's 'Nel cor più non mi sento', WoO70
Mikhail Pletnev *pf*
DG ② 457 493-2GH2 (152 minutes: DDD) Ⓕ
Recorded 1997

From the very first notes of the *Dressler* Variations – Beethoven's first-known composition, dating from 1782 – it is clear that Pletnev is a master of piano texture, and that he is going to use his mastery not only to ravish the ear but also to delight the mind. His nuances in the baby-simple Swiss theme and its artless variations, lasting barely three minutes in total, are quite delicious. At the opposite extreme, the grand set of 24 Variations on Righini's 'Venni amore' comes across as a dry run for later cycles such as the *Eroica* or even the *Diabelli* Variations, both in overall design and in certain idiosyncratic details. Technical tours de force abound here, and Pletnev negotiates them all not only with phenomenal pianistic aplomb but, where appropriate, with dry wit. This makes for a fascinating glimpse into the laboratory of the 20-year-old Beethoven's mind.

In the two early Rondos Pletnev is freer than some might wish with the notated dynamics, phrasing and articulation, and his touch suggests at times that he is thinking more of Scarlatti than of Beethoven. Nevertheless the most startling moments of whimsy in these pieces are not his but the composer's. By contrast, in the Vienna-period Rondos of Op 51 (actually much earlier works than that opus number suggests) Pletnev seems to be thinking forward to the age of Lisztian rhetoric. But the fact that he is never satisfied with the default response to the surface of the music is much to be welcomed, and almost always his initiatives are stylish and effective.

Similarly the bagatelles radiate openness to all sorts of possibilities, from which you can be fairly sure that one of the less obvious and more delightful is going to be selected. In some instances Brendel finds more of a rough-and-tumble edginess; but Pletnev's range of touch and tonal nuance outstrips them both and brings rewards of its own, as in the proto-Schubertian touches of Op 119.

Instrument and recording quality are as near to ideal as we are entitled to expect, and the authority of Barry Cooper's annotations adds to the attractions of an outstanding issue.

Diabelli Variations

33 Variations on a Waltz by Diabelli, Op 120

Alfred Brendel *pf*
Philips 426 232-2PH (53 minutes: DDD) Ⓕ
Recorded 1988

Stephen Kovacevich *pf*
Philips Concert Classics 422 969-2PCC Ⓑ
(54 minutes: ADD). Recorded 1969

Here is a treat, indeed; for in Brendel and Kovacevich we have two of the gramophone's finest interpreters of the *Diabelli* Variations. Brendel has now recorded the work three times. His live 1977 recording of the work, made by Philips in collaboration with the BBC, is still something of a landmark. The piano itself may sound a trifle battle-weary by the end, but the performance is a *tour de force*, a finely thought-out reading seemingly improvised into life with astonishing fire and intellectual acumen. By contrast, this 1988 recording is a calmer affair and this relates not so much to tempos but the general mood. We are off the hustings and back in the study. This version is more measured as befits a reading that works its way slightly more circumspectly to the newly poised expressiveness of the final variations, the concluding Minuet now an even more sophisticated essay in sublime gracefulness.

The reissue of Kovacevich's famous recording does, however, present a considerable challenge to Brendel. The reissue is at bargain-price and though the booklet is bereft of notes, the CD has the full range of cueing points and the sound has almost as much clarity and bloom as the 1988 rival. Kovacevich was a pupil of Dame Myra Hess and his performance has a clarity, poise and vitality that has commended itself to more than one generation of collectors over the past 30 years. It is a performance that avoids other people's mistakes – whilst teaching us to relish uncomplicated skill. Try the Variations Nos 25-27 and you will find playing that is sensitive and exciting but quite unselfregarding; and even where Kovacevich adopts slow tempos, as in Var 14, there is always light in the texture and the rhythms are cleanly sculpted. Where the *Diabelli* is concerned one version can never be enough but Kovacevich remains the safest recommendation.

Diabelli Variations. 32 Variations on an Original Theme in C minor, WoO80
Benjamin Frith *pf*
ASV Quicksilva CDQS6155 (62 minutes: DDD) Ⓢ
Recorded 1990 ◯◯

This bargain on ASV's super-budget Quicksilva label offers a currently almost unbeatable coupling of the *Diabelli* Variations and the *32 Variations on an Original Theme*. Benjamin Frith is one of those artists whose musical perceptions are not to be doubted, and whose playing is almost never troubled by technical blemishes, and certainly not here. In short, both performances are masterly, the interpretations clearly thought through, concentrated in tension and feeling. With excellent recording this disc is unsurpassed, even by Brendel who, of course, has his own insights to offer in the *Diabelli*. But then so has Frith, and very impressive they are too.

Further listening
Six Variations in F on an Original Theme, Op 34. Six Variations in D, Op 76. 15 Variations and a Fugue on an Original Theme in E flat, Op 35, 'Eroica'
Coupling: **Schumann** Etudes symphoniques, Opp 13 and posth
Sviatoslav Richter *pf*
Olympia OCD339 (77 minutes: ADD) Ⓕ

Fantastic performances: the *Eroica* Variations end with Richter playing most pianists under the table. A disc not to be missed.

Complete Piano Sonatas

No 1 in F minor, Op 2 No 1; **No 2** in A, Op 2 No 2; **No 3** in C, Op 2 No 3; **No 4** in E flat, Op 7; **No 5** in C minor, Op 10 No 1; **No 6** in F, Op 10 No 2; **No 7** in D, Op 10 No 3; **No 8** in C minor, Op 13, 'Pathétique'; **No 9** in E, Op 14 No 1; **No 10** in G, Op 14 No 2; **No 11** in B flat, Op 22; **No 12** in A flat, Op 26; **No 13** in E flat, Op 27 No 1, 'quasi una fantasia'; **No 14** in C sharp minor, Op 27 No 2, 'Moonlight'; **No 15** in D, Op 28, 'Pastoral'; **No 16** in G, Op 31 No 1; **No 17** in D minor, Op 31 No 2 'Tempest'; **No 18** in E flat, Op 31 No 3; **No 19** in G minor, Op 49 No 1; **No 20** in G, Op 49 No 2; **No 21** in C minor, Op 53, 'Waldstein'; **No 22** in F, Op 54; **No 23** in F minor, Op 57 'Appassionata'; **No 24** in F sharp, Op 78; **No 25** in G, Op 79; **No 26** in E flat, Op 81*a*, 'Les adieux'; **No 27** in E minor, Op 90; **No 28** in A, Op 101; **No 29** in B flat, Op 106, 'Hammerklavier'; **No 30** in E, Op 109; **No 31** in A flat, Op 110; **No 32** in C minor, Op 111

Piano Sonatas Nos 1-32
Alfred Brendel *pf*
Philips ⑩ 446 909-2PH10 (656 minutes: DDD) Ⓕ
Recorded 1994-96; No 29 live in February 1995 ◯◯

Also available separately – *442 124-2PH*: Nos 1-3 (70 minutes). *446 624-2PH*: Nos 4, 15 and 20 (65 minutes). *446 664-2PH*: Nos 5-7 (59 minutes). *442 774-2PH:* Nos 8-11 (75 minutes). *438 863-2PH:* Nos 12-14 and 19 (60 minutes). *438 134-2PH:* Nos 16-18 (72 minutes). *438 472-2PH:* Nos 21, 22 and 28 (68 minutes). *442 787-2PH:* Nos 23-25 and 27 (59 minutes). *446 093-2PH*: Nos 26 and 29 (62 minutes). *446 701-2PH*: Nos 30-32 (66 minutes)

Intensity is very much the order of the day in this latest sonata cycle, a throwing open of the gates, with a far greater use of declamatory effects and rhetorical tropes than was the case in either of his two earlier cycles. Nos 4, 15 and 20: Brendel's reading of the *Pastoral* has changed – and its status has stratospherically soared – in two interrelated respects. In the first place, the two outer movements are both slower than on either the 1960s Turnabout or 1970s Philips recordings. Some will think the opening movement too slow, but that would be to ignore the thrilling way he now opens up the musical argument. What we have here is not some amiable musical ramble; rather, it is a multi-layered music-drama in which the pianist's relish in debating the issues the music is already asking itself makes for the most exhilarating kind of listening. Nos 12-14 and 19: Beethoven's description of the two Op 27 sonatas as *quasi una fantasia* may refer primarily to structure, but it is the element of the fantastic that is most missing: in No 13 the quirky turns of harmony and texture in the opening *Andante-Allegro* or the surprise return of the *Adagio* just before the end, in the 'Moonlight' (No 14) the equally surprising appearance of the light-footed Minuet after the sad, introverted musing of the opening *Adagio*. No, for Op 27 it's in the 1960s cycle that you find him at his most penetrating.

Nos 16-18: The highlight of Op 31 here is the Tempest: it is a perceptive reading in which the thematic threads scattered across the piece are revealed with great artistry. Nos 21, 22 and 28: Brendel displays a technical mastery and visionary quality which surpasses his own previous fine recordings of these three sonatas. In the *Waldstein* (No 21), his sense of line and standard of pianism falls only marginally short of Gilels's superb 1972 version. Nos 23-25 and 27: Something about the proceedings in these recordings has resulted in an unwelcome monumental quality being imparted to the music. It comes and goes; at its worst it makes you feel Beethoven is being set down on tablets of stone rather than borne aloft. As to the sound, which is predominantly neutral, we are quite close to the instrument – Brendel's sing-along is audible in the first movement of Op 90 – and the sonorities tend to register as chunky and rather airless. Yet, in Op 90 Brendel makes the sun come out magically at the beginning of the second movement, after a true pianissimo at the close of the first. It is this performance along with that of the Appassionata that are the best here.

Nos 26 and 29: Brendel said that this was the last recording of the *Hammerklavier* Sonata we would have from him. He felt that this one, given in Vienna in the Musikverein, was good enough to be 'a decent way of leaving the piece'. There can be no doubt about that for Brendel is at his very best. The fusion of sound and sense is thrilling, the pianism marvellous – an object-lesson in how technique, at this level, is a matter of knowing what you're doing and of fortune favouring the brave. Hats off! The recording is a good one, and the distance from the sound is just right, with a wide dynamic range defined at all levels. Brendel in *Les adieux* – less agitated, warmer and more relaxed than many players – is very enjoyable, but the gem of these two is the *Hammerklavier*.

Nos 30-32: What does one do about a performance so satisfying that, after it, even single well-honed sentence seems an irrelevance? Retire, possibly, and devote oneself to a more useful and benign trade such as growing vegetables. So much, then, for his Op 109. As for Op 111, a brute of a thing to interpret, Brendel has always been one of its most lucid exponents, neither stalling the introduction, which he plays with a well-nigh ideal blend of grandeur and impetus, nor mismanaging the shifting pulses of the subsequent *Allegro con brio ed appassionato*. Brendel plays the whole of Op 110 superbly too. His playing is lucidity itself, in a way that seems at once natural, moving, and true to the letter of Beethoven's text.

Piano Sonatas Nos 1-32
Richard Goode *pf*
Nonesuch ⑩ 7559-79328-2 (608 minutes: DDD) Ⓜ
Recorded 1990s ●●

Until the last few years Richard Goode was active principally as an ensemble player in chamber music, a field in which he excels. There is some unevenness of achievement in his playing but the level, in general, is wonderfully high, with no lapses from grace. Everything demands assessment in the company of the best there is. The interpretation of the A major Sonata, Op 101, is one of the finest ever put on record. Reservations? You may have a doubt as to whether all the playing represents everything Goode is capable of: sometimes he disappoints, slightly, by appearing to hold back from the listener the boldness and fullness of communication the greatest players achieve. One might say that, for all their insight and illumination, some of the performances lack the final leap and a degree of transcendence. A quality often to be observed in Goode is allure. Maybe that is why his playing is so very likeable: the finish of his playing, technical and musical, is immaculate but on top of that he is exciting. His sound always makes you listen. His feeling for it and for fine gradations of sound from one end of his wide dynamic range to the other are those of a virtuoso and inform everything he does. And when he's more obviously on virtuoso territory, he responds to the demands for brilliance and thrilling projection as to the manner born. He is constantly inside the music, and what a lively, cultivated, lucid and stimulating guide he is. There is nothing diffident or half-hearted about the way he makes this cycle of Beethoven resound wonderfully, the earlier sonatas appearing as no less masterly or characteristic of their composer than the later.

Piano Sonatas Nos 1-32 🄷
Artur Schnabel *pf*
EMI Références mono ⑧ CHS7 63765-2 Ⓜ
(605 minutes: ADD). Recorded 1932-38 ●●

Schnabel was almost ideologically committed to extreme tempos; something you might say Beethoven's music thrives on, always provided the interpreter can bring it off. By and large he did. There are some famous gabbles in this sonata cycle, notably at the start of the *Hammerklavier*, with him going for broke. In fact, Schnabel also held that 'It is a mistake to imagine that all notes should be played with equal intensity or even be clearly audible. In order to clarify the music it is often necessary to make certain notes obscure.' If it is true, as some contemporary witnesses aver, that Schnabel was a flawless wizard in the period pre-1930, there is still plenty of wizardry left in these post-1930 Beethoven recordings. They are virtuoso readings that demonstrate a blazing intensity of interpretative vision as well as breathtaking manner of execution. Even when a dazzlingly articulate reading like that of the *Waldstein* is home and dry, the abiding impression in its aftermath is one of Schnabel's (and Beethoven's) astonishing physical and imaginative daring. And if this suggests recklessness, well, in many other instances the facts are quite other, for Schnabel has a great sense of decorum.

He can, in many of the smaller sonatas and some of the late ones, be impeccably mannered, stylish and urbane. Equally he can be devilish or coarse. At the other extreme, he is indubitably the master of the genuinely slow movement. Listen to the way that from the earliest sonatas to the final movement of No 32, he is able to reconcile a calm and concentrated slowness with a breathing pulse and stirring inner life that is beyond the wit of most latter-day imitators.

For the recorded sound, CD is a godsend. There is nothing that can be done about the occasional patch of wow or discoloration but, in general, the old recordings come up very freshly.

Piano Sonatas Nos 1-32
Wilhelm Kempff *pf*
DG Dokumente mono ⑧ 447 966-2GDO8 (511 minutes: ADD). Includes bonus disc, 'Wilhelm Kempff – An All-Round Musician'.
Recorded 1951-56

Wilhelm Kempff was the most inspirational of Beethoven pianists. Those who have cherished his earlier stereo cycle for its magical spontaneity will find Kempff's qualities even more intensely conveyed in this mono set, recorded between 1951 and 1956. Amazingly the sound has more body and warmth than the stereo, with Kempff's unmatched transparency and clarity of articulation even more vividly caught, both in sparkling *Allegros* and in deeply dedicated slow movements. If in places he is even more personal, some might say wilful, regularly surprising you with a new revelation,the magnetism is even more intense, as in the great *Adagio* of the *Hammerklavier* or the final variations of Op 111, at once more rapt and more impulsive, flowing more freely.

The bonus disc, entitled 'An All-Round Musician', celebrates Kempff's achievement in words and music, on the organ in Bach, on the piano in Brahms and Chopin as well as in a Bachian improvisation, all sounding exceptionally transparent and lyrical. Fascinatingly, his pre-war recordings of the Beethoven sonatas on 78s are represented too. Here we have his 1936 recording of the *Pathétique*, with the central *Adagio* markedly broader and more heavily pointed than in the mono LP version of 20 years later.

Piano Sonatas – Nos 1-32; E flat, WoO47 No 1; F minor, WoO47 No 2; D, WoO47 No 3. Andante favori in F, WoO57
Malcolm Bilson, Tom Beghin, David Breitman, Bart van Oort, Ursula Dütschler, Zvi Meniker, Andrew Willis *fps*
Claves ⑩ CD50-9707/10 (689 minutes: DDD)
Recorded 1996

It is easy to point out the fortepiano's shortcomings, especially in the middle to late works of Beethoven. It isn't simply that the tone – somewhere between a small upright piano and a harpsichord – takes a lot of getting used to. There's the limited sustaining power – pitifully limited in the singing high notes of the first-movement *Allegro* of *Les adieux*, or the lilting Menuetto of No 7. Could this really be the sound Beethoven heard in his head, or was his imagination already straining ahead of its time? But the instruments included in this set were the kind of pianos at which Beethoven played and composed. He knew their capabilities and limitations better than we do. There may be good reasons for preferring the modern concert grand, but reject the fortepiano utterly and you miss revelations. For a start, some passages sound surprisingly beautiful: the ethereal trills and pulsations in the finale of No 32; the ecstatic final climax (again trill-dominated) of No 30. The players – respectively Tom Beghin and Malcolm Bilson – deserve a lot of the credit, of course, but these moments do show how responsive fortepianos can be, even in late Beethoven.

Then there are passages where Beethoven's instrument actually scores above the modern piano. Textures like the racing left-hand quavers in the *Scherzo* of No 12 can be transformed – rarely before has this sounded so incisive and gripping. Then there's the so-called *una corda* ('one string') pedal, which turns the usual percussive brightness into something duller and more mysterious. Beethoven clearly asks for this in the slow movement of No 28, requesting a gradual return to full strings in the slow cadenza writing at the end. And all credit to Bilson for bravely taking Beethoven's instructions in the first movement of the *Moonlight* (No 14) at face value ('*pianissimo* throughout and with raised dampers') – the result is, well, at least interesting. The performances most notable for character or musical intelligence turn out to be by Malcolm Bilson. Tom Beghin and Ursula Dütschler are also consistently impressive. Certainly they're never dull; and however quirky Bilson can be on occasion, he avoids the affected rubato of some of his colleagues.

Recording tone varies, suggesting very mixed venues, from relatively spacious rooms to intimate salons; none are too close to the instrument, though. Not a Beethoven sonata set to treasure for all time maybe, but one that offers unique illuminations.

Piano Sonatas

74321-30459-2 – Piano Sonatas Nos 4[b], 13[c], 14[c] and 24[c]
74321-30460-2 – Piano Sonatas Nos 5-7[b] and 26[b]
74321-27762-2 – Piano Sonatas Nos 1-3[a]
74321-27764-2 – Piano Sonatas Nos 8[b], 12[b], 27[b], 28[b]
Alfredo Perl *pf*
Arte Nova Classics 74321-30459/60-2, 27762/64-2 (oas: 73, 72, 73 and 74 minutes: DDD)
Recorded [a]1992-93, [b]1994, [c]1995

Alfredo Perl does not follow the sonatas strictly in sequence: this may irritate some collectors, but it does allow each disc to stand as an independent 'recital' while also forming just one part of the complete journey. There is an enormous amount to celebrate in these performances. The rhythmic power of these works is communicated with a genuine sense of enjoyment, and one of the most striking features of Perl's playing, particularly in the outer movements, is that he never shies away from the *sforzandos* or the *subito pianos* which are so important to Beethoven's style. Indeed, he attacks these dynamic accents and contrasts with such dramatic rigour that certain movements – the finale to the *Moonlight*, for example – are animated with a rare vitality. It is in the more highly charged movements where Perl is most compelling (the outer movements of the *Pathétique*, the opening movement of Op 10 No 1, and the finales of Op 2 No 1 and Op 10 No 2). The A major Sonata, Op 101, receives a tremendous performance, both musically and technically, and the second movement in particular is a marvel of understated virtuosity. In the movements of more lyrical simplicity Perl can be less convincing. In the second movement of Op 90, for example, he does not make the piano sing, and his tone can occasionally sound a little bland. His *fortes*, too, can be rather hard-edged, although the bright recording does not help him here. Perl's tempos have been the cause of some debate: he favours extremes, juxtaposing especially rapid fast movements with protracted slow movements. In Op 101, for example, he follows the march-like second movement, taken dangerously fast, with a particularly drawn-out *Adagio*.

If you wish to sample just one disc from this series to get a flavour of Perl's playing, then try Vol 4 (ranging from the *Pathétique* to Op 101). Perl has entered a hugely competitive field, but once his cycle is complete it could be one of the finest versions by a young pianist to have emerged in recent years.

SBT1188 – Piano sonatas – Nos 1[b]; 3[a]; 32[a] H
SBT1189 – Piano sonatas – Nos 7de; 8[a]; 13[d]; 14[b]
SBT1190 – Piano sonatas – Nos 17[c]; 18[c]; 21[b]; 22[a]
SBT1191 – Piano sonatas – Nos 26[b]; 27[de]; 29[b]
SBT1192 – Piano sonatas – Nos 23[c]; 28[c]; 30[a]; 31[d]
Solomon *pf*
Testament mono/[e]stereo SBT1188-92 Ⓕ
(oas: 73, 78, 80, 78 and 79 minutes: ADD)
Recorded [a]1951, [b]1952, [c]1954, [d]1956

By the autumn of 1956, when a stroke ended Solomon's career at the absurdly early age of 54, he had recorded 18 of the Beethoven piano sonatas, 12 of which had been released. Had his career continued, the cycle would almost certainly have been revised and completed. The immediate rivals would have been the two cycles Wilhelm Kempff recorded for Deutsche Grammophon (mono 1951-56, stereo 1964-65) and the pre-war Schnabel recordings which EMI reissued in its series Great Recordings of the Century in 1963-64. In the event, Solomon's cycle remained incomplete, as did later Emil Gilels's not dissimilar DG cycle.

Some will fret over this but sanguine folk will reflect that all the 'important' sonatas are here in performances that can generally be reckoned 'representative'. Testament's Paul Baily has done a first-rate job on the transfers and the layouts: five CDs, each packed to the gunnels, each logically planned. The only sonata that is significantly out of sequence is Op 111 (No 32) yet that, curiously, is the one performance from among the late, great sonatas which isn't entirely up to scratch. Here one does think back to Schnabel. Alongside Schnabel's not dissimilar reading, Solomon's sounds scampered (in the first movement), lacking in depth (in the second), and oddly unspontaneous, as though haunted by the knowledge of the older reading. The rather hollow-sounding 1951 recording doesn't help.

Op 111 is coupled here (SBT1188) with two of the Op 2 sonatas (Nos 1 and 3), the playing by turns fiery and lucid, gracious and gay. If anything is missing, it is the sense of tragic pathos Schnabel finds in the slow movement of the C major Sonata and his radical recklessness of spirit in the two finales.

The second disc contains celebrated readings of the *Moonlight* (No 14) and the *Pathétique* (No 8). Solomon's reading of the opening movement of the *Moonlight* is famously long-breathed, his reading of the opening movement of the *Pathétique*, and the *Moonlight*'s finale, wonderfully tense and austere.

The remaining three discs are, quite simply, indispensable, Solomon at the peak of his powers as a Beethoven player. In sonata after sonata, we hear virtuosity of the finest and most discriminating kind put at the service of some of the loftiest yet at the same time physically beautiful and physically exciting music known to man. Solomon was famous for the Cistercian clarity of his quick playing (the *Waldstein* – No 21, and *Appassionata* – No 23, sonatas *passim*) and for the concentrated calm of his playing of the great slow movements (this 1952 recording of the *Hammerklavier* – No 29, as fine an example as any). Underpinning both these phenomena is a quality of dynamic control that both gratifies the eye (Beethoven's text lifted off the page with rare precision) and bewitches the ear. It is this latter point which gives Solomon his special ability to define for us that element of unalloyed wonder in Beethoven's writing, those moments when we are brought to what T S Eliot calls 'the still point of the turning world'.

There are minor disappointments on each of these three final discs. The 1951 recording of Op 54 (SBT1190) is dowdily recorded and would almost certainly have been remade had circumstances allowed. Both the 1956 Op 90 (SBT1191) and the 1954 Op 101 (SBT1192) are good without being a match for what we have elsewhere on the discs. In the case of Op 90, this is Solomon's legendary elucidation of the *Hammerklavier* Sonata and his well-nigh definitive account of *Les adieux* (No 26), a performance, humane and vivid, that is fine almost beyond belief.

Piano Sonatas Nos 5 and 32. 32 Variations on an Original Theme in C minor, WoO80
Lars Vogt *pf*
EMI CDC5 56136-2 (55 minutes: DDD) Ⓕ
Recorded 1995 ●

Beethoven in C minor (No 5): now here's a subject worthy of cogitation. Vogt constructs such a journey here, opting to see Beethoven through the prism of three essays in C minor taken from different periods of the composer's career, before, in the concluding measures of Op 111 (No 32), he arrives at what Browning famously called 'my resting-place', 'The C major of this life'. As a concept, this disc is fascinating and delightful, not least because it allows one to set speculation and a spirit of musical and psychological enquiry over 'interpretation' and the tyranny of comparisons.

Here, it is enough to hear and enjoy the disc *through*, for its own sake. As befits a programme of variations and sonata-form movements in C minor and related keys, the playing is brilliant in tempo and tone (the execution more or less flawless), severe yet 'fine' when needs be: as in the hauntingly beautiful phrases in rising sequence shortly after the start of the slow movement of the Fifth Sonata. The playing in the outer movements of this sonata is not, in itself, especially witty, but the rapidity and precision of his delivery of Beethoven's lines constitute a form of pleasure in their own right.

The EMI recording is very brilliant, a touch light-headed perhaps, though with a very respectable bass presence. This isn't soul music – at least, not until the concluding movement of No 32. Its main aim is to divert, challenge, and delight; and in that it succeeds magnificently.

Piano Sonatas Nos 8-11
Stephen Kovacevich *pf*
EMI CDC5 56586-2 (70 minutes: DDD). Ⓕ
Recorded 1997 ●

There are performances that take you through a familiar work as though you were hearing it for the first time. Stephen Kovacevich's version of Beethoven's *Pathétique* is one of those. It's hard to analyse what it is that makes it so fresh. On the face of it, nothing about his interpretation is strikingly or provocatively 'new' – no unusual tempos or articulation of phrases. But there's so much life, evident in crisp, muscular rhythms, *crescendos* that draw you forward in your seat, and tender, confidential lyricism. The recording helps, bringing out the power and brilliance, without losing sense of the subtlety of the playing in more intimate passages. There are similar qualities in the other three sonatas – though not always so consistently. Energy and humour in the *Andante* variations and *Scherzo* finale of Op 14 No 2 seem just right; but the opening *Allegro* could perhaps be a little lighter and more intimate. The Rondo finale of Op 11 starts a little soberly – but wit and the lighter touch aren't absent for long. The rest of the performance (especially the first two movements) makes one wonder why this sonata so rarely turns up in concert programmes. There were no causes for critical doubt in Op 14 No 1, only pleasure, and renewed wonder at Beethoven's brilliance and originality. That's typical of Kovacevich's playing. He's no pianistic egoist, using Beethoven's ideas as a medium to demonstrate his own genius. He wants you to love the music as he does. When combined with such refinement of technique, energy, sense of colour and imagination, it's an attitude that is particularly compelling.

Beethoven Piano Sonatas Nos 8, 23 and 31 🅗
Handel Keyboard Suite in D minor, HWV428 – Prelude; Air and Variations; Presto. Chaconne and Variations in G, HWV435
Edwin Fischer *pf*
APR Signature mono APR5502 (72 minutes: AAD). Ⓜ
Recorded 1931-38 ●●

On this invaluable disc are some of Fischer's finest and most legendary performances. His very first published recording (1931) of the Handel Chaconne, for example, was made at a time when his matchless *leggiero* and radiant tone were unimpeded by obvious blemishes or erratic pianism. Both this performance and that of the pieces from the Suite No 3 are endowed with an improvisatory magic, a strength and grace and supreme assurance.

Fischer commences the *Pathétique* with a scrupulous adherence to Beethoven's *fp* marking, a sudden shift of sound that is fascinatingly modernist or prophetic. The *Allegro di molto e con brio* is exactly that, dancing with an irrepressible lightness and urgency; and if one listens to the slow octave descent just before the final outburst one will hear a rapt 'all-passion-spent' quality, something that Fischer was able to achieve with supreme naturalness, without even a hint of artifice or calculated effect. All past vicissitudes are finally resolved in Op 110 in what is a blaze of heroic glory, and time and time again he makes you pause to consider key points and details that have somehow eluded others. There is here a richness and humanity that was uniquely Fischer's.

Piano Sonatas Nos 8, 14, 15, 17, 21, 23 and 26
Alfred Brendel *pf*
Philips Duo ② 438 730-2PM2 (152 minutes: ADD). Ⓜ
Recorded 1970-77 ●

Piano Sonatas Nos 8 and 23. Choral Fantasia in C minor, Op 80. Bagatelles – Op 33 Nos 3 and 5; Op 119 Nos 2, 7 and 9; Op 126 Nos 1, 4 and 6 🅗
Sviatoslav Richter *pf*
Russian State Academic Choir; Moscow Radio Symphony Orchestra / Kurt Sanderling
Melodiya mono 74321 29462-2 (80 minutes: ADD). Ⓜ
Recorded 1952-60

The Philips reissue, containing seven of Beethoven's most popular named sonatas admirably played by Alfred Brendel, is in every way an outstanding bargain, and is well worth obtaining, even if duplication is involved. All the performances are authoritative and offer consistently distinguished playing, while the recording is very realistic indeed. The *Tempest* resonates in the memory and the central movements of the *Pastoral* are most beautifully shaped. The *Pathétique*, *Moonlight* and *Appassionata* all bring deeply satisfying readings that are compellingly conceived and freshly executed.

This set can be recommended without any reservations whatsoever. The booklet-notes with the Melodiya reissue claim that Richter's live 1960 Moscow *Appassionata* is his favourite among his recorded performances of the work, and from the elemental power that it unleashes one can well believe it. The *Pathétique* is magnificently implacable, while the Choral Fantasia is a remarkable curiosity – with its cavernous acoustic, a fierce recording, the text in Russian, and sung with intimidating gusto. As to the mono sound, it is acceptable.

Beethoven Piano Sonata No 14
Brahms Variations on a Theme by Paganini, Op 35
Franck Prélude, choral et fugue
Evgeni Kissin *pf*
RCA Victor Red Seal 09026 68910-2 Ⓕ
(57 minutes: DDD). Recorded 1997

Strange how many top-flight pianists find it difficult to achieve a natural delivery in the opening movement of the *Moonlight*. With some it's a case of exaggerated hesitation on the upbeats; with Kissin it's a tendency to place the melody fractionally before the left-hand octaves, the reverse of the old left-before-right mannerism. This is vaguely unsettling at first, then positively distracting once you realize the cause. The young Russian does little to temper his strongly projected sound for the intimacy of the recording studio; occasionally climaxes have more metal in the tone than some may like, even in a relatively undemonstrative piece such as the second movement of the Beethoven. Nor does he make concessions as regards sustained intensity of phrasing or ostentatiously grand rubato, especially in the Franck. Yet how much richness of experience you'd be missing if you resist Kissin's manner. And who would want to resist it anyway, when the sense of intellectual, emotional and pianistic identity with the music is so strong? Listen to the lonely arching-up of the lines in Beethoven's first movement as they win temporary freedom from the opening broken chords; or their long-term destination in the defiant arpeggios in the finale, here wonderfully articulate and full of strength; or the sensitivity to each cross-current in Franck's chromatic maelstrom; or the authority of every one of the Brahms *Variations*; or the dexterity of the notorious 7th and 11th variations from Book Two. Listen to these and then say that this is anything other than a wonderful disc. If you do, it can only be that you are allergic to the forcefully projected piano tone. To which one can only say that there are others just as forceful, but very few who have comparable musical insights to project. This is modern piano playing at its finest. The recording quality is of the finest too.

Piano Sonatas Nos 14-18. Variations on an Original Theme in F, Op 34. Seven Bagatelles, Op 33 **H**
Artur Schnabel *pf*
Pearl mono ② GEMMCDS9123 (141 minutes: AAD) Ⓜ
Recorded 1933 **OO**

Heavy background hiss is a small price to pay for Schnabel's immediacy and quality, and both of these discs, the original material transferred with a courageous candour and honesty, do much to convince one that Beethoven and Schnabel are, indeed, synonymous. How characteristic is that gruff but musicianly refusal in No 14 of all undue solemnity, all notion of romantic, moonlit effusion. Such robust eloquence will hardly appeal to those who long for a prolonged gaze into the infinite, but the balance of sense and sensibility provides a superbly authoritative alternative. Of course, there are moments when Schnabel's impetuosity, his embattled rather than fluent resolution of purely pianistic problems, can cause momentary confusion. Yet the odd snatched phrase or telescoped rhythm pales into oblivion given Schnabel's overall achievement, his salty brio and the profound eloquence of his slow movements (has anyone played the central *Adagio* of No 17 so directly yet so speculatively?). His technique, while undeniably erratic, was brilliant; and every page pulses with a vividness and rough-hewn vitality that are somehow pure Schnabel, pure Beethoven.

Time and again he wears his immense learning lightly and in, say, the dazzling wit and repartee of No 16 the dust of ages seems to fall away before one's very eyes and ears. The Op 33 *Bagatelles* also prove that Schnabel was as much at home in concentrated aphorism as in lengthy working-out. So, true Beethoven lovers will treasure these discs, even when they turn to a different sort of enlightenment from Wilhelm Kempff, Schnabel's nominated heir. But then Schnabel and Kempff are like North and South Poles of interpretation, and both are indispensable.

Piano Sonatas Nos 16-18
Stephen Kovacevich *pf*
EMI CDC5 55226-2 (64 minutes: DDD). Ⓕ
Recorded 1994 **O**

The Op 31 Sonatas offer a wonderful way into the Beethoven sonatas, not least because they have done unusually well on record. And what to buy? Well, this offering from Stephen Kovacevich from his Beethoven sonata cycle is very brilliant, an exceptional record in every way. There is stiff competition from Brendel and Richard Goode, to name just two, but Kovacevich finds a middle way that seems effortlessly right. His tempo in the E flat Sonata's *Menuetto* is more or less exactly what one imagines a *moderato e grazioso* should be, and it serves Minuet and Trio equally well.

The preceding *Scherzo* is a touch fiercer than Goode's or Brendel's, the finale a show-stopping *Presto con fuoco*. In the *Tempest*, Kovacevich's playing can be as angry as his rivals but it is always terrifically focused. EMI has been obliged to take on board some pretty ferocious playing. The recording occasionally threatens to fray at the edges but never quite does. War-weary and battle-hardened, it bears these marvellous performances triumphantly home.

Piano Sonatas Nos 19, 20, 22, 23, 30, 31 and 32
Sviatoslav Richter *pf*
Philips ② 438 486-2PH2 (122 minutes: DDD). Ⓕ
Recorded 1992 **OO**

Piano Sonatas Nos 18 and 28. Two Rondos, Op 51. Piano Trio in B flat, Op 97, 'Archduke'[a]. Quintet for Piano and Wind in E flat, Op 16[b]
Sviatoslav Richter *pf*
[a]members of the **Borodin Quartet**; [b]members of the **Moraguès Quintet** Ⓕ
Philips ② 438 624-2PH2 (131 minutes: DDD).
Recorded 1986-92 Ⓕ

There are times in a reviewer's working life when he or she folds away the notebook, discards the score, and just listens – the performance demands it. This was one such event. Those whose chief pleasure as critics is to pounce on minute blemishes would no doubt have a joyous time here – Richter is no chromium-plated perfectionist. But to go glitch-hunting in the face of playing of this quality would surely require a heroic degree of insensitivity. Granted, Richter would hardly be Richter if there wasn't something bizarre to pick out, and there is one detail that does call for comment. In the Quintet for piano and wind, Op 16, Richter and the four members of the Moraguès Quintet repeat not only the first movement exposition, but the exposition plus the slow introduction. For those who listen for structural signposts it is disorientating; and yet it is all so wonderfully played – the colour, the vitality, the sense of creative give-and-take between the players are all you could wish for in this sunny, young piece.

Throughout these two sets the sheer aliveness of the playing can be breathtaking – and that's no exaggeration. It doesn't matter whether the territory is the most searching late Beethoven or an early, 'easy' sonata (Beethoven's own description) such as the G minor, Op 49 No 1. One could make endless lists of favourite details – little touches that show how thorough Richter's understanding is, but what finally distinguishes Richter's Beethoven is a quality ... the word is 'improvisatory': it is as though you were hearing the music not merely played, but composed. This is what holds the attention even when Richter's conscious decisions go against what you expect – the slow tempos in the *Scherzo* and Fugue of Op 110, for instance.

These four discs form a valuable counterweight to the modern nostalgists' claim that great playing – and especially great Beethoven playing – is a thing of the remote past. The transfers serve Richter excellently: intrusive audience noise is minimal, in fact in Op 111 you might only realize that there is an audience at all when clapping and cheering thunders in at the end. The engineering is good.

Piano Sonatas Nos 21, 24 and 31
Stephen Kovacevich *pf*
EMI CDC7 54896-2 (53 minutes: DDD). Recorded 1992 Ⓕ ●

Few pianists today – not Brendel, not Ashkenazy, not Serkin – can free themselves of self-awareness enough to find the tender simplicity of the opening *Moderato cantabile* of Beethoven's Op 110. Kovacevich can, and he goes on to fill each moment of figuration and trilling with light. His finale has a mesmeric inwardness generated by the seemingly infinite nuances he can find in a single repeated note. A steadiness of purpose in the *Arioso* leads naturally into the quiet self-assurance of the effortless building of the Fuga. The coupling – with the little Op 78 and the *Waldstein* – makes for a sensitively built recital in its own right. Again, Kovacevich's skill at drawing the listener in marks the Op 78 Sonata, with its effervescent figurework and spontaneous major-minor changes. The same nimble fingerwork, over a thrumming bass, makes the *Waldstein* positively tingle with life: Kovacevich's joy in the physical excitement and momentum of the writing is equalled by his strength in delineating the song at its heart.

Piano Sonatas Nos 21, 23 and 26
Emil Gilels *pf*
DG 419 162-2GH (68 minutes: ADD). Recorded 1970s Ⓕ ●●

This reissue couples the *Waldstein*, the *Appassionata*, and *Les adieux*, and immediately establishes a claim to being one of the most desirable of all Beethoven piano sonata reissues. Perhaps there is something rather chilly and understated about Gilels's reading of the *Waldstein*'s brief slow movement (by contrast, his playing of the slow movement of *Les adieux* is ravishing), but Beethoven must take some of the blame here, too. Throughout these three sonatas Gilels plays the music with an architect's sense of structure, great technical brilliance, and that uncanny blend of intellectual attack and intellectual distance which give his recordings their peculiar force and distinction. The digital transfers are brilliant and true. The opening of *Les adieux* sounds a trifle muted and there is some tape background, but the ear dismisses this as rapidly as, initially, it picks it up.

Piano Sonatas Nos 27-32 🅗
Solomon *pf*
EMI Références mono/stereo ② CHS7 64708-2 (141 minutes: ADD). Recorded 1951-56 Ⓜ ●●●

Solomon's 1952 recording of the *Hammerklavier* Sonata is one of the great recordings of the century. At the heart of his performance there is as calm and searching an account of the slow movement as you are likely to hear this side of the Great Divide. And the outer movements are also wonderfully well done. Music that is so easy to muddle and arrest is here fierily played; Solomon at his lucid, quick-witted best.

The CD transfer is astonishing. It is as though previously we have merely been eavesdropping on the performance; now, decades later, we are finally in the presence of the thing itself. It is all profoundly moving. What's more, EMI has retained the juxtaposition of the 1969 LP reissue: Solomon's glorious account of the A major Sonata, Op 101 as the *Hammerklavier*'s proud harbinger. We must be grateful that Solomon had completed his recording of these six late sonatas before his career was abruptly ended by a stroke in the latter part of 1956.

The Sonatas, Op 90 and Op 110, were recorded in August 1956. The warning signs were – in retrospect – already there; yet listening to these edited tapes one would hardly know anything was amiss. There is the odd fumble in the *Scherzo* of Op 110; but, if anything, the playing has even greater resolve, both in Op 110 and in a songful (but never sentimental) account of Op 90. The recordings of Opp 109 and 111 date from 1951. Sonata, Op 109, is very fine; Op 111 is – by Solomon's standards – a shade wooden in places, both as a performance and as a recording. Still, this is a wonderful set, and very much a collectors' item.

Piano Sonatas Nos 27[a], 28[b] and 29[c]
Sviatoslav Richter *pf*
Praga PR254022 (75 minutes: ADD). Ⓜ
Item marked [a] recorded 1965, [b]1986, [c]1975

These entirely unedited performances feel not only live but somehow extraordinarily real. Not that Richter ever gives the impression of playing for the microphone, and his vision of musical structures remains constant whether he is in the studio or the concert hall. Nevertheless the atmosphere within which that vision is realized differs from venue to venue, and in Prague it seems to have been extraordinarily conducive. This is outstanding Beethoven playing, though frustratingly the 1965 *Hammerklavier* has a little memory black-out at 8'20" in the first movement, without which it might have grown into something even more extraordinary.

Awards 1977

Piano Sonatas Nos 28-32
Maurizio Pollini *pf*
DG The Originals ② 449 740-2GOR2 Ⓜ
(126 minutes: ADD)
Recorded 1975-77

This reissued DG Originals set makes an exceptionally neat package. Consistent praise has been heaped on these recordings since they won the Instrumental Record Award way back in 1977. One of Pollini's greatest strengths is his ability to stand up to the accumulated momentum of Beethoven's structure, but he can also build on it so as to leave the impression of one huge exhalation of creative breath. In the first movement of the *Hammerklavier* the astonishing technical assurance has you right on the edge of your seat with excitement. His controlled vehemence is without rival in the outer movements, and though he does not get right to the bottom of No 29's poetry, his far-sighted phrasing and paragraphing is again remarkable (hear the build-up to the finale recapitulation and resist it if you can!).

In the last three sonatas there are others who stop to peer deeper into some of the psychic chasms, but Pollini's mastery of integration and continuous growth, and his ability to hold potentially conflicting musical demands in balance, are again sources of wonderment. In terms of the qualities just mentioned, who is Pollini's equal? Other than small touches of pre-echo in Op 111, there is nothing here to distract from the exalted quality of both the music and the playing.

Egmont – incidental music, Op 84

Pilar Lorengar *sop* **Klaus-Jürgen Wussow** *spkr*
Vienna Philharmonic Orchestra / George Szell
Decca The Classic Sound 448 593-2DCS (48 minutes: ADD). Text and translation included. Ⓜ
Recorded 1969

As a simple demonstration of what it is to conduct a great orchestra properly, George Szell and the Vienna Philharmonic in the *Egmont* music will do very nicely – at the moment of Egmont's execution, this uniquely imaginative man could create an entire drama, not out of the music, but out of the silence. It is, indeed, a classic set that is likely even now to remain unsurpassed for many years to come. Some may object to short measure but it will appeal to the tidy-minded library builder. In any case, why should a great recording have to rub shoulders with some distracting fill-up? The original 1969 recording was indeed in 'classic sound' – sound, that is, which comes from a great orchestra directed and balanced *at source* by a great conductor (not by the engineers) in a hall that is entirely sympathetic to the matter in hand. In the circumstances, there is little Decca's engineers can usefully do to 'improve' the sound, apart, that is, from reassert and redefine once and for all the peerless quality of the original. This they have done. The result: perfection. And all this lavished on words and music which – the overture apart – might not be given the time of day were the name of Beethoven not associated with it. Here, though, it makes compelling listening from first to last.

An die ferne Geliebte

Awards 1999

Sechs Gellert Lieder, Op 48. Lieder – Op 52: No 3, Das Liedchen von der Ruhe; No 4, Mailied; Op 75: No 2, Neue Liebe, neues Leben; No 3, Aus Goethes Faust; Op 83: No 1, Wonne der Wehmut; No 2, Sehnsucht. Adelaide, Op 46. An die Hoffnung, Op 94. An die ferne Geliebte, Op 98. Klage, WoO113. Der Liebende, WoO139. An die Geliebte, WoO140
Stephan Genz *bar* **Roger Vignoles** *pf*
Hyperion CDA67055 (69 minutes: DDD) Ⓕ
Texts and translations included
Recorded 1998

The young baritone Stephan Genz is in the first bloom of his youthful prime. Beethoven's setting of Goethe's 'Mailied' (Op 52 No 4), with its lightly breathed, springing words, could have been written with Genz in mind. Roger Vignoles, Genz's regular accompanist, contributes an irresistible bounding energy and even a sense of mischief to one of Beethoven's most spontaneous yet subtle settings, 'Neue Liebe, neues Leben'; and an elusive sense of yearning is created as the voice tugs against the piano line in 'Sehnsucht'. The six *Gellert Lieder* form the centrepiece of this recital: Beethoven's song-cycle, *An die ferne Geliebte*, its grand finale.

The intensity of Genz's cry 'Is there a God?' in *An die Hoffnung*, at the start of the disc, gives some indication of the *gravitas* he brings to his firmly enunciated 'spiritual songs' of Gellert. Genz and Vignoles have here reinstated a number of the original verses omitted by Beethoven in the first printed edition, creating a greater sense of balance and proportion within the set. The concluding song-cycle is quite simply one of the best performances currently available. Fresh and bright of tone, awe-filled and beautifully paced and scaled, Genz's singing is modulated exquisitely from song to song by Vignoles's sentient piano accompaniment.

Cantatas

Cantata on the death of the Emperor Joseph II, WoO87. Cantata on the accession of the Emperor Leopold II, WoO88. Opferlied, Op 121*b*. Meeresstille und glückliche Fahrt, Op 112
Janice Watson, Judith Howarth *sops* **Jean Rigby** *mez* **John Mark Ainsley** *ten* **José van Dam** *bass-bar* **Corydon Singers and Orchestra / Matthew Best**
Hyperion CDA66880 (80 minutes: DDD). Ⓕ
Texts and translations included. Recorded 1996

Beethoven was only 19 when he was commissioned to write this 40-minute cantata on the Emperor's death. It was never performed, the musicians claiming it was too difficult, and remained buried for almost a century. Arguably Beethoven's first major masterpiece, it was one of his few early unpublished works of which the master approved. When he came to write *Fidelio*, he used the soaring theme from the first of the soprano arias here, 'Da stiegen die Menschen an's Licht', for Leonore's sublime moment in the finale, 'O Gott! Welch' ein Augenblick'. The tragic C minor power of the choruses framing the work is equally memorable. Dramatic tension is then kept taut through all seven sections, with recitatives indicating the young composer's thirst to write opera. Matthew Best conducts a superb performance, fresh, incisive and deeply moving, with excellent soloists as well as a fine chorus. In this first cantata the solo quartet simply contribute to the opening and closing choruses.

The second cantata, only a little more than half the length of the first, was written soon after, when Leopold II had succeeded as Emperor. It is apt to have the two works presented successively, when one seems to develop out of the other. This second work is less ambitious, expressing less deep emotions, yet it brings fascinating anticipation of later masterpieces. Much more specific is the way that the finale of the cantata, 'Heil! Stürzet nieder, Millionen', clearly anticipates the choral finale of the Ninth Symphony (even with the word 'Millionen'), a point reinforced by the key of D major. The two shorter pieces, both dating from Beethoven's difficult interim period between middle and late, with Jean Rigby as soloist in the *Opferlied*, make a generous fill-up, performed with equal dedication. With plenty

of air round the chorus, the recording has ample weight yet is transparent enough to clarify even the heaviest textures. A revelatory issue.

'Missa solemnis', Op 123

Mass in D, Op 123, 'Missa solemnis'

Charlotte Margiono *sop* **Catherine** Ⓟ
Robbin *mez* **William Kendall** *ten*
Alastair Miles *bass* **Monteverdi Choir;**
English Baroque Soloists /
Sir John Eliot Gardiner
Awards 1991 Archiv Produktion 429 779-2AH Ⓕ
(72 minutes: DDD). Text and translation included. Recorded 1989 ●●●

The *Missa solemnis* is generally agreed to be one of the supreme masterpieces of the 19th century, but attempts to record a genuinely great performance have over many years run into difficulties. Usually the greatness itself is flawed, perhaps in the quality of the solo singers or in passages where the conductor's approach is too idiosyncratic or momentarily not up to the challenge of Beethoven's inspiration. The strain upon the choir, especially its sopranos, is notorious; similarly the technical problems of balance by producer and engineers. This performance mixes discipline and spontaneous creativity, the rhythms are magically alive and the intricate texture of sound is made wonderfully clear. The great fugues of the *Gloria* and *Credo* achieve at the right points their proper Dionysiac sense of exalted liberation. Gardiner uses a choir of 36 and an orchestra of 60 playing on period instruments, aiming at a 'leaner and fitter' sound. With Gardiner, the exceptional clarity of his smaller body of singers and players, their meticulous responsiveness to direction and concentrated attention to detail is impressive; yet one is aware of it *as* a performance. Sometimes, as in the first sounding of drums and trumpets signifying war, Gardiner's additional intensity brings a real gain.

Missa solemnis. Choral Fantasia in C, Op 80
Elisabeth Söderström *sop* **Marga Höffgen** *contr* **Waldemar Kmentt** *ten* **Martti Talvela** *bass* **Daniel Barenboim** *pf* **New Philharmonia Chorus and Orchestra; John Alldis Choir / Otto Klemperer**
EMI ② CMS7 69538-2 (100 minutes: ADD) Ⓜ
Texts and translations included.
Recorded 1960s ●●

Suspicions began to dawn in the very first bars that this might be not just a good but a rather great performance. The growth of the sustained theme-note in the *Kyrie* tells of power and purpose, and the measured development of the movement induces confidence that all is in safe hands. Doubts begin to creep in about the middle of the *Gloria*. Isn't the 'Qui tollis' section too … perhaps 'plodding' overstates, and 'syllabic' isn't quite right either, but too much a matter of advance note-by-note? Then 'plod' becomes the inescapable word when Klemperer starts the 'In gloria Dei' fugue in such ponderous style and at such a laboured tempo that one goes back again to Gardiner. Perhaps it is the old notion of fugue as an 'academic' form, meaning that it is weightily serious to start with and can only get more so. This is the pattern for the great fugues of the *Credo* in Klemperer's recording, and the stern majesty thus established seems to chide away with almost puritan severity any suggestion of dance-movement in the 'Et ascendit'. Other matters come into question, such as the use of the soloists in the *Sanctus* 'Osanna', and indeed the actual choice of soloists, for Söderström and Höffgen both have wrong sorts of vibrancy for this, while Kmentt lacks power for the 'Et homo factus est', and Talvela, good in the *Agnus*, has the wrong voice for the *Benedictus*. So criticisms mount up. But greatness remains, and this is felt in the work of the chorus. The disc is a marvellous monument to its great trainer, Wilhelm Pitz. No doubt that Klemperer and the sense of occasion fired the chorus to give this recording its enduring life. However, it's doubtful whether the chorus would make this impression if it was recorded today for in nearly all modern recordings of such works the choir is too recessed to be the vivid, immediate human presence it is here. The *Choral Fantasia*, included on the second disc, is a well-chosen fill-up. Sadly, it's a performance without humour. Sound, fine in the *Fantasia*, is less comfortable in the *Missa*: sometimes a little harsh, and a little furry in soft passages. The vivid presence of that choir more than compensates.

Beethoven Missa solemnis[a]. Symphony No 7 in A, Op 92 **Cherubini** Anacréon – Overture **Mozart** Symphony No 35 in D, 'Haffner', K385 H

a**Zinka Milanov** *sop* a**Kerstin Thorborg** *mez* a**Koloman von Pataky** *ten* a**Nicola Moscona** *bass* a**BBC Choral Society; BBC Symphony Orchestra / Arturo Toscanini**

BBC Legends/IMG Artists mono ② BBCL4016-2 (145 minutes: ADD). Recorded live in 1939 Ⓜ OO

It hardly seems credible that with all the commentary written about Beethoven and Toscanini's view of him, this reading of the *Missa solemnis* should have remained unissued for so long. And yet here it is, sounding not at all bad for its years and upstaging even a celebrated 1940 NBC broadcast performance that has circulated on various labels and that Naxos is planning to release very soon. The principal virtues of this BBC reading include a superbly balanced solo quartet (better matched than the 1940 line-up), fervent singing from the BBC Choral Society and the symphonic slant of Toscanini's conducting. Although the leading impression is of unspeakable power held in check, some of the most impressive moments are also the quietest. Two passages from the *Gloria* are especially telling: the lead-in to the 'Qui tollis peccata' episode (4'43") and that thrilling moment (9'48") where Beethoven reduces his forces to a whisper before catapulting us back with what sounds like a quick blast of *Fidelio* and a massive choral fugue. This is a triumph of a performance, significantly broader than the NBC recording of 1953 (though the two *Credos* last an identical 17'58"), and better balanced than the 1940 broadcast. There, the chorus is rather less good, phrasing is marginally less pliant and the brass and timpani tend to hog the limelight. A fourth (unofficial) version – set down live in New York in 1935 with a solo team that includes Martinelli, Rethberg and Pinza – is grander still, but poorly recorded.

The transfer eschews excessive de-hissing for a quiet sea of surface noise that soon ceases to matter, and although the overall sound profile emerges as rather murky (certainly in comparison with the relatively clear post-war RCA recording), the performance is so consistently gripping, that you're soon drawn in. Toscanini's audible singing is further proof of his ecstatic involvement. To encounter the *Missa solemnis* at such a high level of interpretative excellence is a unique privilege, and the only complaint is that by failing to fit the work on to a single disc BBC Legends forces an unfortunate break in concentration. Still, there are compensating fill-ups, all of which are worth hearing. The Seventh Symphony's principal attraction is a warmly voiced *Allegretto* second movement, but, as a whole, the performance falls short of the fastidious tailoring that distinguishes Toscanini's fabulous 1936 New York Philharmonic Symphony recording. Then again, Mozart's *Haffner* is not dissimilar to its RCA New York predecessor though the Minuet's Trio is especially lovely in this BBC recording. Cherubini's cumulatively powerful *Anacréon* Overture is given a peach of a performance and the sound is surprisingly good.

Missa solemnis P

Eva Mei *sop* **Marjana Lipovšek** *contr* **Anthony Rolfe Johnson** *ten* **Robert Holl** *bass*

Arnold Schönberg Choir; Chamber Orchestra of Europe / Nikolaus Harnoncourt

Teldec Ultima ② 0630-18945-2 (81 minutes: DDD). Text and translation included. Recorded live in 1992 Ⓑ OO

There are many marvellous performances in the catalogue of Beethoven's great Mass. Gardiner catches the greatness, rises to it with his uncanny freshness of perception, and secures a performance produced virtually without fault. Levine on DG, with what we would probably still call 'conventional' forces (but of totally unconventional magnificence), presents a large-scale performance, not universally liked, but one which impresses you almost unequivocally on every hearing. And here is Harnoncourt: very different from either of the others, but having at least equally upon it the stamp of devotion and of high attainment. Choir and orchestra achieve wonderful precision and clarity of articulation; they are sensitive to the needs of shading, to the ever-shifting balance of the parts, and to the purpose of cross-rhythms which at first may look like anarchy. The soloists, all of them meeting their immense individual challenges, also work intelligently as a quartet. It might be good simply to stop there and say, 'Enjoy it'. But once comparisons start, such simplicity begins to melt. There is no doubt that Gardiner's performance is more brightly, sharply, recorded. Returning to Harnoncourt after listening to a few minutes of that is to feel a relative remoteness of contact with the sound. Moving then to Levine, there is again a more immediate presence in the sound. Yet Harnoncourt in this three-way comparison emerges as a kind of halfway-house between Gardiner and Levine, and not quite as colourful as either. It may well be that an undecided reader may opt for Gardiner finally for the much more mundane reason that his performance is confined to a single disc (and after all it was *Gramophone* Record of the Year in 1991). Yet, listening again to the *Credo*, there is something almost military in the way Gardiner's people march along, and, as Harnoncourt stresses, the whole Mass is above all 'an appeal for peace'. Harnoncourt's is a performance of great integrity: that is, it is a complete, consistent whole, and all its parts are sound.

Mass in C, Op 86

Mass in C, Op 86. Ah! perfido, Op 65. Meeresstille und glückliche Fahrt, Op 112 **P**
Charlotte Margiono *sop* **Catherine Robbin** *mez* **William Kendall** *ten* **Alastair Miles** *bar* **Monteverdi Choir; Orchestre Révolutionnaire et Romantique / Sir John Eliot Gardiner**
Archiv Produktion 435 391-2AH (62 minutes: DDD). Ⓕ
Recorded 1989-91 **OO**

Gardiner's genius is plentifully in evidence here. Of course it is true that the opening movement, the *Kyrie eleison*, is a plea for mercy. But its opening bars speak of comfort: there is almost the simple good faith of a quiet, very Germanic carol about them. Gardiner sets a mood of deliberate seriousness, with lowered period, pitch and a tempo rather slower than that suggested by Beethoven's direction: *Andante con moto, assai vivace, quasi allegretto ma non troppo*. He also appears to have encouraged the soloists, especially the soprano, to shape and shade the phrases, so intensifying the feeling of seriousness and deliberation. Happily, this policy prevails for only a short time, and to some extent the music itself goes out to meet it. As the second *Kyrie* (following the *Christe*) moves towards its climax, the *fortissimo* brings suspensions where the alto part grinds against the soprano, and then come sudden *fortissimos* with intense modulations and momentary discords, all of which are particularly vivid in this performance. What follows has the same exhilarating quality as that which was so applauded in Gardiner's *Missa solemnis* and, just as he did there, Gardiner is constantly illuminating detail while maintaining an apparently easy natural rightness throughout.

Again, an outstanding contribution is made by the Monteverdi Choir. Splendidly athletic, for instance, are the leaps of a seventh in the fugal 'Hosanna'. The tone-painting of *Meeresstille* finds them marvellously alert and vivid in articulation. *Ah! perfido* brings a similar sense of renewal: there is not even a momentary suspicion of concert routine, but rather as though it is part of an exceptionally intense performance of *Fidelio*. Charlotte Margiono sings the angry passages with the concentration of a Schwarzkopf, and brings to those that are gentler-toned a special beauty of her own. Other soloists in the Mass sing well if without distinction. Distinction is certainly a word to use of the disc as a whole.

Fidelio

Inga Nielsen *sop* Leonore; **Gösta Winbergh** *ten* Florestan; **Alan Titus** *bar* Don Pizarro; **Kurt Moll** *bass* Rocco; **Edith Lienbacher** *sop* Marzelline; **Herwig Pecoraro** *ten* Jaquino; **Wolfgang Glashof** *bass* Don Fernando; **Péter Pálinkás** *ten* First Prisoner; **József Moldvay** *bass* Second Prisoner
Hungarian Radio Chorus; Nicolaus Esterházy Sinfonia / Michael Halász
Naxos ② 8 660070/1 (114 minutes: DDD). Ⓢ
Text included. Recorded 1998 **OO**

Naxos has an uncanny knack for choosing the right artists for its operatic ventures. On this occasion, four of the singers are among the better known in the field, each judiciously cast. Halász, who has already conducted an excellent *Zauberflöte* for the company, projects every facet of the score, inspiring his forces to live every moment of the plot in words and music, making it seem new-minted. This isn't an interpretation in the romantic, quasi-philosophical mode of Furwängler or Klemperer, rather one that alerts the mind and ear to the human agony of it all.

In those respects it challenges the hegemony of Maazel's forceful mid-price set on Decca, the admired, early-stereo Fricsay, also at mid-price and Mackerras at full price, the last-named vocally outclassed in almost every case by this super-bargain Naxos. Nielsen follows her exciting Salome on Chandos with an impressive assumption of the very different character of Leonore: what the two readings have in common is a close identification with the character in hand. This Leonore is no projection of subservient femininity but a tormented wife seeking to save her husband, her plight expressed in every key phrase. She doesn't provide the heroic sounds of a Nilsson (Maazel) or all the warmth of Rysanek (Fricsay), but her slimmer, more compact tone exactly fits this performance as a whole. Winberg is a Florestan equal to his Leonore in vocal and interpretative assets. Not even Heppner (Davis) or Seiffert (Harnoncourt), among modern interpreters, sings the role better. His voice poised between the lyrical and the heroic, his tone warm, his technique firm, Florestan's scene can seldom have been so satisfyingly sung and enacted. In the ensuing ensembles, he is just as convincing. Evil is represented arrestingly in the powerful declamation and imposing tone of Titus as Pizarro, Goodness by the sympathetic but seriously unsteady Don Fernando of Glashof. As Marzelline, Edith Lienbacher is something of a discovery, catching the eagerness, also the sense of nerves a-jangle predicated by the part. The Jaquino, Herwig Pecoraro, is more than adequate.

The dialogue, rather drastically foreshortened, is well spoken by all and intelligently directed. The orchestral and choral singing need fear no comparisons, and the recording has plenty of presence, no tricks. So this is undoubtedly a performance that fulfils almost all the exigent demands made on its principals and – at the price – should be eagerly sought after. Even in absolute terms, its most notable predecessors are matched, if not surpassed, by this daring newcomer.

Fidelio

Christa Ludwig *mez* Leonore; **Jon Vickers** *ten* Florestan; **Walter Berry** *bass* Don Pizarro; **Gottlob Frick** *bass* Rocco; **Ingeborg Hallstein** *sop* Marzelline; **Gerhard Unger** *ten* Jaquino; **Franz Crass** *bass* Don Fernando; **Kurt Wehofschitz** *ten* First Prisoner; **Raymond Wolansky** *bar* Second Prisoner

Philharmonia Chorus and Orchestra / Otto Klemperer

EMI Great Recordings of the Century ② CMS5 67364-2 (128 minutes: ADD). Notes, text and translation included. Recorded 1962 Ⓜ

If you accept Klemperer's broad, metaphysical view of *Fidelio*, his account of Beethoven's only opera is also a classic. On its own terms it is superb, as are the Philharmonia's playing and the recording, but it lacks the theatrical intensity of some other versions, notably Maazel's (Decca) and Halász's recent Naxos set. That kind of intensity is there in Klemperer's own Budapest recording (in Hungarian on Hungaroton) and in an off-the-air recording of his 1961 Covent Garden production. Legge made the mistake of replacing Jurinac, in this 1962 set, with Ludwig, a wonderful singer but not as natural a Leonore as Jurinac. Similarly, Hotter's raging Pizarro is not quite matched by Berry's. Vickers' searing, slightly sentimentalised Florestan is common to both. When Klemperer returned to Covent Garden in 1968, Silja was his Leonore, and no one who saw and heard those performances, the conductor's operatic swan-song, will ever forget the occasion – as Richard Osborne says in his perceptive notes. He fails to point out, though – a small but important matter – that Schwarzkopf speaks Marzelline's dialogue for Hallstein.

Fidelio

Charlotte Margiono *sop* Leonore; **Peter Seiffert** *ten* Florestan; **Sergei Leiferkus** *bar* Pizarro; **László Polgár** *bass* Rocco; **Barbara Bonney** *sop* Marzelline; **Deon van der Walt** *ten* Jaquino; **Boje Skovhus** *bar* Don Fernando; **Reinaldo Macias** *ten* First Prisoner; **Robert Florianschütz** *bass* Second Prisoner

Arnold Schoenberg Choir; Chamber Orchestra of Europe / Nikolaus Harnoncourt

Teldec ② 4509-94560-2 (119 minutes: DDD). Notes, text and translation included. Ⓕ

Recorded 1994

Everything Harnoncourt touches leaves one with a sense of a country rediscovered: we listen to the piece in hand with new ears. So it is again here. Beethoven's sole but intractable opera has seldom emerged from the recording studio, or indeed the theatre, with such clarity of texture, such promptness of rhythm, such unity of purpose on all sides. This is a reading that gives full play to winds and horns, making one aware, whether it's in the Overture, Pizarro's aria, Leonore's big scena or the Prelude to Act 2, just how important they are to the structure and character of each movement. Where tempos are concerned, Harnoncourt is almost bound to be controversial somewhere. If many speeds are to their advantage just on the measured side of the customary, as in the Dungeon quartet, allowing us for once to hear every strand of the argument, that for 'O namenlose Freude' is uncommonly moderate. At this pace, Leonore and Florestan seem to be conducting a gentle exchange of deeply felt emotions on an interior level rather than allowing their pent-up emotions to burst forth in an explosion of joy, as is more usual.

The dialogue is delivered in an understated fashion. Two vocal interpretations stand out for excellent singing and pungent characterization. Once Leiferkus's Pizarro takes centre-stage the action lifts on to a new, more tense plane. This vicious little dictator with his incisive diction, spoken and sung, and his biting, vital voice is a commanding presence. But Evil is up against an equally arresting advocate of Good in Margiono's gloriously sung and read Leonore. Hers isn't the quasi-dramatic soprano usually associated with the part, but she never sounds strained or overparted in the context of a more lyrical, smaller-scale performance. Seiffert fills Florestan with more refulgent tone than any other tenor on recent recordings – the high tessitura of his aria's close causes him no distress at all – but one has to admit that there is little of the *Schmerz* in the tone found, quite differently, in the recording of Vickers (Klemperer). In that sense, though, he fits into Harnoncourt's well-ordered scheme of things. There has, however, been a major piece of miscasting where Don Fernando is concerned. A role that needs a solid bass with strong low notes has been cast with a high baritone who sounds anything but authoritative. Harnoncourt has opted for a professional chamber choir to second the superb Chamber Orchestra of Europe. The fact has to be faced that until this recording, this opera hadn't received a really satisfying recording for at least 20 or so years and the old favourites are beginning to show their age. By the side of the superb Teldec recording, the Klemperer and Maazel sound less than immediate.

Additional recommendation

Fidelio

Nilsson Leonore **McCracken** Florestan

Krause *Don* Pizarro **Böhme** Rocco

Vienna Philharmonic Orchestra / Maazel

Decca Double 448 104-2DF2

(119 minutes: ADD: 11/96) Ⓑ

A fine and often overlooked recording with Nilsson on superb form as the heroine. McCracken is a suitably impassioned Florestan and Maazel generates real electricity 'in the pit'.

Leonore

Leonore **P**

Hillevi Martinpelto *sop* Leonore; **Kim Begley** *ten* Florestan; **Matthew Best** *bass* Pizarro; **Franz Hawlata** *bass* Rocco; **Christiane Oelze** *sop* Marzelline; **Michael Schade** *ten* Jaquino; **Alastair Miles** *bass* Don Fernando; **Robert Burt** *ten* First Prisoner; **Colin Campbell** *bar* Second Prisoner
Monteverdi Choir; Orchestre Révolutionnaire et Romantique / Sir John Eliot Gardiner
Archiv Produktion ② 453 461-2AH2
(138 minutes: DDD). Notes, text and translation included. Recorded 1996 Ⓕ ●

Romain Rolland described Beethoven's *Leonore* as 'a monument of the anguish of the period, of the oppressed soul and its appeal to liberty'. John Eliot Gardiner, in the first complete recording of *Fidelio*'s predecessor for more than two decades, reveals musically and verbally how the early, more radical opera has worked its spell on him, too. This, he says, is Beethoven struggling to recover the revolutionary fervour of his Bonn years; this is the score where the direct expression of spontaneous emotion, rather than the nobility of philosophical abstraction, is really to be found. The slower musical pace of *Leonore* is counterbalanced by a stronger narrative thrust and the actor, Christoph Bantzer, contributes a sprightly narration which interleaves, deftly and movingly, brief asides from the likes of Wordsworth, Goethe and Hölderlin. And then, of course, there is the music.

The *Leonore* No 2 Overture is distinguished by the telling contrasts Gardiner draws between brooding strata of strings and the pearly light of the woodwind; and a reversal of the first two numbers gives Christiane Oelze a head start as a radiant Marzelline. The trio (Rocco, Marzelline and Jaquino) which prepares the Quartet, 'Mir ist so wunderbar', does tend to impede the momentum but it has a telling effect on the beat of the work's human heart, and Gardiner's sensitivity to its pulse throughout makes good any shortfall in dramatic impetus. The D major March which introduces Act 2 is here restored to its original place for the first time since the première. With brass and timpani making menacing circumstance out of what can be mere pomp, it makes the entry of Don Pizarro darker still. Matthew Best is, in articulation if not in range, one of the most blood-curdling Pizarros on disc, just as Alastair Miles is one of the noblest Don Fernandos. 'Komm, Hoffnung' reveals the resilience and steady, gleaming core of Hillevi Martinpelto's Leonore. There are times when one craves a fiercer edge of passion; but, with the equally sharply focused tenor of Kim Begley, it is a joy to hear 'O namenlose Freude' perfectly paced, and really *sung*. This Florestan sings his great aria without *Fidelio*'s vision of an 'Engel Leonore': Begley, no Heldentenor after all, is well suited to the constant, dark minor key of this 'Lebens Frühlingstagen', which presages Gardiner's triumphant – and often surprising – finale.

Vincenzo Bellini

Italian 1801-1835

GROVE *Bellini was given piano lessons by his father, and could play well when he was five. At six he wrote a Gallus cantavit and began studying composition with his grandfather. After a few years his sacred pieces were being heard in Catania churches and his ariettas and instrumental works in the salons of aristocrats and patricians. In 1819 he went to Naples to study at the conservatory, entering the class of the director, Nicola Zingarelli, in 1822. In 1825 his opera semiseria, Adelson e Salvini, was produced at the conservatory. Its success led to commissions from the Teatro S Carlo and from La Scala, Milan.*

Bellini's first opera for Milan, Il pirata (1827), instantly laid the foundation of his career, and with it began his fruitful collaborations with the librettist Felice Romani and the tenor GB Rubini. From 1827 to 1833 Bellini lived mostly in Milan, and during this time his operas, including La sonnambula and Norma, earned him an international reputation, while he himself went through a passionate love affair with Giuditta Cantù, the wife of a landowner and silk manufacturer, Ferdinando Turina. Bellini's amatory entanglements have been romanticized in popular literature but the realities are less creditable.

In 1833 Bellini visited London, where four of his operas were performed with great success at the King's Theatre and Drury Lane. He then proceeded to Paris, where he was commissioned to write I puritani for the Théâtre-Italien and formed a close acquaintance with Rossini and got to know Chopin and other musicians. I puritani enjoyed a genuine triumph in January 1835, and Bellini was appointed a Chevalier de la Légion d'honneur. He decided to remain in Paris and formulated several projects for his future there, but in August 1835 he fell ill and the following month he died, from 'an acute inflammation of the large intestine, complicated by an abscess of the liver' according to the post-mortem report.

Bellini's importance to posterity is as a composer of opera, especially opera seria; his other works can be ignored without great loss. His first influences were the folksong of Sicily and Naples, the teaching of Zingarelli and, above all, the music of Rossini. The Naples performance of Rossini's Semiramide in 1824 was one of the most decisive musical experiences of his student years, and the novel lyrical style of his early operas represented a sentimentalization and heightening of Rossinian lyricism, which in Il pirata broadens to include forceful and dramatic emotions. With this opera Bellini became one of Italy's most influential composers; Donizetti and Pacini, Mercadante and Verdi all learnt from him.

The quintessential feature of Bellini's operatic music is its close relationship with the text. He did not look for musical delineation of character, but the content and mood of each scene are given thorough-going musical interpretation and the text is precisely declaimed. His melodic style, of which the famous 'Casta diva' in Norma is a perfect example, is characterized by the building of broad melodic curves from small (usually two-bar) units.

While his treatment of rhythm is more conventional, his melodies are supported by some colourful harmony and reticent though effective orchestration. More than any other Italian composer of the years around 1830, Bellini minimized the difference between aria and recitative by introducing a large number of cantabile, aria-like passages into his recitative. His expressive range goes far beyond the delicate, elegiac aspects of his art, which have been frequently overemphasized.

I Capuleti ed i Montecchi

I Capuleti ed i Montecchi. Lorenzo
Edita Gruberová *sop* Giulietta; **Agnes Baltsa** *mez* Romeo; **Dano Raffanti** *ten* Tebaldo;
Gwynne Howell *bass* Capellio; **John Tomlinson** *bass*
Royal Opera House Chorus and Orchestra, Covent Garden / Riccardo Muti
EMI ② CMS7 64846-2 (130 minutes: DDD). Text and translation included. Recorded live in 1984 Ⓜ ●

Muti and his two principals, caught at white heat on the stage of Covent Garden, offer a rendition of Bellini's supple, eloquent score that gives the work a new definition and standing in the Bellini canon. Away from the limbo of studio recording, the music lives at a heightened level of emotion and the sound reflects a true opera-house balance. Muti persuades his singers and the Royal Opera House players to noble utterance. Baltsa's Romeo has a Callas-like conviction of phrase and diction: here is a Romeo who will go to his death for the love of his Juliet. Who wouldn't when that role is sung so delicately and affectingly as by Gruberová, then at the height of her powers, as was Baltsa? Raffanti's open-throated Italian tenor is just right for Tebaldo's bold incursions. Gwynne Howell and John Tomlinson contribute effectively to what is an engrossing performance.

Norma

Maria Callas *sop* Norma; **Christa Ludwig** *mez* Adalgisa; **Franco Corelli** *ten* Pollione;
Nicola Zaccaria *bass* Oroveso; **Piero De Palma** *ten* Flavio; **Edda Vincenzi** *sop* Clotilde
Chorus and Orchestra of La Scala, Milan / Tullio Serafin
EMI ③ CMS7 63000-2 (161 minutes: ADD). Notes text and translation included. Recorded 1960 Ⓜ ●●

Norma Ⓗ
Maria Callas *sop* Norma; **Ebe Stignani** *mez* Adalgisa; **Mario Filippeschi** *ten* Pollione; **Nicola Rossi-Lemeni** *bass* Oroveso; **Paolo Caroli** *ten* Flavio; **Rina Cavallari** *sop* Clotilde
Chorus and Orchestra of La Scala, Milan / Tullio Serafin
EMI Callas Edition mono ③ CDS5 56271-2 (160 minutes: ADD). Notes, text and translation included. Recorded 1954 Ⓕ ●●

Norma may be considered the most potent of Bellini's operas, in its subject – the secret love of a Druid priestess for a Roman general – and its musical content. It has some of the most eloquent music written for the soprano voice. The title-role has always been coveted by dramatic sopranos, but there have been few in the history of the opera who have completely fulfilled its considerable vocal and histrionic demands: in recent times the leading exponent has been Maria Callas. Is the 1960 recording better or worse than the 1954 recording? The answer cannot be put in a word. But those who heard Callas sing Norma at Covent Garden in 1953-54, and then again, slim, in 1957, will know the difference. The facts are that in 1954 the voice above the stave was fuller, more solid and more certain, but that in 1960 the middle timbres were more beautiful and more expressive; and, further, that an interpretation which was always magnificent had deepened in finesse, flexibility and dramatic poignancy.

The emphasis you give to these facts must be a matter of personal opinion. Certainly Callas's voice lets her down again and again, often when she essays some of her most beautiful effects. The F wobbles when it should crown a heart-rending 'Oh rimembranza'; the G wobbles in an exquisitely conceived 'Son io' – and yet how much more moving it is than the simpler, if steadier *messa di voce* of the earlier set. There are people who have a kind of tone-deafness to the timbres of Callas's later voice, who don't respond to one of the most affecting and eloquent of all sounds. They will stick to the earlier set. But ardent Callas collectors will probably find that it is the later one to which they will be listening again and again, not unaware of, not even unflinching from, its faults, but still more keenly responsive to its beauties.

'Casta Diva', by the way, is sung in F, as in 1954 – not in the original G, as in the Covent Garden performances of June 1953. (There is no point in fussing about Bellini's keys; the composer's favourite Amina, Malibran, used to put 'Ah non giunge' down a full fourth.) The big duet with Adalgisa is again down a tone, 'Deh! con te' in B flat, 'Mira, o Norma' in E flat, and the change is once again effected in the recitative phrase 'nel romano campo'. Callas does not decorate the music. Adalgisa, a soprano role, is as usual taken by a mezzo. Ludwig blends beautifully with Callas in the low-key 'Mira, o Norma' (though her downward scales are as ill-defined as her colleague's). She is no veteran Adalgisa, but youthful and impetuous except when she lets the rhythm get heavy, and Serafin does nothing to correct her.

On the earlier set, Stignani is a worthy partner whilst Filippeschi is rough but quite effective. On both sets, Serafin restores the beautiful quiet coda to the 'Guerra' chorus, and on both sets, Callas disappointingly does not float over the close of that slow rising *arpeggio*. It is a pity that Serafin did not restore the second statement (solo cello and woodwinds) of the *con dolore* melody that opens Act 2 – even though Bellini was right to cut it for the theatre. In the later set, the conducting is spacious, unhurried, elevated and eloquent. Only in his handling of the mounting tension and the two great climaxes and releases of the finale, might you prefer the earlier version. The La Scala playing is superlative, and the recording is excellent.

I puritani

Montserrat Caballé *sop* Elvira; **Alfredo Kraus** *ten* Arturo; **Matteo Manuguerra** *bar* Riccardo; **Agostino Ferrin** *bass* Giorgio; **Júlia Hamari** *mez* Enrichetta; **Stefan Elenkov** *bass* Gualtiero; **Dennis O'Neill** *ten* Bruno; **Ambrosian Opera Chorus; Philharmonia Orchestra / Riccardo Muti**
EMI ③ CMS7 69663-2 (172 minutes: ADD). Notes, text and translation included. Recorded 1979 Ⓜ ●

I puritani 🄷
Maria Callas *sop* Elvira; Giuseppe di Stefano *ten* Arturo; **Rolando Panerai** *bar* Riccardo; **Nicola Rossi-Lemeni** *bass* Giorgio; **Aurora Cattelani** *mez* Enrichetta; **Carlo Forti** *bass* Gualtiero; **Angelo Mercuriali** *ten* Bruno
Chorus and Orchestra of La Scala, Milan / Tullio Serafin
EMI mono ② CDS5 56275-2 (142 minutes: ADD). Notes, text and translation included. Recorded 1953 Ⓕ ●●

I puritani
Dame Joan Sutherland *sop* Elvira; **Luciano Pavarotti** *ten* Arturo; **Piero Cappuccilli** *bar* Riccardo; **Nicolai Ghiaurov** *bass* Giorgio; **Anita Caminada** *mez* Enrichetta; **Gian Carlo Luccardi** *bass* Gualtiero; **Renato Cazzaniga** *ten* Bruno
Chorus of the Royal Opera House, Covent Garden; London Symphony Orchestra / Richard Bonynge
Decca ③ 417 588-2DH3 (174 minutes: ADD). Notes, text and translation included. Recorded 1973 Ⓕ ●

Were *I puritani* to be produced as frequently as *La bohème*, one could still spend a lifetime of opera-going and not come upon a performance as distinguished as any of these. Obviously all are desirable, and still more obviously, as far as most of us are concerned, all cannot be had. It may be simplest and safest to allow personal preferences for one or other of the three great ladies to settle the matter: all are at their characteristic best and each has her own special gift to bring to the role. *Puritani* is a tenor's opera as well as a soprano's. Di Stefano, who partnered Callas so well in Puccini, is out of his element here. His untidy approach to notes from below, his uncovered upper register and wide-open vowels cause one again to regret the loss of that elegance imparted to some of his earlier recordings. He is never merely bland and can often be exciting, but comparison with either Kraus or Pavarotti in the other recordings shows him at a disadvantage. Both of these tenors make a particularly lovely thing of the solo 'A una fonte' in Act 3, and do impressively well in the bel canto test-piece, 'A te, o cara'. For the baritones, Panerai with Callas has most character in his voice, though both the others have good solid tone and offer no offence to the vocal line even if they fail to caress or excite it.

Perhaps the conductors can decide the issue. Bonynge and Serafin are brisker than Muti, who takes a languorous approach, no bad thing in Bellini as long as there is tenderness and sensitivity, as indeed there is. All secure good orchestral playing, Bonynge having a little extra liveliness, Serafin a little more weight. So the conductors are unlikely to be the deciding factor after all, and one turns to the question of recorded sound. The Callas version from 1953, by now 'historic', lacks the detailed clarity of the others yet is still remarkably vivid and full-bodied, not obviously dated. The EMI sound in the Muti recording perhaps has more opera-house atmosphere than the Decca, which compensates with brighter definition.

No, it is back to the three great ladies. But here again the account is largely predictable. Caballé, often exquisite, especially in the quieter music, loses quality in loud high passages and has not much sparkle in the cabaletta, 'Vien, diletto'. Callas constantly amazes. The thrill of the first sound of her voice at the start of the great solo scene, the sadness which underlies the gaiety of the *Polonaise*, the affection of her verse in the final duet – all have the stamp of greatness. On the other hand there are occasional sour or raw high notes, where in Sutherland's performance these are the crowning glory. She also sings with feeling, phrases broadly, invests her *fioriture* with unequalled brilliance, but commands less dramatic intensity than her rivals. Clearly, objectivity is getting us nowhere: time to fall back on pure personal prejudice.

La sonnambula

La sonnambula 🄷
Maria Callas *sop* Amina; **Nicola Monti** *ten* Elvino; **Nicola Zaccaria** *bass* Count Rodolfo; **Fiorenza Cossotto** *mez* Teresa; **Eugenia Ratti** *sop* Lisa; **Giuseppe Morresi** *bass* Alessio; **Franco Ricciardi** *ten* Notary
Chorus and Orchestra of La Scala, Milan / Antonino Votto
EMI Callas Edition mono ② CDS5 56278-2 (121 minutes: ADD). Notes text and translation included. Recorded 1957 Ⓕ ●●

La sonnambula, first performed in Milan in 1831, was once the most popular opera in England. Dramatically it is a tepid mix which might be subtitled *The mistakes of a night* if that did not suggest something more amusing than what actually takes place. Musically, the promise of a brilliant finale keeps most people in their seats until the end, and there are half-a-dozen charming, sometimes exquisite items on the way. But it is all a little insubstantial, and much depends upon the performance, especially that of the soprano. The name of Maria Callas is sufficient to guarantee that there will be a particular interest in the work of the heroine. As usual, her individuality is apparent from the moment of her arrival. Immediately a character is established, not an insipid little miss but a woman with a potential for tragedy. This is the pattern throughout and much has exceptional beauty of voice and spirit. Nicola Monti has all the sweetness of the traditional lyric tenor. Nicola Zaccaria sings the bass aria gracefully, and carrying off her small role with distinction is Fiorenza Cossotto, at the start of her career. The orchestral playing is neat, the conducting sensible and the recording clear.

La sonnambula

Dame Joan Sutherland *sop* Amina; **Nicola Monti** *ten* Elvino; **Fernando Corena** *bass* Count Rodolfo; **Margreta Elkins** *mez* Teresa; **Sylvia Stahlman** *sop* Lisa; **Giovanni Foiani** *bass* Alessio; **Angelo Mercuriali** *ten* Notary

Chorus and Orchestra of the Maggio Musicale Fiorentino / Richard Bonynge

Decca Grand Opera ② 448 966-2DMO2 (136 minutes: ADD). Notes, text and translation included. Ⓜ

Recorded 1962

La sonnambula was Bonynge's and Sutherland's first Bellini recording. Sutherland's Amina in the early 1960s was sung with extraordinary freedom and exuberance. It is difficult to describe her in the role: it is felt. She does not touch a thrilling nerve of passion as Callas can; but in the final scene – a wonderfully sustained and imaginative piece of dramatic, as well as delicate and brilliant singing – she is very moving. Far more so, in fact, than Callas, who overloaded 'Ah! non credea' and made 'Ah non giunge' too artful. It's no good comparing Sutherland with Callas at this late stage – but it is inevitable where this is concerned, especially as the Elvino, Nicola Monti, sings the role on both sets. No Sutherland admirer is going to convert to Callas in this opera, but it is quite fascinating to find that one's remembered reactions sometimes wrong. Callas does superb things in the coloratura of 'Sovra il sen', Sutherland is full of dramatic fire in the scene in the inn – the tone, the note-shaping is simply exquisite. Bonynge excels in conducting the choruses.

George Benjamin

British 1960

GROVE *Benjamin studied at the Paris Conservatoire with Messiaen and at Cambridge with Goehr: Ligeti and Boulez have been other influences. He first came to attention with the vividly imagined orchestral piece Ringed by the Flat Horizon (1980); this was consolidated with A Mind of Winter (1981) for soprano and small orchestra and At First Light for chamber ensemble (1982).*

Sudden Time

Sudden Time[a]. Upon Silence[b]. Upon Silence[c]. Octet[d]. Three Inventions[d]

[bc]**Susan Bickley** *mez* [a]**London Philharmonic Orchestra,** [bd]**London Sinfonietta,** [c]**Fretwork / George Benjamin**

Nimbus NI5505 (65 minutes: DDD). Texts included. Ⓕ

Recorded 1994-96

Sudden Time, originally issued as a CD single, is here reissued in the context of a range of other works which underline its distinctive textural refinement and expressive conviction. *Upon Silence* (1993) is a setting for mezzo-soprano and five viols of a poem by Yeats in which textures of exceptional subtlety reflect a response to the text which is captivating in its blend of spontaneity and stylization. The alternative version, with the viols replaced by a septet of violas, cellos and double-basses is no less imaginative, while obviously lacking the unique quality – old instruments used in an entirely viable modern way – of the original.

Three Inventions (1994) has ear-opening instrumental effects on every page, but these never detract from the essential processes of argument and cogent form-building in music perhaps more urgently expressive (especially in the third piece) than anything else of Benjamin's. With the astonishingly precocious *Octet*, written in 1979, when the composer was 18, and with highly effective recordings of definitive performances, this disc is an outstanding success.

Antara

Ringed by the flat horizon[a]. A Mind of Winter[b]. At first light[c]. Panorama[d]. Antara[e]

[b]**Penelope Walmsley-Clark** *sop* [e]**Sebastian Bell,** [e]**Richard Blake** *fls* [c]**Gareth Hulse** *ob* [b]**Paul Archibald** *tpt* [a]**Ross Pople** *vc* [e]**Pierre-Laurent Aimard,** [e]**Ichiro Nodaira** *pfs*

[a]**BBC Symphony Orchestra / Mark Elder,** [bce]**London Sinfonietta / George Benjamin** [d]*electronics*

Nimbus NI5643 (71 minutes: DDD). Text included. Ⓕ

Recorded 1985-86

This reissue is a necessary and valuable complement to Nimbus's earlier Benjamin CD (see above), which was built around compositions from the 1990s. But between March 1979, when *Ringed by the flat horizon* was begun, and March 1987, when *Antara* was completed, foundations of remarkable potential were well and truly laid, and it is fascinating to be able to trace that process through four such different works. There are, of course, five items on the disc, but the two minutes 24 seconds of *Panorama* – a beguiling, all-too-brief indication of Benjamin's work using pre-recorded tape – form a study for *Antara* rather than a wholly independent conception. The overall impression is certainly one of progress, in that the accomplished but in some ways rather stiff procedures to be heard in *Ringed by the flat horizon* led directly to the magnificently fluent setting of Wallace Stevens in *A Mind of Winter*, in which lucid instrumental textures provide the ideal foil for a brilliantly resourceful vocal line. In *At first light*, the stylistic spectrum opens up further, with clear hints of Varèse and even Xenakis in those more expressionistic facets of the Benjamin armoury which remain so striking in his later pieces. A stronger dose of expressionism would have been welcome in *Antara*, whose intricate blending of the electroacoustic and normally acoustic (the product an IRCAM spell) has not so far been followed up by Benjamin. This disc is an essential document of the music of our time.

Sir Richard Rodney Bennett

British 1936

GROVE *Richard Rodney Bennett studied at the Royal Academy of Music (1953-57) and with Boulez in Paris (1957-9), though his public career as a composer had begun before this. At 16 he was writing 12-note music, and the period with Boulez encouraged him towards Darmstadt techniques. But in the 1960s he recovered more conventional aspects to develop a style of Bergian expressionism (e.g. in his opera The Mines of Sulphur, 1965); his opera Victory was given at Covent Garden in 1970. His subsequent output is large, including many concertos, settings of English poetry, chamber music, and, notably, big Romantic film scores. A musician of great versatility, he has worked as a jazz pianist (several of his scores of the 1960s are in a sophisticated jazz style) and has played and arranged American popular music.*

Guitar Concerto

Bennett Guitar Concerto[a]
Arnold Guitar Concerto, Op 67[b]
Rodrigo Concierto de Aranjuez[c]
Julian Bream *gtr* **Melos Ensemble / [c]Sir Colin Davis**
RCA Julian Bream Edition 09026 61598-2
(62 minutes: ADD). Item marked [a] recorded in 1972, [b]1959, [c]1963 Ⓕ

This is an enjoyable demonstration both of Julian Bream's skills and of how he has stimulated composers to extend the guitar's repertoire. Sir Richard Rodney Bennett's Guitar Concerto was written in 1970 and Bream was its dedicatee. Bennett sensibly uses a chamber ensemble whose scope for intimacy matches that of the guitar itself. Over its 20-minute length, it contains many flexible dialogues between solo instrument and ensemble, some especially good woodwind and percussion scoring, all carried through with this composer's usual technical skill. Besides inventive textures, there is a good variety of moods, and the guitar even finds a place in some boisterous outbursts during the work's later stages. The music deserves the fine performance it receives and the performance deserves the excellent recording. Sir Malcolm Arnold's Concerto was written for Bream in 1957. Bream made his record in partnership with the composer – directing the Melos Ensemble – two years later and the results are in every way definitive. The recording was made for RCA by Decca engineers and is beautifully balanced and strikingly warm and atmospheric.

The other coupling is Bream's first stereo recording of the Rodrigo *Concierto de Aranjuez* with Colin Davis in charge of the accompaniment (he went on to record it several more times). There are many, many versions of the Rodrigo available and, while some may cheerfully be passed over, it has long been both difficult and pointless to nominate any of the remaining ones as 'the best'. This, however, can certainly be included in their number.

Film Music

Murder on the Orient Express – Suite. Far from the Madding Crowd – Suite. Lady Caroline Lamb – Elegy[a]. Tender is the Night – Nicole's Theme. Enchanted April – Suite[b]. Four Weddings and a Funeral – Love Theme
[a]**Philip Dukes** *va* [b]**Cynthia Miller** *ondes martenot*
BBC Philharmonic Orchestra / Rumon Gamba
Chandos Movies CHAN9867 (70 minutes: DDD) Ⓕ
Recorded 2000

Anyone who has heard Richard Rodney Bennett's score with John Tavener for *Gormenghast* (Sony) will know that he possesses a natural flair for composing within the constraints of the medium, whether big screen or small. The concept of presenting the music in suites (no credit here for the arrangers) makes the best possible case for it, circumventing the problems encountered on the original soundtracks where fragmentation sometimes marrs enjoyment.

It is a measure of Bennett's standing in the film world that all these scores were issued on disc concurrently with the film. The earliest of them, *Far from the Madding Crowd* (1967, MGM – nla), belongs to another era sonically speaking, but on this sumptuously recorded Chandos disc one can imagine oneself back in that state-of-the-art Odeon, Marble Arch, as the curtains parted to reveal Hardy's Dorset landscape on its giant curved screen, with Bennett's wistful unaccompanied theme for flute answered by oboe on the soundtrack.

Like that film, *Lady Caroline Lamb* was presented on its initial run as a road-show attraction, with an Overture, Entr'acte and Exit Music on the soundtrack, played respectively before the showing, during the intermission and after the film. The Suite reveals RRB's fondness for a lyrical line at its most impassioned, with Philip Duke's eloquent viola playing going to the heart of the story of this aristocratic lady's doomed affair with Byron. A harpsichord touches in the picture of cobbled streets in 19th-century London.

Enchanted April moves us to the sunshine of Italy where the colours of the percussion and ondes martenot lend a sweet fragrance to the scene. Elgar's *Chanson de matin* makes an unexpected but entrancing appearance. When concentrating on the music without visual distractions it is easier to note the discreet Love Theme for *Four Weddings and a Funeral*. Beginning on low flute with broken chords on the harp, it subtly underlines the weddings and the funeral where John Hannah reads Auden's poem *Stop all the Clocks*.

From television comes *Tender is the Night – Nicole's Theme*, a popular foxtrot, '20s style, representing Scott Fitzgerald's ill-fated character Nicole Diver, inspired by his wife Zelda. Period dance music plays a part, too, in *Murder on the Orient Express*, where Yuri Torchinsky, leader of the BBC Philharmonic, catches to a tee that sweet sound so characteristic of Oscar Grasso, leader of Victor Silvester's ballroom orchestra.

Conductor Rumon Gamba knows just how to levitate Bennett's celebrated train waltz theme, and the response of his orchestra throughout this disc suggests that they can turn their hand to the idiom of this music at the flick of a wrist.

Alban Berg

Austrian 1885-1935

GROVE *Berg wrote songs as a youth but had no serious musical education before his lessons with Schoenberg, which began in 1904. Webern was a pupil at the same time, a crucial period in Schoenberg's creative life, when he was moving rapidly towards and into atonality. Berg's Piano Sonata Op 1 (1908) is still tonal, but the Four Songs Op 2 (1910) move away from key and the Op 3 String Quartet (1910) is wholly atonal; it is also remarkable in sustaining, through motivic development, a larger span when the instrumental works of Schoenberg and Webern were comparatively momentary. Berg dedicated it to his wife Helene.*

Then came the Five Songs for soprano Op 4 (1912), miniatures setting poetic instants by Peter Altenberg. This was Berg's first orchestral score, and though it shows an awareness of Schoenberg, Mahler and Debussy, it is brilliantly conceived and points towards Wozzeck – and towards 12-note serialism, notably in its final passacaglia. More immediately Berg produced another set of compact statements, the Four Pieces for clarinet and piano Op 5 (1913), then returned to large form with the Three Orchestral Pieces Op 6 (1915), a thematically linked sequence of prelude, dance movement and funeral march. The prelude begins and ends in the quiet noise of percussion; the other two movements show Berg's discovery of how traditional forms and stylistic elements (including tonal harmony) might support big structures.

In May 1914 Berg saw the Vienna première of Büchner's Woyzeck and formed the plan of setting it. He started the opera in 1917, while he was in the Austrian army (1915-18), and finished it in 1922. He made his own selection from the play's fragmentary scenes to furnish a three-act libretto for formal musical setting: the first act is a suite of five character pieces (five scenes showing the simple soldier Wozzeck in different relationships), the second a five-movement symphony (for the disintegration of his liaison with Marie), the third a set of five inventions on different ostinato ideas (for the tragedy's brutally nihilist climax). The close musical structuring, extending to small details of timing, may be seen as an analogue for the mechanical alienness of the universe around Büchner's central characters, though Berg's music crosses all boundaries, from atonal to tonal (there is a Mahlerian interlude in D minor), from speech to song, from café music to sophisticated textures of dissonant counterpoint. Wozzeck had its première in Berlin in 1925 and thereafter was widely produced, bringing Berg financial security.

His next work, the Chamber Concerto for violin, piano and 13 wind (1925), moves decisively towards a more classical style: its three formally complex movements are still more clearly shaped than those of the op.6 set and the scoring suggests a response to Stravinskian objectivity. The work is also threaded through with ciphers and numerical conceits, making it a celebration of the triune partnership of Schoenberg, Berg and Webern.

Then came the Lyric Suite for string quartet (1926), whose long-secret programme connects it with Berg's intimate feelings for Hanna Fuchs-Robettin – feelings also important to him in the composition of his second opera, Lulu (1929-35). The suite, in six movements of increasingly extreme tempo, uses 12-note serial along with other material in projecting a quasi-operatic development towards catastrophe and annulment.

The development of Lulu was twice interrupted by commissioned works, the concert aria Der Wein on poems by Baudelaire (1929) and the Violin Concerto (1935), and it remained unfinished at Berg's death: his widow placed an embargo on the incomplete third act, which could not be published or performed until 1979. As with Wozzeck, he made his own libretto out of stage material, this time choosing two plays by Wedekind, whom he had long admired for his treatment of sexuality. Dramatically and musically the opera is a huge palindrome, showing Lulu's rise through society in her successive relationships and then her descent into prostitution and eventual death at the hands of Jack the Ripper. Again the score is filled with elaborate formal schemes, around a lyricism unloosed by Berg's individual understanding of 12-note serialism. Something of its threnodic sensuality is continued in the Violin Concerto, designed as a memorial to the teenage daughter of Mahler's widow.

Violin Concerto

Berg Violin Concerto
Stravinsky Violin Concerto in D **Ravel** Tzigane[a]
Itzhak Perlman *vn*
Boston Symphony Orchestra / Seiji Ozawa;
[a]New York Philharmonic Orchestra / Zubin Mehta
DG The Originals 447 445-2GOR (57 minutes: ADD/[a]DDD). Recorded 1978 Ⓜ **OO**

Perlman's account of the Berg Violin Concerto with the Boston orchestra under Ozawa has long occupied a respected place in the catalogue. The original reviewer in Gramophone in March 1980 was completely convinced by Perlman's 'commanding purposefulness'. As to the recording, he wrote that 'though Perlman's violin – beautifully caught – is closer than some will like, there is no question of crude spotlighting'. Twenty years later and in a different competitive climate, his verdict ('These are both performances to put with the very finest') still holds good. Perlman is also a little too close in the *Tzigane*, the recording of which sets him very firmly front-stage again. All the same, this is playing of stature and is still among the best available versions. There are, however, more desirable recordings now available of the Stravinsky Concerto.

Berg Violin Concerto **Rihm** Gesungene Zeit
Anne-Sophie Mutter *vn*
Chicago Symphony Orchestra / James Levine
DG 437 093-2GH (52 minutes: DDD). Ⓕ
Recorded 1992 ●

One of the very few 12 note pieces to have retained a place in the repertory, Berg's Violin Concerto is a work on many levels. Behind the complex intellectual façade of the construction is a poignant sense of loss, ostensibly for Alma Mahler's daughter, Manon Gropius, but also for Berg's own youth; and behind that is a disconcerting mixture of styles which resists interpretation as straightforward Romantic consolation. Not that performers need to go out of their way to project these layers; given a soloist as comprehensively equipped as Anne-Sophie Mutter and orchestral support as vivid as the Chicago Symphony's they cannot fail to register. Their recording makes a fine demonstration-quality recording alternative to the version of Krasner and Webern.

Awards 1991

Violin Concerto. H
Lyric Suite (original version)
Louis Krasner *vn* **Galimir Quartet**
(Felix Galimir, Adrienne Galimir *vns*
Renee Galimir *va* Marguerite Galimir *vc*);
BBC Symphony Orchestra / Anton Webern
Testament mono SBT1004 (57 minutes: ADD) Ⓕ
Recorded 1936 ●●●

This is an extraordinary issue of more than mere documentary interest. Krasner commissioned the Violin Concerto and had just given the first performance at the 1936 ISCM Festival in Barcelona (with Hermann Scherchen conducting) only three months after Berg's death. Webern was to have conducted on this occasion but withdrew at the last moment much to the consternation of the BBC who had booked him for the following month with (it would seem) some misgivings. Fortunately adequate rehearsal time had been allotted and the players of the BBC Symphony Orchestra proved more expert in coping with the score than their Barcelona colleagues. Webern had appeared on a number of occasions with the BBC orchestra, but no recording of him survives in the BBC Archives. Berg's death had shocked the musical world, though not as much as the death of the 18-year-old Manon Gropius had shaken the composer, who wrote the concerto as a memorial to her. The disc is exceptionally well documented and includes some interesting notes by Krasner himself.

What strikes one most about this performance is its glowing intensity. There is no sense of the bar-line or of the music ever being 'moved on'; time seems to stand still and yet there is also a natural sense of musical pace. The surface noise on this recording, made before an invited audience in the Concert Hall of Broadcasting House, London, cannot disguise the care with which the textures are balanced and the finesse of the wind players. This was only the work's second performance and yet the players sound as if they had lived with the music all their lives. It has all the anguish and poignancy this music demands and Krasner is an eloquent exponent. The opening bars suffer from some minor audience coughs and the surface noise and moments of distortion call for a tolerance that is well worth extending. The Galimir Quartet specialized in contemporary music and its playing has commendable ensemble and dedication. Unfortunately its pioneering account of the *Lyric Suite*, recorded shortly before the performance of the Violin Concerto took place, was hampered by a very dry acoustic and this must have deterred many listeners. It was the only version for many years and in spite of its musical excellence cannot have made many new friends for the work. The dry sound is worrying, of course, but that should not deter collectors from acquiring this remarkable issue.

Lyric Suite

String Quartet, Op 3. Lyric Suite (original version)
Alban Berg Quartet (Günther Pichler, Gerhard Schulz *vns* Thomas Kakuska *va* Valentin Erben *vc*)
EMI CDC5 55190-2 (46 minutes: DDD). Ⓕ
Recorded 1991-92

This disc brings into focus Berg's two masterpieces for the medium. EMI offers a broad perspective, the four players very forward and distinct. Details may at times seem too intrusive for the good of an integrated interpretation, and the concern to make every emotional nuance tell risks spilling the music over into melodrama. The Berg Quartet probes the extremes of the music determinedly, and their unfailingly bright sound can sometimes seem larger than life. However, there's no doubting the emotional power of the recording.

Piano Sonata, Op 1

Berg Piano Sonata, Op 1
Schoenberg Drei Klavierstücke, Op 11. Sechs Klavierstücke, Op 19. Fünf Klavierstücke, Op 23. Piano Suite, Op 25. Klavierstücke, Op 33*a* and Op 33*b*
Webern Variations, Op 27
Peter Hill *pf*
Naxos 8 553870 (79 minutes: DDD). Ⓢ
Recorded 1996 ●●

When interviewed by *Gramophone* back in September 1989, Peter Hill said he felt he had things to say about the Schoenberg piano works which had not been said on record. Here is the complete vindication of that statement. These are scrupulously prepared performances, with all the polyphonic strands clarified and all the myriad articulation marks respected. In order to accommodate that detail and let it speak musically, Hill takes tempos on the relaxed side of Schoenberg's frequently rather manic metronome indications. The first two of the Op 11 pieces gain a gravity that might have surprised the composer, and the fourth piece of Op 23 loses some of the suggested *schwungvoll* character. Yet there is no lack of brilliance and velocity in such pieces as the Gigue from Op 25, and time and again Hill's thoughtfulness and search for expressiveness and beauty of sound justify his spacious approach.

Hill probes with equal subtlety, sympathy and high intelligence in the Webern Variations, while in the Berg Sonata, Hill's unforced lyricism, inwardness and flexibility of phrasing are again immensely appealing. Apart from its amazing value for money, Naxos's first-rate recording quality, Peter Hill's own lucid booklet-essay, and what sounds like an ideally regulated instrument, all contribute to the outstanding success of this issue.

Seven Early Songs

Three Orchestral Pieces, Op 6. Seven Early Songs. Der Wein

Anne Sofie von Otter *mez* **Vienna Philharmonic Orchestra / Claudio Abbado**

DG 445 846-2GH (49 minutes: DDD). Texts and translations included. Recorded 1992-93 Ⓕ ●

Anne Sofie von Otter included the *Seven Early Songs* on a recital disc, a programme glowing in the sunset of German romanticism. Singing with orchestra, von Otter naturally works on a larger scale. The words are more firmly bound into the vocal line; there is not the detailed give-and-take that is possible with a pianist. But the outline of her interpretation remains that of a true Lieder singer, always lighting upon unexpected subtleties of colour and emphasis to inflect the poetry. In all this Abbado is an equal partner. Von Otter needs careful accompaniment in the concert hall if she is to dominate an orchestra and Abbado, in co-operation with DG's technical team, has produced a balance that never drowns her, but still sounds fairly natural. In *Der Wein*, Berg's late concert aria, von Otter and Abbado catch the lilt of the jazz rhythms. In the *Seven Early Songs* are they a touch too cool? Perhaps, but in the final song, 'Sommertage', they throw caution to the winds and end the cycle on a passionate high.

Abbado has recorded the *Three Orchestral Pieces* before and his 1970s recording has long been one of the standard versions of this work. The opportunity to see how his thoughts have developed since then brings more surprises than one might have expected. In short, his outlook is progressing from the Italianate to the Germanic. No doubt the influence of the Vienna Philharmonic Orchestra has much to do with this and their marvellously eloquent playing is one of the prime attractions of the disc. In their company Abbado finds more depth and complexity in the music than before, although that does mean that the March loses the Bartókian attack and driving rhythms that made his first version so exciting.

Berg Seven Early Songs
Korngold Liebesbriefchen, Op 9 No 4; Sterbelied, Op 14 No 1; Gefasster Abschied, Op 14 No 4; Drei Lieder, Op 18; Glückwunsch, Op 38 No 1; Alt-spanisch, Op 38 No 3; Sonett für Wien, Op 41
R Strauss Wie sollten wir geheim sie halten, Op 19 No 4; Ich trage meine Minne, Op 32 No 1; Der Rosenband, Op 36 No 1; Hat gesagt – bleibt's nicht dabei, Op 36 No 3; Meinem Kinde, Op 37 No 3; Befreit, Op 39 No 4; Die sieben Siegel, Op 46 No 3

Anne Sofie von Otter *mez* **Bengt Forsberg** *pf*

DG 437 515-2GH (64 minutes: DDD). Texts and translations included. Recorded 1991-93 Ⓕ ●●

The chosen Strauss songs here are gentle and affectionate, a mood in which von Otter is often at her best. Not that, having captured a mood, she is content to let it lie dully over as much as a verse or a line. In *Der Rosenband* she is always sensitive to the modulations; in *Ich trage meine Minne* the voice darkens with the change of tonality in verse two; in *Wie sollten wir geheim sie halten* she captures the subdued excitement of the opening as she does the frank exultation of the close. For lightness of touch, the Op 38 songs endear themselves among the Korngold group: *Glückwunsch* has an unaffected, comfortable way with it, and *Alt-spanisch* (with its reminiscence of 'On yonder hill there stands a maiden') is an absolute charmer.

At the centre of the recital are the *Seven Early Songs* of Alban Berg. The first, 'Nacht', which is also the longest and most readily memorable, is taken rather more slowly than usual, but gaining in its subtler evocations of the mists and then the silvered mountain paths. Von Otter's draining the voice of all vibrato also helps to create the sense of watchful stillness, just as in the sixth song, 'Liebesode', it makes for an almost other-worldly dreaminess, deepening to a full-bodied passion as the rose scent is borne to the love-bed. Always the mezzo-soprano voice is resourcefully used, able to colour deeply at such points, to float a pure head-tone in 'Traumgekrönt' or launch to a simply radiant high A in 'Die Nachtigall'.

Five Orchestral Songs, Op 4

Fünf Orchesterlieder nach Ansichtskartentexten von Peter Altenberg, Op 4. Lyric Suite (arr cpsr; originally for string quartet). Lulu – Symphonie

Juliane Banse *sop* **Vienna Philharmonic Orchestra / Claudio Abbado**

DG 447 749-2GH (54 minutes: DDD). Texts and translations included. Recorded 1994 Ⓕ ●●

Claudio Abbado's account of *Lulu* is ravishingly beautiful, with a warmly poetic ardour to Alwa's music that so few real-life singers can give it (the 'Hymne', too, is genuinely hymn-like). The concluding scene has a dark, passionate vehemence and pity that are deeply moving. Any suspicion that he might be overbeautifying the music is erased by the hectic, almost garish drama of the second movement ostinato and the sober gravity that both he and Juliane Banse bring to the 'Lied der Lulu'. Banse is admirable in the *Altenberg* Lieder, too: expressive, unhampered by the range of the vocal line, and bringing to the last song a wide-spanning lyricism that seems almost a foretaste of Geschwitz's death-song in *Lulu*. Aside from a slightly blunted edge, even a slight loss of wit, in its opening movement, the *Lyric Suite* has the same admirable combination of richness and orchestral detail as the *Altenberg* Lieder – in the central movement Abbado demonstrates that clarity and a marking of *misterioso* are not incompatible – and the third movement, as it should be, is the Suite's emotional nub: the Vienna Philharmonic's strings respond with glowing passion. One can say no better of the recording than that it sounds as though Abbado did his own balancing.

Lulu

(orchestration of Act 3 completed by Friedrich Cerha)
Teresa Stratas *sop* Lulu; **Franz Mazura** *bar* Dr Schön, Jack; **Kenneth Riegel** *ten* Alwa; **Yvonne Minton** *mez* Countess Geschwitz; **Robert Tear** *ten* The Painter, A Negro; **Toni Blankenheim** *bar* Schigolch, Professor of Medicine, The Police Officer; **Gerd Nienstedt** *bass* An Animal-tamer, Rodrigo; **Helmut Pampuch** *ten* The Prince, The Manservant, The Marquis; **Jules Bastin** *bass* The Theatre Manager, The Banker; **Hanna Schwarz** *mez* A Dresser in the theatre, High School Boy, A Groom; **Jane Manning** *sop* A 15-year-old girl; **Ursula Boese** *mez* Her Mother; **Anna Ringart** *mez* A Lady Artist; **Claude Meloni** *bar* A Journalist; **Pierre-Yves Le Maigat** *bass* A Manservant
Paris Opéra Orchestra / Pierre Boulez
DG The Originals ③ 463 617-2GOR2 Ⓜ
(172 minutes: ADD). Notes, text and translation included. Recorded 1979 **OOO**

Now here's a masterpiece that fulfils all the requirements for a commercial smash hit – it's sexy, violent, cunning, sophisticated, hopelessly complicated and emotionally draining. *Lulu* was Berg's second opera and easily matches his first – *Wozzeck* – for pathos and dramatic impact. The meaningful but gloriously over-the-top story-line, after two tragedies by Frank Wedekind, deserves acknowledgement. Lulu, mistress of Dr Schön, is married to a medical professor. An artist also has the hots for her, but just as his passion gets out of hand, her husband walks in, catches them approaching the act and dies of shock. She marries the artist, who learns about Dr Schön and kills himself; then she marries the jealous Dr Schön, and eventually kills *him*. Smuggled out of prison by an adoring lesbian, she sets up home in Paris with Schön's son, gets blackmailed and ends up in London as one of Jack the Ripper's victims! And that's not the half of it, but we'll spare you the rest.

What matters is that Berg's music is magnificent, romantic enough to engage the passions of listeners normally repelled by 12-tone music, and cerebral enough to keep eggheads fully employed. It's opulent yet subtle (saxophone and piano lend the score a hint of jazz-tinted decadence), with countless telling thematic inter-relations and much vivid tonal character-painting. Berg left it incomplete (only 390 of the Third Act's 1326 bars were orchestrated by him), but Friedrich Cerha's painstaking reconstruction is a major achievement, especially considering the complicated web of Berg's musical tapestry. This particular recording first opened our ears to the 'real' Lulu in 1979, and has transferred extremely well to CD.

The booklet contains a superb essay by Boulez which in itself is enough to stimulate the interest of a potential listener. The performance is highly distinguished. Teresa Stratas is an insinuating yet vulnerable Lulu, Yvonne Minton a sensuous Gräfin Geschwitz and Robert Tear an ardent artist. Dr Schön is tellingly portrayed by Franz Mazura, Kenneth Riegel is highly creditable as Schön's son and that Boulez himself is both watchful of detail and responsive to the drama, hardly needs saying. It's not an easy listen, but it'll certainly keep you on your toes for a stimulating, even exasperating evening.

Additional recommendation
Lulu (without Act 3)
Lear Lulu **Fischer-Dieskau** Dr Schön
Coupling: Wozzeck
Orchestra of the Deutsche Oper, Berlin / Böhm
DG ③ 435 705-2GX3 (216 minutes: ADD: 1/93) Ⓑ
Böhm's beautifully shaped, romantic view of the opera is well worth hearing for Fischer-Dieskau's fascinating Dr Schön and Evelyn Lear's Lulu even though the three act version has greater allure these days.

Wozzeck

Franz Grundheber *bar* Wozzeck; **Hildegard Behrens** *sop* Marie; **Heinz Zednik** *ten* Captain; **Aage Haugland** *bass* Doctor; **Philip Langridge** *ten* Andres; **Walter Raffeiner** *ten* Drum-Major; **Anna Gonda** *mez* Margret; **Alfred Sramek** *bass* First Apprentice; **Alexander Maly** *bar* Second Apprentice; **Peter Jelosits** *ten* Idiot **Vienna Boys' Choir; Vienna State Opera Chorus; Vienna Philharmonic Orchestra / Claudio Abbado**
DG ② 423 587-2GH2 (89 minutes: DDD). Notes, text and translation included. Recorded live in 1987 Ⓕ **O**

A live recording, in every sense of the word. The cast is uniformly excellent, with Grundheber, good both at the wretched pathos of Wozzeck's predicament and his helpless bitterness, and Behrens as an outstandingly intelligent and involving Marie, even the occasional touch of strain in her voice heightening her characterization. The Vienna Philharmonic responds superbly to Abbado's ferociously close-to-the-edge direction. It is a live recording with a bit of a difference, mark you: the perspectives are those of a theatre, not a recording studio. The orchestra is laid out as it would be in an opera-house pit and the movement of singers on stage means that voices are occasionally overwhelmed. The result is effective: the crowded inn-scenes, the arrival and departure of the military band, the sense of characters actually reacting to each other, not to a microphone, makes for a grippingly theatrical experience. This version has a raw urgency, a sense of bitter protest and angry pity that are quite compelling and uncomfortably eloquent.

Wozzeck
Eberhard Waechter *bar* Wozzeck; **Anja Silja** *sop* Marie; **Heinz Zednik** *ten* Captain; **Alexander Malta** *bass* Doctor; **Horst Laubenthal** *ten* Andres; **Hermann Winkler** *ten* Drum-Major; **Gertrude Jahn** *mez* Margret; **Alfred Sramek** *bass* First Apprentice; **Franz Waechter** *bar* Second Apprentice; **Walter Wendig** *ten* Idiot
Vienna State Opera Chorus; Vienna Philharmonic Orchestra / Christoph von Dohnányi

Schoenberg Erwartung, Op 17
Anja Silja *sop* **Vienna Philharmonic Orchestra / Christoph von Dohnányi**
Decca ② 417 348-2DH2 (123 minutes: DDD). Ⓕ
Notes, texts and translations included
Recorded1979

Wozzeck is an expressionist score, not a late romantic one; there is a danger that once the hideous difficulties of playing it have been mastered, an orchestra (especially if that orchestra be the Vienna Philharmonic, perhaps) will be tempted by the obvious, just-under-the-surface kinships with Mahler to play it as though it were Mahler. Dohnányi's outstanding performance falls into this trap once in a while. Dohnányi's version is more beautiful in orchestral texture, more sophisticated in recording technique, at times more subtle in its pacing than Abbado's account, but both his principal singers sound strained, Waechter severely so. Dohnányi's *Wozzeck* is easier to listen to than Abbado, and it is refreshing to return to it whenever you want a more comfortable perspective or a more Straussian view of the work (and the inclusion of a decent but not outstandingly vivid account of Schoenberg's *Erwartung* makes it better value than its other rivals), but compared to the Abbado it is studio-bound, with all the singers in word-enhancing, but illusion-shattering, close-up.

Luciano Berio

Italian 1925

GROVE *Berio studied with his father and grandfather, both organists and composers, and with Ghedini at the Milan Conservatory in the late 1940s. In 1950 he married the American singer Cathy Berberian, and the next year at Tanglewood he met Dallapiccola, who influenced his move towards and beyond 12-note serialism in such works as his Joyce cycle Chamber Music for voice and trio (1953). Further stimulus came from his meetings with Maderna, Pousseur and Stockhausen in Basle in 1954, and he became a central member of the Darmstadt circle. He directed an electronic music studio at the Milan station of Italian radio (1955-61), at the same time producing Sequenza I for flute (1958, the first of a cycle of solo explorations of performing gestures), Circles (1960, a loop of Cummings settings for voice, harp and percussion) and Epifanie (1961, an aleatory set of orchestral and vocal movements designed to show different kinds of vocal behaviour). These established his area of interest: with the means and archetypes of musical communication.*

For most of the next decade he was in the USA, teaching and composing, his main works of this period including the Dante-esque Laborintus II for voices and orchestra (1965), the Sinfonia for similar resources (1969, with a central movement whirling quotations round Mahler and Beckett) and Opera (1970), a study of the decline of the genre and of Western bourgeois civilization. Two more operas, La vera storia (1982) and Un re in ascolto (1984), came out of his collaboration with Calvino. Other works include Coro (1976), a panoply of poster statements and refracted folksongs for chorus and orchestra, and numerous orchestral and chamber pieces.

Concerto II, 'Echoing Curves'

Rendering. Concerto II, 'Echoing Curves'. Quattro versioni originali della 'Ritirata notturna di Madrid'
Andrea Lucchesini *pf*
London Symphony Orchestra / Luciano Berio
RCA Victor Red Seal 09026 68894-2 (68 minutes: DDD). Recorded 1995 Ⓕ

Reworking takes many different forms with Berio. The simplest kind is to be heard here in the maddeningly repetitive but gloriously witty fusing together of Boccherini's four versions of his successful pot-boiler, *Ritirata notturna di Madrid*. On a much grander scale comes *Rendering*, which works around Berio's orchestration of the sketches for Schubert's 10th Symphony. At 35 minutes this is a big piece – the composer's own reading is phrased throughout with special sensitivity, and relishes the gentle and strange discontinuities between Schubert and Berio with absorbing delicacy. Berio is at his best, and most distinctive, when the composer he reworks is Luciano Berio. *Concerto II, 'Echoing Curves'*, from 1988-89, is a rich, complex elaboration of a work for piano and ensemble called *Points on the curve to find* ... from 1974. More Boulezian than much Berio in its slow-moving tissue of clusters, trills and *tremolandos*, its shimmering textures conjure up remarkable density and luminosity, and the music is perfectly shaped to prepare a finely graded 'dying fall'. The performances have absolute authorial conviction, and the 'big hall' sound is plushy without excessive resonance.

Coro

Cologne Radio Chorus and Symphony Orchestra / Luciano Berio
DG 20th Century Classics 423 902-2GC Ⓜ
(57 minutes: ADD). Recorded 1980

The entire concept of *Coro* depends on pairings, which can emphasize both the differences and the similarities between each member of the pair. Thus each of the 40 choral singers is paired with an instrumentalist (they sit together in performance), while the text pairs 'folk' poetry – the 'tribal' expression of concern with such universals as love and death – with 'art' poetry – the individual expression of a single poet, Neruda, who turns poetry towards an explicitly political content. *Coro* returns regularly to several of its texts, but most persistently to Neruda's line 'Come and see blood in the Streets'. Whether or not Berio intends to preach a sermon on the need for individuals to engage in collective action, the music is undeniably forceful, and also well varied. The opening, in the composer's most lyric vein, shows how important repetition will be, and also reveals the kind of melodic patterns which increasingly evoke Stravinsky's *Les noces* as the work proceeds. *Les noces* also comes to mind during the more dance-like episodes, and in the denser, more impassioned sections Berio's own post-Stravinskian 'ritualism' is evident.The texture of *Coro* may seem overloaded in places, and the text itself is often submerged by the sheer complexity of the competing musical lines. But the work avoids the episodic diffuseness of some of Berio's other large-scale compositions, and is hampered neither by a spoken narration nor an electronic tape. Its diverse elements are skilfully integrated, and the result is a highly personal, yet urgently communicative statement, persuasively performed and well recorded. In fact, *Coro* emerges as one of Berio's best and most ambitious works of synthesis.

Recital I for Cathy

Berio Recital I for Cathy[a]. 11 Folk Songs[b]
Weill (arr Berio. Sung in English) Die Dreigroschenoper – Ballade von der sexuellen Hörigkeit. Mario Galante – Le grand Lustucru. Happy End – Surabaya-Johnny
Cathy Berberian *mez*
[a]**London Sinfonietta;** [b]**Juilliard Ensemble / Luciano Berio**
RCA Victor Gold Seal 09026 62540-2
(65 minutes: ADD). Texts included. Ⓜ
Recorded 1972 ●●

These are classic recordings that no contemporary music enthusiast or Berberian/Berio admirer will want to be without. This disc could be regarded as a fitting tribute to Cathy Berberian and her inimitable vocal genius. As an artist she was unique. As a champion of contemporary music (particularly music by her one-time husband Luciano Berio) she was second to none – not only for her interpretative prowess but also the inspirational quality of her highly individual style; many composers (including Stravinsky) wrote music specifically with her voice in mind.

The recordings gathered together here were all composed, or arranged for her, by Luciano Berio. The two principal items are perhaps among the most famous of the Berberian/Berio collaborations. *Recital I for Cathy* makes use of Berberian's dramatic training in a composition in which the vocalist, frustrated by the non-appearance of her pianist, struggles through the programme whilst simultaneously sharing a Beckett-like stream-of-consciousness monologue with her audience. Berberian's performance here is a monumental *tour de force*. Another example of the extraordinary qualities of Berberian's voice can be found in the celebrated *Folk Songs* of 1964.

The three songs by Kurt Weill reveal Berberian as a natural Weill interpreter (perhaps the best since Lotte Lenya). They are something of a find, this being their first ever release on disc. All in all, this is a wonderful tribute to a phenomenal talent.

Sequenzas

Awards 1999

Sequenzas – I-VIII, IX*a*, IX*b* and X-XIII, 'Chanson'
Luisa Castellani *sop* **Sophie Cherrier** *fl* **Lazlo Hadady** *ob* **Alain Damiens** *cl* **Pascal Gallois** *bn* **Christian Wirth** *alto sax* **Gabriele Cassone** *tpt* **Benny Sluchin** *tbn* **Jeanne-Marie Conquer** *vn* **Christophe Desjardins** *va* **Frédérique Cambreling** *hp* **Elliot Fisk** *gtr* **Florent Boffard** *pf* **Teodoro Anzellotti** *accordion*
DG ③ 20/21 457 038-2GH3 (158 minutes: DDD) Ⓕ
Recorded 1994-97 ●●●

Berio's ongoing sequence of solo compositions complements his larger-scale vocal and orchestral works in various productive ways. That does not make the *Sequenzas* 'miniatures', however: one of the most recent, No 12 for bassoon (1995), is at 18 minutes also the longest, and even the shortest (No 1, for flute, at just over six minutes) offers a distillation which, for all its elegance, is far from lightweight. Berio has come a long way since 1958, when No 1 was written, yet the flexible eloquence with which he imbues some ordinary avant-garde gestures in that piece is early evidence of a distinctive quality of thought which was to mature and intensify in the years ahead. Five years on, in No 2 for harp (1963), the instrument's conventionally genteel image is transformed into vivid confrontations between the seductive and the aggressive, and this formula is developed still more radically in No 3 for female voice (1965). No 4 (1966) is also highly expressionistic, concentrating on the brittle, dense textures of which the piano is capable, rather than seeking to spin a long, connected line. No 5 for trombone (1965), by contrast, is a haunting exploration of the instrument's 'voice', as well as of the voice of the player, the use of long, slow *glissandos* a model for the more elaborate treatment of the device in the bassoon *Sequenza* 30 years later.

That all the performers on these discs – most are members of the Ensemble Inter-Contemporain – are on top of challenging material goes without saying. They might not always stick to the letter of dynamic markings, but the spirit of the music is always vividly conveyed, and the recordings are good. Of the later *Sequenzas*, none is finer than the staggeringly virtuosic No 6 for viola (1967) charting Berio's complex response to the Paganinian romantic heritage, and No 8 for violin (1976) where Bach replaces Paganini as model in a piece with enough of the grandeur and sense of inevitability of Bach's great Chaconne to justify the comparison. With the short No 7 for oboe (1967) Berio hit on the strategy of placing the instrument's intensely volatile line against a single sustained tone (off-stage or electronic), and a comparable effect is used in No 10. Here the trumpet occasionally plays into an open grand piano, which catches and transforms the resonance to create ethereal echo-effects. No 9 from 1980 (for clarinet, and also for saxophone) is to some extent an experiment in constraint, limiting the melodic materials and developing dialogues between varied repetitions, while No 11 (1988) for guitar wittily explores the ways in which the instrument's own limitations can be exploited and challenged. With No 12's superbly long-drawn out but never monotonous bassoon lament, and No 13 for accordion (also 1995) revealing the instrument's capacity for delicate and poetic, as well as brusque, even sinister utterance, it is clear that Berio's interest in putting single instruments under the spotlight was as strong in the mid-1990s as it had been nearly 40 years before.

These discs are a wonderful reminder of why Berio's music matters, and a definitive document of a very special 20th-century achievement.

Sinfonia

Sinfonia. Eindrücke
Regis Pasquier *vn*
New Swingle Singers; French National Orchestra / Pierre Boulez
Erato MusiFrance 2292-45228-2 (45 minutes: DDD). Recorded 1980s Ⓕ ⭘

This was the first complete recording of Berio's *Sinfonia*. Until this, this absorbing and bewilderingly complex work was available only in the four-movement version that Berio himself prepared in 1969 for the first performance with the Swingle Singers and the New York Philharmonic Orchestra (once available on CBS); less than happily coupled with Bartók's *Music for strings, percussion and celesta*). Within a few months, Berio had completed a fifth and final movement which, though ostensibly an appendix, arguably stands as the apotheosis of the entire work; for it is genuinely a 'sounding together' (sinfonia) of the preceding movements, a rich sequence of reminiscences, just as the celebrated third movement leads us through memories of the standard orchestral repertoire in a kind of stream of subconsciousness. To hear the work in its completed form is nothing short of a revelation, and for this reason alone Boulez's performance must be said to supersede Berio's own. To complete the disc he has chosen one of Berio's less-familiar orchestral works, *Eindrücke* ('Impressions') of 1973-74. This is a complete contrast: a vast monody, projected by the string orchestra against the stuttering interjections and lingering trills of the wind and percussion, a stark and uncompromising conception. Again, the reading is a powerful one. This is a most important issue, far too good to miss.

Further Listening
Solo Piano Works
Cinque Variazioni; Wasserklavier; Sequenza IV; Rounds; Erdenklavier; Luftklavier; Feuerklavier; Brin; Leaf; Petite Suite
Arden *pf*
New Albion NA089CD (49 minutes: DDD) Ⓕ
No longer available in the UK, but try the internet
Berio's piano music is characteristically probing in the way it seeks out new approaches to keyboard sonority. This disc, which includes *Sequenza IV* – his most extended solo piano work – is an essential addition to the discography

Hector Berlioz French 1803-1869

GROVE *As a boy Berlioz learnt the flute, guitar and, from treatises alone, harmony (he never studied the piano); his first compositions were romances and small chamber pieces. After two unhappy years as a medical student in Paris (1821-23) he abandoned the career chosen for him by his father and turned decisively to music, attending Le Sueur's composition class at the Conservatoire. He entered for the Prix de Rome four times (1827-30) and finally won. Among the most powerful influences on him were Shakespeare, whose plays were to inspire three major works, and the actress Harriet Smithson, whom he idolized, pursued and, after a bizarre courtship, eventually married (1833). Beethoven's symphonies too made a strong impact, along with Goethe's Faust and the works of Moore, Scott and Byron. The most important product of this time was his startlingly original, five-movement Symphonie fantastique (1830).*

Berlioz's 15 months in Italy (1831-32) were significant more for his absorption of warmth, vivacity and local colour than for the official works he wrote there; he moved out of Rome as often as possible and worked on a sequel to the Symphonie fantastique (Le retour à la vie, renamed Lélio in 1855) and overtures to King Lear and Rob Roy, returning to Paris early to promote his music. Although the 1830s and early 1840s saw a flow of major compositions – Harold en Italie, Benvenuto Cellini, Grande messe des morts, Roméo et Juliette, Grande symphonie funèbre et triomphale, Les nuits d'été – his musical career was now essentially a tragic one. He failed to win much recognition, his works were considered eccentric or 'incorrect' and he had reluctantly to rely on journalism for a living; from 1834 he wrote chiefly for the and the Gazette musicale and the Journal des débats .

As the discouragements of Paris increased, however, performances and recognition abroad beckoned: between 1842 and 1863 Berlioz spent most of his time touring, in Germany, Austria, Russia, England and elsewhere. Hailed as an advanced composer, he also became known as a leading modern conductor. He produced literary works (notably the Mémoires) and another series of musical masterpieces – La damnation de Faust, the Te Deum, L'enfance du Christ, the vast epic Les troyens (1856-58; partly performed, 1863) and Béatrice et Bénédict (1860-62) – meanwhile enjoying happy if short-lived relationships with Liszt and Wagner. The loss of his father, his son Louis (1834-67), two wives, two sisters and friends merely accentuated the weary decline of his last years, marked by his spiritual isolation from Parisian taste and the new music of Germany alike.

A lofty idealist with a leaping imagination, Berlioz was subject to violent emotional changes from enthusiasm to misery; only his sharp wit saved him from morbid self-pity over the disappointments in his private and professional life. The intensity of the personality is inextricably woven into the music: all his works reflect something in himself expressed through poetry, literature, religion or drama. Sincere expression is the key – matching means to expressive ends, often to the point of mixing forms and media, ignoring pre-set schemes. In Les troyens, his grand opera on Virgil's Aeneid, for example, aspects of the monumental and the intimate, the symphonic and the operatic, the decorative and the solemn converge. Similarly his symphonies, from the explicitly dramatic Symphonie fantastique with its idée fixe (the theme representing his beloved, changed and distorted in line with the work's scenario), to the picturesque Harold en Italie with its concerto element, to the operatic choral symphony cum tone poem Roméo et Juliette, are all characteristic in their mixture of genres. Of his other orchestral works, the overture Le carnaval romain stands out as one of the most extrovert and brilliant. Among the choral works, Faust and L'enfance du Christ combine dramatic action and philosophic reflection, while the Requiem and Te Deum exploit to the full Berlioz's most spacious, ceremonial style.

Though Berlioz's compositional style has long been considered idiosyncratic, it can be seen to rely on an abundance of both technique and inspiration. Typical are expansive melodies of irregular phrase length, sometimes with a slight chromatic inflection, and expressive though not tonally adventurous harmonies. Freely contrapuntal textures predominate, used to a variety of fine effects including superimposition of separate themes; a striking boldness in rhythmic articulation gives the music much of its vitality. Berlioz left perhaps his most indelible mark as an orchestrator, finding innumerable and subtle ways to combine and contrast instruments (both on stage and off), effectively emancipating the procedure of orchestration for generations of later composers. As a critic he admired above all Gluck and Beethoven, expressed doubt about Wagner and fought endlessly against the second-rate.

Overtures

Overtures – Les francs-juges, Op 3. Waverley, Op 1. King Lear, Op 4. Le carnaval romain, Op 9. Béatrice et Bénédict. Le corsaire, Op 21. Benvenuto Cellini
Staatskapelle Dresden / Sir Colin Davis
RCA Victor Red Seal 09026 68790-2 (74 minutes: DDD). Recorded 1997 Ⓕ **OO**

Berlioz's seven overtures fit comfortably into an hour and a quarter, in performances that reflect Sir Colin's long absorption with music that remains difficult, original, surprising. The most extrovert, the Ball Scene in *Le carnaval romain*, is exhilaratingly played, but done so without the strenuous attempts after excitement at all costs, through speed and volume, which are all too familiar. The music is more interesting than that, its tensions more dramatic. What are perhaps the two hardest overtures to play successfully, *Waverley* and *King Lear*, benefit from some understatement, especially in the quieter sections when, particularly in *Lear*, a sense of trouble animates the music. As elsewhere, Berlioz's melodies made out of awkward rhythms and uneven metres call for a skilled hand: nowhere is this more evident than at the opening of *Benvenuto Cellini*, whose oddity does not immediately strike the listener but whose 'rightness' is proved by its wonderful verve. Davis handles this superbly, as in different vein he does the soft music answering the opening of *Le carnaval romain*, in which he is given some beautiful playing (especially from the cor anglais) by the Dresden orchestra. It responds to his understanding of the different levels of tension and expression, as well as different dynamic levels, at which Berlioz can make his effects, such as at the start of *Les francs-juges*. Sometimes a slight emphasis in the accompaniment, even the touch of warmth on a single note, can illuminate much in the melody. It is all beautifully done.

Harold in Italy, Op 16

Harold in Italy. Tristia, Op 18.
Les Troyens à Carthage – Act 2, Prelude
Nobuko Imai *va* **John Alldis Choir; London Symphony Orchestra / Sir Colin Davis**
Philips 416 431-2PH (70 minutes: ADD). Texts and translations included. Recorded 1969-80 Ⓕ **OO**

Berlioz was much influenced by the British romantic poet, Byron, and his travels in Italy – where he went in 1831 as the winner of the Prix de Rome – led him to conceive a big orchestral work based on one of Byron's most popular works, *Childe Harold's Pilgrimage*. Like Berlioz's earlier *Symphonie fantastique*, *Harold in Italy* was not only a programme work but brilliantly unconventional and imaginative in its structure and argument. A commission from the great virtuoso, Paganini, led him to conceive a big viola concerto, but the idea of a Byronic symphony got in the way of that. Though there is an important viola solo in the symphony as we know it – richly and warmly played on Davis's recording by Nobuko Imai – it is far from being the vehicle for solo display that Paganini was wanting. Sir Colin Davis's 1975 performance, beautifully transferred to CD, emphasizes the symphonic strength of the writing without losing the bite of the story-telling. The shorter works are also all valuable in illustrating Berlioz's extraordinary imagination. Excellent sound on all the different vintage recordings.

Harold in Italy. Tristia, Op 18 P
Gérard Caussé *va* **Monteverdi Choir; Orchestre Révolutionnaire et Romantique / Sir John Eliot Gardiner**
Philips 446 676-2PH (60 minutes: DDD). Text and translation included. Recorded 1994 Ⓕ ⚬⚬

It is to Gardiner's credit that, like Davis, he conveys that element of wildness without ever slackening control. With Gardiner dynamic contrasts are extreme, far more strikingly so than in most period-instrument performances, and some of the *pianissimos* from the ORR strings are ravishing. The central *Canto religioso* of the second movement of the Pilgrims' hymn provides a remarkable instance, with the arpeggios *sul ponticello* of the solo viola far more eerie than usual. Gardiner's soloist, Gérard Caussé, uses vibrato sparingly. Yet for the smooth phrases of Harold's theme, the work's motto, Caussé consciously produces warm tone. It is a fine solo performance, but not so dominant that one feels the lack of a soloist in the last three-quarters of the finale. It is there that Gardiner's reading, intense from the start, reaches white heat, and it is worth noting that there, as in the rest of the performance, his speeds are never excessively fast. Altogether a thrilling performance, highly recommendable to those who would not normally consider a version with period instruments.

In the three movements of *Tristia* Gardiner, using his own Monteverdi Choir, gives equally refreshing performances, and here the dynamic contrasts are more extreme than in Davis's analogue recording. So the epilogue to the 'Hamlet Funeral March', the third of the three movements, is the more chilling and broken in mood for the extreme hush of the *pianissimo*.

Harold in Italy[a]. Le corsaire – Overture[b]. King Lear – Overture[c]. Trojan March[d] H
[a]**Frederick Riddle** *va* [abd]**Royal Philharmonic Orchestra;** [c]**BBC Symphony Orchestra / Sir Thomas Beecham**
BBC Legends/IMG Artists mono BBCL4065-2 (72 minutes: ADD). Recorded live in [a]1956, [b]1951, [c]1954 and [d]1951 Ⓜ ⚬⚬

These radio recordings of Beecham in full flight could not be more welcome, particularly when his studio recordings of Berlioz with the RPO – including the works listed here have disappeared from the current catalogue. The mono sound here is limited but beefy and immediate, with fine transfers by Paul Baily, even though the opening *Corsaire* Overture is taken from an acetate disc, not a tape. What above all hits one hard from first to last is that Beecham in such live performances of Berlioz conveyed a manic intensity, a red-blooded thrust that brings out to the full the characterful wildness in this ever-original composer, making almost any rival seem cool.

So, the *Corsaire* Overture has a fierceness and thrust entirely apt to the Byronic subject, culminating in a swaggering climax that verges on the frenetic. It will have you laughing with joy. You find a similar approach in Beecham's studio performances of this overture, but this is even more uninhibited in its excitement. *King Lear* – with the BBC Symphony Orchestra, not the RPO – surges with warmth in the lyrical first half, before similarly building excitement in the *Allegro*.

Harold in Italy, recorded in 1956 in the dry acoustic of the Usher Hall, Edinburgh, with the dynamic range compressed so as to magnify *pianissimos*, as at the very start, is specially valuable for having as soloist Beecham's chosen leader of his viola section, Frederick Riddle. It was Riddle who made the first recording of the Walton Viola Concerto in 1937 with the composer conducting, arguably still the finest ever interpretation, and here his expressive warmth and responsiveness to Beecham's volatile inspiration make up for the sort of intonation problems that the viola at that period always seemed to invite, even with players of this calibre. Here more than ever Beecham's ability to mould his phrasing, even when as in the 'Pilgrim's March' the score specifies detached notes, helps to draw the ear.

The pauseful tenderness of the *Adagio* section just after the start of the finale, before the 'Orgy of the Brigands' gets going, is similarly magnetic, thanks to both conductor and soloist, bringing out the parallel in the review of themes with the finale of Beethoven's Ninth. The *Trojan March* makes a swaggering encore, a performance the more electrifying for being recorded at the opening concert of the Colston Hall in Bristol in 1951. As in the rest, one can consistently visualise those Beecham whiskers bristling.

Symphonie fantastique, Op 14

Symphonie fantastique[a]. Roméo et Juliette, Op 17[b] – Love scene; Queen Mab scherzo
[a]**Concertgebouw Orchestra;** [b]**London Symphony Orchestra / Sir Colin Davis**
Philips Solo 446 202-2PM (80 minutes: ADD). Recorded 1974 and 1968 Ⓜ ⚬

This classic performance comes up well again on CD, the sound a little hard at times but everything clear and in place. With what appears to be well over 50 versions of the work available, choice is certainly wide, though there are a good many, some of them by famous names, that pay more attention to the names in question than to Berlioz's still astonishing romantic vision. Davis remains among those conductors who can seek out the individualities in Berlioz with unerring judgement: the telling emphasis that troubles a 'normal' cadence, the lean on a phrase that corrupts it, the crack of a rhythm that makes this March one which ends on the scaffold. The orchestra is, of course, modern, that is to say not 'period' in any form (it does, incidentally, include the extra part for the cornet which Berlioz added, not, in many opinions, much to the music's advantage). Those who prefer period instruments, which can indeed reveal colours something near to those heard by Berlioz, deeply influencing the music's actual invention, will prefer the fine performance by John Eliot Gardiner (below); others can feel themselves as safe in Davis's hands as any – or rather, as skilfully led on a dangerous experience.

Berlioz Symphonie fantastique
Dutilleux Métaboles
Paris Opéra-Bastille Orchestra / Myung-Whun Chung
DG 445 878-2GH (67 minutes: DDD). Ⓕ
Recorded 1993

Not many versions of the *Symphonie fantastique* rival Myung-Whun Chung's in conveying the nervously impulsive inspiration of a young composer, the hints of hysteria, the overtones of nightmare in Berlioz's programme. He makes one register it afresh as genuinely fantastic; the volatile element in this perennially modern piece is something which Chung brings out to a degree rarely known before, and that establishes his as a very individual, sharply characterized version with unusually strong claims. Such an approach as Chung's might easily have sounded fussy or self-indulgent, but the rapport between the conductor and the Bastille orchestra is so complete that all the subtleties of expression, the highly complex rubato, sound natural and spontaneous, regularly making one register this – despite the nationality of the conductor – as a very French performance. Only at the start of the finale does tension momentarily slacken, and Chung's fast tempo for the clarinet's grotesque version of the motto theme challenges the players to the limit, again conveying wildness. The conclusion brings all the expected thrills in its impulsiveness, with the bass drum vividly caught.

The coupling is original, the set of five brief and brilliant pieces which Dutilleux wrote for Szell and the Cleveland Orchestra in 1964. Chung's view is both poetic and atmospheric, bringing out the subtly contrasting timbres in each piece, with the different sections of the orchestra brought together in the final *Presto*, where Chung relishes the marking 'Flamboyant', underlining jazzy syncopations in fractional anticipation to make this an exciting and volatile reading. This is a makeweight to welcome, for it is sure to surprise and delight.

Symphonie fantastique
Orchestre Révolutionnaire et Romantique / Sir John Eliot Gardiner
Philips 434 402-2PH (53 minutes: DDD). Ⓕ
Recorded 1991

In his preface, Gardiner sets out the issues again, and claims to 'recreate as closely as the available documentation permits the sound and atmosphere of the first performance'. Even if we have here only an approximation to the sounds of the first performance, that is a good starting point. Gardiner's performance is in some ways sharper than Roger Norrington's (whose own groundbreaking performance is available on EMI), and more insistent on detail. This can lead to overphrasing, though he does almost nothing that cannot be justified from Berlioz's intricately, often oddly, marked score. Both performances are of endless fascination and enjoyment. Norrington is, in general, more concerned to use his recovered instrumental sounds to shape a performance of the kind with which we are familiar, cleaning everything up and presenting it afresh. Gardiner is perhaps more interested in the kind of performance with which Berlioz might have startled his audience that December night in 1830. So he plays the music with an extra emphasis on sudden flicks of phrasing, an extra abruptness in the stamp of a rhythm or the snap of an interrupting chord, a concern for the extreme. Who can tell what the instruments really sounded like? What matters is that we have, to set beside other well-loved performances with a modern orchestra, this one that takes us very close to the sound world out of which Berlioz created a completely new kind of music.

Symphonie fantastique, Op 14. Béatrice et Bénédict – Overture[a]
London Symphony Orchestra / Sir Colin Davis
LSO Live LSO0007CD (65 minutes: DDD). Ⓢ
Recorded live in 2000

It is not far short of 40 years since Sir Colin Davis with the LSO made his first electrifying recording of Berlioz's *Symphonie fantastique*, and since then he has recorded it twice more for Philips. The differences between the four performances indicate little or no change in the conductor's approach, but sharply reflect contrasts between the different orchestras, and of different recording acoustics.

The LSO version of 1963, marginally brisker than the others, is the sharpest and most incisive of the four, with the 'March to the Scaffold' given a thrilling bite, helped by cleanly focused Philips sound, which for all its age still sounds fresh and vivid, with very clear stereo separation. The Concertgebouw reading is warmer and richer thanks mainly to the players and their hall, while the 1991 digital version from Vienna is even weightier, though at times less tense.

The latest LSO version, recorded at a slightly lower level with less immediate sound, is in many ways the subtlest of the four, conveying more mystery, with *pianissimos* of extreme delicacy beautifully caught. There is an overall gain too from having a live recording of a work with such an individual structure, with its hesitations and pauses. In overall timings it is marginally longer than earlier versions, maybe also reflecting the conditions of a live performance, even though some of this must have been put together from rehearsal tapes as there is no applause at the end.

The *Béatrice et Bénédict* Overture is taken from the complete recording of the opera on the same LSO Live label, and makes both a welcome bonus and a tempting sampler. Though the disc comes at super-budget price, it offers splendid notes by David Cairns, author of the definitive, prize-winning biography of the composer.

La damnation de Faust, Op 24

Susan Graham *sop* **Thomas Moser** *ten* **José van Dam** *bass-bar* **Frédéric Caton** *bass;* **Chorus and Orchestra of Opéra de Lyon / Kent Nagano**
Erato ② 0630-10692-2 (122 minutes: DDD). Ⓜ
Text and translation included. Recorded 1994 ●

New versions of *Faust* appear regularly, but it is rare to encounter one as good this. At its centre is a perception of Berlioz's extraordinary vision, in all its colour and variety and humour and pessimism, and the ability to realize this in a broad downward sweep while setting every detail sharply in place. *La damnation* is a work about the steady failure of consolations in a romantic world rejecting God, until all Faust's sensations are numbed and Mephistopheles has him trapped in the hell of no feeling. Every stage of the progress is mercilessly depicted here. The chorus is brilliant in all its roles, offering in turn the lively charms of peasant life, raptures of faith in the Easter Hymn, beery roistering in Auerbach's Cellar that grows as foul as a drunken party, cheerful student Latin bawls; later they sing with delicacy as Mephistopheles's spirits of temptation and finally become a vicious pack of demons. Nagano takes the Hungarian March at a pace that grows hectic as the dream of military glory turns hollow. It is all brilliantly realized.

There is the same care for orchestral detail. Nagano seems to be conducting from the New Berlioz Edition score, and he uses his imagination with it. He has an unerring sense of tempo, balancing weight of tone against speed, and he can light upon the telling contrapuntal line, or point a detail of instrumental colour (like the viola tremolo that 'betrays' the will-o'-the-wisps as the devil's creatures) or even a single note (like the snarl in the Ride to the Abyss), elements that give Berlioz's marvellous orchestration its expressive quality. José van Dam is an outstanding Mephistopheles, curling his voice round phrases with hideous elegance, relishing the mock-jollity of the Serenade and the Song of the Flea, taunting Faust with lulling sweetness on the banks of the Elbe, yet also disclosing the sadness of the fallen spirit. Thomas Moser sings gravely and reflectively as he is first discovered on the plains of Hungary, and rises nobly to the challenge of the Invocation to Nature (*très large et très sombre*, as Berlioz wanted), but is almost at his finest in the many recitative passages as he twists and turns in Mephistopheles's tightening grasp. Susan Graham does not match these two superb performances, but she sings her two arias simply and well. This version sets Nagano among the outstanding Berlioz conductors of the day.

L'enfance du Christ, Op 25

Jean Rigby *mez* **John Aler, Peter Evans** *tens* **Gerald Finley, Robert Poulton** *bars* **Alastair Miles, Gwynne Howell** *basses;* **St Paul's Cathedral Choir; Corydon Singers and Orchestra / Matthew Best**
Hyperion ② CDA66991/2 (101 minutes: DDD). Text Ⓕ
and translation included. Recorded 1994 ●

Best treats *L'enfance du Christ* as overtly operatic, not so much by cast movements or varied microphone placings as by his pacing of the action and by encouraging his artists to throw themselves wholeheartedly into the emotions of the story. He gets off to a tremendous start with a superb reading by a black-voiced Alastair Miles as a Herod haunted by his dream and startled into belligerent wakefulness by the arrival of Polydorus. Later, there is desperate urgency in the appeals for shelter by Joseph (an otherwise gently lyrical Gerald Finley), harshly rebuffed by the chorus. And, throughout, there are spatial perspectives – the soldiers' patrol advancing (from practically inaudible pizzicatos) to centre stage and going off again; a beautifully hushed and atmospheric faraway 'Amen' at the end. The angels' warning to the Holy Family in Part 1, however, is miscalculated by the voices being too distantly placed for their words to be audible. Balance in general is excellent, a notable passage being the duet in the tender scene at the manger. The clear enunciation (in very good French) of nearly everyone is a plus point. The chorus's response to the mood and meaning of words is always alert and sensitive, matched by the nuanced orchestral playing. The scurrying of the Ishmaelite family to help, played really *pianissimo*, is vividly graphic; and their home entertainment on two flutes and a harp, which can mark a drop in the interest, here has great charm. But overall it is Best's pacing which makes this recording distinctive. This recording of Berlioz's appealing work well stands comparison with its much-praised predecessors.

L'enfance du Christ[a]. Tristia, Op 18 – Méditation religieuse; La mort d'Ophélie. Sara la baigneuse, Op 11. La mort de Cléopâtre
Elsie Morison, Anne Pashley *sops* **Sir Peter Pears, Edgar Fleet** *tens* **John Cameron** *bar*
John Frost, Joseph Rouleau *basses*
St Anthony Singers; [a]Goldsbrough Orchestra; English Chamber Orchestra / Sir Colin Davis
Double Decca ② 443 461-2DF2 (142 minutes: ADD). Ⓜ
Recorded [a]1960 and 1967 ●●

Despite advances in recording since 1960, highly commended performances by other conductors of *L'enfance du Christ*, and another by Colin Davis himself 16 years later, many Berliozians still retain a special affection for his original version, now 40 years old. At the time of the recording he had only recently shot into the limelight as a conductor and was in the first flush of a youthful enthusiasm for Berlioz, of whom he became an outstanding interpreter.

There is an electric excitement in the scene of Herod and the soothsayers, the Goldsbrough Orchestra (which was shortly to be reborn as the English Chamber Orchestra) responding alertly, under Davis's guidance, to the drama of the situation; and even before that, there is a sense of veiled mystery in the Roman soldiers' nocturnal rounds. But he was also fortunate in his cast: Peter Pears as a most expressive narrator, adapting his tone to each aspect of the story,

Elsie Morison with her light soprano, perfectly suggesting Mary's youthful purity and innocence, John Cameron as a solicitous Joseph, and Joseph Rouleau skilfully changing his timbre to double as the tormented Herod and the kindly Ishmaelite father. One or two reservations remain: the duet between Mary and Joseph in Part 1 is not well balanced, the baritone swamping the soprano; and choral intonation is not always as exact as we have come to expect from present-day chorus standards. But overall this is a fine reading. Criticism must be made, however, of the fact that no texts are provided for any of the works here. These pieces appear only rarely in the catalogue; *La mort de Cléopâtre* has had some distinguished later interpreters, including Dame Janet Baker and Yvonne Minton, but Anne Pashley has a fine sense of the dramatic, and is superbly backed up by Davis and the orchestra.

L'enfance du Christ, Op 25[a]. Sara la baigneuse, Op 11[b]. Mélodies, 'Irlande', Op 2 – No 2, Hélène[b]; No 4, La belle voyageuse[c]; No 6, Chant sacré[d]
Quartetto e coro dei maggi[e]
[a]**Susan Graham,** [c]**Susanne Mentzer** *mezzos* [ad]**John Mark Ainsley,** [a]**Gordon Getz** *tens* [a]**François Le Roux** *bar* [a]**Philip Cokorinos,** [a]**Andrew Wentzel,** [a]**Marc Belleau** *basses* **Montreal Symphony** [abde]**Chorus and Orchestra / Charles Dutoit**
Decca ② 458 915-2DH2 (120 minutes: DDD)
Texts and translations included. Ⓕ
Recorded [a]1995 and 1996

Sir Colin Davis in both his recordings (Philips, 1976 and L'Oiseau-Lyre – now Decca, 1960) takes a more direct view of *L'enfance du Christ*. Though in no way lacking in warmth, his readings are a shade more austere, a very valid view in a devotional work in which Berlioz regularly relies on understatement, rare for him. Dutoit, with his warm approach, gives extra bite to the drama in passages of recitative, and generally his speeds tend to be a shade faster.

Most striking of all is the contrast between the different approaches in the most celebrated passage, the 'Shepherds' Farewell'. At one extreme is Sir John Gardiner on Erato (1987) – his phrasing carefully moulded and expansive – and Davis who is almost as slow; at the other is Jean-Claude Casadesus on Naxos (1996), who almost turns the 3/8 *Allegretto* into a dance. He has justification in the metronome marking (dotted crotchet equals 50), which Dutoit comes near to matching, too, adopting a flowing speed that remains devotional.

Dutoit's expressive warmth is most notable in the ensembles with the Virgin Mary and Joseph which, with the subtlest control of dynamic shading – from the chorus and soloists – are ravishingly beautiful. Susan Graham is superb as Mary, giving a performance no less heartfelt than Dame Janet Baker's incomparable one for Davis on Philips, but lighter; while François Le Roux is a clear, idiomatic Joseph. And as the Narrator John Mark Ainsley is equally fresh and idiomatic in his extended passages of recitative.

The sound is spectacularly fine, beautifully balanced, achieving admirable clarity in a warmly atmospheric acoustic. The Montreal players excel themselves; the woodwind is fresh and biting, the brass ripe and rounded, the strings full and warm. The off-stage effects are beautifully done, too. Interestingly, one of the most obvious differences between the two Davis versions comes in the off-stage chorus of angels, warning Mary and Joseph of the danger from Herod – the Decca is rather too close, the Philips rather too distant – where Dutoit's balance is ideal, distant but clear and well focused.

Among the other soloists, Philip Cokorinos as Herod may not have a very distinctive baritone, and is a little gruff, but he conveys the king's changing emotions vividly. In Herod's long aria describing his disturbing dreams one even feels pity for the suffering monarch. And after all, it is the soothsayers who give him the idea of slaughtering the Innocents, which he then takes up enthusiastically. Yet no one quite matches the masterly characterisation of José van Dam on the Gardiner set. Andrew Wentzel as the Ishmaelite father may not quite match the finest rivals on other sets, but his contribution is hardly a weakness, and Marc Belleau is outstanding in the tiny role of Polydorus.

The couplings provide an attractive and valuable makeweight, including three of the *Irlande* songs, Op 2, in their orchestral form (only one of them, 'La belle voyageuse', is otherwise available in that format). Here Susanne Mentzer is the fine soloist, and Sara la baigneuse comes in the very rare version for triple chorus and orchestra. Rarest of all is the so-called *Quartetto e coro dei maggi*, not a quartet at all but a straight chorus for the Magi, exhilarating in its devotional ecstasy. In harness with *L'enfance du Christ* it makes a specially apt item, otherwise unavailable.

Though the best rival versions of *L'enfance* can in various ways be recommended, the Davis Philips set is a benchmark recording. Nevertheless, this set establishes a formidable claim to first choice when, in addition to the warmth and bite of the reading, the digital sound is so sumptuous.

Grande messe des morts, Op 5

Richard Lewis *ten* **Royal Philharmonic Chorus and Orchestra / Sir Thomas Beecham** Ⓗ
BBC Music Legends mono BBCL4011-2
(78 minutes: ADD). Text and translation included. Ⓜ
Recorded live in 1959

Almost 60 years to the day since his first Berlioz performance, Beecham conducted the *Grande messe des morts* in the Albert Hall. Though the *Dies irae* thunders out tremendously, and the 'Lacrymosa' has a wonderful snap on the offbeat chords, it is the quieter movements that characterize what is, after all, a Requiem Mass. Beecham's response to them is with a lifetime's devotion to one of the composers who had been closest to his heart. The 'Quid sum miser' has an enchanting clarity; the long, hushed end of the 'Offertoire', as Berlioz lingers over the gently alternating notes that suffuse the invention, is finely judged; the *Sanctus* is eloquently sung by Lewis and the splendid chorus; the return of the opening 'Te decet hymnus', near the close of the whole work, is sublime. Such things are not achieved without the attention to detail with which Beecham used to complain people did not credit him. How wrong. His orchestral parts were always covered with powerful blue pencil marks and the signature 'TB', so that it was impossible to mistake intentions which players would then shape for him in rehearsal (and which he was capable of nerve-rackingly contradicting in performance). Here, the detail is exquisite. Occasionally he takes his own view, not Berlioz's, about phrasing; and the orchestra contains not a whiff of an ophicleide. No matter. This is a recording of a great occasion – full in recording, scarcely bothered by audience noise – but also of a marvellous performance.

Grande messe des morts[a]. Symphonie funèbre et triomphale[b]

Ronald Dowd *ten* [a]**Wandsworth School Boys' Choir;** b**John Alldis Choir; London Symphony Chorus**a and **Orchestra / Sir Colin Davis**

Philips ② 416 283-2PH2 (127 minutes: ADD). Notes,texts and translations included. Ⓕ
Recorded 1969 ●●

Berlioz's Requiem is not a liturgical work, any more than the *Symphonie funèbre* is really for the concert hall; but both are pieces of high originality, composed as ceremonials for the fallen, and standing as two of the noblest musical monuments to the French ideal of a *gloire*. The Requiem is most famous for its apocalyptic moment when, after screwing the key up stage by stage, Berlioz's four brass bands blaze forth 'at the round earth's imagin'd corners'; this has challenged the engineers of various companies, but the Philips recording for Sir Colin Davis remains as fine as any, not least since Davis directs the bands with such a strong sense of character. He also gives the troubled rhythms of the *Lacrymosa* a stronger, more disturbing emphasis than any other conductor, and time and again finds out the expressive counterpoint, the emphatic rhythm, the telling few notes within the texture, that reveal so much about Berlioz's intentions. The notorious flute and trombone chords of the *Hostias* work admirably. Ronald Dowd is a little strained in the *Sanctus*, but the whole performance stands the test of time and of other competing versions. The same is true of the *Symphonie funèbre et triomphale*, which moves at a magisterial tread and is given a recording that does well by its difficult textures. A fine coupling of two remarkable works.

Grande messe des morts[a]. Veni creator. Tantum ergo. Messe solennelle – Resurrexit[b]

Bortnyansky/Berlioz Pater Noster. Adoremus

[a]**John Mark Ainsley** *ten* **Montreal Symphony Chorus and** [ab]**Orchestra / Charles Dutoit**

Decca ② 458 921-2DH2 (110 minutes: DDD). Ⓕ
Texts and translations included. Recorded 1997 ●

Following his formidable Decca series of major Berlioz recordings, above all *Les Troyens*, Dutoit here tackles the *Grande messe des morts*. The massive and gloriously resonant Montreal forces are here clearly defined: the sessions were not at the now-legendary venue of the church of St Eustache but at St Jerome, a venue just as sympathetic. If the quality of sound is what strikes home first, the interpretation, too, offers a powerful alternative to the fine versions by Davis, Levine and Previn. As in *Les Troyens*, Dutoit favours speeds generally a degree or two more flowing than those rival versions. The Montreal choral sound, too, both here and throughout, is more beautifully integrated than with Davis or Levine; it's a question of ensemble as well as of recording balance, as the recording gives unrivalled weight in the climaxes. Even so, the sound and the performance in the Previn version are fine.

Where the singing of the Montreal Symphony Chorus does not quite match that of the classic Davis version, or of the Previn, is in attack: the performance is often a degree more relaxed, less bitingly dramatic. You could say that Dutoit's is above all a comforting performance rather than a disturbing one, and at flowing, urgent speeds it is one which is held strongly together both in structure and argument. There is also the question of the tenor soloist in the *Sanctus*. The Levine offers Pavarotti, no less, just as the earlier Barenboim offers Domingo (both DG), where Davis has Ronald Dowd and Previn has Robert Tear. It goes without saying that John Mark Ainsley sings with great sensitivity, but the refined, very English sound will not please everyone, and the recording brings out a pronounced vibrato. Even so, the contrast both with other movements and march-like 'Hosanna' within the *Sanctus* are strongly established.

The fill-ups, all of them rare pieces, are welcome, if not especially generous. The two pieces for women's choir – *Veni creator* unaccompanied, *Tantum ergo* with organ – reveal Berlioz at his simplest, and touchingly so. Sir John Eliot Gardiner offers this version of the 'Resurexit' as a supplement to his complete recording of the newly rediscovered *Messe solennelle*, and although it is a more biting performance it suffers from over-reverberant recording, and Dutoit's is far better focused. When it comes to a final recommendation for the *Grande messe des morts*, the classic Davis has unique claims: a revelatory performance, still at full price – at least as a separate issue – after more than 30 years, but with an ideal coupling in the *Symphonie funèbre et triomphale*. The Previn also has a very strong claim with its superb performance and recording, now offered as a bargain two-disc package in EMI's Forte series, with the very generous coupling of Previn's strongly symphonic account of the *Symphonie fantastique*. Yet Dutoit will for many be a first choice, above all for the sound, and certainly it goes to the top of the list of digital versions.

Messe solennelle

Messe solennelle (also includes revised version of Resurrexit) **P**

Donna Brown *sop* **Jean-Luc Viala** *ten* **Gilles Cachemaille** *bar*

Monteverdi Choir; Orchestre Révolutionnaire et Romantique / Sir John Eliot Gardiner

Philips 442 137-2PH (61 minutes: DDD). Text and translation included. Recorded live in 1993 Ⓕ **OO**

The reappearance of Berlioz's lost Mass of 1824 is the most exciting musical discovery of modern times. To an incredulous meeting of the New Berlioz Edition in 1992 the General Editor, Hugh Macdonald, announced that a Belgian choirmaster, Frans Moors, had made contact with news of an improbable find in an Antwerp organ loft. A few days later, Prof Macdonald reported back from Antwerp that this was indeed the *Messe solennelle* which Berlioz alleged that he had burnt after a couple of performances: in fact, he had given a copy to a Belgian friend, going on to use some of the music elsewhere. John Eliot Gardiner with his Monteverdi Choir and Orchestre Révolutionnaire et Romantique gave performances in Bremen, Vienna, Madrid, Rome and Westminster Cathedral. This is a live recording of that last, thrilling occasion.

Why did Berlioz abandon the work? Only the *Resurrexit* was retained, though it was rewritten: both versions are included here. Some of it, but not much, is dull: the *Offertory* and *Sanctus* sit rather stolidly with the rest. He was unfair on what he denounced in an angry scribble on the MS as an 'execrable' fugue. Some is disconcertingly awkward, and Gardiner tells in the notes to this record of his and the singers' and players' confusion – until they all came together and suddenly the music made sense. The best of the work is superb: among this one may count the *Incarnatus*, the *O Salutaris* and the lovely *Agnus Dei*. The latter was too good to lose, and survives in another form in the *Te Deum*. So do other ideas: it was at first disconcerting to hear the chorus singing 'Laudamus te. Benedicimus te' to the Carnival music from *Benvenuto Cellini*, more so than to hear the slow movement of the *Symphonie fantastique* in the beautiful *Gratias*.

Once these and other associations are overcome, the work coheres remarkably well. Yet perhaps it did not do so well enough for Berlioz, and perhaps he was dissatisfied with the conjunction of some rather academic music with ideas that were too original, indeed too beautiful, to make a satisfying whole. All the same, no wonder the precocious 20-year-old was embraced after the first performance by his teacher, old Le Sueur, with the promise that he would be a great composer. Who knows whether he might have been made to think twice about abandoning the work had he heard a performance such as this. This applies to the wonderful Monteverdi Choir, to the orchestra, and above all to Gardiner himself. There will doubtless be more performances, even if it is not likely to be a repertory work. In any case, this is a recording of a great musical event, not to be missed.

Les nuits d'été, Op 7

Les nuits d'été. Herminie

Mireille Delunsch *sop* **Brigitte Balleys** *mez*

Orchestre des Champs-Elysées, Paris / Philippe Herreweghe

Harmonia Mundi HMC90 1522 (54 minutes: DDD). Texts and translations included. Recorded 1994 Ⓕ **OO**

It is not fanciful to hear decided pre-echoes in *Herminie* of Cassandra's fateful, searing music (quite apart from the very obvious dry-run for the *Symphonie fantastique*'s main motif). This extraordinary work of 1828, almost as arresting as its near-contemporary *Cléopâtre*, receives a grand rendering from Mireille Delunsch, who sings it in a compact, direct manner. Her tone is narrow and focused, her French diction clear. Herreweghe and his orchestra adopt a lean sound, surely close to that of Berlioz's time. Delunsch enters into the inner agony of the distraught, frustrated Herminie with a will. All in all, her interpretation is absorbing from start to finish. The recording imparts a slight glare to her tone as it does to that of Balleys in the much more familiar *Nuits d'été*, but that is hardly enough to detract from what is an idiomatic, unfussy reading. Her voice does not luxuriate in the more sensual moments of the cycle as does Régine Crespin's in her famous version (reviewed below) but it has a clarity of profile and a definition of phrase and, where strength of feeling is called for, Balleys provides it, as in 'Au cimitière' and 'Absence'. This makes a sensible pairing with the cantata. What may also influence your choice is, again, Herreweghe's lean, well-pointed support which often emphasizes, rightly, the striking originality of Berlioz's scoring.

Berlioz Les nuits d'été[a]

Ravel Shéhérazade[a] **Debussy** Trois chansons de Bilitis[b] **Poulenc** Banalities[b] – Chansons d'Orkenise; Hôtel[c]. La courte paille[b] – Le carafon; La reine de coeur[c]. Chansons villageoises[b] – Les gars qui vont à la fête. Deux poèmes de Louis Aragon[b]

Régine Crespin *sop* [b]**John Wustman** *pf*

[a]**Suisse Romande Orchestra / Ernest Ansermet**

Decca Legends 460 973-2DM (68 minutes: ADD). Texts and translations included. Items marked [a] recorded 1963, [bc] 1967 Ⓜ **OOO**

Crespin's *Nuits dété* has always been the interpretation by which others have been assessed and, listening to it again, there is no reason to challenge the verdict. In terms of idiomatic and natural French, languorous tone and understanding of the poetry's and the music's meaning, it stands above all other versions without any question. Even Dame Janet Baker's appreciable reading (now available at bargain price on HMV Classics) sounds a trifle affected in its vocal grammar besides Crespin's, particularly as regards the determinedly bright, jolly tone employed by the British artist in the first and last songs, whose joyous moods Crespin encompasses without resort to contrivance. Crespin's tempos are also ideally chosen. The only drawback to her version is the sometimes slack accompanying of Ansermet, not that Barbirolli is ideal in that respect. Crespin's *Shéhérazade* is even more in a class of its own than her account of the Berlioz too. As soon as she launches seductively into 'Asie' we know that singer and music are perfectly matched, and the last two songs are even better. As if this were not enough, we have Crespin's *Chansons de Bilitis* from a later recital, a performance that wonderfully suggests the distant lassitude of poem and music, and a group of Poulenc from the same 1969 record of which the sad, elegiac 'C' (*Deux poèmes*), that lament for a France torn apart by war, is the plum. Anyone who thinks that some of Crespin's successors fully understand how to interpret *mélodies* needs to hear this record to be reminded of the authentic style adumbrated here.

Les nuits d'été. Benvenuto Cellini – Tra la la ... Mais qu'ai-je donc?. Les Troyens – Je vais mourir ... Adieu, fière cité. Béatrice et Bénédict – Dieu! Que vien-je d'entendre? ... Il m'en souvient. La damnation de Faust – D'amour l'ardente flamme

Susan Graham *mez* **Royal Opera House Orchestra, Covent Garden / John Nelson**

Sony Classical SK62730 (61 minutes: DDD). Texts and translations included. Recorded 1996-97 Ⓕ OO

It would be hard to imagine a more inspiriting and rewarding display of Berlioz singing than this from a singer who has the composer's style in her voice and heart. Running the gamut of Berlioz's writing for the female voice Graham manages to explore and deliver the soul of each of her chosen pieces, her voice – firm yet vibrant, clear yet warm – responding interpretatively and technically to the appreciable demands placed on it by this programme. In *Les nuits d'été*, she faces the greatest challenge from revered favourites and meets it head on, catching in almost every respect the varied moods of each song. Her French pronunciation is excellent and she uses the language to evoke the atmosphere of each song without a hint of exaggeration. Marguérite's nobly impassioned solo from *Damnation* is confidently voiced, managing in the studio to conjure up all the heroine's longing, quite arrestingly so at 'Je suis à ma fenêtre'. Throughout the piece Graham maintains a wonderfully secure tone and a long line. The noble dignity of her account of Dido's farewell, in particular at the recollection of the love duet, is deeply moving, and Béatrice's equivocal thoughts about her lover are another triumph, the touch of the martial at 'Les Mores triomphaient' nicely contrasted with the sensual tone of the repeated 'Il m'en souvient'. The fleeter, lighter side of Graham's art is caught in the rapturous cabaletta to Béatrice's aria and in Ascanio's excitable aria from *Benvenuto Cellini*, both dispatched securely. Nelson and the LSO provide idiomatic support, and the recording catches the full colour of the singer's performances. Here is a disc as thoughtfully planned as it is executed.

Roméo et Juliette, Op 17

Daniela Barcellona *mez* **Kenneth Tarver** *ten* **Orlin Anastassov** *bass*
London Symphony Chorus and Orchestra / Sir Colin Davis

LSO Live LSO0003CD (99 minutes: DDD). Recorded live in January 2000 Ⓢ OO

This recording of Berlioz's masterpiece builds in important ways on what Sir Colin has revealed to us in his two previous versions, both for Philips, and preserves what by any reckoning was an electrifying event at the Barbican. The recording was edited from two separate concerts, so ironing out irritating flaws of the moment, while offering the extra dramatic thrust of a live performance. That is most strikingly illustrated in the concluding chorus, a passage that has often been felt to let the rest of the work down, but which here provides an incandescent climax, silencing any doubts. That said, the differences between this live recording and Davis's two studio ones are less a question of interpretation than of recording balance and quality. Davis's view of the work has remained fundamentally unchanged, though his speeds at the Barbican are marginally broader until the concluding sections from Juliet's funeral onwards, which now flow more easily. The live recording may not match in opulence either the 1993 one with the Vienna Philharmonic or the 1968 one with the LSO, for the Barbican acoustic is drier. Yet the refinement of the sound this time, with orchestra and chorus set at a slight distance, brings *pianissimos* of breathtaking delicacy, focused in fine detail. Not only the Love scene but the choral recitatives gain greatly from that, as does the lovely passage before the Love scene where the Capulets return home after the party. The three young soloists are first-rate, characterising strongly. It will be a pity if having this on the LSO Live label, with its limited availability, reduces its circulation, yet everyone will appreciate the benefit of getting such a fine modern recording at so reasonable a price.

Roméo et Juliette

Olga Borodina *mez* **Thomas Moser** *ten* **Alastair Miles** *bass*
Bavarian Radio Chorus; Vienna Philharmonic Orchestra / Sir Colin Davis

Philips ② 442 134-2PH2 (96 minutes: DDD). Text and translation included. Recorded 1993 Ⓕ O

Davis's return to Berlioz's highly demanding dramatic symphony is more than welcome (he first recorded it in 1968, also for Philips). He has not substantially rethought what was by some way the finest recorded performance, but he has lived through the music again and been allowed by the recording to clarify what was before in places obscure. But the gains are also musically more positive. Thomas Moser sings the vocal version of 'Queen Mab' with a verve and wit that make it all sound easy, which it is not. Olga Borodina is excellent in the 'Strophes', phrasing with a long but internally detailed line which is essentially Berliozian, and adding just the right throb of vibrato when he lovingly asks for it at the sacred word 'Shakespeare'.

Alastair Miles has more difficulty with the problematic role of Friar Laurence, and his French is less secure than that of the others, but this cantata finale, never the strongest part of the work, stands up well and he leads it firmly, supported by the excellent chorus. Davis himself makes of this as good a case as possible for a reconciliatory conclusion to a whole symphonic experience, one whose variety as well as quasi-symphonic cohesion he understands better than any other conductor.

Roméo et Juliette
Catherine Robbin *mez* **Jean-Paul Fouchécourt** *ten* **Gilles Cachemaille** *bar*
Monteverdi Choir; Orchestre Révolutionnaire et Romantique / Sir John Eliot Gardiner
Philips ② 454 454-2PH2 (136 minutes: DDD).
Text and translation included. Includes earlier variants. Ⓕ
Recorded 1995

If not exactly a 'variorum' edition, Gardiner's is one that adds to the standard version much of the discarded music that has been rescued (often from under *collettes*, glued-on pieces of paper). Track programming will allow listeners to chart their preferred course through the work, 'standard' or so-called 'original' or Gardiner's own mixture of the two. Briefly, the main differences are as follows. Berlioz expanded the original Prologue so as to bring in more glimpses of music later to be heard and the revised 'Queen Mab' *Scherzo* has a more strongly composed ending. This Second Prologue seems not to have been orchestrated, and it is, here, by Oliver Knussen with a quick Berliozian ear. The finale had the most alterations; they are mostly concerned with shortening Friar Laurence's sermon which is all the better for it. This often maligned finale is more than justified in Gardiner's performance.

Gilles Cachemaille's voice is a little light for Père Laurence but he has an intelligent perception of the part, and sings with an affecting ruefulness as well as firmness. The 'Strophes' are attractively sung by Catherine Robbin, a light contralto such as Berlioz would have known. Jean-Paul Fouchécourt throws off the difficult Queen Mab *Scherzetto* with the panache he might bring to a comic opera aria. Robbin is probably using more vibrato than singers of the day would have done. The question of how much vibrato would have been used by a Paris orchestra of the time is arguable; Gardiner is almost certainly right to discourage it. Yet he also appears to discourage *portamento*, which was coming in as an expressive device. It may partly account for him pressing the music rather hard in consequence, where Davis can allow the great rapturous phrases to unfold more naturally.

Gardiner also presses the 'Queen Mab' *Scherzo* hard, whereas Davis floats the phrases on the light, speeding tempo. But he gives 'Romeo in the Tomb of the Capulets' a brilliantly eloquent account and his reading of the Ball is vigorous and exuberant, even if it does lack the whiff of foreboding which Davis scents in it. No listener with a care for Berlioz will want to be without Gardiner's remarkable set. Sir Colin's recordings are more devoted to the inward emotions, and touch more eloquently on the tragedy of young love destined never to flourish, but never to fade. There is sufficient room for both views of a wonderful work.

Te Deum

Te Deum, Op 22
Roberto Alagna *ten* **Marie-Claire Alain** *org*
European Union and Maîtrise d'Antony Childrens Choirs; Orchestre de Paris Chorus; Orchestre de Paris / John Nelson
Virgin Classics VC5 45449-2 (58 minutes: DDD). Ⓕ
Recorded 2000

It is surprising that the Berlioz *Te Deum* has been relatively neglected on disc in comparison with his other major works, the more so when it so conveniently fits onto a single CD. This latest version has John Nelson as an incisive, understanding conductor of Berlioz, revelling in the weight of choral sound, balancing his forces beautifully. He is helped here by fuller, more brilliant, more detailed digital sound than on previous versions.

The organ sound may be less transparent than it might be, but the authentic French timbre of the Cavaillé-Coll organ of the Madeleine in Paris blends beautifully in the ensemble, and Marie-Claire Alain, as one might expect, is the most idiomatic soloist, making her non-French rivals seem rather square by comparison. It makes for luxury casting, too, to have Roberto Alagna as an imaginative, idiomatic tenor soloist in the prayer, 'Te ergo quaesumus', warmly persuasive and full of temperament.

An additional plus-point for the new issue, even in relation to Sir Colin Davis's now classic version for Philips, is not only the fuller, more open recorded sound but the interesting bonus provided. The two extra instrumental movements included here were written by Berlioz expressly for performances celebrating victory, both with military overtones.

It is good to have them both, even if they are intrinsically far less valuable than the usual choral movements. A Prelude, inserted before the third movement, 'Dignare', uses one of the work's main themes in *fugato*, while at the very end the performance is rounded off with a March for the Presentation of the Colours that in its bold, even corny military style reminds one of the *Symphonie funèbre et triomphale*. On CD one can easily leave either of them out, yet Berlioz, even at his most populist, never fails to grab the listener's attention.

Béatrice et Bénédict

Béatrice et Bénédict
Susan Graham *sop* Béatrice; **Jean-Luc Viala** *ten* Bénédict; **Sylvia McNair** *sop* Héro; **Catherine Robbin** *mez* Ursule; **Gilles Cachemaille** *bar* Claudio; **Gabriel Bacquier** *bar* Somarone; **Vincent Le Texier** *bass* Don Pedro; **Philippe Magnant** *spkr* Léonato
Lyon Opera Chorus and Orchestra / John Nelson
Erato MusiFrance ② 2292-45773-2
(111 minutes: DDD). Notes, text and translation included. Recorded 1991 Ⓕ ●

We have to note that the title is not a French version of *Much Ado about Nothing*, but that it takes the two principal characters of Shakespeare's play and constructs an opera around them. The comedy centres on the trick which is played upon the protagonists by their friends, producing love out of apparent antipathy. Much of the charm lies in the more incidental matters of choruses, dances, the magical 'Nocturne' duet for Béatrice and Héro, and the curious addition of the character Somarone, a music-master who rehearses the choir in one of his own compositions. There is also a good deal of spoken dialogue. Perhaps surprisingly, the extra dialogue is a point in its favour, for it is done very effectively by good French actors and it makes for a cohesive, Shakespearian entertainment. John Nelson secures a well-pointed performance of the score, and with excellent playing by the Lyon Orchestra. Susan Graham and Jean-Luc Viala are attractively vivid and nimble in style, and Sylvia McNair makes a lovely impression in Héro's big solo. The veteran Gabriel Bacquier plays the music-master with genuine panache and without overmuch clownage. There is good work by the supporting cast and the chorus and the recording is finely produced.

Les Troyens

Ben Heppner *ten* Enée; **Michelle DeYoung** *mez* Didon; **Petra Lang** *mez* Cassandre; **Sara Mingardo** *mez* Anna; **Peter Mattei** *bar* Chorèbe; **Stephen Milling** *bass* Narbal; **Kenneth Tarver** *ten* Iopas; **Toby Spence** *ten* Hylas; **Orlin Annastassov** *bass* Ghost of Hector; **Tigran Martirossian** *bass* Panthée; **Isabelle Cals** *mez* Ascagne; **Alan Ewing** *bass* Priam; **Guang Yang** *mez* Hécube; **Andrew Greenan** *bass* First sentry; **Roderick Earle** *bass* Second sentry; **Bülent Bezdüz** *ten* Hélénus; **Leigh Melrose** *bass* A Trojan soldier/Mercure; **Mark Stone** *bar* A Greek Chieftain;
London Symphony Chorus and Orchestra / Sir Colin Davis
LSO Live ④ LSO0010 (240 minutes: DDD)
Recorded live in 2000 Ⓢ ●●

Colin Davis's 1969 recording remains a landmark event, the first time this grand opera of Meyerbeerian length, spectacular *éclat* and Wagnerian artistic ambition had found its way complete onto LP. It effectively changed views about Berlioz the opera composer and orchestral genius (although not necessarily in France where he is still disparaged) and has for many remained the yardstick by which all later performances have been judged. Although studio recorded, it was based on the Covent Garden casting of the day – Jon Vickers' heroic Enée and Josephine Veasey's voluptuous Didon – with a couple of Frenchmen to boost the ranks of lesser Trojans and Carthaginians. The one important piece of non-Covent Garden casting was the Swedish soprano Berit Lindholm's Cassandre, a major blot on an otherwise classic recording, of whom it is scarcely possible to find a good word, except, perhaps, for the 'sheer vocal energy and dramatic involvement' praised by David Cairns in his article on *Les Troyens* in Alan Blyth's *Opera on Record Volume 2*.

In the same article, Cairns reveals that Régine Crespin – at the time the reigning French diva – was not considered for Cassandre in the 1969 recording because of her identification with a potted two-disc version (French EMI, 8/66 – nla) in which she sang 'what was left of the roles of Cassandra and Dido'. More's the pity, because in the substantial extracts of both parts included on those LPs – once available on a single 78-minute mid-price EMI Studio CD (4/94 – nla) – she displays the virtues which all of her successors in both roles most notably lack: vocal distinction, personal charisma, a regal bearing and, of course, eloquent French.

The tantalising glimpses of Crespin's Cassandre and Didon belong to a now lost tradition which none of the singing on the new LSO disc quite emulates – with the possible exception, that is, of the delightful young French mezzo Isabelle Cals, who makes of Enée's son Ascagne a characterful 'enfant semblable à Cupidon' (as Didon's sister, Anna calls him in the Act 4 quintet). Part for part, however, the LSO have assembled a cast which challenges without comprehensively surpassing that of the earlier Davis recording.

Some of the *comprimario* singers are without doubt their predecessors' superiors: the handsome-voiced Peter Mattei is a nobler-toned, more youthful and romantic-sounding Chorèbe in his fraught interview with his 'vierge adorée', Cassandre; Sara Mingardo's sumptuous contralto is luxury casting for Didon's sister beside the admirable but plain Heather Begg. And as the Carthaginian court poet, Iopas, Kenneth Tarver's tone catches the microphone just that bit more sweetly than Ian Partridge's in 'O blonde Cérès', his flattering comparison of his queen with the Goddess of plenty and prosperity. There's not much to choose between Toby Spence and Ryland Davies as the Phrygian sailor Hylas, except that the younger singer is perhaps even more touching in his plaintive song of homesickness at the opening of Act 5.

Any account of *Les Troyens*, however, stands or falls by the casting of the three central characters – Cassandre, Enée and Didon – and this the LSO has done with exceptional results. Michelle DeYoung was originally assigned Cassandre, but was 'promoted' to Didon when Olga Borodina fell ill. Her replacement as

Cassandre, the German dramatic mezzo Petra Lang, was a revelation at the Barbican, a passionate prophetess, thrilling in her imprecations against the Greeks and heroic in her suicide as Troy is consumed in flames at the close of Act 2. Her French has a slightly 'thick' Germanic flavour, but she makes every word tell and she has the grand rhetorical manner Berlioz learned from Gluck and Cherubini to the manner born.

It's hard to imagine today – vocally at least – a more musical, more romantic, more impetuous Enée than Ben Heppner who brings real stylish distinction and heroic bravura to bear. If he lacks the theatrical temperament and the anguish Jon Vickers brings to Enée's music at his moment of truth in Act 5, he also lacks the older Canadian's vocal mannerisms and technical defects.

About Michelle DeYoung's Didon is not quite so successful. Her big, bright-toned voice is less warm than Veasey's and she has a tendency to 'yowl' on climactic notes. She doesn't really convey Didon's regal bearing either: her imperiousness that of a bossy housekeeper rather than a great founding Queen. That said, she rises to a magnificent 'Adieu, fier cité' and works herself into a Medea-like rage when she threatens to serve a dismembered Ascagne as her perjured lover's dinner in the preceding recitative. For such a young singer – this was her first encounter with Didon – this is a signal, if far from perfect, achievement. What really makes this issue indispensable is Davis's conducting of an LSO on incandescent form. The 'world's greatest Berlioz conductor' seems to become ever more convinced of the greatness of this astonishing score and revels, with greater conviction than ever, in its magical orchestral effects – the atmosphere of sun-soaked North African sensuality and impending doom is palpably evoked in a superlative account of the 'Royal Hunt and Storm' – and its grand theatrical rhetoric. Nor does he patronise the light-hearted passages of the score: the ballet of labourers and artisans, and the little Shakespearean duet for the grumbling Trojans who are perfectly content to stay in Carthage with their new-found women. For Davis and his orchestra – and the splendid immediacy of the live recording – this account of *Les Troyens* is first choice at any price. For £20, it's almost a give-away – with a full French-English libretto and an authoritative note by Cairns – so even if you have the classic Philips set this is a must-buy. Snap up the Crespin if you can find it though as well.

Les Troyens

Françoise Pollet *sop* Dido; **Gary Lakes** *ten* Aeneas; **Deborah Voigt** *sop* Cassandra; **Gino Quilico** *bar* Corebus; **Hélène Perraguin** *mez* Anna; **Jean-Philippe Courtis** *bass* Narbal; **Michel Philippe** *bass* Pantheus; **Catherine Dubosc** *sop* Ascanius; **Jean-Luc Maurette** *ten* Iopas; **René Shirrer** *bar* Priam's ghost, First Soldier; **Claudine Carlson** *mez* Hecuba; **John Mark Ainsley** *ten* Hylas; **Marc Belleau** *bass* Hector's ghost, Second Soldier, Greek Captain; **Gregory Cross** *ten* Sinon; **Michel Beuachemin** *bass* Mercury; **Montreal Symphony Chorus and Orchestra / Charles Dutoit**

Decca ④ 443 693-2DH4 (238 minutes: DDD). Notes, text and translation included. Ⓕ
Recorded 1993 ●●

Davis's first *Les Troyens* remained unchallenged for a quarter of a century. Then came Dutoit and the Montreal Symphony Orchestra, who have established themselves as second to none in the French repertory. Add to that a largely French-speaking cast, on balance even more sensitive and tonally more beautiful than Davis's, plus two minor but valuable textual additions, and the advantage of the new over the old is clear. Interpretatively, the contrasts between Dutoit and Davis are quickly established at the very start.

Dutoit launches in at high voltage, more volatile than Davis, conveying exuberance consistently preferring faster speeds. The advantage of Dutoit's faster speeds comes not just in thrilling *Allegros*, but in flowing *Andantes*. So Cassandra's first solo is more persuasively moulded at a flowing speed, with Deborah Voigt far warmer than Berit Lindholm for Davis, both in her beauty of tone and in her *espressivo* phrasing. In 'La prise de Troie' such a moment as the clash of arms within the Trojan horse comes over more dramatically with Dutoit thanks to his timing, and there is more mystery before the arrival of Hector's ghost at the beginning of Act 2. For completeness Dutoit includes the brief prelude that Berlioz wrote for the garbled 1863 performances of the second part of the opera, but not intended to be given in the full five-act version. In sequence here, one immediately registers the drop in inspiration, but on CD the track is easily programmed out.

The other textual addition comes in Act 1. After the Andromache scene – with a clarinet solo of breathtaking gentleness from the Montreal player – there is an extra scene lasting six minutes which the Berlioz scholar, Hugh Macdonald, editor of the Bärenreiter score, has orchestrated from the surviving piano score. In what he describes as 'a somewhat breathless episode' Sinon, a Greek spy, convinces King Priam that the horse is a gift to Pallas Athene and must be brought inside the city. Not only does the scene give an individual role to King Priam, it provides a motivation for the disastrous decision to take in the horse. Berlioz ripped the scene out of the full score at a late stage, simply to shorten Act 1. The minor disadvantage is that the entry of Aeneas with his dire news of Laocoon and the serpents is not so dramatic when it follows another busy scene rather than the stillness of the Andromache scene. The role of Cassandra's lover, Corebus, is taken by Gino Quilico, in rich, firm voice. As Aeneas Gary Lakes is the most experienced of all today's tenors in this role. His big advantage over Jon Vickers, most of all in the great love scene with Dido in Act 3, is that he shades his voice far more subtly. Though the role of Dido very often goes to a mezzo, here Decca firmly opts for a soprano, Françoise Pollet. Very much attuned to the idiom, she sings consistently with full, even tone, so that, matching Dutoit's expressiveness and the richness of the Montreal sound, she brings out the feminine sensuousness of the role more than a mezzo normally would.

Throughout the opera Dutoit's degree of rhythmic freedom, notably in heavily syncopated passages, intensifies the controlled frenzy behind much of the most dramatic writing, and here Dido's hysteria, like Cassandra's earlier on, is most tellingly conveyed. There is barely a weak link in the rest of the huge cast. Catherine Dubosc makes a breathily boyish Ascanius, and Gregory Cross sings with sharp clarity in the tenor role of the spy, Sinon. John Mark Ainsley, though not quite so free of tone as usual on top, makes a sensitive Hylas in the sailor song of Act 5; and the high tessitura of the other tenor role of Iopas strains Jean-Luc Maurette uncomfortably at the top, bringing unsteadiness. As recorded, Michel Philippe as Pantheus sounds unsteady too, but that is very much the exception.

As for the chorus, though on balance the Covent Garden Chorus for Davis sings with even crisper ensemble, the passionate commitment of the Montreal Chorus matches the fire of Dutoit's reading. This is a thrilling set to have one marvelling afresh at the electric vitality of Berlioz's inspiration, and marvelling too that the formidable problems of recording so massive a work have been accomplished so confidently.

Additional recomendation

Les Troyens

Veasey Dido **Vickers** Aeneas **Lindholm** Cassandra **Glossop** Corebus

Wandsworth School Boys' Choir; Chorus and Orchestra of the Royal Opera House, Covent Garden / Sir Colin Davis

Philips ④ 416 432-2PH4 (241 minutes: ADD) Ⓕ

A classic recording, but at full price the new LSO Live set will be first choice (see the review above).

Lord Gerald Berners

British 1883-1950

GROVE *English composer, writer and painter Lord Berners was essentially self-taught. He was honorary attaché in Rome (1911-19), where he came to know Stravinsky and Casella. In 1919 he succeeded to the barony, and thereafter was an eccentric English gentleman. His early works are mostly small and ironical (chiefly songs and piano pieces), close to Les Six; later he wrote ballets, including The Triumph of Neptune (1926), Luna Park (1930) and A Wedding Bouquet (1936).*

The Triumph of Neptune

The Triumph of Neptune. L'uomo dai baffi. Valses bourgeoises. Polka (both orch Lane)

English Northern Philharmonia, Royal Ballet Sinfonia / David Lloyd-Jones

Marco Polo 8 223711 (69 minutes: DDD). Recorded 1996 Ⓕ

A biography of Berners arrived at last in 1998 (Mark Amory, *Lord Berners: The Last Eccentric*; Chatto & Windus). Unfortunately the emphasis on his eccentricity caused several uninformed reviewers to regard that as the main thing rather than his music – a problem Satie understood. The present release is the complete version of Berners's first ballet, *The Triumph of Neptune*, so it breaks new ground and unlike the Suite (Beecham recorded it twice – his second version is on Sony), where the numbers were reordered, it allows us to follow the original sequence of dances. *The Triumph of Neptune* is certainly Berners's best-known orchestral work – parts of it fitted well into the Last Night of the Proms in 1993 – and the Suite scintillates with the infectious enjoyment of all his theatre scores. It is well worth having the full version now, even if some of the scoring sounds heavy and the orchestral playing is not always as clean as it should be. *L'uomo dai baffi* ('The man with a moustache') was a ballet for puppets put on in Rome, where Berners lived, in 1918. It looks as if his friend and colleague, Alfredo Casella, may have scored five of Berners's early piano pieces for chamber group and so Philip Lane has added the remaining two. This makes a convincing set and brings these established documents of avant-garde piano music into another medium, although there are odd disagreements between the piano scores and the chamber versions. Lane has also orchestrated the only one of Berners's three sets of piano duets he didn't score himself – the enchanting *Valses bourgeoises* of 1919 – and a solo piece, the *Polka*, which was used in the Cavalcanti film, *Champagne Charlie*. It is a joy to hear these old favourites in full orchestral colour and Lane has done an excellent job. These performances with the Royal Ballet Sinfonia are some of the most lively on the CD.

Songs • Solo piano works

Polka. Le poisson d'or. Dispute entre le papillon et le crapaud. Trois petites marches funèbres. Fragments psychologiques. March. The expulsion from Paradise. Valse. Lieder Album[a]. Trois chansons[a]. Three English Songs[a]. Dialogue between Tom Filuter and his man by Ned the Dog Stealer[a]. Three Songs[a]. Red Roses and Red Noses[a]. Come on Algernon[a]

[a]**Ian Partridge** *ten* **Len Vorster** *pf*

Marco Polo 8 225159 (52 minutes: DDD). Texts and translations included. Recorded 1998 Ⓕ

The minuscule, dejected, lovelorn *Le poisson d'or*, based on Lord Berners' own poem, has a distant Debussian inheritance, while the *Trois petites marches* and *Fragments psychologiques* are Satie-esque, and not just for their bizarre titles. Yet they, too, have a distinct avant-garde precocity, and 'Un soupir' (the third of the *Fragments*) brings a pensive dolour all its own. Berners' sense of fun erupts in the simulated German *Lieder Album* (the seriousness underpinned with a twinkle), and the French *Trois chansons* are naturally idiomatic, with 'La fiancée du timbalier' engagingly light-hearted. The English songs are most winning. *Tom Filuter*'s dialogue changes mood chimerically, and the *Three Songs* of 1921 are like a re-discovery of the English folksong idiom, while the sentimental *Red Roses and Red Noses* has an endearingly flowing lyrical line. It is followed by the irrepressible *Come on Algernon*, about the insatiable Daisy, who always 'asked for more!', a perfect music-hall number, written for the film *Champagne Charlie*. It makes a delightful pay-off to end the recital.

Ian Partridge obviously relishes all of the stylistic changes like a vocal chameleon. His words are clear, as well. Len Vorster backs him up splendidly and is completely at home in the solo piano music. The recording is truthful, but Berners' vignettes are not best served up as a banquet in themselves: they are much more enticing as an aperitif, or a dessert following other music. But their individuality is in no doubt, and they certainly ought to be featured more often in recital programmes.

Le carrosse du Saint-Sacrement

Le carrosse du Saint-Sacrement[a]. Fanfare[b]. Caprice péruvien[c]

[a]**Ian Caddy** *bass* Viceroy; [a]**Alexander Oliver** *ten* Martinez; [a]**John Winfield** *ten* Balthasar; [a]**Cynthia Buchan** *mez* La Périchole; [a]**Thomas Lawlor** *bar* Thomas d'Esquivel; [a]**Anthony Smith** *bass* Bishop of Lima; [a]**BBC Scottish Symphony Orchestra / Nicholas Cleobury;** [b]**Royal Ballet Sinfonia / Gavin Sutherland;** [c]**RTE Sinfonietta / David Lloyd-Jones**

Marco Polo 8 225155 (79 minutes: DDD). Notes, text and translation included. Recorded [a]1983, [c]1995 and [b]1999 Ⓕ

Lord Berners has now arrived in style! All his music is available on CD; all his published writings are back in print; and Mark Amory's biography has gone into a second edition. So it was high time to add Berners' one-act opera, neglected from its 1924 Paris première under Ansermet until the BBC Radio 3 revival in 1983, which is issued here for the first time.

The libretto is adapted from a short story by Merimée, also used in Offenbach's *La Périchole*. Berners' attractive score has his fingerprints such as the rhythms of his cynical 'Funeral March for a Rich Aunt' and Spanish effects, daringly close to Chabrier (track 6, 18'08"), to suit the Peruvian setting. The leading lady, La Périchole, is a young actress carrying on with the jealous, gout-ridden Viceroy. Their extended duet in Scene 4 develops as a fascinating alliance of scoundrels. At the end of it, she prises the Viceroy's brand-new coach out of him so that she can parade in it to the cathedral and eclipse her rivals in Lima. After a spectacular ride, including a collision, she upstages everyone by giving the carriage to the church to take the sacrament to the dying.

Chris de Souza's excellent radio production used a translation by Adam Pollock of the French libretto. The diction of all the characters is clear: everyone is well cast, especially Cynthia Buchan and Ian Caddy. The *Caprice péruvien* is a later compilation based on music from the opera. Both orchestras are adequate, decently recorded, but above all *Le carrosse* is an enchanting discovery in British comic opera.

Leonard Bernstein

American 1918-1990

GROVE *Bernstein studied at Harvard and the Curtis Institute and was a protégé of Koussevitzky. In 1944 he made his reputation as a conductor when he stepped in when Bruno Walter was ill; thereafter he was associated particularly with the Israel PO(from 1947), the Boston SO and the New York PO (musical director, 1958-69), soon achieving an international reputation, conducting in Vienna and at La Scala. During his tenure the New York PO flourished as never before. A gifted pianist, he often performed simultaneously as soloist and conductor. At the same time, he pursued a career as a composer, cutting across the boundaries between high and popular culture in his mixing of Mahler and Broadway, Copland and Bach. His theatre works are mostly in the Broadway manner: they include the ballet Fancy Free (1944) and the musicals Candide (1956) and West Side Story (1957). His more ambitious works, many of them couched in a richly chromatic, intense post-Mahlerian idiom, often have a religious inspiration, for example the 'Jeremiah' Symphony with mezzo (1942), 'Kaddish', with soloists and choirs (1963) and the theatre piece Mass (1971).*

Fancy Free

Candide – Overture. West Side Story – Symphonic Dances. On the Waterfront – Symphonic Suite. Fancy Free

New York Philharmonic Orchestra / Leonard Bernstein

Sony Classical Bernstein Century SMK63085 (69 minutes: ADD). Recorded 1960-63 Ⓜ **OO**

When Bernstein died, there was a widespread feeling that he had tried to do too much, and yet, in these days of crossover and musical pluralism, his reckless eclecticism might best be seen as prophetic: his film- and show-derived concert music is more popular than ever and these performances have long been considered definitive. All but *Fancy Free* were taped in New York's Manhattan Center in the early 1960s, a problematic venue in which the original sound engineers sought to reconcile the close-miking of individual sections and sometimes individual players with a substantial reverberation period. The results have a synthetic, larger-than-life quality which suits most of the music here. The exception is the Overture to *Candide*, a more driven sort of reading, the brashness of Broadway insufficiently tempered by the rapid figurations of Rossini, the academicism of Brahms, the *joie de vivre* of Offenbach: subtler details tend to disappear into a fog of resonance. In the Symphonic Dances from *West Side Story*, the players eschew the customary shouts in the

'Mambo' but it is doubtful whether there will ever be a more idiomatic reading of what was then essentially 'new music'. The score, by no means a straightforward 'greatest hits' selection, had only recently been unveiled, with Lukas Foss conducting, at a gala concert intended to raise funds for the New York Philharmonic pension fund. Here certainly was the 'aura of show business' which so irked Harold Schonberg, the influential music critic of the *New York Times*: Bernstein's own recording from March 6th has the quality of an unanswerable rejoinder. *On the Waterfront* is if anything even more intense, its lyrical core dispatched with an overwhelming ardour. Last up is what is almost the best of all possible *Fancy Frees*. It was originally sung in inimitable style by Billie Holiday.

Symphony No 2

Bernstein Symphony No 2, 'The Age of Anxiety'
Bolcom Piano Concerto
Marc-André Hamelin *pf* **Ulster Orchestra / Dimitry Sitkovetsky**
Hyperion CDA67170 (59 minutes: DDD) Ⓕ
Recorded 2000

After Hamelin's fantastic virtuosity in the outrageously difficult Godowsky *Studies on Chopin's Etudes* (for which he won the *Gramophone* Instrumental Award 2000) these two works for piano and orchestra are – for him – mere bagatelles. But this is an impressive release since it contains the most convincing account of Bernstein's Symphony No 2 (1949) in recent years, benefiting from a richer sound than Kahane under Litton.

The whole piece is Bernstein's obsessive response to Auden's poem *The Age of Anxiety*, published the year before, about four characters struggling to sort themselves out in New York City. Even though Auden apparently disliked it, you can increasingly hear Bernstein's Symphony as saturated with the poem, its ideas and atmosphere. Often programmatic, it represents a particularly original approach to piano and orchestra and is personal in countless ways – the gentleness of the soft opening and its mystical descending scale, the precisely engineered variations, memorable tunes, a splendid jazzy *Scherzo* and so on. Hamelin and the Ulster Orchestra in fine form under Sitkovetsky deliver a well-paced and cogent performance right up to the deliberately inflated, optimistic ending.

Bolcom is one of the most idiosyncratic American composers of the next generation. His 1976 Piano Concerto draws widely on various types of popular music, which he has always performed so superbly. The Concerto was written in memory of Bolcom's teacher, Milhaud, who would have loved it. The opening movement is captivatingly serene until the blue notes get out of hand; the slow movement is more stable and serious; but the finale comes over as a riotous celebration of Americana. Unfortunately Bolcom intended it to be ironic as a kind of anti-bicentennial tribute. But tunes like these have a habit of occupying centre stage on their own terms. Hamelin is again utterly scrupulous and idiomatic and delivers all the musical styles with supreme confidence – nobody could have mixed them up like Bolcom.

Chichester Psalms

Songfest[a]. Chichester Psalms[b]
[a]**Clamma Dale** *sop* [a]**Rosalind Elias,** [a]**Nancy Williams** *mezzos* [a]**Neil Rosenshein** *ten* [a]**John Reardon** *bar* [a]**Donald Gramm** *bass* [b]soloists from the **Vienna Boys' Choir;** [b]**Vienna Jeunesse Choir;** [a]**National Symphony Orchestra of Washington,** [b]**Israel Philharmonic Orchestra / Leonard Bernstein**
DG 415 965-2GH (62 minutes: ADD). Texts and, where appropriate, translations included Ⓕ
Recorded 1977

'I, too, am America', is the message of Leonard Bernstein's orchestral song-cycle *Songfest*. The subject of the work is the American artist's emotional, spiritual and intellectual response to life in an essentially Puritan society, and, more specifically, to the eclecticism of American society and its many problems of social integration (blacks, women, homosexuals and expatriates). As expected from a composer/conductor equally at home on Broadway or in Vienna's Musikverein, the styles range widely. The scoring is colourful, occasionally pungent, always tuneful. Bernstein's soloists are well chosen and sing with feeling. This vivid live recording of the *Chichester Psalms* offers the full orchestral version and the performers all give their utmost.

Bernstein Chichester Psalms **Barber** Agnus Dei, Op 11 **Copland** In the Beginning. Four Motets – Help us, O Lord; Have mercy on us, O my Lord; Sing ye praises to our King
Dominic Martelli *treb* **Catherine Denley** *mez* **Rachel Masters** *hp* **Gary Kettel** *perc* **Thomas Trotter** *org* **Corydon Singers / Matthew Best**
Hyperion CDA66219 (54 minutes). Texts included Ⓕ
Recorded 1986

Half of this programme is devoted to unaccompanied choral music by Copland: *In the Beginning*, a striking 15-minute 'Creation' for mixed four-part chorus and solo mezzo (which is eloquently executed by Catherine Denley) written in 1947, and three of four short motets he composed in 1921, while studying with Nadia Boulanger in Paris. The performance of the *Chichester Psalms* recorded here uses Bernstein's own reduced (but very effective) instrumentation of organ, harp and percussion, but follows the composer's New York precedent in employing a mixed chorus – although the illusion of a cathedral choir is persuasively conveyed. It is very impressive.

The singing of the Corydon Singers under Best is very fine, and the vivid recording, which gives the voices a pleasant bloom while avoiding the resonance of King's College Chapel, reproduces the instrumental accompaniment, notably the percussion, with electrifying impact. Best's soloist is Dominic Martelli, and very sweetly he sings too. The disc is completed by Barber's setting of the *Agnus Dei* from 1967 and is an arrangement of the famous *Adagio for Strings* which made his name when Toscanini performed it in New York in 1938. This is an imaginative and enterprising programme, extremely well sung and vividly recorded.

Candide (1988 final version)

Jerry Hadley *ten* Candide; **June Anderson** *sop* Cunegonde; **Adolph Green** *ten* Dr Pangloss, Martin; **Christa Ludwig** *mez* Old lady; **Nicolai Gedda** *ten* Governor, Vanderdendur, Ragotski; **Della Jones** *mez* Paquette; **Kurt Ollmann** *bar* Maximilian, Captain, Jesuit father; **Neil Jenkins** *ten* Merchant, Inquisitor, Prince Charles Edward; **Richard Suart** *bass* Junkman, Inquisitor, King Hermann Augustus; **John Treleaven** *ten* Alchemist, Inquisitor, Sultan Achmet, Crook; **Lindsay Benson** *bar* Doctor, Inquisitor, King Stanislaus; **Clive Bayley** *bar* Bear-Keeper, Inquisitor, Tsar Ivan
London Symphony Chorus and Orchestra / Leonard Bernstein
DG ② 429 734-2GH2 (112 minutes: DDD) Ⓕ
Notes and text included. Recorded 1989 ●●●

Here it is – all of it – musical comedy, grand opera, operetta, satire, melodrama, all rolled into one. We can thank John Mauceri for much of the restoration work: his 1988 Scottish Opera production was the spur for this recording and prompted exhaustive reappraisal. Numbers like 'We Are Women', 'Martin's Laughing Song' and 'Nothing More Than This' have rarely been heard, if at all. The last mentioned, Candide's 'aria of disillusionment', is one of the enduring glories of the score, reinstated where Bernstein always wanted it (but where no producer would have it), near the very end of the show. Bernstein called it his 'Puccini aria', and that it is – bittersweet, long-breathed, supported, enriched and ennobled by its inspiring string counterpoint. And this is but one of many forgotten gems.

It was an inspiration on someone's part (probably Bernstein's) to persuade the great and versatile Christa Ludwig and Nicolai Gedda (in his sixties and still hurling out the top Bs) to fill the principal character roles. To say they do so ripely is to do them scant justice. Bernstein's old sparring partner Adolph Green braves the tongue-twisting and many-hatted Dr Pangloss with his own highly individual form of *Sprechstimme*, Jerry Hadley sings the title role most beautifully, *con amore*, and June Anderson has all the notes, and more, for the faithless, air-headed Cunegonde. It is just a pity that someone didn't tell her that discretion is the better part of comedy. 'Glitter and Be Gay' is much funnier for being played straighter, odd as it may sound. Otherwise, the supporting roles are all well taken and the London Symphony Chorus has a field-day in each of its collective guises.

Having waited so long to commit every last note (or thereabouts) of his cherished score to disc, there are moments here where Bernstein seems almost reluctant to move on. His tempos are measured, to say the least, the score fleshier now in every respect: even that raciest of Overtures has now acquired a more deliberate gait, a more opulent tone. But Bernstein would be Bernstein, and there are moments where one is more than grateful for his indulgence: the grandiose chorales, the panoramic orchestra-scapes (sumptuously recorded), and of course, that thrilling finale – the best of all possible Bernstein anthems at the slowest of all possible speeds – and why not (prepare to hold your breath at the choral *a cappella*). You are unlikely to be disappointed by this disc.

On the Town

Frederica von Stade *mez* Claire; **Tyne Daly** *sngr* Hildy; **Marie McLaughlin** *sop* Ivy; **Thomas Hampson** *bass* Gabey; **Kurt Ollmann** *bar* Chip; **David Garrison** *sngr* Ozzie; **Samuel Ramey** *bass* Pitkin; **Evelyn Lear** *sop* Madame Dilly; **Cleo Laine** *sngr* Nightclub singer
London Voices; London Symphony Orchestra / Michael Tilson Thomas
DG 437 516-2GH (75 minutes: DDD) Ⓕ
Notes and text included. Recorded 1992. ●●●

On the Town is a peach of a show, a show which hums along on the heat of its inspiration, a show rejoicing in the race of time, but regretful of its passing, a show which lovingly encapsulates those transitory moments seized and then lost amidst the impatient, pulsating heart and soul of the lonely city – the Big Apple. On two amazing nights Michael Tilson Thomas and this starry cast brought New York City to the Barbican in London. Recording this semi-staged performance live must have been a nightmare for DG's engineers, but one wonders if they might not have pulled off a more up-front balance for the voices. Only Cleo Laine gets to be really intimate with her bluesy nightclub song 'Ain't got no tears left'. You'll hang on every breath Laine takes. Many of the notes are threadbare, but who needs notes when you've got instincts like hers? The major roles are happily well cast. Samuel Ramey was an inspired choice for Claire's monumentally boring boyfriend, Pitkin. His 'Song', a masterpiece of arch formality, is very funny indeed. In performance, Tyne Daly's cab-driving Hildy knocked 'em in the aisles with her huggable personality, and the three sailors, Gabey, Chip, Ozzie – Thomas Hampson, Kurt Ollmann, David Garrison – are just perfect. Not only are they well matched vocally but you could put them on any stage and never look back. Hampson's two big numbers – 'Lonely Town' and 'Lucky to be Me' – are handsomely sung with careful avoidance of that peculiarly 'operatic' articulation. The real heroes of this dizzy enterprise are Tilson Thomas and the London Symphony Orchestra, every last player a character. John Harle's soaring, throaty sax and rhythms are so hot, tight and idiomatic that you'd never credit this wasn't an American band. The playing here is stunning; there's no other word for it.

West Side Story

West Side Story
Dame Kiri Te Kanawa *sop* Maria (Nina Bernstein); **José Carreras** *ten* Tony (Alexander Bernstein); **Tatiana Troyanos** *mez* Anita; **Kurt Ollmann** *bar* Riff; **Marilyn Horne** *mez* Off-stage voice; **composite chorus and orchestra from 'on and off' Broadway / Leonard Bernstein**
DG 457 199-2GH (77 minutes: DDD). Ⓕ
Notes and texts included. Recorded 1984 OO

If the job of a 'crossover' record is to shatter preconceptions on both sides of any musical fence, then this is the greatest ever. Not all the *aficionados* of Broadway musicals are going to warm to *de facto* operatic treatment of West Side Story: not all opera-lovers or devotees of Bernstein as star-conductor are going to rate *West Side Story* as an equivalent to opera. But any listener who keeps any sort of open mind, forgetting the constriction of barriers, must recognize this historic disc as superb entertainment and great music-making on every level, with an emotional impact closely akin to that of a Puccini opera and an intensity of excitement to match anything from disco to *The Rite of Spring.* That of course is the doing of Leonard Bernstein as conductor as well as composer. It is astonishing that before this recording he had never conducted his most famous work. Interviewed by John Rockwell of the *New York Times* during the sessions, Bernstein noted how difficult it was to cast *West Side Story*, and said that in a recording 'I decided to go for sound'.

Dame Kiri Te Kanawa may not be a soprano one would cast as Maria on stage, yet the beauty of the voice, its combination of richness, delicacy and purity, brings out the musical strengths of Bernstein's inspiration. Similarly, with José Carreras as Tony, it is self-evident to point out how such a voice brings out the pure beauty of the big melodies like 'Maria' or 'Tonight', but even a sharp number like his first solo, 'Something's coming', with floated *pianissimos* and subtly-graded *crescendos* allied to sharp rhythms, makes it more clearly a question-mark song, full of expectation, more than just a point number. Marilyn Horne is in glorious voice, while Tatiana Troyanos will surprise you as Anita with the way she could switch her naturally beautiful operatic voice into a New York throaty snarl. Troyanos, it appears, was brought up in exactly the area of the West Side, where the story is supposed to be set, which makes her natural affinity with the idiom less surprising. Kurt Ollmann, American too, as Riff equally finds a very confident balance between the traditions of opera and those of the musical. Diction may not always be so clear as with less rich-toned singers, but Carreras manages a very passable American accent and Dame Kiri a creditable Spanish-American one. The speed with which the piece moves is astounding, not just as superb entertainment but as a Shakespearean tragedy modernized and intensified.

West Side Story
Tinuke Olafimihan Maria; **Paul Manuel** Tony; **Caroline O'Connor** Anita; **Sally Burgess** Off-stage voice; **Nicholas Warnford** Riff; **Julie Paton** Rosalia; **Elinor Stephenson** Consuela; **Nicole Carty** Francisca; **Kieran Daniels** Action; **Mark Michaels** Diesel; **Adrian Sarple** Baby John; **Adrian Edmeads** A-rab; **Garry Stevens** Snowboy; **Nick Ferranti** Bernardo **chorus and National Symphony Orchestra / John Owen Edwards**
TER ② CDTER2 1197 (101 minutes: DDD). Ⓕ
Recorded 1993

This recording of *West Side Story* is something of an achievement. The set starts with the major advantage of being inspired by a production at the Haymarket, Leicester, so that many of the cast are really inside their roles. They have youth on their side, too. Paul Manuel from that company may not have a large voice, but his sympathetic portrayal of Tony, both in his solos and duets with Maria, makes one feel that he identifies totally with the part. Moreover, the way in which he can float a high note, as at the end of the alternative film version of 'Something's Coming' puts him on a par with Carreras (for Bernstein). His Maria, Tinuke Olafimihan, is a gem. Her ability to interact with him and express the laughter and the tragedy of the heroine is very real. At the heart of the 'Somewhere' ballet, Sally Burgess voices the lovers' plea for peace with a magnificent rendition of its famous soaring tune. Nicholas Warnford as leader of the Jets gives no less than his rival in the tricky 'Cool' sequence and Jet song. John Owen Edwards directs Bernstein's score as if he believes in every note. He has imparted to his players the very pulse that sets this music ticking.

Wonderful Town

Kim Criswell *sop* Ruth; **Audra McDonald** *sop* Eileen; **Thomas Hampson** *bar* Baker; **Brent Barrett** *sngr* Wreck; **Rodney Gilfry** *bar* Guide, First Editor, Frank; **Carl Daymond** *bar* Second Editor, Chick Clark; **Timothy Robinson** *ten* Lonigan; **Michael Dore** *bass* First Man, Cadet, Third Cop, Villager; **Lynton Atkinson** *ten* Second Man, Second Cop; **Simone Sauphanor** *sngr* First Girl; **Melanie Marshall** *mez* Second Girl; **Kimberly Cobb** *sngr* Violet; **Robert Fardell** *sngr* First Cop
London Voices; Birmingham Contemporary Music Group / Sir Simon Rattle
EMI CDC5 56753-2 (67 minutes: DDD). Ⓕ
Notes and text included. Recorded 1996-98 OO

The Birmingham Contemporary Music Group, with key brass and sax personnel bumped in from the West End, play the Overture with great attitude, trumpets with the throttle full out and a bevy of saxes licking everyone into shape. But check out the Original Cast album (on Sony) and it's faster, tighter – not much, but enough to sound like NYC in the fast lane; crude and sassy with plenty of grime in the mix. Accept the fact that Rattle's is a pristine *Wonderful Town*, temporarily divorced from its smart book

(Joseph Fields and Jerome Chodorov), out of context, and, to some extent, out of its element, and you'll have a good time. No one in the Original Broadway Cast can come within spitting distance of the vocal talent assembled here. Kim Criswell's Ruth has to live with Rosalind Russell's keys – in the bass-baritone range. Where Russell had about three notes in her voice – all dubious – Criswell has them all but doesn't have too much occasion to use them. So she works the lyric of 'One Hundred Easy Ways' a little harder than Russell – a piranha to Russell's shark. Audra McDonald as Sister Eileen uses every part of her versatile voice, wrapping it round a lyric like the two are inseparable, and sings 'A Little Bit in Love' with such contentment that it's as if she's giving herself a big, well-deserved hug. It's a gorgeous voice and the microphone loves her. It loves Thomas Hampson, too, and though he will never quite erradicate the 'formality' from his delivery he's rarely sounded quite so unassuming as here imagining his 'Quiet Girl'.

Of the big set-pieces, 'Conversation Piece' sounds as if it could have been lifted from a performance of the show. When the village kids get in on the action that's quite a stretch for Simon Halsey's London Voices. Now and again you catch their English choral tradition, but not long enough for it to get in the way. 'Conga!' sounds sufficiently inebriated and they sound right at home on 'Christopher Street'. You get slightly more *Wonderful Town* for your money with Rattle (a couple of reprises for a start). Don Walker's feisty orchestrations get more of an airing with the addition of 'Conquering New York', a dance number which demonstrates how ready Lenny was to raid his bottom drawer by reusing *Prelude, Fugue and Riffs*.

Franz Adolf Berwald

Swedish 1796-1868

GROVE *Swedish composer and violinist Berwald is the most individual and commanding musical personality Sweden has produced. He was the son of CFG Berwald (1740-1825), a violinist of German birth who studied with F. Benda and played in the Stockholm court orchestra. Franz was a violinist or violist in the orchestra (1812-28) and probably studied composition with its conductor, JBE Dupuy. He disowned all his early works, which in their bold modulations show Spohr's influence, except a Serenade for tenor and six instruments (1825) and the fine Septet (?1828). He cherished operatic ambitions but failed to stir much interest in any of his works except Estrella de Soria (1841, performed 1862); The Queen of Golconda was not staged until 1968. In fact he was never properly recognized in his own country.*

He made his greatest contribution to the repertory in his orchestral compositions of the 1840s, above all the four symphonies: the Sinfonie singulière (1845) is the most original, but all share vigorous freshness, formal originality (he sometimes used cyclic forms) and warm harmony and textures, especially in slow movements. His chamber works (two piano quintets, four piano trios and two string quartets), which occupied his main attention from 1849 to 1859, are often Mendelssohnian in style and show real command of form and idiom. Berwald pursued several business interests (he ran an orthopedic institute, a glassworks and a sawmill) and was active as a polemical writer on social issues from 1856. Although he was made professor of composition at the Swedish Royal Academy in 1867, the discovery of his work was a 20th-century phenomenon. His brother August (1798-1869) was also a violinist and composer, and a granddaughter, Astrid, a leading Swedish pianist.

Symphonies

Symphonies – No 1 in G minor, 'Sinfonie sérieuse'; No 2 in D, 'Sinfonie capricieuse'; No 3 in C, 'Sinfonie singulière'; No 4 in E flat. Konzertstück for Bassoon and Orchestra

Christian Davidsson *bn* **Malmö Symphony Orchestra / Sixten Ehrling**

BIS ② CD795/6 (131 minutes: DDD). Ⓕ

Recorded 1996

As one would expect, given Sixten Ehrling's excellent account of the *Singulière* and the E flat Symphonies with the LSO for Decca way back in the late 1960s and his no less impressive 1970 Swedish Radio version of the *Sérieuse*, the performances are *echt*-Berwald. Ehrling gives us plenty of space without ever lingering too lovingly. Even apart from the *tempo giusto*, one feels rather more comfortable with Ehrling's handling of phrasing and balance. He is very attentive to dynamic markings and sometimes, as at the beginning of the *Sinfonie singulière*, *pianissimo* becomes *pianopiano-pianissimo*! The recording reproduces these dynamic extremes flawlessly. The Malmö Concert Hall where this set was made has a good acoustic. The recordings are generally excellent, though there seems to be more back-to-front perspective and air around the players in the *Singulière* and E flat Symphonies than in the *Sérieuse*. On the whole, the recording is truthful and vivid, and the soloist in the *Konzertstück* is excellently balanced. One has to conclude that Ehrling and his fine players bring us closer to the spirit of this music than do any of the current rivals.

Chamber works

Piano Trio No 2 in F minor. Quartet for Piano and Wind in E flat. Grand Septet in B flat

Gaudier Ensemble (Richard Hosford *cl* Robin O'Neill *bn* Jonathan Williams *hn* Marieke Blankestijn *vn* Iris Juda *va* Christoph Marks *vc* Stephen Williams *db* Susan Tomes *pf*)

Hyperion CDA66834 (67 minutes: DDD). Ⓕ

Recorded 1995

The Septet is innovative and anticipates the *Sinfonie singulière*, in enfolding the *Scherzo* into the body of the slow movement, and its invention is delightfully fresh. The Gaudier Ensemble brings elegance and finesse not only to the Septet but also to its companions. The early E flat

Quartet for piano and wind of 1819 is more conventional in its formal layout and is musically less interesting, but there are also touches of that intelligence and wit that illumine all Berwald's music and the piece shines in the Gaudier's hands. The much later F minor Piano Trio of 1851 is more substantial and an unqualified delight. The writing is full of original touches and rhythmic vitality. Its placid surface is disturbed by all sorts of characteristic flourishes: in the theme of the slow movement there is one of the sudden and unexpected modulations for which Berwald's contemporaries were always berating him. Susan Tomes handles the demanding piano part with exemplary skill and taste. It is all hugely enjoyable and well recorded too.

Heinrich Biber Bohemian 1644-1704

GROVE *Biber is important for his works for the violin, of which he was a virtuoso. In the mid-1660s he entered the service of the Prince-Bishop of Olomouc who maintained an excellent Kapelle at his Kromeríž castle. By 1670 Biber had moved to the Salzburg court Kapelle, becoming Kapellmeister in 1684. His formidable violin technique is best seen in the eight Sonatae violino solo with continuo (1681), where brilliant passage-work (reaching 6th and 7th positions) and multiple stopping abound in the preludes, variations and elaborate finales. Most of the Mystery (or Rosary) Sonatas (c1676, for violin and bass) require scordatura tuning: by linking the open strings to the key the sonority and polyphonic possibilities of the violin were increased. The unaccompanied Passacaglia here, built on 65 repetitions of the descending tetrachord, is the outstanding work of its type before Bach. Besides other violin works (which include a Battalia, with strings and continuo), Biber composed sacred music (in a cappella style as well as large-scale concertato works for solo and ripieno voices), 15 school dramas, three operas (only Chi la dura la vince, 1687, survives) and much instrumental ensemble music (often for unusual combinations including brass). Especially notable are the Requiem in F minor, the Missa Sancti Henrici (1701), the 32-part Vesperae (1693), the motet Laetatus sum (1676), and the Sonata S Polycarpi for eight trumpets and timpani. Biber may have composed the 53-part Missa salisburgensis (1628) formerly attributed to Benevoli.*

Balletti

Arias a 4 in A. Ballettae a 4 violettae. Balletti a 6 in C. Balletti lamentabili a 4 in E minor. Harmonia Romana. Trombet undt musicalischer Taffeldienst

Ars Antiqua Austria / Gunar Letzbor *vn*

Symphonia SY95143 (75 minutes: DDD). Ⓕ

Recorded 1995

The baroque palace of Kremsier was the summer residence of Prince-Bishop Karl Liechtenstein-Kastelkorn of Olmütz. He was an ardent music lover and during his rule, which lasted from 1664 to 1695, the palace library acquired what is now recognized as a precious collection of manuscripts. This programme features some of the ensemble music by Biber from the Kremsier source, though the authenticity of the *Harmonia Romana* anthology, some of whose dances are on the disc, has not been established. Never mind, the sequence put together by violinist and director, Gunar Letzbor, is entertaining and very well executed by Ars Antiqua Austria. Most of the music is for strings but there are contributions from variously sized recorders, too, as well as some splendidly gruff, earthy and inebriate interjections from bass, Michael Oman, as the Nightwatchman. Nowadays, he'd be 'taken in' for making that kind of racket in public.

Letzbor has built his programme around an idea of a Carnival Feast at the Bishop's court. It goes something like this: the Bishop enters to a fanfare – dance music greets the guests – a nightwatchman passes by – table music during dinner – dancing – the nightwatchman passes by once more, this time drunk – peasant dancing – midnight, the end of Carnival and the beginning of Lent. The revelry is concluded by the 12 strokes of midnight sounded on what sounds like a school bell. The notion comes off well, for Letzbor's scheme allows for a degree of musical contrast, both of sound and, above all, of mood. Biber's dances are enchanting for the fullness of their character and for their rhythmic bite, and Ars Antiqua brings them to life with vigour, imagination and style. In short, the group offers us well over an hour of first-class entertainment in which only the Bishop's festive board and the contents of his cellar are not shared with us. The disc is superbly recorded, too.

Battalia a 10 in D

Biber Battalia a 10 in D[c]. Passacaglia in C minor[a]. Sonata violino solo representativa in A[c]. Harmonia artificiosa – Partita in C minor[c] **Locke** Canon 4 in 2[c]. The Tempest[c] **Zelenka** Fanfare in D[b]

[a]**Luca Pianca** *lte* [b]**Innsbruck Trumpet Consort;** [c]**Il Giardino Armonico / Giovanni Antonini** *rec*

Teldec 3984-21464-2 (68 minutes: DDD). Ⓕ

Recorded 1998 **oo**

Biber's *Battalia* has arguably become the most celebrated programmatic suite of the 17th century with its easy Bohemian juxtaposition of poignant airs and almost choreographic stage music. Too often we hear each implicit detail exaggerated to death; here, Il Giardino Armonico conveys each movement within the bounds of courtly decorum. The group's leader, Enrico Onofri, provides a memorable and effective gimmick in the March as he walks from right to left and disappears into the distance. His playing in the *Sonata violono solo representativa* is impressive and acutely characterized: the Cuckoo is positively charming, the Frog leaps in a spontaneous counterpoint of improvised special effects and the Hen and the Cock fly by the seats of their pants with a stirring full-throttled sound and thrilling technical precision. Such qualities are also apparent in the remarkable *Harmonia artificiosa* of 1696. Composed for two violas d'amore, this is a beguiling work. Il Giardino Armonico generates a ringing, almost orchestral palette – darkened by a tenor chalumeau – upon which float these soft-grained viole. Less agreeable is the Allemande which is fussily handled and never quite allowed to bed down into its natural harmonic rhythm; the 'Aria variata' that ends the suite has reflective sobriety nonchalantly sacrificed for Mediterranean effervescence. This is both the strength and weakness of Il Giardino in northern and central European repertoire, exemplified in Locke's music for *The Tempest*, from which a majestic orchestral suite can be wrought. The musical ideas are impressive, but too often miscast with ill-suited outbursts imposed on such temperate dances. Overall though, this is a dynamic and distinctive programme with some brilliant performances.

Violin Sonatas

Eight Sonatas for Violin and Continuo (1681). Sonata violino solo representativa in A. Sonata, 'La Pastorella'. Passacaglia for Solo Lute. Mystery Sonatas – Passacaglia in G minor **P**

Romanesca (Andrew Manze *vn* Nigel North *lte/theorbo* John Toll *hpd/org*)

Harmonia Mundi ② HMU90 7134/5 Ⓕ

(127 minutes: DDD). Recorded 1993-94 ○○○

While the more famous *Mystery Sonatas* have quickly found friends, the 1681 set is still largely unknown. Yet what is immediately noticeable from this première recording of the sonatas is that Biber is not only a legendary virtuoso, probably never bettered in the 17th or 18th centuries, but one of the most inventive composers of his age: bold and exciting, certainly but also elusive, mercurial and mysterious. The majority of the works comprise preludes, arias and variations of an unregulated nature: improvisatory preludes over naked pedals and lucid arias juxtaposing with eccentric rhetorical conceits are mixed up in an unpredictable phantasm of contrast, and yet at its best it all adds up to a unified structure of considerable potency. Andrew Manze is the protagonist *par excellence* for music which requires a considered response to complement the adventurous spirit of the virtuoso. In short, this is masterful playing in which Manze has the confidence not to overcharacterize Biber's volatile temperament. Hence the preludes are sweet and restrained, yet there is also a held-back, almost smouldering quality, which is skilfully pitched against the free-wheeling energy of the fast music.

Sonatae tam aris quam aulis servientes

Rare Fruits Council / Manfredo Kraemer *vn*

Auvidis Astrée E8630 (67 minutes: DDD). Ⓕ

Recorded 1997

A more radiant and gratifyingly robust collection of baroque instrumental works would be hard to imagine. These 12 sonatas (which broadly translate as 'sonatas suitable for altar or court') juxtapose pieces for a rich five- or six-part string palette – pursuing an exhilarating, intensely-wrought, sophisticated and unpredictable musical rhetoric – with quasi-concerted and swaggering trumpets. Unlike some of the other printed collections, in which boxes of tricks can sometimes over-prevail, this one comprises highly compelling and accessible music: the satisfying textural surety and tunefulness of Sonata IV is a case in point and so too is the noble ecclesiastical *alla breve* conclusion to Sonata VI (marvellously shaped here).

The secret for performers is to let the antiquated contrapuntal dance-infused music ring, to allow it to unfold as if each contrasted section meant something greater than its mere existence. The emotive, almost physical impact of Biber in his best colours is lavishly exuded in the Rare Fruits Council's strongly projected account. It takes a glowing, colourful and uncomplicated approach, espousing a textural breadth and rhythmic thrust underpinned by a deep violone (8ft bass), theorbo and harp. The playing is often dazzling here – the trumpet sound is peerless, round and coppery – and the total concept unfussy (though this occasionally applies to tuning also).

Mystery Sonatas **P**

John Holloway *vn* **Davitt Moroney** *org/hpd* **Tragicomedia** (Stephen Stubbs *lte/chitarrone* Erin Headley *va da gamba/lirone* Andrew Lawrence-King *hp/regal*)

Virgin Classics Veritas

② VCD7 59551-2 (131 minutes: DDD) Ⓕ

Recorded 1989 ○○○

Biber was among the most talented musicians of the late 17th century. He was a renowned violinist and his compositions, above all for the violin, are technically advanced and strikingly individual. The 15 *Mystery Sonatas* with their additional *Passacaglia* for unaccompanied violin were written in about 1678 and dedicated to Biber's employer, the Archbishop of Salzburg. Each Sonata is inspired by a section of the Rosary devotion of the Catholic Church which offered a system of meditation on 15 Mysteries from the lives of Jesus and His mother. The music is not, strictly speaking, programmatic though often vividly illustrative of events which took place in the life of Christ. All but two of the 16 pieces require *scordatura* or retuning of the violin strings; in this way Biber not only facilitated some of the fingerings but also achieved sounds otherwise unavailable to him. The Sonatas are disposed into three groups of five: Joyful, Sorrowful and Glorious Mysteries whose contrasting states are affectingly evoked in music ranging from a spirit reflecting South German baroque exuberance to one of profound contemplation. John Holloway plays with imaginative sensibility and he is supported by a first-rate continuo group whose instruments include baroque lute, chitarrone, viola da gamba, a 15-string lirone, double harp and regal.

Litaniae de Sancto Josepho

Biber Litaniae de Sancto Josepho. Sonata Sancti Polycarpi. Fidicinium sacro-profanum – Sonata XI P
Bertali Sonata a 13. Sonata Sancti Placidi
Muffat Missa in labore requies
Cantus Cölln; Concerto Palatino / Konrad Junghänel
Harmonia Mundi HMC90 1667 (69 minutes: DDD). Ⓕ
Texts and translations included.Recorded 1998

Cantus Cölln's main priority has always been to promote largely unexplored vocal repertoire of the 17th century from the German lands and central Europe. The mainstay of this disc is two substantial works probably composed for special feasts in the luxurious recesses of Salzburg Cathedral during the 1670s and 1680s. Both are rarities to the catalogue. Biber's *Litaniae de Sancto Josepho* were written in 1677 for the founding of the Fraternity of St Joseph, a well-heeled group of local worthies, by all accounts. Textural imagination is built around contrasted solo and tutti vocal dispositions emboldened by trumpet obbligatos.

Cantus Cölln and the pre-eminent cornett and sackbutters, Concerto Palatino, are plainly in their element, blazing a thrilling trail of dynamic declamation, yet the seamless shaping in the solo litany, 'present at Nativity and servant of Christ', provides the essential lyrical contrast to extended and full-throttled opulence. Muffat's 24-part Mass of multiphonic strings, cornetts, trombones and trumpets perhaps hangs less convincingly, both as a work and in performance. The Mass was long thought to have been written by another (it is Muffat's only surviving vocal work) but the 'Et incarnatus' has the hallmark of the composer's control of harmonic direction and tightly wrought inner-part writing. The 'Crucifixus' is really extraordinary, almost Viennese at the end of the next century (Haydn actually owned the autograph for a while). As with so much 17th-century innovation, one wishes that it went on for a little longer. Once again, the performances here want for little. One could quibble with the occasionally limited dynamic range (Biber's *Sonata Sancti Polycarpi* for eight trumpets is too smoothed out at the edges and lacks the raw nobility of brass on their 'uppers' before battle) but this is a stunning achievement by any standards. The fragrant instrumental pieces relieve the danger of homogeneous overkill and leave the listener relishing the next irresistible mosaic.

Requiem a 15 in A

Biber Requiem a 15 in A P
Steffani Stabat mater
Marta Almajano, Mieke van der Sluis *sops*
John Elwes, Mark Padmore *tens* **Frans Huijts** *bar*
Harry van der Kamp *bass*
Chorus and Baroque Orchestra of the Dutch Bach Association / Gustav Leonhardt
Deutsche Harmonia Mundi 05472 77344-2
(64 minutes: DDD). Texts and translations included. Ⓕ
Recorded 1994

This Requiem may have been performed at the funeral in 1687 of Biber's employer, Max Gandolph von Khuenberg, Archbishop of Salzburg. It is sonorous, stirring and noble and these qualities are at once encountered in the work's richly colourful opening, 'Requiem aeternam dona eis' and to an even greater extent in the wrathful 'Dies irae'. This is a splendid section which inspires Leonhardt and his musicians to deliver it with fearful fervour. But the piece as a whole has clearly captured his imagination and he makes much of the drama. The occasions which prompted grand, ceremonial gestures of the kind which we encounter here must have been quite awe-inspiring since much of the music is redolent of processional solemnity highlighted by dashes of brilliant colour – the scoring includes trumpets and three trombones as well as the standard woodwind and strings.

The companion piece on the disc is of a different hue. In his intimate and contemplative setting of the *Stabat mater*, Biber's Italian contemporary Steffani matches the text with grief-stricken vocal declamation and agonized string suspensions. The scoring is much more modest and subdued than that required for the Requiem. Even so, its emotional content is at least as affecting as Biber's more public demonstration of the Catholic faith. Leonhardt has picked a fine ensemble of vocalists, notably Marta Almajano and Mieke van der Sluis. The Chorus and Baroque Orchestra of the Dutch Bach Association perform well throughout and the programme, offering two starkly different baroque visions of heaven, is richly rewarding.

Missa Bruxellensis

Missa Bruxellensis P
La Capella Reial de Catalunya; Le Concert des Nations / Jordi Savall
Alia Vox AV9808 (52 minutes: DDD). Text included. Ⓕ
Recorded 1999

Modern technology and expert engineering allow us to bask in Biber's magnificent-sounding and spaciously conceived masses, complete with all the glistening attention to detail, the visceral *tutti* impact and the delicate textural contrasts which constitute some of baroque music's most opulent expressions of earthly potency. Salzburg Cathedral provided exceptional acoustical possibilities. As with the *Missa Salisburgensis*, which has recently been recorded successfully by both Paul McCreesh and Ton Koopman, Biber, in his *Missa Bruxellensis* could satisfy the potentate by adorning the unique status of Salzburg as the court with everything. The problem, however, with *Missa Bruxellensis* – so called since it was discovered in Brussels – is that it appears to serve its purpose more as a professional job than as a vehicle for extended inspiration. Even so, a world première recording of a monumental work by a major composer is not to be sniffed at, especially when directed by Jordi Savall. He lets Biber's score roll out unassumingly; even if at the expense of fine tuning and exacting ensemble, the final sections of the *Credo* are immensely stylish, and the 'Miserere' from the *Gloria* has the dignity of a spontaneous event rather than a contrived vignette. The recorded sound has a mixed success, taken from sessions held in the original location; there is a natural sense of the cathedral acoustic, though not, happily, at the expense of immediacy in the solo sections. Less satisfactory are the strident upper frequencies, in particular the solo sopranos. Gripes aside, this will delight collectors who relish fortress-like recordings.

Gilles Binchois French c1400-1460

GROVE *Binchois was one of the three leading musical figures of the first half of the 15th century (with Dufay and Dunstable). Organist at Ste Waudru, Mons, from 1419, he was granted permission to move to Lille in 1423 and apparently entered the service of William Pole, Earl of Suffolk, soon after. Later in the 1420s he joined the Burgundian court chapel where he was much honoured and appointed a secretary to the court (c1437). He held prebends in Bruges, Mons, Cassel and Soignies, where he finally retired; there he was appointed provost of the collegiate church of St Vincent (1452), though he continued to receive a pension from the Burgundian court.*

Although Binchois name was mentioned in contemporary literature only alongside Dufay's, his works had a more independent reputation and, though less widely circulated than Dufay's, were very popular. Six of his songs survive in keyboard arrangements; tenor lines of two or three were used to make basse danses, and numerous compositions from the mid- and late 15th century, including three mass cycles (Ockeghem's Missa 'De plus en plus', Bedyngham's Missa 'Dueil angoisseux' and the anonymous mass-motet cycle 'Esclave puist il devenir'), were based on his works. The fact that many of his compositions survive in only one source, and that most of those were compiled in southern Europe, far from the Burgundian court, suggests that much of his work may be lost or survive only anonymously. His songs, mostly rondeaux, remain within the conventions of refined courtly tradition. They are nearly all for a single-texted upper voice supported by an untexted tenor in longer notes a fifth lower in range and a contratenor in the same range or a little lower. They are characterized by effortless, graceful melodies, uncomplicated rhythms and carefully balanced phrases. His sacred music tends to be more conservative. No complete mass cycle by him has survived, though some of the mass movements can be paired on the basis of similarity. He wrote only one isorhythmic motet, and many of his smaller sacred works are purely functional.

Songs

Triste plaisir et douleureuse joie. Amours merchi de restout mon pooir. Je me recommande humblement. En regardant vostre tres doulx maintiens. Se la belle n'a le voloir. Je vous salue. Adieu mes tres belles amours. De plus en plus. Lune tres belles. Les tres doulx yeux. Amoureux suy et me vient toute joye. Adieu, adieu, mon joieulx souvenir. Jamais tant. Adieu, m'amour et ma maistresse. Dueil angoisseus. Pour prison ne pour maladie. Filles à marier
Ensemble Gilles Binchois / Dominique Vellard *ten*
Virgin Classics Veritas VC5 45285-2
(60 minutes: DDD). Texts and translations included. Ⓕ
Recorded 1996-97

Binchois's songs have rarely appeared in any quantity on CD, yet the booklet-notes to this timely offering set out an objective case for considering Binchois a more significant song composer than his more famous contemporary, Dufay. If one turns to the music, the reasons for Dufay's greater popularity are equally obvious: Binchois's songs yield their secrets more slowly, and operate within a more limited expressive ambit. They demand repeated listening, whereas Dufay's songs tend to make their impact at first hearing. Thus it is all the more important for recordings of Binchois's music to bear repeated listening as well. This one certainly fulfils that requirement, and there is sufficient variety of scoring to sustain interest from song to song. Perhaps the crux of interpreting Binchois is whether to match his fabled restraint in performance, or to coax the songs' expressivity to the surface. Dominique Vellard seems to prefer the former approach, which relies for its effectiveness on the innate vocal qualities of his singers. For the most part, they respond admirably. The special artistry of Lena Susanne Norin is a cause for celebration; Anne-Marie Lablaude's contributions are lighter in tone, but graceful and supple, yet you do wonder whether a more impassioned delivery of the text might not be appropriate – particularly in *Dueil angoisseus*, surely one of the finest poems set to music in the 15th century. And it continues to be puzzling that certain stanzas are shorn of their text to allow for instrumental participation. The Binchois discography makes up in quality for what it lacks in quantity, and notwithstanding these reservations, this disc sits comfortably in a distinguished niche of the repertory.

Sir Harrison Birtwistle British 1934

GROVE *Birtwistle studied at the Royal Manchester College of Music (1952-55), where Davies and Goehr were fellow students, interesting themselves in contemporary and medieval music. He then worked as a clarinettist and schoolteacher for brief periods; in 1975 he was appointed music director at the National Theatre. His works suggest comparison with Stravinsky in their ritual form and style, and sometimes with Varèse in the violence of their imagery (as in the opera Punch and Judy, 1968, a savage enactment of pre-social behaviour). In the 1970s, however, he began to work musical blocks into long, gradual processes of change (The Triumph of Time for orchestra, 1972), then to develop networks of interconnected pulsings beneath such processes (Silbury Air for small orchestra,*

1977; agm for voices and orchestral groups, 1979). His biggest work of this period was the opera The Mask of Orpheus (1973-83, performed 1986), a multi-layered treatment of the myth.

Harrison's Clocks

Joanna MacGregor *pf*
SoundCircus SC004 (26 minutes: DDD). Ⓜ
Recorded 1998

Even if Harrison Birtwistle was not knowingly named after John Harrison, the 18th-century clockmaker discussed in Dava Sobel's recent best-seller *Longitude*, his recurrent concern with musical mechanisms whose 'ticking' regularity is the perfect foil for other, much less predictable elements, makes him the ideal composer to celebrate the pioneer of navigational chronometers. The recurring patterns which dominate the first of these five pieces (composed in 1998) are deceptive in that they create a relatively mild-mannered, even static effect, with contrast confined to brief episodes marking the movement's main formal divisions. But if this leads you to expect a sequence of neo-classical toccatas, the explosive fragmentation of the second piece will soon disabuse you, and in the hair-raisingly intense third movement the implacable power of the composer's invention takes the breath away. Joanna MacGregor meets the demands with interest, bringing the music vividly to life, and the recording is excellent. Indispensable.

The Mask of Orpheus

Awards 1998

Jon Garrison *ten* Orpheus: Man; **Peter Bronder** *ten* Orpheus: Myth, Hades; **Jean Rigby** *mez* Euridice: Woman; **Anne-Marie Owens** *mez* Euridice: Myth, Persephone; **Alan Opie** *bar* Aristaeus: Man; **Omar Ebrahim** *bar* Aristaeus: Myth, Charon; **Marie Angel** *sop* Aristeus: Oracle of the Dead, Hecate; **Arwel Huw Morgan** *bar* Caller; **Stephen Allen** *ten* Priest, First Judge; **Nicholas Folwell** *bar* Priest, Second Judge; **Stephen Richardson** *bass* Priest, Third Judge; **Juliet Booth** *sop* Woman, First Fury; **Philippa Dames-Longworth** *sop* Woman, Second Fury; **Elizabeth McCormack** *mez* Woman, Third Fury; **Ian Dearden** *sound diffusion*
BBC Singers; BBC Symphony Orchestra / Sir Andrew Davis, Martyn Brabbins
NMC NMCD050 (three discs: 162 minutes: DDD) Ⓜ
Notes and text included. Recorded 1996 ●●●

Birtwistle's opera is about the Orpheus myth, but the familiar story has been fragmented. Each of the principal characters is represented by two singers and a (silent) dancer, and much of what happens is not directly described in the libretto. Without following the libretto you will not be able to follow all of what is being sung; at times very little (the text is sometimes broken up; some passages, including much of Act 3, are sung in an invented language). Rituals are often at their most powerful when they appeal to the imagination rather than to reason, and here the sense of ritual is awesomely powerful: solemn and often gravely beautiful in Act 1, much tougher and more complex but also hugely exciting in Act 2 and with a formidable, gathering sense of culmination in Act 3. It is an extraordinarily patterned opera, with many varied repetitions, all meticulously labelled ('First Structure of Decision', 'Second Time Shift' and so on) in the score. The ritual repetitions, the elaborate patternings and allegorical structures make their own effect. In the boldest of these, the 17 'arches' over which Orpheus passes in his quest for Euridice in Act 2, Birtwistle aids comprehension by quite extensive use of speech. But the music says far more than the sometimes enigmatic words, and the ceremonial retelling of the whole story in Act 3, would perhaps have less impact if the words of the song verses were comprehensible. Birtwistle communicates his refracted but gripping myth with, above all, orchestral colour: an orchestra of wind, percussion and plucked instruments (plus tape, sampler and a small chorus) used with vivid mastery. The sheer sound of this opera is quite haunting and moving. *The Mask of Orpheus* is a masterpiece, and this performance is fully worthy of it. There are no weak links at all in the extremely fine cast. Although it is unfair to single out any singer for special mention, Jon Garrison's portrayal of Orpheus the Man is outstanding. The recording, direct and pungent but by no means lacking in atmosphere (the electronic tape is pervasive in the right sense: it is the voice of Apollo), leaves nothing to be desired.

Punch and Judy

Awards 1980

Stephen Roberts *bar* Punch; **Jan DeGaetani** *mez* Judy, Fortune-teller; **Phyllis Bryn-Julson** *sop* Pretty Polly, Witch; **Philip Langridge** *ten* Lawyer; **David Wilson-Johnson** *bar* Choregos, Jack Ketch; **John Tomlinson** *bass* Doctor
London Sinfonietta / David Atherton
Etcetera ② KTC2014 (103 minutes: ADD Ⓕ
Notes and text included. Recorded 1980 ●●●

Punch and Judy was composed in the mid 1960s, and since this recording first appeared on Decca we have had the remarkable 1984 Opera Factory production of the work, directed by David Freeman, seen on stage and television. As Punch, Stephen Roberts is less consistently menacing and 'over the top' in vocal demeanour than Opera Factory's Omar Ebrahim. But Roberts remains a very satisfying interpreter of a part which is far from uniformly aggressive in character and in which a kind of crazy vulnerability offsets the ritual violence. In fact the general excellence of the singers on this set is impressive, with a spectacular contribution from Phyllis Bryn-Julson.

In the light of Birtwistle's finest later works especially the opera *The Mask of Orpheus* and such pieces as *Secret Theatre* and *Earth Dances*, *Punch and Judy* can seem relatively anonymous in style, at least in those places which offer the kind of brittle, fragmented textures found in many composers at that time. Yet these are only moments, and as a whole the opera loses none of its powerful and sustained impact when compared with Birtwistle's more mature compositions. If anything, its startling primitivisms stand out more vividly, while its not inconsiderable moments of reflection and lyricism acquire an enhanced poignancy. The performance gains immeasurably from the alert control of David Atherton and the superlative musicianship of the London Sinfonietta. The analogue recording may lack depth, but it is as clear and immediate as this throat-grabbing music demands.

Georges Bizet French 1838-1875

GROVE *Bizet was trained by his parents, who were musical, and admitted to the Paris Conservatoire just before his tenth birthday. There he studied counter-point with Zimmerman and Gounod and composition with Halévy, and under Marmontel's tuition he became a brilliant pianist. Bizet's exceptional powers as a composer are already apparent in the products of his Conservatoire years, notably the Symphony in C, a work of precocious genius dating from 1855 (but not performed until 1935). In 1857 Bizet shared with Lecocq a prize offered by Offenbach for a setting of the one-act operetta Le Docteur Miracle; later that year he set out for Italy as holder of the coveted Prix de Rome.*

During his three years in Rome Bizet began or projected many compositions; only four survive, including the opera buffa, Don Procopio (not performed until 1906). Shortly after his return to Paris, in September 1861, his mother died; the composer consoled himself with his parents maid, by whom he had a son in June 1862. He rejected teaching at the Conservatoire and the temptation to become a concert pianist, and completed his obligations under the terms of the Prix de Rome. The last of these, a one-act opéra comique, La guzla de l'emir, was rehearsed at the Opéra-Comique in 1863 but withdrawn when the Théâtre-Lyrique director, who had been offered 100 000 francs to produce annually an opera by a Prix de Rome winner who had not had a work staged, invited Bizet to compose Les pêcheurs de perles .

Bizet completed it in four months. It was produced in September 1863, but met with a generally cool reception: an uneven work, with stiff characterization, it is notable for the skilful scoring of its exotic numbers. In the ensuing years Bizet earned a living arranging other composers' music and giving piano lessons. Not until December 1867 was another opera staged - La jolie fille de Perth, which shows a surer dramatic mastery than Les pêcheurs. It received a good press but had only 18 performances.

1868 was a year of crisis for Bizet, with more abortive works, attacks of quinsy and a re-examination of his religious stance; and his attitude to music grew deeper. In June 1869 he married Geneviève, daughter of his former teacher, Halévy, and the next year they suffered the privations caused by the Franco-Prussian war (Bizet enlisted in the National Guard). Bizet found little time for sustained composition, but in 1871 he produced the delightful suite for piano duet, Jeux d'enfants (some of it scored for orchestra as the Petite Suite), and he worked on a one-act opera, Djamileh. Both the opera and Daudet's play L'arlésienne, for which Bizet wrote incidental music, failed when produced in 1872, but in neither case did this have anything to do with the music.

Bizet was convinced that in Djamileh he had found his true path, one which he followed in composing his operatic masterpiece, Carmen. Here Bizet reaches new levels in the depiction of atmosphere and character. The characterization of José, his gradual decline from a simple soldier's peasant honesty through insurbordination, desertion and smuggling to murder is masterly; the colour and vitality of Carmen herself are remarkable, involving the use of the harmonic, rhythmic instrumental procedures of Spanish dance music, to which also the fate-laden augmented 2nds of the Carmen motif may owe their origin. The music of Micaela and Escamillo may be less original, but the charm of the former and the coarseness of the latter are intentional attributes of the characters. The opera is the supreme achievement of Bizet and of opéra comique, a genre it has transformed in that Bizet extended it to embrace passionate emotion and a tragic end, purging it of artificial elements and embuing it with a vivid expression of the torments inflicted by sexual passion and jealousy. The work, however, was condemned for its 'obscene' libretto, and the music was criticized as erudite, obscure, colourless, undistinguished and unromantic. Only after Bizet's death was its true stature appreciated, and then at first only in the revised version by Guiraud in which recitatives replace the original spoken dialogue (it is only recently that the original version has been revived). The reception of Carmen left Bizet acutely depressed; he fell victim to another attack of quinsy and, in June 1875, to the two heart attacks from which he died.

Symphony in C

Symphony in C. Overture in A (ed d'Almeida). Patrie, Op 19. La jolie fille de Perth – Suite
Montreal Symphony Orchestra / Charles Dutoit
Decca 452 102-2DH (72 minutes: DDD). Ⓕ
Recorded 1995

The early Overture in A minor/major is a rarity; it is an oddly proportioned work in four sections, the second a sudden brief theatrical storm, the substantial third an expressive Italian *Andante* (which Dutoit shapes most lovingly): it ends in an energetic but more conventional finale. The work was never heard in Bizet's lifetime. The same fate befell his Symphony, written in the same year: in fact, it was not performed until 80 years later. It is hard to resist the delicately exotic *Adagio*, the fresh, vigorous *Scherzo*, or the compelling vivacity of the finale, with its Schubertian key-shifts. One of its themes was to reappear in the sparkling opera buffa *Don Procopio* composed five years later: that in turn furnished the *Serenade* borrowed for *La jolie fille de Perth*, the orchestral suite from which was put together by Bizet's publishers after the composer's death. The title of *Scènes bohémiennes* springs from the fourth movement, which anticipates the gipsy dance in *Carmen*. Splendidly vivid playing throughout, and recording too (at times even too bright).

Symphony in C[a]. L'Arlésienne[b] – Suites Nos 1 and 2 **H**
[a]**French National Radio Symphony Orchestra;** [b]**Royal Philharmonic Orchestra / Sir Thomas Beecham**
EMI CDC7 47794-2 (65 minutes: ADD). Ⓕ
Recorded 1956-59. **oo**

In Beecham's hands the Symphony in C is made to sound wonderfully songful and although the French orchestral playing is less than ideally polished, the *joie de vivre* of Beecham's performance is irresistible. What makes this disc doubly desirable are the marvellous RPO wind solos (and, of course, the haunting strings in the *Adagietto*) in *L'Arlésienne*. The performances of these two suites stand head and shoulders above present CD competition, their loving finesse mixes evocative magic (the 'Intermezzo' of No 2) with wonderful rhythmic vivacity (the closing 'Farandole'). The refurbishing of the recordings is remarkably successful, especially *L'Arlésienne*.

Carmen

Teresa Berganza *sop* Carmen; **Plácido Domingo** *ten* Don José; **Ileana Cotrubas** *sop* Micaëla; **Sherrill Milnes** *bar* Escamillo; **Yvonne Kenny** *sop* Frasquita; **Alicia Nafé** *mez* Mercédès; **Robert Lloyd** *bass* Zuniga; **Stuart Harling** *bar* Moralès; **Gordon Sandison** *bar* Dancaïre; **Geoffrey Pogson** *ten* Remendado
Ambrosian Singers; London Symphony Orchestra / Claudio Abbado
DG ③ 427 885-2GX3 (157 minutes: ADD) Ⓜ
Notes, text and translation included
Recorded 1977 **oo**

This notable recording followed immediately on the famous Faggioni production at the 1977 Edinburgh Festival, a staging finely observed enough still to remain with those who were there. In it Berganza declared her aim of rescuing the role from bad traditions and from its insults to Spanish womanhood. Her reading was restrained, haughty, but no less attractive and haunting for that. She developed the character, as she does on the recording, from carefree gipsy to tragic woman and, in doing so, is scrupulous in her obedience to Bizet's notes, rhythms and dynamics. Nothing is exaggerated yet nothing is left out in this sensuous but never overtly sensual portrayal, bewitchingly sung. Maybe you don't feel the full engagement of her emotions in her entanglement with José, but better a slight reticence than overacting. Migenes, on the Maazel set, is more immediately seductive, and occasionally more varied in tonal colouring, but Berganza is the more subtle artist. She works in keen rapport with Abbado, who brings clarity of texture, Mediterranean fire and intense concentration to the score. You may find more elegance, more Gallic wit in, say, Beecham's famous EMI set, but only Maazel of other conductors comes near Abbado's emphasis on close-knit ensemble and histrionic strength – and both their sets come as the result of experience of 'real' performances. Domingo benefits here, as on the Maazel in the same way, being more involved in affairs. Like his Carmen, he sometimes lacks variety of colour in his singing, but its sheer musicality and, in the last two acts, power, count for much. Sherrill Milnes is at once virile and fatuous as Escamillo should be. Cotrubas makes a vulnerable, touching Micaëla. The dialogue is heavily foreshortened compared to rival sets. Abbado chooses some of the questionable Oeser alternatives, but – apart from the one in the finale – they are not disturbing. The recording is first-rate.

Carmen
Julia Migenes *mez* Carmen; **Plácido Domingo** *ten* Don José; **Faith Esham** *sop* Micaëla; **Ruggero Raimondi** *bass* Escamillo; **Lilian Watson** *sop* Frasquita; **Susan Daniel** *mez* Mercédès; **Jean-Philippe Lafont** *bar* Dancäire; **Gérard Garino** *ten* Remendado; **François Le Roux** *bar* Moralès; **John Paul Bogart** *bass* Zuniga
French Radio Chorus; French Radio Children's Chorus; French National Orchestra / Lorin Maazel
Erato ③ 2292-45207-2 (151 minutes: DDD). Notes, Ⓕ
text and translation included. Recorded 1992 **oo**

Too many recordings of *Carmen* have blown up the work to proportions beyond its author's intentions but here Maazel adopts a brisk, lightweight approach that seems to come close to what Bizet wanted. Similarly Julia Migenes approaches the title part in an immediate, vivid way, exuding the gipsy's allure and suggesting Carmen's fierce temper and smouldering eroticism; she develops the character intelligently into the fatalistic person of the card scene and finale. Her singing isn't conventionally smooth but it's compelling throughout. Plácido Domingo has made Don José very much his own, and here he sings with unstinting involvement and finesse. Ruggero Raimondi is a macho Toreador though Faith Esham is a somewhat pallid Micaëla.

Carmen
Béatrice Uria-Monzon *mez* Carmen; **Christian Papis** *ten* Don José; **Leontina Vaduva** *sop* Micaëla; **Vincent le Texier** *bass-bar* Escamillo; **Maryse Castets** *sop* Frasquita; **Martine Olmeda** *mez* Mercédès; **Franck Leguérinel** *bar* Dancaïre; **Thierry Trégan** *ten* Remendado; **Olivier Lallouette** *bass* Moralès; **Lionel Sarrazin** *bass* Zuniga; **Paul Renard** *spkr* Lillas Pastia
Bordeaux CNR Children's Choir; Bordeaux Theatre Chorus; Bordeaux Aquitaine Orchestra / Alain Lombard
Auvidis Valois ② V4734 (142 minutes: DDD) Ⓕ
Notes, text and translation included. Recorded 1994 **o**

Having a French singer in the title-role is one of the advantages of this set. Béatrice Uria-Monzon is a full-bodied Mediterranean mezzo: her Carmen is bold and earthy, with thrilling contralto-like tone for such important moments as the 'Tra-la-la' replies to her interrogators in Act 1. She handles the dialogue with Don José very well, before the Séguidille, in which she pretends that, like him, she is from Navarre (this is usually cut). This weight of voice rather tells against her where charm is concerned, with the 'Chanson bohème' sounding haughty rather than festive. The version of *Carmen* used here reverts to spoken dialogue rather than the spurious recitatives. Leontina Vaduva is a good Micaëla but Christian Papis's Don José isn't really a match for either of his leading ladies. In 'Parle-moi de ma mère' he exhibits an unfortunate beat in the voice that makes it all sound too tragic, although he can produce effective, soft notes, as at the end of 'Là bas, là bas'. One has nothing but sympathy for Carmen's preference for Vincent le Texier's Escamillo whose performance is the best among the other principals. This is a well-recorded, authentically French *Carmen*, conducted with flair by Alain Lombard.

Carmen

Victoria de los Angeles *sop* Carmen; **Nicolai Gedda** *ten* Don José; **Janine Micheau** *sop* Micaëla; **Ernst Blanc** *bar* Escamillo; **Denise Monteil** *sop* Frasquita; **Marcelle Croisier** *mez* Mercédès; **Monique Linval** *sop* Mercédès; **Jean-Christoph Benoit** *bar* Dancaïre; **Michel Hamel** *ten* Remendado; **Bernard Plantey** *bass* Moralès; **Xavier Depraz** *bass* Zuniga; **Les Petits Chanteurs de Versailles; French National Radio Choir and Symphony Orchestra / Sir Thomas Beecham** H

EMI Great Recordings of the Century

③ CMS5 67357-2 (162 minutes: ADD). Ⓜ

Recorded 1958/9. ○○○

This classic Beecham set stands the test of time, sparkling, swaggering and seducing in a way that is uniquely Beecham's. It now comes in the EMI Great Recordings of the Century series, with brightened, freshened and clarified sound. As Richard Osborne points out in his brilliant, informative note, there were serious problems at the sessions – a second series was organised 15 months after the first (hence the two Mercédès) – but you would never realise there had been difficulties, either from the performance or the firmly focused, spacious recording in which the atmospheric off-stage effects are vividly caught.

What is so individual is the way that Beecham points rhythms to captivate the ear, as well as his persuasive moulding of phrases. Witness the sensuous way he coaxes the string phrase leading into the second half of the Don José/Micaëla duet in Act 2, 'Parle-moi de ma mère!' (disc 1, track 9, 3'47"). In those qualities Beecham is matched by Victoria de los Angeles in the title-role.

Osborne reveals that Beecham's original choice of heroine was the Swedish mezzo Kerstin Meyer. After all, de los Angeles – Mimì in Beecham's *Bohème* recording – is hardly an obvious candidate for such a fire-eating role. But there is far more to Carmen than is conveyed in that conventional approach, and de los Angeles instantly establishes her as a seductive, provocative character with wickedly sparkling eyes. In her opening solo, the Habanera, her delicious downward *portamento* on 'Je t'aime' is irresistible.

The Carmen quality which de los Angeles does not have in her regular armoury, though, is a snarl. Instead she consistently uses her golden tone to tantalise and provoke, as in the magically sultry moment leading into 'Là-bas dans la montagne' in her Act 2 duet with José just after the Flower song (disc 2, track 13). At that point Beecham, too, subtly pressing the music forward, is a fellow magician. Then at the very end, in Act 4, de los Angeles does finally muster a snarl in the culminating phrase 'laisse-moi passer' ('Well stab me then, or let me pass').

In a way, Nicolai Gedda's portrait of Don José is just as remarkable. He was at his peak, and sings not just with refinement and imagination but with deep passion, leading one on in the widest expressive range in the Flower song. Janine Micheau makes a bright, clear Micaëla, very French in tone, and Ernst Blanc, if not the most characterful Escamillo, makes the bullfighter a forthright, heroic character, singing with firm, clear tone. The rest of the cast, all French, make an excellent team, as is clear in ensembles: the sparkling account of the Act 2 Quintet or the opening of the Card scene, or the swaggering march ensemble as the smugglers depart in Act 3 (disc 3, track 6). A magic set now made all the more enticing in this mid-price reissue.

Les pêcheurs de perles

Barbara Hendricks *sop* Leïla; **John Aler** *ten* Nadir; **Gino Quilico** *bar* Zurga; **Jean-Philippe Courtis** *bass* Nourabad

Toulouse Capitole Chorus and Orchestra / Michel Plasson

EMI ② CDS7 49837-2 (127 minutes: DDD). Notes, text and translation included. Recorded 1989 Ⓕ ○

Let a tenor and a baritone signify that they are willing to oblige with a duet, and the cry will go up for *The Pearl Fishers*. It's highly unlikely that many of the company present will know what the duet is about – it recalls the past, proclaims eternal friendship and nearly ends up in a quarrel – but the melody and the sound of two fine voices blending in its harmonies will be quite sufficient. In fact there is much more to the opera than the duet; and the EMI recording goes further than previous versions in giving a complete account of a score remarkable for its unity as well as for the attractiveness of individual numbers. It is a lyrical opera, and the voices need to be young and graceful. Barbara Hendricks and John Aler fulfil those requirements, she with a light, silvery timbre, he with a high tenor admirably suited to the tessitura of his solos. The third main character, the baritone whose role is central to the drama, assumes his rightful place here: Gino Quilico brings true distinction to the part, and his aria in Act 3 is one of the highlights. Though Plasson's direction at first is rather square, the performance grows in responsiveness. It is a pity the accompanying notes are not stronger in textual detail, for the full score given here stimulates interest in its history. One of the changes made in the original score of 1863 concerns the celebrated duet itself, the first version of which is given in an appendix. It ends in a style that one would swear owed much to the 'friendship' duet in Verdi's *Don Carlos* – except that Bizet came first.

Additional recommendation

Les pêcheurs de perles

Cotrubas Leïla **Vanzo** Nadir

Paris Opera Orch / Prêtre

Classics for Pleasure CD-CFP4721 Ⓑ

(104 minutes: ADD: 10/91)

Worth hearing for Cotrubas's Leïla. Alain Vanzo's voice had lost some of its bloom by the late 70s when this was made. Prêtre's conducting is somewhat lacking in magic.

Sir Arthur Bliss British 1891-1975

GROVE *Bliss Studied with Wood at Cambridge and served in the army in France. Immediately after World War I he made a mark with works using nonsense texts and brittle Les Six-style irony (Rout, 1920), but successive orchestral works (A Colour Symphony, 1922; Introduction and Allegro, 1926; Music for Strings, 1935) established him as Elgar's successor. His three ballets (Checkmate, 1937 ; Miracle in the Gorbals, 1944 ; Adam Zero, 1946), a notable score for the film Things to Come (1935) and his opera The Olympians (1949) express his feelings for high drama and atmosphere. Among his other works are concertos for piano (1938), violin (1955) and cello (1970), songs, chamber and piano music, and choral works (notably the choral symphony Morning Heroes, 1930). In 1953 he was appointed Master of the Queen's Music.*

Cello Concerto, T120

Cello Concerto, T120. Music for Strings, T54. Two Studies, T16

Tim Hugh *vc* **English Northern Philharmonia / David Lloyd-Jones**

Naxos 8 553383 (64 minutes: DDD). Ⓢ

Recorded 1995.

This is a first-rate performance of Bliss's Cello Concerto from Tim Hugh, stylishly and sympathetically partnered by David Lloyd-Jones and the English Northern Philharmonia. The work is a delightful creation, ideally proportioned, impeccably crafted and full of the most beguiling invention. Hugh plays with commanding assurance, great beauty of tone and rapt commitment, and the accompaniment is sprightly and sensitive to match. What makes this release indispensable to all Bliss admirers is the inclusion of the *Two Studies*. These date from 1921 and were believed lost until they turned up in the composer's papers after his death in 1975. The first is a memorably chaste, coolly serene affair, scored with delicious poise, whereas the second is an energetic, good-humoured and occasionally face-pulling romp. That just leaves the tremendous *Music for Strings*, and here, alas, is where reservations have to be raised. This superb score displays and demands a formidable technical facility and Bliss's exhilaratingly well-judged writing would surely test any string section. It would be idle to pretend that the hard-working strings of the English Northern Philharmonia are ideally secure protagonists. Lloyd-Jones's clear-headed, expressive interpretation serves the work well but in the finale's crucial introductory bars do you feel that his approach is oddly perfunctory. The Cello Concerto and the *Two Studies* alone though, will probably be enticement enough for many listeners. The recorded sound is excitingly realistic.

Checkmate – suite

Bliss Checkmate – suite

Lambert Horoscope – suite **Walton** Façade – Suites Nos 1 and 2

English Northern Philharmonia / David Lloyd-Jones

Hyperion CDA66436 (74 minutes: DDD). Ⓕ

Recorded 1990

What a joy to welcome on CD, a major British ballet score (comparable in appeal to Walton's *Façade* with which, happily, it is coupled). Constant Lambert's *Horoscope* is a highly individual score that is somehow very English. It is played here with striking freshness and expansiveness. Lloyd-Jones responds to Bliss's lyricism very warmly. What makes this disc particularly enticing is the inclusion of the two *Façade* suites, welcome away from the spoken poems. This is music that in a witty performance can make one smile and even chuckle. So it is here, especially the 'Tango Pasodoble' with a delicious lilt for 'I do like to be beside the seaside' contrasting with its Offenbachian gusto, the 'Swiss Yodelling Song' with its droll Rossini quotation and refined mock-melancholy, and the irresistibly humorous 'Polka' that just manages not to be vulgar. All are ideally paced and the solo wind playing is a delight. The recording is near perfect.

A Colour Symphony

A Colour Symphony. Adam Zero

English Northern Philharmonia / David Lloyd-Jones

Naxos 8 553460 (74 minutes: DDD). Ⓢ

Recorded 1995

David Lloyd-Jones's exciting and idiomatic account of *A Colour Symphony* proves easily more than a match for all current competition, including the composer's own 1955 recording so spectacularly transferred by Dutton Laboratories. Speeds are judged to perfection – nicely flowing for the first and third movements, not too hectic for the flashing *Scherzo* – and countless details in Bliss's stunning orchestral canvas are most deftly attended to. Phrasing is sensitive and affectionate, solo work is consistently excellent (the slow movement's delicate woodwind arabesques are exquisitely voiced), and tuttis open out superbly in what is technically the finest recording to date from Naxos (magnificently keen-voiced horns throughout). Whereas *A Colour Symphony* was inspired by the heraldic associations of four different colours (one for each movement), the theme of *Adam Zero* is the inexorable life-cycle of humankind. In its entirety, this 1946 ballet score does admittedly have its occasional *longueurs*, but for the most part Bliss's invention is of high quality. Certainly, the vivid exuberance and theatrical swagger of numbers like 'Dance of Spring' and 'Dance of Summer' have strong appeal. Equally, the limpid beauty of both the 'Love Dance' and the hieratic 'Bridal Ceremony' which immediately ensues is not easily banished, while the darkly insistent 'Dance with Death' distils a gentle poignancy which is most haunting.

A Knot of Riddles

Pastoral, 'Lie strewn the white flocks', T46[a].
A Knot of Riddles[b]. Music for Strings, T54[c]
[a]**Sybil Michelow** *mez* [b]**John Shirley- Quirk** *bar*
[a]**London Bruckner-Mahler Choir;** [ab]**London Chamber Orchestra / Wyn Morris;** [c]**London Philharmonic Orchestra / Sir Adrian Boult**
EMI British Composers CDM5 67117-2
(76 minutes: ADD). Texts included. Ⓜ
Recorded [ab]1970 and [c]1974 ●

These are Sumptuous transfers of three classic Bliss recordings. Although there is no shortage of fine versions of the *Pastoral* and the *Music for Strings*, there is only one alternative version of Bliss's *A Knot of Riddles* at present (see below), which makes this reissue all the more desirable. The *Pastoral* dates from 1928 and is dedicated to Elgar, who was supportive during Bliss's early career. Sybil Michelow gives beautiful renderings of Bliss's settings of Jonson, Fletcher, Nichols and Poliziano, while Norman Knight brings Pan to life with his fine flute and piccolo solos. The song-cycle *A Knot of Riddles* dates from 1963 and is a setting for baritone (here John Shirley-Quirk in fine voice) of Kevin Crossley-Holland's translation of seven Anglo-Saxon riddles. The subject gave Bliss a forum for some effective and inventive tone-painting, and Wyn Morris and his team respond to the music most effectively. *Music for Strings* is now amply represented, and with this disc Boult now holds the baton on no less than four of the currently available recordings. This classic version from 1974 has been much admired over the years and Boult's obvious affection for the work shines. A disc to be welcomed by all Bliss enthusiasts.

Two American Poems[ag]. Seven American Poems[cg]. Angels of the Mind[ag]. The Ballads of the Four Seasons[ag]. A Knot of Riddles[chi]. Two Love Songs[cg]. Two Nursery Rhymes[aef]. Three Romantic Songs[bg]. Three Songs[bg]. Four Songs[adf]. At the Window[bg]. Auvergnat[bg]. A Child's Prayer[ag]. Elegiac Sonnet[bhi]. The Fallow Deer at the Lonely House[bg]. The Hammers[bg]. Rich or Poor[cg]. Simples[bg]. Three Jolly Gentlemen[ag]. 'Tis time, I think, by Wenlock Town[bg]. The Tramps[cg]. When I was one-and-twenty[cg]. The Tempest[bcg] – The Storm; Overture and Act 1, Scene 1
[a]**Geraldine McGreevy** *sop* [b]**Toby Spence** *ten* [c]**Henry Herford** *bar* [d]**Leo Phillips** *vn* [e]**Michael Collins** *cl* [f]**John Lenehan** *pf* [g]**Kathron Sturrock** *pf* [h]**Nash Ensemble /** [i]**Martyn Brabbins**
Hyperion ② CDA67188/9 (123 minutes: DDD). Ⓕ
Texts included. Recorded 1998 ●

Nearly all of Sir Arthur Bliss's songs are here (only a few orchestral ones are omitted) but they are of uneven quality and are presented in almost random order, with no sense given of Bliss's development as a songwriter. It was a mistake to include the *Two Love Songs*, which are in fact the vocal movements of Bliss's beautiful *Serenade* for baritone and orchestra. Kathron Sturrock, throughout a wonderfully musical and responsive accompanist, does her best to make Bliss's piano reductions seem pianistic; but despite her they just sound clumpy. The finest songs here are mostly on the second disc. Kathleen Raine's poems drew the best from the composer – simple eloquence, bold, shining gestures and memorable images including a fine nocturne: they are masterly, and would alone make investigating this pair of discs worthwhile. Geraldine McGreevy sings them simply, purely and very movingly, as she does the progression from lyric charm to bare strength of *The Ballads of the Four Seasons*. Also on CD2 is *The Tempest*; this vivid storm scene is all that survives of some 1921 incidental music to Shakespeare's play, set with striking originality for two voices, trumpet, trombone and five percussion players. Things of such quality are rarer on CD1, though the *Three Songs* to poems by W H Davies are all strong, Bliss's setting of *When I was one-and-twenty* has a blithe insouciance, and several of the other sets contain pleasing discoveries, like the elegantly witty 'A Bookworm' from *A Knot of Riddles* or the charming 'Christmas Carol' that opens *Four Songs*. McGreevy is the best of the singers, but both Herford and Spence are committed advocates. The best of these songs (about half) are of a quality to make their present neglect seem inexplicable.

Ernest Bloch Swiss/American 1880-1959

GROVE *Bloch studied with Dalcroze in Geneva, in Brussels (1897-99) and with Knorr in Frankfurt (1900). In 1916 he went to the USA, thereafter spending most of his time there (he took citizenship in 1924). He also taught at Cleveland (1920-25), San Francisco (1925-30) and Berkeley (1940-52). His early works are eclectic: the opera Macbeth (1910) draws on Strauss, Musorgsky and Debussy. Then came a period of concern mostly with Jewish subjects (Schelomo for cello and orchestra, 1916), followed by a vigorous neo-classicism (Piano Quintet No 1, 1923; Concerto grosso No 1 for strings and piano, 1925). He returned to epic compositions in the 1930s with the Sacred Service (Avodath hakodesh, 1933) and the Violin Concerto (1937). His last works represent a summation of his career and lean towards a less subjective style.*

America

America. Concerto grosso No 1
Patricia Michaelian *pf* **Seattle Symphony Chorale and Orchestra / Gerard Schwarz**
Delos DE3135 (61 minutes: DDD). Text included. Ⓕ
Recorded 1993

Ernest Bloch's 'Epic Rhapsody for Orchestra', *America*, is a warming musical flight across the history of the United States, and uses the anthem of the same name as a leitmotif that helps bind English, American Indian and Jewish-style themes into a homogeneous, accessible whole. There are three variegated movements, each a dramatic tone-poem reflecting such universal ideas as 'Struggle and Hardships' or 'Hours of Joy – Hours of Sorrow' (the second movement's subtitle), with the third visiting the world of jazz and culminating in a full-throated choral celebration of the anthem. However, Bloch's 'programme' is fairly specific. *America* might be best described as a great film score that never was, a highly emotive thanksgiving from a man who had only recently arrived in his new home, with tender references to such favourites as *John Brown's Body* and *Dixie*. There are also veiled references to other of Bloch's works, including *Schelomo* and the delightful *Concerto grosso* that Gerard Schwarz programmes as *America*'s coupling. Demonstration standard sound.

Symphony in C sharp minor

Symphony in C sharp minor. Schelomo
Torleif Thedéen *vc* **Malmö Symphony Orchestra / Lev Markiz** Ⓕ
BIS CD576 (78 minutes: DDD). Recorded 1990-92

Bloch's early symphony is an endearing and at times impressive showcase for a young composer (he was 23) endowed by nature and nurture with all the gifts save individuality (though there are hints in the later movements that that too is on the way). He can write impressively strong, expansive melodies, develop them with real ingenuity and build them into monumental climaxes. Climax-building, indeed, is what young Bloch seems most interested in at this stage, that and a love for all the rich contrasts of colour and texture that a big orchestra can provide. He is so adept at pulling out still more stops when you thought there could hardly be any left that one is scarcely ever made impatient by the occasional feeling that this or that movement could have ended two or three minutes earlier.

It's a pleasure, too, to listen for fulfilled echoes of that youthful exuberance in the mature 'biblical rhapsody' *Schelomo*. Just as Lev Markiz adroitly avoids any impression of overpadded grossness in the symphony, so he and his fine soloist find more than richly embroidered oriental voluptuousness in this portrait of King Solomon; there is gravity and even poignancy to the music as well, and Thedéen's subtle variety of tone colour provides shadow and delicacy as well as richness. The recording is excellent.

Violin Sonatas / Cello Suites

Violin Sonatas – No 1; No 2, 'Poème mystique'. Suite hébraïque. Abodah. Melody
Miriam Kramer *vn* **Simon Over** *pf*
Naxos 8 554460 (75 minutes: DDD). Ⓢ
Recorded 1998. ●

Baal Shem[a]. From Jewish Life[a]. Méditation hébraïque[a]. Solo Cello Suites Nos 1-3
Peter Bruns *vc* [a]**Roglit Ishay** *pf*
Opus 111 OPS30-232 (67 minutes: DDD). Ⓕ
Recorded 1999

Bloch's unaccompanied Cello Suites are late works that, while taking an obvious cue from Bach, still have plenty to say. The First Suite (1956) opens with a 'Prelude' before progressing to a lively *Allegro* which, in terms of style, isn't too far removed from the racy 'folkisms' of Kodály's solo Sonata. The typically Blochian slow movement calls for simultaneous bowed and *pizzicato* playing, and the work closes with an appealing 'Gigue'. Both the First Suite and contemporaneous Second were dedicated to the distinguished Canadian cellist Zara Nelsova. No 2 is more chromatic than the First, Bloch widening his expressive vocabulary (the second movement is especially dramatic) and making greater technical demands on his soloist. The German cellist Peter Bruns takes everything in his stride and his grainy, nicely modulated tone helps focus the music's manifold rhythms and colours. Bach hovers nearest the Third Suite (1957), whereas memories of *Schelomo* are most pronounced in the *Méditation hébraïque*. While Bruns isn't quite in Piatigorsky's league for quietly stated eloquence in the opening 'Prayer' from Bloch's suite *From Jewish Life*, he plays beautifully and makes a cogent case for the cello version of *Baal Shem*'s 'Nigun'.

Miriam Kramer's programme might usefully serve as a sort of 'Bloch starter-pack', with the delightful *Suite hébraïque* as its tuneful opener. 'Rapsodie', the Suite's first movement, harbours a noble melody reminiscent of top-drawer Max Bruch and Kramer's performance of it could hardly be more heartfelt. Both violin sonatas are given extremely good performances, that of the Second particularly fine especially in the ecstatic, double-stopped statements of the central theme. The combination of Kramer's musicianship and Naxos's price will be irresistible to most repertory explorers.

John Blow
British 1649-1708

GROVE *Blow was trained as a Chapel Royal chorister and then worked as organist of Westminster Abbey, 1668-79. In 1674 he both became a Gentleman of the Chapel Royal and succeeded Pelham Humfrey as Master of the Children; from 1676 he was also an organist there. Henry Purcell served an apprenticeship under him and many others were influenced by his teaching.*

The 1680s and 1690s were his most productive years as a composer. While still active at the Chapel Royal (where he was named official composer in 1700), he was Almoner and Master of the Choristers at St Paul's Cathedral in 1687-1703, and in 1695 he returned to Westminster Abbey as organist, succeeding Purcell.

Blow was the most important figure in the school of musicians surrounding Purcell and a composer of marked individuality. His music uses a wide range of idioms and reflects his interest in structure. Foremost in his sacred output are c100 anthems, mostly verse anthems (some with instrumental movements); the powerful coronation work God spake sometime in visions (1685) combines features of both types. Blow also wrote several services and Latin sacred works. Most of his odes were written for court occasions; among the others are works for St Cecilia's Day such as Begin the song (1684). The highly original and poignant miniature opera Venus and Adonis (1685), also for the court, was his only dramatic work. A well-known part of his output was his secular vocal music, comprising c90 solo songs and several duets, catches etc; the Ode on the Death of Mr Henry Purcell (1696), a duet with instruments, is notable for its expressiveness. Blow's instrumental works include organ voluntaries and some 70 harpsichord pieces.

Vocal Works

Blow Sonata in A. Ground in G minor. Fugue in G minor. Suite in G. Ground in C minor. An Ode on the Death of Mr Henry Purcell[ab] P
Purcell Birthday Ode, Z331 – Sweetness of Nature[ab]. Here let my life[a]. Oedipus – Music for a while[a]. St Cecilia's Day Ode, Z328 – In vain the am'rous flute
[aba]**Gérard Lesne,** [b]**Steve Dugardin** *countertens*
La Canzona (Pierre Hamon, Sébastien Marq *recs* Elisabeth Joyé *clav* Philippe Pierlot *va da gamba* Vincent Dumestre *theorbo*)
Virgin Veritas VC5 45342-2 (64 minutes: DDD). Ⓕ
Texts and translations included ●

The teacher who has even one pupil who becomes even more distinguished than himself is fortunate; in Purcell, Blow had one such. And when that pupil's death precedes his own he has cause for genuine grief, as Blow did. One of Purcell's songs, here alternated with instrumental pieces by Blow, contains the line 'Nor let my homely death embroider'd be with scutcheon or with elegy', but it is one with which Blow and others could not concur. In a programmatic tour de force Blow's profoundly beautiful vocal tribute to Purcell comes at the end. Few countertenors are as finely matched in artistry and vocal quality as Lesne and Dugardin who, in both the solo songs and duets, wring every drop of emotion from the texts with sincerity, technically effortless *messa di voce* and admirably clear diction. In Blow's *Ode on the death of Mr Henry Purcell*, the risk that the recorders may cover the singers is avoided here. The instrumental support faithfully shadows every vocal nuance throughout. Much of Blow's instrumental music was unpublished in his time and has remained unrecorded – some first-time pieces here. Where violins were originally specified, as in the A major Trio Sonata, in this recording they are replaced by recorders, and the harpsichord Suite in G minor is a modern compilation from various sources. Altogether this album is pure, unalloyed delight.

God spake sometime in visions. How doth the city sit solitary. The Lord is my shepherd. God is our hope and strength. I beheld and lo! a great multitude. Turn thee unto me, O Lord. Blessed is the man. Lift up your heads. O Lord I have sinned. O give thanks unto the Lord. O Lord, thou hast searched me out. Cry aloud and spare not. Lord, who shall dwell in thy tabernacle. I said in the cutting off of my days P
Robin Blaze *counterten* **Joseph Cornwell, William Kendall** *tens* **Stephen Varcoe, Stephen Alder** *bars*
Winchester Cathedral Choir / David Hill; The Parley of Instruments / Peter Holman
Hyperion ② CDA67031/2 (116 minutes: DDD). Ⓕ
Texts included. Recorded 1995

In choosing a range of Blow's best and most representative anthems, Peter Holman and David Hill have had quite a task on their hands: Blow was even more prolific than Purcell in this domain. They have sensibly cast their critical eyes over those works written in the 'golden' age of Charles II, several of whose reputations go before them. The dignity and sobriety of the fine coronation anthem *God spake sometime in visions* is a joy to behold, and it is given a grand and spacious reading here. David Hill, ever the choral director to sustain and shape a line, is peerless in the opening paragraph. Here, as in other distinguished works like *I beheld and lo!*, the success of these performances is determined by deft recognition of the structural strengths and solecisms of Blow's music. He is helped by a pleasing integration between soloists, choir and instruments. Blow's particular attraction is a disarming tunefulness and an idiomatic simplicity of expression. *O Lord I have sinned* has a distinctive Purcellian flavour with its chromatic inflexions and unpredictable contrapuntal movement, yet it fails to plumb the depths as in the similar type of piece which became something of a Purcell speciality. Indeed, for all Blow's quality there are several works here that just miss the mark despite their distinctive place in English Restoration musical life. Nevertheless, this is without doubt an important addition to the English Orpheus series.

Blow I was glad when they said unto me
Boyce Lord, thou hast been our refuge
Handel Utrecht Te Deum and Jubilate, HWV278-79
Julia Gooding, Sophie Daneman *sops* **Edward Burrowes, Timothy Burtt, Alastair Cook** *trebs* **Robin Blaze, Ashley Stafford** *altos* **Rogers Covey-Crump, Mark Le Brocq** *tens* **Andrew Dale Forbes** *bass*
St Paul's Cathedral Choir; The Parley of Instruments / John Scott
Hyperion CDA67009 (74 minutes: DDD). Ⓕ
Texts included. Recorded 1997

Anyone who has tried to listen to music in St Paul's Cathedral might be forgiven for hesitating before buying a recording made there: however, by some magic the Hyperion engineers have succeeded in producing a recording that is a model of clear sound, even in the fullest tuttis, while at the same time capturing something of the cathedral ambience. This CD happily celebrates the tercentenary, which fell in 1997, of the official opening of the cathedral, offering three of the finest pieces written for performance there. The Blow anthem was written for the opening event and also to give thanks for the Peace of Ryswick. It is an attractive work, including a countertenor duet, exquisitely done here by Robin Blaze and Ashley Stafford, and a tenor solo sung fluently and with much refined detail by Rogers Covey-Crump, supported by a pair of obbligato trumpets. The Boyce anthem was written in 1755 for the Festival for the Sons of the Clergy, still held annually at St Paul's; again, there is distinguished solo singing from Covey-Crump in the expressive 'Yea, like as a father pitieth his own children', and from Blaze in 'The eyes of all wait upon thee'; but perhaps the most appealing number is the trio sung here, in very accomplished style, by three of the boys. And there are rousing choral Hallelujahs to end with.

However, the main item is Handel's *Te Deum and Jubilate* for the Peace of Utrecht, given at St Paul's in 1713 and Handel's first serious venture into Anglican church music. Although modelled on Purcell and Croft, it has something of the freshness and vitality of the church music Handel had recently composed in Italy, even if the constraints of the English anthem manner caused him to work on a smaller canvas – few of the individual movements run much over two minutes or so. It is a colourful piece, full of original ideas, and it is done here under John Scott, the incumbent St Paul's organist, with great vitality, breadth, excellent discipline and clear verbal articulation. The St Paul's boys sing in a fresher, less inhibited style than some, with a distinctive edge to their tone. Sopranos are used for the solos here, with Julia Gooding and Sophie Daneman singing with delicacy, and the other soloists, plus the bass Andrew Dale Forbes, shine again. A disc worthy of its subject.

Venus and Adonis

Rosemary Joshua *sop* Venus; **Gerald Finley** *bar* Adonis; **Robin Blaze** *counterten* Cupid, Second Grace; **Maria Cristina Kiehr** *sop* Shepherdess, First Grace; **Christopher Josey** *counterten* Huntsman, First Shepherd; **John Bowen** *ten* Second Shepherd; **Jonathan Brown** *bass* Third Shepherd, Third Grace **Clare College Choir, Cambridge; Orchestra of the Age of Enlightenment / René Jacobs** P

Harmonia Mundi HMC90 1684 (51 minutes: DDD). Ⓕ

Texts included. Recorded 1998

Historically in the shadow of Purcell's *Dido*, *Venus and Adonis* is fast becoming a recognized masterpiece of small-scale baroque drama. Blow draws considerable inspiration from French chamber opera both in matters of constitution and balance, though *Venus and Adonis* is still a distinctly English work with its poised, understated dialogue and an emotional denouement where Adonis's death from the tusks of a boar is touchingly tender in its measured, if demonstrative grief; the effect is not far removed from Dido's lament, though Purcell's tragic vein is ultimately untouchable. There are, however, some superb examples of indigenous word-setting and declamatory *arioso* which put Blow in the Purcell bracket in several instances, not least in Cupid's forthright scene-setting, sung with increasing assurance by Robin Blaze.

Indeed, René Jacobs surrounds himself with many fine singers here, all of whom he marshals in lively and responsive performances. Rosemary Joshua is an irresistable Venus, who wastes not a word either in colourful representation or vocal suppleness, and Gerald Finlay's reflective longing accords with Jacobs's elegant and full-flavoured direction. There is a nobility in the initial exchanges between the protagonists which is elevated by a doleful shimmer of recorders, which augurs much in its funereal symbolism. These responsive instrumental interjections from the OAE are even more effective in 'Hark, hark the rural music sounds'. This admirable recording puts the work on another footing entirely.

Luigi Boccherini
Italian 1743-1805

GROVE *The son of a cello or double bass player, Boccherini made his public début as a cellist at 13. After studying in Rome, he worked intermittently at the Viennese court, 1757-64. In 1760 he began to catalogue his compositions (though excluding cello sonatas, vocal music and certain other works). In 1764-66 he worked in Lucca, where he composed vocal music and in 1765 reputedly arranged the first string quartet performances in public. On tour with the violinist Filippo Manfredi in Paris, 1767-68, he had his six string quartets op.1 and six string trios Op 2 published. In 1769 the duo arrived in Madrid, where Boccherini became composer and performer to the Infante Don Luis. Up to the time of Luis death in 1785 he composed chamber music for his court, notably string quintets for two violins, viola and two cellos. From 1786, as chamber composer to Prince (later King) Friedrich Wilhelm of Prussia, he sent string quartets to the Prussian court, though probably never went there.*

The chief representative of Latin instrumental music during the Viennese Classical period, Boccherini was especially prolific in chamber music: he wrote well over 120 string quintets, nearly 100 string quartets and over 100 other chamber works. At first he used a standard Italian idiom, but with unusually ornate melodies and frequent high cello writing. Later, reflecting his isolated position, his style became more personal, with delicate detail, syncopated rhythms and rich textures; he sometimes used cyclic forms. The orchestral music includes several virtuoso cello concertos and over 20 symphonies; the vocal works include an opera, two oratorios and a Stabat mater (1781).

Cello Concertos

Cello Concertos – No 4 in C, G477; No 6 in D, G479; No 7 in G, G480; No 8 in C, G481
Tim Hugh *vc* **Scottish Chamber Orchestra / Anthony Halstead** Ⓢ
Naxos 8 553571 (74 minutes: DDD). Recorded 1995 ●

This is a winner of a disc, the first of a series covering all 12 of Boccherini's cello concertos, beautifully performed on modern instruments but with concern for period practice and superbly recorded. Though each concerto has its individual delights the formula in all four works is similar, with strong, foursquare first movements, slow movements that sound rather Handelian and galloping finales in triple time. One minor snag is a confusion over numbering. Naxos calls its first selection of works Nos 1-4, whereas in *Gramophone* and on the *Gramophone* Database the new numbering above is used.

Many collectors will be concerned about the Boccherini Cello Concerto beloved of generations in Grützmacher's corrupt edition. Many years ago Jacqueline du Pré was questioned about choosing it for her recording: she promptly justified herself, saying, 'But the slow movement is so lovely.' She was quite right, as her classic recording makes clear, but that movement was transferred from another work, in fact No 7 in G, one of the four works here. Tim Hugh's dedicated account of this lovely G minor movement is a high spot of this issue, with rapt, hushed playing not just from the soloist but also from the excellent Scottish Chamber Orchestra under Anthony Halstead. Hugh offers substantial cadenzas not just in the first movements of each work, but in slow movements and finales too, though none is as extended as the almost two minute meditation in the G minor slow movement. Halstead, as a period specialist and a horn virtuoso as well as a conductor, matches his soloist in the dedication of these performances, clarifying textures and encouraging Hugh to choose speeds on the fast side, with easily flowing slow movements and outer movements which test the soloist's virtuosity to the very limit, without sounding breathless. Not just for those who know only the old Grützmacher concerto, all this will be a delightful discovery.

Cello Concertos – No 3 in D, G476; No 7 in G,G480; No 9 in B flat, G482. Concert aria – Se d'un amor tiranno, G557 **P**
Marta Almajano *sop* **Limoges Baroque Ensemble / Christophe Coin** *vc*
Auvidis Astrée E8517 (62 minutes: DDD). Recorded 1993 Ⓕ

Christophe Coin throws off in the deftest fashion the typical Boccherinian filigree figuration, the little ornamental flourishes perfectly placed and timed, the numerous stratospheric excursions above the treble stave sweet-toned and delicate. And with it he shows a command of Boccherini's style, affectionately graceful, sometimes with a faintly quizzical air. The tone of Coin's instrument is light and translucent, and with this small orchestra the sound in the solos, which are anyway lightly accompanied, is particularly sweet: in the first movement of G482 (the concerto known from the Grützmacher version) the unassuming handling of the virtuoso writing has a special kind of charm and the rather grander manner called for in the D major work G476 is also very happily caught, not without a hint of the romantic at times, for Coin is no austere stylist. The aria that completes his disc is a large-scale duet for cello, in its full concerto manner, and soprano; the lines are full of eloquent appoggiaturas and there is some beguiling duetting for the voice and the instrument. Marta Almajano has a big, clear top register and plenty of drama to her singing.

Simply Baroque **P**
Boccherini Cello Concertos – No 5 in D, G478; No 7 in G, G480 **Bach** Cantatas: No 22, Jesus nahm zu sich die Zwölfe: Choral – Ertöt' uns durch dein' Güte; No 136, Erforsche mich, Gott, und erfahre mein Herz: Choral – Dein Blut, der edle Saft; No 147, Herz und Mund und Tat und Leben: Choral – Jesu bleibet meine Freude; No 163, Nur jedem das Seine: Aria – Lass mein Herz die Münze sein; No 167, Ihr Menschen, rühmet Gottes Liebe: Choral – Sei Lob und Preis mit Ehren. St Matthew Passion, BWV244 – Erbarme dich. Orgel-Büchlein – Ich ruf' zu dir, BWV639. Schübler Chorales – Kommst du nun, Jesu, von Himmel herunter, BWV650. Orchestral Suite No 3 in D, BWV1068 – Air (all arr Koopman)
Yo-Yo Ma *vc* **Amsterdam Baroque Orchestra / Ton Koopman** *hpd/org*
Sony Classical SK60680 (69 minutes: DDD). Recorded 1998 Ⓕ ●

This appealing compilation is extremely imaginative: nine movements from Bach sensitively arranged for cello and chamber orchestra, plus an attractive pair of Boccherini cello concertos. Yo-Yo Ma's Stradivarius was altered for the occasion by luthier Charles Beare (using a baroque bridge, a tail-piece in place of an end-pin and gut strings), and Ma uses a baroque bow. As superior 'light' listening goes, it is difficult to think of a happier 70 minutes' worth. It also provides an ideal 'soft-option' introduction to the sound of period instruments. The *St Matthew Passion*'s 'Erbarme dich' becomes a cleverly worked duet for violin and cello, always flowing and discreet, aided by responsive strings and a tactile lute continuo. Ton Koopman's harpsichord brushes *Jesu Joy of Man's Desiring* into action with a flourish, answered by a mellifluous mix of solo cello, strings and winds. Bassoon and cello join forces for a swaggering 'Lass mein Herz die Münze sein', before the brief chorale 'Dein Blut, der edle Saft' (decorously embellished by a recorder). Last comes the inevitable 'Air' from the Third Orchestral Suite, tellingly arranged (as a duet for cellos) and superbly played. In fact, Koopman's 'second' cello – his lead cellist Jaap ter Linden – is every bit as eloquent as the star act. Listening to the two Boccherini works on this marvellous CD remind you again of Ma's uncanny technical facility, at once elegant and unselfconsciously virtuosic. Ton Koopman provides the cadenzas and the performances are pure delight.

Symphonies

Symphonies, Op 37 – No 1 in C, G515; No 3 in D minor, G517; No 4 in A, G518 Ⓟ
Academia Montis Regalis / Luigi Mangiocavallo
Opus 111 OPS30-168 (55 minutes: DDD). Ⓕ
Recorded 1996 ●●

'Sinfonie a grande orchestra', says Boccherini's own catalogue, in description of his Op 37, a set of four symphonies written in 1786-87 (only the three recorded here survive). Here they are played by a rather *piccola* orchestra yet the performance is brilliant and effective, with its very light and translucent textures conveying the detail with remarkable clarity. All the music sparkles with life – specially effective movements are the finale of the C major, with its curiously fragmented textures, and the *Andante* of the A major, one of Boccherini's loveliest orchestral slow movements, with the gentle and graceful melancholy of its oboe theme. There are attractive minuets here too – listen to the exquisitely played bassoon solo in the Trio of the D minor work or the oddly ambiguous rhythms in the C major. The conductor paces the music well and brings plenty of spirit and vivacity to the quick movements. In general this is an outstanding disc.

String Quintets

String Quintets, Op 25 – No 1 in D minor, G295; No 4 in C, G298; No 6 in A minor, G300. Ⓟ
String Quintet, Op 11 No 5 – Minuet
Europa Galante (Fabio Biondi, Enrico Casazza *vns* Ernesto Braucher *va* Maurizio Naddeo, Antonio Fantinuoli *vcs*)
Virgin Veritas VC5 45421-2 (60 minutes: DDD). Ⓕ
Recorded 1999 ●●●

The frustration of those who seek to identify Boccherini's works by their opus numbers may end in their being taken into care by sympathetic men in white coats. The first three of the six string sextets listed in his own catalogue as Op 25 were first published as Op 36, No 4, as Op 47 No 9, and No 6 as Op 47 No 5. The six of his Op 11, from the Fifth of which the 'amputated' and very famous Minuet is taken, appeared as Op 13 and his own Op 13 became Op 20.

Thank goodness for Gérard, here also the annotator, by whom be guided when in any doubt! Given that Boccherini wrote 100 string quintets it is not surprising that none of the three from Op 25 on this disc has any other listed recording. These three quintets serve as a persuasive introduction to his music, full of melodic invention, harmony that knows when and for how long to remain static or flowing, or ready to spring surprises, great variety of form (but rarely by the sonata-form 'book'), and a kaleidoscope of sounds that could have been imagined only by an accomplished and venturesome virtuoso – which Boccherini was of the cello.

If the music itself is persuasive it becomes irresistible in these performances on period instruments (or copies thereof) at slightly lower pitch than today's standard, wielded by players of the highest calibre and sensitivity. The Font family quartet with whom Boccherini played at the Madrid court of Don Luis must have revelled in these quintets; in these recordings we come as close to sharing that experience as it is possible to get. An absolute must.

Cello Sonatas

Cello Sonatas – No 2 in C minor, G2*b*[b]; No 4 in A, G4[a]; No 10 in E flat, G10[a]; No 17 in C, G17[a]; No 23 in B flat, G565[b]
Richard Lester *vc* [a]**David Watkin** *vc continuo* [b]**Chi-Chi Nwanoku** *db*
Hyperion CDA66719 (67 minutes: DDD). Ⓕ
Recorded 1994 ●

Richard Lester's slightly impetuous playing of these sonatas seems to capture very happily their character: their somewhat wayward invention, their sense of being formalized versions of a cellist's improvisations. Yet beneath it is a strong rhythm and a very sure compositional technique. The music is very high lying: the cellist has prolonged spells in high thumb positions with quite rapid passagework, and these Lester executes with great brilliance and crispness. The opening movement of the C major sonata is a particularly fine piece, with its pensive moments and its sudden flights of fancy; there is an eloquent central *Largo* and a dashing, witty finale. The E flat work has jaunty syncopations, the A major a first movement of particular brilliance and again there is an intensely expressive slow movement. The final sonata here is the B flat work that was evidently the model for the outer movements of the famous Boccherini-Grützmacher Concerto. Lester's bowing is vigorous, his tone warm and sharply defined with very little vibrato. Usually these sonatas are accompanied by a keyboard but here the practice of using another string instrument is preferred. In two sonatas a double-bass is used: the effect is a bit gruff, with something of a chasm between top and bottom when the cello is in its upper reaches. The two cellos are much more persuasive, especially when the second is as supportively played as it is here.

Harpsichord Sonatas, G25-30

Six Sonatas for Harpsichord with Violin, G25-30 Ⓟ
Jacques Ogg *hpd* **Emilio Moreno** *vn*
Glossa GCD920306 (77 minutes: DDD). Ⓕ
Recorded 2000 ●

Boccherini originally wrote these six sonatas for violin and fortepiano but eventually published them, with modifications, for violin and harpsichord. This may have been for commercial reasons, since he was at that time (1768) in Paris where the harpsichord was still in greater favour – though their dedicatee, Mme Brillan de Jouy, was a talented player of both keyboard instruments. The freedom of the writing in the violin parts confirms that her partner, André Noël Pagin, was no less gifted. They remain his only works for this instrumental combination. These are not sonatas in the fully 'classical' sense – thematic material often reappears in different keys but is not significantly developed, and two of the six have only two movements.

If the essence of Boccherini's music were to be summed up in a single word, it would be 'elegance' – of melodic invention, harmony and idiomatic writing for whatever instruments. All this is evident in these sonatas, beautifully played and recorded with an intimacy suggestive of that of the salons in which they were performed in their own time. For the most part the music is lightly pleasing but in the *Adagio* of G25 and the *Largo* of G26 it digs more deeply. The warm sound of Jacques Ogg's harpsichord (by Adlam Burnett, after Blanchet) and the lower pitch to which the instruments are tuned, make it a sympathetic partner to Emilio Moreno's violin (Antonio Gagliano, Naples, *c*1760). This is a most desirable disc and, moreover, the only available recording of these sonatas.

Stabat mater, G532

Boccherini Stabat mater, G532 (1800 vers)[a]
Astorga Stabat mater[b]
Susan Gritton, [a]**Sarah Fox** *sops* **Susan Bickley** *mez*
Paul Agnew *ten* [b]**Peter Harvey** *bass*
[b]**The King's Consort Choir; The King's Consort / Robert King**
Hyperion CDA67108 (73 minutes: DDD). Ⓕ
Texts and translations included. Recorded 1998 ●

These settings of the same text by two Italian composers (more exactly, Sicilian in the case of Astorga), who spent much of their lives in Spain, vary from each other both by the different groupings of the lines into movements and by the stylistic changes that had taken place in music in the course of the at least half century that separates them. Astorga's earlier setting has a good deal more contrapuntal writing, especially in three of its four choruses, as well as some diversity of style: more ornate in the double duet 'Quis est homo' and, in particular, the extremely florid, almost operatic, final 'Amen', but gently pathetic in the instrumental introduction and the soprano solo 'Sancta mater'. Intensity of feeling is heard in the duet stanza voicing the desire to weep with the distraught Mary, and the chorus sings expressively throughout, though 'Virgo virginum praeclara' sounds altogether too cheerful, and in the initial chorus the tenor line obtrudes rather edgily. Boccherini's is by far the more remarkable and beautiful setting. Originally written in 1781 for solo soprano, it was expanded in 1800 for three solo voices: fears that this could lead to a more 'symphonic' sound are dispelled by King's use of only seven instrumentalists. Robert King has a fine team of vocalists who on the whole blend well, an important consideration since only four of the 11 sections of the work are single-voice settings. The anguished melancholy of the opening and the grave serenity of the ending enclose a finely planned diversity of treatments, from the intense 'Quae moerebat' or the lyrical 'Fac ut portem' (both admirably sung by Sarah Fox) to the vigorous 'Tui nati' or the vehemently passionate 'Fac me plagis vulnerari' (for all three singers). The performance is accomplished and polished, but the recording venue tends to amplify singers' higher notes out of proportion.

Arrigo Boito

Italian 1842-1918

GROVE *Boito is best remembered for his one completed opera, Mefistofele, and for his collaborations with Verdi. He studied composition and aesthetics at the Milan Conservatory, then travelled, meeting Verdi in Paris. In Milan from 1862, and associated with the Scapigliatura, a radical literary movement, he wrote ironic poetry and erudite criticism decrying the state of Italian art. Although the first version of the five-act Mefistofele had a catastrophic première under his own direction in 1868, with revisions the work triumphed at Bologna, Venice and, in 1881, La Scala. It was through the efforts of the publisher Giulio Ricordi in 1879 that a successful Shakespearean collaboration, and what was to be a deepening friendship, began between Verdi and Boito. The librettos for Otello (1887) and Falstaff (1893), the second even more polished than the first, are remarkable for their fidelity to Shakespeare, sense of proportion, wit and vividness. His other well-known librettos include those for La Gioconda (set by Ponchielli,1876) and for the 1881 revision of Verdi's Simon Boccanegra. In the 1890s Verdi encouraged Boito to complete his own second opera, Nerone, but he never did, lacking the confidence and musical proficiency to realize his ambitions (the work was performed in an edited version in 1924). As a music critic in the 1860s, he praised Mendelssohn and Meyerbeer and treated Verdi with respect; later he was less than enthusiastic about Wagner and showed antipathy for Richard Strauss.*

Mefistofele

Cesare Siepi *bass* Mefistofele; **Mario del Monaco** *ten* Faust; **Renata Tebaldi** *sop* Margherita; **Floriana Cavalli** *sop* Elena; **Lucia Danieli** *mez* Marta, Pantalis; **Piero De Palma** *ten* Wagner, Nerco H
Chorus and Orchestra of the Santa Cecilia Academy / Tullio Serafin
Decca Grand Opera ② 440 054-2DMO2 (141 minutes: ADD). Notes, text and translation included. Ⓜ
Recorded 1958 ●

This recording has in Siepi a real Italian bass with a fine sense of line and a genuine enjoyment of Boito's words. Phrases that are often merely snarled are here truly sung, and Siepi's is the only devil to suggest in the quartet that he is trying to seduce Martha, and that he will very probably succeed. There is incisiveness and grain there, too, to add menace to his suavity. Tebaldi gives one of the best accounts of 'L'altra notte' on record, strongly sung and very touching in its suggestion of grieving guilt. Del Monaco sings 'Dai campi, dai prati' without the slightest acknowledgement of its poetry, but the splendour of the sound and his instinctive feeling for *legato* have their own allure, and they give nobility to his finely phrased 'Giunto sul passo estremo'. The recording doesn't allow Serafin to make a sonic spectacular of the outer scenes, but his care for Boito's often rather old-fashioned *cantabile*, his quirky rhythms and orchestral colours is scrupulous throughout.

Alexander Borodin

Russian 1833-1887

GROVE *As a youth Borodin developed parallel interests in music and chemistry, teaching himself the cello and qualifying in medicine (1856); throughout his life music was subordinated to his research and his activities as a lecturer (from 1862) at the Medico-Surgical Academy in St Petersburg. His predilection for the music of Mendelssohn and Schumann, together with his acquaintance with Musorgsky, Cui, Rimsky-Korsakov, Liszt and above all Balakirev gave shape to his compositional efforts. It was mainly through Balakirev's influence that he turned towards Russian nationalism, using Russian folksong in his music; he was one of 'The Five', the group eager to create a distinctive nationalist school.*

Borodin's earliest completed works include the First Symphony in E flat (1867), showing a freshness and assurance that brought immediate acclaim, and No 2 in B minor (1876) which, though longer in the making, is one of the boldest and most colourful symphonies of the century, in the Russian context a mature, symphonic counterpart to Glinka's Ruslan and Lyudmila. The piece contributing most to his early fame, however, especially in western Europe, was the short orchestral 'musical picture' On the Steppes of Central Asia (1880; dedicated to Liszt). Among the important chamber pieces, including those works which give the lie most clearly to charges of inspired dilettantism still sometimes brought against him, are the early Piano Quintet in C minor (1862) – already showing the supple lyricism, smooth texture, neat design and heartfelt elegiac quality of his most characteristic music - and the two string quartets, the second famous for its beautiful Nocturne, with their craftsmanship and latent muscularity. His most substantial achievement was undoubtedly the opera Prince Igor (written over the period 1869-87; completed and partly orchestrated by Rimsky-Korsakov and Glazunov). Despite its protracted creation and weak, disjointed libretto (Borodin's own), it contains abundant musical richness in its individual arias, in its powerfully Russian atmosphere and its fine choral scenes crowned by the barbaric splendour of the Polovtsian Dances.

Symphonies

Symphonies – No 1 in E flat; No 2 in B minor; No 3 in A minor. Prince Igor – Overture; Dance of the Polovtsian Maidens; Polovtsian Dances. String Quartet No 2 in D – Notturno (orch N Tcherepnin). In the Steppes of Central Asia. Petite Suite (orch Glazunov)
Torgny Sporsén *bass* **Gothenburg Symphony Chorus and Orchestra / Neeme Järvi**
DG ② 435 757-2GH2 (148 minutes: DDD). Ⓕ
Recorded 1989-91

While it is possible to imagine performances of even greater power and finesse in this strangely unfashionable repertoire, Järvi's Borodin set is arguably the best in recent years. The extravagant layout means we get not just the symphonies but a rich supplement of orchestral works, including even the *Petite Suite* as arranged by Glazunov. Another rarity, Nikolay Tcherepnin's orchestration of the famous *Notturno* will astonish those familiar with the chaste original: Tcherepnin transforms it into an exotic Scriabin-like tableau, almost as remote from Borodin as its kitschy *Kismet* mutation. The more recognizable *Steppes* are negotiated with ample eloquence and the *Prince Igor* excerpts include a brief contribution from the great Khan himself, reminding us of the music's original operatic context. The main works are equally persuasive. Järvi plays the First Symphony for all its worth, with DG's big, resonant sound boosting the work's symphonic credentials. The unfinished Third is also tougher and more dramatic than usual, no mere pastoral reverie in Järvi's interventionist view. The Second Symphony is rather different, suitably epic and yet unusually long-drawn and thoughtful. Thus, the *Scherzo* is bubbling but sensibly articulate, while the *Andante* is daringly broad with a superbly sensitive horn solo.

String Quartet No 2 in A

Borodin String Quartet No 2[a]
Shostakovich String Quartet No 8 in C minor, Op 110[a]
Tchaikovsky String Quartet No 1 in D, Op 11[b]
[a]**Borodin Quartet** (Rostislav Dubinsky, Jaroslav Alexandrov *vns* Dmitri Shebalin *va* Valentin Berlinsk, *vc*); [b]**Gabrieli Quartet** (Kenneth Sillito, Brendan O'Reilly *vns* Ian Jewel *va* Keith Harvey *vc*)
Decca 425 541-2DM (76 minutes: ADD). Ⓜ
Recorded [a]1962 and [b]1976

A slightly curious compilation (two Russian performances from 1962, one English from 1976) but attractive and very good value. The Borodin Quartet plays its eponymous composer's affectionate tribute to his wife with a charming demureness shading the ardour, and in the sharply characterized finale manages even to hint that Shostakovich will be the next composer on the programme. He is, and its reading of his Eighth Quartet is nobly expressive as well as exhaustingly virtuoso. As a tiny bonus for Shostakovich scholars there is even an interesting variant reading towards the end of the third movement. If you have not heard the Gabrieli's

Tchaikovsky before, you will probably like it a great deal: properly chamber-scale, in colour as well as tone of voice, and nice underlining of the lyricism even in Tchaikovsky's most exuberant pages. The recordings still sound very well.

Prince Igor

Mikhail Kit *bar* Igor; **Galina Gorchakova** *sop* Yaroslavna; **Gegam Grigorian** *ten* Vladimir; **Vladimir Ognovenko** *bass* Prince Galitzky; **Bulat Minjelkiev** *bass* Khan Kontchak; **Olga Borodina** *mez* Kontchakovna; **Nikolai Gassiev** *ten* Ovlour; **Georgy Selezniev** *bass* Skula; **Konstantin Pluzhnikov** *ten* Eroshka; **Evgenia Perlasova** *mez* Nurse; **Tatyana Novikova** *sop* Polovtsian Maiden; **Kirov Opera Chorus and Orchestra / Valery Gergiev**
Philips ③ 442 537-2PH3 (209 minutes: DDD).
Notes, text and translation included. Ⓕ
Recorded 1993 ●

Prince Igor, even after 18 years of work, remained unfinished at Borodin's death in 1887, and it was finally completed by Rimsky-Korsakov and Glazunov. Borodin's main problem with *Prince Igor* was the daunting task of turning what was principally an undramatic subject into a convincing stage work. In many ways he never really succeeded in this and the end result comes over more as a series of epic scenes rather than a musical drama. Despite this, however, one is left with an impression of a rounded whole, and it contains some of Borodin's most poignant and moving music, rich in oriental imagery and full of vitality. Curious things happen long before the official surprises of this vitally fresh *Prince Igor*, not least in the Overture, where Gergiev takes the horn's beautiful melody at a very slow pace. Gergiev is anxious to prepare us for the weighty events which follow and his particular point with the theme is to relate it to its place in the opera as the heart of Igor's great aria. There, in league with the bass-baritonal timbre of Gergiev's prince, Mikhail Kit, it solemnly underlines the fact that this is an aria of potency frustrated, sung by a hero who spends most of the opera in captivity; and that is further emphasized by a second aria which no listener will ever have heard before. It is the most significant of the passages discovered among Borodin's papers, rejected by Rimsky-Korsakov in his otherwise sensitive tribute to Borodin's memory but specially orchestrated for this recording by Yuri Faliek.

The other problem with the *Prince Igor* we already know is the way that Act 3 rather weakly follows its much more imposing Polovtsian predecessor. Gergiev obviates both that, and the problem of too much time initially spent in Igor's home town of Putivl, by referring to a structural outline of Borodin's dating from 1883 which proposes alternating the Russian and Polovtsian acts. In the theatre, we might still want the famous Polovtsian *divertissement* as a centrepiece; but on the recording the new order works splendidly, not least because Gergiev is at his fluent best in the scenes of Galitzky's dissipation and Yaroslavna's despair, now making up the opera's Second Act. While Borodina executes Kontchakovna's seductive chromaticisms with astonishing breath control and focus of tone, Bulat Minjelkiev's Kontchak is a little too free and easy, at least next to Ognovenko's perfectly gauged Galitzky, a rogue who needs the extra rebellion music of the more recent version to show more threatening colours. There's just the right degree of relaxation, too, about his drunken supporters Skula and Eroshka. It takes two Russian character-singers to make sense of this pair – 'with our wine and our cunning we will never die in Russia', they tell us truthfully – and their comical capitulation on Igor's return wins respect for Borodin's daring happy-end transition here. It's beautifully paced by Pluzhnikov, Selezniev and their conductor, and crowned by a choral cry of joy which brings a marvellous rush of tearful adrenalin. That leaves us with Gorchakova, so touching in Yaroslavna's first aria but not always projecting the text very vividly and clearly not at her best in the big scena of the last act. Still, in terms of long-term vision, orchestral detail and strength of ensemble, Gergiev is ahead of the competition.

Dmitry Bortnyansky

Ukrainian 1751-1825

GROVE *Bortnyansky studied in Italy from 1769; his first operas were given there, 1776-78. Returning to Russia in 1779, he became Kapellmeister at the St Petersburg court and in 1796 director. His many Russian sacred pieces (later edited by Tchaikovsky) are notable for their Italianate lyricism and skilful counterpoint. He also wrote operas, cantatas and instrumental pieces, notably a Sinfonia concertante (1790).*

Sacred Concertos

Sacred Concertos – No 17, How amiable are thy tabernacles, O Lord of hosts!; No 18, It is a good thing to give thanks unto the Lord; No 19, The Lord said unto my Lord: sit thou at my right hand; No 20, In thee, O Lord, do I put my trust; No 21, He that dwelleth in the secret place of the most high; No 22, The Lord is my light and my salvation; No 23, Blessed is the people that know the joyful sound
Russian State Symphonic Cappella / Valéry Polyansky
Chandos CHAN9840 (66 minutes: DDD). Ⓕ
Texts and translations included. Recorded 1989-90 ●

Bortnyansky has been mostly ignored in the West until quite recently. Tchaikovsky's disparaging comments on editing his sacred concertos also show he was not universally appreciated in his native Russia, but he has never lost his place in the repertoire of the Russian Orthodox Church, and, as the magnificent series of recordings under Polyansky shows, these works are finely crafted pieces with an endless variety of invention.

This is Volume 3, and it contains some real gems. Concerto No 19 is a *locus classicus* of

Bortnyansky's considerable lyrical power, though he also employs his neo-baroque fugal writing to impressive effect, but No 20 is even more convincing, each movement containing a sub-structure characterised by different musical moods. Tchaikovsky complained that the concertos used 'stagey or even operatic' techniques, and that is quite true, but it is done, as one may hear in No 22 (at just over eight minutes the shortest here), with consummate elegance. The Russian State Symphonic Cappella understand this music, in all its manifestations, completely, responding to its subtlest nuances.

Rutland Boughton British 1878-1960

GROVE *Boughton studied briefly at the RCM but was mostly self-taught. While teaching in Birmingham (1905-11) he developed his ideas on the basis of Wagner and William Morris socialism, and put them into practice at his Glastonbury festivals (1914-27), where several of his operas were first produced, including The Immortal Hour (1914); this had immense success when staged in London in 1922. After the collapse of the Glastonbury venture he retired to farm, write and compose, and in 1945 completed his Arthurian cycle of five operas, in which Wagnerianism gives way to a simpler folk-song manner.*

The Immortal Hour

Roderick Kennedy *bass* Dalua; **Anne Dawson** *sop* Etain; **David Wilson-Johnson** *bar* Eochaidh; **Maldwyn Davies** *ten* Midir **Geoffrey Mitchell Choir; English Chamber Orchestra / Alan G Melville**
Hyperion ② CDD22040 (125 minutes: DDD). Ⓜ
Notes and text included. Recorded 1983

The Immortal Hour is part of theatrical folklore: in London in the early 1920s it ran, unprecedentedly, for 216 consecutive performances and, shortly afterwards, for a further 160 at the first of several revivals; within a decade it had been played a thousand times. Many in those audiences returned repeatedly, fascinated by the other-worldly mystery of the plot (it concerns the love of a mortal king, Eochaidh, for the faery princess Etain and the destruction of their happiness by her nostalgic longing for the Land of the Ever Young) and by the gentle, lyrical simplicity of its music. In the bleak aftermath of 1918, with civil war in Ireland, political instability at home and the names of Hitler, Mussolini and Stalin emerging from obscurity into the headlines, what blessed escapism this blend of Celtic myth and folk-tinged pentatonic sweetness must have been. Boughton's score still has the power to evoke that world, immediately and effortlessly. The libretto by 'Fiona McLeod' (the *nom de plume* of William Sharp) is post-Rossetti high kitsch, often veering into bathos or becoming embarrassingly over-heated, but it does grope towards something uncomfortably deep in the human psyche, the potentially schizoid fracture-zone between physical and spiritual.

It is quiet, sweet music, muted in colour and softly plaintive, and whenever the plot demands more than this the opera sags. Midir, the visitant from the Land of the Ever Young who lures Etain away from the mortal world, really needs music of dangerously heady, Dionysiac incandescence, but Boughton's vocabulary can run to nothing more transported than the prettily lilting Faery Song and to some pages of folksy lyricism with a few showy high notes. No less seriously the music has little dramatic grip. Despite all this, and the consequent evocation of a mythology that is at times a lot closer to Never-Never-Land than to Tir-na-n'Og, *The Immortal Hour* does have a quality, difficult to define, that is genuinely alluring. It is there in the touching purity of Etain's music (and how movingly Anne Dawson sings the role). It is there in the moments of true darkness that the music achieves: Dalua, the tormented Lord of Shadow conjures up something of the sombre shudder of the supernatural world. The performance could hardly speak more eloquently for the opera. Alan G Melville allows the music to emerge from and retreat into shadowy silences, all the principal singers are accomplished and the superb chorus has been placed so as to evoke a sense of space. The recording seldom suggests the studio: it is easy to imagine being in the 'dark and mysterious wood' at the world's end where the drama is set.

Lili Boulanger French 1893-1918

GROVE *Boulanger studied at the Paris Conservatoire and won the Prix de Rome. Her composing life was short but productive: most important are her psalm settings and other large-scale choral works in a strong, subtle style.*

Psalms

Psalms – 24[b]; 129[d]; 130, 'Du fond de l'abîme'[abd]. Pour les funérailles d'un soldat[cd]. D'un soir triste. D'un matin du printemps. Vieille prière bouddhique[bd]
[a]**Sonia de Beaufort** *mez* [b]**Martial Defontaine** *ten* [c]**Vincent le Texier** *bar* [d]**Namur Symphonic Chorus; Luxembourg Philharmonic Orchestra / Mark Stringer**
Timpani 1C1046 (67 minutes: DDD). Texts and translations included. Recorded 1998 Ⓕ ●

The name of the remarkable teacher and conductor Nadia Boulanger is famous throughout the musical world, but her sister Lili (six years younger), phenomenally gifted – she was the first woman to win the Premier Prix de Rome (while Nadia had attained only a Second Prix) – showed promise of at least equal distinction. Always of delicate health, her death at the age of 24 was a tragedy for music. Apart from works written in her early teens, which she later destroyed, her composing career lasted a mere seven years; but the quality of these compositions is arresting.

Except for parts of *D'un matin du printemps*

(originally for violin and piano, and orchestrated only two months before her death), a grave, even sombre air permeates her works, which are heavily tinged with modal thinking. Her idiom is strong, with a bold harmonic sense and an individual feeling for scoring (her stirring Psalm 24, for example, has the unusual combination of brass, timpani, harp and organ with the male voices): the beatific ending of Psalm 129 is heart-easing after the earlier harshness of 'Hard as they have harried me, they have not overcome me' (words significantly applicable to her own determined spirit). Her choral works are comparable to the best of Roussel or Honegger, but her Psalm 130 (dedicated to her father's memory), with its exotic scale and chromaticisms, has more affinity with Bloch and is, without much doubt, a masterpiece. A disc not to be missed.

Faust et Hélène

Awards 2000

D'un matin du printemps. D'un soir triste. Faust et Hélène[a]. Psalm 24[b]. Psalm 130, 'Du fond de l'abîme'[c]
[a]**Lynne Dawson** *sop* [c]**Ann Murray** *mez* [a]**Bonaventura Bottone,** [bc]**Neil MacKenzie** *tens* [a]**Jason Howard** *bar* [bc]**City of Birmingham Symphony Orchestra Chorus; BBC Philharmonic Orchestra / Yan Pascal Tortelier**
Chandos CHAN9745 (74 minutes: DDD) Ⓕ
Texts and translations included. Recorded 1999 ○○○

This disc largely duplicates Mark Stringer's programme noted above (inevitably, since in her mere 24 years of life Lili's output was limited). The performances here are first-class, and splendidly recorded too. The eloquent sombreness of *D'un soir triste* tugs at the heart, *D'un matin de printemps* is deliciously airy and optimistic, *Psalm 24* is given tremendous attack by orchestra and chorus (full marks for articulation of words!) and the powerful *Psalm 130* is presented as the masterly, heartfelt work it is. The major work here, though, is the 30-minute cantata *Faust et Hélène* in its first recording. No wonder that it won the 1913 Premier Prix de Rome: the jury must have been thunderstruck by the maturity of this entry from a 19-year-old. It blends lyricism of striking beauty, rapturous fervour, emotional anguish and tense drama with, for a young composer, an astonishing sureness of touch in overall structure, freshness of invention, technical brilliance and imaginative scoring. It seems to have inspired the present performers, among whom it is almost invidious to praise Bonaventura Bottone.

Pierre Boulez

French 1925

GROVE *Boulez studied with Messiaen at the Paris Conservatoire (1942-45) and privately with Andrée Vaurabourg and René Leibowitz, inheriting Messiaen's concern with rhythm, non-developing forms and extra-European music along with the Schoenberg tradition of Leibowitz. The clash of the two influences lies behind such intense, disruptive works as his first two piano sonatas (1946, 1948) and Livre pour quatuor for string quartet (1949). The violence of his early music also suited that of René Char's poetry in the cantatas Le visage nuptial (1946) and Le soleil des eaux (1948), though through this highly charged style he was working towards an objective serial control of rhythm, loudness and tone colour that was achieved in the Structures for two pianos (1952). At this time he came to know Stockhausen, with whom he became a leader of the European avant garde, teaching at Darmstadt (1955-67) and elsewhere, and creating one of the key postwar works in his Le marteau sans maître (1954). Once more to poems by Char, the work is for contralto with alto flute, viola, guitar and percussion: a typical ensemble of middle-range instruments with an emphasis on struck and plucked sounds. The filtering of Boulez's earlier manner through his 'tonal serialism' produces a work of feverish speed, unrest and elegance.*

In the mid-1950s Boulez extended his activities to conducting. He had been Barrault's musical director since 1946 and in 1954 under Barrault's aegis he set up a concert series, the Domaine Musical, to provide a platform for new music. By the mid-1960s he was appearing widely as a conductor, becoming chief conductor of the BBC SO (1971-74) and the New York PO (1971-78). Meanwhile his creative output declined. Under the influence of Mallarmé he had embarked on three big aleatory works after Le marteau, but of these the Third Piano Sonata (1957) remains a fragment and Pli selon pli for soprano and orchestra (1962) has been repeatedly revised; only a second book of Structures for two pianos (1961) has been definitively finished. Other works, notably Eclat/Multiples for tuned percussion ensemble and orchestra, also remain in progress, as if the open-endedness of Boulez's proliferating musical world had committed him to incompleteness. Only the severe memorial Rituel for orchestra (1975) has escaped that fate.

Since the mid-1970s Boulez has concentrated on his work as director of the Institut de Recherche et Coordination Acoustique/Musique, a computer studio in Paris where his main work has been Répons for orchestra and digital equipment.

... explosante-fixe ...

12 Notations[a]. Structures pour deux pianos, Livre 2[b]. ... explosante-fixe ...[c]
[c]**Sophie Cherrier,** [c]**Emmanuelle Ophèle,** [c]**Pierre-André Valade** *fls* [ab]**Pierre-Laurent Aimard,** [b]**Florent Boffard** *pfs* **Ensemble InterContemporain, Paris / Pierre Boulez**
DG 445 833-2GH (70 minutes: DDD). Ⓕ
Recorded 1993-94

Though he may well disapprove of the designation, in ... *explosante-fixe* ... Pierre Boulez has written one of the great flute concertos of the 20th or any other century. At nearly 37 minutes it is also probably the longest, and the expansiveness of the score, dating from 1991-3, gives the lie to all those persistent tales about Boulez's reluctance to compose. He has never lacked for ideas: he has just been unusually fastidious in his concern to do those ideas full justice. This is music of prodigious melodic inventiveness – and if you believe Boulez incapable of lyricism, try ... *explosante-fixe* ... from as early as 1'50". It shares a relish for regular rhythmic patterns with other later works (*Messagesquisse*, *Répons*), but its primary concern is with the possibility of enhancing natural sound by electronic means. There are no sound effects, no funny noises, but a subtle enrichment of pitch and tone colour as the principal flute and its two satellites interact with ensemble and electronics in music that moves absorbingly between turbulence and poetic reflection in Boulez's uniquely personal way.

This is a brilliantly engineered recording; the only regret is that it wasn't possible to present it as a sequence of tracks cued to a fuller commentary in the notes. No less engaging are the performances of *Notations* and *Structures*, *Livre 2*, the former revealing the very early Boulez's debts to Debussy, Stravinsky and Bartók, the latter displaying the full, formidable power of his still-youthful originality. For both books of *Structures* one still has to turn to the pioneering recording by the Kontarsky brothers on Wergo, but *Livre 2* can well stand alone, and here Pierre-Laurent Aimard and Florent Boffard provide a finely characterized reading, as gripping in explosiveness as in restraint, and the pianos are recorded with exemplary naturalness. This is a superb disc. The energy and sensitivity of the works here put a great deal of other contemporary music deeply in the shade, and performances and recordings are equal to the music's stature.

Répons

Répons. Dialogue de l'ombre double[a]

[a]**Alain Damiens** *cl* **Frédérique Cambreling** *hp* **Vincent Bauer** *vib* **Daniel Ciampolini, Michel Cerutti** *perc* **Dimitri Vassilakis, Florent Boffard** *pfs* **Ensemble InterContemporain / Pierre Boulez**

DG 20/21 457 605-2GH (61 minutes: DDD). Ⓕ
Recorded 1996

In 1981, *Répons* was hailed as a breakthrough in the integration of instruments and electronics in a dynamic sound continuum. It is thus not only groundbreaking but also supremely relevant as a model of what it was possible to do creatively with sound in the late 20th century. The version here is the third, from 1984 although further expansions are always possible. A 24-piece ensemble is enclosed by the audience, who are in turn surrounded by six instrumental soloists, a physical immersion in sound startlingly conveyed here by the *spatialisateur* computer programme. Only the soloists are electronically transformed, and these 'real time' processes make the musical textures as sensuous as they are complex. Within this convincing overall trajectory, two sections – track 5, with the piano accumulating layers of sound at a relentless rate, and track 10, where the soloists' spiralling resonances carry their own expressive current – are as satisfying musically as anything Boulez has achieved. *Dialogue de l'ombre double* introduces a theatrical dimension, the clarinet's electronic double gradually becoming more mobile and more 'real' than the actual soloist.

Rituel in memoriam Bruno Maderna

Rituel in memoriam Bruno Maderna[a]. Eclat/Multiples[b]

[a]**BBC Symphony Orchestra,** [b]**Ensemble Intercontemporain / Pierre Boulez**

Sony Classical SMK45839 (52 minutes: ADD/DDD). Ⓜ
Recorded 1976-82

Whatever is involved in the 20-bit technology used by Sony Classical to enhance the original CBS recordings of these works, the result is a very immediate and clear (if not especially deep) sound-picture. The sound does justice to a disc that can be recommended without reservation: magisterial performances by fine musicians of two masterworks by a leading contemporary composer. Boulez's casting off of post-Debussian refinements in *Eclat/Multiples* is enormously invigorating, and there is little of the stately, Messiaen-like processional writing that dominates *Rituel*. Here two very different facets of Boulez's musical personality come into mutually illuminating confrontation, and this recording is frustrating only to the extent that the work itself remains unfinished. Boulez, it seems, finds it no easier to complete compositions in his later style than he did in the 1960s. Maybe what is most radical about him is that Western music's traditional concern with preparing and achieving a definitive ending has ceased to be necessary. In which case, of course, the conclusiveness with which *Rituel* draws to a close could represent a concession to convention that he now regrets. In its CD transfer *Rituel* seems more than ever in thrall to the chiming, clattering percussion spread through the orchestra, which shepherds the various instrumental groups like so many anxious guardians. The source of *Rituel* lies in Boulez's tribute to Stravinsky, and the music – a massive public act of mourning, not a private expression of grief – is in some respects more appropriate as a memorial for the great Russian than for the genial Maderna. Solemn, hieratic, carved from blocks of harmonic marble by a master musical sculptor, *Rituel* is a fitting homage for a composer who learned to keep his emotions under strict control.

Sur Incises

Anthèmes 2[a]. Messagesquisse[b]. Sur Incises[c]

[a]**Hae-Sun Kang** *vn* [ab]**Jean-Guihen Queyras** *vc* [a]**Andrew Gerzso** *elec* [bc]**Ensemble InterContemporain / Pierre Boulez**

DG 20/21 463 475-2GH (66 minutes: DDD). Ⓕ
Recorded 1999

Combine three pianos and three harps with a range of metal percussion, and the result is like a single, magically enhanced keyboard, intensely resonant, but with the kind of incisive, cutting edge to the sound suggested by the title *Sur*

Incises. *Incises* was a piano piece on which Boulez based this 37-minute work, composed between 1996 and 1998. It's divided into two substantial movements or – as Boulez ironically titles them – 'Moments', implying that the immediate event and context matter more than the way events and contexts combine to create large-scale forms. Yet there's unambiguous evidence of larger-scale shaping in the way the second 'Moment' offers a wider range of more broadly characterised material than the first, and it builds to a stunning climax in which boiling cascades of sound erupt volcanically, before the cooling and calming process through which *Sur Incises* ends.

This is a fine example of Boulez's post-*Répons* idiom, which grows as much from the concerns of his very earliest compositions as from more recent preoccupations. Nevertheless, for all its richness, the range of tone colours in *Sur Incises* is narrower than in those later works which involve electroacoustics, and this dimension is represented here by the relatively small-scale *Anthèmes 2* of 1997. There's a consistent intimacy about the interaction of the live violin and the electronics which culminates in a final section (tracks 13-15) notable for its light-hearted dialogue, involving arabesques and scales of a kind the younger Boulez would probably have shunned as unforgivably frivolous. Here the dialogue is part of the marvellously apt process of development by which the music finds ever more imaginative variations for its basic material.

This supremely well-performed and engineered disc is completed by the short 'sketched message' for seven cellos which Boulez wrote to celebrate Paul Sacher's 70th birthday in 1976. The music brilliantly characterises those oppositions between refinement and ferocity which form the essence of Boulez's distinctive style. An outstanding contemporary music release.

Piano Sonatas

Piano Sonatas Nos 1-3
Idil Biret *pf* Ⓢ
Naxos 8 553353 (64 minutes: DDD). Recorded 1995 ⭘

It sometimes seems as if Boulez has spent a lifetime paying the penalty for having found composition so easy as a young man. The first two piano sonatas, works of his early twenties, are formidably assured in technique and tremendously rich in ideas. Those sections of the Third Sonata released for performance sound cold and tentative by comparison. Or is it that the Third Sonata's much more extreme rejection of tradition is itself a triumph, an authentic modernity that stands out the more prominently for its individualism? Such thoughts are inspired by Idil Biret's absorbing disc. In the first movement of the First Sonata the broader picture proves to be well fleshed-out, the argument kept on the move, the young composer's impatience and arrogance palpable in Biret's steely touch and the rather dry but never merely harsh recorded sound. The Second Sonata is no less confidently played. Is it in the Second Sonata's diverse finale that premonitions of the Third Sonata's rejections of continuity begin to appear? Quite possibly – and yet the power of the Second Sonata suggests why such experiments as No 3 represents could never be a last word for Boulez. This disc is not the first to bring us the three sonatas together, but Biret's musical persuasiveness, and the up-to-date sound, earn it a strong recommendation.

Pli selon pli

Awards 1983

Phyllis Bryn-Julson *sop*
BBC Symphony Orchestra / Pierre Boulez
Ultima 8573-84248-2 Ⓑ
(68 minutes: DDD)
Recorded 1981 ⭘⭘⭘

Pli selon pli, composed between 1957-62, is one of the great pillars of post-war musical modernism. It is also as exciting in its moment-to-moment shifts of colour and contour, and as compelling in its command of large-scale dramatic design as anything composed since the great years of Schoenberg and Stravinsky. Easy, no: enthralling and rewarding – yes. This is no grand, single-minded work in the great Germanic symphonic tradition, but a sequence of distinct yet balanced responses to aspects of the great symbolist poet Mallarmé. On his second recording of the piece, Boulez is prepared to let the music expand and resonate, the two large orchestral tapestries enclosing three 'Improvisations', smaller-scale vocal movements in which the authority and expressiveness of Phyllis Bryn-Julson is heard to great advantage. The sound is brilliantly wide-ranging and well balanced, and while the contrast between delicacy and almost delirious density embodied in *Pli selon pli* does take some getting used to, to miss it is to miss one of modern music's most original masterworks. His first version has a special historical status as embodying the composer's view of the work near the time of its actual completion, when forcefulness, and even ferocity, seemed to count for more as foils to the music's moments of relative restraint than the sustained densities so strongly emphasized in the Erato recording.

William Boyce

British 1711-1779

GROVE *Boyce was a St Paul's Cathedral chorister and an organ pupil of Maurice Greene, also studying with Pepusch. From 1734 he held organist's posts in London and from 1736 was a composer to the Chapel Royal, writing anthems and services. His oratorio David's Lamentation over Saul and Jonathan (1736) was followed by his first dramatic works, including a short opera, Peleus and Thetis (by1740), The Secular Masque (1746) and the highly successful pastoral The Chaplet (1749), the first of a series of works for Drury Lane theatre. Increasing deafness hindered him – his last stage work was Heart of Oak (1759) – but his output in other vocal genres continued, and as Master of the King's Musick from 1757 he composed over 40 court odes. Among his few instrumental works are 12 trio sonatas (1747), Eight Symphonys (from ode and opera overtures, 1735-41, published 1760) and Twelve Overtures (1770). Boyce was among the finest and most respected English composers of his time, though his Baroque idiom had become old-fashioned by the end of his life. His music has a fresh vigour, especially evident in fugues, dance movements and expressive vocal writing. The owner of a valuable music library, he gained lasting fame for his Cathedral Music (1760-73), an edition of earlier English services by Orlando Gibbons, Purcell and others.*

Eight Symphonies, Op 2

The English Concert / Trevor Pinnock *hpd* 🅿
Archiv Produktion 419 631-2AH (60 minutes: DDD). Ⓕ
Recorded 1986 ⊙

William Boyce's eight Symphonys (his own spelling) are not symphonies in the modern sense but a collection, issued for concert use, of overtures he had composed over nearly 20 years for theatre pieces and court odes. They represent English 18th-century music at its unpretentious best, notably in their formal unorthodoxy. The performances are a delight – cleanly articulated, decisive in rhythm, just in tempo. The French overture-like movements that open Nos 6 and 7 are crisp and brilliant; the more Italianate first movements, like those of Nos 2 and 4, have a splendid swing. And the tone of gentle melancholy behind the fine, expansive D minor first movement of No 8 is particularly well caught. Three of the symphonies have middle movements marked *Vivace*, which often leads conductors into unsuitably quick tempos; but Pinnock obviously knows that, in 18th-century England, *Vivace* meant a speed not much above *Andante*, and for once these movements make proper sense: they are lively, to be sure, but not fast. It was a mistake, though, to play the repeats in the slow movement of No 1 as flute solos (admirably though they are done) – there is no authority for this and the effect is foreign to orchestral music. That aside, now that the more recent Hogwood recording has been deleted, this one comfortably surpasses any rivals in terms both of style and accomplishment. The sound of the modest-sized band is brightly and truly reproduced too.

Peleus and Thetis

Peleus and Thetis. Corydon and Miranda. Incidental music – Florizel and Perdita; Romeo and Juliet 🅿
Julia Gooding, Philippa Hyde *sops* **Robin Blaze** *counterten* **Joseph Cornwell** *ten* **Andrew Dale Forbes** *bass* **Jilly Bond, Jack Edwards** *spkrs* **Opera Restor'd / Peter Holman** *hpd*
Hyperion CDA66935 (68 minutes: DDD). Ⓕ
Texts included. Recorded 1996

Boyce was in his time one of the leading theatre composers. *Peleus and Thetis* is a short masque, based on a simple story reminiscent of *Acis and Galatea*, except that here the jealous Jupiter resigns his amorous claims on Thetis on learning that her son would outshine his father (he was of course Achilles). Among the best moments are Peleus's spirited song of defiance, Jupiter's fine, richly contrapuntal one of renunciation and the lovers' duet at the end. Boyce's music has a flavour all its own, and at its best a very appealing one; Peter Holman conducts the piece in lively fashion, and uses singers with a good command of the style. Two of the other items are incidental music to Shakespeare productions. The little amorous competition of Mopsa and Dorcas for *The Winter's Tale* (in *Florizel and Perdita*) recall Purcell. It is sung here in something of a brogue, which would probably be more persuasive on stage than on a recording. Then there is a dirge for Romeo and Juliet, a touching, richly harmonized setting of words as Juliet's body is carried across the stage. The 'Pastoral interlude', *Corydon and Miranda*, in which a shepherd chooses between rival claimants for his love, consists of four airs, mostly in a simple, melodious style, but a final fiery one for the girl who loses, linked by recitative, and a final chorus. It isn't great music, but it is tuneful, in a very English way, and it shows sensitivity to the words and their sense. A very agreeable disc.

David's Lamentation

David's Lamentation over Saul and Jonathan (Dublin vers[a] and London vers excs[b]). Ode for St Cecilia's Day[c] 🅿
[c]**Patrick Burrowes** *treb* **William Purefoy,** [a]**Andrew Watts** *countertens* [ab]**Richard Edgar-Wilson** *ten* [c]**Michael George** *bar* **New College Choir Oxford; Hanover Band / Graham Lea-Cox**
ASV Gaudeamus CDGAU208 (80 minutes: DDD). Ⓕ
Recorded 1999

This third disc in ASV's excellent Boyce series offers a wholly unfamiliar work, indeed one that shows an unfamiliar side of the composer. In *David's Lamentation over Saul and Jonathan*, written in 1736, when he was 24, Boyce is in elegiac vein. It starts with a sombre G minor overture, using the typical 'lamentation' bass, falling chromatically, and that is followed by a succession of choruses and airs, in sorrowful tone and minor keys, telling the tale of Israel's defeat and the deaths of Saul and Jonathan – and the slaying of the Amalekite. Of course, it is hardly on the emotional or dramatic scale of Handel's oratorio of three years later (of which the action of this work forms an episode), but Boyce's musical language is, on its more modest canvas, telling, and the work is full of moving and affecting ideas.

The version given here, as the main text, incorporates Boyce's revisions for a Dublin performance in 1744 (sensibly, the altered numbers are also included in their original form as an appendix). Boyce in more familiar vein is represented by the Cecilian ode. Graham Lea-Cox, as before, directs this music with authority and obvious affection; the rhythms are sturdy, and the particular flavour of the music of perhaps the greatest English 18th-century composer is happily captured.

He is helped by a capable band, the admirable choir of New College, and an accomplished team of soloists. Michael George is in good voice and gets his best chance in the ode, with his energetic account of 'In war's fierce alarms'; and Richard Edgar-Wilson shows a full, elegant tenor in his airs in the cantata. Of the two high men's voices William Purefoy produces some soft and sweet-toned, uncommonly even singing, and Andrew Watts, higher in tessitura, fine in line, excels in the poignant numbers. Overall, then, a most enjoyable disc.

Joly Braga Santos

Portuguese 1924-1988

GROVE *Braga Santos studied with Luis de Freitas Branco, who was a great influence on him, and has worked in Lisbon as a composer, conductor teacher (at the conservatory) and critic. At the end of the 1950s his music became affected by newer European trends; his works include operas, symphonies and concertos.*

Symphonies Nos 1 and 5

Portuguese Symphony Orchestra / Alvaro Cassuto
Marco Polo 8 223879 (67 minutes: DDD). Ⓕ
Recorded 1997

Portugal has never figured large in our musical consciousness in England, and until very recently the name of Joly Braga Santos had been all but unrepresented in the catalogue. His output was considerable and the disc suggests that a symphonist of some stature has been overlooked. His First Symphony, created in 1946 at the age of 22 in memory of those fallen in the Second World War, is couched in a largely modal idiom with some kinship to Sibelius and, more particularly, Vaughan Williams, and reveals a gift for structure, highly effective orchestration and for the writing of long, flowing melodic lines. But the Fifth Symphony of 20 years later (which won a UNESCO prize) – of which there *was* once a Decca LP recording – is a totally different matter. Scored for a huge orchestra including a percussion section of 12 who in the fascinating second movement handle an absolute forest of marimbas, it colourfully reflects the composer's visit to Mozambique (then a Portuguese colony) and is written in a wilder, completely atonal but not dodecaphonic idiom – though it ends unexpectedly on a chord of F major. The composer's close friend Alvaro Cassuto, director since its foundation in 1993 of the Portuguese Symphony Orchestra, has moulded it into a body of international quality: its deeply committed performances here impressively make us aware of Braga Santos. Fantastic recorded sound, especially in the Fifth's massive, cataclysmic finale.

Symphonies Nos 3 and No 6

Symphonies Nos 3 and No 6[a]
[a]**Ana Ester Neves** *sop* [a]**São Carlos National Theatre Chorus; Portuguese Symphony Orchestra / Alvaro Cassuto**
Marco Polo 8 225087 (65 minutes: DDD). Ⓕ
Text and translation included. Recorded 1997 ⭘

Here we have one work from each of Brago Santos's two contrasting compositional periods. Symphony No 3 (written in 1949) is bound together by a number of common motifs: it is a closely reasoned, strikingly scored work of modal tendencies (occasionally bringing Vaughan Williams to mind); the *Allegro* section of its finale is centred on a brilliant double fugue. A strong, virile symphony whose stature can be ranked with Sibelius – not to be missed! His Sixth (and last) symphony (1972) is in one movement but several sections, and is curiously disparate in character and idiom. For two-thirds of its length it is purely orchestral, aggressively atonal and disjunctive, with numerous angry outbursts; then it suddenly changes tack to a more consonant choral section and a peaceful, entirely tonal movement for soprano, both settings (in the Galician tongue) of poems by the 16th-century Camões. In both works, performance and recording are first-rate.

Johannes Brahms German 1833-1897

GROVE *Brahms studied the piano from the age of seven and theory and composition (with Eduard Marxsen) from 13, gaining experience as an arranger for his father's light orchestra while absorbing the popular alla zingarese style associated with Hungarian folk music. In 1853, on a tour with the Hungarian violinist Reményi, he met Joseph Joachim and Liszt; Joachim, who became a lifelong friend, encouraged him to meet Schumann. Brahms's artistic kinship with Robert Schumann and his profound romantic passion (later mellowing to veneration) for Clara Schumann, 14 years his elder, never left him. After a time in Düsseldorf he worked in Detmold, settling in Hamburg in 1859 to direct a women's chorus. Though well known as a pianist he had trouble finding recognition as a composer, largely owing to his outspoken opposition – borne out in his D minor Piano Concerto Op 15 – to the aesthetic principles of Liszt and the New German School. But his hopes for an official conducting post in Hamburg (never fulfilled) were strengthened by growing appreciation of his creative efforts, especially the two orchestral serenades, the Handel Variations for piano and the early piano quartets. He finally won a position of influence in 1863-64, as director of the Vienna Singakademie, concentrating on historical and modern a cappella works. Around this time he met Wagner, but their opposed stances precluded anything like friendship. Besides giving concerts of his own music, he made tours throughout northern and central Europe and began teaching the piano. He settled permanently in Vienna in 1868.*

Brahms's urge to hold an official position (connected in his mind with notions of social respectability) was again met by a brief conductorship – in 1872-73 of the Vienna Gesellschaftskonzerte – but the practical demands of the job conflicted with his even more intense longing to compose. Both the German Requiem (first complete performance, 1869) and the Variations on the St Antony Chorale (1873) were rapturously acclaimed, bringing international renown and financial security. Honours from home and abroad stimulated a spate of masterpieces, including the First (1876) and Second (1877) Symphonies, the Violin Concerto (1878), the songs of Opp 69-72 and the C major Trio. In 1881 Hans von Bülow became a valued colleague and supporter, 'lending' Brahms the fine Meiningen court orchestra to rehearse his new works, notably the Fourth Symphony (1885). At Bad Ischl, his favourite summer resort, he composed a series of important chamber works. By 1890 he had resolved to stop composing but nevertheless produced in 1891-94 some of his best instrumental pieces, inspired by the clarinettist Richard Mühlfeld. Soon after Clara's death in 1896 he died from cancer, aged 63, and was buried in Vienna.

Fundamentally reserved, logical and studious, Brahms was fond of taut forms in his music, though he used genre distinctions loosely. In the piano music, for example, which chronologically encircles his vocal output, the dividing lines between ballade and rhapsody, and capriccio and intermezzo, are vague; such terms refer more to expressive character than to musical form. As in other media, his most important development technique in the piano music is variation, whether used independently (simple melodic alteration and thematic cross-reference) or to create a large integrated cycle in which successive variations contain their own thematic transformation (as in the Handel Variations).

If producing chamber works without piano caused him difficulty, these pieces contain some of his most ingenious music, including the Clarinet Quintet and the three string quartets. Of the other chamber music, the eloquent pair of string sextets, the serious C minor Piano Quartet Op 60 (known to be autobigraphical), the richly imaginative Piano Quintet and the fluent Clarinet Trio Op 114 are noteworthy. The confidence to finish and present his First Symphony took Brahms 15 years for worries over not only his orchestral technique but the work's strongly Classical lines at a time when programmatic symphonies were becoming fashionable; his closely worked score led him to be hailed as Beethoven's true heir. In all four symphonies he is entirely personal in his choice of material, structural manipulation of themes and warm but lucid scoring. All four move from a weighty opening movement through loosely connected inner movements to a monumental finale. Here again his use of strict form, for example the ground bass scheme in the finale of the Fouth Symphony, is not only discreet but astonishingly effective. Among the concertos, the four-movement Second Piano Concerto in B flat – on a grandly symphonic scale, demanding both physically and intellectually – and the Violin Concerto (dedicated to Joachim and lyrical as well as brilliant) are important, as is the nobly rhetorical Double Concerto.

Brahms's greatest vocal work, and a work central to his career, is the German Requiem (1868), combining mixed chorus, solo voices and full orchestra in a deeply felt, non-denominational statement of faith. More Romantic are the Schicksalslied and the Alto Rhapsody. Between these large choral works and the many a cappella ones showing his informed appreciation of Renaissance and Baroque polyphony (he was a diligent collector, scholar and editor of old music) stand the justly popular Zigeunerlieder (in modified gypsy style) and the ländler -like Liebeslieder waltzes with piano accompaniment. His best-loved songs include, besides the narrative Magelone cycle and the sublime Vier ernste Gesänge, Mainacht, Feldeinsamkeit and Immer leiser wird mein Schlummer.

Violin Concerto in D, Op 77

Violin Concerto. Violin Sonata No 3 in D minor, Op 108
Maxim Vengerov *vn*
Chicago Symphony Orchestra / Daniel Barenboim *pf*
Teldec 0630-17144-2 (62 minutes: DDD). Ⓜ
Recorded live in 1997-98 **OO**

Until this recording, Maxim Vengerov's success had rested largely on the Russian romantic and 20th-century repertory, but here he tackles one of the most formidable war-horses of the central repertory, and emerges equally triumphant. It is a live recording, and it has the feel of one in its tension, the sense of immediate, spontaneous expression, the magnetism, the excitement. It is a performance of extremes, just as felicitous in bravura as in lyrical purity, with wide tonal contrasts. It adds to the feeling of freshness and new discovery that Vengerov uses a formidable cadenza he has written himself. In the slow movement he is light and flexibly songful, with rubato sounding completely natural, and the finale, taken fast, has a joyful swagger, with a little agogic hesitation before the accented chord each time in the third phrase of the theme, which underlines its folk-like quality. The coupling is an inspired one too, with Barenboim in a double role, freely spontaneous. As for Vengerov, he brings out the mystery in the sonata, as well as the power. The recording of both works is clear and full, with the violin not unduly spotlit.

Brahms Violin Concerto
Schumann Violin Concerto in D minor, Op posth
Joshua Bell *vn*
Cleveland Orchestra / Christoph von Dohnányi
Decca 444 811-2DH (68 minutes: DDD). Ⓕ
Recorded 1994 **O**

Bell's first entry in the Brahms instantly reveals the soloist's love of bravura display, his gift for turning a phrase individually in a way that catches the ear, always sounding spontaneous, never self-conscious. Regularly one registers moments of new magic, not least when, in the most delicate half-tones, *pianissimos* seem to convey an inner communion, after which the impact of bravura *fortissimos* is all the more dramatic. He rounds off the movement with his own big cadenza and a magically hushed link into the coda, rapt and intense. The slow movement, sweet and songful, gains too from Bell's love of playing really softly, not least in stratospheric registers. In the finale the vein of fantasy is less apparent. Next to others this can seem a little plain. Dohnányi and the Cleveland Orchestra provide weighty and sympathetic support and the generous Schumann coupling in another commanding performance adds to the attractions of the disc. There too Dohnányi and the Cleveland Orchestra add to the weight and dramatic impact of a performance that defies the old idea of this as an impossibly flawed piece, with Bell bringing out charm as well as power. The central slow movement has a rapt intensity rarely matched, and the dance-rhythms of the finale have fantasy as well as jauntiness and jollity, with Bell again revelling in the bravura writing. The recording is full-bodied and well balanced.

Violin Concerto. Double Concerto in A minor, Op 102
Gidon Kremer *vn* **Clemens Hagen** *vc*
Royal Concertgebouw Orchestra / Nikolaus Harnoncourt
Teldec 0630-13137-2 (69 minutes: DDD). Ⓜ
Recorded live in 1996-97 ●●

A radical rethink of two great concertos and as good a justification as any for repertoire duplication. These captivating performances illustrate Harnoncourt's habitual fondness for tapered phrase-shaping and pin-sharp articulation. Kremer's first entry in the Violin Concerto is bold and forceful, and yet listen to his sensitive handling of the triplets at 4'43" or his knowing interpretation of Brahms's prescribed *piano lusingando* at 14'50" and the degree of his perception soon registers. He plays a startlingly original 1903 cadenza by Enescu and takes a swift view of the *Andante*, albeit one that is both lissom and flexible. The finale, on the other hand, suggests the impulsive gaiety of a Hungarian dance (the charming 'hiccup' that characterizes the opening theme is fairly typical), with fast speeds and rugged textures. Generally, it is a more daring, less overtly 'virtuoso' Violin Concerto than other versions.

In the Double Concerto Clemens Hagen employs a subtle, variegated tonal palette and Harnoncourt underlines the concerto's symphonic dimensions (especially in the first movement). The *Andante* second movement moves on, lasting 6'06", and the effect suggests parallels with the piano *Intermezzos*. Intimate interludes abound but one senses, above all, great strength of purpose, particularly in the return of the first theme. Harnoncourt, Kremer, Hagen and the orchestra invest both concertos with a wealth of insights, leaving nothing to chance but within a highly spontaneous interpretative framework. Like Harnoncourt's Brahms symphonies, they will usefully supplement – if not always challenge – other fine (perhaps sweeter-toned) recordings. The sound is pleasingly ambient, with precious few coughs or extraneous noises and no applause.

Brahms Violin Concerto
Tchaikovsky Violin Concerto in D, Op 35
Jascha Heifetz *vn*
Chicago Symphony Orchestra / Fritz Reiner
RCA Victor Living Stereo 09026 61495-2 Ⓜ
(64 minutes: ADD). Recorded 1955 and 1957 ●

This combination appears unbeatable. You may think that Reiner starts the opening tutti at an extraordinarily quick speed – until you remember that he is going to accompany no less a virtuoso than Heifetz, so he is merely taking it to match his soloist's performance. You will like this if you think that this concerto is too often played in the kind of 'autumnal' manner often attributed to Brahms's compositions but which really should not apply to many of them. With Heifetz it is played with respect but without any kind of reverent hushed awe. The slow movement is lovely and the finale is a winner, the playing of an exuberant young man, yet Heifetz was over 50 when he made this record. Reiner conducts the fast movement with a fiery rhythmic impetus that incandescently matches the exhilarating, yet unforced bravura of his great soloist. It is confident throughout – and just listen to his real *staccato*, a rare thing from violinists.

The RCA recording comes up extraordinarily well – although the soloist is balanced forwardly, he is naturally focused and the Chicago acoustic ensures a convincing concert-hall balance. If anything, the remastering of the Tchaikovsky is even more remarkable, considering that originally Heifetz was apparently placed right up against the microphone. One soon adapts to the closeness when the fiddle-playing is so peerless; and Heifetz colours Tchaikovsky's melodies ravishingly. The gentle Russian melancholy of the *Canzonetta* is perfectly caught, too.

Piano Concertos

No 1 in D minor, Op 15; **No 2** in B flat, Op 83

Piano Concertos Nos 1 and 2.
Seven Piano Pieces, Op 116
Emil Gilels *pf*
Berlin Philharmonic Orchestra / Eugen Jochum
DG The Originals ② 447 446-2GOR2 Ⓜ
(125 minutes: ADD). Recorded 1972-75 ●●

The booklet-notes make reference to the original *Gramophone* review, in which Gilels and Jochum were praised for 'a rapt songfulness that in no way detracts from Brahms's heroism, and so comes closer to that unique and complex combination of attitudes that for me is Brahms more than any other performances of these concertos I have ever heard, on records or otherwise'. One might add that Jochum and the Berlin Philharmonic make plain sailing where others struggle with choppy cross-currents (admittedly sometimes to Brahms's advantage) and that the recordings don't sound their age. Other interpreters have perhaps probed a little deeper here and there; neither concerto rests content with a single interpretation, the Second especially. As for the Seven Piano Pieces, Gilels viewed the opus as a single piece, a musical novella in several chapters.

Piano Concertos[a] Nos 1 and 2. Scherzo in E flat minor, Op 4. Four Ballades, Op 10. Eight Pieces, Op 76
Stephen Kovacevich *pf*
London Symphony Orchestra / Sir Colin Davis
Philips ② 442 109-2PM2 (141 minutes: ADD/DDD). Ⓜ
Recorded [a]1979 and 1983 ●

This performance of the First is extremely fine. Stephen Kovacevich brings to it a vast amount of eloquence, tenderness and lyrical feeling and he is more poetic and imaginative than most of his rivals. In the slow movement there is much inwardness of feeling, without any attempt either to over- or understate the leonine, combative side of the solo part. Sir Colin Davis and the LSO give him sympathetic support and it is only a pity that although the balance between soloist and orchestra is well judged, the overall sound is opaque. If the recording had been as distinguished as the solo playing, this would have been a truly outstanding reading. But for those who are prepared to make allowances for the sound recording, this No 1 offers huge musical rewards. However, the Second must be numbered among the very finest available, and the recording is far more successful. This is every bit as well balanced as its companion but detail is infinitely more transparent. The performance combines poetic feeling and intellectual strength in no small measure. The first movement unfolds without any false urgency and momentum; it is spacious, autumnal, reflective as well as majestic. The second movement is sparkling and fresh and it is difficult to recall a more beautiful account of the slow movement. In the *Più adagio* section he is quite magical, and in the bars that precede this, he is rapt and poetic without going over the top There is wit, delicacy and poetry in the finale, too. Some may feel that it is almost too relaxed and smiling, but he captures the lambent qualities of texture. As with the First Concerto, Davis provides impeccable support throughout and the unnamed cellist in the slow movement plays with both tenderness and nobility.

In the E flat minor *Scherzo* and the *Ballades* Kovacevich's playing reminds you strongly that this was the music of a pianist-composer, writing for the instrument with a keener ear for texture and tone colour than he is often given credit for. The *Scherzo*, for instance, is not just big and burly all the way through, but sufficiently lithe and crystalline in the recurrent main theme to bring home the full contrast of the sumptuously sustained second trio. He is just as keen in response to the exploratory textures of the *Ballades*. The eight pieces of Op 76 pre-echo the intimate keyboard confessions of Brahms's last years – especially No 3 which Kovacevich plays with delicacy and tenderness. Throughout the solo works Kovacevich stresses the composer's impressionability more than his intensity. But as imagination is coupled with the most scrupulous regard for the letter of the text, the musical results are refreshing. The recorded sound is clear.

Brahms Piano Concerto No 1[a] Ⓗ
Franck Symphonic Variations[b] **Litolff** Concerto symphonique No 4 in D minor, Op 102 – Scherzo[b]
Sir Clifford Curzon *pf*
[a]**London Symphony Orchestra / George Szell;**
[b]**London Philharmonic Orchestra / Sir Adrian Boult**
Decca Legends 466 376-2DM (74 minutes: ADD). Ⓜ
Recorded [a]1962, [b]1955 ●●

It is debatable as to whether there is any other recording of the D minor Concerto that so instantly takes fire and which burns thereafter with so pure and steady a flame. To all outward appearances, Curzon and Szell were an oddly contrasted couple; yet they worked wonderfully well together, in Mozart and here in Brahms. The 1962 recording still comes up phenomenally well, despite some occasional muzzling of the orchestra's bass texturing. A merciful muzzling, you might think, given the frequency with which Szell detects and detonates the small arsenal of explosive devices Brahms has hidden in the undergrowth. We obviously don't lack great recordings of this concerto but this 1962 Decca version remains as collectable as any. The fill-ups to this repackaged CD are also welcome. The Franck is beginning to sound its age technically but the performance is charming. As for the Litolff, it's a gem of a performance, well recorded.

Awards 1993

Piano Concerto No 1. Zwei Gesänge, Op 91
Stephen Kovacevich *pf* **Ann Murray** *mez*
Nobuko Imai *va* **London Philharmonic Orchestra / Wolfgang Sawallisch**
EMI CDC7 54578-2 (59 minutes: DDD) Ⓕ
Texts and translations included ●●●

This is an altogether exceptional account of this leonine, beautiful, but often elusive work. It is one of those profoundly musical performances, thought out in a myriad small details, that at the same time flows freely and spontaneously from the minds and imaginations of musicians for whom the work is no longer a thing to be mastered but an experience to be wonderingly relived. The disc also offers the most imaginative and raptly performed fill-ups imaginable on a Brahms concerto record. The concerto over, Kovacevich is joined by mezzo-soprano Ann Murray and viola player Nobuko Imai for two of Brahms's greatest songs: his setting of Rückert's beautiful eventide poem *Gestillte Sehnsucht* and the sublime *Geistliches Wiegenlied*, a lullaby to the Christ child that bleakly foreshadows the agony that is to come. How wonderfully this song casts its shadow back over the concerto, making us ponder afresh the spiritual meaning of its great slow movement. As for that slow movement, it has rarely been more sensitively played or recorded than here. Kovacevich performs the music with astonishing fine-toned inwardness – playing fabulously underpinned by the LPO's awed, extraordinarily hushed accompaniment.

Piano Concerto No 1. Three Piano Pieces, Op 117
Leif Ove Andsnes *pf*
City of Birmingham Symphony Orchestra / Sir Simon Rattle
EMI CDC5 56583-2 (64 minutes: DDD). Ⓕ
Recorded 1998

Rattle's CBSO players match desk for desk the leading rivals in this formidable, thrilling and superbly directed account of the D minor Concerto. The sonorities are full and dark, the string sound centred in the violas and cellos. The timpani playing is also outstanding, with superb articulation of the hallmark trills, themselves flawlessly matched to the huge answering trills of soloist and full orchestra. It is an expressive performance which also has tremendous drive and contrapuntal clarity, the agogic shifts never drawing attention to themselves. The *pianissimo* string playing in the slow movement has to be heard to be believed, intensely quiet yet with a 'nerve' in it (as Pavarotti once said of Karajan's *pianissimo*). The performance is not in any way in thrall to urbanity and polish. True, it is not as self-evidently weighty as that older generation of players – Arrau and Backhaus, for example – whose phrasing of a Brahms melody, as it were, takes you by the elbow. You notice this more in Andsnes's fill-up, the Op 117 *Intermezzos*, where No 2 is exquisitely done, a hauntingly lovely reverie, but where No 1 is inclined to be mannered, and the opening of No 3 is not at all ominous. The performance of the concerto, however, is certainly not lacking in *gravitas* or power. Indeed, the more you hear it the more aware you are of just how formidable Andsnes's playing is technically, and how mature emotionally. The recording is of demonstration quality. Aided by that, the Concerto has about it a true sense of 'occasion', with beauties, excitements and moments of torrential splendour.

Brahms Piano Concerto No 1[a] Ⓗ
Mozart Piano Concerto No 23 in A, K488[b]
Sir Clifford Curzon *pf*
National Symphony Orchestra / [a]Enrique Jordá, [b]Boyd Neel
Dutton Laboratories Essential Archive mono Ⓑ
CDEA5507 (72 minutes: ADD). Recorded 1945

Since Sir Clifford Curzon's recorded output is a slim volume of finely crafted work, there is nothing here that is not germane. The Brahms gets prime billing on the CD cover which initially may not seem like a good idea. Jordá's conducting is sensitive and sure-footed but workmanlike rather than inspired, the playing of the National Symphony Orchestra marvellous in places but not 100 per cent reliable. (The horns are specially fallible.) Yet, for all that, you will find yourself listening spellbound to Curzon's playing. This is the Curzon who, aged 39, was only emerging into the full light of an international career after a long and inspiring apprenticeship with such teachers as Artur Schnabel and Nadia Boulanger. Indeed, it is that very *emergent* quality which gives his performance a freshness and shy-voiced eloquence that sets the young Brahms vividly and appealingly before us.

It is the Mozart, though, which ravishes sense. This is a performance of rare lucidity and grace which has about it all the clarity and radiance of a revealed truth. It is also marvellously well accompanied. Boyd Neel was a master of clear texturing and balanced tempos. This isn't the Boyd Neel Orchestra itself, but it sounds like it. No doubt it contained many old friends. At the time there were stern things said about surface noise and extraneous whines on the original 78s of the Brahms. Dutton's flawless transfers suggest that Mike Dutton is either a miracle-worker or has had access to better copies. The Mozart seems to have been in pretty good sound from the very start. Happily so, since, in the last resort, the recording of the Brahms *is* a period relic. The Mozart, by contrast, is timeless. Which is why this is to be treasured as well as enjoyed.

Piano Concerto No 2. Four Ballades, Op 10
Emil Gilels *pf*
Berlin Philharmonic Orchestra / Eugen Jochum
DG Classikon 439 466-2GCL (77 minutes: ADD). Ⓑ
Recorded 1972

This has excitement, breadth of vision, warmth and humanity in perfect balance. Gilels and Jochum bring such warmth and humanity to the score as well as a magisterial authority that they carry all before them. But Gilels can also be tender and delicate as well, as the slow movement and finale shows: the prevailing calm of the slow movement is exquisite and the Berlin solo cello contributes a good deal to its effect, while much of the playing in the finale is of the utmost delicacy. This is a great bargain and if you have not acquired Gilels's Second already, it is a 'must', whatever other versions you may already have. The digital remastering for CD has been entirely beneficial. The overall sound is fresher, the bass resonance very slightly modulated, but the rich Brahmsian textures remain satisfyingly full and the piano timbre is focused and natural. Moreover, we have extra bounty in Gilels's *Ballades*, again with good sound quality.

Piano Concerto No 2
Maurizio Pollini *pf*
Berlin Philharmonic Orchestra / Claudio Abbado
DG 453 505-2GH (49 minutes: DDD). Ⓕ
Recorded live in 1995

Pollini's and Abbado's Second is among the most formidably single-minded on record. This does not mean a chilling exclusivity, one that, humanly speaking, omits too much in its quest for a crystalline perfection. On the contrary, the sense is of a granitic reading stripped of all surplus gesture, preening mannerism or overt display, intent only on the unveiling of a musical or moral truth. Again, this is hardly the sort of performance which allows you to savour this or that pianistic luxury, and there will be listeners who, more in love with pianism than with great music-making, will turn away.

Their opening at once suggests a promise of the epic journey to come and in that moment when, as Tovey once put it, 'the air seems full of whispering and the beating of mighty wings' their performance achieves a rare sense of transcendence, of an inspiration above and beyond the printed page. Again, in the *Scherzo* or *Allegro appassionato* Brahms's octave and double-note play at 5'00" is less an opportunity for technical wizardry than a scarifying musical commentary. It is also doubtful whether many artists have achieved such sublimity in the *Andante* (not forgetting the Berlin Philharmonic's most eloquent but unsung cellist) where they combine, most notably in the *Più adagio*, to create an astonishing sense of 'the still centre of the turning world'. Their way, too, with Brahms's 'great and child-like finale' (Tovey again) has a tensile strength that forbids all dalliance.

This recording is a memento of a grand and almost palpable occasion that stunned its audience – there is never a sneeze or sniffle – into submission. Here, surely, is a performance above the vagaries of changing taste and fashion.

Piano Concerto No 2[a]. Lieder, Op 105[b]
Stephen Kovacevich *pf* **Ann Murray** *mez*
London Philharmonic Orchestra / Wolfgang Sawallisch
EMI CDC5 55218-2 (62 minutes: DDD). Texts and translations included. Recorded [a]1993, [b]1994 Ⓕ ●

Brahms's song of the dying girl, 'Immer leiser wird mein Schlummer', recalls with tender pathos the ghostly half-remembered outline of the theme of the slow movement of the Second Piano Concerto. It is one of five songs that make up his Op 105 Lieder and it is marvellous to have not only this song so sympathetically performed by Ann Murray and Stephen Kovacevich but the whole group. Three of the songs are decently represented on record – 'Immer leiser', the thrilling 'Auf dem Kirchhofe' and the soaringly lovely 'Wie Melodien zieht es mir'. But until this you would have sought in vain the group as a group. This is a pity when the third song, the folksy 'Klage', makes so delightful a foil to its immediate neighbours, and when the final song, 'Verrat', is such a splendid example of a ballad about homicide, treated by the mature Brahms with a subtlety we don't always find in some of his more bloodcurdlingly dramatic earlier settings.

The rest of the performance is very fine, yet that isn't to say this disc has it all its own way. In the first place, there is still formidable competition from Kovacevich's own 1979 recording. The impression is that at times the newer performance is cooler and more detached than the LSO/Davis version. This may in part be an impression fostered by the EMI recording which seems thinner-toned and marginally more distant than the Philips. But it is also the conducting. True, No 2 doesn't begin with the furnace fully stoked. That said, there's a touch of coolness about the orchestral playing in the all-important first-movement exposition and development (things get better in the re-exposition). The fact is, though, that Sawallisch produces a less full-bodied, less emotionally weighty reading of the orchestral part than Davis.

The slow movement is here noticeably quicker. Since Brahms marks it *Andante* and since Kovacevich's playing has an even more musing feel to it, you could judge this an advantage. Gilels and Kovacevich with Davis are all slower and more intense. The finale is also quicker by a hair's breadth; but this can tip the scales between success and failure. Kovacevich again plays it with great buoyancy, brilliance and charm. It is playing after the manner of Solomon; and it just about works, despite Sawallisch pushing Brahms's *Allegretto* marking to its limit.

Double Concerto

Double Concerto. Piano Quartet No 3 in C minor, Op 60
Isaac Stern *vn* **Jaime Laredo** *va* **Yo-Yo Ma** *vc*
Emanuel Ax *pf*
Chicago Symphony Orchestra / Claudio Abbado
CBS Masterworks MK42387 (68 minutes: DDD). Recorded 1986 Ⓕ ●

The grave, declamatory utterances at the beginning of the Double Concerto tell us much about the nature of what will follow. They can also reveal a great deal about the two soloists who enter in turn with solo cadenzas separated by thematic orchestral material. It is the much younger man, Yo-Yo Ma, who brings out most strongly the noble gravity of the composer's inspiration, while the relatively veteran Isaac Stern is more melodious and spontaneous-sounding. The music's steady but unhurried paragraphs are very well handled by Abbado and the excellent Chicago Symphony Orchestra is responsive and pretty faithfully balanced with the soloists. This is a performance to satisfy rather than to thrill, but satisfy it does. The recording is rich and rather reverberant.

The powerful C minor Piano Quartet is also well played and provides a substantial partner to the concerto. Apparently Brahms once said that it had the mood of a man thinking of suicide, but it's nothing like as gloomy as that would suggest.

Brahms Double Concerto
Schumann Cello Concerto in A minor, Op 129
Ilya Kaler *vn* **Maria Kliegel** *vc*
National Symphony Orchestra of Ireland / Andrew Constantine
Naxos 8 550938 (59 minutes: DDD). Recorded 1994 Ⓢ

The Brahms and Schumann concertos make an excellent and apt coupling, here given warmly spontaneous-sounding performances, very well recorded. The violinist, Ilya Kaler, is as clean in attack and intonation as Maria Kliegel. Kliegel in her opening cadenza allows herself full freedom, but any feeling that this is to be an easygoing, small-scale reading is dispelled in the main *Allegro*, which is clean and fresh, sharp in attack, helped by full-bodied sound. Kaler and Kliegel make the second subject tenderly expressive without having to use exaggerated rubato. Similarly there is no self-indulgence in the soaring main melody of the central *Andante*, but no lack of warmth or tenderness either. The finale is then unhurried but has dance-rhythms so beautifully sprung and such delicate pointing of phrases that any lack of animal excitement is amply replaced by wit and a sense of fun.

In the Schumann Kliegel takes a spacious, lyrical view of the first movement, using a soft-grained tone at the start with wide vibrato. She then builds up the power of the performance, and with Constantine providing sympathetic accompaniment, the spontaneous expression is most compelling. So, too, is the simple, dedicated playing in the central *Langsam*, and, as in the Brahms, Kliegel brings witty pointing to the finale, not least in the second subject. The balance of the soloists is good.

21 Hungarian Dances

Stuttgart Radio Symphony Orchestra / Georges Prêtre

Forlane UCD16770 (57 minutes: DDD). Ⓕ
Recorded 1997

Georges Prêtre has been honorary guest conductor of the Stuttgart Radio Symphony Orchestra since 1995 and he brings a touch of Gallic flamboyance to these delightful, variously orchestrated dances. The playing is mostly spirited and responsive, and the recording pleasantly blended save that the brass are sometimes a mite recessed. The First *Hungarian Dance* is bouncy and keenly accented; the Fourth features a novel 'question-and-answer' effect between the two halves of the principal melody; the Fifth is more elegant than rustic; the 10th pleasingly vivacious; the 14th broad and bold (almost like a majestic fragment from one of Brahms's larger orchestral works); the 16th warmly impassioned (with some of the best string-playing on the disc) and the 20th employs some telling rubato. There is also a 'CD-ROM/extra multimedia' rehearsal and concert track – six minutes' worth – for use with your PC. An enjoyable disc.

Serenades

Brahms Serenade No 1 in D, Op 11
Stenhammar Serenade in F, Op 31
Royal Stockholm Philharmonic Orchestra / Sir Andrew Davis

Finlandia 3984-25327-2 (79 minutes: DDD). Ⓕ
Recorded 1998

It is a lovely idea to pair these two delightful works, though most collectors who fancy Brahms's First *Serenade* will probably also want the Second. Yet the pairing with Stenhammar suggests many interesting points of contrast, not least a questing inventiveness that recalls Sweden's other estimable early symphonist, Franz Berwald. The very opening has a breezy, extrovert quality that recalls early Nielsen, but thereafter the twists and turns in Stenhammar's writing are more reminiscent of Sibelius, even Strauss or Reger. The waltz-like 'Canzonetta' is quietly melancholic, and the *Scherzo* is impishly playful (save for a sombre second episode that initially sounds like *Deep River*). The 'Notturno' fourth movement has the sort of absorbing fairy tale atmosphere that recalls the glittering masterpieces of Rimsky's school. Stenhammar's original design incorporated six rather than five movements, but Davis makes as strong a case as anyone for the revision. He offers a lean, keen-edged reading that keeps squarely to the plot; the playing is expressive and energetic, and the recording captures it well.

The Brahms is an altogether more relaxed piece and is here given a fresh, unmannered reading, vigorous in the opening *Allegro molto*, bouncy in the closing Rondo and with plenty of light and shade between. Rather than make points merely for the sake of it, Davis keeps to a workable interpretative mean and has his players perform as if in a chamber ensemble. Again, the sound is unexceptional but pleasing.

Complete Symphonies

Staatskapelle Dresden / Kurt Sanderling

RCA Victor Classical Navigator ③ 74321 30367-2 (aas: 197 minutes: ADD). Recorded 1971-72
74321 21285-2: No 1. Tragic Overture, Op 81. 74321 17894-2: Nos 2 and 3. 74321 24206-2: No 4. Variations on a Theme by Haydn, Op 56*a*, 'St Antoni Chorale' Ⓑ

Kurt Sanderling has recorded the Brahms symphonies twice (his first set, with the Berlin Symphony Orchestra, is available on Capriccio), but what started out as solid, patient and well built broadened significantly, and in doing so stressed the epic element that was always implicit in the first recordings: the first movement of the later First Symphony is slower than its predecessor by over two minutes. Sanderling's great strength is in the way he handles Brahms's choppy, obdurate string writing, whether in the First Symphony's strutting first movement *Allegro* or the opening *Allegro non troppo* of the Fourth. Tempos are consistently held firm, the lyrical passages allowed their due only within a solid structural frame (the Third Symphony's middle movement, for example) and first-movement repeats omitted. As ever, it's the Third Symphony that underlines specific interpretative differences between conductors – the first movement especially, a vigorous *Allegro con brio* that, for some reason or other, defeats even the greatest maestros. Sanderling takes a majestic, even marmoreal option that seems misguided: the gestures are grand, certainly, but the music remains rooted to earth. And if ever a piece said 'come fly with me', it is the first movement of Brahms's Third Symphony.

So, summing up, Sanderling is sturdy, intelligently phrased, warmly played, fairly well recorded (the strings are a little grainy) and supplemented by equally well-considered accounts of the *Haydn* Variations and *Tragic Overture*.

Symphonies Nos 1-4. Variations on a Theme by Haydn. Tragic Overture, Op 81. Academic Festival Overture, Op 80. Hungarian Dances – No 1 in G minor; No 3 in F; No 10 in F. Serenades – No 1 in D, Op 11; No 2 in A, Op 16
Concertgebouw Orchestra / Bernard Haitink
Philips Bernard Haitink Symphony Edition ④
442 068-2PB4 (291 minutes: ADD). Ⓑ
Recorded 1970-80

Concertgebouw standards at the time of Haitink's survey (1970-80) left little to be desired. Perhaps the clarinets don't always overcome reservations about their tone and intonation with the sensitivity of their phrasing; but the horns invariably do, and more often than not Brahms's favourite instrument is a source of joy in these recordings, blazing gloriously at appropriate moments (especially in the Fourth Symphony), or opening up and sustaining huge vistas in the 'dawn' of the First's finale. As to the strings, Haitink's insistence on firmly defined (though never over-emphatic) rhythms from the bass-lines up is altogether exceptional; there are countless examples, but most memorable of all is the cellos' and basses' ostinato that sees the Second Symphony's finale in the home straight. What an articulate, integrated Brahms sound this is, too; a case of conductor and engineers easily achieving their aims working in a familiar acoustic. The only movement you may initially find overly sober is the first of the Third Symphony, taken very broadly, though it is determined and imposing, and the launching of the coda is stupendously powerful. All in all, there is no better way of getting to know Brahms's orchestral works on a budget.

Symphonies Nos 1-4. Variations on a Theme by Haydn. Academic Festival Overture. Tragic Overture
Berlin Philharmonic Orchestra / Nikolaus Harnoncourt
Teldec ③ 0630-13136-2 (214 minutes: DDD). Ⓕ
Recorded live in 1996-97

Any fears that Nikolaus Harnoncourt's Brahms will be quirky, provocative or abrasive can be dispelled. There are interpretative novelties (freshly considered articulation and clarified counterpoint) and the Berlin strings project a smooth, curvaceous profile. Harnoncourt makes a beeline for the brass, and the horns in particular. The live recordings have remarkable presence and are mostly cough-free.

The *Haydn* Variations serves as a useful sampler for Harnoncourt's Brahms style as a whole, with an unforced vitality and many salient details subtly underlined. The First Symphony's opening *Un poco sostenuto* seems a trifle soft-grained but the pounding basses from bar 25 are beautifully caught and the first-movement *Allegro* is both powerful and broadly paced. The *Andante sostenuto* slow movement is both limpid and conversational, with trance-like dialogue between oboe and clarinet and sparing use of vibrato among the strings. Harnoncourt makes real chamber music of the third movement, though he drives the trio section to a fierce climax, and the finale's first accelerating pizzicatos are truly *stringendo poco a poco* – the excitement certainly mounts, but only gradually. The main body of the movement generates high tension and moments are overwhelmingly exciting.

The Second Symphony's first movement is relatively restrained. Harnoncourt's strategy is to deliver a sombre exposition and a toughened development. Again, the slow movement is fluid and intimate, with some tender string playing. The third movement's rustling trio is disarmingly delicate and the finale, tightly held, keenly inflected and heavily accented: the coda threatens to break free and the effect is thrilling.

First impressions of Harnoncourt's Third suggest a marginal drop in intensity, yet the first movement's peroration is so powerful that one retrospectively suspects that everything prior to it was mere preparation. The middle movements work well but the rough-hewn, flexibly phrased finale really 'makes' the performance.

Like the Third, the Fourth opens with less import than some of its older rivals, yet the development intensifies perceptibly, the recapitulation's hushed *piano dolce* opening bars are held on the edge of a breath and the coda is recklessly headstrong. The slow movement has some heartfelt moments, the top-gear *Scherzo* is quite exhilarating and the finale, forged with the noble inevitability of a baroque passacaglia. Ultimately, Harnoncourt delivers a fine and tragic Fourth. The two overtures are hardly less absorbing. Harnoncourt's Brahms is the perfect antidote to predictability and interpretative complacency.

Symphonies Nos 1-4
South West German Radio Symphony Orchestra / Sergiu Celibidache
DG ③ 459 635-2GH3 (166 minutes: ADD). Includes bonus disc of rehearsal of Symphony No 4. Ⓕ
Recorded live in 1974-76

Most performances conducted by Sergiu Celibidache (or Celi as he was popularly known) harbour at least one incomparable 'Celi moment', and this set includes plenty. He could galvanize, mesmerize, enrapture and insinuate even the most bizarre interpretative ideas into your consciousness. As a musical magician, he was peerless; but as an exponent of the Classics, he constantly courted controversy. He abandoned the recording studio soon after the war, and it is only thanks to his son and family that the flood of pirate Celi CDs can at last be challenged by superior authorized alternatives. This particular set is better played and better produced than anything before it. The recorded balance is excellent. Textures are transparent (the woodwinds especially), instrumental perspectives are unusually true and the incredible force of fully scored passages is never compromised.

The First Symphony is awe-inspiring. The coda is broad, but it never drags and the slow movement is a minor miracle. It is another one of those moments, but there are more in store, notably in the finale, where slowly interweaving violin desks achieve a perfect *diminuendo*. Another occurs around the famous horn episode, where horns answer each other with incredible power. The celebrated string melody is leisurely and serene, but the tempo soon picks up and the rest of the movement is pure joy. All in all, this must be counted among the most imposing Brahms Firsts currently available.

Celi frequently alters Brahms's written dynamics. For example, near the beginning of the Second Symphony, where the strings take the lead, the horns remain much in evidence. The slow movement builds to an epic climax at 8'47" where full winds and brass declaim above a slow-moving tide of first-violin semiquavers, and the finale's accelerating coda is immensely exciting. Indeed, the whole score enjoys an unusually cogent interpretation.

By contrast, parts of the Third Symphony sound decidedly odd, yet there are some wonderful moments: the quieter episodes in the central development, the fire of the string playing in the recapitulation and the delicate balance of forces elsewhere. The Third's principal 'Celi moment' happens at 7'46" into the second movement, at the point where the strings draw a broad expressive arch, played here with the greatest intensity and mesmerizing control. The finale receives a relatively straightforward reading, often at white heat and again with some first-rate string playing. But, viewed as a whole, this is not a Brahms Third to live with.

For the Fourth Symphony, in addition to the complete performance, we are treated to a full rehearsal of the opening *Allegro non troppo* where a fully 'fired-up' Celi takes the greatest pains over matters of rhythm and articulation. The slow, sweet centre of the movement is addressed in almost mystical terms, far more effectively in concert than in the rehearsal. Cumulatively, the Fourth Symphony is taut, intimate, transparent and rich in incident, and only sometimes deprived of the 'long' view. Remarkable, inspiring, exasperating – Celibidache was all of these, and more. And if the overall approach was sometimes excessively interventionist, you learn so much from listening that eccentricities soon cease to register. These discs enshrine the work of a man who obviously loved every note of Brahms's symphonies and was not afraid to express it in interpretative terms.

Symphonies - Nos 1-4. Tragic Overture, Op 81. Variations on a Theme by Haydn, 'St Antoni Chorale', Op 56*a*

Philharmonia Orchestra / Arturo Toscanini

Testament mono ③ SBT3167 (200 minutes: ADD). Ⓕ
Recorded live in 1952 **OO**

The concerts recorded here preserve the two legendary occasions in the autumn of 1952 when in a Brahms cycle at the Royal Festival Hall Toscanini conducted the Philharmonia Orchestra, then only six years old but already the front runner among London orchestras. The recording itself, now legendary, has generated pirated versions, but never before has the original made by EMI, under the supervision of Walter Legge, been officially released – remastered for Stewart Brown's Testament label by the brilliant transfer specialists of EMI. The result is a revelation. This new set brings the clearest of demonstrations that the RCA recordings of Toscanini and the NBC Symphony Orchestra made during the last years of his life (including his Brahms cycle of the very same 12-month period) give only an imperfect picture of a conductor who at the time, and for a generation or so previously, was almost universally counted the greatest in the world. That reputation has been eroded over the years, but this issue may help to put the record straight.

Take for example the quite different NBC version of No 3 that he recorded in New York barely a month after this performance: as Alan Sanders says in his illuminating note, a 'rhythmically staid recording which entirely lacked the lyricism and eloquence of the Philharmonia performance'. His description points to the marked contrasts, not only in No 3 but in all four symphonies. Whereas the New York performances, resonant and superbly drilled, have a hardness and rigidity, with the dynamic contrasts ironed out, thus eliminating *pianissimos* (partly a question of recording balance), the Philharmonia's consistently bring a moulding of phrase and subtlety of *rubato* which bears out the regular Toscanini instructions to 'Sing!'. And in contrast with most Toscanini recordings, the hushed playing is magical. The New York players, by comparison, seem to have forgotten how to respond to the finer subtleties of this notorious taskmaster among conductors. The extra flexibility of the Philharmonia performances over the NBC has an interesting effect on tempo too. Whereas in No 1 the NBC speeds of 1951 are faster, not just than those of the Philharmonia but of the 1941 NBC performance, in the other three symphonies the Philharmonia timings tend to be a degree quicker, notably in No 3, where for example the *Andante* flows far better.

Walter Legge fought hard to get these live recordings officially issued, but everything was against him, not least contractually. Testament is to be congratulated on at least sorting out so successfully what has long been a frustrating tangle.

Brahms Symphonies Nos 1[a] and 2-4[b]. Variations on a Theme by Haydn[a]. Hungarian Dances[a] – No 1 in G minor; No 3 in F; No 10 in F **Beethoven** Overtures – Coriolan, Op 62[a]; Leonore No 2, Op 72[b] **H**

[a]Vienna Philharmonic Orchestra; [b]Berlin Philharmonic Orchestra / Wilhelm Furtwängler

EMI Références mono ③ CHS5 65513-2 Ⓜ
(219 minutes: ADD). Recorded 1948-56 **OO**

These are extraordinary performances, the Third and Fourth Symphonies especially. In the Fourth it is almost as though Furtwängler, to a Berlin audience in 1948, were saying 'You *still* don't believe that this symphony is an appalling tragedy? Listen!' It is desperately serious from the very beginning: austere, big-phrased, with sober grace amidst the intensity, but also suspense, troubled anxiety. The coda is wildly turbulent, and ends in blackness. The slow movement begins in an unearthly hush, soon giving way to expressive warmth, but the rejoinder of the strings is unutterably poignant: the movement is a mourning procession, relieved only by vain defiance. And the *Scherzo*, which Brahms marked *giocoso*? More like grim determination. The finale is baleful, the strings returning to their intense eloquence, the chorale subdued and prayer-like, the fierce conflict terribly urgent, ending in bleak despair.

You might find the Third Symphony even more disturbing. Furtwängler notices all the music's hushed shadows; he explores them, lingers in them, and on emerging you realize that the *Andante*'s serenity is not untroubled, that clouds are often apt to fall across the music's warm colours. The finale has a funereal tread, the noble string theme is determined, not relaxed or exuberant; there is a feverish quality that leaves the coda hushed.

In the First Symphony there is a palpable sense of Brahms confronting the shade of Beethoven. The theme of the finale is not radiant at its first appearance: after an almost distraught slow movement and a strangely unstable *Scherzo* (the whole symphony takes up where the *first* movement of Beethoven's Ninth left off, not its fourth) that theme will have to struggle for its victory. And thus, Furtwängler seems to say, the forest horns at the outset of the Second Symphony, the huge energy of its first movement, the intense, impulsive romanticism of its *Adagio*; hence the exuberant robustness of the finale: Brahms has earned this romantic richness by what he achieved in the First Symphony. Subjective? Of course, and anyone who objects to interpretations so subjective that they can rule out alternative views may dislike them very much indeed. But if one of a conductor's functions is to reveal the composer's intentions, another is to convince you that those intentions matter. Furtwängler's Third has the power to make you question whether it is as ripely autumnal as most seem to think; his Fourth could keep you awake at night; all four symphonies have a visionary urgency that can sweep you along with it.

They are all live recordings, with some audience noise; the strings are a bit acid at times, the climaxes occasionally dense, but you would probably gladly put up with far worse for performances as toweringly eloquent as these.

Symphony No 1

Brahms Symphony No 1
Schumann Symphony No 1 in B flat, Op 38, 'Spring'
Berlin Philharmonic Orchestra / Herbert von Karajan
DG The Originals 447 408-2GOR (76 minutes: ADD). Ⓜ
Recorded 1964 and 1971

The first of Karajan's three Berlin Brahms cycles was, by general consent, his finest for DG. As to which was Karajan's finest 'phase' in general (if such a thing is calculable), only time will tell. Few would deny that this Brahms C minor Symphony has a 'halcyon days' feel. It is certainly present in the first two movements, the drive established in the main *Allegro* of the first (no repeat) allowing Karajan to relax for the second theme without loss of purpose. The second movement, ideally mobile, evolves freely and seamlessly, with masterfully graded wide dynamic contrasts felt rather than fashioned. Here, as elsewhere, this orchestra's tone production is even, rich and rounded. So far, so good. In the third movement, bar-by-bar dynamic contrasts are smoothed out, with the route to the Trio's climax taken as one very gradual *crescendo*. The finale's 'daybreak' is broad and awe-inspiring (with horn pitching that may be deemed not quite true). Karajan here has gauged tempo, dynamics and accentuation so the strings can articulate without strain; all very impressive, but his *Allegro*'s progress is thus relatively short on attack, energy and the ability to fly.

The more you hear Karajan's Schumann First Symphony, the more convinced you may be that it is spring cultivated and monitored under laboratory conditions. The most unsettling of those conditions is an 'effect' common to a number of his 1970s DG Berlin recordings, namely, for a fairly closely balanced orchestra (particularly the strings, which are not entirely glare-free), as dynamic levels drop, to walk off several paces into a glowing Berlin sunset. The 'effect' also exaggerates the conductor's own contrasts, neither exactly redolent of the vitality and freshness of spring: the resolutely robust and measured delivery of the rustic *forte*, and the carefully crafted confection of his *dolce* piano

---

Symphony No 1. Gesang der Parzen, Op 89
Berlin Radio Chorus; Berlin Philharmonic Orchestra / Claudio Abbado
DG 431 790-2GH (58 minutes: DDD). Ⓕ
Recorded 1990

Abbado's tempos are generally broad: his first movement (without its repeat) boldly emphatic but he never stints on affection, and few would find fault with his warm, lyrical handling of the beautiful *Andante*, 'sostenuto', indeed! He ventures between the score's little nooks and crannies, highlighting small details without impeding the music's flow or weakening the performance's structure. When the finale breaks from *Più andante* to *Allegro non troppo, ma con brio*, Abbado really goes for the burn, very much as Furtwängler did before him. It's a truly inspired reading, grand but never grandiose; appreciative of Brahms's thick-set orchestration, but never stodgy. The fill-up is of enormous import, and opens with one of the composer's most inspired musical gestures: a bold, burgeoning *Maestoso*, anticipating the words 'The gods should be feared/by the human race ...'. *Gesang der Parzen* is a setting of a particularly unsettling poem by Goethe, one that warns how the uplifted have particular reason to fear the gods, those who 'turn their beneficent eyes away from whole races.' Abbado surely sensed the terrible truth of that prophecy, and his reading of Op 89 breathes a deeply disquieting air.

Brahms Symphony No 1 Ⓗ
Wagner Siegfried Idyll. Siegfried – Siegfried's horn-call
Dennis Brain *hn*
Philharmonia Orchestra / Guido Cantelli
Testament mono SBT1012 (62 minutes: ADD). Ⓕ
Recorded 1947-53

Cantelli conducts an interpretation which is free of any idiosyncrasy. Yet there is an extraordinary electricity in his conducting, a sense of concentration and conviction which lifts the performance into one of the greatest ever set down on record. The fiery young Italian makes the vintage Philharmonia play in an inspired fashion, and the 1953 mono recording is very acceptable. A slightly edgy string sound betrays the 1951 origin of the *Siegfried Idyll* recording, but the performance has a tenderness, warmth and eloquence which has never been surpassed. Dennis Brain's exuberant horn-call completes a very desirable Testament disc.

Symphonies Nos 2 and 3

Symphonies Nos 1[a] and 3[b] Ⓗ
[a]**London Symphony Orchestra / Hermann Abendroth;** [b]**Vienna Philharmonic Orchestra / Clemens Krauss**
Biddulph WHL052 (75 minutes: ADD). Ⓜ
Recorded [a]1928, [b]1930

Symphonies Nos 2[a] and 3[b]
[a]**New York Symphony Orchestra / Walter Damrosch;** [b]**London Symphony Orchestra / Hermann Abendroth**
Biddulph WHL053 (79 minutes: ADD).
Recorded [a]1928, [b]1927 Ⓜ Ⓗ

Thank heavens for such independent labels as Biddulph and others like it, for were it not for their sterling efforts, valuable performances such as these would be lost. Much as we prize the Brahms of Furtwängler, Toscanini, Klemperer and Walter, anyone with active critical faculties – and the ability to listen 'through' old sound – is likely to enjoy Krauss, Abendroth or Damrosch virtually as much. All three conductors reflect a performing style that might well have been recognized by the composer himself. Flexibility is a constant attribute, though the three orchestras featured produce very different pooled sonorities. A good many of Abendroth's post-war East German recordings have latterly found their way on to CD, but most collectors will have first encountered the conductor through these Brahms 78s with the LSO. The original sound quality – although generally well balanced – is cramped and mono-dimensional, but the transfers make the best of a difficult job.

The First Symphony opens magisterially. The main body of the first movement is pliable but energetic, whereas the *Andante sostenuto* second movement flows nicely and the finale generates considerable visceral excitement. Abendroth leans on the initial upbeat of the big string tune then pushes forwards. Occasionally the tempo seems too fast, but the effect of Abendroth's approach is rugged and impulsive. The LSO's strings are more expressive than its rather acid woodwinds, the cellos being especially fine – notably in the glorious melody at the centre of the Fourth Symphony's *Andante moderato*. As in the First Symphony, wide tempo fluctuations are conspicuous but convincing, save perhaps in the Passacaglia where the flow is sometimes impeded. Most of Brahms's dynamics are faithfully observed and Abendroth's treatment of the interrelationship of the movements perceptive.

Clemens Krauss was even more celebrated as an opera conductor than Abendroth, and his symphonic records are few and far between. This Vienna Philharmonic account of the Third is distinguished by taut string playing, glorious contributions from the horn section and an unselfconscious approach to rubato. You could easily imagine that anyone who learned the *Andante* from this recording will have found all subsequent versions pallid and unconvincing. Krauss's handling of the opening bars – where violas, cellos and basses answer woodwinds and horns – suggests the intimacy of chamber music. Rarely has the writing breathed more naturally, or the underlying sentiment been more precisely gauged. Although some of the finale's faster passages are a little uncoordinated, the driving force of Krauss's approach marks a telling contrast with the symphony's reflective coda.

Among Walter Damrosch's many claims to musical fame are the first American performances of Brahms's Third and Fourth Symphonies, and his New York recording of the Second is in some respects the most interesting of the set. The second subject is very broadly paced, but the highlight of the performance is the *Adagio non troppo* slow movement, a minutely observed reading full of tender incident. On the debit side, violins tend to lack body at anything above *mezzo-forte* and some will question the finale's very fast speeds (especially later on in the movement). But viewed as a whole, Damrosch's Brahms Two is both lyrical and lively, a quietly individual reading that repays close scrutiny.

With fine transfers and expert annotation, these CDs provide an invaluable historical supplement to existing recommendations. You may not always agree with what you hear, and yet all four performances should significantly extend your knowledge of these wonderful works.

Symphonies Nos 2 and 3
Columbia Symphony Orchestra / Bruno Walter
Sony Classical Bruno Walter Edition SMK64471 Ⓜ
(75 minutes: ADD). Recorded 1960

Bruno Walter (1876-1962) was, quite simply, a lovely man, gentle and kind beyond the ordinary (though his kindness did not extend to anything that compromised his artistic standards). He was always a fine interpreter of Brahms's music, which seemed so suited to his temperament, for Brahms, too, was also a deeply human person. So there was an empathy between the two and Walter responded to the music with his whole heart. In an interview shortly before his death, he gave an account of how the character of Brahms interpretations had changed during his lifetime. Performances seemed to him to have become warmer, more expansive: the Brahms of his youth had been muscular, firmly classical, even a little acerbic. This statement may be of more value for what it tells us about Walter's own development than about Brahms interpretations, and certainly these recordings tend to confirm this viewpoint. Whatever Walter's conception of the work as a whole, song-themes are always allowed to open out with glorious effect. There is something almost pianistic about Walter's subtle flexibility of tempo: this, one imagines, is how Brahms might have envisaged it as he played through these works on the piano

Phrasing too has a marvellous feeling of controlled freedom about it: dynamics may rise and fall considerably during a short phrase, and yet Walter's shaping of longer lines is always masterly. The whole second group of the Second Symphony is like one huge, evolving tune with one point of climax and one final resolution. Perhaps there could be more tautness and inner tension in some of the *allegros*, but the generosity and sensitivity of Walter's readings more than compensate: emphasis is upon the lyrical continuity of the music – Brahms the Schubertian rather than Brahms the Beethovenian – and it is none the worse for that. The recordings have come up marvellously in their digital remastering, gaining clarity and depth. Unfortunately the treble frequencies still sound harsh but that's the problem with technology – it has a habit of revealing the naked truth!

Symphony No 2. Academic Festival Overture
New York Philharmonic Orchestra / Kurt Masur
Teldec 9031-77291-2 (50 minutes: DDD). Ⓜ
Recorded 1992

Masur brings affection to the symphony. In the first movement he maintains a strong sense of line, and paces the music more objectively than Haitink. The structure is clearer, but there's also an unforced lyricism. The *Adagio* has a natural ebb and flow, and Masur makes the listener aware of the music's shape and argument very clearly. After a neatly pointed *Allegretto* the finale is given a beautifully balanced, strongly argued reading which eschews superficial excitement, but satisfies through the feeling of a symphonic argument brought to a logical conclusion. To sum up, Haitink caresses the music with more subjective warmth than Masur, whose reading by no means lacks affection, but is more architectural and objective. The New York Philharmonic responds to Masur with highly sensitive, very accomplished playing, and Teldec's attractively warm but clearly recorded disc is completed by a genial, uplifting *Academic Festival Overture*.

Symphony No 2. Alto Rhapsody, Op 53
Marjana Lipovšek *contr* **Ernst Senff Choir; Berlin Philharmonic Orchestra / Claudio Abbado**
DG 427 643-2GH (60 minutes: DDD). Ⓕ
Recorded 1988

These sessions took place before the BPO elected Abbado as its Chief Conductor, but the orchestra responds to him with unmistakable enthusiasm. The BPO's sound under Abbado is different from the Karajan sound. It still has a wonderful depth and sonority, but whereas Karajan encouraged a homogeneous, ultra-refined quality Abbado persuades the orchestra to play with more separated, slightly lighter textures and greater translucency.

In the symphony's first movement Abbado opts for a good, spacious middle-of-the-road tempo, and lets the music unfold easily and lyrically, but with affectionate care. The music-making is quite unidiosyncratic and direct, but develops genuine fire and passion at climaxes. In the second movement the basic tempo is even a little on the slow side, but there is still an appealing lightness and a quiet, glowing quality in the orchestral sound. Abbado gently but firmly persuades the music on, maintaining an adroit balance between warmth of expression and clarity. The third movement has good balance and clarity, too, and if the middle section lacks its customary eager, crisp quality there is still plenty of vitality in the movement overall. There is just a slightly tame feel to the finale, and the climax doesn't quite have its usual impact. But in general it's a most satisfying performance of the symphony, very well recorded, adorned by Lipovšek's singing in the *Alto Rhapsody*. This has good tone and good sense – perhaps a slightly dry-eyed quality too – and Abbado's characterful conducting is impressive.

Symphony No 3. Tragic Overture, Op 81.
Schicksalslied, Op 54
Ernst-Senff Choir; Berlin Philharmonic Orchestra / Claudio Abbado
DG 429 765-2GH (68 minutes: DDD). Ⓕ
Recorded 1989

This disc is gloriously programmed for straight-through listening. It gets off to a cracking start with an urgently impassioned *Tragic Overture* in which the credentials of the Berlin Philharmonic to make a richly idiomatic, Brahmsian sound are substantially reaffirmed. A wide-eyed, breathtaking account of the *Schicksalslied* ('Song of Destiny') follows to provide sound contrast before the wonders of the Third Symphony are freshly explored. This is a reading of the Symphony to be savoured; it is underpinned throughout by a rhythmic vitality which binds the four movements together with a forward thrust, making the end inevitable right from the opening bars. Even in the moments of repose and, especially, the warmly-felt *Andante*, Abbado never lets the music forget its ultimate goal. Despite this, there are many moments of wonderful solo and orchestral playing along the way in which there is time to delight, and Abbado seems to bring out that affable, Bohemian-woods, Dvořák-like element in Brahms's music to a peculiar degree in this performance. The Symphony is recorded with a particular richness and some may find the heady waltz of the third movement done too lushly, emphasized by Abbado's lingering tempo. Nevertheless, this is splendid stuff, and not to be missed.

Symphonies Nos 3 and 4

London Classical Players / Sir Roger Norrington Ⓓ
EMI CDC5 56118-2 (73 minutes: DDD). Ⓕ
Recorded 1995 ●

This Third is a trail-blazing performance, rather than an interpretation that's had time to mature, and not everything is fully convincing: the transition to the first movement's more relaxed second group could certainly have been more flexible. But on the whole Norrington is far from rigidly metronomic; the contrast between dramatic, urgent *allegro* and the more reflective *un poco sostenuto* passage at the heart of the movement is particularly telling. And as the symphony progresses the insights seem to come more and more frequently. The *Andante* second movement is refreshingly expressive. There are similar fine things in the third movement; not least the horn solo in the recapitulation: Norrington uses 19th-century valve horns, but the tone is appreciably different from what we expect today – warmer, less penetrating, and with an indefinable woodland character as the horn sounds through softly rustling leaves. It is this sylvan stillness (not quite serenity) that returns in the symphony's closing pages.

The opening out of the orchestral sound in the Fourth Symphony is reminiscent of the marvellously alive 1935 Toscanini/BBC Symphony Orchestra recording on EMI. Norrington's version is nowhere near as compelling (the relaxed pace at the opening was surprising), but it is full of fine things: the pungent sound of the woodwind choir announcing the slow movement, the warm, confidential tone of the wooden flute at the heart of the finale, and those rasping, but never over-powering trombones. So, not perfection – but surely that was never Norrington's aim. As in all his best performances and recordings he has thrown down a gauntlet. Are we going to go on deferring to tradition – and at the same time grumbling about how uninspiring most modern Brahms orchestral performances are? Or are we going to face up to the possibility that a composer's scores and recorded remarks, and the testimonies of his contemporaries, could be an even more valuable source of insight into the music than even the greatest recordings of the past? Listen to these recordings without prejudice and your idea of The Brahms Sound will never be quite the same again.

Symphony No 4

Vienna Philharmonic Orchestra / Carlos Kleiber
DG The Originals 457 706-2GOR (40 minutes: DDD). Ⓜ
Recorded 1981 ●●

Carlos Kleiber's charismatic 1981 Vienna recording – a classic of sorts and still sounding exceptionally well – continues to stand its ground. Significantly, Kleiber's recording marked the 100th reissue in DG's Originals series and a crossing at the technological divide between analogue and digital. The CD comes handsomely packaged with a 112-page, full-colour 'Compactotheque' résumé of the whole series, complete with 'quotes from the critics'. But, to return to the music. From the beginning, Kleiber keeps the speed fairly steady. In the first movement's coda, he scores over many of his rivals with prominent horns and a particularly exciting conclusion. He opens the second movement in a rather perfunctory manner, but the Vienna cellos make a beautiful sound in the *piano dolce* second subject. In the *Scherzo*, Kleiber pulls back for the two accented notes that dominate the first theme, an interesting gesture that lends the music an appropriately swaggering gait. This, arguably, is his finest movement – also from 4'48", where he keeps the timpani's triplets crystal-clear, then pushes his horns very much to the fore. Overall, Kleiber in the Fourth is the knight with shining breast-plate, bold, handsome, outgoing, relatively straightforward and (this will court controversy) perhaps just a little superficial.

Symphony No 4[a]. Warum ist das Licht gegeben, Op 74 No 1. Fest- und Gedenksprüche, Op 109. Three Motets, Op 110
Leipzig Radio Men's Chorus; [a]Leipzig Gewandhaus Orchestra / Herbert Blomstedt
Decca 455 510-2DH (71 minutes: DDD). Texts and Ⓕ
translations included. Recorded 1996 ●

Herbert Blomstedt homes in on relative subtleties and the small print, as sympathetic a Brahmsian as any. As early as the ninth bar, he pushes both the tempo and the volume. He is utterly responsive to Brahms's finer dynamics – for example the mysterious *pianissimo* string figurations at 5'23". He treats the first movement as a structure viewed from within and the second movement – with a telling *legato* – effects a subtle transition to *pianissimo* winds. Blomstedt plays by the book, though his finale is more flexible than many – and rather less dramatic, certainly in the *forte* opening chords. He broadens the tempo more for the flute solo at 97 (not necessarily a virtue) and his re-entrance to 'tempo 1' later on is less of a jolt, tempo-wise, though he is by then noticeably faster than at the beginning of the movement. The final reckoning is easily summed up: Blomstedt excels in the lyrical, equivocal sides of the score, thinking through each passage with great sensitivity though always with an ear for structure. The couplings are some of Brahms's finest *a cappella* choruses. Indeed, it was something of an inspiration to tail an 'act that no one could follow' (the catastrophic ending of the Fourth Symphony) with a chorus based on Job's despair. The harmonically 'old world' *Fest- und Gedenksprüche* remind us of Brahms's interest in early music, and the opening verse of the last of the Motets, Op 110 – 'When we are in direst need and know not where to turn' – has a meaningful harmonic complexity that is light years ahead of its time. It marks a beautifully sung conclusion to an extremely fine disc, one that enjoys the added advantage of excellent sound and that includes a performance of the Fourth Symphony that stands its ground even in comparison with the exalted benchmark versions reviewed elsewhere in this section.

String Sextets

No 1 in B flat, Op 18; **No 2** in G, Op 36

String Sextets Nos 1 and 2
Raphael Ensemble (James Clark, Elizabeth Wexler *vns* Sally Beamish, Roger Tapping *vas* Andrea Hess, Rhydian Shaxson *vcs*)
Hyperion CDA66276 (74 minutes: DDD). Ⓕ
Recorded 1988 ●●

Completed after the First Piano Concerto, but still comparatively early works, the Sextets are typified by lush textures, ardent emotion, and wonderfully memorable melodic lines. The first is the warmer, more heart-on-the-sleeve piece, balancing with complete naturalness a splendidly lyrical first movement, an urgent, dark set of intricate variations, a lively rustic dance of a *Scherzo*, and a placidly flowing finale. The Second Sextet inhabits at first a more mysterious world of half-shadows, occasionally rent by glorious moments of sunlight. The finale, however, casts off doubt and ends with affirmation. Both works are very susceptible to differing modes of interpretation, and the Raphael Ensemble has established distinctive views of each, allowing the richness of the texture its head without obscuring the lines, and selecting characteristically distinct tone qualities to typify the two works. The recording is clear and analytic without robbing the sound of its warmth and depth. An impressive recording début for this ensemble.

String Sextet No 1. Piano Trio No 1 in B, Op 8[a] 🄷
[a]**Pablo Casals, Madeline Foley** *vcs* [a]**Isaac Stern, Alexander Schneider** *vns* **Milton Katims, Milton Thomas** *vas* a**Dame Myra Hess** *pf*
Sony Classical Casals Edition mono SMK58994 Ⓜ
(77 minutes: ADD). Recorded 1952 ●

Casals is, of course, the lynch-pin. A charismatic presence, he embraces each work with the passion of a devoted horticulturist tending his most precious flowers. Being a proud humanitarian, Casals had long refused to step foot in Franco's Spain, and it was Alexander Schneider who coaxed him from self-imposed retirement for a series of music festivals in the French town of Prades – hence these recordings. This is a majestic, big-boned account of the early B flat Trio and a sublime version of the sun-soaked B flat Sextet, one of the glories of the Casals Edition. If you need a prime sampling of the Casals manner at its most inspired, then try the Sextet's second movement and note his sullen, ghostly tone at 8'32" – like some ancient bard relaying a solemn but wise message.

Clarinet Quintet in B minor, Op 115

Brahms Clarinet Quintet
Mozart Clarinet Quintet in A, K581
Alessandro Carbonare *cl* **Luc Héry, Florence Binder** *vns* **Nicolas Bône** *va* **Muriel Pouzenc** *vc*
Harmonia Mundi Les Nouveaux Interprètes
HMN91 1691 (70 minutes: DDD). Ⓑ
Recorded 1997

The coupling of these two supreme masterpieces among clarinet quintets is surprisingly rare, coming as a rule in reissues of vintage recordings. Here, by contrast, we have a recording of talented young performers in Harmonia Mundi's budget-price series, Les Nouveaux Interprètes. The Italian, Alessandro Carbonare, produces exceptionally beautiful, liquid tone colours over the widest dynamic range, evidently a result of the development work he has undertaken with the clarinet manufacturers, Selmer. What is specially striking is Carbonare's ability to produce extreme, ear-catching *pianissimos*, making the slow movements of both works the high points, and with his entries in all the movements of the Brahms magically gentle. In the Mozart *Larghetto* he very tastefully elaborates the main melody on its reprise without diminishing the tenderness of his playing. The four string players are not quite so distinctive, but provide sympathetic support, though the recording at times gives an edge to the violin tone, which then tends to sound thin next to the clarinet. The one slight irritation is that the recording from time to time picks up the clicking of Carbonare's keys. A most desirable coupling.

Clarinet Quintet. String Quartet No 2 in A minor, Op 51 No 2
Karl Leister *cl* **Leipzig Quartet** (Andreas Seidel, Tilman Büning *vns* Ivo Bauer *va* Matthias Moosdorf *vc*)
Dabringhaus und Grimm MDG307 0719-2 Ⓕ
(71 minutes: DDD). Recorded 1996

One of the most attractive qualities of this version of a well-loved quintet is the skill with which the artists, abetted by the record producer, have integrated the clarinet into the string textures. Having listened more creatively than any other composer to Mozart's example, Brahms allows the clarinet to become part of the tone colour in the string ensemble; and he has also followed the implications, as not all his interpreters seem to understand. Here, the little falling third theme, one of his lifelong obsessions, moves in and out of the musical texture with wonderful subtlety, so that the return of the opening figure at the very end needs no special emphasis but is a natural conclusion. Leister is an artist of long skill and experience, and also of great musical intelligence; the qualities tell. They also mean that there is no need to confer upon the performance anything approaching the sentimentality which can afflict it, in the name of 'nostalgia' as the old composer looks affectionately back on his life's work. This is quite a robust performance, clearly appreciated by the enthusiastic young string quartet, who give a suitably matching account of the Op 51 work. There are, of course, any number of performances of the quintet, but this is a unique one.

Clarinet Quintet. Trio for Horn, Violin and Piano in E flat, Op 40
Reginald Kell *cl* **Aubrey Brain** *hn* **Rudolf Serkin** *pf*
Busch Quartet (Adolf Busch, Gosta Andreasson *vns* Karl Doktor *va* Hermann Busch *vc*)
Pearl mono GEM0007 (63 minutes: ADD).
Recorded 1937 and 1933

There is no need, at this remove of time, for further praise to be lavished on these performances. This account of the Horn Trio remains at, or very near, the top of any list of recorded rivals. HMV's recording of this somewhat idiosyncratic combination of instruments survives well and has been cleanly, honestly transferred. However, the performance of the Clarinet Quintet will give you even deeper pleasure. Where nowadays do we hear playing of such emotional range, such probing intensity? Here the Busch Quartet and Reginald Kell out-sing and outsearch most rivals in the work's autumnal aspect but also make everything seem alive and doubly intense with their fierce and intense response to the music's wild mood-swings. It helps to have a clarinettist who can coo like a dove and exult like a gipsy; but, in the end, the performance's genius rests in the players' profound and unflinching identification with Brahms's shifting moods.

Clarinet Quintet. Clarinet Trio in A minor, Op 114
Thea King *cl* **Karina Georgian** *vc* **Clifford Benson** *pf*
Gabrieli Quartet (Kenneth Sillito, Brendan O'Reilly *vns* Ian Jewel *va* Keith Harvey *vc*)
Hyperion CDA66107 (65 minutes: DDD).
Recorded 1983

These players' tempo in the Clarinet Quintet is more leisurely than most of their rivals. In the faster flanking movements of the trio, a stronger forward drive might not have come amiss. On the other hand, the group allows itself time to savour every bar to the full. The first thing that strikes you about both these performances is the warmth of heart underlying them. You will respond easily to their quality of good-natured, unforced civility. The ensemble is excellent, with the clarinet very much one of the team, never assuming the role of soloist in a quasi-chamber concerto. Thea King's phrasing is unfailingly perceptive and stylish, and her undemonstrative, wise artistry in both works is most appealing. In the Trio, the sumptuous-sounding cello is impressive, which at times makes you feel that Brahms could just as well have called the work a cello trio. This is a disc which will bear frequent repetition. Playing such as this, committed and serious, yet at the same time relaxed and spontaneous, is not easy to contrive in the recording studio, and Hyperion has done well to capture these interpretations on the wing. The sound is very good indeed, mellow and natural.

Brahms Clarinet Quintet in B minor, Op 115
Mozart Clarinet Quintet in A, K581
David Shifrin *cl* **Emerson Quartet** (Philip Setzer, Eugene Drucker, *vns* Lawrence Dutton *va* David Finckel *vc*)
DG 459 641-2GH (70 minutes; DDD).
Recorded 1996-97

David Shifrin and the Emerson play both works easily, sweetly and leaning affectionately where the melody line calls for an extra spot of emphasis. Here, flexibility and precision form a helpful alliance. In Mozart's first movement (played with its repeat intact), the strings tense effectively for the development and the recapitulation is nicely inflected. The *Menuetto* opens with a real spring to the rhythm; the viola is notably supple at 2'50" into the *Andante con variazione* and the seemingly endless phrase that precedes the final return of the opening theme can rarely have been more beautifully played on disc. The Brahms is similarly sensitive, with the strings dipping considerately as the clarinet makes his first entry. Everything ebbs and flows; there are numerous varieties of dynamic shading, and the onset of the first movement's development could hardly be gentler. Note, too, the intimately shared string lines at the beginning of the *Adagio* and how, a little later on (ie at 2'48"), Shifrin sings his sullen reference back to the Quintet's opening theme. The gipsy interludes are more reflective than fiery, in keeping with the tempered melancholy of the performance as a whole. The last two movements are sonorous and colourful, the sound consistently fine.

Clarinet Quintet. Horn Trio in E flat, Op 40
Reginald Kell *cl* **Aubrey Brain** *hn* **Rudolf Serkin** *pf*
Busch Quartet (Adolf Busch, Gösta Andreasson *vns* Karl Doktor *va* Hermann Busch *vc*)
Testament mono SBT1001 (65 minutes: AAD).
Recorded 1938 and 1933

In today's musical climate it is hard to believe the upheaval and opposition aroused in the mid-1930s by Reginald Kell's adoption of vibrato for the clarinet, which was customarily played 'straight' and rather pale in colour. But his warm, sensuous tone won the approbation of Furtwängler and other conductors and wind players, and soon of the public also; and his approach became largely accepted as the norm. It is difficult to describe the impact of that Clarinet Quintet when it was first heard in 1938, with Kell's first *dolce arpeggio* rising like a benison. That performance, with Kell and the Busch Quartet beautifully integrated and balanced, and with infinitely subtle gradations of tone, became a classic at once. With most, if not quite all, the surface sound now eliminated, it entrances all over again. The disc also contains the Horn Trio with Aubrey Brain (a distinguished and influential player later overshadowed by the fame of his son Dennis) who, as always with him, employed the narrow-bore French horn – he regarded the German-type instrument now universal as 'too euphonium-like': though the former was more risky to play, Aubrey was uncommonly sure-footed and rarely split a note (never in this recording). This performance starts rather stiffly and cautiously, and the first movement takes wing only intermittently (with Adolf Busch as the vitalizing force); and keen ears will not be happy with the tuning of the piano nor the horn's accommodation to it. The *Adagio*, too, lacks convincing continuity; but the performance is just saved from being merely an interesting piece of historical documentation by the tremendous verve of the finale.

Piano Quintet in F minor, Op 34

Awards 1980

Maurizio Pollini *pf* **Quartetto Italiano** (Paolo Borciani, Elisa Pegreffi *vns* Dino Asciolla *va* Franco Rossi *vc*)
DG 419 673-2GH (43 minutes: AAD) Ⓕ
Recorded 1979 ○○○

Most Brahms enthusiasts would agree that the Piano Quintet is his most exciting chamber work, and when it is supported by a quite unusually exciting performance it really does carry all before it. In this recording you will find an exceptional degree of inspiration in the music and the playing. If you'll forgive the cliché, Pollini will sweep you off your feet. This is a fascinating performance from noteworthy musicians and Pollini is very much in the driving seat. He dominates this Piano Quintet, at times perhaps a little more than he should, but this does give the performance a special quality. This is partly due to the rather variable balance which quite often makes the piano sound close and the strings a long way off. When Pollini is letting fly you cannot always hear the lower strings; too often you feel that he is a soloist, the strings the accompaniment. The slow movement is marvellous. Most of it sounds like a piano solo because it is written that way (and how beautifully Pollini plays it). The admirable Quartetto Italiano contributes to the full, notably in the *Scherzo* which receives the most exuberant and thrilling performance imaginable. And what an absolutely stunning movement it is when played like this! But all four movements have an almost mesmeric tension, a positively creative musicality; your attention is gripped, your absorption demanded as of right. The sound is splendidly rounded and full, especially the piano tone.

Brahms Piano Quintet
Henze Piano Quintet
Peter Serkin *pf* **Guarneri Quartet** (Arnold Steinhardt, John Dalley *vns* Michael Tree *va* David Soyer *vc*)
Philips 446 710-2PH (66 minutes: DDD). Ⓕ
Recorded 1995 ○

Henze's Piano Quintet, in three relatively compact movements, develops a dialogue that is often dense but avoids the tendency to diffuseness sometimes found in his larger compositions. The piano shares ideas with the strings as well as standing apart from them, and, as with all Henze's best work, emotional intensity leads directly to troubled, never-quite-serene lyricism. Even though there are moments of rhetorical overemphasis, moods of uneasy nostalgia and unquiet agitation are much more characteristic, especially in the urgently flowing, almost triumphantly assertive finale, with its satisfyingly abrupt ending. Henze's Quintet is given a fine performance by its dedicatees, and the conviction with which its rapidly shifting moods and textures are realized creates some regret that more Henze, or another 20th-century piano quintet, was not included on the disc. Not that the performance of the Brahms is likely to disappoint. But there are so many recommendable versions available. Both the Brahms and the Henze are recorded in a way which favours breadth of perspective over intimacy, but this seems entirely right, given the grand style of the playing.

Brahms Piano Quintet
Schubert Piano Quintet in A, D667, 'Trout'
Sir Clifford Curzon *pf* **Amadeus Quartet** (Norbert Brainin, Siegmund Nissel *vns* Peter Schidlof *va* Martin Lovett *vc*); **James Edward Merrett** *db*
BBC Legends ② BBCL4009-2 (82 minutes: ADD). Ⓜ
Recorded live in 1974 and 1971 ○

If you put this set on at the end of a long day you will feel as if a new day has begun. Such is the power of great music-making ... and these performances are indeed 'great'. Granted, the 1971 recording of the Schubert sounds marginally better than the 1974 Brahms, but the visceral excitement generated by the Brahms Quintet has to be heard to be believed. It would be fairly easy to imagine a tidier performance, but not one that is more spontaneous or inspired. Sir Clifford Curzon's grand vision registers within a few bars of the opening movement and heats to near-boiling point by the start of the recapitulation (from about 10 minutes in). The emotional temperature rises even higher for the second movement. The distinction of the performance resides in the co-operation of all five players, which reaches unprecedented heights in the finale. No wonder the audience explodes: it is doubtful that anyone present has heard a finer performance since. Both Quintets include their important first-movement repeats. The *Trout*'s repeated exposition is even more exciting than its first statement, and there is some gentle tempo acceleration during the development. True, the strings make a fractionally late entrance at the beginning of the *Andante*, but the vitality of the *Scherzo* would be hard to beat, while the Theme and Variations features notable playing from Lovett. There's an amusing spot of premature congratulation when applause momentarily breaks in at the end of the *Allegro giusto*'s exposition, but it soon withers to silence for a joyous finale. Here the recording rather favours the strings, but better that than have the piano drown everyone else out. Wonderful stuff, all of it.

Horn Trio in E flat, Op 40. Piano Quintet
Nash Ensemble (Marcia Crayford, Elizabeth Layton *vns* Roger Chase *va* Christopher van Kampen *vc* Frank Lloyd *hn* Ian Brown *pf*) Ⓜ
CRD CRD3489 (73 minutes: DDD). Recorded 1991

It would be hard to imagine more amiable performances of these two strongly characterized Brahms works. The Nash Ensemble's comfortable approach is intense as well as warm, plainly derived from long experience performing this music in concert. The speeds in both works are markedly slower than on other versions, and the ensemble is a degree less polished, but in their expressive warmth they are just as magnetic, with a sense of continuity that the higher-powered readings do not always convey.

The romanticism of the Nash approach comes out particularly strongly in the opening *Andante* of the Horn Trio, with the horn soloist, Frank Lloyd, producing an exceptionally rich, braying tone, reminiscent of Dennis Brain. After relaxed accounts of the first three movements the galloping finale is given with great panache. Thanks partly to the CRD recording, the Nash performances sound satisfyingly beefy, almost orchestral, though some may find the full-bodied sound a degree too reverberant, with the piano rather in front of the strings. The disc can be strongly recommended, particularly as this is the only available coupling of these two works.

String Quintets

No 1 in F, Op 88; **No 2** in G, Op 111

Walter Trampler *va* **Juilliard Quartet** (Robert Mann, Joel Smirnoff *vns* Samuel Rhodes *va* Joel Krosnick *vc*)
Sony Classical SK68476 (59 minutes: DDD). Ⓕ
Recorded 1995

What playing! Listen to how the Juilliard Quartet tackles the Second Quintet's opening: the pulse is vibrant, articulation is clean but never exaggerated, chords are properly weighted and at the development's shimmering first bars at 5'54" – absolute rapture. The *Adagio*'s sombre outer sections are both expressive and transparent and one has to cite the opening bars of the *Un poco Allegretto* third movement as among the most perfect examples of instrumental voicing ever heard on a chamber music record: *everything* tells, and yet the phrasing remains mobile and expressive. The First Quintet is virtually as good, with a warmly cosseted account of the first movement's waltz-like second set and an impressive build-up of tension from, say, 6'41" – one of the most Dvořákian passages in all of Brahms. Readers who only know the Juilliard Quartet from its lean, intense and tonally fragile RCA/CBS recordings of the late 1950s and early 1960s will find these performances far warmer and more 'European' in tone – although a binding intelligence is common to virtually all of the group's recordings (even through various changes of personnel).

String Quintets Nos 1 and 2
Gérard Caussé *va* **Hagen Quartet** (Lukas Hagen, Rainer Schmidt *vns* Veronika Hagen *va* Clemens Hagen *vc*)
DG 453 420-2GH (59 minutes: DDD). Ⓕ
Recorded 1996 ○

The affirmative *Allegro* that launches the Second String Quintet on its course is exhilarating and the recording by the augmented Hagen Quartet greets the air like an unexpected sunbeam. This particular recording combines clarity and substance; nothing is left to chance and the end result is notably colourful, both in tone and in feeling. The First Quintet is crisply pointed, with crystalline textures, a pleasantly laid-back account of the first movement's lovely second set and a finely tensed development section. Furthermore, the heavily contrapuntal finale is played with great precision and rhythmic *élan*. Both performances include first-movement exposition repeats and both represent the Hagens' 'stylistic grid' at its most convincing, with vividly attenuated dynamics, occasional volatility, a consistent sense of line, impressive internal clarity, equal distribution of voices and a remarkable degree of concentration. Very well recorded and expertly annotated.

Piano Quartets

No 1 in G minor, Op 25; **No 2** in A, Op 26; **No 3** in C minor, Op 60

Awards 1991

Isaac Stern *vn* **Jaime Laredo** *va* **Yo-Yo Ma** *vc* **Emanuel Ax** *pf*
Sony Classical ② S2K45846 Ⓕ
(128 minutes: DDD)
Recorded 1986-89 ○○○

The piano quartets belong to the middle of Brahms's life. They have all the power and lyricism that we associate with his music; but alongside a wealth of melodic and harmonic invention there are some shadows: all we know of Brahms's life suggests that he was never a happy man. Even if this is reflected in the music, and especially the C minor Quartet, all is kept in proportion and there is no overt soul-bearing. These quartets are big pieces which often employ a grand manner, though less so in No 2 than the others. For this reason, the present performances with their exuberant sweep are particularly telling, and although no detail is missed the players offer an overall strength. Top soloists in their own right, they combine their individual gifts with the ability to play as a well-integrated team. The recording is close but not overwhelmingly so.

Piano Quartet No 1. Four Ballades, Op 10
Emil Gilels *pf* members of the **Amadeus Quartet** (Norbert Brainin *vn* Peter Schidlof *va* Martin Lovett *vc*)
DG The Originals 447 407-2GOR Ⓜ
(65 minutes: ADD). Recorded 1970 and 1975 ○

This is an outstanding performance of Brahms's G minor Piano Quartet, unforgettable for its spontaneity and uninhibited romantic warmth and verve. The booklet reminds us that this 1971 recording made history since 'a contract between an artist from the Soviet Union and a Western label was a sensational event in cultural diplomacy'. Reproduced with respect for the sound quality of its time, the playing has a glowing strength and intensity throughout. Only in the first movement's opulent textures does the keyboard occasionally dominate. From Gilels we're also given a maturely unhurried, essentially 'inward' recording of Brahms's four youthful *Ballades*. A bargain.

String Quartets

No 1 in C minor, Op 51 No 1; **No 2** in A minor, Op 51; **No 3** in B flat, Op 67

Alban Berg Quartet (Günter Pichler, Gerhard Schulz *vns* Thomas Kakuska *va* Valentin Erben *vc*)
EMI ② CDS7 54829-2 (102 minutes: DDD). Ⓕ
Recorded 1991 ●

Whereas the C minor and B flat major Quartets were recorded at sessions in a Swiss church, the A minor Quartet is a live concert performance, as applause confirms. All three works emerge not only with technical fluency and finish but also with quite exceptional immediacy and vividness. The first and last movements of No 1 spring at you with all the drama Brahms invariably drew from C minor. Yet the music's cajoling lyricism is very lovingly cherished too. The players' wide dynamic range is faithfully reproduced right down to the most intimate confidence – and of course the ensuing *Romanze*, very tenderly and delicately interwoven, brings still stronger proof of their awareness of the eloquence of *pianissimo* in all its variations of colour and character. In the B flat Quartet (No 3), which shares the first disc, they at once capture its carefree rustic verve with their bold dynamic contrasts and relish of the composer's rhythmic teasing. For the *Andante*'s confident F major song Pichler finds a glowing fervour. The A minor Quartet, recorded at St Petersburg's Palais Yusopov, monopolizes the second disc – some might think a little extravagantly since the playing time is only just 35 minutes. Tonal production is no less clear and true, even if just a shade less vibrant and lustrous than in that resonant Swiss church. Or maybe this impression can be attributed to the players, in their desire to convey the work's retreat into a more elusive, wistful world that they evoke with effortless fluency, fluidity and grace. In sum, a strongly recommended issue for anyone wanting a keen-edged reminder of this composer's warm and vulnerable romantic heart.

String Quartets Nos 1 and 2
Cleveland Quartet (William Preucil, Peter Salaff *vns* James Dunham *va* Paul Katz *vc*)
Telarc CD80346 (68 minutes: DDD). Ⓕ
Recorded 1993

Though the Cleveland Quartet has changed both its leader and viola player in recent years, all the old tonal opulence is still very much there. So is all the old fire, and equally, the determination to wring the last drop of expression from even the most intimate confession. In short, you would be unlikely to meet a more overtly romantic composer than the Brahms you meet here. In the C minor Quartet's *Romanze* some might in fact prefer the very mellow but more emotionally reticent Borodin Quartet, or the Alban Berg with their ethereally withdrawn *pianissimo*. In the bolder flanking movements it is as compulsive as the highly-strung, impressionable Alban Berg while often finding a broader, suaver, melodic sweep. The venue was its favoured Mechanics Hall at Worcester, Massachusetts, a warmly reverberant building – as the sheer fullness of the sound makes plain.

Brahms String Quartet No 3
Schubert String Quintet in C, D956
Miloš Sádlo *vc* **Smetana Quartet** (Jiří Novák, Lubomír Kostecký *vns* Milan Skampa *va* Antonín Kohout *vc*) Ⓕ
Testament SBT1120 (75 minutes: ADD). ●

This documents the prime of a fine ensemble that sprang to life in wartime Prague and retired from active service in 1989. The beauty of tone, balancing of chords, dynamic shading, precision of ensemble and matching vibrato were, for most of the time, as much in evidence in the 1960s and early 1970s as in the 1950s. This disc exhibits some supremely distinguished string quartet playing, but whether readers will unanimously warm to each featured interpretation is another matter. The Schubert Quintet has many admirable virtues, including absolute internal clarity, genial characterization of the first movement's second subject and the whole of the finale, rhythmic stability and excellent sound quality. But the original producer had insisted that the players employ a single swift tempo for both the inner and the outer sections of the *Adagio*, an option that will strike some as needlessly pedantic.

The Brahms Op 67 coupling is less controversial, although no less musical, either: inner voices are crystal-clear and the first movement is nearer to a genuine *Vivace* than in many better-known performances. Only the *Andante*'s opening is rather foursquare. Sound quality tends to vary between sessions but the transfers are truly state-of-the-art.

Clarinet Trio in A minor, Op 114

Brahms Clarinet Trio in A minor, Op 114 🄷
Holbrooke Clarinet Quintet No 1 in G, Op 27 No 1
Weber Clarinet Concertino in E flat, J109
Reginald Kell *cl* **Anthony Pini** *vc* **Louis Kentner** *pf* **Willoughby Quartet** (Louis Willoughby, Kenneth Skeaping *vns* Aubrey Appleton *va* Vivian Joseph *vc*); **orchestra / Walter Goehr**
Testament mono SBT1002 (54 minutes: ADD). Ⓕ
Recorded 1941

In the rapturous love-duet between clarinet and cello in the *Adagio* of the Clarinet Trio, Reginald Kell's tonal warmth and beauty seem more than ever appropriate. Elsewhere in this work, though, despite his liquid sound and finesse of dynamics he is all but outshone by the eloquent lyricism and passion of that superb player Anthony Pini (listen to his statement of the *Allegro*'s second subject). Together with Kentner's understanding collaboration, never over-assertive but always supportive, an admirably cohesive team is formed, alive to Brahms's interplay of interest and changes of mood.

Kell is the star of the Quintet by Josef Holbrooke which has fallen into total neglect, and frankly the present diffuse work (concocted out of previous compositions in the most extraordinary way) will not prompt much revaluation of his status. Nevertheless, it offers great opportunities for *cantabile* clarinet playing in the central Canzonet and for fluent virtuosity in the finale, and Kell excels in both (though the latter finds weaknesses in the Willoughby Quartet).

Not unexpectedly the Weber *Concertino*, every clarinettist's party-piece, finds Kell displaying, besides an easy technical brilliance, beauty of tone, a charming sense of phrase and sensitive dynamic nuances. Walter Goehr's orchestral accompaniment is clean and fully alert.

Brahms Clarinet Trio in A minor, Op 114
Frühling Clarinet Trio in A minor, Op 40
Schumann Märchenerzählungen, Op 132.
Kinderszenen, Op 15 – Träumerei (arr Hough)
Michael Collins *cl* **Steven Isserlis** *vc*
Stephen Hough *pf*
RCA Red Seal 09026 63504-2 (69 minutes: DDD). Ⓕ
Recorded 1998

Here is a conversation between kindred spirits for whom musical phrasing and mellifluous tone production are evident priorities. Even when playing quietly, Stephen Hough exhibits an acute sense of tonal colour: try from 2'23" into Brahms's finale, where he posits the main idea and his colleagues respond with like minds. Hough's transcription of Schumann's 'Träumerei' might appear an old-fashioned appendage to an otherwise enterprising programme. And yet the musical result – where Michael Collins holds the main melody line until near the end of the piece, when Steven Isserlis takes over just for a couple of bars – is utterly captivating.

If the Brahms is 'the fruit of profound maturity' (to quote Isserlis's often entertaining booklet-note), Schumann's four *Märchenerzählungen* – performed here with a cello in place of the original viola – combine forcefulness with a certain fragility. For example, the *Lebhaft und sehr markiert* second movement opens emphatically, then skips off in heady abandon before settling to a mood where the two elements – dark resolution and aerial fantasy – combine.

The third major work in this well-planned romantic programme is by Lvov-born Carl Frühling (1868-1937), a gifted composer who, according to Isserlis, partnered celebrated artists of the day and died in poverty. Many of Frühling's works still await discovery (literally, as no one knows their precise whereabouts) but the Trio here is full of lovely things. Yes, it is eclectic, but anyone with an ear for Chausson, Korngold, Godowsky or Kreisler will love it. The finale is an ideal sampling point, especially 5'25" where Isserlis bows a wistful motive and Hough responds with music that momentarily edges towards Liszt's 'Vallée d'Obermann'.

A highly imaginative programme characterized above all by fine balancing – musically, interpretatively and technically.

Piano Trios

No 1 in B, Op 8; **No 2** in C, Op 87;
No 3 in C minor, Op 101

Piano Trios Nos 1-3. Horn Trio in E flat, Op 40.
Clarinet Trio in A minor, Op 114
Richard Hosford *cl* **Stephen Stirling** *hn* **Florestan Trio** (Anthony Marwood *vn* Richard Lester *vc* Susan Tomes *pf*)
Hyperion ② CDA67251/2 (137 minutes: DDD). Ⓕ
Recorded 1997 ●

Aided by an especially clear, vivid, yet spacious recording, the Florestan Trio and their two colleagues allow us to hear far more of this music than usual – the elaborate decoration of Op 114's *Adagio*, or the sinister detail of the more delicate passages in Op 8's *Scherzo*. Much of the credit for this goes to Susan Tomes; her playing is an object-lesson in sensitivity and in matching the other voices. Balance and blend are a special feature of these performances. Anthony Marwood and Richard Lester match their sounds perfectly for the lovely duet passages in the slow movements of Op 8 and Op 101. What is less expected, and less usual, is the matching of violin and horn, cello and clarinet. But perhaps the single outstanding feature of all the performances is the way the music is shaped. It's not only that the phrases are projected clearly and expressively – the approach moves outwards to encompass the music's larger paragraphs and, indeed, whole movements. These are very desirable recordings, then. Pires, Dumay and Wang (DG) offer big-toned performances on the grand scale of Opp 8 and 87, splendidly recorded. It's not easy to choose between them and the wholehearted, but more intimate approach of the Florestan.

Piano Trios Nos 1 and 2
Augustin Dumay *vn* **Jian Wang** *vc*
Maria João Pires *pf* Ⓕ
DG 447 055-2GH (67 minutes: DDD). Recorded 1995 ●

In the Chinese cellist Jian Wang, the duo of Augustin Dumay and Maria João Pires have found themselves a true soul mate as this, their first disc of piano trios together, engagingly shows. The B major Trio doesn't quite topple the Chungs' recording, still at the very top of the list; but it comes pretty near it. The *Scherzo*'s trio, likewise, pulls back to form a slow, soupy centrepiece. Here the rubato is a little mannered, lacking perhaps the instinctive lilt of other versions. Everything, though, can be traded in for the sheer wonder of this *Adagio*. As slow as any on disc, it reveals the real empathy between Dumay and Wang in moments of great beauty where the Milstein legacy in Dumay's playing is wonderfully apparent. For the C major Trio, Dumay, Pires and Wang offer a generally broad, spacious performance, and a suppleness of repartee in the slow movement's variations which matches their fluency of invention. The *Scherzo*'s niggling is as compact and securely balanced as any, before the players glide, then stride, into the bright sunlight of the Trio.

Cello Sonatas

No 1 in E minor, Op 38; **No 2** in F, Op 99

Heinrich Schiff vc **Gerhard Oppitz** *pf*
Philips 456 402-2PH (55 minutes: DDD). Ⓕ
Recorded 1996 ●●

Brahms's cello sonatas make for an ideal coupling, and not merely because there are only two of them. The differences between them are significant, both in terms of tone and character – the First being fairly mellow and soft-spoken, the Second full of bold contrasts. Oppitz is already well known for some excellent Brahms recordings, primarily the solo works, and his subtlety follows through in this recording. Schiff and Oppitz enjoy a warm, intimate acoustic (at Reinstadl, Neumarkt in Germany) that suits the fastidiously articulated profile of their performances. In the Second Sonata's *Allegro vivace* first movement their handling of the eerie F sharp minor development is particularly fine, and Schiff's vibrant pizzicatos near the start of the *Adagio affettuoso* create precisely the sort of sound world that Brahms must have envisaged. Schiff and Oppitz are also enjoyable in the First Sonata's elegant *Allegretto quasi Menuetto* and in the way they slowly edge into the third movement of the Second Sonata. This coupling is a delight; comely music-making much enhanced by a fine balance of head and heart.

Cello Sonatas Nos 1 and 2
Mstislav Rostropovich *vc* **Rudolf Serkin** *pf*
DG 410 510-2GH (58 minutes: DDD). Ⓕ
Recorded 1982 ●

Our younger generation of cello soloists seems to favour a tone production which balances a refined upper range with a middle and lower register that is strong and well focused, rather than expansively rich and resonant. Readers will not need to be told that Rostropovich's solo image is definitely not of this ilk: his musical personality is in every sense larger than life and in this magnificent coupling of the cello sonatas, in partnership with Rudolf Serkin, the very forward balance of the recording exaggerates this impression in the most vivid way. By comparison the piano image – to the right of and behind the cello – is more reticent in timbre and seldom matches Rostropovich's rich flood of sound, which is not, of course, to suggest that Serkin fails to project the music, merely that the microphone placing makes Rostropovich very much the dominating artist. This passionately warm-hearted and ripely Brahmsian music-making almost overwhelms the listener in its sheer impact. But with playing of this calibre, with both artists wonderfully attuned to each other's responses, every nuance tells and Brahms's bold melodic lines soar out from the speakers to capture the imagination, and provide an enthralling musical experience in each and every work.

Cello Sonatas Nos 1 and 2 **P**
Peter Bruns *vc* **Olga Tverskaya** *fp*
Opus 111 OPS30-144 (52 minutes: DDD). Ⓕ
Recorded 1996

This highly accomplished pair opt for the kind of sound that Brahms himself would have envisaged when writing for these two instruments. The German cellist, Peter Bruns, plays a Venetian Tononi of 1730 in partnership with the Erard grand piano, built at their London factory around 1850, chosen by the Russian-born Olga Tverskaya. It's not hard to understand why this Tononi was Casals's favourite concert instrument (according to the booklet) for 12 years: its glorious tonal plangency would melt a stone. The Erard has a clear-cut translucency that yet never seems undernourished or edgy throughout a very considerable range. The artists themselves cannot be overpraised for their finely attuned balance throughout both sonatas: not even in the low-lying string line in the finale of the earlier, more classically conceived E minor work, or the richer keyboard textures of its successor, is the cello overpowered. Nor is any detail in Brahms's closely interwoven dialogue overlooked: your ear is always where it ought to be thanks to their intimate give and take. Have no fear that concern for period sound in any way cools their approach. What ultimately makes this very truthfully recorded disc so enjoyable is the immediacy and intensity of their personal response to the composer's warm romantic heart. Every note speaks in a way that can scarcely fail to touch your own.

Viola Sonatas

No 1 in F minor, Op 120 No 1; **No 2** in E flat, Op 120 No 2

Brahms Viola Sonatas Nos 1 and 2
Schumann Märchenbilder, Op 113
Lars Anders Tomter *va* **Leif Ove Andsnes** *pf*
Virgin Classics VC7 59309-2 (60 minutes: DDD). Ⓕ
Recorded 1991

Although the last piece of Schumann's *Märchenbilder* has generally been regarded as a little gem, the first three – and especially the two faster middle movements – have been criticized for repetitively patterned figuration that can sometimes sound obsessive. But such is the imaginative vitality of these two Norwegian artists that there's no such danger here. There's an irresistible buoyancy in the springy dotted rhythms of No 2 as well as true urgency in the scurrying semiquaver triplets of No 3, while the regret-tinged opening reflection and the heart-easing, lullaby-like 'Abschied' are both phrased with loving tenderness. Thanks to Schumann's comparatively light keyboard texture Tomter and Andsnes achieve a more subtly balanced partnership here than in the two Brahms sonatas. Though unfailingly attentive to softer confidences in these, the young Andsnes nevertheless often strikes you as more assertive in response to louder dynamic markings than the pleasingly incandescent but not outsize-toned Tomter, as his forceful *marcato* in the fifth (*allegro*) variation of the E flat Sonata's finale makes very clear. At moments of heightened challenge he's inclined to forget that the low-voiced viola has not quite the tonal penetration of the clarinet which inspired these works. That said, there's infinitely more to praise than to question in these works too. Fundamentally, both players are discerning musicians, keenly anxious to convey the ageing Brahms's autumnal nostalgia. The recording is clear and truthful.

Violin Sonatas

No 1 in G, Op 78; **No 2** in A, Op 100;
No 3 in D minor, Op 108

Itzhak Perlman *vn* **Vladimir Ashkenazy** *pf*
EMI Great Recordings of the Century CDM5 66893-2 Ⓜ
(70 minutes: DDD). Recorded 1983

If anyone doubts that these three sonatas represent Brahms at his most blissfully lyrical, then this is an essential set to hear. The trouble-free happiness of these mellow inspirations, all written after the main body of Brahms's orchestral music had been completed, comes over richly and seductively in these fine performances. In their sureness and flawless confidence, they carry you along cocooned in rich sound. Perlman consistently produces rich, full-bodied tone, an excellent illustration being the way that he evokes a happy, trouble-free mood in the melody which opens the second movement *Adagio* of No 3. The obverse of this is that with such consistent richness and warmth, the three sonatas come to sound more alike than they usually do, or maybe should, a point which comes out the more from playing them in sequence. It is true that Perlman does quite often play softly, but for some tastes he is placed too close to the microphone, and the actual dynamic level stays rather high, however gently he is playing. This is not to say that with sharp imagination and with superbly clean articulation from the pianist, these performances lack range of expression, and one thinks especially of the rhythmic pointing, which gives a Hungarian or a Slavonic tang to such passages as the first contrasting episode in the 'raindrop' finale of No 1 or the contrasting *Vivace* passages in the second movement of No 2, where the last pizzicato reprise is made totally delectable. These performances are both distinctive and authoritative. The recording is bright, with a good sense of atmosphere to give bite to the piano tone without diminishing the warmth of Perlman's violin.

Violin Sonatas Nos 1-3
Pamela Frank *vn* **Peter Serkin** *pf*
Decca 455 643-2DH (69 minutes: DDD). Ⓕ
Recorded 1996

Pamela Frank's free-spirited, lean, lightly bowed and subtly variegated tone production is thoroughly eventful and thought-provoking. Both she and Peter Serkin make a nutritious meal out of the First Sonata's opening *Vivace ma non troppo*, supple and low-key but action-packed, with Serkin's quiet trills meaningfully mirroring Frank's shuddering double-stopped arpeggios. The *Adagio* is delicate, limpid and sensitively set up by Serkin; note, too, Frank's meticulously graded chords and her chaste playing of the finale's opening theme. The first page of the Second Sonata finds her adapting her lean but strong tone to the music's mellower sound world, with Serkin offering her colourfully pedalled support. True, Serkin's pedalling sometimes registers on the recording as mechanical action, but you soon get used to it. In the Third Sonata, the balance of power shifts from Frank to Serkin. But there is delicacy aplenty, too – not least in the *Scherzo*. The *Adagio* is very slow, effectively so for most of its duration though some might feel that the more flowing tempo chosen by some of Frank's best rivals is more appropriate. The recordings are intimate and realistic. Of modern digital, single-disc recordings of this repertoire, this is one of the best.

Violin Sonatas Nos 1-3
Augustin Dumay *vn* **Maria João Pires** *pf*
DG 435 800-2GH (72 minutes: DDD). Ⓕ
Recorded 1991

Of the numerous recordings of the violin sonatas available, Dumay and Pires easily deserve to be considered amongst the best, for their playing is consistently mature, stylistically homogeneous and, above all, refined. They never waste a note of the music, and yet it is always allowed to unfurl naturally. A reflective eloquence at the opening of the G major Sonata sets the mood for the entire CD. Pires contributes many lovely delicate touches and there is great breadth to her phrasing when this is required. The first movement of the A major work may be slightly slack in its cohesiveness, but in the *Andante tranquillo* that follows one realizes that the duo sees Brahms above all else as a lyrical dreamer. Only in the D minor Sonata does one feel the darkly intense aspect of the composer's character and here the *Presto agitato* finale is everything it should be in terms of tempo and storminess. The recorded sound is pleasant on the ear, without being ideal. The piano tone is a bit muffled and wanting in colour; this is especially apparent when the two instruments are playing together. But overall this is a release of considerable distinction.

Solo piano works

Variations on a Theme by Paganini, Op 35[b]. Variations and Fugue on a Theme by Handel, Op 24[b]. Four Ballades, Op 10[b]. Variations on a Theme by Schumann, Op 9. Variations on an Original Theme, Op 21 No 1. Variations on a Hungarian Song, Op 21 No 2. Waltzes, Op 39. Two Rhapsodies, Op 79[b]. Piano Sonatas – No 1 in C, Op 1; No 2 in F sharp minor, Op 2; No 3 in F minor, Op 5[b]. Scherzo in E flat minor, Op 4. Piano Pieces – Op 76; Op 116; Op 117; Op 118[b]; Op 119. Hungarian Dances[a]
Julius Katchen, [a]Jean-Pierre Marty *pfs*
Decca London ⑥ 455 247-2LC6 Ⓑ
(388 minutes: ADD). Recorded 1962-66 OO

Items marked [b] are also available on
Double Decca ② 452 338-2DF2 Ⓑ

The American pianist Julius Katchen made his name in the early 1950s and died in 1969, but although one thinks of him as a distinguished figure from the last generation, it is salutary to realize that he would probably be performing today if his career had not ended when he was only 42. Even so, his legacy of recordings reminds us of his gifts and the breadth of his repertory, and the present Brahms cycle has distinction.

It begins with an account of the *Paganini* Variations that gives ample proof of his assured technique: the playing tells us at once that the challenging variations in sixths (Nos 1 and 2 in Book 1) held no terrors for him, and the athleticism here is matched by a fluency in the *leggiero* writing of the variation that follows. In general, though, he makes one more aware of a keyboard virtuoso in this work, rather than a poet; there are other performances which balance these two qualities more finely. Tempos tend to rapidity, too, and the piano sound tends to have a hardish brilliance. However, he does bring a gentler quality to the three other sets of variations here, not least in his freer use of rubato and tonal nuance, as witness (say) the serene Variations Nos 11-12 in the big *Handel* set, where the recording from three years earlier is easier on the ear. Here, as elsewhere, there is a little tape hiss, but not enough to distract.

Poetry is to be found in good measure in Katchen's playing of the *Four Ballades*, Op 10. These pieces belie the composer's youth in their deep introspection, though the pianist takes a brisk view of the *Andante con moto* tempo in No 4. The 16 Waltzes of Op 39 are attractive too in their crispness and charm, and the early *Scherzo* in E flat minor has the right dour vigour. The three sonatas are also impressive in their strong, energetic interpretative grasp, though one could wish that the first-movement repeat of No 1 had been observed. Also, slow movements could have a still more inward quality to convey that brooding self-communion which is so characteristic of this composer (though that of Sonata No 3 in F minor is pretty near it). But the great F minor Sonata is spacious and thoughtful as well as leonine, and this is a noble performance, well recorded in 1966.

The shorter pieces are finely done also. Katchen is in his element in the Two Rhapsodies of Op 79, balancing the stormy and lyrical qualities to perfection. The *Fantasias*, Op 116, are not so well recorded (the sound is a bit muffled). However, the playing is masterly, with tragedy, twilight mystery and storm and stress fully playing their part and giving a golden glow to such pieces as the lovely E major *Intermezzo* which is No 6 of the set and the A major *Intermezzo*, Op 118 No 2. Possibly more sensuous gipsy charm could be found in, say, the B minor *Capriccio* of Op 76, but it is very attractive playing and the playful C major *Intermezzo* in Op 119 is delightful, as is the tender lullaby that begins Op 117.

Only the first 10 of the 21 Hungarian Dances exist in the composer's own (very difficult) version for piano solo, and in the others, written for piano duet, Katchen is joined by Jean-Pierre Marty; there's plenty of fire here and much to enjoy. Altogether, this Brahms set is a fine memorial to Katchen and a worthy issue.

Two Rhapsodies, Op 79. Three Intermezzos, Op 117. Six Piano Pieces, Op 118. Four Piano Pieces, Op 119
Radu Lupu *pf*
Decca 417 599-2DH (71 minutes: ADD). Ⓕ
Recorded 1970s

Here are 71 minutes of the finest Brahms piano music, played by one of the outstanding Brahms exponents of our day. What is most treasurable about it is the quiet rapture of some of the most quintessentially Brahmsian moments; for example, the way Lupu sleepwalks into the last section of Op 117 No 3 and the revelation in Op 118 No 2 that the inversion of the theme is even more beautiful than its original statement. The Op 79 *Rhapsodies* are perhaps a fraction less memorable. Decca's recording sounds a little bottom-heavy, in the manner of certain Ashkenazy records of this vintage, and in the heavier textures of the *Rhapsodies* Lupu compounds the problem by reinforcing the bass with octaves and even fifths. Still, this remains as fine a selection of Brahms's piano works as you are likely to find on one disc.

Variations and Fugue on a theme by Handel, Op 24. Variations on a theme by Paganini, Op 35[a]. Eight Piano Pieces, Op 76[b]. Two Rhapsodies, Op 79[b]. Fantasias, Op 116. Three Intermezzos, Op 117. Six Piano Pieces, Op 118. Four Piano Pieces, Op 119.
[a]Adam Harasiewicz, Stephen Kovacevich, [b]Dinorah Varsi *pfs*
Philips Duo 442 589-2PM2 (157 minutes: ADD/DDD). Ⓜ
Recorded 1969-85

Despite strong competition, in Opp 116, 117 and 119 Kovacevich is first choice. He finds the intimacy of the *Intermezzos* without self-conscious search and in the stormier *Capriccios* and

Rhapsodies blends enormous verve with rock-like stability and strength. These are performances that go right to the composer's innermost, secretive heart. In Op 118 Kovacevich finds a melting tenderness for No 2, a lovely textural lightness for No 4 with its mystical Trio, and the gracious liquidity for No 5. The desolate opening and closing sections of No 6 in their turn are beautifully phrased and deeply moving. In the *Paganini* Variations Adam Harasiewicz doesn't quite send the temperature soaring but his accuracy of detail at certain more hair-raising moments such as Nos 6 and 7 of Book Two must not be underestimated. Recommended.

Brahms Piano Sonata No 3   ▥
Liszt La leggierezza, S144 No 2a. Années de pèlerinage, Première Année, S160, 'Suisse' – Au bord d'une source[a]. Hungarian Rhapsody No 15 in A minor, S244[b] **Schumann** Carnaval, Op 9
Solomon *pf*
Testament mono SBT1084 (79 minutes: ADD).   Ⓕ
Recorded 1952; item marked [a] recorded 1930,
[b]1932   ●●

Solomon's 1952 recordings of Schumann's *Carnaval* and the Brahms Sonata in F minor are essential for the desert island, so this well-produced Testament compilation, generously filled out with Liszt, recommends itself. If you've heard tell of Solomon's reputation but don't know his work, or perhaps know only his Beethoven, snap it up. The sound has come up astonishingly well, also in the Liszt pieces which were made in 1930 and 1932. Solomon's performance of 'Au bord d'une source' is a match for Liszt's poetic inspiration, as few recordings of it are. Technical address and refinement on this level constitute a small miracle.

Brahms Piano Sonata No 3. Intermezzos[a] – E flat, Op 117 No 1; C, Op 119 No 3
Schubert Piano Sonata No 21 in B flat, D960[a]
Sir Clifford Curzon *pf*
Decca The Classic Sound 448 578-2DCS   Ⓜ
(77 minutes: ADD). Recorded 1962, [a]1972   ●●

It took wild horses to drag Curzon into the studio, at least in his last years, and he was a record company's nightmare when it came to agreeing what might be issued. One could say that Curzon was not a natural pianist, yet he developed a technique which admirably served the force of his will: and when the two were in harness and in good shape the transcendental aspects of his playing could produce an indelible musical experience. These recordings have lost none of their freshness. The little holes and imperfections are quite unimportant because at every moment Curzon is conveying an exactitude of character and sense. His sound 'speaks' and persuades you to listen to something precise. Nothing is generalized. Yet the overview is there as well as the detail, particularly in the Schubert.

As with every great pianist, the quality of his sound is distinctive: tightly focused, crystalline, refulgent. With his sovereign control of line and

timing, the pianism seems at all times to be perfectly weighted and to have everything within its sights. You could say that about other great interpreters, no doubt, but there is a special attractiveness about Curzon's ability to delight the senses while penetrating to the heart of the matter. When he was on form he could talk of the most serious things while singing at you like a nightingale. How crude most performances of the Brahms F minor Sonata seem when compared with his. All the climaxes well up from within (and how they glow), yet its scale and range are thrillingly made manifest.

This is terrific value at mid-price. The sound is fair to good in both the big pieces – and only slightly inferior in the earlier recording. The two Brahms *Intermezzos* are in a very dry acoustic as if Curzon had recorded them at home (perhaps he did?); but so they were on the original LP.

---

16 Waltzes, Op 39. 10 Hungarian Dances
Idil Biret *pf*
Naxos 8 550355 (52 minutes: DDD).   Ⓢ
Recorded 1992

Both the *Waltzes* and the *Hungarian Dances* are extremely demanding in their two-hand form, and in the latter collection one could often believe that the 20 fingers of two duettists must be involved, so many notes are being played in all registers (for an example, try No 8 in A minor). However, the technical problems hold no terrors for this pianist and her performances are convincing and attractive. What more need be said about this playing of music in which Brahms portrayed, in turn, sophisticated Vienna and untamed Hungary? Well, not a great deal. The quicker *Waltzes* have plenty of vivacity, and the slower ones are lyrical in an aptly Viennese manner. Tempos, textures, phrasing, rubato and pedalling are well managed and the playing has a very convincing blend of subtlety and simplicity. She treats these 16 pieces as a sequence, as Brahms's key structure allows, and leaves relatively little gap between them. The *Hungarian Dances* have a darkly surging Magyar energy and sound that are very pleasing: indeed, Biret seems totally at home in this music. The recording is a bit larger than life, but perfectly acceptable.

Motets

Two Motets, Op 74. Fest- und Gedenksprüche, Op 109. Three Motets, Op 110. Missa Canonica. Two Motets, Op 29
RIAS Chamber Choir, Berlin / Marcus Creed
Harmonia Mundi HMC90 1591 (61 minutes: DDD).   Ⓕ
Texts and translations included. Recorded 1994-95

These are wonderful pieces, which, hearing, you would suppose to be all heart, looking at, you think must be all brain, and in fact are compounded of both, the one feeding upon and stimulating the other. In no other department of his work is Brahms quite so conscious of his heritage. Writing in the midday of romanticism, he finds the great formal, contrapuntal tradition not a weight upon him but a refreshment. He draws upon Schütz as upon Bach, and from the Italian polyphonists and masters of the double choir as well as from his own German background. The innocent ear would never suspect the mathematical intricacies, the sheer musical logic, and yet it tells, even without conscious recognition: one senses the workmanship, and the emotion which would in any case go out to greet such strong, vivid word-setting is immeasurably enhanced. A striking example is provided by the three movements, all that survive, from the *Missa Canonica*, undertaken in 1856. The *Sanctus* is set in deeply reverential mood and, like the flowing triple-time *Benedictus*, betrays nothing of its origin as an academic exercise. The *Agnus Dei* is overtly polyphonic, yet that too gives way to a gently lyrical mode, in the 'Dona nobis pacem'. They were published in 1984 and this is their first recording. The motets, of course, have been recorded many times and very well too, yet, on balance, no more satisfyingly than they are here. The RIAS Chamber Choir produces a fine quality of homogeneous tone and, under Marcus Creed, shows itself fully responsive to both words and music. This disc carries a strong recommendation, especially for its inclusion of the surviving *Missa Canonica* fragments.

Gesänge

Gesänge – Op 17; Op 42; Op 104. Sieben Lieder, Op 62. Deutsche Volkslieder, WoO33 – In stiller Nacht

Stefan Jezierski, Manfred Klier *hns* a**Marie-Pierre Langlamet** *hp*

RIAS Chamber Choir, Berlin / Marcus Creed

Harmonia Mundi HMC90 1592 (62 minutes: DDD). Ⓕ
Texts and translations included. Recorded 1995-96

The RIAS Chamber Choir's blend of voices is impeccable and the tone-quality perfectly lovely. They are sensitive to word and phrase, responding all as one to their conductor's shading and shaping. Their performances give pleasure enough for one to ask nothing further. The sheer beauty of sound preserves the gentle, romantic qualities of the music faithfully; and there is never any question of dullness, for text and music are both lovingly tendered. The pieces themselves always have more to them than one at first thinks, and the sureness of Brahms's feeling for choral sound impresses immediately. All are unaccompanied save Op 17, where the harp and horns bring a delightful enrichment. This is quiet, late-night listening, of the kind that helps to ease the day into retrospective contentment.

Liebeslieder

Liebeslieder, Op 52. Neue Liebeslieder, Op 65. Three Quartets, Op 64

Edith Mathis *sop* **Brigitte Fassbaender** mez **Peter Schreier** *ten* **Dietrich Fischer-Dieskau** *bar*

Karl Engel, Wolfgang Sawallisch *pfs*

DG 423 133-2GH (55 minutes: DDD). Texts and translations included. Recorded 1982 Ⓕ

These delightful works will be eagerly snapped up by lovers of these seemingly simple but, in fact, quite complex settings for one, two or four voices. The performances are thoroughly idiomatic, both as regards the singers and pianists, with full value given to the words and their meaning. It is not merely a question of fine singing, which with this quartet one may more or less take for granted: the subtlety and charm of the interpretations makes what can all too often be a dreary sequence of three-four numbers into a poetic response to the nature of the waltz. There is an intelligent give-and-take between the soloists, so that voices move in and out of the limelight, as the skilful recording allows, and an extra dimension of the music is disclosed here that is too often obscured. The immediate sound is here a great advantage. This is a very worthwhile and welcome reissue of a most attractive individual record.

Brahms Liebeslieder, Op 52

Rossini Soirées musicales – La promessa; La partenza; La regata veneziana; La pesca

Tchaikovsky Duets, Op 46 – No 1, Evening; No 3, Tears; No 4, In the garden; No 6, Dawn

Heather Harper *sop* **Dame Janet Baker** *mez*

Sir Peter Pears *ten* **Thomas Hemsley** *bar*

Claudio Arrau, Benjamin Britten *pfs*

BBC Music Legends/IMG Artists Britten the Performer BBCB8001-2 (62 minutes: ADD). Ⓜ
Recorded 1968-71

Another archive treasure mined from the catacombs of Broadcasting House comes blinking into the sunlight. A reminder, on this occasion, of the old Aldeburgh where the concert hall became a drawing-room peopled with genius and we, the far-flung radio audience, eavesdropped for a precious hour or so in the privacy of our own homes. The programme is odd, but a joy: the product of taste and knowledge, and a profound pleasure in music-making. First, Brahms's *Liebeslieder* with Claudio Arrau, no less, partnering Britten at the keyboard. It had not been planned as such; cancellations had caused the hosts to shuffle the musical house guests. The result is a performance of great strength and spontaneity, the two pianists – the engine-room of this thoroughly 'instrumental' work – playing with a singleness and singularity of spirit that takes the breath away. Brahms occasionally allows solo voices to shine. Here the tones of Baker and Pears shine characteristically through. In the end, though, it is (as it should be) the power and charm of the whole ensemble that provides the pleasure.

The Tchaikovsky songs, four of the six duets, Op 46, he wrote for his niece, Tatyana Davïdova, are sung in English and are thus as accessible as 'Come into the garden, Maud'. Heather Harper and Dame Janet Baker, accompanied by Britten, sing them grandly, without inhibition, but it is the piano writing that tends to catch the imagination. Finally, there is Rossini, four of *Les soirées musicales*. Should the singing be quite so declamatory? Perhaps not, until one realizes just how grand and funny something like the performance of 'La partenza' really is; Baker imperiously parodying the heroic style, Britten's playing of the 22-second postlude a model of enigmatic humour. At one level, this, and the performance of 'La regata veneziana' which concludes the programme, are high parody. It is in the mordant postlude to 'La partenza', however, that we have 'Essence de Rossini', distilled to a recipe of the composer's own making by Britten himself in another of those acts of musical empathy which made him one of the wonders of the musical world.

Lieder

Brahms Lieder – Op 32; Op 72; Op 94
Liszt Tre Sonetti di Petrarca, S270. Die Loreley, S273. O lieb, so lang du lieben kannst, S298. Es muss ein Wunderbares sein, S314
Thomas Quasthoff *bar* **Justus Zeyen** *pf*
DG 463 183-2GH (80 minutes: DDD). Texts and translations included. Recorded 1999 Ⓕ ◉

Quasthoff treats Brahms's Op 32 as a quasi-cycle, where most singers cherry-pick *Wie rafft ich mich auf in der Nacht* ('Up I jumped in the night'), *Du sprichst, dass ich mich täuschte* ('You said I was mistaken') and the ecstatic *Wie bist du, meine Königin* ('My queen, you are so wondrous'). The nine songs that comprise the set are linked thematically: lost love and quintessentially German romantic *Todessehnsucht* ('longing for death') loom large in the emotional foreground. If this means a lack of variety, Quasthoff minimises the effect with the poetry of his singing and deeply considered inflexion of the German language. His voice, a pure lyric baritone with darker accents, is not dissimilar to that of Fischer-Dieskau's – and the older singer is an obvious interpretative model – although its upper register sounds more robust, so that in a turbulent song such as *Wehe, so willst du mich wieder* ('Alas, would you enclose me, restraining fetters?') he doesn't hector as Fischer-Dieskau tends to.

Apart from Quasthoff's virtues, the disc's main attraction is his partnership with young pianist Justus Zeyen, who has transposed the first (tenor) version of Liszt's Petrarch Sonnets into the keys of the second (baritone) version for Quasthoff. But it is his exquisite playing which enhances the desirability of this disc: his twinkling arpeggios depicting the 'Melodischer Wandel der Sterne' ('Melodious movement of the stars') in *Wie rafft ich* or his subtle mood-painting in Liszt's justly celebrated *Die Loreley* and *O lieb, so lang du lieben kannst* ('Liebestraum'). Unlike Fischer-Dieskau and Barenboim in their Brahms edition, Quasthoff does not disdain to sing the fourth song of Op 94, *Sapphische Ode*, usually reserved for female singers. Many will prefer Fischer-Dieskau and Barenboim in this music, but Quasthoff's and Zeyen's rapt account of *Wie bist du, meine Königin* is treasurable: the singer exhales the repeated exclamations of 'Wonnevoll' ('Rapturous') with intoxicating exaltation, the pianist underlining the sentiment with playing of rare sensitivity.

Zigeunerlieder, Op 103 – Nos 1-7 and 11. Dort in den Weiden, Op 97 No 4. Vergebliches Ständchen, Op 84 No 4. Die Mainacht, Op 43 No 2. Ach, wende diesen Blick, Op 57 No 4. O kühler Wald, Op 72 No 3. Von ewiger Liebe, Op 43 No 1. Junge Lieder I, Op 63 No 5. Wie rafft' ich mich auf in der Nacht, Op 32 No 1. Unbewegte laue Luft, Op 57 No 8. Heimweh II, Op 63 No 8. Mädchenlied, Op 107 No 5. Ständchen, Op 106 No 1. Sonntag, Op 47 No 3. Wiegenlied, Op 49 No 4. Zwei Gesänge, Op 91[a]
Anne Sofie von Otter *mez* **Bengt Forsberg** *pf*
[a]**Nils-Erik Sparf** *va*
DG 429 727-2GH (61 minutes: DDD). Texts and translations included. Recorded 1989 Ⓕ ◉

Many of the Lieder here are but meagrely represented in current catalogues, so that this recital is all the more welcome, particularly in view of the perceptive musicality of both singer and pianist. They show a fine free (but unanimous!) flexibility in the *Zigeunerlieder*, with a dashing 'Brauner Bursche' and 'Röslein dreie' and a passionate 'Rote Abendwolken'; but there is also lightness, happy in 'Wisst ihr, wann mein Kindchen', troubled in 'Lieber Gott, du weisst'; and von Otter's coolly tender tone in 'Kommt dir manchmal in den Sinn' touches the heart. Also deeply moving are the profound yearning and the loving but anxious lullaby in the two songs with viola obbligato (most sensitively played). Elsewhere, connoisseurs of vocal technique will admire von Otter's command of colour and *legato* line in the gravity of *O kühler Wald*, the stillness of *Die Mainacht* and the intensity of *Von ewiger Liebe*, and her lovely *mezza voce* in the *Wiegenlied* and the partly repressed fervour of *Unbewegte laue Luft*; but to any listener her remarkable control, her responsiveness to words and, not least, the sheer beauty of her voice make this a most rewarding disc, aided as she is by Forsberg's characterful playing.

---

49 Deutsche Volkslieder, WoO33 – Ach, englische Schäferin; Ach Gott, wie weh tut Scheiden; All' mein' Gedanken; Da unten im Tale; Dort in den Weiden steht ein Haus; Du mein einzig Licht; Erlaube mir, fein's Mädchen, Es Ging ein Maidlein zarte; Es reit' ein Herr und auch sein Knecht; Es ritt ein Ritter; Es steht ein' Lind'; Es war ein Markgraf über'm Rhein; Es wohnet ein Fiedler; Feinsliebchen, du sollst mir nicht barfuss geh'n; Gar lieblich hat sich gesellet; Gunhilde lebt' gar stille und fromm; Ich stand auf hohem Berge; Ich weiss mir'n Maidlein hübsch und fein; In stiller Nacht, zur ersten Wacht; Jungfräulein, soll ich mit euch geh'n; Mein Mädel hat einen Rosenmund; Mir ist ein schön's braun's Maidelein; Sagt mir, O schönste Schäf'rin mein; Die Sonne scheint nicht mehr: Wach' auf mein' in Herzensschöne; Schönster Schatz, mein Engel; Soll sich der Mond nicht heller scheinen; Wie komm'ich denn zur Tür herein?
Stephan Genz *bar* **Roger Vignoles** *pf*
Teldec 3984-23700-2 (59 minutes: DDD). Texts and translations included. Recorded 1998 Ⓜ ◉◉

This is another outright winner from Genz and Vignoles. Even in the pieces calling for two voices, Genz is not really outdone: his variation in timbre subtly differentiates in each case between two characters, and the unity of purpose predicated by one singer's voice has its own validity. In any case, Genz's absolute and innate gift for natural and spontaneous interpretation is reason enough to recommend this issue. The late William Mann, in examining the sources of these pieces, showed that many weren't folksongs at all but 19th-century inventions, some by Brahms himself, but the innocent ear would find it hard to discern which was authentic and which contemporaneous with the composer, such is Brahms's wonderful gift for writing in folk mode, as in 'Erlaube mir, fein's Mädchen'. This is one of the most winning pieces here, enhanced by the artless simplicity and charm of Genz's singing. His attractively straightforward approach is just as welcome in many other songs such as 'Es steht ein' Lind' and 'Ach, englische Schäferin'. With Vignoles nimble and characterful at the piano, and a perfect recording, this is a must-buy unless you insist on the (almost) complete set available from EMI.

Ein deutsches Requiem, Op 45

Elisabeth Schwarzkopf *sop* **Dietrich Fischer-Dieskau** *bar* **Philharmonia Chorus and Orchestra / Otto Klemperer**

EMI Great Recordings of the Century CDM5 66903-2 (69 minutes: ADD). Notes, text and translation included. Recorded 1961 Ⓜ ●●●

Brahm's *German Requiem*, a work of great concentration and spiritual intensity, is rather surprisingly, the creation of a man barely 30 years old. Klemperer's reading of this mighty work has long been famous: rugged, at times surprisingly fleet and with a juggernaut power. The superb Philharmonia is joined by its excellent chorus and two magnificent soloists – Schwarzkopf offering comfort in an endless stream of pure tone and the superb solo contribution from Fischer-Dieskau, still unequalled, taking us closer to the work's emotional, theological and musical sources than any other. Digital remastering has not entirely eliminated tape noise, but the engineers appear to have encountered few problems with the original tapes. A uniquely revealing account of the work.

Ein deutsches Requiem 🅿

Charlotte Margiono *sop* **Rodney Gilfry** *bar* **Monteverdi Choir; Orchestre Révolutionnaire et Romantique / Sir John Eliot Gardiner**

Philips 432 140-2PH (66 minutes: DDD). Text and translation included. Recorded 1990 Ⓕ ●●

Gardiner's performance is notable for its intensity and fervour and for the superb singing of his choir: splendidly firm and secure attacks and phrasing, always with fine tonal quality, meticulous attention to dynamic nuances, and alertness to verbal meaning and nuance. The solo baritone is a real find: an admirably focused voice with cleanly projected words and sensitive tonal gradations: if the soprano, pure-voiced and consoling, seems slightly less distinguished, it may be that she is set a trifle too far from the microphone. Pains have been taken to bring out contrapuntal strands with clarity, in both the chorus and the orchestra; and here the employment of period instruments and of selective string vibrato makes a significant contribution. In the past Gardiner has been accused of minimizing the spiritual quality of religious works; but not in this outstanding performance.

Ein deutsches Requiem

Harolyn Blackwell *sop* **David Wilson-Johnson** *bar* **London Symphony Chorus and Orchestra / André Previn**

LSO Live LSO0005CD (66 minutes: DDD). Text and translation included. Recorded 2000 Ⓑ

A version of the *German Requiem*, fresh and concentrated, to confound even more strikingly than usual the jaundiced strictures notoriously piled on it by Bernard Shaw. With incandescent singing from the London Symphony Chorus, finely shaded over the widest dynamic range, this performance emphasises the drama of the piece in high contrasts. Any idea of longueurs in these seven movements could not be more completely dispelled. Brahms's markings may be predominantly measured, but Previn, by choosing flowing tempos, never for a moment lets them sag as they so easily can.

Previn has long shown what a fine Brahmsian he is, not least in this taxing work (his superb 1986 Teldec recording was a revelation). What the timings reveal here is that, however dedicated the performance is, Previn's speeds are markedly faster than most. The overall timing is over 10 minutes less than two fine rival versions from Karajan (DG, 1964 and 1983) and almost as much less than Abbado (DG – live, 1992).

Nor is there any hint of haste, just dramatic intensity to devotional ends. So the entry of the chorus in the setting of the Beatitudes in the first movement, 'Selig sind' ('Blessed are they that mourn'), is as extreme as I have ever heard it, yet when the following setting of Psalm 126 erupts on the word 'Freude', Joy, the *fortissimo* is thrilling in its bite. Just as bitingly dramatic are the climaxes in the second movement on the words 'Denn alles Fleisch es ist wie Gras' ('For all flesh is as the grass'), with the *crescendos* on the repeated timpani beats superbly caught, adding a frisson of excitement to the fearful message. Then on the words 'Aber des Herrn Wort' ('But the Word of the Lord'), leading to a vigorous *fugato*, the suddenness of the *forte* attack has you sitting up. Equally, the vision of the Last Trump in the sixth movement could not be more dramatic. In every way this performance has you registering the words with new intensity.

The impact of the chorus is all the greater when the recording gives the impression of a relatively compact group – perhaps more a question of the Barbican acoustic rather than actual size. In *pianissimos* it almost feels like a chamber group, but the *fortissimos* bite home far more tellingly than in recordings where the chorus is set in a more reverberant acoustic.

The soloists are equally responsive. David Wilson-Johnson's tone is not perhaps very beautiful, but the plaintive quality and his feeling for the words make it a most compelling performance, and Harolyn Blackwell in 'Ihr habt nun Traurigkeit' conveys in the sweetness of her tone a tender vulnerability. Altogether an outstanding, fresh and revealing version of a much-recorded work, at bargain price.

Havergal Brian

British 1876-1972

GROVE *Largely self-taught, Brian won success at the beginning of the century as a composer of large-scale choral and orchestral pieces, but then was forgotten until a revival of interest began in the 1950s. Meanwhile, without prospect of performance, he had continued to write big works, including an opera The Tigers (1916-30), the 'Gothic' Symphony with soloists, choirs and brass bands (1927) and the four-hour concert opera Prometheus Unbound (1944). In his last years he became most productive, writing 27 symphonies after the age of 70, his heavy Romantic style growing more compact and elliptical.*

Symphony No 1 in D minor, 'Gothic'

Eva Jenisová *sop* **Dagmar Pecková** *contr* **Vladimir Dolezal** *ten* **Peter Mikulás** *bass* **Slovak Philharmonic Choir; Slovak National Theatre Opera Chorus; Slovak Folk Ensemble Chorus; Lucnica Chorus; Bratislava Chamber Choir; Bratislava Children's Choir; Youth Echo Choir; Czechoslovak Radio Symphony Orchestra, Bratislava; Slovak Philharmonic Orchestra / Ondrej Lenard**
Marco Polo ② 8 223280/1 (111 minutes: DDD) Ⓕ
Text and translation included. Recorded 1989

The *Gothic* (1927) is legendary for its length, for its everything-but-the-kitchen-sink scoring and for having been left unperformed for decades. The tiny handful of hearings since its belated première have not wholly dispelled that image; indeed they have fuelled dismissal of Brian as an incompetent visionary, a self-taught composer whose reach far exceeded his grasp and who, creating in a vacuum of non-performance was unable to check his impractical imaginings with his ear. Admiration for Brian's boldness and inventive daring was mingled with exasperation that his teeming textures and wildly complex proliferations seemed self-defeating, that at his most exultant or would-be mystical the plethora of lines and instrumental colours simply congealed into a grey opacity. And there was the sheer barnstorming quality of the piece, too: the piling of climax upon climax, especially in the gigantic setting of the *Te Deum* which forms the Symphony's Part 2 (Part 1, for orchestra alone, is almost conventionally scored; it is Part 2 that requires triple chorus, soloists, four brass bands and practically everything else you can think of. But in a performance as good as this one, the real reasons for the Symphony's long neglect soon become apparent. The choral writing is almost unbelievably difficult, but with choral singing as splendidly prepared as that of the seven choirs assembled here, the remarkable precision of Brian's ear is unarguably demonstrated. In a sympathetic performance the huge choral climaxes are not simply repetitive; they chart the successive emotions of the text, from jubilance, through panic dread, to a moving expression of trust, humble and chastened. Hence the title.

Yes, it is a fine performance, fine enough to dispose of two other possible reservations about the piece: that it is simply too long, and in any case falls apart in the middle. The performance, indeed, has one of the Symphony's own characteristics: it is sure enough and strong enough for the occasional slack page and the evident fact that Brian was learning his mastery as he went along (the first movement is less assured than the others) to matter hardly at all. And how hugely the Slovak singers, to say nothing of the virtuoso first trumpet and splendid brass section, enjoy this not wholly unaccustomed idiom. A towering achievement; recorded, a touch of acidity aside, with fine clarity and spaciousness.

Symphony No 2 in E minor

Symphony No 2. Festival Fanfare
Moscow Symphony Orchestra / Tony Rowe
Marco Polo 8 223790 (55 minutes: DDD). Ⓕ
Recorded 1996

Built over a resourcefully deployed group of ostinato figures and upon the pounding of three sets of timpani and two pianos, the *Scherzo* of Brian's Second Symphony rises to a climax of extraordinary ferocity dominated by bellowing, stereophonically-placed horns. He wanted 16 of them; here he gets eight, and the effect is very nearly as overwhelming as he had planned. This is followed by a 20-minute slow finale, constructed from a sequence of sombre and striking phrases: a grandiose and epic funeral march in effect, but incorporating within it moments of noble, Sibelius-like darkness, a superb central lament for richly sonorous strings and, after a vast, triple climax, an epilogue of frozen poignancy. It is a movement that would convince even those most dubious of Brian's gifts that he was a composer touched by genius. If you are less convinced by the first two movements this may be partly due to Brian's habit, characteristic of this stage of his career, of writing extremely dense counterpoint, in which the primacy of a particular theme isn't always immediately obvious on first hearing. You sense, too, that the orchestra and conductor on this disc, so obviously bowled over by and committed to the third and fourth movements, were perplexed by the first and second. Lines that you sense should be presented with real eloquence emerge here rather half-heartedly, squarish of rhythm; once or twice they have difficulty in emerging at all from Brian's luxurious textures. Nor is the recording, which in the symphony is on the dull, flat side, much of a help. But the latter half of this symphony is so superb that it is likely to convince you that the first half is worth persevering with. The ceremonious *Fanfare*, late Brian and thus terse, non-repetitive but cumulative, provides a further, rousing inducement.

Symphonies Nos 4, 12, 17 and 32

Symphonies Nos 4, 'Das Siegeslied'[a], and 12[b]
[a]Jana Valásková *sop* **[a]Slovak Philharmonic Chorus; [a]Brno Philharmonic Chorus; [a]Cantus Choir; [ab]Bratislava Radio Symphony Orchestra / Adrian Leaper**
Marco Polo 8 223447 (61 minutes: DDD). Ⓕ
Recorded 1992

Symphonies Nos 17 and 32. In Memoriam. Festal dance
Ireland National Symphony Orchestra / Adrian Leaper
Marco Polo 8 223481 (60 minutes: DDD) Ⓕ
Recorded 1992

Havergal Brian's Fourth Symphony, *Das Siegeslied* ('The Song of Victory'), is a stentorian setting of one of the most bloodthirsty of the Psalms, written (in German) in 1933 by a composer whose close involvement with German music and ideas was central to his imagination. It's easy to read the work, as Malcolm MacDonald's note accompanying this recording does, as a desperate warning against nationalist arrogance and militarism. But isn't it something even more alarming? The moment at which this question becomes most insistent is the passage in which Brian sets the most repulsive verse of the entire Psalm, 'That thy foot may be dipped in the blood of thine enemies, and the tongue of thy dogs in the same'. Brian harps on the verse, repeating it for close on five minutes, building with weirdly ingenious canons and ostinatos a sinister mantra of exultation in vengeance.

Most of the big moments of the symphony have this disturbing dual quality. Antidotes are there: in a beautiful, phenomenally difficult unaccompanied chorus in the first movement; in the fabulously strange music, almost impassive yet radiantly sensuous, with which the soprano soloist in the second movement responds to one of the symphony's most catastrophic descents from raucousness into the abyss; and in the hugely complex chorale fantasy on a theme very close to Luther's own *Ein feste Burg* that precedes the finale's culminating sequence of barbarous triumphs. But those triumphs are so savage and so mercilessly piled on that one cannot avoid being relieved when the symphony ends.

How clever, then, of Marco Polo to have twinned it with one of Brian's tersest structures. The 12th symphony is a work in which he never repeats himself, rigorously excluding all connective tissue, proceeding by statement and counter-statement alone to a single, superbly intransigent movement that says in 11 minutes almost as much as the Fourth seems to manage in 50. It forces you to go back and try to make sense of the Fourth. On the second of these releases is the sombre, battle-riven 17th – a locus classicus for studying Brian's technique of progress through metamorphosis rather than 'development', and his last work, the 32nd. In this he refused to pay the symphony an autumnal farewell, choosing instead to earn his eloquent coda by strenuous endeavour, through music of Nielsen-like conflict and one of the most haunted of his characteristic funeral marches. Of the couplings, the grandly stated *In Memoriam* is a three-movement symphony in all but name, fusing Bruckner and the slow march music in *Parsifal* with scoring of lucid richness. There's no denying that Brian's music is 'difficult', but any lingering suspicion that his neglect led to a crabbed and arcane 'private' language will not withstand a couple of intent hearings of either of these discs. Marco Polo are doing us a great service in providing such assured, decently recorded performances in shrewdly devised couplings that make the process of coming to terms with Havergal Brian as easy as it can be.

Symphonies Nos 11 and 15

Symphonies – No 11[a]; No 15[b]. For Valour[b]. Doctor Merryheart[a]
National Symphony Orchestra of Ireland / [a]Adrian Leaper, [b]Tony Rowe
Marco Polo 8 223588 (77 minutes: DDD). Ⓕ
Recorded [a]1993 and [b]1997

Symphony No 11 is in three movements, strangely proportioned: six minutes of noble, slow counterpoint followed by a jovial *Scherzo* more than twice as long, which incorporates graceful 'slow-movement material' before finally *becoming* a slow movement. The march-finale, despite being tripartite, lasts barely four minutes. No 15, by contrast, is in a single movement (though in three spans, fast-slow-fast) and is developed from a single theme. In fact, the ungainly-looking No 11 feels like a unity, largely because of the use of a couple of brief motto ideas, most obviously to unify the strong contrasts of the central movement, but also in fact linking the seemingly quite unrelated outer ones. No 15 is still more impressive, though its mood is difficult to read. 'Relaxed and extrovert' is the description in Malcolm MacDonald's notes; 'a work of power and tenderness' was how the composer saw it. The regular tread that runs throughout, the audible relatedness of all the ideas despite strange contrasts, give it an enigmatic, at times a sinister quality that is most compelling. Though probably the strongest piece here, the magnificent elegy that opens No 11 will win friends more readily.

The two overtures are very varied, too. *For Valour* (a more celebratory, less martial piece than its title implies) is a huge sonata-form *allegro*, hints of Elgarian *nobilmente* punctuating its Straussian exuberance, all three of its main ideas industriously spawning subsidiaries. *Doctor Merryheart* begins with a similar profusion of themes but then turns into a set of seven overlapping variations in which Brian affectionately but mercilessly parodies Strauss's *Don Quixote* and *Ein Heldenleben*. The performances are enthusiastic and accomplished and the recording is rich but clean. A good introduction to Brian's bewildering variety.

Frank Bridge British 1879-1941

GROVE *Bridge studied with Stanford at the RCM (1899-1903) and made a reputation as a chamber musician (a violist) and conductor. His early works, including the orchestral suite The Sea (1911), the symphonic poem Summer (1914) and much chamber music, are close to Bax and Delius, but after World War I he developed rapidly. His Third (1926) and Fourth (1937) Quartets are highly chromatic, reflecting his admiration for Berg, though his music remained distinctively English. Also remarkable is the contrapuntal vigour and energy of his later orchestral works, which include the rhapsody Enter Spring (1927), Oration with solo cello (1930) and Phantasm with solo piano (1931). None of his more adventurous music was much regarded until the 1970s, his fame resting largely on his having been Britten's teacher.*

The Sea, H100

The Sea, H100. Summer, H116. Cherry Ripe, H119*b*. Enter Spring, H174. Lament, H117
Royal Liverpool Philharmonic Orchestra / Sir Charles Groves
EMI British Composers CDM5 66855-2 Ⓜ
(60 minutes: ADD). Recorded 1975

An ideal introduction to the music of Frank Bridge, this much-loved programme was always one of the highlights of Sir Charles Groves's Liverpool tenure, and its reappearance is more than welcome. Although a handful of individual performances – most notably Vernon Handley and the Ulster Orchestra in a stunningly engineered account of *The Sea* (on Chandos) – may have surpassed them in terms of poetic rapture and beguiling finish, Groves's clear-headed, stirringly sympathetic *Enter Spring*, though at times a little too sturdy on its pins, easily outranks the competition. The transfer is the same as that used for an earlier mid-price EMI Studio offering from 1989, and the finished article sounds as resplendent and full-bodied as ever (if, perhaps, with a touch less background hiss than before). Don't miss this reissue.

Bridge The Sea, H100[a]. Enter Spring, H174[b]
Britten The Building of the House, Op 79[c]
Holst Egdon Heath, H172[d]. A Fugal Concerto, H152[e]
[e]**Richard Adeney** *fl* [e]**Peter Graeme** *ob* [c]**East Anglian Choirs;** [ace]**English Chamber Orchestra,** [b]**New Philharmonia Orchestra,** [d]**London Symphony Orchestra /** [abcd]**Benjamin Britten,** [e]**Imogen Holst**
BBC Legends/IMG Artists Britten the Performer
[d]mono/stereo BBCB8007-2 (70 minutes: ADD) Ⓕ
Recorded live in [d]July 1961, [bc]June 1967, [a]June1971 and [e]June 1969

Britten conducts the music of his beloved mentor and teacher, Frank Bridge, with a heart-warming dedication. From the outset his radiant interpretation of *The Sea* grips with its pungent elemental force, mastery of the singing line and unforgettably rapt poetic instinct. The supple naturalness of the phrasing is a thing of wonder throughout, nowhere more so than during the strings' ineffably tender reprise of the main theme of 'Moonlight'. Similarly, Britten's faithful conception of *Enter Spring* possesses a fresh-faced capriciousness, cogent sweep and expressive ardour to make one fall in love all over again with Bridge's exuberant vision. As in *The Sea*, one senses an acute concern for the grander scheme: how shrewd of Britten to hold something in reserve during the joyful clangour of the paragraph beginning at fig 30 (12'34"), thereby minimizing the danger of the same material sounding uncomfortably blatant when it returns in all its swaggering pomp at the close. And what reserves of poignant tenderness he conjures from his hard-working New Philharmonia strings in the ecstatic central portion. Britten's sparky *The Building of the House* Overture launches proceedings in dashing fashion. This was only its second performance (the world première having taken place two days earlier), and one readily overlooks the chorus's sharp initial entry in view of the quick-witted tension generated elsewhere. Britten's 1961 Orford Church performance of Holst's *Egdon Heath* brings with it some occasional insecurity from the LSO, yet his eloquent direction distils exactly the right chill and the interpretation as a whole evinces a compelling dignity, patience and lucidity. Finally Holst's daughter, Imogen, presides over a wonderfully poised and serene account of her father's engaging *Fugal Concerto* from a June 1969 concert at Blythburgh Church. Recordings of varying vintage have all come up very freshly.

Suite for string orchestra, H93

Suite for string orchestra, H93. There is a willow grows aslant a brook, H174. The Two Hunchbacks, H95. Threads, H151. Rosemary, H68*b*. Canzonetta, H169. Berceuse, H8. Serenade, H23
Britten Sinfonia / Nicholas Cleobury.
Conifer Classics 75605 51327-2 (63 minutes: DDD). Ⓕ
Recorded 1997

Nicholas Cleobury and the admirable Britten Sinfonia give what is, on balance, the most shapely and unaffectedly eloquent realization of Frank Bridge's delectable Suite for strings (1908) yet committed to disc. Not only are these fine artists scrupulously faithful to the letter and spirit of the score, their perceptive treatment of the haunting third movement in particular distils a fragrant, other-worldly atmosphere that looks forward to the first of Bridge's *Two Poems* (after Richard Jefferies) of seven years later. Similarly impressive is Cleobury's acutely sensitive rendering of that miniature masterpiece, *There is a willow grows aslant a brook* (1927). Cleobury not only brings out the human anguish in this extraordinary essay, but there's a refinement of texture and suppleness of expression about this dedicated music-making that is deeply moving.

Conifer also gives us two specimens of Bridge's incidental music. He employs Belgian folk melodies to match the setting of *The Two Hunchbacks* and the results are very endearing. Likewise the two intermezzos from Frank Stoyton's three-act comedy entitled *Threads* (1921). Four miniatures round off the release, including the *Two Entr'actes*, published in 1939, otherwise known as *Rosemary* (originally the second of the *Three Sketches* for piano from 1906) and *Canzonetta* (first conceived for piano under the title of *Happy South* following a Mediterranean holiday in 1926). A first-rate anthology, ripely recorded.

String Sextet in E flat, H107

Bridge String Sextet in E flat, H107 **Goossens** Concertino, Op 47. Phantasy Sextet, Op 37
Academy of St Martin in the Fields Chamber Ensemble (Kenneth Sillito, Malcolm Latchem, Rita Manning, Robert Heard *vns* Robert Smissen, Stephen Tees *vas* Stephen Orton, Roger Smith *vcs*)
Chandos CHAN9472 (59 minutes: DDD). Ⓕ
Recorded 1995

This admirable programme presents three fine chamber offerings, excellently realized. Goossens's high-quality invention and effortless craft are strikingly evident in the *Concertino*, here performed in its original 1928 guise for string octet and also the elegantly structured *Phantasy Sextet* of 1923. Scored for three violins, one viola and two cellos, this impressive composition is consistently fertile, tightly knit and confidently conceived for the medium. Bridge's Sextet is laid out for the more traditional line-up comprising pairs of each instrument, and is at once the most ambitious and sumptuous of the composer's early chamber offerings. Perhaps the most striking music can be found in the central *Andante con moto*, a wistfully lilting threnody which itself frames a brief *Scherzo* of nervy propulsion. As usual with Bridge, the elegant formal design, captivating lyrical flow and satisfying cogency yield huge pleasure. The playing is splendid, the sound and balance impeccable.

String Quartets

No 1 in E minor, 'Bologna', H70; **No 2** in G minor, H115; **No 3**, H175; **No 4**, H188

String Quartets – Nos 2 and 3
Bridge Quartet (Catherine Schofield, Kaye Barker *vns* Michael Schofield *va* Lucy Wilding *vc*)
Meridian CDE84311 (58 minutes: DDD). Ⓕ
Recorded 1996 ●

The string quartets of Frank Bridge are some of the most rewarding in the repertoire and here the composer is, on the whole, eminently well served by this eponymous group. In the glorious Second Quartet of 1915, the Bridge Quartet acquit themselves well. Theirs is a thoughtful rendering which, in its comparatively restrained manner, will undoubtedly give pleasure. By the time we reach the superb Third Quartet of 1926, Bridge's command of the medium is total. This score is one of his most searching, deeply felt utterances. The musicians impress it with the honest and hard-working integrity of their playing; however, you may feel that they fight rather too shy of the darker emotional undertow of Bridge's expressionist vision – the intellectual sinew and questing harmonic scope of this marvellous creation are perhaps not as comprehensively conveyed here as one would wish. A most pleasing coupling, however, boasting very good recorded sound quality.

Piano Trio No 2

Phantasy Trio in C minor, H79. Piano Trio No 2, H178. Miniatures – H88: Romance; Intermezzo; H89: Valse russe; Hornpipe
Bernard Roberts Trio (Andrew Roberts *vn* Nicholas Roberts *vc* Bernard Roberts *pf*)
Black Box BBM1028 (57 minutes: DDD). Ⓕ
Recorded 1995

These are utterly sympathetic, beautifully prepared performances from this fine family group, whose line-up comprises the distinguished pianist Bernard Roberts and his two sons, Andrew and Nicholas.

The centrepiece is the Second Piano Trio, a truly magnificent creation that Anthony Payne has justly hailed as 'one of the masterpieces of 20th-century English, indeed European chamber music'. Cast in two interlinked movements, it is a work of searing intensity and astounding individuality, whose November 1929 première provoked a shockingly ignorant and hurtful response from some quarters of the British musical establishment. Compared with the Dartington Trio on a rival Hyperion issue, these dedicated newcomers take a more restrained, less lingering view of this troubled music. Some will crave an altogether more palpable sense of numbing loss in the unnerving *Andante molto moderato* slow movement than the Bernard Roberts Trio chooses to convey; and the work's towering final climax perhaps lacks that last ounce of cumulative power and epic breadth. No matter, this is a shapely, thoroughly convincing conception all the same.

Winner of the 1907 Cobbett Composition Prize, the *Phantasy* Trio in C minor inhabits an entirely different world, its elegant arch-shaped form, superior craftsmanship and generous lyrical flow being typical of Bridge's early output. The present group gives a splendidly taut, agreeably unmannered account of this lovely piece, and lavishes similarly deft and affectionate treatment upon four of the nine *Miniatures* for piano trio published in three sets between 1909 and 1915 (the opening 'Romance' is a particularly touching morsel). The sound is admirably vivid, though the piano timbre is perhaps just a touch clangorous. In all, a most desirable acquisition.

Cello Sonata in D minor, H125

Bridge Cello Sonata **Schubert** Sonata for Arpeggione and Piano in A minor, D821
Mstislav Rostropovich *vc* **Benjamin Britten** *pf*
Decca The Classic Sound 443 575-2DCS Ⓜ
(52 minutes: ADD). Recorded 1968 oo

The Maltings, Snape, July 1968: Britten was greeting two of his dearest musical friends and mentors; Rostropovich was making two important discoveries. This reissue is a major historic document, demonstrating the special nature of the musical relationship between composer, cellist and the music which they were performing. Rostropovich's is certainly the dominant voice at the start of the Frank Bridge Sonata, though both cello and piano go on to flex the work's Bergian muscles to the full in a recording which eavesdrops on every movement of the finger, every breath in the body. Schubert's *Arpeggione* Sonata was new to Rostropovich. In the broad, exploratory charting of its territory, Britten and Rostropovich enjoy many a moment of – if not drooling – then licking their lips over its more delectable turns of melody and harmonic contours. They make us stand and stare at much we might have missed: every time its opening melody recurs, it seems reinvented, and Britten's delight in peeping out when least expected from the 'cradle' Rostropovich said that he had created for him, throws many an idea into bright new relief. Britten as Lieder accompanist comes to the fore, of course, in the slow movement. Here Rostropovich does make a meal of it, and it will be something of a relief to most listeners, one suspects, to move into the clearer air of the finale. Even here, though, the bite as well as the bark of the *furiant* episodes is something else.

Bridge Cello Sonata. Four Short Pieces, H104 – Spring Song. Melodie, H99. Scherzo, H19*a*
Britten Cello Sonata, Op 65
Steven Doane *vc* **Barry Snyder** *pf* Ⓕ
Bridge BCD9056 (52 minutes: DDD). Recorded 1994

Bridge's two-movement Cello Sonata of 1917 is very English in its rich eloquence, although there is an affinity with Fauré, a composer with whom Bridge shared qualities of quietly glowing passion and unerring craftsmanship. The sonata's deeply emotional second movement is masterly, and this performance by the American duo of Steven Doane and Barry Snyder is warmly sympathetic and thoroughly enjoyable. The Bridge miniatures that accompany it are equally effective. Britten's Sonata, written for Rostropovich, is equally unconventional in having five movements, of which Nos 2, 4 and 5 each last less than three minutes but are none the less characterful and telling. This duo also responds keenly to the younger man's crisper invention and here is another strong yet sensitive performance. If you want these two sonatas together this attractive disc provides a safe recommendation. The recording favours the cello, but is otherwise faithful and pleasing.

Benjamin Britten British 1913-1976

GROVE *Britten studied with Frank Bridge as a boy and in 1930 entered the RCM. In 1934 he heard Wozzeck and planned to study with Berg, but opposition at home stopped him. The next year he began working for the GPO Film Unit, where one of his collaborators was Auden: together they worked on concert works as well, Auden's social criticism being matched by a sharply satirical and virtuoso musical style (orchestral song cycle Our Hunting Fathers, 1936). Stravinsky and Mahler were important influences, but Britten's effortless technique gave his early music a high personal definition, notably shown in orchestral works (Bridge Variations for strings, 1937; Piano Concerto, 1938; Violin Concerto, 1939) and songs (Les illuminations, setting Rimbaud for high voice and strings, 1939).*

In 1939 he left England for the USA, with his lifelong companion Peter Pears; there he wrote his first opera, to Auden's libretto (Paul Bunyan, 1941). In 1942 he returned and, partly stimulated by Purcell, began to concentrate on settings of English verse (anthem Rejoice in the Lamb and Serenade for tenor, horn and strings, both 1943). His String Quartet No 2 (1945), with its huge concluding chaconne, also came out of his Purcellian interests, but the major work of this period was Peter Grimes (1945), which signalled a new beginning in English opera. Its central character, the first of many roles written for Pears, struck a new operatic tone: a social outcast, he is fiercely proud and independent, but also deeply insecure, providing opportunities for a lyrical flow that would be free but is not. Britten's gift for characterization was also displayed in the wide range of sharply defined subsidiary roles and in the orchestra's sea music.

However, his next operas were all written for comparatively small resources (The Rape of Lucretia, 1946 ; Albert Herring, 1947; a version of The Beggar's Opera, 1948 ; The Little Sweep, 1949), for the company that became established as the English Opera Group. At the same time he began writing music for the Aldeburgh Festival, which he and Pears founded in 1948 in the Suffolk town where they had settled (cantata St Nicolas, 1948; Lachrymae for viola and piano, 1949). And in this prolific period he also composed large concert works (The Young Person's Guide to the Orchestra, 1946; Spring Symphony with soloists and choir, 1949) and songs.

The pattern of his output was thus set, though not the style, for the operas show an outward urge to ever new subjects: village comedy in Albert Herring, psychological conflict in Billy Budd (1951), historical reconstruction in Gloriana (1953), a tale of ghostly possession in The Turn of the Screw (1954), nocturnal magic in A Midsummer Night's Dream (1960), a struggle between family history and individual responsibility in Owen Wingrave (1971) and, most centrally, obsession with a doomed ideal in Death in Venice (1973), the last three works being intermediate in scale between the chamber format of Herring and The Screw, and the symphonic fullness of Budd and Gloriana, both written for Covent Garden. But nearly all touch in some way on the themes of the individual and society and the violation of innocence. Simultaneous with a widening range of subject matter was a widening musical style, which came to include 12-note elements (Turn of the Screw) and a heterophony that owed as much to oriental music directly as it did to Mahler (cycle of 'church parables', or ritualized small-scale operas: Curlew River, The Burning Fiery Furnace, The Prodigal Son, 1964-68).

Many of these dramatic works were written for the Aldeburgh Festival, as were many of the instrumental and vocal works Britten produced for favoured performers. For Rostropovich he wrote the Cello Symphony (1963) as well as a sonata and three solo suites; for Pears there was the Hardy cycle Winter Words (1953) among many other songs, and also a central part in the War Requiem (1961). His closing masterpiece, however, was a return to the abstract in the String Quartet No 3 (1975).

Britten was appointed a Companion of Honour in 1952, to the Order of Merit in 1965, and was awarded a life peerage in 1976.

Piano Concerto in D, Op 13

Piano Concerto. Violin Concerto, Op 15
Mark Lubotsky *vn* **Sviatoslav Richter** *pf*
English Chamber Orchestra / Benjamin Britten
Decca London 417 308-2LM (67 minutes: ADD). Ⓜ
Recorded 1970

Just after Britten's performances were released on LP in 1971, the composer admitted with some pride that Sviatoslav Richter had learned his Piano Concerto 'entirely off his own bat', and had revealed a Russianness that was in the score. Britten was attracted to Shostakovich during the late 1930s, when it was written, and the bravado, brittleness and flashy virtuosity of the writing, in the march-like finale most of all, at first caused many to be wary of it, even to think it somehow outside the composer's style. Now we know his music better, it is easier to accept, particularly in this sparkling yet sensitive performance. The Violin Concerto dates from the following year, 1939, and it, too, has its self-conscious virtuosity, but it is its rich nostalgic lyricism which strikes to the heart and the quiet elegiac ending is unforgettable. Compared to Richter in the other work, Mark Lubotsky is not always the master of its hair-raising difficulties, notably in the *Scherzo*, which has passages of double artificial harmonics that even Heifetz wanted simplified before he would play it (Britten refused), but this is still a lovely account. Fine recordings, made at The Maltings at Snape.

Piano Concerto. Soirées musicales, Op 9. Matinées musicales, Op 24
Ralf Gothóni *pf*
Helsingborg Symphony Orchestra / Okko Kamu
Ondine ODE825-2 (71 minutes: DDD). Ⓕ
Recorded 1994

A perceptive, at times daring, always thought-provoking account of Britten's Piano Concerto. Indeed, pungent characterization reigns, especially in the two middle movements. Here the 'Waltz' is teased out with sly seduction by Okko Kamu and his excellent Swedish group, yet at the same time the ominous undertones of this music have never been more unnervingly projected. Even more distinctive is Ralf Gothóni's provocatively expansive way with the opening of the 'Impromptu'. Britten's theme here emerges like some ravishingly intimate meditation, its quasi-improvisatory air compellingly conveyed. Yet such is the magnetic concentration of Gothóni's playing that the line never falters, and the rest of the movement is again memorably realized. We are also offered the concerto's original slow movement, a sharply inventive, capricious 'Recitative and Aria' (which Britten withdrew in 1945). No complaints about the fizz and bravura on show in the opening 'Toccata', nor about the finale, whose *largamente* climax struts forth in superbly grim fashion. Welcome contrast comes with the two Rossini-inspired suites, and Kamu does them both proud. The orchestral playing in Helsingborg has poise, affection and wealth of tender expression in the two most reflective numbers (the 'Canzonetta' from *Soirées* and 'Nocturne' from *Matinées*). Ondine's sound throughout is simply first-rate.

Young Apollo, Op 16

Young Apollo[a]. Double Concerto in B Minor[b]. Two Portraits[c]. Sinfonietta, Op 1[d]
[b]**Gidon Kremer** *vn* [bc]**Yuri Bashmet** *va* [a]**string quartet** (Lyn Fletcher, Dara De Cogan *vns* Tim Pooley *va* Peter Worrall *vc*) [a]**Nikolai Lugansky** *pf*
Hallé Orchestra / Kent Nagano
Erato 3984-25502-2 (59 minutes: DDD). Ⓕ
Recorded 1998 ⭘

This absorbing release contains three world-première recordings. Most striking is the Double Concerto, the short score of which the gifted 18-year-old completed by the early autumn of 1932. That same summer Britten also produced his 'official' Op 1, the dazzlingly inventive *Sinfonietta* for 10 instruments. The two works have plenty in common both formally and stylistically: notably at the outset of the *Sinfonietta*'s central *Andante lento* there's the soloistic nature of the two violins' expressive dialogue. The 'orchestral' version of the *Sinfonietta* heard here, dating from 1936, incorporates a full complement of strings as well as a second horn part.

Colin Matthews fashioned a performing edition of the Double Concerto from Britten's helpfully detailed sketches, the piece receiving its première at the 1987 Aldeburgh Festival. While not quite showing the effortless fluency and innovative thematic guile of the *Sinfonietta*, it remains an astonishing work for one so young, with numerous examples of sparky, head-turning inspiration. Likewise, the *Two Portraits* make intriguing listening. Composed in August 1930 (just a couple of months prior to his first term at the RCM), the first is a 'sketch for strings describing David' (David Layton, a close friend of the 16-year-old Britten at Gresham's School), whose emotional vehemence and harmonic restlessness nod towards Janáček and even Berg. There are tantalizing pre-echoes too of the 'Wiener Walzer' movement from the *Frank Bridge* Variations when the music switches into 3/4 time at 5'38". By contrast, its partner is a restrained self-portrait (subtitled 'E B B') for solo viola and strings, whose dignified main theme possesses an almost Holstian sobriety. Only the seven-minute 'fanfare' for piano and orchestra, *Young Apollo*, fails to improve much with repetition. Nagano directs a set of performances which are beyond praise in their luminous refinement and blistering commitment; all three distinguished soloists are on unimpeachable form. Erato's sound quality is sumptuously realistic to match.

Violin Concerto in D minor, Op 15

Violin Concerto[a]. Symphony for Cello and Orchestra, Op 68[b]

[a]**Rebecca Hirsch** *vn* [b]**Tim Hugh** *vc* **BBC Scottish Symphony Orchestra / Takuo Yuasa** Ⓢ

Naxos 8 553882 (68 minutes: DDD). Recorded 1997

Rebecca Hirsch follows up her invaluable coupling of the two Rawsthorne violin concertos for Naxos with this no less likeable account of Britten's superb essay in the form. Not only does she (for the most part) make light of the solo part's fiendish technical difficulties, her playing evinces a beguiling lyrical beauty that is breath-taking. By the side of both Ida Haendel and Lorraine McAslan, Hirsch perhaps lacks the last ounce of fiery temperament (and there are a handful of tiny misreadings that might prove irksome on repetition), but generally she is a convincing, characterful advocate. In the *Cello Symphony*, Tim Hugh displays a profound musicality, great subtlety of tone and affecting lyrical ardour that puts in mind Steven Isserlis's account with Richard Hickox, though not quite achieving the dark-hued individuality and unremitting logic of that distinguished 1987 production. Nor does it displace dedicatee Rostropovich's blisteringly intense, composer-directed versions of this gritty masterpiece, but Hugh's achievement is considerable and he more than holds his own alongside the formidable roster of current rivals.

Takuo Yuasa draws an eloquent response from the BBC Scottish SO. However, at the Violin Concerto's opening *Moderato con moto*, some leisurely tempos tend to undermine the purposeful thrust of the whole. Apart from one or two uncomfortably hard-edged tuttis, sound and balance are very good indeed.

Cello Symphony

Britten Cello Symphony **Walton** Cello Concerto

Julian Lloyd Webber *vc*

Academy of St Martin in the Fields / Sir Neville Marriner

Philips 454 442-2PH (71 minutes: DDD). Ⓕ

Recorded 1996 **oo**

This is an inspired coupling of two works, closely parallel in the careers of their composers, each reflecting the mastery of a great Russian cellist (respectively Rostropovich and Piatigorsky), but which could hardly be more sharply contrasted. Julian Lloyd Webber in an illuminating note makes that very point, and the passionate commitment of his playing in both works confirms his views. Not only is the power of each piece fully laid out, the beauty is presented as never before on disc, helped by sumptuous, beautifully balanced sound.

On any count this is the finest, most formidable disc that Julian Lloyd Webber has yet given us. In the Britten it almost goes without saying that, like his rivals on disc, Lloyd Webber cannot quite command the power and thrust of Rostropovich. That said, Lloyd Webber and Sir Neville Marriner, helped by the far greater dynamic range of the recording, not only convey the extraordinary originality of Britten's scoring in a way beyond any rival, but find an extra warmth. In the Walton, Lloyd Webber is individual and imaginative in his phrasing – he is outstanding in the deeply meditative statement of the theme in the variation finale – and the sumptuousness of the Philips sound makes this exceptionally warm, while the sparky complexity of the central *Scherzo* is thrillingly clear. This performance confirms this post-war work as vintage Walton, the equal of his pre-war concerto masterpieces for viola and violin. In both pieces Lloyd Webber makes light of the formidable technical difficulties. This project has involved him deeply, and he has been wonderfully well served by his collaborators.

Simple Symphony, Op 4

Prelude and Fugue, Op 29. Lachrymae, Op 48*a*. Elegy. Simple Symphony. Variations on a theme of Frank Bridge, Op 10

Lars Anders Tomter *va* **Norwegian Chamber Orchestra / Iona Brown**

Virgin Classics VC5 45121-2 (78 minutes: DDD). Ⓕ

Recorded 1988-91

The *Frank Bridge* Variations are finely disciplined, strongly characterized and benefit from sumptuous engineering. The hushed intensity achieved in such variations as the 'Adagio' and 'Chant' recalls Britten's own remarkable interpretation – and there can be no higher praise than that! In the *Simple Symphony* the infectious 'Playful Pizzicato' could perhaps have been given with a greater sense of fun; elsewhere, though, there can be no complaints about the outer movements (both wonderfully crisp and vital), whilst the lovely 'Sentimental Sarabande' has surely seldom enjoyed such tenderly expressive advocacy. The *Prelude and Fugue* is brought off with exhilarating poise and panache, and it is difficult to imagine a more eloquent contribution than that of violist Lars Anders Tomter in the early solo *Elegy* and haunting, Dowland-inspired *Lachrymae*. Consistently superior sound, Michael Oliver's admirable booklet-notes and an uncommonly generous playing time add to the considerable attractions of this release.

Sinfonia da Requiem, Op 20

Cello Symphony, Op 68[a]. Sinfonia da Requiem[b]. Cantata misericordium, Op 69[c]
Mstislav Rostropovich *vc* **Sir Peter Pears** *ten* **Dietrich Fischer-Dieskau** *bar*
[a]**English Chamber Orchestra,** [b]**New Philharmonia Orchestra,** [c]**London Symphony Chorus** and **Orchestra / Benjamin Britten**
Decca London 425 100-2LM (75 minutes: ADD). Ⓜ
Text and translation included. Recorded 1964 ●●

This disc offers two of Britten's finest works, the *Cello Symphony* and the *Sinfonia da Requiem*. The latter was written in 1940 and is one of the composer's most powerful orchestral works, harnessing opposing forces in a frighteningly intense way. From the opening drumbeat the *Sinfonia* employs a sonata form with dramatic power, although the tone is never fierce or savage; it has an implacable tread and momentum. The central movement, 'Dies irae', however, has a real sense of fury, satirical in its biting comment – the flutter-tongued wind writing rattling its defiance. The closing 'Requiem aeternam' is a movement of restrained beauty. On this recording from 1964 the New Philharmonia play superbly.

The Cello Symphony, written in 1963 as part of a series for the great Russian cellist Mstislav Rostropovich, was the first major sonata-form work written since the *Sinfonia*. The idea of a struggle between soloist and orchestra, implicit in the traditional concerto, has no part here; it is a conversation between the two. Rostropovich plays with a depth of feeling that has never quite been equalled in other recordings and the playing of the English Chamber Orchestra has great bite. The recording too is extraordinarily fine for its years. The *Cantata misericordium* was written in 1962 as a commission from the Red Cross. It takes the story of the Good Samaritan and is scored for tenor and baritone soloists, chorus, string quartet and orchestra. It is a universal plea for charity and in this performance receives a powerful reading. This release is a must for any Britten enthusiast.

The Young Person's Guide ..., Op 34

The Young Person's Guide to the Orchestra. Simple Symphony, Op 4a. A Spring Symphony, Op 44 – Spring, the sweet spring. Noyes Fluddeb – Noye, Noye, take thou thy company ... Sir! heare are lions. Serenade for Tenor, Horn and Strings, Op 31 – Nocturne. Folk Songs – The Plough Boy; Early One Morning. Billy Budd – Interlude and Sea Shanties. A Ceremony of Carols, Op 28 – Adam lay i-bounden. A Hymn to the Virgin. War Requiem – Lacrimosa. Peter Grimes – Interlude (Dawn)
Sir Peter Pears *ten* **Barry Tuckwell** *hn* **various soloists; choirs, choruses and orchestras, London Symphony Orchestra**, ab**English Chamber Orchestra / Benjamin Britten** *pf*
b**Norman Del Mar**
Decca 436 990-2DWO (74 minutes: ADD). Ⓜ
Recorded 1963-68

This reissue includes the composer's own 1963 recording of *The Young Person's Guide to the Orchestra* with the LSO and his complete 1968 ECO version of the *Simple Symphony*. The latter is delightfully fresh and is unforgettable for the joyful bounce of the 'Playful Pizzicato', helped by the resonant acoustic of The Maltings, Snape. In *The Young Person's Guide*, without the now somewhat rather dated text, he adopts quick, demanding tempos, with more spacious ones for the more introspective sections. This is beautiful playing, possessing wit and brilliance, with all kinds of memorable touches. Even if this transfer is a little dry in sonority, this disc is invaluable for these two performances alone. As a bonus we are also offered 10 short excerpts from other major Britten works.

String Quartets

String Quartets – No 2 in C, Op 36; D (1931); F (1928)
Sorrel Quartet (Gina McCormack, Catherine Yates *vns* Vicci Wardman *va* Helen Thatcher *vc*)
Chandos CHAN9664 (74 minutes: DDD). Ⓕ
Recorded 1998 ●

The Sorrel Quartet can claim a significant 'first' in its account of the recently resurrected F major Quartet from 1928. At 15, Britten was nothing if not precocious, and although the ideas in this substantial piece offer few hints of his mature style, he was already using the medium to excellent effect. Three years later, in the D major Quartet which has been a repertory item since Britten revised it in 1974, there are signs of a more individual voice; this is an attractive performance, well shaped and effectively characterized. Nevertheless, it is on the interpretation of the Quartet No 2 that the disc must be judged. The Sorrel's naturalness and feeling for line are much in evidence. Tempos for the first movement are broader than most rivals, but they serve an approach which makes a virtue of reticence, and still manages to be quite gripping. It has just about the best sound currently available (with The Maltings, Snape, providing an ideal acoustic), and the otherwise unrecorded F major Quartet adds strength to the recommendation of this noteworthy disc.

String Quartet No 3, Op 94. Alla marcia. Quartettino. Simple Symphony, Op 4
Maggini Quartet (Laurence Jackson, David Angel *vns* Martin Outram *va* Michal Kaznowski *vc*)
Naxos 8 554360 (65 minutes: DDD). Ⓢ
Recorded 1997

This second volume of the Maggini Quartet's Britten series amply fulfils the promise of the first. As before, the recording, made in St Martin's Church, East Woodhay (near Newbury) favours blend and immediacy: the leading full-price alternative, recorded at Snape by the Sorrel Quartet for Chandos, has a richer atmosphere and a stronger sense of space, but, as interpretations, the Maggini's versions need fear nothing from the current competition. The major work here is the late Third Quartet, a score whose extreme contrasts of mood and texture, ranging from rapt serenity to explosive bitterness, are the more difficult to make convincing for the extraordinary economy of means which the ailing Britten summoned. The Maggini are hard to beat in the conviction they bring to all aspects of what is a notably well-focused, technically polished account. Their choice of basic tempos for the tricky outer movements is ideal, and they relish the elements of parody elsewhere without descending into caricature. This disc also provides the only currently available version of the early but radical *Quartettino*, and the quartet version of the *Simple Symphony*.

Solo Cello Suites

No 1, Op 72; **No 2**, Op 80; **No 3**, Op 87

Solo Cello Suites Nos 1 and 2. Cello Sonata, Op 65
Mstislav Rostropovich *vc* **Benjamin Britten** *pf*
Decca London 421 859-2LM (68 minutes: ADD). Ⓜ
Recorded 1961-69 ●●●

This is a classic recording of the Cello Sonata, with Rostropovich and the composer playing with an authority impossible to surpass, and is here coupled with the unaccompanied First and Second Cello Suites. The suggestive, often biting humour, masks darker feelings. However, Britten manages, just, to keep his devil under control. Rostropovich's and Britten's characterization in the opening *Dialogo* is stunning and their subdued humour in the *Scherzo-pizzicato* also works well. In the *Elegia* and the final *Moto perpetuo*, again, no one quite approaches the passion and energy of Rostropovich. This work, like the two Suites, was written for him and he still remains the real heavyweight in all three pieces. Their transfer to CD is remarkably successful; it is difficult to believe that these recordings were made in the 1960s.

Solo Cello Suites Nos 1-3
Jean-Guihen Queyras *vc*
Harmonia Mundi Les Nouveaux Interprètes HMN91 Ⓑ
1670 (65 minutes: DDD). Recorded 1998 ●

Britten's three Cello Suites have all the strength of musical character to sustain a permanent place in the repertory. Inspired by the personality, and technique, of Mstislav Rostropovich, they are remarkable for the way in which they acknowledge yet at the same time distance themselves from the great precedent of Bach's Cello Suites. The best performers (like Rostropovich himself, though he has never recorded No 3) are equally at ease with the music's Bach-like contrapuntal ingenuity and its lyric intensity, where Britten's own most personal voice is heard. Queyras has such a fine sense of phrase that his slower speeds do not sound unconvincing, and his playing – technically superb – has an impressive consistency of style. The quality of the recording is another plus, with the close focus needed to ensure that all the details tell, and the occasional tap of the bow and other non-musical noise an acceptable intrusion. The only disappointment came in the final track, with the Russian Prayer for the Dead that ends Suite No 3. Here, of all places, Queyras is simply too fast. Nevertheless, this lapse is not so great as to deprive the disc of a place in this guide.

A Spring Symphony, Op 44

A Spring Symphony[a]. Cantata Academica, Op 62[b]. Ⓗ
Hymn to St Cecilia, Op 27[c]
Jennifer Vyvyan *sop* **Norma Procter, Helen Watts** *contrs* **Sir Peter Pears** *ten* **Owen Brannigan** *bass* **[a]Emanuel School Boys' Choir; [a]Chorus and Orchestra of the Royal Opera House, Covent Garden / Benjamin Britten; London Symphony [bc]Chorus** and **[c]Orchestra / George Malcolm**
Decca London 436 396-2LM (74 minutes: ADD). Ⓜ
Texts and translation included. Recorded 1960-61 ●●

Britten's performance of the *Spring Symphony* fairly leaps out of one's loudspeakers, and the 1960 sound is as crisp and alive as the performance and the work itself. In the last two pieces George Malcolm's direction is as vivid as Britten's elsewhere. The *Cantata Academica* (1959) is one of Britten's happiest pieces, bubbling over with warmth, jollity and good fellowship. Indeed the Latin title is only one of mock-solemnity. Try 'Tema seriale con fuga' to hear how this composer could make living music out of the most perniciously academic device of our troubled century. Further high points are Owen Brannigan's marvellously pompous bass aria and the boisterous 'Canone ed ostinato'. The performance of the *Hymn to St Cecilia* is skilful, idiomatic and touching.

A Spring Symphony[a]. Hymn to St Cecilia.
Five Flower Songs, Op 47
Alison Hagley *sop* **Catherine Robbin** *mez* **John Mark Ainsley** *ten* **[a]Choristers of Salisbury Cathedral; Monteverdi Choir; [a]Philharmonia Orchestra / Sir John Eliot Gardiner**
DG 453 433-2GH (62 minutes: DDD). Ⓕ
Texts included ●

John Eliot Gardiner directs a memorable and thoroughly invigorating account of Britten's vernal paean. From the start, one registers the exceptional refinement and transparency of his approach, to say nothing of the exciting realism of DG's sound. No praise can be too high for the marvellously nimble and extremely well-focused contribution of the Monteverdi Choir or the Philharmonia's superbly disciplined response throughout. The Choristers of Salisbury Cathedral also emerge with great credit. High-spots abound: the smiling, easy sway of 'Spring, the sweet Spring' (whose bird-call cadenzas are delightfully attended to); an exceptionally perceptive 'Waters above', whose truly *pppp diminuendo* conclusion leads magically into 'Out on the lawn I lie in bed'; the terrific bounce and clean-limbed swagger of the triptych comprising Part 3 (both 'Fair and fair' and 'Sound the flute' come close to perfection); and, of course, the joyous, bank holiday clangour of the finale (splendidly dapper and affirmative on this occasion), with its heart-stopping appearance of 'Sumer is icumen in' – a moment which never fails to send shivers down the spine (though the four horns might perhaps have cut through the orchestral fabric just a touch more than they do here?). Gardiner's soloists are very good, if perhaps not quite a match for the finest. Ainsley stands out for his honeyed tone, and the intelligence of his word-painting always catches the attention, as does the warmth and projection of Alison Hagley's soprano Overall, then, while not displacing the composer's classic recording, Gardiner's version can hold its own against all-comers and should give much pleasure to seasoned Brittenites. Both *a cappella* fill-ups are also a treat: an exquisitely poised and supremely touching *Hymn to St Cecilia*, followed by the delicious *Five Flower Songs*.

Hymn to St Cecilia, Op 27

Rejoice in the Lamb, Op 30. Te Deum in C. Jubilate Deo in C. Antiphon, Op 56*b*. A Hymn to the Virgin. Festival Te Deum, Op 32. Missa brevis in D, Op 63. Hymn to St Peter, Op 56*a*. A Hymn of St Columba. Prelude and Fugue on a Theme of Vittoria. Hymn to St Cecilia
St John's College Choir, Cambridge / Christopher Robinson with **Ian Farrington** *org* Ⓢ
Naxos 8 554791 (74 minutes: DDD)

As with other recent records from St John's, there is a freshness, almost a feeling of adventure and a sense that all this choral discipline (plentifully in evidence) is an easy yoke. These are excellent performances, the opening item setting a standard which is to be maintained throughout. Buoyant rhythms, precise accentuations and well-pointed contrasts are features of the singing; and the playing of Ian Farrington in accompaniments that are often difficult and always demanding of maximum alertness, is outstanding. Outstanding, too, is the contribution of the trebles. In tone they preserve the traditional John's sound, without exaggerating its so-called continental element. But what impresses most is the sense of imaginative involvement. It is there, for instance, in the *Kyrie* of the *Missa brevis*, and most of all in the 'I cannot grow' section of *A Hymn to St Cecilia*. To this they bring a distinctive excitement, a wide-eyed, breathlessly playful feeling of childlike wonder. The programme itself is highly attractive. The 'hymns' are fully developed compositions, and the canticles are notably independent of tradition (for instance, a quietly meditative note of praise is struck at the start of both Te Deums). The *Missa brevis* makes inventive use of its forces; and *Rejoice in the Lamb*, a masterly expression of the liberal spirit, never ceases to amaze with its evocation of the cat Jeoffry, valiant mouse and staff-struck poet. Also interesting is Britten's single published solo for organ, the *Prelude and Fugue on a theme of Vittoria* – more striking in the prelude, more fascinating in the fugue. Recorded sound is not as vivid as the performances, but this remains a very likeable disc.

AMDG

AMDG. Choral Dances from 'Gloriana'. Chorale after an Old French Carol. Five Flower Songs, Op 47. A Hymn to the Virgin. Sacred and Profane, Op 91
Polyphony / Stephen Layton
Hyperion CDA67140 (62 minutes: DDD). Ⓕ
Recorded 1999-2000 **OO**

The programme is delightful and the choir excellent. If bought 'on spec', without deliberations over rival recordings, pauses for comparisons or calculations concerned with the possibility of duplicating this item or that, the disc could surely not fail to please.

AMDG presents as formidable a challenge to its singers as any of Britten's compositions for unaccompanied choir. In fact that is sometimes suggested as the reason why, having written it for an expert group in 1939 and realising that its chances of frequent performance were slim, Britten never prepared the work for publication. It's a pity he couldn't have heard Stephen Layton's Polyphony! Even more than the Finzi Singers, their predecessors on record, they have worked it into the system so that they have the sense of it clearly in their mind and can make the word-setting fresh and spontaneous. 'God's Grandeur' (*allegro con fuoco*) has the fire: the Finzis seem almost cautious by comparison. In 'The Soldier' Polyphony catch the swing of the triplets and dotted notes with more panache and make more of the words. Then, taking a slightly slower tempo than the Finzis, they bring out the tender lyricism (sopranos and tenors in octaves) in 'Prayer II' and grasp more decisively the *con moto*, *Vivace* and *Avanti!* markings in 'O Deus, ego amo te'.

In the *Five Flower Songs* Polyphony have a slight advantage (these distinctions are all 'slight' in the normal degrees of comparison because all of the performances are of a remarkably high standard) over The Sixteen (Collins – nla) in that theirs is a rather younger tone and their numbers (or maybe the record sound) allow them to convey more sense of round-the-table intimacy. In the *Choral Dances from 'Gloriana'*, The Sixteen may well be found preferable on account of the version they use, involving solo tenor and harp. With the straightforward choral version Polyphony improve on the Finzi Singers' performance with crisper rhythms and a clearer acoustic. The ethereal and rarely heard *Chorale after an old French Carol* has, in comparison with the only other available recorded version, under Hickox, a greater share of heavenly light (and lightness); and *Sacred and Profane*, like *AMDG* a work for virtuosos, is given with wonderful confidence and imagination.

Additional recommendation
AMDG
Couplings: Hymns – to St Peter, Op 56a; of St Columba;

to the Virgin; to St Cecilia, Op 27. Rejoice in the Lamb, Op 30. Choral Dances from 'Gloriana'
Finzi Singers / Spicer with **Lumsden** *org*
Chandos CHAN9511 (67 minutes: DDD: 4/97). Ⓕ
Texts included

Very enjoyable performances from this expert choir, successfully directed by Paul Spicer. Andrew Lumsden's ear-catching contributions might make up your mind.

Songs

Harmonia Sacra – Lord! I have sinned; Hymn to God the Father; A Hymn on Divine Musick. This way to the Tomb – Evening; Morning; Night. Night covers up the rigid land. Fish in the unruffled lakes. To lie flat on the back with the knees flexed. A poison tree. When you're feeling like expressing your affection. Not even summer yet. The red cockatoo. Wild with passion. If thou wilt ease thine heart. Cradle song for Eleanor. Birthday song for Erwin. Um Mitternacht. The Holy Sonnets of John Donne, Op 35
Ian Bostridge *ten* **Graham Johnson** *pf*
Hyperion CDA66823 (65 minutes: DDD). Texts included. Recorded 1995 Ⓕ

Bostridge is in the royal line of Britten's tenor interpreters. Indeed his imaginative response to words and music may come closer than any to Pears himself. He is heard here in a veritable cornucopia of by and large unfamiliar and even unknown songs (the Donne cycle apart), mostly from the earliest period of Britten's song-writing career when his inspiration was perhaps at its most free and spontaneous. The three settings from Ronald Duncan's *This way to the Tomb* nicely match that poet's florid, vocabulary-rich style as Britten was to do again two years later in *Lucretia*, with 'Night', based on a B minor ground bass, a particularly arresting piece. The Auden settings, roughly contemporaneous with *On this Island*, all reflect Britten's empathy with the poet at that time. The third, *To lie flat on the back*, evinces Britten's gift for writing in racy mode, as does *When you're feeling like expressing your affection*, very much in the style of *Cabaret Songs*. Much deeper emotions are stirred by the two superb Beddoes settings (*Wild with passion* and *If thou wilt ease thine heart*), written when the composer and Pears were on a ship returning home in 1942. *The red cockatoo* itself is an early setting of Waley to whom Britten returned in *Songs from the Chinese*.

All these revelatory songs are performed with full understanding and innate beauty by Bostridge and Johnson, who obviously have a close artistic rapport. They form a lengthy and rewarding prelude to their shattering account of the Donne Sonnets. They are as demanding on singer and pianist as anything Britten wrote, hence their previously small representation in the catalogue. Both artists pierce to the core of these electrifying songs, written after, and affected by, Britten's visit to Belsen with Menuhin in 1945 shortly after the war's end. The recording which catches the immediacy of these riveting performances complete one's pleasure in this richly satisfying issue.

Britten Four Cabaret Songs. When you're feeling like expressing your affection. On this Island – As it is, plenty. Blues (arr Runswick) – The Spider and the Fly; Blues; The clock on the wall; Boogie-Woogie
Porter Paris – Let's do it. Gay Divorce – Night and Day. Leave it to Me – My heart belongs to daddy. Miss Otis Regrets. Nymph Errant – The Physician
Jill Gomez *sop* **Martin Jones** *pf* **instrumental ensemble** (David Roach *cl/sax* Graham Ashton *tpt* Beverley Davison *vn* Chris Lawrence *db* John Constable *pf* Gregory Knowles *perc*)
Unicorn-Kanchana DKPCD9138 (52 minutes: DDD). Ⓕ
Texts included. Recorded 1992

Britten's cabaret songs were written for the singing actress Hedli Anderson; there were more than four, but these are the only ones published so far. The texts by Auden are full of the spirit that William Coldstream described, writing of one of Anderson's performances, 'teaching of carefree lucidity and the non-avoidance of banality'. *When you're feeling like expressing your affection* which is published and performed here for the first time is one of the results of Auden and Britten's work for the GPO in the 1930s. Apart from references to 'any telephone kiosk' and 'Press button A' it would still serve well as an encouragement to make use of the telephone. 'As it is, plenty' from *On this Island*, being also in the ironic popular-music style, rounds off the group nicely. Jill Gomez's performances are perfect in every nuance, her beautiful tone, clear diction and just hinted-at irony, never overdoing it, give the songs the exact weight they need. The Cole Porter encores and Daryl Runswick's arrangements of four *Blues* by Britten complete what is, without doubt, a quite delicious record.

Serenade, Op 31

Serenade[a]. Les illuminations[b]. Nocturne, Op 60[c] **H**
Sir Peter Pears *ten* **Alexander Murray** *fl* **Roger Lord** *cor ang* **Gervase de Peyer** *cl* **William Waterhouse** *bn* **Barry Tuckwell** *hn* **Dennis Blyth** *timp* **Osian Ellis** *hp* acstrings of the **London Symphony Orchestra;** [b]**English Chamber Orchestra /** [abc]**Benjamin Britten**
Decca London 436 395-2LM (73 minutes: ADD). Ⓜ
Texts included. Recorded 1959-66 **OO**

No other instrument was more important to Britten than the human voice and, inspired by the musicianship and superb vocal craftsmanship of his closest friend, Peter Pears, he produced an unbroken stream of vocal works of a quality akin to those of Purcell. Three of his most haunting vocal pieces are featured on this wonderful CD. The performances date from between 1959 and 1966 with Pears in penetratingly musical form, even if the voice itself was by now a little thin and occasionally unsteady. The ECO and LSO are superb in every way. The recordings are vintage Decca and excellent for their time. This welcome mid-price reissue is strongly recommended.

Serenade[a]. Our Hunting Fathers, Op 8. Folk-song arrangements – Oliver Cromwell; O waly waly
Ian Bostridge *ten* [a]**Marie Luise Neunecker** *hn*
Britten Sinfonia / Daniel Harding; [a]Bamberg Symphony Orchestra / Ingo Metzmacher
EMI CDC5 56871-2 (58 minutes: DDD). Texts and translations included. Recorded 1996-97 Ⓕ

On each hearing, Britten's *Serenade* still has the power to astonish anew for its amazingly apt setting of the diligently chosen poems and for the deftly woven, dazzling horn part written for Dennis Brain. There is something inevitable and predestined about these pieces, as though they existed for all time, an impression enhanced by this performance. Bostridge is spontaneous and immediate in his responses to text and music. One small reservation concerns a weakness in the lower register in the Keats Sonnet, 'Oh soft embalmer of the still night'. In the horn contribution, Neunecker is as lithe and full-toned as any that has gone before. Metzmacher follows tradition in tempo matters and his players are alive to every nuance of the diaphanous scoring. This compilation also offers an interesting conspectus of the composer when young and culminates in the early, quirky masterpiece, *Our Hunting Fathers*, written in 1936 under the influence of Auden and echoes of terrible events in Germany. Ian Bostridge's well-known affinity with the composer's music and his virtue of verbal illumination are amply demonstrated here. The folk-song settings receive pertinent readings, the first plangent, the second skittish, as is appropriate to their texts.

Sonnets of John Donne, Op 35

Seven Sonnets of Michelangelo, Op 22. The Holy Sonnets of John Donne. Winter Words, Op 52
Justin Lavender *ten* **Julian Milford** *pf*
Carlton Classics 30366 0056-2 (66 minutes: DDD). Texts and translations included. Ⓜ
Recorded 1996

The highlight of this recording is the *Donne* Sonnets, where Lavender has the advantage, over other Britten tenor interpreters to date, of an Italianate metal in his tone, just what these dramatic, even heroic settings call for. He also has the range and technique to make them sound less intractable, vocally speaking, than they often seem, which is not to imply that he is unable to fine away his tone to a silvery line as required by that great Schubert-like song, 'Since she whom I lov'd'. Together with Milford's eager response to the stringent challenge to his technical resources, this is a convincing reading.

That Italianate sound also serves Lavender well in the more extrovert *Michelangelo* Sonnets. These are sung with a fine feeling for line and verbal colouring. In *Winter Words*, intelligently as he enters into the quirky, intense world of this wonderful cycle, he doesn't quite match Philip Langridge on Collins (currently unavailable) in tonal management or verbal acuity, but the difference is slight and, with Milford again a resourceful and vital partner, this is an interpretation to cherish. The recording ambience sometimes lends a slight edge to the singer's tone, but as a whole this issue is recommendable on every count.

Phaedra, Op 93

Phaedra. Lachrymae, Op 48*a*. Sinfonietta, Op 1. The Sword in the Stone. Movement for Wind Sextet. Night Mail – End sequence
Jean Rigby *mez* **Nigel Hawthorne** *narr* **Roger Chase** *va* **Nash Ensemble / Lionel Friend**
Hyperion CDA66845 (65 minutes: DDD). Ⓕ
Text included. Recorded 1995

A chronologically wide-ranging Britten programme performed with unerring sensitivity and much quiet insight. The *Movement* for wind sextet (here receiving its première recording) dates from 1930. Britten composed it during his last term at Gresham's School and annotator Philip Reed suggests that a hearing of Janáček's identically scored *Mládí* may have acted as a spur. The *Sinfonietta*, which Britten completed two years later while still a student at the Royal College of Music, represents a remarkable achievement for one so young. Amazingly inventive and concise, it bears a dedication to his mentor, Frank Bridge, whose tangily pastoral idiom can be discerned in the rapt central *Andante*. The Nash Ensemble's account could hardly be bettered: in this same movement, for example, how perceptively Friend and his colleagues gauge (and sustain) the mood of gentle rapture, and how effortlessly they handle the almost Sibelian transition into the 'Tarantella' finale. Britten's and Auden's unforgettable collaboration for the end sequence from the documentary *Night Mail* dates from 1936 when both artists were briefly employed by the GPO Film Unit. Remarkably, this is its first commercial recording – and a marvellous one it is, too, with Nigel Hawthorne the exemplary reciter. Three years later, Britten was approached by the BBC to write the incidental music for an adaptation of T H White's *The Sword in the Stone*. Scored for a small ensemble, the suite abounds in witty motivic borrowings from Wagner's *Ring*. The disc opens with a persuasive rendering of *Phaedra* from Jean Rigby. Eloquently though she responds, her contribution is perhaps not quite as characterful or involving as that of, say, Dame Janet Baker (the work's dedicatee) or Felicity Palmer. The sound and balance are first-rate. An excellent anthology.

An American Overture, Op 27

An American Overture. King Arthur – Suite (arr Hindmarsh). The World of the Spirit (arr Hindmarsh)
Susan Chilcott *sop* **Pamela Helen Stephen** *mez* **Martyn Hill** *ten* **Stephen Varcoe** *bar* **Hannah Gordon, Cormac Rigby** *spkrs*
Britten Singers; BBC Philharmonic Orchestra / Richard Hickox
Chandos CHAN9487 (79 minutes: DDD). Ⓕ
Text included. Recorded 1995-96

The performance of the Coplandesque *An American Overture* by Hickox and the excellent BBC Philharmonic has exemplary polish, commitment and dash. The remaining items owe their revival to the efforts of Paul Hindmarsh. Britten wrote his incidental music for a BBC radio dramatization of the King Arthur legend in 1937. It was the first of his 28 radio commissions and contains much high-quality invention. Hindmarsh has fashioned the 23-year-old composer's inventive inspiration into a terrific four-movement orchestral suite lasting some 25 minutes, which Hickox and the BBC PO duly devour with audible relish.

The 'radio cantata' *The World of the Spirit* dates from May 1938. Commissioned by the BBC as a successor to *The Company of Heaven* (1937), it intersperses sung and spoken texts chosen by R Ellis Roberts. Again, Britten's fertile compositional powers are much in evidence. The work contains a whole string of memorable numbers, from the lilting barcarolle-like treatment of Emily Brontë's 'With wide-embracing love', via the joyful strut and swagger of Part 2's concluding 'The Spirit of the Lord' with its unmistakable echoes of Walton's *Belshazzar's Feast*, to a strikingly imaginative setting of Gerard Manley Hopkins's *God's Grandeur*, a poem which also features in Britten's unaccompanied choral suite of a year later entitled *A M D G*. Framing the 42-minute edifice are two radiant settings of the Whitsuntide plainsong, *Veni Creator Spiritus* – an idea possibly inspired by a recent encounter with Mahler's Eighth Symphony at the Queen's Hall in a performance given under Sir Henry Wood. The recording is superbly wide in its range and offers a realistic quality.

A Ceremony of Carols, Op 28

A Ceremony of Carols. Missa brevis in D, Op 63. A Hymn to the Virgin. A Hymn of St Columba, 'Regis regum rectissimi'. Jubilate Deo in E flat. Deus in adjutorum meum

Sioned Williams *hp* **Westminster Cathedral Choir / David Hill** with **James O'Donnell** *org* Hyperion CDA66220 (49 minutes: DDD). Texts included. Ⓕ
Recorded 1986 ●

A Ceremony of Carols sets nine medieval and 16th-century poems between the 'Hodie' of the plainsong Vespers. The sole accompanying instrument is a harp, but given the right acoustic, sensitive attention to the words and fine rhythmic control the piece has a remarkable richness and depth. The Westminster Cathedral Choir performs this work beautifully; diction is immaculate and the acoustic halo surrounding the voices gives a festive glow to the performance. A fascinating *Jubilate* and *A Hymn to the Virgin*, whilst lacking the invention and subtlety of *A Ceremony*, intrigue with some particularly felicitous use of harmony and rhythm. *Deus in adjutorum meum* employs the choir without accompaniment and has an initial purity that gradually builds up in texture as the psalm (No 70) gathers momentum. The *Missa brevis* was written for this very choir and George Malcolm's nurturing of a tonal brightness in the choir allowed Britten to use the voices in a more flexible and instrumental manner than usual. The effect is glorious. St Columba founded the monastery on the Scottish island of Iona and Britten's hymn sets his simple and forthright prayer with deceptive simplicity and directness. The choir sings beautifully and the recording is first-rate.

War Requiem, Op 66

War Requiem[a]. Sinfonia da Requiem, Op 20. Ballad of Heroes, Op 14[b]

Heather Harper *sop* **[a]Philip Langridge, [b]Martyn Hill** *tens* **John Shirley-Quirk** *bar* **[a]St Paul's Cathedral Choir; London Symphony Chorus and Orchestra / Richard Hickox**

Chandos ② CHAN8983/4 (125 minutes: DDD) Ⓕ
Texts and translations included ●●●

Britten's *War Requiem* is the composer's most public statement of his pacifism. The work is cast in six movements and calls for massive forces: full chorus, soprano soloist and full orchestra evoke mourning, supplication and guilty apprehension; boys' voices with chamber organ, the passive calm of a liturgy which points beyond death; tenor and baritone soloists with chamber orchestra, the passionate outcry of the doomed victims of war. The most recent challenger to the composer's classic Decca version offers up-to-date recording, excellently managed to suggest the various perspectives of the vast work, and possibly the most convincing execution of the choral writing to date under the direction of a conductor, Richard Hickox, who is a past master at obtaining the best from a choir in terms of dynamic contrast and vocal emphasis. Add to that his empathy with all that the work has to say and you have a cogent reason for acquiring this version even before you come to the excellent work of the soloists. In her recording swan-song, Harper at last commits to disc a part she created. It is right that her special accents and impeccable shaping of the soprano's contribution have been preserved for posterity.

Shirley-Quirk, always closely associated with the piece, sings the three baritone solos and duets with rugged strength and dedicated intensity. He is matched by Langridge's compelling and insightful reading, with his notes and words more dramatic than Pears's approach. The inclusion of two additional pieces, neither of them short, helps to give this version an added advantage even if the *Ballad of Heroes* is one of Britten's slighter works.

War Requiem, Op 66

Stefania Woytowicz *sop* **Sir Peter Pears** *ten* **Hans Wilbrink** *bar* **Wandsworth School Boys' Choir; Melos Ensemble; New Philharmonia Orchestra and Chorus / Carlo Maria Giulini**

BBC Legends/IMG Artists BBCL4046-2 (79 minutes: Ⓜ
ADD). Texts included. Recorded live in 1969 ●●●

This performance is a revelation. Philip Reed, in his authoritative note, points out that, unbeknown to many, Britten and Giulini had a mutual respect for and an admiration of each other's work. Here they combine to give a performance that is a true Legend, as this BBC series has it. Giulini's reading is as dramatic and viscerally exciting as any rival version. The music leaps from the page new-minted in his thoroughgoing, histrionically taut hands, the rhythmic tension at times quite astonishing. For instance, the sixth movement, 'Libera me', is simply earth-shattering in its effect, every bar, every word, every instrument sung and played to the hilt – and so it is throughout, with the live occasion added to the peculiar, and in this case peculiarly right, acoustics of the Albert Hall adding its own measure of *verité* to the inspired occasion.

The performance of the New Philharmonia forces, under the man who was at the time their favourite conductor after Klemperer, is at once technically assured and wholly dedicated. Only perhaps the classic Decca recording comes near equalling it in this respect, and that doesn't quite have the electrifying atmosphere, what Reed calls 'the remarkable spirit embodied in this exceptionally interesting and moving performance', found on this astonishing occasion. Nor have the Wandsworth Boys' Choir, placed up in the Hall's gallery, been surpassed.

The soloists also seem to realise the special quality of the occasion. Pears surpasses even his own creator's reading on the Decca set, singing with the sustained concentration and vocal acuity that were so much his hallmarks in Britten's music. The Polish soprano Stefania Woytowicz, who at the time made something of a speciality of this work, has very much the vocal timbre of Vishnevskaya, for whom the part was written, and perhaps a shade more sensitivity. She is certainly the best soprano on any version, and Wilbrink, a notable Pelléas around this period at Glyndebourne, comes near being the best baritone. He may not be quite as varied or subtle as Decca's Fischer-Dieskau, nor as confident as Chandos's Shirley-Quirk, but he has a more beautiful voice than either, with a plangency in his tone that is so right for this music, and his carefully wrought enunciation of the words, the unidiomatic English not inappropriate, is eloquent at all times, but nowhere more so than at 'I would go up and wash them from sweet wells' in the final movement.

Most of all it is the sum of the parts that so impresses with this release, as does the truthfulness of the sound, preferable to the wide range but sometimes artificial reverberation of the Chandos set. Then the – single – disc comes at mid-price to complete one's satisfaction in its exhumation from the archives.

War Requiem

Galina Vishnevskaya *sop* **Sir Peter Pears** *ten*
Dietrich Fischer-Dieskau *bar*
Simon Preston *org* **Bach Choir; Highgate School Choir; Melos Ensemble; London Symphony Orchestra / Benjamin Britten**
Decca ② 414 383-2DH2 (132 minutes: DDD). Texts and translations included. Includes previously unreleased rehearsal sequence. Recorded 1963 Ⓕ **OO**

Decca has used the most recent digital and Cedar technology to improve the original sound, under the overall supervision of veteran technician James Lock. This is one of the great performances of recording history. As an imaginative bonus, Decca – with the approval of the Britten estate – gives us the first issue of a long rehearsal tape. This was made by the producer John Culshaw without Britten's approval. When Culshaw presented it to the composer on his 50th birthday, Britten was 'appalled', considering it 'an unauthorised invasion of a territory exclusively his own and his performers', as Donald Mitchell relates in the booklet. Now Mitchell believes that we should be allowed 'to assess the tape as a contribution to our knowledge of him [Britten] as a performer and interpreter of his own music and to our understanding of the *War Requiem* itself.'

Throughout this fascinating aural document you hear evidence of Britten's vision of his own music, his astonishing ear for timbre and intimate details, above all his wonderful encouragement of all his forces, culminating in his heart-warming words of thanks at the end of the sessions, not to mention his tension-breaking humour and a couple of sharp comments from Vishnevskaya, who is unsurpassed as soprano soloist. The merit of this ground-breaking performance and recording is that it so arrestingly conveys Britten's intentions. We are lucky now to have not only the composer's irreplaceable reading refurbished, but also his commentary suggested by the rehearsal sequences.

Albert Herring

Sir Peter Pears *ten* Albert Herring; **Sylvia Fisher** *sop* Lady Billows; **Johanna Peters** *contr* Florence Pike; **John Noble** *bar* Mr George; **Owen Brannigan** *bass* Mr Budd; **Edgar Evans** *ten* Mr Upford; **April Cantelo** *sop* Mrs Wordsworth; **Sheila Rex** *mez* Mrs Herring; **Joseph Ward** *ten* Sid; **Catherine Wilson** *mez* Nancy; **English Chamber Orchestra / Benjamin Britten**
Decca London ② 421 849-2LH2 (138 minutes: ADD). Ⓕ
Notes and text included. Recorded 1964.

Having shown us the grim and nasty side of Aldeburgh life at the beginning of the 19th century in *Peter Grimes*, Britten had fun with its parochial aspects at the end of the century in his comic opera *Albert Herring*. For some tastes, it has proved too parochial. This tale of the mother-dominated shop assistant who is elected May King because of his virtue, is slipped a laced drink at his crowning and goes off for a night on the tiles, after which he asserts himself repels some who otherwise admire the composer because of its self-regarding whimsicality. The possible cure for these people is to listen to Britten's own recording, here marvellously transferred to CD and showing again what a genius John Culshaw was at making records of opera. Britten finds all the humour in the piece, but he gives it a cutting-edge and is totally successful in conveying the proximity of comedy to tragedy in the remarkable ensemble where Albert is thought to have been killed. With the English Chamber Orchestra on peak form, all kinds of Bergian echoes in the score are revealed and some, too, of Verdi's *Falstaff* (Act 3). There is also Sir Peter Pears's brilliant performance as Albert, a genuine piece of perceptive singing-acting. Britten takes some passages at Rossinian speeds, and in the touching love music for Sid and Nancy finds a true lyrical vein. As for the outright comic episodes, such as Lady Billows's speech, the composer of *Paul Bunyan* and the Pyramus and Thisbe episode in *A Midsummer Night's Dream* needed no lessons in how to extract every bit of musical wit from what he had composed. The cast is well-nigh ideal. If only Britten had written more comic operas

Billy Budd

Peter Glossop *bar* Billy Budd; **Sir Peter Pears** *ten* Captain Vere; **Michael Langdon** *bass* John Claggart; **John Shirley-Quirk** *bar* Mr Redburn; **Bryan Drake** *bar* Mr Flint; **David Kelly** *bass* Mr Ratcliffe; **Gregory Dempsey** *ten* Red Whiskers; **David Bowman** *bar* Donald; **Owen Brannigan** *bass* Dansker; **Robert Tear** *ten* Novice; **Robert Bowman** *ten* Squeak; **Delme Bryn-Jones** *bar* Bosun; **Eric Garrett** *bar* First Mate; **Nigel Rogers** *ten* Maintop; **Benjamin Luxon** *bar* Novice's Friend; **Geoffrey Coleby** *bar* Arthur Jones
Ambrosian Opera Chorus; London Symphony Orchestra / Benjamin Britten
The Holy Sonnets of John Donne, Op 35. Songs and Proverbs of William Blake, Op 74
Sir Peter Pears *ten* **Dietrich Fischer-Dieskau** *bar* **Benjamin Britten** *pf*
Decca London ③ 417 428-2LH3 (205 minutes: ADD).
Notes and text included. Ⓕ
Recorded 1961 ●●

Billy Budd is remarkable in having been composed for male voices, yet not once is there any lack of colour or variety. Britten marvellously supports the tenor, baritone and bass protagonists with extraordinary flair in the use of brass and woodwind. This was the last operatic recording John Culshaw produced for Decca and he again showed himself unsurpassed at creating a theatrical atmosphere in the studio. Although there have been several striking and brilliant stage productions of this opera in recent years, not to mention Nagano's recording, it must also be said that both technically and interpretatively this Britten/Culshaw collaboration represents the touchstone for any that follows it, particularly in the matter of Britten's conducting. Where Britten is superb is in the dramatic tautness with which he unfolds the score and his unobtrusive highlighting of such poignant detail as the use of the saxophone after the flogging. His conducting of the choral scenes, particularly when the crew are heard singing below decks while Captain Vere and his officers are talking in his cabin, is profoundly satisfying and moving. Most of all, he focuses with total clarity on the intimate human drama against the background of life aboard the ship.

And what a cast he had, headed by Peter Pears as Vere, conveying a natural authoritarianism which makes his unwilling but dutiful role as 'the messenger of death' more understandable, if no more agreeable. Peter Glossop's Billy Budd is a virile performance, with nothing of the 'goody-goody' about him. Nor does one feel any particular homo-eroticism about his relationship with Michael Langdon's black-voiced Claggart: it is a straight conflict between good and evil, and all the more horrifying for its stark simplicity. Add to these principals John Shirley-Quirk, Bryan Drake and David Kelly as the officers, Owen Brannigan as Dansker and Robert Tear and Benjamin Luxon in the small roles of the novice and his friend, and one can apply the adjective 'classic' to this recording with a clear conscience. Also on the discs are two of Britten's most sombre song-cycles, the *Donne Sonnets* and the *Blake Songs and Proverbs*, the former with Pears, the latter with Fischer-Dieskau, and both incomparably accompanied by Britten. They make ideal complements to *Billy Budd*. This is without doubt a vintage set.

Billy Budd
Simon Keenlyside *bar* Billy Budd; **Philip Langridge** *ten* Captain Vere; **John Tomlinson** *bass* John Claggart; **Alan Opie** *bar* Mr Redburn; **Matthew Best** *bass-bar* Mr Flint; **Alan Ewing** *bass* Lt Ratcliffe; **Francis Egerton** *ten* Red Whiskers; **Quentin Hayes** *bar* Donald; **Clive Bayley** *bass* Dansker; **Mark Padmore** *ten* Novice; **Richard Coxon** *ten* Squeak; **Timothy DuFore** *bar* Bosun; **Christopher Keyte** *bar* Bosun; **Richard Whitehouse** *bar* Second Mate, Gunner's Mate; **Daniel Norman** *ten* Maintop; **Roderick Williams** *bar* Novice's Friend, Arthur Jones; **Alex Johnson** *treb* Cabin Boy
Tiffin Boys' Choir; London Symphony Chorus and Orchestra / Richard Hickox
Chandos ③ CHAN9826 (165 minutes: DDD). Notes, text and translation included. Ⓕ
Recorded 1999 ●

Britten's score is so often praised that we tend to neglect the distinction of Forster and Crozier's libretto, sung in this set with unerring conviction by its three principals. Keenlyside and Langridge deserve special mention for their arresting sensitivity throughout the final scenes, when they make the utterances of Billy and Vere so poetic and moving: refined tone allied to eloquent phrasing – the epitome of English singing at its very best. Keenlyside has a voice of just the right weight and an appreciation of how Billy must be at once sympathetic and manly. From first to last you realise the lad's personal magnetism in vocal terms alone, explaining the crew's admiration for his qualities. Langridge is the complete Vere, suggesting the man's easy command of men, his poetic soul, his agony of mind at the awful decision placed in his hands to sacrifice Billy. At the opposite end of the human spectrum, Claggart's dark, twisted being and his depravity of thought are ideally realised by Tomlinson, give or take one or two moments of unsteadiness when his voice comes under pressure. In supporting roles there is also much to admire. Mark Padmore conveys all the Novice's terror in a very immediate, tortured manner. Clive Bayley's Dansker is full of canny wisdom. Alan Opie is a resolute Mr Redburn. Matthew Best's is an appropriately powerful Mr Flint, though his large, gritty bass-baritone records uneasily. Hickox conducts with all his old zest for marshalling large forces, searching out every cranny of this highly evocative score, and the London Symphony forces respond with real virtuosity. Chandos's skilful recording captures the large-in-scale while not overlooking pertinent detail, too. Speeds now and again sound a shade too deliberate, and there's not always quite that sense of an ongoing continuum you feel in both of Britten's readings, which are by and large tauter, especially in the account taken from the 1951 première on VAI. But the Chandos, using the revised two-act version, comes into most direct competition with Britten's later Decca set. The latter still sounds well, though inevitably it hasn't the aural range of the Chandos recording. Yet nobody will ever quite catch the creative tension the composer brings to his own work. For all that, the Chandos set benefits from this trio of imaginative singers, and most newcomers will be satisfied with its appreciable achievement.

Billy Budd (four-act version)

Thomas Hampson *bar* Billy Budd; **Anthony Rolfe Johnson** *ten* Captain Vere; **Eric Halfvarson** *bass-bar* John Claggart; **Russell Smythe** *bar* Mr Redburn; **Gidon Saks** *bass* Mr Flint; **Simon Wilding** *bass* Mr Ratcliffe; **Martyn Hill** *ten* Red Whiskers; **Christopher Maltman** *bar* Donald; **Richard Van Allan** *bass* Dansker; **Andrew Burden** *ten* Novice; **Christopher Gillett** *ten* Squeak; **Matthew Hargreaves** *bass* Bosun; **Ashley Holland** *bass* First Mate; **Simon Thorpe** *bar* Second Mate, Arthur Jones; **Robert Johnston** *ten* Maintop; **William Dazeley** *bar* Novice's Friend

Manchester Boys' Choir; Northern Voices; Hallé Choir and Orchestra / Kent Nagano

Erato ② 3984-21631-2 (148 minutes: DDD). Ⓜ
Notes and text included. Recorded live in 1997

This recording is an exciting achievement; it restores to circulation the original, four-act version of the score. The crucial difference between this and Britten's two-act revision is a scene at the close of what is here Act 1, in which 'Starry' Vere addresses his crew and is hailed by them as the sailors' champion, thus establishing the relationship between captain and foretopman. It is thus an important scene though musically not particularly distinguished. One can quite see why Britten wanted a tauter two-act drama. Nagano gives us a wonderfully full-bodied, accurate and detailed account of the many-faceted score. There are electrifying moments, not least the battle scene, where the listener feels very much in the middle of things, and the end of Act 3 where those tremendous and ominous series of chords represent Vere telling Budd of the sentence of death. Britten, in his studio recording, prefers a leaner sound and a slightly tauter approach all-round – in his hands you feel the tension of the personal relationships even more sharply than with Nagano. Hampson is very good, singing with all his customary beauty of voice and intelligence of style, though he imparts a touch of self-consciousness that goes against the grain of the writing. Halfvarson, as Budd's antagonist, the evil Claggart, gives us a mighty presence, singing with power and bite, though not always a steady tone. Rolfe Johnson sings his heart out as he presents Vere's tormented soul. For the rest, Gidon Saks makes a dominant Mr Flint, the sailing-master, Richard Van Allan, is here, predictably, a characterful Dansker, and Andrew Burden stands out as a properly scared Novice, far preferable to Tear's placid reading on Decca. The sum here is greater than the parts, and this set can be heartily recommended. In Manchester's Bridgewater Hall, where the recording was made (though, to judge by the absence of background noise, there must have been sessions without an audience), the orchestral contribution was, apparently, exceptionally clear. That has been carried over into the amazingly wide spectrum of sound on the recording: indeed sometimes the orchestra is simply too loud.

Curlew River

Sir Peter Pears *ten* Madwoman; **John Shirley-Quirk** *bar* Ferryman; **Harold Blackburn** *bass* Abbot; **Bryan Drake** *bar* Traveller; **Bruce Webb** *treb* Voice of the Spirit

English Opera Group / Benjamin Britten and **Viola Tunnard**

Decca London 421 858-2LM (69 minutes: ADD). Ⓜ
Text included. Recorded 1965 **OO**

Curlew River captured completely the composer's fascination with the Japanese Noh play on which it was based. It was an inspired idea to locate the action in East Anglia, so one has the clash and intermingling of East and West with an immediacy that reflects the keenness of Britten's response to both. The recording, produced by John Culshaw, was made in Orford Church (is there an aircraft overhead near the start?). The atmosphere of this unforgettable occasion is preserved. The procession of monks at the beginning and end comes towards us and recedes, just as if we were sitting in a pew. Peter Pears's performance as the Madwoman is one of his finest and most touching, while John Shirley-Quirk and Bryan Drake are equally authoritative as the Ferryman and Traveller. The voice of the Madwoman's dead son is devoid of the sentimentality that might have been a peril if any treble other than Bruce Webb had sung it, and the inventive and beguiling orchestral score is marvellously played. With the composer and Viola Tunnard directing the performance, this is in a class of its own.

Curlew River

Philip Langridge *ten* Madwoman; **Thomas Allen** *bar* Ferryman; **Gidon Saks** *bass* Abbot; **Simon Keenlyside** *bar* Traveller; **Charles Richardson** *treb* Voice of the Spirit

London Voices; Academy of St Martin in the Fields / Sir Neville Marriner

Philips 454 469-2PH (70 minutes: DDD). Notes and Ⓕ text included. Recorded 1996

Until now, nobody has wanted to challenge the hegemony of Britten's magical performance, but the newer performance is given almost as much presence and perspective by Erik Smith as John Culshaw achieved in the Decca version. Marriner and his hand-picked team of instrumentalists follow in the tradition of the Britten-led performance, exposing the extreme originality of the composer's reworking of the Japanese play, the results as mesmeric and concentrated as they should be. The spare beauty of the scoring and the subtlety of the interaction between voices and instruments is as convincing as one could wish, so there's little to choose here between the two readings. Because the Madwoman was one of Pears's greatest achievements and fitted his voice like the proverbial glove, his interpretation remains *hors concours*. Langridge is a perceptive enough artist not to ape Pears. He treats the part in an inward, dreamy manner, more intimate and personal than Pears's hieratical approach, just as valid in its way and finely executed. As the strong-willed Ferryman, Thomas Allen almost matches Shirley-Quirk's firm, acutely enunciated portrayal: there is just that much more youthful sap in Shirley-Quirk's voice. On the other hand Keenlyside far surpasses his predecessor as the more ruminative Traveller, singing with the strong, vibrant tone and sharply etched *legato* for which he is famed. Gidon Saks is a suitably grave Abbot, and the London Voices sing securely and solemnly as the Monks. The newer recording obviously has a greater range than the old one; both are sensitively directed to capture the work's very special ethos. Those who have the old one can probably remain satisfied, but newcomers and those seeking another view of the piece, should certainly consider this invaluable, carefully crafted and eloquent newcomer.

Death in Venice

Sir Peter Pears *ten* Gustav von Aschenbach; **John Shirley-Quirk** *bar* Traveller, Elderly Fop, Old Gondolier, Hotel Manager, Hotel Barber, Leader of the Players, Voice of Dionysus; **James Bowman** *countertenor* Voice of Apollo; **Kenneth Bowen** *ten* Hotel Porter; **Peter Leeming** *bass* Travel Clerk; **Neville Williams** *bass-bar* **Penelope MacKay** *sop* Strolling Players; **Iris Saunders** *sop* Strawberry-seller

English Opera Group Chorus; English Chamber Orchestra / Steuart Bedford

Decca London ② 425 669-2LH2 (145 minutes: ADD). Ⓕ Notes and text included. Recorded 1973

In his insert-notes, Christopher Palmer has pertinent things to say about the sexual climate of Britten's last opera, *Death in Venice*; but these seem to become of less consequence as one listens to the music. Its potency and inventiveness create this opera's disturbing and intense atmosphere, each episode heightened dramatically by instrumental colouring. Under Bedford's direction each scene is fully integrated into a fluent and convincing whole. This recording was made while Britten was very ill; it omits Aschenbach's first recitative ('I have always kept a close watch over my development as a writer ...'), given as an optional cut in the vocal score, which was published after the recording was made, by which time Britten had changed his mind about this cut and wished it had been included in the recording. Pears's Aschenbach, a very English conception, is a masterly performance, matched by John Shirley-Quirk's assumption of the six characters who are Aschenbach's messengers of death and the Voice of Dionysus.

Gloriana

Awards 1994

Dame Josephine Barstow *sop* Queen Elizabeth I; **Philip Langridge** *ten* Earl of Essex; **Della Jones** *mez* Lady Essex; **Jonathan Summers** *bar* Lord Mountjoy; **Alan Opie** *bar* Sir Robert Cecil; **Yvonne Kenny** *sop* Penelope; **Richard Van Allan** *bass* Sir Walter Raleigh; **Bryn Terfel** *bass-bar* Henry Cuffe; **Janice Watson** *sop* Lady-in-waiting; **Willard White** *bass* Blind ballad-singer; **John Shirley-Quirk** *bar* Recorder of Norwich; **John Mark Ainsley** *ten* Spirit of the Masque; **Peter Hoare** *ten* Master of Ceremonies **Welsh National Opera Chorus and Orchestra / Sir Charles Mackerras**

Argo ② 440 213-2ZHO2 (148 minutes: DDD) Ⓕ Notes and text included. Recorded 1992

Four decades on from the ill-fated première of Britten's Coronation opera where, instead of the staid pageant expected by the bejewelled and stiff audience assembled for a royal gala, they were given an intimate study of the ageing Queen's torment as she copes with the conflict of private emotions in the midst of public pomp, *Gloriana* has now at last been given a complete recording on CD. Mackerras presents it here with the utmost conviction, drawing together the motivic strands of the score into a coherent whole (not an altogether easy task), appreciating the contrast of the public and private scenes, exposing the sinews of the writing for the two principal characters, and drawing superb playing from his own WNO Orchestra. Josephine Barstow crowns her career with her performance as Queen Elizabeth, commanding the opera by her vocal presence, her imposing, vibrant tone, her vital treatment of the text, and her attention to detail. Philip Langridge projects all the vehement impetuosity of Essex but also, in the famous lute songs, the poetic ardour of the handsome if unruly Earl. There is much discerning interpretation elsewhere and the recording is worthy of the performance. Any small reservations are as nothing before the triumph of the achievement as a whole.

A Midsummer Night's Dream

Alfred Deller *counterten* Oberon; **Elizabeth Harwood** *sop* Tytania; **Sir Peter Pears** *ten* Lysander; **Thomas Hemsley** *bar* Demetrius; **Josephine Veasey** *mez* Hermia; **Heather Harper** *sop* Helena; **John Shirley-Quirk** *bar* Theseus; **Helen Watts** *contr* Hippolyta; **Owen Brannigan** *bass* Bottom; **Norman Lumsden** *bass* Quince; **Kenneth Macdonald** *ten* Flute; **David Kelly** *bass* Snug; **Robert Tear** *ten* Snout; **Keith Raggett** *ten* Starveling; **Richard Dakin** *treb* Cobweb; **John Prior** *treb* Peaseblossom; **Ian Wodehouse** *treb* Mustardseed; **Gordon Clark** *treb* Moth; **Stephen Terry** *spkr* Puck
Choirs of Downside and Emanuel Schools; London Symphony Orchestra / Benjamin Britten
Decca London ② 425 663-2LH2
(144 minutes: ADD). Notes and text included. Ⓕ
Recorded 1966 ●●

Brian Asawa *counterten* Oberon; **Sylvia McNair** *sop* Tytania; **John Mark Ainsley** *ten* Lysander; **Paul Whelan** *bar* Demetrius; **Ruby Philogene** *mez* Hermia; **Janice Watson** *sop* Helena; **Brian Bannatyne-Scott** *bass* Theseus; **Hilary Summers** *contr* Hippolyta; **Robert Lloyd** *bass* Bottom; **Gwynne Howell** *bass* Quince; **Ian Bostridge** *ten* Flute; **Stephen Richardson** *bar* Snug; **Mark Tucker** *ten* Snout; **Neal Davies** *bar* Starveling; **David Newman** *treb* Cobweb; **Claudia Conway** *sop* Peaseblossom; **Sara Rey** *sop* Mustardseed; **Matthew Long** *treb* Moth; **Carl Ferguson** *spkr* Puck **New London Children's Choir; London Symphony Orchestra / Sir Colin Davis**
Philips ② 454 122-2PH2 (148 minutes: DDD) Ⓕ
Notes and text included. Recorded 1995 ●

The Philips set is in almost every respect immediate and present, almost to a fault, yet there are few if any attempts at suggesting the perspectives you hear on the 34-year-old Decca set for the composer. For instance, on Decca, Puck seems to be everywhere, yet on the newer version you are in the front stalls listening to an enjoyable concert with little attempt to simulate a stage. That may have influenced the often leisurely pacing of Davis's reading. Everything is heard with great clarity, the sensuousness of Britten's ravishing score, with all its mysterious harmonies and sonorities, is fully realized, action and reaction among the singers are keenly heard, yet something of the midsummer magic of Britten's direction eludes Davis and his team. On Decca we hear this music fresh-minted, unadorned; in Davis's hands the work is viewed through a tougher, more modern prism. One wonders if any members of the LSO today were in the orchestra under the composer back in 1966: they are certainly as acute if not more so in their playing than their predecessors. As for pacing, if you try either Oberon's 'I know a bank' or Tytania's solo 'Come, now a roundel and a fairy song' you will hear how much tauter is Britten's approach, Davis allowing his singers more licence. In the case of McNair this gives her space to develop what is a knowingly sophisticated approach to her role, even more evident in her sensual account of the Act 2 solo 'Hail, mortal, hail'. Her singing is lovely, but it is an earthly reading where Elizabeth Harwood for Britten suggests a more other-worldly Queen of the Fairies.

Similarly the luscious, vibrant voice of the American countertenor Brian Asawa is very different from Deller's ethereal delicacies. Like McNair's singing, Asawa's, taken on its own terms, is most seductive, but disconcerting at first hearing. Puck is also upfront, not so much puckish as rough-hewn. With Bottom we meet another thought-provoking interpretation. Lloyd makes the weaver sound more high-born than his predecessor. This is almost a noble craftsman, with no hint of the rustic portrayed unforgettably by Owen Brannigan, the role's creator, who savours the text so lovingly. Lloyd scores with his splendidly resonant account of 'O grin-look'd night' in the play. One thing is sure: there has never been a more amusing Flute than Ian Bostridge (hilarious as Thisbe) or a better sung Quince than Gwynne Howell. Another plus for Davis is the casting of the lovers with young singers in their early prime, a small advance on the Britten set. In particular, Philogene's ripe mezzo as Hermia and Ainsley's ardent tenor as Lysander stand out as ideal interpretations. Neither Hippolyta nor Theseus matches the regal authority of Helen Watts and Shirley-Quirk on the composer's set. You will derive a great deal of pleasure from the newcomer with its exemplary recording and careful preparation on all sides. It is now the prime recommendation for a modern set. But the Decca remains as fresh and inspired as the day it was made; Britten's taut, disciplined yet magical reading unsurpassed.

Noye's Fludde / The Golden Vanity

Noye's Fludde
Owen Brannigan *bass* Noye; **Sheila Rex** *mez* Mrs Noye; **David Pinto** *treb* Sem; **Darian Angadi** *treb* Ham; **Stephen Alexander** *treb* Jaffett; **Trevor Anthony** *spkr* The Voice of God; **Caroline Clack** *sop* Mrs Sem; **Maria-Thérèse Pinto** *sop* Mrs Ham; **Eileen O'Donnovan** *sop* Mrs Jaffett
Chorus; English Opera Group Orchestra; An East Suffolk Children's Orchestra / Norman Del Mar

The Golden Vanity, Op 78
Mark Emney *treb* Captain; **John Wojciechowski** *treb* Bosun; **Barnaby Jago** *treb* Cabin-boy; **Adrian Thompson** *treb* Captain; **Terry Lovell** *treb* Bosun; **Benjamin Britten** *pf* **Wandsworth School Boys' Choir / Russell Burgess**
Decca London 436 397-2LM (66 minutes: ADD) Ⓕ
Texts included. Recorded 1961 and 1966

Britten wrote these two works for children, yet one must not imagine that they are cosy and (in the pejorative sense) childish. Many of Britten's friends thought that there remained much of the child in him, and this clearly comes out in the boisterous high spirits of some of this music. By and large, *Noye's Fludde* and *The Golden Vanity* are happy works. *Noye's Fludde* makes invigorating listening. This 1961 performance, recorded in Orford Church where it had its première three years before (at the 1958 Aldeburgh Festival), is immensely vivid and one responds to the enthusiasm of the young singers and instrumentalists. All of the children of East Suffolk seem to be involved in the enterprise: consorts of recorders, bands of bugles, peals of handbell ringers, plenty of violins, a few lower strings, seven percussion players, child soloists, and a choir as big as you like, enough to give full representation to the 49 different species of animal mentioned in the text. Then three grown-ups, and the English Chamber Orchestra. The skill and imaginative power with which Britten has used these forces defy adequate description. There are inevitably rough edges in the singing and playing, but the spirit is there in abundance. The same is true of *The Golden Vanity*, and although there's more conscious vocal skill in the singing of the Wandsworth School Boys' Choir, it never gets in the way of the presentation, which bubbles with life.

Peter Grimes

Awards 1986

Sir Peter Pears *ten* Peter Grimes; **Claire Watson** *sop* Ellen Orford; **James Pease** *bass* Captain Balstrode; **Jean Watson** *contr* Auntie; **Raymond Nilsson** *ten* Bob Boles; **Owen Brannigan** *bass* Swallow; **Lauris Elms** *mez* Mrs Sedley; **Sir Geraint Evans** *bar* Ned Keene; **John Lanigan** *ten* Rector; **David Kelly** *bass* Hobson; **Marion Studholme** *sop* First Niece; **Iris Kells** *sop* Second Niece H

Chorus and Orchestra of the Royal Opera House, Covent Garden / Benjamin Britten

Decca ③ 414 577-2DH3 (144 minutes: ADD) Ⓕ
Notes and text included. Recorded 1958 ooo

Philip Langridge *ten* Grimes; **Janice Watson** *sop* Ellen Orford; **Alan Opie** *bar* Captain Balstrode; **Ameral Gunson** *mez* Auntie; **John Graham-Hall** *ten* Bob Boles; **John Connell** *bass* Swallow; **Anne Collins** *contr* Mrs Sedley; **Roderick Williams** *bar* Ned Keene; **John Fryatt** *ten* Rector; **Matthew Best** *bass* Hobson; **Yvonne Barclay** *sop* First Niece; **Pamela Helen Stephen** *mez* Second Niece

London Symphony Chorus; City of London Sinfonia / Richard Hickox

Chandos ② CHAN9447/8 (147 minutes: DDD) Ⓕ
Notes and text included. Recorded 1995 oo

The Decca set has long been regarded as the definitive recording which, in 1958, introduced this opera to many listeners and one which has never been superseded in its refinement or insight. Britten's conducting, lithe, lucid and as inexorable as 'the tide that waits for no man', reveals his work as the complex, ambiguous drama that it is. Peter Pears, in the title-role which was written for him, brings unsurpassed detail of nuance to Grimes's words while never losing sight of the essential plainness of the man's speech. The rest of the cast form a vivid portrait gallery of characters. The recording is as live and clear as if it had been made yesterday and takes the listener right on to the stage. The bustle of activity and sound effects realise nicely Britten's own masterly painting of dramatic foreground and background. For Hickox on Chandos there is Langridge's tense, sinewy, sensitive Grimes. Predictably he rises to the challenge of the Mad scene; this is a man hugely to be pitied, yet there is a touch of resignation, of finding some sort of peace at last, after all the agony of the soul. His portrayal is tense and immediate and a match for that of Pears in personal identification – listen to the eager touch at 'We strained in the wind'.

The next composite heroes are the members of the chorus. Electrifying as their rivals are, the LSO singers, trained by Stephen Westrop, seem just that much more arresting, not least in the hue-and-cry of Act 3, quite terrifying in its immediacy as recorded by Chandos. Hickox's whole interpretation has little to fear from the distinguished competition. Many details are placed with special care, particularly in the Interludes and the parodistic dances in Act 3, and whole episodes, such as the Grimes/Balstrode dispute in Act 1, have seldom sounded so dramatic. Once or twice one would have liked a firmer forward movement, as in the fifth Interlude (Britten's own direction of this Passacaglia is that bit more urgent), but the sense of total music-theatre is present throughout and it's excitingly laid before us by the City of London Sinfonia and the recording. Of the other soloists, the one comparative disappointment is Janice Watson's Ellen Orford. She sings the part with tone as lovely as any of her rivals on disc and with carefully wrought phrasing and is very much part of a convincing team but doesn't have the experience to stand out from the village regulars and sound important, as Ellen should. Britten's set remains *hors concours* (the composer's own taut conducting is unsurpassed), but that recording stretches over three CDs. Hickox is the finest of the modern recordings: as sound it is quite spectacular, vast in range, with well-managed perspectives and just enough hints of stage action to be convincing.

Additional recommendation

Peter Grimes

Vickers Peter Grimes **Harper** Ellen Orford

Royal Opera House Chorus and Orchestra / C Davis

Philips 432 578-2PM2 (146 minutes: ADD: 11/91) Ⓜ

A mid-price alternative which enshrines the wonderfully drawn Grimes of Jon Vickers and the touching, immensely human Ellen of Heather Harper. Colin Davis's conducting too displays his love of the score.

The Turn of the Screw

Sir Peter Pears *ten* Prologue, Quint; **Jennifer Vyvyan** *sop* Governess; **David Hemmings** *treb* Miles; **Olive Dyer** *sop* Flora; **Joan Cross** *sop* Mrs Grose; **Arda Mandikian** *sop* Miss Jessel **English Opera Group Orchestra / Benjamin Britten** H

Decca London mono ② 425 672-2LH2 Ⓕ
(105 minutes: ADD). Notes and text included.
Recorded 1955 oo

As Sir Colin Davis has shown on Philips, there is room for an alternative interpretation of this remarkable work, but this superb first recording will remain as documentary-historical evidence of the highest importance and value. Will there ever be a better performance, let alone recording, of *The Turn of the Screw* than this by the original cast, recorded less than four months after the 1954 Venice première? Christopher Palmer contributes a stimulating essay to the booklet with this reissue, in which he faces squarely all the implications of this choice of subject by Britten as far as what Palmer calls his 'intellectual paedophilia' is concerned. It is a valid and provocative comment, and was a useful contribution to the growing body of Britten criticism. This score is Britten at his greatest, expressing good and evil with equal ambivalence, evoking the tense and sinister atmosphere of Bly by inspired use of the chamber orchestra and imparting vivid and truthful life to every character in the story. As one listens, transfixed, all that matters is Britten's genius as a composer. Jennifer Vyvyan's portrayal of the Governess is a classic characterization, her vocal subtleties illuminating every facet of the role and she has the perfect foil in Joan Cross's motherly and uncomplicated Mrs Grose. The glittering malevolence of Pears's Quint, luring David Hemmings's incomparable Miles to destruction; the tragic tones of Arda Mandikian's Miss Jessel; Olive Dyer's spiteful Flora – how fortunate we are that these performances are preserved. As with all of the Decca/Britten reissues, the transfer is a triumph.

The Turn of the Screw
Philip Langridge *ten* Prologue; **Robert Tear** *ten* Quint; **Helen Donath** *sop* Governess; **Michael Ginn** *treb* Miles; **Lilian Watson** *sop* Flora; **Ava June** *sop* Mrs Grose; **Heather Harper** *sop* Miss Jessel
Orchestra of the Royal Opera House, Covent Garden / Sir Colin Davis
Philips ② 446 325-2PH2 (108 minutes: ADD) Ⓕ
Notes and text included. Recorded 1981 ●

Davis yields little if anything to the composer's in realizing the taut, claustrophobic feeling of the score. The players of the ROH Orchestra are quite as alert as Britten's chamber ensembles to the minutiae of the fastidious instrumentation, bringing out the genius of Britten's variation form. Davis unerringly pinpoints the change from the lyrical euphony of some of the earlier scenes and the sinister, otherworldly suggestions of the later ones. The cast stands comparison with its rivals – though Tear, for all his competence, cannot quite match the peculiarly haunting quality of Pears's tone as Quint in a role specifically tailored to Britten's partner. Tear doesn't attempt to double with the Prologue, here sung with predictable intelligence and refined poetic expectancy by the young Langridge. Donath very properly lets a note of nervous agitation enter into her tone and evinces full understanding of the Governess's predicament, 'Lost in my labyrinth' rightly given as a whispered, interior monologue, though she doesn't build all the tensions as unerringly as Vyvyan (Britten). Heather Harper, herself an erstwhile Governess, is a rightly hard-bitten Miss Jessel. Ava June is even more articulate than her teacher Joan Cross as Mrs Grose. Lilian Watson makes a vivid Flora, but Michael Ginn doesn't suggest the paradox of evil in innocence as David Hemmings so amazingly does on Decca. The years make one newly aware of the historic importance of Britten's own reading but each version is wholly worthy of this score.

Sébastien de Brossard

French 1655-1730

GROVE *Lexicographer and composer Sébastien de Brossard was maître de chapelle at Strasbourg Cathedral, 1687-98, then held a similar post in Meaux, where he composed sacred music, chiefly motets. He was among the first in France to write violin sonatas, and his French cantatas are among the few based on biblical subjects. Of his writings on music the most important is his Dictionnaire (1701, rev. 1703), the first of its kind in France. His extensive library is now in the Bibliothèque Nationale, Paris.*

Grands Motets

In Convertendo Dominus. Miserere mei, Deus. Canticum eucharisticum pro pace
Delphine Collot, Catherine Padaut *sops* **Jean-Paul Fouchécourt, Gilles Ragon** *tens***Olivier Lallouette, Jérôme Corréas** *basses***Accentus Chamber Choir; Limoges Baroque Ensemble / Christophe Coin**
Auvidis Astrée E8607 (76 minutes: DDD) Ⓕ
Texts and translations included. Recorded 1995

The name of Sébastien de Brossard usually appears in music history books only when its owner is being quoted in his capacity as a revealing theorist and lexicographer. As a composer, mainly of church music, his achievements are less often considered next to those of notable contemporaries such as Charpentier and Lalande, but in 1995 the Centre de Musique Baroque de Versailles devoted one of its annual short festivals to him, and this recording arises from that occasion. The three *grands motets* – large-scale pieces for choir, soloists and orchestra – are surprisingly eventful music, seemingly conceived more for entertainment than for liturgical edification. *Canticum eucharisticum pro pace*, a 40-minute show-piece written to celebrate the joining of Strasbourg to France, depicts God/Louis XIV as both angry war hero and generous peacemaker, and even includes a dramatic solo for a singer representing the voice of God. The other two motets, too, contain interesting contrasts and a few good descriptive moments of their own. The performances are refined and attractive, even if the choir is occasionally a little unfocused.

Petits Motets

O Jesu! quam dulce nomen tuum, SdB24[a]. O plenus irarum dies!, SdB31[b]. Beati immaculati, SdB49[c]. Silentium dormi, SdB52[d]. Miserere mei, SdB53[e]
[ace]**Cyrille Dubois** *treb* [bc]**Alain Buett** *bar* [d]**Hervé Lamy** *bass-bar* **Juan-Sebastian Lima** *theorbo* **Jean-Marie Quint** *vc* [e]**Maîtrise de Caen / Robert Weddle** *org*
Assai 207582 (55 minutes: DDD) Ⓕ
Texts and translations included. Recorded 1999 ⭘

Brossard's *Petits motets* exemplify the fluent melodic style and intimacy of the genre at its most engaging. Cyrille Dubois is a seasoned treble with an astonishingly natural flair for the conventions and declamatory 'délicatesse' of the French baroque. Put simply, there isn't anyone quite like him. The idiom is in his blood. As the opening motet, *O Jesu! quam dulce nomen tuum* reveals, Dubois places notes with the accuracy and nonchalance of an old pro, naturally colouring vowels and embellishing cadences without a morsel of fear. The equivalent performance by Isabelle Desrochers (Astrée Naïve, 1997) conveys little of the incandescence of the text. Dubois is joined by the expressive and resonant bass of Alain Buett, who is a commanding presence in the harrowing and harmonically daring *O plenus irarum dies!* (*O day full of wrath!*); Weddle, leading from the organ a sensitive continuo accompaniment to a lilting *tripla* for the merciful Christ, judges the music's Italianate contrasts with sensual relief.

The fine duo motet, *Beati immaculati*, is sweetly set by Brossard (who reckoned it was his best motet), and Dubois and Buett have a rollicking time in a splendid performance. *Silentium dormi* suffers in comparison: the tenor, Hervé Lamy, is not in the same league vocally. Finally, we have an unpretentious and musicianly performance of a *Miserere*, for treble, vocal consort and continuo. Again, few will doubt that treble singing of this quality, guided so intelligently, adds a delectable frisson to French baroque music. A strong recommendation.

Max Bruch

German 1838-1920

GROVE *Bruch studied with Hiller and Reinecke and had some success with his cantata Frithjof Op 23 (1864) before taking posts in Koblenz, Sondershausen, Liverpool and Breslau. Official recognition came in 1891 when he became professor at the Berlin Academy. Although he composed three operas, his talent lay in epic expression; during his lifetime the secular choral works Odysseus and Das Feuerkreuz, with their solid choral writing and tuneful style, sometimes showing affinities with folk music, were considered particularly significant. Only his violin concertos (especially the appealing No 1 in G minor), the Scottish Fantasy for violin and orchestra and the Kol nidrei for cello and orchestra Op 47 have remained in the repertory.*

Violin Concertos

No 1 in G minor, Op 26; **No 2** in D minor, Op 44; **No 3** in D minor, Op 58

Violin Concertos Nos 1-3. Scottish Fantasy, Op 46. Serenade in A minor, Op 75. Konzertstück in F sharp minor, Op 84. Adagio appassionato, Op 57. In memoriam, Op 65. Romance in A minor, Op 41
Salvatore Accardo *vn*
Leipzig Gewandhaus Orchestra / Kurt Masur
Philips Silver Line ③ 432 282-2PSL3 Ⓜ
(214 minutes: ADD). Recorded 1977

This three-disc set contains all the major *concertante* works for violin and orchestra. They are quite marvellously played by Salvatore Accardo, admirably accompanied by the Leipzig Gewandhaus Orchestra under Kurt Masur. The G minor Concerto is clearly the most concentrated in its inspiration but there are plenty of attractive ideas elsewhere in this anthology. Certainly the Second and Third Concertos prove to have many memorable pages, especially when the advocacy is so persuasive. Bruch originally intended to use the description 'concerto' for both the *Konzertstück* and the relatively lightweight but charming *Serenade*, but thought better of it. The very enjoyable *Allegro appassionato* and *Romanze* are both admirably described by their titles, while *In memoriam*, which Bruch considered the finest of all these works, is undoubtedly inspired. We all know the *Scottish Fantasy* is brimming with engaging invention and Accardo's acount is full of warmth and colour. The only snag – and it should not deter the enthusiastic collector – is that this issue proves an exception to the usual excellence of the Philips sound balance. Possibly because of the resonant acoustics of the Leipzig Gewandhaus, the engineers have been tempted to place their microphones too close to the soloist. With remastering, this creates a dominating effect and brings a degree of shrillness at times to the solo timbre. It can be mitigated by a roll-off treble control; otherwise it is best to play these recordings at not too high a level. Then the poetry of the solo playing and the rich orchestral tapestry combine to captivate the ear in this lovely music.

Bruch Violin Concerto No 1[a]
Beethoven Violin Concerto in D, Op 61[b]
Kyung Wha Chung *vn*
[a]**Royal Concertgebouw Orchestra;** [b]**London Philharmonic Orchestra / Klaus Tennstedt**
EMI CDC7 54072-2 (70 minutes: DDD) Ⓕ
[b]Recorded live in 1989 ⭘⭘

Kyung Wha Chung has recorded both of these central concertos before, but in this generous and attractive coupling these EMI performances not only have the benefit of more modern sound but are more spontaneous in their expressive warmth. The Bruch was recorded in the studio and reflects Chung's growing ease in a recording environment. Notoriously, she dislikes the constraints of recording, when she is so essentially spontaneous in her expressiveness. Here her expressive rubato is freer, so that in the first movement the opening theme is more impulsive, and her freedom in the second subject vividly conveys the sort of magic you find in her live performances. The slow movement brings extreme contrasts of dynamic and expression from orchestra as well as soloist, and the finale is again impulsive in its bravura. The Beethoven is a live recording. Chung sustains spacious speeds very persuasively indeed. She is freely flexible in her approach to Beethoven, as Tennstedt is too, but magnetically keeping an overall command. The element of vulnerability in Chung's reading adds to the emotional weight, above all in the slow movement, which in its wistful tenderness is among the most beautiful on disc. As for the outer movements, they are full of flair, with a live event bringing few if any penalties in flaws of ensemble or other blemishes. Altogether, an exceptionally attractive release.

Bruch Violin Concerto No 1
Mendelssohn Violin Concerto in E minor, Op 64
Maxim Vengerov *vn* **Leipzig Gewandhaus Orchestra / Kurt Masur** Teldec 4509-90875-2 Ⓜ
(51 minutes: DDD). Recorded 1993 ○

As one might expect with Mendelssohn's own orchestra, the Leipzig Gewandhaus, under Kurt Masur, there is a freshness and clarity in the Mendelssohn which ideally matches the soloist's playing, at once keenly felt and expressive but clean and direct, with articulation of diamond precision and fine tonal shading. If anyone has ever thought this work at all sentimental, this shatters any such idea, and Masur encourages a flowing speed in the central *Andante*, which brings out the songfulness of the main theme. It is consistent with this approach that in his expressiveness Maxim Vengerov is more inclined to press ahead than to hold back, so that with a dashingly fast speed for the finale one is left breathless at the end. The slow movement of the Bruch gains from being taken at a flowing speed, and Vengerov finds a rare depth of expressiveness, which makes the movement a meditation rather than simply a lyrical interlude. With outstanding recorded sound, warm yet clear and detailed, there is now no more recommendable disc of this coupling.

Violin Concerto No 1. Scottish Fantasy
Cho-Liang Lin *vn*
Chicago Symphony Orchestra / Leonard Slatkin
CBS Masterworks SK42315 (53 minutes: DDD) Ⓕ
Recorded 1986 ○○

This is a radiantly beautiful violin recording, ravishing in the combination of passion and purity, strength and dark, hushed intensity. There are quite a number of virtuoso violinists with a special affection for Bruch's *Scottish Fantasy* and Lin's warm and committed performance plainly indicates comparable involvement. He is prepared to play with the gentlest possible *pianissimo* and the engineers provide a balance which allows you fully to appreciate this, the natural balance being particularly welcome. The orchestral sound is warm and atmospheric in CBS's Chicago manner, slightly diffused but with the solo instrument nicely distinct. Although Lin may be a fraction less volatile, he is even more firmly positive in bravura passages, producing double-stopping of astonishing purity and precision, with the cleanest possible articulation in dazzling passagework. He actually makes the *Scottish Fantasy* seem compact. This is a work that is not only rather diffuse in its four-movement construction, it lasts a full half-hour, but this performance make you want to hear it again at once, so many moments of delight does it bring. If Lin scores a distinct point or two over his rivals, it is most clearly in the dashing finale, not least when at the end its bravura fades into a dreamy cadenza which Lin plays with a celestial purity and repose. Slatkin's and the Chicago Symphony Orchestra's accompaniments are outstanding.

Bruch Violin Concerto No 2 **Goldmark** Violin Concerto No 1 in A minor, Op 28
Nai-Yuan Hu *vn* **Seattle Symphony Orchestra / Gerard Schwarz**
Delos DE3156 (60 minutes: DDD) Ⓕ
Recorded 1993-94

Hu is a virtuoso in the best sense of that word, with uncommon lyrical gifts, who can shape phrases with a sense of gentle rapture and coax his violin to produce the most lovely sounds. Even though the Bruch was specifically written for Sarasate, neither of these warm-hearted concertos impresses primarily by its brilliance. Here both gain from the understanding partnership attained by Hu with Schwarz and his excellent Seattle orchestra within a kindly acoustic. Having attended the première of Bruch's Second Concerto, Brahms wrote to Simrock: 'Hopefully a law will not be necessary to prevent any more first movements being written as an *Adagio*. That is intolerable for normal people.' Bruch's riposte was, 'If I meet with Brahms in heaven, I shall have myself transferred to Hell'. He could not understand why the popularity of the First Concerto precluded performance of the others, 'which are just as good if not better'. Certainly Hu's superb reading here bears out the composer's evaluation of the Second. The ardently simple presentation of the glorious main theme of that maligned *Adagio* goes right to the heart.

Clarinet and Viola Concerto, Op 88

Clarinet and Viola Concerto in E minor, Op 88. Romance, Op 85. Eight Pieces, Op 83
Paul Meyer *cl* **Gérard Caussé** *va* **François-René Duchâble** *pf* **Orchestra of the Opéra National de Lyon / Kent Nagano**
Erato 2292-45483-2 (65 minutes: DDD) Ⓕ
Recorded 1988

The Double Concerto and the Eight Pieces both stem from Bruch's later years as a composer, by which time he was ill and tiring, also embittered and resentful of the successes being enjoyed by Strauss and Debussy (the latter 'an unqualified scribbler'). His Concerto is not only a backward-looking and inward-looking work: it is the music of a weary composer with little more to say but the habit of a lifetime in saying it. The technique does not fail, though the last movement is thinly stretched; the manner is still lyrical, and makes graceful use both of the solo instruments and of the accompaniments. This is unusually disposed so that the chamber orchestra of the first movement gradually swells in numbers until it is virtually a full symphony orchestra for the finale. Some problems ensue for the viola, which is in any case cast in a secondary role to the clarinet. Parity is restored with the *Eight Pieces*, though Bruch wrote them for the talents of his son Max Felix, a gifted clarinettist whose performance of these pieces earned him favourable comparison with the great Richard Mühlfeld from the conductor Fritz Steinbach. They are pleasant pieces, sometimes drawing on the tonal companionship which Mozart discovered the instruments to have in his *Kegelstatt* Trio, sometimes contrasting them with opposing kinds of music.

Scottish Fantasy

Bruch Scottish Fantasy
Lalo Symphonie espagnole, Op 21
Tasmin Little *vn* **Royal Scottish National Orchestra / Vernon Handley**
HMV Classics HMV5 73041-2 (68 minutes: DDD) Ⓑ
Recorded 1996 ●

It is an excellent idea to couple Bruch's evocation of Scotland with Lalo's of Spain, both works in unconventional five-movement *concertante* form. Tasmin Little takes a ripe, robust and passionate view of both works, projecting them strongly, as she would in the concert hall, but neither is she lacking in poetry. Her leisurely speeds give her freedom to point rhythms infectiously and play with an extra degree of individuality in her phrasing, daringly using *portamentos* or agogic hesitations in a way that adds to the character of the reading. Little has the gift of sounding totally spontaneous on disc, with no feeling of strict studio manners. In this she is here greatly helped by the splendid, keenly polished playing of the Scottish orchestra under Vernon Handley, a most sympathetic partner. Handley is also excellent in pointing the rhythms of the fast movements of the Lalo, matching his soloist, and the recording is superb, with brass in particular vividly caught.

Symphonies

No 1 in E flat, Op 28; **No 2** in F minor, Op 36; **No 3** in E, Op 51

Symphonies Nos 1-3
Cologne Gürzenich Orchestra / James Conlon
EMI ② CDS5 55046-2 (103 minutes: DDD) Ⓕ
Recorded 1992-93

Bruch's three symphonies are works whose rather reticent melodic style, at times dense scoring and formal stiffness, need affectionate help if their genuine qualities are to emerge and outweigh their flaws. Carefully handled there is real romantic charm (and some agreeably brusque sturdiness) to the first movement of the Third Symphony; its *Adagio* has sonorous solemnity and an ardent climax, and its *Scherzo* exhibits some fire. The Second Symphony, its over-extended finale apart, is stronger still. Conlon and his Cologne players cannot always disguise passages of awkwardly coarse scoring, but their sound, though full, is lean and that is in itself an advantage. Conlon is also able to relax into Bruch's genial melodies, to linger and shape them with affectionate rubato. For anyone wanting all the symphonies of this neglected but likeable composer, this set is all in all a pretty safe recommendation.

Anton Bruckner Austrian 1824-1896

GROVE *Bruckner was the son of a village schoolmaster and organist, with whom he first studied and for whom he could deputize when he was ten. His father died in 1837 and he was sent at 13 as a chorister to the St Florian monastery where he could study organ, violin and theory. He became a schoolmaster-organist, holding village posts, but in 1845 went to teach at St Florian, becoming organist there in 1851. During these years he had written masses and other sacred works. In 1855 he undertook a counterpoint course in Vienna with the leading theorist, Simon Sechter; the same year he was appointed organist at Linz Cathedral. He continued his studies almost to the age of 40, but more crucial was his contact, in 1863, with Wagner's music – first Tannhäuser, then Tristan und Isolde; these pointed to new directions for him, as the Masses in D minor, E minor and F minor, and Symphony No 1, all written in 1864-68, show.*

In 1868, after Sechter's death, he was offered the post of theory teacher at the Vienna Conservatory, which he hesitantly accepted. In the ensuing years he travelled to Paris and London as an organ virtuoso and improviser. In Vienna, he concentrated on writing symphonies; but the Vienna PO rejected No 1 as 'wild', No 2 as 'nonsense' and 'unplayable' and No 3 as 'unperformable'. When No 3 was given, it was a fiasco. No 4 was successfully played, but No 5 had to wait 18 years for a performance and some of No 6 was never played in Bruckner's lifetime. He was criticised for his Wagnerian leanings during the bitter Brahms-Wagner rivalries. His friends urged him to make cuts in his scores (or made them for him); his lack of self-confidence led to acquiescence and to the formal distortion of the works as a result. Late in his life he revised several of his earlier works to meet such criticisms.

Bruckner taught at a teacher-training college, 1870-74, and at Vienna University – after initial opposition – from 1875. Only in the 1880s did he enjoy real success, in particular with Symphony No 7; his music began to be performed in Germany and elsewhere, and he received many honours as well as grants from patrons and the Austrian government. Even in his last years, he was asked to rewrite Symphony No 8, and when he died in 1896 No 9 remained unfinished.

Bruckner was a deeply devout man, and it is not by chance that his symphonies have been compared to cathedrals in their scale and their grandeur and in their aspiration to the sublime. The principal influences behind them are Beethoven and Wagner. Beethoven's Ninth provides the basic model for their scale and shape, and also for their mysterious openings, fading in from silence. Wagner too influenced their scale and certain aspects of their orchestration, such as the use of heavy brass (from No 7 Bruckner wrote for four Wagner tubas) and the use of intense, sustained string cantabile for depth of expression. His musical forms are individual: his vast sonata-type structures often have three rather than two main tonal areas, and he tends to present substantial sections in isolation punctuated by pregnant silences. Huge climaxes are attained by remorseless reiterations of motifs, or, in the Adagios, by the persistent use of swirling figural patterns in the violins against which a huge orchestral tutti is inexorably built up, often with ascending phrases and enriching harmonies. Secondary themes often have a chorale-like character, sometimes counterpointed with music in dance rhythms. Slow movements are often planned (as in Beethoven's Ninth) around the alternation of two broad themes. Scherzos are in 3/4, often with the kind of elemental drive of that in Beethoven's Ninth; they carry hints of Austrian peasant dances, and some of the trios show ländler-like characteristics. From No 3 onwards, Bruckner's symphonies each end with a restatement of the work's opening theme. Because of their textual complications, Bruckner's symphonies have mostly been published in two editions: the Sämtliche Werke series (ed R Haas and others) usually give the work as first written, the Gesamtausgabe (ed L Nowak and others) the revised and cut versions.

Complete Symphonies

No 0 in D minor, 'Die Nullte'; **No 1** in C minor; **No 2** in C minor; **No 3** in D minor; **No 4** in E flat, 'Romantic'; **No 5** in B flat; **No 6** in A; **No 7** in E; **No 8** in C minor; **No 9** in D minor

Symphonies – Nos 1 (Linz version), 2, 3 (1889 version, ed Nowak), 4-7, 8 (ed Haas) and 9
Berlin Philharmonic Orchestra / Herbert von Karajan
DG ⑨ Karajan Symphony Edition 429 648-2GSE9 Ⓜ
(520 minutes: ADD/DDD). Recorded 1975-81

Karajan's understanding of the slow but powerful currents that flow beneath the surfaces of symphonies like the Fifth or Nos 7-9 has never been bettered, but at the same time he shows how much more there is to be reckoned with: strong emotions, a deep poetic sensitivity (a Bruckner symphony can evoke landscapes as vividly as Mahler or Vaughan Williams) and a gift for singing melody that at times rivals even Schubert. It hardly needs saying that there's no such thing as a perfect record cycle, and Karajan's collection of the numbered Bruckner symphonies (unfortunately he never recorded 'No 0') has its weaknesses. The early First and Second Symphonies can be a little heavy-footed and, as with so many Bruckner sets, there's a suspicion that more time might have been spent getting to know the fine but elusive Sixth. However, none of these performances is without its major insights, and in the best of them – particularly Nos 3, 5, 7, 8 and 9 – those who haven't stopped their ears to Karajan will find that whatever else he may have been, there was a side to him that could only be described as 'visionary'. As for the recordings: climaxes can sound a touch overblown in some of the earlier symphonies, but overall the image is well focused and atmospheric. A valuable set, and a landmark in the history of Bruckner recording.

Symphonies Nos 0-9
Concertgebouw Orchestra / Bernard Haitink
Philips Bernard Haitink Symphony Edition ⑨
442 040-2PB9 592 minutes: ADD) Ⓑ
Recorded 1963-72

Right from the start of Haitink's cycle, you sense here is a man who briefed his team, read the map and is raring to go. The cycle began in 1963 with Symphony No 3. The playing is alert, rousing even, though inclined to edginess. This is partly to do with the sound of the post-war Concertgebouw (marginally more Francophone in those days), partly a matter of an as yet not-quite-symbiotic bond between Haitink and the players. The Fourth Symphony followed in 1965. This suggests some deepening and refining of the bond between conductor and orchestra and is a very fine performance. The *Scherzo* is particularly exciting. The Ninth Symphony (also 1965) came surprisingly early in the cycle. The performance explains why. Both conductor and orchestra play the symphony as if in the grip of a deep compulsion. The orchestral response alone has a terrific explicitness and immediacy. As for Haitink, he plays the work very dramatically, as a symphonic psycho-drama, 'a vastation', as thinkers and theologians of Bruckner's time often termed breakdown and purgation of the spirit.

When it comes to the great central tetralogy, Symphonies Nos 5-8, there are some problems. Most problematic is the Eighth Symphony. The Seventh has a quick first movement; but it survives. Not so the Eighth. The first movement just about hangs together, thanks to some finely concentrated playing at critical junctions. But the *Scherzo* is absurdly quick, as is the finale. Haitink's account of the Sixth Symphony is less of a problem than it is with some rivals. The recording is exceptionally fine – everything thrillingly immediate, finely 'terraced'. The *Adagio* always sounded well and so it remains, the keening Dutch oboe and bright trumpets the perfect foil for the Rembrandt-colourings of the strings and lower brass. Symphonies Nos 1, 2, 5 and 6 were the last to be recorded. (Haitink actually ended with this rousing account of No 1.) They are all very fine. This is one of the best Fifths ever made; dramatic where Karajan is epic but fascinatingly alive and well integrated. The Second Symphony also receives an exceptional performance (the text, as elsewhere in the cycle, is Haas). Philips's CD remastering realizes just how vivid and astonishingly natural these Concertgebouw-played, Concertgebouw-made recordings are. You will need a supplementary account of the Eighth, but this hardly matters when the set is remastered, at a knock-down price.

Symphonies Nos 3-9. Choral Works
[ab]**Dame Margaret Price** *sop/mez* [b]**Doris Soffel** *mez* [a]**Christel Borchers** *contr* [a]**Claes H Ahnsjö,** [b]**Peter Straka** *tens* [a]**Karl Helm,** [b]**Matthias Hölle** *basses* [ab]**Munich Philharmonic Chorus;** [a]**Munich Bach Choir; Munich Philharmonic Orchestra / Sergiu Celibidache**
EMI ⑬ Celibidache Edition CDS5 56688-2
(712 minutes: ADD/DDD). Texts and translation included. Recorded live 1982-95 Ⓕ

Also available separately – *CDC5 56689-2* (66 minutes): No 3 (ed Nowak). *CDC5 56690-2* (79 minutes): No 4 (ed Haas). ② *CDS5 56691-2* (90 minutes): No 5 (ed Haas). *CDC5 56694-2* (66 minutes): No 6 (ed Haas). ② *CDS5 56695-2* (114 minutes): No 7 (ed Haas); Te Deum[a]. ② *CDS5 56696-2* (104 minutes): No 8 (ed Nowak). ② *CDS5 56699-2* (113 minutes): No 9 (ed Nowak). Rehearsal sequences. *CDC5 56702-2* (77 minutes): Mass No 3 in F minor[b]

As a thinker, Celibidache was part genius, part crank. (This Bruckner set reveals both aspects.) A bizarre aggregation of musical, spiritual and quasi-scientific ideas led him to believe that because of what he called 'epiphenomena' – the need for each note to sound, resonate and return – it was necessary to place round the music an inordinate amount of space: 'The richer the music, the slower the tempo.' It is Celibidache's overriding preoccupation with slowness, with temporal space, which helps conjure forth what has got to be one of the greatest Bruckner performances recorded – this 1987 account of the Fourth Symphony, a truly towering act of the re-creative imagination – and several that are well-nigh interminable. His initial tempos are often quite sprightly. It is when he gets to the second and third subjects – to the great *Gesangsperiode* in each movement – that he drops down many more gears than most Bruckner conductors would dare imagine. What Celibidache gives us, in effect, is a sequence of slow movements within the symphonic continuum. In each case, the slow movement itself is the crown (what a revelation his reading of the slow movement of the Sixth Symphony is!), the dark sun at the centre of the Bruckner universe around which the *adagio* sections of the opening and closing movements (and the third movement Trio) slowly circle. The problems come in the Seventh, Eighth and Ninth Symphonies. The Haas edition of the Eighth Symphony (Celibidache uses the slightly shorter Nowak edition) gives an estimated playing time of 78 minutes. Many conductors are quicker than this. Some are slower. But even these are as the flash of a swallow's wing alongside the dinosaur flap of Celibidache's record-breaking 104 minutes. The performance of the Seventh Symphony is almost as odd. Here Haas gives an estimated playing time of 68 minutes. Par for the course is nearer 62 or 63 minutes. Celibidache takes nigh on 80. Since the symphonies and the F minor Mass are available separately, the performances to acquire are those of the Fourth and Sixth Symphonies. The Fifth, too, if you don't already have one of Jochum's performances or Karajan's 1975 Berlin recording to which the Celibidache is surprisingly close in tempo and style, even though the manner of the music-making is a good deal earthier.

The ensemble playing, even in the best performances, is not faultless. Celibidache occasionally has trouble getting woodwind and brass in together; the solo flute can play like a seraph but the flutes *en masse* are tentative, and the clarinet playing is chancy. The brass playing is generally first-rate, but it is the strings that one comes back to. The recordings have weight, warmth and immediacy. The choral works, though, fare less well; in the *Te Deum*, the choir is a misty irrelevance and although you hear more of it in the F minor Mass, neither the recording nor the choral or solo singing is in the top flight. Despite Celibidache's occasional flashes of insight, there are better versions of both works to be had elsewhere. The transfers have been well done. Applause (rarely instantaneous, Celibidache clearly had his public well trained) is separately banded, and the pauses between movements are 'live', and feel right in context. Thus we have the best of all worlds, live music-making sensitively preserved on record.

Symphony No 1

Symphony No 1 (Linz version). Te Deum
Jessye Norman *sop* **Yvonne Minton** *mez* **David Rendall** *ten* **Samuel Ramey** *bass***Chicago Symphony Chorus and Orchestra / Daniel Barenboim**
DG Galleria 435 068-2GGA (70 minutes: DDD) Ⓜ
Text and translation included. Recorded 1980

There is still a relative lack of choice when it comes to single CDs of the boisterous First Symphony in its original Linz version, so the reissue of this Chicago recording under Barenboim is a most attractive choice, particularly if you don't mind adding to your collection a superb – eloquently sung, expertly played, exceptionally well-recorded – account of Bruckner's mighty *Te Deum.* In the symphony, Barenboim is witty, affectionate and vital and the Chicago playing is sumptuous. Here and there one might long for the countrified tread of Eugen Jochum, a German Bruckner conductor of the old school, but one can understand DG's desire to give the best of this Barenboim Bruckner cycle another airing. Warmly recommended if the coupling suits.

Symphonies Nos 1 (ed Carragan) and 3 – Bewegt, quasi Andante (1876 version)
Royal Scottish National Orchestra / Georg Tintner
Naxos 8 554430 (76 minutes: DDD) Ⓢ
Recorded 1998 ●

Some of the outstanding performances in the late Georg Tintner's Naxos Bruckner series have been of the early symphonies. 'Your young men shall see visions,' says the Prophet Joel. It has been Tintner's skill to conjure vision by marrying sharpness of detail and youthful diction with a daring breadth of utterance. He did this in his recording of the Symphony No 3 and he does it again here in a fine account of the First recorded in Glasgow's Henry Wood Hall with the RSNO at the top of its considerable form.

Timings of individual movements confirm a broad reading, as broad as Václav Neumann's on his old Leipzig set (nla). But where Neumann's performance ended up sounding soulful and ponderous, Tintner's is as fresh as could be. Bruckner called this a 'cheeky little minx' of a symphony. Tintner shows it to be that, and more. (Bruckner's own generally unavailing pursuit of cheeky post-pubescent minxes clearly fed a rich and lively fantasy life which the symphony vividly charts. Or so Freudians might have us believe.)

The announcement that this is the 'world première recording' of the 'unrevised Linz version' shouldn't cause seasoned collectors to throw out cherished extant recordings of the 1866 'Linz' (as opposed to 1890-91 'Vienna') version. The emendations Bruckner made in 1877 to the 1866 text are fairly minor. That said, future interpreters may want to follow Tintner in using this plainer Haas/Carragan edition rather than the 1955 Nowak edition which, in typically meddling style, incorporates the 1877 changes into the original text. The added plainness of the orchestration at the very end of the symphony is absolutely right for a peroration that is both prompt and ingenious.

Though it receives no banner headlines, the fill-up is rather more intriguing textually. It is the largely forgotten 1876 revision of the original 1873 version of the *Adagio* of the Third Symphony. The changes include a quicker tempo, a gentle elaboration of the violin figurations near the start, and a disastrous attempt to underpin the lead to the final climax with a new *Tannhäuser*-like violin accompaniment. Since this is funny in the wrong way, it could be said nicely to complement the main work on the disc which is funny (and fun) in all the right ways.

Symphony No 2

Symphony No 2 (ed Carragan)
National Symphony Orchestra of Ireland / Georg Tintner
Naxos 8 554006 (71 minutes: DDD) Ⓢ
Recorded 1996 ●●

This exceptional recording by veteran Austrian conductor Georg Tintner is in a league of its own. It is a beautifully shaped performance, characterfully played and vividly recorded. What's more, it is, in effect, a gramophone 'first', for though the original, 1872 version of Bruckner's Second Symphony has been recorded elsewhere this is the first to reach a wider market. Not that the differences between editions are hugely significant. What the earlier 1872 version principally offers is the reversal of the order of the two inner movements (the *Scherzo* now comes before the *Andante*), a full clutch of repeats in the *Scherzo* and Trio, a rather longer development section in the finale, various small changes to the orchestration and the absence of some of the more meretricious tempo markings. What is appealing about the 'full monty' is the feeling it gives of the symphony's Schubertian pedigree: heavenly length joining hands with a deep sense of melancholy and melodic *Angst*. Which brings us to Tintner's reading of the symphony, which is shrewd and affectionate, tellingly phrased and beautifully paced, the moves away from and back to the basic pulse nicely handled. This is Bruckner conducting of the old school. There is also something reassuringly old-fashioned about the playing of the National Symphony Orchestra of Ireland. The entire orchestra has the character of a well-to-do country cousin who is blessedly innocent of the more tiresome aspects of metropolitan life. This is an exceptional recording.

Symphony No 2 (ed Haas)
Saarbrücken Radio Symphony Orchestra / Hiroshi Wakasugi
Arte Nova Classics 74321 27770-2 Ⓢ
(61 minutes: DDD). Recorded 1992

Budget-price Bruckner is something of a rarity in the record catalogues; super-budget Bruckner more or less unheard of. Hiroshi Wakasugi's performance of the Second Symphony is a delight. He plays the complete text and plays it with fluency and affection. He has a keen eye for the letter of the score, a keen ear for its Schubertian sonorities, and an even keener instinct for the flow and continuity of its rhythms and the logic of the whole. This couldn't replace the Karajan but anyone happening upon this disc is likely to find a friend for life, in both the music and its performance.

Symphony No 3

Symphony No 3 (1877 version)
Vienna Philharmonic Orchestra / Bernard Haitink
Philips 422 411-2PH (62 minutes: DDD) Ⓕ
Recorded 1988 ●●

This is the least perfect of the nine symphonies, though not the least magnificent. As a symphonic project it is both magnificent and characteristic. Unfortunately, the sweep of the musical vision outdistanced Bruckner's ability to control it structurally; in 1889 he returned to the text and radically revised it. For most Bruckner scholars, however, the 1877 text is the ideal. 'It is stylistically purer,' Robert Simpson has written 'and though its construction leaves much to be desired, its weaknesses are exacerbated, not propped, by the crude remedies of the later version.' The 1877 is the version to collect. The finale's polka subject, which has a certain sly wit and grace in Haitink's Concertgebouw recording, retains a certain slyness and grace but with the Vienna Philharmonic it is more the slyness and grace some of us associate with that old darling of Chancery Lane, Mr Horace Rumpole. This newer recording, like the playing, is immensely forceful. Haitink, dedicated Brucknerian that he is, makes a wonderful job of the work without resort to all those unseemly cuts, revisions and re-orchestrations that most of his rivals rely on. He is a Brucknerian bold and true, and the Vienna Philharmonic, the brass in particular, plays gloriously, with particular thrust, spontaneity, and weight of tone in the much disputed finale.

Symphony No 3 (1873 version)
Royal Scottish National Orchestra / Georg Tintner
Naxos 8 553454 (78 minutes: DDD) Ⓢ
Recorded 1998

This original (1873) version of Bruckner's Third is his longest symphony, a work of epic intent filled with youthful fire. It has rarely been recorded and is rarely played, yet this is the work as it was meant to be heard. Had Robert Haas's fully prepared and engraved edition of the 1873 version not been incinerated in a raid on Leipzig in 1944 (happily, an uncorrected proof later turned up in Winterthur) the work's recorded history might have been very different. In the event it was not until 1977 that the Bruckner/Haas edition finally appeared in print, edited by Nowak, since when it has been recorded by Inbal and Norrington (nla). The Inbal recording is admirable in almost every way, a consistently satisfying version orchestrally and technically. What it lacks is the danger and visionary daring of parts of Tintner's reading. The contrast is most marked in the first movement where Tintner, like Inbal but unlike Norrington, judges the written instruction *Gemässigt, misterioso* ('Moderate, mysterious') to be all-important, taking the *alla breve* instruction as a secondary consideration. Yet he goes further than Inbal. As early as fig A (1'23"), it is clear that persistence of pulse is not a priority. Tintner conducts the Third Symphony as he (and, indeed, all other good Brucknerians) would conduct the Fifth. It makes for a revelatory reading of the first movement. Clock-watchers will no doubt be fascinated by the relative statistics: Norrington 18'48", Inbal 24'00", Tintner 30'34". In fact, the Tintner doesn't seem slow. Vivid yet profound are the words that most immediately come to mind. It is Tintner at his greatest.

The sound he draws from the Royal Scottish National Orchestra – the strings in particular – has an almost Sibelian spareness to it, as does the recording, where space has been cleared for tuttis that are clear, fierce, and unclaustrophobic. Clearing space involves keeping the orchestra slightly at a distance, at some cost to the winds – and the woodwinds in particular – in the two outer movements and in the otherwise wonderfully vibrant and beautifully paced *Scherzo* and Trio. The finale makes less of a mark. The playing of the polka in the crucial polka-cum-chorale seems to be under-rehearsed, bland and uninvolved; a pity since this juxtaposition of dance hall and funeral rite is one of Bruckner's most graphic inventions.

Symphony No 4

Vienna Philharmonic Orchestra / Karl Böhm
Decca Legends 466 374-2DM (68 minutes: ADD) Ⓜ
Recorded 1973. ●●●

Böhm's VPO account of the Fourth Symphony has the unmistakable stamp of greatness. It was made in the Sofiensaal in Vienna with its helpful acoustic; for though one can detect a whisper of tape-hiss if you put your ear against the loudspeaker, in almost every other way the sound is realistic and warm. There is a roundness in the brass tone with plenty of bite and fullness but no unwanted rasp – especially important in this symphony. Böhm's Fourth is at the head of the field irrespective of price. The warmth as well as the mystery of Bruckner are far more compellingly conveyed in Böhm's spacious view than with any other conductor.

Awards 1999

Symphony No 4
Berlin Philharmonic Orchestra / Günter Wand
RCA Victor Red Seal 09026 68839-2 Ⓕ
(69 minutes: DDD)
Recorded live in 1997 ●●●

The pacing of each movement is majestic, not too fast, in the first movement; a slow, contemplative tread in the second; animated, but capable of opening out into something more leisurely in the *Scherzo*; varied, but with the sense of an underlying slow pulse in the finale. Wand allows himself some fairly generous rubato from time to time, halting slightly on the high unaccompanied cello phrase in the first movement second subject. From the start there's something about Wand's performance that puts it in a different league from rival recordings. There's the depth and richness of the string sound in the opening *tremolo*. A few seconds later the Berlin Philharmonic's principal horn intones the opening phrases so magically and majestically that it's hard to believe one isn't listening to a real voice – a superhuman larynx, not just a contraption of brass and valves. Of course the sound is, to some extent, the orchestra's own, but there is a feeling that the players are giving extra for Wand, something with more inner life; and the unaffected eloquence and shapeliness of the phrasing is all Wand. It carries you along even when the rubato ought to jar, as it does sometimes in other versions. This is a concert performance, and it feels like one. Things that work in concert – the once-off live inspiration – aren't always ideal solutions on a repeatable commercial recording. Take Wand's big *ritardando* at the fleeting reference to Brünnhilde's Magic Sleep motif in the finale – the effect might pall after a couple of playings. But then he does ease very effectively into the weird *pianissimo* cello and bass figures that follow, triplet quavers gradually *becoming* triplet crotchets. The sound quality is excellent.

Symphony No 4
Philadelphia Orchestra / Wolfgang Sawallisch
EMI CDC5 55119-2 (67 minutes: DDD) Ⓕ
Recorded 1993 ●

The Philadelphians have always had their special sound, nurtured and lovingly preserved down the years by Stokowski, Ormandy and Muti; and to judge by this fine Bruckner Fourth it is something that Sawallisch will not willingly forgo. Indeed, the genius of this particular reading lies in its protean quality, the very way the sound is so interestingly adapted and applied. The Fourth is an odd work. Popular, certainly, but popular for certain specific moments: the mistily romantic opening, the fine hunting *Scherzo* and the finale's magnificent peroration. The finale does not so much round off the work as propose the kind of grounds on which it might originally have been built. Which is where Sawallisch's reading, and the Philadelphians' realization of it, is so interesting. Apart from one passage midway through the slow movement, where the mood darkens and the music mysteriously broods, the first two movements can have an almost straightforwardly classical feel. This seems to be Sawallisch's view, and the Philadelphia playing here is lucid and eloquent. How different is the finale! Here we are deep in the Wagnerian forest – the dramatic change of mood graphically registered. What sounded at first light like just another Bruckner Fourth has proved to be anything but. The recording is glorious.

Symphony No 4
Royal Concertgebouw Orchestra / Nikolaus Harnoncourt
Teldec 0630-17126-2 (65 minutes: DDD) Ⓕ
Recorded live in 1997

If you're expecting something controversial – something to fulminate against – you'll probably be disappointed. Harnoncourt's interpretation of Bruckner Fourth is nothing like as provocative as his Beethoven. It is relatively fast, but not startlingly so. If Harnoncourt's first movement is more gripping, more like a symphonic drama than usual, that has more to do with the crisp, clear rhythmic articulation than with the number of crotchets per minute. The solo woodwind and horn playing that follows is lovely, expansive enough; what else would one expect from the Concertgebouw in Bruckner? This is an unusually compelling Bruckner Fourth – exciting throughout the first movement and *Scherzo*, and in passages like the problematical Brucknerian Ride of the Valkyries that erupts after the finale's bucolic second theme. In many more traditional Bruckner performances the bass often seems to move in sustained, undifferentiated pedal points. In Harnoncourt's version one is often aware of a deep pulsation – like the throbbing repeated notes that open the finale – continuing, however discreetly, while the tunes unfold above. To hear the finale's second theme in this version is to be reminded that Bruckner was an excellent dancer, light on his feet until he was nearly 70. Of course one shouldn't confuse the man with the musical personality, but why should Bruckner always sound heavy, sedentary, as though slowly digesting a gigantic meal? Harnoncourt provides us with the light-footedness, while allowing the music to unfold at its own speed, to take time. There's no question that Nikolaus Harnoncourt must be considered a serious contender in Bruckner.

Symphony No 4 (ed Haas)
Berlin Philharmonic Orchestra / Herbert von Karajan
EMI Karajan Edition CDM5 66094-2 Ⓜ
(70 minutes: ADD). Recorded 1970-71

There was always something very special about Karajan's EMI recordings of the Fourth and Seventh Symphonies with the Berlin Philharmonic Orchestra. Both works had, of course, been in Karajan's repertory for many years, though it was not until 1970 that he made his first recordings of either work. The recording of the Fourth is one of the finest ever made in Berlin's Jesus-Christus Kirche, the church's clear but spacious acoustic allowing the Berlin playing to be heard in all its multicoloured, multi-dimensional splendour.

Symphony No 5

Staatskapelle Dresden / Giuseppe Sinopoli
DG 469 527-2GH (77 minutes: DDD) Ⓕ
Recorded live in 1999 ●●●

Publishers publish 'study' scores, but no marketing guru has ever come up with the idea of the 'study' recording. They exist, of course: recordings which do us the singular honour of providing an interpretation while at the same time allowing us to hear all the notes. This doesn't suit every piece of music ('Gentleman,' Richard Strauss once said, 'Give me an *impression* of the music!'), nor does it suit all listeners. Here we have a study recording par excellence, as close as we have come on record to being provided with a sound facsimile of the symphony's printed page.

Such an undertaking requires immense discipline from the orchestra, the balance engineer (Klaus Hiemann) and the conductor. On this form the Staatskapelle Dresden have no peer. The sound is characterful, the ensemble exact, the concentration absolute. There must be a quarter of a million notes in this symphony and we hear practically all of them more or less flawlessly delivered. (A hair's-breadth wobble by a player it would be invidious to identify is an event in itself.)

Like Sinopoli's Bruckner Nine recording, the engineering is intensely concentrated: not cold as such but fiercely analytical. It entirely suits the Fifth, arguably the most intricately crafted of all Bruckner's symphonies. The myriad ways in which themes combine and recombine is a source of endless fascination, albeit one hitherto best examined in the silence of the study.

Sinopoli is here more the alpha-quality Kapellmeister than the Bruckner 'interpreter'. The text is his passion, his trust in it is absolute, his patience immense. The first movement is one of Bruckner's most subtle and elusive. So much of it is marked to be delivered in an undertone, with *p*, *pp*, and *ppp* the principal markings. Cynics will argue that Bruckner wrote these in because he did not trust the orchestras and conductors of his time, a theory Sinopoli gives us every reason to doubt.

After the enigma that is the first movement, Sinopoli senses a somewhat easier, more sunlit mood in the *Adagio*, the limbo-like moments of stasis notwithstanding. He is wary, however, of what some conductors see as the Upper Austrian folksiness of the *Scherzo*. 'A formidable human power directly faced with heedless gaiety' is how Robert Simpson sums up this music, exactly how Sinopoli appears to see it, too.

The finale resolves fugue, chorale and a host of earlier considerations into a glorious home-coming, a process greatly helped here by Sinopoli's refreshingly swift, clear, beautifully integrated treatment of the main exposition. How splendidly this helps clarify and energise the argument later on! There is here an inevitability about the proceedings that has everything to do with the performance (the orchestra, in the tumultuous final pages, is supremely poised and perfectly balanced), without the performance in any way drawing attention to itself. It is Bruckner and the impeccable logic of his musical thinking we are listening to (and very moving it proves to be).

Among rival versions, Karajan's 1976 Berlin recording, though rather grander in manner, comes closest to this (though the CD transfers have always seemed foggy and recessed). Welser-Möst's doesn't quite operate on this level and, in any case, is now eclipsed technically and orchestrally. Those who prefer the thrills and spills of a 'real' performance (the Sinopoli maybe live but it doesn't seem so) will no doubt prefer Horenstein's 1971 Proms performance. But that is a very different kind of experience, more overtly dramatic, more mundane. Sinopoli's Bruckner Fifth has all the beauty of a great mathematical proof.

Symphony No 5 (ed Nowak)
London Philharmonic Orchestra / Franz Welser-Möst
EMI CDC5 55125-2 (70 minutes: DDD) Ⓕ
Recorded live in 1993 ⭘

Welser-Möst has looked, listened, and decided 'enough is enough'. Enough pussy-footing around the Fifth as though it were some sacred monolith, enough of circumspection. This is a sensual and exciting performance, certainly not for those of a nervous disposition or those who genuinely seek the longer view such as Karajan provides. Welser-Möst's reading is more in the Jochum style where analysis doesn't drive out passion, where what is contemplated in the study doesn't entirely predetermine what is experienced in performance. Welser-Möst takes risks with the finale, where the fugue is driven fiercely on, and in the *Adagio* where his observation of the *alla breve* marking gives a generous pendulum-swing to the crotchet-triplet accompaniment. This can make for a reading that is unconsidered and overquick, but not here. The play of two against three is beautifully realized as the basis for one of the most richly expressive of all recorded accounts of this movement. In general, he favours an almost Beethoven-like drive and directness. Yet there is plenty of space around the lyric subjects and chorales. In the first movement the gearing of the transitions whereby this is achieved is especially elaborate. He is most obviously himself, the boy from Linz, in the *Scherzo* and Trio. It begins fiercely, as Bruckner requires, but then opens out in a wonderfully broad lolloping Upper Austrian dance. The London Philharmonic plays gloriously throughout and the engineers get superb results from the Vienna Konzerthaus auditorium.

Symphony No 6

Bruckner Symphony No 6 (ed Haas)
Wagner Wesendonk Lieder
Christa Ludwig *mez*
New Philharmonia Orchestra / Otto Klemperer
EMI CDM5 67037-2 (77 minutes: ADD) Ⓜ
Recorded 1964 and 1968 ⭘⭘⭘

Alleluias are in order. This is the finest – nay, the only wholly acceptable – account of Bruckner's Sixth Symphony on record. Quite why this terse, searching and exhilarating symphony has so eluded interpreters is difficult to establish; suffice it to say that Klemperer's performance, made in London's Kingsway Hall over eight sessions in November 1964, is masterly from first note to last. It is a performance by turns lofty tender and serene, but it is, above all, a structurally cogent performance and within the compass of its steady-treading tempos an intensely exciting one. Back in 1965, it was hailed as glorious – the Klemperer Bruckner style majestic, magisterial, magnificently architectural – at its very finest, and time has dimmed neither the performance nor EMI's superbly articulate recording which reproduces with clarity and immediacy the marvellously transparent textures of Klemperer's reading, the fabulous string traceries and the stark beauty of woodwind and brass playing. All this comes up very vividly on this reissue. Walter Legge disbanded the

Philharmonia in 1964 and eight months on, one senses the players – every jot of their former expertise in place – in doubly determined mood. The performance has immense backbone, yet in the *Scherzo* and the fantastic echoing Trio section the playing marries clarity with immense subtlety. Here and in the slow movement, Klemperer demonstrates that you don't have to be effete to be tender, sensitive or profound. This is a performance that no Brucknerian can afford to miss. This latest CD reissue also has historical significance, the Ludwig/Klemperer *Wesendonk* interpretation having something of a classic status. Surprisingly, Klemperer's speeds are on the fast side, and he is occasionally perfunctory, but Ludwig's singing is dark and meaningful, the tone refulgent. Her account is illuminating, even if on the heavy side, but it is compelling in its urgency and elevation, with correspondingly warm support from conductor and orchestra.

Symphony No 7

Concertgebouw Orchestra / Bernard Haitink
Philips Solo 446 580-2PM (65 minutes: ADD) Ⓜ
Recorded 1979 ⭘

Bernard Haitink's 1979 Concertgebouw account of Bruckner's Seventh Symphony was a change from and an advance on his 1966 Concertgebouw recording. Broader in pace and warmer-toned, it retained much of the earlier reading's classical integrity while also paying more attention to the music's Schubertian aspect. Haitink does not go as far down that particular road as Karajan does in his deeply reflective, pantheistically charged 1971 Berlin Philharmonic version. The velvet sonorities of the Berlin performance will not please everyone, though it has to be said that the Berliners' quiet, affective glow of colour is part and parcel of a reading which is deeply thought through and of a piece with itself. (The *Adagio* is especially fine, more *innig* than the Haitink and more of a piece.) But the return of this later Haitink recording to the catalogues is both timely and welcome for those in search of a fine, middle-of-the-road, mid-price recording of the symphony.

Symphony No 7 (ed Haas)
Berlin Philharmonic Orchestra / Herbert von Karajan EMI Karajan Edition CDM5 66095-2 Ⓜ
(68 minutes: ADD). Recorded 1970-71 ⭘

'Glowing' is an apt word with which to describe this account of the Seventh. Very much *sui generis*, this is arguably the most purely beautiful account of the symphony there has ever been on record. Other readings may surge and carol more than this but none captures so intense a sense of spiritual longing within the context of a calm yet unerringly sure articulation of the symphonic structure. Oddly, the recording has moments of slightly wispy string sound which sound wispier here than they did on EMI's earlier less spacious, less full-bodied – digital remastering. That, though, is not enough to undermine the recommendation as such.

Symphony No 7 (ed Haas)
Vienna Philharmonic Orchestra / Herbert von Karajan
DG Karajan Gold 439 037-2GHS (66 minutes: DDD) Ⓕ
Recorded 1989 ⭘

The Vienna Philharmonic features on what was Karajan's last recording, an idiomatic account of the Seventh Symphony, lighter and more classical in feel than either of his two Berlin recordings yet loftier, too. As for the Original-image bit-processing you need go no further than the first fluttered violin *tremolando* and the cellos' rapt entry in the third bar to realise how ravishingly 'present' the performance is in this reprocessing. Or go to the end of the symphony and hear how the great E major peroration is even more transparent than before, the octave drop of bass trombone and bass tuba 13 bars from home the kind of delightfully euphoric detail that in 1989 only the more assiduous score-reader would have been conscious of hearing. This remastered Bruckner Seventh is definitely pure gold.

Symphony No 7 (ed Haas)
Royal Scottish National Orchestra / Georg Tintner
Naxos 8 554269 (66 minutes: DDD) Ⓢ
Recorded 1997

Since there are no recommendable budget, let alone super-budget recordings of Bruckner's Seventh Symphony, this will do nicely. It is a finely schooled performance, chaste and discreet, with a notable reading of the *Adagio* which lies at the heart of the work. Tintner sees this very much as a piece, the first (G major) climax finely achieved, the later, greater climax splendidly 'placed'. The coda, Bruckner's lament for the dead Wagner, is played relatively swiftly, touchingly and without bombast. In general, his reading of the score is loyal without being in any sense dull or hidebound. In an ideal world, the playing of the first violins would be more consistently secure *in alt*. In particular, you have the feeling that both the players and the engineers (the engineering is generally excellent) would have benefited from a chance to refine and tidy parts of the performance of the first movement. A notable bargain, none the less.

Symphony No 8

Symphony No 8 (ed Haas)
Vienna Philharmonic Orchestra / Herbert von Karajan
DG ② 427 611-2GH2 (83 minutes: DDD) Ⓕ
Recorded 1988 ⭘⭘⭘

As if by some strange act of providence, great conductors have often been remembered by the immediate posthumous release of some fine and representative recording. With Karajan it is the Eighth Symphony of Bruckner, perhaps the symphony he loved and revered above all others.

It is the sense of the music being in the hearts and minds and collective unconscious of Karajan and every one of the 100 and more players of the Vienna Philharmonic that gives this performance its particular charisma and appeal. It is a wonderful reading, every bit as authoritative as its many predecessors and every bit as well played but somehow more profound, more humane, more lovable if that is a permissible attribute of an interpretation of this work. The end of the work, always astonishing and uplifting, is especially fine here and very moving. Fortunately, it has been recorded with plenty of weight and space and warmth and clarity, with the additional benefit of the added vibrancy of the Viennese playing. The sessions were obviously sufficiently happy for there to shine through moments of spontaneous eloquence that were commonplace in the concert hall in Karajan's later years, but which recordings can't always be relied upon to catch.

Symphony No 8

Symphony No 8 (ed Nowak)
Vienna Philharmonic Orchestra / Carlo Maria Giulini
DG ② Masters 445 529-2GMA2 (88 minutes: DDD) Ⓜ
Recorded 1984 ●●

Giulini's performance of the Eighth can confidently be claimed as also being among one of the great Bruckner recordings of the age. It is an immensely long-breathed performance, yet it is of a piece with itself and the music it serves. It is a reading that is suffused from start to finish with its own immutable logic, cast and voiced, you might say, like a great tenor bell. The playing of the Vienna Philharmonic is similarly whole: luminous as though lit from within, immensely strong, yet flawless in every aspect of tone and touch. You might argue that Giulini's case is helped by his use of the tidied Nowak text; that Karajan, in his last and greatest recording, goes one stage further by conjuring from the fuller Haas edition a performance of even greater grandeur and sweep. But the two are not in contention. Both are miracles sufficient unto themselves; the Karajan a shade earthier, perhaps, a shade rougher-hewn than the Giulini which glows, in this magnificent transfer, like Carrara marble lit by the evening sun.

Symphony No 9

Berlin Philharmonic Orchestra / Daniel Barenboim
Teldec 9031-72140-2 (63 minutes: DDD) Ⓕ
Recorded live in 1990 ●

This is an outstanding version of Bruckner's Ninth Symphony – and no surprise, given Barenboim's evident sympathy for the work in concert performances over the past three decades. Like Karajan's reading on DG, it is essentially a 'central' account of the score that attempts neither extreme breadth of utterance nor sharp-edged drama. Rather it is a reading that combines long lines, flowing but astutely nuanced, and sonorities that are full-bodied yet always finely balanced. The outer movements have great rhetorical and emotional power; the *Scherzo* is thunderous and glinting by turns. The *Adagio* begins very slowly but, for once, Barenboim gets away with it, the movement growing organically rather than remaining still-born near the start. This is a live performance and, as you would expect, it is superbly executed, the playing every bit as fine as it is on the Karajan recording. But even that doesn't compete with the natural splendours of the Teldec. This is superb Bruckner sound, spacious and clear, with strings, woodwind and brass at once unerringly 'placed' and finely matched. Given good engineering and the kind of astute playing we have from Barenboim and the Berliners, the Philharmonie is far from being the acoustic lemon it is sometimes said to be. This is currently a front-runner for this symphony.

Symphony No 9
Vienna Philharmonic Orchestra / Carlo Maria Giulini
DG 427 345-2GH (68 minutes: DDD) Ⓕ
Recorded 1988 ●

Giulini's Ninth is an idiosyncratic reading – nearly seven minutes longer than Karajan's – but it has about it a kind of immutable breadth and boldness of utterance that is not to be gainsaid. Despite the slowness, there is very much the sense of his being the master of his own brief. As a concept it is quite different from the musically dynamic readings of others. In the first movement's main *Gesangsperiode* it can seem dangerously broad with the Vienna strings rather tensely following the contours of Giulini's protracted beat. Here the wary score-watcher may notice some unevenness in ensemble though, that said, this is a reading which should be patiently heard rather than proof-read. The *Scherzo* is very effective, with drive and dynamism. After that, the orchestra is at its finest in the concluding *Adagio*, not only the Viennese horns, but the entire ensemble in the difficult broad transitions and terrifying C sharp minor climax. The recording is magnificent.

Symphony No 9
Berlin Philharmonic Orchestra / Herbert von Karajan
DG Galleria 429 904-2GGA (62 minutes: ADD) Ⓕ
Recorded 1976 ●●

Karajan's 1976 recording has long been something of a classic, capturing the conductor and the Berlin Philharmonic on top form. From the opening of the titanic first movement to the final grinding dissonance of the lofty *Adagio* Karajan's control of phrase lengths, tempo and rhythmic swing are gloriously apparent. This beautifully recorded performance seems refreshingly urgent, cohesive and properly threatening. Exceptionally vivid, it was sometimes difficult to tame on LP, but the CD version gives unalloyed pleasure.

Symphony No 9
Berlin Philharmonic Orchestra / Günter Wand
RCA Red Seal 74321 63244-2 (62 minutes: DDD) Ⓕ
Recorded live 1995-97 ●

Symphony No 9. String Quintet in F – Adagio (arr Stadlmair)
Leipzig Gewandhaus Orchestra / Herbert Blomstedt
Decca 458 964-2DH (77 minutes: DDD) Ⓕ
Recorded 1995-97

Symphony No 9
Royal Scottish National Orchestra / Georg Tintner
Naxos 8 554268 (60 minutes: DDD) Ⓢ
Recorded 1997

On this occasion, it is the octogenarians who have it. Blomstedt's account of the Ninth is clear and methodical in its approach but there never seems to be a great deal *behind* the notes. (In the outer movements, at least: the *Scherzo* is fine.) Nor is the Leipzig playing all one might hope for in terms of weight of tone or precision of intonation. In the titanic string passage in the first movement (bar 333ff) Blomstedt's Leipzig strings are all but swamped by the brass. Not so the SNO strings under Tintner, though neither orchestra at this point is any real match for Wand's BPO. Decca's Leipzig recording seems clean enough, though the timpani are not always audible (*piano* registers as *pianissimo*, *pianissimo* barely registers at all). The best thing on the Decca is a sensitive and lyrical account of the sublime *Adagio* from Bruckner's String Quintet. Tintner's account of the symphony, though, is very fine, a disc to be purchased with confidence by those who have been investing in this (generally) excellent budget-price series. His account of the *Scherzo* and Trio is as quick and glintingly malevolent as Horenstein's on his famous old 1954 Vox recording (nla), his reading of the outer movements logical yet searching, too. There is, for example, nothing maudlin or long-drawn about his treatment of the final *Adagio*, yet the sense of troubled nobility of utterance is everywhere there, right through to the slightly tremulous quality of the horns' long-held final chord.

In the *Scherzo*, Wand is slower than Tintner or Blomstedt; this works perfectly well in context, though, the Trio is, by any reckoning, disappointingly flaccid. This, however, is the only flaw in a performance that is otherwise remarkably similar to Tintner's in its sense of the work's mingled spirituality and drama but played by the Berliners with a power, spontaneity and depth of tone that neither of the rival orchestras can quite match. This is not to say that the Berliners' playing is inch-perfect. It isn't. What transforms their performance, lifting it on to the very highest level, is that special visceral quality which has long been bedded deep in the orchestra's collective unconscious. Karajan used to talk of the players taking wing and shifting direction 'like a flock of birds'. A great conductor will allow this to happen without in any sense relinquishing his grasp of the larger argument. Wand's is just such a performance, marvellously directed but with moments of sublime frenzy and sublime quiet. So powerful a performance could easily produce a slightly cluttered recording. In fact, the RCA recording is first-rate, the best of the three. It is rich and immediate, yet marginally clearer in the depiction of those troublesome timpani entries than the otherwise excellent Naxos. This is Wand's third recording of the Ninth. It surpasses his own earlier Cologne and live North German RSO performances, though it does not supersede all else that has gone before. However, it will no doubt be avidly collected by concert and radio audiences who have recently been marvelling at his Bruckner conducting in Edinburgh, London and elsewhere.

String Quintet in F

String Quintet in F. Intermezzo in D minor. Rondo in C minor. String Quartet in C minor **P**
L'Archibudelli (Vera Beths, Lisa Rautenberg *vns* Jürgen Kussmaul, Guus Jeukendrup *vas* Anner Bylsma *vc*) Sony Classical Vivarte SK66251 Ⓕ
(76 minutes: DDD). Recorded 1994

'Bruckner is long, he takes time,' remarked Anner Bylsma in a *Gramophone* interview in March 1995; not exactly controversial, but it is important in understanding his, and his ensemble's, approach to the Quintet. The first movement in particular is more spacious than any other version. But there is more to it than tempo. What matters here is the subtlety of phrasing and fineness of the shading, giving vitality and inner intensity to patterns that can easily sound repetitive, especially at this speed. Much of the Quintet is marked *p*, *pp* or *ppp*; L'Archibudelli shows how magically suggestive so many of the quiet passages can be and how important it is to respect those dynamic gradings. They also make the work as a whole sound as unified and sublimely purposeful as the best of the symphonies. As for coupling: the 22-minute student Quartet, with its hints of Mendelssohn and rather more obvious debt to Haydn, is beautifully played, and there is more than one pre-echo of greater things to come. The spaciousness of the Sony sound suits the Quintet especially well, the more obviously 'chamber' textures of the Quartet perhaps less so.

Masses

No 1 in D minor; **No 2** in E minor; **No 3** in F minor

Masses – Nos 1[a], 2 and 3[ba]
Edith Mathis, [b]Maria Stader *sops* **[a]Marga Schiml, [b]Claudia Hellmann** *mezzos* **[a]Wiesław Ochman, [b]Ernst Haefliger** *tens* **[a]Karl Ridderbusch, [b]Kim Borg** *basses* **Bavarian Radio Chorus and Symphony Orchestra / Eugen Jochum**
DG ② The Originals 447 409-2GOR2
(148 minutes: ADD). Text and translation included. Ⓜ
Recorded [a]1963, [b]1971 and [c]1972 ●●

Like Bruckner, Eugen Jochum came from a devout Catholic family and began his musical life as a church organist. He would have known the Mass texts more or less inside out, which explains why his readings focus not on the sung parts – which, for the most part, present the text in a relatively foursquare fashion – but on the orchestral writing which, given the gloriously full-bodied playing of the Bavarian orchestra, so lusciously illuminates familiar words. He approaches the Masses with many of the same ideas he so eloquently propounds in his recordings of the symphonies and the music unfolds with a measured, almost relaxed pace which creates a sense of vast spaciousness. This can have its drawbacks: one is so entranced by the beautifully moulded orchestral introduction to the *Benedictus* from the D minor Mass that the entry of a rather full-throated Marga Schiml comes as a rude interruption. DG's transfers are extraordinarily good – they really seem to have produced a sound which combines the warmth of the original LP with the clarity of detail we expect from CD.

Mass No 1. Te Deum in C
Joan Rodgers *sop* **Catherine Wyn-Rogers** *contr* **Keith Lewis** *ten* **Alastair Miles** *bass* **Corydon Singers and Orchestra / Matthew Best** with **James O'Donnell** *org*
Hyperion CDA66650 (67 minutes: DDD). Texts and translations included. Recorded 1993 Ⓕ

Earth shaking is the only way to describe Bruckner's great *Te Deum* – literally and metaphorically with, on this disc, the thundering Westminster Cathedral organ (sensitively superimposed). The considerably enlarged Corydon Singers sing with consummate skill, rooting out the subtleties and nuances of Bruckner's magnificent score yet always faithful to Matthew Best's thrusting, athletic direction. It is followed with a performance of the D minor Mass of extraordinary power and strength. From the dazzling orchestral colour and the electrically charged climaxes piling in one on top of the other, to the opulent writing for voices encompassing a vast array of human emotions, Bruckner's debt to Wagner is everywhere apparent. This is very much Bruckner the symphonist – the orchestra dominates the work – and this orchestra produces playing of the very highest calibre.

Mass No 3. Psalm 150 in C
Juliet Booth *sop* **Jean Rigby** *mez* **John Mark Ainsley** *ten* **Gwynne Howell** *bass* **Corydon Singers and Orchestra / Matthew Best**
Hyperion CDA66599 (68 minutes: DDD). Texts and translations included. Recorded 1992 Ⓕ

The F minor Mass can certainly be regarded as being among the finest music Bruckner ever created. The intensity of religious feeling is heightened rather than diminished by the sumptuous orchestral support, and the soaring melodies and opulent harmonies are somehow purified and enriched by the devotional character of these familiar texts. Matthew Best's performance, by understating the music's abundant richness, gives tremendous point to the inner conviction of Bruckner's faith. His orchestra, brought together for this recording but sounding as if it has been playing this music all its days, plays with commendable discretion, balancing admirably with a relatively small choral body. As with everything the Corydon Singers and Best turn their hands to, it is an impeccable performance, infused with real artistry and sensitive musicianship. Enhanced by the glorious solo voices from a high-powered team this is a CD of rare depth and conviction.

Mass No 3 (ed Nowak). Te Deum
Jane Eaglen *sop* **Birgit Remmert** *contr* **Deon van der Walt** *ten* **Alfred Muff** *bass* **Linz Mozart Choir; London Philharmonic Orchestra / Franz Welser-Möst**
EMI CDC5 56168-2 (79 minutes: DDD). Texts and translations included. Recorded 1995 Ⓕ

Welser-Möst's quartet of soloists, for all their manifest strengths, give the impression of trying a little too hard for their own good. Yet the sheer, almost operatic, spectacle of Welser-Möst's riveting performance of the Mass should not be missed. Raw excitement on an almost primeval level sets the scene for the exhilarating *Te Deum*. Here again Welser-Möst goes at it with all guns blazing. Joakim Svenhedren treats us to a ravishing solo violin obbligato in the 'Aeterna fac' but this is only the briefest of respites in a performance which sweeps all before it in a consuming whirlwind of energy. Best and the Corydons find a greater depth to this music than Welser-Möst and his team. But if it's sheer, unbridled excitement you want nothing beats this.

Te Deum

Bruckner Te Deum
Verdi Messa da Requiem
Leontyne Price, Leonie Rysanek *sops* **Hilde Rössl-Majdan, Christa Ludwig** *mezzos* **Fritz Wunderlich, Giuseppe Zampieri** *tens* **Walter Berry** *bass-bar* **Cesare Siepi** *bass* **Vienna Singverein; Vienna Philharmonic Orchestra / Herbert von Karajan**
EMI Salzburg Festival Edition mono ② CMS5 66880-2 (107 minutes: ADD). Recorded live in 1960 and 1958 Ⓜ

Karajan recorded these works more than once in the studio, in better sound, yet these live recordings made at Salzburg have their own validity in the vast Karajan discography because they catch performances undoctored in any way by the conductor or others, and recorded, obviously, at a single stretch. The Verdi was recorded in the Felsenreitschule. In spite of Karajan's many better-recorded versions, we would recommend listening to this one because you will be rewarded with a more immediate experience than with those recorded in the studio (the 1967 film done at La Scala apart). Everything here seems that much more vivid, more spontaneously felt than in the studio. It is true there are a few noises off, including one incident that sounds like a member of the audience falling off their perch, and some questionable intonation among the soloists, but these are worth tolerating for Karajan's visionary reading, one also strong on orchestral detail. His Vienna forces are on tremendous form, alive to the nuances Karajan wants us to hear and to his overview of the work's structure.

Heading the solo team is Rysanek, her only recording of this piece. After a tentative start she soon finds her most responsive form, with the arching phrases of 'Salva me' finely taken, a beautifully floated entry at 'Huic ergo' and an even more ethereal one at 'Sed' in the 'Domine Jesu Christe' movement. She may lack some of the dramatic bite needed for the 'Libera me' but compensates with warmth and sensitivity in the reflective moments. Ludwig is as ever strength personified in the mezzo solos. Zampieri – Vienna's tame Italian tenor at the time and a favourite with the conductor – sings with vibrant tone and great feeling, although his dynamic range is limited. Siepi is his firm sympathetic self on the bass line. The Verdi is complemented by the 1960 Bruckner recorded in the new Festspielhaus, a performance of breadth and conviction, adorned by the singing of Price and the youthful Wunderlich. The sound of the Verdi is reasonable, of the Bruckner very good, albeit still mono The notes offer contemporary reviews. Gottfried Kraus, as always in these archive sets from Austria, places everything in context.

Ignaz Brüll

Austrian 1846-1907

GROVE *Brüll was a close friend of Brahms, for and with whom he often played. Brüll wrote chamber and orchestral music, many songs and 10 operas, of which Das goldene Kreuz (1875) was his greatest success.*

Piano Concertos

Piano Concertos – No 1 in F, Op 10; No 2 in C, Op 24. Andante and Allegro, Op 88
Martin Roscoe *pf* **BBC Scottish Symphony Orchestra / Martyn Brabbins**
Hyperion CDA67069 (73 minutes: DDD) Ⓕ
Recorded 1998

Ignaz Brüll is remembered today for two things: first his hugely successful opera *Das goldene Kreuz*, and secondly, for being a member of Brahms's circle in Vienna. His association with Brahms has to some extent militated against an independent evaluation of his work, something this recording should go some way towards redressing. Brüll was an early developer (the booklet contains a photograph of him aged 24 with a six-inch beard!) and his two piano concertos are youthful works. The first was written when he was just 14, and it shows an incredible fertility of ideas and maturity of formal and orchestral handling. The first movement is bold and passionate, and the finale is witty and brilliant, but it is the powerful central *Andante* that most impresses. The Second Concerto, written when Brüll was 22, is a more accomplished work, with a stronger melodic vein and more varied and imaginative orchestral writing. The *Andante and Allegro*, Op 88 (1902), is a more mature work, the lyrical first section (based on an earlier unpublished song) offset by a sparkling finale. The performances are exemplary, full of warmth and character from soloist and orchestra. Roscoe's muscularity and authoritative firmness of style are complemented by his delicacy and range of colour. And the BBC Scottish Symphony Orchestra offers tonal refinement and some lovely woodwind playing. All this is helped by the full and clean recorded sound – the clarity, balance and tonal blending are magnificent.

Gavin Bryars

British 1943

GROVE *Bryars studied philosophy at Sheffield University and music privately; in the 1960s he played in jazz groups and since 1970 he has lectured at Leicester Polytechnic. A leading experimental composer, influenced by Cage and Satie, he first wrote for indeterminate forces (The Sinking of the Titanic, 1969), but more recently his music has been influenced by theories of literature; it is often repetitive and witty. His opera Medea was staged in 1984.*

Cello Concerto

Cello Concerto, 'Farewell to Philosophy'. One Last Bar, Then Joe Can Sing. By the Vaar
Julian Lloyd Webber *vc* **Charlie Haden** *db* **Nexus** (Bob Becker, Bill Cahn, Robin Engelman, Russell Hartenberger, John Wyre *perc*)**English Chamber Orchestra / James Judd**
Point Music 454 126-2PTH (75 minutes: DDD) Ⓕ
Recorded 1995

Rather like Sibelius's *Swan of Tuonela*, Gavin Bryars's 1995 Cello Concerto (or *Farewell to Philosophy*, to quote its Haydn-inspired subtitle) emerges from among shadows, its solo line climbing sadly and patiently until the long first section takes its leave among *Parsifal*-style string figurations. Section two is more animated, at least initially (timpani set the scene), until the mood darkens again; the fifth recalls the orchestration of Haydn's *Philosopher* Symphony ('pairs of English and French horns playing alternating *legato* phrases, muted violins and unmuted lower strings accompanying with *staccato* quavers'), and the sixth, blurring dissonances and a softly chiming bell. The *Farewell* connection, again after Haydn, greets the tender final section with its progressive reduction of forces, a haunting 20th-century parallel to the various *fin de siècle* swan-songs of Franz Liszt. Lloyd Webber's tone seems perfectly suited to the job, being full-bodied and expressive but relaxed enough to blend with the components of a predominantly dark accompaniment.

One Last Bar, Then Joe Can Sing (1994) was an Arts Council commission for the percussion quintet Nexus and, to quote Bryars himself, 'is a reflexion on aspects of percussion history, both personal and musical'. The work's opening takes as its starting-point the last bar at the end of the first part of Bryars's opera *Medea*, then calls on varieties of tuned percussion (the glow of marimbas in contrast to the glitter of high bells), prompts some haunting modulations and fades to a tranquil coda. *By the Vaar* (a river in Flanders and the scene of another Bryars opera) was written for – and is performed by – jazz bass-player Charlie Haden, whose specific sound (he uses gut strings) inspired a husky, mellow 'extended *adagio*'. Much of the solo work is played pizzicato which of course underlines the jazz element, while bass clarinet, percussion and strings set up a warming backdrop It's a nice piece, but the Cello Concerto is rather more than that, and *One Last Bar, Then Joe Can Sing*, more still.

Cadman Requiem

Cadman Requiem. Adnan Songbook. Wonderlawn – Epilogue
Valdine Anderson *sop* **The Hilliard Ensemble; Fretwork; Gavin Bryars Ensemble / Dave Smith**
Point Music 462 511-2 (61 minutes: DDD) Ⓕ
Texts included. Recorded 1997

Gavin Bryars is primarily concerned to let instruments and voices sound naturally, irrespective of the historical associations that these sounds may carry. When his music is as well performed and recorded as on this disc, it achieves a power and inevitability that is rare in new music. The voice seems to suit Gavin Bryars's compositional approach. The very presence of a singer accords a subjective intensity that nicely complements the unwavering, dry-eyed clarity of Bryars's instrumental writing. Bryars says he attempts to write vocal material that will highlight the unique character of each singer's voice and that all the vocal works are being performed on this recording by the specific singers he had in mind. His writing for The Hilliard Ensemble does reconstitute the characteristic four-part sound, but they are also given every opportunity to be appreciated as soloists.

In composing the *Adnan Songbook* for the young British soprano Valdine Anderson, Bryars could almost have used Richard Strauss as a model, so expressive is his treatment of her highest tessitura. On the other hand, the blunt, even artless handling of the text and instrumental accompaniment is typical of Bryars. It is this oblique mixture of understatement and expressive warmth that makes the work so original. *Cadman Requiem* is also very impressive. Dedicated to the sound engineer Bill Cadman, who died in the Lockerbie aircrash in 1988, the piece was recorded with its two ensembles, Fretwork and The Hilliard Ensemble, facing each other. The resulting rich blend of timbres, well captured by the recording, makes for arresting listening. Overall, a hauntingly beautiful album that provides compelling evidence of the recent resurgence in Bryars's work.

Ferruccio Busoni

Italian/German 1866-1924

GROVE *Born to musician parents, an Italian father and a German mother, Busoni appeared from the age of eight as a pianist. In 1876 the family settled in Graz, where he had lessons with Wilhelm Mayer and produced his first published works. He then moved to Vienna, where he came to know Goldmark and Brahms, to Leipzig and eventually Berlin in 1894. Until he was 40 his output consisted mostly of piano and chamber music, including arrangements of Bach (these were eventually published in seven volumes). But in 1902 he began conducting concerts of modern music, including works by Debussy, Bartók, Sibelius and himself, and his music began to open itself to a wider range of influence. He adopted an aesthetic of 'junge Klassizität', by which he intended a return to the clarity and purely musical motivation of Bach and Mozart; yet such works as his* Elegien *(1907), the virtuoso* Fantasia contrappuntistica *(1910) and the Second* Sonatina *(1912), all for piano, show his awareness of the latest developments including Schoenberg's most recent music, along with his reverence of the past. His* Sketch of a new Aesthetic of Music *(1907) looks forward with enthusiasm to the use of microtones and electronic means.*

The unresolved conflicts in his musical mind between futurism and classical recovery, Italian vocality and German substance, Lisztian flamboyance and Mozartian calm all inform his larger works, which include a Piano Concerto with choral finale (1904), several works on American Indian themes and operas – the E.T.A. Hoffmann fantasy Die Brautwahl *(1912), a commedia dell'arte double bill of* Arlecchino *and* Turandot *(1917) and the unfinished* Doktor Faust *(1924), where the protagonist's search after knowledge and experience is finally assuaged when he gives birth to a new future.*

Piano Concerto, K247

Marc-André Hamelin *pf*
Men's Voices of the City of Birmingham Symphony Chorus and Orchestra / Mark Elder
Hyperion CDA67143 (72 minutes: DDD) Ⓕ
Recorded 1999 **OO**

Busoni's Piano Concerto has never become a repertoire piece. It fits awkwardly into a concert programme, due to its length and its choral finale, and the extreme difficulty of its solo writing cannot quite disguise the fact that it's really more of a symphony with an elaborate piano part than a real concerto. This new recording might just change all that, for like no other performance (not even Garrick Ohlsson's stunning account on Telarc) it proves what a richly enjoyable piece it is. Without in the least understating the grandeur of the central movement (or its Faustian pointers to Busoni's later style), it finds humour not only of the gallows kind in the first *Scherzo* (even a touch of irony to its nostalgic centre), while the brilliant tarantella second *Scherzo* is often very funny indeed: Busoni celebrates his Italian ancestry, but at times bursts into helpless laughter at it as well. Hamelin obviously loves the work's opportunities for grand romantic pianism and barnstorming, and he has a fine ear for its stark boldness. Elder is splendidly eloquent, from the nobly Brahmsian introduction to the full-throatedly sung finale. Both are at their best in the central *Pezzo Serioso*, which is grand and grave, but alert to the presence of Chopin as well as Liszt. The recording is warm and spacious, the piano at times just a touch (but forgivably) close. This is a remarkable performance.

Additional recommendation

Piano Concerto, K247

Ogdon *pf* **John Alldis Choir, Royal Philharmonic Orchestra / Revenaugh**

HMV Classics HMV5 73857-2 (69 minutes: ADD: 9/00) Ⓢ

John Ogdon's pioneering 1968 recording of this marathon work was among the very finest of his records. It's a hugely impressive interpretation and a steal at super-bargain price

Arlecchino

Robert Wörle *ten* Arlecchino (Peter Matič *spkr*) Leandro; **Marcia Bellamy** *mez* Colombina (Katharina Koschny *spkr*); **René Pape** *bass* Ser Matteo del Sarto; **Siegfried Lorenz** *bar* Abbate Cospicuo; **Peter Lika** *bass* Dottor Bombasto**Berlin Radio Symphony Orchestra / Gerd Albrecht**

Capriccio 60 038 (67 minutes: DDD). Notes and synopsis included. Recorded 1992 Ⓕ

Albrecht's *Arlecchino* is one of the finest readings of a Busoni opera yet committed to disc. He projects a great feeling of drama and dramatic pace (as well as the *commedia dell'arte* aspects of the opera) and seems to have absorbed the Busoni spirit successfully; the presence of Busoni's final masterpiece, *Doktor Faust*, is exceptionally strong. Marcia Bellamy is well suited to the role of Colombina, and there are some exceptionally good performances from René Pape, Siegfried Lorenz and Peter Lika in the roles of Matteo, Abbate Cospicuo and Dottor Bombasto. The master-stroke, however, is the casting of Robert Wörle in both the Arlecchino and Leandro roles, an inspired idea and one which is delivered with great aplomb and panache. Albrecht draws superb orchestral playing from the Berlin Radio Symphony Orchestra (especially in the wind and brass departments), and the recording is well balanced and atmospheric.

Die Brautwahl

Siegfried Vogel *bass* Voswinkel; **Carola Höhn** *sop* Albertine; **Graham Clark** *ten* Thusman; **Vinson Cole** *ten* Lehsen; **Pär Lindskog** *ten* Baron Bensch; **Roman Trekel** *bar* Leonhard; **Günter von Kannen** *bar* Manasse

Chorus of the Deutsche Staatsoper, Berlin; Staatskapelle Berlin / Daniel Barenboim

Teldec ② 3984-25250-2 (116 minutes: DDD)

Notes, text and translation included. Recorded live in November 1993 Ⓕ ●

Busoni's first mature opera occupied him for seven years (1905-11). He may not have been as natural a man of the theatre as Richard Strauss, but *Die Brautwahl* has plenty of fine music in it – at times foreshadowing the splendours of *Doktor Faust*. This 1992 Berlin production used a version made by Antony Beaumont, whose completion of *Doktor Faust* was a great success. As Beaumont explains in the booklet, we get only about two-thirds of the whole, and all aspects of the opera's subject-matter may not be ideally balanced. This 'fantastic comedy' is based on a story by E T A Hoffmann, with the climactic scene in which a bride is chosen (hence the title) leaning heavily on *The Merchant of Venice*. The action is set in Berlin, but there are echoes of Wagner's Nuremberg in the text and characterization. Musically, Busoni keeps his distance from Wagner, though he fails to match the potent lyricism and needle-sharp comic timing of Verdi's *Falstaff*, one of his ideals. Even so, the music is attractive, and ranges widely in character, as adept at depicting the sinister musings of Manasse as the romantic longings of the bride-to-be Albertina or the serio-comic tussles between Thusman and Leonhard, the mysterious manipulator of events. This performance is a strong one, with a certain, untroublesome amount of stage noise. No doubt reflecting the staging, the recording occasionally recesses the singers, but the energy and command of Barenboim's conducting are never in doubt. The energy does not mean that anything is rushed, and the romantic episodes are warmly moulded, the scenes of fantasy properly attentive to matters of colour and texture. Roman Trekel, a warm yet dramatically resonant baritone, makes a strong impression as Leonhard. He is the perfect foil to Graham Clark, who tackles the role of Thusman with relish, and with considerable technical skill in music which demands lyrical sensitivity as well as comic agility.

Doktor Faust

Dietrich Henschel *bar* Doktor Faust; **Markus Hollop** *bass* Wagner, Master of Ceremonies; **Kim Begley** *ten* Mephistopheles; **Torsten Kerl** *ten* Duke of Parma; **Eva Jenis** *sop* Duchess of Parma; **Detlef Roth** *bar* Soldier; **William Dazeley** *bar* Natural Philosopher; **Eberhard Lorenz** *ten* Lieutenant; **Frédéric Caton** *bass* Theologian; **Jérôme Varnier** *bass* Jurist; **Dietrich Fischer-Dieskau** *spkr* Poet **Geneva Grand Theatre Chorus; Chorus and**

Orchestra of the Opéra National de Lyon / Kent Nagano
Erato ③ 3984-25501-2 (196 minutes: DDD) Ⓜ
Notes, text and translation included.
Recorded 1997-98 ⭘

'Sooner or later there must be a new recording of *Doktor Faust*', declared Michael Oliver, welcoming the CD reissue of the 1969 DG version – heavily cut, but with Dietrich Fischer-Dieskau in the title-role. This new recording, not only provides the full, uncut text, as completed by Busoni's pupil Philipp Jarnach soon after the composer's death, but also offers as supp\lements Antony Beaumont's very different realizations of parts of the opera's later stages. So complete is this version, indeed, that it includes the spoken prologues and epilogues, with Fischer-Dieskau providing a poignant link to that earlier recording. Given that Beaumont worked from sketches and other information of which Jarnach was unaware (or chose to ignore), there can be no question as to which of the two is the more genuinely Busonian, and the extended closing scene in Beaumont's version has a persuasive gravity and sense of fulfilment quite different from Jarnach's more terse yet slightly melodramatic completion. Nevertheless, it will take a sensibility more refined than most not to be swept away by the sheer visceral power of Jarnach's rendering of the death of Faust. Dietrich Henschel displays considerable style and stamina during his two extended monologues in the opera's final stages, and although his singing isn't entirely free of straining for effect, or of bluster, the character's tortured humanity is vividly conveyed.

Kim Begley makes a considerable success of the other principal role, although, in an ideal world, Mephistopheles would manage more variety – the loudness would be a little less consistent. But Begley tackles the many demanding aspects of the part with panache and, in the scintillating ballad, wit and menace are in perfect balance. Other parts are adequately taken, though the singers are not always responsive to the dramatic importance of often quite brief musical segments, and articulation of the German text varies in clarity and accuracy. This variability is one reason why the performance takes some time to take wing: another, more fundamental reason concerns the nature of the recording itself.

This is not the first of Kent Nagano's Erato releases from Lyon to have an element of dryness in the sound. At times, principal voices are backwardly placed, and even when they are not one suspects (playing the discs at 'normal' volume) that the brilliance of the orchestral sound is being damped down in order to ensure their audibility, in ways which increase the occasionally opaque impression of Busoni's harmonic writing. Nevertheless, Nagano's shaping of this extremely demanding and intricate score is neither inflexible nor inexpressive. *Doktor Faust* can at last be heard in a recording, that, in the end, reaches and reveals its essence.

Dietrich Buxtehude

German c1637-1707

GROVE *Buxtehude's first studies were under his father, who held posts as organist in Hälsingburg and Helsingor (Elsinore), as did Buxtehude himself between c1657 and 1668, when he became organist at the Marienkirche at Lübeck, one of the most important posts in north Germany; he was also appointed Werkmeister (general manager) of the church. Later that year he married Anna Margarethe Tunder, his predecessor's daughter. Besides his normal duties on Sundays and feast days, he reinstated the practice of giving Abendmusik concerts in the church on five Sunday afternoons each year. These events attracted much interest and drew JS Bach from Arnstadt in Advent 1705.*

Surviving texts from the Abendmusik performances show that he composed a number of oratorio-like works, but none has survived. The bulk of his known sacred music consists of cantatas or sacred concertos, the latter often settings of psalm texts, consisting of contrasting sections in which each line of the text is treated with a new motif. He used a concertato style, for voices and continuo (sometimes with other instruments), in which the motifs are treated in dialogue in a manner related to the Venetian polychoral style; there are also arioso sections. Buxtehude wrote a number of chorale settings, commonly with the melody in the soprano but with instrumental accompaniment and interludes; in ensemble settings he used the chorale motet style, in the manner of a sacred concerto but with motifs from the chorale melody, and he also set chorales with the melody in one voice and instrumental counterpoints. His sacred arias are mostly in strophic or varied strophic form, with a fluent, sometimes Italianate melodic style. Some extended vocal works, akin to Bach's cantatas, combine movements in the sacred concerto style with others of the aria type.

Most of Buxtehude's instrumental music is for the organ: about half consists of freely composed music, often using a toccata-like section with several fugues and incorporating virtuoso passage-work, while half consists of chorale settings, some of the variation and fantasia types, but mostly highly unified settings of a single stanza of the chorale with a richly ornamented melody. He composed suites and other music for the harpsichord; his courantes are variations of the allemandes and the gigues are loosely fugal. French influence is noticeable. He also wrote several variation sets. The only works published in his lifetime were two collections each of seven sonatas, for violins, viola da gamba and harpsichord continuo (seven more sonatas survive in MS); they are closer to the German tradition of improvisatory viol playing than to the Corelli tradition, with movements in contrasting tempo and texture. They include ground bass movements and fugues, usually only in two parts as the viol part is not always independent of the bass. Especially in his sacred vocal works and his organ music, Buxtehude represents the climax of the 17th-century north German school, and he significantly influenced Bach.

Harpsichord Works

Harpsichord Works, Volumes 1-3 **P**
8 224116: Toccata in G, BuxWV165. Canzona in C, BuxWV166. Fugue in B flat, BuxWV176. Auf meinen lieben Gott, BuxWV179. Wie schön leuchtet der Morgenstern, BuxWV223. Canzonetta in A minor, BuxWV225. Suites – C, BuxWV226; D minor, BuxWV233. Aria in A minor, BuxWV249 Ⓕ

8 224117: Canzona in G, BuxWV170. Canzonetta in G, BuxWV171. Fugue in C, BuxWV174. Nun lob mein Seel' den Herren, BuxWV215. Suites – No 10 in E minor, BuxWV235; No 18 in G minor, BuxWV242. Courant zimble in A minor, BuxWV245. More Palatino, BuxWV247 **P** Ⓕ

8 224118: Prelude and Fugue in G, BuxWV162. Canzonetta in D minor, BuxWV168. Suites – No 13 in F; BuxWV238; No 19 in A, BuxWV243. La capricciosa, BuxWV250 **P**
Lars Ulrik Mortensen *hpd*
Da Capo ③ 8 224116/7/8 Ⓕ
(oas: 52, 53 and 54 minutes: DDD). Recorded 1998 ●

Trying to determine for which instrument – organ, harpsichord or clavichord – Buxtehude's keyboard works were intended is a difficult exercise, since in the 17th century they were largely interchangeable. Reasonably enough, Mortensen includes in his survey all but those works which demand pedals – and few of these pieces seem to call for the greater degree of *sostenuto* possible on the organ. In all three discs he uses a fine Ruckers-type instrument tuned in mean-tone temperament, and arranges his programmes effectively to illustrate the wide range of Buxtehude's art, though the contrapuntal facility that drew Bach to trudge 200 miles to hear him is everywhere apparent. On Volume 1 Buxtehude's influence is most conspicuous in the Toccata, whose dashing initial declamation and subsequent *tremolos* prefigure Bach's D major Toccata; then a series of extraordinary rising modulations leads to a long fugue (which changes metre just before the end). The popular Fugue in C (Vol 2) is a jolly gigue, worthy to stand beside Bach's *Fugue à la gigue*. Equally appealing to Bach must have been Buxtehude's inventiveness, illustrated on the second and third volumes by three sets of variations. More extensive than Sweelinck's set, the 12 on *More Palatino* (whose theme is majestically expounded) show a wide variety of moods and treatments; but the 32 on *La capricciosa* – a *bergamesca* dance whose melody will be recognized as one of the tunes quoted in the Quodlibet of the *Goldberg Variations* – is without doubt among the finest of pre-Bachian variation sets. It also calls for very considerable virtuosity – which Mortensen, in his clean-cut, well controlled playing supplies brilliantly. The recordings vividly capture Mortensen's strongly rhythmic and engaging playing, whose zest is particularly apparent in the gigues in which Buxtehude delighted. These are enthusiastically recommended discs, especially volume 3 for *La capricciosa*, which is a great acquisition to the recorded repertoire.

Vocal works

Nimm von uns, Herr, BuxWV78. Jesu, meines Lebens Leben, BuxWV62. Mit Fried und Freud, ich fahr dahin, BuxWV76. Führwahr, er trug unsere Krankheit, BuxWV31. Herzlich lieb, hab' ich dich o Herr, BuxWV41. Der Herr ist mit mir, BuxWV15
Claron McFadden *sop* **Franciska Dukel** *mez* **Jonathan Peter Kenny** *counterten* **Marius van Altena** *ten* **Stephan MacLeod** *bass* **Collegium Vocale; The Royal Consort; Anima Eterna Orchestra / Jos van Immerseel**
Channel Classics CCS7895 (65 minutes: DDD) Ⓕ
Texts included. Recorded 1994

The North German middle ground between chorale *concertato* and the early cantatas of Bach is an interesting one, especially in the hands of composers of Buxtehude's stature. In these cantatas the disparate textual elements of bible passage, hymn and devotional poetry are complemented by the composer's skill in drawing together the comparably disparate musical ones of sonata, concertato principles, aria and chorale. That in itself might give these cantatas only an ephemeral charm, but Buxtehude was a musician who was gifted in the art of word-painting and, above all, in the expression of deep, often grief-stricken emotions. He could be brilliant, too, in his lyrical approach to texts, but it is an all-pervading melancholy which seems to characterise most strongly much that is most profound in his sacred vocal music. These six works demonstrate Buxtehude's formal versatility with two large-scale chorale cantatas; a beautiful ostinato-based strophic aria, with an almost startling dissonance; the famous, austere and highly contrapuntal *Canticum Simeonis* (*'Mit Fried und Freud'*) which Buxtehude performed at his father's funeral in 1674; and two *concertante* pieces, one consisting of a sinfonia and multisectional aria, the other of a sinfonia, aria and alleluia. The performances respond to the highly charged emotional outpouring of these works but can lack polish. However, the music is first-rate (the ostinato- and chaconne-based movements make particularly strong appeal) and Immerseel's direction is stylish and sensitive. The cantata texts are in German only but there is a translation of Immerseel's interesting introductory essay.

Membra Jesu nostri, BuxWV75 **P**
Bach Collegium Japan / Masaaki Suzuki
BIS CD871 (59 minutes: DDD). Text and translation included. Recorded 1997 Ⓕ

Buxtehude's *Membra Jesu nostri patientis sanctissima* is a cycle of seven cantatas, each one of which is an address to a different Member of the Body of Christ crucified, implicit in the work's title. It has been well represented in the catalogue but this recording offers an impressive addition. Indeed, in respect of ensemble and expressive *gravitas* it is, perhaps, the most convincing of them all, but the pleasure of this deeply felt reading, for some readers, may be diluted by too reverberant an acoustic. If you were present in such a building and able to sense other aspects of its ambience you might feel differently. But in the context of a CD, one would like to hear more detail, above all from the string instruments. Even so, there is no mistaking the technical skill and sensibility with which these artists have realized the tender, agonized suspensions and expressive power of these beautiful pieces. Only the intimacy of the music suffers. The solo vocal contributions are almost uniformly strong, and there are electrifying moments in the ensemble singing as, for example, in the limpid, perfectly balanced textures of the 'Ad ubera portabimini' which concludes the second cantata of the cycle. Despite reservations, this version is on balance the first recommendation.

William Byrd

British 1543-1623

GROVE *Brought up in London, Byrd was a pupil of Tallis. In 1563 he became Organist and Master of the Choristers at Lincoln Cathedral and married there in 1568. Though he remained at Lincoln until c1572 he was a Gentleman of the Chapel Royal from 1570 and its organist from 1575 (at first jointly with Tallis). In London he rapidly established himself as a composer, gaining influential friends and patrons and earning favour with Queen Elizabeth, who granted him a patent (with Tallis) in 1575 for the printing and marketing of part-music and MS paper. After his wife's death in the 1580s he remarried. He and his family were often cited as Catholic recusants, but he continued to compose openly for the Roman church. In 1593 Byrd moved to Essex, where he spent the rest of his life and was frequently involved in property litigation. His reputation was very high: he was described as 'Father of British Music'. Morley and Tomkins were among his pupils.*

Much of Byrd's vast and varied output was printed during his lifetime. His sacred music ranges widely in style and mood, from the florid and penitential motets of the Cantiones sacrae to the concise and devotional ones in the Gradualia (motet sections intended to form an impressive scheme of complete Mass Propers). His secular songs predate the true madrigal; they use intricate, flowing counterpoint derived from an earlier English style (eg Tallis, Taverner) and range from solemn lamentations to exuberant jests. His instrumental music is specially important: the many consort songs greatly influenced the later lute ayre, while the virginal pieces are unparalleled in richness of invention and contrapuntal brilliance. In all the genres in which he wrote Byrd was both traditionalist and innovator, channelling continental ideas into a native English tradition, and his expressive range was unusually wide for his day. He wrote for both Catholic and Anglican churches with equal genius.

Chamber works

Byrd Fantasia a 6. Pavan and Galliard – Kinbourough Good, MB32. The Queen's Alman, MB20, 'Hugh Ashton's Ground'. Pavan and Galliard a 6. Pavan and Galliard, MB14. Browning. Pavan a 5. The Carman's Whistle, MB36. The Irish March, MB94. My Lord of Oxenford's Maske. Pavan, MB17. A Fancie, MB25. Praeludium and Ground. Pavan and Galliard, MB60 **Anonymous** Pavans – Mille regretz; Belle qui tiens ma vie
Capriccio Stravagante / Skip Sempé *hpd*
Auvidis Astrée E8611 (73 minutes: DDD) Ⓕ
Recorded 1997

This is technically superb and musically distinctive. Skip Sempé and his musicians grab hold of each piece and play it in a way that leaves no doubt why it was chosen; that is, they have something new and interesting to say musically about each work. The sound is also wonderful: Sempé plays on a Skowroneck harpsichord that he enthusiastically describes as 'one of the first truly admirable harpsichords of the 20th century'; the viols and the recorder group are beautifully recorded, with every detail of the dense polyphony clear. So this is the kind of disc you could play to almost any music-lover as a way of explaining that Byrd is not just a great composer but one of the greatest. On the other hand, those who know the music may well feel a touch uncomfortable. While Sempé plays with often truly dazzling skill and virtuosity, many may wish that his pavans were a touch steadier. He also has a slightly mannered way of overdotting cadential bass figurations. The ensemble pieces are sometimes heavily orchestrated: the great six-part *Fantasia* that opens the disc, for example, has recorders and continuo instruments added to the viols as though to underline contrasts that some would think were already there in the music. Caveats apart, this is an invigorating disc which gives you a new understanding of some of the finest masterpieces of English music.

Byrd Fantasia a 5, BE17/8. Browning a 5, BE17/10. Fantasias a 6, BE17/13-14. In Nomines a 5, BE17/19-22 **Mico** Fancies a 4 Nos 4*a*, 5-7, 9, 10, 14, 18 and 19. Pavans a 4 Nos 2-4
Phantasm (Laurence Dreyfus, Wendy Gillespie, Jonathan Manson, Markku Luolajan-Mikkola, *viols*) with **Martha McGaughey, Alison McGillivray** *viols*
Simax PSC1143 (60 minutes: DDD) Ⓕ
Recorded 1996

The odd juxtaposition of Byrd's very finest chamber music with pieces by Richard Mico may seem rather like pairing late Beethoven with Vanhal; but it works extremely well here. Though Mico has been little regarded, much of his music shows absolute mastery (his Pavan No 4 is in some ways one of the most perfect and beautiful examples of the simple eight-bar pavane); it was eminently worth devoting half a disc to this obscure but lovely composer and bringing it to the public by associating it with Byrd. The Mico selection includes two pieces that are by no means certainly his (*Fancies* Nos 18 and 19); but they are still glorious pieces. Phantasm plays this music with immaculate control and balance, finding many telling details that might elude less careful musicians. Some listeners may be a touch less happy with the Byrd, feeling that the honeyed sounds cover certain details, that the speed of *Browning* loses the work's harmonic and contrapuntal magic, that the myriad changes in the grand six-voice *fantasias* could benefit from greater lightness of touch. But that would be like saying that only the English can perform Elgar idiomatically. What Phantasm brings to this music is a clear and unusual view of the music. Moreover, they present what is absolutely the best of Byrd's consort work, omitting the troublesome first *In Nomine* and the less perfect first six-part *Fantasia*. The four *Fantasias* and the four *In Nomines* on this disc are the core of Byrd's claim to stand among the world's greatest composers of chamber music. The performances convincingly support that claim.

Complete Keyboard Works

23 Pavans and Galliards (with two additional Pavans and five Galliards). 14 sets of Variations. 11 Fantasias. 11 Grounds. Nine Preludes. Miscellanea and variant versions P

Awards 2000

Davitt Moroney *chbr org/clav/hpd/muselar virg/org*

Hyperion ⑦ CDA66551/7 (497 minutes: DDD) Ⓜ

Recorded 1991-97 ooo

The three volumes of keyboard music added in 1950 as an afterthought to Edmund Fellowes's edition of Byrd have only slowly made their full impact as containing one of the most remarkable and innovative repertories in the history of music. A much-needed new edition by Alan Brown (1969-71) was followed by Oliver Neighbour's important critical study (1978), which perhaps for the first time made it absolutely clear that Byrd was not at all just another of the 'Elizabethan Virginalists' but stood head and shoulders above all his contemporaries – in range, in contrapuntal technique, in melodic invention and above all in formal control and imagination. Davitt Moroney has completed the picture by presenting the entire body of music on seven CDs. The results here are definitive and a triumph for all concerned. Moroney absolutely has the music in his hands, head and soul. There are so many glorious details in his playing that it is hard to know where to begin in its praise: with the wonderful clarity of the part-writing; with the superb energy of the playing; with the glittering virtuosity; with the ability to vary the colours and move from the ineffably light and whimsical to the seriously confrontational; with the constant delicate flexibility of his metre; or with his compelling grasp of Byrd's often difficult formal designs.

Moroney approached this Everest of a project over many years, in constant consultation with Brown and particularly Neighbour (who – appropriately enough – plays the 'third hand' for the duet *Fantasia* on Disc 4). Disc 3 was recorded in 1991 on the Ahrend organ at Toulouse; Discs 1 and 4 in 1992 at Ingatestone Hall, seat of one of Byrd's great patrons, Lord Petre; the remainder in 1996-7 at Fontevraud. The various engineers have coped well with the different places and occasions. Six different instruments are used to vary the colour and to fit the different styles of the music. The most novel is the muselar virginal, a marvellously earthy instrument with a refreshingly noisy action. The others are plainly chosen with loving care. A harpsichord by Hubert Bédard (after Ruckers) tends to be used for the lighter pieces, while he chooses one by Reinhard von Nagel (after Couchet) for some of the more serious works. Neatly enough, the set ends with a prelude already heard on Ahrend's Toulouse organ, now played on four different instruments in turn (omitting only the chamber organ). Alongside all of this, Moroney has provided the most detailed set of notes: 200 pages of wide-ranging erudition (in English and French) including a key to the 'BK' numbers of the Brown edition which are used throughout his running prose. Apart from a biographical essay, disquisitions about Byrd's organs, the best way to tune, loving descriptions of the instruments (including the paintings on his muselar virginal) and much else, he devotes an essay to each of the pieces – never less than 100 words and quite often around 1000 words. He also includes helpful references to Alan Brown's edition and Oliver Neighbour's critical study. So when you have got through the 497 minutes needed to listen to the discs, you still have several hours of reading to do. Enjoy.

Cantiones Sacrae

Cantiones Sacrae (1575) – Tribue, Domine. Siderum rector. Domine secundum. Fantasias – C; D. Attollite portas. Miserere mihi. Aspice Domine. Peccantem me quotidie. Salvator mundi II. O lux, beata Trinitas

New College Choir, Oxford / Edward Higginbottom with **Timothy Morris** *org* CRD CRD3492

(64 minutes: DDD). Texts and translations included. Ⓜ

Recorded 1994

There is so much wonderful six-part writing in this attractive selection from the 1575 *Cantiones Sacrae* that such a medium appears in a new light, particularly when performed by the choir and in the acoustic of New College Chapel – where, as Edward Higginbottom reminds us, they 'have been rehearsing for 500 years'. The beauty and balance of the musical architecture is constantly conveyed to the listener, particularly in the six-part writing. It doesn't matter whether these compositions were intended for liturgical or domestic use, or as a noble offering to the Queen: from a purely musical point of view they are superb. To give a single example, the little Vespers hymn *O lux, beata Trinitas* displays consummate craftsmanship through the ingenious use of the number three – three high, then three low voices, three diverse voices, a canon three-in-one, three strophes, triple time, and so on, building up to a tremendous final 'Amen'. The point made by this recording is that it all sounds natural, uncontrived, magnificent. The three organ pieces are a welcome addition: with their brilliant fingerwork and gentle registrations they present a charming and lively contrast to the vocal settings.

Gradualia

Gradualia – Volume 1: Saturday Lady Masses in Advent. Domine quis habitabit. Omni tempore benedic Deum. Christe redemptor omnium. Sermone blando a 3. Miserere. Ne perdas cum impiis. Lamentations of Jeremiah. Christe, qui lux es a 5. Christe qui lux es a 4. Sanctus. Audivi vocem de caelo. Vide Dominum quoniam tribulor. Peccavi super numerum (all ed Skinner)
The Cardinall's Musick; Frideswide Consort
(Caroline Kershaw, Jane Downer, Christine Garratt, Jean McCreery *recs*) **/ Andrew Carwood**
ASV Gaudeamus CDGAU170 (70 minutes: DDD) Ⓕ
Texts and translations included. Recorded 1996

This is a great start to The Cardinall's Musick's project to record Byrd's complete output. On the disc, some of the shorter motets are entrusted to The Cardinall's' habitual instrumental accomplices, the Frideswide Consort. A full list of sources is given for each piece, along with appropriate editorial commentary. Since Byrd set certain texts a number of times, such precision seems only sensible. Much of this music is new to the CD catalogue, and even in this selection of largely unpublished motets, there are impressive finds (the nine-voice *Domine quis habitabit*, for instance). This repertory is the mother's-milk of English choristers, and of the younger generation of English vocal ensembles The Cardinall's Musick remains perhaps the closest to that tradition outside of actual choral establishments. So they respond to Byrd with a suavity and confidence born of longstanding acquaintance. The expansive penitential pieces, such as the early *Lamentations*, are far removed from the small-scale forms of the *Gradualia*. The Cardinall's Musick respond effectively to these different functions and moods, and the recording complements them admirably.

Gradualia – Volume 2: Nativity of our Lord Jesus Christ – Puer natus est; Viderunt ... omnes fines terrae; Dies sanctificatus; Tui sunt coeli; Viderunt omnes fines terrae; Hodie Christus natus est; O admirabile commercium; O magnum mysterium. Ave regina caelorum. O salutaris hostia. Confitemini DomiNo In exitu Israel (with Sheppard and Mundy). Laudate pueri Dominum. Decantabat populus. Deus in adjutorium. Ad Dominum cum tribularer (all ed Skinner)
The Cardinall's Musick / Andrew Carwood
ASV Gaudeamus CDGAU178 (73 minutes: DDD) Ⓕ
Texts and translations included. Recorded 1996 ●

This second volume of The Cardinall's Musick's Byrd edition is, if anything, more impressive than the first. It may be a matter of programming, for the works recorded here seem to be of a higher overall calibre: even an obviously experimental piece such as *O salutaris hostia* could have been included on merit alone – yet this appears to be its first recording. Complete surveys sometimes turn up items of lesser interest, yet they also allow one to hear pieces that might have difficulty in finding a home elsewhere: witness the responsory, *In exitu Israel*, an intriguing collaborative effort by Byrd and his contemporaries, Mundy and Sheppard. Finally, one can judge for oneself the authenticity of works that modern scholarship has deemed doubtful (such as the opening *Ave regina caelorum*). Most of the pieces here involve male altos on the top line. The centrepiece is a collection of Propers from the *Gradualia* of 1607, this time for the Nativity. As on their first set, Skinner's and Carwood's decision to structure each volume around a set of Propers proves an astute piece of programming, integrating shorter items as it does (such as the various *Alleluia* settings) within a framework that allows them their own space. The singers are on very fine form indeed. It takes confidence to carry off *O salutaris hostia*, whose fierce false relations could so easily have sounded merely wilful. Only in the final, extended settings does the pace flag: the disc's last moments are rather ponderous. That aside, this is a disc to delight Byrd-lovers everywhere.

Masses

Masses – for Three Voices; for Four Voices; for Five Voices (ed Skinner). Fantasias[a] – in G, 'A Voluntary for My Ladye Nevell'; in D minor; C, 'A Fancie for My Ladye Nevell' Ⓟ
[a]**Patrick Russill** *org* **The Cardinall's Musick / Andrew Carwood**
ASV Gaudeamus CDGAU206 (79 minutes: DDD) Ⓕ
Texts and translations included.
Recorded 1999 and [a]2000 ●●●

This is incomparable music by one of the greatest English composers and it was high time for someone to take a fresh look at these works in the light of more recent research and of changing attitudes to performance practice.

Byrd had composed his three settings of the Ordinary of the Mass in troubled times for the small recusant Catholic community that still remained in England in spite of persecution. The settings would have been sung, in all probability, during festive, albeit furtive, celebrations of the old time-honoured Roman liturgy, in private chapels in the depths of the country, at places such as Ingatestone, the seat of Byrd's principal patron, Sir John Petre. Andrew Carwood has recorded them in the Fitzalan Chapel of Arundel Castle, a small but lofty building with a clear resonance that enables the inner voices of the part-writing to come through straight and clean. It hasn't the aura of King's College Chapel, but is probably easier to manage than, say, Winchester Cathedral or Merton College Chapel.

Carwood uses two voices to a part in all three Masses. In comparison with rival recordings he is alone in selecting high voices for the three-part Mass, transposed up a minor third, which introduces a note of surprising lightness and grace. He, too, is alone in taking the initiative of using an all-male choir for the four-part Mass – alto, tenor, baritone, bass. This close, low texture, together with the transposition down an augmented fourth, adds a fitting sense of gravity to the performance. In particular, it heightens the poignancy of such passages as the 'dona nobis pacem' in the *Agnus Dei*, with its series of suspensions in the drooping phrases leading to the final cadence. This is a world away from the slick performance of Dutch ensemble Quink (the four-part Mass, in 1985), who canter here like young colts to the last chord without a trace of emotion, every note precisely in its place, with a perfect blend and utter clarity, but missing entirely one essential dimension: an understanding of what it all means and in what context it was composed. The Sixteen under Harry Christophers (the four-part Mass, in 1989 – 1/91, nla – and the five-part Mass, in 1988), like The Cardinall's Musick, achieve a sense of gravity at this same point by a well-calculated tempo. The Tallis Scholars (recently reissued by Gimell) perform musically, with near perfection, but generate less feeling for the sense of the text. King's (under David Willcocks, 1959 and 1963) flow into every phrase of each Mass – in particular those of this passage in the four-part Mass – with consummate art and beauty, rising to a climax and then sinking gently to a close.

That dimension of understanding, however, is precisely what this new recording by The Cardinall's Musick seems to demonstrate. Theirs is a simplicity of style that belies simplistic criticism. Vibrato is used sparingly: 40 years on, some listeners might consider the constant use of it by a King's Choir of the late 1950s almost too overpowering. Carwood chooses his tempos with care, avoiding the modern tendency to speed everything up inordinately. David Hill, with his huge Winchester Cathedral choir, occasionally succumbs to the temptation. But Hill, like Christophers, had the excellent idea of interspersing pieces of the Proper from Byrd's *Gradualia*. Yet Carwood and The Cardinall's Musick have made their mark with the depth of their understanding. The interesting historical note on the whole background is a good pointer to what the listener may experience as the music unfolds.

Masses – Three Voices; Four Voices; Five Voices. Motet – Ave verum corpus a 4 **P**

The Tallis Scholars / Peter Phillips

Gimell CDGIM345 (67 minutes: DDD) Ⓕ

Recorded 1984 **OO**

Byrd was a fervently committed Roman Catholic and he helped enormously to enrich the music of the English Church. His Mass settings were made for the many recusant Catholic worshippers who held services in private. They were published between 1593 and 1595 and are creations of great feeling. The contrapuntal writing has a much closer texture and fibre than the Masses of Palestrina and there is an austerity and rigour that is allowed to blossom and expand with the text. The beautifully restrained and mellow recording, made in Merton College Chapel, Oxford, fully captures the measure of the music and restores the awe and mystery of music that familiarity can dim.

Mass for Five Voices (with Propers for the Feast of Corpus Christi). Gradualia ac cantiones sacrae: Part 2 – Corpus Christi. Gradualia seu cantionum sacrarum, liber secundum: Votive Mass for the Blessed Sacrament – Ab ortu solis; Alleluia: Cognoverunt discipuli

Winchester Cathedral Choir / David Hill

Hyperion CDA66837 (73 minutes: DDD). Texts and translations included. Recorded 1995 Ⓕ

On this CD the five movements of Byrd's Mass for five voices are interspersed with the five pieces of the Proper for the Feast of Corpus Christi. We can therefore transport ourselves back in time to the end of the 16th and beginning of the 17th century, and imagine their being performed, in early summer, at a live celebration of Mass in one of the great houses of the Catholic nobility. Winchester Cathedral Choir has purposely sought out an enclosed space in the great cathedral to make this recording, so that the sound captures something of the immediacy of singers performing in a small hidden room. One is particularly struck by the quality of the trebles – the slight edge to the gentle tone of very young singers – and also by the teamwork of the whole choir. The secret of this recording lies in its unity of theme and in its understanding of Byrd's triumphant statements of belief, expressed in music of great tenderness as well as strength.

Music for Holy Week and Easter

Plorans plorabit. Passio Domini nostri Jesu Christe secundum Johannem[a]. Adoramus te[bc]. Vespers for Holy Saturday[a]. Mass Propers for Easter Day. Haec dies. Angelus Domini. Mane vobiscum. Post dies octo. Christus resurgens

The Cardinall's Musick / Andrew Carwood [a]*ten* with [b]**Robin Tyson** *counterten* [c]**Patrick Russill** *org*

ASV Gaudeamus CDGAU214 (76 minutes: DDD) Ⓕ

Texts and translations included. Recorded 2000 **OOO**

The sixth volume of The Byrd Edition is a landmark recording, covering most of Byrd's Holy Week and Easter music, from the *St John's Passion* choruses for Good Friday to the Octave day of Easter, and including miniature Vespers at the end of the Easter Vigil, and the whole of the Proper of the Mass for Easter Day.

The opening motet *Plorans plorabit*, recalling the Lamentations chanted earlier in the week, is a stern reminder of the recusant atmosphere in which Byrd lived out his religious beliefs. The straightforward Passion choruses are rightly set into their proper context, an edition of *St John's Passion* prepared by Byrd's Roman contemporary, Guidetti. Admirably sung,

Carwood maintains throughout a remarkable balance between drama and restraint. A gentle consort song, *Adoramos te*, fills the space in the listener's imagination between the burial of Christ and his rising from the dead. The miniature Vespers follow, sung, almost with bated breath, to Byrd's simple three-part settings of the two antiphons, with a correction of Bretts' suggested psalm-tone for the single – and shortest – psalm.

The Mass *Resurrexi* is exhilarating, with surging themes, rhythmic interplay and bursts of joy. Byrd, unable to resist word-painting suggestive of earthquake at the Offertory, introduces here a note of merriment into a particularly serious liturgy, and doesn't entirely avoid it elsewhere. Thankfully it was under- rather than overplayed. The solemn final four-part processional *Christus resurgens* is a triumphant re-statement of the Easter: total joy.

Consort Songs

O Lord, within thy tabernacle. Quis me statim. With Lilies White. Wretched Albinus. Blame I Confess. Ye Sacred Muse. Rejoice unto the Lord. Fair Britain Isle. In Nomines a 5, BE17 Nos 18-22. Browning a 5, BE17 No 10. Fantasia a 5, BE17 No 8. Praeludium and Ground a 5

Gérard Lesne *counterten* **Ensemble Orlando Gibbons** (Wieland Kuijken, Kaori Uemura, Anne-Marie Lasla, Sylvie Moquet, Jérôme Hantaï *viols*)

Virgin Classics Veritas VC5 45264-2 Ⓕ

(65 minutes: DDD). Recorded 1996

The five *In Nomines* reveal the growing maturity and control over form of the inventive fledgling Byrd, though you will need to shuffle tracks to follow it in sequence. This is the only CD where the *In Nomines* are coupled with Byrd's consort songs. Of the other instrumental items, the *Praeludium and Ground* are treated with winsome lightness but the 20 remarkable variations on *Browning* hang more heavily than is suggested by the words of either version of the tune (the other is *The leaves be green*). Solemnity is the prevailing mood of the consort songs, four of them laments. *Wretched Albinus* refers to the disgracing of the Earl of Essex, attributed to a 'silly woman' – the same Queen Elizabeth whose protection of Byrd from anti-Catholic laws is obliquely celebrated in *Rejoice unto the Lord*, the only cheerful oasis in this desert of sorrow. Fortunately the sorrow is expressed in magnificent music of which *Ye Sacred Muse*, Byrd's tribute to the recently deceased Tallis, is the jewel in the crown. Magnificent vocal music calls for a matching singer and Gérard Lesne fills that requirement to the full. First-class recording and excellent booklet-notes provide additional reasons for acquiring this disc.

All in a garden green. La volta No 1 in G, 'Lady Morley'. O mistress mine I must. Wolsey's Wild. O Lord, how vain are all our delights. Psalmes, Sonets and Songs – Who likes to love; My mind to me a kingdom is; Farewell, false love. Triumph with pleasant melody. Truth at the First. Ad Dominum cum tribularer. Cantiones sacrae – Attollite portas; da mihi auxilium; Domine secundum actum meum; Miserere mihi, Domine Ⓟ

Sophie Yates *virg* **I Fagiolini / Robert Hollingworth; Fretwork**

Chandos Chaconne CHAN0578 (73 minutes: DDD)

Texts and translations included Ⓕ

Recorded 1994 ⊙

This disc adopts an imaginative approach to programming Byrd's music by presenting works in different genres grouped together to demonstrate a single stage in his development. It includes Latin motets, keyboard dances and variations on popular songs of the day, and sacred and secular songs (and a dialogue) with viols. There is so much here that wins our admiration: the dazzling contrapuntal elaboration of *Attollite portas*, the close-knit texture of *Da mihi auxilium* and the massive *Ad Dominum cum tribularer*; the exuberant variations on *O mistress mine* (neatly played by Sophie Yates) and Byrd's melodic gift in the strophic *O Lord, how vain.* The singers' adoption of period pronunciation of English – so that, for example, 'rejoice' emerges as 'rejwace' – affects the tuning and the musical sound, it is claimed here, but without rather clearer enunciation the point remains not proven. Probably more upsetting to many will be the Anglicized pronunciation of Latin. The viol consort gives quiet, stylish support and is well balanced, the Fagiolini sopranos occasionally 'catch the mike' on high notes (eg in the passionate pleas of *Miserere mihi, Domine*), and the recorded level of the virginals might have been a little higher without falsifying its tone. But these are very minor criticisms of a most rewarding disc.

John Cage

American 1912-1992

GROVE *Cage left Pomona College early to travel in Europe (1930-31), then studied with Cowell in New York (1933-34) and Schoenberg in Los Angeles (1934): his first published compositions, in a rigorous atonal system of his own, date from this period. In 1937 he moved to Seattle to work as a dance accompanist, and there in 1938 he founded a percussion orchestra his music now concerned with filling units of time with ostinatos (First Construction (in Metal), 1939). He also began to use electronic devices (variable-speed turntables in Imaginary Landscape No 1, 1939) and invented the 'prepared piano', placing diverse objects between the strings of a grand piano in order to create an effective percussion orchestra under the control of two hands. He moved to San Francisco in 1939, to Chicago in 1941 and back to New York in 1942, all the time writing music for dance companies (notably for Merce Cunningham), nearly always for prepared piano or percussion ensemble. There were also major concert works for the new instrument: A Book of Music (1944) and Three Dances (1945) for two prepared pianos, and the Sonatas and Interludes (1948) for one.*

During this period Cage became interested in Eastern philosophies, especially in Zen, from which he gained a treasuring of non-intention. Working to remove creative choice from composition, he used coin tosses to determine events (Music of Changes for piano, 1951), wrote for 12 radios (Imaginary Landscape No 4, also 1951) and introduced other indeterminate techniques. His 4'33" (1952) has no sound added to that of the environment in which it is performed; the Concert for Piano and Orchestra (1958) is an encyclopedia of indeterminate notations. Yet other works show his growing interest in the theatre of musical performance (Water Music, 1952, for pianist with a variety of non-standard equipment) and in electronics (Imaginary Landscape No 5 for randomly mixed recordings, 1952; Cartridge Music for small sounds amplified in live performance, 1960), culminating in various large-scale events staged as jamborees of haphazardness (HPSCHD for harpsichords, tapes etc, 1969). The later output is various, including indeterminate works, others fully notated within a very limited range of material, and pieces for natural resources (plants, shells). Cage also appeared widely in Europe and the USA as a lecturer and performer, having an enormous influence on younger musicians and artists; he wrote several books.

The Seasons

The Seasons. Suite for Toy Piano[a]. Concerto for Prepared Piano and Orchestra[b]. Seventy-Four (Versions A and B)[c]
Margaret Leng Tan [a]*toy pf*/[b]*prepared pf* **American Composers Orchestra / Dennis Russell Davies**
ECM New Series 465 140-2 (76 minutes: DDD) Ⓕ
Recorded [ab]1999 and [c]2000 ⭘

This is an enchanting CD, every item a sheer delight. Margaret Leng Tan worked with Cage in the last decade of his life and her earlier recordings show a special sympathy for Cage's keyboard music. The second of her New Albion CDs included the piano solo version of *The Seasons*, and Cage was honest enough to admit to her that he had help from Virgil Thomson and Lou Harrison in making the orchestral version recorded here. The result is Cage at his most poetic, evoking each of the four seasons in lovely changing colours. There are two realisations of one of the last of what are called Cage's 'Number Pieces', *Seventy-Four*, written specially for the American Composers Orchestra a few months before his death in 1992. This seamless garment of sustained sound in two overlapping parts is an immensely moving document from a unique human being at the end of his life. Anyone who responds to the spiritual minimalism of Pärt, Górecki or Tavener will understand, especially in these dedicated performances. The *Concerto for Prepared Piano* (1951) takes its rightful place as the major classic for the transformed instrument with orchestra – a status emphasised by this fastidious performance with its delicate sonic tapestry, including discreet radio, all reflecting Cage's absorption with oriental philosophy. Tan has recorded the *Suite for Toy Piano* (1948) before. This time the sound is closer, you can hear her in-breath just before some movements, and we could have done with more precise rhythms. Lou Harrison's orchestration is perfectly in the spirit and it makes a fascinating complement – Cage writing memorable tunes! This disc shows that much of Cage has now entered the mainstream and that his music is unique.

Sonatas and Interludes

Sonatas and Interludes
Aleck Karis *prepared pf*
Bridge BCD9081A/B (65 minutes: DDD) Ⓕ
Recorded 1997
Includes bonus disc of Cage reading his lecture 'Composition in Retrospect'

Pianists now yearn to record Cage's *Sonatas and Interludes* the way actors were supposed to want to play Hamlet. What emerges is that prepared pianos can sound very different. The latest contender, the American Aleck Karis, plays the opening Sonata more briskly than most and overall has a lively rhythmic sense – and these are American rhythms after all. Some pianists have had trouble with Cage's calligraphy and get the exposed third note of the Fourth Sonata wrong. Karis is right with an A – not a B – in this fully notated work. His sense of swing is again utterly idiomatic in the Fifth Sonata, and the Eighth, which starts with such a poetic figure, is lovely and dreamy. When it comes to the spacious opening of the Twelfth Sonata, one of Karis's preparations is twanging and feels in danger of working loose. But these are details, and Karis's performance of the cycle is as attractive as any. With Cage's 1982 lecture added as a free bonus disc, this is a good buy.

Music for Piano

Music for Piano – 1; 2; 3; 4-19; 20; 21-36; 37-52; 53-68; 69-84; 85. Music for ... Two Pianos I/II; Three Pianos; Four Pianos; Five Pianos. Electronic Music for Two Pianos
Steffen Schleiermacher *pf*
Dabringhaus und Grimm ② MDG613 0784-2 Ⓕ
(153 minutes: DDD). Recorded 1996

This set is devoted to the *Music for Piano* series almost entirely written in the 1950s, which is neglected and mostly unavailable. One can see why performers have found these pieces less attractive. After Cage's crisis year of 1952, which saw him produce the so-called silent piece *4'33"*, he was obsessed with removing his own tastes and desires from his compositions. Before he became fully committed to the I Ching's random numbers he marked out blotches and imperfections in the manuscript paper he was using as a way of getting the notes. Cage said he looked at his paper and suddenly realized that all the music was there. This procedure also settled the density of notes on the page. In the whole series the performer is left to decide dynamics and pace in a continuity dominated by single notes. If this sounds austere, we are reckoning without the ingenuities of Schleiermacher. Cage specifies various types of sound production, apart from the use of the keys: primarily plucking the strings from inside or muting them. As in Schleiermacher's prepared piano recordings, the quality of sound has been most carefully considered. A muted low note or a single plucked string can be marvellously evocative in conjunction with conventionally produced pitches. The ambience of the prepared piano is not far away. Further, Schleiermacher avails himself of Cage's provision for several of these pieces to be played together, which he does at intervals in the series. Since we have heard the same pieces solo, the superimposed versions bring back familiar material in a fascinating way. There are discoveries too, since *Music for Piano 85* is not listed in *Grove*, and *Electronic Music for Two Pianos* extends the palette refreshingly at the end of the second CD. Fastidiously researched and performed, Schleiermacher says he has taken the pieces seriously. In so doing he has begun a new chapter of virtually unknown Cage.

Litany for the Whale

Litany for the Whale. Aria No 2. Five. The Wonderful Widow of Eighteen Springs. Solo No 22. Experiences No 2. Thirty-six Mesostics re and not re Marcel Duchamp. Aria (arr Hillier). The Year Begins to Be Ripe
Theatre of Voices (Paul Elliott, Andrea Fullington, Allison Zelles, Terry Riley *vocs* Alan Bennett *voc/closed pf* Shabda Owens *voc/electronics*) / **Paul Hillier** *voc*
Harmonia Mundi HMU90 7187 (72 minutes: DDD) Ⓕ
Texts included. Recorded 1995

This is a landmark for Cage, Paul Hillier's group and everyone else. Hillier says he has been interested in Cage for years and here his own considerable advocacy has turned Cage into a troubadour of our global village. The Theatre of Voices' collection jumps right in at the deep end with *Litany for the Whale* (1980), a 25-minute monody with two uncannily similar voices (Alan Bennett and Paul Elliott) using only five notes in antiphonal phrases. Shut your eyes and this ritual could almost be Gregorian chant. The scope narrows to three notes in *The Wonderful Widow*, where the closed piano part is slightly subdued, and the same three recur in *Thirty-six Mesostics* (organized like an acrostic but down the middle), spoken by American minimalist Terry Riley and sung by Hillier. Cage's *Aria* (1958), for Cathy Berberian, has been associated with one voice but this realization for seven voices and electronic sounds is thoroughly idiomatic. *Experiences* No 2, another monody to a poem by E E Cummings is beautifully sung by Andrea Fullington, but the precisely notated pauses are not always accurate. *Aria* No 2 is a fastidious mix of extended vocal techniques by Alan Bennett with weather sounds. Cage convinces us of the musical beauty of rainfall, water and thunder. *Five* is a vocal version of one of Cage's late number pieces. This type of sustained writing is ideal for voices and there are meditative qualities in all these performances. The close-microphone breathing in *Solo* No 22 is, like everything else here, artistic and well engineered.

Antonio Caldara Italian c1670-1736

GROVE *Caldara was a chorister at St Mark's, Venice, and proficient on the viol, cello and keyboard. In the 1690s he began writing operas, oratorios and cantatas; his trio sonatas opp. 1 and 2 (1693, 1699) are his only known instrumental chamber works. He served as maestro di cappella da chiesa e dal teatro to the Duke of Mantua, 1699-1707, and maestro di cappella to Prince Ruspoli in Rome between 1709 and 1716, meanwhile composing for other cities. From 1716 until his death he was vice-Kapellmeister at the Viennese court. He was much favoured there for his dramatic works, cantatas liturgical music and oratorios; latterly he also composed stage works for the Vienna Carnival, for court celebrations and for Salzburg. His output (over 3000 works, almost all vocal) was one of the largest of his generation. His operas and oratorios make him a central figure in the creation of music drama in the tradition of Metastasio, many of whose texts he was the first to set.*

Maddalena ai piedi di Cristo

Awards 1997

Maria-Cristina Kiehr, Rosa Dominguez *sops* **Bernarda Fink** *contr* **Andreas Scholl** *counterten* **Gerd Türk** *ten* **Ulrich Messthaler** *bass* **Schola Cantorum Basiliensis / René Jacobs**
Harmonia Mundi ② HMC90 5221/2 Ⓕ
(126 minutes: DDD). Notes, text and translation included. Recorded 1995. ●●●

Caldara was the most prolific and famous oratorio composer of his day and this one, written around 1700, is wonderfully rich in fresh and attractive invention. Practically devoid of external action, it is dramatically tense and concentrates on the struggle between the forces of good and evil, the sinner Magdalen being urged towards penitence by her sister Martha; the roles of Christ and a Pharisee are considerably smaller. The work opens arrestingly, with an agitated sinfonia followed by the hypnotic aria 'Dormi, o cara': then come another 27 brief *da capo* arias with their associated recitatives. There is no lack of variety: some arias are accompanied only by a continuo instrument; others are furnished with different usages of the five-part strings. René Jacobs furthers the dramatic impact by his pacing; and his casting is flawless. He has the highly effective idea of differentiating the parts of Earthly and Celestial Love by allocating the former to a mezzo and the latter to a countertenor. Both are excellent, but so are all the participants. It seems almost invidious to single out highlights but one must cite the aria 'Diletti' for Magdalen (Kiehr) and the succeeding ornate 'Vattene' for Martha (Dominguez) and, even more, two florid arias from Scholl and two delivered passionately by Fink. You are urged to acquire this disc.

Joseph Canteloube

French 1879-1957

GROVE *Canteloube studied with d'Indy at the Schola Cantorum and collected and arranged folksongs from throughout France, especially from his native province (four volumes of Chants d'Auvergne for voice and orchestra, 1923-30). He also wrote two operas and other works.*

Chants d'Auvergne

Canteloube Chants d'Auvergne – La pastoura als camps; Baïlèro; L'ïo de rotso; Ound' onorèn gorda; Obal, din lou Limouzi; Pastourelle; L'Antouèno; La pastrouletta è lo chibaliè; La delïssádo; N'aï pas iéu de mio; Lo calhé; Lo fiolaïré; Passo pel prat; Lou boussu; Brezairola; Maluros qu'o uno fenno. Jou l'pount d'o Mirabel; Oï, ayaï; Pour l'enfant; Chut, chut; Pastorale; Lou coucut; Postouro sé tu m'aymo; Quand z-éyro petituono; Té, l'co tèl; Uno jionto postouro; Hél beyla-z-y-dau fél; Obal, din lo combuèlo; Là-haut, sur le rocher; Lou diziou bé
Villa-Lobos Bachianas brasileiras No 5
Dame Kiri Te Kanawa *sop* **English Chamber Orchestra / Jeffrey Tate**
Double Decca ② 444 995-2DF2 (111 minutes: DDD) Notes, text and translation included. Ⓜ
Recorded 1982-83

Te Kanawa's richly sensuous approach to these delightful songs is very seductive, especially when the accompaniments by Jeffrey Tate and the ECO are so warmly supportive and the sound so opulent. Her account of the most famous number, 'Baïlèro', must be the most relaxed on record, yet she sustains its repetitions with a sensuous, gentle beauty of line, supported by lovely wind playing from the orchestra which seems to float in the air. There is a resonance given to the sound, which means that certain of the brighter, more obviously folksy numbers, lose a little of their rustic sharpness. However, the overall effect is very appealing, particularly when her voice (recorded in the early 1980s) is so young and fresh. As an encore we are offered the Villa-Lobos *Bachianas brasileiras* No 5, an 'Aria' for soprano and cellos. She sings this in Portuguese and the result is ravishing, almost decadent at its softly intoned reprise. An enticing disc.

Canteloube Chants d'Auvergne, Volume 2 – La pastoura als camps; Baïlèro; L'ïo dè rotso; Ound' onorèn gorda; Obal, din lou Limouzi; L'Antouèno; La pastrouletta è lo chibaliè; N'aï pas iéu de mio; Lo calhé; Maluros qu'o uno fenno; Pour l'enfant; Quand z-éyro petituono; Hél beyla-z-y-dau fél; Là-haut, sur le rocher; Lou diziou bé
Emmanuel Chansons bourguignonnes du Pays de Beaune, Op 15 – Quand j'ai sôti de mon villaige; Il était une fille, une fille d'honneur; Le pommier d'Août; Noël; Complainte de Notre Dame; Aidieu, bargeire!
Dawn Upshaw *sop* **Orchestra of the Opéra de Lyon / Kent Nagano**
Erato 0630-17577-2 (63 minutes: DDD). Texts and translations included. Recorded 1996 Ⓕ ●

Chants d'Auvergne – Baïlèro; L'ïo dè rotso; Ound' onorèn gorda; Obal, din lou Limouzi; L'Antouèno; La delïssádo; N'aï pas iéu de mio; Lo calhé; Lo fiolaïré; Passo pel prat; Brezairola; Oï, ayaï; Pour l'enfant; Chut, chut; Lou coucut; Tè, l'co, tè!; Uno jionto postouro; La pastoura als camps; Pastourelle; La pastrouletta è lo chibaliè; Lou boussu; Malurous qu'o uno fenno; Jou l'pount d'o Mirabel; Pastorale
Frederica von Stade *mez* **Royal Philharmonic Orchestra / Antonio de Almeida**
Sony Classical Essential Classics SBK63063 Ⓑ
(73 minutes: DDD). Recorded 1980s

Maurice Emmanuel's arrangements of his local Burgundian folk-songs are antecedents to what Canteloube was to do a decade or two later. This is the second disc that Dawn Upshaw has devoted primarily to Canteloube's *Songs of the Auvergne*. Upshaw and Nagano seem to have taken a conscious decision to re-establish a link with the music's folk texts and banish as much sentimentality as they can. Their 'Baïlèro' is keenly dramatized and refuses to wallow. The simple 'Pour l'enfant' is bright-eyed with detail; and 'L'ïo dè rotso' is given a more sarcastic edge than usual. In general, there is a grittiness here that sets it apart from most recordings, with Upshaw's determination to put across the words and Nagano's restraint in the orchestra, encouraging cool strings to let the bright Lyon wind section pipe through clearly. The Sony selection with Frederica von Stade is an old friend. Two sets of recordings have been combined and all the best-known songs are here in more conventional performances than are found on the Erato disc. Von Stade varies her tone according to the sense of each song, but the overall mood is less sharp, more comfortable if you like, than with Upshaw. The RPO sounds a lot richer than its Lyon counterpart and, at slower speeds, Antonio de Almeida provides big-orchestra accompaniments, where Nagano prefers chamber-music detail. You will probably find that the consoling romanticism of the *Songs of the Auvergne* on this tried-and-trusted disc is more what you had in mind.

André Caplet

French 1878-1925

GROVE *Caplet studied at the Paris Conservatoire (1896-1901) and started his career as a conductor, in Paris and at the Boston Opera (1910-14). Debussy was a great influence on him, and a friend, Caplet being entrusted with the orchestration of Le martyre de St-Sébastien (1911), of which he conducted the first performance. His compositions became more individual, and even extraordinary in their melodic contours and effects of colour. His main works include the Conte fantastique after Poe for harp and strings (1919), the cello concerto Epiphanie (1923) and Le miroir de Jésus for women's voices, harp and strings (1923).*

Légende pour orchestre

Caplet Suite persane – Nihavend. Légende pour orchestre. Marche triomphale et pompière
Debussy (orch Caplet) Children's Corner. Pagodes. Suite bergamasque – Clair de lune
Rheinland-Pfalz State Philharmonic Orchestra / Leif Segerstam
Marco Polo 8 223751 (56 minutes: DDD) Ⓕ
Recorded 1987

The valuable services rendered by André Caplet to Debussy – besides the pieces orchestrated here he also completed *Gigues* and *Boîte à joujoux*, scored the *Martyre de Saint-Sébastien* and conducted its first performance – have overshadowed his own gifts as a composer. Colour plays a large part in Caplet's early (1901) *Nihavend*, despite its having originally been scored only for double wind quintet: it is a kind of Rimskian passacaglia or set of variations on a simple, and apparently authentic, Persian melody. The *Légende*, four years later, is also an orchestral expansion, from a nonet: a solo saxophone has a prominent role in both versions. Highly charged emotionally and clearly structured, it is disquieting in mood: like the previous piece, it has nothing Debussian about it. The Debussy items are well done, especially *Pagodes*, which culminates in a shimmering web of exotic sound with its celesta, string trills and *glissandos* in contrary motion from two harps.

Conte fantastique

Conte fantastique[a]. Les prières[b]. Deux divertissements[c]. Deux sonnets[d]. Septet à cordes vocales et instrumentales[e]
[be]**Sharon Coste,** [de]**Sandrine Piau** *sops* [e]**Sylvie Deguy** *mez* [acd]**Laurence Cabel** *hp* **Ensemble** [abe]**Musique Oblique**
Harmonia Mundi Musique d'abord HMA190 1417 Ⓑ
(55 minutes: DDD). Recorded 1992

Few listeners will fail to respond to the evocative opening of the chamber version of André Caplet's *Conte fantastique* for harp and strings based on Poe's *Masque of the Red Death*. It is dramatic too, but far from lurid in its menace, with the harp chiming to represent Death. The other three major works on this disc are even more appealing and often quite ravishing. The composer makes a memorable success of the combination of voices, harp and string quartet, helped by lovely singing, sensitive playing, and warmly atmospheric sound. Two solo *Divertissements* for harp make a central interlude. If you enjoy Ravel's chamber music, you will be captivated by this Caplet anthology.

Manuel Cardoso

Portuguese 1566-1650

GROVE *Cardoso was at Évora Cathedral choir school and in 1588 joined the Carmelite convent in Lisbon, becoming choir director and organist. He also served the future King John IV at Vila Viçosa. His many published masses and motets show his mastery of the Palestrinian contrapuntal style; numerous other works were lost in the Lisbon earthquake of 1755.*

Missa Miserere mihi Domine

Missa Miserere mihi Domine. Magnificat Secundi Toni
Ensemble Vocal Européen / Philippe Herreweghe
Harmonia Mundi HMC90 1543 (52 minutes: DDD) Ⓕ
Texts and translations included
Recorded 1994

One wonders what the 17th-century Portuguese composer Manuel Cardoso, who was for most of his life a monk at a Carmelite monastery in Lisbon, would have made of the idea that his music would enjoy a revival at the dawning of the 21st century. This recording of his *Missa Miserere mihi Domine* (a first) from the Ensemble Vocal Européen is a further – and very welcome – contribution to our knowledge and appreciation of the flowering of sacred polyphony in Portugal in the first half of the 17th century, music that, seen in a wider European context, seems 'out of phase with its time' (to quote the accompanying notes). With music as fine as this, however, any latter-day perception of an unbroken line of musical progress seems completely irrelevant. Cardoso's setting, highly reminiscent of Victoria with its never-ending sequence of suspensions, is up there with the best. Only the more straightforward, five-voice *Magnificat* lightens the tone of a disc that otherwise wallows in glorious misery.

The choir sings superbly, responding sensitively to the words and creating a full and sonorous sound that well suits Cardoso's music. Full credit, too, must be accorded to Herreweghe – and the Harmonia Mundi technicians – for achieving such an exceptionally satisfactory balance between the voice parts.

Elliott Carter

American 1908

GROVE *Carter studied at Harvard (1926-32), at the Ecole Normale de Musique in Paris (1932-35) and privately with Boulanger. Back in the USA he worked as musical director of Ballet Caravan (until 1940) and as a teacher. From boyhood he had been acquainted with the music of Schoenberg, Varèse, Ives and others, but for the moment his works leaned much more towards Stravinsky and Hindemith: they included the ballets Pocahontas (1939) and The Minotaur (1947), the Symphony No 1 (1942) and Holiday Overture*

(1944). However, in his Piano Sonata (1946) he began to work from the interval content of particular chords, and inevitably to loosen the hold of tonality. The development was taken further in the Cello Sonata (1948), already characteristic of his later style in that the instruments have distinct roles.

A period of withdrawal led to the First Quartet (1951), a work of complex rhythmic interplay, long-ranging atonal melody and unusual form, the 'movements' being out of step with the given breaks in the musical continuity: effectively it is a single unfolding of 40 minutes' duration. It was followed by exclusively instrumental works of similar complexity, activity and energy, including the Variations for orchestra (1955), the Second Quartet (1959), the Double Concerto for harpsichord and piano, each with its own chamber orchestra (1961), the Piano Concerto (1965), the Concerto for Orchestra (1969), the Third Quartet (1971) and the Brass Quintet (1974). At that point Carter returned to vocal composition for a triptych of works for soloist and ensemble: A Mirror on which to Dwell (1975), Syringa (1978) and In Sleep, in Thunder (1981), with words by Elizabeth Bishop, John Ashbery and Robert Lowell respectively. But he has also continued the output of large instrumental movements with A Symphony of Three Orchestras (1976), the piano solo Night Fantasies (1980), the Triple Duo (1983) and Penthode for small orchestra (1985). His String Quartet No 4 (1986) is in a simpler style.

Piano Concerto

Piano Concerto. Concerto for Orchestra.
Three Occasions
Ursula Oppens *pf* **South West German Radio Symphony Orchestra / Michael Gielen**
Arte Nova Classics 74321 27773-2 Ⓢ
(62 minutes: DDD). Recorded 1992

Oppens and Gielen have collaborated in a recording of the Piano Concerto before, and their long familiarity with the work brings an air of confidence to an account which is admirable in its feeling for the essential character as well as the formal logic of a score whose shoals of notes will defeat all but the most dedicated of interpreters. Gielen's ability to bring a convincing sense of shape and a persuasive expressive profile to complex music is no less apparent in an admirable reading of the *Concerto for Orchestra*. Again and again, the solo lines marked in the score are brought out, although the recording isn't able to give ideal clarity to the highly detailed string writing (a compositional problem, perhaps). But Gielen's is as compelling a presentation of this turbulent yet strangely affirmative music as one could hope to hear.

In *Three Occasions* Gielen (in what appears to be a public performance, though the booklet makes no mention of it) is weighty, perhaps to excess in the often delicate third piece. Nevertheless, the interpretation is full of character, and the orchestra confirms its excellence in this demanding repertory. Recommended, despite the inadequate insert-notes.

Symphonia

Symphonia: sum fluxae pretium speia.
Clarinet Concerto[b]
[b]**Michael Collins** *cl* [a]**BBC Symphony Orchestra,** [b]**London Sinfonietta / Oliver Knussen**
DG 20/21 459 660-2GH (64 minutes: DDD) Ⓕ
Recorded 1998 ooo

Carter's three-movement *Symphonia* (1993-96) seems certain to provide the crowning glory to his orchestral output, just as his recent chamber opera *What Next?* should prove the summit of his vocal works. Nevertheless, *Symphonia*'s 45 minutes are not a mere distillation of the techniques and moods developed over the previous half-century or so, and while it is not radically innovative it has plenty of challenges to offer: and not only to orchestral players! The 'I' of *Symphonia*'s subtitle – 'I am the child of flowing hope' – is a 'charming, wanton, inconstant, beautiful, gleaming and noble' bubble, the subject of Richard Crashaw's extraordinary Latin poem *Bulla*. Carter transforms this image into a musical celebration of modernist instability and unpredictability: but in so doing he makes a permanent statement in a masterwork which deserves to endure, and to be heard and reheard. In Knussen's supremely authoritative interpretation, the sound quality has been meticulously managed in order to help the listener trace those gradually emerging and steadily unfolding arcs of eloquent melody. It takes time to appreciate how *Symphonia*'s extraordinary variety of pace contributes to the music's melodic and harmonic coherence. The Clarinet Concerto, written soon after *Symphonia*'s completion, is more immediately approachable, an exuberant tribute to Boulez's seminal *Domaines* in the way it moves the soloist around in dialogue with various well-contrasted instrumental groups. This performance will leave you breathless with admiration, not only for Carter's inventiveness but also for the brilliance with which the score is realized by these dedicated artists.

String Quartets

Awards 1999

String Quartet No 5. Duo. Cello Sonata. Fragment. Figment. 90+
Ursula Oppens *pf* **Arditti Quartet** (Irvine Arditti, Graeme Jennings *vns* Garth Knox *va* Rohan de Saram *vc*)
Auvidis Montaigne MO782122 Ⓜ
(76 minutes: DDD). Recorded 1996 ooo

There is a 47-year time-span for the compositions on this hugely rewarding disc, and comparison of the earliest and most recent works underlines that, for Carter, there has been no turning back. While casting a few glances over its shoulder at the fast-disappearing world of neo-classicism, the Cello Sonata (1948) is well on the way to Carter's own personal brand of modernism, and the Fifth String Quartet (1994-95) is a notably intense distillation of that arrestingly personal style. The quartet is by some way the toughest item included, a lattice of eloquently shaped, persistently diverse fragments, whose moments of continuity are the more telling for their rarity. This is the kind of musical discourse in which silence can be as highly charged as sound, and there's little of the kind of loquacious yet never incoherent exuberance that makes the Cello Sonata such a joy, and which is realized to admiration in this superbly characterised performance by Rohan de Saram and Ursula Oppens. An even more powerful shaping of dialogue in terms of a constantly shifting kaleidoscope of similarities and differences can be heard in the *Duo* for violin and piano (1973-74). Irvine Arditti and Ursula Oppens ensure that the music's epic voyage grips as strongly as ever, even though the dryish recording makes their reading sound almost superhumanly effortless. With three of Carter's typically resourceful late miniatures, rather clinically but very clearly recorded, and all played with outstanding sympathy and technical skill, this is an indispensable Carter release.

Giuseppe Cavallo

Italian ?-1684

GROVE *Almost nothing is known about Cavallo. Active in 17th-century Naples – one of the musical capitals of Europe in the 17th and 18th centuries – he was a student of important Neopolitan composer Francesco Provenzale and in 1675 succeeded him as maestro di canto at the Conservatorio di S Maria di Loreto until his death in 1684. The exceptional quality of his surviving music has ensured its resurrection.*

Il giudizio universale

Roberta Andalò, Roberta Invernizzi *sops* **Stefano di Fraia, Rosario Totaro, Giuseppe de Vittorio** *tens* **Giuseppe Naviglio** *bass* **Cappella de' Turchini / Antonio Florio** P

Opus 111 OPS30-262 (55 minutes: DDD) Ⓕ

Text and translation included. Recorded 1999

Cavallo or Cavalli (probably not the famous Venetian, and anyway 'o' and 'i' were as interchangeable in the 17th century as sonata and canzona) was a twilight figure who is thought to have frequented the monastic order of 'Oratorio di Napoli', maybe as a priest. What we know for certain is that the institution attracted thousands of manuscripts from leading composers in the city. *Il giudizio universale*, or 'The Last Judgement', is something of a rarity in the collection since the majority of 'spiritual melodramas' or 'oratorios' are now lost.

Written in 1681, *Il giudizio* was probably performed by one of the established conservatories in Naples. Its demands are unusual: short, swiftly interchanging sections of instrumental ritornellos and pairs of protagonists, be they angels, mortals, damned souls or blessed souls, all expostulating on their precarious condition. This contrasts strongly with other oratorios of the period, such as Stradella's *Giovanni Battista*, in which action is more markedly offset against extended, reflective lyricism. This is a 'hot to trot' theatrical *mélange*.

The musical characterisation is unquestionably the work of an accomplished composer who can, in cricketing parlance, play down the right line. Cavallo has a tendency to work a strong musical idea for as long as the text demands. Only some of the recitatives test his (and our) patience, but these are in Part 2, preparing the way for the all-important sorting of the saved and the damned. This is where bold colouring, a strong harmonic presence and attractive tunefulness lead us to a skilful five-part choral conclusion, complete with imitation 'last trumpet' calls. Before that, Antonio Florio expertly guides his receptive soloists to rapturous arias for the saved souls and descending chromatic figures for the 'howling amidst horrid lakes'. There is something terrifying about Cavallo's fire-and-brimstone Christ, who seems so resolutely trapped in the spirit of Jeremiah; and something comic about the saved souls gloating, 'Go now, you damned' – a kind of 'we're all right Jack, on yer bike'. It relieves the formulaic and stilted juxtaposition of good and evil which not even the ebullient musical shading of Cavallo can entirely conquer.

The singing, apart from occasional lapses in intonation, is commanding and atmospheric. The first soprano, Roberta Invernizzi, is vocally mesmerising and the ensemble carefully matched. The strings sparkle and then soften with the doubled recorders to match the instrumental palette to the theatrical commentary. It all makes for an engrossing experience. For just under an hour, a perfect college production alternative to *Dido*. Recommended.

Emmanuel Chabrier

French 1841-1894

GROVE *Chabrier was trained as a lawyer and worked in the Ministry of the Interior until 1880, meanwhile developing his talents as a pianist and improviser, studying composition, publishing piano pieces and writing light stage works. His friends included Verlaine, Manet, Fauré, Chausson, d'Indy and Duparc, who encouraged his admiration for Wagner. He produced several imaginative operas, among which the Wagnerian Gwendoline (1885) and the graceful opéra comique Le roi malgré lui (1887) were favourably received in Germany. He is best known for his sparkling orchestral rhapsody España (1883), but his natural talent for the lyric, the comic and the colourful is most apparent in his piano works, notably the Impromptu (1873), the ten Pièces pittoresques (1881), the Bourrée fantasque (1891) and the Valses romantiques (1883); they show free treatment of dissonance, modality, bold harmonic contrasts, rhythmic verve and dynamic inventiveness, and inspired subsequent generations of French composers, particularly Ravel.*

Suite pastorale

Suite pastorale. Habanera. España. Larghetto. Prélude pastoral. Joyeuse marche. Gwendoline – Overture. Le roi malgré lui – Fête polonaise
Ronald Janezic *vn* **Vienna Philharmonic Orchestra / Sir John Eliot Gardiner**
DG 447 751-2GH (66 minutes: DDD) Ⓕ
Recorded 1995 ●●

For more than 40 years the Detroit Symphony Orchestra/Paul Paray recording on Mercury has held top place in our affections when Chabrier's orchestral music is wanted. Now Gardiner has entered the orchestral fray, and aided by superbly responsive playing by the Vienna Philharmonic and first-class recording that, while warm, leaves all detail clear, sweeps the board with a wonderful set of outstanding and quite exuberant performances. The early *Larghetto* for horn and orchestra is the least characteristic of the composer, being a long-breathed, lyrical piece in the romantic tradition: it is played with quiet mastery by Ronald Janezic. But the *Suite pastorale* of five years later is quintessential Chabrier. Poulenc described the 'Idylle' as being as heady as one's first kiss; and light-footed as the 'Danse villageoise' is here, with telling cross-accents and a splendidly rowdy end, and spruce the 'Scherzo-valse', given subtle rhythmic flexibility, it is 'Sous bois', lush in tone, which is utterly enchanting. *España*, that ever-fresh centrepiece, is enormously ebullient; but for all its verve, its internal balance is excellent throughout, the brass brilliant but never drowning out the ornamental subsidiary phrases. In contrast, the *Habanera* is suitably languorous.

The Overture to *Gwendoline* – the nearest Chabrier came to Wagnerism – has one clinging to the edge of one's seat in the agitated urgency of the opening and the blazing ferocity of its final pages; and Gardiner brings well-managed rubato to the noisy orgy of the *Roi malgré lui* scene. Judging by the speed at which he takes it, he seems to have had French *chasseurs* in mind for the brash *Joyeuse marche*, which the orchestra obviously enjoyed. Altogether an exhilarating disc.

Chabrier España. Suite pastorale. Joyeuse marche. Bourrée fantasque. Le roi malgré lui – Fête polonaise; Danse slave. Gwendoline – Overture 🄷
Roussel Suite in F, Op 33
Detroit Symphony Orchestra / Paul Paray
Mercury 434 303-2MM (68 minutes: ADD) Ⓜ
Recorded 1957-60

Paray's classic Chabrier collection radiates a truly life-enhancing spontaneity, an all-too-rare commodity today. His *España* has to be one of the most twinklingly good-humoured ever committed to disc – an account overflowing with rhythmic panache and unbuttoned exuberance – whilst the adorable *Suite pastorale* has rarely sounded so fresh-faced and disarming, even if Paray's very swift 'Sous bois' does take some getting use to. The excerpts from *Le roi malgré lui* are dispatched with memorable theatrical charisma and huge gusto, qualities which extend to a blistering rendition of the remarkable, almost feverish overture to *Gwendoline*. But Paray reserves perhaps his finest achievement for the uproarious *Joyeuse marche* and *Bourrée fantasque* (an astonishingly quick-witted, vital conception). The orchestra respond with irrepressible spirit and characteristic Gallic poise, and the Mercury engineering astonishes in its intrepidly wide range of dynamic and full-blooded brilliance (just sample those hefty bass-drum thwacks towards the end of *España*). All this and Roussel's bustling, neo-classical *Suite* too! An irresistible confection.

Cécile Chaminade French 1857-1944

GROVE *Chaminade studied privately with Godard and other Conservatoire teachers and gave her first public concert at 18. She wrote several major works in the 1880s, including an orchestral suite, a symphonie dramatique Les amazones, a Concertstück for piano and orchestra and an opéra comique; thereafter she wrote little besides piano pieces and songs, music of considerable charm, perhaps influenced by what was expected of a woman composer. She toured widely, several times in England (from 1892) and in the USA (1908).*

Piano works

Piano Sonata in C minor, Op 21. Rigaudon, Op 55 No 6. Les Sylvains, Op 60. Arabesque, Op 61. Prelude in D minor, Op 84 No 3. Troisième valse brillante, Op 80. Inquiétude, Op 87 No 3. Quatrième valse, Op 91. Valse-Ballet, Op 112. Album des enfants – Book 1, Op 123: No 4, Rondeau; No 5, Gavotte; No 9, Orientale; No 10, Tarantelle; Book 2, Op 126: No 1, Idylle; No 2, Aubade; No 9, Patrouille; No 10, Villanelle. Le passé, Op 127 No 3. Cortège (Fragment), Op 143. Sérénade espagnole, Op 150
Peter Jacobs *pf* Hyperion CDA66846 Ⓕ
(74 minutes: DDD). Recorded 1995 ●

Cécile Chaminade's craftsmanship, talent for graceful melodic inventiveness, easy natural charm and effective keyboard writing are indisputable even by those whose tastes are for more elaborate or more solid fare. This volume from Peter Jacobs offers eight of her children's pieces of Opp 123 and 126 – small but far from the conventional pap so often palmed off on children, as is shown by the scintillating *Tarantelle* (which is not all that easy!). There are more substantial concert works here too: the emotional *Le passé*, the once very popular *Sérénade espagnole* which Kreisler took up, and the immensely engaging *Troisième valse brillante*. Since Chaminade is usually thought of as a miniaturist, however, the big eye-opener here is a relatively early C minor Sonata which, if not a masterpiece, reveals that as well as knowing her Chopin and Schumann she had a firm sense of form and an enviable abundance of ideas; the lyrical *Andante* is unexpectedly thoughtful, and the spirited finale goes well beyond Norman Demuth's rather patronizing remark that she was 'nearly a genius who knew what and how to write for pianists of moderate ability' – which perhaps is best exemplified here in a brilliant D minor *Prelude* that sounds harder than it is. As before, Peter Jacobs shows himself to be fluent, clean fingered, elegantly delicate where required, and able to invest the music with fine nuances of tone and pace – an ideal interpreter of Chaminade.

Gustave Charpentier

French 1860-1956

GROVE *Charpentier studied at the Lille Conservatory and with Massenet in Paris, developing a passion for the bohemian life of Montmartre and a distaste for authority, also winning the Prix de Rome in 1887. In Rome he wrote the orchestral suite Impressions d'Italie, the symphony-drama La vie du poète and the first act of his most famous work, the opera Louise (1900). His growing reputation and the expected scandal of its theme of women's liberation made Louise a success; it anticipated Puccini's verismo works but also recalls Gounod and, in its leitmotifs and harmony, Wagner. In 1913 he had short-lived success with his last opera, Julien, further operas of the 'people' being projected but not completed. He was founder of the Conservatoire Populaire Mimi Pinson, which gave free musical tuition to midinettes from 1902.*

Louise

Berthe Monmart *sop* Louise; **André Laroze** *ten* Julien; **Louis Musy** *bar* Father; **Solange Michel** *mez* Mother**Paris Opéra-Comique Chorus and Orchestra / Jean Fournet** H

Philips mono ③ 442 082-2PM3 (163 minutes: ADD)
Notes, text and translation included. Ⓜ
Recorded 1956

This recording has an air of authority and authenticity throughout. All the principals were members of the company at the Opéra-Comique during the 1950s, when Jean Fournet was its Music Director. Berthe Monmart may not be the soprano of one's dreams, but her singing is full of charm, and she achieves complete conviction. All the singers have well-nigh perfect diction – essential in this supreme example of French *verismo*. What genius Charpentier mustered for this one work. When the Father makes his entrance in Act 1, to his 'tired' music and asks if the soup is ready, the psychological portrait is completed – mother/father/daughter, caught in this early picture of youth in rebellion. Musy's career had begun in the 1920s, and he had sung the entire baritone repertory at the Opéra-Comique before becoming its director of productions. André Laroze is the real thing – a French tenor. In the duet that follows 'Depuis le jour' he and Monmart get up steam in fine ecstatic fashion. Fournet's pacing of the score achieves excitement at the climactic moments, the lovers' duets, Louise's almost hysterical apostrophe to Paris in the closing scene, while making the faintly mystical opening of Act 2 a miniature poem. The mono sound is amazingly vivid – you are swept along by its fresh sense of theatricality.

Louise (abridged version)

Ninon Vallin *sop* Louise; **Georges Thill** *ten* Julien **André Pernet** *bass* Father; **Aimée Lecouvreur** *mez* Mother; **Christiane Gaudel** *mez* Irma **Rougel Chorus; Orchestra / Eugène Bigot**

Nimbus Prima Voce mono NI7829 Ⓕ
(69 minutes: ADD). Recorded 1935

The première of *Louise* took place at the Opéra-Comique in April 1900 and it now seems to be back in fashion for its centenary. With this in mind, this reissue of Nimbus's transfer of this beloved 'abridged version' made by the composer in 1935 is timely. At the very first moment, the spell works, with Georges Thill's clarion voice calling up the hill in Montmartre for his lover. As can be seen in Abel Gance's famous film of the opera, made in 1938, Thill was a trifle stiff as an actor, visually, but the power and passion of his vocal acting is heart-stopping. Until you've heard him you don't know what heroic French tenors can be like. Vallin's voice was sometimes described as mezzo-soprano and her version of 'Depuis le jour' is robust, with more urgency than many modern sopranos. The scenes chosen here concentrate on Louise, Julien and Louise's father – her mother and all those extras and crowds don't get much of a hearing. The final scene, the row between Louise and her father – the first resounding blow struck for modern feminism in a modern opera – is the greatest moment in this recording, Vallin and André Pernet generating enough electricity to light up the Eiffel Tower. The sound is very well reproduced. This adorable opera is heard to great advantage in Fournet's complete recording, but this glimpse of the opera, under the composer's supervision, is one of the most delightful and important of all historic recordings.

Marc-Antoine Charpentier

French 1643-1704

GROVE *Charpentier studied in Rome, probably with Carissimi, whose oratorios he introduced into France. On his return to Paris he was employed as composer and singer by the Duchess of Guise and also collaborated with Molière in the theatre. In the early 1680s he entered the service of the grand dauphin, for which Louis XIV granted him a pension in 1683, and he was for a time music teacher to Philippe, Duke of Chartres (later Duke of Orleans and Regent of France). Perhaps also in the 1680s Charpentier became attached to the Jesuit church of St Louis in Paris, and from 1698 until his death he held the important post of maître de musique of the Saint-Chapelle, for which he wrote some of his most impressive works.*

Charpentier's church music was based initially on mid-century Italian models, but soon incorporated French modes of expression – the 'official' grandeur of the grand motet; the declamatory manner of the court air and Lullian récit; the 'popular' simplicity of noëls; and an often elaborately ornamented melodic line. Charpentier was the only Frenchman of his time to write oratorios of any quality. His theatre compositions are even more indebted to French models, and he was an important composer of airs sérieux and airs à boire.

Concert pour quatre violes, H545

Concert pour quatre parties de violes, H545. Il faut rire et chanter: Dispute de bergers, H484. La pierre philosophale, H501. Airs – Ah! Qu'ils sont courts les beaux jours, H442. Ah qu'on est malheureux, H443. Ah, laissez-moi rêver, H441. Auprès du feu l'on fait l'amour, H446. Ayant bu du vin claret, H447. Charmantes fleurs naissez, H449*b*. En vain rivaux assidus, H452. Fenchon, la gentile Fenchon, H454. Non, non je ne l'aime plus, H455. Quoi! Je ne verrai plus, H461. Quoi! rien ne peut vous arrêter, H462. Rentrez, trop indescrets soupirs, H464. Sans frayeur dans ce bois – Chaconne, H467. Tristes déserts, sombre retraîte, H469 P

Sophie Daneman, Adèle Eikenes, Patricia Petibon *sops* **Paul Agnew, Andrew Sinclair, François Piolino** *tens* **David le Monnier** *bar* **Alan Ewing** *bass* **Ensemble Orlando Gibbons; Les Arts Florissants / William Christie**

Erato 3984-25485-2 (74 minutes: DDD) Ⓕ
Texts and translations included ●

Here is a delightfully constructed programme, of which only the tenderly expressive *Concert pour quatre parties de violes* has made previous appearances on disc. But it is the way in which William Christie has dispersed its six movements irregularly within a longer sequence of mainly continuo airs for one and two solo voices that lends particular charm to the programme, ensuring at the same time a consistently high and diverting musical interest. The four-strand string *Concert* is a piece of outstanding merit, beautifully crafted and affectingly expressive. Ensemble Orlando Gibbons plays with tonal warmth, rhythmic suppleness and insight into the subtle inflective nuances present in each and every section of the piece. The texture is light and transparent, which it needs to be in order to disclose the sheer beauty of the harmonies and phrase contours. After the *Concert* it is the *airs sérieux*, all but one of which are supported solely by continuo, that most readily engage your interest.

The odd one out is *Charmantes fleurs naissez* for two sopranos and, in this performance, sporting two recorders. It's a ravishing piece, sung with sensibility by Sophie Daneman and Adèle Eikenes. Daneman's performance of it is accomplished, her subtle blend of theatre and chamber styles paying off handsomely. Paul Agnew has four solo airs which he sings with declamatory elegance and a feeling for their expressive intensity. The *à boire* element is represented by three lively airs for two- and three-voice ensembles. The remaining items – *La pierre philosophale*, a short *divertissement*, and a single *scène pastorale, Il faut rire et chanter: Dispute de bergers* – date from the 1680s and both are musically delightful. *La pierre philosophale* is a comedy by Thomas Corneille and Donneau de Visée, for which Charpentier provided music for one of its five acts. If we mention a Menuet for a little gnome, and a chorus, during which another rises out of the ground, you will quickly get an idea of the high seriousness of the spectacle. Charpentier's contribution probably saved the day. Living up to its name, there is much laughter and singing in the *Dispute de bergers*. The story-line is Indian paper-thin, but Charpentier's score is characteristically animated and entertaining. Christie brings it to life with all his customary flair and the performance is captivating from start to finish. In short, this disc is a winner.

Leçons de Ténèbres du Vendredi Saint

Agnès Mellon *sop* **Ian Honeyman** *ten* **Jacques Bona** *bar* **Il Seminario Musicale / Gérard Lesne** *counterten* Virgin Classics Veritas VC7 59295-2 (71 minutes: DDD). Texts and translations included. Ⓕ Recorded 1994 P

Charpentier wrote many settings of the *Tenebrae*, or *Leçons de Ténèbres* as they were known in France, and they invariably inspired him to great heights of expressive intensity. Their texts come from the *Lamentations of Jeremiah the Prophet*, but are interspersed with affective, ornamental, melismatic phrases inspired by letters of the Hebrew alphabet. In addition to the *Leçons* the sequence includes Antiphons and Responses as well as plainchants with their faburdens for the Psalms, and occasional instrumental ritornellos. Not quite all of this music is by Charpentier. There are, for instance, pieces by Nivers, one of the greatest French organists of the time, included in the sequence; but though most of the assembled chants with their harmonizing faburdens were common property of the Catholic Church throughout Europe, one faburden at least is by Charpentier (H156). The French baroque *Leçons de Ténèbres* are deeply moving, with their distinctive blend of Italian monodic *lamentazioni* and French *airs de cour*. The idiom allows for dramatically highly charged effects and, in the hands of Charpentier, such effects are often realized with thrilling suspensions, dissonances and impassioned declamation. Indeed, with Charpentier one often senses the composer's love for, and experience in writing for, the stage in the many theatrical gestures and in his vividly pictorial handling of the texts. Certainly this highly emotive blend of sacred and secular ingredients resulted in music of extraordinary intensity, none of which is lost on Gérard Lesne and his ensemble, Il Seminario Musicale. They are sensible to the myriad expressive nuances suggested by the texts and realized in music of reflective intensity.

Messe pour les trépassés, H2

Messe en la mémoire d'un prince **P**

Charpentier Messe pour les trépassés, H2[a]. Motet pour les trépassés, H311[b]. Miserere mei , H193[b]
Couperin Les carillons de Paris[c]
Roberday Fugue et Caprice VIII[c]
[a]**Caroline Pelon** *sop* [a]**Pascal Bertin** *counterten* [a]**Hans Jörg Mammel** *ten* [a]**Jean-Claude Sarragosse** *bass* [c]**Jean-Marc Aymes** *org* [ab]**Namur Chamber Choir,** [ab]**Ensemble La Fenice / Jean Tubéry** *rec*
Virgin Classics Veritas VC5 45394-2
(63 minutes: DDD). Texts and translations included. Ⓕ
Recorded 1999

This recording is the product of a close and fruitful collaboration between scholars (including the late Jean Lionnet, Jean Duron and Catherine Cessac) and performers. Together they have given us a deeply moving requiem service that reflects the latest thinking in period style. The performances are simple and dignified, like a rather exquisite string of pearls. The succession of musical forms, textures, instruments and voices is breathtaking and complex (track 14). Charpentier created individual musical architectural structures to enhance the individual lines of the Latin texts (performed here with a period accent), exploiting seemingly endless combinations of voices (apparently eight) and instruments (cornetts, recorders, violins, cello or bass viol, serpent, bassoon, lute, harpsichord and organ). To complete the sense of a religious occasion, church bells are rung at the beginning and organ music by Charpentier's distinguished contemporaries, Louis Couperin and François Roberday, has been interleaved. The performances suit the notional occasion, and so while – appropriately – no one voice stands out among the solo singers, as a choir they produce strong clean lines, consistently in tune despite the challenge posed by the unusual period temperament of the organ. The finely tuned continuo instrumentation (tracks 12 and 14) and the added ornamentation (in the violin parts of, for example, tracks 5, 18 and 21) are stunning refinements worthy of a jeweller.

Mass, H1

Te Deum, H147. Mass, H1. Precatio pro filio regis, H166. Panis quem ego dabo, H275. Canticum Zachariae, H345, 'Benedictus Dominus Deus'
Le Concert Spirituel / Hervé Niquet
Naxos 8 553175 (57 minutes: DDD). Texts and translations included. Recorded 1996 Ⓢ

This early Mass is a beautiful piece, intimately scored for voices with two melody instruments and continuo. Charpentier's vocal requirements consist of pairs of sopranos, alto, tenor and bass soloists, with a four-part chorus that splits into two four-part entities for the 'Pleni sunt coeli…Hosanna' of the *Sanctus*. The Mass is harmonically richly inventive with passages of vivid word-painting. Taken as a whole the work is generously endowed with subtle inflexions, a pervasive element of contemplation, and effectively varied rhythmic juxtapositions which enliven the text and hold our attention. Conductor Hervé Niquet has appropriately included an Offertory, *Precatio pro filio regis*, and an Elevation, *Panis quem ego dabo*, to conform with standard practice.

The *Te Deum*, for four soloists, four-part choir and *colla parte* instruments, is not that one for which Charpentier is renowned but a smaller, later piece belonging to the last years of his life. Modest in scale it may be but musically it is impressive and emotionally satisfying. The choir and instrumentalists of Le Concert Spirituel are on their usual lively form. Some of the solo vocal contributions are more focused than others but the choir maintains a high standard of vocal blend and secure intonation. The recorded sound is very good indeed and Niquet directs with stylistic assurance.

Vesper psalms / Magnificat, H72

Charpentier Beatus vir, H221. Laudate pueri, H149. Laetatus sum, H216. Nisi Dominus, H150. Lauda Jerusalem, H210. Ave maris stella, H60. Magnificat, H72. Salve regina, H24 **Nivers** Antiphonarium Monasticum, Antiennes I-VI
Le Concert Spirituel / Hervé Niquet
Naxos 8 553174 (61 minutes: DDD). Texts and translations included. Recorded 1995 Ⓢ

This release offers a liturgical reconstruction of the Vespers office. The five Vesper psalms and *Magnificat* belong to different periods in Charpentier's life and the six antiphons are by his organist-composer contemporary, Nivers. The reconstruction works well and Le Concert Spirituel, under Hervé Niquet, demonstrates its rapport with Charpentier's music. The vocal sound is fresh and the wide range of musical *Affekt* shows off a greater diversity of tonal colour. Tenors and basses incline towards a roughness of timbre here and there yet, overall, the bright and full-blooded choral sound is pleasing and vital. Some may find the recording balance of the psalms and canticle a fraction too close, creating the atmosphere of a drawing-room Vespers rather than one in more spacious, ecclesiastical surroundings. The antiphons fare much better in this respect, having a deeper aural perspective. This is a richly rewarding programme of music which never disappoints.

Actéon

Awards 1982/3

Dominique Visse *counterten* Actéon; **Agnès Mellon** *sop* Diane; **Guillemette Laurens** *mez* Junon; **Jill Feldman** *sop* Arthébuze; **Françoise Paut** *sop* Hyale; **Les Arts Florissants Vocal Ensemble**
La Comtesse d'Escarbagnas/ Le Mariage Forcé – Ouverture
Michel Laplénie *ten* **Philippe Cantor** *ten* **Les Arts Florissants Instrumental Ensemble / William Christie**
Harmonia Mundi Musique d'abord HMA195 1095 Ⓑ
(47 minutes: ADD). Recorded 1981 **ooo**

One always feels rather sorry for poor old Actaeon; if you remember, he was caught hiding in the bushes while the Goddess Diana and her followers were bathing. Without being given much of an opportunity to explain himself, Diana turns him into a stag, whereupon he is torn to pieces by his own hounds. Charpentier's little vignette opera is an astonishingly rich score containing most, if not all, the ingredients of a tragédie-lyrique. There is a profusion of fine choruses and dances but an overture which departs somewhat from the standard Lullian pattern. *Actéon* is made up of six short scenes well contrasted with one another. The first of them is musically the most colourful with appealing evocations of *La chasse* and a riotous dance as the hunters go in search of their quarry. The second scene is much gentler with a tender air for Diana, pastoral reflections from her followers and a recurring chorus of nymphs which recalls passages in Blow's *Venus and Adonis*. Jill Feldman as Arthebuze, one of Diana's attendants, is admirably languid in her air disdaining love's ardour. Scene 3 discloses a pensive Actéon who, whilst reflecting on matters of the heart, stumbles upon Diana and her retinue in a state of *déshabillé*. Actéon's defence is touching and is delicately portrayed by Dominique Visse; but it's all to no avail and, with a splash of water, Diane, sung by Agnes Mellon, turns him into a stag. The fourth tableau begins with Acteon's horrifying discovery as he gazes into his reflection in a lake: 'A horrible fur enwraps me', he cries and, at this point Visse cleverly alters the character of his voice: 'Ma parole n'est plus qu'une confuse voix.' A poignant symphonie follows. In the fifth tableau Actéon is torn to pieces by his own hounds and, in the sixth and final scene, Junon imperious as ever explains to the hunters what they have just done. A chorus of grief mingled with anger sung by Acteon's followers brings this little *opera de chasse* to an end.

Christie directs the work from beginning to end with conviction and assurance. The action is well paced and there is an intensity of expression, a fervour, which gives a touching emphasis to the drama.

Médée

Lorraine Hunt *sop* Médée; **Bernard Deletré** *bass* Créon; **Monique Zanetti** *sop* Créuse; **Mark Padmore** *ten* Jason; **Jean-Marc Salzmann** *bar* Oronte; **Noémi Rime** *sop* Nérine P
Les Arts Florissants / William Christie
Erato ③ 4509-96558-2 (195 minutes: DDD) Ⓕ
Texts and translations included. Recorded 1994 OO

Lorraine Hunt's Medea is something of a *tour de force*. She invests every word with meaning and produces the widest range of colour to express all the emotional nuances in Medea's complex character – jealousy, indignation, tenderness, sorrow, fury, malignity and outright barbarism: she is especially outstanding in Act 3, one of the most superb acts in all baroque opera, in which she has no fewer than four great monologues, the first with affecting chromatic harmonies, the second accompanied by feverish rushing strings, the third the sombre 'Noires filles du Styx' with its eerie modulations, the fourth with dark orchestral colours. Charpentier's orchestration and texture, indeed, are wonderfully effective: string writing varies between extreme delicacy (beautifully played here) and savage agitation; the cool sound of the recorders is refreshing and the many dances featuring recorders and oboes are enchanting. As Jason, Mark Padmore, a real *haute-contre*, sings with admirable ease and intelligence and the tragic Creusa, poisoned by the vengeful Medea is the light-voiced Monique Zanetti, the very embodiment of youthful innocence and charm: her death scene, still protesting her love for Jason, is most moving. A notable detail in all the principals, incidentally, is their absorption of *agréments*, with Hunt showing special mastery in this regard. There is a large cast for the numerous minor roles, all well taken; and the chorus sings cleanly and with evident commitment. All told, a considerable achievement, and a triumph for Christie.

Ernest Chausson French 1855-1899

GROVE *Chausson grew up in comfortable and cultured circumstances but turned to music only after being trained in law. Studying with Massenet at the Paris Conservatoire, he came under Franck's influence and visited Germany to hear Wagner. His friends in Paris included Mallarmé, Debussy, Albéniz and Cortot. He died prematurely in a cycling accident but his output reflects his growing maturity from dependence on Massenet, Franck and Wagner, seen in the prettiness of early songs and the orchestration of the symphonic poem Viviane (1882), to a more elaborate, intensely dramatic style in the Poème de l'amour et de la mer (1882-93) and the opera Le roi Arthus (1886-95), and finally to a period of serious melancholy which produced the Turgenev-inspired Poème op.25 for violin and orchestra (1896) and some concise chamber music. Once criticised for being vague and Wagnerian, his music took on a more classical expression from about 1890, when he turned towards older Gallic and Italian resources and to Couperin and Rameau.*

Soir de Fête, Op 32

Symphony in B flat, Op 20. Viviane, Op 5. Soir de fête, Op 32. La têmpete – Air de danse; Danse rustique
BBC Philharmonic Orchestra / Yan Pascal Tortelier
Chandos CHAN9650 (67 minutes: DDD) Ⓕ
Recorded 1997 O

There are at least two misconceptions to put right about Franck's arguably most gifted pupil. The first, which this disc dispels admirably, is that the majority of Chausson's music, in the manner of his *Poème*, is endlessly melancholic or elegiac. And the second, which Tortelier's disc doesn't dispel quite so well, is that in his orchestral writing Chausson never managed to free himself from Wagner's embrace. Never *entirely* perhaps, but by the time the 43-year-old composer came to write his last orchestral piece, the nocturnal *Soir de fête* included here, his escape from Wagner was well underway, and who knows where it might have led, had it not been for his tragically early death the following year? The outer sections of *Soir de fête* have something about them of 'the vibrating, dancing rhythms of the atmosphere' of Debussy's later *Fêtes*. The programme as a whole, the overall richness of the orchestral process – whether Wagnerian, Franckian, Straussian (as in the Arthurian sorcerer Merlin's final enchantment by Viviane) or Chaussonian – is well served by the full-bodied sound of Tortelier's BBC Philharmonic. The Symphony, like Franck's, is cyclical, but not otherwise as indebted to the older composer as is often suggested. There are none of Franck's organ-loft sonorities anywhere in Chausson's wonderfully variegated, open-air orchestration. Tortelier here gives us the finest modern recording of the Symphony now available. Each movement is superbly built, and Chandos's recording is truly impressive although in the excerpts from Chausson's incidental music for *The Tempest*, the sound is perhaps a little bulky.

Poème, Op 25

Poème, Op 25 (arr cpsr). Piano Trio in G minor, Op 3. Andante et Allegro. Pièce, Op 39

Charles Neidich *cl* **Philippe Graffin** *vn* **Gary Hoffman** *vc* **Pascal Devoyon** *pf* **Chilingirian Quartet** (Levon Chilingirian, Charles Sewart *vns* Asdis Valdimarsdottir *va* Philip de Groote *vc*)

Hyperion CDA67028 (62 minutes: DDD) Ⓕ

Recorded 1997

The opulent sound of this disc is ideal for Chausson; it especially suits the impassioned early Trio. Devoyon plays the demanding piano part in the grand style, yet the strings are never swamped. In particular, Philippe Graffin's sensuous, unforced tone sails above the texture without any of the strenuous feeling we experience in other performances. All three players sound completely at home, whether in the rhetorical gestures of the work's big moments, or the poised delicacy of the second movement. This Trio, though an early work, is already fully characteristic of Chausson – the way the carefree, day-in-the-country atmosphere at the start of the finale is gradually overtaken by tragic portents very strongly shows his melancholic nature. The *Andante et Allegro* is less individual, but here, too, the performance rises to the occasion – and beyond. Neidich's playing is quite remarkable for its breadth of expression in the *Andante* as well as for the extraordinarily brilliantly articulated *Allegro*. Hoffman and Devoyon are equally convincing in the beautiful, dreamy *Pièce* for cello and piano The most novel aspect of the disc, paradoxically, concerns the most familiar music: this is the first recording of a newly rediscovered version of the *Poème*, with string quartet and piano accompaniment. As a chamber work, the music's essentially intimate tone is felt more strongly, and Graffin gives a plangent account of the solo part, with something of that sense of freedom that Ysaÿe, the work's sponsor, would certainly have conveyed. The only trouble with the arrangement is the loss of perspective between the soloist and an 'orchestra' led by another solo violin. But the Chilingirian and Devoyon play the sustained 'tutti' music beautifully.

Carlos Chávez Mexican 1899-1978

GROVE *Chávez studied with Ponce (1910-14) and Ogazón (1915-20) but was self-taught as a composer, being most influenced by his experience of Indian culture. A visit to Europe in 1922-3 was unproductive, but his first trip to the USA (1923-4) began a close association: in 1926-8 he lived in New York and formed friendships with Copland, Cowell and Varèse. On his return to Mexico he became founder-director of the Mexico SO (1928-48) and director of the National Conservatory (1928-33), having a decisive influence on Mexican cultural life. His works include seven symphonies (the Sinfonía india is no.2, 1936) and two Aztec ballets (El fuego nuevo, 1921; Los cuatro soles, 1925). He was a master of orchestration, particularly of wind writing, and explored concerto writing; characteristic are the four Soli (1933-66) for small groups and orchestra.*

Piano sonatas

Sonatas – No 2; No 6. Cinco caprichos. Seven Pieces. 10 Preludes

Hsuan-Ya Chen *pf*

Elan ② CD82406 (123 minutes: DDD) Ⓕ

Recorded 1998

Chávez's piano music presents a very different picture of the composer from that we are familiar with through his orchestral music, even the more abstract later symphonies (Vox). There are precious few indications of the folkloric exoticism of the *Sinfonía india* in the five works played here, indeed little enough to suggest their Mexican origin.

The three large movements of the Second Sonata (1919-20) possess a Lisztian bravura which persuaded Ignaz Friedman, no less, to arrange for its publication in 1923. By that time Chávez was moving to a more modernistic, angular style in a series of miniatures (the second, *Solo*, just 28 bars in length; the sixth, *Paisaje*, a mere 13) collated in 1930 as the *Seven Pieces* and published by Henry Cowell six years later. The *10 Preludes* (1937) are radically different again. Starting out as a set based on the seven Gregorian modes, Chávez exchanged the percussive, overtly colouristic manner of earlier pieces for a more contrapuntal style, extending to 'a kind of bimodality in the eighth and a mixture of modality-tonality' in the final pair. Deceptively simple-sounding, the *Preludes* form a wonderfully expressive sequence that deserves exposure in the recital room.

So, too, does the excellent *Cinco caprichos* (1975), his final solo piano work. The quicker, odd-numbered movements are capricious indeed, twisting and turning through a variety of moods, offset by the second and fourth, with their evocative bass-up writing for the left hand. The biggest surprise, though, is the Sixth Sonata which is incongruously (for 1961) but convincingly Mozartian in every fibre, but without a hint of pastiche. If ever a work was meant to be heard with the innocent ear then this is it. Across a full half-hour Chávez recreates the spirit of the classical sonata, however modern the inner structure. The variation-finale takes up more than half the duration, building calmly into a most impressive edifice. Hsuan-Ya Chen, whose doctoral dissertation was on Chávez's piano music, plays with admirable authority in what is the first of an exceptionally promising series. Elan's sound is nicely clear and resonant.

Luigi Cherubini

Italian 1760-1842

GROVE *Cherubini was a dominant figure in French musical life for half a century. At 18, with 36 works (mainly church music) to his credit, he began a period of study with Sarti in Bologna and Milan (1778-80). The resulting Italian operas he produced in Italy and London (1784-85), and his work as an Italian opera director (1789-90) in Paris (where he had settled in 1786), pale in significance next to the triumphant première of his second French opera, Lodoïska (Paris, 1791). He was appointed inspector at the new Institut National de Musique (from 1795 the Conservatoire), his status soon being enhanced by the successes of Médée (1797) and Les deux journées (1800). As surintendant de la musique du roi under the restored monarchy, he turned increasingly to church music, writing seven masses, two requiems and many shorter pieces, all well received (unlike his later operas). National honours, a commission from the London Philharmonic Society (1815) and the directorship of the Conservatoire (1822) and completion of his textbook, Cours de contrepoint et de fugue (1835), crowned his career.*

Cherubini's importance in operatic history rests on his transformation of merely picturesque or anecdotal opéra comique into a vehicle for powerful dramatic portrayal (eg Médée's depiction of psychological conflict) and for the serious treatment of contemporary topics (Lodoïska's realistic heroism; social reconciliation in Les deux journées). His best church music, notably the C minor Requiem (specially admired by Beethoven, Schumann, Brahms and Berlioz), unites his command of counterpoint and orchestral sonority with appropriate dramatic expression, while his non-vocal works, chiefly the operatic overtures, Symphony in D and six string quartets, make their effect through the creative use of instrumental colour.

Mass No 1 in C minor

Mass No 1 in C minor. Marche funèbre
Corydon Singers; Corydon Orchestra / Matthew Best
Hyperion CDA66805 (54 minutes: DDD). Text and translation included. Recorded 1995 Ⓕ

It would be an oversimplification to suggest that Matthew Best emphasizes the Beethoven rather than the Berlioz aspect of the main work here; but he does seem less interested in the fascinating use of colour as an element in the actual invention than in the rugged moral strength and the force of the statements. The recording reflects this emphasis, and is firm and clear without being especially subtle over orchestral detail. The choir delivers the *Dies irae* powerfully, and much dramatic vigour is recalled in the fugue traditionally reserved for 'Quam olim Abrahae'. Berlioz, however, was satirical about Cherubini's fugues, and saved his admiration for the wonderful long *decrescendo* that ends the *Agnus Dei*. This is beautifully controlled here. Best includes the tremendous *Marche funèbre*, inspiration here again for Berlioz. Best handles this superbly, opening with a merciless percussion crash and sustaining the pace and mood unrelentingly. It sounds more original than ever, a funeral march that, rather than mourn or honour, rages against the dying of the light.

Requiem in C minor

Requiem in C minor[a]. Marche funèbre
[a]Gruppo Vocale Cantemus; Italian Swiss Radio [a]Chorus and Orchestra / Diego Fasolis
Naxos 8 554749 (56 minutes: DDD) Ⓢ
Text and translation included. Recorded 1996

Cherubini's C minor Requiem was admired by both Berlioz and Beethoven, with good reason, since both owed a great deal to a work that is not far short of a masterpiece. For Beethoven, the music's rugged strength and the force of the statements held much; Berlioz, often mocking and unfair to Cherubini, responded warmly to the use of instrumental colour as part of the actual invention (and took the monotone chanting that movingly ends the *Agnus Dei* for Juliet's funeral cortège in his *Romeo and Juliet*). To oversimplify, if Christoph Spering and his Cologne artists (Opus 111) give a more colourful, 'Berliozian' performance, Matthew Best and the Corydon Singers (Hyperion) and players respond to the 'Beethovenian' aspect of the music. There is, of course, much more to it than that. Both are excellent performances.

So is the present one. Certainly it has more of an emotional charge in the 'Dies irae' than Spering's which, once the trump has sounded, gathers the voices with nervous intensity rather than the urgent drama that both Best and Fasolis discover. Best and Fasolis also produce great vigour for the 'Quam olim Abrahae' fugue. No-one can make very much of the *Sanctus*, a surprisingly weak movement; all respond sensitively to the strange 'Pie Jesu', Best and Fasolis with rather sharper definition of phrasing.

All three open with the tremendous *Marche funèbre*, another piece that inspired Berlioz when he came to write his *Hamlet* funeral march. Excellent as the new performance is, those who acquired Best, in particular, can rest content.

Medea

Sylvia Sass *sop* Medea; **Veriano Luchetti** *ten* Jason; **Kolos Kováts** *bass* Creon; **Klárá Takács** *mez* Neris; **Magda Kalmár** *sop* Glauce; **József Gregor** *bass* Captain of the Guard; **Veronika Kincses** *sop* First Maid; **Katalin Szökefalvi-Nagy** *mez* Second Maid **Budapest Symphony Orchestra; Hungarian Radio and Television Chorus / Lamberto Gardelli**
Hungaroton ② HCD11904/5 (137 minutes). Notes, Ⓕ and text and translation included. Recorded 1977

Medea has so many of the makings of a cult-opera (rare performances, most of them 'legendary', weighty critical respect and no familiar tunes) that one may well approach it with misgivings. Happily, it speaks for itself on first acquaintance and strengthens the impression on each renewal. Occasionally a sequential-figure is over-used, or a spasm of tonic-dominant routine momentarily arrests the striking creativity; sometimes (the final bars may be a case in point) there comes a disappointment in the power of the music to match the drama. But the vigour and sublimity of the writing go further than merely commanding respect: it is a moving, strongly concentrated opera, akin in spirit and inventiveness to Beethoven and Berlioz, and much more central to the operatic tradition than its performing (and recording) history would suggest.

Its association in our time with Maria Callas brings that comparison to mind almost as a reflex. But her commercially recorded version was never a completely satisfying memento, its greatness having to free itself from evident vocal fatigue. Here, Gardelli conducts a more integrated performance, his orchestra is more responsive and his chorus better disciplined. Among Callas's associates, the Creon and Neris were well below standard, while their opposite numbers, Kolos Kováts and the richly endowed Klárá Takács, are admirable. Magda Kalmár, slightly edgy on high notes but generally firm and fresh, deals competently with Glauce's difficult aria, and the strenuous role of Jason brings out a forceful individuality in Luchetti beyond what we normally expect from him. For Sass herself, if she were to be remembered in the future by one single recording, this it should surely be. It was first issued in 1978 when her voice was at its best and the style less given to exaggeration than in more recent times. She distorts some vowels and provides an uneasy moment or two, but the achievement remains impressive. She captures the humanity as well as the horror, and has the intensity of a vivid, distinctive vocal personality so essential for the recording of such a role. In this she is helped by the recorded balance which favours the soloists.

Fryderyk Chopin Polish 1810-1849

GROVE *The son of French émigré father (a schoolteacher working in Poland) and a cultured Polish mother, Chopin grew up in Warsaw, taking childhood music lessons (in Bach and the Viennese Classics) from Wojciech Zywny and Jósef Elsner before entering the Conservatory (1826-29). By this time he had performed in local salons and composed several rondos, polonaises and mazurkas. Public and critical acclaim increased during the years 1829-30 when he gave concerts in Vienna and Warsaw, but his despair over the political repression in Poland, coupled with his musical ambitions, led him to move to Paris in 1831. There, with practical help from Kalkbrenner and Pleyel, praise from Liszt, Fétis and Schumann and introductions into the highest society, he quickly established himself as a private teacher and salon performer, his legendary artist's image being enhanced by frail health (he had tuberculosis), attractive looks, sensitive playing, a courteous manner and the piquancy attaching to self-exile. Of his several romantic affairs, the most talked about was that with the novelist George Sand – though whether he was truly drawn to women must remain in doubt. Between 1838 and 1847 their relationship, with a strong element of the maternal on her side, coincided with one of his most productive creative periods. He gave few public concerts, though his playing was much praised, and he published much of his best music simultaneously in Paris, London and Leipzig. The breach with Sand was followed by a rapid deterioration in his health and a long visit to Britain (1848). His funeral was attended by nearly 3000 people.*

No great composer has devoted himself as exclusively to the piano as Chopin. By all accounts an inspired improviser, he composed while playing, writing down his thoughts only with difficulty. But he was no mere dreamer – his development can be seen as an ever more sophisticated improvisation on the classical principle of departure and return. For the concert-giving years 1828-32 he wrote brilliant virtuoso pieces (eg rondos) and music for piano and orchestra the teaching side of his career is represented by the studies, preludes, nocturnes, waltzes, impromptus and mazurkas, polished pieces of moderate difficulty. The large-scale works – the later polonaises, scherzos, ballades, sonatas, the Barcarolle and the dramatic Polonaise-fantaisie – he wrote for himself and a small circle of admirers. Apart from the national feeling in the Polish dances, and possibly some narrative background to the ballades, he intended notably few references to literary, pictorial or autobiographical ideas.

Chopin is admired above all for his great originality in exploiting the piano. While his own playing style was famous for its subtlety and restraint, its exquisite delicacy in contrast with the spectacular feats of pianism then reigning in Paris, most of his works have a simple texture of accompanied melody. From this he derived endless variety, using wide-compass broken chords, the sustaining pedal and a combination of highly expressive melodies, some in inner voices. Similarly, though most of his works are basically ternary in form, they show great resource in the way the return is varied, delayed, foreshortened or extended, often with a brilliant coda added.

Chopin's harmony however was conspicuously innovatory. Through melodic clashes, ambiguous chords, delayed or surprising cadences, remote or sliding modulations (sometimes many in quick succession), unresolved dominant 7ths and occasionally excursions into pure chromaticism or modality, he pushed the accepted procedures of dissonance and key into previously unexplored territory. This profound influence can be traced alike in the music of Liszt, Wagner, Fauré, Debussy, Grieg, Albéniz, Tchaikovsky, Rachmaninov and many others.

Piano Concertos

No 1 in E minor, Op 11; **No 2** in F minor, Op 21

Awards 1999

Piano Concertos Nos 1 and 2
Martha Argerich *pf* **Montreal Symphony Orchestra / Charles Dutoit**
EMI CDC5 56798-2 (69 minutes: DDD) Ⓕ
Recorded 1998 ○○○

Martha Argerich's first commercially released recordings of the Chopin concertos were for DG; No 1 in 1968, No 2 in 1978. Here she revisits both concertos and offers an act of re-creative daring, of an alternating reverie and passion that flashes fire with a thousand different lights. Indeed, her earlier performances are infinitely less witty, personal and eruptive, less inclined to explore, albeit with the most spontaneous caprice and insouciance, so many new facets, angles and possibilities. Now, everything is accomplished without a care for studios and microphones and with a degree of involvement that suggests an increase rather than a diminution of her love for these works. The recordings are impressively natural and if Dutoit occasionally seems awed if not cowed into anonymity by his soloist (the opening tuttis to the slow movements of both concertos are less memorable than they should be) he sets off Argerich's charisma to an exceptional degree. Argerich's light burns brighter than ever. Rarely in their entire history have the Chopin concertos received performances of a more teasing allure, brilliance and idiosyncrasy.

Piano Concertos Nos 1 and 2. Mazurkas – F minor, Op 63 No 2; F minor, Op 68 No 4 Waltz in E minor, Op posth
Evgeni Kissin *pf* **Moscow Philharmonic Orchestra / Dmitri Kitaienko**
RCA Victor Red Seal 09026 68378-2 Ⓜ
(71 minutes: ADD). Recorded live in 1984

Here is a live example of just what is possible from a 12-year-old genius. These performances, taken from a 1984 Moscow concert, are among the most phenomenally assured and meteoric of any on record. Every page blazes with youthful confidence and a stylistic know-how that would be astonishing from a pianist twice Kissin's age. Even at that age he possessed the peculiar attributes of Russian pianism at its greatest, with flawless, even strength and the most full-bodied *cantabile*. True, there are moments (the opening of the F minor Concerto's central *Larghetto*) where he sounds too relentlessly upfront, and doubtless when he re-records these concertos in his maturity he will find an even wider spectrum of colour and nuance. However, it is doubtful whether he will ever surpass the infallible, propulsive brilliance of these performances. The sound is immaculate.

Piano Concertos Nos 1 and 2
Murray Perahia *pf*
Israel Philharmonic Orchestra / Zubin Mehta
Sony Classical SK44922 (76 minutes: DDD) Ⓕ
Recorded live in 1989 ●

Perahia has never made any secret of his liking for the 'inspirational heat-of-the-moment' of a live performance as opposed to a studio recording, where 'sometimes things get tame'. As enthusiastic audience applause (discreetly rationed on the disc) makes plain, these two concertos were recorded live at Tel Aviv's Mann Auditorium. Whether they were subsequently 'doctored' we don't know, but the finished product brings us a Perahia miraculously combining exceptional finesse with an equally exceptional urgency. In all but the finale of No 1 (where Pollini on EMI beats him by a minute) his timings throughout both works are considerably faster than most of his rivals on disc. Was this prompted by 'inspirational heat-of-the-moment'? Or was it a deliberate attempt to come closer than others do to the surprisingly briskish metronome markings printed in the Eulenburg scores? The two slow movements are distinguished by exquisitely limpid *cantabile* and superfine delicacy of decorative detail while again conveying urgent undercurrents. But in a guessing-game perhaps it would be the two finales that would most betray the identity of the soloist. Not only are they faster, but also of a more scintillating, *scherzando*-like lightness. The recording is first-rate.

Piano Concertos Nos 1 and 2
Polish Festival Orchestra / Krystian Zimerman *pf*
DG ② 459 684-2GH2 (82 minutes: DDD) Ⓜ
Recorded 1999 ●

Krystian Zimerman was in his early twenties when he recorded the Chopin concertos for DG two decades ago, with Carlo Maria Giulini conducting the Los Angeles Philharmonic. For his long-anticipated remakes he directs the Polish Festival Orchestra from the keyboard, an ensemble he founded and trained from scratch. Are the results worth all the extraordinary effort (and no doubt expense) that went into this project? In many ways, yes. Helped by DG's exquisite engineering, Chopin's oft-maligned orchestrations emerge with the clarity of a venerable painting scrubbed clean and fully restored. Not one string phrase escapes unaccounted for. Every dynamic indication and accent mark is freshly considered, and each orchestral strand is weighed and contoured in order for each instrument to be heard, or, at least, to make itself felt. Some listeners may find the strings' ardent vibrato and liberal *portamentos* more cloying than heartfelt, yet the vocal transparency Zimerman elicits from his musicians underscores the crucial influence of *bel canto* singing on this composer. If he downplays many of Chopin's dynamic surges and enlivening accents, he compensates with carefully pinpointed climaxes in both concertos' slow movements. The slow timings, incidentally, have less to do with fast versus slow than the pianist's insidiously spaced *ritardandos* and broadening of tempos between sections. More often than not he lets his right hand lead, rather than building textures from the bottom up, or bringing out inner voices as Argerich does in her more forceful, impulsive renditions. By contrast, some of Zimerman's salient expressive points have calcified rather than ripened with age. Having said that, he has clear ideas of what he wants, and commands the formidable means to obtain the desired results, both at the keyboard and in front of his hand-picked musicians. Of the many offerings made to celebrate Chopin's 150th anniversary, Zimerman's achievement stands out.

Piano Concertos Nos 1[a] and 2[b] **H**
Noel Mewton-Wood *pf* **[a]Netherlands Philharmonic Orchestra, [b]Zurich Symphony Orchestra / Walter Goehr**
Dante Historical Piano Collection HPC105 Ⓕ
(69 minutes: ADD). Recorded *c*1951 and 1948

Inconsolable after the death of his partner Bill Fredricks, Noel Mewton-Wood (1922-53) committed suicide and robbed the world of a musical genius. Born in Melbourne, he included, in his London-based career, work with Schnabel, a début (in Beethoven's Third Concerto) with Sir Thomas Beecham, the frequent replacement of Benjamin Britten as Peter Pears's musical collaborator and, mercifully for the present generation, the making of several recordings taken from his eclectic and enterprising repertoire.

Amazingly, in his incomparably sensitive and robust hands, the Chopin concertos seem as though heard for the first time, their passions and intimacies virtually re-created on the spot. Who of today's pianists would or could risk such candour or phrase and articulate Chopin's early intricacy with such alternating strength and delicacy? The sympathetic insert-notes (in French only) suggest parallels with Solomon, Anatole Kitain and Murray Perahia, yet as with all truly great artists, Mewton-Wood's playing defies comparison, however exalted. No more vital or individual performances exist on record. The orchestra is hardly a model of precision or refinement, but the recordings have come up remarkably well.

Piano Concerto No 1. Ballade in G minor, Op 23 . Nocturnes, Op 15 – No 1 in F; No 2 in F sharp minor. Nocturnes, Op 27 – No 1 in C sharp minor; No 2 in D flat. Polonaise No 6 in A flat, Op 53, 'Heroic'
Maurizio Pollini *pf* **Philharmonia Orchestra / Paul Kletzki**
EMI Studio Plus CDM5 66221-2 (73 minutes: ADD) Ⓜ
Recorded 1960-68 **OO**

This disc is a classic. The concerto was recorded shortly after the 18-year-old pianist's victory at the Warsaw competition in 1959. Nowadays we might expect a wider dynamic range to allow greater power in the first movement's tuttis, but in all other respects the recording completely belies its age, with a near perfect balance between soloist and orchestra. This is, of course, very much Pollini's disc, just as the First Concerto is very much the soloist's show, but effacing as the accompaniment is, Pollini's keyboard miracles of poetry and refinement could not have been achieved without one of the most characterful and responsive accounts of that accompaniment ever committed to tape. The expressive range of the Philharmonia on top form under Kletzki is throughout exceptional, as is the accord between soloist and conductor in matters of phrasing and shading. The solo items are a further reminder of Pollini's effortless bravura and aristocratic poise.

Piano Concerto No 2. Preludes, Op 28
Maria João Pires *pf* **Royal Philharmonic Orchestra / André Previn**
DG 437 817-2GH (74 minutes: DDD) Ⓕ
Recorded 1992 **OO**

Here, beautifully and responsibly partnered by Previn and the RPO, and recorded with the greatest warmth and clarity, Pires gets the treatment she deserves. What gloriously imposing breadth as well as knife-edged clarity she brings to each phrase and note. The intricacy and stylishness of her rubato remind us that the inspiration behind the F minor Concerto was Constantia Gladkowska, a young singer and Chopin's first love. Listen to Pires's *fioritura* in the heavenly *Larghetto* or her way of edging into the finale's scintillating coda and you will gasp at such pianism and originality. Indeed, the opening of her finale may surprise you with its dreaminess (*Allegro vivace*?) but as with all great pianists, even her most extreme ideas are carried through with unshakeable conviction and authority.

Pires's 24 Preludes, too, remind us that she is the possessor of one of the most crystalline of all techniques. More importantly, her way with the more interior numbers among Chopin's teeming and disparate moods is of exceptional drama and intensity. Understatement plays little part in her conception and those who prefer the more classically biased playing of artists such as Pollini are in for some surprises. You will rarely hear Chopin playing of greater mastery or calibre. In her own scrupulously modern way she surely embodies the spirit of the great pianists of the past; of Kempff, Edwin Fischer and, most of all, Cortot.

Piano Concertos Nos 1 and 2 (chamber versions)
Fumiko Shiraga *pf* **Jan-Inge Haukås** *db* **Yggdrasil Quartet** (Fredrik Paulsson, Per Oman *vns* Robert Westlund *va* Per Nyström *vc*)BIS CD847
(72 minutes: DDD). Recorded 1996 Ⓕ

This is one of the most exciting Chopin recordings in recent years because it confronts and deepens the uneasiness that Chopin lovers have with his concertos. They are more comfortable as chamber works, the chamber works he never succeeded in writing when he confronted that form head on. If you find Chopin's ideas inflated when cast in orchestral form, this recording will remove the last traces of doubt. Pianist Fumiko Shiraga has reduced the scope of the music, and wisely so. The heroism and grandeur is of the sort one finds in Schumann's piano-chamber context, the dynamic and expressive extremes that Shiraga achieves are no less compelling than a pianist unleashed against a large orchestra. Shiraga doubles in some tutti passages – a surprise at first, but again a wise decision. She adds gravity and fullness to the Yggdrasil Quartet's excellent accompaniment while remaining hidden, diligently underscoring but never overbearing.

Cello Sonata

Piano Trio in G minor, Op 8. Cello Sonata in G minor, Op 65. Introduction and Polonaise brillant in C, Op 3 (versions for pf, vc and pf, arr Feuermann)
Pamela Frank *vn* **Yo-Yo Ma** *vc* **Emanuel Ax, Eva Osinska** *pfs* Sony Classical SK53112 Ⓕ
(72 minutes: DDD). Recorded 1989-92

This most welcome reminder of the 'chamber music' Chopin starts with his G minor Piano Trio (1828-29) dedicated to his compatriot, the would-be composer-cum-cellist, Prince Radziwill. Rarely has it enjoyed what might be termed 'bigger-named' rescue on disc. For even if Chopin's beloved piano gets the best of it, a performance as imaginatively characterised as this makes you salute the teenage work anew. Despite the procrustean (for Chopin) demands of sonata-form, the minor-key challenges of the opening *Allegro con fuoco* are conveyed with appealing urgency before the amiable grace of the *Scherzo*, the smouldering romance of the *Adagio sostenuto* and the dance-like gaiety of the finale. Shortly after accepting the Trio's dedication, Prince Radziwill invited Chopin to stay at his country estate – hence the Op 3 *Polonaise brillant* in C (the slow introduction came later) for the Prince to play with his bewitching 17-year-old pianist daughter. Here, Yo-Yo Ma chooses Emanuel Feuermann's reworking of the cello part – as Chopin himself might well have enhanced it with decorative *fioriture* had the Prince's fingers been as agile as his daughter's. More importantly, the disc offers what is thought to be this work's first recording in a solo-piano version, recently discovered by the Polish pianist-musicologist Jan Weber. It is played with spirited affection by Weber's pupil, Eva Osinska. The mature Cello Sonata receives a tactfully balanced, persuasively fluid performance from Ma and Ax that ranks with the best of its rivals. The recording is vivid and true.

Cello Sonata in G minor, Op 65. Polonaise brillante in C, Op 3 (ed Feuermann). Grande duo concertante in E on themes from Meyerbeer's 'Robert le Diable'. Nocturne in C sharp minor, Op posth (arr Piatigorsky). Etude in E minor, Op 25 No 7 (arr Glazunov). Waltz in A minor, Op 34 No 2 (arr Ginzburg). Etude in D minor, Op 10 No 6 (arr Glazunov)
Maria Kliegel *vc* **Bernd Glemser** *pf*
Naxos 8 553159 (64 minutes: DDD) Ⓢ
Recorded 1994

Here are Chopin's complete works for cello and piano complemented by an intriguing garland of encores. Performed with a relish inseparable from youth, impressively balanced and recorded, this is a notable offering, particularly at Naxos's super-bargain price. Clearly, Kliegel and Glemser have few reservations concerning the sonata's surprisingly Germanic overtones. Recognizably Chopin in virtually every bar there remains an oddly Schumannesque bias, particularly in the finale's tortuous argument – an irony when you consider that Chopin had so little time for his adoring colleague. Yet this awkward and courageous reaching out towards a terser form of expression is resolved by both artists with great vitality and, throughout, they create an infectious sense of a live rather than studio performance.

Kliegel and Glemser are no less uninhibited in Chopin's earlier show-pieces, written at a time when the composer had a passing passion for grand opera and for what he dismissed as 'glittering trifles'. Their additions (transcriptions by Glazunov, Piatigorsky and Ginzburg) remind us how singers, violinists and cellists beg, borrow or steal Chopin from pianists at their peril. As Chopin put it, 'the piano is my solid ground; on that I stand the straightest', and his muse has proved oddly and magically resistant to change or transcription. Still, even though the selection often suggests an alien opacity, the performances are most warmly committed.

'Cello Waltzes', Volume 1
Etude in C sharp minor, Op 25 No 7 (arr Glazunov). Grande valse brillante in D, Op 18 (arr Davïdov). Mazurkas – G minor, Op 67 No 2; C, Op 67 No 3; A minor, Op 67 No 4; A minor, Op 68 No 2; B flat, Op posth (arr Wispelwey/Lazić). Preludes, Op 28 – No 2 in A minor; No 3 in G; No 4 in E minor; No 6 in B minor; No 7 in A (arr Wispelwey/Lazić). Waltzes – No 2 in A flat, Op 34 No 1; No 3 in A minor, Op 34 No 2; No 5 in A flat, Op 42 (arr Davïdov). Nocturne No 20 in C sharp minor, Op posth (arr Piatigorsky). Introduction and Polonaise brillante in C, Op 3. Cello Sonata in G minor, Op 65 – Scherzo
Pieter Wispelwey *vc* **Dejan Lazić** *pf*
Channel Classics CCS16298 (59 minutes: DDD) Ⓕ
Recorded 1999 and 2000 **OO**

Chopin's music, so beautifully conceived for the piano's sonority and technique, is treacherous territory for an arranger. But a good case can be made for transcription to Chopin's next most favoured instrument, the cello, and Pieter Wispelwey makes it in his lively, eccentric booklet-notes. The performances, full of verve and expressive sensitivity, provide an even stronger argument. The *valse* arrangements by the 19th-century cellist Davïdov transform Chopin's pianistic evocations into virtuoso cello pieces, most spectacularly so in the case of Op 34 No 1, with its rocketing scales and sparkling passagework. That the original character often changes – the repeated-note figure at the start of Op 18 has a quite different effect when articulated by a bouncing bow – seems not to matter when the music sounds so idiomatic in its new dress.

Glazunov's beautiful arrangement of the famous slow Etude from Op 25 and Piatigorsky's version of the Nocturne are just as successful. The artists' own arrangements are simpler in scope. The middle section of Op 68 No 2 is even left, most effectively, as a piano solo. The Mazurkas are, no doubt, specially chosen for their appropriateness as cello pieces, and the lyrical Preludes sound most impressive, if more overt and operatic than usual. Only the third Prelude seems a mistake; the semiquavers are a cellistic tour de force, but the long notes added to the piano bass introduce an earthbound quality that's certainly not there in the original.

Very good recorded sound, brilliant and imaginative cello playing; and Dejan Lazić, still in his early twenties, moves easily from sensitive, discreet accompanist to ebulliant soloist in the Op 3 Polonaise.

Four Ballades

No 1 in G minor, Op 23; **No 2** in F, Op 38;
No 3 in A flat, Op 47; **No 4** in F minor, Op 52

Awards 1995

Ballades Nos 1-4. Mazurkas – No 7 in F minor, Op 7 No 3; No 13 in A minor, Op 17 No 4; No 23 in D, Op 33 No 2. Waltzes – No 1 in E flat, Op 18; No 5 in A flat, Op 42; No 7 in C sharp minor, Op 64 No 2. Etudes, Op 10 – No 3 in E; No 4 in C sharp minor. Nocturne No 1 in F, Op 15
Murray Perahia *pf*
Sony Classical SK64399 Ⓕ
(61 minutes: DDD). Recorded 1994 ○○○

This is surely the greatest, certainly the richest, of Perahia's many exemplary recordings. Once again his performances are graced with rare and classic attributes and now, to supreme clarity, tonal elegance and musical perspective, he adds an even stronger poetic profile, a surer sense of the inflammatory rhetoric underpinning Chopin's surface equilibrium. In other words the vividness and immediacy are as remarkable as the finesse. And here, arguably, is the oblique but telling influence of Horowitz whom Perahia befriended during the last months of the old wizard's life. Listen to the First *Ballade*'s second subject and you will hear rubato like the most subtle pulsing or musical breathing. Try the opening of the Third and you will note an ideal poise and lucidity, something rarely achieved in these outwardly insouciant pages. From Perahia the waltzes are marvels of liquid brilliance and urbanity. Even Lipatti hardly achieved such an enchanting lilt or buoyancy, such a beguiling sense of light and shade. In the mazurkas, too, Perahia's tiptoe delicacy and tonal irridescence (particularly in Op 7 No 3 in F minor) make the music dance and spin as if caught in some magical hallucinatory haze. Finally, two contrasting *Etudes*, and whether in ardent lyricism (Op 10 No 3) or shot-from-guns virtuosity (Op 10 No 4) Perahia's playing is sheer perfection. The recording beautifully captures his instantly recognizable, glistening sound world.

Ballades Nos 1-4. Barcarolle in F sharp, Op 60. Berceuse in D flat, Op 57. Scherzo No 4 in E, Op 54
Evgeni Kissin *pf*
RCA Red Seal 09026 63259-2 (62 minutes: DDD) Ⓕ
Recorded 1998

Kissin plays Chopin with a rhetorical drama, intensity and power that few could equal, an astonishing achievement which shines like a beacon of light. His technique is of an obliterating command, enough to make even his strongest competitors throw up their hands in despair, and yet everything is at the service of a deeply ardent and poetic nature. Listen to his slow and pensive *Andantino* in the Second *Ballade*, its rhythm or thought-pattern constantly halted and checked, the following *presto* storms of such pulverizing force that they will make even the least susceptible hackles rise and fists clench as Jove's thunder roars across the universe. The first subject of the First *Ballade* is daringly slow and inward-looking, the start of the glorious Fourth evoking the feelings of a blind man when first granted the gift of sight, while the *Berceuse* is seen through an opalescent pedal haze that creates its own hallucinatory and rarified atmosphere. The final page of the *Barcarolle* – always among music's most magical homecomings – is given with an imaginative brio known to very few, and the Fourth *Scherzo* is among the most Puckish and highly coloured on record. The recordings are less than ideally beautiful but more than adequate.

Ballades Nos 1-4. Barcarolle. Fantaisie in F minor, Op 49
Krystian Zimerman *pf* Ⓕ
DG 423 090-2GH (60 minutes: DDD)
Recorded 1987

With Zimerman there is total surrender to the impulse of the moment. Each piece comes up with all the immediacy of a brand-new discovery. His is musical story-telling at its most arrestingly dramatic, reproduced with a richness and warmth of sonority to match the playing. In the First *Ballade* the way he sustains a feeling of self-evolving growth is admirable. The intensity of his involvement is apparent (even in his breathing) right from the start, but as in all four he holds so very much in reserve for impassioned outbursts to come. No 2 allows him to give full rein to his liking for the boldest contrasts of both dynamics and tempo, though its two great storms are all the more powerful for not being rushed. And how beautifully he dissolves tumult into the last, plaintive minor-key recall of the opening theme – even if allowing himself a little license in achieving his ends. In the A flat *Ballade* his delight in the unexpected C major tonality in bars 29 to 35 is wholly irresistible, as indeed is his very simple, quiet opening. In the F minor *Ballade* he surely overdoes the pause on that G flat melody note (which Chopin marks only with a *tenuto*) in bar 56. But he plays almost as if composing the music as he goes along. His *Barcarolle* is richly sensuous and passionate. As for the *Fantasie*, rarely will you hear this music given stronger undertones of patriotic protest, pride, and even prayer. The introduction is surely too slow, and here Zimerman reacts too literally to the score's every dot and rest. But though slightly affected in effect, its ominous spirit accords with his disturbed conception of the work as a whole.

Ballades[f] – No 3 in A flat, Op 47; No 4 in F minor, Op 52. Etude in E, Op 10 No 3[a]. Grande Valse Brillante in D, Op 18[f]. Nocturnes – No 2 in E flat, Op 9 No 2[d]; No 8 in D flat, Op 27 No 2[e]; No 13 in C minor, Op 48 No 1[g]; No 15 in F minor, Op 55 No 1[f]; No 19 in E minor, Op 72 No 1[e]. Scherzos – No 2 in B flat minor, Op 31[g]; No 4 in E, Op 54[c]. Waltz No 7 in C sharp minor, Op 64 No 2[b]
Shura Cherkassky *pf*
BBC Legends/IMG Artists BBCL4057-2 Ⓜ
(76 minutes: ADD/[c]DDD). Recorded live in [a]1970, [b]1978, [c]1991, [d]1980, [e]1983, [f]1987 and [g]1988 ●●

A compilation such as this would be outstanding in any context. That it comes at a time when Decca's series of live Cherkassky recordings has not only dried up but also been deleted (shame!) makes it all the more welcome. Aficionados will not need to be told that Cherkassky was a pianist for whom the epithet 'magician' might have been invented. How he managed to play so freely, in every dimension of the pianist's art, and yet (usually) without violence to the music, is something that would challenge the powers of the subtlest analyst and the most imaginative essayist to convey. Even in his favourite repertoire he seemed to be constantly surprised and enthralled by every turn the music took, while another part of his musicianship stood guarantor of coherence and inevitability. Best not to enquire too deeply. Best simply to marvel.

Not that everyone would agree with that assessment; and certainly Cherkassky's studio recordings often found the magic dimmed. There were even live appearances that seemed to support the sceptics more than the believers. But this Chopin selection is overwhelmingly a delight. The Nocturnes float as if on a magic carpet, the Waltzes are as affectionate as they are elegant (with wicked *echt*-Cherkasskian voicings in the C sharp minor), the Ballades seem to follow some secret narrative thread, and the Scherzos are shot through with daring, yet never self-serving, nuances.

Total consistency is not to be expected: the end of the F minor Ballade, the central section of the Etude, and several passages in the Op 31 Scherzo are uncomfortably strenuous. Yet those very same pieces have moments of heart-stopping inspiration, and the E major Scherzo – recorded a decade ago on Cherkassky's 82nd birthday – is technically the most wizardly performance of them all. The recordings come from seven different occasions, and the quality of the instruments is variable. The pianos in London's Queen Elizabeth Hall and, especially, the Queen's Hall, Edinburgh sound poorly regulated, affecting three of the Nocturnes. But this remains a CD to cherish.

Etudes

Etudes, Opp 10 and 25
Maurizio Pollini *pf* DG 413 794-2GH Ⓕ
(56 minutes: ADD). Recorded 1972 ●

The 24 *Etudes* of Chopin's Opp 10 and 25, although dating from his twenties, remain among the most perfect specimens of the genre ever known, with all technical challenges – and they are formidable – dissolved into the purest poetry. With his own transcendental technique (and there are few living pianists who can rival it) Pollini makes you unaware that problems even exist – as for instance in Op 10 No 10 in A flat, where the listener is swept along in an effortless stream of melody. The first and last of the same set in C major and C minor have an imperious strength and drive, likewise the last three impassioned outpourings of Op 25. Lifelong dislike of a heart worn on the sleeve makes him less than intimately confiding in more personal contexts such as No 3 in E major and No 6 in E flat minor from Op 10, or the nostalgic middle section of No 5 in E minor and the searing No 7 in C sharp minor from Op 25. Like the playing, so the recording itself could profitably be a little warmer at times, but it is a princely disc all the same.

Etudes, Opp 10 and 25
Vladimir Ashkenazy *pf*
Decca 414 127-2DH (63 minutes: ADD) Ⓕ
Recorded 1975

These are excellent performances of some two dozen pieces, offering a feast of beautiful playing, and with very realistic sound. Hear the controlled impulsiveness with which Ashkenazy throws off Op 10 No 9, or his perfect wedding of the stormy inner and lyrical outer sections of Op 10 No 3. Other notable points include the finely judged flow of Op 25 No 1, the elegant celerity of Op 25 No 9 and his lovely singing of the left-hand melodies of Op 25 Nos 5 and 7. They have been digitally remastered from analogue originals but sound quality is of a consistently high standard.

Fantasie, Op 49

Fantasie in F minor, Op 49. Waltzes – No 2 in A flat, Op 34 No 1; No 3 in A minor, Op 34 No 2; No 5 in A flat, Op 42. Polonaise No 5 in F sharp minor, Op 44. Nocturnes – No 1 in C sharp minor, Op 27 No 1; No 2 in D flat, Op 27 No 2; No 10 in A flat, Op 32 No 2. Scherzo No 2 in B flat minor, Op 31
Evgeni Kissin *pf*
RCA Victor Red Seal 09026 60445-2 Ⓕ
(67 minutes: DDD). Recorded live in 1993

Evgeni Kissin's playing at 21 (when these performances were recorded) quite easily outmatches that of the young Ashkenazy and Pollini – and most particularly in terms of the maturity of his musicianship. The programme launches off with a reading of the great F minor *Fantasie*, which, though a bit measured, is integrated to perfection. The power and determination of the performance certainly make one sit up and listen, but at the same time it would be difficult not to be moved by the heartfelt lyricism of the melodic passages. Although Kissin may be a little unsmiling in the three waltzes, at least he has admirable sophistication in being able to add interest to the interpretations. His control in the tricky A flat, Op 42, is quite amazing. The *Nocturne* in C sharp minor is a jewel. This reading is among the most darkly imaginative and pianistically refined on disc. The disc ends with a powerfully glittering performance of the Second *Scherzo*.

Mazurkas

Nos 1-64: Op 6 Nos 1-4 **(1-4)**; Op 7 Nos 1-5 **(5-9)**; Op 17 Nos 1-4 **(10-13)**; Op 24 Nos 1–4 **(14-17)**; Op 30 Nos 1-4 **(18-21)**; Op 33 Nos 1-4 **(22-25)**; Op 41 Nos 1-4 **(26-29)**; Op 50 Nos 1-3 **(30-32)**; Op 56 Nos 1-3 **(33-35)**; Op 59 Nos 1-3 **(36-38)**; Op 63 Nos 1-3 **(39-41)**; Op 67 Nos 1-4 **(42-45)**; Op 68 Nos 1-4 **(46-49)**; Op posth **(50-64)** Ⓗ

Mazurkas Nos 1-51
Artur Rubinstein *pf*
RCA Victor Red Seal ② 09026 63050-2 Ⓑ
(140 minutes: ADD). Recorded 1960s OO

Recording in the studio, rather than at a live concert, quite naturally leads to a safe and uniform approach, which does not really serve the inspired inventiveness of the music. In some ways these recordings suffer from this. If one compares Rubinstein's readings here with those that he recorded on 78rpm records in 1938-39 (reviewed overleaf), one immediately notices that an element of fantasy and caprice has given way to a more sober view of the music. The *Mazurkas* are so intricate in their variety of moods that the successful pianist has to be able to treat each one as a definite entity, contrasting the emotional content within the context of that particular piece. Rubinstein, with his serious approach, lends the music more weight than is usual and he wholly avoids trivializing it with over-snappy rhythms. With him many of the lesser-known *Mazurkas* come to life, such as the E flat minor, Op 6 No 4, with its insistent little motif that pervades the whole piece. His phrasing is free and flexible and he has utter appreciation of the delicacy of Chopin's ideas. He does not, however, take an improvisatory approach. Rubinstein judges to perfection which details to bring out so as to give each piece a special character. He convinces one that he has made this music his own. When you hear Rubinstein tackle the C sharp minor Mazurka, Op 53 No 3, you at once know that he fully comprehends the depth of this, perhaps the greatest of all of them. He ranges from the pathos of the opening to a persuasive tonal grandeur in the more assertive parts, and yet is able to relate the two. The recording has a number of blemishes: the piano is too closely recorded, the loud passages are hollow-toned, especially in the bass, and little sparkle to the sound.

Mazurkas Nos 1-52, 55, 56, 59-62
Vladimir Ashkenazy *pf*
Double Decca 448 086-2DF2 Ⓑ
(143 minutes: DDD/ADD). Recorded 1976-85 OO

Vladimir Ashkenazy made his integral set of the *Mazurkas* over a decade. He has always played outstandingly. He does so again here, giving complete satisfaction. The set includes all those published posthumously and the revised version of Op 68 No 4; so his is the most comprehensive survey in the current catalogue. Ashkenazy memorably catches their volatile character, and their essential sadness. Consider, for example, the delicacy and apparently untrammelled spontaneity with which he approaches these works. He shows the most exquisite sensibility, each item strongly, though never insistently characterised. His accounts of the Mazurkas, Op 6 and Op 7, for instance, offer a genuine alternative to Rubinstein. Nine pieces in all, they were Chopin's first published sets and their piquancy, the richness of their ideas, is here made very apparent. One is given a sense of something completely new having entered music. Although there are fine things in all the groups, Op 24 is the first Mazurka set of uniformly high quality and No 4 is Chopin's first great work in the genre. On hearing them together like this one appreciates the cumulative effect which the composer intended, and Ashkenazy makes a hypersensitive response to their quickly changing moods. The recorded sound has the warmth, fullness and immediacy typical of this series, with a nice bloom to the piano tone. About two-thirds are digital and all are believably natural in balance and timbre.

Mazurkas Nos 1-51[a]; No 23 in D, Op 33 No 2[b]; No 35 in C minor, Op 56 No 3[e]; No 41 in C sharp minor, Op 63 No 3[f]. Waltzes – No 2 in A flat, Op 34 No 1[c]; No 7 in C sharp minor, Op 64 No 2[d] Ⓗ
Artur Rubinstein *pf*
Naxos Historical mono ② 8 110656/7 Ⓢ
(137 minutes: ADD)
Recorded [cd]1928-30, [bef]1930-32 and [a]1939 OOO

Nocturnes[a] – Opp 9, 15, 27, 32, 37, 48, 55, 62 and 71. Scherzos[b] – Opp 20, 31, 39 and 54 Ⓗ
Artur Rubinstein *pf*
Naxos Historical mono ② 8 110659/60 Ⓢ
(132 minutes: ADD). Recorded [b]1932 and [a]1936-37 ●●●

The Mazurkas – coupled with the *Barcarolle*, *Berceuse*, Polonaises Nos 1-7 and *Andante spianato and Grand polonaise*: all recorded 1938-39 – are also available on EMI Références mono ③ CHS7 64697-2 Ⓕ

At the risk of sparking controversy, one can only say that such playing makes a mockery of present-day standards. A reminder of the cruel adage 'if it is not done easily it is not worth doing', all these performances prove that Rubinstein played the piano as naturally as a bird flies or a fish swims. He was, quite simply, in his element, and never more so than in Chopin.

Who else has given us the Nocturnes with such ravishing inwardness, pianistic sheen and a *bel canto* to rival the finest singer? Decorative *fioriture* are spun off like so much silk, and whether or not you consider Op 15 No 2 'inseparable from champagne and truffles' and Op 27 No 1 a portrait of 'a corpse washed ashore on a Venetian lagoon', or hear the nightingales of Nohant in Op 62 No 1 and the chant of the monks of Valdemosa in Op 15 No 3 and Op 37 No 1, you can hardly remain unaffected by Rubinstein's unique artistry. His feline ease in the double-note flow of Op 37 No 2, or the way he lightens the darkness of the great C minor Nocturne without losing an ounce of its tragedy, all form part of the genius that made him the most celebrated of all Chopin pianists.

Rubinstein's Mazurkas are equally the stuff of legends. Chopin's most subtle and confessional diary, they transcend their humble origins and become in Rubinstein's hands an ever-audacious series of miniatures extending from the neurasthenic to the radiant, from Chopin's nagging child (Op 17 No 3) to the unfurling of proud ceremonial colours (Opp 63 No 1). What heartache he conveys in Op 63 No 3; and when has Op 67 No 3 been more intimately confided, its banal association with *Les sylphides* more blissfully resolved? Chopin's final composition, Op 68 No 4, becomes a valediction encouraging rather than forbidding weeping, Rubinstein's *rubato* the caressing magic that created a furore at his unforgettable recitals.

Finally the Scherzos, played with an outrageous but enthralling disregard for safety. Only a pedant will underline the odd mis-hit or pockmark within the context of such sky-rocketing bravura and poetic impulse. As an added bonus there are additional recordings of three Mazurkas and two Waltzes, the A flat Op 34 No 1 alive with dizzying virtuoso trickery. The sleeve-note writer may comically mistake the Mazurkas for the Polonaises in referring to Schumann's oft-misquoted description, 'guns [*sic*] buried in flowers', but that is a mere spot on Naxos's blazing sun. No more life-affirming Chopin exists.

Nocturnes

No 1 in B flat minor, Op 9; **No 2** in E flat, Op 9; **No 3** in B, Op 9; **No 4** in F, Op 15; **No 5** in F sharp, Op 15; **No 6** in G minor, Op 15; **No 7** in C sharp minor, Op 27; **No 8** in D flat, Op 27; **No 9** in B flat, Op 32; **No 10** in A flat, Op 32; **No 11** in G minor, Op 37; **No 12** in G, Op 37; **No 13** in C minor, Op 48; **No 14** in F sharp minor, Op 48; **No 15** in F minor, Op 55; **No 16** in E flat, Op 55; **No 17** in B flat, Op 62; **No 18** in E, Op 62; **No 19** in E minor, Op 72; **No 20** in C sharp minor, Op posth; **No 21** in C minor, Op posth

Nocturnes Nos 1-19
Maria João Pires *pf* DG ② 447 096-2GH2 Ⓕ
(109 minutes: DDD). Recorded 1996 ●●●

Passion rather than insouciance is Pires's keynote. Here is an intensity and drama that scorn all complacent salon or drawing-room expectations. How she relishes Chopin's central storms, creating a vivid and spectacular yet unhistrionic contrast with all surrounding serenity or 'embalmed darkness'. The *con fuoco* of Op 15 No 1 erupts in a fine fury and in the first *Nocturne*, Op 9 No 1, Pires's sharp observance of Chopin's *appassionato* marking comes like a prophecy of the coda's sudden blaze. Chopin, she informs us in no uncertain terms, was no sentimentalist. More intimately, in Op 15 No 3 (where the music's wavering sense of irresolution led to the sobriquet 'the Hamlet Nocturne') Pires makes you hang on to every note in the coda's curious, echoing chimes, and in the *dolcissimo* conclusion to No 8 (Op 27 No 2) there is an unforgettable sense of 'all passion spent', of gradually ebbing emotion. Pires with her burning clarity has reinforced our sense of Chopin's stature and created a new range of possibilities (showing us that there is life after Rubinstein). Naturally, Rubinstein's legendary cycles possess a graciousness, an ease and elegance reflecting, perhaps, a long-vanished *belle époque*. Yet moving ahead, one has no hesitation in declaring Maria João Pires among the most eloquent master-musicians of our time.

Nocturnes Nos 1-19. Waltz in C sharp minor, Op 64 No 2. Piano Concertos Nos 1 and 2 Ⓗ
Artur Rubinstein *pf*
London Symphony Orchestra / Sir John Barbirolli
EMI Références mono ② CHS7 64491-2 Ⓜ
(161 minutes: ADD). Recorded 1931-37 ●●●

Rubinstein's 1936-37 cycle of the *Nocturnes* still serves as a yardstick for all subsequent rivals. Listening to just two, namely Op 37 No 2 and Op 48 No 1, is enough to arouse excitement. The former has a unique finesse and drama, especially where Rubinstein returns from a stormy and heroic central section without as much as a hair out of place, while the latter is full of the most natural and telling rubato, aided by perfect timing and inimitable refinement of tone. Although his later versions could boast virtually as much composure, they hadn't quite this degree of ardour and inner tension. The First

Concerto is similarly stylish, its outer movements full of brilliant but often subtle fingerwork, its *Romanze* coolly poetic. The Second is perhaps less wholly satisfying; although undeniably a virtuoso, the Rubinstein of 1931 hadn't quite balanced impulse and control with the precision timing that he achieved a few years later. There's an extra, too – an elegant performance of the C sharp minor Waltz, clean-fingered and particularly winning, and although earlier than any other recording in the set, somehow more prophetic than its companions of the 'aristocratic' Rubinstein of post-war years. It just shows that chronology isn't always a reliable gauge for artistic development. The transfers are superb, but some 78 surfaces are more pronounced than others.

Polonaises

No 1 in C sharp minor, Op 26; **No 2** in E flat minor, Op 26; **No 3** in A, Op 40, 'Military'; **No 4** in C minor, Op 40; **No 5** in F sharp minor, Op 44; **No 6** in A flat, Op 53, 'Heroic'; **No 7** in A flat, Op 61, 'Polonaise-fantaisie'; **No 8** in D minor, Op 71; **No 9** in B flat, Op 71; **No 10** in F minor, Op 71; **No 11** in B flat minor; **No 12** in G flat; **No 13** in G minor; **No 14** in B flat; **No 15** in A flat; **No 16** in G sharp minor

Polonaises Nos 1-7. Andante spianato and Grande Polonaise in E flat, Op 22 H
Artur Rubinstein *pf*
Naxos Historical mono 8 110661 (64 minutes: ADD) Ⓢ
Recorded 1934-35 ●●●

Here, in all their glory, are Rubinstein's 1934-35 recordings of Chopin's six mature Polonaises framed by examples of his early and late genius (Opp 22 and 61 respectively). Together with his early discs of the Mazurkas, Scherzos (EMI) and Nocturnes, these performances remain classics of an unassailable calibre, their richness and character increased rather than diminished by the passage of time.

For Schumann, the Polonaises were 'canons buried in flowers' and whether epic or confiding, stark or florid their national and personal fervour is realised to perfection by Rubinstein. Listen to the *Andante spianato* from Op 22 and you will hear a matchless *cantabile*, a tribute to a *bel canto* so often at the heart of Chopin's elusive and heroic genius. Try the central *meno mosso* from the First Polonaise and witness an imaginative freedom that can make all possible rivals sound stiff and ungainly by comparison. The A major Polonaise's colours are unfurled with a rare sense of its ceremonial nature and the darker, indeed tragic, character of its sombre C minor companion is no less surely caught. The two 'big' Polonaises, Opp 44 and 53, are offered with a fearless bravura (you can almost hear the audience's uproar after Rubinstein's thunderous conclusion to the latter), rhythmic impetus and idiomatic command beyond criticism.

The simple truth is that Rubinstein played the piano as a fish swims in water or a bird flies through the air, free to phrase and inflect with a magic peculiarly his own, to make, in Liszt's words, 'emotion speak, weep and sing and sigh'. The sound may seem dated but Naxos's transfers are excellent, and to think that all this is offered at a bargain price…

Polonaises Nos 1-16. Allegro de concert in A, Op 46. Etudes – F minor, Op posth; A flat, Op posth; D flat, Op posth. Tarantelle in A flat, Op 43. Fugue in A minor. Albumleaf in E. Polish Songs, Op 74 – Spring. Galop marquis. Berceuse. Barcarolle. Two Bourrées
Vladimir Ashkenazy *pf*
Double Decca ② 452 167-2DF2 Ⓑ
(145 minutes: DDD/ADD). Recorded 1974-84

Ashkenazy's Chopin hardly needs any further advocacy. His distinguished and virtually complete survey rests alongside the Rubinstein recordings in general esteem. The 16 *Polonaises* were not recorded in sets but individually, or in small groups, which is one reason why they sound so fresh, with Ashkenazy striking a sensitive artistic balance between poetic feeling and the commanding bravura that one takes for granted in the more extrovert pieces, with their Polish patriotic style. The recordings (even within groupings of opus numbers) vary between analogue and digital, and the recording venues are as different as the Kingsway Hall, St John's, Smith Square, and All Saints, Petersham; but the realism of the piano sound is remarkably consistent. A series of shorter pieces is included on the second disc and the playing is always distinguished. Among the major items, the gentle *Berceuse* is quite melting, while the *Allegro de concert* and *Barcarolle* are hardly less memorable.

Polonaises Nos 1-7
Maurizio Pollini *pf*
DG The Originals 457 711-2GOR (62 minutes: ADD) Ⓜ
Recorded 1975 ●●

This is Pollini in all his early glory, in expertly transferred performances. Shorn of all virtuoso compromise or indulgence, the majestic force of his command is indissolubly integrated with the seriousness of his heroic impulse. Rarely will you be compelled into such awareness of the underlying malaise beneath the outward and nationalist defiance of the *Polonaises.* The tension and menace at the start of No 2 are almost palpable, its storming and disconsolate continuation made a true mirror of Poland's clouded history. The C minor *Polonaise*'s denouement, too, emerges with a chilling sense of finality, and Pollini's way with the pounding audacity commencing at 3'00" in the epic F sharp minor *Polonaise* is like some ruthless prophecy of every percussive, anti-lyrical gesture to come. At 7'59" Chopin's flame-throwing interjections are volcanic, and if there is ample poetic delicacy and compensation (notably in the *Polonaise-fantaisie*, always among Chopin's most profoundly speculative masterpieces), it is the more elemental side of his genius, his 'canons' rather than 'flowers' that are made to sear and haunt the memory.

Other pianists may be more outwardly beguiling, but Pollini's magnificently unsettling Chopin can be as imperious and unarguable as any on record. That his performances are also deeply moving is a tribute to his unique status.

Preludes, Op 28

No 1 in C; No 2 in A minor; No 3 in G; No 4 in E minor; No 5 in D; No 6 in B minor; No 7 in A; No 8 in F sharp minor; No 9 in E; No 10 in C sharp minor; No 11 in B; No 12 in G sharp minor; No 13 in F sharp; No 14 in E flat minor; No 15 in D flat; No 16 in B flat minor; No 17 in A flat; No 18 in F minor; No 19 in E flat; No 20 in C minor; No 21 in B flat; No 22 in G minor; No 23 in F; No 24 in D minor; No 25 in C sharp minor; Op 45; No 26 in A flat, Op posth

Preludes Nos 1-26[a]. Barcarolle[b]. Polonaise No 6[c]. Scherzo No 2 in B flat minor, Op 31[d]
Martha Argerich pf
DG Galleria 415 836-2GGA (62 minutes: ADD) Ⓜ
Recorded [a]1977, [b]1961, [c]1967, [d]1975 ●

Professor Zurawlew, the founder of the Chopin Competition in Warsaw, was once asked which one of the prize-winners he would pick as having been his favourite. The answer came back immediately: 'Martha Argerich'. This disc could explain why. There are very few recordings of the 24 Preludes (Op 28) that have such a perfect combination of temperamental virtuosity and compelling artistic insight. Argerich has the technical equipment to do whatever she wishes with the music. Whether it is in the haunting, dark melancholy of No 2 in A minor or the lightning turmoil of No 16 in B flat minor, she is profoundly impressive. It is these sharp changes of mood that make her performance scintillatingly unpredictable. In the *Barcarolle* there is no relaxed base on which the melodies of the right hand are constructed, as is conventional, but more the piece emerges as a stormy odyssey through life, with moments of visionary awareness. Argerich is on firmer ground in the *Polonaise*, where her power and technical security reign triumphant. The CD ends with a rippling and yet slightly aggressive reading of the second *Scherzo*. This is very much the playing of a pianist who lives in the 'fast lane' of life. The sound quality is a bit reverberant, an effect heightened by the fact that Argerich has a tendency to overpedal.

Preludes Nos 1-24. Scherzos – No 1 in B minor, Op 20; No 2 in B flat minor, Op 31; No 4 in E, Op 54
Håvard Gimse pf
Naim Audio NAIMCD028 (73 minutes: DDD) Ⓕ
Recorded 1999 ●

Håvard Gimse is a Norwegian pianist who studied with Jiří Hlinka (Leif Ove Andsnes's teacher) and whose Chopin lives and breathes with the most engaging poetry, fluency and vitality. Here is the sort of Chopin playing one so often looks for in vain, individual yet without recourse to heavy-handed idiosyncrasy and with a rare

capacity for revealing the fine musical grace and proportion behind some of Chopin's most volatile and audacious pages. Even the jaded teacher at an Australian conservatory who once complained that Chopin's scherzos were weak because repetitious (he surely missed the point: Chopin's revolutionary insistence, his way of forcing home his points without change or modulation achieves its own sense of menace) might have delighted in the play of light and shade, the sheer variety Gimse brings to Chopin's mischievous and declamatory distortion of the term 'scherzo'. This is true of *Scherzos* Nos 1 and 2, less so of the mercurial major-key flight of No 4. Here Gimse's rhythm is delightfully deft, his texture bubbling and oxygenated. Listen to the virtuoso flick of the phrase at 4'21" in the Second *Scherzo* or, equally, to the poetic inwardness of the Fourth and 15th Preludes. You won't hear the nervous aplomb of, say, Cortot in a Prelude (No 16) he was fond of calling 'The Road to the Abyss' (Music & Arts), and Martha Argerich drives a fiercer bargain in the storming No 12 (DG). But, overall, Gimse's style is sufficiently personal to make all such comparisons irrelevant. The recordings are excellent and this is definitely a pianist to watch.

Chopin 24 Preludes[a] **Mendelssohn** Ⓗ
(arr Rachmaninov) A Midsummer Night's Dream[b] – Scherzo **Prokofiev** Suggestion diabolique, Op 4 No 4[c]
Rachmaninov Lilacs[d]. Moment musical in E minor, Op 16 No 4[e] . Preludes – G, Op 32 No 5[f]; B minor, Op 32 No 10[g] **Schumann** Kinderszenen, Op 15[h]
Stravinsky Etude, Op 7 No 4[i] **Vallier** Toccatina[j] **Weber** Piano Sonata No 1 in C – Rondo, 'Perpetuum mobile'[k]
Benno Moiseiwitsch pf
Testament SBT1196 (78 minutes: ADD) Ⓕ
Recorded [h]1930, [i]1938, [b]1939, [g]1940, [ad]1948, [cjk]1950, [ef]1956 ●●

Chopin Four Ballades – No 1 in G minor, Op 23[a]; Ⓗ
No 2 in F, Op 38[b]; No 3 in A flat, Op 47[c]; No 4 in F minor, Op 52[d]. Nocturne No 2 in E flat, Op 9 No 2[e]. Polonaise No 9 in B flat, Op 71 No 2[f]. 24 Preludes, Op 28[g]
Benno Moiseiwitsch pf
APR APR5575 (77 minutes: ADD). Recorded [ac]1938 Ⓕ and 1939, [e]1940, [f]1943, [bd]1947, [g]1948 ●●

Benno Moiseiwitsch's love affair with the piano spawned numerous fine recordings, though few match this superlative 1948 set of Chopin's Preludes. The first Prelude is candid and forthright, whereas No 4's *Largo* projects an outspoken top line (and note how sensitively Moiseiwitsch negotiates the accompaniment's constantly shifting harmonies). De-synchronised chords mark the opening of Prelude No 6, while the same Prelude's quiet close *segues* almost imperceptibly into the gnomic A major (a parallel sense of transition marries Preludes 10 and 11). Bryce Morrison, in his booklet-notes for Testament, singles out No 16 for its dexterity, but the more oratorical Nos 18 and 22 are particularly notable too for their especially keen sense of narrative.

But the greatness of these performances lies beyond detail. Much of the magic resides in Moiseiwitsch's ability to balance close-up and landscape, cultivating the individual phrase while keeping an eye on whole paragraphs. His touch, pedalling and attention to contrapuntal side-play are remarkable. These are profoundly individual readings that positively teem with incident. But which CD to choose? Transfer-wise, Testament achieves a marginally clearer sound frame, APR a touch more warmth (with a tad more surface noise). One minor criticism of Testament's disc: there is a very slight drop in pitch between the end of the 14th Prelude and the beginning of the 15th – not a full semitone, but noticeable enough to trouble those with perfect or relative pitch. APR's transfer is spot-on.

Choosing between the two programmes is more problematic. APR's all-Chopin sequence includes fluent, attentively voiced accounts of the four Ballades, the Fourth a first-ever release. Odd smudges hardly matter in the face of such compelling musicianship. In the B flat Polonaise it's fascinating to compare Moiseiwitsch with fellow-Leschetizky-pupil Ignaz Friedman, the one restrained and elegant, the other (Friedman) pointed and rhythmically fierce. Likewise in the A flat Ballade, where Friedman invests the 'Galloping Horse' second set (Sir Winston Churchill's description) with extra impetus, Moiseiwitsch's musical manners are far milder. The early E flat Nocturne is mercifully unmannered and perfectly paced.

Testament's makeweights highlight Moiseiwitsch's virtuosity, most memorably in Rachmaninov's re-working of the *Scherzo* from the *Midsummer Night's Dream*, which is heard to even better advantage than on the arranger's own recording. So much happens, so quickly and at so many dynamic levels, you can hardly credit the results to a single pair of hands. A Rachmaninov sequence includes a stereo G major Prelude (Op 32 No 5) and a justly famous 1940 account of the sombre B minor Prelude, Op 32 No 10. His primary-coloured 1930 recording of *Kinderszenen* is a joy. In contrast, lightning reflexes benefit textually bolstered Weber and the dry wit of Prokofiev, Stravinsky and John Vallier.

Those fancying an 'Essential Moiseiwitsch' collection should plump for Testament, though Chopin's magnificent Ballades are a significant enough draw to push the scales in APR's direction. It really is a matter of repertory preferences. Both discs are extremely well annotated.

Scherzos

No 1 in B minor, Op 20; **No 2** in B flat minor, Op 31; **No 3** in C sharp minor, Op 39; **No 4** in E, Op 54

Chopin Scherzos Nos 1-4
Schumann Bunte Blätter, Op 99
Sviatoslav Richter *pf*
Olympia OCD338 (75 minutes: ADD) Ⓕ
Recorded 1970-77

Remarkably well recorded considering the source, one performance after another here is so memorable as to rank among the best versions around of the piece in question. There is nothing amidst all the glorious playing here that will not keep your attention galvanized to the music. Richter is not usually thought of as a very credible Chopin player, and yet he strides through the four *Scherzos* with an abundance of technique and deftly coloured textures that make this version a definite front-runner. His Chopin is finely controlled, spaciousness being the watchword rather than overt passion. His Schumann, on the other hand, has always been dazzling, because he has a temperament that convincingly responds to the extreme swings in mood. Many of the *Bunte Blätter* are amazingly fast and unnerving. Don't miss these performances if you like this repertoire.

Scherzos Nos 1-4
Ivo Pogorelich *pf*
DG 439 947-2GH (42 minutes: DDD) Ⓕ
Recorded 1995

Love him or hate him, Pogorelich guarantees a response. Chopin for the faint-hearted this is not; original, provocative, challenging, daring, it emphatically is. Nevertheless, if Pogorelich's most unconventional ideas approach wilful eccentricity, the rewards far outweigh any reservations. True, if they weren't reinforced by such transcendental pianism Pogorelich's interpretations wouldn't carry nearly the same authority or conviction; but it is precisely the marrying of his imaginative scope with his extraordinary technical resource that opens up such startling expressive possibilities.

The first and second *Scherzos* show the juxtaposition of extremes at its most intense, stretching the limits of the musically viable. Predictably, the outer sections of the B minor *Scherzo* are incredibly fast, possessed with an almost demonic drive, while the central Polish carol (*Sleep, little Jesus*) is unusually slow and luxuriously sustained. But such extremes, of character as much as tempo, place enormous tension on the musical structure, and this is most evident in the B flat minor *Scherzo*. Make no mistake, Pogorelich's playing is astounding, from the imperious opening to the lingering and ravishing middle section, where his sublime lyrical simplicity is of the deepest inward poetry. The contrasts inherent in the Third *Scherzo* are surprisingly underplayed, the showers of descending arpeggios taken quite slowly, eschewing the element of virtuosity. In the more elusive E major *Scherzo* Pogorelich captures the capricious mood perfectly.

To sum up a recording like this is not easy. For all the hugely seductive pianistic allure, some may find Pogorelich's probing individualism too overwhelming. There are more ideas crammed into under 42 minutes than on many discs almost twice the length, although most collectors will still feel short-changed by the playing time. This may not be Chopin for every day, but the force of

Pogorelich's musical personality subtly and irrevocably shapes one's view of the music. He has also been given a wonderfully clear and immediate recorded presence. A truly extraordinary disc.

Waltzes

No 1 in E flat, Op 18; **No 2** in A flat, Op 34 No 1; **No 3** in A minor, Op 34 No 2; **No 4** in F, Op 34 No 3; **No 5** in A flat, Op 42; **No 6** in D flat, Op 64 No 1; **No 7** in C sharp minor, Op 64 No 2; **No 8** in A flat, Op 64 No 3; **No 9** in A flat, Op 69 No 1; **No 10** in E minor, Op 69 No 2; **No 11** in G flat, Op 70 No 1; **No 12** in F minor, Op 70 No 2; **No 13** in D flat, Op 70 No 3; **No 14** in E minor, Op posth; **No 15** in E, Op posth; **No 16** in A flat, Op posth; **No 17** in E flat, Op posth; **No 18** in E flat, Op posth.; **No 19** in A minor, Op posth

---

Waltzes Nos 1-14
Artur Rubinstein *pf*
RCA Red Seal 09026 63047-2 (50 minutes: ADD) Ⓑ
Recorded 1960s ●

There has in recent years been a tendency to take Rubinstein's imposing series of Chopin recordings from the mid-1960s for granted, but to hear them digitally refurbished soon puts a stop to that. His tone does not have much luxuriance, being quite chiselled; yet a finely tuned sensibility is evident throughout. This is at once demonstrated by his direct interpretation of Op 18, its elegance explicit. His reading of Op 34 No 1 is *brillante*, as per Chopin's title. In Op 34 No 2 Rubinstein judges everything faultlessly, distilling the sorrowful yet cannily varied grace of this piece. The two finest here are Opp 42 and 64 No 2, and with the former Rubinstein excels in the unification of its diverse elements, its rises and falls of intensity, its hurryings forward and holdings back. This is also true of his reading of Op 64 No 2, the yearning of whose brief *più lento* section is memorable indeed. The sole fault of this issue is that conventional programming leads to the mature Waltzes, which were published by Chopin himself, coming first, the lesser, posthumously printed, items last. Not all of these latter are early but they have less substance than Opp 18-64, and should come first.

Waltzes Nos 1-17 Polonaises – G minor, Op posth; B flat, Op posth
Allan Schiller *pf*
ASV Quicksilva CDQS6149 (60 minutes: DDD) Ⓢ
Recorded 1994

Allan Schiller's playing has a wholesomely musical, straightforward directness that could be described as quintessentially English. Far more sparing than his rivals in resorting to cajoling rubato, he avoids personal idiosyncrasies of all kinds so that the music, as printed, can tell its own tale. The recording itself has a similar unforced naturalness to it. That said, sometimes Schiller's well-trained, obedient fingers are a little too impersonal in more nostalgic moods – Op 64 No 2 in C sharp minor, Op 69 No 1 in A flat (inspired by a youthful love, Maria Wodzinska) and even Op 69 No 2 in B minor. In several more agile contexts a little more light-fingered fancy and charm would not have come amiss. However, in both contexts Schiller's imagination seems to be given freer rein as the set progresses. And he certainly comes close to the truth in the spirited Op 70 No 1 in G flat, as is indeed also the case in the warmly benign posthumous E flat major Waltz with which he concludes. Both *Polonaises* are played with an engaging youthful purity of sound and sentiment.

Waltzes Nos 1-14. Mazurka in C sharp minor, Op 50 No 3. Barcarolle. Nocturne in D flat, Op 27 No 2 🄷
Dinu Lipatti *pf*
EMI Great Recordings of the Century mono
CDM5 66904-2 (65 minutes: ADD) Ⓜ
Recorded 1947-50 ●●●

As an erstwhile pupil of Cortot, it was perhaps not surprising that Lipatti always kept a special place in his heart for Chopin. And thanks, primarily, to the 14 Waltzes, played in a non-chronological sequence of his own choosing, it is doubtful if the disc will ever find itself long absent from the catalogue. Like the solitary *Mazurka*, they were recorded in Geneva during his remarkable renewal of strength in the summer of 1950. The *Nocturne* and *Barcarolle* date back to visits to EMI's Abbey Road studio in 1947 and 1948 respectively. Just once or twice in the Waltzes you might feel tempted to question his sharp tempo changes for mood contrast within one and the same piece – as for instance in No 9 in A flat, Op 69 No 1. However, for the most part his mercurial lightness, fleetness and charm are pure delight. His *Nocturne* in D flat has long been hailed as one of the finest versions currently available. And even though we know he himself (one of the greatest perfectionists) was not completely happy about the *Barcarolle*, for the rest of us this glowing performance has a strength of direction and shapeliness all its own. In fuller contexts there is just a trace of plumminess in the recorded sound.

Waltzes Nos 1-19
Vladimir Ashkenazy *pf*
Decca 414 600-2DH (56 minutes: ADD/DDD) Ⓕ
Recorded 1976-83

No one has served Chopin's cause more faithfully than Ashkenazy. He always preferred miscellaneous programmes which, while wholly understandable from his own point of view, occasionally posed problems for the collector wanting conveniently packaged sets of this or that genre in its entirety. So hats off to Decca for this reissue. All 19 known waltzes are here, including the last six posthumous publications. Rubinstein and Lipatti have long been the heroes in the sphere of the waltz. Ashkenazy must now join their number. From all three of these outstanding artists the waltzes emerge as true 'dance poems'. Ashkenazy also finds the ideal, translucent sound world for this composer, without excessive weight in the bass or injudicious use of the right pedal. What lessons he can teach certain younger contenders about exaggerated point-making (especially in the spotlighting of inner parts), and whirlwind spontaneity in faster numbers achieved without loss of grace or finesse. There is no need to be worried by any suggestion of inconsistency arising from date, level or system of recording.

Piano Sonatas

No 1 in C minor, Op 4; **No 2** in B flat minor, Op 35; **No 3** in B minor, Op 58

Piano Sonatas Nos 2 and 3. Etudes – Op 10 Nos 1-12 (two versions); Op 25 Nos 1-12 (two versions). Waltzes Nos 1-14. Ballades Nos 1-4. Preludes Nos 1-24. Impromptus Nos 1-3. Nocturnes Nos 2, 4, 5, 7, 15 and 16. Polonaise No 6. Berceuse (two versions). Fantasie in F minor, Op 49. Tarantelle in A flat, Op 43. Barcarolle. Chants polonais, Op 74 – No 2, Spring (trans Liszt); No 12, My darling; No 14, The ring. Piano Concerto No 2 H

Alfred Cortot *pf* **orchestra / Sir John Barbirolli**

EMI mono ⑥ CZS7 67359-2 (429 minutes: ADD) Ⓜ

Recorded 1920-43

Has there ever been a more bewitching or endearing virtuoso than Alfred Cortot? His touch was of a crystalline clarity, his coloration alive with myriad tints and hues. Combined with a poetic passion that knew no limits, such qualities created an idiosyncrasy and style that usually survived a fallible and bewilderingly confused keyboard mechanism. His left hand in particular had a way of drifting in and out of focus and leading a wayward and disobedient life of its own. Yet Cortot's famous errors surely resulted not from incompetence, but from his nervous, high-pitched intensity; a sheer involvement that could easily cloud his composure or unsettle his equilibrium. Importantly, Chopin's elusive essence emerged, for the greater part, unscathed from his inaccuracy and caprice.

Here on six glorious CDs is Cortot's Chopin in all its infinite richness and variety. The transfers are outstanding, with no attempt made to mask the glitter of his brilliance in the interests of silent surfaces or to remove other acoustical hiccups. Although not everything is included, the selection is wonderfully enterprising and judicious, with several alternative performances of the same work offered for perusal. The only quibble is the preference shown for the 1942 set of the *Preludes* when the earlier 1933 recording seems to be infinitely superior. The 1931 B minor Sonata is far superior to a later version from 1933. Cortot's 1933 B flat minor Sonata is also a far cry from one made in 1953, where his powers failed him almost totally and is, indeed, of a dizzying aplomb and brio.

There is elaboration in the Second *Ballade*, the volcanic interjections ablaze with added notes, and in the opening of the last and glorious Fourth *Ballade* there is a convulsive leap across the rhythm.

However, the gem is surely the Third *Ballade* with the opening pages played as if improvised on the spot, the figuration foaming and cascading with a freedom and liberality unknown to most players. The F minor *Fantasie* also suggests that Cortot never compromised where his intensity of vision was concerned. Cortot's *Barcarolle* is as insinuating as it is blisteringly intense, even though the hectic rush through the final pages shows him at his least eloquent. In the *Etudes* (the 1934 is preferable to the 1942 set; both are included) he reaches out far beyond mere pedagogical concerns. The final and awe inspiring Op 25 No 12, too, is not the *cantus firmus* of a traditional view but an elemental declamation and upheaval.

In the waltzes there is a near operatic freedom in the melody of Op 42 with its cunning mix of duple and triple rhythm, a charming decorative aside at bar 20 in the E flat, Op 18 (only in the 1943 version), and a puckish mercurial touch throughout that banishes all possible monotony from so many pieces in three time. There is a comically confused start to the A flat, Op 64 No 3, and an unholy muddle at the end of the final Waltz in E minor. The Second Concerto, heard in Cortot's own arrangement or refurbishment with some marginal re-texturing here and there, shows him at his most excitingly rhetorical. Barbirolli's accompaniment may be rumbustious rather than subtle, yet the music sounds as if newly minted, alive in all its first audacious ardour and novelty. Six *Nocturnes* are included in the set and while hardly examples of the stylistic purity to which we have become accustomed in the post-Cortot era, are brilliantly alive with his own heady alternative. You will not easily find a more absorbing box-set of piano discs.

Piano Sonatas Nos 2[a] and 3[b]. Scherzo No 3 in C sharp minor, Op 39[c]

Martha Argerich *pf*

DG 419 055-2GGA (56 minutes: ADD) Ⓜ

Recorded [a]1975, [b]1967, [c]1961 **OO**

This consolidates and confirms (if confirmation were necessary) our sense of a unique vision and virtuosity. Here, simply and assuredly, is one of the most magisterial talents in the entire history of piano playing. She is hardly a comfortable companion, confirming your preconceptions. Indeed, she sets your heart and mind reeling so that you positively cry out for respite from her dazzling and super-sensitive enquiry. But again, in the final resort, she is surely a great musician first and a great pianist second. From her, Chopin is hardly the most balanced or classically biased of the romantics. Argerich can tear all complacency aside. How she keeps you on the *qui vivre* in the Second and Third Sonatas. Is the Funeral March too brisk, an expression of sadness for the death of a distant relative rather than grief for a nation? Is the delicate rhythmic play at the heart of the Third Sonata's *Scherzo* virtually spun out of existence? Such qualms or queries tend to be whirled into extinction by more significant felicities. Who but Argerich, with her subtle half-pedalling, could conjure so baleful and macabre a picture of 'winds whistling over graveyards' in the Second Sonata's finale, or achieve such heart-stopping exultance in the final pages of the Third Sonata (this performance is early Argerich with a vengeance, alive with a nervous brio). And if her free spirit leaves us tantalized, thirsting for Chopin's First, Second and Fourth as well as his Third *Scherzos*, for example, she has also left us overwhelmingly enriched, for ever in her debt.

Chopin Piano Sonata No 3. Polonaise in A flat, 'Heroic', Op 53
Schumann Kinderszenen, Op 15. Papillons, Op 2
Alex Slobodyanik *pf*
EMI Debut CDZ5 73500-2 (69 minutes: DDD) Ⓑ
Recorded 1998

Alex Slobodyanik (the son of Alexander Slobodyanik, a celebrated pianist of the '60s and '70s) is Russian-born but American-based and the possessor of a truly prodigious talent. His Schumann *Papillons* are among the most engaging on record, delicate and piquant in No 4, immaculately virtuosic in No 6 and with the sort of haunting nuance and *cantabile* in No 7 that usually only comes later in a pianist's career. Rarely has carnival night (the coda) died away more magically, its gaiety lost in a mist of distant chimes, while Slobodyanik's *Kinderszenen* shows a no less breathtaking rapport with Schumann's poetry. His 'Dreaming' (made very much the nodal and expessive centre of the cycle) is memorable, while 'Child Falling Asleep' evolves into a lullaby of exquisite joy and pain, of childhood revisited through adult eyes and perceptions. Chopin's Third Sonata begins more flamboyantly, if no less poetically, with a fierce thrust that is hardly *maestoso*, yet contains such zest and ardour that one listens as if mesmerised. There is no repeat – the authenticity of the first-movement repeats in either of the mature sonatas is in any case debatable – and, throughout, some of Chopin's most richly ornate pages are allowed to blossom and expand in glorious profusion (the reverse of the gaunt and death-haunted Second Sonata). Again, there is absolutely no sense of the studio, but rather of live and immediate responses caught on the wing. Only a touch of diffidence mars the A flat *Polonaise*, yet even here the playing reveals the most exceptional refinement and musicianship. The English-based recordings are virtually ideal and, overall, this is a début of débuts.

Piano Sonatas Nos 1-3
Vladimir Ashkenazy *pf*
Decca Ovation 448 123-2DM (76 minutes: ADD) Ⓜ
Recorded 1976-81

Ashkenazy's grouping of the three sonatas is particularly valuable as he makes such a good case for the early (1827) C minor Sonata, and his account of No 3 is undoubtedly very fine, with an excitingly spontaneous account of the last movement. But it is the 'Funeral March' Sonata that one especially remembers. He obviously identifies with the music profoundly and after the concentration of the first two movements the dazzling finale seems the more mercurial. The analogue piano recording is very real and vivid.

Piano Sonatas Nos 2 and 3
Maurizio Pollini *pf*
DG 415 346-2GH (52 minutes: DDD) Ⓕ
Recorded 1986 ●

These two magnificent romantic sonatas are Chopin's longest works for solo piano The passion of the B flat minor Sonata is evident throughout, as is its compression (despite the overall length) – for example, the urgent first subject of its first movement is omitted in the recapitulation. As for its mysterious finale, once likened to 'a pursuit in utter darkness', it puzzled Chopin's contemporaries but now seems totally right. The B minor Sonata is more glowing and spacious, with a wonderful *Largo* third movement, but its finale is even more exhilarating than that of the B flat minor, and on a bigger scale. Pollini plays this music with overwhelming power and depth of feeling; the expressive intensity is rightly often disturbing. Magisterial technique is evident throughout and the recording is sharp-edged but thrilling.

Piano Sonatas Nos 2 and 3
Murray Perahia *pf*
Sony MK76242 (50 minutes: ADD) Ⓕ
Recorded 1974 ●

Listening to Murray Perahia's Chopin Sonatas, you have the impression of an unusually searching mind at work behind the fine fingers. The catalogue has long offered more urgently driven performances but with his deliberate tempo and his very lightly pedalled texture, Perahia draws attention to a host of hidden subtleties – harmonic and rhythmic, as well as inner voices – often merely glossed over. Just now and again you might be prompted to feel that pursuit of detail encourages shorter-lapped phrasing than we often hear, that it breaks the music's broader sweep. But if so, that is a small price to pay for revelations of such beauty. Chopin specialists will find much of interest in the text he uses for the *Largo* (or rather its central *sostenuto* section) of the B minor Sonata, incidentally one of the loveliest things on the disc. The CD transfer is good enough even if the acoustic lacks ideal spaciousness.

Piano Sonatas Nos 2 and 3. Fantasie in F minor, Op 49
Artur Rubinstein *pf*
RCA Victor Red Seal 09026 63046-2 Ⓜ
(61 minutes: ADD). Recorded 1960s

In the Chopin sonatas it is difficult to think of which performance to choose as the greatest. Aside from the Funeral March itself, Rubinstein's account of the Second Sonata is a bit too imperious; the Third is much more thrilling, with considerable technical risks being taken both in the first movement and the finale. His own feeling for quiet nuances in the *Largo* of this work is quite superb, and here too Pollini on DG achieves an innocence that is disarming. Pollini's disc is the most perfect, both in terms of the pianist's technical accomplishment and the lucid piano sound, with nothing that offends the ear. The middle treble range in Rubinstein's piano sound has a hollow resonance. Rubinstein tackles the F minor *Fantasie* in rather a heavy-handed manner, with more power than searching drama. To sum up this release, if you want your Chopin sonatas balanced and formally cohesive, then Rubinstein is for you.

Piano Sonata No 2. Nocturnes Nos 5, 13, 18 and 20. Barcarolle. Scherzo No 2
Mikhail Pletnev *pf*
Virgin Classics VC5 45076-2 (68 minutes: DDD) Ⓕ
Recorded 1988

These are superb and audacious performances. Love them or hate them you will never – not for a minute, not for a second – remain indifferent. Is his *Barcarolle* daringly free or scrupulously true to both the music's outer and inner manifestation? Dare one mention a glaring rhythmic distortion in the closing octaves, a vulgarization of Chopin's nobility in the second bar of the C minor *Nocturne*, or question the *forte* rather than *pianissimo* start to the *doppio movimento* in the same *Nocturne*? Such questions are asked in a spirit of awe rather than impertinence and are, in any case, invariably silenced by Pletnev's technical and musical imperiousness. The Second Sonata will have experts (and particularly Polish experts) locked in furious debate when not mesmerized by the spine-tingling drama Pletnev achieves at the start of the first-movement development, the sinister underlying waltz rhythm he finds in the *Scherzo*, the chillingly exact 'timpani' rolls in the Funeral March and, most of all, the terrifying miasma emanating from the finale. Rarely, too, has the *Nocturnes'* erotic undertow surfaced so tellingly through their civilized veneer. In short, not since Michelangeli's heyday has Chopin been played with such compulsive brilliance, individuality and pianistic mastery. The recordings capture Pletnev's sound world to perfection and are of optimum range and clarity.

Piano Sonata No 3. Mazurkas Nos 36-38. Nocturne No 4. Polonaise No 6. Scherzo No 3
Martha Argerich *pf*
EMI CDC5 56805-2 (52 minutes: ADD) Ⓕ
Recorded 1965

Argerich's pianism is notable for its remarkable combination of seemingly effortless technical resource and temperamental volatility. For all the combustibility of the mixture, however, the vehemence of Argerich's playing is seldom exploited to the disadvantage of the extraordinary subtleties of her art. Moreover, despite the self-imposed limits she places on the repertory she performs, such is the spontaneity of her approach that each of her interpretations, no matter how familiar in broad outline, is characterised by a profusion of contrasting details beneath the surface. In the B minor Sonata she omits the first-movement repeats. Such a formal contraction can, of course, contribute to the momentum with which the movement unfolds. Ironically, however, Argerich seems to some extent to rein in the propulsive power for which she has been renowned, even at this stage in her career, appearing instead to be seeking at every turn to exploit a deeply-felt exprssive lyricism to offset the febrile intensity of the most energetic figurational devices. This has the virtue of allowing us a less hectic view of subsidiary elements within the music, which elsewhere can too often be overwhelmed by the sheer turbulance of the action. Some of the most satisfying playing on the disc comes in her account of the Op 59 *Mazurkas*. There is a vulnerability as well as an affecting wistfulness about the playing which captures the elusiveness of the idiom, with its harmonic ambiguities, with rare acuity. At the other end of the scale, the excitement she generates in the A flat *Polonaise* is of an order that goes far beyond mere effect. If these accounts do not necessarily outstrip her other recordings, they nevertheless offer an intriguing insight into ongoing 'work in progress' from a pianistic giant whose artistry continues to fascinate and perplex.

Piano Sonata No 3. Mazurkas – A minor, Op 17 No 4; B flat minor, Op 24 No 4; D flat, Op 30 No 3; D, Op 33 No 2; C sharp minor, Op 50 No 3; C, Op 56 No 2; F sharp minor, Op 59 No 3; B, Op 63 No 1; F minor, Op 63 No 2; C sharp minor, Op 63 No 3; F minor, Op 68 No 4
Evgeni Kissin *pf*
RCA Victor Red Seal 09026 62542-2 Ⓕ
(65 minutes: DDD). Recorded live in 1993 ●

Kissin is among the master-pianists of our time, and in poise and maturity all these performances seem light-years away from colleagues twice his age. What magnificence and assertion he finds in the B minor Sonata's opening, what menace in the following uprush of chromatic scales, his deliberate pedal haze capturing one of Chopin's most truly modernist moments. Kissin may relish left-hand counter-melody in the return of the second subject and elsewhere, yet such detail is offered within the context of the whole. A momentary failure of concentration at 1'04" in the *Scherzo* comes as reassuring evidence of human fallibility but elsewhere one can only marvel at a manner so trenchant, musicianly and resolutely unsentimental. The equestrian finale is among the most lucid on record and concludes in a controlled triumph that has the audience cheering to the heavens. The 12 *Mazurkas* are no less remarkable for their strength and discretion. Everything is unfolded with complete naturalness and authority. Kissin's rubato is beautifully idiomatic yet so stylishly applied that you are only aware of the finest fluctuations of pulse and emotion. Few other pianists have gone to the heart of the matter with such assurance (always excepting Artur Rubinstein). The recording captures Kissin's clear, unnarcissistic sonority admirably and audience noise is minimal.

Piano Sonata No 3. Polonaise-Fantaisie in A flat, Op 61. Nocturne No 1. Scherzo No 4. Barcarolle. Ballade No 4
Nelson Goerner *pf*
EMI Debut CDZ5 69701-2 (77 minutes: DDD) Ⓑ
Recorded 1996

Nelson Goerner is Argentinian, a student of Maria Tipo, and devotes his most personal and inflammatory recital to Chopin's later masterpieces. How fearlessly he launches the B minor Sonata's imperious opening, never using Chopin's *maestoso* instruction as an excuse for undue rhetoric or inflation. Even the startling sense of hiatus in the first movement repeat (can this really be authentic?) makes sense given such intensity. His second movement *Scherzo* is as colourful as it is volatile and in the *Largo* the playing is, again, gloriously free-spirited and keenly felt. His transition out of the *Polonaise-Fantaisie*'s central *Più lento*, back to Chopin's principal idea, shows a compelling sense of the composer's depth and introspection, and if his choice of the Fourth *Scherzo* is surprising, given such seriousness, he is brilliantly attuned to one of Chopin's most elusive and mercurial major-key flights of fancy. The C minor *Nocturne* pulses with profound elegy, its central octaves fired off like so many ceremonial cannons, and Goerner makes something very special out of the Fourth *Ballade*'s coda, tempering Chopin's bravura with fine melodic intricacy. EMI has provided this most personal and distinctive artist with an impressively bold and spacious recording.

Muzio Clementi Italian/British 1752-1832

GROVE *Clementi trained first in Rome, but in 1766-7 went to Dorset, England, to study the harpsichord. Moving to London in 1774, he became conductor at the King's Theatre and from 1770 gave concerts, often including his well-known keyboard sonatas Op 2 (1779).*

Clementi travelled widely as a pianist in 1780-85, and in 1781 took part in a piano contest with Mozart in Vienna. In 1785-1802 he was a frequent piano soloist in London (notably at the Grand Professional Concerts) and conductor of his own symphonies, but in the 1790s he was overshadowed by the visiting Haydn. He was in great demand as a teacher. In 1798 he established a music publishing and piano-making firm, touring Europe (initially with his pupil John Field) as its representative in 1802-10. Among the firm's publications were major works by Beethoven. Clementi continued to conduct his symphonies in London and abroad; his last major works were three piano sonatas Op 50 (1821).

Foremost in Clementi's large output are c70 keyboard sonatas, spanning some 50 years. Counterpoint, running figuration and virtuoso passagework are constant elements. The earliest (some with violin) generally have two movements, but three are normal from c1782. Dramatic writing (which strongly influenced Beethoven) appears increasingly, and works such as Op 13 (1785) feature motivic unity and powerful expression. The sonatas of after c 1800 tend to be more diffuse. Only six of the symphonies and one piano concerto (1796) survive. Clementi also wrote keyboard duets, chamber music and two influential didactic works, Introduction to the Art of Playing on the Piano Forte (1801) and the comprehensive keyboard collection Gradus ad Parnassum (1817-26).

Keyboard Sonatas

Keyboard Sonatas – F minor, Op 13 No 6; F, Op 33 No 2; G minor, Op 34 No 2. Musical Characteristics, Op 19 – Preludio I alla Haydn; Preludio I alla Mozart. Capriccio in B flat, Op 17. Fantasie with Variations, 'Au clair de lune', Op 48 Ⓟ
Andreas Staier *fp*
Teldec Das Alte Werk 3984 26731-2 Ⓕ
(68 minutes: DDD). Recorded 1999 ○○○

One is inclined to think of Clementi as a rather dry composer, however brilliant and ingenious. There is nothing remotely dry about this CD, which is full of expressive and often powerful music. Partly it is the instrument: on the fortepiano Clementi's music has a sharpness of impact that it lacks on a modern grand, and also a gently poetic, often almost mysterious ring that carries overtones of early romanticism, especially in some of the slower music. But the chief responsibility belongs with Andreas Staier, who is clearly fired by the music and discovers so many layers of expression in it – and shows, with his intellectual control, such a grasp of its structures and shapes its detail so powerfully.

Essentially he plays three sonatas with a framework of single pieces surrounding them. Two of those pieces come from Clementi's *Musical Characteristics*, a group of short preludes published in 1787 and imitating Haydn and Mozart as well as Sterkel, Kozeluch and Vaňhal. Interestingly, these lively pieces indicate the features of the two composers that Clementi regarded as distinctive. Then there is a *Capriccio*, a charming piece demanding (and receiving) crisp and athletic fingerwork, and incorporating songs (by Hook and Paisiello) from a play running in London at the time. The final item is a brilliant and imaginative fantasy on *Au clair de lune*, which Clementi varies in some highly inventive ways. This is a late work, from about 1820, and its style is comparable with mature Beethoven.

Of the three sonatas, the last (Op 33 No 2, 1794) is an elegantly written piece, in effect in two movements, of which the first is vigorously developed. Staier is masterly in his command of Clementi's dialectic and of the slightly quirky character of some of his themes, as in this finale. Op 34 No 2 is a big G minor work: its first movement has a sombre slow introduction preceding (and later interrupting) a fiery *Allegro* of great energy. The *Adagio* draws beautifully shapely and pointed playing from Staier, and the finale, another elaborate and extended movement, is impassioned music, powerfully done. The first of the sonatas, the earlier F minor work (1785), seems in some ways the most 'romantic' in feeling, with its *Allegro agitato* pensively, rather freely played, carrying hints of menace and darkness (enhanced by Staier's sensitive pedalling and misty textures), its eloquent *Largo*, where the melodic line is enunciated with real pathos, and its stormy final *Presto*. In all, Staier's reconciliation of the poetic and imaginative content of this music, with his command of its structure and its arguments, makes this one of the most impressive fortepiano discs in memory.

Piano Sonatas – B flat, Op 24 No 2; F sharp minor, Op 25 No 5; B minor, Op 40 No 2; D, Op 40 No 3
Nikolai Demidenko *pf*
Hyperion CDA66808 Ⓕ
(69 minutes: DDD). Recorded 1994

Several recent excellent releases – on period and modern instruments – have done much to counter Mozart's evaluation of Clementi as a 'mere mechanicus'. For those who remain unconvinced, this issue (on a modern piano) provides a comprehensive demonstration of the composer's skill and imagination that should ensure an enthusiastic following. The B flat Sonata, Op 24 No 2, which Clementi played at Joseph II's court in December 1781, is an exuberant exhibition piece. Demidenko's spontaneous keyboard virtuosity and delightful variety of touch underlines the music's surprising diversity. Indeed, the soft lighting of his performances in general heightens the emotional impact of his interpretations. Two of the Op 40 Sonatas offer remarkable illustrations of Clementi's dramatic and expressive power. Demidenko's performance of the dazzling D major Sonata reveals its potent cocktail of Beethovenian boldness and Mozartian *dolce* in the first movement, and luxuriates in its poignant, improvisatory melody and rich harmony in the second. However, Demidenko's tonal range, technical polish and musical intelligence are even more impressive in the B minor Sonata. Here, his apt characterization of the first movement's turbulent mix of icy reserve and fiery bravura, and deft handling of the second movement's fusion of *adagio* and finale, compellingly evoke the music's spirit of fantasy.

Louis-Nicolas Clérambault

French 1676-1749

GROVE *Like his father Dominique (c1644-1704) and earlier members of the family, Clérambault served the French court. From 1714 he was organist of the Maison Royale de St Cyr (a school near Versailles) and at St Sulpice, Paris, and, from 1719, the Jacobins. He was considered one of France's finest players. His first harpsichord collection (1704) is wholly in the French style, but many of his other works combine French and Italian elements. Most notable are his 25 French cantatas (1710-43), some simple, others dramatic and intense. His other works include violin solo and trio sonatas, organ music and many motets. Clérambault's sons César François-Nicolas (d1760) and Evrard Dominique (1710-90) were both organists; the former succeeded to his father's posts and probably composed cantatas.*

Cantatas

La mort d'Hercule. Poliphème. Sonatas – No 2, 'La félicité'; No 5, 'Chaconne'; No 6, 'L'impromptu'; No 7, 'La magnifique'
Luc Coadou *bass* **Les Solistes du Concert Spirituel** (Jocelyn Daubigney *fl* Patrick Cohën-Akenine, Hilary Metzger *vns* Blandine Rannou *hpd*)
Naxos 8 553743 (66 minutes: DDD). Texts and translations included. Recorded 1996 Ⓢ

Les Solistes du Concert Spirituel perform two of Clérambault's chamber cantatas for bass, interspersed with instrumental compositions. Luc Coadou has chosen from two of Clérambault's five anthologies, published between 1710 and 1726. *Poliphème* comes from the First Book, and *La mort d'Hercule* from the Third. He is responsive to the many expressive details of text and music, but his voice does not always settle comfortably in the centre of his notes, and the pervading tonality is established more by implication than precision. Strikingly declamatory though the *Hercules* piece is, it is not, perhaps, one of Clérambault's most inspired cantatas, and certainly not among the most immediately accessible of them. The imagery contained in the *Polyphemus* text seems to have sparked off Clérambault's imagination, and, indeed, that of Coadou. Clérambault paints a touching picture of the Cyclops's despair in an 'Air fort et tendre', gently accompanied by a flute which perfectly mirrors his melancholy. The other pieces are instrumental 'Simphonies', some with fanciful, allusive titles.

Orphée. Léandre et Héro. Harpsichord Suite No 2 in C minor. Sonata prima in G, 'Anonima'. Simphonie à cinq in G minor
Sandrine Piau *sop* **Les Solistes du Concert Spirituel** (Jocelyn Daubigney *fl* Patrick Cohën-Akenine, Martha Moore *vns* Alix Verzier *va da gamba* Catherine Arnoux *viol* Blandine Rannou *hpd*)
Naxos 8 553744 (62 minutes: DDD). Texts and translations included. Recorded 1996 Ⓢ

These chamber cantatas, *Orphée* and *Léandre et Héro*, are captivating pieces which reveal Clérambault's sensitivity in setting texts and endorse his reputation as, perhaps, *the* master of the *cantate française*. *Orphée*, contained in the First of his five anthologies of cantatas, is often regarded as Clérambault's masterpiece, but *Léandre et Héro*, from the Second Book, at times hardly seems inferior. Sandrine Piau is no stranger to this subtly inflected repertoire and sings with passion and a lively sense of style. Her voice is clear, lightly textured and attractive, and she pays close attention to textural detail. *Léandre et Héro*, inspired by the touching love-story of Hero and Leander, is similarly scored to *Orphée*, that is, for high voice with violin, flute and continuo. Perhaps Clérambault, notwithstanding a splendidly vigorous *air de tempête*, never quite achieves the expressive variety of *Orphée*, but *Léandre* is graced by music of strong character, admirably realized by Piau. The remaining items are instrumental and add to a satisfying programme, well performed.

Motets

Panis angelicus, C131. Exultet omnium, C112. Domine salvum fac regem, C152. Domine ante te, C158. O deliciis affluens, C109. Magnificat. Salve regina, C114. O piisima, o sanctissima, C135. Domine salvum, C157 P

Gérard Lesne *counterten* **Mark Padmore** *ten* **Josep-Miquel Ramon i Monzó** *bass* **Il Seminario Musicale**

Virgin Classics Veritas VC5 45415-2 (63 minutes: DDD). Recorded 1999 Ⓕ oo

Here are six very good reasons to get better acquainted with the music of Nicolas Clérambault. The qualities so admired in his cantatas – think no further than *Orphée* – are amply evident in these motets for three male voices, flute, violins and continuo, which celebrate in turn the Virgin Mary, Louis XV and Saint Sulpice (Clérambault was organist at the Parisian church named after him from 1715). The Clérambault authority Catherine Cessac rightly places these works among the finest of their kind from the first half of the 18th century.

The presence of the concertante flute in the opening motet, *Panis angelicus*, C131, at once alerts the listener to the fashionableness of Clérambault's music. But the rather secular impression (then also very fashionable) gained from the occasionally rustic, strummed accompaniment in the otherwise uplifting hymn of praise, *Exultet omnium*, C112, and a hint of the flirtatious in the 'Stella matutina' of *O delicii affluens*, C109, should be attributed more to the exuberance of Il Seminario Musicale than the composer. Clérambault himself was a masterful accompanist to judge from his beautifully crafted bass lines, which are both melodic in themselves and harmonically memorable.

Clérambault's attention to the texts – their meanings and their rhythms – is also impressive. The rhetorical qualities of the *Domine salvum*, C152, the 'Quia fecit' of the *Magnificat*, C136, and the *Domine salvum*, C157, the antiphony in the *Domine*, C158, the melismas in the 'Tecum cantemus domino' of *O deliciis affluens*, in the (almost Handelian) 'Et exultavit' of the *Magnificat*, and the chromatic suspensions in *O piisima, o sanctissima*, C135, draw the listener to the texts. But the crowning work on this disc is the *Salve regina*, C114: the groaning and weeping of the 'Ad te clamamus', the catchy 'Eya ergo' and the powerful downward sequences ('O clemens, o pia, o dulcis Virgo Maria') make for compelling listening.

The performers deserve the highest praise for their part in bringing this music to life. In addition to delivering superbly judged solos (especially in the *Magnificat*), Gérard Lesne, Mark Padmore and Josep-Miguel Ramon i Monzó – their Latin properly tinged with French – join in exquisitely executed duos and trios (for example, in the Simphonie of the *Exultet omnium*, the 'Et misericordia ejus' and 'Gloria Patri' of the *Magnificat* and the 'Ad te clamamus' of the *Salve regina*). The skilful instrumentalists of Il Seminario Musicale, particularly the bass player, Richard Myron, contribute sensitively and spiritedly. The recording is clear and resonant, allowing the listener greater access to the subtleties of Clérambault's remarkable music than could ever have been enjoyed by 18th-century worshippers at the cavernous Saint Sulpice.

Eric Coates

British 1886-1957

GROVE *Coates studied at the Royal Academy of Music, worked as an orchestral viola player, and wrote light orchestral music and c100 songs. He is best known for the suite London (1933) and The Dam Busters march from his film score.*

Light orchestral works

Saxo-Rhapsody. Wood Nymphs. Music Everywhere (Rediffusion March). From Meadow to Mayfair. The Dam Busters – march; London. Cinderella – Phantasy. London Again **Royal Liverpool Philharmonic Orchestra / Sir Charles Groves** The Merrymakers – Miniature Overture. Summer Days – At the dance. By the Sleepy Lagoon. The Three Men – Man from the sea. The Three Bears – Phantasy **London Symphony Orchestra / Sir Charles Mackerras** Calling all Workers – March. The Three Elizabeths **City of Birmingham Symphony Orchestra / Reginald Kilbey** H

HMV Classics ② HMV5 72327-2 (129 minutes: ADD) Ⓑ Recorded 1956-71

Eric Coates reached a vast public through the use of his music as signature tunes for radio programmes, and the cinema furthered the cause with the huge success of *The Dam Busters* march. There is much more to his music, though, than mere hit themes. Suites such as *London, London Again, From Meadow to Mayfair* and *The Three Elizabeths* offer a wealth of delights and are all the better for the juxtaposition of their contrasted movements. The two tone-poems for children, *Cinderella* and *The Three Bears*, are splendidly apt pieces of programme music – simple to follow, ever charming, never trite. The miniature overture *The Merrymakers* and the elegant waltz 'At the dance' are other superb pieces of light music, whilst the *Saxo-Rhapsody* shows Coates in more serious mood. Throughout there is a rich vein of melody, and an elegance of orchestration that makes this music to listen to repeatedly with ever increasing admiration. The three conductors and orchestras featured adopt a no-nonsense approach that modestly suggests that his music should not be lingered over, never taken too seriously. Considering that the Mackerras items were first issued in 1956 (the rest being from 1968-71), the sound is of astonishingly good and remarkably uniform quality. This is a veritable feast of delightful music and, at its low price, a remarkable bargain.

Sweet Seventeen. Summer Afternoon. Impressions of a Princess[a]. Salute the Soldier. Two Light Syncopated Pieces. For Your Delight. The Unknown Singer[a]. I Sing to You. Coquette. Over to You. Idyll. Under the Stars. By the Tamarisk. Mirage. Last Love. The Green Land[a]
[a]**Peter Hughes** *sax* **BBC Concert Orchestra / John Wilson**
ASV White Line CDWHL2107 (79 minutes: DDD) Ⓜ
Recorded 1996

The title of these pieces won't ring much of a bell with any but the most avid Coates fans. Indeed, four pieces are here recorded for the first time. But what delights there are! It goes without saying that Coates's craftsmanship is in evidence from start to finish. Yet so often, one wonders just *why* a particular piece never quite made it in the way his most popular works did. Isn't *Summer Afternoon* every bit as delightful as *By the Sleepy Lagoon*? And wouldn't *Salute the Soldier* have served just as well as other marches as a radio signature tune? Most simply, aren't *Under the Stars*, *For Your Delight* and others just simply such utter charmers? The BBC Concert Orchestra plays beautifully, and the conductor seems thoroughly imbued with the Coates style. The recorded sound is crisp and clean, too. You are urged to sample the pleasures of this splendid collection.

Songs

Rise up and reach the stars; At vesper bell; The young lover; The grenadier; Four old English songs; Because I miss you so; Sigh no more, ladies; Tell me where is fancy bred; The fairy tales of Ireland; Music of the night; Betty and Johnny; The mill o' dreams; When I am dead; The little green balcony; Ship of dream; The outlaw's song; Your name; Beautiful lady moon; Princess of the dawn. First meeting
Richard Edgar-Wilson *ten* **Michael Ponder** *va* **Eugene Asti** *pf*
Marco Polo 8 223806 (69 minutes: DDD) Ⓕ
Texts included. Recorded 1994

Richard Edgar-Wilson has a natural, free-ranging and expressive tenor voice, his words coming through with complete clarity, while Eugene Asti revels in Coates's luxurious accompaniments. Such is the consistency of Coates's luxurious accompaniments. Such, moreover, is the consistency of Coates's inspiration and musicianship that, though these are not his best-known songs, the selection here is still immensely enjoyable. At the most obviously popular end of the spectrum *The grenadier* has one of those rousing Fred Weatherly lyrics after the fashion of *Stonecracker John*, while at the more ambitious end are some delightfully fresh Shakespeare settings, as well as the short song-cycle *The mill o' dreams*. The songs *Because I miss you so*, *The fairy tales of Ireland* and *Music of the night* are particularly lovely compositions. By way of variety the collection also includes a piece for viola and piano that Coates composed for his teacher Lionel Tertis. This gives producer Michael Ponder a chance to step into the limelight, which he deserves for this diverting collection.

Aaron Copland American 1900-1990

GROVE *Copland studied with Goldmark in New York and with Boulanger in Paris (1921-24), then returned to New York and took a leading part in composers organisations, taught at the New School for Social Research (1927-37) and composed. At first his Stravinskian inheritance from Boulanger was combined with aspects of jazz (Music for the Theatre, 1925) or with a grand rhetoric (Symphonic Ode, 1929), but then he established an advanced personal style in the Piano Variations (1930) and orchestral Statements (1935). Growing social concerns spurred him towards a popular style in the cowboy ballets Billy the Kid (1940) and Rodeo (1942), but even here his harmony and orchestral spacing are distinctive. Another ballet, Appalachian Spring (1944) – a continuous movement towards a set of variations on a Shaker hymn – brought a synthesis of the folksy and the musically developed.*

Other works from the 'Americana' period include the Lincoln Portrait for speaker and orchestra (1942), the Fanfare for the Common Man (1942), the 12 Poems of Emily Dickinson for voice and piano (1950), two sets of Old American Songs (1950-52) and the opera The Tender Land (1954). But there were also more complex developments, especially among the chamber and instrumental works: the Piano Sonata (1941), Violin Sonata (1943), Piano Quartet (1950) and Piano Fantasy (1957). In the orchestral Connotations (1962) and Inscape (1967) he completed a journey into serialism, though again the sound is individual. Other late works, including the ballet Dance Panels (1963), the String Nonet (1960) and the Duo for flute and piano (1971), continue the cool triadic style. He was conductor, speaker and pianist, a generous and admired teacher, and author of several books, among them Music and Imagination (1952).

Clarinet Concerto

Clarinet Concerto. Connotations. El salón México. Music for the Theatre
Stanley Drucker *cl* **New York Philharmonic Orchestra / Leonard Bernstein**
DG 431 672-2GH (74 minutes: DDD) Ⓕ
Recorded live in 1989 **OO**

This is a real scoop for Copland enthusiasts. These recordings reveal Bernstein and the

NYPO on top form in the kind of music they find absolutely natural. The least familiar piece, *Connotations*, may be the place to start since Bernstein brings it off splendidly. It was commissioned for the opening of the Lincoln Center in 1962 and Copland may have been disappointed that the piece failed to win friends. This recording makes an eloquent plea for Copland's most extended serial work on orchestral scale. The language is unrelievedly dissonant, harking back to the 1920s in New York. There is even a near quotation from Copland's Piano Variations and a solo piano enters with glacial chords like ice-blocks followed by rapt strings and some gentle groans from Bernstein. The rest of this disc is just as rewarding and all in Copland's popular manner. *Music for the Theatre* (1925) sets the style for much of later Copland – and gave Bernstein some ideas too. The style is absolutely right and so is *El salón México* which Bernstein knew from making the piano arrangement shortly after it was composed. Both these performances are as good as any available and well recorded too. The Clarinet Concerto is another bonus in Stanley Drucker's interpretation. Perhaps Bernstein overdoes the Mahler aspects of the first movement but not seriously. Drucker throws in a few bends; the balance at 6'14" nearly loses the soloist; but the drive towards the end is really exciting. In view of the riches of the CD as a whole, this is probably the performance of the Clarinet Concerto to have, along with excellent performances of the three other works.

Piano Concerto

Piano Concerto. Orchestral Variations. Short Symphony. Symphonic Ode
Garrick Ohlsson *pf*
San Francisco Symphony Orchestra / Michael Tilson Thomas
RCA Victor Red Seal 09026 68541-2 (66 minutes: DDD). Recorded 1996 Ⓕ ●●

According to Virgil Thomson, jazz was Aaron Copland's 'one wild oat'. Page after page of *Music for the Theatre* and its first cousin, the 1926 Piano Concerto, featured here, read like the blueprints for symphonic dance to come. A bold proclamation passes between trumpets and trombones, a 'fanfare for …'; but before you can finish the sentence, a dramatic cut to the wide shot: a glorious lyric effusion, its sights set on yet another gleaming skyline. Brave new world or lonely town? The quizzical solo piano isn't entirely sure, but the yearning grows: rhapsody in blue. Ohlsson kicks into this rhythm-bending mood-swing with terrific aplomb, and the San Francisco Symphony stretches every sinew to get its long limbs co-ordinated. Tilson Thomas has the players well blooded in the ways of this music: it's slick, it's tight, but it still retains that sense of wilful precariousness. It's hard to imagine that the *Orchestral Variations* were ever laid down in anything but orchestral terms, their sonority and harmony stretched from top to bottom of the score in spare, spacey chords. Then you remember that in its ground-breaking piano original it was as if the keyboard had been surrealistically elongated. It has the look of a modern metropolis in sound: lean, clean, oblique. *Symphonic Ode* – Copland's first big orchestral piece after the Piano Concerto – goes onwards and upwards in sky-scraping, octave-leaping tower blocks of sound. It's so very much a young man's America, alternately monolithic and toughly contrapuntal. A jazzy hint of misbegotten adolescence, a reflective heart and a tremendous conclusion as implacable as the US Constitution. The performance *knows* just how good it is. Deep-set, blockbusting recording. A winner.

Symphony No 3

Copland Symphony No 3[a]
Hanson Symphony No 2, 'Romantic'[b]
[a]**Dallas Symphony Orchestra / Eduardo Mata**
[b]**Saint Louis Symphony Orchestra / Leonard Slatkin**
HMV Classics HMV5 73544-2 (72 minutes: ADD) Ⓑ
Recorded 1986 ●

This release is a superb coupling of two of the very greatest American symphonies. Mata's account of the Copland may seem understated when compared with Bernstein's – the *scherzo* has a taut, spare energy but much less weight, while the slow movement has a fine intensity, capable of relaxing into grace and lyrical purity but never approaches Bernstein's transported, slightly Thespian poignancy. The colours of the finale are bright and crisp, the mood exhilaratingly joyous, but the sudden grinding of brakes and the gaze into the abyss beneath all this exuberance is less of a shock than in Bernstein's version. In short, the work does not seem quite such a huge gesture of a symphony in Mata's hands, but in compensation for this the quieter emotions are more gravely stated (the first movement, after all, is marked 'with simple expression', and throughout the work Mata often comes closer to this injunction than Bernstein). The strings in the *scherzo*'s trio section, too, have a hushed lyricism that is more touching than Bernstein's heartfelt but rather over-the-top eloquence, while the reminder of this mood at the centre of the slow movement seems a natural progression and even the most fully-scored pages of the finale are never harsh or densely opaque as they sometimes are with Bernstein. Mata's players are not quite a match for the NYP but they are splendidly recorded; DG's live recording glares rather at times.

Turning to the coupling, anyone who has been moved by the Barber *Adagio for strings* must respond to the yearning lyricism of the string writing of Hanson's *Romantic* Symphony, composed for the Boston Symphony Orchestra's 50th anniversary in 1930. This splendid work has real tunes – the *Andante* is its melodic focal point. It is convincing structurally, too, with the finale quoting earlier themes succinctly and powerfully (it is neither too long or too rhetorical) and without false optimism. Some will find Hanson's harmonic language not daring enough, but his music communicates. This performance is very fine. Perhaps, it has rather less grip and fervour than the composer's own, but it has breadth and a natural response to the atmosphere of the piece, while the orchestral playing is committed and fresh and the spacious acoustics add to the evocative effect.

Symphony No 3. Appalachian Spring. Fanfare for the Common Man
Minnesota Orchestra / Eiji Oue
Reference Recordings RR-93CD (72 minutes: DDD) Ⓕ
Recorded 2000 ●●

As an opening salute, the *Fanfare for the Common Man* makes a good centenary tribute and prepares listeners for its appearance in the finale of the Third Symphony. It also shows off the prowess of the Minnesota brass. The version of *Appalachian Spring* here is the suite, not the full ballet, and it is well paced under Oue although occasionally lacking attack in the strings, for example at 15'22", where Copland said he wanted 'bitten out *marcato*'.

The Third Symphony (1944-46) followed straight on from *Appalachian Spring*, with Copland extending that idiom into an epic symphony very much affected by the post-war American mood and providing a vehicle for Koussevitzky. Copland's Third is surely the finest American symphony after Ives, and has eclipsed that other once-famous Third – by Roy Harris. The Copland used to seem exaggerated, but now, with so much Mahler around, that is no longer the case. The work is spaciously proportioned, which comes over well here.

Significant earlier versions have been Copland's rather understated treatment with the New Philharmonia and, of course, Bernstein's much better projected interpretation on DG, considered by some the best.

Yet Oue's approach is compelling throughout, falling midway between Copland's objectivity and Bernstein's dramatisation. The soft, long lines of the first movement move inexorably towards the first climax, and Copland's translucent scoring tells in its purely personal way. The *scherzo* is a controlled riot, again showing off the brass – the orchestra's best feature – and the finale is convincing. Of the Third Symphony this is – although the orchestra is not flawless – among the best recordings since Bernstein. The recorded sound is spectacular too.

Ballets

Appalachian Spring. Billy the Kid. Rodeo
San Francisco Symphony Orchestra / Michael Tilson Thomas
RCA Red Seal 09026-63511-2 (77 minutes: DDD) Ⓕ
Recorded 1999 ●●●

For *Appalachian Spring* Tilson Thomas boldly opts for the rarely heard full orchestral version of the complete ballet score (Slatkin does likewise on his quite admirable 1985 recording with the St Louis Symphony, on HMV Classics or part of an all-Copland 'twofer' on EMI Double Forte). This includes an extra 10 or so minutes of fretful, dark-hued music omitted from the familiar suite (try from around 22'), after which that glorious final statement of *Simple Gifts* seems to emerge with even greater éclat and emotional release than usual. Elsewhere, these newcomers distil all the tender poetry and dewy freshness you could wish for, while bringing a marvellously supple spring and athletic purpose to any faster music.

Under Tilson Thomas, the suite from *Billy the Kid* opens with a real sense of 'once upon a time' wonder, the illimitable expanses of the prairie stretching out before our very eyes. The ensuing street scene soon generates an infectious rhythmic snap, and there's a wonderfully affecting contribution from the SFSO's principal trumpet during the card game at night (sample from 11'45" onwards). Best of all is 'Billy's death' (17'36"), as poignantly intoned as you've ever heard it. Absolutely no grumbles, either, about the four *Rodeo* dance episodes. Tilson Thomas sees to it that 'Buckaroo Holiday' packs all the requisite punch and high-kicking swagger, while the two middle numbers ravish the ear in their disarming beauty. Moreover, the concluding 'Hoe-Down' goes with terrific, toe-tapping gusto, though the orchestra's delirious whoops of delight may perhaps strike some listeners as rather too much of a good thing.

Boasting some opulent, exhilaratingly expansive sonics, this is one corker of a release.

El salón México[a]. Danzón cubano[b]. An Outdoor Overture[b]. Quiet City[b]. Our Town[b]. Las agachadas[a]. Fanfare for the Common Man[b]. Lincoln Portrait[b]. Appalachian Spring – suite[b]. Rodeo – Four Dance Episodes[b]. Billy the Kid – orchestral suite[b]. Music for Movies[c]. Letter from Home[b]. John Henry[b]. Symphony No 3[c]. Clarinet Concerto[d]
Benny Goodman *cl* **Henry Fonda** *narr* **[a]New England Conservatory Chorus; [b]London Symphony Orchestra; [c]New Philharmonia Orchestra; [d]Columbia Symphony Orchestra / Aaron Copland**
Sony Classical ③ SM3K46559 (226 minutes: ADD) Ⓜ
Recorded 1963-76

This offers a welcome gathering of a lot of Copland's own performances. Only *Las agachadas* ('The shake-down song') for unaccompanied chorus is new to the British catalogue; this is a rather lame performance and nobody would buy the three-CD set for that. The oldest recording is the Clarinet Concerto with Benny Goodman – the second of the two he made under Copland. *Lincoln Portrait* with Henry Fonda is disappointing, but apart from earlier recordings in Spanish and Portuguese, this, made in 1968, is the only one under Copland. He was surprisingly modest about interpretation and wrote (in *Copland on Music*; New York: 1960): 'Composers rarely can be depended upon to know the correct tempi at which their music should proceed'. All the same it is a pleasure to have Copland as both composer and interpreter in some of his most delightful shorter works such as *Letter from Home*, *John Henry*, *Quiet City* and *An Outdoor Overture*. All told, this is an economical way to build up a collection of his performances which provide such an insight into his personality.

El salón México. Dance Symphony. Fanfare for the Common Man. Rodeo – Four Dance Episodes. Appalachian Spring – suite
Detroit Symphony Orchestra / Antál Dorati
Decca Ovation 430 705-2DM (74 minutes: DDD) Ⓜ
Recorded 1980s

This glorious disc shows how well Antál Dorati assimilated the music of Aaron Copland. The big-boned swagger of 'Buckaroo Holiday' from *Rodeo* with its vision of open spaces and clear blue skies is established straightaway in Dorati's performance with keen rhythmic drive and fine orchestral articulation. The 'Hoe Down' is properly exciting while the other two dance episodes are wonderfully expressive. In the 1945 suite of *Appalachian Spring* Dorati secures marvellous phrasing and dynamics but tends to understate the score's poetic elements. Decca's exemplary sound quality is of demonstration standard in *Fanfare for the Common Man*, as it is in the enjoyable curtain-raiser, the sturdy, big-hearted *El salón México*. Dorati's vast experience as an interpreter of Stravinsky and Bartók pays fine dividends in Copland's gruesome *Dance Symphony*. A most welcome mid price release.

Piano Quartet

Movement[a]. Two Pieces[a]. Vitebsk[b]. Piano Quartet[c]. Sextet[d]
[d]**Michael Collins** *cl* [bcd]**Martin Roscoe** *pf*
[ad]**Vanbrugh Quartet** ([bc]Gregory Ellis, Keith Pascoe *vns* [c]Simon Aspell *va* [bc]Christopher Marwood *vc*)
ASV CDDCA1081 (65 minutes: DDD) Ⓕ
Recorded 1999

This fine collection of Copland's small output of chamber music offers the first British recording of *Movement*, a characteristically introspective piece from his student years in Paris which shares a theme with the *Symphony for Organ and Orchestra*. The *Two Pieces* (1928) are also rarities well worth having, the rapid second one embodying to perfection the ideals of Nadia Boulanger's teaching.

Then there are the three major chamber works, starting with *Vitebsk*, the 1929 trio based on a Jewish folk theme. This is a commanding performance, which makes the most of the off-key quarter-tones and is thoroughly adroit in the central *Allegro*. The Sextet is a genuine chamber piece, although it was an arrangement of the *Short Symphony* which was found too difficult for most orchestras in 1933 and had to wait until 1944 for its American première. With Collins and Roscoe the Vanbrugh give an accomplished performance of the Sextet's sparklingly affirmative rhythms.

The Piano Quartet (1950) is in the same slow-quick-slow layout as *Vitebsk*. Like the final slow movement of the Piano Sonata its outer movements have a sublime immobility. Written while Copland was working on his great cycle, *Twelve Poems of Emily Dickinson*, the first two movements of this impressive quartet enter new territory, Copland tentatively exploring serial techniques before Stravinsky did. A few exposed string phrases lack finesse, and some soft details in the piano are almost lost – at the end of the first movement and more seriously at the end of the last movement when the dissonant note in the last chord is inaudible. But this is a valuable collection, well worth acquiring to have all these works together, played – and recorded – like this.

Additional recommendation
Piano Quartet
Couplings: Violin Sonata. Duo for Flute and Piano. Rodeo – suite (arr cpsr)
Jeanne Baxtresser *fl* **Glenn Dicterow, Charles Rex** *vns* **Rebecca Young** *va* **Alan Stepansky** *vc* **Israela Margalit** *pf*
EMI Anglo-American Chamber Music CDC5 55405-2 Ⓕ
(77 minutes: DDD: 10/96)

An account of the Piano Quartet which does full justice to its striking integrity and admirable ambition. Stylish and imaginative playing in the couplings adds to this fine disc

---

Arcangelo Corelli Italian 1653-1713

GROVE *Corelli studied in Bologna from 1666, and was admitted to the Accademia Filarmonica at 17. By 1675 he was in Rome, where he became the foremost violinist and a chamber musician to Queen Christina of Sweden, to whom he dedicated his 12 trio sonatas da chiesa Op 1 (1681). His 12 trio sonatas da camera Op 2 (1685) were dedicated to Cardinal Pamphili; Corelli was his music master, 1687-90. His next patron, Cardinal Pietro Ottoboni, received the dedication of the trio sonatas Op 4 (1694). Corcilli came to dominate Rome musical life, and also directed opera performances there and in Naples. After 1708 he retired from public view.*

Corelli was the first composer to derive his fame exclusively from instrumental music. His works were immensely popular during his lifetime and long afterwards, and went through numerous reprints and arrangements (42 editions of the op.5 violin sonatas had appeared by 1800). They were seen as models of style for their purity and poise. His small output – six published sets and a few single pieces – contains innovations of fundamental importance to Baroque style, reconciling strict counterpoint and soloistic violin writing, and using sequential progressions and suspensions to give a notably modern sense of tonality. Distinctions between 'church' (abstract) and 'chamber' (dance) idioms are increasingly blurred in his sonatas. The op.6 concerti grossi (1714) resemble trio sonatas with orchestral reinforcement and echo effects. They were especially popular in England, preferred even to Handel's concertos well into the 19th century. There were many imitations of Corelli's music, notably of the folia variations in the violin sonata Op 5 No 12 (1700), and some composers used his music as a springboard; Bach borrowed a theme from the trio sonata Op 3 No 4 (1689) for an organ fugue. As a violinist Corelli was the finest, most influential teacher of his day; as an ensemble director he imposed high standards of discipline.

Concerti grossi

12 Concerti grossi, Op 6 – No 1 in D; No 2 in F; No 3 in C minor; No 4 in D; No 5 in D flat; No 6 in F; No 7 in D; No 8 in G minor; No 9 in F; No 10 in C; No 11 in B flat; No 12 in F **P**

Awards 1989

The English Concert / Trevor Pinnock

Archiv Produktion ② 459 451-2ATA2 (130 minutes: DDD). Recorded 1988 Ⓜ ooo

In his working life of about 40 years Corelli must have produced a great deal of orchestral music, yet the 12 *Concerti grossi*, Op 6, form the bulk of what is known to have survived. Their original forms are mostly lost but we know that those in which they were published in Amsterdam by Estienne Roger had been carefully polished and revised by the composer – and that they were assembled from movements that had been written at various times. The first eight are in *da chiesa* form, the last four in *da camera* form – without and with named dance movements respectively, and the number of their movements varies from four to seven. Each features the interplay of a group of soloists, the *concertino* (two violins and a cello) and the orchestra, the *ripieno*, the size of which Corelli stated to be flexible. These are without doubt masterpieces of their genre, one that was later developed by, notably, Bach and Handel, and they are rich in variety. The scores leave scope for embellishment, and the players of The English Concert take full advantage of them.

Trio Sonatas

Trio Sonatas, Op 3[a] – F; D; B flat; B minor; D minor; G. Trio Sonatas, Op 4[b] – C; G minor; A; D; A minor; E **P**

Jakob Lindberg *theorbo* **Purcell Quartet** (Catherine Mackintosh, [a]Elizabeth Wallfisch, [b]Catherine Weiss *vns* Richard Boothby *vc*); **Robert Woolley** [a]*hpd*/[b]*org*

Chandos Chaconne CHAN0526 (76 minutes: DDD) Ⓕ Recorded 1990s

Corelli's chamber music was reprinted 84 times during his lifetime and 31 more during the rest of the 18th century, a record that most composers would find enviable even today. The Sonatas of Op 3 are *da chiesa*, those of Op 4 are *da camera* (with dance-titled movements); the recording contains the first six of each set – the remaining ones are on another disc (Chandos CHAN0532), should you (as is probable) be tempted to add them to your collection. They are small gems: most have four movements and their durations range from five-and-a-half to seven-and-a-half minutes, within which they pack a wealth of invention, pure beauty and variety of pace and mood. Surviving evidence suggests that they were played at a much lower pitch than today's standard, the lower string tension adding warmth and opulence to the sound. Catherine Mackintosh takes full advantage of the works' opportunities for pliant phrasing and added embellishments; Elizabeth Wallfisch 'converses' with her in her own characteristic way, whilst Catherine Weiss follows her example more closely. The Purcell Quartet's oneness of thought and timing is a joy to hear and the recording is superb in all respects.

William Cornysh British 1468-1523

GROVE *After being at court (from 1494) Cornysh became Master of the Children at the Chapel Royal, a post he held until his death. From 1509 he was the leading figure in the plays and entertainments that enlivened court life. In 1513 he made the first of several visits to France with the Chapel Royal, in Henry VIII's retinue. Several of his sacred vocal works are in the Eton Choirbook; their style ranges from the flamboyance of the Stabat mater to the simplicity of the Ave Maria Mater Dei. His notable secular partsongs (in MSS are similarly versatile, Yow and I and Amyas being simple and chordal and A robyn a three-part canon apparently incorporating elements of pre-existent melody. Several other musicians with the surname Cornysh were active in the late 15th century and early 16th.*

Magnificat

Salve regina. Ave Maria, mater Dei. Gaude virgo mater Christi. Magnificat. Ah, Robin. Adieu, adieu, my heartes lust. Adieu courage. Woefully arrayed. Stabat mater

The Tallis Scholars / Peter Phillips

Gimell CDGIM014 (65 minutes: DDD). Texts and translations included. Recorded 1988 Ⓕ

Cornysh's music is a riot of abundant, often seemingly wild melody, constantly in search of wanton, abstract, dare-devil ideas. Take, for example, the extraordinary conclusion to the five-part *Magnificat*, where pairs of voices are challenged with music of gradually increasing complexity, peaking in an exchange of quite hair-raising virtuosity between the sopranos – and all this just for the words 'and ever shall be, world without end'! As far as the sacred works are concerned, The Tallis Scholars respond magnificently to Cornysh's audacious imagination. Theirs is a majestic and glorious sound, to be relished in full in the *Stabat mater*, a huge piece that survives incomplete and for which the late Frank Harrison composed treble parts that may even trump Cornysh himself in their sheer bravura. Marginally less striking in The Tallis Scholars' performances are the short part-songs and the carol *Woefully arrayed*, robbed as they are here of some of their latent expressiveness and strength by being sung (admittedly very beautifully) in an inappropriately resonant building, and in rounded modern English vowels rather than their brighter, more robust Tudor equivalents. But judged as a whole this disc must be reckoned an outstanding success.

François Couperin French 1668-1733

GROVE *Couperin was the central figure of the French harpsichord school. He came from a long line of musicians, mostly organists, of whom the most eminent was his uncle, Louis Couperin, though his father Charles (1638-79) was also a composer and organist of St Gervais. François succeeded to that post on his 18th birthday; his earliest known music is two organ masses. In 1693 he became one of the four royal organists which enabled him to develop his career as a teacher through his court connections. He was soon recognized as the leading French composer of his day through his sacred works and his chamber music and, from 1713, his harpsichord pieces. In 1716 he published an important treatise on harpsichord playing and the next year he was appointed royal harpsichordist.*

Among the music Couperin composed for Louis XIV's delectation were his Concerts royaux, chamber works for various combinations. He had written works in his own elaboration of trio-sonata form in the 1690s following the Italianate style of Corelli but retaining French character in the decorative lines and rich harmony. Later, he published these alongside French-style groups of dances as Les nations; they include some of his emotionally most powerful music. He was much concerned with blending French and Italian styles; he composed programmatic tributes to Lully and Corelli and works under the title Les goûts-réünis. He also wrote intensely expressive pieces for bass viol.

But it is as a harpsichord composer that Couperin is best known. He published four books with some 220 pieces, grouped in 27 ordres or suites. Some movements are in the traditional French dance forms, but most are character pieces with titles that reflect their inspiration: some are portraits of individuals or types, some portray abstract qualities, some imitate the sounds of nature. The titles may also be ambiguous or metaphorical, or even intentionally obscure. Most of the pieces are in rondeau form. All are elegantly composed, concealing a complex, allusive and varied emotional world behind their highly wrought surface. Couperin took immense pains over the notation of the ornaments with which his harpsichord writing is sprinkled and animated. These, and his style generally, are expounded in his L'art de toucher le clavecin.

Couperin's children were also musicians: Nicholas (1680-1748) succeeded his father at St Gervais, and probably composed, while Marie-Madeleine (1690-1742) was probably an abbey organist and Marguerite-Antoinette (1705- c1778) was active as a court harpsichordist, c1729-1741

Pièces de clavecin

L'art de toucher le clavecin – Prelude No 6 in B minor. **P**
Troisième livre de pièces de clavecin – Treizième ordre; Quatorzième ordre; Quinzième ordre

Robert Kohnen *hpd* **Barthold Kuijken** *fl*
Accent ACC9399D (64 minutes: DDD) Ⓕ
Recorded 1993

Kohnen's playing is rhythmically incisive, fastidious in detail – Couperin was hot on that – and full of character. If, on first acquaintance, his realization of Couperin's vignette 'Les lis naissans' (*Ordre* No 13) seems a shade spiky then his lyrical approach to the flowing 6/8 melody of the rondeau 'Les rozeaux', which follows, reassures us that Kohnen does have the poetry of the music at heart, and intends that it should be so. Less appealing are Kohnen's somewhat intrusive vocal introductions to 'Les folies françoises'. This information is provided in the booklet so it hardly needs to be reiterated. In a concert recital such snatches of actuality can be effective; on a disc, after repeated listening, they become an unwelcome interruption. Occasional departures from the norm in the following two *ordres* are of an altogether more agreeable nature. In 'Le rossignol-en-amour' (*Ordre* No 14) Kohnen takes Couperin up on his suggestion to use a transverse flute, played here with a beautifully rounded tone by Barthold Kuijken. Likewise, in the jaunty rondeau, 'La Julliet', the trio texture is realized by flute and harpsichord rather than the more usual two-harpsichord texture. This piece is beautifully done, as is the subtly bell-like 'Carillon de Cithère' which follows it. In short, a stylish and entertaining release which is as likely as any to draw the cautious listener into Couperin's refined, allusory and metaphor-laden idiom.

Leçons de ténèbres

Trois leçons de ténèbres. Laetentur coeli et exultet. Magnificat anima mea. Victoria! Christo resurgenti
Les Talens Lyriques (Véronique Gens, Sandrine Piau *sops* Emmanuel Balsa *va da gamba*) / **Christophe Rousset** *org*
Decca 466 776-2OH (65 minutes: DDD). Texts and translations included. Recorded 1999 Ⓕ **OO**

Couperin's superb settings for solo voices and continuo of the sombre Tenebrae lessons for the Wednesday of Holy Week were composed around 1715. Their exquisitely drawn melodies and anguished but dignified chromaticisms will come as a surprise to listeners used to seeing Couperin only as an urbane, perhaps even rather frivolous court harpsichord composer. In their sheer power and beauty the *Leçons de ténèbres* rate among the highest musical achievements of the baroque period.

This recording features two of France's leading baroque sopranos. Both sing with a refined sense of vocal intensity learned in the baroque stage repertoire, bringing a declamatory flavour to the *Leçons*' recitatives, heart-rending laments and occasional apocalyptic outbursts, while also demonstrating in the more free-flowing music (in particular the vocalise-like settings of the Hebrew letters which head each section of text) consummate control and poise. Sandrine Piau's voice is the lighter and purer of the two; that of Véronique Gens is somewhat darker, heavier and has a touch more vibrato, yet when the two of them come together in the Third *Leçon* they blend surprisingly well. The gamba-and-organ accompaniments are both tasteful and unobtrusive (typically so for the serious-minded Christophe Rousset). By comparison, William Christie's harpsichord accompaniments on Erato are more interventionist and less earnest, their greater range of textural options helping to push Les Arts Florissants sopranos Patricia Petibon and Sophie Daneman into readings which are decidedly more sprightly and text-aware. The Decca release is considerably more generous than the Erato, filled out to a more respectable length in joyous vein by two additional two-voice motets (for Easter and St Bartholomew's days respectively) and a substantial *Magnificat*.

Bernhard Crusell Finnish 1775-1839

GROVE *Crusell studied the clarinet from the age of eight and at 12 joined a military band in Sveaborg; in 1791 he went to Stockholm where he became a court musician two years later. He studied the clarinet in Berlin in 1798 with Tausch and in 1803 went to Paris to study composition with Gossec and Berton and the clarinet with Lefèvre. He later held posts as music director in the Swedish court chapel and royal regiment. His compositions include three clarinet concertos (1811, 1816, 1829), an air and variations for clarinet and a Concertante for clarinet, bassoon and horn (1816); he also wrote chamber music, including three clarinet quartets (1812, 1816, 1823), an opera Den lilla Slafvinnan (1824, Stockholm) and 12 songs. He was a fluent composer with a fresh vein of melody. He also made Swedish translations of operas by Mozart, Rossini and others.*

Clarinet Concertos

Crusell Clarinet Concerto No 2 in F minor, 'Grand' **Baermann** Adagio in D flat **Rossini** Introduction and Variations in C minor **Weber** Concerto Concertino in C minor, J109
Emma Johnson *cl* **English Chamber Orchestra / Sir Charles Groves** Ⓕ
ASV CDDCA559 (55 minutes: DDD). Recorded 1985

It was this Crusell Grand Concerto which Emma Johnson played when she won the BBC Young Musician of the Year competition in 1984. That occasion was the first time she had played a concerto with a full symphony orchestra, and her special affection for the piece, her total joy in each of the three movements, comes over vividly in this performance. The uninhibited spontaneity of her playing, exactly matching a live performance, brings an extra compulsion and immediacy of expression. Emma Johnson in each movement translates the notes with very personal phrasing and expression, always taking risks and bringing them off. This is a daring performance, naughtily lilting in the outer movements, happily songful in the *Andante pastorale* of the slow movement. In the three shorter pieces Johnson may not have the same technical perfection, but the free expressiveness could not be more winning. Her moulding of *legato* melodies in the Weber and Rossini works, as well as the Baermann, brings warm expressiveness, with free rubato and sharp contrasts of tone and dynamic. The orchestral sound is full and bright, with Groves a lively, sympathetic accompanist.

Clarinet Concertos – No 1 in E flat, Op 1; No 2 in F minor, Op 5; No 3 in B flat, Op 11
Kari Kriikku *cl* **Finnish Radio Symphony Orchestra / Sakari Oramo**
Ondine ODE965-2 (64 minutes: DDD) Ⓕ
Recorded 2000 ●

With full, bright, immediate sound, the Finnish clarinettist Kari Kriiku gives dazzling performances of these three delightful clarinet concertos. In many ways he is even more daring than the two excellent rivals Karl Leister (BIS) and Emma Johnson (ASV and Regis Records), regularly choosing speeds that stretch virtuosity to the limit, particularly in the finales. Those of Nos 1 and 2 may be marked *allegretto* merely, but Kriiku, by choosing exceptionally fast speeds, brings out an extra *scherzando* quality, often sharp and spiky, in which Crusell's characteristically dotted rhythms are delightfully crisp. The almost impossibly rapid tonguing never seems to get in the way of detailed characterisation. Leister in the finale of No 2 comes near to matching Kriiku's fast speed, but the result is far plainer, and generally Leister's readings are remarkable for the smoothness and liquid tone of his playing.

Johnson in her recordings is altogether more relaxed, regularly adopting speeds rather broader, extremely so in the *Alla Polacca* which ends No 3. Consistently, her pointing of rhythm brings out the fun in the writing, and in her comparably broad approach to slow movements she finds extra poetry, at times bringing out the links with the slow movement of Mozart's late masterpiece. Partly as a result of the immediacy of the recording, Kriiku's *pianissimos* are not as extreme, yet in flair and panache Kriiku is second to none, superbly supported by the crisp, purposeful playing of the Finnish National Radio orchestra under Sakari Oramo.

An excellent disc, guaranteed to win friends for these sparkling works.

Jean-Henri D'Anglebert
French 1635-1691

GROVE *In 1662 D'Anglebert succeeded Chambonnières as harpsichordist to Louis XIV, a post he officially held until his death. His Pièces de clavecin (1689) contains four suites of dances (three beginning with unmeasured preludes) complemented by transcriptions of popular tunes, arrangements of works by Lully, and five organ fugues that show a firm grasp of contrapuntal techniques. The volume contains a comprehensive table of ornaments, with many new signs that passed into general usage, and ends with a short treatise on keyboard harmony.*

Pièces de clavecin

Pièces de clavecin – A minor; C; D; D minor; G; G minor Ⓟ
Christophe Rousset *hpd*
Decca L'Oiseau-Lyre ② 458 588-2OH2 (159 minutes: DDD). Recorded 1996 Ⓕ

Jean-Henri d'Anglebert is one of the three most important figures of the influential French harpsichord school of the 17th century, yet his music, like that of his immediate predecessor as court harpsichordist to Louis XIV, Chambonnières, is not nearly as well represented on disc as that of the triumvirate's third member, Louis Couperin. Its relative lack of popularity probably has to do with the musical preoccupations of our own time, for in d'Anglebert's music, for all its stylistic and technical assurance, we find less of the touching melancholy and haunting expressiveness with which Couperin can speak to us across the ages. By comparison, d'Anglebert seems more a prisoner of his own time and place, namely the courtly surroundings of Versailles where, if seriousness was still a requirement, so too was an approach which is less subjective, less fragile, and consequently probably less striking to modern ears. D'Anglebert it was, however, who took harpsichord music forward, expanding its expressive range and weight – he appears to have been the first French keyboard composer to write a set of variations – and paving the way for the keyboard achievements of François Couperin, Rameau, and even Bach. For all harpsichordists, then, he is a composer not to be ignored.

That this set claims to be the 'complete' harpsichord works is a little misleading. For example, owners of the 'complete works' published in 1975 by Heugel will notice that while all the published pieces appear, be they d'Anglebert originals or transcriptions, only genuine d'Anglebert works are included from the manuscript sources. In view of the undoubted documentary value (and intent) of this recording, it seems a shame that Decca does not see fit to give more information.

Turning to the performances, Christophe Rousset is in many ways the ideal harpsichordist for this music. Sympathetic to d'Anglebert – he considers his output to be 'a jewel of French music' – he possesses both the serious temperament and the exquisite technique his music demands. D'Anglebert's works must be among the most ornament-encrusted in existence, yet Rousset never struggles in this complex of *tremblements*, *ports de voix* and *chutes*, executing them instead with unfailing poise and control, whichever hand or finger they lie under. (The harpsichord, a beautifully prepared 1629 Ruckers, must likewise be commended for meeting the tough demands made on it by so many notes.) Ornaments aside, however, Rousset's overall touch is in any case positively aristocratic, producing a rich and gently sonorous tone which never clatters and never jangles. His elegant realisations of the unmeasured preludes are an utter delight. It is true that spontaneity is not high on his list of attributes – he springs few interpretative surprises and sticks rigorously to the text, adding scarcely a single decoration of his own – but nobody could deny that this is harpsichord-playing of an extremely high level of refinement.

Claude Debussy French 1862-1918

GROVE *Debussy studied with Guiraud and others at the Paris Conservatoire (1872-84) and as prizewinner went to Rome (1885-7), though more important impressions came from his visits to Bayreuth (1888, 1889) and from hearing Javanese music in Paris (1889). Wagner's influence is evident in the cantata La damoiselle élue (1888) and the Cinq, poèmes de Baudelaire (1889) but other songs of the period, notably the settings of Verlaine (Ariettes oubliées, Trois mélodies, Fêtes galantes, set 1) are in a more capricious style, as are parts of the still somewhat Franckian G minor String Quartet (1893); in that work he used not only the Phrygian mode but also less standard modes, notably the whole-tone mode, to create the floating harmony he discovered through the work of contemporary writers: Mallarmé in the orchestral Prélude à 'L'après-midi d'un faune' (1894) and Maeterlinck in the opera Pelléas et Mélisande, dating in large part from 1893-5 but not completed until 1902. These works also brought forward a fluidity of rhythm and colour quite new to Western music.*

Pelléas, with its rule of understatement and deceptively simple declamation, also brought an entirely new tone to opera - but an unrepeatable one. Debussy worked on other opera projects and left substantial sketches for two pieces after tales by Poe (Le diable dans le beffroi and La chûte de la maison Usher), but nothing was completed. Instead the main works were orchestral pieces, piano sets and songs.

The orchestral works include the three Nocturnes (1899), characteristic studies of veiled harmony and texture ('Nuages'), exuberant cross-cutting ('Fêtes') and seductive whole-tone drift ('Sirènes'). La mer (1905) essays a more symphonic form, with a finale that works themes from the first movement, though the centrepiece ('Jeux de vagues') proceeds much less directly and with more variety of colour. The three Images (1912) are more loosely linked, and the biggest, 'Ibéria', is itself a triptych, a medley of Spanish allusions. Finally the ballet Jeux (1913) contains some of Debussy's strangest harmony and texture in a form that moves freely over its own field of motivic connection. Other late stage works, including the ballets Khamma (1912) and La boîte à joujoux (1913) and the mystery play Le martyre de St Sébastien (1911), were not completely orchestrated by Debussy, though St Sébastien is remarkable in sustaining an antique modal atmosphere that otherwise was touched only in relatively short piano pieces (e.g.'La cathédrale engloutie').

The important piano music begins with works which, Verlaine fashion, look back at rococo decorousness with a modern cynicism and puzzlement (Suite bergamasque, 1890; Pour le piano, 1901). But then, as in the orchestral pieces, Debussy began to associate his music with visual impressions of the East, Spain, landscapes etc, in a sequence of sets of short pieces. His last volume of Etudes (1915) interprets similar varieties of style and texture purely as pianistic exercises and includes pieces that develop irregular form to an extreme as well as others influenced by the young Stravinsky (a presence too in the suite En blanc et noir for two pianos, 1915). The rarefaction of these works is a feature of the last set of songs, the Trois poèmes de Mallarmé (1913), and of the Sonata for flute, viola and harp (1915), though the sonata and its companions also recapture the inquisitive Verlainian classicism The planned set of six sonatas was cut short by the composer's death from rectal cancer.

Orchestral Works

Images. Berceuse héroïque[a]. Danse sacrée et danse profane[b]. Jeux. Nocturnes. Marche écossaise sur un thème populaire. Prélude à l'après-midi d'un faune. La mer. Première rapsodiec[b]

Awards 1980

Vera Badings *hp* [c]**George Pieterson** *cl* **Concertgebouw Orchestra /** [a]**Eduard van Beinum, Bernard Haitink**

Philips Duo ② 438 742-2PM (141 minutes: ADD) Ⓜ

Recorded [b]1957, 1976-79 **○○○**

Philips has repackaged Haitink's late-1970s recordings on two CDs for the price of one. Space has also been found for Debussy's last orchestral work, the short *Berceuse héroïque* conducted by Eduard van Beinum (in excellent 1957 stereo). In every respect this package is a genuine bargain. In *La mer*, like the 1964 Karajan on DG Galleria, there is a concern for refinement and fluidity of gesture, for a subtle illumination of texture; and both display a colourist's knowledge and use of an individually apt variety of orchestral tone and timbre. It is the wind playing that you remember in Haitink's *Images*: the melancholy and disconsolate oboe d'amore in 'Gigues'; and from 'Ibéria', the gorgeous oboe solo in 'Les parfums de la nuit', and the carousing clarinets and raucous trumpets in the succeeding holiday festivities. And here, as elsewhere in the set, the Concertgebouw acoustic plays a vital role. Haitink's *Jeux* is slower and freer than average, and possessed of a near miraculous precision, definition and delicacy. The jewel in this set, for many, will be the *Nocturnes*, principally for the purity of the strings in 'Nuages'; the dazzling richness and majesty of the central procession in 'Fêtes'; and the cool beauty and composure of 'Sirènes'. Haitink opts for an ethereal distance; there may be passages where you are unsure if they are singing or not, but the effect is magical.

Debussy La mer. Prélude à l'après-midi d'un faune
Ravel Daphnis et Chloé – Suite No 2. Boléro

Berlin Philharmonic Orchestra / Herbert von Karajan

DG Galleria 427 250-2GGA (64 minutes: ADD) Ⓜ

Recorded 1964-65 **○○○**

Karajan never concealed his passion for French music and these masterpieces of French orchestral music are masterly; beautifully recorded too. Controlled and aristocratic, they show a scrupulous regard for the composers' wishes. The sound of the Berlin strings is sumptuous, with detail well placed and in a generally natural perspective. It is a joy to relish the beauty of the playing in such clear, well-defined sound. It has that indefinable quality that one can more readily recognize than describe, a magic that makes one forget the performer and transports one into the composer's world. You can either be seduced by some of the most sheerly beautiful orchestral sound recorded, or appreciate it for its wide-ranging imagery and its properly mobile pacing; whichever, it is one of the great recorded *La mers* and one of the classics of the gramophone. Karajan's interpretation of *Prélude à l'après-midi d'un faune* remains one of the most beautiful readings committed to record – the first flute, Karlheinz Zöller, plays like a wizard. *Boléro* is slow and steady (but Karajan risks floating the early solos). This is also a ravishing account of the Second Suite from *Daphnis et Chloé*.

La mer. Nocturnes. Première rapsodie. Jeux

Franklin Cohen *cl* **Cleveland Chorus and Orchestra / Pierre Boulez**

DG 439 896-2GH (71 minutes: DDD) Ⓕ

Recorded 1991-93 **○**

No one, we would submit, is the equal of Karajan in 1964 as a colourist in *La mer*, although few have had the Berlin Philharmonic's rich and varied palette to deploy on it. And very few are Karajan's equal in relating Debussy's detailed tempo indications. Boulez's speed for 'Jeux de vagues' was, and still is, too leisurely by half, and the orchestra seems to be here – untypically – on auto-pilot. Boulez does at least forge ahead in the middle of the second half's gathering wave. But for the remaining 56 minutes of music-making on this disc, there is nothing but praise. Boulez conducts *Jeux* with obvious authority and passionate urgency, without lingering unduly in its moments of fantasy and sophisticated sensuality. In the clarinet *Rapsodie* and *Nocturnes* there is a quite fabulous subtlety and variety of pace, texture and colour. From the latter, 'Nuages' is more mobile than is common and 'Fêtes' is rather more gentle than usual (with a perfectly judged distance for the trumpets at the start of the central procession). Boulez greatly varies the vowels from phrase to phrase in the chorus's *vocalise* in 'Sirènes', sometimes within a phrase, in a manner that is both haunting and hypnotic, and which is entirely consistent with the music's dynamic. The Cleveland ladies' pitching is beyond criticism, as is Franklin Cohen's clarinet-playing. There is also a grace and poise about this singing and playing and the 20-odd years of Boulez's experience with the work show, too, in his now more moderate slowings and suspensions. The sound is warm and full.

Nocturnes – Nuages; Fêtes. Prélude à l'après-midi d'un faune. Le martyre de Saint-Sébastien – symphonic fragments. La mer H
Philharmonia Orchestra / Guido Cantelli
Testament mono SBT1011 (67 minutes: ADD) Ⓕ
Recorded 1954-55 ⦿

The death of Guido Cantelli in an air crash at the age of 36 in 1956 was a terrible loss. In a career lasting just 13 years he made his way right to the top of his profession, although at the end of his life he was still developing and maturing, and would surely have been one of the most important artists of our time. Fortunately he made a number of superlative recordings over a period of seven years and this disc, which contains all his Debussy, shows why concert audiences in the 1950s were bowled over by him.

It is a pity that he never conducted all three *Nocturnes*, for 'Nuages' flows beautifully and expressively and he chooses just the right tempo for 'Fêtes'. He does not press this piece too hard as most conductors do, and its colour and piquant personality thus flower freshly and easily. *L'après-midi* is also given plenty of room to breathe: the playing cool, elegant, beautifully poised, yet very eloquent. In *La mer* Cantelli avoids the ham-fisted, overdramatic approach of so many conductors, and instead we have a performance with clear, gleaming textures. The first movement ebbs and flows in a movingly poetic fashion: every detail makes its effect and everything is perfectly in scale. The middle movement is taken quite briskly, but phrasing is hypersensitive and appropriately fluid. In the last movement there is plenty of drama and excitement, although climaxes are kept within bounds in a way which paradoxically makes for a greater effect than if they were given Brucknerian proportions, as they often are.

During Cantelli's lifetime *Le martyre de Saint-Sébastien* was strangely regarded as a tired, feeble work, yet he conducted the 'Symphonic fragments' quite frequently. His approach is very much of the concert hall in that he gives the four pieces a life of their own rather than relating them to the unfolding drama. However, he still captures the music's peculiarly fervent, religious-cum-exotic flavour very effectively. The Philharmonia plays with extraordinary subtlety, and the recordings sound very well indeed.

Prélude à l'après-midi d'un faune[a]. Images[b]. Jeux[c]. Danse sacrée et danse profane[d]
[b]**František Kimel** *ob* [d]**Karel Patras** *hp* **Czech Philharmonic Orchestra / Serge Baudo**
Supraphon Archiv SU3478-2 (70 minutes: ADD) Ⓜ
Recorded 1966 and 1977 ⦿

Serge Baudo's Debussy collection brings together three of the most outstanding recordings Supraphon gave us in the analogue era. Indeed the rich, balmy sound is perfect for the ravishing Czech playing in the *Prélude à l'après-midi d'un faune*, with a wonderfully limpid flute solo, and Baudo letting the music flow onwards in the most natural way. Debussy's translucent colours gleam vividly at the very opening of *Images*, and the piquant oboe solo is ear-catching. 'Les parfums de la nuit' waft softly and languorously in the evening breeze, and the opening of 'Le matin d'un jour de fête' is hauntingly mysterious before the orchestra blazes into life. Finest of all is *Jeux*, always an elusive work on record, but here presented with richly glowing colouristic magic, ravishingly seductive string textures, and a subtle feeling for the music's ebb and flow. The transfer is ADD, and if you are one of those collectors who think that a digital CD can't transfer analogue hall ambience and decay properly, sample this.

String Quartet

Debussy String Quartet in G minor, Op 10 **Ravel** String Quartet in F **Webern** String Quartet (1905)
Hagen Quartet (Lukas Hagen, Rainer Schmidt *vns* Veronika Hagen *va* Clemens Hagen *vc)*
DG 437 836-2GH (70 minutes: DDD) Ⓕ
Recorded 1992-93

The first movement of the Debussy is taken fastish, but its passionate urgency convinces and it is not forced tonally or tempo-wise. Indeed, the playing is beautifully polished, and this fine ensemble also fully understands the emotional world of the music, the slow movement (again more flowing than usual) offering an acid test which they pass easily. The finale is thrilling. In the Ravel, the playing is sensitive and skilful. Webern's one-movement Quartet was inspired by a painting entitled 'Evolving, Being, Passing Away', and the music begins with a motif akin to Beethoven's 'Muss es sein?' figure in his String Quartet, Op 135. The scenario here is predictable: youthfully Germanic heart-searching and struggle, but with little that is memorable, and ultimately somewhat constipated. Still, this performance is persuasive, and the work deserves to be heard when played as well as this. The recorded sound is excellent.

Debussy String Quartet in G minor, Op 10
Ravel String Quartet in F
Quartetto Italiano (Paolo Borciani, Elisa Pegreffi *vns* Piero Farulli *va* Franco Rossi *vc*)
Philips Silver Line 420 894-2PSL (57 minutes: ADD) Ⓜ
Recorded 1968 ⦿

Coupling the Debussy and Ravel String Quartets has become a cliché of the record industry, but as someone has said, a cliché is only a great truth made stale by repetition, and these two wonderful pieces do make a satisfying pair. The account of them by the Quartetto Italiano is over 30 years old but none the worse for that. They are marvellously vital performances in which intensity of feeling does not preclude refinement. The only quibble is about the high-level transfer to CD which may send you reluctantly to the volume control of your amplifier. But when the necessary adjustment is made, the result as sound is satisfactory and the playing good enough to make this Philips issue a first choice at medium price in these works despite its age.

Piano Trio

Debussy Piano Trio in G **Fauré** Piano Trio in D minor, Op 120 **Ravel** Piano Trio in A minor
Florestan Trio (Anthony Marwood *vn* Richard Lester *vc* Susan Tomes *pf*)
Hyperion CDA67114 (66 minutes: DDD) Ⓕ
Recorded 1999 ➊

The Florestan Trio has the ability to adapt its style to different kinds of music without any loss of conviction. After Brahms and Schumann comes this French disc showing it equally adept at entering the 1880 salon world of Debussy's youthful Trio, Ravel's brilliant exotic idiom, and the intimate, intense thoughts of Fauré's old age. In the quicker movements Susan Tomes's playing is remarkably light and precise. The finale of the Fauré, for example, has a *scherzando* quality that throws into relief the seriousness of the strings' initial gesture. The string players are always ready to modify their sound to produce special expressive effects – the eerily quiet unison passage in Fauré's *Andante* (track 2, 2'54") or the vibrato-less duet in the Ravel *Passacaille* (track 10, 5'15") – sounding wonderfully remote and antique. The clarity of the Hyperion recording allows the fantastical detail in the Ravel *Pantoum* to emerge. In the Debussy, the Florestan favour elegance rather than trying to search out expressive depths. Their freshness, imagination and purposeful directness makes this a top choice.

Sonata for Flute, Viola and Harp

Sonata for Flute, Viola and Harp[a]. Prélude à l'après-midi d'un faune (arr Samazeuilh)[b]. Syrinx[b]. La flûte de Panc. Chansons de Bilitis[d]
[cd]**Irène Jacob** *spkr* **Philippe Bernold,** [d]**Mathieu Dufour** *fls* [a]**Gérard Caussé** *va* [ad]**Isabelle Moretti,** [d]**Germaine Lorenzini** *hps* **Ariane Jacob** [b]*pf*/[d]*celesta*
Harmonia Mundi HMC90 1647 (50 minutes: DDD) Ⓕ
Texts included.

The high point of this disc is a beautifully sensitive performance of Debussy's elusive late sonata, a 'terribly sad' work according to the composer himself, but also containing in its latter two movements an uneasy kind of high spirits born of desperation. The opening and close of the first movement provide two of those haunting moments at which French composers seem to excel. Philippe Bernold is a player of delicate, refined tone whose descents to the edge of sound are hypnotic in their effect; and with his two partners the performance rivals those recordings hitherto cherished as yardsticks – the classic Melos of 1962 and the Nash of 1991. Bernold captures the spirit of rapture in *Syrinx*, which is heard both in its usual form as an unaccompanied solo and as it was originally intended, as incidental music to a play, *Psyché*. Unfortunately Irène Jacob, who reads the text admirably, is too distantly placed in relation to the flute. The same criticism applies to the erotic *Chansons de Bilitis* poems. It was Debussy's own idea to make a transcription for flute and piano of the *Prélude à l'après-midi d'un faune*; but imaginatively as Samazeuilh wrote this and Ariane Jacob plays the piano part, the sensuous magic of this score suffers from this reduction of colour.

Violin Sonata

Debussy Violin Sonata **Franck** Violin Sonata in A **Ravel** Berceuse sur le nom de Gabriel Fauré. Pièce en forme de habanera. Tzigane
Augustin Dumay *vn* **Maria João Pires** *pf*
DG 445 880-2GH (56 minutes: DDD)
Recorded 1993 Ⓕ

There is a spacious, eloquent view here of Franck's Sonata, in which Dumay's sweet tone also has the requisite strength; as for Pires, she accompanies where necessary and yet can offer a partner's contribution too, as well as being equal to the composer's considerable pianistic demands. Although the recorded balance favours the violinist, the brilliant second movement is very effective, as is the flowing canonic finale, in which the players rightly think in long phrases. Debussy's emotionally fragile world fares even better: this playing has the right flexibility of time and tone, and the rapidly shifting moods of this essentially sad music, so different from Franck's with its emotional assurance, are unerringly captured; and the sound is excellent here. Dumay and Pires are also at home in Ravel's music with its delicate tenderness and – in *Tzigane* at least – glittering virtuosity.

Cello Sonata

Debussy Cello Sonata in D minor
Britten Cello Sonata, Op 65
Schumann Fünf Stücke im Volkston, Op 102
Mstislav Rostropovich *vc* **Benjamin Britten** *pf*
Decca The Classic Sound 452 895-2DCS Ⓜ
(51 minutes: ADD). Recorded 1961 ➊➊➊

Rostropovich was second only to Sir Peter Pears as a Britten catalyst, inspiring some of his finest instrumental works as well as some of his most memorable accompanying. Or should we say partnering, for soloist and accompanist are so well matched, and respect each other so much, that the rigid role-play of leader and follower is joyously over-ruled, turning chamber music into a dramatic experience which suggests the dialogue of two actors. This is particularly evident in the temperamental caprice of the Debussy Sonata, where the range of colour drawn by Britten from the keyboard, in response to Rostropovich's own, has to be heard to be believed. Their spontaneously attuned rubato throughout, as well as their rhythmic vitality in the finale, are further sources of delight. Rostropovich and Britten are also indisputable winners in Schumann's five folk-style pieces (even though No 2, marked *langsam*, is questionably fast), much more at one with each other as well as with the rustic simplicity and strength of the music itself. Regardless of more recent recordings, Rostropovich remains the real heavyweight in the Britten Sonata – it's a classic. It's difficult to believe the recording is nearly 40 years old. This disc can confidently be hailed as a collector's piece, likely to survive in the gramophone archives for all time.

Debussy Cello Sonata
Bridge Cello Sonata in D minor, H125. Four Short Pieces, H104 – Meditation; Spring song
Dohnányi Cello Sonata in B flat minor, Op 8
Bernard Gregor-Smith *vc* **Yolande Wrigley** *pf* Ⓕ
ASV CDDCA796 (68 minutes: DDD). Recorded 1992

The *commedia dell'arte* inspiration of the Debussy Cello Sonata can be appreciated on minimal acquaintance, but the highly individual formal structure of the work and its extraordinary variety of mood and content present huge challenges not easily met in live performance; and the Sonata can seem even more unattainable on disc. Bernard Gregor-Smith and Yolande Wrigley take up the challenge in this very fine performance of lyrical elegance, and not a little rococo irony and wit. Speeds are on the fast side, but there is no lack of refinement and flexibility in the playing, with superb bravura displays from Gregor-Smith in the finale. Whilst the performance of the Debussy is generally excellent, the centrepiece is the fervent and frequently heroic account of the Sonata in B flat by Ernö Dohnányi. The work is seldom performed, and Gregor-Smith's fine-toned and dexterous reading deserves high praise. The Frank Bridge Cello Sonata is a personal expression of grief and outrage, dating from the final year of the First World War, and shares a common tonality with the Debussy. Its broad paragraphs dictate the interpretative approach, but the work receives a fluent and idiomatic reading, reserving the last degree of energy for the poignantly rhetorical closing pages of the piece. The disc also includes two characteristic Bridge miniatures, again eloquently played by this expert husband-and-wife duo. They have been faithfully, if not brilliantly recorded. As for the playing, however, the skill of execution is matched by a refined insight into each work, lending a rare equilibrium to a superb recital of unusual perception and eloquence.

En blanc et noir

En blanc et noir. Petite suite. Nocturnes (arr Ravel) – Nuages; Fêtes. Six épigraphes antiques. Lindaraja
Katia and **Marielle Labèque** *pf duet/pfs*
Philips 454 471-2PH (58 minutes: DDD) Ⓕ
Recorded 1996

Katia and Marielle Labèque give a Debussy programme which is stylish and scintillating. Whatever sparkles and delights is here in abundance. Playing with a fierce, recognizably French clarity and verve they make you doubly aware of the extraordinary force of nature that consumed Debussy during his final years. Faced with the outbreak of war, the possible destruction of his beloved France and his own terminal illness, he composed, among other masterpieces, his *En blanc et noir*, a wild dreamscape containing some of his most startling and original music. And if the Labèques play with an electrifying bravura, they are no less enviably refined, registering every detail of the score with scrupulous precision and sensitivity. They are no less dazzling in the more openly endearing *Petite suite* and if 'Fêtes' (from the *Nocturnes*) explodes in an orgy of brilliance, such open display is poetically balanced in *Epigraphes antiques*, where the duo are hauntingly memorably. Time and again they show how the finest insights are only available to pianists liberated from all difficulty, who are free to concentrate on a purely musical discourse. The recordings are immaculate and combined with the Labèque sisters' verve and pianistic aplomb provide a special, crystalline experience.

Complete Piano Works

Awards 1996

Préludes, Books 1[a] and 2[a]. H
Pour le piano[a]. Estampes[a] . Images, Sets 1a and 2a. Children's Cornera. 12 Etudes. D'un cahier d'esquisses. Rêverie. Valse romantique. Masques. L'isle joyeuse. La plus que lente. Le petit nègre. Berceuse héroïque. Hommage à Haydn. Danse bohémienne. Mazurka. Deux Arabesques. Nocturne. Tarantelle styrienne. Ballade. Suite bergamasque. Fantaisie (recorded live)
Walter Gieseking *pf* **Hessian Radio Orchestra, Frankfurt / Kurt Schröder**
EMI mono ④ CHS5 65855-2 (276 minutes: ADD) Ⓜ
Recorded 1951-55 ●●●

The complete Préludes with items marked [a] are also available on HMV Classics ② HMVD5 73192-2 Ⓑ
and (Préludes only) on EMI Great Recordings of the Century CDM5 67233-2 Ⓜ

Gieseking's insight and iridescence in Debussy are so compelling and hypnotic that they prompt either a book or a blank page – an unsatisfactory state where criticism is concerned! First and foremost, there is Gieseking's sonority, one of such delicacy and variety that it can complement Debussy's witty and ironic desire to write music 'for an instrument without hammers', for a pantheistic art sufficiently suggestive to evoke and transcend the play of the elements themselves ('the wind, the sky, the sea…'). Lack of meticulousness seems a small price to pay for such an elemental uproar in 'Ce qu'a vu le vent d'ouest', and Puck's elfin pulse and chatter (*pp aérian*) are caught with an uncanny deftness and precision. The final

Debussian magic may not lie in a literal observance of the score, in the unfailing dotting and crossing of every objective and picturesque instruction, yet it is the start or foundation of a great performance. More domestically, no one (not even Cortot) has ever captured the sense in *Children's Corner* of a lost and enchanted land, of childhood re-experienced through adult tears and laughter. 'Pour les tierces', from the *Etudes*, may get off to a shaky start but, again, in Debussy's final masterpiece, where pragmatism is resolved into a fantasy undreamed of even by Chopin, Gieseking's artistry tugs at and haunts the imagination. Try 'Pour les sonorités opposées', the expressive centre of the *Etudes*, and you may well wonder when you have heard playing more subtly gauged or articulated, or the sort of interaction with a composer's spirit that can make modern alternatives seem so parsimonious by comparison. So here is that peerless palette of colour and texture, of a light and shade used with a nonchalantly deployed but precise expertise to illuminate every facet of Debussy's teeming and insinuating imagination. An added bonus, a 1951 performance of the *Fantaisie* for piano and orchestra (an ecstatic and scintillating work, played here with a life-affirming chiaroscuro), completes an incomparable set of discs. The transfers are a triumph, with an immediacy much less obvious in the originals. These records should be in every musician's library.

Préludes

Awards 1994

Préludes – Books 1 and 2
Krystian Zimerman *pf*
DG ② 435 773-2GH2 Ⓜ
(84 minutes: DDD)
Recorded 1991 ooo

Two discs, retailing at a high mid-price and playing for a total of 84 minutes? The playing and the recording had better be in the luxury class. Fortunately they are. Zimerman is the very model of a modern virtuoso. His overriding aim is vivid projection of character. His quasi-orchestral range of dynamic and attack, based on close attention to textual detail (there are countless felicities in his observation of phrase-markings) and maximum clarity of articulation, is the means to that end. As a result, he draws out the many connections in this music with the romantic tradition, especially in pianistic *tours de force* such as 'Les collines d'Anacapri', 'Ce qu'a vu le vent d'ouest' and 'Feux d'artifice', which are treated to a dazzling Lisztian *élan*. The instrument he has selected is itself something of a star and DG's recording combines opulence with razor-sharp clarity. At the other extreme Zimerman displays an exquisite refinement of touch that makes the quieter pieces both evocative and touching. Such sensitively conceived and wonderfully executed Debussy playing stands, at the very least, on a level with a classic recording such as Gieseking's.

Préludes – Books 1 and 2ª. Images. Children's Corner
Arturo Benedetti Michelangeli *pf*
DG ② 449 438-2GH2 (128 minutes: ADD/ªDDD) Ⓕ
Recorded 1971-88 o

Of Debussy playing his own music Alfredo Casella said 'he made the impression of playing directly on the strings of the instrument with no intermediate mechanism – the effect was a miracle of poetry'. This is not Michelangeli's way. He can certainly be poetic and produce miracles but his manner is not ingratiating. Generalized 'atmosphere' doesn't interest him. His superfine control is put at the service of line and movement, above all, and the projection of perspectives. He gives you a sense not just of foreground and background but of many planes in between. Michelangeli was capable of a transcendental virtuosity that had nothing to do with playing fast and loud and everything to do with refinement, and it is very much in evidence here – in many *Préludes* and especially in the first two *Images* of the Second Book. The clarity of texture and the laser-like delineation can sometimes be disconcerting if you're accustomed to a softer, more ethereal style, but they have a way of making Debussy's modernism apparent and thrilling. He sounds here as if he has had nothing to do with the 19th century. The *Images* and *Children's Corner* are among the finest versions ever recorded. But in some of the *Préludes*, particularly in Book 1, the sound is rather close and dry – maybe how Michelangeli wanted it. He uses as little pedal as he can get away with. There are people who regard Gieseking as unparalleled in this music, but after a quarter of a century the best of Michelangeli, similarly, will run and run. Today's generation of Debussy pianists will be expected to work from a less corrupt text, quite rightly, but they will have far to go before they can rival the penetrating qualities of Michelangeli's Debussy at its best. He could take your breath away and he was illuminating in this repertoire in a rare way.

Images

Images. Le petit nègre. Children's Corner. La plus que lente. Valse romantique. Tarantelle styrienne. Mazurka. Suite bergamasque. Hommage à Haydn. Elégie. Berceuse héroïque. Page d'album. Etudes. Etude retrouvée
Jean-Yves Thibaudet *pf*
Decca ② 460 247-2DH2 (151 minutes: DDD) Ⓕ
Recorded 1994-98

Jean-Yves Thibaudet's Debussy cycle is a cornucopia of delights. Whatever sparkles and enchants is here in super-abundance. The 12 *Etudes* could hardly be presented more personally or vivaciously. Nos 6 and 7 are marvels of bright-eyed irony and humour while Nos 8 and 9 contrast a haunting alternation of lassitude and hyperactivity with razor-sharp cascades of repeated notes. Thibaudet's timing in the central *lento, molto rubato* of No 12 (which, as Roger Nichols tells us in his excellent notes, shows

Debussy as more than a 'soft-centred voluptuary drifting through life on a cloud of disembodied dissonances') is memorably acute and, throughout, you are made more than aware of a pianist with a penchant for spare pedalling and a superfine brilliance far remote from, say, Gieseking's celebrated, opalescent magic. Thibaudet brings a pristine, spine-tingling quality to every bar. He takes a brisk hand to the *Children's Corner* suite (*allegro* rather than *allegretto* in 'Serenade for the Doll', hardly *modérément animé* in 'The Snow is Dancing') but even here his spruce technique and vitality are never less than enlivening. In the *Suite bergamasque* he dances the 'Menuet', so to speak, with an unusual sense of its underlying grace and gravity and his 'Clair de lune' is exceptionally silvery and transparent. Both books of *Images* are given with a rare sense of epiphany or illumination, of flashing fins and sunlight in 'Poissons d'or' and of a timeless sense of archaism in 'Hommage à Rameau'. Given such palpable relish, early works (the *Ballade* and *Danse*, for example) hardly emerge as 'sins of Debussy's youth', their key influences still evident. And anyone doubting Thibaudet's teasing wit should hear him in the *Valse romantique* and *Mazurka*, Debussy's sophisticated memory of his beloved Chopin. The *Etude retrouvée* provides an enchanting bonus and encore, and Decca's presentation and sound are, respectively, lavish and natural. If you want to hear Debussy newminted, with air-spun and scintillating textures, Thibaudet is your man.

Awards 1990

Images – Sets 1 and 2. D'un cahier d'esquisses. L'îsle joyeuse. Deux arabesques. Hommageà Haydn. Rêverie. Page d'album. Berceuse héroïque
Zoltán Kocsis *pf* Philips 422 404-2PH Ⓕ
(62 minutes: DDD)
Recorded 1988 ●●●

Suite bergamasque. Images oubliées. Pour le piano Estampes
Zoltán Kocsis *pf* Philips 412 118-2PH Ⓕ
(55 minutes: DDD). Recorded 1983

Zoltán Kocsis stands out as an especially idiomatic exponent of Debussy's piano style. On the first disc here, he plays four relatively early sets of pieces of which all but the *Suite bergamasque* are in the composer's favourite triptych form that he also used in *La mer*. The rarity here is the *Images oubliées*, pieces dating from 1894 that Debussy left unpublished, doubtless because he reworked material from them in the *Estampes* and very obviously in the Sarabande of *Pour le piano*, but they are fine in their own right and here we can compare the different treatments of the similar ideas.

The second recital also offsets the familiar with the less known. It also brings playing of exceptional finesse, and at times of exceptional brilliance and fire. The main work is *Images*, its two sets completed in 1905 and 1907 respectively, by which time the composer was already master of that impressionistic style of keyboard writing so different from anything before. For superfine sensitivity to details of textural shading Kocsis is at his most spellbinding in the first two numbers of the second set, 'Cloches à travers les feuilles' and 'Et la lune descend sur le temple qui fût'. He is also successful in reminding us of Debussy's wish to 'forget that the piano has hammers' in the atmospheric washes of sound that he conjures (through his pedalling no less than his fingers) in *D'un cahier d'esquisses*. The sharp clear daylight world of *L'îsle joyeuse* reveals a Kocsis exulting in his own virtuosity and strength as he also does in the last piece of each set of *Images*, and even in the second of the two familiar, early *Arabesques*, neither of them mere vapid drawing-room charmers here. The recording is first rate. Both discs are highly recommendable.

Etudes

Etudes – Books 1 and 2
Mitsuko Uchida *pf* Philips 422 412-2PH Ⓕ
(47 minutes: DDD). Recorded 1989 ●

The harmonic language and continuity of the *Etudes* is elusive even by Debussy's standards, and it takes an artist of rare gifts to play them 'from within', at the same time as negotiating their finger-knotting intricacies. Mitsuko Uchida is such an artist. On first hearing perhaps rather hyperactive, her playing wins you over by its bravura and sheer relish, eventually disarming criticism altogether. This is not just the finest-ever recorded version of the *Etudes*; it is also one of the finest examples of recorded piano playing in modern times, matched by sound quality of outstanding clarity.

Le martyre de Saint-Sébastien

Awards 1993

Sylvia McNair *sop* **Ann Murray** *mez* **Nathalie Stutzmann** *contr* **Leslie Caron** *narr* **London Symphony Chorus and Orchestra / Michael Tilson Thomas**
Sony Classical SK48240 Ⓕ
(66 minutes: DDD). Text and translation included. Recorded 1991 ●●●

'Archers aim closely, I am the target; whoever wounds me the most deeply, loves me the most. From the depths I call forth your terrible love ... again ... again! ... AGAIN!' cries the Saint in ecstasy. What Oscar Wilde did to the story of Salome, so the Italian writer D'Annunzio did to the story of Saint Sebastian (a young Roman officer ordered to be killed by his own archers because of his sympathy for persecuted Christians). This was the first modern recording, not of the complete play (which lasted five hours!), but of an intelligent and effective reduction of the written text using the Saint as narrator, and incorporating all of an hour's worth of Debussy's incidental music. And it must be deemed a triumph. Leslie Caron's Saint is quietly intense and a model of restraint; Sylvia McNair's *vox coelestis* is just that, a gift from

God; and the chorus and orchestra respond with total conviction to Tilson Thomas's committed direction. The sheer sorcery of Debussy's music, benefits enormously from the acoustic of, appropriately, All Saints Church in Tooting, London.

Pelléas et Mélisande

Jacques Jansen *bar* Pelléas; **Irène Joachim** *sop* Mélisande; **Henri Etcheverry** *bar* Golaud; **Paul Cabanel** *bass* Arkel; **Germaine Cernay** *mez* Geneviève; **Leila ben Sedira** *sop* Yniold; **Emile Rousseau** *bass* Shepherd; **Armand Narçon** *bass* Doctor **H**

Yvonne Gouverné Choir; symphony orchestra / Roger Desormière

EMI Références mono ③ CHS7 61038-2

(196 minutes: ADD). Booklet with translation included. Ⓜ

Recorded 1941 ●

The strength of the performance owed much to the fact that Irène Joachim, Jacques Jansen and Henri Etcheverry had already sung the work many times under Desormière at the Opéra-Comique. Irène Joachim had studied the role of Mélisande with its creator, Mary Garden; and both she and Jansen had been coached by Georges Viseur, who with Messager had been the *répétiteur* for the opera's first performance. Jansen with his free, youthful-toned production and Joachim with her silvery voice and intelligent response to every verbal nuance, set standards for the doomed lovers that, though nearly equalled, have never been surpassed; but even more impressive is Etcheverry's interpretation of Golaud, a role in which, arguably, he has yet to be rivalled. Leila ben Sedira gives one of the most convincing portrayals ever heard of the child Yniold; and Germaine Cernay and Paul Cabanel (who alone is just a trifle free with the text in places) fill the parts of the older characters with distinction. In this recording, the placing of the voices is such that every single word is crystal-clear. More important every word is invested with meaning by a native French cast – in other versions allowances sometimes need to be made for non-French singers – which had immersed itself totally in the emotional nuances and overtones of the text. Every shade of expression is caught, but nevertheless the overall feeling is of subtle Gallic understatement – with Golaud's self-tormenting jealousy and Pelléas's final inability to resist declaring his love for his brother's mysterious, fey wife creating the great emotional climaxes.

Keith Hardwick's alchemy in transforming these old recordings into sound of improved quality (and with only minimal vestiges of the 78rpm surfaces) is nothing short of amazing. He has not, of course, been able to correct the thin 1941 recording of the woodwind, but one soon comes to terms with the dated instrumental sound because of Desormière's inspired pacing and moulding of the score, the committed orchestral playing, and the well-nigh perfect casting.

Pelléas et Mélisande

Claude Dormoy *ten* Pelléas; **Michèle Command** *sop* Mélisande; **Gabriel Bacquier** *bar* Golaud; **Roger Soyer** *bass* Arkel; **Jocelyne Taillon** *mez* Geneviève; **Monique Pouradier-Duteil** *sop* Yniold; **Xavier Tamalet** *bass* Doctor, Shepherd

Burgundian Chorus; Orchestra of the Opéra de Lyon / Serge Baudo

RCA Opera ② 74321 32225-2 Ⓑ

(147 minutes: ADD). Synopsis and text included.

Recorded 1978 ●

There have been many fine historic recordings of *Pelléas et Mélisande*: reissues have included Desormière's of 1941 and Cluytens's of 1956. The excellence of this performance from Baudo leaves one wondering why it took the best part of 20 years to reappear. Baudo produces a warm sound from the Lyon orchestra, knows how to shape Debussy's subtle phrases, and is notably good at making use of silences. He is fortunate to have a cast without a single weak member. It is often the case that the central figure of Golaud, tortured by blind jealousy, steals the show, but Gabriel Bacquier is superb, capturing every nuance from tenderness to abrupt anger (at the news of the loss of the ring) or agonized frustration beside Mélisande's deathbed. Michèle Command, here at an early stage of her career, and entirely free from the undue weightiness that has sometimes characterised her work since, makes a shy, fey Mélisande who remains an enigmatic figure; she invests the famous solo about her long hair with a sense of melancholy.

The big surprise of this set is the Pelléas, a sensitive singer who seems, inexplicably, to have appeared in only one other recording (*The Merry Wives of Windsor*), made in the year before this – in a bass role! Listed here as a tenor, he is more a high baritone (which is appropriate for the part), just occasionally sounding a trifle stretched on a high note. The part of Arkel is given nobility by Roger Soyer; and the Yniold sounds convincingly childlike. Care has been taken in the production, as can be heard in the hollower acoustic of the scene in the vaults; only the perspective of the sailors on the unseen ship – always a problem in recordings – is a little uncertain. Make no mistake: this is a very rewarding version of this masterpiece, and as a two-disc bargain-price issue is a real snip.

Pelléas et Mélisande

François Le Roux *bar* Pelléas; **Maria Ewing** *sop* Mélisande; **José van Dam** *bar* Golaud; **Jean-Philippe Courtis** *bass* Arkel, Shepherd; **Christa Ludwig** *mez* Geneviève; **Patrizia Pace** *sop* Yniold; **Rudolf Mazzola** *bass* Doctor

Vienna State Opera Chorus; Vienna Philharmonic Orchestra / Claudio Abbado

DG ② 435 344-2GH2 (148 minutes: DDD). Notes, text and translation included. Recorded 1991 Ⓕ

This superb issue challenges the finest. The warmth of the VPO strings in the very first bars holds out a promise that is never disappointed: the orchestra, subtle but positively glowing, is responsive to every one of Debussy's dynamics and rises to the most intense of climaxes in the emotional high spots of Act 4. Abbado directs a sensitive and flexible reading, rather faster than usual in some places – impelled by the dramatic situation, he pushes ahead when Golaud flares up on hearing that Mélisande has lost his ring, and in that terrible scene when little Yniold is made to spy on his stepmother. José van Dam is an artist who, in whatever he undertakes, leaves one reaching for superlatives: in this performance his Golaud is a character on a dangerously short fuse, heavy with menace in his first warning to Pelléas, quickly losing control with Yniold, and lashing himself into a frenzy at the 'grande innocence' of Mélisande's eyes, leading him to seize her by her long hair. Maria Ewing makes the hapless heroine less of a wimp than she is sometimes represented, and in a remarkable way nuances and colours her every word with meaning. She is tender to Golaud when he suffers a slight wound, sweet but very erotic in the Act 3 soliloquy as she combs her hair, and bursts out in suddenly awakened passion at the fatal nocturnal parting from Pelléas. Or is it so sudden? We notice that her words to him at the end of Act 1, 'Oh! Pourquoi partez-vous?', are delivered not ingenuously, as with some interpreters of the part, but already with a vague yearning.

Le Roux's Pelléas sounds young, fresh and ardent, his singing is refined, his words are meaningful, and he conveys Pelléas's unease in the sinister scene with Golaud in the cavern. (The only slight shortcoming in the whole recording is when his eventual declaration of love is almost lost under orchestral reverberation.) The casting of the aged Arkel has often been a weakness in the past: either he is not entirely accurate or he emerges as just dull. Here the intelligence of Courtis makes of him a figure akin to wise old Gurnemanz in *Parsifal*, an opera much in Debussy's mind. Patrizia Pace makes a very credible child, and that no pains were spared in the production is suggested by the fact that no less an artist than Christa Ludwig takes the tiny part of Geneviève. Even those with either of the other recommendations of the opera are urged not to miss this one.

Additional recommendations

Pelléas et Mélisande

Henry Pelléas **Alliot-Lugaz** Mélisande

Montreal Symphony Orchestra / Dutoit

Decca 430 502-2DH2 (151 minutes: DDD: 3/91) Ⓕ

A fine modern alternative to the Abbado with Didier Henry and Colette Alliot-Lugaz a touching central pair. Dutoit conducts his superb Montreal orchestra with great style – sumptuously recorded.

Stilwell Pelléas **von Stade** Mélisande

Berlin Philharmonic Orchestra / Karajan

EMI CMS5 67057-2 (162 minutes: ADD: 11/99) Ⓜ

A controversial recording: too 'hot-house' for some but full of breathtaking playing and a heartbreakingly touching pair of lovers. This was clearly a labour of love for the great Austrian conductor.

Rodrigue et Chimène

(recons Langham Smith and orch Denisov)

Laurence Dale *ten* Rodrigue; **Donna Brown** *sop* Chimène; **Hélène Jossoud** *mez* Iñez; **Gilles Ragon** *ten* Hernan; **Jean-Paul Fouchécourt** *ten* Bermudo; **José van Dam** *bass-bar* Don Diègue; **Jules Bastin** *bass* Don Gomez; **Vincent le Texier** *bass-bar* King; **Jean-Louis Meunier** *ten* Don Juan d'Arcos; **Jean Delescluse** *ten* Don Pèdre de Terruel

Chorus and Orchestra of the Opéra de Lyon / Kent Nagano

Erato ② 4509-98508-2 (109 minutes: DDD) Ⓜ

Notes, text and translation included. Recorded 1993-94

It may come as a surprise to many who treasure the unique magic of *Pelléas et Mélisande* that Debussy toyed with some 30 other plans for operas, and two years before *Pelléas* had all but completed his first operatic venture. Debussy very soon realised that the libretto's blustering tone was alien to his ideals of half-hinted action in short scenes, and became increasingly restive, finally abandoning it and claiming that it had been accidentally destroyed. In reality it survived complete in a sketch in short score, though some pages have since been lost. Richard Langham Smith reconstructed the work from the manuscripts in the Piermont Morgan Library in New York, it was completed and orchestrated, with a remarkable insight into Debussian style, by Edison Denisov, and in 1993 it was presented by the Opéra de Lyon to mark the opening of its new house. Inconsistencies of style reveal something of Debussy's uncertainties and doubts over a subject inappropriate for him. There is little in Act 3 that would lead anyone to identify him as the composer, and virtually the only sections of the work with a harmonic idiom that was later to become characteristic of him are Rodrigue's and Chimène's mutual declaration of love at the start of Act 1, the orchestral prelude to Act 2 and the unexpected quiet interlude that precedes Rodrigue's mortal challenge to his beloved's father Don Gomez, who had shamed his own father. Debussy is less at home with the choral scene leading up to the angry conflict between the two initially friendly houses, the heroic and warlike atmosphere of much of Act 2, and the bombastic assembling of the royal court; but all these are tackled, if not with individuality, at least with vigour. Don Gomez's death scene is affecting, and the unaccompanied choral requiem for him makes an effective close to Act 2.

Unlike *Pelléas*, there are a number of extended set pieces for the singers, including Rodrigue's dutiful dilemma, Don Diègue's hymn to the concept of honour, Chimène's lament for her father and her final anguish as she is torn between love and hate for Rodrigue. As a performance and recording, this is in the highest class. Nagano's orchestra plays for him with finesse, and the work is cast from strength. Laurence Dale is a near-perfect Rodrigue – youthful, ardent and sensitive to changes of mood; Donna Brown makes a passionate

Chimène, though occasionally just too close to the microphone for sudden outbursts; and José van Dam is his reliable self, with nobility in his voice. Clarity of enunciation throughout (except, at times, from the chorus) is to be applauded.

Léo Delibes

French 1836-1891

GROVE *A church, organist until 1871, Delibes was drawn to the theatre, first writing light operettas in the style of his teacher Adolphe Adam (roughly one a year from 1856 to 1869), then becoming chorus master at the Théâtre-Lyrique and the Opéra. He is best known for his appealing classical ballets Coppélia (1870), with its charming character numbers, and the tuneful but more sophisticated Sylvia (1876), both admired by Tchaikovsky. Meyerbeer's influence is evident in his serious opera Jean de Nivelle (1880), and a gift for witty pastiche in his dances for Hugo's play Le roi's'amuse (1882). His masterpiece is Lakmé (1883), a highly successful opera indebted to Bizet and memorable for its oriental colour, strong characterization and fine melodies.*

Coppélia

Orchestra of the Opéra de Lyon / Kent Nagano
Erato ② 4509-91730-2 (99 minutes: DDD) Ⓕ
Recorded 1993

Though the text played complete may be straightforward Delibes, the interpretation announces itself as being anything but straightforward. Every phrase, every accent, every nuance seems to be newly considered, without losing the feel for the action on the stage. The overriding impression here is of the rightness and naturalness of Nagano's reading. The rare quality of the performance is evident at once from the way the music lights up at the *cantando* section in the 12th bar of the Prelude. Later, in Act 2, the Boléro has a rare dash and brio, while the opening March of Act 3 has a similarly compelling onward momentum. The sequence of speciality dances that makes up most of the final Act is delightfully turned, with a quite heavenly viola solo in 'La Paix' and a thrilling final Galop Anyone who loves this music should make a point of hearing Nagano's outstanding reading.

Coppélia[a]. Sylvia H
London Symphony Orchestra / Anatole Fistoulari; [a]Minneapolis Symphony Orchestra / Antál Dorati
Mercury Living Presence ③ 434 313-2MM3 Ⓜ
(173 minutes: ADD). Recorded 1957-58

The quality of sound here is astonishing for recordings over 40 years old. Nor do the attractions stop at there. These always were highly regarded performances of two of the most attractively tuneful ballets ever composed. Moreover, both conductors here had a great deal of experience in, and feeling for, the ballet style and this is evident in their handling of the scores. Both extract playing that is gracious and brilliant in turn, if just occasionally lacking the final degree of finesse, and in such passages as Fistoulari's vigorous 'Les chasseresses' or Dorati's 'Musique des automates' one can scarcely fail to be won over. It is only fair to mention that this record ing of *Sylvia* is itself not absolutely complete, since it lacks the 'Pas des esclaves' and 'Variation-Valse' from the Act 3 'Divertissement'. On its own terms though, the reissue represents a most compelling offering.

Sylvia

Delibes Sylvia
Saint-Saëns Henry VIII – Ballet-divertissement
Razumovsky Sinfonia / Andrew Mogrelia
Naxos ② 8 553338/9 (114 minutes: DDD) Ⓢ
Recorded 1995

Of Delibes's two full-length ballets, *Coppélia* is the more obviously popular, the one with the bigger tunes and the greater number of recordings. However, *Sylvia* is also a superbly crafted score, full of haunting melodies. Andrew Mogrelia's Naxos series is one to be collected and treasured: there is loving care applied to selection of tempos, shaping of phrases, orchestral balance and refinement of instrumental detail. Here you thrill to *Sylvia*'s Act 1 Fanfare, marvel at the control of tempo and refinement of instrumental detail in the 'Valse lente' and 'Entrée du sorcier', and revel in the sheer ebullience of Sylvia's return in Act 2. The inclusion of the ballet music from Saint-Saëns's *Henry VIII* was an admirably enterprising move, even though it doesn't amount to anything major apart from the 'Danse de la gitane', being essentially a collection of mock 'Olde Britishe' dances. All the same, a quite remarkable bargain.

Lakmé

Natalie Dessay *sop* Lakmé; **Gregory Kunde** *ten* Gérald; **José van Dam** *bass-bar* Nilakantha; **Delphine Haidan** *mez* Mallika; **Franck Leguérinel** *bar* Frédéric; **Patricia Petibon** *sop* Ellen; **Xenia Konsek** *sop* Rose; **Bernadette Antoine** *sop* Mistress Bentson; **Charles Burles** *ten* Hadji
Toulouse Capitole Chorus and Orchestra / Michel Plasson
EMI ② CDS5 56569-2 (144 minutes: DDD) Ⓕ
Text and translation included. Recorded 1997

Opera audiences in 19th-century Paris may never have visited India, but they loved to dream about it. After the successes enjoyed by *Les pêcheurs de perles* and *Le roi de Lahore* Delibes knew what he was doing when he chose to set an adaptation of Pierre Loti's exotic Indian novel *Rarahu* and duly scored a hit with his opera *Lakmé* at the Opéra-Comique in 1883. The opera is nothing without a star in the title-role. Natalie Dessay is certainly that and yet she never fails to remember that Delibes's heroine must be fragile and sensitive. Her Bell Song, brilliantly sung, is also intent on telling a story. Her singing of the death scene, with its delicate *fil de voce* perfectly poised each time the high A comes round, is heartfelt and leaves no doubt that this is a Lakmé who deserves to go to heaven. EMI found a worthy tenor to partner her. Gregory Kunde, as Gérald, is at ease at the top of his voice. At the first entrance of the colonial Brits, Frédéric describes Gérald as a poet and Kunde lives up to the promise by phrasing his opening solo, 'Fantaisie aux divins mensonges', with poetic sensibility. In the duets he and Dessay are tender young love personified. The supporting cast is also a decent one. Michel Plasson gives the music room to breathe and is able to conjure a dreamy atmosphere in the scenes of romance. His Toulouse orchestra is adequate, if not exceptional, and the recording is of a good standard. What reason is there to resist?

Additional recommendation

Lakmé

Sutherland Lakmé **Vanzo** Gérald

Monte-Carlo Opera Orchestra / Bonynge

Decca Double 460 741-2DF2 (138 minutes: ADD: 4/99) Ⓜ

One for Sutherland fans (don't even try to understand her French) or those wanting a mid-price set. The largely French cast helps convey the spirit of this elusive score.

Frederick Delius

British 1862-1934

GROVE *Delius's father lent him money to set up as a citrus grower in Florida (1884-86), where he had lessons with Thomas Ward; he then studied at the Leipzig Conservatory (1886-8) and met Grieg. He settled in Paris as a man of bohemian habits, a friend of Gauguin, Strindberg, Munch and others, until in 1897 he moved to Grez with Jelka Rosen, later his wife. There he remained.*

He had written operas, orchestral pieces and much else before the move to Grez, but nearly all his regularly performed output dates from afterwards while looking back to the musical and other experiences of earlier years: the seamless flow of Wagner, the airier chromaticism of Grieg, the rich colouring of Strauss and Debussy, the existential independence of Nietzsche. His operas A Village Romeo and Juliet (1901) and Fennimore and Gerda (1910) are love stories cast in connected scenes and examining spiritual states within a natural world. Nature is important too in such orchestral pieces as In a Summer Garden (1908), A Song of the High Hills (with wordless chorus, 1911) or A Song of Summer (1930), though there are other works in which the characteristic rhapsodizing is made to serve symphonic forms, notably the Violin Concerto (1916) and three sonatas for violin and piano (1914, 1923, 1930). The choral works include two unaccompanied, wordless songs 'to be sung of a summer night on the water' (1917), the large-scale A Mass of Life with words from Nietzsche (1905) and a secular Requiem (1916). In the early 1920s he grew blind and paralysed as a result of syphilitic infection, and his last works were taken down by Eric Fenby.

Violin and Piano Concertos

Fantastic Dance. A Dance Rhapsody No 1[a]. A Dance Rhapsody No 2. A Song of the High Hills. Three Preludes. Zum Carnival

Maryetta Midgley *sop* **Vernon Midgley** *ten* **Eric Parkin** *pf* **Ambrosian Singers**

Royal Philharmonic Orchestra / Eric Fenby, [a]Norman Del Mar

Unicorn-Kanchana Souvenir UKCD2071 Ⓜ

(65 minutes: DDD). Recorded 1981-90

Irmelin Prelude. A Song of Summer. A Late Lark. Piano Concerto in C minor[a]. Violin Concerto[b]

Anthony Rolfe Johnson *ten* **Ralph Holmes** *vn* **Philip Fowke** *pf* **Royal Philharmonic Orchestra / Eric Fenby, [a]Norman Del Mar, [b]Vernon Handley**

Unicorn-Kanchana Souvenir UKCD2072 Ⓜ

(71 minutes: DDD). Recorded 1981-90

Koanga – La Calinda (arr Fenby). Idyll: Once I passed through a populous city. Songs of Sunset. A Village Romeo and Juliet – The Walk to the Paradise Garden[a]

Felicity Lott *sop* **Sarah Walker** *mez* **Thomas Allen** *bar* **Ambrosian Singers**

Royal Philharmonic Orchestra / Eric Fenby, [a]Norman Del Mar

Unicorn-Kanchana Souvenir UKCD2073 Ⓜ

(73 minutes: DDD). Recorded 1981-90 ●

The unique insight that the late Eric Fenby would bring as an interpreter of Delius was the reason for many of these Unicorn recordings, but we owe the idea and its realization to their producer, the late Christopher Palmer. As well as providing Delians with some of the most illuminating text on the music, Palmer, in the studio, and especially in a work like *A Song of the High Hills*, was able to put his understanding (and Fenby's, of course) into practice. You don't need the score of *A Song of the High Hills* to tell you that the passage from 9'54" represents 'The wide far distance, the great solitude'. That to which you are listening – totally spellbound – could be nothing else (and by nobody else).

Ralph Holmes's recording of the Violin Concerto (with Vernon Handley) is a warm, leisurely reading. The Piano Concerto, as recorded here, is a grand showstopper in the best romantic piano concerto tradition, yet Fowke and Del Mar alert you to all the Delian reverie in the making (the dynamic range of Fowke's piano is colossal). But the outlay for Vol 2 is justified by Anthony Rolfe Johnson alone, in the all too brief six minute-long *A Late Lark* ('one of Delius's works that is surely entirely without flaw', as Trevor Harvey put it in his original review).

In Vol 3, Fenby's control in *Songs of Sunset* does not always match his insight (choral work is often sloppy and too distantly recorded); the recent Hickox, or the 1957 Beecham is to be preferred. But without Fenby in the recording studio (or at Grez!), we would never have had *Idyll*: Whitman texts combined with a late reworking of music from an earlyish opera, *Margot la Rouge*, to provide a reflective then rapturous love duet that looks back to Delius's Paris as well as to his *Paris* – this makes Vol 3 indispensable, especially as sung and played here. And a very considerable bonus to be found in Vol 3 is Del Mar's previously unissued *Walk to the Paradise Garden*. This is not the Beecham version for reduced orchestra, as stated in the otherwise excellent notes, though it incorporates many of Beecham's dynamics and tempo indications. It is, most assuredly, a *Walk* on the grandest (11'00" to Beecham's 8'38"), most passionate scale (there's not a bar-line in earshot, either), and turns out to be yet another of these three discs' memorials to inspired Delians who died in our, but before their, time.

On Hearing the First Cuckoo in Spring

Brigg Fair. In a Summer Garden. Paris: The Song of a Great City. On Hearing the First Cuckoo in Spring. Summer Night on the River. A Village Romeo and Juliet – The Walk to the Paradise Garden
BBC Symphony Orchestra / Sir Andrew Davis
Teldec British Line 4509-90845-2 (F)
(77 minutes: DDD). Recorded 1992

This *Brigg Fair* is unique. What a lovely surprise to hear real London sparrows sharing the air space of St Augustine's Church with Delius's translated Lincolnshire larks (flute and clarinet) in the opening minutes of the work, albeit much more distantly. Very effective too are those almost still pools of string sound (early morning mists?), given the extended boundaries of this acoustic, and the familiar warmth and depth of tone Davis draws from the orchestra's strings. In the final magnificently broad climax (pealing bells, for once, very clear), you cannot fail to be impressed by the depth, coherence and articulacy of the sound – hallmarks, indeed, of the entire disc. Davis's strings come into their own in the *Walk to the Paradise Garden*. For *In a Summer Garden*, Davis mutes his strings more often than Delius asks; but the reading's delicacy of texture and hazy, suffusing warmth are difficult to resist.

Brigg Fair, RTVI/16[a]. Koanga[b] – La Calinda (arr Fenby). Hassan[c] – Closing scene. Irmelin Prelude, RTVI/27[b]. Appalachia, RTVII/2[d] (H)
[c]**Jan van der Gucht** *ten* [c]**Royal Opera House Chorus, Covent Garden;** [d]**BBC Chorus;** [a]**Symphony Orchestra;** [bcd]**London Philharmonic Orchestra / Sir Thomas Beecham**
Naxos Historical mono 8 110906 (66 minutes: AAD). (S)
Recorded [a]1928-29 and 1938

There always was a unique alchemy between the art of Sir Thomas Beecham and the music of Frederick Delius, and you can detect it in every bar of this remarkable January 1938 recording of *Appalachia*. It is, quite simply, a performance to cherish, its beaming dedication, wistful heartache and rapt wonder leaving the listener in no doubt about Sir Thomas's boundless love for a work that served as his introduction to the composer (he later recalled how the 1907 London première under Fritz Cassirer left him 'startled and electrified'). By July 1938, Beecham and the LPO had committed to disc the three remaining items that eventually made up The Delius Society's lavishly presented third and final volume of the composer's music issued by Columbia Records; suffice it to say, *La Calinda* skips along entrancingly here, while no true Delian could fail to respond to Beecham's ineffably poignant way with both the closing scene from *Hassan* and the lovely *Irmelin Prelude*.

Naxos's curtain-raiser, *Brigg Fair*, was recorded towards the end of the previous decade. Some seven months separated the two days required to produce a reading of unforgettable tenderness and bewitching poetry (the results of an even earlier session in July 1928 having been rejected altogether), although some will still hold an ever-so-slight preference for the second of Sir Thomas's three versions (a gloriously intuitive display with the newly formed RPO from November 1946).

David Lennick's transfers have been admirably managed, *Appalachia* now sounding rather more open and full-bodied than on a rival Dutton compilation. Throw in a lively and informative booklet-essay from Lyndon Jenkins, not to mention the absurdly low price-tag, and it should be abundantly clear that this is a self-recommending issue.

Additional recommendation
Orchestral Works
Brigg Fair – An English Rhapsody. Dance Rhapsody No 2. On Hearing the First Cuckoo in Spring. Summer Night on the River. A Song Before Summer. Intermezzo (arr Fenby). Irmelin Prelude. Sleighride. Summer Evening (ed & arr Beecham). Florida Suite (rev & ed Beecham) – Daybreak, Dance
Royal Philharmonic Orchestra / Beecham
EMI Great Recordings of the Century
CDM5 67552-2 (77 minutes: ADD) (M)

Brigg Fair A Song Before Sunrise. Songs from the Norwegian. Hassan – excerpts. Dance Rhapsodies Nos 1 and 2. On Hearing the First Cuckoo in Spring. Summer Night on the River. Danish Songs. Irmelin Prelude.
Suddaby *sop* **Thomas** *contr*
Royal Philharmonic Orchestra / Beecham
Dutton CDLX7028 (77 minutes: ADD) (M)
Two superb reissues containing superlative performances from Beecham and the RPO, both beautifully remastered and at mid-price. At least one of these discs of these should be on every classical enthusiast's shelf.

Cello Sonata

Delius Cello Sonata. Caprice and Elegy. Hassan – Serenade (arr Fenby). Romance
Grieg Cello Sonata in A minor, Op 36. Intermezzo in A minor, CW118
Julian Lloyd Webber *vc* **Bengt Forsberg** *pf*
Philips 454 458-2PH (66 minutes: DDD) (F)
Recorded 1996

The links between Grieg and Delius are many, which makes this a very apt and attractive coupling, bringing together all the works each composer wrote for this medium. This is Julian

Lloyd Webber's second recording of the Delius Cello Sonata. The overall duration this time is almost two minutes shorter, and the easier flow goes with a lighter manner and a less forward balance for the cello. The result in this freely lyrical single-movement structure is more persuasive, with greater light and shade, and just as much warmth in the playing. Bengt Forsberg's variety of expression and idiomatic feeling for rubato consistently match those of his partner. The *Caprice and Elegy* of 1930 inspire equally free and spontaneous performances, and it is particularly good to have the tuneful *Romance* of 1898, which inexplicably remained neglected for 80 years till Lloyd Webber revived it. The Grieg Sonata, too, among the most inspired and intense of his longer works, prompts magnetic playing, again with more light and shade than is common, helped by not having the cello spotlit, in a natural recording acoustic. The lyrical *Intermezzo* provides an attractive makeweight. Though a very high proportion of the music here is reflective, the meditative intensity of the playing sustains it well.

Violin Sonatas Nos 1-3. Cello Sonata
Ralph Holmes *vn* **Julian Lloyd Webber** *vc*
Eric Fenby *pf*
Unicorn-Kanchana Souvenir UKCD2074 Ⓜ
(65 minutes: ADD/DDD). Recorded 1972-81

This is selfless, utterly dedicated music-making, always spontaneous-sounding yet never losing the organic thread of Delius's remarkable, free-flowing inspiration. There is a slight fragility to Holmes's distinctive, silvery tone that is extremely moving, and Fenby, though no virtuoso practitioner, accompanies with intuitive sympathy. The recording of the piano (the instrument used is the three-quarter Ibach grand left to Fenby by Delius himself) remains a touch boxy and wanting in bloom, though the balance is otherwise natural and the overall effect nicely intimate. In the Cello Sonata Lloyd Webber and Fenby adopt a mellow, notably ruminative approach. Dedicatee Beatrice Harrison's 1926 recording with Harold Craxton should be sought out by all discerning Delians, for through the surface crackle emerge a rapt wonder, generous flexibility and instinctive sense of line that are something special. A small textual observation of note: Lloyd Webber (like Harrison before him) eschews the cello's final D major chord.

Violin Sonatas

Violin Sonatas – B; Nos 1-3
Tasmin Little *vn* **Piers Lane** *pf*
Conifer Classics 75605 51315-2 (77 minutes: DDD) Ⓕ
Recorded 1997

Tasmin Little's Delian instincts are formidable, here amply confirmed by Conifer's rewarding coupling. The wonderful First Sonata receives big-hearted, confident advocacy here. These marvellously sensitive performers strike a near-ideal balance between flexibility and purposeful concentration, even by the standards of Holmes and Fenby. Little and Lane are not out of place in such august company. Likewise, the Second Sonata is given a commandingly articulate, thoughtful interpretation that never once threatens to hang fire. In the Third Sonata Little's playing glows with fervour and understanding. Moreover, she and Lane see to it that the fine Sonata in B major (1892) emerges in infinitely convincing fashion. To both outer movements they bring fiery propulsion as well as a firm sense of direction, while the haunting central processional of the lovely *Andante molto tranquillo* (which so impressed Grieg) captures the imagination. The recording is full-bodied, though the piano focus could be sharper within a church acoustic that is too expansive for such intimate repertoire. The sessions (as Little relates in her touching notes) were lent an extra poignancy by the news of Eric Fenby's death on the first day of recording.

Sea Drift

Awards 1994

Sea Drift. Songs of Sunset. Songs of Farewell
Sally Burgess *mez* **Bryn Terfel** *bass-bar*
Waynflete Singers; Southern Voices; Bournemouth Symphony Chorus and Orchestra / Richard Hickox
Chandos CHAN9214 (77 minutes: DDD) Ⓕ
Texts included. Recorded 1993 ●●●

Sea Drift is a sublime conjunction of Whitman's poetry and Delius's music describing love, loss and unhappy resignation, with the sea (as Christopher Palmer put it) as 'symbol and agent of parting'. Written in 1903-04 (the same years as Debussy's *La mer*), it is surely Delius's masterpiece; right from the swaying opening bars its spell is enduring and hypnotic. Hickox in his second recording of the work now gives us the finest recorded post-Beecham *Sea Drift*. The shaping of the opening falling woodwind figures at a slow tempo more than usually (and very beautifully) portends the sad turn of events; and the climax is broad and superbly co-ordinated. Terfel's bar-by-bar characterization (and glorious voice), conveys the full expressive range of the role from impassioned appeal to gentle call without artifice; and the choral singing is superb. The whole is recorded with warmth, spaciousness, depth and clarity.

Songs

Fennimore and Gerda – Intermezzo. Lebenstanz, RTVI/15. An Arabesque, RTII/7[bc]. Sakuntala[b]. The Page Sat in the Lofty Tower[a]. In Bliss we Walked with Laughter[a]. Two Brown Eyes[a]. I Hear in the Night[a]. Two Danish Songs, RTV/21 – The Violet[b]; Autumn[a]. Seven Danish Songs, RTIII/4[a]. Summer Landscape, RTV/24[b]
[a]**Henriette Bonde-Hansen** *sop* [b]**Johan Reuter** *bar*
[c]**Danish National Opera Chorus;** [c]**Aarhus Chamber Choir; Aarhus Symphony Orchestra / Bo Holten**
Danacord DACOCD536 (70 minutes: DDD) Ⓕ
Texts and translations included. Recorded 2000

This collection of Delius's Danish inspirations, beautifully performed and recorded, makes a delightful disc, including as it does rarities that are otherwise unavailable. Even if 'masterworks' is a bit of an exaggeration, the pieces here all show Delius at his most characteristic, drawing on his deep sympathy for Scandinavia and its culture.

Significantly, the performances under Bo Holten tend to be faster and often more passionate than those on rival recordings, such as in Unicorn's admirable Delius Collection.

An Arabesque dates from 1911, but all the other vocal items were written much earlier. In many ways the conventional picture we have of Delius, as the blind and paralysed composer of his later years, is misleading, failing to reflect what we know of the younger man, active and virile, a point that Bo Holten has clearly registered. It is good to have the *Seven Danish Songs* of 1897 as a group in Delius's own sensuous orchestrations. The self-quotations in the ballad-like 'Irmelin Rose' are the more telling in orchestral form, and the most beautiful song of all, 'Summer Nights', is magically transformed in its atmospheric evocation of a sunset.

Delius also orchestrated two separate Danish songs, 'The Violet' and *Summer Landscape* as well as *Sakuntala*, prompting Holten to orchestrate the five other Danish songs, which here form another orchestral cycle. These, too, are more beautiful than with piano, even though Holten is less distinctive than Delius himself in his use of orchestral colour, notably in woodwind writing. All these songs are sung in the original language, where the Unicorn series opted for the English translations which Delius either made himself or approved. The two singers here may not be as characterful as such British soloists as Felicity Lott, Sarah Walker or Thomas Allen (in *An Arabesque*), but they both have fresh young voices, clear and precise, with Henriette Bonde-Hansen shading her bright soprano down to the gentlest *pianissimos*. The choral singing, too, is excellent in *An Arabesque*.

The *Fennimore and Gerda* 'Intermezzo' (drawn from two of that opera's interludes) is relatively well known, but *Lebenstanz* ('Life's Dance'), inspired by a play of Helge Rode, is a rarity, originally conceived in 1899, otherwise available only on Unicorn conducted by Norman Del Mar. Here, too, Holten opts for marginally faster speeds in a piece depicting (in the composer's words) 'the turbulence, the joy, energy, great striving of youth'. The dance sections – one of them surprisingly Straussian – are punctuated by typically reflective passages, and the depiction of death at the end is peaceful and not at all tragic.

The Aarhus Symphony Orchestra responds warmly to Holten's idiomatic direction, and the refined playing is quite closely balanced in a helpful acoustic.

Five Partsongs (1887). Her ute skal gildet staa. Irmelin Rose (arr Lubin). On Craig Dhu. Wanderer's Song. Midsummer Song. The splendour falls on castle walls. Two Songs for Children. To be sung of a summer night on the water. A Village Romeo and Juliet – The dream of Sali and Vrenchen (arr Fenby). Appalachia – Oh, Honey, I am going down the river (arr Suchoff). Irmelin – Away; far away to the woods. Hassan – Chorus behind the scenes; Chorus of Beggars and Dancing Girls

Joanna Nolan *sop* **Stephen Douse** *ten* **Andrew Ball** *pf* **Mark Brafield** *org* **Elysian Singers of London / Matthew Greenall**

Somm Recordings SOMMCD210 (50 minutes: DDD) Ⓕ Texts and translations included. Recorded 1992

Delius had a special relationship with the collective human voice, and the songs here are presented chronologically, which allows us to follow pleasurably the development of his style. The extracts from *A Village Romeo and Juliet* and *Appalachia* prolong what would otherwise be a rather brief encounter and their accompaniments also provide contrast of timbre, but they do need to be heard in context to 'take off'. The 'essential' Delius comes with *On Craig Dhu* – experience of nature not so much tinged by melancholy as perceived through it; a haunting evocation in grey; and the setting of Tennyson's *The splendour falls on castle walls*, as characteristically Delius as Britten's setting of it, in his *Serenade*, is Britten. Though the singing itself deserves a generally warm welcome, not all Delius's chromatic wanderings are as confidently charted as they might be. The sopranos seem the strongest contingent, and the ones most often in the expressive spotlight (maybe they also excite more resonance, and with it prominence, from the generously reverberant location). Nor are the soloists ideal, the tenor sounding unhappy in the higher regions of the second of the two songs, *To be sung of a summer night on the water*. And on occasions, as in the first of those two songs, one might have wished for more varied pacing and dynamic shading from the conductor. But the world of Delius performance is one where devotees are used to taking the roundabouts with the swings, and this is the only all-Delius collection of its kind on the market.

A Mass of Life

A Mass of Life[a]. Requiem[ba]

[a]**Joan Rodgers,** [b]**Rebecca Evans** *sops* [a]**Jean Rigby** *mez* [a]**Nigel Robson** *ten* **Peter Coleman-Wright** *bar* **Waynflete Singers; Bournemouth Symphony Chorus and Orchestra / Richard Hickox**

Chandos ② CHAN9515 (129 minutes: DDD). Texts Ⓕ and translations included. Recorded 1996

This is only the third commercial recording of *A Mass of Life*. The previous two recordings were the 1952 Beecham (no longer available) and the 1971 Groves on EMI. You might imagine modern recording would best place this vast canvas between your loudspeakers. And yes, Hickox's dynamic peaks are marginally higher, his perspectives marginally wider and deeper. Actually, some of this has as much to do with Hickox's own pacing and shading as the engineering. In general, this 'idealized' light- and air-filled sound brings a sharper, bright presence for the chorus, and such things as the piccolo trilling atop the final 'Hymn to Joy'. What it doesn't bring is the sense of performers in a specific acoustic space. But the chorus shines in the prominent role which the Chandos balance gives them, with ringing attack for all entries where it is needed, and singing as confident as it is sensitive, even if one has to make the odd allowance for not quite perfect pitching on high (Delius's demands are extreme) and moments where they are too loud. The soloists are fine; Hickox's baritone has a good line in stirring, virile address, though little of Benjamin Luxon's nobility, inwardness and true *legato*. What makes the Hickox *Mass* preferable to the Groves (but only just) is the conductor's inspired handling of each part's central dance panels. Hickox makes you believe in them, with a judicious drive, lift to the rhythms, and really incisive, eager singing and playing. As a coupling, Hickox has only the second-ever commercial recording of the Requiem: more Nietzsche, but this time dogma not poetry, all the more unpalatable/embarrassing (regardless of your faith) for being in English, but containing much unique Delius.

Henry Desmarest French 1661-1741

GROVE *As a boy chorister in the royal chapel Desmarest became a disciple of Lully. He maintained court links and his first opera was given at Versailles in 1682. Later he was maître de chapelle at a Jesuit college. An amorous imbroglio led to his exile in 1699, and in 1701 he took a court post in Madrid. From 1707 he was surintendant de la musique to the Duke of Lorraine at Lunéville, where he expanded musical activities. He wrote c20 stage works; the tragédies lyriques, such as Iphigénie en Tauride (1704), use more adventurous harmony and more flexible recitative than Lully's. His other works include impressive grands motets, cantatas, airs and sonatas.*

Grands Motets Lorrains

Grands Motets Lorrains – Usquequo, Domine; Lauda Jerusalem; Domine, ne in furore P
Sophie Daneman, Rebecca Ockenden *sops* **Paul Agnew** *ten* **Laurent Slaars** *bar* **Arnaud Marzorati** *bass* **Les Arts Florissants / William Christie**
Erato 8573-80223-2 (68 minutes: DDD) Ⓕ
Texts and translations included. Recorded in 2000 OO

If Henry Desmarest has not yet joined other French baroque composers among the ranks of the Great Rediscovered, here is a disc which ought to help him on his way. These three *grands motets* were composed between 1708 and 1715, the early years of his time as musical director to the court of the Duke of Lorraine. Scored for soloists, choir and orchestra, each is a multi-sectional psalm-setting lasting about 20 minutes. What is immediately striking is not only how strong-boned and well-written the music is, but also how contrasted; here are moments of supreme tenderness (for instance, the setting of 'He giveth snow like wool' in *Lauda Jerusalem*), powerful intensity ('How long shall I take counsel in my soul' in *Usquequo, Domine*), robust grandeur (the final chorus of *Lauda Jerusalem*) and uplifting rhythmic vigour (the corresponding movement in *Domine, ne in furore*). And if a tendency towards melancholy is unsurprising given that two of these psalm-texts are penitential, who is to say that we are not also witnessing a reflection of the unhappy circumstances of this composer's life?

Such music could not have fallen into better hands than those of those arch-revivers William Christie and Les Arts Florissants. Christie's talent – as in his opera conducting – is to see the work as a totality and not just as a string of separate movements, with the result that the music never fails to punch its full expressive weight, never marks time. With Sophie Daneman and Paul Agnew excellent among the soloists, and choral singing which remains unfailingly vivid and alert throughout, these are vibrant performances that do not put a foot wrong. The recording is clear and nicely balanced, though an unusual profusion of extraneous noises is an irritant. Even so, this is a must-buy for French baroque fans.

Ernö Dohnányi Hungarian 1877-1960

GROVE *Dohnányi studied with Thomán and Koessler at the Budapest Academy (1894-7) and came quickly to international eminence as both pianist and composer. After teaching at the Berlin Hochschule (1905-15) he returned to Budapest and worked there as pianist, teacher, conductor and composer. His influence reached generations in all spheres of musical life and he is considered one of the chief architects of 20th-century Hungarian musical culture; he championed the music of Bartók and Kodály. He also toured internationally as a pianist, ranking among the greatest of his time, and as a conductor (his pupils included Solti). He left Hungary in 1944 and in 1949 settled in the USA. His works are in a Brahmsian style, crossed with Lisztian virtuosity and thematic transformation; they include two symphonies (1901, 1944), two piano concertos (1898, 1947), two piano quintets (1895, 1914) and two violin concertos (1915, 1950), the popular Variations on a Nursery Song for piano and orchestra (1914) and three string quartets (1899, 1906, 1926).*

Violin Concerto No 2

Dohnányi Violin Concerto No 2 in C minor, Op 43
Bartók Violin Concerto No 2, Sz112
Mark Kaplan *vn* **Barcelona Symphony Orchestra / Lawrence Foster**
Koch International Classics 37387-2 Ⓕ
(70 minutes: DDD). Recorded 1996

Throughout Dohnányi's immensely likeable Second Violin Concerto, the general idea is to keep the solo line as busy and as prominent as possible, even to the extent of dispensing with orchestral violins. The first movement features a furious *fugato*, Straussian tutti passages and Kreislerian solo writing. The *Scherzo* recalls Reger at his most mischievous, and the slow movement has a warmth that is reminiscent of Brahms. A spirited finale features a novel cadenza with solo horn and the overall effect of the concerto is of spontaneous invention bursting at the seams. Mark Kaplan's idiomatically luscious performance is given alert support from Lawrence Foster's Barcelona orchestra, and the recording is more than acceptable. Kaplan's Bartók is equally forceful and the partnership with Foster works particularly well when soloist and orchestra indulge in vigorous banter. This is a strong, spontaneous and warmly felt reading, flexible in gesture and with the added interest of Bartók's brassy original coda – a more powerful ending than the revision, albeit without any contribution from the soloist.

Symphony No 1

Symphony No 1 in D minor, Op 9.
American Rhapsody, Op 47
BBC Philharmonic Orchestra / Matthias Bamert
Chandos CHAN9647 (67 minutes: DDD) Ⓕ
Recorded 1998

The First Symphony is a fascinating if uneven work. Sundry influences spontaneously spring to mind: Tchaikovsky, Brahms and Richard Strauss. The five-movement structure has its obvious models in Beethoven and Berlioz, but the scoring, although tending towards Wagnerian sonorities, is frequently individual, and so is the 23-year-old Dohnányi's command of symphonic argument. Bamert offers a broad reading, with much drama, most notably at the beginning of the *Scherzo* and the furious *fugato* passage 12'00" into the finale, where the BBC lower strings 'dig in' with a vengeance. Bamert and Chandos also offer us an excellent performance of the much later *American Rhapsody* (1950 as opposed to 1900 for the Symphony). Here, Dohnányi's sound world recalls the Delius of *Appalachia* and the *Florida* suite and his use of American traditional tunes are reminiscent of Charles Ives's Second Symphony. If all this sounds as if Dohnányi didn't have an original idea in his head, it is certainly not meant to. The references are intended to focus superficial similarities but should not mask the fact that Dohnányi had plenty to say, and said it well. As for the recording, it is in the demonstration class.

Variations on a Nursery Theme

Dohnányi Variations on a Nursery Theme, Op 25
Brahms Piano Concerto No 1 in D minor, Op 15
Mark Anderson *pf* **Hungarian State Symphony Orchestra / Adám Fischer** Ⓕ
Nimbus NI5349 (75 minutes: DDD). Recorded 1994

Mark Anderson gives a glittering performance of the Dohnányi, and a spontaneous one at that; he is superbly accompanied by Adám Fischer and the Hungarian State SO. Nimbus's recording is admirable in everything but the backward placing of the woodwind in general and the bassoons in particular. One thing that the Dohnányi *Variations* share with the D minor Brahms Concerto is a passionate minor key opening. Again Fischer and his Hungarian orchestra are quite superb, the playing incisive and gloweringly vivid. It is a measure, too, of the accord that exists between conductor and soloist that the pianist enters the fray with the perfectly groomed musical manners of a soloist in a baroque concerto. And it is the logic of Anderson's playing, his sweet reasonableness, that holds the attention, even though Brahmsians may find Anderson a shade light-toned in bravura passages. The Brahms obviously faces tough competition, but the Dohnányi is without doubt a fine performance in its own right.

Der Schleier der Pierrette – Pierrot's Love-lament; Waltz-rondo; Merry Funeral March; Wedding waltz. Suite in F sharp minor, Op 19. Variations on a Nursery Theme, Op 25[a]
[a]**Howard Shelley** *pf* **BBC Philharmonic Orchestra / Matthias Bamert**
Chandos CHAN9733 (70 minutes: DDD) Ⓕ
Recorded 1998

Here's the very first recording of *The Veil of Pierrette*, four scenes from a mimed entertainment dating from 1908-9. The best movement is the exuberant 'Wedding Waltz' (track 21), rumbustious music, carefree and beautifully scored. The rest consists of a fairly serious prelude, a waltz parody (less memorable than the finale) and a mischievous 'Merry Funeral March'.

Dohnányi's penchant for quality musical entertainment bore popular fruit with his perennially fresh *Variations on a Nursery Theme*. Howard Shelley's performance is a model of wit and style, blending in with the orchestra whenever the moment seems right and employing an ideal brand of *rubato*. Bamert's conducting is properly portentous in the Introduction and charming elsewhere, whether in the music-box delights of the fifth variation, the animated bustle of the sixth or the seventh's novel scoring (plenty for the bassoons and bass drum). Kocsis and Fischer's is still marginally the best version overall, but Shelley and Bamert are no less musical.

Lovely, too, is the F sharp minor Suite, especially the opening *Andante con variazioni* which seems to straddle the worlds of Dvořák and Elgar (try the serene string choirs from 9'35"). The stamping *Scherzo* brings to mind the *Scherzo* from Bruckner's Ninth, and the tuneful Rondo finale has a striking resemblance to a key passage in the *Rondo-burleske* in Mahler's Ninth. As with the rest of this admirable series, the music is a constant delight and Chandos has come up with a dazzlingly realistic recording. A peach of a disc – though if you're arachnophobic, try to avert your eyes from the CD and booklet cover!

Sextet

Dohnányi Sextet in C, Op 37a
Fibich Quintet in D, Op 42
Endymion Ensemble (Mark van de Wiel *cl* Stephen Stirling *hn* Krysia Osostowicz *vn* [a]Iris Juda *va* Jane Salmon *vc* Michael Dussek *pf*) Ⓕ
ASV CDDCA943 (66 minutes: DDD). Recorded 1995

Both composers employ their chosen resources with great expertise, Dohnányi in a richly harmonized Sextet that opens among the clouds and ends in a mood of dance-like exuberance, Fibich with a more conventional structure and a genial stream of melody. Each work owes something to Brahms although in the case of Fibich's Quintet, Schumann seems as much in evidence, not only through the score's specific melodic complexion, but also in a *Scherzo* that features two contrasting trios. Smetana is another possible point of reference, especially at the start of the finale, although – as Jan Smaczny usefully points out in his excellent booklet-note – the younger Fibich 'often anticipated the achievements of the elder composer'. Dohnányi's Sextet is a far darker piece, opening as it does among rolling string arpeggios and toughening for a fairly tense development. The 'Intermezzo' second movement suggests (at least initially) Brahms as siphoned through the imagination of Schoenberg, whereas the eventful third movement suddenly breaks into a rhythmically upbeat finale that sounds as much Afro-Caribbean as Hungarian, albeit with a luscious 'big' tune to offset the fun. The Endymion Ensemble does both Fibich and Dohnányi proud and the recordings are excellent.

Piano Quintets

Piano Quintets[a] – No 1 in C minor, Op 1; No 2 in E flat minor, Op 26. Suite in the Old Style, Op 24
[a]**Vanbrugh Quartet** (Gregory Ellis, Elizabeth Charleson *vns* Simon Aspell *va* Christopher Marwood *vc*);
Martin Roscoe *pf*
ASV CDDCA915 (70 minutes: DDD). Recorded 1994 Ⓕ

Dohnányi's First Piano Quintet, Op 1, written when the composer was only 18, is a work of abounding confidence and energy that is played here with suitable verve and exuberance. Roscoe and the Vanbrugh Quartet luxuriate in lush, romantic textures in the first movement, and delight in the melodic exchanges of the warmly expressive *Adagio*. Moreover, their expression of Hungarian flavour, evident in the *Scherzo*'s jaunty cross-rhythms and the engagingly dance-like finale, has considerable charm. The Second Quintet, written some 19 years later, shows a striking advance in technique. Sensitive evocation of atmosphere in the first movement by Roscoe and the Vanbrugh Quartet highlights both Dohnányi's more searching harmonic language and his remarkably fresh and imaginative approach to form. The performers deftly blend the *Intermezzo*'s faintly Viennese character with the flamboyant toccata material, and the final movement's fusion of slow movement and finale is ingeniously turned from sombre minor to radiant major. Both the quintets display Dohnányi's considerable pianistic skills; the *Suite in the Old Style* provides further evidence with a highly effective display of the composer's parody of baroque keyboard techniques. Roscoe's evident sympathy for his music contributes to this arrestingly persuasive account, which fully exploits the work's rich variety of style and technique. Newcomers to Dohnányi's music will find much to enjoy in this disc of repertoire that clearly deserves to be much better known.

String Quartets

Dohnányi String Quartets – No 2 in D flat, Op 15; No 3 in A minor, Op 33
Kodály Intermezzo
Lyric Quartet (Patricia Calnan, Harriet Davies *vns* Nick Barr *va* David Daniels *vc*) Ⓕ
ASV CDDCA985 (60 minutes: DDD). Recorded 1996

Dohnányi's output is nothing if not rich in contrasts: both slow movements of these appealing quartets are visited by animated, mood-changing faster sections, stormy and passionate in the Second Quartet and skittish in the Third. The earlier quartet is the more wholesomely romantic of the two, with a *Presto acciacato* second movement that recalls the orchestral storm sequence at the beginning of Wagner's *Die Walküre*. The Second Quartet's heart is in its poignant slow movement finale which incorporates references to previous movements. Dohnányi's musical language suggests something of Strauss, Brahms and Mendelssohn, with the Third Quartet's cynically argumentative first movement providing the grittiest musical activity on the disc. The earliest work programmed is by Kodály, a pleasant but uncharacteristic *Intermezzo* from 1905 that the Lyric Quartet performs – like everything else – with gusto and warmth.

Gaetano Donizetti Italian 1797-1848

GROVE *Donizetti was of humble origins but received help and a solid musical education (1806-14) from Mayr, producing apprentice operas and many sacred and instrumental works before establishing himself at Naples with La zingara (1822). Here regular conducting and a succession of new works (two to five operas a year) marked the real start of his career. With the international triumph of Anna Bolena (1830, Milan) he freed himself from Naples; the further successes of L'elisir d'amore and Lucrezia Borgia (1832, 1833, Milan), Marino Faliero (1835, Paris) and the archetype of Italian Romantic opera, Lucia di Lammermoor (1835, Naples), secured his pre-eminence. Some theatrical failures, however, as well as trouble with the censors and disappointment over losing the directorship of the Naples Conservatory to Mercadante, caused him to leave for*

Paris, where besides successful French versions of his earlier works he brought out in 1840 La fille du régiment and La favorite. His conducting of Rossini's Stabat mater (1842, Bologna) and enthusiasm in Vienna for Linda di Chamounix (1842) led to his appointment as Kapellmeister to the Austrian court. Declining health began to affect his work from this time, but in Don Pasquale (1843, Paris) he produced a comic masterpiece, and in the powerful Maria di Rohan (1843, Vienna), Dom Sébastien, roi di Portugal (1843, Paris) and Caterina Cornaro (1844, Naples) some of his finest serious music.

Donizetti's reputation rests on his operas: in comedy his position has never been challenged but in the tragic genre, though his work sums up a whole epoch, no single opera can be considered an unqualified masterpiece. His works survive through the grace and spontaneity of their melodies, their formal poise, their effortless dramatic pace, their fiery climaxes and above all the romantic vitality underlying their artifice. Like Bellini, Donizetti epitomized the Italian Romantic spirit of the 1830s. Having imitated Rossini's formal, florid style for ten years (1818-28) he gradually shed heavily embellished male-voice parts, conceiving melodies lyrically and allowing the drama to determine ensemble structures. From 1839 his style was further enriched by fuller orchestration and subtler, more varied harmony. If he contributed nothing so distinctive to the post-Rossinian tradition as Bellini's 'heavenly' melody, he still showed a more fluent technique and a wider-ranging invention, from the brilliant to the expressive and sentimental. He was particularly responsive to the individual qualities of his singers, including Persiani (Lucia), Pasta and Ronzi de Begnis (Anna Bolena, Maria Stuarda, Roberto Devereux), the baritone Giorgio Ronconi and the tenors Fraschini and Moriani (L'elisir d'amore, Lucia). Although his practical facility and readiness to adapt scores themselves constructed of 'spare-part' set forms once brought criticism, since 1950 revivals and reassessment as well as a fuller understanding of the theatrical practices of his day have restored Donizetti to critical and popular favour.

Concertos

Sinfonia in G minor (recons Päuler). Sonata in C minor (orch Hoffmann). Oboe Sonata in F (orch Hoffmann). Concerto for Violin, Cello and Orchestra in D minor (recons Wojciechowski). Cor Anglais Concerto in G. Clarinet Concertino in B flat (recons Meylan). Sinfonia in D minor (recons Andreae)
Budapest Camerata / László Kovács
Marco Polo 8 223701 (64 minutes: DDD) Ⓕ
Recorded 1994

This is an intriguing issue of instrumental concertos, recorded for the first time. As in his string quartets, Donizetti's dramatic flair and imaginative instrumentation provide the main points of interest, while the G major Concerto for cor anglais – a theme and variations – allows us to sample Donizetti's formal ingenuity and thematic invention. After a crisp performance of the buoyant G minor *Sinfonia*, the Budapest Camerata offers a group of solo concertos featuring a variety of instruments. The C minor flute *Concertino* and F major oboe *Concertino* – originally intended as instrumental sonatas – are presented in Wolfgang Hoffmann's sensitive orchestrations. Contrasts (textural, dramatic and dynamic) are well defined, with admirably clear recording. The exuberant *allegros* are not especially profound, but Donizetti's slow movements are often most effective. The D minor Concerto for violin, cello and orchestra is the longest and most impressive work here. The Budapest Camerata balances solo and ensemble forces with subtle refinement throughout this charming piece, whose brief *Andante* has genuine pathos, and smiling finale has engaging wit.

Anna Bolena

Maria Callas *sop* Anna Bolena; **Nicola Rossi-Lemeni** *bass* Enrico VIII; **Giulietta Simionato** *mez* Giovanna Seymour; **Gianni Raimondi** *ten* Riccardo Percy; **Plinio Clabassi** *bass* Rochefort; **Gabriella Carturan** *mez* Smeton; **Luigi Rumbo** *ten* Hervey **Chorus and Orchestra of La Scala, Milan / Gianandrea Gavazzeni** Ⓗ
EMI mono ② CMS5 66471-2 (140 minutes: ADD)
Notes, text and translation included. Ⓜ
Recorded live in 1957

One of Callas's unique qualities was to inspire an audience with the sense of a great occasion, and to key-up a sympathetic conductor into the production of something to match her own intensity and the public's expectations. Here she gives one of her finest performances. The first impression is a vocal one, in the sense of the sheer beauty of sound. Then, in the first solo, 'Come innocente giovane', addressing Jane Seymour, she is so clean in the cut of the voice and the style of its usage, delicate in her *fioriture*, often exquisite in her shading, that anyone, ignorant of the Callas legend, would know immediately that this is an artist of patrician status. There are marvellous incidental moments, and magnificent *crescendos*, into, for instance, 'per pietà delmio spavento' and 'segnata è la mia sorte', culminating in the Tower scene.

Unfortunately, the singers at her side hardly measure up. Simionato has a splendid voice that nevertheless bumps as it goes into the low register and is not reliably steady in many passages, while the manner is too imperious and unresponsive in expression. The tenor role, of the ineffectual lover Percy, has been reduced by Gavazzeni's cuts, but Gianni Raimondi makes limited impression in what remains; and, as the King, Rossi-Lemeni produces that big but somewhat woolly tone that became increasingly characteristic. Even so, the great ensembles still prove worthy of the event, and the recording, which is clear without harshness or other distortion, conveys the special quality of this memorable evening at the opera with remarkable vividness and fidelity. For those who insist on a modern recording, there is an imaginatively conducted 1994 performance on Nightingale Classics by Elio Boncompagni, with Edita Gruberová in the title-role. But this Callas/Gavazzeni set is in a different class altogether.

Don Pasquale

Renato Bruson *bar* Don Pasquale; **Eva Mei** *sop* Norina; **Frank Lopardo** *ten* Ernesto; **Thomas Allen** *bar* Malatesta; **Alfredo Giacomotti** *bass* Notary**Bavarian Radio Chorus; Munich Radio Orchestra / Roberto Abbado**
RCA Victor Red Seal ② 09026 61924-2
(120 minutes: DDD). Notes, text and translation included. Recorded 1993 Ⓕ

Roberto Abbado balances equably the witty and more serious sides of this score, finding a gratifying lightness in the 'A quel vecchio' section of the Act 1 finale and creating a delightful sense of expectancy as Pasquale preens himself while awaiting his intended bride. Abbado plays the score complete and respects Donizetti's intentions. This set has many strengths and few weaknesses. Pasquale is usually assigned to a veteran singer and with Bruson you hear a voice hardly touched by time and a technique still in perfect repair. Apart from weak low notes, he sings and acts the part with real face, and his vital diction is a pleasure to hear. He works well with Thomas Allen's nimble, wily Malatesta, an inspired piece of casting. Like Bruson, Allen sings every note truly and relishes his words. Eva Mei's Norina is an ebullient creature with a smile in her tone. The edge to her voice seems just right for Norina though others may find it tends towards the acerbic under pressure. Her skills in coloratura are as exemplary as you would expect from a reigning Queen of Night. Lopardo is that rare thing, a tenor who can sing in an exquisite half-voice, yet has the metal in his tone to suggest something heroic in 'E se fia', the cabaletta to 'Cercherò lontana terra', which in turn is sung in a plangent, loving way, just right. The recording here is exemplary.

L'elisir d'amore

Angela Gheorghiu *sop* Adina; **Roberto Alagna** *ten* Nemorino; **Roberto Scaltriti** *bar* Belcore; **Simone Alaimo** *bar* Dulcamara; **Elena Dan** *sop* Giannetta; **Chorus and Orchestra of the Opéra National de Lyon / Evelino Pidò**
Decca ② 455 691-2DHO2 (123 minutes: DDD)
Notes, text and translation included Ⓕ
Recorded 1996

This work, ideally combining the needs of comedy and sentiment, has always been a favourite of opera goers. This set catches these contrasting moods to perfection under Pidò's alert, affectionate conducting, not least because the recording is based on live performances at the Lyon Opera. The main interest is on how our most sought-after operatic pairing fare in the central roles. Gheorghiu presented her credentials as Adina at Covent Garden prior to this recording; some found her dramatically a shade shrewish in the part, but Adina is a feisty, temperamental girl, and a touch of steel doesn't seem inappropriate. It makes her capitulation when she realizes the true depth of Nemorino's feelings that much more moving. She provides plenty of flirtatious fire in the early scenes and turns Nemorino away with determination, making her intentions clear in pointed attack in the recitative, but her concern for him is never far below the surface and comes to the fore in her colloquy with Dulcamara. All this is conveyed in singing that matches warmth with pointed diction and fleet technique, essential at Pidò's sometimes racy speeds.

Alagna's Nemorino is almost on the same level. He enjoys himself as the lovelorn yokel, one with a vulnerable soul as he shows at his moment of greatest heartbreak, 'Adina, credimi' in the Act 1 finale. His sense of fun is obvious in the bottle-shaking episode when he thinks he has found the elixir of the title. The two Italians in the lower roles are admirable. Scaltriti may not be as preening as some Belcores but he sings the part with a firmness that older singers miss. Alaimo is a naturally witty Dulcamara and never indulges in unwanted *buffo* mugging.

The Erato set, at mid-price, presents formidable opposition. Devia is a less wilful, less vivid Adina than Gheorghiu, but her style is, if possible, even more idiomatic. There's not much to choose between the other roles, but as a whole the Decca sounds the more lifelike reading, worth every penny of the asking price.

L'elisir d'amore
Mariella Devia *sop* Adina; **Roberto Alagna** *ten* Nemorino; **Pietro Spagnoli** *bar* Belcore; **Bruno Praticò** *bar* Dulcamara; **Francesca Provvisionato** *mez* Giannetta; **Tallis Chamber Choir; English Chamber Orchestra / Marcello Viotti**
Erato ② 4509-98483-2 (129 minutes: DDD) Ⓜ
Notes, text and translation included
Recorded 1992

This set is a delight, making one fall in love all over again with this delightful comedy of pastoral life. Roberto Alagna, disciple of Pavarotti, sings Nemorino with all his mentor's charm and a rather lighter tone appropriate to the role. He also evinces just the right sense of vulnerability and false bravado that lies at the heart of Nemorino's predicament. He is partnered by Mariella Devia who has every characteristic needed for the role of Adina. With a fine sense of buoyant rhythm, she sings fleetly and uses the coloratura to enhance her reading. She can spin a long, elegiac line where that is needed, and her pure yet full tone blends well with that of her colleagues. She also suggests all Adina's high spirits and flirtatious nature. The other principals, though not as amusing in their interpretations as some predecessors, enter into the ensemble feeling of the performance. All are helped by the lively but controlled conducting of Viotti and by the ideal recording.

L'elisir d'amore (sung in English)
Mary Plazas *sop* Adina; **Barry Banks** *ten* Nemorino; **Ashley Holland** *bass* Belcore; **Andrew Shore** *bar* Dulcamara; **Helen Williams** *sop* Giannetta
Geoffrey Mitchell Choir; Philharmonia Orchestra / David Parry
Chandos Opera in English Series ② CHAN3027 (133 minutes: DDD). Notes and text included. Ⓕ
Recorded 1998

'Prima la musica' no doubt, but in this instance the words should perhaps take their share of the credit first. The late Arthur Jacobs, who was an expert on Arthur Sullivan, provides a translation that might almost be the work of W S Gilbert. A resourceful vocabulary and a keen ear for verbal rhythms are its main technical assets, and a natural sense of humour rather than the untiring facetiousness of a self-conscious clever-dick is the source of its wit. Dulcamara ('my learning academical, both physical and chemical') is of course a Gilbertian figure to start with, so the translator is not forcing an entrance for his hobby-horse, and though he makes free with the Italian (the original verses of the finale, for instance, have nothing about protecting dogs from rabies), his inventions are all in the spirit of the thing. The Gilbertian element emerges again when Andrew Shore, in the Barcarolle, sings his part of 'elderly Senator' in the tones of Sir Henry Lytton. Generally he gives a well-sung, gracefully-turned portrayal of the mountebank, as does Ashley Holland for Sergeant Belcore. The lovers have light, well-matched voices, Mary Plazas avoiding the pert, hard character-note and vocal tone that can make Adina so unsympathetic, and Barry Banks giving particular pleasure with the freedom and clarity of his upper notes.

The Geoffrey Mitchell Choir sounds alert, precise and fresh-voiced as ever, and the playing of the Philharmonia under David Parry calls for special remark: from the Overture onwards (with its delightfully chirruping woodwind) there are passages in the score that find a flavour, their own by rights but usually lost because not sought-out. The recording, dedicated to the memory of Sir Geraint Evans, is one of the series' best.

La favorita

Fiorenza Cossotto *mez* Leonora; **Luciano Pavarotti** *ten* Fernando; **Gabriel Bacquier** *bar* Alfonso; **Nicolai Ghiaurov** *bass* Baldassare; **Ileana Cotrubas** *sop* Ines; **Piero de Palma** *ten* Don Gasparo; **Chorus and Orchestra of the Teatro Comunale, Bologna / Richard Bonynge**
Decca Grand Opera ③ 430 038-2DM3 (168 minutes: ADD). Text and translation included Ⓜ
Recorded 1974

La favorita's lack of popularity has been attributed to the lack of an important soprano role, which is a pity, for it really is a very fine opera. Though there are passages where it fails to rise to the situation, and unfortunately the final duet is one of them, it has much in it that goes to the heart within the drama, and it is richly supplied with melody and opportunities for fine singing. The opportunities are well taken here. The recording has Pavarotti in freshest voice. That understates it: his singing is phenomenal. Wherever you care to test it, it responds. Of the two best-known solos, 'Una vergine' in Act 1 is sung with graceful feeling for line and the shape of the verses; the voice is evenly produced, of beautifully pure quality and with an excitingly resonant top C sharp. Throughout the opera he gives himself sincerely to the role dramatically as well as vocally. Cossotto, who in her absolute prime was one of the most exciting singers ever heard, is just fractionally on the other side of it here; she still gives a magnificent performance, gentle as well as powerful, in a part she made very much her own at La Scala. The role of Alfonso attracted all the great baritones in the time when the opera was heard regularly. Here, Gabriel Bacquier sings with a somewhat colourless tone. Yet Alfonso emerges as a credible character, a man of feeling, whose 'A tanto amor' has, in context, a moving generosity of spirit and refinement of style. Ghiaurov brings sonority, Cotrubas sweetness, Piero de Palma character.

The chorus is poorly recorded but that may be to its advantage. The orchestra does well under Bonynge, especially in the 20-minute stretch of ballet music which would be 10 too many if less well played. Recorded sound is fine; the booklet contains a brief note, synopsis and text with a not unamusing translation.

La fille du régiment

Joan Sutherland *sop* Marie; **Luciano Pavarotti** *ten* Tonio; **Spiro Malas** *bass* Sulpice; **Monica Sinclair** *contr* Marquise; **Edith Coates** *contr* Duchess; **Jules Bruyère** *bass* Hortensius; **Eric Garrett** *bar* Corporal; **Alan Jones** *ten* Peasant
Chorus and Orchestra of the Royal Opera House, Covent Garden / Richard Bonynge
Decca ② 414 520-2DH2 (107 minutes: ADD)
Notes, text and translation included Ⓕ
Recorded 1968 **OO**

Even Joan Sutherland has rarely, if ever, made an opera recording so totally enjoyable and involving as this. With the same cast (including chorus and orchestra) as at Covent Garden, it was recorded immediately after a series of live performances in the Royal Opera House, and both the comedy and the pathos come over with an intensity born of communication with live audiences. That impression is the more vivid on this superb CD transfer. As with some of Decca's early CD transfers, you could do with more bands to separate items and it strikes one as odd not to indicate separately the most spectacular of Luciano Pavarotti's contributions, his brief but important solo in the finale to Act 1, which was the specific piece which prompted the much-advertised boast 'King of the High Cs'. For those who want to find it, it comes at

2'58" in band 13 of the first disc. Dazzling as the young Pavarotti's singing is, it is Sutherland's performance which, above all, gives glamour to the set, for here in the tomboy Marie she found a character through whom she could at once display her vocal brilliance, her ability to convey pathos and equally her sense of fun. The reunion of Marie with the men of her regiment and later with Tonio makes one of the most heartwarming operatic scenes on record. The recording is one of Decca's most brilliant, not perhaps quite so clear on inner detail as some, but equivalently more atmospheric. Though there are one or two deliberately comic touches – such as Edith Coates's last cry of 'Quelle scandale' – that get near the limit of vulgarity, the production is generally admirable. The sound at once takes one to the theatre, without any feeling of a cold, empty studio.

Lucia di Lammermoor

Maria Callas *sop* Lucia; **Ferruccio Tagliavini** *ten* Edgardo; **Piero Cappuccilli** *bar* Enrico; **Bernard Ladysz** *bass* Raimondo; **Leonard del Ferro** *ten* Arturo; **Margreta Elkins** *mez* Alisa; **Renzo Casellato** *ten* Normanno; **Philharmonia Chorus and Orchestra / Tullio Serafin**
EMI Callas Edition ② CDS5 56284-2 (142 minutes).
Notes, text and translation included. Ⓕ
Recorded 1959

Callas was certainly more fallible here than in her first Lucia for Serafin in 1953, but the subtleties of interpretation are much greater; she is the very epitome of Scott's gentle, yet ardently intense heroine, and the special way she inflects words and notes lifts every passage in which she is concerned out of the ordinary gamut of soprano singing. In that sense she is unique, and this is certainly one of the first offerings to give to an innocent ear or a doubter to help convince them of Callas's greatness. The earlier part of the Mad scene provides the most convincing evidence of all. Then the pathos of 'Alfin son tua', even more that of 'Del ciel clemente' are here incredibly eloquent, and the coloratura is finer than it was in 1953, if not always so secure at the top. Tagliavini, after a rocky start, offers a secure, pleasing, involving Edgardo. Cappuccilli, then in his early prime, is a forceful but not insensitive Enrico, Bernard Ladysz a sound Raimondo. Serafin is a far more thoughtful, expressive Donizettian than his rivals on other sets, confirming this as the most persuasive account of the opera ever recorded.

Lucia di Lammermoor
Cheryl Studer *sop* Lucia; **Plácido Domingo** *ten* Edgardo; **Juan Pons** *bar* Enrico; **Samuel Ramey** *bass* Raimondo; **Jennifer Larmore** *mez* Alisa; **Fernando de la Mora** *ten* Arturo; **Anthony Laciura** *ten* Normanno; **Ambrosian Opera Chorus; London Symphony Orchestra / Ion Marin**
DG ② 435 309-2GH2 (138 minutes: DDD)
Notes, text and translation included. Ⓕ
Recorded 1990

With Studer and Domingo in the leading roles, this version is certainly fit as a whole to stand alongside its eminent predecessors. The fine deep colours of the orchestra, the sturdy dramatic cohesion and well-wrought climaxes, are well brought out; passages traditionally omitted are in place (and deserve to be). The role of Lucia's confidante is sung with distinction by Jennifer Larmore, and though Juan Pons could do with more bite to his tone and Samuel Ramey with more expressiveness in his vocal acting these have their strengths too. Studer combines beautiful tone, technical accomplishment and touching pathos. Details include an extended cadenza in the Mad scene, which ends on a not too exposed high E flat (D being the ceiling elsewhere). Domingo triumphantly overcomes the difficulties such a role must pose at this stage of his career: Edgardo di Ravenswood in this recording is as firmly at the centre of the opera as is its eponymous heroine.

Additional recommendation
Lucia di Lamermoor
Callas Lucia **di Stefano** Edgardo
Berlin RIAS Symphony Orchestra / Karajan
EMI mono CMS5 66438-2 (119 minutes: ADD: 2/91R) Ⓜ
Live Recording

This is a live recording of a great event: two great musicians striking sparks of each other. Karajan directs a white-hot performance and Callas sings with a passion rarely conveyed on disc.

Maria Stuarda

(sung in English)
Janet Baker *mez* Maria Stuarda; **Rosalind Plowright** *sop* Elisabetta; **David Rendall** *ten* Leicester; **John Tomlinson** *bass* Talbot; **Alan Opie** *bar* Cecil; **Angela Bostock** *sop* Anna; **English National Opera Chorus and Orchestra / Sir Charles Mackerras**
Chandos Opera in English Series ② CHAN3017 (136 minutes: ADD). Notes and English text included. Ⓜ
Recorded live in 1982

This revival celebrates the association of Janet Baker and Charles Mackerras within the context of the ENO company and one of its most memorable productions. For those who saw this, the set will call the stage back to mind with wonderful vividness; but the appeal goes well beyond that, preserving a performance stamped with the strong individuality that confers the status of a gramophone classic. This brought a personal triumph for Janet Baker and it impresses afresh by the distinctiveness of her vocal characterization. It is not every singer who reflects, or re-creates, the distinctive identities through vocal colour and 'registration'. Everyone who was there will remember the 'Royal bastard!' in confrontation with Elizabeth, but equally powerful, and more regal, is her command – 'Be silent! Leave me!' – to the Lord Chancellor of England who brings to Fotheringay news of her condemnation to death. By contrast, the quieter moments can be immensely moving, as, for instance, in the line in which she acknowledges an unexpected generosity in her great opponent. In that role, Rosalind Plowright gives what surely must have been one of the supreme performances of her career. The writing for Elizabeth makes immense demands of the singer, and in these fearsome opening solos the technical challenges are triumphantly met, the voice thrillingly ample, the quality in full bloom.

John Tomlinson's massive bass commands attention (which it does not then always reward with evenness of production). The male soloists have not the most grateful of roles, but Alan Opie's Cecil shows its quality in the duet with Elizabeth, and David Rendall endows the ineffectual Leicester with plenty of Italianate ardour. The chorus has limited opportunities, and has certainly been heard to better advantage on other occasions. A word of warning must be added concerning texts which involve cuts and adaptations. The transpositions are defended as standard practice when an exceptional mezzo-soprano (such as Malibran) took a soprano role, in the present instance merely conforming to the lower orchestral pitch of Donizetti's time. However, it is unlikely that at this date the set would be bought or rejected with this kind of consideration foremost. What remains are the strong positives, most notably the vitality of Mackerras's conducting and the glory of Baker's singing. Also, for those to whom this is a priority, the opera is given in clear English.

Poliuto

Franco Corelli *ten* Poliuto; **Maria Callas** *sop* Paolina; **H** **Ettore Bastianini** *bar* Severo; **Nicola Zaccaria** *bass* Callistene; **Piero de Palma** *ten* Nearco; **Rinaldo Pelizzoni** *ten* Felice; **Virgilio Carbonari, Giuseppe Morresi** *basses* Christians **Chorus and Orchestra of La Scala, Milan / Antonino Votto**

EMI mono ② CMS5 65448-2 (111 minutes: ADD) Notes, text and translation included. Ⓜ
Recorded live in 1960

This is the first appearance of this recording in the official canon, by incorporation into EMI's Callas Edition; and the quality is certainly an improvement on the previous 'unofficial' incarnation. The sound is clear and faithful to the timbre of the voices, which are slightly favoured in the balance at the expense of the orchestra. With it comes unforgettable testimony to what was clearly a great night at La Scala. Its place in the Callas history owes less to the importance of this new role in her repertory than to the triumph of her return to the house she had left in high dudgeon in 1958. The part of Paolina in this Roman tragedy is restricted in opportunities and leaves the centre of the stage to the tenor. In other ways it suits her remarkably well, the Second Act in particular involving the heroine in grievous emotional stress with music that here runs deep enough to give it validity. There is a big part for the chorus, which sings with fine Italian sonority. Nicola Zaccaria, La Scala's leading *basso cantabile*, has not quite the sumptuous quality of his predecessors, Pasero and Pinza, but is still in their tradition. Ettore Bastianini is rapturously received and, though wanting in polish and variety of expression, uses his firm and resonant voice to exciting effect. The tenor *comprimario*, Piero de Palma cuts a by no means inadequate vocal figure by the side of Corelli, who is mostly stupendous: it is not just the ring and range of voice that impress, but a genuinely responsive art, his aria 'Lasciando la terra' in Act 3 providing a fine example. It is for his part in the opera, quite as much as for Callas's, that the recording will be valued.

Rosmonda d'Inghilterra

Renée Fleming *sop* Rosmonda; **Bruce Ford** *ten* Enrico II; **Nelly Miricioiu** *sop* Leonora di Guienna; **Alastair Miles** *bass* Gualtiero Clifford; **Diana Montague** *mez* Arturo; **Geoffrey Mitchell Choir; Philharmonia Orchestra / David Parry**

Opera Rara ② ORC13 (150 minutes: DDD). Notes, text and translation included. Recorded 1994 Ⓕ

Donizetti's 41st opera shows the confident mastery of form that can make useful, unselfconscious innovations, and there is scarcely more than a single item in which he seems not to be writing with genuine creativity. The performance could hardly be improved. David Parry conducts with what feels like a natural rightness and the playing of the Philharmonia is of unvaryingly high quality – the Overture is one of Donizetti's best, and the orchestral score shares interest on equable terms with the voice-parts. These include two virtuoso roles for sopranos, who in the final scene confront each other in duet. As Rosmonda, the immured and misled mistress, Renée Fleming shows once again that not only has she one of the most lovely voices in our time but that she is also a highly accomplished technician and a sympathetic stylist. Nelly Miricioiu is the older woman, the Queen whose music encompasses a wide range of emotions with an adaptable vocal character to match. She fits the Second Act more happily than the First, where for much of the time the tone appears to have lost its familiar incisive thrust. Bruce Ford is an excellent, incisive Enrico, and Alastair Miles makes an authoritative father and councillor as Clifford. The *travesto* role of Arturo is taken by the ever welcome Diana Montague, and it is good to find that a solo has been dutifully included for 'him' in Act 2, even if it is a less than inspired piece of music. The only complaint with the recording concerns balance, which sometimes accords prominence and recession in a somewhat arbitrary way. The opera and performance, however, are strong enough to take that on board.

John Dowland British c1563-1626

GROVE *Dowland became a Catholic while serving the English ambassador in Paris (1580-84) and in 1588 graduated at Oxford. In 1592 he played the lute to the queen, then travelled in Europe, visiting the courts of Brunswick, Kassel, Nuremberg and cities in Italy, where he met Marenzio. He was back in London in 1597, then became a lutenist at the Danish court (1598-1603, 1605-6). On his return he served Lord Walden (1609-12) and eventually achieved his ambition, the post of court lutenist, in 1612. He had been awarded a doctorate by 1621 and played at James I's funeral in 1625. He was succeeded by his son Robert (c 1591-1641), also known for the lute collections he edited.*

Though known in his day as a virtuoso lutenist and singer, Dowland was also a prolific, gifted composer of great originality. His greatest works are inspired by a deeply felt, tragic concept of life and a preoccupation with tears, sin, darkness and death. In the best of his 84 ayres for voice and lute (published mainly in 4 vols., 1597, 1600, 1603, 1612), he markedly raised the level of English song, matching perfectly in music the mood and emotion of the verse; in his best songs, such as In darknesse let mee dwell, he freed himself of almost all conventions, accompanying the singer's strange, beautiful melody with biting discords to express emotional intensity to an extent unsurpassed at the time. His 70-odd pieces for solo lute include intricate polyphonic fantasias, expressive dances and elaborate variation sets; foremost among his other instrumental music is the variation set Lachrimae, which contains the famous 'Semper Dowland semper dolens', characterizing his air of melancholy. But he could also write in a lighter vein, as in the ballett-like Fine Knacks for Ladies. He also wrote psalm settings and spiritual songs.

Lachrimae, or Seaven Teares

Christopher Wilson *lte* **Fretwork** (Wendy Gillespie, Richard Campbell, Julia Hodgson, William Hunt, Richard Boothby *viols*) P

Virgin Classics Veritas VC5 45005-2 Ⓕ
(60 minutes: DDD). Recorded 1987-89 ●

Did Dowland ever expect this collection to be played in its entirety, at one sitting? If so, in what order? Whatever your own 'answers' to these unanswerable questions may be, you can easily impose them on any of the various integral versions on CD. Fretwork's reissue presents them as an entirety, with the dances in their original published order – the whole book 'as is'. The performances are laudable in their characterization (of the pavans in particular), discreet embellishment of the dances, clarity of detail (the product of pleasantly dry string sound and acoustic) and overall balance, in which the lute is neither forced into the background nor obtrusive. Christopher Wilson adds a firmly propulsive edge to the dances. This is the best available version of Dowland's monumental work, graced with Peter Holman's splendid notes and blessed with superbly engineered recording.

Lute Works

A fancy, P73. Pavana Dowlandi Angli. Doulands rounde battell galyarde, P39. The Erle of Darbies galiard, P44. Mistris Norrishis delight, P77. A jig, P78. Galliard, P76. Une jeune fillette, P93. Gagliarda, P103. Squires galliard. A fancy, P72. Sir Henry Umptons funerall. Captayne Pipers galliard, P88. A fantasie, P1
Bacheler (arr ?) The Earl of Essex galliard, P89
Moritz, Landgrave of Hessen (arr Dowland?) Pavin **Joachim Van Den Hove** Pavana Lachrimae **Holborne** Hasellwoods galliard **R Dowland** Sir Thomas Monson, his Pavin and Galliard. Almande
Paul O'Dette *lte*
Harmonia Mundi HMU90 7164 (73 minutes: DDD) Ⓕ
Recorded 1996

Given the odd transmission of John Dowland's lute music, any 'complete' recording of it is inevitably going to include a fair number of works that can have had little to do with him. Paul O'Dette has boldly put most of these together in his fifth and last volume, adding for good measure the three surviving works of the master's son, Robert Dowland. O'Dette is engagingly candid in expressing his views about the various works and their various degrees of authenticity. The only works he seems to think authentic are the *Sir Thomas Monson* pavan and galliard that survive only under the name of Robert Dowland. The collection is none the less fascinating for all that. They are nearly all thoroughly worthwhile pieces, some of them very good indeed (including the one now agreed to be by Holborne and the one O'Dette thinks likely to be by Daniel Bacheler); and he ends with what he considers a late adaptation of one of Dowland's most famous fantasies. O'Dette continues to show that in terms of sheer freedom of technique he is hard to challenge among today's lutenists: the often complicated counterpoint is always crystal clear; and he invariably conveys the strongest possible feeling for the formal design of the works. He plays with a thoughtfulness and control that are always invigorating. Anyone who is fascinated by the work of the prince of lutenists will want to have this disc.

Almains – Sir John Smith his Almain, P47; My Lady Hunsdons Puffe, P54. Ballads and Other Popular Tunes – Fortune, P62; Go from my Window, P64; My Lord Willoughby's Welcome Home, P66*a*; Walsingham, P67; Robin, P70. Fantaisies – Fantasie, P1*a*; Forlorne Hope Fancye, P2. Galliards – Captaine Digorie his Galliard, P19; Frog Galliard, P23*a*; Melancholy Galliard, P25; Mignarde, P34; The King of Denmarke his Galliard, P40; The most sacred Queene Elizabeth, her Galliard, P41*a*; Can she excuse, P42; Galliard to Lachrimae, P46. Jigs, Corantos, Toys – Mistris Winters Jumpe, P55; Mrs Vauxe's Gigge, P57; The Shomakers Wife, P58. Pavans – Piper's Pavan, P8; Semper Dowland Semper Dolens, P9; Lachrimae, P15. Preludium, P98 P
Nigel North *lte* Ⓕ
Arcana A36 (72 minutes: DDD). Recorded 1995

The disc contains 24 items, but of the 42 in Robert Dowland's anthology of 1610 Dowland contributed only seven, not all of which are included here. If this disappoints anyone who might expect a direct connection between the album's title, 'Lute Lessons' and that of Robert Dowland's book, there is more than ample compensation in the marvellous quality of playing on this disc, and in the appearance of 'Volume 1' on the cover, suggesting that it may herald yet another integral set of Dowland's lute works. If this should be the case we should have a clear market-leader in the field. The present disc is quite simply superb. Whilst North's fingers are always ready to dance to Dowland's more joyous tunes, they sometimes take a little longer to allow the more contemplative music plenty of breathing space, as in *Semper Dowland* and *Forlorne Hope Fancye*, delivered with the utmost eloquence. His readiness to embellish is unequalled in quantity, quality and the smoothness with which it blends into the lines. Nor does anyone put rubato to more telling use. In his *Musick's monument* (1674) Thomas Mace describes the 'sting' – vibrato – as an ornament, and though there is no evidence that the resource was used in earlier times, North's application of it is so effective that it is hard to believe that it was not; added to his beautiful tone, it is without doubt a potent aid to expressiveness.

Preludium, P98. Fantasias – P6; P71. Pavans – Lachrimae, P15; The Lady Russell's Pavan, P17; Pavana Johan Douland, P94; La mia Barbara, P95. Galliards – Frog Galliard, P23; Galliard (upon a galliard by Dan Bachelar), P28; The Lord Viscount Lisle, his Galliard, P38; The Earl of Essex, his Galliard, P42a; Galliard to Lachrimae, P46; A Galliard, P82; Galliard on 'Awake sweet love', P92. An Almand, P96. My Lord Willoughby's Welcome Home, P66a. Loth to departe, P69. The Shoemakers Wife, a Toy, P58. Coranto, P100. Come away, P60 **P**

Paul O'Dette *lte*

Harmonia Mundi HMU90 7163 (64 minutes: DDD) Ⓕ

Recorded 1995

Cadential trills played on one string are a recurrent problem for performers; the less well equipped use a *rallentando* or slurr them, whilst guitarists tend to play them across two strings. No one is more adept at delivering them cleanly and in tempo than O'Dette. It is in the suppleness of his phrasing, clarity of his contrapuntal lines and attention to the functional purpose of every note, that O'Dette is pre-eminent – and has the edge over Lindberg. This disc has all the virtues of its predecessors, and though it is doubtful that the Earl of Essex would have been happy to dance his galliard at O'Dette's pace, you can share the sentiment of its last track – you will be loath to leave it.

Lute Songs

The First Booke of Songes or Ayres – If my complaints could passions moue; Can she excuse my wrongs with vertues cloake; Deare if you change ile neuer chuse againe; Go Cristall teares; Sleepe wayward thoughts; All ye whom loue or fortune hath betraide; Come againe: sweet loue doth now enuite; Awake sweet loue thou art returnd. The Second Booke of Songs or Ayres – I saw my Lady weepe; Flow my teares fall from your springs; Sorrow sorrow stay, lend true repentant teares; Tymes eldest sonne, old age the heire of ease; Then sit thee down, and say thy 'Nunc Dimitis'; When others sings 'Venite exultemus'; If fluds of tears could clense my follies past; Fine knacks for Ladies, cheap, choise, braue and new; Come ye heavie states of night; Shall I sue, shall I seeke for grace

Paul Agnew *ten* **Christopher Wilson** *lte*

Metronome METCD1010 (59 minutes: DDD) Ⓕ

Texts included. Recorded 1995

Lovesongs and Sonnets of John Donne and Sir Philip Sidney

G Tessier In a grove most rich of shade. **Dowland** O sweet woods, the delight of solitarie-nesse. Sweete stay a while, why will you? Preludium. **Morley** Who is it that this darke night. **Coprario** Send home my long strayde eies to mee. **A Ferrabosco II** So breake off this last lamenting kisse. **Corkine** The Fire to see my woes for anger burneth. 'Tis true, 'tis day, what though it be? **Hilton II** A Hymne to God the Father. **Anonymous** Come live with me. So breake off this last lamenting kisse. Goe my flocke, goe get you hence. Goe and catch a fallinge star. O deere life when shall it be. Sir Philip Sidney's Lamentacion. Dearest love I doe not goe

Paul Agnew *ten* **Christopher Wilson** *lte*

Metronome METCD1006 (62 minutes: DDD) Ⓕ

Texts included. Recorded 1994

In the Dowland, Paul Agnew is light of step in the quicker songs, and he languishes longer than most over the variously sorrowful ones. Many of his choices now enjoy 'pop' status, but his inclusion of the beautiful trilogy of which 'Tymes eldest sonne' is the first part is particularly welcome. He receives the most sensitive of support from Wilson, clearly articulated, warm in tone, and perfectly complementary in completing the contrapuntal textures – neither intrusively nor coyly balanced with the voice. Dowland's lute songs have generated many fine recordings, as they richly deserve, and here is one more, beautifully presented, with a booklet containing first-class annotation and all the texts. Love is a familiar peg on which to hang a song recital, and if there is a further focus it is usually on the composer of the music; Agnew and Wilson turn the tables, for once, by spotlighting the writers of the texts, namely Sir Philip Sidney and John Donne. Sidney's sonnets *Astrophel and Stella*, written between 1581 and 1583, may have been addressed to the daughter of the Earl of Essex but she was unwillingly married to Lord Rich in 1581, so Sidney may have had in mind the daughter of Sir Francis Walsingham, whom he married in 1583. The emotional range of Donne's *Songs and Sonets* may also mirror the fluctuating fortunes of his own, basically happy marriage. In both cases the operative word is 'may'. To the good features of the recording of the Dowland songs are to be added notably clearer diction and some graceful embellishments from Agnew, and two well-chosen lute solos by way of interludes from Wilson.

Guillaume Dufay French c1400-1474

GROVE *Dufay was acknowledged by his contemporaries as the leading composer of his day. Having been trained as a choirboy at Cambrai Cathedral, where he probably studied under Loqueville, he seems to have entered the service of the Malatesta family in Pesaro some time before 1420. Several of his works from this period were written for important local events. After returning briefly to Cambrai and establishing links with Laon, where he held two benefices, he was a singer in the papal choir in Rome from 1428 until 1433, when he became associated with the Este family in Ferrara and the Dukes of Savoy. He rejoined the papal choir (1435-7), and composed the famous motet Nuper rosarum flores for the dedication of Brunelleschi's dome of Florence Cathedral in 1436, but spent his later years (apart from 1451-8, when he was again in Savoy) at Cambrai, where he was visited as a celebrity by such musicians as Binchois, Tinctoris and Ockeghem. Although he composed up to his death, most of his late works are lost.*

Working in a period of relative stability in musical style, Dufay achieved distinction rather by consummate artistry than bold innovation. More than half his compositions, including most of his antiphons, hymns, Magnificats, sequences and single items of the Mass, are harmonizations of chant, with the melody usually in the upper part. Most of his motets are imposing compositions written to celebrate a political, social or religious event; four- and five-part textures, often alternating with duos, are common, two or more texts may be set simultaneously, and isorhythm is sometimes used. Others, in a three-voice, treble-dominated style, are more direct and intimate expressions of religious sentiment. Moving from early paired mass movements to the developing form of the cyclic tenor mass, he was apparently the first to base a cycle on a secular melody. Outstanding among his masses is the Missa 'Ave regina celorum', perhaps his last composition. He also composed secular songs, three-quarters of them rondeaux. As an artist of international fame, he is represented in some 70 MSS in many countries.

Complete secular music

Timothy Penrose *counterten* **Rogers Covey-Crump, John Elwes, Paul Elliott** *tens* **Paul Hillier, Michael George** *bars*
Medieval Ensemble of London / Peter Davies and **Timothy Davies**
L'Oiseau-Lyre 452 557-2OC5 (321 minutes: ADD) Ⓑ
Texts and translations included. Recorded 1980

The passage of time has not diminished the grandeur of the achievement of the Medieval Ensemble of London. The opportunity of hearing the entire corpus of Dufay's songs from the same interpretative perspective is irreplaceable – it is doubtful that any record company today would be willing to undertake such an ambitious project. More than just the scope of Dufay's invention, it is its astonishing consistency that strikes the listener – nearly every song has something to delight, to intrigue, to teach. The rough chronology, traced from first to last, is a programme in itself, beginning with the jaunty, seemingly effortless songs of his youth, catchy and dazzling by turns, to the increasingly involving works of maturity, culminating in the sublime poise of his last years.. Although the ensemble doesn't always match Dufay's phenomenal consistency, it's hard to argue with a line-up that includes Paul Elliott, Rogers Covey-Crump and John Elwes, all of them in their prime. And yes, one can disagree with the odd phrase here, spot a fluffed note among the instrumentalists (or, more rarely, the singers), or wonder at some surprising glitches in the CD transfer but with the last song, the beautiful, canonic *Les doleurs* lingering in the mind's ear, one accepts the series's limitations as its many virtues endure. Every serious collector should have this.

Missa S Jacobi

Awards 1999

Missa S Jacobi. Rite majorem Jacobum canamus. Balsamus et munda cera. Gloria 'Resurrexit dominus' and Credo 'Die Maria'. Apostolo glorioso
The Binchois Consort (Mark Chambers, David Gould, Fergus McLusky, Robin Tyson *countertens* James Gilchrist, Chris Watson, Andrew Carwood, Edwin Simpson *tens*) /
Andrew Kirkman
Hyperion CDA66997 (67 minutes: DDD) Ⓕ
Texts and translations included. Recorded 1997 ●●●

In what is only their second CD, The Binchois Consort shows absolute mastery of Dufay's difficult early style, with immaculate balance, wonderfully free phrasing, and crystalline clarity. Moreover in the *Missa S Jacobi* Andrew Kirkman shows an uncanny ability to set the perfect tempo every time, so that the music emerges with its full force. The *Missa S Jacobi* is an odd but supremely important work. It is one of two early Dufay Mass cycles that have rarely been recorded, partly because they are less obviously part of the grand tradition than his later four-voice cantus firmus Masses. And this one is particularly difficult because its many different textures and styles present a severe challenge if it is not to seem fragmented and incoherent. Here it stands as a glorious masterpiece, its nine movements spanning over 40 minutes, with the various styles acting as necessary contrast and culminating in the famous Communion that Heinrich Besseler many years ago argued was the earliest example of *Fauxbourdon* writing. Strangely, two of the motets work less well: both the earlier *Rite majorem* and the later *Balsamus* seem to go too fast for the details to have their full effect, perhaps because they are so strikingly different in style from the other works performed here. And it seems a touch perverse to use the now fashionable 'old French' pronunciation of Latin, particularly in a motet composed for a papal ceremony (even if the original singers would have been Franco-Flemish): in all his early motets the text seems centrally important, and this kind of pronunciation loses too many of the consonants. But the Italian-texted *Apostolo glorioso* is again quite superb, as is the astonishing *Gloria* and *Credo* pair. Briefly, then, this is as close to a perfect Dufay CD as any available.

Missa 'Se la face ay pale'

Missa 'Se la face ay pale'. Gloria ad modum tubae. Chanson 'Se la face ay pale'
Early Music Consort of London / David Munrow
Virgin Veritas Edition VER5 61283-2
(45 minutes: ADD). Texts and translations included. Ⓜ
Recorded 1973

A good number of Munrow's first performances remain unsurpassed. One would single out Dufay's Mass *Se la face ay pale* in this regard. Nowadays, tempos might be slightly brisker, and voices used in preference to instruments on the lower parts; but only compare the serene tranquillity of the *Kyrie I* with the exhilaration at the end of the *Credo*: here are poetry and variety in abundance. For this, one of the most significant of 15th-century Mass cycles, there is still no convincing alternative performance on CD. The earlier more 'medieval' *Gloria ad modum tubae* is performed here with tenor sackbuts on the lower lines, and two countertenors (Bowman and Brett) descanting above in cheerful canon; quite the most convincing account of the piece available, and a good beginning to the disc.The disc concludes with the chanson *Se la face ay pale* in its original three-part version.

Magnificat sexti toni

Nuper rosarum flores. Alma redemptoris mater II. Letabundus. Ecclesie militantis. Magnificat sexti toni. Benedicamus Domino II. Recollectio Festorum Beate Marie Virginis: Plainchant for Vespers I
Pomerium / Alexander Blachly
Archiv Produktion 447 773-2AH (60 minutes: DDD) Ⓕ
Texts and translations included. Recorded 1995-96

Pomerium here presents a new addition to our knowledge of Dufay's music, the set of plainchants he wrote for a new feast, the Recollection of the Feasts of the Virgin Mary, composed in 1458. The work is fascinating in many ways: as one of the very few cases of liturgical chant by a named composer, let alone the greatest composer of his age; as an example of Dufay's work in his full maturity (he was perhaps 60 years old at the time he composed it), and entirely different from what we know of his late polyphony; and as a case of unambiguously dated chant composition. Pomerium performs only the music for the First Vespers, a mere fragment of the whole feast. Perhaps there could have been more than four singers for these chants: elegant though the performance is, it hardly sounds like a cathedral *schola*. But the longer pieces are particularly persuasive: the hymn *Gaude redempta* and the Responsory *Surge propera*. For the rest, they provide the addition of two of Dufay's most famous motets and a group of very rarely heard polyphonic liturgical works, particularly the glorious *Letabundus* setting and the *Magnificat* in the sixth tone, which is sung with a superb degree of lucidity. Pomerium sings with men and women, showing an attractive vibrant energy, with everything neatly controlled. The sound in the Grotto Church of Notre Dame, New York, is well captured.

Paul Dukas French 1865-1935

GROVE *Dukas studied with Guiraud at the Paris Conservatoire (1881-89) and became a friend of Debussy, d'Indy and Bordes. His Franckian leanings are evident in his first published work, the overture Polyeucte (1891), though Beethoven is also suggested, as again in his Symphony in C (1896). But the symphonic scherzo L'apprenti sorcier (1897) is more individual, not least in its augmented-triad and diminished-7th harmonies, which influenced Stravinsky and Debussy. The next years were devoted to the opera Ariane et Barbe-Bleue (1907), though at the same time he produced two piano works of Beethovenian range and power: the Sonata in E flat minor and the Variations, interlude et final sur un thème de Rameau. Dukas self-criticism constricted his later output. Apart from the exotic ballet La péri (1912) he published only a few occasional works. He cultivated craftsmanship to an extreme degree and his orchestration has been widely admired and imitated. His voluminous criticism reveals an unusual breadth of sympathy and he was a conscientious editor of Beethoven, Couperin, Rameau and Scarlatti and an admired teacher at the Conservatoire.*

L'apprenti sorcier

L'apprenti sorcier. Symphony in C. La péri
French National Orchestra / Leonard Slatkin
RCA Red Seal 09026 68802-2 (71 minutes: DDD) Ⓕ
Recorded 1996

In the best of Franckian traditions, Dukas's three-movement Symphony is as abstract as his *Sorcerer's Apprentice* is vividly narrative. Both works are from the mid-1890s. And from more than a decade later, the ballet *La péri* is something else again. A *poème dansée* in which glittering Russian Nationalist orientalism, and later Salome's Dance, merge with French late romantic impressionism, the end result hinting at, among other things, Ravel's *La valse* to come. The orchestration is a wonder; Dukas himself said he wanted it to be like 'a kind of dazzling, translucent enamel'. Here, as always in Slatkin's best work, the structure is powerfully attended to, the texture has a beautiful sheen, and the whole disc confirms him as a quite exceptional stylist. In the weighting and scale of the orchestral sound, and the way lines and surface detail are projected, accentuated and articulated,

Slatkin sounds marginally more French than Tortelier (below), with the textures and timbres a degree more vibrant and varied. His orchestra is French, of course, and his recording is also noticeably less reverberant. And all of these elements enhance the listener's appreciation of the Symphony's brilliantly active, flaring orchestration and its fundamentally classical stance. While Tortelier's perspectives may indeed be deeper in the shimmering landscapes and poetic melancholy of the slow movement, Slatkin's performance on the whole is slightly better geared and 'gathered'.

Dukas L'apprenti sorcier **Saint-Saëns** Symphony No 3 in C minor, Op 78, 'Organ'
Simon Preston *org* **Berlin Philharmonic Orchestra / James Levine** Ⓕ
DG 419 617-2GH (47 minutes: DDD)

James Levine and the Berlin Philharmonic Orchestra, on cracking form, offer a performance of Saint-Saëns's Third Symphony which is still among the best available. The balance between the orchestra and organ, here played powerfully by Simon Preston, is well judged and the overall acoustic very convincing. Levine directs a grippingly individual reading, full of drama and with a consistently imaginative response to the score's detail. The organ entry in the finale is quite magnificent, the excitement of Preston thundering out the main theme physical in its impact. The music expands and blossoms magnificently, helped by the spectacular dynamic range of the recording. Levine's choice of coupling is a happy one, especially as his account of Dukas's masterpiece is still the best in the catalogue. Levine chooses a fast basic tempo, but justifies his speed by the lightness of his touch and, of course, the clean articulation and rhythmic bounce of the Berlin Philharmonic playing help considerably. The climax is thrilling, but Levine reserves something for the moment when the sorcerer returns to quell the flood. Levine must have had Disney's imagery in his mind in the closing pages of the story, for the picture of the crestfallen Mickey handing back the broom to his master springs readily to mind. In all, it provides a marvellous finish to an exhilarating listening experience.

Dukas L'apprenti sorcier (arr Rabinovitch)
Ravel La valse (arr cpsr)
R Strauss Symphonia domestica, Op 53 (arr Singer)
Martha Argerich, Alexandre Rabinovitch *pfs*
Teldec 4509-96435-2 (62 minutes: DDD) Ⓕ
Recorded 1995

Dukas's *L'apprenti sorcier* and Ravel's *La valse* both inhabit worlds of exuberant nightmare, and although one can marvel at the concentrated wit and verve of Argerich and Rabinovitch, it is their uncanny evocation of unsettled states where all equilibrium is lost and the 'ceremony of innocence' is well and truly drowned that forms the most lasting impression. Such vividness brings parts of *La valse* to a near standstill before accelerating away and achieving an effect not unlike suddenly applied centrifugal force. The opening quivers with unease, the commencement of a vision where even the most opulent Viennese gaiety and extravagance is menacingly clouded and distorted.

The Dukas, too, develops from sinister hints to a situation diabolically out of control yet one sustained by both players with an iron grip made all the more remarkable when you consider the immense virtuoso resources involved. Otto Singer's skilful version of Strauss's *Symphonia domestica* hardly transcends its orchestral origin yet it is illuminated at every point – whether in rhetorical uproar or in flickering, Lisztian half-lights – through playing of an overwhelming brio and crystalline clarity. If anything Argerich's blow-torch incandescence has increased rather than diminished over the years. The recordings are close but unconfined, capturing faithfully the remarkable, dazzling impact of these performances.

Symphony in C major

Symphony in C. Polyeucte – overture
BBC Philharmonic Orchestra / Yan Pascal Tortelier
Chandos CHAN9225 (56 minutes: DDD) Ⓕ
Recorded 1993 ●

Before *L'apprenti sorcier*, the tradition Paul Dukas was following was that of César Franck, and he was also heavily influenced by the Wagnerianism which held French composers in thrall during that period. Both models can be discerned in the overture *Polyeucte*: nevertheless, and despite extensive Wagnerian use of the brass, there is a clarity (even delicacy in the third of its five sections) and an imaginative sense of colour which are individual to him. The finely crafted Symphony composed four years later, in 1896 – daringly in C major at a time when tonality was undergoing such general buffeting – shows Dukas as essentially a classicist, although the middle section of the central movement reveals that Nature romanticism had not passed him by. The eloquent performance here gives the vigorous first movement a splendid *élan* while also luxuriating in the Franckian secondary subjects, there is lovely warm, lyrical playing and sensitive nuance in the second movement, and the finale (even more Franckian in its harmonic thinking) bubbles over with nervous energy. Exemplary recording quality.

Piano Sonata in E flat minor

Dukas Piano Sonata in E flat minor
Dutilleux Piano Sonata **Schmitt** Deux mirages
John Ogdon *pf*
EMI Matrix CDM5 65996-2 (79 minutes: ADD) Ⓜ
Recorded 1972

The first of Schmitt's *Mirages*, written in 1920 and published in memory of Debussy, is a haunting, elaborately textured elegy; the second, a ferocious rendering of the story of

Mazeppa's tragic ride, was dedicated to Cortot. One wonders whether he would ever have had the technique to play it: Ogdon, however, revels in its enormous demands. His fluency and limpid clarity are to be admired, too, in the Dutilleux Sonata, whose spiky first movement veers from fragile delicacy to pounding *fortissimo* chords; its slow movement (headed 'Lied') is deeply moving in its intensity; and rather more diatonicism marks the final massive chorale, with its brilliant ensuing variations. The main work here, however, is the big Dukas Sonata, written at the turn of the century, and advanced for its time. It has always been hailed by French critics as a masterpiece, but despite that it is not very often performed, at least in this country. The sonata's Franckian harmonic and melodic traits are combined with a pianistic exuberance which suits Ogdon's temperament admirably, as does the demonic *Scherzo*, but this is also balanced by his air of mystery in its trio section and by his tonal purity in the quiet slow movement. This release brings home to us just how outstanding a pianist we lost.

John Dunstaple British c1390-1453

GROVE *Dunstaple is acknowledged as the most eminent of the Englishmen who strongly influenced the generation of Dufay and later continental composers. Little is certainly known about his career; he was probably not the John Dunstavylle who was at Hereford Cathedral, 1419-40, but may have been in the service of the Duke of Bedford before 1427. He was in the service of Queen Joan of Navarre, second wife of Henry IV, 1427-36, and was serviteur et familier domestique in the household of Henry, Duke of Gloucester, in 1438. In the late 1430s he held lands in northern France. There is evidence that he was also an astronomer. He was buried at St.Stephen's, Walbrook, where his epitaph described him as 'prince of music'.*

Most of his surviving music is in continental sources. 51 compositions are consistently stated in MS sources to be his, but many others, anonymous or with conflicting ascriptions, are probably by him. Stylistically, his music can be divided into four categories: isorhythmic works in which a plainchant tenor forms the lowest of three or four parts; non-isorhythmic works based on a plainchant that may be in any of the three parts; works in 'free treble' or 'ballade' style, consisting of a freely composed melodic line (which may however incorporate traces of elaborated plainchant) and two slower supporting parts; and declamatory works in a syllabic style with careful accentuation of the text. Two of the earliest mass cycles, Rex seculorum and Da gaudiorum premia, are ascribed to him in some sources and some of his other mass movements may originally have belonged to complete cycles. Most of his works are in three parts, except for the isorhythmic motets which are mostly in four, and, while nearly all begin in triple time, there is often a change to duple near the middle and sometimes a shorter return to triple towards the end. His melodies are characterised by stepwise and triadic movement, and the harmony, reflecting the English predilection for 3rds and 6ths, is predominantly consonant.

Vocal Works

Awards 1996

Descendi in ortum meum. Ave maris stella. Gloria in canon. Speciosa facta es. Sub tuam protectionem. Veni, Sancte spiritus / Veni creator spiritus. Albanus roseo rutilat / Quoque ferundus eras / Albanus domini laudus. Specialis virgo. Preco preheminencie / Precursor premittitur / textless / Inter natos mulierum. O crux gloriosa. Salve regina mater mire. Missa Rex seculorum

Orlando Consort

Metronome METCD1009 (74 minutes: DDD) Ⓕ

Texts and translations included. Recorded 1995 ●●●

This disc contains three of Dunstaple's well-known motets – *Preco preheminencie*, *Veni veni* and *Albanus* – but the rest are rarely performed. For some of the delicious antiphons, it is hard to see why: *Salve regina mater mire* is particularly striking – one of those pieces that sounds far more impressive than it looks on the page. There are also some total novelties. The canonic *Gloria* was discovered in Russia: it is a massively inventive work that adds a substantial new dimension to our knowledge of Dunstaple. And *Descendi in ortum meum*, though discovered and published a quarter of a century ago, surely stands as the latest known work of its composer: a magnificent piece that builds an entirely new kind of edifice with the materials of his characteristic style. Most impressive of all, though, is the Mass, *Rex seculorum*, which ends the disc. This may or may not be by Dunstaple – which is probably why it has never been recorded. Whoever the composer, though, it is a key work in the history of the polyphonic mass cycle, brimming with invention. The Orlando Consort has a wonderfully forward style that beautifully matches the music and helps the listener to understand why Dunstaple achieved such an enormous reputation on the continental mainland. If they are occasionally a touch rough, these are classic performances that will be hard to challenge.

Henri Duparc French 1848-1933

GROVE *Duparc studied the piano and composition with Franck, writing works that he later destroyed; this loss, together with a crippling psychological condition that caused him to abandon composition at the age of 36, has resulted in a legacy of just 13 songs (composed 1868-84). An important influence is Wagner, seen in the ambitious harmonic structure of Chanson triste and the shifting chromaticism of Soupir. Yet Duparc's feeling for poetic atmosphere and the craftsmanship he used to communicate it, as in the sinister drama of La manoir de Rosemonde, were unique, giving the French mélodie a rare musical substance and emotional intensity. From 1885 he led a quiet life, remaining close to Ernest Chausson and cultivating his aesthetic sensibility through reading and drawing.*

Mélodies

L'invitation au voyage. Sérénade florentine. Extase. Chanson triste. Le manoir de Rosemonde. Lamento. Au pays où se fait la guerre. La fuite. La vague et la cloche. Sérénade. Testament. Phidylé. Romance de Mignon. Elégie. Le galop. Soupir. La vie antérieure
Danielle Borst *sop* **François Le Roux** *bar*
Jeff Cohen *pf*
REM REM311049 (63 minutes: DDD). Texts and translations included. Recorded 1987 Ⓕ

If you consider Duparc's songs the most rewarding in the French language you will rejoice at this issue. Without hesitation, we would say Le Roux's are the most successful performances of these masterpieces in miniature since the war. In his foreword to this issue the veteran composer Henri Sauguet comments: 'The interpretations of François Le Roux and Danielle Borst are remarkable, not just for their vocal qualities and their emotional commitment but also for their exemplary use of words, which illustrates perfectly the profound unity of poetry and music.' That almost says all that needs to be said, at any rate about Le Roux who has the lion's share of the burden. His voice can sometimes take on a rough edge but his understanding of the Duparc idiom is second to none, rivalling that of Panzéra and Bernac in the distant past, precisely because he realizes what French can convey when it is sung with a scrupulous care over diction. Added to that he and his admirable pianist, Jeff Cohen, seem almost always to find exactly the right tempo for each *mélodie*, not indulging in the excessively slow speeds adopted by some non-Francophone singers today. Le Roux is partnered in *La fuite* by Borst, another dedicated Duparcian who catches some of its trance-like beauty. The recorded sound is ideal. A 'must' for anyone interested in great performances of *mélodies*.

Marcel Dupré

French 1886-1971

GROVE *Dupré studied with Guilmant, Vierne and Widor at the Paris Conservatoire (1902-14), returning as professor of organ (1926-54) while also serving as organist of St Sulpice (1934-71) and appearing internationally as a recitalist. His works introduced a Lisztian virtuosity and a contemplative modality into organ music; he also wrote religious symphonic poems. Alain and Messiaen were among his pupils.*

Organ Works

Complete Organ Works, Volume 9
Entrée, méditation, sortie, Op 62. Les nymphéas, Op 54. Suite bretonne, Op 21. Poème héroïque, Op 33 (arr cpsr)
Jeremy Filsell *org*
Guild GMCD7188 (63 minutes: DDD) Ⓕ
Recorded on the organ of St Boniface Episcopal Church, Florida, USA in 1998 ●

It's sometimes the case that the reputation of great composers rests on a handful of works. With Dupré it's the two symphonies, the Op 7 Preludes and Fugues and the *Noël* Variations for which he's best known, but these compositions form a tiny proportion of his entire output. One of the many benefits of Guild's series is the discovery of hidden treasures, and much of the music on Volume 9 deserves to be heard more frequently.

The revelation here is *Les nymphéas*. This is a beautiful work, even as original as Debussy's *Images*, *Nocturnes* or the quieter moments of *Jeux*. It would make a marvellous orchestral suite; indeed, much of Dupré's organ writing has a quasi-orchestral character, and reflects his love and knowledge of the vast tonal palette of 20th-century instruments. You can also tell that, like Messiaen, he was an experienced writer of piano and chamber music.

We're indebted to Filsell for his special arrangement of *Les nymphéas* for this CD, and for his excellent performances throughout this volume. The choice of the organ at St Boniface, Florida, was a good one as it provides sensuous colours for the softer movements, plus glockenspiel effects for the *Suite bretonne*. The playing is backed up by fine recorded sound and comprehensive programme notes. There's no doubt that this series is setting the standard for Dupré interpreters of the future and will be a landmark in the history of organ recordings.

Complete Organ Works, Volume 10
Le chemin de la croix, Op 29
Jeremy Filsell *org*
Guild GMCD7193 (56 minutes: DDD) Ⓕ
Recorded 1998 ●●

Complete Organ Works, Volume 11
Vêpres du commun des fêtes de la Sainte-Vierge, Op 18. Choral et Fugue, Op 57. Regina coeli, Op 64
Vocal Quartet; Jeremy Filsell *org*
Guild GMCD7198 (55 minutes: DDD) Ⓕ
Recorded 1998 ●●

Complete Organ Works, Volume 12
79 Chorales, Op 28
Jeremy Filsell *org*
Guild GMCD7203 (72 minutes: DDD) Ⓕ
Recorded 1998 ●●
All recorded on the organ of St Boniface Episcopal Church, Sarasota, Florida, USA

Thinking about 20th-century French music after Debussy and Ravel, the names of Messiaen and the members of Les Six would probably spring to mind. However, at the same time organists like Vierne, Tournemire, Alain, Langlais and Dupré himself were writing music every bit as original and as intense as the aforementioned composers. One of the many benefits of Guild's series (which concludes with these three volumes) is the opportunity to discover just how fine a composer Dupré was. Perhaps more than any of his contemporaries he managed to embrace both the sacred and the secular with utter conviction.

Le chemin de la croix is one of his major works and is a landmark piece of musical drama. One can hear links with the *Symphonie-Passion* of six years earlier, and David Gammie in his comprehensive accompanying notes points out the influence of these works on Duruflé's Requiem and Messiaen's *Les corps glorieux*. Filsell gives a suitably dramatic performance with some telling *rallentandos* at climactic moments.

All three compositions on Volume 11 were inspired by Gregorian chant, and each movement is preceded on this CD by the singing of the verse on which it's based. The vocal quartet includes the CD's producer Adrian Peacock and Filsell himself – an inspired and appropriate piece of programming. Listening to Filsell's flowing, atmospheric playing it's easy to imagine oneself sitting in a vast, incense-laden Parisian church, with glorious improvised music coming from the west-end *grand orgue*.

Dupré is remembered for writing music of extreme technical complexity, but Volume 12 shows that he was well capable of composing pieces for organs and organists of modest resources. The 79 *Chorales* take hymn tunes which were all used by Bach as the basis for chorale-preludes. Many of Dupré's chorales are effective Bachian pastiches, but a handful of them have the unmistakable 20th-century French idiom. Again, Filsell's performances are beyond reproach, and he shows that Dupré was able to match JSB for solemnity and piety.

As is so often the case Naxos provides healthy competition, and Volume 11 of its Dupré series has a very fine performance of *Le chemin de la croix* from Mary Preston. She brings a greater clarity to the music, helped by the drier acoustic of the Meyerson Symphony Center at Dallas. However, Filsell in the more resonant acoustic of St Boniface Church, Sarasota, Florida brings more warmth, passion and drama to his interpretations, and this, coupled with Gammie's excellent insert-notes sways the balance in favour of the Guild series.

In all 12 volumes Filsell's playing has been consistently superb, and what has been most impressive is that his virtuosity has always been the servant of the music. The St Boniface organ may not have the *éclat* of a Cavaillé-Coll, but its clarity and attack enhance Dupré's complex textures, and the recordings are suitably warm and atmospheric. We must salute Filsell for one of the greatest achievements in organ recordings.

Prelude and Fugue in F minor, Op 7 No 2. Cortège et Litanie, Op 19 No 2. Symphonie- Passion, Op 23. Symphony No 2 in C sharp minor, Op 26. Evocation, Op 37 – Allegro deciso
John Scott *org*
Hyperion CDA67047 (71 minutes: DDD). Recorded on the organ of St Paul's Cathedral, London in 1998 Ⓕ

This is an impressive release on every account. As we have come to expect from John Scott, the playing is superb – that perfect combination of technical virtuosity and intense musicianship which is so rare among organists – and numerous Hyperion recordings from the cavernous St Paul's over the past 15 years have fine-tuned its engineering to such an extent that we no longer admire the sound, *per se*, but find that the acoustic positively enhances it. That awesome echo, as the final chord of Scott's vehement account of the *Symphonie-Passion* is cast adrift to fend for itself in the cathedral's vastness, adds a tangible sense of presence. Yet the clarity is there; the precision of Scott's fingerwork is captured in microscopic detail in his stunning performance of the Second Symphony's 'Preludio' and 'Toccata' movements. The Prelude and Fugue receives a richly atmospheric performance which makes you wonder why it is that this deeply moving piece, with its strong melodic ties with the popular Requiem, has been so overshadowed by its companions. Musically, technically and emotionally these are truly distinguished recordings.

Suite bretonne, Op 21. Symphonie- Passion, Op 23. Symphony No 2 in C sharp minor, Op 26. Variations sur un vieux Noël, Op 20
Thomas Trotter *org*
Decca 452 478-2DH (74 minutes: DDD)
Played on the Skinner organ, Princeton University Chapel, New Jersey, USA. Recorded 1995 Ⓕ

Thomas Trotter's Decca recording is a welcome addition to the Dupré discography, consisting as it does of four of the finest compositions. Dupré's own recordings were marked by their clarity of articulation, rock-steady rhythm and a willingness to disregard his own tempo and metronome indications. Like Dupré, Trotter isn't afraid to play faster than the printed speeds; this adds to the drama of *Symphonie-Passion* and the sense of fun in the *Noël* Variations. Trotter's flair for pacing is evident in the outer movements of the Second Symphony; he knows exactly when to hold back and give the music space, and when to surge ahead to telling effect. Dupré's registration markings are scrupulously observed, and Trotter contributes his own ideas of colour with magical effect towards the end of 'Nativité' (*Symphonie-Passion*) and 'Berceuse' (*Suite bretonne*). The recorded sound of the organ, which has all the appropriate colours and suitable grandeur, may be a little too recessed for some tastes. However, if you find the sound acceptable, then this disc, with its excellent accompanying booklet, can be warmly recommended as a thrilling experience.

Maurice Duruflé French 1902-1986

GROVE *Duruflé studied with Tournemire, whose deputy at SteClotilde he became, and then at the Paris Conservatoire (1920-28) with Gigout and Dukas. In 1930 he was appointed organist of*

StEtienne-du-Mont and he toured internationally as a recitalist. His works are few, in a vivid modal style, and include a Requiem (1947).

Requiem

Duruflé Requiem, Op 9[a] **Fauré** Requiem, Op 48[b]
[a]**Ann Murray** *mez* [a]**Thomas Allen** *bar* [b]**Mary Seers** *sop* [b]**Michael George** *bass* [b]**John Scott** *org*
Corydon Singers; English Chamber Orchestra / Matthew Best
Hyperion CDA67070 (78 minutes: DDD). Text and translation included. Recorded 1985-87 Ⓕ

Matthew Best favours Duruflé's compromise version of his Requiem (with strings, harp and trumpets). The combination of chamber ensemble with solo organ lines (sometimes not entirely convincing) makes for some problems of balance – there is a lack of bass in parts of the *Domine Jesu Christe*, the trumpets' plainchant is overloud in the *Kyrie*, and the first 'Hosanna' in the *Sanctus* is inaudible; but for the performance itself there can be nothing but praise – soloists, chorus, orchestra and organ are all first-class – the Corydon Singers offer expressive singing, with a wide dynamic range and remarkably clear words; and Best shapes the work expressively and sensitively. In Fauré's Requiem Best uses either John Rutter's reconstruction of the pre-publication state of Fauré's score, or something very closely resembling it, but the resulting performance sounds quite different to Rutter's own (reviewed under Fauré). He chooses slightly but perceptibly slower speeds for a start (save in the *In Paradisum*, which is a little faster than Rutter's). More significantly, he uses a larger, warmer, less grainy string force which together with a spacious acoustic and exceptionally refined choral singing gives a honeyed glow to the music which many will find a very acceptable compromise between the slightly austere leanness of Rutter's own presentation of his edition and the somewhat cumbrous opacity of the 1900 score.

Duruflé Requiem. Prélude et Fugue sur le nom d'Alain, Op 7. Quatre Motets sur des thèmes grégoriens, Op 10 **Fauré** Requiem, Op 48. Cantique de Jean Racine, Op 11. Messe basse **Poulenc** Mass in G. Salve Regina. Exultate Deo. Litanies à la vierge noire
Jonathon Bond, Andrew Brunt, Robert King *trebs* **Benjamin Luxon** *bar* **Christopher Keyte** *bass* **St John's College Choir, Cambridge; Academy of St Martin in the Fields / George Guest** with **Stephen Cleobury** *org*
Double Decca ② 436 486-2DF2 (149 minutes: ADD) Ⓜ
Recorded 1969-76

Here is almost two-and-a-half hours of bliss. These are recordings to set aside for the time when, as the prayer says, 'the busy world is hushed'. Asked to characterise Fauré's and Duruflé's Requiems as compared with others, we might suggest words such as 'delicate', 'restrained', 'meditative', 'undramatic'; but that last would be a mistake. These performances certainly do not go out of their way to 'be' dramatic or anything else other than faithful to the music, but one is struck by the power exercised by those rare moments that rise to a *forte* and above. The choir is surely at its best, the trebles with their fine clear-cut, distinctive tone, the tenors (so important in the Fauré) graceful and refined without being precious, the altos exceptionally good, and only the basses just occasionally and briefly plummy or obtrusive in some way. The Poulenc works further test a choir's virtuosity yet in the extremely difficult Mass, the choir seems secure, and in the *Salve Regina* they catch the necessary tenderness. The treble soloists sing beautifully, Christopher Keyte dramatizes almost too convincingly in Duruflé's 'tremens factus', and Benjamin Luxon, his production less even, builds finely in Fauré's *Libera me*. Stephen Cleobury, the organist throughout, contributes an admirably played solo written by Duruflé as a tribute to the young organist Jehan Alain, killed early in the war. These recordings have a vividness, certainly in the choral sound, that modern recordings generally lack.

Duruflé Requiem[a] **Fauré** Requiem, Op 48[b]
[a]**Kiri Te Kanawa,** [b]**Lucia Popp** *sops* **Siegmund Nimsgern** *bass-bar* **Ambrosian Singers;** [a]**Desborough School Choir;** [a]**New Philharmonia Orchestra,** [b]**Philharmonia Orchestra / Sir Andrew Davis**
Sony Classical Essential Classics SBK67182 Ⓑ
(79 minutes: ADD). Recorded 1977

These recordings, made within six months of each other with substantially the same forces and in the same church, were issued separately but obviously go together. Both had outstandingly good reviews in *Gramophone* and although textural matters have arisen to enrich the choice and complicate the issue, if what were then regarded as the standard versions (in full orchestral score) are required, then the recommendations can remain. Davis's superiority over more recent versions is especially apparent in the Duruflé. His way with the opening is typical: the flow, the gentle wave-like motion, is beautifully caught and in the 'Libera me' he discovers the full richness of Duruflé's colours. Kiri Te Kanawa sings with feeling and is incomparably lovely in sheer sound. There may be misgivings about the sound produced in remastering, but it settles down (or one's ears do).

Henri Dutilleux

French 1916

GROVE *Dutilleux studied with the Gallons, Büsser and Emmanuel at the Paris Conservatoire (1933-8), where he was appointed professor in 1970 after periods with French radio (1943-63) and at the Ecole Normale de Musique (from 1961). His first works suggest influences from Debussy, Ravel, Roussel and Honegger, but he developed as an isolated and independent figure, producing a relatively small output of great breadth and originality, predominantly of instrumental works; they include two symphonies (1950, 1959) and other orchestral pieces, piano music and the string quartet Ainsi la nuit (1976).*

Cello Concerto

Cello Concerto, 'Tout un monde lointain'. Métaboles. Mystère de l'instant
Boris Pergamenschikov *vc* **BBC Philharmonic Orchestra / Yan Pascal Tortelier**
Chandos CHAN9565 (60 minutes: DDD) Ⓕ
Recorded 1997

This is the third issue in the Chandos Dutilleux series with the BBC Philharmonic and Yan Pascal Tortelier. The virtues of those earlier issues remain evident here, with meticulously prepared, well-played performances, and recordings carefully adapted to the coloristic subtlety and textural delicacy of the music. *Métaboles* is particularly tricky to bring off, but this version is admirable in the way it builds through some dangerously episodic writing to underline the power of the principal climaxes, though a more sharply delineated sound picture could have reinforced these contrasts even more appropriately. Boris Pergamenschikov is an eloquent soloist in the Cello Concerto. Tortelier's account of *Mystère de l'instant* – using a full orchestral complement of strings – is excellently done. As with *Métaboles*, the structure is shaped with great flexibility and feeling for its ebb and flow, and this emerges as a highly dramatic score, despite the inherent reticence of Dutilleux's style.

Violin Concerto

Dutilleux Violin Concerto, 'L'arbre des songes'. Timbres, espace, mouvement. Deux Sonnets de Jean Cassou (orch cpsr) **Alain** (orch Dutilleux) Prière pour nous autres charnels
Olivier Charlier *vn* **Martyn Hill** *ten* **Neal Davies** *bar* **BBC Philharmonic Orchestra / Yan Pascal Tortelier**
Chandos CHAN9504 (58 minutes: DDD) Ⓕ
Texts and translations included. Recorded 1996 ○

Timbres, espace, mouvement (1978, revised 1991) can be counted as Dutilleux's best orchestral composition, at once rooted in tradition yet persistently sceptical about conventional 'symphonic' values. It's a tricky score to bring off, and Tortelier is successful in negotiating its twists and turns of form. In the Violin Concerto (1985) Tortelier again favours a symphonic approach, and very effective it is too, with a soloist who is authoritative without being overly self-assertive. In the rival Decca recording (reviewed below) Pierre Amoyal is more intense in tone, with a volatility from which all sense of effort has not been completely purged. Is the Charlier/Tortelier version too staid, or does this richly perfumed music demand a response that keeps its more flamboyant qualities under firmer control than that provided by the Decca team? Amoyal and Dutoit make the more immediate impact, but it could be that Charlier and Tortelier prove more satisfying in the longer run. The Chandos disc also includes Dutilleux's orchestral arrangement of his Cassou settings, and also his orchestration, made in 1944, of Jehan Alain's touching prayer. Well-characterised contributions from Martyn Hill and Neal Davies complete this valuable release.

Violin Concerto, 'L'arbre des songes'. Cello Concerto
Pierre Amoyal *vn* **Lynn Harrell** *vc* **French National Orchestra / Charles Dutoit**
Decca 444 398-2DH (51 minutes: DDD) Ⓕ
Recorded 1993

The Cello Concerto, first performed in 1970, was written for Rostropovich, and Lynn Harrell boldly confronts this formidable precedent; there is certainly no sense of undue reticence or constraint in his playing. The many technical challenges present no problems: more significantly, Harrell the interpreter has the full measure of the music's tricky blend of boldness and delicacy. From the start of the 'very free and flexible' first movement the undertones of mystery and menace which reflect the music's source in Baudelaire's poetry are fully in evidence, and Harrell has the advantage of first-class recorded sound. The cello is placed well forward, but the orchestra is never recessed to compensate. The Violin Concerto builds on the sultry, surreal Baudelairean spirit of the Cello Concerto – the 'tree' of the title seems tropical, the 'dreams' mainly unquiet – and Pierre Amoyal, with admirable support from Dutoit and the FNO, succeeds brilliantly in shaping the rhapsodic solo line with a mixture of intensity and fantasy, so that the piece works well as both structure and expression. Here, too, the production team has ensured that the concerto's rich textures can be heard without strain or artificiality. The whole enterprise can be warmly recommended.

Complete Symphonies

Awards 1994

Symphonies – No 1; No 2, 'Le double'
BBC Philharmonic Orchestra / Yan Pascal Tortelier
Chandos CHAN9194 Ⓕ
(60 minutes: DDD)
Recorded 1993 ○○○

This pair of relatively early works by Henri Dutilleux, completed in 1951 and 1959 respectively, show him poised to inherit the Honegger/Martinů strand of the symphonic tradition. Yet, while an almost Simpsonian *élan* in the first movement of No 2 promises a rich vein for further exploration, the Stravinskian strategies of the finale, ending with a virtual recomposition of the chorale that concludes the *Symphonies of Wind Instruments*, reveals a more modernist tendency, and leads away from the well-made, tonally-resolving symphony altogether. With their broad thematic vistas and persuasive adaptations of traditional forms, Dutilleux's symphonies offer considerable rewards to interpreters and listeners alike. Yan Pascal Tortelier and the BBC Philharmonic allow the music all the space it needs in strongly characterised, rhythmically well-sprung performances with uniformly excellent solo playing in No 2, and the sound is rich and natural.

The Shadows of Time

Joel Esher, Rachael Plotkin, Jordan Swaim *trebs*
Boston Symphony Orchestra / Seiji Ozawa
Erato (special price) 3984-22830-2 (22 minutes: DDD)
Recorded live in 1998

Boldly, Erato gambled that the interest and appeal of the first substantial work by Henri Dutilleux for almost a decade would justify this issue of a CD single. We can only commend the enterprise and the finely engineered recording. *The Shadows of Time* is an unambiguously emotional, even angry work, and may well stand as the musical testament of a composer who, while seeking to celebrate 'the unity of time and place' (as his brief note accompanying the disc puts it), can only do so from the basis of considerable pessimism about the ability of the real world to achieve the kind of harmonious, classical ideals to which he, as an artist, aspires. Pessimism and anger are most explicit in the way the first and last sections depict the inexorable passage of time, and in the increasing density and urgency of the orchestral lament which explodes out of a central episode in which childrens' voices repeat the questions, 'Why us? Why the star?'. This is a reference to Anne Frank and 'all the innocent children of the world', Dutilleux declares, yet there is nothing mawkish here, rather an almost *Wozzeck*-like pathos in the way the music searches for consolation without, in the end, quite achieving it. By the time of these performances Ozawa, his orchestra and the three assured young singers, had achieved absolute authority in this often testing music. The result is a moving and memorable document of a very special occasion, and a very special work.

Antonin Dvořák Bohemian 1841-1904

GROVE *Dvořák studied with Antonín Liehmann and at the Prague Organ School (1857-9). A capable viola player, he joined the band that became the nucleus of the new Provisional Theatre orchestra, conducted from 1866 by Smetana. Private teaching and mainly composing occupied him from 1873. He won the Austrian State Stipendium three times (1874, 1876-7), gaining the attention of Brahms, who secured the publisher Simrock for some of his works in 1878. Foreign performances multiplied, notably of the Slavonic Dances, the Sixth Symphony and the Stabat mater, and with them further commissions. Particularly well received in England, Dvořák wrote The Spectre's Bride (1884) and the Requiem Mass (1890) for Birmingham, the Seventh Symphony for the Philharmonic Society (1885) and St Ludmilla for Leeds (1886), besides receiving an honorary doctorate from Cambridge. He visited Russia in 1890, continued to launch new works in Prague and London and began teaching at the Prague Conservatory in 1891 (where Joseph Suk was among his most gifted pupils). Before leaving for the USA he toured Bohemia playing the new Dumky Trio. As director of the National Conservatory in New York (1892-5) he taught composition, meanwhile producing the well-known Ninth Symphony ('From the New World'), the String Quartet in F, the String Quintet in E flat and the Cello Concerto. Financial strain and family ties took him back to Prague, where he began to write symphonic poems and finally had his efforts at dramatic music rewarded with the success of the fairytale opera Rusalka (1901). The recipient of honours and awards from all sides, he remained a modest man of simple tastes, loyal to his nationality.*

In matters of style Dvořák was neither conservative nor radical. His works display the influences of folk music, mainly Czech (furiant and dumky dance traits, polka rhythms, immediate repetition of an initial bar) but also ones that might equally be seen as American (pentatonic themes, flattened 7ths); Classical composers whom he admired, including Mozart, Haydn, Beethoven and Schubert; Wagner, whose harmony and use of leitmotifs attracted him; and his close friend Brahms (notably his piano writing and mastery of symphonic form). Despite his fascination with opera, he lacked a natural instinct for drama for all their admirable wit and lyricism, his last five stage works rank lower than his finest instrumental music. Here his predilection for classical procedures reached its highest level of achievement, notably in the epic Seventh Symphony, the most closely argued of his orchestral works, and the Cello Concerto, the crowning item in that instrument's repertory, with its characteristic richness and eloquence, as well as in the popular and appealing Ninth Symphony and the colourful Slavonic Dances and Slavonic Rhapsodies. Among his chamber works, landmarks are the String Sextet in A Op 48, a work in his national style which attracted particular attention abroad; the F minor Piano Trio Op 65, one of the climaxes of the more serious, classically 'Brahmsian' side of his output - unlike the E minor Op 90, a highly original series of dumka movements alternately brooding and spirited; the exuberant Op 81 Piano Quintet; and several of the string quartets, notably the popular 'American' Op 96, with its pentatonic leanings, and the two late works, the deeply felt op.106 in G and the warm and satisfying Op 105 in A flat.

Cello Concerto

Dvořák Cello Concerto **Tchaikovsky** Variations on a Rococo Theme, Op 33
Mstislav Rostropovich *vc* **Berlin Philharmonic Orchestra / Herbert von Karajan**
DG The Originals 447 413-2GOR (60 minutes: ADD) Ⓜ
Recorded 1968 **ooo**

This splendid disc offers a coupling that has justifiably held its place in the catalogue at full price (both on LP and CD) for over 30 years. The upper surface of the CD itself is made to look like a miniature reproduction of the original yellow label LP – complete with light reflecting off the simulated black vinyl surface. There have been a number of outstanding recordings of the Dvořák Concerto since this DG record was made, but none to match it for the warmth of lyrical feeling, the sheer strength of personality of the cello playing and the distinction of the partnership between Karajan and Rostropovich. Any moments of romantic licence from the latter, who is obviously deeply in love with the music, are set against Karajan's overall grip on the proceedings. The orchestral playing is superb. You have only to listen to the beautiful introduction of the secondary theme of the first movement by the Principal Horn to realise that the BPO is going to match its illustrious soloist in eloquence, while Rostropovich's many moments of poetic introspection never for a moment interfere with the sense of a spontaneous forward flow. The recording is as near perfect as any made by DG in that vintage analogue era. The CD transfer has freshened the original and gives the cello a highly realistic presence, and if the passionate *fortissimo* violins lose just a fraction in fullness, and there seems to be, comparably, just a slight loss of resonance in the bass, the sound picture has an impressively clear and vivid focus.

In the coupled Tchaikovsky *Rococo* Variations, Rostropovich uses the published score rather than the original version. However, he plays with such masterly Russian fervour and elegance that any criticism is disarmed. The music itself continually demonstrates Tchaikovsky's astonishing lyrical fecundity, as one tune leads to another, all growing organically from the charming 'rococo' theme. The recording here is marvellously refined. The description 'legendary' is not a whit too strong for a mid-price reissue of this calibre.

Dvořák Cello Concerto **Herbert** Cello Concerto No 2 in E minor, Op 30
Yo-Yo Ma *vc* **New York Philharmonic Orchestra / Kurt Masur**
Sony Classical SK67173 (61 minutes: DDD) Ⓕ
Recorded 1995

Ma's and Masur's version of the Dvořák is among the very finest, matched by few and outshining most, including Ma's own previous version with Maazel and the Berlin Philharmonic (also available on Sony Classical). It is fascinating to compare Ma's two versions, the newer one more readily conveying weight of expression despite the less spotlit placing of the soloist, more disciplined yet more spontaneous-sounding. This time Ma's expressiveness is simpler and more noble, and the recording (made in Avery Fisher Hall, New York), once a trouble-spot for engineers, is fuller and more open than the Berlin one, cleaner in tuttis, with only a touch of unwanted dryness on high violins. Ma and Masur together encompass the work's astonishingly full expressive range, making it the more bitingly dramatic with high dynamic contrasts. The Victor Herbert Concerto here receives a high-powered performance, but one which does not overload the romantic element with sentiment, whether in the brilliant and vigorous outer movements or in the warmly lyrical slow movement. Ma's use of rubato is perfectly judged, with the slow movement made the more tender at a flowing speed. The finale is then given a quicksilver performance, both brilliant and urgent. Herbert's concerto, first given in 1894, was almost certainly what prompted Dvořák to write his own concerto later that same year, triumphantly demonstrating the viability of the genre.

Additional recommendations

Cello Concerto

Coupling: Symphony No 9
Casals *vc* **Czech Philharmonic Orchestra / Szell**
Dutton CDEA5002 (74 minutes: ADD: 1/96) Ⓑ

Casals's legendary 1937 account of the Dvořak concerto, described at the time as 'seemingly played with a sword rather than a bow', still exercises a powerful effect. Szell's bitingly powerful performance of the New World makes this transfer particularly desirable.

Coupling: Elgar Cello Concerto.
Fournier *vc* **Berlin Philharmonic Orchestra / Szell; Wallenstein**
DG Galleria 423 881-2GGA (65 minutes: ADD: 11/88) Ⓜ

The third of Fournier's three accounts, and for some the most satisfying. Of the dozens of recordings of this work, this still stands as a first-class recommendation.

Couplings: **Bruch** *Kol Nidrei*. **Tchaikovsky** Variations on a Rococo Theme.
Starker *vc* **London Symphony Orchestra / Dorati**
Mercury Living Presence 432 001-2MM Ⓜ
(64 minutes: DDD: 3/91)

Janos Starker's admirers will not want to be without this issue, for there is much that is eloquent and moving in the Dvořák. The recorded sound a little harsh, though.

Couplings: **Saint-Saëns** Cello Concerto No 1. Le Carnival des animaux – excerpt. **Fauré** Elegie. Berceuse. **Ravel** Pièce en forme de habanera. **Debussy** Rêverie.
Fournier *vc* **Lush, Moore** *pfs* **Philharmonia / Kubelik; Susskind**
Testament SBT1016 (77 minutes: ADD: 7/93) Ⓕ

This is the first (1948) of Fournier's three recordings of the Dvořák. Here Fournier's customarily aristocratic, beautifully fashioned playing has in addition a quality of spirituality and strength of communication which lift his performance to great heights.

Coupling: Piano Concerto
Rostropovich *vc* **Maxián** *pf* **Czech Philharmonic Orchestra / Talich**
Supraphon Historical 11 1901-2 (77 minutes: ADD: 3/94) Ⓜ

A wonderful performance from a young Rostropovich under the veteran Vaclav Talich. Surely no other reading has quite the poignancy and depth of expression found here in a perfect combination of youth and experience.

Violin Concerto

Dvořák Violin Concerto in A minor, B108. Mazurek, B90 **Sarasate** Concert Fantasy on Carmen, Op 25. Zigeunerweisen, Op 20
Akiko Suwanai *vn* **Budapest Festival Orchestra / Iván Fischer**
Philips 464 531-2PH (55 minutes: DDD) Ⓕ
Recorded 1999 ●●●

No one could doubt the virtuoso flair of Akiko Suwanai the moment she starts playing Sarasate's *Zigeunerweisen*. This is just the sort of persuasive playing that this sequence of Liszt-inspired gypsy doodlings demands, if it is not to seem too long and self-indulgent. In 1990 Suwanai was the youngest-ever winner of the Tchaikovsky Competition in Moscow, and though she has made few discs she plainly has just the qualities to make her a magnetic recording artist.

As in *Zigeunerweisen*, so in the parallel Sarasate *Fantasy* based on Bizet's themes in *Carmen*, she uses the most daring dynamic and tonal range, in extreme *pianissimos* seeming to be communing with herself. In a big concert hall such an extreme would hardly project, but recording is different, and the result is magical, with the boldness of her rhythmic attack just as impressive.

Dvořák's dance-based *Mazurek* makes an apt and colourful link to the main work in which Suwanai is even more daring, urgent and volatile, than Maxim Vengerov. None of the artists on this disc may be Slavonic, but this is a version of the Violin Concerto which, at speeds on the fast side, notably in the finale, brings out the Slavonic flavours more vividly than ever, with Fischer and his superb Hungarian orchestra matching the fiery energy of the soloist.

Again this is a performance marked by daringly extreme *pianissimos*, notably in the opening statement of the main theme in the slow movement, a hushed meditation no less intense for being taken at a naturally flowing speed, bringing an overall timing a full two minutes less than in Vengerov's weightier version. The finale is marked *Allegro non troppo*, where you could well argue that Suwanai's very fast speed is a genuine *Presto*, relating the movement to the hectic fling of Dvořák's G minor *Slavonic Dance*. A marginally more relaxed speed – with Vengerov and others – allows more spring in the *furiant* rhythms, but the excitement of such a daring approach as Suwanai's is undeniable.

The recording is excellent, as we have come to expect of Philips issues from this source, with the soloist only marginally spotlit.

Dvořák Violin Concerto[a] **Elgar** Violin Sonata in E minor, Op 82[b]
Maxim Vengerov *vn* [b]**Revital Chachamov** *pf*
[a]**New York Philharmonic Orchestra / Kurt Masur**
Teldec 4509 96300-2 (58 minutes: DDD) Ⓕ
Recorded [b]1995 and [a]live in 1997 ●●●

This makes a winning coupling, unexpected though it may be. Maxim Vengerov, always an inspirational artist, gives positive, passionate performances of both works, finding a purposeful logic in music that can in lesser hands seem wayward. He is helped in the Dvořák Violin Concerto by being recorded live (in Avery Fisher Hall): though the orchestra sound a little congested, the violin is beautifully caught, the daringly wide dynamic and tonal range of Vengerov's playing on his 1723 Stradivarius being fully exploited. He is masterly in conveying the sharp changes of mood in this unconventionally shaped work, at one moment purposeful, at another deeply reflective. This, more than most rivals – even Tasmin Little and Itzhak Perlman – conveys an improvisational quality, intensifying the Slavonic flavours, making the music sparkle, bringing out the fun and fantasy.

The slow movement is yearningly beautiful, heartstoppingly tender thanks to Vengerov's use of the subtlest half-tones, while the finale is as light and resilient as a Slavonic dance. In this, Masur is the most sympathetic accompanist, persuading his American players to evoke the music's Czech flavours.

In some ways, particularly for the British listener, the Elgar Sonata is an even more exciting choice of work, and certainly it gives wonderful promise of what this inspired young virtuoso will do when he tackles the Elgar Violin Concerto, as surely he must. In the Sonata one finds a similarity of approach on an excellent rival version from Lydia Mordkovich on Chandos. Both artists naturally respond to the improvisational quality that, like the Concerto, the work's sharp changes of mood invite.

In the central *Andante*, the most elusive of the three movements, they make the music flow more easily than either Kennedy (at the beginning of his career) or Menuhin, finding plenty of fantasy, not least in the tricky little upward flourishes. Mordkovich may respond a little more readily to the elegiac quality of this late work, but Vengerov's big, bold manner in the outer movements brings out the music's masterfully testing original effects and sonorities which reflect the fact that Elgar was himself a violinist, loving what a violin can do.

The pianist, Revital Chachamov, makes an ideal partner, and the recording is nicely balanced. What a pity we have had to wait so long for these two outstanding performances, maybe because no one thought of putting them together sooner.

Additional recommendations
Violin Concerto
Coupling: Suk Fantasy
Suk *vn* **Czech Philharmonic Orchestra / Ançerl**
Supraphon SU1928-2 (69 minutes: ADD: 6/64[R]) Ⓜ
A distinguished performance from this all-Czech line-up.

Coupling: Romance in F minor
Perlman *vn* **London Philharmonic Orchestra / Barenboim**
EMI CDC7 47168-2 (45 minutes: ADD: 1/88) Ⓕ
A performance full of warmth, virtuosity and eloquence. The disc also has the benefit of this glorious *Romance*.

Coupling: **Lalo** Symphonie espagnole.
Tetzlaff *vn* **Czech Philharmonic Orchestra / Pešek**
Virgin Classics VM5 61910-2 (63 minutes: DDD) Ⓜ
What is remarkable about Tetzlaff's performances of both these works is the quicksilver lightness of the passagework, which brings out the element of fantasy.

Coupling: **Glazunov** Violin Concerto.
Zimmermann *vn* **London Philharmonic Orchestra / Welser-Möst**
EMI CDC7 54872-2 (52 minutes: DDD: 3/94) Ⓕ
A fresh, relatively lightweight rather than full-blown romantic approach marks Frank Peter Zimmermann's account out as a refreshing alternative to seriously consider.

Czech Suite

Czech Suite, B93. Festival March, B88. The Hero's Song, B199. Hussite, B132
Polish National Radio Symphony Orchestra / Antoni Wit
Naxos 8 553005 (65 minutes: DDD) Ⓢ
Recorded 1993-94

Wit's achievement, especially in *The Hero's Song*, is considerable. This colourful, rather sprawling tone-poem was Dvořák's last orchestral work and is not an easy piece to bring off. Wit finds genuine nobility in it, while his gentle, mellow way with the lovely *Czech Suite* also gives much pleasure. The opening 'Praeludium' is just a touch sleepy, but there is no want of lyrical affection or rhythmic bounce elsewhere and the whole performance radiates an idiomatic, old-world charm that really is most appealing. As for the *Hussite* overture, Wit's clear-headed reading impressively combines dignity and excitement. Given such finely disciplined orchestral playing, the results are again both eloquent and characterful. All of which just leaves the rousing *Festival March* of 1879, splendidly done here, with the excellent Katowice brass sounding resplendent in their introductory call-to-arms. Recordings throughout possess a most agreeable bloom and transparency.

Legends

Legends, B122. Nocturne in B, B47. Miniatures, B149. Prague Waltzes, B99
Budapest Festival Orchestra / Iván Fischer
Philips 464 647-2PH (68 minutes: DDD) Ⓕ
Recorded 1999 **OO**

Dvořák's 1881 *Legends* are like Brahmsian *Slavonic Dances* – intimate music, mostly reflective and invariably light-hearted. One might also think in terms of the scherzos from Dvořák's symphonic and chamber pieces, where elements of the dance are weighted with a certain gravitas. The eighth *Legend* occasionally anticipates the Seventh Symphony's *Scherzo*, and the sixth, parts of the Eighth Symphony. This is the Dvořák of woodland and foliage, eventful, piquantly scored and with generously nostalgic codas.

Iván Fischer has often professed a deep fondness for 'Dvořák miniatures', and his affection registers afresh in performances that combine certain old-style expressive devices (there are plentiful violin *portamentos*) with taut execution and acute feeling for the shape of a phrase. In the fourth, at the point where the main subject reappears on the strings (4'36"), Fischer grants unusual prominence to the trumpet counter-melody. The second's gorgeous opening shows the Budapest strings off to fine advantage, and the ninth's arched first subject benefits from Fischer's sense of musical line. Two of the best alternative versions – Kubelík on DG (indivisibly wedded to Dvořák's *Stabat mater*) and Karel Sejna (Supraphon) – are taken from analogue sources, whereas Jiri Bělohlávek's 1996 recording for the Czech label Clarton is, like Fischer's, captured in fine digital sound. Bělohlávek's strength lies primarily with the natural responses of his players, virtues that he harnesses in performances that are as warm and self-effacing as the music itself. Fischer is more of an ideas man, and if some of his charm sounds more applied than Bělohlávek's, that's not to suggest that it is in any way superficial or phoney. In short, Fischer's performances have real character. Sir Charles Mackerras and Raymond Leppard also run this new Philips release pretty close, though the Budapest orchestra's added flavouring is hard to resist.

The remainder of Fischer's programme is somewhat lighter, excepting the beautiful *Nocturne* which Dvořák re-worked from earlier chambermusic sources. Fischer's performance is seamless and fluid, noticeably swifter than Dorati's Detroit recording for Decca and just a fraction less sensitive. Choosing between the two inclines one marginally towards the Dorati, but in the case of the *Prague Waltzes*, Fischer's extra gaiety and panache win the day. He also makes a strong case for playing the 'Terzettos' for two violins and viola as 'miniatures' for an augmented version of the same instrumental combination. The first piece works particularly well.

No sensitive listener will fail to respond to this enchanting programme, especially as the playing and conducting are so consistently imaginative. To call it 'light' music is to court the misguided notion that the *Legends* (in particular) fail to tap our deeper responses. 'Gentle' would be a better word and, once you've taken the music to heart – which is not difficult – 'indispensable' would be another.

Additional recommendation
Legends
Coupling: Stabat mater.
English Chamber Orchestra / Kubelík; various artists
DG 453 025-2GTA2 ② (129 minutes: ADD: 8/77R) Ⓜ
Newly-minted conducting from a great Dvořákian, with the ECO responding to the manner born.

Slavonic Dances, B83 and B147

Cleveland Orchestra / George Szell
Sony Classical Essential Classics SBK48161 Ⓑ
(74 minutes: ADD)
Recorded 1963-65

This reissue is something of a revelation. Both discs have been lovingly remastered and the quality is an amazing improvement over the old LPs. The remastering engineers seem to have discovered a whole 'bottom octave' in the sound, which before had appeared to lack richness and weight to support the brilliant upper range. The *Slavonic Dances* are offered as Szell recorded them, with no repeats cut, so the phenomenal orchestral virtuosity is revealed in all its glory. There is much evidence of the conductor's many captivatingly affectionate touches of rubato and, throughout, this large orchestra follows Szell's every whim, with playing full of lyrical fervour and subtlety of nuance, wonderful precision and a lilting rhythmic pulse. The recordings were made within the acoustics of Cleveland's Severance Hall, usually a pair of dances at a time. The result is infectiously spontaneous and we cannot recommend this disc too highly; even if the close balance prevents any real *pianissimos* to register, the dynamic range of the music-making is still conveyed.

Slavonic Dances
Russian National Orchestra / Mikhail Pletnev
DG 447 056-2GH (72 minutes: DDD) Ⓕ
Recorded 1994 ●

Though Pletnev has Slavonic musicians, the results are not quite traditionally Czech, with refinement and crispness of ensemble the keynotes rather than earthier qualities. His is a distinctive and highly enjoyable version of Dvořák's colourful dances. These are, after all, works which for all their lack of pretension are open to all kinds of subtleties of interpretation, with different views totally valid. At times with such refined playing one might even dub Pletnev's approach as Mozartian, with elegance a regular element, and with even the wildest *furiants* kept under control. The crispness of ensemble and clarity of texture give a sharpness of focus that avoids any idea that these are performances lacking in bite, though after the Previn one might well feel they are on the cool side, with the extrovert joy of the music rather underplayed. So the *Dumka* lament of the second dance is lighter and cooler than with Previn, charming rather than warmly expressive. Dynamic contrasts are sharply defined through all the dances, and Pletnev and his Russian players consistently make one marvel at the beauty of the instrumentation.

Additional recommendations
Slavonic Dances
Czech Philharmonic Orchestra / Sejna
Supraphon SU1916-2 (72 minutes: ADD: 11/61R) Ⓜ
Sejna secures some wonderfully lithe and vivacious playing from his superb Czech band – an exhilarating treat.

Bavarian Radio Symphony Orchestra / Kubelík
DG The Originals 457 712-2GOR (71 minutes: ADD) Ⓜ
Inspirationally re-creative, scrupulously prepared performances under Kubelík's intensely charismatic direction.

Complete Symphonies

No 1 in C minor, B9, 'The Bells of Zlonice'; **No 2** in B flat, B12; **No 3** in E flat, B34; **No 4** in D minor, B41; **No 5** in F, B54; **No 6** in D, B112; **No 7** in D minor, B141; **No 8** in G, B163; **No 9** in E minor, B178, 'From the New World'

Symphonies Nos 1-9. Scherzo capriccioso, B131. Overtures – In nature's realm, B168; Carnival, B169; My home, B125*a*
London Symphony Orchestra / István Kertész
Decca ⑥ 430 046-2DC6 (431 minutes: ADD) Ⓑ
Recorded 1963-66 ●●

István Kertész recorded the Dvořák symphonies during the mid-1960s and his integral cycle was quick to achieve classic status, with his exhilarating and vital account of the Eighth Symphony rapidly becoming a special landmark in the catalogue. The original LPs, with their distinctive Bruegel reproduction sleeves are now collectors' items in their own right, but these magnificent interpretations became available again in 1992, in glitteringly refined digitally remastered sound, and it is a tribute to the memory of this tragically short-lived conductor that this cycle continues to set the standard by which all others are judged. Kertész was the first conductor to attract serious collectors to the early Dvořák symphonies which, even today are not performed as often as they should be; and his jubilant advocacy of the unfamiliar First Symphony, composed in the composer's twenty-fourth year, has never been superseded. This work offers surprising insights into the development of Dvořák's mature style, as does the Second Symphony. Kertész shows that Symphonies Nos 3 and 4 have much more earthy resilience than many commentators might have us believe, insisting that Dvořák's preoccupation with the music of Wagner and Liszt had reached its zenith during this period. The challenging rhetoric of the Fourth has never found a more glorious resolution than here, with Kertész drawing playing of quite gripping intensity from the London Symphony Orchestra.

The Fifth Symphony, and to a still greater extent, its glorious successor, Symphony No 6, both reveal Dvořák's clear affinity with the music of Brahms. Kertész's superb reading of the Sixth, however, shows just how individual and naturally expressive this underrated work actually is, whilst the playing in the great climax of the opening movement and the vigorous final peroration remains tremendously exciting, even almost 30 years after the recording first appeared. In the great final trilogy, Kertész triumphs nobly with the craggy resilience of the Seventh Symphony, and his buoyant ardour brings a dynamic thrust and momentum to the Eighth Symphony, whereas his *New World* is by turns indomitable and searchingly lyrical. The six-disc set also offers assertive and brilliant readings of the Overtures *Carnival*, *In nature's realm* and the rarely heard *My home*, together with a lucid and heroic account of the *Scherzo capriccioso*.

These definitive performances have been skilfully reprocessed, the sound is astonishingly good, even by modern standards, and the playing of the London Symphony Orchestra is often daringly brilliant under the charismatic direction of one of this century's masters of the podium.

Additional recommendations

Complete Symphonies

Coupling: Carnival Overture. The Wood Dove. Scherzo capriccioso.

Berlin Philharmonic Orchestra; Bavarian Radio Symphony Orchestra / Kubelík

DG 463 158-2GB6 ⑥ (425 minutes: ADD: 10/88) Ⓑ

Kubelík's accounts of the last three symphonies have long been highly praised for their freshness, natural lyrical warmth and lack of self-conscious idiosyncrasy and the earlier works show much the same qualities.

Symphonies Nos 1-3

Philips Duo 446 527-2PM2 ② (140 minutes: ADD: 3/96) Ⓜ

Symphonies Nos 4-6

Coupling: Hussite. My Home.

Philips Duo 446 530-2PM2 ② (149 minutes: ADD: 3/96) Ⓜ

Symphonies Nos 7-9

Coupling: Legends

Philips Duo 456 327-2PM2 ② Ⓜ

(158 minutes: ADD: 1/70R, 3/73R)

London Symphony Orchestra / Rowicki, London Philharmonic Orchestra / Leppard

Plentiful character, infectious dedication and trenchant symphonic strength are the hallmarks of Rowicki's underrated cycle, one of the unsung treasures of the Philips catalogue.

Symphonies Nos 3

Vienna Philharmonic Orchestra / Myung-Whun Chung

DG 449 207-2GH (71 minutes: DDD) Ⓕ

Recorded 1995 ◉

An impressive coupling. Myung-Whun Chung takes an affectionately fleet-of-foot view of the Third Symphony. With the Vienna Philharmonic on their toes throughout (and audibly enjoying themselves), Chung's reading is notable for its newly minted freshness and intelligent sense of proportion. So we find that the opening *Allegro moderato* emerges in shapely, sensitive fashion, yet with no lack of cumulative intensity at its close. In the ideally flowing slow movement Chung locates both dignity and drama. Again, phrasing is always imaginative and thoughtful, while the stately central processional has never sounded more luminously refined. The performance of the Seventh is an interpretation of red-blooded fervour and rugged contrasts, whose dramatic impact is greatly heightened by the burnished glow of the VPO's contribution, to say nothing of DG's enormously ripe close-knit sound. In Chung's pungently characterful, ever flexible hands, the first movement progresses with pleasing dignity and purpose, nowhere more striking than in the coda where his decision not to press ahead too soon pays handsome dividends. Equally, Chung sees to it that the sublime second subject really takes wing both times round, the Viennese warmth and charm much in evidence. The succeeding *Poco adagio* is distinctive, with an almost Brucknerian hush and concentration. Whatever Chung's *Scherzo* slightly lacks in home-grown, idiomatic lilt, the arresting vigour and clean-limbed transparency of the playing provide fair compensation. What's more, the anxious Trio is voiced with unusual clarity, its many subtle details set in bold relief. The storm-tossed finale is magnificent, a conception of irresistible rigour and muscular conviction.

Symphony No 5

Symphony No 5. Othello, B174. Scherzo capriccioso

Oslo Philharmonic Orchestra / Mariss Jansons

EMI CDC7 49995-2 (64 minutes: DDD) Ⓕ

Recorded 1989 ◉

Of all the romantic composers, it is probably Dvořák who best evokes a sunlit, unspoiled and relatively untroubled picture of 19th century country life. Light and warmth radiate from his Fifth Symphony, composed in just six weeks when he was in his early thirties. It has been called his 'Pastoral Symphony', and it is easy to see why, especially in a performance as fresh and sunny as this. Mariss Jansons brings out the expressiveness and heart of the music without exaggerating the good spirits and playful humour that are so characteristic of the composer, and one would single out for praise the fine wind playing of the Oslo Philharmonic Orchestra (and not least its golden-toned horns) were it not for the fact that the strings are no less satisfying. The lyrical *Andante con moto* brings out the fine interplay of the instrumental writing, the bouncy *Scherzo* is uninhibited without going over the top and the exciting finale has plenty of momentum. The other two pieces are nicely done, the *Scherzo capriccioso* having both lilt and vigour and the rarely played *Othello* overture (a late work) being a suitably dramatic response to Shakespeare's tragedy. The recording is warm and clear.

Additional recommendation

Symphony No 5

Coupling: Three Slavonic Rhapsodies

Czech Philharmonic Orchestra / Sejna

Supraphon SU1917-2 (75 minutes: ADD: 4/58R) Ⓜ

Irreproachably idiomatic music-making, evincing both tingling vitality and fresh-faced wonder – a classic, life-enhancing document.

Symphony No 6

Symphony No 6. The wild dove

Czech Philharmonic Orchestra / Jiří Bělohlávek

Chandos CHAN9170 (63 minutes: DDD) Ⓕ

Recorded 1992

Bělohlávek has referred to his Czech orchestra's 'singing art of playing' and its 'mellow sound' and it is indeed Bohemia's woods, fields and wildlife, rather than energetic village green festivities, that linger in the memory here. Perhaps you shouldn't expect a Czech Philharmonic performance to 'go' or leap about excitedly in the manner of Kertész's with the LSO; in these days of high adrenalin, high contrast and high definition, there's a lot to be said for a less assertive and vigorous approach, always artlessly sung, and for this orchestra's Old World timbres a Brahmsian fireside glow, for example, to the Symphony's first movement second subject on cellos and horns (beautifully eased in by Bělohlávek). These horns, always more rounded in tone than their rasping counterparts in London (Kertész), bear an obvious family resemblance to the woodwind, not only in timbre, but also in the use of vibrato (again, that 'singing art of playing'). And the 'silver moon' flute is one of this disc's principal joys. Bělohlávek also projects the drama of *The wild dove* with relish. Chandos, as ever, guarantees a sepia-toned warmth throughout.

Symphonies Nos 6 and 8
Vienna Philharmonic Orchestra / Myung-Whun Chung
DG 469 046-2GH (77 minutes: DDD) Ⓕ
Recorded 1999 **OO**

Drawing playing of infectious eagerness and disarming poise from his distinguished band, Myung-Whun Chung directs an exhilaratingly purposeful and memorably fresh account of the Sixth. The wonderful opening *Allegro non tanto* at once sets the template for Chung's mobile, yet affectionately pliant approach. Unfortunately there's no repeat, but, by way of compensation, Chung does impart a riveting expectancy to the start of the development section: try from the *sempre molto tranquillo* marking at bar 191 (3'49") through to fig D (4'50") – just one of many paragraphs that readily stir the imagination. Likewise, the succeeding *Adagio* enshrines an unusually flowing conception, though there's no gainsaying the flexibility and poetry of Chung's conducting, not to mention the chamber-like intimacy and concentration of the VPO's sublimely poised response (such heart-warming *dolce* tone from the first violins).

Chung's *Scherzo* must be just about the swiftest on disc. With the VPO absolutely on its toes, the effect is undeniably exciting, though more of those delicious *ben marcato* violas cutting through the texture at 0'40", 1'52" and 6'03" would have been welcome. On the other hand, Chung's dare-devil tempo does throw into sharper relief both the blissful innocence of the *Trio* (with its sublime piccolo writing) as well as the deceptively relaxed launch pad of the finale. The latter movement is paced to perfection, its giddy coda as thrillingly judged as any. In fact Chung's Sixth is the best we've had in years, meriting a place way up there alongside the likes of Kubelík, Rowicki and Ančerl.

Chung's earlier Gothenburg SO Eighth for BIS was full of good things, but this April 1999 remake operates at an altogether higher level of intensity. The first movement is a generously moulded, spontaneous-sounding affair, its sunshine and storm gauged with arresting flair. The slow movement, though not as distinctive as Harnoncourt's 'back to nature' restoration, is very fine indeed, its dark-hued eloquence counterbalanced by a touching lyrical simplicity. Elsewhere, the *Allegretto grazioso* is a great success, its *Trio* etched with open-mouthed wonder, while the scampering coda fairly chortles with mischief. The finale, too, brings plenty of incident, not least that grandly theatrical *ritenuto* for the trombones' four-bar flourish at fig M or 4'45" (by no means the only instance where memories of Talich and Kubelík came flooding back).

DG's sound is immensely ripe and full-bodied, this great orchestra's burnished glow and mahogany-like timbre exceptionally well captured. However, some tuttis (especially in the Eighth) may fall a little too aggressively on the ears for some tastes, and at times the ample Musikverein acoustic precludes the last ounce of clarity. No matter, Chung's remains a cherishable pairing overall.

Additional recommendation
Symphony No 6
Coupling: Symphony No 7
Czech Philharmonic Orchestra / Sejna
Supraphon SU1918-2 (74 minutes: ADD: 6/54[R]) Ⓜ
Sejna's Sixth remains a miracle of joyous musicality and endearing spontaneity; the Seventh is less compelling, though still cherishable.

Coupling: Hussite. My Home. Carnival
Czech Philharmonic Orchestra / Ançerl
Supraphon 11 1926-2 (75 minutes: ADD) Ⓜ
One of the most distinguished versions of a simply glorious symphony, intelligent observation and purposeful thrust in perfect accord.

The Wild Dove
Coupling: The Water Goblin. The Noon Witch. The Golden Spinning-Wheel
Czech Philharmonic Orchestra / Chalabala
Supraphon SU3056-2 (80 minutes: ADD) Ⓜ
Extraordinarily atmospheric readings, full of narrative flair – *The Water Goblin* enjoys particularly fervent advocacy.

Symphony No 7

Symphonies Nos 7-9[a]. Symphonic Variations, B70[b]
[a]Concertgebouw Orchestra; [b]London Symphony Orchestra / Sir Colin Davis
Philips Duo ② 438 347-2PM2 (139 minutes: ADD) Ⓜ
Recorded [a]1977-78, [b]1968 **OO**

Colin Davis's magnificent Amsterdam Dvořák Seventh remains one of the most compellingly taut available: gloriously played and paced to perfection, it has a dark, searing intensity wholly apt for this, the Czech master's most tragic utterance; certainly, only a select handful of rivals on disc have matched this performance's irresistible symphonic drive. The Eighth is excellent, too: it is notable for its keen vigour, textural transparency and unfailing sense of purpose – only a little more nudging affection might not have gone amiss. Davis's finely-sculpted *New World* (first-movement repeat included) is another powerful, involving affair – the sublimely articulate orchestral response alone ensures enormous pleasure. Although not as endearingly flexible or evocative a reading as some would prefer, Davis's directness is always refreshing and never brusque. The result: an impressively cogent, concentrated conception. Apart from some distractingly close balancing in the finale of No 8, all three symphonies are blessed with Philips engineering of the highest analogue quality. Davis's 1968 version of the masterly *Symphonic Variations* is very fine: sounding admirably fresh still, it's an effective and unfussy rendering.

Symphony No 7. Nocturne in B, B47.
The water goblin
Czech Philharmonic Orchestra / Jiří Bělohlávek
Chandos CHAN9391 (69 minutes: DDD) Ⓕ
Recorded 1992

Bělohlávek is a lucid, sure-footed guide through Dvořák's mightiest symphonic utterance, and his sympathetic direction combines both warm-hearted naturalness as well as total fidelity to the score (dynamics are scrupulously attended to throughout). If it sounds just a little under-energized next to other vividly dramatic accounts, the sheer unforced eloquence and lyrical fervour of the playing always give enormous pleasure. Certainly, the first movement's secondary material glows with affectionate warmth, whilst the sublime *Poco adagio* emerges seamlessly, its songful rapture and nostalgic vein captured as to the manner born by this great orchestra (listen out for some gorgeous work from the principal flute, clarinet and horn). The *Scherzo* trips along with an infectious, rhythmic spring, as well as an engaging poise and clarity; moreover, the dark-hued unsettling Trio (a casualty in so many rival performances) is handled with equal perception. The finale, too, is immensely pleasing, marrying symphonic thrust with weighty rhetoric rather in the manner of Colin Davis's distinguished Amsterdam account. The closing bars are very broad and imposing indeed. All in all, a performance of considerable dignity and no mean stature, benefiting from vibrant Chandos engineering. The symphony is followed by a long-breathed, slumbering account of the *Nocturne* (gloriously played by the Czech PO strings) and the disc concludes with a fine *Water goblin*. Again, the orchestral response is as disciplined and poised as you could hope to hear.

Additional recommendation
Symphonic Variations
Coupling: Carnival. The Water Goblin. Scherzo capriccioso. Hussite. My Home. The Noon Witch. Othello. The Golden Spinning-Wheel. In Nature's Realm
London Symphony Orchestra / Kertész
Decca Double ② 452 946-2DF2 Ⓜ
(156 minutes: ADD: 8/98)
Superb performances; snap them up at mid price.

Symphony No 8

Symphony No 8. The wood dove
Scottish National Orchestra / Neeme Järvi
Chandos CHAN8666 (57 minutes: DDD) Ⓕ
Recorded 1987

Neeme Järvi and the SNO's account of the Eighth Symphony underlines the expressive warmth of the piece, the rhapsodic freedom of invention rather than any symphonic tautness. That the result seems so warm and natural is due above all to the responsiveness of the SNO players who seem to feel Järvi's wonderfully free rubato and affectionate moulding of phrase with collective spontaneity. It is a joy to have the sort of rubato that you expect from a solo performer so freshly transferred to the orchestra, with such precision and without any feeling of mannerism, not even of the kind that Karajan's comparable moulding with the Berlin Philharmonic sometimes induces. The score, of course, to take an obvious example, is marked *allegro con brio* from the first bar, and anyone wanting a more firmly structured reading will be happier with a version such as the Davis/Philips. But Järvi is here doing no more than follow a long-established performing tradition, and one which in a performance such as his – always purposeful, marked by strong dramatic contrasts – hardly sounds wayward, persuasive rather. Though he allows himself fair breadth, Järvi's speeds are never eccentric. The finale is marginally slower than usual, but Järvi's relaxation goes with a control of tension that almost suggests the telling of a story, easy and natural in its sharp changes of mood. In all four movements the incidental delights are many, with charm a regular ingredient.

In *The wood dove*, as in the symphony, Järvi's feeling for the rhapsodic side of Dvořák's invention makes for a persuasive performance, warm and colourful. The Chandos sound has a characteristic bloom.

Symphonies Nos 8 and 9
Berlin Philharmonic Orchestra / Rafael Kubelík
DG The Originals 447 412-2GOR (73 minutes: ADD) Ⓜ
Recorded 1972

These accounts are quite magnificent and their claims on the allegiance of collectors remain strong. Their freshness and vigour remind one of what it was like to hear these symphonies for the first time. The atmosphere is authentic in feeling and the sense of nature seems uncommonly acute. Kubelík has captured the enthusiasm of his players and generates a sense of excitement and poetry. The playing of the Berlin Philharmonic is marvellously eloquent and, as is often the case, a joy in itself. The woodwinds phrase with great poetic feeling and imagination, and all the departments of this great orchestra respond with sensitivity and virtuosity. The recording has great dynamic range and encompasses the most featherweight string *pianissimos* to the fullest orchestral tutti without discomfort. The listener is placed well back in the hall so that the woodwind, though they blend beautifully, may seem a little too recessed for some tastes, though it should be said that there is no lack of vividness, power or impact. The balance and the timbre of each instrument is natural and truthful; nothing is made larger than life and Kubelík has a natural warmth and flexibility. This will remain high on any list of recommendations for it has a vernal freshness that is wholly reviving.

Additional recommendations

Symphony No 8

Coupling: Cello Concerto[a]

Halle Orchestra / Barbirolli

[a]Tortelier *vc* **[a]London Symphony Orchestra / [a]Previn**

HMV Classics HMV5 73454-2 (75 minutes: ADD: 5/79[R]) Ⓢ

The Eighth shows the inimitable Halle/Barbirolli partnership at its most inspirationally fresh. Here is truly life-enhancing, hugely spontaneous music-making.

Coupling: The Noon Witch.

Concertgebouw / Harnoncourt

Teldec 3984 24487-2 (51 minutes: DDD: 12/99) Ⓕ

A typical Harnoncourt interpretation with a freshness of approach and attention to colour and detail that spell winner.

Symphony No 9

Symphony No 9[a]. American Suite[b]

[a]Vienna Philharmonic Orchestra / Kyrill Kondrashin; [b]Royal Philharmonic Orchestra / Antál Dorati

Decca 430 702-2DM (63 minutes: DDD) Ⓜ

Recorded 1979-83

Kondrashin's *New World* caused something of a sensation when originally transferred to CD. Here was a supreme example of the clear advantages of the new medium over the old and the metaphor of a veil being drawn back between listener and performers could almost be extended to a curtain: the impact and definition of the sound is really quite remarkable and the acoustics of the Sofiensaal in Vienna are presented as ideal for this score. The upper strings have brilliance without edginess, the brass – with characteristically bright VPO trumpets – has fine sonority as well as great presence, the bass is firm, full and rich and the ambience brings luminosity and bloom to the woodwind without clouding.

Symphony No 9[a].

Slavonic Dances B83: No 6 in D, No 8 in G minor; B147: No 2 in E minor

New York Philharmonic Orchestra / Kurt Masur

Apex 85738 1085-2 (60 minutes: DDD) Ⓢ

Recorded in [a]1991 ●

Although Avery Fisher Hall's notoriously unhelpful acoustic is reflected in the relatively dry sound, the Teldec engineers have done wonders in giving it not only a fair bloom but in conveying an extreme dynamic range. The slow movement of this performance is particularly fine, with *pianissimos* that have you catching your breath.

Anyone who has ever attended a recording session of this repertory work will know what problems are created by the need to get the woodwind chords precise enough at the start of both the first two movements. It is a tribute to Masur and the players that a live performance – apparently taken from one concert and not edited from other sources, unless it was a previous rehearsal – should achieve a precision of ensemble to rival that of a studio performance. The slow movement is outstanding, with Masur's very straight, simple phrasing conveying an emotional intensity quite as deep as with a more overtly expressive style.

Masur's very direct manner in the fast movements brings strong, dramatic results, but with very forward sound, and with percussion standing out (the timpani almost deafening at times) the results may be too aggressive for some. Though phrasing is sympathetic, and Masur allows a natural easing for the third theme in the first movement, this is not among the warmer readings of this much recorded work. Yet with an attractive coupling of three Slavonic Dances winningly done, ending with the best-known of all, the G minor Furiant, B83 (Op 46) No 8, it makes a valuable addition to what might be counted an over-long list. Masur does incidentally, even in this live performance, observe the exposition repeat in the first movement.

Dvořák Symphony No 9. American Suite in A, B190

Smetana Má vlast – Vltava

Prague Symphony Orchestra / Libor Pešek

Classic fM The Full Works 75605 57043-2 Ⓜ

(71 minutes: DDD). Recorded 1998

Symphony No 9. The Water Goblin, Op 107

Royal Concertgebouw Orchestra / Nikolaus Harnoncourt

Teldec 3984-25254-2 (64 minutes: DDD) Ⓕ

Recorded live in October 1999 ●

Harnoncourt has some distinguished Concertegbouw forebears, not least structure-conscious Sir Colin Davis and combustible Antál Dorati (both Philips). This, though, beats them all. Auspicious happenings register within the first few pages: carefully drawn woodwind lines; basses that calm meticulously from fierce *fortissimo* to tense *pianissimo*; provocative bassoons and an effortless passage into the lovely flute melody at 2'58". At the start of the development section *piano* violins really are played *leggiero* (lightly), a significant detail that most rivals gloss over. The exposition repeat is taken and, more unusually, is the *Scherzo*'s repeat after the *Trio*. Middle and lower voices (bassoons, violas, horns) are granted their full flavour and the violin desks are divided. Harnoncourt's *Largo* is something of a minor miracle – take the string passage three minutes in and the gently stressed second-violin line at 3'06". Undulating clarinets register against shimmering string *tremolandos* and, beyond the beautifully judged approach to the *Meno* passage (bar 78), you suddenly hear quiet second-violin *pizzicato* chords (7'00") that you almost never notice in concert. The *Scherzo*'s tight *staccato* really dances and, as elsewhere, dynamics are fastidiously graded. The finale itself never sags, and for the home strait Harnoncourt treads a course somewhere between the printed *Allegro con fuoco* and the expressive broadening that Dvořák later sanctioned. The closing bars are played with epic resolve. Most admirable about Harnoncourt's Dvořák is its close proximity to nature: barely a minute passes that isn't somewhere touched by verdure or sunshine.

Compared to Pešek's earlier recording with the Royal Liverpool Philharmonic, his Prague Symphony re-make is faster, fresher and more spontaneous. Again, the first-movement repeat is observed and while some speeds catch the Prague players sounding somewhat hard-pressed (the first movement's development and part of the *Scherzo* are a mite breathless) a compensating sense of excitement suits the impulsive nature of the music. Pesek's 10'12" *Largo* is at times more like a *Larghetto* (Harnoncourt clocks up 12'17") but the mood is right (more elegiac than solemn) and the finale is full of vigour. For recording quality, Teldec yields the greater warmth, Classic FM the sharper 'edge'.

For the couplings, Harnoncourt gives us *The Water Goblin*, the most folk-like of Dvořák's Erben tone-poems where, as in the Symphony, middle voices (in this case ominous and darkly shaded) rise to the fore and the stamping outer sections are played with great rhythmic bite. Pešek makes winsome music of the lovely *American Suite*, adding a forthright 'Vltava' (faster by a minute than his Liverpool recording) into the bargain. First-timers will find nothing to complain about here, but if you think that you know the *New World* back-to-front then Harnoncourt will have you thinking again.

Additional recommendations

Symphony No 9

Coupling: Othello. In Nature's Realm.

Czech Philharmonic Orchestra / Ançerl

Supraphon SU1927-2 (70 minutes: ADD) Ⓕ

A truly great, remarkably unforced interpretation, consistently illuminating and displaying an iron grip unmatched on disc.

Coupling: Carnival. Smetana The Bartered Bride – Overture. Weinberger Schwanda the Bagpiper – excerpts.

Chicago Symphony Orchestra / Reiner

RCA Living Stereo 09026 62587-2 Ⓜ
(64 minutes: ADD: 8/95)

This legendary partnership gives a delectably fresh, exquisitely poised *New World* – ravishing Chicago strings in the Largo.

Piano Quintet in A

Piano Quintet in A, B155a. Piano Quartet No 2 in E flat, B162

András Schiff *pf* **Panocha Quartet** (Jiří Panocha, aPavel Zejfart *vns* Miroslav Sehnoutka *va* Jaroslav Kulhan *vc*)

Teldec 0630-17142-2 (72 minutes: DDD) Ⓕ
Recorded 1997

The ease of musical passage in Dvořák's Second Piano Quartet was confirmed by the composer himself, who once confessed that the melodies positively 'surged' upon him. Indeed, the endless cello line that opens the second movement would have done even Wagner proud (in principle if not in style) and the dramatic opening *Allegro con fuoco* is similarly well endowed in terms of melody. Any sensitive listener sampling the first movement's haunting coda will encounter some of the most ravishing modulations in the whole of Dvořák's voluminous output. András Schiff and the Panocha Quartet seem acutely alive to most of this varied musical incident. Articulation is crisp (especially from the pianist) and the general approach is rhythmically alert, with lively characterization all round in the 'folky' finale. The better-known Second Piano Quintet is rather more relaxed, though Schiff's detail-studded playing again engages one's interest and the important first-movement repeat allows us a few seconds' worth of extra music that most rival versions omit. Generally, the pianist has the strongest musical voice; very occasionally with the Panocha inner voices could be more clearly defined.

Piano Quintet in A, B155. String Quintet in G, B49

Gaudier Ensemble (Marieke Blankestijn, Lesley Hatfield *vns* Iris Juda *va* Christoph Marks *vc* Stephen William *db* Susan Tomes *pf*)

Hyperion CDA66796 (66 minutes: DDD) Ⓕ
Recorded 1995

The pianist here is Susan Tomes, who matches even Pressler in imagination, encouraging a performance lighter than that for DG, full of mercurial contrasts that seem entirely apt. For example, in the second movement *Dumka* there is more light and shade, and the *Scherzo* sparkles even more, leading to a jaunty, exuberant finale. The G major String Quintet, the earliest of the two which Dvořák wrote, the one with extra double-bass, is similarly lighter than the Chilingirian Quartet on Chandos. The Chilingirian is just as strongly characterised as the Gaudier, with a firmer, fuller tone. Marieke Blankestijn's violin is thinner than Levon Chilingirian's, but it can be just as beautiful, as in the lovely high-floating second subject of the slow movement. A fine disc.

Piano Quintet[a]. Piano Quartet No 2 in E flat, B162

Menahem Pressler *pf* **Emerson Quartet** (Eugene Drucker, [a]Philip Setzer *vns* Lawrence Dutton *va* David Finckel *vc*)

DG 439 868-2GH (75 minutes: DDD) Ⓕ
Recorded 1993

If the Piano Quintet with its wealth of memorable melody is by far the better-known, Pressler and the Emersons demonstrate how the Piano Quartet, sketched immediately after the other work and completed two years later in 1889, is just as rich in invention and in some ways even more distinctive in its thematic material. If there is one movement that above all proves a revelation, it is the *Lento* of the Quartet. Opening with a duet for cello and piano, it is here played with a rapt, hushed concentration to put it among the very finest of Dvořák inspirations. The performance of the Quintet, too, is comparably positive in its characterization. Many will prefer the easier, even warmer reading from Domus in the Piano Quartet, which is neatly if not so generously coupled with the much earlier Piano Quartet in D, B53. In this music it is not always the high-powered reading that makes its mark most persuasively, and the Hyperion sound for Domus is far warmer than the DG New York recording for this disc, which gives an unpleasant edge to high violins, making the full ensemble rather abrasive. None the less, if the volume is curbed, one can readily enjoy these passionate and intense accounts of two of Dvořák's most striking chamber works.

String Quintet in G

String Quintets – G, B49; E flat, B180.
Intermezzo in B, B49
Chilingirian Quartet (Levon Chilingirian, Mark Butler *vns* Louise Williams *va* Philip De Groote *vc*); **Simon Rowland-Jones** *va* **Duncan McTier** *db*
Chandos CHAN9046 (69 minutes: DDD) Ⓕ
Recorded 1990-91

Dvořák's G major String Quintet is thoroughly engaging. Originally in five movements, Dvořák subsequently removed the 'Intermezzo' second movement, revising and publishing it separately eight years later as the haunting *Nocturne* for string orchestra. Enterprisingly, this Chandos disc includes that 'Intermezzo' in its original string quintet garb. The E flat Quintet from 1893, on the other hand, is a wholly mature masterpiece. Completed in just over two months during Dvořák's American sojourn, it replaces the double-bass of the earlier Quintet with the infinitely more subtle option of a second viola. Brimful of the most delightfully fresh, tuneful invention, the score also shares many melodic and harmonic traits with the popular *American* Quartet – its immediate predecessor. The Chilingirian Quartet, ideally abetted by double-bassist Duncan McTier and violist Simon Rowland-Jones, are enthusiastic, big-hearted proponents of all this lovely material, and the excellent Chandos recording offers both a realistic perspective and beguiling warmth.

Additional recommendation
String Quintet in G
Coupling: Serenade, Op 44.
Lincoln Center Chamber Music Society / Shifrin
Delos DE3152 (66 minutes: DDD: 8/95) Ⓕ

A strongly communicative, memorably perceptive reading of a marvellous work, expertly engineered into the bargain.

Piano Quartets

Piano Quartets – No 1 in D, B53; No 2 in E flat, B162
Domus (Krysia Osostowicz *vn* Timothy Boulton *va* Richard Lester *vc* Susan Tomes *pf*)
Hyperion CDA66287 (70 minutes: DDD) Ⓕ
Recorded 1987

These are two very enjoyable works. Hans Keller's description of the opening pages of the E flat Quartet as 'childish' is staggering – this from the leading campaigner against 'posthumous critical torture'! Childlike would be much more suitable, and this appealing characteristic is well brought out by the members of Domus: Susan Tomes's descent from incisive *fortissimo* clarity to *pianissimo* mystery in the opening bars is a delight, and fully prophetic of the kind of musicianship we're to hear. Two other unforgettable moments from this performance: the lovely return of the first movement second subject, with its heart-easing B major/E flat major modulation – very sensitive use of rubato here – and cellist Richard Lester's richly expressive solos at the beginning of the *Lento*. The D major Quartet is a delightful, if not fully mature piece – it does tend to rely rather heavily on sequence and repetition. Domus makes sure we don't miss any of its virtues, but it doesn't force anything: the timing in the magical opening shift from D major to B major is finely judged, and Dvořák's wonderfully effortless melodies are affectionately shaped and shaded; admirable too the way Susan Tomes finds so much beauty in what often looks like conventionally decorative piano writing. In general the sound is very pleasing, intimate enough to draw one right into the performances without being intimidating, even in the somewhat histrionic second theme of the E flat Quartet's *Lento*. A richly rewarding disc.

Piano Quartet No 2 in E flat, B162[a]. Violin Sonatina in G, B183[b]. Four Romantic Pieces, B150[b]
Isaac Stern *vn* [a]**Jaime Laredo** *va* [a]**Yo-Yo Ma** *vc* [a]**Emanuel Ax**, [b]**Robert McDonald** *pfs*
Sony Classical SK62597 (69 minutes: DDD) Ⓕ
Recorded 1996 ○

This Sony production of the great E flat Piano Quartet fully matches the rival Schiff/Panocha recording (recorded later but released earlier), although it is perhaps rather less natural in terms of overall aural perspective: Sony's close-miked recorded balance is in contrast to the recital-hall sound stage favoured by Teldec.

Schiff is a more colourful player than Emanuel Ax (occasionally to the point of affectation), but Ax's crisp, dancing pianism is just as effective and his handling of the assertive episodes in the first two movements never stints on drama. The Czech strings are marginally sweeter than their American counterparts, the Americans more gently inflected, whereas Yo-Yo Ma's handling of the winding melody that opens the second movement has an achromatic, inward quality that is uniquely distinctive. Schiff's recording honours the finale's repeat (Ax's doesn't) but neither team opts to play the long exposition repeat in the first movement.

Teldec's near-ideal coupling of Dvořák's Second Piano Quintet – also the choice of

Menahem Pressler with the Emerson Quartet – will please economy-conscious collectors who require the two masterpieces on the same CD. Domus and Josef Suk offer the likeable but less memorable First Piano Quartet. Both discs feature fine performances (Domus's is the more intimately stated option), but it would be a great shame to miss out on Stern's Indian summer recordings of the two violin works, especially as Robert McDonald's accompaniments are models of discreet musical reportage.The piano parts of either work have never been more perceptively played, though Stern's melding of impishness and tonal chastity is no less seductive. A sparing use of *portamento* signals his vintage pedigree, though expressive overkill is never on the agenda. Only the Sonatina's *Scherzo* might have benefited from being pushed up a notch or two in tempo (it is after all marked *molto vivace*), but the *Larghetto* is most poetically addressed, and the last of the *Romantic Pieces* tellingly sustained. True, the tonal grain in Stern's playing was tougher a few years earlier, but the gain in wisdom and repose more than compensates.

Complete String Quartets

No 1 in A, B8; **No 2** in B flat, B17; **No 3** in D, B18; **No 4** in E minor, B19; **No 5** in F minor, B37; **No 6** in A minor, B40; **No 7** in A minor, B45; **No 8** in E, B57; **No 9** in D minor, B75; **No 10** in E flat, B92; **No 11** in C, B121; **No 12** in F, B179, 'American'; **No 13** in G, B192; **No 14** in A flat, B193

String Quartets Nos 1-14; F, B120 (Fragment). Cypresses, B152. Quartettsatz. Two Waltzes, B105
Prague Quartet (Břetislav Novotny, Karel Přibyl *vns* Lubomír Malý *va* Jan Sírc *vc*)
DG ⑨ 463 165-2GB9 (589 minutes: ADD) Ⓑ
Recorded 1975-77 ∞

Like Schubert, Dvořák turned to the string quartet early in his career. The three complete quartets included in Vol 1 (Nos 1-3) show considerable facility in writing for strings (after all, Dvořák was a violinist), but it took him some time to arrive at a fully idiomatic quartet style: the first movement of No 2 for instance wouldn't lose much by being orchestrated. Dvořák also had to learn to rein in his natural expansiveness: the Third Quartet spins out its modest material to an astonishing 70 minutes – the first movement alone is longer than the whole American Quartet! The outer movements of the No 4 in E minor (Vol 2) show him concentrating admirably, though the later shortened version of the central *Andante religioso* is a considerable improvement. So the interest of Vol 1 (three discs) is largely musicological. Despite this, with playing so fresh and authoritative even the impossibly long-winded Third Quartet has rewards to offer. Each performance has a strong sense of purpose, but that doesn't mean an inability to enjoy all those charming Dvořákian byways. Technically the playing is admirable, though you may be surprised at the scrunch at the climax of No 1's slow movement – very untypical. Nevertheless, the enjoyment increases strongly through Vol 2. The violin cavatina in the *Andante* of the Fifth Quartet has just the right gentle lilt – recommended to the unconverted. Listening to the Prague in the fine first movement of No 7 one realizes how what looks on the page like very simple music can come glowingly to life in the right hands – and the way they handle the slightly tricky *poco più mosso* at the second subject is very impressive. The finest work in Vol 2 (discs 4-6) is undoubtedly the D minor Quartet, No 9. Volume 3 contains three gems: the E flat Quartet (No 10), the *American* and No 13 in G major – the outstanding work of the collection. The Prague are very sensitive to dynamic contrast (Dvořák's markings are often surprisingly detailed). Another good sample extract might be the opening of the G major's slow movement; strong, intense playing here, and fine command of long phrasing – and what marvellous music! So don't let the size of this set put you off. There's plenty of fine music on these nine well-filled discs, all of it more than well performed and the recordings are generally creditable.

String Quartet No 12

Dvořák String Quartet No 12. Cypresses, B152 – Nos 1, 2, 5, 9 and 11 **Kodály** String Quartet No 2, Op 10
Hagen Quartet (Lukas Hagen, Annette Bik *vns* Veronika Hagen *va* Clemens Hagen *vc*) Ⓕ
DG 419 601-2GH (61 minutes: DDD)

The Hagen Quartet never exaggerates, and there are moments (like the lead back to the first subject in the first movement of the *American*) where the beauty and poise of the playing really do take the breath away. There's astonishing elegance and subtlety here (not to mention technical precision), but the playing may strike you as rather too cosmopolitan in manner to allow any expression of purely national feeling. And it isn't just a question of mood: there are places where the Hagen's concern to emphasize folk characteristics is evident (the little 'blue' appoggiatura which leader Lukas Hagen appends to the recitative theme of Kodály's second movement for instance), but it somehow sounds a little studied. Quite simply, the playing may strike you as over-refined: rough edges are smoothed down: abrupt transitions are, where possible, delicately eased into. The *Scherzo* of the *American* Quartet is full of sudden changes in dynamics and texture: the Hagen has a tendency to cushion the surprise by making a rapid but perceptible *crescendo* or *decrescendo*. Effectively this puts a distance between the listener and the music – all very civilized of course, but ultimately perhaps muffling the sharpness of human contact. The Hagen plays down the accents in the finale theme of the Dvořák (obviously not wanting to spoil the effect of that wonderfully rarefied *pianissimo*). You would never suspect that Dvořák's dynamic contrasts are actually quite extreme. But the playing is winning, and the coupling is interesting. Over-cultivated it may be, but it has plenty to tell us about this music. Even so, CD buyers looking for one authoritative recording of Dvořák's most popular quartet have yet to receive a wholly satisfying recording.

String Quartets Nos 12 and 13
Vlach Quartet, Prague (Jana Vlachová, Ondřej Kukal *vns* Petr Verner *va* Mikael Ericsson *vc*) Ⓢ
Naxos 8 553371 (69 minutes: DDD). Recorded 1995

On the face of it, the credentials of the Vlach Quartet of Prague would seem to be impeccable – the group's leader, Jana Vlachová, is the daughter of the great Josef Vlach – and, indeed, the players make a most pleasing impression on this vividly recorded Naxos coupling. They certainly produce a beguilingly rich, beautifully blended sound and bring to this music a big-hearted, songful fervour as well as textural mastery. What is more, Dvořák's characteristic, chugging cross-rhythms are handled with particular felicity. Interpretatively, their approach contrasts strongly with other readings in that the Vlach team adopt a coaxing, lyrically expressive stance (with the gorgeous slow movement of the *American* a highlight). In the case of the masterly G major Quartet, these gifted newcomers show fresh insights (they are especially perceptive in those wistful reminiscences at the heart of the finale).

Additional recommendation
String Quartet Nos 12, American', and 13
Lindsay Quartet
ASV CDDCA797 (66 minutes: DDD) Ⓕ
Utterly dedicated, typically probing accounts from the Lindsays; the great G major Quartet comes off especially well here.

Piano Trios

Piano Trios – No 3 in F minor, B130; No 4 in E minor, B166, 'Dumky'
Florestan Trio (Anthony Marwood *vn* Richard Lester *vc* Susan Tomes *pf*)
Hyperion CDA66895 (68 minutes: DDD). Recorded 1996 Ⓕ

A favourite and appropriate pairing – Dvořák's most passionate chamber work in harness with one of his most genial. The F minor Piano Trio (1883) was contemporaneous with the death of Dvořák's mother; it anticipates something of the storm and stress that characterises the great D minor Seventh Symphony (1884-5) and the Florestan Trio serves it well. All three players allow themselves plenty of expressive leeway and yet the musical line is neither distorted nor stretched too far. The second movement *Allegretto* is truly *grazioso* and the qualifying *meno mosso* perfectly judged. The finale is buoyant rather than especially rustic, whereas the more overtly colourful *Dumky* Trio inspires a sense of play and a vivid suggestion of local colour – 2'45" into the third movement, for example, or 1'25" into the fourth. Throughout the performance, the manifest 'song and dance' elements of the score (heartfelt melodies alternating with folk-style faster music) are keenly projected. The recordings are first-rate, as are the insert-notes. If you're after a subtle, musically perceptive coupling of these two works, then you could hardly do better.

Violin Sonata in F

Violin Sonata in F, B106. Ballad in D minor, B139. Four Romantic Pieces, B150. Violin Sonatina in G, B183. Nocturne in B, B48*a* (arr cpsr)
Anthony Marwood *vn* **Susan Tomes** *pf*
Hyperion CDA66934 (67 minutes: DDD) Ⓕ
Recorded 1997 ⦿

This delectable release enshrines music-making of sensitivity and eloquence. Marwood may not produce as luscious a sound as that of some of his rivals, but his subtly variegated tone colouring more than compensates; Tomes, too, displays the deftest touch throughout. The F major Sonata receives a wonderfully pliable reading, full of imaginative touches. You will especially warm to their unhurried, yet purposeful way with the opening movement (Dvořák's *ma non troppo* marking ideally judged). The beautiful ensuing *Poco sostenuto* has both Brahmsian warmth and hushed intimacy; the finale is joyous and articulate. Marwood's and Tomes's account of the captivating *Sonatina* is less 'glamorous' and high-powered than the Gil and Orli Shahams' 1995 account on DG – and altogether more personable as a result. Try from the *Scherzo* (track 3) to hear Marwood and Tomes at their sparkling best. Similarly, the second of the *Four Romantic Pieces* has an earthy tang reminiscent of Janáček, while the *Allegro appassionato* third movement unfolds with just the right flowing ardour. Hyperion also offers the haunting *Nocturne* in B major and a sombre, vividly characterised *Ballad* in D minor from 1884. This anthology must now take the palm, not least in view of the marvellously realistic and impeccably balanced recording.

Additional recommendation
Violin Sonata. Violin Sonatina. Romantic Pieces
Shaham, G *vn* **Shaham, O** *pf*
DG 449 820-2GH (52 minutes: DDD: 5/97) Ⓕ
Highly proficient, sensitive playing from the brother-and-sister partnership of Gil and Orli Shaham.

Requiem Mass

Requiem Mass, B165. Mass in D, B153
Pilar Lorengar *sop* **Neil Ritchie** *treb* **Erzesébet Komlóssy** *contr* **Andrew Giles** *counterten* **Robert Ilosfalvy, Alan Byers** *tens* **Tom Krause** *bar* **Robert Morton** *bass* **Nicholas Cleobury** *org* **Ambrosian Singers; Christ Church Cathedral Choir, Oxford / Simon Preston; London Symphony Orchestra / István Kertész**
Double Decca ② 448 089-2DF2 (138 minutes: ADD) Ⓜ
Texts and translations included. Recorded 1968

Kertész's Requiem dates from 1968 and on all counts but one, it surpasses Karel Ančerl's classic 1959 set, reissued on DG in 1995 and coupled with Fischer-Dieskau's 1960 set of Dvořák's *Biblical Songs* with Jörg Demus. The exception is the rather too soft-grained singing of Pilar Lorengar as compared with the clear, more vibrant soprano of Maria Stader. But Lorengar's singing is particularly sensitive and appealing in the quieter passages. The lovely quality of Robert Ilosfalvy's voice tells beautifully in 'Liber scriptus proferetur' and in the opening section of the quartet, 'Recordare, Jesu pie'. Dvořák distributes short passages among the soloists impartially. They combine beautifully in the quartet, and the chorus with them in 'Pie Jesu Domine'. The hero of the occasion is Kertész. He gets choral singing and orchestral playing of the finest quality. It is abundantly evident that he cherishes a great love for this work. The Mass in D (sung in the original version with organ) sits well with the Requiem; Simon Preston produces a fine, well-balanced performance, with the Christ Church choristers on excellent form.

Stabat mater

Stabat mater. Psalm 149
Lívia Aghová *sop* **Marga Schiml** *contr* **Aldo Baldin** *ten* **Luděk Vele** *bass* **Prague Children's Choir; Prague Philharmonic Choir; Czech Philharmonic Orchestra / Jiří Bělohlávek**
Chandos ② CHAN8985/6 (96 minutes: DDD).Notes, texts and translations included. Recorded1991 Ⓕ ●

The 10 sections of the *Stabat mater* are well laid out for the different vocal and instrumental forces and so avoid the monotony which might seem inherent in this contemplative and deeply sombre text. This performance was recorded in Prague Castle, and in it we feel the full dignity and drama of the work, an oratorio in all but name. The four solo singers convey genuine fervour and one feels that their sound, which is quite unlike that of British singers, must be akin to what the composer originally imagined. If they are a touch operatic, that doesn't sound misplaced and they perform well together, as in the second verse quartet 'Quis est homo'. The choral singing is no less impressive, and indeed the whole performance under Bělohlávek gets the balance right between reverent simplicity and intensity of feeling. Psalm 149 is a setting of 'Sing unto the Lord a new song' for chorus and orchestra and its celebratory mood provides a fine complement to the other work.

Additional recommendation
Stabat mater
Coupling: Legends
Mathis *sop* **Reynolds** *mez* **Ochman** *ten* **Shirley-Quirk** *bar* **Bavarian Radio Chorus and Symphony Orchestra; English Chamber Orchestra / Kubelík**
DG 453 025-2GTA2 ② (129 minutes: ADD: 3/78R) Ⓜ
This warm-hearted work well deserves all the care and attention lavished upon it by the performers, who respond with evident enthusiasm to Kubelík's inspiring direction.

Mass in D

Dvořák Mass in D, Op 86 **Eben** Prague Te Deum 1989 **Janáček** Our Father
Dagmar Masková *sop* **Marta Benacková** *mez* **Walter Coppola** *ten* **Peter Mikulás** *bass* **Lydie Härtelová** *hp* **Josef Ksica** *org* **Prague Chamber Choir / Josef Pancík**
ECM New Series 449 508-2 (59 minutes: DDD) Ⓕ
Texts and translations included. Recorded 1993

This imaginative coupling brings together three fine pieces of Czech church music in skilled and sympathetic interpretations. Dvořák's Mass has received a number of good recorded performances; this one, in the original 1887 version with organ, has a very well-matched quartet of soloists who blend smoothly with each other and with the chamber choir. It is a work of particular intimacy and charm, and these qualities mark this performance. Janáček's setting of the Lord's Prayer dates from 1906, and is in turn a meditative piece, not without vivid illustrative touches appropriate to a work originally designed to accompany a sequence of devotional pictures; and Petr Eben's *Prague Te Deum* coincided, in 1969, with a moment of apparent release from political oppression. It has something of Janáček's suddenness in the invention, and a graceful melodic manner. Each of these works is in its way inward, personal and reflective, but they all share a Czech character; and this is well related to Czech history by Antonín Pešek in an exceptionally interesting, long essay setting the country's church music in its historical and religious context.

Rusalka

Renée Fleming *sop* Rusalka; **Ben Heppner** *ten* Prince; **Franz Hawlata** *bass* Watergnome; **Dolora Zajick** *mez* Witch; **Eva Urbanová** *sop* Foreign Princess; **Iván Kusnjer** *bar* Hunter, Gamekeeper; **Zdena Kloubová** *sop* Turnspit; **Lívia Aghová** *sop* First Woodsprite; **Dana Burešová** *mez* Second Woodsprite; **Hana Minutillo** *contr* Third Woodsprite **Kühn Mixed Choir; Czech Philharmonic Orchestra / Sir Charles Mackerras**
Decca ③ 460 568-2DHO3 (163 minutes: DDD) Ⓕ
Notes, text and translation included
Recorded 1998 ●●●

Renée Fleming's tender and heart-warming account of Rusalka's Invocation to the Moon reflects the fact that the role of the lovelorn water-nymph, taken by her in a highly successful production at the Met in New York, has become one of her favourites. Ben Heppner also has a special relationship with the opera, for the role of the Prince was the first he studied in depth as a student. He has sung it repeatedly since then, often opposite Renée Fleming, and both he and Charles Mackerras have long harboured the ambition to make a complete recording. The joy of this magnificent set, which won *Gramophone*'s Record of the Year

1999, is that in almost every way it fulfils every expectation and more, offering a recording with glowing sound that more than ever before reveals the richness and subtlety of Dvořák's score. As interpreted by Fleming and Mackerras, Rusalka's big aria at the start of Act 3, when having been rejected by the Prince, she seeks consolation in returning to the water, is as poignantly beautiful as the more celebrated Invocation to the Moon in Act 1, when she laments over loving a human. In addition, the climactic moments bring glorious top-notes, firm and true up to B flat and B. Heppner, like Fleming, conveys his special affection for this music, unstrained up to top C, combining heroic power with lyric beauty. Dolora Zajick as the Witch, Jezibaba, is characterful and fruity. Franz Hawlata as the Watergnome, Rusalka's father, is firm and dark, bringing a Wagnerian weight to the role. The engineers also thrillingly capture the off-stage effects so important in this opera, with the Watergnome balefully calling from the lake. Even the smaller roles have been cast from strength, all of them fresh, true and idiomatic. The clear-toned First Woodsprite, Lívia Aghová, is a leading soloist in the Prague National Theatre, as is Eva Urbanová, the firmly focused mezzo who plays the Foreign Princess. Similarly, Iván Kusnjer (Hunter and Gamekeeper) is a noted Simon Boccanegra. Strikingly, there is not a hint of a Slavonic wobble from any of the singers. In the orchestra, too, the Czech horns are consistently rich and firm. And if anyone is worried about having four non-Czech principals, they are as idiomatic as any rivals, with three of them – Fleming, Zajick and Hawlata – helped by having Czech forebears.

The final glory of the set lies in the warmly understanding conducting of Charles Mackerras. It may seem surprising that such a specialist in Czech music is only now tackling his first complete Dvořák opera recording, but in every way this matches and even outshines his supreme achievement in the Decca series of Janáček operas. In those you had the Vienna Philharmonic, but here the Czech Philharmonic is both a degree more idiomatic and just as opulent in tone, with superb solo work. The strings produce ravishing sounds, refined and transparent in the lovely evocations of water, often with instruments muted. He is helped there by the rich Decca recording, giving a keen sense of presence. The balance between voices and orchestra is well managed, with voices never drowned, though one oddity of the recording – which will not trouble everyone – is that characters tend to emerge on the scene with an initial phrase or two heard from off-stage.

Rusalka

Milada Subrtová *sop* Rusalka; **Eduard Haken** *bass* Watergnome; **Marie Ovčačíková** *contr* Witch; **Ivo Zídek** *ten* Prince; **Alena Míková** *mez* Foreign Princess; **Jadwiga Wysoczanská** *sop* First Woodsprite; **Eva Hlobilová** *sop* Second Woodsprite; **Věra Krilová** *contr* Third Woodsprite; **Ivana Mixová** *sop* Turnspit; **Václav Bednář** *bar* Hunter, Gamekeeper
Prague National Theatre Chorus and Orchestra / Zdeněk Chalabala
Supraphon ② SU0013-2 (149 minutes: ADD) Ⓕ
Notes, text and translation included. Recorded 1961 ⓞ

This excellent set boasts Eduard Haken, one of the great interpreters of the Watergnome, in robust voice, infusing the character with a rueful gentleness as well as a firmness of utterance. Ivo Zídek as the Prince was in his mid-thirties and in his prime at the time of this recording, singing ardently and tenderly and with a grace of phrasing that matches him well to Milada Subrtová's Rusalka. Hers is a beautiful performance, sensitive to the character's charm as well as to her fragility and pathos. The Slavonic tradition of the old watersprite legend places her in the line of the suffering heroine and it is a measure of Dvořák's success that her delicate appeal holds throughout quite a long opera, and her sinuous but never oversensual lines and the piercing harmony associated with her give her a unique appeal. Subrtová sings the part with unfaltering sensitivity. Zdeněk Chalabala, who died only a couple of months after completing this recording, handles the score with great tenderness and an affection that shines through every bar. This is a beautiful performance. The recording comes up remarkably well, too.

The Jacobin

Václav Zítek *bar* Bohuš; **Vilém Přibyl** *ten* Jiří; **Daniela Sounová** *sop* Terinka; **Karel Průša** *bass* Count Vilém; **René Tuček** *bar* Adolf; **Marcela Machotková** *sop* Julie; **Karel Berman** *bass* Filip; **Beno Blachut** *ten* Benda; **Ivana Mixová** *mez* Lotinka
Kantilena Children's Chorus; Kühn Chorus; Brno State Philharmonic Orchestra / Jiří Pinkas
Supraphon ② 11 2190-2 (155 minutes: ADD). Notes, Ⓕ text and translation included. Recorded 1977

This was the first (and, so far, only) recording of Dvořák's charming village comedy – for the Jacobin of the title is not here a political activist but a young man, Bohuš, returning from exile in Paris to his stuffy old father, Count Vilém. The sub-plots include all manner of misunderstandings, and set in the middle of them is the touching figure of Benda, the fussy, rather pedantic but wholly moving music-master. Dvořák is known to have had in mind his own boyhood teacher, Antonín Liehmann, whose daughter gives her name, Terinka, to Benda's daughter. Beno Blachut celebrated his 64th birthday during the making of this set. His was a long career, as well as one of great distinction; he is still well able to get round the lines of this part, and gives an affecting picture of the old musician, never more so than in the rehearsing of the welcome ode. This is an idea that has cropped up in opera before, but it is charmingly handled here. Václav Zítek sings Bohuš pleasantly and Marcela Machotková trips away lightly as Julie. Vilém Přibyl sounds less than his most energetic, though his voice is in good fettle; and there is some lack of drive from Jiří Pinkas, who might have done more to bring out the often witty touches in Dvořák's scoring. Never mind: this revived version of a delightful piece can be safely recommended.

Kate and the Devil

Anna Barová *contr* Kate; **Richard Novák** *bass* Devil Marbuel; **Miloš Ježil** *ten* Shepherd Jirka; **Daniela Suryová** *contr* Kate's mother; **Jaroslav Horáček** *bass* Lucifer; **Jan Hladík** *bass* Devil the Gate-keeper; **Aleš Stáva** *bass* Devil the Guard; **Brigita Sulcová** *sop* Princess; **Natália Romanová** *sop* Chambermaid; **Pavel Kamas** *bass* Marshall; **Oldřich Polášek** *ten* Musician **Brno Janáček Opera Chorus and Orchestra / Jiří Pinkas**

Supraphon ② 11 1800-2 (119 minutes: AAD). Notes, Ⓕ text and translation included. Recorded 1979

Though this was never one of the best Supraphon recordings, it is perfectly serviceable. The plot is complicated, and broadly speaking concerns the bossy Kate who, finding herself a wallflower at the village hop, angrily declares that she would dance with the Devil himself. Up there duly pops a junior devil, Marbuel, who carries her off to hell, where her ceaseless chatter wearies Lucifer himself. The diabolical company is only too happy to allow the shepherd Jirka to remove her again. Jirka, attractively sung by Miloš Ježil, also manages to help the wicked but later repentant Princess to escape the Devil's clutches, and all ends well. The work has a proper coherence, and much good humour besides. Anna Barová's Kate is strong and full of character, but manages not to exclude the charm that should underlie her rantings at Marbuel, who is handsomely sung by Richard Novák. Brigita Sulcová similarly makes much of the not very sympathetic Princess. Jaroslav Horáček enjoys himself hugely as Lucifer and Jiří Pinkas accompanies them well.

Sir George Dyson British 1883-1964

GROVE *Dyson studied at the Royal College of Music (1900-04) and later taught there (director from 1938), and at several schools. His works include choral and orchestral pieces (notably The Canterbury Pilgrims, 1931) and books.*

The Canterbury Pilgrims

Awards 1997

The Canterbury Pilgrims. In Honour of the City. At the Tabard Inn
Yvonne Kenny *sop* **Robert Tear** *ten* **Stephen Roberts** *bar* **London Symphony Chorus and Orchestra / Richard Hickox**
Chandos ② CHAN9531 Ⓕ (118 minutes: DDD). Texts included. Recorded 1996 **ooo**

It seems extraordinary that Dyson's *Canterbury Pilgrims* had to wait so long for a première recording. This superb offering from Hickox of this full-length cantata based on the Prologue to Chaucer's *Canterbury Tales* bears out its reputation as Dyson's masterpiece. This is a fresh, openly tuneful work, aptly exuberant in its celebration of Chaucer. Following the scheme of Chaucer's Prologue, Dyson in his 12 movements, plus Envoi, presents a sequence of portraits, deftly varying the forces used, with the three soloists well contrasted in their characterizations and with the chorus acting as both narrator and commentator, providing an emotional focus for the whole work in two heightened sequences, the sixth and twelfth movements, moving and noble portraits of the two characters who aroused Dyson's deepest sympathy, the Clerk of Oxenford and the Poor Parson of a Town. If the idiom is undemanding, with occasional echoes of Vaughan Williams's *A Sea Symphony* and with passages reminiscent of Rachmaninov's *The bells*, the cantata sustains its length well. Sensibly, *At the Tabard Inn*, the concert overture which Dyson wrote in 1943, basing it on themes from the cantata, is given first.

Outstanding among the soloists is Robert Tear who not only characterises brilliantly but sings with admirable fullness and warmth. The beautiful, fading close, when Tear as the Knight begins the first tale, moving slowly off-stage, is most atmospherically done. Yvonne Kenny and Stephen Roberts sing well too, but are less distinctive both in timbre and expression.

The London Symphony Chorus sings with incandescent tone, superbly recorded, and with the orchestra under Hickox – an ideal advocate – brings out the clarity and colourfulness of Dyson's instrumentation. *In Honour of the City* provides the perfect fill-up. Like the main work, it uses a modern-language version of a middle-English text. The idiom is very similar to that of the Chaucer work, music designed for a good amateur chorus, fresh, direct and tuneful, again with Hickox drawing glowing sounds from chorus and orchestra.

Hanns Eisler German 1898-1962

GROVE *Eisler studied with Schoenberg (1919-23) and in 1925 began teaching in Berlin, where his left-wing political sympathies became more acute. He grew critical of his early works, which had sprung directly from Schoenberg, and wrote political songs. In 1930 he began a collaboration with Brecht (notably with Die Massnahme, 1930, and Die Mutter, 1931), which continued after both men went into exile in the USA; there he also produced many film scores. In 1950 he returned to Berlin and applied himself to the problems of creating music for a socialist state: his solution was to write functional music almost exclusively, including film scores, incidental music and songs, in a strenuous diatonic style still motivated by the Schoenbergian coscience of his youth.*

Suites for Orchestra

Suites for Orchestra – No 2, Op 24, 'Niemandsland'; No 3, Op 26, 'Kuhle Wampe'; No 4, Op 30, 'Die Jugend hat das Wort'; No 5, Op 34, 'Dans les rues'. Balladen – Op 18: Ballade vom Nigger Jima; Op 22: Ballade von der Wohltätigkeit; Ballade von der Säckeschmeissern; Op 41: Das Lied vom SA-Mann. Die Rundköpfe und die Spitzköpfe, Op 45 – Lied von der belebenden Wirkung des Geldes; Die Ballade vom Wasserrad. Ideal und Wirklichkeit
Ensemble Modern / Heinz Karl Gruber *bar*
RCA Victor Red Seal 74321 56882-2 (70 minutes: DDD). Texts and translations included. Ⓕ
Recorded 1998

This is Hanns Eisler conveying anger, derision or fierce joviality at the top of his voice, and very enjoyable it is, if perhaps a little exhausting after 70 minutes. Bourgeois greed, capitalist market-manipulation, American colour prejudice, the Nazis' betrayal of their own supporters – these are the subjects of his songs, delivered by Gruber with the sort of raucous relish that Eisler so much appreciated in Ernst Busch, his close collaborator in the 1930s, when all these songs were written. So were many of Eisler's film scores, from which the four suites derive. They are scored, like the songs, for an ensemble of wind and percussion, with piano, banjo, two cellos and double-bass, closely resembling what would have been termed a 'jazz band' in the Germany of that period. And much of the music uses jazz elements, too, chosen for its energy and stridency, but also setting Eisler's grave or sober, often strikingly economical lyricism in sharp contrast. It is good amidst all the hectic energy to be reminded of that element, so central to Eisler's output as a whole.

The very last piece here is irresistible. It dates from 1956, and is a world-weary song about how everyone ends up with second best, if that ('You fancy a tall, slim one, but what you get is short and fat. C'est la vie! In the days of the Emperor we imagined a republic. And now we've got one ...'). Gruber has encouraged his players (though from the sound of it they hardly needed urging) to produce sounds that are as far from the gentility of the concert hall as his own voice is remote from that of a Lieder recital: clarinets wail, saxophones leer, trombones rasp, and all are recorded with maximum, in-your-face directness.

Hollywood Songbook

Awards 1999

In den Weiden. Frühling. Speisekammer 1942. Auf der Flucht. Über den Selbstmord. Die Flucht. Gedenktafel für 4000 Soldaten. Epitaph. Spruch. Ostersonntag. Der Kirschdieb. Hotelzimmer 1942. Die Maske des Bösen. Zwei Pascal Lieder. Die letzte Elegie. Winterspruch. Fünf Elegien. Nightmare. Hollywood-Elegie No 7. Der Schatzgräber. Panzerschlacht. L'automne californien. Fünf Anakreontische Fragmente. Erinnerung an Eichendorff und Schumann. Sechs Hölderlin-Fragmente. Der Mensch. Vom Sprengen des Gartens. Die Heimkehr. Die Landschaft des Exils. Der Sohn. An den kleinen Radioapparat
Matthias Goerne *bar* **Eric Schneider** *pf*
Decca 460 582-2DH (70 minutes: DDD) Ⓕ
Texts and translations included. Recorded 1998 ●●●

This is a hugely impressive issue of major importance. Goerne has obviously been smitten by these wonderful, neglected songs: he calls them 'the 20th century *Winterreise*', and in performances as gripping as these it is hard to contradict him. They are Eisler's songs of exile, written in Hollywood while the Germany for which he felt both passionate revulsion and deep nostalgia sank into the abyss. Most of the 46 short songs are settings of poems by Brecht, some written specifically for Eisler, but they also incorporate 'mini-cycles' to texts by Mörike and Eichendorff, two poems by Blaise Pascal (set in English) and one or two others including a single poem by Eisler himself. The songs are not here sung in the order in which Eisler eventually published them, but the sequence chosen makes poignant dramatic sense, chronicling Brecht's and Eisler's horror at what was happening in Germany, their flight and exile, their reaction to the alien world of Hollywood and meditations on Germany's vanished past, hideous present and uncertain future. As performed here, the cycle ends with a loving homage to Schubert, 'On Watering the Garden', followed by the haunting and moving 'Homecoming', a vision of Berlin obliterated by bombardment, and by the intense and characteristically Eislerian lyricism of 'Landscape of Exile'.

These works demand a prodigious expressive range from any singer who undertakes them. Goerne can sing 'On Suicide' with a mere thread of sound without ever losing the quality of his voice but can then swell in an instant to a formidable *fff* for the last syllable of the terrifying final line ('People just throw their unbearable lives away'). The sheer beauty of his voice is just what those many homages to the Lied tradition need. His English is pretty good, his diction immaculate, and he makes a memorably sinister thing of the seventh *Hollywood Elegy* (set in English; Brecht's German original is lost), that horrifying image of a man sinking in a swamp with a 'ghastly, blissful smile'. Goerne's is a masterly and profoundly moving achievement. Eric Schneider's accompaniment is first-class and the recording is excellent.

Edward Elgar

British 1857-1934

GROVE *Elgar had violin lessons in Worcester and London but was essentially self-taught, learning much in his father's music shop. From the age of 16 he worked locally as a violinist, organist, bassoonist, conductor and teacher, also composing abundantly though not yet very individually: the accepted corpus of his works belongs almost entirely to the period after his 40th birthday.*

His first attempt to establish himself in London was premature. He moved there with his wife Alice in 1889, but in 1891 they returned to Malvern, and he began to make a reputation more steadily with choral works: The Black Knight, The Light of Life, King Olaf and Caractacus. These were written within a specifically English tradition, but they were influenced also by German music from Weber, Schumann and Mendelssohn to Brahms and Wagner. The orchestral Enigma Variations (1899), in which each variation portrays a different friend of Elgar's, then proclaimed the belated arrival of a fully formed original style, taken further in the oratorio The Dream of Gerontius (1900), where the anxious chromaticism of a post- Parsifal manner is answered by the assurances of the Newman text: Elgar was himself a Roman Catholic, which may have been one cause of his personal insecurity.

Cello Concerto

Cello Concerto. Sea Pictures, Op 37
Jacqueline du Pré *vc* **Janet Baker** *mez* **London Symphony Orchestra / Sir John Barbirolli**
EMI CDC5 56219-2 (54 minutes: ADD) Ⓕ
Recorded1965 ●●●

Issued in 1965 and one of EMI's best-sellers ever since, these Elgar recordings make the most cherishable of couplings. Though both Jacqueline du Pré and Janet Baker were already well established and widely appreciated in 1965, this disc marked a turning point for both of them in their recording careers. With Barbirolli so warm-hearted and understanding an accompanist to each, these are both in every sense classic performances that can never be replaced. Jacqueline du Pré's Elgar has been all the more appreciated since her tragic illness took her away. In principle her *espressivo* may be too freely romantic, but the slow movement and epilogue remain supreme in their intensity, conveying in whispered *pianissimos* of daring delicacy an inner communion, while the bravura of the brilliant passages remains astonishing from an artist who was still only 20.

Equally, the young Janet Baker translated the work into something greater than had been appreciated before. Until this recording, *Sea Pictures* had tended to be underprized even among Elgarians; but the passion, intensity and sheer beauty of this performance with each of the five songs sharply distinct rebutted any idea that – in reflection of verse of varying quality – it had anything of sub-standard Elgar in it. It is a work which you will probably never be able to listen to again without hearing in your mind Janet Baker's deeply individual phrasing on this disc. What strikes you more than anything else is the central relevance to Baker's whole career of the last stanza in 'Sabbath morning at sea', a radiant climax. 'He shall assist me to look higher' says the Barrett Browning poem, and the thrust of meaning as she sings it invariably conveys a *frisson* such as you rarely get on record. The CD transfer is valuable for clarifying the sound, but it adds little to the original LP. The sound in the Cello Concerto exactly matches the LP sound, and the precise placing makes the soloist all the more vivid. The precision of CD makes more apparent the slight discrepancy between the sides, with *Sea Pictures* a degree fresher and fuller and with more bloom on the sound. The slight sibilant emphasis is not the fault of the transfer, but also comes on the LP.

Elgar Cello Concerto[a] **Bloch** Schelomo[a]
Kabalevsky Cello Concerto No 2 in G, Op 77[b]
Tchaikovsky Variations on a Rococo Theme in A, Op 33[c]. Nocturne, Op 19 No 4[c]. Pezzo capriccioso, Op 62[c]. Andante cantabile, Op 11[c]
R Strauss Don Quixote[d]
Steven Isserlis *vc* [a]**London Symphony Orchestra / Richard Hickox;** [b]**London Philharmonic Orchestra / Andrew Litton;** [c]**Chamber Orchestra of Europe / Sir John Eliot Gardiner;** [d]**Minnesota Orchestra / Edo de Waart**
Virgin Classics VBD5 61490-2 (51 minutes: DDD) Ⓜ
Recorded 1988

Cellists are apt to 'come of age' in recordings of the Elgar. Isserlis was no exception. This is a wonderful account of the Concerto – brave, imaginative, individual – indeed, quite the most personal in its perception of the piece since the treasurable Du Pré on EMI. And that, you will appreciate, is saying something though not, we hasten to add, that the two readings are in any outward sense similar. Far from it. With Isserlis, the emotional tug is considerably less overt, the emphasis more on shadow and subtext than open heartache. Yet the inner-light is no less intense, the phrasing no less rhapsodic in manner than Du Pré. On the contrary. This is free-range Elgar all right, and like Du Pré it comes totally without affectation. Both Isserlis and Du Pré take an appropriately generous line on the first movement's sorrowful song, with Isserlis the more reposeful, the more inclined to open out and savour key cadences. The *Scherzo* itself is quite simply better played than on any previous recording; the articulation and definition of the semiquaver 'fours' would, we are sure, have astonished even the composer himself. From a technical point of view Isserlis is easily the equal, and more, of any player currently before us. And if you still feel that Du Pré really did have the last word where the epilogue is concerned, then listen to Isserlis sinking with heavy heart into those pages preceding the return of the opening declamation. He achieves a mesmerizing fragility in the bars marked *lento* – one last backward glance, as it were – and the inwardness of the final *diminuendo* is something to be heard and remembered. Hickox and the LSO prove model collaborators and it almost goes without saying that they bring all their well-oiled skills to bear on the outrageous biblical climaxes of Bloch's soulful *Schelomo*; trumpets and horns positively outreach themselves. Isserlis does not stint himself either, pouring forth his darkest and most impassioned colours. Thanks also to an impeccably balanced recording, the integration, the give and take between soloist and orchestra in one of Elgar's most perfectly crafted scores, is seamless. Don't on any account miss these performances.

Elgar Cello Concerto **Dvořák** Cello Concerto in B minor, B191
Maria Kliegel *vc* **Royal Philharmonic Orchestra / Michael Halász** Ⓢ
Naxos 8 550503 (73 minutes: DDD)

The technical accomplishment of Kliegel's playing is balanced by a richness of musical insight which will not disappoint. The boldness of the opening soliloquy recalls Du Pré at her finest, and yet Kliegel shares a yet deeper cup of grief in the world-weariness of the main first subject, carried with noble conviction. She takes a more improvisatory view in the lilting second group than Du Pré, though Schiff (Philips) is the most convincing of all in the transition back to the 9/8 at the close of the movement. The *Scherzo* is brilliantly done, and at a very fast tempo, but the conductor Michael Halász overlooks Elgar's precisely noted *A tempo* indication in response to the soloist's cantabile *largamente* statements at the end of each main section. The effect is not only tedious, but is quite the reverse of the composer's intention, clearly stated in the score. The *Adagio* is thoughtfully played, avoiding unwelcome posturing or empty affectation, though Kliegel is, if anything, a little too cool and dispassionate here. The finale is superbly paced, with the rumbustious militarism of the orchestration never allowed to dominate. The passage in which the soloist leads the orchestral cellos in a grand reprise of the main *allego* theme is not as exciting as it could be, but the transition to the elegiac mood of the final pages is unerringly convincing. The recording was made at Henry Wood Hall, and is full bodied and emphatic in major tuttis, yet one might have wished the overall balance to favour the soloist more than it does.

Elgar Cello Concerto in E minor, Op 85[a] Ⓗ
Bruch Kol nidrei, Op 47[b] **Dvořák** Cello Concerto[c]
Pablo Casals *vc* [a]**BBC Symphony Orchestra / Sir Adrian Boult;** [b]**London Symphony Orchestra / Sir Landon Ronald;** [c]**Czech Philharmonic Orchestra / George Szell**
EMI Références mono CDH7 63498-2 (75 minutes: ADD). Recorded 1936-45 Ⓜ ●

It scarcely seems necessary to write anything further about Casals's famous recordings of the Dvořák and Elgar concertos, which have long been recognized as classics of the recorded repertoire. The former, destined to mark a standard for generations, and seemingly played with a sword rather than a bow, still exercises a powerful effect: the incandescent solo playing is so mesmeric that one can accept the rather harsh and dry orchestral sound which betrays its age (from 1937). Some of Casals's passionate quality may have been due to his decision to break out of his self-imposed restricted activities caused by the Spanish civil war: the astute Fred Gaisberg, hearing that he had consented to appear with Szell in Prague, talked them into making a recording the day after the concert. *Kol nidrei* is a quietly eloquent, broad reading of this meditation, deftly accompanied by Landon Ronald. About Casals's Elgar there has always been controversy: his reading was heavily criticized as over-emotional ('un-English') when he first played it in London before the war, but when he returned in 1945 and performed it, according to Boult, in exactly the same way, it was said that 'in the deeply meditative sections ... it reached an Elgarian mood of wistfulness that few artists understand'. In the light of subsequent performances by other famous cellists this raises an interesting point for discussion, from which we here prudently excuse ourselves.

Additional recommendation
Coupling: **Lutosławski** Cello Concerto
Wispelwey *vc* **Netherlands Radio Philharmonic Orchestra / Van Steen**
Channel Classics CCS12998 (54 minutes: DDD: 7/99) Ⓕ
His utterly sympathetic performance of the Elgar displays both elasticity and plentiful re-creative fantasy. A notable achievement in every way.

Violin Concerto in B minor

Elgar Violin Concerto
Vaughan Williams The lark ascending
Kennedy *vn* **City of Birmingham Symphony Orchestra / Sir Simon Rattle**
EMI CDC5 56413-2 (72 minutes: ADD) Ⓕ
Recorded 1997 ●

Astonishingly, in the case of the first two movements at least, this release, recorded during the week following a live concert at Birmingham's Symphony Hall in July 1997, fully re-creates the heady excitement of that memorable event. From every conceivable point of view – authority, panache, intelligence, intuitive poetry, tonal beauty and emotional maturity – Kennedy surpasses his 1985 *Gramophone* Award-winning EMI Eminence recording (now on HMV Classics). The first movement is a magnificent achievement all round, with tension levels extraordinarily high for a studio project. Rattle launches the proceedings in exemplary fashion, his direction passionate, ideally flexible and texturally lucid (the antiphonally divided violins help). The CBSO, too, is on top form. But it's Kennedy who rivets the attention from his commanding initial entry onwards. There's no hiding in this of all scores and Kennedy penetrates to the very essence of 'the soul enshrined within' in his melting presentation of the 'Windflower' theme – Elgar's *dolce semplice* realized to tear-spilling perfection. The slow movement is almost as fine. What poise and dedication these artists bring to this rapt meditation. Only the finale oddly dissatisfies. Not in terms of technical address or co-ordination (both of which are stunning); rather, for all the supreme accomplishment on show, the results are not terribly moving. Despite any lingering doubts about this last movement we are still left with an enormously stimulating and marvellously well-engineered display. The fill-up is a provocative account of *The lark ascending*, which Kennedy (whose tone is ravishing) and Rattle spin out to a (surely unprecedented?) 17-and-a-half minutes.

Violin Concerto[a]. Cello Concerto[b] **H**
[a]Yehudi Menuhin *vn* **[b]Beatrice Harrison** *vc* **[a]London Symphony Orchestra, [b]New Symphony Orchestra / Sir Edward Elgar**
EMI Great Recordings of the Century mono
CDM5 66979-2 (75 minutes: AAD). Recorded 1932 Ⓜ and 1928 ○○○

Elgar's conducting for Menuhin in the Violin Concerto's opening orchestral tutti is quite magnificent, as is his solicitous, attentive accompaniment throughout the work. Menuhin's youthful, wonderfully intuitive musicianship in fact needed little 'instruction', as is well known, and the success of the recording may be judged from the fact that there have been few periods in the years since it was first issued when it has not been available in some shape or form. Beatrice Harrison first studied the Cello Concerto for an abridged, pre-electric recording with Elgar conducting. So impressed was the composer then that he insisted that Harrison should be the soloist whenever he conducted the work again. Their authoritative performance is deeply felt and highly expressive, but it has a quality of nobility and stoicism which comes as a refreshing change from some overindulgent modern performances. After EMI had made the first LP transfer of the Menuhin Violin Concerto for the composer's centenary in 1957 the original matrices were destroyed. When Anthony Griffith made a fresh transfer in the early 1970s using improved technology the results were at the same time better and worse, for Griffith was obliged to work with commercial pressings. In going back to the 1957 tape for this transfer EMI's engineers have on balance made the right decision, for although the 1957 engineers did not quite capture all the body of the originals there is an impressive clarity in their transfer, now brightened a little more for CD. Griffith's 1970s transfer of the Harrison/Elgar Cello Concerto was impressively managed, and this reissue has given still more presence to the sound without any sense of falsification.

Additional recommendation
Violin Concerto
Kennedy *vn* **London Philharmonic Orchestra / Handley**
EMI Eminence CD-EMX2058 (54 minutes: DDD: 12/84[R]) Ⓜ
Also available on HMV Classics
Kennedy's superb first recording of the Elgar Violin Concerto won the Gramophone Record of the Year in 1985. Now at bargain price don't miss it.

Enigma Variations

Enigma Variations. Cockaigne Overture, Op 40. Introduction and Allegro, Op 47. Serenade for Strings
BBC Symphony Orchestra / Sir Andrew Davis
Teldec British Line 9031-73279-2 (74 minutes: DDD) Ⓜ
Recorded 1991

These are four of the best Elgar performances on disc available. First, the recording is superb, with near-perfect balance and a really natural sound (listen to the brass in the final climax of 'Nimrod' on track 15). Second, the playing of the BBC Symphony Orchestra is first-rate. Andrew Davis's conducting of all four works is inspired, as if he had forgotten all preconceived notions and other interpretations, gone back to the scores and given us what he found there. In *Cockaigne*, for example, the subtle use of *ritardando*, sanctioned in the score, gives the music that elasticity which Elgar considered to be an ideal requisite for interpreting his works. The poetry and wit of this masterpiece emerge with renewed freshness. As for the *Enigma* Variations, instead of wondering why another recording was thought necessary, you will find yourself rejoicing that such a fine performance has been preserved to be set alongside other treasured versions. Each of the 'friends pictured within' is strongly characterised by Davis, but without exaggeration or interpretative quirks. Tempos are just right and the orchestral playing captures the authentic Elgarian sound in a manner Boult would have recognized. Similarly, in the *Introduction and Allegro*, how beautifully the string quartet is recorded, how magical are the gentle and so eloquent pizzicatos which punctuate the flow of the great melody. The fugue is played with real zest and enjoyment. This is music on a large scale and is played and conducted in that way, whereas the early *Serenade* is intimate and dewy-eyed and that is how it sounds here.

Enigma Variations. Falstaff. Grania and Diarmid – Incidental Music; Funeral March
City of Birmingham Symphony Orchestra / Sir Simon Rattle
EMI British Composers CDC5 55001-2 Ⓕ
(79 minutes:DDD). Recorded 1992-93

Rattle gives us perhaps the most meticulously prepared and subtly blended *Falstaff* ever committed to disc. This conductor's keen intellect and almost fanatical fidelity to the letter of the score team up to produce the most invigorating, wittily observant results. It is, however, a bit like viewing a pristinely restored portrait of Shakespeare's fat knight, whereas Barbirolli presents us with the lovable, vulnerable creature of flesh and blood himself – his epilogue really does touch to the marrow every time. In *Enigma* the results are always enjoyable and refreshing, with myriad details in Elgar's lovingly-woven, orchestral canvas adroitly pinpointed. A fine, deeply-felt performance. The most completely successful item here is the glorious *Grania and Diarmid* incidental music: the magnificent 'Funeral March' is one of Elgar's most inspired creations and Rattle gauges its brooding melancholy most eloquently. Balance is impeccable (and the transfer level comparatively low) in all three works, although the quality in *Falstaff* isn't quite as rich and glowing as it is elsewhere. Overall, this is an exceedingly stimulating release.

Enigma Variations[a]. Falstaff[b]
[a]**Philharmonia Orchestra,** [b]**Hallé Orchestra /**
Sir John Barbirolli
EMI Studio CDM7 69185-2 (65 minutes: ADD) Ⓜ
Recorded 1962 and 1964 ○

This disc restores to the catalogue at a very reasonable price two key Elgar recordings of works which Barbirolli made very much his own. Barbirolli brought a flair and ripeness of feeling to the *Enigma* with which Elgar himself would surely have identified. Everything about his performance seems exactly right. The very opening theme is phrased with an appealing combination of warmth and subtlety, and variation after variation has a special kind of individuality, whilst for the finale Barbirolli draws all the threads together most satisfyingly. *Falstaff* is a continuous, closely integrated structure and again Barbirolli's response to the music's scenic characterization is magical while he controls the overall piece, with its many changes of mood, with a naturally understanding flair. The original recordings perhaps sounded more sumptuous but on CD there is more refined detail and greater range and impact to the sound.

Enigma Variations[a]. Pomp and Circumstance
Marches, Op 39[b]
[a]**London Symphony Orchestra,** [b]**London**
Philharmonic Orchestra / Sir Adrian Boult
EMI CDM7 64015-2 (55 minutes: ADD). Recorded Ⓜ
1970 and 1976 ○○

Adrian Boult's 1970 recording of the *Enigma* Variations offers similar riches to those of Barbirolli with the additional bonus of a slightly superior recorded sound. Boult's account has authority, freshness and a beautiful sense of spontaneity so that each variation emerges from the preceding one with a natural feeling of flow and progression. There is warmth and affection too coupled with an air of nobility and poise, and at all times the listener is acutely aware that this is a performance by a great conductor who has lived a lifetime with the music. One need only sample the passionate stirrings of Variation 1 (the composer's wife), the athletic and boisterous 'Troyte' variation, or the autumnal, elegiac glow that Boult brings to the famous 'Nimrod' variation to realise that this is a very special document indeed. The LSO, on top form, plays with superlative skill and poetry and the excellent recording has been exceptionally well transferred to CD. The *Pomp and Circumstance* Marches, recorded six years later with the London Philharmonic Orchestra, are invigoratingly fresh and direct – indeed the performances are so full of energy and good humour that it is hard to believe that Boult was in his late eighties at the time of recording! A classic.

Additional recommendations
'Enigma' Variations
Couplings: Cockaigne. Serenade. Salut d'amor
Baltimore Symphony Orchestra / Zinman
Telarc CD80192 (62 minutes: DDD: 10/90) Ⓕ
  An impressive performance. Zinman has the feel for the ebb and flow, the elasticity of the music, and he obtains idiomatic playing from the excellent Baltimore SO.

Further listening
Stenhammer Serenade in F, Op 31
Couplings: Piano Concerto No 2 in D minor, Op 23.
Florez och Blanzeflor, Op 3
Wixell *bar* **Solyom** *pf*
Munich Philharmonic Orchestra; Swedish Radio
Symphony Orchestra/ Westerberg
EMI Matrix CDM5 65081-2 (73 minutes: ADD: 5/94) Ⓕ
  The Serenade is arguably Stenhammar's masterpiece. In its Overture the writing is vibrant and luminous and full of subtly changing textures and colours.

Reger Four Symphonic Poems after Arnold Böcklin, Op 128
Coupling:Variations and Fugue on a Theme of JA Hiller,
Op 100
Royal Concergebouw Orchestra / Järvi
Chandos CHAN8794 (67 minutes: DDD: 3/90) Ⓕ
  Strongly recommended, especially to those who think they don't like Reger; how could anyone not like 'The Hermit playing the violin' from the Poems, or not respond to the Variations' breathtaking encyclopedia of orchestral resource?

Pomp and Circumstance

Pomp and Circumstance, Op 39 – No 1 in D[a]; Ⓗ
No 2 in A minor[a]; No 3 in C minor[b]; No 4 in G[a];
No 5 in C[b]. The Dream of Gerontius, Op 38 –
Prelude[c]. Serenade in E minor, Op 20[d]. Improvisation
No 4[f]. Salut d'amour, Op 12[e]. Chanson de nuit,
Op 15 No 1[e]. Chanson de matin, Op 15 No 2[b].
Land of Hope and Glory[b]. Cockaigne, Op 40[a]
[a]**BBC Symphony Orchestra,** [b]**London Symphony**
Orchestra, [c]**Royal Albert Hall Orchestra,** [d]**London**
Philharmonic Orchestra, [e]**New Symphony**
Orchestra / Sir Edward Elgar[f] *pf*
HMV Classics mono HMV5 74001-2 Ⓑ
(77 minutes: ADD). Recorded 1926-33 ○

With the magnificent Elgar Edition now deleted by EMI – three volumes of three discs each – it is good to have such an engaging sampling as this. Available through HMV stores and the HMV website, it comes as a welcome supplement to the three separate discs, recently issued in EMI's British Composers series, which offer the two symphonies and other works.

The five *Pomp and Circumstance* marches are taken from recordings of different vintages. The earliest, No 3, made in 1927, is thinner in sound than No 5, recorded in 1930 when it was new, and Nos 1, 2 and 4. Those are among Elgar's last recordings, made with the BBC Symphony Orchestra in 1932 and 1933. As with the *Cockaigne Overture*, also performed by the then recently founded BBC Symphony Orchestra, the sound as transferred is splendidly full-bodied, the Elgarian trombones rasping out wonderfully well. As for the performances, one can almost see Elgar's great moustache bristling at the panache of the playing, and the delightful lilt he gives to such a motif as the Dvořákian theme in No 3.

Broadly, as ever, Elgar favours speeds on the fast side, here and elsewhere, but then allows ripely romantic expansion in big expressive moments, as in the dedicated account of the *Gerontius* Prelude. Recorded live in 1927 at the Royal Albert Hall, that comes in limited but wonderfully atmospheric sound, leading on to the tenor's first entry. Setting the seal on this issue are two of the shortest and most moving items – one of the strangely intense piano improvisations he recorded for HMV with uninhibitedly splashy playing, and the brief account of *Land of Hope and Glory* he recorded with the LSO for a Pathé newsreel at the opening of the EMI Studios in Abbey Road in 1931. That brings a gruff but moving speech from Elgar: 'Gentlemen, please play this tune as though you've never heard it before.' That alone is worth the money.

Symphonies

No 1 in A flat, Op 55; **No 2** in E flat, Op 63; **No 3** in C minor, Op 88

Symphony No 1^{a}. Falstaff, Op 68^{b} H
London Symphony Orchestra / Sir Edward Elgar
EMI CDM5 67296-2 (80 minutes: ADD) Ⓜ
Recorded ^{a}1930 and ^{b}1931 OO

Symphony No 2 H
London Symphony Orchestra / Sir Edward Elgar
EMI CDM5 67297-2 (57 minutes: ADD) Ⓜ
Recorded 1927 OO

Cello Concerto in E minor, Op 85^{a}. Cockaigne, Op 40^{b}. Falstaff, Op 68^{c} – Interludes. Froissart, Op 19^{d}. In the South, Op 50^{e} H
^{a}**Beatrice Harrison** *vc* ^{d}**London Philharmonic Orchestra;** ^{b}**Royal Albert Hall Orchestra;** ^{e}**London Symphony Orchestra;** ^{ac}**New Symphony Orchestra / Sir Edward Elgar**
EMI CDM5 67298-2 (75 minutes: ADD) Ⓜ
Recorded ^{b}1926, ^{a}1928, ^{c}1929, ^{e}1930 and ^{d}1933 OO

The blockbuster coupling here (clocking in at nearly 80 minutes to boot) has to be that of the First Symphony and *Falstaff*, both of which receive readings that leave you gasping in wonder at the astonishing vitality, entrancing poetry and (above all) daring flexibility of Elgar's conducting. Certainly, this is a *Falstaff* brimful of humanity, irresistible narrative flair and (at the close) heart-rending poignancy. As for the symphony, never was there a more wistful treatment of the *Scherzo*'s enchanting trio section ('play it like something you hear down by the river,' Elgar used to say), while the work's thrilling closing pages have surely never resounded with greater cumulative swagger.

Similarly, the composer's 1927 version of the Second Symphony enshrines another inspirational display, its huge expressive fervour and blistering intensity shining like a beacon across the decades. First-timers should listen out for the generous use of *portamento*, to say nothing of the staggering reserves of *sostenuto* tone Elgar draws from the LSO strings (hardly a top-ranking group at the time). Recorded over just one day, this rapt performance was rush-released in time for Elgar's 70th birthday on June 2. Six weeks later, Elgar re-made the first side of the *Rondo* third movement (producer Fred Gaisberg having in the meantime noticed 'foreign noises' in the original take), and it was from those July 1927 sessions that the tantalising five-minute rehearsal sequence derives (the unique shellac pressing of which Elgar was extremely fond of playing to visitors at his home).

The third disc kicks off with a rivetingly characterful *Froissart* from February 1933 (with Elgar at the helm of Beecham's formidable, recently formed LPO), followed by an astoundingly charismatic *Cockaigne* with the Royal Albert Hall Orchestra (Elgar's very first recording for the electric microphone, set down in April 1926). Exhilarating is the only word to describe the 1930 account of *In the South* with the LSO, the music's thrusting grandeur and intimacy of feeling seamlessly integrated into a searingly cogent whole. We also get an agreeably bluff, aptly rustic rendering of the two 'Dream Interludes' from *Falstaff*, and the anthology concludes with Beatrice Harrison's big-hearted, wonderfully touching 1928 performance of the Cello Concerto.

The First Symphony's scherzo still sounds pretty uncongenial (though at least someone at EMI has taken the opportunity to tidy up that horrendous side-join at 4'20" that defaced its full-price predecessor). Otherwise, the sound is often remarkably vivid, with a commendable truthfulness of timbre on the third disc not quite matched by the first two (containing the symphonies and *Falstaff*).

Symphony No 1

Awards 1977

Symphony No 1. Serenade for Strings. Chanson de nuit, Op 15 No 1. Chanson de matin, Op 15 No 2
London Philharmonic Orchestra / Sir Adrian Boult
EMI CDM7 64013-2 (70 minutes: DDD) Ⓜ
Recorded 1968-76 OOO

Boult in Elgar on CD: the combination is irresistible, particularly when in addition to the symphony it comes with substantial and valuable makeweights. The 1976 recording of the symphony is among the last that Boult made of Elgar, a noble, unforced reading with no hint of extreme speeds in either direction. In Boult's view the flow of the music is kept free and direct, with *rallentandos* and *tenutos* reduced to the minimum in the links between sections. The sound in this digital transfer is first-rate, every bit as fine as the original LP. The brass is gloriously full, which with Elgar is one of the main necessities. On the fill-ups, more than in the symphony, the analogue original is revealed in the degree of tape-hiss, noticeable but not distracting, and if anything the 1973 recording of the Serenade brings sound even more vivid in its sense of presence than that of the bigger ensemble. Boult so naturally conveys the tenderness and delicacy of the inspiration, and so it is too in the two shorter pieces from 1968 with violin tone noticeably less full and rounded but still sweet enough. The couplings will for many be irresistible.

Symphony No 1 in A flat, Op 55. Introduction and Allegro, Op 47 (2 versions). Elegy, Op 58 (2 versions). Variations on an Original Theme, 'Enigma', Op 36. Bavarian Dances, Op 27 – Lullaby (H)
Hallé Orchestra / Sir John Barbirolli
Dutton Laboratories Barbirolli Edition ② CDSJB1017 (M)
(117 minutes: ADD). Recorded 1947 and 1956 ○○○

This splendid two-disc collection brings together most of the Elgar recordings that Barbirolli made with the Hallé Orchestra at its peak in the early post-war period, not just in the late '40s for HMV, but in the mid-'50s, when for a time they had a contract with Pye. These are generally more urgent readings than those he made later, often more passionate, and freer in *rubato*. All richly merit their reissue here.

Most cherishable of all is Barbirolli's glorious 1956 recording for Pye of the First Symphony, a performance which even Barbirolli rarely matched for its passionate intensity. Recorded in a single day it is more spontaneous in its expressiveness than his remake with the Philharmonia for HMV in 1962. On LP it had limited currency over the years, and appeared on CD for only a very short time on the briefly revived Nixa label. Here at last it appears in full-bodied and immediate stereo sound, transforming what we had before.

Interpretatively, it is typical of Barbirolli in its expressive freedom, with speeds often on the broad side, notably in the heavenly *Adagio*, as deeply felt as Elgar's own recording of 26 years earlier, but more spacious. Barbirolli's control of Elgarian climax through all four movements, notably in the finale, is unerring, and the brass is richly caught.

That comes on the first of the two discs, together with stereo versions of the *Introduction and Allegro* and *Elegy* recorded with the Symphony in December 1956. They make a fascinating contrast with the mono versions of those same two works made for HMV in 1947 and included on the second disc – never previously available in any format since their original issue on 78. The stereo versions are fuller-toned, but the 1947 reading of the *Introduction and Allegro* – the third of the six he recorded over the years – is, in its relative spareness, even more athletic and incisive, despite moments of breathlessness in the fugue.

The 1947 mono version of the *Enigma* Variations also makes an intriguing contrast with both his later recordings; it is at once more urgent and more volatile than either the 1956 Hallé version for Pye or the best-known version, that of 1962 for EMI, with the Sinfonia of London and the Allegri String Quartet. Both Hallé versions have soloists from the orchestra less prominently balanced, and rightly so.

This issue includes not only a highly informative note by Michael Kennedy, but a valuable Barbirolli/Elgar discography, complete with dates but no identification of orchestras. No Elgarian should miss this unique issue.

Additional recommendations
Symphony No 1
Couplings: Introduction and Allegro. Elegy. *'Enigma'* Variations. Bavarian Dances.
Hallé Orchestra / Barbirolli
Dutton Barbirolli Edition CDSJB1017 ② (M)
(117 minutes: DDD: A/00)
The best of Barbirolli's Hallé Elgar recordings, with a valuable discography and excellent notes. Don't miss this.

Symphony No 2

Symphony No 2. In the South. Pomp and Circumstance, Op 39 – Marches 1, 3 and 5
BBC Symphony Orchestra / Sir Andrew Davis
Teldec Ultima 0630 18951-2 (70 minutes: DDD) (B)
Recorded 1992 ○

In what is his finest achievement on record to date, Andrew Davis penetrates right to the dark inner core of this great symphony. In the opening *Allegro vivace e nobilmente*, for example, how well he and his acutely responsive players gauge the varying moods of Elgar's glorious inspiration: be it in the exhilarating surge of that leaping introductory paragraph or the spectral, twilight world at the heart of this wonderful movement, no one is found wanting. In fact, Davis's unerring structural sense never once deserts him, and the BBC Symphony Orchestra simply plays its heart out. Above all, though, it's in the many more reflective moments that Davis proves himself an outstandingly perceptive Elgarian, uncovering a vein of intimate anguish that touches to the very marrow; in this respect, his account of the slow movement is quite heart-rendingly poignant – undoubtedly the finest since Boult's incomparable 1944 performance with this very same orchestra – while the radiant sunset of the symphony's coda glows with luminous beauty. Prefaced by an equally idiomatic, stirring *In the South* (and aided throughout by some sumptuously natural engineering), this is an Elgar Second to set beside the very greatest. In every way a treasurable release.

Symphony No 2
BBC Philharmonic Orchestra / Sir Edward Downes
Naxos 8 550635 (56 minutes: DDD) (S)
Recorded 1993 ○

Here is further proof that Edward Downes is an Elgarian to be reckoned with. This account of the Second Symphony is up there with the very best. In the first movement, Downes steers a gloriously clear-sighted course: here is the same unexaggerated, splendidly authoritative conception heard from this conductor in the concert hall. Unlike some rivals on record, Downes resists the temptation to give too much too soon, and this feeling of power in reserve lends an extra cumulative intensity to the proceedings; indeed, the coda here is absolutely thrilling. The ensuing *Larghetto* sees Downes striking a near-perfect balance between introspection and heart-warming passion. Both the *Rondo* and finale are ideally paced – the former not too hectic, the latter flowing to perfection, culminating in an epilogue of rare delicacy. Throughout, the BBC Philharmonic plays outstandingly for its former chief: the orchestra's golden-toned cello section must be singled out for special praise. Just a touch more clarity in tuttis, and the recording would have been ideal. In sum, a deeply sympathetic Elgar Second, definitely the preferred budget version, possessing qualities to match any rival. At Naxos price, it's surely a must for all Elgarians.

Additional recommendations

Symphony No 2

Couplings: Sospiri. Elegy

Hallé Orchestra; New Philharmonia / Barbirolli

EMI British Composers CDM7 64724-2 Ⓜ

(66 minutes: ADD: 2/94)

Barbirolli's superb second recording of the Second Symphony. No one conveys the welling emotion of the second movement quite so candidly: tears spill from those violin glissandos at the climax.

Couplings: Symphony No 1. Pomp and Circumstance March No 5

Philharmonia / Haitink

EMI Double Forte ② CZS5 69761-2 Ⓜ

(118 minutes: DDD: 10/97)

The cumulative intensity of Haitink's interpretation is overwhelming in its clear-sightedness and emotional impact; moreover, the Philharmonia respond with refinement and dedication.

Coupling: Serenade

Hallé Orchestra / Loughran; Academy of St Martin in the Fields / Marriner

ASV Quicksilva CDQS6087 (70 minutes: DDD: 8/93) Ⓢ

This super-budget Elgar Second is surely well worth anyone's money. The Halle respond with commendable, sure-footed discipline and their playing lacks nothing in whole-hearted application or fervour.

Further listening

Suk Asrael Symphony, Op 27

Bavarian Radio Symphony Orchestra / Kubelík

Panton 81 1101-2 (64 minutes: ADD: 1/94) Ⓕ

A wholly compelling imaginative intensity and interpretative flair of a true poet of the rostrum.

Parry Symphony No 5

London Philharmonic Orchestra / Bamert

Chandos CHAN8955 (57 minutes: DDD: 9/91) Ⓕ

Bamert's treatment of the symphony is broad and particularly impressive in the slow movement. The orchestra plays with thrilling conviction.

Symphony No 3

Bournemouth Symphony Orchestra / Paul Daniel

Naxos 8 554719 (55 minutes: DDD) Ⓢ

Recorded 1999 **OO**

How thrillingly urgent Elgar's unforgettably gaunt introductory bars sound here – a magnificent launch-pad for an interpretation of unswerving dedication, plentiful character and purposeful intelligence. Audibly galvanised by Paul Daniel's fervent direction, the Bournemouth orchestra responds with infectious eagerness, notable polish and, most important, all the freshness of new discovery. In these newcomers' hands there's a rhythmic snap and athletic drive about the mighty opening movement that genuinely exhilarate. Where Davis perhaps scores over Daniel is in the spiritual, 'inner' dimension he brings to those ineffably beautiful bars at the start of the development section. Come the succeeding *Allegretto*, and Daniel's approach is more urgent, less evocative. By the way, in this same movement (4'34") the solo viola's G sharp crotchet is now trilled – just one of a clutch of subtle emendations Payne has since incorporated into the score since Sir Andrew Davis's première recording on NMC. The anguished slow movement welds a penetrating textural and harmonic clarity to a noble strength that is very moving. Best of all is the finale, which now emerges in a rather less piecemeal fashion than it does under Davis. Particularly good is the dark swagger that Daniel locates in both those *nobilmente* paragraphs beginning at bars 68 and 253 (2'36" and 10'01" respectively), while the closing bars are magical, the final soft tam-tam stroke disappearing into the ether like some vast unanswered question. Tony Faulkner's sound is excellent in every respect. In sum, another Elgar jewel in the Naxos crown: absolutely not to be missed.

Additional recommendation

Symphony No 3

BBC Symphony Orchestra / A Davis

NMC NMCD053 (56 minutes: DDD: 3/98) Ⓕ

An eloquent, profoundly involving performance with handsome, indeed demonstration-worthy sound.

Further listening

Schmidt Symphony No 4

Coupling: Variations on a Hussar's Song

London Philharmonic Orchestra / Welser-Möst

EMI CDS5 55518-2 (72 minutes: DDD: 1/96) Ⓕ

Welser-Möst shows great feeling for and sympathy with this music and carries his fine players with him.

Violin and Piano Works

Romance in C minor, Op 1. Pieces, Op 4 – No 1, Idylle; No 3, Virelai. Mazurka in C minor, Op 10 No 1. Salut d'amour. Bizarrerie in G minor, Op 13 No 2. Chanson de nuit. Chanson de matin. La capricieuse, Op 17. Gavotte in A. Etude-Caprice (cpted Reed). Serenade. May Song. In Hammersbach. Carissima. Adieu. Etudes characteristiques

Marat Bisengaliev *vn* **Benjamin Frith** *pf*
Black Box BBM1016 (67 minutes: DDD) Ⓕ
Recorded 1998

Born in 1962, Marat Bisengaliev hails from Kazakhstan and is a prize-winning graduate from the Moscow Conservatory. On the evidence of this most enjoyable disc he is a violinist of great technical accomplishment and communicative warmth, and he generates a really fine rapport with the admirable Benjamin Frith. As the opening *Romance* (with its striking echoes of the finale from Schumann's Fourth Symphony) immediately reveals, these artists bring an affectingly uncloying, totally unforced naturalness of expression to this charming repertoire. Even such well-worn nuggets as the two *Chansons* and *Salut d'amour* emerge with a new-minted freshness. Only in *La capricieuse* do you feel that the rubato lacks the last ounce of spontaneity. Elsewhere, the programme usefully plugs a number of gaps in the Elgar discography, not least the delectable *Bizarrerie*, Op 13 No 2 (companion piece to *Mot d'amour*), *Virelai* (1884) and a cheeky *Gavotte* from the following year. The winsome *In Hammersbach* will be more familiar as the second of the *Three Bavarian Dances* (though it began life as the third of six partsongs that went to make up the 1895 *Scenes from the Bavarian Highlands*). Eagle-eyed enthusiasts will also have spotted two world-première recordings in the contents listed above: it was left to violinist W H Reed to complete the *Etude-Caprice* that Elgar first sketched as long ago as 1877, while the ferocious difficulty of the five solo *Etudes characteristiques* of 1878 has long put off any potential champions on disc (and Bisengaliev rises to the challenge with fearless aplomb). Piano tone seems a touch metallic at the outset, but the ear soon adjusts, and balance within the generous church acoustic is generally excellent.

Elgar Violin Sonata in E minor, Op 82
Finzi Elegy in F, Op 22 **Walton** Violin Sonata
Daniel Hope *vn* **Simon Mulligan** *pf*
Nimbus NI5666 (62 minutes: DDD) Ⓕ
Recorded 2000 ○○○

It is good to find so responsive a young violinist as Daniel Hope turning to British music. As with his earlier Nimbus issues of Schnittke, Shostakovich and others he conveys his enthusiasm not just in his playing but in the informative notes that he himself provides. The coupling of the violin sonatas by Elgar and Walton is a most satisfying one, not unique on disc, and one which provides fascinating parallels. The Finzi *Elegy* is a very apt makeweight, the only surviving movement from a projected Violin Sonata written in a hectic period for the composer at the beginning of the Second World War.

The Elgar elicits a performance of high contrasts both in dynamic range – with Hope using daringly extreme *pianissimos* – and in flexibility of tempo. So in the first movement the opening at an urgent speed gives way to a very broad reading of the second subject, hushed and musingly introspective. Yet such freedom of expression goes with deep concentration, so that the structure is still firmly held together.

In the slow movement Hope, rather like Lydia Mordkovitch in her superb Chandos version, rejects the idea of this enigmatic movement and an interlude, bringing out gravity in his dark violin tone. In the finale, too, Hope conveys an improvisational quality, again using the widest dynamic range, finely matched by Simon Mulligan – like Hope, a Menuhin protégé.

Lorraine McAslan with John Blakely on ASV Quicksilva gives a lighter reading, generally faster with less extreme contrasts, and so it is too in the Walton Sonata. Menuhin in both the Elgar and the Walton brings out the virtuoso side of the writing, big and bold if not so detailed as Hope. The two movements are both among the longest of any of Walton's multi-movement works, and again, with big contrasts and concentrated expression, Hope and Mulligan hold the structure firmly together.

In the Variation second movement Mulligan, matching Hope, finds an improvisational quality in the dropping fourth motif which rounds off each of the contrasted variations. With slow music outweighing fast there is a danger that it will seem to end inconclusively, but Hope and Mulligan rise superbly to the challenge of the long eighth variation, like a deeply reflective barcarolle, leading into a dazzling coda, full of flair. With Hope's sweet, finely focused violin tone beautifully caught in the Nimbus recording – full and warm but less reverberant than some – and well-balanced against the piano, it makes an outstanding recommendation.

The Black Knight

The Black Knight, Op 25. Scenes from the Bavarian Highlands, Op 27
London Symphony Chorus and Orchestra / Richard Hickox
Chandos CHAN9436 (61 minutes: DDD) Ⓕ
Texts included. Recorded 1995

The Black Knight is a large-scale, red-blooded choral setting of Longfellow's translation of a German poem by Ludwig Uhland. Elgar completed it in 1893 and it provided him with his first big success – especially in the Midlands, where it was gratefully taken up by many choral societies. The text tells of a sinister, unnamed 'Prince of mighty sway', whose appearance at the King's court during the feast of Pentecost has disastrous consequences. Elgar's score boasts much attractive invention, some of it strikingly eloquent and prescient of greater offerings to come. The choral writing is always effective, the orchestration already vivid and assured. Richard Hickox and his combined London Symphony forces are dab hands at this kind of fare and their performance has great bloom and spaciousness. Similarly, in the tuneful, vernally fresh *Scenes from the Bavarian Highlands* (given here with the orchestral accompaniment

Elgar supplied in 1896), Hickox and his colleagues respond with commendable spirit and pleasing polish. Typical of Chandos, the recording is bright and clear, tonally beyond reproach and with just the right balance between choir and orchestra.

The Kingdom

The Kingdom, Op 51[a]. Coronation Ode, Op 44[b]
[a]**Margaret Price,** [b]**Felicity Lott** *sops* [a]**Yvonne Minton** *mez* [b]**Alfreda Hodgson** *contr* [a]**Alexander Young,** [b]**Richard Morton** *tens* [a]**John Shirley-Quirk,** [b]**Stephen Roberts** *bars* [a]**London Philharmonic Choir and Orchestra / Sir Adrian Boult;** [b]**Cambridge University Musical Society Chorus,** [b]**Choir of King's College Cambridge;** [b]**New Philharmonia Orchestra / Philip Ledger**
EMI British Composers ② CMS7 64209-2 (130 minutes: ADD) Ⓜ ●

Boult was a passionate admirer of *The Kingdom* and, as ever, the unaffected devotion and sheer authority of his advocacy is hard to resist. The two formidable contenders in the work are Leonard Slatkin and Richard Hickox. All three performers have much going for them. In short, Boult enjoys the strongest team of soloists, Hickox obtains the most disciplined and full-bodied choral work, and Slatkin secures the finest orchestral playing – indeed, the LPO are on inspired form, responding with an exemplary sensitivity, commitment and concentration which also marked out Slatkin's magnificent account of the Symphony No 2 set down with this same group some 17 months later. Slatkin also benefits from perhaps the best engineering, with Boult's Kingsway Hall production now sounding just a little pale and hard-edged in comparison. Where the EMI release really comes up trumps, though, is in the shape of its generous fill-up, Philip Ledger's superb, swaggering reading of the *Coronation Ode*. Ultimately, then, the Boult, must take the palm, especially at mid price, though no devoted Elgarian should miss hearing Slatkin's gloriously lucid conception either.

Additional recommendation
The Kingdom
Couplings: Sospiri. Sursum corda
Marshall, Palmer *sops* **Davies** *ten* **Wilson-Johnson** *bar* **London Symphony Chorus and Orchestra / Hickox**
Chandos ② CHAN8788/9 (108 minutes: DDD: 2/90) Ⓕ
Particularly impressive and moving from 'The Breaking of the Bread'; the orchestra play with fire and sensitivity.

The Light of Life

Judith Howarth *sop* **Linda Finnie** *mez* **Arthur Davies** *ten* **John Shirley-Quirk** *bar* **London Symphony Chorus and Orchestra / Richard Hickox**
Chandos CHAN9208 (63 minutes: DDD). Text included. Recorded 1993 Ⓕ

In the glorious orchestral 'Meditation' Hickox's conducting demonstrates a noble flexibility, sensitivity to dynamic nuance and feeling for climax. Equally the engineering, sumptuous yet detailed, comes close to the ideal. The LSO and Chorus contribute to proceedings in exemplary, disciplined fashion. As The Blind Man, Arthur Davies could hardly be more ardent, but his slightly tremulous timbre will not be to all tastes. John Shirley-Quirk, so eloquent and firm-toned a Jesus for Groves (on EMI) back in 1980, now shows signs of unsteadiness in the same part. On the other hand, Linda Finnie and Judith Howarth make a creditable showing. Hickox's reading excels in precisely the areas where the Groves was deficient, and vice versa. If you already have the Groves reissue, hang on to it, for it is by no means outclassed by the Hickox. However, for anyone coming to this underrated score for the first time, Hickox's must now be the preferred version.

Sea Pictures

Sea Pictures, Op 37. The Music Makers
Felicity Palmer *mez* **London Symphony Chorus and Orchestra / Richard Hickox**
EMI British Composers CDM5 65126-2 (62 minutes: DDD). Texts included. Recorded 1986 Ⓜ

These idiomatic Elgar performances from Richard Hickox well merit their mid-price resuscitation within EMI's British Composers series. Hickox's admirable London Symphony Chorus impresses in matters of intonation and diction. Felicity Palmer sings commandingly, though her contribution in *The Music Makers* doesn't always generate the tear-laden intensity the part requires. However, Hickox doesn't quite match Sir Andrew Davis's Teldec account – he evinces a personal identification with Elgar's inspiration that is rather special. In the *Sea Pictures*, however, Hickox and Palmer form an intelligent, distinctive partnership, less endearing, perhaps, than many would like in 'In Haven' and 'Where corals lie', yet tough and dramatic in 'Sabbath morning at sea' and 'The swimmer'. It is a thrusting, unsentimental view which is most refreshing. The orchestral playing is excellent.

The Dream of Gerontius

The Dream of Gerontius, Op 38[a]. Sea Pictures[b]
Janet Baker *mez* [a]**Richard Lewis** *ten* [a]**Kim Borg** *bass* [a]**Hallé Choir;** [a]**Sheffield Philharmonic Chorus;** [a]**Ambrosian Singers;** [a]**Hallé Orchestra,** [b]**London Symphony Orchestra / Sir John Barbirolli**
EMI British Composers ② CMS5 73579-2 (122 minutes: ADD). Texts included. Recorded 1964-65 Ⓜ ●●

This *Gerontius* very much belongs to the Angel of Janet Baker and the conducting of Barbirolli here giving another example of that instinctive rapport which filled the few precious recordings they made together. Barbirolli penetrated to the core of the work's spirituality. In showing his affection for it, he was liable to embark on slow tempos and unmarked *ritardandos*. Whether one accepts these or finds them self-indulgent rather depends on one's mood. The Prelude at once announces the intensity of feeling Barbirolli brings to the whole work. He is superb with his choir. Though it may not be as impressive a body as that on some other sets, it sings with perhaps the greatest character and conviction of all. Thank goodness it's given a forward recording. The Hallé is a superb instrument in Barbirolli's hands and Janet Baker is superb. We hear all the tenderness and eloquence one expects from an Angel, and a radiance balanced by other-worldliness. Her skill with the text is unrivalled. It comes to the fore in the description of St Frands's stigmata and in the whole dialogue with Gerontius. The farewell is the very epitome of serene consolation. Richard Lewis declaims 'Take me away' with the proper terror and utters a quite beautiful 'Novissima hora est' but elsewhere is less communicative and shows less spontaneity than for Sargent 10 years earlier. The cold from which he was said to be suffering seems occasionally evident. Perhaps it accounts for the very audible cough at the start of the 'Be merciful' chorus, just after he has stopped singing. If Kim Borg's Priest and Angel of the Agony are an acquired taste because of his peculiar accenting of the English language it's one worth acquiring. He has all the authority for the first role, the supple expression for the second. Many, many years ago this set found its way into many people's hearts, as it deserves, and they will be delighted to have it so arrestingly refurbished. Like so many other accounts of this piece, it is its own justification because everyone concerned was obviously inspired by the glorious music to give of his and her very best.

The Dream of Gerontius[a]. Cello Concerto[b] **H**
Gladys Ripley *contr* **Heddle Nash** *ten* **Dennis Noble** *bar* **Norman Walker** *bass* **Paul Tortelier** *vc*
Huddersfield Choral Society; [b]BBC Symphony Orchestra; [a]Liverpool Philharmonic Orchestra / Sir Malcolm Sargent
Testament mono ② SBT2025 (120 minutes: ADD) Ⓕ
Text included. Recorded 1945-53 ●

This pioneering set of *Gerontius* has come up newly minted in these superbly engineered transfers taken from 78rpm masters. That only enhances the incandescence and fervour of the reading itself, in virtually all respects the most convincing the work has received. Sargent's conducting, influenced by Elgar's, is direct, vital and urgently crafted with an inborn feeling for the work's ebb and flow and an overall picture that comprehends the piece's spiritual meaning while realizing its dramatic leanness and force. Heddle Nash's Gerontius is unrivalled in its conviction and inwardness. He was encouraged by Elgar in 1930 to take the part and sang it under the composer's baton in 1932 to his satisfaction. By 1945 the work was in Nash's being; he sang it from memory and had mastered every facet of interpreting it. Such phrases as 'Mary pray for me', 'Novissima hora est' and 'My soul is in my hand, I have no fear' come from and go to the heart. 'Take me away' is like a searing cry of pain from the depth of the singer's soul. Gladys Ripley is a natural and communicative Angel throughout, her flexible and appealing tone always a pleasure to hear. The Liverpool Philharmonic lives up to its reputation at the time as the country's leading orchestra (in particular the sonorous string section) and the members of the Huddersfield Choral Society sing as if their lives depended on the outcome. Tortelier's Cello Concerto presents the classical approach as compared with the romantic one of Du Pré, and is the best of Tortelier's readings of the work on disc, with his tone and phrasing at their firmest and most telling. A considered and unaffected reading among the best ever committed to disc.

Further listening
Schmidt Das Buch mit sieben Siegeln
Oelze *sop* **Kallisch** *contr* **Andersen, Odinius** *tens* **Pape, Reiter** *basses* **Winklhofer** *org*
Bavarian Radio Chorus and Symphony Orchestra / Welser-Möst
EMI ② CDS5 56660-2 (107 minutes: DDD) Ⓕ
Live recording

The singing throughout is impressive and the sensitive orchestral response reflects belief in this visionary work.

The Spirit of England

The Spirit of England, Op 80. Give unto the Lord, Op 74. O hearken thou, Op 64. The Snow, Op 26 No 1. Land of Hope and Glory (arr Fagge)
Dame Felicity Lott *sop* **London Symphony Chorus; Northern Sinfonia / Richard Hickox**
EMI British Composers CDM5 65586-2 Ⓜ
(52 minutes: DDD). Texts included. Recorded 1987

Hickox adopts a purposeful approach to the great wartime cantata, *The Spirit of England*. Many collectors got to know this compassionate and moving score through Sir Alexander Gibson's extremely fine 1976 recording (originally made for RCA, now reissued at mid-price on Chandos). Gibson's spacious and eloquent interpretation enshrined one of his very finest achievements in the studio, and possibly this EMI rival doesn't match it in sheer depth of feeling. That said, Hickox draws magnificent singing from the London Symphony Chorus, and his mobile reading compensates with a fervour to which many will positively respond. The fillers are all worth having, especially the sublime coronation Offertory from 1911, *O hearken thou*. The production lacks nothing in transparency and amplitude, though in *The Spirit of England* one craves a more expansive acoustic.

'Elgar's Interpreters on Record'

Crown of India – March of the Mogul Emperors[a]. **H**
The Dream of Gerontius[b] – My work is done[bc] (2 recordings); It is because then thou didst fear[c]; I see not those false spirits[b]; We now have passed the gate[b]; Softly and gently[b]. The Saga of King Olaf, Op 30 – And King Olaf heard the cry![d]. The Apostles, Op 49 – By the Wayside[e]. Caractacus, Op 35[f] – Leap, leap to light; O my warriors. O hearken thou, Op 64[g].

The Starlight Express[h] – O children, open your arms to me; There is a fairy hides in the beautiful eyes; I'm everywhere; My Old Tunes; Dustman, Laugher's Song. Songs (arr. Haydn Wood)[i] – Like to the damask rose; Queen Mary's song; Shepherd's Song, Op 16 No 1; Rondel, Op 16 No 3. The shower, Op 71 No 1[j]

[e]Dora Labbette, [h]Alice Moxon *sops* **[b]Dame Clara Butt, [c]Kathleen Ferrier** *contrs* **[b]Maurice d'Oisly, [d]Tudor Davies, [e]Hubert Eisdell** *tens* **[e]Dennis Noble, [e]Harold Williams, [h]Stuart Robertson** *bars* **[f]Peter Dawson** *bass-bar* **[e]Robert Easton** *bass* **[c]Gerald Moore** *pf* **[a]Black Diamonds Band; [b]New Queen's Hall Orchestra / Sir Henry Wood; [d]Symphony Orchestra / Sir Eugene Goossens; [e]Hallé Orchestra / Sir Hamilton Harty; [f]Orchestra / Sir John Barbirolli; [g]St George's Chapel Choir, Windsor / Sir Walford Davies; [i]Light Symphony Orchestra / Haydn Wood; [j]Glasgow Orpheus Choir / Sir Hugh Roberton**

Dutton Laboratories Elgar Society mono CDAX8019 Ⓑ (76 minutes: ADD). Recorded 1912-48

This wonderful collection of recordings, made for the most part in Elgar's own lifetime, has not only authenticity of period; for those born into that time it is something to be played and savoured where no absurdity of unmeasured response will be wondered at, or, ever so kindly, derided. The voices of the soloists, for instance. A snigger at Dame Clara Butt's Angel in *The Dream of Gerontius* would incite thoughts of murder. Those five who sing the Beatitudes and commentary in *The Apostles*, they too are so wonderfully of their period, and fine singers too. Tudor Davies, fiery as a Welsh Martinelli in his declamation of Olaf's saga, or Peter Dawson, exponent of 'singing that *was* singing' in *Caractacus*: these also are part of the sacred book. Kathleen Ferrier's test recording is movingly lovely to hear again, as is the Glasgow Orpheus Choir. In fact, not forgetting some of the less likely contents, this is an anthological treasure. Wondrously clean transfers have been mastered by Dutton Laboratories. Just hear that first track, the *Crown of India* March, and make a guess at the date; or, listening with perfect clarity to that record from *The Apostles*, recall how the light blue label whizzed round amid the gunge and dust bequeathed by the second-hand shop whence it came. Everything is for congratulations here, including John Knowles's fine booklet-notes.

George Enescu Romanian 1881-1955

GROVE *Enescu studied at the Vienna Conservatory (1888-94) and at the Paris Conservatoire (1895-9). Paris remained the centre of his professional life, though he spent much time in Romania as a teacher and conductor. He is regarded as the greatest and most versatile Romanian musician and was widely admired as a violinist. Apart from the two Lisztian Rhapsodies roumains for orchestra (1901) his music has been neglected, perhaps partly because of the complexity and diversity of his stylistic allegiances: Romanian folk music is a recurrent influence, but so too are Wagner and Reger and early Schoenberg. His output includes the opera Oedipe (1936), five symphonies (1905, 1914, 1921, 1934, 1941) and much chamber music.*

Poème roumain

Poème roumain, Op 1. Vox maris, Op 31[a]. Vox de la nature, Op posth

[a]Florin Diaconescu *ten* **George Enescu Bucharest Philharmonic [a]Choir and Orchestra / Cristian Mandeal**

Arte Nova Classics 74321 65425-2 Ⓢ (62 minutes: DDD). Recorded 1997

If all you know of Enescu are his First *Romanian Rhapsody* and Third Violin Sonata, then the 26-minute symphonic poem *Vox maris* – which preoccupied its composer for some 20 years – will likely come as a profound shock. Even Scriabin would have drowned in these waters with their pungent harmonic cross-currents, exotic colours and densely crowded textures. Enescu's orchestra is huge: quadruple woodwinds, six horns, four trumpets, three trombones, tuba, timpani, percussion (five players), two harps, piano and off-stage chorus. There is a form of sorts (slow-fast-slow) and the opening recalls the romanticised antiquity of Pfitzner's *Palestrina*, but the overwhelming impression is of vast, tonal tidal waves that ultimately defeat the sailor of the story (a death at sea) and draw cries of 'Miserere, Domine' from the soprano. Tolling horn lines recall Sibelius's *Tapiola* while the desolate closing moments suggest the sucking of shingle against distant thunder and a hollow wind. Enescu's expansive *Romanian Poem* is an outrageously precocious essay for a teenager, redolent of Saint-Saëns in its slow first section and with elements of Romanian dance in the second. Viewed purely as music, one thinks of Liszt (primarily) and that upcoming First *Romanian Rhapsody*. Of the available versions this release packs the weightiest wallop and is certainly the best recorded. *Voix de la nature*, an unfinished torso, emerges as a close-knit tapestry of sound that, like *Vox maris*, has an air of ancient legend about it. A good deal happens during its eight-and-a-half minutes, but the petered-out ending offers no clues as to where the music might have been going. The interpretation is convincing (though the playing isn't front-rank), the sound excellent and the musical journey well worth making. At a fiver, you won't find a cheaper ticket to a more interesting destination.

String Quartets, Op 22

String Quartets, Op 22 – No 1 in E flat; No 2 in G

Ad Libitum Quartet (Adrian Berescu, Serban Mereuta *vns* Bogdan Bisoc *va* Filip Papa *vc*)

Naxos 8 554721 (74 minutes: DDD) Ⓢ
Recorded 1999

There's something peculiarly appealing about delving among the pages of an expansive, imaginatively written string quartet. Schoenberg, Reger and Hindemith all composed them; even Dvořák let his ideas ramble for an hour-long Third Quartet, but Enescu's 1920 First Quartet crams so much into 45-odd minutes that even two or three hearings barely scratch its surface. The massive, harmonically complex first movement is cast in sonata form, though the extended stream of consciousness that dominates the development section embraces all manner of colours and nuances. It's a veritable forest of invention, fairly Brahmsian in texture, organic in its thinking (themes thread easily from one to another) and frequently dramatic.

The second movement incorporates sundry embellishments and effects (including the use of *sul ponticello*), and the finale features variations on a march-like theme. It will make wonderful if challenging listening for anyone who values quality ideas above economical structuring.

Although the two quartets share the single opus number (22), they're years apart chronologically, aeons if you consider their contrasting styles. The Second Quartet was Enescu's penultimate work and breathes the heady aroma of Romanian folk music, especially in the slow movement and finale, which recall the world of the far better-known Third Violin Sonata. Shorter than the First Quartet by almost half, the Second feels tighter and more agile. Again, Enescu employs *sul ponticello*; harmonics too, while certain parts of the work (the second movement in particular) seem to have taken on board something of the colour scheme that Bartók employed for his Fifth Quartet. At other times Enescu seems surprisingly closer to Schoenberg than to Bartók.

The Ad Libitum Quartet do a fabulous job. They attend to Enescu's endless technical demands with a devotion that translates to apparent effortlessness. That in itself is a real achievement, and their generally soft-spoken, conversational mode of playing is in marked contrast to the tougher-grained Voces Quartet on Olympia, another good group, marginally more intense than Ad Libitum, more angular in their phrasing but hardly flattered by a hard analogue recording. CPO's Quatuor Athenaeum Enesco are also accomplished, swifter than the Ad Libitum in the Second Quartet and more resonantly recorded. But despite their freewheeling way with the First Quartet's third movement, viewed overall, their command of nuance is less comprehensive than Ad Libitum's, and their tempo transitions less effective. In sum, Naxos's superior production is a secure top recommendation and unbeatable value too. You simply have to try it.

Einar Englund — Finnish 1916-1999

GROVE *Englund studied with Palmgren and Carlsson at the Helsinki Academy (1933-41), with Copland at Tanglewood, and in Russia, where he was impressed by Prokofiev and Shostakovich. His works include five symphonies (1946-77), concertos and piano pieces.*

Symphonies

Symphonies – No 2, 'Blackbird'; No 4, 'Nostalgic'. Piano Concerto No 1[a]
[a]Niklas Sivelöv *pf* **Turku Philharmonic Orchestra / Jorma Panula**
Naxos 8 553758 (76 minutes: DDD) Ⓢ
Recorded 1996

The late Einar Englund is the finest Finnish symphonist between Sibelius and Kokkonen, and the *Blackbird* Symphony is one of his best. One can hear why he so named it from the woodwind writing, particularly the solos for flute, although he grew wary of emphasising the title in later life. One of the most attractive features of all his music is its orchestration. Panula's account is superbly played, with excellent sound. The Fourth (1976), written in memory of Shostakovich, is less epic, though no less inventive. A chamber symphony for strings and percussion, its most effective movement is the sparkling but macabre *Scherzo*, 'Tempus fugit', haunted by the chiming of bells and the manic ticking of some outlandish clock. Here, as well as in the darkly poetic third span, 'Nostalgia', and concluding 'Epilogue', Panula finds great poetry. Naxos's centrepiece, though, is the first of Englund's two piano concertos, otherwise unavailable, written for a competition in 1955 – which it won. Englund's own recording disappeared from the catalogue long ago, but Niklas Sivelöv proves a fine advocate.

Symphonies – No 4, 'Dedicated to the Memory of a Great Artist'; No 5, 'To the Memory of JK Paasikivi'. The Great Wall of China
Tampere Philharmonic Orchestra / Eri Klas
Ondine ODE961-2 (65 minutes: DDD) Ⓕ

The first cycle of Englund's seven symphonies is finally completed here (after 10 years and under its third conductor) with the Fourth and Fifth and an exuberantly parodistic theatre suite. Paavo Pohjola set the pace in the Fourth Symphony (1976) in the 1980s (Finlandia – nla); not until 1993 did a second appear, from Geza Szilvay's fine youth orchestra. Well-phrased and zestful, especially in the 'Tempus fugit' *scherzo*, Szilvay's focus on detail (in some places still the most finely realised) sacrificed momentum, a failing his rivals avoid. Panula plumbed deepest in the slow movement 'Nostalgia', though there is very little difference between his account and Klas's; both set a more realistic tempo in the finale than Szilvay. Finlandia's still excellent recording is edged out by Ondine's.

The Fifth Symphony (1977) was recorded on LP by Jukka-Pekka Saraste; Englund once said this was too fast, so he would probably have approved of Klas's better-judged version. Although titled *Sinfonia Fennica* ('Finnish' Symphony) and dedicated to the memory of President Paasikivi, the composer claimed it contained more of his wartime experiences than his famous *War* Symphony (No 1, 1946). In a bold, riveting single span, its full orchestration pairs very effectively with the strings-and-percussion of No 4.

The suite from the incidental music to Max Frisch's *The Great Wall of China* (1949) is great fun. *Pace* the booklet-note, Englund parodied Shostakovich specifically in four of the eight movements, not just the March. 'The Green Table Tango' and 'Rumba' reveal what an adept light/jazz composer he also was (under the pseudonym, Marcus Eje). The Tampere band are really put through their paces here and come through very well. If Panula's Naxos disc is still perhaps the best introduction to Englund's music, this disc should certainly be the next stop.

Manuel de Falla   Spanish 1876-1946

GROVE *Falla studied in Cádiz. and from the late 1890s in Madrid, where he was a pupil of Tragó for the piano and Pedrell for composition. In 1901-3 he composed five zarzuelas in the hope of making money; then in 1905 came his first important work, the one-act opera La vida breve, which he revised before its first performance, in Paris in 1913. He had moved to Paris in 1907 and become acquainted with Dukas, Debussy, Ravel, Stravinsky and Albéniz, all of whom influenced his development of a style using the primitive song of Andalusia, the cante jondo, and a modern richness of harmony and colour. This was not an immediate achievement: he wrote little before returning to Madrid in 1914, but then came the piano concerto Noches en los jardines de España (1915) and the ballets El amor brujo (1915) and El sombrero de tres picos (1919), the latter presented by Dyagilev and designed by Picasso.*

Like Stravinsky a few years before, he turned to a much sparer style and to the format of touring theatre in El retablo de maese Pedro (1923). He also began to concern himself with the medieval, Renaissance and Baroque musical traditions of Spain, reflected in his Concerto for harpsichord and quintet (1926). Most of the rest of his life he devoted to a vast oratorio, Atlántida, on which he worked in Granada (where he had settled in 1919) and after 1939 in Argentina. With Albéniz and Granados he was one of the first Spanish composers to win international renown and the most gifted of the three.

Harpsichord Concerto

Harpsichord Concerto. El sombrero de tres picos
Maria Lluisa Muntada *sop* **Tony Millan** *hpd* **Jaime Martin** *fl* **Manuel Angulo** *ob* **Joan-Enric Lluna** *cl* **Santiago Juan** *vn* **Jorge Pozas** *vc* **Spanish National Youth Orchestra / Edmon Colomer**
Auvidis Valois V4642 (56 minutes: DDD) Ⓕ
Recorded 1989

Falla's *El sombrero de tres picos* ('The three-cornered hat') started life as a 'mimed farce', but Diaghilev then persuaded the composer to revise and enlarge it as a one-act ballet for his company which had its première in London in 1919. Besides the orchestra, it features a soprano solo warning wives to resist temptation and cries of 'Olé' from men's voices representing a bull-ring crowd. Much of the score consists of dances such as the fandango and seguidilla, while the finale is a jota. This performance by Maria Lluisa Muntada and the Spanish National Youth Orchestra, playing under the direction of its founder Edmon Colomer, brings to us all the vivid colours, intense melodies and vigorous rhythms that together evoke that southernmost province of Spain which is Andalusia. These artists clearly love and understand this music and they bring tremendous gusto to the famous 'Miller's Dance' (the longest single number) with its chunky chords getting louder and faster. The Harpsichord Concerto, completed in 1926, shows us another side of Falla and was among the first 20th-century compositions for the instrument. It is less obviously Spanish in style and instead more neo-classical – indeed, Stravinsky was probably the chief model – although we may detect an Iberian element in its directness and even toughness. With just five instruments playing alongside the soloist, it is really a chamber work, but the writing is so powerful that the composer's title is doubtless justified. Here, too, the playing is fine and the recording of both these works is full-blooded and atmospheric.

Noches en los jardines de España

Falla El amor brujo – ballet (complete)[a]. Noches en los jardines de España[b] **Rodrigo** Concierto de Aranjuez[c]
[a]**Huguette Tourangeau** *mez* [c]**Carlos Bonnell** *gtr* [b]**Alicia de Larrocha** *pf* [ac]**Montreal Symphony Orchestra / Charles Dutoit**; [b]**London Philharmonic Orchestra / Rafael Frühbeck de Burgos**
Decca Ovation 430 703-2DM (71 minutes: DDD) Ⓜ
Recorded 1980-83 ●

Decca's hugely enjoyable disc of Spanish music includes Rodrigo's most famous work, the *Concierto de Aranjuez* which has never lost its popularity since its Barcelona première in 1940. Here Carlos Bonnell imparts a wistful, intimate feeling to the work, aided by a thoughtful accompaniment from Charles Dutoit's stylish Montreal Orchestra. The famous string tune in the *Adagio* enjoys a fulsome rendition. Dutoit's beautifully played interpretation of *El amor brujo* captures the wide range of emotions that this fiery, mysterious piece requires and his performance of the famous 'Ritual Fire Dance' must be among the best in the catalogue. A cooler mood is captured in *Nights in the gardens of Spain* with Alicia de Larrocha as the distinguished soloist. Her smooth, effortless playing matches the mood of the piece exactly and de Burgos's accompaniment with the London Philharmonic is equally sympathetic, with ripe tone colour and careful dynamics. Those unfamiliar with these great Spanish works will be hard pressed to find a better introduction than this superbly recorded disc.

Albéniz (orch Halffter). Rapsodia española, Op 70 **Falla** Noches en los jardines de España **Turina** Rapsodia sinfónica, Op 66
Alicia de Larrocha *pf* **London Philharmonic Orchestra / Rafael Frühbeck de Burgos**
Decca 410 289-2DH (52 minutes: DDD) Ⓕ
Recorded 1983

The three magically beautiful nocturnes which make up Falla's *Nights in the gardens of Spain* express the feelings and emotions evoked by contrasted surroundings, while Albéniz's enjoyably colourful *Rapsodia española* is a loosely assembled sequence of Spanish dances such as the *jota* and the *malagueña*. Like Falla's *Nights* the work was conceived as a piano solo, but this disc contains a version with orchestra arranged by Cristóbal Halffter. The disc is completed by Turina's short, two-part work for piano and strings. All three pieces are excellently performed, but it is the Falla work which brings out the quality of Larrocha's artistry; her ability to evoke the colour of the Spanish atmosphere is remarkable. Frühbeck de Burgos supports her magnificently and persuades the LPO to produce some very Latin-sounding playing. The recording is suitably atmospheric.

Noches en los jardines de España[a]. El sombrero de tres picos[b]
[b]**Jennifer Larmore** *mez* **Chicago Symphony** [b]**Chorus and Orchestra /** [a]**Plácido Domingo,** [b]**Daniel Barenboim** [a]*pf*
Teldec 0630-17145-2 (63 minutes: DDD). Text and translation included. Recorded live 1997 Ⓜ

All the key recordings of Falla's magically luminous nights spent in exotic Spanish gardens are quite old now, although still excellent, so a splendid new version is very welcome indeed. Barenboim and Domingo make a wonderfully understanding partnership, wafting the great Chicago orchestra into the Spanish night with its balmy warmth, and glittering background of flamenco dance rhythms. The rustling opening of the evocation of the 'Generalife' is beautifully managed by Domingo, and Barenboim's crystal-clear entry somehow suggests the water flowing in those astonishing centuries-old Moorish fountains. The orchestral detail is full of subtle colouring, and the ebb and flow of tempo and tension seem totally spontaneous. The central 'Danza lejana' glimmers and glitters and leads into the final sequence with sparkling pianistic dash and a most volatile response from the Chicago players. The languorous closing pages create a richly sensuous sunset-like apotheosis, Domingo's expansive *rallentando* boldly underlined by the piano. Daniel Barenboim conducts *The Three Cornered Hat* which opens with a fierce, brash briskness from trumpet and timpani, and Jennifer Larmore is a vibrant if not especially individual soloist. Again this superb orchestra revels in the vivid colouring and flashing rhythms, and no less so in the gentler moments. The live recording is full-blooded, yet has plenty of transparency. Strongly recommended.

El sombrero de tres picos

El amor brujo[a]. El sombrero de tres picos[b]. La vida breve – Interlude and Dance
[b]**Teresa Berganza** *sop* [a]**Marina de Gabarain** *mezzo* **Suisse Romande Orchestra / Ernest Ansermet**
Decca Legends 466 991-2DM (69 minutes: ADD) Ⓜ
Recorded [a]1955 and 1961 ○○○

Ansermet's vintage 1961 recording of *El sombrero de tres picos* with the Suisse Romande Orchestra is an electrifyingly great performance and the sound remains in the top demonstration class – four decades after it was made!

Ansermet's opening with hard-sticked timpani, extrovert trumpeting and fervently spirited 'Olés' creates an altogether different sound world of dramatic primary colours and rhythmic pungency. He has the advantage of the characterful Teresa Berganza as his soloist, and the ballet swings along spontaneously, with infectious zest, the Swiss orchestra on its toes and clearly enjoying every minute. Every detail of Falla's superb score is sharply and richly focused, the colours lighting up radiantly. Just try the opening of Ansermet's 'Neighbours' Dance' to hear just how this music should be played, while the horn and cor anglais fanfares which announce the gutsy 'Miller's Dance' could not be more commanding. The finale just grabs the listener, and carrries the music along with thrilling impetus to make a thrillingly expansive climax. This is a truly marvellous performance and the spectacular Victoria Hall recording, produced by James Walker and remastered by Andrew Wedman could hardly be better had it been made yesterday.

Ansermet's *El amor brujo* is very early stereo (1955) and not as opulent as *El sombrero*, but it still sounds remarkably lustrous. The performance is not quite as distinctive as its companion, but is still brightly etched, 'El círculo mágico' being quite bewitching; and the strings as well as the horns bring splendid bite to the 'Fire Dance'. The finale does expose the weakness of the Suisse Romande Orchestra in the middle strings, but it's none the less passionately played. A reissue fully worthy of its legendary status.

Atlántida (arr E Halffter)[a]. El sombrero de tres picos[b]
[a]**Enriqueta Tarrés,** [b]**Victoria de los Angeles** *sops* **Anna Ricci** *mez* **Eduardo Giménez** *ten* **Vincente Sardinero** *bar* [a]**Children's Chorus of Our Lady of Remembrance;** [a]**Spanish National Chorus and Orchestra;** [b]**Philharmonia Orchestra / Rafael Frühbeck de Burgos**
EMI Matrix ② CMS5 65997-2 (146 minutes: DDD) Ⓜ
Texts and translations included.Recorded 1963-77

Not even the devoted efforts of Falla's pupil Ernesto Halffter could succeed in making a convincing whole of the oratorio his master left in a jumble of disorganized fragments. Both textually and musically it remains a disparate collection of ideas that the composer, through ill-health and the depression caused by the cumulative effects of the Spanish civil war, an unhappy refuge in Argentina and then the great European war, was for over two decades unable to muster into order. Yet it was conceived with the most elevated of aims – a mystic 're-emergence' of submerged Atlantis signifying a celebration of Spain's extending the bounds of Christianity. There is much splendid music in the widest diversity of styles, particularly for the chorus who, with a baritone narrator, carries the main weight of the work. Sardinero is a noble-voiced narrator, Ricci brings pathos to her solo as the dying Queen Pyrene; in the charmingly folk-like 'Isabella's dream' a steadier line than Tarrés produces would have been preferable. The chorus, which has some of the most impressive sections, is mostly good, and the orchestra provides useful support. In view of its troubled genesis, the work is inevitably flawed, and some people might prefer merely a suite of its finest sections; but the full Halffter reconstruction, now accepted as definitive, gives us a glimpse of the masterpiece *Atlántida* might have been. There have been other excellent performances of the ever-fresh *Three-cornered hat*, but none better than this imaginative and scintillating reading by Frühbeck and the Philharmonia. So vivacious and idiomatic is the playing, so flexible and alive to all the score's sly, witty allusions, and so subtle are the nuances, that the stage-pictures seem to be conjured up before our eyes. The recording is as vivid as the performance. Terrific!

Gabriel Fauré

French 1845-1924

GROVE *Fauré was trained at the Ecole Niedermeyer (1854-65) as organist and choirmaster, coming under the influence of Saint-Saëns and his circle while working as a church musician (at Rennes, 1866-70; St Sulpice, 1871-3; the Madeleine, from 1874) and giving lessons. Though he met Liszt and was fascinated by Wagner, he sought a distinctive style in his piano pieces and numerous songs, which had to be composed during summer holidays. Recognition came slowly owing to the modernity of his music. In 1892 he became national inspector of the provincial conservatories, and in 1896 chief organist at the Madeleine and composition teacher at the Conservatoire, where his pupils included Ravel, Koechlin, Roger-Ducasse, Enescu and Nadia Boulanger; from 1905 to 1920 he was the Conservatoire's resolute and influential director, becoming celebrated for the vocal and chamber master-pieces he produced until his death.*

Fauré's stylistic development can be traced from the sprightly or melancholy song settings of his youth to the bold, forceful late instrumental works, traits including a delicate combination of expanded tonality and modality, rapid modulations to remote keys and continuously unfolding melody. Widely regarded as the greatest master of French song, he produced six important cycles (notably the novel La bonne chanson op.61) and three collections each of 20 pieces (1879, 1897, 1908). In chamber music he enriched all the genres he attempted, while his works for piano (chiefly nocturnes, barcarolles and impromptus) embody the full scope of his stylistic evolution. Among his few large-scale works, the popular and delicately written Requiem op.48 and the 'song opera' Pénélope (1913) are noteworthy.

Dolly Suite

Pelléas et Mélisande, Op 80 (with Chanson de Mélisande – orch Koechlin). Three Songs, Op 7 – Après un rêve (arr vc/orch Dubenskij). Pavane, Op 50. Elégie, Op 24. Dolly Suite, Op 56 (orch Rabaud)
Lorraine Hunt *sop* **Jules Eskin** *vc* **Tanglewood Festival Chorus; Boston Symphony Orchestra / Seiji Ozawa**
DG 423 089-2GH (56 minutes: DDD). Texts and translations included. Recorded 1986 Ⓕ

Fauré's music for Maeterlinck's play *Pelléas et Mélisande* was commissioned by Mrs Patrick Campbell and to the usual four-movement suite Ozawa has added the 'Chanson de Mélisande', superbly sung here by Lorraine Hunt. Ozawa conducts a sensitive, sympathetic account of the score, and Jules Eskin plays beautifully in both the arrangement of the early song, *Après un rêve*, and the *Elégie*, which survived from an abandoned cello sonata. The grave *Pavane* is performed here in the choral version of 1901. *Dolly* began life as a piano duet, but was later orchestrated by the composer and conductor Henri Rabaud. Ozawa provides us with a pleasing account of this delightful score and the recording is excellent.

Masques et bergamasques, Op 112. Ballade, Op 19. Pavane, Op 50. Fantaisie, Op 79. Pénélope – Overture. Elégie, Op 24. Dolly Suite (orch Rabaud)
Richard Davis *fl* **Peter Dixon** *vc* **Kathryn Stott** *pf*
BBC Philharmonic Orchestra / Yan Pascal Tortelier
Chandos CHAN9416 (72 minutes: DDD) Ⓕ
Recorded 1995

The biggest *concertante* work here, the *Ballade* of 1881, is Fauré's orchestration of his piano piece of the same name; it is gentle music that persuades and cajoles in a very Gallic way. Though not an overtly virtuoso utterance, it makes its own exacting technical demands on the soloist, among them being complete control of touch and pedalling. The highly-regarded Fauréan Kathryn Stott meets these with consistent success. *Masques et bergamasques*, which takes its title from Verlaine's sad, mysterious poem *Clair de lune*, is a late stage work that the composer himself described as melancholy and nostalgic, but it is hardly romantic, being instead pointedly neo-classical in character and shape, recalling Bizet's youthful C major Symphony and Grieg's *Holberg Suite*. The playing here under Yan Pascal Tortelier is very satisfying, as are the elegant flute solos of the exquisitely delicate *Pavane*, performed here without the optional chorus, and in *Dolly*. The rarely heard Overture to the opera *Pénélope* is also effectively presented here. There's little rhetoric and no bombast in Fauré's art, but how civilized he was, and what sympathetic interpreters serve him here! The recording is warm yet also delicate.

Ballade, Op 19

Fauré Ballade, Op 19 **Franck** Symphonic Variations, Op 46 **d'Indy** Symphonie sur un chant montagnard français in G, Op 25
François-Joël Thiollier *pf* **National Symphony Orchestra of Ireland / Antonio de Almeida**
Naxos 8 550754 (55 minutes: DDD) Ⓢ
Recorded 1993

The renamed RTE Symphony Orchestra, a match for its more recorded counterpart in Ulster, taped this programme in their Dublin concert hall (acoustically clean, bright and airy, but warm, if this disc's sound is representative). François-Joël Thiollier's playing is individual, often impulsive but always idiomatic, helped by the sensitive, guiding hand of a conductor well acquainted with the music. A more high-profile production would probably have retaken those passages where piano and orchestra co-ordination is occasionally fractionally awry, such as in the last variation of the Franck, but it might also have seemed less spontaneous. Thiollier's rubato is always distinctive and attractive; the style, particularly and crucially in the Fauré, properly fluid. Both the piano and the orchestra's woodwind are discreetly prominent, but internal balances are generally excellent. There are no budget-price competitors in this repertoire that reproduce with such beauty of tone.

Piano Quintets

Awards 1995

Piano Quintets – No 1 in D minor, Op 89; No 2 in C minor, Op 115
Domus (Krysia Osostowicz *vn* Timothy Boulton *va* Richard Lester *vc* Susan Tomes *pf*); **Anthony Marwood** *vn*
Hyperion CDA66766 (60 minutes: DDD) Ⓕ
Recorded 1994 ○○○

This is not music that yields up its secrets easily. Indeed, despite pages pulsing with all of Fauré's sustained radiance and energy the abiding impression is of music of such profound introspection that the listener often feels like an interloper stumbling into an essentially private conversation. But perseverance reaps the richest rewards and moments like the opening of the D minor Quintet where Fauré achieves what is referred to in the insert-notes as a 'rapt weightlessness', or the closing pages of the C minor Quintet's *Andante moderato* send out resonances that finally embrace the entire work. The otherworldly dance commencing the finale of the First Quintet, the wild catch-as-catch-can opening and elfin close of the C minor Quintet's *Allegro vivo* or the grave serenity of the following *Andante moderato*; all these are surely at the heart of Fauré's simultaneously conservative and radical genius. Simply as a person Fauré remained conscious of an elusiveness that baffled and tantalized even his closest friends, companions who felt themselves gently but firmly excluded from his complex interior world. Domus fully suggests this enigma yet plays with such ardour and *élan* that the composer himself would surely have been delighted ('people play me as if the blinds were down'). The recordings are superb.

Piano Quartets

Awards 1986

Piano Quartets – No 1 in C minor, Op 15; No 2 in G minor, Op 45
Domus (Krysia Osostowicz *vn* Robin Ireland *va* Timothy Hugh *vc* Susan Tomes *pf*)
Hyperion CDA66166 Ⓕ
(62 minutes: DDD) ○○○

The First Piano Quartet reveals Fauré's debt to an earlier generation of composers, particularly Mendelssohn. Yet already it has the refined sensuality, the elegance and the craftsmanship which were always to be hallmarks of his style and it is a thoroughly assured, highly enjoyable work which could come from no other composer's pen. The Second Quartet is a more complex, darker work, but much less ready to yield its secrets. The comparatively agitated, quicksilver *Scherzo* impresses at once, however, and repeated hearings of the complete work reveal it to possess considerable poetry and stature. Just occasionally one could wish that the members of Domus had a slightly more aristocratic, commanding approach to these scores, but overall the achievement is highly impressive, for their playing is both idiomatic and technically impeccable. The recording is faithful and well balanced.

Works for Cello

Romance in A, Op 69[b]. Elégie, Op 24[b]. Cello Sonatas[b] – No 1 in D minor, Op 109; No 2 in G minor, Op 117. Allegretto moderato[a]. Sérénade, Op 98[b]. Sicilienne, Op 78[b]. Papillon, Op 77[b]. Andante[c]
Steven Isserlis, [a]**David Waterman** *vcs* [b]**Pascal Devoyon** *pf* [c]**Francis Grier** *org*
RCA Victor Red Seal 09026 68049-2 Ⓕ
(62 minutes: DDD). Recorded 1993-94

This, surely, is the most 'complete' of Fauré's complete works for cello yet to appear. Isserlis has unearthed the original version of the *Romance*, Op 69 (entitled *Andante*), with a sustained, chordal accompaniment for organ in place of the piano's broken chordal semiquavers, and a gracious flourish from the cello by way of adieu. Mystically accompanied by Francis Grier at the organ of Eton College Chapel, the cello's song, restored to the church, seems to acquire more depth. But let it be said at once that in the familiar version of this work, as throughout the disc, Pascal Devoyon is a partner in a thousand, keenly aware of Isserlis's respect for the 'discretion, reticence and restraint' once hailed as the hallmarks of Fauré's style. In fact only in the noble *Elégie* do we discover the full breadth and richness of this cello's (a 1745 Guadagnini) tonal range. A world war, plus the private trauma of incipient deafness, helps to explain the yawning gulf between the miniatures and the two sonatas of 1918 and 1922. Skipping through the score of the First you notice that only once does Fauré use a dynamic marking above a *forte*, relying on the word *espressivo* to elicit just that little extra intensity at moments of climax. This is appreci-ated by both artists, most movingly in the central *Andante*. In the first movement, how-ever, it is Devoyon's piquant accentuation that brings home the music's menace. The urgency and *Elégie*-evoking heart-throb of the G minor work again benefit from the immediacy of key-board characterization, and the variety of keyboard colour, underpinning this poetically introspective cellist's fine-spun line.

Violin Sonatas

No 1 in A, Op 13; No 2 in E minor, Op 108

Fauré Violin Sonatas Nos 1 and 2[a] **Franck** Violin Sonata in A[b]
Arthur Grumiaux *vn* [a]**Paul Crossley**, [b]**György Sebok** *pfs*
Philips Musica da Camera 426 384-2PC Ⓜ
(73 minutes: ADD). Recorded 1979 ○○

Those Fauré-lovers who long prayed for a CD reissue of the two sonatas from Grumiaux and Paul Crossley won't be disappointed. The sound itself is pleasing – better, even, than it was on LP. And there is a radiance in the playing suggesting an unerring understanding of structure and style that somehow goes hand in hand with the joyous spontaneity of new discovery. The hyper-sensi-tive suppleness of Grumiaux's shading and phrasing is a particular delight, as is his aware-ness that just as much of the musical message comes from the piano – particularly in the Sec-ond Sonata. As for Crossley, not for nothing has he come to be recognized as one of this country's most dedicated Fauré specialists. It would cer-tainly be difficult to over-praise the subtlety of the two artists' interplay in both works. Inciden-tally, their immediacy of response often finds outlet in a slightly faster tempo than most of their rivals, not least in both slow movements, where they rise more urgently to moments of heightened excitement (perhaps even too urgently in the *Andante* of the Second Sonata). Despite the slightly plummier-sounding repro-duction of György Sebok's piano, there is also much pleasure to be found in the open-hearted warmth brought by both artists to the Franck Sonata, where you have the impression that Gru-miaux himself might have put aside a silken Strad in favour of a throatier Guarnerius.

Violin Sonatas Nos 1 and 2. Morceau de concours. Andante in B flat, Op 75. Romance in B flat, Op 28. Berceuse, Op 16

Pierre Amoyal *vn* **Pascal Rogé** *pf*
Decca 436 866-2DH (65 minutes: DDD) Ⓕ
Recorded 1992

These radiant early and late masterpieces are unforgettable reflections of Fauré's first roman-tic ardour and his subsequent, deeply courageous journey through the most remote and interior regions of both soul and mind. Amoyal and Rogé are superbly challenging and authentic at every level. The opening *Allegro molto* from the First Sonata becomes a tumul-tuous rush of events, a committed alternative to more 'classical' or staid readings, while the *Andante* is kept firmly on the move. Yet how stellar is Rogé's way with the *a tempo* and *dolcis-simo* at 2'36", and what an Elysium both players find as the music sinks to its final resting place. The *Allegro vivo*, on the other hand, could hardly be more nimble, a true catch-as-catch-can with a delightful relishing of Fauré's constantly shifting and mischievously altered phrase lengths. Again, in the Second Sonata, both violinist and pianist play with rare individ-uality and unanimity, Amoyal's sweet and slightly nasal tone complemented by Rogé's greater fullness. Their *Andante* is, again, coolly paced but elsewhere there is a powerful recogni-tion of Fauré's strength and delicacy and the way his ceaseless flow of ideas is so often tinged with irony and unease. For their encores Amoyal and Rogé give us three miniatures in which salon clichés are effortlessly and, indeed, magically transformed. Even the *Berceuse*'s passing resem-blance to the *Eton Boating Song* seems sublime rather than unfortunate. The recordings are excellent and the entire recital should do much to erase notions (sadly, still current) of Fauré as a poor country cousin of Ravel and Debussy.

Complete Works for Piano

Five Impromptus. Impromptu, Op 86. Thème et Variations in C sharp minor, Op 73. Romances sans paroles, Op 17. Quatre valses-caprices. 13 Barcarolles. Ballade in F sharp, Op 19. 13 Nocturnes. Souvenirs de Bayreuth[a]. Pièces brèves, Op 84. Dolly, Op 56[a]. Nine Préludes, Op 103. Mazurka in B flat, Op 32
Kathryn Stott, [a]**Martin Roscoe** *pfs*
Hyperion ④ CDA66911/4 (297 minutes: DDD) Ⓜ
Recorded 1994 ○○

Fauré's piano works are among the most subtly daunting in all keyboard literature. Contradict-ing his diffidence ('it seems that I repeat myself constantly'), they possess, on the contrary, an astonishing scope. Encompassing Fauré's entire creative life, they range through an early, finely wrought eroticism via sporting with an aerial virtuosity as teasing and light as the elements themselves (the *Valses-caprices*) to the final deso-lation of Fauré's last years. There, in his most powerful works (*Barcarolles* Nos 7-11, *Nocturnes* Nos 11-13), he faithfully mirrors a pain that 'scintillates in full consciousness', a romantic agony prompted by increasing deafness and a lack of recognition that often seemed close to oblivion. Few compositions have reflected a darker night of the soul, and Fauré's anguish, expressed in both numbing resignation and unbridled anger, could surely only be exorcized by the articulation of such profound and disturbing emotional complexity. The task for the pianist, then, is immense, but in Kathryn Stott Fauré has a subtle and fearless champion. How thrilled Fauré would have been by the sheer immediacy of Stott's responses. Time and again she throws convention to the winds, and although it would be surprising if all her performances were consistent successes, disappointments are rare. Sometimes her rubato and luxuriant pedalling soften the outlines of Fauré's starkest, most austere utterances. The 12th and 13th *Nocturnes*, for example, are surely too loosely controlled to achieve their fullest drama and focus. But such quibbles remain quibbles. How Stott relishes a modern Steinway's opulent transformation of the harp's thin and glittering textures in the Sixth *Impromptu*, and the *Mazurka* has rarely been spun off with such a truly virtuoso insouciance. The Fourth *Nocturne* is gloriously supple, and the 13 *Barcarolles* show Stott acutely responsive to passion and finesse alike. The *Pièces brèves*, too, are played with rare affection. A true and dedicated Francophile (though with a very wide repertoire), Stott is among the more stylish and intriguing of the younger generation of pianists. For *Souvenirs de Bayreuth* and *Dolly* she is robustly partnered by Martin Roscoe.

La naissance de Vénus

L'absent, Op 5 No 3. Après un rêve, Op 7 No 1. Au cimetière, Op 51 No 2. Les berceaux, Op 23 No 1. Cantique de Jean Racine, Op 11. La chanson du pêcheur, Op 4 No 1. Les Djinns, Op 12. Madrigal, Op 35. La naissance de Vénus, Op 29. Pavane, Op 50. Pleurs d'or, Op 72. Puisqu'ici-bas, Op 10 No 1. Le ruisseau, Op 22. Le secret, Op 23 No 3. Sérénade toscane, Op 3 No 2. Tarentelle, Op 10 No 2

Isabelle Eschenbrenner, Brigitte Lafon, Sylvie Pons *sops* **Anna Holroyd** *contr* **Adrian Brand, Bruno Ranc** *tens* **Jacques Bona** *bass* **Bo Yuan** *db* **Jean-Claude Pennetier** *pf* **Louis Robilliard** *org* **Ravel Quartet** (Giovanni Battista Fabris, Reiko Kitahama *vns* Zoltán Tóth *va* Jean-Michel Fonteneau *vc*) **Solistes de Lyon-Bernard Tétu / Bernard Tétu**

EMI CDC5 56728-2 (74 minutes: DDD). Texts and translations included. Recorded 1998 Ⓕ

La naissance de Vénus, the 'scène mythologique' that gives this CD its title, was composed by Fauré for an amateur choral society. The piece is in one movement lasting nearly 23 minutes, including parts for soprano, alto, tenor and bass soloists. The opening immediately reminds you of Fauré's piano writing at its finest, a beautiful slow melody that acts as a prelude to the first choral section. In this the scene is set with a glowing dawn which seems to onlookers to herald some divine occurrence. Another piano interlude, in a barcarolle rhythm, precedes the appearance of Venus from the waves. The bass announces that Jupiter himself is there to greet his daughter. It's a surprise to find Jupiter cast as a tenor – perhaps the original group dictated who should be assigned which role. Jupiter's catalogue of all the delights Venus will bestow on the world forms the centre of the cantata. The choir re-enter to cry 'Salut à toi' – they are on 'tu-toi' terms with the goddess immediately. She answers with a soaring phrase over the chorus, assuring them that 'the sad life of the most humble being can become the most enviable'. This is a real discovery and Bernard Tétu and his chorus with Jean-Claude Pennetier at the piano give a reading which suggests all the lost charm of private small-scale choral singing that belongs to the world of the late 19th-century Paris salons. Bruno Ranc, who is Jupiter, also sings four of Fauré's best-known *mélodies* in the ensuing recital. There are many more sophisticated performances on disc of *Après un rêve* and *Au cimetière* but there is a freshness and simplicity about this whole CD, juxtaposing choral items (including *Les Djinns*, a Victor Hugo poem evoking a nightmare of howling and wailing) with duets and solo numbers. *La naissance de Vénus*, which has never before been recorded, is a must for Fauré collectors, and others will find this a charming, gentle and haunting disc.

Mélodies

Le papillon et la fleur, Op 1 No 1. Op 3 – No 1, Seule!; No 2, Sérénade toscane. L'absent, Op 5 No 3. Op 8 – No 1, Au bord de l'eau; No 3, Ici-bas. Op 10 – No 1, Puisqu'ici-bas; No 2, Tarentelle. La fée aux chansons, Op 27 No 2. Op 39 – No 2, Fleur jetée; No 3, Le pays des rêves; No 4, Les roses d'Ispahan. Nocturne, Op 43 No 2. Clair de lune, Op 46 No 2. Op 51 – No 1, Larmes; No 2, Au cimetière. Arpège, Op 76 No 2. Accompagnement, Op 85 No 3. Le plus doux chemin, Op 87 No 1. Le don silencieux, Op 92. Chanson, Op 94. C'est la paix!, Op 114. Vocalise-étude. Pelléas et Mélisande – Chanson de Mélisande

Sarah Walker *mez* **Malcolm Martineau** *pf*

CRD CRD3477 (68 minutes: DDD). Texts and translations included. Recorded 1991 Ⓜ

Starting with an early song, and a charmer, *Le papillon et la fleur* has the young Fauré with (so it seems) a head full of Schubert, as the piano enters with a ripple of *Die Forelle* and waltzes away into something more like *Seligkeit*. Here, that rather crusty quality in Sarah Walker's louder tones is something of a liability. Still, if this is the initial reaction it is not one that prevails for long. It is hard to imagine the *Nocturne* and *Au bord de l'eau* more beautifully sung, the first entering a very private world, the second catching perfectly the relaxed, reflective mood, and both benefiting from the softened, warmed tone of the singer and her excellent accompanist. The programme follows no chronological order. This has the advantage that the best-known songs can be distributed fairly evenly, with *Clair de lune*, *Les roses d'Ispahan* and *Aurore* mingled here with some from the 1870s and others that extend into the 20th century. These include the frank emotion of the postwar *C'est la paix!* and *Le don silencieux* which Sarah Walker sings so affectionately to the haunting accompaniment of those wistfully unfulfilled harmonies. Most haunting of all, perhaps, is Mélisande's song, in English, written for Mrs Patrick Campbell in 1889.

Requiem

Requiem[a]. Pavane, Op 50
[a]**Robert Chilcott** *treb* [a]**John Carol Case** *bar* [a]**King's College Choir Cambridge; New Philharmonia Orchestra / Sir David Willcocks**
EMI CDM7 64715-2 (42 minutes: ADD). Text and translation included. Recorded 1967 Ⓜ OO

This is the Fauré Requiem to come home to. It is tempting to describe it as a recording as near as can be to absolute perfection from start to finish. It has still not been overtaken on its own ground. The textual dimension of course is new since then, and if an earlier version of the score is wanted, the smaller orchestra being in some ways preferable, then the recording by the Cambridge Singers under the text's editor, John Rutter, might be tried instead. But for what we used to mean by the Fauré Requiem in days when ignorance (of textual complications) was bliss, then this is still the best. Willcocks neither sentimentalizes nor hurries; the choir (especially in respect of its tenors) is on top form; Robert Chilcott sings the *Pie Jesu* with the most touchingly beautiful purity and control, and John Carol Case brings to his solos a style that exactly matches that of the famous choir. If anything, time has enhanced appreciation, for the recorded sound compares so favourably, giving due prominence to the choir and obtaining an immediacy of sound that these days is exceptional. The only matter for regret is that the *Pavane* was not performed in its choral version, but as it is such an exquisite composition in either form the regret is short-lived.

Awards 1985

Requiem (original version – ed Rutter). Motets – Ave verum corpus; Tantum ergo; Ave Maria; Maria, Mater gratiae. Cantique de Jean Racine, Op 11 (orch. Rutter). Messe basse
Caroline Ashton, Ruth Holton *sops* **Stephen Varcoe** *bar* **Simon Standage** *vn* **John Scott** *org* **Cambridge Singers; City of London Sinfonia / John Rutter**
Collegium COLCD109 (63 minutes: ADD/DDD) Texts and translations included. Recorded 1984 Ⓕ OOO

Fauré began his Requiem in 1885, under the impact of the death of his father, but the work did not take on the form in which we now know it until 15 years later. The familiar 1900 score, therefore, cannot really be regarded as 'definitive'; it is a compromise, rather, between Fauré's original conception and what his publisher no doubt saw as the practicalities of concert performance. It is Fauré uncompromised that John Rutter has sought to restore in his edition of the seven-movement 1892 version, and his performance of it, using a chamber orchestra, a small choir and, in the 'Pie Jesu', a soprano who could easily be mistaken for a treble (Fauré's own early performances used a boy soloist) is a most convincing argument for accepting this score as more 'authentic' than the customary 1900 version.The differences are audibly obvious, and most are no less obviously improvements. The almost omnipresent organ (John Scott's registrations are beautifully clean and transparent) now sounds more like a continuo instrument than (as can easily happen with the 1900 score) an unwelcome thickening of an already dark orchestra. Above all, one is more aware than in any other recording that the sound in Fauré's head when he conceived the work was not that of a conventional orchestra but the rich, dark graininess of divided violas and cellos, the radiant luminosity of the work provided not by violins or woodwind but by the voices. It is thus more unified than the later revision as well as being more intimate. Rutter's chorus is a fine one, immaculate of diction and pure of line; Stephen Varcoe's light and unforced baritone could well be just what Fauré had in mind and Caroline Ashton's absolute purity in her brief solo is most moving. The recording is excellent. The *Messe basse* and four motets were added to this reissue to make quite a generous CD coupling. If you listen to these in sequence (including his blandly dozy account of the *Cantique*) you may well find it a slow and sweetly sad *diminuendo* from the Requiem: more of the same but not quite so good.

Fauré Requiem[a]. Messe basse[b]. Cantique de Jean Racine[b] **Vierne** Pièces de fantaisie. Suite No 1, Op 51 – Andantino[c] **Séverac** Tantum ergo[d]
[a]**Lisa Beckley** *sop* [a]**Nicholas Gedge** *bass-bar* [abd]**Oxford Schola Cantorum;** [a]**Oxford Camerata / Jeremy Summerly** with [abc]**Colm Carey** *org*
Naxos 8 550765 (60 minutes: DDD). Texts and translations included. Recorded 1993 Ⓢ

One could say at once that this is a highly competitive recording of the Fauré Requiem but in fact it stands on its own because of the version it presents and the edition it uses. Most of the available recordings are of the final 1900 version. This one, meanwhile, is of an edition by Denis Arnold (1983) based on the original version but incorporating the two additional movements. On first impulse, the word arising is 'austere'. Certainly the flashes of gold and scarlet made by the few but highly effective brass entries in the familiar versions are missed; the harp is notably absent from the *Sanctus*, and that wispy, high solo violin (1894) is now a less other-worldly presence at normal on-the-stave pitch. The instrumental colours are dark*ish*, yet not sombre, and are lightened by the sunlight stippling of the organ in the *In Paradisum*. With the voices added, the effect is of a subtler beauty, still more distinctively itself than even the 1894 score.

The performance of the Requiem and the *Messe basse* is admirable, with excellent playing by Jeremy Summerly's Oxford Camerata, and fresh-voiced, sensitively attuned choral singing from Oxford Schola Cantorum. Authenticity extends now to French pronunciation of the Latin ('luceat eis' very French indeed). The rather flaccid organ solo by Vierne, written as a sight-reading exercise for his pupils, is finely played by Colm Carey. The *Tantum ergo* by Séverac is a haunting, carol-like little piece, beautifully sung, and Fauré's *Cantique de Jean Racine* makes a perfect conclusion.

Robert Fayrfax British 1464-1521

GROVE *Fayrfax was a Gentleman of the Chapel Royal by 1497, graduated MusB (1501) and MusD (1504) at Cambridge and was incorporated DMus at Oxford (1511). From 1509 until his death he was senior lay clerk there, and received many payments from Henry VIII for music MSS. 29 compositions by him survive (more than by any other English composer of his generation), including two Magnificats, ten votive antiphons and secular pieces. He is important for his cultivation of the cyclic mass, of which six of his are known, all except one are based on a plainsong cantus firmus in the tenor of the full sections. His music is less elaborate than that of Cornysh and Taverner and uses restrained, carefully wrought melodic lines.*

Magnificat, 'O Bone Ihesu'

Magnificat, 'O Bone Ihesu'. Missa, O Bone Ihesu. Salve regina. Most clere of colour. I love, loved and loved wolde I be. Benedicite! What dreamed I? (all ed Skinner)

The Cardinall's Musick / Andrew Carwood

ASV Gaudeamus CDGAU184 (76 minutes: DDD) Ⓕ

Texts and translations included. Recorded 1996 ●

The Cardinall's Musick put the focus here around Fayrfax's Mass *O bone Ihesu*. Tragically, only a single voice survives of the antiphon that was probably its model, so in that respect their recording cannot be complete, unless David Skinner is prepared to indulge in the massive and quixotic task of reconstruction for this and other fragmentary survivals. But fascinatingly we do have a glorious *Magnificat* built on the same materials, one of the most widely distributed of all early Tudor works. By far the most commanding performance here is of that *Magnificat*: wonderfully controlled and perfectly tuned. The group is slightly rougher in the Mass and in the *Salve regina* – a work that, as David Skinner's useful note points out, stands rather apart from the style we otherwise know from Fayrfax and which may be one of his earliest surviving works. Intriguingly, this is the piece that seems to show the strongest debts to composers from the continental mainland (especially Brumel), giving important insights into the evolution of his music. Similarly, the three songs presented here, in performances that are skilled but slightly wooden, show a remarkable affinity with other mainland music, particularly that of Alexander Agricola. These little three-voice works, with their beautifully evocative texts, can without any doubt be counted among the glories of early Tudor music.

Missa Regali ex Progenie

(Ed Skinner). Antiphona Regali ex Progenie. Missa Regali ex Progenie. Lauda Vivi Alpha et O. Magnificat Regali. Alas, for lak of her presens. That was my woe Ⓟ

The Cardinall's Musick / Andrew Carwood

ASV Gaudeamus CDGAU185 (78 minutes: DDD) Ⓕ

Texts and translations included. Recorded 1997

Fayrfax's *Missa Regali ex Progenie* and *Magnificat Regali* are both early works, written before 1504, perhaps to impress his royal patron, and both, particularly the Mass, show signs that the composer had yet to settle into his stride. The longer, wordy movements of the Mass (the *Gloria* and *Credo*) seem elusive, as though he were note-spinning rather than weaving the contrapuntal texture, even if the hallmarks of greatness are all there. The Cardinall's Musick, with its by now almost instinctive understanding of his music, gives as convincing a performance as anyone could, or likely will, for some considerable time to come.

The votive antiphon *Lauda Vivi Alpha et O*, with its coda in praise of Henry VIII, probably dates from the time of or shortly after his coronation in 1509. This extended homage to the Virgin is rich in textural resonances, and a double meaning of 'O rosa gratie redolentissima' ('Most sweetly-scented rose') was surely intended. Here the long-drawn-out vocal lines, shifts in scoring, intellectual transitions of harmony of Fayrfax's mature style are much in evidence and the work's richness is given its full due by The Cardinall's Musick. The contrast between this fully-blown rose of a piece and the closed, but equally perfectly formed rosebud that is the duo 'That was my woe' is striking: it was a long way from ceremonial homage to semi-private entertainment in Tudor London. It is sung with perfection by Robin Blaze and Steven Harrold. All in all, a definite success story, and credit must go to ASV for having the courage (given the commercial pressures of today's CD market) to see this project through. Projects such as this enrich our lives.

Morton Feldman American 1926-1987

GROVE *Feldman studied with Riegger and Wolpe and from 1950 was closely associated with Cage; he also gained much from contact with New York painters. In 1972 he joined the faculty of the State University of New York, Buffalo. His consistent concern was with quiet, pure and open-textured music, sometimes elastically notated (as in the Projection series of 1950-51) but more often fully written out. The Viola in my life series (1970-71) and Rothko Chapel (1971) are the best known of his works. Several later pieces are extremely long, for example the First String Quartet (1979) which lasts c 100 minutes and the Second (1983), intended to last six hours.*

Piano and Orchestra

Coptic Light. Cello and Orchestra. Piano and Orchestra
Robert Cohen *vc* **Alan Feinberg** *pf* **New World Symphony Orchestra / Michael Tilson Thomas**
Argo 448 513-2ZH (74 minutes: DDD) Ⓕ
Recorded 1995

Tilson Thomas has been quoted as saying he thought Feldman's music was still greatly underestimated given it was so beautiful and important. *Piano and Orchestra* (1975) is a single contemplative span, a kind of anti-concerto, with just one brief aggressive outburst somewhat anticipated by menacing *crescendos* to which the piano remains impervious. It is all poetically executed – with luscious orchestral sound too.

Cello and Orchestra (1972) uncannily anticipates Tavener's hit *The Protecting Veil* with its high sustained writing for the cello. A not entirely dissimilar spiritual atmosphere pervades the work and we are reminded that Feldman himself at this time said that he regarded his music as elegiac, symbolizing a state of mourning – for the Holocaust, civilization or Western culture. The continuity is beautifully imagined with cello melisma periodically obliterated by gentle clusters. There is a loud brass chord at 9'38" and the ending settles itself down to oscillations between two chords and finally single notes. *Coptic Light* (1986), a New York Philharmonic commission written during Feldman's last year, owes its title to the composer's fascination with the patterning of oriental carpets. Listening to the work, you can imagine this multicoloured source and so this late piece is more static: the patterns barely vary for long stretches. With these scrupulous and well-recorded performances Tilson Thomas helps to ensure that Feldman is no longer underestimated.

Palais de Mari

Feldman Palais de Mari
Wuorinen Piano Sonata No 3. Bagatelle. Capriccio
Alan Feinberg *pf*
Koch International Classics 37308-2 Ⓕ
(65 minutes: DDD). Recorded 1994

Alan Feinberg is an exemplary type of late 20th-century, usually American, pianist who can swing the best *Kitten on the Keys* in the business. The Wuorinen works, all from the 1980s, are in the tough New York dialect of the post-Webern school but, with playing like this from Alan Feinberg, and so vividly recorded, they provide some scintillating listening. Whatever the music, Feinberg brings his own kind of commitment and panache to bear – a winning combination. You can imagine his fans wanting to buy anything he records because of this powerful impact. The often cataclysmic Sonata No 3 was written for Feinberg but the *Bagatelle* – if you can imagine anything by Wuorinen being a mere bagatelle – at least starts in poetic mode, quietly. So does the *Capriccio*, which opens with a Brahmsian expressiveness, albeit via Schoenberg: by the end the piano sounds as though it is under attack.

The very late Feldman piece is a bonus, a relentlessly quiet oasis thrown into sharp relief in such a welter of hyperactivity. *Palais de Mari* was commissioned by Bunita Marcus, but it is only a third the length of *For Bunita Marcus* written in the previous year. Feinberg's performance of *Palais* has every detail of the score in place and he brings his unique qualities to this mesmerizingly rapt meditation, where events take the form of the occasional dry chord in a liquid landscape. This disc comes strongly recommended to Feldman enthusiasts.

Rothko Chapel

Piano and Orchestra[a]. Durations II[b]. Rothko Chapel[c]
[c]**Julie Moffat** *sop* [c]**Ulrich Koch** *va* [b]**Rohan de Saram** *vc* [a]**Roger Woodward,** [b]**Yvar Mikashoff** *pfs* [c]**Klangforum Wien;** [a]**Saarbrücken Radio Symphony** [c]**Chorus and Orchestra /** [a]**Hans Zender,** [c]**Beat Furrer**
Col Legno Collage WWE1CD 20506 Ⓜ
(60 minutes: ADD). Recorded live in [a]1975, [b]1986 and [c]1994 **OO**

Routine Investigations. The Viola in my Life – I and II. For Frank O'Hara. I met Heine on the Rue Fürstenberg
Ensemble Recherche
Naïve Montaigne MO782126 (60 minutes: DDD) Ⓜ
Recorded 1991-3 **OO**

Recordings of Morton Feldman continue to appear, with both these discs worth attention from newcomers to his unique idiom. Increasing concert performances would be equally welcome, though without sustained concentration, the live experience is rendered futile.

Such is the case with *Durations II*, the poise of De Saram's and Mikashoff's account cancelled out by offstage interference. This 1960 piece typifies the calm abstraction of earlier Feldman: the remaining works date from the first half of the 1970s, when a new emotional ambience, intuition if you will, infuses the compositional process. The first two *The Viola in my Life* works are masterpieces of discreet characterisation; to which the wordless mezzo in *I met Heine on the Rue Fürstenberg* adds a wry twist, as if evoking that imagined encounter. Vocalise plays a more complex role in *Rothko Chapel*, perhaps the masterwork of Feldman's middle phase, its rapt contemplation enhanced by the introduction of a soprano melisma and a pastoral viola melody from the composer's past. The sometimes threatening choral dynamics aptly evoke the brooding introspection of Rothko's canvases. As with late Nono, this is spiritual music without religious connotations.

For Frank O'Hara brings an emphasis on instrumental unisons, and punctuating silences. It could be said that while Cage conceptualised silence, Feldman personalised it. The formal demarcation in *Piano and Orchestra* is that between sound and silence, the 'soloist' more a pacifier of the orchestra's fleeting gestures of aggression. This is the bleakest of these works, anticipating the Beckett-inspired pieces of Feldman's last years. *Routine Investigations* is its emotional pendant, the sudden crescendoing tones having an emotive quality rare in his music.

There can be little but praise for Ensemble Recherche's immaculate performances. The Woodward/Zender première of *Piano and Orchestra* must yield in expressive subtlety to Feinberg and Tilson Thomas, but the Col Legno release is still essential for the well-nigh perfect account of *Rothko Chapel*. As Kyle Gann aptly comments in the Montaigne notes, '...the amazing quality of his aural balance in these middle works makes them uniquely precious for the Feldman fan.' And one day, one hopes, for many others too.

John Field

Irish 1782-1837

GROVE *Field's early musical training came from his father and from Tommaso Giordani in Dublin, after which he was apprenticed to Muzio Clementi in London. He probably studied with Salomon. By 1801 he had established a reputation as a concert pianist and published his first important works, the piano sonatas Op 1. As a result of a successful continental tour with Clementi (1802-3) he remained in St Petersburg, becoming an idol of fashionable society there and in Moscow, teaching, giving concerts and composing until 1823, when illness overwhelmed him; he died in Moscow, having made one return visit to London and to other European cities.*

During his lifetime Field was known chiefly for the sensitivity of his playing, especially his expressive touch, singing phrases and extreme delicacy, a striking contrast to the fashion for virtuoso display. This legendary playing style was supported by the publication of his 17 nocturnes, each a self-sufficient piece evoking a dreamy mood of sadness consoled; song-like in manner and texture, they anticipated Chopin's pieces of the same type by nearly 20 years and influenced Liszt and Mendelssohn. Among Field's other, more numerous works, the most important are the rondos and fantaisies for piano, the Kamarinskaya variations (1809) and the Air russe varié for piano duet (1808), and the seven piano concertos. At his best, he was the equal of any of the Romantic pianist-composers.

Piano Concertos

No 1 in E flat, H27; No 3 in E flat, H32
Benjamin Frith *pf* **Northern Sinfonia / David Haslam**
Naxos 8 553770 (52 minutes: DDD) Ⓢ
Recorded 1996

Benjamin Frith presents a very formidable challenge to rival versions, at super-budget price. Both works are played with effortless fluency, plus all the immediacy and freshness of new discovery. In No 1 Frith is acutely responsive to the delicate charm of the Scottish-inspired (*'Twas within a mile of Edinboro' Town*) slow movement. He makes one aware of Field's teasing delight in the unexpected in the smiling outer movements, to which he brings a wide range of tone, and piquant accentuation in the last. There is warm, sympathetic support from the Northern Sinfonia under David Haslam. The performers revel in the composer's surprises of modulation, rhythm and orchestral colouring, while from the soloist there is not a trace of the perfunctory in passagework. The recording (in a resonant venue) might be thought overforward and full, but it remains a true bargain.

Piano Concertos – No 2 in A flat, H31; No 3 in E flat, H32 **P**
Andreas Staier *fp*
Concerto Köln / David Stern
Teldec 3984-21475-2 (62 minutes: DDD) Ⓕ
Recorded 1998

For those who love the sound and capabilities of the modern piano, the fortepiano's thinner tone, distinctive timbre and more intimate dynamic scope (or, put another way, the lack of power) take some adjusting to. But once one is attuned to its tonal and colouristic possibilities, the daring nature of the piano writing emerges with striking force. Take the soloist's first entry in the Second Concerto, where the virtuosic power and originality delivers its full intended frisson and physicality when heard on an instrument being pushed to its limit. Andreas Staier is a brilliant pianist who allies dazzling technical élan to his acute musical insight and imagination. In the outer movements, his fingerwork is as precise and crystalline as his musical intelligence, with passagework assuming a quasi-melodic purpose, elevated to the level of what Gerald Abraham called 'significant line'.

The slow movement of the A flat Concerto, a brief contrasting *molto espressivo* song without words, is played with unaffected simplicity and clarity of line, while in the E flat major Concerto, Staier follows Field's own practice of interpolating one of his nocturnes as a slow movement by playing the well-known work in C minor. Staier is a most poetic and inspiring advocate, yet the success of these performances is as much due to the extraordinary clarity and impact of the Concerto Köln's orchestral playing. There is such an infectious generosity of spirit, such vivid character and crispness, with beautifully poised wind playing and a real bite from the brass and timpani. Try the opening of the finale of the Second Concerto, where, after the lilting melody is presented by the soloist, the full orchestra respond with invigorating gusto and rusticity, never losing their tonal blend or refinement. The recorded sound, too, is wonderfully clear and detailed.

Nocturnes

No 1 in E flat, H24; **No 2** in C minor, H25; **No 3** in A flat, H26; **No 4** in A, H36; **No 5** in B flat, H37; **No 6** in F, H40; **No 7** in C, H45; **No 8** in A, H14E; **No 9** in E flat, H30; **No 10** in E minor, H46B; **No 11** in E flat, H56A; **No 12** in G, H58D; **No 13** in D minor, H59; **No 14** in C; **No 15** in C, H61; **No 16** in F, H62A

Nocturnes Nos 1-15
Roberto Mamou *pf* Ⓕ
Pavane ADW7110 (64 minutes: DDD)

Nocturnes Nos 1-16 🅿
Joanna Leach *fp*
Athene ATHCD1 (76 minutes: DDD) Ⓕ
Recorded 1990-91

The Tunisian-born pianist Roberto Mamou achieves an often exemplary middle course between drama and understatement and he stresses Field's closeness to, rather than his remoteness from, Chopin. The recordings are satisfactory and this is an appealing issue. Joanna Leach performs on square pianos by Stodart, Broadwood and Thomas D'Almaine dating from 1823 to 1835 and, most persuasively, suggests an intimacy and transparency hard to parallel on more modern, brilliant and forceful instruments. The ear is quickly attuned to the sound, to the radically different pedalling Leach refers to in her excellent notes, and to a cloudy but appropriate and often hypnotic resonance. Melody and accompaniment (at the very heart of this music) are more closely entwined than on today's instruments, offering a greater sense of Field's harmonic subtlety. There are some extraneous noises, inseparable from period instruments, but so far from distracting attention they somehow add to the potent atmosphere of these performances. A fascinating pair of issues.

Gerald Finzi British 1901-1956

GROVE *Finzi studied privately with Farrar (1914-16) and Bairstow (1917-22) and lived most of his life in the country. Influenced by Elgar and Vaughan Williams as well as his teachers, he developed an intimate style and concentrated on songs, particularly settings of Hardy. Other works include a clarinet concerto (1949) and Dies natalis for high voice and strings (1939).*

Clarinet Concerto

Clarinet Concerto in C minor, Op 31. Five Bagatelles, Op 23 (orch Ashmore). Love's Labour's Lost – Soliloquies Nos 1-3. A Severn Rhapsody in D minor, Op 3. Romance in E flat, Op 11. Introit in F, Op 6
Robert Plane *cl* **Lesley Hatfield** *vn* **Northern Sinfonia / Howard Griffiths**
Naxos 8 553566 (71 minutes: DDD) Ⓢ
Recorded 1995 ●

This is a highly accomplished, indeed commanding performance of Finzi's gorgeous Clarinet Concerto from Northern Sinfonia principal, Robert Plane. With his bright, singing tone and effortless technical mastery, there's no shortage of intuitive poetry from Plane in the sublime central *Adagio*. Howard Griffiths's conducting is exemplary. We also get an atmospheric account of Lawrence Ashmore's idiomatic orchestration of the *Five Bagatelles* (with the poignant 'Romance' a highlight), as well as exquisitely drawn renderings of both the *Romance* for strings and 'Three Soliloquies' from Finzi's incidental music for a 1946 BBC production of *Love's Labour's Lost*. The fragrant, very early *Severn Rhapsody* (1923) makes a welcome return to the catalogue under Griffiths's deeply felt advocacy, and Lesley Hatfield makes a touching soloist in the radiant *Introit* (the slow movement of a withdrawn Violin Concerto from 1925-27). The sound and balance are extremely truthful, though the acoustic may be a little over-resonant for some tastes. Really helpful presentation too. All in all, a remarkable bargain.

Love's Labour's Lost – Suite, Op 28. Clarinet Concerto in C minor, Op 31. Prelude in F minor, Op 25. Romance in E flat, Op 11
Alan Hacker *cl* **English String Orchestra / William Boughton** Nimbus NI5101 (65 minutes: DDD) Ⓕ
Recorded 1987

There are several other Finzi issues available which include the Clarinet Concerto. Alan Hacker, however, encompasses all his colleagues' virtues, providing special insights and revelling in the brilliant writing. He also adds something extra – an almost mystical realization of the music's poetic vision which is deeply moving. This is in spite of the fact that the string-playing sometimes lacks polish and precision. Finzi wrote incidental music for a BBC production of *Love's Labour's Lost* and expanded it for a later open-air production. It is tuneful, graceful music, but one cannot feel that the stage was Finzi's world. The disc is completed by two interesting early pieces for strings, the *Prelude* and *Romance*, both wholly characteristic of the composer and very well played.

Violin Concerto

Violin Concerto[b]. Romance in E flat, Op 11[b]. Prelude in F minor, Op 25[b]. In Years Defaced[a] – To a Poet a Thousand Years Hence (orch C Matthews); When I Set Out for Lyonnesse (orch cpsr); In Years Defaced (orch Roberts); Tall Nettles (orch Alexander); At a Lunar Eclipse (orch Weir); Proud Songsters (orch Payne)
[a]**John Mark Ainsley** *ten* [b]**Tasmin Little** *vn*
City of London Sinfonia / Richard Hickox
Chandos CHAN9888 (55 minutes: DDD) Ⓕ
Texts included. Recorded [b]1999 and [a]2000 ●●

Finzi began work on his Concerto for small orchestra and solo violin in 1925, dedicating it to Sybil Eaton (a talented young violinist and the object of the 24-year-old composer's unrequited love). He harboured considerable doubts about the opening movement, however, and when Eaton eventually premièred the piece in May 1927 with Sargent and the British Women's Symphony Orchestra, the Queen's Hall audience heard only the second and third movements. When Vaughan Williams confirmed that he would programme the concerto at a Bach Choir concert the following year, Finzi penned another first movement. Neither he nor the critics found much to please them, though, and the concerto was not heard again in its entirety until the present artists' revival in 1999 in Southampton's Turner Sims Concert Hall. The work's highlight undoubtedly remains the central, characteristically rapt *Molto sereno* that Finzi later recast as his Op 6 *Introit*. Of the two vigorous flanking movements the finale leaves the stronger impression, but the concerto thoroughly deserves its new lease of life, and Little and Hickox's sparkling and stylish advocacy will win it many new friends.

There's another first recording in the guise of the song-cycle, *In Years Defaced*. Only one number, the 1928-32 setting of Hardy's 'When I set out for Lyonnesse', was actually orchestrated by Finzi, and, in an effort to place it in a more programme-friendly context, the Finzi Trust commissioned five contemporary composers to choose a song that might benefit from the extra colour an orchestral palette can provide. The resulting sequence is a joy from start to finish. Without compromising her own strongly recognisable idiom, Judith Weir sheds new light on Finzi's bleakly beautiful response to Hardy's 'At a lunar eclipse' (the links with Holst's *Egdon Heath* never clearer) – and the same goes for Colin Matthews' treatment of the cycle's hauntingly timeless opener, 'To a poet a thousand years hence'. Elsewhere, Anthony Payne's exquisitely judged scoring of 'Proud songsters' shares stylistic fingerprints with his masterly elaboration of the sketches for Elgar's Third Symphony; more unexpectedly, Christian Alexander's arrangement of 'Tall Nettles' (written when Finzi was just 19) brings cherishable pre-echoes of VW's *A Pastoral Symphony*. Ainsley is a potent, irreproachably sensitive presence throughout this imaginative and rewarding creation which, as Jeremy Dale Roberts observes in the booklet, enshrines 'a coherent work of touching intensity'. Again, Hickox and the City of London Sinfonia accompany to the manner born and are no less responsive to the radiant string textures of the chaste, rather Bachian *Prelude* and more emotive *Romance*. Lovely, airy sound and exemplary presentation further enhance the appeal of this disc.

Dies natalis

Dies natalis, Op 8. Intimations of Immortality, Op 29
John Mark Ainsley *ten* **Corydon Singers and Orchestra / Matthew Best**
Hyperion CDA66876 (67 minutes: DDD). Texts included Ⓕ
Recorded 1996 ●●

What is central, and essential, is the capacity of Finzi's music to grow in the listener's mind over long years, deepening in appeal, strengthening in the conviction of its purpose. Moreover, these performances are marvellously good at clarifying the strengths. Rather more than their predecessors, they clarify structure and texture. The soloist is more distinctly focused in the recording-balance, and this makes an important difference when the poet's words are such a vital element. Ainsley sings with grace and clarity. The small choir conveys a restrained presence in the *Intimations*; but for much of the time this kind of halo over the sound is appropriate, and in certain important passages the fewer numbers help to compensate with clearer definition. Highly recommended.

Choral Works

All this night, Op 33. Let us now praise famous men, Op 35. Lo, the full, final sacrifice, Op 26. Magnificat, Op 36. Seven Part-songs, Op 17. Though did'st delight my eyes, Op 32. Three Anthems, Op 27. Three Short Elegies, Op 5. White-flowering days, Op 37
Finzi Singers / Paul Spicer with **Harry Bicket** *org*
Chandos CHAN8936 (79 minutes: DDD)
Texts included. Recorded 1990

To the listener who seeks music in which the fastidious limitation of its means is itself some guarantee of the depth of its purposes, Finzi will always be rewarding. This is true of all the works collected here. Some, such as the first and last, *God is gone up* and *Lo, the full, final sacrifice*, are relatively well known, though not necessarily the most satisfying. There are some fine shorter pieces including the unaccompanied *Seven Poems of Bridges* and the *Three Drummond Elegies* that delight as word-settings. 'White-flowering days', to words by Edmund Blunden, comes from *A Garland for the Queen*, the Coronation gift of 10 composers in 1953, none happier than this in catching the fresh hopefulness of the time. Best of all perhaps is the *Magnificat*, which also had its first British performance in that year. It is heard here in its original version with organ, beautifully played on this disc and providing a more spiritual association than the orchestral accompaniment added later. The Finzi Singers are sensitive, assured and accurate; their tone is uniformly good, and they convey a sense of personal involvement in the music. The sound and presentation are well up to the rest.

César Franck Belgian/French 1822-1890

GROVE *Franck, French composer, teacher and organist of Belgian birth, was intended by his ambitious father for a career as a piano virtuoso. He studied at the Liège (1830-35) and Paris (1837-42) conservatories but found his true vocation only later through organist's appointments in Paris, chiefly that of Ste Clotilde (from 1858) and part-time teaching. His improvisatory skill attracted notice and led to his first major work, the remarkable Six pièces (1862), though another decade passed before he was appointed organ professor at the Conservatoire. From the mid-1870s until his death his creative powers lasted unabated. He wrote large-scale sacred works, notably the oratorio Les béatitudes (1879), and several symphonic poems such as Le chausseur maudit (1882) and Psyché (1888). But his achievements are evident especially in the symphonic, chamber and keyboard works in which he made one of the most distinguished contributions to the field by any French musician. Here, in the Piano Quintet (1879), the Prélude, choral et fugue for piano (1884), the Violin Sonata (1886), the Symphony in D minor (1888) and the String Quartet (1889), his inherent emotionalism and a preoccupation with counterpoint and traditional forms found a balance, in turn decisively impressing his band of disciples, from Duparc, d'Indy and Chausson to Lekeu, Vierne, Dukas and Guilmant. Features of his mature style, indebted alike to Beethoven, Liszt and Wagner, are his complex, mosaic-like phrase structures, variants of one or two motifs; his rich chromaticism, often put to structural use in the 'chord pair'; and his fondness for cyclic, tripartite forms.*

Symphony in D minor

Franck Symphony in D minor[a]
Mendelssohn Symphony No 5 in D, 'Reformation', Op 107[b]
[a]**Berlin Radio Symphony Orchestra,** [b]**Berlin Philharmonic Orchestra / Lorin Maazel**
DG The Originals 449 720-2GOR (64 minutes: ADD) Ⓜ
Recorded 1961

This CD preserves a phenomenon: a living Legend in the making. Appreciative insert-notes describe features of Maazel's work of the period – freshness of vision and youthful vitality tempered by a feeling for line and a classical poise – to which might be added a more timeless Maazel characteristic: a sensational command of the orchestra. Both orchestras were at their then (1961) finest, and there are countless examples of expressive shaping, pointing (the Mendelssohn second movement) and shading (the shadowed mystery at the start and centre of the Franck). Just occasionally, you are aware of command over-exercised: the finale of the Franck has one or two radical swells and drastic *diminuendos* and *pianissimos* (the extent of the dynamic control seems an end in itself). And some of Maazel's more racy tempos are questionable. The very mobile *Allegretto* central movement of the Franck works like a dream (it is seraphic rather than sentimental). But the finale of the Mendelssohn? This is admittedly a 'problem' movement, inclined to sound foursquare if not dispatched with a certain dash. Maazel's quick march here solves the problem, but leaves little room for airy celebration and final elation. The recordings (and doubtless their remastering) contribute to the lean-and-hungry impression of the performances: always superbly clear (the windband sonorities in the Mendelssohn symphony, and their wide disposition, are thrilling), but wanting warmth and space in *fortissimo* tuttis (those of the Franck are often strident and hectoring).

Symphony in D minor. Symphonic Variations[a]. Les Eolides
[a]**Louis Lortie** *pf* **BBC Philharmonic Orchestra / Yan Pascal Tortelier**
Chandos CHAN9875 (62 minutes: DDD) Ⓕ
Recorded 2000 ⭘

With so many versions of the Symphony and the *Symphonic Variations* available, it is surprising that these two favourite orchestral works are not coupled together more often. Here Tortelier adds an attractive bonus in the evocative tone-poem *Les Eolides*.

The statistic to note about Tortelier's reading of the Symphony is that overall it is no less than five minutes shorter than both the Karajan and Chailly versions, both also coupled with the *Symphonic Variations*, and almost three minutes shorter than the Monteux. The result is not a reading in any way perfunctory, rushed or trivial, but one made fresher, eliminating any suspicion of the glutinous or sentimental, helped by a cleanly defined yet atmospheric recording.

The Symphony's slow introduction, promptly repeated, is all the more effective for being taken at a flowing speed, with no feeling of haste, and the main *Allegro* is fresh and alert, less smooth than with either Karajan or Chailly. However, Monteux's account, which has a very different coupling (*Petrushka*), still strikes one as the most idiomatic performance of all, bitingly dramatic, too, with the 1959 sound astonishingly full and vivid.

Tortelier is far closer to Monteux in his feeling for the idiom than either Karajan or Chailly, both taking a weighty view. In tempo Tortelier is very similar to Karajan and Monteux in the central *Allegretto*, with fine gradations of dynamic and a slightly raw-sounding cor anglais adding to the freshness. It is in the finale that Tortelier is most distinctive, his fast, urgent speed for the *Allegro non troppo* challenging the players of the BBC Philharmonic to produce exciting rather than genial results.

Louis Lortie is the excellent soloist in the *Symphonic Variations*, spontaneously poetic in the slow sections, sparkling and light in the *scherzando* finale. Tortelier is again at his most warmly understanding in *Les Eolides*, a work that can seem wayward, but which here is made light and fanciful in its luminously scored evocation of the breezes of heaven. Again Tortelier reinforces his outstanding claims as an interpreter of the French romantic repertory.

Piano Quintet

Franck Piano Quintet in F minor[a] **Mozart** Clarinet Quintet in A, K581[b] **R Strauss** Capriccio – Prelude[c]
Amadeus Quartet (Norbert Brainin, Siegmund Nissel *vns* Peter Schidlof *va* Martin Lovett *vc*) [b]**Gervase de**

Peyer *cl* [a]**Clifford Curzon** *pf* [c]**Cecil Aronowitz** *va* [c]**William Pleeth** *vc*
BBC Legends/IMG Artists amono BBCL4061-2 Ⓜ (77 minutes: ADD). Recorded live in [a]1960, [b]1966 and [c]1971 ●●●

Rarely can a case for live rather than studio performances have been made more persuasively than by the present disc, a study in contrasts if ever there was one. The Amadeus Quartet was celebrated for its homogeneity (accusations from critics of a plush or de luxe style were rare), yct this superb ensemble could easily accommodate other radically different players, and here Curzon's legendary nervous intensity is accentuated by the Amadeus, who join him in a performance of the Franck Quintet so super-charged it virtually tears itself apart. Taken from a 1960 Aldeburgh Festival concert it eclipses all others (even Curzon's revelatory Decca disc). Curzon and his colleagues hurl themselves at music which clearly they see as hardly needing a cooling agent. How free and rhapsodic is Curzon's reply to the Amadeus's opening *dramatico*, and what a savage explosion of pent-up energy from all the players at 7'22"! Intonation may suffer at 3'12" in the finale's equestrian nightmare, but the concluding pages are overwhelming, and Curzon's darting *crescendos* at 3'56" and 58" are like snarls of defiance.

At the opposite end of the spectrum is Mozart's Clarinet Quintet, that assuaging and elusive glory of the repertoire, played with all Gervase de Peyer's serenity and elegance. Yet again, the performance is essentially live, and has the sort of vitality and imaginative subtlety less easy to achieve or even countenance in the studio. And the same could be said of Cecil Aronowitz and William Pleeth, who join the Amadeus for Strauss's Prelude to *Capriccio*, aptly described in the notes as 'a sumptuous effusion of very late romanticism'. The recordings (1960-71) are vivid and immediate, and odd noises off only add to the sense of occasion. Finally, a word of warning; this performance of the Franck is not for late-night listening: you'll sleep more peacefully after the Mozart.

Violin Sonata

Debussy Violin Sonata. Sonata for Flute, Viola and Harp **Franck** Violin Sonata in A **Ravel** Introduction and Allegro
Kyung-Wha Chung *vn* **Osian Ellis** *hp* **Radu Lupu** *pf* **Melos Ensemble**
Decca 421 154-2DM (67 minutes: ADD) Ⓜ
Recorded 1962-77 ●●●

Here we have masterpieces from the French tradition in excellent performances that have won the status of recording classics. Kyung-Wha Chung and Radu Lupu are a fine duo who capture and convey the delicacy and poetry of the Franck Sonata as well as its rapturous grandeur, and never can the strict canonic treatment of the great tune in the finale have sounded more spontaneous and joyful. They are no less successful in the different world of the elusive Sonata which was Debussy's last work, with its smiles through tears and, in the finale, its echoes of a Neapolitan tarantella. The 1977 recording is beautifully balanced, with a natural sound given to both the violin and piano. The Melos Ensemble recorded the Ravel *Introduction and Allegro* 15 years before, but here too the recording is a fine one for which no allowances have to be made even by ears accustomed to good digital sound; as for the work itself, this has an ethereal beauty that is nothing short of magical and Osian Ellis and his colleagues give it the most skilful and loving performance. A wonderful disc and a must buy.

Prélude, choral et fugue

Prélude, choral et fugue. Prélude, aria et final. Grand caprice. Les plaintes d'une poupée. Danse lente. Choral No 3 in A minor (arr Hough)
Stephen Hough *pf*
Hyperion CDA66918 (68 minutes: DDD) Ⓕ
Recorded 1996 ●

Hough has a dream-ticket combination of virtues – astonishing agility, a faultless ear for texture, fine-tuned stylistic sensibility and an exceptional understanding of harmonic and structural tensions. He acknowledges all Franck's nuances, notated and implied, without ever disturbing the broader flow; he gives full rein to the heroic Lisztian cascades, without ever tipping over into melodrama. The only hint of a nit to be picked would be that the *fortissimo* arpeggiations in the 'Choral' don't ring as resonantly as they might. One can't imagine the calm at the end of the 'Aria' being better judged. In their very different ways the almost comical bravura of the *Grand caprice* and the salon charm of the *Danse lente* and *Les plaintes d'une poupée* are extremely difficult to bring off with success. Yet anyone who has followed Hough's recording career will know that this sort of thing is meat and drink to him. As for his own transcription of the A minor *Chorale*, the unavoidable adjective is 'awesome'.

Organ Works

Pièce héroïque in B minor. Cantabile in B. Fantaisie in A. Grande pièce symphonique in F sharp minor, Op 17. Pastorale in E, Op 19. Fantaisie in C, Op 16. Prélude, fugue et variation in B minor, Op 18. Trois chorales – No 1 in E; No 2 in B minor; No 3 in A minor. Prière in C sharp minor, Op 20. Final in B flat, Op 21
Marie-Claire Alain *org*
Erato ② 0630-12706-2 (152 minutes: DDD). Recorded on the Cavaillé-Coll organ, Saint-Etienne, Caen, France in 1995 Ⓜ

Alain is a completely involved communicator. More than anyone else she delves into the very soul of these works. Thus we have an intensely prayerful *Prière*, a majestically statuesque *Grande pièce symphonique* while the *Chorales* are delivered with an unexpected degree of fervour; perhaps the Third is a shade overfervent since some of the semiquaver figurations lack absolute clarity – something which after one or two hearings serves to heighten the excitement but which might, after repeated listening, become irritating. This is a highly authoritative release not just in terms of playing but also in Alain's accompanying notes. The Caen organ is a particularly fine specimen of a Cavaillé-Coll, dating from 1884 – 25 years after the St Clotilde organ for which Franck wrote much of this music. The recording captures it, and the church's atmosphere, effectively.

Harold Fraser-Simon

British 1872-1944

After an early career in shipping, Fraser-Simon became known as a songwriter. Then, beginnng with Bonita (1911) he composed a series of stage shows, the most successful of which was The Maid of the Mountains, running for 1352 performances. He also wrote A Southern Maid (1917) and Our Peg (1919) and collaborated with Ivor Novello in Our Nell (1924) but none were as successful. Fraser-Simon also wrote the ballets A Venetian Wedding (1926) and The Nightingale and the Rose (1927); he subsequently set children's texts, including incidental music for Kenneth Grahame's Toad of Toad Hall, settings from Alice in Wonderland, six volumes of songs from AA Milne's When We Were Very Young and the most popular, Christopher Robin is Saying his Prayers and Christopher Robin at Buckingham Palace.

The Maid of the Mountains

Janis Kelly *sop* Teresa; **Christopher Maltman** *bar* Beppo; **Michael George** *bass* Baldassare; **Richard Suart** *bass* Tonio; **Sally Burgess** *mez* Vittoria; **Donald Maxwell** *bar* General Malona; **Joanna Gamble** *mez* Angela; **Jeanette Ager** *sop* Gianetta; **Michael Bundy** *bar* Pietro; **Tom Taylor** *voc* **Mayor of** Santo; **New London Light Opera Chorus; New London Orchestra / Ronald Corp**

Hyperion CDA67190 (80 minutes: DDD) Ⓕ

Text included. Recorded 2000 **OO**

Let's confess that this is at times a somewhat odd score, with a curiously perfunctory Act 1 finale and a leading man (Baldassare) who merely recites his musical numbers. An absolutely complete performance will expose such weaknesses as much as the strengths. But the strengths of a work that set a London long-running record are considerable.

The principal numbers go to the Maid and the brigand Beppo, parts created by José Collins and Thorpe Bates, who were both fine singers. Janis Kelly and Christopher Maltman give their numbers full value, most obviously the hit number 'Love Will Find a Way', quite gloriously sung here by Kelly. They also share three interpolated hit numbers by James W Tate, among them the lovely 'Paradise for Two'. Hearing the score at leisure, one can also relish lesser numbers such as the splendidly catchy duet 'Dirty Work' or the lovely Act 3 Barcarolle.

What particularly distinguishes this recording is its use of full chorus and orchestra, playing the original orchestrations. In the way Ronald Corp lets the music breathe, one really senses the opulence of the original production and the full flavour of what can only struggle through the acoustic sound of 83 years ago. Altogether this is a quite outstandingly successful re-creation of the work. Sceptics will carp, but it is a hugely important contribution to preserving our British musical theatre heritage. One can envisage the romantic hit numbers providing rich material on the air waves for some time to come.

Girolamo Frescobaldi

Italian 1583-1643

GROVE *Frescobali studied with Luzzaschi at Ferrara, where he also came under Gesualdo's influence. Soon after 1600 he went to Rome where in 1607 he became organist of S Maria in Trastevere. The same year he travelled with his patron, Guido Bentivoglio, to Brussels, but his experience of this centre of keyboard music left little imprint on him, except perhaps in the fantasias of 1608. In July 1608 Frescobaldi was elected organist of St Peter's, Rome; during the following years he was employed also by Cardinal Pietro Aldobrandini and other patrons.*

In 1615 Frescobaldi secured a position with Duke Ferdinando Gonzaga at Mantua, but after three months he returned to Rome, remaining there until 1628 when he became organist at the Medici court in Florence. By the time he returned once more to Rome, in 1634, his fame was international and he was moving in the highest circles of patronage. In 1637 Froberger came from Vienna to study with him. Little is known of his other pupils, but his influence on keyboard playing and composition remained important for a century or more.

Frescobaldi is remembered chiefly for his keyboard music, much of which was published in 12 volumes (1608-14) with toccatas, canzonas, ricercares, dances and variations. The most famous is Fiori musicali (1635), with pieces for use in the Mass: the Kyrie-Christe unit from the Ordinary, toccatas to be played during the Elevation and other pieces corresponding to items of the Proper (introit, gradual, offertory, communion). Bach owned a copy and learnt from it.

Frescobaldi's vocal music is of relatively small importance. His sacred works, including c40 motets, mostly for one to three voices and continuo, show none of the complexity and expressive intensity of the keyboard works. Perhaps his most characteristic vocal music is in an early volume of madrigals (1608), but two volumes of Arie musicali published during his years in Florence (1630) are also of interest.

Il primo libro di madrigali

Concerto Italiano / Rinaldo Alessandrini **P**

Opus 111 OPS30-133 (53 minutes: DDD). Texts and translations included. Recorded 1995 Ⓕ

This story, which has a happy ending, is a curious one. Frescobaldi, in Antwerp with his Roman patron in 1608, was commissioned by a local printer to produce his first and indeed only book of madrigals. The collection seems to have little impact on contemporaries. It was never reprinted either North or South of the Alps, and in our own times its existence gradually became submerged under the weight of Frescobaldi's reputation as a composer for the keyboard. Those interested in pursuing the matter discovered that the only known surviving copy lacks one of its voice-parts. Frescobaldi's *Primo libro* seemed set fair to remain a footnote in the textbooks rather than a musical reality.

All that changed with the discovery of a complete set of partbooks, then in a private library, a challenge that Rinaldo Alessandrini has now taken up by both editing and recording the music. The distinctive sound and approach of his Concerto Italiano will be familiar to all enthusiasts for Italian music of the Monteverdi period (and above all for the music of Monteverdi himself), and their many admirers will not be disappointed with the result. Their instinctive feel for the diction, sound and sense of the Italian language married to a sophisticated and dynamic interpretational approach brings out all the rhetorical subtleties of Frescobaldi's extraordinary music, with its obvious parentage in the madrigals of Gesualdo and Monteverdi.

This is virtuoso madrigal singing at its most exhilarating, all the more effective for being sometimes (but not on all tracks) imaginatively underpinned by continuo instruments. The real revelation here is not so much the Concerto Italiano, whose powerfully moving performances we have come to expect, but Frescobaldi's madrigals; no one with a soul should miss them.

Giovanni Gabrieli

Italian c1553/6-1612

GROVE *Giovanni Gabrieli, like his uncle Andrea Gabrieli, with whom he studied, worked briefly at the Munich court (c 1575-8) and in 1585 he became organist of St Mark's, Venice, and of the confraternity of S Rocco, posts he held for the rest of his life. After Andrea's death, he edited many of his works for publication. His own fame and influence were widespread and crucial, notably in northern Europe - Schütz was among his many pupils - and he represents the highest point of the High Renaissance Venetian school. He composed motets and mass movements (Symphoniae sacrae, 1597, 1615, MSS), instrumental ensemble music (1597, 1615, MSS) and organ works (1593, MSS), as well as a few madrigals (1587 and anthologies). Much of his sacred ceremonial music exploits the architecture of St Mark's, using contrasting groups of singers and players to create cori spezzati effects, but often in a more intense and dissonant style than his uncle's. His music for wind ensemble is lively and colourful and includes up-to-date concertato writing; the organ ricercares are in a well-developed and specific keyboard style.*

Canzonas

Sacrae symphoniae (1597) – Canzon a 8: primi toni, septemi toni (2), noni toni, duodecimi toni; Canzon a 10: primi toni, duodecimi toni, echo duodecimi toni; Sonata octavi toni, a 12.Canzoni (1608) – Canzon seconda a 4. Canzoni et Sonate (1615) – Canzon a 7: V, VI. Canzon a 8: VIII, X-XII; Canzon XIV, a 10; Canzon XVI, a 12. Ricercar del primo tono P

Concerto Palatino / Bruce Dickey, Charles Toet

Harmonia Mundi HMC90 1688 (76 minutes: DDD) Ⓕ

Recorded 1998

Gabrieli's instrumental music is as evocative of the sonorous interior spaces of St Mark's Basilica and the grandeur of the Venetian Renaissance as his better-known large-scale motets, yet they are not so often performed except as 'fillers'. This single-minded recording, which above all provides an opportunity to re-evaluate the canzonas, will bring a number of surprises to many. One is the sheer variety of styles and techniques which Gabrieli deploys, even among the early pieces which might be thought to be written in a comparatively limited idiom. Not so, for this early group ranges from the sparkling Canzon septimi toni, which achieves its effect by adopting all the characteristics of the double-choir motet, to the far more serious Canzon noni toni, which plays with chromatic inflection, another vocal device, as a way of making its effect. Although the double-choir technique and quasi-counterpoint are still the mainstay of the pieces from the 1615 collection, there are also intrusions of idiomatic writing, as with the exuberant passagework for cornetts in the Canzon VIII.

As might be expected, Concerto Palatino are well up to the challenges. These readings are characterised by just the kind of sensitive articulation and modulated phrasing that is often absent in performances of this repertory. Above all there is a sense of kaleidoscopic colour, a subtlety of interpretation based on exploration of the variety of texture in Gabrieli's writing, which stands in contrast to the more usual 'block-buster' performances relying on sudden dynamic shifts and full brilliance. Highly recommended for specialists and newcomers alike.

Sacrae Symphoniae

The 16 Sonatas and Canzonas from Sacrae symphoniae. Toccata quinti toni. Three Toccatas. Intonatione del noni toni P

His Majesties Sagbutts and Cornetts / Timothy Roberts *org*

Hyperion CDA66908 (75 minutes: DDD) Ⓕ

Recorded 1997

Giovanni Gabrieli is arguably the earliest composer to write a significant body of instrumental music to a formula which can be said to be truly idiomatic and timelessly palatable. The *Sacrae symphoniae* publication of 1597 is a mixed set of vocal and instrumental pieces and, in its grand design, preserves a glorious heyday of textural opulence, intimate and playful dialogue between galleries and unashamedly ostentatious virtuosity. His Majesties Sagbutts and Cornetts have augmented their chamber consort to form, as cornettist David Staff proudly proclaims, 'the largest group of cornett and sagbutt players to have been assembled from one city since the 17th century'. These wonderful 16 canzonas and sonatas make up the complete instrumental music of the 1597 collection. In essence it is the extensive juxtaposition between sombre blocks and glittering small-scale exchanges which gives the music its seminal quality of moving both inevitably and eventfully towards a self-assured resolution, befitting its aristocratic gait. Having a 'moderator' (in this case the fine keyboardist, Timothy Roberts), as opposed to an artistic director, is pragmatic and democratic but there is the odd moment where a strong artistic presence at the helm would have, ironically perhaps, empowered the musicians towards a more flexible and varied approach to articulation and colour. That said, there are some glorious and majestic sounds here: you can fly to the buzzing *Canzon duodecimi toni a 10*, bathe in the fragrant harmonic mosaic of the three-choir *Canzon quarti toni a 15* and relish elsewhere the peculiarly delicate and sweet sounds of this ensemble. Overall, a notable and distinctive achievement. Recommended to a broad listenership.

'A Venetian Coronation, 1595'

G Gabrieli Intonazioni – ottavo tono; terzo e quarto toni; quinto tono alla quarta bassa[a]. Canzonas – XIII a 12; XVI a 15; IX a 10. Sonata VI a 8 pian e forte. Deus qui beatum Marcum a 10[c]. Omnes gentes a 16[c] **A Gabrieli** Intonazioni – primo tono[a]; settimo tono[b]. Mass Movements[c] – Kyrie a 5-12; Gloria a 16; Sanctus a 12; Benedictus a 12. O sacrum convivium a 5[c]. Benedictus Dominus Deus sabbaoth[ab] (arr Roberts) **Bendinelli** Sonata CCCXXXIII. Sarasinett[a] **M Thomsen** Toccata I

[a]**James O'Donnell,** [b]**Timothy Roberts** *orgs* **Gabrieli** [a]**Consort and Players / Paul McCreesh**

Virgin Classics Veritas VC7 59006-2 (71 minutes: DDD). Texts and translations included Ⓕ ooo

The coronation of a new Doge of Venice was always a special occasion, and never more so than when Marino Grimani (1532-1605) was elected to that office. We do not know what music was played then, but the whole ceremony is notionally and credibly reconstructed in this recording by Paul McCreesh and his cohorts. The recording was made in Brinkburn Priory, a church whose acoustic (aided by deft manipulation of the recording controls) is spacious enough to evoke that of the Basilica of St Mark, the site of the original event. Space *per se* is vital to the music of the Gabrielis, who excelled in using it by placing instrumental and vocal groups in different parts of the building – which thereby became an integral part of the music. A fine selection of music that *could* have been played then is enhanced by the opening tolling of a bell, a *crescendo* marking the leisurely approach of the ducal procession, and the impression of architectural space created by changing stereo focus. It would be difficult to speak too highly of the performances, supplemented by first-class annotation, in this memorable recording. A trip to Venice would cost a lot more than this disc but, though you could visit the real St Mark's, it would not buy you this superb musical experience.

'Music for San Rocco'

G Gabrieli Symphoniae sacrae (1615) – Jubilate Deo a 10; Misericordia tua a 12; Suscipe clementissime a 12; In ecclesiis a 14; Buccinate in neomenia a 19. Intonazioni – del nono tono; duodecimo tono. Canzoni et Sonate – Canzon XIV a 10; Sonata XVIII a 14, Sonata XIX a 15; Sonata XX a 22; Sonata XXI per tre violini. Timor et tremor a 6. Magnificat a 33 (arr Keyte). Domine Deus meus a 6 **Barbarino** Audi, dulcis amica mea. Ardens est cor meum

Timothy Roberts *org* **Gabrieli Consort and Players / Paul McCreesh**

Archiv Produktion 449 180-2AH (78 minutes: DDD) Ⓕ Texts and translations included. Recorded 1995

The words 'Venice' and 'splendour' were simply made to go together and are certainly brought together in this recording entitled 'Music for San Rocco'. Paul McCreesh and his team of advisers have taken Thomas Coryat's description, Coryats Crudities, of the 1608 festivities in honour of St Roch as the starting-point for this concert programme, which was performed in the magnificent Scuola Grande di San Rocco, famous for its sequence of paintings by Tintoretto. The programme explores a wide range of works by Gabrieli, from the more intimate motets with organ accompaniment right through the spectrum to the extraordinary 33-part Magnificat reconstructed for the occasion by Hugh Keyte. The sheer magnificence of the sound of massed cornetts and sackbuts, blending so harmoniously with the voices, clearly struck Coryat, and is equally irresistible the best part of four centuries later. This is where the Gabrieli Consort and Players came in some years ago when one could only wonder at McCreesh's logistical abilities in bringing together the required number of chamber organs and so on. The group has, of course, gone from strength to strength, exploring a wide range of repertory, but they clearly retain a strong affinity with Gabrieli's music. The singing and playing are quite superb, securely and compellingly flamboyant. It's difficult to single out individuals but one must mention David Hurley who sings the remarkable solo motets by Barbarino with great poise. For the sheer splendour of the music, and the excellence of the performances, this recording is a must.

Francesco Geminiani

Italian 1687-1762

GROVE *Geminiani studied in Rome with Corelli and A Scarlatti, and in 1711 became leader of the opera orchestra in Naples. Settling in London in 1714, he earned instant success as a violin virtuoso and became one of the most influential teachers (of the violin and composition). He published a series of instrumental works, starting with the highly acclaimed violin sonatas Op 1 (1716). In the 1730s he made two lengthy visits to Ireland, and later spent time in the Netherlands and Paris. He settled in Dublin in 1759, giving his last known concert in 1760.*

Geminiani's principal works are solo sonatas and concerti grossi. His model was Corelli, but he composed with originality, writing for a wider range of solo instruments and using a more sonorous and chromatic idiom; his music is more expressive and dramatic than Corelli's (though still contrapuntal). Most works have the traditional four-movement plan still popular in England. The violin sonatas Op 1 and Op 4 (1739) are especially difficult to play, and include cadenzas. Geminiani revised the former set as trio sonatas (c1757), and also made arrangements of others of his works. His 45 concerti grossi have a concertino of two violins, viola and cello; they include arrangements of sonatas by Corelli.

Concerti grossi

Geminiani Concerti grossi (after Corelli, Op 5)[a]. P
Cello Sonata in D minor, Op 5 No 2[b] **Corelli/Geminiani** Sonata for Violin and Cello in A, Op 5 No 9a[c]
[bc]**David Watkin** *vc* [b]**Alison McGillivray** *vc* [b]**Richard Egarr** *hpd* [a]**Academy of Ancient Music / Andrew Manze** [c]*vn*
Harmonia Mundi ② HMU907261/2 Ⓕ
(144 minutes: DDD). Recorded 1998-99 OO

Eighteenth-century English music lovers, it seems, were obsessed with the music of Corelli, in particular his concerti grossi; Manze's notes quote a lovely account of how, when the Op 6 concertos were first published in 1714, one London orchestra of gentlemen amateurs, led by a Mr Needler, could not stop themselves from playing through all 12 at one sitting. They remained Corelli's only published concertos, however, so it is not hard to see what a welcome sight the works presented on this disc must have been when they first appeared in the mid-1720s; immensely skilful arrangements by Corelli's London-based pupil Francesco Geminiani of the master's 12 violin sonatas, Op 5, they were to all intents a new set of Corelli concertos.

Well, what held for Londoners back then should hold equally well for baroque enthusiasts today; these ingeniously crafted concerti grossi are a true delight, their musical effectiveness in no way compromised by their origins. Listeners familiar with Corelli's Op 5 will doubtless have fun spotting what Geminiani has done with them (which goes well beyond straightforward orchestration, while keeping the results utterly true to Corelli's spirit); those who do not know the originals can just sit back and enjoy the music for what it is, which is to say bright, tuneful and invigorating.

Where Manze's particular success lies is in conjuring the atmosphere of the past and in the sheer joyousness and freshness which these performances convey. It is as if Mr Needler and his friends were before us, revelling in an unexpected Corellian bonus. Listen to the Academy of Ancient Music lustily laying into the thick chords in the final movement of Concerto No 4, dragging back the tempo and then charging off again, and you can almost see the complicit grins on their faces; or the way in which the ending of the well-known *La folia* (Concerto No 12) sweeps them up into a fit of orchestral scrubbing, to be capped by an excited ornamental whinny from Manze's violin.

Manze is as free with his embellishments elsewhere in the set, throwing in double-stops, blue notes and all manner of flourishes with an abandon which will not be to everyone's taste (recalling more than ever the oft-quoted description of him as 'the Gidon Kremer of the baroque violin'), but which one cannot help feeling contributes hugely to the enthusiastic tenor of the music-making as a whole. The orchestra itself is in fine form, offering up a full sound whose occasional slight rawness is no bad thing in performances of such strength, directness and honesty.

Roberto Gerhard

Spanish/British 1896-1970

GROVE *Gerhard studied in Barcelona with Granados and Pedrell and in Vienna and Berlin with Schoenberg (1923-8), returning to Barcelona to take an active part in musical life. His compositions from this period are few: they include the Schoenbergian Wind Quintet (1928), the cantata L'alta naixenç;a del rei en jaume (1932) and the ballet Ariel (1934). In 1939 he left Spain and eventually settled in England, where he became much more productive, in a distinctly Spanish style. There were three more ballets (Don Quixote, 1941; Alegrias, 1942; Pandora, 1944), an opera (The Duenna, 1947), the symphony Homenaje a Pedrell (1941) and songs, besides the Violin Concerto (1943), which looks back to the early atonal works and forward to the dynamic, boldly colourful, serial compositions of his last two decades.*

This late development was rapid, from the Schoenbergian style of the First Quartet (1955) to the athematic, block-form, effect-filled Second (1962). It can be seen too in the cycle of four symphonies (1953, 1959, 1960, 1967) and the Concerto for Orchestra (1965), which move towards a Varèsian sound-drama (the Third Symphony has the sub-title 'Collages' and includes tape). Other late works include electronic pieces, much incidental music and pieces for ensemble (Concert for Eight, 1962; Hymnody, 1963; Libra, 1968; Leo, 1969).

Symphony No 2

Symphony No 2. Concerto for Orchestra
BBC Symphony Orchestra / Matthias Bamert
Chandos CHAN9694 (55 minutes: DDD) Ⓕ
Recorded 1997

Although the avowed purpose of Gerhard's *Concerto for Orchestra* (1965) was to highlight the orchestra as an entity rather than its constituent sections or instruments, and while it may not have the immediate universal appeal of, say, Kodály's or Bartók's works with the same title (written in a very different idiom some 20 or so years earlier), it has never been surpassed for its imaginative handling of instrumental sonorities or for its virtuoso demands on the players. It has to be said right away that this is a stunning performance: not merely does the BBC SO rise spectacularly to the work's demands, but Bamert shows himself exceptionally skilful at securing internal balances. It is worth quoting Gerhard's own words: 'My favourite listener is one who does not read explanatory programme notes ... I stand by the *sound* of my music, and it is the sound that must make the sense ... a work of music takes shape only in the mind of the listener.' Gerhard's Second Symphony has been represented on disc only by the revised version (*Metamorphosis*) which had had to be completed by Alan Boustead (available on Auvidis Montaigne); although Gerhard may have felt the original too cerebral, it was at least all his, and tough going as it undoubtedly is, it is very welcome to all interested in the mental processes of this quite exceptional musician. The opening of the work's second section, with its clicking percussion, is hauntingly mysterious, and the final nightmare palindrome *Scherzo* (of which only a fraction exists in the Boustead version) is one of his most astonishing creations. With first-class recording throughout, this must be regarded as an essential disc for all admirers of Gerhard.

Symphony No 4, 'New York'

Symphony No 4, 'New York'. Pandora Suite
BBC Symphony Orchestra / Matthias Bamert
Chandos CHAN9651 (54 minutes: DDD) Ⓕ
Recorded 1997

Roberto Gerhard attached *New York* to the title of his Fourth Symphony (1967) because it was commissioned for performance there. Thirty years on, the music's frequent recourse to imposing brass clusters suggests common ground with Varèse's *Déserts* (1954), and its subtext of urban menace and decay. Varèse would probably have scorned the way Gerhard introduces allusions to Catalan folk music as a way of humanising his bleak landscape, and the two kinds of material do indeed seem distinctly uneasy associates. But that might have been Gerhard's point; not to integrate atonal symphonism and nostalgic folklorism, but to let them stand side by side as symbols of a fractured culture and an uprooted life. Matthias Bamert and the BBCSO provoke such thoughts through the cogency and clarity with which they project the symphony's constant shifts of mood: and the sound has rather greater range and presence than that of Víctor Pablo Pérez's well-conceived reading for Auvidis Montaigne. The Chandos coupling, the suite from the ballet *Pandora*, was written a quarter of a century before the symphony, and here folklorism is at the heart of music which has nothing to do with mere exoticism. This wartime score is as redolent of deep, dark feelings as anything Gerhard ever wrote. Good though the Auvidis Montaigne version of *Pandora* is, this one is better recorded, and lingers even more potently in the mind's ear.

Piano Trio

Piano Trio. Cello Sonata. Chaconne. Gemini
Cantamen (Caroline Balding *vn* Jo Cole *vc* Timothy Lissimore *pf*)
Metier MSVCD92012 (77 minutes: DDD) Ⓕ
Recorded 1995

Between Gerhard's Piano Trio, written in 1918 at the age of 22, and *Gemini*, composed nearly half a century later, yawns a stylistic gulf that almost defies credence; but of the genuineness of his convictions in each case there is no question. The sensuous warmth of the Trio demonstrates the influence of Ravel, with clear reminiscences of the Frenchman's String Quartet in the finale. The second movement is exquisitely seductive, and Cantamen plays the whole work with tenderness and sympathy. Five years later, everything was to change when Gerhard went to study in Vienna with Schoenberg; but his perpetually enquiring mind and ultrasensitive ear, along with his strong sense of Catalan identity, led him to temper the dodecaphonic system, so that later works broke free of serial dogma and frequently incorporated references to Spanish turns of phrase. This is so in the 1956 Cello Sonata which, for all the trenchant energy of its outer movements, is never less than euphonious: its deeply lyrical slow movement is beautifully shaped by Jo Cole. The *Chaconne* for solo violin is more uncompromising in idiom but Caroline Balding fulfils its virtuosic demands with distinction. *Gemini*, with its plucked piano strings and keyboard clusters, its violin scurries and its frenetic outbursts, shows Gerhard's love of experimentation in sonorities and the two instruments are presented as antagonists rather than partners. The performance has real fire and conviction.

George Gershwin

American 1898-1937

GROVE *Gershwin was essentially self-taught. He was first a song plugger in Tin Pan Alley and an accompanist. In his teens he began to compose popular songs and produced a succession of musicals from 1919 to 1933 (Lady, be Good!, 1924; Oh, Kay!, 1926; Strike up the Band, 1927; Funny Face, 1927; Girl Crazy, 1930); the lyrics were generally by his brother Ira (1896-1983). In 1924 he became famous: he wrote Rhapsody in Blue as a concerto for piano and Paul Whiteman's jazz band. Its success led him to devote increasing energy to 'serious' composition. His more ambitious works include the*

Piano Concerto in F (1925) and the tone poem An American in Paris (1928). But he continued composing for the musical theatre, and some of his most successful musicals (Strike up the Band, Girl Crazy, Of Thee I Sing) date from this period. In 1934-5 he wrote his 'American folk opera' Porgy and Bess, which draws on African-American idioms; given on Broadway, it was only a limited success. Gershwin went to Hollywood in 1936 and wrote songs for films. He was a sensitive songwriter of great melodic gifts and did much to create syntheses between jazz and classical traditions in his concert music and black folk music and opera in Porgy and Bess.

Piano Concerto in F major

Piano Concerto in F. Porgy and Bess – symphonic suite. Second Rhapsody
Aalborg Symphony Orchestra / Wayne Marshall *pf*
Virgin Classics VM5 61243-2 (72 minutes: DDD) Ⓜ
Recorded 1995

Wayne Marshall makes his first entry in the Piano Concerto and, in the space of a bar or two, you hear a quick wit and a cool head, the ability to convey (just as Gershwin strove to do) the jazzman's freewheeling, rhapsodic manner alongside a concert pianist's formality. Where Gershwin sits back in the wee small hours spinning yet another of his blue tunes, Marshall is in no hurry to go anywhere. And yet there's a very real sense of the imperative, too, a 'something's coming' kind of feeling. When it comes, it's a special moment. So, too, is Gershwin's grandiose recapitulation (and Marshall goes all the way with that). Generally, the Aalborg Symphony is well up on the style – no mean achievement when the orchestra can so easily sound like a dead-weight in this piece. But then, Marshall's 'Jack-be-nimble' approach is plainly infectious, encouraging reflexes from his band that are as quick and sparky as his own. The pulse of the Roaring Twenties was racy and capricious. But there was always time to dream. That's the tenor of Marshall's performance. The same is true of his dashing account of the *Second Rhapsody*. Again the contrasts are strong, the manner spontaneous – impulsive, Manhattan-brash to a degree – though Marshall never lets us forget that these are luxury goods. Gershwin's shot-silk climaxes (Hollywood dreams indeed), with all their audacious modulations and fruity horn counterpoints (nobody played with wrong-note harmonies like Gershwin), are played for all they're worth. There's also a spirited account of the Robert Russell Bennett *Porgy and Bess* Suite, as felicitous (real delicacy of atmosphere as 'Clara' emerges from the opening street cries) as it is robust (that's quite a hurricane that blows through Catfish Row).

Rhapsody in Blue

Gershwin An American in Paris. Rhapsody in Blue **H**
Grofé Grande Canyon Suite
New York Philharmonic Orchestra / Leonard Bernstein *pf*
Sony Classical SMK63086 (64 minutes: ADD) Ⓜ
Recorded 1958-59

Bernstein conducted and played the music of Gershwin with the same naturalness as he brought to his own music. Here, *An American in Paris* swings by with an instinctive sense of its origins in popular and film music; no stilted rhythms or four-squareness delay the work's progress, and where ripe schmaltz is wanted, ripe schmaltz is what we get, devoid of all embarrassment. *Rhapsody in Blue* is playful and teasing, constantly daring us to try to categorize its style, and then confounding our conclusions. Although the solo passages from individual players are beautifully taken, the orchestra captures the authentic flavour of Gershwin's and Bernstein's idiom, and Bernstein pushes them to transcend the printed scores. His own playing in the *Rhapsody* is tantalizingly unpredictable. The recording is clear and bright, perhaps a touch hard-edged, and a little of the richness of the original LP issue might have been preferred by some, especially as the editing is now made more obvious.

'Gershwin Fantasy'

Fantasy on Porgy and Bess (arr Courage). Three Preludes (arr Heifetz). A Damsel in Distress – Nice work if you can get it. Girl Crazy – But not for me (both arr Tunick); Embraceable you; I got rhythm. Show Girl – Liza. Tip-Toes – Sweet and low-downa. Goldwyn Follies – Love is here to stay (all arr Brohn)
Joshua Bell *vn* **George Gershwin** *pf* **London Symphony Orchestra / John Williams** *pf*
Sony Classical SK60659 (55 minutes: DDD). Ⓕ
Recorded 1997. Item marked a incorporates composer's 1926 piano roll

In the 1920s George Gershwin used to encounter Jascha Heifetz at smart New York parties, and the two sometimes improvised violin-piano duets. Heifetz urged Gershwin to compose a major concert work for him, but Gershwin never got around to it. After the composer's death, Heifetz himself arranged five songs from Porgy and Bess as well as Gershwin's three Preludes for piano. These transcriptions and arrangements are the springboard for this CD.

John Williams has arranged eight songs from Porgy into a 20-minute Fantasy, somewhat in the manner of Sarasate's assaults on Carmen and other 19th-century operas. It comes as something of a surprise to hear "Bess, you is my woman now" in such a high key, but Joshua Bell takes on the wailing "My man's gone now" and of course "Summertime" to make a very convincing virtuoso effect.

Heifetz's transcriptions of the Preludes sound so natural that one would believe that Gershwin had composed them that way, whereas Williams's arrangements of some other show- and film-tunes seem to look forward more to the style of Grappelli. This is a light-hearted, sunny disc, which makes huge demands on Bell as soloist but none at all on the listener – it's sheer pleasure.

Gershwin Piano Rolls

Akst Jaz-o-mine[a] **Berlin** For Your Country and My Country[ac] **Conrad** Singin' the Blues ('till My Daddy Comes Home)[a] **Frey** Havanola[a] **O Gardner** Chinese Blues[d] **Gershwin** La La Lucille – From Now On[a] Rialto Ripples[a] **B Grant** Arrah Go On I'm Gonna Go Back to Oregon[a] **Kern** Zip Goes a Million – Whip-Poor-Will[a] **Matthews** Pastime Rag No 3[e] **M Morris** Kangaroo Hop[a] **Pinkard** Waitin' for Me[a] **Schonberg** Darling[ab] **Schonberger** Whispering[a] **Various** Greenwich Village Follies of 1920 – Just Snap Your Fingers at Care[a] **P Wendling** Buzzin' the Bee[a]
[a]**George Gershwin,** [b]**Cliff Hess,** [c]**Rudy Erlebach,** [d]**Bert Wynn,** [e]**Fred Murtha** *pfs*
Nonesuch 7559-79370-2 (42 minutes: DDD)
Derived from piano rolls cut between 1916 and 1921. Ⓕ
Recorded 1992-93

There are some curiosities here but only two numbers are by Gershwin himself. The first of these is *Rialto Ripples*, a catchy rag Gershwin wrote in collaboration with Will Donaldson and put on to a roll in September 1916. It is fascinating to compare Gershwin's own 1916 performance with the sheet music published a year later. The roll has much more of the ragtime idiom in oom-pah left-hand chords and even reveals a few misprints in the score. Another ragtime connection is the 1916 roll, under one of Gershwin's pseudonyms (Fred Murtha), of *Pastime Rag No 3*, one of only five polished rags in different styles by black composer Artie Matthews. Again there are interesting differences between the sheet music published in the same year and Gershwin's roll – he doesn't play repeats but he returns to the A strain at the end. He doesn't seem to know what to do with the 'stoptime' effect (1'21") in Strain C and just holds the pedal down. The rest of the song arrangements, which sometimes employ two players, show the ragtime background of this piano style, especially in the earlier rolls. These are also good examples of the techniques of the roll arrangers, who hyped it all up by adding notes to create the effect of a whole team of pianists.

Solo Piano Works

Of Thee I Sing – Prelude[a]; Jilted. Second Rhapsody[a]. The Shocking Miss Pilgrim – For you, for me, for evermore. Cuban Overture[a]. Pardon My English – Isn't it a pity? Variations on 'I got rhythm'[a]. Catfish Row[a]. Shall we dance? – Let's call the whole thing off[a]; They can't take that away from me[a]. Goldwyn Follies – Our love is here to stay
Jack Gibbons *pf*
ASV White Line CDWHL2082 (77 minutes: DDD) Ⓜ
Items marked [a] arr Gibbons. Recorded 1992-93

This disc is mostly comprised of Gibbons's own arrangements, based on Gershwin's film music, two-piano pieces, and in the case of the 'Catfish Row' *Porgy and Bess* suite, his orchestrations. The longest work is the *Second Rhapsody*, composed for a scene in the Gershwins' first Hollywood movie, *Delicious* (from which the best-known song is 'Blah, blah, blah'). The film starred Janet Gaynor and Charles Farrell, and in this sequence the heroine wanders frightened through Manhattan – it might be rechristened *A Scotswoman in New York*. George Gershwin referred to the main tune as his 'Brahmsian theme' but today no one would mistake it for anything but Gershwin. 'For you, for me', one of the melodies salvaged from their files by Ira Gershwin and used 10 years after George's death, emerged in the 1947 film *The Shocking Miss Pilgrim*. Ira and Kay Swift hoped it would be a gold-mine and rated the tune higher than any among Gershwin's unpublished songs. The solo version of the *Cuban Overture* is Gibbons's own adaptation of Gershwin's four hand arrangement; like the 'Catfish Row' suite it makes formidable demands on the pianist and Gibbons gives them both virtuoso performances. The recital ends with three of the standards Gershwin wrote in Hollywood during the last months of his life. 'They can't take that away from me' must be a strong contender for the great songs of the 20th century, and no one hearing 'Our love is here to stay' can doubt that a premonition of death lingered somewhere in the composer's heart in the autumn of 1936.

Porgy and Bess

Awards 1989

Willard White *bass* Porgy; **Cynthia Haymon** *sop* Bess; **Harolyn Blackwell** *sop* Clara; **Cynthia Clarey** *sop* Serena; **Damon Evans** *bar* Sportin' Life; **Marietta Simpson** *mez* Maria; **Gregg Baker** *bar* Crown **Glyndebourne Chorus; London Philharmonic Orchestra / Sir Simon Rattle**
EMI ③ CDS5 56220-2 (189 minutes: DDD) Ⓕ
Notes and text included. Recorded 1988 OOO

The company, orchestra and conductor from the outstanding 1986 Glyndebourne production recreate a very real sense of Gershwin's 'Catfish Row' community on this complete recording. Such is its atmosphere and theatricality, we might easily be back on the Glyndebourne stage. From the very first bar it's clear just how instinctively attuned Rattle and this orchestra are to every aspect of a multi-faceted score. The cast, too, are so *right*, so much a part of their roles, and so well integrated into the whole, that one almost takes the excellence of their contributions for granted. Here is one beautiful voice after another, beginning in style with Harolyn Blackwell's radiant 'Summertime', which at Rattle's gorgeously lazy tempo, is just about as beguiling as one could wish. Willard White conveys both the simple honesty and inner-strength of Porgy without milking the sentiment and Haymon's passionately sung Bess will go wherever a little flattery and encouragement take her. As Sportin' Life, Damon Evans not only relishes the burlesque elements of the role but he really *sings* what's written a lot more than is customary. But the entire cast deliver throughout with all the unstinting fervour of a Sunday revivalist meeting. Sample the final moments of the piece – 'Oh Lawd, I'm on my way' – if that doesn't stir you, nothing will.

Carlo Gesualdo
Italian c1561-1613

GROVE *A nobleman and amateur musician, Gesualdo is notorious for having his first wife and her lover murdered in 1590; he married Leonora d'Este of Ferrara three years later. While at the Ferrarese court (1594-6) he played the lute and showed a passion for music and came to be accepted as a serious composer. He eventually retired to his castle at Gesualdo, sunk into a deep melancholy from which music alone could provide relief. His music was strongly influenced by Luzzaschi and Nenna, particularly the former in his use of serious, expressive, richly worked music even for quite light texts. He took great pains over word setting, allowing texts to be clearly heard and strongly expressed. Much of the music in his six madrigal books (1594-1611) and three sacred books (1603-11) uses unexpected harmonies and changes of key, dissonances and striking chromaticism in a highly original way, usually prompted by the emotions of the texts. Stravinsky made arrangements of some of his madrigals.*

Madrigals

Ahi, disperata vita. Sospirava il mio cor. O malnati messaggi. Non t'amo, o voce ingrata. Luci serene e chiare. Sparge la morte al mio Signor nel viso. Arde il mio cor. Occhi del mio cor vita. Mercè grido piangendo. Asciugate i begli ochi. Se la mia morte brami. Io parto. Ardita Zanzaretta. Ardo per te, mio bene. Instrumental items – Canzon francese. Io tacerò. Corrente, amanti **P**

Les Arts Florissants / William Christie

Harmonia Mundi HMC90 1268 (55 minutes: DDD) Ⓕ

Texts and translations included

To many, Gesualdo is known above all for the *crime passionnel* which left his wife and her lover impaled on the same sword, but the notion that his highly-charged music is the product of a tortured and unstable mind is, no doubt, over-romanticized. For this foray into the schizophrenic world of Gesualdo's five-voice madrigals, Les Arts Florissants have selected their programme from the last three books, pieces in which the highly-mannered and exaggerated aspects of the composer's style reach their most extreme expression. Nevertheless, we should not think of all these works being undifferentiated in style, and one of the fascinations of this disc, which has been very carefully planned, is the insight it offers into the gradual emergence and sharpening of the features which characterise Gesualdo's late madrigalian manner. Some of those elements can already be heard in *Sospirava il mio cor* from the Third Book, and by the last tracks they are present, with all their compositional distortions in full dress. William Christie and Les Arts Florissants are no strangers to the aesthetic of the Italian madrigal in its last decades. This recording, like so many of their productions, is full of surprises on both the large and small scales. The first, of a general kind, is the decision to add continuo accompaniments *avant la lettre*. This is justifiable on historical grounds, though less certain is the precise way it has been done with some passages within a piece still left *a cappella*. What is less justifiable, if only on artistic grounds, is the performance of two madrigals on instruments alone (*Io tacerò* and *Corrente, amanti*); it makes little sense to attempt such highly charged word-driven music in this way. What may also surprise is the rather understated, almost classically-pure character of the interpretations, though it is a relief that the calculatedly neurotic and deliberately out-of-tune manner so often turned out for Gesualdo has here been eschewed. These are technically very fine and dramatically convincing and coherent readings which are certainly preferable to any other recordings of Gesualdo's madrigals currently available.

Gesualdo Asciugate i begli occhi. Beltà, poiché t'assenti. Canzone del Principe. Gioite voi col canto. Languisce al fin. Mercè grido piangendo. Moro, lasso, al mio duolo. Se la mia morte brami. Se vi duol il mio duolo. S'io non miro non moro. Tu m'uccidi, o crudele **P**
Luzzaschi Madrigals, Book 5 – Lungi da te cor mio; Ahi cruda sorte mia; Itene mie querele **Monte** Di mie dogliose note **Montella** Se lontana voi sete
Nenna Occhi miei che vedeste
Concerto Italiano (Elisa Franzetti, Monica Piccinini, Elisabetta Tiso *sops* Rosa Domínguez *mez* Alessandro Carmignani *conterten* Gianluca Ferrarini, Paolo Fanciullacci *tens* Sergio Foresti *bass* Mara Galassi *hp* Andrea Damiani *theorb*) **/ Rinaldo Alessandrini**

Opus 111 OPS30-238 (68 minutes: DDD) Ⓕ

Texts and translations included. Recorded 1999 **OO**

The first impression from this CD is that Rinaldo Alessandrini's Gesualdo lacks the burnished warmth of his Monteverdi. The acoustic is less resonant, and the exactitude of the singers' tuning makes it cold, at times almost claustrophobic; in other words the tone has been judged just about perfectly. We begin with perhaps the most famous madrigal of them all, *Moro, lasso, al mio duolo*, and the tendency to downplay the dramatic potential of those famous chromatic audacities sets the tone from the start. Indeed, some may find the understatement surprising. However, these interpretations have real staying power, a narrative persuasiveness that unfolds with repeated listening (while making clear the fragmentation at the heart of the music).

Concerto Italiano's approach does Gesualdo more favours than the histrionics that his music can so readily invite. The same is true of Alessandrini's insert-notes (co-written with Iain Fenlon), which start from the premise that Gesualdo was a real artist, not a musical shock-tactician, nor a composer-cum-psychopath, nor yet a one-trick pony. It is true that similar strategies recur from work to work: for example the sensuous settings of words addressed to the beloved – 'dolcissimo cor mio', 'Dolce del cor tesoro', both rendered as sensually as possible – and the contrasts with harsher sentiments that immediately follow. It would be absurd to claim for Gesualdo a range to which he probably never aspired. As it is, could anyone guess how the penultimate syllable of the phrase 'potessi dirti pria ch'io mora' (in *Mercè grido piangendo*) resolves? That a major chord can be so jarring sums up Gesualdo's art very neatly, and here as elsewhere the singers find unsuspected poignancy in a pause or a breath.

The disc begins and ends with madrigals from composers whom Gesualdo admired. However, these performances are not quite so convincing: they are weighed down by the continuo (harp and theorbo), which is absent from the performances of Gesualdo, and the timbre of the soprano Alessandrini uses for these pieces is white and rather strained. But his Gesualdo really is indispensable.

Tenebrae responses

Responsoria et alia ad Officium Hebdonadae Sanctae spectantia **P**

Taverner Choir / Andrew Parrott

Sony Classical SK62977 (67 minutes: DDD). Text and translation included. Recorded 1996 Ⓕ

Gesualdo's *Tenebrae* have a distinguished discography – the Hilliard Ensemble's recording of all three days of the *Triduum sacrum* for ECM achieved considerable popularity. This recording from the Taverner Choir is no less compelling, and it includes the plainsong which ought to frame Gesualdo's polyphony, an essential detail which the Hilliards left out. The composer's tough vision comes across all the more forcefully, betraying not a hint of complacency. Liturgical reconstruction is a rock on which many fine performances have foundered, but can be very effective when the plainchant is interpreted as consciously as the polyphony. There is no suggestion of auto-pilot in the way the plainsong is delivered: no lush, rounded cadences, but carefully chosen voices whose pleasing edge keeps the music firmly anchored to earth. Listening to the polyphony, one is struck by the care with which Parrott has chosen his singers. The countertenors in particular seem to rise out of the chest-tone of the lower voices: a 'bottom-up' approach to timbre more typical of continental ensembles than of English ones. It has always been a great strength of Parrott's that he ensures that the stable core of singers comprising the Taverner Choir can adapt its sound to the music under consideration. And right from the first polyphonic entry, the acerbic quality of Gesualdo's chordal progressions have a dynamism that is deeply involving. Those who treasure the Hilliards' recording need not fear duplication, and for the first-time buyer one can recommend either version.

Orlando Gibbons British 1583-1625

GROVE *Gibbons came from a musical family and was a chorister (1596-8) and student (1599-1603) at King's College, Cambridge. He joined the Chapel Royal in c 1603 and was one of its organists by 1615 (senior organist, 1625). In 1619 he became a virginal player at court and in 1623 organist at Westminster Abbey. He took the MusB at Cambridge (1606) and the DMus at Oxford (1622). One of the most important English composers of sacred music in the early 17th century, he wrote several Anglican services, popular in their day, and over 30 anthems, some imposing and dramatic (e.g. O clap your hands), others colourful and most expressive (See, the word is incarnate; This is the record of John). His instrumental music, also important, includes over 30 elaborate contrapuntal viol fantasias and over 40 masterly keyboard pieces. His madrigals (1612) are generally serious in tone (eg The Silver Swanne).*

Vocal Works

O clap your hands. Great Lord of Lords. Hosanna to the Son of David. Prelude in G[a]. Out of the deep. See, see, the Word is incarnate. Preludes – No 3 in D minor, MBXX/3[a]. Lift up your heads. Almighty and everlasting God. First (Short) Service – No 6, Magnificat; No 7, Nunc dimittis. Second Service – No 3, Magnificat; No 4, Nunc dimittis. Fantazia of four parts[a]. O God, the king of glory. O Lord, in Thy wrath rebuke me not

Oxford Camerata / Jeremy Summerly with [a]**Laurence Cummings** *org*

Naxos 8 553130 (65 minutes: DDD). Texts included. Ⓢ Recorded 1994

The Oxford Camerata provides a representative selection of choral works by Gibbons, together with three of his organ pieces. The programme is introduced by a bright and busy performance of the eight-part *O clap your hands*, followed by the noble verse anthem *Great Lord of Lords* – and it is pleasing to hear in this piece, and in the other verse-anthems, the rich timbre of the countertenor Robin Blaze, a welcome acquisition for the Camerata, which has a great deal of vocal talent in its make-up. They tackle the gently moving *See, see, the Word is incarnate* with great confidence, together with the First and Second Services and the quiet collects with all the knowledge and aplomb of cathedral lay clerks or choral scholars from Oxford and Cambridge. Laurence Cummings plays two short preludes, the one in G major – a real test of agility – from *Parthenia* and that in D minor from Benjamin Cosyn's *Virginal Book*. The *Fantazia of four parts* is a most extraordinary work, quite hard to steady and control. Nevertheless, it is a welcome addition to the programme.

Pavan and Galliard a 6. Fantasia a 2 No 1. Go from my window. Fantasias a 6 – Nos 3 and 5. Fantasia a 4 No 1 'for the great double bass'. Galliard a 3. In Nomine a 4. Pavan and Galliard in A minor, 'Lord Salisbury'. Prelude in G. Masks – Lincoln's Inn mask; The Fairest Nymph. Alman in G. Behold, thou hast made my days. Glorious and powerful God. The First Set of Madrigals and Mottets – Daintie fine bird; Faire is the rose; I weigh not fortune's frown; I see ambition never pleased; I feign not friendship where I hate; The silver swanne

Tessa Bonner *sop* **Timothy Roberts** *keybds* **Red Byrd; Rose Consort of Viols**
Naxos 8 550603 (68 minutes: DDD) Ⓢ
Recorded 1992

Beautifully performed and finely recorded, this selection of Gibbons's music is especially attractive for its variety. At its richest it presents writing for voice and viols combined, five parts to each, or for viols alone, sometimes in six parts. In lightest, most transparent texture there is a charming piece for two viols. Three keyboard instruments are used for solos: virginals, harpsichord and organ. A soprano also sings solos to viol accompaniment. Moods and styles vary correspondingly. The *Masks* and *Alman* for virginals have a high-spirited, almost popular manner; the Fifth *Fantasia* includes some unusual chromaticism and harmonic developments that for a while almost anticipate Purcell. Tessa Bonner sings with unvibrant purity; but most striking here is the pronunciation. It is one of the distinguishing marks of this curiously named group, Red Byrd, that they sing such music with vowel-sounds modified to fit theories about the English in which it would originally have been sung. Thus the 'daintie fine bird' tells 'oi sing and doy', and the 'u' acquires a sort of umlaut in *I weigh not fortune's frown*, 'weigh' and 'frown' also having a measure of rusticity. Perhaps it is a good idea, but it does increase the desirability of printed texts in the booklet. The instrumental music is finely played, the viols avoiding any imputation of belonging to the squeeze-and-scrape school, and Timothy Roberts's keyboard solos are particularly skilful, in *legato* and fluency.

Second Service (ed Higginbottom) – Te Deum Laudamus; Jubilate Deo; Magnificat; Nunc dimittis. Anthems – O Lord, in Thy wrath rebuke me not. O God, the king of glory. Glorious and powerful God. Sing unto the Lord. O clap your handsr. See, see, the Word is incarnate. Organ works – Fantasia of four parts. A Fancy in A. A Fancy for a double organ
David Burchell *org* **New College Choir, Oxford / Edward Higginbottom**
CRD CRD3451 (66 minutes: DDD). Texts included. Ⓜ
Recorded 1987

Of all the English composers of the Shakespearian age, Gibbons is in many ways the easiest to love. But he can also be the easiest to destroy by taking too solemn an approach to his delicate lines. The New College Choir offers what seems to be the ideal sound quality. All the voices are mellow and light – which may well surprise and initially disconcert those accustomed to a more stentorian reading of the bass solo that opens Glorious and powerful God, for example. To match this, Edward Higginbottom prefers dancing tempos, occasionally thereby covering a much-treasured detail, but in general stressing the range of colours and rhythms that are so vital to this music. His organist, David Burchell, adds to the effect with his limpid and stylish playing. Higginbottom also gives us an important treat in reconstructing the incomplete Te Deum and Jubilate of the large Second Service. This is impressive and wonderful music; but, more than that, the complete Second Service is, at some 24 minutes, the longest and grandest conception that survives from Gibbons. It is very good to have; and it is doubly good to hear the massive and varied Te Deum moulded so sensitively.

Umberto Giordano Italian 1867-1948

GROVE *Giordano studied with Serrao at the Naples Conservatory between 1880 and 1890 and was commissioned, after showing promise in a competition, to write an opera: this was Mala vita, a verismo opera of some violence and crudity, given at Rome in 1892. After another failure (an old-fashioned romantic melodrama), he moved to Milan, where his Andrea Chenier was given, at La Scala, in 1896; with its French Revolutionary subject and its fervent, assertive style, it was an immediate success and has remained popular in Italy and beyond. Comparable success, at least in Italy, was met by Fedora (1898, Milan), but of his seven later operas only the comic Il re (1929, Milan), which was taken up by coloratura sopranos, enjoyed any real success although he remained a master of the intense, vehement, Massenet-influenced, theatrically effective style that gives Andrea Chenier its appeal.*

Andrea Chénier

Luciano Pavarotti *ten* Andrea Chénier; **Leo Nucci** *bar* Gerard; **Montserrat Caballé** *sop* Maddalena; **Kathleen Kuhlmann** *mez* Bersi; **Astrid Varnay** *sop* Countess di Coigny; **Christa Ludwig** *mez* Madelon; **Tom Krause** *bar* Roucher; **Hugues Cuénod** *ten* Fleville; **Neil Howlett** *bar* Fouquier-Tinville, Major-domo; **Giorgio Tadeo** *bass* Mathieu; **Piero De Palma** *ten* Incredible; **Florindo Andreolli** *ten* Abate; **Giuseppe Morresi** *bass* Schmidt; **Ralph Hamer** *bass* Dumas **Welsh National Opera Chorus; National Philharmonic Orchestra / Riccardo Chailly**
Decca ② 410 117-2DH2 (107 minutes: DDD). Notes, Ⓕ text and translation included. Recorded 1982-84

Whatever else, this is undoubtedly the best-recorded and probably the best-conducted *Chénier* yet. Chailly overconducts the score, drawing attention to himself rather than to Giordano, but by and large he is sympathetic to both the score and his singers. *Chénier* isn't easy to interpret; it bustles along busily all the time, but not always with much distinction or to any very strong purpose. For the many and important small roles, Decca has assembled half a dozen old faithfuls in various states of vocal health. Varnay goes rather over the top as the old Countess in Act 1. The three *comprimario* tenors, whose combined ages must be more than 200, all make the mark with Piero De Palma the most potent as the spy Incredible, an object-lesson in acting with the voice. Giorgio Tadeo, a *buffo* bass of distinction, here turns himself into the nasty Mathieu. Krause is an honourable Roucher. But Christa Ludwig is better than any, making old Madelon's brief appearance into a moving vignette. Of the younger singers, Kathleen Kuhlmann is a rather anonymous Bersi, while Neil Howlett is a snarling Fouquier-Tinville.

But *Chénier* stands or falls by its three principals. All three here perform eloquently. Pavarotti tends to rasp his way through the Improvviso, but improves no end in his first love duet with Maddalena, and defies the court in Act 3 with real heroism. But it is in the final act that his tone recaptures its old refulgence in his poetic musings and death-going duet. Again and again a phrase will set Caballé apart as a uniquely subtle artist. There are occasionally those self-regarding mannerisms that she indulges in, also a want of sheer tonal weight, but you will warm to her portrayal. Nucci's Gérard is excellent, a nice balance between line and punch. Pavarotti and Caballé enthusiasts will need to have this set; others should perhaps endeavour to hear the pros and cons of Levine.

Andrea Chénier

Plácido Domingo *ten* Andrea Chénier; **Renata Scotto** *sop* Maddalena; **Sherrill Milnes** *bar* Carlo Gérard; **Michael Sénéchal** *ten* Incredible; **Maria Ewing** *mez* Bersi; **Gwendolyn Killebrew** *mez* Madelon; **Jean Kraft** *mez* Countess; **Allan Monk** *bar* Roucher; **Terence Sharpe** *bar* Fléville; **Stuart Harling** *bass* Fouquier-Tinville; **Isser Bushkin** *bass* Schmidt; **Malcolm King** *bass* Dumas; **Piero De Palma** *ten* Abate; **Nigel Beavan** *bass-bar* Maestro di casa; **Enzo Dara** *bar* Mathieu **John Alldis Choir; National Philharmonic Orchestra / James Levine**

RCA ② 74321 39499-2 (114 minutes: ADD). Notes, text and translation included. Recorded 1976 Ⓜ

Choosing between these two recordings, it might seem sensible to start with the tenor in the title-role, and here a strong inclination would be to plump for RCA and Domingo: he is in splendid voice, with a touch of nobility to his manner that makes for a convincing portrayal of a poet. Pavarotti (Chailly) begins with a rather leather-lunged Improvviso, but he later finds poetry in the role as well, especially when responding to his soprano, Caballé, who is rather stretched by the more exhausting reaches of her role and sounds audibly grateful for the occasional opportunities he gives her to float rather than belt a high-lying phrase. However, Pavarotti is an *Italian* tenor, and his Italianate sense of line adds one per cent or so of elegance to some phrases that even Domingo cannot match. Caballé does many things beautifully, and her fine-spun *pianissimos* and subtle shadings only occasionally sound mannered, but the role is undeniably half-a-size too big for her. So it is for Scotto, you might say, and a hint of strain is audible once or twice, in her timbre rather than her phrasing. It is her phrasing, indeed, that tips the balance back to RCA: Scotto is as subtle a vocalist as Caballé, but she gives meaning and eloquence to every phrase without ever breaking the long line, which one cannot always say of the Spanish soprano. Matters are about even as far as the baritones are concerned: Milnes acts admirably, but refrains from over-acting, and the voice is rich and characterful. In the supporting cast, but RCA's striking Bersi, vividly characterised Incredible, and their Roucher, too, are not outmatched (only their Madelon, both fruity and acid – a grapefruit of a voice – is disappointing). A lot of people will enjoy the huge energy and bustle of Levine's direction. It is vividly characterful, but a shade exhausting and overassertive. The flow of the music seems more natural in Chailly's hands, and orchestral detail is clearer. The Decca recording, too, is warmer.

Fedora

Magda Olivero *sop* Fedora; **Mario del Monaco** *ten* Loris; **Tito Gobbi** *bar* de Siriex; **Leonardo Monreale** *bass* Lorek, Nicola; **Lucia Cappellino** *sop* Olga; **Virgilio Carbonari** *bass* Borov; **Silvio Maionica** *bass* Grech; **Piero de Palma** *ten* Rouvel; **Peter Binder** *bar* Kiril; **Dame Kiri Te Kanawa** *sop* Dmitri; **Riccardo Cassinelli** *ten* Desire; **Athos Cesarini** *ten* Sergio; **Pascal Rogé** *pf* Boleslao Lazinski **Monte-Carlo Opera Chorus and Orchestra / Lamberto Gardelli**

Zandonai Francesca da Rimini: Act 2 – E ancora sgombro il campo del comune? ... Date il segno, Paolo, date ... Un'erba io m'avea, per sanare ... Onta et orrore sopra[abde]. Act 3 – No, Smadragedi, no! ... Paolo, datemi pace! ... Ah la parola chi i miei occhi incontrano[ab]. Act 4 – Ora andate ... E così, vada s'è pur mio destino[abc]

[a]**Magda Oliviero** *sop* Francesca; [b]**Mario del Monaco** *ten* Paolo; [c]**Annamaria Gasparini** *mez* Biancofiore; [d]**Virgilio Carbonari** *bass* Man-at-arms; [e]**Athos Cesarini** *ten* Archer **Monte-Carlo Opera Orchestra / Nicola Rescigno**

Decca Grand Opera ② 433 033-2DM2 (132 minutes: ADD). Notes, texts and translations included. Recorded 1969 Ⓜ

The music in *Fedora* is richly textured orchestrally and finely written for the voices, and this recording made in 1969 is notable for the singing of both Magda Olivero and Mario del Monaco, who, despite being in their mid-fifties, bring tremendous verve, vocal resource and dramatic skill to their roles. Tito Gobbi has less to do as the diplomat de Siriex, but gives him character, and another plus is the playing of Pascal Rogé, who performs the non-singing role of the Polish pianist and spy Boleslao Lazinski in Act 2 who, while performing, eavesdrops on a dialogue between Loris and Fedora. This exchange is a marvellous example of verismo writing and singing, and so is their final scene with her death. The set opens with excerpts from another opera, Zandonai's *Francesca da Rimini* with the same two excellent principals. The recordings are clear and and fresh-sounding .

Madame Sans-Gene

Mirella Freni *sop* Caterina; **Giorgio Merighi** *ten* Lefebvre; **Mauro Buda** *bar* Napoleone; **Andrea Zese** *bar* Fouche; **Valter Borin** *ten* Neipperg; **Antonio Feltracco** *ten* Vinaigre, Despreaux; **Marzia Giaccaia** *sop* Toniotta, Carolina; **Muriel Tomeo** *sop* Giulia;

Federica Bragaglia *sop* Principessa Elisa, La Rossa; **Valerio Marletta** *bar* De Brigole; **Riccardo Ristori** *bar* Gelsomino, Roustan; **Alfio Grasso** *bar* Leroy; **Muriel Tomao** *sop* Madame Bulow
Modeno Teatro Comunale Chorus; Emilia Romagna 'Toscanini' Symphony Orchestra / Stefano Ranzani
Dynamic CDS247 (123 minutes: DDD) Ⓕ
Notes, text and translation included
Recorded live in 1999

In the not-so-distant past most 'serious' musicians thought Giordano beneath notice while opera-goers of a certain kind felt he was everything they stood for. He was passionate and melodious; he gave his singers something to sing, and, under the right circumstances, genuine thrills were to be had. He was also considered to be out of the common run: the aristocrat of verismo, with Chenier's 'Improvviso' as the thinking-man's 'Nessun dorma'.

This opinion was usually based on *Andrea Chenier* and (with slightly less conviction) *Fedora*. Otherwise a few excerpts from one or two lesser-known operas were gratefully heard but did not allay suspicions that a wider acquaintance might prove disheartening. Meanwhile, this set from the Italian-based company, Dynamic, invites us all to think again. The plot of *Madame Sans-Gene* is a rather charming variant on the theme of the Emperor's clothes; it is also about a star-struck girl who learns sense and returns to home and boyfriend. The première at La Scala in 1929 failed to impress, though Toscanini conducted and Toti Dal Monte sang the leading role; apparently Giordano was almost found guilty of modernism. To us now, the score is elegantly lyrical and lively, modern in relation to Chenier as (say) *Gianni Schicchi* is in relation to *Manon Lescaut*; and, as far as its position in the body of his work is concerned, *Gianni Schicchi* might be a fair analogy.

Madame Sans-Gene is also a comedy. The story takes a serious turn in Act 3, which for a while seems about to topple over into tragedy. Napoleon, previously a figure in the background, appears in person and in a bad mood, but is charmed and shamed into a talk about old times with the genial heroine and all ends well. At first Madame Sans-Gene, so-called, seems to be one of those tireless life-and-soul-of-the-party people who can be so wearing, but she develops into less of a turn and more of a character, while her chirpy vocal line eventually settles for a more rewarding warmth and lyricism. She even has a kind of 'Improvviso' herself, a spirited solo in which instead of playing the gracious hostess to a lot of stuck-up women she tells them their fortune in no uncertain terms.

It is understandable that the role should be attractive to a star soprano who late in her career looks for something out of the way in which much is accomplished by personality. Mirella Freni's voice is still full-bodied and to a large extent pure in quality, but for many years now has forfeited the firm evenness of its prime. She gives a genuine performance – and (not far off her 64th birthday) a remarkable one. The best singing, however, is that of the tenor, Giorgio Merighi. Martinelli sang the role at the premiere in 1915, and something of that incisive tone and ardent address are recaptured here. Mauro Buda as Napoleon shows an almost tenorial baritone which it would be good to hear in a part with more opportunities. Maestro Ranzani conducts with spirit. As a recording this is a great deal more satisfactory than the currently available alternative, taken from an Italian radio transmission in 1957.

Mauro Giuliani

Italian 1781-1829

GROVE *In Vienna from 1806, Giuliani became famous as the greatest living guitarist, teaching, performing and composing a rich repertory for the guitar. He was also a cellist, playing in the première of Beethoven's Symphony no.7 (1813). In 1814 he became honorary chamber musician to Napoleon's second wife. He returned to Italy in 1819 and was patronized by the nobility. His works include three guitar concertos, sonatas, studies and variations for solo guitar, quartets and many duos (with flute or violin) for guitar and songs.*

Guitar Concerto No 1

Giuliani Guitar Concerto No 1 in A, Op 30
Schubert Sonata for Arpeggione and Piano in A minor, D821 (arr Williams)
John Williams *gtr* **Australian Chamber Orchestra**
Sony Classical SK63385 (52 minutes: DDD) Ⓕ
Recorded 1998

The guitar has played a part in several adaptations of the Schubert A minor Sonata, substituting for either the arpeggione or the piano, but never before with a string orchestra in the supporting role, reversing the bowed/percussive relationship. Good arranging does not consist of literal adherence to the original score but, as here, in making small changes to take advantage of the new instrumentation. Rarely has such a transmutation been accomplished with greater conviction. Put any doubts or prejudices you may have on the back burner and prepare to enjoy familiar beauty in new clothing. The Giuliani is familiar in every respect – except that of interpretation. What we have in this recording is the recognition of the relationship between instrumental and vocal music in Giuliani's work; it is apparent in his (and others') frequent adaptation of operatic music for the guitar, but has more or less escaped the attention of guitarists on record. The vocal quality of the writing is fully realized here, producing what might even be regarded as the first stylistically faithful recording of the First Concerto. The performances from both John Williams and the Australian Chamber Orchestra are exemplary and praise should also extend to the engineers who recorded them with such clarity and ideal balance. If you already have these works, don't let it deter you from adding this revelatory one to your collection.

Philip Glass American 1937

GROVE *Glass studied at the Juilliard School and with Boulanger in Paris (1964-66) and worked with the Indian musicians Ravi Shankar and Alla Rakha. His minimalist works of 1965-68 (eg Two Pages) are 'experimental and exploratory' but later ones, for his own amplified ensemble, are more complicated (eg Music in Fifths). Since 1975 his works have nearly all been for the theatre. When Einstein on the Beach was given at the Met (1976) he became famous; further full-scale operas, Satyagraha (1980), Akhnaten (1984), The Making of the Representative for Planet 8 (1988) and The Voyage (1992), chamber operas and music theatre works followed. One of the most popular serious composers in the USA, he has also performed in rock and jazz.*

Symphony No 2

Symphony No 2. Orphée – Interlude. Concerto for Saxophone Quartet and Orchestra
Raschèr Saxophone Quartet (Carina Raschèr *sop sax* Harry Kinross White *alto sax* Bruce Weinberger *ten sax* Kenneth Coon *bass sax*) **Vienna Radio Symphony Orchestra, Stuttgart Chamber Orchestra / Dennis Russell Davies**
Nonesuch 7559-79496-2 (69 minutes: DDD) Ⓕ
Recorded 1996

Glass is not a symphonist in the conventional sense, but then nor was Messiaen. Glass himself has indicated that his large-scale orchestral works are conceived with their probable role in the conventions of concert programming (and, presumably, recording) in mind. This sounds outrageously manipulative when stated explicitly, but it is of course nothing more than a description of the context of the symphonic form since its inception, which conveniently returns us to square one. Glass has also said that he devoted his earlier career to subtracting elements from his music and is now deciding what to put back in. In the case of this symphony, the specified element is polytonality, the presence of which in much 20th-century music (Glass cites Honegger, Milhaud and Villa-Lobos in his booklet-note) is perhaps taken for granted. However, when it is added into this stripped-down and austere idiom, the results are certainly quite striking. The opening movement recalls the prelude to *Akhnaten*, the third and final movement reprises the chattering arpeggios of the composer's earlier works, closing with an exciting – and, indeed, viscera-loosening – *crescendo*.

After recovering during the snippet from *Orphée*, we come to the marvellous Concerto. Conceived for performance either as a quartet or in this quartet-plus-orchestra version, this is a gloriously animated work, almost Coplandesque in many respects, yet remaining true to Glass's own vision. Despite being presented as the secondary work on this disc, its presence makes the whole recommendable.

Symphony No 3

Symphony No 3[a]. The CIVIL WarS – Interludes Nos 1 and 2[a]. The Voyage – Mechanical Ballet[b]. The Light[b]
[a]**Stuttgart Radio Symphony Orchestra,** [b]**Vienna Radio Symphony Orchestra / Dennis Russell Davies**
Nonesuch 7559-79581-2 (61 minutes: DDD) Ⓕ
Recorded 1999

Comparing Glass's Third Symphony with his Second finds the forces reduced from full orchestra to strings, the overall timing reduced by virtually half and the number of movements increased from three to four. Glass No 2 is long-breathed, atmospheric and occasionally suggestive of Brucknerian vistas, whereas Glass No 3 is texturally lean and harmonically more adventurous than much of the composer's previous work. It also seems to have taken in influences from some fairly unexpected sources.

The first movement is sombre and march-like while the second, which is built on compound meters, kicks out in all directions, switching to a gutsy *staccato* at 2'59". Of course, the pulse is constant (Glass wouldn't be Glass if that had changed) but the tone has altered, sometimes sidling nearer to Sibelius, sometimes a stone's throw from Shostakovich. At the start of the brief finale, there's even a hint of Kurt Weill ('Anger' from the *Seven Deadly Sins*), but one thing is for sure: if you play the Symphony blind, you might never guess that it's by Glass.

The stylistic shift from mellow, arpeggiated dreamscape (a familiar Glassian aura that holds sway for most of *The Light*) to a sort of ecstatic acerbity, follows through to the rest of the work. But there's another presence – less of a surprise, perhaps – later in the long third movement when the Arvo Pärt of *Cantus* seems to join the fray (try from around 8'03").

The idea of external influence extends to the interludes from *The CIVIL WarS*, where, as annotator David Wright advises us, Tchaikovsky's *Nutcracker* gets a look in, particularly in the Second Interlude with its pas-de-deux-like downward scales. 'Mechanical Ballet' (from *The Voyage*) and the expansive (21-minute) *The Light* are rather more what you'd expect from Glass: haunting narratives, always on the move yet tinged with melancholy. But even if you don't care for Glass's more familiar 'arpeggiated' style, do try the Third Symphony. It's certainly different, and the performance is excellent.

Itaipú

The Canyon. Itaipú[a]
Atlanta Symphony [a]**Chorus and Orchestra / Robert Shaw**
Sony Classical SK46352 (56 minutes: DDD) Ⓕ
Recorded 1990 ●

Space is central to the work of most composers who have cultivated minimalist techniques: Reich Górecki, Kancheli, MacMillan, Bryars and Glass all employ it as an essential creative constituent, and all have in some way managed to reclaim it for our own claustrophobic imaginations. The idea of spacious natural vistas has always been central to the work of Glass. *Itaipú* and *The Canyon* are the second and third of his 'portraits of nature', the former being a commission from the Atlanta Symphony Orchestra and Chorus, while the latter was composed specifically for the Rotterdam Philharmonic. Itaipú is located on the Paraná River, which in turn forms the border between Brazil and Paraguay. It is the location of a massive hydro-electric dam with individual generators large enough to house a full symphony orchestra. So it's little wonder that Itaipú provided Glass with instant inspiration. The score itself is divided into four separate sections and calls on substantial orchestral and choral forces. Although consistent with Glass's other work, *Itaipú* has an especially dark, rugged tonal profile. The hub of the work – 'The Dam' itself – is in the third movement, where brass and winds abet a pounding ostinato and a series of modulations redolent of such scenically aware late-romantics as Sibelius, Bruckner and Roy Harris. It's one of the most arresting passages in Glass's output and gives a vivid impression of the dam's overwhelming physical presence. *Itaipú* sets Guarani Indian texts, although Glass intended that the words support the music, rather than vice versa.

The Canyon is purely orchestral, and much shorter. It's built around two basic ideas, with a jagged middle section that heats up for a powerful climax. Less heavily scored than *Itaipú*, *The Canyon* utilises a large array of percussion, which Glass exploits with his usual ear for nuance. But *Itaipú* is the disc's main 'event' – a patient, cumulatively powerful essay, easily assimilated and well enough crafted to repay repeated listening. Those who find certain other of Glass's works monotonous and uneventful would do well to sample it. The recordings are cleanly balanced, the performances neat. Recommended, especially to those not normally 'behind Glass'.

La Belle et la Bête

Janice Felty *mez* La Belle; **Gregory Purnhagen** *bar* La Bête, Avenant, Ardent, Port Official; **John Kuether** *bass* Father, Usurer; **Ana Maria Martinez** *sop* Felicie; **Hallie Neill** *sop* Adelaide; **Zheng Zhou** *bar* Ludovic
Philip Glass Ensemble / Michael Riesman
Nonesuch ② 7559-79347-2 (89 minutes: DDD)
Notes, text and translation included. Ⓕ
Recorded 1994 O

This is one of Philip Glass's most innovative and impressive works. It isn't exactly an opera, but nor is it film music; cantata is the nearest term, yet even that won't really convey the idea. What Glass has done is to make a setting of the script for Jean Cocteau's 1946 film *La Belle et la Bête*, using every word as it is spoken in the film, but having it sung, the whole thing designed to be performed in concert, with a print of the film being projected silently. Of all Cocteau's movies, *La Belle et la Bête* is visually the most stylised, with its images of the Beast's castle, and the Vermeeresque settings for the family home of the merchant whose search for a rose to give to his youngest daughter sets off the nightmarish story. Cocteau described his film as 'the illustration of the border that separates one world from the other'. For all its surreal photography and extravagant décor by Christian Bérard (the apparently living, arms-bearing candelabra, poking out from the wall, have influenced hundreds of interior decorators), the dialogue in the film is delivered in a naturalistic way. The words are sung in an ethereal way, and the music itself trembles with characteristic Glass motifs.

La Belle et la Bête hovers somewhere between genteel beat music and Messiaen-influenced *mélodie* and defies categorization. As Beauty, Janice Felty's voice matches the image of Josette Day in the film, but Gregory Purnhagen's light baritone would never suggest Jean Marais, whose smoky tones were such an inspiration to Cocteau. Most people prefer the Beast with his hairy face and claws to the rather effete-looking Prince Charming who emerges at the end, and Glass's music seems to make an ironic commentary on this transformation. Well worth investigating.

Alexander Glazunov

Russian/USSR 1865-1936

GROVE *Glazunov studied privately with Rimsky-Korsakov (1879-81) and had his First Symphony performed when he was 16. He became a member of the circle around the patron Belyayev, who took him to meet Liszt in Weimar, and in 1899 was appointed to the St Petersburg Conservatory, which he directed from 1905 until leaving the Soviet Union in 1928. During these later years he composed relatively little: the bulk of his output, which includes nine symphonies, much else for orchestra, the ballet Raymonda (1897) and seven quartets, dates from before World War I. He has a significant place in Russian music in that he reconciled Russianism and Europeanism. He absorbed Balakirev's nationalism, Rimsky-Korsakov's orchestral virtuosity, Tchaikovsky's lyricism, Borodin's epic grandeur and Taneyev's contrapuntal skill.*

Violin Concerto

Glazunov Violin Concerto
Dvořák Violin Concerto in A minor, B108
Frank Peter Zimmermann *vn* **London Philharmonic Orchestra / Franz Welser-Möst**
EMI CDC7 54872-2 (52 minutes: DDD) Ⓕ
Recorded 1993

It is characteristic of Frank Peter Zimmermann that, even in two Slavonic blockbusters among violin concertos, he draws out the lighter qualities, tackling the most formidable passagework with quicksilver agility and precision, and finding tenderness and poetry in the big melodies rather than juicy romanticism. If at first you find such a relatively lightweight approach leaves you short on panache and bravura, you should quickly come to enjoy the freshness of Zimmermann's view. His very assurance, too, with clean, seemingly effortless articulation and intonation even in the most formidable passages of double-stopping, may rob the performances of something in sheer excitement, but the purely musical qualities provide ample compensation. Zimmermann, for all his emotional restraint and his refusal to use a big fat tone in the main lyrical themes, is hardly too cool for the music. With Welser-Möst and the LPO providing clean, sympathetic accompaniments to match the soloist, his rubato is free and natural without self-indulgence. Zimmermann's observance of *pianissimo* markings, normally disregarded, brings magical moments. One catches the breath when the *Tranquillo* theme returns in the Glazunov, and the whole of the slow movement of the Dvořák is intensely beautiful. In the latter's finale, it makes up in its sense of fun for any lack of flamboyance. The marking is, after all, *Allegro giocoso*, and his similar avoidance of vulgarity in the finale of the Glazunov equally results in a carefree, lilting performance, with admirably clear triplets in the closing passage. So although these performances – with the soloist balanced naturally, not spotlit – may not please traditionalists looking for blockbusting qualities, anyone fancying this apt but unusual coupling should certainly investigate.

Glazunov Violin Concerto **Tchaikovsky** Violin Concerto in D, Op 35
Maxim Vengerov *vn* **Berlin Philharmonic Orchestra / Claudio Abbado**
Teldec 4509-90881-2 (55 minutes: DDD) Ⓕ
Recorded 1995 ●

This seems to be the only disc coupling what might reasonably be counted as the two greatest romantic Russian violin concertos: if Vengerov's reading of the Tchaikovsky emerges clearly as a leading contender among many superb versions, in the Glazunov he turns this warhorse concerto from a display piece into a work of far wider-ranging emotions. This Tchaikovsky immediately establishes itself as a big performance in the manner and in the range of dynamic of the playing. For all his power, and his youthfully eager love of brilliance, Vengerov is never reluctant to play really softly, and how magical that often is. Each theme in turn is sharply characterised, with dynamic contrasts cleanly established. The central Canzonetta is full of Russian temperament, with Vengerov freer in his rubato than most rivals, but conveying such natural unforced expressiveness there is nothing self-conscious about it. The finale is fast, light and sparkling, with articulation breathtakingly clean to match the transparency of the orchestral textures as controlled by Abbado. Vengerov rounds the performance off with an explosion of excitement such as one might expect in the concert hall but not often in the recording studio. The Glazunov is if anything even more remarkable, with Vengerov making you appreciate afresh what a wonderful and varied sequence of melodies Glazunov offers. It is characteristic of Vengerov how he shades and contrasts his tone colours. He reserves his big, romantic tone for the third theme, where most rivals let loose sooner with less subtle results. As in the Tchaikovsky, rubato is free but always spontaneous-sounding, and the lolloping fourth section brings some delicious *portamento*. Predictably the dashing final section is spectacular in its brilliance, with orchestral textures fresh and clean.

Suite caractéristique

Suite caractéristique in D, Op 9. Le chant du destin, Op 84. Deux Préludes, Op 85
Moscow Symphony Orchestra / Igor Golovschin
Naxos 8 553857 (75 minutes: DDD) Ⓢ
Recorded 1996 ●

Le chant du destin (1907) opens with and is dominated by a sombre two-phrase theme which reminds one incongruously of Gershwin's song, *'s Wonderful*, only the mood and colouring is utterly different. The music is eloquently presented, but rather outstays its welcome. The eight-movement *Suite caractéristique* from two decades earlier is vintage Glazunov, an orchestral transcription of piano pieces. Slavic melancholy characterises the 'Introduction', which serves to usher in an engaging 'Danse rustique'. The central, delicately scored 'Pastorale' is particularly charming and the following 'Danse orientale' is at first piquant, in the best Russian pseudo-oriental manner, but reaches an expansive climax, and the gentle beginning of the 'Elégie' is followed by a passionate interjection (in a surprisingly Tchaikovskian manner). The grand closing 'Cortège' makes a resplendent, very Russian ending. The two *Préludes* date from 1906 and 1908 respectively. One remembers, in a grave, valedictory mood, Vladimir Stassoff; the second (much more extended) opens surprisingly like Tchaikovsky's *Francesca da Rimini* and this curious leitmotif dominates the early part of the piece, which later produces a gentle, disconsolate chorale and a sonorously Wagnerian coda. It is played most impressively, as indeed is the *Suite*. The recording is good too.

The Seasons

Glazunov The Seasons – ballet, Op 67
Tchaikovsky The Nutcracker – ballet, Op 71[a]
[a]**Finchley Children's Music Group; Royal Philharmonic Orchestra / Vladimir Ashkenazy**
Decca ② 433 000-2DH2 (131 minutes: DDD) Ⓕ
Recorded 1989-90 ●

One cannot think of a happier coupling than Glazunov's complete *Seasons* – perhaps his finest and most successful score – with Tchaikovsky's *Nutcracker*. Glazunov's delightful ballet, with even the winter's 'Frost', 'Hail', 'Ice' and 'Snow', glamorously presented, and the bitterness of a Russian winter quite forgotten are, like the scenario of the *Nutcracker*, part of a child's fantasy world. Glazunov's twinklingly dainty scoring of the picturesque snowy characters is contrasted with the glowing summer warmth of the 'Waltz of the cornflowers and poppies', and the vigorously thrusting tune (perhaps the most memorable theme he ever wrote) of the Autumn 'Bacchanale'. Tchaikovsky's ballet is beautifully played by the RPO; there is much finesse and sparkle, and the lightest and most graceful rhythmic touch from Ashkenazy. The conductor's affection for the score and his feeling for Tchaikovsky's multi-hued orchestral palette is a constant delight to the ear. Yet the big *Pas de deux* brings a climax of Russian fervour. The recording is properly expansive here; made at Walthamstow, it sets everything within a glowing acoustic ambience. The aural richness and glowing woodwind detail of the recording of *The Seasons* is most impressive.

Piano Works

Four Preludes and Fugues, Op 101. Prelude and Fugue in D minor, Op 62. Prelude and Fugue in E minor (1926)
Stephen Coombs *pf*
Hyperion CDA66855 (60 minutes: DDD) Ⓕ
Recorded 1995

Piano Sonata No 2 in E minor, Op 75. Prelude and Two Mazurkas, Op 25. Two Impromptus, Op 54. Idylle, Op 103. Barcarolle sur les touches noires. Song of the Volga Boatmen, Op 97 (arr Siloti). In modo religioso, Op 38. Triumphal March, Op 40[a]. Pas de caractère, Op 68 (all arr cpsr)
Stephen Coombs *pf* **[a]Holst Singers / Stephen Layton**
Hyperion CDA66866 (70 minutes: DDD) Ⓕ
Recorded 1995

The third disc in Stephen Coombs's series is devoted to Glazunov's six essays in the form of the prelude and fugue. It begins and ends with intricately wrought homages to Bach – the first, of 1899, darker and much more chromatic than the last, a wholesome specimen revealing none of the problems of the composer's declining years. The Op 101 set is both freer and more fantastical in its fugal treatments. Taken as a whole, it seems to be Glazunov's towering achievement in any field, working its way from the restless A minor No 1, with its hyper-Elgarian sequences, and the capricious No 2, to the C minor Prelude and Fugue – swooning Tchaikovskian romanticism within the perspectives of Bach and Chopin – and on to a thoroughly diatonic C major celebration – hard-earned victory indeed. Coombs meets the challenge unflinchingly; there's a little too much use made of the sustaining pedal in the earlier chromatic welters, but the later stages are both appropriately lucid and bright.

The fugue at the heart of the Second Sonata's finale does give the listener an extra taste of his contrapuntal genius, and it's all the more welcome in a sea of romantic rodomontade. That, though, is clearly what Glazunov felt the piano sonata was all about – and he does it with style: the E major transformation of the scherzo theme towards the end of this exhaustingly busy Second Sonata is a fine stroke. The rest of Vol 4 either ties up loose ends, following Glazunov along the road of whimsical, radiant Chopin stylization, or throws in some enjoyable novelties. Coombs's orchestral thunder comes in useful for the weighty transcription of a *Triumphal March* for the Chicago Columbian Exposition; when the Holst Singers enter with their 'Slava, Columbus's, it's probably just as well that the recording presents them as a solid backdrop to the busy piano part, not a wall in front of it. Glazunov's handling of *John Brown's Body* shows a surprising wit and spirit, and the serious transcription of the *Song of the Volga Boatmen* that follows, with its shades of Mussorgsky's 'Bydlo', makes a surprising contrast – one of many that will surely raise this composer's status immeasurably.

Reyngol'd Glière

Ukraine/USSR 1875-1956

GROVE *Glière studied at the Moscow Conservatory, where he became professor of composition (1920-41). His works, in the Russian epic tradition of Borodin and Glazunov, include three symphonies (the third subtitled 'Il'ya Muromets', 1911), concertos (one for coloratura soprano, 1943) and ballets (notably The Red Flower), as well as operas on central Asian themes using indigenous musical traditions, and chamber and piano music.*

Symphony No 2

Symphony No 2 in C minor, Op 25. The Red Poppy – Ballet Suite, Op 70
New Jersey Symphony Orchestra / Zdenek Macal
Delos DE3178 Ⓕ
(73 minutes: DDD). Recorded 1995

This performance of Glière's colourful late-romantic Second Symphony is extremely satisfying, with a fine blend of transparency and warmth. Glière never puts a foot wrong, but that's because he's going along trails blazed for him by others long before 1908. Although the romantic parts of *Firebird* are audibly just round the corner, here the magic is tamed and the amount of repetition can even become slightly irksome. The New Jersey cor anglais plays with peerless refinement in the slow movement, and Macal coaxes suave phrasing from his musicians. Delos could have made its disc indispensable by choosing something less well known than the *Red Poppy* Suite as a filler; but for newcomers to the composer this is certainly a necessary work. Delos makes a big pitch about the 'Virtual Reality' recording quality. Ultimately destined for Surround Sound Home Theatre reproduction, it involves, amongst other things, a careful choice of venue, slightly more than usual spatial separation of players in the hall, and a pragmatic approach to multi-miking.

Concerto for Coloratura Soprano

Ginastera Harp Concerto, Op 25 **Glière** Harp Concerto, Op 74. Concerto for Coloratura Soprano and Orchestra, Op 82
Eileen Hulse *sop* **Rachel Masters** *hp* **City of London Sinfonia / Richard Hickox**
Chandos CHAN9094 (65 minutes: DDD) Ⓕ
Recorded 1992

Glière was among the comparatively few front-rank Russian composers who stayed on in their homeland after the 1917 Revolution. The music he composed there adopted a middle-of-the-road conservative style which helped him to steer clear of the more viscous controversies of the 1920s and 1930s. The Concertos for harp and coloratura soprano date from 1938 and 1942 respectively, and are unashamedly ingratiating, high-grade mood-music, here played and recorded in a manner that those with a sweet tooth should find irresistible. The Harp Concerto by Ginastera is made of sterner stuff, but only slightly – it's Bartókian acerbities are tempered by an engaging Latin American swing. Again the performance is crisp and bouncy, but in this instance the reverberant recording takes something of the edge off the rhythmic bite.

Mikhail Glinka

Russian 1804-1857

GROVE *Having come to know rural folk music in its purer forms, and receiving an unsystematic musical education in St Petersburg and on his sojourn in Italy (1830-33), Glinka neither inherited a tradition of sophisticated composition nor developed a distinctive and consistent personal style. But he exerted a profound and freely acknowledged influence on Balakirev, Rimsky-Korsakov, Mussorgsky, Borodin and Tchaikovsky, as well as on Prokofiev and Stravinsky. His first important compositions, written in Berlin (1834), where he studied briefly with Siegfried Dehn, were a Capriccio for piano duet and an unfinished symphony, both applying variation technique to Russian themes. It was his opera A Life for the Tsar (1836; originally Ivan Susanin) that established him overnight as Russia's leading composer. Though its national character derives from melodic content alone (mostly merely quasi-Russian), it is nevertheless significant for its novel, expressive Russian recitative and for its use of the leitmotif. His next opera, Ruslan and Lyudmila (1842), based on Pushkin's fantastic, ironic fairy-tale, was less well received, being structurally unsuited to the stage and musically haphazard, yet it contains elements of striking originality, including Chernomor's grotesque little march, pungent touches of chromatic colour, exuberant rhythms, the use of the whole-tone scale and the 'changing background' technique for folktune presentation. Inspiring the oriental and 'magic' idioms of later Russian composers, this opera proved to be seminal in the history of Russian music. At Paris (1844-5) Glinka enjoyed Berlioz's music and in Spain (1845-47) folk music and fresh visual impressions; two Spanish Overtures resulted, exceeded in inventiveness however by the kaleidoscopic orchestral variations Kamarinskaya (1848). Among the rich legacy of his songs, the Pushkin settings Where is our rose?, I recall a wonderful moment, Adèle and The toasting cup are particularly fine.*

Orchestral Works

Capriccio brillante on the 'Jota aragonesa'. Souvenir d'une nuit d'été à Madrid. Symphony on Two Russian Themes. Overture in D. Kamarinskaya. Valse-fantaisie. Ruslan and Lyudmila – Overture; Dance; Chernomor's March
BBC Philharmonic Orchestra / Vassily Sinaisky
Chandos CHAN9861 (71 minutes: DDD) Ⓕ
Recorded 2000

Following on the heels of ASV's selection of Glinka's orchestral music, with the Armenian Philharmonic under Loris Tjeknavorian, comes this more comprehensive survey. Both conductors include the two 'Spanish Overtures', the *Valse-fantaisie* and *Kamarinskaya* in closely matched performances. Sinaisky is rather faster and brighter in the first 'Spanish Overture', *Capriccio on the jota aragonesa*, and in the second, *Souvenir d'une nuit d'été*, he reflects more subtly the French grace that also lies within the music, where Tjeknavorian goes for greater verve and colour. Both conductors give good, vivid performances of the *Valse-fantaisie* and *Kamarinskaya*, with recordings that do justice to Glinka's brilliant and delicate orchestration.

Thereafter the repertory parts company. Tjeknavorian gives the rest of his record up to a suite of six pieces from *A Life for the Tsar*, consisting of the overture and finale plus four of the Polish dances. Sinaisky prefers *Ruslan and Lyudmila*, with a lively performance of the overture and then the Act 3 dances and the dwarf Chernomor's grotesque little march. This gives him room for the early Overture in D minor, which does not often feature on records, and for the *Symphony on Two Russian Themes*. The work survives in only a single movement, but fascinatingly and attractively anticipates *Kamarinskaya*. Those who bought the Tjeknavorian record will surely be feeling few regrets, but for a highly enjoyable introduction to Glinka's orchestral music, indeed to his whole original way of thinking and its relevance for Russian music, this Chandos disc is the one to go for.

Ruslan and Lyudmila

Vladimir Ognovienko *bass-bar* Ruslan; **Anna Netrebko** *sop* Lyudmila; **Mikhail Kit** *bar* Svetozar; **Larissa Diadkova** *mez* Ratmir; **Gennadi Bezzubenkov** *bass* Farlaf; **Galina Gorchakova** *sop* Gorislava; **Konstantin Pluzhnikov** *ten* Finn; **Irina Bogachova** *mez* Naina; **Yuri Marusin** *ten* Bayan; **Chorus and Orchestra of the Kirov Theatre / Valery Gergiev**
Philips ③ 446 746-2PH3 (202 minutes: DDD)
Notes,text and translation included. Ⓕ
Recorded live in 1995 **oo**

With Gergiev, the playing rises well above the reliability of long-practised routine; indeed, the Overture, always a winner, has quite exceptional brilliance and exhilaration. Later, the performance is just as remarkable for its refinement of detail and for sensitivity in the meditative, tender passages which enrich the musical score as they do the humanity of this operatic fairy-tale. The principals act with the professionalism of those brought up in a rigid school; they know their job and proceed accordingly. The Ruslan (Ognovienko) is an ample bass-baritone, the Farlaf (Bezzubenkov) a sturdy bass with a neat capacity for patter, Bayan (Marusin) a tenor with tense tone, slightly flat intonation, especially memorable as the bardic figure who holds in thrall an audience with a longer attention-span than might be counted on today. Larissa Diadkova's Ratmir made a strong impression in the 1995 Edinburgh Festival and it is good to hear her here. Gorchakova brings glamour of voice to Gorislava, and Netrebko is outstanding.

Christoph Gluck Bohemian 1714-1787

GROVE *Gluck's father was a forester in the Upper Palatinate (now the western extreme of Czechoslovakia); Czech was his native tongue. At about 14 he left home to study in Prague, where he worked as an organist. He soon moved to Vienna and then to Milan, where his first opera was given in 1741. Others followed, elsewhere in Italy and during 1745-46 in London, where he met Handel's music. After further travel (Dresden, Copenhagen, Naples, Prague) he settled in Vienna in 1752 as Konzertmeister of the Prince of Saxe-Hildburghausen's orchestra, then as Kapellmeister. He also became involved in performances at the court theatre of French opéras comiques, as arranger and composer, and he wrote Italian dramatic works for court entertainments. His friends tried, at first unsuccessfully, to procure a court post for him; but by 1759 he had a salaried position at the court theatre and soon after was granted a royal pension.*

He met the poet Calzabigi and the choreographer Angiolini, and with them wrote a ballet-pantomime Don Juan (1761) embodying a new degree of artistic unity. The next year they wrote the opera Orfeo ed Euridice, the first of Gluck's so-called 'reform operas'. In 1764 he composed an opéra comique, La rencontre imprévue, and the next year two ballets; he followed up the artistic success of Orfeo with a further collaboration with Calzabigi, Alceste (1767), this time choreographed by Noverre; a third, Paride ed Elena (1770), was less well received.

Gluck now decided to apply his new ideals to French opera, and in 1774 gave Iphigénie en Aulide (as well as Orphée, a French revision of Orfeo) in Paris; it was a triumph, but also set the ground for a controversy between Gluck and Italian music (as represented by Piccinni) which flared up in 1777 when his Armide was given, following a French version of Alceste (1776). Iphigénie en Tauride followed in 1779 – his greatest success, along with his greatest failure, Echo et Narcisse. He now acknowledged that his career was over; he revised Iphigénie en Tauride for German performance, and composed some songs, but abandoned plans for a journey to London to give his operas and died in autumn 1787, widely recognised as the doyen of Viennese composers and the man who had carried through important reforms to the art of opera.

Gluck's opera reforms - they are not exclusively his own, for several other composers (notably Jommelli and Traetta, both like Gluck French-influenced) had been working along similar lines – are outlined in the preface he wrote, probably with Calzabigi's help, to the published score of Alceste. He aimed to make the music serve the poetry through its expression of the situations of the story, without interrupting it for conventional orchestral ritornellos or, particularly, florid and ornamental singing; to make the overture relevant to the drama and the orchestration apt to the words; to break down the sharp contrast between recitative and aria: 'in short to abolish all the abuses against which good sense and reason have long cried out in vain '. Orfeo exemplifies most of these principles, with its abandonment of simple recitative in favour of a more continuous texture (with orchestral recitative, arioso and aria running into one another) and its broad musical-dramatic spans in which different types of solo singing, dance and choral music are fully integrated. It also has a simple, direct plot, based on straightforward human emotions, which could appeal to an audience as the complicated stories used in contemporary opera seria, with their intrigues, disguises and subplots, could not. He had a limited compositional technique, but one that was sufficient for the aims he set himself. His music can have driving energy, but also a serenity reaching to the sublime. His historical importance rests on his establishment of a new equilibrium between music and drama, and his greatness on the power and clarity with which he projected that vision; he dissolved the drama in music instead of merely illustrating it.

Arias

Gluck Paride ed Elena – O del mio dolce ardor. Orfeo ed Euridice – Che puro ciel!; Che farò senza Euridice. Alceste – Non vi turbate **Haydn** Il mondo della luna – Una donna come me. Orlando Paladino – Ad un sguardo, a un cenno solo. La fedeltà premiata – Deh soccorri un'infelice **Mozart** Le nozze di Figaro – Voi che sapete. Don Giovanni – Batti, batti; Vedrai, carino; In quali eccessi…Mi tradì quell'alma ingrata. Lucio Silla – Dunque sperar…Il tenero momento. La finta giardiniera – Dolce d'amor compagna. La clemenza di Tito – Ecco il punto, oh Vitellia…Non più di fiori

Anne Sofie von Otter *mez* **The English Concert / Trevor Pinnock** *hpd*

Archiv Produktion 449 206-2AH (71 minutes: DDD) Ⓕ
Texts and translations included. Recorded 1995

For the sake of both vocal and family well-being, Anne Sofie von Otter has always followed the wise course of self-rationing in opera. This disc, an entirely personal selection of arias from the Viennese classical period, means all the more to her including, as it does, arias sung by dramatic and passionate women 'most of whom', von Otter admits in the accompanying notes, 'I have never performed on stage and, alas, probably never will'. They include *La clemenza di Tito*'s Vitellia whom von Otter has irresistibly observed in her own role as Sesto: here she at last voices her guilt at implicating Sesto in her crime of passion, and expresses that unique fusion of sadness and desperation of 'Non più di fiori' in the eloquent company of Colin Lawson's basset-horn, followed by Gluck's Alceste, again keenly observed by von Otter in a *comprimario* role. Her lyric mezzo is perfectly suited to that grave Gluckian passion of 'Non vi turbate'. Gluck's Orfeo is, of course, familiar to von Otter at first hand, and here The English Concert's introduction to the accompanied recitative which precedes 'Che farò' creates exquisitely the 'nuova serena luce' of the Elysian fields against which von Otter's grief, affectingly ornamented, is the darker, the more plangent. The Mozart arias evoke memorable stage and concert performances by von Otter: a Cherubino whose phrasing combines with that of the wind soloists to create the warm breath of tender burgeoning sensuality in 'Voi che sapete'; a Cecilio (*Lucio Silla*) whose coloratura captures the thrilled anticipation of that 'tenero momento'; and a moustachioed Ramiro (*La finta giardiniera*) who pays ecstatic *cantabile* tribute to the power of love.

Alceste

Teresa Ringholz *sop* Alcestis; **Justin Lavender** *ten* **P** Admetus; **Jonas Degerfelt** *ten* Evander; **Miriam Treichl** *sop* Ismene; **Lars Martinsson** *bar* Herald; Voice of Apollo; **Adam Giertz** *treb* Eumelo; **Emilie Clausen** *treb* Aspasia; **Johan Lilja** *bass* High Priest; Hercules; God of the Underworld; **Mattias Nilsson** *bar* Bandit **Drottningholm Court Theatre Chorus and Orchestra / Arnold Östman**

Naxos ③ 8 660066/8 (147 minutes: DDD). Notes, text and translation included. Recorded 1998 Ⓢ

Almost all critics of Gluck's two versions of *Alceste* – the Italian original, first given in Vienna in 1767, and the French revision or recomposition given in Paris in 1776 – regard the latter as superior: musically richer, more flexible, dramatically more persuasive, deeper in its treatment of the emotions and the humanity of the two central characters. But this performance of the Italian version treats the 1767 text on its own terms. Like the original *Orfeo*, the original *Alceste* is an opera pared down, in accordance with Gluck's and his librettist Calzabigi's reform principles, to deal with just a single issue: it is concerned exclusively with Alceste's sacrifice of her life to save that of her husband, Admeto, King of Thessaly, and the emotions that each of them and those around them feel. The French version introduces a third main character, Hercules, who goes to Hades to bring Alceste back: true to Euripedes, but dramatically arbitrary. In the Italian version, it is Apollo who intervenes to restore her, which in 18th-century opera is much more plausible: the power of love, as expressed in the music (and experienced by the audience), persuades the gods to set things right. The performance here is deftly paced and transparent in its textures. There is no portentousness about Arnold Östman's direction. It begins with an urgent, vital overture, with strongly marked phrasing and with textures that give the wind, including the brass, plenty of prominence. This performance captures the quiet nobility of the ceremonial music; and the choral singing has a good deal of warmth and expressiveness – and there is plenty of it, often in dialogue with the principals (the Act 2 dialogue between Alceste, determined on death, and the Infernal Spirits – reminiscent of Orpheus's in Act 2 of *Orfeo* is particularly powerful). The Drottningholm orchestra ensures that the detail of accompanying textures is clearly heard, and it plays gently and lightly in the dances.

The cast is mostly made up of quite young singers. Teresa Ringholz has a voice of modest dimensions, which she uses in a natural way, with little vibrato, firm, surely tuned, clear and well focused. She catches Alceste's increasingly passionate determination, at the close of Act 1, as her resolution to die to save her husband hardens, with its magnificent climax in 'Ombre, larve'; her monologue in the forest early in Act 2, with flute and oboe, is movingly sung and so is the aria, with cor anglais obbligato, where she sings of dying of happiness. Her controlled manner – there is no outburst of grief when she bids her children farewell at the end of the act, for example – catches well the stylised nature of Gluck's expression. Justin Lavender, as Admeto, is slightly less successful. He has a generous tenor – fuller and weightier than that of the other tenor, Jonas Degerfelt, who sings gracefully and also with vitality – and he brings to the music a good deal of passion that occasionally threatens to go beyond the scale of the performance as a whole. The smaller roles are very adequately done. This recording conveys effectively the intensity and the integrity of Gluck's vision.

Armide

Mireille Delunsch *sop* Armide; **Charles Workman** **P** *ten* Renaud; **Laurent Naouri** *bar* Hidraot; **Ewa Podles** *mez* Hate; **Françoise Masset** *sop* Phénice, Mélisse; **Nicole Heaston** *sop* Sidonie, Shepherdess, Lucinde; **Yann Beuron** *ten* Artémidore, Danish Knight; **Brett Polegato** *bar* Ubalde; **Vincent le Texier** *bar* Aronte; **Magdalena Kožená** *mez* Pleasure; **Valérie Gabail** *sop* Naiad **Choeur des Musiciens du Louvre; Les Musiciens du Louvre / Marc Minkowski**

Archiv Produktion ② 459 616-2AH2 (139 minutes: DDD). Notes, text and translation included. Recorded live in 1996 Ⓕ ●

'Perhaps the best of all my works', said Gluck of his *Armide*. But this, the fifth of his seven 'reform operas', has never quite captured the public interest as have *Orfeo*, *Alceste*, the two *Iphigénies* and even *Paride ed Elena*. Its plot is thinnish, concerned only with the love of the pagan sorceress Armide, princess of Damascus, for the Christian knight and hero Renaud, and his enchantment, disenchantment and finally his abandonment of her; the secondary characters have no real life. But *Armide* has two features that set it apart. One is the extraordinary soft, sensuous tone of the music; Gluck said that it was meant 'to produce a voluptuous sensation', and that if he were to suffer damnation it would be for the passionate love duet in Act 5. And certainly his orchestral writing here has a warmth, a colour and a richness going far beyond anything in his other reform operas (apart from parts of *Paride ed Elena*). Secondly, there are several great solo dramatic scenes, two of them for Armide herself: the opera's closing scene, in which she rails furiously at Renaud's treachery, and one at the end of Act 2, where, discovering him asleep and torn between love and hatred of her enemy, she cannot bring herself to kill him.

The success of *Armide*, then, depends critically on the Armide herself. Here it goes to Mireille Delunsch, who brings to it a good deal of intensity where it is needed but does not have command of a wide range of tone, and does not seem to make much use of her words. There is some graceful singing in the softer music and the scene where she cannot bring herself to kill Renaud is finely done, with a firm line, clear detail and a degree of passion, but neither here nor in the invocation of Hate is there a great deal of agitation or emotional tension. The closing scene is of course powerfully done, and is also conducted with plenty of fire. This is a very adequate performance by Delunsch though a little short of a thrilling one. Renaud is sung by Charles Workman, in a strong tenor, sounding almost baritonal in his opening scene with Artémidore but then singing the sleep song, 'Plus j'observe ces lieux', with soft, sweet tone and much delicacy. The lovers' duet in Act 5 is sung gently and with much charm. Among the other singers, Ewa Podles of course makes a strong impression as Hate with her large and steady voice – and some remarkable music to sing. Françoise Masset and Nicole Heaston sing Armide's confidantes and various smaller roles; Heaston in particular sings with delicacy and allure. Laurent Naouri shows a pleasant, firm baritone as Hidraot, and Yann Beuron (whose lyrical high tenor and clarity of diction give especial pleasure) and Brett Polegato sing the two lesser male roles.

Marc Minkowski makes much of the score's colour and flow. He uses a substantial orchestra which, however, plays lightly and flexibly and with rhythmic spring, and there is some excellent solo woodwind playing (notably the flute solos, from Kate Clark). He has a tendency towards quickish tempos: here and there, and especially in some of the dances (of which a few are omitted), he could have given the music a little more space. But he certainly keeps the score moving along well, is attentive to the accompanying figures and to the characterization of individual numbers – there are jolly and lively pieces here as well as impassioned ones – and he draws some alert and spirited singing from the chorus.

Iphigénie en Aulide

Lynne Dawson *sop* Iphigénie; **José van Dam** *bass* Agamemnon; **Anne Sofie von Otter** *mez* Clytemnestre; **John Aler** *ten* Achille; **Bernard Deletré** *bass* Patrocle; **Gilles Cachemaille** *bass* Calchas; **René Schirrer** *bass* Arcas; **Guillemette Laurens** *mez* Diane; **Ann Monoyios** *sop* First Greek woman, Slave; **Isabelle Eschenbrenner** *sop* Second Greek woman **Monteverdi Choir; Lyon Opéra Orchestra / Sir John Eliot Gardiner**

Erato ② 2292-45003-2 (132 minutes: DDD). Notes, Ⓕ text and translation included. Recorded 1987 ●●

Gluck's first reform opera for Paris has tended to be overshadowed by his other *Iphigénie*, the *Tauride* one. But it does contain some superb things, of which perhaps the finest are the great monologues for Agamemnon. On this recording, José van Dam starts a little coolly; but this only adds force to his big moment at the end of the Second Act where he tussles with himself over the sacrifice of his daughter and – contemplating her death and the screams of the vengeful Eumenides – decides to flout the gods and face the consequences. To this he rises in noble fashion, fully conveying the agonies that Agamemnon suffers.

The cast in general is strong. Lynne Dawson brings depth of expressive feeling to all she does and her Iphigénie, marked by a slightly grainy sound and much intensity, is very moving. John Aler's Achille too is very fine, touching off the lover and the hero with equal success, singing both with ardour and vitality. There is great force too in the singing of Anne Sofie von Otter as Clytemnestre, especially in her outburst 'Ma fille!' as she imagines her daughter on the sacrificial altar. John Eliot Gardiner's Monteverdi Choir sings with polish, perhaps seeming a little genteel for a crowd of angry Greek soldiers baying for Iphigénie's blood. But Gardiner gives a duly urgent account of the score, pressing it forward eagerly and keeping the tension at a high level even in the dance music. A period-instrument orchestra might have added a certain edge and vitality but this performance wants nothing in authority. Securely recommended.

Iphigénie en Tauride

Christine Goerke *sop* Iphigénie; **Vinson Cole** *ten* Pylade; **Rodney Gilfry** *bar* Oreste; **Sharon Baker** *sop* 1st Priestess, Greek woman; **Jayne West** *sop* 2nd Priestess, Diana; **Stephen Salters** *bar* Thoas; **Mark Andrew Cleveland** *sngr* Scythian; **Mark Risinger** *sngr* Minister of the Sanctuary; **Boston Baroque / Martin Pearlman** Ⓟ

Telarc Classics ② CD80546 (134 minutes: DDD) Ⓕ Text and translation included. Recorded 1999 ●●

'With Gluck, there's a long sweep to the drama,' says Martin Pearlman towards the end of his illustrated introductory talk about *Iphigénie en Tauride*, included here at the end of the second CD. It is obvious from his performance that this is how he sees the work; and it is his capacity to sustain that 'long sweep' that makes this version so compelling and so powerful.

Gluck's masterpiece plunges straight into the drama, the mini-overture quickly breaking into a storm scene, the storm at sea in which Orestes and Pylades are thrown up on the Scythian shore, but symbolising, too, the storm raging in Iphigenia's soul. Pearlman, using period instruments (this recording is the first to do so), draws vivid and dramatic playing from his admirable group, and he is particularly successful, too, in the various dances in the course of the opera, which, beautifully alive and springy in rhythm, never for a moment permit the drama to flag – they emerge as an integral part of it, as Gluck intended, not as decorative interludes. With these clear textures, Gluck's orchestral colouring comes across sharply as, too, does the lofty, hieratic quality of the work. There is tenderness as well, and it is thanks partly to Pearlman's sensitive timing of the declamatory music that the opera's climactic moment – the sacrifice scene, where brother and sister at last recognise each other – is so intense and poignant.

Although it lies quite high, the role of Iphigenia is often assigned to a mezzo, as if to heighten the intensity. Christine Goerke is a true soprano, which allows softer tones and more femininity than one generally hears, but there is metal in her voice, too (she does not altogether forgo vibrato), and the weight of the tragedy is by no means underplayed: listen to 'O malheureuse Iphigénie' – enhanced by the fine line of the oboe obbligato – or to her impassioned singing of the noble aria at the beginning of Act 4. Rodney Gilfry provides a strong, manly Orestes, not heavy but successful in conveying the tortures he is suffering. Vinson Cole gives a sympathetic reading of Pylades – lyrical, shapely and expressively phrased. Stephen Salters makes a vigorous Thoas, not as rampagingly barbaric as he is sometimes drawn. There is excellent choral singing.

The principal existing recordings both have rather starrier casts. Muti's is a big, modern opera-house performance, powerful and exciting, Gardiner's more stylish, more concentrated dramatically. Both have Sir Thomas Allen's superlative Orestes and for Gardiner Diana Montague is an outstanding Iphigenia. But this new set, in which Gluck's 'long sweep' is so well captured and the work's scale so tellingly conveyed without prejudicing its range and intensity of feeling, is just about first choice.

Orfeo ed Euridice

Derek Lee Ragin *counterten* Orfeo; **Sylvia McNair** *sop* Euridice; **Cyndia Sieden** *sop* Amore P
Monteverdi Choir; English Baroque Soloists / Sir John Eliot Gardiner
Philips ② 434 093-2PH2 (89 minutes: DDD) Ⓕ
Notes, text and translation included. Recorded 1991 ●

This version of *Orfeo*, played on period instruments and following the original text, has a degree of spiritual force to which other recordings scarcely aspire, and that is to the credit primarily of the conductor, John Eliot Gardiner. It begins with a taut, almost explosive account of the overture, moves to a deeply sombre opening chorus and then a *ballo* of intense expressiveness, finely and carefully moulded phrases (but plenty of air between them) and a lovely translucent orchestral sound. Every one of the numerous dances in this set, in fact, is the subject of thoughtful musical characterization, shapely execution and refined timing of detail. Derek Lee Ragin excels as Orpheus; the sound is often very beautiful, the phrasing extraordinarily supple and responsive for a countertenor voice. Eurydice is sung clearly and truly, and with due passion, by Sylvia McNair – she delivers 'Che fiero momento' and some of the recitative, with a considerable degree of force – and the casting of Cyndia Sieden, with her rather pert, forward voice, as Amore proves to be very successful.

Orfeo ed Euridice (abridged recording) H
Kathleen Ferrier *contr* Orfeo; **Ann Ayars** *sop* Euridice; **Zoë Vlachopoulos** *sop* Amore
Glyndebourne Festival Chorus; Southern Philharmonic Orchestra / Fritz Stiedry
Dutton Laboratories Essential Archive mono Ⓑ
CDEA5015 (63 minutes: ADD). Recorded 1947 ●

Nothing like comparisons for putting things in perspective. 'What a horrible sound!' you may think at the beginning of this, and then, if you try the 1992 reissue in Decca's Ovation series, you may decide that it is relatively Elysian after all. The Decca is edgy, acid and crackly. Dutton has eliminated the crackles and to some extent rounded the edginess; the acid tone of the violins is presumably beyond remedy unless through a top-cut of the kind that would draw scandalised condemnation from practically every reviewer except this one. However, the sound remains unpleasing though it is certainly a great deal better than its predecessor. Dutton improves on the previous version also by including everything in the original set. Missing on Ovation are the dance at the start of Act 2, the flute solo ('Dance of the Blessed Spirits'), Euridice's 'Quest'asilo dolce e beato', and the first, concerted, 'Trionfi, amore' passage in the finale. The omissions are pointless and the restorations to be welcomed.

Towards the performance itself you cannot fail to warm. The text is the hybrid Ricordi version that was most commonly in use at the time and which is now usually disowned in favour of either Vienna, Paris or Berlioz. In these excerpts it coheres, and the effect of the abridgement is concentrated and moving. Stiedry's speeds, especially the urgent 'Che farò', are likely (as Alan Blyth says in his notes) now to seem 'right', far more than they did at the time. The beauty of Ferrier's singing will often go straight to the heart – in 'Euridice non è più ed io respiro ancor' for instance. Her Italian is clear and serviceable but unmistakably English, with a slight tendency ('Millay paynay') towards diphthong. Her colleagues are better in this respect and sing very agreeably throughout. The chorus has a less impersonal sound than is usual nowadays, but is not all that well recorded. Yet these are minor matters. The set goes into the library, and stays there, for its noble and intensely human Orfeo.

Additional recommendation

Orphée et Eurydice

von Otter Orfeo **Hendricks** Euridice **Fournier** Amor

Lyon Opera Orchestra / Gardiner

EMI CDS5 56885-2 (89 minutes: DDD: 2/90) Ⓕ

Berlioz's edition of Gluck's masterpiece (sung of course in French) receives powerful advocacy from Sir John Eliot Gardiner, Anne Sofie von Otter and Barbara Hendricks. As a total interpretation of the work, this set is more penetrating than any other in the catalogue.

Leopold Godowsky

Polish/American 1870-1938

GROVE *An American pianist and composer of Polish birth, Godowsky toured widely from the age of nine, making his American début in Boston in 1884. Tours of the USA and Canada followed and until 1900 he taught in Philadelphia and Chicago. Until World War II he continued to appear in Europe; his reputation as a Chopin interpreter was not enhanced by a series of elaborate Studies on the Etudes. His concert career ended in 1930.*

53 Studies on Chopin's Etudes

Awards 2000

Marc-André Hamelin *pf*

Hyperion ② CDA67411/2 Ⓕ

(158 minutes: DDD)

Recorded 1998-99 ○○○

Godowsky's 53 studies on Chopin's 27 studies are the *ne plus ultra* of romantic intricacy. Godowsky's wily disclaimer that, far from wanting to 'improve' on Chopin's matchless originals, he merely wished to extend the parameters of technique, hardly convinces purists, who dismiss his *magnum opus* as an outrageous gilding of the lily, an unforgivable powdering and rouging of Chopin's genius. For others, Godowsky's ingenuity, his ear-tickling wit and elegance, create edifices, indeed 'miracles of rare device'. But if heated debate still rages around the music, the quality of Marc-André Hamelin's long-awaited two-disc recording is entirely uncontroversial. Rarely can such a gargantuan task – truly a labour of Hercules – have been accomplished with such strength, grace and agility, with an ease bordering on nonchalance. His virtuosity is pre-eminent because it is so musical, and it is impossible to think of another living pianist who could have carried off this enterprise with comparable success.

In lesser hands these *Etudes* can seem overweight, so bedecked with finery that they can scarcely move. With Hamelin, even the densest, seemingly impenetrable textures are kept as light as air and everything is mobile, fluent and adroit. Readers suspicious of this dazzling enterprise should try *Etudes* Nos 1, 7, 14, 25, 33, 42 and 45 to see if they possess a true taste for decadence. Meanwhile, Jorge Bolet's stately selection (nla) and Carlo Grante's more than able three-disc recording are effortlessly eclipsed. And so, to evoke Schumann, it's 'hats off, gentlemen' to this handsomely presented and finely recorded set: to Hyperion, to producer Andrew Keener and most of all to Marc-André Hamelin who crowns his already awe-inspiring discography with a truly phenomenal achievement.

Alexander Goehr

British 1932

GROVE *Goehr's father, the conductor Walter Goehr, brought the family to England in 1933, and Alexander studied with Hall at the Royal Manchester College (1952-5), where fellow students included Birtwistle and Davies. He then followed Messiaen's classes at the Paris Conservatoire (1955-56). Family and education thus fitted him to marry Schoenbergian with post-Webernian influences, which he did in two cantatas, The Deluge (1958) and Sutter's Gold (1960), and in instrumental pieces of this period. With the Violin Concerto (1962) and Little Symphony (1963) he moved into a broader style made possible by greater understanding of serialism. His first opera, Arden Must Die (1967), is a morality on the borders of Weill, and a triptych of music-theatre pieces (1968-70) also shows a concern with social behaviour. Orchestral and chamber works of this period move still closer to the ethos of the two Viennese schools, but in doing so display a more confident individuality (String Quartet No 3, 1976). His second opera, Behold the Sun (1985), is about the clash between revolutionary and established thought in 16th-century Germany. In 1976 he became professor of music at Cambridge.*

Arianna

Ruby Philogene *sop* Arianna; **Angela Hickey** *mez* Venus, Dorilla; **Juliet Schiemann** *sop* Cupid; **Lawrence Zazzo** *counterten* Bacchus; **Timothy Dawkins** *bass* Jupiter, First Messenger; **Philip Sheffield** *ten* Theseus; **Jeremy Huw Williams** *bar* Counsellor; **Andrew Hewitt** *ten* Herald; **Stephen Rooke** *ten* Second Messenger **Arianna Ensemble / William Lacey**

NMC ② NMCD054 (132 minutes: DDD) Ⓕ

Recorded live in 1996

The title-page of *Arianna* describes it as a 'lost opera by Monteverdi, composed again by Alexander Goehr'. Precisely. At its heart is Ariadne's lament, all that survives of Monteverdi's score, some of its phrases lightly modified, richly and movingly sung by Ruby Philogene. The vocal line is embedded in an elaborate instrumental texture in Goehr's own manner, in which the modernism he grew up with (his father, the conductor Walter Goehr, was a pupil of Schoenberg) is enriched with a modality that owes a lot to

Goehr's own teacher, Olivier Messiaen, but a good deal also to Monteverdi himself. Whether Monteverdi ever set these lines we may never know. Goehr has set them effectively and very beautifully, in Monteverdi's manner: a reminder that although Schoenberg watched over Goehr's cradle, so did Monteverdi – Walter Goehr, who both edited and performed his works, was one of the pioneers of the Monteverdi revival.

Indeed, at times, it is as though Goehr and Monteverdi had collaborated on this opera, the vocal lines, brilliant toccatas and madrigalesque choruses often sounding very much like the earlier composer, even the instrumentation suggesting that Claudio Monteverdi has been so deeply excited by the sound of the modern keyed flute, the soprano saxophone and bass clarinet that he cannot resist using them. Often you sense the two composers absorbedly recognizing affinities. Goehr's score is at once a loving homage, an entrancing game, and a vivid evocation for the 1990s of how dazzling, fast-moving and emotionally hard-hitting Monteverdi's lost original must have been to its first audiences in 1608. But it could only have been written in our time and only, you conclude, by Alexander Goehr.

The soloists are almost without exception excellent. Philip Sheffield's eloquent Theseus, Jeremy Huw Williams's Counsellor, and the Messengers of Timothy Dawkins and Stephen Rooke stand out, even in the company of Ruby Philogene's tremendous Ariadne, and William Lacey is clearly a conductor of real gifts. The live recording is admirable.

Berthold Goldschmidt

German 1903-1996

GROVE *A British conductor and composer of German origin, Goldschmidt studied with Schreker in Berlin (1922-25) and moved to England in 1935; he conducted the Glyndebourne company at the Edinburgh Festival. His works, in many genres, have connections with Busoni, Weill and Shostakovich.*

Concertos

Clarinet Concerto[a]. Violin Concerto[b]. Cello Concerto[c]
[a]Sabine Meyer *cl* **[b]Chantal Juillet** *vn* **[c]Yo-Yo Ma** *vc*
[a]Berlin Komische Opera Orchestra / Yakov Kreizberg; [b]Philharmonia Orchestra / Berthold Goldschmidt; [c]Montreal Symphony Orchestra / Charles Dutoit
Decca Entartete Musik 455 586-2DH Ⓕ
(67 minutes: DDD). Recorded 1990s ●

The oblivion into which these three concertos fell after their premières in the 1950s is puzzling. Their style, even by the standards of 40-odd years ago, is not 'advanced', but they make original use of traditional forms. The first movement of the Cello Concerto, for example, has half a dozen themes instead of the expected two, but the ideas are subtly related so that the overall impression is of a richly fertile but disciplined invention: there is not the slightest hint of garrulity, nor any sense that the music is derived from Hindemith, whom at a few moments it superficially resembles. In the corresponding movement of the Clarinet Concerto each idea grows out of its predecessor, all of them flowering from a gently lyrical opening which repeatedly returns, sounding beautifully different at each recurrence. It is partly this shrewd and practised but quite unobtrusive craftsmanship that gives these pieces their unmistakably personal flavour, their ability to encompass a wide range of mood and texture within a short movement.

The finale of the Clarinet Concerto includes nimbly pattering scherzo material, gracious lyricism, athletic energy and jovial exuberance, but they are unified, not merely juxtaposed. Goldschmidt's lyricism is firm and strong, and a fast movement does not have to relax to incorporate it. The slow movement of the Violin Concerto is marked *Andante amoroso*, but its beauty is grave and ample, not languishing. All three of these concertos, in fact, are strong and rich enough to repay repeated listening. The Violin Concerto was recorded after a series of performances by Chantal Juillet that so impressed Goldschmidt that he dedicated the neglected 40-year-old work to her. Although he did not live to see the release of that recording he had the satisfaction of knowing that it was being delayed until it could be coupled with his other two concertos. Juillet's reading of 'her' concerto is a splendid one, but the others here are no less fine, and all three are admirably recorded.

Nicolas Gombert

Flemish c1495-c1560

GROVE *Probably a native of Flanders and possibly a pupil of Josquin (he composed a déploration on Josquin's death, 1545), Gombert was a singer (from 1526) and maître des enfants (from 1529) in Emperor Charles V's court chapel, with which he travelled in Europe and for which he also served unofficially as composer. He was canon of Notre Dame, Tournai, by 1534. By 1540 he had been dismissed from the imperial chapel but was probably pardoned (and granted a benefice) c1552. Highly regarded by his contemporaries as a great innovator, he favoured dense textures and often used dark, rich timbres. He used pervading imitation more consistently than anyone of his own or an earlier generation, creating textures in which the voices tend to be equally important. All but two of his ten extant masses elaborate existing motets or chansons. His motets (over 160 survive) (from books, 1539, 1541, many in collections), are his most representative works, each phrase of text having its own expressive motif worked through the texture. Other sacred works include eight fine Magnificats and multi-voice works. His chansons (over 70) are like the Netherlands motet only more animated and often conceived on a broad scale. His music continued to be printed until long after his death.*

Missa Tempore paschali

Missa Tempore paschali. Magnificat octavi toni. Adonai, Domine Iesu Christe. In illo tempore loquente Jesu. O Rex gloriae
Henry's Eight / Jonathan Brown
Hyperion CDA66943 (65 minutes: DDD). Texts and translations included. Recorded 1996 Ⓕ ○

This disc reinforces the impression of Gombert as the most involving composer of his generation; the booklet-note aptly describes his music as a cross between the imitative processes of Josquin's generation and the seamless style of Ockeghem. The *Missa Tempore paschali* is thought to be a fairly early work, whereas the *Magnificat* is one of a set that probably dates from Gombert's last years. The Mass is most ambitious, culminating in a 12-voice *Agnus Dei* modelled on Brumel's Mass, *Et ecce terrae motus*. The singing is confident and assured, with a good grasp of large-scale form in the *Credo*. The final *Agnus Dei* seems to crown the Mass in a more credible manner. An added feature is the more inventive, and highly convincing, use of false relations in the readings prepared for Henry's Eight by John O'Donnell. The result has invigorating harmonic incident throughout. The Mass is complemented by some of the composer's most well-known works; the motet, *In illo tempore* is particularly lovely and Henry's Eight respond with some particularly sensitive singing. Those familiar with their very English, yet full-bodied sound won't be disappointed; those who aren't can start here. In Henry's Eight Gombert has found worthy champions.

Henryk Górecki

Polish 1933

GROVE *Górecki studied with Szabelski at the Katowice Conservatory (1955-60) and with Messiaen in Paris. His music has connections with Penderecki, but its deepest affinities are with ancient Polish religious music, and it often shows a saintly simplicity. Most of his works are for orchestra or chamber ensemble; they include the chamber trilogy Genesis (1963) and three symphonies, the third of which achieved striking public success in the early 1990s.*

Symphony No 2, 'Copernican'

Symphony No 2, 'Copernican', Op 31[a]. Beatus vir, Op 38
[a]Zofia Kilanowicz *sop* **Andrezej Dobber** *bar* **Silesian Philharmonic Choir; Polish Radio Choir; Polish National Radio Symphony Orchestra / Antoni Wit**
Naxos 8 555375 (67 minutes: DDD) Ⓢ
Recorded 2000

Górecki composed his Second Symphony in 1972 in response to a commission to mark the 500th anniversary of the birth of the Polish astronomer Nicolas Copernicus. It possesses a certain Janus-like quality in that it forms a bridge between his earlier 'modernist' works and his later 'reductionist' style, into which the ubiquitous Third Symphony falls. The Second Symphony comprises two movements, the first glancing back to the dissonance of earlier works, the second looking forward to more tonal pastures in which the seeds of the Third Symphony are in abundant evidence. The opening movement, while uncompromising in its intensely dramatic and violent gesture, nevertheless has a strong sense of purpose and direction, a gigantic 'birthing' push, one could say, from darkness to light. The second movement sets words from Copernicus's *De revolutionibus orbium coelestium* describing God's creation of the sun, the moon and the stars before finally culminating in an iridescent halo of sustained strings. Górecki's *Copernican* Symphony is an unsung masterpiece, and a greater and more impressively constructed work than the Third Symphony.

Beatus vir was composed in 1977 in response to a commission to mark the 900th anniversary of the martyrdom of the Bishop of Cracow, Stanisław of Szczepanów. The opening page are particularly striking and there are some marvellously scored moments in the remaining 24 minutes or so, though it does not attain the stature of the Second Symphony. That said, this disc is thoroughly recommended to anyone wanting to expand their appreciation of Górecki beyond the Third Symphony. The *Copernican* Symphony more than justifies the price of the disc alone and the performances and recorded sound throughout are exceptionally fine.

Symphony No 3

Awards 1993

Symphony No 3, 'Symphony of Sorrowful Songs', Op 36
Dawn Upshaw *sop* **London Sinfonietta / David Zinman**
Nonesuch 7559-79282-2 Ⓕ
(54 minutes: DDD). Recorded 1991 ○○○

Górecki's Third Symphony has become legend. Composed in 1976, it has always had its champions and admirers within the contemporary music world, but in 1993 it found a new audience of undreamt-of proportions. A few weeks after its release, this Elektra Nonesuch release not only entered the top 10 in the classical charts, but was also riding high in the UK Pop Album charts. It has since become the biggest selling disc of music by a contemporary classical composer. The Symphony, subtitled *Symphony of Sorrowful, Songs* was composed during a period when Górecki's musical style was undergoing a radical change from avant-garde serialism to a more accessible style firmly anchored to tonal traditions. The Symphony's three elegiac movements (or 'songs') form a triptych of laments for all the innocent victims of World War Two and are a reflection upon man's inhumanity to man in general. The songs – including a poignant setting of an inscription scratched by a girl prisoner on the wall of her cell in a Gestapo prison – are beautifully and ethereally sung by Dawn Upshaw, and David Zinman and the London Sinfonietta provide an intense and committed performance of the shimmering orchestral writing. The recording quality is excellent.

Symphony No 3, 'Symphony of Sorrowful Songs', Op 36[a]. Three Pieces in Old Style
[a]**Zofia Kilanowicz** *sop* **Katowice Radio Symphony Orchestra / Antoni Wit**
Naxos 8 550822 (66 minutes: DDD). Text and translation included. Recorded 1993 Ⓢ ⭘

No matter how we evaluate the worth of Górecki's Third Symphony, this piece has done more than any other large-scale contemporary work to stimulate interest in modern music. Up to now the Symphony's strongest allies (apart from Classic FM and the media generally) have been Dawn Upshaw, the London Sinfonietta and David Zinman, whose silken, sensuous and hypnotically intense Elektra-Nonesuch recording helped smooth the way for its wider acceptance. And this new Naxos recording is virtually as good. The performance is exceptionally fine, although the acoustic is more resonant than Elektra's, the orchestral choirs less closely balanced and Antoni Wit isn't as meticulous as Zinman in his observance of minor details. Interpretatively, Wit leaves the more austere impression. His relative inwardness squares convincingly with the symphony's harrowing texts and 'Sorrowful Songs' sub-title. If spectacular singing is your main priority, then Upshaw's is the vocal tour de force. Zofia Kilanowicz displays stronger lower registers and a brilliant, bleached-white soprano that reflects the score's innate pathos, its sense of shock. Her enunciation is more idiomatic, while her partial suspension of vibrato is a powerful interpretative ploy. What is most impressive about this performance is its spirituality; and given the overall excellence of the recording, the conducting and the singing, it is strongly recommended, particularly to those who have yet to discover the Symphony's hypnotic sound-world. It is also commended to those who do know the work but who find Upshaw and Zinman too 'plush' and, most importantly, to those whose distaste for popularism has inhibited a serious assessment of the Symphony's sterling virtues.

Kleines Requiem für eine Polka

Kleines Requiem für eine Polka, Op 66[a]. Harpsichord Concerto, Op 40[b]. Good Night, 'In memoriam Michael Vyner', Op 63
Dawn Upshaw *sop* **Sebastian Bell** *fl* **John Constable** *pf* **Elisabeth Chojnacka** *hpd* **David Hockings** *perc* **London Sinfonietta / [a]David Zinman, [b]Markus Stenz**
Nonesuch 7559-79362-2 (59 minutes: DDD) Ⓕ
Recorded 1993-94 ⭘

Like a small café huddled within the shadow of some ancient church, Górecki's *Kleines Requiem für eine Polka* (1993) evokes feelings of paradox. The opening movement suggests distracted tranquillity. This is followed by a grating *Allegro* which approximates the sort of vicious 'knees-up' that Shostakovich penned whenever he bared his teeth at empty celebration. Later, we are back within the tranquil interior of Górecki's imagination – and it's there that we stay until the work ends. The *Kleines Requiem für eine Polka* displays a profundity expressed via the simplest means. It is a pity, then, that the Harpsichord Concerto breaks the mood so quickly: one's initial impression is of a further violent 'episode' from the first work, although the stylistic contrast breaks the illusion soon enough. This is probably the most famous 20th-century harpsichord concerto after Falla's. Bach served as its creative prime mover, while Elisabeth Chojnacka is its dedicatee and most celebrated interpreter. Here she revels in the piece's playful aggression. It's an unrelenting display and in total contrast to *Good Night*, Górecki's deeply felt memorial to one of his staunchest supporters, Michael Vyner. The language is sombre, but never merely mournful. Mostly quiet and contemplative, *Good Night* is scored for alto flute, piano and tam-tam with Dawn Upshaw intoning Hamlet's 'flights of angels' in the closing movement. The work ends in a spirit of veiled ritual with a sequence of quiet gong strokes. The performance and recording are consistently fine.

Choral Works

Miserere, Op 44[a]. Amen, Op 35[a]. Euntes ibant et flebant, Op 32[a]. My Vistula, grey Vistula, Op 46[b]. Broad waters, Op 39[b]
[a]**Chicago Symphony Chorus;** [a]**Chicago Lyric Opera Chorus / John Nelson;** [b]**Lira Chamber Chorus / Lucy Ding**
Nonesuch 7559-79348-2 (67 minutes: DDD) Ⓕ
Texts and translations included. Recorded 1994

Miserere is an intensely spiritual, prayerful work in which Górecki responds with heartfelt passion to the political events of 1981 (a sit-in by members of Rural Solidarity which ultimately led to the democratization of Poland). It is as intellectually demanding and emotionally compelling as anything by Górecki released on disc. Lovers of the Third Symphony will fall under its spell straight away, but it should gain respect from those less easily swayed by the opulent orchestral textures of that work, for here Górecki is using what is probably his favourite medium, the unaccompanied choir. The voices enter in a series of layered thirds until all ten parts begin an electrifying ascent through the word 'Domine' to the work's climax which, with the first statement of 'Miserere', suddenly bathes us in a quiet chord of A minor – a moment as devastatingly effective as an orchestra full of banging drums and crashing cymbals. John Nelson directs a hypnotic performance full of impact, his choral forces emotionally committed and technically excellent. The recording itself is not technically excellent – there are a number of persistent background rattles and bangs. The church where the recording was made suffers from a cloudy acoustic and there is a haze of surface noise. In the end, it only serves to reinforce this grainy aural picture of those dark times in Poland's recent history.

Górecki Totus tuus, Op 60. Amen, Op 34 **Pärt** Magnificat. The Beatitudes **Tavener** Magnificat. Nunc dimittis. Funeral Ikos **Anonymous** Plainchant – Alma redemptoris mater. Ave Maria. Regina caeli laetare. Alleluia, venite ad me. Beati mundo corde. Requiem aeternam. Ego sum resurrectio et vita. In paradisum
David Goode *org* **Choir of King's College, Cambridge / Stephen Cleobury**
EMI CDC5 55096-2 (59 minutes: DDD). Texts and translations included. Recorded 1994 Ⓕ ●●

This disc links the music of these three composers in an illuminating way. The contemporary pieces are separated by soberly sung plainchant which acts as a kind of sorbet to cleanse the palate between the various dishes. The performances of Górecki's *Totus tuus* and *Amen* are technically superb, and can rarely have been sung with such absolute control: similarly Tavener's *Funeral Ikos* is performed with perfect pacing and tuning. Yet these three pieces lack spontaneity. They are too polite, perhaps, so that the Górecki works never quite catch fire, and the Tavener never really moves one. The response is more convincing in the Tavener *Collegium Regale* canticles, sung with virtuoso flair and the Pärt *Magnificat* and *The Beatitudes*. Here the performances have just that element of flexibility lacking in the other pieces, for all their beauty of sound. Pärt's intimate austerity is well served in the care with which his melodies are shaped and the dynamic levels maintained.

François-Joseph Gossec

Belgian/French 1734-1829

GROVE *In Paris Gossec was a violinist in La Pouplinière's orchestra, c1751-62, as well as a composer. In 1762-70 he directed the Prince of Condé's theatre at Chantilly, from c 1766 also serving the Prince of Conti; meanwhile he composed opéras comiques, notably Les pêcheurs (1766, Paris). He founded the Concert des Amateurs in 1769 and directed it until 1773; the orchestra was one of Europe's finest. In 1773-77 he was a director of the Concert Spirituel. From 1775 he held posts at the Opéra and presented various stage works there; the ballets were the most successful. From 1784 he directed the new Ecole Royale de Chant. At the Revolution he directed the band of the Garde Nationale and wrote numerous Revolutionary works for large forces. After 1799 his output declined, and he concentrated on teaching at the Conservatoire.*

Gossec's c50 symphonies, showing many Mannheim traits, are his most important works and contributed significantly to the development of the genre in France. One of them (1761) was among the first French orchestral works to use clarinets. Novel effects of scoring also appear in his Messe des morts (1760) and oratorio La nativité; (1774). He also wrote other sacred works, songs, symphonies concertantes, chamber music and treatises.

Symphonies

Symphonies, Op 5 – No 2 in E flat, B26; No 3 in D, B27, 'Pastorella'. Symphonies, Op 12 – No 5 in E flat, B58; No 6 in F, B59; D, B86
London Mozart Players / Matthias Bamert
Chandos CHAN9661 (67 minutes: DDD) Ⓕ
Recorded 1997 ●

François-Joseph Gossec, born in what is now Belgium, was the leading instrumental composer in Paris during the second half of the 18th century. He wrote some 50 symphonies, much admired in their time, and very attractive they are too. The two symphonies from his Op 5, of the early 1760s, are lively, Italianate pieces in four movements; there is a charming if inventively slightly ordinary *Romanza* in one of them, and a particularly jolly Minuet and a spirited, well worked out finale in the other. But some of the musical ideas seem static and anonymous. The later compositions, two from his Op 12 of 1769 and one from the mid-1770s, are in three movements, and altogether more interesting. The *Andantino* of the one in F has some very poetic writing and rich textures; the E flat work has a solemn, elevated slow introduction and an *Andante* with real pathos; while the one in D is a big piece with trumpets, a martial first movement and a sombre second, then a cheerful finale. Matthias Bamert directs the performances with energy and commitment. Anyone interested in the byways of the classical or late pre-classical era should give this disc a hearing.

Louis Moreau Gottschalk

American 1829-1869

GROVE *At 13 Gottschalk went to Paris for piano and composition lessons, and by 19, through the success of his 'Creole' piano pieces Bamboula, La savane and La bananier (the so-called Louisiana trilogy), his name was a household word throughout Europe. He was hailed as the New World's first authentic musical spokesman and his keyboard virtuosity was compared with Chopin's. After another charming genre piece, Le mancenillier (1851), and tours of Switzerland, France and Spain, 1850-52, he made his New York début. In touring the USA to increase his income, 1853-56, he catered ever more to the public taste for sensational effects (eg in Tournament Galop and The Last Hope). His most fruitful period, 1857-61, was spent in the Caribbean, where in relative seclusion he wrote some of his finest works, including Souvenir de Porto Rico, Ojos criollos (four hands), the Symphony no.1 ('La nuit des tropiques') and the one-act opera Escenas campestres. A second extended tour of the USA, 1862-65, produced little but the well-known Dying Poet and the duet La gallina. From his last years in South America, feverishly devoted to concert-giving, the most notable works are Pasquinade, the Grand scherzo and the Grande tarantelle for piano and orchestra. Although not an 'advanced' composer, Gottschalk was sensitive to local colour and often used quotation as both a musical and psychological device, as well as syncopated rhythms and jagged melodic lines – all traits associated with later music.*

Piano Works

O ma charmante, épargnez-moi, RO182. Grande fantaisie triomphale sur l'hymne national brésilien, RO108. Melody in D flat. Bamboula, RO20. The Dying Poet, RO75. Grande étude de concert, RO116, 'Hercule'. The last hope, RO133. Murmures éoliens, RO178. Symphony No 1, RO5, 'La nuit des tropiques' – Andante (arr Napoleão). La chute des feuilles, RO55. Tournament Galop, RO264
Philip Martin *pf*
Hyperion CDA66915 (73 minutes: DDD) Ⓕ
Recorded 1996 ●

It is not only the playing here which gives such satisfaction, but the whole package is stylishly produced – Rousseau on the booklet cover and fine notes from Jeremy Nicholas. The piano sound from the fastidious Hyperion team is flawless. Martin, operating in a context where some pianists can hardly play softly at all, has a ravishing *pianissimo*. This makes *O ma charmante* and the perennial – but highly original – *The last hope* simply enchanting. Gottschalk is a real melodist. Martin understands the intimacies of the salon but he also lacks nothing in his transcendental virtuosity. The more flamboyant numbers, such as *Tournament Galop* prove this. About 10 years after Gottschalk's death, his pianist colleague, Artur Napoleão, made a piano arrangement of the first movement of Symphony No 1 (*Night in the tropics*) which Martin includes here. It is slightly drab compared with the orchestral version and soon feels repetitive. But don't let that put you off this outstanding continuation of Martin's Gottschalk series.

La colombe, RO60. La moissonneuse, RO173. Le songe d'une nuit d'été, R0240. Pensée poétique. L'étincelle, RO80. Souvenir de Cuba, R0245. La gitanella, RO103. Morte!!, RO174. Polonia, R0210. Fantôme de bonheur, R094. Forest Glade Polka, R098. Ossian ballades, RO187. Ricordati, RO227. Reflets du passé, R0223. Apothéose, RO8
Philip Martin *pf*
Hyperion CDA67118 (72 minutes: DDD) Ⓕ
Recorded 1999

Piano Works for Two and Four Hands
Réponds-moi, RO225[a]. Printemps d'amour, RO214[a]. Marche de nuit, RO151[a]. Ses yeux, RO234[a]. La jota aragonesa, RO130[a]. Le bananier, RO21[a]. Ojos criollos, RO184[a]. Orfa, RO186[a]. L'étincelle, RO80[a]. Marche funèbre, RO148[a]. La gallina, RO100[a]. Radieuse, RO217[a]. Grande tarantelle, RO259[a]. Souvenir d'Andalousie, RO242[b]. Le banjo, RO22[b]. Grand scherzo, RO114[b]. Pasquinade, RO189[b]. Berceuse, RO27[b]. Tournament Galop, RO26[b]. Mazurka. Union, RO269[b]. The Last Hope, RO133[b]. Scherzo-romantique, RO233[b]. Le mancenillier, RO142[b]. The Dying Poet, RO75[ab]
[a]**Nerine Barrett**, [b]**Alan Marks** *pfs*
Nimbus ② NI7045/6 (107 minutes: DDD) Ⓜ
Recorded 1984-91

It was once necessary to explain who Gottschalk was. Now the proud American virtuoso from New Orleans has taken his place as a composer of some of the most colourful and charming romantic piano music – thanks largely to Martin's advocacy in this immaculately produced Hyperion series. Compared with Gottschalk's syncopated masterpieces such as *Souvenir de Porto Rico*, which ends Volume 1, this collection may be slighter, but every track is a delight. Martin's feeling for this music is so convincing and the recorded sound so ideal that even the more trivial pieces are a joy – Gottschalk appears as a real melodist. A superficial crowd-pleaser such as *Apothéose* is good for a laugh. But *Morte!!* is moving in its simplicity with, as elsewhere, more *staccato* than Gottschalk specified. At times this makes the piano texture sound like Satie but it is particularly effective in the funeral bell sections (3'35"; 4'27") of this lamentation.

The piano duets on the two-disc set from Nimbus feature the magnificent team of Marks and Barrett, well recorded, who sparkle in infectious enjoyment of this vivid music. Try the Cuban syncopations of tracks 1 and 11. The Nimbus CD notes needed bringing up to date (the writer is Wilfrid Mellers) while the informative Hyperion booklet by Jeremy Nicholas takes advantage of two new monographs on Gottschalk.

Charles François Gounod

French 1818-1893

GROVE *Gounod studied privately with Reicha and at the Paris Conservatoire with Halévy (counterpoint) and Le Sueur (composition), winning the Prix de Rome in 1839. At Rome (1840-42) he was deeply impressed by the 16th-century polyphonic music (particularly Palestrina's) he heard in the Sistine Chapel and wrote some rather austere masses; for a time a church organist in Paris, he considered joining the priesthood. The climax of his liturgical work came in 1855 with the florid Messe solennelle de Ste Cécile, a favourite setting scarcely superseded by his 12 later ones (1870-92). Meanwhile he wrote a Gluckian, then a Meyerbeerian opera, both failures; the succeeding five, all first performed at the Théâtre-Lyrique, are the works by which he is remembered, namely the small-scale Le médecin malgré lui (1858) and Philémon et Baucis (1860), the triumphant Faust (1859), in which sensitive musical characterization and a refreshing naturalness set new standards on the French operatic stage, and the major successes Mireille (1864) and Roméo et Juliette (1867).*

In 1870 Gounod took refuge in England from the Franco-Prussian War, staying some four years to exploit the English demand for choral music. The first conductor of the Royal Albert Hall Choral Society (1871), he produced dozens of choruses and songs. But he experienced considerable intrigue in his private life, effectively marking the end of his fruitfulness as a composer. His oratorios for Birmingham, La rédemption and Mors et vita, if banal and facilely emotional, were nonetheless successful. Gounod's influence on the next generation of French composers, including Bizet, Fauré and especially Massenet, was enormous. Tchaikovsky and later Poulenc, Auric and Ravel admired his clean workmanship, delicate sentiment, gift for orchestral colour and, in his best songs, unpretentious lyrical charm.

Symphonies

Symphony No 1 in D. Symphony No 2 in E flat
Orchestra of St John's, Smith Square / John Lubbock
ASV CDDCA981 (65 minutes: DDD) Ⓕ
Recorded 1996 and 1993

Gounod's symphonies are not brow-furrowing and do not represent any advance in symphonic thought beyond Schumann and Mendelssohn, but they reveal Gounod in the Gallic tradition of elegantly crafted works with a light touch. The melodious, classically built and even witty First Symphony, with its delicate second-movement fugue and vivacious finale, is not to be peremptorily brushed aside. The longer Second Symphony makes an attempt to sound more serious, especially in the first movement and the dramatic *Scherzo* – the cantilena of the *Larghetto* is beautifully shaped here – but high spirits return in the finale. John Lubbock and his St John's orchestra are adept at the crisply neat treatment that this music demands. His wind section is outstanding, but in the finale of No 1 the violins too show real virtuosity. A warm but clean recorded sound adds to our pleasure.

Mélodies

Où voulez-vous aller?[a]. Le soir[a]. Venise[a]. Ave Maria[b]. Sérénade[b]. Chanson de printemps[a]. Au rossignol[b]. Ce que je suis sans toi[a]. Envoi de fleurs[a]. La pâquerette[b]. Boléro[b]. Mignon[a]. Rêverie[a]. Ma belle amie est morte[b]. Loin du pays[b]. Clos ta paupière[a]. Prière[b]. L'absent[a]. Le temps des roses[a]. Biondina[c]. The Worker[c]. A lay of the early spring[c]. My true love hath my heart[b]. Oh happy home! Oh blessed flower![c]. The fountain mingles with the river[a]. Maid of Athens[c]. Beware! The Arrow and the Song[a]. Ilala: stances à la mémoire de Livingston[c]. If thou art sleeping, maiden[c]
[a]**Dame Felicity Lott** *sop* [b]**Ann Murray** *mez*
[c]**Anthony Rolfe Johnson** *ten* **Graham Johnson** *pf*
Hyperion ② CDA66801/2 (136 minutes: DDD) Ⓕ
Texts and translations included. Recorded 1993

This well-filled two-CD set is surely the most wide-ranging single issue of Gounod's *mélodies*. The first of the discs confirms the commonly held view of Gounod. Almost without exception the songs are pleasing and sentimental, a sweetly scented posy of hymns to flowers, of reveries and serenades. The selection includes two settings of poems that Berlioz had used in *Les nuits d'été*, plumbing the depths of the poetry, where Gounod is content to skim across the surface. In chronological order, the songs show how little Gounod's music deepened, but also how evergreen was his inspiration in melody and harmony.

To turn to the second disc is to have all one's prejudices overturned. This comprises non-French settings, for which Gounod dons first Italian garb for the song-cycle *Biondina*, and then English for a group of ten songs written during his stay in London in the 1870s. The Italian cycle is a delight. It would be impossible to guess the composer, as Gounod exchanges his customary flowing themes and rippling arpeggios for an ardent, Tosti-like vocal line over dry *staccato* chords. Anthony Rolfe Johnson catches its mix of sunny lyricism and Gallic sensitivity to perfection. The English songs are even more unusual, ranging from the Victorian ballad style of *The Worker* to a bizarre musical tribute to Livingstone, *Ilala*. All three singers are on their best form, Rolfe Johnson bringing an air of intimate seductiveness to Byron's *Maid of Athens*.

Faust

Richard Leech *ten* Faust; **Cheryl Studer** *sop* Marguerite; **José van Dam** *bar* Méphistophélès; **Thomas Hampson** *bass* Valentin; **Martine Mahé** *mez* Siébel; **Nadine Denize** *sop* Marthe; **Marc Barrard** *bar* Wagner; **French Army Chorus; Toulouse Capitole Choir and Orchestra / Michel Plasson**
EMI ③ CDS5 56224-2 (204 minutes: DDD). Notes, Ⓕ
text and translation included. Recorded 1991 ●

Richard Leech as the eponymous hero sings his part with the fresh, eager tone, the easy *legato*, the sense of French style that it has so badly been wanting all these years, certainly since Nicolai Gedda essayed the role on the now rather aged Cluytens/EMI sets from 1953 and 1958. Gedda's voice may be more lyrical in the role, but Leech encompasses it with less effort, and creates a real character. It is extremely distinguished singing. Beside him he has an equally impressive loved one in Studer and antagonist van Dam. Studer finds herself another amenable *métier* in Gounod; her Marguérite is not only sung with innate musicality, firm tone and expressive phrasing but also with a deep understanding of this style of French music in terms of nuance and the lighter touch. The Jewel song is a treasure; the King of Thulé, even more, the sad solo in Marguerite's chamber are touching. In the latter this Marguérite really captures the sense of hopelessness combined with longing for the absent lover. To add to one's satisfaction her French seems faultless. Van Dam achieves so much more by subtlety of accent and by care over note values than have basses, mostly from eastern Europe in modern times, by over-egging the pudding. Here is a resolute, implacable Devil with a firm, even tone to second the insinuating characterization. His voice may have dried out a little, but he remains a paragon of a stylist in all he attempts. The three French-speaking singers excel in subsidiary roles. Thomas Hampson is in places overextended as Valentin, a role that needs experience and perfect French.

Plasson almost but not quite kills the score with kindness. He so loves the piece that his tempos, especially in the more reflective moments, such as the start of the Garden scene, become much slower than the score predicates and demands. Against that must be set his respect for the minutiae of Gounod's often inspired writing for orchestra and a general warmth that lights the score from within. It was an inspired stroke to invite the French Army Chorus to sing the Soldiers' Chorus, delivered with such verve as to make it seem unhackneyed.

Faust
Jerry Hadley *ten* Faust; **Cecilia Gasdia** *sop* Marguerite; **Samuel Ramey** *bass* Méphistophélès; **Alexander Agache** *bar* Valentin; **Susanne Mentzer** *mez* Siébel; **Brigitte Fassbaender** *mez* Marthe; **Philippe Fourcade** *bass* Wagner; **Welsh National Opera Chorus and Orchestra / Carlo Rizzi**
Teldec ③ 4509-90872-2 (211 minutes: DDD). Notes, text and translation included. Recorded 1993 Ⓕ

Where Gounod is at his most inspired this version of his most popular work is more than commendable. Most notable are the solos for Marguerite and Faust, the Garden scene, the vignette in Marguerite's room that used to be regularly cut, and the Prison scene. The tender, sweet-toned and idiomatically French singing and style of Gasdia and Hadley quite exceed expectations in these days of homogenised and uniform interpretation. These two principals step outside those predictable parameters to give us readings of high individuality, favouring their grateful music with delicately etched line, varied dynamics and real involvement in their characters' predicaments. Both their happiness and later remorse are eloquently expressed. Gasdia gives a well-nigh faultless performance – light-hearted, elated in the Jewel song, ardent in the Garden duet, ecstatic in the bedtime solo that follows, ineffably sad in her 'Il ne revient pas'. She is no less touching when she has lost her reason. Subtle timbres, poised high notes inform all her singing. Hadley, with the ideal weight of voice for Faust, has done nothing better. 'Je t'aime' at the first meeting with Marguerite is whispered in wonder. In the love duet he sings to her as a gentle lover, caressing his music, and Gasdia replies in kind.

The good news continues with Mentzer. She sings both Siébel's regular solos with vibrant, properly virile tone, the quick vibrato attractive. It's a real coup to have Fassbaender as Marthe, making so much of little. Ramey is the one singer to give a standardised performance. His Méphisto is as soundly and resolutely sung as one would expect from this sturdy bass, but it doesn't have the Francophone smoothness and subtlety of other interpretations. The only drawback is the often lax conducting. Rizzi conducts an often alarmingly slow account of the score and in compensation the more exciting passages are given rather too much verve. However, he is aware of the sensuous nature of Gounod's scoring and the WNO Chorus and Orchestra are excellent. The recording is open, full of presence and well balanced.

Faust (sung in English)
Paul Charles Clarke *ten* Faust; **Mary Plazas** *sop* Marguerite; **Alastair Miles** *bass* Méphistophélès; **Gary Magee** *bar* Valentin; **Diana Montague** *mez* Siébel; **Sarah Walker** *mez* Marthe; **Matthew Hargreaves** *bass* Wagner; **Geoffrey Mitchell Choir; Philharmonia Orchestra / David Parry**
Chandos Opera in English Series ③ CHAN3014 (208 minutes: DDD). Notes and text included. Recorded 1998 Ⓕ

After listening to this *Faust*, one can feel something very like awe. The structure is massive, the workmanship infinitely thorough, the boldness of stroke (dramatic and musical) almost breathtaking. And the winning numbers come up as in some dream-world lottery. No doubt the performance contributes to the awe. That is because it is in many ways a very good one, and partly because it underlines seriousness and grandeur. But it appears that David Parry has joined the swelling ranks of the slowcoaches. The Church scene and Faust's solo in the garden, for instance, are probably the slowest on record, and in the Ballet music the second dance (marked *adagio* but not *lento*) goes half as slow again as the metronome marking. Happily, there is nothing boring about it. This recording and its production keep the stage in view, and it is particularly good to have the chorus in such clear focus.

The principals, too, form a strongly gifted team. Paul Charles Clarke, the Faust, is an interesting tenor, thrustful both in tone and manner yet capable of gentleness and delicacy. He never lets us forget that this is *his* story; when he sings everything counts. By comparison, Alastair Miles's Méphistophélès seems a mild-mannered type with reserves of authority and a magnificent voice. Vocally he is very impressive, the fine texture of his voice showing up to great advantage, his production admirably firm and even, his style unfailingly musical. The absence of overt devilry may pass as a virtue, but the absence of character is surely taking the disguise too far. Gounod's Mephisto is a joker, a man of the world and an exhibitionist; this one, rarely in the spotlight, loses it entirely when Marthe enters the garden in the person of Sarah Walker.

The Valentin, Gary Magee, has a fine, vibrant baritone and rises well to his high notes and big moments. Diana Montague is an excellent Siébel (and how she rises to hers). The Marguerite, Mary Plazas, is totally likeable, ingenuous but not winsomely so, touchingly sincere in her love and her loss, clean in the scale-work of her Jewel song, a little underpowered in the grand melody of the Church scene, but having a powerful high C in reserve. The English version by Christopher Cowell reads well, sounds natural and does not affect the artless colloquialism that can be an embarrassing feature of modern translations.

Additional recommendation
Faust
Nash Faust **Licette** Marguerite **Easton** Mephistopheles
BBC Choir; symphony orchestra / Beecham; Raybould
Dutton Laboratories mono ② 2CDAX2001 Ⓜ
(138 minutes: ADD: 5/94)

Recorded in 1929-30 Beecham's English version enshrines two wonderful performances by Heddle Nash and Miriam Licette, regular partners in these roles. They are object lessons in style and diction. Beecham conducts with the lightest of touches.

Roméo et Juliette

Plácido Domingo *ten* Roméo; **Ruth Ann Swenson** *sop* Juliette; **Alastair Miles** *bass* Frère Laurent; **Kurt Ollmann** *bar* Mercutio; **Susan Graham** *sop* Stephano; **Alain Vernhes** *bar* Capulet; **Sarah Walker** *mez* Gertrude; **Paul Charles Clarke** *ten* Tybalt; **Christopher Maltman** *bar* Paris; **Erik Freulon** *bar* Gregorio; **Toby Spence** *ten* Benvolio; **David Pittman-Jennings** *bar* Duc; **Dankwart Siegele** *bass* Frère Jean; **Bavarian Radio Chorus; Munich Radio Orchestra / Leonard Slatkin**
RCA Victor Red Seal ② 09026 68440-2
(156 minutes: DDD). Notes, text and translation included. Recorded 1995 Ⓕ ●

Thanks to the advocacy of Leonard Slatkin and his team, Gounod's romantic work, *Roméo et Juliette*, seems the epitome of the well-made French 19th-century opera. Swenson shows a true empathy for the shape and feeling of a Gounod phrase. At the start, in the famous Waltz song, she announces her gifts. Besides singing this showpiece with technical confidence, a full, rounded tone and refined delicacy in coloratura, she shows an understanding of the girl's youthful vivacity yet tempers that with inner feeling in the 'Loin d'hiver' passage. The fear at having to enter the tomb of Tybalt in the solo at the end of Act 4, so often omitted in the opera house, is graphically expressed; as are the last, desperate utterances as she eagerly grasps the *poignard* to join her beloved in Elysium. Her French, though not perfect, is well learnt, and quite adequate to support her impressive portrayal. She seems to have inspired Domingo back to almost his best, youthful form. Roméo's famous aria is sung with growing ardour and full resonance. The outburst against Tybalt when he has killed Mercutio is heroic to a fault. But the golden tenor is still able to soften in the duets in response to this Juliette. Only once or twice the strain on high betrays the advancing years. Two principals of such calibre deserve and, by and large, get worthy support and all are brought together into a firm ensemble by Slatkin's direction. He brings all the bitter-sweetness out of the Entr'actes by which Gounod obviously set so much store, cares for the composer's refined orchestration and shapes the set pieces with an unerring ear for matching tempos.

What more can you ask for? Well, a chorus and orchestra that respond with a like mind, and that's what we have here. Most of the original 1873 score is in place, except for the first three movements of the Wedding tableau, often omitted. To complete our pleasure the recording is near faultless. The voices are up-front, but never to the detriment of the orchestra.

Percy Grainger

American/Australian 1882-1961

Grainger studied with Knorr and Kwast at the Hoch Conservatory in Frankfurt (1895-99), where he became linked with Balfour Gardiner, Quilter and C Scott, and settled in London in 1901. Another close friend was Grieg. During the next decade he appeared widely as a concert pianist; he also took part in the folksong movement, collecting and arranging numerous songs. He was an unconventional man, in his attitudes, his lifestyle and his music where he experimented with a variety of techniques, including rhythm freed from regular metre, polytonality, improvisation and highly unusual instrumentation. In 1914 he moved to the USA, where he taught in Chicago and New York; he visited Australia several times, helping the establishment of the Grainger Museum at Melbourne. His large output, complicated by the fact that he often made several versions of a piece, includes both original works and folksong arrangements. He has suffered the fate of being remembered more for what he called his 'fripperies' (Country Gardens, Handel in the Strand, Molly on the Shore) than his larger works, but even in them his originality of spirit comes through.

The Warriors

Grainger The Warriors **Holst** The Planets, H125[a]
[a]women's voices of the **Monteverdi Choir; Philharmonia Orchestra / Sir John Eliot Gardiner**
DG 445 860-2GH (68 minutes: DDD) Ⓕ
Recorded 1994 ●

Grainger's *magnum opus*, *The Warriors*, was the 'music for an imaginary ballet', a commission set up by Sir Thomas Beecham for Diaghilev's Ballets Russes, but one which failed to materialise. Grainger wrote it anyway, of course, his imagination running riot with visions of a great tribal pageant, a 'wild sexual concert', the ghostly clans of all humankind spirited together in celebration of life's prime. *The Warriors* was his corrective, a symphony of dissolution. It is excessive, vulgar, as strange as it is beautiful. Above all, it's the rhythmic excitement of the piece that is so totally irresistible. Gardiner's classical and pre-classical explorations have, by necessity of style, set great store by rhythmic matters, and what a boon they are in *The Planets*. It's Gardiner's insistence upon precise articulations that keeps fleet-footed 'Mercury' so airborne, that brings the opening of 'Jupiter' into such sharp relief, making it shine all the brighter. There are other moments where a little more theatrical rhetoric would not have gone amiss: is the controlled fury of 'Mars' perhaps a shade too controlled? But the marmoreal beauty of 'Venus' and 'Neptune' (a ravishing texture descending from the gleam of celeste to an organ pedal sunk too deep to fathom), the sensitivity of the Philharmonia's playing, duly leave their impression. The recorded sound is superb.

Grainger In a Nutshell. Train Music (ed Rathburn). The Warriors. Lincolnshire Posy. Country Gardens, BFMS22 (rev 1950) **Debussy** (orch Grainger) Pagodes **Ravel** (orch Grainger) La vallée des cloches[a]
City of Birmingham Symphony Orchestra / Sir Simon Rattle
EMI CDC5 56412-2 (70 minutes: DDD). Recorded [a]1990 and 1996 Ⓕ ●

This is a marvellous Grainger anthology. Rattle surpasses Richard Hickox's commendable account of *In a Nutshell* in terms of rhythmic point and bracing character and makes us even more aware of the originality of Grainger's vision. *The Warriors* is handsomely served on CD by Geoffrey Simon and John Eliot Gardiner (see above). Rattle's stunning version of *The Warriors* possesses a mastery of texture and irresistible choreographic flair to remind us of the piece's ballet origins. *Country Gardens* is quirkily scored, harmonically eventful and hugely entertaining. The delectable arrangements of Ravel's *La vallée des cloches* and Debussy's *Pagodes* are quite captivating in their imaginative sonorities and both receive exquisite treatment here. *Train Music* is an intriguing torso, dating from 1901, which the ambitious teenage composer began to score for an orchestra of about 150 players. It's heard here in a reduced orchestration by the American Grainger authority, Eldon Rathburn. Finally, we are given an exceptionally perceptive *Lincolnshire Posy*. Not only do the fabulous blend and immaculate intonation of the CBSO's wind and brass take the breath away, but Rattle's interpretation is also full of insight. Most remarkable of all is 'Rufford Park Poachers', full of tragic grandeur; 'Lord Melbourne', too, is memorable, acquiring a fierce, hard-edged intensity. Both the recording and presentation are immaculate.

Miscellaneous Orchestral Works

Green Bushes, BFMS12. Lord Maxwell's Goodnight, BFMS14 (both ed Barry Peter Ould). Hill Song No 2. The Merry King, BFMS39[a]. Eastern Intermezzo. Colonial Song, S1. Spoon river, AFMS2. The Power of Rome and the Christian Heart. The Immovable Do. County Derry Air, BFMS29. Ye Banks and Braes O' Bonnie Doon, BFMS31. English Dance No 1
[a]**Paul Janes** *pf* **BBC Philharmonic Orchestra / Richard Hickox**
Chandos CHAN9839 (70 minutes: DDD) Recorded 1999 Ⓕ ●●

Here's a recipe guaranteed to delight Grainger acolytes and inquisitive newcomers alike: a liberal sprinkling of old friends (the majority intoxicatingly 'dished up' for large orchestra), three of the composer's most ambitious creations and no less than four world première recordings.

Falling into the last two categories comes the giddily inventive *English Dance* No 1 (the sketches for which date as far back as 1899, and the riotous final item here). Bearing the inscription 'For Cyril Scott with long love', this is the work of which Gabriel Fauré exclaimed: 'It's as if the total population were a dancing.' Hickox and company have already set down this remarkable piece in its final scoring from 1924-29; the present orchestration dates from 1906-09 and wears an even more exuberantly colourful demeanour than its successor.

Originally conceived in 1907 for 24 winds (in which guise it can be heard on Chandos), the bracing, somewhat Delian *Hill Song* No 2 is played in its final incarnation from 1948 for symphony orchestra (but dispensing with violins, trombones and tuba). That same year, Grainger accepted a commission for an even more ambitious wind-band creation, *The Power of Rome and the Christian Heart*, based on ideas from as far back as 1918 and given here with the optional string parts. It's an imposing, oddly moreish affair, whose second half borrows material from the 1943 orchestral essay *Dreamery* (Chandos) as well as the first movement ('The Power of Love') of the marvellous *Danish Folksong Suite*.

From a clutch of indelible favourites, to be singled out are the well-upholstered 1919 orchestration of the supremely touching *Colonial Song*, *Green Bushes* (in a particularly opulent version from 1905-06) and that memorably tangy 1920 harmonisation of the *Irish Tune from County Derry*. Comparative rarities include Grainger's uniquely piquant May 1933 arrangement for 'tuneful percussion' of his *Eastern Intermezzo* (better known, perhaps, as the fourth movement of his *Youthful Suite*) and *The Merry King* (based on a West Sussex folksong and featuring some enjoyably extravagant piano writing).

Hickox secures a set of performances that are simply past praise in their combination of stylish swagger and heartwarming commitment to the cause. Wonderful Chandos sound, too, irrepressibly vivid, utterly truthful in timbre and spectacularly wide-ranging. Terrific stuff!

Youthful Suite. Molly on the Shore, BFMS1. Irish Tune from County Derry, BFMS15. Shepherd's Hey, BFMS16. Country Gardens. Early one Morning, BFMS unnum. Handel in the Strand, RMTB2. Mock Morris, RMTB1. Dreamery (ed Ould). The Warriors (ed Servadei)
BBC Philharmonic Orchestra / Richard Hickox
Chandos Grainger Edition CHAN9584 (75 minutes: DDD). Recorded 1997 Ⓕ ●

Featuring some ripe, beautifully clean-cut sonics, this collection is a great success for all involved. As the opening, chest-swelling 'Northern March' of the *Youthful Suite* immediately shows, Hickox draws playing of infectious swagger from the ever-excellent BBC Philharmonic (marvellous brass sounds especially). The suite boasts some striking invention, not least in the central 'Nordic Dirge' (a hauntingly eloquent processional, incorporating plenty of 'tuneful percussion') and a winsome, at times almost Ivesian 'English Waltz'. There follow seven of

Grainger's most popular miniatures in the orchestrations Gershwin made for Leopold Stokowski. Hickox gives us Grainger's original thoughts and a delectable sequence they comprise, full of truly kaleidoscopic textural and harmonic variety. By the side of Rattle's CBSO version, Hickox's *Country Gardens* is perhaps marginally lacking in twinkling good humour and entrancing lightness of touch, but his infectious energy and evident affection more than compensate. *Dreamery*, described by Grainger as 'Slow Tween-Play' (an epithet which, annotator Barry Peter Ould suggests, 'could be construed as his particular term for an intermezzo'), appears here in the extended orchestral version.

For *The Warriors*, Hickox uses a new critical edition prepared by the Australian Grainger authority, Alessandro Servadei. Grainger's orchestral palette has never sounded more gloriously extravagant than here. Then again, this impression is just as much a tribute to Hickox's performance, which is breathtaking in its virtuosic brilliance and stunning co-ordination.

Music for Wind Band

The Power of Rome and the Christian Heart. Children's March: Over the Hills and Far Away, RMTB4. Bell Piece[a]. Blithe Bells. The Immovable Do. Hill Songs – No 1; No 2. County Derry Air, BFMS29. Marching Song of Democracy

[a]James Gilchrist *ten* **Royal Northern College of Music Wind Orchestra / Timothy Reynish, Clark Rundell**

Chandos Grainger Edition CHAN9630 Ⓕ
(65 minutes: DDD). Recorded 1992-97 ●

Rundell's compelling realization of the extraordinary *Hill Song* No 1 – regarded by Grainger as one of his finest achievements and performed here in its original guise for (wait for it!) two piccolos, six oboes, six cors anglais, six bassoons and double-bassoon – was actually made by BBC Manchester back in 1992; the remaining items date from 1997 and benefit from the splendid sound and balance achieved by Chandos. As well as the *Hill Song* No 1, we get the 1929 scoring of its pithier successor from 1907.

Another of Grainger's most striking wind-band compositions opens the disc, namely the 12-minute *The Power of Rome and the Christian Heart*. Its central section will be familiar as the six-and-a-half-minute orchestral piece, *Dreamery* (both works were completed in 1943), while its closing measures utilise material from the first movement ('The Power of Love') of the *Danish Folk-song Suite*. Both the *Children's March* and *Bell Piece* feature some unexpected vocal contributions. In the latter – a charming 'ramble' on John Dowland's *Now, O now I needs must part* – Grainger incorporates a bell part specially written for his wife, Ella. The delightfully piquant arrangements of *Blithe Bells* and *The Immovable Do* date from March 1931 and November/December 1939 respectively. These fine players equally revel in the 'scrunchy' harmonies of the eventful version of *Irish Tune from County Derry* (made in 1920 for military band and pipe-organ). That just leaves the boisterous *Marching Song of Democracy* (in a transcription that dates from July 1948), which Rundell again directs as to the manner born. All in all, this is a most entertaining and stimulating release.

Keyboard Works

Piano Music for four hands, Volume 3
Rondo. Crew of the Long Dragon. Fantasy on George Gershwin's 'Porgy and Bess'. Ye Banks and Braes, BFMS32. Tiger-Tiger, KS4/JBC9. Walking Tune, RMTB3. **C Scott** Three Symphonic Dances. **Delius** A Dance Rhapsody No 1, RTVI/18. **Grieg** Knut Lurasens Halling II. **Addinsell** Festival. **Le Jeune** La Bel'aronde. **Gershwin** Girl Crazy – Embraceable you (all trans Grainger)

Penelope Thwaites, John Lavender *pfs*

Pearl SHECD9631 (78 minutes: DDD) Ⓕ
Recorded 1989-1991

Volume 3 of Grainger's music for four hands (Volume 2 is no longer available) contains short original compositions and a number of his transcriptions. These latter are fascinating in their admirable combination of scrupulous fidelity and creative rethinking for an entirely different medium. You would not necessarily think that a transcription, even for two pianos, of Delius's First *Dance Rhapsody* could possibly work with any real degree of success. However, the reality is that it works so well that some may even prefer Grainger's version to the original. In the *Porgy and Bess Fantasy* he treats the tunes with loving respect, but as a pianist he cannot help seeing different ways of presenting them: the very big gestures in 'My man's gone now'; a searching little prelude to 'It ain't necessarily so' implying all sorts of interesting things that Grainger could have done with that slithery little tune if he weren't obliged to play it straight – which he then does, and with sparkling enjoyment.

Grainger Jutish Medley, DFMS8. Colonial Song, S1. Molly on the Shore, BFMS1. Harvest Hymn. Spoon River, AFMS1. Country Gardens, BFMS22. Walking Tune, RMTB3. Mock Morris, RMTB1. Ramble on Themes from Richard Strauss's 'Der Rosenkavalier'. Shepherd's Hey, BFMS4. Irish Tune from County Derry, BFMS6. Handel in the Strand, RMTB2. The Hunter in his career, OEPM4. Scotch Strathspey and Reel, BFMS37. In a Nutshell Suite – No 4, The Gum-suckers March. The Merry King, BFMS38. In Dahomey **Stanford** (arr Grainger) Four Irish Dances, Op 89 – No 1, A March-Jig; No 4, A Reel

Marc-André Hamelin *pf*

Hyperion CDA66884 (73 minutes: DDD) Ⓕ
Recorded 1996

This is perhaps one of the most riveting and satisfying anthologies of Grainger's music. Hamelin's superb control and artistry just about sweep the board if you're looking for a disc that not only brings you all the old favourites but also explores some of the less familiar music, such as Grainger's arrangements of two of Stanford's

Irish Dances, the Cakewalk Smasher, *In Dahomey* or some of the rather less familiar folk-music settings such as *The Merry King* – the latter a delightful discovery. The deceptive ease with which Hamelin presents these pieces is quite breathtaking. The *Irish Tune from County Derry*, for instance, contains some exacting problems which call on the pianist to play *ppp* in the outer fingers and *mf* with the middle in order to bring out the melody which Grainger places almost entirely within the middle register of the piano, and yet Hamelin makes it sound incredibly natural. His subtle control of melodic voicing can also be heard in, among other pieces, the marvellous *Scotch Strathspey and Reel* and the *Jutish Medley* and in the gorgeous *Ramble on Themes from Richard Strauss's 'Der Rosenkavalier'*, Hamelin's mastery of the pedal (especially the seldom used middle pedal) is a real delight. This is a very desirable Grainger anthology.

Songs

David of the White Rock[a]. Died for Love, BFMS10[a]. The Sprig of Thyme, BFMS24[a]. Willow, Willow, OEPM1[a]. Near Woodstock Town[a]. Early one morning[a]. In Bristol Town (arr Gibbs)[d]. Songs of the North[a] – No 2, This is no my plaid; No 3, Turn ye to me; No 4, Skye Boat Song; No 5, Weaving Song. The Bridegroom Grat[a]. The Land O' the Leal[a] (both arr Ould). Proud Vesselil[a] (ed Thwaites). Under a bridge[ac]. Hubby and Wifey, DFMS5[ac]. The Lonely Desert-Man sees the Tents of the Happy Tribes, RMTB9[abc]. Colonial Song[ab]. The Only Son, KS21[ab]. The Love Song of Har Dyal, KS11[ac]. A Song of Autumn[a]. Five Settings of Ella Grainger[a]. O Glorious, Golden Era[a]. Little Ole with his Umbrella[a]. Variations on Handel's 'The Harmonious Blacksmith'[a] (ed Ould). Harvest Hymn[ae]. After-word[a]

Della Jones *mez* [a]**Penelope Thwaites** *pf* with [b]**Mark Padmore** *ten* [c]**Stephen Varcoe** *bar* [d]**George Black** *gtr* [e]**John Lavender** *pf*

Chandos Grainger Edition CHAN9730 Ⓕ
(74 minutes: DDD). Texts included. Recorded 1998 ⭘

Again Grainger amazes, amuses, arouses, intrigues. These 'Songs for mezzo' originate in Britain (with an excellent sequence of Scottish songs), Jutland and Australia. Some are folk-songs collected in the early years of the century; two have words by Kipling, five by Ella, Grainger's wife, and some have no words at all. The latter are fortifying antidotes to those text-merchants who think that song is essentially 'about' the communication of words, whereas everybody knows that you sing (la-la, dee-dee, as in these of Grainger) because a tune has taken your fancy and singing it makes you feel better.

It is really Della Jones's record, or hers and that of the admirable Penelope Thwaites. But the menfolk appear occasionally and always to effect. Mark Padmore is a resourceful tenor with hints here that he has in reserve a vibrant, rather Italianate body of tone. This emerges in *The only son* (the dream of Mowgli the wolfman). Better than that, however, is *The Lonely Desert-Man sees the tents of the Happy Tribes*, where the tenor has the 'Lonely Man' theme, and the two other voices sing a song of happiness and innocence.

Della Jones hereself is a natural for Grainger: she has the spirit to match, and, like him, a certain ambiguity in her forthrightness, so that at times we're not quite sure about what is serious and what is a bit of fun. The *Colonial Song* ('Sentimental No 1') is unashamedly nostalgic, but with an element of send-up too: in the piano solos especially a joyful passage of inspired improvisation that is both a joke and 'for real'. Also for real is the prime quality of this disc, with 15 tracks 'première recordings' and 14 'première recordings in this version'.

Rudyard Kipling Settings – Dedication, KS1, Dedication II; Anchor Song; The Widow's Party, KS7; Soldier, Soldier; The Sea-wife; Ganges Pilot; The First Chantey; The Young British Soldier. Three Settings of Robert Burns. Songs of the North – Fair Young Mary, SON7; The Woman are a Gane Wud, SON9; My Faithful Fond One, SON10; O'er the Moor, SON12. The Power of Love, DFMS4. The Twa Corbies. A Reiver's Neck-Verse. Lord Maxwell's Goodnight, BFMS14

Martyn Hill *ten* **Penelope Thwaites** *pf*

Chandos Grainger Edition CHAN9610 Ⓕ
(69 minutes: DDD). Texts included ⭘

Grainger cared for neither rules nor forms; he wrote what he wanted and for whom he wanted, and one sees him flinging down collar and tie to do it. A singer probably needs to shed a few inhibitions in coping with these songs, and if Martyn Hill had any to start with he has got rid of them like the discarded collar and tie. He gives magnificent performances, and is matched by Penelope Thwaites who seems unerringly to make sense of the idiosyncratic piano parts. Some are folk-songs or settings of Burns, and in at least one of these – *Afton Water* – a comparison with Britten's way with folk-song inevitably comes to mind, Grainger being similarly determined and single-minded in working out his concept, but exquisite in the delicacy of his murmurous water-colouring. Then in others he stands almost in reproach of Britten, for the traditional melody so 'takes' him that he wants little more than to present it, lovingly, almost reverently, in its own unadorned beauty. As for the eight poems of Kipling – one of them being set twice – they inspire him with a sense of strange, fierce compassion and unquenchable energy: 'ballads' as they are, surely too close to brutally humorous reality to be regarded as being acceptable in the drawing-room'ballad' musical-evenings of the age.

The song with two settings is *Dedication*, or 'Mother o' mine', a poem in passionately bad taste that must have meant something special to Grainger (with that mother o' his). Martyn Hill sings with fine abandon, especially in the first version with its desperately high-lying phrases at the start and its ultimate abasement. To the 'character' songs – *The Widow's Party* and the relentless *Young British Soldier* for instance – he brings an unfailingly right touch, directed by a sense of passionate, imaginative conviction.

His voice is not now beautiful, at any rate not above a *mezzo-forte*; but it is pliant and resourceful, and at times capable of most lovely 'pure' singing. He has made many good recordings, but this, surely, is his masterpiece.

The Power of Love, DFMS4. Early one morning. Scherzo. Random Round, RMTB8. O Gin I Were Where Gadie Rins, SON13. Skye Boat Song, SON3. Danny Deever, KS12. Irish Tune from County Derry (all ed Ould). Mock Morris, RMTB1. Died For Love, BFMS10 (ed Perna). Love Verses from 'The Song of Solomon'. Shepherd's Hey, RMTB3.The Three Ravens, BFMS41. Youthful Rapture. The Merry King, BFMS39 (ed Rogers). Dollar and a Half a Day, SCS2. Molly on the shore, BFMS1
Susan Gritton *sop* **Pamela Helen Stephen** *mez* **Mark Tucker** *ten* **Stephen Varcoe** *bar* **Tim Hugh** *vc* **Joyful Company of Singers; City of London Sinfonia / Richard Hickox**
Chandos Grainger Edition CHAN9653 Ⓕ
(62 minutes: DDD). Texts included. Recorded 1998 ○

Once considered the musical equivalents of Betjeman's 'chintzy chintzy cheeriness', *Molly on the shore*, *Mock Morris* and *Shepherd's Hey* now raise a delighted smile in appreciation of their energy, wit, skill, grace and joy. Like most of the items here, they are short pieces, and it would be unthinkable to call any of them 'major works'. But in each instance, for the space of three or four minutes, Grainger is the Jupiter of composers: the unfeigned, unforced, Bringer of Jollity. He is other things as well. In all of his folksong arrangements there is scarcely one which at some moment does not make the heart jump, as (for instance) he feels his way towards the secretive beauty of the *Brigg Fair* tune in *Died For Love* or as he commits himself with unstinting sympathy and inflamed musical imagination to the protest of *Dollar and a Half*. His *Random Round*, meant for improvisation but eventually (in 1943) written out, begins as casual fun and ends in something very like ecstasy. Among the soloists, Susan Gritton brings a pure tone and a ready understanding, and Stephen Varcoe leads a haunting performance of *The Three Ravens*. The Joyful Company of Singers deserves to remain so, and with Richard Hickox, the City of London Sinfonia sound as though they are playing for pleasure too. With fine sound and a good booklet, the disc is a stayer.

Awards 1996

I'm Seventeen Come Sunday, BFMS8. Brigg Fair, BFMS7. Love Verses from 'The Song of Solomon'. The Merry Wedding. Shallow Brown, SCS3. Father and Daughter. My Dark-Haired Maid, 'Mo Nighean Dhu'. The Bride's Tragedy. Irish Tune from County Derry, BFMS5. Scotch Strathspey and Reel, BFMS28. The Lost Lady Found, BFMS33. The Three Ravens, BFMS41. Danny Deever. Tribute to Foster
Monteverdi Choir; English Country Gardiner Orchestra / Sir John Eliot Gardiner
Philips 446 657-2PH (75 minutes: DDD) Ⓕ
Texts included. Recorded 1994-95 ○○○

The really startling thing about all these settings is the way in which Grainger unlocks the *inner* life of each text, each melody. He'll digest it, understand it, respect it, and then in his response – which is nothing if not personal – he'll elaborate, creating as little or as much subtext as is appropriate. Like Britten, in his folk-song settings, Grainger knew how and when to get out of the way. The plaintive *Brigg Fair* is no more, no less than the tenor solo and chiefly wordless chorus will allow us – a tune so precious to Grainger that even the harmony is almost an intrusion. Then there is the classic *Londonderry Air* – no words, just voices – a harmony that is so rich, so expressive, so integrated, that it always shrouds the melody in the imagination. Then what, you may ask, could be more extraordinary than the *Love Verses from 'The Song of Solomon'*? Well, *Shallow Brown* for a start, which is astounding. A sea shanty with the reach of a spiritual, it is set as the sailors will have yelled it, the vocal line stretching and distorting, straining to be heard over furious oceanic *tremolandos* in guitars and strings. This is a fabulous disc. John Eliot Gardiner may have inherited some of his joy in this music from his great-uncle, Balfour Gardiner (one of the 'Frankfurt Gang', which included Grainger). He is hot in his response to its rhythmic zest as are his wonderfully articulate and impeccably tuned Monteverdi singers and players. The singing is, by turns, fleet, spry, fireside-cosy cathedral-rich – or plain raucous. The recorded sound is brilliant and revealing.

Enrique Granados

Spanish 1867-1916

GROVE *Granados studied in Barcelona with Pedrell and in Paris (1887-89), then returned to Barcelona to work as a teacher, pianist and composer. His greatest success came with the piano suite Goyescas (1911), a sequence of highly virtuoso studies after paintings by Goya he expanded them to form an opera of the same title, produced in New York in 1916. His other works include songs, orchestral pieces and more piano music.*

Danzas españolas

12 Danzas españolas, Op 37. 7 Valses poéticos
Alicia de Larrocha *pf*
RCA Victor Red Seal 09026 68184-2 Ⓕ
(68 minutes: DDD). Recorded 1994 ○

Alicia de Larrocha, that incomparable interpreter of the Spanish repertoire, is here revisiting many of her favourite musical haunts. And if some of her former edge and fire, her tonal and stylistic luxuriance are now replaced by more 'contained' and reflective qualities, her warmth and affection remain undimmed. Her rubato, while less lavishly deployed than before, is potent and alluring, and each and every dance is played with rare naturalness, ease and authority.

But if a touch of sobriety occasionally blunts the fullest impact of these fascinating, most aristocratic idealizations of local Spanish life and colour, the actual playing is never less than masterly. The *Valses poéticos* are offered as an engaging encore. The recordings have much less range and reverberance than her previous ones on Decca; however, all lovers of this repertoire will want to add this to their collection.

Goyescas

Granados Goyescas **Albéniz** Iberia. Navarra
Alicia de Larrocha *pf*
Double Decca ② 448 191-2DF2 (141 minutes: ADD) Ⓜ
Recorded 1972-76 **OO**

Alicia de Larrocha has been playing these works, the greatest in the repertoire of Spanish piano music, all her life. Complete technical assurance in these extremely demanding works has now become taken for granted, and Larrocha is not unique in mastering their terrors; but though there have been other distinguished interpreters, her readings have consistently remained a touchstone. She employs plenty of subtle rubato but possesses the ability to make it sound as natural as breathing. In the true sense of that much-misused word, this is classical playing, free from any superimposed striving for effect but responding fully to the music's sense of colour; and even in the densest of textures she is able to control conflicting tonal levels. *Goyescas,* which can tempt the unwary into exaggerated 'expressiveness', brings forth a wealth of poetic nuance, without losing shape – as for instance in the splendid 'El amor y la muerte'. The recorded quality throughout always was good and here emerges as fresh as ever. Anyone who does not already possess these recordings in one of their previous issues should not hesitate to acquire them now – all the more since the two discs together cost the same as one full-price one.

Goyescas. El pelele
Eric Parkin *pf*
Chandos CHAN9412 (61 minutes: DDD) Ⓕ
Recorded 1993

The Granados *Goyescas* are profoundly Spanish in feeling, but the folk influence is more of court music than of the flamenco or *cante hondo* styles which reflect gipsy and Moorish influence. A direction in the score at the beginning of the *Goyescas* is *con garbo y donaire* ('with charm and elegance'). The description aptly fits Parkin's performances. His readings have an element of free rubato, but this is never excessive, and it serves to underline the improvisatory nature of these pieces. Aided by a clean technique in this sometimes complex texture he gives persuasive performances that also contain much poetry. He captures the dignified flamboyance of the traditional dance in the 'Fandango by candlelight', carefully observing the direction *avec beaucoup de rythme*. Two of the hardest tests for a pianist in this collection of Goyesque studies are the preservation of coherence in the long 'Serenata del espectro' and the avoidance of mawkishness in 'La maja y el ruiseñor': Parkin emerges successfully from both. A piano with bright top octaves was perhaps not the ideal instrument for this recording, but there is no lack of colour or nuance from the performer.

Alexandr Grechaninov

Russian/American 1864-1956

Grechaninov studied at the Moscow Conservatory (1881-90) and with Rimsky-Korsakov at the St Petersburg Conservatory (1890-93) and worked as a piano teacher and folksong arranger; in 1910 he received a pension for his liturgical music. But that ceased with the Revolution, and in 1925 he settled in Paris, moving to the USA in 1929. His large output (nearly 200 opus numbers) includes operas, five symphonies, masses, songs and piano music.

Piano Trios

No 1 in C minor, Op 38; No 2 in G, Op 128
Bekova Sisters (Elvira Bekova *vn* Alfia Bekova *vc* Eleonora Bekova *pf*)
Chandos CHAN9461 (53 minutes: DDD) Ⓕ
Recorded 1996

Composed in 1906, Grechaninov's First Piano Trio is a typical product of Russia's 'Silver Age': typical in its expert, school-of-Rimsky craftsmanship, typical in its languishing lyricism, typical in its fundamental complacency. The first movement draws heavily on the figurations from Tchaikovsky's Fourth Symphony but divests them of all emotional immediacy or dangerous intensity. This makes for pleasant, undemanding listening, and throws into relief the achievements of Rachmaninov, Scriabin and Stravinsky. But don't expect more than that. Grechaninov is one of several candidates for the label of 'the Russian Brahms'. That fits him as unsatisfactorily as it does Taneyev or Glazunov, but the finale of his Second Trio at least shows why it sticks. This playful, yet sturdy and well-crafted music has a feel of 1881 rather than 1931. Composed in California, at two removes from the Russia its composer had left six years earlier, its childlike escapism is touching, and its sounds agreeable and rewarding to play. Strong, enjoyable, upfront performances from the talented Bekova sisters; the recording is well lubricated with resonance, but not absurdly so.

All-Night Vigil

All-Night Vigil, Op 59. Nunc dimittis, Op 34 No 1. **P**
The Seven Days of the Passion, Op 58 – No 3, In Thy Kingdom[a]; No 6, Now the Powers of Heaven
[a]**James Bowman** *counterten* **Holst Singers / Stephen Layton**
Hyperion CDA67080 (63 minutes: DDD) Texts and translations included. Recorded 1998 Ⓕ **OO**

Grechaninov's music has begun once more to be performed and recorded as it deserves. There are excellent discs available of several of his Liturgies, Masses, the oratorio *The Seven Days of the Passion* and also his orchestral music. The *All-Night Vigil* is an outstanding achievement. Like Rachmaninov's famous setting, it is a selection of texts from the services of Vespers and Matins celebrated as a Vigil, though in current parish practice this lasts rather less than an entire night. Grechaninov sets fewer texts: the duration of the work is just over 47 minutes. Here we find the sustained chordal writing and slow-moving melodies oscillating around a few notes familiar from Rachmaninov, but Grechaninov has his own distinctive harmonic vocabulary, and his writing is less text-driven. Chant is an inspiration, but is also used in a different way from Rachmaninov: none is quoted in its entirety, the composer preferring instead to use fragments of various chants which are combined and juxtaposed with considerable freedom. He is a master of texture: listen to the astonishing darkness of sound produced by the scoring for lower voices in *Ot yunosti moyeya*, for example. Overall there is a feeling of luminosity in the writing, however, as well as an undeniable grandeur, to which the exclusive use of brilliant major keys contributes greatly. To round off the disc we are given three other liturgical works, including a dramatic setting of the Beatitudes (sung at the Divine Liturgy) with James Bowman as soloist. The Holst Singers under Stephen Layton are superb: they have a complete mastery of the style and the fine, rich choral timbre which the music demands. Very highly recommended.

Edvard Grieg — Norwegian 1843-1907

GROVE *Grieg studied with EF Wenzel at the Leipzig Conservatory (1858-62), where he became intimately familiar with early Romantic music (especially Schumann's), gaining further experience in Copenhagen and encouragement from Niels Gade. Not until 1864-65 and his meeting with the Norwegian nationalist Rikard Nordraak did his stylistic breakthrough occur, notably in the folk-inspired Humoresker for piano Op 6. Apart from promoting Norwegian music through concerts of his own works, he obtained pupils, became conductor of the Harmoniske Selskab, projected a Norwegian Academy of Music and helped found the Christiania Musikforening (1871), meanwhile composing his Piano Concerto (1868) and the important piano arrangements of 25 of Lindeman's folksongs (Op 17, 1869). An operatic collaboration with Bjornson came to nothing, but his incidental music to Ibsen's Peer Gynt (1875), the most extensive and best known of his large compositions, produced some of his finest work. Despite chronic ill-health he continued to tour as a conductor and pianist and to execute commissions from his base at Troldhaugen (from 1885); he received numerous international honours. Among his later works, The Mountain Thrall Op 32 for baritone, two horns and strings, the String Quartet in G minor Op 27, the popular neo-Baroque Holberg Suite (1884) and the Haugtussa song cycle Op 67 (1895) are the most distinguished.*

Grieg was first and foremost a lyrical composer; his Op 33 Vinje settings, for example, encompass a wide range of emotional expression and atmospheric colour, and the ten opus numbers of Lyric Pieces for piano hold a wealth of characteristic mood-sketches. But he also was a pioneer, in the impressionistic uses of harmony and piano sonority in his late songs and in the dissonance treatment in the Slåtter Op 72, peasant fiddle-tunes arranged for piano.

Piano Concerto

Grieg Piano Concerto in A minor, Op 16[b]
Debussy Préludes – Book 1[a]
Arturo Benedetti Michelangeli *pf* [b]**New Philharmonia Orchestra / Rafael Frühbeck de Burgos**
BBC Legends/IMG Artists [b]mono/[a]stereo
BBCL4043-2 (69 minutes: DDD/ADD) Ⓜ
Recorded live in [b]1965 and [a]1982 ●●●

Somehow you feel it must be possible to deliver the hackneyed opening flourishes of the Grieg Concerto with real abandon and impetuosity, to get the orchestra to respond to them with genuine ardour, then for the soloist to combine flow, virtuoso dash, fantasy and noble eloquence and to crown the structural highpoints in a way that lifts you out of your seat. Yet until you hear a performance like this one you may never quite believe it can be done. A sense of joyous rhapsody buoys up Michelangeli's playing from first note to last, yet everything is founded on a bedrock of high intelligence, taste and natural authority. Witness too the fabulous tone-colours he draws from the instrument. His slow movement is by turns balmy and ecstatic, and the finale has terrific drive. Scarcely a phrase that does not sound newly minted; never a note that sounds contrived or unspontaneous. And the virtuosity...! If your hair is not standing on end in the finale's coda you need an urgent medical check-up. Forget the boxy recording and the hissy background. This is a performance that entirely merits the hysterical cheers that greet it.

Seventeen years on, Michelangeli's Debussy also provokes rapturous applause, but in this instance it was probably partly a tribute to his by this time legendary status – he was 63 and rapidly becoming as famous for his cancellations as for his performances. Of course there are marvels of pianism here, but an air of calculation hangs over much of the playing, all the more apparent when heard straight after the dumbfounding Grieg Concerto. Those who have Michelangeli's 1978 DG studio version will find little to prefer here, apart, perhaps, from the slightly warmer acoustic.

Grieg Piano Concerto[a]. Piano Sonata in E minor, Op 7[b] **Schumann** Piano Concerto in A minor, Op 54[a]
[a]**Stephen Kovacevich,** [b]**Zoltán Kocsis** *pfs*
BBC Symphony Orchestra / Sir Colin Davis
Philips 446 192-2PM (78 minutes: [a]ADD/[b]DDD) Ⓕ
●

Stephen Kovacevich's natural, intimately poetic phrasing, his delicately glistening fingerwork and his bravura and rhythmic virility, too, when required (as in Grieg's finale) must be noted first. Yet it is difficult to recall any other performance in which pianist, conductor and orchestra are in closer or more subtly balanced and shaded accord than in this classic account. Every participant sounds as personally involved as they would in chamber music-making. The sound quality has not the forward brightness of present-day reproduction. But its old-world mellowness seems just right for performances as loving as these. For good measure we're even given an encore – though there is no mention of it in the accompanying booklet-notes – and from a different pianist. But Zoltán Kocsis's account of Grieg's early E minor Sonata is sufficiently incisive and characterful to justify resurgence.

Grieg Piano Concerto **Schumann** Piano Concerto in A minor, Op 54
Murray Perahia *pf* **Bavarian Radio Symphony Orchestra / Sir Colin Davis**
Sony Classical SK44899 (60 minutes: DDD) Ⓕ
Recorded live in 1987 and 1988 **OO**

Despite the hazards, Murray Perahia delights in the inspirational heat-of-the-moment of a live recording. Though there are no claps, coughs or shuffles to confirm the presence of an audience, we're told that both concertos were recorded live at Munich's Philharmonie Gasteig. Of the two works, the Grieg is better served by the immediacy and warmth of Perahia's response, whether through rhythmic bite in livelier dance tempo or total surrender to lyrical nostalgia elsewhere. Never is there the slightest sacrifice of artistic sensitivity or keyboard finesse. You will be delighted that someone so dedicated to Mozart, Beethoven and the light-fingered Mendelssohn could so patently revel in Grieg's unabashed sentiment and bravura. His Schumann is no less ardent. In the spirited finale, as throughout the Grieg, any collector would be as happy with this performance as that of Kovacevich for Philips. But in the first two movements, where Schumann speaks more personally, it is Kovacevich who finds a simpler, more confiding note – as well as more artfully weaving the piano into the comparatively light texture as if it were part of the orchestra instead of a spot-lit outsider. Davis goes all the way in both works to uphold Perahia in his open-hearted point-making, and the Bavarian Radio Symphony Orchestra gives him all he asks. The sound is more arrestingly clear-cut than the old Philips, which is still pleasing for its mellowness and balance.

Grieg Piano Concerto[a] **Schumann** Piano Concerto in A minor, Op 54[a]. Romance in F sharp, Op 28 No 2. Vogel als Prophet, Op 82 No 7 **Palmgren** West-Finnish Dance, Op 31 No 5. Refrain de berceau **H**
Benno Moiseiwitsch *pf* [a]**Philharmonia Orchestra / Otto Ackermann**
Testament mono SBT1187 (70 minutes: ADD) Ⓕ
Recorded 1941, [a]1953 **O**

Few pianists have played the silken aristocrat more engagingly than Benno Moiseiwitsch. His outward impassivity (celebrated in a Savage Club cartoon) hid an imaginative delicacy and stylish nonchalance often mistaken for diffidence. Playful, individual, debonair, occasionally mischievous (why not expand on the last pages of the Grieg Concerto's cadenza if you feel like it?), he invariably had one more surprise up his sleeve than you expected. Both the Grieg and Schumann Concertos were central to Moiseiwitsch's immense repertoire and, as with so many other Russian pianists, Schumann remained his greatest love. His opening to the Schumann Concerto is understated (like a great actor throwing away his lines), but his projection of the principal theme has a matchless tonal bloom and subtlety. The *espressivo* at 1'43" is, again, vintage Moiseiwitsch, and how many other pianists have eased their way through the central A flat dreams with such unaffected charm? In the opening of the Intermezzo he is delightfully *grazioso*, emphasising the *staccatos* as much as the manifold feelings and colours, and in the finale his play of light and shade are, again, inimitable Moiseiwitsch. The Grieg Concerto, too, sounds newly minted, with markings such as *tranquillo e cantabile* observed with special affection. The catalogue may be filled with more openly confrontational performances but Moiseiwitsch, who took music more by stealth than storm, elegantly eclipses the readings of so many more assertive keyboard tigers. For encores there are classic performances of Palmgren (a composer Moiseiwitsch made his own) and Schumann. Ackermann's partnership is arguably more able than inspiring, but Testament's transfers of recordings dating from 1941 to 1953 are superb.

Peer Gynt Suites

Grieg Peer Gynt – Suites Nos 1 and 2, Opp 46 and 55. Holberg Suite, Op 40 **Sibelius** Legends, Op 22 – No 2, The Swan of Tuonela. Kuolema – Valse triste, Op 44. Finlandia, Op 26
Berlin Philharmonic Orchestra / Herbert von Karajan
DG Karajan Gold 439 010-2GHS (78 minutes: DDD) Ⓜ
Recorded 1981-84 **OO**

Very impressive indeed. Comparing the LP and CD formats, the greater definition and presence of the latter tells, particularly at the bass end of the spectrum. Somehow one feels that one could stretch out and touch the players, so vivid is the sound. In the *Peer Gynt* movements, there is much greater range and separation. *Peer Gynt* is most beautifully done. At times you might think the wind could have been a shade more distant, particularly in the 'By the seashore' movement but there is no want of atmosphere here – quite the contrary! Not to put too fine a point on it, this is a marvellous recording. In the *Holberg Suite*, the sound has marvellous clarity and definition as well as exemplary range. For some tastes it may be a little too sophisticated but one's admiration for it remains undimmed. The playing throughout is beautifully cultured and there is wonderful lightness and delicacy. The present issue is Karajan's third account of 'The Swan of Tuonela' and it is regrettable that he never committed to disc the four *Legends* in their entirety. It is as powerful and atmospheric an account as ever recorded, and the remaining two pieces, 'Valse triste' and *Finlandia*, reinforce one's feeling that this partnership has never been equalled. The stirring account of *Finlandia* is incredibly wide-ranging – the orchestral playing is really in a class of its own.

Grieg Peer Gynt – Suites Nos 1 and 2, Opp 46 and 55
Saeverud Peer Gynt, Op 28 – Suites Nos 1 and 2
Anne-Margrethe Eikaas *sop*
Norwegian Radio Orchestra / Ari Rasilainen
Finlandia 0630-17675-2 (74 minutes: DDD) Ⓕ
Recorded 1996 ◉

To juxtapose the *Peer Gynt* music of Grieg and Saeverud on record is such an obvious idea that it is astonishing that no one has thought of it before. It was inevitable that there should be a reaction against the pictorialism and romanticism of Grieg's *Peer Gynt*, particularly after the upheaval of the Second World War and the Nazi occupation of Norway, and when Saeverud was approached by Hans Jacob Nilsen to compose his incidental music, it was for a realistic production shorn of sentiment and glamour. Saeverud's score for the play has no vestige of romanticism, not a trace of gentility, and its musical language is robust and uncouth. It is full of character, whether it is in 'Peerludium', the portrayal of the cocky Peer himself, the wild and lascivious 'Anitra' (nothing demure about her) or the splendidly earthy 'Devil's Five-hop' and the equally brilliant 'Dovretroll jog'. The Norwegian Radio Orchestra is a highly accomplished body with great refinement of colour and tone, and Ari Rasilainen draws splendid, well-characterised playing from them. The familiar Grieg suites are hardly less fine. The recording is refined.

Holberg Suite. Two Elegiac Melodies, Op 34. Peer Gynt – Suites Nos 1 and 2. Two Lyric Pieces
Academy of St Martin in the Fields / Sir Neville Marriner
Hänssler Classic 98 995 (66 minutes: DDD) Ⓕ
Recorded 1994 ◉

The clean ruggedness of Grieg's music comes across well here. Indeed, there is much to praise: the sheer zest of the opening *Allegro vivace* of the *Holberg Suite* and, in the same five-movement work, the way Marriner and his players convey the necessary 'period' quality. The *Two Elegiac Melodies* are also fine; the second of them is the poignant 'Last spring' and features some movingly hushed playing from the violins. The incidental music to *Peer Gynt*, which follows, has a similarly attractive freshness. One gets the impression that this is the kind of music that the ASMF can play beautifully at the drop of a hat, but beautiful playing it remains, with nothing routine about it. Even the well-worn 'Morning' in Suite No 1 sounds as fresh as if it were the morning of the world, and one could not ask for a more loving account of 'Solveig's Song'. The two transcriptions of the *Lyric Pieces* are also evocative, with fine oboe playing in the first, 'Evening in the mountains'. The recording is richly reverberant but permits detail to emerge.

Peer Gynt – Suites: No 1, Op 46; No 2, Op 55. In Autumn, Op 11. Symphonic Dances, Op 64
City of Birmingham Symphony Orchestra / Sakari Oramo
Erato 8573-82917-2 (74 minutes: DDD) Ⓕ
Recorded 2000 ◉

As soon as the strings respond to the flute near the beginning of *Peer Gynt*'s 'Morning' – longingly leaning on an expressive *ritardando* – you sense this is a quality production. Done to death it may be, but Grieg's vernal score still holds the potential to seduce, enthral and entertain. Here, charm and drama form a seductive alliance. Sakari Oramo has an architect's sense of proportion and an athlete's sense of pacing. He also knows how to shape and colour musical textures. Ase's death ends with a full-bodied *pianissimo* while the bassoon counter-subject that follows Peer through 'The Hall of the Mountain King' can rarely have sounded more mischievous. Rather than push an unworkable *accellerando*, Oramo moves with stealth, tightening the rhythm as he goes, letting in an element of swagger before speeding for the final chase. 'Ingrid's Lament' enjoys powerfully drawn basses and an unusually dramatic climax and 'Peer Gynt's Journey Home' allows ample space for the elements to rage. Note how, at around 1'14", woodwinds goad lower strings into action and the ensuing tumult gradually gains momentum. As for 'Anitra' and the 'Arabian Dance', both benefit from the CBSO's vivid but unforced characterisations.

In the booklet-notes we learn that the Concert Overture *In Autumn* takes its point of departure from a song called *Autumn Storms*. And if there's one aspect of Oramo's performance that pips Beecham's stereo version to the post, it's a feeling of what one might call 'weatheredness'. True, the superb recording helps, but so do Oramo's rock-steady control of rhythm and sense of atmosphere.

The *Symphonic Dances* are by turns lyrical or exuberant, the last of them – the partially pensive A minor – being faster than Järvi's thinner-sounding Gothenburg version by a good two minutes. The Birmingham orchestra are consistently responsive to Oramo's very specific demands. Rather than rest on laurels left them by Sir Simon Rattle, they have taken Oramo's cue for a rather different brand of instrumental projection, weightier than before perhaps, less concerned with textual minutiae and rather more inclined to flair at the nostrils.

Credible rivals are headed by piquant Sir Thomas in *Peer Gynt* and *In Autumn*, and by Järvi in the *Symphonic Dances*. Oramo's Grieg matches both, being less fussy than keen-eared and with a sense of play that does credit both to Ibsen's dramatic prompt and the folk-music roots of the concert works.

Norwegian Dances

Norwegian Dances, Op 35. Lyric Suite, Op 54. Symphonic Dances, Op 64
Gothenburg Symphony Orchestra / Neeme Järvi
DG 419 431-2GH (68 minutes: DDD) Ⓕ ●

These recordings have just been reissued in a six-CD bargain box of Grieg's complete orchestral works: DG 471 300-2GB6 ●●

Grieg's music has that rare quality of eternal youth: however often one hears it, its complexion retains its bloom, the smile its radiance and the youthful sparkle remains undimmed. Though he is essentially a miniaturist, who absorbed the speech rhythms and inflections of Norwegian folk melody into his bloodstream, Grieg's world is well defined. Both the *Norwegian Dances* and the *Symphonic Dances* were originally piano duets, which Grieg subsequently scored: Järvi conducts both with enthusiasm and sensitivity. In the *Lyric Suite* he restores 'Klokkeklang' ('Bell-ringing'), which Grieg omitted from the final score: it is remarkably atmospheric and evocative, and serves to show how forward-looking Grieg became in his late years. The recording is exceptionally fine and of wide dynamic range; the sound is very natural and the perspective true to life.

String Quartets

Grieg String Quartets – No 1 in G minor, Op 27; No 2 in F, CW146 **Schumann** String Quartet No 1 in A minor, Op 41 No 1
Petersen Quartet (Conrad Muck, Gernot Süssmuth *vns* Friedemann Weigle *va* Hans Jakob Eschenburg *vc*)
Capriccio 10 476 (75 minutes: DDD) Ⓕ
Recorded 1993

Grieg String Quartet No 1 in G minor, Op 27
Mendelssohn String Quartet No 2 in A minor, Op 13
Shanghai Quartet (WeiGang Li, HongGang Li *vns* Zheng Wang *va* James Wilson *vc*)
Delos DE3153 (64 minutes: DDD) Ⓕ ●
Recorded 1993

Since Grieg owed much to Schumann, coupling their quartets seems a good idea. These G minor and A minor Quartets were written when the composers were in their thirties, although Grieg was a few years older. Yet it is his work that sounds more youthfully passionate, while the Schumann is a rather self-conscious homage to his friend Mendelssohn and classical models. The Petersens invest the Grieg G minor Quartet with *gravitas* and are skilful in linking the disparate sections of its structure. Their recording has a natural balance and an impressively wide dynamic rang; it also copes well with Grieg's forceful, semi-orchestral string writing. The whole performance has vigour and tenderness in good proportion, and a truly Scandinavian feeling. The unfinished F major Quartet is another sensitive performance and the work sounds no more incomplete than Schubert's *Unfinished* Symphony. The Schumann is no less enjoyable; the artists are fully inside his idiom and make a consistently beautiful and meaningful sound. The Shanghai Quartet's brightly lit account of the Mendelssohn suggests a rich store of interpretative potential. Theirs is a sizzling, multi-coloured performance. The Grieg coupling is, if anything, even finer, with an *Allegro molto* first movement that truly is *ed agitato*, a warming *Romanze* and a superbly characterised *Intermezzo*. It is arguably the most compelling performance of this endearing score since the original Budapest Quartet's trail-blazing HMV 78s from 1937. It is richly recorded.

Violin Sonatas

No 1 in F, Op 8; **No 2** in G, Op 13; **No 3** in C minor, Op 45

Augustin Dumay *vn* **Maria João Pires** *pf*
DG 437 525-2GH (70 minutes: DDD) Ⓕ
Recorded 1993 ●

Grieg's violin sonatas span his creative life, the first two dating from his early twenties, before his Piano Concerto, and the Third Sonata of 1887 belonging to the last decade of his life. Augustin Dumay brings to this music a youthful *seigneur*, manifest in the impetuosity, charm and command of his playing. He and Maria João Pires are at their considerable best in the G major Sonata, with its vivid first movement, lilting *Allegretto* and triumphant finale – whose conclusion they lift to the skies. The recording does full justice to Dumay's silky and resourceful tone. Pires is rightly an equal partner, and both artists bring an infectiously fresh response to the music. The finale of the C minor Sonata, which anticipates Sibelius in its urgency and elemental force, is compellingly played.

Violin Sonatas Nos 1-3
Henning Kraggerud *vn* **Helge Kjekshus** *pf*
Naxos 8 553904 (67 minutes: DDD) Ⓢ
Recorded 1996

This disc gives us consistently enjoyable performances. The two young Norwegians play with idiomatic style, and give the impression of absorbing and expressing every aspect of the music. Their eagerness at the start of Op 8's first *Allegro* sets the tone; the *doloroso* opening of Op 13, the delicacy and serenity of the E major section of that sonata's middle movement, and the exciting 'Hall of the Mountain King' atmosphere they generate in the finale of Op 45 – these are just a few of the places where Kraggerud and Kjekshus convince us they've found exactly the right sound and manner of expression. Dumay and Pires on DG are magnificently recorded, causing one to regret the slight lack of brilliance in the Naxos recording and wish that the violin in particular had been given a more glamorous presence. They are as deeply involved as the Norwegians but play with far greater freedom. However, Kraggerud's account of the 'big tune' in the last movement of Op 45, respecting all Grieg's marks of expression and phrasing, has a nobility that Dumay, more heart-on-sleeve and cavalier about dynamics and slurs, misses. The Naxos disc is, in short, highly recommendable – as a contrast to Dumay/Pires or simply as an excellent bargain.

Piano Works

Volume 1: Piano Sonata in E minor, Op 7. Funeral March for Rikard Nordraak, CW117. Melodies of Norway – The sirens' enticement. Stimmungen, Op 73. Transcriptions of Original Songs I, Op 41 – No 3, I love thee. Four Humoresques, Op 6. Four Piano Pieces, Op 1
Einar Steen-Nøkleberg *pf*
Naxos 8 550881 (72 minutes: DDD) Ⓢ
Recorded 1993

Volume 2
Two Improvisations on Norwegian Folksongs, Op 29. Melodies of Norway – A Ballad to Saint Olaf. 25 Norwegian Folksongs and Dances, Op 17. Transcriptions of Original Songs II, Op 52 – No 2, The first meeting. 19 Norwegian Folksongs, Op 66
Einar Steen-Nøkleberg *pf*
Naxos 8 550882 (70 minutes: DDD) Ⓢ
Recorded 1993

Volume 3
Four Album Leaves, Op 28. Six Poetic Tone-pictures, Op 3. Melodies of Norway – Iceland. Three Pictures from life in the country, Op 19. Three Pieces from 'Sigurd Jorsalfar', Op 56 – Prelude. Ballade in G minor, Op 24, 'in the form of variations on a Norwegian melody'
Einar Steen-Nøkleberg *pf*
Naxos 8 550883 (64 minutes: DDD) Ⓢ
Recorded 1993 ○

Volume 4: Holberg Suite, Op 40. Melodies of Norway – I went to bed so late. Six Norwegian Mountain Melodies, CW134. Peer Gynt Suite No 1, Op 46 – Morning. 17 Norwegian Peasant Dances, Op 72
Einar Steen-Nøkleberg *pf*
Naxos 8 550884 (71 minutes: DDD) Ⓢ
Recorded 1993

These are the first four volumes of a complete Grieg cycle which stretches to no fewer than 14 discs. Since all of them are at super-budget price they make a very competitive alternative to other complete or near-complete surveys. Einar Steen-Nøkleberg came into prominence during the 1970s and won numerous Norwegian and other prizes. He was professor of the piano at the Hanover Musikhochschule for a number of years and is the author of a monograph on Grieg's piano music and its interpretation.
8 550881: The first disc juxtaposes early pieces, the Sonata, Op 7, the Op 6 *Humoresques* and the *Funeral March for Rikard Nordraak*, all written in the mid-1890s with his very last piano work, *Stimmungen* (or 'Moods'), Op 73. He plays these bold and original pieces with great flair and understanding. Whatever its limitations there is much greater range in Grieg's piano music than is commonly realised and Steen-Nøkleberg is attuned to the whole spectrum it covers, whether in the Bartókian 'Mountaineer's Song' from the Op 73 to the charm and innocence of the *Allegretto con grazia*, the third of the *Humoresques*, Op 6. *8 550882*: The *19 Norwegian Folksongs* (1896) are remarkable pieces as Grieg himself knew. He wrote to the Dutch composer, Julius Röntgen, of having 'put some hair-raising chromatic chords on paper. The excuse is that they originated not on the piano but in my mind.' Readers will recognise No 14 as the source of the theme for Delius's *On hearing the first cuckoo in spring*. Steen-Nøkleberg plays them with great tonal finesse and consummate artistry.
8 550883: The most substantial work on this disc is the *Ballade* which Grieg wrote on his parents' death. This recording can hold its own with the best in this healthy area of the catalogue – even if there are moments when Steen-Nøkleberg seems too discursive. Yet what an imaginative colour he produces in the *Adagio* variation when the music suddenly melts *pianissimo*.
8 550884: The *Norwegian Peasant Dances* are amazing pieces for their period, and though their audacity and dissonance were later overtaken by Bartók, they still retain their capacity to surprise. The playing conveys the extraordinary character and originality of these pieces as do few others. The smaller pieces contained on this disc – as well as on its companions – are full of rewards.

Piano Sonata in E minor, Op 7. Six Poetic Tone-pictures, Op 3 – Nos 4-6. Four Album Leaves, Op 28 – No 1 in A flat; No 4 in C sharp minor. Agitato. Lyric Pieces – Book 3, Op 43; Book 5, Op 54
Leif Ove Andsnes *pf*
Virgin Classics VC7 59300-2 (72 minutes: DDD) Ⓕ
Recorded 1992

Andsnes was 22 when he recorded Grieg's Sonata – exactly the composer's age when he wrote it. Despite the heroic opening, Andsnes does not save the first movement from sounding repetitive. It is the two inner movements that display real character and imagination and the pianist rises to the occasion in both. The finale is stunningly played. He is to be heard at his very best in the *Lyric Pieces*, Op 43. One relishes the glinting colours in 'Butterfly', the simple heart-felt yearnings of 'Solitary Wanderer' and the delightful twittering energy of the 'Little Bird'. Here is a pianist with sufficient insight and subtlety not to feel the need to prettify the music. This well-crafted CD has pleasant piano sound, not overclose in impact.

Lyric Pieces – Arietta, Op 12 No 1. Berceuse, Op 38 No 1. Butterfly, Op 43 No 1. Solitary Traveller, Op 43 No 2. Album Leaf, Op 47 No 2. Melody, Op 47 No 3. Norwegian Dance, 'Halling', Op 47 No 4. Nocturne, Op 54 No 4. Scherzo, Op 54 No 5. Homesickness, Op 57 No 6. Brooklet, Op 62 No 4. Homeward, Op 62 No 6. In ballad vein, Op 65 No 5. Grandmother's Minuet, Op 68 No 2. At your feet, Op 68 No 3. Cradle Song, Op 68 No 5. Once upon a time, Op 71 No 1.

Puck, Op 71 No 3. Gone, Op 71 No 6.
Remembrances, Op 71 No 7
Emil Gilels *pf*
DG The Originals 449 721-2GOR (56 minutes: ADD) Ⓜ
Recorded 1974 ●●●

Here, surely, is a classic recording, one of calibre and status for all time. Rarely can a great artist have declared his love with such touching candour. By his own admission Gilels discovered in Grieg's *Lyric Pieces* a 'whole world of intimate feeling' and at the sessions where these were recorded fought tirelessly to capture their intricate mix of innocence and experience. The results are of an unblemished purity, grace and contained eloquence. He brings the same insight and concentration to these apparent trifles as he did to towering masterpieces of the classic repertoire. The programme proceeds chronologically and one can appreciate the gradual but marked development in Grieg's harmonic and expressive language – from the folk-song inspired early works to the more progressive and adventurous later ones. Gilels's fingerwork is exquisite and the sense of total involvement with the music almost religious in feeling. Never can Debussy's sniping estimate of Grieg', 'a pink bonbon filled with snow' (or DG's dreary accompanying notes), have seemed wider of the mark. The recordings remain as impeccable as the playing. This is a disc for everyone's desert island.

Peer Gynt

Peer Gynt – The Bridal March passes by; Prelude; In the Hall of the Mountain King; Solveig's Song; Prelude; Arab Dance; Anitra's Dance; Prelude; Solveig's Cradle Song. Symphonic Dance, Op 64 – Allegretto grazioso. In Autumn, Op 11. Old Norwegian Romance with Variations, Op 51 **H**
Ilse Hollweg *sop* **Beecham Choral Society; Royal Philharmonic Orchestra / Sir Thomas Beecham**
EMI Great Recordings of the Century CDM5 66914-2 Ⓜ
(77 minutes: ADD)
Recorded 1957 ●●

Grieg's incidental music was an integral part of Ibsen's *Peer Gynt* and from this score Grieg later extracted the two familiar suites. This recording of excerpts from *Peer Gynt* goes back to 1957 but still sounds well and is most stylishly played. Included is the best known ('Anitra's Dance' is a delicate gem here) together with 'Solveig's Song' and 'Solveig's Cradle Song'. Beecham uses Ilse Hollweg to advantage, her voice suggesting the innocence of the virtuous and faithful peasant heroine. There is also an effective use of the choral voices which are almost inevitably omitted in ordinary performances of the two well-known orchestral suites: the male chorus of trolls in the 'Hall of the Mountain King' are thrilling, and the women in the 'Arab Dance' are charming. The other two pieces are well worth having too; *Symphonic Dances* is a later, freshly pastoral work, while the overture *In Autumn* is an orchestral second version of an early piece for piano duet. This reissue is further enhanced by the first release in stereo of the *Old Norwegian Romance*.

Songs

Awards 1993

Haugtussa, Op 67. Two brown eyes, Op 5 No 1. I love but thee, Op 5 No 3. A swan, Op 25 No 2. With a waterlily, Op 25 No 4. Hope, Op 26 No 1. Spring, Op 33 No 2. Beside the stream, Op 33 No 5. From Monte Pincio, Op 39 No 1. Six Songs, Op 48. Spring showers, Op 49 No 6. While I wait, Op 60 No 3. Farmyard Song, Op 61 No 3
Anne Sofie von Otter *mez* **Bengt Forsberg** *pf*
DG Grieg Anniversary Edition 437 521-2GH Ⓕ
(68 minutes: DDD). Texts and translations included.
Recorded 1992 ●●●

With performances like this, Grieg in his celebratory year emerged as a first-rank composer in this genre. Anne Sofie von Otter is at the peak of her powers, glorying in this repertoire. Take the *Haugtussa* cycle. Von Otter projects her imagination of the visionary herd-girl with absolute conviction. She is no less successful in the German settings that follow. The sad depths of *One day, my thought* from Six Songs, Op 48, also set memorably by Wolf in his *Spanish Songbook*, the hopelessness of Goethe's *The time of roses* (Op 48 No 5), a setting of great beauty, are encompassed with unfettered ease, but so are the lighter pleasures of *Lauf der Welt*. Even the familiar *A dream* (Op 48 No 6) emerges as new in von Otter's daringly big-boned reading. Throughout, her readings are immeasurably enhanced by the imaginative playing of Bengt Forsberg. They breathe fresh life into *A swan* and in the almost as familiar *With a waterlily*, another superb Ibsen setting, the questing spirit expressed in the music is marvellously captured by the performers. And there are more pleasures to come. A superb account of *Hope*, a wistful, sweetly voiced and played account of *Spring*, the charming, teasing *While I wait* and a deeply poetic reading of the justly renowned *From Monte Pincio* are just three more definitive interpretations. This should be regarded as a 'must' for any collector of songs, indeed any collector.

Further Listening
Orchestral Songs
Bonney *sop* **Stene** *mez* **Hagegård** *bar* **Tellefsen** *narr*
Gothenburg Symphony Chorus and Orchestra / Järvi
DG Classikon 469 026-2GCL (61 minutes: DDD: 8/00). Ⓑ
A collection of orchestral songs beautifully sung by Barbara Bonney (especially) and Håkan Hagegård. Neeme Järvi's direction is first-class, as is the recording

Francisco Guerrero

Spanish 1528-1599

GROVE *Guerrero was a pupil of Morales. He also taught himself the vihuela, harp, cornett and organ. He was maestro de capilla of Jaén Cathedral (1546-9) and then vice-maestro (1551) and maestro (1574-99) of Seville Cathedral. He visited Rome (1581-82), Venice and the Holy Land (1588-89). The most important 16th-century*

Spanish composer of sacred music after Victoria, he published 18 masses and c150 motets; because of their singable, diatonic lines, they remained in use in Spanish and Spanish-American cathedrals for more than two centuries after his death. He also published secular songs; many other works survive in anthologies and MSS. His brother Pedro (bSeville, c1520), his first teacher, was also a composer.

Missa de la Batalla Escoutez

Missa de la Batalla Escoutez[ab]. Pange lingua[a]. In exitu Israel[ab]. Duo Seraphim[a]. Regina coeli[b]. Magnificat[a]. Conditor alme siderum[a]
[a]**Westminster Cathedral Choir;** [b]**His Majestys Sagbutts and Cornetts / James O'Donnell**
Hyperion CDA67075 (72 minutes: DDD). Texts and Ⓕ translations included. Recorded 1998   ○○

Despite his suggestive name, Guerrero's parody of Janequin's *La Bataille de Marignan* is not the work of a fighting man: fanfares and alarums are definitely off the agenda while he develops, in an often rather sober manner, the smooth counterpoint of his model. Only in the 'Osanna' does Guerrero let rip, a moment seized on with gusto by the choir and His Majestys Sagbutts and Cornetts. Guerrero spent his career at Seville Cathedral, where the chapter was one of the first in Spain to agree to the establishment of a permanent, salaried wind band to participate in processions and at other points in divine worship.

Bruno Turner, in his fine notes, explains that the instruments (shawms, cornetts, sackbuts, dulcian and organ) are used in the Mass to 'colour and enhance the variety of the different movements, but without going to the speculative lengths of modern orchestrations.' The instruments subtly double the voices, adding depth to the sound, and strengthening major cadence points. Particularly striking is the earthy tone of the *bajón* (dulcian) reinforcing the bass-line in proto-continuo fashion. In fact, it is in the other items on this CD that the combination of voices and instruments really comes into its own. The setting of the psalm *In exitu Israel* experiments with Guerrero's forces (including cornetts and recorders which the shawmists were also expected to play), resulting in an opulence of sound more readily associated with Venetian music of the period. But this isn't just an exercise in applied musicology. These are well-paced, intelligent performances that get inside the skin of Guerrero's marvellous music. Don't be surprised to find yourself humming the Spanish chant for the hymn *Conditor alme siderum* after this compelling rendition. The musicianship is superb, the technical element entirely satisfactory and satisfying.

Missa pro defunctis

Guerrero Missa pro defunctis[a]. Hei mihi. Libera me Ⓟ
Cabezón Tiento sobre Ad Dominum cum tribularer
Esquivel In paradisium **Josquin Desprez**
Pater noster
Orchestra of the Renaissance / Michael Noone with [a]**Simon Davies** *ten* [a]**Josep Cabré** *bar*

Glossa GCD921402 (79 minutes: DDD) [a]Interspersed with Plainchant. Texts and translations included.   Ⓕ
Recorded 1999   ○

This recording is a reconstruction of Guerrero's Requiem Mass as it might have been performed in Seville Cathedral to honour the passing of its *maestro di capilla* in 1599. To listen to the full sequence unfold from the opening processional (here played by the minstrels), with chanted items fully integrated, is fascinating. Of all the liturgical ceremonies at the end of the 16th century, the polyphonic Requiem Mass was the one that remained closest to plainchant; the structure of its texts requires the constant alternation of the two media, and the chant itself is embedded in the polyphonic elaboration to a far greater extent than in other Mass settings. Don't skip the chanted items on this CD; they are superbly sung by Josep Cabré and Simon Davies and add depth, hinting at the highly sophisticated and solemn ceremonial of the ritual for the Dead. The contrast with Guerrero's magisterial polyphony is often striking, even dramatic – the Offertory, *Domine Jesu Christe*, for example. The effect on this recording is the greater for the use of wind instruments – and harp – as vocal accompaniment. This is done with greater refinement and success than on any of the Orchestra of the Renaissance's discs to date: the combinations and distribution of instruments is convincing, whether the voices are supported by just organ and dulcian or the full complement of cornett, shawms and sackbust. The pacing is generally just right; Noone's tempos are measured, appropriately solemn but never lugubrious. Nothing feels rushed, but the intensity is there. The CD is well produced, with clear, informative notes.

Reynaldo Hahn
Venezuelan/French 1875-1947

🐝 *Hahn studied with Massenet at the Paris* GROVE *Conservatoire. While in his teens he gained a reputation as a composer of songs, which he sang to his own accompaniment in fashionable salons, gaining admittance to Proust's circle. But after 1900 he concentrated on the theatre, as conductor (at the Opéra from 1945) and as a composer of ballets, operas and operettas (Ciboulette, 1923; Mozart, 1925).*

Songs

A Chloris. Le rossignol des lilas. L'enamourée. Trois jours de vendange. Etudes latines – Lydé; Tyndaris; Phyllis. Les fontaines. Automne. Infidélité. Dans la nuit. D'une prison. Quand la nuit n'est pas étoilée. Fumée. Le printemps. Je me souviens. Quand je fus pris au pavillon. Paysage. Fêtes galantes. Nocturne. Mai. L'heure exquise. Offrande. Si mes vers avaient des ailes
Susan Graham *sop* **Roger Vignoles** *pf*
Sony Classical SK60168 (62 minutes: DDD). Texts Ⓕ and translations included. Recorded 1998   ○○

A pupil of Massenet and Saint-Saëns, Hahn wrote over 30 stage works, as well as orchestral and chamber compositions and a first-class book on the interpretation of French song. He also conducted Mozart at Salzburg, was music critic of *Le Figaro*, and after the Second World War directed the Paris Opéra. But the record catalogue at least has done him proud, not least with this pleasurable collection. Susan Graham brings to it a voice of lovely quality, excellent French and – in keeping with Hahn's own insistence – gives overriding importance to clarity of enunciation, the verbal meaning governing the vocal colour. It is certainly better to savour these songs a few at a time, but the programme has been well put together to show Hahn's range, from the Bachian pastiche of *A Chloris* or the antique simplicity of *Lydé* to the adventurous harmonic progressions of *Fumée*, *Le printemps* or *Je me souviens*, from the despairing pathos of *D'une prison* to the light-heartedness of *Quand je fus pris au pavillon*, from the quiet rapture of *Nocturne* to the passion of *Dans la nuit* (a splendid miniature). His outstanding gift for lyricism is evident throughout; *Le rossignol des lilas*, for example, is enchanting. Susan Graham perfectly captures these songs' elegant intimacy with a wealth of nuance, from the gentle tone of *L'enamourée* to the fullness of *L'automne*; and the way she floats the words 'l'heure exquise' is haunting. Roger Vignoles provides most sensitive partnership throughout: he has more scope in songs like *Les fontaines* or *Dans la nuit*, but equally noteworthy is his subtle treatment of the repeated pattern of *Infidélité*.

Douze rondels. Etudes latines. Si mes vers avaient des ailes. Paysage. Rêverie. Offrande. Mai. Infidélité. Seule. Les cygnes. Nocturne. Trois jours de vendange. D'une prison. Séraphine. L'heure exquise. Fêtes galantes. Quand la nuit n'est pas étoilée. Le plus beau présent. Sur l'eau. Le rossignol des lilas. A Chloris. Ma jeunesse. Puisque j'ai mis ma lèvre. La nymphe de la source. Au rossignol. Je me souviens. Mozart – Air de la lettre. O mon bel inconnu – C'est très vilain d'être infidèle. Ciboulette – C'est sa banlieue; Nous avons fait un beau voyage. Une revue – La dernière valse

Dame Felicity Lott *sop* **Susan Bickley** *mez* **Ian Bostridge** *ten* **Stephen Varcoe** *bar* **Graham Johnson, Chris Gould** *pfs* **London Schubert Chorale / Stephen Layton**

Hyperion ② CDA67141/2 (134 minutes: DDD) Ⓕ

Texts and translations included. Recorded 1995 ●

The two cycles, *Douze rondels* and *Etudes latines*, are linked by a common fascination with the past. The *Douze rondels* were composed to poems in a medieval metre, which allowed Hahn to try his hand at pastiche madrigals and courtly ballads. The *Etudes latines* cast their gaze back still further in time to classical antiquity. For Hahn, as for Debussy in his *Bilitis* songs and Ravel in *Daphnis et Chloé*, that era seemed to represent the ultimate in purity and sensuality rolled into one. This collection of ten songs is a real discovery and rivals late Fauré, both in its refinement and mesmerizing simplicity of utterance. The three main singers divide the songs between them. Apart from a few moments when one would like a more substantial tone, Stephen Varcoe's light baritone suits Hahn very well and he is a refreshingly unaffected interpreter, who sings with grace and feeling. Susan Bickley is better at the larger canvas of a piece like *Quand la nuit n'est pas étoilée* than the more intimate songs but the most celebrated pair of all Hahn's *mélodies* goes to Dame Felicity Lott, whose sympathy for the French style could have no happier outlet. Both *Si mes vers avaient des ailes* and *L'heure exquise* are included here, the latter if not an hour, then at least two-and-a-half minutes that are truly exquisite. They are both beautifully sung and are undisturbed by the discomfort around the top of the stave that sometimes mars Lott's singing elsewhere. At the end, she offers four operetta solos as an encore. Graham Johnson's accompaniments are as sensitive as ever. The piano could have been placed a little closer, but the voices have been well captured.

George Frederic Handel

German/British 1685-1759

GROVE *Handel was the son of a barber-surgeon who intended him for the law. At first he practised music clandestinely, but his father was encouraged to allow him to study and he became a pupil of Zachow, the principal organist in Halle. When he was 17 he was appointed organist of the Calvinist Cathedral, but a year later he left for Hamburg. There he played the violin and harpsichord in the opera house, where his Almira was given at the beginning of 1705, soon followed by his Nero. The next year he accepted an invitation to Italy, where he spent more than three years, in Florence, Rome, Naples and Venice. He had operas or other dramatic works given in all these cities (oratorios in Rome, including La resurrezione) and, writing many Italian cantatas, perfected his technique in setting Italian words for the human voice. In Rome he also composed some Latin church music.*

He left Italy early in 1710 and went to Hanover, where he was appointed Kapellmeister to the elector. But he at once took leave to take up an invitation to London, where his opera Rinaldo was produced early in 1711. Back in Hanover, he applied for a second leave and returned to London in autumn 1712. Four more operas followed in 1712-15, with mixed success; he also wrote music for the church and for court and was awarded a royal pension. In 1716 he may have visited Germany (where possibly he set Brockes's Passion text); it was probably the next year that he wrote the Water Music to serenade George I at a river-party on the Thames. In 1717 he entered the service of the Earl of Carnarvon (soon to be Duke of Chandos) at Edgware, near London, where he wrote 11 anthems and two dramatic works, the evergreen Acis and Galatea and Esther, for the modest band of singers and players retained there.

In 1718-19 a group of noblemen tried to put Italian opera in London on a firmer footing, and launched

a company with royal patronage, the Royal Academy of Music; Handel, appointed musical director, went to Germany, visiting Dresden and poaching several singers for the Academy, which opened in April 1720. Handel's Radamisto was the second opera and it inaugurated a noble series over the ensuing years including Ottone, Giulio Cesare, Rodelinda, Tamerlano and Admeto. Works by Bononcini (seen by some as a rival to Handel) and others were given too, with success at least equal to Handel's, by a company with some of the finest singers in Europe, notably the castrato Senesino and the soprano Cuzzoni. But public support was variable and the financial basis insecure, and in 1728 the venture collapsed. The previous year Handel, who had been appointed a composer to the Chapel Royal in 1723, had composed four anthems for the coronation of George II and had taken British naturalization.

Opera remained his central interest, and with the Academy impresario, Heidegger, he hired the King's Theatre and (after a journey to Italy and Germany to engage fresh singers) embarked on a five-year series of seasons starting in late 1729. Success was mixed. In 1732 Esther was given at a London musical society by friends of Handel's, then by a rival group in public; Handel prepared to put it on at the King's Theatre, but the Bishop of London banned a stage version of a biblical work. He then put on Acis, also in response to a rival venture. The next summer he was invited to Oxford and wrote an oratorio, Athalia, for performance at the Sheldonian Theatre. Meanwhile, a second opera company ('Opera of the Nobility', including Senesino) had been set up in competition with Handel's and the two competed for audiences over the next four seasons before both failed. This period drew from Handel, however, such operas as Orlando and two with ballet, Ariodante and Alcina, among his finest scores.

During the rest of the 1730s Handel moved between Italian opera and the English forms, oratorio, ode and the like, unsure of his future commercially and artistically. After a journey to Dublin in 1741-42, where Messiah had its première (in aid of charities), he put opera behind him and for most of the remainder of his life gave oratorio performances, mostly at the new Covent Garden theatre, usually at or close to the Lent season. The Old Testament provided the basis for most of them (Samson, Belshazzar, Joseph, Joshua, Solomon, for example), but he sometimes experimented, turning to classical mythology (Semele, Hercules) or Christian history (Theodora), with little public success. All these works, along with such earlier ones as Acis and his two Cecilian odes (to Dryden words), were performed in concert form in English. At these performances he usually played in the interval a concerto on the organ (a newly invented musical genre) or directed a concerto grosso (his Op 6, a set of 12, published in 1740, represents his finest achievement in the form).

During his last decade he gave regular performances of Messiah, usually with about 16 singers and an orchestra of about 40, in aid of the Foundling Hospital. In 1749 he wrote a suite for wind instruments (with optional strings) for performance in Green Park to accompany the Royal Fireworks celebrating the Peace of Aix-la-Chapelle. His last oratorio, composed as he grew blind, was Jephtha (1752); The Triumph of Time and Truth (1757) is largely composed of earlier material. Handel was very economical in the re-use of his ideas; at many times in his life he also drew heavily on the music of others (though generally avoiding detection) - such 'borrowings' may be of anything from a brief motif to entire movements, sometimes as they stood but more often accommodated to his own style.

Handel died in 1759 and was buried in Westminster Abbey, recognised in England and by many in Germany as the greatest composer of his day. The wide range of expression at his command is shown not only in the operas, with their rich and varied arias, but also in the form he created, the English oratorio, where it is applied to the fates of nations as well as individuals. He had a vivid sense of drama. But above all he had a resource and originality of invention, to be seen in the extraordinary variety of music in the Op 6 concertos, for example, in which melodic beauty, boldness and humour all play a part, that place him and JS Bach as the supreme masters of the Baroque era in music.

Concerti grossi

Op 3, HWV312-17; **Op 6**, HWV319-30

Concerti grossi, Opp 3 and 6
Vienna Concentus Musicus / Nikolaus Harnoncourt
Teldec ④ 4509-95500-2 (237 minutes: ADD/DDD) Ⓑ
Recorded 1982-85

The somewhat perfunctory look of these recoupled reissues (there are no insert-notes and precious little information about the recordings) masks just what extraordinary music-making lies within. It took a long time for Harnoncourt's prodigious musical personality to be recognised for what it is. And it is true that these recordings come from a time when even Harnoncourt's supporters were finding him a little too eccentric to handle. But listening now to these searching, unceasingly imaginative performances of Handel's finest instrumental music, you can't help feeling that Harnoncourt was (as he has been so often) simply ahead of his time. Here he shows the very creative freshness and insight that have characterised his Beethoven.

The fact is that there is ferocious creativity in every bar. Every opening slow movement is the prelude to a drama, every fugue a precisely related episode. You can find imposing examples of the former in Op 6 No 5 (its opening solo violin notes are like being tickled under the nose with a feather) or Op 6 No 6 (like the start of some great operatic scena), and stunning demonstrations of the latter in Op 3 No 3 or Op 6 No 1 (both broadly painted but leading to very different types of climax). There is hardly a place where Handel's music is allowed to lie down or just play itself; Harnoncourt is everywhere busy with thunderous dynamic contrasts, stomping dance rhythms or the sort of vivid articulation that at one moment has us enthralled by a grippingly minimal *staccato*, at another swept up by the warm embrace of a sudden but grandly *legato* phrase (quite a Harnoncourt trademark, this).

The Vienna Concentus Musicus plays for the most part with a virtuosity and precision that is well highlighted by the slightly dry but transparent acoustic in which they are recorded, and that is so typical of Teldec's 1980s Das Alte Werk recordings. There are a few places where the basic pulse seems oddly uncertain (most off-puttingly, perhaps, at the very beginning of the whole set, in the opening bars of Op 3 No 1), but elsewhere Harnoncourt's control of every aspect of the music is tight, his involvement total. To him this is big music, and these are big performances. Of course, there is no denying that they sound eccentric, even now. Not everything works and we would hesitate to recommend them as one's only encounter with this music. But their consistent and often audacious probing at the music's meaning is a spirit-reviving antidote to what by comparison seems like bland cautiousness on the part of some of Harnoncourt's rivals. Whether you actually like it or not (and we certainly can't guarantee that you will), this re-release performs the double and timely favour of reminding us that this man was always a genius of some kind, and of putting before us more convincingly than ever a Handel we can associate with Beethoven's judgement of him as 'the greatest of composers'.

Concerti grossi, Op 3 **P**
Tafelmusik / Jeanne Lamon
Sony Classical Vivarte SK52553 (60 minutes: DDD) Ⓕ
Recorded 1991

This is a fine issue impressive for its stylistic fluency and infectious response to Handel's music which could not disappoint anyone. Tafelmusik plays only the six concertos of which Handel's authorship is undisputed. This version, in respect of finesse and vitality, has the edge over the competition. Where Tafelmusik scores is in the sheer virtuosity of its playing and the easy gracefulness of its phrasing. Strong accents are not overemphasised and, though vigorous, there is nothing aggressive in this approach to the music. Tafelmusik includes a plucked string instrument among the continuo colloquium; they have large reinforcements at the top and bottom of the string texture and the performances have great radiance. The disc is beautifully recorded.

Concerti grossi, Op 6 Nos 1-4 **P**
The English Concert / Trevor Pinnock Ⓕ
Archiv Produktion 410 897-2AH (42 minutes: DDD)

Nos 5-8 **P**
The English Concert / Trevor Pinnock Ⓕ
Archiv Produktion 410 898-2AH (61 minutes: DDD)

Nos 9-12 **P**
The English Concert / Trevor Pinnock Ⓕ
Archiv Produktion 410 899-2AH (58 minutes: DDD)

Trevor Pinnock's accounts contain much that is satisfying: polished ensemble, effectively judged tempos, a natural feeling for phrase, and a buoyancy of spirit which serves Handel's own robust musical language very well. Crisp attack, a judicious application of appoggiaturas and tasteful embellishment further enhance these lively performances. Pinnock varies the continuo colour by using organ and harpsichord and also includes Handel's autograph (though not printed) oboe parts for Concertos Nos 1, 2, 5 and 6; where they occur a bassoon is sensibly added to fulfil the customary three-part wind texture of the period. The recorded sound is clear and captures faithfully the warm sonorities of the instruments.

Concerti grossi, Op 6 Nos 1-5 **P**
Collegium Musicum 90 / Simon Standage *vn* Ⓕ
Chandos Chaconne CHAN0600 (62 minutes: DDD)
Recorded 1996

Concerti grossi, Op 6 Nos 6-9 **P**
Collegium Musicum 90 / Simon Standage *vn* Ⓕ
Chandos Chaconne CHAN0616 (58 minutes: DDD)
Recorded 1997

Concerti grossi – Op 6 Nos 10-12; C, HWV318, 'Alexander's Feast' **P**
Collegium Musicum 90 / Simon Standage *vn*
Chandos Chaconne CHAN0622 (56 minutes: DDD) Ⓕ
Recorded 1997

The first disc of the ever-fresh Op 6 *Concerti grossi* includes the oboe parts that Handel later added to Nos 1, 2, 5 and 6. The performances are brimful of vitality, and the clean articulation and light, predominantly detached style give the music buoyancy and help to bring out Handel's often mischievous twinkle in the eye. Speeds are generally brisk, with boldly vigorous playing, but Standage's team can also spin a tranquil broad line. Dynamics, throughout, are subtly graded and natural-sounding, and except in one final cadence ornamentation is confined to small cadential trills. On the second disc, except, rightly, in the sombre colours in the splendid Sixth (G minor) Concerto – here with oboe and the agreeable addition of a theorbo to the continuo – there is a general air of cheerfulness about the performances that is most engaging. The fugue in No 7 is wittily buoyant, the *Allegro* in No 9 borrowed from the *Cuckoo and the nightingale* Organ Concerto could scarcely be more high-spirited, the final Passepied of No 6 and the Hornpipe of No 7 are spring-toed; and Standage's feeling for convincing tempos is nowhere better shown than in the long Musette of No 6, which too often, in other hands, can drag. Phrasing everywhere is shapely, and the surprise chords that interrupt the flow of No 8's Allemande are admirably 'placed'. A thoroughly enjoyable disc, cleanly recorded.

On the final disc the playing is always on its toes – positively twinkling in dance movements such as the concluding fugal gigue of No 12. The final two concertos, No 11 in particular, also give Simon Standage an opportunity to shine as a soloist; his *ad lib* sections are tastefully done, without excesses, and his semiquavers in the variants of the A major *Andante* are featherlight. Dynamics everywhere are well contrasted in a natural way, and the tempos are very nicely judged; a slightly faster repeat of the first half of No 10's fifth movement suggests the splicing of a different take. As a fill-up, we are presented with the *Alexander's Feast* Concerto grosso, for which the string group is joined by oboes and bassoon. The excellent concertino of two violins and cello is thrown into high relief and the *Allegro* movements are performed with delightful spring.

12 Concerti grossi, Op 6 **P**
Academy of Ancient Music / Andrew Manze *vn*
Harmonia Mundi ② HMU90 7228/9 Ⓕ
(157 minutes: DDD). Recorded 1997 ●

With one stride, Harmonia Mundi has stolen a march on Chandos Chaconne's rival set of Handel's Op 6 with Simon Standage's Collegium Musicum 90; by juggling with the order, the 12 concertos have been accommodated on only two CDs. The AAM is on sparkling form, clearly enjoying itself under Andrew Manze's leadership. Performances are invigoratingly alert, splendidly neat (all those semiquaver figurations absolutely precise) and strongly rhythmical but not inflexible, with much dynamic gradation which ensures that phrases are always tonally alive and sound completely natural (even if more subtly nuanced than Handel's players ever dreamt of). Manze's basically light-footed approach is particularly appealing, and he sees to it that inner-part imitations are given their due weight. Speeds are nearly all fast, occasionally questionably so (though exhilarating), as in the first *Allegro* of No 1, the big *Allegro* of No 6 and the *Allegro* in No 9. But Manze successfully brings out the character of all the movements, and the listener can't fail to love the vigorous kick of his No 7 hornpipe. He is mostly sparing in embellishing solo lines except in Nos 6 and 11. Altogether this is an issue of joyous vitality.

Organ Concertos, Op 4

No 1 in G minor; No 2 in B flat; No 3 in G minor; No 4 in F; No 5 in F; Op 7 – No 1 in B flat; No 2 in A; No 3 in B flat; No 4 in D minor; No 5 in G minor; No 6 in B flat. Harp Concerto in B flat, Op 4 No 6 **P**
Paul Nicholson *org* **Frances Kelly** *hp*
The Brandenburg Consort / Roy Goodman *hpd*
Hyperion ② CDA67291/2 (154 minutes: DDD) Ⓕ
Recorded 1996

This recording was made at St Lawrence Whitchurch on the organ which Handel must certainly have played and which has recently been admirably restored. Under Paul Nicholson's hands, the organ sounds well. There is plenty of brightly glittering passagework – in the second movement of Op 4 No 1, for example, or the *Allegro* of Op 4 No 2 – and rich diapason sound in such movements as the passacaglia-like first of Op 7 No 1; while the softer side of the instrument is particularly appealing in Op 4 No 5, where Nicholson, doubtless conscious that this is a transcription of a recorder sonata, draws from it some very sweet sounds. It has of course a mechanical action, and here and there the incidental noise may be rather disconcerting. Still, it is authentic, so possibly we should be grateful to have it so clearly reproduced. There is some very lively and at times virtuoso playing from Nicholson in the quick movements, with sturdy rhythms, and some of the dance movements too go with a good swing.

Nicholson gives good, precise accounts of the various solo fugues and the transcriptions and improvisatory movements used here when Handel offered merely an ad lib. He is a thoughtful player; his added ornamentation is always musical and intelligent, and stylish too, and his treatment of the natural caesuras in the music is always dictated by the structure. In several movements, however, overdeliberate orchestral phrasing or accentuation can be damaging. This happens quite often and it sometimes affects Nicholson's playing. Op 4 No 6 is played on the harp, with some very delicate timing from Frances Kelly. The recording is bright and clear, capturing happily the acoustic of this moderate-sized church.

Water Music, HWV348-50

Water Music. Music for the Royal Fireworks **P**
Le Concert des Nations / Jordi Savall
Auvidis Astrée ES9920 (74 minutes: DDD) Ⓜ
Recorded 1993 ●

Of the period-instrument couplings of these two 'elemental' suites, particularly the *Fireworks Music*, Savall's must be placed at the top of the list. It is, however, strange that though the booklet-notes acknowledge that the *Water Music* falls into 'three suites' and that the Suite in G major was probably played during supper, the recorded performance ends with that in F major (described as 'Suite II') preceded by the rest ('Suite I') – neither the published nor the 'logical' order. The movements from the earlier Concerto in F are not included and there is also the familiar retitling and juggling with the order of movements. What splendid performances these are though, spirited, clean-edged and elegantly embellished – by a solo trumpet in the *Adagio* of the Overture of the *Fireworks Music*, where the preceding section is repeated as marked. The orchestral force is substantial, and the comparatively high-level recording and generous acoustic give a deliberate sense of being close to the performers – just as, on the Thames, King George I may have been in a barge adjacent to the musicians – rather than of hearing them from the riverside.

Water Music. Music for the Royal Fireworks
Scottish Chamber Orchestra / Nicholas McGegan
Classic fM The Full Works 75605 57044-2 Ⓜ
(68 minutes: DDD). Recorded 1998 ●

Classic fM has introduced the 'layman' to a great deal of accessible art music, often in the form of detached movements; any fear that extension of the process via The Full Works series might involve a measure of 'dumbing down' is dispersed by this recording. The only punch that is pulled here is that modern instruments and pitch are used, but Nicholas McGegan is too wise and experienced to allow that to count for much. He places Handel's *Water Music* Suites in the order usually accepted as appropriate to a single excursion along the Thames – F major on the outward journey, D major on the way back, and the gentler G major during supper – one that is equally effective in a recording. Identifying the movements by their titles provides the usual occupation for a relaxed winter's evening, but no matter – the music is magnificent in whatever order it is played, and by whatever titles it bears. The flanking Suites are recorded in a more spacious acoustic, as befits the postulated outdoor location of their original performances. The beginning and end of the *Music for the Royal Fireworks* are ablaze with the brilliant sounds of the trumpets and drums that the King loved. Authentic or not, these beautifully balanced performances are most enjoyable.

Water Music **P**
Simon Standage, Elizabeth Wilcock *vns*
The English Concert / Trevor Pinnock *hpd*
Archiv Produktion 410 525-2AH (54 minutes: DDD) Ⓕ
Recorded 1983 **OO**

Whatever the circumstances were which prompted Handel to write his *Water Music*, it is highly unlikely that George I ever witnessed performances matching up to this one. These are sparkling performances of the three groups of movements which comprise the *Water Music*. Tempos are well judged and there is a truly majestic sweep to the opening F major French overture; that gets things off to a fine start but what follows is no less compelling with some notably fine woodwind playing, so often the disappointing element in performances on period instruments. In the D major music it is the brass department which steals the show and here, horns and trumpets acquit themselves with distinction. Archiv Produktion has achieved a particularly satisfying sound in which all strands of the orchestral texture can be heard with clarity. In this suite the ceremonial atmosphere comes over particularly well with some resonant brass playing complemented by crisply articulated oboes. The G major pieces are quite different from those in the previous groups, being lighter in texture and more closely dance-orientated in character. They are among the most engaging in the *Water Music* and especially, perhaps, the two little 'country dances', the boisterous character of which Pinnock captures nicely. Pinnock's is still the best performance of the *Water Music* on the market.

Water Music. Il pastor fido – Suite, HWV8c **P**
Tafelmusik / Jeanne Lamon *vn*
Sony Classical Vivarte SK68257 (76 minutes: DDD) Ⓕ
Recorded 1995 **O**

The jubilant spirit of the *Water Music* is splendidly captured here. This Canadian group has a good grasp of Handelian style, and lots of energy; there is plenty of vigour to its playing but no roughness. There are many nicely and unobtrusively managed details of timing and accent, yet always perfectly natural and justified from within. The tempos in the main are on the quick side but not hurried. The flowing *Andante* for the famous Air, which so readily becomes sticky if done slowly, is particularly likeable; here it sounds just right and no less expressive than usual. Only the D major *Lentement* seems heavy and ponderous, and perhaps the *Bourrée* that follows is also a little clumsily done. The horn playing, recorded well forward, is particularly impressive – clean and clear, with a fine ring; it would have sounded well across the Thames. The movements are done here with the F major music first, then the D major and G major mixed, an unusual arrangement these days but one that probably has Handel's authority: and it works well. Tafelmusik gets through the *Water Music* in some 52 minutes, and there is room for a substantial suite of dances from the second version of *Il pastor fido*, when Handel added ballet music for the French dancer Marie Sallé and her troupe. These are charming and lively pieces and the final Chaconne, with its inventive textures, is particularly appealing. The sound here is a shade middle- and bottom-heavy, rather more so than in *The Water Music*, but again the playing is splendidly fresh and spirited.

Music for the Royal Fireworks

Music for the Royal Fireworks. Concertos – F, HWV331; D, HWV335*a*. Passacaille, Gigue and Minuet in G. Occasional Suite in D (both arr Pinnock) **P**
The English Concert / Trevor Pinnock *hpd*
Archiv Produktion 453 451-2AH (60 minutes: DDD) Ⓕ
Recorded 1996

Trevor Pinnock uses George II's preferred scoring rather than Handel's – that is, just wind and percussion. What we know about the first performances of the work seems to indicate that Handel had his way and strings were used, along with a massed wind; probably the wind version was never heard in Handel's day. Well, here it is, with 24 oboes, 12 bassoons, double bassoon, nine each of trumpets and horns and six percussion. It's certainly rousing stuff, and a noble noise. With his direct and unaffected rhythm, Pinnock sets up a sturdy momentum for the Overture and the effect is grand and imposing. The dances too receive straightforward performances, with plenty of spirit and energy. This disc offers some welcome rarities. The F major Concerto is made up of versions of two movements from the D major part of the *Water Music*, here in F major; one is the movement generally labelled in the 18th century 'Mr Handel's Water Peice', again, with some interesting and very characteristic differences from the familiar version and the other is the *Alla Hornpipe*. In between Pinnock plays, as a slow movement, an *Adagio* from Op 3 No 5. The D major Concerto consists of what are probably early versions – less purposefully shaped, but again with some highly characteristic touches – of two movements from the *Fireworks Music* with a version of a movement from a violin sonata, on the organ, in between. The Passacaille, Gigue and Minuet come from a trio sonata and the *Occasional Suite* draws on the *Occasional Oratorio* overture, the *Ariodante* ballet and music composed for *Joshua* and *Alessandro Severo*. It all works pretty well, although some of the music in this last is not the most distinguished of Handel. But the concertos especially are well worth having, and certainly George II's vision of the *Fireworks Music* is to be relished in its way.

Music for the Royal Fireworks. Concerti a due cori – No 1 in B flat, HWV332; No 2 in F, HWV333; No 3 in F, HWV334 **P**

Tafelmusik / Jeanne Lamon *vn*

Sony Classical Vivarte SK63073 (66 minutes: DDD) Ⓕ

Recorded 1997

It hasn't been done before, but it makes excellent sense to devote a CD to the three *Concerti a due cori* and the *Music for the Royal Fireworks*. Here the *Fireworks Music* is done in the form, with strings as well as wind, that Handel preferred. The less familiar *Concerti a due cori* were composed in the late 1740s for use in the intervals of oratorio performances. They borrow freely from other works – in particular *Messiah* (at the time scarcely known to London audiences) and *Belshazzar* – and some movements seem a little odd in shape because the structure is dictated, in the originals, by the texts; but they are cheerful, outgoing pieces and make very attractive listening, undemanding but, typically, touching here and there on deeper feeling.

These performances are splendidly spirited and enjoyable on every plane. Tafelmusik tends to favour speedy tempos in Handel. In the *Fireworks Music* 'La paix' is taken steadily but it is all very nicely judged, and the jauntiness they bring to the main *Allegro* of the overture is particularly likeable, making it a shade more detached than usual to good effect. Handel's directions for the repeats in the dance movements are decidedly ambiguous, and Tafelmusik makes sensible decisions of its own which don't always quite accord with the instructions but work perfectly well. Once or twice there is a stylish lilt, almost a hint of *inégalité*, in the dances.

The band sounds a big one, but the strings are only 5.6.3.3.2, with a fair number of wind – six oboes, three bassoons, four horns and three trumpets, with percussion (their collective intonation is as good as one has any right to expect). In the concertos, there is some first-rate wind playing and there is a fine, earthy ring from the horns throughout. One or two tempos may strike you as quickish; no one would think of singing 'And the glory of the Lord' as fast as Tafelmusik plays Handel's transcription of it, but after all there's no reason why it shouldn't be done this way on instruments.

Orchestral and Ballet Music

Orchestral and Ballet Music from Alcina, Ariodante, Arminio. Berenice, Rinaldo, Rodelinda and Serse **P**

Collegium Musicum 90 / Simon Standage *vn*

Chandos Chaconne CHAN0650 (67 minutes: DDD) Ⓕ

Recorded 1999

Handel's music is never more winsome than when it is written for special occasions, not least operas. Several of the items in this programme are arias, but they are not sung. Like today's musicals, though not for calculated commercial reasons, some became what we would now term pops, and Handel reworked them as instrumental pieces, so no liberty has been taken here in presenting them in that form. The charm of this music has not escaped the notice of others in recording studios, but it has never been more persuasively captured than it is by Collegium Musicum 90. Other recordings exist of the complete operas and some of the individual instrumental items, but *Arminio* is represented by only one aria; there is nothing run-of-the-mill about the fugal subject of the Overture, or its treatment, and the Minuet is winsome and light of step. Collegium Musicum 90 fields a team of 32 players but their sound is marvellously light and transparent even when in full flood, and their use of period instruments (or copies thereof) leads also to a natural, revelatory balance. Flawless recording and excellent notes by Standage complete an outstanding issue.

Trio Sonatas

Trio Sonatas, Op 5, HWV396-402 – No 1 in A; No 2 in D; No 3 in E minor; No 4 in G; No 5 in G minor; No 6 in F; No 7 in B flat **P**

London Baroque

Harmonia Mundi HMC90 1389 (69 minutes: DDD) Ⓕ

Recorded 1991

Handel's publisher, Walsh, printed the six Trio Sonatas, Op 2, in about 1730, following them up in 1739 with seven further trios which he published as the composer's Op 5. In each set Handel offered a choice of melody instruments though the writing suggests that he had violins foremost in mind. The performances by London Baroque are poised, well shaped and susceptible to the subtle nuances of Handel's part-writing. Ingrid Seifert and Richard Gwilt are partners of long standing and their even dialogue, sometimes grave, sometimes lively and at other times playful, serves the music effectively. Tempos are well judged and phrases are eloquently shaped and articulately spoken. In all this the violinists are sympathetically supported by the continuo players who make their own vital contribution to clear textures and overall balance. Recorded sound is appropriately intimate, serving the sound character of the instruments themselves and evoking a chamber music ambience. The music, it hardly need be said, maintains a high level of craftsmanship and interest which will surely delight listeners.

Trio Sonatas – Op 2 No 5 in G minor, HWV390; Op 5 Nos 4 and 7. Tra le fiamme, HWV170. Notte placida e cheta, HWV142 **P**

Catherine Bott *sop* **Caroline Kershaw, Jane Downer** *recs/obs* **Nigel Amherst** *violone* **Jonathan Manson** *vc* **Purcell Quartet** (Catherine Mackintosh, Catherine Weiss *vns* Richard Boothby *va da gamba/vc* Robert Woolley *hpd*)

Chandos Chaconne CHAN0620 (70 minutes: DDD) Ⓕ

Texts and translations included. Recorded 1997 ○

The idea of alternating trio sonatas with cantatas is a happy one, based perhaps on the idea that people play CDs for pleasure and not simply for reference. The two cantatas presented here are rarities on record. *Tra le fiamme* is a spectacularly scored piece, its textures enriched by a viola da gamba obbligato (probably composed for a visiting virtuoso) and wind instruments (recorders in some numbers, oboes in another) as well as strings. *Notte placida e cheta* is a delightful evocation of night, sleep and amorous reflection, with its opening aria full of sinuous, voluptuous interweaving violin lines and its soft, gently accompanied recitatives; it ends – a slightly rude awakening, perhaps, to chime with the words – with a fugal aria in which the singer takes one of the four contrapuntal parts along with the violins and the bass. Catherine Bott sings them very responsively, both to the words and to the sense of Handel's lines, with neatly placed detail and some attractively floated phrases. The viol obbligato is done in accomplished style by Richard Boothby who supplies much of the continuo harmony with multiple stops. In the Trio Sonatas there is some splendidly athletic playing from the violins of the Purcell Quartet, which plays with its usual spruce rhythms and conversational give and take; in several movements, such as the second and the fourth of Op 2 No 5 or the second of Op 5 No 7, the cello joins in on equal terms (its rushing semiquavers come out rather prominently in the recording). There is some gently eloquent playing in the *Adagio* of the Op 2 Sonata and the Purcellian *Passacaille* in Op 5 No 4, and nicely sprung rhythms in the dances in the Op 5 pieces. These are probably the most appealing performances currently available of these works.

Recorder Sonatas

Sonatas for Recorder and Continuo – No 1 in G minor, HWV360; No 2 in A minor, HWV362; No 3 in C, HWV365; No 5 in F, HWV369; No 6 in B flat, HWV377. Sonata for Flute and Continuo No 3 in B minor, HWV367*b* **P**

Marion Verbruggen *rec/fl* **Jaap ter Linden** *vc* **Ton Koopman** *hpd/org*

Harmonia Mundi HMU90 7151 (58 minutes: DDD) Ⓕ

Recorded 1994 ○

These are very lively, musically intelligent performances. The recorder playing is outstandingly fine, sweet in tone, pointed in articulation, perfectly tuned, technically very fluent, and informed by a good understanding of the art of ornamentation. Add to that the fact that Marion Verbruggen has a real command of Handel's language and you will realise that this CD is out of the ordinary. Some of Ton Koopman's accompaniments are a little busy (half are on the organ, half on the harpsichord), but it's all part of the sense of lively music-making that runs through this attractive disc.

Flute Sonatas

No 1 in E minor, HWV359*b*; No 2 in G, HWV363*b*; No 3 in B minor, HWV367*b*; No 4 in A minor, HWV374; No 5 in E minor, HWV375; No 6 in B minor, HWV376; No 7 in D, HWV378; No 8 in E minor, HWV379 **P**

Barthold Kuijken *fl* **Wieland Kuijken** *va da gamba* **Robert Kohnen** *hpd*

Accent ACC9180 (73 minutes: DDD) Ⓕ

Recorded 1991 ○

In this recording of solo flute sonatas Barthold Kuijken plays pieces unquestionably by Handel as well as others over which doubt concerning his authorship has been cast in varying degrees. Certainly not all of the pieces here were conceived for transverse flute – there are earlier versions of HWV363*b* and 367*b*, for example, for oboe and treble recorder, respectively; but we can well imagine that in Handel's day most, if not all, of these delightful sonatas were regarded among instrumentalists as more-or-less common property. Barthold Kuijken, with his eldest brother Wieland and Robert Kohnen, gives graceful and stylish performances. Kuijken is skilful in matters of ornamentation and is often adventurous, though invariably within the bounds of good taste. Dance movements are brisk and sprightly though he is careful to preserve their poise, and phrases are crisply articulated. This is of especial benefit to movements such as the lively *Vivace* of the B minor Sonata (HWV367*b*) which can proceed rather aimlessly when too *legato* an approach is favoured; and the virtuosity of these players pays off in the *Presto (Furioso)* movement that follows. In short, this is without doubt a delightful disc which should please both Handelians and most lovers of baroque chamber music.

Keyboard Suites

HWV426-33 – No 1 in A; **No 2** in F; **No 3** in D minor; **No 4** in E minor; **No 5** in E; **No 6** in F sharp minor; **No 7** in G minor; **No 8** in F minor. HWV434; **HWV436-41 – No 1** in G minor; **No 2** in D minor; **No 3** in D minor; **No 4** in E minor; **No 5** in B flat; **No 6** in G; **No 7** in D minor; **No 8** in G minor

Awards 1997

Keyboard Suites, HWV426-33 Nos 2, 3 and 5. Chaconne in G, HWV435 **D Scarlatti** Keyboard Sonatas – B minor, Kk27; D, Kk29; E, Kk206; A, Kk212; C sharp minor, Kk247; D, Kk491; A, Kk537

Murray Perahia *pf*

Sony Classical SK62785 Ⓕ

(69 minutes: DDD). Recorded 1996 ○○○

In his projection of line, mass and colour Perahia makes intelligent acknowledgement of the fact that none of this is piano music, but when it comes to communicating the forceful effects and the brilliance and readiness of finger for which these two great player-composers were renowned, inhibitions are thrown to the wind. Good! Nothing a pianist does in the *Harmonious Blacksmith* Variations in Handel's E major Suite, or the Air and Variations of the D minor Suite could surpass in vivacity and cumulative excitement what the expert harpsichordist commands, and you could say the same of Scarlatti's D major Sonata, Kk29; but Perahia is extraordinarily successful in translating these with the daredevil 'edge' they must have. Faster and yet faster! In the Handel (more than in the Scarlatti) his velocity may strike you as overdone; but one can see the sense of it. It is quite big playing throughout, yet not inflated. Admirable is the way the piano is addressed, with the keys touched rather than struck, and a sense conveyed that the music is coming to us through the tips of the fingers rather than the hammers of the instrument. While producing streams of beautifully moulded and inflected sound Perahia is a wizard at making you forget the percussive nature of the apparatus. There are movements in the Handel where the musical qualities are dependent on instrumental sound, or contrasts of sound, which the piano just can't convincingly imitate. And in some of the Scarlatti one might have reservations about Perahia's tendency to idealise, to soften outlines (hard to avoid, given the piano's capacity for nuance) and to make the bite less incisive.

You could of course raise a more fundamental objection and say that it begs the question: why do it on the piano at all? If you can't bear to hear it on anything other than the harpsichord this record won't be for you. But Perahia is an artist, not just a pianist, and if you don't rule out of court the prospect of these composers *transcribed* for the piano, he has an experience to offer that is vivid and musically considered at the highest level – and not at all second-best. The virtuosity is special indeed, and there is not a note that hasn't been savoured.

Keyboard Suites, HWV426-33 Nos 1[b], 2-3[a], 4[b], 5[a], 6-7[b] and 8[a]

[a]**Sviatoslav Richter,** [b]**Andrei Gavrilov** *pfs*

EMI Double Forte ② CZS5 69337-2 Ⓜ

(119 minutes: ADD). Recorded live in 1979 **OO**

Keyboard Suites, HWV434; HWV436-41 Nos 1[a], 2-3[b], 4[a], 5[b], 6[a], 7[b] and 8[a] **Beethoven** Piano Sonata No 17 in D minor, Op 31 No 2, 'Tempest'[a]

[a]**Sviatoslav Richter,** [b]**Andrei Gavrilov** *pfs* EMI Double Forte ② CZS5 69340-2 (119 minutes: ADD) Ⓜ

Recorded live in 1979 **O**

Even by Sviatoslav Richter's Tours Festival standards, 1979 was a red-letter year. Then, partnered by his dazzling young compatriot Andrei Gavrilov, he played Handel's 16 Suites, offering performances of such quality that long-familiar reservations concerning their provenance and overall success evaporated as if by magic. From Richter and Gavrilov these baroque chains of dances emerge with an unforgettable wit and vitality. Listen to Gavrilov in the First Suite's opening Prelude and you will hear an authentic as well as spirited emulation of the extempore style. Yet it is in the slow movements that Gavrilov achieves his greatest effect. In such hands, the Sarabande from the Seventh Suite becomes Handel's 'black pearl', if you like, and in the same grave and ceremonial dances from Suites Nos 11 and 13, the music emerges like great mysterious pools of light.

Richter's genius has rarely sounded more imperturbable and, whether he is playful and resilient in, say, the Fifth Suite's Gigue or poised and tonally translucent – a model of sense and sensibility – in the *Air con Variazione*, you are always aware of the musical artist first and the transcendental pianist second. Tempos are judicious rather than extreme, and even the most determined Beckmesser will surely find himself abandoning pencil and paper and succumbing to the spell of such serenity and affection. Finally, as a further reminder of Richter's unique stature there is his legendary 1961 disc of Beethoven's D minor Sonata, Op 31 No 2. Rarely can Beethoven's suggestion that we should read Shakespeare's *The Tempest* (a metaphysical fantasy concerned with the mystery of death and rebirth) have seemed more teasing or obtuse. In any event, from Richter the music retains its mystery, its eloquence 'contained' to the point of enigma. Richter 'does' so little and the result is hauntingly pure and distilled. The recordings, though occasionally showing their age, have been beautifully transferred.

Keyboard Suites, HWV426-33 – Nos 1 and 7; **P**
HWV438 – No 4 in D minor. Chaconne in G, HWV435. Prelude in D minor. The Lady's Banquet – Sonata in C; Capriccio in F, HWV481; Preludio ed Allegro in G minor, HWV574; Fantaisie in C, HWV490

Olivier Baumont *hpd*

Erato 0630-14886-2 (63 minutes: DDD) Ⓕ

Recorded 1995

A splendid disc, imbued with freshness and vitality. Employing three different instruments – a Flemish harpsichord (1652) by Couchet, a shallower, 'dustier'-toned anonymous Italian instrument of 1677, and a wonderfully rich 1707 French instrument by Dumont – all tuned to a pitch a whole tone lower than that of today, Olivier Baumont presents two of Handel's 1720 'grand suites', the D minor Suite from the 1733 collection, which is seldom heard, the great C major Chaconne (one of Handel's favourites), which Baumont plays with every variant repeated, and a handful of very early shorter pieces. Two things in particular are striking about these performances – Baumont's stylishness and spontaneous-sounding skilful free decorations of Handel's text (not only in repeats but, for example, in the minor-key variants of the Chaconne). Definitely a disc to raise one's spirits.

Cantatas

Il delirio amoroso, 'Da quel giorno fatale', HWV99. La Lucrezia, HWV145. Tra le fiamme, HWV170 **P**

Magdalena Kožená *mez* **Les Musiciens du Louvre / Marc Minkowski**

Archiv Produktion 469 065-2AH (67 minutes: DDD) Ⓕ

Recorded 1999

The Czech soprano Magdalena Kožená brings to these Handel cantatas a sense of drama quite out of the ordinary. That is clear at the very start, in the recitative that begins *Delirio amoroso*, where she invests every word with meaning in her timing and colouring of the notes. But it is most telling in her fine performance of *Lucrezia*. In the exceptionally beautiful and tragedy-laden F minor aria, 'Già superbo del mio affanno', she draws a long line, of great intensity, encouraged by Handel's bold chromatics and his appoggiaturas; and she goes on, in the second aria, taken at a testing speed, to sing with passion and agility. The passacaglia-like aria that follows is equally telling, but the most striking moment falls at the opening of the final number, just six bars of quite heart-rendingly soft singing, as Lucretia faces death ('Gia nel seno comincia').

Delirio amoroso, too, has some fine things. The overture is a bit scurried and the exuberant first aria is by no means improved by the solo violinist's indulgent (and unimaginatively repetitive) *rubato* in his lengthy solos – a piece this long, and with so much repeated material, really needs much stricter rhythmic discipline, although his duetting with Kožená is a brilliant piece of musical trapeze. She does well in the difficult 'Per te lasciai la luce', high and sustained, with obbligato cello, and in the delightful third aria with recorders (a precursor of 'Hush, ye pretty warbling quire'). Her voice, which is not free of vibrato but has a pleasant natural ring and vitality, proves equally pleasing in the remaining cantata, *Tra le fiamme*, another colourful piece, which Minkowski directs with a light touch and Kožená sings with particular athleticism in the final aria, 'Voli per l'aria', with the viola da gamba scrubbing away. Three really fine pieces here, then, in performances that show different facets of Kožená's singing but above all establish her as someone who lives the music and puts it across with real conviction.

Chandos Anthems

No 4*a*, HWV249*a*, 'O sing unto the Lord'; No 6, HWV251, 'As pants the hart'; No 11, HWV256, 'Let God arise'

Ensemble William Byrd; Académie Sainte-Cécile / Graham O'Reilly

L'Empreinte Digitale ED13072 (57 minutes: DDD) Ⓕ

Texts included ○

Graham O'Reilly is clearly a fine musician with a keen and true feeling for this music. He uses very small forces, modelled on those Handel is likely to have had available to him; the Académie Sainte-Cécile has five violins, no violas, two cellos and a double-bass, with one oboe and one bassoon, with just the solo singers (soprano, tenor and bass in two of the anthems, with an extra tenor in the other). This produces not only lucid and well-balanced textures but also an intimacy of atmosphere that the more traditional type of choral performances rules out. It also allows O'Reilly to phrase the music sensitively. Listen for example to the opening Sonata of *O sing unto the Lord*, with its slightly detached articulation and its gently sprung rhythms, or to the vigorous but poised Sonata beginning *As pants the hart*. The sound in the first chorus here has an almost sensuous quality, with its rich suspensions and chromaticisms; and later, in 'Why so full of grief', taken at a nicely measured tempo, the effect is of highly expressive, devotional chamber music. In *Let God arise* there is some happy interplay between soprano and oboe in 'Let the righteous be glad', and spirited ensemble singing in the closing items. The recording is beautifully clear.

Arias

María Bayo

No se emenderá jamás, HWV140. Tra le fiamme, HWV170. Alcina – Sì; son quella!; Tornami a vagheggiar; Mi restano le lagrime. Giulio Cesare – V'adoro, pupille; Che sento? Oh Dio!; Se pietà di me non senti; Da tempeste il legno infranto. Rinaldo – Lascia ch'io pianga **P**

María Bayo *sop* **Capriccio Stravagante / Skip Sempé**

Auvidis Naïve E8674 (64 minutes: DDD). Texts and translations included. Recorded 1999 Ⓕ ○○

Bayo starts with an aria that is always a sure winner, Cleopatra's triumphal celebration in *Giulio Cesare* of her brother's defeat and her conquest (amorous, of course) of Caesar: Bayo sings 'Da tempeste' with tremendous vivacity, precise articulation and beautifully clean pitching. In 'V'adoro, pupille', from much earlier in the same opera, she is gently seductive, conveying just a hint of sensual languor, singing on a chamber-music scale with a delicately colourful accompaniment from Capriccio Stravagante under Skip Sempé. In 'Se pietà', one of the more tragic utterances, at a dark moment in the opera, she is not over-intense, but the tone is richer, the lines expressively shaped. The performance of the cantata *Tra le fiamme* is notable for the brilliance and accuracy of Bayo's duetting in the opening aria with the obbligato viola da gamba. She sings 'Lascia ch'io pianga' with a refined line, but perhaps more vibrato than one might wish, and there is some gently alluring ornamentation in the *da capo*. As a Spaniard, she naturally includes Handel's little Spanish cantata, *No se emenderá jamás*, a light piece with guitar accompaniment, which is delicately done: this seems to be its only current recording with a soprano. Of the arias from *Alcina*, Morgana's 'Tornami a vagheggiar' is a delight for its high spirits and Bayo's easy, natural mode of delivery. 'Mi restano le lagrime', where Alcina faces her downfall, is done with pathos and poignancy – and again in the *da capo* her ornamentation allows for heightening of the expression.

David Daniels

Ariodante – E vivo ancora ... Scherza infida in grembo al drudo. Giulio Cesare – Cara speme, questo core; Va tacito e nascosto; L'angue offeso mai riposa; Al lampo dell'armi; Dall' ondoso periglio...Aure, deh, per pietà. Rinaldo – Cara sposa; Venti, turbini, prestate. Rodelinda – Pompe vane di morte!...Dove sei?; Vivi tiranno!. Serse – Fronde tenere...Ombra mai fù. Tamerlano – A dispetto

David Daniels *counterten* **Orchestra of the Age of Enlightenment / Sir Roger Norrington**

Virgin Classics Veritas VC5 45326-2 (69 minutes: DDD). Texts and translations included. Ⓕ
Recorded 1998

The ever-increasing popularity of Handel and his contemporaries, and their employment of alto castratos, has encouraged the development of countertenors capable of similar vocal feats to the original interpreters of the heroic roles in these works. Among these David Daniels can certainly be counted as a leading contender. He displays and deploys his talent here in a wide range of arias reflective and dramatic. His amazing technique runs through Tamerlano's virtuoso 'A dispetto' and Bertarido's 'Vivi tiranno!' without a blemish in the sound and with every division in its place yet part of a confidently delivered whole: by and large Daniels's runs and embellishments are smoothly accomplished. In more reflective pieces such as Giulio Cesare's 'Aure, deh, per pietà' (he also tackles Sesto's 'Cara speme' from *Giulio Cesare*, a particularly liquid, subtle piece of singing), Bertarido's 'Dove sei?' and Ariodante's sad lament, 'Scherza infida', written for the great Senesino, he uses his impeccable Italian to express wide-ranging emotions. Throughout, Roger Norrington and the Orchestra of the Age of Enlightenment give excellent support. The recording is blameless so there is every reason for readers to sample this fine exposition of the countertenor's art.

Véronique Gens

Armida abbandonata, HWV105. Agrippina condotta a morire, HWV110. La Lucrezia, HWV32

Véronique Gens *sop* **François Fernandez, Mira Glodeanu** *vns* **Les Basses Réunies** (Bruno Cocset *vc* Pascal Monteilhet *theorbo* Blandine Rannou *hpd* Richard Myron *db*)

Virgin Classics Veritas VC5 45283-2
(53 minutes: DDD). Texts and translations included. Ⓕ
Recorded 1996

Composed during Handel's youthful years in Italy, these cantatas contain some of the boldest music he ever wrote, and certainly amongst the most passionate. They are not set to the pastoral, amorous texts that were widely favoured: two of them deal with tragic episodes in Roman history (the rape of Lucretia and the condemnation to death of Agrippina by her son Nero), the other, after Tasso, with the betrayal of Armida.

These performances by Véronique Gens amply capture this passionate character. She brings to them a full, warm, large voice, not entirely without hints of vibrato, but handled with real feeling for style; she uses the words and their sound effectively, phrases expressively and sometimes subtly, varies her colour a good deal, and brings particular emotional energy to the recitatives. *Lucrezia* draws some remarkably intense singing from her, in the highly chromatic F minor aria and in the lament-like 'Alla salma infedel'. In this lament, the main continuo accompaniment is assigned to the theorbo, which emphasises the intimate tone of the music. The violin playing in *Armida* is also particularly enjoyable – brilliant in the *furioso* recitative, stylish and sweet-toned in 'Venti, fermate'. They play with admirable spirit and rhythmic spring in the lively second aria of *Agrippina*, too, where again Gens sings commandingly, impassioned in the first aria ('Orrida, oscura'), with lightness in the second and then with much intensity in the beautiful 'Come, o Dio!' and also in the concluding recitatives. Les Basses Réunies supplies excellent continuo support. In all, highly impressive performances of some superlative music.

Ann Murray

Alcina – Mi lusinga il dolce affetto; Verdi prati, selve amene; Stà nell'Ircana. Ariodante – E vivo ancora?... Scherza infida; Dopa notte. Giulio Cesare – Va tacito e nascosto; Se in fiorito ameno prato; Piangerò, la sorte mia; Dall' ondoso periglio...Aure, deh, per pietà. Serse – Fronde tenere e belle...Ombra mai fù; Se bramate d'amar, chi vi sdegna; Crude furie degl'orrido abissi

Ann Murray *mez* **Orchestra of the Age of Enlightenment / Sir Charles Mackerras**

Forlane UCD16738 (75 minutes: DDD). Texts and translations included. Recorded 1994 Ⓕ

The cautious tread of the watchful huntsman, with the lovely dialogue of voice and basset-horn in Caesar's first aria, makes a delightful beginning, and as the recital proceeds one realises afresh what variety of mood and manner will be found in almost any collection of arias by Handel. These range from the simple ease and beneficence of 'Verdi prati' to the florid outburst of the frustrated Xerxes in 'Crude furie'. In between are Cleopatra's lament, Caesar's love song, Ariodante's sadness and his new-found joy. The musical interest is unfailing wherever one looks, in rhythm, harmonic poignancy, or the scoring – the solo violin as woodbird in 'Se in fiorito ameno prato' or in the basset-horn of 'Va tacito'.

Handel and Mackerras have long been associated, and with the Orchestra of the Age of Enlightenment he provides the singer with a stylish accompaniment that is never assertive or doctrinaire but scrupulous in its care for phrasing and texture. Ann Murray responds with singing which has not only her customary expressiveness and energy but also a generally well-preserved beauty of tone that has not always been so characteristic. Occasionally a harsher, less firmly placed tone threatens to emerge, as at the start and *da capo* of 'Stà nell' Ircana', but such moments are short-lived and instead she encourages a mellower, warmer sound which also has the advantage of being precise in its focus. The voice is quite closely recorded.

Dorothea Röschmann

Handel German Arias, HWV202-10[a] **Telemann** Ⓟ
Musique de table – 'Paris' Quartets: G, E minor
[a]**Dorothea Röschmann** *sop* **Academy for Ancient Music, Berlin**
Harmonia Mundi HMC90 1689 (79 minutes: DDD) Ⓕ
Texts and translations included. Recorded 1998 ∞

Handel's nine *German Arias* are not as well known nor as often recorded as they deserve, perhaps because, being devotional music, they are generally rather solemnly, even earnestly sung. Dorothea Röschmann sings them delightfully. There is no want of seriousness, or intensity, where it is called for. The instrumental support is highly polished, but arguably too varied in colour: what is the justification for switching bass instruments for an aria's middle section? The obbligato part is shared between violin, flute and oboe: the oboe seems to be a mistake in the high part of 'Meine Seele', with a rather squealy effect – although Röschmann's exuberance at 'Alles jauchzet, alles lacht' ('all rejoice, all laugh') is happy. The Telemann 'Paris' quartets set off the arias well. Some of the playing in the E minor work is a little sober, but the lively G major is done in lively and elegant fashion, with spruce rhythms. But it is Röschmann's Handel that is the real joy: listen to 'Die ihr aus dunklen Grüften' and you won't be able to resist it.

Bryn Terfel

Judas Maccabaeus – I feel the Deity within ... Arm, arm, ye brave!. Te Deum in D, 'Dettingen' – Vouchsafe, O Lord. Samson – Honour and arms scorn such a foe. Berenice – Si, tra i ceppi e le ritorte. Alcina – Verdi prati, selve amene. Orlando – O voi del mio poter…Sorge infausta una procella. Acis and Galatea – I rage, I melt, I burn!…O ruddier than the cherry. Semele – Where'er you walk. Alexander's Feast – Revenge, revenge, Timotheus cries…Behold a ghastly band. Giulio Cesare – Va tacito e nascosto. Serse – Fronde tenere…Ombra mai fù. Messiah – Thus saith the Lord…But who may abide?; Why do the nations?; Behold I tell you a mystery…The trumpet shall sound
Bryn Terfel *bass-bar* **Scottish Chamber Orchestra / Sir Charles Mackerras**
DG 453 480-2GH (73 minutes: DDD). Texts and translations included. Recorded 1995 Ⓕ

'I feel', sings Terfel with assurance in his voice matching the solemnly, expectantly, ceremonious opening bars; and then, the second time, 'I feel', but now with the awed conviction of one who has experienced 'the Deity within'. The adjustment, the change of expression, is small, and no doubt when described sounds obvious enough; but it is typical of the imaginative intelligence Terfel brings. Comparing recordings, one hears authority in early versions, something more mystical in recent ones, but never such alertness as in Terfel. And what of his singing, his voice-production, his care for *legato*? As to the latter, conflict always lurks as expressive emphasis, shading and verbal naturalism assert their rights in the face of pure beauty and the evenness of the singing-line. Terfel is one in whom the rival claims work their way to a compromise, though if one side has to win it will generally be the expressive element. A good example of the compromise is the second track, the 'Vouchsafe, O Lord', quietly and simply sung, preserving the movement's unity and yet with a power of feeling that, at 'let thy mercy lighten upon us', is as overtly emotional as an operatic aria. The adapted arias, 'Where'er you walk', 'Verdi prati' and 'Ombra mai fù', justify their inclusion readily enough, and it is good to hear Terfel in the solos from *Messiah*. The singing here incorporates a good deal of embellishment, some of it of Mackerras's devising. He is an excellent conductor for Terfel, sharing with him an appreciation of the zest in Handel. The Scottish Chamber Orchestra appears to share it too, and the recording, though made in the resonant Usher Hall, is vivid and clean.

Alexander Balus, HWV65

Lynne Dawson, Claron McFadden *sops* **Catherine Denley** *mez* **Charles Daniels** *ten* **Michael George** *bass* **New College Choir, Oxford; The King's Consort and Choir / Robert King** Ⓟ
Hyperion ② CDA67241/2 (156 minutes: DDD) Ⓕ
Notes and text included. Recorded 1997

Alexander Balus has never been one of Handel's more popular oratorios. That is mainly because its plot is by modern standards lacking in drama and motivation, and accordingly does not call forth the vein of his music that nowadays has the strongest appeal. It tells a tale of treachery by Ptolomee, King of Egypt, against Alexander, King of Syria and the husband of his daughter Cleopatra (no relation to the famous one), who is allied to the Jews, under Jonathan. *Alexander Balus* is essentially a sentimental drama, in which the interest centres on the various characters' emotional reactions to their situations, amatory, political and religious, and these are rather static in the first two acts but much more powerful in the more eventful third with the deaths of both Alexander and Ptolomee. To an 18th-century audience it would have had resonances in terms of contemporary politics and religion, and in particular it explains, by analogy with English Protestantism, the seemingly smug attitude taken up by the Jews: everything would have been all right if only they had the right religion. Understanding its background helps you to understand why the music is as it is, so it is something of a pity that the otherwise informative booklet-note here touches on none of this.

Here we have a very capable, idiomatic, sensibly cast performance under Robert King. The choruses are especially accomplished. The New College Choir, supported by men from The King's Consort Choir, is confident, bright-toned and vigorous, clean in line and well balanced. Lynne Dawson sings beautifully in her firm and resonant soprano and her usual poised and unaffected style. Her singing of the lamenting music in the final act is particularly moving. Cleopatra has a couple of duets, one with some attractive interplay with the secondary character Aspasia, sung with much assurance by Claron McFadden. As Alexander, Catherine Denley sings with much confidence and directness in music that isn't all of special individuality. Jonathan is sung fluently and warmly, but very plainly, by Charles Daniels. Lastly there is Michael George, who is ideally suited to the villainous Ptolomee, with his forceful (but always musical) manner and the touch of blackness in his tone. The orchestral playing is accomplished, and often rather carefully shaped. The recitative moves at a steady but natural pace; ornamentation is generally modest. All Handelians will want to acquire this set, and others should not be put off by the indifferent press *Alexander Balus* has received from time to time.

Alexander's Feast, HWV75

Alexander's Feast. Concerto grosso in C, HWV318, 'Alexander's Feast' **P**
Donna Brown *sop* **Carolyn Watkinson** *contr* **Ashley Stafford** *counterten* **Nigel Robson** *ten* **Stephen Varcoe** *bar* **Monteverdi Choir; English Baroque Soloists / Sir John Eliot Gardiner**
Philips ② 422 053-2PH2 (98 minutes: DDD) Ⓕ
Text included. Recorded live in 1987 ●

Alexander's Feast was the first work Handel set by a major English poet (Dryden) and the first time he allotted the principal male part to a tenor instead of the castrato heroes of his Italian operas. These factors, combined with fine music, scored with great brilliance and imagination, ensured the immediate success of *Alexander's Feast*. It is strange that nowadays it is seldom performed so this recording would have been very welcome even had it not been so full of vitality and so stylishly performed. The Monteverdi Choir and the soloists are all Gardiner regulars, and the English Baroque Soloists have ample opportunities to shine – especially the violins, although the natural horns' lusty entry in the bucolic 'Bacchus, ever fair and young' is exhilarating.

L'Allegro, il Penseroso HWV55

Awards 1987

Patrizia Kwella, Marie McLaughlin, Jennifer Smith *sops* **Michael Ginn** *treb* **Maldwyn Davies, Martyn Hill** *tens* **Stephen Varcoe** *bar* **Monteverdi Choir; English Baroque Soloists / Sir John Eliot Gardiner** **P**
Erato ② 2292-45377-2 Ⓜ
(116 minutes: ADD). Notes, text and translation included. Recorded 1980 ●●●

The score of *L'Allegro, il Penseroso ed il Moderato* is presented virtually complete. The soprano aria 'But O, sad virgin' is omitted, which if you look at the marvellous opening for two cellos, seems savage indeed, but the music does rather lose its way in the long decorative passages for both voice and instruments, and its absence need not be regretted. The band is small and so is the superbly alert chorus. Playing and singing constantly delight by their delicacy. The three soprano soloists sound poised and clean-cut. Jennifer Smith's high notes are an especial joy. Handel wanted a boy treble for two arias and presumably knew that their words were never very clear; this one produces some pretty sounds. The succession of charming miniatures is interrupted in the middle of Part 2 by more substantial items and a blaze of brilliant coloratura from several soloists. Martyn Hill's 'These delights' is triumphantly good, and the choral singing here is excitingly precise. The final chorus in Part 2, a fugue with four subjects, is sublime, but he did not bother himself unduly with the final chorus in Part 3. But in general this is very likeable music, its charm, conciseness and emphasis on word-painting unlike anything else in Handel. The sound quality is very good.

L'Allegro, il penseroso ed il moderato, HWV55 **P**
Lorna Anderson, Susan Gritton, Claron McFadden *sops* **Paul Agnew** *ten* **Neal Davies** *bass* **The King's Consort Choir; The King's Consort / Robert King**
Hyperion ② CDA67283/4 (138 minutes: DDD) Ⓕ
Text and translation included. Recorded 1999

This is the first truly complete recording of Handel's delectable pastoral ode. Milton's two complementary poems, skilfully interleaved by Charles Jennens, offer a wealth of graphic, sensuous imagery; and the composer responded in a series of vignettes celebrating the English landscape with a freshness and fidelity of observation encountered in the paintings of Gainsborough and the poetry of James Thomson. The early numbers of *L'Allegro* – literally 'the cheerful man' – have a spontaneous exuberance barely matched in Handel's output, while much of the music of *Il penseroso* ('The melancholy man') attains a contemplative ecstasy found elsewhere only in parts of *Theodora*. The whole work is suffused with an almost pantheistic sense of wonder and delight in the natural world. For Part 3, *Il moderato*, Jennens offered a rational, very 18th-century reconciliation of Milton's two extreme temperaments. While alive to the *al fresco* gaiety of numbers such as 'Mirth, admit me of thy crew' and 'O let the merry bells', Robert King gives full value to the tranquil reflectiveness that lies at the core of the work, favouring broad tempos and gravely expressive phrasing. Occasionally, as in the soprano aria 'Straight mine eye hath caught new pleasures' and the pictorial accompanied recitative that follows, his approach seems a shade too reverential. But for the most part he directs this glorious music with affection and relish, abetted by vivid orchestral playing (the many obbligatos, notably from flute, horn and cello are invariably superb) and a typically responsive contribution from the chorus.

Susan Gritton is a soprano of rare accomplishment, with a warm, pure, yet highly individual timbre and a wonderful feeling for the broad Handelian line. Both the *scena* 'Come pensive nun' and the romantic nocturne 'Oft on a plat of rising ground', with its haunting evocation of 'the far-off curfew', are intensely moving; and, with the cellist Jane Coe, Gritton makes an eloquent case for the long florid aria 'But O! sad virgin', omitted in the Gardiner recording. Lorna Anderson, if a mite less secure above the stave, brings an appealing plangent tone to the nightingale aria 'Sweet bird' (done complete here, whereas Gardiner makes drastic cuts) and a trancelike absorption to the sublime 'Hide me from Day's garish eye'. Some slightly odd vowel sounds apart, Claron McFadden's bright, eager tones and nimble coloratura serve the more extrovert arias well; Neal Davies is sturdy in his bucolic hunting number and mellifluous in his minuet aria in *Il moderato*; and Paul Agnew is personable and stylish, though his *legato* is rather shown up by Susan Gritton's in 'As steals the morn'.

Apollo e Dafne, HWV122

Apollo e Dafne, 'La terra e liberata'. Crudel tiranno amor, HWV97 **P**

Nancy Argenta *sop* **Michael George** *bass*
Collegium Musicum 90 / Simon Standage
Chandos Chaconne CHAN0583 (58 minutes: DDD) Ⓕ
Texts and translations included. Recorded 1994

Handel's *Apollo e Dafne* is a difficult work to put in context. Completed in Hanover in 1710 but possibly begun in Italy, its purpose is not clear, while as secular cantatas go it is long (40 minutes) and ambitiously scored for two soloists and an orchestra of strings, oboes, flute, bassoon and continuo. But this is not just a chunk of operatic experimentation: it sets its own, faster pace than the leisurely unfolding of a full-length baroque stage-work, yet its simple Ovidian episode, in which Apollo's pursuit of the nymph Dafne results in her transformation into a tree, is drawn with all the subtlety and skill of the instinctive dramatic genius that Handel was. This recording features the expert Handelian voices of Nancy Argenta and Michael George, and both convey their roles convincingly. Argenta's hard, clear tone seems just the thing for the nymph, who is not required to be especially alluring but who does have to sound quick to anger and (literally) untouchable; and George strikes the right note as Apollo, bragging loudly at the opening of his superior skill in archery to Cupid before succumbing more gently, and in the end extremely touchingly, to Cupid's arts. The orchestra is bright and efficient (though without ever creating a very big sound), and the pacing of the work seems just right. This is superb Handel then, and as if that were not enough there is a bonus in the form of a shorter cantata for soprano and strings, *Crudel tiranno amor*. It is a beautiful piece indeed, and Argenta performs it perfectly.

Deborah, HWV51

Yvonne Kenny, Susan Gritton *sops* **Catherine Denley** *mez* **James Bowman** *counterten* **Michael George** *bass* **New College Choir, Oxford; Salisbury Cathedral Choristers; The King's Consort / Robert King** **P**
Hyperion ② CDA66841/2 (140 minutes: DDD). Text included. Recorded 1993 Ⓕ

Deborah, written in 1733, was the first oratorio composed for the entertainment of London theatre audiences. It is also a compound of numerous earlier works, including the Chandos and Coronation Anthems, the *Brockes Passion* and the *Ode for the Birthday of Queen Anne*, and in putting *Deborah* together in this manner, Handel was less successful than he usually was in creating a unified work – though the librettist and indeed the Bible itself have to be assigned some of the blame. It is, however, worth revival. It begins with an overture different from the one usually heard: a fine, stirring D major trumpety piece, with a concluding minuet that was to find a place in the *Fireworks* Music. There are some noble choruses, several of which are in five or even eight voices, giving Handel the opportunity for grand effects. The chief interest rests with the choruses. Here they are very well sung by the combined forces of 32 trebles, eight countertenors, six tenors and eight basses, who produce a lot more sound than you might expect. Robert King's control of this group and the polish he imparts to the choral singing, with its clearly projected lines and its firmness of tone is admirable, as is Michael George's warm and resonant contribution as Abinoam and Catherine Denley's firm, direct and stylish singing of the music of the unfortunate Sisera. The orchestral playing is polished; the recorded sound is more reverberant than might be ideal.

Dixit Dominus, HWV232

Dixit Dominus. Laudate pueri Dominum, HWV237
Saeviat tellus, HWV240. Salve regina, HWV241
Annick Massis *sop* **Magdalena Kožená** *mez*
Choeur des Musiciens du Louvre; Les Musiciens du Louvre / Marc Minkowski
Archiv Produktion 459 627-2AH (78 minutes: DDD) Ⓕ
Texts and translations included. Recorded live 1998 **OO**

These pieces, written in Handel's early twenties, embody a kind of excitement and freedom, and a richness of ideas, that come from his contact with a different tradition and a sudden realisation that the musical world was larger and less constricted than he had imagined, tucked away in provincial middle and north Germany: and that he was exhilarated by the discovery. You can positively hear him stretching his musical wings in this music. And it certainly does not fail to take off in these very lively performances. The quickish tempos habitually favoured by Marc Minkowski are by no means out of place here. The *Saeviat tellus*, although little recorded, is pretty familiar music as Handel recycled most of it, notably the brilliant opening number in *Apollo e Dafne* and the lovely 'O nox dulcis' in *Agrippina*. This is a solo motet, as too is the *Salve regina*, notable for the expressive vocal leaps and chromatic writing in the 'Ad te clamamus' and the solo organ and string writing in the 'Eia ergo' that follows. *Laudate pueri*, which uses a choir, is another fresh and energetic piece: the choir of the Musiciens du Louvre do their pieces in rousing fashion, and there is some happy oboe playing, as well as fine singing from Kožená, earlier on, in particular in the hugely spirited 'Excelsus super omnes'. The biggest item is of course the *Dixit Dominus*, where the choir sings very crisply. The illustrative settings of 'ruinas' tumbling down through the registers, and the 'conquassabit' that follows, are truly exciting; and the long closing chorus is done with due weight at quite a measured pace. These are splendid performances that truly capture the spirit of these marvellous pieces.

Israel in Egypt, HWV54

Libby Crabtree, Susan Gritton *sops* **Michael Chance, Robert Ogden** *countertens* **Ian Bostridge** *ten* **Stephen Varcoe, Henry Herford** *basses* **Angela East** *vc* **Alastair Ross** *hpd* **James Vivian** *org* **King's College Choir, Cambridge; The Brandenburg Consort / Stephen Cleobury**

Decca ② 452 295-2DH2 (126 minutes: DDD) Ⓕ
Text and translation included. Recorded 1995 ⭘

Israel in Egypt is an experimental one-off, since no other Handel oratorio shows such a heavy imbalance in favour of choruses over arias and recitatives. Handel himself seems to have seen it as a miscalculation not worth repeating; after the lukewarm reception which attended its première in London in 1739 he quickly amended it by importing arias from other works, and when he revived the work in 1756 he replaced the first of its three parts with a new, largely *pasticcio* concoction.

Subsequently, the oratorio became known almost entirely by Parts 2 and 3 – 'Exodus' and 'Moses' Song' – and gained justifiable popularity for its thrilling *echt*-Handelian choruses, as well as for typically tender moments such as the alto aria 'Thou shalt bring them in'. The original Part 1 – basically the 1737 funeral anthem for Queen Caroline, minimally adjusted from 'The Ways of Zion do mourn' to become 'The Lamentations of the Israelites for the Death of Joseph' – was in the meantime consigned to obscurity, from whence it has rarely emerged, even in its independent state.

The first recording to restore *Israel in Egypt* to triptych condition was Andrew Parrott's with the Taverner Consort and Players in 1989. The two make an interestingly complementary pair. Parrott's is a typical product of the British period-performance scene of the time, with a virtuoso, mixed professional choir delivering a brisk, lean and incisive reading, backed up by such stalwart baroque soloists as Nancy Argenta, Anthony Rolfe-Johnson and David Thomas. It is very accomplished, but in places it is underpowered and lacking in atmosphere.

The King's performance offers something different. The spacious chapel acoustic cannot help but bring a greater grandeur to proceedings, of course, but the presence of a choir of men and boys also forges an unmistakable aural link with the English choral tradition – which one assumes is what Handel himself was attempting to tap into when he put in all these choruses in the first place. It works wonders above all for Part 1, the erstwhile anthem, which in these evocative surroundings begins, at least, to escape the torpor which its static, overwhelmingly slow choruses can create. The principal gain in Parts 2 and 3, on the other hand, is in sheer weight. True, there is less textural clarity than in the Parrott (the alto line sometimes struggles to be heard), but the hammerblows of 'He smote all the first-born of Egypt', for instance, though blunter than Parrott's, are certainly mightier. The downside, inevitably, is a comparative lack of vocal precision in the choir; fast passagework, such as in 'I will sing unto the Lord', is clouded compared to the Taverner Consort, and the boys sound tired in 'But the waters overwhelmed their enemies'.

Elsewhere, however, Cleobury shows a surer touch than Parrott in some of the less bombastic descriptive music; the orchestral breezes of the soprano aria 'Thou didst blow with the wind' are bracingly real, while good spatial separation among the violins lends such verisimilitude to 'Their land brought forth frogs' that you almost feel that one of the little blighters is going to plop onto your head at any minute. Cleobury also has a strong solo line-up, better matched than Parrott's team, though for the latter the ever-stern David Thomas is surely more of a natural for the duet 'God is a man of war' than the more gentlemanly Stephen Varcoe.

On balance, the vote just about goes to Cleobury though both have their virtues. But it is worth pointing out that for those who (probably along with Handel) consider that all the best music resides in Parts 2 and 3, a very strong rival exists in John Eliot Gardiner's vivid and superbly executed performance with the Monteverdi Choir, recorded live in 1990.

Israel in Egypt, HWV54

Nancy Argenta, Emily Van Evera *sops* **Timothy Wilson** *counterten* **Anthony Rolfe Johnson** *ten* **David Thomas, Jeremy White** *basses* **Taverner Choir and Players / Andrew Parrott** 🅿

Virgin Classics Veritas ② VMD5 61350-2 Ⓜ
(135 minutes: DDD). Text included. Recorded 1989

Israel in Egypt, of all Handel's works, is the choral one *par excellence* – so much so, in fact, that it was something of a failure in Handel's own time because solo singing was much preferred to choral by the audiences. Andrew Parrott gives a complete performance of the work, in its original form: that is to say, prefaced by the noble funeral anthem for Queen Caroline, as adapted by Handel to serve as a song of mourning by the captive Israelites. This first part is predominantly slow, grave music, powerfully elegiac; the Taverner Choir shows itself to be firm and clean of line, well focused and strongly sustained. The chorus has its chance to be more energetic in the second part, with the famous and vivid Plague choruses – in which the orchestra too plays its part in the pictorial effects, with the fiddles illustrating in turn frogs, flies and hailstones. And last, in the third part, there is a generous supply of the stirring C major music in which Handel has the Israelites give their thanks to God, in some degree symbolizing the English giving thanks for the Hanoverian monarchy and the Protestant succession. Be that as it may, the effect is splendid. The solo work is first-rate, too, with Nancy Argenta radiant in Miriam's music in the final scene and distinguished contributions from David Thomas and Anthony Rolfe Johnson.

Jephtha, HWV70

Awards 1989

Lynne Dawson, Ruth Holton *sops* **Anne Sofie von Otter** *mez* **Michael Chance** *counterten* **Nigel Robson** *ten* **Stephen Varcoe** *bar* **Alastair Ross** *hpd* **Paul Nicholson** *org* **Monteverdi Choir; English Baroque Soloists / Sir John Eliot Gardiner** **P**

Philips ③ 422 351-2PH3 (158 minutes: DDD) Ⓕ
Text included. Recorded live in 1988 ●●●

Jephtha has the same basic story as several eastern Mediterranean myths familiar to the opera-goer (in *Idomeneo* and *Iphigénie en Aulide*, for example), of the father compelled to sacrifice his child. Jephtha's daughter Iphis is not in the event sacrificed: when Abraham-like, her father has shown himself willing to perform God's will, and she has shown herself ready to accept it, an angel happily intervenes and commutes her sentence to perpetual virginity. But not before the tragic situation has provoked some of the noblest music Handel wrote. From the moment that Jephtha sees that it is his daughter who has to fall victim to his improvident oath, the music, hitherto on a good but not outstanding level, acquires a new depth, above all in the sequence at the end of Act 2. This recording does the work full justice. It could scarcely have been better cast. Nigel Robson seems ideal as Jephtha. He has due weight as well as vigour, style as well as expressive force. Lynne Dawson's Iphis is also a real success. Sometimes this role is done in a girlishly 'innocent' vein; she does more than that, establishing the character in the appealing love duet in Part 1. Her firm, well-focused, unaffected singing is just right for this role.

The other outstanding contribution comes from Michael Chance as Hamor, her unfortunate betrothed. His first song, 'Dull delay', is beautifully measured and delicately shaped, and indeed all his singing is impeccably musicianly, attentive to the words too: his declamation of the recitative is a model. Stephen Varcoe sings Zebul's music with due resonance and spirit, and Anne Sofie von Otter makes a distinguished contribution in Storgè's music: 'Scenes of horror' has a splendid attack and depth of tone, and 'Let other creatures die!' is spat out with rare power. Ruth Holton makes a pleasantly warm and mellifluous angel. The Monteverdi Choir is in fine voice: vigorous in attack, precise in ensemble, firm in tone at all dynamic levels, responsive to all that Gardiner asks of them. Here and there one might cavil at some of the dynamic shaping in the choruses, for example in 'Doubtful fear' in Act 3; and the Overture can be a trifle fussy in detail. But the broad vision of the work, the rhythmic energy that runs through it and the sheer excellence of the choral and orchestral contributions speak for themselves. Cuts are very few, and amply justified by authentic precedent. This recording is firmly recommended as likely to be the standard version of this great work.

Joseph and his Brethren, HWV59

Yvonne Kenny *sop* **Catherine Denley** *mez* **Connor Burrowes** *treb* **James Bowman** *counterten* **John Mark Ainsley** *ten* **Michael George** *bass* **New College Choir, Oxford; The King's Consort Choir; The King's Consort / Robert King** **P**

Hyperion ③ CDA67171/3 (164 minutes: DDD) Ⓕ
Text included. Recorded 1996

There has never been a complete, professional recording of *Joseph and his Brethren*, a neglect out of proportion to the merits of its music. It is full of good and characteristic things, and there are several scenes, including the extended denouement in the last act, that are very moving. The work begins splendidly, with an unusual overture heralding a deeply felt opening scene for Joseph, languishing in an Egyptian prison. The setting of his prophecy is effective, with seven bars of darting arpeggios for the years of plenty and seven of sparse harmonic writing, *adagio*, for the famine years. The rest of Act 1 celebrates Joseph's foresight, preferment and marriage to Asenath, Pharaoh's daughter. The highlights of Act 2 include a prison scene for Simeon, an agonised G minor accompanied recitative and aria, a beautiful, nostalgic idyll for Joseph, and scenes for Joseph with his brothers which incorporate a splendid outburst from Simeon, an aria from Benjamin and a moving chorus from the brothers, a sustained prayer and a richly worked fugue.

The soloists dispatch all this music with spirit and accuracy. Of course, the central figure is James Bowman in the very demanding title-role. He is in excellent voice, full, rich and duly agile in the rapid music. *Joseph* is well suited to Robert King's way of conducting Handel. This is not a specially dramatic performance, but carefully moulded, well balanced, intelligently paced. The choir produces a sound that is bright and firm and the singing is resolute, although the attack is soft-edged rather than incisive. King is particularly good at shaping the dynamics in a natural and unanimous way.

Messiah, HWV56

Dorothea Röschmann, Susan Gritton *sops* **Bernarda Fink** *contr* **Charles Daniels** *ten* **Neal Davies** *bass* **Gabrieli Consort and Players / Paul McCreesh** **P**

Archiv Produktion ② 453 464-2AH2
(132 minutes: DDD). Text included. Ⓕ
Recorded 1996 ●●

The Gabrieli Consort and Players are as responsive and professional a group as you will find. McCreesh has assembled solo singers with broad mainstream experience and Handel's choruses encapsulate all the vitality and litheness of the modern English vocal consort at its best. More than that, McCreesh is a natural dramatist and all his singers respond magnificently to the evangelical fervour. McCreesh's expression is candid and immediate, if not imparted with the unfolding spirituality of Suzuki, or fragrancy of Christie; his is a particular musicianship which reaches out, quite Sargent-like in the robust swagger of 'And the Glory', the grand leisurely 'Amen' and almost elegiac enunciation in 'Comfort ye' – perhaps too static for some but Charles Daniels's supreme control has us holding our breath.

McCreesh, in employing, for the most part, the Foundling Hospital version of 1754, treats us to a second soprano. His casting serves him well with two incandescent performances: Susan Gritton is suitably unmollifiable in 'a refiner's fire' though she turns on the intensity in 'I know that my Redeemer liveth'. Dorothea Röschmann provides a similarly bright edge and in both cases, we are treated to singing of real technical finesse. Bernarda Fink's heady and rasping contralto may not appeal to everyone but 'He was despised' leaves one in little doubt of Jennens's starkest sentiments. Neal Davies is sure-footed and impressive. The energy and focused proclamation of this reading will win many friends: whilst tempos may appear hard-pushed, there is a consistency and rooted concentration to proceedings, always thoroughly engaged. Recorded sound is resonant but also close, and fairly compressed in its livelier moments.

Messiah **P**

Arleen Auger *sop* **Anne Sofie von Otter** *mez* **Michael Chance** *counterten* **Howard Crook** *ten* **John Tomlinson** *bass* **The Choir of the English Concert; The English Concert / Trevor Pinnock**

Archiv Produktion ② 423 630-2AH2 (150 minutes: DDD). Text included. Recorded 1988 Ⓕ ●●

How authentic is authentic? Trevor Pinnock and The English Concert, while using period instruments, are guaranteed to appeal very widely to traditional lovers of Handel's masterpiece, who might as a rule opt for a performance using modern instruments. Pinnock gets the best of both worlds. One of the most distinctive points is that, even more than his rivals, he brings out the impact of timpani and trumpets, above all in the 'Hallelujah' and 'Amen' choruses. In that he stirs the blood in a way that even Sargent would have envied. Another distinctive point is that a genuine, dark, firm, bass soloist has been chosen, John Tomlinson, who is ripely resonant here. Traditionalists who lament the lack of dark bass tone and the predominance of baritonal shades in Handel today will doubtless raise a cheer, and if it comes to authenticity, Handel must surely have been thinking of just such a voice, rather than anything thinner or more discreet. Not only Tomlinson but Arleen Auger too will delight listeners of all Handelian persuasions. She has one of the sweetest, most ravishing soprano sounds on any of the current versions, and the warmth of expressiveness, whether strictly authentic or not, brings many of the most memorable moments in the whole performance. Try the close of 'I know that my Redeemer liveth', where the dramatic contrasts of dynamic are extreme and masterfully controlled, without a hint of sentimentality. The male alto, Michael Chance, also outshines his direct rivals in artistry and beauty of tone, but he is given only a proportion of the alto numbers. The majority are given to Anne Sofie von Otter. Hers is another beautiful voice, finely controlled. The recording is one of the finest available, with plenty of bloom and with inner clarity never making textures sound thin or overanalytical.

Messiah **H**

Dame Isobel Baillie *sop* **Gladys Ripley** *contr* **James Johnston** *ten* **Norman Walker** *bass* **Huddersfield Choral Society; Liverpool Philharmonic Orchestra / Sir Malcolm Sargent**

Dutton Laboratories Essential Archive mono ② 2CDEA5010 (146 minutes: ADD) Ⓑ

Recorded 1946 ●

From the 1940s until the early 1960s one of the greatest of regular British musical events (every bit as important as the Proms) was Malcolm Sargent's *Messiah*. He conducted it up and down the country, always to packed houses; and indeed for one to be able to attend the performance at Huddersfield Town Hall needed very special connections (ideally with a member of the choir), for tickets were scarcer than an invitation to Buckingham Palace! It was easier to go to the final London performance with the Royal Choral Society on Good Friday, which was unabridged, and involved both afternoon and evening sessions! Otherwise Sargent usually omitted – as he does on this recording – three numbers from Part 2 and four from Part 4. Even then, the performance time was two-and-a-half hours without the interval. Apart from spacious tempos, Sargent had his own ideas about Handelian style. Today we usually listen to a quite different kind of *Messiah*, brisker, often exchanging grandeur for exhilaration; so it is heart-warming to have the opportunity to return to a great tradition that Sargent kept alive for so many years.

This is made possible by one of Dutton Laboratories' most miraculous 78rpm transfers – the finest ever heard taken from 78s of any music – of Sargent's extraordinarily vivid and expansive recording (the most spontaneous of the three he made). The four splendid soloists – that queen of oratorio sopranos, Dame Isobel Baillie; the rich-voiced Gladys Ripley; the warmly lyrical James Johnson; and the vibrant Norman Walker are right inside their parts. But the star of the performance is undoubtedly Isobel Baillie. Her first entry in 'There were shepherds' is a truly ravishing moment, while her gloriously beautiful 'I know that my Redeemer liveth' has never been surpassed on record. Sargent opens the work with a sumptuous presentation of the Overture, while his tempos for the choruses now sound very slow to ears used to 'authenticity'. Sargent believed deeply in this music and he carried the listener with him. The hushed close of 'All we like sheep' almost brings tears to the eyes. The sound itself is truly astounding! In its original 78rpm format this set sold more than 120,000 copies in America alone, and it cost a great dealof money in those days. At bargain price it is an ideal investment for anyone who relishes an old-fashioned, large-scale approach to Handel's *Messiah*.

The Occasional Oratorio, HWV62

Susan Gritton, Lisa Milne *sops* **James Bowman** *counterten* **John Mark Ainsley** *ten* **Michael George** *bass* **New College Choir, Oxford; The King's Consort / Robert King** 🅿
Hyperion ② CDA66961/2 (144 minutes: DDD) Ⓕ
Text included. Recorded 1994

The occasion that called forth this work was the Jacobite rising of 1745 and its impending defeat. The Duke of Cumberland's victory at Culloden was yet to come. Handel, anticipating it, hit off the mood of the moment with a rousing piece full of appeals to patriotic feeling, partly through the traditional identification between the English Protestant culture of Hanoverian times with that of the biblical Hebrews. Much of the music comes from existing works, notably *Israel in Egypt*. The 'plot' pursues the familiar route of Anxiety-Prayer-Victory-Jubilation, but the work lacks the unity of theme and purpose of the great dramatic oratorios; if, however, you value Handel primarily because the music is so splendid you will find a lot to relish here. King rises to the challenge of this sturdier side of Handel's muse and produces playing and singing full of punch and energy, and with that command of the broad Handelian paragraph without which the music lacks its proper stature.

The grand eight-part choruses, with the choir properly spaced, antiphonally, over the stereo span, make their due effect. King has a distinguished solo team. John Mark Ainsley's singing is particularly touching in the highly original 'Jehovah is my shield', where the rocking figures in the orchestra eventually turn out to symbolise sleep. Also very enjoyable is Susan Gritton's soprano, a sharply focused voice with a fine ring and due agility in the lively music and handled with taste and a keen feeling for the shape of phrases in the contemplative airs. A fine set.

Saul, HWV53

Lynne Dawson, Donna Brown *sops* **Derek Lee Ragin** *counterten* **John Mark Ainsley, Neil Mackie, Philip Salmon, Philip Slane** *tens* **Alastair Miles, Richard Savage** *basses* **Monteverdi Choir; English Baroque Soloists / Sir John Eliot Gardiner** 🅿
Philips ③ 426 265-2PH3 (159 minutes: DDD) Ⓕ
Recorded live in 1989 ●

Saul is considered by many to be one of the most arresting music dramas in the English language, even though it is officially classed as an oratorio. In it Handel explores in some psychological depth the motivation of his characters, most notably that of the eponymous anti-hero, whose tantrums caused by envy and by his searching for supernatural intervention are all vividly delineated; as is the friendship of David and Jonathan and the different characters of Saul's daughters, Merab and Michal. In yet another compelling performance of Handel under his baton, John Eliot Gardiner – in this live recording made at the Göttingen Handel Festival in Germany – fulfils every aspect of this varied and adventurous score, eliciting execution of refined and biting calibre from his choir and orchestra. Alastair Miles captures Saul in all his moods. John Mark Ainsley and Derek Lee Ragin are affecting as Jonathan and David; so are Lynne Dawson and Donna Brown as Michal and Merab. There are a few cuts, but not serious enough to prevent us from making a firm recommendation.

Solomon, HWV67

Andreas Scholl *counterten* **Inger Dam-Jensen, Susan Gritton, Alison Hagley** *sops* **Susan Bickley** *mez* **Paul Agnew** *ten* **Peter Harvey** *bass* **Gabrieli Consort and Players / Paul McCreesh** 🅿
Archiv Produktion ③ 459 688-2AH3
(161 minutes: DDD). Notes and text included. Ⓕ
Recorded 1998. ●●

Solomon is universally recognised as one of Handel's finest masterpieces, not only with magnificent choruses, but more importantly containing rapturous love music, nature imagery, affecting emotion and, in Part 2, the vividly portrayed dramatic scene of Solomon's famous judgement over the disputed infant. This is in fact the only dramatic part of the oratorio; and each of the female characters appears in only one of the work's three parts. Paul McCreesh, responsive to the work's stature, employs an orchestra of about 60 (including a serpent as the bass of the wind group, and incidentally instructing the horns to play with their bells up to produce a more pungent tone) and presents the oratorio in the original 1749 version, full and uncut. It has been argued that even in so splendid a work Handel was fallibly human enough to include some dead wood. McCreesh, however, stoutly defends Handel's original structural balance. In one respect, though, he does depart from Handel's intentions. By the time *Solomon* was written, Handel was using no castratos in his oratorios, and the title-role in this case was deliberately designed for a mezzo-soprano; but here the chance to secure the pre-eminent countertenor Andreas Scholl was irresistible. The colour of Handel's predominantly female vocal casting (only Zadok and the smaller-part Levite being exceptions) is thus slightly modified. This historical infidelity is one of the few reservations that could be made about the set, which is a notable achievement.

McCreesh is fortunate in his cast, too. Predictably, Scholl becomes the central focus by his beauty of voice (conspicuously in 'When the sun o'er yonder hills'), calm authority, charm ('What though I trace') and intelligent musicianship throughout. Inger Dam-Jensen, as Solomon's queen, sounds suitably ecstatic in the florid 'Blessed the day' and amorous in 'With thee th'unsheltered moor', and her duet with Solomon flows with easy grace. The confrontation between the two harlots in Part 2 is brilliantly characterised by Alison Hagley as the tenderly maternal one (her 'Can I see my infant gored?' is most moving) and Susan Bickley as the inhumanly vengeful one. And to Susan Gritton falls the sublime 'Will the sun forget to streak', with its wonderful unison oboe-and-flute obbligato. As the high priest Zadok, Paul Agnew shines in the ornate 'See the tall palm'. A more positive and audible keyboard continuo would have been welcome but this is a minor shortcoming, and the effect of the performance as a whole is deeply impressive, with such things as 'Will the sun', the grave interlude to 'With pious heart' and the elegiac chorus 'Draw the tear from hopeless love' haunting the listener's mind.

Susanna, HWV66

Awards 1991

Lorraine Hunt, Jill Feldman *sops* **Drew Minter** *counterten* **Jeffrey Thomas** *ten* **William Parker** *bar* **David Thomas** *bass* **Chamber Chorus of the University of California, Berkeley; Philharmonia Baroque Orchestra / Nicholas McGegan** P
Harmonia Mundi ③ HMU90 7030/2 Ⓕ
(178 minutes: DDD). Notes and text included.
Recorded live in 1989. ooo

Here is a case of the most astonishing neglect by the record companies. *Susanna* was neglected even by Handel, who revived it only once, in his last year, after the première performances of 1749. *Susanna* tells the tale from the Apocrypha of the two Elders who, espying a beautiful and virtuous woman about to bathe, decide when she rejects their advances to denounce her as an adultress; she is sentenced to death and saved only when Daniel comes to judgement and restores her to her loving husband. This performance confirms that it is a deeply serious work, with no more than a flicker of comedy in the representation of the Elders. In a long opening scene the marital happiness of Susanna and Joacim is firmly established, to provide a context for Susanna's virtue and morality. When Joacim departs, Susanna is struck with foreboding, marvellously expressed in an accompanied recitative and an aria, in B minor with rich, five-part strings, in which a new tone enters, grave yet glowing and steadfast: 'Bending to the throne of glory' is one of Handel's noblest utterances, as sung here by Lorraine Hunt. Then enter the Elders, artfully characterised by Handel: a tenor, capable of a graceful paean to love and nature ('Ye verdant hills'), and eager to woo Susanna; and a bass, whose music is more fiery and whose inclinations are more violent. These are cleverly cast: Jeffrey Thomas is brilliantly successful at infusing the tenor music with insinuating sensuality that perfectly catches the character's lasciviousness, while David Thomas sings the bass's music with a sharpness of line and a graphic expression of the music and its sense that seem truly menacing.

Drew Minter makes a musical Joacim, gentle in tone and phrasing, perfectly tuned; the part is perhaps a shade high-lying for him. His tone lacks the firm centre that might be ideal here, especially for the fiery aria at the end of the Second Act, but the delicate control of his singing gives pleasure. He and the Susanna, Lorraine Hunt, match extraordinarily well. Her soprano may not be the most beguiling, but her singing achieves great power and tonal concentration in the great expressive arias that are the heart of the work, to which she truly rises – and her bathing aria at the beginning of Part 2 has an apt touch of languor. Jill Feldman's singing of the Attendant's arias, and later of Daniel's, is duly fresh and stylish, possibly a shade shrill in sound though apt enough for these youthful roles.

There is some first-rate choral singing, marked by strong, direct rhythms and firm lines, very telling in the vigorous fugal movements. The Philharmonia Baroque Orchestra produces a warmer sound than many baroque bands but with welcomely little of surface gloss; they are excellently disciplined and their articulation is pleasantly incisive. Nicholas McGegan's feeling for tempo and for the sense of the music seems to be unerring, and the power and the springiness of the rhythms he sets in the big choral numbers lends them true grandeur. An excellent recording, a first-rate accompanying booklet: you will obtain great pleasure from this set.

Theodora, HWV68

Lorraine Hunt *sop* **Jennifer Lane** *mez* **Drew Minter** *counterten* **Jeffrey Thomas** *ten* **Nigel Rogers** *ten* **David Thomas** *bass* **Chamber Chorus of the University of California, Berkeley; Philharmonia Baroque Orchestra / Nicholas McGegan** P
Harmonia Mundi ③ HMU90 7060/2
(170 minutes: DDD). Text included. Ⓕ
Recorded 1991 o

If contemporary audiences were put off by the theme of martyrdom, we should be grateful that the self-righteous piety of Morell's libretto inspired some of Handel's finest music here, with the added bonus of both the original and revised versions of 'Symphony of Soft Musick'. This recording can be wholeheartedly recommended. David Thomas as Valens, the Roman governor, opens the proceedings with a firm and resolute tone and later gives the bloodthirsty 'Racks, gibbets, sword and fire' much menace. Lorraine Hunt was an inspired choice for the taxing title-role: the top notes of 'Angels ever bright and fair' are celestially floated, while she finds great intensity in 'With darkness deep', the emotional centre of the work. Drew Minter gives a mellifluous and characterful account of Didymus, a Roman officer recently converted to Christianity who attempts to save Theodora. Listen to their duet, 'To Thee, Thou glorious Son', to hear how winningly they blend their voices. Praise too for Jeffrey Thomas as Septimius, particularly in his elegant ornamentation in the virtuoso aria 'Dread the fruits of Christian folly', only occasionally showing strain in the wide leaps in 'From virtue springs'. Jennifer Lane is also impressive as Irene (described in the libretto simply as 'A Christian') – despite being burdened with some of Morell's most trite utterances. Nicholas McGegan has at his command a highly skilled orchestra and excellent choir, chooses tempos which are unfailingly apt, supporting and giving weight to the vocal lines.

Opera arias and duets

Alessandro – Overture; Sinfonia; Che vidi?; No, più soffrir; Placa l'alma; Solitudine amate...Aure, fonti; Pur troppo veggio...Che tirannia d'Amor; Svanisci, oh reo timore...Dica il falso. Admeto, Re di Tessaglia – Il ritratto d'Admeto; La sorte mia vacilla; Quest'è dunque la fede...Vedrò fra poco. Riccardo Primo, re di Inghilterra – Morte vieni...A me nel mio rossere...Quando non vede. Siroe, re di Persia – A costei, che dirò?; L'aura non sempre; Si diversi sembianti...Non vi piacque, ingiusti dei. Tolomeo, re di Egitto – E dove, e dove mai...Fonti amiche; Ti pentirai, crudel **P**

Catherine Bott, Emma Kirkby *sops* **Brandenburg Consort / Roy Goodman**

Hyperion CDA66950 (76 minutes: DDD). Texts and translations included. Recorded 1997 Ⓕ **OO**

It was a happy idea to assemble a selection of Handel's arias written for the two sopranos whose famous rivalry coloured the last years of the first Royal Academy. Francesca Cuzzoni – impersonated here by Catherine Bott – was Handel's principal soprano from 1723, creating among other roles Cleopatra and Rodelinda. Faustina Bordoni – her roles here go to Emma Kirkby – arrived in 1726 and the two sang together in several operas including five new ones by Handel, all represented on this recording. Both were superlative singers and each had a characteristic style. Cuzzoni was praised for her clear and sweet high notes, her use of rubato, her control of volume and above all for her affecting expression. Bordoni, whose voice lay slightly lower, was admired for her fine articulation, flexibility in divisions and ornamentation, and passion and expression in slow arias.

In his music composed for them, Handel clearly differentiated between their capacities, as this disc illustrates. The 'rival queens' first sang together in *Alessandro*, which is the opera most fully represented here. There are two of Cuzzoni's arias, one brilliant piece with rapid divisions, which Bott throws off in splendidly free fashion, and a pathetic one, a typical F minor *siciliano*, taken very slowly here, allowing plenty of time for some expressive (but restrained) elaboration in the *da capo*. Of Faustina's music we have the exquisite *scena* that opens Act 2, including the aria, 'Aure, fonti', and the lively one with which the act closes. The aria typifies, in the way it demands and rewards precisely detailed singing, Handel's writing for her, and Kirkby's refinement of detail is remarkable. There is beautifully managed interplay between the singers in the *Alessandro* duet; they seem to feed one another with opportunities. The programme is imaginatively put together and Roy Goodman is a prompt and stylish accompanist.

Acis and Galatea, HWV49b

Norma Burrowes *sop* Galatea; **Anthony Rolfe Johnson** *ten* Acis; **Martyn Hill** *ten* Damon; **Willard White** **P**

Acis and Galatea, HWV49*b*

Sophie Daneman *sop* Galatea**; Paul Agnew** *ten* Acis**; Patricia Petibon** *sop* Damon**; Alan Ewing** *bass* Polyphemus**; Joseph Cornwell** *ten* Coridon**; François Piolino, David Le Monnier, Andrew Sinclair** *tens*

Les Arts Florissants / William Christie

Erato ② 3984-25505-2 93 minutes: DDD) Ⓕ

Texts included **OO**

Christie has elected to give a 'chamber version' of the work, that is, with forces akin to those Handel used for his original Cannons performances: probably five singers and between seven and a dozen instrumentalists (Christie actually has a couple of auxiliary tenors, which is understandable: the ensembles call for just one soprano, three tenors – one possibly a countertenor – and a bass). He does not however follow the original Cannons text, adding a choral 'Happy we' after the duet, and assigning the role of Damon to a soprano: these changes are not without Handelian authority, but it comes from his 1739 revival, which embodied other departures and used much larger forces. Never mind: there is nothing that any modern conductor would do that is half as shocking as the violences that Handel himself did to Acis on some of its revivals – and that should mute purist complaint.

Christie strongly emphasises the work's central division. He adopts rather speedy tempos throughout Act 1 (that is, up to 'Happy we'), which is concerned with pastoral love: Acis's 'Where shall I seek' and Damon's 'Shepherd, what art thou pursuing?' don't seem, respectively, like Larghetto and Andante, but the urgency and the joy of the lovers' mutual desire is strongly caught. In Act 2, where Polyphemus's shadow falls over their love, the sparkle and vitality give way to the pathetic and the elegiac. Christie's tempos here are steady, and his shaping of the act seems to me something of a departure: its climaxes here come not in 'The flocks shall leave the mountains' (when Acis is killed) and 'Heart, the seat of soft delight' (when he is immortalised as a river) – arguably the most powerful musical numbers – but in the ensembles, 'Mourn, all ye Muses!' and 'Must I my Acis still bemoan', where the sustained, refined, gentle singing of Christie's ensemble lends the music an emotional weight that it does not usually achieve (enhanced in 'Must I my Acis' by the preservation of the slowish tempo at the point, 'Cease, Galatea, cease to grieve', where most conductors press forward).

There are other, mostly smaller, points where Christie does new and different things, and some will not like all of them (examples are the horrid choral trill in 'Oh the pleasure of the plains!', at 3'31", and the top B flat a little later; the added orchestral coda in 'Happy we'; the acceleration during 'Wretched lovers', at 3'26"; or least of all the substitution of watery recorder for incisive oboe in 'Would you gain the tender creature'). Christie's orchestra is evidently one-to-a-part, as Handel's may have been: this seems to produce a slightly oboe-heavy balance in some items, and in the lightly scored pieces – such as 'Would you gain' – the continuo line seems overweighted.

The opening scenes, then, are done more lustily, in two senses, than usual. The choral opening is remarkably hearty and robust. Sophie Daneman sings Galatea with something more than stylised pastoral sensuality: there is real intensity in her airs, with a pretty warbling recorder, very chirrupy, and sharply moulded phrasing, and particular sensuality in 'As when the dove'. If her 'Heart, the seat', at the end, seems to carry rather less emotional weight, that is part of the overall reading of the work. Paul Agnew makes an elegant Acis in Act 1, with an eager 'Where shall I seek' and 'Love in her eyes sits playing' done with quiet passion. 'Love sounds th'alarm', later, is lively but not quite stirring. Patricia Petibon's Damon is prettily sung, with a nice ring to the voice, in Act 1, but her Act 2 air, 'Consider, fond shepherd', taken rather slowly, is marred by uncertainty in her English pronunciation and in her command of idiom. Joseph Cornwell's single air, as Coridon, with recorder, is not specially interestingly done. Alan Ewing's Polyphemus, done with spirit and humour in a well-focused, firm-edged voice and articulated with precision, is excellent.

Sir John Eliot Gardiner's version made in 1976 long held the field in this work, and to some extent still does, although Robert King's smaller-scale reading has many virtues too. Christie's new version may not be everyone's answer but it is a polished and strongly characterised performance, finely recorded, and is certainly the first we would urge anyone to try.

Admeto, Re di Tessaglia

René Jacobs *counterten* Admeto; **Rachel Yakar** *sop* Alceste; **Ulrik Cold** *bass* Ercole, Apollo; **Rita Dams** *mez* Orindo; **James Bowman** *counterten* Trasimede; **Jill Gomez** *sop* Antigona; **Max van Egmond** *bar* Meraspe, A Voice; **Il Complesso Barocco / Alan Curtis** P

Virgin Classics Veritas ③ VMT5 61369-2 (217 minutes: ADD). Notes, text and translation included. Recorded 1979 Ⓕ

This reissue is the first *Admeto* on CD. It is full of fine things, particularly in its music for the two women – Alceste, the nobly self-sacrificing wife of King Admetus, and Antigona, the princess he had once wooed but then rejected, who now returns after the supposed death of Alceste. The plot, then, is akin to the familiar one of Gluck's *Alceste*, but with an extra sub-plot that allows for touches of wit and irony (it was based on a Venetian libretto) and insights into human character. When it was first released, the recording was something of a pioneer as regards the use of period instruments and performing conventions. Things have moved on, of course: it seems a bit dated now, heavier in manner than most Handel opera recordings of recent years – for example, the recitatives are slowish, and the bows spend more time on the strings than is customary now. And some of the cast are not wholly at home in a baroque style where little vibrato is wanted. One thinks in particular of Rachel Yakar, but although her articulation and attack are not always ideally clean she does bring a good deal of spirit to some of the arias, for example her Act 3 'Là dove gli occhi io giro'.

Jill Gomez's lighter, bell-like voice is, however, more convincingly Handelian: she sings Antigona's music charmingly and with due agility, and expressively too in the beautiful Act 2 *siciliana*. James Bowman is in his best voice as Trasimede, Admetus's brother who loves Antigona. René Jacobs, however, lacks the heroic tones and the incisiveness that the role demands. Ulrik Cold makes a strong Ercole, with appropriately sturdy, masculine tone, and Meraspe is neatly and very stylishly sung by Max van Egmond. Alan Curtis's direction is attentive to matters of style, but he sometimes lets the bass-line plod. Even so, Handelians need not hesitate.

Agrippina

Della Jones *mez* Agrippina; **Derek Lee Ragin** *counterten* Nero; **Donna Brown** *sop* Poppea; **Alastair Miles** *bass* Claudius; **Michael Chance** *counterten* Otho; **George Mosley** *bar* Pallas; **Jonathan Peter Kenny** *counterten* Narcissus; **Julian Clarkson** *bass* Lesbo; **Anne Sofie von Otter** *mez* Juno; **English Baroque Soloists / Sir John Eliot Gardiner** P

Philips ③ 438 009-2PH3 (217 minutes: DDD)
Notes, text and translation included. Ⓕ
Recorded 1991-92 OO

Agrippina is Handel's Venetian opera, composed in 1709 for the S Giovanni Gristostomo theatre, where it was evidently and deservedly a great success. Handel drew on its music, but he never revived it: its scheme, with a large number of short and lightly accompanied arias, is very much of its time and its place. Yet *Agrippina* is a very effective piece, if directed with due vitality (as it is here), and it is full of appealing music in a wide variety of moods. Any admirer of countertenor singing should be prepared to buy the set for Michael Chance's singing alone. But in fact there are two other countertenors here who are well worth hearing, especially Derek Lee Ragin, whose high-lying voice and sensitive, thoughtful phrasing serve Nero's music admirably. His last aria, a brilliant piece with colourful instrumental writing, as he renounces Poppea in expectation of the imperial crown, is breathtakingly done, fiery singing with very precise execution of the divisions. The third of the countertenors is Jonathan Peter Kenny as Narcissus, rather softer in tone and line, who provides some particularly musical singing in his Act 2 aria.

Della Jones gives a masterful performance in the title-role. Her music is very varied in mood: there are several brief and catchy little pieces, which she throws off with spirit, but also some larger-scale numbers, such as the marvellous C minor aria near the end of Act 1 (although totally insincere in sentiment), which is done with great vigour, and the noble, invocation-like 'Pensieri, voi mi tormentate', another of the opera's high points, to which she brings much intensity. Donna Brown as Poppea makes the most of a role with much lively and appealing music. Alastair Miles's full and resonant bass – the part goes down to cello C – brings due weight of authority to the emperor Claudius; Pallas is done by a clean, lightish but nicely firm baritone, George Mosley, and Julian Clarkson contributes some very neat singing in the role of Lesbo. Anne Sofie von Otter comes in as a *dea ex machina* at the very end, not to rescue the situation but to honour the marriage of Poppea and Otho – which she does in style. John Eliot Gardiner is a fine and very experienced conductor of Handel and he has a sure feeling for tempo and for the character of each movement. The orchestral playing is beyond reproach. The text followed is that of the Chrysander edition. This recording is comfortably among the half-dozen finest recordings of Handel operas.

Alcina

Arleen Auger *sop* Alcina; **Eiddwen Harrhy** *sop* Morgana; **Kathleen Kuhlmann** *mez* Bradamante; **Della Jones** *mez* Ruggiero; **Patrizia Kwella** *sop* Oberto; **Maldwyn Davies** *ten* Oronte; **John Tomlinson** *bass* Melisso; **Opera Stage Chorus; City of London Baroque Sinfonia / Richard Hickox** **P**

EMI ③ CDS7 49771-2 (217 minutes: DDD). Notes, text and translation included. Recorded 1985 Ⓕ ●

Alcina, musically and dramatically, is among the finest of Handel's operas. This set must certainly have a strong claim to be reckoned one of the best sung of Handel opera recordings. There is no member of the cast who is not a Handelian of high quality and natural sense of style. What Arleen Auger loses in sheer brilliance of tone or technique she makes up by the sweetness and musicality of her voice. Her big central aria in Act 2, 'Ah! mio cor!', is best of all, for its intensely musical singing and purity of tone. Auger is at her best in the early part of the opera, lacking in the later part the edge that can give full force to the scorned sorceress's angry music. Della Jones in the *primo uomo* role of Ruggiero, excels in the incisive music, like her two arias in Act 1 and the one in Act 3, though this last is rushed and becomes a shade hectic in feeling (and there is some wild ornamentation). She gives a fine performance too of the lovely 'Mi lusinga', well focused in tone, strongly expressed yet always stylish. But the sensuous beauty of castrato tone needed for the finest of her arias, the incomparable 'Verdi prati' perhaps understandably, eludes her; it is, however, well done, if marred at the end by the solecism of a large, romantic *rallentando*. For Kathleen Kuhlmann, the Bradamante, there can be nothing but warm praise. She has a splendid natural sense of how to give direction to the music, she throws off the semiquaver passages with clarity and fire, and conveys the character's qualities admirably with her firm line and heroic manner. The smaller roles are taken by established British Handel singers of the middle generation.

The choral numbers are also well done, if with what sounds like a larger group than is appropriate for the music. The orchestral playing is generally very capable. There are, however, reservations about the direction, especially on matters of tempo. One sometimes feels that Richard Hickox hasn't got a very dependable instinct for tempo in Handel – the slower music is often exaggeratedly slow, the fast sometimes driven – or that he characterises the music very effectively. In sum, then, a recording with many merits, principally vocal ones. The recorded quality is a little variable: sometimes the acoustic seems hugely spacious, at other times more conventional. There is an excellent booklet. As a whole there can be little doubt that this *Alcina*, in its style and its completeness, comfortably surpasses its recorded predecessors.

Additional recommendation

Alcina

Fleming Alcina **Graham** Ruggiero **Kuhlmann** Bradamante **Les Arts Florissants / Christie**

Erato 8573-80233-2 (191 minutes: DDD: 3/00) Ⓕ

Luxury casting and Christie's stylish direction make this alternative well worth considering. For vocal splendour this takes the palm but Hickox's version has a more idiomatic feel to it and a more appropriate scale.

Ariodante

Awards 1996

Lorraine Hunt *sop* Ariodante; **Juliana Gondek** *sop* Ginevra; **Lisa Saffer** *sop* Dalinda; **Jennifer Lane** *mez* Polinesso; **Rufus Müller** *ten* Lurcanio; **Nicolas Cavallier** *bass* King of Scotland; **Jörn Lindemann** *ten* Odoardo; **Wilhelmshaven Vocal Ensemble; Freiburg Baroque Orchestra / Nicholas McGegan** **P**

Harmonia Mundi ③ HMU90 7146/8 (202 minutes: DDD). Notes, text and translation included. Recorded 1995 Ⓕ ●●●

This recording, made with the cast from the Göttingen Festival in 1995 (largely American singers who have collaborated with McGegan in his Californian performances), seems at least the equal of the best he has done before. The quality of the music is of course a factor: *Ariodante* is one of the richest of the Handel operas. It begins with a flood of fine numbers, mostly love music for the betrothed pair, Ariodante and the Scottish princess Ginevra – she is introduced in a wonderfully carefree aria, he in a gentle, exquisite slow arietta; then they have a very individual and beautiful love duet, and each goes on to a more jubilant aria. But the plot thickens and the music darkens with Polinesso's machinations, designed to impugn her fidelity: thus Act 2 contains music of vengeance and grief (above all the magnificent 'Scherza infida!' for Ariodante, a G minor aria with muted upper and pizzicato lower strings, and soft bassoons), while the final act shows all the characters *in extremis*, until the plot is uncovered and equilibrium restored.

This is also one of Handel's few operas with extensive ballet; each act includes some splendid and ingeniously tuneful dance music. McGegan directs in his usual spirited style. There is a real theatrical sense to his conducting: this is one of those opera sets where, after the overture, your spine tingles in expectation of the drama. Lorraine Hunt's soprano seems warm and full for a castrato part, but her line is always well defined and she has a delightfully musical voice. A fine set.

Ariodante **P**

Anne Sofie von Otter *mez* Ariodante; **Lynne Dawson** *sop* Ginevra; **Veronica Cangemi** *sop* Dalinda; **Ewa Podles** *mez* Polinesso; **Richard Croft** *ten* Lurcanio; **Denis Sedov** *bass* King of Scotland; **Luc Coadou** *ten* Odoardo; **Choeur des Musiciens du Louvre; Les Musiciens du Louvre / Marc Minkowski**

Archiv Produktion ③ 457 271-2AH3 (178 minutes: DDD). Text and translation included. Ⓕ

Recorded 1997 ○

Lynne Dawson is the star of this show – and perhaps the leading Handel opera soprano today. In Act 2, where Ginevra finds herself inexplicably rejected and condemned by everyone, Dawson brings real depth of tone and feeling to her E minor lament, 'Il mio crudel martoro'; in the final act she shines in the desolate miniature 'Io ti bacio' and brings much fire to the outburst 'Sì, morro'. But she never transgresses the canons of baroque style. Von Otter, too, has much marvellous music – the aria 'Scherza infida' is one of Handel's greatest expressions of grief – and she sings it beautifully, but she is not really at one with this idiom and seems to lack a natural feeling for the amplitude of Handel's lines. She tries, perhaps, to do too much with them in terms of shaping and detailed expression.

Yet of course there is much to enjoy here too, the beauty of the actual sound, the immaculate control, the many telling and musicianly touches of phrasing. But the noble, climactic triumphant aria, 'Dopo notte' doesn't have quite the effect it should. For that, however, Minkowski is partly to blame. Carried away, it almost seems, by the passion of the music, he is often inclined to go at it baldheaded, too fast and with a ferocity of accent, especially in the bass lines, that seems foreign to the style and dangerously close to ugly. This happens in several of Ariodante's numbers, including this last aria, but also in the scene that opens Act 3, first in the dark-toned D minor Sinfonia and then in the extraordinary C minor aria, 'Cieca notte', with its extravagant leaps in the violin part and its jerky rhythms.

Veronica Cangemi makes a charming Dalinda, light, spirited and duly agile, with some gently pathetic expression in the delightful *siciliana* song early in Act 2. Ewa Podles brings her large, resonant voice to Polinesso's music; the Lurcanio, Richard Croft, is a sturdy tenor, rather heavy in tone and at times almost baritonal. The King of Scotland's fatherly music is done with due fullness and warmth by Denis Sedov, who covers the two-octave range with comfort and resonance and brings due nobility to his *siciliana* aria in Act 2. Despite the driven quality of Minkowski's performance, especially in the high dramatic music of the latter part of the opera, the sheer passion of this set does give it claims to be considered first choice. The admirable McGegan performance is possibly a safer buy, and in some respects it is a more stylish performance, but the singing here, Lynne Dawson's above all, is on balance superior.

Athalia

Awards 1987

Joan Sutherland *sop* Athalia; **P**
Emma Kirkby *sop*Josabeth; **Aled Jones** *treb* Joas; **James Bowman** *counterten* Joad; **Anthony Rolfe Johnson** *ten* Mathan; **David Thomas** *bass* Abner; **New College Choir, Oxford; Academy of Ancient Music / Christopher Hogwood**

L'Oiseau-Lyre ② 417 126-2OH2 (122 minutes: DDD) Ⓕ

Notes and text included. Recorded 1985 ○○○

Athalia, composed for Oxford in 1733 to a libretto that draws on Racine's play, tells of the usurping, apostate Jewish queen, Athalia, and her overthrow when the prophet Joad and his wife Josabeth bring the true heir, the boy Joas, to the throne. The action is feebly handled by Handel's librettist, Samuel Humphreys (in particular it is never made clear what happens to Athalia in the end, or why); but several of the characters are quite strong and Handel grasps the opportunities offered him for striking music.

Athalia fares best of all, musically, as one would expect; and it was a brilliant stroke of imagination to ask Joan Sutherland to take this role in the present recording. She is a great Handelian, but is scarcely a figure one expects to see in early-music circles. In the event, the slight disparity of approach between her and the other members of the cast serves ideally to symbolise the separation of Athalia from her fellow-Israelites. Sutherland uses more vibrato than the others in the cast, but the singing is truly magnificent in its grandeur and its clear, bell-like, perfectly focused tone. Athalia's part is not a large one, with only two full-length arias; the second, 'My vengeance awakes me', is an energetic piece which she throws off with enormous spirit. Among the rest, Emma Kirkby is on her very best form, singing coolly, with poised musicianship, and with quite astonishing technical command at times. Listen to 'Through the land', in Act 2, where the voice is beautifully balanced with two recorders and violins, the passagework perfectly placed, the oddly shaped phrases pitched with sureness, the thrilling a delight. Her Act 1 aria 'Faithful cares' is finely done too, in spite of a hint of clumsiness in the accompaniment once or twice.

James Bowman, as Joad, has his moments, and always sounds well. David Thomas is dependable in the often very vigorous music for the priest, Abner; and as Athalia's priest, Mathan, Anthony Rolfe Johnson sings in shapely fashion. The boy Joas is sung, as it should be, by a boy, in this case Aled Jones, who gives a very controlled, exact performance, perhaps rather careful but of intense tonal beauty. The choral singing is a little variable. At its best, for example in the chorus that opens the Second Act, it is first-rate, spirited, forthright and accurate, but in certain of the others there is an air of the routine. There is much good, crisp orchestral playing, though some of the AAM's less positive characteristics are evident: an occasional moment of unsure ensemble, and a lack of broad shaping. These are however perfectionist quibbles: these two discs, excellently recorded, give an admirable and often striking realization of a choice work.

Flavio

Jeffrey Gall *counterten* Flavio; **Derek Lee Ragin** *counterten* Guido; **Lena Lootens** *sop* Emilia; **Bernarda Fink** *contr* Teodata; **Christina Högman** *sop* Vitige; **Gianpaolo Fagotto** *ten* Ugone; **Ulrich Messthaler** *bass* Lotario; **Ensemble 415 / René Jacobs** **P**
Harmonia Mundi ② HMC90 1312/3
(156 minutes: DDD). Notes, text and translation included. Recorded 1989 Ⓕ

Flavio is one of the most delectable of Handel's operas. Although it comes from his 'heroic' period, it is rather an ironic tragedy with a good many comic elements. Does that sound confusing? – well, so it is, for you never know quite where you are when King Flavio of Lombardy starts falling in love with the wrong woman; this starts as an amusing idle fancy but develops into something near-tragic, since he imperils everyone else's happiness, ultimately causing the death of one counsellor and the dishonour of another. The delicately drawn amorous feeling is like nothing else in Handel, and in its subtle growth towards real passion and grief is handled with consummate skill. The opera, in short, is full of fine and exceptionally varied music, and it is enhanced here by a performance under René Jacobs that, although it takes a number of modest liberties, catches the moods of the music surely and attractively, with shapely, alert and refined playing from the admirable Ensemble 415. And the cast is strong. The central roles, composed for two of Handel's greatest singers, Cuzzoni and Senesino, 18th-century superstars, are sung by Lena Lootens, a delightfully natural and expressive soprano with a firm, clear technique, and the countertenor Derek Lee Ragin, who dispatches his brilliant music with aplomb and excels in the final aria, a superb minor-key expression of passion. The singers also include Bernarda Fink as the lightly amorous Teodata and Christina Högman, both fiery and subtle in the music for her lover, and the capable Jeffrey Gall as the wayward monarch. Altogether a highly enjoyable set, not flawless but certainly among the best Handel opera recordings.

Giulio Cesare

Awards 1992

Jennifer Larmore *mez* Giulio Cesare; **Barbara Schlick** *sop* Cleopatra; **Bernarda Fink** *mez* Cornelia; **Marianne Rørholm** *mez* Sextus; **Derek Lee Ragin** *counterten* Ptolemy; **Furio Zanasi** *bass* Achillas; **Olivier Lallouette** *bar* Curio; **Dominique Visse** *counterten* Nirenus **P**
Concerto Cologne / René Jacobs
Harmonia Mundi ③ HMC90 1385/7 (243 minutes: DDD). Notes, text and translation included Ⓕ
Recorded 1991 **ooo**

Handel's greatest heroic opera sports no fewer than eight principal characters and one of the largest orchestras he ever used. Undoubtedly this, and the singing of Francesca Cuzzoni (Cleopatra) and Senesino (Caesar), helped to launch *Giulio Cesare* into the enduring popularity that it enjoys to this day. But it is primarily the quality of the music, with barely a weak number in four hours of entertainment, that has made it such a favourite with musicians and audiences. Here the period instruments are an immediate advantage in giving extra 'bite' to the many moments of high drama without threatening to drown the singers in *forte* passages.

This performance is a particularly fine one with an excellent cast; Caesar, originally sung by a castrato, is here taken by the young mezzo, Jennifer Larmore. She brings weight and integrity to the role, seemingly untroubled by the demands of the final triumphant aria, 'Qual torrente'. Occasionally her vibrato becomes intrusive, but that is a minor quibble in a performance of this stature. Handel could just as well have called his opera 'Cleopatra' as it is she who is the pivotal element in the drama, a role taken here by Barbara Schlick. One of Handel's most vividly developed characters, this many faceted woman is represented by Schlick with acuity and imagination, ranging from the haunting pathos of 'Piangerò', where she occasionally seems stretched on the top notes, to the exuberant virtuosity of 'Da tempeste' in the final act. If Cleopatra represents strength in a woman, then Cornelia is surely the tragic figure, at the mercy of events. Her first aria, 'Priva son', here taken very slowly, shows Bernarda Fink to be more than equal to the role, admirable in her steady tone and dignity of character. Derek Lee Ragin's treacherous Ptolemy is also memorable, venom and fire injected into his agile voice. A first-rate cast is supported by René Jacobs and Concerto Cologne on fine form, though the continuo line is sometimes less than ideally clear. The recording is excellent.

Giulio Cesare (sung in English: ed Mackerras)
Dame Janet Baker *mez* Giulio Cesare; **Valerie Masterson** *sop* Cleopatra; **Sarah Walker** *mez* Cornelia; **Della Jones** *mez* Sextus; **James Bowman** *counterten* Ptolemy; **John Tomlinson** *bass* Achilles; **Christopher Booth-Jones** *bar* Curio; **David James** *counterten* Nirenus; **English National Opera Chorus and Orchestra / Sir Charles Mackerras**
Chandos Opera in English Series ③ CHAN3019
(183 minutes: DDD). Notes and English text included. Ⓕ
Recorded 1984 ●

This opera was a personal triumph for Dame Janet. As Caesar, she arms the voice with an impregnable firmness, outgoing and adventurous. Valerie Masterson shares the honours with Dame Janet, a Cleopatra whose bright voice gains humanity through ordeal. The tinkle of surface-wear clears delightfully in her later arias, sung with a pure tone and high accomplishment. As a total production, *Julius Caesar* was an outstanding achievement in ENO's history. Strongly cast, it had a noble Cornelia in Sarah Walker, a high-spirited Sesto in Della Jones, and in James Bowman a Ptolemy whose only fault was that his voice lacked meanness of timbre appropriate to the odious character. John Tomlinson's massive bass also commands attention. At the time of this recording the cuts and adaptations in the texts were severely condemned in some quarters. Mackerras's conducting is impeccable and the opera is given in clear, creditable English.

Theodora, HWV68

Susan Gritton *sop* **Susan Bickley** *mez* **Robin Blaze** *counterten* **Paul Agnew, Angus Smith** *tens* **Neal Davies** *bass* **Gabrieli Consort and Players / Paul McCreesh** Ⓟ
Archiv Produktion ③ 469 061-2AH3
(184 minutes: DDD). Text and translation included Ⓕ
Recorded 2000 ●●●

Handel's penultimate oratorio, *Theodora*, was a failure in his own time. Until relatively recently it remained a rarity, but over the last few years it has come to be recognised as a masterpiece, although quite different in mood and treatment from most of his more familiar oratorios. In their note on the work in the booklet here, Ruth Smith and Paul McCreesh draw attention to the then newish concept of the heroine, in the age of sensibility, paralleling Theodora's plight with those of the fictional heroines Clarissa and Pamela: a fascinating notion that puts Handel or at least his librettist, Morell, in the avant-garde of their time, and certainly invites one to listen to the music with a different awareness.

And this recording encourages attentive listening to the subtleties of the work, because it is done with such affection, care and refinement. There is nothing sensational about it, no singer who overwhelms you with brilliance or virtuosity. But the solo music, all of it, is finely sung. Theodora herself is taken by Susan Gritton, who has justly won golden opinions recently, and will win more here for a great deal of lovely, clear and musicianly singing, with a quiet seriousness and unaffected intensity that are ideally suited to the role. The detail – of phrasing, articulation, the placing of stresses, the degree to which notes are sustained – is impeccable. Her presence at the centre of the tragic drama elevates it as a whole. Listen to her charming singing of the *siciliana* 'The pilgrim's home', for instance, or to the quietly rapt performance of her first air in the final act, 'When sunk in anguish and despair'.

Irene, her fellow Christian, is sung with scarcely less distinction by Susan Bickley, coolly expressive in most of her music, more passionate in 'Defend her Heaven' in Act 2, a shapely performance with subtleties of timing. Didymus, originally a castrato role (very rare in oratorios), is sung by Robin Blaze, whose focused, even-toned countertenor – not a hint of the traditional hoot – serves well: this is fluent singing, with no great depth of tone, but very steady and controlled, with the detail precisely placed. As Septimius, Paul Agnew is in good voice, firm and full in tone, phrasing the music elegantly (although the Act 3 air is unconvincing, too bouncy and cheerful for the situation). Lastly, there is Neal Davies as the Roman ruler, Valens, whose excellent singing makes as persuasive a case as can be imagined for torturing Christians – his is a pleasantly grainy voice, with considerable warmth and fullness of tone, well suited to a figure representing authority, and he despatches the divisions with assurance.

Ornamentation is appropriate and tasteful, largely confined to *da capo* sections and to the occasional appoggiatura, trill or flourish – truly ornamental, in fact. McCreesh takes the recitative at a natural and relaxed pace. His main contribution, however, is in the well-sprung rhythms he draws from his Gabrieli singers and players, in the way he allows the lines to breathe, and in the sense of purpose and direction he imparts to the bass-line. Add to this a keen sense of the right pace for each number, and a confident, precise chorus, well balanced (8.8.6.5) both in itself and in relation to the orchestra (26 strings, with oboes and bassoons at least doubled), and you have the recipe for what seems to be an outstanding reading of this noble work.

The Christie Glyndebourne version is available only on video (NVC), and two of the three CD recordings in the catalogue are heavily and unjustifiably cut. So the only serious competitor is McGegan's, with the admirable Lorraine Hunt in the title-role; but this new one is generally more strongly cast and more natural in its direction and its pacing, and is the one to choose.

Orlando

Patricia Bardon *mez* Orlando; **Rosemary Joshua** *sop* Angelica; **Hilary Summers** *contr* Medoro; **Rosa Mannion** *sop* Dorinda; **Harry van der Kamp** *bass* Zoroastro **Les Arts Florissants / William Christie** Ⓟ
Erato ③ 0630-14636-2 (168 minutes: DDD) Ⓕ
Notes, text and translation included. Recorded 1996

Christie is very much concerned with a smooth and generally rich texture and with delicacy of rhythmic shaping. His management of the recitative could hardly be bettered and moments of urgency or of other kinds of emotional stress are tellingly handled. Sometimes he favours a rather sustained style in the arias, making the textures seem airless and heavy, and the lines within them too smooth. However, to set against it there is his exceptional delicacy of timing, his careful but always natural-sounding moulding of cadences and other critical moments in the score. Not many Handel interpreters show this kind of regard for such matters and it is certainly a delight to hear Handel's music so lovingly nurtured; also, of course, it helps the singers to convey meaning. The cast is very strong. The title-role is taken by a mezzo, Patricia Bardon, who draws a very firm and often slender line, with that gleam in her tone that can so enliven the impact of a lowish mezzo – the famous Mad scene is magnificent. The Sleep scene, with very sweet, soft-toned playing of the *violette marine*, is lovely.

Hilary Summers offers a very sensitively sung Medoro, pure and shapely in line. Harry van der Kamp makes a finely weighty Zoroastro, with plenty of resonance in his lower register; the last aria in particular is done in rousing fashion. As Angelica, Rosemary Joshua's musicianship comes through in her attractive phrasing and timing. Rosa Mannion's Dorinda is no less full of delights, catching the character to perfection. Hogwood's lighter orchestral textures are appealing but the refinement of detail in the newer set is equally admirable.

Radamisto

Ralf Popken *counterten* Radamisto; **Juliana Gondek** *sop* Zenobia; **Lisa Saffer** *sop* Polissena; **Dana Hanchard** *sop* Tigrane; **Monika Frimmer** *sop* Fraarte; **Michael Dean** *bass-bar* Tiridate; **Nicolas Cavallier** *bass* Farasmane; **Freiburg Baroque Orchestra / Nicholas McGegan** *hpd* **P**

Harmonia Mundi ③ HMU90 7111/3 (190 minutes: DDD). Notes, text and translation included. Recorded 1993 Ⓕ

Radamisto was Handel's first opera for the Royal Academy of Music, the company set up in 1719 under his musical directorship to put London opera on a secure basis (as optimistic a notion then as now). It is a tale of dynastic doings in post-classical Thrace, with King Tiridate of Armenia forsaking his wife Polissena because he becomes enamoured of Zenobia, Radamisto's queen; Radamisto and Zenobia go through various trials, but 'after various Accidents, it comes to pass, that he recovers both Her and his Kingdom'. It is easy enough to poke fun at plots such as these, but the score of *Radamisto*, one of Handel's richest, is its justification. Handel certainly knew how to 'wow' the London audiences on these big occasions. In the Second Act particularly, one arresting number follows another; Radamisto's 'Ombra cara', which has been claimed as the finest aria Handel ever wrote, falls early in the act, and towards the end there is a wonderful sequence, chiefly of minor-key numbers, as the emotional tensions mount, culminating in a duet for the apparently doomed lovers. The Third Act, although dramatically less powerful, is also full of colourful and characterful music, including a noble quartet which Handel clearly remembered 30 years later when composing *Jephtha*. Any Handelian will relish the constantly alert playing, the strong dramatic pacing and the weight given to the orchestral textures, and the excellent cast.

Rinaldo

David Daniels *counterten* Rinaldo; **Cecilia Bartoli** *mez* Almirena; **Gerald Finley** *bar* Argante; **Luba Orgonasova** *sop* Armida; **Bejun Mehta** *counterten* Christian Sorcerer; **Mark Padmore** *ten* Herald; **Daniel Taylor** *counterten* Eustazio; **Bernarda Fink** *contr* Goffredo; **Catherine Bott** *sop* Siren I; **Ana-Maria Rincón** *sop* Donna; Siren II; **Academy of Ancient Music / Christopher Hogwood** **P**

Decca L'Oiseau-Lyre ③ 467 087-2OHO3 (179 minutes: DDD). Recorded 1999 Ⓕ ●

In a sense, *Rinaldo* is at once Handel's most familiar and unfamiliar opera: familiar because, as his lavish first stage work for London, it has been much written about both by modern historians and by the composer's contemporaries; unfamiliar because the Handel opera revival of recent years has largely passed it by. Although there are numerous recordings of its two hit slow arias – 'Lascia ch'io pianga' and 'Cara sposa' – this is its first complete studio recording for over 20 years. It may not be Handel's most dramatically effective work (Act 3 marks time rather), and its magic effects and transformation scenes no doubt make it a tricky prospect for opera companies, but in many ways its rich orchestration and impressive set-piece arias make it an opera ideal for recording. That much makes this release a welcome sight already; add the de luxe cast Decca has assembled for the purpose and it begins to look irresistible.

Top of the bill come David Daniels as the eponymous crusader knight and Cecilia Bartoli as his love Almirena. Daniels' heart-stopping countertenor voice is one of the marvels of our age. It is not big, and though he is technically untroubled by the virtuoso runs of the quicker arias, some may feel that it lacks some of the heroic power expected of a warrior; but there is an inner strength to it, and in the love music he is utterly convincing. In 'Cara sposa', his lament for the abducted Almirena, the milk and honey really flows and we know we are in the presence of something special. Bartoli is equally impressive in her own way, though her singing is less well suited to Handel. Of course, she can deliver the most demanding music with almost frightening ease and force and, as ever, she throws herself into her role, but one cannot not help thinking that a more natural and unaffected style would have been more appropriate for arias such as 'Lascia ch'io pianga' and 'Augeletti che cantate'. Others may disagree.

The rest of the cast is almost unwaveringly strong. Daniel Taylor is slightly less technically secure or forceful than the others (which is hardly a criticism), but he does well enough with what is the opera's least effective role as Goffredo's brother Eustazio.

Christopher Hogwood's direction is typically neat and good-mannered. He is not, dare one say, a natural opera conductor – others may have found more magic in the enchanted gardens and more sensuality in the sirens who lure Rinaldo, and you sometimes get the feeling that he is rushing the singers at important moments – but he has an unerring sense of tempo in Handel and the opera as a whole is well paced. The Academy of Ancient Music play to a high standard, backed up by a startlingly virtuoso performance (by the tape editor?) on the Drottningholm thunder machine and by some genuine birdsong at the beginning of Act 2, recalling the fact that live birds were introduced into the theatre at the work's première.

Competition for this recording consists of Jean-Claude Malgoire's pioneering account from 1977, and from a performance recorded live under John Fisher at La Fenice in 1989. The latter is notable for having an impressive Marilyn Horne in the title-role, but little else; some 50 minutes of music have been cut, and the sound is, at its worst, 'live'. The former is altogether a better piece of work – it features notable singing from, among others, Carolyn Watkinson as Rinaldo and Ileana Cotrubas as Almirena – but it suffers some less distinguished contributions lower down the cast, as well as from the effects of an 'early' baroque orchestra, and in general it treads a bit too carefully throughout. Decca's newcomer may not be the last word on the opera, but for all-round standard of performance and production it currently wins hands down and it will take some beating.

Rodelinda

Sophie Daneman *sop* Rodelinda; **Daniel Taylor** *counterten* Bertarido; **Adrian Thompson** *ten* Grimoaldo; **Catherine Robbin** *mez* Eduige; **Robin Blaze** *counterten* Unulfo; **Christopher Purves** *bass* Garibaldo; **Raglan Baroque Players / Nicholas Kraemer** *hpd* P

Virgin Classics Veritas ③ VCT5 45277-2
(173 minutes: DDD). Notes, text and translation included. Recorded 1996 Ⓕ ●

Composed just after *Giulio Cesare* and *Tamerlano*, *Rodelinda* must rank in many people's top half-dozen of the Handel operas, with its complex plot of dynastic intrigue revolving around the powerful, steadfast love of Bertarido (the ousted king of Milan) and his queen Rodelinda: just the kind that unfailingly drew strong music from Handel. Nicholas Kraemer gives a very direct and unaffected reading of this score. The pacing is sensible, if anything slightly on the slow side (at least by recent standards of Handel opera conducting), especially perhaps in the recitative; the playing of the Raglan Baroque Players is alive and rhythmically well sprung, with a firmly defined bass-line. There is some modest ornamentation in the *da capo* sections of the arias. What you don't get very strongly is much sense of urgency or boldness, of an unfolding drama, or indeed of the musical characterization of individual numbers. There is just a hint here of the 'concert in costume'. Its star is Sophie Daneman. The voice is bright and intense, very firm in focus, dead sure in pitch, with only the faintest and most discriminatingly used hint of vibrato. It is ideally suited to Rodelinda's character, as the poignant singing of her lovely, elegiac opening aria makes clear – and that is immediately followed by a defiant one, vigorously thrown off. Adrian Thompson is also particularly enjoyable as the would-be usurper Grimoaldo. Thompson's easy and natural delivery, his natural feeling for the shape of Handel's phrases and his elegant manner make all his music a pleasure to listen to, and perhaps especially his final aria, which is a delight.

Catherine Robbin sings Eduige's music with spirit and rhythmic life. The two castrato roles, Bertarido and Unulfo, are taken by countertenors. Daniel Taylor is a very accomplished singer, even-toned and accurate, well able to realise the pathos of Bertarido's prison scene (a B flat minor aria, *Largo*; though he doesn't quite rise to the drama of the accompanied recitative that follows), and the famous 'Dove sei' is touchingly done. But this role was written for Senesino, one of the great expressive singers of his day, and Taylor (or indeed the countertenor voice) isn't quite capable of conveying emotion on the scale the music demands. Unulfo's rather smaller part is neatly and clearly done – and some exceedingly awkward passagework is surely negotiated in his Act 1 aria – by Robin Blaze, although the general effect is rather bland and sober. Christopher Purves takes the role of the villainous Garibaldo capably but is rather strident at the top. This may not be the most dramatic of Handel opera recordings, but it gives an excellent account of the music and there is some first-rate singing – and in one of the very finest and most compelling of the Handel operas.

Rodrigo

Rodrigo (ed Curtis) P

Gloria Banditelli *mez* Rodrigo; **Sandrine Piau** *sop* Esilena; **Elena Cecchi Fedi** *sop* Florinda; **Rufus Müller** *ten* Giuliano; **Roberta Invernizzi** *sop* Evanco; **Caterina Calvi** *mez* Fernando; **Il Complesso Barocco / Alan Curtis** *hpd*

Virgin Classics Veritas ② VCD5 45897-2
(155 minutes: DDD). Notes, text and translation included. Recorded 1997 Ⓕ

The music of Handel's Italian years has a unique freshness, a boldness of invention, a novelty in textures and lines – characteristics which distinguish his first Italian opera, *Rodrigo*, written in 1707 for the Medici court at Florence (the

Medici had had a share in inviting Handel to Italy). This recording restores all that survives of the lyrical music, with one item composed in a more-or-less Handelian manner by Curtis and other Handel music imported to fit the original text. Curiously, the dances (recorded by Barbirolli, Lewis and others) are not included here, and – presumably in the interest of keeping the set to two CDs – there are many large cuts in the recitative. As a result some quite important sections are omitted and the often very close succession of lyrical numbers gives a slightly misleading impression of the opera. Even so the recording of this fine, often very moving and mostly inspiriting piece is warmly welcome.

Like most Italian operas of its time, it is essentially a succession of arias, mostly shorter ones than those of Handel's mature operas. As so often with Handel, much of the finest music comes in Act 2, with a pair of arias for Esilena (the second a furious outburst), and at the beginning of the next act, with Rodrigo and Esilena apparently facing death, Handel finds that marvellous vein of pathos familiar in his later operas. Alan Curtis, a man of the theatre, keeps the score moving along at a good pace. He conducts, as it were, from a 17th-century standpoint, with a flexibility over accent and metre that allows the music to move unusually freely. Yet he is rather predictable in his use of cadential *rallentandos*, and there are points where the orchestral discipline is a shade loose. He gives the singers a good deal of time in some of the recitative, and lets them elaborate the *da capo* sections rather more fully, and with less concern for the original line, than one sometimes would wish.

Sandrine Piau sings Esilena's part beautifully, with much attention to detail, to timing and to phrasing, as well as with fluency and with a richness of tone unusual for her. Gloria Banditelli makes a sturdy Rodrigo, direct and accurate, and very controlled in the fast semiquaver passages. She gives an elegant account of 'Dolce amore' at the end of Act 2. Elena Cecchi Fedi perhaps overdoes the characterization of Florinda as a shrew, singing shrilly at times and with rather more shouting and pouting than is consistent with musical enjoyment. But the singing is powerful and brilliant in its way. Roberta Invernizzi, as Evanco sings musically and expressively (try the little *siciliano* aria at the beginning of Act 3). Rufus Müller turns in a confident but rather ordinary performance as Florinda's brother Giuliano. There is competent and spirited playing from Il Complesso Barocco, and there are excellent notes from Anthony Hicks and Curtis.

Serse

Judith Malafronte *mez* Serse; **Jennifer Smith** *sop* Romilda; **Brian Asawa** *counterten* Arsamene; **Susan Bickley** *mez* Amastre; **Lisa Milne** *sop* Atalanta; **Dean Ely** *bar* Ariodate; **David Thomas** *bass* Elviro; **Hanover Band and Chorus / Nicholas McGegan** Ⓟ

Conifer Classics ③ 75605 51312-2 (177 minutes: DDD). Notes, text and translation included. Recorded 1997 Ⓕ

Handel's *Serse* has proved to be one of the most popular of his operas over recent years – certainly in England. Wit may not be a part of most people's image of Handel's operas, and rightly: but from time to time, and especially when he was using a libretto of Venetian origins, Handel and his London librettists permitted themselves touches of ironic humour and sometimes rather more than that – *Serse* has one truly comic character, a servant, and King Xerxes himself is in some degree made a figure of fun by his unruly amorous whims. But as in all the best comedy, the situations give rise to serious emotion too, and in Act 2 of *Serse*, when events provoke first Xerxes, then Romilda (whom he thinks he loves) and then Amastre (who loves him) into forceful expressions of passion, touchingly followed by a gentle aria from Xerxes's brother Arsamene (Romilda's true lover), the music springs into real life and enters more than a purely entertaining plane. Otherwise, however, it is inclined to be elegant, thin-textured and short-breathed. Although the cast here isn't obviously starry it is evenly accomplished and the performance holds together very well under Nicholas McGegan's assured direction. His own personal touch is unmistakable – the light textures, quickish tempos, spruce rhythms, dapper cadences, faintly ironic tone – and it works well for this opera, perhaps better than it does for a big heroic piece. The soloists are exemplary, too. This set must surely be the choice for anyone wanting a stylish version of this lively and appealing work.

Teseo

Eirian James *mez* Teseo; **Julia Gooding** *sop* Agilea; **Della Jones** *mez* Medea: **Derek Lee Ragin** *counterten* Egeo; **Catherine Napoli** *sop* Clizia; **Jeffrey Gall** *counterten* Arcane; **François Bazola** *bar* Sacerdote di Minerva; **Les Musiciens du Louvre / Marc Minkowski** Ⓟ

Erato ② 2292-45806-2 (148 minutes: DDD) Ⓜ
Texts and translations included. Recorded 1992

Teseo was Handel's third opera for London, given at the beginning of 1713. Exceptionally, its libretto was based on a French original, written by Quinault for Lully; it is a spectacular piece, in five acts, with Medea (after the events of *Médée*) and Theseus (before the events of *Hippolyte* or the Ariadne operas) as its central characters. It is Medea who, as slighted lover and jealous sorceress, provides the principal musical thrills; but the score is, in any case, an unusually rich and inventive one, with much colourful orchestral writing even before she turns up at the beginning of Act 2. When she does, she introduces herself with a *Largo* aria, 'Dolce riposo', of a kind unique to Handel in its depth of poetic feeling, with a vocal line full of bold leaps above throbbing strings and an oboe obbligato; but, lest we should think her docile, Medea hints at her true colours in the ensuing C minor aria, and by the end of the act she is singing furious recitative and fiery, incisive lines – real sorceress music. Her biggest scene comes at the start of the final act, a *Presto* vengeance aria, packed with raging rapid semiquavers. Handel scored the opera for a more varied orchestra than usual; there are recorders, flutes, oboes, bassoons and trumpets called for. The arias themselves tend to be rather shorter than usual for Handel. The work needs first-rate singing, and by and large receives it here. The role of Medea falls to Della Jones, a singer with a superb technique and a remarkable ability to identify with the role; she truly lives Medea's part and brings to it great resources of spirit and technique. Except when allowed to play too fast, too loudly or too coarsely, the Musiciens du Louvre are impressive. Several numbers are accompanied with only a continuo instrument, to good effect. The recitative always moves well, and appoggiaturas are duly observed.

Howard Hanson American 1896-1981

GROVE *Hanson studied with Goetschius in New York and became director of the Eastman School (1924-64), where he was an influential teacher and founded the Institute of American music; he also promoted modern American music through his work as a conductor. His own music shows the influence of Sibelius, Grieg and Respighi (his teacher in Rome in the early 1920s). Among his works are seven symphonies, symphonic poems, choral pieces, chamber and piano music and songs.*

Symphonies

Symphonies – No 2, Op 30, 'Romantic'; No 4, Op 34, 'The Requiem'. Elegy in memory of Serge Koussevitzky
Jena Philharmonic Orchestra / David Montgomery
Arte Nova Classics 74321 43306-2 Ⓢ
(60 minutes: DDD). Recorded 1996

Here is enticingly off-the-beaten-track repertory from this new super-budget label. The Fourth (*Requiem*) was apparently Hanson's own favourite of his seven symphonies. Inscribed 'in memory of my beloved father', it is a darkly intense, neo-Sibelian outpouring which won the composer the first Pulitzer Prize given to music in 1944. The tuneful, opulently scored *Romantic* (No 2) has remained a firm favourite with American orchestras and audiences since its première in November 1930 under Serge Koussevitzky. More recently, its use on the soundtrack of the 1979 feature-film *Alien* won Hanson an entirely new band of admirers. The *Elegy* (1956) is a supremely touching memorial to a close friend and great conductor to whom American music this century owes an incontestably profound debt of gratitude. Performances are capable and shapely, and the sound is very good too. The orchestra responds with plenty of enthusiasm to David Montgomery who knows his way round these scores. That said, nothing here poses a serious challenge to Gerard Schwarz and the splendid Seattle Symphony in terms of orchestral finesse or interpretative insight: Montgomery's provincial band inevitably don't possess the ingratiating tonal lustre and sheer muscle of their American counterparts, while Schwarz's direction displays just that little bit of extra commitment to the cause. None the less, at its absurdly low price, this issue will find many new friends for Hanson's ripely romantic vision.

Symphony No 1 in E minor, 'Nordic', Op 21. Merry Mount Suite. Pan and the Priest, Op 26. Rhythmic Variations on Two Ancient Hymns
Nashville Symphony Orchestra / Kenneth Schermerhorn
Naxos 8 559072 (61 minutes: DDD) Ⓢ

Another Hanson landmark in the unstoppable Naxos series, American Classics. The least-known piece here is the *Rhythmic Variations*, considered lost until recently and cited as such in the *New American Grove*. This seems distinctly careless of someone, since Hanson recorded this late work himself in 1977. It is serenely spacious, utterly diatonic but no great rediscovery.

The *Nordic* Symphony was completed when Hanson was in Rome studying with Respighi – stylistically it brings Sibelius south to Italy. The Nashville performance can be compared with the Seattle orchestra under that fine Hanson interpreter, Gerard Schwarz. Schermerhorn is more spacious, taking a good two minutes longer overall – no bad thing in such hyperactive music as it constantly strives towards the next climax. Schwarz is faster in the final *Allegro* but both performances are exciting and well recorded: the issue is settled by coupling and, of course, price.

There are many attractive features in the *Merry Mount Suite* – Charleston syncopation in the 'Children's Dance' and characteristic Hanson harmony oscillating between two chords at the start of the ecstatic 'Love Duet'. All supremely operatic but the stage work still remains in limbo. *Pan and the Priest*, a vivid symphonic poem reaching pagan intensity, completes a bargain Hanson package that's well recorded, too.

Symphonies – Nos 2, 4 and 6; No 7, 'A Sea Symphony'. Fantasy Variations on a Theme of Youth. Elegy in memory of Serge Koussevitzky. Serenade, Op 36. Mosaics
Carol Rosenberger *pf* **New York Chamber Symphony Orchestra; Seattle Symphony Chorale and Orchestra / Gerard Schwarz**
Delos ② DE3705 (136 minutes: DDD) Ⓜ
Recorded 1988-92

Gerard Schwarz's red-blooded 1988 account of the Second Symphony (*Romantic*) remains a match for any rival. Schwarz and his excellent Seattle band do full justice to its dark opulence, concision and organic power. Similarly, there's no missing the communicative ardour and clean-limbed security of Schwarz's lucid reading of the Sixth. Commissioned in 1967 by the New York Philharmonic for their 185th anniversary season, it boasts a formidable thematic economy and intriguing formal scheme of which Hanson himself was justifiably proud. Its successor,

A Sea Symphony from 1977, sets texts from Walt Whitman's *Leaves of Grass*. In the unashamedly jubilant finale Hanson fleetingly quotes from his *Romantic* Symphony of more than four decades earlier: it is a spine-tingling moment in a score of consummate assurance and stirring aspiration. Schwarz's traversal finds the Seattle Symphony Chorale on rousing form. We also get exemplary renderings of the pretty 1945 Serenade for flute, harp and strings (a gift for Hanson's wife-to-be, Margaret Elizabeth Nelson) and characteristically inventive *Fantasy Variations on a Theme of Youth* from 1951 (with Carol Rosenberger a deft soloist), both these featuring Schwarz directing the New York Chamber Symphony. The present warm-hearted accounts of both the *Elegy in memory of Serge Koussevitzky* and *Mosaics* (which is a highly appealing set of variations written in 1957 for Szell and the Cleveland Orchestra) need not fear comparison with the composer's own Mercury recordings. The engineering is wonderfully ripe.

Solo Piano Works

Sonata in A minor, Op 11. Two Yuletide Pieces, Op 19. Poèmes érotiques, Op 9. Three Miniatures, Op 12. Three Etudes, Op 18. Enchantment. For the First Time. Slumber Song
Thomas Labé *pf*
Naxos 8 559047 (76 minutes: DDD) Ⓢ
Recorded 1999

Much of this CD is an orgy of romantic piano music. Admirers of Hanson's *Romantic* Symphony (Arte Nova) or his one-time smash-hit opera *Merry Mount* (Naxos) will surely devour this collection, which includes unknown and unpublished music. A first impression is that the earliest works here, written around 1920, have the sort of ecstatic luxuriance that might be expected of a pupil of Respighi. But this influence came later since Hanson didn't start his three-year residence in Rome until 1921. His background was Swedish and there's a Nordic, Sibelian intensity about his whole approach, although the fulsome piano style clearly stems from Liszt.

The earliest piece is probably the *Slumber Song*, a pure salon morsel, and the latest is the suite *For the First Time*; this is known in Hanson's still current 1962 orchestral recording (Mercury), but the restrained piano version (1970) works admirably in the Schumann-to-MacDowell tradition of an extended set of character pieces. The three *Poèmes érotiques* (the fourth has disappeared) are what Hanson called his 'first studied attempt at psychological writing'. They are powerful in a surging melodic style where in several pieces the climaxes stem from an almost Tchaikovskian cathartic need to unburden tensions.

The striking three-movement Sonata (1918) has had to be completed from the composer's shorthand by Thomas Labé since it was never published, although Hanson performed it in 1919. The vivid improvisatory keyboard writing, at times extravagantly rhetorical, causes Labé to hit the piano rather hard in the last two movements. One can understand his enthusiasm, but there are times when a little more *cantabile* might have helped. However, nothing must detract from the real service that this CD does in bringing Hanson's piano music to public attention for the first time.

Merry Mount

Lawrence Tibbett *bar* Wrestling Bradford; **Göta Ljungberg** *sop* Lady Marigold Sandys; **Gladys Swarthout** *mez* Plentiful Tewke; **Edward Johnson** *ten* Sir Gower Lackland; **Alfredo Gandolfi** *bar* Myles Brodrib; **Giordano Paltrinieri** *ten* Jonathan Banks, **Arnold Gabor** *bar* Faint-not-Tinker; **James Wolfe** *sngr* Samoset; **Irra Petina** *mez* Desire Annable; **Louis d'Angelo** *bar* Praise-God-Tewke; **Chorus and Orchestra of the Metropolitan Opera, New York / Tullio Serafin** 🄷
Naxos Historical mono ② 8 110024/5 Ⓑ
(126 minutes: ADD). Recorded live in 1934 ●

Hanson's only opera was a considerable success when first given. It provided a major role for Tibbett (Wrestling Bradford) and included other luminaries of the international opera scene. This is the first opportunity to register the impact of the entire opera. The recording itself is a lucky scoop taken from 78rpm acetate and metal discs of the broadcast originally in the possession of Tibbett. No doubt technical wonders have been worked on the original sound but the result is still patchy, although, with announcements, commentary and applause included, the recording has a powerful sense of occasion. The story started with a grisly episode in New England history (about 1625) concerning feuding Puritan and Cavalier colonists. This was made the basis of a slender short story by Nathaniel Hawthorne and considerably embroidered in a libretto by Richard L Stokes, which was published separately before the opera had even been staged. The crowd scenes gave Hanson the opportunity to write some magnificent choruses, and the dances before the maypole in Act 2 (scene 1) were so exciting at this première that they stopped the show. When Bradford gives his soul to the devil (scene 3) the choral and orchestral panoply is as vivid as anything in the Shakespeare film scores of Walton, and similar in style.

Tibbett is magisterial in conveying all the horrors of repressive Puritanism souring into devil-worship but Göta Ljungberg (Marigold/Astoreth) is resplendent in her lyrical role, specially the climactic Act 3 lament (track 14). Their joint immolation must have made a convincing peroration on stage, judging by the reports of 50 curtain calls. What is remarkable is that a composer with so little experience in the theatre could deliver such an operatic grand opera. It has everything opera houses normally – like star roles, crowd scenes, violence and spectacle. This is a very worthwhile release and let's hope it leads to a revival.

Karl Amadeus Hartmann

German 1905-1963

GROVE *Hartmann studied with Haas at the Munich Academy (1924-27), with Scherchen and with Webern (1941-42). After the war he started the Musica Viva festival in Munich to present music that had been banned during the Nazi years, and most of his published works date from after this period. They include most importantly a cycle of eight symphonies (1936, 1946, 1947, 1949, 1950, 1953, 1958, 1962), which have a Brucknerian breadth while suggesting the influences of Reger, Berg, Stravinsky, Bartók and Blacher. He also wrote several concertos and vocal music including a chamber opera Simplicius Simplicissimus (1949), a strongly expressive work combining popular song, chorale and psalm-like recitation with symphonic method.*

Symphonies

Symphonies – Nos 1[a], 2 – Adagio[b], 3[c], 4-6[b], 7 (1957-58)[d] and 8[b]. Gesangsszene (1963)
Doris Soffel *contr* **Dietrich Fischer-Dieskau** *bar*
Bavarian Radio Symphony Orchestra / [a]Fritz Rieger, [b]Rafael Kubelík, [c]Ferdinand Leitner, [d]Zdenek Macal Ⓕ
Wergo ④ WER60187-50 (225 minutes: ADD) ●

In the 1930s Hartmann was beginning to establish a reputation, but was forced to withdraw himself and his works from public musical life as a known opponent of the Nazi regime. During the war he destroyed or radically revised most of his output up till then, and these eight symphonies (five of which are based on, or are revisions of, earlier works) appeared between 1946 and his death in 1963. Together they show his broad sympathies with the 20th-century masters. You can hear the presence of Bruckner in the monumental sense of structure, of Reger in the densely chromatic counterpoint and an intense, tortured lyricism derived from Berg. There is a tribute to the neo-classical Stravinsky in the Fifth Symphony, and more than a hint of Bartók in the irresistible momentum of the fugues that conclude the Sixth. Mahler is present in the Whitman settings of the First Symphony, significantly entitled Attempt at a Requiem and in the upheavals of the first movement of the Eighth. The spectral Funeral March in Webern's Pieces, Op 6, haunts sections of the First, Third and Eighth Symphonies.

Whether Hartmann managed to forge a demonstrably personal idiom is questionable. What is indisputable is the power of Hartmann's music to communicate, and its capacity to fascinate. On the debit side, not all the vigorously contrapuntal sections of the later works avoid sounding academic. The dates of these live recordings are not given, but they are all naturally balanced, with excellent clarity – Hartmann's torrents of tuned percussion are thrillingly captured. The Bavarian Radio Symphony Orchestra plays with polish and conviction.

Symphony No 4. Concerto funèbre[a]. Chamber Concerto[b]
[a]Isabelle Faust *vn* **[b]Paul Meyer** *cl* **[b]Petersen Quartet** (Conrad Muck, Gernot Sussmuth *vns* Friedemann Weigle *va* Hans-Jakob Eschenburg *vc*)
Munich Chamber Orchestra / Christoph Poppen
ECM New Series 465 779-2 (78 minutes: DDD) Ⓕ

When Hartmann opted for internal exile during the Nazi era, he took with him some key influences from the free musical world. Beam up around 0'33" into the third movement of the 1939 *Concerto funèbre* (track 3) and you have a virtual quote from the first movement of Bartók's 1934 Fifth String Quartet. Hartmann completed his Chamber Concerto for Clarinet, String Quartet and String Orchestra in 1935, seven years after Bartók wrote his Fourth Quartet – which in turn barges headlong into Hartmann's second movement (0'07" into track 9, an unmistakable reference to the Quartet's finale).

In the Chamber Concerto the melodic and structural profile of the first movement follows the profile of Kodály's 1933 *Dances of Galánta* (try following through from 1'09" until around 3'22" into track 8, taking particular note of the clarinet line). The language of the work is Magyar-inspired (even aside from the *Galánta* references) and the scoring lively and luminous.

The *Concerto funèbre* opens with a quotation (which is fully acknowledged this time) of the Hussite chorale 'Ye Who are God's Warriors', best known to Brits for its use in Smetana's *Má vlast*. The reference commemorates the Nazi betrayal of Czechoslovakia, though Hartmann's anger finds controlled expression in the *Allegro di molto* third movement.

The Fourth Symphony is scored for strings and frames a lively *Allegro di molto* with two profound *Adagios* that, again, draw you in by virtue of their intense arguments. All three performances do Hartmann proud. Isabelle Faust's eloquent playing of the *Concerto funèbre* draws maximum effect from extremes in mood and temperature. Thomas Zehetmair and the drier-toned André Gertler are her strongest competitors, though neither is in any way preferable. Rafael Kubelík offers an admirably pliant live account of the Fourth Symphony, and while Ingo Metzmacher's Fourth is occasionally more intense than this version under Christoph Poppen (especially in the unison opening pages), Poppen's central *Allegro* has the stronger sense of propulsion.

With fine sound and imaginative programming, this is the ideal Hartmann primer.

Sir Hamilton Harty

Irish 1879-1941

GROVE *Harty held organist's posts in Ireland and in 1900 moved to London. After early success as a composer and accompanist he turned to conducting, working with the LSO and becoming conductor of the Hallé Orchestra, 1920-33; he gave new British music and British premières of Strauss, Mahler (including the Ninth*

Symphony) and Shostakovich. He then worked with London orchestras. He was a noted Berlioz interpreter and made arrangements of popular Handel works; his own compositions include an attractive Irish Symphony, a Violin Concerto, chamber and vocal works, some written for his wife, the soprano Agnes Nicholls.

An Irish Symphony

An Irish Symphony. In Ireland. With the Wild Geese
National Symphony Orchestra of Ireland / Prionnsías O'Duinn
Naxos 8 554732 (57 minutes: DDD) Ⓢ
Recorded 1996

Back in 1996, Chandos cannily repackaged their enterprising and hugely enjoyable Harty series with Bryden Thomson and the Ulster Orchestra at mid-price, the third and final volume of which contains the same three items featured here plus an utterly delightful rendering of the boisterous *Comedy Overture* for good measure. The two conductors' approaches complement each other well. Thomson brings the greater epic grandeur and narrative flair to *With the Wild Geese*, yet Prionnsías O'Duinn's rather more urgent reading develops a fine thrust and red-blooded drama in the faster music, while not missing out on the touching melancholy of the lyrical episodes. The Dublin orchestra are on similarly responsive form in *An Irish Symphony*, of which O'Duinn gives another unmannered, chipper and thoroughly personable account. He imparts a mischievous swagger to 'The Fair Day' (the symphony's impish *scherzo*) and a likeable vigour to the opening movement, 'On the Shores of Lough Neagh', where he knocks nearly two minutes off Thomson's timing. Perhaps Thomson's more affectionately relaxed manner pays greater dividends in the charming fantasy for flute, harp and orchestra, *In Ireland*, where the principals from the NSOI have not quite the grace and character of their Belfast counterparts.

Whatever, both discs are thoroughly recommendable – and neither will break the bank! Chris Craker's production values for Naxos are first-rate, though Chandos's outstandingly realistic Ulster Hall sound has the edge in terms of airy bloom and sheer sumptuousness.

Jonathan Harvey

British 1939

GROVE *Harvey studied at Cambridge, privately with Erwin Stein and Hans Keller, and with Babbitt at Princeton (1969-70). He has taught at the universities of Southampton (1964-77) and Sussex. His early music shows enthusiasms ranging from Britten and Messiaen to Stockhausen and Davies, but since the early 1970s he has developed a more integrated style and has emerged as an outstanding composer of electronic music (Mortuos plango, vivos voco, 1980). Later pieces include Madonna of Winter and Spring (1986).*

Madonna of Winter and Spring

Madonna of Winter and Spring[a]. Percussion Concerto[b]. Song Offerings[c]
[c]**Penelope Walmsley-Clark** *sop* [b]**Peter Prommel** *perc* [ab]**Netherlands Radio Philharmonic Orchestra / Peter Eötvös;** [c]**London Sinfonietta / George Benjamin**
Nimbus NI5649 (78 minutes: DDD). Text and translation included. [ac]Recorded 1998 and [b]live in 1997 Ⓕ

This is an impressive disc indeed: a strong cast, a varied programme, and music of great integrity and beauty. In relation to many British scores that have garnered recent critical praise, Harvey more than holds his own. The three pieces – two of them recorded here for the first time – date from the 1980s and '90s. Each introduces a 'foreign' element to the orchestra in a slightly different way. There are elements of the competitive streak between soloist and orchestra in the Percussion Concerto; in *Song Offerings* relations between the two elements are more symbiotic, as one might expect; but in *Madonna of Winter and Spring*, the most extended piece here, the 'foreign' element is assumed by synthesisers and electronics. This piece, in particular, sums up Harvey's preoccupations: the interaction of the different media, and the programmatic elements derived from the composer's faith.

At intervals the orchestra recedes, creating electro-acoustic 'windows' reminiscent of similarly mixed-media scores (Birtwistle and Boulez come to mind); at others, individual instruments appear in a quasi-soloistic context, adding an extra dimension to the orchestral texture. Moreover, the quality of these interpretations gives this recording a special appeal. The electro-acoustic element is well captured, and conveys something of the spatial imaging mentioned in the composer's insert-notes.

All three pieces receive committed, dynamic interpretations: if particular performers deserve mention, they are the Netherlands Radio PO, percussionist Peter Prommel, and Penelope Walmsley-Clark, whose faultless diction and intonation are a wonder to hear and make the performance of *Song Offerings* particularly effective. If only contemporary music could always enjoy such advocacy.

Choral Works

I love the Lord. Carols. Lauds (with **Paul Watkins** *vc*). Sobre un éxtasis alte contemplación. Come, Holy Ghost. O Jesu, nomen dulce. Two Fragments. The Angels. Forms of Emptiness **The Joyful Company of Singers / Peter Broadbent**
ASV CDDCA917 (63 minutes: DDD). Texts and translations included. Recorded 1994 Ⓕ

Compare Jonathan Harvey's *Come, Holy Ghost* with one of his large-scale instrumental works and you might suspect that they are the work of different Jonathan Harveys, one providing short pieces for cathedral choirs, the other active on the avant-garde concert scene. So it is a particular virtue of this disc that by providing such a generous cross-section of Harvey's choral music it makes it easier to hear how the two Harveys are in fact one far-from-inconsistent composer. Since Harvey himself has progressed from choir school to electronic studio it is not so surprising that his music can relate to both worlds so effectively, and most of the compositions here takea fresh look at aspects of the English cathedral tradition without attempting to force those aspects into an unholy alliance with modernist techniques, and technologies. From the early *Fragments* (1966) to *The Angels* (1994) we can hear versions of the kind of contemplative intensity that informs some of Harvey's finest concert works (for example, Bhakti), and these choral pieces are never poor relations. The short Sobre un éxtasis alte contemplación works within its own essential sounds, and in exploring speech as well as song it develops the more dramatic dialogue to be found in the larger-scale *Forms of Emptiness* (1986) and *Lauds* (1987). In such compositions, with their highly diverse textures, spiritual and sensual elements are brought into purposeful conjunction. The Joyful Company of Singers prove to be the ideal interpreters to project all facets of this often quite challenging music.

Joseph Haydn Austrian 1732-1809

GROVE *Haydn, the son of a wheelwright, was trained as a choirboy and taken into the choir at St Stephen's Cathedral, Vienna, where he sang from c1740 to c1750. He then worked as a freelance musician, playing the violin and keyboard instruments, accompanying for singing lessons given by the composer Porpora, who helped and encouraged him. At this time he wrote some sacred works, music for theatre comedies and chamber music. In c1759 he was appointed music director to Count Morzin; but he soon moved, into service as Vice-Kapellmeister with one of the leading Hungarian families, the Esterházys, becoming full Kapellmeister on Werner's death in 1766. He was director of an ensemble of generally some 15-20 musicians, with responsibility for the music and the instruments, and was required to compose as his employer – from 1762, Prince Nikolaus Esterházy – might command. At first he lived at Eisenstadt, c30 miles south-east of Vienna by 1767 the family's chief residence, and Haydn's chief place of work, was at the new palace at Eszterháza. In his early years Haydn chiefly wrote instrumental music, including symphonies and other pieces for the twice-weekly concerts and the prince's Tafelmusik, and works for the instrument played by the prince, the baryton (a kind of viol), for which he composed c125 trios in 10 years. There were also cantatas and a little church music. After Werner's death church music became more central, and so, after the opening of a new opera house at Eszterháza in 1768, did opera. Some of the symphonies from c1770 show Haydn expanding his musical horizons from occasional, entertainment music towards larger and more original pieces, for example Nos 26, 39, 49, 44 and 52 (many of them in minor keys, and serious in mood, in line with trends in the contemporary symphony in Germany and Austria). Also from 1768-72 come three sets of string quartets, probably not written for the Esterházy establishment but for another patron or perhaps for publication (Haydn was allowed to write other than for the Esterházys only with permission); Op 20 clearly shows the beginnings of a more adventurous and integrated quartet style.*

Among the operas from this period are Lo speziale (for the opening of the new house), L'infedeltà delusa (1773) and Il mondo della luna (1777). Operatic activity became increasingly central from the mid-1770s as regular performances came to be given at the new house. It was part of Haydn's job to prepare the music, adapting or arranging it for the voices of the resident singers. In 1779 the opera house burnt down; Haydn composed La fedeltà premiata for its reopening in 1781. Until then his operas had largely been in a comic genre; his last two for Eszterháza, Orlando paladino (1782) and Armida (1783), are in mixed or serious genres. Although his operas never attained wider exposure, Haydn's reputation had now grown and was international. Much of his music had been published in all the main European centres; under a revised contract with the Esterháza his employers no longer had exclusive rights to his music.

His works of the 1780s that carried his name further afield include piano sonatas, piano trios, symphonies (nos.76-81 were published in 1784-85, and Nos 82-7 were written on commission for a concert organization in Paris in 1785-86) and string quartets. His influential Op 33 quartets, issued in 1782, were said to be 'in a quite new, special manner': this is sometimes thought to refer to the use of instruments or the style of thematic development, but could refer to the introduction of scherzos or might simply be an advertising device. More quartets appeared at the end of the decade, Op 50 (dedicated to the King of Prussia and often said to be influenced by the quartets Mozart had dedicated to Haydn) and two sets (Opp 54-55 and 64) written for a former Esterházy violinist who became a Viennese businessman. All these show an increasing enterprise, originality and freedom of style as well as melodic fluency, command of form, and humour. Other works that carried Haydn's reputation beyond central Europe include concertos and notturnos for a type of hurdy-gurdy, written on commission for the King of Naples, and The Seven Last Words, commissioned for Holy Week from Cadíz Cathedral and existing not only in its original orchestral form but also for string quartet, for piano and (later) for chorus and orchestra.

In 1790, Nikolaus Esterházy died; Haydn (unlike most of his musicians) was retained by his son but was free to live in Vienna (which he had many times visited) and to travel. He was invited by the impresario and violinist JP Salomon to go to London to write an opera, symphonies and other works. In the event he went to London twice, in 1791-92 and 1794-95. He composed his last 12 symphonies for performance there, where they enjoyed great success; he also wrote a symphonie concertante, choral pieces, piano trios, piano sonatas and songs (some to English words) as well as arranging British folksongs for publishers in London and Edinburgh. But because of intrigues his opera, L'anima del filosofo, on the Orpheus story, remained unperformed. He was honoured (with an Oxford DMus) and fêted generously, and played, sang and conducted before the royal family. He also heard performances of Handel's music by large choirs in Westminster Abbey.

Back in Vienna, he resumed work for Nikolaus Esterházy's grandson (whose father had now died); his main duty was to produce masses for the princess's nameday. He wrote six works, firmly in the Austrian mass tradition but strengthened and invigorated by his command of symphonic technique. Other works of these late years include further string quartets (Opp 71 and 74 between the London visits, op.76 and the Op 77 pair after them), showing great diversity of style and seriousness of content yet retaining his vitality and fluency of utterance; some have a more public manner, acknowledging the new use of string quartets at concerts as well as in the home. The most important work, however, is his oratorio The Creation in which his essentially simple-hearted joy in Man, Beast and Nature, and his gratitude to God for his creation of these things to our benefit, are made a part of universal experience by his treatment of them in an oratorio modelled on Handel's, with massive choral writing of a kind he had not essayed before. He followed this with The Seasons, in a similar vein but more a series of attractive episodes than a whole.

Haydn died in 1809, after twice dictating his recollections and preparing a catalogue of his works. He was widely revered, even though by then his music was old-fashioned compared with Beethoven's. He was immensely prolific: some of his music remains unpublished and little known. His operas have never succeeded in holding the stage. But he is regarded, with some justice, as father of the symphony and the string quartet: he saw both genres from their beginnings to a high level of sophistication and artistic expression, even if he did not originate them. He brought to them new intellectual weight, and his closely argued style of development laid the foundations for the larger structures of Beethoven and later composers.

Piano Concertos

Piano Concertos – in G, HobXVIII/4; in F, HobXVIII/3; in D, HobXVIII/11
Norwegian Chamber Orchestra / Leif Ove Andsnes *pf*
EMI CDC5 56960-2 (54 minutes: DDD) Ⓕ
Recorded 1998 ○○○

Like Emanuel Ax on Sony, Leif Ove Andsnes confines himself to the three concertos that have been fully authenticated. Had the works generally known as 'the Haydn piano concertos' been these three and not a rag-bag of juvenilia and pieces attributed to Haydn, the canon might have been more highly thought of than has often been the case. That said, even the slightest work can dazzle and delight if it is performed as well as these are here. Where Ax's performances have a slightly monochrome feel to them, everything tapped out (there is much audible fingerwork) with the same well-adjusted mix of energy and sensibility, Andsnes's playing is altogether more various while at the same time being perfectly at one with itself stylistically. Ax's Franz Liszt Chamber Orchestra is the more idiomatic of the two ensembles in the D major Concerto's *Rondo all'Ungarese* but that is just about the only occasion on which it has the edge over Andsnes's stylish and highly articulate Norwegian Chamber Orchestra; and, even here, Andsnes himself scores points for a less noisy plunge into the interlude in D minor and a more sunlit and finely flighted way with the episode which follows. The Norwegian players are never afraid to play full out, a strategy which the explicit but carefully balanced recording is happy to underwrite.

Thus the players make much of the 'look here, young man' chromaticisms in the first movement of the D major Concerto as the piano chatters irrepressibly on; and they contribute decisively to the superbly articulated – nay, revelatory – performance of the G major Concerto with which the disc begins. After a splendidly jaunty account of the first movement, Andsnes pushes this G major Concerto to its limits with a decidedly skilfully shaped account of the glooming C major slow movement and a dashing account of the concluding *Presto*. Andsnes's playing of the *Largo cantabile* of the F major Concerto – the concerto's centrepiece and its *raison d'être* – is the very embodiment of sweetness and light. All in all, few could doubt that this is a simply marvellous disc.

Cello Concertos

No 1 in C, HobVIIb/1; **No 2** in D, HobVIIb/2

Cello Concertos Nos 1 and 2
Truls Mørk *vc* **Norwegian Chamber Orchestra / Iona Brown**
Virgin Classics VC5 45014-2 (50 minutes: DDD) Ⓕ
Recorded 1991 ○

Playing a rare early 18th-century Domenico Montagnana cello, Truls Mørk brings an unusual lyrical tenderness to these perennially popular concertos. He can certainly produce a big, gutsy tone where appropriate, as in his imposing initial entry in the C major work; and the agility of his bowing is never in question, as you can hear in the finale of the same concerto, where he responds eagerly to the dramatic and comic potential of Haydn's bravura episodes, with their wide leaps and *staccato* repeated notes. But what lingers in the mind is the delicacy and suppleness of Mørk's *cantabile* phrasing and his beautiful range of colour in piano dynamics. Listen, for instance, to his veiled, dusky tone in the first-movement development of the C major, his sudden withdrawn *pianissimo* in the slow movement, the bow barely brushing the string, or his gravely eloquent shaping of the D major's *Adagio*. The very leisurely first movement, with its (for Haydn) unusually slow harmonic rhythms, mingles elegance, animation and just the right degree of expressive freedom (rubato acutely judged, here as elsewhere) while the finale, which can be a lumbering bore, dances with a lithe, airy grace. The expert Norwegian Chamber Orchestra accompanies crisply and attentively, though oboes and horns get a slightly raw deal in the resonant church acoustic. Among the rival versions of these concertos, several are outstanding, but Mørk can hold his own; and in some moods you might well prefer his fresh, sweet-toned, uncommonly gracious performances before all others.

Cello Concertos Nos 1 and 2. Sinfonia concertante in B flat, HobI/105. Symphony No 13 in D – Adagio cantabile
Steven Isserlis *vc* **Douglas Boyd** *ob* **Matthew Wilkie** *bn* **Marieke Blankestijn** *vn* **Chamber Orchestra of Europe / Sir Roger Norrington**
RCA Victor Red Seal 09026 68578-2 Ⓕ
(75 minutes: DDD). Recorded 1996 ○

What a versatile artist Steven Isserlis is. Having made his name as a sympathetic interpreter of a wide variety of romantic and modern music, here he shows he can be just as persuasive in 18th-century repertoire. His stylistic awareness is evident in beautiful, elegant phrasing, selective use of vibrato and varied articulation, giving an expressive range that never conflicts with the music's natural language. In the cello concertos he is helped by an extremely sensitive accompaniment, stressing the chamber musical aspects of Haydn's pre-London orchestral writing. The *Adagios* are taken at a flowing speed, but Isserlis's relaxed approach means they never sound hurried. The *Allegro molto* finale of the C major Concerto, on the other hand, sounds poised rather than the helter-skelter we often hear. Mørk's vivacious, imaginative performances characterise the music very strongly, but some may prefer Isserlis's and Norrington's lighter touch and greater refinement. And this is not taking into account the extras – the lovely symphony movement (a cello solo throughout) and what many may find the highlight of the disc – the *Sinfonia concertante*. The first movement's tuttis have excessively prominent added dynamics that detract from the music's vigour and grandeur, but the serenade-like *Andante*, the robust and witty finale and, throughout, the conversational exchanges of the four soloists, are an unalloyed delight.

Cello Concertos Nos 1 and 2
Academy of St Martin in the Fields / Mstislav Rostropovich *vc*
EMI CDC7 49305-2 (49 minutes: ADD) Ⓕ
Recorded 1975 ○○

This deserves a place on any collector's shelf. With Rostropovich directing from the bow the ASMF sounds a little less sturdy than usual, a little more lithe in the First Concerto. The scale of its first movement is little short of perfection: everything a *Moderato* should be, with Rostropovich humming along nonchalantly with the lightest of breaths in its second theme. He is leisurely in the *Adagio*, playing it as an extended meditation which exists almost outside time. Without ever losing the life of the melodic line, Rostropovich progresses as slowly as it is humanly possible to do without total stasis; and, to wonderfully joyful effect, breaks all records for speed in the finale. Every note, every sequential phrase is there in its place, secured by glintingly true intonation and needle-sharp dramatic timing. The almost complete absence of physical stick and finger sound which Rostropovich and his engineers manage between them makes the latter two movements of the Second Concerto a most pleasing experience. Rostropovich takes deep, long breaths: the surface of his slow movement is glassy, every fragment of bowing and phrasing given the microscopic hair-pin treatment. For his deep, instinctive understanding of scale, and for Britten's cadenzas, many collectors' preferences in these concertos will remain with Rostropovich.

Trumpet Concerto

Trumpet Concerto in E flat, HobVIIe/1[a]. Cello Concerto in D, HobVIIb/2[b]. Violin Concerto No 1 in C, HobVII[c]
[a]**Wynton Marsalis** *tpt* [c]**Cho-Liang Lin** *vn* [b]**Yo-Yo Ma** *vc* [a]**National Philharmonic Orchestra / Raymond Leppard;** [b]**English Chamber Orchestra / José Luis Garcia;** [c]**Minnesota Orchestra / Sir Neville Marriner**
CBS Masterworks MK39310 (59 minutes: DDD) Ⓕ ○

The American trumpeter Wynton Marsalis has all the fluency one could wish for and an instrument allowing a full three octaves to be displayed in his own cadenza to the first movement. Although this is an efficient performance, it in no way approaches the class of the next one. The cellist Yo-Yo Ma is very different as a performer: though equally a master of his instrument, and indeed a virtuoso who seems incapable of producing an ugly sound or playing out of tune, one feels a deep emotional involvement in all he does. In addition, the recording in the D major Cello Concerto is unusually faithful in blending the cello well into the ensemble without ever covering it. Ma is supported by the excellent English Chamber Orchestra and the qualities of integration and ensemble under their leader's direction are all that one could wish for. In the C major Violin Concerto the skilful Cho-Liang Lin has the benefit of a most sympathetic conductor in Neville Marriner, but he cannot match Ma's subtlety and commitment.

Overtures – Acide e Galatea; Lo speziale; Le pescatrici; L'infedeltà delusa; Philemon und Baucis; Der Götterrath; Il ritorno di Tobia; Der Feuersbrunst; L'incontro improvviso; Il mondo della luna **Vienna Haydn Sinfonietta / Manfred Huss** Ⓟ
Koch Schwann 317232 (61 minutes: DDD) Ⓕ
Recorded 1994

The Haydn Sinfonietta's stylish, vigorous approach – enhanced by period instruments and exemplary recording – creates striking portrayals of the repertoire under review. Here, listeners are given the opportunity to sample overtures from Haydn's theatrical music composed between 1762 and 1777 in an absorbing illustration of life at Esterházy. The Sinfonietta's arresting vitality in *Acide e Galatea*, *Le pescatrici*, *Lo speziale* and *Il mondo della luna*, underlines this music's originally festive purpose; while suitably majestic performances of *L'infedeltà delusa* and *Philemon und Baucis* attest to their presentation before the Empress Maria Theresia. Increased intensity in minor-key pieces such as *Der Götterrath*, with its grand depiction of the 'Council of the Gods' (an allegory for the Hapsburg family), and *Il ritorno di Tobia* highlight Haydn's overtly dramatic writing. Brighter, more startling colours are brilliantly projected by these musicians in an aptly fiery account of *Der Feuersbrunst* and the exotic *L'incontro improvviso* which conjures up vivid images of a Turkish harem. With potent contrast between rhythmically taut energy in the fast movements and elegant sensitivity in the imaginatively scored slow ones, this disc is a winner.

Six Scherzandos, HobII/33-38
Vienna Haydn Sinfonietta / Manfred Huss
Koch Schwann 314432 Ⓕ
(52 minutes: DDD). Recorded 1993

The *Six Scherzandos* which Haydn wrote in 1761 to impress his new patron, Prince Paul Anton Esterházy, exhibit all the typical characteristics of the composer's mature style. Each of these miniature symphonies presents the four movements of the classical symphony with a degree of thematic and formal concentration associated with Beethoven's Op 126 *Bagatelles* and, ultimately, with the works of Anton Webern. Moreover, their sequence here creates a compelling musical cycle. The abounding vitality and subtle sensitivity with which Manfred Huss and the Vienna Haydn Sinfonietta perform this music emphasises its remarkable formal and instrumental variety, highlighting the startling emotional intensity created by its sudden changes of mood. Sample the vivacious opening *allegros*, the rugged minuets, the affecting *adagios*, and the brief, energetic finales. Ensemble is impeccably balanced throughout, and the recorded sound is vividly clear and natural.

Complete Symphonies

No 1 in D; **No 2** in C; **No 3** in G; **No 4** in D; **No 5** in A; **No 6** in D, 'Le matin'; **No 7** in C, 'Le midi'; **No 8** in G, 'Le soir'; **No 9** in C; **No 10** in D; **No 11** in E flat; **No 12** in E; **No 13** in D; **No 14** in A; **No 15** in D; **No 16** in B flat; **No 17** in F; **No 18** in G; **No 19** in D; **No 20** in C; **No 21** in A; **No 22** in E flat, 'Philosopher'; **No 23** in G; **No 24** in D; **No 25** in C; **No 26** in D minor, 'Lamentatione'; **No 27** in G; **No 28** in A; **No 29** in E; **No 30** in C, 'Alleluja'; **No 31** in D, 'Hornsignal'; **No 32** in C; **No 33** in C; **No 34** in D minor; **No 35** in B flat; **No 36** in E flat; **No 37** in C; **No 38** in C; **No 39** in G minor; **No 40** in F; **No 41** in C; **No 42** in D; **No 43** in E flat, 'Mercury'; **No 44** in E minor, 'Trauersinfonie'; **No 45** in F sharp minor, 'Farewell'; **No 46** in B; **No 47** in G, 'Palindrome'; **No 48** in C, 'Maria Theresia'; **No 49** in F minor, 'La passione'; **No 50** in C; **No 51** in B flat; **No 52** in C minor; **No 53** in D, 'Imperial'; **No 54** in G; **No 55** in E flat, 'Schoolmaster'; **No 56** in C; **No 57** in D; **No 58** in F; **No 59** in A, 'Fire'; **No 60** in C, 'Il distratto'; **No 61** in D; **No 62** in D; **No 63** in C, 'La Roxelane'; **No 64** in A, 'Tempora mutantur'; **No 65** in A; **No 66** in B flat; **No 67** in F; **No 68** in B flat; **No 69** in C, 'Loudon'; **No 70** in D; **No 71** in B flat; **No 72** in D; **No 73** in D, 'La chasse'; **No 74** in E flat; **No 75** in D; **No 76** in E flat; **No 77** in B flat; **No 78** in C minor; **No 79** in F; **No 80** in D minor; **No 81** in G; **No 82** in C, 'L'ours'; **No 83** in G minor, 'La poule'; **No 84** in E flat; **No 85** in B flat, 'La reine'; **No 86** in D; **No 87** in A; **No 88** in G, 'Letter V'; **No 89** in F; **No 90** in C; **No 91** in E flat; **No 92** in G, 'Oxford'; **No 93** in D; **No 94** in G, 'Surprise'; **No 95** in C minor; **No 96** in D, 'Miracle'; **No 97** in C; **No 98** in B flat; **No 99** in E flat; **No 100** in G, 'Military'; **No 101** in D, 'Clock'; **No 102** in B flat; **No 103** in E flat, 'Drumroll'; **No 104** in D, 'London'.

Symphonies – Nos 1-104; 'A' in B flat; 'B' in B flat. Sinfonia concertante in B flat, HobI/105, 'No 105'
Philharmonia Hungarica / Antál Dorati
Decca 448 531-2LC33 (33 discs: ADD) Ⓑ
Recorded 1969-73 ●

Dorati's famous integral recording of all 104 of the published Symphonies now returns in a Decca bargain box containing 33 CDs. It still holds its place in the catalogue as the only complete set to contain everything Haydn wrote in this medium, including the Symphonies 'A' and 'B', omitted from the original numbering scheme because at one time they were not thought to be symphonies at all. The survey also encompasses additional alternative movements for certain works (notably Nos 53 and 103) and alternative complete versions of the *Philosopher* Symphony and No 63, which are fascinating. The remastering confirms the excellence of the vintage Decca sound. No more needs to be said, except that the one minus point in these very convincing modern-instrument performances is Dorati's insistence on measured, often rustic tempos for the minuets. For those who can run to the complete series this is self-recommending – a source of inexhaustible pleasure.

Early Symphonies

Symphonies Nos 6-8
Northern Chamber Orchestra / Nicholas Ward
Naxos 8 550722 (59 minutes: DDD) Ⓢ
Recorded 1993

Although this disc doesn't offer any revelations, there's quite a lot to enjoy in the popular Times of Day trilogy, with their colourful and entertaining *concertante* writing. The Northern Chamber Orchestra is a lively, responsive group, and fields a personable bunch of soloists – deft work from flute and violin, for instance, in the finales of Nos 6 and 7, an eloquent cello in the *Andante* of No 8, and nicely turned cameos from the double-bass in the Trios of *Le midi* and *Le soir*. The minuets could move with a nimbler spring, and the slow movements, especially that of *Le matin*, are sometimes short on delicacy and fantasy, with a dearth of truly soft playing. But *Allegros* are bright-eyed and propulsive, with ample verve and virtuosity in the finales. The horns are sometimes unduly discreet, but in general the full, immediate recording is very acceptable. No one staking a fiver on this disc could possibly be disappointed.

Symphonies Nos 22, 29 and 60
Northern Chamber Orchestra / Nicholas Ward
Naxos 8 550724 (60 minutes: DDD) Ⓢ
Recorded 1992-93

In the *Philosopher*, Ward and the NCO (using modern instruments) present a spacious, elegantly phrased account of the title-character's personality. Ward's idiomatic feeling for Haydn's style produces a subtly balanced, appealingly smooth-lined performance. The E major Symphony, No 29, offers Ward and the NCO the chance to explore Haydn's attractive variety of instrumental forces and powerful opposition of major and minor. The programme culminates with No 60 (*Il distratto*). Here, Ward controls his orchestra with customary deftness to make the music's overtly descriptive elements especially telling. Haydn's comic depiction of the protagonist's absent-mindedness is vividly portrayed in the two outer movements, and distinctive thematic characterization effectively heightens the dramatic contrasts in the Minuet and *Adagio*, in a winning performance that fully captures the composer's infectious wit.

Symphonies Nos 22, 86 and 102
City of Birmingham Symphony Orchestra / Sir Simon Rattle
EMI CDC5 55509-2 (68 minutes: DDD) Ⓕ
Recorded 1994 ●

Rattle establishes a middle path between traditional and period styles of performance. In addition, the idea of coupling symphonies from different periods of Haydn's career – not new but relatively rare – is refreshing, and has here produced an issue that one can warmly recommend to anyone simply wanting a representative Haydn symphony disc. The limited vibrato and light phrasing used by the strings throughout these performances set them apart from most others using modern instruments, giving them extra freshness and transparency. So in the *Adagio* of No 102, elegant at a flowing speed, the solo cello is clearly defined, and the Minuet brings the strongest contrast of all with modern-instrument rivals, exuberantly turned into a scherzo at one-in-a-bar. No 86, the fifth of the 'Paris Symphonies', is similarly refreshing, and here too Rattle refuses to rush his first movement in the name of authenticity. The main *Allegro* is marginally more relaxed than that of Dorati (on Decca). By contrast Rattle's *Presto* for the finale is hectic, and one marvels at the agility of the Birmingham horns in their repeated triplets. In the square rhythms of the opening *Adagio* of No 22, Rattle achieves elegance without sacrificing the chunky strength of the chorale on cor anglais, and this symphony, unlike later ones, finds Rattle using harpsichord continuo. The helpful acoustic of Symphony Hall, Birmingham, sets the seal on the disc's success with warm, clear sound.

Symphonies Nos 26, 35, 38, 39, 41-52, 58, 59, 65 **P**
Orchestra of the Age of Enlightenment / Frans Brüggen
Philips ⑤ 462 117-2PH5 (389 minutes: DDD) Ⓜ
Recorded 1996 ●

Although increasingly rejected by scholars, the label *Sturm und Drang* is still widely used to describe the symphonies Haydn wrote during the late 1760s and early 1770s. Storm and stress is, of course, most evident in the half-dozen minor-key symphonies of this period. Several of the major-key works here also have their share of turbulence, above all No 46, in the (for late 18th-century audiences) bizarre key of B major. Others, though, employ the cheerful, Italianate musical language of the day with a new force, originality and, as in movements like the 'limping' Minuet of No 58, comic eccentricity. No 42 in D has an unprecedented amplitude and harmonic breadth, No 43 a mingled fire and reflective lyricism, while No 48, the erroneously named *Maria Theresia*, is one of the noblest and most imposing in a line of 18th-century C major ceremonial symphonies. Stormy, majestic or playful, virtually every work here reflects Haydn's restless exploration of the symphony's expressive and intellectual potential during these years.

These symphonies have been well served by previous period-instrument recordings, but this set – 19 works on five discs – more than holds its own. Brüggen is the most 'romantic' of the conductors in this repertoire: and he has little truck with the smart tempos and clean-cut phrasing favoured by Hogwood and Weil, in particular. Outer movements are often broad and Brüggen phrases the lyrical music as expressively as any traditional conductor, and reveals a strong control of cumulative symphonic tensions. Slow movements are shaped with all the refinement and chamber-musical delicacy heard on Pinnock's recordings, and often with more affection. In one or two of the faster movements Brüggen's tempo is arguably a notch too expansive, above all in the first movement of the C major, No 41. He also shows an intermittent fondness for shading away at cadences, notably in the opening movement of the *Lamentatione*, No 26. Equally controversial is his speeding up for the trios of several of the minuets, most blatantly in that of *La Passione*, though his tempos for the minuets themselves are thoughtfully chosen, ranging from the measured, elegiac No 26 to the stinging one-in-a-bar quasi-*Scherzo* of No 52. The beautiful, melancholy Minuet of

No 46 is much broader than on any rival period version, to its advantage; and Brüggen hilariously heightens the 'limping' effect in the Minuet of No 58 with outrageous unmarked *sforzandos*.

Brüggen eschews a harpsichord continuo, though he rightly reinforces the bass-line with a clearly audible bassoon. And he omits second-time repeats in all but a few sonata movements, a small price to pay for an average of nearly four symphonies per disc. Brüggen's performances, though occasionally questionable, are the most individual in their shaping and characterization. The playing of the OAE is brilliant and refined (it was criminal not to name the superlative horn players), and the recording is natural, detailed and atmospheric. If you're still undecided, this set – five well-filled discs for the price of four – offers a serious price advantage over the other contenders.

Symphonies Nos 50, 54-57 and 60 Ⓟ
Academy of Ancient Music / Christopher Hogwood
L'Oiseau-Lyre ③ 443 781-2OH3 (179 minutes: DDD) Ⓕ
Recorded 1993

These six symphonies date from 1773-74, when the intensity of Haydn's musical language during the preceding years was being tempered with a new urbanity and a deliberately calculated popular appeal. The older style is represented by the *Adagios* of Nos 54 and 56, with their spacious lines and rarefied atmosphere. Typical of the newer, more 'accessible' manner is the obscurely nicknamed *Schoolmaster*, No 55, with its droll, *faux-naïf* variation slow movement and its catchy finale, a deft and witty amalgam of variation, rondo and sonata forms.

The little-known No 57 also aims at popular effect in its theme-and-variation slow movement, its stomping *Ländler*-Minuet and *Prestissimo* finale suggesting a riotous comic opera imbroglio. The spirit of *opera buffa* permeates several movements here, including the opening *Presto* of No 54, a symphony Hogwood opts to perform in its original version – that is, without the slow introduction and the enhanced scoring for flutes, trumpets and timpani. Two of the other symphonies, both in C major with high horns, trumpets and timpani, have overt theatrical connections: No 50 probably started life as the introduction to *Der Götterrath*, the lost prologue to the marionette opera *Philemon und Baucis*, while the burlesque six-movement *Il distratto*, No 60, originated as incidental music to a farce centring on an 'absent-minded' hero – hence the music's frequent air of distractedness and comic inconsequentiality. Hogwood has thought carefully about the precise character of each movement, chooses his tempos shrewdly and is always alive to felicitous details of wind colour or inner string writing. Abetted by marvellously lithe, incisive playing from the Academy of Ancient Music, he gives a viscerally exciting reading of No 56, the finale dispatched with phenomenal panache at the fastest possible tempo. Here, and in Nos 50 and 60, brass and timpani rasp and thunder to thrilling effect. The finale of No 57 is likewise breathtaking, not only in its accuracy at high speed but also in its delicacy and point. Aided by notably sweet, refined string playing, the filigree writing in Nos 54 and 57 is exquisitely realised. The recording is clean, immediate and well balanced.

Symphonies Nos 55-69
Austro-Hungarian Haydn Orchestra / Adám Fischer
Nimbus ⑤ NI5590/4 (317 minutes: DDD) Ⓢ
Recorded 1996-97

With a fair sprinkling of named symphonies, and one or two whose theatrical associations render them eccentric in symphonic terms – as, for example, the six-movement *Il distratto*, No 60 – this makes a most attractive collection, with no hint of routine in any of the performances. In the helpful acoustic of the Haydnsaal of the Esterházy Palace at Eisenstadt, the sound is at once warmly atmospheric and intimate, with high contrasts of dynamic and texture. Fischer's fine control of dynamics is repeatedly illustrated in the subtlety of echo phrases, clear but unexaggerated. Fischer uses modern rather than period instruments. As he explains in the booklet, his players, carefully chosen from the leading orchestras of Vienna and Budapest, are happier with the instruments with which they have grown up. Also, the orchestra is designed to provide an alternative to period groups, based as it is 'on this living tradition of Austro-Hungarian music-making'.

This set offers a very agreeable alternative to the full period sound, when the strings are relatively sparing with vibrato, and most strikingly the characteristic Viennese oboes and horns stand out so vividly, with fine separation. Inevitably comparisons are to be made with Antál Dorati's classic, pioneering 33-disc set with the Philharmonia Hungarica. In important ways, not just in the extra fullness of the digital sound, the new performances improve on the old, notably in the brisker speeds for minuets. Fischer tends to prefer speeds in slow movements a fraction more flowing than those of Dorati, while outer movements are regularly a degree more relaxed than with the older conductor. Fischer's springing of rhythm is always persuasive, so that at no point does his chosen speed seem too slow, even if those dedicated to period practice might well prefer the more hectic *prestos* and *prestissimos* of the earlier set. Generally exposition or first-half repeats are observed, but not second-half repeats, though inexplicably the exposition repeat is not observed in the first movement of No 61.

Generally these are performances which register Haydn's humour more clearly than does Dorati's, even in the *Sturm und Drang* symphonies such as Nos 58 and 59 (*Fire*). Fischer may not point the humour of the tuning-up joke in the finale of No 60 quite as well as Dorati, but Fischer brings out the distinctive timbres in No 67, with the extraordinary fading out on string phrases *col legno* in the long slow movement, and the hurdy-gurdy effect underlined in the equally eccentric writing for two violins in the third-movement Trio. The bargain price adds to the appeal of the set.

Symphonies Nos 82-87
Orchestra of the Eighteenth Century / Frans Brüggen
Philips ② 462 111-2PH2 (143 minutes: DDD)   Ⓕ
Recorded 1996   ●

Haydn's so-called *Paris* Symphonies, written in 1785-6 for the famed orchestra of the Concert de la Loge Olympique, have fared pretty well on CD: there are three rival period-instrument accounts from Sigiswald Kuijken, Roy Goodman and Bruno Weil respectively. Brüggen is crisp and vital in the *allegros*, yet always allows the music plenty of breathing space. And his phrasing of the lyrical themes is more expressively moulded than on any of these rival versions. The main theme of No 85's opening *Vivace*, for instance, glides with a feline grace, and the first movement of No 84 has an airy, dancing elegance. Yet Haydn's dramatic coups, such as the barbaric dissonances in the first movement of No 82, are played for all they're worth; and throughout Brüggen shows a shrewd grasp of long-range structure, knowing just when to tighten the screws (as in the fiercely modulating developments in the finales of Nos 83 and 85, both unusually tense and truculent here, and the thrilling, brassy codas to the finales of Nos 82 and 86). He judges nicely the pace and character of each of the minuets, too, ranging from the red and gold pomp of No 82 to the brisk and breezy No 85, with its whiplash accents and whooping high horns. And, predictably, his phrasing in the slow movements is more affectionate, more highly nuanced, than on any of the competing versions. Also, his tempos here are all aptly chosen.

It would be rash, perhaps, to recommend an outright 'winner' among period versions of the *Paris* Symphonies when all competitors have so much going for them, but Brüggen would get the vote, for his stronger sense of drama in sonata movements, for his more expressive phrasing, and for his superlative wind players, who in refinement and imagination eclipse all their rivals. The live Philips recordings are remarkably consistent, combining transparency with a pleasing ambient warmth.

Symphonies Nos 93, 94, 97 and 99-101
Concertgebouw Orchestra / Sir Colin Davis
Philips Duo ② 442 614-2PM2 (ADD/DDD)   Ⓜ
Recorded 1975-81   ●●

Symphonies Nos 95, 96, 98 and 102-104
Concertgebouw Orchestra / Sir Colin Davis
Philips Duo ②442 611-2PM2 (ADD/DDD)   Ⓜ
Recorded 1975-81   ●●

A superb achievement. It's nigh-on impossible to imagine better 'big-band' Haydn than one encounters here on Colin Davis's four well-filled CDs. His direction has exemplary sparkle (try the superb opening movement of the

Miracle Symphony) and sensitivity (witness his eloquent moulding of No 98's great *Adagio*). Minuets are never allowed to plod, outer movements have an ideal combination of infectious zip and real poise, and the humour is always conveyed with a genial twinkle in the eye. Quite marvellous, wonderfully unanimous playing from the Amsterdam orchestra, too (the woodwind contributions are particularly distinguished), with never a trace of routine to betray the six-year recording span of this acclaimed project. The Philips engineering, whether analogue or digital, is of the very highest quality, offering a natural perspective, gloriously full-bodied tone and sparkling textures within the sumptuous Concertgebouw acoustic. Invest in this set: it will yield enormous rewards for years to come.

Symphonies Nos 103 and 104   Ⓟ
La Petite Bande / Sigiswald Kuijken
Deutsche Harmonia Mundi 05472-77362-2   Ⓕ
(57 minutes: DDD). Recorded 1995

In the slow movements of these symphonies Kuijken is more gracious and reflective than his rivals, with affectionate touches of timing; and he leaves you in no doubt that the central *minore* section is the most awesome, physically powerful music in any 18th-century symphonic slow movement. Kuijken's grave, steady tread in the C minor-major theme and variations of No 103 is also appealing, he brings a swaggering grandeur to the final C major variation and shapes with tenderness the quiet string phrases that usher in the coda – a sudden and magical change of atmosphere. In the minuets, conversely, Kuijken is appreciably faster than most, especially in No 103, where at his headlong tempo the flicking 'Scotch snap' figures tend to be blurred. He is genial and gamesome in the opening *Allegro con spirito* of No 103 and broad yet thrilling in the finale. No 104 opens with a magnificently imposing, portentous introduction, and both the first *Allegro* and the finale are strong and spirited, the urgent drama of the developments powerfully limned. The recorded sound has an attractive spaciousness and bloom, if not total clarity: inner string parts are not always ideally defined and both horns and bassoons at times seem underbalanced. Kuijken's interpretations, vividly realised by his 35-strong orchestra (particularly delectable work from first flute and first oboe), can be recommended to anyone seeking these symphonies in period performances that do ample justice to the music's boldness and imaginative reach.

Otte Notturni, HobII/25-32

Marten Root *fl* Michael Niesemann *ob*   Ⓟ
Mozzafiato (Charles Neidich, Ayako Oshima *cls*
William Purvis, Stewart Rose *hns* Marji Danilow *db*)
L'Archibudelli (Vera Beths, Lucy van Dael *vns*
Jürgen Kussmaul, Guus Jeukendrup *vas*
Anner Bylsma *vc*)
Sony Classical Vivarte SK62878 (77 minutes: DDD) Ⓕ
Recorded 1996

Between 1788 and 1790 Haydn was commissioned to write a set of *Notturni* for a curious and complex instrument, the *lira organizzata*, a kind of hurdy-gurdy with an inbuilt miniature organ. On the rare occasions when these works are aired today, the two *lire* parts are taken by flute and oboe, following Haydn's own practice in his London concerts. In six of the *notturni* the *lire* are complemented by clarinets, horns, violas, cello and double-bass, while in two (Hob Nos 27 and 28) clarinets are replaced by violins. All are on a miniature scale, with, usually, three brief movements (fast-slow-fast). The *Notturni*, for all their brevity and lightness of touch, are beautifully crafted, often sophisticated in their harmony and motivic development and exquisitely scored, with kaleidoscopically varied colours that at times recall Mozart's wind serenades.

Most of the finales are racy rondos, full of quickfire instrumental interplay; an exception is that of No 29, one of Haydn's ingenious amalgams of fugue and sonata form. Slow movements are often pastoral in feeling, with touches of sensuous chromaticism; one or two, though, touch a deeper vein, above all the brooding, dark *Adagio* of No 27, probably reflecting Haydn's increasing melancholy and loneliness in his final year at Esterháza in 1790. This *Adagio* is taken very flowingly here. The players' technical finesse is matched by their pointed, shapely phrasing, their care for blend and dovetailing and their palpable delight in Haydn's witty raillery. Here and there the horns could have brayed out more rudely; but otherwise balance is excellent, and the recorded sound vivid and immediate.

Divertimentos

Divertimentos – G, HobII/1; D, HobII/D22 Add; G, HobII/9 **P**

Vienna Haydn Sinfonietta / Manfred Huss

Koch Schwann 312862 (57 minutes: DDD) Ⓕ
Recorded 1994

In this set of *Divertimentos*, Manfred Huss rightly takes every opportunity to highlight the Vienna Haydn Sinfonietta's excellent soloist and ensemble skills in performances of abounding vitality. The period-instrument sound – emphasised by a full, bright recording – does have the occasional rough edge, but this only adds power and piquancy to these compelling accounts. Huss and his team vividly bring out the striking baroque colours in the G major *Divertimento* (HobII/1), conveying the music's startling array of expressive moods with elegant phrasing in the slow movements, and further underlining the score's rich stylistic diversity in the theme and variations of the finale. In the D major *Divertimento*, on the other hand, Huss deftly balances bravura horn writing and strings to reveal the full sparkle and textural variety of this robust piece. Listen to the enchanting discourse between the horns in the slow movement, or the dazzling virtuosity from everyone in the finale.

Until recently, the unfortunate state of the sources for the G major *Divertimento* (HobII/9) had made modern performances impossible. Yet, with the discovery of new material, Huss and the Haydn Sinfonietta display the work's infectious vivacity with exquisite playing, thus restoring this splendid music to the repertory. Serene poise in the slow movement contrasts *cantabile* melody and pizzicato accompaniment, and the piece culminates in a finale of arresting vigour.

Flute Quartets

Cassation in F, HobII/20. Divertissement in B flat, HobII/B4. Flute Quartet in A, HobII/A4. Notturno No 1 in C, HobII/25

Linos Ensemble

Capriccio 10 719 (68 minutes: DDD). Recorded 1994 Ⓕ

These highly polished, enthusiastic performances generate a compelling immediacy. What's more, the diverse choice of pieces amply shows the excellent soloistic skills of Linos's members and its deftly balanced ensemble, while close recording presents this group's eloquence and fresh vitality in fine, clear detail. The delightful, open-air qualities of this repertoire are exemplified by the F major *Cassation*, whose good humour is captured with buoyant vigour in the opening *Allegro*; with stately elegance in the two minuets, affecting melodiousness in the *Adagio*, and an engaging swing in the final rondo. The extrovert B flat *Divertissement* offers a charming display of fluent, conversational playing, a style which the Linos exploits to particular effect in the lively alternation of different instrumental groupings in the elegant A major Quartet for flute and strings. Ultimately, the infectiously high-spirited, effervescent exchanges between flute and oboe in the witty C major *Notturno* sum up the allure of this entertaining issue.

Complete String Quartets

Op 1 – No 1 in B flat, 'La chasse'; **No 2** in E flat; **No 3** in D; **No 4** in G,; **No 5** in E flat; **No 6** in C. **Op 9 – No 1** in C; **No 2** in E flat; **No 3** in G; **No 4** in D minor; **No 5** in B flat; **No 6** in A. **Op 20,** 'Sun' – **No 1** in E flat; **No 2** in C; **No 3** in G minor; **No 4** in D; **No 5** in F minor; **No 6** in A. **Op 33 – No 1** in B minor; **No 2** in E flat, 'Joke'; **No 3** in C, 'Bird'; **No 4** in B flat; **No 5** in G; **No 6** in D. **Op 42** in D. **Op 50 – No 1** in B flat; **No 2** in C; **No 3** in E flat; **No 4** in F sharp minor; **No 5** in F, 'The Dream'; **No 6** in D, 'Frog'. **Op 54 – No 1** in G; **No 2** in C; **No 3** in E. **Op 55 – No 1** in A; **No 2** in F minor; **No 3** in B flat. **Op 64 – No 1** in C; **No 2** in B minor; **No 3** in B flat; **No 4** in G; **No 5** in D, 'The Lark'; **No 6** in E flat. **Op 71** – No 1 in B flat; **No 2** in D; **No 3** in E flat. **Op 74 – No 1** in C; **No 2** in F; **No 3** in G minor, 'Rider'. **Op 76 – No 2** in D minor, 'Fifths'; **No 3** in C, 'Emperor'; **No 4** in B flat, 'Sunrise'. **Op 77 – No 1** in G; **No 2** in F

Op 0; Op 1 – Nos 1[a], 2, 3, 4[a] and 6 in C[a]; Op 2 – Nos 1, 2[a], 4[a] and 6; Op 9; Opp 17, 20, 33, 42[a], 50[a], 54, 55, 64, 71, 74, 76, 77 and 103

Angeles Quartet (Kathleen Lenski, Steven Miller, [a]Sara Parkins *vns* Brian Dembow *va* Stephen Erdody *vc*)

Philips (21 discs) 464 650-2PX21 Ⓜ
(140 minutes: DDD). Recorded 1994-99 **OO**

The most relevant comparisons for this newcomer are the Aeolian Quartet on Decca and the Kodály Quartet on Naxos. The all-digital Naxos series features performances that are, in the main, musically reliable and technically proficient. But turn back to the 1973-76 Aeolian series and every work becomes an event, every quirk of harmony, rhythm or timing is etched with maximum relish.

Comparative disc layouts begin to differ from CD 3, and the Angeles omit *The Seven Last Words*, a work which, beautiful though it is, was not originally written for string quartet. Recordings-wise, Philips favours a warm, open sound, balanced much as you would hear it from the centre stalls in a smallish-size concert hall. Decca's analogue recordings are closer, dryer, more sensitive to extraneous noise and commonly balanced in favour of Emanuel Hurwitz's first violin. It's a clear and intimate sound frame and the leader bias actually suits the divertimento-style early quartets, but Philips's more refined engineering makes for less strenuous listening in extended (ie concert-length) sessions. A handful of edits (audible more through headphones than on speakers) are the only blots on Philips's otherwise immaculate aural landscape.

The svelte texture of the Angeles' pooled sound, their consistent evenness in full chords and the musical like-mindedness of individual players, whether in excited *presto*s or in shared rubato is admirable. As to contrasts in playing styles, think of the relatively smooth-toned Juilliard or Emerson Quartets (Angeles) as compared with the internally differentiated Amadeus Quartet (Aeolian). There are a few textual differences – accompanying figures that fall 1'15" into the *Adagio* of Op 0 are played *pizzicato* by the Angeles and *arco* by the Aeolians, and an appoggiatura in the first movement of Op 54 No 1 (Angeles) is ironed out to full note value by the Aeolians; other such differences centre primarily on musical repeats, and in that respect the Aeolians are marginally more generous. The Angeles are generally lighter, faster and subtler in their use of tone colouring whereas the Aeolians' roster of virtues includes strong (even emphatic) characterisation, consistently flexible phrasing and a more pungent approach to rhythm.

Surfing the set for good sampling points brings us, initially, to the early quartets, where both groups sport some superb first-violin solo work, tastefully inflected with Lenski, more candidly expressive with Hurwitz. A particularly telling comparison is provided by the quietly contrapuntal Minuet of Op 17 No 1, where the Angeles' seamless *legato* contrasts against the Aeolians' near *staccato*. The exquisite *Adagio* of Op 20 No 6 is another good place to compare, the Angeles with their perfectly timed pauses, warm cello line and overall restraint set against the more romantic, even rhapsodic, Aeolian. Listening to the first bars of Op 33 No 1 is like eavesdropping on a small gathering mid-conversation, where the cello line gradually gains in urgency. The Angeles' *sotto voce* handling of the *scherzo* to Op 33 No 3 is wonderful: it's rather more pensive than the Aeolians and marks much more of a contrast with the chirping trio.

Op 50 No 4's *Andante* anticipates the dramatic interjections that trouble various late Schubert slow movements. Both groups are effective here, though when the cello marks an expected change of key two minutes or so into the movement, it's the Aeolian's Derek Simpson who makes the biggest impact: you can almost see the rosin erupt from his strings. In Op 50 No 5 late Beethoven springs more readily to mind, but there the Angeles' extra speed and restraint is more effective. Note how beautifully they negotiate the quiet alternation between upper and lower voices towards the end of Op 50 No 6's *Poco adagio* and the sudden blossoming that follows. Then again, Op 54 No 1's mobile *Allegretto* second movement harbours the potential to switch from tenseness to lyrical effusiveness, which the Angeles exploit to the full, as they do for the rhapsodising *Adagio* of Op 54 No 2. Late Beethoven is evoked once more, this time the Cavatina from Op 130.

Beam up around three minutes into the *Adagio* of the *Lark* Quartet (Op 64 No 5) and you'll note how skilfully the Angeles cue a *ritardando*, while the bracing finale to Op 74 No 3 has just the right bounce to offset all the breathless excitement. The *Sunrise* Quartet (Op 76 No 4) opens like a spring flower (never more so than in the Angeles' ecstatically controlled performance) and Op 77 No 1's cheeky *Allegro moderato* bounds in with perfectly modulated high spirits.

Turning to other competition, the Lindsays, Amadeus, Vienna Konzerthaus, Quatuor Mosaïques, Pro Arte and Takács, all have added substantially – and characterfully – to the Haydn quartet discography, and all have their value. However, in this particular context it really is a head-to-head contest between two 'complete' sets similarly presented.

Richard Wigmore contributes detailed annotation, quite different from Lindsay Kemp's overview for Decca, but just as useful and equally well-written. The Angeles appeal perhaps primarily for their restrained expressiveness and consistent attention to detail. Philips's superior recording is another bonus. The Aeolians generate more immediate heat but, ultimately, the Angeles' intelligence and cooler blending pay the higher musical dividends. Personal taste will be a crucial deciding factor, but one thing is sure: you simply must invest in one or the other.

String Quartets: Op 1 No 1. Op 20 Nos 2 and 5. Op 50 No 3. Op 54 Nos 1-3. Op 64 Nos 3 and 4. Op 74 No 3. Op 76 Nos 3 and 4. Op 77 No 2 **H**
Pro Arte Quartet (Alphonse Onnou, Laurent Halleux *vns* Germain Prévost *va* Robert Maas *vc*)
Testament mono ③ SBT3055 (229 minutes: ADD) Ⓕ
Recorded 1931-38 ●

String Quartets: Op 1 No 6. Op 20 Nos 1 and 4. Op 33 Nos 2, 3 and 6. Op 50 No 6. Op 55 Nos 1 and 3. Op 64 No 6. Op 71 No 1. Op 74 Nos 1 and 2. Op 77 No 1 **Hoffstetter** String Quartets, Op 3 – No 4 in B flat; No 5 in F **H**

Pro Arte Quartet (Alphonse Onnou, Laurent Halleux *vns* Germain Prévost *va* Robert Maas *vc*)
Testament mono ④ SBT4056 (243 minutes: ADD) Ⓕ
Recorded 1931-38 ●

The Pro Arte Quartet's first London appearance in 1925 prompted *The Times* to declare, 'One has never heard it surpassed, and rarely equalled, in volume and beauty of tone, in accuracy of intonation and in perfection of balance between the parts' – and that could well be the verdict on these sets. The musicians' tempos invariably seem just right and their phrasing has an inner life that is extraordinarily potent. Alphonse Onnou and Laurent Halleux were superbly matched, and Halleux often led in their early days. Such virtuosity as the quartet exhibits is effortless and totally lacking in ostentation. Of course, the actual sound is dated – the string tone is wanting in bloom and freshness – but the ear soon adjusts, though one might wish that these transfers could have given us a little more space between movements.

String Quartets, Op 1

String Quartets, Op 1 Nos 1-6
Petersen Quartet (Conrad Muck, Gernot Sussmuth *vns* Friedemann Weigle *va* Hans-Jakob Eschenburg *vc*)
Capriccio ② 10 786/7 (99 minutes: DDD) Ⓕ
Recorded 1995-96 ●

The history of the string quartet in effect began with these cheerful, compact *Divertimenti a quattro*, as the composer titled them; and though they contain only spasmodic hints of future glories, their freshness and exuberance make for highly pleasurable listening. All are in five movements, with two contrasted Minuets placed second and fourth, the former a leisurely *Minuetto galante*, the latter brisker and earthier, with the *sansculotte* two-part writing and octave doublings found in Haydn's later minuets right through to the Op 76 Quartets. As in the early piano sonatas, the trios usually turn to the comic minor, often with striking effect – for example in the violins' canonic imitations in the fourth movement of No 4, or the eloquent chromaticism in the second movement of No 5. The slow movements are accompanied arias for the first violin, often touching in their innocence and candour, while the ebullient *Presto* outer movements delight in quirkily irregular phrase-lengths, quick-fire repartee and contrasts of texture and register – the kind of music that led po-faced North German critics to accuse Haydn of debasing the art with 'comic fooling'.

The Petersen Quartet responds vividly to the music's youthful verve, with polished ensemble, keen attack and a wide spectrum of colour and dynamics. Purists may raise an eyebrow at the special effects the players deploy in repeats, especially in minuets – added touches of imitation, pizzicato and even *col legno*. But the young Haydn, famed for his mischievous humour, may have enjoyed these liberties. The recording combines clarity with an attractive church resonance.

String Quartets, Op 9

String Quartets, Op 9 Nos 1, 3 and 4
Kodály Quartet (Attila Falváy, Tamás Szabó *vns* Gábor Fias *va* János Devich *vc*)
Naxos 8 550788 (52 minutes: DDD) Ⓢ
Recorded 1993

String Quartets, Op 9 Nos 2, 5 and 6
Kodály Quartet (Attila Falváy, Tamás Szabó *vns* Gábor Fias *va* János Devich *vc*) Ⓢ
Naxos 8 550787 (58 minutes: DDD). Recorded 1993

Overshadowed by four dozen later masterpieces, Haydn's Op 9 has usually received short shrift from both players and commentators. Least neglected of the set is the D minor, No 4, described by Hans Keller as 'the first great string quartet in the history of music'. The minor mode at this period (1769-70) invariably drew something special from Haydn, and this work stands apart from the others for its intensity of expression, its mastery of texture and development and the sheer character of its ideas. The opening *Allegro moderato* could well have been at the back of Mozart's mind when he came to write his own great D minor Quartet, K421. Of Nos 1-5 it is true that there are *longueurs*, nowhere more so than in the stiff, gawky opening movements of Nos 1-3, and the routine set of variations that opens No 5. But there are compensations elsewhere: in the terse, resourceful and (especially in No 3) witty finales; in the varied minuets, ranging from the high-stepping No 5, with its alfresco octave doublings, to the suave, chromatically subtle No 2; and in several of the slow movements. The Kodály Quartet is, as ever, a sympathetic Haydn exponent, impressing with its slightly old-fashioned warmth of sonority, the natural musicality of its phrasing and its care for blend, balance and intonation, though the boomy church acoustic hardly helps.

String Quartets, Op 20

Awards 1993

String Quartets, Op 20 Nos 1-6 **P**
Quatuor Mosaïques (Erich Höbarth, Andrea Bischof *vns* Anita Mitterer *va* Christophe Coin *vc*)
Auvidis Astrée ② E8802 Ⓕ
(147 minutes: DDD). Recorded 1990 ●●●
Also available separately: E8785 – Nos 1, 5 and 6. E8786 – Nos 2-4

The Op 20 String Quartets date from the composer's so-called *Sturm und Drang* period, though Haydn's increasingly frequent use of the more dramatic and 'serious' minor mode in these pieces can perhaps be attributed just as much to the fruitful influence of the three operatic projects he had been working on just a few years previously. Moreover, these quartets reveal a greater preoccupation with counterpoint than any of his music to that date, and the great fugal finales of Nos 2, 5 and 6 clearly herald the consummate craftsman so overwhelmingly displayed in the mature quartets to come.

Incidentally, the Op 20 set's nickname *Sun* derives from the illustration on the handsome title-page of the Hummel edition of this music, at the top of which peers out the sun-god's head. These wonderfully flexible performances display an altogether breathtaking refinement, sensitivity and illumination. Indeed, in terms of expressive subtlety, imaginative intensity and sheer depth of feeling, the Mosaïques' achievement in these marvellous works is unmatched.

String Quartets, Op 20 Nos 1, 3 and 4
The Lindsays (Peter Cropper, Ronald Birks *vns* Robin Ireland *va* Bernard Gregor-Smith *vc*)
ASV CDDCA1027 (79 minutes: DDD) Ⓕ
Recorded 1997

String Quartets, Op 20 Nos 2, 5 and 6
The Lindsays (Peter Cropper, Ronald Birks *vns* Robin Ireland *va* Bernard Gregor-Smith *vc*)
ASV CDDCA1057 (66 minutes: DDD) Ⓕ
Recorded 1998

The Lindsays are Haydn interpreters of rare understanding and communicative flair. Their characterization is bold and decisive, enhanced by a scrupulous observation of the composer's expression and dynamic markings. Faster movements tend to be more urgent, less ruminative, than those from the Quatuor Mosaïques. The *zingarese* cross-rhythms of No 4's Minuet have an abrasive edge, and the *Presto e scherzando* finale is no mere frolic in The Lindsays' hands – its wit can scathe and sting, and the closing theme, with its gipsy *acciaccaturas*, has an almost manic insistence. Elsewhere The Lindsays bring an ideal warmth and lyricism to the opening movement of No 1, characteristically phrasing in long, eloquent spans, and a quixotic energy to the outer movements of the G minor, No 3, where the Quatuor Mosaïques is broader and tougher. In the Minuet of No 3 The Lindsays' singing line and flexibility of pulse realise to the full Haydn's searching harmonic progressions; and the lulling E flat Trio is exquisitely floated, with the players venturing an even more hushed, absorbed tone colour on the repeat. Each of the slow movements reveals dedication and profound identification. The players vindicate their dangerously slow tempo in the sublime *Affettuoso e sostenuto* of No 1 with the breadth and intensity of their phrasing, subtlety of colour and feeling for harmonic flux. Conversely, the slow movements of No 3 and, especially, No 4 are more flowing than with the Quatuor Mosaïques yet no less moving. As ever, the occasional moment of impure intonation and marginally imprecise ensemble is a small price to pay for performances of such colour, character and spontaneity. The Lindsays observe all the important marked repeats and the recording is vivid and truthful.

Characterization of the sharply contrasted Nos 2, 5 and 6 is invariably vivid, phrasing is alive and inventive, and the players combine a scrupulous care for Haydn's dynamic and expression markings with a strong feeling for the music's larger contours. The opening movement of the C major has a bold, exhilarating sweep together with an acute response to such moments as the magical dip towards E flat near the end of the exposition (1'46"), where they find a wonderful withdrawn quality of tone. They underline the operatic associations of the *Adagio*, with Peter Cropper bringing a vocal eloquence to his consolatory E flat *cantabile* (from 3'04"); and in the closing fugue, where Haydn wears his learning with supreme nonchalance, they play with captivating lightness and delicacy, the dynamic held down to *sotto voce* until the final send-off, as the composer requests. The F minor, Haydn's most tragic quartet, and the sunny, extrovert A major are no less compelling. Listen, for instance, to the variety of expression The Lindsays bring to the F minor's Minuet, to their dreamy lilt and beautifully judged *rubato* in the *Adagio*, or to the dancing, *scherzando* spirit of No 6's opening movement. And both final fugues are intensely vital within their prescribed *sotto voce* dynamic; that in No 6 delightfully skittish. Equally enjoyable is the *Adagio* of No 6, for Peter Cropper's tender, spontaneously inflected line, the pointing of the beautiful viola part (particularly telling from 3'50") and, again, the subtle tonal shading in response to harmonic flux.

String Quartets, Op 33

String Quartets, Op 33 Nos 1, 2 and 4
The Lindsays (Peter Cropper, Ronald Birks *vns* Robin Ireland *va* Bernard Gregor-Smith *vc*)
ASV CDDCA937 (62 minutes: DDD) Ⓕ
Recorded 1994

The Lindsays' is chamber-music-making of unusual re-creative flair, untouched by the faintest hint of routine. In their uncommonly grave, inward readings of the slow movements of the E flat and B flat Quartets they sustain a daringly slow tempo magnificently, phrasing in long, arching spans, always acutely sensitive to harmonic movement, as in their subtle colouring of Haydn's breathtaking tonal excursions in No 4. Beethoven is evoked in The Lindsays' swift, mordant reading of No 1's epigrammatic *Scherzo*: rarely have the waspish part-writing and the abrupt, disconcerting contrasts in dynamics and articulation been so vividly realised. Typically, it makes the most of the complete change of mood and texture in the major-key Trio, finding an almost Viennese sweetness of tone and phrase, complete with touches of *portamento*. The finale, fast, fierce, utterly uncomical, has a distinct whiff of the Hungarian *puszta* here, both in the wild gipsy figuration from 0'10" and the mounting passion of the sequence in the development. The Lindsays bring an ideal spaciousness and flexibility to the urbane, quietly spoken first movement of the E flat Quartet, No 2, taking due note of Haydn's *cantabile* marking. In the finales of this Quartet and No 4 they bring vital, inventively varied phrasing, palpably relishing Haydn's exuberance and comic sleight of hand. Here, as occasionally elsewhere, it's easy to overlook the odd moment of rhythmic unsteadiness or impure intonation for the sake of such characterful music-making.

String Quartets, Op 33 Nos 3, 5 and 6
The Lindsays (Peter Cropper, Ronald Birks *vns* Robin Ireland *va* Bernard Gregor-Smith *vc*)
ASV CDDCA938 (61 minutes: DDD) Ⓕ
Recorded 1995 **oo**

The Lindsays eclipse all-comers in range of colour, vital, creative phrasing and emotional penetration. They respond gleefully to the subversive comedy that pervades each of the three works – most overtly in the Slavonic-influenced finale of *The Bird* (No 3), and in the outrageous *Scherzo* of No 5, where with explosive *sforzandos* and sly touches of timing it relishes to the full Haydn's rhythmic and dynamic mayhem. But time and again in this music wit is suddenly suffused with poetry; and The Lindsays bring a glancing delicacy and grace of interplay to, say, the startling tonaldeflexions in the opening *Vivace assai* of No 6. With The Lindsays' slower-than-usual tempo and wonderfully tender, contained *sotto voce*, the second movement of No 3, where Haydn transmutes the Minuet-scherzo into a hymn, becomes the expressive core of the quartet. The variation finales of Nos 5 and 6 can easily seem anticlimactic. Here, though, the players' rhythmic point and inventively varied phrasing and dynamics (repeats are never mere repetitions) make the music consistently compelling. The Lindsays play from the Henle Urtext edition, which corrects tempo markings and numerous details of phrasing in the unreliable Peters and Eulenburg editions; and it observes both repeats in sonata movements – particularly important in the first movement of *The Bird*, where the four-bar lead-back to the development adds yet another point of harmonic subtlety. The Lindsays constantly provoke you to respond afresh to Haydn; to his wit and comic exuberance, his inexhaustible inventiveness and his often unsuspected profundity.

String Quartets, Op 33 Nos 1, 4 and 6 **P**
Quatuor Mosaïques (Erich Höbarth, Andrea Bischof *vns* Anita Mitterer *va* Christophe Coin *vc*)
Auvidis Astrée E8570 (60 minutes: DDD) Ⓕ
Recorded 1996 **o**

From the teasingly timed initial upbeat of the D major Quartet, No 6, the Quatuor Mosaïques' performances have all the familiar hallmarks: inventive phrasing, subtly varied colour, a sure sense of organic growth and a spontaneous-sounding delight in Haydn's inspired unpredictability. Tempo and manner in the opening *Vivace assai* of No 6 are, typically, gentler than that of the equally imaginative Lindsays, the articulation lighter and more delicate, as you would expect from period strings. It catches ideally the music's glancing *scherzando* spirit, with a delightfully eager, quick-witted give-and-take between the instruments. Like The Lindsays, the Mosaïques vividly plays up the contrast between the perky, high-stepping D major theme and alternating D minor melody. But the Mosaïques flexes the tempo more freely and plays with the length of Haydn's upbeats, to witty or pathetic effect. In the *Andante* of the B minor Quartet the Mosaïques arguably overdoes the whimsical hesitations. However, its unusally reflective way with this movement, and the sense of remoteness it brings to the strange, spare second theme is very appealing. As for the undervalued B flat Quartet, it is a delight throughout, from the puckish opening movement, with its quasi-improvisatory freedom (The Lindsays are fiercer and more brittle here) to the comic exuberance of the finale; the vitality and point of the inner voices' semiquavers in the finale's G minor episode are typical of the character the Mosaïques brings to seemingly routine accompanying figuration. In sum, this disc is another winner from this period-instrument quartet. The recording has an attractive ambient warmth.

Awards 1996

String Quartets, Op 33 Nos 2, 3 and 5 **P**
Quatuor Mosaïques (Erich Höbarth, Andrea Bischof *vns* Anita Mitterer *va* Christophe Coin *vc*)
Auvidis Astrée E8569 (61 minutes: DDD) Ⓕ
Recorded 1995 **ooo**

The Mosaïques, at a rather slower tempo than usual, find in the theme-and-variation finale of the G major Quartet, No 5, an unsuspected reflective tenderness. The theme itself is played with a characteristic touch of flexibility and a gentle lift to the dotted rhythms; in the first variation Erich Höbarth shapes his decorative semiquavers *fioriture* with apparently spontaneous fantasy; the luminous, high-lying textures of the second are exquisitely realised; and even the *Presto* send-off has a delicacy and whimsy in keeping with what has gone before. The Mosaïques' readings of the slow movements in the so-called *Joke* (No 2) and *Bird* (No 3) Quartets are again outstanding in their grave tenderness, their sensitivity to harmonic flux and the improvisatory freedom Erich Höbarth brings to his ornamental figuration. The *Bird*, in particular, receives as searching a performance as ever heard: in the first movement the players steal in almost imperceptibly, respond vividly to the music's richness and wit, and bring a spectral *pianissimo* to the mysterious lull in the development. The Slavonic finale, one of several movements to benefit from the lighter, more flexible period bows, goes with terrific fire and panache. In the opening *Allegro* of the *Joke* they take to heart Haydn's *moderato e cantabile* qualification, phrasing fluidly and expansively, with a vital and delicate interplay between the voices. The finale, like that of No 5, is unusually graceful, with the notorious ending deliciously managed. In sum, this truthfully recorded disc has playing that marries uncommon style, technical finesse (tuning, blend and balance suffering little by comparison with the finest modern-instrument quartets) and re-creative flair.

String Quartet, Op 42

Haydn String Quartet, Op 42
Schumann String Quartet No 3 in A, Op 41 No 3
Shostakovich String Quartet No 3 in F, Op 73
Allegri Quartet (Peter Carter, David Roth *vns* Jonathan Barritt *va* Bruno Schrecker *vc*)
Naim Audio NAIMCD016 (73 minutes: DDD) Ⓕ
Recorded 1996

The beauty of these readings is that they mean what they say. There is no hint of any over-earnestness and the programme has been very carefully chosen. Haydn's exquisite Op 42 is given an especially winning rendition, the *Andante ed innocentemente* first movement donning a degree of understatement that reflects its equivocal personality. Following Haydn's Op 42 with Shostakovich's Op 73 was an inspired idea: the former ends quietly and the latter opens with a sort of distracted innocence, marking time before the real drama starts. The argument suddenly intensifies, playfully, provocatively, though characterization is cleverly differentiated. In the second movement, Prokofiev is an obvious point of reference and there has rarely been a more delicately pointed account of the weird, tiptoe *staccato* passage that emerges out of the first idea. The third movement is a striking precursor of the 10th Symphony's violent 'Stalin' *Scherzo*, the slow movement redolent of the 12th Symphony's noble opening and the long finale ending in a mood of veiled mystery. Above all, this is profoundly natural playing and the recordings maintain a realistic 'small concert-hall' ambience throughout. The disc ends with an affectionate, flexible performance of Schumann's loveliest string quartet. The opening *Andante espressivo* sets the mood while the ensuing second set (1'19") is limpid and rapturous, and the finale – which in some hands can seem repetitive – is given precisely the right degree of rhythmic emphasis. Again one senses wholehearted identification between the repertoire and its interpreters – and while one may question the wisdom of mixed-repertory CD programmes, this one is so well planned and well played, that it can be recommended even to those who already own recordings within cycles.

String Quartets, Op 54

String Quartets, Op 54 Nos 1-3
The Lindsays (Peter Cropper, Ronald Birks *vns* Robin Ireland *va* Bernard Gregor-Smith *vc*) Ⓕ
ASV CDDCA582 (66 minutes: DDD) ●●

All three quartets are in the usual four-movement form but they contain many surprises: in No 1, the false recapitulation in the first movement, the dark modulations in the following sonata-form *Allegretto* and the Hungarian gipsy flavour (anticipated in the Minuet) and mischievousness of the final rondo. No 2 has a rhapsodic fiddler in its second movement, a nostalgic minuet with an extraordinarily anguished trio, and an *Adagio* finale in which a *Presto* section turns out to be no more than an episode.

A notable feature of No 3 is its ternary-form *Largo cantabile*, the centre of which is more like a mini-concerto for the first violin; 'Scotch snaps' pervade the Minuet, and pedal points the finale. The performances (and the recording) are superb, marked by unanimity, fine tone, suppleness of phrasing, and acute dynamic shaping; in the second movement of No 1 there are hushed passages whose homogeneity and quality of sound are both quite remarkable. Overall, this recording is irresistible.

String Quartets, Op 55

String Quartets, Op 55 Nos 1-3
The Lindsays (Peter Cropper, Ronald Birks *vns* Robin Ireland *va* Bernard Gregor-Smith *vc*)
ASV CDDCA906 (64 minutes: DDD) Ⓕ
Recorded 1994 ●

Most immediately striking of the trilogy is the F minor work, No 2, with its searching double variations on related minor and major themes (a favourite form in Haydn's later music), spiky, rebarbative second movement *Allegro* and strangely spare contrapuntal Minuet. The A major, No 1, has much of this key's traditional brilliance, with ample scope for the leader's creative virtuosity in the outer movements and the stratospheric trio of the minuet; in contrast the noble, wonderfully scored *Adagio cantabile* prefigures the profound slow movements of Haydn's final years. The more inward-looking No 3 in B flat is specially remarkable for the varied recapitulations in the flanking movements, astonishingly free and inventive even for Haydn, and the subtle chromatic colouring in all four movements which may just owe something to the quartets Mozart had dedicated to Haydn three years earlier.

Here and there The Lindsays' intonation is less than true, especially from the leader, but as so often with this group, this is a small price to pay for performances of such colour and penetration. The balance, as with many recent quartet recordings, is a shade closer than ideal but the overall sound picture is very acceptable.

String Quartets, Op 64

String Quartets, Op 64 Nos 1-3
Kodály Quartet (Attila Falvay, Tamás Szabo *vns* Gábor Fias *va* János Devich *vc*)
Naxos 8 550673 (64 minutes: DDD) Ⓢ
Recorded 1992

String Quartets, Op 64 Nos 4-6
Kodály Quartet (Attila Falvay, Tamás Szabo *vns* Gábor Fias *va* János Devich *vc*)
Naxos 8 550674 (65 minutes: DDD) Ⓢ
Recorded 1992

The so-called *Lark* (No 5), with its soaring opening melody and *moto perpetuo* finale, is perhaps the most immediately fetching of all Haydn's quartets. But No 6 is at least as fine, with its intimate and intensely argued opening movement, its poignant, exquisitely textured *Andante* and a finale full of instrumental fooling and insouciant contrapuntal virtuosity. Of the other works, No 2 is one of Haydn's most astringent pieces, from its tonally deceptive opening to the mordant, unsettling humour of the finale. Quartets Nos 3 and 4 return to a more familiar vein of sociable wit. Both are endlessly subtle and surprising in their arguments, with *cantabile* slow movements of peculiar candour and eloquence. Quartet No 1, the least favoured of the six is certainly the plainest in its thematic ideas. But it is an absorbing, immensely sophisticated piece, exploring an astonishing range of textures; the recapitulation of the leisurely first movement opens up marvellous new harmonic vistas, while the central development of the finale is a canonic *tour de force*. The Kodály Quartet has rightly won plaudits for its wonderfully civilized playing; mellow and lyrical, far removed from the highly-strung brilliance cultivated by many modern quartets. Ensemble and intonation are first-class, tempos generally spacious, with broad, natural and beautifully matched phrasing. It is at its very finest where Haydn is at his most searching; and the Quartets Nos 2, 5 and 6 each receive outstanding, deeply considered performances. In one or two movements the Kodály's penchant for slowish tempos leads to a slight dourness. Against that, it brings a deliciously lazy *Ländler* lilt, enhanced by the first violin's *portamentos*, to the Trio of No 6, and a grave, inward intensity to each of Haydn's slow movements. The recording, made in a Budapest church, is resonant and less intimate than is ideal in this music.

String Quartets, Op 64

String Quartets, Op 64 Nos 1-3 **P**
Salomon Quartet (Simon Standage, Micaela Comberti *vns* Trevor Jones *va* Jennifer Ward Clarke *vc*)
Hyperion CDA67011 (69 minutes: DDD) Ⓕ
Recorded 1995 ●

String Quartets, Op 64 Nos 4-6 **P**
Salomon Quartet (Simon Standage, Micaela Comberti *vns* Trevor Jones *va* Jennifer Ward Clarke *vc*)
Hyperion CDA67012 (60 minutes: DDD) Ⓕ
Recorded 1995 ●

These are predictably stylish, clean-limbed readings of the quartets Haydn composed in his final months at Eszterházy, just before his first visit to London. As Peter Holman points out in his informative note, the Op 64 works are generally less demonstrative, less 'public' in tone than the quartets that precede and follow them. The Salomon brings to them an aptly relaxed, intimate manner, with the familiar hallmarks of lucid textures, vital phrasing and a natural feeling for the music's conversational interplay. Tempos in the outer movements tend to be quite spacious, allowing the Salomon ample room for manoeuvre. They are particularly enjoyable in No 5, where Simon Standage shows an inventive variety of inflexion in the first movement's *Lark* theme – there's a beautiful sense of lyrical repose, for instance, when the theme appears for the only time in a full *legato* texture near the start of the development; and the unhurried tempo in the finale allows for much more meaningful phrasing than in the slick, virtuoso performances one often hears – again, the players' light, airy articulation is a delight here. The Salomon's observant, sympathetic readings, beautifully recorded, make a highly persuasive case for all these works.

String Quartets, Op 71 Nos 1-3
Kodály Quartet (Attila Falvay, Tamás Szabo *vns* Gábor Fias *va* János Devich *vc*) Ⓢ
Naxos 8 550394 (62 minutes: DDD). Recorded 1989

String Quartets, Op 74 Nos 1-3
Kodály Quartet (Attila Falvay, Tamás Szabo *vns* Gábor Fias *va* János Devich *vc*) Ⓢ
Naxos 8 550396 (63 minutes: DDD). Recorded 1989

The Kodály Quartet plays with self-evident joy and an easy neatness of ensemble. There is never a hint of routine and the intercommunication is matched by enormous care for detail. Just sample the elegant *Andante* with variations which form the slow movement of Op 71 No 3, or the witty Minuet which follows, or any of the consistently inspired Op 74 set. The hushed intensity of playing in the *Largo assai* of Op 74 No 3 is unforgettable. The recordings are wholly natural and balanced within a well-judged acoustic; the sound is of the highest quality and documentation is excellent. At their modest price this pair of CDs is irresistible.

String Quartets, Op 76

String Quartets, Op 76 Nos 1-6 **H**
Tátrai Quartet (Vilmos Tátrai, Mihály Szücs *vns* György Konrád *va* Ede Banda *vc*)
Hungaroton ② HCD12812/3-2 (128 minutes: ADD) Ⓕ
Recorded 1964-65

Your reaction to this receiving our top recommendation may be, for heaven's sake, why not a modern recording in stereo? Play them and you will know the answer. The performances are breathtaking – for each player's sensitivity and brilliance, their intimately interwoven ensemble and, most of all, their revelatory characterization. Even the recording is remarkable for its age. When writing these six works in his mid-sixties Haydn was at the peak of his powers. You will be bowled over as much by their unpredictable ingenuity as by their startling range and variety of experience – extending from Croatian merrymaking on the village green to visionary regions scarcely explored more searchingly by Beethoven. The Tátrai's musical response is very immediate. This finds outlet in readiness to risk fast tempos for livelier movements (always with a touch of virtuoso brilliance when needed) as well as great intensity in slow movements – not least as exemplified in the unforgettable revelations of the last three. Pungency of accentuation and clarity of articulation also contribute to its youthful vividness, as does, even more, its wide range of dynamics and colour – so arrestingly demonstrated in the dramatic opening movement of No 2. Though the sound quality may not compare with the best on offer today, its clarity is admirable: microphones seem less close than on many modern recordings, permitting everything to emerge in better perspective. But it's Haydn's genius that overwhelms you, and just as Haydn's own imagination seems progressively to take wing in the course of the six works, so does the players' own commitment.

String Quartets, Op 76 Nos 1-3
The Lindsays (Peter Cropper, Ronald Birks *vns* Robin Ireland *va* Bernard Gregor-Smith *vc*)
ASV CDDCA1076 (75 minutes: DDD) Ⓕ
Recorded 1998-99 ●

These are among the finest Haydn quartet recordings heard in years, performances which will quickly establish themselves as classics of the genre. They are consistently a degree more refined in texture and control of dynamic than the Lindsays' earlier live recordings, and the ensemble is more polished. Yet the feeling of spontaneity is just as intense as before, with Haydn's witty moments being pointed even more infectiously, as in the finale of Op 76 No 2 where in the main theme the little upward *portamentos* at the end of the eighth bar are delectably timed on each occurrence. The studio sound is fuller, too, and far better balanced, so that one can register far more clearly than before the first violin's rapid triplets in the finale of the *Emperor*; it is ideally crisp articulation. Matching the new performances of the *Fifths* and the *Emperor*, The Lindsays' account of Op 76 No 1 is just as strongly characterised. The sense of fun in the opening *Allegro con spirito* is deliciously brought out, leading on to an account of the sublime *Adagio*, both dedicated and refined, which conveys a Beethovenian depth of expression, making most rivals sound superficial.

String Quartets, Op 76 – Nos 4-6
Lindsay Quartet (Peter Cropper, Ronald Birks *vns* Robin Ireland *va* Bernard Gregor-Smith *vc*)
ASV CDDCA1077 (78 minutes: DDD) Ⓕ
Recorded 1999 ●●

Here, in the last three Op 76 quartets, you have Haydn interpretations that bring forth the full range of expression in these inspired works of his official retirement. They are not just polished and refined but communicate with an intensity that simulates live performance. No 5 in D was one of the works which The Lindsays recorded earlier live at the Wigmore Hall, but the extra subtlety this time means that rhythms are a degree more liltingly seductive, in which humour is more delightfully pointed, as in the repeated cadence-figure at the start of the finale, with comic pauses beautifully timed.

The quiet opening of No 4, which gave rise to the nickname *Sunrise*, gently insinuates itself before the full thrust of the *Allegro* takes over; with its heightened contrasts, it could not be more captivating. Most strikingly, too, the slow movements in each of these three quartets are given a visionary intensity, matching The Lindsays' treatment of the slow movement of No 1 in the companion disc.

Here is music from the last years of Haydn's career – written soon after his return to Vienna from his second brilliantly successful visit to London – which in these performances has you thinking forward to middle or late Beethoven and the new world of the 19th century. So the *Adagio* of No 4 brings a hymn-like dedication, not least in the dark E flat minor episode, and the astonishing modulations in the *Fantasia* slow movement of No 6 convey the tingle of new discovery, with magical *pianissimos* for contrast. This was a work which for Donald Tovey marked a tailing-off of inspiration, but one registers the opposite with The Lindsays, when the *adagio* Fantasia gives way to such witty treatment both in the *presto* Minuet (in fact a *scherzo*), with its weird leaps, and the *Allegro spirituoso* finale.

With refined sound that draws out the subtleties of balance between these players, here is another disc of Haydn from The Lindsays that sets the highest standards.

String Quartets, Op 76 Nos 2-4
Alban Berg Quartet (Günter Pichler, Gerhard Schulz *vns* Thomas Kakuska *va* Valentin Erben *vc*)
EMI CDC5 56166-2 (66 minutes: DDD) Ⓕ
Recorded 1993-94

This disc is uncommonly fine, above all the performance of the D minor, No 2. The Berg takes both outer movements more spaciously than most of its rivals. The opening *Allegro* is tough and austere, the players thinking and phrasing in long spans, bringing an urgent sweep to the development and a true sense of climax to the coda. And with its broader tempo the Berg realises details like the repeated hairpin *crescendos* on the sequence of tied notes in the second group. In the Berg's hands the Hungarian-tinged finale has great trenchancy and symphonic weight, with an imaginative variety of colour and accent.

The *Emperor* and the *Sunrise* are hardly less fine, marrying impressive formal control with a vivid sense of character and felicity of detail: listen, for instance, to the subtle timing and hushed, veiled tone at the sudden dip to E flat in the first movement of No 3; the rapt tenderness and breadth of phrase in the sublime *Adagio* of the *Sunrise*, the melody unfolding in a single unbroken span; or the deft management of the progressive speed increases in the finale of the same work. The leader's very fluid, ruminative phrasing in the Quartet's opening makes it seem even more than usual like a slow introduction, with the first phrase stealing in magically from nowhere. At its best, especially in No 2, the Berg brings rare imaginative insight to this inexhaustible music. The recording is both clear and sympathetic.

String Quartets, Op 77

String Quartets – Op 77 Nos 1 and 2; Op 103 in D minor (unfinished) **P**
Quatuor Mosaïques (Erich Höbarth, Andrea Bischof *vns* Anita Mitterer *va* Christophe Coin *vc*) Ⓕ
Auvidis Astrée E8800 (62 minutes: DDD)

Anyone who thinks that period-instrument performance means austerity and coolness should listen to this disc. Here is playing full of expressive warmth and vigour. The opening of Op 77 No 1 is done duly gracefully, but with a sturdy underlying rhythm and the *Scherzo* is crisp and alive. Then the first movement of the F major work is beautifully done, with many sensitive details; and the lovely second movement is ideally leisurely, so that the players have ample room for manoeuvre and the leader makes much of his opportunities for delicate playing in the filigree-like high music. The players show a real grasp of structure and illuminate the key moments with a touch more deliberation or a little additional weight of tone. These performances, clearly recorded, are competitive not merely within the protected world of 'early music' but in the bigger, 'real' world too!

Seven Last Words, Op 51

The Lindsays (Peter Cropper, Ronald Birks *vns* Robin Ireland *va* Bernard Gregor-Smith *vc*)
ASV CDDCA853 (71 minutes: DDD) Ⓕ
Recorded 1992 **OO**

This performance by the Lindsays is magical. There are few groups who could sustain these seven slow movements, each lasting about 10 minutes, and yet give them such variety of intensity, colour and mood. Haydn revealed himself as a visionary composer in the way he set about creating these seven miniature tone-poems for string quartet. The work is divided into nine sections comprising seven slow movements each describing one of the final utterances of Christ on the Cross together with a slow introduction and a final *Presto con tutta la forza* which depicts the earthquake which occurred when 'the veil of the temple was rent in twain'. Some may not find it a disc to be listened to from beginning to end; they may need substantial breaks between one movement and the next.

Seven Last Words, Op 51[a] (interspersed with Seven Gregorian Responsories for Holy Week[b])
[a]**Carmina Quartet** (Matthias Enderle, Susanne Frank *vns* Wendy Champney *va* Stephan Goerner *vc*)
[b]**Schola Romana Lucernensis / Father Roman Bannwart**
Claves 50-2002 (74 minutes: DDD). Text and translation included. Recorded 1999-2000 Ⓕ

Haydn's *Seven Last Words* was designed for performance in Holy Week, in the Santa Cueva grotto in Cádiz, with discourses from the bishop on each of the seven utterances followed by Haydn's musical meditation. Originally these were orchestral pieces, not the string quartet versions (arranged by Haydn to widen access to the music) which are more often given today. Haydn was concerned that 'seven *Adagios*' would be exhausting to the listener, and would probably not have favoured performance of them without a break. The idea of interspersing them with Holy Week Gregorian responsories is certainly an appropriate solution.

The group singing them here is a mixed choir, although we hear either the men or the women, never the two together. They sing in a carefully moulded style, cadences softly rounded off; ensemble is precise, from the women especially. The Carmina Quartet plays with a remarkably wide range of expression. The Introduction is quite fiercely done, and the 'Terremoto' at the end has a violence and is taken at a pace that almost obscures the pulse of the music.

In between, they play the 'seven *Adagios*' (as Haydn called them – actually three *Largos*, two *Graves*, a *Lento* and an *Adagio*) as they would any other Haydn slow movement. The first is quite relaxed and lyrical, although its accents are well marked, and it has touches of added ornamentation. Refinement and delicacy of line characterise the second, and the third, the E major meditation on 'Mother, behold thy son', is done with much tenderness.

In the fourth their realisation of Haydn's notated ornaments – the appoggiaturas in bars 2 and 4, and at several points later – are oddly perverse and disturbing: one played short, the other long, although the second phrase is a clear echo of the first. No 5 ('I thirst') again draws some very telling soft playing from the quartet, but also pained *forzato* accents, and there is forceful expression of 'Consummatum est', along with moments of tenderness (for example, the G major modulation near the end). They play the E flat No 7 with the sense of calm and fulfilment that Haydn surely sought. Their tempos, generally, are well chosen, perhaps faster at times than many quartets take these pieces, but this helps bridge the gulf between Haydn's normal mode of expression and the special significance of this remarkable music.

Piano Trios, Hob XV

Hob XV – No 1 in G minor; **No 2** in F; **No 5** in G; **No 6** in F; **No 7** in D; **No 8** in B flat; **No 9** in A; **No 10** in E flat; **No 11** in F minor; **No 12** in E minor; **No 13** in C minor; **No 14** in A flat; **No 15** in G; **No 16** in D; **No 17** in F; **No 18** in A; **No 19** in G minor; **No 20** in B flat; **No 21** in C; **No 22** in E flat; **No 23** in D minor; **No 24** in D; **No 25** in G, 'Gipsy Trio'; **No 26** in F sharp minor; **No 27** in C; **No 28** in E; **No 29** in E flat; **No 30** in E flat; **No 31** in E flat minor; **No 32** in G; **No 34** in E; **No 35** in A; **No 36** in E flat; **No 37** in F; **No 38** in B flat; **No 39** in F; **No 40** in F; **No 41** in G; **No C1** in C; **No f1** in E flat

Piano Trios: HobXIV – No 6 in G; No C1 in C; HobXV – Nos 1-2, 5-32, 34-41, C1 and f1. Hob XVI – No 6 in G. Hob*deest* – D
Beaux Arts Trio (Isidore Cohen *vn* Bernard Greenhouse *vc* Menahem Pressler *pf*)
Philips ⑨ 454 098-2PB9 Ⓑ
(394 minutes: ADD)
Recorded 1970-79 ●●●

Haydn's trios are essentially accompanied keyboard sonatas, with the cello wedded to the keyboard bass almost throughout; this lack of cello independence has deterred many groups from investigating their musical riches. Not, fortunately, the Beaux Arts, whose acclaimed complete cycle accumulated by stealth during the 1970s and has now reappeared on nine mid-price discs. A dozen of the works date from the 1760s, or even earlier, and offer little more than rococo charm, though the G minor (No 1 in Hoboken's catalogue), with its neo-baroque severity, is a notable exception. But the majority of the trios date from the 1780s and 1790s and contain some of Haydn's most imaginative, lyrical and harmonically adventurous music.

Two outstanding works from the 1780s are the E minor, No 12, with its passionate, closely worked opening *Allegro*, and No 14 in A flat, with its exquisitely tender *Adagio* in a remote E major that leads without a break into one of Haydn's most hilariously quixotic finales. The 14 magnificent trios of the 1790s range from relaxed, intimate pieces like the E flat, No 29, through the sombre, almost tragic F sharp minor, No 26, to the C major, No 27, unsurpassed in the whole series for its intellectual and virtuoso brilliance. Finest of all, perhaps, are the E major, No 28, with its radiant outer movements and its astonishing central E minor *passacaglia*; and the E flat, No 30, with its noble, lyrically expansive first movement, its deep-toned, often richly chromatic *Andante* and its glorious German-dance finale.

The Beaux Arts' playing throughout is vital, refined, and sharply responsive to the music's teeming richness and variety. The early trios were conceived for harpsichord, though such is the deftness and delicacy of Menahem Pressler's touch here that there is no question of the music being overpowered by the modern Steinway. In the later trios the players catch beautifully the leisurely, almost improvisatory feel of many of the opening movements, and bring a ruminative intensity, and a wonderful quality of soft playing to the great slow movements, while the finales have immense brio, wit and virtuosity, with ideally clean, crisp articulation from Pressler.

Occasionally in the earlier works the Beaux Arts sounds a touch oversophisticated for this guileless music – the opening violin solo in No 2 is a case in point. And there are a few disappointments in the later trios – the first movement of the great F sharp minor, No 26, sounds too lightweight, even skittish while, conversely, in the *passacaglia* of No 28 they take a ponderous view of Haydn's *Allegretto*. But there's a feast of superlative, little-known music here, most of the playing is remarkably felicitous, and the recording has Philips's customary warmth and refinement. £60 or so may seem a lot to fork out all at once, but no one is likely to regret the investment – this set will last a lifetime.

Piano Trios: HobXV – Nos 18, 24, 25 and 29
Vienna Piano Trio (Wolfgang Redik *vn* Marcus Trefny *vc* Stefan Mendl *pf*)
Nimbus NI5535 (60 minutes: DDD) Ⓕ
Recorded 1997 ●

The *Gipsy* Trio, No 25, may have been written in and for London, but this ensemble's short, snappy bowing, stomping piano accents and instinctive fluctuations of tempo and pulse in the finale, locate the work in the grape-treading, Romany heart of the Burgenland. The steps of the dance shape and pervade the E flat Trio, too, in the jaunty rhythms of the opening *Allegretto*, and the boisterous and cross-accented Allemande of its finale. Among countless delights in these bold performances is the sensitivity to the power of silence, and the short, hushed half-tones within the long-breathed lines of the *Andante* of the A major Trio. And, not least, the perceptive understanding and judgement of the shifting qualities of an *Allegro* which so well supports the structure of the outer movements of the D major, as well as enabling many a clearly articulated yet fanciful variation in the *Gipsy* Trio. These recordings are close, sometimes breathy, always thrillingly true.

Piano Trios: HobXV – Nos 27-30 **P**
Vera Beths *vn* **Anner Bylsma** *vc* **Robert Levin** *fp*
Sony Classical Vivarte SK53120 (74 minutes: DDD) Ⓕ
Recorded 1992 ●●

These are truly magnificent pieces, full startling originality, and conceived on a grand scale – not simply long but composed with a remarkable spaciousness to their ideas and working-out. These performances do them ample justice, with their very brilliant and stylish pianism and a beautifully held instrumental balance: clearly Bylsma doesn't see Haydn's cello parts as routine stuff. Robert Levin, using a McNulty copy of a 1780 piano by J A Stein, produces playing of great vitality and delightful crispness, and puts across powerfully the intellectual force and the argumentative character of the music. This is outstandingly keen and vital musicianship, excellently recorded.

Piano Sonatas

Piano Sonatas: HobXVI – Nos 1-20, 28-62. HobIX – No 8, Seven Menuets from 'Kleine Tänze für die Jugend'. HobXVII – No 1, Capriccio in G; No 2, 20 Variations in A; No 3, 12 Variations in E flat; No 4, Fantasia in C; No 5, Six Variations in C; No 6, Variations in F minor; No 7, Five Variations in D; No 9, Adagio in F. Seven Last Words
John McCabe *pf*
Decca London ⑫ 443 785-2LC12 Ⓑ
(873 minutes: ADD). Recorded 1974-77 ●●●

McCabe's recordings of Haydn's piano sonatas represent one of the great recorded monuments of the keyboard repertoire. Sample any of the discs in this budget-price set and you will immediately become aware of the immense treasures on offer. The special qualities McCabe brings to his performances benefit from a composer's awareness of musical content, pursuing the structural argument with acute perceptions. Thus, assisted by the rich resonance and tonal subtlety of the modern piano, McCabe provides a consistently stylish view of Haydn's developing musical persona that comprehensively exploits this repertoire's inherent expressive potential. Spare textures and astonishing formal concentration in the earliest works establish a perfect balance between structure and content, and McCabe's crisp, poised playing enables the music to make its own potently expressive impact. The middle-period sonatas demonstrate Haydn's further experimentation and consolidation of style and technique. Harpsichord textures, reminiscent of Scarlatti, are still apparent in works such as the A flat Sonata (No 31), but so, too, are new influences. For instance, McCabe luxuriates in the *Sturm und Drang* characteristics of the G minor Sonata (No 32), penetrating to the core of the musical fabric to release the full power of the score's passion.

Haydn's piano sonatas reach a supreme level of refinement in the late works, and McCabe responds with suitably spacious playing, sensitive to the music's richer 'orchestral' colours. He brings a connoisseur's touch to the impressionistic harmonic effects in the first movement of the C major Sonata (No 60); his sinuous phrasing underlines the Schubertian flavour of the opening *Andante* to the D major Sonata (No 61); he charmingly points the Beethovenian syncopation in the same work's *Scherzo* and ultimately achieves the perfect balance between content and design in the magisterial E flat Sonata (No 62). McCabe's consummate poise between foreground motivic activity and structural background is equally remarkable in the separate keyboard pieces, which certainly add to the appeal of this set.

His outstanding performances of both *Seven Last Words* and the ingeniously constructed F minor Variations are obvious highlights; but try, also, the enchanting *Adagio*, and the charming selection of dances, which provide further evidence of Haydn's mastery of miniature forms. The vividly clear 1970s recordings have retained all the clarity for which they are justly renowned and McCabe's performances set the standards against which others will be judged.

Awards 1987

Piano Sonatas: HobXVI – No 20 in C minor; No 49 in E flat; No 34 in E minor; No 32 in B minor; No 42 in D; No 48 in C; No 51 in D; No 50 in C; No 52 in E flat; No 40 in G; No 37 in D. No 4, Fantasia in C. No 6, Variations in F minor. No 9, Adagio in F

Alfred Brendel *pf*

Philips ④ 416 643-2PH4 (205 minutes: ADD/DDD) Ⓕ

Booklet included. ●●●

The sonatas collected in this set are some magnificent creations, wonderfully well played by Alfred Brendel. Within the order and scale of these works Haydn explores a rich diversity of musical languages, a wit and broadness of expression that quickly repays attentive listening. It is the capriciousness as much as the poetry that Brendel so perfectly attends to; his playing, ever alive to the vitality and subtleties, makes these discs a delight. The sophistication innate in the simple dance rhythms, the rusticity that emerges, but above all, the sheer *joie de vivre* are gladly embraced. Brendel's continual illumination of the musical ideas through intense study pays huge dividends. The recording quality varies enormously between the different works and though the close acoustic on some of the later discs could be faulted for allowing one to hear too much of the keyboard action, it certainly brings one into vivid contact with the music.

Piano Sonatas: HobXVI – G minor, No 44; C minor, No 20; E minor, No 34; G, No 40; C, No 48; E flat, No 49; C, No 50; D, No 51; E flat, No 52. HobXVII – No 4, Fantasia in C

András Schiff *pf*

Teldec ② 0630-17141-2 (147 minutes: DDD) Ⓕ

Recorded 1997 ●

András Schiff has consistently championed Haydn, not only the sonatas but also the glorious late piano trios. He has, though, long delayed recording any of the sonatas, but this two-disc set, offering the last five sonatas plus four of the finest earlier ones, has been worth the wait. If his way with Haydn tends to be more intimate, less robust and less gleefully subversive than Alfred Brendel's, Schiff is equally acute in his responses to the music's drama, wit and poetry, and in his control of narrative line. His 'centred' tone and limpid, subtly coloured soft playing are a constant delight, as is his variety of articulation and nuance. He plays all the marked repeats, embellishing and dramatizing them as appropriate; and he is alive to Haydn's manipulations of silence, timing pauses and fermatas with an ear for their exact comic or dramatic significance.

As for the great C minor Sonata, Schiff's is one of the most searching readings on record: the outer movements combine refinement of detail with bold dramatic contrasts and a terrific overall sweep. The finale, a notch slower than Brendel's, is also more impassioned and disturbing, rising (especially in the repeat) to a final climax of desperate intensity. Schiff's virtuoso technique – and his understanding of Haydn's silences – pays special dividends in a dazzling performance of the C major *Fantasia*. And he wonderfully realises the richness and sophistication of the final three sonatas. In the first movement of the C major, where Haydn conjures miracles from his initial vision of dry bones, Schiff's playing is as crisp and as vividly orchestrated as Brendel's. Schiff is also more spacious in the E flat sonata, a magnificent, probing reading which realises the music's reach, poetry and harmonic daring as completely as any. The recording captures the beautiful, luminous sonorities of his Bösendorfer, and provides just the right amount of space around the sound.

Piano Sonatas: HobXVI – A, No 26; B minor, No 32; C sharp minor, No 36; D, No 37; E flat, No 49
Leif Ove Andsnes *pf*
EMI CDC5 56756-2 (58 minutes: DDD) Ⓕ
Recorded 1997

This disc offers delectable performances of five shrewdly contrasted works: two troubled, trenchant minor-key sonatas from the 1770s juxtaposed with a pair of lightweight pieces from the same period and culminating in the great E flat Sonata. Andsnes is responsive to the individual character of these sonatas, to their richness and variety of incident, and their sheer unpredictablility. With his wide spectrum of colour and dynamics he makes no apologies for using a modern Steinway. But his playing, founded on a pellucid *cantabile* touch and diamantine passagework, marries classical refinement and clarity with a spontaneous exuberance, a sense that the next phrase is yet to be created. Repeats are never merely repetitions, and Andsnes is always ready to add stylish and witty touches of embellishment. The opening movements of both minor-key sonatas have a lithe, sinewy urgency, above all in the vehement sequences of their developments, together with a rare delicacy of nuance: and here, as elsewhere, you notice how alive and concentrated is his *piano* and *pianissimo* playing. Andsnes brings a bright, buoyant yet lyrical approach to the E flat Sonata's outer movements, to the wonderful *Adagio* a limpid line, a subtly flexed pulse and, in the B flat minor central episode, a true sense of passion. With few provisos this is just the sort of playing – joyous, imaginative, involving – to win Haydn's sonatas a wider following. The recording of the E flat, made in a church in Oslo, has slightly more ambient warmth than that of the remaining sonatas, recorded at EMI's Abbey Road studios. But throughout, the piano sound is natural and present without being too closely miked.

Haydn Piano Sonatas: HobXVI – A, No 30; E flat, No 52 **Schubert** Piano Sonata No 14 in A minor, D784. Marche militaire No 1 in D, D733 (arr Tausig)
Evgeni Kissin *pf*
Sony Classical SK64538 (62 minutes: DDD) Ⓕ
Recorded 1994

Enormously enjoyable! This is Haydn playing of high style and verve – also affectionate, articulate, colourful and expressive – and its vitality seems authentic even when Kissin asks you to admire the means with which he achieves it. This is not wilful or eccentric playing. By the end of the A major work, an engaging and (even by Haydn's standards) unconventional sonata, you feel its stature has been enhanced, which is just as it should be. Kissin meets the greater challenge of Haydn's last Sonata equally well. The breadth as well as the brilliance of the first movement is there, and its warmth; his tempo may be a little brisker than usual but it still allows for weight. The last movement *Presto* really is breakneck, at a speed which would be unwise, not to say unrealistic, for most others; once again, the impression is of allure allied to perfectly judged dramatic tension and articulate speech. Maybe he sustains the phrases of the *Adagio* with less success: they tend to emerge a bar at a time instead of as an arching span. How difficult this is to do when tone on the piano dies so quickly. But it is precisely this kind of growth and building through sentences and long paragraphs – and through silences – that he manages so well in the first movement of the Schubert sonata. Admire here what you will: the unforced, perfectly scaled range of dynamics and attacks; the motivating force of the left hand, so often neglected by those who see interest only in the right; the sensitivity to harmonic movement, again, and to the smallest shifts of colour and weight; the infallible timing and marvellous rhythm in all aspects; the voicing and vitality of the texture from top to bottom. Above all, there is a commanding vision of the whole. The finale is equally fine. The recording balance is not too close; the sound pleasingly open and natural.

Piano Sonatas: HobXVI – C, No 35; C sharp minor, No 36; D, No 37; E flat, No 38; G, No 39
Jenö Jandó *pf*
Naxos 8 553128 (62 minutes: DDD) Ⓢ
Recorded 1993

The exquisite, classical balance evident in these six keyboard sonatas makes them especially rewarding examples of the composer's exploitation of the piano's broad expressive range and rich textural variety. This volume in Jenö Jandó's complete edition presents these pieces in a compelling, modern-instrument version. For example, there is brilliance and sparkle in the opening movements of the D major and E flat Sonatas; warmth and dramatic intensity in the slow movements (most notably in the baroque echoes of the Sonatas in C major and D major), and an appealing blend of wit and elegance in finales such as the third movement of the D major Sonata. Most remarkable, though, is the G major Sonata, where Jandó's precision and sensitive balance of linear and harmonic dimensions convey the work's concerto character and Haydn's imaginative approach to form. Try Jandó's engaging account of the opening *Allegro*, his deft balance of the slow movement's effective blend of major and minor, and his exuberant virtuosity in the finale.

Piano Sonatas: HobXVI – E flat, No 49; C, No 50; D, No 51; E flat, No 52
Jenö Jandó *pf*
Naxos 8 550657 (62 minutes: DDD) Ⓢ
Recorded 1992

The keyboard sonatas which Haydn originally intended for piano, such as the four considered here, show the composer's exploration of the instrument's capacity for greater dynamic variation. Jandó is sensitive to the relationship between motif and dynamics which is particularly evident in the E flat and D major Sonatas respectively. Aided by clear recorded sound, Jandó's warmth in the lyrical passages provides a dramatic contrast to his crisp, positive approach in the livelier music. Jandó's glittering technique has a high profile in the other two sonatas in the programme. His well-turned readings are uncontroversial, but they lack nothing in excitement. Sample the finale of the E flat Sonata, where the wealth of expressive detail at an extremely fast tempo is breathtaking.

Masses

Missa Sancti Bernardi de Offida in B flat, HobXXII/10, **P** 'Heiligmesse'. Mare Clausum, HobXXIVa/9. Insanae et vanae curae. Motetti de Venerabili Sacramento, HobXXIIIc/5*a-d*. Te Deum in C, HobXXIIIc/2
Jörg Hering *ten* **Harry van der Kamp** *bass*
Tölz Boys' Choir; Tafelmusik / Bruno Weil
Sony Classical SK66260 (63 minutes: DDD). Texts Ⓕ and translations included. Recorded 1994

A special attraction for Haydn lovers is the first-ever recording of the unfinished ode *Mare Clausum*, commissioned in 1794 by Haydn's English friend Lord Abingdon, and abandoned when the nobleman was imprisoned for libel. The gauche, crudely chauvinistic verses, trumpeting England's sovereignty of the sea, should make the most hardened Europhobe blush. But the two numbers Haydn completed are worthy of his ripest style: a noble F major bass aria with rich, inventive writing for woodwind, authoritatively sung by Harry van der Kamp, and a D major chorus whose verve and contrapuntal power presage the late Masses and oratorios. Under Bruno Weil's spirited direction both the Tölz Boys' Choir, with their bright-edged, slightly breathy tone, and the period orchestra, Tafelmusik, is on first-rate form here and throughout this enterprisingly planned disc. It includes the thrilling, majestic, late *Te Deum* and the motet *Insanae et vanae curae*, adapted from a 'storm' chorus in the oratorio *Il ritorno di Tobia*.

Weil's reading is eagerly responsive to the music's drama, with taut rhythms, sharp dynamic contrasts and keen instrumental detailing; and he maintains the initial pulse through the tranquil D major section. Between these masterpieces the four little *Motetti de Venerabili* from the 1750s (another recorded first) inevitably sound tame, for all their easy tunefulness and skilful marshalling of rococo cliché. The largest work on the disc is, of course, the so-called *Heiligmesse*, first of the six magnificent Mass settings of Haydn's old age. This receives an energetic, uplifting reading, with brisk tempos, fresh, incisive choral work and strongly etched orchestral colours. In one or two sections Weil can drive too hard and Harry van der Kamp sometimes overwhelms the excellent boy soloists. But there is no doubting the vigour and joyfulness of Weil's reading, nor the skill and commitment of his forces. Quite apart from its pioneering value, this is an inspiring Haydn collection whose appeal is enhanced by vivid sound.

Mass No 1, Missa Sunt bona mixta malis, HobXXII/2 **P** – Kyrie; part of Gloria. Non nobis, Domine, HobXXIIIa/1. Ave regina in A, HobXXIII*b*/3. Responsoria de Venerabilis, HobXXIIIc/4*a-d*. Responsorium ad absolutionem in D minor, HobXXII*b*/1. Salve regina in E, HobXXIII*b*/1. Mass No 7 in B flat, HobXXII/7, Missa brevis Sancti Johannis de Deo ('Little Organ Mass')
Marie-Claude Vallin, Ann Monoyios *sops*
Tölz Boys' Choir; L'Archibudelli (with **Anner Bylsma** *vc* **Anthony Woodrow** *db* **Bob van Asperen** *org*);
Tafelmusik / Bruno Weil
Sony Classical Vivarte SK53368 (60 minutes: DDD)
Texts and translations included. Ⓕ
Recorded 1992-93

This is the first appearance on disc of two recent Haydn discoveries, the brief Offertorium *Non nobis, Domine* and fragments (the *Kyrie* and part of the *Gloria*) of a Mass *Sunt bona mixta malis*. But its real charms lie in two works for solo soprano, choir and orchestra composed to mark the entry into convent life of Therese Keller whom Robbins Landon suggests was Haydn's great love. Be that as it may, what seeps out of every pore is a warmth and sincerity, something akin to profound inner happiness, which makes one wonder just how deep Haydn's love was for the devout Therese Keller.

Marie-Claude Vallin captures the essential innocence of the *Ave regina*; her voice has a naive, almost childlike quality, although in her ethereally soaring high notes and fluent trills there is no doubting her technical command. Ann Monoyios has an altogether fuller, more mature quality as befits the more intense *Salve regina*. Bruno Weil's support for these two delightful singers is as unobtrusive as it is sympathetic. His excellent team of musicians (not forgetting splendid work from the recording team) are allowed to relax in performances which seem almost to float on air, so graceful and effortless does it sound. Add to this a performance of the *Little Organ Mass* (No 7) of rare poise and elegance and you have a disc of real beauty.

Masses – No 1*a* in G, HobXXII/3, 'Missal rorate coeli **P** desuper'; No 13 in B flat, HobXXII/13, 'Schöpfungsmesse' (with alternative setting of the Gloria)
Susan Gritton *sop* **Pamela Helen Stephen** *mez*
Mark Padmore *ten* **Stephen Varcoe** *bar*
Collegium Musicum 90 Chorus; Collegium Musicum 90 / Richard Hickox
Chandos Chaconne CHAN0599 (62 minutes: DDD) Ⓕ
Texts and translations included. Recorded 1995 ●

The *Creation* Mass is no less resplendent or searching than, say, the *Nelson* Mass or the *Harmoniemesse*, a glorious affirmation of Haydn's reverent, optimistic yet by no means naive faith. Even by Haydn's standards, the work is startling in its exploitation of colourful and dramatic key contrasts, as in the sudden swerve from F major to an apocalyptic *fortissimo* D flat at 'Judicare vivos'; the *Benedictus*, characteristically, moves from serene pastoral innocence (shades of 'With verdure clad' from *The Creation*) to urgent intensity in its central development; and the sublime G major *Agnus Dei* has a profound supplicatory fervour extraordinary even among the composer's many memorable settings of this text.

This reading eclipses previous recordings in the quality of its choir and soloists, the subtlety of Hickox's direction and the vividness and transparency of the recorded sound. In faster movements like the *Kyrie* and the openings of the *Gloria* and *Credo* Hickox strikes just the right balance between dignity and happy, pulsing energy, relishing each of Haydn's dramatic *coups*; and he brings a marvellous clarity and verve, and a sure sense of climax, to the chromatically inflected fugues in the *Gloria* and at 'Dona nobis pacem'. Abetted by his first-rate orchestra, Hickox is always alive to the felicities of Haydn's scoring, while the 24-strong professional choir is superbly responsive throughout.

We also get the alternative version of the *Gloria*, and the ultra-compressed (6'49") and instantly forgettable *Missa rorate coeli desuper*, which David Wyn Jones, in his excellent note, wryly describes as 'a reminder of how perfunctory church music in 18th-century Austria could be'. It is neatly dispatched by Hickox and his forces, but inevitably comes as an anticlimax.

Masses – No 6 in G, 'Missa Sancti Nicolai', HobXXII/6; No 9 in B flat, 'Missa Sancti Bernardi von Offida' ('Heiligmesse'), HobXXII/10

Lorna Anderson *sop* **Pamela Helen Stephen** *mez* **Mark Padmore** *ten* **Stephen Varcoe** *bar* **Collegium Musicum 90 / Richard Hickox**

Chandos Chaconne CHAN0645 (62 minutes: DDD) Ⓕ Text and translation included.

With fresh, inspiriting work from soloists, chorus and orchestra, the performance of the so-called *Heiligmesse* captures the symphonic impetus and the spiritual and physical exhilaration of this gloriously life-affirming music. Hickox opts for Haydn's original scoring, minus the horn parts and the enhanced parts for clarinets that he (or someone with his approval) later added for a performance in Vienna's Court Chapel.

Hickox is ever responsive to the drama and colour of Haydn's orchestral writing, while the 24-strong chorus sings with firm, well-nourished tone over a wide dynamic range and a real care for the meaning of the text. The many high-lying entries are always true, never strained or overblown, and the sopranos rise unflinchingly to their frequent high B flats. The soloists have less to do here than in Haydn's other late Masses: but, led by the plangent, beseeching soprano of Lorna Anderson, they sing with a chamber-musical grace and intimacy both in the fervently contrapuntal 'Gratias' and in the 'Et incarnatus est', set as a canon on one of those tender, heart-easing melodies that are such a feature of Haydn's late style. The appealing *Missa brevis* is cast in the 'pastoral' key of G major. With prominent parts for high horns, it draws on musical imagery traditionally associated with Advent and the Nativity – most obviously in the swaying 6/4 metre and assuaging parallel thirds of the *Kyrie*, which, unusually in his Masses, Haydn repeats for the 'Dona nobis pacem'. Again, the soloists make their mark both individually and in ensemble, with Anderson floating a beautiful line in the 'Gratias' and Mark Padmore launching the expressive G minor 'Et incarnatus est' with gently rounded tone and graceful phrasing. The recorded sound is clear, spacious and carefully balanced, combining vivid orchestral detail with plenty of impact from the chorus.

Masses – No 7 in B flat, HobXXII/7, Missa brevis Sancti Johannis de Deo ('Little Organ Mass'); No 12 in B flat, HobXXII/12, 'Theresienmesse' **P**

Janice Watson *sop* **Pamela Helen Stephen** *mez* **Mark Padmore** *ten* **Stephen Varcoe** *bar* **Collegium Musicum 90 Chorus; Collegium Musicum 90 / Richard Hickox**

Chandos CHAN0592 (60 minutes: DDD) Texts and translations included. Recorded 1995 Ⓕ ⭘

Hickox generates the physical and spiritual elation essential to this music, calling to mind Haydn's own much-quoted remark that whenever he praised God his heart leapt with joy. In the glorious *Theresienmesse* of 1799 Hickox's manner is particularly fine in the exultant, springing *Gloria* and the rough-hewn vigour of the *Credo*. He understands, too, the Mass's dramatic and symphonic impetus, bringing a powerful cumulative momentum to the sonata-form 'Dona nobis pacem' and thrillingly tightening the screws in the closing pages. The choir is placed forward, though never at the expense of orchestral detail, keenly observed by Hickox. His uncommonly well-integrated solo quartet framed by the sweet-toned Janice Watson and the gentle, mellifluous Stephen Varcoe, sings with a chamber-musical grace and refinement in the 'Et incarnatus est' and the *Benedictus*. And their supplicatory tenderness in the 'Dona nobis pacem' contrasts arrestingly with the choir's urgent demands for peace. Hickox also captures the peculiar serenity and innocence of the much earlier *Missa brevis Sancti Johannis de Deo*, or *Little Organ Mass*, its intimacy enhanced here by the use of solo strings. A disc guaranteed to refresh the spirit.

Mass No 10 in C, HobXXII/9, 'Missa in tempore belli'. Te Deum in C, HobXXIIIc/1. Te Deum in C, HobXXIIIc/2. Alfred, König der Angelsachsen, HobXXX/5 – Aria des Schutzgeistes; Chor der Dänen

Nancy Argenta *sop* **Catherine Denley** *mez* **Mark Padmore** *ten* **Stephen Varcoe** *bar* **Jacqueline Fox** *spkr* **Collegium Musicum 90 Chorus and Orchestra / Richard Hickox**

Chandos Chaconne CHAN0633 (64 minutes: DDD) Texts and translations included. Recorded 1997 Ⓕ ⭘

Few other conductors on disc convey so happily the mingled drama, symphonic power and spiritual exhilaration of these glorious works than Richard Hickox. He is fully alive to the ominous unease that permeates the great *Mass in Time of War*, but while others strive for maximum dramatic and rhetorical effect, Hickox directs the Mass with a natural, unforced sense of phrase and pace. His tempos in the *Kyrie* and the opening of the *Gloria* are animated, yet never at the expense of dignity; and at the end of the *Credo* the prospect of the life to come rouses Hickox and his forces to a blaze of dancing jubilation.

The playing of Collegium Musicum 90, led by Simon Standage, is polished and athletic, with detail sharply etched, while the chorus sings with fresh tone and incisive attack. The four soloists are well matched in the anxious C minor *Benedictus*; elsewhere Nancy Argenta brings a pure, slender tone, and a graceful sense of phrase to the *Kyrie*, while in the 'Qui tollis' Stephen Varcoe deploys his mellow baritone with real sensitivity, abetted by the eloquent solo cello of Richard Tunnicliffe. The fill-ups, all but one sharing the Mass's C major, trumpet-and-drum sonorities, are imaginatively chosen. The two *Te Deum* settings epitomise the immense distance Haydn travelled during his career, the rococo exuberance and strict species counterpoint of the little-known early work contrasting with the grandeur, sweep and massive, rough-hewn energy of the 1799 setting.

The two numbers of incidental music Haydn completed for the play *King Alfred* in 1796, shortly before embarking on the Mass, are a real collectors' item. Argenta sings the first hymn-like E flat aria with chaste elegance, while choir and orchestra palpably enjoy themselves in the following number, a rollicking, brassy celebration of the Danes' victory over the Anglo-Saxons. In sum, a winner of a disc: enterprising planning, invigorating performances and first-class recorded sound, with an ideally judged balance between chorus and orchestra.

Mass No 11 in D minor, HobXXII/11, 'Nelson'. Te Deum in C, HobXXIIIc/2 Ⓟ

Dame Felicity Lott *sop* **Carolyn Watkinson** *contr* **Maldwyn Davies** *ten* **David Wilson-Johnson** *bar* **The English Concert and Choir / Trevor Pinnock**

Awards 1998

Archiv Produktion 423 097-2AH (50 minutes: ADD) Ⓕ
Texts and translations included ●●●

The British Admiral had ousted the Napoleonic fleet at the Battle of the Nile just as Haydn was in the middle of writing his *Nelson* Mass. Although the news could not have reached him until after its completion, Haydn's awareness of the international situation was expressed in the work's subtitle, 'Missa in Augustiis', or 'Mass in times of fear'. With its rattle of timpani, pungent trumpet calls, and highly strung harmonic structure, there is no work of Haydn's which cries out so loudly for recording on period instruments; and it is the distinctive sonority and highly charged tempos of this performance which set it apart. The dry, hard timpani and long trumpets bite into the dissonance of the opening *Kyrie*, and the near vibrato-less string playing is mordant and urgent. The fast-slow-fast triptych of the *Gloria* is set out in nervously contrasted speeds, and the *Credo* bounces with affirmation. Just as the choral singing is meticulously balanced with instrumental inflexion, so the soloists have been chosen to highlight the colours in Pinnock's palette.

Mass No 14 in B flat, HobXXII/14,'Harmoniemesse'. Salve regina in E, HobXXIII*b*/1

Nancy Argenta *sop* **Pamela Helen Stephen** *mez* **Mark Padmore** *ten* **Stephen Varcoe** *bar* **Collegium Musicum 90 Chorus; Collegium Musicum 90 / Richard Hickox**

Chandos Chaconne CHAN0612 (59 minutes: DDD) Ⓕ
Texts and translations included. Recorded 1996 ●

Haydn's first major work, the *Salve regina* of 1756, is here juxtaposed with his last, the *Harmoniemesse* of 1802, so-called because of its exceptionally full scoring for woodwind. The gulf between the two works, in sophistication, mastery and emotional range, is predictably vast. Yet, in their very different ways, both reconcile the formal liturgical conventions of their era with the expression of Haydn's own life-affirming religious faith. Hickox and his forces ideally capture this sense of celebratory spiritual energy. Tempos are lively, rhythms alert and vital. In the Mass Hickox generates an exhilarating symphonic momentum in, say, the opening sections of the *Gloria* and *Credo*, and, aided by an outstandingly clear, well-balanced recording, realises to the full such dramatic *coups* as the sudden swerve into A flat in the recapitulation of the 'Benedictus' and the martial fanfares that slew the music from D major to B flat at the start of the 'Dona nobis pacem'. The steely-edged valveless trumpets are thrilling here; and elsewhere the wind players do rich justice to Haydn's glorious, inventive writing, nicely balancing rusticity and refinement.

Nancy Argenta's innocent, bell-like tones and graceful sense of line are heard to touching effect in the 'Et incarnatus est' of the Mass. In the *Salve regina*, she also reveals her deft, fluent coloratura technique. No great depths in this youthful work, of course: but Haydn's setting of the Marian antiphon is elegant and affecting, with a command of shapely, Italianate melody and a feeling for dramatic contrast. This is certainly the most memorable work of Haydn's from the 1750s and aptly complements Hickox's fervent, inspiring reading of the *Harmoniemesse*.

The Seasons, HobXXI/3

Barbara Bonney *sop* **Anthony Rolfe Johnson** *ten* **Andreas Schmidt** *bar* **Monteverdi Choir; English Baroque Soloists / Sir John Eliot Gardiner** Ⓟ

Archiv Produktion ② 431 818-2AH2
(127 minutes: DDD). Text and translation included Ⓕ
Recorded 1990 ●●

The comparative unpopularity of Haydn's *The Seasons* when considered against *The Creation* is understandable perhaps, but it is not all that well deserved. Less exalted its subject and libretto may be, but its depiction of the progress of the year amid the scenes and occupations of the Austrian countryside drew from its composer music of unfailing invention, benign warmth and constant musical-pictoral delights. As usual, John Eliot Gardiner and his forces turn in disciplined, meticulously professional performances, though the orchestra is slightly larger – and consequently a tiny bit less lucid – than the sort you might nowadays find playing a classical symphony. The choir, however, performs with great clarity and accuracy, and brings, too, an enjoyable sense of characterization to their various corporate roles. The soloists all perform with notable poise and intelligence: Barbara Bonney's voice is pure and even, Anthony Rolfe Johnson sounds entirely at ease with the music, and Andreas Schmidt is gentle-voiced but certainly not lacking in substance. Perhaps in the end this is a performance which just lacks that last inch of necessary warmth to make it unbeatable, but it's a first-rate recommendation none the less.

The Creation

Awards 1997

Die Schöpfung (The Creation), HobXXI/2 **P**
Sylvia McNair, Donna Brown *sops*
Michael Schade *ten* **Rodney Gilfry, Gerald Finley** *bars*
Monteverdi Choir; English Baroque Soloists / Sir John Eliot Gardiner
Archiv Produktion ② 449 217-2AH2 Ⓕ
(101 minutes: DDD). Text included
Recorded 1995 **ooo**

With Gardiner's first down-beat it is obvious that Chaos's days are numbered. Not that 'days' (strictly speaking) are in question till the mighty words have been spoken, and then, in this performance, what an instantaneous blaze! No premonitory intimation (of pre-echo in the old days whereas now even the faintest stirring in the ranks of the choir will do it), but a single-handed switching-on of the cosmic power-grid and a magnificently sustained C major chord to flood the universe with light. This is one of the great characteristics here: the superbly confident, precise attack of choir and orchestra. Enthusiasm, then, in plenty; but how about the *mystery* of Creation? It is certainly part of the aim to capture this, for the bass soloist's 'Im Anfange' ('In the beginning') with *pianissimo* chorus has rarely been so softly and so spaciously taken: the Spirit that moved upon the face of the waters is a veiled, flesh-creeping presence, felt again in the first sunrise and the 'softer beams with milder light' of the first moon. Even so, others have incorporated this element more naturally. Gardiner has an excellent Raphael in Gerald Finley, and gains from having extra singers for Adam and Eve, especially as the Eve, Donna Brown, brings a forthright style doubly welcome after the somewhat shrinking-violet manner and breathy tone of Sylvia McNair's Gabriel. On the whole, Gardiner is sound: yet his is a fun *Creation* and a real enrichment of the library. Against others of comparable kind, Gardiner stands firm as an easy first choice: a re-creator of vision, a great invigorator and life-enhancer.

Die Schöpfung (The Creation) **P**
Ann Monoyios *sop* **Jörg Hering** *ten*
Harry van der Kamp *bass* **Tölz Boys' Choir; Tafelmusik / Bruno Weil**
Sony Classical Vivarte ② SX2K57965 Ⓑ
(91 minutes: DDD). Text and translation included
Recorded 1993

Bruno Weil's reading, using a period orchestra of up to 45 players and an all-male choir of similar strength, is above all a luminous, joyous affair, with generally fleet tempos, nimble, dancing rhythms and a richly communicated sense of delight in the work's sublime, pre-lapsarian innocence. Tafelmusik equals and sometimes surpasses rival period orchestras in the point and relish of its playing, and the Tölz Boys' Choir sings with brio, accuracy and characteristically fresh, bright-edged tone; textures in the great contrapuntal choruses are lucidly sifted, yet the climaxes pack a proper punch. Weil's direction mingles a sense of spontaneous discovery with a strong feeling for shape and structure and a sharp ear for Haydn's wonderful orchestral detail. Weil's eager, vital pacing and judgement of tempo relationships almost invariably feel right, though occasionally you long for a deeper sense of mystery and reverence.

The three soloists are all stylish singers, clean of line and tone (vibrato used quite sparingly) and notably flexible in coloratura. They make their mark in recitative and aria, and blend and balance unusually well in ensemble. If Ann Monoyios's soprano lacks the hint of tonal depth ideally required by the central part of 'Nun beut die Flur', her purity, freshness and shapely sense of phrase are delectable. And like her male colleagues, she ornaments tastefully at fermatas and cadences. Jörg Hering is a compact, elegant tenor with no hint of bleat or strain. The best-known of the solo trio, Harry van der Kamp, can become parched at the top of his compass, and occasionally spoils his *legato* through verbal over-emphasis. But he has amply resonant low notes. To sum up, Weil conveys most infectiously the work's unique joy and exhilaration. The recording has a fine depth of perspective and an almost ideal balance between voices and orchestra.

Armida

Jessye Norman *sop* Armida; **Claes Hakon Ahnsjö** *ten* Rinaldo; **Norma Burrowes** *sop* Zelmira; **Samuel Ramey** *bass* Idreno; **Robin Leggate** *ten* Ubaldo; **Anthony Rolfe Johnson** *ten* Clotarco
Lausanne Chamber Orchestra / Antál Dorati
Philips ② 432 438-2PH2 (140 minutes: ADD) Ⓕ
Recorded 1978

Armida, widely considered Haydn's finest opera, is based on a familiar literary classic adopted for opera by numerous other composers: what is surprising is that in his setting Haydn reverted to *opera seria* style, with no *buffo* characters, very few ensembles and extensive *secco* recitatives. Dramatic action is minimal: for three acts Rinaldo lingers under the spell of the enchantress Armida despite all the efforts of fellow-Crusaders to recall him to his mission. The work's static nature, however, casts the emphasis on its musical qualities, and in this regard *Armida* is of the highest standard. The enchantress herself, personified by the redoubtable Jessye Norman, has the widest range of emotions to portray, from tenderness to rage; Ahnsjö as Rinaldo produces a fine *legato* and very accurate florid passagework, but his low register rather lets him down; Ramey shows laudable firmness and flexibility; and Burrowes's fresh youthful charm is very appealing. Another strength is the alert orchestral playing. The most notable features of the opera are three long through-composed sequences and imaginative scoring: the scene in the magic forest, where Rinaldo at last, to Armida's fury, breaks free from her spell, is masterly, and in itself is sufficient to compel a revision of the too common neglect of Haydn as an operatic composer.

L'anima del filosofo

L'anima del filosofo, ossia Orfeo et Euridice **P**
Uwe Heilmann *ten* Orfeo; **Cecilia Bartoli** *mez* Euridice, Genio; **Ildebrando d'Arcangelo** *bass* Creonte; **Andrea Silvestrelli** *bass* Pluto; **Angela Kazimierczuk** *sop* Baccante; **Roberto Scaltriti** *bar* First Chorus; **Jose Fardilha** *bass* Second Chorus; **Colin Campbell** *bar* Third Chorus; **James Oxley** *ten* Fourth Chorus
Chorus and Orchestra of the Academy of Ancient Music / Christopher Hogwood
L'Oiseau-Lyre ② 452 668-2OHO2 Ⓕ
(124 minutes: DDD) Notes, text and translation included. Recorded 1996 ⚫

Christopher Hogwood here builds his band on the model of those prevalent in late 18th-century London theatres. Not only does his phrasing and articulation discover no end of both witty and poignant nuances, but the grave austerity of the string playing, and the plangency of the early woodwind instruments are eloquent advocates of an opera whose uncompromisingly tragic ending (even the seductive Bacchantes perish) owes more to Ovid and Milton than to operatic tradition. Hogwood also remembers that Haydn was writing for a Handelian London choral tradition: his chorus, be they cast as Cupids, Shades or Furies, have robust presence and sculpt their lines with firm muscle. Cecilia Bartoli takes the role of Euridice. In her very first aria, 'Filomena abbandonata', she understands and eagerly re-creates the type of coloratura writing which simultaneously fleshes out the central nightingale simile and incarnates the single word 'crudeltà'. Her unmistakable, melting half voice comes into its own as emotion first clouds reason, only to create the fatal emotional extremes to which she gives voice so thrillingly. Uwe Heilmann is just the tenor of rare agility and wide vocal range vital for this particular Orfeo. The minor parts are strongly profiled: Ildebrando d'Arcangelo is a stern, noble Creonte, Andrea Silvestrelli a fearsome, stentorian Pluto – and there's even a convincing *strepito ostile* off-stage as Euridice's abduction is attempted in Act 2. Beyond the detail, it is the poignancy of the musical drama at the heart of this strange, grave *Orfeo* which Hogwood reveals with such sympathetic and imaginative insight.

L'isola disabitata, HobXXVIII/9

Ying Huang *sop* Silvia; **Susanne Mentzer** *mez* Costanza; **John Aler** *ten* Gernando; **Christopher Schaldenbrand** *bar* Enrico
Padova Chamber Orchestra / David Golub

Arianna a Naxos, HobXXVI*b*/2
Susanne Mentzer *mez* **David Golub** *pf*
Arabesque ② Z6717-2 (121 minutes: DDD). Notes, Ⓕ texts and translations included. Recorded 1997

L'isola disabitata may be the least viable of all Haydn's operas in the theatre, but it contains some memorable, richly worked music, not least the strenuous, impassioned G minor Overture. The heroine, Costanza, a latter-day Ariadne, has two eloquent *Adagio* arias, though their tone is grave and dignified rather than, as their texts suggest, truly tragic. The music for Costanza's husband, Gernando, abducted by pirates 13 years earlier and now returned to the desert island to rescue his wife and her sister, is also slow and soulful, though his one extended aria, 'Non turbar' (Act 2), provides the emotional climax of the opera. Costanza's younger sister Silvia, who has grown up on the island as an ingenuous child of nature, is charmingly portrayed in her opening number; and Gernando's companion Enrico, with whom Silvia inevitably falls in love at first meeting, expresses his devotion to his friend in a sturdy, confident aria with ringing high horns. The opera's most obviously attractive number is the splendid final quartet, with elaborate *concertante* parts for violin, cello, flute and bassoon symbolizing each of the four characters. David Golub secures merely decent playing from the Padova Chamber Orchestra, which admittedly is not helped by the cavernous acoustic, but his soloists are excellent. As Costanza Susanne Mentzer sings with intense, burnished tone and a fine breadth of phrase; Ying Huang sings quite beautifully, with pure, sweet tone, naturally graceful phrasing and a fullness in the lower register. John Aler's personable tenor has plenty of sap as Alva; and the young baritone Christopher Schaldenbrand makes a notable recording début as Enrico, warm and deep of tone and elegant of line.

Arabesque adds the great tragic cantata *Arianna a Naxos*. If other singers have brought to the music more vivid colours and a greater sense of vulnerability and desperation, Susanne Mentzer sings very impressively, with a grandeur that never let you forget that Ariadne was the daughter of Minos

Johann Heinichen German 1683-1729

GROVE *Initially an advocate, German composer and theorist Heinichen composed music for the Weissenfels court, then moved to Leipzig (1709), where he presented operas and directed a collegium musicum. He also worked at Zeitz and Naumburg. In 1710-16 he lived in Italy and had two operas staged in Venice in 1713. From 1717 he was Kapellmeister (with JC Schmidt) at the Dresden court. He wrote serenatas, cantatas, sacred works, and instrumental music for the court, combining German, French and Italian features; his concertos and sonatas are italianate, with unusual instrumental combinations and sonorities. He wrote two versions of a thoroughbass treatise, the second (1728) among the major musical writings of the period.*

Concertos

Awards 1993

Concertos – C, S211; G, S213; G, S214,'Darmstadt'; S214, Venezia'; G, S215; G, S217; F, S226; F, S231; F, S232; F, S233; F, S234; F, S235. Serenata di Moritzburg in F, S204. Sonata in A, S208. Movement in C minor, S240 P

Musica Antiqua Köln / Reinhard Goebel

Archiv Produktion ② 437 549-2AH2 (137 minutes: DDD). Recorded 1992 Ⓕ ○○○

Johann David Heinichen was a contemporary of Bach and one of an important group of musicians employed by the Dresden court during the 1720s and 1730s. As well as being an inventive composer, Heinichen was also a noted theorist and his treatise on the continuo bass was widely admired. All the music collected here was probably written for the excellent Dresden court orchestra and most of it falls into that rewarding category in which north and central German composers were pre-eminent. Vivaldi had provided effective models but the predilection for drawing upon other influences, too, gives the concertos of the Germans greater diversity. Heinichen admittedly does not so readily venture into the Polish regions whose folk-music gives such a piquancy to Telemann's concertos and suites, but the wonderful variety of instrumental colour and deployment of alternating 'choirs' is every bit as skilful. Your attention will be held from start to finish. Much of the credit for this must go to Reinhard Goebel and his impeccably drilled Musica Antiqua Köln. Some of these pieces might well seem less entertaining in the hands of less imaginative musicians and it would be untruthful to claim that everything here is of uniform interest; there is an element of routine passagework, especially in the wind writing from time to time, but by far the greater amount of this music is of high interest and very entertaining. Each concerto fields its own distinctive wind group drawing variously upon recorders, flutes, oboes, bassoons and horns, the latter always in pairs, in addition to *concertante* parts in many of them for one or more violins and cellos. There is little need to say more. The recorded sound is first-rate, and Goebel's painstaking essay is fascinating to read.

Hans Werner Henze German 1926

GROVE *Henze studied at a music school in Brunswick and, after war service, with Fortner at the Institute for Church Music in Heidelberg (1946-48). At first he composed in a Stravinskian neo-classical style (First Symphony, 1947), but lessons with Leibowitz in 1947-48 encouraged his adoption of 12-note serialism. Unlike such contemporaries as Stockhausen, however, he held his music open to a wide range of materials. Occasionally he made his obeisance to Darmstadt (Second Quartet, 1952), but his large, varied output of this period also shows the continuing importance to him of neo-classicism, Schoenbergian or Bergian expressionism and jazz. Nor was he dismissive of old forms or, in particular, the theatre: he conducted the Wiesbaden ballet (1950-53) and composed ballets (Jack Pudding, 1951; Labyrinth, 1951) and operas (Boulevard Solitude, 1952).*

In 1953 he moved to Italy, where his music became more expansive, sensuous and lyrical and he concentrated on a sequence of operas (König Hirsch, 1956; Elegy for Young Lovers, 1961) and cantatas (Kammermusik, 1958; Cantata della fiaba estrema, 1963). The climax to this period came with a rich and elaborate but also dynamic treatment of The Bacchae in the opera The Bassarids (1966), followed by a period of self-searching; that was externalised in the Second Piano Concerto (1967) and eventually gave rise to an outspoken commitment to revolutionary socialism. Henze visited Cuba (1969-70), where he conducted the first performance of his Sixth Symphony, incorporating the tunes of revolutionary songs. He also developed a bold, poster style in music-theatre works (El Cimarrón, 1970), leading to his dramatization of class conflict in the opera We Come to the River (1976).

But he was also continuing his exploration of an expressionist orchestral sumptuousness in such works as Heliogabalus imperator (1972) and Tristan (1974), and an enjoyment in reinterpreting old musical models (Aria de la folía española for chamber orchestra, 1977). Later works, including the opera The English Cat (1983) and the Seventh Symphony (1984), continue his highly personal synthesis of past and present, lyricism and rigour.

Piano Concerto No 2

Piano Concerto No 2[a]. Telemanniana

[a]**Rolf Plagge** *pf*

North-West German Philharmonic Orchestra / Gerhard Markson

CPO999 322-2 (62 minutes: DDD). Recorded [a]1997 and 1995 Ⓕ ○

In an interview with Oliver Knussen for DG's 1996 reissue of the Second Piano Concerto (1967), Henze stated he felt it had 'made a breakthrough towards a vaster area of musical expression'. Manifest through every bar of this rich and intense score is a sense of release and discovery, of standing on the brink of a new musical landscape utterly different from what had gone before. Henze only had a couple of years to explore this before the storm over *The Raft of the Medusa* burst around his head, changing irrevocably the course of his career. Not until the Seventh Symphony did a very different Henze begin to approach the position the Second Piano Concerto had indicated.

But it would be wrong to read into the Concerto's explosive character a harbinger of the political storms and stresses to come. Henze's music reflected the outcome of musical decisions and dissatisfactions, a desire for change, in which the impact of Japanese Gagaku music is of much consequence. The Concerto forms 'the bridge between the Bacchants and Maenads of *The Bassarids* to the dying soldiers and workers of *The Raft of the Medusa*'. The epilogue is yet another example in his output of music inspired by poetical forms; in this case the 129th sonnet of Shakespeare, a writer who has inspired several of Henze's finest works.

Henze wrote the Concerto for Christoph Eschenbach, who premièred it in 1968, recording it under the composer's direction in London two years later. That performance still sounds splendid and has unassailable authority, but should not deter anyone from investigating this newcomer, which is brilliantly played and prepared. If Eschenbach and Henze occasionally wring more excitement out of the notes, Plagge and Markson are only just behind, and CPO's terrific recording captures even more of the subtle orchestral detail. The orchestra also turns in a very fine performance of Henze's Suite of Telemann arrangements, written in the same year as the Concerto. Gerd Albrecht's account on Koch (coupled with Casella's *Scarlattiana*) has long been unavailable, but Markson's has the edge anyway. Recommended with enthusiasm.

Symphony No 9

Berlin Radio Chorus; Berlin Philharmonic Orchestra / Ingo Metzmacher

EMI CDC5 56513-2 (56 minutes: DDD). Text and translation included. Recorded live in 1997 Ⓕ

Henze's Ninth Symphony deals with his experience of Nazi Germany and it is dedicated 'to the heroes and martyrs of German anti-Fascism'. All seven of its movements are choral, settings of poems by Hans-Ulrich Treichel, themselves based on the novel by Anna Seghers, *The Seventh Cross*. The novel tells of seven prisoners, condemned to be crucified, who escape from a concentration camp. Six are recaptured; after a series of horrifying experiences the seventh manages to reach freedom by boarding a Dutch ship on the Rhine. The first movement, 'The Escape', is not an exciting action scene but a portrayal of abject, pitiful terror; in its successor, 'Among the Dead', the delirious prisoner finds himself in a no man's land of shadows. There is a brief, savage portrayal of the persecutors, then the trees from which the crosses will be made sing lyrically of their own beauty before they are ruthlessly hacked down. Now the fate of one of the other prisoners is described; he is an artist, and as he dies, 'I...the wounded eagle, spread my wings and fly once more over the only land I have'. At this point what is marked in the score as a *gran canto*, a grave, plangent string melody, rises with poignant eloquence in the strings. The penultimate movement, much the longest of the seven, is a hideous nightmare drama set in a cathedral, where the exhausted prisoner has hidden at night. Christ will not reply to his prayers; all he can hear is the voices of the dead (12 soloists, placed at the opposite end of the hall from the orchestra and choir), raptly and horribly praising the voluptuous pleasures of torture and martyrdom. 'The Rescue', finally, provides the huge contrast of rich, calm, multi-layered polyphony, but though the prisoner has survived, the horror remains. The extremest of emotions are explored and extremes are needed to express them. The lines are often tortuous or angular, the textures often dense.

This is a live recording of the first performance. The chorus is not large and is placed well behind the main body of the orchestra. The recording balance does not always compensate for this, and at times it is difficult to follow both the choral counterpoint and the words. Despite this the cumulative impact is shockingly powerful. It is a piece that one senses Henze has been steeling himself to write for years, and its eloquence catches you by the throat.

Undine

London Sinfonietta / Oliver Knussen with **Peter Donohoe** *pf*

DG ② 453 467-2GH2 (103 minutes: DDD) Ⓕ

Recorded 1996 **OO**

Henze's *Undine* (or *Ondine*, as Frederick Ashton's ballet for which it was written is called) is easily his most approachable score, filled with melody, magically delicate evocation and humour. When the ballet first appeared, in October 1958, the music was dismissed by some critics as an eclectic and derivative mish-mash, and it makes no effort to disguise its indebtedness to, in particular, the neo-classical Stravinsky. What we have been missing all these years, this committed performance demonstrates, is a score that pays homage to the whole tradition of classical dance and the music written for it, a score whose richness is out of all proportion to the chamber orchestra it uses. That richness ranges from a quite magnificently sonorous evocation of the sea, via the stately wedding music in Act 2, to the deliciously tongue-in-cheek miniature piano concerto that accompanies the quite irrelevant but entertaining *divertissement* in Act 3. The second *divertissement*, that is: disastrously for the otherwise poetic scenario about a water-nymph's fatal love for a human, Ashton insisted on two of them. But the heart of the ballet is the subtle, quietly iridescent music associated with Ondine herself.

Ashton's ballet was described as a 'concerto' for Margot Fonteyn who was its inspiration, and much of Henze's score is a sort of portrait of 'the radiant centre of the whole ballet...this wonder floating, almost, above the ground', as Henze described her at the time. It is his achievement that the concluding passacaglia, even after those interpolations, is so moving as Ondine, knowing that her kiss will kill her beloved, is nevertheless irresistibly drawn to embrace him. Knussen's performance is so good that you can almost imagine your own staging, and it is superbly recorded.

Nachtstücke und Arien

Drei sinfonische Etüden. Quattro poemi. Nachtstücke und Arien[a]. La selva incantata[a]
[a]**Michaela Kaune** *sop* **North German Radio Symphony Orchestra / Peter Ruzicka**
Wergo WER6637-2 (61 minutes: DDD) Ⓕ
Recorded 1999

This attractive compilation fills significant gaps in the current discography of Henze's earlier compositions. The main work, *Nachtstücke und Arien*, dates from 1957, and mortally offended avant-garde puritans at its première by its revival of full-blooded lyricism, less than 10 years after Strauss's *Four Last Songs* was supposed to have said a final farewell to such self-indulgence. As the interview printed in the booklet makes clear, Henze is still bitter about his treatment by the progressive German establishment at the time, but there is nothing bitter about this sumptuous, at times explosively dramatic music. It comes across well in this performance, Michaela Kaune singing with poise and, where necessary, an apt operatic flair. The recorded sound throughout is adequate, though not especially well defined.

Like the other works on the disc, *Nachtstücke und Arien* owes far more to the post-romantic *espressivo* of Berg and Schoenberg than it does to Strauss. It is most directly indebted to Henze's own opera *König Hirsch*, the major work of the 1950s in which he gave his new-found love of melody the fullest rein. With *La selva incantata* (The enchanted forest), from 1991, we find Henze revisiting *König Hirsch* and recasting some of its most characterful music in purely orchestral form. *Three Symphonic Studies* and *Four Poems* for orchestra were both written in the 1950s (the former was revised in 1964), and although less fully rounded than *Nachtstücke und Arien*, they all have Henze's typical blend of turbulent emotionalism and spacious, questing lyricism.

In the relatively extended first *Study* the risk of aimless drifting is not altogether avoided. But this lapse is corrected with interest in the shorter, more tightly controlled *Poems*. The romantic resonances confirm how fruitful the experience of composing for the theatre, and at the same time engaging with earlier German traditions, had become for Henze. Those resonances continue in most of his finest later works, but the well-shaped, idiomatic performances on this disc let you hear some of their earliest manifestations.

Six Songs from the Arabian

Six Songs from the Arabian. Three Auden Songs
Ian Bostridge *ten* **Julius Drake** *pf*
EMI CDC5 57112-2 (57 minutes: DDD). Ⓕ
Texts and translations included. Recorded 2000 **OO**

Henze says that he doesn't accept commissions any more, but he was clearly eager to break his rule in this case: he was so impressed by Bostridge's voice and artistry that the music of this new cycle was 'more or less all written down in my head' before he had decided on which texts to use. With the exception of the sixth song (by Hafiz, translated by Rückert) and four quoted lines from Goethe in the first, the poems are Henze's own and, he insists, drawn from real life.

Henze has been visiting the East coast of Africa for several years and the bold sailor Selim and the tragically abandoned Fatuma are both people that he knows. The cycle certainly has the quality of personal experience: in the third, 'A Daybreak', the sense of patient waiting in velvet darkness for the first signs of dawn is tangible; in the elegantly sinister second, 'The Praying Mantis', you are quite sure that Henze has watched her horrible courtship intently. They are very big songs (about eight minutes each, on average), strongly dramatic and very beautiful, especially the fourth ('Caesarion') and the last ('Paradise'). They are extremely but not impossibly demanding: 'not impossibly' because although they stretch Bostridge they do so with an absolute understanding of his strengths and qualities. The keyboard writing, too, makes virtuosic demands at times, and Drake is as equal to them as to the cycle's tropical colours and bold imagery; fittingly, the cycle is dedicated to him as well as to Bostridge. Splendidly recorded, this is an oustanding achievement.

Louis Hérold French 1791-1833

GROVE *Hérold studied at the Paris Conservatoire with Louis Adam, Kreutzer, Catel and Méhul (who became the dominant influence on his style), composing his first opera in Italy in 1814. For several years he had difficulty finding adequate texts and his works frequently failed. Not until the delightful Marie (1826) did he score a triumphant success, meanwhile working as an accompanist at the Théâtre-Italien in Paris and later as singing coach at the Opéra, where he composed music for five ballets, including La somnambule and La fille mal gardée. The two operas for which he is remembered - Zampa, ou La fiancée de marbre (1831; originally Le corsaire) and the finer Le pré aux clercs (1832) – were both popular successes, the first full of effective theatrical situations and showing the brilliant tenor Chollet to advantage, the second treating thoughtfully a controversial subject. Such accomplished scores suggest that had Hérold lived longer, he might have fulfilled his ambitions to compose grand opera.*

La fille mal gardée

La fille mal gardée – excerpts (arr Lanchbery)
Orchestra of the Royal Opera House, Covent Garden / John Lanchbery
Decca Ovation 430 196-2DM (51 minutes: ADD) Ⓜ
Recorded 1962 ●

The Royal Ballet's *La fille mal gardée* remains a source of perpetual delight, not least for the music that John Lanchbery arranged largely from Hérold's patchwork score for the 1828 version. The Clog dance is the obvious highlight; but there are felicitous moments throughout, with snatches of Rossini, Donizetti *et al* cropping up all over the place. This recording is the original one that Lanchbery conducted when the ballet proved such a success in the Royal Ballet's repertoire in 1960. More recently he has recorded the score complete; and ballet lovers will consider this fuller version essential. However, others will find that the complete score rather outstays its welcome by comparison with this constantly uplifting selection. A most compelling recommendation.

Hildegard of Bingen

German 1098-1179

GROVE *German composer, abbess and mystic Hildegard of Bingen's writings include much lyrical and dramatic poetry which has survived with monophonic music. The Symphonia armonie celestium revelationum contains musical settings of 77 poems arranged according to the liturgical calendar. The poetry is laden with imagery and the music, based on a few formulaic melodic patterns, is in some respects highly individual. Her morality play Ordo virtutum contains 82 melodies in a more syllabic style. She also wrote medical and scientific treatises, hagiography and letters and recorded her many visions.*

Vocal Works

Favus distillans. Et ideo puelle. O tu illustrata. O vos angeli. Studium divinitatis. O ignee Spiritus. O rubor sanguinis. O orzchis Ecclesia. O gloriosissimi lux vivens angeli. Rex noster promptus est. Deus enim in prima muliere. De patria. Sed diabolus in invidia. Nunc gaudeant materna viscera Ecclesia
Sinfonye (Jocelyn West, Vivien Ellis, Stevie Wishart, Emily Levy, Vickie Couper, Julie Murphy); **members of the Oxford Girls' Choir**
Celestial Harmonies 13127-2 (62 minutes: DDD) Ⓕ
Texts and translations included ●

Stevie Wishart succeeds in putting Hildegard's music across chiefly by her imaginative choice of singers, which includes quite young girls. The tuneful, unsophisticated timbre of the youngest voices – as, for example, that of Vickie Couper in *Deus enim in prima muliere* – acts as a foil to the sturdy chest voices of the older women – which have a quality of their own, somewhat akin to that of Hungarian folk singers. Such contrasts seem to be typical of the whole Hildegardian picture. Hildegard herself was made up of contrasts: she is ecstatic and at the same time quietly tender; she can be passionate while maintaining a sense of decorum; she is erotic but also chaste. One could do without the hurdy-gurdy and dispense with the drones and the improvised organum. What is left is a penetration of Hildegard's music which rarely comes through in other interpretations. One thinks particularly of the composer's portrayal of the mystery of the Incarnation in *O tu illustrata* and also, particularly, of the remarkably sustained lines of ecstasy in *O vos angeli* – this extraordinary outpouring ranging over two octaves, but which yet has shape and structure for all Hildegard's protestations that she had never studied her art formally.

A Feather on the Breath of God
Columba aspexit. Ave, generosa. O ignis spiritus Paracliti. O Jerusalem. O Euchari, in leta vita. O viridissima virga. O presul vere civitatis. O Ecclesia
Awards 1982/3
Gothic Voices / Christopher Page with **Doreen Muskett** *symphony*
Robert White *reed drones*
Hyperion CDA66039 (44 minutes: DDD) Ⓕ
Recorded 1981 ●●●

Here is a collection of choice gems from one of the greatest creative personalities of the Middle Ages. We have limited means of assessing how these inspired pieces were performed in Hildegard's time; but the refreshingly unsophisticated timbre of the four sopranos and the reedy, almost boyish, vocal quality of the contralto are convincing enough to transport the listener right back to the unpolluted atmosphere of Hildegard's cloister. Most to be savoured are the unaccompanied items, amounting to 50 per cent of the total. Indeed, since the notes go out of their way to tell us that 'distractions such as the intrusion of instrumental decorations' were to be avoided, then why did the producer go out of his way to introduce symphony and reed drones in the performance of the other 50 per cent? However, this is a delightful recording. When it was first released it sparked new interest in the music of the Middle Ages by a broader audience and it remains a jewel in Hyperion's crown.

Ordo Virtutum (arr Thornton/Gaver). Symphoniae – O quam magnum miraculum; O felix anima; O quam mirabilis Ⓟ
Sequentia Vocal and Instrumental Ensembles / Barbara Thornton, Benjamin Bagby *vocs*
Elizabeth Gaver *vn*
Deutsche Harmonia Mundi ② 05472 77394 2 (92 minutes: DDD). Notes, texts and translations Ⓕ
included. Recorded 1997 ●

This masterly production, undoubtedly the fruit of maturity and experience, strikes the listener at once by its note of calm self-confidence. Peter Dronke's assertion that the likeliest occasion for the original performance was the consecration of Hildegard's new monastery on the Rupertsberg in the spring of 1152 is made with conviction. There would have been a part to sing for each of the 20 nuns that made up Hildegard's community of *moniales*. Dronke defends the introduction of instruments (in this recording three medieval fiddles, flute and organistrum) by quoting a letter from the impassioned pen of Hildegard herself. He suggests that the characters may have been costumed in garments resembling those depicted in the illuminations of Hildegard's other theological work, *Scivias*. The subject-matter – the strife experienced by the Soul (Anima) assailed by the devil but strengthened and finally victorious through recourse to the Virtues – would not have been unfamiliar to nuns who, once clothed in the robes of their Profession, followed the Rule of St Benedict, enrolled in his 'school of sanctity'. The recording, therefore, is faced with the task of trying to reproduce a festive occasion of much solemnity and depth of meaning, not a mere medieval jollity. The achievement is total. The singing is open and fluid and the rhythmic interpretation convincingly flexible. The instrumental interludes do not disturb the onward flow of the drama: rather, they broadly punctuate the text. This is indeed a recording worthy of marking the 900th anniversary of the birth of Hildegard!

Vespers – Deus in adjutorium meum intende; O aeterne Deus; Spiritus Sanctus vivificans vita; O magne Pater; Caritas abundat in omnia; Lesung; O vis aeternitatis; O ignis Spiritus Paracliti; O quam mirabilis – Magnificat; Kyrie and Pater noster; O presul vere civitatis; O Jerusalem, aure civitas

Scholars of St Hildegard, Eibingen / Johannes Berchmans Göschl, Sr Christiane Rath, OSB

Ars Musici AM1203-2 (69 minutes: DDD). Texts and Ⓕ translations included. Recorded 1997

Here is Hildegard sung by Benedictine *moniales*! They're from St Hildegard's Abbey, Eibingen, a modern abbey, founded around 1900, above the site of Hildegard's own monastery. These nuns are living the same life as that of Hildegard's community, singing daily the same Benedictine Office, breathing the same air and trying to capture the spirit of their great 12th-century predecessor. This is more than a mere anthology. It cannot properly be described as a reconstructed office. The structure of Vespers is used here to place a somewhat random selection of pieces in a plausible context. The chosen antiphons do, in fact, look as if they are intended to be sung with psalmody: they appear in the sources with their corresponding *evovae* (psalm-tone ending) – not always, let it be whispered, the most correct or appropriate ending – and they represent really lovely, rather unusual tones, beautifully sung by these Benedictines, who chant office psalms regularly and with understanding. As for their interpretation of Hildegard's music, this is influenced, but not unduly so, by some of the findings of semiology.

Paul Hindemith German 1895-1963

GROVE *Hindemith studied as a violinist and composer (with Mendelssohn and Sekles) at the Hoch Conservatory in Frankfurt (1908-17) and made an early reputation through his chamber music and expressionist operas. But then he turned to neo-classicism in his Kammermusik No 1, the first of seven such works imitating the Baroque concerto while using an expanded tonal harmony and distinctively modern elements, notably jazz. Each uses a different mixed chamber orchestra, suited to music of linear counterpoint and, in the fast movements, strongly pulsed rhythm.*

During this early period Hindemith lived as a performer: he was leader of the Frankfurt Opera orchestra (1915-23, with a break for army service), and he played the viola in the Amar-Hindemith Quartet (1921-9) as well as in the first performance of Walton's Viola Concerto (1929). Much of his chamber music was written in 1917-24, including four of his six quartets and numerous sonatas, and he was also involved in promoting chamber music through his administrative work for the Donaueschingen Festival (1923-30). However, he also found time to compose abundantly in other genres; including lieder (Das Marienleben, to Rilke poems), music for newly invented mechanical instruments, music for schoolchildren and amateurs, and opera (Cardillac, a fantasy melodrama in neo-classical forms). In addition, from 1927 he taught at the Berlin Musikhochschule.

His concern with so many branches of music sprang from a sense of ethical responsibility that inevitably became more acute with the rise of the Nazis. With the beginning of the 1930s he moved from chamber ensembles to the more public domain of the symphony orchestra, and at the same time his music became harmonically smoother and less intensively contrapuntal. Then in the opera Mathis der Maler (preceded by a symphony of orchestral excerpts) he dramatised the dilemma of the artist in society, eventually opposing Brechtian engagement and insisting on a greater responsibility to art. Nevertheless, his music fell under official disapproval, and in 1938 he left for Switzerland, where Mathis had its first performance. He moved on to the USA and taught at Yale (1940-53), but spent his last decade back in Switzerland.

His later music is in the style that he had established in the early 1930s and that he had theoretically expounded in his Craft of Musical Composition (1937-39), where he ranks scale degrees and harmonic intervals in order from most consonant (tonic, octave) to most dissonant (augmented 4th, tritone), providing a justification for the primacy of the triad. His large output of the later 1930s and 1940s includes concertos (for violin, cello, piano, clarinet and horn) and other orchestral works, as well as sonatas for most of the standard instruments. His search for an all-encompassing, all-explaining harmony also found expression in his Kepler opera Die Harmonie der Welt.

Cello Concerto

Cello Concerto. The Four Temperaments
Raphael Wallfisch *vc* **Howard Shelley** *pf*
BBC Philharmonic Orchestra / Yan Pascal Tortelier
Chandos CHAN9124 (52 minutes: DDD) Ⓕ
Recorded 1992

These two concertos, both from Hindemith's maturity (1940), make a good pairing. The outwardly conventional Cello Concerto contrasts a relatively small voice (the cello) which carries the work's lyrical message, with a large orchestra used initially for active statements delivered with great power. Hindemith's plan would seem to be gradually to reconcile these apparently contradictory modes of address. *The Four Temperaments* is a concerto for piano and string orchestra, a much more evenly balanced combination, using theme and variations form to integrate and relate the contrasted 'humours'. Hindemith's treatment of his material appears to argue that all temperaments, whatever the dominant disposition, are closely related. His portraiture, in fact, reveals characterization of great depth and dimension. Performances are superbly accomplished, indeed this is the finest of many currently available recordings of *The Four Temperaments*. And Chandos has resisted the temptation to move in on the soloist in the Cello Concerto. The sound is open and spacious.

Violin Concerto

Violin Concerto[a]. Symphonic Metamorphosis on Themes of Carl Maria von Weber[b]. Mathis der Maler[c]
David Oistrakh *vn* [ab]**London Symphony Orchestra / [a]Paul Hindemith, [b]Claudio Abbado [c]Suisse Romande Orchestra / Paul Kletzki**
Decca Enterprise 433 081-2DM (77 minutes: ADD) Ⓜ
Recorded 1962 and 1968 ●●

Hindemithians who can afford to be choosy about the *Mathis der Maler* Symphony and the *Symphonic Metamorphosis* will immediately recognise the superiority of the full-price Blomstedt readings. Consistently spectacular 1960s Decca sound adds allure to the merely proficient performances on offer here. What makes this medium-price disc indispensable, however, is the 30-minute Violin Concerto with Oistrakh playing at his legendary best and the composer conducting. The late Deryck Cooke, in his original *Gramophone* review, wrote of Oistrakh as 'superbly poised and eloquent...and as performed here the Concerto shows that behind Hindemith's stony neo-classical facade beats a romantic German heart'. Listening to this recording it's hard to understand the concerto's relative neglect but easy to imagine current star violinists finding Oistrakh's an impossible act to follow. The 1962 sound gives Oistrakh a discreet dominance, and the engineers flatten out the slow movement's central climax, but thankfully there are no other allowances that need be made for this preservation of what can only be described as a classic recording.

Wind Concertos

Clarinet Concerto. Horn Concerto. Concerto for Trumpet, Bassoon and Strings. Concerto for Flute, Oboe, Clarinet, Bassoon, Harp and Orchestra
Walter Buchsel *fl* **Liviu Varcol** *ob* **Ulrich Mehlhart** *cl* **Carsten Wilkening** *bn* **Reinhold Friedrich** *tpt* **Marie Luise Neunecker** *hn* **Charlotte Cassedanne** *hp* **Brigitte Goebel** *spkr* **Frankfurt Radio Symphony Orchestra / Werner Andreas Albert**
CPO CPO999 142-2 (70 minutes: DDD) Ⓑ
Recorded 1990-93

Hindemith's four wind concertos (1947-49) have never enjoyed the success of the *Kammermusik* concertos with which they have much in common; that for clarinet came first, to a commission from Benny Goodman and its lack of overt display may have militated against its popularity. Ulrich Mehlhart's performance more than bears comparison with that of any rival, and is served by the best sound. The 1949 Horn Concerto was written for Dennis Brain. If not quite in Brain's class, Marie Luise Neunecker's is nevertheless a fine, highly musical account. The declamation of Hindemith's poem in praise of the horn, inscribed over its wordless setting, may be thought intrusive. The other two concertos (both 1949) are rarities indeed, not until now commercially available in the UK. In them, Hindemith most nearly approaches his 1920s manner, for instance in the woodwinds and harp Concerto with the finale's quotations from Mendelssohn's *Wedding March*, occasioned by his silver anniversary. In the Clarinet and Horn Concertos, Albert's tempos are brisker than the composer's own; in all four works the soloists and Frankfurt orchestra are committed advocates.

Mathis der Maler / Metamorphosis

Mathis der Maler. Trauermusik[a]. Symphonic Metamorphosis on Themes of Carl Maria von Weber
[a]**Geraldine Walther** *va* **San Francisco Symphony Orchestra / Herbert Blomstedt**
Decca 421 523-2DH (55 minutes: DDD) Ⓕ
Recorded 1987 ●●

The charge sometimes levelled against Hindemith of being dry and cerebral utterly collapses in the face of Blomstedt's evidence as presented on this disc. Masterly craftsmanship and virtuosity there is in plenty; but the powerful emotions of *Mathis der Maler* and the festive high spirits of the *Symphonic Metamorphosis* could not be denied except by those who have wilfully chosen to close their ears. Each of the three movements of the *Mathis* Symphony is based on a panel of Grünewald's great Isenheim altar. The eventual glorious illumination of 'The angels' folk-tune, the poignant slow movement and the blazing triumphant Alleluias after the desperate struggle with the demons in the finale are imbued with a searing intensity in Blomstedt's performance, which also presents Hindemith's elaborate web of counterpoints with the utmost lucidity. For brilliant and joyously ebullient orchestral writing few works are able to match that based on Weber's piano duets and his *Turandot* overture: here the San Francisco Symphony Orchestra's woodwind and brass sections have a field day. In addition, this warmly recommended disc contains a heartfelt performance of the very moving and quite beautiful elegy on the death of King George V, *Trauermusik*. It is tenderly played, with Geraldine Walther as a sweet-toned soloist and a full, rich sonority from the San Francisco strings.

Symphonic Metamorphosis on Themes of Carl Maria von Weber. Mathis der Maler. Nobilissima Visione
Philadelphia Orchestra / Wolfgang Sawallisch
EMI CDC5 55230-2 (71 minutes: DDD) Ⓕ
Recorded 1994

The Philadelphia players for Sawallisch give taut performances that simply outclass much of the competition. Another plus point is the unusual running order that achieves a better musical balance, starting with the most brilliant piece, the *Symphonic Metamorphosis*, and increasing in weight to the resounding brass Alleluias at the climax of the *Mathis* Symphony. Sawallisch's interpretations rank with Blomstedt in the *Mathis* Symphony and *Symphonic Metamorphosis*. Though many will prefer the leaner sound of the San Francisco Orchestra, EMI's sound for Sawallisch is relatively recessed. Given the spacious acoustic of Memorial Hall and the conductor's largeness of vision this is entirely apposite, with no loss of detail.

Kammermusiken

Awards 1993

Kammermusiken – No 1, Op 24 No 1; No 2; No 3, Op 36 No 2; No 4, Op 36 No 3; No 5, Op 36 No 4; No 6, Op 46 No 1; No 7, Op 46 No 2. Kleine Kammermusik No 1 for Wind Quintet, Op 24 No 2
Konstanty Kulka *vn* **Kim Kashkashian** *va* **Norbert Blume** *va d'amore* **Lynn Harrell** *vc* **Ronald Brautigam** *pf* **Leo van Doeselaar** *org*
Royal Concertgebouw Orchestra / Riccardo Chailly
Decca ② 433 816-2DH2 (138 minutes: DDD) Ⓕ
Recorded 1990 ○○○

Even were the performances and recordings not outstanding (and they are) this would be a very valuable set. Hindemith's series of *Kammermusik* ('Chamber Music') began in 1921 as an iconoclastic response to the hyper-intense emotionalism of German 'Expressionist' music over the previous 15 years. It continued until 1927, at which point he began to rationalise the harmonic and expressive foundations of his style. This, then, is neo-classicism with a German accent and as such it was to be a vital force in sweeping away the cobwebs of late romanticism; Walton, Prokofiev, Shostakovich and Britten were among those who, however indirectly, would feel the benefit. The music is also immensely enjoyable in its own right. Hindemith cheekily throws together disparate idioms and sheer force of personality is all that guards against anarchy. All this is done with more than half an eye on the performers' enjoyment of recreation, and the fine array of artists assembled by Chailly savour every detail. Recording quality is exemplary.

Kammermusiken – Nos 1, 4 and 5
Kolja Blacher *vn* **Wolfram Christ** *va* **Berlin Philharmonic Orchestra / Claudio Abbado**
EMI CDC5 56160-2 (55 minutes: DDD) Ⓕ
Recorded 1996 ○

First impressions do not always prove reliable; when you first listen to these performances you may be underwhelmed. The opening chords seem not nearly grotesque enough, the tempo too relaxed. Persistence, though, has its rewards: by the end you will be won round – the performances are really excellent. Where the *Gramophone* Award-winning Chailly underlines the music's 1920s radicalism, Abbado takes a broader line, rather as the composer might have done in, say, the 1940s. He is well served by his band and soloists – violinist Kolja Blacher especially has the edge over any of his rivals – as well as the sound which varies its focus for each work. For example, No 1 (1922), scored for 12 instruments with no soloist, is closely miked to give a real chamber feel, while Nos 4 and 5 (1924-25) sound more like orchestral works. For those already in possession of the Chailly (reviewed above), this disc may be redundant; if the thought of all seven at once is too daunting, this is the place to start. Recommended with enthusiasm.

String Quartets

Hindemith String Quartet No 3, Op 22 H
Prokofiev String Quartet No 2 in F, Op 92
Walton String Quartet in A minor
Hollywood Quartet (Felix Slatkin, Paul Shure *vns* Paul Robyn *va* Eleanor Aller *vc*)
Testament mono SBT1052 (74 minutes: ADD) Ⓕ
Recorded 1951

Although many accounts of the Prokofiev have appeared over the years, none has approached, let alone surpassed, the Hollywood version of the Second Quartet. The same would no doubt apply to the Hindemith but for the fact that there have been fewer challengers. What a wonderful feeling for line these players had, what an incredible, perfectly matched and blended ensemble – and how well these transfers sound! That goes for the Walton, too: there is no other account of it that makes so positive a case for it.

Violin Sonatas

Violin Sonatas – E flat, Op 11 No 1; D, Op 11 No 2; E (1935); C (1939)
Ulf Wallin *vn* **Roland Pöntinen** *pf* Ⓕ
BIS CD761 (56 minutes: DDD). Recorded 1995 ○

The E major Sonata of 1935 is brief (under 10 minutes long – as is Op 11 No 1) and not complex, yet it is familiar Hindemith from first note to last. The C major work (1939) is more complex and grave, and probably the finest of them. The longest sonata – and most conservative in idiom – is that in D major. Both Op 11 works were written in 1918 while Hindemith was on active service, and are remarkable for bearing few traces of either the grimness of the Great War or Hindemith's personal voice. Both deserve wider currency. This issue is also welcome in including the fragmentary abandoned finale of Op 11 No 1, a rustic dance not in keeping with the symmetry of the whole. The sweet-toned Ulf Wallin is fully attuned to Hindemith's wavelength and Pöntinen provides exemplary support. The recording is typical BIS (ie excellent). A splendid disc.

Viola Sonatas

Viola Sonatas – F, Op 11 No 4; Op 25 No 4; C (1939). Nobilissima visione – Meditation. Trauermusik

Paul Cortese *va* **Jordi Vilaprinyó** *pf* **Philharmonia Orchestra / Martyn Brabbins** Ⓕ

ASV CDDCA978 (70 minutes: DDD). Recorded 1993

The late-romantic lyricism of the early F major Sonata, Op 11 No 4, comes over as slightly saccharine, with a tendency for the extremes to be evened out – a common problem with works from Hindemith's most radical decade. But in the more acerbic Second, Op 25 No 4 (1922), Cortese's warmth is persuasive. He is at his best in No 3 (1939), where he gives a performance of real depth that edges out even the composer's own from the top spot – though some might prefer a quicker pace. This can be recommended as first choice in the sonatas and *Meditation* (from *Nobilissima visione*). The *Trauermusik* is a bonus, though it does not supplant the Walther-Blomstedt version.

Requiem for those we love

When Lilacs Last in the Door-yard Bloom'd (Requiem for those we love)

Jan DeGaetani *mez* **William Stone** *bar* **Atlanta Symphony Chorus and Orchestra / Robert Shaw**

Telarc CD80132 (62 minutes: DDD). Text included. Recorded 1986 Ⓕ

Hindemith's Requiem is a setting of Whitman's poem – the lilacs piled on President Lincoln's coffin as it was taken across the country after his assassination just as the Civil War was over, the thrush ('voice of uttermost woe') symbolizing his own mourning, and the then fallen Western star (hailed at Lincoln's inauguration as a good omen) – further layers of association were added when, 80 years later almost to the day, President Roosevelt died as the Second World War was coming to an end. It includes a tragedy-laden sinfonia, arias, recitatives, marches, a massive double fugue and a passacaglia. It is not, however, the great technical virtuosity – in places as close-packed as Whitman's verse – which leaves the most lasting impression, but the haunting beauty of much of the setting.

Robert Shaw gives a superlative and moving performance of the work and receives an outstandingly vivid recording. He knows the work perhaps more intimately than anyone (having commissioned it from Hindemith in 1945 for his Collegiate Chorale in New York), and he makes the most of every expressive nuance, every shade of dynamics, though without losing the overall shape. There is greater subtlety in the playing of the prelude than ever before; the big brass chords have weight and fullness without stridency (a splendid outburst at 'the tolling bells' perpetual clang'), and the orchestral playing generally is first-rate; it would scarcely be possible to find a more sympathetic baritone than William Stone, an unforced lyrical singer with clean technique and exemplary enunciation, or a sweeter or purer-voiced mezzo than Jan DeGaetani; and the chorus is wonderfully alert to the words and has a fine command of tone colour. Add all these factors together and you will understand why this disc should be added to your collection.

Das Unaufhörliche

Ulrike Sonntag *sop* **Robert Wörle** *ten* **Siegfried Lorenz** *bar* **Berlin Radio Children's Choir; Berlin Radio Chorus and Symphony Orchestra / Lothar Zagrosek**

Wergo ② WER6603-2 (95 minutes: DDD). Text and translation included. Recorded 1995 Ⓕ

The oratorio *Das Unaufhörliche* ('The One Perpetual'), setting a poem by Gottfried Benn, was Hindemith's longest concert work. It never established itself in the repertoire (although Boult conducted the UK première as early as 1933). *Das Unaufhörliche* is cast in three parts, the first describing the 'one perpetual' itself, the second its effect on diverse areas of activity (including art, science and love), the third Humankind's reaction away from it and final acquiescence: 'Ever expansion and eternal change'. How closely Hindemith accorded with Benn's viewpoint – they later fell out over Benn's Nazi sympathies – is a matter for conjecture, but his evanescent score matched the poem's expansiveness of theme and nobility of utterance. In this alone it pointed the way to *Mathis der Maler*, for there is nothing here akin to the *Kammermusiken* or *Neues vom Tage* (a smash-hit in Berlin at the time).

This is the work's first recording and the performance is a fine one with good sound. Flies in the ointment? Soprano Ulrike Sonntag, who seems too often to be straining for her notes and whose intonation is not always secure, and Wergo's failure to provide a translation of Benn's spoken introduction, recorded in 1932 and included as the final track. These are quibbles, however, and should not deter anyone from investing in this important release.

Further Listening

Mass

Coupled with: Zwölf Madrigale – Eines Narren, eines Künstlers Leben; An eine Tote; An einen Schmetterling; Magisches Rezept; Es bleibt wohl, was gesagt wird; Kraft fand zu Form. Lieder nach alten Texten, Op 33

Danish National Radio Choir / Gronostay

Chandos CHAN9413 (52 minutes: DDD) Ⓕ

Texts and translations included

If not quite capturing the spirit of the missal, Hindemith's Mass is still an evocative, exploratory setting. This is Uwe Gronostay's second, beautifully sung recording of the work, (his first, on Globe, is unavailable in the UK).

Sancta Susanna

Sancta Susanna

Susan Bullock *sop* Susanna; **Della Jones** *mez* Clementia; **Ameral Gunson** *mez* Old Nun; **Mark Rowlinson** *spkr* Farmhand; **Maria Treedaway** *spkr* Maid **Leeds Festival Chorus**

Drei Gesänge, Op 9. Das Nusch-Nuschi, Op 20 – Dances. Tuttifäntchen – Suite

Susan Bullock *sop*

BBC Philharmonic Orchestra / Yan Pascal Tortelier

Chandos CHAN9620 (70 minutes: DDD). Notes, text Ⓕ and translations included. Recorded 1997

Sancta Susanna is one of the three early stage works Hindemith composed in the wake of the First World War, its companions being *Mörder, Hoffnung der Frauen* (1919) and *Das Nusch-Nuschi* (1920), based on a play for Burmese marionettes and represented here by its dances. Hindemith earned a living in the Frankfurt Opera during this period and so it is natural that he nurtured operatic ambitions. *Sancta Susanna* enjoyed a certain notoriety during its time. Fritz Busch refused to conduct its première on account of its blasphemous plot. It tells briefly of a young nun, Susanna, inflamed by the legend she hears from Sister Clementia, of a girl coming naked to the altar to embrace the lifesize figure of Christ on the Cross. For this blasphemy she is buried alive. Aroused and undeterred Susanna strips off and rips the covering from Christ's torso. She is terrified when a huge spider falls on to her head from the crucifix and, horrified by her deed, begs the nuns to wall her up. A drastic cure for arachnophobia or blasphemy!

The opera is short, concentrated, highly imaginative and resourceful in its use of sonority; and its expressionist musical language is so powerful that one feels at the end of its barely 23 minutes that one has heard a much longer piece. It is superbly done here. No praise can be too high for the singers and for the delicacy, eloquence and power of the playing that Yan Pascal Tortelier draws from his orchestra. The recorded sound is of demonstration quality in its unforced naturalness. The gorgeous Straussian *Drei Gesänge*, Op 9, are very vehement and passionate and at times wildly over the top but their assured craft and confident ambition is breathtaking. Susan Bullock performs them with thrilling panache. They are written for a large orchestra and there is little of what we think of as Hindemith in them. Nor is there much in *Tuttifäntchen*, a children's pantomime first performed in Darmstadt in 1922. The dances from *Nusch-Nuschi* are expertly done. There is some extraordinary music here.

Mathis der Maler

Roland Hermann *bar* Mathis; **Josef Protschka** *ten* Albrecht; **Gabriele Rossmanith** *sop* Regina; **Sabine Hass** *sop* Ursula; **Harald Stamm** *bass* Riedinger; **Heinz Kruse** *ten* Hans Schwalb; **Victor von Halem** *bass* Lorenz von Pommersfelden; **Hermann Winkler** *ten* Wolfgang Capito; **Ulrich Hielscher** *bass* Truchsess von Waldberg; **Ulrich Ress** *ten* Sylvester von Schaumberg; **John Cogram** *ten* Der Pfeiffer des Grafen von Helfenstein; **Marilyn Schmiege** *mez* Helfenstein

North German Radio Chorus; Cologne Radio Chorus and Symphony Orchestra / Gerd Albrecht

Wergo ③ WER6255-2 (166 minutes: DDD). Notes Ⓕ and text included. Recorded 1990

The masterpiece, *Mathis der Maler*, is one of the pinnacles of 20th-century German opera. It has become axiomatic to see in it a parable of the times, with Hindemith using the turbulent world of 16th-century Germany to mirror the Nazi Reich and his place in it. But in reality *Mathis* is a spiritual and historical opera, not a political one. Rudolf Stephan in his essay for Wergo plays down the political angle; if Hitler had not risen to power until, say, 1936, one doubts that *Mathis* would have turned out much different. Gerd Albrecht's acquaintance with Hindemith's music goes back to the early 1960s, before the composer's death. Hindemith even sanctioned some retouching of the orchestration in *Mathis* made by Albrecht for a festival performance, though it is not made clear whether Albrecht has applied this here, nor to what extent. Rarely have Hindemith's often heavy textures sounded so clear.

As to the music, is not the brief concluding 'Alleluia' duet that crowns the sixth tableau one of *the* great moments in 20th-century opera? You will be convinced from your first hearing of it. There are fine moments aplenty in Albrecht's reading, not least where familiar passages from the *Mathis* Symphony surface and precipitate some of the most intense music of the opera. Roland Hermann is, perhaps, a shade stolid in places as the painter (though his world-weariness in the final scene is just right); Josef Protschka makes a most authoritative Cardinal, acting as a perfect foil to Hermann's Mathis. They head a fine cast, supported by some lusty singing and playing from the combined forces of Cologne and North German Radios.

Mathis der Maler

Dietrich Fischer-Dieskau *bar* Mathis; **James King** *ten* Albrecht; **Gerd Feldhoff** *bass* Lorenz von Pommersfelden; **Manfred Schmidt** *ten* Capito; **Peter Meven** *bass* Riedinger; **William Cochran** *ten*

Schwalb; **Alexander Malta** *bass* Truchsess von Waldburg; **Donald Grobe** *ten* Sylvester von Schaumberg; **Rose Wagmann** *mez* Ursula; **Urszula Koszut** *sop* Regina; **Trudeliese Schmidt** *mez* Countess Helfenstein

Bavarian Radio Chorus and Symphony Orchestra / Rafael Kubelík

EMI ③ CDS5 55237-2 (183 minutes: ADD). Notes, text and translation included. Recorded 1977 Ⓕ

Comparing Albrecht with Kubelík's reissued version shows that honours are fairly even; choosing between them would depend largely on one's keenness for individual names. Neither version is perfect, but both are very fine. Albrecht, who makes one or two minor but noticeable cuts, has the benefit of more modern sound, but EMI's for Kubelík has transferred well. The choruses in particular are excellent, although Albrecht's seem tame in the famous 'Temptation of St Antony' scene when set next to Kubelík's devilish-sounding Bavarians. Comparison of the casts yields a mixed picture; many listeners will prefer Fischer-Dieskau as Mathis to the rather raw-voiced Hermann; for many this will be the crucial criterion, but Wergo does have the better of some other principals. The roles of Schwalb and his daughter encapsulate the predicament: for EMI, William Cochran is more imposing than Heinz Kruse as the peasant leader but Wergo's Gabriele Rossmanith is sweeter and younger-toned as Regina. For Albrecht, their first appearance seems to be a mid-afternoon stroll and not the convincing escape from pursuit that Kubelík effects here (first disc, track 4). Despite the urgings of sentiment, neither set outclasses the other. For most, choice will rest on preferences for cast members. Those who love this score will want both.

Alun Hoddinott British 1929

GROVE *Hoddinott studied at University College, Cardiff, and privately with Benjamin, returning to Cardiff as lecturer in 1959; in 1967 he became professor, and founded the Cardiff Festival of 20th-century Music. His music is essentially tonal though not diatonic, in a vigorous style that has roots in Bartók, Rawsthorne and Hindemith. His large output consists mostly of orchestral and chamber music (symphonies, concertos, sonatas), but he has also written operas and choral music.*

Symphonies

Symphonies – No 2, Op 29[a]; No 3, Op 61[b]; No 5, Op 81[c]

[ab]London Symphony Orchestra / [a]Norman Del Mar, [b]David Atherton; [c]Royal Philharmonic Orchestra / Sir Andrew Davis

Lyrita SRCD331 (74 minutes: ADD) Recorded 1967-73 Ⓕ

Alun Hoddinott is one of the best, most resourceful of living British symphonists, and the return to the catalogue of three demonstrations of that fact is welcome. What is meant by 'resourceful' is well illustrated by this coupling. The Second Symphony, from 1962, is apparently in a conventional four-movement layout, but in fact the outer movements investigate the arch-like or palindromic forms that Hoddinott was to make much use of later. Its successor is in two movements, but both are in two parts, with opening and closing *adagios* reflecting each other across the two intervening quick sections. The Fifth Symphony has a finale of six panels, each slow section having a faster 'pair'. Its first movement (again there are only two) is described by the composer as an 'interrupted passacaglia'; the effect is of craggy, splendidly stormy music continually encroaching upon lyricism. Excellent performances, mostly decent recordings.

Leopold Hofmann Austrian 1738-1793

GROVE *After a period as Kapellmeister at St Peter's, Vienna, Hofmann became court keyboard teacher (1769); from 1772 he was second court organist and also Kapellmeister at St Stephen's Cathedral. He enjoyed wide fame as both player and composer. His many sacred works (including over 30 masses) combine Austrian Baroque and Neapolitan traits, while his c55 symphonies are in a galant style. Among his other works are Lieder, concertos and chamber music.*

Cello Concertos

Cello Concertos – D, B:D3; C, B:C3; D, B:D1; C, B:C1

Northern Sinfonia / Tim Hugh *vc* Ⓢ

Naxos 8 553853 (68 minutes: DDD) Recorded 1996

The supremacy of Haydn and Mozart has always cast a shadow over the other Viennese composers of their time. In his day Leopold Hofmann, Kapellmeister at St Stephan's Cathedral from 1772, was one of the most eminent, as a composer of church music, symphonies, concertos and chamber works. His cello concertos – there are eight in all – belong to the 1760s or early 1770s, much the time of the Haydn C major Concerto, which they resemble in style. They are attractive, agreeable pieces, technically and formally assured if without very much individuality. The longest of the four concertos here, the one catalogued as D3, is more mature in style than the others and makes greater demands on the soloist. Tim Hugh's advocacy certainly makes the revival of these concertos worthwhile. He brings a very sound modern technique to the music, throwing off the rapid passages with evident ease, and there is a breadth to his phrasing that gives some amplitude to Hofmann's writing. His intonation is faultless, his tone full and warm, and he brings a keen feeling for *galant* expression to the slow movements. There is vivacity in the quick movements too. The Northern Sinfonia plays responsively. Those who relish good cello playing, should try this disc.

Violin Concertos

Violin Concertos – B flat, B:Bb1; A, B:A2. Concerto for Violin, Cello and Strings in G, B:G1
Lorraine McAslan *vn* **Tim Hugh** *vc*
Northern Chamber Orchestra / Nicholas Ward Ⓢ
Naxos 8 554233 (60 minutes: DDD). Recorded 1997

For a composer long represented in the catalogue only by a concerto that masqueraded as Haydn's (Hob VII*f*:D1), this is a welcome issue of orchestral works, admirably edited and presented by the New Zealand scholar Allan Badley. These Viennese concertos, probably from the 1760s, are *galant* works, with florid solo parts and elaborate lines, a leisurely harmonic pace and a good deal of sequence, but they are shapely and effective music, with tenderness in the slow movements – and also wit: the finale of the B flat Concerto is especially ingenious and beguiling. Then there is the double concerto, for violin and cello, which has much attractive dialogue and duetting, rather in the manner of the Mozart violin-viola *Sinfonia concertante*. The *Adagio* here is also eloquent. The performances are excellent, with clean, perfectly tuned and expressive violin playing from Lorraine McAslan. Tim Hugh plays equally securely and with a keen sense of style. Tempos are well chosen by Nicholas Ward who obtains spruce accompaniments from the Northern Chamber Orchestra.

Joseph Holbrooke British 1878-1958

GROVE *A pupil of Corder at the Royal Academy of Music, Holbrooke was influenced by Wagner and early Strauss. His large output, dating mostly from the beginning of the century, includes operas (among them the huge trilogy The Cauldron of Anwyn), symphonies, symphonic poems, chamber music and much for piano.*

Piano Concerto No 1

Holbrooke Piano Concerto No 1, Op 52, 'The Song of Gwyn ap Nudd' **Wood** Piano Concerto in D minor
Hamish Milne *pf* **BBC Scottish Symphony Orchestra / Martyn Brabbins**
Hyperion CDA67127 (69 minutes: DDD) Ⓕ
Text included. Recorded 1999

Holbrooke's ambitious First Piano Concerto is by some margin the most impressive orchestral piece of his we have yet encountered on disc. Dubbed a symphonic poem by its creator, it follows the narrative of a poem based on a Welsh legend by his patron Lord Howard de Walden entitled *The Song of Gwyn ap Nudd*. Yet, as annotator Lewis Foreman observes, the work can also be appreciated perfectly well as a red-blooded romantic concerto in the grand tradition. There's no denying the deft resourcefulness and vaulting sweep with which Holbrooke handles proceedings. It receives outstandingly eloquent and tirelessly committed treatment in this performance.

The coupling is the D minor Piano Concerto by Haydn Wood (1882-1959), who, before he made his name in the field of light music, was a gifted violinist and composition pupil of Stanford at the Royal College of Music. Indeed, it was Stanford who conducted the Queen's Hall première of Wood's big-boned D minor Concerto in July 1909. The work is an altogether more straightforward, less individual confection than it's partner. Grieg's Concerto is the obvious template, and there are plentiful stylistic echoes throughout of Tchaikovsky, Rachmaninov and MacDowell. The opening movement is full of effective display and boasts a ravishing secondary idea. Tuttis incline to overthickness, yet there's some delightfully transparent scoring elsewhere. The finale starts promisingly but tends to lose its way. By far the best music comes in the central *Andante* – a genuinely haunting, deeply felt essay, boasting some wistfully fragrant orchestral sonorities. Not a great work, by any means, but incurable romantics will devour it. All told, this must be counted as an exemplary release.

Robin Holloway British 1943

GROVE *Holloway studied with Goehr (from 1960) and at Cambridge, where in 1974 he was appointed lecturer. His large output covers many genres (including numerous songs) and shows a remarkable command of diverse styles: some pieces lovingly reinterpret Romanticism (Scenes from Schumann for orchestra,1970); others are strikingly positive in their modernism (The Rivers of Hell for chamber ensemble,1977). His first opera, Clarissa, a study of rape, was given by the English National Opera in London in 1990.*

Concertos for Orchestra

Awards 1994

Second Concerto for Orchestra, Op 40
BBC Symphony Orchestra / Oliver Knussen
NMC NMCD015M (34 minutes: DDD) Ⓜ
Recorded 1993

A North African holiday was the initial stimulus for Robin Holloway's *Second Concerto for Orchestra*. The extremes of contrast, he tells us ('opulence and austerity, richness and drabness, brilliant light and dense shadow...And above all, the noises...the polyphony of hammering, tapping, thudding, tinkling, bashing ...'), haunted him and were soon demanding to be turned into music. At the same time, the experience seems to have set him off on a more enigmatic, private voyage through his, and our musical past. We hear a few particularly aching bars from Act 2 of *Tristan* and rather more of Chopin's F sharp major *Barcarolle*; while a strange, broken tune on muted trombone metamorphoses neatly into Parry's *Jerusalem*. It's bewildering, but gripping at the same time. Holloway can swerve from lush, late romanticism to strident modernism and back again with the alarming quickness of an opium dream; but as with any really revelatory dream, the more you probe it, the more lucid it seems. There are few contemporary orchestral works about which you will feel, on reaching the end, that you want to go back and soak in the experience all over again, and then go away somewhere and ponder its riddles.

The members of the BBC Symphony Orchestra play as though each one of them were engaged on his or her own voyage of discovery – this is the kind of piece that will expose weakness or lack of conviction in every section of an orchestra. Oliver Knussen's triumph in pulling it all together, and then shaping and shading it so lovingly, is just one of the technically miraculous aspects of this disc; another is that the production team have somehow turned BBC Maida Vale Studio No 1 into a fine, spacious acoustic, with teeming details beautifully focused. It all adds up to a quite fascinating disc.

Third Concerto for Orchestra, Op 76
London Symphony Orchestra / Michael Tilson Thomas
NMC NMCD039 (45 minutes: DDD) Ⓕ
Recorded live in 1996

The first ideas for No 3 came during a trip through South America – sound pictures of Lake Titicaca, riotous New Year's Day celebrations in the Bay of Bahia, the slow train-crossing of the Great Brazilian Swamp and the huge, satanic slag heap at the Potosì Silver Mine. Holloway jotted them all down on the spot: then his notebook was stolen, and it took another 13 years to recall them and finish the piece. By then, of course, the alchemical processes of memory had transformed the original musical impressions into something quite different. What might have been simply a descriptive tone-poem finally emerged as a powerful and unusual musical argument – a huge slow movement, with a moderately fast dance-like finale, which evolves from tiny scraps of motifs (there is hardly a 'theme' in sight). And yet much of the original 'illustrative' character of the piece remains.

String and woodwind textures recall dense, overripe rain forest foliage; the dark, 'sluggish' first movement suggests the movement of a vast, slow, muddy river; extravagant sensuousness contrasts with clangorous bells or craggy brass. This recording, based on its 1996 première, is quite an achievement. It is rare for a conductor and an orchestra to show such a compelling grasp of the shape and atmosphere of a work at its first performance. Technically the sound has none of the usual problems associated with a live recording – virtually no intrusive noise, good balance, warm tone.

Fantasy-Pieces on...'Liederkreis'

Holloway Fantasy-Pieces on the Heine 'Liederkreis' of Schumann, Op 16. Serenade in C, Op 41*b*
Schumann Liederkreis, Op 24
Toby Spence *ten* **Ian Brown** *pf*
Nash Ensemble / Martyn Brabbins
Hyperion CDA66930 (75 minutes: DDD). Text and translation included. Recorded 1996 Ⓕ

A contemporary composer takes a 19th-century classic – Schumann's song-cycle *Liederkreis* – and sets it in a musical frame of his own devising: a short, astringent 'Praeludium' and four extended movements, the style hovering between pure homage and what the composer calls 'phantasmagorical collage'. Certainly sufficient to cause hackles to rise! But the result, entitled *Fantasy-Pieces on the Heine 'Liederkreis' of Schumann* is uniquely fascinating, haunting and increasingly rewarding the more one goes back to it. Brief though it is, the 'Praeludium' is just enough to tell the ear that the performance of *Liederkreis* that follows (very persuasive in this recording) is not going to be the whole story. Holloway picks up magically on Schumann's ending, in a short movement, 'Half asleep' (what follows is, at times, intensely dream-like). Then come an *Adagio*, a *Scherzo* and a finale – on one level, symphonic, on another, an intricate series of references and cross-references based on Schumann's songs (not all from *Liederkreis*). The manner drifts between masterful irony and fleeting moments of intense self-revelation. *Liederkreis* remains *Liederkreis*, and yet something profound and (in the wider sense) modern is added. The Serenade in C is a kind of post-modern *divertimento*. Scored for the same forces as Schubert's Octet, it alternates, charmingly and teasingly, between sensuous Viennese cosiness, something closer to the salon Elgar, and delightful, end-of-the-pier vulgarity – though with a more acerbic harmonic colouring from time to time. Play a short extract to a musical friend and he/she might well date it before the First World War. But nothing is ever what it seems for very long; the disruptive subtlety of *Fantasy-Pieces* is here too, despite the seeming holiday feeling. Splendid performances from the Nash Ensemble – colourful, precise and sensitive to Holloway's kaleidoscopic shifts in mood. The recordings are quite excellent: the change in perspective for the Schumann songs makes perfect aural sense.

Vagn Holmboe

Danish 1909-1996

GROVE *Holmboe studied with Hoffding and Jeppesen in Copenhagen, and with Toch in Berlin, then returned to Copenhagen to work as a teacher (at the conservatory), critic and composer. He is the leading Danish symphonist after Nielsen (he has composed 11, 1935-82) and composer of a series of 14 string quartets (1949-75), regarded as the most important Scandinavian contributions to the genre since World War Two. He has also written operas, vocal and chamber music. His style is unproblematic if not immediately accessible, influenced by Nielsen, Hindemith and Stravinsky.*

Chamber Concertos

Chamber Concertos – No 7 for Oboe and Chamber Orchestra, Op 37; No 8 for Orchestra, Op 38, 'Sinfonia concertante'; No 9 for Violin, Viola and Orchestra, Op 39

Max Artved *ob* **Mikkel Futtrup** *vn* **Tim Frederiksen** *va* **Danish Radio Sinfonietta / Hannu Koivula**

Da Capo 8 224086 (62 minutes: DDD) Ⓕ
Recorded 1997 OO

While Holmboe remained audibly the same composer, Holmboe the concerto writer had a very different agenda from Holmboe the symphonist, and nowhere does that become more apparent than in No 8 (1945), subtitled *Sinfonia concertante*, a splendid chamber-orchestral concerto yet also a direct precursor of the magnificent *First Chamber Symphony* (1953). Internal cohesion seems to be No 8's *raison d'être*, not the interplay of soloist(s) and tutti found in, for instance, Nos 7 (1944-45) and 9 (1945-46). The Eighth also stands a little apart from its companions by virtue of its more Hindemithian aspect. The arch-form first movement of No 7, for oboe, has in its outermost sections distinct pre-echoes of the humane luminosity that infuses so much of the music of Holmboe's last three decades, and – as does the second of No 8 – nimbly synthesises elements of multiple movements within a single span as do several of the symphonies. No 9 is more conventional, a delightful two-part invention in three movements for violin and viola, with orchestral accompaniment in the outer spans only. The performances are exemplary, the sound clear if very slightly studio-bound. A definite must-buy for Holmboe enthusiasts.

Chamber Concertos – No 10 for Orchestra, Op 40; No 11 for Trumpet and Orchestra, Op 44; No 12 for Trombone and Orchestra, Op 52; No 13 for Oboe, Viola and Orchestra, Op 67

Max Artved *ob* **Ole Edward Antonsen** *tpt* **Jacques Mauger** *tbn* **Tim Frederiksen** *va* **Danish Radio Sinfonietta / Hannu Koivula**

Da Capo 8 224087 (75 minutes: DDD) Ⓕ
Recorded 1997 O

Chamber Concerto No 10 (1945-46) is a bracing early example of Holmboe's metamorphosis technique, its nine sections acting like variations within a traditional concerto format: the sections in pairs respectively form an introduction and three 'movements', with the last acting as coda. The concerto is described on the back of the jewel-case as being 'for wood-brass-gut and orchestra': in the official Hanson catalogue, 'Wood-brass-gut' – in Danish *Trae-messing-tarm* – is the subtitle, the concerto being listed as the composer's second (of three) for orchestra. Nos 11-13 (1948, 1950 and 1955-56) are conventional in layout. The gem of the disc is No 13, for the unusual combination of oboe and viola (for the most part playing as a pair in intertwining lines). This is music suffused by that wonderful Nordic light so prevalent in Holmboe's later works, beguiling and beautifully played. Although Da Capo's recording is a mite studio-bound, this is a fine disc.

Chamber Concertos – No 11 for Trumpet and Orchestra, Op 44; No 12 for Trombone and Orchestra, Op 52; Tuba and Orchestra, Op 127. Intermezzo concertante, Op 171

Håkan Hardenberger *tpt* **Christian Lindberg** *tbn* **Jens Bjørn-Larsen** *tuba* **Aalborg Symphony Orchestra / Owain Arwel Hughes** Ⓕ

BIS CD802 (55 minutes: DDD). Recorded 1995

The Trumpet Concerto has a leanness of texture and neo-classical air that will surprise those familiar with Holmboe's symphonies. Hardenberger's first entry creates an electricity that is maintained throughout the work – indeed, the disc as a whole. No 11's tripartite design recurs, condensed into a single movement, in No 12: a brief, expressively crucial slow section framed by a large-boned *Allegro* (rather grave in character in the trombone work), and a good-humoured, rollicking finale. The Tuba Concerto (1976), by contrast, requires a full orchestral complement, its one integrated span bearing little semblance of traditional three-movement form. It is the most dramatic and exploratory work here, both in mood and sonority, the demands of which on tuba virtuosos over the years have occasioned it to be played in slightly differing versions, especially with regard to the taxing cadenza. The short *Intermezzo concertante* reaffirms that the tuba really can sing. Wonderful music, wonderfully performed and recorded.

Symphonies

Symphonies – No 11, Op 144; No 12, Op 175; No 13, Op 192

Aarhus Symphony Orchestra / Owain Arwel Hughes Ⓕ

BIS CD728 (63 minutes: DDD). Recorded 1994

Few who have invested in this series so far can doubt that these are among the most commanding symphonies to have emerged in post-war Europe. Some might even argue that they are *the* finest since Sibelius and Nielsen. All credit to Owain Arwel Hughes and the Aarhus orchestra for their committed advocacy and to BIS for recording them in such vivid, naturally balanced sound. The 11th, composed in 1980, is quintessential Holmboe, and its atmosphere resonates in the mind long after you have heard it. To quote Knud Ketting's notes, 'the symphony's climax in dynamic and emotional terms comes in the second movement and it then slowly retreats within itself…[it] is cast as a strong arch, which impresses at first hearing, and commands increasing admiration on closer acquaintance'. The arabesque that opens the symphony seems to come from another world and the transparent, luminous textures communicate the sense of a spiritual quest that one rarely encounters in modern music. The 12th is a taut, well-argued piece, and is, like its two companions on this disc, in three movements. No one listening to the 13th, written at the instigation of Owain Arwel Hughes, would think that it was the work of an 85-year-old. Of course, there have been other octogenarian symphonies but none that sounds quite so youthful or highly charged as this one.

Symphonic Metamorphoses

Symphonic Metamorphoses – No 1, Op 68, 'Epitaph'; No 2, Op 76, 'Monolith'; No 3, Op 80, 'Epilog'; No 4, Op 108, 'Tempo variabile'
Aalborg Symphony Orchestra / Owain Arwel Hughes Ⓕ
BIS CD852 (75 minutes: DDD). Recorded 1996 ⭘

In form the symphonic metamorphosis is an offshoot of the symphonic fantasia (but of a radically different ilk to Sibelius's *Pohjola's Daughter*), each of these four very different from its companions. The vigour and luminous orchestration of the symphonies are present, as are many of the internal developmental processes, but not the level of integration. Holmboe's priorities here are unlike those of many others of his pieces, yet the music coheres perfectly on its own terms. Hughes is fully inside Holmboe's idiom, whether in the single-minded determination of *Monolith* or in the magnificent and visionary *Epilog*, one of the composer's most searching utterances, prefiguring both the Ninth Symphony (1969) and *Requiem for Nietzsche*. This is extraordinary music.

String Quartets

String Quartets – No 10, Op 102; No 11, Op 111; No 12, Op 116
Kontra Quartet (Anton Kontra, Boris Samsing *vns* Peter Fabricius *va* Morten Zeuthen *vc*)
Da Capo 8 224101 (67 minutes: DDD) Ⓕ
Recorded 1997

These works are worthy of comparison with the best in 20th-century cycles. True, Holmboe's idiom was less overtly pioneering or sensational (in the best sense of the word) than his peers, yet his quartets are no less visionary or searching. The crucial difference was his uncommon humanity, which refracts through his music like light through a prism, with no place for Shostakovich-type desolation. The 10th Quartet (1969) is serious in tone but always positive in spirit. Cast as a diptych, the constituent sections (fast-slow-fast, and slow-fast) together form a five-movement arch design to which he would often return later – as in No 12 (1973). The 10th is typically subtle and seems to grow and develop with each re-hearing. The same is true of No 11 (1972). Do not be fooled by its comparative brevity (just over 18 minutes), the subtitle (*Quartetto rustico*) or the light, bird-like twitterings of the opening *Allegro leggiero* into believing it a relaxation or something merely diverting: it is just as purposeful as any of its fellows, even if it smiles throughout. No 11's *Andante tranquillo* third movement is another of Holmboe's wonderful creations combining Nordic light with sublime counterpoint. The 12th has two such spans, and is one of his finest quartets. The opening *Allegro robusto* has a Bartókian air reminding us that eastern European folk music was a lasting influence, while the work's final bars, unusually, resolve on a question mark. The Kontra Quartet has the idiom under its skin, though the clear recording is not exactly spacious. Still, a fine disc.

String Quartets – No 13, Op 124; No 14, Op 125; No 15, Op 135
Kontra Quartet (Anton Kontra, Boris Samsing *vns* Peter Fabricius *va* Morten Zeuthen *vc*)
Dacapo 8 224127 (59 minutes: DDD) Ⓕ
Recorded 1997-98

Holmboe's Quartets Nos 13 and 14 were composed back-to-back in 1975, but are as different as chalk and cheese. No 13 is in the five-movement structure that he favoured at this time. Right from the opening gentle but severe dissonance, the work moves with complete sureness of touch into a new landscape. Jakob Levinson in his booklet-note comments on its Janus-like aspects: how it is 'at once more rigorous and freer', looking back to earlier symmetries and forward to the different tack taken by No 14 and its successors. The appeal of that new direction accounts, presumably, for his carrying on straight afterwards with No 14. Cast in six short movements gathered into groups of three, then two, with the *Allegro vivace* finale (the longest single movement) separate, it grows inexorably from the severe, almost Bach-like opening solo for the first violin. The movements have something of the character of variations, but are thoroughly integrated. The grave, concentrated No 15 (1977-78) has at its heart the *Funèbre* third movement, a searching and dramatic funeral march, motifs from which are taken up in the finale. The Kontra's performances are excellent and Dacapo's recording is clear. A great disc.

Gustav Holst

British 1874-1934

GROVE *Holst studied at the Royal College of Music with Stanford, and in 1895 met Vaughan Williams, to whom he was close for the rest of his life. From 1905 he taught at St Paul's Girls' School in Hammersmith.*

Like Vaughan Williams, he was impressed by English folksong, but also important was his reading in Sanskrit literature (chamber opera Savitri, composed1908; Choral Hymns from the Rig Veda, 1912) and his experience of the orchestral music of Stravinsky and Strauss (he had played the trombone professionally). In The Planets (1916) he produced a suite of seven highly characterful movements to represent human dispositions associated with the planets in astrology, and his interest in esoteric wisdom is expressed too in his cantata The Hymn of Jesus (1917). But his very varied output also includes essays in a fluent neo-classicism (A Fugal Concerto for flute, oboe and strings, 1923; Double Violin Concerto, 1929), a bare Hardy impression (Egdon Heath, 1927) and operas.

Egdon Heath

A Somerset Rhapsody, H87. Beni Mora, H107. Invocation, H75. A Fugal Overture, H151. Egdon Heath, H172. Hammersmith, H178
Tim Hugh *vc* **Royal Scottish National Orchestra / David Lloyd-Jones**
Naxos 8 553696 (69 minutes: DDD) Ⓢ
Recorded 1996

This superb recording was made in the Henry Wood Hall in Glasgow. Lloyd-Jones has as his two weightiest items the Hardy-inspired *Egdon Heath*, arguably Holst's finest work, as well as the prelude and fugue, *Hammersmith*, comparably dark and intense. In the latter he chooses the wind-band version, achieving a subtlety of shading in phrasing and dynamic amply to justify that striking choice. The Naxos sound is vividly atmospheric while letting one hear inner detail. Lloyd-Jones generally adopts flowing speeds and is objective in his interpretation while bringing out to the full the tenderness and refinement of the writing. Particularly beautiful is the performance of *A Somerset Rhapsody* which opens the disc, with the cor anglais solo ravishingly played. The six works are neatly balanced, three dating from before the climactic period of *The Planets* and *The Hymn of Jesus*, and three after. Particularly valuable is the atmospheric *Invocation* for cello and orchestra of 1911, rather dismissed by Imogen Holst, but here given a yearningly intense, deeply thoughtful performance with Tim Hugh as soloist. This is a highly recommendable offering, whether for the dedicated Holstian or the newcomer wanting to investigate more characteristic work outside *The Planets*.

Additional recommendations

A Somerset Rhapsody
Couplings: Beni Mora. A Fugal Overture. Hammersmith. Japanese Suite. Scherzo
London Philharmonic Orchestra; London Symphony Orchestra / Boult
Lyrita SRCD222 (62 minutes: ADD: 7/92) Ⓕ

Conducted by one of the composer's greatest friends and staunchest advocate, this release is still of the front rank.

Somerset Rhapsody and Egdon Heath
Couplings: Brook Green Suite. Vaughan Williams In the Fen Country. Five Variants of Dives and Lazarus. Norfolk Rhapsody No 1
Bournemouth Sinfonietta / Del Mar; various artists
HMV Classics HMV5 73461-2 Ⓜ
(66 minutes: DDD/ADD: 2/81[R])

The *Somerset Rhapsody* builds from the quietest of beginnings to a fine climax – a vivid recording.

The Planets, H125

Holst The Planets[a]
Elgar Variations on an Original Theme, Op 36, 'Enigma'[b]
[a]Geoffrey Mitchell Choir; [a]London Philharmonic Orchestra, [b]London Symphony Orchestra / Sir Adrian Boult
EMI Studio Plus CDM7 64748-2 (78 minutes: ADD) Ⓜ
Recorded [a]1978, [b]1970 ●

Boult's long association with *The Planets* is well known (since the famous first run-through – for it can scarcely have been more – at the Queen's Hall in 1919). This splendid set from 1978 has been admirably remastered. Boult, in the composer's words, 'first made the *Planets* shine' and he always had something special to say about the music on all his recordings. Apart from public performances, he made five recordings of the work, and this is considered by many to have been the finest. Boult's interpretation varied very little throughout his long association with the work, only being temporarily shaken when he heard the reissue of Holst's own very different 1926 performance. However, he stuck to his own view which the composer thoroughly approved of.

The actual performance has an indefinable 'rightness' about it, a supreme authority that makes it difficult to imagine the score being interpreted in any other way. Has 'Mars' ever resounded with more terrifying ferocity since? We very much doubt it. In 'Venus' the playing has a translucent beauty, while the impish 'Mercury' really sparkles. 'Jupiter' has marvellous exuberance and sparkle, its big tune lent enormous dignity and humanity. 'Saturn', too, is paced to perfection (the central climax has a massive inevitability about it), and 'Uranus' goes about his mischievous antics with terrific swagger. In 'Neptune' one notes again the exquisite poise of the orchestral response, and the choir contributes admirably. If you've never heard Boult's *Planets*, we urge immediate investigation of this set! Plenty of *Enigma* recordings have been added to the catalogue since 1970 when this recording was made, but none has surpassed it in authority and fidelity. Just listen to the clarity of detail – nothing overdone, but so many little touches that give this familiar music a freshness that projects its originality. There is also a slightly elegiac feel to the phrasing here as if Boult, no sentimentalist, was nevertheless aware that his *Enigma* days must inevitably be numbered. Yet the faster variations have the vitality and brio that one might expect from a younger conductor. The LSO's performance is excellent and the recording too.

Awards 1987

The Planets Women's voices of the **Montreal Symphony Chorus and Orchestra / Charles Dutoit**
Decca Penguin 460 606-2DP Ⓑ
(53 minutes: DDD)
Recorded 1986 ●●●

The Planets is undoubtedly Holst's most famous work and its success is surely deserved. The musical characterization is as striking as its originality of conception: the association of 'Saturn' with old age, for instance, is as unexpected as it is perceptive. Bax introduced Holst to astrology and while he wrote the music he became fascinated with horoscopes, so it is the astrological associations that are paramount, although the linking of 'Mars' (with its enormously powerful 5/4 rhythms) and war also reflects the time of composition. Throughout, the work's invention is as memorable as its vivid orchestration is full of infinite detail. No recording can reveal it all but this one comes the closest to doing so. Dutoit's individual performance is in a long line of outstanding recordings.

The Planets[a] (includes extra version of Neptune with original ending). Lyric Movement **C Matthews** Pluto
Tim Pooley *va* **Hallé Orchestra** and
[a]**Choir** (Women's Voices) **/ Mark Elder**
Hyperion CDA67270 (75 minutes: DDD) Ⓕ

Unusually popular repertoire for Hyperion; but the special interest here is *Pluto*, commissioned by the Hallé's outgoing director Kent Nagano to illustrate the eighth planet, discovered only in 1930. For proper effect, though, it obviously demands a decent *Planets*, which happily it receives. If the Hallé lack the glitz and sheen of Dutoit's and Karajan's orchestras, then they offer a warmly idiomatic sound which suits their new director Mark Elder's generally expansive yet detailed approach, and the full-blooded, rather forward recording.

Mars, with balefully clear percussion, steers a middle way between the machine-gun tempo favoured by the composer and Haitink's leaden grimness (Philips – nla). *Venus* and *Mercury* are sensuous, even lingering, but *Jupiter* is refreshingly vibrant and dancing. Tension slackens somewhat in *Saturn*, but spaciousness and detail make more sense of *Uranus* than usual, although the transcendent organ *glissando* is somewhat underwhelming.

Neptune is suprisingly lush, a distinctly fleshly Mystic with a chorus as alluring as ethereal. Which, in the main version here, fades out to *Pluto* – a flashing *scherzo*, inspired by the rushing particles of the so-called 'solar wind'. Matthews wisely avoids Holstian pastiche, linking it to the original by tempo – Holst's favoured 5/4 – and sound; celesta, glockenspiel and jittery percussion create fleeting reminiscences of the other planets. The result is appealing, postmodern but lyrical, yet ultimately unsatisfying.

Like a spectacularly modern wing grafted onto a classic building, it stimulates by contrast, yet the uneasy lack of unity diminishes both. A separate piece, linked companionably rather than umbilically, might have been a rather more effective choice. As the composer disarmingly admits, Pluto's planetary status is pretty dubious, anyway. The *Lyric Movement*, with a fine soloist, raises hopes for some more rare Holst from this particular team.

The Planets. Egdon Heath, H172
BBC Symphony Chorus and Orchestra /
Sir Andrew Davis
Teldec British Line 4509-94541-2 (64 minutes: DDD) Ⓜ
Recorded 1993

This is a mightily impressive account of *The Planets*. The high spot of Davis's reading is undoubtedly 'Saturn', whose remorseless tread has rarely seemed more implacable. Aided by orchestral playing that is both memorably concentrated and rapt, Holst's textures in the closing section acquire a breathtaking translucency, and how memorably the BBC SO brass thrusts home the terrifying central climax at 5'34". 'Neptune', too, is exceptionally successful: ethereally delicate *tremolando* harps set the scene for a tone picture of exquisite beauty, graced by choral work of notable purity from the women of the BBC Symphony Chorus. Elsewhere, 'Mercury' darts hither and thither in suitably impish fashion. 'Venus' is cool and chaste: if the BBC violins can't quite command the bloom and sheen of the very finest groups, the liquidity and poise of the woodwind are most striking. The burst of energy at the close of 'Jupiter' is genuinely exhilarating. The spectacularly ample sound certainly makes the mischievous antics of 'Uranus' a feast for the ears, and Davis handles the coda superbly, plunging the listener into a world which is unnerving in its bleakness. Davis shows comparable perception in the similarly remote terrain of *Egdon Heath*. He succeeds in conveying much of the sombre intensity of Holst's cloud-hung evocation.

The Hymn of Jesus, H140

The Hymn of Jesus, H140[a]. First Choral Symphony, H155[b]
[b]**Felicity Palmer** *sop* [a]**St Paul's Cathedral Choir;**
[a]**London Symphony Chorus; London Philharmonic**
[b]**Choir and Orchestra /** [a]**Sir Charles Groves,**
[b]**Sir Adrian Boult**
EMI British Composers CDM5 65128-2
(72 minutes: ADD). Texts included. Ⓜ
Recorded 1974 and 1977

When it first appeared in 1978, Groves's account of *The Hymn of Jesus* was generally rated a finer effort than Boult's 1961 Decca recording. The authority and honesty of the former's direction is impressive. True, orchestral discipline could at times be tighter, but the choral singing is never less than very commendable. It should, however, be pointed out that Groves's achievement has since been outshone by Richard Hickox (reviewed overleaf), who in turn cannot quite match the extraordinary fervour and intensity of Sir Malcolm Sargent in his pioneering 1944 account. The really good news here, though, is Boult's powerful 1974 première recording of the awesome *Choral Symphony*. This was one of Holst's most ambitious, imaginative and questing creations, still under-appreciated to this day. It contains pages that are among the most original he conceived, not least the opening

'Invocation to Pan' and extraordinarily intense setting of the *Ode on a Grecian Urn*. The sound in both items is satisfyingly full and immediate.

Seven Partsongs

Seven Partsongs, H162. A Choral Fantasia, H177. A Dirge for Two Veterans, H121. Ode to Death, H144
Patricia Rozario *sop* **London Symphony Chorus; Joyful Company of Singers; City of London Sinfonia / Richard Hickox**
Chandos CHAN9437 (59 minutes: DDD) Ⓕ
Texts included. Recorded 1994

It is the First World War that is the unnamed, ever-felt presence here. 'I float this carol with joy, with joy to thee O Death', chants Walt Whitman with that willed mystical intoxication that proved so surprisingly attractive to both Holst and Vaughan Williams, composers who could face reality soberly enough and in Holst's case often with a bleak, spare beauty of sound that takes and bestows only a hard-won comfort. Listening even to the relatively 'light' and partially happy Bridges settings (the *Seven Partsongs*), one becomes aware of a hollow, half-anxious feeling, located in that mysterious area of midriff wherein these undefined apprehensions take their dwelling. With it comes a musician's cherishing of silence, as though the music which intrudes upon it must be most finely attuned if it is to justify the presumption. Death emerges from its temporary hiding place in the seventh ('Assemble, all ye maidens') and then, for the rest of the recital, comes into its kingdom. Most explicitly, the *Dirge for Two Veterans* takes up the 'full-keyed bugles' of war, and that was written in the last months of 1914. In the *Ode to Death* (1931) and even the partsongs for women's voices, it is surely the dreadful sadness of that war which fills the hollow places and so, for comfort, enhances the apprehension of beauty in music. The programme has a very special value, and the performances are worthy of it.

The Cloud Messenger

The Cloud Messenger, H111[aef]. The Hymn of Jesus, H140[ef]. A Choral Fantasia, H177[bdg]. A Dirge for Two Veterans, H121[dg]. Ode to Death, H144[eg]. Ave Maria, H49[c]. Motets, H159-60[c] – The Evening-Watch. This have I done for my true love, H128[c]. Seven Partsongs, H162[bdg]. O lady, leave that silken thread, H4[c]. Short Partsongs, H13[c] – Soft and gently through my soul. The autumn is old, H1[c]. Winter and the birds, H App I/40[c]
[a]**Della Jones** *mez* [b]**Patricia Rozario** *sop* [c]**Finzi Singers / Paul Spicer;** [d]**Joyful Company of Singers; London Symphony** [e]**Chorus and** [f]**Orchestra,** [g]**City of London Sinfonia / Richard Hickox**
Chandos Two for One ② CHAN241-6 Ⓜ
(147 minutes: DDD). Recorded 1990 ●

The Cloud Messenger is a 43-minute work of considerable imaginative power. Before its previous single issue release it had been virtually forgotten since its disastrous première under the baton of Holst himself in 1913. It shows the composer already working on an epic scale – something which casts light on the subsequent eruption of *The Planets*. It is marvellous to have the work on disc, though it is, as you might expect, uneven. Those who admire the ascetic rigour of Holst's later music may share the reservations of Imogen Holst and find the score disappointingly 'backward'. There are certainly echoes of Vaughan Williams's *A Sea Symphony* and several older models. On the other hand, the glittering approach to the sacred city on Mount Kailasa and the stylised orientalism of the climactic dance are new to British music; another world, the world of 'Venus', is foreshadowed in the closing pages. The text is Holst's own translation from the Sanskrit. One of the few incontrovertible masterpieces in Holst's output, the familiar *Hymn of Jesus* has seldom received a better performance on disc, although the grand acoustics of London's St Jude's impart a certain warm imprecision – the choral singing itself is splendidly crisp – which can blunt the impact of Holst's acerbic harmonies.

Arthur Honegger

French/Swiss 1892-1955

GROVE *Honegger studied from 1911 at the Paris Conservatoire, then returned to Switzerland for military service (1914-15), though Paris remained his home. He was a member of Les Six, and set Cocteau's libretto in his stylised opera Antigone (1927), but he had no time for Satie or for the group's flippancy: he was acutely aware of artistic responsibility and took his guidelines from Bach and Beethoven. His harmony, though fundamentally tonal, is often dense and wide-ranging, set in motion by a vigorous rhythmic propulsion that suggests Baroque formality wielding modern means: that is the manner of his oratorio-style stage works, including Le roi David (1921) and Jeanne d'Arc au bûcher (1938). His other works include five symphonies (1930, 1941, 1946, 1946, 1951), three 'symphonic movements' (Pacific 231, 1923; Rugby, 1928; No 3, 1933), chamber pieces, songs and much incidental music.*

Symphonies

No 1 in C; **No 2** for Strings and Trumpet obbligato in D, H153; **No 3**, H186, 'Liturgique'; **No 4** in A, H191, 'Deliciae basiliensis' **No 5** in D, H202, 'Di tre re'

Symphonies Nos 1-5. Three Symphonic Movements – No 1, H53; 'Pacific 231'; No 2, H67, 'Rugby', H67
Bavarian Radio Symphony Orchestra / Charles Dutoit
Erato Ultima ② 3984-21340-2 (141 minutes: DDD) Ⓑ
Recorded 1982-84 ●

Although a pupil of d'Indy, and someone who may have both learned too much from 1920s Stravinsky and Prokofiev, Honegger is very obviously next generation, musically, and in his response to not one, but two world wars. The music is harmonically daring (there's plenty of writing in two keys at once), dealing in sometimes consecutive, at others simultaneous, but always very bold and often very moving contrasts – gesturally graphic grim realities and possible deliverance or almost escapism – all within a neo-classical framework. Dutoit is perhaps rather better at the often seraphic beauty of the deliverance and escapism – for example, the haven of the Fourth Symphony is the single most successful performance here – than he is with the music's muscular driving force and dark power. Nevertheless his cycle is a considerable achievement, and the Munich recordings, though not as vividly present as some, are faultlessly balanced and satisfyingly natural. In short, at the price, an attractive starting-point for the Honegger symphonies. Minimal insert-notes, as you'd expect from these Ultima reissues.

Honegger Symphonies Nos 2 and 3
Stravinsky Concerto in D
Berlin Philharmonic Orchestra / Herbert von Karajan
DG The Originals 447 435-2GOR (72 minutes: ADD) Ⓜ
Recorded 1969 ○○○

Karajan's performances of these Honegger symphonies enjoy legendary status – and rightly so. This recording remains in a class of its own for sheer beauty of sound and flawless ensemble. The French critic, Bernard Gavoty, once spoke rather flightily of Karajan 'transcending emotions and imparting to them that furnace heat that makes a work of genius give off light if brought to the desired temperature' – but it's true! There is a luminous quality and an incandescence about these performances. The Stravinsky Concerto in D major was written within a year of the *Symphonie liturgique* and may perhaps be a little too 'cultured' and not spiky enough for some tastes. The lightness of touch, sprightliness of rhythm and flawless ensemble of the Berlin Philharmonic Orchestra are an absolute joy in themselves.

Symphony No 2, H153. Three Symphonic Movements Nos 1-3. Pastorale d'été, H31. Monopartita, H204
Zurich Tonhalle Orchestra / David Zinman
Decca 455 352-2DH (70 minutes: DDD) Ⓕ
Recorded 1998

With the Symphony for strings David Zinman gives us a handful of shorter orchestral pieces ranging from the well-known to a comparative rarity, the *Monopartita*. This was Honegger's last orchestral work and has even been referred to as a Sixth Symphony which has imploded. It finds the composer at his most resourceful: one of its episodes hints at the slow movement of the *Deliciae basiliensis* Symphony. The Tonhalle does not offer string playing that can match Karajan's Berlin Philharmonic, but Zinman can more than hold his own against most comers. He gets responsive and sensitive playing from the orchestra. A finely characterised *Pastoral d'été* and a *Pacific 231* that sounds as if it is coming in on time, and very good Decca sound enhance the attractions of this issue.

Symphonies Nos 3 and 5. Three Symphonic Movements – No 1
Danish National Radio Symphony Orchestra / Neeme Järvi
Chandos CHAN9176 (57 minutes: DDD) Ⓕ
Recorded 1992

There is a resemblance in the Fifth to the opening bars (with their triads in contrary motion) to Milhaud's *Moses* and one wonders whether it was a deliberate tribute or merely fortuitous. Be that as it may, the Fifth remains one of Honegger's most individual scores, and this recording serves it well. There is nothing restrained here and even if the finale does not quite match the sheer exhilaration and gusto of Serge Baudo's wonderful Supraphon account from the early 1960s (which now sounds far more full bodied in its new transfer), the Järvi is not far behind: moreover it is very well recorded. So, too, is the rest of the programme and although the playing of the Danish orchestra for Järvi in the Third does not outshine that of the BPO for Karajan this is a very convincing and compelling account. The *Pacific 231* also thunders mightily along the track.

Jeanne d'Arc au bûcher

Françoise Pollet, Michèle Command *sops* **Nathalie Stutzman** *contr* **John Aler** *ten* **Marthe Keller, Georges Wilson, Pierre-Marie Escourrou, Paola Lenzi** *narrs* **Chorus and Children's Voices of French Radio; French National Orchestra / Seiji Ozawa**
DG 429 412-2GH (69 minutes: DDD). Text and translations included. Recorded live in 1989 Ⓕ

Honegger described *Joan of Arc at the stake* as a 'dramatic oratorio', but it is almost impossible to categorise, the two chief characters – Joan and Brother Dominc – being speaking parts, but with a chorus, a children's chorus, and a curiously constituted orchestra including saxophones instead of horns, two pianos and, notably, an ondes martenot which, with its banshee shriek, bloodcurdlingly reinforces the climax as Joan breaks her earthly chains. The action is partly realistic, partly symbolic, unfolding in quasi-cinematic flashbacks. The musical techniques and styles employed by Honegger are extraordinarily varied, with humming and shouting besides singing, and with elements of polyphony, folk-song, baroque dances and jazz rhythms; yet all is fused in a remarkable way to produce a work of gripping power and, in the final scenes, almost intolerable emotional intensity: the beatific *envoi* 'Greater love hath no man ...' is a passage that catches the throat and haunts the mind. Ozawa captured the work's dramatic forces in this public performance, which has been skilfully recorded; Marthe Keller vividly portrays Joan's bewilderment, fervour and agony, John Aler makes a swaggering Procus, and Françoise Pollet is radiant-voiced as the Virgin. Even more than *Le roi David*, this is Honegger's masterpiece.

Alan Hovhaness American 1911-2000

GROVE *Hovhaness studied with Converse at the New England Conservatory. His earliest music, though Romantic in harmony, reflects his interest in Renaissance style; from 1943 he began to incorporate elements of his Armenian heritage, and in the 1950s, when he travelled widely, he embraced non-Western and experimental procedures. From c1960 he took a keen interest in Japanese and Korean music, which affected his style; only in the 1970s did he return to a more Western style, richer and more spacious. An individual feature is his way of treating elements (harmony, tone colour etc) as either predominant or else neutral; any note may be exclusively linear, vertical, textural or rhythmic. Most of his work is broadly religious in inspiration; he is enormously prolific, having reached his first 60 symphonies in the mid-1980s, with corresponding production in other orchestral music, choral and solo vocal works, piano and chamber music.*

Khaldis, Op 91

Khaldis, Op 91[a]. Mount Katahdin, Op 405[b]. Fantasy, Op 16[c]
[ab]**Martin Berkofsky,** [c]**Alan Hovhaness** *pfs*
[a]**William Rohdin,** [a]**Dan Cahn,** [a]**Francis Bonny,** [a]**Patrick Dougherty** *tpts* [a]**Neal Boyar** *perc*
Crystal CD814 (52 minutes: ADD) Ⓕ
Recorded [c]1970, [a]1972 and [b]1999

Khaldis (1951) has a connection with the late Hovhaness's well-known *St Vartan* symphony (1950) in their common use of a quartet of trumpets: the composer wanted a piece he could play with them and a percussionist alone. It is a striking work – named from the god of the universe of the pre-Armenian Urarduan people – full of volcanic, apocalyptic visions. The even-movement structure has the feel of a set of studies rather than an integrated concerto, the brass tending to play en bloc and one movement scored as if for some primordial trio of giants.

The sonata *Mount Katahdin* (1986-87) does not sound almost a career later than *Khaldis*. The four movements resemble the sequence of a Bach orchestral suite, with the imposing opening 'Solenne', half as long again as the rest of the work, succeeded by three tiny movements, lighter in character and acting as foils for the first. The central 'Jhala of Larch Trees' is particularly lovely. Berkofsky plays with evident love and conviction, and these are persuasive performances, whether from 1972 (*Khaldis*, previously released on Poseidon – nla) or 1999 (*Mount Katahdin*). Most fascinating of all is Hovhaness's own account of the *Fantasy*, written *c*1936 and also once available on a Poseidon LP. A mesmeric performance of a mesmeric piece, the 10 sections or 'steps' built from Indian ragas utilise Cowellesque devices such as playing the strings inside the instrument with fingers, plectrum, marimba mallet or timpani stick. The sound overall is acceptable but the remastered *Khaldis* and *Fantasy* are a touch lacking in depth.

Symphonies

Khrimian Hairig, Op 49. The Holy City, Op 218. Psalm and Fugue, Op 40*a*. Kohar, Op 66. Symphony No 17, Op 203, 'Symphony for Metal Orchestra'
Chris Gekker *tpt* **Manhattan Chamber Orchestra / Richard Auldon Clark**
Koch International Classics 37289-2 (53 minutes: DDD). Recorded 1995 Ⓕ

The lengthiest offering here (at just over 20 minutes) is the *Symphony for Metal Orchestra* (the 17th of Hovhaness's 67 symphonies) which was composed in 1963 shortly after a visit to Japan. Scored for the singular combination of six flutes, three trombones and metallic percussion, its four contemplative movements incorporate elements of Japanese *gagaku* music together with sounds inspired by the Shó (a Japanese mouth-organ, here imitated by the flutes). Rather more rewarding is *The Holy City*, a highly evocative, nine-and-a-half-minute essay for trumpet, harp, chimes and strings dating from 1967 and full of atmospheric sonorities. Chris Gekker is the superb trumpet soloist both here and in the serene, yet deceptively purposeful *Khrimian Hairig* (composed in 1944 and revised four years later), which takes its name from 'a heroic Armenian priest'. The glowing string textures in the *Psalm and Fugue* (1941) cast quite a spell, as do the hypnotic, mantra-like melodic lines of *Kohar* (1946), another Armenian-inspired creation, scored for flute, cor anglais, timpani and strings. Richard Auldon Clark and his New York group give outstandingly sympathetic performances. Really excellent sound, too.

String Quartets

Hovhaness Four Bagatelles, Op 30. String Quartets – No 1, Op 8, 'Jupiter'; No 3, Op 208 No 1, 'Reflections on my Childhood'; No 4, Op 208 No 2, 'The Ancient Tree'. Suite from String Quartet No 2 – Gamelan in Sosi Style; Spirit Murmur; Hymn
Z Long Song of the Ch'in
Shanghai Quartet (WeiGang Li, HongGang Li *vns* Zheng Wang *va* James Wilson *vc*) Ⓕ
Delos DE3162 (69 minutes: DDD). Recorded 1994 ●

The likeable First Quartet of 1936 boasts, like Mozart's *Jupiter* Symphony, a four-part fugue of impressive rigour (hence the work's subtitle). Next come three out of the seven pithy movements that comprise the Second Quartet from 1952: the concluding 'Hymn' is a particularly affecting creation. The Third and Fourth Quartets were inspired by childhood memories. The former basks in a soothing, supplicatory glow, with some occasional touches of Eastern promise (aural reminders of the composer's Armenian roots), whereas its more nostalgic companion is a sweetly lyrical essay of beguiling euphony and striking resonance.

Delos's collection begins with the haunting, perfectly crafted *Four Bagatelles* (delightful miniatures, these) and ends with *Song of the*

Ch'in by the Chinese composer, Zhou Long: the 'ch'in' is a traditional Chinese zither and this imaginative, fastidiously conceived piece from 1985 attempts to convey the piquant sounds of that ancient instrument through the 'modern' medium of the string quartet. These are consistently pure-toned, beautifully rapt performances from the talented young Shanghai Quartet, and Delos's sound is warm and true.

Herbert Howells British 1892-1983

Howells studied with Stanford and Wood at the Royal College of Music, where he taught from 1920 almost to his death. He also succeeded Holst at St Paul's Girls' School (1932-62) and was professor of music at London University. His music is within an English diatonic tradition embracing Elgar, Walton and Vaughan Williams. The earlier works include two piano concertos and chamber pieces, but most of his music is choral, including c15 anthems, a concert Requiem (Hymnus Paradisi, 1938, first performed 1950), masses, anthems and motets and some fine songs. Deeply tinged by the English choral tradition, Howells's music reflects a subtle and fastidious craftsman who was capable of a restrained, individual eloquence.

Piano Concertos

Piano Concertos[a] – No 1 in C minor, Op 4; No 2 in C, Op 39. Penguinski
[a]**Howard Shelley** *pf* **BBC Symphony Orchestra / Richard Hickox**
Chandos CHAN9874 (71 minutes: DDD) Ⓕ
Recorded 2000 ●

An astonishing revelation, especially to anyone who still thinks of Herbert Howells as a nostalgic English rhapsodist, more at home in an organ loft than a concert hall. The First Piano Concerto is very early (1914 – Howells was 22); it has not been performed for many years because its last few bars are missing (John Rutter has provided them). It reveals the young Howells as more Russian than English – the dazzlingly flamboyant keyboard writing is strongly reminiscent of Rachmaninov – and with hardly a trace of English reserve as he brandishes theme after theme, intensifying many of them to heights of impassioned eloquence. And yet in this quite uncharacteristic student work there are a few hints of his later reticence, one being the very opening, where double-basses, then horn, then low woodwind hesitantly suggest a splendid theme which only then arrives, sweeping nobly in the strings. One or two lyrical paragraphs also suggest the 'real' Herbert Howells. But who, the Second Piano Concerto demands, was he? This work was abused at its première (one critic shouted 'Thank God that's over!') and Howells, deeply wounded, withdrew it immediately. Indeed, although it's a lot closer to 'real' Howells in its rhapsodic lyricism, there's another quality (labelled in the score 'hard and bright') which is angular, sometimes dissonant, tough and determined.

Surely we shall get closer to the real Howells, favourite pupil and lifelong admirer of the arch-conservative Stanford, in *Penguinski*, from its title an obvious satire on Stravinsky? But in fact the sidelong glances at him are admiring and affectionate, and the robust humour is Howells' own. There is more to him than we had imagined, this disc entertainingly demonstrates, and his stature is increased, not diminished, by the realisation that he was once an exuberant romantic, that his ears were sharp and that he had a sense of humour. Enthusiastic, virtuoso, very slightly rough-cornered performances and a sumptuously rich recording.

Threnody

King's Herald. Paradise Rondel. Fantasia[a]. Threnody[a]. Pastoral Rhapsody. Procession
[a]**Moray Welsh** *vc* **London Symphony Orchestra / Richard Hickox**
Chandos CHAN9410 (58 minutes: DDD) Ⓕ
Recorded 1995 ●

This delightful, moving disc offers a whole sequence of orchestral works which for whatever reason Howells hid from the world. Only since his death have such pieces as these emerged, and one can only marvel that so accomplished and imaginative a writer for the orchestra should have let any of them be buried. Howells completed the short score of *Threnody* with piano accompaniment in 1935, his first task after his son's death. Probably planned as the slow movement of a three-movement cello concerto, it is given here in the orchestration made by Christopher Palmer for the Howells centenary concert in 1992. More direct in style and structure, it is an effective pendant to the *Fantasia*, with the two movements together forming a rhapsodic concerto lasting almost half an hour.

The other major piece is the *Pastoral Rhapsody*, written earlier in 1923 and more conventionally English except for a radiant climax with anglicised echoes of *Daphnis* and *Petrushka*. In his note Lewis Foreman speculates that Howells may have let the piece be forgotten after a couple of performances, feeling that Vaughan Williams's *Pastoral* Symphony was too close a model. In fact the *Rhapsody* is totally distinct, and so is the *Paradise Rondel*, named after a Cotswold village: a generally vigorous movement dating from 1925, which over a shorter span is full of sharp contrasts, including one passage which in its addition of a piano offers clear echoes of the 'Russian Dance' from *Petrushka*.

The collection opens with the boldly extrovert *King's Herald*, bright with Waltonian fanfares. Drawn from a brass band piece of 1934, it was arranged for orchestra as a Coronation offering in 1937. *Procession*, which closes the sequence, is the earliest work here, adapted from a piano piece written in 1920, and in this orchestration of 1922 brings more echoes of *Petrushka*, again reflecting Howells's response to appearances in

London by Diaghilev's Ballets Russes. Helped by rich, atmospheric sound, Hickox draws performances both brilliant and warmly persuasive from the LSO, with Moray Welsh a movingly expressive soloist in the concertante works.

Suite for Orchestra, 'The B's'

Suite for Orchestra, 'The B's'. Three Dances[a]. In Green Ways[b]
[b]**Yvonne Kenny** *sop* [a]**Lydia Mordkovitch** *vn*
London Symphony Orchestra / Richard Hickox
Chandos CHAN9557 (65 minutes: DDD). Text and translation included. Recorded 1996 Ⓕ

Both *The B's* (1914) and *Three Dances* (1915) are from Howells's student days. The former is a delightful orchestral suite celebrating Howells's circle of closest friends at the Royal College of Music, each of the five movements bearing as its subtitle the nickname of a colleague. As with many of Howells's student offerings, the infectious confidence and sheer craft are remarkable. Completed just a couple of months after *The B's*, the *Three Dances* for violin and orchestra reveal a similarly assured touch and engaging charm. Perhaps the most captivating of the set is the wonderfully serene *Quasi lento*, with its long-breathed melody of seraphic loveliness. By contrast the first dance is all sunny, carefree vigour and the brief third somewhat akin to a boisterous Irish jig. Lydia Mordkovitch plays with enormous fervour, but in the middle dance she doesn't have quite the radiance or security of RLPO leader Malcolm Stewart on Hyperion; Hickox's accompaniment, too, is marginally 'bluffer' than that of Handley's, though still full of appealing bonhomie. *In Green Ways* had its origins in a song-cycle for high voice and small orchestra written the same year as the *Three Dances*. In 1928 Howells extensively revised his earlier thoughts, and the set exists in two versions, one with piano and another with orchestral backing. It takes its name from a collection of poetry by James Stephens, whose poem 'The Goat Paths' forms the emotional kernel of the whole sequence in Howells's sublime treatment. Yvonne Kenny sings radiantly, with Hickox and the LSO as model partners. The airy recording complements this hugely enjoyable release.

Organ Sonata No 2

Organ Sonata No 2. Six Pieces (1940-45)
Graham Barber *org*
Priory PRCD524 (67 minutes: DDD) Ⓕ
Recorded on the organ of Hereford Cathedral in 1995

These are powerful, authoritative performances which ooze the spirit of Howells – that odd mixture of emotional detachment with a hint of deep personal passion, an undercurrent of tragedy and an almost improvisatory fluidity of structure. The Sonata has a formal structure which makes it easy to follow while the *Six Pieces* give such a kaleidoscopic array of organ colours that the ear is continually enchanted. The Hereford organ is a lovely instrument. Priory has, in focusing the microphones on the organ, expunged much of the building's aural ambience, but the sound is an utter delight to the ear.

Evening Services

Evening Services – G; Collegium Sancti Johannis Cantabrigiense; New College, Oxford; Collegium Regale; Sarum; York. Magnificat and Nunc Dimittis
The Collegiate Singers / Andrew Millinger with **Richard Moorhouse** *org*
Priory PRCD745 (65 minutes: DDD) Ⓕ
Recorded 2000

Howells wrote 20 settings of the evening canticles, which, with their brothers of the morning, will occupy five discs in this useful, boldly conceived, enterprise. Despite giving it a warm welcome, however, one can't help wishing the series had been arranged chronologically. Paul Andrews's introduction tells of three periods (1918-41, 1945-57, 1966-75) and so from the start interests us in Howells's development. This first volume duly opens with the first setting, but it is followed by the Sarum Service of 1966, and the programme continues to jump around so that the opportunity for which the essay prepared us is withdrawn.

That initial setting, the freshly vigorous work of the Stanford pupil, sets out on the long life's musical journey with bone and muscle. The gentler passages have a light-footed grace, and in exultation the spirit flares; this is the music of purposeful movement, where the more 'Howells' he becomes the more the firm lines of the Stanford pupil dissolve, and the nearer he draws to a music of mystical stasis. The opening of the Collegium Regale *Magnificat* has something of this, the great thing being that he can still pull out of it (with the strong-boned 'He hath shown strength with his arm', for instance). It would have been good to follow the order of composition, seeing which parts of his musical system he developed and which he left unexercised.

The other slightly hesitant, or faltering, element in this welcome release concerns the choice of a choir of mixed voices. The women scrupulously adhere to the tonal ideal, but boy trebles and male altos have a distinctive quality, and Howells's own sound is less distinctive without them. It is an extremely good choir, and they are under careful, intelligent direction, yet making a chance comparison with the choir of Bristol Cathedral in the G major setting one can't help rejoicing in a character (individual as a face) which those trebles possessed and for which the Collegiate sopranos substitute a collective identity somewhat de-personalised.

The recorded sound is fine, balance between choir and the excellent organist is well judged, and the acoustic resonance is sufficient to form an appropriate setting while preserving the clear articulation. The selection here includes two première recordings (the York Service and the 1941 setting for men's voices, performed, as the score suggests, by women). The most colourful and frequently heard, the Collegium Regale, brings this first volume to an exciting close.

Requiem

Choral and Organ Works. Requiem[a]. Collegium Regale – Communion Service[ab]. St Paul's Service[ab]. Like as the hart[a]. Long, long ago[a]. Take Him, Earth, for Cherishing[a]. Organ Rhapsody No 3[b]. Paean[b]
[b]Ian Farrington *org* **[a]St John's College Choir, Cambridge / Christopher Robinson**
Naxos 8 554659 (76 minutes: DDD). Texts included Ⓢ
Recorded 1999

Howells, probably more than any other composer, extended the cathedral repertoire in the 20th century. Here his music is performed by one of the best choirs. Under Christopher Robinson, St John's has preserved its distinctive character (the bright tone of its trebles a famous part of it) and, as this record demonstrates, has gained in vigour and clarity of purpose. Immediately notable is the choice of relatively quick speeds. Howells sometimes appears to invite a relaxed style of performance which is not to his advantage. In the Requiem, directions such as 'slowly but with flexible rhythm' and *quasi lento* are themselves fairly flexible, and timings vary (St John's, in the first, 1'38" to the Finzi Singers' 2'40", on Chandos, and in the second *Requiem aeternam* St John's 3'07", Finzi Singers 4'13").

In both, particularly the second, St John's secures the more concentrated attention. Moreover, its tempo suits the acoustic. This applies to a similar comparison with the Choir of King's College in its more reverberant chapel, singing the Communion Service dedicated to it: the more opulent sound matches the broader tempo, St John's achieving (as in the *Sanctus*) clearer effects within a narrower spectrum. Their discs also have in common the *Rhapsody No 3* for organ, and whereas the expansive performance at King's includes a murmurous *pianissimo* next-thing-to-silence, the quicker, more sharply defined one at St John's has a dramatic urgency. The choice of programme is particularly happy, with one of the lesser-known Evening Services (the 'St Paul's') and one of the best-known of Howells's anthems (*Like as the hart*).

Additional recommendation
Requiem
Couplings: Take him, earth, for cherishing.
Vaughan Williams Mass in G minor. Te Deum
Coxwell, Seers *sops* **Chance** *counterten* **Salmon** *ten*
J Best *bass* **Corydon Singers / M Best**
Hyperion CDA66076 (DDD: 10/87) Ⓕ
A fine performance of the *Requiem* and attractive couplings.

Hymnus Paradisi

Hymnus Paradisi[a]. A Kent Yeoman's Wooing Song[b]
Joan Rodgers *sop* **[a]Anthony Rolfe Johnson** *ten*
[b]Alan Opie *bar* **BBC Symphony Chorus and Orchestra / Richard Hickox**
Chandos CHAN9744 (65 minutes: DDD) Texts included. Recorded 1998 Ⓕ

Hymnus Paradisi[a]. Concerto for Strings[b]
[a]Heather Harper *sop* **aRobert Tear** *ten*
[a]Bach Choir; [a]King's College Choir, Cambridge; [a]New Philharmonia Orchestra / Sir David Willcocks; [b]London Philharmonic Orchestra / Sir Adrian Boult
EMI British Composers CDM5 67119-2 Ⓜ
(74 minutes: ADD). Text included. Recorded 1970-73 ◉

Both versions of the *Hymnus Paradisi* are fine, so choice may depend on the couplings. *A Kent Yeoman's Wooing Song* is claimed as a première recording, while the Concerto for Strings has two earlier versions. Both have a vigour of mood and movement which brings the listener back to earth after the ecstatic spirituality of the *Hymnus*. Nobody with a real love of Howells will wish to be without either of these extra pieces. The Concerto was written around the central slow movement, an elegy composed four years earlier after the death of Elgar, who was a personal friend. The outer movements are marked *Allegro assai vivace* and *Allegro vivo (ritmico e giocoso)*, but their vitality is expressed not so much through speed and jollity as by the vigorous musical mind that instinctively works through counterpoint. The *Yeoman's Song* (first performed, in orchestral form, in 1953) originated as a wedding present for Sir Keith Falkner in 1930: very much of the English pastoral school, it would no doubt have been derided as such in its own time, whereas a later audience, less bothered about trends in the 1930s, can accept it more readily for the delightful thing it is. So, both couplings being desirable, choice has not been simplified after all. In the *Hymnus Paradisi*, the new recording has sharper definition, Willcocks from 1970 having a 'fatter' sound. In two movements (Nos 4 and 5) Willcocks is significantly faster and the performance gains from that. More important, he conducts a more impassioned account: the *crescendos* have more intensity and even the *tranquillo* has an emotional concentration, less evident in the Hickox recording, fine as that is. Decisive is the radiant singing of Heather Harper. Joan Rodgers (Hickox) is a lovely singer, and long admired, but the quick vibrato on high notes does not suit here. Harper is ideal; the part might have been written for her. Rolfe-Johnson sings sensitively, as does Robert Tear but with voice in fresher bloom. To sum up, for any Howells fan the rash expenditure on both discs would be amply rewarded.

Missa Sabrinensis

Janice Watson *sop* **Della Jones** *mez* **Martyn Hill** *ten*
Donald Maxwell *bar*
London Symphony Chorus and Orchestra / Gennadi Rozhdestvensky
Chandos CHAN9348 (76 minutes: DDD). Text and translation included. Recorded 1994 Ⓕ ◉

Along with the Stabat mater this 'Mass of the Severn', the river which together with the Wye defined the composer's homeland, shows even more than *Hymnus Paradisi*, the extraordinary, even daunting accomplishment of Howells's complex choral-orchestral polyphonic technique and harmonic language. In *Hymnus Paradisi* and the *Stabat mater* Howells movingly delineates spiritual and sensual responses to the grief of loss. The *Missa Sabrinensis* naturally encompasses a wider, different emotional spectrum, but without sacrificing self-consistency or intensity. It is unique, in English music, analogous perhaps to Janáček's *Glagolitic Mass*, though it could hardly be more different in temper and texture. A richly imploring Kyrie (subtly reworked for the Agnus Dei), a 20-minute Gloria of magnificent range and brilliantly balanced lyricism and exaltation, an exquisitely delicate Benedictus – all this is Howells at his most characteristic and inspired. Perhaps the rhetoric of the Sanctus is less convincing; and the Credo is uneven, yet this still contains fine music, including the most exalted passage in the work, at the words 'Et unam sanctam catholicam et apostolicam Ecclesiam'. The performance isn't always ideal. In the proliferating polyphonic complexes Rozhdestvensky is rather too broad-brush in matters of detail. And the generous-spirited chorus sometimes sound a degree under-prepared or under-directed – or both.

Of the soloists, an authoritative Martyn Hill and outstanding Janice Watson more than compensate for less certain colleagues. But the dominant impression of the performance – helped by a spacious, warm recording – is Rozhdestvensky's full-blooded communication of the rich emotional content, impulsively pointing-up the extremes, the climactic conflagrations, the fragrant lyrical pastures.

Johann Hummel Austrian 1778-1837

GROVE *A child prodigy and a pupil of Mozart (Vienna, 1786-8), Hummel undertook an extended tour (1789-92) throughout northern Europe with his father, arousing particular interest in England, where he met Haydn. Back in Vienna he studied with Albrechtsberger, Salieri and Haydn, giving lessons to support himself. He held a position as Konzertmeister to Prince Nikolaus Esterházy (1804-11) and, after a period of writing piano and chamber music for Vienna, returned to the concert platform. He was Kapellmeister in Stuttgart (1816-18) and Weimar (from 1819), where he conducted the court theatre and many concerts, knew Goethe and other luminaries and still had time to teach and compose; he toured regularly as a pianist and worked tirelessly on his important piano method (1828). The climax of his career came in 1830 with a trip to Paris and London. Despite his public and financial success - he had an excellent business sense and systematised multinational music publishing – he remained a warm and simple person. His playing was praised for its clarity, neatness, evenness, superb tone and delicacy, products of his preference for the light-toned Viennese piano; he excelled at improvisation. Ferdinand Hiller was among his pupils. Hummel wrote some of the finest music of the last years of Classicism, with ornate Italianate melodies and virtuoso embroidery; his later music shows more expression and variety, including imaginative harmony and long flights of lyricism.*

Piano Concertos

Piano Concerto No 4 in E, Op 110. Double Concerto in G, Op 17
Hagai Shaham *vn*
London Mozart Players / Howard Shelley *pf*
Chandos CHAN9687 (63 minutes: DDD) Ⓕ
Recorded 1998 ●

Shelley is outstanding in this music, blending classical and romantic elements perfectly. These two concertos are wonderfully infectious. The E major occupies a kind of bridge between Mozart and Chopin, although Mozart's depth and subtlety are in a different vein. Hummel is more of a show-off, and his music almost smiles at you, its charm and sparkle eschewing any pretentiousness. Throughout, Shelley conveys the music's *joie de vivre*, revelling in the figurative passagework. The Double Concerto may have been inspired by Mozart's *Sinfonia concertante*, K365; it doesn't have the same harmonic or lyrical variety as the E major Concerto, but it is a charming work, especially when so persuasively played. Shelley's well-proportioned piano part is perfectly complemented by Hagai Shaham's sweet-toned violin. Shelley fulfils his dual role admirably, and the London Mozart Players respond well to his playing and conducting. The recorded sound is first-rate. A lovely disc.

Concertino in G, Op 73. Piano Concerto No 5 in A flat, Op 113. Gesellschafts Rondo in D, Op 117
London Mozart Players / Howard Shelley *pf*
Chandos CHAN9558 (59 minutes: DDD) Ⓕ
Recorded 1997

These are decorous rarities played with an assured brilliance and affection. Hummel's Mozartian rather than Chopinesque bias declares itself most obviously in his Op 73 *Concertino*, though even here the figuration has a recognizably Hummelian froth and sparkle. Too charming to be vacuous, such surface brio has little in common with Mozart's depth and subtlety, and for music of greater romantic range and ambition we turn to the A flat major Concerto, with its fuller scoring and lavishly decorated solo part. Lovers of a finespun, operatic cantilena will warm to the central 'Romanze'. The *Gesellschafts Rondo* (offered here in a première recording) commences in solemn *Adagio* vein before turning to a bustling and ceremonious *Vivace*. It may be that Hummel 'puffed, blew and perspired' when he played but he won the admiration of Chopin (a hard master to please) and his sheer style is infectious when projected with such unfailing expertise by Howard Shelley in his dual role as pianist and conductor. The Chandos recordings are exceptionally well balanced.

Awards 1987

Piano Concertos – No 2 in A minor, Op 85; No 3 in B minor, Op 89
Stephen Hough *pf*
English Chamber Orchestra / Bryden Thomson
Chandos CHAN8507 (66 minutes: DDD) Ⓕ ●●●

This is a staggering disc of Hummel's piano concertos played by Stephen Hough. The most obvious comparison is with the piano concertos of Chopin, but whereas those works rely on the grace and panache of the piano line to redeem an often lacklustre orchestral role, the Hummel works have finely conceived orchestral writing and no shortage of original ideas. The piano part is formidable, combining virtuosity of a very high order with a vigour and athleticism that does much to redress Hummel's somewhat tarnished reputation. The A minor Concerto is probably the better known of the works here, with a thrilling rondo finale, but the B minor is no less inventive with some breath-taking writing in the piano's upper registers. This disc makes strong demands to be heard: inventive and exciting music, a masterly contribution from Stephen Hough, fine orchestral support from the ECO under Thomson and a magnificent recording.

Piano Trios

Piano Trios – E flat, Op 12; G, Op 35; G, Op 65; E flat, Op 96
Beaux Arts Trio (Ida Kavafian *vn* Peter Wiley *vc* Menahem Pressler *pf*)
Philips 446 077-2PX (69 minutes: DDD) Ⓜ
Recorded 1996 ●

These are delightful, intelligent and witty performances of some very attractive music. The Op 12 work is fresh and untroubled, taking delight in the easy mastery of counterpart that was one of Hummel's qualities, and the Beaux Arts Trio plays it with a lively sense of enjoyment that suits it ideally. Hummel was not a profound composer, but he was an immensely talented one and the variety of his invention is remarkable. He never forgot Mozart, as can be heard in the G major Trio of 1811, and he kept an ear on current developments without changing his essentially classical approach to music. Romantic ideas were accommodated rather than imitated or seriously taken up. The Beaux Arts players understand the balance well, and do excellent justice to all these works.

Solo Piano Works

Rondo in E flat, Op 11. Piano Sonata No 2 in E flat, Op 13. Capriccio in F, Op 49. Variations on a theme from Gluck's 'Armide' in F, Op 57. Bagatelles, Op 107 – La contemplazione; Rondo all'ungherese. La bella capricciosa, Polonaise in B flat, Op 55
Howard Shelley *pf*
Chandos CHAN9807 (73 minutes: DDD) Ⓕ
Recorded 1999 ●

This attractive recital shows several sides of Hummel's creative personality, from the classical sonata to the fanciful early romantic character piece, with a good deal of virtuosity thrown in. Most relishable are some of the more contemplative items – including the 'Contemplazione' from his Op 107 bagatelles, a beautiful piece that takes a short theme as its starting point and weaves a poetic fabric around and beyond it. The other bagatelle here, the 'Rondo all'ungherese', is quite a different piece, exploiting ideas of gipsy themes and rhythms with a good deal of wit. Both respond splendidly to Howard Shelley's playing, his attentive shaping, his sense of the music's poetry, his springy rhythms. These are latish works, from the mid 1820s; the rather earlier *Capriccio*, Op 49, is another particular success, notable for Shelley's exquisite timing and aristocratic poise in the slow music and his brilliant fingerwork in the fast.

The recital begins with the earliest piece, an 1804 *Rondo* to which Shelley brings crisp phrasing, precise ornaments and happily judged touches of *rubato*. He ends with a sonata of 1805, more classical than much of what has gone before: easy to say that the style is Beethovenian with less exalted content, but the central *Adagio* is a fine piece with a vein of nobility of its own. The other items are the ingenious Gluck variations, in which Shelley shows a fine command of piano sonorities and rhythms, as well as ample brilliance in the closing pages, and the polonaise *La bella capricciosa*, which moves from a gentle, unassuming start to a coruscating finish. The recording is a model of clear and rich piano tone.

Englebert Humperdinck

German 1854-1921

GROVE *Humperdinck studied at the Cologne Conservatory (1872-76) and at the Royal Music School in Munich (1877-79), meeting Wagner in Naples and assisting him with Parsifal at Bayreuth (1881-82). After interludes in Paris, Spain, Cologne and Mainz (working for B Schotts Sohne), he moved to Frankfurt as a teacher and opera critic, also writing his most famous work, Hänsel and Gretel (1890-93; given its début at Weimar under Richard Strauss); by 1900 he was in Berlin, teaching, composing operas and writing Shakespearean incidental music (among his most successful work). The operatic version of Königskinder, another characteristic piece in his naive, folklike style, was first performed in New York in 1910; like Hänsel und Gretel it started from simple song settings and went through an intermediate stage to a full opera, showing Wagnerian harmonic and textural influences.*

Hänsel und Gretel

Elisabeth Grümmer *sop* Hänsel; **Elisabeth Schwarzkopf** *sop* Gretel; **Maria von Ilosvay** *mez* Gertrud; **Josef Metternich** *bar* Peter; **Anny Felbermayer** *sop* Sandman, Dew Fairy; **Else Schürhoff** *mez* Witch 🄷

Choir of Loughton High School for Girls; Bancroft's School Choir; Philharmonia Orchestra / Herbert von Karajan
EMI Great Recordings of the Century mono ② CMS5 67061-2 (108 minutes: ADD). Notes, text and translation included. Recorded 1953 Ⓜ

This new CD transfer has opened up the mono sound, putting air round the voices and instruments, giving presence. Where EMI's earlier transfer of this set (nla) sounds disappointingly flat, a little gauzy, damped down, this one is brighter, clearer, fuller, with textures clarified. The voices too are better defined and separated. A full stereo recording would have been better still, but it was this recording which Walter Legge would often cite in conversation, when he mounted his curious hobby-horse, questioning the value of stereo over mono. The scene he picked on was where children hear the cuckoo in the forest: there the distancing of the cuckoo-call does indeed simulate stereo atmosphere, but that is far clearer this time than last. As for the performance, it remains a classic, with Karajan plainly in love with the music, and with the two principals singing immaculately. This is not for those who resist the child-voice inflexion of Schwarzkopf and Grümmer, but everyone else will register the mastery in singing and acting. The thinness of Anny Felbermayer's voice as the Sandman is an unwelcome contrast, but this is otherwise a satisfyingly Germanic team, and it is good to have it sounding so fresh.

Additional recommendation
Hänsel und Gretel
Fassbaender Hänsel **Popp** Gretel **Vienna Philharmonic Orchestra / Solti**
Decca ② 455 063-2DMO2 (108 minutes: ADD: 11/88) Ⓜ
A fine mid-price alternative though there's nothing cut-price about the casting. Fassbaender and Popp are delightful in the title roles and other treats include Walter Berry as the Father and the lovely Norma Burrowes as the Sandman. Solti draws gorgeous playing from the VPO.

Sigismondo d'India Italian c1582-1629

GROVE *As a young man d'India travelled in Italy, notably to Florence, and in 1611 he became chamber music director at the Turin court; he left in 1623, working in Modena and Rome. His five books Le musiche (1609-23) contain chamber monodies, varied in style but often of great emotional intensity, and duets; he also published eight volumes of madrigals (1606-24), some highly chromatic and expressive, villanellas and motets.*

Il terzo libro de madrigali

La Venexiana (Rossana Bertini, Nadia Ragni *sops* Giuseppe Maletto, Sandro Naglia *tens* Daniele Carnovich *bass* Paul Beie *lte* Franco Pavan *theorbo* Fabio Bonizzoni *hpd*) **/ Claudio Cavina** *counterten*
Glossa GCD920903 (57 minutes: DDD). Texts and translations included. Recorded 1997 Ⓕ

D'India's Terzo libro closely resembles Monteverdi's Fifth Book. Both contain a number of pieces incorporating a basso continuo, and both close with a series of madrigals in which the independent bass plays an essential rather than a merely decorative role. In these, the most forward-looking pieces in both collections, the bass becomes the foundation of a structure characterised by that polarity between lower and upper voices that is the hallmark of the new 17th-century manner. There are other similarities too, such as in the choice of texts, with both composers showing a keen interest in Tasso and Guarini, while d'India's Canzone di lontananza strongly recalls Monteverdi's Lamento d'Arianna. Monteverdi apart, d'India's most obvious stylistic debts are to the music of the Neapolitan school, and above all to the late madrigals of Gesualdo. The language of most of the madrigals in d'India's Third Book is highly rhetorical and discontinuous even to the point of fragmentation, with sudden shifts of mood and colour. La Venexiana has a full-blooded and mosaic-like approach which maintains its intensity even across the frequent silences in the narrative. D'India's is a vivid language of gesture, made up of individual pristine moments, and the ensemble's carefully shaded punctuation of the architecture of the whole is telling and dramatic.

Vincent d'Indy French 1851-1931

GROVE *D'Indy studied with Lavignac from 1865 and with Franck at the Paris Conservatoire from 1872, becoming Franck's staunchest adherent. From here he gained his devotion to what he saw as the standards of German symphonism and in 1894 he was the leading founder of the Schola Cantorum, set up as a Franckist conservatory. In his own music he insisted on logical construction, preferring sonata and variation forms, though his scoring could be brilliant and his contrapuntal skill is often at the service of airiness rather than density. He also contrasted Wagnerism (three Wallenstein overtures, 1873-81) with use of folksongs from the Ardèche (Symphonie sur un chant montagnard franc;ais for piano and orchestra, 1886). Other works include two more symphonies (1903, 1916-18), the symphonic variations Istar (1896), operas (Le chant de la cloche, 1883, performed 1912; Fervaal, 1897 ; L'étranger, 1903), motets, songs, chamber and piano music.*

Symphonies

Symphony No 2 in B flat, Op 57. Souvenirs, Op 62
Monte Carlo Philharmonic Orchestra / James DePreist
Koch International Classics 37280-2 (64 minutes: DDD). Recorded 1994 Ⓕ

D'Indy's Second Symphony (1902-03) is a mighty utterance, epic in ambition and scale, yet tightly knit too. However, for all the intellectual strength of the writing, there is also plenty of tenderness and nobility on display. D'Indy's scoring, too, is rich and colourful. This is, in short, a most imposing and rewarding piece, and anyone who has ever fallen under the spell of the symphonies of, say, Chausson, Dukas or Magnard should hasten to make its acquaintance. The coupling on this Koch disc is *Souvenirs*, an eloquent and moving poem for orchestra from 1906 which d'Indy dedicated to his wife Isabelle, who had died the previous year. James DePreist presides over a finely prepared, characterful pair of performances and the Monte Carlo Philharmonic, though not of the first rank, responds with striking commitment, while the recording has great warmth and naturalness.

Symphony No 3, Op 70, 'de bello gallico'. Saugefleurie, Op 21. Souvenirs, Op 62
Strasbourg Philharmonic Orchestra / Theodore Guschlbauer
Auvidis Valois V4686 (72 minutes: DDD) Ⓕ
Recorded 1992

Souvenirs is a haunting, imaginatively scored tone-poem that starts with what sounds like a ghostly premonition of Shostakovich's 11th Symphony, then proceeds to varieties of chromatic lyricism that recall the Debussy of *Pelléas* and the lone Symphony of Ernest Chausson. The Third Symphony, a highly inventive commentary on aspects of the Great War, suggests a specific programme and is an ambiguous, loosely constructed piece that extends one's limited experience of its composer. Guschlbauer's broadly sympathetic readings are more appreciative of the music's *lent et calm* than its *vif et agité*. Essential listening for incurable romantics.

John Ireland British 1879-1962

GROVE *Ireland studied at the Royal College of Music, first as a pianist, then as a composer under Stanford (1897-1901), under whom he gained command of a solid Brahmsian style radically altered during the next two decades by the impressions of Debussy, Ravel and Stravinsky. The result was a sequence of lyrical piano pieces, but also substantial chamber works, including two piano trios (1906, 1917) and two violin sonatas (1909, 1917). Meanwhile he served as organist and choirmaster at St Luke's, Chelsea (1904-26), later returning to the RCM to teach (1923-39). Postwar works include the symphonic rhapsody Mai-Dun (1921, one of many works suggestive of English landscape), the Piano Concerto (1930), a classic of 20th-century English music, and Legend for piano and orchestra (1933).*

A Downland Suite

A Downland Suite (arr Ireland and Bush). Orchestral Poem in A minor. Concertino pastorale. Two Symphonic Studies (arr Bush)
City of London Sinfonia / Richard Hickox
Chandos CHAN9376 (64 minutes: DDD) Ⓕ
Recorded 1994 ⚬

Hickox gives a sensitive account of the *Downland Suite* and extracts great expressive intensity from the glorious second movement 'Elegy'. The *Concertino pastorale* is another fine work, boasting a most eloquent opening 'Eclogue' and tenderly poignant 'Threnody', towards the end of which Ireland seems to allow himself a momentary recollection of the haunting opening phrase of his earlier orchestral prelude, *The Forgotten Rite*. In 1969 Ireland's pupil, Geoffrey Bush, arranged two sections of the score for the 1946 film *The Overlanders* which were not incorporated into the 1971 concert suite compiled by Sir Charles Mackerras. The resulting, finely wrought *Two Symphonic Studies* were recorded many years ago by Sir Adrian Boult for Lyrita – no longer available – and Hickox proves just as sympathetic an interpreter, whereas the *Orchestral Poem* in A minor is here receiving its recorded début. This is a youthful essay, completed in 1904, some three years after Ireland's studies with Stanford. It is a worthy rather than especially inspiring effort, with hardly a glimpse of the mature manner to come, save for some particularly beautiful string writing. Hickox makes out a decent enough case for it. However, with rich, refined Chandos sound, this is most enjoyable.

Violin Sonatas

Violin Sonatas – No 1 in D minor; No 2 in A minor. Bagatelle. Berceuse. Cavatina. The Holy Boy (arr cpsr)
Paul Barritt *vn* **Catherine Edwards** *pf*
Hyperion CDA66853 (66 minutes: DDD) Ⓕ
Recorded 1995 ⚬

After many years of neglect by the record companies, Ireland's glorious Second Violin Sonata of 1917 at last appears to be coming into its own again. Here is a satisfying, passionate, superbly disciplined reading that communicates strongly, especially in the lovely *Poco lento quasi adagio* slow movement. Barritt and Edwards put not a foot wrong in the ambitious 1909 Cobbett Prize-winning First Violin Sonata. The rest of the disc is filled with all the four pieces which comprise the remainder of Ireland's output for violin and piano The good-humoured *Bagatelle* (1911) bears a dedication to Marjorie Hayward, who participated in the belated 1913 première of the First Sonata (with Ireland at the piano). Both the *Berceuse* (1902) and *Cavatina* (1904) are early miniatures – tuneful, pretty and unpretentious offerings. Finally, *The Holy Boy* receives radiant advocacy. Recording quality is clean and intimate; balance seems eminently well judged.

Violin Sonatas – No 1 in D minor[a]; No 2 in A minor[b] H
Phantasie Trio in A minor[c]. The Holy Boy[d]
[ac]**Frederick Grinke**, [b]**Albert Sammons** *vns*
[cd]**Florence Hooton** *vc* [ab]**John Ireland**, [c]**Kendall Taylor**, [d]**Lawrence Pratt** *pfs*
Dutton Laboratories Historic Epoch mono CDLX7103 Ⓜ
(73 minutes: ADD). Recorded 1930-45? ⚬⚬

Such was the overwhelming critical acclaim that greeted the March 1917 première of John Ireland's Second Violin Sonata that the 37-year-old composer's reputation was cemented virtually overnight. The performers on that momentous occasion were the legendary Albert Sammons and pianist William Murdoch. Some 13 years later, Sammons finally set down his thoughts on this glorious music for Columbia with Ireland himself at the piano. Quite why this valuable document has never seen the light of day until now is something of a mystery, so all gratitude to Dutton for granting a long overdue lease of life to a nobly spacious rendering of such palpable depth of feeling and unerring insight. As for the First Violin Sonata, Frederick Grinke's 1945 Decca recording (again with the composer) continues to strike as, quite simply, the most perceptive interpretation of this endearing early offering ever encountered, possessing a compelling sweep, gentle ardour and tingling concentration that grip from first measure to last. For the November 1938 recording of the single-movement *Phantasie Trio* in A minor Grinke was joined by cellist Florence Hooton and pianist Kendall Taylor. Here is yet another cherishable display, the playing wonderfully alive and always radiating a most winning understanding and spontaneity. As a delectable postscript Hooton teams up with Lawrence Pratt for an affectingly full-throated performance of *The Holy Boy* (still Ireland's most popular miniature). Good, if not exceptional transfers, the spookily quiet background is obtained at the expense of some naturalness of timbre. Urgently recommended all the same.

Additional recommendation
Violin Sonatas Nos 1 and 2
Couplings: Fantasy-Sonata. Cello Sonata. The Holy Boy. Phantasie Trio. Trios Nos 2 and 3
Mordkovitch *vn* **Georgian** *vc* **Brown** *pf*
Chandos ② CHAN9377/8 (147 minutes: DDD: 12/95) Ⓕ
Whole-hearted, affectionate performances.

Solo piano works

Merry Andrew. The towing-path. Rhapsody. Two Pieces (1924-5). Decorations. Leaves from a Child's Sketchbook. The darkened valley. Sonatina. Three Pastels. Two Pieces (1921). Summer evening
John Lenehan *pf*
Naxos 8 553889 (71 minutes: DDD) Ⓢ
Recorded 1996 ○

Nostalgia is Ireland's keynote, his pantheistic and wistful Gallic delicacy subsumed into a wholly English reticence. On this release there is a strong feeling of how purely local influences (Pangbourne and the Thames Valley in *The towing-path*, Le Fauvic beach, Jersey in 'The Island Spell', to take two examples) are transcended to become statements of wider poetic import. The large-scale *Rhapsody*, with its powerful Fauréan overtones, is relished by John Lenehan, a strong, sympathetic interpreter, and time and again he makes you wonder at works aptly described as 'some of the most appealing English piano music written this century, too long neglected.'

Sarnia. London Pieces. In Those Days. Prelude in E flat. Ballade. Columbine. Month's Mind
John Lenehan *pf*
Naxos 8 553700 (60 minutes: DDD) Ⓢ
Recorded 1995 ○

The pleasures here are many. John Lenehan is a very accomplished performer: not only is his technical address impeccable, but he also has a strikingly wide dynamic range and sophisticated variety of tone colour, both of which he uses to poetic effect throughout. That Lenehan has a real affinity for Ireland's muse is immediately evident from his raptly intimate delivery of the gentle opening diptych, *In Those Days*. Similarly, in the extraordinarily imaginative, harmonically questing *Ballade* of 1929 Lenehan rises superbly to the elemental fury of the remarkable central portion, with its brooding echoes of the 'Northern' Bax from the same period. Elsewhere, *Columbine* is a treat, as is the ravishing *Month's Mind* and the haunting Prelude in E flat. Lenehan's supremely affectionate and articulate advocacy will surely win Ireland many friends.

Additional recommendation
London Pieces
Couplings: In Those Days. Leaves from a Child's Sketchbook. The darkened valley. Two Pieces. Equinox. Sonatina. Prelude. Ballade. Greenways
Parkin *pf*
Chandos CHAN9140 (74 minutes: DDD: 6/93) Ⓕ
The best of Ireland's piano music, revealing a subtle, nostalgic sensibility driven by something more urgent.

Decorations Couplings: The Almond Tree. Preludes. Rhapsody. The Towing-Path. Merry Andrew. Summer Evening. Sonata in E/E minor
Parkin *pf*
Chandos CHAN9056 (72 minutes: DDD: 8/92) Ⓕ
Parkin's grasp of the subtle invocations of the Sonata and his total mastery of its technical demands is superb.

Charles Ives American 1874-1954

GROVE *Ives was influenced first by his father, a bandmaster who had libertarian ideas about what music might be. When he was perhaps 19 (the dating of his music is nearly always problematic) he produced psalm settings that exploit polytonality and other unusual procedures. He then studied with Parker at Yale (1894-98) and showed some sign of becoming a relatively conventional composer in his First Symphony (1898) and songs of this period. He worked, however, not in music but in the insurance business, and composition became a weekend activity - but one practised assiduously: during the two decades after his graduation he produced three more symphonies and numerous other orchestral works, four violin sonatas, two monumental piano sonatas and numerous songs.*

The only consistent characteristic of this music is liberation from rule. There are entirely atonal pieces, while others are in the simple harmonic style of a hymn or folksong. Some are systematic and abstract in construction; others are filled with quotations from the music of Ives's youth: hymns, popular songs, ragtime dances, marches etc Some, like the Three Places in New England, are nostalgic; others, like the Fourth Symphony, are fuelled by the vision of an idealist democracy. He published his 'Concord' Sonata in 1920 and a volume of 114 songs in 1922, but composed little thereafter. Most of his music had been written without prospect of performance, and it was only towards the end of his life that it began to be played frequently and appreciated.

Symphony No 2

Symphony No 2. Robert Browning Overture
Nashville Symphony Orchestra / Kenneth Schermerhorn
Naxos 8 559076 (67 minutes: DDD) Ⓢ
Recorded 2000

Ives' Second Symphony is not as well served on CD as might be expected. Bernstein gave the première in 1951 some 40 years after the work's composition. His 1958 recording, showing its age, is still available and so is his live recording from 1987. Listening again, Tilson Thomas with the Concertgebouw stands up well but there is little competition from Järvi with the Detroit and Somary with the Nuremberg.

What's new about this Nashville release is that it uses Jonathan Elkus's edition made for the Charles Ives Society for both works. The main difference for the listener is that the exposition of the second movement of the Symphony is repeated – from 3'37" to 7'10". That this helps the overall balance in this extended, somewhat repetitive movement is debatable. When it comes to Bernstein, he quite unnecessarily cut 16 measures from the last movement. His tempos may be considered slow in the third and fourth movements, but in both his recordings the work luxuriates in a way that nobody else achieves.

The *Robert Browning Overture* is one of Ives' most visionary pieces, with declamatory trumpet parts that make Scriabin's *Poème de l'extase* seem reticent. The mystical calm of the opening is memorably caught in the Nashville performance; the energetic passages are vivid, although some textures inevitably get submerged. It is a great relief to have the obvious errors in the score corrected. This puts earlier recordings such as Stokowski's beyond the pale and it's well worth buying this CD for the *Browning Overture* alone, although both works in these carefully-considered editions make a bargain pair.

Symphony No 2. The Gong on the Hook and Ladder. Tone Roads – No 1. A Set of Three Short Pieces – Largo cantabile, Hymn. Hallowe'en. Central Park in the Dark. The Unanswered Question
New York Philharmonic Orchestra / Leonard Bernstein
DG 429 220-2GH (68 minutes: DDD) Ⓕ
Recorded 1987-88 **oo**

Although Bernstein thought of Ives as a primitive composer, these recordings reveal that he had a deep understanding of, his music. The Second Symphony (written in 1902 and first performed in 1951) is a glorious work, still strongly rooted in the 19th century yet showing those clear signs of Ives's individual voice that are largely missing from the charming but lightweight First Symphony. Bernstein brings out all its richness and warmth without wallowing in its romantic elements, and he handles with utter conviction the multi-textures and the allusions to popular tunes and snatches from Bach, Brahms and Dvořák, to name but a few. The standard of playing he exacts from the NYPO, both here and in the disc's series of technically demanding shorter pieces, is remarkably high with the depth of string tone at a premium and the engineers retain this to a degree unusual in a live recording. An essential disc for any collection.

String Quartets

String Quartets No 1, 'From the Salvation Army'; No 2. A set of three short pieces – Scherzo, 'Holding Your Own' **Barber** String Quartet, Op 11
Emerson Quartet
(Eugene Drucker, Philip Setzer *vns* Lawrence Dutton *va* David Finckel *vc*) Ⓕ
DG 435 864-2GH (65 minutes: DDD) **o**

The First Quartet (1896) is a student work, saturated in hymn-tunes: each movement was probably used as an organ voluntary. But, like the Third Symphony, it assembles an affectionate archive of religious forms of musical expression ranging from mystical intensity to almost ecstatic fervour. The Fugue, which forms the first movement of the First Quartet, crops up again as the third movement of the Fourth Symphony. In the performance the Emerson has everything under control even if the third movement is slightly cold. Ives's Second Quartet (1913) is wildly different. With the first movement called 'Discussions' and the second 'Arguments' there is free scope for all Ives's photographic realism with textures as violent as middle-period Bartók later on. The Emerson brings hard-edged attack to the 'Arguments' but the ironic 'Andante Emasculata', a burlesque cadenza at 0'43", and similar moments are a little short-changed. The last movement, 'The Call of the Mountains', has a real chill when it opens largely without vibrato: and it climaxes resoundingly on 'Nearer my God', linking this peroration to the last movement of the Fourth Symphony. The Scherzo is a rarity – a brief comic study in rhythmic juxtapositions with the occasional diatonic tune sticking out of the melée. A fine, well-recorded performance.

Elisabeth Jacquet de la Guerre

French 1666/67-1729

GROVE *Elisabeth-Claude Jacquet de la Guerre was the daughter of Claude Jacquet (d 1702), member of a well-known family of harpsichord makers and organists. An accomplished harpsichordist with a talent for improvisation, she became a protégée of Louis XIV and Mme de Montespan. She wrote music for the Théâtres de la Foire. Her surviving music includes a ballet, an opera Cephale et Procris (1694), three collections of cantatas (1708- c1715), solo and trio sonatas with violin and bass viol, and two sets of Pièces de clavecin (1687, 1707). She was among the first in France to use the sonata and cantata genres, was the only woman to write a tragédie lyrique and among the earliest to publish harpsichord collections.*

Pièces de clavecin

Awards 1999

Premier livre de pièces de clavecin. Pièces de clavecin **P**
Carole Cerasi *hpd*
Metronome METCD1026 Ⓕ
(79 minutes: DDD)
Recorded 1997 ●●●

Elisabeth Jacquet was remarkable. A member of a family of musicians, at the age of only five she attracted the benevolent attention of Louis XIV by her harpsichord playing, and subsequently was taken under the wing of his favourite, Mme de Montespan. At 18 she married the organist Marin de la Guerre and became famous for the concerts she gave at her home, in which her powers of improvisation were greatly admired. She wrote trio sonatas, an opera, violin sonatas, and two books of *Cantates françaises* on Old Testament subjects. Her first book of harpsichord pieces was published as early as 1687 and contains in its four suites, apart from partly unmeasured Louis Couperin-like preludes, sequences of dances that have real individuality and feeling for expressive harmony, a very unusual *Tocade* (to open the F major Suite) and a couple of chaconnes. Twenty years later, after a series of family deaths, she produced two more harpsichord suites 'that can be played on the violin'. All this music is performed with flair, vitality, panache and character by the Swedish-born harpsichordist Carole Cerasi. Her playing on a rich-toned Ruckers instrument (originally single-manual but with a *ravalement* to two manuals by Hemsch in 1763) is deeply impressive and rewarding, and a model of clarity.

Leos Janáček Moravian 1854-1928

GROVE *Janáček was a chorister at the Augustinian 'Queen's' Monastery in Old Brno, where the choirmaster Pavel Križkovský took a keen interest in his musical education. After completing his basic schooling he trained as a teacher and, except for a period at the Prague Organ School, he spent 1872-79 largely as a schoolteacher and choral conductor in Brno. In 1879 he enrolled at the Leipzig Conservatory, where he developed his interest in composition under the strict and systematic supervision of Leo Grill. After a month in Vienna he returned to Brno in May 1880; there he became engaged to one of his pupils, Zdenka Schulzová, whom he married in July 1881.*

In Brno, Janáček took up his former activities, and also founded and directed an organ school and edited a new musical journal, Hudební listy. After composing his first opera, Šárka, he immersed himself in collecting Moravian folk music, which bore fruit in a series of orchestral suites and dances and in a one-act opera, The Beginning of a Romance. This was favourably received in 1894, but Janáček withdrew it after six performances and set to work on Jenůfa.

During the long period of composition of Jenůfa (1894-1903), Janáček rethought his approach to opera and to composition in general. He largely abandoned the number opera, integrated folksong firmly into his music and formulated a theory of 'speech-melody', based on the natural rhythms and the rise and fall of the Czech language, which was to influence all his ensuing works and give them a particular colour through their jagged rhythms and lines. Jenufa was soon followed by other operatic ventures, but his reputation in Brno was as a composer of instrumental and choral music and as director of the Organ School. Outside Moravia he was almost unknown until the Prague première of Jenůfa in 1916. The creative upsurge of a man well into his 60s is explained partly by the success of Jenůfa in Prague and abroad, partly by his patriotic pride in the newly acquired independence of his country, and perhaps most of all by his passionate, though generally distant, attachment to Kamila Stösslová, the young wife of an antique dealer in Pisek, Bohemia.

Between 1919 and 1925 Janáček composed three of his finest operas, all on subjects with special resonances for him: Káťa Kabanová with its neglected wife who takes a lover, The Cunning Little Vixen with its sympathetic portrayal of animals (and particularly the female fox), and The Makropoulos Affair with the 'ageless' woman who fascinates all men. Each was given first in Brno and soon after in Prague. His 70th birthday was marked by a doctorate from the Masaryk University in Brno. Early in 1926 he wrote the Sinfonietta for orchestra, characteristic in its blocks of sound and its forceful repetitions, and later that year his most important choral work, the Glagolitic Mass. While performance of his music carried his fame abroad, he started work on his last opera, From the House of the Dead, which he did not live to see performed. It received its première in April 1930 in a version prepared by his pupils Bretislav Bakala and Osvald Chlubna.

Janáček's reputation outside Czechoslovakia and German-speaking countries was first made as an instrumental composer. He has since come to be regarded not only as a Czech composer worthy to be ranked with Smetana and Dvořák, but also as one of the most substantial and original opera composers of the 20th century.

Taras Bulba

Janáček Taras Bulba. The Cunning Little Vixen – Suite **V Novák** Slovak Suite, Op 32 **H**
Czech Philharmonic Orchestra / Václav Talich
Supraphon Historical mono 11 1905-2 Ⓜ
(71 minutes: AAD). Recorded 1953-54 ●●

Talich's *Taras Bulba* is hugely imposing. Aided by playing of brazen fervour from the Czech PO, his reading has a rare dignity, culminating in an apotheosis of overwhelming grandeur and majesty (magnificent brass sounds). Not that there's any want of energy and momentum: in Talich's hands, the battle scenes of the first two tableaux possess thrilling snap and vigour. Some might crave a leaner, harder-edged orchestral sonority, but the impact and stature of this music-making is not in question. It's followed by the affectionate orchestral suite from *The Cunning Little Vixen* which Talich himself compiled in 1937. Of course, not all Janáčekians will approve of the great conductor's 'sensualising' of the original instrumentation, but many collectors will be grateful to have this classic 1954 recording restored to circulation at long last, and its sense of enchantment and magical atmosphere remain utterly intoxicating. The Novák coupling is an unmitigated delight. Talich's wonderful conception has all the tangy affection and lithe, rhythmic punch one could wish for, but he also locates and taps into a vein of tangible, old-world nostalgia that is extremely moving. If you don't already know these lovely scores, we urge immediate investigation, for you won't ever hear better performances than these.

String Quartets

String Quartets – No 1, 'Kreutzer Sonata'; No 2, 'Intimate Letters' Along an Overgrown Path (1906-08) – Suite No 1

Radoslav Kvapil *pf* **Talich Quartet** (Petr Messiereur, Jan Kvapil *vns* Jan Talich *va* Evzen Rattai *vc*)

Calliope CAL9699 (73 minutes: DDD) Ⓕ

Recorded 1986 ●

This recording does not give a true balance, and in places the sound itself is rather grey. At first blush, too, the Talich Quartet's manner can seem tentative. Yet this is exactly what is right. The music is sudden, questing, unpredictable, by turns mysterious, vehement in its emotions, passionately lyrical. The whole programme of the Second Quartet, with its reference in the title to secret affections, indicates the extraordinariness of the emotion for the younger woman that overcame Janáček; and its exceptional and impossible nature finds ideal expression in the idiom of Janáček's astonishing final years. The Talich Quartet suggests secrecy, fear even, in the quick shifts between musical gestures; yet it can allow Janáček's beautiful phrases declaring his full heart to find passionate expression. It is a more restrained manner of playing than that adopted by other groups, and it can make its effect by skilful understatement; but repeated hearings increasingly find it to yield subtle and true performances of both works. Room is also found for the First Suite of *Along an Overgrown Path*. Kvapil is direct and eloquent in his approach to Janáček's oblique statements and half-hidden memories, both passionate and tragic; but he never overstates, and his allusive manner is very effective indeed.

Pohádka

Pohádka. Presto in E minor. Violin Sonata. Capriccio. Concertino

Pierre Amoyal *vn* **Gary Hoffman** *vc* **Mikhail Rudy** *pf* members of **L'Orchestre de l'Opéra National de Paris / Sir Charles Mackerras**

EMI CDC5 55585-2 (72 minutes: DDD) Ⓕ

Recorded 1995 ●

This is an odd assemblage of Janáček's late chamber music, but the music itself is capable of an oddity which does not dim with time. Mikhail Rudy contrasts well the eccentricity of the left-hand *Capriccio*, never losing sight of its contained lyricism, with the more approachable lyricism of the *Concertino* In this he is ideally supported by Mackerras, whose expert judgement of the weight and pace and contrasts of the music never falters. Much of the secret in bringing off this difficult, haunting music lies in a sense of timing, together with something more, a long-acquired skill in contrasting textures dramatically, which has itself something to do with timing, at any rate with a sense of dramatic cut and thrust. The violin and cello works, themselves very different in their more romantic natures, are finely handled by Amoyal and Hoffman, with Rudy a sympathetic and supportive partner. There are now many different versions of each of these works, none in this exact compilation. It is certainly one that can be strongly recommended.

Janáček Pohádka

Kodály Cello Sonata, Op 4

Liszt Elégies – No 1, S130; No 2, S131. La lugubre gondola, S134

Anne Gastinel *vc* **Pierre-Laurent Aimard** *pf*

Auvidis Valois V4748 (50 minutes: DDD) Ⓕ

Recorded 1995

This is an imaginative piece of programme planning, with arrangements of Liszt's *Elégies* and *La lugubre gondola* separated by Kodály's Sonata and Janáček's *Pohádka*. Liszt, writing in the 1870s and early 1880s, sounds as modern as either of the two composers writing in 1910; and indeed there is much in his augmented-chord harmony and his fondness for unusual scales that influenced Kodály, while Janáček also admired him and used his religious music for teaching. This is romantic music outside the mainstream of European musical romanticism. Gastinel and Aimard give performances as intelligent as these juxtapositions suggest, oblique and dark in the linking figure of Liszt, especially with *La lugubre gondola*, one of the most extraordinary late piano pieces. Kodály's sonata is played with a quiet intensity, rhapsodic in manner but strongly held together by the clarity of emphasis on the motto theme and its musical implications. Janáček's pieces can sound sharper and quirkier than here, and in such performances make their point more strongly; but this playing is of a piece with the whole approach. Gastinel has a clean, resinous tone, and a strong sense of line; she is well partnered by Aimard, and the recording is balanced.

Piano Sonata / In the Mists

Piano Sonata 1.X.1905, 'From the Street'. Along an Overgrown Path. In the Mists. Thema con variazioni, 'Zdenka'
Rudolf Firkušný *pf*
DG 20th Century Classics 429 857-2GC Ⓜ
(79 minutes: ADD). Recorded 1971 ●

Janáček's only piano sonata has a history almost as dramatic as the events which inspired it. Its subtitle, *From the Street*, commemorates a student demonstration in which a 20-year-old worker was killed, an event which so outraged Janáček that he wrote a three-movement sonata as an expression of his feelings. Before the première in 1906 he burnt the third movement and after a private performance in Prague he threw the remaining movements into a river. It is only thanks to the pianist, Ludmil Tučkova, who had copied out the first two movements, that the work survives. The underlying theme of Firkušný's approach to this work (who may claim historical authenticity as he studied with Janáček) is anger, turning the first movement into a defiant roar of fury whilst the slow movement has an inherent restlessness, bitterness never far below the surface. Much of the same characteristics can be found in the other works – *Along an Overgrown Path* and the masterly *In the Mists* – although he occasionally overloads these delicate little pieces with dramatic power. The early Theme and Variations are conventionally romantic but impeccably played. This disc represents playing of the highest class with full notes and tracking details.

Diary of one who disappeared

(two versions) H
[a]**Nicolai Gedda,** [b]**Beno Blachut** *tens* [a]**Véra Soukupová,** [b]**Stěpánka Stěpánová** *mezzos* [a]**Prague Radio Chamber Chorus;** [b]**Czech Singers Chamber Chorus;** ab**Josef Páleníček** *pf*
Supraphon [a]stereo/[b]mono SU0022-2
(73 minutes: DDD/AAD). Text and translation included. Recorded [b]1956 and [a]1984 Ⓜ

Here is a highly interesting enterprise: two parallel performances of Janáček's song-cycle, both recorded in Prague, but one being the classic version with Beno Blachut made in 1956, the other hitherto unknown in this country and made in 1984 by Nicolai Gedda. Blachut, who despite his heroic use of his voice kept it in good order throughout a long career, was then in his early forties, and in his prime; Gedda, another singer who has preserved his voice carefully, was in his sixtieth year. Any lover of Janáček's music is strongly urged to acquire this striking record. The commentary, by the distinguished scholar Jiří Vysloužil, makes no bones about preferring Blachut, observing that 'what may have displeased some critics, including even those abroad, was the operatic style of Gedda's interpretation'. It is easy enough to see what he means: for instance, in No 6, translated as 'Hey there my tawny oxen', as the young man ploughing has his head set afire by a glimpse of the gipsy girl in the bushes, Gedda gives the climactic phrase 'v jednom je plameni' an Italianate fervour where Blachut develops the song's passion more steadily towards the phrase, which can therefore be less strenuously emphasised. Even so, Gedda's vocal elegance and eloquence have their own appeal; and his Russian background has long helped him towards a deep understanding of music in the Slavonic repertory. His is a superb performance of a work that can well sustain a new approach, whatever loyalties there may be to Blachut's identification with the work. Listeners have a unique opportunity here for getting, literally, two for the price of one and enjoying the comparisons. A lynch-pin of both performances is Josef Páleníček.

Glagolitic Mass

Glagolitic Mass[a]. Sinfonietta, Op 60[b]
Felicity Palmer *sop* **Ameral Gunson** *mez* **John Mitchinson** *ten* **Malcolm King** *bass* **Jane Parker-Smith** *org* [a]**City of Birmingham Chorus and Orchestra;** [b]**Philharmonia Orchestra / Sir Simon Rattle**
EMI Great Recordings of the Century CDM5 66980-2
(62 minutes: DDD). Text and translation included. Ⓜ
Recorded 1980s ●

'I am not an old man, and I am not a believer – until I see for myself.' Thus Janáček replied angrily to a critic after the première of his *Glagolitic Mass*. This is a gritty, masterful performance of a jagged, uncomfortable masterpiece. Its unusual title stems from the script of the ancient Slavonic text (*Glagol*) which Janáček set to music. Rattle's is a full-blooded, urgent view of the work, with particularly fine solo contributions from Felicity Palmer and John Mitchinson. That the language is an unfamiliar one is occasionally evident in the chorus, though they, like the orchestra, give totally committed performances under Rattle's inspired leadership. Also included on this disc is the *Sinfonietta* (originally entitled 'Military Sinfonietta', reflecting in the brass-heavy scoring of the work). It is as much a study in orchestration as form with the melody of the fourth movement appearing unaltered no less than 14 times, changed only in orchestral colour. It is brilliantly played here, with the 12 trumpets coming up gleaming in the final climax. An enticing proposition!

Janáček (ed Wingfield) Glagolitic Mass (original version)
Kodály Psalmus Hungaricus, Op 13[a]
Tina Kiberg *sop* **Randi Stene** *contr* **Peter Svensson** *ten* **Ulrik Cold** *bass* **Per Salo** *org* [a]**Copenhagen Boys' Choir; Danish National Radio Choir and Symphony Orchestra / Sir Charles Mackerras**
Chandos CHAN9310 (63 minutes: DDD). Texts and translations included. Recorded 1994 Ⓕ ●●

Mackerras's version of the *Glagolitic Mass* is of particular interest as it embodies one of the reconstructions that have been painstakingly made of Janáček's original intentions in different works as his stature has drawn greater scholarly interest. This one has been made by Paul Wingfield. He has gone into the nature of his restorations in great detail in his excellent monograph on the work in the Cambridge Music Handbooks series (CUP: 1992), and summarises them in his note to this recording. Briefly, they involve the playing of the Intrada at the beginning and the end, in the Introduction a very complex rhythmic pattern and in the 'Gospodi pomiluj' ('Kyrie') use of quintuple metre instead of the familiar four-in-a-bar, and fierce timpani interjections in the wild organ solo. There are other points; but in any case, most interested listeners will care less for them in detail than for the heightened force and impact of the music. This it certainly now (or once again) has. These matters make it the more regrettable that, despite marvellous handling of the work by Mackerras, there are problems with a quartet of soloists that is less than exciting, and a recording that even with the most modern techniques can obscure the detail and clarity. This should not detract from the interest of the disc, which every lover of the work will surely want to hear. Those who acquire it will have the additional benefit of a fine performance of Kodály's *Psalmus Hungaricus*, though the restored Mass is naturally the occasion here for recommendation and choice.

The Cunning Little Vixen

Awards 1983

The Cunning Little Vixen. The Cunning Little Vixen – orchestral suite (arr V Talich)
Lucia Popp *sop* Vixen, Young vixen; **Dalibor Jedlička** *bass* Forester; **Eva Randová** *mez* Fox; **Eva Zikmundová** *mez* Forester's wife, Owl; **Vladimír Krejčik** *ten* Schoolmaster, Gnat; **Richard Novák** *ten* Priest, Badger; **Václav Zítek** *bar* Harašta; **Beno Blachut** *ten* Pásek; **Ivana Mixová** *mez* Pásek's wife, Woodpecker, Hen; **Libuše Marová** *contr* Dog; **Gertrude Jahn** *mez* Cock, Jay; **Eva Hríbiková** *sop* Frantik; **Zuzana Hudecová** *sop* Pepik; **Peter Saray** *treb* Frog, Grasshopper; **Miriam Ondrášková** *sop* Cricket
Vienna State Opera Chorus; Bratislava Children's Choir; Vienna Philharmonic Orchestra / Sir Charles Mackerras
Decca ② 417 129-2DH2 (109 minutes: DDD) Ⓕ
Notes, text and translation included
Recorded 1981 ●●●

Janáček used the most unlikely material for his operas. For *The Cunning Little Vixen* his source was a newspaper series of drawings, with accompanying text, about the adventures of a vixen cub and her escape from the gamekeeper who raised her. The music is a fascinating blend of vocal and orchestral sound – at times ludicrously romantic, at others raw and violent. Mackerras's Czech training has given him a rare insight into Janáček's music and he presents a version faithful to the composer's individual requirements. In the title-role, Lucia Popp gives full weight to the text while displaying all the richness and beauty of her voice. There is a well-chosen supporting cast of largely Czech singers, with the Vienna Philharmonic to add the ultimate touch of orchestral refinement. Decca's sound is of demonstration quality.

Additional recommendation
The Cunning Little Vixen (sung in English)
Coupling: Taras Bulba
Watson Vixen **Montague** Fox **Allen** Forester
Royal Opera House Chorus and Orchestra / Sir Simon Rattle
EMI CDS7 54212-2 (120 minutes: DDD: 3/92) Ⓕ
Live recording

Rattle's version is extremely well cast and is worth considering if you want to overcome the language barrier in an opera that in every way draws you into the drama.

House of the Dead / Makropulos ...

Awards 1980

From the House of the Dead[a]. Mládí[b]. Nursery rhymes[c] **Dalibor Jedlička** *bar* Goryanchikov; **Jaroslava Janská** *sop* Alyeya; **Jiří Zahradníček** *ten* Luka (Morosov); **Vladimir Krejčík** *ten* Tall Prisoner; **Richard Novák** *bass* Short Prisoner; **Antonín Svorc** *bass-bar* Commandant; **Beno Blachut** *ten* Old Prisoner; **Ivo Zídek** *ten* Skuratov; **Jaroslav Souček** *bar* Chekunov, Prisoner acting Don Juan; **Eva Zigmundová** *mez* Whore; **Zdeněk Soušek** *ten* Shapkin, Kedril; **Václav Zítek** *bar* Shishkov; **Zdeněk Švehla** *ten* Cherevin, A Voice
Vienna State Opera Chorus; Vienna Philharmonic Orchestra / Sir Charles Mackerras; [c]London Sinfonietta Chorus; [bc]London Sinfonietta / David Atherton
Decca ② 430 375-2DH2 (123 minutes: DDD/ADD) Ⓕ
Notes, texts and translations included.
Recorded 1980 ●●●

The Makropulos Affair. Lachian Dancesa
Elisabeth Söderström *sop* Emilia Marty; **Peter Dvorský** *ten* Albert Gregor; **Vladimir Krejšík** *ten* Vítek; **Anna Czaková** *mez* Kristina; **Václav Zítek** *bar* Jaroslav Prus; **Zdeněk Švehla** *ten* Janek; **Dalibor Jedlička** *bass* Kolenatý; **Jiří Joran** *bass* Stage technician; **Ivana Mixová** *contr* Cleaning woman; **Beno Blachut** *ten* Hauk-Sendorf; **Blanka Vitková** *contr* Chambermaid
Vienna State Opera Chorus; Vienna Philharmonic Orchestra / Sir Charles Mackerras; aLondon Philharmonic Orchestra / François Huybrechts
Decca ② 430 372-2DH2 (118 minutes: ADD) Ⓕ
Notes, text and translation included. Recorded 1978

From the House of the Dead (the 1980 *Gramophone* Record of the Year) was here recorded for the first time in its proper, original version; and this revealed it as even more of a masterpiece – a work, indeed, to count among the handful of masterpieces of 20th-century opera. The loss of the final chorus, a sentimental addition, is but the most striking of the clarifications: throughout, the sound is sharper, the textures are sparer, and this serves to sharpen the effect and to give the singers more clearly differentiated support. The cast are led, nominally, by Goryanchikov, but the character is not really the hero of an opera that has no heroes and in which all are heroes, though Dalibor Jedlička sings him warmly and well. The prisoners are skilfully contrasted in Janáček's writing so as to make an apparently random yet actually well-structured group, and there is not a weak performance among them.

The Makropulos Affair has, of course, very much a heroine, in the tragic figure of Emilia Marty; and here Elisabeth Söderström gives one of her greatest recorded performances. She succeeds amazingly in conveying the complexity of the character, the elegance yet flinty cynicism, the aloofness yet vulnerability, the latent warmth that can flower into such rich expressive phrases and then be reined in with a sense of nervy panic. She is only really alarmed by Prus, the most formidable of the men around her, powerfully sung by Václav Zítek; for poor silly Hauk-Sendorf, another captivating little vignette from Beno Blachut, she has amused tenderness. Mackerras is again masterly: the opera operates in many ways at a much swifter pace, with the narrative speeding by in a series of graphic strokes whose sharpness of characterization can need familiarity for its full impact. This is a recording to set among great performances of it. As with *From the House of the Dead*, there is an essay by John Tyrrell that not only gives the listener the best possible introduction to the opera but is also a contribution to scholarship. The fill-ups, *Mládi* and the *Nursery rhyme*, come from David Atherton's splendid 1981 set of five LPs devoted to Janáček; the *Lachian Dances* set is a rather less successful companion to *Makropulos*.

Jenůfa

Elisabeth Söderström *sop* Jenůfa; **Wieslaw Ochman** *ten* Laca; **Eva Randová** *mez* Kostelnička; **Petr Dvorskü** *ten* Steva; **Lucia Popp** *sop* Karolka; **Marie Mrazová** *contr* Stařenka; **Václav Zitek** *bar* Stárek; **Dalibor Jedlička** *bass* Rychtar; **Ivana Mixová** *mez* Rychtarka; **Vera Soukopová** *mez* Pastuchyňa, Tetka; **Jindra Pokorná** *mez* Barena; **Jana Janasová** *sop* Jano

Vienna State Opera Chorus; Vienna Philharmonic Orchestra / Sir Charles Mackerras

Decca ② 414 483-2DH2 (130 minutes: DDD) Ⓕ

Recorded 1982 **OOO**

Janáček's first operatic masterpiece is a towering work, blending searing intensity with heart-stopping lyricism. It tells of Jenůfa and the appalling treatment she receives as she is caught between the man she loves and another who finally comes to love her. But dominating the story is the Kostelnička, a figure of enormous strength, pride and inner resource who rules Jenůfa's life and ultimately kills her baby. Randová's characterization of the role of the Kostelnička is frightening in its intensity yet has a very human core. The two men are well cast and act as fine foils to Söderström's deeply impressive Jenůfa. The Vienna Philharmonic plays beautifully and Mackerras directs magnificently. The recording is all one could wish for and the booklet is a mine of informed scholarship.

Káťá Kabanová. Capriccio[a]. Concertino[a]

Elisabeth Söderström *sop* Kátá Kabanová; **Petr Dvorsky** *ten* Boris; **Naděžda Kniplová** *contr* Kabanicha; **Vladimír Krejčík** *ten* Tichon; **Libuše Márová** *mez* Varvara; **Dalibor Jedlička** *bass* Dikoj; **Zdeněk Svehla** *ten* Kudrjáš; **Jaroslav Souček** *bar* Kuligin; **Jitka Pavlová** *sop* Glaša; **Gertrude Jahn** *mez* Fekluša

Vienna State Opera Chorus; Vienna Philharmonic Orchestra / Sir Charles Mackerras; [a]Paul Crossley *pf* a**London Sinfonietta / David Atherton**

Decca ② 421 852-2DH2 (140 minutes: ADD) Ⓕ

Notes, text and translation included.

Recorded 1976-78 **OOO**

Kátá, a free spirit, is imprisoned by marriage into, and domicile with, a family in a provincial Russian town on the Volga. The family is manipulated by her mother-in-law, a widow whose sole obsession is with her status. The only son (Kátá's husband) is spineless, and Kátá looks for escape in love. She finds the love, but true escape only in suicide. Janáček focuses on his heroine, giving her at least two of the most moving scenes in opera: the first where, to music of shimmering, seraphic beauty she describes her childhood imagination given free rein by sunlight streaming through the dome in church; and the second in the last scene where, after confessing her adultery, she concludes that 'not even God's own sunlight' gives her pleasure any more. Söderström has the intelligence and a voice which guarantees total credibility; and of the superb all-Czech supporting cast one might only have wished for a slightly younger-sounding sister-in-law. Mackerras obtains the finest playing from the VPO; and Decca reproduces the whole with clarity, atmosphere, ideal perspectives and discernible stage movement – only a detectable levelling of the score's few extreme *fortissimos* points to the recording's vintage. As a bonus, Decca adds the late chamber concertos, both excellently performed and engineered, and equally essential Janáček.

Josquin Desprez French c1440-1521

GROVE *Josquin was a singer at Milan Cathedral in 1459, remaining there until December 1472. By July 1474 he was one of the 'cantori di capella' in the chapel of Galeazzo Maria Sforza. Between 1476 and 1504 he passed into the service of Cardinal Ascanio Sforza, whom he probably accompanied in Rome in 1484. His name first appears among the papal chapel choir in 1486 and recurs sporadically; he had left the choir by 1501. In this Italian period Josquin reached artistic maturity.*

He then went to France (he may also have done so while at the papal chapel) and probably served Louis XII's court. Although he may have had connections with the Ferrara court (through the Sforzas) in the

1480s and 1490s, no formal relationship with the court is known before 1503 when, for a year, he was maestro di cappella there and the highest-paid singer in the chapel's history. There he probably wrote primarily masses and motets. An outbreak of plague in 1503 forced the court to leave Ferrara (Josquin's place was taken by Obrecht, who fell victim in 1505). He was in the north again, at Notre Dame at Condé, in 1504; he may have been connected with Margaret of Austria's court, 1508-11. He died in 1521. Several portraits survive, one attributed to Leonardo da Vinci.

Josquin's works gradually became known throughout western Europe and were regarded as models by many composers and theorists. Petrucci's three books of his masses (1502-14) reflect contemporary esteem, as does Attaingnant's collection of his chansons (1550). Several laments were written on his death (including Gombert's elegy Musae Jovis), and as late as 1554 Jacquet of Mantua paid him tribute in a motet. He was praised by 16th-century literary figures (including Castiglione and Rabelais) and was Luther's favourite composer.

Josquin was the greatest composer of the high Renaissance, the most varied in invention and the most profound in expression. Much of his music cannot be dated. Generally, however, his first period (up to c1485) is characterised by abstract, melismatic counterpoint in the manner of Ockeghem and by tenuous relationships between words and music. The middle period (to c1505) saw the development and perfection of the technique of pervasive imitation based on word-generated motifs. This style has been seen as a synthesis of two traditions: the northern polyphony of Dufay, Busnois and Ockeghem, in which he presumably had his earliest training, and the more chordal, harmonically orientated practice of Italy. In the final period the relationship between word and note becomes even closer and there is increasing emphasis on declamation and rhetorical expression within a style of the utmost economy.

His many motets span all three periods. One of the earliest, the four-part Victimae paschali laudes (1502), exemplifies his early style, with its dense texture, lack of imitation, patches of stagnant rhythm and rudimentary treatment of dissonance. Greater maturity is shown in Planxit autem David, in which homophonic and freely imitative passages alternate, and in Absalon, fili mi, with its flexible combination of textures. His later motets, such as In principio erat verbum, combine motivic intensity and melodic succinctness with formal clarity; they are either freely composed, four-part settings of biblical texts, or large-scale cantus firmus pieces. Transparent textures and duet writing are common.

Josquin's 18 complete masses combine elements of cantus firmus, parody and paraphrase techniques. One of the earliest, L'ami Baudichon, is a cantus firmus mass on a simple dance formula the simplicity of melody and rhythm and the clarity of harmony and texture recall the Burgundian style of the 1450s and 1460s. Fortuna desperata, on the other hand, is an early example of parody. Canonic writing and ostinato figures are features. His last great masses, notably the Missa de beata virgine and the Missa 'Pange lingua', were preceded by works in which every resource is deployed with bravura.

Josquin's secular music comprises three settings of Italian texts and numerous chansons. One of the earliest, Cela sans plus, typifies his observance of the formes fixes and the influences of the Burgundian styles of Busnois and Ockeghem. Later works, such as Mille regretz, are less canonic, the clear articulation of lines and points of imitation achieved by a carefully balanced hierarchy of cadences. Some, like Si j'ay perdu mon ami, look forward to the popular 'Parisian' chanson, of Janequin.

Songs and Instrumental Music

Master of Musicians – Songs and instrumental music by Josquin des Prez, and his pupils and contemporaries

Josquin Adieu mes amours[b]. Bergerotte savoysienne[c]. Comment peult avoir joye. De tous biens pleine – à 3; à 4. Dido – Fama malum à 4[abcd]; Dulces exuviae à 4. El grillo[abcd]. Faulte d'argent[ab]. Je me complains[bc]. Mille regretz[abcd]. Pauper sum ego[d]. Petite camusette[ab]. Pleine de dueil[bc]. Se congié prens[ab] – Recordans de mia segnora; à 6. Si j'avoys Marion. Si j'ay perdu mon amy – à 3; à 4. Le villain **Agricola** Se congié prens **Alonso** La tricotea[abd] **Anon** Belles tenés moi[c] **Févin** Faulte d'argent[c] **Gerle** Mille regretz **Isaac** Agnus Dei[d] – à 5; à 3 **Japart** Se congié prens[c] **Orto** Si j'ay perdu mon amy **Le Roy** Tordion **Spinacino** Adieu mes amours **Susato** Bergeret sans roche. Pavan Mille regretz – à 3; à 4 **Vinders** Lamentatio super morte Josquin des Prez[cd]
[a]**Belinda Sykes** *contr* [b]**John Potter** *ten* [c]**Jennie Cassidy** *mez* [d]**Robert Evans** *bar* **London Musica Antiqua** (John Bryan *rec/crumhn/viol* Alison Crum *rec/crumhn/viol/hp* Jacob Heringman *viol/lte/gtr* Roy Marks *crumhn/viol* Rebecca Miles *rec*) **/ Philip Thorby**
Signum SIGCD025 (68 minutes: DDD). Texts and translations included. Recorded 2000 Ⓕ ●

The secular music of Josquin has not always been very successful in recordings. Many of the pieces are very short – some can seem like exercises for something else, and others make little sense unless they are understood in the wider context of other settings based on the same material. The last problem is solved here by the inclusion of a lot of the related settings alongside those of Josquin. And the recording solves the first problem by unapologetically offering no fewer than 37 tracks, with the pieces grouped together so they flow cleanly from one to the next; it also resists some of the more outgoing pieces, so that the whole disc occupies a consistent sound world.

That sound world is mostly a gentle one, with the lines flowing quite fast in an easy playing style that can occasionally lose a few details but compensates with clarity of design. The musicians also cultivate a sound that favours vivacity and flair over constant attention to all the details of intonation; but that, too, is good, because everything is lively and full of variety. The instruments used range from viols and lutes to an ensemble of recorders and even one of crumhorns (played with an admirable restraint). And the singers offer all the variety of tone-colour one might expect from a group spearheaded by John Potter.

Many pieces here have never been recorded before; and the disc has the twin benefits of being remarkably accessible for easy listening as well as providing a marvellous basis for the closer understanding that can come from following the insert material carefully. Most enjoyable.

Masses

Josquin Desprez Missa L'homme armé super voces musicales. Missa L'homme armé sexti toni
Anonymous L'homme armé
The Tallis Scholars / Peter Phillips
Gimell CDGIM019 (74 minutes: DDD) Ⓕ
Text and translation included
Recorded 1989 ○

Towards the end of the Middle Ages it became customary to use popular secular melodies instead of the plainchant themes as the basis for polyphonic Masses. One such was the 15th-century melody *L'homme armé* ('Beware of the armed man'), a melody that may have originated as a crusader song. These settings would provide endless opportunities for a composer to demonstrate his contrapuntal skills. In the first of Josquin's two settings, *Super voces musicales*, he uses the tune over and over again, beginning each time on successive ascending degrees of the six-note scale *Ut re mi fa sol la*, so that it rises higher and higher as the Mass progresses. Sometimes the melody appears back to front from halfway through the piece on to the end. In the *Sexti toni* Mass the tune is transposed so that F rather than G is the final note. The listener's enjoyment is in no way lessened by all this contrapuntal ingenuity. The music flows along with unsurpassed ease and beauty, displaying that unique quality of seeming inevitability which characterises all great music. It is well matched by the expertise and enthusiasm of The Tallis Scholars and the first-class recording.

Awards 1987

Missa Pange lingua. Missa La sol fa re mi
The Tallis Scholars / Peter Phillips
Gimell CDGIM009 (62 minutes: DDD) Ⓕ
Recorded 1986 ○○○

This is absolutely superb. We must accept that Josquin is unlikely to have heard this music with two ladies on the top line, but they do it so well that only a fundamentalist would mark the disc down for that. It should also be said that the least successful performance on the entire disc is in the opening *Kyrie* of this Mass where there is a certain brutality in the approach; and although The Tallis Scholars make much of the 'Benedictus' and the last *Agnus Dei*, there may still be better ways of doing it. On the other hand, as just one example among many, these were the first musicians to make the 'Osanna' truly successful and understand why Josquin should have chosen to compose it that way. But they sing even better in the Mass, *La sol fa re mi*. Again and again in the singing one has the feeling that Josquin's lines are projected with an understanding and clarity that have rarely been heard before. The *La sol fa re mi* of the title denotes (among other things) the melodic passage which appears over 200 times in the course of the work with its intervals unchanged – which may not seem a recipe for the kind of music one would want to hear. But Josquin treats his material with such astonishing sophistication that you are rarely aware of the melodic fragment as such; and Phillips is scrupulously careful never to emphasise the melody except in places – such as the end of the second 'Osanna' – where it is clearly intended to work as an ostinato. This performance shows that the *La sol fa re mi* belongs with the greatest works of its era.

Josquin Desprez Missa de beata virgine
Mouton Nesciens mater. Ave Maria virgo serena. Ave sanctissima Maria. O Maria piissima. Ave Maria gemma virginum
Theatre of Voices / Paul Hillier
Harmonia Mundi HMU90 7136 (53 minutes: DDD) Ⓕ
Texts and translations included. Recorded 1993 ○

Jean Mouton was a composer who, in the eyes of 16th-century musicians, most successfully challenged the peerless Josquin Desprez. So it was a good idea to assemble a programme that juxtaposes the two composers: for Josquin it is his most successful Mass; and for Mouton a group of motets on the same theme – varied but all of them luscious and exhilarating. Effectively Paul Hillier divides up the Mass, as it would have been divided in a celebration, and puts Mouton's motets into the gaps. This works particularly well, the constant juxtaposition of the two similar yet contrasting styles clarifying one's perception of both composers. The music is also superbly performed. The 15 singers of the Theatre of Voices are effortlessly clear, wonderfully in tune and beautifully balanced. You hear the lines and spaces of Josquin just as you hear the immaculately modulated colours of Mouton; and that is partly because the singers have such good control of a range of vocal timbre. But beyond that there is an energy in the performances that keeps everything marvellously alive: even if you occasionally feel that Hillier takes the music a touch briskly, there is constant delight in the shapes that result. An issue of true distinction.

Missa Gaudeamus. Recordare virgo Mater. Regina caeli. Missa Ave maris stella. Virgo salutiferi/Ave Maria
A Sei Voci; Maîtrise des Pays de Loire / Bernard Fabre-Garrus *bass*
Auvidis Astrée E8612 (68 minutes: DDD). Texts and translations included. Recorded 1997 Ⓕ

Bernard Fabre-Garrus has long been experimenting with different ways of performing renaissance polyphony. It seems that each of his recordings offers a new sound; and in this particular case his novelty is to use the children of the Maîtrise des Pays de Loire – both boys and girls – to sing the top line of Josquin's Mass *Gaudeamus*. This is one of Josquin's most rhythmically intricate works, so there is a major challenge here; just occasionally the rhythms slip a little. But to compensate for that there is a stirring energy to their singing; and part of the elegance of Fabre-Garrus performances has always been in his fluid, linear approach to polyphony, which works splendidly here. Moreover, with just six singers on the three lower lines, he always manages to produce a beautifully clear and balanced texture. This is a very successful and exciting performance of one of Josquin's most stunning masterpieces. His astonishingly varied treatment of the *Gaudeamus* melody ranges from straight imitation through unusually long-held tenor notes (that have a stunning effect on the work's harmonic rhythm), via bravura exercises in ostinato, to the heart-stopping modulations of the final *Agnus Dei*. The plainchants are sung with an unusual lucidity and energy. The motets include the rarely heard *Recordare virgo Mater*, which gives a special opportunity for the children to sing in three parts; and they end with a superlatively eloquent and clear performance of one of Josquin's most famous five-voice motets, *Virgo salutiferi*.

Dmitry Kabalevsky

Russian/USSR 1904-1987

GROVE *Kabalevsky had a liberal education, wrote poetry and painted and showed promise as a pianist. The family moved to Moscow in 1918, where he studied the piano with Selyanov and from 1925 at the Moscow Conservatory with Catoire and Myaskovsky, the latter a formative influence; in 1932 he returned to teach at the conservatory (full professor from 1939). He was also involved in organizational and union activities, and worked in the music publishing house. The period 1932-41 was prolific, with much dramatic music (including the first version of his opera Colas Breugnon) and the first three symphonies. In the war years he turned to topical works on heroic patriotism. After the party decree of 1948 he worked towards a more lyrical idiom, as seen in his concertos of the ensuing years; later he worked in operetta and topical cantatas. Kabalevsky occupied an important role in Soviet music, as writer, spokesman on cultural policy, teacher and administrator as well as composer.*

Cello Concerto No 2

Kabalevsky Cello Concerto No 2 in G, Op 77
Khachaturian Cello Concerto
Rachmaninov (trans Rose) Vocalise, Op 34 No 14
Mats Lidström *vc* **Gothenburg Symphony Orchestra / Vladimir Ashkenazy** *pf*
BIS CD719 (65 minutes: DDD) Ⓕ
Recorded live in 1995

This coupling offers performances of two works which, if not masterpieces, are still sufficiently rewarding to be in the regular concert repertory. Ashkenazy creates an evocative opening atmosphere for the first movement of the Kabalevsky, when after mysterious string pizzicatos the soloist steals in with a gentle, singing tone. The soliloquy continues, for the work's unusual structure, with its three unbroken sections linked by cadenzas, invites an improvisational approach well understood by Mats Lidström. The Khachaturian Concerto opens with a flamboyantly coloured orchestral declamation before the cello sails off with vigorous animation. This is followed by a sinuous Armenian theme from the wind which the cello takes up ruminatively, with well-judged *espressivo*. Yet it is the energetic main theme that dominates and the soloist is carried along on its impetus, while ardently recalling the secondary material, finally leading to an exciting sequential coda. The finale offers the busy, rumbustious Khachaturian we know so well from the Violin Concerto. This composer's major works (with the exception of the Violin Concerto) can seem rather inflated, but here the combined concentration of Lidström and Ashkenazy minimises this impression. As an encore we are given a beautiful, restrained account of Rachmaninov's *Vocalise*. The recording is of high quality and well balanced, but a shade over-resonant, though the ear adjusts.

Mauricio Kagel

Argentinian 1931

GROVE *Kagel, a self-taught as a composer, worked in Buenos Aires as a conductor and in films before moving to Cologne in 1957; he has taught at the Musikhochschule there since 1974. The first work he completed in Europe was Anagrama for voices and instruments (1958), using all sorts of improper vocal sounds in textures of Boulezian fastidiousness; this absurd combination of strict form and unconventional, subversive ingredients has remained characteristic. Many of his works are explicitly theatrical: at one extreme they include pieces for the opera house (Staatstheater, 1971; Die Erschöpfung der Welt, 1985) and radio dramas, though in other works the instrumentalists' actions are the drama (Match for two cellists and percussionist, 1964). The intention is often satirical, to examine ways in which music is used as psychological therapy, marketable commodity, religious devotion, subject of learned expertise etc. Several works have also been filmed by the composer (eg Ludwig van, 1970).*

Auftakte, sechshändig

Auftakte, sechshändig. Phantasiestück. Serenade. Transición II
L'Art Pour l'Art (Astrid Schmeling *fl* Michael Schräder *gtr* Hartmut Leistritz *pf* Nils Grammersdorf, Matthias Kaul *perc*)
CPO CPO999 577-2 (67 minutes: DDD) Ⓜ
Recorded 1997

This refreshingly different disc enables collectors to catch up with Kagel, increasingly valued for his humane and unaggressive occupation of those more progressive regions of musical activity which often seem to be the sole preserve of the solemn and the pretentious. At the same time, there's much more to Kagel's music than skittishness and satire. *Transición II* for piano, percussion and tape (1958-59) takes up the idea of 'modulating' between live and recorded sound in textures of continuous discontinuity. Though Kagel could easily devise the kind of expressionistic flurries of activity that were the avant-garde calling-card of the late 1950s, there is already an unusually playful quality to the sound manipulation. The music may be dry, but it is also bracing, and this essential sprightliness, allied to wry good humour come to the fore in his later, more personal works. In *Phantasiestück* for flute and piano (1987-88), Kagel shows his willingness to flirt with instrumental cliché without sliding into inconsequence, and moments of Gallic winsomeness are offset by more sardonic sound effects. In the *Serenade* for flute, guitar and percussion (1994-95) the expressive range is even wider. The whole piece (lasting a substantial 24 minutes) is held together by intricate, beguiling displays of ingenuity, and there's a fine-tuned feeling for textural subtlety which never flags, even if some of the more basic ideas outstay their welcome. Finally, *Auftakte, sechshändig* for piano and percussion (1996) offers a more concentrated narrative in which pitched and unpitched materials wrestle to dominate the enthralling course of events. It's difficult to imagine more persuasive performances, and all the recordings are good.

'1898'

'1898'[a]. Music for Renaissance Instruments[b]
[a]**Hauptschule Peter-Griess- Strasse Children's Choir;** [a]**Köln-Flittard,** [b]**Collegium Instrumentale / Mauricio Kagel**
DG 20/21 459 570-2GX (74 minutes: ADD) Ⓜ
Recorded 1967-73 ●

Mauricio Kagel's *1898* was commissioned by DG to celebrate the company's 75th anniversary. Taking its title from the year the firm came into being, *1898*, in a typical Kagel inversion, sets out to re-create the intense, wiry sound of early gramophone recordings. The work reflects 19th-century musical culture, which, as the composer writes, was 'a time when one inhaled tonally and exhaled atonally.' The whole piece is conceived as a kind of two-part invention. The players are presented with the same two staves of music and the exact instrumental doublings of each line is only established in rehearsals. Then 22 children aged 10-13 from the Hauptschule Peter-Griess-Strasse in Cologne are brought in. The children's untrained vocal improvisations range from wonderfully off-key melodies to cruel bouts of bittersweet laughter that seem almost to mock the rest of the music, adding a whole new level of texture and meaning to *1898*. Four 'Stroh' string instruments were designed for the piece to Kagel's specifications, which combine attributes from both the string and brass families of instruments in a bizarre way, their keening, magnified screeching noises a distinctive feature of *1898*'s sound world. Conceived with the physical attributes of the gramophone record in mind, *1898* has two sides, each lasting around 25 minutes. This music is so intense that one should perhaps treat *1898* exactly like a gramophone record – stopping the CD after the first movement and taking a break before embarking on the second movement.

Yet the playing here is so extraordinarily sensitive and poignant that it makes for compelling listening, with the characteristically incisive contributions of the percussionist Christoph Caskel beautifully captured on this recording. In *Music for Renaissance Instruments*, a large ensemble of crumhorns, bombards, renaissance trombones, viols and a raucous positive organ are given a good work-out. This piece is, as Kagel writes, 'pervaded with the breath of the past' even while breaking the taboos of its time. It is the particular genius of this composer that he has never been afraid to 'inhale'.

Giya Kancheli Georgian 1935

GROVE *Kancheli studied at the Tbilisi Conservatory (1958-63), where he has taught since 1972. He is recognised as one of the most radical thinkers in Georgian music. His works, using folk music, include six symphonies (1967-81), jazz pieces and musicals.*

Liturgy for Viola and Orchestra

Liturgy for Viola and Orchestra, 'Mourned by the Wind'. Bright Sorrow
Ian Ford, Oliver Hayes *trebs* **France Springuel** *vc* **Cantate Domino Chorus; I Fiamminghi / Rudolf Werthen**
Telarc CD80455 (72 minutes: DDD) Ⓕ
Recorded 1996 ●

Givi Ordzhonikidze, the editor of a well-known book on Shostakovich, was one of Kancheli's closest friends and staunchest supporters, and it was the sense of loss after his death in 1984 that prompted the composition of the heart-rendingly beautiful *Liturgy* (subtitled *Mourned by the Wind*). The other inspiration was Yuri Bashmet, for this four-movement lament was originally a Viola Concerto. It goes superbly on the cello too, thanks to France Springuel's passionate advocacy, and in this form it inevitably invites comparisons with Tavener's *The Protecting Veil*.

A common feature of these two pieces is that they can seem almost unbearably moving if they catch you in the right mood and yet almost unbearably protracted if they don't. Yet for all the obvious gestures of lamentation and assuaging, *Liturgy* is not a tear-jerking piece. In fact the texture is for the most part quite transparent, and Kancheli constantly steers away from potentially manipulative clichés on to stonier paths. The more intense the urge towards consolation the more the sense of inconsolability grows; as a result the blind rage which erupts in the second and fourth movements is painfully intense. The Flemish orchestra gives a wonderfully controlled performance and Telarc's recording quality is superb. *Bright Sorrow* again draws from the bottomless well of lamentation which is the ex-USSR composer's special curse and privilege. It bears the dedication, 'To children, the victims of war', hence the choice of two boy soloists to intone phrases from Goethe, Shakespeare, Pushkin and the contemporary Georgian poet, Galaktion Tabidze, symbolizing the innocent victims of the last world war addressing themselves to the present-day generation. The soloists sing only slow, fragmented lines, conveying the fragility of innocence. The overall concept of polyglot texting and the fusion of pacifism and religiosity reflects a conscious admiration for Britten's *War Requiem*. The second half of the work seems to be gaining strength and optimism, but these are soon obliterated, leaving behind only a heart-broken crippled waltz. Highly recommended, whether or not you already have the Kancheli 'bug'.

...à la Duduki

...à la Duduki. Trauerfarbenes Land
Vienna Radio Symphony Orchestra / Dennis Russell Davies
ECM New Series 457 850-2 (57 minutes: DDD) Ⓕ
Recorded 1997 ●

... *à la Duduki* (a 'duduki' is a Georgian folk-reed instrument) should prove the ideal introduction to Kancheli's current style. And while a momentary encounter might suggest familiar territories revisited (vast terrains sparsely but dramatically populated), the musical material is more immediately striking, the scoring more texturally variegated, and the time sequences – even the rhetorical uses of silence – quite different from those in Kancheli's other recent work. Furthermore, echoes of modern jazz frequently fall within earshot. *Trauerfarbenes Land* ('Country the Colour of Mourning') employs a large orchestra and is different again, being nearly twice as long as ... *à la Duduki* and darker in tone. The opening has solo piano and *fortissimo* trombones hammer what sounds like a recollection of Carl Ruggles before six significant quavers (which turn up again later, in different hues and keys) mark a dramatic dynamic contrast. Time and again Kancheli's penchant for 'cliff-hanger' climaxes bring us to the edge of a towering aural precipice. This is the music of personal displacement: desolate, spacious, occasionally cryptic, and with sudden pangs of sweetened nostalgia that flutter across the canvas like torn diary jottings tossed by the wind. Dennis Russell Davies and producer Manfred Eicher conjure between them a precision-tooled sound picture where every grade of nuance is meticulously reported. Performance standards are unusually high throughout, so much so that it's hard to imagine either work being better played. An exceptional release of some extraordinarily powerful music.

Lament

Lament (Music of mourning in memory of Luigi Nono)
Maacha Deubner *sop* **Gidon Kremer** *vn*
Tbilisi Symphony Orchestra / Jansug Kakhidze
ECM New Series 465 138-2 (42 minutes: DDD) Ⓕ
Text and translation included. Recorded 1998

Music of lamentation has long been Kancheli's preoccupation, and this *Lament*, inscribed to the memory of Luigi Nono, has all the familiar Kancheliian moods: damaged soulfulness, peremptory outbursts and transfigured sadness, invoked aphoristically yet stretched to a hypnotic unbroken 42-minute span. Initial dots of sound on the solo violin grow into painfully sweet bursts of melody, suggesting a context only the composer himself knows and which the listener has to grope towards. Meanwhile a non-vibrato singer intones prayerful fragments. Kremer's violin becomes an eloquent voice; Maacha Deubner's soprano becomes a celestial instrument. Just as you sense the need for new ideas, the orchestra's sculpted orchestral chords gain a pulverizing force, and before long all hell breaks loose. The slight residual rawness of the Tbilisi brass is a treasurable authentic feature here, and the entire score is conducted faithfully by the man who knows Kancheli's music better than any musician alive. Eventually the text of Hans Sahl's poem, *Strophen* (Verses), reveals the underlying substance. The recording quality is first-rate.

Reinhard Keiser German 1674-1739

GROVE *Keiser wrote operas for Brunswick from c1693 and in 1694 became court chamber composer. From 1696-97 he was Kapellmeister at Hamburg, and from 1700-01 also Kapellmeister to the Schwerin court. As joint director of the Hamburg Theater-am-Gänsemarkt, 1702-7, he presented 17 of his own operas. Der Carneval von Venedig (1707), which included local dialect, was especially successful. He remained active in Hamburg until 1718. After a period as a guest Kapellmeister at Stuttgart he served intermittently at Copenhagen. He was back in Hamburg by 1723 and in 1728 became Kantor of the cathedral. The Singspiel Der hochmüthige, gestürtzte und wieder erhabene Croesus (1730), a version of a 1710 opera, was among his last stage works.*

Keiser was the central and most original figure in German Baroque opera, and wrote over 80 stage works. Most have serious German texts, which cover a wide range of subjects and often include allegorical or comic elements. They are notable for their dramatic flavour and skilful characterisation. Italian and French musical elements appear (including Italian arias from 1703), with dramatic recitatives and ariosos, varied aria forms and inventive instrumentation. His several Passions, oratorios and cantatas show similar features. Among his other works are sacred music and trio sonatas. Handel drew heavily on his works in his own.

Croesus

Roman Trekel *bar* Croesus; **Werner Güra** *ten* Atis; **Salomé Haller** *sop* Clerida; **Brigitte Eisenfeld** *sop* Trigesta; **Johannes Mannov** *bass* Cyrus; **Markus Schäfer** *ten* Eliates; **Dorothea Röschmann** *sop* Elmira; **Graham Pushee** *counterten* Halimacus; **Johanna Stojković** *sop* Nerillus; **Klaus Häger** *bass* Orsanes; **Kwangchul Youn** *bass* Solon; **Kurt Azesberger** *ten* Elcius; **Hanover Boys' Choir; Berlin RIAS Chamber Choir; Akademie für Alte Musik Berlin / René Jacobs**
Harmonia Mundi ③ HMC90 1714/6 Ⓕ
(188 minutes: DDD). Recorded 1999 ○○○

Reinhard Keiser was principal opera composer at Hamburg's celebrated Theatre on the Goose-market from 1697 to 1704 and from 1707 to 1718, returning intermittently, under Telemann's direction, between 1722 and 1735 when he retired after the death of his wife. During the first of these periods, a young man called Georg Friedrich Händel joined his theatre's orchestra and during his temporary absence composed three operas for the Goosemarket opera house, including *Almira* (1705) to a libretto set by Keiser.

Keiser's opera, given the catchy title *Die Unbeständigkeit weltlicher Ehre und Reichthums der hochmüthige/gestürzte/und wieder erhabene Croesus* ('The inconstancy of earthly glory and riches of the proud, deposed and rehabilitated Croesus') at its first performance in 1711, is called by the *New Grove* one of 'a handful of masterpieces' and René Jacobs concurs in his evangelising essay, 'Why Produce *Croesus* today'? printed in Harmonia Mundi's lavish booklet. The answer to Jacobs's rhetorical question lies in the quality of the music, which will come as a delightful surprise to baroque lovers who know Keiser by reputation rather than from his work. He looms large, of course, in the Handel biography, and the leading Handel scholar, Winton Dean, has commented that Keiser's operatic music left an indelible mark on that of the younger composer.

What makes *Croesus* particularly interesting is that it survives complete only in a version made by Keiser in 1730, at a time when Handel's operas were already well known at the Goose-market Theatre. There is another fascinating Handelian link, too, in that there is a striking similarity of atmosphere between Keiser's *Croesus* and Handel's *Serse* (1738). (Both are based on libretti by the Venetian poet, Nicola Minato, and the plots of both operas are quite similar.)

For the 1730 *Croesus*, Keiser replaced 37 of the 51 concerted numbers – it constitutes virtually a different work – and adapted at least three of the leading roles for different voice-types. This was standard baroque practice, but it leads Jacobs into some spurious claims: because in the 1730 version the title role of the rich King of Lydia is taken by a baritone, Jacobs has transposed the part of his adviser, the Greek philospoher Solon, from tenor to low bass on the dubious grounds that 'Croesus is younger and must therefore have a higher voice'. But old men were often assigned to tenors during this period. Jacobs can't touch a baroque opera without intervention of this kind – remember his ghastly, wrong-headed decision to have Giove-as-Diana in Cavalli's *Calisto* played in drag and sung by the bass Giove in falsetto. At least Solon is a minor part, but the transposition of the part of Atis – a baritone in 1711, a soprano castrato in 1730 – for tenor seems fairly pointless now when heroes sung by high voices are readily accepted by audiences.

Apart from these adjustments – he admits, too, that 'the conductor lent a hand in the arrangement of the recitatives' – Jacobs opts for the 1730 version because the 1711 original survives incomplete. The music itself is sheer bliss from first to last, and has a succession of variously characterised arias – the most exquisite are alloted to the heroine Elmira, ravishingly sung by Dorothea Röschmann, the most moving to the deposed Croesus (Roman Trekel) in his prison or facing his death in the flames of a sacrificial fire. The beauties of the work are manifold – the beginning of Act 2 is a pastoral scene in which peasants sing folksongs, and there is a delicious chorus for the peasant children extolling the joys of kissing lips as sweet as nuts. Suffice it so say that anyone who has almost all of Handel's operas will be delighted and fascinated by Keiser's.

The solo singing is uniformly first class, with eloquent performances from Trekel as Croesus, and from Werner Güra as his dumb son Atis, whose speech – and articulacy – is restored by the shock of an assassination attempt on his father. Klaus Häger as Elmira's villainous, unwanted admirer is first-class, too. There are also vivid contributions from Graham Pushee (Atis's confidant, Halimacus), Salomé Haller (the alternative love interest, Clerida) and the performers of the two comic servants, Brigitte Eisenfeld (Trigesta) and Kurt Azesberger (Elcius). This is another outstanding Jacobs resurrection and a great baroque operatic discovery too.

Albert Ketèlbey British 1875-1959

GROVE *Ketèlbey appeared as a solo pianist and conducted internationally. He was a popular composer of light orchestral pieces (In a Monastery Garden, 1915; In a Persian Market, 1920).*

In a Persian Market

In a Monastery Garden[a]. The Adventurers. Chal Romano Suite romantique. Caprice pianistique. The Clock and the Dresden Figures. Cockney Suite – No 3, At the Palais de Danse; No 5, Bank Holiday. In the Moonlight. Wedgwood Blue. Bells across the meadows. Phantom melody. In a Persian Market[a]
[a]**Slovak Philharmonic Male Chorus; Bratislava Radio Symphony Orchestra / Adrian Leaper**
Marco Polo 8 223442 (74 minutes: DDD) Ⓕ
Recorded 1992 ○

What a splendid CD! The obvious favourites (*In a Monastery Garden*, *In a Persian Market*, *Bells across the meadows*) are played with a grace and sensitivity that never invites unfavourable comparison with earlier recordings of the same pieces. If others in the same somewhat maudlin vein (*In the Mystic Land of Egypt*, *In a Chinese Temple Garden*, *Sanctuary of the Heart*) are missing, it is to give us the opportunity to hear some of Ketèlbey's unjustly overshadowed compositions. And what delights there are! Over-exposure to Ketèlbey's more stereotyped, highly perfumed compositions has disguised what varied and inventive music he composed. Once you acquaint yourself with the charms of *The Clock and the Dresden Figures*, *In the Moonlight* and the invigorating open-air spirit of *Chal Romano*, you will want to hear them again and again. Not to mention the equally invigorating overture *The Adventurers*, the elegant *Suite romantique* and the sparkling *Caprice pianistique* – and what a pity we are restricted to just two movements of the *Cockney Suite*. It is a pity, too, that the generally excellent notes should perpetuate the myth that 'Ketèlbey' was a pseudonym. But, no matter. With the playing, the conducting and the recording of a high standard, this is a collection that absolutely demands to be heard.

Aram Khachaturian

Russian/USSR 1903-1978

GROVE *Khachaturian, a bookbinder's son, at first studied medicine; he received his musical education comparatively late, studying the cello and composition under Myaskovsky at the Moscow Conservatory (1929-37). He came to wider notice in 1936 with his Piano Concerto and his Violin Concerto (1940), and was active from 1937 in the Union of Soviet Composers. Most of his best-known works, including the ballet Gayane, date from the 1940s. In common with other Soviet composers, he was subject to official criticism in 1948; but his colourful, nationally tinged idiom was far removed from modernistic excess. He concentrated on film music in the ensuing years, and took up conducting and teaching (at the Gnesin Institute and the Conservatory). His later works include 'concert rhapsodies' which re-interpret concerto form. His career represents the Soviet model of the linking of regional folklorism with the central Russian tradition; his Armenian heritage is clear in his melodies and his vitality, but in disciplined form. His greatest strengths lie in colourful orchestration and effective pictorialism.*

Piano Concerto

Piano Concerto. Dance Suite. Five Pieces for Wind Band – Waltz; Polka
Dora Serviarian-Kuhn *pf* **Armenian Philharmonic Orchestra / Loris Tjeknavorian**
ASV CDDCA964 (59 minutes: DDD) Ⓕ
Recorded 1995 ⭘

In the Piano Concerto Dora Serviarian-Kuhn and her Armenian compatriot, Loris Tjeknavorian, are in every way first-class: both identify naturally with the sinuous oriental flavour of the melodic lines and understand that the outer movements need above all to convey thrusting vitality; here there is plenty of drive and rhythmic lift. But what primarily makes this performance memorable is Serviarian-Kuhn's sense of fantasy, so that her various cadential passages, for all their brilliance, are charismatically quixotic rather than merely bravura displays. The other works on the disc are small beer. The 'Waltz' for wind band has an engaging carousel flavour; the somewhat vulgar 'Polka' which follows roisterously suggests the circus. The *Dance Suite* goes through the usual Khachaturian routines with which he likes to clothe his agreeable but at times rather insubstantial Armenian folk ideas. Easily the most memorable movement is the first and much the longer of the two Uzbek dances, which opens gently and touchingly: the reprise, with its haunting cor anglais solo, has a genial Nordic feeling. The closing 'Lezghinka', too, is rather jolly, but repetitive. The performances here are excellent and they are vividly recorded.

Violin Concerto

Khachaturian Violin Concerto in D minor
Tchaikovsky (arr Glazunov) Méditation, Op 42 No 1
Itzhak Perlman *vn*
Israel Philharmonic Orchestra / Zubin Mehta
EMI CDC7 47087-2 (46 minutes: DDD) Ⓕ
Recorded 1983 ⭘

Khachaturian's concerto is a work of considerable charm, beautifully written. Shostakovich once pointed out that a 'natural and folk idiom' was evident in everything his friend wrote, and Khachaturian's Armenian origin is evident in the melodic and harmonic contours of the lilting second theme in the first movement and the *Andante sostenuto* that follows. It goes without saying that Itzhak Perlman plays this work with total technical command and persuasive feeling, and the result is most enjoyable, even if one feels in some places, such as the first movement's long cadenza, that musical inspiration is being spread rather thin. The finale, however, is predictably exciting. The Tchaikovsky *Méditation* coupling is well worth having, both for its intrinsic quality and also because it was originally planned as the slow movement of his own Violin Concerto. There is good accompaniment from Mehta and the Israel Philharmonic Orchestra and a bright recording.

Gayaneh – Suite No 2

Khachaturian The Widow of Valencia – Suite. Gayaneh – Suite No 2
Tjeknavorian Danses fantastiques
Armenian Philharmonic Orchestra / Loris Tjeknavorian Ⓕ
ASV CDDCA884 (65 minutes: DDD) ⭘

Khachaturian's *The Widow of Valencia* is an early work (1940), yet already reveals the composer's fund of good tunes. He admitted its lack of authentic Spanishness and while the 'Introduction' opens with flashing southern Mediterranean gusto, it soon makes way for a sultry Armenian melody of best local vintage. However, why worry? Altogether this is a most winning suite, without a dull bar, piquantly scored and brilliantly presented by an orchestra which is completely at home and clearly enjoying themselves. They also give us another suite, comprising six indelible numbers – for the most part little known – from Khachaturian's masterpiece, *Gayaneh*. Tjeknavorian's own *Danses fantastiques* frequently burst with energy and the gentler dances have that Armenian flavour so familiar in *Gayaneh*. Brilliant playing in glittering yet spacious sound.

Spartacus – Ballet suites Nos 1-3

Royal Scottish National Orchestra / Neeme Järvi
Chandos CHAN8927 (63 minutes: DDD) Ⓕ
Recorded 1990

Khachaturian's ballet, *Spartacus*, first produced in 1956, was a judicious and highly successful artistic response to the demands of Soviet populist realism. For its dramatic narrative of a Roman slave rebelling against his captors, eventually to be betrayed and killed, the composer created a score of striking vitality, at once full-blooded and crude, passionate and tuneful, and yet individual. The ballet's most famous number, the 'Adagio of Phrygia and Spartacus', is justly popular. Elsewhere there are many expressions of joyous extroversion and scenes of wild revelry, in which the music erupts with great energy, for example the 'Entrance of the Merchants' and the wild 'Dance of the Pirates', both in Suite No 2. The scene of 'The Market' which opens Suite No 3 has enormous bustle. The romantic side of the score is full of languid sensuality: the Gaditanian Maidens are deliciously and decadently alluring, and the 'Dance of the Egyptian Girl' is hardly less seductive. Those who enjoy the 'Sabre Dance' from *Gayaneh* will respond to the vigorous 'Dance of a Greek Slave' with its rhythmic bite. Järvi and his Scottish players respond exuberantly to the near vulgarity of the unbuttoned animation and revel in the lusher evocations. The resonant acoustics of the Henry Wood Hall, Glasgow, cast a rich ambient glow over Khachaturian's vivid primary colours. Recommended.

Oliver Knussen British 1952

GROVE *Knussen studied in London and with Schuller at Tanglewood. His works display a fine ear for complex textural blendings; they include three symphonies (1967, 1971, 1979) and the operas Where the Wild Things Are (1983) and Higglety Pigglety Pop! (1985).*

Horn Concerto

Flourish with Fireworks, Op 22. The Way to Castle Yonder, Op 21a. Two Organa, Op 27. Horn Concerto, Op 28. Music for a Puppet Court, Op 11. Whitman Settings, Op 25. '... upon one note', Fantazia after Purcell
Lucy Shelton *sop* **Barry Tuckwell** *hn* **London Sinfonietta / Oliver Knussen**
DG 449 572-2GH (45 minutes: DDD). Text included. Ⓕ
Recorded 1995

This is a sample of what Knussen has written since his two one-act operas *Where the Wild Things are* (1984) and *Higglety Pigglety Pop!* (1985), a period during which, he says, he has come to prefer being 'bewitched for a few minutes than hypnotised for an hour'. Bewitching these short pieces certainly are. The *Flourish* has lyrical substance as well as the appropriate 'occasional' brilliance. *The Way to Castle Yonder* is a very brief suite from *Higglety Pigglety Pop!*, but also a vivid orchestral tone-poem in its own right. The *Organa* are fine examples of his love of fantasy, ingenious pieces that use a 12th-century technique to modern ends with such audible logic and lucid instrumentation that you want to hear both again immediately. Something similar happens in *Music for a Puppet Court*, two solutions to puzzle-canons by the Tudor composer John Lloyd flanking further developments of the same material. The lengthiest works here are both in a sense dreams. '*... upon one note*' is a day-dream from which Knussen is awoken by Purcell. The Horn Concerto is a beautiful, allusive dream about all the worlds that the solo horn can evoke, from woodland poetry to dark menace. Knussen is a masterly orchestrator. This disc will give unalloyed pleasure.

Higglety Pigglety Pop!

Cynthia Buchan *mez* Jennie; **Lisa Saffer** *sop* Potted Plant; Baby; Mother Goose; **Rosemary Hardy** *sop* Rhoda; Voice of Baby's Mother; **Christopher Gillett** *ten* Cat-Milkman; High voice of Ash-tree **David Wilson-Johnson** *bass-bar* Pig-in-Sandwich Boards; Low voice of Ash-tree **Stephen Richardson** *bass-bar* Lion

Where the Wild Things Are
Lisa Saffer *sop* Max; **Christopher Gillett** *ten* Wild Thing with Beard; Goat Wild Thing; **David Wilson-Johnson bass-bar** Rooster Wild Thing; **Stephen Richardson bass-bar** Bull Wild Thing; **Mary King** *mez* Mama; Tzippy; **Quentin Hayes bass** Wild Thing with Horns
London Sinfonietta / Oliver Knussen
DG 20/21 ② 469 556-2GH2 (102 minutes: DDD) Ⓕ
Notes and texts included

The stories and drawings of Maurice Sendak upon which both these operas are based explore a vein of surreal dreaming and of the delight that children take in both fantasy and disorder, and all of these things appeal to something close to the centre of Oliver Knussen's creativity. An obvious model for both operas is Ravel's *L'enfant et les sortilèges*, and Knussen shares Ravel's pleasure in mechanisms that work immaculately well. He also has much of Ravel's mastery of orchestration, and one of the most enjoyable aspects of both scores is their kaleidoscopic sequence of brilliantly imagined and faultlessly executed instrumental textures. Ravel has foolishly been accused of heartlessness, and it is as untrue of Knussen as it is of him. Knussen's music reveals profundities and a childlike awe in Sendak that you might not have suspected.

The Ash-tree in *Higglety Pigglety Pop!*, for example, is at one level a straightforward comic character ('You are taller than I am', says the Sealyham terrier Jennie; 'Sixty feet taller, to be precise', replies the tree, primly), but Knussen's setting of its words for two singers, tenor and bass, and his evocative orchestra make of it a magic voice of nature as well. The Lion in the same opera is a relative of the amiable beast in *The Wizard of Oz*, but at the same time formidable. Knussen's *Wild Things*, roaring gibberish, are anarchically comic and their 'Wild Rumpus' hugely inventive fun, but they have also the musical equivalent of the pointed teeth and glaring yellow eyes that Sendak gave them; and something of pathos when the child Max leaves them on their island. Knussen's quotations (a magnificent blast of Mussorgsky as Max is crowned King of the Wild Things; a demure Mozartian musical box to introduce the fiendish Baby in *Higglety*) are for adults, of course, as are the cunning stylistic references in *Higglety*'s finale, but in the best sense both of the operas are for children of all ages, or indeed for any listener who is inclined to respond to wonder, humour and meticulous intricacy.

Both recordings were made following staged performances, and have benefited from it: the singers (unfair to single out any of them: they are all first class) are audibly enjoying themselves a great deal, and the orchestra takes no less obvious pleasure in Knussen's magical sounds.

Zoltán Kodály   Hungarian 1882-1967

GROVE *Kodály was brought up in the country, he knew folk music from childhood and also learnt to play the piano and string instruments, and to compose, all with little tuition. In 1900 he went to Budapest to study with Koessler at the Academy of Music, and in 1905 he began his collaboration with Bartók, collecting and transcribing folksongs. They also worked side by side as composers, and Kodály's visit in 1907 to Paris, bringing back Debussy's music, was important to them both: their first quartets were played in companion concerts in 1910, marking the emergence of 20th-century Hungarian music.*

Kodály, however, preferred to accept rather than analyse folk material in his music, and his style is much less contrapuntal and smoother harmonically. His major works, notably the comic opera Háry János, the Psalmus hungaricus, the 'Peacock' Variations for orchestra and the Dances of Marosszék and Galánta draw on Magyar folk music (unlike Bartók, he confined himself to Hungarian material). His collecting activity also stimulated his work on musical education, convincing him of the value of choral singing as a way to musical literacy. He taught at the Budapest Academy from 1907, and after World War Two his ideas became the basis of state policy, backed in part by his own large output of choral music, much of it for children, as well as other exercise pieces, and was widely used as a model abroad.

Symphony in C

Symphony in C. Summer Evening. Magyar Rondo
Christopher Warren-Green *vn* **Philharmonia Orchestra / Yondani Butt** Ⓕ
ASV CDDCA924 (54 minutes: DDD). Recorded 1994

Kodály's only Symphony has an engagingly pastoral quality, with mild but memorable thematic material, lively – even somewhat overwrought – musical arguments and notably scenic orchestration. Yondani Butt presents a volatile view of the piece, with weighty textures and a fairly intense delivery, especially in the first movement's emphatic development section. The slow movement, an elegiac *Andante* based on folk-style motives, is appealingly atmospheric, while the fresh-faced finale generates plenty of rustic excitement. *Summer Evening* underlines the music's alternation of dance and reverie, whereas Butt's invigorating performance of the rarely heard but strangely more-ish *Magyar Rondo* (shades of Bartók's *Romanian Folk Dances*) has the Philharmonia playing like a generously augmented gipsy band, with stylish solo work from Christopher Warren-Green. Enthusiasm and sincerity are much in evidence throughout this well-recorded concert, while the odd spot of executive ruggedness is fairly appropriate to the music's outdoor character.

Dances from Galánta

Háry János – concert suite. Dances of Marosszék. Variations on a Hungarian folksong, 'The Peacock'. Dances from Galánta
Montreal Symphony Orchestra / Charles Dutoit
Decca 444 322-2DH (77 minutes: DDD) Ⓕ
Recorded 1994

Dutoit presents a warmly persuasive reading of *Háry János*. In the fifth movement, 'Intermezzo', the big *tenutos* in this very nationalistic piece are winningly timed. The instrumental solos are imaginatively played by the Montreal principals, as is, for example, the saxophone in the final Funeral March section of the fourth movement, the 'Battle and Defeat of Napoleon'. The *Peacock* Variations benefit even more than *Háry János* from the opulent Montreal sound, most of all in the glorious climax of the finale, which with Dutoit has tremendous panache. In the two sets of *Dances* Dutoit is warmly sympathetic in his springing of rhythms and moulding of phrases. For this apt, generous coupling of Kodály's four most popular orchestral pieces Dutoit stands a clear first choice.

Dances from Galánta[a]. Dances of Marosszék[a]. Háry János[a] – concert suite; The Flute-Playing Hussar; The Old Woman; The Jewish family; Háry riding Lucifer; The two gipsies. Dancing Song[b]. St Gregory's Day[c]. See the gipsies[b]
[b]Budapest Children's Choir Magnificat; [c]Kecskemét Children's Choir Miraculum; [a]Budapest Festival Orchestra / Iván Fischer
Philips 462 824-2PH (66 minutes: DDD). Texts and translations included. Recorded 1998 Ⓕ OO

Iván Fischer and his Hungarian band join the most august company in this wonderful repertoire. As both sets of dances amply demonstrate, Fischer's Budapest Festival Orchestra is no less virtuosic than Ormandy's dazzling Philadelphians or Ferenc Fricsay's exemplary Berlin RSO, and its impassioned playing melds an earthy physicality, tangy exuberance and improvisatory flair to consistently telling effect. Add to the mix Fischer's wittily observant direction (an abundance of affectionate *rubato* in the opening section of the *Marosszék Dances* especially, allied to a generous quotient of 'gipsy' slides from the strings elsewhere), and the results are irresistible. Similarly, their *Háry János* Suite is immensely engaging. After a spectacularly good introductory 'sneeze', Fischer sees to it that Kodály's great arcs of melody are truly *espressivo cantabile* as marked. It's followed by an unusually propulsive, chipper 'Viennese Musical Clock' and affectingly gentle 'Song' (less heart-on-sleeve than Fricsay's, and – praise be – no spot-lit cimbalom either). Napoleon's battlefield antics are hilariously depicted (splendidly bolshy trombones), while Fischer's thrusting 'Intermezzo' has joyous swagger. Moreover, for all the giddy festivities of the brassy 'Entrance of the Emperor and his Court', Fischer still manages to extract plenty of ear-burning detail (such as the horns' arresting harmony at 1'08"). Five miniatures from the original *Singspiel* are also included, programmed separately from the suite; in 'The two gipsies' Fischer shares fiddling duties with Gábor Takács-Nagy. Last but not least we get three choral offerings from 1925-9, which are delivered with captivating freshness and charm by the two admirable children's choirs here. A peach of an issue, complemented by an irrepressibly vivid and wide-ranging Philips recording.

Cello Sonatas

Solo Cello Sonata, Op 8. Cello Sonata, Op 4. Three Chorale Preludes (after Bach)
Maria Kliegel *vc* **Jenö Jandó** *pf*
Naxos 8 553160 (64 minutes: DDD) Recorded 1994-95 Ⓢ O

Maria Kliegel rises to the challenge of Kodály's Solo Sonata with considerable gusto: harmonics, *glissandos*, *sul ponticello*, fiery arpeggios – all are expertly employed and delivered via a nicely rounded tone. Kliegel's lustrous account of the *Adagio* (to be played *con grand espressiono*) underlines harmonic similarities with late Liszt and the folky, one-man-band finale has ample panache. The appreciative booklet-note relates Bartók's enthusiasm for the Solo Sonata's 'unusual and original style…[and] surprising vocal effects'. In fact, no other work by Kodály is so profoundly Bartókian in spirit. The Sonata, Op 4, is a far milder piece, though forthright expressive declamation sits at the centre of the first movement and the second is infused with the spirit of folk music. Kliegel and Jenö Jandó are in musical accord, and the recording is very good – although if you listen to the 'Bach-Kodály' tracks and wait for the Solo Sonata to start, you'll note a huge expansion in the cello's recorded profile. The three *Chorale Preludes* that open the programme are 'attributed Bach' and enjoy the rich trimmings of a thunderous piano part (Busoni-cum-Liszt, with a snatch of Bartók for good measure) and a warm flood of tone from Kliegel. All in all, then, a fine bargain, and a well-planned coupling.

Laudes organi and Missa brevis

Kodály Laudes organi. Missa brevis
Janáček (ed Wingfield) Mass in E flat
Andrew Reid *org*
Westminster Cathedral Choir / James O'Donnell
Hyperion CDA67147 (73 minutes: DDD). Texts and translations included. Recorded 1999 Ⓕ OO

Janáček begun his Mass around 1908, left it to gather dust for 20 years, then turned it into the first draft of the *Glagolitic Mass*. After his death a pupil, Vilém Petrúelka, attempted a reconstruction which, as Paul Wingfield unsubtly points out, was no good. Wingfield's own version draws substantially on the original draft of the *Glagolitic Mass* to the extent of including a complete movement (the *Sanctus*) from it. Clearly Janáček knew best, and the only distinguishing moments are those bits recognisably from the *Glagolitic Mass*. Unquestionably, though, both the *Missa brevis* and *Laudes organi* are among Kodály's most inspired creations. Yet new recordings of favourite works are prone to disappoint. Not this one. If anything, this stunning performance, crowned by Andrew Reid's masterly organ playing, raises this setting of dog-Latin verses in praise of the organ and commissioned by the American Guild of Organists even higher. About 20 years before *Laudes organi*, the *Missa brevis* was first performed in this version for organ and chorus (it was originally an organ solo) in a bomb shelter during the 1944-45 Siege of Budapest. From such an inauspicious start, the work has fared remarkably well on record and this release represents an undoubted climax. It's a simply glorious performance and, in short, should not be missed.

Erich Wolfgang Korngold

Austro/Hungarian 1897-1957

GROVE *Korngold, an American composer of Austro-Hungarian origin, was the son of the music critic Julius Korngold (1860-1945). He studied with Zemlinsky and had spectacular early successes with his ballet Der Schneemann (1910, Vienna) and operas Violanta (1916) and Die tote Stadt (1920). In 1934 he went to Hollywood and wrote some fine film scores. After World War II he wrote orchestral and chamber pieces, including a Violin Concerto and Symphony in F sharp, in a lush, Romantic style.*

Violin Concerto

Korngold Violin Concerto[a]. **Rózsa** Violin Concerto, Op 24[b], Tema con variazioni Op 29a[b]. **Waxman** Fantasy on Bizet's 'Carmen'[c].
Jascha Heifetz *vn* **Gregor Piatigorsky** *vc* [b]**Chamber Orchestra;** [a]**Los Angeles Philharmonic Orchestra / Alfred Wallenstein;** [b]**Dallas Symphony Orchestra / Walter Hendl;** [c]**RCA Victor Symphony Orchestra / Donald Voorhees**
RCA Victor Gold Seal [ac]mono/[b]stereo
09026 61752-2 (70 minutes: ADD) Ⓜ
Recorded 1946-63

Heifetz's legendary recording of the Korngold Concerto serves a double purpose: as an effective introduction to Korngold's seductive musical style, and as the best possible example of Heifetz's violin artistry. The work itself was written at the suggestion of Bronislaw Huberman, but it was Heifetz who gave the première in 1947. It calls on material that Korngold had also used in three of his film scores (he was at the time composing for Hollywood), although the way he welds the themes into a three-movement structure is masterly enough to suggest that the concerto came to him 'of a piece'. The very opening would be enough to seduce most listeners, unless – that is – they have an aversion to the film music of the period. Miklós Rózsa's Concerto has its roots in the composer's Hungarian soil, and echoes of Bartók are rarely absent. But whereas Korngold's score is taken from movie music, Rózsa's (or parts of it) became a film score – namely, *The Private Life of Sherlock Holmes*. Rózsa's self-possessed, skilfully written *Tema con variazoni* was taken, in 1962, from a much larger work then in progress, but Heifetz and Piatigorsky play it in a reduced orchestration. As to the *Carmen Fantasy* by Franz Waxman (another notable film composer), its luscious tunes and frightening technical challenges were written with the great violinist very much in mind. It's a stunning piece of playing, and wears its years lightly. The other recordings sound far better, and the Rózsa items are in stereo. Marvellous stuff!

Additional recommendation
Couplings: Much Ado about Nothing, Op 11 – Maiden in the Bridal Chamber; Dogberry and Verges; Intermezzo; Hornpipe **Barber** Violin Concerto, Op 14
Shaham *vn* **London Symphony Orchestra / Previn** *pf*
DG 439 886-2GH (71 minutes: DDD: 9/94). Ⓕ
Shaham is yearningly warm without sentimentality, clean and precise in attack. The suite from *Much ado about nothing* provides a delightful and apt makeweight.

Symphony in F sharp

Symphony in F sharp, Op 40. Einfache Lieder, Op 9 – No 1, Schneeglöckchen; No 3, Ständchen; No 4, Liebesbriefchen; No 6, Sommer. Die tote Stadt – Glück, das mir verblieb
Barbara Hendricks *sop* **Philadelphia Orchestra / Franz Welser-Möst**
EMI CDC5 56169-2 (63 minutes: DDD) Ⓕ
Recorded 1995

Franz Welser-Möst's view of Korngold's magnificent Symphony is less expansive than other interpretations, especially in the weighty *Adagio* slow movement, but he is no less impressive for that. His account is curvaceous and 'filmic', but one has less of an image of Errol Flynn sailing the high seas when that wonderful horn theme appears in the *Scherzo*. The sombre *Adagio* is superbly controlled and beautifully crafted. Elsewhere, he generates a huge degree of rhythmic incisiveness from his players – the fleet-footed *Scherzo* for instance, or the daring-do finale. Although not wearing its heart on its sleeve, Welser-Möst's reading is not lacking in passion. Barbara Hendricks's ravishing accounts of four of the six *Einfache Lieder* and the famous Marietta's Lied from *Die tote Stadt* make an excellent foil to the symphony.

Sursum corda

Sursum corda, Op 13. Die kleine Serenade ('Baby Serenade'), Op 24. Der Schneemann – Prelude; Serenade. Die tote Stadt – Prelude to Act II[a]. Das Wunder der Heliane – Interlude
[a]**Karen Robertson** *sop* [a]**Tibor Pazmany** *org* **Linz Bruckner Orchestra / Caspar Richter**
ASV CDDCA1074 (62 minutes: DDD) Ⓕ
Recorded 1999

This disc is an absolute must for newcomers to Korngold's music. Richter presents a beautifully rounded and balanced programme, headed by a virtuosic, highly charged account of the Prelude to Act 2 from the opera *Die tote Stadt*, with a finely sung, if brief contribution from soprano Karen Robertson. Although there's no film music by Korngold on this disc, the symphonic overture *Sursum corda* (dating from the same period as *Die tote Stadt*), with its uplifting, heroic themes, did eventually provide material for the film score to *The Adventures of Robin Hood* some 18 years later. Richter and his players deliver a wonderfully impassioned and incident-packed performance. The 'Baby Serenade' was composed shortly after the birth of Korngold's second son Georg, and is a delightful five-movement suite describing a day in the life of his baby son. Korngold's perceptive and often humorous sketches are brilliantly matched in a performance that simply exudes affection and fun – check out the wonderfully characterised performances in the jazzy 'Baby tells a story', track 6. Two extracts from the remarkably early ballet *Der Schneemann* (including the ravishing 'Serenade') follow, and the disc is nicely rounded off with the orchestral Interlude from *Das Wunder der Heliane* – more voluptuous playing in what must be some of Korngold's most voluptuous music. Excellent sound: a disc not to be missed.

Suite, Op 23

Korngold Suite, Op 23
Schmidt Piano Quintet in G
Joseph Silverstein, Joel Smirnoff *vns* **Michael Tree** *va* **Yo-Yo Ma** *vc* **Leon Fleisher** *pf*
Sony Classical SK48253 (75 minutes: DDD) Ⓕ
Recorded 1991 and 1993

Paul Wittgenstein's many commissions for piano left-hand (he lost his right arm during the First World War) significantly enriched the 20th-century's musical repertoire, and Sony's superb CD bears witness to two of the finest. Both date from the inter-war years, Korngold's Suite being a product of 1930 and Schmidt's Quintet – one of three that he composed for Wittgenstein – from 1926. Korngold's sensual 'Lied' (the Suite's fourth movement) is the musical equivalent of death by chocolate, while the homely tones of Schmidt's *Adagio* are no less lovely in their way. Both tug insistently at the heart-strings, yet they are very different. Korngold also gives us a purple-hued waltz and a pungent 'Groteske' with a buttermilk centre. His is a music ripe to bursting point, although at the same time it is also wickedly subtle and immensely clever. Schmidt's first movement has a second set that could have strayed from an undiscovered Brahms sextet, with piano writing that is unexpectedly prophetic of Bartók's Third Concerto. His third movement opens like a Brahms piano miniature, and continues in the manner of Reger. Both works feature delightful finales, Korngold's being a set of variations on a tender theme. Sony's stellar line-up gives Schmidt's Quintet the outing of its life: you will wait impatiently to replay the two middle movements. Fleisher's beautifully graded playing is granted affectionate support from Silverstein and his colleagues, supple but sweet-centred and very well balanced. A hugely enjoyable coupling.

Suite, Op 23. Piano Quintet in E, Op 15
Claire McFarlane, Jan Peter Schmolck *vns* **Schubert Ensemble of London** (Simon Blendis *vn* Douglas Paterson *va* Jane Salmon *vc* William Howard *pf*)
ASV CDDCA1047 (69 minutes: DDD) Ⓕ
Recorded 1997

This supremely stylish interpretation of Korngold's Op 23 Suite (1930) has a very great deal to commend it, occupying a satisfying middle ground between the Czech Trio's endearingly homely view and the far more grandly virtuosic (and, in the heavenly fourth-movement 'Lied', self-consciously protracted) approach espoused by Sony's starry team. Not for the first time on disc, William Howard's decidedly superior brand of pianism is a very real boon, and the whole performance radiates an affection and gentle purposefulness that are genuinely appealing. Anyway, Korngoldians will surely want to acquire this ASV coupling for the marvellous Piano Quintet, which here receives a reading that marries refreshing spontaneity to notable architectural elegance. Dating from 1921 and composed just after *Die tote Stadt*, it's an exuberantly confident offering cast in three movements. These artists audibly revel in Korngold's taxing, yet sumptuously rewarding writing, and the recording is handsome and true.

Piano Trio in D, Op 1. Suite, Op 23
Jana Vlachová *vn*
Czech Piano Trio (Dana Vlachová *vn* Jan Páleníček *vc* Milan Langer *pf*)
Supraphon SU3347-2 (62 minutes: DDD) Ⓕ
Recorded 1997

Supraphon's well-recorded version of the Suite is remarkably fast. Where this Czech team scores over recorded rivals is in the 'Lied', which Korngold asks to be played *Nicht zu langsam*. Their timing is a nifty 3'09". The coupling is Korngold's outrageously precocious – and utterly unmissable – Op 1 Piano Trio. No other musical 12-year-old could have penned such a memorable – and meaningful – opening theme (a sure premonition of Korngold's film scores), not to mention the *Scherzo*'s Trio and the brief *Larghetto* third movement. Astonishing! It is no surprise that, following the Trio's New York première, W J Henderson wrote (in the New York *Sun*), 'if we had a little boy of 12 who preferred writing this sort of music to hearing a good folk tune or going and out and playing in the park, we should consult a specialist.' Fortunate for us, folk tunes and football took second place to chronicling some quite marvellous musical ideas.

Violin Sonata

Violin Sonata in D, Op 6. Sonett für Wien, Op 41. Much Ado About Nothing – Dogberry and Verges; Intermezzo; Hornpipe; Bridal Morning. Das Wunder der Heliane – Gesang der Heliane. Der Schneemann – Serenade. Die tote Stadt – Glück, das mir verblieb; Mein Sehnen, mein Wähnen (all arr cpsr). Märchenbilder, Op 3 – The Gnomes (arr Révay)
Detlef Hahn *vn* **Andrew Ball** *pf*
ASV CDDCA1080 (70 minutes: DDD) Ⓕ
Recorded 2000

This is an indispensable disc gathering together the complete works for violin and piano, including no fewer than three world-première recordings. In addition, the whole venture is made all the more indispensable for the superb performances throughout.

The disc opens with the remarkably early, but technically and emotionally mature, Violin Sonata in D – a ravishing work that certainly ranks among Korngold's major compositions. It was composed in 1912 at the suggestion of Carl Flesch and Artur Schnabel, and was first performed by them in 1913. The Sonata is lyrical and expansive and has all the characteristics of

Korngold's melodic and harmonic idiom – there's certainly nothing apprentice about this piece. Hahn and Ball give a beautifully crafted performance indeed and have truly absorbed the essence of this masterly score.

Korngold's suite of incidental music for *Much Ado About Nothing* has enjoyed a certain amount of currency in its original orchestral version, but less so in Korngold's own arrangement for violin and piano heard here. The transition works marvellously, being ideally suited to the intimacy of chamber music. The second movement, 'Dogberry and Verges', a grotesque march depicting the two drunken night-watchmen, pays passing homage to Korngold's childhood idol Gustav Mahler, and elsewhere in the suite (still essentially an early work, written in 1919) there are constant intimations of the film scores of later years.

The remainder of the disc is devoted to smaller arrangements of works, including two extracts from the opera *Die tote Stadt* and one from *Das Wunder der Heliane* as well as the gorgeous song setting *Sonett für Wien* (In Memoriam), Op 41, the theme of which Korngold also used in the 1946 film *Escape Me Never*. Hahn and Ball are once again most persuasive; only in the 'Serenade' from *Der Schneemann* is a certain amount of charm lost through their slightly impulsive choice of tempo. Excellent sound recording – another highly recommendable issue in ASV's Korngold series.

Die Kathrin

Melanie Diener *sop* Kathrin; **David Rendall** *ten* François; **Robert Hayward** *bass-bar* Malignac; **Lilian Watson** *sop* Chou-Chou; **Della Jones** *mez* Monique **BBC Singers; BBC Concert Orchestra / Martyn Brabbins**

CPO ③ CPO999 602-2 (162 minutes: DDD). Notes, text and translation included. Recorded 1997 Ⓕ

In the mid-1970s, when the revival of Korngold's music got underway, not even the most ardent enthusiast can have imagined that one day all of his operas would be given commercial recordings. That, however, is what has been achieved with this, the first modern performance and recording of his last stage work. *Die Kathrin* is separated by 10 years from its predecessor, *Das Wunder der Heliane*. Between *Heliane* and *Die Kathrin*, Korngold's career had changed. From being the wunderkind of the 1910s, he had developed into the film composer and arranger of large-scale operettas. If *Heliane* is the most grandiose of his operas, *Die Kathrin* is the most unpretentious; Korngold had thought of labelling it a folk-opera. The story is simple. The hero, François, is a singer who has been conscripted into the army. He falls in love with Kathrin, leaving her pregnant. She loses her job, follows him to Marseilles, where in a vaguely *Tosca*-like plot-twist François is implicated in the murder of the villain, who has actually been shot by one of the cabaret girls. Five years pass, François returns to find Kathrin and his child. The opera ends with a rapturous love duet. The music is full of typically lush Korngold scoring. In the night-club scene, obligatory in any 1930s opera, there are two catchy numbers, and Korngold brings in such fashionably jazzy instruments as a trio of saxophones and a banjo. The cast is exceptionally strong. Diener has just the right weight of voice for Kathrin, and Rendall makes François into a very positive hero. In the night-club scene, Watson and Jones are suitably exotic as the good-time girls, while Hayward conveys the nasty side of things as Malignac. Brabbins brings out the essentially Puccinian side of the score; in its structure the opera resembles *La rondine* more than a little: *verismo* didn't die with *Turandot*. Devotees of Korngold's music won't need any encouragement. Those with a taste for tuneful, romantic opera, sometimes bordering on operetta, should give it a chance.

Fritz Kreisler

Austrian 1875-1962

GROVE *After study at the Vienna Conservatory and the Paris Conservatoire Kreisler toured the USA (1888-89). Real recognition came in 1899, after a concert with the Berlin PO under Nikisch. His London début was in 1902 and in 1910 he gave the première of Elgar's Concerto. He lived in Berlin, 1924-34, and in 1939 settled in the USA, becoming an American citizen in 1943. His last concert was in 1947. Kreisler played with grace, elegance and a sweet, golden tone with a pronounced vibrato. His repertory included brief pieces of his own, some of them semi-pastiche pieces which he initially ascribed to composers such as Tartini and Pugnani, some of them sugary Viennese morsels, all beautifully written to display brilliant, subtle and expressive violin playing.*

Compositions and Arrangements

Original Compositions and Arrangements – works by Kreisler and arrangements of works by Bach, Brandl, Dvořák, Falla, Glazunov, Heuberger, Poldini, Rimsky-Korsakov, Schubert, Scott, Tchaikovsky and Weber
Fritz Kreisler *vn* with various artists
EMI Références mono CDH7 64701-2 (78 minutes: ADD). Recorded 1930-38 Ⓜ

Kreisler Praeludium and Allegro in the style of Pugnani. Schön Rosmarin. Tambourin chinois, Op 3. Caprice viennois, Op 2. Précieuse in the style of Couperin. Liebesfreud. Liebesleid. La Gitana. Berceuse romantique, Op 9. Polichinelle. Rondino on a theme by Beethoven. Tempo di Menuetto in the style of Pugnani. Toy Soldier's March. Allegretto in the style of Boccherini. Marche miniature viennoise. Aucassin and Nicolette, 'Canzonetta medievale'. Menuet in the style of Porpora. Siciliano and Rigaudon in the style of Francoeur. Syncopation
Joshua Bell *vn* **Paul Coker** *pf*
Decca 444 409-2DH (63 minutes: DDD) Recorded 1995 Ⓕ

Years of 'encore' employment have guaranteed the cult longevity of Kreisler's music – certainly among violinists. The repertoire on Kreisler's disc consists of his own pieces and a large number of arrangements. Some of the latter are pretty feeble musically, yet the great violinist's unique artistry and magical tone-quality shine through. Sometimes he does not land right in the middle of a note, but always plays with the timing and phrasing of a great singer. Nothing is routine or set in his playing, which has a continual feeling of discovery and freshness. The transfers are excellent. Joshua Bell learned Kreisler from his teacher, the late Josef Gingold, and yet his approach is anything but 'old school'. He habitually avoids the pitfalls of imitation, flashiness and patronizing overkill, preferring instead to revisit the music with modern ears. His *Caprice viennois* is light years removed from the composer's own, a fresh-faced, strongly characterised reading that trades sentimentality for just a hint of jazz. And of course there's that inseparable twosome, *Liebesfreud* and *Liebesleid*, the latter in particular displaying Bell's tone at its most alluring. The longest piece on the disc is the *Praeludium and Allegro in the style of Pugnani* which Bell gives 'the full treatment', deftly pointing the *Allegro*, relishing passagework and double-stopping with impressive accuracy. Some pieces seem indivisible from Kreisler's own very individual tone and phrasing, *Polichinelle*, for example, and *Marche miniature viennoise*, both of which paraded the sort of personalised rubato, timing and tone-production that have for so long seemed part of the music's very essence. Here and in a few other instances, Bell's brighter, more overtly virtuosic approach doesn't quite catch the music's period charm and yet a mini-masterpiece like the rarely heard *Berceuse romantique* (a sort of Fauré-Korngold synthesis) displays ample style, subtlety and affection of phrasing. Bell's smooth, witty and keenly inflected readings make for elevated entertainment: they may not replace the composer's own, but they do provide a youthful and in many ways illuminating alternative. The recordings are excellent, but Coker's fine accompaniments occasionally seem overprominent.

Viennese Rhapsody

Albéniz/Kreisler Tango, Op 165 No 2 **Dvořák/Kreisler** Slavonic Dances – B78: No 2 in E minor; B145: No 2 in E minor **Falla/Kreisler** La vida breve – Danse espagnole **Granados/Kreisler** Andaluza, Op 37 No 5 **Kreisler** Caprice viennois, Op 2. Tambourin chinois, Op 3. Berceuse romantique, Op 9. Viennese Rhapsodic Fantasietta. Zigeuner-capriccio. La gitana. Polichinelle. Aucassin and Nicolette. Liebesleid. Liebesfreud. Slavonic Fantasie **Scott/Kreisler** Lotus Land, Op 47 No 1 **Wieniawski/Kreisler** Etude-Caprice in A minor, Op 18 No 4

Leonidas Kavakos *vn* **Péter Nagy** *pf*

BIS CD1196 (71 minutes: DDD) Ⓕ

Recorded 2000 **OO**

Leonidas Kavakos's Kreisler is authentic in the best meaning of that term, namely a keen approximation both of the music's spirit and of the composer's inimitable playing style. Few Kreisler recitals have recalled, in so much minute detail, the warmth, elegance and gentlemanly musical manners of the master himself.

It was an inspired idea to open the programme with that nostalgic evocation of Old Vienna, the eight-minute *Viennese Rhapsodic Fantasietta*, a Korngold sound-alike that cannot waltz without smiling wistfully or even shedding the odd tear. Kavakos has mastered that lilting 3/4 to a T. His tone is uncannily familiar – cooler and less vibrant perhaps than Kreisler's own during the earlier part of his recording career but with a similarly consistent (though never overbearing) vibrato. The varieties of bowing, slides, attack and articulation are all reminiscent of an inimitable model. More remarkable still is Kavakos's ability to tease a phrase this or that side of the barline – not in any obvious way, but subtly enough to notice without having it register on a metronome. But don't imagine that these performances are mere imitations: an individual personality does come through, it's just that a Kreislerian accent has become part of the mix – at least for the purposes of this recital. Kavakos was a pupil of another fine Kreisler exponent, Joseph Gingold, and the teaching obviously paid off.

The programme has been very well chosen, ending with what are surely Kreisler's three most famous miniatures – *Liebesleid*, *Liebesfreud* and *Caprice viennois* – and with a peppering of transcriptions beforehand. The *Slavonic Fantasie* after Dvořák is among the most interesting, incorporating as it does the first of the four *Romantic Pieces*. Cyril Scott's *Lotus Land* is haunting and exotic, while Kreisler's own *Zigeuner-capriccio* provides a fine example of Kavakos's slightly melancholy puckishness. Péter Nagy's stylish accompaniments add yet more flavour to the menu. All in all a super programme, beautifully recorded.

Ernst Krenek

Austro/American 1900-1991

GROVE *Krenek, an American composer of Austrian origin, studied in Vienna and Berlin with Schreker, who was an influence on his early works (Symphonies Nos 1-3, 1921-22). After a visit to Paris, he began to emulate Stravinsky's neo-classicism, producing an eclectic style out of which, with the addition of mild jazz elements, he wrote his opera Jonny spielt auf (1926), a spectacular success in its day. He followed it up with more jazz operas, including Leben des Orest (1930), and then assimilated 12-note serialism in his most ambitious opera, Karl V (1938). In 1938 he moved to the USA, where he taught and continued to compose prolifically, his later works including further operas: Pallas Athene weint (1955), Der goldene Bock (1964), Sardakai (1970). Nearly all his music since Karl V is serial, several works of the 1950s and 1960s being abstract speculations in the technique. In scope and style his music embraces almost all the major trends, displayed in a highly accomplished technique.*

Songs

O Lacrymosa, Op 48. Stella's Monolog, Op 57. Die Nachtigall, Op 68. Fünf Lieder, Op 82. Four Songs, Op 112. The Flea, Op 175. Wechselrahmen, Op 189

Christine Schäfer *sop* **Axel Bauni** *pf*

Orfeo Musica Rediviva C373951A (67 minutes: DDD) Ⓕ Texts and translations included. Recorded 1994

In this entertaining recital, the chronological arrangement of the songs affords a fair view of Krenek's stylistic development across nearly 40 years (1926-65). Quite a development it was, from the radiant *O Lacrymosa*, three further musings by Rilke on the Virgin Mary, to the near-volcanic *Wechselrahmen* ('Changing Settings'), to poems by Emil Barth. In musical style, *O Lacrymosa* is clearly suggestive of Hindemith's *Das Marienleben*. More individual is *Stella's Monolog* (1928), on lines from Goethe's play *Stella*. Cast as a dramatic scena, this compositional *tour de force* has a wide range of moods, some of *buffa*-like airiness at odds with the text's romantic ardour, suggesting a send-up. When in 1937 Krenek came to set five brief stanzas by Kafka, he had finally embraced Schoenberg's 12-note method. The Kafka songs, Op 82, as well as those of Op 112 (1946-47, setting Gerard Manley Hopkins) show a concomitant spareness of texture, but his setting of Donne's *The Flea* (1960) is wonderfully exuberant, while *Wechselrahmen*'s extremity of expression is entirely apposite given Krenek's tirelessly adventurous spirit. Christine Schäfer is a sympathetic interpreter; a touch shrill in the topmost registers, her voice is big enough to cope with these songs' widely varying demands. Axel Bauni gives first-class support and the recording sounds bright and truthful. This release is a must for anyone remotely interested in Lieder, of the 20th century or any other.

Johann Kuhnau

German 1660-1722

GROVE *German composer and theorist Kuhnau studied in Dresden and Zittau, where he briefly served as Kantor and organist, and then at Leipzig, where in 1684 he became organist at the Thomaskirche and, in 1701, Kantor. His secular vocal music is all lost, but many sacred works survive, mostly cantatas, anticipating the style of Bach, his successor: they show lyrical vocal writing, powerful fugues and dramatic contrasts of texure which stress the rhetorical sense. He published four sets of keyboard pieces, including two sets called Clavier-Übung (each with seven suites, one set in the major keys and one in the minor) and, his best-known work, the Biblical Sonatas, which describe in music, sometimes naively but with enterprising use of the harpsichord's resources, the emotional states aroused by particular stories from the Bible.*

Tristis est anima

Ihr Himmel jubilirt von oben. Weicht ihr Sorgen aus dem Hertzen. Gott, sei mir gnädig nach deiner Güte. Wie schön leuchtet der Morgenstern. Tristis est anima mea. O heilige Zeit

Deborah York *sop* **Gary Cooper** *org* **The King's Consort Choir; The King's Consort / Robert King**

Hyperion CDA67059 (75 minutes: DDD). Texts and Ⓕ translations included. Recorded 1998

Johann Kuhnau was Cantor at St Thomas's, Leipzig until his death, crossing paths with Bach and inspiring the younger man to borrow the title *Clavier-Übung* for the prime repository for Bach's published keyboard works. Out of Bach's shadow, Kuhnau stands tall as a polymath of a sort that had almost ceased to exist in the pragmatic social climate of the 17th-century musician: lawyer, novelist, philosopher, theorist, linguist and musician. This splendid and varied cross-section of his choral music leaves us in no doubt that Kuhnau is far more than merely a confident practitioner who followed the plot of changing fashion. Through a keen sense of assimilation comes a singular, mainly sober, yet highly accomplished church composer. *Gott, sei mir gnädig* is a fine, evocative work full of rhetorical detail and inference, whilst in *Wie schön leuchtet der Morgenstern* the declamation straddles the concentrated world of the Bach motet, *Komm, Jesu, komm*, yet punctuated by the secular ostentation and chuckling horns of another world.

Robert King and his consort of singers and players highlight the multi-layered references in Kuhnau's cantatas, from the graceful Bach-aria lilt of *Weicht ihr Sorgen*, with the sympathetic colouring, if questionable diction, of Deborah York offset by an affectionate and responsive band of strings and unison oboes, to the decidedly pietist world of the *accompagnato* recitative in *Wie schön leuchtet*. The beguiling and antiquated *Tristis est anima mea* is worth its weight in gold. Vocally colourful (all the soloists are on fine form, especially Robin Blaze and Peter Harvey) and instrumentally outstanding, this is an important recording of a woefully neglected figure whose music has real stature.

György Kurtág

Romanian 1926

GROVE *Kurtág studied with Veress and Farkas at the Budapest Academy (1946-55) and with Milhaud and Messiaen in Paris (1957); in 1967 he began teaching at the Budapest Academy. His works are few and mostly short, suggesting a combination of the most abstract Bartók and late Webern, though with a strong lyrical, expressive force (and sometimes ingenious wit). Most of his compositions are for chamber forces, sometimes with solo voice. Among the best known are The Sayings of Péter Bornemisza (1968), a 'concerto' for soprano and piano in 24 short movements, and Messages of the Late RV Troussova (1980) for soprano and orchestra. Some of his pieces (eg 15 songs, 1982) use the cimbalom.*

String Quartets

Aus der Ferne III. Officium breve, Op 28. Ligatura, Op 31*b*. String Quartet, Op 1. Hommage à Mihály András (12 Microludes), Op 13
Keller Quartet (András Keller, János Pilz *vns* Zoltán Gál *va* Ottó Kertész *vc*) **Miklós Perényi** *vc* **György Kurtág** *celesta*
ECM New Series 453 258-2 (49 minutes: DDD) Ⓕ
Recorded 1995

This disc, devoted exclusively to Kurtág's music for string quartet, is of great significance, and both performance and recording are equal to the enterprise. The Keller Quartet has secure technique as well as emotional commitment, while ECM has provided a warm yet spacious acoustic for this expressive music. The journey begins with Kurtág's Op 1 of 1959, in a world, dominated by expressionistic fragmentation, of which he is clearly the master. Eighteen years later, in the Op 13 *Microludes*, Kurtág has perfected his own personal style, in which small, separate forms are linked together, and the music's allusions – to Bartók and Webern, in particular – are subsumed into a lyrical, dramatic discourse. The fruits of Kurtág's long apprenticeship are most evident here in the superb *Officium breve* of 1988-89, a miracle of textural imagination and musical thought whose richly varied language is distilled further into the two miniatures – *Ligatura* (also 1989) and *Aus der Ferne* (1991). By now Kurtág's music is characterised by a concentrated homogeneity, and by a harmony whose tensions, and stability, are the result of bringing convergence and divergence into confrontation. The result is memorable, and these fine recordings provide immensely rewarding listening.

Játékok

Játékok – excerpts from Books 1-5 and 8. Transcriptions from Machaut to Bach – No 46, Gottes Zeit ist die allerbeste Zeit (Bach: BWV106); No 48, Aus tiefer Not (Bach: BWV687); No 50, Trio Sonata in E flat (Bach: BWV525/1); No 52, O Lamm Gottes unschuldig (Bach: BWV*deest*)
György Kurtág, Márta Kurtág *pf duet*
ECM New Series 453 511-2 (50 minutes: DDD) Ⓕ
Recorded 1996

If any contemporary composer can persuade the musical world that compositions of between 30 seconds and four minutes in length are the natural vehicle for progressive post-tonal music, and therefore for the music of the future, that composer is Kurtág. This sequence of compositions, the longest of which lasts just over five minutes, offers a very special experience. The disc contains a selection from Kurtág's ongoing sequence of 'games' (*Játékok*) for solo piano and piano duet. They are a mixture of studies and tributes, not explicitly pedagogic in *Mikrokosmos* mode, but ranging widely in technical demands and style, from fugitive fragments, in which even the smallest element tells, to the extraordinary flamboyance of a *Perpetuum mobile* containing nothing but *glissandos*. Most are sombre in tone, and even the more humorous items, like the furiously constrained 'Beating – Quarrelling', have a bitter side to them. For access to another musical world, Kurtág has included four of his Bach transcriptions, music whose serenity and confidence speaks immediately of utter remoteness from the real present. Yet there is no nostalgia: Bach was then, and Kurtág is now.

The performances risk overprojection but they are supremely characterful, and the close-up recording reinforces the impression of music that is mesmerically persuasive in its imagination and expressiveness. If only even more of these pieces had been included!

Pierre de La Rue Flanders c1460-1518

GROVE *La Rue was a tenor at Siena Cathedral (1482/3-85) and at 's-Hertogenbosch Cathedral (1489-92). He served the Burgundian court chapel and went with Philip the Fair to Spain (1501-3, 1506); on his journeys he met leading composers in France and Germany. Later he worked at Marguerite of Austria's court in Mechelen and in Archduke Karl's private Kapelle (1514-16). La Rue stands alongside Josquin, Obrecht, Isaac, Compère and Brumel as one of the leading Flemish composers of the period, and is significant for the extent and diversity of his work, as well as for its quality and individuality. Central to his outpost are his masses (which include 31 cycles, two Kyries and five Credos); they feature cantus firmus treatments (La Rue preferred plainchant to secular models), canon and simple two-voice sections used to contrast with the fuller four- and five-voice texture. Most of his motets are for four voices; his chansons are usually for four voices and range in style from the late-Burgundian type with textless lower parts to the 16th-century type with vocal parts of equal design. He also composed seven Magnificats and a set of Lamentations. His music, which is probably closest to Josquin's in style, influenced the succeeding generation.*

Missa de feria

Missa de feria. Missa Sancta Dei genitrix. O domine, Jesu Christe. Pater de caelis. Regina caeli. Salve regina
Gothic Voices (Catherine King *alto* Steven Harrold, Julian Podger, Leigh Nixon *tens* Stephen Charlesworth, Donald Greig *bars*) **/ Christopher Page** with **Shirley Rumsey, Christopher Wilson** *ltes*
Hyperion CDA67010 (66 minutes: DDD). Texts and translations included. Recorded 1997. Ⓕ

Pierre de la Rue comes across as an inherently serious composer, his music reminiscent of the weightier Trappist ales of his homeland (the term 'specific gravity' describes it very well).

This holds not only for works that are richly scored (the five-voice *Missa de feria* and the six-voice *Pater de caelis*, a jewel among renaissance motets) but also for those having the more usual four-voice layout, like the Mass *Sancta Dei genitrix*. Of the composers of his generation, La Rue comes perhaps closest to incorporating the qualities of textural and formal 'seamlessness' associated with Ockeghem in the previous generation, and with Gombert in the next.

Christopher Page observes in his sensitive annotations that La Rue's music 'does not buzz with the open fifths and octaves so familiar to the singers of Gothic Voices from medieval music'. Here, the group sounds less brittle than it sometimes does, although tempos are still comparatively brisk in relation to many recordings of Franco-Flemish polyphony. The determination to adapt its sound to the needs of the music marks Gothic Voices out from many ensembles for early polyphony, and cannot be overpraised; yet on this recording there are signs that its careful search for the 'right' sound in this repertory has not quite reached equilibrium. One suspects that Gothic Voices' treble-dominated sound, appropriate to so much medieval music (especially that in which it has specialised), is not quite so suited to early renaissance polyphony in which all voices have equal prominence. Above all, the ebb and flow of La Rue's music (so masterfully in evidence in *Pater de caelis*) does not elicit the same measure of give-and-take from the singers. It is as though they were (collectively) still feeling their way into an unfamiliar idiom. But what price intellectual curiosity, or the thrill of new discoveries? Gothic Voices' risk-taking has been praised before, and if the results are not quite as satisfying here, they may represent the first stage of a new exploration. Meanwhile, the beauty and integrity of La Rue's music warrant a strong recommendation.

Edouard Lalo French 1823-1892

GROVE *Lalo studied at the Lille Conservatory and in Habeneck's class at the Paris Conservatoire. As a violinist and teacher in Paris in the 1850s he showed an unfashionable inclination towards chamber music, playing Classical string quartets and composing string trios and a noteworthy quartet. During the 1870s he attracted attention for his instrumental works, especially for the Symphonie espagnole (1874), a five-movement violin concerto, and the powerful Cello Concerto (1877). After disappointment at the poor reception of his opera Fiesque (1866-67), he took up stage music again in 1875, winning success with Le roi d'Ys (1888), on which his operatic fame has rested; his ballet score Namouna (1881-82) became popular as a series of orchestral suites. Among the hallmarks of Lalo's music, the vigour of which stands in contrast to the style of Franck's pupils and the impressionists, are his strongly diatonic melody, piquant harmony and ingenious orchestration.*

Violin Concerto

Violin Concerto in F, Op 20[a]. Concerto russe, Op 29[a]. Scherzo. Le roi d'Ys – Overture
[a]**Olivier Charlier** *vn* **BBC Philharmonic Orchestra / Yan Pascal Tortelier**
Chandos CHAN9758 (72 minutes: DDD) Ⓕ
Recorded 1998

This collection opens splendidly with a spankingly good performance of the Overture to *Le roi d'Ys*, with its melodrama, brassy splashes and a rather memorable swooning cello solo. It has all the gusto and panache of a Beecham performance and is certainly the finest account on disc since Paray's old Mercury version. Then come the two *concertante* violin works, both written with Sarasate in mind (separated by the comparatively familiar *Scherzo*, given here with rumbustious zest). Why are they not better known? The Violin Concerto has plenty going for it, a nicely coloured palette, a disarmingly nostalgic lyrical melody to haunt the first movement, followed by a delightful, songful *Andante*, which Olivier Charlier plays with engaging delicacy. But the real surprise here is the *Concerto russe*, virtually another *Symphonie espagnole*, but with Slavic rather than Spanish ideas, and very good ones too. It opens sonorously, and the soloist makes a touching entry with a chorale-like theme, which is later echoed by the orchestra. When the *Allegro* really moves off, the *Symphonie espagnole* come immediately to mind. The lovely slow movement, the 'Chant russe', opens with another chorale and the violin steals in with a genuine Russian folk tune, which (with its rhythmic snaps) astonishingly reminds one of the Bruch *Scottish Fantasy*. Charlier plays it most tenderly and the result is gently ravishing. The 'Intermezzo', with its off-beat timpani interjections and catchy main theme, is delicious, rhythmically sparkling in Charlier's hands, and there is another luscious secondary theme to come in the middle. The finale opens with a burst of sombre Slavonic passion from the strings, and another folk melody arrives. Soon the music quickens, culminating in a vivacious conclusion, with Charlier's contribution always lightly sparkling. Highly recommended.

Cello Concerto

Lalo Cello Concerto in D minor[a]
Saint-Saëns Cello Concerto in A minor, Op 33[b]
Schumann Cello Concerto in A minor, Op 129[a]
János Starker *vc* **London Symphony Orchestra / [a]Stanislaw Skrowaczewski, [b]Antál Dorati**
Mercury 432 010-2MM (65 minutes: ADD) Ⓜ
Recorded 1962-64 **OO**

Starker's playing is exemplified by a highly individual blend of intensity and specialised musical intelligence which has been misconstrued as cool detachment rather than interpretative integrity. His formidable intellectual, as well as technical assimilation of the Schumann Cello Concerto, presents it with rare *ipso facto* cogency. Starker's reading has an elemental pulse and fearless zeal; despite his dubious insertion of a cadenza, this remains a truly valiant performance. Lalo's Cello Concerto receives a similarly massive reading, and few recorded accounts can approach Starker's emphatic gravity in the opening *Allegro maestoso*, but the prelude, marked *Lento*, is simply over-dramatised. There is the expected relaxation in the second subject, but the relentless dynamism of this turbulent movement is fearlessly maintained. There are some fine woodwind contributions, too, in the central Intermezzo, and Starker moderates his vibrato to great effect in the dream-like *Andantino* sections, while his quicksilver brilliance in the finale could not offer greater contrast. Starker's reading of Saint-Saëns's First Concerto dates from 1964, and is in many ways exemplary in its studied clarity. The gripping urgency of the opening is well sustained, with only marginal repose found in the lyrical secondary theme, whilst the soloist's effortless facility in the difficult double-stopped passage later is also noteworthy. Here, then, are some highly individual, occasionally provocative, and yet never less than totally valid, accounts of three seminal works of the cello literature. That these performances are now almost 40 years old seems scarcely credible, given the transparency and range of the sound, whilst from a historical standpoint they form a vivid document of one of the great cellists of the century, heard at the height of his powers.

Lalo Cello Concerto
Massenet Fantaisie **Saint-Saëns** Cello Concerto No 1 in A minor, Op 33
Sophie Rolland *vc* **BBC Philharmonic Orchestra / Gilbert Varga**
ASV CDDCA867 (65 minutes: DDD) Ⓕ
Recorded 1993 ●

Sophie Rolland's performance of the Lalo Concerto is surely as fine as any recorded. It opens with great character, thanks to Gilbert Varga's strong accompaniment, and the solo playing is joyously songful. But Rolland is at her finest as she plays her introduction to the finale with commanding improvisatory spontaneity. The orchestra bursts in splendidly and she shows her technical mettle with some bouncing bowing in the attractive closing Rondo. The Saint-Saëns Concerto brings similar felicities. Massenet's *Fantaisie* opens dramatically and is rhythmically vital, flowing onwards boldly to produce a winningly sentimental yearning melody which the soloist clearly relishes. A cadenza then leads to a charming, very French Gavotte, and the piece ends jubilantly. It really is a find, and it could hardly be presented more persuasively. The recording is near perfect.

Cello Concerto in D minor[a]. Cello Sonata[b]. Chants russes, Op 29[b]
Maria Kliegel *vc* [b]**Bernd Glemser** *pf*
[a]**Nicolaus Esterházy Sinfonia / Michael Halász**
Naxos 8 554469 (60 minutes: DDD) Ⓢ
Recorded 1998

Maria Kliegel views the Concerto as a strong, dramatic work, and she has just the qualities – impressive, powerful tone and brilliant technique – to bring it off. The early exchanges with the orchestra establish her heroic presence, which she then relaxes to give a soft, delicate account of the second theme, lending to this expansive movement an unusually wide range of expression. The orchestral interruptions sound suitably stern and implacable – although the many loud, *staccato* chords for full orchestra become somewhat wearisome. This is partly Lalo's fault, but whereas on some other versions, Yo-Yo Ma's, for instance (Sony – nla), they're played without too much emphasis, here they are hammered out, the effect increased by a slightly boomy acoustic.

The second movement is taken quite slowly, its melancholy mood made more intense than usual, with the sound of the charming major-key *scherzo* sections again slightly spoilt by over-resonant bass. The finale is excellent; a robust, serious approach allied to energetic, bouncy rhythms. Throughout, the orchestra sounds warmly romantic, the important solo wind parts full of character.

The Sonata, too, is well worth hearing. Written 20 years before the Concerto, it's still a fully mature work, mixing grand Lisztian gestures with classical formal outlines and ingenious, colourful harmony. Kliegel and Glemser play with fine style and intense commitment, encompassing the high romanticism and, in the outer movement, Lalo's characteristically forceful rhythmic manner. *Chants russes* is an arrangement of the middle movement of the *Concerto russe* for violin – it's very effective as a cello piece. Kliegel's soft, refined sound near the end is especially memorable.

Symphonie espagnole

Lalo Symphonie espagnole, Op 21[a]
Vieuxtemps Violin Concerto No 5 in A minor, Op 37[b]
Sarah Chang *vn* [a]**Royal Concertgebouw Orchestra,** [b]**Philharmonia Orchestra / Charles Dutoit**
EMI CDC5 55292-2 (52 minutes: DDD) Ⓕ
Recorded [a]live in 1995, [b]1994

Vieuxtemps's Fifth Violin Concerto opens disarmingly, but the tutti gathers strength in Dutoit's hands before Chang steals in silkily and proceeds to dominate the performance with her warm lyricism and natural, flowing rubato. In a performance like this it remains a small-scale work to cherish, for it hasn't a dull bar in it. The recording is warm and full, the balance treating the relationship between the violin and the excellent Philharmonia Orchestra as an equal partnership. The *Symphonie espagnole* is altogether more ambitious, but Lalo's inventive Spanishry holds up well throughout the five movements. How attractive is the Concertgebouw acoustic for the fanfare-like opening – giving it weight as well as point. Again Dutoit's approach is full of impetus so that when the malagueña secondary theme arrives, it makes a shimmering contrast. The delicious piping woodwind *crescendo* and *decrescendo* which begins the finale sets the scene for scintillating salterello fireworks from the soloist. The dash into the home straight brings vociferous applause, which makes one realise that the concentration and spontaneity of the performance has been helped by the presence of an audience, who aren't apparent until this point. Certainly the splendidly resonant Concertgebouw sound and perfect balance would never have given the game away.

Lalo Symphonie espagnole
Dvořák Violin Concerto in A minor, B108
Christian Tetzlaff *vn* **Czech Philharmonic Orchestra / Libor Pešek**
Virgin Classics VC5 45022-2 (63 minutes: DDD) Ⓕ
Recorded 1992-93 ◉

This is a unique and generous coupling, and if Virgin Classics' decision to record Tetzlaff in Prague was dictated by the obvious advantage in having Dvořák's compatriots accompanying in his Violin Concerto, the Czech Philharmonic's playing under Pešek proves just as idiomatic in the Spanish dance rhythms of Lalo as in Czech dances, with crisp ensemble and rhythm deliciously sprung. What is especially remarkable about Tetzlaff's performances of the *Symphonie espagnole* as well as the Violin Concerto, is the quicksilver lightness of the passagework, which brings out the element of fantasy; in that he is helped by a recording balance which does not spotlight the soloist as sharply as in most other versions. In both works, Tetzlaff's concentration makes for a sense of spontaneity, leading one on magnetically. With delectable pointing of rhythm and phrase Tetzlaff makes the Lalo more subtly winning than it often is, helped by the extra transparency of textures.

Constant Lambert British 1905-1951

GROVE *Lambert entered the Royal College of Music when he was 17, and was becoming well known by the time he was 20. He was the first English composer commissioned by Dhiagilev (Romeo and Juliet, 1926), initiating a lifelong association with ballet as a conductor and composer: he wrote Pomona (1927) for Nizhinska and Horoscope (1938) for the Vic-Wells Ballet, of which he was founder musical director (from 1931). But he also wrote concert pieces, preferring unconventional genres and anti-traditional tastes for jazz and Stravinsky: such works include The Rio Grande for piano, chorus and orchestra (1927), the Concerto for piano and nonet (1930-31) and the choral orchestral 'masque' Summer's Last Will and Testament (1932-5). He stood in sharp relief against the background of English musical life and had wide-ranging interests. A lively critic, he wrote the stimulating Music Ho! a Study of Music in Decline (1934).*

Piano Concerto

Concerto for Piano and Chamber Orchestra[a]. Merchant Seamen Suite. Pomona. Prize-Fight
[a]**David Owen Norris** *pf* **BBC Concert Orchestra / Barry Wordsworth**
ASV White Line CDWHL2122 (66 minutes: DDD) Ⓜ
Recorded 1998 ◉◉

More gaps in the Lambert discography are enterprisingly plugged by these sensitive and shapely performances, which display most agreeable dash and commitment. The Piano Concerto recorded here is not that unnervingly bleak 1930-31 creation for soloist and nine players but one from 1924 that remained in short score, never to be heard in the composer's lifetime. Not only is the concerto brimful of striking invention and tightly organised, it also plumbs expressive depths, not least in the *Andante* slow movement which contains music as achingly poignant as any Lambert penned. David Owen Norris does full justice to the glittering solo part, and he receives splendid support from Barry Wordsworth and the BBC Concert Orchestra. *Prize-Fight* (Lambert's first ballet score) is earlier still, begun in 1923, completed the following year and overhauled one last time in 1927. Lasting just under nine minutes, it's a veritable romp, pungently scored in the manner of Satie and Milhaud, and with something of the anarchic spirit of Georges Auric's deliciously daft contributions to those glorious Ealing Comedies. In point of fact, Lambert had long been a connoisseur of the silver screen before he finally embarked on his first film score in 1940, for a flag-waving documentary entitled *Merchant Seamen*. Two years later, he compiled the present five-movement suite, and a superior specimen it is. *Pomona*, of course, we've had before. Wordsworth's spacious realisation occasionally lacks something in sheer effervescence and dry wit). Slower numbers, however, are invested with a stately *gravitas* that works well enough, save for the 'Passacaglia', which is inclined to drag. This is a most enjoyable and valuable compilation and the recording is vivid and truthfully balanced.

Tiresias

Tiresias. Pomona
English Northern Philharmonia / David Lloyd-Jones with [a]**Michael Cleaver** *pf*
Hyperion CDA67049 (72 minutes: DDD) Ⓕ
Recorded 1998 ◉

Constant Lambert's *Tiresias* was commissioned for the Festival of Britain in 1951 and the subject had been preoccupying the composer for over 20 years. In the event, the ailing Lambert struggled to meet his July deadline and called upon colleagues like Robert Irving, Alan Rawsthorne, Elisabeth Lutyens, Gordon Jacob, Denis Apivor, Humphrey Searle and Christian Darnton to help him finish the orchestration. Lambert directed eight performances in all, but the work was coolly received and he died the following month, just two days before his 46th birthday. The instrumentation of *Tiresias* calls for neither violins nor violas and features a notably varied battery of percussion as well as an important role for piano obbligato (brilliantly played here by Michael Cleaver). The music has a dark-hued intimacy and at times starkly ritualistic demeanour which probably baffled that glitzy first-night audience. However, Lambert's achievement is ripe for reassessment, and David Lloyd-Jones's meticulously prepared realization allows us to revel anew in the score's many effective set-pieces. Stravinsky and Ravel are prime influences, but the work is suffused with that distinctive mix of keen brilliance and bleak melancholy so characteristic of its creator. The present account is all one could wish for.

Pomona (1927) is much earlier and altogether lighter in tone. Deftly scored for a chamber orchestra of 34 instrumentalists, *Pomona* comprises eight delightfully inventive numbers whose neo-classical spirit breathes very much the same air as that of Stravinsky and Les Six from the same period. Again, the performance is first rate and the sound quite admirable.

Romeo and Juliet

The Bird Actors. Pomona. Romeo and Juliet
Victoria State Orchestra / John Lanchbery
Chandos CHAN9865 (56 minutes: DDD) Ⓕ
Recorded1999 ●

John Lanchbery's enjoyably lithe account of *Pomona* with a well-drilled State Orchestra of Victoria occupies a middle ground between the sturdier, at times unhelpfully sluggish manners of Barry Wordsworth and the BBC Concert Orchestra (whose mid-price ASV compilation remains essential listening for David Owen Norris's eloquent resuscitation of the teenage Lambert's astonishingly precocious 1924 Piano Concerto) and the altogether more touchingly graceful and witty approach espoused by David Lloyd-Jones and the admirable English Northern Philharmonia.

The really good news here is the CD début of *Romeo and Juliet*, one of only two ballet scores that Diaghilev commissioned from British composers for his Ballets Russes (the other being Lord Berners' *The Triumph of Neptune*, also staged in 1926). In his helpful booklet essay, Peter Dickinson relates how the 20-year-old Lambert openly confronted Diaghilev when he learnt that his preferred set designer, Christopher Wood, had been replaced by Max Ernst and Joan Miró, and that the impresario had reworked Nijinska's original choreography himself. It's a frothy romp firmly in the Stravinsky/Poulenc/Milhaud mould – and a brilliantly confident achievement for a 20-year-old student – but, strange to relate, there's barely a glimpse of the sheer expressive scope of either *Pomona* or *The Rio Grande* (not to mention the Piano Concerto). We've long needed a worthy successor to Norman Del Mar's affectionate Lyrita version with the ECO (nla); happily, Lanchbery and company have plugged the gap with notable success. Not only does the orchestral playing evince infectious zest and unswerving dedication to the cause, Lanchbery directs with palpable relish throughout.

There's also a sparkling curtain-raiser in the guise of *The Bird Actors*, a three-minute overture whose title comes from a poem by Sacheverell Sitwell and which originally began life as the finale of an even earlier ballet entitled *Adam and Eve* (which in turn sowed the seeds for much in *Romeo and Juliet*). The sound throughout is lively and full-bodied, without perhaps being in the very top flight.

Rued Langgaard Danish 1893-1952

Aged 11 Langgaard made his début in Copenhagen as organist and improviser. A series of trips to Berlin led to the performance of his hour-long Symphony No 1 (1908-11) by the Berlin PO in 1913. The musical community in Denmark, however, regarded the highly productive but reserved and solitary composer with scepticism. After his opera Antikrist was turned down by Copenhagen's Royal Theatre in 1925, he turned his back on modernism and openly criticised Danish musical life and Nielsen's influence on it. His Straussian music, coloured by religion and symbolism, did not concur with the anti-Romantic and sober attitude dominant in Denmark around 1930. Interest in his work was reawakened in the 1960s, Music of the Spheres in particular being seen as anticipating the avant-garde music of the '60s.

Music of the Spheres

Music of the Spheres. Four Tone Pictures
Gitta-Maria Sjöberg *sop* **Danish National Radio Choir and Symphony Orchestra / Gennadi Rozhdestvensky**
Chandos CHAN9517 (53 minutes: DDD) Ⓕ
Recorded 1996 ●

With Rozhdestvensky at the helm, Chandos presents what is probably this composer's most important – certainly most original – work, *Music of the Spheres* (1916-18). So radical did its sonic experiments seem even in the late 1960s that Ligeti no less, when inspecting the score, quipped that he had merely been a 'Langgaard imitator' all along. The manipulation of blocks of sound rather than conventional thematic development does have much in common with trends in post-Second World War avant-garde composition (though stemming from impressionism), but other contemporaries of Langgaard's, such as Schoenberg and Scriabin, had traversed similar terrain at least in part. The main difference between Langgaard and Ligeti lies in the former's reliance on a fundamentally tonal language, however eccentrically deployed, and *Music of the Spheres* seems in hindsight to be a bridge between two other highly virtuosic scores with celestial connotations: Holst's *The*

Planets and Ligeti's *Atmosphères*. The *Tone Pictures* (1917) were written alongside this extraordinary work, yet possess none of its stature: four charming songs, they seem effusive and outmoded by comparison. Chandos's sound is of demonstration quality.

The End of Time

The End of Time, BVN243[a]. From the Song of Solomon, BVN381[b]. Interdikt, BVN335.
Carl Nielsen, Our Great Composer, BVN355[c]
[ab]**Nina Pavlovski** *sop* [ab]**Stig Andersen** *ten*
[a]**Per Høyer** *bar* [b]**Per Salo** *org*
Danish National Radio [abc]Choir and Symphony Orchestra / Gennadi Rozhdestvensky
Chandos CHAN9786 (60 minutes: DDD). Texts and translations included. Recorded 1999 Ⓕ

The End of Time, a concert suite dating from 1939-40, is based on the original 1921-23 version of the opera *Antikrist*. It's a cantata in four movements (a prelude and three self-contained 'arias') to which Langgaard made further revisions as he assembled it, the whole making a highly effective work that doesn't betray its origins. The text as retained also illustrates, in brief, the radical differences between the two versions of the opera. The shorter *From the Song of Solomon* (1949) is one of his last works, and typically strays very little from the Straussian opulence of the opening. There is more than a touch of Wagner in the latter stages. Langgaard's selective use of the Biblical text had a moralistic point that was aimed at what he felt to be the degenerate Danish society of the time. The orchestral *Interdikt* (1947-48) is targeted rather more personally; specifically, at the interdict he believed the Danish musical establishment had placed on him. It is quintessential Langgaard – eruptive, memorable and not a note too long. The role of the organist is an acute autobiographical touch. *Carl Nielsen, Our Great Composer* (1948; the title is also the complete text) presents the less attractive, paranoid side of his creative persona. This sarcastic little hymn is pure doggerel (catchy, though), attacking Nielsen's posthumous pre-eminence. Rozhdestvensky has the measure of Langgaard's idiom, and secures top-notch performances, while Chandos's sound quality is both rich and clear.

Libby Larsen

American 1950

Larsen studied at the University of Minnesota, where her teachers included Argento. Determined to find a role for the composer outside academe, in 1973 she co-founded with the composer Stephen Paulus the Minnesota Composers Forum (known as the American Composers Forum since 1996). Adventurous without being self-consciously avant-garde, Larsen has written in all genres. Her style is noted for its energy, optimism, rhythmic diversity, colourful orchestration, liberated tonality without harsh dissonance, and pervading lyricism. Although she has written abundantly for orchestras and mixed ensembles, she is attracted in particular to the qualities of the voice – in this she betrays the influence of Argento.

Symphonies Nos 1 and 3

Symphonies – No 1, 'Water Music'; No 3, 'Lyric'. Parachute Dancing. Ring of Fire
London Symphony Orchestra / Joel Revzen
Koch International Classics 37370-2 Ⓕ
(57 minutes: DDD). Recorded 1996

This is a terrific disc. From the very first bars of the invigorating *Water Music* Symphony (1984), one is drawn irresistibly into Larsen's sound world and left in no doubt that here is a composer who has made the art of symphonic writing very much her own. On the evidence of the present collection, her principal musical antecedents seem to be Sibelius, Stravinsky and the American symphonic composers of the mid-20th century. But there is much more that is distinctively her own, and the result is a muse full of zest and vim. True, *Water Music* is more a sinfonietta than a symphony, but it is very accomplished. One can almost 'hear liquid', as it were, and this is the finest water music since Respighi's *Fountains*. The Third Symphony (1991) is an electric score. *Ring of Fire* (1995) is no less involving, a brilliant tone-poem inspired by lines from T S Eliot's *Little Gidding*. The performances from the LSO take wing, with everyone clearly at home with the idiom.

Solo Symphony. Marimba Concerto, 'After Hampton'[a]. Deep Summer Music
[a]**John Kinzie** *mari* **Colorado Symphony Orchestra / Marin Alsop**
Koch International Classics 37520-2 Ⓕ
(58 minutes: DDD)

Libby Larsen is probably best known in this country for the disc featuring her *Water Music* and *Lyric* symphonies (reviewed above), while recently the coupling of two song sets and the *String Symphony* was warmly recommended in *Gramophone*. Larsen's orchestral music is very approachable, attractively scored, with frequent – fleeting – resonances of other composers, whether Reich and the Copland of *Quiet City* in *Deep Summer Music* (1983) or Stravinsky in the Marimba Concerto (1992). The third movement of her *Solo Symphony* (1999, her Fifth) has a distinctly Bernsteinian tang. While Larsen's voice may not be the most distinctive, the use she makes of her materials marks her out as an outstandingly gifted composer.

The *Solo Symphony*, commissioned by the Colorado Symphony (who give it here in a performance of exemplary virtuosity), is exciting, serious-minded yet fun, both orchestral display piece and genuine symphony, and like the Fourth a touch Pistonesque. The 'Solo' of the title can be taken to mean both individual players or melodic lines – Larsen is fundamentally a melodist – but also the listener, whom the composer has described as being 'the true soloist'.

John Kinzie is the nimble marimba player in the Concerto *After Hampton* (1992, referring to the mallet percussionist Lionel Hampton). Beneath the surface glitter, Larsen investigates the nature of the concerto form, with the soloist merging in and out of the orchestral texture, and forming a mini-ensemble with the percussion. Koch's continuing advocacy of Larsen is unreservedly to be praised and this release receives a warm recommendation.

Orlande de Lassus

Franco/Flemish 1532-1594

GROVE *Lassus served Ferrante Gonzaga of Mantua from c1544, accompanying him to Sicily and Milan (1546-49). He worked for Constantino Castrioto in Naples, where he probably began to compose, then moved to Rome to join the Archbishop of Florence's household, becoming maestro di cappella of St John Lateran in 1553. After returning north, to Mons and Antwerp, where early works were published (1555-56), he joined the court chapel of Duke Albrecht V of Bavaria in Munich as a singer (1556). He married in 1558. Although a Catholic, he took over the court chapel in 1563 and served the duke and his heir, Wilhelm V, for over 30 years, until his death. In this post he consolidated his position by having many works published and travelling frequently (notably to Vienna and Italy, 1574-79), establishing an international reputation. The pope made him a Knight of the Golden Spur in 1574.*

One of the most prolific and versatile of 16th-century composers, Lassus wrote over 2000 works in almost every current genre, including masses, motets, psalms, hymns, responsorial Passions and secular pieces in Italian, French and German. Most of his masses are parody masses based on motets, chansons or madrigals by himself or others; the large number of Magnificats is unusual. His motets include didactic pieces, ceremonial works for special occasions, settings of classical texts (some secular, e.g. Prophetiae Sibyllarum, 1600), liturgical items (offertories, antiphons, psalms, eg Psalmipoenitentiales, 1584) and private devotional pieces. He issued five large volumes of sacred music as Patrocinium musices (1573-76), and after his death in 1594 his sons assembled another (Magnum opus musicum, 1604).

Admired in their day for their beauty, technical perfection and rhetorical power, the motets combine the features of several national styles – expressive Italian melody, elegant French text-setting and solid northern polyphony – enhanced by Lassus's imaginative responses to the texts. His secular works reveal a cosmopolitan with varied tastes. The madrigals range from lightweight villanellas (Matona mia cara) to intensely expressive sonnets (Occhi, piangete); the chansons include 'patter' songs and reflective, motet-like works; and among the German lieder are sacred hymns and psalms, delicate love-songs and raucous drinking-songs. This versatility and this wide expressive range place Lassus among the most significant figures of the Renaissance period.

Lassus's sons Ferdinand (c1560-1609) and Rudolph (c1563-1625) also served the Bavarian court chapel and were responsible for assembling many of their father's works for publication. Ferdinand succeeded to his father's post at court; Rudolph composed much sacred music.

Madrigals

Libro de villanelle, moresche, e altre canzoni. Madrigals – Tutto 'l dì piango; Sol'e pensoso i più deserti campi; O Lucia miau; Madonna mia pietà
Concerto Italiano / Rinaldo Alessandrini
Opus 111 OPS30-94 (59 minutes: DDD) Ⓕ
Texts and translations included. Recorded 1994

This wickedly funny disc was released to coincide with the quincentenary of Lassus's death. Here Concerto Italiano gets a chance to let its hair down: the result is as hilarious as one could have hoped. The singers get inside both the meaning *and* the sound of the words, transfiguring musical texts that are (at times) purposefully naive. They also capture the incipient, slightly worrying hysteria that pervades many of these pieces. Psychologically, this is well judged: as Lassus's letters show, Italian is the language of his manic phases, just as French corresponds to his depressive ones. Apart from some indispensable anthology numbers such as 'Matona mia cara' from the *Libro de villanelle*, the most convincing performances are those of the *moresche*. A few more serious items are thrown in for the sake of contrast. These are the only disappointing pieces in the set, too slow for comfort by some margin – but then again, the rather archaic madrigal, *Madonna mia pietà* is delivered with real passion. The humour here is more often allusive than explicit, and as often lavatorial as genuinely bawdy. Those familiar with French *chanson* texts will probably have seen worse. Besides, one cannot help but respond to Lassus's evident relish at setting these dubious gems.

Lagrime di San Pietro

Ensemble Vocal Européen / Philippe Herreweghe
Harmonia Mundi HMC90 1483 (60 minutes: DDD) Ⓕ
Texts and translations included. Recorded 1993 ●

Lassus completed his swan-song days before his death in 1594. The decision to set 20 stanzas from Luigi Tansillo's unfinished meditation on 'the tears of St Peter' must have been a highly personal one. The poet's portrayal of a man driven nearly insane with remorse allowed Lassus to exorcise the mental illness that engulfed him in his last years. The result is perhaps his most moving work, for there is in these *madrigali spirituali* a distilled mannerism that evokes the understated passion of late-period Brahms. Philippe Herreweghe captures the detached expression of pain that makes this music so haunting. This is partly a matter of vocal timbre:

individually the singers' tone is a shade cool, but collectively they sound full-bodied. Their interpretative acuteness is best illustrated by their approach to rubato: Herreweghe ever so slightly *stretches* the pulse when the voices achieve a poignant inflexion or come to a standstill. Such moments acquire an intensity that clearly identifies them as the key moments in a psychological drama, making the cycle as a whole compulsive listening. Quite simply, Herreweghe's singers achieve something that is very, very special indeed.

Masses

Missa Entre vous filles. Missa Susanne un jour. Infelix ego
Oxford Camerata / Jeremy Summerly
Naxos 8 550842 (68 minutes: DDD). Text and translation of *Infelix ego* included. Recorded 1993 Ⓢ

The Masses *Entre vous filles* and *Susanne un jour* show Lassus at his best, full of variety and invention, music of an immediate impact; in fact, they display exactly the same qualities as the better-known motets. The Oxford Camerata has understood this well, taking considerable care with the nuances of the text and really enjoying the music's rich sonorities. Sometimes a slight imprecision in the playing of chords is detectable, but this is more than outweighed by the sense of melodic contour and the powerful, somewhat dark and austere sound which conveys so well the spirit of the music. With over 68 minutes of some of the finest 16th-century polyphony available at such a low price, no one should hesitate to buy this disc.

William Lawes British 1602-1645

GROVE *William Lawes, the younger brother of Henry Lawes, was probably a chorister at Salisbury Cathedral until the Earl of Hertford placed him under the tutelage of his own music master, John Coprario. In 1635 Lawes was appointed 'musician in ordinary for the lute and voices' to Charles I, though he was probably in Charles's service before then. In 1642 he enlisted in the royalist army and accompanied the king on campaigns; he was killed during the battle to relieve the garrison at Chester.*

Lawes was a gifted, versatile and prolific composer. The stylised dance suite is the basic vehicle for his chamber music, often with a preceding fantasia or pavan. In his viol consorts he exhibited late Renaissance traits, but the larger part of his chamber music uses violins in the concertante style of early Baroque violin music with continuo. It includes the 'Harpe' consorts, a unique collection of variation suites for violin, bass viol, theorbo and harp. Of Lawes's vocal music, over 200 songs are extant, many of them composed for court masques and other theatrical entertainments. He is considered the leading English dramatic composer before Purcell. Much of his church music – c50 anthems and ten sacred canons or rounds – is also of high quality, The Lord is my Light being one of the finest verse anthems of its period.

Royall Consorts

Royall Consorts – No 2 in D minor; No 4 in D; No 5 in D; No 8 in C; No 10 in B flat Ⓟ
The Greate Consort (Anne Schumann *vn* Emilia Benjamin, Reiko Ichise *va da gambas* Elizabeth Kenny, William Carter *theorbos*) **/ Monica Huggett** *vn*
ASV Gaudeamus CDGAU147 (68 minutes: DDD) Ⓕ
Recorded 1996 ●

These formalised dances give us a less familiar view of this composer: the broody cavalier reflecting, in exquisitely fashioned thematic strains, the unequivocal decorum of musical conceits in Charles I's cultivated time-bomb of a court. The soft-grained and unforced string timbre of The Greate Consort is underpinned by delightfully subtle and undemonstrative theorbo playing. For some, the characterization in, say, the Aires of Consort No 4 will seem a touch under-explored but given the Pavan's wonderful concentration of seamless allusions, gently passed back and forth, the sense of an integral suite is strongly and vitally projected. Monica Huggett leads by example with tonal sweetness and exemplary musicianship. Rare qualities indeed, and treasure from which she has effected chamber music playing of the very highest quality.

Jean-Marie Leclair French 1697-1764

GROVE *French composer and violinist Leclair was initially a dancer. He lived from 1723 in Paris, where he became a prominent soloist and began producing violin sonatas (from 1723). He also appeared abroad, and in 1733 became ordinaire de la musique du roi at the French court. In 1738-43 he served the court of Orange in the Netherlands and (in 1740-43) Franc;ois du Liz at The Hague. He then lived mainly in Paris, where he was murdered (probably by his nephew).*

Foremost in Leclair's output are over 60 solo, duet and trio sonatas for violin. In these he imbued the Italian style with French elements more successfully than most of his contemporaries, using short ornamented phrases and colourful harmonies; the idiom reflects his own virtuoso technique. He also composed concertos, minuets, suites etc, ballet music, an opera (Scylla et Glaucus, 1746) with many striking features and other vocal music. He was an influential teacher and is considered the founder of the French violin school.

Violin Concertos

Flute Concerto No 3 in C, Op 7. Violin Concertos – Op 7: No 4 in F; No 6 in A. No 2 in A, Op 10 Ⓟ
Rachel Brown *fl*
Collegium Musicum 90 / Simon Standage *vn*
Chandos Chaconne CHAN0564 (65 minutes: DDD) Ⓕ
Recorded 1994 ●

Of the violin concertos here, Op 10 No 2 is the richest harmonically. The solo instrument in Op 7 No 3 is Leclair's stated alternative of flute, the only one of his 12 violin concertos to be so designed. Accordingly, it lacks the double-stopping so much favoured by this greatly admired violinist-composer. Otherwise it exploits the graceful sequential passagework found in the other concertos, though here with a fuller accompanying texture, with more movement in inner parts. Rachel Brown's playing throughout is deliciously cool and poised. Virtuoso violin fireworks abound in the vigorous first movements of the other two Op 7 concertos here and the ebullient finale of the A major (the start of whose first movement has a Vivaldian resonance): as expected, Simon Standage throws off their difficulties with panache and an apparent ease that allows him also to add stylish embellishments of his own. The extensive multiple-stopping on which the elegant minuet-like Aria of Op 7 No 6 relies is performed with well-nigh impeccable intonation.

Violin Concertos – Op 7: No 1 in D minor. Op 10: No 3 in D; No 4 in F; No 6 in G minor **P**
Collegium Musicum 90 / Simon Standage *vn*
Chandos Chaconne CHAN0589 (59 minutes: DDD) Ⓕ
Recorded 1995 ●

This disc contains Leclair's most vivacious and attractive works, played with great élan, sensitivity and neatness, and recorded with exemplary clarity and balance. The concertos represent a high-water mark in 18th-century violin technique, with extensive double-stopping, an extended range that soars up to heights scarcely ventured previously, rapid scales and flying arpeggios, and elaborate figurations of all kinds. To all of this Standage brings a seasoned virtuosity which he places totally at the service of the music's grace: his bowing in particular commands admiration. From the stylistic viewpoint these concertos are interesting for their mingling of French and Italian elements. There are Vivaldian unisons, but French dance forms for the middle movements – a pair of minuets in the D minor, minuets *en rondeau* in the G minor, a pair of gavottes with unusual interplay between solo and tutti in the F major, and an ornate solo line over supporting reiterated chords in the D major. Standage adds spontaneous embellishments of his own on repeats.

Violin Sonatas

Violin Sonatas, Op 1 – No 1 in A minor; No 3 in B flat; No 8 in G; No 9 in A **P**
François Fernandez *vn* **Pierre Hantaï** *hpd* **Philippe Pierlot** *va da gamba*
Auvidis Astrée E8662 (64 minutes: DDD) Ⓕ
Recorded 1995

Leclair's Op 1 set was so successful when it was first published in 1723 that it had to be reprinted four times. Though the technical demands it makes on the violinist are considerable, the composer himself was at pains not to employ virtuosity as an end in itself and to condemn the 'trivialisation' of players who exaggerated the speed of quick movements. Leclair also, like Couperin, was insistent that performers should not add ornamentation of their own – though in the four sonatas here only the initial *Adagio* of No 3 is much decorated. Rather did he place emphasis on 'le beau chant' – expressive *cantabile*, which is well exemplified in the first movements of Nos 1, 8 and 9. The crisp *Allegro*, with its rapid dipping across strings, and the *Largo* of No 3 make play with multiple stopping, including double trills, and there is vigorous cross-string work too in the ebullient Giga of No 1. Leclair shows himself fond of the rondeau form with long episodes, and the Sarabande of No 9 is a set of variations. This last has an athletic gamba line, as does the whole of the G major Sonata; and the alert and positive continuo playing here (from both gamba and harpsichord) is a special pleasure. But naturally the main spotlight falls on François Fernandez, whose lively, pointed bowing, delicate and sprightly fast movements and graceful slow ones (like the gentle G major Musette) do full justice to Leclair's attractive invention.

Franz Lehár Austro/Hungarian 1870-1948

GROVE *The son of a military bandmaster and composer, Lehár studied in Prague with Foerster and Fibich and followed his father in an army career. In 1902 he resigned to work in Vienna as a conductor and composer, notably of operettas, achieving spectacular international success with Die lustige Witwe (1905), Der Graf von Luxemburg (1909) and Zigeunerliebe (1910). These and others restored the fortunes of the Viennese operetta and opened the genre to a greater musical and dramatic sophistication. After World War One his time seemed to have passed, but then came new successes, many written for Richard Tauber: Paganini (1925), Der Zarewitsch (1927), Friederike (1928), Das Land des Lächelns (1929) and Giuditta (1934). His other works include waltzes, marches and songs.*

Waltzes / Overtures

Gold und Silber, Op 79. Wiener Frauen – overture. Der Graf von Luxemburg – Waltz; Waltz Intermezzo. Zigeunerliebe – overture. Eva – Wär' es auch nichts als ein Traum von Glück; Waltz Scene. Das Land des Lächelns – overture. Die lustige Witwe – concert overture **H**
Zurich Tonhalle Orchestra / Franz Lehár
Beulah mono 1PD16 (58 minutes: ADD) Ⓕ
Recorded 1947 ●

These were the 77-year-old composer's last recordings. Most were reissued on LP (latterly on the Eclipse label), but here they are for the first time complete. Mostly the selections represent obvious items from Lehár's melodic output. However, the inclusion of the *Wiener Frauen* overture is an especial joy, representing Lehár at his less familiar but most melodic and inventive. The operetta's principal character was a piano tuner, and the overture includes an ingenious passage where one hears the piano being tuned up before launching into one of Lehár's most luxuriant and beautiful waltzes.

In his excellent notes Malcolm Walker aptly describes these recordings as, in a sense, Lehár's last will and testament. Slower and more indulgent than his earlier recordings they may be; but never for a moment the slightest bit ponderous. Rather they are full of nostalgia, wonder and joyful pride – lovingly caressed performances by a master melodist, master orchestrator and master conductor. The transfers have been excellently done from original shellac discs. Filtering may be required to minimise hiss; but it is more than worthwhile for uniquely beautiful recordings of some of the most heavenly melodies ever created.

Concertino for Violin and Orchestra

Tatjana – Prelude, Act 1; Prelude, Act 2; Prelude, Act 3; Russian Dances. Fieber. Il guado. Concertino for Violin and Orchestra in B flat minor. Eine Vision: meine Jugendzeit. Donaulegenden, 'An der grauen Donau'
Robert Gambill *ten* **Latica Honda-Rosenberg** *vn* **Volker Banfield** *pf* **North German Radio Philharmonic Orchestra / Klauspeter Seibel**
CPO CPO999 423-2 (70 minutes: DDD). Texts and translations included. Recorded 1996-97 Ⓑ

This splendidly produced collection will surprise and delight. Lehár's mastery of the orchestra has never been in doubt; and here is further evidence of his technical accomplishment. Such touches of the operetta composer as are here are of the more ambitious operetta scores such as *Zigeunerliebe*. More often it is Wagner, Richard Strauss and Korngold who come to mind. Throughout, the music is tastefully and evocatively written, and with a supreme confidence in the handling of a large orchestra. *Tatjana* was an early operatic attempt of which Lehár was especially fond, and its preludes and dances capture the starkness of its Siberian setting. *Il guado* ('The ford') and the concert overture *Eine Vision* are works from the *Lustige Witwe* years, when Lehár was still seeking to determine in which direction his future lay. The former is a symphonic poem with some attractively rippling writing for the piano, the latter a recollection of the Bohemian countryside of his youth. The elegant *Concertino* for violin and orchestra, which has been recorded previously, is a student work that demonstrates his affection for his own instrument. *Fieber* is the starkest piece in the collection – a bitter First World War portrayal of a soldier in the throes of a deadly fever. *Donaulegenden* gives glimpses of the familiar waltz-time Lehár, but a Lehár looking back sadly at a bygone age. What other operetta or waltz composer could have written music as powerful, gripping and spine-tingling as this? Do try it!

Songs

Aus längst vergang'ner Zeit. Sieben Karst-Lieder. Reiterlied 1914. Nur einer. Erste Liebe. Der Thräne Silberthau! Sehnsucht, heimliches Verlangen. Die du mein alles bist. Das lockende Lied. Schau mich an, sei mir gut. Schillernder Falter. Ich liebe dich! Frauenherz, du bist ein kleiner Schmetterling! Wenn eine schöne Frau befiehlt. Liebesglück. Geträumt! Die ganze Welt dreht sich um die Liebe
Gabriele Rossmanith, Heidi Wolf *sops* **Iris Vermillion** *mez* **Jürgen Sacher** *ten***Jens-Peter Maintz** *vc* **Cord Garben** *pf*
CPO CPO999 432-2 (62 minutes: DDD) Ⓜ
Texts and translations included. Recorded 1996

This collection of songs is a revelation. It is proof that, though Lehár found fame in operetta, he could readily have succeeded in more serious fields. Those serious ambitions are shown in the earliest items here – in *Aus längst vergang'ner Zeit*, an emotional song about faded youth, or in the *Karst-Lieder*, songs that evoke the Croatian landscape where he was stationed as bandmaster in the early 1890s. That Lehár's serious ambitions outlasted his early operetta successes is exemplified by the wartime laments, *Reiterlied 1914* and *Nur einer*. Though he thereafter concentrated on more popular, sentimental numbers, he never lowered his standards of musicianship. *Das lockende Lied* is a taxing coloratura test-piece, but in *Wenn eine schöne Frau befiehlt*, written for Richard Tauber, there is a delicious touch of syncopation.

The sheer variety of these songs is astonishing. There are glorious melodies, too, in the entrancing *Erste Liebe*, in the slow waltz *Ich liebe dich!*, with its haunting solo cello part, and in *Frauenherz, du bist ein kleiner Schmetterling!*, a capricious little number finished at 4.30 one morning just before the première of his *Paganini*. That, for all its diversity, the collection never seems less than an entity is a tribute to accompanist Cord Garben and his refreshingly youthful team of singers. This really is a quite irresistible release!

Giuditta (sung in English)

Deborah Riedel *sop* Giuditta; **Jerry Hadley** *ten* Octavio; **Jeffrey Carl** *bar* Manuele Biffi, Antonio; **Andrew Busher** *spkr* Duke; **Naomi Itami** *sop* Anita; **Lynton Atkinson** *ten* Pierrino; **William Dieghan** *ten* Sebastiano
English Chamber Orchestra / Richard Bonynge
Telarc CD80436 (78 minutes: DDD). Text included. Ⓕ Recorded 1996

Giuditta was Lehár's last stage work and the peak of his compositional development. Written for the Vienna State Opera, it is a highly ambitious score, containing some fiendishly difficult vocal writing and using a large orchestra featuring mandolin and other exotic instruments. For this recording some two hours of music have been compressed into 78 minutes by means of snips here and there and the omission of a couple of subsidiary numbers. The piece has a *Carmen*-like story, about the disenchanted wife of an innkeeper who persuades a soldier to desert, before eventually abandoning and ruining him as she goes from lover to lover. The best-known number is Giuditta's 'On my lips every kiss is like wine', here gloriously sung by Deborah Riedel; the leading male role was written for Tauber, and there are some marvellous and demanding tenor solos, equally superbly sung by the impressive Jerry Hadley. Despite writing for the opera house, Lehár remained faithful to his formula of interspersing the music for the principal couple with sprightly dance numbers for a comedy pair, here in the hands of Naomi Itami and Lynton Atkinson. Assisted by Richard Bonynge's lilting conducting, these contribute richly to the appeal of the recording.

Das Land des Lächelns

Anneliese Rothenberger *sop* Lisa; **Harry Friedauer** *ten* Gustl; **Nicolai Gedda** *ten* Sou-Chong; **Renate Holm** *sop* Mi; **Jobst Moeller** *bar* Tschang
Bavarian Radio Chorus; Graunke Symphony Orchestra / Willy Mattes
EMI ② CMS5 65372-2 (87 minutes: ADD) Ⓜ
Recorded 1967 ●

The great glory of this *Das Land des Lächelns*, Lehár's portrayal of the clash of western and eastern cultures, is the singing of Nicolai Gedda, who brings off 'Dein ist mein ganzes Herz' and the other Richard Tauber favourites to quite splendid effect. Anneliese Rothenberger is on excellent form vocally and full of charm, and she and Gedda make an excellent partnership. Renate Holm is a smiling Mi and the other principals, chorus and orchestra all play their full parts. Willy Mattes is an experienced and sympathetic conductor of operetta. The score here is, of course, not identical with that given in London when the operetta was first produced there in 1931. Apparently, Tauber was in and out of the cast every other day, providing his understudy, Robert Naylor, with plenty of opportunities. The show only had a short run in London on its first appearance. It seems that it was Tauber rather than Lehár that people wanted to hear. This reissue should be in every Viennese operetta collection.

Die lustige Witwe

Cheryl Studer *sop* Hanna; **Boje Skovhus** *bar* Danilo; **Bryn Terfel** *bass-bar* Zeta; **Rainer Trost** *ten* Camille; **Barbara Bonney** *sop* Valencienne; **Uwe Peper** *ten* Raoul; **Karl-Magnus Fredriksson** *bar* Cascada; **Heinz Zednik** *ten* Njegus; **Richard Savage** *bar* Bogdanowitsch; **Lynette Alcantara** *sop* Sylviane; **Philip Salmon** *ten* Kromow; **Constanze Backes** *mez* Olga; **Julian Clarkson** *bass* Pritschitsch; **Angela Kazimierczuk** *sop* Praškowia
Wiener Tschuschenkapelle; Vienna Philharmonic Orchestra / Sir John Eliot Gardiner
DG 439 911-2GH (80 minutes: DDD). Notes, text and translation included. Recorded 1994 Ⓕ ●●

This is one of those great operetta interpretations that is committed to record once in a generation if one is lucky. Gardiner's approach is on an altogether more inspired plane than his rivals. In the Viennese rhythms, he shows himself utterly at home – as in the Act 2 Dance scene, where he eases the orchestra irresistibly into the famous waltz. But there are also countless instances where Gardiner provides a deliciously fresh inflexion to the score. The cast of singers is uniformly impressive. If Cheryl Studer's 'Vilja' isn't quite as assured as some others, her captivatingly playful 'Dummer, dummer Reitersmann' is typical of a well-characterised performance. As Danilo, Boje Skovhus acquits himself well with a polished performance and he offers a natural, more human characterization than his rivals, while Barbara Bonney is superb. Not the least inspired piece of casting comes with Bryn Terfel, who transforms himself outstandingly well into the bluff Pontevedran ambassador. As for Gardiner's personally selected chorus, they make Monteverdi to Montenegro and Pontevedra seem the most natural transition in the world. DG's recorded sound has an astonishing clarity and immediacy, as in the way the piccolos shriek out at the Widow's Act 1 entrance or in the beautiful *pianissimo* accompaniment to the 'Vilja-Lied'.

Die lustige Witwe **H**
Dame Elisabeth Schwarzkopf *sop* Hanna; **Erich Kunz** bar Danilo; **Anton Niessner** *bar* Zeta; **Nicolai Gedda** *ten* Camille; **Emmy Loose** *sop* Valencienne; **Josef Schmidinger** *bass* Raoul; **Ottakar Kraus** *bar* Cascada
Philharmonia Orchestra and Chorus / Otto Ackermann
EMI mono CDH7 69520-2 (72 minutes: ADD) Ⓕ
Recorded 1953 ●●●

In this star-studded performance from the previous generation to Gardiner's, the music emerged as one of the great classics of light opera. Emmy Loose has exactly the right appealing kind of voice for the 'dutiful wife' who plays with fire, and Nicolai Gedda is a superb Camille, sounding extraordinarily like Tito Schipa at his best. His high notes ring out finely and his caressing lyrical tones would upset a far better-balanced woman than the susceptible Valencienne. These two sing their duets beautifully, both excelling in the second act duet, in which Gedda has the lion's share. Nothing in this recording, except Schwarzkopf's 'Vilia', is so ravishing as his soft tone in the second half of the duet ('Love in my heart is waking'), which begins 'Sieh' dort den kleinen Pavillon' ('See over there the little pavilion') which is perhaps the loveliest in the score. Erich Kunz has not the charm but more voice and a perfect command of the style the music requires; and he is very taking in the celebrated Maxim's song. He speaks the middle section of the little song about the Königskinder possibly because the vocal part lies uncomfortably high for him; and perhaps his rich laughter would not be considered quite the thing in the diplomatic service. But his is, in most ways, a very attractive and lively performance. The Baron's part was probably much written up for George Graves but here what little he has to do is done well by Anton Niessner.

Elisabeth Schwarzkopf sings Hanna radiantly and exquisitely. She commands the ensembles in no uncertain manner and makes it clear that the 20-million-francs widow would be a personage even if she had only 20 centimes. It is a grand performance, crowned with the sensuous, tender singing of the celebrated waltz in Act 3. The chorus singing is first-rate and its Viennese abandon sounds absolutely authentic, whatever its address. Otto Ackermann conducts with total understanding, and notable sympathy for the singers, and the members of the Philharmonia Orchestra play like angels for him. The recording is as good as one can reasonably expect and, very important in such a score, the string tone is lovely throughout. In addition, the balance between orchestra and voices could not be better.

Jón Leifs
Icelandic 1899-1968

GROVE *Leifs studied in Leipzig (1916-22) and conducted various German orchestras. He wrote orchestral, vocal and piano music based on Icelandic folk music, which he championed.*

Organ Concerto

Concerto for Organ and Orchestra, Op 7[a]. Dettifoss, Op 57[b]. Fine II, 'Farewell to Earthly Life', Op 56[c]. Variazioni pastorale, Op 8

[a]Björn Steinar Sólbergsson *org* **[b]Loftur Erlingsson** *bar* **[c]Reynir Sigurdsson** *vib*
[b]Hallgrím's Church Motet Choir; Iceland Symphony Orchestra / En Shao Ⓕ
BIS CD930 (56 minutes: DDD). Recorded 1998-99 ●

Leifs began writing his Organ Concerto (1917-30) with the central Passacaglia (which takes up two-thirds of the whole work), which only gradually achieves the explosive style (with premonitions of *Hekla*) of the brief outer movements. Well received at its 1935 première in a Nazi-arranged Nordic music festival, the concerto was execrated later once the Jewish connections of Leifs's wife had become known. A piece long heard-of but unheard, the present performance reveals the concerto to be a truly original and virile utterance. Björn Steinar Sólbergsson gives a consummate rendition of what sounds like a monstrously difficult solo part.

The orchestra is given music of unusual delicacy (for this composer) in the *Variazioni pastorale* (on a theme from Beethoven's *Serenade*, also Op 8), though the pastoralism is more redolent of Roy Harris than Beethoven. In this work, also completed in 1930, Leifs's real voice again emerges gradually, and the return of Beethoven's theme at the close is wonderfully surreal – though the tonal framework remains more conventional than in the later works. *Fine II* (1963) is one of two orchestral endings Leifs penned for his unfinished Edda oratorio, *Twilight of the Gods*. *Dettifoss* (1964) is the third of Leifs's tone paintings (the others are *Geysir* and *Hekla*) of Icelandic natural wonders, though here he conceived of a dialogue between poet Einar Benediktsson and the huge waterfall rather than straight depiction. Thumpingly good performances from all concerned, captured in spectacular sound to match the landscape.

Hekla

Elegy, Op 53[c]. Hekla, Op 52[bc]. Icelandic Overture, Op 9[ac]. Loftr-Suite, Op 6*a*[c]. Réminiscence du Nord, Op 40[c]. Requiem, Op 33*b*[a]

[a]Hallgrím's Church Motet Choir; [b]Schola Cantorum; [c]Iceland Symphony Orchestra / En Shao
BIS CD1030 (65 minutes: DDD). Texts and translations included. Recorded 1998-99 Ⓕ

Hekla (1961) is, like *The Rite of Spring*, enormously complex in texture, such that it is practically impossible to achieve a truly definitive account in which everything can be heard. Highlight one passage and another is likely to be submerged. So it proves when comparing recordings of it. The bells that feature prominently early on do not ring out in this newcomer, although rather more other detail does than in the competitors. En Shao's is a more measured approach and the benefits of the slower speeds outweigh any minor losses. The rival accounts from Leif Segerstam and Paul Zukofsky are still very fine, but this new release is the one to have. It is a signal tribute to Leifs's growing popularity that all but one of the works here have alternatives to compare them with, even if with the *Loftr-Suite* (1915-25) only of the 'Funeral March'. En Shao and Petri Sakari (Chandos) are fairly close in terms of expressive intent and tempo here, as indeed they are in the exuberant if loosely constructed *Icelandic Overture* (1926). The latter work and the extended and searching *Réminiscence du Nord* for strings (1952) have a flavour suggestive of Roy Harris about them, which is remarkable given that the Overture pre-dates the American's famous Third Symphony by some 12 years. The *Elegy* for strings (1961, in memory of his mother) and Requiem show the private side to Leifs not heard much in works composed in his more 'public' manner. The *Elegy* is less interesting, however deeply felt, than *Réminiscence du Nord* or Requiem (1947, to a non-liturgical text assembled by Leifs). The motet is without doubt a gem, a lullaby to a dead child whom the parent seems frightened to wake. Beneath the surface gentleness is an undertow of dissonance like a barely suppressed howl of anguish.

Kenneth Leighton
British 1929-1988

GROVE *Leighton studied at Oxford and with Petrassi in Rome, and in 1970 was appointed professor at Edinburgh University. His music is in a 12-note but fundamentally diatonic style; its romanticism is expressed in lyrical melody, instrumental colour and virtuoso solo writing. It includes Catholic church music, concertos, chamber and instrumental pieces.*

God's Grandeur

God's Grandeur. What love is this of thine?. Give me wings of faith[a]. Crucifixus pro nobis, Op 38[a]. Lully, lulla, thou little tiny child, Op 25*b*. Mass, Op 44[a]. Laudate pueri, Op 68

Finzi Singers / Paul Spicer with
[a]**Andrew Lumsden** *org*

Chandos CHAN9485 (71 minutes: DDD). Texts and translations included. Recorded 1993 Ⓕ

There is a fine unease in Kenneth Leighton, a sense that fulfilment, musical and spiritual, must be striven for, that nothing worthwhile is gained without what Hardy called 'a full look at the worst'. Every new phrase in these choral settings sounds like the outcome of innumerable rejections: nothing is facile. In several of them, comfort is found – in *God's Grandeur* 'There lives the dearest freshness', in *What love is this of thine?* 'Oh, that thy love might overflow my heart' – and with it a sweetness that means so much more when hard won out of bleakness. He is a composer for the pilgrimage – not joyless by any means, but serious. In this excellent programme never does anything (not even of a bar's length) compromise this integrity. In date the works range from a student composition, his fine, independent setting of the Coventry Carol, to the anthem, *What love is this of thine?*, written not very long before his death. In style, rhythm, melody, harmony, counterpoint and the expert management of choral sound, all contribute, taking turn as a principal source of life and interest. The performances have all that could be desired in textual responsiveness and technical control. Somewhere among the sopranos is a voice (or it may be two voices) which at a *forte* has a worn or otherwise obtrusive edge); but clearly all members are valuable singers, as is shown by the ample supply of soloists from the ranks. Most of the works here are sung *a cappella*, those that are not being accompanied with clarity and discretion by Lumsden. The acoustic of All Saints', Tooting, is resonant but not excessively so for such a programme as this. This disc is a most welcome addition to the catalogue.

Ruggiero Leoncavallo

Italian 1858-1919

GROVE *Italian composer and librettist Leoncavallo studied literature at Bologna University. The failure of an early opera, I Medici (1893), conceived as the first of a Renaissance trilogy (unrealised) and written for Giulio Ricordi who rejected it, prompted him, in a defiant quest for fame, to write the poem and music of Pagliacci (Milan, 1892), the single work for which he is widely known. In its economy and consistent impetus, notably with the commedia dell'arte playlet and the Zola-inspired prologue invoking naturalism, the opera represents a skilful exploitation of the 1890s verismo trend; it made Leoncavallo a celebrity overnight. That success was never repeated. However, he set La bohème (1897) in opposition to Puccini and the sentimental Zazà (1900) was favourably received. One of the first composers to become involved with gramophone records, he wrote the popular song Mattinata (recorded by Caruso,1904) and conducted Pagliacci (1907), both for the G and T Company.*

Pagliacci

José Cura *ten* Canio; **Barbara Frittoli** *sop* Nedda; **Carlos Alvarez** *bar* Tonio; **Simon Keenlyside** *bar* Silvio; **Charles Castronovo** *ten* Beppe; **Adrian Folea** *ten* First Villager; **Gert Jan Alders** *bass* Second Villager; **National Children's Choir; Netherlands Radio Choir; Royal Concertgebouw Orchestra / Riccardo Chailly**

Decca 467 086-2DH (73 minutes: DDD) Ⓕ
Recorded 1999 ○○○

The big point in favour of this new version of *Pagliacci* is the glorious playing of the Royal Concertgebouw Orchestra under their long-time music director. If Riccardo Chailly in previous *verismo* opera recordings – with Italian opera orchestras – has tended to sound aggressive and paradoxically not fully Italianate, this is quite different. The opening orchestral prelude instantly alerts you to the refinement of the playing, not just in the polished ensemble but in the subtle shading of tone and dynamic. The wonder is that with the Concertgebouw players responding warmly to their director the result sounds totally natural and idiomatic in its phrasing and *rubato*, while letting one hear the piece with new clarity, making one marvel at the beauty and subtlety of Leoncavallo's orchestration, matching that of Puccini. When speeds in ensembles are on the fast side, the results are never breathless. Rather, they tingle with excitement, and the *scherzando* wit of much of the writing comes over with new point. The brilliant, incisive singing of the Netherlands Radio Choir also has one marvelling afresh at the complexity of the choral writing in the sparkling ensembles which frame the piece.

Happily Decca has lined up a first-rate cast to match. José Cura's voice has not quite the glowing freshness it once had, having acquired something of a baritonal quality, but there is little of the roughness which mars his deeply disappointing recital of Verdi arias for Erato. The feeling for detail as well as the heroic power make his reading of Canio strong and intense, far more than the loud rant it can become even with leading tenors. 'Vesti la giubba' is nicely shaped, moving without being too lachrymose, and Cura reserves his finest singing of all for the climactic 'No! Pagliaccio non son' at the end.

Barbara Frittoli proves an excellent choice as Nedda, giving a finely detailed performance, with singing on almost every phrase showing that she has rethought the role and its implications, rather as Callas did in her classic performance, but with more sensuous, more beautiful tone. Soon after her first entry, leading up to her Balatella with the birds, she produces a ravishing top A on the phrase 'O che bel sole' (track 7, 1'04"), responding to the marking *dolce*.

Another rising star, Carlos Alvarez, with his big heroic baritone, makes an impressive Tonio from the Prologue onwards, even if he does not sound as sinister as some in his menaces. He is well contrasted in scale and timbre with Simon Keenlyside as Nedda's lover Silvio, lighter and more lyrical. The *pianissimo* close to Silvio's big duet with Nedda could not be subtler from either singer, while Charles Castronovo as Beppe in the final Play scene sings with comparable refinement.

There are few digital versions of this perennially popular opera not marred by poor recording if not flawed singing, and so this new one is particularly welcome. Vintage versions may offer individual performances of each role which in various ways outshine these, but in the power, beauty and refinement of the Royal Concertgebouw's playing we have something incomparable, enhanced by Decca's rich, spacious and brilliant recording.

Carlo Bergonzi *ten* Canio; **Joan Carlyle** *sop* Nedda; **Giuseppe Taddei** *bar* Tonio; **Rolando Panerai** *bar* Silvio; **Ugo Benelli** *ten* Beppe **OO**

Mascagni Cavalleria rusticana
Fiorenza Cossotto *mez* Santuzza; **Carlo Bergonzi** *ten* Turiddu; **Giangiacomo Guelfi** *bar* Alfio; **Adriane Martino** *mez* Lola; **Maria Gracia Allegri** *contr* Lucia
Chorus and Orchestra of La Scala, Milan / Herbert von Karajan

Opera Intermezzos: **Verdi** La traviata – Prelude, Act 3. **Puccini** Manon Lescaut – Intermezzo. Suor Angelica – Intermezzo. **Schmidt** Notre Dame – Intermezzo. **Massenet** Thaïs – Méditation (with Michel Schwalbé *vn*). **Giordano** Fedora – Intermezzo. **Cilea** Adriana Lecouvreur – Intermezzo. **Wolf-Ferrari** I gioiello della Madonna – Intermezzo. **Mascagni** L'amico Fritz – Intermezzo
Berlin Philharmonic Orchestra / Herbert von Karajan
DG ③ 419 257-2GH3 (198 minutes: ADD). Notes, texts and translations included. Recorded 1965 Ⓕ

Pagliacci is also available on a single disc: DG The Originals 449 727-2GOR (78 minutes: ADD) Ⓜ

Cav and Pag, as they are usually known, have been bedfellows for many years. Lasting for about 75 minutes each, both operas have similarities. Each concerns the passions, jealousies and hatred of two tightly knit communities – the inhabitants of a Sicilian town and the players in a travelling troupe of actors. *Cavalleria rusticana* ('Rustic chivalry') concerns the triangular relationship of mother, son and his rejected lover. Played against a rich musical tapestry, sumptuously orchestrated, the action is played out during the course of an Easter day. Bergonzi is a stylish, ardent Turiddu whose virile charms glitter in his every phrase and Fiorenza Cossotto makes a thrilling Santuzza motivated and driven by a palpable conviction; her contribution to the well-known Easter hymn scene is gripping. But the real hero of the opera is Karajan, whose direction of this powerful work is magnificent. Conviction and insight also instil *Pagliacci* with excitement and real drama. A troupe of actors arrives to give a performance of a *commedia dell'arte* play. The illustration of real love, life and hatred is portrayed in the interplay of Tonio, Silvio, Nedda and her husband Canio. As the two rivals, Caro Bergonzi and Giuseppe Taddei are superb. Taddei's sinister, hunch-backed clown, gently forcing the play-within-the-play closer to reality until it finally bursts out violently is a masterly assumption, and Karajan controls the slow build-up of tension with a grasp that few conductors could equal. The Milan La Scala forces respond wholeheartedly and the 1965 recording sounds well. The third disc is filled by a selection of very rich, very soft-centred opera intermezzos.

Pagliacci
Giuseppe di Stefano *ten* Canio; **Maria Callas** *sop* Nedda; **Tito Gobbi** bar Tonio; **Rolando Panerai** bar Silvio; **Nicola Monti** *ten* Beppe **OO**

Mascagni Cavalleria rusticana **H**
Maria Callas *sop* Santuzza; **Giuseppe di Stefano** *ten* Turiddu; **Rolando Panerai** *bar* Alfio; **Anna Maria Canali** *mez* Lola; **Ebe Ticozzi** *contr* Lucia
Chorus and Orchestra of La Scala, Milan / Tullio Serafin
EMI mono ② CDS5 56287-2 (141 minutes): ADD. Notes, texts and translations included. Ⓕ
Recorded 1954

The sound here is much more confined than on the Karajan set, though more immediate. Serafin conducts swifter-moving performances, yet ones quite as notable as Karajan's for pointing up relevant detail. All four interpretations carry with them a real sense of the theatre and are quite free from studio routine. It is difficult to choose between the casts on these two sets. Callas lives the characters more vividly than anyone. The sadness and anguish she brings to Santuzza's unhappy plight are at their most compelling at 'io piango' in 'Voi lo sapete' and at 'Turiddu mi tolse' in her encounter with Alfio, where the pain in Santuzza's heart is expressed in almost unbearable terms. As Nedda, she differentiates marvellously between the pensiveness of her aria, the passion of her duet with Silvio, and the playfulness of her *commedia dell'arte* acting. One unforgettable moment among many is when her tone shivers on the word 'lurido' as she sees Tonio leaving, then becomes all smiling a moment later as she greets her love with 'Silvio!' Her partner in both operas is di Stefano They work up a huge lather of passion in the big *Cavalleria* duet, and the tenor is wholly believable as the caddish

Turiddu. In the immediacy of emotion of his Canio, it is the tenor's turn to evoke pity. Di Stefano does it as well as any Canio on record without quite having the heroic tone for the latter part of the opera. Panerai is a strong Alfio on the Serafin set, but Guelfi, with his huge voice, is possibly better suited to this macho part. It is impossible to choose between the two Tonios, both pertinently cast. Taddei plays the part a little more comically, Gobbi more menacingly. Callas or Karajan enthusiasts will have no difficulty making their choice. Others may be guided by quality of sound. With either you will be ensured hours of memorable listening.

Pagliacci (sung in English)
Dennis O'Neill *ten* Canio; **Rosa Mannion** *sop* Nedda; **Alan Opie** *bar* Tonio; **William Dazeley** *bar* Silvio; **Peter Bronder** *ten* Beppe
Geoffrey Mitchell Choir; Peter Kay Children's Choir; London Philharmonic Orchestra / David Parry
Chandos Opera in English Series CHAN3003 (80 minutes: DDD). Notes and text included. Ⓕ
Recorded 1997

'Hello…Hello' is the neat rendition of 'Si può…si può', presumably unthinkable in the days which produced 'A word allow me' as its translation. 'A slice of life as we live it' replaces 'life with its laughter and sorrow', 'Will ye hear then the story?' becomes 'Now you know what we're here for', and 'Ring up the curtain' (can't do much about that) is now 'Bring up the curtain'. Two others: at the point in the Nedda-Silvio duet which inspired Fred Weatherly's couplet 'For such a passion/The whip's the fashion', Edmund Tracey wisely renounces rhyme in favour of 'I tamed him nicely ... I gave him a beating', and 'Put on your costume' (this is almost like rewriting *The Book of Common Prayer*) does for 'On with the motley'.

The text is one thing, the performance another. Opera singers are trained to pronounce their words in a very pure English which nowadays sounds more upper-class than it did not so long ago when all 'official' pronunciation was 'pure' in this sense. The 'slice of life' involves travelling players and villagers, but they all sound like ladies and gentlemen: it takes some of the verity out of *verismo*. Dennis O'Neill's Canio is fine as to vocal resource and avoidance of cheapness; but 'Un tal gioco' wants ironical bite, 'Vesti la giubba' more sense of occasion, 'No, Pagliaccio non son' more tension, bitterness and (at one point) sweetness. Rosa Mannion is an admirable Nedda, and both baritones do well, Alan Opie excellent in the Prologue, William Dazeley a lyric baritone of pleasing quality and tasteful style. The off-stage serenade is nicely sung by Peter Bronder, and the chorus is fine. David Parry's conducting has grown in authority, and in the climax (menace in the accompaniment to 'No, Pagliaccio' for instance) more than fulfils expectations. With effective work by producer and sound engineers, this *Pagliacci* will much enhance appreciation of the opera.

Anatoli Liadov Russian 1855-1914

GROVE *Liadov, a pupil of Rimsky-Korsakov at the St Petersburg Conservatory, showed promise and developed a lasting interest in counterpoint; from 1878 he taught at the conservatory (Prokofiev and Myaskovsky were among his pupils), also making appearances as a conductor. In the 1870s he was associated with 'The Five', and in the 1880s with the Belyayev circle. Many of his pieces are based on pre-existing motifs (folksongs, other composers' themes, a cantus firmus) or rely on a programme, revealing his sense of orchestral colour and gift for musical characterization (notably in the orchestral works Baba-Yaga, ?1891-1904, and Kikimora, 1909); later works, including the symphonic poem Skorbnaya pesn (1914), experiment with extended tonality. A series of charming piano miniatures is still in the repertory. Procrastination, indolence and self-doubt prevented him from completing a work of any size or scope.*

The Enchanted Lake

Liadov The Enchanted Lake, Op 62
Mussorgsky Boris Godunov – I am sick at heart[a]
Tchaikovsky Marche slave, Op 31. Capriccio italien, Op 45. Eugene Onegin – Waltz; Polonaise
Kirov Theatre [a]Chorus and Orchestra / Valery Gergiev
Philips 442 775-2PH (54 minutes: DDD)
Recorded 1993. Includes a bonus sampler CD of previous recordings from the Kirov Theatre forces conducted by Gergiev Ⓕ

Liadov's orchestral pieces have always had a tenuous hold on the repertory, and afford glimpses of an exceptional talent. In the shifting harmonies and dissolving textures of *The Enchanted Lake*, which shimmers atmospherically, there is not only acknowledgement of *Siegfried*'s Forest Murmurs but anticipation of Scriabin and even Schoenberg. It was a novel idea to have the Kirov orchestra's 'Russian Spectacular', the title of this disc, open to the rich aural canvas of *Boris Godunov*'s 'Coronation Scene' as refashioned by Shostakovich, complete with tolling bells, weighty brass and generous cymbal spray. The sound is big and generalised, the conducting more majestic than excitable – which usefully serves to minimise the contrast with *Marche slave*, a comparatively lyrical statement with a sad-eyed account of the principal theme and lightweight, almost balletic sequences thereafter. Gergiev never drives too hard, while his artful shaping of *Eugene Onegin*'s 'Polonaise' incorporates sensitive handling of the central section. Likewise in the Waltz, where the cello line is affectionately moulded. *Capriccio italien* is thoughtfully held together, with much deft passagework in the closing tarantella.

There's a bonus CD, made up of snippets from Gergiev's various Russian stage work recordings for Philips; nothing earth-shattering, but a nice cross-section. This is a good, well-planned (if hardly generous) programme, warmly recorded.

Gyorgy Ligeti

Hungarian 1923

GROVE *Ligeti studied with Farkas, Veress and Járdányi at the Budapest Academy, where he began teaching in 1950. During this period he followed the prevailing Kodály-Bartók style in his works while also writing more adventurous pieces (First Quartet, 1954) that had to remain unpublished. In 1956 he left Hungary for Vienna. He worked at the electronic music studio in Cologne (1957-8) and came to international prominence with his Atmosphères (1961), which works with slowly changing orchestral clusters. This led to teaching appointments in Stockholm (from 1961), Stanford (1972) and Hamburg (from 1973).*

Meanwhile he developed the 'cloud' style in his Requiem (1965) and Lontano for orchestra (1967), while writing an absurdist diptych for vocal soloists and ensemble: Aventures (1966) and Nouvelles aventures (1966). His interests in immobile drifts and mechanical processes are seen together in his Second Quartet (1968) and Chamber Concerto (1970), while the orchestral Melodien (1971) introduced a tangle of melody. The combination of these elements, in music of highly controlled fantasy and excess, came in his surreal opera Le grand macabre (1978). His subsequent output has been diminished by ill-health, although it includes a Horn Trio (1982) in which perverse calculation is carried into Romanticism. Other later works include Monument, Selbstporträt, Bewegung, for two pianos (1976), two pieces for harpsichord (1978), two Hungarian studies for chorus (1983) and a book of piano studies (1985).

Concertos

Violin Concerto[a]. Cello Concerto[b]. Piano Concerto[c]
[a]Saschko Gawriloff *vn* **[b]Jean-Guihen Queyras** *vc* **[c]Pierre-Laurent Aimard** *pf*
Ensemble InterContemporain / Pierre Boulez
Awards 1995
DG 439 808-2GH (67 minutes: DDD). Ⓕ
Recorded 1992-93 ●●

The Violin Concerto (1992) is music by a composer fascinated with Shakespeare's *The Tempest*: indeed, it might even prove to be a substitute for Ligeti's long-mooted operatic version of the play. There are plenty of 'strange noises', the result not just of Ligeti's latter-day predilection for ocarinas, but of his remarkable ability to play off natural and artificial tunings against each other. This work is superior to the Piano Concerto because the solo violin is so much more volatile and poetic as a protagonist, an animator who 'fires up' the orchestra, functioning as a leader at odds with the led. Saschko Gawriloff is a brilliantly effective soloist, and well served by a sharply defined yet expressive accompaniment – Boulez at his most incisive – and a totally convincing recording. The other works are played and recorded with similar success. The Cello Concerto (1966) is a particularly powerful reminder of the strengths of the earlier Ligeti, where simple, basic elements generate anything but minimal consequences.

The Ligeti Project, volume 1
Melodien. Chamber Concerto. Piano Concerto[a]. Mysteries of the Macabre[b] (arr Howarth)
[b]Peter Masseurs *tpt* **[a]Pierre-Laurent Aimard** *pf*
ASKO Ensemble; Schönberg Ensemble / Reinbert de Leeuw
Teldec New Line 8573 83953-2 (64 minutes: DDD). Ⓕ
Recorded 1999 ●

It is good that Teldec has picked up where Sony left off in issuing a complete edition of Ligeti's authorized works. *Melodien*, in particular, has been ill-served on disc: surprisingly so, as its 13 minutes are a microcosm of Ligetian practice at its most refined and accessible, the transitions between apparent activity and real stasis magically effected. The ASKO Ensemble has greater dynamic nuance than the London Sinfonietta's pioneering account (Decca – nla), reaffirming just why this music has had such an impact on a generation of European (not least British) composers. Equally influential, the Chamber Concerto has been better represented. This paring down to essentials of the harmonic and textural mesh familiar from earlier works, out of which melodic lines can then reassert themselves, is deftly achieved with no little humour. Compared with Boulez, de Leeuw feels a shade deadpan, but 'Calmo' has real plangency and 'Movimento' is pungently mechanistic.

Whether through familiarity or a more integrated balance with the orchestra, Aimard does not quite recapture the sense of daring in his 1992 account of the Piano Concerto, notably the opening *Vivace*'s freewheeling polyrhythms and the fractured energy of the fourth movement, where Boulez's precision still allows for a more spontaneous interplay. Yet the *Lento*'s folk inflections are fervently expressive, and the overall impression is of a work that seems far more unsettling than it did a decade ago: a sure sign of interpretative flexibility and musical durability.

It was a neat touch to sign off with Elgar Howarth's *Macabre* paraphrase. Masseurs is as fully equipped as Håkan Hardenberger (Philips – nla) to deliver the necessary pyrotechnics, while this first recording with ensemble accompaniment gives the music a more strident feel, in keeping with its operatic context. Ligeti can feel well served.

String Quartets

String Quartets – No 1, 'Métamorphoses nocturnes'; No 2
Artemis Quartet (Heime Müller, Natalia Prischepenko *vns* Volker Jacobsen *va* Eckart Runge *vc*)
Ars Musici AM1276-2 (43 minutes: DDD). Ⓕ
Recorded 1999 ●

It may seem odd to observe that Ligeti's quartets have been a part of the 'canon' for some time; the Second is over 30 years old, and the First received its première only in the 1970s. Yet few string quartets of the late 20th century are as often performed as these, and it was only a matter of time before one of the up-and-coming younger ensembles took up the challenge thrown down by the Arditti Quartet in their recent re-recording of both pieces for Sony (their earlier reading on Wergo dates from the late 1970s).

The First Quartet, *Métamorphoses nocturnes*, dates from Ligeti's Hungarian period, and the evident debt to Bartók notwithstanding, his approach to mass and textural transformation is recognisable to anyone familiar with his later music. There have been several recordings apart from the two Arditti versions, including a disappointingly glib reading from the Hagen Quartet. To their credit, the Artemis let the music breathe, and make much of Ligeti's impish humour: both works are theatrical and benefit from being 'played up', which the Artemis do perhaps more freely than the Ardittis.

But the real test comes with the Second Quartet, where the Arditti's pre-eminence is more obvious (the first recording, by the work's dedicatees the LaSalle Quartet, is no longer available) and the composer's demands rather fiercer. Here the acoustic makes a perceptible difference. The Arditti's ambience is very resonant and has been recorded at a certain distance – presumably a lesson learnt from the Wergo session, which was miked so closely that one heard the players' tense breathing. This brings a psychological distance to the performance, and slightly blurs the sudden cuts and changes of texture on which the musical drama depends.

The Artemis are miked more closely than the Sony recording, but the sound still allows for some beautifully differentiated, 'atmospheric' timbres (like the 'organ-stops' of bar 71, first movement). There is also a more palpable sense of immediacy, and a more riotous climax in the most abrupt passages (the *ferocissimo* fourth movement, most obviously). True, the drier acoustic gives them less cover when immediate contrasts are called for, but this never detracts from the sense of technical security. Also, the durations are closer to those prescribed in the score, where the Ardittis take things much faster despite the greater resonance afforded them by the acoustic (in fact all the Arditti's recent re-recordings have tended to be perceptibly faster than the first recordings). The Artemis offer a sufficiently different view from the Ardittis to make for an unmissable alternative. First-time buyers may defer to the Arditti's pedigree, but they need not hesitate to start here.

Horn Trio

Horn Trio[a]. Six Bagatelles[b]. 10 Pieces[b]. Sonata for Solo Viola[c]

[a]**Marie Luise Neunecker** *hn* [a]**Saschko Gawriloff** *vn* [c]**Tabea Zimmermann** *va* [a]**Pierre-Laurent Aimard** *pf* [b]**London Winds** (Philippa Davies *fl* Gareth Hulse *ob* Michael Collins *cl* Robin O'Neill *bn* Richard Watkins *hn*)

Sony Classical SK62309 (71 minutes: DDD). Ⓕ
Recorded 1994-96 ●

This issue presents music from the 1950s and 1960s (*10 Pieces*, *Bagatelles*) to the 1980s and 1990s (Horn Trio, Viola Sonata). Those looking for a specific reason to buy this disc need look no further than the account of the Horn Trio, Ligeti's homage to Brahms, a work which has become a classic of its kind. What distinguishes this version is the astonishing horn-playing of Marie Luise Neunecker – the impression of near-effortlessness and breadth of dynamic range she conveys are unlikely to be bettered. As to her companions, they have both recorded the Trio before, and their experience is audible.

This interpretation is especially effective at projecting the music's multiple levels and layers. As to its expressive power, even those who find Ligeti's later music problematic can hardly deny the poignant, tragic beauty of the concluding *Lamento*. The two sets of wind pieces are given polished, bravura performances by London Winds. The *Bagatelles* are among the composer's most convincing music from his pre-Western period; as to the *10 Pieces*, they plough the same furrow as those two masterpieces from the same year (1968), the Second String Quartet and *Continuum* for harpsichord (and the *Chamber Concerto*, begun the following year); but they are altogether more lightweight, their brevity almost provocative when heard against the broader canvas of those other works. Provocative in a very different way is the Viola Sonata, completed in 1994. Listen to Tabea Zimmermann's commanding and expressive playing, and hear a composer for whom confounding the critics' expectations has always been second nature.

Etudes

Etudes – Book 1; Book 2; Book 3. Musica ricercata

Pierre-Laurent Aimard *pf*

Sony Classical SK62308 Ⓕ
(65 minutes: DDD). Recorded 1995 ●●

Let us salute Pierre-Laurent Aimard first – not just a modern music specialist but an artist of phenomenal gifts, and excellently recorded here. First impressions of the music are likely to be of its immediacy. The complexities are a problem only for the pianist – whatever the sources of Ligeti's inspiration, his ideas serve only a musical/poetic purpose. Central to these dazzling pieces is his longstanding interest in composing with layers of material in different metres or different tempos and in producing what he calls 'an illusion of rhythm'; evident, too, are his more recent preoccupations with modern mathematics, in particular the young science of dynamical systems which seeks to explain the precarious balance between pattern and chaos, order and disorder. Ligeti's powerful imagination is fuelled by many things, but there is no question of having to have a special key to enter his world. The music is enough. There are 15 *Etudes* so far, in two books plus the beginning of a third, and as with the collections of Chopin and Debussy there is a good deal to be gained from hearing each book in sequence. The example of Liszt might also come to mind, who opened up a world of sound on the piano as Chopin before him had done, and as Debussy was to do. When we reach the end of Ligeti's Book 2, apparently at the limits of pianistic possibilities and expression, there can be no doubt that Ligeti's *Etudes* belong with the greatest piano music of this or any other century. They are amazing.

Le grand macabre

Sibylle Ehlert *sop* Venus, Gepopo; **Laura Claycomb** *sop* Amanda; **Charlotte Hellekant** *mez* Amando; **Derek Lee Ragin** *counterten* Prince Go-Go; **Jard van Nes** *contr* Mescalina; **Graham Clark** *ten* Piet the Pot; **Willard White** *bass* Nekrotzar; **Frode Olsen** *bass* Astradamors; **Martin Winkler** *bar* Ruffiak; **Marc Campbell-Griffiths** *bar* Schobiak; **Michael Lessiter** *bar* Schabernack; **Steven Cole** *ten* White Minister; **Richard Suart** *bass* Black Minister
London Sinfonietta Voices; Philharmonia Orchestra / Esa-Pekka Salonen
Sony Classical Ligeti Edition ② S2K62312
(102 minutes: DDD). Text and translation included. Ⓕ
Recorded live in 1998

Le grand macabre, a comedy about the end of the world, an elaborate game of musical time-travel, an ambiguous dance on the brink of an abyss, looks more and more like the key opera of the end of the 20th century. Direct comparison between this version and Elgar Howarth's splendid 1987 Wergo performance is difficult, because Ligeti extensively revised the score in 1996, and it is that 'final version', as he calls it, that is recorded here. He has made a number of cuts, a great deal of what was originally spoken dialogue is now sung and there have been many changes to the scoring, making it more practical but also thinning it out. The reduction of spoken dialogue and the lightening of the orchestral texture make life a little easier for the singers (though not for the soprano singing Gepopo, which Ligeti has described as an attempt to out-Zerbinetta Zerbinetta) and for the players. The whole performance is rather more assured than Howarth's (his was recorded at a concert, Salonen's during a series of staged performances with presumably much longer rehearsal time) and the score's beauties are more lovingly polished. It now sounds rather closer to a 'normal' opera and, perhaps inevitably, lacks a degree of Howarth's alarming impact.

Interestingly enough, it is Salonen's performance, sung in English to a French audience (Howarth's was in German, his audience Austrian), that draws more laughs at the jokes. As Gepopo Sibylle Ehlert is spectacularly virtuoso and Willard White's gravity is effective in the role of Nekrotzar. Graham Clark is hugely exuberant as Piet the Pot, and Steven Cole and Richard Suart make a splendid double-act of the two Ministers. Jard van Nes and Frode Olsen are perhaps inhibited by the English language from making Mescalina and Astradamors as grotesque as they can be, though both sing well, as does every other member of the cast. The recording, like the performance, is a little more comfortable, rather less in-your-face, than Howarth's. This version is the one to have – Ligeti's revisions are all improvements, and the performance is a fine one – but the older one has a shade more of the quality that Ligeti says he has hoped for in stage productions of the opera, that of 'demoniacal farce'.

Further Listening
Ligeti Aventures
Couplings: Nonsense Madrigals. Mysteries of the Macabre. Nouvelles Aventures. Der Sommer. Three Weores Songs. Five Arany Songs. Four Wedding Dances
Soloists; Philharmonia Orchestra / Salonen
Sony Classical SK62311 (72 minutes: DDD: 1/97) Ⓕ

A richly entertaining collection; in some ways a sort of autobiography, ranging from Ligeti's early folk-song arrangements and settings of the safely 'classic' poet Janos Arany to the 'non-tonal but diatonic' *Nonsense Madrigals*, which are are hugely inventive, sometimes very funny.

Magnus Lindberg

Finnish 1958

Following piano studies, Lindberg entered the Sibelius Academy where his composition teachers included Rautavaara and Heininen. Heininen encouraged his pupils to explore the works of the European avant-garde, and this led c1980 to the founding of the informal grouping known as the Ears Open Society, through which Lindberg and his contemporaries aimed to encourage a greater awareness of mainstream modernism. Lindberg's compositional breakthrough came with two large-scale works, Action-Situation-Signification (1982) and Kraft (1983-85). Action, the work in which Lindberg first turned to musique concrète, led to his founding with Esa-Pekka Salonen the experimental Toimii Ensemble. This group, in which he plays piano and percussion, has provided him with a laboratory for his sonic development. During the late 1980s Lindberg's music approached a new modernist classicism, in which many of the communicative ingredients of a vibrant musical language (harmony, rhythm, counterpoint, melody) were reinterpreted. Key scores in this period were the orchestral/ensemble triptych Kinetics (1988), Marea (1989-90) and Joy (1989-90), reaching fulfilment in Aura (1993-94) and Arena (1994-95). Recent works, including Feria (1997), Fresco (1997) Cantigas (1999) the Cello Concerto (1999) and most recently Gran Duo (2000) have established Lindberg's international reputation as one of Finland's leading orchestral composers.

Aura

Aura[a]. Engine[b]
[b]**London Sinfonietta,** [a]**BBC Symphony Orchestra / Oliver Knussen**
DG 20/21 463 184-2GH (51 minutes: DDD). Ⓕ
Recorded [b]1997 and [a]1998

Few contemporary composers have established themselves as orchestral composers with the conviction of Magnus Lindberg, whose career over the past 15 years has seen him forge a personal style in this most potential-filled medium. Back in 1985, *Kraft* defined an approach to the orchestra overflowing with new and challenging ideas. The intervening years saw those ideas streamlined, even simplified, but not compromised, so that the generous span of *Aura*, completed in 1994, forms the natural climax of an exploratory and liberating decade.

Playing for some 37 minutes, *Aura* falls into four continuous sections (tracked separately here), defined as much by variety of incident as by contrast in character. A lengthy gathering of, and focusing on salient ideas leads to a powerfully sustained phase of monumental imagery and grandeur worthy of Bruckner, before a 'scherzo' of great cumulative energy overspills into a 'finale' which draws together the conflicting elements into a peroration of Sibelian inevitability. Decidedly, but not intrinsically, symphonic, Lindberg's ideas are not so sharply defined, or evolve so organically, that they form a genuinely symphonic discourse. Listening to this work in parallel with Per Nørgård's Fifth Symphony (Chandos) and its searing, masterly layering of harmonic and rhythmic densities, confirms that Lindberg is ghosting the medium rather than remaking it. *Aura* is gripping music even so, and Knussen's control over both the smallest detail and the broader soundscape, galvanising the BBC Symphony into playing of real class, makes the listening experience the more riveting.

Engine (1996) stands in absolute contrast: progressing in sharply defined textural blocks, with more than a hint of verse and refrain, this is Lindberg the constructivist, assembling a mosaic which resolves with satisfying unexpectedness. With first-rate playing from the London Sinfonietta, this is a disc which can only enhance Lindberg's stature.

Thomas Linley II British 1756-1778

GROVE *One of England's most precocious musicians, Linley studied with Boyce, then became Nardini's violin pupil in Florence (1768-71), where he met Mozart (1770). Returning to England, he performed in Bath and London and from 1773 was leader at Drury Lane theatre. He composed prolifically, writing stage works (the first, 1775, with his father), sacred music, an Ode on the Spirits of Shakespeare (1776), songs etc, violin sonatas and 20 or more violin concertos. His works are fluent and imaginative; his death (in a boating accident) was a great loss to English music.*

The Song of Moses

The Song of Moses. Let God Arise

Julia Gooding, Sophie Daneman *sops* **Robin Blaze** *counterten* **Andrew King** *ten* **Andrew Dale Forbes** *bass* **Holst Singers; The Parley of Instruments / Peter Holman** *hpd*

Hyperion CDA67038 (67 minutes: DDD). Text included. Recorded 1997 Ⓕ

English music in the second half of the 18th century did not quite know where to go. In one direction lay the Handelian oratorio tradition, while in the other there was the new, continental *galant* style, as introduced to the country by J C Bach. The kind of synthesis of these two which Haydn and Mozart achieved may have lain beyond the capabilities of most composers, but in England many were in any case happy simply to place them side by side in the same work. That is just what Thomas Linley junior did in his oratorio, *The Song of Moses*, composed in 1777 for the Drury Lane Theatre, and here recorded for the first time. As the title suggests, it sets out on a Handelian path, with imposing and dramatic choruses, fugues and Hallelujahs not in any way uninfluenced by *Israel in Egypt*, yet in its arias and duets the style is wholly up to date and in a charmingly tuneful English way at that. More striking still, however, is the ease with which both styles are handled by their 21-year-old composer, whose death by drowning a year later was a genuine loss to English music.

The performance (which Peter Holman claims as probably the first since 1778) does it full justice. Sophie Daneman seems technically the more comfortable of the two excellent female soloists, but Julia Gooding's charming vocal quality also somehow sounds just right in this English repertoire. The stars of the show, however, are the Holst Singers; true, there are occasional weaknesses in the inner parts, but on the whole the choir is well drilled and impressively resounding in its descriptions of the Egyptians' misfortunes. The anthem, *Let God Arise*, composed for the 1773 Three Choirs Festival, is a more frankly Handelian piece and is also a rather less interesting one. In *The Song of Moses*, on the other hand, we have a real find.

Franz Liszt Hungarian 1811-1886

GROVE *Liszt was taught the piano by his father and then Czerny, establishing himself as a remarkable concert artist by the age of 12. In Paris he studied theory and composition with Reicha and Paer; he wrote an opera and bravura piano pieces and toured France, Switzerland and England before ill-health and religious doubt made him reassess his career. Intellectual growth came through literature, and the urge to create through hearing opera and especially Paganini, whose spectacular effects Liszt transferred to the piano in original works and operatic fantasias. Meanwhile he gave lessons and began his stormy relationship (1833-44) with the (married) Countess Marie d'Agoult. They lived in Switzerland and Italy and had three children.*

The greatest pianist of his time, Liszt composed some of the most difficult piano music ever written and had an extraordinarily broad repertory, from Scarlatti onwards; he invented the modern piano recital. To help raise funds for the Bonn Beethoven monument, he resumed the life of a travelling virtuoso from 1839-47; he was adulated everywhere he went. In 1848 he took up a full-time conducting post at the Weimar court, where, living with the Princess Carolyne Sayn-Wittgenstein, he wrote or revised most of the major works for which he is known, conducted new operas by Wagner, Berlioz and Verdi and, as the teacher of Hans von Bülow and others in the German avant-garde, became the figurehead of the 'New German school'. In 1861-9 he lived mainly in Rome, writing religious works (he took minor orders in 1865); from 1870 he journeyed regularly between Rome, Weimar and Budapest. He remained active as a teacher and performer to the end of his life.

Two formal traits give Liszt's compositions a personal stamp: experiment with large-scale structures (extending traditional sonata form, unifying multi-movement works), and thematic transformation, or subjecting a single short idea to changes of mode, rhythm, metre, tempo or accompaniment to form the thematic basis of an entire work (as in Les préludes, the Faust-Symphonie). His 'transcendental' piano technique was similarly imaginative, springing from a desire to make the piano sound like an orchestra or as rich in scope as one. In harmony he ventured well beyond the use of augmented and diminished chords and the whole-tone scale; the late piano and choral works especially include a strikingly advanced chromaticism.

Piano works make up the greater part of Liszt's output; they range from the brilliant early studies and lyric nature pieces of the first set of Années de pèlerinage to the finely dramatic and logical B minor Sonata, a masterpiece of 19th-century piano literature. The piano works from the 1870s onwards are more austere and withdrawn, some of them impressionistic, even gloomy (Années, third set). Not all the piano music is free of bombast but among the arrangements, the symphonic transcriptions (notably of Berlioz, Beethoven and Schubert) are often faithful and ingenious, the operatic fantasias more than mere salon pieces.

Liszt invented the term 'sinfonische Dichtung' (symphonic poem) for orchestral works that did not obey traditional forms strictly and were based generally on a literary or pictorial idea. Whether first conceived as overtures (Les préludes) or as works for other media (Mazeppa), these pieces emphasize musical construction much more than story-telling. The three-movement Faust Symphony too, with its vivid character studies of Faust, Gretchen and Mephistopheles, relies on technical artifice (especially thematic transformation) more than musical narrative to convey its message; it is often considered Liszt's supreme masterpiece. Although he failed in his aim to revolutionise liturgical music, he did create in his psalm settings, Missa solemnis and the oratorio Christus some intensely dramatic choral music.

Piano Concertos

No 1 in E flat, S124; **No 2** in A, S125

Piano Concertos Nos 1ª and 2ª.
Beethoven Piano Sonatas Nos 10, 19 and 20
Sviatoslav Richter *pf* **London Symphony Orchestra / Kyrill Kondrashin**
Philips 50 Great Recordings 464 710-2PM Ⓜ
(70 minutes: ADD). Recorded ª1961 and 1963 ●●●

These were recognised as classic performances virtually from their first appearance. They are characterised not only by the intense expressiveness of Richter's playing, but also by very careful balances of orchestral texture which hitherto had not been much apparent in recordings of these works. Throughout, the emphasis is on poetic insight, dramatic impact, and these interpretations have in these and other regards exerted a considerable influence. Yet even if sensitive readings of Liszt's concertos are now less rare, this in no way weakens the impression made by Richter's and Kondrashin's. In short, these are among the great Liszt recordings.

Piano Concertos Nos 1 and 2. Totentanz, S126
Krystian Zimerman *pf*
Boston Symphony Orchestra / Seiji Ozawa Ⓕ
DG 423 571-2GH (56 minutes: DDD) ●

This is playing in the grand manner. From the start of First Concerto you are aware of a consciously leonine approach. This is no bad thing either; for the music really calls for it. Zimerman even deliberately takes risks in a few technically perilous places where some of his colleagues, at least in the studio, play safe; and indeed his octaves in the opening cadenza are an example. The result sounds spontaneous and, yes, even brave. Ozawa and the orchestra are behind the soloist in all this. Not only do lyrical sections sing with subtlety, the big passages also are shapely. There is plenty of drive in this Concerto. In the Second Concerto Zimerman adopts a different approach; he evidently considers it a more poetic piece and the playing style, strong though it is, is to match. Finely though he handles the gentler music, there are odd sniffs and hums in the *molto espressivo* passage following the D flat major cello solo, and also in the last of the work's quiet sections. In the gorgeously grisly *Totentanz*, both the music and the playing should make your hair stand on end. The sound has a depth that suits the music and the piano is especially impressive. Zimerman's freshness (he reminds us that this is a young man's music), and the coupling, makes this disc a most desirable one.

Piano Concertos Nos 1 and 2. Totentanz
Alfred Brendel *pf*
London Philharmonic Orchestra / Bernard Haitink
Philips Silver Line 426 637-2PSL (56 minutes: ADD). Ⓜ
Recorded 1976

Few pianists have ever made a more persuasive case for Liszt than Alfred Brendel. He penetrates far below the surface of the composer's emotional vortex and surface rhetoric. This set shows him at his very finest and Bernard Haitink conducts the London Philharmonic Orchestra with comparable distinction; indeed it is orchestral playing of the highest calibre. The disc opens with the Second Piano Concerto, sounding wonderful from the very first bar, and the coupling, the E flat Concerto and the rarer *Totentanz*, are hardly any less memorable, combining brilliance with warmth and subtlety of keyboard colouring. The recording, too, is very good, if not quite so richly textured as more modern recordings.

Liszt Piano Concerto No 1
Chopin Piano Concerto No 1 in E minor, Op 11
Martha Argerich *pf*
London Symphony Orchestra / Claudio Abbado
DG The Originals 449 719-2GOR (56 minutes: ADD). Ⓜ
Recorded 1968

These performances, in DG's beautifully refurbished sound, remain as fanciful and coruscating as the day they were made. Argerich's fluency and re-creative spark dazzle and dumbfound to a unique degree but, given her reputation for fire-eating virtuosity, it is perhaps necessary to say that both performances quiver with rare sensitivity as well as drama. Time and again she gives a telling and haunting poetic counterpoint to her, arguably, more familiar way of trailing clouds of virtuoso glory. Abbado partners his mercurial soloist as to the manner born, finding (in the Chopin in particular) a burgeoning sense of wonder where others sound dry and foursquare.

Additional recomendation
Piano Concertos
Couplings: Fantasia on Hungarian Folk Themes, S123
Chopin Andante spianato and Grande polonaise in E flat, Op 22
Richter *pf* **London Symphony Orchestra / Kondrashin**
BBC Legends/IMG Artists mono BBCL4031-2 Ⓜ
(69 minutes: ADD: 4/00). Live recording

Richter's London début concerts in July 1961 were the sensation of the season, and the Liszt piano concertos at the Royal Albert Hall were the climax. Solos are miked very close by today's standards but only in this respect do the concertos yield to the famous Philips studio versions, made a little later during the same London visit.

A Dante Symphony

A Dante Symphony, S109[a]. Années de pèlerinage – deuxième année, S161, 'Italie' – No 7, Après une lecture du Dante (fantasia quasi sonata)[b]
[a]**Berlin Radio Women's Chorus;** [a]**Berlin Philharmonic Orchestra / Daniel Barenboim** [b]*pf*
Teldec 9031-77340-2 (67 minutes: DDD). Ⓜ
Item marked [a] recorded live in 1992

This disc proves conclusively that the *Dante Symphony* (a contemporary of the *Faust Symphony*) is no longer one that needs its apologists. Tone, full and rounded, firm and true, and rock-steady pacing elevate the symphony's opening beyond its all too familiar resemblance to a third-rate horror-film soundtrack. As the symphony progresses, together with the countless examples of Berlin tone and artistry filling out, refining or shaping gestures in often revelatory ways, one becomes aware of Daniel Barenboim's skill in maintaining the large-scale tension he has created. And that is a very real achievement.

As for the final choral Magnificat, if Liszt owed Wagner a debt of gratitude for persuading him to conclude the symphony with the 'noble and softly soaring' bars that precede a more noisily affirmative appended coda, in Barenboim's Magnificat (and much else in the symphony), it is Wagner's debt to Liszt that is more readily apparent; the *Parsifal*ian radiance of these final pages is unmistakable. More importantly, for once they sound convincingly conclusive. The *Dante* Sonata was recorded with the kind of risk-taking abandon and occasionally less than perfect execution that you might expect from a live event. Improvisatory, impulsive and full of extreme contrasts, Barenboim's *Dante* Sonata is vividly pictorial. The instrument itself (closely miked and widely spaced) sounds larger than life. This recording is, in a word, riveting. The recording of the symphony is spacious, focused and expertly balanced.

A Faust Symphony, S108

A Faust Symphony
Kenneth Riegel *ten*
Tanglewood Festival Chorus; Boston Symphony Orchestra / Leonard Bernstein
DG The Originals 447 449-2GOR (77 minutes: ADD). Ⓜ
Recorded 1976

David Gutman's absorbing booklet-note for the Leonard Bernstein release informs us that at a particular Tanglewood concert in 1941 (August 8) Bernstein scored a triumph in modern American repertoire and Serge Koussevitzky conducted the first two movements of *A Faust Symphony*. Some 20 years later Bernstein himself made a distinguished recording of the work, faster than this superb 1976 Boston remake by almost five minutes yet ultimately less involving. The passage of time witnessed not only an easing of tempo but a heightened response to individual characters, be it Faust's swings in mood and attitude, Gretchen's tender entreaties or the unpredictable shadow-play of 'Mephistopheles'. Orchestral execution is first-rate, the strings in particular really showing their mettle (such biting incisiveness), while Bernstein's pacing, although often slower than average, invariably fits the mood. The sound too is far warmer and more lifelike than its rather opaque New York predecessor, although when it comes to the tenor soloist in the closing chorus, Kenneth Riegel is rather strident.

A Faust Symphony
András Molnár *ten*
Hungarian State Choir; Orchestra of the Franz Liszt Academy / András Ligeti Ⓢ
Naxos 8 553304 (73 minutes: DDD). Recorded 1994

There's a lot right with this performance, not least being its outspoken acknowledgement of Faust's stormy character. Liszt's first-movement portrait receives zestful advocacy, less polished than some, perhaps, but fired by immense gusto. The recording, too, is endowed with plenty of body, while András Ligeti's vocal promptings vie with Toscanini's in *La bohème*!

Gretchen is quite comely and Ligeti effectively traces both her darker moods and those passages associated with Faust's yearning. Mephistopheles is more angry than 'ironico' and if you want confirmation of Ligeti's Lisztian mettle, then try from 5'49" through the following minute or so: it is quite thrilling. True, woodwind pointing isn't as vivid as under, say, Leonard Bernstein, but there is certainly no lack of enthusiasm. The Orchestra of the Franz Liszt Academy gives its all and the Hungarian State Choir makes noble music of the final chorus, even though András Molnár's wobbly tenor proves to be something of a distraction. It's a compelling if flawed production, less carefully prepared than its best rivals but more spontaneous than most.

Hungarian Rhapsodies, S359

(Orch cpsr/Doppler) – **No 1** in F minor (piano No 14); **No 2** in D minor (piano No 2 in C sharp minor); **No 3** in D (piano No 6 in D flat); **No 4** in D minor (piano No 12 in C sharp minor). **No 5** in E minor (piano No 5); **No 6** in D, 'Carnival in Pest, (piano No 9 in E flat)

Hungarian Rhapsodies Nos 1-6
Budapest Festival Orchestra / Iván Fischer
Philips 456 570-2PH (60 minutes: DDD). Ⓕ
Recorded 1997 ●●

Fischer's idiomatic foray into this well-worn repertoire is distinguished by tonal lustre and high spirits, with the authentic gipsy violin of József 'Csócsi' Lendvay lending a touch of added spice to No 3 (i.e. the piano No 6) and a tangy cimbalom much in evidence throughout. Rubato is legion, though more improvisatory than schmaltzy. Even if you have never particularly liked Doppler's version of the Second, Fischer's performance is so vivid, so imaginative of phrasing, that you may well be won over. Charm is in generous supply everywhere. There is plenty of power, too, with meaty brass and growling *crescendos* at the start of No 4, and a riot of colour to close No 6. Fischer's *Hungarian Rhapsodies* are as frisky as foals and as flavoursome as goulash, as dashing and as dancing as anyone might want. They are further aided by excellent, full-bodied sound.

Tone poems

Ce qu'on entend sur la montagne, S95. Tasso, S96. Les Préludes, S97. Orpheus, S98. Prometheus, S99. Festklänge, S101. Mazeppa, S100
London Philharmonic Orchestra / Bernard Haitink
Philips ② 438 751-2PM2 (127 minutes: ADD). Ⓜ
Recorded 1968-71

Héroïde funèbre, S102. Die Ideale, S106. Mephisto Waltz No 1, S514, 'Der Tanz in der Dorfschenke'; No 2, S110. Hungaria, S103. Hamlet, S104. Hunnenschlacht, S105. Von der Wiege bis zum Grabe, S107
London Philharmonic Orchestra / Bernard Haitink
Philips ② 438 754-2PM2 (131 minutes: ADD). Ⓜ
Recorded 1968-71

The 12 'numbered' symphonic poems date from Liszt's rich maturity, with the lean, near-expressionist *Von der Wiege bis zum Grabe* ('From the Cradle to the Grave') following on after a period of some 25 years. Haitink's readings have an abundance of personality. In *Héroïde funèbre*, for example, his dangerously slow tempo exceeds Liszt's prescribed timing by some seven minutes: it is a terrifying vision, superbly sustained and beautifully played. He also copes manfully with the more explosive aspects of *Hamlet, Prometheus* and *Hunnenschlacht*, and his way with the scores' many reflective episodes is entirely winning.

Elsewhere, he sorts through the complexities of Liszt's colourful orchestration with a cool head and a warm heart, etching the frequent examples of 'nature music' much as he does Wagner's and keeping abreast of each tone-poem's narrative trail. True, some of Liszt's *marcatos, impetuosos, appassionatos* and *agitatos* are occasionally brought to heel, but then others aren't – and we have Liszt's blessing for flexibility in what he himself terms 'the degree of sympathy' that conductors employ for his work. What matters is that Haitink has us enter Liszt's world direct, rather than through the distorting mirror of the conductor's own ego. It is a volatile sequence, yes, and not without its *longueurs*, but it remains an essential musical confrontation for all students of the romantic orchestra and an accurate pointer to where Tchaikovsky, Smetana and countless others found significant musical sustenance. With excellent sound and commonsense documentation, these two sets will provide hours of aural adventure.

Tasso, S96. Trois Odes funèbres, S112
Berlin Radio Men's Chorus; Berlin Radio Symphony Orchestra / Karl Anton Rickenbacher
Koch Schwann 317682 (57 minutes: DDD). Ⓕ
Recorded 1994

Rickenbacher's is a strong and sombre reading of *Tasso* that responds to the powerful opening – much the best music in a very uneven work – and does well with the minuet passage and with the later pages in which Liszt is at his most assertive and least creative. Nevertheless, the record has a claim on Lisztians for the inclusion, as what appears to be a first recording, of three very fine works that have lain neglected. Two are personal elegies, moving laments on the death of his son Daniel and his eldest daughter Blandine. 'Les morts', a so-called Oration for Orchestra for Daniel, makes use of a chorus to intone, during the work, words by the Christian thinker who at one stage profoundly affected Liszt, the Abbé Lammenais. 'La notte', for Blandine, is based on *Il penseroso*, from the Italian book of the *Années de pèlerinage*, but also includes some haunting Hungarian reminiscences. He asked for these two works to be played at his funeral. Dying half-ignored in Bayreuth, he went to his grave without any proper music. The *Odes* were not performed until 1912. The third is a kind of pendant to *Tasso*, and uses some of its themes. The *Odes* are strong and moving works, perhaps difficult to programme in concerts even individually. To have them available at last, in an ideal recording, in very sympathetic performances, is a cause for some gratitude.

Piano Sonata in B minor, S178

Liszt Piano Sonata. Hungarian Rhapsody No 6
Brahms Two Rhapsodies, Op 79
Schumann Piano Sonata No 2 in G minor, Op 22
Martha Argerich *pf*
DG Galleria 437 252-2GGA (64 minutes: ADD). Ⓜ
Recorded 1963-72 ○○○

No one could accuse Martha Argerich of unstructured reverie or dalliance and her legendary DG performance of the Liszt Sonata from 1972 suggests a unique level of both technical and musical achievement. Her prodigious fluency unites with a trail-blazing temperament, and Valhalla itself never ignited to such effect as at the central *Andante*'s central climax. Both here and in the final *Prestissimo* there are reminders that Argerich has always played octaves like single notes, displaying a technique that few if any could equal. There are times when she becomes virtually engulfed in her own virtuosity yet this is a performance to make other pianists turn pale and ask, how is it possible to play like this? Argerich's Schumann, too, is among her most meteoric, headlong flights. In terms of sheer brilliance she leaves all others standing yet, amazingly, still allows us fleeting glimpses of Eusebius (the poetic dreamer in Schumann, and one of his most dearly cherished fictions). The Brahms and Liszt *Rhapsodies*, taken from Argerich's very first 1963 DG disc, are among the most incandescent yet refined on record. The sound, when you bother to notice it, is excellent. (The Liszt and Brahms works, are also included in a compilation disc reviewed in the Collections section; refer to the Index.)

Piano Sonata. Nuages gris, S199a. Unstern: sinistre, disastro, S208. La lugubre gondola, S200, No 1a. R W – Venezia, S201[a]
Maurizio Pollini *pf*
DG 427 322-2GH (46 minutes: DDD). Items marked [a] Ⓕ
recorded live in 1988

No prizes for predicting that this Liszt B minor Sonata is technically flawless and beautifully structured. What may come as more of a shock (though not to those who have followed Maurizio Pollini's career closely) is its sheer passion. To say that he plays as if his life depended on it is an understatement, and those who regularly accuse him of coolness should sit down in a quiet room with this recording, a decent hi-fi system and a large plateful of their own words. The opening creates a sense of coiled expectancy, without recourse to a mannered delivery, and Pollini's superior fingerwork is soon evident. His virtuosity gains an extra dimension from his ability at the same time to convey resistance to it – the double octaves are demonstrably a fraction slower than usual and yet somehow feel faster, or at least more urgent.

There is tensed steel in the very fabric of the playing. By the two-minute mark so much passion has been unleashed one is bound to wonder if it has not all happened too soon. But that is to underestimate Pollini's unerring grasp of the dramatic structure and its psychological progression from paragraph to paragraph; it is also to underestimate his capacity to find extra technical resources when it would seem beyond the power of flesh and blood to do so. Another contributing factor, which for some listeners may take more adjusting to, is his determination to maintain the flow in lyrical paragraphs, at tempos slightly more forward-looking and with breathing-spaces slightly less conspicuous than usual. Throughout the performance floods of feeling and dams of intellectual will-power vie with one another to extraordinarily compelling effect. The final page is pure mastery, a fitting conclusion to a spell-binding performance. It seems not so much that Pollini has got inside the soul of the music but that the music has got inside him and used him, without mercy, for its own ends. In Pollini's hands *Unstern* certainly has a fine inexorable tread and *La lugubre gondola* and *R W – Venezia* are both beautifully weighted. The audience (a rather restive one) adds nothing to the sense of involvement in any of the three live recordings. The background ambience changes suddenly in *La lugubre gondola*. Still, after such a classic account of the Sonata, anything would have been an anti-climax.

Piano Sonata. Two Légendes, S175. Scherzo and March, S177
Nikolai Demidenko *pf*
Hyperion CDA66616 (67 minutes: DDD). Ⓕ
Recorded 1992

Even in an impossibly competitive field Demidenko's Liszt Sonata stands out among the most imperious and articulate. His opening is precisely judged and once the Sonata is under its inflammatory way his virtuosity is of a kind to which few other pianists could pretend. The combination of punishing weight and a skittering, light-fingered agility makes for a compulsive vividness yet his economy in the first *cantando espressivo*, sung without a trace of luxuriance or indulgence, is no less typical. There are admittedly times when he holds affection at arm's length, but just as you are wondering why he commences the central *Andante* so loudly he at once withdraws into a wholly apposite remoteness or reticence. Earlier, his pedalling is deeply imaginative. Predictably, the fugue is razor-sharp and in the storming pages just before the retrospective coda the sense of concentration becomes almost palpable. The final climax, too, is snapped off not only with a stunning sense of Lisztian drama but also with an even truer sense and understanding of Liszt's score and instructions.

Demidenko's couplings are no less autocratic and refined, with a capacity to make seemingly arbitrary ideas sound unarguable. His *Légendes* are far from benign or, indeed, Franciscan, yet his tautness and graphic sense of their poetic power carry their own authority. Finally, Demidenko is in his element in the *Scherzo* and March's diablerie, music which coming after the two *Légendes*, affects one like an upside-down crucifix, or some dark necromancy. The recording is outstanding and Demidenko's intimidating dynamic range emerges without even a trace of distortion.

Piano Sonata. Années de pèlerinage – Deuxième année, Italie, S161: Après une lecture du Dante (fantasia quasi sonata). Harmonies poétiques et religieuses, S173 No 7, Funérailles. Gnomenreigen, S145 No 2
Mikhail Pletnev *pf*
DG 457 629-2GH (67 minutes: DDD). Ⓕ
Recorded 1997

Mikhail Pletnev provides us with a seasoned and nuanced reading of the great B minor Sonata. There is throughout a great sense of ease and luxury, amply displaying his congenial affection for the music's intimate voices. The *Dante* Sonata is, on the whole, rather less successful. The *Dante* Sonata works by accumulation of sound-mass, and Pletnev's occasionally brittle tone works against the music's almost geological accumulation of force. A touch more evenness to the *tremolo* playing would also give the performance some of the luminescence that it lacks in the upper range. A quirky reading of *Gnomenreigen*, giving it a strangely grim humour, and a powerful traversal of the 'Funérailles', fills out the recording. Dedicated Lisztians will be happier with more conventionally romantic performances but fans of Pletnev's sinewy keyboard determination will find that there is much on this release to please them.

Transcendental Etudes

12 Etudes d'exécution transcendante, S139
Jenö Jandó *pf* Ⓢ
Naxos 8 553119 (64 minutes: DDD). Recorded 1994

The 12 *Transcendental Etudes* are the ultimate test of quasi-orchestral virtuosity and of the capacity to achieve nobility and true eloquence. Jandó perhaps lacks diabolic *frisson* in the more ferocious numbers but his performances, overall, are not disfigured by wilful, sensational attributes or hysteria. No 1 is dramatically pointed, an impressive curtain-raiser, and he can hell-raise with assurance in 'Mazeppa'. His 'Feux follets' hardly sparks with the brilliance of, say, some of the full-blooded accounts of certain Russian artists, but even when it hardly modulates from study to tone-poem it is still more than capable (higher praise than you might think where such intricacy is concerned). He flashes an impressive rapier at the start of 'Eroica' and there is plenty of swagger and facility in the so-called 'Appassionata' *étude*. 'Chasse-neige', too, proceeds with a fine sense of its menacing start to a howling, elemental uproar before returning to distant thunder. Jandó is less assured in introspection, yet it has to be said that all-encompassing versions of the *Transcendental Etudes* are hard to come by. Jandó is impressively recorded.

Totentanz

Impromptu in F sharp, S191. Nuages gris, S199. La lugubre gondola, S200 Nos 1 and 2. Unstern: sinistre, disastro, S208. Totentanz, S525. Danse macabre (Saint-Saëns), S555. Réminiscences des Huguenots (Meyerbeer), S412
Arnaldo Cohen *pf* Ⓢ
Naxos 8 553852 (71 minutes: DDD). Recorded 1996

Arnaldo Cohen is as poetically and imaginatively intrepid as he is technically coruscating, and all these performances offer refinement and ferocity in equal proportion. Few pianists could identify or engage so closely with music which hovers on the edge of silence or extinction (*Nuages gris, La lugubre gondola* Nos 1 and 2), or which sparks and sports with a truly devilish intent (*Danse macabre*, *Totentanz* and so on). In the *Danse macabre* the music emerges from Cohen's fingers supercharged with malevolence. On the other hand he can send the F sharp *Impromptu* spiralling into a true sense of its ecstasy, or momentarily inflect *Nuages gris* in a manner that accentuates rather than detracts from its abstraction and economy. He makes something frighteningly bleak out of *Unstern* (or 'Evil Star'), with its savagely dissonant climax and its unresolved hymnal solace, yet is no less at home in *Réminiscences des Huguenots*, dismissing ambuscades of treacherous skips, octaves and every other technical terror with a telling mix of verve and nonchalance. These, then, are performances of rare lucidity, virtuoso voltage and trenchancy, and all quite excellently recorded.

19 Hungarian Rhapsodies, S244

No 1 in C sharp minor; **No 2** in C sharp minor; **No 3** in B flat; **No 4** in E flat; **No 5** in E minor, 'Héroïde-Elégiaque'; **No 6** in D flat; **No 7** in D minor; **No 8** in F sharp minor, 'Capriccio'; **No 9** in E flat, 'Carnival in Pest'; **No 10** in E; **No 11** in A minor; **No 12** in C sharp minor; **No 13** in A minor; **No 14** in F minor; **No 15** in A minor 'Rákóczy'; **No 16** in A minor, 'For the Munkascy festivities in Budapest'; **No 17** in D minor; **No 18** in F sharp minor, 'On the occasion of the Hungarian Exposition in Budapest'; **No 19** in D minor

Hungarian Rhapsodies Nos 1-19. Rhapsodie espagnole, S254
Roberto Szidon *pf*
DG ② 453 034-2GTA2 (156 minutes: ADD). Ⓜ
Recorded 1972

This well-known set has been in and out of the catalogue a number of times in various formats, always to considerable acclaim. And the performances are every bit as good as everybody has always said. Although individual readings of isolated *Rhapsodies* may surpass Szidon's, taken as a whole this is certainly the most pleasurable set available. Szidon's technique is especially geared towards clarity of passagework and rhythmic precision and he also possesses a convincingly dreamy temperament that enables the slow passages to emerge with a rare distinction. His technical mastery is in no doubt and this is playing of great flair, with a natural idiomatic feeling for rubato. The *Rapsodie espagnole* is a welcome bonus. The recorded sound is acoustically sympathetic and vivid.

Hungarian Rhapsodies Nos 2 and 9. Ballade No 2 in B minor, S171. Bénédiction de Dieu dans la solitude, S173 No 3. Berceuse, S174. Polonaise in C minor, S223 No 1. Scherzo and March, S177 **H**
Louis Kentner *pf*
APR mono APR5514 (79 minutes: ADD). Ⓜ
Recorded 1937-41 **OO**

This glorious recital is a timely reminder of Louis Kentner's greatness, his richness and enterprise during his heyday. Here is playing which in its life-affirming sweep and opulence makes accusations concerning Liszt's theatricality doubly misleading. What expansiveness, what true *molto espressivo* Kentner achieves in the Second *Hungarian Rhapsody*, what poetic warmth and freedom in the more heartfelt, soaring melodies of the First *Polonaise* and Second *Ballade*. True, some may find him more luxuriant than devotional in the *Bénédiction* (a reminder, perhaps, that the temporal and spiritual aspects of Liszt's life were opposite sides of the same coin) but the personal charisma and magnetism are in any case a far cry from our own age where one pianist is so easily mistaken for another. In the *Scherzo and March*, where Liszt sardonically raises hell-fire, Kentner's mastery is unassailable, and his elegance in the ravishing *Berceuse* (so closely modelled on Chopin yet so far from his classic economy) again evokes a time when pianists were indeed kings of the keyboard. Above all, these performances show a patrician ease that makes you sit back and marvel, and forget a later period in Kentner's life when his playing so sadly became a parody of its former quality. Superb transfers.

Hungarian Themes ..., S242

Complete Solo Piano Music, Volume 29
Hungarian Themes and Rhapsodies, S242
Leslie Howard *pf*
Hyperion ② CDA66851/2 (159 minutes: DDD). Ⓕ
Recorded 1993

When listening to these 22 pieces, officially entitled *Magyar Dalok* and *Magyar Rapszódiák*, you at once realize you've heard many a snatch of them before. And not surprisingly, for they are in fact the source of most of what eventually emerged as Liszt's world-wide best-sellers, the *Hungarian Rhapsodies*. The composer revels in the lavishly decorative, cimbalom-coloured, improvisational style of the gipsies, in the process making demands on the pianist variously described by Leslie Howard in his insert-notes as 'devil-may-care, frighteningly difficult, frenetic, hand-splitting' and so on. Whether because of Liszt's own waning interest in platform pyrotechnics, or the fact that only he could really bring them off, simplification and formal condensation seem to have been primary aims when recasting these first flings as *Hungarian Rhapsodies*. But as Howard reveals, there are losses as well as gains in the maturer Liszt. Despite moments of protracted rodomontade there is a vast amount of enjoyment to be had.

Années de pèlerinage

Première année, S160, 'Suisse'; Deuxième année, S161, 'Italie'; Troisième année, S163

Années de pèlerinage – Première année[a]. Venezia e Napoli, S162[b]
Sergio Fiorentino *pf*
APR APR5583 (72 minutes: ADD). Ⓜ
Recorded [b]1962 and [a]1963 **O**

The third volume of Sergio Fiorentino's early Liszt recordings made during the 60s unites the contemplative (Volume 1) and the virtuoso (Volume 2). For in the first book of the *Années de pèlerinage*, composed while Liszt journeyed through Switzerland with Marie d'Agoult, his mistress of the moment, you can hear in 'Le mal du pays' stark alternations of heroism and despair, a prophecy of darker things to come. Even 'Orage', most daunting of octave *études*, is more notable for far-reaching dissonance than mere display, an iconoclasm looking far into the future. Elsewhere, in 'Chapelle de Guillaume Tell', Liszt celebrates Switzerland's national hero with alpine horns echoing across the mountains, while 'Au lac de Wallenstadt' prompted the ever susceptible Marie d'Agoult to hear 'the melancholy cadence of oars'.

Fiorentino's performances are of a rare virtuosity and imaginative delicacy, and one doubts whether the sense of bells ringing gently and exultantly through the crystalline Swiss air in 'Les cloches de Genève' has often been caught more evocatively (*con somma passione*). He rightly makes the gloomy and Byronic 'Vallée d'Obermann' the nodal and expressive centre of the cycle, fully justifying and sustaining his audaciously slow tempo (it is, after all, marked *lento*) and, throughout, his performances are alive with the sort of fantasy and freedom that eluded Jorge Bolet in his more cautious *Gramophone* Award-winning Decca recording (12/84). Sadly Fiorentino recorded only one work from the official Italian *Annèe* ('Sposalizio') so this disc ends with its supplement, *Venezia e Napoli*, a garland of encores that show off his poetic resource and, in the 'Tarantella', quicksilver brilliance to perfection. Fiorentino's early Saga recordings often suggested an enviable, if occasionally flippant facility, but here he is at his finest; even when he playfully tampers with the score (in 'Les cloches de Genève) it is usually to Liszt's advantage. The transfers have come up trumps, though Bryan Crimp could do little to erase some pitch flutter in the original Delta discs.

Années de pèlerinage – Première année; Deuxième année; Troisième année. Venezia e Napoli, S162
Lazar Berman *pf*
DG ③ 437 206-2GX3 (176 minutes: ADD). Ⓜ
Recorded 1977 ⭘

Liszt's three volumes of *Années de pèlerinage* are rarely recorded complete, largely because many pianists remain baffled by the dark-hued prophecy and romanticism of the third and final book. Berman's resource here is remarkable and his performance of the entire book is hauntingly inward and sympathetic to both the radiance of 'Les jeux d'eau à la Villa d'Este' and to Liszt's truly dark night of the soul (*lamentoso, doloroso* and so on), and to his desolate lack of spiritual solace elsewhere. He is hardly less persuasive in the first two books. 'Chapelle de Guillaume Tell' is a true celebration of Switzerland's republican hero with alpine horns ringing through the mountains, while in 'Au lac de Wallenstadt' Berman's gently undulating traversal is truly *pianissimo* and *dolcissimo egualamente*. His 'Orage' is predictably breathtaking, and in the gloomy Byronic 'Vallée d'Obermann' the severest critic will find himself mesmerized by Berman's free-wheeling eloquence. These superb recordings have been finely remastered.

Années de pèlerinage – Deuxième année
Jorge Bolet *pf*
Decca 410 161-2DH (51 minutes: DDD). Ⓕ
Recorded 1982

The exceptionally wide dynamic range Bolet uses in this work is most faithfully conveyed. So, too, is the lovely sound he produces throughout. There is necessarily much pedalling in, for example, his ardent reading of 'Sposalizio', yet clarity is always complete. Also here are a beautiful, dark-toned realization of 'Il penseroso', and a piquant one of 'Canzonetta del Salvator Rosa'. The piano truly sings in the 'Sonetti', and all three receive ideal performances – hear the last page of No 104, for instance. Bolet's long-drawn-out, though never excessive, sweetness in these pieces sets off the acrid *Dante* Sonata, of which an almost alarmingly vivid performance is given. As well as embodying a fresh response to a wide range of moods this is obviously a great feat of pianism.

Additional Recommendation
Années de pèlerinage – Deuxième année, S161: Après une lecture du Dante
Couplings: Valse oubliée No 4, S215. Mephisto Waltzes Nos 1, 2 and 4. Die Zelle in Nonnenwerth, S534bis. Ballade No 2 in B minor, S171. Harmonies poétiques et réligieuses, S173 – No 9, Andante lagrimoso
Leif Ove Andsnes *pf*
EMI CDC5 70022-2 (74 minutes: DDD: 03/01). Ⓕ

Leif Ove Andsnes's *Dante* Sonata is outstandingly well paced and his Ballade excitingly coloured and powerfully projected. Overall this is a high-class recital, one that will make an effective addition to any non-specialist collection

Song transcriptions

Complete Solo Piano Music, Volume 15
Adelaïde, S466. Sechs geistliche Lieder, S467. An die ferne Geliebte, S469. Lieder von Goethe, S468 (Beethoven). Lieder, S547 (Mendelssohn). Lieder, S485 (Dessauer). Er ist gekommen in Sturm und Regen, S488. Lieder, S489 (Franz).Two songs, S554 (Rubinstein). Lieder von Robert und Clara Schumann, S569. Provenzalisches Lied, S570. Two songs, S567. Frühlingsnacht, S568. Widmung, S566 (Schumann)
Leslie Howard *pf*
Hyperion ② CDA66481/2 (147 minutes: DDD). Ⓕ
Recorded 1990

Few composers have ever shown a more insatiable interest in the music of others than Liszt, or devoted more time to transcribing it for the piano. Here Howard plays 60 of Liszt's 100 or so song transcriptions, including several by the lesser-known Dessauer, Franz and (as composers) Anton Rubinstein and Clara Schumann, alongside Beethoven, Mendelssohn and Robert Schumann. The selection at once reveals Liszt's variety of approach as a transcriber no less than his unpredictability of choice. Sometimes, as most notably in Beethoven's concert aria, *Adelaïde*, the keyboard virtuoso takes over: he links its two sections with a concerto-like cadenza as well as carrying bravura into an amplified coda. Mendelssohn's *On wings of song* brings imitative subtleties all his own, while the fullness of heart of Schumann's *Dedication* and *Spring Night* is likewise allowed to expand and overflow. But after the dazzling pyrotechnics of many of his operatic arrangements, the surprise here is the self-effacing simplicity of so much included. The five songs from Schumann's *Liederalbum für die Jugend* are literal enough to be played by young children. Even his later (1880) fantasy-type transcriptions of Rubinstein's exotic *The Asra* has the same potent economy of means, characterizing his own original keyboard music in advancing years. Howard responds keenly to mood and atmosphere, and never fails, pianistically, to emphasize the 'singer' in each song – in response to the actual verbal text that Liszt was nearly always conscientious enough to write into his scores. The recording is clean and true.

Petrarch Sonnets

Complete Solo Piano Music, Volume 21
Soirées musicales, S424. Soirées italiennes, S411. Nuits d'été à Pausilippe, S399. Tre sonetti del Petrarca, S158. Venezia e Napoli, S159. La serenata e L'orgia (Grande fantaisie sur des motifs des Soirées musicales), S422. La pastorella dell'Alpi e Li marinari (Deuxième fantaisie sur des motifs des Soirées musicales), S423
Leslie Howard *pf*
Hyperion ② CDA66661/2 (157 minutes: DDD). Ⓕ
Recorded 1991-92

The two discs comprising Vol 21 of Howard's enormous cycle remind us of the young Liszt's love affair with Italy, the spotlight now falling primarily on frolics with Rossini, Mercadante and Donizetti in lighter, lyrical vein. The special interest of the two original sets of pieces included, i.e. the three *Sonetti del Petrarca* and the four *Venezia e Napoli*, is that Howard introduces them as first written (*c*1839 and 1840 respectively) before Liszt's characteristically painstaking later revisions. There is much to enjoy in the playing itself, especially in simpler contexts when gondolas glide through calm waters, or lovers dream, or shepherds dance. Melody, so important throughout, is nicely sung. And whether in filigree delicacy or exuberant zest (as in excitable Venetian regattas) to his translucent delicacy in the upper reaches of Gounod's Rêverie. Apart from a slightly metallic touch above a certain dynamic level in the treble, the recorded sound quality can best be described in a nutshell as ripe.

Opera transcriptions / paraphrases

Complete Solo Piano Music, Volume 30

Oberon – Overture, S574 (Weber). Fantasia on themes from Le nozze di Figaro and Don Giovanni, S697 (Mozart). Ernani Paraphrase, S432. Miserere du Trovatore, S433. Rigoletto Paraphrase, S434. Réminiscences de Boccanegra, S438 (Verdi). Valse de concert sur deux motifs du Lucia et Parisina, S214/3 (Donizetti). Réminiscences de Robert le diable (Meyerbeer) – Cavatine; Valse infernale, S413. Les Adieux – Rêverie sur un motif de Roméo et Juliette, S409 (Gounod). Schwanengesang and Marsch from Hunyadi László, S405 (Erkel). Lohengrin – Elsa's Bridal Procession, S445/2; Two Pieces, S446. Fantasy on themes from Rienzi, S439 (Wagner)

Leslie Howard *pf*

Hyperion ② CDA66861/2 (153 minutes: DDD). Ⓕ

Recorded 1993

Liszt's operatic outings range from literal transcriptions, such as the opening *Oberon* Overture, to the most free fantasias, like that on motives from *Rienzi* at the end of the disc. The sequence is artfully planned to provide the maximum contrast between Liszt as lion and dove, with four of the 16 items earmarked as 'first recordings'. Of these, the Gounod *Roméo et Juliette* Rêverie is a tender, nocturne-like idyll that not for a second outstays its welcome. Liszt scholars may nevertheless be still more grateful for Howard's rescue of the other three, and first and foremost the nearly 22-minute long Fantasia on themes from *Le nozze di Figaro and Don Giovanni*, the 'almost-complete' manuscript of which Howard has now himself completed for performance and publication. Though self-indulgently protracted (as Busoni surely realized when preparing his own shortened version), its thematic interweavings *en route* still take your breath away. With Verdi and Wagner we are on more familiar ground, where it goes without saying that Howard has formidable CD rivals. But throughout the disc there is a spaciousness in his characterization that far more often than not compensates for momentary technical strain or loss of finesse. His tonal range is certainly wide, ranging from the deep, dark, brooding intensity he finds for the *Ernani* and *Il trovatore* excerpts

Douze Grandes Etudes, S137

Complete Solo Piano Music, Volume 34

Douze Grandes Etudes, S137. Morceau de salon, S142

Leslie Howard *pf*

Hyperion CDA66973 (76 minutes: DDD). Ⓕ

Recorded 1994

In this first recording of the concert version of the *Douze Grandes Etudes* (1837), Leslie Howard brings his customary technical wizardry to bear on this outrageously difficult music in an arresting virtuoso display that demonstrates Liszt's consummate skill at transforming musical material. Moreover, despite Liszt's exhortation that only the later revisions of the studies should be played, there is a great deal to recommend the 1837 set, as these performances attest. The extreme technical demands of these pieces have led to critical scorn, but the challenges they contain are not designed merely for display, but are the result of the composer's comprehensive exploitation of the piano's expressive capabilities. Saint-Saëns said that 'in Art a difficulty overcome is a thing of beauty' and, in the present instance, Howard's own triumph over the monumental difficulties posed by these pieces reveals the astonishing beauty of Liszt's 'orchestral' use of tone colour and sparkling virtuosity.

Christus, S3

Henriette Bonde-Hansen *sop* **Iris Vermillion** *mez* **Michael Schade** *ten* **Andreas Schmidt** *bar* **Cracow Chamber Choir; Stuttgart Gächinger Kantorei Stuttgart Radio Symphony Orchestra / Helmuth Rilling**

Hänssler Classic Exclusive Series ③ CD98 121 (162 minutes: DDD). Text and translation included. Ⓕ

Recorded live in 1997

Christus is essentially a contemplative work and so could really be said to exist in a different timescale to most music. Much of the opening part, the 'Christmas Oratorio', uses very simple melody and harmony, and is studiously undramatic. Helmuth Rilling does well not to charge it with too much colour, and, if listened to as meditation rather than drama, what can seem static takes on a positive atmosphere as a group of long reflections on the Christmas events. This is a far cry from the sensational Liszt of the early virtuoso years, even from the creative ventures of the previous decade, not yet reaching the terse, inward pieces of the last years. There is greater drama in the middle part, 'After Epiphany', especially in the superb scene of Christ walking on the water. Although there is still the suggestion that a wonder is being contemplated, Liszt stirs up a terrific storm. This part also includes the beautiful setting of the

Beatitudes, sung by Andreas Schmidt with a degree of uncertainty which he entirely sheds when he comes to pronounce the sentences in Part 3 ('Passion and Resurrection') for the scene of the Agony in the Garden. Liszt here turns to his most intense chromatic idiom. The long *Stabat mater* is beautifully controlled by Rilling. His soloists support him well, though Iris Vermillion can seem rather operatic; Henriette Bonde-Hansen sings with a beautiful, clear tone. The recording does excellent justice to Liszt's wide-ranging orchestration. *Christus* is not a work for every day, nor for every conductor. It is done justice in this sympathetic, patient performance.

Antonio Literes Spanish 1673-1747

GROVE *Literes was a bass viol player to the royal choir in Madrid and from 1693 bassist of the royal chapel. He became known as the leading court composer, writing zarzuelas (notably Accis y Galatea, 1708), secular cantatas, an oratorio and a considerable amount of sacred music.*

Los elementos

Marta Almajano *sop* El Ayre, La Aurora; **Lola Casariego** *mez* La Tierra; **Anne Grimm** *sop* El Agua; **Xenia Meijer** *mez* El Fuego; **Jordi Ricart** *bar* El Tiempo
Al Ayre Español / Eduardo López Banzo
Deutsche Harmonia Mundi 05472 77385-2 (61 minutes: DDD). Notes, text and translation included. Recorded 1997 Ⓕ

This disc is fascinating for the insight it affords into this little-explored territory of the Spanish baroque, *Los elementos*. Subtitled 'opera armonica al estilo ytaliano', the work is not really an opera, more perhaps an extended prologue, or *loa*, that possibly originally introduced another theatrical entertainment, whether an opera proper or a play with or without music. So little is known about the origins of *Los elementos* that it is difficult to categorize or contextualize at present. What is absolutely clear is the influence of the Italian style that pervaded the Spanish court towards the end of the 17th century. The succession of recitatives and arias in *Los elementos* is occasionally disrupted by the introduction of the indigenous verse-and-refrain form of *estribillo* and *coplas*; even here the musical style is wholeheartedly Italian, which makes the use of castanets (for the most part in the tutti sections) seem totally anachronistic.

Apart from this quibble, however, the performance is generally excellent with a strong line-up of Spanish singers. The roles of the four elements are taken by four female voices, while the figure of Tiempo (Time) is here sung by the Catalan baritone Jordi Ricart. Literes gives his soloists plenty of opportunity to shine, seemingly quite at home with the virtuoso aria as well as with the lyrical style of recitative characteristic of music for the Spanish theatre. In the first part of the piece the properties of the four elements – air, earth, fire and water – are described, giving the composer plenty of scope for contrast, while the portrayal of the gradual arrival of dawn – and the ways in which each of the elements is affected – is equally vividly drawn. Literes proves himself to be a composer of imagination and secure technique and Eduardo López Banzo's choice of tempos is mostly convincing. The playing is fine (the continuo occasionally over-exuberant), and the overall sound is very good. This disc is particularly recommended to anyone with an interest in baroque music (and not just Spanish music) for the quality of the work and the contribution this recording makes to a richer and fuller picture of the musical past.

Pietro Locatelli Italian 1695-1764

GROVE *Locatelli studied the violin in Rome and in 1717-23 played in the basilica of S Lorenzo in Damaso. He was appointed to the Mantuan court in 1725 but gave concerts elsewhere (especially Germany), gaining a high reputation; his playing was noted for its virtuosity and sweetness. From 1729 he worked mostly as a teacher and orchestral director in Amsterdam. Locatelli wrote almost exclusively sonatas and concertos. The first of his four concerto grosso sets (1721) is the most Corellian (particularly its Christmas Concerto); his later music is more progressive. His influential L'arte del violino (1733) contains 12 solo violin concertos in a Venetian idiom like Vivaldi's and 24 caprices for solo violin. Among Locatelli's other works are solo and trio sonatas.*

10 Sonatas, Op 8

Locatelli Trio (Elizabeth Wallfisch *vn* Richard Tunnicliffe *vc* Paul Nicholson *hpd*); **Rachel Isserlis** *vn* Ⓟ
Hyperion ② CDA67021/2 (116 minutes: DDD). Recorded 1994 Ⓕ

There is a sense of the decadent about the music of Locatelli. But decadence, we all know, can be quite fun, and it would be an austere spirit that took little pleasure in these sonatas and especially the playing of them here. This two-disc set of his Op 8 (published in 1744) contains six violin sonatas and four trio sonatas, three for two violins and continuo and one using the much less common combination of violin, cello and continuo. A number of them have a slowish movement and most end with a quick triple-metre piece, again in brilliant violinistic style. The most attractive is No 5, with its interesting gestures and hints of wit in the second movement. The most demanding is No 6 with its final minuet with variations, quite breathtaking (and improbably set in E flat, a perverse gesture): here Elizabeth Wallfisch clambers unruffled through the technical thickets, which include an extraordinary variation with trills on one string and moving parts on another and dashes from one end of the compass to the other and back again, and much more besides. This is amazing violin playing of a kind of virtuosity rarely heard from a period instrument player. The three trio sonatas for two violins are not virtuoso music in quite the same way, and musically not generally very inventive. The performances are admirable; no one who admires good violin playing will want to miss Wallfisch's crisp, rhythmic playing.

Matthew Locke British 1621-1677

GROVE *Locke was a chorister and secondary at Exeter Cathedral, where he became friendly with Christopher Gibbons. In 1653 he and Gibbons wrote the music for James Shirley's masque Cupid and Death and in 1656 he joined with others in writing the music (all lost) for Davenant's opera The Siege of Rhodes, in which he also sang. After the Restoration in 1660 he was awarded three posts at court, to which in 1662 he added that of organist to the queen (facilitated by his conversion to Roman Catholicism). He continued to write for the theatre and also engaged in a polemical exchange with Thomas Salmon over the latter's proposals for a new form of musical notation.*

Locke's importance lies in his chamber music and dramatic music, which influenced Purcell's. His consort music and other ensemble works, mainly suites and separate dances, display robust and daring melody, harmony and form, as well as a conscious preoccupation with contrasting rhythms, tempos and dynamics. Although sometimes experimental, it is the work of a gifted and inspired craftsman. His extant sacred music, while not as maturely conceived, is often of high quality. His dramatic music, best represented by Cupid and Death, the masque in The Empress of Morocco (1673) and the vocal music for Psyche (1675), shows a sure dramatic instinct, especially in the recitatives and in several of the curtain tunes. Locke's other music includes the well-known pieces 'ffor His Majesty's Sagbutts and Cornetts', probably performed on the eve of Charles II's coronation, and Melothesia (1673), a collection of keyboard works with an important preface giving the first extant English rules for realising a figured bass.

Consort of Fower Parts

Consort of Fower Parts. Duos – No 1 in D; No 2 in C **P**
Fretwork (Wendy Gillespie, Richard Campbell, William Hunt, Julia Hodgson, Susanna Pell, Richard Boothby *viols*); **Nigel North** *lte* **Paul Nicholson** *org/spinet*
Virgin Classics Veritas VC5 45142-2 Ⓕ
(67 minutes: DDD). Recorded 1990

Locke is capable of some exquisite music and Fretwork here are loving advocates. Experienced as they are in the performance of so much of the finest English consort music of the 17th century from Byrd to Purcell, Fretwork are particularly well placed to discriminate between the elusive properties in an age of subtle, abstract ideals. In the Ayre of No 4 and the equivalent in Suites Nos 2 and 6, there is a simplicity of utterance entirely appropriate to Locke's delightful tunefulness, as does the disarming warmth of expression in the opening movements of the major-key works. Fretwork's intonation is perfect. There is a considered and deft use of a variety of continuo instruments, not to mention two attractive *Duos* for bass viols, which break up the prevalent quartet texture. Locke's special language shines as brightly here as one can remember.

Consort of Fower Parts, Suites Nos 1-6. **P**
The Flatt Consort – Suite No 1 in C minor
Phantasm (Laurence Dreyfus, Wendy Gillespie, Jonathan Manson, Markku Luolajan-Mikkola *viols*)
Global Music Network GMNC0109 Ⓕ
(55 minutes: DDD) ○

Matthew Locke, the irascible and xenophobic Anglo-Catholic, is usually remembered in the 'predecessor of Purcell' category, a classification that is easy to understand when listening to works such as the four-movement consort suites on this disc, composed around the 1650s. Each has an opening *fantasie* full of the brooding, angular and often dissonant expressiveness one associates with Purcell's own later viol fantasies, and Purcell is known to have admired Locke, composing an elegy on his death in 1677. But Locke had a personality of his own: the dances – courantes, ayres and sarabandes – that follow the *fantasies* in each suite have an idiosyncratic rhythmic snap to them that is guarantee of that. Writing in the booklet, Laurence Dreyfus also draws attention to Locke's 'striking muscularity' and also to his 'purest lyricism and...most generous warmth', dubbing his work 'true music of consolation'. Changeable and abrupt though it may at first seem, it is certainly music that grows on you with repeated listenings.

Phantasm play with their customary expertise. Their combination of vibrant tone quality and strong rhythmic attack allows them to make the most of Locke's mercurial musings, bringing lyrical gravity to the *Fantasies* and an exhilarating spring to the faster dances. A fairly close recording helps, giving them at times the clarity and substance almost of a string quartet. By comparison the equally accomplished Fretwork have a thinner and less defined sound, and their performances are less consistent in offering moment-to-moment excitement. Their generally more subdued approach has power to charm, as does their enlivening use of archlute, organ or spinet continuo in some of the suites, but for me it is Phantasm who tend to make more of this intriguing music. It is a pity, though, that GMN have not provided better tracklistings.

Alonso Lobo Spanish c1555-1617

GROVE *Lobo, a choirboy at Seville Cathedral, studied at Osuna University and was a canon there by 1591. He assisted Guerrero at Seville Cathedral from 1591, becoming maestro de capilla of Toledo Cathedral in 1593 and of Seville in 1604. He published masses and motets, some for double choir (1602); many other sacred works are in MSS. Victoria esteemed him as an equal and he was long regarded as one of the finest Spanish composers.*

Missa Maria Magdalene

Lobo Missa Maria Magdalene. O quam suavis est, Domine. Quam pulchri sunt. Ave regina caelorum. Versa est in luctum. Credo quod Redemptor. Vivo ego, dicit Dominus. Ave Maria
Guerrero Maria Magdalene
The Tallis Scholars / Peter Phillips
Gimell CDGIM031 (63 minutes: DDD). Ⓕ
Texts and translations included

Alonso Lobo has mainly become known for one work, his setting of the funerary *Versa est in luctum*. This is undoubtedly a masterpiece of its kind but to have it placed alongside other pieces from Lobo's 1602 collection (one of the six Masses in the volume, and all seven motets) affords a welcome chance to assess his composition skills more fully. Lobo's music is sonorous in a manner that is direct and unfussy in effect, though often highly expressive, and always structured with the utmost technical control. Take, for example, Lobo's *Ave Maria*, an 8-in-4 canon (in other words, four more voices are generated from the original quartet) which emanates a sense of absolute serenity. In fact, each of the motets explores a different aspect of the compositional techniques brought to the genre, and the Mass is equally fine, Lobo making the spacious textures of the motet, *Maria Magdalene* by his teacher Guerrero a distinguishing feature of his own setting of the Ordinary. The Tallis Scholars are on superb form, the overall sound vibrant and immediate with solo sections providing contrast through a more introspective approach. Even if you've never bought a CD of late-Renaissance polyphony, try this one. You'll be bowled over.

Carl Loewe

German 1796-1869

GROVE *Loewe, a pupil of Türk at Halle, began composing songs and instrumental pieces at an early age, also singing his own ballads to great acclaim. Among his finest early solo vocal works are settings of Goethe's Erlkönig (1818) and Byron's Hebrew Melodies (Opp 4, 5, 13 and 14). He was a prolific composer in many media, but his other works, including the operas (notably Emmy, 1842) and oratorios, string quartets and piano works (in particular some programmatic sonatas and the tone poem Mazeppa, Op 27), were not as acclaimed as his narrative songs. Their accompaniments and modified strophic style, incorporating dramatic and lyrical passages, make a vivid impression (eg Archibald Douglas, Op 128); the fairy element in many of his folklore settings (eg Herr Oluf and Tom der Reimer) creates colour and melodic interest. From 1820 to 1865 Loewe worked in Stettin as a conductor, organist and teacher, yet it was through his recital tours that he won international fame; the Viennese called him 'the north German Schubert'.*

Lieder

Die drei Lieder, Op 3 No 3. Elvershöh, Op 118 No 2. Der Woywode, Op 49 No 1. Die nächtliche Heerschau, Op 23. Der letzte Ritter, Op 124. Tom der Reimer, Op 135. Odins Meeresritt, Op 118. Waffenweihe Kaiser Heinrich's IV, Op 122
Andreas Schmidt *bar* **Cord Garben** *pf*
CPO CPO999 253-2 (65 minutes: DDD). Ⓜ
Recorded 1994 ●

This opening volume in CPO's Loewe Edition contains only one really well-known ballad, *Tom der Reimer*, sung here with a devotion to the words and to their dramatic import. This is an essential quality for these ballads, and Andreas Schmidt's control of the portrayal of character and of the often sensational unfolding of events is superb. He and his pianist, Cord Garben (sometimes set rather far back and not sufficiently clear in articulation), have a sure instinct for Loewe's structures, for the movement from one section or tempo into another, for the telling surprise modulation, for the decorative touches in the melody, so that these fine works are not merely a string of events but a dramatic experience. Apart from the spooky ballads, such as *Elvershöh* and others which were said to have gripped Loewe's listeners as he sang them himself at the piano, a strong vein which he explored was the historical narrative. There is a chilling delivery of the ballad embodying that popular 19th-century image, the dead troops reviewed by their dead general – in this case, Napoleon. This is an excellent beginning to a major enterprise.

Kleiner Haushalt, Op 71. Die Heinzelmännchen, Op 83. Heinrich der Vogler, Op 56 No 1. Das Vaterland, Op 125 No 2. Der Nöck, Op 129 No 2. Fünf Lieder, Op 145. Prinz Eugen, der edle Ritter, Op 92. Archibald Douglas, Op 128
Kurt Moll *bass* **Cord Garben** *pf*
CPO CPO999 306-2 (58 minutes: DDD). Texts and translations included. Recorded 1994 Ⓜ

Kurt Moll has all the attributes that go to make a fine Loewe singer, not only the splendidly flexible bass voice that can darken the grim songs (plunging to a strong low E), brighten the cheerful ones and colour all the detail of the ballads vividly, but nimbleness of wit as well as gravity, a sense of comedy as well as dignity. The delightful Rückert *Kleiner Haushalt* is a real comic *tour de force*; at the other end of his recital, *Archibald Douglas* has an impetus that is dramatic but adroitly skirts the melodramatic. He makes a compelling narrative of *Heinrich der Vogler*, changing tone and manner for the lyrical songs that make up the *Fünf Lieder*, Op 145 and in 'Der Feind' deftly sketching the animals who all shy away from their common enemy approaching through the wood – a man.

Drei Balladen, Op 1 – Edward; Erlkönig. Drei Balladen, Op 2 – Herr Oluf. Drei Balladen, Op 3 – Elvershöh; Die drei Lieder. Lieder, Gesänge, Romanzen und Balladen, Op 9 – Book 1: Wandrers Nachtlied; Book 3: Ich denke dein; Book 8: Türmwachter Lynkeus zu den Füssen der Helena; Lynkeus, der Türmer, auf Fausts Sternwarte singend; Gutmann und Gutweib. Drei Balladen, Op 20. Die Gruft der Liebenden, Op 21. Zehn Geistliche Gesänge, Op 22 – Book 1: Gottes ist der Orient!. Drei Balladen, Op 44 – Der getreue Eckart; Der Totentanz. Drei Balladen, Op 56 – Heinrich der Vogler. Drei Balladen, Op 59 – Der Schatzgräber. Zwölf Gedichte, Op 62 – Book 1: Süsses Begräbnis; Hinkende Jamben. Kleiner Haushalt, Op 71. Vier Legenden, Op 75 – Der heilige Franziskus. Sechs Gesänge, Op 79 – Frühzeitiger Frühling. Fünf Lieder, Op 81 – In Vorübergehen. Prince Eugen, Op 92 Drei Balladen, Op 97 – Der Mohrenfürst auf der Messe. Odins Meeresritt, Op 118. Drei Gesänge, Op 123 – Trommelständchen; Die Uhr. Archibald Douglas, Op 128. Drei Balladen, Op 129 – Der Nöck. Tom der Reimer, Op 135*a*. Fünf Lieder, Op 145 – Meeresleuchten. Canzonette. Freibeuter. Wenn der Blüten Frühlingsregen

Dietrich Fischer-Dieskau *bar* **Jörg Demus** *pf*

DG ② 449 516-2GX2 (156 minutes: ADD). Texts and Ⓜ translations included. Recorded 1968-79 **OO**

All the best-known ballads are included here, magnificently sung by a great artist at the height of his powers. *Edward*, *Herr Oluf*, *Heinrich der Vogler*, *Prince Eugen*, *Der Zauberlehrling*: these and others are sung with a wonderful sense of the graphic, conveyed through an appreciation of the colour of the words that never descends into overemphasis and that is beautifully attuned to Loewe's illustrative manner. Fischer-Dieskau and Demus are ideal partners, Demus responding quickly and with an ear for the sinister that often marks the piano writing and its subtle use of motive. Not just a composer of ballads, Loewe was also a Lieder writer in the great German tradition, and this is too often overlooked, but not by Fischer-Dieskau.

Two songs alone, from this magisterial collection, are witness to Loewe's stature. They are settings of the wonderful poems from the second part of *Faust* in which Lynceus, the lynx-eyed watcher on the tower, sees the magical appearance, of Helen of Troy herself. He, incarnating the gift of the perception of visual beauty, after a life of watching from his tower can conceive of nothing that could surpass this wonder; and, in the second song, hymns his gratitude to the gift of sight. Loewe's two settings are beautiful responses to the poetry of a great artist with the gift of an ideal simplicity. These two songs alone should persuade the responsive listener to make the exploration.

Op 1 – No 1, Edward; No 3, Erlkönig. Alles ist eitel, Op 4 No 4. Op 9 – Book 1: No 3, Über allen Gipfeln ist Ruh; No 4, Der du von dem Himmel bist; Book 8: No 1, Turmwächter Lynceus zu den Füssen der Helena; No 2, Lynceus der Helena seine Schätze darbeitend; No 3, Lynceus auf Fausts Sternwarte singend. Hochzeitlied, Op 20 No 1. Der Bergmann, Op 39. Die Begegnung am Meeresstrande, Op 120. Der Asra, Op 133. Findlay. Wandrers Nachtlied

Christoph Prégardien *ten* **Cord Garben** *pf*

CPO CPO999 417-2 (66 minutes: DDD). Texts and Ⓜ translations included. Recorded 1997 **O**

Christoph Prégardien has many of the qualities called for by Loewe's songs and ballads, and awareness of the demands made by a composer with a far wider range than is sometimes allowed. He can be eerie in the blood-curdling *Edward* and again in *Erlkönig* (songs that thrilled Wagner), especially by his sensitive and discreet articulation of the words within the melodic line. *Edward* is powerfully impelled towards the realization of the murder with softly anguished calls of the repeated 'O!'. The Erl-King's threat of force is the more sinister for the underemphasis of the key word, 'Gewalt'; and the whole uneasy alternation between major and minor, as spirit and human worlds contest, is delicately balanced until the final, terrible triumph of the Erl-King's major third in the climactic discord.

These are, without doubt, superb performances. The amiable cycle of five songs about a miner, *Der Bergmann*, is lightly and touchingly handled, with a lively contribution from Cord Garben. Prégardien deploys his eloquence of line to fine effect in the Goethe songs. The two *Wandrers Nachtlied* settings, which are beautifully sung here, are as remarkable as any in the repertory. Still more could be said of the *Lynceus* triptych. Dazzled by his glimpse of Helen of Troy, in the last of the songs the watcher on the tower gives thanks for the gift of sight that has brought him so many marvels. Far-ranging arpeggios spread the world beneath him, and a rapt melodic line, wonderingly enunciated by Prégardien, is a prayer of thanks. Here is one of the great German Lieder.

Paolo Lorenzani Italian 1640-1713

GROVE *Lorenzani was a chorister in the Cappella Giulia in the Vatican and a pupil of Benevoli. After an early career as maestro di cappella in Rome and Messina, he fled during the wars of 1678 to Paris and became an important figure in the struggle to gain recognition for Italian music and thus to break Lully's monopoly. He gained the support of Louis XIV (who helped him become director of the queen's music) and leading aristocrats (who arranged performances of his dramatic music, notably the pastorale Nicandro e Fileno in 1681), but after Queen Marie-Thérèse's death in 1683 his influence waned, despite successful Roman-style oratory performances he arranged as maître de chapelle to the Theatine order (from 1685) and an opera, Orontée, given at Chantilly. In 1694 he returned to Italy as director of the Cappella Giulia. Although rooted in the Roman tradition, his style was readily adaptable to French taste, and the instrumental writing particularly shows Lully's influence. Among his surviving works are airs, cantatas, motets (a set of 25 was published) and a mass and Magnificat, both for two choirs.*

Grands motets

Antienne à la Vierge. Motet pour l'élévation. Motet pour tous les temps. Dialogue entre Jésus et l'Ame. Motet pour les confesseurs. Litanies à la Vierge
Le Concert Spirituel / Hervé Niquet
Naxos 8 553648 (63 minutes: DDD). Texts and translations included. Recorded 1997 Ⓢ

Paolo Lorenzani was a Roman-born composer who towards the end of the 17th century spent 16 years in France, where he tried to raise the profile of Italian music. In this he had little success, especially as in doing so he inevitably came up against the machinations of the tyrannical Lully; indeed their rivalry seems to have become quite acrimonious, and eventually Lorenzani returned to Italy to finish his days as director of the Cappella Giulia at the Vatican. This rarity to the catalogue offers five of the *grands motets* for soloists, choir, violins and continuo which he published in Paris in 1693, plus a *Litany of Our Lady* for voices and continuo which he probably wrote when back in Rome. The lack of success the *motets* enjoyed at the time – for all that the King liked them and that they were very much in the French style – no doubt hastened Lorenzani's departure, but listening to them now, musico-political distractions put aside, it is hard to understand why they should have failed; this is highly attractive music, easily on a par with that of some of the better-known *grand motet* composers of the time, and there is some clever responsiveness to text as well.

The performances, too, are very enjoyable. Hervé Niquet's experience in this type of music pays off in a well-balanced and lithe ensemble, good stand-out solos, and an intelligent, quick-witted approach to the music's interpretation. Lorenzani may not be a forgotten genius exactly, but his music is well worth unearthing. Lully has plenty to answer for.

Antonio Lotti

Italian c1667-1740

Lotti, a pupil of Legrenzi in Venice, became an organist at St Mark's in 1690, eventually becoming maestro di cappella (1736). He also taught at the Ospedale degli Incurabili (Galuppi was one of his pupils); he wrote sacred music for both institutions. From 1692 he composed operas, mostly serious: he presented c30, the last four (1717-19) in Dresden. His large output includes oratorios, secular cantatas, duets, madrigals, instrumental pieces and numerous masses, motets and psalms. Most of his sacred choral works have no orchestral accompaniment; many, such as a Miserere of 1733, remained in use long after his death. His output bridges the late Baroque and early Classical styles and his late works are notable for their elegance and skilful counterpoint.

Madrigals

Duetti, terzetti e madrigali a più voci, Op 1 – Inganni dell'umanità; Lamento di tre amanti; La vita caduca; Moralità d'una per la; Incostanza femminile; Lontananza insopportabile; Funerale della speranza; Crudeltà rimproverata, Giuramento amorosa; Querela amorosa; Incostanza della sorte Scherzo d'amore; Capriccio; Supplica ad amore
Il Complesso Barocco / Alan Curtis *hpd*
Virgin Classics Veritas VC5 45221-2 (78 minutes: DDD). Texts and translations included. Ⓕ
Recorded 1996

A Venetian contemporary of Vivaldi, Lotti's association with St Mark's lasted all of his working life, nearly 60 years. The madrigal enjoyed a revival at the turn of the 18th century; what fascinates here is the music's hybrid nature and its flexibility. The texture is largely imitative, with each text-line having its own melodic point; but alongside this convention are Lotti's contemporary-sounding harmonic touches. They are a source of unexpected delight, especially in this vivacious and spirited interpretation. This is music of high vocal virtuosity, requiring the utmost agility in execution and deftness of characterization: on that count Il Complesso Barocco can hardly be faulted, though admittedly the higher voices are perhaps slightly less sure-footed in their extreme registers. The continuo, spearheaded by Curtis, is equally natural and unfussy (though in the more richly scored pieces the organ may be a touch obtrusive). There can be few better opportunities to broaden (or to make) one's acquaintance with Lotti.

Requiem

Requiem in F. Credo. Miserere
Balthasar-Neumann Choir and Ensemble / Thomas Hengelbrock
Deutsche Harmonia Mundi 05472 77507-2 Ⓕ
(68 minutes: DDD). Recorded 1998

Lotti's Requiem Mass in F major is considered by Thomas Hengelbrock the most important Requiem before Mozart's. The piece is full of expressive contrast and rendered the more fascinating by Lotti's affection for a quasi-Palestrina style on the one hand and his skill in deploying more up-to-date techniques on the other. This Requiem is essentially in the late baroque idiom, occasionally recalling certain of Vivaldi's larger sacred vocal pieces. The sections differ from the sequence usually encountered in later 18th-century Requiem Masses. There is neither *Sanctus*, 'Benedictus' nor *Agnus Dei*, but instead a very extended 'Dies irae' as well as a much shorter 'Requiem aeternam', *Kyrie* and Offertory. Full of theatrical gestures, supple polyphony, warmly seductive harmony and some beautiful melodies, the Requiem holds attention from start to finish. The contrasts are often striking, as between the hushed opening section and the awesome introduction to the 'Dies irae'. The *a cappella Miserere* is sung with clarity and finesse. The five-movement *Credo* is a supple piece for choir and strings with some affecting, shimmering harmonies in the 'Crucifixus'. As well as full Mass settings, Lotti seems also to have favoured separate autonomous sections such as this, themselves subdivided into short units. The splendid performances bring this highly-charged music to life.

Jean-Baptiste Lully

Italian/French 1632-1687

GROVE *A French composer of Italian birth, Lully was taken from Florence to Paris in 1646 by Roger de Lorraine, Chevalier de Guise, who placed him in the service of his niece, Mlle de Montpensier. At her court in the Tuileries Lully got to know the best in French music and, despite his patroness's dislike of Mazarin and her involvement in the Fronde, he was no stranger to Italian music either. After the defeat of the Frondists, Mlle de Montpensier was exiled to St Fargeau. Lully obtained release from her service and on the death of his friend Lazzarini, in 1653, was appointed Louis XIV's compositeur de la musique instrumentale. From 1655 his fame as dancer, comedian and composer grew rapidly, and his disciplined training of the king's 'petite bande' earned him further recognition. In 1661 he was made surintendant de la musique et compositeur de la musique de la chambre and in 1662 maître de la musique de la famille royale. By then he was a naturalised Frenchman, and in July 1662 he married Madeleine Lambert.*

Lully then collaborated with Molière on a series of comédies-ballets which culminated in Le bourgeois gentilhomme (1670). After that he turned to opera, securing the privilege previously granted to Perrin and forestalling potential rivals with oppressive patents granted by the king. He chose as librettist Philippe Quinault, with whom he established a new and essentially French type of opera known as tragédie lyrique. Between 1673 and 1686 Lully composed 13 such works, 11 of them with Quinault.

During this time Lully continued to enjoy the king's support. His greatest personal triumph came in 1681 when he was received as secrétaire du Roi. After the king's marriage to Mme de Maintenon in 1683 life at court took on a new sobriety; it was perhaps in response to this that Lully composed much of his religious music. During a performance of his Te Deum in January 1687 he injured his foot with the point of a cane he was using to beat time. Gangrene set in, and within three months he died, leaving a tragédie lyrique, Achille et Polyxène, unfinished.

At his death Lully was widely regarded as the most representative of French composers. Practically all his music was designed to satisfy the tastes and interests of Louis XIV. The ballets de cour (1653-63) and the comédies-ballets (1663-72) were performed as royal entertainments, the king himself often taking part in the dancing. The tragédies lyriques (1673-86) were kingly operas par excellence, expressing a classical conflict between la gloire and l'amour; Louis himself supplied the subject matter for at least four of them and certainly approved the political sentiments of the prologues. Lully's music was correspondingly elevated, in the stately overtures, the carefully moulded 'récitatif simple' and the statuesque choruses; many of the airs, too, draw as much attention to the galant mores of the court as to the stage action. Finally, the Versailles grand motet, of which the Miserere is an outstanding example, was designed to glorify the King of France as much as the King of Heaven.

Suites

L'Orchestre du Roi Soleil

Première Suite: Le bourgeois gentilhomme. Deuxième Suite: Le divertissement royal. Troisième Suite: Alceste

Le Concert des Nations / Jordi Savall

Alia Vox AV9807 (64 minutes: DDD) Ⓕ

Recorded 1999 ●

Le Concert des Nations offers here a compendium of Lully's music from the heyday of the court of Louis XIV (widely assumed to have been at Versailles, but in fact from before the move from Paris). The pieces, drawn from a variety of Lullian sources to make up three entertainments (or *divertissements*), provide Savall with opportunities to present his musicians in Lully's spectrum of ensemble textures. The players respond to the rhythmic vitality of the music, adding ornamentation with tremendous precision and flair (might Lully have censored it, one wonders?), but the secret of the obvious success of this recording is the rightness of the tempos, whether for a dance, a battle, a gust of wind or a funeral. Those who saw the film *Tous les matins du monde* (or own the CD of the soundtrack) will be familiar with Lully's 'March pour la Cérémonie turque' and will immediately hear the difference even a few years has made to Savall: the playing on this new recording more effectively captures the military character without caricaturing the janissary element. The real stars of the recording, however, are the percussion players, Michèle Claude and Pedro Estevan, whose command of the possibilities for accompanying this repertory would have impressed even Lully (there are almost no indications given in the scores themselves). Whole evenings of Lully are still an acquired taste, but a recording of highlights as good as this is something anyone who enjoys baroque music would wish to own.

Acis et Galatée

Jean-Paul Fouchécourt *ten* Acis; **Véronique Gens** *sop* Galatée; **Monique Simon** *sop* Diane, Second Naiad; **Jean-Louis Meunier** *ten* Comus; **Howard Crook** *ten* Apollon, Télème, Priest of Juno; **Françoise Masset** *sop* Scylla, Dryad; **Rodrigo del Pozo** *counterten* Tircis; **Mireille Delunsch** *sop* Aminte, Abundance; First Naiad; **Laurent Naouri** *bar* Polyphème; **Thierry Félix** *bar* Neptune, Sylvan **Choeur des Musiciens du Louvre; Les Musiciens du Louvre / Marc Minkowski** Ⓟ

Archiv Produktion ② 453 497-2AH2

(107 minutes: DDD). Notes, text and translation included. Recorded 1996 Ⓕ ●●

Acis et Galatée was Lully's last completed opera, and one of his greatest. A *pastoral héroïque* performed in 1686 to entertain the Dauphin during a hunting party at the Duc de Vendôme's château, it employs many features of his *tragédies en musique* – vocal ensembles, instrumental movements and an enhanced use of the orchestra in general; and each act contains a *divertissement* with choruses and dances. One of the glories of the score is the concluding *passacaille*, which with instrumental sections builds up from single voices to chorus. There is also a small but affecting chaconne for Galatea in Act 2; but another glorious moment is the lengthy scene in which she discovers the body of her lover and calls on her father, Neptune, who guarantees Acis immortality by transforming him into a river. The opera is prefaced by a prologue in which various gods and a personification of Abundance flatter the king and his son: points of special interest are the riches of the scoring at Apollo's entrance and the charm of the dances – in fact the whole prologue is permeated by dance rhythms. The classical story of the cyclops destroying his young rival was given a typically French slant and topical moral by making Galatea initially play hard to get, in contrast to the simple, unaffected love of shepherds and shepherdesses (though the haughty Scylla is an exception). In the main body of the opera Lully ensures vitality by constantly, and extremely effectively, changing metre.

Marc Minkowski brings out all the drama of the work by thoughtful treatment of the verbal text, intelligent pacing and varied instrumental articulation and weight: especially striking are the rough sonorities of the march in which Polyphemus first appears, and the intensity of the lovers' angry confrontation in Act 2. Jean-Paul Fouchécourt projecting the image of an ardent youthful lover, and Véronique Gens that of a passionate goddess, are both excellently cast, but Laurent Naouri almost steals the scene from them with his fearsomely powerful Polyphemus: Howard Crook contributes valuably in various roles, though he is ill at ease in the very highest register. There is considerable finesse in the chorus singing, and the theorbo continuo, working overtime, is admirable. An altogether splendid performance of a masterpiece.

Witold Lutosławski Polish 1913-1994

GROVE *LutosLawski studied with Maliszewski at the Warsaw Conservatory (1932-37) and soon made his mark as a pianist and composer, though few works from before 1945 have been published. He then developed a clear, fresh tonality related to late Bartók displayed in the Little Suite for orchestra (1951), the Concerto for Orchestra (1954) and the Dance Preludes for clarinet and piano (1954). But that style was short-lived: in the late 1950s he was able to essay a kind of serialism (Funeral Music for strings, 1958) and to learn from Cage the possibility of aleatory textures, where synchronization between instrumental lines is not exact (Venetian Games for chamber orchestra, 1961). Most of his subsequent works were orchestral, fully chromatic, finely orchestrated in a manner suggesting Debussy and Ravel, and developed from an opposition between aleatory and metrical textures. These include his Second (1967), Third (1983) and Fourth (1993) symphonies, concertos for cello (1970) and for oboe and harp (1980), and settings of French verse with chorus (Three Poems of Henri Michaux, 1963), tenor (Paroles tissées, 1965) and baritone (Les espaces du sommeil, 1975). During this period he was also internationally active as a teacher and conductor of his own music.*

Cello Concerto

Cello Concerto. Livre pour orchestre. Novelette. Chain 3
Andrzej Bauer *vc*
Polish National Radio Symphony Orchestra / Antoni Wit Ⓢ
Naxos 8 553625 (73 minutes: DDD). Recorded 1995

This is an excellent disc; fine music, well played and recorded, and all at the special Naxos price. The earliest composition, *Livre* (1968), was the first work completed by Lutosławski after the Second Symphony, and it shows him at his freshest and boldest, as if relieved to be free (if only temporarily) from the burden of one of music's weightiest traditions. With its well-nigh surreal juxtapositions of strongly contrasted materials, and the unusual ferocity of its tone – the 'book' in question must have been of the blood and thunder variety – *Livre* reveals a Lutosławski quite different from the relatively benign, ironic master of the later works. Coming immediately after *Livre*, the Cello Concerto has an even wider expressive range: indeed, in the balance it achieves between lamenting melodic lines and mercurial scherzo-like writing, coupled with a tendency to home in on crucial pitch-centres, it sets out the basic elements of the composer's later style. This performance owes a great deal to Antoni Wit's skilful shaping of the music's alternations between relatively free and precise notation, and this skill is even more evident in the remaining orchestral scores. *Novelette*, completed in 1979, is Lutosławski's response to his first American commission; it is far more cogent and concentrated than its title might lead you to expect. *Chain 3* (1986) is one of the best later works, let down only by some rather perfunctory quasi-tonal harmony near the end. But this does not undermine the impression the disc as a whole conveys of some of the most characterful and individual music of the last 30 years.

Symphonies

Symphony No 1. Chantefleurs et Chantefables[a]. Jeux vénetiens. Postlude No 1. Silesian Triptych[a]
[a]**Olga Pasiecznik** *sop* **Polish National Radio Symphony Orchestra / Antoni Wit**
Naxos 8 554283 (73 minutes: DDD). Ⓢ
Recorded 1996-97

Juxtaposing Lutosławski's early Symphony No 1 with the late *Chantefleurs et Chantefables* reinforces the fundamentally French associations of this composer's very personal musical voice; to contemplate how the symphony's exuberant embrace of a Roussel-like idiom was complemented, more than 40 years later, by the subtle Ravellian overtones of *Chantefleurs et Chantefables* is to recognize that the radical gestures of *Jeux vénetiens* (1961) have worn less well than Lutosławski's more 'conservative' qualities. Indeed, the wild piano cadenza in *Jeux vénetiens* now evokes the high jinks of Ibert's *Divertissement* rather than the liberated avant-garde ethos of more determinedly progressive musical minds. The downbeat ending is far more memorable.

Olga Pasiecznik's singing is outstanding, especially in *Chantefleurs*, where she easily surpasses Dawn Upshaw in subtlety and Antoni Wit turns in strongly characterized, well-shaped accounts of all the scores. The playing is eloquent as well as energetic, and although, as with earlier Naxos volumes, the recordings are rather glassy and generalized, the music's range of colour and variety of texture is never in doubt. With such a well-filled disc, why did Naxos decide to include the first of the Three Postludes? The composer himself was clearly happy for the piece to appear on its own, but in a series with pretensions to completeness the full set is surely a must.

Further Listening

Szymanowski Symphony No 4, 'Symphonie Concertante'
Coupling: Symphony No 2, Op 19
Shelley *pf* **BBC Philharmonic Orchestra / Sinaisky.**
Chandos CHAN9478 (56 minutes: DDD: 10/96) Ⓕ

Bigness of gesture, one of Sinaisky's strong suits, fits this work well, and the growth from delicacy to eloquence in the slow movement is as well managed as the barbaric power that sweeps the finale to an exciting conclusion. A very fine performance from Howard Shelley, too.

Symphonies – No 1; No 2. Symphonic Variations. Funeral music. Concerto for Orchestra. Jeux vénitiens. Livre pour Orchestre. Mi-parti
Polish National Radio Symphony Orchestra / Witold Lutosławski
EMI Double Forte ② CZS5 73833-2 Ⓑ
(149 minutes: ADD). Recorded 1976-77 ●

This is a straight reissue of two EMI Matrix issues, one which contained the symphonies, *Symphonic Variations* and *Funeral music*, the other with the *Concerto for Orchestra*, *Jeux vénitiens*, *Livre pour Orchestre* and *Mi-parti*. The works illustrate Lutosławski's progress from relatively traditional to relatively radical styles. The *Concerto for Orchestra* fully deserves to stand alongside Bartók's slightly earlier, similarly exuberant essay in the genre, and this performance, by turns punchy and passionate, proves that Lutosławski was not always an overly reticent conductor of his own scores. The playing and recording lack some of the refinement of Barenboim's Chicago version, but it has an attractively raw energy, the composer contemplating 'youthful' excesses with enjoyment rather than embarrassment. Hearing *Jeux vénitiens* immediately after the concerto supports the argument that Lutosławski's change of direction, around 1960, risked losing much that was most substantial in his earlier music. The aleatory jam sessions of *Jeux vénitiens* seem especially dated in this rather cluttered, airless recording, but at least the performance doesn't attempt to add spurious solemnity to a liberating *jeu d'esprit*. *Livre* and *Mi-parti* are both much finer works, and the blend of formal mastery with vivid, well-contrasted materials – especially in *Mi-parti* – offers one of the most satisfying and distinctive musical experiences of recent times.

The first two symphonies, *Symphonic Variations* and *Funeral music* share an acute sense of texture, with the *Symphonic Variations* (1938) serving as a sort of changing room where the composer busily experiments with all manner of musical dress. The *Funeral music* for Bartók (1956-58) is a powerful synthesis of original thought and active homage, with plentiful reminders of the master himself – especially of his *Divertimento* for strings. The real groundbreaker, however, is the Second Symphony, a seething, structured mass in two parts: the first, nervous and diffuse (with strikingly original passagework for piano and percussion), the second initially dense, but ultimately ethereal.

With performances that are authoritative and engaging, this bargain-priced reissue is an indispensable Lutosławski release.

Further Listening

Penderecki Orchestral Works
Wilkomirska *vn* **Palm** *vc* **Blumental** *hpd* **Krakow Philharmonic Choir; Polish National Radio Symphony Orchestra; London Symphony Orchestra / Penderecki**
EMI ② Double Forte CZS5 74302-2 Ⓑ
(148 minutes: ADD: 8/01)

These performances underline the composer's strengths as a conductor concerned to bring out the dramatic immediacy of his scores.

Concerto for Orchestra

Concerto for Orchestra. Funeral Music. Mi-parti
BBC Philharmonic Orchestra / Yan Pascal Tortelier
Chandos CHAN9421 (55 minutes: DDD). Ⓕ
Recorded 1993 ●●

Tortelier's virtues as a conductor – expressive warmth allied to a special rhythmic buoyancy – are generously apparent in a sizzling account of the *Concerto for Orchestra*. The musical flow is firmly controlled, yet the effect is never inflexible, and the technical precision and the alertness of the playing is something for the listener to revel in. The sound is bright, well differentiated dynamically, and even if the BBC's Manchester studio lacks some of the depth and atmosphere of Chicago's Orchestra Hall, as caught in Barenboim's version, this recording is generally more vivid, in keeping with a performance which has precisely the kind of bite and energy that the score demands. It is good that Chandos and

Tortelier chose *Mi-parti* to complete the disc, since of all Lutosławski's later instrumental works this one makes out the best possible case for his radical change of technique around 1960.

Concerto for Orchestra. Symphony No 3
Chicago Symphony Orchestra / Daniel Barenboim
Erato 4509-91711-2 (58 minutes: DDD). Ⓕ
Recorded live in 1992

Lutosławski's Third Symphony was commissioned by the Chicago SO and first performed by them under Sir Georg Solti in 1983, but only nine years later did the orchestra record the work. None of the versions made in the interim can equal Barenboim's blend of refined detail and cumulative power, and the Erato recording is also more faithful to the dynamics marked in the score. The *Concerto for Orchestra*, completed almost 30 years before the symphony, is comparatively conservative in style, but it possesses ample substance to match its panache. It also remains a formidable challenge to an orchestra. As with the symphony, Barenboim's strength is the large-scale creation and sustaining of tension, and the recording contains the heavy climaxes without draining them of clarity or impact.

Chantefleurs et Chantefables

Chantefleurs et Chantefables. Preludes and Fugue. Five Songs. Chain 1
Solveig Kringelborn *sop* **Norwegian Chamber Orchestra / Daniel Harding**
Virgin Classics VC5 45275-2 (73 minutes: DDD). Ⓕ
Texts and translations included ●

Chantefleurs et Chantefables, Lutosławski's penultimate work, was heard as a late and exquisite flowering of lyricism, prompted in part by the French language, in part by the delicately fresh evocations of childhood wonder that he found in Robert Desnos's poems. It was by no means unheralded: it has obvious ancestors in the *Five Songs* to Polish texts that Lutosławski wrote over 30 years earlier but which have seldom been heard since, no doubt because of their language. They are very beautiful, with gratefully lyrical vocal lines over strikingly evocative orchestral textures (strings, two harps, piano, timpani and percussion) that are complex in technique but lucidly 'readable' to the ear. Solveig Kringelborn, who gave the first performance of *Chantefleurs et Chantefables* under the composer's direction, sounds just as much at home in Polish as in French.

The two purely instrumental works here are quite as absorbingly coupled. The seven Preludes are played in the order in which they are printed in the score, but for all the disparate material they contain it is obvious that Lutosławski composed them with great care so that they would make equal but different sense played in any order. The extended 'Fugue' (quotation marks inserted because although it isn't really a fugue it has the feeling of one), a remarkable work from 1972, is clearly an ancestor of the three *Chains* that followed in the 1980s. *Chain 1*, for 14 instruments, progresses from a sequence of crisp, lively, at times almost neoclassical 'events' to a climax of density (ultimately a 12-note chord) in which until the very last moment every line is clearly distinguishable. These are quite admirable performances and recordings, with the Norwegian Chamber Orchestra responding with enthusiasm and warmth to Lutosławski's implicit demands that they should play as though they were an ensemble of soloists. Daniel Harding's love for this music is apparent in his care for balance, vivid sonority and the sheer range (from eloquent intensity to touching tenderness) of Lutosławski's lyricism.

Edward MacDowell

American 1860-1908

GROVE *MacDowell studied the piano in Paris (with Marmontel), Wiesbaden and Frankfurt (Carl Heymann), as well as composition (with Raff, at the Hoch Conservatory in Frankfurt), taking his first post at the Darmstadt Conservatory. Liszt heard his First Modern Suite and First Piano Concerto and strongly encouraged him; by 1884 German firms had published 10 of his works. After several years in Wiesbaden he moved to Boston in 1888 to pursue a performing career. His Second Piano Concerto and First and Second Orchestral Suites won success there and in New York, and he was increasingly accepted as a leading figure in American musical life. Compositions of the Boston years included his popular Woodland Sketches, Sonata tragica and Sonata eroica and the Six love Songs. In 1896 he became the first professor of music at Columbia University; besides organizing the new department, he conducted a New York men's glee club and composed some of his best piano music - Sea Pieces, the Third and Fourth Sonatas, New England Idyls - and many male choruses. He left Columbia in 1904 but continued to teach privately; after his death his summer home at Peterborough, New Hampshire, was converted into an artists' colony (still active).*

MacDowell was a Romantic by temperament, with a musical imagination shaped by nature and literature (notably poetry and Celtic and Nordic legends). His style derives largely from Schumann, Liszt, Wagner, Raff and especially Grieg and, though not innovatory, influential or distinctively American, retains a certain melodic freshness and attractive orchestral colouring.

Piano Concertos

Piano Concertos – No 1 in A minor, Op 15[a]; No 2 in D minor, Op 23[a]. Hexentanz, Op 17 No 2[a]. Romance for Cello and Orchestra, Op 35[b]
[a]**Stephen Prutsman** *pf* [b]**Aisling Drury Byrne** *vc* **National Symphony Orchestra of Ireland / Arthur Fagen**
Naxos 8 559049 (56 minutes: DDD). Ⓢ
Recorded 1999

Music of another time, another age, the MacDowell piano concertos can, in the right hands, seem more endearing than quaint or overblown. Both may satisfy conventional notions of dark and light, of tragedy and skittishness, but their heart-easing, lavishly decorated themes understandably attracted Liszt.

Stephen Prutsman, a brilliant and versatile pianist, plays with ease and fluency, tossing aside the *Presto* movements from both concertos with an enviable sheen, though arguably without a necessarily committed or potent romanticism. Suave and engaging in the Grieg-haunted *Andante tranquillo* from the A minor Concerto, he loses his poise in the deeply welling *più mosso, con passione* from the D minor Concerto's first movement, and it is here, in particular, that one misses Van Cliburn's unforgettable warmth and virtuosity (RCA – nla). No pianist has played this concerto with such magisterial command or emotional generosity; indeed, it sounds as if it was written for him. Eugene List, too, shows a higher degree of involvement than Prutsman, though it must be admitted that the latter's occasional reticence results from Naxos's recessed sound, which irons out much sense of dynamic perspective or variety. Too often Prutsman is confined to the shadows when he should be centre-stage. The National Symphony Orchestra of Ireland has its uneasy moments, but world-première recordings of the *Hexentanz*, in an arrangement for piano and orchestra, and the *Romance* for cello and orchestra make this a tempting issue.

Six Poems after Heine, Op 31

Piano Sonata No 4 in E minor, Op 59, 'Keltic'. Forgotten Fairy Tales, Op 4. Six Poems after Heine, Op 31. 12 Virtuoso Etudes, Op 46

James Barbagallo *pf* Ⓕ

Marco Polo 8 223633 (65 minutes: DDD)

Edward MacDowell's star may have faded to near oblivion over the years. Yet even when his very personal and oddly touching voice seems stifled by deference to outmoded European ideals he still provides enough poetic and psychological interest to make James Barbagallo's affectionate tribute more than worthwhile. The rough-and-tumble of academic life, with its hard-nosed, political jockeying for position, was ill-suited to MacDowell's gentle nature and his professorship at Columbia was short-lived. The gems of this release are without doubt the six Op 31 *Poems after Heine*, their charm and piquancy evoking Scottish castles, nightingales and a shepherd boy 'crowned with golden sunshine'. The *Forgotten Fairy Tales*, too, have their moments but the 12 *Virtuoso Etudes* are somewhat less interesting than their title might imply: the 'Polonaise' is truly awful and the 'Valse triste' an unengaging mixture of whimsy and complacency. However, 'Wilde Jagd', with its sinister chromatic undertow, is effective and there is much homely lyricism elsewhere. Although the *Keltic* Sonata urges us on with instructions such as 'with tragic pathos', the music is overwhelmed by Grieg's influence and by too many tub-thumping, inflated gestures. Overall, Barbagallo is more persuasive in intimacy than in brilliance. That aside, he is unfailingly warm-hearted in his approach.

Guillaume de Machaut

French c1300-1377

GROVE *Machaut entered the service of John of Luxembourg, King of Bohemia, as a royal secretary, c1323. The king helped him to procure a canonry in Reims, which was confirmed in 1335; Machaut settled there c1340, although he continued in royal service until the king's death (1346). He then served various members of the French high nobility, including John, Duke of Berry, his later years being dedicated to the manuscript compilation of his works.*

With his prolific output of motets and songs, Machaut was the single most important figure of the French Ars Nova. He followed and developed the guidelines of Philippe de Vitry's treatise Ars nova and, in particular, observed Vitry's unprecedented advocation of duple time in many of his works, even in his setting of the Ordinary of the Mass. Only in some of his lais and virelais and the Hoquetus David did he consistently adhere to 13th-century rhythmic patterns and genres. His own rhythmic style is novel in its use of variety and motivic interest, particularly through syncopation, and in his development of isorhythmic techniques: all but three of his 23 motets, and four of the movements of the Messe de Nostre Dame –one of the earliest polyphonic settings of the Mass Ordinary – are isorhythmic. In secular music, Machaut set a wide range of poetic forms, all of which are illustrated in his long narrative poem, the Remede de Fortune (probably an early work). While the relationship between text and music is most closely observed in the monophonic lais and virelais, a highly flexible approach is adopted in the three-voice motets so that the subtle treatment of the text avoids the symmetricality of complete isorhythm. More progressive features of Machaut's style - an increased awareness of tonality, the use of unifying rhythmic motifs – are found in his polyphonic settings of rondeaux and ballades, while melodic considerations are to the fore in his virelais.

Messe de Nostre Dame

Messe de Nostre Dame. Je ne cesse de prier (Lai 'de la fonteinne'). Ma fin est mon commencement

Hilliard Ensemble / Paul Hillier

Hyperion CDA66358 (54 minutes: DDD). Texts and translations included Ⓕ

Machaut's *Messe de Nostre Dame* is the earliest known setting of the Ordinary Mass by a single composer. Paul Hillier avoids a full reconstruction on this release: his deference to 'authenticity' restricts itself to the usage of 14th century French pronunciation of the Latin. His ensemble sings two to a part, with prominent countertenors. It is arguable whether the musicians sing the chant at too fast a tempo but they are smooth and flexible and the performance as a whole is both fluid and light in texture. Also included on this release are two French compositions. The wonderful *Lai 'de la fonteinne'* is admirably sung by three tenors and is pure delight – providing food for the heart as well as for the intellect. The rather more familiar *Ma fin est mon commencement*, with its retrograde canon, completes this admirable Hyperion disc.

Songs

Tant doucement me sens emprisonnes. Comment puet on. De Fortune. More qui oo jo nc vous voy. De quanque amours. Je ne cuit pas qu'onques. Liement me deport. Je puis trop bien. Certes mon oueil. En amer a douce vie. Hé dame de valour. Une vipere. Ma fin est mon commencement. De toutes flours
Orlando Consort (Robert Harre-Jones *counterten* Charles Daniels, Angus Smith *tens* Donald Greig *bar*)
Archiv Produktion 457 618-2AH (78 minutes: DDD). Texts and translations included. Ⓕ
Recorded 1997

This is unique: a disc devoted entirely to Machaut's songs, all performed with voices alone. Only the texted line in the manuscripts is sung with text; the rest are vocalized. While this has been the accepted orthodoxy in many circles for some years, nobody has previously quite had the courage to do it for an entire 78 minutes. It works very well, not least because the sheer skill of the Orlando Consort leaves one speechless: everything is immaculately tuned, balanced and phrased; the music is flawlessly edited; absolutely nothing seems to impede the flow of the music. What some listeners may feel is that the texts are not quite sufficiently projected. Particularly in the four-voice pieces you need to listen carefully to distinguish the texted line, which is after all the 'main' voice in any of these songs. But that becomes a lot easier if you follow the texts in the booklet: suddenly the ear can focus on the texted line. And that seems important. The choice of works is also excellent, with an emphasis on pieces that are rarely heard.

Sir Alexander Mackenzie

British 1847-1935

GROVE *Mackenzie studied in Germany and at the Royal Academy of Music, by 1865 becoming known in Edinburgh as a violinist and conductor. In the 1880s he won a reputation as one of England's leading composers, chiefly with the oratorio The Rose of Sharon (1884). From 1885 he lived in London, conducting the Novello Oratorio Concerts and, from 1888, serving as an influential principal of the RAM he also conducted for the Philharmonic Society (1892-9) and occasionally for the Royal Choral Society, making a tour of Canada in 1903. He received a knighthood (1895) and created KCVO (1922). A workmanlike composer, Mackenzie produced successful choral works, vocal settings (many of Scottish poets) and descriptive orchestral pieces, often imaginative and satisfying if also somewhat derivative.*

Scottish Concerto,

Mackenzie Scottish Concerto, Op 55
Tovey Piano Concerto in A, Op 15
Steven Osborne *pf*
BBC Scottish Symphony Orchestra / Martyn Brabbins
Hyperion CDA67023 (62 minutes: DDD). Ⓕ
Recorded 1998

From the horns' call-to-arms at the outset of the piece to the irrepressible merrymaking of the closing pages, Edinburgh-born Sir Alexander Mackenzie's *Scottish Concerto* (1897) spells firm enjoyment, and it is astonishing that it is only here receiving its first recording. Cast in three movements, each of which employs a traditional Scottish melody, it is a thoroughly endearing and beautifully crafted work which wears its native colours without any hint of stale cliché or cloying sentimentality; indeed, the canny wit, genuine freshness and fertile imagination with which Mackenzie treats his material are in evidence throughout the work.

By contrast, Edinburgh-based Sir Donald Tovey's Piano Concerto (1903) exhibits a rather more formal demeanour, its three movements brimful of youthful ambition and possessing a very Brahmsian solidity and dignity. Certainly, there's plenty to admire in the imposing, lucidly structured first movement, which boasts a development section of impressive emotional scope and satisfying rigour. Tovey's idiomatically assured writing is not always entirely untouched by a certain academic earnestness, but on the whole any unwanted stuffiness is deftly kept at bay. In fact, repeated hearings only strengthen one's admiration for this work.

No praise can be too high for Steven Osborne's contribution, while the excellent Martyn Brabbins draws a splendidly stylish and alert response from his fine BBC group. Sound and balance are excellent too.

James MacMillan

British 1959

GROVE *MacMillan studied at Edinburgh University and then with Casken at Durham University. In 1990 he became affiliate composer of the Scottish Chamber Orchestra he has since become visiting composer for the Philharmonia (London) and artistic director of its Contemporary Music Series. His music is noted for its energy and emotional power, its religious and political content and its references to Scottish folk music. Recent works include The Beserking (1990), a piano concerto for Peter Donohoe; Sinfonietta (1991); and Veni, Veni, Emmanuel (1992), a percussion concerto for Evelyn Glennie.*

The Confession of Isobel Gowdie

The Confession of Isobel Gowdie. Tryst
BBC Scottish Symphony Orchestra / Jerzy Maksymiuk
Koch Schwann 310502 (54 minutes: DDD) (F)

Awards 1993

This time the publicity doesn't exaggerate. The première of *The Confession of Isobel Gowdie* at the 1990 Proms was a 'spectacular triumph' – nothing less – and this with an audience drawn largely (one presumes) by Beethoven's Fourth Symphony and Sibelius's Violin Concerto. But success can fade with alarming rapidity. What matters now is that several years later, away from the uplift of that extraordinary reception, *The Confession of Isobel Gowdie* tells its story as stirringly as ever. If MacMillan's programme (the martyrdom of a Scottish Catholic 'witch') seems overpictorial, no problem; the progression from rapt modal string threnody (complete with keening *glissandos*) through mounting violence to the re-emergence and transformation of the modal lament is as easy to follow as the 'narrative' of a Mahler symphony – and the after-effect isn't actually all that dissimilar.

Others may be bothered by undisguised echoes of other composers: Copland, Messiaen, Stravinsky, Ives, the famous single-note *crescendo* from Berg's *Wozzeck* ... but the fact that they are undisguised is part of their strength – that and the way in which they are so obviously drawn into the argument. Of course the quality of the performance matters, and Maksymiuk and his orchestra give the kind of penetrating performance which (usually) only comes from long involvement. *Tryst* also emerges well: the forces may be smaller, but the head-on confrontation of violence with calmer, more humane sounds again generates a compelling musical drama, and the ending, though less spectacular than Isobel Gowdie's final one-tone immolation, works both as an imaginative conclusion and as a challenge to go back and dig deeper. Away with caution! Give this a try.

Tryst

Tryst[a]. Adam's Rib[b]. They Saw the Stone had been Rolled Away[a]. Í (A Meditation on Iona)[a]
[b]Scottish Chamber Orchestra Brass; [a]Scottish Chamber Orchestra / Joseph Swensen (F)
BIS CD1019 (59 minutes: DDD).

This is the third recording of *Tryst* – extraordinary for a contemporary orchestral work. But its individuality is still as striking now as when it first appeared more than 10 years ago: especially so in this taut, gripping version. MacMillan touches, as warmly and directly as Mahler. The sounds can be violent, acerbic or prickly (as indeed they can in Mahler!); the keening string lament at the heart of the work isn't always easy on the ear, and yet it all speaks – it is plainly the work of someone who urgently wants to tell us something. So too are the performances. Joseph Swensen brings the passionate enthusiasm to *Tryst*, and to *Í*, that has made his concerts with the Scottish Chamber Orchestra such events in Scotland. *Í* (pronounced 'ee') is a quite astonishing work. The subtitle, 'A Meditation on Iona', might suggest something romantically atmospheric, with soft, lilting Celtic accents. In fact this is hard, intense, sometimes eerie music: a tribute to St Columba, the muscular, fiercely contentious monk who brought Christianity to Scotland and founded the monastic college of Iona – perhaps also a reminder of St Paul's words about working out one's salvation with 'fear and trembling'.

Along with this come two short, brooding pieces, which are dominated by the sound of brass: *Adam's Rib* and *They saw the Stone had been Rolled Away*, the latter giving more than a foretaste of MacMillan's Symphony, *Vigil* – the concluding part of the trilogy *Triduum*. As with *Triduum*, the success is total: powerful, concise works, powerfully and understandingly performed, in crisp, clear recordings.

Veni, veni, Emmanuel

Veni, veni, Emmanuel[a]. After the tryst[b]. '... as others see us ...'[c]. Three Dawn Rituals[c]. Untold[c]
[a]Evelyn Glennie *perc* **[b]Ruth Crouch** *vn* **[b]Peter Evans** *pf* **[ac]Scottish Chamber Orchestra / [a]Jukka-Pekka Saraste, [c]James MacMillan** (F)
Catalyst 09026 61916-2 (68 minutes: DDD).

Taking the Advent plainsong of the title as his basis, MacMillan reflects in his continuous 26-minutes sequence the theological implications behind the period between Advent and Easter. The five contrasted sections are in a sort of arch form, with the longest and slowest in the middle. That section, 'Gaude, Gaude', expresses not direct joy as the Latin words might suggest but a meditative calm, using the four relevant chords from the plainsong's refrain as a hushed ostinato. Over that the soloist on the marimba plays an elaborate but gentle and intensely poetic cadenza. The main sections on either side are related dances based on hocketing repeated notes and full of jazzy syncopations, with powerful sections for Advent and Easter respectively framing the work as a whole. The plainsong emerges dramatically as a chorale at the climax of the second dance-section, a telling moment.

The composer's descriptive notes are most helpful and detailed, but they deliberately keep quiet about the coda, where MacMillan brings off another dramatic coup. After the soloist has worked through the widest range of percussion in the different sections, there is a gap when players in the orchestra pick up and start playing little jingling bells, and the soloist progresses up to the big chimes set on a platform above the rest of the orchestra. The very close of the work brings a crescendo of chimes intended to reflect the joy of Easter in the Catholic service and the celebration of the Resurrection. Disappointingly though, the preparatory jingles are gentle and discreet, and even the final chimes are devotional rather than exuberant, working to a crescendo which could have been bigger and more sustained. Even so, this is a magnificent representation of one of the most striking and powerful works written by any British composer of the younger generation.

Mass

A New Song[ab]. Mass[ab]. Christus vincit[a]. Gaudeamus in loci pace[b]. Seinte Mari moder milde[ab]. A Child's Prayer[a]. Changed[ab]
[a]**Westminster Cathedral Choir / Martin Baker** with [b]**Andrew Reid** *org*
Hyperion CDA67219 (66 minutes: DDD). Ⓕ
Texts and translations included. Recorded 2000 **OO**

MacMillan's choral music is more often than not a direct response to his own Christian faith. The *Mass* recorded here was commissioned by Westminster Cathedral for the 'Glory of God in the Millennium Year of the Jubilee' and unlike MacMillan's two previous Masses (the *St Anne Mass* and the *Galloway Mass*), which were composed for congregational use, was specifically written for performance by a professional choir. It is through-composed and this provides a sense of structure, continuity and flow that greatly enhances its accessibility when heard out of context – on disc rather than celebrated. That MacMillan intended the *Mass* for practical use is apparent by his choice of vernacular rather than the Latin text. His often eclectic style is very much in evidence; the score glimmers with echoes of Howells and Duruflé, especially in the *Kyrie* and in his often quasi-orchestral organ writing, but in general it is MacMillan's own individual voice that shapes this impressive and deeply felt setting. The *Gloria* contains some particularly effective music, not least some marvellously atmospheric organ writing, and the crepuscular *Agnus Dei* lingers in the mind long after the final notes die away.

Of the remaining works on the disc, *A New Song* (a setting of Coverdale's translation of Psalm 96) and *A Child's Prayer* (dedicated to the victims of the Dunblane tragedy) stand out as particularly fine examples of MacMillan's choral writing. As an added bonus we are treated to the wonderfully translucent organ solo *Gaudeamus in loci pace*, beautifully performed by Andrew Reid. Performances throughout are exceptionally fine, the recorded sound radiantly atmospheric. A must.

Albéric Magnard French 1865-1914

GROVE *Magnard, of a serious disposition, produced severe, formalistic works – mainly orchestral and chamber music and operas – taking Wagner, Beethoven, Gluck and his teacher d'Indy as models. Canon and fugue pervade much of his output, though the Third Symphony (1896) and the opera Bérénice (1909), his masterpiece, show a refreshing clarity of scoring and a lyric simplicity.*

Symphonies

Symphonies – No 1 in C minor, Op 4. No 2 in E, Op 6
BBC Scottish Symphony Orchestra / Jean-Yves Ossonce
Hyperion CDA67030 (67 minutes: DDD). Ⓕ
Recorded 1997 **O**

Symphonies – No 3 in B flat minor, Op 11. No 4 in C sharp minor, Op 21
BBC Scottish Symphony Orchestra / Jean-Yves Ossonce
Hyperion CDA67040 (73 minutes: DDD). Ⓕ
Recorded 1997 **O**

The name of Albéric Magnard began to impinge on the record public only 30 years ago, and there have been recordings of three of his symphonies, the opera *Guercoeur*, and a five-disc set of his chamber music and songs; but he seems doomed to be a composer whose music (highly praised by several contemporaries) survives only via the gramophone: his impact on the concert life of this country has been virtually nil, and he has not been much better served in his native France. Not that he would have cared overmuch: during his life (brought to an abrupt end at the start of the First World War by German invaders who set fire to his country house) he made little attempt to get his music performed, being paranoically sensitive to any suspicion of nepotistic influence, as his father was a powerful newspaper proprietor. By all accounts he was a withdrawn and austere person, and perhaps in keeping with that image his music is not for the casual listener who looks for facile attractiveness, but in a somewhat Teutonic way is rewarding for the serious-minded in its skilfully crafted and thoughtfully lyrical character.

The First Symphony (1890) shows the unmistakable influence of Wagner in the *religioso* slow movement. Despite the adoption of the cyclic principle championed by his teacher Vincent d'Indy, under whose watchful eye the work was written and who must have smiled approvingly at his pupil's fluent contrapuntal technique, Magnard's proliferation of ideas threatens structural continuity, especially in the first movement. In contrast to that movement's initial brooding atmosphere, the Second Symphony begins more sunnily and spiritedly (but with a spacious second-subject paragraph), and the following *Scherzo* (which replaced an earlier fugue) is a bucolic 'Danses' tinged with introspection. The emotional core of the symphony is the luxuriant *Chant varié*, and the work ends in an almost light-hearted mood. The Third Symphony's striking organum-like opening leads to an *Allegro* by turns vigorous and contemplative. Next comes a *Scherzo* headed 'Danses' (as in the previous symphony), a mocking soufflé with a wistful central section – an altogether captivating movement that is anything but austere. The movingly tense slow movement's long lines are subverted by menacing outbursts that build to a stormy climax before subsiding; and there is a finale which combines exuberance and lyricism with a return to the symphony's very first theme. This is certainly the work to recommend to newcomers to Magnard. Several years elapsed before the appearance of his last symphony in 1913, and by then his overall mood had darkened. The turbulent passion that characterizes the first movement, presented in dramatically colourful orchestration, is also mirrored in the finale: between them come a highly individual *Scherzo* with strange oriental-type passages and a lengthy, anguished slow movement. The BBC Scottish Symphony Orchestra is on splendid form throughout and their efforts have been recorded in exemplary fashion.

Gustav Mahler Austrian 1860-1911

From 1875 to 1878 Mahler was at the Vienna Conservatory, where he studied the piano, harmony and composition. After that he attended university lectures, worked as a music teacher and composed Das klagende Lied, *a cantata indebted to the operas of Weber and Wagner but also showing many conspicuously Mahlerian features.*

In 1880 he accepted a conducting post at a summer theatre at Bad Hall, and was engaged in a similar capacity in 1881 and 1883 at the theatres in Ljubljana and Olomouc. In autumn 1883, he became music director at Kassel. He found conditions uncongenial, but an unhappy love affair with one of the singers led to his first masterpiece, the song cycle Lieder eines fahrenden Gesellen, *and the inception of the closely related First Symphony.*

Early in 1885 Mahler secured the post of second conductor at the Neues Stadttheater in Leipzig, to begin in July 1886. The intervening year he spent at the Landestheater in Prague, where he had the opportunity of conducting operas by Gluck, Mozart, Beethoven and Wagner. At Leipzig, in January 1887, he took over the Ring *cycle from Arthur Nikisch, who fell ill, and convincingly established among critics and public his genius as an interpretative artist. The following year he completed Weber's unfinished comic opera* Die drei Pintos *(its successful performances in 1888 made Mahler famous and provided a useful source of income) and fell in love with the wife of Weber's grandson. It was through the Webers that he discovered in 1887 the musical potential of* Des Knaben Wunderhorn, *a collection of folklike texts by Arnim and Brentano which provided Mahler with words for all but one of his songs for the next 14 years.*

Disagreements with colleagues led to Mahler's resignation at Leipzig in May 1888 and to his dismissal a few months later from Prague, but within a few weeks he secured a far more important appointment at the Royal Opera in Budapest. His first year there was overshadowed by the illness and deaths of his parents and his sister. Though he was successful in bringing the opera house into profit and improving standards and repertory, the imminent appointment of an Intendant with artistic control made his situation untenable; he resigned and became first conductor at the Stadttheater, Hamburg. Despite a stifling artistic atmosphere and a heavy workload, Mahler returned to composition and at his summer retreat in the Salzkammergut completed the Second and Third Symphonies. 1895 brought both tragedy, when his youngest brother committed suicide, and success, with the première of the Second Symphony in Berlin in December. Now a conductor of international stature and a composer of growing reputation, he turned his attention to the Vienna Hofoper. The main obstacle was his Jewish origins; so he accepted Catholic baptism in February 1897 and was appointed Kapellmeister at two months later.

At Vienna Mahler brought a stagnating opera house to a position of unrivalled brilliance. In 1901 he had a villa built at Maiernigg on the Wörthersee in Carinthia, where he spent the summers composing. In 1902 he married Alma, daughter of the artist Emil Jakob Schindler, and though their life together was not untroubled the security benefited his creative life. At Maiernigg he completed Symphonies Nos 5-8 and in 1904 the Kindertotenlieder, *settings of five poems by Rückert on the death of children. The death of Mahler's own elder daughter, Maria, from scarlet fever three years later left him distraught.*

In Vienna Mahler was surrounded by radical young composers, including Schoenberg, Berg, Webern and Zemlinsky, whose work he supported and encouraged. His propagation of his own music, however, aroused opposition from a section of the Viennese musical establishment, and when the campaign against him, led by an anti-semitic press, gained momentum he turned to New York, where he spent his last winters as conductor, first of the Metropolitan Opera and, from 1910, of the New York PO. He continued to spend the summers in Europe, where he undertook further conducting and completed the valedictory Ninth Symphony and Das Lied von der Erde. *This last, a setting of six Chinese poems in German translation, took the shape of a large-scale symphony for two voices and orchestra but Mahler, whose fear of death and sense of fate had been intensified by the diagnosis of a heart condition in 1907, refused to number the work 10, citing Beethoven, Schubert and Bruckner. He did, however, start work on a 10th symphony, but died before he could complete it.*

Although as a conductor Mahler achieved fame primarily in opera, his creative energies were directed almost wholly towards symphony and song. Even in the early Das klagende Lied, *there are stylistic features to be found in his mature music, for example the combining of onstage and offstage orchestras, the association of high tragedy and the mundane, the drawing on folksong ideas and the dramatic-symbolic use of tonality. This last reappeared in his early masterpiece, the* Lieder eines fahrenden Gesellen, *which has an evolutionary tonal scheme paralleling the changing fortunes of the travelling hero. In the 1890s Mahler was much influenced by the* Wunderhorn *poems, in his symphonies as well as his songs, for he often used song to clarify an important moment in the structure of a symphony, for example 'Urlicht' in No 2, which he found himself unable to continue after writing the imposing first movement. No 3 is more idiosyncratic; again, its dramatic scheme evolved with recourse to song and chorus. No 4 returns to tradition, in a first movement of rare wit and subtlety; here the poetic idea is the progress from experience to innocence (with a Wunderhorn song finale). While No 2, 'The Resurrection', moves from C minor to E flat, No 4 goes from G major to the 'heavenly' E major. Parody, irony and satire are important in Mahler's thinking during these years, with popular invention (like the children's round in no.1 and the march tunes of No 3) and elements of distortion.*

Nos 5, 6 and 7 are sometimes regarded as a trilogy, although No 5 is a heroic work, with a narrative running from its opening funeral march through the agitated Allegro to a Scherzo and a triumphant conclusion. The symphony moves from C sharp minor to D major. No 6, a tragic work – and in many musicians' view, his greatest symphony for its equilibrium between form and drama - begins and ends in A minor; the finale makes it clear that there is no escape for the implied hero and indeed his death is symbolically enacted in the movement's shattering climax. The shape of No 7, which moves from E minor to C major, is less satisfying; possibly, with its dark, nocturnal middle movement, it is consciously built round the poetic concept of darkness moving towards the light of the finale. The largest-scale of Mahler's symphonies is No 8, the so-called 'Symphony of a Thousand', in which the second part is a vast synthesis of forms and media embodying the setting of the final scene of Goethe's Faust as an amalgam of dramatic cantata, oratorio, song cycle, Lisztian choral symphony and instrumental symphony. This public pronouncement was followed by one of his most personal, Das Lied von der Erde, influenced in its vocal writing and woodwind obbligatos by Mahler's new interest in Bach. His last two symphonies return to the four-movement scheme of the middle-period ones, incorporating extensions of the character movements of his earlier works with the new type of slow first movement (followed up in the unfinished 10th) and ending with an Adagio in a mood of profound resignation. Mahler's extension of symphonic form, of the symphony's expressive scope and the use of the orchestra (especially the agonised timbres he obtained by using instruments, particularly wind, at the top of their compass) represent a pained farewell to Romanticism; different aspects were followed up by the Second Viennese School, Shostakovich and Britten.

Complete Symphonies

No 1 in D; **No 2** in C minor, 'Resurrection'; **No 3** in D minor; **No 4** in G; **No 5** in C sharp minor; **No 6** in A minor; **No 7** in E minor; **No 8** in E flat, 'Symphony of a Thousand'; **No 9** in D; **No 10** in F sharp minor

Symphonies – No 1[a]; No 2[b] (with **Cheryl Studer** *sop* **Waltraud Meier** *mez* **Arnold Schoenberg Choir**); No 3[b] (**Jessye Norman** *sop* **Vienna Boys' Choir; Vienna State Opera Chorus**); No 4[b] (**Frederica von Stade** *mez*); No 5[a]; Nos 6[c] and 7[c]; No 8[a] (**Studer, Sylvia McNair, Andrea Rost** *sops* **Anne Sofie von Otter** *mez* **Rosemarie Lang** *contr* **Peter Seiffert** *ten* **Bryn Terfel** *bass-bar* **Jan-Hendrik Rootering** *bass* **Tölz Boys' Choir; Berlin Radio Chorus; Prague Philharmonic Chorus**) Nos 9[b] and 10[b] – Adagio

[a]**Berlin Philharmonic Orchestra;** [b]**Vienna Philharmonic Orchestra;** [c]**Chicago Symphony Orchestra / Claudio Abbado**

DG ⑫ 447 023-2GX12 (718 minutes: ADD/DDD). Texts and translations included. Ⓜ

Recorded 1977-94

The current pre-eminence of Gustav Mahler in the concert hall and on disc is not something that could have been anticipated – other than by the composer himself. Hard now to believe that his revival had to wait until the centenary celebrations of his birth in 1960. And yet by 1980 he was more widely esteemed than his longer-lived contemporaries Sibelius and Strauss and could suddenly be seen to tower over 20th-century music much as Beethoven must have done in a previous age. (Not that he hadn't been there all along: the music of Berg, Shostakovich, Britten and even Copland bears witness to this, disparately but resonantly Mahlerian.) By this time too, a new generation of conductors had come to the fore, further transforming our perceptions of the composer. Claudio Abbado is arguably the most distinguished of this group and, while his interpretations will not satisfy every listener on every occasion, they make an excellent choice for the library shelves, when the price is reasonably competitive and the performances so emblematic (and arguably central to our understanding) of Mahler's place in contemporary musical life.

Of the alternatives, Haitink's package has the fewest expressive distortions while Bernstein's is the most ceaselessly emotive of them all; neither has Abbado's particular combination of qualities. It is probably no accident that Donald Mitchell's notes for this set are focused on the nature of Mahler's 'modernity'. For it is that ironic, inquisitive, preternaturally aware young composer who haunts this conductor's performances. Not for Abbado the heavy, saturated textures of 19th-century romanticism, nor the chilly rigidity of some of his own 'modernist' peers. Instead an unaffected warmth and elegance of sound allows everything to come through naturally – in so far as the different venues and DG's somewhat variable technology will permit – even in the most searingly intense of climaxes.

Increasingly these days, Abbado is presenting Mahler as a fluent classicist, less concerned to characterize the surface battle of conflicting emotions than to elucidate the underlying symphonic structure. The lack of Solti's brand of forthright theatricality can bring a feeling of disappointment. But even where he underplays the drama of the moment, sufficient sense of urgency is sustained by a combination of well-judged tempos, marvellously graduated dynamics and precisely balanced, ceaselessly changing textures. The propulsion comes from within. For those still put off by Mahler's supposed vulgarity the unhurried classicism of these readings may well be the most convincing demonstration of the composer's absolute integrity.

It was in November 1907 that Mahler famously told Sibelius that 'the symphony must be like the world. It must embrace everything.' And perhaps it is only today that we see this as a strength rather than a weakness in his music. He wrote music that is 'about' its own past while at the same time probing into all our futures, music that is so all-embracing and communicates with such directness that we can make it 'mean' whatever we want it to, confident that we alone have really understood the code. Abbado lacks Bernstein's desire to explore these limitless possibilities every time he mounts the podium, but some will count that as a blessing. These are committed and authoritative performances.

New York Philharmonic – The Mahler Broadcasts 1948-82

Symphonies – No 1 (recorded live in 1959)[ac]; No 2 (**Kathleen Battle** *sop* **Maureen Forrester** *contr* **Westminster Choir;** rec 1982)[afm]; No 3 (**Yvonne Minton** *mez* **Camerata Singers; Little Church around the Corner Boys' Choir; Trinity Church Boys' Choir; Brooklyn Boys' Choir** rec 1976)[adm]; No 4 (**Irmgard Seefried** *sop* rec 1962)[ah]; No 5 (rec 1980)[akm]; No 6 (rec 1955)[ag]; No 7 (rec 1981)[ae]; No 8 (**Frances Yeend, Uta Graf, Camilla Williams** *sops* **Martha Lipton, Louise Bernhardt** *contrs* **Eugene Conley** *ten* **Carlos Alexander** *bar* **George London** *bass-bar* **Schola Cantorum; Public School No 12 Boys' Choir, Manhattan;** rec 1950)[bj]; No 9 (rec 1962)[ac]; No 10 – Adagio; Purgatorio (rec 1960 and 1958)[ag]. Lieder eines fahrenden Gesellen (**Dietrich Fischer-Dieskau** *bar* rec 1964)[ai]. Das Lied von der Erde (**Kathleen Ferrier** *contr* **Set Svanholm** *ten* rec 1948)[bl]

[a]New York Philharmonic Orchestra, [b]Philharmonic Symphony Orchestra of New York / [c]Sir John Barbirolli, [d]Pierre Boulez, [e]Rafael Kubelík, [f]Zubin Mehta, [g]Dimitri Mitropoulos, [h]Sir Georg Solti, [i]William Steinberg, [j]Leopold Stokowski, [k]Klaus Tennstedt, [l]Bruno Walter

New York Philharmonic mono/[m]stereo

⑫ NYP9801/12 (903 minutes: ADD). Also contains interviews and reminiscences about Mahler

Available at $225 (plus postage and packing) at selected Tower Records stores or by mail order; in North America call (toll free) 1-800-557-8268; worldwide 1-317-781-1861; web: www.newyorkphilharmonic.org

Not your average collection of Mahler symphonies, but one which, with pride, charts in words and music, the impact of the composer's final two years (1909-11) in and on New York and the important part the city's orchestra subsequently played in spreading the Mahler message. One might argue that Walter and Mitropoulos would have pioneered and propagated Mahler performance in New York even if the composer had never set foot in the place. But if you have the Mahler connection, and the tradition, then why not make it work for you? That is what the orchestra has done here, and the result, though highly priced, has the potential for being equally highly prized by Mahler historians and dedicated collectors alike (English speaking ones, as there are no translations of the many valuable features in the booklets' 500-odd pages). One of the booklets contains a list of all the NYPO's Mahler performances since 1904, pin-pointing the broadcasts where tapes 'are known to exist', and it is from these tapes that this compilation was chosen.

In making the choices, consideration was given to the New York players' own views and memories of the concerts or conductors (printed in the booklet); and to featuring symphonies from conductors who never took them into the studio (Barbirolli in the First, Mitropoulos in the Sixth and 10th, Stokowski in the Eighth). Bernstein is conspicuous by his absence, but it would seem that rights are not currently available for the release of his Mahler broadcast tapes. We hear, though, from the man whose Mahler was Bernstein's model; and Mitropoulos's 1960 Sixth Symphony must have been a hard act for Bernstein to follow. Follow it Bernstein did, with an equally powerful but more protean New York Sixth (from 1967, now on Sony Classical), yet Mitropoulos delivers the symphony's integrity and unpalatable truths with a grim and arguably more compelling single-mindedness. Apart from the slow movement (placed second, and gloriously played), there is little relief from the symphony's burdened, battering march to tragedy. Latterly interpreters have also been more protean in the Eighth's expansive Faust fantasy, and it would be idle to pretend that other conductors don't make more than Stokowski of the contrasts explicitly indicated in Mahler's score (angels that dance as well as sing, 'freed from earthly stress'). Stokowski in 1950 opted for an unusually moderate range of tempos (starting with a swift *Andante*), and it is impossible to say whether he was playing safe, attempting to dignify the folksy inspiration, or bringing us something of the manner in which Mahler himself conducted the work (Stokowski was present at the Eighth's Munich world première in 1910). Whatever the case, along the way there are as many attractions as there are inevitable insecurities, and it is worth hearing, not least for the First Part of the symphony, which bears the unmistakable stamp of greatness, and the sound is a marvel for its years.

The earliest recording here is a vital, controlled and incisive 1948 *Das Lied von der Erde* from Walter, with Kathleen Ferrier making her American début. Set Svanholm tends to press ahead of the beat, but it is a rare pleasure to hear the tenor songs as resolutely conquered and characterized. As for Ferrier's contribution, there is little to choose between this and her famous 1952 Decca Vienna account made with a more relaxed Walter. The later recording perhaps presents the richer portrait of a unique vocal phenomenon, and a cathartic release of emotion in the final pages not matched in New York (where the manner is closer to the score's indication of something a little more serene and understated). Aptly enough for this enterprise, applause has been retained at the end of the works, even if, in the case of *Das Lied*, one wishes that the audience had waited a few seconds longer. But audience noise during the music can be frustrating. Time may well be standing still at the start of Barbirolli's 1959 First Symphony, but the audience is still finding its way to the seats, and letting loose coughs often enough for some of them to blot out Mahler's birdcalls.

Matters improve, possibly because, as one of the concert's critical notices informs us, only part of the audience stayed to the end. And the part that did was witness to some engaging features, such as the pronounced, and for the time, deeply unfashionable string *portamentos* (even Stokowski, in his Eighth, opts for discreet slides), and a *Scherzo* with big boots and rustic charm laid on by the barrow-load. The *Scherzo* of Barbirolli's 1962 New York Ninth Symphony is of a consistently coarser cut than his 1964 Berlin studio recording for EMI, and arguably benefits from it, though there is little evidence for the booklet's general assessment of the Berlin Ninth as 'rather disengaged from the work's churning emotions'. And the brightly analytical (and stereo) Berlin recording does allow clearer perception of the details of – future archival revelations apart – Barbirolli's finest taped Mahler symphony interpretation. Solti's Fourth Symphony (also 1962), as we know from his two Decca studio recordings, was unexpectedly graceful, with a long-breathed slow movement, and admirable discipline and refinement, even if that refinement streamlines the work's bolder colours and sardonic edge.

All the New York recordings enjoy good balances; those already mentioned are all in very decent, if occasionally pale, mono sound. The stereo tapings aren't ideally flattering to New York's violins, but benefit from a wider dynamic range (especially the Boulez Third Symphony). For a live recording, the deployment of the various on- and off-stage forces in Mehta's 1982 Second is a major achievement. This was a special occasion for all involved (the orchestra's 10,000th concert), and although Mehta's is neither a particularly lofty nor radical view of the work, the excitement in the hall (as one musician explains it in the booklet, 'the players turning each other on') has transferred to disc admirably. The pleasures of Boulez's 1976 performance of the Third Symphony include a typical (and often very sensuous) cultivation of inner workings, concern for outer structure, very precisely graded dynamics, and a strikingly individual rubato (the opening of the finale's hymn, a mesmerizing example). Rarely has the sudden tumult and its immediate aftermath at the end of the third movement – proclamatory brass receding over shimmering strings – cast such a spell. Never mind the horns' tremors in their hushed upper reaches here: as this performance progresses, you gradually become aware of a real time context and continuity almost impossible to create in the studio. Tennstedt had the ability, at the moment of performance, to persuade listeners that the music could and should sound no other way, and his 1980 New York Fifth Symphony runs the full gamut of 'no tomorrow' intensity, intervention, riotous colour and perfectly formed details.

In contrast, the years between Kubelík's Bavarian Radio Seventh (recorded for DG in 1970) and this 1981 New York account appear to have prompted a radical rethink. Or maybe Kubelík is responding to the extra heft of the New York orchestra and ephemeral concert conditions to push out the boundaries. Still recognizable, if moderated, are the sharp features and deliberately soured tone lending menace to both the second and third movements, and an *Andante amoroso* cajoled into a diversion of wonderfully graceful, fresh-voiced charm. But the much broader manner maximizes the far-flung sonorities, in the first movement, at the expense of line and general decorum. You may react differently, particularly if you agree with criticisms of Kubelík's Munich Mahler as lightweight. We mentioned pride at the beginning of this review, and from the general level of playing in this set, it is entirely justified. Naturally there are fluffs, early entries and an occasional rubato prompting untidiness, but the vast majority demonstrates a level of professionalism and innate ability to produce the right sort of sound at the right time that have made and maintained the orchestra as one of the world's ideal Mahler instruments. As to the two-hour-long sequence of audio interviews by William Malloch, 'I Remember Mahler' (New York players' first-hand experiences under Mahler, recorded in the early 1960s), these undoubtedly benefit from editing, but their complete presentation here corresponds with the comprehensive nature of the project, and allows a few more anecdotes currency as cherishable Mahler memorabilia.

Symphonies – Nos 1 and 2 (**Elly Ameling** *sop* **Aafje Heynis** *contr* **Netherlands Radio Chorus**); No 3 (**Maureen Forrester** *contr* **St Willibrord Church Boys' Choir; Netherlands Radio Chorus**); No 4 (**Ameling**); Nos 5-8 (**Ileana Cotrubas, Heather Harper, Hanneke van Bork** *sops* **Birgit Finnila** *mez* **Marianne Dieleman** *contr* **William Cochran** *ten* **Hermann Prey** *bar* **Hans Sotin** *bass* **St Willibrord and Pius X Children's Choir; Collegium Musicum Amstelodamense; Amsterdam Toonkunst Choir; Amsterdam Stem des Volks Choir**); No 10 – Adagio
Concertgebouw Orchestra / Bernard Haitink
Philips Bernard Haitink Symphony Edition
⑩ 442 050-2PB10 (692 minutes: ADD). Ⓜ
Recorded 1962-71 ●

If space is at a premium, this set is undeniably attractive, though the multilingual illustrated booklet dispenses with texts and translations and several symphonies are awkwardly spread between discs. For a generation of record buyers it was these sane, lucid, sometimes (as it now seems) insufficiently demonstrative Concertgebouw readings that represented a way into music previously considered unacceptable in polite society. Haitink's phrasing has an appealing natural simplicity, his rhythmic almost-squareness providing welcome reassurance. The preoccupation with conventional symphonic verities of form and structure does not preclude striking beauty of sound and the recordings have come up well in the remastering. There is some residual hiss. Haitink's early No 1 (1962), his first taping of a Mahler symphony, is usually reckoned the least satisfactory of his career. Not that it is without interest for the Concertgebouw's reedy woodwinds and vibrato-laden trumpets lend specific character and charm to what is otherwise a comparatively featureless reading. True, the third movement doesn't quite work: Haitink's attempts at 'Jewishness' are so self-conscious that the results sound rhythmically suspect, not quite together rather than convincingly ethnic. The real problem is the boxed-in sound, uncharacteristically rough-and-ready with none of the cool tonal lustre which characterized subsequent LPs from this source.

The Fourth receives a similarly straightforward account with a wonderfully hushed *Poco adagio* and few if any of the aggressive mannerisms which have marred more recent versions. The restraint can border on inflexibility at times. The first movement lacks a certain element of fantasy with everything so very accurate and together, and, while Elly Ameling makes a lovely sound in the finale, the orchestra's animal caricatures are not really vulgar enough, the sense of wonder and awe in the face of heaven rather muted at the close. Though inevitably lacking the gut-wrenching theatricality and hallucinatory colour of Bernstein, the Seventh has none of the staidness and rigidity that occasionally prompts doubts about Haitink's Mahlerian credentials. Now accommodated on a single CD, it emerges as a high point of the series, second only to the celebrated Ninth. The opening is deceptively cool and brooding; thereafter the interpretation is unexpectedly driven and intense, even if Mahler's fantastical sonorities are left to fend for themselves. Only those who feel the nth degree of nightmarish 'exaggeration' to be vital to the expression of the whole need have any doubts. The finale is effectively held together but should perhaps sound more hollow than this.

To sum up: if you must have the Mahler symphonies under a single conductor, Haitink could arguably be the man to go for. His objectivity will not spoil you for alternative readings. Nevertheless you would not want to miss out on Bernstein, unrelenting in his desire to communicate the essentials of these scores, taking his cue from Mahler's remark that 'the symphony must be like the world. It must be all-embracing'. Haitink is more circumspect, the music's vaunting ambition knowingly undersold.

Symphony No 1

Symphony No 1. Lieder eines fahrenden Gesellen
Dietrich Fischer-Dieskau *bar*
Bavarian Radio Symphony Orchestra / Rafael Kubelík
DG The Originals 449 735-2GOR (67 minutes: ADD).
Text and translation included. Ⓜ
Recorded 1967

Rafael Kubelík is essentially a poetic conductor and he gets more poetry out of this symphony than almost any other conductor who has recorded it. Although he takes the repeat of the first movement's short exposition, it is strange that he should ignore the single repeat sign in the *Ländler* when he seems so at ease with the music. Notwithstanding a fondness for generally brisk tempos in Mahler, Kubelík is never afraid of rubato here, above all in his very personally inflected account of the slow movement. This remains a delight. The finale now seems sonically a little thin, with the trumpets made to sound rather hard-pressed and the final climax failing to open out as it can in more modern recordings. The orchestral contribution is very good even if absolute precision isn't guaranteed.

Dietrich Fischer-Dieskau's second recording of the *Lieder eines fahrenden Gesellen* has worn rather less well, the spontaneous ardour of his earlier performance (with Furtwängler and the Philharmonia – now reissued on EMI) here tending to stiffen into melodrama and mannerism. There is of course much beautiful singing and he is most attentively accompanied, but the third song, 'Ich hab' ein glühend Messer', is implausibly overwrought, bordering on self-parody. By contrast, Kubelík's unpretentious, Bohemian approach to the symphony remains perfectly valid. A corrective to the grander visions of those who conduct the music with the benefit of hindsight and the advantages of digital technology? Perhaps.

Mahler Symphony No 1
Berg (orch Verbey) Piano Sonata, Op 1
Royal Concertgebouw Orchestra / Riccardo Chailly
Decca 448 813-2DH (70 minutes: DDD). Ⓕ
Recorded 1995

Chailly gives us a straightforward symphonic overview in which the more overtly programmatic elements are never allowed to threaten the work's structural integrity. Lest it be thought that this implies 'worthy but dull', two things give this performance a very special appeal: the quality of the orchestral playing and the scrupulous attention paid to phrasing and dynamics. The first movement is particularly fresh. How often do we get a genuine *ppp* from the horns before the *cantabile* melody of the cellos and the active part of the development. No doubt the two middle movements will be too emotionally reticent for some: that second movement hardly evokes a peasants' merrymaking, while the third is purged of rusticity, its more bizarre and hysterical elements reduced to a series of incidental if novel orchestral effects. And yet, where a lesser orchestra might have sounded plain, the Royal Concertgebouw imbues the music with real character. The ending goes very well indeed, the horns correctly prominent, the all-too-common percussive thwack on the final crotchet conscientiously eschewed. Chailly's enterprising coupling is much more convincing than you might suppose and much more relevant than another *Blumine*. The recording quality is excellent.

Symphony No 1
Concertgebouw Orchestra / Leonard Bernstein
DG 427 303-2GH (56 minutes: DDD). Ⓕ
Recorded live in 1987 ●●

Bernstein's basic view of the First Symphony underwent very little change over the years. How acutely he hears Mahler's early-morning silence. The rising sixth for two oboes in bar 15 is like a deep intake of breath from this rapt observer; the richly harmonized horns some bars later are truly *espressivo*, their dreamy reverie broken only by the sudden *ff* pizzicatos (like a startled animal) which Bernstein points up so vividly a bar later. You will love, too, the way in which the chiming harp tells as we move into the uneasy middle section: the chilling entry of tuba and bass drum at fig 13 casts an appropriately long, ominous shadow across the proceedings.

All this is most beautifully and subtly chronicled by the Concertgebouw players. How warmly and generously their strings phrase the wayfarer's music: it takes a great Mahler orchestra and a great Mahler conductor to imply so much suppleness and freedom within the bar without actually labouring the rubato. Their exhilaration in the coda (the euphoric explosion of brass fanfares is hair-raising) is second to none, and again it is the way in which the phrasing spontaneously sings that proves so uplifting. Needless to say, Bernstein gilds the proverbial lily somewhat in the Trio: 'Viennese' isn't the word, and he obviously believes (and why not?) that Mahler simply felt it unnecessary to mark in all the *portamento* – the opening violin phrases being one case in point. There has never been an account of the finale like this one. Masterly control and abandon (such as could only happen in a live performance) go hand in hand: the ferocious onslaught of the opening pages, the touch of rhetoric in the brass declamations of bars 6 and 19, the intense energy in the strings. Then, in repose, the lovingly attended second subject where Bernstein's light and shade in phrasing and dynamics is uniquely affecting. And so on to the tumultuous conclusion. Impressively recorded, this is an almost impossible act to follow.

Symphony No 2

Awards 1988

Arleen Auger *sop* **Dame Janet Baker** *mez*
City of Birmingham Symphony Chorus and Orchestra / Sir Simon Rattle
EMI ② CDS7 47962-8 (86 minutes: DDD) Ⓕ
Text and translation included.
Recorded 1986 ●●●

Where Simon Rattle's interpretation is concerned, we must go into the realm of a giant Mahlerian like Klemperer. For we are dealing here with conducting akin to genius, with insights and instincts that cannot be measured with any old yardstick. Rattle's sense of drama, of apocalyptic events, is so strong that at the final chords one is awed. None of this could have been achieved, of course, without the CBSO, which here emerges as an orchestra of world class. With such supple and rich string-playing, such expressive woodwind and infallibly accurate and mellow-toned brass, could anyone, coming upon this recording unawares, be blamed for identifying these players as belonging to Vienna, Berlin or Chicago? Attention to dynamics is meticulous throughout and contributes immeasurably to the splendour of the performance. A double *pianissimo* is really that, so when triple *forte* comes along its impact is tremendous. Some of the outstanding features of the performance can be pinpointed: the haunting beauty of the *portamento* horn-playing and the strings' sensitive and perfectly graded *glissandos* at fig 23; the magical entry of flute and harps just after fig 3 in the second movement (and, incidentally, the two harps really sound like two throughout, which is rarer than one might think); and the frightening eruption of the two *fortissimo* drum notes just after fig 51 in the same movement. Then, in the finale, there are the superb woodwind trills, the sense of mounting terror at fig 8. Dame Janet Baker is at her most tender in 'Urlicht', with Arleen Auger as the soul of purity in the finale. The CBSO Chorus is magnificent. Indeed the whole finale is an acoustic triumph. This in a spiritual class of its own and the recording is superb.

Symphony No 2
Elisabeth Schwarzkopf *sop* **Hilde Rössl-Majdan** *mez* **Philharmonia Chorus and Orchestra / Otto Klemperer**
EMI Great Recordings of the Century CDM5 67235-2 Ⓜ
(72 minutes: ADD). Text and translation included. ●

You emerge from Klemperer's first movement unharrassed, unbruised, unsettled in the knowledge that this extraordinary music has something much more to yield. You miss those elements of high-risk, the brave rhetorical gestures, the uncompromising extremes, in Klemperer's comparatively comfortable down-the-line response. He knocks minutes off most of the competition (yes, it is a fallacy that Klemperer was always slower), paying little or no heed to Mahler's innumerable expressive markings in passages which have so much to gain from them. Take, for example, the magical shift to remote E major with the *ppp* emergence of the second subject where Klemperer allows himself no lassitude whatsoever in the rubato despite Mahler's explicit requests to the contrary. Likewise the grisly procession of cellos and basses which begins the approach to the awesome climax of the development. How little Klemperer makes of their cadaverous first entry or Mahler's long backward glance just prior to the coda.

But then, come the deceptive second movement minuet, something happens, the performance really begins to find its space. Klemperer's scherzo is ideally big-boned with fine rollicking horns and a lazy trio with lovely old-world close-harmony trumpets. And the finale, growing more and more momentous with every bar, is possessed of a unique aura. Not everyone is convinced by Klemperer's very measured treatment of the Judgement Day march. The grim reaper takes his time but the inevitability of what is to come is somehow the more shocking as a result. Klemperer's trumpets peak thrillingly in the bars immediately prior to the climax itself – and what a seismic upheaval (literally terrific) he and his orchestra pull off at this point. The rest is sublime: marvellous spacial effects, off-stage brass and so on, an inspirational sense of the music burgeoning from the moment the chorus breathe life into Klopstock's Resurrection Ode. It a pity that in those days so many technical blemishes were allowed to make it through to the final master (the glaringly early bassoon entry in bar 12 of the first movement, for example), though EMI's digital remastering of this almost legendary reading is superb.

Symphony No 3

Norma Procter *contr* **Wandsworth School Boys' Choir; Ambrosian Singers; London Symphony Orchestra / Jascha Horenstein**
Unicorn-Kanchana Souvenir ② UKCD2006/7
(97 minutes: ADD). Text and translation included. Ⓜ
Recorded 1970 ●

Horenstein's interpretation of the Third Symphony is an outstanding example and its reissue on CD at mid-price is a major addition to the Mahler discography. No other conductor has surpassed Horenstein in his total grasp of every facet of the enormous score. Even though the London Symphony Orchestra strings of the day were not as powerful as they later became, they play with suppleness and a really tense sound, especially appropriate in the kaleidoscopic first movement, where changes of tempo and mood reflect the ever-changing face of nature. Horenstein gives the posthorn solo to a flügelhorn, a successful experiment. His light touch in the middle movements is admirable, and Norma Procter is a steady soloist in 'O Mensch! Gib acht!', with the Wandsworth School Boys' Choir bimm-bamming as if they were all Austrian-born! Then comes the *Adagio* finale, its intensity and ecstasy sustained by Horenstein without dragging. The recording is not as rich as more recent ones, but it is still a classic.

Symphony No 3. Four Rückert Lieder. Kindertotenlieder
Martha Lipton *mez* **Dietrich Fischer-Dieskau** *bar* **Women's chorus of the Schola Cantorum; Boys' Choir of the Transfiguration; New York Philharmonic Orchestra / Leonard Bernstein**
Sony Classical ② SM2K61831 (142 minutes: ADD). Ⓜ
Recorded 1962.

Few who experienced Bernstein's passionate advocacy of Mahler's musical cause in the 1960s were left untouched by it. These recordings date from those years and the flame of inspiration still burns brightly about them almost 40 years later. The CBS recordings were clearly manipulated, but the sound – at best, big and open but trenchant and analytically clear – suited Mahler's sound world especially well. Bernstein's account of the Third Symphony is as compelling an experience and as desirable a general recommendation now as when it first appeared. The New Yorkers are on scintillating form under the conductor they have most obviously revered in the post-war period. This is a classic account, by any standards. Bernstein himself is a subtle and self-effacing pianist. Fischer-Dieskau scales the musical heights in several of the *Rückert* Lieder.

Symphony No 4

Symphony No 4[a]. Lieder eines fahrenden Gesellen[b]
[a]**Judith Raskin** *sop* [b]**Frederica von Stade** *mez* [a]**Cleveland Orchestra / George Szell;** [b]**London Philharmonic Orchestra / Sir Andrew Davis**
Sony Classical Essential Classics SBK46535 Ⓑ
(75 minutes: ADD/DDD). Recorded 1966 ●●

Collectors who waited for years in anticipation of the reappearance on CD of Szell's famous Cleveland Fourth Symphony will not be disappointed. Sony Classical has come through with a pristine digital remastering of the open and exceptionally well-balanced Columbia original. Some hardening of tone under pressure was always a problem, even on LP, but on the whole you would never credit that this was a 1960s recording. As to the performance, the assurance and precision of its execution is something quite remarkable – an orchestra in the very peak of condition: ensemble absolutely unanimous, rubato finely turned to a man, not a blemish in earshot. There is no better tribute to Szell's achievements in Cleveland. Some people have found it dispassionate and calculated in effect and would willingly sacrifice some of the precision for a greater sense of spontaneity at the moment of performance (Szell was always at his best in the concert hall). That's a very subjective reaction, of course, and the cool, pellucid beauty of Szell's Cleveland strings in the slow movement is beyond dispute. The *Lieder eines fahrenden Gesellen* are strong and characterful readings which will provide much pleasure. They sound fresh and alert, and the tone colouring is quite beautifully controlled.

Symphony No 4
Kathleen Battle *sop*
Philharmonic Orchestra / Lorin Maazel
Sony Classical SMK39072 (61 minues: DDD). Ⓜ
Recorded 1983 ●●

Kathleen Battle sings the symphony's rapt coda in a consciously intimate manner which might roughly be dubbed the 'Listen with Mother' style. By that, no offence is intended. Maazel's version is a very inward-looking one, and in saying that we merely point to the fact that it is a very Viennese performance; in Vienna, Mahler's Vienna or Maazel's introspection is an unavoidable condition of being. What's more, only in Vienna will you hear string and, in its special way, wind playing such as is provided here for Maazel in the long-drawn slow movement – it is simply 22-and-a-half minutes of unadulterated pleasure. Maazel has always conducted the symphony's first movement in a relaxed, springy, Bruno Walter-ish way. Away from the score, the ear that is innocent of Mahler's many abstruse changes of tempo may think them rather artificial; but the playing of the VPO is such that one listens, hypnotized. It is difficult not to be tempted by the general ease, introspection and near-morbid nostalgia of the Maazel. The sound, as you would expect of a recording made in Vienna's Musikvereinsaal, is very satisfying.

Symphony No 4
Amanda Roocroft *sop*
City of Birmingham Symphony Orchestra / Sir Simon Rattle
EMI CDC5 56563-2 (59 minutes: DDD). Ⓕ
Recorded 1997

Rattle springs two big surprises in the first four bars. The first tempo might initially strike you as *over*cautious, but check Mahler's score, and note the words: *Bedachtig – Nicht eilen* ('Cautious; prudent – don't hurry'). In keeping with the accepted view among seasoned Mahlerians that the *poco ritard* in the third bar does not apply to the sleigh bells, Rattle then effects a fleeting moment of disarray as the bells jangle roughshod over this elegant turn into the first theme. A gauche, childlike moment. But then comes the real surprise. The tempo for this charming theme-with-airs (marked *gemachlich* – 'leisurely') is faster, not slower, than the opening tempo. Leisurely, yes, but eager too. The adventure playground of Mahler's youth is up and running. The benefits of this become plainer as the movement unfolds. The second subject sounds completely new (the CBSO cellos manage to persuade us that they've only just discovered it). The first horn is youth's magic horn, the woodwinds beckon raucously. And all the while those startling swings of mood and manner just happen – no rhyme, no reason; just a child's fancy. But beware the bogeyman fiddler. His dance of death – all the sharper, all the more sour (remember he's tuned up a tone) for being so flatly dispatched – comes as a timely reminder that childhood fears are no less real for being the stuff of fairy-tales. Rattle contrasts this beautifully with the rubicund Trio. The transfiguration at its heart, swathed in woozy *portamento*, is quite simply gorgeous. So, too, the opening of the slow movement, the cellos' legato so fine as to suggest little or no contact with the strings. Rattle's reading is perhaps the most inquisitive (and therefore the most intriguing) of recommendable versions.

Symphony No 5

New Philharmonia Orchestra / Sir John Barbirolli
EMI CDM5 66910-2 (74 minutes: ADD). Ⓜ
Recorded 1969 **OO**

Sir John Barbirolli's Fifth occupies a special place in everybody's affections: a performance so big in spirit and warm of heart as to silence any rational discussion of its shortcomings. Some readers may have problems with one or two of his sturdier tempos. He doesn't make life easy for his orchestra in the treacherous second movement, while the exultant finale, though suitably bracing, arguably needs more of a spring in its heels. But against all this, one must weigh a unity and strength of purpose, an entirely idiomatic response to instrumental colour and texture (the dark, craggy hues of the first two movements are especially striking); and most important of all that very special Barbirollian radiance, humanity – call it what you will. One point of interest for collectors – on the original LP, among minor orchestral mishaps in the *Scherzo*, were four bars of missing horn obbligato (at nine bars before fig 20). Not any more! The original solo horn player, Nicholas Busch, has returned to the scene of this momentary aberration (Watford Town Hall) and the absent bars have been ingeniously reinstated. There's even a timely grunt from Sir John, as if in approval. Something of a classic, then; EMI's remastering is splendid.

Symphony No 5
Royal Philharmonic Orchestra / Daniele Gatti
Conifer Classics 75605 51318-2 (70 minutes: DDD). Ⓕ
Recorded 1997 **O**

Don't let the very opening put you off. Daniele Gatti's Mahler is an expertly prepared eruption of youthful enthusiasm, a display of heart-on-sleeve lyricism. He takes his cue from Mahler's injunction that the upbeat triplets of the trumpet theme should be played somewhat hurriedly, in the manner of military fanfares, and throughout the movement he is wont to place the material in inverted commas. In the subsequent movements, no one is likely to confuse Gatti's flexible rubato with mere mannerism. The wide dynamic range is impressive but subtlety of inflexion is the conductor's trump card. So while the second movement is an almost frantic and at times formidably loud *tour de force*, the famous *Adagietto* is uncommonly slow and sensitive. For the most part, too, Gatti coaxes a properly middle-European sound out of his wind and brass, and, if the RPO's strings cannot yet match those of Vienna, Berlin or Amsterdam, their sound is nevertheless surprisingly full and rich. Indeed, the musicians sound so grandly confident that the few lapses that are evident seem worse than they are. The finale is again thrillingly extrovert, quite without heaviness. In short, this is something of a triumph for all concerned. The production team makes the very best of London's Henry Wood Hall. Above all else, Gatti deserves high praise for what must be counted the freshest, most natural-sounding Fifth that we have had for a long time.

Symphony No 5
Vienna Philharmonic Orchestra / Leonard Bernstein
DG 423 608-2GH (75 minutes: DDD). Ⓕ
Recorded live in 1987 **OO**

Bernstein's tempo for the Funeral march in the first movement of the Fifth Symphony became slower in the 23 years that separated his New York CBS recording from this one, made during a performance in Frankfurt. The strings only passage at fig 15 in the first movement is exquisitely played, so is the long horn solo in the *Scherzo*. And there is one marvellously exciting moment – the right gleam of trumpet tone at one bar before fig 29 in the second movement. Best of all is Bernstein himself, here at his exciting best, giving demonic edge to the music where it is appropriate and building the symphony inexorably to its final triumph.

Thanks to a very clear and well-balanced recording, every subtlety of scoring, especially some of the lower strings' counterpoint, comes through as the conductor intended. One is made aware of the daring novelty of much of the orchestration, of how advanced it must have sounded in the early years of this century. Here we get the structure, the sound and the emotion. The *Adagietto* is not dragged out, and the scrupulous attention to Mahler's dynamics allows the delightfully silken sound of the Vienna strings to be heard to captivating advantage, with the harp well recorded too. Bernstein is strongest in Mahler when the work itself is one of the more optimistic symphonies with less temptation for him to add a few degrees more of *Angst*.

Symphony No 5
Berlin Philharmonic Orchestra / Claudio Abbado
DG 437 789-2GH (69 minutes: DDD). Ⓕ
Recorded live in 1993 ●●

The *Adagietto* is suddenly, almost imperceptibly, there. It is the hallmark of any great performance of the symphony, and Abbado is in among the very select few as these magical bars materialize. It might even be the most beautiful, the most subtly inflected account of the movement we have yet heard on disc. How spontaneously the restless heart leaps with Mahler's central diversion; the breathless *pianopianissimo* to a barely grazed *glissando* towards the close is out of this world. So too the huge central *Scherzo*, another of those testing movements separating natural Mahlerians from the would-bes. The key here is patience – respect for space, silence, atmosphere. And the charm. Not even Bernstein quite matches Abbado's relish of the finale's airborne fantasy: it's that delicate balance between tip-toeing sweetness and light and inherently rugged, foot-stomping good humour. Abbado takes an appreciably more dispassionate view of the first movement than Bernstein (doesn't everybody?). Abbado steps back from the tragedy, his funeral march determined to keep up appearances, maintain dignity, the voice (so to speak) cracking only under the stress of Mahler's accentuation. There's a suitably rash development and a splendidly morbid military wind band sound when the march returns centre-stage. Bernstein is at his most wilfully exciting in the second movement. And fine though Abbado is, no one peaks at the climax – the shining trumpet-led premonition of the finale's chorale – quite like Bernstein. Both are special performances (nothing less could challenge the supremacy of Bernstein), both conductors and both orchestras right inside the spirit and sound of this score.

Symphony No 6

Symphony No 6. Kindertotenlieder
Thomas Hampson *bar* **Vienna Philharmonic Orchestra / Leonard Bernstein**
DG ② 427 697-2GH2 (115 minutes: DDD). Ⓕ
Recorded live in 1988 ●

Mahler's tragic Sixth Symphony digs more profoundly into the nature of man and Fate than any of his earlier works, closing in desolation, a beat on the bass drum, a coffin lid closing. Bernstein's reading was at a concert, with all the electricity of such an occasion, and the VPO responds to the conductor's dark vision of Mahler's score with tremendous bravura. Fortunately, the achingly tender slow movement brings some relief, but with the enormous finale lasting over 30 minutes we must witness a resumption of a battle to the death. The coupling is a logical one, for the *Kindertotenlieder* takes up the theme of death yet again. But it is in a totally different, quieter way: these beautiful songs express a parent's grief over the loss of a child, and although some prefer a woman's voice, the sensitive Thomas Hampson makes a good case here for a male singer. The recording of both works is so good one would not know it was made 'live', particularly as the applause is omitted.

Symphony No 6[a]. Kindertotenlieder[b]. Rückert-Lieder[c]
[bc]**Christa Ludwig mez Berlin** [a]**PhilharmonicOrchestra / Herbert von Karajan**
DG The Originals ② 457 716-2GOR2 Ⓜ
(129 minutes: ADD). Recorded 1974-75 ●●

Karajan's classic Sixth confirmed his belated arrival as a major Mahler interpreter. Only Bernstein, in his more emotive, less consciously beautifying way, left recorded performances of comparable strength and conviction. Karajan's understanding of Mahler's sound world – its links forward to Berg, Schoenberg and Webern as opposed to retrospective links with Wagner – is very acute. Combining this with a notable long-term control of rhythm, Karajan is sustains not only the composer's lucidly stated tragic case but also Mahler's exploration of materials drawn from different sound worlds and even, in the Scherzo, from different areas of the inherited musical tradition. This Scherzo is a masterly achievement by composer, conductor, and orchestra alike. Also, the engineers have tidied up the very end of the symphony, where the bass tuba's entry over drum and *ff pizzicato* basses no longer betrays quite so obviously its origin as part of a separate take. The *Rückert Lieder* are memorably sung by Christa Ludwig who is eloquently supported by the Berlin wind players who are recorded with gratifying immediacy.

Symphony No 7

Chicago Symphony Orchestra / Claudio Abbado
DG Masters 445 513-2GMA (79 minutes: DDD). Ⓕ
Recorded 1984 **OO**

Abbado's account of Mahler's Seventh Symphony was always a highlight of his cycle and remains the ideal choice for collectors requiring a central interpretation in modern sound. Steering a middle course between clear-sightedness and hysteria, and avoiding both the heavy, saturated textures of 19th-century romanticism and the chilly rigidity of some of his own 'modernist' peers, he is, as the original review reported, 'almost too respectable'. That said, it is all to the good if the forthright theatricality and competitive instincts of the Chicago orchestra are held in check just a little. Even where Abbado underplays the drama of the moment, a sufficient sense of urgency is sustained by a combination of well-judged tempos, marvellously graduated dynamics and precisely balanced, ceaselessly changing textures. For those put off by Mahler's supposed vulgarity, the unhurried classicism of Abbado's reading may well be the most convincing demonstration of the music's integrity. This is a piece Abbado continues to champion in concert with performances at the very highest level.

Symphony No 7
New York Philharmonic Orchestra / Leonard Bernstein
Sony Classical Bernstein Century Edition SMK60564 Ⓜ
(80 minutes: ADD). Recorded 1965

We are often assured that great conductors of an earlier generation interpreted Mahler from within the Austrian tradition, encoding a sense of nostalgia, decay and incipient tragedy as distinct from the in-your-face calamities and neuroses proposed by Leonard Bernstein. Well, this is one Bernstein recording that should convince all but the most determined sceptics. It deserves a place in anyone's collection now that it has been transferred to a single disc at mid-price. The white-hot communicative power is most obvious in the finale which has never sounded more convincing than it does here; the only mildly questionable aspect of the reading is the second *Nachtmusik*, too languid for some. The transfer is satisfactory, albeit dimmer than one might have hoped. It sounds historic, but historic in more ways than one.

Symphony No 7
City of Birmingham Symphony Orchestra / Sir Simon Rattle
EMI CDC7 54344-2 (77 minutes: DDD). Ⓕ
Recorded live in 1991 **O**

You may wonder about the choice of venue – The Maltings, Snape: a great sounding hall – one of the most natural and focused in the world – but for Mahler? Well, there are times here where the hefty tuttis of the outer movements sound fit to burst at the seams. The tonal quality is first-class, the immediacy is to some extent exciting; one can see right into the phantasmagorical scoring of the inner movements – a clear, gently ambient sound serving both intimacy and atmosphere. Last things first. The finale is for once a sensation. From the quasi baroque splendour of the opening procession right through to a coda which truly flings wide its glorious excess (outreaching trumpets, horns and celestial cowbells), the adrenalin really pumps. Rattle pulls off a mad kind of coherence, a wholeheartedly vulgar apotheosis of Viennese dance with no apologies for Mahler's seemingly irrational changes of gear and direction. Even the most unruly transitions are met head-on with ferocious energy (the only way), episodes falling over each other in the jostling for centre-stage. The characterization is acute, the colours wonderfully garish (just listen to the squally clarinet trills at 2'48" – hair-raising). Mahler was not one to mince his notes, and neither is Rattle.

Not even Bernstein is as uncompromising in the *Scherzo*. The nightmare comes quickly into focus: the shrieking *glissando* on two clarinets at 00'28" is at once surreal, a flash of grinning skull behind the face. Rapier violin *sforzandos* claw the texture, an emaciated string bass slithers from behind a bellowing tuba, the contra-bassoon grunts and snorts, the strings really relish their grotesque waltz. The dynamic extremes are vicious. Rattle is unique in making it sound thus. On either side of these grisly goings on, the two *Nachtmusiks* could hardly be more beguiling. Poetic sonorities abound. Only the first movement slightly disappoints. Structurally, sonically, it is impressive – organic and elemental. The CBSO violins are right inside that second subject and as harps draw back the veil on Mahler's central idyll, they could hardly sing more sweetly. But whilst Rattle pulls off the somewhat corny recapitulation with aplomb, there isn't the almost euphoric release that one experiences with Bernstein. But trombones proudly take command in the coda and the first trumpet's fearless ascent to his high-stopped *f* into Tempo 1 brings a genuine tingle of excitement. Few orchestras play the score this well; few conductors have explored it so exhaustively. Against these considerations, any reservations count for little.

Symphony No 8

Heather Harper, Lucia Popp, Arleen Auger *sops* **Yvonne Minton** *mez* **Helen Watts** *contr* **René Kollo** *ten* **John Shirley-Quirk** *bar* **Martti Talvela** *bass* **Vienna Boys' Choir; Vienna State Opera Chorus; Vienna Singverein; Chicago Symphony Orchestra / Sir Georg Solti**
Decca 460 972-2DM (80 minutes: ADD). Text and Ⓜ
translation included. Recorded 1971 **OO**

Of the so-called classic accounts of the Eighth Symphony, it is Solti's which most conscientiously sets out to convey an impression of large forces in a big performance space, this despite the obvious resort to compression and other forms of gerrymandering. Whatever the inconsistencies of Decca's multi-miking and overdubbing, the overall effect remains powerful even today. The remastering has not eradicated all trace of distortion at the very end and, given the impressive flood of choral tone at the start of the 'Veni creator spiritus', it still seems a shame that the soloists and the Chicago brass are quite so prominent in its closing stages. As for the performance itself, Solti's extrovert way with Part 1 works tremendously without quite erasing memories of Bernstein's ecstatic fervour. In Part 2, it may be the patient Wagnerian mysticism of Tennstedt that sticks in the mind. Less inclined to delay, Solti makes the material sound more operatic. Yet for its gut-wrenching theatricality and great solo singing, Solti's version makes a plausible first choice – now more than ever. Also, it has been squeezed onto a single CD, albeit at premium price.

Awards 1987

Symphony No 8 $

Elizabeth Connell, Edith Wiens, Dame Felicity Lott *sops* **Trudeliese Schmidt, Nadine Denize** *contrs* **Richard Versalle** *ten* **Jorma Hynninen** *bar* **Hans Sotin** *bass* **Tiffin Boys' School Choir; London Philharmonic Choir and Orchestra / Klaus Tennstedt**

HMV Classics ② HMVD5 73068-2 Ⓑ
(82 minutes: DDD). Notes included.
Recorded 1986 OOO

Mahler's extravagantly monumental Eighth Symphony, which is often known as the *Symphony of a Thousand*, is the work that raises doubts in even his most devoted of admirers. Its epic dimensions, staggering vision and sheer profligacy of forces required make it a 'difficult work'. Given a great live performance it will sway even the hardest of hearts; given a performance like Tennstedt's, reproduced with all the advantages of CD, home-listeners, too, can be mightily impressed (and so, given the forces involved, will most of the neighbourhood!) – the sheer volume of sound at the climax is quite overwhelming. The work seeks to parallel the Christian's faith in the power of the Holy Spirit with the redeeming power of love for mankind and Tennstedt's performance leaves no doubt that he believes totally in Mahler's creation. It has a rapt, almost intimate, quality that makes his reading all the more moving. The soloists are on excellent form and the choruses sing with conviction.

Symphony No 8 H

Joyce Barker, Beryl Hatt, Agnes Giebel *sops* **Kerstin Meyer** *mez* **Helen Watts** *contr* **Kenneth Neate** *ten* **Alfred Orda** *bar* **Arnold Van Mill** *bass* **BBC Chorus; BBC Choral Society; Goldsmith's Choral Union; Hampstead Choral Society; Emanuel School Boys' Choir; Orpington Junior Singers; London Symphony Orchestra / Jascha Horenstein**

BBC Legends/IMG Artists ② BBCL4001-7 (101 minutes: ADD). Recorded live in 1959. Includes an interview with Jascha Horenstein by Alan Blyth Ⓜ

This is the first official release of Jascha Horenstein's celebrated Royal Albert Hall concert of March 20, 1959. It was a curtain-raiser for the centenary cycle mounted by the BBC at the behest of Robert Simpson. The work had been given before in the UK under Sir Henry Wood and Sir Adrian Boult, but it was the present performance that began the indigenous Mahler boom, transfixing not only the nearly 6000 enthusiasts who packed the hall but a wider listenership beyond. When Leonard Bernstein came to conduct and record the work in London a few years later, the groundwork had already been laid. Not that Horenstein was a Mahlerian of the modern age. A conductor steeped in the German tradition, he made his début in the 1920s with the Vienna Symphony Orchestra in a programme that included Mahler's First Symphony. He brings to his readings of the composer a weight and certainty that can initially disappoint those accustomed to a more thrustful approach. In other words, don't be put off by the apparently lukewarm opening, the English choral society coloration of the choirs and the dodgy contribution of the second soprano. The performance quickly finds its feet and acquires its own metaphysical brand of tension. Part 2 is if anything even finer. The orchestral preamble is superbly wrought.

There are some incidental problems, but these are scarcely worth mentioning when the cumulative power of the final build-up is so immense and the recording expands so impressively, encompassing an authentic blaze of choral sonority. For once the Royal Albert Hall really comes into its own, and the transfer is better than one dared hope. The coughers are sometimes intrusive, yet there are aspects of Horenstein's performance that no studio-made version can quite rival. This was his finest hour and happily the two-CD set includes a vintage interview to put the achievement in context; there are also authoritative booklet-notes by Bernard Keeffe.

Symphony No 9

Awards 1984

Berlin Philharmonic Orchestra / Herbert von Karajan

DG Karajan Gold ② 439 024-2GHS2 Ⓕ
(85 minutes: DDD)
Recorded live in 1982 OOO

Awards 1981

Symphony No 9. Kindertotenlieder. Five Rückert-Lieder

Christa Ludwig *mez* **Berlin Philharmonic Orchestra / Herbert von Karajan**

DG Double ② 453 040-2GTA2 Ⓜ
(132 minutes: ADD)
Recorded 1979-80 OOO

Mahler's Ninth is a death-haunted work, but is filled, as Bruno Walter remarked, 'with a sanctified feeling of departure'. Rarely has this symphony been shaped with such understanding and played with such selfless virtuosity as it was by Herbert von Karajan and the BPO. Choice between the 1982 Karajan classic and the analogue studio recording is by no means easy. Both versions won *Gramophone* Awards in their day, but, whereas the low-profile, mid-price reissue of the analogue LP has Christa Ludwig's magisterial *Kindertotenlieder* and *Rückert-Lieder*, the live account preserves the look and price bracket of the original package. There is no extra music. The performance remains a remarkable one, with a commitment to lucidity of sound and certainty of line. There is nothing dispassionate about the way the Berlin Philharmonic tears into the *Rondo-Burleske*, the agogic touches of the analogue version ironed out without loss of intensity. True, Karajan does not seek to emulate the passionate immediacy of a Barbirolli or a Bernstein, but in his broadly conceived, gloriously played *Adagio* the sepulchral hush is as memorable as the eruptive climax. The finesse of the playing is of course unmatched.

For this Karajan Gold reissue, the tapes have been picked over to open up the sound and do something about the early-digital edginess of the strings. There is still some occlusion at climactic points; and if those strings now seem more 'plasticky' than fierce, it is impossible to say whether the conductor would have approved. Karajan came late to Mahler and yet, until the release of his (rather more fiercely recorded) 1982 concert relay, he seemed content to regard his earlier studio performance as perhaps his finest achievement on disc. The attraction is greatly enhanced by Christa Ludwig's carefully considered Mahler performances of the mid-1970s. The voice may not be as fresh as it was when she recorded the songs in the late 1950s, but there are few readings of comparable nobility. Ludwig articulates the text with unrivalled clarity and 'In diesem Wetter' at least is positively operatic. How much of the grand scale should be attributed to Karajan? It is difficult to say; the voice is sometimes strained by the tempos. This collection is not to be missed.

Mahler Symphony No 9
R Strauss Metamorphosen, AV142
Vienna Philharmonic Orchestra / Sir Simon Rattle
EMI ② CDS5 56580-2 (108 minutes: DDD). Ⓕ
Recorded live in 1993 and 1997

This may not be a Mahler Ninth for all seasons and all moods, but how thrilling it is to hear the score projected at white heat! Even if Sir Simon Rattle is less frankly emotive than a Barbirolli or a Bernstein, his is still a performance that goes for broke – fidgety, raw and intense. Listeners exclusively committed to the eloquent lucidity of Karajan should perhaps give it a wide berth. This is at various times the loudest, softest, fastest and slowest Mahler Ninth on disc. There are passages where the nuancing is *echt*-Viennese (with some pronounced string *portamentos*, as towards the very end of the work), others where the music is driven forward harshly and with surprising rigidity. There are big rhetorical effects which threaten to reduce a glorious symphonic canvas to a series of neurotic episodes, others where the power and commitment of the playing take the breath away. Test the waters – if you can – with the first movement. This is overwhelming, edge-of-the-seat stuff, yet ultimately a little monochrome. Despite the impulsive, agitated approach, the mood of brutal obstinacy is oppressively sustained. In music that responds equally to the tragic subjectivity of a Bernstein and the elevated sense of eternal calm evoked by Karajan, Rattle continues to press home the attack, conveying rather an unquenched commitment to life. Nor does he seek the kind of linear clarity delivered by Bruno Walter, whose remastered stereo recording is much more revealing than its previous LP incarnations. If in the final analysis, the vehemence of execution is not always allied to the generosity of spirit you find in the great performances of the past, is that any more than a recognition that we live in different times? There is little space to discuss the Strauss, except that there is a sense in which it tells the same story, abandoning the familiar berth of Karajan-inspired smoothness for altogether choppier seas. Rattle's music-making lives in the here and now and the immediacy of the performance – passionate but dry-eyed – is gripping.

Symphony No 9
Berlin Philharmonic Orchestra / Sir John Barbirolli
EMI Studio CDM7 63115-2 (78 minutes: ADD). Ⓜ
Recorded 1964
Also available on HMV Classics HMV5 74364-2 Ⓑ

This remastered transfer to CD supports the views of those who regard it as one of the classic interpretations, worthy to be ranked with Walter's and Karajan's. There is an almost imperceptible tape hiss to remind us of the recording's age; otherwise the late Kinloch Anderson's sensitive production wears well. The rapport between Sir John and the Berliners is obvious in the warmth, flexibility and richness of the playing, with the principal horn in particular movingly expressive. Barbirolli's shaping of the great first movement, like a broad arch, has all the intensity that one so admired in his conducting and also an architectural structure for which he did not always receive full credit. The savagery of the *Rondo Burleske* is a feature of this performance with Mahler's scoring sounding years ahead of its time. Barbirolli takes fewer than 23 minutes over the *Adagio*-finale, with the result that the melodic pulse never falters. The string playing here is wonderfully heartfelt.

Symphony No 10

Awards 2000

Berlin Philharmonic Orchestra / Sir Simon Rattle
EMI CDC5 56972-2 (77 minutes: DDD) Ⓕ
Recorded live in 1999

Rattle previously recorded Deryck Cooke's performing version of Mahler's incomplete 10th in June 1980 and the passionate sensitivity of his reading helped win over a sceptical public at a time when we were much less keen to tamper with the unfinished works of dead or dying artists. These days, it's almost as if we see in their unresolved tensions some prophetic vision of the life to come. Over the years, Rattle has performed the work nearly 100 times, far more often than anyone else. Wooed by Berlin, he repeatedly offered them 'Mahler ed Cooke' and was repulsed. He made his Berlin conducting début with the Sixth. But, after the announcement in June 1999 that he had won the orchestra's vote in a head-to-head with Daniel Barenboim, he celebrated with two concert performances of the 10th. It's a composite version that is presented here. As always, Rattle obtains some devastatingly quiet string playing, and technical standards are unprecedentedly high in so far as the revised performing version is concerned. Indeed, the danger that clinical precision will result in expressive coolness is not immediately dispelled by the self-confident meatiness of the violas at the start. We are not used to hearing the line immaculately tuned with every accent clearly defined. The tempo is broader than before and, despite Rattle's characteristic determination to articulate every detail, the mood is, at first, comparatively serene, even Olympian. Could Rattle be succumbing to the Karajan effect? But no – somehow he squares the circle. The neurotic trills, jabbing dissonances and tortuous counterpoint are relished as never before, within the context of a schizoid *Adagio* in which the Brucknerian string writing is never undersold.

The conductor has not radically changed his approach to the rest of the work. As you might expect, the scherzos have greater security and verve. Their strange hallucinatory choppiness is better served, although parts of the fourth movement remain perplexing despite the superb crispness and clarity of inner parts. Rattle allows himself some satiric palm-court stylization hereabouts, also pointing the parallels with the 'Trinklied' from *Das Lied*. More than ever, everything leads inexorably to the cathartic finale, brought off with a searing intensity that has you forgetting the relative baldness of the invention. Several conductors now impose a long *glissando* on the upward thrust of the heart-wrenching sigh that concludes the work; Rattle has no truck with this. But then the 10th is a work in progress in which the conductor has every right to innovate (Rattle now cuts out a drum stroke to pass seamlessly from the fourth to the fifth movement for example). Berlin's Philharmonie is not the easiest venue: with everything miked close, climaxes can turn oppressive but the results here are very credible and offer no grounds for hesitation. In short, this new version sweeps the board even more convincingly than the old. According to reports of the first night, Rattle was called back and accorded two Karajan-style standing ovations after the orchestra had left the stage. There is no applause here, but it is not difficult to imagine such a scene. Rattle makes the strongest case for an astonishing piece of revivification that only the most die-hard purists will resist. This release is strongly recommended.

Symphony No 10 (ed Cooke)
Berlin Radio Symphony Orchestra / Riccardo Chailly
Decca 466 955-2DH (79 minutes: DDD) Ⓕ
Recorded 1986 ●

This, the third incarnation of Riccardo Chailly's 1986 studio recording, is the first to fit its 79 minutes onto a single sound carrier. It's about time too, for, with James Levine (RCA – nla), Eliahu Inbal (Denon – nla) and Kurt Sanderling (never released domestically) all out of the UK catalogue, only Chailly has a real chance of threatening Sir Simon Rattle's *Gramophone* Award-winning monopoly. In terms of recorded sound, Chailly is ahead on points: his orchestra (and inevitably you'll notice his violas) may lack the deep-pile of the Berlin Philharmonic, but his strings are sympathetically laid out in the warm acoustic of the Jesus-Christus Kirche.

Interpretatively speaking, Chailly is, unsurprisingly, on the cool side, though one never has the feeling that he is merely going through the motions. Reviewing the set on its first appearance, Michael Kennedy had an intriguing take on this, suggesting that 'Chailly accepts the Tenth as a fait accompli. For him, it exists, there are no points to prove, nothing about which to be on the defensive'. Today one might add that the reticence is of a piece with what we know of Chailly's subsequent Mahler conducting, while the text itself has continued to evolve as Cooke's confederates continue their search for an ideal version. Indeed, part of the collectability of Chailly's reading, for admirers of Mahler ed Cooke, will be the many points at which he departs from Rattle's solutions and/or follows the score published in 1976 as opposed to the 1989 revision of it.

Thus, where Rattle enlivens the denouement of the first *Scherzo* with a cymbal clash, Chailly in the mid-'80s is being literal: the effect was not restored until the 1989 edition. On the other hand, Chailly gives us the chance to hear xylophone and side drum parts subsequently excised from the fourth movement. Rattle, like Sanderling, cuts out a (not-so-muffled) drum stroke to pass seamlessly from the fourth to the fifth movement; this isn't explicitly authorised score-wise, although it has made such good sense in performance that unsuspecting listeners might attribute an editing fault to the Chailly. In the finale, the Italian is not among those who underwrite the return of the *Adagio*'s dissonant 'break-down' chords with added percussion, and he surely has a point.

Swings and roundabouts? Even for those not interested in the minutiae, this represents a worthwhile addition to the collection – a Tenth to live with perhaps – and there are authoritative notes from David Matthews, one of the confederates mentioned above.

Das Lied von der Erde

Violeta Urmana *mez* **Michael Schade** *ten*
Vienna Philharmonic Orchestra / Pierre Boulez
DG 469 526-2GH (61 minutes: DDD). Text and translation included. Recorded 1999 Ⓕ

This performance can be welcomed as something quite out of the ordinary, indeed a reading to place among the best the piece has ever received. Never has the score sounded so precisely articulated, so finely balanced or so translucent. For this, equal praise should go to Boulez, to the Vienna Philharmonic and to the recording team working in the Musikvereinsaal. To that, one should add Boulez's customary command of structure and his perhaps more recently acquired ability to expound a work in hand with all his own clarity of thought while retaining its emotional content. Here, at speeds closer to those of Walter than of most modern conductors, he allows the music to speak for itself, at the same time quite avoiding the tendency to lingering and sentimentality inherent in slower performances.

The other overwhelming asset is Violeta Urmana's marvellous realisation of the mezzo songs. Not since Ludwig for Klemperer has one experienced the feeling of being enveloped by a tone at once refulgent and warm, a style well-nigh ideal in line and breath control yet at the same time deeply expressive. Phrase after phrase pours from Urmana's throat with effortless ease. She may not bring quite the emotional charge of Ferrier, even more Baker (for Leppard), to the songs but she runs them pretty close, and the great Farewell is simply heart-rending as delivered by her, Boulez and the VPO.

Schade compensates us for his slightly dry tone by his sensitive projection of the text. He is more in the vein of the incomparable Patzak for Walter and Richard Lewis for Reiner than the sappy-toned but slightly less characterful Wunderlich for Klemperer (though I still find his tempos sluggish by comparison with Walter and Reiner). Come the last song, though, Klemperer and Ludwig, and Baker with Leppard still hold sway. In any case if you want state-of-the-art sound, rather important in this work, there is no contest: Boulez wins hands down and, with the Vienna Philharmonic playing the work as to the manner born, this is a winner.

Das Lied von der Erde

Kathleen Ferrier *contr* **Julius Patzak** *ten*
Vienna Philharmonic Orchestra / Bruno Walter Ⓜ
Decca Legends 466 576-2DM (ADD).
Recorded 1952

Astonishingly, one might be in the hall with the VPO and these remarkable artists. If what we hear on this transfer from the master tapes in the fifth song is significantly different from what Bruno Walter heard as tenor, solo violin and flute raptly commune, it would be surprising. Equally astounding is the way the transferred recording conveys the weight and body of the VPO's tone. How easily can we now appreciate the passion, drive, and guile of Walter's conducting, with its subtle colourings and barely perceptible rubatos. The post-war VPO winds, the oboe especially, may strike some as curiously nasal. Yet it is the very complexity and idiosyncrasy of the orchestral timbres which help give this reading its special interest. No one has conducted or played the elusive third movement better; the pace is ideal, and Patzak outpoints every rival except possibly Wunderlich on the Klemperer recording. Beyond this there is Ferrier, an artist born to sing this music and singing it here at a time so close to her own death as to make this a truly harrowing song of farewell.

Das Lied von der Erde

Christa Ludwig *mez* **Fritz Wunderlich** *ten*
Philharmonia Orchestra, New Philharmonia Orchestra / Otto Klemperer
EMI CDM5 66892-2 (64 minutes: ADD). Ⓜ
Recorded 1964-66

In a famous BBC TV interview Klemperer declared that he was the objective one, Walter the romantic, and he knew what he was talking about. Klemperer lays this music before you, even lays bare its soul by his simple method of steady tempos (too slow in the third song) and absolute textural clarity, but he doesn't quite demand your emotional capitulation as does Walter. Ludwig does that. In the tenor songs, Wunderlich cannot match Patzak, simply because of the older singer's way with the text; 'fest steh'n' in the opening song, 'Mir ist als wie im Traum', the line plaintive and the tone poignant, are simply unsurpassable. By any other yardstick, Wunderlich is a prized paragon, musical and vocally free. So natural is the sound on the revived EMI that it easily beats the mono Decca. With voice and orchestra in perfect relationship and everything sharply defined, the old methods of the 1960s have nothing to fear here from today's competition. These two old recordings will never be thrust aside; the Walter for its authority and intensity, the feeling of being present on an historic occasion, the Klemperer for its insistent strength and beautiful singing.

Additional recommendations

Das Lied von der Erde

Baker *mez* **King** *ten* **Concertgebouw Orchestra / Haitink**
Philips 432 279-2PSL (66 minutes: ADD:10/76R). Ⓜ
Also on Philips Duo, coupled with Symphony No 9:
② 462 299 2PM2 (146 minutes: DDD: 4/99) Ⓑ
and on Eloquence 468 182-2 Ⓢ

The most compellingly individual reading of the contralto songs ever put on record, matched by Haitink's deeply felt conducting. For Janet Baker fans it will be first choice

King *ten* **Fischer-Dieskau** *bar* **Vienna Philharmonic Orchestra / Bernstein**
Decca Legends 466 381-2DM (67 minutes: ADD: 5/89R) Ⓜ

An interpretation to make the nerve-ends tingle, with some extraordinary emotional insights. Fischer-Dieskau sings magnificently and the Vienna Phil responds to Bernstein's impassioned direction with superfine playing

Hodgson *contr* **Mitchinson** *ten* **BBC Northern Symphony Orchestra / Horenstein**
BBC Legends/IMG Artists BBCL4042-2
(73 minutes: ADD: 4/00). Recorded live Ⓜ

Horenstein gives us a deeply eloquent, valedictory reading. Its sustained intensity, revelatory attention to orchestral detail and wonderful overview of the work deserves to be set beside classics by Walter, Klemperer and Reiner

Baltsa *mez* **König** *ten* **London Philharmonic Orchestra / Tennstedt**
HMV Classics HMV5 73468-2 (67 minutes: DDD: r/d).
Text and translation included. Ⓑ

The LPO under Klaus Tennstedt play with alternating intensity and delicacy throughout, and Klaus König proves one of the best tenor soloists on disc. Quite a bargain

Das klagende Lied

(complete version including 'Waldmärchen')
Susan Dunn *sop* **Markus Baur** *boy alto* **Brigitte Fassbaender** *mez* **Werner Hollweg** *ten* **Andreas Schmidt** *bar* **Städtischer Musikverein Düsseldorf; Berlin Radio Symphony Orchestra / Riccardo Chailly**
Decca 425 719-2DH (64 minutes: DDD). Text and translation included. Recorded 1989 Ⓕ

Few would realize that *Das klagende Lied* is the work of a teenager. Mahler's first significant work is as self-assured as anything he was to write in later life. Indeed enthusiastic Mahlerians will recognize here passages which crop up in other works, most notably the Second Symphony. Those same Mahlerians might not recognize much of this recording, however, since only two movements of *Klagende Lied* are usually performed: the 30-minute first movement is considered too rambling. But no one could arrive at that conclusion from this tautly directly, electrifying performance, and it contains wonderfully imaginative music, including some delightful forest murmurs.

For this movement alone this CD is a must for any Mahler fan, but more than that this is a spectacular recording of a one-in-a-million performance. The soloists, choir and orchestra achieve near perfection under Chailly's inspired direction, and the decision to substitute for the marvellous Brigitte Fassbaender a boy alto (Markus Baur) to represent the disembodied voice of the dead brother is pure genius. His weird, unnatural voice provides a moment of sheer spine-tingling drama.

Des Knaben Wunderhorn

Des Knaben Wunderhorn – Revelge[b]. Das irdische Leben[a]. Verlor'ne Müh[ab]. Rheinlegendchen[a]. Der Tamboursg'sell[b]. Der Schildwache Nachtlied[ab]. Wer hat dies Liedlein erdacht?[a]. Lob des hohen Verstandes[b]. Des Antonius von Padua Fischpredigt[b]. Lied des Verfolgten im Turm[ab]. Trost im Unglück[ab]. Wo die schönen Trompeten blasen[a]
[a]Elisabeth Schwarzkopf sop [b]Dietrich Fischer-Dieskau bar London Symphony Orchestra / George Szell
EMI Great Recordings of the Century CDM5 67236-2 (50 minutes: ADD). Texts and translations included. Ⓜ
Recorded 1968 ●●●

EMI's classic recording made in 1968 by Schwarzkopf, Fischer-Dieskau and Szell more or less puts all rivals out of court. Even those who find Schwarzkopf's singing mannered will be hard pressed to find more persuasive versions of the female songs than she gives, while Fischer-Dieskau and Szell are in a class of their own most of the time. Bernstein's CBS version, also from the late 1960s but with less spectacularly improved sound than EMI now provide, is also very fine, but for repeated listening Szell, conducting here with the kind of insight he showed on his famous Cleveland version of the Fourth Symphony, is the more controlled and keen-eared interpreter. Also, few command the musical stage as Fischer-Dieskau does in a song like 'Revelge' where every drop of irony and revulsion from the spectre of war is fiercely, grimly caught. Strongly recommended.

Lieder aus Des Knaben Wunderhorn
Jard van Nes *contr* **John Bröcheler** *bass* **Arnhem Philharmonic Orchestra / Roberto Benzi**
Ottavo OTRC79238 (55 minutes: DDD). Ⓕ
Texts included. Recorded 1992

Jard van Nes is a natural for Mahler, vocally and interpretatively. Particularly admirable is her fresh, spontaneous approach, free from both the shadow of past performance or awe before such familiar songs. She catches ideally the folk-like charm of 'Rheinlegendchen' and 'Wer hat dies Liedlein erdacht?'. She is also appropriately earthy in 'Das irdische Leben', then marvellously tender as the distant lover in 'Des Schildwache Nachtlied'. Her unadorned mastery of word and tone cannot be praised too highly – listen to the *keck* delivery of 'Verlor'ne Muh': just right – and she crowns her performance with her grave utterance in 'Urlicht'. Bröcheler is among the best, characterizing 'Lob des hohen Verstandes' with vivacity and revelling in St Antony's sermon. Benzi and his orchestra never make the mistake of over-egging the pudding. Although the detail is all clearly projected and keenly played, in a perfectly balanced recording, the music is kept on the move.

Kindertotenlieder / Rückert-Lieder

Kindertotenlieder[a]. Rückert-Lieder[b]. Lieder eines fahrenden Gesellen[a]
Dame Janet Baker *mez* **[a]Hallé Orchestra, [b]New Philharmonia Orchestra / Sir John Barbirolli**
EMI CDM5 66981-2 (65 minutes: ADD). Ⓕ
Texts and translations included ●

The songs of the *Lieder eines fahrenden Gesellen* ('Songs of a Wayfarer') are quoted from Mahler's First Symphony and the fresh, springtime atmosphere is shared by both works. The orchestration has great textural clarity and lightness of touch. The *Kindertotenlieder*, more chromatically expressive than the earlier work, tap into a darker, more complex vein in Mahler's spiritual and emotional make-up. The *Rückert-Lieder* are not a song-cycle as such but gather in their romantic awareness and response to the beauties of the poetry a unity and shape that binds them. Baker and Barbirolli reach a transcendental awareness of Mahler's inner musings. Barbirolli draws from the Hallé playing of delicacy and precision, establishing a clear case for having this CD in your collection.

Kindertotenlieder. Rückert-Lieder. Lieder eines fahrenden Gesellen. Lieder aus Des Knaben Wunderhorn – Das irdische Leben; Des Antonius von Padua Fischpredigt; Urlicht
Brigitte Fassbaender *mez* **Deutsches Symphony Orchestra, Berlin / Riccardo Chailly**
Decca 425 790-2DH (71 minutes: DDD). Ⓕ
Texts and translations included. Recorded 1988-89 ○

Fassbaender's emotionally charged way of singing is ideally matched to Mahler yet she is just as able to smile and sing gently, wittily. It is in the dramatic declamation, however, that the true flavour of her singing is caught. Throughout the *Fahrenden Gesellen* it is the immediacy, fearlessness of attack and her particular intensity, that make these readings so arresting. The swiftish speeds throughout keep sentimentality at bay; so does Chailly's and the orchestra's biting precision and light touch. Similar characteristics inform a deeply eloquent interpretation of *Kindertotenlieder*. The world-weary tone and verbal illumination in the first song catch at the heart and suggest the personal responsibility for the children's deaths on the part of the protagonist. Baker/Barbirolli, with the singer in lovely voice, must be a 'safer' recommendation than the more daring Fassbaender, but the latter is an inviting proposition – and a searing experience.

Mahler Lieder und Gesänge – No 1, Frühlingsmorgen; No 2, Erinnerung; No 3, Hans und Grethe; No 7, Ich ging mit Lust durch einen grünen Wald; No 11, Ablösung im Sommer; No 12, Scheiden und Meiden. Rückert-Lieder – Ich atmet' einem linden Duft; Liebst du um Schönheit; Blicke mir nicht in die Lieder; Ich bin der Welt abhanden gekommen
Marx Hat Dich die Liebe berhürt. Maienblüten. Und gestern hat er mir Rosen gebracht. Venetianisches Wiegenlied. Wofür **R Strauss** Acht Lieder aus Letzte Blätter, Op 10 – No 3, Die Nacht; No 8, Allerseelen. Sechs Lieder aus Lotusblättern, Op 19 – No 4, Wie sollten wir geheim sie halten; No 6, Mein Herz ist stumm. Vier Lieder, Op 27 – No 1, Ruhe, meine Seele; No 4, Morgen. Nachtgang, Op 29 No 3. Meinem Kinde, Op 37 No 3. Begegnung, AV72
Katarina Karnéus *mez* **Roger Vignoles** *pf*
EMI Debut CDZ5 73168-2 (64 minutes: DDD). Ⓑ
Recorded 1998 ○○

This is an outright winner. Karnéus's absolutely natural voice has an ideal warmth of tone and she connects completely with the text. Karnéus begins with a group that confirms her as an ideal interpreter of Strauss Lieder. She is impressive when deep feelings are invoked by the composer, as in 'Ruhe, meine Seele' and 'Morgen', and both these pieces are all the better for being given without the slow tempos and excess of sentiment commonly imposed on them today. The sincere simplicity evinced here is so much more relevant and moving, especially when the phrasing and the German is, as everywhere on the issue, so exemplary, the movement between notes, using gentle *portamento*, so admirable. In the Mahler, there's ebullience and good humour, even a smile in the voice, in 'Ich ging mit Lust' and 'Hans und Grethe', a rich vein of heartfelt, inner feeling so appropriate to 'Liebst du um Schönheit' and 'Ich bin der Welt'. Though in the latter song one misses the orchestral clothing usually encountered, Vignoles consoles us for its absence with his subtle, soft-grained, finely judged playing. Again the rich, even tone and response to the texts add an extra dimension to one's pleasure, particularly in the touching *Venetian Lullaby* which closes a profoundly satisfying programme. The recording is well balanced. The only drawback is that to get texts and translations you are directed to EMI's web site, but don't let that stop anyone acquiring this recital, a real 'must buy' for Lieder lovers.

Marin Marais French 1656-1728

GROVE *Marais, the central figure in the French bass viol school, spent his life in Paris, much of it in royal service. A pupil of Sainte-Colombe and protégé of Lully, he composed four operas (1693-1709 - notably Alcione, 1706, famous for its storm scene) that form an important link between Lully and Campra. But his greatest significance lies in his five collections of music for one to three bass viols (1686-1725), comprising over 550 pieces. As well as the usual dances, they include character pieces that are among his finest works, and they possess an eloquence and refinement of line and richness of ornamental detail that perfectly display the qualities of his instrument. The Pieces en trio (1692) are recognised as the first appearance of the trio sonata in France.*

Alcyone – Suites

Le Concert des Nations / Jordi Savall Ⓟ
Auvidis Astrée ES9945 (53 minutes: DDD). Ⓜ
Recorded 1993 ○

As one of the greatest exponents of the solo viol tradition perfected by Marais, Savall focuses his insights upon this music and interprets the scoring as Marais might have done. He experiments with all the chamber-music combinations of the day and, typically, hazards some of his own, particularly in the Chaconne. Occasionally, Savall uses winds and sometimes miscalculates his effects, as in the 'Bourrée pour les Bergers et Bergères'. His command of Maraisian ornamentation is, however, everywhere evident and indeed very welcome because of the constant melodic echoes of the solo repertoire in the opera score. With chamber music come more transparent textures, revealing the harmonic and textural richness of the post-Lullian style; cross-rhythms, syncopations and sequences have more impact. By contrast, the opera performances can often sound sluggish and four-square. Savall also includes music that was left out of the opera recording, including the delicately syncopated 'Air pour les Faunes et les Driades' from the Prologue, the exquisitely scored Sarabande, with its beautifully shaded cadences, and the Gigue from Act 1 as well as the 'Sarabande pour les Prêtresses de Junon' from Act 2. In the Prologue and the March and Air 'pour les Matelots' in Act 3, Savall orchestrates passages that were once vocal solos to maintain the proportions of the movements.

Pièces de viol

Le labyrinthe & autres histoires

Pièces de viole – Deuxième livre: Cloches ou carillon; La polonaise; Sarabande à l'espagnol; Chaconne en rondeau; Troisième livre: Plainte; La musette; La guitarre; Quatrième livre: Rondeau Le bijou; Le tourbillon; Le labyrinthe; Cinquième livre: Le tombeau pour Marais le cadet; La georgienne dite La maupertis; Le jeu du volant; Prélude en harpegement; Marche persane dite La sauvigny

Paolo Pandolfo *bass viol* **Mitzi Meyerson** *hpd* **Thomas Boysen** *theorbo/gtr*

Glossa GCD920404 (67 minutes: DDD). Ⓕ
Recorded 1999 ●●

Paolo Pandolfo stands alone in his generation as the master of his instrument and of a repertory that depends upon a deep affinity for its socio-historical context. Labyrinths form the theme of this recording: Louis XIV's passion for them, the monumental *Labyrinthe* Marais composed to amuse him, and the labyrinthine character of Marais' output when taken as a whole. Pierre Jacquier has contributed a thought-provoking essay and Pandolfo (rather courageously) offers notional monologues related to the *pièces* he selected to represent a hypothetical route through Marais' musical maze. The CD begins, appropriately enough, with a freely expressed prélude (almost *non-mesuré*) that sets the tone for the recording and ends with a playfully unstuffy performance of a chaconne. Along the way there are spine-tingling allusions to a harp, bells, a musette and a guitar; a yearning polonaise, a lascivious sarabande and a pompous Persian march. A breathless game of badminton (*Le jeu du volant*), a surgical procedure (vividly narrated in period voice by François Fauché) and a hallucinogenic whirlwind, a delicate lament and a eulogy provide momentary diversion. But in Pandolfo's hands none eclipse the dramatically conceived and passionately realized *Labyrinthe* itself.

It isn't simply that Pandolfo is completely at ease with the instrument and the idiom; he creates new sounds and new combinations of effects with his continuo forces (in *Cloches ou carillon* and *La musette*) – sounds and effects not precisely notated in the music and probably unimagined by Marais, but within the scope and idiom of the instruments. Pandolfo himself can play so softly, almost without attack, so clearly, so quickly and yet so apparently effortlessly. He can play a chord a dozen different ways, and he appears to relish the 'growl-ish' effects the lower strings of the bass viol can produce, making them sound truly beautiful and even exotic. The second viol, the harpsichord, theorbo, two baroque guitars and array of percussion instruments provide Pandolfo with an astonishingly fresh palate of instrumental colour in which to swathe his interpretations. So expertly has the ensemble been recorded that for once the CD listener can truly imagine himself among the privileged few invited to the king's private rooms at Versailles. This is a thrilling disc.

Pièces de viole, Livre 2 – Part 1: Ballet en rondeau; Couplets de folies; Prélude; Cloches ou carillon. Part 2: Prélude lentement; Chaconne en rondeau; Tombeau pour M de Ste Colombe; Prélude; Allemande; Courante; Pavan selon de goût des anciens compositeurs de luth; Gavotte; Rondeau en vaudeville; Gigue; Chaconne; Fantaisie

Markku Luolajan-Mikkola, Varpu Haavisto *vas da gamba* **Eero Palviainen** *lte* **Elina Mustonen** *hpd* Ⓕ

BIS CD909 (73 minutes: DDD). Recorded 1997

The most substantial pieces here are the set of variations of *La folia*, and the *Tombeau pour M de Ste Colombe* in memory of Marais's mentor. His idiom embodies a paradox that is peculiarly French, in that it demands a very high technical standard, yet its proper expression requires the utmost restraint. The young Finnish viol-player, Markku Luolajan-Mikkola, is a founder-member of Phantasm. Here he holds his own with elegance and reserve, although in the slower pieces one might have wished for more rhythmic flexibility. The continuo section consists of another viol-player, and a theorbo or harpsichord (though in the variations on *La folia*, the two are combined). This works well for the most part, though the high partials of the harpsichord tend to drown the viols: the lute is far less obtrusive. The problem of balance also intrudes when the soloist is in the lower range. But as an introduction to Marais's art this is hard to fault – try his Pavan 'in the style of the bygone lute composers': a real treat.

Pièces de viole, Quatrième Livre – Marche tartate; Sarabande; La tartarine; Les fêtes champêtres; Gigue la fleselle; Rondeau le bijou; Le tourbillon; L'uniforme; Allemande pour le sujet; Gigue pour la basse; Allemande l'asmatique; Muzette; Caprice ou Sonate; Le labyrinthe; Allemande la bizare; La minaudiere; Allemande la singuliere; L'arabesque; Allemande la superbe; La reveuse; Marche; Gigue; Le badinage; Deux Allemandes

Christophe Coin, Vittorio Ghielmi *bass viols* **Christophe Rousset** *hpd* **Pascal Monteilhet** *theorbo/gtr*

L'Oiseau-Lyre 458 144-2OH (78 minutes: DDD). Ⓕ
Recorded 1996

To bring the subtleties of music intended to be perceived as in a *goût étranger* to life, a performer must first master the traditional French baroque style. Christophe Coin has done that, both technically and musically, to a degree matched by no other viol player of today. This recording encompasses an astonishing range of moods and effects: he sings ('Fêtes champêtres'), he swaggers ('La fleselle'), he soars ('Caprice'). He revels in the resonance of Marais's exquisite chordal writing ('Sarabande' and 'Muzette') and takes time when it suits the music – always just the right amount (too much would sap the music, too little would betray a lack of *sensibilité* and too frequent would render his performances clichéd). He can be rhetorical ('Fêtes champêtres') but is equally at home with the saucy 'Tartarine'. He is a virtuoso of the first rank (amply in evidence in the 'Tourbillon' and the marathon 'Labyrinthe'), paying attention to the smallest detail – the syncopations of the allemandes ('L'asmatique' and 'La singuliere'), the echoes in the majestic 'Marche tartate' and the graceful 'Arabesque'. He conjures visions in the Rameau-esque 'Minaudiere' and the 'Allemande la superbe'.

Central to French viol playing is mastery of the melancholy; so much of the repertory is in minor keys and within the range of the human voice. For performers it is the most revealing of all musical 'affects' and Coin has the character and conviction never to allow it to degenerate into self-indulgence. In his hands such pieces as the rondeaux popularized in the film, *Tous les matins du monde* ('L'arabesque', 'Le reveuse' and 'Le badinage'), and 'Le bijou' are elegant and poetic. With a fine team of accompanists, Rousset (always moulding his playing to Coin's bow strokes, notably in the 'Allemande la bizare'), Ghielmi (whose shuddering low notes in the 'Rondeau le bijou' are especially effective) and Monteilhet (whose guitar playing contributes so much to the 'Sarabande'), Coin provides entertainment you will want to revisit again and again, and sets new standards for viol players today.

Luca Marenzio

Italian 1553/4-1599

GROVE *Possibly a pupil of Contino in Brescia, Marenzio moved to Rome in c1574 and served cardinals and other wealthy patrons (including Luigi d'Este) until 1586. During these years he published copiously and gained an international reputation. He travelled in 1587, visiting Verona, and briefly served Ferdinando de' Medici in Florence, where in 1589 he composed intermedi for the ducal wedding festivities. He returned to Rome later that year, residing with the Duke of Bracciano untilc 1593, when he entered Cardinal Cinzio Aldobrandini's service; he held a Vatican apartment in 1594. In 1595-6 he visited the Polish court, returning to Rome in 1598.*

One of the most prolific madrigalists of the period, Marenzio published over 400 madrigals and villanellas in at least 23 books (1580-99). They range widely, from light pastorals to serious sonnets (these mostly from later years), and are notable for their striking mood- and word-painting. They long remained popular in Italy and elsewhere, especially England. His motets, though less well known, also feature much verbal imagery and religious symbolism.

Madrigals

Madrigali a 4vv ... libro primo
Concerto Italiano (Rossana Bertini *sop* Claudio Cavina *counterten* Giuseppe Maletto *ten* Sergio Foresti *bass* Mara Galassi *hp* Andrea Damiani *lte*) / **Rinaldo Alessandrini**
Opus 111 OPS30-117 (62 minutes: DDD). Ⓕ
Texts and translations included. Recorded 1994

What Concerto Italiano reveals to us is that four-part writing in this expressive and varied milieu makes a virtue out of its limitations: Marenzio capitalizes on exposed dialogues between voices and textural brittleness. Classicism (in the broadest musical sense synonymous with four-part writing long before Bach chorales or Haydn quartets) is what Alessandrini is seeking to impart in this clear juxtaposition of fluent canzonets with intimate rhetoric. The music is so subtly shaded, both by Marenzio and the singers, that unless you are a reincarnated madrigalist this should be experienced in small doses. There is just the same commitment and concentration to the extensive detail in the music. Just observe how much care has gone into *Chi vol udire i miei sospiri in rime* with its beautifully paced *crescendo* on the word 'sospiri' (sighs), the almost imperceptible sketching of the pulse and other wonderful liberties with rhythmic inflexion. So much of this innate understanding is of course expressed through the singers' native tongue (what life those watery vowels bring to Petrarch's later-to-be-famous *Zefiro torna*) and a warm changeable Mediterranean breeze which unselfconsciously manipulates the temperature. None of this would count for much were the ensemble not highly refined in purely abstract terms and this is perhaps the best yet in that respect. Only rarely does the soprano's rich and penetrating tone cause one to worry and when it does this is usually because of a slight tendency to flatness. A small concern in a very fine release.

Frank Martin

Swiss 1890-1974

GROVE *Martin, the son of a Calvinist minister, was deeply impressed by a performance of the St Matthew Passion he heard at the age of 10. He studied with Joseph Lauber and worked from 1926 with Jaques-Dalcroze, then in his Piano Concerto no.1 (1934) and Symphony (1937) adopted Schoenbergian serialism while retaining an extended tonal harmony that looked to Debussy: the mature fusion of these elements into a style marked by dissonant chords, smooth part-writing and 'gliding tonality' did not come until the dramatic chamber oratorio Le vin herbé (1941), soon followed by two larger oratorios, In terra pax (1944) and Golgotha (1948), as well as by the Petite symphonie concertante for harp, harpsichord, piano and strings (1945) and the Sechs Monologe aus 'Jedermann' (1943, orchestrated 1949). In 1946 he moved to the Netherlands; he also taught at the Cologne Musikhochschule (1950-57). His later works include the operas Der Sturm (1956, Vienna Staatsoper) and Monsieur de Pourceaugnac (1963, Geneva), a large-scale Requiem (1972) and many concertante pieces, among them concertos for violin and harpsichord (both 1952) and a second for piano (1969).*

Maria-Triptychon

Der Sturm – Overture; Mein Ariel, hast du, der Luft nur ist; Ein feierliches Lied; Hin sind meine Zauberei'n. Maria-Triptychon. Sechs Monologe aus Jedermann
Linda Russell *sop* **David Wilson-Johnson** *bar* **Duncan Riddell** *vn* **London Philharmonic Orchestra / Matthias Bamert**
Chandos CHAN9411 (68 minutes: DDD). Ⓕ
Recorded 1994

The *Maria-Triptychon* was written in the late 1960s in response to a request from Wolfgang Schneiderhan for a work for violin, soprano and orchestra that he could perform with his wife, Irmgard Seefried. Although their recording under the composer himself emanating from a Swiss Radio tape is authoritative, it does not match this Chandos recording in sheer beauty of sound. Linda Russell sings the solo part with great sympathy and intelligence, and Duncan Riddell assumes the mantle of Schneiderhan with no mean success. The transparency of texture that the Chandos team achieves shows this visionary score in the most favourable light. It makes a stronger impression than in any earlier performance, thanks to the dedication of the LPO and its conductor. Bamert distils a strong atmosphere and sense of mystery in all these scores. David Wilson-Johnson is on impressive form in the *Jedermann* Monologues (one of the great song-cycles of the century). His is as perceptive and moving an account as any – and he is no less impressive in the magical *Der Sturm*.

Mass for Double Choir

Awards 1998

Martin Mass for Double Choir. Passacaille
Pizzetti Messa di requiem. De profundis
Westminster Cathedral Choir / James O'Donnell *org*
Hyperion CDA67017 (71 minutes: DDD) Ⓕ
Texts and translations included
Recorded 1997 ○○○

These are magnificent performances. Written in 1922, the *Agnus Dei* being added four years later, the Mass is one of Martin's most sublime compositions. Surprisingly it gains enormously from using boys' rather than female voices and although one might think women naturally score over boys in terms of understanding and maturity, it is a measure of James O'Donnell's achievement with Westminster Cathedral Choir that the gain in purity and beauty is at no time at the expense of depth and fervour. This is an altogether moving and eloquent performance, often quite thrilling and always satisfying. This disc brings us a fine performance by O'Donnell of the *Passacaille* and the Pizzetti *Messa di Requiem*, also composed in 1922. The received wisdom is that it is in his *a cappella* music that Pizzetti is at his finest and in his 1951 monograph Guido Gatti spoke of his setting as 'the most serene and lyrical of all ... from Mozart's to Gabriel Fauré's'. Serene and lyrical it most certainly is, and it will come as a revelation to those encountering it for the first time. There is a fervour and a conviction about the Westminster performances of the Requiem and the 1937 *De profundis*. The luminous tone this choir produces in both these inspired works will ring in your ears long after you have finished playing this splendidly recorded disc.

Requiem

Elisabeth Speiser *sop* **Ria Bollen** *contr* **Eric Tappy** *ten* **Peter Lagger** *bass* **Lausanne Women's Chorus; Union Chorale; Ars Laeta Vocal Ensemble; Suisse Romande Orchestra / Frank Martin**
Jecklin Disco JD631-2 (47 minutes: ADD). Text and translation included. Recorded live in 1973 Ⓕ

Astonishingly, this beautiful score still remains grievously neglected – it deserves to be heard as often as the Fauré Requiem. The work comes from Martin's last years, and was inspired, he tells us, by three cathedrals – St Mark's in Venice, the Montreale in Palermo and the Greek temples of Paestum near Naples. It is a work of vision and devotion of spirit, and casts a strong spell. It is one of those pieces that leaves you with a feeling of enormous tranquillity. The musical language is familiar enough, for there are the same subtle shifts of colour and harmony that you will find in Martin's *Petite Symphonie concertante*. However, there is a dramatic power (*Dies irae*) and a serenity (*In Paradisum*) that are quite new. The short *In Paradisum* is inspired and has a luminous quality and radiance that are quite otherworldly. Martin certainly put all his consummate musical skills into this score with organ and orchestra of equal importance. He conducts a completely dedicated and authoritative performance: it might well be improved upon in one or two places in terms of ensemble or security, but the spirit is there. The Swiss Radio recording is eminently truthful and well balanced, and offers a natural enough acoustic.

Bohuslav Martinů Bohemian 1890-1959

GROVE *Martinu studied at the Prague Conservatory (1906-10), then worked as a teacher and orchestral violinist before going to Paris in 1923. There he studied with Roussel and developed a neo-classical style, sometimes using jazz (La bagarre, 1926; Le jazz, 1928, both for orchestra). He began to apply himself to Czech subjects (ballet Špalíček, 1933; operas The Miracles of Mary, 1935, Comedy on the Bridge, 1937 ; Field Mass for male voices, wind and percussion,1939), but not exclusively: this was also the period of his fantasy opera Julietta (1938) and of numerous concertos. In 1940 he left Paris, and the next year arrived in New York, where he concentrated on orchestral and chamber works, including his first five symphonies. From 1948 his life was divided between Europe and the USA: this was the period of his Sixth Symphony (1953), Frescoes of Piero della Francesca for orchestra (1955) and opera The Greek Passion (1961). He was one of the most prolific composers of the 20th century, imaginative in style, with energetic rhythms and powerful, often dissonant harmony, but uneven in quality.*

Symphonies

Symphonies Nos 1 and 2
Bamberg Symphony Orchestra / Neeme Järvi Ⓕ
BIS CD362 (61 minutes: DDD)

Symphonies Nos 3 and 4
Bamberg Symphony Orchestra / Neeme Järvi Ⓕ
BIS CD363 (63 minutes: DDD)

Symphonies Nos 5 and 6
Bamberg Symphony Orchestra / Neeme Järvi Ⓕ
BIS CD402 (59 minutes: DDD). Recorded 1988

Despite his travels throughout his formative years as a composer, Martinů remained a quintessentially Czech composer and his music is imbued with the melodic shapes and rhythms of the folk-music of his homeland. The six symphonies were written during Martinů's America years and in all of them he uses a large orchestra with distinctive groupings of instruments which give them a very personal and unmistakable timbre. The rhythmic verve of his highly syncopated fast movements is very infectious, indeed unforgettable, and his slow movements are often deeply expressive, most potently, perhaps, in that of the Third Symphony which is imbued with the tragedy of war. The Bamberg orchestra plays marvellously and with great verve for Järvi, whose excellently judged tempos help propel the music forward most effectively. His understanding of the thrust of Martinů's structures is impressive and he projects the music with clarity. The recordings are beautifully clear, with plenty of ambience surrounding the orchestra, a fine sense of scale and effortless handling of the wide dynamic range Martinů calls for. It is enthusiastically recommended.

Further Listening
Madetoja Symphonies Nos 1-3
Couplings: Comedy Overture. Kullervo. The Ostrobothnians – Suite. Okon Fuoko – Suite.
Finnish Radio Symphony Orchestra / Segerstam; Tampere Philharmonic Orchestra / Rautio
Finlandia ② 4509-99967-2 (150 minutes: DDD) Ⓑ
Madetoja was a one-time pupil of Sibelius and his symphonies breathe much the same. Worth investigating.

Symphony No 4. Memorial to Lidice. Field Mass[a]
[a]**Ivan Kusnjer** *bar* **Czech Philharmonic** [a]**Chorus and Orchestra / Jirí Bělohlávek**
Chandos CHAN9138 (65 minutes: DDD). Ⓕ
Text and translation included

It is doubtful whether the luscious, intricately-scored pages of the big-hearted Fourth Symphony have ever sounded more opulent. This is, for the most part, glorious playing, intoxicating in its richness (what strings!) and sure-footed poise. Bělohlávek has an unexpectedly playful, almost balletic way with the *Scherzo*; the trio section, too, has a most appealing delicacy and engaging sense of innocence. Reservations? Well, greater bite and tighter focus to Chandos's reverberant sound picture would have been better. More crucially, though, there is some lack of intensity and temperament: you just don't sense the anguish behind the engulfing climax of the slow movement, whilst the finale could certainly do with more unbuttoned exuberance and head-spinning exhilaration. Järvi has the more winning rhythmic flair, though in terms of orchestral polish he honestly can't hold a candle to Bělohlávek's super-refined ensemble. In other words, we still await a truly convincing modern recorded account of this wonderful symphony. Bělohlávek's account of the *Field* Mass, on the other hand, is an undoubted success. It is wonderfully fervent, boasting a noble-toned, impassioned contribution from the baritone, Ivan Kusnjer, and disciplined, sonorous work from the men of the Czech Philharmonic Chorus. Chandos's recording captures it all to perfection: blend and focus impeccably combined. The moving *Memorial to Lidice* completes this ideally-chosen triptych. Bearing a dedication 'To the Memory of the Innocent Victims of Lidice', Martinů's score was written in response to the notorious mass-destruction of that village by the Nazis in June 1942. One of the composer's most deeply-felt creations, this is an eight-minute orchestral essay of slumbering power, incorporating at its climax a spine-chilling quotation from Beethoven's Fifth. It, too, receives sensitive advocacy here.

Chamber works

Piano Quartet. Quartet for Oboe, Violin, Cello and Piano Viola Sonata. String Quintet
Joel Marangella *ob* **Isabelle van Keulen, Charmian Gadd, Solomia Soroka** *vns* **Rainer Moog, Theodore Kuchar** *vas* **Young-Chang Cho, Alexander Ivashkin** *vcs* **Daniel Adni, Kathryn Selby** *pfs* Ⓢ
Naxos 8 553916 (73 minutes: DDD). Recorded 1994

The Quartet for oboe, violin, cello and piano is a highly attractive piece in the busy yet unfussy neo-classical style that Martinů made so much his own. Its opening theme is quite captivating, but all three movements have charm. The other music is hardly less delightful. The Viola Sonata is an eloquent work from the mid-1950s, composed three years after the *Rhapsody-Concerto* for the same instrument and orchestra. These were vintage years in Martinů's creativity. The String Quintet is the earliest work, dating from his Paris years, and shows the influence of Roussel. Although the first movement is perhaps not top-drawer Martinů, the slow movement is most imaginative. The performances are often touched with distinction and are never less than eminently serviceable. Adni could perhaps be a little more supple in the Piano Quartet of 1942 though in general he plays with spirit. There is plenty of air round the players and the recording is lifelike and well balanced.

Works for Violin and Piano, Volumes 1 and 2
Volume 1: Sonatas – C, H120; D minor, H152; No 1, H182. Concerto, H13. Elegy, H3. Impromptu, H166. Five Short Pieces, H184.
Volume 2: Sonatas – No 2, H208; No 3, H303. Sonatina, H262. Seven Arabesques, H201. Ariette-Vocalise, H188a. Czech Rhapsody, H307. Sept études rythmiques, H202. Intermezzo, H261. Five Madrigal Stanzas, H297
Bohuslav Matoušek *vn* **Petr Adamec** *pf*
Supraphon ② SU3412-2 (121 and 111 minutes: DDD). Recorded 1996 and 1997 Ⓕ ●

A handsome undertaking, which gathers together for the first time all 16 of Martinů's compositions for violin and piano. Supraphon's decision to present the music in more or less chronological order makes it all the easier to chart a fascinating stylistic journey spanning some 36 years. The 19-year-old Martinů wrote his impassioned *Elegy* (enigmatically subtitled 'Evil Returns') in 1909, and the comparatively straightforward violin writing contrasts dramatically with the piano's big-boned, unashamedly dramatic contribution. Strangely, the following year's Concerto proves to be anything but. Indeed, one wonders whether its title was a leg-pull on the young composer's part, for its 27-minute progress totally eschews any ostentatious display in favour of a sunny simplicity and open-hearted playfulness. With the ambitious Sonata in C from 1919, we encounter an increasing confidence and fluency, though there's still little sign of the composer's mature voice.

Volume 2 kicks off with the winsome *bonne-bouche* of 1930, the *Ariette-Vocalise*, while the following year saw the creation of the concise and poised Second Violin Sonata, *Seven Arabesques* and the similarly engaging and pithy *Sept études rythmiques* (the latter pair designed for teaching purposes). The 1937 *Sonatina*, too, was conceived for students (in this case, the very young, for it can be played entirely in first position) and radiates a treasurable serenity and joy. Likewise, the four attractive pieces that comprise the *Intermezzo* (again, from 1937) were designed for aspiring young fiddlers everywhere. Composed in New York during 1943, the *Five Madrigal Stanzas* bear an inscription to a certain amateur violinist by the name of Professor Albert Einstein. The altogether more meaty Third Sonata was penned towards the end of 1944 and possesses an impressive thematic resource and pungent emotional scope that relate it to this figure's Symphonies Nos 3-5 from the same period. That just leaves the Kreisler-dedicated *Czech Rhapsody* of 1945, an exuberant and virtuosic essay, full of unquenchable optimism. Violinist Bohuslav Matoušek and pianist Petr Adamec form a consistently stylish and sympathetic partnership, and the recordings are rich and airy to match, though piano focus could at times ideally be sharper. A notable achievement.

Piano Sonata

Bagatelle, H323. Dumka No 3, H285bis. Fantasie a toccata, H281. The Fifth Day of the Fifth Moon, H318. Piano Sonata, H350. Eight Préludes, H181
Eleonora Bekova *pf*
Chandos CHAN9655 (60 minutes: DDD). Recorded 1997-98 Ⓕ

Martinů hardly wrote the sort of music where every note is worth its weight in gold. Criticized for his failure to sense that 'all kinds of heterogeneous elements mixed together do not constitute an independent style', he unsettlingly reminds you of an actor happiest when adopting a wide variety of masks but uncomfortable when compelled to be himself. Yet, as the powerful Sonata and *Fantasie a toccata* show, Martinů was capable of a genuine eloquence and stature beyond a merely elegant and impersonal expertise. As Graham Melville-Mason tells us in his notes, the Sonata was much admired by Rudolf Serkin, who programmed it alongside Beethoven's *Hammerklavier* Sonata. Eleonora Bekova's performances show a uniform and unswerving command. Her full-blooded sonority and technique proclaim her Moscow training and, musically enriched by her success in chamber music, she makes light of every difficulty. Whether in chic Parisian asides directed at jazz and ragtime (the First and Second *Préludes*), in the greater weight and substance of the Sonata (which has, perhaps surprisingly, failed to enter the mainstream repertoire beside the sonatas of, say, Copland, Janáček, Barber and Dutilleux, for example) or in a garland of encores including the perky, tantalizingly brief *Bagatelle*, her performances are exemplary. Chandos's excellent sound, too, makes this a prime issue.

The epic of Gilgamesh

Eva Depoltová *sop* **Stefan Margita** *ten* **Ivan Kusnjer** *bar* **Ludek Vele** *bass* **Milan Karpíšek** *spkr*
Slovak Philharmonic Choir and Orchestra / Zdeněk Košler
Marco Polo 8 223316 (56 minutes: DDD). Translation included. Recorded 1989 Ⓕ ●

This is one of Martinů's greatest works, completed in 1955, a month or so before the three *Frescoes of Piero della Francesca*. It tells how Gilgamesh, King of Uruk, hears about the warrior Enkidu, a primitive, at home among the works of nature with only animals as friends. He sends him a courtesan to whom he loses his innocence; the King then befriends him but they fight before their friendship is really cemented. The second and third parts of the oratorio centre on the themes of death and immortality; the second tells of Enkidu's death and Gilgamesh's grief, his plea to the gods to restore Enkidu and his search for immortality, and the third records his failure to learn its secrets. It is almost impossible to hear the chilling episode of the last words of Enkidu's ghost ('Yes, I saw') with its subtly changing vocal colours without a feeling of awe. With its evocation of a mysterious past, use of spoken narrative and distinctive sound world, it is inevitable that it should be compared with Honegger's *Le roi David*. But *Gilgamesh* is far stronger and its invention far more sustained and powerful. The performance is in Czech as is the narration, which should not limit the dissemination of this disc, for the music deals with universal themes and is Martinů at his most profound and inspired. There are no weaknesses in the cast (the Gilgamesh of Ivan Kusnjer is very impressive), and the chorus and orchestra respond very well to Zdeněk Košler's direction. The recording maintains a natural balance, and the resonant acoustic is used to good advantage.

Giuseppe Martucci Italian 1856-1909

GROVE *Martucci studied at the Naples Conservatory. As a touring piano virtuoso, he won praise from Liszt and Anton Rubinstein in 1874, but from 1880-81 was professor of the piano (in 1902, director) at the Naples Conservatory. He was an enthusiastic conductor of the German (sometimes English and French) repertory in Naples and Bologna, where he was director of the Liceo Musicale (1886-1902). Besides piano music, he composed distinctive chamber works, often Schumannesque or Elgarian in their gentle lyricism and caprice (eg the popular Notturno, Op70 No 1, and Novelletta, Op 82 No 2); his attractive Second Symphony has been called 'the starting point of the renaissance of non-operatic Italian music'.*

Nocturne

Martucci Nocturne, Op 70 No 1.
La canzone dei ricordi
Respighi Il tramonto
Brigitte Balleys *mez* **Lausanne Chamber Orchestra / Jésus López-Cobos**
Claves CD50-9807 (51 minutes: DDD). Ⓜ
Recorded 1997

Martucci, once director of conservatoires in both Bologna and Naples, and conductor of the first performance in Italy of *Tristan*, is a curious case of a composer totally unfamiliar to the UK's concert life but surprisingly well represented on disc. His warmly nostalgic and tender *Nocturne* would make a worthy alternative to the Mahler *Adagietto* or Barber's overplayed *Adagio*; and the seven poems of his elegiac cycle, *La canzone dei ricordi* are haunting examples of a refined Italian lyricism a world away from his contemporary, Puccini. The setting of Shelley's *Il tramonto* by Martucci's pupil Respighi is suitably poignant but more lush in texture. The admirable Brigitte Balleys sings with her accustomed artistry, but from time to time her voice 'catches' the mike: the playing of the Lausanne Chamber Orchestra is seductively affectionate.

Pietro Mascagni Italian 1863-1945

GROVE *Mascagni studied with Ponchielli and Saladino at the Milan Conservatory (1882-84), then worked as a touring conductor and wrote Guglielmo Ratcliff (c1855). His next opera was the one-act Cavalleria rusticana, which was staged in Rome in 1890 and won him immediate international acclaim: it effectively established the vogue for verismo. None of his later operas was anything like so successful, though some numbers from L'amico Fritz (1891) and the oriental Iris (1898) have survived in the repertory. Later works include the comedy Le maschere (1901), the unexpectedly powerful Il piccolo Marat (1921) and Nerone (1935), this last testifying to his identification with fascism.*

Cavalleria rusticana

Renata Scotta *sop* Santuzza; **Plácido Domingo** *ten* Turiddu; **Pablo Elvira** *bar* Alfio; **Isola Jones** *mez* Lola; **Jean Kraft** *mez* Lucia **Ambrosian Opera Chorus; National Philharmonic Orchestra / James Levine**
RCA Red Seal 74321 39500-2 (71 minutes: ADD).
Notes, text and translation included. Ⓕ
Recorded 1978

This was a strong contender in an overcrowded field when it was first released. You would be hard pressed to find either a more positive or a more intelligent Turiddu or Santuzza than Domingo or Scotto. Scotto manages to steer a precise course between being too ladylike or too melodramatic. She suggests all the remorse and sorrow of Santuzza's situation without resorting to self-pity. Her appeals to Turiddu to reform could hardly be more sincere and heartfelt, her throbbing delivery to Alfio, 'Turiddi mi tolse l'honore', expresses all her desperation when forced to betray her erstwhile lover, and her curse on Turiddu, 'A te la mala pasqua', while not resorting to the lowdown vigour of some of her rivals, is filled with venom. Domingo proved how committed he was to his role when the part was first given to him at Covent Garden in the mid-1970s. He gives an almost Caruso-like bite and attack to Turiddu's defiance and (later) remorse, and finds a more appropriate timbre than Bergonzi (for Karajan on DG, reviewed under Leoncavallo). He also delivers the Brindisi with an appropriately carefree manner, oblivious of the challenge awaiting him. Pablo Elvira's Alfio is no more than adequate, and the other American support is indifferent. Levine's direction, as positive as Karajan's, is yet quite different. He goes much faster, and time and again catches the passion if not always the delicacy of Mascagni's score. He is well supported by the superb National Philharmonic Orchestra. With a bright and forward recording, this reading of the work is wholly arresting.

Cavalleria rusticana (sung in English)
Nelly Miricioiu *sop* Santuzza; **Dennis O'Neill** *ten* Turiddu; **Phillip Joll** *bar* Alfio; **Diana Montague** *mez* Lola; **Elizabeth Bainbridge** *mez* Lucia
Geoffrey Mitchell Choir; London Philharmonic Orchestra / David Parry
Chandos Opera in English CHAN3004
(79 minutes: DDD). Notes and text included. Ⓕ
Recorded 1997

One of the most magical beginnings in opera is beautifully played here, and at this early stage one is not getting restive over the slow speeds. Dennis O'Neill sings his *siciliana* like a lover, with touches of an imaginative tenderness that are rare if not unique in this music. His voice distances effectively, and very effective too is the mingling of the church bells with the singing of the off-stage chorus. Santuzza, Nelly Miricioiu, must have been born in another village, but that doesn't matter; her voice has some raw patches but that also troubles less than it might as she brings such concentrated feeling to the part. On the other hand, when the Alfio arrives one can't go on saying that it doesn't matter: it does. We want a vibrant Italianate voice if possible, and a firm one at least. Elizabeth Bainbridge is a vivid Mamma Lucia, but Diana Montague, immensely welcome as a singer, has quite the wrong voice-character for Lola, who should be either the local Carmen or a shallow, pert flirt. Still, for those collecting Chandos's Opera in English series this is not to be missed. The drama keeps its hold, the grand old melodies surge, the score reveals more of its inspired detail, and the English language (in Edmund Tracey's translation) does itself worthwhile credit.

Jules Massenet French 1842-1912

GROVE *Massenet entered the Conservatoire at the age of 11 as a piano pupil of Adolphe Laurent. He later studied harmony with Reber and composition with Ambroise Thomas, winning the Prix de Rome in 1863. In Rome he got to know Liszt and, through him, Constance de Sainte Marie, who became his pupil and, in 1866, his wife. The following year his opera La grand'tante was given at the Opéra-Comique, and in1873 Marie-Magdeleine at the Théâtre de l'Odéon initiated a series of drames sacrés based on female biblical characters. Many of his secular operas, too, are in effect portraits of women.*

In 1878 Massenet was made a teacher of composition at the Conservatoire, where he remained all his life, influencing many younger French composers, including Charpentier, Koechlin, Pierné and Hahn. In his own music he began to move away from the suave, sentimental melodic style derived from Gounod and to adopt a more Wagnerian type of lyrical declamation. The change is apparent in Manon (1884), which placed Massenet in the forefront of French opera composers, and still more in Werther (1892).

But as early as 1877, in Hérodiade, Massenet had begun to modify the symmetry and loosen the syntax of his melodies to give them a more speaking, intimate, conversational character. Repetitions are usually masked or transferred to the orchestra while the voice takes a lyrical recitative line in the Wagnerian manner; literal repetitions are carefully calculated to provide an insistent, emotional quality. Often his melodies have a swaying, hesitant character (9/8 or 6/8) – first and most effectively used in Act 1 of Manon to express a girl's hesitant yet delighted awareness of her own charms. By Werther, the relationship of voice and orchestra is more sophisticated, and that opera contains clear examples of Massenet's dissolution of formal melody into rhapsodic recitative-like writing as evolved by Wagner. Massenet's music is harmonically conservative, rarely venturing beyond modest chromaticisms; rhythmically, it is original in the variations he uses to give the melody a more caressing, intimate character. He had a characteristically French ear for orchestral nuance. Though primarily a lyrical composer, he was also a master of scenes of action, as for example at the opening of Manon.

After Sapho (1897) Massenet scored few major successes. His conception of opera became outdated long before his death and his position as France's leading opera composer was finally challenged when Debussy's Pelléas et Mélisande was given at the Opéra-Comique in 1902.

Don Quichotte

Don Quichotte[a]. Scènes alsaciennes[b]
Nicolai Ghiaurov *bass* Don Quichotte; **Régine Crespin** *sop* Dulcinée; **Gabriel Bacquier** *bar* Sancho Panza; **Michèle Command** *sop* Pedro; **Annick Dutertre** *sop* Garcias; **Peyo Garazzi** *ten* Rodriguez; **Jean-Marie Fremeau** *ten* Juan
[a]**Suisse Romande Chorus and Orchestra / Kazimierz Kord;** [b]**National Philharmonic Orchestra / Richard Bonynge**
Decca ② 430 636-2DM2 (133 minutes: ADD).
Notes, text and translation included. Ⓜ
Recorded 1978 ●

This heroic comedy was Massenet's last big success (in 1910, when he was 68). People who think of him as only a salon composer should listen to the start of Act 1, set in a Spanish town square at fiesta time; the opening music bursts out of the loudspeakers like that of Verdi's *Otello*, although here the mood is joyous, with tremendous rhythmic verve and gusto. In fact, this opera is closer to Verdi's *Falstaff*, with the same admixture of gentler serious moments amidst the comic bustle and intrigue, and of course, here again the central character is a comic yet lovable figure. The recording, made by a British team in Geneva in 1978, still sounds well although orchestral detail could be clearer.

As for the performance by mainly Swiss forces under Kazimierz Kord, and with a Bulgarian bass in the title role (written for Chaliapin), one can only praise it for its idiomatic realization of a 'Spanish' opera by a gifted French composer for the theatre. Though Régine Crespin may be too mature vocally for Dulcinée, the object of the elderly Don Quixote's adoration, she sings splendidly and few will find this a serious weakness. Nicolai Ghiaurov rightly makes Quixote himself a real person, touching and dignified as well as comic, and Gabriel Bacquier gives a rounded portrayal of his servant Sancho Panza, so that Quixote's death scene in the company of his old friend comes across as particularly strong. The lively and tuneful *Scènes alsaciennes* with Bonynge make a fine fill-up.

Hérodiade

Nadine Denize *mez* Hérodiade; **Cheryl Studer** *sop* Salomé; **Ben Heppner** *ten* Jean; **Thomas Hampson** *bar* Hérode; **José van Dam** *bass-bar* Phanuel; **Marcel Vanaud** *bar* Vitellius; **Jean-Philippe Courtis** *bass* High Priest; **Martine Olmeda** *mez* Young Babylonian; **Jean-Paul Fouchécourt** *ten* Voice in the Temple **Toulouse Capitole Chorus and Orchestra / Michel Plasson**

EMI ③ CDS5 55378-2 (166 minutes: DDD). Notes, text and translation included. Recorded 1994 Ⓕ ●

Written in 1880, *Hérodiade* is typical of the early grand operas with which Massenet courted popularity. It offers five magnificent roles to singers who have the wherewithal to make the most of them, with some glorious show-pieces which are – as always with Massenet – gratefully written for the voice. It is impossible to say whether Massenet consciously took Verdi's *Aida* as a model, but we do know that he put in his request for tickets to see the first performance at the Palais Garnier while he was orchestrating *Hérodiade*. The similarities are inevitable, as both operas are descendants of Meyerbeer. There are copious ballets, mystic off-stage chanting, grand choral finales and exotic settings of Eastern promise. Michel Plasson conducts the opera uncut and has the advantage of a good studio recording. He is not one for taking an objective view of the music and there are times when he rushes frenetically ahead, as if he is as possessed by the lurid goings-on in the drama as the characters on stage. The sense of atmosphere is palpable. In Plasson's hands the heavy chords at the opening of Act 3 resound with a potent mysticism that presages Klingsor's castle (Massenet knew his Wagner too). In fact, we are at the dwelling of Phanuel the sorcerer, a less threatening proposition. José van Dam is marvellous in this big solo, leaning on the opening words of 'Dors, ô cité perverse' with a sinister gleam in his voice that sends shivers down one's back. Silvery pure in tone, Studer's Salomé throws herself into the drama with lustful abandon and Heppner phrases the music with remarkable breadth and seems to have heroic top notes to spare.

Manon

Angela Gheorghiu *sop* Manon; **Roberto Alagna** *ten* Des Grieux; **Earle Patriarco** *bar* Lescaut; **José van Dam** *bass-bar* Comte des Grieux; **Nicolas Rivenq** *bar* De Brétigny; **Gilles Ragon** *ten* Guillot; **Anna Maria Panzarella** *sop* Poussette; **Sophie Koch** *mez* Javotte; **Susanne Schimmack** *mez* Rosette; **Nicolas Cavallier** *bar* Innkeeper; **Chorus and Symphony Orchestra of La Monnaie / Antonio Pappano**

EMI ③ CDS5 57005-2 (163 minutes: DDD). Ⓕ
Notes, text and translation included.
Recorded 1999 ●●●

EMI has had the good sense to build this set around Pappano's own company at La Monnaie, a Francophone group of singers who give an authentic flavour that non-French-speaking performers cannot hope to match. The piece is given absolutely complete, including the ballet (splendidly played), although it's a shame room had not been found for Gheorghiu to record the Fabliau, alternative to the Gavotte, as an appendix.

Nothing of the myriad character of Massenet's popular work escapes Pappano's eye and ear. He has a near-perfect idea of how to pace the score and he persuades his orchestra and chorus to play and sing with the utmost respect for pertinent detail, so important in Massenet, and to follow, as do the soloists, the many expressive markings demanded by the composer. The attention to detail is evident everywhere. The big scenes at Amiens and the Cours-la-Reine have just the élan and spirit called for too. Plasson, on a rival EMI set, made in Toulouse in 1982, is almost but not quite as convincing.

Gheorghiu's is a Manon to savour in practically every respect. Suitably coquettish in her first solo, she turns ruminative, plangent for her second, 'Voyons, Manon'. The farewell to her little table is inward and pensive, tone subtly shaded with the 'larmes dans la voix' so admired in native French singers. To the Gavotte and the recitative preceding it, Gheorghiu brings the outward aplomb and, in the second verse, the hint of sadness required. The prayer at St Sulpice has all the urgency and the sense of apprehension as to how Des Grieux, now a servant of the church, will respond to her. Once she reaches him, 'N'est-ce plus ma main' could hardly be more seductive. And the Act 4 solo, in the gambling room at Hotel Transylvanie, is as nervously fevered in its love of gambling as it should be.

Throughout these solos, Gheorghiu prudently follows Massenet's scrupulous instructions as to dynamics and phrasing with unforgettable results, not to mention the sheer glory of her singing as such, outclassing her compatriot, the sensitive Ileana Cotrubas, who recorded the role for Plasson too late in her career.

If Alagna doesn't quite equal his wife's example, he is an ardent, French-sounding Des Grieux, always suggesting the Chevalier's obsessive love for his 'Sphinx étonnant'. He is rightly overwhelmed by his first sight of Manon, and carries her off to Paris with romantic verve. The Dream, finely phrased as it is, hasn't quite the individuality that Ansseau, Heddle Nash (in the famous pre-war broadcast now on Dutton) or Gedda and others, brought to it, mainly because his tone has become a shade occluded. At St Sulpice, it rings out more truly. 'Ah fuyez, douce image' begins in nicely reflective fashion and the B flat climaxes are suitably impassioned. In most respects he surpasses the ageing Kraus for Plasson, even when he isn't quite as elegant.

Earle Patriarco, a young American baritone, proves an excellent Lescaut, keen with the text and properly cynical in manner. His first solo, at Amiens, begins the real action with theatrical flair. 'A quoi bon l'économie' is neat, with the 'O Rosalinde' section rightly sentimental. His French is faultless. Still better is José van Dam as Le Comte (he sang the part for Plasson), words shaped so meaningfully onto tone, his spoken contribution faultlessly timed. Rivenq's De Brétigny is characterful, but his voice is too much like Patriarco's. Ragon is suitably nasty as the old roué, Guillot, and makes the most of the text.

All the smaller parts are enthusiastically taken, small decorations on a masterly interpretation. Given an exemplary recording for balance and presence, this set is about as good as you'll get today (or maybe any day) of this adorable piece.

Many will have an affection for the 1956 EMI set with Victoria de los Angeles's *nonpareil* of a Manon and Monteux as her elegant conductor, but the work is cut, the recording is dated. And some will continue to treasure the ancient 1928-29 Columbia set now on Malibran, with Féraldy and Rogatchewsky as the most attractive of lovers, but this new version is the one to introduce a new generation to a work of which Beecham declared: 'I would give up all the *Brandenburgs* for *Manon* and would think that I had profited by the exchange.'

Massenet Manon[a] **Berlioz** Les nuits d'été, Op 7[b] **H**
Debussy La damoiselle élue[c]
Victoria de los Angeles *sop* Manon; [c]**Carol Smith** *mez*; [a]**Henri Legay** *ten* Des Grieux; [a]**Michel Dens** *bar* Lescaut; [a]**Jean Borthayre** *bass* Comte des Grieux; [a]**Jean Vieuille** *bar* De Brétigny; [a]**René Hérent** *ten* Guillot; [a]**Liliane Berton** *sop* Poussette; [a]**Raymonde Notti** *sop* Javotte; [a]**Marthe Serres** *sop* Rosette; [c]**Radcliffe Choral Society; Boston Symphony Orchestra / Charles Munch;** [a]**Opéra-Comique Choir and Orchestra / Pierre Monteux**
Testament mono ③ SBT3203 (213 minutes: ADD). Ⓕ
Texts and translations included. Recorded in 1955

One of the first classic opera recordings of the LP era here makes a welcome return to the catalogue. As EMI now has its highly praised new set of *Manon* with Gheorghiu and Alagna, it has fallen to Testament to bring back this earlier HMV set. Compared to its previous CD release, the sound here has been carefully restored with greatly reduced hiss, a less wiry treble and firmer bass – a successful facelift for a *Manon* who no longer sounds her age.

Recorded in mono in 1955, the set fell at a unique point in the opera's history on disc. Previous recordings from the 78rpm era had captured the special Opéra-Comique spirit for posterity, but they hold limited sonic appeal to present-day collectors; later recordings have up-to-date sound, but their international casts generally cannot claim the same sense of style. Only with this 1955 set do we get the best of both worlds. All the basic elements of the performance were provided by the Théâtre National de l'Opéra-Comique, while de los Angeles and Monteux bring a dash of international glamour. It makes an excellent combination which is never likely to be repeated.

Already at the time a practised exponent of Manon on stage, de los Angeles makes a vivid heroine, allowing us to *see* every expression passing across her face, almost as if we were watching a video. Maybe the role lies a little high for her, but de los Angeles surprised herself on the day of recording by hitting the high D in the Cours-la-Reine scene. Monteux's skill in his native French repertoire is second to none, and he brings exemplary sparkle to the music. The attack of the less-than-first-class Opéra-Comique orchestra at big moments like the end of the Saint-Sulpice duet is electric.

It would be possible to find fault with various members of the supporting cast, but that is to miss the point. They sing with a grace and wit that nobody from outside the Opéra-Comique tradition can replicate easily. Henri Legay did not have a great tenor voice, but the poetry and the passion of Des Grieux come as second nature to him. Michel Dens' lively Lescaut and Jean Borthayre's serious Comte des Grieux are no less idiomatic; and the delectably perfumed Guillot of René Hérent is a collector's item in the best sense of the term, as he had been singing this role with the company since his début in 1918. The cast communicate the text with exemplary clarity.

Last time round on CD this *Manon* was coupled with a later recording by de los Angeles of Chausson's *Poème de l'amour et de la mer*. Testament has chosen more contemporaneous fillers. She is charming in both, and Charles Munch makes a worthy partner for her. For the opera itself there is now a clear choice between this reissue and EMI's fine new Pappano set. Opera collectors will probably want both.

Ileana Cotrubas *sop* Manon; **Alfredo Kraus** *ten* Des Grieux; **Gino Quilico** *bar* Lescaut; **José van Dam** *bass-bar* Comte des Grieux; **Jean-Marie Frémeau** *bar* De Brétigny; **Charles Burles** *ten* Guillot; **Ghyslaine Raphanel** *sop* Poussette; **Colette Alliot-Lugaz** *sop* Javotte; **Martine Mahé** *mez* Rosette; **Jacques Loreau** *bar* Innkeeper **Toulouse Capitole Chorus and Orchestra / Michel Plasson**
EMI ③ CDS7 49610-2 (154 minutes: DDD). Notes, Ⓕ text and translation included. Recorded 1982

Plasson's version of Massenet's most popular opera would be hard to improve upon. The performance is a genuine piece of company-work, particularly welcome as the company is French and can call upon such gifted singers as Colette Alliot-Lugaz and Charles Burles to take principal supporting roles. Excellent are the brother and father, frequently underestimated as both singing and acting parts but here played with distinction of voice and style by Gino Quilico and José van Dam. It is with the two leading roles that some qualifications have to be introduced among the general praise. Manon and Des Grieux, whatever their sins, have youth on their side, which is something Ileana Cotrubas and Alfredo Kraus in 1982 could not quite claim. Kraus is still marvellously clear in tone, firm in production and resonant throughout his extensive range, but he has developed a way of allowing the emotion to take too external a form of expression and occasionally the music requires a somewhat richer timbre. Cotrubas is usually fine until a high note approaches, affecting the ease and steadiness – and sometimes the charm – of her singing. Even so, both give deeply felt, extressively nuanced performances, presenting genuine characers and not stereotypes. Plasson conducts a performance that is both vigorous and delicate, and production and recorded sound are excellent.

Thaïs

Renée Fleming *sop* Thaïs; **Thomas Hampson** *bar* Athanaël; **Giuseppe Sabbatini** *ten* Nicias; **Estefano Palatchi** *bass* Palémon; **Marie Devellereau** *sop* Crobyle; **Isabelle Cals** *mez* Myrtale; **Enkelejda Shkosa** *mez* Albine; **Elisabeth Vidal** *sop* La Charmeuse; **David Grousset** *bass* Servant; **Bordeaux Opera Chorus; Bordeaux-Aquitaine National Orchestra / Yves Abel**

Decca ② 466 766-2DHO2 (147 minutes: DDD). Ⓕ
Text and translation included. Recorded 1997-98 OO

At last – a modern recording of *Thaïs* with a soprano who can sing the title-role. Heaven knows why it took so long. It is not as though a recording is as tricky as a stage production, where the casting department needs to find a singer as glamorous and daring as the role's creator, Sybil Sanderson, who famously exposed her breast at the première in 1894. All we need on disc is a soprano with a fabulously beautiful voice, idiomatic French, a sensuous *legato*, pure high notes up to a stratospheric top D, and the ability to leave every listener weak at the knees. Where was the problem?

Renée Fleming makes it all sound so easy. Her success a couple of years ago at the Opéra Bastille in Paris with Massenet's Manon showed that she has an affinity for this composer. As Thaïs, a role with a similar vocal profile, she proves equally well cast. Within minutes of her entrance it is clear that neither of the other sets from the last 25 years will be able to touch her. Fleming simply has a vocal class that puts her in a different league from the unsteady Beverly Sills on Maazel's EMI set or the outrageously voiceless Anna Moffo on the now long-forgotten set from RCA (nla). There is just enough individuality in her singing to give Fleming's Thaïs a personality of her own, and vocal loveliness brings a bloom to her every scene. When she bids farewell to Athanaël with the words 'We shall meet again in the heavenly city', we believe her. Few other sopranos today could float up to the top A with such angelic grace.

The Athanaël she leaves behind is Thomas Hampson, who is her match in sensitivity and roundness of tone. Their duet at the oasis in the desert is beautifully sung, every word clear, every phrase shaped with feeling. (Thanks to Yves Abel it does not become a wallow even in the final bars, where every conductor must be tempted to squeeze out the last drop of sentimentality.) If only Hampson were equally good at getting beneath the skin of the operatic characters he plays. In the case of Athanaël there is plenty of psychological complexity down there to uncover, but Hampson seems unwilling to engage the character's dark side. Even where Massenet loads the vocal score with helpful comments like 'd'une voix sourde et terrible' or 'avec une furie soudaine' he remains even-tempered to a fault. So much beautiful and shapely singing is almost more than this frighteningly intense role deserves.

None of the other characters in *Thaïs* is important enough to influence a choice of recording. Giuseppe Sabbatini makes an appealing Nicias without quite putting across the glamour of the playboy in the few minutes at his disposal. Marie Devellereau and Isabelle Cals duet nicely as Crobyle and Myrtale and are joined by the elegant Elisabeth Vidal effortlessly walking the vocal tightrope above them in the high-lying role of La Charmeuse. Enkelejda Shkosa, a young mezzo to watch, adds a touch of luxury casting in the small role of the abbess, Albine.

Occasionally, one regrets that Abel does not have the New Philharmonia at his disposal, as Maazel does, but the subtlety of colour and accent that he draws from the Orchestre National Bordeaux-Aquitaine are a world apart from Maazel's constant up-front aggression. The famous 'Méditation', elegantly played by the young French violinist Renaud Capuçon, and featuring swoony background chorus is a dream. Add in a first-class Decca recording and it will be clear that this new *Thaïs* has pretty well everything going for it. The only competition in the current catalogue is Maazel's unlovely EMI set. So, with an affectionate glance back to Renée Doria's Thaïs in Decca's early '60s set and Gabriel Bacquier's Athanaël for RCA, Abel and company comfortably sweep the board.

Werther

Awards 1981

José Carreras *ten* Werther; **Frederica von Stade** *mez* Charlotte; **Thomas Allen** *bar* Albert; **Isobel Buchanan** *sop* Sophie; **Robert Lloyd** *bass* Bailli; **Malcolm King** *bass* Bailli's friend; **Paul Crook** *ten* Bailli's friend; **Linda Humphries** *sop* Kätchen; **Donaldson Ball** *bar* Brühlmann **Royal Opera House Orchestra, Covent Garden; Children's Choir / Sir Colin Davis**

Philips ② 416 654-2PH2 (131 minutes: AAD/ADD) Ⓕ
Notes, text and translation included
Recorded 1980 OOO

The ebb and flow of word and music, the warm, tremulous life of the string playing, and the pacing of each *tableau vivant* is handled so superbly by Sir Colin Davis that there is not a single moment of *longueur*. The Royal Opera House orchestra plays at its very best: the solo detail and the velocity of its every response to Massenet's flickering orchestral palette operates as though with heightened awareness under the scrutiny of the laser beam. The casting polarizes this Werther and this Charlotte. José Carreras is very much a Werther of action rather than of dream, of impetuous self-destruction rather than of brooding lyricism. The real *élan* he brings to lines like 'Rêve! Rêve! Extase! Bonheur!' is more impressive than the conjuring of 'l'air d'un paradis', where the voice can be overdriven at the top. So far as style, line and inflection are concerned, Frederica von Stade's performance can hardly be faulted. Her voice is the very incarnation of Charlotte's essential simplicity of character; but there are times when one could perhaps wish for a darker *tinta* to find the shadows in the role, and to bring a greater sense of the undercurrent of emotional conflict as it grows towards the last two acts. Thomas Allen finds unusual breadth in this Albert, noting the slightest giveaway flutter in the line: when he sings 'j'en ai tant au fond du coeur' one does actually begin to believe that there may be depths there of which one is too often kept ignorant. Isobel Buchanan's is a small-scale and a straightforward Sophie, a real 'oiseau d'aurore'.

Werther

Jerry Hadley *ten* Werther; **Anne Sofie von Otter** *mez* Charlotte; **Gérard Théruel** *bar* Albert; **Dawn Upshaw** *sop* Sophie; **Jean-Marie Frémeau** *bar* Magistrate; **Gilles Ragon** *ten* Schmidt, Brühlmann; **Frédéric Caton** *bass* Johann; **Geneviève Marchand** *sop* Kätchen
Chorus and Orchestra of the Opéra National de Lyon / Kent Nagano
Erato ② 0630-17790-2 (121 minutes: DDD). Ⓜ
Notes text and translation included. Recorded 1995

The opening scene of this recording promises very well; the orchestra certainly knows how to play Massenet, and Nagano avoids the extremes of quasi-*verismo* style that can mar this essay in masochistic, unrequited passion. Jerry Hadley suggests convincingly the impulsive, romantic young poet. As Charlotte, Anne Sofie von Otter has just the right balance between sounding young (she's meant to be 20) but emotionally mature. She and von Stade (Davis) are among the finest interpreters of the role. Dawn Upshaw makes a very positive, flirty Sophie and Gérard Théruel a good Albert. There is a grandeur about the Davis recording which this version doesn't quite attain. However, von Otter and Hadley sound every bit as dramatic, but in a more intimate, neurotic way.

Werther

John Brecknock *ten* Werther; **Dame Janet Baker** *mez* Charlotte; **Patrick Wheatley** *bar* Albert; **Joy Roberts** *sop* Sophie; **Harold Blackburn** *bass* Magistrate; **Terry Jenkins** *ten* Schmidt; **John Tomlinson** *bass* Johann; **Nigel Waugh** *bar* Brühlmann; **Janice Andrew** *mez* Käthchen
English National Opera Chorus and Orchestra / Sir Charles Mackerras
Chandos Opera in English Series ② CHAN3033
(130 minutes: ADD). Notes and English text included. Ⓕ
Recorded live in December 1977

John Copley's production, on which this live recording is based, effectively put *Werther* into the operatic repertory in London. Although it had had a single Covent Garden performance in 1894, and had been staged at Sadler's Wells in the early 1950s (when Norman Tucker's translation, sung here, was first used), *Werther* had never caught on in Britain. Of all Massenet's operas, it is the one that has now achieved the greatest respectability. The recording is dominated by Dame Janet Baker's Charlotte. Her penultimate role with the English National Opera, she brings to the part all her intensity, with a clarity of diction that is almost embarrassing at moments, lines such as 'I might just as well give the children their supper' gaining a weight that the music can't generally support. Throughout the 1970s she gained in authority and confidence as a stage actress, although some excursions into the soprano territory had already begun to introduce a hint of strain into the voice above the stave. She was one of the greatest singing-actresses of the second half of the 20th century, and like *any* fine singer she was always at her best in her own language. Although some of her operatic performances in Italian find her in robust form, her English-language performances demonstrate even more just why she was so special.

John Brecknock as Werther has a moment or two of strain in Act 1, but in the great confrontations with Charlotte in the last two scenes, he rises to a performance of passion and strength that equals Baker's. Patrick Wheatley and Joy Roberts provide good support as Albert and Sophie, while the young John Tomlinson is a vivid Johann. The company at the Coliseum at this time had an integrity and confidence that must have been mostly due to Sir Charles Mackerras's leadership. The whole performance sweeps along with an inevitability that is seldom achieved in the recording studio. The sound quality is excellent considering that these are broadcast tapes over 20 years old. A special word of praise for the ENO orchestra's wind and brass sections, which achieve an authentic French sound that often eludes British orchestras.

Werther H

Georges Thill *ten* Werther; **Ninon Vallin** *mez* Charlotte; **Marcel Roque** *bar* Albert; **Germaine Féraldy** *sop* Sophie; **Armand Narçon** *bass* Bailli; **Henri Niel** *ten* Schmidt; **Louis Guenot** *bass* Johann
Cantoria Children's Choir; Chorus and Orchestra of the Opéra-Comique, Paris / Elie Cohen
EMI Références mono ② CHS7 63195-2
(121 minutes: ADD). Notes, text and translation Ⓜ
included. Recorded 1931

If you want to hear just how thoroughly prepared, technically secure, idiomatic and deeply felt French singing could be between the wars, you need only listen to this wonderful performance, here brought to new life on this excellent EMI transfer. The reading shows the benefits of singers sticking to their own language and singing repertory they knew through and through. Vallin develops her portrayal unerringly. The placing of her tone, the way she moves naturally with the music and the consistently warm and steady tone – these are things to treasure. Thill's tone is just as glorious and true as his partner's, his enunciation of the text pleasing and unaffected. Each of Werther's many solos receive a near-ideal reading, with the voice at once plangent and virile. Perhaps what one marvels at more than anything is the way both singers scrupulously follow Massenet's copious markings of feeling and dynamics. The singers surrounding this sovereign pair are no less pleasing. Roque provides a mellow baritone and just the right amount of concern as the solid Albert. Narçon starts off the opera splendidly as a jovial Bailli. Féraldy is pert and lively as Sophie, with the light, airy soprano the role calls for but seldom gets. Elie Cohen's conducting has elegance, balance and passion – but passion that never becomes overheated as it does in some modern interpretations. Tempos are perfectly judged and Cohen avoids heavy-handed lingering that doesn't allow Massenet to speak for himself. A classic set. The sound is adequate.

Additional recommendation

Werther

Alagna *Werther* **Gheorghiu** *Charlotte* **London Symphony Orchestra / Pappano**

EMI CDS5 56820-2 (128 minutes: DDD: A/99) Ⓕ

For those wanting a modern recording of *Werther* this is first choice mostly because of Alagna's heroic assumption of the title-role; Gheorghiu, for all her dramatic commitment and fine singing, sounds overstretched. Pappano and the LSO are on top form.

Nicholas Maw British 1935

GROVE *Maw studied with Berkeley at the Royal Academy of Music (1955-58) and Boulanger and Deutsch in Paris (1958-59). He has taught in England and the USA. His music represents the extension of a solid tonal tradition, traceable back through Britten, Tippett, Bartók and Strauss, all influences on a style of fresh vigour. Among his works are two comic operas, One Man Show (1964) and The Rising of the Moon (1970), orchestral pieces and chamber music. His monumental orchestral work Odyssey was given in 1987.*

Violin Concerto

Joshua Bell *vn*

London Philharmonic Orchestra / Sir Roger Norrington Ⓕ

Sony Classical SK62856 (42 minutes: DDD). ●

For over a quarter-of-a-century, Maw has been investigating those lines of musical development that were left dangling when modernism cut them. He's not so much writing 'neo-Brahms' or 'neo-Strauss' as exploring the enticing paths that they opened up but which post-Schoenbergians have not pursued. The enormous orchestral *Odyssey* that he began in the early 1970s (impressively recorded by Sir Simon Rattle and the City of Birmingham Symphony Orchestra on EMI) has had many satellites and successors, but the roots of his mature style have never been clearer than in this concerto, written for a virtuoso of the most archetypally romantic instrument of them all. It is a concerto that Joseph Joachim would have loved as much as Joshua Bell so evidently does. Full of warmly eloquent melody, the concerto is fundamentally lyrical in all four of its movements, but there is vital energy too, plentiful opportunity for sparkling virtuosity, many beautifully expressive orchestral solos and, in the *Scherzo* and finale especially, magnificently rich multi-layered climaxes. The performance is remarkably fine, the recording clean but not clinical. A violin concerto for all who love the violin and its music.

La Vita Nuova

Ghost Dances. La Vita Nuova. Roman Canticle

Carmen Pelton *sop* **William Sharp** *bar*

Twentieth Century Consort / Christopher Kendall

ASV CDDCA999 (65 minutes: DDD). Texts and translations included. Recorded 1995 Ⓕ

Maw's originality may not be the kind that leaps up and yells in your face; but original he certainly is. He can draw on influences as diverse as Britten and Richard Strauss in *La Vita Nuova*, blend elements of Schoenberg's *Pierrot* and Stravinsky's *Petrushka* with the sounds of Latin American and African folk instruments in *Ghost Dances*, and still come up with something that feels like nobody else. The sound of the soprano's sultry tonal phrases in *La Vita Nuova* is a long way from the eerie tone of the African Kalimba at the end of *Ghost Dances* – beautifully described by Malcolm MacDonald in his notes as 'like a phantom piano played with a bony finger'. And yet in context they are obviously the same composer: a romantic with a fertile imagination and a superb technical palate, who clearly delights in enticing and surprising the ear. The performances are of outstanding warmth and finesse. The sound world of *La Vita Nuova* emerges with such richness and depth that it's hard to believe that only 10 instruments are playing and Carmen Pelton has a strong sense of the way the vocal lines soar and dip over long periods. William Sharp is eloquent and quite distinct throughout the short *Roman Canticle*. And everything in *Ghost Dances* seems as clear as it should be, with no loss of atmosphere – an excellent recording. It adds up to a perfect introduction to a composer who offers genuine, long-term rewards, not instant, transient gratification.

Hymnus

Hymnus[a]. Little Concert[b]. Shahnama[b]
[a]Oxford Bach Choir; [a]BBC Concert Orchestra, [b]Britten Sinfonia / Nicholas Cleobury Ⓕ
ASV CDDCA1070 (74 minutes: DDD).

Hymnus is firmly rooted in the tradition of large-scale English choral works, full of luminous harmonies, rich choral textures and fine, eminently singable lines. The music is compelling, accessible and distinctive and the choral writing clearly designed to be demanding yet well within the scope of a large amateur choral society. Maw wrote it in 1996 to mark the centenary of the 200-voice Oxford Bach Choir and, as it was intended primarily to display a large chorus, there are no solo parts and the orchestral accompaniment is relatively discreet.

The net result of this is that the choir has virtually no respite throughout the work's 33-minute duration, which probably accounts for the sense of tiredness and strain that permeates this recording. Climaxes (and there are a great many of those in the work) appear to overstretch the choir while the gentler passages fail to exhibit the kind of precision and polish which characterizes the choir's live performances. The BBC Concert Orchestra also seems to be lacking that final polish, but much of this may well be attributed to a strangely boxy and claustrophobic recording. It is a splendid work and there are some worthy performers, all of which deserve rather better than this.

The other two works on the disc more than compensate for any shortcomings to be found in *Hymnus*. Nicholas Daniel produces an amazing range of moods and colours – from the exquisitely lyrical to the robustly athletic – in the *Little Concert* for oboe, two horns and strings, while the atmospheric and evocative *Shahnama*, nine brief movements inspired by an 11th-century Persian epic, is beautifully captured in Nicholas Cleobury's nicely spaced and tautly directed performance.

Billy Mayerl

British 1902-1959

Mayerl studied in the junior department of Trinity College of Music (1914-19) and worked as a pianist for silent filme and in hotel bands playing American popular music. His first composition Egyptian Suite was published in 1919. In 1921 he joined Bert Ralton's band (later called the Savoy Havana Band) which regularly broadcast in the early years of the BBC. In 1926 he left that band for the music hall and founded his own school of music which pioneered teaching by post, using records. With Nippy (1930) his career moved to music theatre and he composed and directed several musical comedies which were successful at the time. He was a regular broadcaster before World War Two but the War marked the end of his celebrity. He continued as a performer despite ill health and was editor of The Light Music Magazine (1957-58).

Solo keyboard works

Mayerl Crystal Clear. Orange Blossom. Piano Exaggerations. Pastorale Exotique. Wistaria. Canaries' Serenade. Shy Ballerina. Puppets Suite, Op 77. Piano Transcriptions – Body and Soul; Deep Henderson; Tormented; Sing, you sinners; Cheer up; Have you forgotten?; The object of my affection; Is it true what they say about Dixie?; I need you; Love was born; I'm at your service **Parkin** Mayerl Shots, Sets 1 and 2. A Tribute to Billy Mayerl
Eric Parkin *pf*
Priory PRCD544 (80 minutes: DDD). Ⓕ
Recorded 1995

Nobody since the master himself has come anywhere near Parkin's easy technical mastery and fastidious musicianship in this delightful music. Some pianists hit the more demanding pieces quite hard: Parkin, like Mayerl, knows better and his playing is consistently light and subtle. This has always been his approach, allied to a faultless sense of pace and rhythm. However, Mayerl, apart from perfecting the piano novelty, also contributed to the English pastoral tradition, which Parkin knows equally well. *Shy Ballerina* is charmingly done with rubato which would be quite out of place in Mayerl's rhythmic numbers. The three-movement *Puppets Suite* is a *tour de force*. As a bonus on this generous 80-minute CD Parkin puts in two sets of his own pieces called *Mayerl Shots*. He explains that, as a result of practising lots of Mayerl, further ideas surfaced spontaneously in a similar idiom. These are all fluent tributes and there are even quotations for the specialists. The piano sound is sharp and clear. Essential listening.

Mayerl Scallywag. Jasmine. Oriental. Minuet for Pamela. Fascinating Ditty. Funny Peculiar. Chopsticks. Carminetta. Mignonette. Penny Whistle. Piano Transcriptions – Me and my girl; Blue velvet; Sittin' on the edge of my chair; The pompous gremlin; My heaven in the pines; Alabamy bound; Stardust; Please handle with care; Two lovely people; Two hearts on a tree; You're the reason why. Studies in Syncopation, Op 55 – Nos 7, 10, 14, 15 and 18
Parkin Mayerl Shots, Set 3
Eric Parkin *pf*
Priory PRCD565 (76 minutes: DDD). Ⓕ
Recorded 1995

This release, 'Scallywag', has its own discoveries, notably the *Studies in Syncopation*, which parallel Bartók's *Mikrokosmos* in this field. There are three books of six pieces each, dating from 1930-31, and Parkin plays five of them, proving that they are not just exercises but real music. There are gems in the transcriptions – Carmichael's *Stardust*, Mayerl's own 'You're the reason why' from his 1934 show *Sporting Love*, and a forgotten but lovely tune by Peter York called *Two hearts on a tree*. The Spanish *Carminetta* is Mayerl's equivalent of Joplin's *Solace*. And there is real comedy – totally appreciated and effectively realized by Parkin – in *Chopsticks* and *Penny Whistle*. In addition Parkin gives us his own response to Mayerl in a similar idiom – a third set of his *Mayerl Shots*. The recording is adequate although there is occasionally some background noise.

Piano Transcriptions, Volume 3

There's a small hotel; The mood that I'm in; So rare; I'm always in the mood for you; Turkey in the straw; For only you; Thanks for the memory; The Highland Swing; I got love; Amoresque; There's rain in my eyes; Patty cake, patty cake, baker man; Blame it on my last affair; I have eyes; Like a cat with a mouse; Phil the Fluter's Ball; Fools rush in; Peg o' my heart; All the things you are; The Musical Earwig; Transatlantic Lullaby; Tell me I'm forgiven; Japanese Juggler; Poor little rich girl
Eric Parkin *pf*
Priory PRCD468 (63 minutes: DDD). Ⓕ
Recorded 1993

This is pure 1930s music. This is not Mayerl as the lightning-fingered whizz-kid of the 1920s, although many of the transcriptions are tricky enough: it's the style he taught through the Billy Mayerl School of Music, a success story here and abroad until the war. These transcriptions – popular songs of the period arranged in Mayerl's inimitable English accent – are a wonderful encapsulation of an era and they transcend it – as long as they are played like this. The demands on the performer are similar to studying the style of the period at any time. Classically trained pianists have to work hard to play Joplin, Gershwin and Mayerl. But Mayerl belongs to them, as long as their left hand is strong enough, because this is basically a notated tradition rather than an improvised one. Parkin understands it all – the effortless lilt, the light touch, not too much pedal, nothing overdone, everything speaking for itself.

John McCabe British 1939

GROVE *McCabe studied at the Royal Manchester College and with Genzmer in Munich, then returned to England to work as a pianist, critic and composer; in 1983 he became director of the London College of Music. His works, in an extended tonal style relating to Hartmann and Nielsen, include three symphonies (1965, 1971, 1978), much other orchestral music, chamber and keyboard pieces.*

Edward II

Royal Ballet Sinfonia / Barry Wordsworth
Hyperion ② CDA67135 (114 minutes: DDD). Ⓕ
Recorded 1999

Commissioned by the Stuttgart Ballet, choreographed by David Bintley and first given in April 1995, *Edward II* is the third of McCabe's ballet scores and draws its story-line from Christopher Marlowe's eponymous drama and the medieval courtly satire, *Le roman de Fauvel*. Quite apart from the meaty intrigue, complex character relationships and psychological pathos of the plot, McCabe's music communicates with an expressive fervour that is captivating. It's not just the superbly judged orchestration (colourful extras include triple woodwind and electric guitar) and wealth of memorable invention that impress. Above all, it's McCabe's ability to forge his tightly knit material into a dramatically convincing and organically coherent whole that marks him out as a composer of exceptional gifts. No praise can be too high for Barry Wordsworth's fluent, pungently theatrical direction, not to mention the unstinting application of the excellent Royal Ballet Sinfonia (which has truly assimilated McCabe's idiom into its bloodstream). Tony Faulkner's excitingly truthful Walthamstow sound allies razor-sharp focus to a most pleasing bloom, too.

Symphonies

Symphony No 2[a]. Notturni ed alba[b].
The Chagall Windows[c]
[b]**Jill Gomez** *sop* [ab]**City of Birmingham Symphony Orchestra / Louis Frémaux;** [c]**Hallé Orchestra / James Loughran**
EMI British Composers CDM5 67120-2 Ⓜ
(75 minutes: ADD). Text included. Recorded 1972-75

Commissioned by the Hallé Concerts Society for its 1974-5 season, *The Chagall Windows* exhibits a truly symphonic purpose throughout its 12 interlinked, beautifully proportioned contrasting sections (each of Marc Chagall's famous stained-glass windows in Jerusalem, photographs of which originally sowed the seeds for the work in the composer's mind back in the early 1960s, depicts one of the 12 Tribes of Israel). This fine first recording under James Loughran was made over the two days immediately preceding the Manchester world première (on January 9, 1975). The hauntingly lyrical song-cycle *Notturni ed alba*, first heard at the 1970 Three Choirs Festival in Hereford, is an uninterrupted setting for soprano and large orchestra of four medieval Latin poems based around the topic of night. It remains an intoxicating creation, full of tingling atmosphere and slumbering passion. Even more compelling is the Second Symphony from the following year. This is yet another one-movement structure of uncommon elegance and dazzling orchestral resource, and is performed here with total sympathy by its dedicatees, Louis Frémaux and the Birmingham orchestra. Stuart Eltham's engineering sounds superbly vivid still. An altogether exemplary reissue.

Symphony No 4, 'Of Time and the River'. Flute Concerto[a]
[a]**Emily Beynon** *fl* **BBC Symphony Orchestra / Vernon Handley** Ⓕ
Hyperion CDA67089 (56 minutes: DDD).

John McCabe's Fourth Symphony, some half an hour in duration, has something Sibelian about its utterly inevitable, ever-evolving progress.

Behind the frequently prodigal surface activity, one is acutely aware of the inexorable tread of a grander scheme – a preoccupation with time mirrored in Thomas Wolfe's novel *Of Time and the River*, from which the work derives its subtitle. The very opening idea is momentarily reminiscent of Britten, and there's a magnificent passage in the second movement that recalls Vaughan Williams at his visionary best. Yet McCabe's score possesses a strong individuality, formal elegance and abundant integrity too. With dedication and scrupulous perception, Handley secures a disciplined and alert response from the BBC SO. The engaging Flute Concerto composed for James Galway in 1989-90 proves both resourceful and communicative. Although it plays for 25 minutes without a break, the work falls into a graspable three-movement scheme, and its sense of drama (allied to a breathtaking mastery of texture and colour) suggests an underlying narrative impulse (not so, according to the composer). There is much that genuinely haunts here, not least the gently lapping opening idea (inspired by watching the play of waves on a Cornish beach), the ravishing dialogue between the soloist and orchestral flutes and the delightful emergence soon afterwards of an entrancingly naive, folk-like theme (heard again on alto flute at the pensive close, magically fading into the ether). Emily Beynon gives a flawless and characterful account of the demanding solo part, and is immaculately partnered by Handley and his BBC forces.

Further Listening
Simpson Symphony No 9
Bournemouth Symphony Orchestra / Handley
Hyperion CDA66299 (68 minutes: DDD: 12/88) Ⓕ

So utterly absorbing is this symphony that one hardly gives a thought to the performance or the recording.

String Quartets

String Quartets Nos 3-5
Vanbrugh Quartet (Gregory Ellis, Elizabeth Charleson *vns* Simon Aspell *va* Christopher Marwood *vc*)
Hyperion CDA67078 (68 minutes: DDD). Ⓕ
Recorded 1998

Here is music of enormous integrity and genuine staying power from an underrated British master, impeccably realized by artists and production crew alike. John McCabe's Third Quartet has both fastidious craft and satisfying logic to commend it, its five movements laid out to form an elegant arch in three parts. The sheer resourcefulness with which McCabe handles his material calls to mind the towering example of such figures as Bartók, Bridge, Britten and Simpson (yes, the music really is that rewarding!), while anyone who loves the Tippett quartets will surely recognize a kindred humanity and tumbling lyricism in, say, the memorable *Lento* episode which launches the 'Passacaglia' finale. The Fourth Quartet dates from three years later (1982) and was composed in joint celebration of two birthdays, namely the Delmé Quartet's 20th and Joseph Haydn's 250th. Cast in one movement and lasting just under 20 minutes, the spectral unison theme heard at the outset fuels nine formidably inventive and contrasting variations, whose ever-evolving progress and ambitious emotional scope again repay the closest scrutiny (an enormous pleasure in a performance as cogent as the present one). A viewing of Graham Sutherland's *The Bees* (a series of copper etchings) provided the impulse for McCabe's Fifth Quartet (1989). Although the prospect of assimilating the work's 14 sections might initially appear somewhat daunting, the composer's unusual formal design falls readily into a more or less 'traditional' three-movement scheme. Uncompromising in its relentless organic growth, the Fifth none the less yields a most ingratiating lyrical flow and vaulting grace. It is, in fact, the most immediately approachable of Hyperion's valuable clutch and, like its no less substantial colleagues, must be deemed a major addition to the catalogue. The Cork-based Vanbrugh Quartet proves to be an inspirational protagonist, its performances being both flawlessly prepared and magnificently authoritative.

Nikolay Medtner Russian 1880-1951

GROVE *Medtner studied the piano under Safonov at the Moscow Conservatory (1897-1900) and had composition lessons with Arensky and Taneyev, though was mostly self-taught. In 1921 he left Russia. He settled in Paris (1925-35), but was out of sympathy with musical developments there and found a more receptive audience in London, where he spent his last 16 years. He belonged in the line of Russian composer-pianists, though his music is close too to the Schumann-Brahms tradition. His works include three piano concertos (1918, 1927, 1943), much solo piano music, three violin sonatas and songs.*

Piano Concertos

No 1 in C minor, Op 33; **No 2** in C minor, Op 50; **No 3** in E minor, Op 60

Piano Concerto No 1. Piano Quintet in C, Op posth
Dmitri Alexeev *pf*
New Budapest Quartet (András Kiss, Ferenc Balogh *vns* Laszlo Barsony *va* Karoly Botvay *vc*); **BBC Symphony Orchestra / Alexander Lazarev**
Hyperion CDA66744 (59 minutes: DDD). Ⓕ
Recorded 1994

For Dmitri Alexeev the First Concerto is Medtner's masterpiece, an argument he sustains in a performance of superb eloquence and discretion. Even the sort of gestures later vulgarized and traduced by Tinseltown are given with an aristocratic quality, a feel for a love of musical intricacy that takes on an almost symbolic force, but also for Medtner's dislike of display. Time and again Alexeev makes you pause to reconsider Medtner's quality, and his reserve brings distinctive reward. The early *Abbandonamente ma non troppo* has a haunting improvisatory inwardness and later, as the storm clouds gather ominously at 11'55", his playing generates all the necessary electricity. How thankful one is, too, for Alexeev's advocacy of the Piano Quintet where, together with his fully committed colleagues, the New Budapest Quartet, he recreates music of the strangest, most unworldly exultance and introspection. Instructions such as *poco tranquillo (sereno)* and *Quasi Hymn* take us far away from the turbulence of the First Concerto (composed in the shadow of the First World War) and the finale's conclusion is wonderfully uplifting. The recordings are judiciously balanced in both works, and the BBC Symphony Orchestra under Lazarev are fully sympathetic.

Awards 1992

Piano Concertos Nos 2 and 3
Nikolai Demidenko *pf* **BBC Scottish Symphony Orchestra / Jerzy Maksymiuk**
Hyperion CDA66580 (74 minutes: DDD) Ⓕ
Recorded 1991 ●●●

This splendid disc is given a fine recording, good orchestral playing from a Scottish orchestra under a Polish conductor and, above all, truly coruscating and poetic playing from the brilliant young Russian pianist Nikolai Demidenko. Medtner was a contemporary and friend of Rachmaninov; he settled in Britain in the 1930s, and like Rachmaninov he was an excellent pianist. But while the other composer became immensely popular, Medtner languished in obscurity, regarded as an inferior imitation of Rachmaninov who wrote gushing music that was strong on gestures but weak on substance. The fact is that he can be diffuse (not to say long-winded) and grandiose, and memorable tunes are in short supply, so that his music needs to be played well to come off. When it is, there is much to enjoy, as here in Demidenko's hypnotically fiery and articulate accounts.

Piano Concertos Nos 2 and 3. Arabesque in A minor, Op 7 No 2. Fairy Tale in F minor, Op 26 No 3 Ⓗ
Nikolay Medtner *pf*
Philharmonia Orchestra / Issay Dobrowen
Testament mono SBT1027 (77 minutes: ADD). Ⓕ
Recorded 1947

The strong Russian flavour of the ornate writing is evident, as is the composer's masterly understanding of the piano. Listening to the composer himself in the Second's first *molto cantabile a tempo, ma expressivo* or the Third's *dolce cantabile* is to be made doubly aware of his haunting and bittersweet lyricism. The streaming figuration in the Second Concerto's *Romanza* is spun off with deceptive ease, a reminder that while Medtner despised obvious pyrotechnics he was a superb pianist. Two exquisitely played encores are included (the ambiguous poetry of the A minor *Arabesque* could be by no other composer), and the 1947 recordings have been superbly remastered.

Piano Concertos – No 1 in C minor, Op 33; No 3 in E minor, Op 60
Konstantin Scherbakov *pf* **Moscow Symphony Orchestra / Vladimir Ziva**
Naxos 8 553359 (70 minutes: DDD). Ⓕ
Recorded 1996

With this recording Naxos completes its Medtner concerto cycle with Scherbakov. To have such romantic richness – once the province of specialists – offered on a bargain label is cause for celebration in itself; to have it performed and recorded with such tireless commitment is a double blessing. That said, the performances on the first disc suffered from the soloist's poetic parsimony and an oppressive ill-balance from Naxos. But this second disc is successful on all counts. Scherbakov, praised by Richter and recently hailed as a 'modern Rachmaninov', is now more attuned to Medtner's widely fluctuating idiom, complementing his unquestioned virtuosity with inwardness and conviction. Sample the passage beginning at 6'30" in the Third Concerto's finale and you will hear the sort of eloquence that warms the hearts of all true Russians. Elsewhere he and his partners are entirely sympathetic to freely associating ideas that sprout wings of the spirit and evolve into endlessly changing hues and patterns contained within a disciplined if idiosyncratic sense of form.

Commissioned by Moiseiwitsch, an early and courageous champion of Medtner's genius, the Third Concerto, subtitled 'Ballade', flows like some primeval river of the imagination, its burgeoning course inspired by Lermontov's *Water Spirit*, while the First Concerto's often epic gestures blend a bittersweet Russian romanticism (and all Medtner's music is a nostalgic idealisation of his native land) with themes of an almost Elgarian cut (10'00" into the opening *Allegro*). Scherbakov's agility at, say, the *con moto* (8'38") is never at the expense of a composer whose bravura is always poetically motivated, and so all lovers of romantic piano concertos need look no further.

There is stiff competition from Alexeev in the First Concerto, to an even greater extent from the *Gramophone* Award-winning Demidenko in the Third (both on Hyperion) and, of course, from the composer himself in the Second and Third Concertos. Yet even at this exalted level Scherbakov more than holds his own.

Violin Sonatas

No 1 in B minor, Op 21; **No 2** in G, Op 44; **No 3** in E minor, Op 57, 'Epica'

Violin Sonatas Nos 1 and 2
Lydia Mordkovitch *vn* **Geoffrey Tozer** *pf*
Chandos CHAN9293 (60 minutes: DDD). Ⓕ
Recorded 1993 ●

Mordkovitch's readings emphasize a lyrical and relaxed approach, and this is particularly so in the lyrical first movement of the short, attractive First Sonata – a little too relaxed perhaps in the outer sections of the lilting second movement

'Danza'. Elsewhere (for instance the *Allegro appassionato* and Finale-Rondo of the Second Sonata), Mordkovitch has an intuitive grasp of structure, allowing the music to unfold with a high degree of ease and direction. These artists are persuasive interpreters of these works and can be strongly recommended to the first-time explorer. Recorded sound is warm and balanced.

Medtner Violin Sonata No 3
Ravel Violin Sonata
Vadim Repin *vn* **Boris Berezovsky** *pf*
Erato 0630-15110-2 (61 minutes: DDD). Ⓕ
Recorded 1996

Of Medtner's three sonatas this is perhaps the most intricately worked and, at over 40 minutes, certainly the most substantial. At times it seems almost too long for its own good and for that reason it needs a very persuasive and masterly performance in order to project its strengths. Fortunately this one is about as persuasive as you can get – Repin is lyrical and passionate and has plenty of fiery temperament for this music, and he is ideally complemented by Berezovsky's equally splendid playing. Much is made of the sonata's lyrical and melodic abundance (the *Scherzo* is delivered with great panache) and Repin's choice of tempo for all movements is expertly judged. In the Ravel, Repin and Berezovsky are perhaps even more impressive. As a vehicle for Repin's talent it shows what a marvellous colourist he is, what exceptional subtlety and nuance he brings to the music and, in the 'Blues' movement especially, the sheer *frisson* he is capable of generating. One cannot understate the superb ensemble playing either, with Berezovsky perfectly attuned to every twist and turn of Repin's playing. The recorded sound is very realistic and naturally balanced.

Eight Mood Pictures

Eight Mood Pictures, Op 1. Three Improvisations, Op 2. Three Novelles, Op 17. Improvisation, Op 31 No 1. Etude 'of medium difficulty'. Three Hymns in Praise of Toil, Op 49
Geoffrey Tozer *pf*
Chandos CHAN9498 (70 minutes: DDD). Ⓕ
Recorded 1995

Dithyramb in E flat, Op 10 No 2. Fairy Tale in F minor, 'Ophelia's song', Op 14 No 1. Sonatas, Op 25 – No 1 in C minor, 'Sonata-Skazka'; No 2 in E minor, 'The Night Wind'. Sonate-Idylle in G, Op 56
Geoffrey Tozer *pf*
Chandos CHAN9618 (72 minutes: DDD). Ⓕ
Recorded 1995

Medtner's piano music contains glories and riches indeed – an unending sense of intricacy from Russia's most subtle and recondite composer. Even when Medtner reminds you of his debt to others (to, say, Brahms and Schumann) he remains inimitably himself, ranging effortlessly from lyric to epic and essaying everything in between. Take the 'Prologue', from Op 1, composed when Medtner was 18 and prefaced by some lines from Lermontov telling of a soul carried to earth by an angel. Such serenity and other-worldly preoccupation are expressed in music of rippling complexity, soaring to declamatory heights before resuming its pensiveness and quiet ecstasy. In total contrast *The Night Wind* Sonata, dedicated to and greatly admired by Rachmaninov, is among the most daunting of all sonatas; of heroic length and ambition. Then there are the *Three Hymns in Praise of Toil*, transcending their seeming workaday proletariat title, their radiant outpouring coloured by a typically Slavic anxiety and unease. 'Nixe' (a water sprite – Op 2 No 1), on the other hand, reminds us of Szymanowski in its exoticism, most notably in a magical and shimmering final retreat. The *Improvisation*, Op 31 No 1 is another of Medtner's finest, most imaginative offerings, and if the *Dithyramb* exults in Brahmsian fullness, its final pages, which seem to engulf the entire keyboard, are of a vehemence peculiar to Medtner.

Playing throughout with an enviable strength, grace and subtlety and with an unfailingly beautiful sonority, Geoffrey Tozer is more than equal to every occasion. Hearing him, for example, in the Sonata, Op 25 No 2 or in the slow movement from the *Sonata-Skazka* (complete with a melody he describes in his excellent notes as 'one of the loveliest Medtner ever wrote'), you will be made more than aware of his warmth and affection as well as his imperturbable fluency and skill. Played with such conviction all this music acquires a haunting idiosyncrasy which repays constant attention, even when, as Tozer engagingly puts it, 'the themes in Medtner's perorations are like guests leaving a party, standing in the doorway with hats and coats on, saying goodbye, but each unwilling to be the first to leave'. The recordings are of the highest quality.

Piano Sonatas

Sonata in F minor, Op 5. Two Fairy Tales, Op 8. Sonata Triad, Op 11. Sonata in G minor, Op 22. Sonatas, Op 25 – No 1 in C minor, 'Sonata-Skazka'; No 2 in E minor, 'The Night Wind'. Sonata-Ballade in F sharp, Op 27. Sonata in A minor, Op 30. Forgotten Melodies – Set I, Op 38; Set II, Op 39. Sonata romantica in B flat minor, Op 53 No 1. Sonata minacciosa in F minor, Op 53 No 2. Sonate-Idylle in G, Op 56
Marc-André Hamelin *pf*
Hyperion ④ CDA67221/4 (279 minutes: DDD). Ⓜ
Recorded 1998 ●

With this classic recording of the 14 piano sonatas, Medtner's star soared into the ascendant. Superlatively played and presented, it effects a radical and triumphant transition from years of indifference to heady acclaim. True, Medtner was celebrated by Rachmaninov as 'the greatest composer of our time' and championed by pianists such as Moiseiwitsch, Horowitz and Gilels, yet his music fell largely on deaf ears. Such irony and enigma lie in the music itself, in its distinctive character, colour and fragrance. Listeners were understandably suspicious of music that yields up its secrets so unreadily, almost as if Medtner wished it to remain in a private rather than public domain. Moments of a ravishing, heart-stopping allure, and heroics on the grandest of scales are apt to occur within an indigestible, prolix and recondite context. On paper (and it is virtually impossible to appreciate or consider Medtner without a score) everything is comprehensible, yet the results are never quite what you expect. Much of the writing, too, is formidably complex, with rhythmic intricacies deriving from Brahms and whimsicalities from Schumann supporting a recognizably Slavic yet wholly personal idiom.

Such writing demands a transcendental technique and a burning poetic commitment, a magical amalgam achieved with delicacy, drama and finesse by Marc-André Hamelin. Interspersing the sonatas with groups of miniatures containing some of Medtner's most felicitous ideas, he plays with an authority suggesting that such music is truly his language. Wherever you turn you will find a stylistic consistency and aplomb that make you realize that mastery of Medtner's difficulties requires a reflex and elegance beyond mere physical preparation, a capacity to absorb, away from the keyboard, a plethora of ideas, and resolve them into an unfaltering lucidity. Hamelin achieves an unfaltering sense of continuity, a balance of sense and sensibility in music that threatens to become submerged in its own passion. Readers uncertain of Medtner's elusive art should try the *Forgotten Melodies* (and most of all 'Alla reminiscenza'), the *Sonata Triad* and, by contrast, the simple Elysium conjured in the first movement of the *Sonate-Idylle*. Such heaven-sent performances will set you journeying far and wide, their eloquence and calibre accentuated by Hyperion's sound, by clarity, warmth and refinement.

Songs

The Angel, Op 1*a*. Winter Evening, Op 13 No 1. Songs, Op 28 – No 2, I cannot hear that bird; No 3, Butterfly; No 4, In the Churchyard; No 5, Spring Calm. The Rose, Op 29 No 6. I loved thee well, Op 32 No 4. Night, Op 36 No 5. Sleepless, Op 37 No 1. Songs, Op 52 – No 2, The Raven; No 3, Elegy; No 5, Spanish Romance; No 6, Serenade. Noon, Op 59 No 1. Eight Songs, Op 24

Ludmilla Andrew *sop* **Geoffrey Tozer** *pf*

Chandos CHAN9327 (60 minutes: DDD). Texts and translations included. Recorded 1993 Ⓕ

Musical Opinion, reviewing the newly published Op 52 in 1931, concluded that, 'very accomplished musician' as he undoubtedly was, Medtner could hardly be considered 'a born song writer': 'These restless, feverish compositions with their incessant chromaticism and modulations are essentially unvocal, though they are dramatic and rhapsodical enough.' It says something for the achievement of Ludmilla Andrew that the 'unvocal' character of Medtner's writing is hardly evident at all, though, to be fair, the first three songs from Op 52 are perhaps the very ones in which the voice is most hard-pressed and in which it is even possible to feel that they might do very well as piano solos. In the 'Serenade' (No 6 in the set), the piano part *is* an accompaniment, and the singer brings to it a charm and delicacy worthy of its dedicatee, Nina Koshetz. Geoffrey Tozer is an excellent accompanist. His playing of 'Winter Evening', with its evocative rustling start, is superb; but always, along with the sheer virtuosity, there is a responsive feeling for mood and coloration. There are songs in which the piano takes over. Yet in many the interest is evenly d istributed, and these are among the most delightful in the repertoire.

Fanny Mendelssohn-Hensel

German 1805-1847

GROVE *Sister of Felix Mendelssohn, Fanny was a gifted pianist and composer of songs (some published under her brother's name), piano music and a few large-scale dramatic works. In the 1830s she became the central figure in a flourishing salon, for which she created most of her compositions and where she performed on the piano and conducted. Her diary and correspondence provide vivid and essential material on the musical life of her time.*

Lieder

Lieder – Opp 1, 7, 9 and 10. Ich wandelte unter den Bäumen. Die Schiffende. Traum. Suleika. Dämmrung senkte sich von oben. Nach Süden. **Mendelssohn** Italien, Op 8 No 3

Susan Gritton *sop* **Eugene Asti** *pf*

Hyperion CDA67110 (72 minutes: DDD). Texts and translations included. Recorded 1999 Ⓕ ⭘

A few single songs by Mendelssohn's sister Fanny have appeared in concert programmes and have registered as pleasant, delightful even, but rather too comfortable and conventional to reward any more sustained attention. This is now proved to be untrue. Heard in sequence, as here, the songs reveal their strength. The melodies are more athletic, the piano parts more varied, the modulations more expressive than one may have thought. The choice of text – more of Goethe than of any other poet – challenges thoughtfulness. There is also a curious feature of the music: though the excellent commentary on the songs often suggests a reminiscence on Fanny's part (of Bach or Schubert or Schumann), the associations in a present-day listener's mind are likely to be forward as often as back. *Die frühen Gräber* (Op 9 No 4), for instance, is compared to 'a Bach organ chorale'; and yet as one searches in the mind to identify a kinship for that unusually deep-toned piano writing, the name which surfaces is not Bach but Brahms. In less sensitive hands than Eugene Asti's this could sound muddy; but his clarity and feeling for rhythm and harmony obviate that. Similarly, a springlike voice such as Susan Gritton's could have confirmed the impression that pleasantness was all, whereas she is remarkably good at deepening the colours (as in *Der Ersehnte*, Op 9 No 1) and concentrating the mind (as in *Im Herbste*, Op 10 No 4). An excellent record: enterprising programme, fresh young artists, fine presentation.

Felix Mendelssohn

German 1809-1847

GROVE *Mendelssohn came from a distinguished intellectual, artistic and banking family in Berlin (the family converted from Judaism to Christianity in 1816, taking the additional name 'Bartholdy'). He studied the piano with Ludwig Berger and theory and composition with Zelter, producing his first piece in 1820; thereafter, a profusion of sonatas, concertos, string symphonies, piano quartets and Singspiels revealed his increasing mastery of counterpoint and form. Besides family travels and eminent visitors to his parents' salon, early influences included the poetry of Goethe (whom he knew from 1821) and the Schlegel translations of Shakespeare; these are traceable in his best music of the period. His gifts as a conductor also showed themselves early: in 1829 he directed a pioneering performance of Bach's St Matthew Passion at the Berlin Singakademie, promoting the modern cultivation of Bach's music.*

A period of travel and concert-giving introduced Mendelssohn to England, Scotland (1829) and Italy (1830-31). In 1833 he took up a conducting post at Düsseldorf, concentrating on Handel's oratorios. Among the chief products of this time were The Hebrides, the G minor Piano Concerto, Die erste Walpurgisnacht, the Italian Symphony and St Paul. But as a conductor and music organizer his most significant achievement was in Leipzig (1835-47), where to great acclaim he conducted the Gewandhaus Orchestra, championing both historical and modern works, and founded and directed the Leipzig Conservatory (1843).

Composing mostly in the summer holidays, he produced Ruy Blas Overture, a revised version of the Hymn of Praise, the Scottish Symphony, the Violin Concerto Op 64 and the fine Piano Trio in C minor (1845). Meanwhile, he was intermittently (and less happily) employed by the king as a composer and choirmaster in Berlin, where he wrote highly successful incidental music, notably for A Midsummer Night's Dream (1843). Much sought after as a festival organiser, he was associated especially with the Lower Rhine and Birmingham music festivals. His death at the age of 38, after a series of strokes, was mourned internationally.

With its emphasis on clarity and adherence to classical ideals, Mendelssohn's music shows alike the influences of Bach (fugal technique), Handel (rhythms, harmonic progressions), Mozart (dramatic characterisation, forms, textures) and Beethoven (instrumental technique), though from 1825 he developed a characteristic style of his own, often underpinned by a literary, artistic, historical, geographical or emotional connection; indeed it was chiefly in his skilful use of extra-musical stimuli that he was a Romantic. His early and prodigious operatic gifts, clearly reliant on Mozart, failed to develop, but his penchant for the dramatic found expression in the oratorios as well as in Ruy Blas Overture, his Antigone incidental music and above all the enduring Midsummer Night's Dream music, in which themes from the overture are cleverly adapted as motifs in the incidental music. The oratorios, among the most popular works of their kind, draw inspiration from Bach and Handel and content from the composer's personal experience, St Paul being an allegory of Mendelssohn's own family history and Elijah of his years of dissension in Berlin. Among his other vocal works, the highly dramatic Die erste Walpurgisnacht, Op 60 (on Goethe's poem greeting springtime) and the Leipzig psalm settings deserve special mention; the choral songs and lieder are uneven, reflecting their wide variety of social functions.

After an apprenticeship of string symphony writing in a classical mould, Mendelssohn found inspiration in art, nature and history for his orchestral music. The energy, clarity and tunefulness of the Italian have made it his most popular symphony, although the elegiac Scottish represents a newer, more purposeful achievement. In his best overtures, essentially one-movement symphonic poems, the sea appears as a recurring image, from Calm Sea and Prosperous Voyage and The Hebrides to The Lovely Melusine. Less dependent on programmatic elements and at the same time formally innovatory, the concertos, notably that for violin, and the chamber music, especially some of the string quartets, the Octet and the two late piano trios, beautifully reconcile classical principles with personal feeling; these are among his most striking compositions. Of the solo instrumental works, the partly lyric, partly virtuoso Lieder ohne Worte for piano (from 1829) are elegantly written and often touching.

Piano Concertos

No 1 in G minor, Op 25; **No 2** in D minor, Op 40; **A minor** (piano and strings); **E; A flat** (both two pianos)

Piano Concertos – Nos 1 and 2. Capriccio brillant in B minor, Op 22. Rondo brillant in E flat, Op 29. Serenade and Allegro giocoso, Op 43
Stephen Hough *pf* **City of Birmingham Symphony Orchestra / Lawrence Foster**
Hyperion CDA66969 (75 minutes: DDD). Ⓕ
Recorded 1997 **OO**

With Stephen Hough's Mendelssohn we enter a new dimension. The soft, stylish arpeggios that open the first work here, the *Capriccio brillant*, announce something special. But this is just a preparation for the First Concerto. Here again, 'stylish' is the word. One can sense the background – especially the operatic background against which these works were composed. The first solo doesn't simply storm away, *fortissimo*; one hears distinct emotional traits: the imperious, thundering octaves, the agitated semiquavers, the pleading appoggiaturas. The revelation is the First Concerto's slow movement: not a trace of stale sentimentality here, rather elegance balanced by depth of feeling. Some of the praise must go to the CBSO and Foster; after all it's the

CBSO violas and cellos that lead the singing in that slow movement. Foster and the orchestra are also effective in the opening of the Second Concerto – too often dismissed as the less inspired sequel to No 1. The first bars are hushed, sombre, a little below the main tempo, so that it's left to Hough to energize the argument and set the pace – all very effective.

Piano Concerto in A minor. Concerto for Violin, Piano and Strings in D minor
Rainer Kussmaul *vn* **Andreas Staier** *fp*
Concerto Köln
Teldec Das Alte Werk 0630-13152-2
(72 minutes: DDD). Ⓕ
Recorded 1996

These two works of Mendelssohn, dating from his early teens, make an excellent coupling, providing generous measure too, when the brilliant boy was writing more expansively than he did in his later concertos. Given that these works were first heard in the Sunday salons at the Mendelssohns' home, it is logical that they should be recorded here not just on period instruments but with a small band of strings, in places one instrument per part. What is less welcome is that the strings of Concerto Köln adopt what might be regarded as an unreconstructed view of period string-playing, so that the orchestral tuttis are rather trying, not least in slow movements, even on an ear well adjusted to period performance.

The soloists, both outstanding, provide a total contrast, and there the violinist, Rainer Kussmaul, is if anything even more impressive than Andreas Staier, for many years the harpsichordist of Concerto Köln and here the director as well as soloist. Throughout the Double Concerto Kussmaul plays with rare freshness and purity, allowing himself just a measure of vibrato, and if Staier takes second place, that is not just a question of balance between the violin and an 1825 fortepiano by Johann Fritz of Vienna, but of the young composer's piano writing, regularly built on passagework, often in arpeggios, rather than straight melodic statements. No doubt that had something to do with the pianos of the day, with their limited sustaining power. That applies to the piano writing in the Piano Concerto too, and it is striking that though each work is astonishing from a composer so young, the Double Concerto, written just a year later, reveals a clear development. The material is not as memorable in either work as it is in such a masterpiece as the Octet of two years later, yet in every movement, and not least the finales of both works, the composer is clearly identifiable as Mendelssohn.

Double Piano Concertos – E; A flat
Benjamin Frith, Hugh Tinney *pfs*
RTE Sinfonietta / Prionnsías O'Duinn
Naxos 8 553416 (74 minutes: DDD). Ⓢ
Recorded 1995

Mendelssohn was 14 when he completed his first two-piano Concerto in E major, and still only 15 when he followed it with a considerably longer (rather too long) and more ambitious second in A flat. Both concertos were first heard at the family's Sunday morning music parties, with the composer's much-loved, slightly older sister, Fanny, at the second piano. As her talents were akin to his own, the two solo parts are indistinguishable in their challenges. And it is to the great credit of Benjamin Frith and Hugh Tinney that without a score at hand, you would be hard-pressed to guess who was playing what. You will be as impressed by their attunement of phrasing in lyrical contexts as by their synchronization in all the brilliant semiquaver passagework in which both works abound. Their uninhibited enjoyment of the imitative audacities of the later work's finale is a real *tour de force*. Under Prionnsías O'Duinn the RTE Sinfonietta plays with sufficient relish to allow you to forget that the recording is perhaps just a little too close. In short, a not-to-be-missed opportunity to explore the precocious young Mendelssohn at super-bargain price.

Violin Concerto in E minor

Mendelssohn Violin Concerto
Bruch Violin Concerto No 1 in G minor, Op 26
Schubert Rondo in A, D438
Kennedy *vn*
English Chamber Orchestra / Jeffrey Tate
EMI CDC7 49663-2 (71 minutes: DDD). Ⓕ
Recorded 1987

These are exceptionally strong and positive performances, vividly recorded. When it comes to the two main works, Kennedy readily holds his own against all comers. His view of the Mendelssohn has a positive, masculine quality established at the very start. He may at first seem a little fierce, but fantasy goes with firm control, and the transition into the second subject on a descending arpeggio (marked *tranquillo*) is radiantly beautiful, the more affecting by contrast with the power of what has gone before. Kennedy is unerring helped by Jeffrey Tate's refreshing and sympathetic support. Though it is the English Chamber Orchestra accompanying, there is no diminution of scale. With full and well-balanced sound, the piece even seems bigger, more symphonic than usual. In the slow movement Kennedy avoids sentimentality in his simple, songful view, and with Tate a devoted Mendelssohnian, the finale sparkles with no feeling of rush. The coda is always a big test in this work, and Kennedy's and Tate's reading is among the most powerful and exciting on record.

The Bruch brings another warm and positive performance, consistently sympathetic, with the orchestra once more adding to the power. Kennedy is more than a match for rival versions, again bringing a masculine strength which goes with a richly expressive yet totally unsentimental view of Bruch's exuberant lyricism as in the central slow movement. The *Rondo* in A major, D438, from 1816, was originally written for solo violin accompanied by string quartet. Performed as here with string orchestra, it in effect becomes another *Concertstück*, following a regular Schubertian form, a substantial *Andante* introduction leading to an *Allegro*, lasting here in all some 16 minutes. The 19-year-old was simply enjoying himself with a flow of ideas that may not be very memorable but which in the hands of performers like this are sweetly entertaining.

String Symphonies

String Symphonies Nos 1, 6, 7 and 12
Nieuw Sinfonietta Amsterdam / Lev Markiz Ⓕ
BIS CD683 (70 minutes: DDD). Recorded 1994

Amazing stuff, brilliantly performed. The first of the symphonies fair bursts from the staves, with a chuckling finale that would surely have delighted Rossini. And although the Sixth Symphony's finale harbours hints of miracles to come, Mendelssohn's mature personality is more comprehensively anticipated in the Seventh. Again, the finale suggests the ebullient, life-affirming manner of the orchestral symphonies, albeit sobered by a spot of fugally formal writing later on. The 12th Symphony opens with a Handelian sense of ceremony, goes on to incorporate a characteristically tender *Andante* and ends with a finale that, to quote Stig Jacobsson's enthusiastic notes, 'dies away to *pizzicato* and a subsequent *accelerando* which recalls Rossini'. This is truly delightful music, the playing both sensitive and exciting, while BIS's sound is impressively full-bodied.

Symphonies / Overtures

Symphonies – No 1 in C minor, Op 11; **No 2** in B flat, Op 52, 'Hymn of Praise'; **No 3** in A minor, Op 56, 'Scottish'; **No 4** in A, Op 90, 'Italian'; **No 5** in D, Op 107, 'Reformation'.
Overtures – Die Hochzeit des Camacho, Op 10; **A Midsummer Night's Dream**, Op 21; **The Hebrides**, Op 26, 'Fingal's Cave'; **Meeresstille und glückliche Fahrt**, Op 27; **The Fair Melusina**, Op 32; **Athalie**, Op 74; **Ruy Blas**, Op 95

Symphonies Nos 1, 2[a] and 3-5. Overtures – The Hebrides; A Midsummer Night's Dream; The Fair Melusina. Octet in E flat, Op 20 – Scherzo
[a]**Elizabeth Connell,** [a]**Karita Mattila** *sops*
[a]**Hans-Peter Blochwitz** *ten*
London Symphony Orchestra / Claudio Abbado
DG ④ 415 353-2GH4 (245 minutes: DDD). Ⓕ
Recorded 1984-85 **OO**

Claudio Abbado gives us a comprehensive collection of the mature symphonies plus three overtures and the orchestral arrangement (in shortened form) of the *Scherzo* from his String Octet, which at the first British performance in 1829 of the Symphony No 1 Mendelssohn substituted for the Minuet third movement. If you have a programming facility on your player, you can quite easily insert that *Scherzo* instead of the Minuet, and the idea of having it as an appendix to the symphony is a good one. The wide-ranging sound comes out most strikingly in Symphony No 2. Abbado conveys a keen sense of joy with a wide expressive range. The yearning 6/8 movement is haunting at Abbado's quite slow speed, and though this speed for the *Andante religioso* brings dangers of sweetness and sentimentality, he avoids them with his warm but unmannered phrasing. Again, in the choral finale Abbado's speeds tend to be relaxed and the sense of joyful release is all the keener, when in response to the tenor's calls of 'Hüter, ist die Nacht bald hin?' ('Watchman, will the night soon pass?') the soprano gives her radiant call of 'Die Nacht ist vergangen ('The night has departed'). Elizabeth Connell is the more tenderly affecting by being placed at the point slightly at a distance, and then the chorus comes in with even more impact to signal the arrival of day. Earlier Connell and the second soprano, Karita Mattila, are nicely matched in the duet with chorus, 'Ich harrete des Herrn' ('I waited on the Lord'). Hans-Peter Blochwitz's tenor may be on the light side for the key tenor part, but the tonal beauty and natural feeling for words and phrasing are a delight. Sois the singing of the London Symphony Chorus, particularly beautiful in the chorale, 'Nun danket alle Gott'. Abbado's expansiveness and the luminous choral sound makes for a rich result.

It is that avoidance of Victorian blandness which is striking in Abbado's accounts of Nos 1 and 5. In No 1 he is tough and biting in the C minor first movement, slower and simpler in the second, returning to a tough, dark manner for the Minuet and finale. This performance has one marvelling that Mendelssohn could have ever have countenanced the idea of the Octet *Scherzo* as substitute, a piece so different in mood.

The first movement of the *Reformation* finds Abbado biting and dramatic, and crisper and again quicker in the second movement *Allegro vivace*. In both the *Scottish* and *Italian* Symphonies Abbado's earlier versions clearly come into contention (these were recorded in 1968 for Decca), but where in the *Scottish* the differences of interpretation are relatively unimportant those in the *Italian* are more striking. Here the outer movements are fractionally faster than before, but that difference brings just a hint of breathlessness in the playing of the LSO, where before it was so sparking. By contrast the noticeably faster speed for the second movement *Andante* this time sounds fresher, and the marginally faster speed for the third movement is preferable. As for the overtures, they too bring fresh and attractive performances, very fast and fleet in the fairy music of *A Midsummer Night's Dream* and with the contrast between first and second subjects of *The Hebrides* underlined.

Symphony No 2 **P**
Soile Isokoski *sop* **Mechthild Bach** *sop* **Frieder Lang** *ten* **Cologne Chorus Musicus; Das Neue Orchester / Christoph Spering**
Opus 111 OPS30-98 (65 minutes: DDD). Text and translation included. Recorded 1993 Ⓕ

The *Hymn of Praise* stands under the shade of Beethoven's *Choral* Symphony, with its considerable length and choral and solo contributions, but it does not reach similar heights of sublimity. What it does possess is an unassuming lyricism, vitality and elegance that is highly attractive. Spering is relaxed in his choice of tempos. In no way, however, does he let the music drag or become sentimental. With clean, crisp textures this is a most refreshing performance, full of incidental beauties. In the main *Allegro* of the first movement as well as in the opening section of the big choral cantata-finale, Spering's speeds are fast but refreshing. The rest is different, not just slower in its speeds, but often more affectionate. The duet for the two soprano soloists, 'Ich harrete des Herrn' ('I waited on the Lord'), is especially beautiful, with Soile Isokoski and Mechthild Bach angelically sweet yet nicely contrasted. The tenor soloist too, Frieder Lang, is exceptionally sweet-toned. The chorus, as recorded in a warm acoustic, are not always ideally clear in inner definition, but the freshness of their singing matches that of the whole performance. Anyone attracted by the advance of period performance into 19th-century repertory should investigate this issue.

Symphonies Nos 3 and 4
London Symphony Orchestra / Claudio Abbado
DG 3-D Classics 427 810-2GDC (71 minutes: DDD). Ⓜ
Recorded 1984 **OO**

Claudio Abbado's coupling of the *Scottish* and *Italian* Symphonies makes a pretty clear first choice for those wanting these works paired together (the full set is reviewed above). The sound is fresh within a pleasing ambience and the performances show this conductor at his very finest. *Allegros* are exhilarating, yet never sound rushed, and the flowing *Adagio* of the *Scottish* is matched by the admirably paced *Andante* in the *Italian*, with the mood of the 'Pilgrim's March' nicely captured. The *Scherzo* of the *Scottish* is a joy, and the recording clarifies textures that can often sound muddled, especially at the exuberant horn arpeggios. Both first-movement exposition repeats are included.

Symphonies Nos 3 and 4 **P**
London Classical Players / Sir Roger Norrington
Virgin Classics VM5 61735-2 (65 minutes: DDD). Ⓜ
Recorded 1989 **O**

Schumann Symphonies – No 3 in E flat, 'Rhenish', Op 97; No 4 in D minor, Op 120 **P**
London Classical Players / Sir Roger Norrington
Virgin Classics VM5 61734-2 (57 minutes: DDD). Ⓜ
Recorded 1989 **O**

Issued originally in 1990 and 1991, both these discs represented an extension of repertory for Norrington and the London Classical Players, moving a stage further in period performances of the central romantic repertory. If in Beethoven Norrington has always been wedded to the doctrine of obeying the composer's challengingly fast metro-nome markings, it is different here. Both in Mendelssohn and in Schumann the outer movements at least are relatively unrushed. It is a special delight to hear textures so lightened and clarified in both the Mendelssohn symphonies – the first movement of the *Italian* skipping infectiously, and the flute articulation wonderfully clean in the *Saltarello* finale.

Here and elsewhere it helps to have a rather less resonant body of strings, so giving extra prominence to brass and woodwind. The different entries in the *Scherzo* of the *Scottish* Symphony are given extra clarity, while the great horn entry in the coda of the finale is gloriously resonant (track 4, 8'05"), a moment to send you heavenwards.

If Mendelssohn as an orchestrator has always been counted a master of transparency, it is so different with Schumann. Yet Norrington in these exhilarating performances – like Sir John Eliot Gardiner in his comprehensive set of the Schumann symphonies – demonstrates that period performance alongside skilful balancing can undermine the old myth, with textures at least as clear as you would expect in Brahms. Again speeds are unexaggerated, even if the three middle movements of the *Rhenish* Symphony flow rather faster than in most performances with modern instruments. The second and third movements become interludes, but the fourth, inspired by a visit to Cologne Cathedral, loses none of its gravity, thanks largely to heightened dynamic contrasts. The Fourth Symphony in its revised version brings similar qualities, with the successive *accelerandos* in the coda to the finale clear and unexaggerated, full of excitement but without hysteria. Two welcome reissues at mid-price.

Symphonies Nos 3 and 4
San Francisco Symphony Orchestra / Herbert Blomstedt
Decca 433 811-2DH (67 minutes: DDD). Ⓕ
Recorded 1989 and 1991 **O**

Blomstedt's *Scottish* impresses most by dint of its joyous vigour (outer movements go with a will), rhythmic bounce (perky winds and razor-sharp strings in the *Scherzo*) and unaffected eloquence (as in his affectionately flowing yet never short-winded third movement *Adagio*). This *Italian*, too, is first-rate. Under Blomstedt the opening *Allegro vivace* positively fizzes along, aided by some quite beautifully sprung string playing, whilst the *Saltarello* finale is articulated with real panache. The middle movements are perhaps marginally less memorable, though again the stylish orchestral response yields much pleasure. Although the symphonies were actually set down some 17 months apart, Decca's admirably consistent sound picture possesses the exemplary clarity and sheen we have now come to expect from this particular source. No one can go far wrong with this disc.

Symphonies Nos 3 and 4. Overture – The Hebrides
Ulster Orchestra / Dimitry Sitkovetsky
Classic fM 75605 57013-2 (77 minutes: DDD). Ⓜ
Recorded 1997

Violinist-turned-conductor, Dimitry Sitkovetsky, here draws from the orchestra superb performances of both symphonies as well as the overture, helped by the outstandingly full and rich recording, made in the Ulster Hall. In a way that challenges and generally outshines many rival discs, Sitkovetsky consistently conveys the feeling of live performances caught on the wing. With speeds beautifully chosen and with rhythms crisp and well sprung, his readings are full of light and shade, warmly dramatic, demonstrating an expressive freedom – notably in pressing ahead – which always sounds natural, never self-conscious. With refined playing from every section, at once tense and polished, textures are exceptionally clear and transparent, so that often obscured inner details are brought out. In that, the full and immediate recording adds to the impact and vivid sense of presence. The strings in particular produce some magical *pianissimos*, reflecting Sitkovetsky's own mastery as an instrumentalist, yet the stormy passages in the first movement of the *Scottish* also have a physical impact that brings out the inspiration from nature to an exceptional degree. Similarly in the *Hebrides* Overture, after a restrained opening, the atmospheric beauty of the writing comes out vividly. A very generous and apt coupling.

Symphony No 3. Overture – The Hebrides; A Midsummer Night's Dream. Incidental music, Op 61: Scherzo; Nocturne; Wedding March **H**
London Symphony Orchestra / Peter Maag
Decca The Classic Sound 443 578-2DCS Ⓜ
(76 minutes: ADD). Recorded 1957-60 **OO**

The Hebrides and the *Scottish* Symphony offer 'Classic' Decca engineering at its best: airy 1960 Kingsway Hall sound with a real sense of perspective drawing the ear in (woodwind set behind strings but without loss of clarity), pinpoint instrumental positioning yet no impression of instruments sealed off from each other, and, for the pre-Dolby period, a remarkable dynamic range, accomplished with low hiss levels and no audible overloading. There is, perhaps, a slight thinness of tone in the middle register, a characteristic that is far more pronounced in the 1957 *Midsummer Night's Dream* excerpts, but the high-key clarity and fizzing presence readily compensate. Maag's intelligent balancing of the orchestra and gauging of the work's proportions and rhetoric do not preclude imaginative handling of their illustrative poetry; in other words, he is a superb Mendelssohnian stylist. Personal rhythmic and dynamic inflexions abound (no doubt eyebrows will rise at such things as his sudden broad delivery of the Mechanicals' clowning in the *Midsummer Night's Dream* Overture). Singing lines are all beautifully wrought, especially that of the symphony's *Adagio*, and its 'martial' sections benefit from discreetly balanced timpani. In *The Hebrides*, the balance and range of the sound allow all those swells (superbly observed) to register in proper proportion – here is both delicate impressionism and all the stormy drive and drama that you could want, putting many more recent rivals in the shade. At the heart of this disc's success is, of course, the playing of the revitalized LSO, responding to some challenging tempos with mainly knife-edge precision of ensemble and superb attack – truly vintage LSO champagne.

A Midsummer Night's Dream

Overture and Incidental Music to A Midsummer Night's Dream, Opp 21 and 61

A Midsummer Night's Dream
Edith Wiens *sop* **Sarah Walker** *mez*
London Philharmonic Choir and Orchestra / Andrew Litton
Classics for Pleasure CD-CFP4593 Ⓑ
(50 minutes:DDD). Recorded 1987

This fine complete version of *A Midsummer Night's Dream* incidental music is a genuine bargain. Andrew Litton not only includes the linking melodramas but makes them seem an essential part of the structure. They are not separately banded, because they prepare for what is to come by echoing what has passed, as in the finale where a grand reprise of the 'Wedding March' and *diminuendo* lead naturally to the brief mentions of the fairy music from the Overture, before the delightful closing chorus, sung with an engaging lyrical felicity. How like Sullivan are the solo vocal lines here! Similarly, fragments of the *Scherzo* (which is played with the lightest touch) are used to anticipate the 'Fairies March'. The Overture is most attractively done, the violins light and dainty and the wide dynamic range making the strongest contrast with the full orchestral tuttis. The engineers have, by clever microphone placing and excellent balance, tamed the reverberation of Walthamstow Assembly Hall so that there is bloom on the sound, yet everything projects naturally and clearly. The woodwind detail is a delight and with excellent soloists the vocal numbers have plenty of character and are in the right scale – too much reverberation and the choruses can sound too heavy. The other orchestral movements are well characterized; the 'Nocturne', with a fine horn solo, is spaciously romantic and the 'Intermezzo', taken fast, has the right *appassionato* feeling without being melodramatic. This recording has everything going for it: freshness of approach, spontaneity of feeling and very good sound indeed.

A Midsummer Night's Dream. Symphony No 4
Kenneth Branagh *spkr* **Sylvia McNair** *sop* **Angelika Kirchschlager** *mez* **Women of the Ernst-Senff Chorus; Berlin Philharmonic Orchestra / Claudio Abbado**
Sony Classical SK62826 (78 minutes: DDD). Text included. Recorded live in 1995 Ⓕ

It makes an attractive package having Mendelssohn's *A Midsummer Night's Dream* music, dramatically presented (with Kenneth

Branagh taking every role from Titania to Puck), very generously coupled with Mendelssohn's most popular symphony. Sony has managed to squeeze in 50 minutes of the *Midsummer Night's Dream* music, which means only a few minor omissions. Some may resist Branagh's style – burring his 'r's for a Mummerset Puck, coming near to an Olivier imitation in Oberon's final speech – but in his versatility he is very persuasive. Having speech over music in melodrama certainly makes sense of the more fragmentary passages of the score. Abbado's performances are a delight, fresh and transparent in the fairy music, with generally fast speeds made exhilarating, never breathless. The chorus is atmospherically balanced, with the two excellent soloists, Sylvia McNair and Angelika Kirchschlager, set more forwardly. The recording, made in the Philharmonie in Berlin, is rather more vivid, a degree less recessed than in the symphony, where the orchestra is placed at a slight distance, an effect one gets used to. In the *Italian* Symphony Abbado's reading has changed little since his earlier LSO version, though here and there, as in the third movement, the phrasing is this time a little more moulded. By any reckoning he remains one of the most persuasive interpreters of this delectable work.

Octet in E flat, Op 20

Octet. String Quintet No 2 in B flat, Op 87
Academy of St Martin in the Fields Chamber Ensemble
Philips 420 400-2PH (63 minutes: ADD). Ⓕ
Recorded 1978

The glorious Octet is a work of unforced lyricism and a seemingly endless stream of melody. The Academy Chamber Ensemble, of fine soloists in their own right, admirably illustrates the benefits of working regularly as an ensemble for they play with uncommon sympathy. The string quintet is a work of greater fervour and passion than the Octet, but it is characterized by the same melodiousness and unfettered lyricism with plenty of opportunities for virtuoso playing, which are well taken. The recordings give a pleasant and warm sheen to the string colour.

String Quintets

String Quintets – No 1 in A, Op 18[a]; No 2 in B flat, Op 87[b]
Raphael Ensemble (Anthony Marwood, Catherine Manson *vns* Timothy Boulton, Louise Williams *vas* [a]Andrea Hess, [b]Michael Stirling *vcs*)
Hyperion CDA66993 (58 minutes: DDD). Ⓕ
Recorded 1997

These quintets – both masterpieces – emanate from opposite ends of Mendelssohn's career, Op 18 being much of a piece with the Overture to *A Midsummer Night's Dream*, Op 87, presenting more ardent lyricism. The Raphael Ensemble's smoothly mellifluous performances and ecstatic involvement is tellingly exemplified in the first movement of Op 18, where converging string lines set up gloriously full textures, whereas the *Scherzo*'s contrapuntal scurryings inspire quiet-voiced virtuosity. Both performances convey the shimmer and bustle of Mendelssohn's string writing without forcing the issue and score full marks for imagination, tonal integration and musicality. The recordings are well-nigh ideal.

String Quartets

String Quartets – No 3 in D, Op 44 No 1; No 4 in E minor, Op 44 No 2; No 5 in E flat, Op 44 No 3
Talich Quartet (Jan Talich Jr, Petr Macecek *vns* Vladimir Bukac *va* Petr Prause *vc*)
Calliope CAL9302 (80 minutes: DDD). Ⓕ
Recorded 2000

Here is a set of brilliant but not dazzling performances of Mendelssohn's Op 44 Quartets: that is to say, they illuminate the music but never blind the listener with empty demonstration of the players' virtuosity. Certainly the speeds are fast, but the fingerwork is so deft and the textures (helped by excellent recording) so lucid that everything Mendelssohn asks for is clear. Of the three works in this marvellous set, it is the third, in E flat (No 5), which stands highest, with one of the finest of all his first movements and an *Adagio* of a pensiveness that the players reflect in their just tempo and in a slight greying of tone. The *scherzo* and the finale (*Allegro con fuoco*) are classic examples of how the rigorous contrapuntal teaching which Mendelssohn received in his youth from old Carl Zelter gave him the technique for music of not merely pace but of wit and ingenuity. It is music to enliven the spirit, and so is this performance of it.

The quartet's sense of tempo serves them well in the D major Quartet, Mendelssohn's own favourite, with a *Menuetto* whose harmonic originality encourages a wistfulness in the playing, and in the E minor Quartet with an *Andante* that keeps gently moving (Mendelssohn particularly marked it *nicht schleppend*, 'not dragging'). One might regret that none of the first movement repeats are observed, but as there is already 80 minutes' music here, such a complaint would be unreasonable. Included in the booklet is a long, excellent historical and descriptive note by Alain Patrick Olivier, which has been translated (as is notoriously not always the case) into good English prose. Altogether an outstanding issue.

String Quartets – E flat (1823); No 1 in E flat, Op 12; No 2 in A minor, Op 13; No 3 in D, Op 44 No 1; No 4 in E minor, Op 44 No 2; No 5 in E flat, Op 44 No 3; No 6 in F minor, Op 80. Andante, Scherzo, Capriccio and Fugue, Op 81 Nos 1-2
Melos Quartet (Wilhelm Melcher, Gerhard Voss *vns* Hermann Voss *va* Peter Buck *vc*)
DG ③ 415 883-2GCM3 (199 minutes: ADD). Ⓜ
Recorded 1976-81

The familiar and misleading cliché of Mendelssohn as the cheerful chappie of early romanticism vanishes at the sound of the F minor Quartet, Op 80. Here is the intensity, anguish and anger that everyone thought Mendelssohn incapable of. His beloved sister Fanny died in May 1847 (his own death was merely months away), and the ensuing summer saw him leave Berlin for Switzerland, where he began to 'write music very industriously'. And what remarkable music it is. Right from the opening *Allegro assai* one senses trouble afoot, an unfamiliar restlessness mixed in with the more familiar busyness. Furthermore the second movement is surely the most fervent and punishing that Mendelssohn wrote – wild, insistent and unmistakably tragic in tone. This gradual intensification and darkening that occurs throughout Mendelssohn's quartet cycle makes it a most revealing guide to his creative development. But much of the earlier music is profoundly 'Mendelssohnian' in the accepted sense of that term: fresh, dynamic, light-textured, beautifully crafted and full of amiable melodic invention.

The very early E flat Quartet, Op posth (composed when Mendelssohn was only 14), although fashioned in the style of Haydn and Mozart, points towards imminent developments – a song-like A minor Quartet, already taking its lead from late Beethoven in the same key, the E flat, Op 12, with its delightful Canzonetta (which was once popular as a separate 'encore') and the eventful Op 44 set, three of Mendelssohn's most concentrated full-scale works. And DG also adds the four separate pieces, Op 81, thus treating us to the entire Mendelssohn string quartet canon. The Melos Quartet comes up trumps with a really superb set of performances – technically immaculate, transparent in tone and full of enthusiasm. The recordings have presence and clarity.

String Quartets Nos 1 and 2 Ⓟ
Quatuor Mosaïques (Erich Höbarth, Andrea Bischof *vns* Anita Mitterer *va* Christophe Coin *vc*)
Auvidis Astrée E8622 (57 minutes: DDD). Ⓕ
Recorded 1997 ●●

Saturated in Beethoven, youthfully experimental – these are still two of the finest string quartets written in the 19th century. Op 13 (actually the first to be composed) is especially original: a turbulent, passionate work framed by a prelude and postlude based on a song – a product of an early love affair. There is nothing superficial about these performances. One senses deep, unforced absorption right from the start of both works. The sound of the gut strings (brightly recorded), and the relatively sparing vibrato, might create problems for one or two listeners; but the expressive manner is not significantly different from most conventional modern performances. There is no suggestion of cultivating 'period style' for its own sake, and no hurried tempos in slow movements – the music always has time to breathe. Both performances are refreshing and stimulating, particularly enjoyable in the 'Intermezzo' movements Mendelssohn provides in place of the scherzo or the more classical minuet.

Piano Trios

Piano Trios – No 1 in D minor, Op 49; No 2 in C minor, Op 66
Vienna Piano Trio (Wolfgang Redik *vn* Marcus Trefny *vc* Stefan Mendl *pf*)
Nimbus NI5553 (55 minutes: DDD). Ⓕ
Recorded 1997

In Stefan Mendl the Vienna Piano Trio has an exceptionally brilliant pianist. Perhaps the spotlight ought not to be quite so much on the keyboard in the first of these two works, in D minor, but his fingerwork is delectably light and frothy. The composer himself, as an effortless prestidigitator, is of course much to blame in giving it so unrelentingly breathless a stream of notes. In the intervening six years before the C minor Trio, Mendelssohn learnt a lot – no doubt never forgetting his friend Hiller's comment that some of the patterned, arpeggio-type figuration in the earlier work was 'old-fashioned'. You need only compare the elfin *Scherzos* of both to appreciate the infinitely subtler scoring of the latter. Subject-matter is likewise more affirmatively contrasted throughout, notably in the chorale-inspired triumphs of the finale. A more forwardly projected, richer cello song would have helped, but general balance in Nimbus's resonant concert hall is better here than in the D minor. And the enthusiastic freshness and vitality of this young team is a constant stimulus (note their daringly fast tempo risked in both *Scherzos*). In sum, plenty to enjoy here.

Cello Sonatas

Cello Sonatas – No 1 in B flat, Op 45; No 2 in D, Op 58. Variations concertantes, Op 17. Assai tranquillo. Song without words, Op 109 Ⓟ
Steven Isserlis *vc* **Melvyn Tan** *fp*
RCA Red Seal 09026 62553-2 (62 minutes: DDD). Ⓕ
Recorded 1994 ●

Isserlis and Tan offer idiomatic, well-turned performances full of freshness and vigour. Try the First Sonata in B flat major (which Mendelssohn wrote for his brother, Paul, in 1838), where the second movement's dual function as scherzo and slow movement is convincingly characterized, and the music's passionate outbursts sound arrestingly potent. Isserlis's and Tan's fine blend of subtlety and panache affectingly conveys the nostalgic mood of the *Variations concertantes*, and culminates powerfully in the work's conclusion. In the D major Second Sonata, Isserlis's and Tan's spontaneity and energy in the outer movements, skilfully controlled variety of timbre and touch in the *Scherzo*, and dramatic opposition of chorale (piano) and recitative (cello) in the third movement sound immensely compelling. In the *Assai tranquillo*, as in the charming *Song without words*, Op 109, sympathetic tonal balance between cello and fortepiano in the softly lit recording brings out the music's sentiment. Isserlis and Tan effectively draw out the work's inconclusive ending to create a telling analogy of the eternal nature of friendship. Excellent balance and crisp, restrained recording helps vividly to evoke this music's romantic atmosphere.

Songs without words

Mendelssohn Lieder ohne Wörter – Op 19: Nos 1, 3 and 5; Op 30: Nos 2 and 6; Op 38: Nos 2, 3 and 6; Op 53 No 4; Op 62 No 2; Op 67: Nos 1, 2 and 4; Op 102 No 5
Bach/Busoni Chorale Preludes – Ich ruf' zu dir, Herr Jesu Christ, BWV639; Wachet auf, ruft uns die Stimme, BWV645; Nun komm, der Heiden Heiland; Nun freut euch, lieben Christen, BWV734
Schubert/Liszt Auf dem Wasser zu singen, D774. In der Ferne, D957 No 6. Ständchen, D889. Erlkönig, D328
Murray Perahia *pf* Ⓕ
Sony Classical SK66511 (66 minutes: DDD) **OO**

These pieces demand above all the ability to project and sustain a singing line, to mould and shape a beautiful and nuanced sound, and to evoke the atmosphere of each poetic inspiration. In short, they demand a pianist of Perahia's sensibility and temperament. The Bach/Busoni Chorale Preludes are played with entirely natural tempos but never allowing the accompaniments, however florid, to sound rushed or agitated. The chorales sing with the most beautiful and luminous tone, and with a wonderfully sustained line. The slower Preludes (*Nun komm, der Heiden Heiland* and *Ich ruf' zu dir, Herr Jesu Christ*) receive a poised lyricism, and the hugely demanding *Nun freut euch, lieben Christen* is articulated with marvellous fleetness and clarity, even if it doesn't quite have Demidenko's dazzling power. In the Mendelssohn selection, Perahia is adept at differentiating melodic strands and the accompanimental figuration, whether in the tricky combination of *legato* and *staccato* in Op 67 No 2, or the ardent poetry of Op 19 No 1, Op 38 No 3 or Op 67 No 1. He is concerned always to maintain a sense of momentum, never wallowing in the slower pieces, and his fingerwork and characterisation in the notorious 'Spinnerlied', Op 67 No 4, are superbly acute. He also brings a smile with the occasional witty throwaway ending.

A natural Schubertian and a pianist of lyrical purity and warmth, Perahia is an obvious candidate for these wonderful Schubert/Liszt song transcriptions, and the results are always engaging, though slightly uneven. *Auf dem Wasser zu singen* is taken faster than usual – in itself no bad thing – but the meticulously phrased accompaniment becomes slightly agitated and detracts from the vein of lyricism. Some sections of *Erlkönig* sound under palpable technical strain, particularly when the music moves to B flat for the difficult left-hand triplets; moreover, the final two chords seem diluted of their sense of despair. Some listeners may feel *In der Ferne* to lack brooding intensity or a Schubertian sense of romantic alienation, but Perahia prefers the more comforting virtues of pianistic beauty and colour. *Ständchen*, too, is utterly beautiful and full of character. The sheer poetry of this disc is something to rejoice in, and Perahia's artistry shines through every bar.

Variations sérieuses

Piano Sonata in E, Op 6. Variations sérieuses in D minor, Op 54. Three Preludes, Op 104*a*. Three Studies, Op 104*b*. Kinderstücke, Op 72, 'Christmas Pieces'. Gondellied in A. Scherzo in B minor
Benjamin Frith *pf*
Naxos 8 550940 (65 minutes: DDD). Ⓢ
Recorded 1994-95

The multiplicity of notes in Mendelssohn's piano music sometimes lays him open to the charge of 'note-spinning'. So what higher praise for Benjamin Frith than to say that thanks to his fluency, tact and fancy, not a single work in this second volume seems to outstay its welcome. The unchallengeable masterpiece, of course, is the *Variations sérieuses*, so enthusiastically taken up by Clara Schumann, and still a repertory work today. Frith characterizes each variation with telling contrasts of tempo and touch without sacrificing the continuity and unity of the whole. Equally importantly, never for a moment does he allow us to forget the *sérieuses* of the title.

No less impressive is his sensitively varied palette in the early E major Sonata (unmistakable homage to Beethoven's Op 101) so often helped by subtle pedalling. But surely the recitative of the *Adagio* at times needs just a little more intensity and underlying urgency. Of the miniatures the six *Kinderstücke* ('Christmas Pieces' – written for the children of a friend) emerge with an unforced charm. As music they lack the romance of Schumann's ventures into a child's world, just as the *Three Studies* do of Chopin's magical revelations in this sphere. However, Frith's fingers never let him down. In the first B flat Study he even seems to acquire a third hand to sustain its middle melody. For sheer seductive grace, the independent *Gondellied* haunts the memory most of all. With pleasantly natural sound, too, this disc is quite a bargain.

Lieder

Lieder – Op 8: No 4, Erntelied; No 8, And'res Maienlied. Op 9: No 6, Scheidend. Op 19*a*: No 1, Frühlingslied; No 2, Das erste Veilchen; No 3, Winterlied; No 4, Neue Liebe; No 5, Gruss; No 6, Reiselied. Op 34: No 1, Minnelied; No 2, Auf Flügeln des Gesanges; No 3, Frühlingslied; No 6, Reiselied. Op 47: No 1, Minnelied; No 2, Morgengrüss; No 3, Frühlingslied; No 4, Volkslied; No 6, Bei der Wiege. Op 57: No 1, Altdeutsches Lied; No 2, Hirtenlied; No 4, O Jugend; No 5, Venetianisches Gondellied; No 6, Wanderlied. Op 71: No 1, Tröstung; No 3, An die Entfernte; No 4, Schilflied; No 5, Auf der Wanderschaft; No 6, Nachtlied. Op 84: No 1, Da lieg' ich unter den Bäumen; No 3, Jagdlied. Op 86: No 1, Es lauschte das Laub; No 4, Allnächtlich im Traume; No 5, Der Mond. Op 99: No 1, Erster Verlust; No 5, Wenn sich zwei Herzen Scheiden. Op posth.: Das

Waldschloss; Pagenlied; Der Blumenkranz; Warnung vor dem Rhein; Schlafloser Augen Leuchte.
Dietrich Fischer-Dieskau *bar* **Wolfgang Sawallisch** *pf*
EMI ② CMS7 64827-2 (95 minutes: ADD). Texts Ⓜ included. Recorded 1970

Mendelssohn's Lieder offer a challenge all their own, and Fischer-Dieskau takes it up with characteristic alacrity. As the majority of these songs are primarily accompanied melody, with little inherent teasing out or biting on the words, the singer is presented with a comparatively empty stage for his recreative imagination to design and pace. There are passing moments (in the Op 47 *Morgengrüss*, for example) when the simplicity and ingenuousness of Mendelssohn's settings seems to frustrate Fischer-Dieskau. These moments, though, are rare. His voice, here in its prime, can draw on an extraordinarily wide palette of colour within the legato of the most timeworn strophic song. Both Fischer-Dieskau and Sawallisch, whose light-filled piano playing shows his real sympathy and understanding for this composer, know just when to move into the salon with Mendelssohn. The four Lenau settings and the little drama of mortality offered in *Das erste Veilchen* are re-created with a perfectly-scaled sense of fleeting ardour and melancholy. Best of all are those little vignettes of the dark mythology of the German folk-soul, those diabolic night rides into the forest which find Mendelssohn at his witchy best, and Fischer-Dieskau at his most virtuosic.

Lieder – Op 8: No 8, And'res Maienlied. No 10, Romanze. Op 9: No 1, Frage; No 5, Im Herbst; No 7, Sehnsucht; No 8, Frühlingsglaube; No 9, Ferne; No 10, Verlust; No 12, Die Nonne. Op 19*a*: No 3, Winterlied; No 4, Neue Liebe. Op 34: No 2, Auf Flügeln des Gesanges; No 3, Frühlingslied; No 4, Suleika; No 5, Sonntagslied. Op 47: No 3, Frühlingslied; No 5, Der Blumenstrauss; No 6, Bei der Wiege. Op 57 No 3, Suleika. Op 71: No 2, Frühlingslied; No 6, Nachtlied. Op 86: No 3, Die Liebende schreibt; No 5, Der Mond. Op 99: No 1, Erster Verlust; No 5, Wenn sich zwei Herzen Scheiden; No 6, Es weiss und rät es doch keiner. Pagenlied, Op posth
Barbara Bonney *sop* **Geoffrey Parsons** *pf*
Teldec 2292-44946-2 (60 minutes: DDD). Texts and Ⓕ translations included. Recorded 1991

The charm of these songs lies in their simple style and almost endless stream of delightful melody. Unlike other Lieder composers Mendelssohn avoided blatant word-painting or vivid characterizations and the most satisfying songs here tend to be settings of texts which do not on the surface offer much scope for musical expression. But while this disc may not give us the very best of Mendelssohn, or indeed the finest examples of 19th-century Lied, the singing of Barbara Bonney makes this a CD not to be missed. Here is a rare example of a singer caught on record at the very height of her technical and artistic powers, able to exercise seemingly effortless vocal control in portraying the subtle colours and understated moods of each songs. The partnership with that ever-sensitive accompanist Geoffrey Parsons is inspired. Listen to how Bonney seems to float ethereally above the rippling piano figures in that most famous of all Mendelssohn songs, *Auf Flügeln des Gesanges* ('On wings of song') – a performance which can surely never have been bettered on record.

Lieder – Op 8: No 7, Maienlied; No 8, And'res Maienlied. Op 9: No 1, Frage; No 2, Geständnis; No 8, Frühlingsglaube. Op 19*a*: No 4, Neue Liebe; No 5, Gruss. Op 34: No 2, Auf Flügeln des Gesanges; No 3, Frühlingslied; No 4, Suleika. Op 47: No 1, Minnelied; No 4, Volkslied. Op 57: No 3, Suleika; No 6, Wanderlied. Op 71: No 4, Schilflied; No 6, Nachtlied. Op 86: No 3, Die Liebende schreibt; No 5, Der Mond. Op 99: No 1, Erster Verlust; No 6, Es weiss und rät es doch keiner. Op posth: Mädchens Klage; Das Waldschloss. Romances (Byron) – There be None of Beauty's Daughters; Sun of the Sleepless
Dame Margaret Price *sop* **Graham Johnson** *pf*
Hyperion CDA66666 (59 minutes: DDD). Texts and Ⓕ translations included. Recorded 1993

This recital wholly dispels any lingering doubts there may be about Mendelssohn as a composer of Lieder. He surpassed even Schubert and Brahms in his understanding of Heine's *Die Liebende schreibt*. At the heart of the recital are the settings of Goethe. Besides *Die Liebende schreibt* the pair include the poignant *Erster Verlust* and the two Suleika settings, neither quite a match for Schubert's inspired versions but valid in their own right, particularly when sung with Price's uninhibited, Lehmannesque ardour. Another facet of the performances, a free-ranging *Schwung*, can be heard in *Frühlingslied* and the familiar *Neue Liebe*. The real discoveries here are the two Byron settings uncovered by Johnson. Mendelssohn understood and knew how to set English and the accentuations here are wholly idiomatic. The recording has great presence. Both singer and pianist are in the room with us, anxious and able to please.

Die erste Walpurgisnacht

Die erste Walpurgisnacht, Op 60. Songs without Words (orch Matthus) – Andante con moto, Op 19 No 1; Allegro di molto, Op 30 No 2; Adagio, Op 53 No 4; Andante grazioso, Op 62 No 6. Lieder (orch Matthus) – Op 34: No 2, Auf Flügeln des Gesanges; No 6, Reiselied. Op 19*a*: No 4, Neue Liebe; No 5, Gruss. And'res Maienlied, Op 8 No 8. Pagenlied, Op posth. Schilflied, Op 71 No 4. Der Mond, Op 86 No 5
Jadwiga Rappé *contr* **Deon van der Walt** *ten* **Anton Scharinger** *bar* **Matthias Hölle** *bass* **Bamberg Symphony Chorus and Orchestra / Claus Peter Flor**
RCA Red Seal 09026 62513-2 (61 minutes: DDD). Ⓕ Texts and translations included. Recorded 1994

The idea of pagans outwitting their Christian oppressors inspired Mendelssohn to pen some of his most mischievous musical invention: Berlioz was extremely impressed and the rumpus that erupts when Druid guards 'come with prods and pitchforks' (track 8) matches the sailors' choruses from *The Flying Dutchman* for visceral excitement. The lighter Mendelssohn has doughty men tiptoe through a woodland retreat to a Puckish *Scherzo* while the closing 'hymn to faith' recalls the Second Symphony and *Elijah*. Claus Peter Flor directs a performance notable above all for its delicacy, its warmth of texture, its excellent solo singing and the energetic drive of the big choruses. The Overture in particular shows Flor's skill at creating a three-dimensional sound stage, shaping and blending, allowing due prominence to salient musical lines without spoiling the overall balance. The fill-ups are eight delightful Lieder interspersed with four of the *Songs without Words*, piquantly scored by Siegfried Matthus with especially imaginative use of harp and high percussion. 'Spring Song' becomes an oboe solo; 'May Breezes' is shared among solo strings and harp; No 20 is passed to the solo horn (alluding unmistakably to *A Midsummer Night's Dream*); 'On Wings of Song' incorporates fluid harp writing, and 'Traveller's Song' restlessly shimmering strings (to fit the autumn wind). Deon van der Walt is the pleasingly mellifluous soloist and Flor is as considerate, authoritative and imaginative as he is in the main work. All in all, a super disc, beautifully engineered.

Elijah

Elijah (sung in English) **P**
Renée Fleming, Libby Crabtree *sops* **Patricia Bardon, Sara Fulgoni** *mezzos* **Matthew Munro** *treb* **John Mark Ainsley, John Bowen** *tens* **Neal Davies** *bar* **Bryn Terfel** *bass-bar* **Geoffrey Moses** *bass* **Edinburgh Festival Chorus; Orchestra of the Age of Enlightenment / Paul Daniel**
Decca ② 455 688-2DH2 (131 minutes: DDD). Ⓕ
Text included. Recorded 1996

Paul Daniel and Bryn Terfel ensure that this is one of the most dramatic performances of the oratorio on disc. The young conductor, with the advantage of a period instrument orchestra and an excellent one at that, has looked anew at the score and as a consequence reveals much of the rhythmic and dynamic detail not always present in other performances, at least those available on CD in English. His accomplishment in terms of pacing and of balance is also praiseworthy, and he earns further marks for using the trio, quartet and double quartet of soloists Mendelssohn asks for in specific pieces, so as to vary the texture of the music. Terfel simply gives the most exciting and vivid account of the prophet's part yet heard. His range, in terms of vocal register and dynamics, is huge; his expression, mighty and immediate, befits a man of Elijah's temperament. As the score demands, anguish, anger and sympathy are there in full measure, displayed in exceptional definition of words, and when this Elijah calls on the Lord for the saving rain, the Almighty could hardly resist such a commanding utterance. Yet there is always the inwardness part of the role demands, not least in 'It is enough': you sense a man at the end of his tether. As far as the other soloists are concerned, for the concerted numbers Daniel has chosen voices that nicely match each other in timbre. The chorus is alert and unanimous in both attack and well thought-through phrasing, but its actual sound can be a little soft-centred, partly because all-important consonants are ignored. In every respect the orchestral playing is exemplary.

Awards 1993

Elijah (sung in German)
Helen Donath, Kerstin Klein *sops* **Jard van Nes** *contr* **Donald George** *ten* **Alistair Miles** *bass* **Leipzig Radio Chorus; Israel Philharmonic Orchestra / Kurt Masur**
Teldec ② 9031-73131-2 Ⓕ
(110 minutes: DDD). Text and translation included. Recorded live in 1992 **OOO**

This is a tremendous performance on almost every count. Never before on disc had the work been treated with such an accent on vivid drama: the Old Testament text and its setting sounds as if it had been created on the spot, all Victorian plush and sentiment disposed of. Nor had any previous recording anything like the immediacy, both choral and orchestral, as this one. The choral singing is fiery, yet disciplined. They sound wholly confident in tone, articulation and accent, responsive to all the roles they have to play, obedient to Mendelssohn's dynamic markings, and totally committed to the discipline imposed on them by Masur's incisive beat. The pace of his reading can be judged by the fact that it takes some 110 minutes over the score as compared with the customary, say, 125. No doubt the live recording has something to do with the sense of electricity in the performance. Chorus and conductor seem to have struck up an ideal rapport with the Israel Philharmonic, on home ground here in every sense. It plays with verve allied to a technical skill capable of keeping up with Masur's exigent demands. In consequence, sections (especially in Part 2) that can seem weak or uninspired in other hands here have a dynamic, driving force that carries all before it. Masur also gains credit for choosing soloists rather than the choir as demanded by Mendelssohn for the trios, quartets and double quartets.

Most of the solo singing is worthy of what surrounds it. With a voice of the right weight and timbre for the part, Alistair Miles sings an honest, strongly limned Elijah. He, more than the other soloists, would sometimes like a little more time than Masur permits him to phrase with more meaning, especially in 'Es ist genug': by and large he stands up well to current competition, both in voice and in delivery. Helen Donath is rightly urgent as the grieving widow, though one or two high notes discolour, and mostly belies her years. There is an excellent boy-like soprano as the Youth. Jard van Nes is even better, making a fiery Queen and singing her solos gravely but without any hint of sentimentality. The blot on the escutcheon is the wiry tenor and tight vibrato of Donald George, whose voice does not record well.

Elijah (sung in German)
Christine Schäfer *sop* **Cornelia Kallisch** *contr*
Michael Schade *ten* **Wolfgang Schöne** *bass-bar*
Stuttgart Gächinger Kantorei; Stuttgart Bach Collegium / Helmuth Rilling
Hänssler Classic ② 98 928 (128 minutes: DDD). Ⓕ
Text and translation included. Recorded 1994

Rilling brings out arrestingly the drama of the piece, turning it into a well-varied, exciting quasi-opera, a far from traditional view of the oratorio. The vicissitudes of the prophet's eventful life, his reaction to events, the challenge to Baal, the encounter with Jezebel, have never sounded so electrifying. For that we have to thank Rilling's disciplined chorus biting in diction, precise and convincing in attack. Yet they can also provide the most sensitive, ethereal tone, as in Nos 28 and 29, trio and chorus, 'Siehe, der Hüter Israels'. In general, every strand of the complex writing for chorus is made clear yet the overall effect is one of spontaneous combustion.

The orchestral playing is no less arresting. Furthermore as Elijah Schöne unerringly or authoritatively captures his many moods. Here is the courageous man of action as he confronts Baal's followers and ironically taunts them, the sense of fiery conviction in 'Ist's nichts des Herrn Wort', of doubt in 'Es ist genug', and finally the wonderful Bachian serenity in 'Ja, es sollen wohl Berge weichen', all evoked in the most positive and imaginative delivery of the text. The voice itself, a firm, expressive bass-baritone, is ideal for the role, one on which the singer has obviously lavished much time and consideration – to excellent effect. The same can be said for Schäfer, who brings a Silja-like conviction to all her work, nowhere more so than in 'Höre Israel'. Anyone hearing her declaim 'Weiche nicht' would never be afraid again. The voice itself is interesting, gleaming and yet not without a fair degree of warmth in the tone. Kallisch is almost as convincing in the mezzo solos and gives us a wonderfully malign portrayal of Jezebel. Schade is a fresh-voiced, communicative Obadiah, and he's another who is vivid with his words, especially so in the juniper tree recitative. The recording, however, is slightly too reverberant, but the added space around the voices doesn't preclude immediacy of impact.

Paulus, Op 36

Juliane Banse *sop* **Ingeborg Danz** *mez* **Michael Schade** *ten* **Andreas Schmidt** *bar*
Stuttgart Gächinger Kantorei; Prague Chamber Choir; Czech Philharmonic Orchestra / Helmuth Rilling
Hänssler Classic ② 98 926 (131 minutes: DDD). Text Ⓕ
and translation included. Recorded 1994

Rilling gives dramatic life to a work that can all too easily ramble episodically. His own revered Stuttgart choir and the Czech forces partnering them make certain that their conviction comes across to us boldly. Each section is firmly integrated into the whole and offers great clarity. Schmidt is excellent with his steady, warm voice and he is completely inside the role. His singing of 'Gott sei gnädig' is both firmly phrased and movingly interpreted. Young Juliane Banse sings her recitatives and solos, especially 'Jerusalem', with notable beauty of tone. The youthful German-Canadian tenor Michael Schade is an artist of the utmost refinement and intelligence. If you already have the Kurt Masur version on Philips (nla) you need not feel you have second-best but if you're a newcomer to the work Schmidt will probably win you over to Rilling.

Aarre Merikanto Finnish 1893-1958

GROVE *Aarre Merikanto, son of the composer Oskar Merikanto (1868-1924), studied with Reger in Leipzig (1912-14) and Vasilenko in Moscow (1915-16), and taught at the Helsinki Academy (1936-58). His opera Juha (1922) invites comparison with Janácek; other works, in a highly coloured, chromatic style, include three symphonies (1916, 1918, 1953), three piano concertos (1913, 1937, 1955) and chamber music.*

Piano Concertos

Piano Concertos Nos 2 and 3. Two Studies. Two Pieces
Matti Raekallio *pf*
Tampere Philharmonic Orchestra / Tuomas Ollila
Ondine ODE915-2 (55 minutes: DDD). Ⓕ
Recorded 1997

While it is undeniably true that the principal legacy of Aarre Merikanto lies in his most pioneering music, dating roughly from the period between 1918 and 1931, his later, more accessible, style yielded works with much to offer. The Second and Third Piano Concertos (from 1937-8 and 1955 respectively; No 1 was written prior to the First World War) are typical of his later output – contrapuntally inventive and impressionistic in scoring. Both have an engaging Prokofievan brio in the brisk outer movements and a Rachmaninovesque romanticism in the lyrical central *adagios*. Yet Merikanto never entirely forsook his adventurous harmonic writing, and especially in the Second the result – allied to considerable formal lassitude – is suggestive of (of all people) Villa-Lobos. Granted it is with a Nordic not a Brazilian accent, but think here of works such as *Momoprecoce* and *Bachiana* No 3 as much as the piano concertos; those who know both will appreciate the similarity. Matti Raekallio is a pianist of real technical ability and musical sensibility. He has the measure of both concertos, and the Second in particular could well become popular as an alternative to Prokofiev's Third or the *Paganini* Rhapsody. The purely orchestral *Two Studies* and *Two Pieces* (1941), though much slighter affairs, are by no means insignificant trifles. Tuomas Ollila secures more than competent performances from the Tampere orchestra, matched by excellent sound. A real delight.

Pan, Op 28

Lemminkäinen, Op 10. Pan, Op 28. Four Compositions. Andante religioso. Scherzo
Tampere Philharmonic Orchestra / Tuomas Ollila
Ondine ODE906-2 (51 minutes: DDD). Ⓕ
Recorded 1997

Aarre Merikanto's career divided broadly into three phases, those of apprentice, radical and conservative, and there are works from each present on this valuable issue. Critical hindsight accords (quite rightly) that the brief radical phase, roughly corresponding to the 1920s, was the most valuable, though at the time Merikanto's modernistic approach – and that of his like-minded contemporaries, Ernest Pingoud and Väinö Raito – was derided. Only one piece here represents this period, the highly accomplished tone-poem, *Pan* (1924), a wonderful, evocative, yet robust score, possessed of a very Nordic brand of impressionism. *Lemminkäinen* (1916), by contrast to *Pan*, seems immature, and rather parochial. A Sibelian shadow lies heavily across its quarter-hour duration, yet without a trace of the older composer's own *Lemminkäinen* tone-poems. There is little of the latter's emotional and psychological depth – or musical range – but instead a prevailing rollicking good humour broken occasionally by quieter, more serious moments. The remaining works all date from the early stages of Merikanto's post-modern period, when he reverted to a simpler, more accessible idiom. The *Four Compositions* (1932), which barely exceed *Pan* in length, nevertheless make a very effective and satisfying set, and whereas the *Andante religioso* (1933) seems like a piece out of context, the *Scherzo* (1937) is entirely convincing on its own. The performances are sympathetic and well recorded.

Olivier Messiaen French 1908-1992

GROVE *Messiaen studied at the Paris Conservatoire (1919-30) with Dukas, Emmanuel and Dupré, and taught there (1941-78) while also serving as organist of La Trinité in Paris. Right from his first published work, the eight Preludes for piano (1929), he was using his own modal system, with its strong flavouring of tritones, diminished 7ths and augmented triads. During the 1930s he added a taste for rhythmic irregularity and for the rapid changing of intense colours, in both orchestral and organ works. Most of his compositions were explicitly religious and divided between characteristic styles of extremely slow meditation, bounding dance and the objective unfolding of arithmetical systems. They include the orchestral L'ascension (1933), the organ cycles La nativité du Seigneur (1935) and Les corps glorieux (1939), the song cycles Poèmes pour Mi (1936) and Chants de terre et de ciel (1938), and the culminating work of this period, the Quatuor pour la fin du temps for clarinet, violin, cello and piano (1941).*

During the war he found himself surrounded by an eager group of students, including Boulez and Yvonne Loriod, who eventually became his second wife. For her pianistic brilliance he conceived the Visions de l'amen (1943, with a second piano part for himself) and the Vingt regards sur l'enfant Jésus (1944), followed by an exuberant triptych on the theme of erotic love: the song cycle Harawi (1945), the Turangalîla-symphonie with solo piano and ondes martenot (1948) and the Cinq rechants for small chorus (1949). Meanwhile the serial adventures of Boulez and others were also making a mark, and Messiaen produced his most abstract, atonal and irregular music in the Quatre études de rythme for piano (1949) and the Livre d'orgue (1951).

His next works were based largely on his own adaptations of birdsongs: they include Réveil des oiseaux for piano and orchestra (1953), Oiseaux exotiques for piano, wind and percussion (1956), the immense Catalogue d'oiseaux for solo piano (1958) and the orchestral Chronochromie (1960). In these, and in his Japanese postcards Sept haïkaï for piano and small orchestra (1962), he continued to follow his junior contemporaries, but then returned to religious subjects in works that bring together all aspects of his music. These include another small-scale piano concerto, Couleurs de la cité céleste (1963), and monumental Et exspecto resurrectionem mortuorum for wind and percussion (1964). Thereafter he devoted himself to a sequence of works on the largest scale: the choral-orchestral La Transfiguration (1969), the organ volumes Méditations sur le mystère de la Sainte Trinité (1969), the 12-movement piano concerto Des canyons aux étoiles (1974) and the opera Saint François d'Assise (1983).

Et exspecto resurrectionem ...

Un sourire[b]. Et exspecto resurrectionem mortuorum[b]. Oiseaux exotiques[a]. La ville d'en-haut[b]. Un Vitrail et des oiseaux[b]
Yvonne Loriod *pf* a**Bavarian Radio Symphony Orchestra,** b**Berlin Radio Symphony Orchestra / Karl Anton Rickenbacher**
Koch Schwann 311232 (70 minutes: DDD). Ⓕ
Item marked [a] recorded 1985, [b]1993

In *Oiseaux exotiques* Messiaen creates a bower-bird's nest of extravagant and endearingly ramshackle ornateness. *Et exspecto resurrectionem mortuorum*, on the other hand, is one of his grandest and simplest structures, with its litany-like repetitions and responses. Placed between these, the three shorter pieces can be seen both as a useful way of programming works that fit awkwardly in concerts or as a series of further illustrations of Messiaen's use of what one might call 'strophic form'. *Un Vitrail et des oiseaux* ('A stained-glass window and birds'), for example, splits a typical chorale-like theme into four strophes, follows each with a varied 'antistrophe' of birdsong, and each of those with a progressively embellished cadenza, ending with a coda and a solemn restatement of all four strophes of the chorale. It is disarmingly simple and yet audibly related to the cumulative nobility of *Et exspecto*. That tiny but lovely homage to Mozart, *Un sourire*, is a miniature example of the same process; so is *La ville d'en-haut*, which can now be heard as a sort of sketch for Messiaen's last vision of eternity, *Eclairs sur L'au-delà*. These five disparate pieces certainly make a satisfying and illuminating programme. *Oiseaux exotiques* (a cheerful racket of a piece) is rather drily recorded; there's more space around the other pieces in the collection. All are very well played, demonstrating proper regard to Messiaen's all-important silences and near-silences as well as his precisely judged juxtapositions.

Chronochromie. La ville d'en-haut. Et exspecto resurrectionem mortuorum
Cleveland Orchestra / Pierre Boulez
DG 445 827-2GH (58 minutes: DDD). Ⓕ
Recorded 1993 ⦿

Boulez has spoken of his pleasure at performing Messiaen with an orchestra relatively unfamiliar with his music. It sounds as though the Cleveland Orchestra must have enjoyed it too. You would expect them to, perhaps, in such a passage as that in the fourth movement of *Et exspecto*, where the two superimposed plainchant melodies return together with the noble 'theme of the depths' – it has great splendour, as does the chorale melody of the finale, rising at the end to a satisfyingly palpable *fffff*. And in this performance of *Chronochromie* you can hear why Messiaen said that certain pages of it were 'a double homage to Berlioz and Pierre Schaeffer [the French pioneer of electronic music]'. Absolute rhythmic precision and the clarity of colour that comes from meticulous balance are among the other pleasures of these performances. They make a most satisfying coupling, too. The recordings are excellent: clean but not clinical and ample in dynamic range.

La transfiguration ...

La transfiguration de Notre Seigneur Jésus-Christ[a]. Et exspecto resurrectionem mortuorum
[a]**Silke Uhlig** *fl* [a]**Oliver Link** *cl* [a]**Michael Sanderling** *vc* [a]**Tobias Schweda** *vib* [a]**Edgar Guggeis** *marimba* [a]**Peter Sadlo** *xylorimba* [a]**Yvonne Loriod** *pf* [a]**North German Radio Chorus; Berlin Radio** [a]**Chorus and Symphony Orchestra / Karl Anton Rickenbacher**
Koch Schwann ② 31216-2 (121 minutes: DDD). Text Ⓕ and translation included. Recorded 1996

Messiaen's *La transfiguration* (1965-9) marked a return to large-scale composition after the more concentrated scores of his middle years. It also enshrined the rediscovery of consonant harmony found to varying degrees in all his subsequent works, and the composer's desire to bring together his most personal features of style makes this a key piece for anyone seeking the essence of Messiaen. Reviewers of the first recording of *La transfiguration* (on Decca under Dorati – nla), were divided as to the merits of the work. This new recording makes a strong case for it, with Rickenbacher and his well-trained forces underlining those respects in which the second of the two seven-movement parts has greater tension and variety than the first. An added virtue is that the music of these later stages does not renounce all reference to that tougher, more genuinely intense style employed by the composer in a middle-period score like *Chronochromie*. There's no shortage of those rapt, swooning melodies which the younger Messiaen tended to assign to the ondes martenot, but we are never allowed to forget that, to the Catholic believer, the Transfiguration was not just something to contemplate with reverential awe, but a mind-boggling drama that changed human history.

The effectiveness of this performance owes much to the spacious yet scrupulously balanced sound, and the presence of Yvonne Loriod (who also took part in the earlier recording) provides a further guarantee of an authentic spirit. Less persuasive is Rickenbacher's approach to *Et exspecto resurrectionem mortuorum*. Koch Schwann's decision to present the five movements as a single track rather underlines the slowness of the proceedings. Written just before *La transfiguration*, it has passages which are – even for Messiaen – unusually static, and forms which are unusually repetitive. Nor do the woodwind players in this performance always pay sufficiently close attention to the dynamic contrasts in the score. The main, and very considerable virtue of this set, then, is that it restores one of Messiaen's most imposing and characteristic works to circulation, and this performance will be hard to beat.

Turangalîla-symphonie

Turangalîla-symphonie. Quatuor pour la fin du temps
Saschko Gawriloff *vn* **Siegfried Palm** *vc* **Hans Deinzer** *cl* **Aloys Kontarsky, Peter Donohoe** *pfs* **Tristan Murail** *ondes martenot*
City of Birmingham Symphony Orchestra / Sir Simon Rattle
EMI ② CDS7 47463-8 (130 minutes: DDD/ADD). Ⓕ
Recorded 1986 ⦿⦿

No longer a rarity in the concert hall, Messiaen's epic hymn to life and love has been lucky on record too. Messiaen's luxuriant scoring presents a challenge for the engineers as much as the players and the EMI team comes through with flying colours. Tristan Murail's ondes martenot is carefully balanced – evocative and velvety, neither reduced to inaudibility nor overmiked to produce an ear-rending screech. Peter Donohoe's piano obbligato is similarly integrated into the orchestral tapestry yet provides just the right decorative intervention. Rattle is at his best in the work's more robust moments like the jazzy fifth movement and the rhythmic passages which recall Stravinsky's *Le Sacre*. But those unfamiliar with Messiaen's extraordinary score should perhaps start with the central slow movement, the beautiful *Jardin du sommeil d'amour*, exquisitely done by the Birmingham team. This *Turangalîla* leaves room, on a second CD, for a distinguished *Quatuor pour la fin du temps*. The music-making here lacks the youthful spontaneity of the main work, but is notable for an unusually slow and sustained performance of the solo-cello movement.

Turangalîla Symphony (1990 revised version)
Pierre-Laurent Aimard *pf* **Dominique Kim** *onde*
Berlin Philharmonic Orchestra / Kent Nagano
Teldec 8573 82043-2 (73 minutes: DDD) Ⓕ
Recorded live in 2000 ●

Turangalîla is a difficult score, and to record it live is risky. Even when the orchestra is the Berlin Philharmonic? Yes, since the work is very far from the centre of their repertoire. Whether despite or because of that risk this is a splendidly exciting performance, more surprisingly it is also for the most part a very accurate and detailed one. The excitement is reflected in fastish tempos, one suspects, to passionate urgency in the second movement, with less justification in the sixth, though here the warmth and bright light of the 'garden of love's slumber' are so beautiful that one is reluctant to complain. The textures and colours of the third movement are finely balanced, as they are even in the headlong exuberance of its successor. Although the precision of the seventh seems to understate its balefulness the complex textures and superimposed rhythms of the ninth are outstandingly clear and fascinating. Throughout one alternates between astonishment that the Berlin Philharmonic seem to have re-invented their sound and (often in passages of massive or exciting brass sonority) gratitude that they haven't.

The soloists are admirable; the extremes of the piano part, in particular, are just what Aimard is good at. Inevitably in a live recording there are one or two imprecisions of balance – the ondes martenot is slightly backward in the fourth movement, and some of the birds with whom Aimard converses in the sixth are rather far back in the shrubbery – but this is among the two or three best accounts of *Turangalîla* available. We would still give primacy to Simon Rattle's version on EMI, and recommend Previn's (also EMI) despite its rather bright sound, but Nagano is ahead of all the others.

Turangalîla Symphony[a]. L'ascension
[a]**François Weigl** *pf* [a]**Thomas Bloch** *ondes martenot*
Polish National Radio Symphony Orchestra / Antoni Wit
Naxos ② 8 554478/9 (107 minutes: DDD). Ⓢ
Recorded 1998

No other 20th-century composition – nothing by Strauss or Scriabin, nothing by Hollywood's finest – outdoes the sublime earthiness of the *Turangalîla* Symphony. It is so unselfconsciously over-the-top as to be in an expressive category of its own: even *The Rite of Spring* seems austere beside it. The trick in performance is for 100 or so musicians to sustain the illusion of transcendent spontaneity for 80 minutes, and with more than 70 CDs under their belt for Naxos alone, you might expect a touch of the perfunctory from the Polish National RSO.

Not a bit of it. With the indefatigable Antoni Wit in charge, the only places where this performance threatens to become routine are in the sixth movement, when more melting woodwind playing can be imagined. But one is willing to sacrifice the last degree of tonal and textural refinement for the strong contrasts and surging intensity offered here, and the sound is typically bold and forwardly balanced. Despite the generalised brightness which seems to be a Naxos trademark these days (so that the various strands of the texture are not ideally defined in very loud passages, and the solo piano grows clangorous here and there), the spirit of the music survives and prospers. The soloists are excellent, and if this particular ondes martenot is less sweetly vibrant than you have come to expect, so much the better: it still supplies the music with its special ecstatic radiance at crucial moments.

Wit's *Turangalîla* doesn't displace André Previn's long-established and greatly admired version – its only rival in lower price categories. Nevertheless, Wit's coupling – an imposing account of Messiaen's early yet already characteristic *L'ascension* – is even more welcome than Previn's pair of Poulenc concertos, and devotees of Naxos's ongoing forays into 20th-century masterworks certainly shouldn't hesitate.

Additional recommendation
Turangalîla Symphony
Couplings: Poulenc Concert Champêtre. Organ Concerto
Beroff *pf* **Loriod** *org* **London Symphony Orchestra / Previn**
EMI Double Forte ② CZS5 69752-2 Ⓑ
(129 minutes: ADD: 6/78[R])
If you're happy with the couplings, Previn's is the top recommendation at less than full price.

Further Listening
Villa-Lobos Chôros No 11
Gothóni *pf* **Finnish Radio Symphony Orchestra / Oramo**
Ondine ODE916-2 (62 minutes: DDD: 12/98) Ⓕ
Villa-Lobos in his usual excitably coloured, hyper-exuberant style, writing in a grandiose loose form that – since few of its vast proliferation of themes are developed – defies analysis but whose overall effect is strangely riveting.

Eclairs sur l'Au-Delà

Orchestra of the Opéra-Bastille, Paris / Myung-Whun Chung
DG 439 929-2GH (66 minutes: DDD). Ⓕ
Recorded 1994

Eclairs sur L'Au-Delà ('Illuminations of the Beyond') was Messiaen's last major work. It is almost a summary, musical and spiritual, of the preoccupations of his preceding 60 years but shows him delightedly discovering not only new birds but also entrancingly new sounds: he has not made such startling use before of the contrabass clarinet (in the huge and complex eighth movement, which culminates in a Great Messiaen Tune of sonorous nobility), nor employed (to evoke the Lyrebird) such vertiginous leaps between sections of the orchestra. In one way, then, it is a series of nostalgic revisits. In the fourth movement, for example, there's a sort of two-minute summary of the extremely dense counterpoint of *Chronochromie*; the sixth recalls the 'Dance of fury for the seven trumpets' in the *Quartet for the end of time*. But there's also a touching sense of Messiaen in his eighties preparing to contemplate the beyond. In the ninth of the 11 movements he writes his last birdsong piece, 25 birds impersonated simultaneously by 18 woodwind instruments: the image is of Christ as the Tree of Life, the birds are the souls of the blessed, and of course they are all singing at once. He then considers 'The path to the invisible': it is a clamorous and insistent piece, one of his great angular toccatas, expressing the very difficulty of keeping to that path. Finally, most movingly, one of his almost motionless, beginningless and endless string chorales, 'Christ, Light of Paradise'. Chung has a fine orchestra, and the immaculate recording made in the Opéra-Bastille sounds spacious.

Etudes de rythme

Six Petites Esquisses d'Oiseaux. Cantéyodjayâ. Quatre Etudes de rythme. Pièce pour le Tombeau de Paul Dukas

Gloria Cheng *pf*

Koch International Classics 37267-2 (49 minutes: DDD). Recorded 1993 Ⓕ

Gloria Cheng is technically fearless and meticulously attentive to complex rhythms, she can sustain a bold melodic line splendidly, and her playing has powerful attack. She is just what the exhilarating but exhausting *Cantéyodjayâ* needs, and she gives it a performance of great *élan* and exciting drama. Similar qualities are needed, of course, in the outer sections of the *Quatre Etudes*, which have all the ferocity that Messiaen asks for. If there is any criticism it is that she tends to mark up Messiaen's quieter dynamics. Thus the famous 'Mode de valeurs et d'intensités', which has a 'mode' of seven degrees of intensity, from *ppp* to *fff*, seems to lack a couple of degrees at the bottom end. However, rarely does one hear this piece sound quite so coherent, and Cheng's concentration in the austere 'Neumes rythmiques' is remarkable. There is fine precision in the *Petites Esquisses*, but again a slight lack of dynamic range at the quieter end of the spectrum means that each bird does not quite, as Messiaen insists, 'have its own aesthetic'. The recital ends with an impressively austere account of Messiaen's elegy for his teacher.

Huit préludes

Huit préludes. Etudes de rythme – No 1, Ile de feu I; No 4, Ile de feu II. Vingt regards sur l'Enfant-Jésus – No 4, Regard de la Vierge; No 10, Regard de l'esprit de joie; No 15, Le baiser de l'Enfant-Jésus

Angela Hewitt *pf*

Hyperion CDA67054 (76 minutes: DDD). Recorded 1998 Ⓕ

Hewitt has few equals in Messiaen. The very early *Préludes* (Messiaen was studying with Dukas when he wrote them) might not seem the ideal repertory in which to demonstrate this, but Hewitt plays them with such exquisitely controlled colour, such clarity and such eager love for the music that, if one had dared think of them as not wholly characteristic one immediately changes one's mind. Indeed they are full, certainly in this performance, of luminous, shot and shaded colours that are typical of the mature Messiaen, and in the final virtuoso number Hewitt seems even to have discovered an early draft for a theme in the *Turangalîla* Symphony. Her melodic lines are strong, her sonorities rich (but her loud playing is never noisy or forced) and she has that crucial quality needed of a Messiaen pianist: patience. Patience to let a chord register and fade, patience never to pre-empt a climax. In the two *Ile de feu* pieces she shows that she can produce hard-edged sonorities as well as subtle ones. And all her gifts as a Messiaen pianist are evident in 'Le baiser de l'Enfant-Jésus': the tempo is patient, the contemplation rapt, the embellishments delicately precise, with a magical change of colour as the sunlit *hortus conclusus* at the centre of the movement is reached. The recording is finely sensitive to the exceptional beauty of Hewitt's sound.

La nativité du Seigneur

La nativité du Seigneur. Le banquet céleste

Jennifer Bate *org*

Unicorn-Kanchana DKPCD9005 (62 minutes: DDD). Recorded on the organ of Beauvais Cathedral in 1980. Ⓕ ●

La nativité du Seigneur comprises nine meditations on themes associated with the birth of the Lord. Messiaen's unique use of registration gives these pieces an extraordinarily wide range of colour and emotional potency and in Jennifer Bate's hands (and feet) it finds one of its most persuasive advocates. Bate was much admired by the composer and is so far the only organist to have recorded his complete works for the instrument. *Le banquet céleste* was Messiaen's first published work for the organ and is a magical, very slow-moving meditation on a verse from St John's Gospel (VI, 56). The faithful recording captures both the organ and the large acoustic of Beauvais Cathedral to marvellous effect.

Vingt regards sur l'enfant Jésus

Pierre-Laurent Aimard *pf*

Teldec ② 3984-26868-2 (116 minutes: DDD). Recorded 1999 Ⓕ ●●

One ought to begin any review of the *Vingt regards* by discussing how well the pianist conveys the cycle's visionary awe and builds its disparate sections into a true cycle. But here the virtuosity is so remarkable that one could well imagine even listeners with a profound distaste for Messiaen – for whom the 15th *Regard* ('The kiss of the infant Jesus') is a by-word for sentimental religiosity – listening open-mouthed. Sheer virtuosity is an important part of the cycle's language: one of the functions of *Regard* No 6 ('By Him all was made') is to astonish, and the power and excitement of Aimard's playing are indeed astonishing. Virtuosity is also desirable if Messiaen's demands for a huge palette of colour and orchestral or super-orchestral sonorities are to be met. In No 14 ('The gaze of the angels') his notes evoke 'powerful blasts of immense trombones' and Aimard's prodigious range of timbre and dynamic provide just the sound that Messiaen must have imagined. It is the same with the 'gongs and oboes, the enormous nasal consort' of No 6 ('Gaze of the prophets, shepherds and wise men'). In the penultimate *Regard* ('I sleep, but my heart is awake'), Messiaen makes a more extreme demand: that in the hushed coda the player should recall a passage from the *Fioretti* of St Francis where 'the angel drew his bow across the string and produced a note so sweet that if he had continued I should have died of joy'. Here the effect is suggested not by virtuosity but intense concentration, stillness and purity of colour.

Even 'The gaze of time' (No 9), that austere exercise in rhythmic canon, emerges as strange but gripping, and 'The kiss of the infant Jesus' is no less sweetly radiant for its florid tendrils being so Lisztian. Could it have been a little slower? Possibly; Aimard's timing is faster than most (nine minutes shorter than Messiaen's specified duration) and a few of his silences could have been held longer but his dazzling technique and fabulous range of colour make this the most spectacular reading of the *Vingt regards* yet.

Poèmes pour Mi

Poèmes pour Mi. Réveil des oiseaux. Sept Haïkaï
Françoise Pollet *sop* **Pierre-Laurent Aimard, Joela Jones** *pfs* **Cleveland Orchestra / Pierre Boulez**
DG 453 478-2GH (72 minutes: DDD). Texts and translations included. Recorded 1990s Ⓕ

All the performances here are excellent, virtuoso indeed, and the recordings are first-class. *Poèmes pour Mi* represent Messiaen at his most lyrically passionate and sensuous, the *Réveil des oiseaux* his 'bird style' at its most intransigent, while the *Sept Haïkaï* stand both for Messiaen's love-affair with Asia and his attempts to convey vivid colour in music. In Françoise Pollet the *Poèmes* get as close as any reading has to Messiaen's specification of a *grand soprano dramatique* as the ideal solo voice. She can sustain a long arch of melody splendidly and, assisted by Boulez's firm control, generates great rhythmic excitement in the fourth and ninth songs of the set. This latter quality gives exhilaration to *Réveil des oiseaux*, as the tangle of exuberant melodies grows ever more complex; Aimard is glitteringly precise here. But it is the *Sept Haïkaï* that are most crucial to Messiaen's later development, with their pairs of movements reflecting each other, their searing saturated colours, their use of juxtaposed 'refrains' and their central homage to the sound of a Japanese orchestra. Boulez has expressed reservations about some of his great teacher's theories, but evidently has few if any about the fantastic sound world imagined by his astonishingly precise ear.

Saint François d'Assise

Dawn Upshaw *sop* L'Ange; **José Van Dam** *bass-bar* Saint François; **Chris Merritt** *ten* Le Lépreux; **Urban Malmberg** *bar* Frère Léon; **John Aler** *ten* Frère Massée; **Guy Renard** *ten* Frère Elie; **Tom Krause** *bar* Frère Bernard; **Akos Banlaky** *ten* Frère Sylvestre; **Dirk d'Ase** *bass* Frère Rufin **Jeanne Loriod, Valerie Hartmann-Claverie, Dominique Kim** *ondes martenots;* **Arnold Schoenberg Choir; Hallé Orchestra / Kent Nagano**
DG 20/21 ④ 445 176-2GH4 (236 minutes: DDD). Notes, text and translation included. Ⓕ
Recorded live 1998

The breakthrough for Messiaen's only opera came with the Salzburg Festival production unveiled in August 1992, Esa-Pekka Salonen conducting. Van Dam and his monks still wore habits, but Peter Sellars's production concept broke with the composer's 'realistic' Umbrian spectacle to put Dawn Upshaw's Angel in a grey business suit, while his trademark video monitors relayed associated imagery. He even invented a second Angel, one who doesn't exist in the score, an Angel who dances and mimes.

Nagano took up the reins for the 1998 Salzburg revival as captured here in DG's live recording, and there is no mistaking the remarkable authority and technical self-confidence of the results. Van Dam's definitive Saint François is a remarkable achievement for an artist on the cusp of his sixth decade and his identification with the role is profound. Upshaw too is well cast, with just enough tonal weight to underpin her fresh, ardent, mobile singing. It's mostly plain sailing in the subsidiary roles, although Malmberg's French is still as dodgy as the choir's. The musicians of the Hallé have been drilled to the peak of perfection, closely scrutinized by vivid, upfront sound that does not always give their glittering sonorities a natural perspective in which to expand. Above all, the set is a triumph for them. All Messiaen's trademarks are here: the birdsong, the modal rigour (especially for the word setting which is crystal clear), the basic triads given new harmonic context and heft, the post-Stravinskian dances. There are also distant echoes of *Boris Godunov* and *Pelléas et Mélisande*.

Uninitiated listeners should perhaps try Act 1 scene 3 (the curing of the leper) where the mosaic construction permits a breathtaking conjunction of ideas from timeless chant through 1960s modernism, to childlike eruptions of joy and premonitions of holy minimalism. Even here, there is only limited dramatic conflict, no development of character as conventionally understood. And yet it scarcely matters so long as you can leave your preconceptions behind and accept Messiaen's ecstatic tableaux as you would the stained-glass windows of a great cathedral. *Saint François d'Assise* can make *Parsifal* seem like an intermezzo, but it exerts a uniquely hypnotic spell. Strongly recommended.

Nikolay Miaskovsky

Russian 1881-1950

GROVE *Miaskovsky studied for a military career but entered the St Petersburg Conservatory (1906-11), where his teachers included Lyadov and Rimsky-Korsakov. He served in the war, and from 1921 taught at the Moscow Conservatory. He was not an innovator but was an influential, individual figure working within the Russian tradition. His large output is dominated by the cycle of 27 symphonies (1908-50), highly regarded in and outside Russia in his lifetime. He also wrote 13 string quartets (1913-49), choral and chamber music.*

Cello Concerto, Op 66

Miaskovsky Cello Concerto in C minor, Op 66
Prokofiev Symphony-Concerto for Cello and Orchestra in E minor, Op 125. (also includes alternative finale)
Truls Mørk *vc* **City of Birmingham Symphony Orchestra / Paavo Järvi**
Virgin Classics VC5 45282-2 (72 minutes: DDD). Ⓕ
Recorded 1997

Whichever way you view it – as attractive repertoire, as dynamic sound, or as distinctive interpretation – this CD is a sure-fire winner. Neither work yields its strongest virtues without encouragement: the Prokofiev responds best to focused solo phrasing and firm handling from the rostrum, while Miaskovsky's concerto can too easily sound discursive. Here, however, musical impact takes effect right from Prokofiev's introductory bars: Paavo Järvi and his players cut a commanding profile and the recording conveys a startlingly realistic sound stage, especially from the lower strings. Truls Mørk might be tagged a 'communicative introvert': his tone is firm and even, his phrasing refined and his poetic musicianship especially suits the Miaskovsky concerto, with its subtle asides and winding musical lines. Again, Järvi comes up trumps with a sympathetic accompaniment and the recording is spectacularly good.

Sinfonietta No 1

Sinfonietta No 1 in B minor, Op 32 No 2. Theme and Variations. Two Pieces, Op 46 No 1. Napeve
St Petersburg Chamber Ensemble / Roland Melia
ASV CDDCA928 (56 minutes: DDD). Ⓕ
Recorded 1994

Miaskovsky's Variations are consistently attractive, as are the shorter works, despite disconcerting reminiscences of the *Skye Boat Song* in the first of the Op 46 Pieces. That's not to say that the music 'holds' you in the way that Stravinsky, Martinů, Honegger or Tippett do. And, as so often with Miaskovsky, there are slack moments where ideas seem to be coming back for no better reason than to fill out a pre-allocated space. The fact remains that if you have got the Miaskovsky bug, or if you want the fullest possible picture of middle-of-the-road Soviet music, you will find confident, full-bodied performances here which are the equal of any.

Darius Milhaud

French 1892-1974

GROVE *Milhaud studied with Widor, Gédalge and Dukas at the Paris Conservatoire and became associated with Claudel, who took him to Rio de Janeiro as his secretary (1916-18): he wrote incidental music for Claudel's translation of the Oresteia (1922), making innovatory use of chanting chorus and percussion; he also drew on Brazilian music in his ballet L'homme et son désir (1918). But Claudel's influence was briefly succeeded by Cocteau's, and he became a member of Les Six; works of this period include the ballet Le boeuf sur le toit (1919). In 1922 he sought out jazz in Harlem and used the experience in another ballet, Le création du monde (1923). Thereafter he travelled widely, taught on both sides of the Atlantic and produced a colossal output in all genres, normally in a style of fluent bitonality. His operas include Les malheurs d'Orphée (composed1925), Le pauvre matelot (1926), Christophe Colomb (1928), Maximilien (1930), Bolivar (1943), David (1952) and Saint Louis (1970). There are also 12 symphonies and much other orchestral music, sacred and secular choral music, 18 quartets and songs.*

La création du monde, Op 81

Harp Concerto, Op 323. Le boeuf sur le toit, Op 58. La création du monde
Frédérique Cambreling *hp*
Lyon Opéra Orchestra / Kent Nagano
Erato MusiFrance 2292-45820-2 (59 minutes: DDD). Ⓜ
Recorded 1992

Here is music to delight, with performances to match. Milhaud's ballet *Le boeuf sur le toit* was written for Jean Cocteau in 1919 and is set in an American bar during the Prohibition period (forbidding the manufacture and sale of alcohol) that was then just beginning. Kent Nagano shows more Gallic taste and sophistication, and the playing is above all musicianly, while the more uproarious moments come over all the more effectively for this very reason. The playing by the accomplished Lyon orchestra is excellent, not least the wind players who have plenty to do. Written four years later, *La création du monde* was one of the first works by a European composer to take its inspiration from African folklore and the raw black jazz that Milhaud heard in New Orleans. This ballet on the creation myth ends with a mating dance and the whole work is powerfully and darkly sensual.

Nagano and his French orchestra bring out all the character of this music and take the jazz fugue in Scene 1 more urgently than usual, to excellent effect. The Harp Concerto dates from 1953, three decades further on into Milhaud's career, and inevitably it has a brighter character, though here, too, there is some jazz influence, if of a gentler kind. Cambreling is a fine player – an ideal interpreter of this uneven but nearly always fascinating composer.

Milhaud Le boeuf sur le toit, Op 58. La création du monde, Op 81
Ibert Divertissement **Poulenc** Les biches – Suite
Ulster Orchestra / Yan Pascal Tortelier
Chandos CHAN9023 (68 minutes: DDD). Ⓕ
Recorded 1991

Here is 1920s French music directed by a conductor who is completely in the spirit of it, and plenty of spirit there is, too. Except for Ibert's *Divertissement*, this is ballet music, and that work too originated in the theatre as incidental music for Eugène Labiche's farce *The Italian Straw Hat*. Poulenc's suite from *Les biches*, written for Diaghilev's ballet company and first heard in Monte Carlo, is fresh and bouncy and stylishly played here, although Chandos's warm recording, good though it is, takes some edge off the trumpet tone; the genial nature of it all makes us forget that it is a unique mix of 18th-century *galanterie*, Tchaikovskian lilt and Poulenc's own inimitable street-Parisian sophistication and charm. As for Ibert's piece, this is uproariously funny in an unbuttoned way, and the gorgeously vulgar trombone in the Waltz and frantic police whistle in the finale are calculated to make you laugh out loud. Milhaud's *Le boeuf sur le toit* also has Parisian chic and was originally a kind of music-hall piece, composed to a scenario by Cocteau. It was while attending a performance of it in London in 1920 that the composer first heard the American jazz orchestra that, together with a later experience of New Orleans jazzmen playing 'from the darkest corners of the Negro soul' (as he later expressed it), prompted him to compose his masterly ballet *La création du monde*. Tortelier and his orchestra understand this strangely powerful music no less than the other pieces. This is a most desirable disc.

Violin Sonatas

Saudades do Brasil, Op 67 – Leme; Ipanema (arr Lévy). Suite for Violin, Viola and Piano, Op 157*b*. Quatre Visages, Op 238. Sonatine for Violin and Viola, Op 226. Sonatas for Viola and Piano – No 1, Op 240; No 2, Op 244. Sonatine for Viola and Cello, Op 378
Paul Cortese *va* **Michel Wagemans** *pf* with **Joaquín Palomares** *vn* **Frank Schaffer** *vc*
ASV CDDCA1039 (78 minutes: DDD). Ⓕ
Recorded 1997

Paul Cortese here brings his rich, warm tone and flawless, rock-steady technique to Milhaud's viola music. Of the seven works presented here, four were written in the 1940s while Milhaud was teaching at Mills College in the USA. Exceptions are the two arrangements from the early *Saudades do Brasil*; the Suite (which includes a jaunty Provençal-flavoured overture, a lyrical 'Divertissement' and an engagingly cheery finale), and the much later sinewy and prickly *Sonatine* for violin and cello (played here with great finesse), which contains an unexpectedly emotional slow movement. Of the four other works, the violin and viola *Sonatine* is easy-flowing small-talk, unmemorable save for the energetic final fugue; *Quatre Visages*, however, reveals Milhaud's sly wit in its characterizations of four women – a sunnily contented Californian, a chatterbox from Wisconsin, an earnest creature from Brussels and a vivacious Parisienne. The First Viola Sonata is one of Milhaud's most endearing works. It has Milhaud indulging to the full his penchant for canonic writing. The Second Sonata is less overtly bracing, and its central *Modéré* is charged with expressive drama, while the finale is a rough-and-tumble which tempts Michel Wagemans, alert as he is, into being much too loud for his partner – as he sometimes is elsewhere, notably in the early Suite. But, all in all, this disc does Milhaud proud.

Scaramouche (arr two pianos)

Le boeuf sur le toit, Op 58*a* (arr cpsr). Scaramouche, Op 165*b*. La libertadora, Op 236*a*. Les songes, Op 237. Le bal martiniquais, Op 249. Carnaval à la nouvelle-orléans, Op 275. Kentuckiana, Op 287
Stephen Coombs, Artur Pizarro *pfs*
Hyperion CDA67014 (62 minutes: DDD). Ⓕ
Recorded 1997

Milhaud was an inveterate traveller, and he absorbed influences from many national styles, illustrated by titles such as *Kentuckiana*, *Le bal martiniquais* and 'Brazileira' (from *Scaramouche*). The music exudes infectious dance impulses, languid geniality, knockabout humour and sheer *joie de vivre*. It may inhabit a limited expressive sphere, but providing you don't expect introspection or searching profundity you won't be disappointed. There is enjoyment at every turn, whether in the foot-tapping 'Brazileira', the Satie-esque simplicity of the 'Valse' from *Les songes*, or the breezy music-hall atmosphere of *Le boeuf sur le toit*, with its forays into polytonality and its wonderfully imaginative piano writing. The performances are exemplary. Stephen Coombs and Artur Pizarro both enjoy the byways of the piano repertory, and, even if Pizarro is the more starry soloist, they are well matched as a duo. Coombs's top part is suitably bright and sharply lit, and is offset by Pizarro's more subtle colouring. They revel in the protracted playfulness of *Le boeuf sur le toit* (the only work here for piano duet, incidentally, although there is if anything a greater wealth of inner detail than in the two-piano works), where their feeling for Hispanic exoticism is matched by their virtuosity. The recorded sound is excellent, as are Robert Matthew-Walker's accompanying notes.

Ernest Moeran British 1894-1950

GROVE *Moeran studied at the Royal College of Music (1913-14) then, after war service, with Ireland (until 1923) who, with Delius, was a dominant influence on his early music. In the early 1930s he retired to the Cotswolds, where he wrote his Symphony in G minor (1937), a work of Nature lyricism drawing on Sibelian thematic methods. His other works, all marked by meticulous craftsmanship, include the Sinfonietta (1944) and orchestral Serenade (1948), concertos for violin (1942) and cello (1945), chamber music and songs.*

String Quartets

String Quartets – No 1 in A minor; No 2 in E flat. String Trio in G
Maggini Quartet (Laurence Jackson, David Angel *vns* Martin Outram *va* Michal Kaznowski *vc*)
Naxos 8 554079 (59 minutes: DDD). Ⓢ
Recorded 1995 ○

The A minor Quartet dates from 1921 when Moeran was a pupil of John Ireland at the Royal College of Music. It is an enormously fluent, folk-song-inspired creation, full of Ravelian poise; indeed the last movement of the three (an exhilarating rondo) owes much to the finale of the French master's F major Quartet. The Maggini Quartets accords the piece wonderfully assured, flexible advocacy. Discovered among Moeran's papers by his widow after his death in 1950, the E flat Quartet appears to be another comparatively early effort. It is cast in just two movements, the second of which is an ambitious linked slow movement and finale, full of ambition and tender fantasy, and containing some truly magical inspiration along the way. Perhaps this movement's intrepid thematic and emotional diversity engendered sufficient niggling doubts in Moeran's mind for him to suppress the whole work. Certainly, in a performance as convinced and convincing as this, its melodic fecundity and unpretentious, 'out of doors' charm will endear it to many. That leaves the masterly String Trio of 1931, which, in its impeccable craft, rhythmic pungency (the opening *Allegretto giovale* boasts a time-signature of 7/8), gentle sense of purpose and unerring concentration (above all in the deeply felt slow movement), represents one of Moeran's finest achievements. The members of the Maggini Quartet reveal a relish for Moeran's exquisitely judged part-writing and give an admirably polished, affectionate rendering. Sound and balance are excellent throughout this enterprising, hugely enjoyable collection.

Further listening
Bax String Quartet No 1
Couplings: Piano Quartet. Harp Quintet
McCabe *pf* **Kanga** *hp* **English String Quartet**
Chandos CHAN8391 (53 minutes: DDD: 4/87) Ⓕ

Dating from 1918, the first movement of Bax's First Quartet conveys an uncomplicated happiness, sunny and mellifluous., while the finale a quite wild Irish dance.

Federico Mompou Spanish 1893-1987

GROVE *Mompou studied in Barcelona and with Motte-Lacroix and Samuel-Rousseau in Paris, where he remained until 1941 except for a return to Barcelona in 1914-21; he then settled in his native city. His output consists almost entirely of small-scale piano pieces and songs in a fresh, naive style indebted to Satie and Debussy; he aimed for maximum expressiveness through minimum means, often achieving a melancholy elegance.*

Música callada

Herbert Henck *pf*
ECM New Series 445 699-2 (63 minutes: DDD). Ⓕ
Recorded 1993

Listening to this disc is rather like entering a retreat. There is a rapt, contemplative atmosphere around these 28 miniatures written between 1959 and 1967 as an attempt to express St John of the Cross's mystic ideal of 'the music of silence'. Practically all slow-moving, using repetition as a structural device but avoiding keyboard virtuosity, and rarely rising even to a *forte*, they seem to acknowledge descent from Erik Satie via the impressionists, though harmonically much freer and sometimes harsher – even, occasionally, stepping inside the area of atonality. No 3 has a childlike innocence in its folkloric theme: Mompou's fascination with bell-sounds finds echoes in Nos 5, 17 and 22. Overall there is a sense of tranquil self-communion which, paradoxically, exerts a strange spell on the listener. Herbert Henck, a specialist in 20th-century music, plays this collection with a tender sensitivity and an ideally suited luminosity of tone, and he is finely recorded. An exceptional and haunting issue, whose sounds seem to hang in the air, as it were.

Preludes

Awards 1998

Cançons i danses – Nos 1, 3, 5, 7, 8 and 9. Preludes – Nos 1, 5, 6, 7, 9 and 10. Cants màgics. Charmes. Variations. Dialogues. Paisajes
Stephen Hough *pf*
Hyperion CDA66963 (77 minutes: DDD) Ⓕ
Recorded 1996 ○○○

The music of Federico Mompou may appear at first to consist of little more than charming, delicately scented but dilettantish salon near-improvisations with marked overtones of Erik Satie; but it is significant that his earliest works (in the 1920s) are imbued with a sense of mystery and wonder. Later he was to progress from an ingenuous lyricism (in the *Songs and dances*) to a profounder contemplation and mysticism, to greater harmonic and keyboard complexity (*Dialogues*) and finally, in the 1946-60 *Paisajes* ('Landscapes'), to a more experimental, less tonal idiom. In the hands of an imaginative pianist like Stephen Hough this other-worldly quality becomes revelatory. Hough's command of tonal nuance throughout is ultra-sensitive, he catches Mompou's wistful moods to perfection, and on the rare occasions when the music lashes out, as in *Prelude* No 7, he is scintillating. In the more familiar *Songs and dances* he is tender in the (mostly melancholy) songs and exhilaratingly crisp rhythmically in the dances. He treats the 'Testament d'Amelia' in No 8 with a good deal of flexibility, and because Mompou declared (and demonstrated in his own recordings) that 'it's all so free', he takes the fullest advantage of the marking *senza rigore* in No 5, which reflects Mompou's lifelong fascination with bell-sounds.

---

12 Préludes. Suburbis. Dialogues. Cants magics. Chanson de berceau. Fêtes lointaines
Jordi Masó *pf* Ⓢ
Naxos 8 554448 (79 minutes: DDD). Recorded 1998

Vol 1 of Jordi Masó's Mompou cycle was given the warmest of welcomes and Vol 2 is no disappointment, either. Everything is presented with crystalline clarity, and if the manner is unusually robust it is never less than musicianly. Directions such as *énergiquement* and *très clair* (Prélude No 2), the *forte* climax of Prélude No 6 or the sudden blaze of anger that erupts in Prélude No 7 are arguably more sympathetically conveyed than Mompou's gentler, more characteristic instructions (*con lirica espressione* in Prélude No 8 or *un peu plus calme* in the second 'Gitanes' from *Suburbis*). It is almost as if Masó, a vibrant and articulate pianist, wished to draw attention away from sentimental or salon associations, and direct us towards Mompou's underlying fervour and what Wilfrid Mellors calls (in his invaluable book *Le jardin retrouvé*) the 'pre-melodic' nature of Mompou's vocal lines (in *Cants magics*) or the evocation of a remote, prehistoric world (see Stephen Hough's notes to his *Gramophone* Award-winning Hyperion disc). Masó's boldness is potent and arresting and his comprehensive undertaking makes comparison with Hough and Martin Jones a marginal issue. So although he is less tonally subtle than Jones, his playing is vital and idiomatic, qualities highlighted by the bright, immediate sound. Vol 3 is eagerly awaited.

Jean-Joseph de Mondonville

French 1711-1772

GROVE *In the 1730s violinist and composer Mondonville was in Lille; then he settled in Paris, where he won fame as soloist and composer. He became sous-maître to the royal chapel in 1740 and intendant in 1744. His music is notable for its imaginative textures. Best known were his sonatas for harpsichord and violin (1734), among the earliest accompanied keyboard music, and those for harpsichord, violin and voice (1748); his 17 grands motets (among the finest since Lalande's and like his, much performed at the Concert Spirituel) and 10 stage works (1742-71) were also popular.*

Six Sonates en symphonies, Op 3

Les Musiciens du Louvre / Marc Minkowski Ⓟ
Archiv Produktion 457 600-2AH Ⓕ
(58 minutes: DDD)

These pieces show Mondonville in a position to offer something unique. He was a violinist first and foremost, and his most important legacy is his Op 3 set of six sonatas for violin and obbligato keyboard of 1734 – among the first of their kind – of which these *Sonates en symphonies* are orchestrations, made by the composer and performed with great success in Paris 15 years later. Put simply, they are pure enjoyment throughout, breathing that spirit of almost pure hedonism which characterizes the most beguiling of mid-18th-century French art. All the symphonies are in three movements, the outer ones being brisk and animated with much busy passagework surviving the transition from solo violin music very effectively, and the middle ones tuneful miniatures evoking the hushed atmosphere of a balmy night scene from a French baroque opera. Minkowski's dramatic skills help him create a magical atmosphere in these, while his galvanizing energy lends boisterous life to the quick movements. The orchestra plays superbly. These are utterly delightful recordings.

Grands motets

Grands motets – Dominus regnavit; In exitu Israel; De profundis Ⓟ
Sophie Daneman, Maryseult Wieczorek *sops* **Paul Agnew, François Piolino** *tens* **Maarten Koningsberger** *bar* **François Bazola** *bass*
Les Arts Florissants / William Christie
Erato 0630-17791-2 (72 minutes: DDD). Texts and translations included. Recorded 1996 Ⓕ ●

Mondonville's *grands motets* were enormously popular for many years at the Concert Spirituel in Paris (of which he was a director for a time). They follow the pattern laid down by Lalande and continued by Rameau, but with more independent instrumental parts and incorporating Italian influences (e.g. *da capo* arias) and operatic elements. These three on psalm texts are deeply impressive. *Dominus regnavit* (1734) was perhaps the earliest of Mondonville's *grands motets* and, besides its polyphonic opening chorus, is notable for two verses entirely for high-register voices and instruments, an operatic *tempête*, and a stunning complex 'Gloria patri'. *De profundis* (1748), written for the funeral of a Chapel Royal colleague, is by its nature sombre, and ends not with the usual 'Gloria patri' but with 'Requiem aeternam' and a fugue. The initial chorus was praised to the sky by contemporaries as 'sublime': other highlights are a baritone aria over a free chaconne bass, and a chorus illustrating 'morning' and 'night' by high and low voices respectively. There is even more illustrative music in the 1755 *In exitu Israel*: what amounts to a dramatic scena, with agitated strings and rushing voices for the 'fleeing sea', dotted figures for the mountains 'skipping like rams', and tremolos and vocal melismas for the 'trembling earth'. The present performances are vivid, with very good soloists, an alertly responsive chorus and a neat orchestra.

Claudio Monteverdi

Italian 1567-1643

GROVE *Monteverdi studied with Ingegneri, maestro di cappella at Cremona Cathedral, and published several books of motets and madrigals before going to Mantua in about 1591 to serve as a string player at the court of Duke Vincenzo Gonzaga. There he came under the influence of Giaches de Wert, whom he failed to succeed as maestro di cappella in 1596. In 1599 he married Claudia de Cattaneis, a court singer, who bore him three children, and two years later he was appointed maestro di cappella on Pallavicino's death. Largely as the result of a prolonged controversy with the theorist GM Artusi, Monteverdi became known as a leading exponent of the modern approach to harmony and text expression. In1607 his first opera, Orfeo, was produced in Mantua, followed in1608 by Arianna. The dedication to Pope Paul V of a grand collection of church music known as the Vespers (1610) indicated an outward looking ambition, and in 1613 Monteverdi was appointed maestro di cappella at St Mark's, Venice.*

There Monteverdi was active in reorganising and improving the cappella as well as writing music for it, but he was also able to accept commissions from elsewhere, including some from Mantua, for example the ballet Tirsi e Clori (1616) and an opera, La finta pazza Licori (1627, not performed, now lost). He seems to have been less active after c1629, but he was again in demand as an opera composer on the opening of public opera houses in Venice from 1637. In 1640 Arianna was revived, and in the following two years Il ritorno d'Ulisse in patria, Le nozze d'Enea con Lavinia (lost) and L'incoronazione di Poppea were given first performances. In 1643 he visited Cremona and died shortly after his return to Venice.

Monteverdi can be justly considered one of the most powerful figures in the history of music. Much of his development as a composer may be observed in the eight books of secular madrigals published between 1587 and 1638. The early books show his indebtedness to Marenzio in particular; the final one, Madrigali guerrieri et amorosi, includes some pieces 'in genere rappresentativo' – Il ballo delle ingrate, the Combattimento di Tancredi e Clorinda and the Lamento della ninfa – which draw on Monteverdi's experience as an opera composer. A ninth book was issued posthumously in 1651.

Orfeo was the first opera to reveal the potential of this then novel genre; Arianna (of which only the famous lament survives) may well have been responsible for its survival. Monteverdi's last opera L'incoronazione di Poppea, though transmitted in not wholly reliable sources and including music by other men, is his greatest masterpiece and arguably the finest opera of the century. In the 1610 collection of sacred music Monteverdi displayed the multiplicity of styles that characterise this part of his output. The mass, written on themes from Gombert's motet In illo tempore, is a monument of the prima prattica or old style. At the other extreme the motets, written for virtuoso singers, are the most thorough-going exhibition of the modern style and the seconda prattica.

Il combattimento di Tancredi e ...

Il combattimento di Tancredi e Clorinda. **P**
Il ballo delle ingrate
Concerto Italiano / Rinaldo Alessandrini *hpd*
Opus 111 OPS30-196 (58 minutes: DDD). Texts and Ⓕ
translations included. Recorded 1998 ●

The graphic realism and dramatic subtlety of both these expanded madrigals are given the most incandescent and powerful readings imaginable here. Concerto Italiano has won many plaudits for its delectable linguistic colouring of the earlier Mantuan madrigal books. *Combattimento*, this *sui generis* dramatic masterpiece from 1624, demonstrates Alessandrini's impeccable instincts for theatrical timing and the *stile concitato*, where extrovert representation of two fighting crusaders has the listener enraptured, not only by the celebrated violence of the figuration, but the poignant foreboding of the Christian knight's discovery that the Saracen warrior whom he has killed is the maiden he loves, in disguise. Stylistically provocative, it is the evocative restraint of Concerto Italiano's expressive world which shuns the self-conscious over-enactment that temporarily stalls even the most established readings. That said, the pace is hot throughout with words spat out by the Testo, or narrator, Roberto Abbondanza. His tenor is dark and often a touch hard-grained but he is remarkable in his dynamic range, contemplative dolour and grounded physicality. He is surrounded by a deeply affecting commentary of well-judged vibrating strings, bright fifths and rhythmic vitality. There are other notable recordings of this great *scena* but the pathos and purity of sentiment of Alessandrini's version have no rival, and the post-baptism, reconciliation scene at the end is given an ethereal fragility by Clorinda, the beguiling Elisa Franzetti.

The other work here, *Il ballo delle ingrate*, was written in 1608 for Monteverdi's patron Duke but the composer revised the original commission and published it as part of the *Madrigali guerrieri e amorosi* 30 years later. Again, the characterization is penetrating, the recitative style unforced and the string players revel in the potent undercurrents of women's fate should they resist love. An irresistible release.

1610 Vespers

Vespro della Beata Virgine (ed Parrott/Keyte) **P**
Taverner Consort; Taverner Choir; Taverner Players / Andrew Parrott
Virgin Classics Veritas Double ② VBD5 61662-2 Ⓑ
(106 minutes: DDD). Recorded 1984 ●

The technical and interpretative problems of the Monteverdi *Vespers* of 1610 are legion. Should the entire volume be performed as an entity, or just the psalms, or perhaps a mixture of psalms and motets? Since the vocal lines in the original publication are heavily ornamented, does this preclude the addition of further embellishment after the manner of contemporary instruction books? Which portions should be sung chorally (and how large should such a 'choir' be?), and which by the soloists? How should the continuo be realized?

Many of these difficulties stem from the ambiguities of the original publication of the *Vespers* which remains the source from which all modern performing editions must be made. Others are caused by uncertainties over 17th-century liturgical practice. In both these areas this recording offers new ideas. Firstly the liturgy. The central controversy raised by the *Vespers* concerns five non-liturgical compositions inserted among the Marian psalms, hymn and 'Magnificat': 'Nigra sum', 'Pulchra es', 'Duo Seraphim', 'Audi coelum' and the 'Sonata sopra Sancta Maria'. These, the sacred *concerti* described on the title-page as 'suitable for the chapels or private chambers of princes', do not conform textually to any known Marian office but occur in Monteverdi's collection in positions normally occupied by psalm antiphons. These apparent contradictions have led some editors to suggest that they should not be performed as part of the *Vespers*. More convincing is the view, followed here, that the *concerti* are substitutes for the antiphons missing from Monteverdi's collections. This view is taken even further by seeing them as antiphon-repeats and inserting plainchant for the missing first strain. This is done for three of the psalms; for the remaining two, contemporary instrumental sonatas by Giovanni Paolo Cima are performed. One effect is to make this version feel more unified and monumental.

Both physically and emotionally the *concerti* are presented here as the focal points of the *Vespers*. Certainly they are the occasion for some of the most spectacular singing on this recording. The essential ingredient here is the performance of Nigel Rogers, surely the most accomplished and convincing singer of the early 17th-century Italian virtuoso repertory. He gives persuasive and seemingly effortless performances in three of the *concerti* in his mellifluous, dramatic yet perfectly controlled manner. In two cases, 'Audi coelum' and 'Duo Seraphim', he is well matched with Andrew King and Joseph Cornwell. By comparison 'Pulchra es', sung by Tessa Bonner and Emma Kirkby, seems rather understated.

One important feature of Andrew Parrott's interpretation is its fundamental conception, historically accurate, of the *Vespers* as chamber work rather than a 'choral' one. Thus only one instrument is used per part, the harpsichord is employed very sparingly, and the basic continuo group is restricted to organ and chitarrone. Following the same principle, one voice per part is taken as the norm. The result is a clarity of texture, evident from the opening bars, which allows correct tempos to be used without stifling often intricate rhythmic features. 'Nisi Dominus', for example, is taken at a lively speed but does not end up sounding rushed as so often happens. 'Lauda Jerusalem' proceeds at a jaunty pace without loss of detail, and 'Laetatus sum' sounds stately without being leaden footed. That these effects can be achieved is largely due to decisions about the size and balance of forces.

Finally, mention should be made of another fundamental choice which represents something of a novelty. Both 'Lauda Jerusalem' and the 'Magnificat' are transposed down a fourth here, as they should be according to the convention relating to the clef combinations in which they were originally notated. This brings all the vocal parts into the tessitura of the rest of the work, and also restores the instruments to their normal ranges. Whether or not the result is less 'exciting' than the version we are used to hearing has only partly to do with questions of musicality. For the rest, one of the lasting virtues of this well-balanced, unobtrusive recording is that it allows us to hear the *Vespers* sounding something along the lines that Monteverdi intended.

Vespro della Beata Vergine
Sophie Marin-Degor, Maryseult Wieczorek *sops*
Artur Stefanowicz, Fabián Schofrin *countertens*
Paul Agnew, Joseph Cornwell, François Piolino *tens* **Thierry Félix, Clive Bayley** *basses*
Les Sacqueboutiers de Toulouse; Les Arts Florissants / William Christie *hpd/org*
Cima Concerti ecclesiastici – Sonata per il violino, cornetto e violone; Sonata per il violino e violone
Members of Les Arts Florissants
Erato ② 3984-23139-2 (100 minutes: DDD). Text and Ⓕ translation included. Recorded 1997

This is in some ways an oddly old-fashioned approach to the 1610 *Vespers*. With a substantial choir and sometimes highly varying orchestration, William Christie creates a warm and glowing sound. Part of his emphasis is on texture and flow, so Monteverdi's often sharp dissonances tend to have a soft edge; and there are some occasionally irrelevant pitches buried in the polyphonic web. He faces the challenge of putting the 'Lauda Jerusalem' and the 'Magnificat' at a pitch-standard a fourth lower than the rest (which he has at a modern concert pitch). And that is where the rich orchestration pays its dividends; the resulting almost impossibly low bass-lines, particularly in the 'Et misericordia' section of the 'Magnificat', sound clear and lucid with their instrumental doubling. He also benefits from the splendid low range of the tenors he uses: they manage to make the 'Gloria Patri' section a true climax to the work, and in particular they give the 'Duo Seraphim' perhaps the most convincing performance available anywhere because they are so beautifully matched. Christie prefaces each of the psalms with a chant introit; and he follows the order of the print except in putting 'Duo Seraphim' before the 'Sonata sopra Sancta Maria'. To fill the gap where Monteverdi put 'Duo Seraphim' he introduces a sonata by Cima, superbly played by a team led by the violinist, François Fernandez; and another excellently performed sonata by Cima separates the 'Lauda Jerusalem' from 'Duo Seraphim'. There is a warmth and generosity here that are undeniably attractive; the movements mentioned go better than anything else available; and everything is done at the level of skill and musicality that we have come to expect from Christie and his group.

Vespro della Beata Virgine – Domine ad adiuvandum; Dixit Dominus; Laudate pueri; Laetatus sum; Nisi Dominus; Lauda Jerusalem (with plainchant antiphons). Magnificat II. Motets – O quam pulchra es. Domine, ne in furore. Ego flos campi. Adoramus te, Christe. Laudate Dominum omnes gentes. Ego dormio, et cor meum vigilat. Christe, adoramus te. Cantate Domino P

Concerto Italiano / Rinaldo Alessandrini

Opus 111 OPS30-150 (75 minutes: DDD). Texts and translations included. Recorded 1996 Ⓕ OO

Rinaldo Alessandrini and the Concerto Italiano have acquired a formidable reputation, above all for their records of Monteverdi madrigals. The kind of knowledge and detailed understanding of the subtleties of both meaning and pronunciation of the Italian language which only a native speaker can possess, and an impressive command of 17th-century vocal styles and techniques are two of the important elements that characterize their distinctive approach. Allied to a profound sense of drama and a lively musicality, these skills have been expertly shaped by Alessandrini to produce some of the finest recordings of this repertory. This makes their foray into Monteverdi's church music all the more intriguing. The first half of the disc is made up of a complete vespers setting assembled from individual pieces published throughout the composer's career. Sung by one voice to a part and richly underpinned by a varied continuo group including theorbos, double harp and contrabass, there is a clarity and intimacy about the result. Details that often disappear in performances with larger forces here speak clearly (the performance of 'Dixit Dominus' from the *Vespers* of 1610 is notable in this respect). The recording is completed by a series of motets including three for solo voice; here it is almost invidious to express preferences, but it is difficult to resist praise for Rossana Bertini's breathtakingly audacious performance of *Laudate Dominum*, invigorated by a good deal of ornamentation executed with great flair and *élan*. This disc brims with revelations and surprises – no serious Monteverdian can afford to be without it.

Madrigals

Il primo libro de madrigali. Settimo libro de madrigali – Tempro la cetra; Tirsi e Clori

The Consort of Musicke / Anthony Rooley

Virgin Classics Veritas VC5 45143-2 (57 minutes: DDD). Texts and translations included. Recorded 1991 Ⓕ

Monteverdi's *Primo libro* of 1587 presents a detailed map of his absorption of contemporary madrigalian styles, and above all of his command of the lighter repertories that had become so popular in Italy during the 1580s. At the same time, there is a bittersweet quality about these pieces, for all that they are so episodically structured. This presages the later books when Monteverdi had moved to the Gonzaga court at Mantua, and had become acquainted with the more adventurous music then being written by composers both there and at Ferrara, inspired by the poetry of Guarini and Tasso. This is the first recording to treat the book in its entirety. Here The Consort of Musicke is on fine form, turning in sensitively wrought and carefully considered accounts, with perfect ensemble and tuning, and the textual details sensitively registered. The disc is rounded off with a number of pieces from the *Settimo libro*, clearly more dramatic in conception and effect, which provide an instructive and dramatic contrast with the madrigals from the first book. The continuo grouping here provides a sturdy and richly textured accompaniment to the soloists, and both instrumentalists and vocalists apply discreet and appropriate ornamentation with style.

Il secondo libro de madrigali P

Concerto Italiano / Rinaldo Alessandrini

Opus 111 OPS30-111 (58 minutes: DDD). Texts and translations included. Recorded 1994 Ⓕ

Captivation begins with the very opening of the first piece on the disc, *Non si levav'anchor l'alba novella*, whose gently growing sense of the awakening dawn is itself a delicately drawn metaphor for transition from the urgent desire of the lovers' final embrace after a night of lovemaking to the gentle pain of their parting. The exquisite bittersweet pathos of the scene, whose every nuance and ambiguity is superbly caught in Alessandrini's vision of Monteverdi's music, sets both the standard and the tone for much of what follows in a number of important ways. First, with the exception of *S'andasse amor a caccia* and *Non giacinto o narcisi*, there are no examples here of the lighter *canzonetta*, such a prominent feature of the musical picture in Italy during the 1580s and a strong presence in the composer's own *Primo libro* of 1587. Secondly, and crucially, almost half the contents of the *Secondo libro* of three years later are settings of poetry by Torquato Tasso, whose *Gerusalemme liberata* was the most significant and influential epic to have been written in Italy since Ariosto's *Orlando furioso*, first published in the early decades of the century. Packed with strong images and bright colours, Tasso's verse was much drawn upon by many composers, including Monteverdi who continued to set it throughout his career. In Alessandrini and the Concerto Italiano, the intimate fusion of words and music which the composer embarks upon in this Second Book, and which was to remain a lifelong preoccupation, is delineated with charm, skill and profound understanding.

Awards 1994

Il quarto libro de madrigali

Concerto Italiano / Rinaldo Alessandrini

Opus 111 OPS30-81 (62 minutes: DDD) Ⓕ

Texts and translations included

Recorded 1993

Monteverdi's Fourth Book of Madrigals, first published in 1603, is a wide-ranging collection of pieces written during the previous 10 years. Originally written for performance before a select audience by an ensemble of professional virtuoso singers, these madrigals, many of which are set to the sensuous, emotional and epigrammatic verses of Guarini and Tasso, show Monteverdi's seemingly inexhaustible ability to unite words and music in expressively effective ways. A complete and profound understanding of textual nuance is, then, central to any successful performance and here the Concerto Italiano begins with a considerable advantage over any group of non-Italians. Some of the finest madrigals in the Fourth Book are those involving direct speech, which allowed Monteverdi to make full use of the court virtuosi, famed for their abilities to combine clear declamation with dramatic gestures and subtle shadings of dynamics and speed. The Concerto Italiano has taken the combined messages of music and history to heart; these are performances infused with a flexible approach to tempo and strong projection of text geared to a determination to allow each detail of the words to speak with due force. The singing style is muscular without losing its ability to move into a gentler mood, the vocal balance good, the sound rich in its lower registers and bright and clear in the upper ones. At its best this record is simply without equal.

Il quinto libro de madrigali

Concerto Italiano / Rinaldo Alessandrini

Opus 111 OPS30-166 (65 minutes: DDD). Texts and Ⓕ translations included. Recorded 1996

There is a modernity about Monteverdi's poetic choices in the Fifth Book which is reflected in an adventurous harmonic and gestural language which pushes the madrigalian vocabulary of Giaches de Wert and Luca Marenzio to new boundaries. As always with Monteverdi, his main preoccupation is with an intimate bonding of words and music in a way which goes beyond the illustrative manoeuvres of traditional madrigalian styles. This aesthetic priority is one which Rinaldo Alessandrini and the Concerto Italiano have done so much to understand and reveal. Enthusiasts for the Concerto's highly dramatic, yet sensitive and subtle approach, will not be disappointed by this disc. The opening diptych, 'Cruda Amarilli/O Mirtillo', sets the tone and style for much of what follows; the pace is stately, the passion being generated by extraordinary dissonances, delineated here with a lingering attention that is truly spine-chilling while still retaining its erotic undertow. Here and elsewhere on this recording, the exactness of the voicing, the gentle underscoring of rhythm and meaning, the authentic sound of the Italian language and the sheer musicality of the final result are united in performances of great expressive power and integrity.

Awards 1998

Il ottavo libro de madrigali – Sinfonia; Altri canti d'amor; Non havea Febo ancora, 'Lamento della ninfa'; Vago augelletto; Perchè t'en fuggi, O Fillide?; Altri canti di Marte; Ogni amante è guerrier; Hor ch'el ciel e la terra; Gira il nemico insidioso Amore; Dolcissimo uscignolo; Ardo, ardo, avvampo, mi struggo

Concerto Italiano / Rinaldo Alessandrini

Opus 111 OPS30-187 (75 minutes: DDD) Ⓕ

Texts and translations included. Recorded 1997

Monteverdi's Eighth Book of Madrigals, issued with the eye-catching title of *Madrigali guerrieri et amorosi* ('Madrigals of Love and War'), was published in 1638. Taking their cue from the prominent position allocated to his cherished *genere concitato* in both the preface and contents of the collection, Rinaldo Alessandrini has made an unusual selection of pieces in which this kind of writing, which in practice involves much rapid chordal repetition, triadic formulas and scale passages to imitate the sounds of war, is prominent. It is a brave choice. The rhetorical gestures of the *genere concitato* are few, simple, obvious and rapidly pall when over-used. Nor are they confined to the *madrigali guerrieri* alone, since the agitation caused by the pains of love can also call them up. The real interpretative difficulty is to invest these moments with sufficient drama and character that they emerge from their somewhat textbook status and come to life. The Concerto Italiano's dramatic readings of the texts involve the familiar devices of severe contrast, occasional changes of pace, subtle underscorings at cadences and the highlighting of dissonant moments. The star performance is 'Hor ch'el ciel e la terra' which begins with a magically poetic evocation of the stillness of the night before settling into a depiction of the lover's pain, achieved through sharp stabbing motions of almost mannerist exaggeration. The Concerto's account of the second part ('Cosi soil d'una chiara fonte viva') is remarkable, not least for its inspired isolation of vocal lines of great lyrical power passed between the voices; it is a revelation.

Chamber Duets

Chamber Duets – Chiome d'oro, bel tesoro; Io son pur vezzosetta pastorella; Non è di gentil core; Non è mai le stelle; O come sei gentile, caro augellino; Ohimè, dovè il mio ben?; O viva fiamma; S'el vostro cor, madonna; Soave libertate; Tornate, o cari baci; Vorrei baciarti, O Filli; Book 8: Mentre vaga Angioletta ogn'anima; O sia tranquill'il mare; Book 9: Bel pastor dal cui bel guardo. Scherzi musicali – Zefiro torna. Non vedrò mai le stelle

Complesso Barocco / Alan Curtis *hpd/org*

Virgin Classics Veritas VC5 45293-2 (68 minutes: DDD). Texts and translations included. Ⓕ

Recorded 1996

Monteverdi's Chamber Duets are of a consistently high quality and include some of his most popular pieces (such as *Zefiro torna*, or the ravishing *Chiome d'oro*). The opening track wonderfully sets the tone, and showcases another of the recording's distinctive features, a particularly full continuo group. As one expects of Complesso Barocco, the standard of interpretation throughout is very high, although some of the more extended pieces seem to lose the thread of the argument, and the male soloists seem almost breathless at the tail-end of certain *passaggi*. The native singers' ease with the language is an essential asset: *Bel pastor*, one of the few duets for unequal voices, is particularly telling in this regard. Moving beyond interpretation, this project brings to the fore Monteverdi's astonishing resourcefulness and diversity of expression: what generous, essential music this is!

L'incoronazione di Poppea

Helen Donath *sop* Poppea; **Elisabeth Söderström** *sop* Nerone; **Cathy Berberian** *mez* Ottavia; **Paul Esswood** *counterten* Ottone; **Giancarlo Luccardi** *bass* Seneca; **Rotraud Hansmann** *sop* Virtue, Drusilla; **Jane Gartner** *sop* Fortune, Pallas, Darmigella; **Maria Minetto** *contr* Nurse; **Carlo Gaifa** *ten* Arnalta; **Philip Langridge** *ten* Lucano; **Enrico Fissore** *bass-bar* Lictor, Mercury; **anonymous** *treb* Love; **Margaret Baker** *sop* Valletto **Vienna Concentus Musicus / Nikolaus Harnoncourt** P
Teldec ④ 2292-42547-2 (215 minutes: ADD).
Notes, text and translation included. Ⓜ
Recorded 1973-74

L'incoronazione di Poppea has always had its staunch admirers, many claiming it to be Monteverdi's greatest masterpiece, even the finest opera of the 17th century. However, what's left of the opera amounts to little more than a vocal score, and even then with some scenes missing, others evidently added by hands other than Monteverdi's own. To turn the sketchy, inadequate sources into something that Monteverdi might have recognized as his work requires not only considerable effort but also more than a little self-confidence. Harnoncourt's production is still the best recording of it ever made. With its strong, sensitive cast and excellent pacing, this is a performance that shows the work's true potential, even if the realization is calculated to raise a few eyebrows – and more so today than when it was first released.

There are reservations about the use of loud wind instruments, above all in vocal contexts, and about the heavy ornamentation that their players use. Even the scoring of the string orchestra is heavy-handed on occasion. These effects are, of course, entirely of Harnoncourt's own making, since there's nothing in the sources to indicate even the size and nature of the orchestra, let alone its deployment. Also, his decision to associate certain timbres with specific situations could be seen as regrettable. Trumpets for the gods is acceptable enough, but there's nothing subtle about the pair of oboes that surfaces to accompany the comic characters. What saves this performance, however, is the fine cast of singers. There's not a single weak link. It was an imaginative move to cast Elisabeth Söderström as Nerone (originally a high castrato role), and one can forgive her palpable femininity on the grounds that she finds so much to convey in her playing of the part. Equally sure of her role as Ottavia is Cathy Berberian. Even the lesser characters are played superbly well – Jane Gartner as Fortune/Darmigella/Pallas, for example, or Philip Langridge as Lucano. It's as if every member of the cast recognizes the latent power of this marvellous music; and that's what makes this recording such an enduring one.

L'incoronazione di Poppea P
Sylvia McNair *sop* Poppea; **Dana Hanchard** *sop* Nerone; **Anne Sofie von Otter** *mez* Ottavia, Fortune, Venus; **Michael Chance** *counterten* Ottone; **Francesco Ellero d'Artegna** *bass* Seneca; **Catherine Bott** *sop* Drusilla, Virtue, Pallas, Athene; **Roberto Balcone** *counterten* Nurse; **Bernarda Fink** *contr* Arnalta; **Mark Tucker** *ten* Lucano, First Soldier; **Julian Clarkson** *bass* Lictor, Mercury; **Marinella Pennicchi** *sop* Love; **Constanze Backes** *sop* Valleto; **Nigel Robson** *ten* Liberto, Second Soldier
English Baroque Soloists / Sir John Eliot Gardiner
Archiv Produktion ③ 447 088-2AH3
(191 minutes: DDD). Notes, text and translation Ⓕ
included. Recorded live in 1993

The central question was always about how much needs to be added to the surviving notes in order to make *Poppea* viable on stage. Gardiner and his advisers believe that nothing needs adding and that the 'orchestra' indeed played only when explicitly notated in the score but that it was a very small group. To some ears this will have a fairly ascetic effect but it is firmly in line with the current scholarly thinking about the opera. To compensate for that asceticism Gardiner has a rich group of continuo players and they play with wonderful flexibility. And Gardiner's spacious reading of the score bursts with the variety of pace one might expect from a seasoned conductor of early opera. Sylvia McNair is a gloriously sensuous Poppea: from her sleepy first words to the final duet she is always a thoroughly devious character, with her breathy, come-hither tones. Complementing this is Dana Hanchard's angry-brat Nerone, less even in voice than one might hope, but dramatically powerful nevertheless. Whether they quite challenge Helen Donath and Elisabeth Söderström for Harnoncourt must remain a matter of opinion, but they certainly offer a viable alternative.

The strongest performances here, though, come from Michael Chance and Anne Sofie von Otter as Ottone and Ottavia, both of them offering superbly rounded portrayals. Again they face severe challenges from Harnoncourt's unforgettable Paul Esswood and Cathy Berberian, but here the challenge is more equal, being on roughly the same grounds. Francesco Ellero d'Artegna is perhaps the most vocally skilled Seneca to date, with a resonant low C, though

Michael Schopper for René Jacobs comes closer to the character of the oddball philosopher with clear political views for which he is happy to die. Catherine Bott is a wonderfully lively Drusilla; and the remainder of the cast are consistently strong. The fact that this was recorded at a public concert is noticeable only from occasional superfluous noises.

L'Orfeo

Laurence Dale *ten* Orfeo; **Efrat Ben-Nun** *sop* Euridice, Music; **Jennifer Larmore** *mez* Messenger; **Andreas Scholl** *counterten* Hope; **Paul Gérimon** *bass* Charon; **Bernarda Fink** *contr* Proserpina; **Harry Peeters** *bass* Pluto; **Nicolas Rivenq** *bar* Apollo
Concerto Vocale / René Jacobs
Harmonia Mundi ② HMC90 1553/4
(120 minutes: DDD). Notes, text and translation included. Recorded 1995

It is clear right from the start, with the almost aggressive snarling brass and thudding drums of the opening Toccata, that René Jacobs's reading of *L'Orfeo* is a full-blooded one. The tone is set almost immediately by Efrat Ben-Nun, whose approach to the two roles that she sings is refreshingly direct and dramatic; her lines are sensitively shaped and phrased, and only the improvised embellishments to the part of Music, at times quite elaborate, could possibly cause any controversy. Among the other soloists Bernarda Fink delivers a convincingly urgent account of Proserpina's appeal at the opening of the Fourth Act, while Harry Peeters's Pluto presents his measured responses with an attractively lyrical authority. Charon's strangely angular lines, with their air of menace appropriate to one who spends time in contact with the Underworld, are expertly managed by Paul Gérimon, who shows himself to be a true Monteverdi bass. René Jacobs's approach to the thorny question of orchestration is robust.

The score is notoriously difficult to interpret in this respect, often contradictory in its indications and in the end any solution can only be judged against some notion of what Monteverdi's sound world might have been. Jacobs's version was originally given at the Salzburg Festival in 1993, and his instrumental resources, based around three continuo instruments spatially separated, are more a reflection of the acoustical properties of a modern pit rather than those of the sort of room in the Ducal Palace in which *L'Orfeo* was first performed. There is nothing necessarily wrong with that, and it has to be said that the result is successful, discriminating and only rarely over-elaborate.

In Laurence Dale in the title-role, Jacobs has found a powerful protagonist, a singer capable of negotiating the sudden changes of emotional state that characterize the part at some of its most critical moments. More to the point, 'Possente spirto' is something of a *tour de force*, conveying the central conception of the power of song with true rhetorical understanding. This is a version of *L'Orfeo* to be reckoned with.

Il Ritorno d'Ulisse in Patria

Christoph Prégardien *ten* Ulisse; **Bernarda Fink** *contr* Penelope; **Christina Högmann** *sop* Telemaco, Siren; **Martyn Hill** *ten* Eumete; **Jocelyne Taillon** *mez* Ericlea; **Dominique Visse** *counterten* Pisandro, Human Fragility; **Mark Tucker** *ten* Anfinomo; **David Thomas** *bass* Antinoo; **Guy de Mey** *ten* Iro; **Faridah Subrata** *mez* Melanto; **Jörg Dürmüller** *ten* Eurimaco; **Lorraine Hunt** *sop* Minerva, Fortune; **Michael Schopper** *bass* Nettuno, Time; **Olivier Lallouette** *bass* Giove; **Claron McFadden** *sop* Giunone; **Martina Bovet** *sop* Siren, Love
Concerto Vocale / René Jacobs
Harmonia Mundi ③ HMC90 1427/9
(179 minutes: DDD). Notes, text and translation included. Recorded 1992

The only surviving manuscript score of this major musical drama, preserved in Vienna, presents an incomplete version of three acts. For this recording, René Jacobs has, within the spirit of 17th century music-making, added more music by Monteverdi and others to expand the work to a satisfying five-act structure suggested by some surviving librettos. He has also considerably expanded the scoring, very much enlivening the instrumental palette that Monteverdi would have had available to him for his original production in Vienna in 1641, and the result is powerful and effective. The extensive cast, led by Christoph Prégardien in the title role, is excellently chosen, not only for vocal quality but also for a convincing awareness of Monteverdi's idiom. Without that, the performance could have seemed tame, and that is nowhere better exemplified than in Act 1, Scene 7 where Ulysses awakes, wondering where he is and what is to happen to him. Prégardien here manages to convey as much depth of feeling as a Pagliaccio yet stays clearly within the bounds of Monteverdi's expressive style. The result is a *tour de force*, one of the many within this production. The adept instrumental contribution certainly helps to maintain variety throughout the work, and an accompaniment suited to the sentiments expressed by the vocalists is always possible with these resources. Ultimately, this production is very much one for our time. It is a practical solution to the problems of performing music of another age, and one that turns out to be inspired, moving and totally compelling.

Cristóbal de Morales

Spanish c1500-1553

GROVE *Morale is recognised as the most important figure in early 16th-century Spanish sacred music. He received his early musical education in Seville and in 1526 was appointed maestro de capilla of Avila Cathedral. In 1531 he resigned and by September 1535 was a singer in the papal chapel in Rome. He left in 1545 and was appointed maestro de capilla at Toledo Cathedral. He then fell ill and in 1547 renounced the position. On returning to*

Andalusia he became maestro de capilla to the Duke of Arcos at Marchena (1548-51). In 1551 he became maestro de capilla at Málaga Cathedral.

His works, almost all liturgical, include over 20 masses, 16 Magnificats, two Lamentations and over 100 motets. The Magnificats, perhaps the best known of his works, are permeated by Gregorian cantus firmi ; his Lamentations are characterised by a sober homophonic style. In his motets he often used chant associated with the text, as a melodic point of departure (eg Puer natus est) or as an ostinato figure (eg the five-voice Tu es Petrus), but he seldom borrowed entire melodies. Their texture is characterised by free imitation with exceptional use of homophonic sections to stress important words or portions of text. The two masses for the dead and the Officium defunctorum are the most extreme examples of Morales's sober style. He had thorough command of early 16th-century continental techniques and his style is better compared to Josquin, Gombert and Clemens than to his Spanish contemporaries. He favoured cross-rhythms, conflicting rhythms, melodic (but not harmonic) sequence and repetition, harmonic cross-relations, systematic use of consecutives and occasional daring use of harmony.

Masses

Missa 'Si bona suscepimus' **Crecquillon** Andreas Christi famulus **Verdelot** Si bona suscepimus
The Tallis Scholars / Peter Phillips
Gimell CDGIM033 (56 minutes: DDD). Texts and translations included. Recorded 1999 Ⓕ OO

Back with their own Gimell label as an independent venture again – as widely reported – The Tallis Scholars move into what is for them new territory: Cristóbal de Morales. He is perhaps the most admired Spanish composer of all time, to judge from the distribution and longevity of his works. But not nearly enough of his music has been recorded: in the current catalogue he occupies only a single column, as against two for Guerrero and three for Victoria. He merits a far larger place in our musical life.

And the six-voice Mass *Si bona suscepimus* appears not to have been recorded before. It was printed in his first book of Masses (1544) and undoubtedly comes from his years in the papal chapel. At first listening, there may be something almost too serene about its flawless counterpoint that flows with effortless invention. But there is an abundance of arresting detail in here, and he uses the six voices with an astonishing variety of textures.

And The Tallis Scholars are up to their usual standards of magnificent sound colour, nicely judged balance and extremely pure intonation. There is nothing overtly Spanish in the performance: they simply sing what is there in the music, without imposing too much externally. They hardly ever rush or slow down severely, preferring to allow the music to unfold at its own flexible pace. That could seem bland until you compare the sound with the introductory five-voice motet of Verdelot on which the Mass is based, or indeed the marvellous Crecquillon motet that ends the disc; these immediately sound quite different (and indeed make you wonder why the Crecquillon motet passed for so long as a work of Morales).

Morales Mass for the feast of St Isidore of Seville. Missa 'Mille regretz'. Emendemus in melius
Guerrero O Doctor optime
Instrumental and organ works by Cabézon, Rogier, Guerrero, Gombert and Santa María
Gabrieli Consort and Players / Paul McCreesh
Archiv Produktion 449 143-2AH (76 minutes: DDD). Ⓕ
Texts and translations included. Recorded 1995

The instrumental *canciones* by Guerrero and Rogier which open the disc are played with delightful sensitivity: one can understand why instrumentalists were so prized in Spanish cathedrals at this time if they played like this. Morales's Mass itself, performed by an all-male consort, is sung splendidly. There is a real feeling for the work's direction (not easily discerned in music so seamlessly polyphonic as Morales) which, in combination with the seductively rich sonority of the choir, make it a performance of genuine stature. The only reservations concern the stodgy singing of the 'Hosanna' which would surely benefit from a lighter, more rhythmic approach. The plainchant is for the feast of St Isidore of Seville, taken from unspecified 16th- and 17th-century sources by Robert Snow. It is sung accompanied by a dulcian, as indeed is the polyphony, common Spanish practice of the time. Instruments and choir come together only in Guerrero's motet, *O Doctor optime*, sung at the Offertory, which is an object lesson in how to achieve blend and balance. Another *canción* by Rogier acts as a recessional, and the disc closes with a short piece by Tomás de Santa María followed by a magnificent performance of Morales's motet *Emendemus in melius*.

Wolfgang Amadeus Mozart

Austrian 1756-1791

GROVE *Mozart, son of Leopold Mozart, showed musical gifts at a very early age, composing when he was five and when he was six playing before the Bavarian elector and the Austrian empress. Leopold felt that it was proper, and might also be profitable, to exhibit his children's God-given genius (Mozart's sister was a gifted keyboard player), so from mid-1763-66 the family set out on a European tour. Mozart astonished his audiences with his precocious skills; he played to the French and English royal families, had his first music published and wrote his earliest symphonies. In 1767 they were off again, to Vienna, where hopes of having an opera by Mozart performed were frustrated by intrigues.*

1770-73 saw three visits to Italy, where Mozart wrote two operas (Mitridate, Lucio Silla) and a serenata for performance in Milan, and acquainted himself with Italian styles. Summer 1773 saw a further visit to Vienna where he wrote a set of string quartets and, on his return, a group of symphonies including Nos 25 in G minor and 29 in A. Apart from a journey to Munich for the première of his opera La finta giardiniera early in 1775, the period from 1774 to mid-1777 was spent in Salzburg, where Mozart worked as Konzertmeister at the Prince-Archbishop's court; his works of these years include masses, symphonies, all his violin concertos, six piano sonatas, several serenades and divertimentos and his first great piano concerto, K271.

In 1777 he was sent, with his mother, to Munich and to Mannheim, but was offered no position (though he stayed over four months at Mannheim, falling in love with Aloysia Weber). His father then dispatched him to Paris: there he had minor successes, notably with his Paris Symphony, no.31, deftly designed for the local taste. But prospects there were poor and Leopold ordered him home, where a superior post had been arranged at the court. He returned slowly and alone; his mother had died in Paris. The years 1779-80 were spent in Salzburg, playing in the cathedral and at court, composing sacred works, symphonies, concertos, serenades and dramatic music. But opera remained at the centre of his ambitions, and an opportunity came with a commission for a serious opera for Munich. He went there to compose it late in 1780; his correspondence with Leopold is richly informative about his approach to musical drama. The work, Idomeneo, was a success. In it Mozart depicted serious, heroic emotion with a richness unparalleled elsewhere in his works, with vivid orchestral writing and an abundance of profoundly expressive orchestral recitative.

Mozart was then summoned to Vienna, where the Salzburg court was in residence on the accession of a new emperor. Fresh from his success, he found himself placed between the valets and the cooks; his resentment towards his employer, exacerbated by the Prince-Archbishop's refusal to let him perform at events the emperor was attending, soon led to conflict, and in May 1781 he resigned, or was kicked out of, his job. He made his living over the ensuing years by teaching, by publishing his music, by playing at patrons' houses or in public, by composing to commission; in 1787 he obtained a minor court post as Kammermusicus, which gave him a reasonable salary and required nothing beyond the writing of dance music for court balls. He earned, by musicians standards, a good income, but lavish spending and poor management caused him financial difficulties. In 1782 he married Constanze Weber, Aloysia's sister.

In his early years in Vienna, Mozart built up his reputation by publishing, playing the piano and, in 1782, having an opera performed: Die Entführung aus dem Serail, a German Singspiel which went far beyond the usual limits of the tradition with its long, elaborately written songs. The work was successful and was taken into the repertories of many provincial companies (for which Mozart was not however paid). In these years, too, he wrote six string quartets which he dedicated to the master of the form, Haydn: they are marked not only by their variety of expression but by their complex textures, conceived as four-part discourse, with the musical ideas linked to this freshly integrated treatment of the medium.

In 1782 Mozart embarked on the composition of piano concertos, so that he could appear both as composer and soloist. He wrote 15 before the end of 1786, with early 1784 as the peak of activity. They represent one of his greatest achievements, with their formal mastery, their subtle relationships between piano and orchestra (the wind instruments especially) and their combination of brilliance, lyricism and symphonic growth. In 1786 he wrote the first of his three comic operas with Lorenzo da Ponte as librettist, Le nozze di Figaro: here and in Don Giovanni (given in Prague, 1787) Mozart treats the interplay of social and sexual tensions with keen insight into human character that - as again in the more artificial sexual comedy of Così fan tutte (1790) - transcends the comic framework, just as Die Zauberflöte (1790) transcends, with its elements of ritual and allegory about human harmony and enlightenment, the world of the Viennese popular theatre from which it springs.

Mozart lived in Vienna for the rest of his life, though he undertook a number of journeys to Salzburg, Prague, Berlin and Frankfurt. The last Prague journey was for the première of La clemenza di Tito (1791), a traditional serious opera written for coronation celebrations, but composed with a finesse and economy characteristic of Mozart's late music. Instrumental works of these years include some piano sonatas, three string quartets written for the King of Prussia, some string quintets, which include one of his most deeply felt works (K516 in G minor) and one of his most nobly spacious (Kn C), and his last four symphonies – one (No 38 in D) composed for Prague in 1786, the others written in 1788 and forming, with the lyricism of No 39 in E flat, the tragic suggestiveness of No 40 in G minor and the grandeur of No 41 in C, a climax to his orchestral music. His final works include the Clarinet Concerto and some pieces for masonic lodges (he had been a freemason since 1784). At his death from a feverish illness whose precise nature has given rise to much speculation (he was not poisoned), he left unfinished the Requiem, his first large-scale work for the church since the C minor Mass of 1783, also unfinished. Mozart was buried in a Vienna suburb, with little ceremony and in an unmarked grave, in accordance with prevailing custom.

Clarinet Concerto in A, K622

Clarinet Concerto. Clarinet Quintet in A, K581
Thea King *basset cl* [b]**Gabrieli String Quartet** (Kenneth Sillito, Brendan O'Reilly *vns* Ian Jewel *va* Keith Harvey *vc*); [a]**English Chamber Orchestra / Jeffrey Tate**
Hyperion CDA66199 (64 minutes: DDD). Ⓕ
Recorded 1985 ●

The two works on this disc are representative of Mozart's clarinet writing at its most inspired; however, the instrument for which they were written differed in several respects from the modern clarinet, the most important being its extended bass range. Modern editions of both the Clarinet Concerto and the Quintet have adjusted the solo part to suit today's clarinets, but Thea King reverts as far as possible to the original texts, and her playing is both sensitive and intelligent. Jeffrey Tate and the ECO accompany with subtlety and discretion in the concerto, and the Gabrieli Quartet achieves a fine rapport with King in the Quintet. Both recordings are clear and naturally balanced, with just enough distance between soloist and listener.

Clarinet Concerto. Oboe Concerto in C, K314
Jack Brymer *cl* **Neil Black** *ob*
Academy of St Martin in the Fields / Sir Neville Marriner
Philips 416 483-2PH (50 minutes: ADD). Ⓕ
Recorded 1973 ∞

For all the classic status of Jack Brymer's recordings with Beecham (available on EMI with various couplings), we would not now choose them in preference to this Marriner version. His recording here is of the highest distinction, coupled with Neil Black's delightful performance of the Oboe Concerto. They are fine performances, even great ones; with Marriner, Brymer seems to have rethought his approach to a work he must have known almost too well. He has shed none of his elegance, but there is a greater touch of wistfulness, a hint of tragedy, which lends the music fuller substance. Even in the finale, there is the suggestion that the liveliness is the more precious for an awareness of a darker element. It is the finest of all the recordings displaying Brymer's art at its greatest in one of the greatest works ever written for the instrument.

Mozart Clarinet Concerto[a]
Spohr Clarinet Concerto No 1 in C minor, Op 26
Weber Clarinet Concerto No 2 in E flat, J118
Ernst Ottensamer *cl/[a]basset cl*
Vienna Philharmonic Orchestra / Sir Colin Davis
Philips 438 868-2PH (72 minutes: DDD). Ⓕ
Recorded 1992

Ernst Ottensamer is a virtuoso with a real sense of style, that is to say a musician with an instinct for the difference between the contained romanticism of Mozart's concerto and the overt but differing romanticism of Spohr and Weber. His tone is rich and warm, with a beautiful depth in the lower registers of the basset clarinet in the Mozart, but also a brilliance that has a bit of a wicked glint to it in Weber's finale compared to the dancing ease of Mozart's. Mozart's *Adagio* is beautifully judged in tempo, a song with a seamless line, while Weber's *Romanza* is taken quite differently, like a wordless operatic aria. Spohr's short *Adagio*, a touchingly simple, direct piece, is charmingly delivered, and elsewhere Ottensamer listens with a careful ear to the woodwind and other lines which in this work intermingle so subtly: he is an old Philharmoniker who shows a proper attention to his colleagues. He is given close, sympathetic support by orchestra and conductor. One of Davis's particular qualities is his ear for the telling simplicities in Mozart, so that here a plain arpeggio springs to life with the clarinet's melody, or a set of repeated notes has a sense of direction towards a cadence. How musically the 'accompaniment' is done. The VPO responds with complete understanding, and the recording engineers have missed nothing.

Additional recommendations
Mozart Clarinet Concerto, K622
Coupled with: Beethoven Violin Concerto (arr Pletnev for cl)
Collins *cl* **Russian National Orchestra / Pletnev**
DG 457 652-2GH (70 minutes: DDD: r/d). Ⓕ

Wonderfully agile playing from Michael Collins on the basset clarinet. His is an elegant but powerful reading, and in the slow movement he is deeply poetic. Pletnev's Russian National Orchestra give refined support

Flute Concertos

No 1 in G, K313/K285c; **No 2** in C, K314/K285d. **Andante in C major**, K315/K285e. **Flute and Harp Concerto** in D, K299/K297c

---

Flute Concerto No 1. Andante. Flute and Harp Concerto
Susan Palma *fl* **Nancy Allen** *hp*
Orpheus Chamber Orchestra
DG 427 677-2GH (58 minutes: DDD). Ⓕ
Recorded 1988

Mozart's G major Flute Concerto is a charming work, not without depth. This is an admirable performance by Susan Palma, a remarkably gifted player who is also a member of the Orpheus Chamber Orchestra, a conductorless ensemble of 24 musicians, who play with skill and unanimity so that all is alert, lithe and yet sensitive. Palma's tone is liquid and bright, with fine tonal nuances. The Concerto for flute and harp was written for the flute-playing Count de Guines to play with his harpist daughter, and combines these two beautiful instruments to fine effect. Again the soloists are highly skilled and, beyond that, their playing is nicely matched, tonally and stylistically. Indeed Palma is as delightful as in the other work and the spacious *Andante* in C major that separates the two concertos, while Nancy Allen makes an exquisite sound and also articulates more clearly than many other harpists. The attractive cadenzas are by Palma and Bernard Rose. The balance between the soloists and the orchestra is natural and the recording from New York's State University has a very pleasing sound.

Flute Concertos Nos 1 and 2. Andante. Flute and Harp Concerto **P**
Konrad Hünteler *fl* **Helga Storck** *hp* **Orchestra of the Eighteenth Century / Frans Brüggen**
Philips 442 148-2PH (78 minutes: DDD). Ⓕ
Recorded 1990s

Konrad Hünteler and Frans Brüggen shape the elegant lines of the G major Concerto with finesse, enhanced by an exceptionally attractive blend between Hünteler's *c*1720 Denner flute and the orchestra's pleasingly fine-grained sound. Hünteler's soft flute sound (atmospherically evoking the human voice) and the orchestra's distinctive period instruments bring added dramatic intensity to this music. Likewise, Hünteler and the orchestra capture the direct charm of the C major *Andante*. The C major concerto is Mozart's arrangement for flute of his Oboe Concerto. For this recording, the 18th-century flute parts have been compared with those for oboe for a more 'authentic' text, and the resulting exquisitely balanced account makes a wholly convincing masterpiece for the flute. Hünteler and Storck, aided by the orchestra's subtle playing, highlight vividly the flute and harp concerto's perfect match of technical and instrumental resources.

Flute and Harp Concerto[a]; Concerto for Bassoon and Orchestra in B flat, K191[b]; Sinfonia concertante in E flat, K297[bc]

[a]**Kate Hill** *fl* [c]**Nicholas Daniel** *ob* [c]**Joy Farrall** *cl* [bc]**Julie Andrews** *bn* [b]**Lucy Wakeford** *hp* [c]**Stephen Bell** *hn* **Britten Sinfonia / Nicholas Cleobury**

Classic fM The Full Works 75805 57038-2 Ⓜ
(74 minutes: DDD). Recorded 1998

A delightful recording in every way. These three works are brimful of Mozartian melody of the most beguiling kind. Julie Andrews, the bassoonist, has a spring in her step from the very opening of her solo concerto – after Nicholas Cleobury has set the pace in his spirited and stylishly turned opening ritornello. Her articulation is most winning: there is geniality here without clowning. The melody of the *Andante* then brings a touchingly doleful mood, while the Minuet finale is so deftly decorated that you cannot help being captivated. The Flute and Harp Concerto (which opens the programme) also swings off elegantly; and what fragility of texture the soloists, Kate Hill and Lucy Wakeford, create between them! The flute playing is quite exquisite in the slow movement, and the harp's delicate filigree brings a sense of caressing to the background embroidery. The finale dances off with great charm. The support provided by the Britten Sinfonia throughout has just the right degree of robustness to set off the airy tracery of the two soloists. The *Sinfonia concertante* is of course a team work and the solo response is first class. In the slow movement the bassoonist winningly takes the lead: the finale brings a delectably light-hearted gait; and how these players enjoy their divisions, with each taking the spotlight in turn, and then chortling in concert most infectiously. The recording is vividly real, the kind that leaps out of the speakers and immediately communicates with the listener. Overall, then, it is highly recommended.

Horn Concertos

No 1 in D, K412; **No 2** in E flat, K417; **No 3** in E flat, K447; **No 4** in E flat, K495

Horn Concertos Nos 1-4. Piano Quintet in E flat, K452 **H**

Dennis Brain *hn*
Philharmonia Orchestra / Herbert von Karajan

EMI mono CDM5 66898-2 (55 minutes: ADD). Ⓕ
Recorded 1953 ●●●

Dennis Brain was the finest Mozartian soloist of his generation. Again and again Karajan matches the graceful line of his solo phrasing (the *Romance* of No 3 is just one ravishing example), while in the *Allegros* the crisply articulated, often witty comments from the Philharmonia violins are a joy. The glorious tone and the richly lyrical phrasing of every note from Brain himself is life-enhancing in its radiant warmth. The *Rondos* are not just spirited, buoyant, infectious and smiling, although they are all of these things, but they have the kind of natural flow that Beecham gave to Mozart. There is also much dynamic subtlety – Brain doesn't just repeat the main theme the same as the first time, but alters its level and colour. His legacy to the next generation of horn players (and those that have followed on afterwards) was to show them that the horn – a notoriously difficult instrument – could be tamed absolutely and that it could yield a lyrical line and a range of colour to match any other solo instrument. He was tragically killed, in his prime, in a car accident while travelling home overnight from the Edinburgh Festival – his driving was as legendary as his playing. He left us this supreme Mozartian testament which may be approached by others but rarely, if ever, equalled, for his was uniquely inspirational music-making, with an innocent-like quality to make it the more endearing. It is a pity to be unable to be equally enthusiastic about the recorded sound. The mono master is, rightly, not given spurious stereo treatment, but the remastering – although the horn timbre, with full Kingsway Hall resonance, is unimpaired – has dried out the strings: added clarity is no fair exchange for loss of amplitude. But this remains a classic recording.

Horn Concertos Nos 1-4. Rondos – D, K514; E flat, K371, 'Concert Rondo' **P**

Anthony Halstead *hn* **Academy of Ancient Music / Christopher Hogwood**

L'Oiseau-Lyre 443 216-2OH (60 minutes: DDD). Ⓕ
Recorded 1993 ●

A particular charm of Halstead's recording lies in cool, understated performances and the variety in his approach to the different concertos: the broader phrasing and longer lines he brings to the more consciously expansive and symphonic K495, for example, the chamber musical playing in K447 (easily the finest of the concertos), and the gentle lyricism in K417. Everywhere, however, he excels with his shapely moulding of the music and his natural, musical way of rounding off phrases. Playing a period horn, he 'makes' the notes that are not natural harmonics by deft movements of his hand in the bell. This technique can lead to the chromatic notes differing sharply in quality from the open ones, but Halstead seems to have more control over tone quality than most natural horn players: the stopped notes sometimes slip in unobtrusively, but where he wants to use colour to stress them, he does so very effectively, with the occasional touch of brassiness or muffling. Clearly his special skill allows him extra options. For the D major Concerto, the last of the four (the correct chronological order is K417, K495,

K447, K412), we are given the Süssmayr version of the finale (the familiar one, written during the Easter after Mozart's death and including a Lamentation plainsong) and a very capable filling-out of Mozart's incomplete autograph version by John Humphries, who also supplies the skilful completion of the skeletal K371 *Rondo*. With the Academy of Ancient Music under Hogwood on form, with well pointed ritornellos and attentive accompaniments, this is a thoroughly enjoyable and musicianly account of these endearing works.

Horn Concertos Nos 1-4. Horn Quintet in E flat, K407/K386*c*
David Pyatt *hn* **Kenneth Sillito** *vn* **Robert Smissen, Stephen Tees** *vas* **Stephen Orton** *vc*
Academy of St Martin in the Fields / Sir Neville Marriner
Erato 0630-17074-2 (70 minutes: DDD). Ⓜ
Recorded 1996

David Pyatt, *Gramophone's* Young Artist of the Year in 1996, provides performances in which calm authority and high imagination fuse; and this disc is ideally placed in the catalogue to comlement the nobility and urbanity of Dennis Brain. Although there can be no direct comparison with Anthony Halstead, Pyatt's is very much in that mode of supple, understated and often witty playing, accompanied by truly discriminating orchestral forces. Soloist and orchestra create a constantly shifting and lively pattern of dynamic relationships. Pyatt makes the music's song and meditation very much his own. Compared with the dark, dream-like *cantabile* of Brain, he offers in the Second Concerto an *Andante* of cultivated conversation and, in the Third, a *Romanza* of barely moving breath and light. His finales trip the light fantastic. The Second Concerto's springing rhythms reveal wonderfully clear high notes; the Third is nimble and debonair without being quite as patrician as Brain's; and the Fourth creates real mischief in its effervescent articulation. The cadenzas by Terry Wooding (to the first movements of the Third and Fourth Concertos) epitomize Pyatt's performances as a whole: longer and more daringly imaginative than those of Brain, while remaining sensitively scaled and fancifully idiomatic. The concertos are imaginatively and unusually coupled with a fine performance of the Horn Quintet in E flat.

Horn Concertos Nos 1-4; E, KAnh98*a*/K494*a*. Rondos for Horn and Orchestra – D, K514 (cptd Süssmayr); E flat, K371. Fragment for Horn and Orchestra in E flat, K370*b* (both reconstr Humphries)
Bournemouth Sinfonietta / Michael Thompson *hn*
Naxos 8 553592 (76 minutes: DDD). Ⓢ
Recorded 1995

This is not just an excellent bargain version of the horn concertos, superbly played and recorded, but a most valuable example of Mozartian scholarship on disc. Michael Thompson, himself directing the Bournemouth Sinfonietta with point and flair, plays the four regular concertos in revised texts prepared by John Humphries, as well as offering reconstructions by Humphries of two movements, designed as the outer movements, an *Allegro*, K370*b* and a *Rondo*, K371, for an earlier horn concerto written soon after Mozart arrived in Vienna. The other *Rondo*, K514, completed by Süssmayr, is the version generally used in modern performances of the second movement of the so-called Horn Concerto No 1, K412. This was in fact the last to be composed, and is less demanding technically for the soloist, both in the key chosen and in the range required.

The *Rondo* played here as the second movement finale of K412 is Humphries's reconstruction from sources recently discovered, much more imaginative than the Süssmayr version. It is a revelation too in the most popular of the concertos, No 4, to have extra passages, again adding Mozartian inventiveness. For example, the tutti in the first movement before the development section is here extended in a charming few extra bars. The most frustrating, if equally illuminating item is the E major Fragment dating from 1785-86, which consists of a magnificent orchestral tutti, longer than usual, leading into only a few bars of horn solo. Thompson, for 10 years the Philharmonia's first horn, is not only technically brilliant, but plays with delectable lightness and point, bringing out the wit in finales, as well as the tenderness in slow movements. As conductor and director, he also draws sparkling and refined playing from the Bournemouth Sinfonietta, very well recorded in clear, atmospheric sound. An outstanding issue for both specialist and newcomer alike.

Oboe Concerto in C, K314/K271k

Oboe Concerto. Flute Concerto No 1. Clarinet Concerto
Nicholas Daniel *ob* **Kate Hill** *fl* **Joy Farrall** *basset cl*
Britten Sinfonia / Nicholas Cleobury
Classic fM 75605 57001-2 (73 minutes: DDD). Ⓜ
Recorded 1997

This collection of Mozart's finest solo woodwind concertos is a winner. All the soloists are distinguished British orchestral players, each having a distinct personality in his or her own right. Joy Farrall's clarinet style combines an easy freedom with warm classical directness. Her performance of the Clarinet Concerto is totally seductive, with Nicholas Cleobury's gracefully phrased opening ritornello setting the scene for the lightly pointed solo entry. Her delicacy of feeling and velvety, luminous timbre immediately cajole the ear, as does the subtlety of her wistful dynamic nuancing. Her fluid line is heard at its most ravishing in the *Adagio*, which is richly echoed by the strings of the Britten Sinfonia; and the delicacy of the reprise is particularly magical. It is followed by a delicious, bubbling finale with lilting secondary material. Nicholas Daniel is hardly less appealing in the more petite Oboe Concerto and his reedy sweetness of timbre never cloys. He, too, is at his finest in the slow movement, while in the infectious closing *Rondo* finale he provides a neatly succinct cadenza. The Flute Concerto is equally delectable, especially the tender *Adagio* which Cleobury moves forward at exactly the right measured pace and which Kate Hill carols so touchingly. The neatly pointed Minuet finale is captivating. The recorded sound is excellent and well balanced over all.

Mozart Oboe Concerto
R Strauss Oboe Concerto in D
Douglas Boyd *ob*
Chamber Orchestra of Europe / Paavo Berglund Ⓕ
ASV CDCOE808 (44 minutes: DDD)

This coupling links two of the most delightful oboe concertos ever written. Mozart's sprightly and buoyant work invests the instrument with a chirpy, bird-like fleetness encouraging the interplay of lively rhythm and elegant poise. Boyd's reading captures this work's freshness and spontaneity beautifully. If the Mozart portrays the sprightly side of the instrument's make-up the Strauss illustrates its languorous ease and tonal voluptuousness. Again Boyd allows himself the freedom and breadth he needs for his glowing interpretation; he handles the arching melodies of the opening movement and the witty *staccato* of the last with equal skill. Nicely recorded.

Complete Piano Concertos

No 1 in F, K37; **No 2** in B flat, K39; **No 3** in D, K40; **No 4** in G, K41; **No 5** in D, K175; **No 6** in B flat, K238; **No 8** in C, K246; **No 9** in E flat, K271, 'Jeunehomme'; **No 11** in F, K413/K387*a*; **No 12** in A, K414/K385*p*; **No 13** in C, K415/K387*b*; **No 14** in E flat, K449; **No 15** in B flat, K450; **No 16** in D, K451; **No 17** in G, K453; **No 18** in B flat, K456; **No 19** in F, K459; **No 20** in D minor, K466; **No 21** in C, K467; **No 22** in E flat, K482; **No 23** in A, K488; **No 24** in C minor, K491; **No 25** in C, K503; **No 26** in D, K537, 'Coronation'; **No 27** in B flat, K595

Piano Concertos Nos 1-27
English Chamber Orchestra / Murray Perahia *pf*
Sony Classical ⑫ SX12K46441 Ⓜ
(608 minutes: ADD/DDD). Recorded 1975-84 ●●

Mozart concertos from the keyboard remain unbeatable. There is a rightness, an effortlessness, about doing the concertos this way which makes for heightened enjoyment. Not that it is the only way; and yet so many of them seem to gain in vividness when the interplay of pianist and orchestra is realized by musicians listening to each other in the manner of chamber music. Provided the musicians are of the finest quality, of course. We now just take for granted that the members of the English Chamber Orchestra will match the sensibility of the soloist. They are on top form here, as is Perahia, and the finesse of detail is breathtaking. Just occasionally Perahia communicates an 'applied' quality – a refinement which makes some of his statements sound a little too good to be true. But this is to be pernickety. The line of his playing, appropriately vocal in style, is exquisitely moulded; and the only reservations one can have are that a hushed, 'withdrawn' tone of voice, which he is little too ready to use, can bring an air of self-consciousness to phrases where ordinary, radiant daylight would have been even more illuminating; and that here and there a robuster treatment of brilliant passages would have been in place. However, the set is entirely successful on its own terms – whether or not you want to make comparisons with other favourite recordings. Indeed, we now know that records of Mozart piano concertos don't come any better played than here.

Piano Concertos Nos 1-27. Rondo in D, K382
English Chamber Orchestra / Daniel Barenboim *pf*
EMI ⑩ CES5 72930-2 (661 minutes: ADD). Ⓜ
Recorded 1967-74 ●

Mozart's piano concertos explore a number of expressive worlds ranging from buoyant youthful elegance – though there are surprises and formal innovations even in the Salzburg works, like the Minuet section that invades the finale of K271 – to the *Sturm und Drang* of the first movements in K466 and K491, the introspection of the slow movements of K467 and K488 and the ineffable poise of K595, the last concerto of all. In their performance it is necessary for a soloist and conductor to be at one interpretatively, or better still to be one and the same person, which is what happens here, just as it would have done in Mozart's own time.

Daniel Barenboim uses cadenzas of his own along with Mozart's, and others by Beethoven arranged by Edwin Fischer (No 20 in D minor) and Wanda Landowska (in the *Coronation* Concerto, No 26). (Barenboim's own may take Mozart rather far in the direction of romanticism.) He gives a legitimate sense of breadth to Mozart's thought that will appeal especially to collectors who have come to these concertos through Beethoven's. At times he can be self-indulgent and seeming to be unconsciously telling us how exquisitely he can turn a phrase, rather than allowing Mozart to speak for himself; but we hasten to say that we feel this only here and there and that not all listeners will agree. The best way to find out whether you do is to listen to this soloist's shaping of a melody in a slow movement, such as the poignant *Adagio* of No 23 in A major; beautiful as this playing is with its ultra-delicate dynamic shading, it could be thought anachronistically romantic in spirit and even narcissistic. Alternatively, but for similar reasons, hear Barenboim in the *Larghetto* of No 27, with its mannered half-tones and hesitations.

Again, the performances of the dramatic D minor and C minor Concertos on the eighth CD in this set, which incidentally are the only ones of the series to have a minor key, will tell you if Barenboim's approach to these works that were admired by Beethoven is too overtly Beethovenian, with their *Sturm und Drang* excessively explosive and the Romance in the D minor a heavy-weight affair, not least where the orchestra is concerned. But it is still Murray Perahia, like Barenboim, directing the excellent ECO, who seems to be closest of all to that radiantly self-revealing and self-giving, and yet still elusive, genius which Mozart demonstrated in this wonderful series of concertos.

Piano Concertos Nos 1-14

Piano Concertos Nos 1-4 🅿
Robert Levin *hpd* **Academy of Ancient Music / Christopher Hogwood**
Decca L'Oiseau-Lyre 466 131-2OH Ⓕ
(60 minutes: DDD). Recorded 1998

'These performances follow the original practice in Salzburg and use an orchestra without cellos', says a note in the booklet. But Neal Zaslaw, in his weighty tome on the Mozart symphonies – *The Compleat Mozart* (W W Norton & Co: 1991) – reckons that between 1767 (the year these works were adapted from the music of other composers) and 1775, that city's orchestra had either one or two cellos. Controversy apart, you are unlikely to miss this instrument here because the bass's line alone is quite rich in sonority. Moreover, Levin plays continuo (as Mozart did) and that helps to fill gaps though he is occasionally a trifle over-enthusiastic.

Best not to be critical about that aspect, however, because these juvenile pieces get what they need: enthusiastic advocacy. The sound of the period ensemble is also very good (no seedy violins) although the harpsichord isn't stable. Sometimes it moves forward and, in K37, wanders to the right. Levin improvises his own cadenzas, as he has consistently done throughout this series. It is his prerogative, and he has managed to stay in style without being imitative.

Hogwood's contribution has its own brand of distinction. For instance, his artistic contouring of phrases (some of them forming only a background) in the *Andante* of K40 offers delicately graded tonal contrasts to the different sort of lyricism that Levin extracts from his percussive instrument. Asperities of timbre are absent, and the succeeding *Presto* has a bubbling verve because all the accents are perfectly judged. Soloist and conductor always interpret the music – and that is real authenticity.

Piano Concertos Nos 9 and 21
English Chamber Orchestra / Murray Perahia *pf* Ⓕ
Sony Classical SK34562 (59 minutes: DDD) ●

Perahia's fine Mozart playing is a feature of the musical scene that has been with us for decades, as this issue reminds us. There is a delightful freshness and crispness as well as the kind of authority that convinces us that this is the only way to perform the music – that is, until another masterly account comes along. Perahia's choice of tempos is a case in point, yet he seems natural rather than merely predictable and one recalls how even fine musicians can often go astray on this matter which Wagner and Stravinsky alike regarded as crucial. Are there any reservations? Well, perhaps the CD sound is just that little bit close and bright, but with music-making of this quality that does not seem to matter.

The grave *Andantino* of No 9 (which Einstein called Mozart's 'Eroica', perhaps in part because of its key) is given weight without exaggeration. In No 21, Perahia does not give the first movement the *maestoso* element which is suggested in some editions: instead there is a delightful flexibility and Leporello-like charm. However, one may possibly feel that the G minor passage before the second subject and the E minor one in the development are too soft and yielding, charming though they are in themselves. Perahia's own cadenza is effective and in keeping with his chosen approach. In the famous *Andante* also, Perahia plays with great feeling and poise.

Piano Concertos Nos 11, 12 and 14
English Chamber Orchestra / Murray Perahia *pf* Ⓕ
Sony Classical SK42243 (70 minutes: ADD/DDD) ●

Piano Concertos Nos 20 and 27
English Chamber Orchestra / Murray Perahia *pf* Ⓕ
Sony Classical SK42241 (63 minutes: ADD/DDD) ●

These discs happily epitomize some of the best qualities of the complete Perahia/ECO set. Always intelligent, always sensitive to both the overt and less obvious nuances of this music, Perahia is firstly a true pianist, never forcing the instrument beyond its limits in order to express the ideas, always maintaining a well-projected singing touch. The superb ECO reflects his integrity and empathy without having to follow slavishly every detail of his articulation or phrasing. K414 and K413 are charming and typically novel for their time, but do not break new ground in quite the way that K449 does. Here, Mozart's success in the theatre may have suggested a more dramatic presentation and working of ideas for this instrumental genre. K595 is a work pervaded by a serenity of acceptance that underlies its wistfulness. Mozart had less than a year to live, and the mounting depression of his life had already worn him down, yet there is still a sort of quiet joy in this music. The vast range of styles, emotions, and forms that these few works encompass are evocatively celebrated in these performances, and admirably captured in civilized recordings.

Piano Concertos Nos 11-13 (arr cpsr)
Patrick Dechorgnat *pf* **Henschel Quartet** (Christoph Henschel, Markus Henschel *vns* Monika Henschel *va* Mathias D Beyer *vc*)
EMI Debut CDZ5 72525-2 (79 minutes: DDD). Ⓑ
Recorded 1995

Writing of these three concertos in 1782, Mozart made an impressive claim: 'They strike a happy medium, neither unnecessarily complex nor overly simple; colourful, pleasant to the ear – but not without substance. At certain moments only the *cognoscenti* will derive any enjoyment from them, but there is something to please the less discriminating too, even if they don't know why.' Heard here in Mozart's own arrangement for piano and string quartet (made for greater accessibility) they make a crystalline, tirelessly inventive trio played with much spirit, articulacy and affection. A faint suspicion that in the opening *Allegro* of K414 (always among Mozart's most economical but endearing works) provided you are clear and tasteful the rest will follow is erased in a most affecting sense of interplay in the *Larghetto* from K413, a grave sense of serenity in the *Andante* from K414 and embellishments that are elegant and discreet throughout. Dechorgnat also achieves a special sense of romantic delicacy in the second subject from the opening movement of K415 and time and again relishes the opportunity for improvisatory freedom and magic in the cadenzas. He is superbly partnered by the Henschel Quartet, and balance and sound are exemplary.

Piano Concertos Nos 12 and 19
London Mozart Players / Howard Shelley *pf*
Chandos CHAN9256 (52 minutes: DDD). Ⓕ
Recorded 1993

These are clear and stylish readings. The playing of Shelley and the London Mozart Players is assured, relaxed and enjoyable, allowing the music to unfold naturally. Shelley demonstrates his fine judgement of tempo, and textures are well served; the recording gives quite a bold sound to his modern piano, but its overall immediacy and warmth are not excessive and the balance is just right. Phrasing also deserves praise: Shelley and his expert team shape the music gracefully without falling into the slightly mannered delivery which can affect other artists in this repertory. Finally, cadenzas have the right balance of freedom and formality. Perhaps the two 'slow' movements here – the quotes are because that of K414 is an *Andante* and K459's is an *Allegretto* – are richer in style than will suit some tastes: they do not sound authentic in period-performance terms, but then this is another kind of performance and perfectly convincing. The recordings are of high quality.

Piano Concertos Nos 15-27

Awards 1984

Piano Concertos Nos 15 and 16
English Chamber Orchestra / Murray Perahia *pf*
Sony Classical SK37824 Ⓕ
(50 minutes: DDD) ooo

This is an interpretation of the highest calibre: Perahia's delicious shaping of even the longest and most elaborate phrases, his unfailingly clear and arresting articulation, and his delicacy and refinement of tone are without parallel. Perahia's attention is, moreover, by no means restricted to the solo parts: even the tiniest details of the orchestral writing are subtly characterized, and the piano and orchestra take on the character of a dialogue – sometimes poignant, often witty or sparklingly humorous. The two works are admirably contrasted: the 15th is largely light and high-spirited, while the first movement of the 16th is almost Beethovenian in its grandeur and purposefulness, and both concertos have typically beautiful slow movements. Recordings are superb.

Piano Concertos Nos 15 and 26 **P**
Robert Levin *fp*
Academy of Ancient Music / Christopher Hogwood
L'Oiseau-Lyre 455 814-2OH (62 minutes: DDD). Ⓕ
Recorded 1997

This disc is particularly interesting for several reasons. Firstly, the fortepiano employed (unsigned) belonged to Mozart himself. Secondly, an earlier version of K450's *Andante* – whose existence is not even mentioned by Köchel, Einstein, Hutchings or *Grove* – with significant differences in the shape of the theme, is included besides the usual one. Thirdly, Robert Levin – by playing along in tuttis, improvising cadenzas, lead-ins and liberal embellishments, providing new left-hand parts for K537 and adopting some of Mozart's original, more difficult readings in K450 – has boldly opted for performances with an element of spontaneity and non-familiarity such as Mozart's own audiences would have experienced. The results are delightfully fresh and vital. The wind are excellent, the finale of K450 is splendidly lightfooted; but in K537 Hogwood might have heeded Richard Strauss's advice not to look encouragingly at the trumpets, who in the first movement are somewhat overenthusiastic. The biggest surprise comes in the slow movement of K537, where Levin often offers a free, but stylish paraphrase of the solo part. There is an A just below middle C on this fortepiano that gives off a curious tinkle whenever it is struck, and in the initial *Allegro* of K537 this can be a bit obtrusive; but it cannot put you off a thoroughly illuminating performance.

Piano Concertos Nos 9 and 17 **P**
Concerto Köln / Andreas Staier *fp*
Teldec Das Alte Werk 4509-98412-2 Ⓕ
(61 minutes: DDD). Recorded 1995

Andreas Staier, speaking of the use of period instruments in this outstanding recording of Mozart's G major Concerto, K453, declares the piece has 'more of the farmyard about it' that way – and he's right. From the braying and bellowing of the mid-phrase *crescendos*, the snuffling and snorting of the bassoons and the hee-hawing of the alternating loud and soft chords, Staier appears throughout it all the delighted child with a favourite picturebook. Conductorless, the string playing in the outer movements of both this and the E flat Concerto is buoyant with daring. The impetus and excitement of both dialogue and modulations in the slow movement of K453 is thrilling – and so is the dialogue within the orchestral writing itself in the finale.

In K271 the music-making has a bracing

immediacy as the almost percussive string playing cuts into the fortepiano's rhetoric, so imaginatively developed in Staier's fingers.

Piano Concertos Nos 17[a] and 21 Ⓕ
Maria João Pires *pf*
Chamber Orchestra of Europe / Claudio Abbado
DG 439 941-2GH (58 minutes: DDD). Item marked [a] recorded live in 1993

It is clear from the opening of the G major Concerto that Claudio Abbado and the Chamber Orchestra of Europe were on good form at this concert in Italy. It springs along, yet unhastily, and the orchestral sound, while full-bodied, has none of the heaviness that detracts from good Mozartian style. Playing what sounds like a modern piano of unusual tonal crispness, Maria João Pires also satisfies, with shapely phrasing and lovely sonorities, and this whole first movement proceeds with both a keen sense of purpose and unmannered grace. The cadenza here is Mozart's own and, of course, a model of what cadenzas in his concertos should be but often are not, in other words suiting the music and not overlong. After these unalloyed pleasures, the touching *Andante* is no less satisfying, elegantly sculptured and with marvellous woodwind playing. The playful, variation-form finale is again perfectly judged, and indeed the performance of the whole concerto offers truly outstanding Mozart playing, among the best on disc and unquestionably in the Perahia class. The recording is worthy of it: beautifully balanced and clear for one taken live while also being refreshingly free of audience noise and applause. The C major Concerto is also excellent, the first movement strong yet not pompous. The famous 'Elvira Madigan' slow movement is not at all romanticized but admirably poised, and the finale springs along.

Piano Concertos Nos 17 and 20
Robert Levin *fp*
Academy of Ancient Music / Christopher Hogwood
L'Oiseau-Lyre 455 607-2OH (61 minutes: DDD). Ⓕ
Recorded 1996

The performance of the D minor Concerto is a major achievement, one of those recordings that has a sense of occasion, a feeling that the artists are creating the music afresh. Well, so they are, to a rather greater extent than usual: Robert Levin improvises the cadenzas and quite a lot else besides. The first-movement cadenza here is a particular triumph. Hogwood and Levin take quite a measured tempo for this movement, and it works very well, giving Levin just the space he needs to shape the music pointedly and with meaning. Here and there he does vary the text more than one might expect. Of course, that is well within his rights, historically speaking, and he never transgresses the boundaries of good taste but at times one might feel there is a little too much ornamentation. In the lighter G major Concerto Levin is truly on sparkling form, playing the outer movements gracefully and wittily – the finale is especially fine, with the basic speed maintained, to brilliant effect. There is some attractive varying of repeats, which is surely what the music asks for. There is elaboration here too, occasional in the first movement, more generous in the *Andante*. These are fine performances, with sensitive and delicate playing from Levin, and admirable support from Hogwood and the AAM; the balance between piano and orchestra seems particularly happily managed, the glittering fortepiano sound coming clearly through the textures but so translucent as to allow woodwind details to be heard sharply.

Piano Concertos Nos 18 and 19
Robert Levin *fp*
Academy of Ancient Music / Christopher Hogwood
L'Oiseau-Lyre 452 051-2OH (59 minutes: DDD). Ⓕ
Recorded 1995

These are thoughtful, strongly characterized performances which make much of the individuality of the works. K456 is taken at rather steady tempos, with soft and sustained textures and gentle colours, and Levin plays it with rare tenderness and delicacy – there are many sensitive touches of timing in the first movement and less of self-conscious brilliance or assertiveness than the music might permit. This rather inward view is very compelling, and it harmonizes happily with the view he and Hogwood take of the slow movement, a G minor set of variations, which on modern instruments is apt to sound decoratively pathetic but not deeply felt, which it certainly does here. There is a good deal of intensity, and of darker colouring: partly the result of the superior blend of sound resulting from the use of the fortepiano. And some of the solo woodwind playing is of a very high order. Then the finale is taken at quite a measured tempo, not at all as a jolly hunting piece, allowing Levin to shape and shade individual phrases effectively. Levin improvises the cadenzas, although sets by Mozart survive for both concertos: his argument that a cadenza should have an element of the unexpected is a strong one. The F major, K459 is a lighter work, in a sense; its airy orchestral textures are quite unlike those of the other concertos, especially K456. This is a lively, almost jaunty performance, but in no way superficial; there are countless delectable touches in Levin's playing as well as lightness and elegance, and the effect is very appealing. Similarly, the slow movement, here an *Allegretto*, is quite relaxed, and there is some lovely woodwind playing, counterpointing gracefully with the piano, all exquisitely audible in this aurally translucent recording; at the end you are left under no illusions about the seriousness and stature of the music.

Piano Concertos Nos 18 and 20
Richard Goode *pf* **Orpheus Chamber Orchestra**
Nonesuch 7559-79439-2 (58 minutes: DDD). Ⓕ
Recorded 1996

With a first-rate balance and quality of sound, here is a Mozart concerto record to transcend considerations of style and stance. The excellence of Richard Goode's playing is not surprising, but the quality of his collaboration with the Orpheus Chamber Orchestra is special: and the beautiful thing about Mozart performance of this calibre is that the two seem inseparable. Of course the freshness and placing of the detail are to be savoured, but it is the long view which holds and persuades. In the D minor Concerto's first movement the brilliant piano writing is so thrilling here because it's projected as being essential to the expression, not just a decoration of it. Goode is particularly impressive in the way he handles the three successive solo statements at the start of the development without slackening pace. They are subtly different in feeling, one from the other, and although he's not the first player to have noticed this, it's characteristic of his distinction to have kept the detail and the overview in balance. He plays his own cadenza in the finale, in place of Beethoven's. He has some good ideas about dynamics in this last movement, and the lightening of mood at the turn to the major key towards the end has rarely sounded such an inspiration – on Mozart's part, of course. The B flat Concerto, K456, is equally enjoyable. The outer movements are brisk and light on their feet, even balletic, but all the colours – and the shadows which pass over the face of the music – are there, just as one wants. Paciness makes for vivacity but never brittleness. At the end, you feel you have had glorious entertainment, and a discourse that has touched on the deepest things. You may well be puzzled as to how Goode achieves so much while appearing to do so little. In this the orchestra matches him, as it also matches his spontaneity.

Piano Concertos Nos 19 and 27
Orpheus Chamber Orchestra / Richard Goode *pf*
Nonesuch 7559-79608-2 (55 minutes: DDD). Ⓕ
Recorded 1996

Given that these concertos were recorded as long ago as April 1996, one can only assume that someone was disconcerted by a slight quirk in the recording. The opening *tutti* of K595 (which comes first on the disc) makes a striking impact, not only thanks to the crisp, alert playing but to the full, bright, immediate recording. The piano enters with similarly full and immediate sound – very different from the more transparent piano sound on a rival Decca release with András Schiff – but then the orchestra seems to move further off. It is an inconsistency of balance that is disconcerting for no more than a moment or two, but might well make a hypercritical artist or producer have reservations.

What matters is the liveness of the experience that Goode and his partners provide. His approach is more purposeful, more direct than that of Schiff, who favours speeds consistently a shade broader than Goode's. The natural weight and gravity of Goode's playing, reflecting his equivalent mastery as a Beethovenian, emerges clearly in such moments as the hushed B minor opening or the development in the first movement of K595, an extraordinary modulation for a movement in B flat major (track 1, 6'25"), or in the opening solo of the *Larghetto* which follows. Not that Goode's Mozart has anything remotely heavy about it in the wrong way. His lightness and wit in the finales of both concertos is a delight, with scale passages rippling infectiously, articulated with sparkling clarity.

In the finale of K459, Goode, like Schiff, opts for a very fast *Allegro assai*, drawing on his phenomenal agility. Some may prefer a slightly more relaxed tempo, such as Murray Perahia, for example, adopts, with more swagger and fun in it, but Goode's playing is thrilling from first to last. In the face of such commanding playing as this, one can only hope that this is not the last Mozart concerto disc that Goode will offer us.

Piano Concerto No 20. Symphony No 38 in D, K504, 'Prague'. Serenade No 13 in G, K525, 'Eine kleine Nachtmusik'. Three German Dances, K605 **H**
Vienna Philharmonic Orchestra / Bruno Walter *pf*
Pearl mono GEMMCD9940 (72 minutes: AAD). Ⓜ
Recorded 1936-37

Bruno Walter was an accomplished pianist, and his solo work in Mozart's D minor Concerto is full of personality. The first movement cadenza by Reinecke is boring, but otherwise there's much to enjoy in this romantic and subjective interpretation. The VPO plays beautifully both here and in the other Mozart works. The *Prague* Symphony has lots of muscle as well as grace and elegance. If you seek a romantic approach to *Eine kleine Nachtmusik*, then Walter's affectionate interpretations will surely give great pleasure, and the little *German Dances* are charmingly played. Pearl has used commercial pressings for the issue, and a certain amount of surface noise is present. Colin Attwell has reproduced the original sound quality very faithfully and straightforwardly, and his transfers are much kinder to the ears than most others from this period.

Piano Concertos Nos 20 and 24
Alfred Brendel *pf* **Scottish Chamber Orchestra / Sir Charles Mackerras**
Philips 462 622-2PH (60 minutes: DDD). Ⓕ

Brendel's conception of Mozart's two minor-key concertos has altered in countless nuances and emphases but little in fundamentals since his 1973 Philips recordings with Marriner. His sensibility, pianistic refinement and sheer questing intelligence remain as compelling as ever. Neither performance will entirely please those who favour a barnstorming approach. More than in 1973, Brendel is at times more concerned to draw out the music's elegiac resignation than to highlight its more obvious passion and turbulence. But more than most pianists he constantly illuminates the smaller and larger shapes of the music with his range of colour and dynamics. In both opening movements, for instance, he brings a speaking eloquence to the piano's initial solo theme and then in the development finds a subtly altered tone of voice, in response to the gradually darkening musical landscape, for each of its reappearances. Another Brendel hallmark is his variety of tone and articulation in rapid passagework, which is purposefully directed in accordance with its place in the overall scheme. As before, he provides apt and spontaneous-sounding embellishments and 'in-filling' at fermatas, this time allowing himself greater freedom in decorating the spare lines of the slow movements; again, he uses his own cadenzas in both concertos, more adventurous in their thematic development than any of Mozart's own surviving examples but otherwise models of style and concision. Both the *Romanze* slow movements unfold at natural, flowing tempos, that in K466 a notch more swiftly than in 1973; and Brendel brings out hints of playfulness here and in the two major-key variations in the finale of K491. Where this new version definitely scores is in the orchestral accompaniments.

In the opening tutti of K491 one can hear the extra character Mackerras brings to the music compared to Marriner – the impact of raw, louring brass (tamed by Marriner) at strategic moments, for instance, or his attentive shaping of inner strands to enhance the tension. The recording has an attractive spaciousness and ambient warmth, though in K491 the keyboard occasionally obscures important thematic ideas on oboes, clarinets and bassoons.

Piano Concertos Nos 23 and 24
Orpheus Chamber Orchestra / Richard Goode *pf*
Nonesuch 7559-79489-2 (56 minutes: DDD) Ⓕ ●

This is the third Mozart CD Richard Goode and the Orpheus Chamber Orchestra have made, and collaborations of this kind must necessarily be rare. The demands this sort of music-making imposes on the players are considerable. But so are the potential rewards. They are evident here in the exceptional focus and concentration of the playing. Polished you might expect it to be, but the allure and spontaneity are a joy. First impressions are likely to be of details of scoring in the orchestral expositions of the first movements, details that may not go unnoticed in other performances but which rarely receive such voicing and definition. The pianist does not disappoint either. Judge him by his first entry in this concerto, in the solo theme: there is none more difficult to get right. Goode has the range, the control and the rhetoric. He passes another difficult test in this first movement by supplying an impressive cadenza. It is an outstanding account of this movement, to be returned to again and again. There is no falling off in the other two either. The way the variations of the finale are presented as all of a piece, without changes of tempo, is admirable. There is flexibility, and they have all the time they need, but Goode lets some of his part run on, convincingly, at points where other pianists usually do the opposite.

The A major, K488, equally well illuminated, has light and air from a different world. There is indeed an airborne quality to the finale, done here with the utmost vivacity, and a hint of that too in the open textures and the easy, glorious buoyancy of the first movement. As with the great interpretations of the past, we are given an object lesson in what the music can yield when an attempt is made to realise as many aspects of it as possible. The recorded sound is exemplary. Credit is also due to Max Wilcox, the producer.

Piano Concertos Nos 23 and 24
Mitsuko Uchida *pf*
English Chamber Orchestra / Jeffrey Tate
Philips Solo 442 648-2PM (58 minutes: DDD). Ⓜ
Recorded 1987-88

These performances from the late 1980s have impressive authority. The balance of sound is a distinctive feature of the recording. How beautifully Mitsuko Uchida plays, and with what freshness and sensibility. Throughout the intimate No 23, the ease with which she releases and projects the expression is a delight. One wants to hear magic communicated in this music and it is there. After the slow movements, the daylight and brio she brings to the finale is lovely, as if to test the reality of the sublime visions which have gone before. This is some of the best playing of Mozart in recent years. It is an all-round achievement that will not quickly be surpassed and no doubt it will occupy a place in the catalogue as one of the best Mozart concerto recordings of our day.

Hers is a thoughtful approach to the great C minor Concerto (No 24). She eschews the overtly *Sturm und Drang* style that is fashionable for the first movement. Perhaps her interpretation is helped too by the balancing of the 'percussive' piano rather far back in a way that reveals good orchestral detail while obscuring nothing contributed by the keyboard. But when she plays her own cadenza the piano appears to come forward; the cadenza itself is fairly convincing at first but goes on too long, wandering stylistically into Beethovenian territory with dreamy recitative and, later, a thumping chord deep in the bass. A poised account of the *Larghetto* and a powerful but well-nuanced finale complete this attractive performance. When you listen to the colour and distinction Jeffrey Tate brings to these works you feel surer still of that. It is the pianist who must make the running, of course, but it is not many in Mozart who get a collaborator of such calibre.

Piano Concertos Nos 23 and 24
Sir Clifford Curzon *pf*
London Symphony Orchestra / István Kertész
Decca The Classic Sound 452 888-2DCS (57 minutes: ADD). Recorded 1968 Ⓜ ●●

In a list of all-time best recordings of Mozart piano concertos these should have a place. The balances of piano with orchestra are just right, and the sound has come up freshly on CD, with air as well as clarity and a nicely truthful character. In the No 24 the wind is not as forward as recordings favour these days, but from the LSO as distinguished soloists and as a wind chorus their contributions tell. Kertész gives Curzon nicely judged support; it sets him off, in a frame, even if it does appear a mite neutral at times and strangely limp in the presentation of the variation theme at the start of the finale of the C minor Concerto. These days, some people might consider the interpretations dated, or unreconstructed. Curzon doesn't decorate the bare, leaping intervals at the close of the slow movement of K488, and he's restrained too in the C minor. But the performances seem to be beyond fashion. The slow movements are especially fine. In the *Larghetto* of No 24, unfolding at an ideal tempo, Curzon gives the impression of walking while he speaks to us. The gravity of the F sharp minor *Adagio* of No 23 is a different thing; but there, again, he is unaffected and completely unsentimental, direct in manner even while projecting the deepest feeling. He reminds us that the best interpreters do not impose but find a way of letting the music speak through them.

Piano Concertos Nos 24 and 25
András Schiff *pf*
Salzburg Mozarteum Camerata Academica / Sándor Végh
Decca 425 791-2DH (63 minutes: DDD). Ⓕ
Recorded 1988

The names of András Schiff and Sándor Végh are distinguished ones in this repertory. The characteristics of these performances are immediately recognizable, though like many good things hard to define. Among them is a generally positive delivery allied to a certain sweetness; listen, for example, to the slow movement of No 24 and the finale of the No 25, whose quality owes much to the presence of players like the flautist Aurèle Nicolet. Then there is the pianist's articulation, sometimes *quasi-staccato* in quick passagework but clear and unfailingly expressive even in rapid fingerwork. The conductor and soloist are adroit in their management of transitions, whether of mood, pace, texture or dynamics, and in any combination, and their tempos are also generally well chosen. The recording in the Salzburg Mozarteum is a good one. Finally, these artists are able to balance the component parts of a movement, and of a whole concerto, skilfully, so that, for example, finales seem to flow naturally from slow movements, just as those movements do from opening ones. Schiff and Végh know how to bring out the joy in this music without sacrificing delicacy, a delicacy without the prettification that we occasionally hear from other pianists. In fact, Schiff brings such tonal finesse on this recording that it is hard to remember he is playing a big modern Bösendorfer. Performances such as his make a good argument for the viability of modern instruments here as an alternative to period ones.

Piano Concertos Nos 9 and 25
Richard Goode *pf*
Orpheus Chamber Orchestra
Nonesuch 7559-79454-2 (63 minutes: DDD). Ⓕ
Recorded 1997 ●●

There is something specially attractive about Richard Goode's occasional collaborations with the Orpheus Chamber Orchestra. The opening of No 25 sounds tremendous, with a leathery thwack to the kettledrums and the orchestra suitably weighty. Although the acoustic is a bit dry, there is a satisfying depth to the sonority, and the balance and placing of the instruments is absolutely perfect. All the colours are vivid. In contrast to many players of the modern instrument, Goode does not pull his punches and makes this first movement a most glorious procession, imposing but never ponderous. His tempo has a propulsive energy and an underlying fitness that makes possible some relaxation of it in the broader paragraphs of the solo part. Wonderful slow movement too, flowing admirably, and it's a tricky one to get right.

This concerto has rarely been recorded so successfully, but the Ninth has been done better. Many of the virtues enjoyed by No 25 apply here also. It needs a different rhetoric, of course, and Goode supplies it, but he waxes and wanes and there's something a shade impersonal about him. The reservations concern the first movement principally, where it's as if he were saying: 'I do not need to attract your attention, this beautiful thing Mozart has made we are going to lay out before you'. One would have preferred him to make us experience it more acutely. However, this is a Mozart concerto disc to give exceptional pleasure. It aims high and wherever you sample it there is no gap between intention and achievement. And what teamwork! Technical precision in ensemble-playing can be brought about readily enough, given rehearsal, but the musical focus sustained here is not something often encountered outside chamber music.

Piano Concerto No 26. Rondos – D, K382; A, K386
English Chamber Orchestra / Murray Perahia *pf*
Sony Classical SK39224 (DDD) Ⓕ
●

This is one of the most distinguished of Perahia's Mozart concerto recordings. The D major Concerto, No 26, is not, perhaps, a work of such individuality as the 12 concertos which preceded it, or the only one which succeeded it (No 27), yet it used to be one of the most popular, probably because it has a convenient nickname (*Coronation*), stemming from the fact that Mozart performed it on October 15, 1790, at the festivities accompanying the coronation of the Emperor Leopold II in Frankfurt am Main. Now, curiously enough, it is not played all that often and of the available recordings, Perahia leads the field: dignified yet never aloof in the first movement, eloquent in the central *Larghetto* (which he decorates tastefully), and marvellously agile and dexterous in the florid concluding *Rondo*. He plays his own characteristically stylish cadenza in the first movement (Mozart's own has not survived, but for many years the one he wrote for an earlier concerto in the same key, K451, was wrongly associated with the *Coronation* Concerto). As a coupling Perahia gives us the two concert *Rondos*: K382 in D, a Viennese alternative finale for the Salzburg D major Concerto, K175; and K386 in A, presumably the original, rejected finale of K414. The A major *Rondo* has had an eventful history, having been cut into pieces in the 19th century for use as greeting cards (!), and patched together subsequently by numerous editors, including Alfred Einstein, Paul Badura-Skoda, Sir Charles Mackerras, and Erik Smith. The version performed here has a different ending which was discovered by Peter Tyson. It was completed by Paul Badura-Skoda and this is its first recording. The performances are sheer delight and, as in the concerto, the ECO plays, quite literally, con amore – a spirit evidently shared by the Sony recording team.

Piano Concerto No 27. Concerto for Two Pianos and Orchestra in E flat, K365/K316*a*
Emil Gilels, Elena Gilels *pfs*
Vienna Philharmonic Orchestra / Karl Böhm
DG Galleria 419 059-2GGA (59 minutes: ADD) Ⓜ
oo

This is the most beautiful of Mozart playing, his last piano concerto given here by Emil Gilels with total clarity. This is a classic performance, memorably accompanied by the VPO and Böhm. Suffice it to say that Gilels sees everything and exaggerates nothing, that the performance has an Olympian authority and serenity, and that the *Larghetto* is one of the glories of the gramophone. He is joined by his daughter Elena in the Double Piano Concerto in E flat, and their physical relationship is mirrored in the quality, and the mutual understanding of the playing: both works receive marvellous interpretations. We *think* Emil plays first, Elena second, but could be quite wrong. The VPO under Karl Böhm is at its best; and so is the quality of recording, with a good stereo separation of the two solo parts, highly desirable in this work.

Violin Concertos

No 1 in B flat, K207; **No 2** in D, K211; **No 3** in G, K216; **No 4** in D, K218; **No 5** in A, K219; **D**, K271*a*

Violin Concertos Nos 1-5[a]. Adagio in E, K261[c]. Rondo in C, K373[a]. Sinfonia concertante in E flat, K364/K320*d*[b]
[a]**Arthur Grumiaux** *vn* [b]**Arrigo Pellicciа** *va*
[ab]**London Symphony Orchestra / Sir Colin Davis;**
[c]**New Philharmonia Orchestra / Raymond Leppard**
Philips Duo ② 438 323-2PM2 (153 minutes: ADD). Ⓜ
Recorded 1961-64

The concertos are also available on Philips 50 Great Recordings, coupled with violin sonatas nos 32 and 35 464 722-2PM2 Ⓜ

These performances of the five standard violin concertos, the *Sinfonia concertante* and a couple of other pieces were much admired when they came out on LP, and they continue to earn praise for their crispness, lightness and eloquence. Grumiaux was also fortunate in his partner in the *Sinfonia concertante*, for Pelliccia is also an expert Mozartian and they give a performance of this beautiful piece that is expressive but still avoids self-indulgent romanticism. In the solo concertos, too, Grumiaux plays cadenzas that suit the music in length and style. Both Sir Colin Davis and Raymond Leppard are sympathetic partners in this repertory, and since the playing of the two London orchestras is no less satisfying, this issue scores all round artistically. The 1960s recordings do not sound their age, and are pleasing save for a little tape hiss and an excess of bass that hardly suits the style of this translucent music. However, that is a small price to pay when so much else is admirable, and Grumiaux's fine tonal palette is well caught.

Violin Concertos Nos 1-5. Serenade No 7 in D, 'Haffner', K250/K248*b* – Andante; Menuetto; Rondo
Pamela Frank *vn* **Zurich Tonhalle Orchestra / David Zinman**
Arte Nova Classics ② 74321 72104-2 Ⓢ
(139 minutes: DDD). Recorded 1997-1999

What a good idea to include the violin concerto movements from the *Haffner* Serenade as a filler, rather than the more usual group of extra movements for violin and orchestra. The Serenade shows the 20-year-old Mozart with his imagination at full stretch; Frank, Zinman and the Zurich orchestra revel in the wit, the sensuous expressiveness and the melodic fecundity of this still neglected music. Pamela Frank gives us, here and throughout the two discs, violin playing of great technical purity. The music speaks to us without any affectation, yet respecting Mozart's indications and such 18th-century conventions as tailing off the weak beats of the bar. She's given a splendidly positive, well-considered accompaniment. The bouncy rhythms and perfect orchestral balance of, say, the opening tutti to K216 establish a sense of *joie de vivre* that carries over into the violin playing.

Zinman's care for detail ensures that nothing of importance is overlooked: on the many occasions where the bass is carried by the second violin or viola these lines are given a bit of extra emphasis to highlight the harmonic movement. The horns deserve special mention; their purity of tone and rhythmic poise give a real sparkle to the outer movements of K207 and to the middle section of the *Haffner* Minuet, spectacularly scored for violin and wind. Zinman has also written the cadenzas (except in K219, where Frank plays the famous Joachim ones) – they're imaginative and stylish, but don't always sound improvisatory enough and occasionally seem too long. Frank has an ability to bring the music to life, and she's supported by an unusually characterful orchestra and very crisp, clear recording. A fantastic bargain.

Violin Concertos Nos 1-5[b]. Rondos[b] – B flat, K269/K261*a*; C, K373. Concertone in C, K190/K186*e*[abce]. Adagio in E, K261[b]. Sinfonia concertante in E flat, K364/K320*d*[dh]. Double Concerto in D, KAnh56/K315*f*[gh]. Sinfonia concertante in A, KAnh104/K320*e*[dfh]
[a]**Richard Morgan** *ob* [b]**Henryk Szeryng,** [c]**Gérard Poulet** *vns* [d]**Nobuko Imai** *va* [e]**Norman Jones,** [f]**Stephen Orton** *vcs* [g]**Howard Shelley** *pf* [b]**New Philharmonia / Sir Alexander Gibson;** [h]**Academy of St Martin in the Fields / Iona Brown** *vn*
Philips Mozart Edition ④ 422 508-2PME4 Ⓜ
(265 minutes: ADD/DDD). Recorded 1960-70

Mozart's violin concertos reflect their creator's love and understanding of an instrument which he played more than capably. They have much in common with Mozart's cassations, divertimentos and serenades, which also highlight the solo violin and have other concerto-like elements in them. But their lightweight means of expression in no way diminishes their long-term appeal, for Mozart filled them to the brim with wonderful ideas. Henryk Szeryng has a relaxed way with these works and the New Philharmonia under Sir Alexander Gibson is alert yet sensitive. Szeryng's tone is unfailingly beautiful with a sweetness that is greatly appealing. His evident affection for these works makes for pleasing listening and the vivid and witty 'Turkish' episode in the finale of No 5 has great spirit. This disc also includes the 'doubtful' but agreeable solo Concerto in D major, K271*a*, together with a rather laid-back account of the *Sinfonia concertante* with Iona Brown and Nobuko Imai as the soloists (beautifully matched and well blended). In addition we have the reconstructions of the incomplete projected Concerto for piano and violin and the single-movement *Sinfonia concertante* in A major for string trio and orchestra. The recordings are satisfying.

Violin Concertos Nos 1, 2 and 5 🅿
Orchestra of the Age of Enlightenment / Monica Huggett *vn*
Virgin Classics Veritas VC5 45010-2 Ⓕ
(77 minutes: DDD). Recorded 1991 ●

These fresh, appealing performances stand up well in an awesomely crowded field. With her gut-strung Amati, Monica Huggett does not, of course, rival modern-instrument virtuosos but these concertos gain much from her sweet, slender tone, her light, buoyant articulation and her beautiful control of colour in *piano* dynamics. The passagework in the opening movements of the first two concertos can seem tedious in high-powered traditional performances; but the lighter period bow and Huggett's deft touches of timing and shading invariably lend wit and point to Mozart's sequences of triplets and semiquavers. The finales of both these concertos are delightfully lithe and airy, while the closing minuet of No 5 is unusually delicate – though there is plenty of gusto in the A minor 'Turkish' episode. In the three slow movements other performances may be more overtly expressive, freer with rubato; but Huggett's purity and poise, her subtle graduations of vibrato and her gentle eloquence of phrase are very persuasive. These performances have a keen feeling for the music's dance rhythms and a sure sense of style in cadenzas and ornamentation. The orchestral contribution is crisp, transparent and nicely detailed. Clear, naturally balanced sound.

Mozart Violin Concerto No 3
Brahms Violin Concerto in D, Op 77[a]
Frank Peter Zimmermann *vn*
Berlin Philharmonic Orchestra / Wolfgang Sawallisch
EMI CDC5 55426-2 (60 minutes: DDD) Ⓕ
Item marked [a] recorded live in 1995

With the string complement of the Berlin Philharmonic reduced, and Sawallisch at his most sparkling, the Mozart is a delight throughout, with a quicksilver lightness in the outer movements very different from the big bow-wow approach that virtuoso violinists used to adopt. More than in the Brahms Zimmermann finds a vein of fantasy, and in the central *Adagio* he plays with a repose and concentration markedly greater than in his live account of the Brahms slow movement. Curiously, it is not until the finale of the Brahms, where Zimmermann seems to acquire an extra degree of daring, that the advantages of live recording come home at all clearly. Till then, his performance seems just a little too well mannered, with his silvery tone pointing a lack of bravura, however brilliant the playing is technically. Yet in the finale not only does the performance take wing, but Zimmermann becomes more individual, as in the little commas of expression he inserts each time in the main Hungarian dance theme.

Violin Concertos Nos 3-5
Camerata Academica Salzburg / Augustin Dumay *vn*
DG 457 645-2GH (75 minutes: DDD). Ⓕ
Recorded 1996 ●

Taking a break from chamber music-making, Augustin Dumay makes his début as soloist and conductor in these vivid and immediate recordings from the Salzburg Mozarteum. The dual role is very much what sets these performances apart. High-fibre, robustly articulated orchestral playing acts as frame and foil for the imaginative *richesse* of Dumay's own free and airy spirit; and the excitement of the players' close mutual engagement gives a real sense of Mozart's youthful energy bursting out of its Salzburg prison walls. Dumay's choice of tempos makes each slow movement appear to breathe the air of another planet: in the G major work, the pizzicato pulse becomes the plucking of a distant lyre, as the bow scarcely seems to shift on the string in a finely suspended song. In the D major, the soloist is *primus inter pares* in a fine weave of wind and strings. And in the A major, whose piercingly true, birdlike first-movement song deliciously anticipates Joachim's larkrise of a cadenza, there is a fluency and sense of wonderment which makes other interpretations seem earthbound by contrast. Dumay can be earthy enough when the occasion demands: in the finales of the D major and A major Concertos, his little moments of rubato make a shapely leg point and stretch forward in a series of high-stepping open-air dances.

Overtures

Overtures – Le nozze di Figaro; Il re pastore; Die Entführung aus dem Serail; Die Zauberflöte; Idomeneo; Der Schauspieldirektor; Bastien und Bastienne; La clemenza di Tito; Lucio Silla; Così fan tutte; La finta giardiniera; Mitridate, Re di Ponto; Don Giovanni
Sinfonia Varsovia / Yehudi Menuhin
Classic fM The Full Works 75605 57032-2 Ⓜ
(63 minutes: DDD). Recorded 1998

This is a highly recommendable issue, offering fresh and alert performances, vividly recorded. Not only that, the choice of overtures is markedly more generous than on any rival disc, including as it does the early pieces, *Il re pastore*, *Bastien und Bastienne* and *Mitridate*. The Overture to *Bastien und Bastienne* may be little more than a flourish, lasting just over a minute and a half, but its opening strikingly anticipates the first theme of the *Eroica*. Like the Overture to *Lucio Silla*, the most inspired of Mozart's teenage operas, the one for *Mitridate* is like a symphony in three movements, just as delightful only even more compact, lasting in all only five and a half minutes. Menuhin's fresh, alert manner at relatively brisk speeds, is most refreshing. And what above all makes this disc compelling is the overall sense of live communication, of players responding in fresh enjoyment. The excellent sound is full and clear with ample bloom.

Serenades

No 3 in D, K185/167*a*; **No 4** in D, K203/K189*b*; **No 5** in D, K204/K231*a*; **No 6** in D, K239, 'Serenata notturna'; **No 7** in D, K250/K248*b*, 'Haffner'; **No 9** in D, K320, 'Posthorn'; **No 10** in B flat for 13 wind instruments, K361/K370*a*, 'Gran Partita'; **No 11** in E flat, K375; **No 12** in C minor, K388/K384*a*; **No 13** in G, K525, 'Eine kleine Nachtmusik'

Serenades – Nos 3 and 4 (with **Iona Brown** *vn*); No 5 (**Kenneth Sillito** *vn*); Nos 6 and 7 (**Iona Brown** *vn*); Nos 9 and 13. Marches – D, K62; D, K189/167*b*; D, K215/K213*b*; D, K237/K189*c*; D, K249; D, K335/K320*a* No 1; D, K335/K320*a* No 2. Cassations – G, K63 (**Kenneth Sillito** *vn*); B flat, K99/K63*a*; D, K100/K62*a*. Divertimento in D, K131. Notturno in D, K286/K269*a*. Galimathias musicum, K32 (**John Constable** *hpd* **Ambrosian Singers**)
Academy of St Martin in the Fields / Sir Neville Marriner
Philips Mozart Edition ⑦ 422 503-2PME7 Ⓜ
(404 minutes: DDD). Recorded 1981-89

The prospective collector must face the fact that although at medium price this set represents a substantial outlay, it is a pretty good investment for a lifetime's listening pleasure. With Sir Neville Marriner and the Academy of St Martin in the Fields we are in sure and sensitive Mozartian hands, and these performances, by and large, penetrate easily to the heart of the music in all its moods and colours. The recordings are good, too, with crisp sound that nevertheless has a bloom of resonance on it, and there is a natural balance between the orchestral forces, which include a harpsichord. In fact this issue offers Philips engineering at its best. Alongside masterpieces such as the big *Posthorn* and *Haffner* Serenades and the incomparably graceful *Eine kleine Nachtmusik* there is something of a ragbag of music here, and seven CDs make for a lot of listening. But there are few disappointments with the way this music is played. The *Galimathias musicum* is an extraordinary mixture of themes, with 17 sections in all making up a cheerful 'quodlibet' medley of popular tunes, including a bagpipe-like one in the Lydian mode (in this case G major with C sharps), which the composer seems to have penned in 1766, aged 10; here also the Ambrosian Singers and a solo harpsichordist make a useful and idiomatic contribution.

Good nature goes together with inventiveness and compositional brilliance in the best of Mozart's entertainment music, and we can only sit back and admire the wealth of ideas that are laid out before us, including instrumental ones – for example, the *Divertimento*, K131 has four horns, as its last *Adagio* reminds us. Nevertheless, for anyone planning consecutive listening there are seemingly unending stretches of D major – every work on the fourth, sixth and seventh discs is in this key, and most of the fifth as well. The *Eine kleine Nachtmusik* on the fifth is the exception, being in G major, and is nicely played though the orchestra seems on the big side and in its second-movement Romance the bass-line is over-weighty. In the *Haffner* Serenade, Iona Brown is a stylish violin soloist, while the small contribution of the posthorn player Michael Laird in the work named after his instrument (listen for him in the second Minuet) is attractive too, as is that of the other wind players.

Serenade No 3[a]. March, K189/K167*b*. Five Contredanses, K609. Notturno in D, K286/K269*a*
[a]**Arvid Engegard** *vn* **Salzburg Mozarteum Camerata Academica / Sándor Végh**
Capriccio 10 302 (66 minutes: DDD). Ⓕ
Recorded 1988-89

The main work here is the big *Serenade*, K185, commissioned by the Antretter family of Salzburg and first performed in August 1773 to celebrate the end of the university year. Like other works of its kind it incorporates a miniature two-movement violin concerto within a loose symphonic framework: an *Andante* designed to display the instrument's powers of cantilena, and a brisk *contredanse* with plenty of opportunities for ear-catching virtuosity. There is also a violin solo in the glum D minor trio of the second minuet. But perhaps the finest movements are the sensuous A major *Andante grazioso*, with its *concertante* writing for flutes and horns, and the rollicking 6/8 finale, preceded by an unexpectedly searching *Adagio* introduction.

The performance by Végh and his hand-picked Salzburg players is affectionate, rhythmically alive and beautifully detailed, with an imaginative, subtly coloured solo violin contribution from Arvid Engegard. The tempo and specific character of each movement is shrewdly judged: the two minuets, for example, are vividly differentiated, the first properly swaggering, with a nice lilt in the trio, the second spruce and quick-witted. Only in the finale is Végh arguably too leisurely, though here too the style and rhythmic lift of the playing are infectious. Végh follows the serenade with deft, colourful readings of five contredanses from Mozart's last year and a beguiling performance of the *Notturno* for four orchestras, exquisitely imagined open-air music, with its multiple echoes fading into the summer night. All in all a delectable disc, offering a varied concert of Mozart's lighter music performed with exceptional flair and finesse. The recording, too, is outstandingly vivid, with the spatial effects in the *Notturno* beautifully managed.

Serenades Nos 6, 12 and 13
Orpheus Chamber Orchestra
DG Galleria 439 524-2GGA (54 minutes: DDD). Ⓜ
Recorded 1985

The *Serenata notturna* (No 6) can easily seem bland but here is attractively vivacious and alert. The use of light and shade is a constant source of pleasure, the playing itself is extremely fine, and it is altogether a splendid account. *Serenade* No 12 is a big piece, being in four movements, and it is played so stylishly and with so much refinement and variety that one never becomes satiated with wind tone, as can happen with more ordinary performances. Of course one wonders at the composer's choice of a minor key for the C minor Serenade (No 12), a work described in Anthony Burton's booklet note as 'dramatic and sombre' which is thus hardly conventional serenade material, but the writer provides no explanation since there is none that fits the facts.

But whatever the mystery of its nature, this is a splendid piece, with a tense first movement and a mirror canon (using inversion) for oboes and bassoons in its Minuet that has been described as suggesting 'the image of two swans reflected in still water'. The finale is a terse set of variations, and indeed it is only the *Andante* (in E flat major) of this Serenade that offers real warmth. Since the recording in a New York location is as successful as the playing, this is the most recommendable version available of this work.

There are many worthy recorded performances of Mozart's most famous *Serenade*, the one that is now universally called *Eine kleine Nachtmusik* (No 13), but this one by the string section of the Orpheus Chamber Orchestra has qualities of refinement and alertness that make it rather special. These players clearly enjoy the music, but bring to it a delightful precision as well as the necessary *joie de vivre* and spontaneity, and each of the four movements is beautifully shaped and characterized, so that this familiar music comes up as fresh as anyone could wish for.

Serenades Nos 6 and 13. Divertimento in D, K136. Adagio and Fugue in C minor, K546
Ferenc Liszt Chamber Orchestra / János Rolla
Hungaroton HCD12471 (50 minutes: ADD/DDD) Ⓕ

The *Eine kleine Nachtmusik Serenade* is a favourite which will never be in any danger of oblivion. The Hungarian Ferenc Liszt Chamber Orchestra plays splendidly with an exceptionally alert style, but with a slightly heavier sound, a slightly solider style, than the Orpheus Chamber Orchestra. Nevertheless, this is to point to minor differences in the two perfectly sensible approaches, not to suggest that either of the performances is in any way materially superior to the other. Another common factor of the two discs is their inclusion, along with the *Nachtmusik*, of *Serenade* No 6. The Divertimento here offers a degree of instrumental contrast, adding a few wind players to the basic orchestra of strings. Perhaps rather more of the built-in different sounds of these two groups could have been made in the present recording; but the *Serenade* remains an enchanting one. The Divertimento, also in D, lacks corresponding colour, but is nevertheless, quite a strong work; and the C minor *Adagio and Fugue* (an arrangement by Mozart himself from a piano duo) offers a very noticeably strong *Adagio*, and a fugue in which Mozart makes one of his few explorations – a successful one – of an earlier contrapuntal idiom.

Serenades Nos 10[a] and 11[b]. Adagio in F, K410/K484*d*
[a]Academy of St Martin in the Fields / Sir Neville Marriner; [b]Holliger Wind Ensemble
Philips Complete Mozart Edition 446 227-2PM Ⓜ
(76 minutes: DDD). Recorded 1984

'A great wind piece of a very special kind': that is how Mozart's Serenade No 10 for 13 instruments was described on its première in March 1784, and with no exaggeration. It has had many excellent recordings in the past, and this one is certainly among the very finest. It is a matter of taste rather than any kind of chauvinism that leads us to prefer English wind players to any others in the world: the compromise they invariably find between a smooth, well-blended sound and individuality of tone and expression seems to be extremely satisfying. The present disc happily exemplifies it. The ensemble sound, which digital recording doubtless captures the more vividly, has a remarkable warmth and richness yet remains clearly defined, with the result that much inner detail comes through. Sir Neville Marriner's interpretation is characteristically both spirited and graceful.

The main *Allegro* of the first movement is quickish yet there seems to be plenty of time for shaping the music; the rhythms are well sprung, the textures lucid. The first trio, for pairs of clarinets and basset-horns is particularly light and happy, and the Ländler-ish lilt of the second one of the second Minuet is nicely caught. It is a pity that in the *Romanze*, again lovingly played and with some finely athletic work from the bassoons in the central section, an evident slip of Mozart's pen is taken seriously and a bar omitted just before the coda. There is much that is exquisite in the variations, above all in the fifth with its wonderful soft textures and the deeply poetic oboe solo above them, played here with great beauty and intensity. The finale is high-spirited, and very neatly played. Heinz Holliger leads his group of wind players in an exceptionally crisp and light-textured reading of the supreme 11th Serenade, marked as you would expect by some quite winningly imaginative oboe solos. Characterizing the lightness of texture is the unusually reedy, thin-sounding clarinet tone, which will not please everyone. Except for the modern pitch it might almost be from period instruments. The Holliger group can sound too metrical, however crisp in pinpoint precision the ensemble is but in the slow movement the melodic lines soar persuasively. The *Adagio* in F major, K410 is a much shorter, light work, but equally appealing in its Mozartian charm and here receives yet another persuasive performance.

Serenade No 11. Harmoniemusik on 'Die Zauberflöte' **P**
(arr Stumpf)
Nachtmusique (Alf Hörberg *cl/basset hn* Danny Bond, Donna Agrell *bns* Claude Maury, Teunis Van der Zwart *hns*) **/ Eric Hoeprich** *cl/basset hn*
Glossa GCD2K0601 (65 minutes: DDD). Ⓜ
Recorded 1996

This recording of K375 uses the relatively rare original version, without oboes. In some ways it makes better sense – the later one with oboes never quite justifies their presence. This performance is thoughtful, euphonious (the chording purer than is usual with period instruments) and very musicianly. The opening movement is taken rather deliberately, the central Adagio rather more quickly than usual and flowing very gracefully. Eric Hoeprich, who directs from the first clarinet, has a beautifully full and round tone and provides many happy details of expressive timing. In both Minuets (the lighter second taken in lively fashion) the tempo is slightly relaxed or the Trio, to good effect, both at the Trio itself and at the da capo. There is some very neat and spirited playing in the finale; the clarinets in particular are tested and show themselves to be duly agile. If some of the emphatic chords in the opening movement are a little too loudly played, which leads to some coarsening of tone, this is nevertheless one of the best available recorded versions of the work, certainly in its sextet form.

The *Zauberflöte* wind arrangements are less familiar than those of the Da Ponte operas and they are particularly enjoyable; more than once the transcription virtually reproduces the original scoring. They follow the same formulae as the others, offering shortened versions of the overture and 13 favourite numbers. The arrangements are for the most part the work of J C Stumpf, although two pieces are indeed performed in other versions, for smaller ensemble, in order to create variety.

Mozart Serenade No 13. Adagio and Fugue in C minor, K546
Anonymous (arr L Mozart) Cassation in G, 'Toy Symphony' **Pachelbel** Canon and Gigue
Academy of St Martin in the Fields / Sir Neville Marriner
Philips 416 386-2PH (52 minutes: DDD). Ⓕ
Recorded 1984-85

Sir Neville Marriner here collects a miscellaneous group of popular classical and baroque pieces in characteristically polished and elegant performances. The only roughness – and that deliberate – is in the extra toy percussion of Leopold Mozart's *Cassation* with its long-misattributed *Toy* Symphony. The anonymous extra soloists enjoy themselves as amateurs might, not least on a wind machine, but what is very hard to take is the grotesquely mismatched cuckoo-whistle, an instrument which should readily be tunable for pitch. *Eine kleine Nachtmusik* brings a performance plainly designed to caress the ear of traditional listeners wearied with period performance. The second movement Romanze is even more honeyed than usual on muted strings. The oddity of the Pachelbel item is that the celebrated Canon – taken unsentimentally if sweetly at a flowing speed – is given a reprise after the fugue. Warm, well-balanced recording.

Divertimentos

Divertimentos – B flat, K287/K271*h*; D, K205/K167*a*
Salzburg Mozarteum Camerata Academica / Sándor Végh
Capriccio 10 271 (59 minutes: DDD). Ⓕ
Recorded 1988 ●

Mozart's Divertimento, K287 is a six-movement work cast on quite a large scale, and is scored for two violins, viola, two horns and bass, a combination which presents some difficulties of balance. One solution is to use a full orchestral string section, but this can bring its own problems, for Mozart demands playing of virtuoso standard in this score, and anything less is ruthlessly exposed. Sandor Végh's smallish string band is of high quality, and has a pleasantly rounded tone quality. The engineers have managed to contrive a satisfactory balance which sounds not at all unnatural, and the sound quality itself is very good. Végh directs an attractive, neatly pointed performance of the work, one which steers a middle course between objective classicism and expressive warmth. The Divertimento, K205, has five movements, but none lasts longer than five minutes, and the work is much shorter and more modest than K287. Scoring in this case is for violin, viola, two horns, bassoon and double bass, to provide another difficult but well resolved problem for the engineers. Végh directs another characterful, delightful performance, to round off a very desirable disc.

Ein musikalischer Spass, K522

Ein musikalischer Spass. Contredanses – C, K587, 'Der Sieg vom Helden Koburg'; D, K534, 'Das Donnerwetter'; C, K535, 'La Bataille'; G, K610, 'Les filles malicieuses'; E flat, K607/K605*a*, 'Il trionfo delle donne'. Gallimathias musicum, K32. German Dances – K567; K605; C, K611, 'Die Leyerer'. March in D, K335 No 1
Orpheus Chamber Orchestra
DG 429 783-2GH (69 minutes: DDD). Ⓕ
Recorded 1989

The celebrated *Musikalischer Spass* ('Musical Joke') which begins the disc is never so crudely funny that it wears thin, but make no mistake, the jokes are there in just about every passage, whether they are parodying third-rate music or wobbly playing, and oddly enough sound still more amusing when the performance is as stylishly flexible as this one by the conductorless Orpheus Chamber Orchestra. One of the tunes here (that of the finale on track four) is that of the BBC's *Horse of the Year* programme – and what a good tune it is, even at the umpteenth repetition as the hapless composer finds himself unable to stop The rest of this programme is no less delightful and includes miniature pieces supposedly describing a thunderstorm, a battle, a hurdy-gurdy man and a sleigh-ride (with piccolo and sleigh-bells). There is also a *Gallimathias musicum*, a ballet suite of dainty little dances averaging less than a minute in length, which Mozart is supposed to have written at the age of 10. Whatever the case this CD, subtitled 'A Little Light Music', provides proof of his genius, though differently from his acknowledged masterpieces. The recording is as refined as anyone could wish yet has plenty of impact.

Symphonies

No 1 in E flat, K16; **No 2** in B flat, K17 (attrib L Mozart); **No 4** in D, K19; **No 5** in B flat, K22; **No 6** in F, K43; **No 7** in D, K45; **No 7*a*** in G, K45*a*/KAnh221, 'Alte Lambach'; **No 8** in D, K48; **No 9** in C, K73; **No 10** in G, K74; **No 11** in D, K84/K73*q*; **No 12** in G, K110/K75*b*; **No 13** in F, K112; **No 14** in A, K114; **No 15** in G, K124; **No 16** in C, K128; **No 17** in G, K129; **No 18** in F, K130; **No 19** in E flat, K132; **No 20** in D, K133; **No 21** in A, K134; **No 22** in C, K162; **No 23** in D, K181/K162*b*; **No 24** in B flat, K182/K173*dA*; **No 25** in G minor, K183/K173*dB*; **No 26** in E flat, K184/K161*a*; **No 27** in G, K199/K161*b*; **No 28** in C, K200/K189*k*; **No 29** in A, K201/K186*a*; **No 30** in D, K202/K186*b*; **No 31** in D, K297/K300*a*, 'Paris'; **No 32** in G, K318; **No 33** in B flat, K319; **No 34** in C, K338; **No 35** in D, K385, 'Haffner'; **No 36** in C, K425, 'Linz'; **No 38** in D, K504, 'Prague'; **No 39** in E flat, K543; **No 40** in G minor, K550; **No 41** in C, K551, 'Jupiter'; **(No 42)** in F, K75; **(No 43)** in F, K76/K42*a*; **(No 44)** in D, K81/K73*l*; **(No 45)** in D, K95/K73*n*; **(No 46)** in C, K96/K111*b*; **(No 47)** in D, K97/K73*m*; **(No 55)** in B flat, KApp214/K45*b*; **F**, KAnh223/K19*a*; **B flat**, K74*g*/KAnh216/C11.03

Symphonies Nos 1-36; Nos 38-47; (No 7*a*) in G, 'Alte Lambach', K45*a*/KAnh221; G, 'Neue Lambach' H
Berlin Philharmonic Orchestra / Karl Böhm
DG ⑩ 453 231-2GX10 (749 minutes: ADD). Ⓑ
Recorded 1959-68

Böhm's vintage Mozart recordings with the Berlin Philharmonic were in fact just as much a pioneering project as Antál Dorati's Haydn symphonic cycle, completed five years later. This was the first attempt on commercial disc to record the whole Mozart symphony cycle, at a time when virtually none of the works before the little known G minor, No 25, were at all familiar even to specialists. What the performances tell us, warm and genial, with bold contrasts of dynamic and well-sprung rhythms, is that for the players as well as the conductor this was a voyage of discovery, and their enthusiasm never wanes. On matters of scholarship these performances may have been supplanted by a whole series of recordings since, but as a welcoming way to investigate Mozart early and late they hold their place, with no hint of routine in the playing. As with Dorati in Haydn, minuets are slow and often heavy by today's standards, but some of the minuets in the early symphonies are taken more briskly, almost as fast *ländlers*. In finales Böhm rarely adopts an extreme speed, but always the springing of rhythm, and the clarity of articulation has the ear magnetized, even with a speed slower than we have grown used to.

When this set was first issued on CD, it involved 12 discs, and it is welcome to have these transfers squeezed on to 10 discs instead, particularly when the sound is fuller and more forward, with good body and presence. There is some inconsistency in the recording quality, but not enough to worry about, and even the earliest reading – of the *Haffner*, made in 1959 – is satisfyingly full-bodied, when one or two of the later ones are rather thinner. All the earlier symphonies were recorded in intensive sessions in 1968, and the present bargain box, unlike the previous, has such information included, as well as essays on Böhm as Mozartian by Peter Cosse and Mozart as symphonist by Heinz Becker. Cosse's memory of Böhm on television drawing a parallel between the slow movement of the Symphony No 1 and part of the unfinished Requiem is delightful. Böhm is inconsistent over such matters as exposition repeats. In the *Prague*, for example, though there is no repeat in the first movement, the exposition repeat is observed in the *Presto* finale, a question, one imagines, of Böhm wanting to balance two exceptionally long earlier movements. Then in No 40 he does observe the first movement repeat, but not in No 39 or the *Jupiter*, and it is probable that with the *Jupiter* the reason is that DG wanted the symphony to fit comfortably on an LP side. Whatever the reason, it means that the last three symphonies have been squeezed on to a single disc of 79 minutes, and only one of the other discs has a timing of less than 70 minutes, and most are over 75. An excellent bargain, for the historical specialist and for all Mozartians.

Symphonies Nos 1, 2, 4 and 5
Abel (formerly attrib Mozart) Symphony, Op 7 No 3
Northern Chamber Orchestra / Nicholas Ward Ⓢ
Naxos 8 550871 (59 minutes: DDD). Recorded 1994

Symphonies Nos 6-10
Northern Chamber Orchestra / Nicholas Ward Ⓢ
Naxos 8 550872 (56 minutes: DDD). Recorded 1993

These two discs of Mozart's first 10 symphonies offer a unique view of the composer's earliest years of apprenticeship as a symphonist. Ward and his orchestra show a sensitive response to the wealth of stylistic influences apparent in these works. Purists may question the inclusion of two of the symphonies, Nos 2 and 3, since neither work is actually by Mozart. The former is attributed to the composer's father, Leopold, while the latter is Mozart's orchestration of C F Abel's E flat Symphony, Op 7 No 3. However, when they are played with such engaging style and elegance as here, these two works add a further important dimension to Mozart's early symphonic output. Where J C Bach's influence is most powerful (Symphonies Nos 1, 4, 5 and 6), the NCO presents the music's contrasting thematic characters with fine clarity, balancing the music's beautifully transparent textures with appropriate lightness of touch. The inclusion of trumpets and drums in the next three symphonies (Nos 7, 8 and 9) announces the young composer's growing brilliance and stature. In these pieces, the NCO moves into a higher gear, revealing Mozart's potent originality, with powerfully dramatic tuttis and expressively sung *andantes*. Mozart made his first trip to Italy in 1770, and the symphony he wrote in Milan that year (No 10) shows his enthusiastic incorporation of Italian stylistic models. Here the NCO's deliciously spacious orchestral playing shows Mozart's ravishing originality, with dramatic opposition of gesture and instrumentation in the exuberant *allegros* and a beguilingly graceful slow movement that winningly displays a keen awareness of the composer's innovative touches. These are indeed splendid performances, admirably complemented by vivid recordings (made in the spacious acoustic of the Concert Hall, New Broadcasting House, Manchester).

Symphonies Nos 15-18
Northern Chamber Orchestra / Nicholas Ward Ⓢ
Naxos 8 550874 (58 minutes: DDD). Recorded 1994

After Mozart returned from his first extended tour of Italy in 1771, he embarked on a number of symphonic projects that show his astonishing assimilation and transformation of the Italian overture, with crisp, transparent orchestration and suppleness of expression. The influence of Sammartini and J C Bach – whose music could be heard at concerts in Salzburg during 1772 when these pieces were written – is especially apparent in the bold thematic gestures and civilized discourse between wind and strings. Nicholas Ward and the NCO bring their customary style and eloquence to this music in performances that evocatively portray its blend of formal unity, radiant vitality and occasionally – as in the rhythmically imaginative finale of the C major Symphony – rustic charm. Opening *allegros* are suitably vivacious, *andantes* are graceful and poignant and the vigorous finales bristle with energy. The first movement of the C major Symphony offers a more potent dramatic formula, with subtly poetic triplets and tense tremolos; however, the highlight of the programme is the F major Symphony (No 18), which Saint-Foix described as 'the first of [Mozart's] great symphonies'. Here, Ward's and the NCO's dramatically compelling account, beautifully presented in a natural, spacious recording, brilliantly highlights the music's operatic qualities.

Symphonies Nos 16-30 **P**
The English Concert / Trevor Pinnock
Archiv Produktion ④ 439 915-2AH4 Ⓕ
(264 minutes: DDD). Recorded 1993-94 ●

This set includes all the symphonies Mozart wrote between the spring of 1772 and the end of 1774, his most prolific period of symphony composition. What is exciting about this set is the sweetness of the period-instrument sound (not at all the same as the sweetness of a modern chamber orchestra) and the suppleness and flexibility The English Concert brings to the music. They play, much of the time, as if it were chamber music, particularly in second subjects – the lyrical passages, that is, where they shape the phrases with a warmth and refinement you hardly expect in orchestral music. Timing is quietly witty, yet not at all contrived or artificial: it is the sort of expressive refinement that depends on listening to one another, not on the presence of a conductor. There is large-scale playing too. The opening of the brilliant D major work, K133 has a splendid swing, with its prominent trumpets, and a real sense of a big, symphonic piece. K184 is duly fiery and its accents are neatly judged. The two final symphonies are both very impressively done: an eloquent rather than a fiery account (though something of that too) of the opening movement of K201, with a particularly euphonious and shapely *Andante*, and the finales of both are done with exceptional vitality and the rhythmic resilience that is characteristic of these performances. In short, quite outstanding performances, unfailingly musical, wholly natural and unaffected, often warmly expressive in the slow music and always falling very happily on the ear, with no trace of the harshness that some think is inevitable with period instruments. They are excellently recorded, with the properly prominent wind balance helping to characterize the sound world of each work.

Symphonies Nos 21-24 and 26
Northern Chamber Orchestra / Nicholas Ward Ⓢ
Naxos 8 550876 (53 minutes: DDD). Recorded 1993

This is a chance to enjoy Mozart's inexhaustibly imaginative assimilation and transformation of Italian operatic models. Ward's balanced orchestral textures reveal Mozart's fragrant orchestration with great clarity in the A major Symphony. Sample the second movement's deftly handled interplay of strings, woodwind and horns, and buoyantly stately Menuetto that culminates effectively in the finale's restless drive. The complete musical satisfaction provided by the four Italian-overture symphonies that comprise the remainder of the programme is due to the fullness and vigour of the orchestration itself, and to the Northern Chamber Orchestra's lively performances. The opening *allegros* and cheerfully effervescent finales bubble with infectious vitality, while the slow movements give the opportunity for more intimate instrumental ensembles. Most impressive, however, is the E flat major work, which originated as the overture to the play *Lanassa*. Here, Ward and the NCO compellingly portray the dramatic violence of the opening *Presto*, the despair of its minor-key *Andante* and the exuberant rhythms of its finale. The recording is atmospheric.

Symphonies Nos 25, 28 and 29
Prague Chamber Orchestra / Sir Charles Mackerras
Telarc CD80165 (78 minutes: DDD). Recorded 1987 Ⓕ

Here are three symphonies from Mozart's late teens, written in Salzburg, in crisply articulated performances. The first of them is a *Sturm und Drang* piece in G minor, a key that the composer reserved for moods of agitation. Mackerras takes the orchestra through the big opening *Allegro con brio* of No 25 with drive and passion, although it is unlikely that Mozart would have expected a Salzburg orchestra in the 1770s to play as fast as this skilful body of Czech players. The gentle *Andante* comes therefore as a relief, though here too Mackerras keeps a firm rhythmic grasp on the music, and indeed a taut metrical aspect is a feature of all three symphonies as played here, so that minuets dance briskly and purposefully and finales bustle. However, the sunlit warmth of the beautiful A major Symphony, No 29, comes through and the bracing view of the other two symphonies is a legitimate one, though giving little or nothing in the direction of expressive lingering, much less towards sentimental indulgence. The Prague Chamber Orchestra is an expert ensemble, not overlarge for this style of music, and the recording is without doubt admirably clear although a little reverberant.

Symphonies Nos 28, 29 and 35
Berlin Philharmonic Orchestra / Claudio Abbado
Sony Classical SK48063 (74 minutes: DDD). Ⓕ
Recorded 1990-91

These are 'big band' versions of Mozart symphonies. Nos 28 and 29 were recorded live in the Philharmonie, the *Haffner* done in the empty concert hall. The Berlin sound is big and weighty, with horns whooping out richly; the result is not just big-scaled but elegant. Abbado is never a mannered Mozartian, but his phrasing and pointing of rhythm is delicately affectionate. The result, while being warm and elegant, also conveys an element of fun, with tempos never allowed to drag. Slow movements are kept flowing, and finales are hectically fast, but played with such verve and diamond-bright articulation that there is no feeling of breathlessness. Abbado is generous with repeats, but he does not attempt the latter-day 'authentic' habit of including repeats in the *da capos* of minuets. With the score of the *Haffner* sparing of repeats, No 29 is by far the longest of the three symphonies here, the young Mozart spreading his wings. The Sony engineers have coped splendidly with the acoustic problems of the Philharmonie to give a full and forward sound, not always ideally clear on detail in tuttis but with good presence.

Symphonies Nos 29, 31-36 and 38-41 **P**
English Baroque Soloists / Sir John Eliot Gardiner
Philips ⑤ 442 604-2PH5 (309 minutes: DDD). Ⓜ
Recorded 1984-89 **OO**

Gardiner took his pilgrimage through the late Mozart symphonies more or less in chronological order over a span of six years. The first disc contains appealing performances of Nos 29 and 33, the former particularly lyrical and shapely, with an eloquent account of the *Andante*, the latter distinguished for its refinement of line and the properly spirited opening movement. Then comes the *Paris*, No 31, a piece designed to show off a virtuoso orchestra, which it duly does in this alert and shapely reading, coupled with No 34, another large-scale piece, in which Gardiner again provides a specially graceful slow movement. In the *Haffner*, *Linz* and *Prague* Symphonies Gardiner is possibly more concerned with classical grandeur than with strong characterization of the ideas. The G minor is the outstanding achievement of the set: the first movement performed with great drive and spaciousness, the second shapely and intense in expression, the finale done with immense vitality, the strings' arpeggios leaping vividly through the texture. The *Jupiter* is almost equally splendid, if slightly flawed by some *piano* effects in the first movement tuttis (this happens too in No 39) where they do not belong, but the crowning glory, the finale, contains many thrilling things. This is probably the version to choose, under any conductor, of these symphonies on period instruments – and perhaps on any instruments.

Symphony No 33. Serenade No 9
Academy of St Martin in the Fields / Iona Brown
Hänssler Classic CD98 129 (59 minutes: DDD). Ⓕ
Recorded 1997

Symphony No 35. Serenade No 7
Academy of St Martin in the Fields / Iona Brown *vn*
Hänssler Classic CD98 173 (72 minutes: DDD). Ⓕ
Recorded 1997

Each disc brings together a middle-period symphony and a contemporaneous Serenade. The sound recording has a sharpness of focus and sense of presence more often associated with the finest analogue recordings of the 1960s and 1970s. It is surprising to find that the venue was Henry Wood Hall, for this sounds rather more intimate than most recordings made there, with plenty of bloom but no excessive reverberation. This is Mozart sound, using modern instruments but with some concern for the crisper manners encouraged by period performance, that in its freshness and beauty makes one want to go on listening. The finale of the Symphony No 33, for example, brings a hectic speed which does not sound at all breathless, with featherlight triplets, and similarly in the finale of the *Posthorn* Serenade with which it is coupled. Exceptionally in that Serenade Iona Brown opts for a more relaxed speed and more moulded style in the lovely minor-key *Andantino* of the fifth movement. The posthorn in the Trio of the second Minuet is this time much more brazen and more forwardly balanced than before. The coupling of the *Haffner* Symphony and *Haffner* Serenade is specially apt. In the Symphony Brown follows the autograph in omitting an exposition repeat. Iona Brown herself is the virtuoso soloist in the Serenade, lighter than ever in the *moto perpetuo* scurryings of the fourth-movement Rondo. For those who continue to resist period performances in this repertory these are very refreshing discs.

Symphonies Nos 35, 36 and 38-41 **H**
Berlin Philharmonic Orchestra / Karl Böhm
DG The Originals ② 447 416-2GOR2 Ⓜ
(146 minutes: ADD). Recorded 1959-66

These performances come from the first ever complete set of Mozart symphonies (reviewed above), and they still represent 'big orchestra' Mozart at its most congenial. The contrast between Böhm's sparkling Mozart, both elegant and vigorous, and the much smoother view taken by Karajan on his countless recordings with the same orchestra, works almost entirely in Böhm's favour here. Interpretatively, these are performances very much of their time, with exposition repeats the exception (as in the first movement of No 40) and with minuets taken at what now seem like lumbering speeds. However, the slow movements certainly flow easily enough, and finales bounce along infectiously. Consistently they convey the happy ease of Böhm in Mozart, even if the recording is beefy by today's standards, not as transparent as one now expects in this repertory, whether on modern or period instruments. There is some inconsistency between the different recordings, all made in the Jesus-Christus Kirche in Berlin. The best sound comes from the sessions in 1966 for the *Linz* and No 39 – satisfyingly full without any perceptible edginess on violins – and the least good from 1959 for the *Prague*, where high violins sound rather fizzy. Yet the very precision of the CD transfers encourages one to highlight such points. In practice most collectors will find the sound more than acceptable enough in all six symphonies to convey the warmth of Böhm in Mozart without distraction.

Symphonies Nos 36 and 38
Prague Chamber Orchestra / Sir Charles Mackerras
Telarc CD80148 (66 minutes: DDD). Ⓕ
Recorded 1987

Mozart wrote his *Linz* Symphony in great haste (five days to be precise), but needless to say there is little evidence of haste in the music itself, except perhaps that the first movement has all the exuberance of a composer writing on the wing of inspiration. The slow movement with its siciliano rhythm certainly has no lack of serenity, although it has drama too. The *Prague* Symphony was written only three years later, yet Mozart's symphonic style had matured and the work is more ambitious and substantial. A glorious spaciousness surrounds Sir Charles's performances. The recording venue is reverberant, yet there is no loss of detail, and the fullness of the sound helps to add weight to climaxes without going beyond the bounds of volume that Mozart might have expected. Sir Charles captures the joy and high spirits that these symphonies embody without in any way undermining their greatness. This vivacity is emphasized by the East European sound of the Prague Chamber Orchestra, with the out-of-doors timbre of its winds which provides a pleasing contrast both with those of the standard British and Germanic orchestras and specialist, authentic ensembles. Mackerras does, however, adopt some aspects of the modern approach to Mozart performance: he includes harpsichord continuo, his minuets are taken trippingly, one-to-a-bar, and he prefers bowing that is crisper, more detached, and pointed. Phrasing and articulation are taken with a natural grace and without overemphasis, dynamics being graded to give drama at the right moments. The very rightness of the result is recommendation enough.

Symphony No 38. Piano Concerto No 25 in C, K503[a]. Ch'io mi scordi di te ... Non temer, amato bene, K505[b]
[b]**Bernarda Fink** *sop* **Lausanne Chamber Orchestra / Christian Zacharias** [ab]*pf*
Dabringhaus und Grimm MDG340 0967-2 Ⓕ
(73 minutes: DDD). Recorded 1999 ●

Here Christian Zacharias successfully experiments with a nicely balanced Mozart group of symphony, aria and concerto. He himself takes multiple roles, conducting a fresh and lively account of the *Prague* Symphony, and acting as piano soloist not only in the Concerto, directing the weighty K503 from the keyboard, but also providing a crisply pointed obbligato in the most taxing of Mozart's concert arias, *Ch'io mi scordi di te*. The sense of freedom and spontaneous enjoyment is enhanced by the clarity of the recording, made in the Metropole, Lausanne. Though tuttis are big and weighty, Zacharias finds rare transparency in lighter passages, and a vivid sense of presence throughout. One of Zacharias's great merits as a Mozart pianist is the crispness of his articulation; he defines each note with jewelled clarity, even in the fastest, trickiest passagework, as in the dashing triplets in the finale of K503.

The Symphony too is given a refreshing performance, with due weight in the first movement and light, crisp articulation in the finale. Some may feel that Zacharias underplays the gravity of the central *Andante*, but nowadays few will object to a flowing tempo such as one expects in a period performance.

In many ways, most striking of all is the concert aria, which comes between symphony and concerto. Bernarda Fink, officially a mezzo, is not just untroubled by the soprano tessitura but gives a most characterful interpretation, pointing words and phrases with delightful individuality. Using her lovely creamy tone colours, Fink here offers one of the most impressive of all versions of this notorious test-piece since Schwarzkopf, rounding off her virtuoso display of coloratura with a perfect trill in an exuberant account of the coda. Her contribution crowns a consistently enjoyable programme.

Symphonies Nos 40 and 41 **P**
The English Concert / Trevor Pinnock
Archiv Produktion 447 048-2AH (73 minutes: DDD). Ⓕ
Recorded 1994

The *Jupiter* is a truly outstanding performance. No 40 is satisfactory but not extraordinary, though the first movement is taken at a true *Molto allegro* while the finale is poised and full of fire. The *Jupiter*, though, is magnificent. The first movement is duly weighty, but energetically paced and its critical junctures timed with a keen sense of their role in the shape of the whole. In the *Andante* Pinnock draws an extraordinarily beautiful, almost sensuous sound from The English Concert and the lines are moulded with tenderness. This, above all, is the quality that distinguishes Pinnock's recordings from all others, this natural and musical sound, deriving from the way the players are intently listening to one another; it is fitting that it reaches its high point in the *Jupiter*. He takes the Minuet at a lively pace and with a fine spring to the rhythm. As for the finale: well, it is decidedly quick, and one has the impression of a performance in which the orchestra is pressed to an extent that its ensemble playing is under stress, though it does of course hold together. It is a very bold, outspoken reading, which leaves one gasping afresh at the music's originality; and the prominence of the woodwind and brass gives different perspectives from usual. It may not be to everyone's taste, but it raises the blood pressure, and the spirits too. The sound of the orchestra is very vivid and clean, with sweet, warm and firm string tone, with the wind well forward.

Clarinet Quintet in A, K581

Clarinet Quintet. String Quartet No 18 in A, K464
Janet Hilton *cl* **The Lindsays** (Peter Cropper, Ronald Birks *vns* Robin Ireland *va* Bernard Gregor-Smith *vc*)
ASV CDDCA1042 (74 minutes: DDD). Ⓕ
Recorded 1998 ○

The Lindsays' interpretation of K464 is entirely persuasive, barring a few minor quibbles – the first movement, though flexible and elegant, is perhaps slightly lacking in urgency and dynamic contrast, the finale, on the other hand, has all the drama and onward thrust one could wish for, but occasionally begins to lose its rhythmic poise. The Lindsays play the quartet complete with all its repeats. If you prefer to have modern instruments in this quartet, go for this recording. The Clarinet Quintet is given with the finesse and care for phrasing and articulation that characterizes all Lindsay Mozart issues. It's good for Mozart to sound suave, and Janet Hilton presents the melody of the *Larghetto* (track 2) with lovely soft articulation, yet the music is more rhetorical and passionate than she allows, and the hint of vibrato only serves further to soften the expression. There are, however, fine features in this performance – the exciting, perfectly controlled first-movement development, a lively, beautifully shaped Minuet, a really melancholic viola in the finale and a splendidly robust concluding *Allegro*. The recording is clear, intimate, but not dry.

String Quintets

String Quintets – No 1 in B flat, K174; No 2 in C minor, K406/K516*b*; No 3 in C, K515; No 4 in G minor, K516; No 5 in D, K593; No 6 in E flat, K614
Arthur Grumiaux, Arpad Gérecz *vns* **Georges Janzer, Max Lesueur** *vas* **Eva Czako** *vc*
Awards 1991
Philips Mozart Edition ③ 422 511-2PME3 Ⓜ
(170 minutes: ADD). Recorded 1973 ○○○

Of the six works which comprise Mozart's complete *oeuvre* for string quintet, that in B flat major, K174, is an early composition, written at the age of 17. It is a well-made, enjoyable work, but not a great deal more than that. The C minor work, K406, is an arrangement by Mozart of his Serenade for six wind instruments, K398. It is difficult not to feel that the original is more effective, since the music seems to sit a little uncomfortably on string instruments. But the remaining four works, written in the last four years of Mozart's life, are a different matter. The last string quintets from Mozart's pen were extraordinary works, and the addition of the second viola seems to have pulled him to still greater heights. It has been suggested that Mozart wrote K515 and K516 to show King Friedrich Wilhelm II of Prussia that he was a better composer of string quintets than Boccherini, whom the King had retained as chamber music composer to his court. There was no response, so he offered these two quintets for sale with the K406 arrangement to make up the usual set of three. K593 and K614 were written in the last year of his life. Refinement is perhaps the word that first comes to mind in discussing these performances, which are affectionate yet controlled by a cool, intelligent sensitivity. The recordings have been well transferred, the quality is warm and expansive and Grumiaux's tone, in particular, is a delight to the ear but all the playing is stylish.

String Quintet No 3. String Quartet No 16 in E flat, K428
Louise Williams *va* **The Lindsays** (Peter Cropper, Ronald Birks *vn* Robin Ireland *va* Bernard Gregor-Smith *vc*)
ASV CDDCA992 (67 minutes: DDD). Ⓕ
Recorded 1995

Here's a fine performance of the great C major Quintet. The Lindsays take the first movement at a true Allegro, so that it bowls along in top gear, the details vivid and sharply etched. Much of this grandest and most spacious movement in Mozart's chamber output is marked to be played softly: in the Lindsays' hands the wonderful counterpoint in the development section can be heard with exceptional clarity as the tension builds up, but not the dynamic. The Andante sounds the more touching for never being over-played, and it's a special pleasure to hear how the most florid passages for first violin and first viola fit effortlessly into the rhythmic scheme. In the finale, Peter Cropper introduces some beautifully played portamentos in the main theme, and the whole movement sounds delightfully witty and happy. The E flat Quartet, K428 is cool and stylish, which suits this enigmatic work rather well. The Lindsays' way of using Mozart's marks of expression and articulation to make the music speak feels absolutely right, especially in their delicate, refined Andante, and it's good to hear the quartet played with all its repeats. The recording has a nice intimate quality.

Flute Quartets

Flute Quartet No 1 in D, K285. Oboe Quartet in F, K370/K368*b*. Clarinet Quintet
Jaime Martin *fl* **Jonathan Kelly** *ob* **Nicholas Carpenter** *cl* **Brindisi Quartet** (Jaqueline Shave, Patrick Kiernan *vns* Katie Wilkinson Krososhunin *va* Anthony Pleeth *vc*)
EMI Debut CDZ5 69702-2 (64 minutes: DDD). Ⓕ
Recorded 1996

Do you like your Mozart refined and graceful? Or robust and spontaneously expressive? A combination of both would be perfect, you may think, but in practice it's not always easy to achieve. The Brindisi Quartet and its three colleagues play with exceptional finesse, and excellent balance and blend, well captured by the recording. These are predominantly light-toned performances, with the phrases shaped convincingly and with unfailing elegance. Their approach seems just about ideal in the Flute Quartet, where the joyful, vivacious atmosphere of the outer movements is enhanced by thoughtful attention to detail. Jaime Martin's sensitive, sensuous flute-playing in the *Adagio* provides a delightful contrast. There are many good things in the other two pieces, too. Jonathan Kelly's virtuosity in the Oboe Quartet's finale is really exciting, as is the brilliant, superbly balanced development section in the Clarinet Quintet's first movement. But there are places where you might long for something less cool and detached. The recording of the Oboe Quartet by Nicholas Daniel and members of the The Lindsays (reviewed further on with the String Quartet No 17 and the Horn Quintet) combine stylishness with strong expression.

Flute Quartets – D, K285; G, K285*a*; C, KAnh171/K285*b*; A, K298
Emmanuel Pahud *fl* **Christoph Poppen** *vn* **Hariolf Schlichtig** *va* **Jean-Guihen Queyras** *vc* Ⓕ
EMI CDC5 56829-2 (59 minutes: DDD)

There may be only one movement of any emotional weight, the B minor *Adagio* of the First Quartet, K285, but in that brief cantilena Pahud finds a mystery and subtlety of dynamic shading that outshine almost any rival. For the rest he consistently conveys the fun in the writing here. The A major work may run the dangerous course of parodying the banalities of the contemporaries whom Mozart despised, but Pahud still finds charm in the invention, helped by the warm, imaginative playing of his string partners. Pahud's lighter, more sparkling playing, with his fresh, clear tone is preferable to Galway's more romantic approach at generally broader speeds, and with phrasing more heavily underlined in characteristically full flute tone. In his 1969 Philips recording William Bennett, with the Grumiaux Trio, adopts speeds similar to Pahud's in crisp, direct and enjoyable readings, but Pahud is more individual in his phrasing and control of dynamic, helped by vivid digital recording with fine presence. Pahud, unlike both Galway and Bennett, observes second-half repeats as well as first in the sonata-form first movements of the first three quartets. Recommended.

Piano Quartets

No 1 in G minor, K478; **No 2** in E flat, K493

Piano Quartets – E flat, K452; Nos 1 and 2 **P**
Sonnerie (Monica Huggett *vn* Emilia Benjamin *va* Alison McGillivray *vc* Gary Cooper *fp*)
ASV Gaudeamus CDGAU212 (76 minutes: DDD).
Recorded 2000 Ⓕ

Sonnerie go one – rather a large one – better than their recorded rivals in the Mozart piano quartets by including an extra work: the piano quartet arrangement (not generally thought to be Mozart's own, but more or less contemporary) of the Quintet for piano and wind. The work, so artfully composed around the sound and capacities of the oboe, clarinet, bassoon and horn, loses the motivation for its particular thematic structure in transcription but is nevertheless a worthwhile bonus.

Not that these performances need any bonus. They have exceptional musical vitality, as though the music is being freshly thought through as it unfolds and the players are newly fired by its ideas. The G minor Quartet in particular is given a large-scale, outspoken performance, vigorous, dark-toned in the first movement, with an almost alarmingly vivid and strongly shaped account of the development section. There is drama in the *Andante*, too, which is expansively done, and the rich implications the players (pianist Gary Cooper most of all) draw from the textures and the harmonies is impressive. The finale of the E flat work, too, is done with great spirit – here the pianist is very much in the driving seat – and there are many happy details of timing and dynamic gradation.

Mozart's wit is beautifully captured in K493, yet this is a deeply serious performance, strongly argued, with the mystery and logic of his unusual modulations fully grasped. The first movement here, taken at a rather steady tempo, is particularly successful, with Cooper taking his time over the expression of its ideas and Monica Huggett and her colleagues playing the lyrical secondary material with much warmth.

Piano Quartets Nos 1 and 2
Isaac Stern *vn* **Jaime Laredo** *va* **Yo-Yo Ma** *vc*
Emanuel Ax *pf*
Sony Classical SK66841 (56 minutes: DDD). Ⓕ
Recorded 1994

There is no shortage of good recordings of this favourite coupling of two Mozart masterpieces, and this grouping of star names offers performances of comparable imagination and insight. In the E flat Quartet, K493, it is not just Isaac Stern and Yo-Yo Ma whose solo entries have one sitting up, but also Jaime Laredo in the rare moments when Mozart gives a solo to his own instrument, the viola. Speeds are beautifully chosen, and in both works the performances convey a happy spontaneity. Emanuel Ax shows what a natural, individual Mozartian he is. The G minor work is in many ways parallel to the great piano concertos of the period, with the piano regularly set against the strings in ensemble, and Ax readily establishes the sort of primacy plainly required, even in such company as this. He is a shade robust at the start of the central *Andante* but in fast music as in slow his gift of pointing rhythms and moulding phrases is consistently persuasive and imaginative. The recording, made in the Manhattan Center, New York, is a degree drier than in many of the current rival versions, but there is ample bloom on the sound, fitting very well in a domestic listening room.

String Quartets

No 1 in G, K80/K73*f*; **No 2** in D, K155/K134*a*; **No 3** in G, K156/K134*b*; **No 4** in C, K157; **No 5** in F, K158; **No 6** in B flat, K159; **No 7** in E flat, K160/K159*a*; **No 8** in F, K168; **No 9** in A, K169; **No 10** in C, K170; **No 11** in E flat, K171; **No 12** in B flat, K172; **No 13** in D minor, K173; **No 14** in G, K387; **No 15** in D minor, K421/K417*b*; **No 16** in E flat, K428/K421*b*; **No 17** in B flat, K458, 'Hunt'; **No 18** in A, K464; **No 19** in C, K465, 'Dissonance'; **No 20** in D, K499, 'Hoffmeister'; **No 21** in D, K575; **No 22** in B flat, K589; **No 23** in F, K590

Awards 1991

String Quartets Nos 1-23
Quartetto Italiano (Paolo Borciani, Elisa Pegreffi *vns* Piero Farulli *va* Franco Rossi *vc*)
Philips Mozart Edition ⑧ 422 512-2PME8 Ⓜ
(474 minutes: ADD)
Recorded 1966-70 ●●●

These classic performances have won praise since they began to appear in 1967. Admittedly, a little allowance has to be made for the sound. For example, it is a touch heavy and close in the 1966 recording of the D minor Quartet that is one of the wonderful set of six that Mozart dedicated to Haydn. In a way, this accords with the playing of the Quartetto Italiano, which is at times rather earnest – and in the first movement of this work, rather deliberate in its pace. But these are the only criticisms of a splendid issue, and the innate seriousness of these fine Italian artists is almost always a plus feature: indeed, they bring an overall intelligence, refinement and, above all, range of interpretative values to this often superb and always attractive music. As for quality of ensemble, they are impeccable. This is still the best general survey of Mozart's string quartets available, and at mid-price the eight discs represent a safe investment that should yield many years of pleasure.

String Quartets No 14-19
Chilingirian Quartet (Levon Chilingirian, Mark Butler *vns* Nicholas Logie *va* Philip de Groote *vc*)
CRD3362: Nos 14 and 15 (59 minutes: ADD).
CRD3363: Nos 16 and 17 (56 minutes: ADD).
CRD3364: Nos 18 and 19 (68 minutes: ADD). Ⓜ
Recorded 1979

For reticent, confidential performances that reach deeply into this wonderful music we suggest you try the Chilingirian Quartet's versions of the 'Haydn' Quartets, first issued on LP in 1980. They effectively move you from a public to a private domain of music-making. The Chilingirian may be slightly less adroit technically than some competitors, the Alban Berg Quartet particularly, especially as regards intonation (Levon Chilingirian is sometimes a bit wayward in this respect); nor does it aspire to the Alban Berg's tonal opulence and power, but its performances of these six inexhaustible works represent some of the most searching, naturally expressive Mozart playing on disc today. Its tendency, in contra-distinction to the Alban Berg, is towards understatement. Tempos are frequently a little slower than average, dynamic contrasts vivid without exaggeration (*fortes* are never harsh or explosive), phrasing is alive and imaginative, yet with no attempt to beautify the moment. In *Allegros*, notably the first movements of Nos 17 and 19, and the finale of No 16, the Chilingirian may appear over-leisurely, slightly lacking in bite and brio; but its uncommonly thoughtful, intimate approach consistently reveals depths and shadows in this music that elude more obviously dynamic performances. Rarely, if ever, will you hear No 18 played with such grace, such gentle, reflective intensity; more than ever its Minuet, spare and absorbed, seems to look forward through Beethoven's Op 18 No 5 to the corresponding movement in the late A minor Quartet, Op 132. And profound reflective tenderness is a quality the Chilingirian consistently brings to the slow movements: listen to its hushed, veiled tone at the start of the *Andante* of No 19, for instance, or the subtly judged ebb and flow of tension in the astonishing chromatic *Andante* of No 16, not, perhaps, *con moto*, as Mozart asks, but haunting in its subdued disquiet. The Chilingirian receives an ideally truthful, rounded recording that reveals with ideal clarity its exceptional care for inner detail. Few other current versions of the 'Haydn' Quartets offer richer rewards.

String Quartets Nos 15-17 and 20
Franz Schubert Quartet (Florian Zwiauer, Helge Rosenkranz *vns* Hartmut Pascher *va* Vincent Stadlmair *vc*)
Nimbus ② NI5455/6 (115 minutes: DDD). Ⓕ
Recorded 1994

Mozart's profound debt to Haydn in the six string quartets he dedicated to the composer (of which the Franz Schubert Quartet here plays K421 and K428) is most evident in their innovative approach to texture. Moreover, the true equality between the four parts – demonstrating a critical relationship between instrumentation and musical substance – has inspired startlingly different interpretative approaches. The Chilingirian Quartet's elegantly refined, charmingly understated accounts convincingly present the music in an intimate, private context. By contrast, like the Alban Berg Quartet, the Franz Schubert Quartet offers more dramatic readings, whose wider dynamic range projects the music in a more public manner. Nimbus's impressively truthful recording reveals the music's varied textures with pellucid clarity in the opening *allegros*, and relatively fast *andantes* imbue the performers' lush ensemble with appropriately increased animation.

The minuets are more passionate than those of the Chilingirian, and the finales are likewise bold and dramatic, with the variation finale of the D minor work, in particular, confirming a satisfying sense of overall unity. Despite their striking contrasts, though, the Franz Schubert Quartet does not quite achieve the extremes of the Alban Berg, whose powerfully arresting 1979 recording of the *Hunt* Quartet (K458) still sounds exceptionally fresh. The Franz Schubert Quartet's comparatively relaxed approach to the first movement, for example, fails to match the Berg's exhilarating evocation of the chase.

Nevertheless, for those who find the latter too highly charged, the Franz Schubert Quartet here offers an alternative whose beautiful textural clarity and vivid thematic detail many will find irresistible. To the *Hoffmeister* Quartet, the Franz Schubert Quartet brings delicacy and finesse, most notably in their dynamic control and contrapuntal clarity. Try them in the first movement's development section, their lucid counterpoint in the second movement's introspective trio (in the tonic minor), their heartfelt expression in the *Adagio*, and their enthralling, symphonic conception of the finale. These distinguished accounts deserve an assured place among the very best.

String Quartet No 17. Oboe Quartet in F, K370/K368*b*. Horn Quintet in E flat, K407/K386*c*
Nicholas Daniel *ob* **Stephen Bell** *hn* **The Lindsays** (Peter Cropper *vn* Ronald Birks *vn/va* Robin Ireland *va* Bernard Gregor-Smith *vc*)
ASV CDDCA968 (68 minutes: DDD). Ⓕ
Recorded 1995

The Lindsays really make the *Hunt* Quartet sparkle. One could describe their approach as middle-of-the-road; they're as meticulous as many period-instrument groups about details of phrasing, and avoid excessive accents and vibrato, yet their sound is modern, and the care over detail doesn't preclude a very spontaneous approach in which the music's feeling is compellingly communicated. In the Oboe Quartet Nicholas Daniel matches the string players' care over articulation and detailed expression, and plays with exceptional technical polish and brilliance. His gleaming tone is capable of great expressive range. The Horn Quintet is perhaps not quite such an individual or remarkable work as the two quartets. And you may find yourself longing for the extra character and beauty that a fine performance with the natural horn would have had. Yet this is a highly recommendable reading, too. The recording is very lifelike, with clear spacing of the instruments.

String Quartets Nos 21 and 23 P
Quatuor Mosaïques (Erich Höbarth, Andrea Bischof *vns* Anita Mitterer *va* Christophe Coin *vc*)
Auvidis Astrée E8659 (60 minutes: DDD). Ⓕ
Recorded 1998 ●

The Mosaïques here turn to Mozart's last quartets; the sheer refinement of its playing – its silk-sewn ensemble and its uncanny ability to sense out the living pulse and pace of a work – comes into its own in the *sotto voce* movements of No 21. A single ascending or descending scale can take on a rare beauty. And when these characteristic scales return to seal the first movement in tiny coda, they are enlivened by the little touches of rubato which breathe air into this performance. That same touch of rubato awakens the spirit of dance in the Menuetto, lifting the heel and pointing the toe. It is details like these which reanimate this music and give the edge of character to the Mosaïques' playing, over and above their rivals in this repertoire. In No 21, the mercurial playing of the Mosaïques, with the light, close harmony and subtly shaded inner voices, which is such a hallmark of this group, combines with a perfectly judged pace for the 6/8 *Allegretto*. Again the Mosaïques takes little moments to catch its breath, so that the hurtling round-dance of a finale leaves us a little less dizzy than it does in the hands of most other groups.

Piano Trios

Awards 1991

Piano Quintet in E flat, K452. Clarinet Trio in E flat, K498, 'Kegelstatt'. Adagio and Rondo in C minor, K617. Adagio in C, K356/K617a. Piano Quartets – No 1 in G minor, K478; No 2 in E flat, K493. Piano Trios – B flat, K254; D minor, K442 (cptd Stadler and Marguerre); No 1 in G, K496; No 3 in B flat, K502; No 4 in E, K542; No 5 in C, K548; No 6 in G, K564

Patrick Ireland, Karl Schouten, Bruno Giuranna *vas* **Jean Decroos** *vc* **Aurèle Nicolet** *fl* **Heinz Holliger** *ob* **Eduard Brunner, Jack Brymer** *cls* **Hermann Baumann** *hn* **Klaus Thunemann** *bn* **Bruno Hoffmann** *glass harmonica* **Beaux Arts Trio** (Isidore Cohen *vn* Bernard Greenhouse *vc* Menahem Pressler *pf*); **Alfred Brendel, Stephen Kovacevich** *pfs*

Philips Mozart Edition ⑤ 422 514-2PME5 Ⓜ

(274 minutes: ADD/DDD). Recorded 1969-87 ○○○

These recordings come from different locations and dates. Four of the five discs offer the two piano quartets and seven piano trios, played by the Beaux Arts Trio who are joined in the quartets by the viola player Bruno Giuranna; these are clearly the centrepiece of the issue and the playing of this fine ensemble is strongly characterful yet thoughtful. These are alert, direct and yet refined performances and earn only praise, although the recording in Philips's favoured Swiss location of La-Chaux-de-Fonds could have placed a little more distance between the players and the listener. But otherwise this clear sound suits the music, and Menahem Pressler's piano tone is well captured.

The D minor Trio which ends the series is not wholly authentic, being mainly Maximilian Stadler's compilation from material found by Mozart's widow Constanze after his death. Before we come to the piano quartets and piano trios, the first disc also has important works in fine performances in which Alfred Brendel and Heinz Holliger are just two of the artists involved (the Quintet for piano and wind was among the composer's favourite works). The first disc also offers two pieces featuring the ravishing sound of the glass harmonica (musical glasses), which is played by its leading exponent, Bruno Hoffmann, and the solo *Adagio* in C major is quite ethereally beautiful, if rather closely recorded. This unique instrument is usefully described and illustrated in the booklet.

Piano Trios – No 1 in G, K496; No 3 in B flat, K502. Divertimento in B flat, K254

Augustin Dumay *vn* **Jian Wang** *vc*
Maria João Pires *pf*

DG 449 208-2GH (73 minutes: DDD). Includes bonus CD featuring short works by Brahms, Franck, Grieg, Ⓕ Mozart and Ravel. Recorded 1995

This disc of early Mozart trios is radiant with the discriminating, fanciful and exuberant music-making which characterizes this rare trio of friends. A *crescendo* of joy shooting up through the opening scalic and arpeggio figures of K496 is answered by finely tapered violin playing and a cello which draws the ear to its contributions long before the true dialogue of the *Andante*. This ensemble finds a truly lilting 6/8 (rather than the illusion of a sturdier 3/4) for the second movement, and the finale is full of a sense of wonder, in its platinum-tipped violin and the drawing back into finely nuanced tones of grey for the sombre fifth variation. For K502, Pires picks up on the forward impetus inherent in the rhythm of the opening theme and in the slow movment her phrasing makes its melody more shapely above the unsurpassed beauty of sustained tone in violin and cello. A delicious performance of the little *Divertimento*, K254 reveals the ancestry of these two trios, and there is another bonus in a 48-minute disc of extracts from the six recordings of Mozart, Brahms, Franck, Ravel and Grieg made over six years by the incomparable duo of Pires and Dumay.

Piano Sonatas

No 1 in C, K279/K189*d*; **No 2** in F, K280/K189*e*; **No 3** in B flat, K281/K189*f*; **No 4** in E flat, K282/K189*g*; **No 5** in G, K283/K189*h*; **No 6** in D, K284/K205*b*; **No 7** in C, K309/K284*b*; **No 8** in A minor, K310/K300*d*; **No 9** in D, K311/K284*c*; **No 10** in C, K330/K300*h*; **No 11** in A, K331/K300*i*; **No 12** in F, K332/K300*k*; **No 13** in B flat, K333/K315*c*; **No 14** in C minor, K457; **No 15** in F, K533/K494; **No 16** in C, K545; **No 17** in B flat, K570; **No 18** in D, K576

Piano Sonatas Nos 1-18. Fantasia, K475

Mitsuko Uchida *pf*

Philips Mozart Edition ⑤ 422 517-2PME5 Ⓜ

(325 minutes: DDD) ○○○

Awards 1991

By common consent, Mitsuko Uchida is among the leading Mozart pianists of today, and her recorded series of the piano sonatas won critical acclaim as it appeared and finally *Gramophone* Awards in 1989 and 1991. Here are all the sonatas, plus the *Fantasia* in C minor, K475, which is in some ways a companion piece to the sonata in the same key, K457. This is unfailingly clean, crisp and elegant playing, that avoids anything like a romanticized view of the early sonatas such as the delightfully fresh G major, K283. On the other hand, Uchida responds with the necessary passion to the forceful, not to say *Angst*-ridden, A minor Sonata, K310. Indeed, her complete series is a remarkably fine achievement, comparable with her account of the piano concertos. The recordings were produced by Erik Smith in the Henry Wood Hall in London and offer excellent piano sound; thus an unqualified recommendation is in order for what must be one of the most valuable volumes in Philips's Complete Mozart Edition. Do not be put off by critics who suggest that these sonatas are less interesting than some other Mozart compositions, for they are fine pieces written for an instrument that he himself played and loved.

Piano Sonatas Nos 1-3 P
Ronald Brautigam *fp* Ⓕ
BIS CD835 (58 minutes: DDD). Recorded 1996

Ronald Brautigam brings uncommon energy and excitement to these sonatas, playing them with a freshness and sense of novelty that few manage to produce for music familiar to most pianists from their schoolroom days. One might find the first movement of K279 a little breathless, perhaps wanting in elegance; Brautigam doesn't always bother to round off a phrase gracefully. But the *Andante* is beautifully played, with much delicacy of timing, just the right vein of sentiment and a fine command of the textures available on the fortepiano. He is indeed masterly in all the slow movements here. In the beautiful F minor middle movement of K280 his understanding of the expressive nature of Mozart's harmony is particularly telling, and in the recapitulation especially he produces an almost Chopinesque poetry with the soft-textured left hand against a right-hand melody: let no one say this isn't Mozartian, for if you can do it as tastefully as this, on the instrument Mozart used, you may be sure Mozart would have done something like it. Mozart might have made the repeats (all of which are observed) a little more elaborate; Brautigam ornaments very little but he does play the music slightly differently second time round in details of timing and shading. There are very few recordings of these sonatas on the fortepiano, and these are extremely musical and imaginative performances.

Piano Sonatas Nos 5, 6 and 10
Maria João Pires *pf*
DG 437 791-2GH (73 minutes: DDD). Ⓕ
Recorded 1990

Maria João Pires presents these sonatas with clear yet lightly pedalled textures and an overall directness that still allows room for tonal and rhythmic flexibility – which, generally speaking, is not overdone. Largely, her playing seems to let the music speak for itself, although of course just offering the notes is not enough and what we here appreciate is the art that actually conceals art. However, one might question the occasional detail: for example, less than a minute into the G major Sonata, Pires's longish trill on the D preceding the second subject is questionable, which gives us a bar with four beats in it instead of three. The *Andante* of the same work begins with repeated Cs that seem too emphatically *staccato*, and its central section is a little overdramatized. The dance movement called *Rondeau en Polonaise* in K284 is on the slow side, though it still holds together, and the variation-form finale varies considerably in pace. Pires consistently observes repeats, including the second halves of movements (thus we get virtually every note of K283 twice), as is indicated. These are clear, commendable performances, and the kind of grace that Pires brings to this music, in which other pianists can sound a touch severe, is most appealing. The recording is pleasing and faithful.

Piano Duets

Piano Sonatas Nos 15 and 16. Fantasia, K475 (all arr Grieg)
Sviatoslav Richter, Elisabeth Leonskaja *pfs*
Teldec 4509-90825-2 (62 minutes: DDD). Ⓜ
Recorded 1993

When Grieg added an accompaniment for a second piano to Mozart's keyboard sonatas, he did it primarily with teaching in mind. It was apparently common practice in the 1880s for teachers to accompany their pupils on a second piano. But the resulting compositions soon found their way into the concert hall where, according to Grieg, 'the whole thing sounded surprisingly good'. And so it does today. In trying to 'impart to several of Mozart's sonatas a tonal effect appealing to our modern ears' Grieg left a telling little document or two on just what those late 19th-century Norwegian ears expected. If the C major 'Sonata facile' seems to sit even more sedately in the drawing-room, then it soon becomes clear that the light glinting through its windows is not a million miles away from that bouncing off the fjord waters which lap around Troldhaugen.

The C minor *Fantasia* becomes a dark salon melodrama (shades of *Bergljot*) which moves from conversation with not a little chromatic prevarication to the hanging of whimsical icicles of figuration around the major-key section. Gently exuberant harmonies cross-weave their way through the sparse trio-sonata-like textures of the opening F major before a trotting bass makes a high-stepping mountain horse of the rondo-finale. These are Mozart-Kugeln with a *bonne bouche* or two of the finest Gravadlax on the side. And if these fond tributes are good enough for Elisabeth Leonskaja and Sviatoslav Richter, who could resist tasting them?

Piano Variations

Piano Variations[a] – G, K24; D, K25; C, K179/K189*a*; G, K180/K173*c*; C, K264/K315*d*; C, K265/K300*e*; F, K352/K374 (with **Koopman**); E flat, K353K/300*f*; E flat, K354/K299*a*; F, K398/K416*e*; G, K455; A, K460/K454*a* (**Koopman**); B flat, K500; D, K573; F, K613. Minuets[c] – F, K1*d*; G/C, K1/K1*e*/K1*f*; F, K2; F, K4; F, K5; D, K94/K73*h*; D, K355/K576*b* (**Uchida**). Fantasia in D minor, K397/K385*g*[b]. Rondos[b] – D, K485; A minor, K511. Adagio in B minor, K540[b]. Gigue in G, K574b. Klavierstück in F, K33*B*c. Capriccio in C, K395/K300*g*[c]. March No 1 in C, K408/K383*e*[c]. Prelude and Fugue in C, K394/K383*a*[c]. Allegros[c] – C, K1*b*; F, K1*c*; B flat, K3; C, K5*a*; G minor, K312/K590*d*; B flat, K400/K372*a* (cpted Stadler). Suite in C, K399/K385*i*[c]. Kleine Trauermarsch in C minor, K453*a*[c]. Andante in C, K1*a*[c]. Fugue in G minor, K401/K375*e*[c] (with **Tini Mathot** *hpd*) [a]**Ingrid Haebler,** [b]**Mitsuko Uchida** *pfs* [c]**Ton Koopman** *hpd* P
Philips Mozart Edition ⑤ 422 518-2PME5 Ⓜ
(274 minutes: ADD/DDD) ●●●

These five mid-price discs offer music of fine and often superb quality in a convenient format. Of the three artists here, two are generally fine and satisfying, though the third is more controversial. Ingrid Haebler was recorded back in 1975, but the piano sound is good and little tape background remains, and her performances of the variation sets, which take up the first three discs, are delicate without cuteness, effortlessly encompassing the music's wide range of moods. Mitsuko Uchida, on the fourth disc, performs individual pieces including the two rondos and the beautiful *Adagio* in B minor in a highly refined manner, a touch over-sophisticated perhaps but still beautiful and expressive and taking full, unashamed advantage of the sound of a modern grand. By contrast, Ton Koopman's disc of minuets and other miscellaneous things is played on a harpsichord at a semitone below modern concert pitch and offers a recording of such immediacy that some will regard it as too bright. Koopman puts gusto into everything he does, but not always to good effect. However, even if grace is in short supply in his performances, they offer ample personality, and any reservations about his playing should not affect the desirability of the set as a whole.

Fantasias

Adagio in B minor, K540. Fantasias – C minor, K396/385f; D minor, K397/K385g; C minor, K475. Gigue in G, K574. Kleiner Trauermarsch in C minor, K453a. Minuet in D, K355/576b. Rondos – D, K485; F, K494; A minor, K511
Christian Zacharias *pf*
Dabringhaus und Grimm MDG340 0961-2 (67 minutes: DDD). Ⓕ

Most of Mozart's single piano pieces are the product of some special stimulus: they are not the daily bread of music-making, like the sonatas, but something rather more piquant. Christian Zacharias groups the pieces interestingly, starting with a D major-based section: the D minor *Fantasia*, the D major *Rondo*, the B minor *Adagio* and the D major *Minuet*, as if making a kind of free sonata of them. He omits the *Allegretto* portion of the *Fantasia* (on the grounds, it seems, that Mozart left it unfinished: the usual 10-bar completion is the work of a publisher – so we forgo some 40 bars of genuine Mozart), and leads directly from the *Fantasia* into the *Rondo*. Ill-advised, perhaps, as the missing *Allegretto* would have provided a much more effective release from the *Fantasia*'s tensions than the *Rondo*, which is quite different in idiom; still, he plays the *Fantasia* very urgently and eloquently, with an appropriately improvisatory feeling. And the *Rondo* is given a taut and brilliant performance, with a keen awareness of the expressive significance of the harmony. The B minor *Adagio* is one of Mozart's darkest, most inward pieces: written at a difficult moment in his life, it invites autobiographical interpretation with its sense of defeat and protest. Zacharias's sombre, subdued performance underlines such thoughts, and in the very chromatic K355 *Minuet*, too, his playing is dark and impassioned.

The C minor *Fantasia*, K396, is a rarity: a completion by Maximilian Stadler of a fragment that Mozart wrote for keyboard and violin. One can't imagine a performance much more persuasive than this; and in the authentic C minor *Fantasia* Zacharias plays beautifully, again with fire in the turbulent sections and with exquisite gentleness in the coolly reflective music such as the B flat episode. The little C minor *Funeral March* is played immediately after the *Fantasia* (Mozart's evident original intention was to follow it with the C minor Sonata, K475). The K494 *Rondo* – more familiar in its revised version as finale of the K533 Sonata – is played in a more relaxed manner; in the A minor *Rondo*, K511, Zacharias beautifully captures the 'sentimental' tone and provides a performance of great delicacy and refinement, again drawing the full depth of expression from Mozart's harmonic subtleties.

Concert Arias

Concert Arias – Ah! se in ciel, benigne stelle, K538; Vorrei spiegarvi, oh Dio!, K418; No, no che non sei capace, K419; Se tutti i mali miei, K83/K73*p*; Popoli di Tessaglia! … Io non chiedo, eterni Dei, K316/K300*b*; Mia speranza adorata … Ah, non sai qual pena sia, K416; Alcandro, lo confesso … Non so d'onde viene, K294; Ma che vi fece, o stelle … Sperai vicino il lido, K368
Natalie Dessay *sop* **Orchestra of the Opéra de Lyon / Theodor Guschlbauer**
EMI CDC5 55386-2 (64 minutes: DDD). Texts and translations included. Recorded 1994 Ⓕ ●

Natalie Dessay's range extends upward far into the leger lines yet without incurring breathiness of a pallid coloration in the lower notes. She has a sylph's grace and lightness, and yet the timbre or character of her voice is thoroughly human. The profusion of scales and more intricate passagework common in some degree to all these pieces finds in her an unostentatious virtuoso, mind and breath giving well-regulated support, and a sensitive feeling for phrase and line making good musical sense throughout. Where vehemence and a dramatic quality of voice are in demand, as in the opening of *Popoli di Tessaglia*, we can find some reassurance in their absence because at least the young singer does not try to force an effect. In less strenuous attack, as in *No, no che non sei capace*, she conveys the energy of a determined spirit yet still has some way to develop as an expressive artist. The more sorrowful and tender phrases of *Se tutti i mali miei*, for example, evoke only a mild response in her. Occasionally, too, Dessay's purity forfeits normal resonance and for what seems to be an involuntary note or two the voice flutes with a kind of disembodied hollowness. An instance occurs just before the second part of *Vorrei spiegarvi*, yet this is such a lovely performance, so graceful in its leisurely interplay of voice and instruments, that grumbling really is out of order. Orchestra, conductor and recorded sound all make their contributions.

Litaniae ...

Mass in C, K257, 'Credo'. Litaniae de venerabili altaris sacramento, K243 **P**

Angela Maria Blasi *sop* **Elisabeth von Magnus** *contr* **Deon van der Walt** *ten* **Alistair Miles** *bass* **Arnold Schoenberg Choir; Vienna Concentus Musicus / Nikolaus Harnoncourt**

Teldec Das Alte Werk 9031-72304-2 (61 minutes: DDD). Notes, texts and translations included. Ⓕ
Recorded 1991

The *Litaniae de venerabili altaris sacramento* of 1775 has powerful claims to be reckoned the finest of Mozart's church works before the C minor Mass and Requiem; but it has never quite had the recognition it deserves. Or the performance: until now, that is. It is clearly a deeply felt work, from the grave, warm opening of the 'Kyrie', through the imposing 'Verbum caro factum' and the graceful 'Hostia' that succeeds it, the 'Tremendum' with its almost Verdian menace and the appealing 'Dulcissum convivium' (a soprano aria with soft textures supplied by flutes and bassoons), the highly original 'Viaticum' and the resourcefully and lengthily developed 'Pignus' to the 'Agnus', a beautiful soprano aria with solo writing for flute, oboe and cello. The performance here under Nikolaus Harnoncourt rightly sees no need to apologize for the stylistic diversity of the work. The issue is made still more attractive by the inclusion of a Mass setting of the same year, one of Mozart's most inventive and original in its textures and its treatment of words. Altogether this must be counted as a very attractive record.

Masses

No 1 in G, K49/K47*d*, 'Missa brevis'; **No 2** in D minor, K65/K61*a*; 'Missa brevis'; **No 16** in C, K317, **'Coronation'; No 18** in C minor, K427/K417a, **'Great'; No 19** in D minor, K626, **Requiem**

Missae breves – G, K49/K47*d*[a]; D minor, K65/K61*a*[b]; D, K194/K186*h*a; C, K220/K196*b*b, 'Spatzenmesse' **P**

[a]**Christine Schäfer,** [b]**Angela Maria Blasi** *sops* [a]**Ingeborg Danz,** [b]**Elisabeth von Magnus** *mezzos* [a]**Kurt Azesberger,** [b]**Uwe Heilmann** *tens* [a]**Oliver Widmer** *bar* [b]**Franz-Josef Selig** *bass* **Arnold Schoenberg Choir; Vienna Concentus Musicus / Nikolaus Harnoncourt**

Teldec Das Alte Werk 3984-21818-2 (69 minutes: DDD). Texts and translations included. Ⓕ
Recorded 1994

These youthful Masses, composed between 1768 and 1775, are among Mozart's most concise – K65, in particular, is a *Missa brevis* with a vengeance. Brevity was *de rigueur* in the Salzburg liturgy and we can hardly blame Mozart for rattling unceremoniously through the long texts of the *Gloria* and *Credo*. With minimal scope for musical development, much of the writing in the two earlier works, especially, is perfunctory – the 12-year-old composer dutifully going through the motions. As so often in late 18th-century Masses, the central mystery of the 'Et incarnatus est – Crucifixus' prompts a more individual musical response; and the *Benedictus* of K65 is a touching little duet for soprano and alto soloists based, surprisingly, on a descending chromatic motif, a traditional trope of lamentation. For all the conventional bustle of their faster movements, the two later Masses are more varied in their textures (though, *pace* the booklet-note, elaborate counterpoint is still at a premium) and more memorable in their ideas. Both the settings of the *Benedictus* have the grace and airiness of 18th-century Austrian churches. But the high point in each work is the *Agnus Dei*, especially that of K194, with its harmonic poignancy and dramatic alternations of solo and chorus. Occasionally Nikolaus Harnoncourt's direction can sound over-insistent – in, say, the *Kyrie* of K49, with its almost aggressive *marcato* articulation. But for the most part he chooses apt, mobile tempos, keeps the rhythms buoyant and characterizes vividly without betraying the music's blitheness and innocence.

The playing of the Concentus Musicus is polished and responsive and the Arnold Schoenberg Choir do all that is asked. Both individually and in consort the soloists make the most of their limited opportunities, with delectable tone and phrasing from the two sopranos, Christine Schäfer and Angela Maria Blasi. The recorded balance is excellent, catching Harnoncourt's sharply etched orchestral detail while giving ample presence to the choir.

Coronation Mass. Vesperae solennes de confessore in C, K339. Epistle Sonata in C, K278/K271*e* **P**

Emma Kirkby *sop* **Catherine Robbin** *mez* **John Mark Ainsley** *ten* **Michael George** *bass* **Winchester Cathedral Choir; Winchester Quiristers Academy of Ancient Music / Christopher Hogwood** with **Alastair Ross** *org*

L'Oiseau-Lyre 436 585-2OH (54 minutes: DDD). Texts and translations included.
Recorded 1990 Ⓕ

It is difficult to think of many recordings of Mozart's church music that so happily captures its character – the particular mixture of confidence, jubilation and contemplation – as Hogwood's. His unfussy direction, broad phrasing, lively but generally unhurried tempos and happy details of timing serve splendidly in the *Coronation* Mass, the finest of Mozart's completed mass settings; the solemnity of the *Kyrie*, the fine swing of the *Gloria* and the energy of the *Credo*, with due pause for its rapt moment at the 'Et incarnatus', all these come over with due effect. Arguably the 'Osanna' is rather quick, but its jubilation is splendid. And the sweetness of the *Benedictus* is ravishing.

Not more so, however, than the *Agnus*, for there, at a decidedly slow tempo, Hogwood allows Emma Kirkby to make the most of this very sensuous music, which she duly most beautifully does. The soloists are altogether an excellent team, with two refined voices in the middle and Michael George a firm and sturdy bass. The inclusion of the K278 Epistle Sonata is a happy notion. The *Vesperae solennes de confessore* is a setting of the five vesper psalms and the *Magnificat*, made in 1780, a year after the Mass, for some church feast in Salzburg. With admirable singing from the choir and a spacious recording with exceptionally good stereo separation that properly conveys the ecclesiastical ambience, this is a disc to treasure.

Masses – Coronation[a]; C minor[b]; Requiem[c]
Helen Donath, [b]Heather Harper *sops* **[a]Gillian Knight, [c]Yvonne Minton** *mezzos* **Ryland Davies** *ten* **[ab]Stafford Dean, [c]Gerd Nienstedt** *basses* ac
John Alldis Choir; London Symphony [b]Chorus and [ab]Orchestra, cBBC Symphony Orchestra / Sir Colin Davis
Philips Duo ② 438 800-2PM2 (135 minutes: ADD). Ⓜ
Recorded [ab]1971, c1967

These seem rather old-fashioned performances nowadays, but they are vigorous and full of conviction and many readers will find them wholly sympathetic. The *Coronation* Mass has a splendidly imposing start, and the two long movements, the *Gloria* and *Credo*, are done with plenty of spirit at rather rapid tempos: the effect is brilliant and affirmative, though with these rather large forces it does seem a shade driven.

The 'Osanna' is also decidedly speedy. There is some really lovely, heartfelt solo singing from Helen Donath, especially in the *Agnus Dei*. The soloists are recorded unnaturally forward, giving the impression of their being very close with a big choir in the distance. The orchestral balance doesn't seem quite right, either, with the trombones in particular too prominent at times. Davis's reading of the C minor Mass is very much more weighty; his interpretations certainly accentuate the difference between these two works, only three or four years apart. The sombre, intense opening can readily be justified, but the heavy 'Domine Deus' and the very slow 'Et incarnatus', beautifully sung though it is, again by Donath, do seem exaggerated, and even if the 'Quoniam' is quickish it seems somewhat ponderously *legato*. There is certainly a feeling for the grandeur of the work and also its drama (listen for example to the *Sanctus*), and the sturdy, forthright 'Benedictus' is effective too.

Donath excels again in the 'Laudamus te' (her semiquaver runs neat and crystalline) and her duetting with Heather Harper in the 'Laudamus te' is very enjoyable, although the voices do not really match well: there are of course arguments either way, for blend or contrast, in music with such close interplay. The performance of the Requiem is also available on a single CD and it is one that has been much, and justly, recommended. It is certainly a rather operatic reading, with much drama and passion and eloquence, and it is very musical and compelling, though some may feel that the variations in tempo and the general consciousness of effect are not what they want in an ecclesiastical work. Again, there is sure and strong choral singing, and Donath shines once more as the soprano, with Ryland Davies in his best voice in the tenor music. These are not, then, the versions of these works that one would necessarily choose first of all, but they are musical and persuasive and, at a moderate price, well worth considering.

C minor Mass (ed Maunder) **P**
Arleen Auger, Lynne Dawson *sops* **John Mark Ainsley** *ten* **David Thomas** *bass* **Winchester Cathedral Choir; Winchester Quiristers; Academy of Ancient Music / Christopher Hogwood**
L'Oiseau-Lyre Florilegium 425 528-2OH
(51 minutes: DDD). Text and translation included. Ⓜ
Recorded 1988

Mozart left unfinished the work that ought to have been the choral masterpiece of his early Viennese years but there is enough of it to make up nearly an hour's music – music that is sometimes sombre, sometimes florid, sometimes jubilant. Christopher Hogwood avoids any charge of emotional detachment in his steady and powerful opening *Kyrie*, monumental in feeling, dark in tone; and he brings ample energy to the big, bustling choruses of the *Gloria* – and its long closing fugue is finely sustained. The clarity and ring of the boys' voices serve him well in these numbers. There is a strong solo team, headed by the late Arleen Auger in radiant, glowing voice and, as usual, singing with refined taste; Lynne Dawson joins her in the duets, John Mark Ainsley too in the trio. But this is essentially a 'soprano mass' – Mozart wrote it, after all, with the voice of his new wife (and perhaps thoughts of the much superior one of her sister Aloysia) in his mind – and Auger, her voice happily stealing in for the first time in the lovely 'Christe', excels in the florid and expressive music of the 'Et incarnatus' (where Richard Maunder has supplied fuller string parts than usual, perhaps fuller than Mozart would have done had he finished the work). Hogwood directs with his usual spirit and clarity.

C minor Mass (ed Eder)
Arleen Auger, Barbara Bonney *sops* **Hans Peter Blochwitz** *ten* **Robert Holl** *bass* **Berlin Radio Chorus; Berlin Philharmonic Orchestra / Claudio Abbado**
Sony Classical SK46671 (53 minutes: DDD). Text and Ⓕ
translation included. Recorded 1990 ●

'Comfortable' is not a fashionable word to use by way of praise; 'disturbing' is. However, Abbado's is comfortable. No doubt part of the warmth is due to another unfashionable feature, the use of a large orchestra not playing on period instruments. That it plays magnificently and that the choir is a particularly fine one will have something to do with it too. Perhaps the balance of the recording overweights the orchestral bass, and a little less reverberance might not come amiss in the hall acoustic, but these are matters of degree, not disqualifying objections. Rather similarly, when it comes to the style of the performance, one might prefer a more jolly, a-hunting-we-will-go bounce for the rhythms of the *Credo*, but again this is a matter of degree for Abbado is not lacking in vitality or colour. Of course if you take the view that the 'Qui tollis' should be like sitting on spikes you will find Abbado too well cushioned and will prefer an alternative version. But there is no feeling of superficiality or blandness in Abbado, and the double choir is well recorded to carry weight and to enforce the pictorial effect of the music. In tempo, too, he judges well. Abbado's singers are well forward and very distinct. Abbado brings a vigorous touch to the *Kyrie* without impairing the profundity. The other great strength is the excellence of the two sopranos. With the happy emulation of the seraphim they place their high As and B flats, their semiquaver runs and long held notes in the 'Domine Deus'. Auger has warmth, Bonney brightness, and she sings the 'Et incarnatus est' with blissfully assured control. There have been many lovely accounts of this work on disc, and few better than here.

C minor Mass (ed Schmitt/Gardiner)
Sylvia McNair *sop* **Diana Montague** *mez*
Anthony Rolfe Johnson *ten* **Cornelius Hauptmann** *bass* **Monteverdi Choir; English Baroque Soloists / John Eliot Gardiner**
Philips 420 210-2PH (54 minutes: DDD). Ⓕ
Text and translation included. ○

Writers on Mozart sometimes take him to task for the alleged mixture of style in the C minor Mass, in particular the use of florid, 'operatic' solo writing amidst all the severe ecclesiastical counterpoint. To object is to misunderstand the nature of Mozart's religion, but it takes a performance as stylistically accomplished as this one to make the point in practice. The usual stumbling-block is the 'Et incarnatus', with its richly embellished solo line and its wind obbligatos. Sung as it is here, by Sylvia McNair, beautifully refined in detail, it is indeed passionate, but passionately devout. McNair is deeply affecting in the 'Christe', taken quite spaciously and set in a measured Kyrie of great cumulative power which also has some fine, clean singing from the Monteverdi Choir.

As with Gardiner's version of the *Requiem* one might wish for the sound of a boys' choir (why go to the trouble of having authentic instruments if you then use unauthentic voices?) but the bright, forward tone of his sopranos is very persuasive. The music is all strongly characterized: the 'Gloria' jubilant, the 'Qui tollis' grandly elegiac with its solemn, inexorable march rhythm and its dying phrases echoed between the choirs, the 'Credo' full of vitality. Some of the 'Cum sancto spiritu' fugue is too heavily accented, though. A confident recommendation.

Requiem (cptd Süssmayr)
Sylvia McNair *sop* **Carolyn Watkinson** *contr*
Francisco Araiza *ten* **Robert Lloyd** *bass*
Chorus and Academy of St Martin in the Fields / Sir Neville Marriner
Philips 432 087-2PH (50 minutes: DDD). Text and translation included. Recorded 1990 Ⓕ ○

Mozart's Requiem may not be wholly Mozart's, as we all know: but performers certainly show no reservations in the power or the conviction they bring to its music, whoever it may be by. This one under Sir Neville Marriner is among the noblest and most powerful of them all; an unusually thoughtful and careful reading. The first thing that strikes you is the passionate nature of the choral singing, right from the start: the Academy chorus sings the beginning almost as if it were a personal protest against death, and the chromaticisms and dissonances of the 'Requiem aeternam' make their due effect. And the 'Kyrie', taken at a vigorous pace, has great energy. The dynamics in the 'Dies irae' are strongly made, almost exaggerated; there is a solemn 'Rex tremendae majestatis', with sharply dotted rhythms, a slow 'Lacrimosa' with detailed shaping, a lively 'Domine Jesu' and an 'Agnus Dei' so grandly sombre that it emerges as the expressive climax of the whole work.

There is superlative solo singing, too – Robert Lloyd in dark and noble voice in the 'Tuba mirum', Sylvia McNair as moving as always with her beautiful sound and refinement of nuance, in that number, in the 'Benedictus' and in the 'Lux aeterna'. The inner voices are quiet satisfactory although Francisco Araiza's expressive taste is possibly not quite in line with that of the others. Possibly the slowish tempos do not work quite so well for the solo ensemble numbers as they do for the choruses: the 'Recordare' seems a shade static, however refined the shaping of the music, and perhaps so too does the 'Benedictus'.

The version used is billed as Süssmayr's, but that is not entirely the whole truth: for example, his trombone parts are sometimes omitted (as in part of the 'Tuba mirum' and the 'Benedictus') and there is a basset horn chromaticism omitted in the 'Agnus' – though that may be simply a mistake. Marriner's Requiem is a powerful and distinctive interpretation of the work: a consistent, considered view of it which has been faithfully and carefully carried through.

Requiem. Ave verum corpus in D, K618 **P**
Anna Maria Panzarella *sop* **Nathalie Stutzmann** *contr* **Christoph Prégardien** *ten* **Nathan Berg** *bass*
Les Arts Florissants / William Christie
Erato 0630-10697-2 (54 minutes: DDD). Ⓜ
Texts and translations included. Recorded 1994 ○

Les Arts Florissants provides a substantial, dramatic reading: the tempo for the 'Requiem aeternam' is slow, but malleable, and Christie is ready to make the most of the changes in orchestral colour or choral texture and indeed to dramatize the music to the utmost. Clearly he has little truck with any notion that this is an austere piece: he sees it as operatic, almost romantic – and the result is very compelling. There are surprising things: 'Quantus tremor', in a very weighty account of the 'Dies irae', for example, is hushed rather than terrifying; the 'Recordare' is slow to the point of stickiness; there are rather mannered *crescendos* in the *Sanctus*; and often cadences are drawn out, for example in the 'Hostias'. The powerful choruses of the Sequence are imposingly done, and the grave 'Lacrimosa' wonderfully catches the special significance not only of the music itself but also of the fact that this is the moment where Mozart's last autograph trails off. The choral singing is sharply etched and generally distinguished: the choir gives a vigorous yet finely dovetailed *Kyrie* fugue and the 'Quam olim Abrahae' is splendidly sturdy. Although the solo singing is not uniformly outstanding the soprano's melting tone is sometimes very appealing, and Prégardien is an excellent stylist; the *Benedictus* is particularly impressive, very shapely and refined. In short, this is a reading full of character and imaginative ideas, very much a conscious modern interpretation of the work and very finely executed. The disc is completed by perhaps the only piece which can reasonably follow the Requiem, the *Ave verum corpus*, in a slow, hushed, rather romantic reading that is undeniably moving.

Requiem. Kyrie in D minor, K341/K368*a* **P**

Sibylla Rubens *sop* **Annette Markert** *contr*
Ian Bostridge *ten* **Hanno Müller-Brachmann** *bar*
La Chapelle Royale; Collegium Vocale
Orchestra of the Champs-Elysées, Paris /
Philippe Herreweghe
Harmonia Mundi HMC90 1620 (54 minutes: DDD).
Texts and translations included. Ⓕ
Recorded live in 1996

This is a direct, unaffected recording of the Süssmayr version of the Requiem, marked by its vigorous choral singing and its strong rhythmic underpinning. Herreweghe is not afraid of slowish, more traditional tempos and his conducting provides its own justification. The opening 'Requiem aeternam' moves with deliberation and a firm, steady tread; so in a different way does the 'Dies irae', but with no lack of energy. The momentum of the 'Rex tremendae majestatis' is quite out of the ordinary; in the 'Confutatis' Herreweghe makes the most of the contrast between the sharp rhythms of the men's voices and the female angelic choir, softening it, however, by easing the tempo from one to the other. The 'Lacrimosa' is unusually impassioned. There is a finely energetic 'Quam olim Abrahae' fugue, in which the Chapelle Royale and Collegium Vocale sing cleanly and vigorously, as they also do in the *Kyrie* fugue. These are of course female sopranos and altos, but steady and concentrated in tone; perhaps here and there the choral sound seems a shade pallid. The clarity of the recording is a delight in the big contrapuntal choruses. The solo quartet too comes across with unusual definition, for example in the 'Recordare' (where there is some passionate singing from them, coupled with pleasantly reedy basset-horn tone) and in the *Benedictus*, which is done with an agreeable flow. Individually, the soloists do some pleasing things and all do well in the 'Tuba mirum'. While not perhaps the most arresting Requiem in the catalogue, this is certainly a very accomplished version, especially for Herreweghe's direction, with its firmness and resilience and its clear sense of shape and direction. The coupling of the fine D minor *Kyrie*, now widely taken to be a relatively late work (in spite of its K number), in a shapely reading, is a happy choice.

Requiem. Symphony No 25 **H**

Lisa della Casa *sop* **Ira Malaniuk** *contr* **Anton Dermota** *ten* **Cesare Siepi** *bass*
Vienna State Opera Concert Choir; Vienna Philharmonic Orchestra / Bruno Walter
Orfeo D'Or mono C430961B (76 minutes: ADD). Ⓕ
Recorded live in 1956

Listening to this is a moving experience. This was Walter's farewell to a festival with which he had been closely associated over 30 years: he conducted there from 1925 to 1937 after which he withdrew because of Austria's Anschluss with Nazi Germany. He returned again in 1946 and off and on, mostly conducting Mahler, until this final meeting with his beloved Mozart. Yet there is nothing sentimental here from a conductor nearing his 80th birthday. As a contemporary critic (Karl Schumann) put it, the little G minor Symphony is given as an 'eerie vision of night and suffering' with consolation coming only in the *Andante*. Of the other work Schumann commented: 'Walter understands the Requiem logically as Catholic church music, as a musical interpretation of the liturgy' and so banishes thoughts about a 'swansong elegy'.

The performance is taut and closely worked. Listen to the counterpoint of 'Quam olim Abrahae' and you will hear the sharp rhythms that characterize the whole. Even so, Walter's beloved VPO displays its warm, ethereal string tone as circumstances allow. Four of the leading soloists of the day contribute positively. Siepi inhabits the bass-line as to the manner born, and della Casa provides tones fit for the contemplation of heavenly matters. In-between Malaniuk's soothing mezzo and Dermota's plaintive tenor are heard to advantage. The one drawback of the performance is the unsteady tone of the Vienna Opera chorus's sopranos. But as a whole, the choral singing is as dedicated as the rest. The recording is in well-focused mono. This was the best of Walter's Requiems and so worth an hour or so of anyone's time.

Opera arias

Cecilia Bartoli
Le nozze di Figaro – Non so più; Voi che sapete; Giunse alfin il momento ... Deh vieni. Così fan tutte – E'amore un ladroncello. Don Giovanni – Vedrai, cariNo La clemenza di Tito – Parto, parto; Deh, per questo; Ecco il punto, o Vitellia ... Non piu di fiori. Concert Arias – Chi sa, chi sa, qual sia, K582; Alma grande e nobil core, K578; Ch'io mi scordi di te?, K505
Cecilia Bartoli *mez* **András Schiff** *pf* **Peter Schmidtl** *basset cl/basset hn* **Vienna Chamber Orchestra / György Fischer**
Decca 430 513-2DH (58 minutes: DDD). Texts and translations included. Recorded 1989-90 Ⓕ

Mozart wrote some of his most appealing music for the mezzo-soprano voice with the roles of Cherubino and Susanna in *Le nozze di Figaro*, Dorabella in *Così fan tutte* and Zerlina in *Don Giovanni* each boasting at least one memorable aria. Alongside these this disc includes a handful of concert arias including *Ch'io mi scordi di te?* which was written for the farewell performance of the great mezzo Nancy Storace with Mozart playing the concertante piano role. Here with as innate an interpreter of Mozart's piano writing as András Schiff and a voice so remarkably self-assured as Cecilia Bartoli's the electricity of that first, historic performance seems almost to be recreated. And, here as elsewhere, György Fischer directs the splendid Vienna Chamber Orchestra with disarming sensitivity while the recording is wonderfully warm and vibrant.

Cecilia Bartoli boasts a voice of extraordinary charm and unassuming virtuosity: her vocal characterizations would be the envy of the finest actresses and her intuitive singing is in itself a sheer delight. But she also brings to these arias a conviction and understanding of the subtleties of the language which only a native Italian could. Listen to the subtle nuances of 'Voi che sapete', the depth of understanding behind Dorabella's seemingly frivolous 'E'amore un ladroncello'; these are not mere performances, but interpretations which cut to the very soul of the music. No Mozart lover should be without this CD.

Cecilia Bartoli

Così fan tutte – In uomini, in soldati; Temerari! ... Come scoglio; Ei parte ... Per pietà, ben mio. Le nozze di Figaro – E Susanna non vien! ... Dove sono; Giunse alfin il momento ... Al desio (K577*a*). Don Giovanni – Batti, batti, o bel Masetto; In quali eccessi ... Mi tradì quell' alma ingrata. Davidde penitente, K469 – Lunghi le cure ingrate. Exsultate, jubilate, K165/K158*a*

Cecilia Bartoli *mez* **Vienna Chamber Orchestra / György Fischer**

Decca 443 452-2DH (61 minutes: DDD). Texts and translations included. Recorded 1993 Ⓕ ●

There are few Italian mezzos, or sopranos for that matter, who sing a lot of Mozart and Bartoli's very Italian characteristics are immediately identifiable: brilliance of execution, vitality of words, sharpness of mind. She tears into the recitative before Donna Elvira's 'Mi tradì' with a blistering fury that leaves most interpreters of the role standing and has no problems with the *fioriture* of the aria itself. Her Fiordiligi has the bite for 'Come scoglio', but comparisons with a variety of lyric sopranos show up a want of depth to the tone, both here and in 'Per pietà'. Her Countess delivers her lines with appropriate aristocratic weight, though one senses her natural temperament being suppressed with difficulty. However much she tries to disguise herself, the real Bartoli is likely to pop her head out.

There are unlikely to be any complaints about her effervescent Despina or Zerlina, both portrayals for which she has stage experience. In the concert hall she is also a spirited interpreter of *Exsultate, jubilate*. From the opening line Bartoli makes other singers seem bland by comparison, getting the Latin words to tingle with a sense of elation that only an Italian-speaker would dare. The orchestral sound might be more firmly focused (the sound picture in 'Batti, batti' has the solo cello close, while the wind struggle to be heard from some deep recess) but Fischer accompanies his soloist with energy and tact.

Natalie Dessay 🅿

Ascanio in Alba, K111 – Dal tuo gentil sembiante. Die Entführung aus dem Serail, K384 – Welcher Wechsel; Traurigkeit ward mir zum Lose; Martern aller Arten. Idomeneo, rè di Creta, K366 – Solitudini amiche; Zeffiretti lusinghieri. Lucio Silla, K135 – Vanne, t'affreta; Ah se il crudel periglio. Zaide, K344 – Ruhe sanft, mein holdes Leben; Tiger! Wetze nur die Klauen. Die Zauberflöte, K620 – O zittre nicht, mein lieber Sohn!; Zum Leiden; Der Hölle Rache; Ach, ich fühl's

Natalie Dessay *sop* **Orchestra of the Age of Enlightenment / Louis Langrée**

Virgin Classics VC5 45447-2 (67 minutes: DDD). Texts and translations included. Recorded 2000 Ⓕ ●●●

Dessay, as her EMI album of French operatic arias amply demonstrated, is an acclaimed star in Vienna, Salzburg, the New York Met and, of course, the French capital, where she is something close to a cult figure. A Mozart album from this delightful singer was obviously overdue, for Dessay has cornered the market in the world's poshest operatic addresses – except Covent Garden and Glyndebourne, of course – as the Queen of Night, whose two arias frame this recital programme. She can be heard in the role complete in William Christie's 1996 recording of *Die Zauberflöte* for Erato, whose 'kind permission' has been sought and acknowledged by Virgin for their re-recording of the Queen's entrance scena and Vengeance aria. Aided by Louis Langrée's marginally faster tempos, Dessay's 'star-blazing' accounts of these famous show-stoppers sound even more vehement than before – the angry staccatos of 'Der Hölle Rache' spat out with blinding accuracy and the *in altissimo* Fs effortlessly, cleanly attained. Unfortunately, the aria's impact is somewhat dulled by coming at the beginning, rather than at the end, of the recorded sequence. The microphone also catches a slight hardening of tone, bordering on shrillness, which is largely absent from the rest of her singing here.

Dessay's light, girlish timbre might not immediately suggest regal imperiousness, but she brings real depth of feeling to 'Zum Leiden bin ich auserkoren' and its magnificent recitative 'O zittre nicht' on the concluding track. Between these mainstay arias of what the Germans call her Parade-Rolle, she selects an enterprising mix of the familiar – a delicate, fragile, touching 'Ach, ich fühl's' suggesting she may soon hanker after the role of the Queen's daughter, Pamina – and the virtually unknown – the fawn's charming but virtuosic aria, 'Dal tuo gentil sembiante' from *Ascanio in Alba* (the *festa teatrale* written for the wedding of the Archduke Ferdinand to Maria Beatrice of Modena, in

Milan, 1771). The instrumental quality of her florid technique is put to marvellous use here, as it is in Giunia's moment of truth in Act 2 of *Lucio Silla*, 'Ah se il crudel periglio'. Perhaps in the theatre one would crave a richer voice, but Dessay colours her tone so effectively that the aria touches all the right emotional spots.

The same is true of Konstanze's back-to-back vocal ordeals from Act 2 of *Die Entführung aus dem Serail*: 'Traurigkeit' is wonderfully expressive, and even though some may prefer a grander sound for this role her technique and musicianship are simply staggering in 'Martern aller Artern'; she gives us the *concertante* aria in full, opening up the cuts Mozart himself made when he realised he had sacrificed the drama to the agile throat of Caterina Cavalieri.

It's intelligent programming to give us two of the arias Mozart wrote for his prototype Konstanze in his unfinished seraglio opera now known by the name of its heroine, Zaide. The gorgeous 'Ruhe sanft' has become a popular favourite, largely thanks to Lucia Popp's wonderful Decca recording with István Kertész in the early 1970s. Dessay's timbre lacks the lamented Czech soprano's creaminess and warmth, but she is so musical and phrases the long, rapturous lines of this celebrated number so exquisitely that Mozartians will be glad of a modern alternative. For contrast, she gives us one of Zaide's less frequently heard solos, the defiant 'Tiger! Wetze nur die Klauen' – and sounds as if her own claws are as sharp as any tiger's. Dessay completes the programme with Ilia's ravishing garden aria, 'Zeffiretti, lusinghieri', and does it captivatingly with limpid, fresh tone and long-breathed melismata.

Langrée has recently garnered glowing credentials as a Mozartian at Glyndebourne, and his beautifully conceived and theatrical accompaniments here demonstrate why. In addition, the period instruments of the Orchestra of the Age of Enlightenment complement the astringency of the soprano's tone.

Renée Fleming

Le nozze di Figaro – Giunse alfin il momento ... Deh, vieni; Giunse alfin il momento ... Al desio di chi t'adora, K577*a*. Don Giovanni – In quali eccessi ... Mi tradì. Die Entführung aus dem Serail – Ach, ich liebte. Il rè pastore – L'amerò, sarò costantea. Die Zauberflöte – Ach, ich fühl's. La finta giardiniera – Geme la tortorella; Crudel, Oh Dio! fermate; Ah, dal pianto, dal singhiozzo. Zaïde – Ruhe sanft, mein holdes Leben. Il sogno di Scipione – Lieve son al par del vento. Nehmt meinen Dank, ihr holden Gönner, K383

Renée Fleming *sop* [a]**Krista Bennion Feeney** *vn* **Orchestra of St Luke's / Sir Charles Mackerras**

Decca 452 602-2DH (60 minutes: DDD). Ⓕ
Recorded 1995

Renée Fleming's exceptionally beautiful voice has a depth to it which first reminds you of de los Angeles in her prime and then, in the context of *Le nozze di Figaro*, of the mistress rather than the maid. It also points up the slight oddity that as regards tessitura (or the 'lie' of the voice) the two roles differ very little, while the voice-characters are nevertheless quite distinct. It suggests also good reasoning on the part of Fleming, who is quoted in an article on the disc as saying 'I wanted to do this high-lying Mozart before it's too late.' She does indeed mingle 'high-lying Mozart' with the medium. In several items she faces the heights and takes them with zest and success. The Germanic use of head-voice in 'Ach, ich liebte' (*Die Entführung*), for instance, is forsworn in favour of a full-bodied voice in the upper notes. In La Fortuna's aria from *Il sogno di Scipione* not only are the C major scales similarly brave and full, but the cadenza is topped with a *staccato* E and G, both *in alt*. But this is the record of more than a singer. Mackerras and the St Luke's Orchestra contribute greatly towards its distinction. The playing of the big scene for Sandrina in *La finta gardiniera*, for instance, is very special indeed. In both the *Zauberflöte* and *Zaïde* arias a fast tempo is chosen, with a loss of the more luxurious loveliness and a gain in 18th-century refinement. In everything, orchestral parts as well as the voice, the sound is suited to the sense, and both provide plentiful delight.

Véronique Gens

Le nozze di Figaro – Non so più cosa son; Porgi, amor. Don Giovanni – Batti, batti; In quali eccessi ... Mi tradì. Così fan tutte – Temerari ... Come scoglio; Ei parte ... Per pietà, ben mio. La clemenza di Tito – Deh per questo istante; Ecco il punto ... Non più di fiori vaghe catene. Oh, temerario Arbace! ... Per quel paterno amplesso, K79/K79*d*. Ch'io mi scordi di te ... Non temer, amato bene, K505*a*

Véronique Gens *sop* **Orchestra of the Age of Enlightenment / Ivor Bolton** with **Melvyn Tan** *fp*

Virgin Classics Veritas VC5 45319-2
(59 minutes: DDD). Ⓕ
Texts and translations included. Recorded 1998 ●

Véronique Gens is one of the most engaging and stylish Mozart sopranos around, as this sampler of her art confirms. Her early training has made her a particularly happy collaborator with the Orchestra of the Age of Enlightenment. Under the exacting baton of Ivor Bolton, they show sharp and eager teeth to match her own highly-strung recitative in 'In quali eccessi'. And this Donna Anna demonstrates more than one-dimensional *Angst* as the orchestra's wind soloists breathe in sympathy with every moment of *palpitando* in Gens's own supple phrasing. There's a similar focus on the emotional potential of breath in a 'Non so più' whose fierce frustration flies out of eloquent consonants. Steady control of breath and tone bring a moving poise to 'Non più di fiori', where Vitellia's horrified introspection finds empathy in Lesley Schatzberger's basset-horn obbligato. And as Sesto, Gens moulds the moist clay of some of Mozart's most beautiful melodic contours in 'Deh, per questo istante'. Two concert arias circle in the orbit of that earlier great *opera seria*, *Idomeneo*: Idamante's 'Non temer', in which Gens sighs poignantly with the dying fall of Melvyn Tan's sweetly articulated fortepiano; and the youthful Arbace aria 'Per quel paterno amplesso', to whose lilting farewell Gens brings eloquent breadth. There's her Countess and Zerlina to enjoy as well and the two exquisitely sculpted and sparingly but powerfully ornamented arias from *Così fan tutte*.

Gundula Janowitz

Ah, lo previdi ... Ah, t'invola, K272. A questo seno ... Or che il cielo, K374. Alma grande e nobil core, K578. Grabmusik, K42*a*/K35*a* – Betracht dies Herz und frage mich. Vado, ma dove? oh Dei!, K583. Bella mia fiamma ... Resta, o cara, K528. Misera! dove son ... Ah! non son io, K369

Gundula Janowitz *sop* **Vienna Symphony Orchestra / Wilfried Boettcher**

DG The Originals 449 723-2GOR (61 minutes: ADD). Ⓜ
Texts and translations included. Recorded 1966

An 'original' is exactly what this disc is, as it reproduces Janowitz's first solo recital record, issued in 1967. Listening back, we can marvel not just at the purity of tone and silken vocal line, but also a refinement of style that marks out a fully formed artist. Highlights include a delicate *Vado, ma dove?* and a performance of *Bella mia fiamma* which lights up the music with the subtlest of colours from within. Some recitatives might have been more dramatic, but Boettcher and the Vienna Symphony Orchestra provide alert accompaniment. There is also a bonus: the original LP did not have room for the ravishing G minor lament 'Betracht dies Herz' from the *Grabmusik*, K42, and that is issued for the first time here, a minor treasure in its own right.

Sumi Jo

Die Entführung aus dem Serail – Martern aller Arten. Die Zauberflöte – Ach, ich fühl's. Vorrei spiegarvi, oh Dio, K418. No, che non sei capace, K419. Ah, se in ciel, benigne stelle, K538. Il rè pastore – L'amerò, sarò costante. Voi avete un cor fedele, K217. Chi sà, chi sà, qual sia, K582. Le nozze di Figaro – Deh vieni, non tardar. Der Schauspieldirektor – Bester Jüngling. Nehmt meinen Dank, ihr holden Gönner, K383. Schon lacht der holde Frühling, K580

Sumi Jo *sop* **English Chamber Orchestra / Kenneth Montgomery**

Erato 0630-14637-2 (65 minutes: DDD). Texts and Ⓕ
translations included. Recorded 1995

Sumi Jo's disc naturally begs comparison with Renée Fleming's (reviewed above). Both singers give delightful performances, and if a contrast claims attention it lies rather more in the instrumental work and perhaps that of the conductors. In 'Ach, ich fühl's' (*Die Zauberflöte*) Mackerras, conducting for Fleming, takes an unusually fast tempo, while Kenneth Montgomery, still quick compared with what became the norm, avoids the suspicion of didacticism. Interestingly, it is Sumi Jo who forfeits elegance in the difficult high run on 'Herzen', while Fleming, at the faster speed, uses her technique to more secure advantage. In *Nehmt meinen Dank* comparison focuses more exclusively upon the singers, for here Fleming is distinctly the more expressive: warmer ('bleibt immer dar'), more responsive ('so feurig, als mein Herz ihn sprich'). Delights abound. Sumi Jo has the apt Susanna voice, and her 'Deh vieni' is delicious. In *Vorrei spiegarvi* the delicate charm is winningly captured, with a beautifully judged interplay between voice and instruments. 'Martern aller Arten' has its scales and broad intervals clearly articulated, with plenty of spirit and never a harsh note. Throughout, this lovely singer is a worthy exponent of the tradition handed on from Mozart's own time.

Vesselina Kasarova

Così fan tutte – Ah, scostati! ... Smanie implacabili. Le nozze di Figaro – Non so più cosa son. Idomeneo – Non ho colpa; Il padre adorato; March of the priests. Mitridate, rè di Ponto – Venga pur, minacci; Già dagli occhi. Don Giovanni – Vedrai, carino; In quali eccessi ... Mi tradì quell'alma ingrata. Lucio Silla – Il tenero momento. La clemenza di Tito – Marcia; Deh per questo istante; Non più di fiori. Io ti lascio, o cara, addio, KAnh245/K621*a*

Vesselina Kasarova *mez* **Staatskapelle Dresden / Sir Colin Davis**

RCA Victor Red Seal 09026 68661-2
(74 minutes: DDD). Texts and translations included. Ⓕ
Recorded 1996

Being the questing, individual spirit Kasarova is, she can be controversial as she breaks new ground in interpretation. She does nothing by halves, so some of these performances could quite easily divide lovers of Mozart singing. However, most of the arias in this vivid recital are thrilling in all the right kinds of ways. Defiant Dorabella, despondent Elvira and confused Vitellia are all unerringly portrayed, but it is in the great castrato roles that Kasarova excels most of all. Both sides of Farnace's character in *Mitridate* are explored in his arias, the first fiercely proud, the single word 'barbaro' saying it all. Then in the second we hear the gently palpitating voice of repentance, 'son pentito'. In Cecilio's aria from *Lucio Silla*, another aspect of Kasarova's singing brings a smile of pleasure – the wonderful variety she brings to her runs. The aria, *Io ti lascio* displays her grave beauty of tone, enhanced by the slightest of vibrations, revealing a singer of high intelligence with the means to fulfil her earnest intents. Who better to partner such an elevated singer than Sir Colin Davis? He provides the know-how of a loving Mozartian, prompt in every phrase, and both the singer and the conductor are seconded by playing of idiomatic firmness from the orchestra. Everything is admirably recorded.

Additional recommendation

Opera arias

Arias from Così fan tutte; Don Giovanni; Idomeneo, rè di Creta and Le nozze di Figaro

Frittoli *sop* **Scottish Chamber Orchestra / Mackerras**

Erato 8573 86207-2 (55 minutes: DDD: 9/01) Ⓕ

Some may find Barbara Frittoli's tone hard with a tendency to shrillness in the upper register (though it brings an exciting edge to her *furiouso* delivery of Elettra's mad scene in *Idomeneo*). In sum, a record for her fans, primarily. Mackerras and the SCO provide luxurious support.

Exsultate, jubilate, K165/K158a

Mozart Exsultate, jubilate. Zaïde – Ruhe sanft, meine holdes Leben. Nehmt meinen Dank, ihr holden Gönner, K383. Mia speranza adorata ... Ah non sai qual pena sia, K416. Vorrei spiegarvi, oh Dio, K418. Ch'io mi scordi di te ... Non temer, amato bene, K505[a]
R Strauss Morgen, Op 27 No 4. Liebeshymnus, Op 32 No 3. Der Rosenband, Op 36 No 1. Wiegenlied, Op 41 No 1. Das Bächlein, AV118
Christine Schäfer *sop* [a]**Maria João Pires** *pf*
Berlin Philharmonic Orchestra / Claudio Abbado
DG 457 582-2GH (65 minutes: DDD). Texts and translations included. Recorded 1997 Ⓕ

Schäfer must now be rated in the royal line of Schwarzkopf, Seefried, Ameling, Popp and most recently Bonney as an interpreter of Mozart and Strauss. Yet, she is, like those renowned singers, very much her own person with her own distinctive voice and style. Her almost vibrato-less, at times slightly acerbic tone won't be to all tastes but her unadorned, clear and imaginative singing of all the Mozart arias holds attention. In *Nehmt meinen Dank*, the single word 'Geduld' carries a wealth of meaning; the whole of K416 has an intense feeling of farewell as Schäfer delivers it and again a single word, 'addio' at the end of the recitative, is drenched in sadness. In *Non temer, amato bene*, with Pires providing an ideal counterpoint to the singer, Schäfer etches into the mind the full import of the emotions being expressed, without a hint of sentimentality. *Ruhe sanft* disarms criticism, so touchingly, simply, is it sung, with the little cadenza before the reprise deftly touched in. The more extrovert pieces, *Exsultate, jubilate* and *Vorrei, spiegarvi* are sung more objectively. Abbado and the BPO support Schäfer in the most refined fashion possible, all the instrumental detail finely honed. They are just as ingratiating in Strauss. Most recent interpreters have had richer, warmer voices than Schäfer's. She is a throwback to, say, Elisabeth Schumann, who sang *Wiegenlied* with the same kind of artless, silvery beauty, combined with a pure, keen line – a real winner. But so is each of these beautifully composed and sung pieces, the texts fully understood so the words are ideally melded with their settings: note especially the extra intensity at the climax of *Liebeshymnus* and the ideal delineation of the elegiac *Morgen*'s reflective mood. Indeed it's in this last song, that one hears, as well as anywhere, the soprano's special gift of plaintive eloquence. The recording could not be better balanced.

La clemenza di Tito

Uwe Heilmann *ten* Tito; **Della Jones** *mez* Vitellia; **Cecilia Bartoli** *mez* Sesto; **Diana Montague** *mez* Annio; **Barbara Bonney** *sop* Servillia; **Gilles Cachemaille** *bar* Publio
Academy of Ancient Music Chorus; Academy of Ancient Music / Christopher Hogwood
L'Oiseau-Lyre ② 444 131-2OHO2 (137 minutes: DDD). Notes, text and translation included. Recorded 1993 Ⓕ

The appeal of *La clemenza di Tito*, if less immediate and less obvious than that of the other operas of Mozart's maturity, is still very powerful and very individual. Hogwood has assembled a quite remarkable cast, with certainly two, perhaps three, outstanding interpretations. First among them must be Cecilia Bartoli, who rightly establishes Sextus as the central character, the one whose actions and whose feelings are the focal point of the drama. The opening number is the duet 'Come ti piace, imponi', where the firm and pure sound of Bartoli's voice, in contrast with the contained hysteria of Vitellia's, at once defines the opera's basis. It is clear from her singing that she reads Sextus, for all his weakness in giving way to Vitellia, as a man of integrity, one of the noblest Romans of them all.

Then there is Della Jones's remarkable Vitellia. There are lots of interesting and emotionally suggestive touches in her singing, which is very committed and very passionate, if not perhaps immaculately tidy – but then, tidiness is no part of Vitellia's persona. Her rich bottom register is magnificent and the top Bs have no fears for her. Uwe Heilmann's Titus is marked by much subtle and finely shaped singing and a keen awareness of how phrasing conveys sense. Occasionally the tone is inclined to be nasal, but that does not interfere with a very sympathetic and often moving reading. Hogwood's keen awareness of what, expressively speaking, is going on in the music, and his refusal to be tied to a rigid rhythmic pulse in order to make it manifest, is one of the strengths of this recording. The recitatives are sung with a great deal of life and awareness of meaning, not simply gabbled through at maximum speed. These, of course, are not Mozart's own work and are usually heavily cut. While some may feel that the inclusion of every note, as in the present version, is an advantage to the opera, others may not unreasonably take the opposite view. At any rate, the discs' tracking is arranged so that a new track begins for each aria, which enables listeners to make their own cuts without difficulty.

La clemenza di Tito
Gösta Winbergh *ten* Tito; **Carol Vaness** *sop* Vitellia; **Delores Ziegler** *mez* Sesto; **Martha Senn** *mez* Anno; **Christine Barbaux** *sop* Servilia; **László Polgár** *bass* Publio
Vienna State Opera Chorus; Vienna Philharmonic Orchestra / Riccardo Muti
EMI ② CDS5 55489-2 (136 minutes: ADD). Notes, texts and translation included. Recorded live in 1988 Ⓕ

Riccardo Muti, oblivious to or at least putting aside attempts at period practice, interprets the work unashamedly as a grand, incisive near-tragedy. Nor is he averse to the players of the Vienna Philharmonic drawing the most sensuous sounds from the score, yet he never indulges Mozart, favouring swiftish, though flexible tempos and sharp rhythms. Muti is also notable for catching the *tinta*, the individual colour, of this work. Listen to the trio of contrasted feeling,

'Quello di Tito', in Act 2 and you'll divine the calibre of this reading, or a little earlier to the way Muti persuades the chorus into the most mellifluous sounds in 'Ah, grazie si rendamo'. Muti's approach is admirably seconded by the generous voices taking the three central roles: Vaness is in her element as Vitellia, alternately amorous, vindictive, scheming and forgiving. Her account is boldly and confidently sung throughout a longish evening. As Sextus, Ziegler is fully the equal of her/his loved one, encompassing both her arias with richly contoured tone and courageously delivered coloratura, all tending to convey Sesto's torture of the mind. The only drawback is a certain similarity in the two singers' refulgent tone.

At the centre of the emotional chasm stands Winbergh's commanding, concerned Tito, perhaps the most heroically sung on any version yet sufficiently flexible for his arias' runs (given a few unwanted aspirates). If the other singers aren't quite in the same category, they are all well in the vocal and dramatic picture. It is good to hear the true sound of a theatre acoustic on this live recording. Of course, on the other hand you have to cope with applause at the end of many numbers and one intrusion, happily only in dry recitative, of an audible aeroplane. In all, then, this is a formidable addition to the work's discography, totally engrossing on its own terms and recommendable as a contender to any newcomer to the piece on disc.

Così fan tutte

Elisabeth Schwarzkopf *sop* Fiordiligi; **Christa Ludwig** *mez* Dorabella; **Hanny Steffek** *sop* Despina; **Alfredo Kraus** *ten* Ferrando; **Giuseppe Taddei** *bar* Guglielmo; **Walter Berry** *bass* Don Alfonso

Philharmonia Chorus and Orchestra / Karl Böhm

EMI ③ CMS7 69330-2 (165 minutes: ADD). Notes, text and translation included. Recorded 1962 Ⓜ ○○○

Così fan tutte is the most balanced and probing of all Mozart's operas, formally faultless, musically inspired from start to finish, emotionally a matter of endless fascination and, in the second act, profoundly moving. It has been very lucky on disc, and besides this delightful set there have been several other memorable recordings. However, Karl Böhm's cast could hardly be bettered, even in one's dreams. The two sisters are gloriously sung – Schwarzkopf and Ludwig bring their immeasurable talents as Lieder singers to this sparkling score and overlay them with a rare comic touch. Add to that the stylish singing of Alfredo Kraus and Giuseppe Taddei and the central quartet is unimpeachable. Walter Berry's Don Alfonso is characterful and Hanny Steffek is quite superb as Despina. The pacing of this endlessly intriguing work is measured with immaculate judgement. The emotional control of the characterization is masterly and Böhm's totally idiomatic response to the music is arguably without peer. However, two modern recordings, using period instruments, do offer stimulating alternative views.

Così fan tutte **P**

Amanda Roocroft *sop* Fiordiligi; **Rosa Mannion** *sop* Dorabella; **Eirian James** *mez* Despina; **Rainer Trost** *ten* Ferrando; **Rodney Gilfry** *bar* Guglielmo; **Carlos Feller** *bass* Don Alfonso

Monteverdi Choir; English Baroque Soloists / Sir John Eliot Gardiner

Archiv Produktion ③ 437 829-2AH3 (134 minutes: DDD). Recorded live in 1992 Ⓕ

Gardiner's is a *Così* with a heart, and a heart in the right place. It comes from a stage performance given in the Teatro Comunale at Ferrara – the city from which the sisters in the story hail – in 1992. The vitality and the communicativeness of the recitative is one result of recording a live performance; it is flexible, conversational and lively, as it ought to be, and the Italian pronunciation is remarkably good considering there isn't a single Italian in the cast. Amanda Roocroft makes a capable Fiordiligi, with a big, spacious 'Come scoglio', and shows real depth of feeling in a very beautiful account of 'Per pietà'; her tone is bright and forward. Rosa Mannion, as Dorabella, acts effectively with her voice in 'Smanie implacabili' and is full of life in her Act 2 aria. The Guglielmo, Rodney Gilfry, is outstanding for his light, warm and flexible baritone, gently seductive in Act 1, showing real brilliance and precision of articulation in 'Donne mie'. Eirian James's Despina is another delight, spirited, sexy and rich-toned, and full of charm without any of the silliness some Despinas show. Period instruments notwithstanding, this is a fairly traditional performance. Gardiner often uses quite generous rubato to highlight the shape of a phrase, and he is alert, as always, to how the orchestral writing can underline the sense.

Così fan tutte **P**

Soile Isokoski *sop* Fiordiligi; **Monica Groop** *mez* Dorabella; **Nancy Argenta** *sop* Despina; **Markus Schäfer** *ten* Ferrando; **Per Vollestad** *bar* Guglielmo; **Huub Claessens** *bass* Don Alfonso

La Petite Bande and Chorus / Sigiswald Kuijken

Accent ③ ACC9296/98 (181 minutes: DDD). Notes, text and translation included. Recorded live in 1992 Ⓕ

Kuijken's live recording is lighter in mood than Gardiner's. Nearly all the tempos are quicker and there is more sense of spontaneity. Mozart very rarely wrote dynamic or accentuation marks into his singers' parts; the singers were expected to learn their music from a repetiteur (or Mozart himself) and take their cues from what they heard in performance. Gardiner has his singers follow, meticulously, the orchestral dynamics; Kuijken leaves them, more or less, to sing with what they hear. This is a symptomatic difference: one performance is highly wrought, the other freer and more natural. The sisters in the Kuijken version are excellently done by Soile Isokoski, even in voice and with an attractive ring, and Monica Groop, again a pleasing and even voice intelligently and musically used. Their duets are very appealing, with a happy sense in 'Prenderò quel brunettino' that they might be getting up to a little mischief. The Alfonso here, Huub Claessens, more baritone than bass, is particularly successful in the recitative, which here again is done with much care for its meaning. A pleasing, lively *Così*, it would be a good recording with which to get to know the opera, whereas the Gardiner is a connoisseur's performance, subtle and sophisticated, and communicating important things about the opera.

Additional recommendation

Così fan tutte

Caballé Fiordiligi **Baker** Dorabella **Cotrubas** Despina **Gedda** Ferrando **Ganzarolli** Guglielmo

Royal Opera House Chorus and Orchestra / C Davis

Philips ③ 422 542-2PME3 (182 minutes: ADD: 2/75R) Ⓜ

The somewhat surprising casting of Caballé and Baker pays rich rewards, indeed the entire cast has a real ensemble feel to it, helped no doubt by Davis's clear direction. A fine mid-price alternative in good sound

Don Giovanni

Eberhard Waechter *bar* Don Giovanni; **Joan Sutherland** *sop* Donna Anna; **Elisabeth Schwarzkopf** *sop* Donna Elvira; **Graziella Sciutti** *sop* Zerlina; **Luigi Alva** *ten* Don Ottavio; **Giuseppe Taddei** *bar* Leporello; **Piero Cappuccilli** *bar* Masetto; **Gottlob Frick** *bass* Commendatore H

Philharmonia Chorus and Orchestra / Carlo Maria Giulini

EMI ③ CDS5 56232-2 (162 minutes: ADD). Notes, text and translation included. Recorded 1959 Ⓕ **OO**

Although this set is over 40 years old, none of its successors is as skilled in capturing the piece's drama so unerringly. It has always been most recommendable and Giulini captures all the work's most dramatic characteristics, faithfully supported by the superb Philharmonia forces of that time. At this stage of Giulini's career, he was a direct, lithe conductor, alert to every turn in the story and he projects the nervous tension of the piece ideally while never forcing the pace, as can so easily happen. Then he had one of the most apt casts ever assembled for the piece. Waechter's Giovanni combines the demonic with the seductive in just the right proportions, Taddei is a high-profile Leporello, who relishes the text and sings with lots of 'face'. Elvira was always one of Schwarzkopf's most successful roles: here she delivers the role with tremendous intensity. Sutherland's Anna isn't quite so full of character but is magnificently sung. Alva is a graceful Ottavio. Sciutti's charming Zerlina, Cappuccilli's strong and Italianate Masetto and Frick's granite Commendatore are all very much in the picture. The recording still sounds well.

Don Giovanni P

Rodney Gilfry *bar* Don Giovanni; **Luba Orgonasova** *sop* Donna Anna; **Charlotte Margiono** *sop* Donna Elvira; **Eirian James** *mez* Zerlina; **Christoph Prégardien** *ten* Don Ottavio; **Ildebrando d'Arcangelo** *bass* Leporello; **Julian Clarkson** *bass* Masetto; **Andrea Silvestrelli** *bass* Commendatore

Monteverdi Choir; English Baroque Soloists / Sir John Eliot Gardiner

Archiv Produktion ③ 445 870 2AH3 (176 minutes: DDD). Notes, text and translation included. Recorded 1994 Ⓕ

John Eliot Gardiner's set has a great deal to commend it. The recitative is sung with exemplary care over pacing so that it sounds as it should, like heightened and vivid conversation, often to electrifying effect. Ensembles, the Act 1 quartet particularly, are also treated conversationally, as if one were overhearing four people giving their opinions on a situation in the street. The orchestra, perfectly balanced with the singers in a very immediate acoustic, supports them, as it were 'sings' with them. That contrasts with, and complements, Gardiner's expected ability to empathize with the demonic aspects of the score, as in Giovanni's drinking song and the final moments of Act 1, which fairly bristle with rhythmic energy without ever becoming rushed. The arrival of the statue at Giovanni's dinner-table is tremendous, the period trombones and timpani achieving an appropriately brusque, fearsome attack. Throughout this scene, Gardiner's penchant for sharp accents is wholly appropriate; elsewhere he is sometimes rather too insistent. As a whole, tempos not only seem right on their own account but also, all-importantly, carry conviction in relation to each other. Where so many conductors today are given to rushing 'Mi tradì', Gardiner prefers a more meditative approach, which allows his soft-grained Elvira to make the most of the aria's expressive possibilities.

As in his other Mozart opera recordings, Gardiner benefits from working with singers whom he knows well. Gilfry's Giovanni is lithe, ebullient, keen to exert his sexual prowess; an obvious charmer, at times surprisingly tender yet with the iron will only just below the surface. Suave and appealing, delivered in a real baritone timbre, his Giovanni is as accomplished as any on disc. Ildebrando d'Arcangelo was the discovery of these performances: this young bass is a lively foil to his master and on his own a real showman, as 'Madamina' indicates, a number all the better for a brisk speed. Orgonasova once more reveals herself a paragon as regards steady tone and deft technique – there is no need here to slow down for the coloratura at the end of 'Non mi dir' – and she brings to her recounting of the attempted seduction a real feeling of immediacy. In 'Or sai chi l'onore' she manages just the right kind of supple urgency. As Anna, Margiono sometimes sounds a shade stretched technically, but consoles us with the luminous, inward quality of her voice and her reading of the role, something innate that cannot be learnt.

Nobody in their right senses is ever going to suggest that there is one, ideal version of *Don Giovanni*; the work has far too many facets for that, but for sheer theatrical *élan* complemented by the live recording, Gardiner is among the best, particularly given a recording that is wonderfully truthful and lifelike.

Don Giovanni

Bo Skovhus *bar* Don Giovanni; **Christine Brewer** *sop* Donna Anna; **Dame Felicity Lott** *sop* Donna Elvira; **Nuccia Focile** *sop* Zerlina; **Jerry Hadley** *ten* Don Ottavio; **Alessandro Corbelli** *bar* Leporello; **Umberto Chiummo** *bass* Masetto, Commendatore

Scottish Chamber Chorus and Orchestra / Sir Charles Mackerras

Telarc ③ CD80420 (183 minutes: DDD). Notes, text and translation included. Recorded 1995 Ⓕ

This set has no astonishing or brilliant individual interpretations, but the whole is full of life and energy and freshness. The Scottish Chamber Orchestra is not a period-instrument group, but Mackerras, as he explains in the accompanying booklet (and as we hear), uses valveless horns and trumpets and something close to period timpani – hence the alarming sound of the opening chords. He also calls for sharper attack and quicker decay from the string players and a very forward wind balance. Tempos are often but by no means always on the fast side. But he also allows his singers plenty of time to phrase their music expressively, for example in the Giovanni-Zerlina scene in the first finale, in the trio at the beginning of Act 2 (some wonderfully sensual orchestral colours here), in Giovanni's serenade, in the great sextet (very powerfully done) and in the cemetery scene, which has a proper sense of the hieratic and yet a knife-edge tension too. In sum, this release is a highly theatrical interpretation that has you right on the edge of your seat.

Umberto Chiummo makes a good, incisive Masetto and a truly formidable Commendatore in the final scenes. Nuccia Focile provides a beguiling Zerlina, with a sweet upper range and more than a touch of sensuousness and charm. Alessandro Corbelli, the Leporello, is a lively, lowish baritone who uses the sound of the words to advantage and can phrase with just the right hint of elegance. His voice is very close, arguably too close, in sound to that of the Giovanni, Bo Skovhus, yet the master-servant relationship is conveyed convincingly. Skovhus's sharp vitality (listen to 'Metà di voi'), his virile Champagne Aria and his deeply sensual *portamentos* in the Serenade stress those aspects of Giovanni's character that underlie the plot. Jerry Hadley offers an Ottavio of some intensity, not the smoothest or most graceful, but stronger in expression than most and Dame Felicity is in full, creamy voice in a role she has often sung with distinction. On the question of versions, Mackerras gives the Prague original first (with 'Dalla sua pace' inserted in Act 1), so if you play the second disc through to the end, you should then skip the first 10 tracks of the third disc to continue; or, if you want the Vienna version, you should skip the last six of the second and pick up at the beginning of the third, where you will hear the rare (and rather silly, though musically agreeable) Zerlina-Leporello duet and Elvira's scene (but not 'Il mio tesoro'). This is an excellent solution for listeners who can be bothered to press a couple of buttons. All round, an immensely enjoyable version of *Don Giovanni*.

Additional recommendation

Don Giovanni

Allen Don Giovanni **Vaness** Donna Anna **Ewing** Donna Elvira **Gale** Zerlina **Lewis** Don Ottavio **Van Allen** Leporello **London Philharmonic Orchestra / Haitink**

EMI ③ CDS7 47037-8 (172 minutes: DDD: 12/84) Ⓕ

Haitink's *Don Giovanni* is considerably more than just a memento of a fine Glyndebourne production. Thomas Allen is a dangerous Giovanni, predatory yet magnetic. Vaness is wonderful as Anna and Ewing is fine Elvira. Richard Van Allen matches his master in charisma.

Die Entführung aus dem Serail

Die Entführung aus dem Serail[a]. Exsultate, jubilate, K165/K158a[b] **H**

Maria Stader *sop* Constanze (Beate Guttmann); **Rita Streich** *sop* Blonde; **Ernst Haefliger** *ten* Belmonte (Sebastian Fischer); **Martin Vantin** *ten* Pedrillo (Wolfgang Spier); **Josef Greindl** *bass* Osmin; **Walter Franck** *spkr* Bassa Selim

[a]**Berlin RIAS Chamber Choir and Orchestra,** [b]**Berlin Radio Symphony Orchestra / Ferenc Fricsay**

DG The Originals [a]mono/[b]stereo ② 457 730-2GOR2 (125 minutes: ADD). Notes, texts and translations included. Recorded 1954 Ⓜ ●

Fricsay was an advocate of crisp, zestful, pared-down Mozart *avant la lettre*. This was the first in his distinguished series of Mozart opera recordings, throughout which he used Berlin Radio forces and singers familiar with his work. They prove formidable advocates. The orchestra, recorded in resonant, honest mono, plays superbly. Stader was a particular favourite with Fricsay. If not the most refulgent of sopranos, she had both the consistency of voice and thoroughness of technique to cope with almost all the demands of Constanze's music. Although one ideally wants a more dramatic singer in the part, her feeling for the shape of a Mozart phrase is always admirable. She is suitably partnered by the fluent, lyrical Haefliger, who also sang Belmonte at Glyndebourne in the 1950s. Rita Streich is the ideal Blonde, singing with pure tone and spirited attack: she has the individuality of voice, the hint of vibrato most attractive, to please the most fastidious listener. Vantin is a more than adequate Pedrillo, who sings his Serenade in an appropriate *mezza voce*. Greindl brings a fully fledged bass to bear on Osmin's music and fills it with a nice combination of vicious sadism leavened by comedy. Although his singing is occasionally marred by intrusive aspirates, he is among the most enjoyable Osmins on disc. Happily he and Streich are allowed to speak their own dialogue so that their Act 2 encounter goes particularly well.

As was a dubious custom with DG at the time, the other singers are doubled by speaking voices that hardly match their own. Those who have come to appreciate Fricsay's many attributes as a conductor will not be disappointed by this reissue, and will gain as a generous bonus Stader's delightful account of *Exsultate, jubilate*. In absolute terms those without *Die Entführung* in their collection should hear this one.

Die Entführung aus dem Serail
Ingrid Habermann *sop* Constanze; **Donna Ellen** *sop* Blonde; **Piotr Bezcala** *ten* Belmonte; **Oliver Ringelhahn** *ten* Pedrillo; **Franz Kalchmair** *bass* Osmin; **Harald Pfeiffer** *spkr* Bassa Selim **Linz Landestheater Choir; Linz Bruckner Orchestra / Martin Sieghart**
Arte Nova Classics ② 74321 49701-2
(115 minutes: DDD). Notes, text and translation included. Recorded live in 1996-97 Ⓢ

This is a real bargain, just about as enjoyable as any performance given by more prominent artists on better-known labels. Recorded live, it is not surprising to find such a natural sense of ensemble among the principals or such a well-integrated account of the score from Sieghart, who is also aware of the latest research on this score in terms of orchestration and small embellishments. His reading is a shade strict and unsmiling, but it has the virtue of keeping the drama on the move in a work that can outstay its welcome in more self-indulgent performances, and the playing of the small band is exemplary. Dialogue is included but kept to the minimum essential to clarify the action. Ingrid Habermann has the dramatic coloratura, the technique and all the notes to encompass the fearful demands of Constanze's role and shows the dramatic resolution it requires. The Polish tenor Piotr Bezcala has also been judiciously cast for his part: his voice is firm and sappy, and he discloses an ability to make his four taxing arias sound relatively simple. One or two unwanted lachrymose moments apart, he is a model of Mozartian style. The Canadian soprano, Donna Ellen, is a mettlesome Blonde, happy in the dizzy heights reached in her first aria. Her Pedrillo is a lively singer but one prone to questionable pitch, particularly in his Serenade. Best of all is the native Austrian, Franz Kalchmair as an Osmin with a rotund, pleasing bass, as happy at the bottom as at the top of his range and he is obviously a formidable actor. The Bassa Selim's role has been severely curtailed; what remains of it is spoken with the appropriate blend of menace and authority by Harald Pfeiffer. The recording is reasonably good.

Idomeneo, re di Creta

Anthony Rolfe Johnson *ten* Idomeneo; **Anne Sofie von Otter** *mez* Idamante; **Sylvia McNair** *sop* Ilia; **Hillevi Martinpelto** *sop* Elettra; **Nigel Robson** *ten* Arbace; **Glenn Winslade** *ten* High Priest; **Cornelius Hauptmann** *bass* Oracle Ⓟ
Monteverdi Choir; English Baroque Soloists / Sir John Eliot Gardiner
Archiv Produktion ③ 431 674-2AH3
(211 minutes: DDD). Notes, text and translation included. Recorded 1990. ***Gramophone*** Award Winner 1991 Ⓕ ●●●

This is unquestionably the most vital and authentic account of *Idomeneo* to date on disc. We have here what was given at the work's first performance in Munich plus, in appendices, what Mozart wanted, or was forced, to cut before that première and the alternative versions of certain passages, so that various combinations of the piece can be programmed by the listener. Gardiner's direct, dramatic conducting catches ideally the agony of Idomeneo's terrible predicament – forced to sacrifice his son because of an unwise row. This torment of the soul is also entirely conveyed by Anthony Rolfe Johnson in the title role to which Anne Sofie von Otter's moving Idamante is an apt foil. Sylvia McNair is a diaphanous, pure-voiced Ilia, Hillevi Martinpelto a properly fiery, sharp-edged Elettra. With dedicated support from his own choir and orchestra, who obviously benefited from a long period of preparation, Gardiner matches the stature of this noble *opera seria*. The recording catches the excitement which all who heard the live performances will recall.

Idomeneo, re di Creta
Plácido Domingo *ten* Idomeneo; **Cecilia Bartoli** *mez* Idamante; **Heidi Grant Murphy** *sop* Ilia; **Carol Vaness** *sop* Elettra; **Thomas Hampson** *bar* Arbace; **Frank Lopardo** *ten* High Priest; **Bryn Terfel** *bass-bar* Oracle
Chorus and Orchestra of the Metropolitan Opera, New York / James Levine
DG ③ 447 737-2GH3 (176 minutes: DDD). Notes, text and translation included. Recorded in 1994 Ⓕ

After Gardiner's lithe, slimline *Idomeneo*, Levine brings us back to a 'traditional' reading, with a big orchestra and a cast starry enough to make the Golden Horseshoe thoroughly happy. There can be little question that this must be the most recommendable recording for those not wanting a period-instrument 'authentic' version. First, however, a word of explanation is needed, in view of the great divergences among current recordings of the opera, to clarify what this consists of. It is more or less the Munich first performance version: we get both arias for Arbace (particularly welcome in view of Thomas Hampson's fine singing), Idamante's acceptance of death 'No, la morte' and Elettra's final venomous 'D'Oreste, d'Aiace', but not Idomeneo's 'Torna la pace' and only the shorter version of his 'Fuor del mar' (with a changed ending). Recitatives are given almost complete, and though words are most expressively coloured throughout, this results in many recitatives almost turning into *ariosos*. Appoggiaturas are applied, if not very consistently, but only one artist, Heidi Grant Murphy, ventures to ornament an aria, in the reprise section of 'Se il padre perdei'. Murphy's Ilia is a gentle, youthful, sweet-voiced *ingénue*; her *fioriture* in 'Zeffiretti' are sung with delicious purity and clarity. Bartoli as Idamante is utterly convincing and deeply involved in every nuance of the character's emotions, and her 'No, la morte' is memorable. Carol Vaness may be forgiven for a rather screamy 'D'Oreste, d'Aiace' but her earlier 'Tutto nel cor' shows the right bitterness and fury, and she persuasively softens her tone when Elettra feels that fate seems to be favouring her. As Idomeneo, Plácido Domingo gives a reading of the nobility and intelligence we might expect from him, one which makes him an outstanding interpreter of the role. Aided by a well-judged production that conveys the various perspectives in the opera, Levine presides over a coherently planned performance satisfying both from the dramatic and the lyrical viewpoints.

Mitridate, re di Ponto

Giuseppe Sabbatini *ten* Mitridate; **Natalie Dessay** *sop* Aspasia; **Cecilia Bartoli** *mez* Sifare; **Brian Asawa** *counterten* Farnace; **Sandrine Piau** *sop* Ismene; **Juan Diego Flórez** *ten* Marzio; **Hélène Le Corre** *sop* Arbate **Les Talens Lyriques / Christophe Rousset** P

Decca ③ 460 772-2DHO3 (179 minutes: DDD).
Notes, text and translation included.
Recorded 1998 Ⓕ

Mozart was not quite 15 when he composed *Mitridate*, as the first carnival opera for the Milan opera house, which was shortly to become La Scala. Operas of that period were composed specifically for the cast that created them: Mozart more than once referred to fitting an aria to the voice as a tailor fitted a suit to the figure. And some of the original cast of *Mitridate* thought their arias ill-fitting: Mozart was required to rewrite several of them. Many of the arias are expansive pieces, with a semi-*da capo*, and make heavy demands on the singers' agility and compass. This set has a starry cast. The *primo uomo* role, Sifare, was written for an unusually high-lying castrato voice. Here it is sung, with great character, by Cecilia Bartoli. Perhaps the finest of her four arias is the slow one in Act 2 with horn obbligato, 'Lungi da te, mio bene', which is sung here with real depth of feeling, shapeliness of line and richness of tone. But her caressing of the phrases in the slow part of her second Act 1 aria, and her exact and clearly articulated semiquaver *fioriture* in the fast part, are a delight too, as they are in her opening number, a virtuoso piece which she dispatches imperiously. The only reservation is that the part does lie very high for her: the top B flats sound strained, and indeed the quality from G upwards is slightly impaired. Still, it is a marvellous performance and she brings to the music a real sense of drama and care for the words and their meaning, in the recitative and the arias.

There is nothing but praise, too, for Natalie Dessay in the prima donna role of Aspasia, beloved of Sifare, lusted after by his brother Farnace, betrothed to their father Mitridate (that more or less summarizes the basis of the plot). Full, creamy tone, brilliantly thrown-off rapid music, a firmly sustained line (try 'Pallid'ombre', in Act 3, taken very slowly), a keen sense of drama, high notes struck loud and clear and bang in the middle: one could ask for nothing more. Her duet with Bartoli, the single concerted number, at the end of Act 2, is a joy: they seem to have all the time in the world for sensitive phrasing and refined detail.

Then Brian Asawa, in the castrato role of Farnace, offers some very fine countertenor singing, with a full, almost throaty tone, not at all in the usual countertenor manner, and extraordinarily even across a wide range. In his final aria (where Farnace repents his misdeeds) there is a powerfully sustained line in what is the longest and possibly the most deeply felt piece in the opera. Sandrine Piau sings tenderly and gracefully in Ismene's rather lighter role.

Giuseppe Sabbatini copes well in the role of Mitridate but does not always manage so happily either in the lyrical music or the expressions of anger. He is inclined to sing too loudly or too softly: there is no comfortable mean. His first aria, 'Se di lauri', the most beautiful piece in the score, is forceful and grandiose where softness and warmth are wanted, and the *pianissimo* recapitulation is not persuasive. Still, this is accurate, technically accomplished and perfectly tuned singing. In the angry arias he is apt to rant; the effect is fiery enough but the sound is not very musical. In the two small roles, Hélène Le Corre sings very pleasantly in Arbate's aria and Juan Diego Flórez shows a substantial, slightly nasal voice in Marzio's. Rousset directs his period instrument band with vigour and conviction.

Le nozze di Figaro

Sesto Bruscantini *bar* Figaro; **Graziella Sciutti** *sop* Susanna; **Franco Calabrese** *bass* Count Almaviva; **Sena Jurinac** *sop* Countess Almaviva; **Risë Stevens** *mez* Cherubino; **Monica Sinclair** *contr* Marcellina; **Ian Wallace** *bass* Bartolo; **Hugues Cuénod** *ten* Don Basilio; **Daniel McCoshan** *ten* Don Curzio; **Gwyn Griffiths** *bar* Antonio; **Jeanette Sinclair** *sop* Barbarina **Glyndebourne Festival Chorus and Orchestra / Vittorio Gui** H

Classics for Pleasure ② CD-CFPD4724 Ⓑ
(158 minutes: ADD). Recorded 1955 ○○○

This comes from what might be termed the second generation of Glyndebourne performances, those dominated by Vittorio Gui, whose approach to Mozart was more volatile, more Italianate, possibly a little less warm than that of his equally individual predecessor, Fritz Busch. This is immediately evident in the Overture, which tells us very definitely that we are to hear a tale of intrigue and emotional turmoil, da Ponte as prominent as Mozart. To achieve his purpose, Gui imported a cast that included three Italians. Bruscantini is a mercurial, light-voiced, mobile Figaro, Calabrese a dark-browed Almaviva, very much a dominant personality in his household (he is also, for the most part, strong and vibrant in tone and excellent in Mozartian diction). Graziella Sciutti, who was to be Glyndebourne's Susanna only in 1958, was brought in for the recording, and a lively, if a little thin-voiced Susanna she proves. Wonderful to hear all three pronouncing their own tongue so pointedly.

For all that, the most compelling reason for obtaining this set is the Countess of the irreplaceable Sena Jurinac, a noble, aristocratic assumption sung in the warmest, most palpitating tones – a lovable singer at the height of her powers. A drawback is Risë Stevens's tired-sounding and unidiomatic Cherubino, but even she fits well enough into the ensemble.

This was one of EMI's earliest stereo efforts, and the placings are well managed, with the sense of intimacy you get in the theatre at Glyndebourne but it has to be said that the orchestral sound now seems a little confined and lacking in bloom. But then – regardless of the countless excellent modern recordings available – listen again to Jurinac's touching 'Dove sono' (sustained at a slow speed) and Gui's very theatrical way with the score and you will know that you will always need to have this set. Gui's matching of tempos is laudable and he draws playing from the RPO, then doubling as the Glyndebourne orchestra, that is at once disciplined and full of character. And this set is an exceptional bargain.

Le nozze di Figaro **P**

Bryn Terfel *bass-bar* Figaro; **Alison Hagley** *sop* Susanna; **Rodney Gilfry** *bar* Count Almaviva; **Hillevi Martinpelto** *sop* Countess Almaviva; **Pamela Helen Stephen** *mez* Cherubino; **Susan McCulloch** *sop* Marcellina; **Carlos Feller** *bass* Bartolo; **Francis Egerton** *ten* Don Basilio, Don Curzio; **Julian Clarkson** *bass* Antonio; **Constanze Backes** *sop* Barbarina

Monteverdi Choir; English Baroque Soloists / Sir John Eliot Gardiner

Archiv Produktion ③ 439 871-2AH3

(179 minutes: DDD). Notes, text and translation included. Recorded live in 1993 Ⓕ

The catalogue of *Figaro* recordings is a long one, and the cast lists are full of famous names. In this version only one principal had more than a half-dozen recordings behind him, and some had none at all. It is a commentary on the astuteness of the casting and on the capacity of a strong conductor to make the whole so much more than the sum of its parts that this version can stand comparison with any, not only for its grasp of the drama but also for the quality of its singing. It is, of course, a period-instrument recording, more evidently so than many under Gardiner. The string tone is pared down and makes quite modest use of vibrato, the woodwind is soft-toned (but happily prominent). The voices are generally lighter and fresher-sounding than those on most recordings and the balance permits more than usual to be heard of Mozart's instrumental commentary on the action and the characters. The recitative is done with quite exceptional life and feeling for its meaning and dramatic import, with a real sense, during much of it, of lively and urgent conversation.

Bryn Terfel and Alison Hagley make an outstanding Figaro and Susanna. Terfel is quite a deep bass-baritone with enough darkness in his voice to sound pretty menacing in 'Se vuol ballare' as well as bitter in 'Aprite un po' quegli occhi'; it is an alert, mettlesome performance – and he also brings off a superlative 'Non più andrai'. Hagley offers a reading of spirit and allure. The interplay between her and the woodwind in 'Venite inginocchiatevi' is a delight, and her cool but heartfelt 'Deh vieni' is very beautiful. Once or twice her intonation seems marginally under stress but that is the price one pays for singing with so little vibrato, and it's worth it. Hillevi Martinpelto's unaffected, youthful-sounding Countess is enjoyable; both arias are quite lightly done, with a very lovely, warm, natural sound in 'Dove sono' especially. Some may prefer a more polished, sophisticated reading, of the traditional kind, but this is closer to what Mozart would have wanted and expected.

Rodney Gilfry provides a Count with plenty of fire and authority, firmly focused in tone; the outburst at the *Allegro assai* in 'Vedrò mentr'io sospiro' is formidable. Pamela Helen Stephen's Cherubino sounds charmingly youthful and impetuous; 'Voi che sapete' is taken a good deal quicker than usual, and with a touch of comedy, and benefits from it. There is no want of dramatic life in Gardiner's direction. His tempos are marginally quicker than most, and the orchestra often speaks eloquently of the drama. Gardiner adopts the Moberly/Raeburn order of events in Act 3. This involves placing 'Dove sono' before, instead of after, the sextet and in the last Act he places Susanna's aria before, instead of after, Figaro's.

Le nozze di Figaro **H**

Cesare Siepi *bass* Figaro; **Hilde Gueden** *sop* Susanna; **Alfred Poell** *bar* Count Almaviva; **Lisa della Casa** *sop* Countess Almaviva; **Suzanne Danco** *sop* Cherubino; **Hilde Rössl-Majdan** *contr* Marcellina; **Fernando Corena** *bass* Bartolo; **Murray Dickie** *ten* Don Basilio; **Hugo Meyer-Welfing** *ten* Don Curzio; **Harald Pröglhöf** *bass* Antonio; **Anny Felbermayer** *sop* Barbarina

Vienna State Opera Chorus; Vienna Philharmonic Orchestra / Erich Kleiber

Decca Legends ③ 466 369-2DM03 Ⓜ

(172 minutes: ADD). Recorded 1955

Erich Kleiber's *Figaro* is a classic of the classics of the gramophone: beautifully played by the Vienna Philharmonic, conducted with poise and vitality and a real sense of the drama unfolding through the music. It's very much a Viennese performance, not perhaps as graceful or as effervescent as some but warm, sensuous and alive to the interplay of character. At the centre is Hilde Gueden, whose Susanna has echoes of Viennese operetta singing although she remains a true Mozartian stylist – her 'Deh vieni' is impeccably graceful and perfectly timed. Lisa della Casa's Countess may not be one of the most dramatic but the voice is full yet focused, and 'Dove sono' is a delight in particular. Suzanne Danco's Cherubino is not exactly impassioned, and is really as much girlish as boyish, but it is still neat and musical singing. The balance among the men is affected by the casting of Figaro with a weightier singer than the Count. But Alfred Poell's Count makes up in natural authority and aristocratic manner what he lacks in sheer power, and he shows himself capable, too, of truly sensual singing in the Act 3 duet with Susanna.

There are excellent performances, too, from Corena's verbally athletic Bartolo and Dickie's alert, ironic Basilio. However, the true star is

Erich Kleiber. The beginning of the opera sets your spine a-tingling with theatrical expectation. Act 1 goes at pretty smart tempos, but all through he insists on full musical value. There is no rushing in the confrontations at the end of Act 2 – all is measured and properly argued through. And everything is truly sung: the singers never skimp on the music to convey the drama; they rather use the music to convey it. With Kleiber and the VPO behind them, they do so utterly convincingly. The sound is satisfactory, for a set of this vintage – and no lover of this opera should be without it.

Additional recommendation

Le nozze di Figaro

Prey Figaro **Mathis** Susanna **Fischer-Dieskau** Count **Janowitz** Countess **Troyanos** Cherubino

Deutsche Oper Orchestra / Böhm

DG The Originals 449 728-2GOR3 Ⓜ

(173 minutes: ADD: 3/97)

A strongly cast opera from 1968 with Böhm a near perfect Mozartian in charge. Fischer-Dieskau and Janowitz are ideally partnered as the aristocrats and Prey and Mathis are a lively pair of young lovers. Troyanos's Cherubino is finely drawn. A mid-price version well worth considering

Zaïde

Lynne Dawson *sop* Zaïde; **Hans-Peter Blochwitz** *ten* Gomatz; **Olaf Bär** *bar* Allazim; **Herbert Lippert** *ten* Sultan Soliman; **Christopher Purves** *bass* Osmin **Academy of Ancient Music / Paul Goodwin** Ⓟ

Harmonia Mundi HMU90 7205 (75 minutes: DDD). Notes, text and translation included. Ⓕ

Recorded 1997

Mozart began composing the work known as *Zaïde* in 1779-80, but left it unfinished, ostensibly because no performance was in prospect, but perhaps also because, very soon after he broke off, he came to see that this rather static kind of musical drama was not the sort of piece he wanted to write. Moreover, the character relationships are difficult to deal with: the libretto and the music (as far as it goes) imply a powerful attraction at the beginning of the opera between Zaïde and Gomatz, but ultimately, in the final scene, which Mozart never reached, they turn out to be brother and sister: very touching, and well attuned to the sensibilities of the time, but cramping to the composer. Nevertheless, the music of *Zaïde* is full of fine things, often foreshadowing not only the similar *Entführung* but also *Idomeneo*. This recording captures its beauties and its depth of feeling beautifully. This is partly because of the sympathetic conducting of Paul Goodwin, who paces it with excellent judgement, bringing to it just the right degree of flexibility, and achieves orchestral textures that are clear and warm – much more so than usual from period-instrument groups. The melodramas, tellingly shaped, perfectly catch the tone of passion. The AAM plays at its best for him (notably, understandably, the principal oboist).

It is hard to imagine a better cast. Lynne Dawson sings the title-role with a frail beauty that is very appealing. Hans-Peter Blochwitz's shapely lines and full, eloquent tone make Gomatz's arias a delight, too; and Herbert Lippert, the second tenor, as the Sultan (in love, or lust, with Zaïde), is almost his match in evenness and lyrical quality. It is also a luxury to have Olaf Bär as Allazim: the music is sung with a refinement of tone and ease of articulation that you don't imagine it has often had before. Christopher Purves sings Osmin cleanly without perhaps quite fully realizing the comedy. In sum, this far excels any previous recording.

Die Zauberflöte

Ruth Ziesak *sop* Pamina; **Sumi Jo** *sop* Queen of Night; **Uwe Heilmann** *ten* Tamino; **Michael Kraus** *bar* Papageno; **Kurt Moll** *bass* Sarastro; **Andreas Schmidt** *bar* Speaker; **Heinz Zednik** *ten* Monostatos; **Lotte Leitner** *sop* Papagena; **Adrianne Pieczonka** *sop* **Annette Kuettenbaum, Jard van Nes** *mezzos* First, Second and Third Ladies; **Max Emanuel Cencic, Michael Rausch, Markus Leitner** *trebs* First, Second and Third Boys; **Wolfgang Schmidt** *ten* **Hans Franzen** *bass* Two Armed Men; **Clemens Bieber** *ten* **Hans Joachim Porcher** *bar* Two Priests **Vienna Boys' Choir; Vienna State Opera Concert Choir; Vienna Philharmonic Orchestra / Sir Georg Solti**

Decca ② 433 210-2DH2 (152 minutes: DDD). Notes, text and translation included. Recorded 1990 Ⓕ **OO**

Sir Georg Solti's relationship with *Die Zauberflöte* is long and illustrious. When, in 1937, he was musical assistant to Toscanini in Salzburg, it was Solti's fingers which conjured the sound from Papageno's glockenspiel. In Salzburg in 1990, Solti turned from rostrum to celesta and duetted with Papageno once again. This recording is a fitting celebration of Solti's own long Mozartian journey. Solti's 1969 recording, also for Decca and available as a three-disc reissue, was praised for its feeling for excitement, where a very slight excess of solemnity or relaxation can be deadly. It is exactly that quality which epitomizes this newer recording: if anything, tempos are even more finely judged, more intuitively moulded to the shape of the score's harmonic dramas and emotional breathing.

Solti's tempos and pacing are in fact the inspiration of this *Flute*. Marginally faster than in 1969, the Overture now springs rather than stings on its way. Sarastro's crew are a merry, totally unpompous lot: there is no more joyful entry than for this Sarastro, truly *mit Freuden* in the finale of Act 1. Solti also pays tribute to the *Flute* as fairy-tale. Largely by pacing, he never allows Schikaneder's little motto couplets (Ladies, Boys, Speaker) to become ponderous moralistic asides: each one bounces into its natural place in the dramatic scheme of things. Solti gives time and space enough, though, for melodically or harmonically self-isolating lines such as Tamino's response to the Speaker, 'Der Lieb' und Tugend Eigentum'; for the vibrancy of the inner string parts for Isis and Osiris and the Armed Men; to Pamina's cry of 'Die

Wahrheit!' – one of the most moving on disc.

Ruth Ziesak's fresh, intelligent performance here restores to Pamina that fusion of innocence and strength, vulnerability and courage which the character and her music demand. With Solti's tempo, and sprung orchestral chords pulsing like a heartbeat, her first pure phrase of 'Bei Männern' catches the breath with delight; her genuflecting cry of pain to Sarastro quite pierces the heart; her 'Ach, ich fühl's' is shaped by deep desperation, not mere melancholy. The casting of Tamino epitomizes a major difference between the two Solti versions. Uwe Heilmann, raw, penetrating and a little Schreier-like of timbre, is a livelier dramatic presence than Stuart Burrows (1969), if not as aristocratic and well-groomed a voice. The 1969 version is singerly: this newer recording primarily dramatic.

By the same token, Hermann Prey's Papageno (1969) is easier to listen to than that of Michael Kraus, who tends to bounce clean off the end of a phrase, and whose chattering quality can be sometimes less purely musical but often more plausible than Prey. This Queen of Night is not merely an Olympia with a crown. Sumi Jo was truly in her ascendant here. A truly rhythmic brightness and glow of melodic phrasing suffuses her singing, and this is considerable relief from the muscular gymnastics of other interpreters on record. Her lunar beauty seems to take its strength, as it surely must, from Sarastro himself. Kurt Moll, appropriately, sings on an entirely other vocal plane: the depth of his voice is fully equal to the breadth of his music. In his musical temple there are indeed many mansions. His slaves and his Monostatos (Heinz Zednik) are ably aided and abetted by the natural, well-paced dialogue, often whispering and wondering, sometimes crackling with tension; never over-directed. Effects, too, both meteorological and avian, surpass those on previous recordings. To sum up, Solti's earlier recording bears up well musically, but it is eclipsed dramatically by the live presence and meticulous recording balance of this newer version.

Die Zauberflöte **P**

Rosa Mannion *sop* Pamina; **Natalie Dessay** *sop* Queen of Night; **Hans-Peter Blochwitz** *ten* Tamino; **Anton Scharinger** *bass* Papageno; **Reinhard Hagen** *bass* Sarastro; **Willard White** *bass* Speaker; **Steven Cole** *ten* Monostatos; **Linda Kitchen** *sop* Papagena; **Anna Maria Panzarella** *sop* **Doris Lamprecht** *mez* **Delphine Haidan** *contr* First, Second and Third Ladies; **Damien Colin, Patrick Olivier Croset, Stéphane Dutournier** *trebs* First, Second and Third Boys; **Christopher Josey** *ten* First Armed Man, First Priest; **Laurent Naouri** *bass* Second Armed Man, Second Priest

Les Arts Florissants / William Christie

Erato ② 0630-12705-2 (150 minutes: DDD). Ⓜ

Notes, text and translation included. Recorded 1995

With a background primarily in the French baroque, William Christie comes to *Die Zauberflöte* from an angle quite unlike anyone else's; yet this is as idiomatic and as deeply Mozartian a reading of the work as any. Interviewed in the booklet-note, Christie says wise things about the work and ways of performing it, and in particular remarks on the unforced singing that is one of his objectives, much more manageable with the gentler sound of period instruments. All of this is borne out by the performance itself, which falls more sweetly and lovingly on the ear than any other. All this gives Christie opportunities to shape the work subtly and sensitively, with finer levels of nuance than are available to most modern performances. Mozartians will relish it, and it will surely prompt fresh thought about the work.

His tempos, for example, often set tradition aside. Many are quickish, but not all: 'Der Hölle Rache' is distinctly slower than usual, deliberate rather than fiery; so in particular is the union of Pamina and Tamino in the second finale, which gives it a *gravitas* that establishes it as the true emotional climax of the work. Yet overall the performance is quick and light-textured – and often quite dramatic. These light and soft textures and graceful phrasing are what above all characterize this recording. Some may find Christie less responsive than many more traditional interpreters to the music's quicksilver changes in mood, yet this is a part of his essentially broad and gentle view of *Die Zauberflöte*. His cast has few famous names. There is of course Hans-Peter Blochwitz, probably the finest Tamino around these days. As Pamina, Rosa Mannion has much charm and a hint of girlish vivacity but blossoms into maturity and indeed passion in 'Ach, ich fühl's' – the final phrases, as the wind instruments fall away and leave her alone and desolate, are very moving. Natalie Dessay's Queen of Night is forthright, clean and well tuned, with ample weight and tonal glitter. The orchestral playing from Les Arts Florissants is polished, and the translucent sound is a joy on the ear. Christie offers a very satisfying, acutely musical view of the work.

Die Zauberflöte **H**

Tiana Lemnitz *sop* Pamina; **Erna Berger** *sop* Queen of Night; **Helge Roswaenge** *ten* Tamino; **Gerhard Hüsch** *bar* Papageno; **Wilhelm Strienz** *bass* Sarasto; **Walter Grossmann** *bass* Speaker, Second Armed Man; **Heinrich Tessmer** *ten* Monostatos, First Armed Man; **Irma Beilke** *sop* Papagena, First Boy; **Hilde Scheppan** *sop* First Lady; **Elfriede Marherr-Wagner** *sop* Second Lady; **Rut Berglund** *contr* Third Lady, Third Boy; **Carla Spletter** *sop* Second Boy; **Ernest Fabbry** *ten* Priest

Favres Solisten Vereinigung; Berlin Philharmonic Orchestra / Sir Thomas Beecham

EMI Références mono ② CHS7 61034-2 (130 minutes: ADD). Notes, texts and translation included.

Also available on Pearl mono GEMMCDS9371. Ⓜ

Recorded 1937-38 **OO**

Beecham's feeling for both the grandeur and the delicacy, and the evident command he has of his forces, ensure attentiveness and delight at every turn. Every appearance of Gerhard Hüsch is a joy: we have had good Papagenos since this, the first of all complete recordings of *Die Zauberflöte*, but he surely remains the best. Tiana Lemnitz sings with such surpassing beauty for so much of the time that the occasional scoop is forgiven. Erna Berger's Queen of Night is firm and technically accomplished, and there are some splendid performances by the Three Ladies. The Tamino is not well cast: Roswaenge lacks finesse though he is a positive enough character. Wilhelm Strienz is literally out of his depth, producing nasty, unresonant low notes and generally sounding more like a Hans Sachs than a Sarastro. Walter Grossmann is a woolly Speaker, and Heinrich Tessmer, perfect as Monostatos, is sadly no use as First Armed Man. The absence of dialogue, as the anonymous writer of EMI's admirable sleeve-note says, 'turns music-dramainto a sort of song-cycle'. Altogether a set to pick one's way through, essential though it is to have it at hand. And this also applies to the Pearl, warily recommending it over its rival with the caution that there is surface-sound (however reduced) and, alas, no text and translation. The Pearl transfer provides the greater enjoyment, although it is true that EMI has all but eliminated the surface-sound; true also that the EMI transfer has greater sharpness of sibilants and 't's with all that that may imply about frequency range.

Additional Recommendation

Die Zauberflöte

Janowitz *sop* Pamina; **Popp** *sop* Queen of Night; **Gedda** *ten* Tamino; **Berry** *bar* Papageno

Philharmonia Chorus and Orchestra / Klemperer

EMI Great Recordings of the Century

② CMS5 67388-2 (134 minutes: ADD: 10/00). Ⓜ

Text and translation included.

A classic set if not quite a 'Great Recording'. Nicolai Gedda is a forthright Tamino, Lucia Popp a *nonpareil* of a Queen of Night and Walter Berry an enchanting Papageno. However, Gundula Janowitz, beautifully as she sings, is a detached Pamina. Note, the dialogue is absent (Otto Klemperer's decision).

Modest Mussorgsky

Russian 1839-1881

GROVE *Mussorgsky's mother gave him piano lessons, and at nine he played a Field concerto before an audience in his parents' house. In 1852 he entered the Guards' cadet school in St Petersburg. Although he had not studied harmony or composition, in 1856 he tried to write an opera the same year he entered the Guards. In 1857 he met Dargomïzhsky and Cui, and through them Balakirev and Stasov. He persuaded Balakirev to give him lessons and composed songs and piano sonatas.*

In 1858 Mussorgsky passed through a nervous or spiritual crisis and resigned his army commission. A visit to Moscow in 1859 fired his patriotic imagination and his compositional energies, but although his music began to enjoy public performances his nervous irritability was not entirely calmed. The emancipation of the serfs in March 1861 obliged him to spend most of the next two years helping manage the family estate; a symphony came to nothing and Stasov and Balakirev agreed that 'Mussorgsky is almost an idiot'. But he continued to compose and in 1863-6 worked on the libretto and music of an opera, Salammbô, which he never completed. At this time he served at the Ministry of Communications and lived in a commune with five other young men who ardently cultivated and exchanged advanced ideas about art, religion, philosophy and politics. Mussorgsky's private and public lives eventually came into conflict. In 1865 he underwent his first serious bout of dipsomania (probably as a reaction to his mother's death that year) and in 1867 he was dismissed from his post.

He spent summer 1867 at his brother's country house at Minkino, where he wrote, among other things, his first important orchestral work, St John's Night on the Bare Mountain. On his return to St Petersburg in the autumn Musorgsky, like the other members of the Balakirev-Stasov circle (ironically dubbed the 'Mighty Handful'), became interested in Dargomïzhsky's experiments in operatic naturalism. Early in 1869 Musorgsky re-entered government service and, in more settled conditions, was able to complete the original version of the opera Boris Godunov. This was rejected by the Mariinsky Theatre and Mussorgsky set about revising it. In 1872 the opera was again rejected, but excerpts were performed elsewhere and a vocal score published. The opera committee finally accepted the work and a successful production was given in February 1874.

Meanwhile Mussorgsky had begun work on another historical opera, Khovanshchina, at the same time gaining promotion at the ministry. Progress on the new opera was interrupted partly because of unsettled domestic circumstances, but mainly because heavy drinking which left him incapable of sustained creative effort. But several other compositions belong to this period, including the song cycles Sunless and Songs and Dances of Death and the Pictures at an Exhibition, for piano, a brilliant and bold series inspired by a memorial exhibition of drawings by his friend Victor Hartmann. Ideas for a comic opera based on Gogol's Sorochintsy Fair also began to compete with work on Khovanshchina; both operas remained unfinished at Musorgsky's death. During the earlier part of 1878 he seems to have led a more respectable life and his director at the ministry even allowed him leave for a three-month concert tour with the contralto Darya Leonova. After he was obliged to leave the government service in January 1880, Leonova helped provide him with employment and a home. It was to her that he turned on February 23, 1881 in a state of nervous excitement, saying that there was nothing left for him but to beg in the streets; he was suffering from alcoholic epilepsy. He was removed to hospital, where he died a month later.

Many of Mussorgsky's works were unfinished, and their editing and posthumous publication were mainly carried out by Rimsky-Korsakov, who to a greater or lesser degree 'corrected' what Mussorgsky had composed. It was only many years later that, with a return to the composer's original drafts, the true nature of his rough art could be properly understood

Pictures at an Exhibition (orch Ravel)

Pictures at an Exhibition (orch Ravel). **A Night on the Bare Mountain** (arr Rimsky-Korsakov)

Pictures at an Exhibition. St John's Night on the Bare Mountain. The destruction of Sennacheriba. Salammbô – Chorus of priestesses[a]. Oedipus in Athens – Chorus of people in the temple[a]. Joshua[b]
[b]**Elena Zaremba** *mez* [a]**Prague Philharmonic Chorus; Berlin Philharmonic Orchestra / Claudio Abbado**
DG 445 238-2GH (65 minutes: DDD). Texts and translations included. Recorded live in 1993 Ⓕ

St John's Night on the Bare Mountain is the original version of *A Night on the Bare Mountain*. Abbado relishes the odd grotesque spurts of colour from the woodwind and Mussorgskian ruggedness. The composer's structural clumsiness is not shirked and the lack of the smooth continuity found in the Rimsky-Korsakov arrangement does not impede the sense of forward momentum; indeed at the close the Russian dance element is emphasized, rather than the sinister pictorialism. The choral pieces are gloriously sung and again Abbado brings out their Russian colour, especially in the glowing yet sinuous 'Chorus of priestesses'. *Joshua* is made to seem a minor masterpiece with its lusty opening (hints of Borodin's Polovtsians) and its touching central solo ('The Amorite women weep'). This is most eloquently sung by Elena Zaremba and the theme is then movingly taken up first by the women of the chorus and then the men, before the exultant music returns. The performance of *Pictures at an Exhibition*, like the choral items, gains from the spacious ambience and sumptuous overall textures. It is very dramatic in its contrasts and very beautifully played.

The refinement and colour of the evocation, so characteristic of Abbado is most touching in 'The old castle', while 'Tuileries' is gently evoked with a flexibly fluid control of tempo. 'Bydlo' opens and closes mournfully, yet reaches a strong, positive immediacy as it finally comes close. The chicks dance with dainty lightness, then the hugely weighty lower orchestral tutti and bleating trumpet response of 'Samuel Goldenberg' demonstrate the extraordinary range of tone this great orchestra can command.

After the scintillating virtuosity of 'Market Place at Limoges' the sonorous Berlin brass makes a tremendous impact in 'Catacombe' and Abbado's tonal and dynamic graduations are astute; then after a ferociously rhythmic 'Baba-jaga' he steadily builds his three-dimensional 'Great Gate at Kiev', losing none of the grandeur of the gentle contrasts of the intoned chorale, with the tam-tam splashes at the end satisfyingly finalizing the effect. A most enjoyable concert: there is nothing routine about anything here.

Mussorgsky Pictures at an Exhibition
Stravinsky The Rite of Spring
Philadelphia Orchestra / Riccardo Muti
EMI Studio Plus CDM7 64516-2 (64 minutes: ADD). Ⓜ
Recorded 1978 ❍

Pictures at an Exhibition was the first commercial recording to do full justice to the sheer range and depth of sonority that the Philadelphia Orchestra could command. The recording venue was the Metropolitan Church of Philadelphia and the generous acoustic of the hall enabled this great orchestra to be heard to best advantage. The lower strings in 'Samuel Goldenberg and Schmuyle' have an extraordinary richness, body and presence, and 'Baba Yaga' has an unsurpassed virtuosity and attack. The glorious body of tone, the richly glowing colours, the sheer homogeneity of the strings and perfection of the ensemble is a consistent pleasure. Muti's reading is second to none and the orchestral playing is breathtaking. There are many other fine recordings of this work but they do not have quite that homogeneity of tone and the extraordinary sheen that is and has been the hallmark of the Philadelphians for many decades. The recording is amazingly lifelike and truthful.

Muti directs a performance of *The Rite of Spring* which is aggressively brutal but yet presents its violence not in coldly clinical terms but with red-blooded conviction. He favours a tempo a degree faster than usual, but no faster than the composer recommends. The great compulsion of the performance lies in his ability to draw playing from his orchestra which is not just precise and brilliant, but passionately committed. Wildness and barbarity are so clearly part of the mixture to a degree not matched by most other recordings, so it is not surprising that Muti's interpretation remains among the front-runners. The recording is gloriously full and dramatic with wide dynamic range and fine separation. The brass and percussion are caught with special vividness helped by one of the most impressive bass responses to be heard in this work.

Mussorgsky Pictures at an Exhibition. A Night on the Bare Mountain
Ravel Valses nobles et sentimentales
New York Philharmonic Orchestra / Giuseppe Sinopoli
DG 429 785-2GH (67 minutes: DDD). Ⓕ
Recorded 1989

Sinopoli's recording of *Pictures at an Exhibition* has great panache and is full of subtle detail and sharply characterized performances. None of this would be possible without the marvellous virtuosity of the New York Philharmonic Orchestra, whose brass section plays with a wonderful larger-than-life sonority and whose woodwind section produces playing of considerable delicacy and finesse, as for example in 'Tuileries' and the 'Ballet of the Unhatched Chicks'. Sinopoli revels in the drama of this work and this is nowhere more noticeable than in his sinister readings of 'Catacombs' and 'Baba-Yaga'. *A Night on the Bare Mountain* is no less impressive, where again the orchestra's flair and virtuosity have an almost overwhelming impact. Less successful are Ravel's *Valses nobles et sentimentales* which are perhaps too idiosyncratic for an individual recommendation despite some superb performances and moments of great beauty. The sound is very well balanced.

Mussorgsky Pictures at an Exhibition Ⓗ
Respighi The Pines of Rome. The Fountains of Rome
Chicago Symphony Orchestra / Fritz Reiner
RCA Victor Gold Seal 09026 61401-2 Ⓜ
(70 minutes: ADD). Recorded 1957-59 ∞

This 1957 *Pictures at an Exhibition* was, alongside Karajan's famous Philharmonia version for EMI (currently out of the catalogue), one of the first two outstanding stereo recordings of this piece. Both records showed the startling instrumental virtuosity which each great orchestra could command. Reiner's performance is full of character, and marvellously played, especially by the famous Chicago brass, although the full string sonority is equally impressive (in 'Goldenberg and Schmuyle', for instance), and besides the spectacle, there are tender moments like the hauntingly nostalgic picture of 'The old castle'. The climax of the closing 'Great Gate of Kiev' is superbly built to produce a very grand final statement, but note also the venom of the attack in the fierce scalic flourish at 1'28" (track 15). The extraordinary thing about this reissue is that the channels are reversed. It is almost unbelievable that this was not noticed. With excellent notes, however, this is an indispensable reissue. (This recording is, incidentally, also included in a compilation disc which is reviewed in the Collections section.)

Reiner's legendary performances of Respighi's *Pines* and *Fountains of Rome* were recorded in Orchestra Hall, Chicago, in 1959. This recording still has the power to astonish, both by the sheer quality of the orchestral playing and the richly translucent sound and incredibly subtle detail. The ecstatic moment when the strings swell out in 'The Pine of the Janiculum' (track 18 – first at 1'53", then even more rapturously at 3'37"), is unforgettable and the portrait of the Villa Medici fountain at sunset has a similar element of rapture, with the bell gently tolling at the end. The wonderful internal balances in the music's quieter passages are a credit to conductor and engineers alike, and of course also to the unique hall acoustics. The playing of the Chicago orchestra is quite glorious and the many touches from the percussion department add to the uniquely atmospheric quality of these remarkable recordings. The big splashes of sound, like the turning on of the Triton Fountain, or great Neptune processional, associated with the Trevi at midday, so spacious in Reiner's hands, are splendidly brought off. But it is the gentle moments that one remembers most, utterly alluring in their soft focus, almost decadent in their glowing seduction of colour.

Pictures at an Exhibition. A Night on the Bare Mountain. Boris Godunov – Symphonic synthesis. Khovanshchina – Act 4 Entr'acte (all arr Stokowski)
BBC Philharmonic Orchestra / Matthias Bamert
Chandos CHAN9445 (69 minutes: DDD). Ⓕ
Recorded 1995

Oliver Daniel (Stokowski's biographer) wrote extensively about doubts expressed by various musicians that Stokowski's orchestral transcriptions were entirely his own work, explaining that Lucien Cailliet (a clarinet player in the Philadelphia Orchestra) did a good deal of the physical work of score-writing. Yet Cailliet himself stated that the conductor and he discussed each piece in detail first, and it is known that Stokowski was always amending the instrumentation in the course of performances. In any case, Cailliet's association with the conductor ended in 1938 and while he might have contributed to the skilfully tailored 24-minute *Boris Godunov* synthesis, the *Pictures at an Exhibition* was all Stokowski's own and *Night on Bald Mountain* (the correct title, and nearer the original Russian meaning) was scored for Disney in 1940. Anyone who has seen *Fantasia* finds the imagery in this last piece unforgettable and the powerfully plangent orchestration (especially the use of percussive effects) is in many respects nearer to Mussorgsky's *St John's Night on the Bare Mountain* than the Rimsky version. It sounds really superb here, as indeed does the *Pictures*. The sombre power of the operatic synthesis, with its Kremlin bells and chanting monks and the haunted portrait of Boris himself, emerges with distinction. The Entr'acte from *Khovanshchina* is even finer, one of Stokowski's most effective transcriptions, rich in sonority and played very movingly under Matthias Bamert.

The vividness of Stokowski's *Pictures* is immensely likeable too, particularly the way in which the orchestration is varied – the unison horns sing out splendidly near the climax of 'Bydlo', while to feature a cor anglais for the main theme in 'The old castle' is quite as telling as Ravel's saxophone, perhaps more so. Stokowski uses the violins rather more than Ravel, as instanced by the opening 'Promenade'. The one moment when Ravel's scoring is truly inspired is the interchange between Goldenburg and Schmuyle; Stokowski has the woodwind echo the solo trumpet and the effect, mockingly piquant though it is, becomes less bleatingly obsequious than Ravel's version. Not surprisingly, the 'Catacombes' sequence makes a sumptuously weighty impact and 'Baba-jaga' is searingly grotesque and bizarrely full of imaginative orchestral comments. Two numbers are omitted: 'Tuileries' and 'Limoges', as Stokowski considered them 'too French' and 'not Mussorgskian'. 'The Great Gate of Kiev', scored for massive forces, including bells and organ, makes a huge final apotheosis – how Stokowski must have revelled in its grand climax.

Pictures at an Exhibition. A Night on the Bare Mountain. Khovanshchina – Prelude, Act 1, 'Dawn over the Moscow River'
Atlanta Symphony Orchestra / Yoel Levi Ⓕ
Telarc CD80296 (50 minutes: DDD). Recorded 1991

When this was released, Telarc established a position for it as sonically the most spectacular set of *Pictures* among the many in the current catalogue. And it is a very fine performance too. The programme opens with *A Night on the Bare Mountain* – the brass sound is special, with great richness and natural bite with no exaggeration. The performance overall is both well paced and exciting. Perhaps Levi's evil spirits are not as satanic as some, but they make an impact and the contrasting melancholy of the closing section is very touching, with the tolling bell nicely balanced and the clarinet solo poignantly taking over from the gently elegiac strings.

The characterization of *Pictures at an Exhibition* is no less successful, although it is an essentially mellower view than, for example, Sinopoli's highly praised DG version with the New York Philharmonic Orchestra. Levi's is a performance where throughout the conductor makes the most of the colour, and brilliant orchestral effects of Ravel's inspired score, revealing much that often goes unheard – the grotesquerie of 'Gnomus' is not accentuated, but one greatly enjoys the attack of the lower strings which are very tangible indeed; a doleful bassoon introduces 'The Old Castle' and the saxophone solo has a satin-like finish on the timbre to produce an elegant melancholy; the woodwind in 'Tuileries' is gentle in its virtuosity. Levi holds back a little for the delicate string entry and the whole piece has a captivating lightness of touch. 'Baba-Yaga' makes a grand entrance, her music much less plangent than with Sinopoli, but again with the orchestral sounds tickling the ear. The reprise is dramatic and weighty and we are led naturally into the great finale, very grandiloquent. The final climax is unerringly built and at the very close the brass and strings produce an electrifying richness and weight of sound, to bring a *frisson* of excitement, with the tam-tam resounding clearly. Then there is silence, and out of it steals the exquisite opening of the *Khovanschchina* Prelude, with its poetic evocation of dawn over the Kremlin. Levi goes for atmosphere above all else and does not make too much of the climax, but the coda with its fragile woodwind halos is most delicately managed. This disc is a first choice if state-of-the-art recording is your prime consideration.

Pictures at an Exhibition (piano)

Mussorgsky Pictures at an Exhibition **H**
Tchaikovsky Piano Sonata in G, Op 37
Sviatoslav Richter *pf*
Melodiya mono 74321 29469-2 (61 minutes: ADD). Ⓜ
Recorded 1956-58

The blend of German and Russian backgrounds must have something to do with the unique power of Richter at his best. Certainly that comes across in the tempering of rhetoric with structural insight which elevates the Tchaikovsky Sonata beyond any other performance of this unwieldy piece; again Richter's sweeping panache and volcanic sense of flow make for a colossal Mussorgsky *Pictures* (Moscow, 1958), far better recorded than the famous, though currently unavailable, live Sofia account. Richter's interpretations in these years had an elemental power and unselfconscious abandon that was refined and tempered in later life. The mono sound is acceptable.

Complete Songs

Boris Christoff *bass* **Alexandre Labinsky, Gerald Moore** *pfs* **French Radio National Orchestra / Georges Tzipine** **H**
EMI Références mono ③ CHS7 63025-2 (191 minutes: ADD). Notes, texts and translations included. Ⓜ
Recorded 1951-56 **000**

This set is undoubtedly one of the all-time glories of the gramophone and should be in any worthwhile song collection. This is unquestionably Boris Christoff's most important legacy. Even on the first disc, in the earlier and slightly less remarkable songs, Mussorgsky offers a range of personalities and emotions as then unknown in Russian song. There are the warlike King Saul, the sad figure of Wilhelm Meister in the *Song of the Old Man* (what we know as 'An die Türen'), the desolate landscape of *The Wind Howls*, the folk-hero, Calistratus. Then we hear a wide variety of styles from the recitative-like *Cast-off Woman* to the gentle lyricism of *Night*. In this last song Christoff produces that magical *mezza voce* of his to suggest the intimacy of the loved one portrayed within. But, by then – the 11th song – he has already given us an amazing palette of sound colours, everything from the utterly ferocious to the gentlest whisper. With the second disc, we come to many of the better-known songs but few of them have ever been better interpreted than here. In *Hopak*, the bass has a rollicking time of it, relishing every word. In *Savishna*, a wonderfully vivid song, he subtly portrays the idiot. He catches the bitter satire of *The Classicist* and the humour of *The Seminarist*, where the Latin recitation is gleefully projected.

The rather weak *Puppet Show* is almost saved here by Christoff's identity with its twists of irony. Then he can change style again to produce a hypnotically sweet tone for *Evening Song*, a tender lyric built on only five notes. But the centrepiece of this disc is, of course, the *Nursery* cycle, where Christoff manages to adapt his big tone for a convincing impersonation of a small boy. He finds yet other voices for the Nurse and for the Mother. This is a *tour de force*. Similarly rewarding are his performances of the *Sunless* and *Songs and Dances of Death* cycles. He catches all the bleak gloom of the first, the histrionic force of the second, where his variety of timbre is once more astonishing, but in the *Songs and Dances* he uses a corrupt orchestration. After these two cycles, Mussorgsky's inspiration seemed to falter, though *On the Dnieper*, a lyrical piece of surpassing beauty, and the ever-popular *Song of the flea*, which ends the set, are remarkable achievements in their way and are here excellently interpreted. Labinsky and Moore are vivid and imaginative partners.

Boris Godunov

Boris Godunov (first version)
Nikolai Putilin *bar* Boris Godunov; **Viktor Lutsiuk** *ten* Grigory; **Nikolai Okhotnikov** *bass* Pimen; **Fyodor Kuznetsov** *bass* Varlaam; **Konstantin Pluzhnikov** *ten* Shuisky; **Nikolai Gassiev** *ten* Missail; **Zlata Bulycheva** *mez* Fyodor; **Olga Trifonova** *sop* Xenia; **Yevgenia Gorokhovskaya** *mez* Nurse; **Liubov Sokolova** *mez* Hostess; **Evgeny Akimov** *ten* Simpleton; **Vassily Gerello** *bar* Shchelkalov; **Grigory Karassev** *bass* Nikitich; **Evgeny Nikitin** *bass* Mityukha; **Yuri Schikalov** *ten* Krushchov

Boris Godunov (second version)
Vladimir Vaneyev *bass* Boris Godunov; **Vladimir Galusin** *ten* Grigory; **Olga Borodina** *mez* Marina; **Nikolai Okhotnikov** *bass* Pimen; **Fyodor Kuznetsov** *bass* Varlaam; **Konstantin Pluzhnikov** *ten* Shuisky; **Nikolai Gassiev** *ten* Missail; **Evgeny Nikitin** *bass* Rangoni, Mityukha; **Zlata Bulycheva** *mez* Fyodor; **Olga Trifonova** *sop* Xenia; **Yevgenia Gorokhovskaya** *mez* Nurse; **Liubov Sokolova** *mez* Hostess; **Evgeny Akimov** *ten* Simpleton; **Vassily Gerello** *bar* Shchelkalov; **Grigory Karassev** *bass* Nikitich; **Yuri Schikalov** *ten* Krushchov; **Andrei Karabanov** *bar* Lavitsky; **Yuri Laptev** *ten* Chernikovsky
Chorus and Orchestra of the Kirov Opera / Valery Gergiev
Philips ⑤ 462 230-2PH5 (306 minutes: DDD). Notes, Ⓜ texts and translations included. Recorded 1997 **OO**

What we have here is, literally, two operas for the price of one. That is to say, the two discs containing Mussorgsky's first *Boris Godunov* and the three containing his second are available at five discs for the normal cost of three. And what we are dealing with is, in a real sense, two operas. First, a brief resumé of the facts. In 1868-69 Mussorgsky composed seven scenes: outside the Novedevichy Monastery, Coronation outside the Kremlin, Pimen's Cell, the Inn, the Tsar's rooms in the Kremlin, outside St Basil's Cathedral, Boris's Death in the Kremlin. When these were rejected by the Imperial Theatres in 1872, he made various revisions. To meet objections about the lack of female roles, Mussorgsky added the two scenes with the Polish princess Marina Mniszek; he also substituted the final Kromy Forest scene for the St Basil's scene (causing a problem by duplicating the episode with the *yurodivy*, or holy fool). He made a large number of adjustments, some of a minor nature, some rather more significant (such as dropping Pimen's narration of the murder of the young Tsarevich), and one huge, the complete rewriting of the original fifth scene, in the Kremlin, sometimes known as the Terem scene (*terem* is an obsolete word meaning a room in a tower). This was the work that he resubmitted, and which was first performed in St Petersburg in 1874. Rimsky-Korsakov's famous version (which does much more than reorchestrate) was first heard in 1896, and for many years superseded its predecessors.

However, it has increasingly been recognized that *Boris* II is not a revision of *Boris* I but a different work, both as regards the view of the central character and his place in the historical narrative, and also as regards the rethought musical technique and sometimes change of idiom which this has brought about. Therefore the present set makes a real contribution to our understanding and enjoyment of Russia's greatest opera. It follows that there have to be two singers of the central role. Putilin (*Boris* I) is in general more capacious in tone, more brooding and lofty, in the Terem scene more embittered and harsh, willing to act with the voice. Vaneyev is a decidedly more immediate and human Boris, tender with his son Fyodor (a touching, engaging performance from Zlata Bulycheva) both in the Terem and at the end, not always as dominating as this Tsar should be but sympathetic, allowing his voice to blanch as death approaches, and especially responsive to the melodic essence of Mussorgsky's speech-delivered lines. This enables him to be rather freer with the actual note values. It does not necessarily matter that much: Mussorgsky changed his mind over various details, and the important thing is to use his notes to create character rather than be too literal with what the different versions propose. Pimen, strongly sung with a hint of the youthful passions that he claims to have abjured, is sung by Nikolai Okhotnikov more or less identically in both performances.

The only character, apart from Boris, to be accorded two singers is Grigory, the False Dmitri. Viktor Lutsiuk (*Boris* I) is strenuous, obsessed, vital; Vladimir Galusin (*Boris* II) can sound more frenzied, and has the opportunity with the addition of the Polish acts to give a convincing portrayal of a weak man assuming strength but being undermined by the wiles of a determined woman. Here, she is none other than Olga Borodina, moodily toying with her polonaise rhythms and then in full sensuous call. Yevgenia Gorokhovskaya is a jolly old Nurse in the *Boris* II Terem scene. The rest of the cast do not really change their interpretations from one *Boris* to another, and indeed scarcely need to do so: it is not really upon that which the differences depend. Liubov Sokolova sings a fruity Hostess, welcoming in Fyodor Kuznetsov a Varlaam who can really sing his Kazan song rather than merely bawling it. Konstantin Pluzhnikov makes Shuisky move from the rather sinister force confronting Boris in the Terem to a more oily complacency in the Death scene: many Shuiskys make less of the part. Evgeny Nikitin is a creepy, fanatical Rangoni, Vassily Gerello a Shchelkalov of hypocritical elegance, Evgeny Akimov a sad-toned Simpleton. Gergiev directs strong, incisive performances, accompanying sympathetically and controlling the marvellous crowd scenes well.

However, it is a pity that he allows fierce whistles completely to drown the speeding violins opening the Kromy Forest scene (the music can be heard only when it returns), and he has not been given sufficient clarity of recording with the chorus. The words are often obscure, even with the boyars in the Death scene, and far too much is lost in the crowd exchanges. This is regrettable for a work that, in either incarnation, draws so much on realistic detail of articulation.

Nevertheless, these five discs form a fascinating set, one which no admirer of this extraordinary creative achievement can afford to ignore.

Boris Godunov

Anatoly Kotcherga *bass* Boris; **Sergei Larin** *ten* Grigory; **Marjana Lipovšek** *mez* Marina; **Samuel Ramey** *bass* Pimen; **Gleb Nikolsky** *bass* Varlaam; **Philip Langridge** *ten* Shuisky; **Helmut Wildhaber** *ten* Missail; **Sergei Leiferkus** *bar* Rangoni; **Liliana Nichiteanu** *mez* Feodor; **Valentina Valente** *sop* Xenia; **Yevgenia Gorokhovskaya** *mez* Nurse; **Eléna Zaremba** *mez* Hostess; **Alexander Fedin** *ten* Simpleton; **Albert Shagidullin** *bar* Shchelkolov; **Wojciech Drabowicz** *ten* Mitukha, Krushchov

Slovak Philharmonic Chorus; Berlin Radio Chorus; Tölz Boys' Choir; Berlin Philharmonic Orchestra / Claudio Abbado

Sony Classical ③ S3K58977 (200 minutes: DDD). Ⓕ

Notes, text and translation included. Recorded 1993 ●

Few conductors have been more diligent than Claudio Abbado in seeking the truth about this vast canvas. He chooses the definitive 1872-74 version, adding scenes, including the complete one in Pimen's cell and the St Basil's scene from 1869. His is a taut, tense reading – grand, virtuosic, at times hard-driven, favouring extremes of speed and dynamics. The orchestra is very much in the foreground, sounding more emphatic than would ever be the case in the opera house. Kotcherga has a superb voice, firmly produced throughout an extensive register. His is a Boris avoiding conventional melodrama and concerned to show the loving father. The ambitious lovers are well represented. Indeed, Larin is quite the best Grigory yet recorded on disc, sounding at once youthful, heroic and ardent, and quite free of any tenor mannerisms. Lipovšek characterizes Marina forcefully: we are well aware of the scheming Princess's powers of wheeler-dealing and of erotic persuasion. The recording is of demonstration standard: it is most potent in the way that it captures the incisive and pointed singing of the combined choruses in their various guises. Here all is vividly brought before us by conductor and producer in the wide panorama predicated by Mussorgsky's all-enveloping vision.

Boris Godunov (arr Rimsky-Korsakov)

Ivan Petrov *bass* Boris Godunov; **Vladimir Ivanovsky** *ten* Grigory; **Irina Arkhipova** *mez* Marina; **Mark Reshetin** *bass* Pimen; **Alexey Geleva** *bass* Varlaam; **Georgy Shulpin** *ten* Shuisky; **Nikolay Zakharov** *ten* Missail; **Yevgeny Kibkalo** *bass* Rangoni; **Valentina Klepatskaya** *mez* Feodor; **Tamara Sorokina** *sop* Xenia; **Yevgeniya Verbitskaya** *mez* Nurse; **Veronika Borisenko** *mez* Innkeeper; **Anton Grigoryev** *bass* Simpleton, Nikitich; **Alexey Ivanov** *bar* Shchelkalov; **Vladimir Valaitis** *bar* Lavitsky; **Yury Galkin** *bass* Chernikovsky; **Leonid Ktitorov** *bass* Mityukha; **Anatoly Mishutin** *ten* Krushchov, Boyar

Chorus and Orchestra of the Bolshoi Theatre, Moscow / Alexander Melik-Pashayev

Melodiya ③ 74321 29349 2 (175 minutes: ADD). Ⓜ

Notes, text and translation included. Recorded 1962 ●

This is certainly the most authentic-sounding version of the Rimsky arrangement so far recorded. Under Melik-Pashayev's conducting, which combines discipline, an innate understanding of the score's rhythmic and melodic requirements and sheer experience in directing the work, it flows onwards in a steady stream of musical and dramatic consistency. Nowhere else will you hear such a cast of singers, steeped in the best tradition of performing the work at the Bolshoi, and at the same time so apt for their given roles. Ivan Petrov isn't at all in the Chaliapin or Christoff (Dobrowen) mould of performing the work: his performance is entirely free of any melodrama and is sung with all the vocal verities observed in a rounded, warm bass. In his more modest way, Petrov invests his role with just as much feeling and drama as his more histrionic rivals – his is a richly rewarding portrayal.

Even better, though, is the Marina of the young Irina Arkhipova. In her case, she has no peer, let alone a better on any other set. The proud carriage of her voice and the finely nuanced character of her loud and soft singing are just what one wants from the ambitious Polish Princess. Her Grigory, Vladimir Ivanovsky, isn't vocally quite in the same class – the voice sounds strained under pressure – but, like everyone else in the cast, he is very much inside his role and declaims it with real, fervent passion. In the Polish act Yevgeny Kibkalo makes an ideally insinuating Rangoni. Mark Reshetin is perfectly cast as grave old Pimen; he is another bass whose tone is well supported and easily produced. Georgy Shulpin has one of those sharp-edged tenors that many British ears abhor, but it seems to be absolutely the right voice for that crepuscular, two-faced boyar. Anton Grigoryev is a plangent, touching Simpleton. Most of the supporting cast is in the same mould, peculiarly Russian, and therefore idiomatic in timbre. Some listeners may well find themselves baulking at the backward recording of the orchestra. The excellent singing of the chorus is vividly caught. The stereo spread is a trifle too marked. If you enjoy Rimsky's admittedly inauthentic scoring, you should seriously consider acquiring this well-remastered Melodiya set.

Boris Godunov (arr Rimsky-Korsakov) **H**

Boris Christoff *bass* Boris, Pimen, Varlaam; **Nicolai Gedda** *ten* Grigory; **Eugenia Zareska** *mez* Marina, Feodor; **André Bielecki** *ten* Shuisky, Missail, Krushchov; **Kim Borg** *bass* Rangoni, Shchelkalov; **Ludmila Lebedeva** *sop* Xenia; **Lydia Romanova** *mez* Nurse, Hostess; **Wassili Pasternak** *ten* Simpleton; **Raymond Bonte** *ten* Lavitsky; **Eugène Bousquet** *bass* Chernikovsky

Choeurs Russes de Paris; French Radio National Orchestra / Issay Dobrowen

EMI Références mono ③ CHS5 65192-2 Ⓜ

(178 minutes: ADD). Recorded 1952 ●

Dobrowen's lean, vivid, acutely shaped direction, benefiting from taut rhythms and fastish tempos, is as vital as that on any version since. Its other main attribute is, of course, Christoff's first complete reading on disc of the tortured Tsar, whose role he sings with an enviable combination of firm tone, vital diction and concentrated histrionics, never overstepping the mark. His assumption of two other parts has always been frowned on, but he so subtly varies his tone – softer, greyer for Pimen, rotundly rollicking for Varlaam – that the tripling only worries in the final scene when Pimen comes face to face with the dying ruler. The contrast of his finely shaded Pimen with Ramey's one-dimensional singing on the Abbado version is most marked. If that were not enough, there is the beauty and ardour of the young Gedda as Grigory to please the ear and Zareska's seductive, vocally appealing Marina. She also sings a likeable Feodor. Kim Borg doubles successfully as Shchelkalov and an oily Rangoni. The choral singing is good. We have heard much better on disc since, but few orchestras, in the West at least, have sounded so Russian as these French players but then few have had the benefit of being tutored by Dobrowen. The digital transfers bring out the excellence of the original engineering.

Khovanshchina

Aage Haugland *bass* Ivan Khovansky; **Vladimir Atlantov** *ten* Andrey Khovansky; **Vladimir Popov** *ten* Golitsin; **Anatolij Kotscherga** *bar* Shaklovity; **Paata Burchuladze** *bass* Dosifey; **Marjana Lipovšek** *contr* Marfa; **Brigitte Poschner-Klebel** *sop* Susanna; **Heinz Zednik** *ten* Scribe; **Joanna Borowska** *sop* Emma; **Wilfried Gahmlich** *ten* Kouzka

Vienna Boys' Choir; Slovak Philharmonic Choir; Vienna State Opera Chorus and Orchestra / Claudio Abbado

DG ③ 429 758-2GH3 (171 minutes: DDD). Notes, text and translation included. Recorded live in 1989 Ⓕ ●●

The booklet-essay suggests that Mussorgsky's music constantly poses a question to his Russian compatriots: 'What are the causes of our country's continuing calamities, and why does the state crush all that is good?'. Anyone who follows today's news from Russia and then experiences this opera will understand what is meant, and while we observe with sympathy we seem no nearer than the citizens of that great, tormented country to finding solutions for its endemic problems. However, Mussorgsky was not the least of those Russian musicians who found lasting beauty in her history and he expressed it in a powerfully dramatic idiom that drew on folk-music and had both epic qualities and deep humanity as well as an occasional gentleness. There is also an element here of Russian church music, since *Khovanshchina* has a political and religious theme and is set in the 1680s at the time of Peter the Great's accession. Since the work was unfinished when Mussorgsky died, performances always involve conjectural work, and the version here – which works convincingly – is mostly that of Shostakovich with the choral ending that Stravinsky devised using Mussorgsky's music. The cast in this live recording is not one of star opera singers, but they are fully immersed in the drama and the music, as is the chorus and the orchestra under Abbado, and the result is deeply atmospheric. The booklet has the Russian text and a translation.

Carl Nielsen

Danish 1865-1931

GROVE *Nielsen had a poor, rural upbringing, though his father was a musician and he learnt to play the violin, brass instruments and the piano. He studied at the Copenhagen Conservatory (1884-6), then continued having lessons with Orla Rosenhoff. In 1890-91 he travelled to Germany, France and Italy, and began his Brahmsian First Symphony (1892); from 1889 to 1905 he played the violin in the Danish court orchestra.*

During the decade from the First Symphony to the Second ('The Four Temperaments', 1902) he developed an extended tonal style, but compacted and classical in its logic: the relatively few works of this period include the string quartets in G minor and E flat, the cantata Hymnus amoris and the opera Saul and David. Here he showed a gift for sharp musical characterisation, pursued in his second opera, the comedy Maskarade (1906) and other works, while his parallel command of large-scale, dynamic forms was affirmed by the Third Symphony (Sinfonia espansiva, 1911) and the Violin Concerto (1911).

From this period he was an international figure and went abroad often to conduct his own music, while working in Copenhagen as a conductor and teacher. At the same time his music became still more individual in its progressive tonality (movements or works ending in a key different from the initial one), 'group polyphony' (the orchestra being treated as an assembly of ensembles in counterpoint), vigorous rhythmic drive and dependence on a harmony not so much of chords as of focal pitches. His chief works were still symphonies (no. 4 'The Inextinguishable', 1916; No.5, 1922) and chamber pieces (F major quartet, 1919; Serenata in vano for quintet, 1914), but he also produced numerous songs and hymn tunes, in addition to incidental scores.

The range of his output remained broad during his last decade, but his textures became still more polyphonic and his ideas still more vividly characterized, bringing a conversational style, intimate or dramatic, to such works as the Sixth Symphony (Sinfonia semplice, 1925), the Wind Quintet (1922) and the concertos for flute (1926) and clarinet (1928). His last works, going still deeper into the great contrapuntal tradition, include the Three Motets (1929) and Commotio for organ (1931).

Violin Concerto, FS61

Awards 1989

Nielsen Violin Concerto[a]
Sibelius Violin Concerto in D minor, Op 47[b]
Cho-Liang Lin *vn*
[a]**Swedish Radio Symphony Orchestra,** [b]**Philharmonia Orchestra / Esa-Pekka Salonen**

Sony Classical SK44548 (69 minutes: DDD). Recorded 1987-88 Ⓕ ●●●

At the time this was the best recording of the Sibelius Concerto to have appeared for more than a decade and probably the best ever of the Nielsen. Cho-Liang Lin brings an apparently effortless virtuosity to both concertos. He produces a wonderfully clean and silvery sonority and there is no lack of aristocratic finesse. Only half-a-dozen years separate the two concertos, yet they breathe a totally different air. Lin's perfect intonation and tonal purity excite admiration and throughout them both there is a strong sense of line from beginning to end. Esa-Pekka Salonen gets excellent playing from the Philharmonia Orchestra in the Sibelius and almost equally good results from the Swedish Radio Symphony Orchestra. This is one of the classic concerto recordings of the century.

Violin Concerto. Flute Concerto. Clarinet Concerto
Toke Lund Christiansen *fl* **Niels Thomsen** *cl*
Kim Sjøgren *vn*
Danish National Radio Symphony Orchestra / Michael Schønwandt
Chandos CHAN8894 (80 minutes: DDD). Ⓕ
Recorded 1990

Kim Sjøgren may not command the purity of tone of Cho-Liang Lin but he has the inestimable advantage of totally idiomatic orchestral support: Michael Schønwandt has an instinctive feeling for this music – and it shows throughout. The perspective between soloist and orchestra is well judged (Sjøgren is never larger than life) and so is the internal balance. In the Flute Concerto, which veers from Gallic wit to moments of great poetic feeling, Toke Lund Christiansen is an excellent soloist. He has no want of brilliance or of authority and his performance is also endowed with plenty of character. Niels Thomsen's account of the Clarinet Concerto is one of the very finest now before the public. If there is any music from another planet, this is it! There is no attempt to beautify the score nor to overstate it: every dynamic nuance and expressive marking is observed by both the soloist and the conductor. Thomsen plays as though his very being is at stake and Michael Schønwandt secures playing of great imaginative intensity from the Danish Radio Orchestra.

Additional Recommendation
Violin Concerto, FS61
Couplings: Flute Concerto, FS119. Clarinet Concerto, FS129
Davies *fl* **Banks** *cl* **Carney** *vn* **Bournemouth Symphony Orchestra / Bakels**
Naxos 8 554189 (79 minutes: DDD: 8/00) Ⓢ

Decent but not high-grade accounts from all concerned. Jonathan Carney proves a thoroughly musical soloist, his sweet-toned contribution at once unforced and affectionate. At Naxos price, it makes an excellent first-time Nielsen buy

Symphonies

No 1 in G minor, FS16; **No 2** FS29, 'The Four Temperaments'; **No 3**, FS60, 'Sinfonia espansiva'; **No 4**, FS76, 'The inextinguishable'; **No 5**, FS97; **No 6**, FS116, 'Sinfonia semplice'

Awards 1991

Symphonies Nos 1, 2 and 3[a]. Maskarade – Overture. Aladdin – Suite, FS89
[a]**Nancy Wait Fromm** *sop* [a]**Kevin McMillan** *bar*
San Francisco Symphony Orchestra / Herbert Blomstedt
Double Decca 460 985-2DF2 Ⓜ
(134 minutes: DDD). Recorded 1989 ●●●

The complete symphonies with Blomstedt / San Francisco SO are also available in a box set: Decca 443 117-2DH3 Ⓕ

Nielsen always nurtured a special affection for his First Symphony – and rightly so, for its language is natural and unaffected. It has great spontaneity of feeling and a Dvořákian warmth and freshness. Blomstedt's recording is vital, beautifully shaped and generally faithful to both the spirit and the letter of the score. The recording is very fine: the sound has plenty of room to expand, there is a very good relationship between the various sections of the orchestra and a realistic perspective. The Second and Third are two of Nielsen's most genial symphonies, both of which come from the earliest part of the century, in performances of the very first order. The Second (1902), inspired by the portrayal of *The Four Temperaments* (Choleric, Phlegmatic, Melancholic, Sanguine) that he had seen in a country inn, has splendid concentration and fire and, as always, from the right pace stems the right character. Moreover the orchestra sounds inspired, for there is a genuine excitement about its playing. Indeed Blomstedt's accounts are by far the most satisfying available. The Third, *Espansiva*, is even more personal in utterance than *The Four Temperaments*, for during the intervening years Nielsen had come much further along the road of self-discovery. His melodic lines are bolder, the musical paragraphs longer and his handling of form more assured. It is a glorious and richly inventive score whose pastoral slow movement includes a part for two wordless voices. Blomstedt gives us an affirmative, powerful reading and in the slow movement, the soprano produces the required ethereal effect. The sound is very detailed and full-bodied, and in the best traditions of the company. Blomstedt's *Espansiva* has greater depth than most accounts; the actual sound has that glowing radiance that characterizes Nielsen, and the tempo, the underlying current on which this music is borne, is expertly judged – and nowhere better than in the finale.

Symphony No 1. Flute Concerto. Rhapsody Overture: An imaginary trip to the Faroe Islands, FS123
Patrick Gallois *fl*
Gothenburg Symphony Orchestra / Myung-Whun Chung Ⓕ
BIS CD454 (63 minutes: DDD). Recorded 1989

This recording of the First Symphony is hardly less fine than that of Blomstedt. Tempos are generally well judged and there is a good feeling for the overall architecture of the piece. It gets off to a splendid start and Chung shapes the second group affectionately. He pulls back further later on, interpreting the *molto tranquillo* as an agogic rather than a character marking. However, he does not put a foot wrong in the slow movement, which has a splendid sense of line, and phrasing which is attentive but never overemphatic. In the *Scherzo* he does pull back fractionally for the wind on their second appearance though not the first time round. The finale is exhilaratingly played. Throughout the work Chung knows how to build up to a climax and keep detail in the right perspective. As always, the Gothenburg Symphony Orchestra plays with enthusiasm and spirit, as if it has always lived with this music and yet, paradoxically, is discovering it for the first time. The Rhapsody Overture, *An imaginary trip to the Faroe Islands*, begins most imaginatively but inspiration undoubtedly flags. The performance of the Flute Concerto is rather special. It is most strongly characterized by Patrick Gallois who plays with effortless virtuosity and an expressive eloquence that is never over- or under-stated. His purity of line in the first movement is quite striking and he has the measure of the poignant coda. His dynamic range is wide, the tone free from excessive vibrato and his approach fresh.

Symphony No 2. Aladdin – Suite, FS89
Gothenburg Symphony Orchestra / Myung-Whun Chung Ⓕ
BIS CD247 (56 minutes: DDD). Recorded 1983

Myung-Whun Chung has a real feeling for this repertoire and his account of the Second Symphony is very fine. Nielsen himself had a strong association with the Gothenburg Symphony Orchestra, and the present orchestra is an enthusiastic and responsive body. Tempos are excellently judged, there is a splendid sense of forward movement and completely idiomatic feeling. The recording is impressive too, with the excellent acoustic of the Gothenburg Hall used to great advantage. Until this release the *Aladdin* music had been out of the catalogue for some time so it was doubly welcome. It certainly receives a beguiling and spirited performance under Chung. The strings produce excellent quality in 'Aladdin's Dream' and the playing is alert and sensitive. A very distinguished set.

Symphonies Nos 2 and 3
National Symphony Orchestra of Ireland / Adrian Leaper
Naxos 8 550825 (68 minutes: DDD). Ⓢ
Recorded 1994

The vital current on which every phrase must be borne in Nielsen needs to flow at higher voltage. This is music which needs to be played at white heat. Well, there is certainly no lack of electricity in Leaper's reading of the Second. He sets a cracking pace for the first movement, the choleric temperament, and hardly puts a foot wrong in its three companions. His tempos in the *Sinfonia espansiva* are well judged and sensible throughout all four of the movements. The finale, where many conductors get it wrong, seems to be just right. These are more than just serviceable performances: they are very good indeed and the Irish orchestra sounds well rehearsed and inside the idiom. You can pay more and do worse although some collectors will think the additional polish one gets from Blomstedt or Myung-Whun Chung is worth the extra outlay. These latter performances continue to grow in stature, and it is no mean compliment to the Naxos versions to say that they give them a very good run for their money. Naxos does not identify the singers in the slow movement of the *Espansiva*. No one investing in this issue and then going on to either of the Blomstedt accounts is going to feel that they have been let down. The recording team secures a very decent balance: well laid-back wind and brass, with good front-to-back perspective and transparency of texture.

Symphonies Nos 3[a] and 5
[a]**Ruth Guldbaek** *sop* [a]**Niels Møller** *ten*
[a]**Royal Danish Orchestra; New York Philharmonic Orchestra / Leonard Bernstein**
Sony Classical The Royal Edition SMK47598 Ⓜ
(71 minutes: ADD). Recorded 1962-65 ⭘

These performances are extremely fine, the finest Fifth ever on record in the opinion of many – it is an essential library supplement. To some tastes it is an overdriven performance and an aggressively balanced recording; to most Nielsen lovers it has charisma and a sense of discovery without ever violating the spirit of the music (Nielsen, it should be remembered, was happy to let great conductors follow their instincts in his music – including Furtwängler in this very work). Overall, this disc shows Leonard Bernstein at something close to his greatest. Under his direction the accompaniments revel in the music, and the understanding between orchestra and both soloists is excellent. In No 5 there is the magnificent playing of the New York Philharmonic Orchestra, with the best side-drum and clarinet solos on record, ensuring that the menace with which Nielsen's humanity has to wrestle is fully embodied. The sense of anticipation Bernstein generates is not the least factor which makes this performance so thrilling – plus the way expectation shades into depression, desperation or exaltation. The Third Symphony is scarcely less fine. The finale is more subtly grasped by Blomstedt, but no one who cares about Nielsen should miss Bernstein in the remaining movements.

Symphonies Nos 3 and 5
Catherine Bott *sop* **Stephen Roberts** *bar*
Royal Scottish Orchestra / Bryden Thomson
Chandos CHAN9067 (71 minutes: DDD). Ⓕ
Recorded 1991

Bryden Thomson and the Royal Scottish Orchestra give fresh and direct readings of the *Espansiva* and the Fifth which are eminently satisfying. At no point are we aware of the conductor interposing himself between composer and listener, and one can sense an evident enthusiasm on the part of the players. This is Nielsen plain and unadorned without any frills. Thomson has a very good feeling for Nielsen's tempos and his account of the finale feels exactly right. All in all, a splendidly sane performance with good singing from the fine soloists in the slow movement.

The Fifth Symphony is another unaffected and straightforward performance that has a great deal going for it – not least the beautiful clarinet playing in the coda, and the thoroughly committed second movement. One is, perhaps, more aware of the beat in the first movement than in Blomstedt's Decca account and it rarely seems to float or sound disembodied as it does with him. However, Thomson achieves very spirited playing from the orchestra and the recordings are very good and present, even if the sound lacks the transparency Decca achieves for Blomstedt. Eminently enjoyable, ardent performances that can hold their head high.

Symphonies Nos 4-6. Little Suite in A minor, FS6[a]. Hymnus Amoris[b]
[b]**Barbara Bonney** *sop* [b]**John Mark Ainsley,** [b]**Lars Pedersen** *tens* b**Michael W Hansen,** [b]**Bo Anker Hansen** *bars*
San Francisco Symphony Orchestra / Herbert Blomstedt; [a]**Danish National Radio Symphony Orchestra /** [a]**Ulf Schirmer**
Double Decca 460 988-2DF2 Ⓜ
(142 minutes: DDD)

The complete symphonies with Blomstedt / San Francisco SO are also available in a box set: Decca 443 117-2DH3 Ⓕ

The Fourth and Fifth are two of Nielsen's most popular and deeply characteristic symphonies. Blomstedt's are splendid performances. The Fourth occupied Nielsen between 1914 and early 1916 and reveals a level of violence new to his art. The landscape is harsher; the melodic lines soar in a more anguished and intense fashion (in the case of the remarkable slow movement, 'like the eagle riding on the wind', to use the composer's own graphic simile). Blomstedt's opening has splendid fire and he is not frightened of letting things rip. The finale with its exhilarating dialogue between the two timpanists comes off splendidly. The Fifth Symphony of 1922 is impressive, too: it starts perfectly and has just the right glacial atmosphere. The climax and the desolate clarinet peroration into which it dissolves are well handled. The recording balance could not be improved upon: the woodwind are well recessed (though clarinet keys are audible at times), there is an almost ideal relationship between the various sections of the orchestra and a thoroughly realistic overall perspective. Blomstedt has a good rapport with his players who sound in excellent shape and respond instinctively to these scores. Blomstedt's account of the Sixth Symphony is a powerful one, with plenty of intensity and an appreciation of its extraordinary vision. It is by far the most challenging of the cycle and inhabits a very different world from early Nielsen. The intervening years had seen the cataclysmic events of the First World War and Nielsen was suffering increasingly from ill health. Blomstedt and the fine San Fransisco orchestra convey the powerful nervous tension of the first movement and the depth of the third, the *Proposta seria*.

Symphonies Nos 4 and 5
Finnish Radio Symphony Orchestra / Jukka-Pekka Saraste
Finlandia 3984-21439-2 (72 minutes: DDD). Ⓕ
Recorded 1997

This is an impressive account of the Symphony No 4 which can hold its own among the very best. The Finnish RSO brings a feeling of urgent intensity to the slow movement and Saraste is attentive to matters of dynamics and phrasing. He builds up the musical argument powerfully to a convincing climax. Nor can No 5 be faulted: it is also powerfully conceived with a strong command of both detail and the overall architecture of the piece. The opening moves but is atmospheric, with careful attention to dynamic nuance and texture. The *tranquillo* section (two bars before fig 24: track 5) is most sensitively handled: it is both poetic and mysterious. The engineers cope admirably with the dryish acoustic of the Helsinki Culture Hall: they produce exemplary clarity and it is only at the ends of movements or in the general pause that precedes the final *Allegro* of No 4 where one becomes aware of this. Among modern recordings, this issue deserves to be recommended alongside Blomstedt's San Francisco coupling. You may even prefer it.

Symphonies Nos 4 and 6
Royal Scottish National Orchestra / Bryden Thomson
Chandos CHAN9047 (70 minutes: DDD). Ⓕ
Recorded 1991

Bryden Thomson's accounts of the Fourth and Sixth call to mind the ardent intensity of the pioneering Danish recordings (no longer available) by Launy Gróndahl and Thomas Jensen, such are their fire. The orchestra plays with total commitment and the underlying violence of No 4 makes a powerful impact, both at the opening and in the finale. But his Sixth is arguably the very finest version of the work on disc, notwithstanding the cultured and splendidly recorded account by Herbert Blomstedt.

Thomson strikes exactly the right tempo for the first movement and the problematic 'Humoreske' has never made better sense. He takes it at a steadier pace than most rival conductors, so that its questioning spirit registers. The third movement, the 'Proposta seria', is both eloquent and searching. Even in a strongly competitive field this splendidly recorded Chandos account brings one closer to this extraordinary work than any other.

Aladdin – Suite, FS89

Aladdin – Suite. Maskarade – Overture; Prelude, Act 2; The Cockerels' Dance. Rhapsody Overture: An imaginary trip to the Faroe Islands, FS123. Helios Overture, FS32. Saga-Drøm, FS46. Pan and Syrinx, FS87
Gothenburg Symphony Orchestra / Neemi Järvi
DG 447 757-2GH (72 minutes: DDD). Ⓕ
Recorded 1995

Järvi gets totally committed playing from his fine orchestra; its members convey the feeling that they all believe in every note they utter. *Aladdin* is given with great spirit and spontaneity. The recording, made by the same team and in the same venue as the orchestra's earlier recording of the work, under Myung-Whun Chung, is excellent, though the 1983 BIS account has marginally greater depth and transparency. In only one instance does Järvi get it wrong and that is in the *Helios Overture*, which is too fast for its sunrise to cast its spell! Thoughts turn to Jupiter where the sun rises every 10 hours. Everything else here calls for applause.

Wind Quintet, FS100

Nielsen Wind Quintet, FS100
Fernström Wind Quintet, Op 59
Kvandal Wind Quintet, Op 34. Three Sacred Folktunes, Op 23*b*
Oslo Wind Quintet (Tom Ottar Andreasson *fl* Lars Peter Berg *ob* Arild Stav *cl* Hans Peter Aasen *bn* Jan Olav Marthinsen *hn*) Ⓢ
Naxos 8 553050 (70 minutes: DDD). Recorded 1993

This is a thoroughly entertaining CD, combining three very different and unfamiliar works with what is probably the finest wind quintet ever penned. The major item here, of course, is the Nielsen: a glorious work which achieves the rare combination of seriousness of expression as well as being utterly relaxed in tone. The Oslo ensemble is a little slower than usual, but its measured tempos are most convincing; indeed, in the finale they highlight musical connections with Nielsen's Fifth and Sixth Symphonies in ways rarely heard. The Swede John Axel Fernström was undeniably a minor composer. If his music does not possess many visionary qualities it is certainly well crafted and his 1943 Quintet is an engaging concert opener. Johan Kvandal from Norway is a weightier proposition and better-known outside of his native country than is Fernström. Kvandal's Quintet, Op 34 (1971), was written for the Oslo ensemble and is serious and high-minded in tone, contrasting effectively with both the Fernström and Kvandal's own *Sacred Folktunes* of 1963. In the Quintet's fast second movement Kvandal adopts a rather Shostakovichian manner, even alluding to the Soviet master's 12th Symphony, though to what purpose is unexplained. The idiomatic playing is reproduced in a slightly flat recording (made in the studios of Norwegian Radio), although the Naxos sound has great immediacy.

String Quartets

No 1 in G minor, FS4; **No 2** in F minor, FS11; **No 3** in E flat, FS23; **No 4** in F, FS36

String Quartets Nos 1 and 2
Oslo Quartet (Geir Inge Lotsberg, Per Kristian Skalstad *vns* Are Sandbakken *va* Oystein Sonstad *vc*)
Naxos 8 553908 (62 minutes: DDD). Ⓢ
Recorded 1998 ●

Nielsen wrote five quartets in all between 1882 and 1919, although two of them exist in different versions, and the opus numbering is contradictory. This may explain why Naxos gets itself into such a pickle over the numbering of the G minor and F minor Quartets here, the second and third he composed (the early D minor of 1882-83 remains unnumbered). The G minor, Op 13 (FS4; 1887-88 but thoroughly rewritten in 1898) is No 1 and the F minor, Op 5 (FS11; 1890) is No 2. The front cover cites the works correctly as 'Quartets No 1, Op 13. No 2, Op 5', but the back cover has 'Quartet No 1 in F minor, Op 5 (Rev 1898)' and 'No 2 in G minor, Op 13 (1890)', managing thus to confuse both dates and numbering. Although in his notes Keith Anderson lays out the composition history quite simply, he refers only to the opus numbers, which should be consigned to oblivion and replaced by the more accurate Fog-Schousboe numbers.

The performances are as clear-sighted as the labelling is a mess. As with the first volume, the Oslo are sympathetic exponents, and do not overlay any extraneous expression on the music as the disappointing Zapolski for Chandos did. Like the almost exactly contemporaneous early Sibelius quartets, there is barely a hint of the familiar, mature Nielsen in either work, but both are well crafted and beautifully written for the instruments. The Oslo seem completely at home in the style, more so than either the Kontra for BIS (who, like the Zapolski, have the benefit of top-quality sound) or Danish (Kontrapunkt) Quartets, making them come alive as none of their rivals manage. The recording is, like Volume 1, a touch confined but not constricted; that aside, this disc can be unreservedly recommended.

String Quartets Nos 3 and 4
Oslo Quartet (Geir Inge Lotsberg, Per Kristian Skalstad vns Are Sandbakken *va* Øystein Sonstad *vc*)
Naxos 8 553907 (57 minutes: DDD). Ⓢ
Recorded 1997

Why is it that quartets of international standing have not taken up the Nielsen quartets (or the Berwald or Stenhammar for that matter). They are marvellous pieces and their neglect outside Scandinavia seems quite unaccountable. This release by the Oslo Quartet is refreshingly straightforward, full of vitality and spirit. Both scores are played with evident feeling but without any intrusive expressive exaggeration. The recordings are a little closely balanced, and as a result *fortissimo* passages can sound a touch fierce and wiry, for example in the closing page or so of the first movement of the F major (seven minutes into track 5). A pity the Oslo doesn't have as well-balanced a recording as Chandos and the Danish engineers provide for the Zapolski. The quartet is scrupulous in observing dynamic markings and gives totally dedicated, idiomatic performances. Artistically it is the finest at any price point.

String Quartets Nos 1-4.
Movements for String Quartet, FS3*c*
Danish Quartet (Tim Frederiksen, Arne Balk-Møller *vns* Claus Myrup *va* H Brendstrup *vc*)
Kontrapunkt ② 32150/1 (138 minutes: DDD). Ⓕ
Recorded 1992

Nielsen composed two quartets and a string quintet during his student years. There was a gap of eight years between the F minor Quartet and the Third, in E flat, Op 14 (FS23) during which Nielsen had written his First Symphony, and another eight before the F major, Op 44 (FS36) saw the light of day. By this time he had written his opera, *Saul and David* and the best part of *Maskarade* as well as the Second Symphony. The Danish Quartet is very sensitive to dynamic nuance and phrases imaginatively. Of course, the F major Quartet goes deeper than the Third. There is a grace, an effortless fluency and a marvellous control of pace. Ideas come and go just when you feel they should; yet its learning and mastery is worn lightly. Though the earlier quartets are not such perfect works of art, they are nevertheless always endearing. The Danish Quartet is completely inside this music and is totally persuasive. In spite of the closely balanced recording this set gives real pleasure and can be recommended with enthusiasm.

Solo piano works

Five Pieces, FS10. Humoresque Bagatelles, FS22. Chaconne, FS79. Suite, FS91. Three Pieces, FS131
Leif Ove Andsnes *pf*
Virgin Classics VC5 45129-2 (54 minutes: DDD). Ⓕ
Recorded 1995

This music on this disc is quite wonderful and deserves the widest dissemination. Although the *Suite* (*Suite luciferique*) was dedicated to Schnabel, the great pianist never played it in public. On record the finest advocate of the piano music was Arne Skjold Rasmussen, whose three-LP set appeared fleetingly in this country in a Vox box during the 1960s. Without the slightest disrespect to him, this music has at last found its true interpreter in the Norwegian Leif Ove Andsnes. He has the measure both of the fresh and charming early pieces, FS10 and 22, and the later more searching, other-worldly *Suite* and the *Three Pieces*. The *luciferique* of the former alludes, incidentally, to the messenger of light, not the prince of darkness, and Nielsen subsequently withdrew the title. This is music of great substance and a deep and powerful originality. Andsnes has such a natural feeling for it that you will probably never find yourself questioning his interpretative judgements. He brings wit and subtlety to pieces like the 'Spinning Top' and 'Jumping Jack' from FS10, and there is always a splendid rhythmic grip, tonal sensitivity and variety of keyboard colour. He communicates real conviction, a feeling that this is the only way this music can sound. There is an impressive eloquence and nobility, and the recorded sound is in every respect exemplary. It is 'present', natural and lifelike. Because this music is unfamiliar, collectors may be cautious or slow in exploring it. To judge from his BBC Proms performance in 1995, Andsnes has quite a following and it is to be hoped that he will lead his admirers on to this music which he has here served so well.

Aladdin

Mette Ejsing *contr* **Guido Paevatalu** *bar*
Danish National Radio Chamber Choir; Danish National Radio Symphony Orchestra / Gennadi Rozhdestvensky
Chandos CHAN9135 (79 minutes: DDD). Text and translation included. Recorded 1992 Ⓕ

Nielsen's music to Adam Oehlenschläger's *Aladdin* comes from 1917-18, and was commissioned for a particularly lavish production of the play at the Royal Theatre in Copenhagen. More than half the music consists of orchestral interludes to accompany processions and dances, most of which come in the Third Act. Many are delightful and endearing, and once heard difficult to get out of one's head. Robert Simpson summed the work up in his Nielsen monograph: 'The market-square in Isfahan where four orchestras play in four different tempos suggesting marvellously the clashing colours, movements and sounds of an eastern market-place is undoubtedly the most striking and original part of the music. Some of it is not very interesting (the rather commonplace Blackamoors' Dance, for instance) but most is intensely perceptive and colourful.' It is full of characteristic Nielsenesque touches, and although it is not the composer at his very best, it offers many irresistible delights. Performance and recording are both superb.

Maskarade

Awards 1999

Aage Haugland *bass* Jeronimus; **Susanne Resmark** *contr* Magdelone; **Gert Henning Jensen** *ten* Leander; **Bo Skovhus** *bar* Henrik; **Michael Kristensen** *ten* Arv; **Kurt Ravn** *bar* Leonard; **Henriette Bonde-Hansen** *sop* Leonora; **Marianne Rørholm** *contr* Pernille; **Johan Reuter** *bar* Night Watchman, Master of the Masquerade; **Christian Christiansen** *bass* Tutor
Danish National Radio Choir and Symphony Orchestra / Ulf Schirmer
Decca ② 460 227-2DHO2 (145 minutes: DDD) Ⓕ
Notes, text and translation included
Recorded 1996 ooo

If you can keep a straight face through the master/servant antics of the club-addicts Leander and Henrik, if you can stay uncharmed by the ageing, repressed Magdelone when she shows she can still cut a caper, if you can stop your foot tapping in the Act 3 Maskarade itself, and if you can remain unmoved by the gentle pathos of the demasking scene, then you're made of very stern stuff. It is, not surprisingly, thoroughly idiomatic. Since the first production in 1906 *Maskarade* has been Denmark's national opera, and all the principals here have the music in their blood. Gert Henning Jensen may be a rather tremulous Leander, but he sounds appropriately youthful, and the love duets with his well-matched Leonora, Henriette Bonde-Hansen, are wonderfully touching. Bo Skovhus is in superb voice as the Figaro-esque Henrik, though an even sharper sense of fun in the characterization would not have come amiss; Michael Kristensen's blockhead Arv is also a paler impersonation than it should be. Aage Haugland is in magnificent voice and almost steals the show in Act 1 as the crusty old Jeronimus; the vulnerable but lovable Magdelone of Susanne Resmark brings a lump to the throat. Ulf Schirmer conducts with excellently judged tempos and a deep affection for the idiom. Above all he has a grasp of the underlying momentum of each act.

This recording uses a score prepared by the government-sponsored Carl Nielsen Edition, which restores traditionally cut or displaced passages and corrects a host of textual and musical details. The resulting play of contrasts and effective large-scale pacing, especially in the supposedly problematic Second and Third Acts, entirely vindicates this full-length version. Having said that, Schirmer does miss a trick or two. The Overture could do with rather more lilt and swagger (the Danish strings could be more full-bodied here); the end of Act 2, where a preview of the Maskarade is heard as if through half-open doors, is too loud; synchronization is initially dodgy in Act 3, as though the chorus can't quite believe the swift tempo; and the choral interpolations in the Tutor's strophic song sound a little contrived. So collectors wedded to the lovable Unicorn-Kanchana Frandsen set (somewhat dimmed in its CD transfer) will find reasons for returning to it; and the richest comedy of all in Act 1 is to be found in the 1954 Grøndahl set on Danacord (whose heavy cuts rule it out as a top recommendation, however). The balance sheet comes out strongly in favour of this Decca set, though, even before taking into account the excellent recording quality and high quality of booklet presentation. This is a life-enhancing comic opera, comparable in many ways to Britten's *A Midsummer Night's Dream*, and it's wonderful to hear the piece done full justice.

Pehr Henrik Nordgren Finnish 1944

Nordgren studied musicology at the University of Helsinki, taking an MA in 1967, and composition as a private student of Joonas Kokkonen from 1965 to 1969. From 1970 to 1973, he studied composition and traditional Japanese music at the Tokio University of Art and Music. Nordgren is a composer who transcends divisions between schools and styles combining, in various ways, elements of twelve-tone technique, Ligetian field technique, the Western tonal tradition, a meditative minimalism related to the music of Arvo Pärt, and Finnish and Japanese folk music. He has acknowledged Shostakovich as a particularly strong influence, but the affinity is one of expressive aims rather than style. Significant works include Euphonie II (1967), The Turning Point (1972) and 10 piano ballades (1972-78) – both of which draw upon Nordgren's interest and study into Japanese traditional music – three symphonies (1974, 1989, 1993) and Beaivi, Ah...áñan (The Sun, My Father) for soloists, choir and orchestra (1987–89) – a setting of poems in the Sámi language. He has also composed a number of concertos, chamber works, a few vocal works and two operas.

Symphonies Nos 2 and 4

Symphonies – No 2, Op 74; No 4, Op 98
Finnish Radio Symphony Orchestra / Juha Kangas
Finlandia 3984-29720-2 (55 minutes: DDD). Ⓕ
Recorded 1999

Cello Concerto No 1, Op 50[a]. Concerto for Strings, Op 54[b]. Violin Concerto No 3, Op 53[c]. Equivocations, Op 55[d]. Nine Kwaidan Ballades[e]
[c]**Kaija Saarikettu,** [d]**Reijo Tunkkari** *vns* [d]**Timo Kangas** *va* [a]**Erkki Rautio** *vc* [d]**Niiles Outakoski** *vc* [d]**Ritva Koistinen** *kantele* [e]**Izumi Tateno** *pf* [abc]**Ostrobothnian Chamber Orchestra / Juha Kangas**
Finlandia Meet the Composer ② 3984 23408-2 (154 minutes: DDD). Ⓜ
Recorded 1984,1990 and 1992-93

The darkly eloquent, recent Fourth Symphony is an ideal introduction to the impressive sound-world of Pehr Henrik Nordgren, though it's more richly scored and denser in texture than anything on the two-disc set (one of Finlandia's valuable Meet the Composer compilations). The Fourth begins turbulently, and often during its course rises to forbidding, dissonantly fraught climaxes. But, as often in his work, the complexity is built from simple constituents – a phrase from *Boris Godunov*, Finnish folk melodies – and at the centre and the end of the symphony the textures clear to reveal a solitary herdsman playing a pipe and a hushed, solemn string chorale. The effect is moving, but the presence of those simple motifs amidst the uproar that surrounds the islands of tense calm gives them a grandeur, even a nobility and the whole work a powerful sense of drama. The Second Symphony (1989) is longer, its contrasts more violent, its unifying elements harder to perceive, but its coherence is striking. Even in a densely complex *tutti* or a texture thinned to nothing more than a string shimmer and a few isolated piano notes the sense of movement and destination is tangible.

On the two-disc set the ideal starting-point is the *Concerto for Strings*. Characteristic of Nordgren again is the way that the first movement is derived from two ideas, one unchanging (a simple, pulsing rhythm), the other a melodic figure which is both extended and simplified, becoming intensely expressive in the process. The central movement is an exciting, virtuoso toccata; the finale a sombre meditation on two simple ideas. Both concertos also build great variety from simple material (the Cello Concerto begins with single notes so precisely judged that a four-note rising phrase from the soloist has real lyrical eloquence), while the gripping *Equivocations* uses the Finnish national instrument, the kantele, to evoke an archaic folk world without ever quoting folk melody.

There is an improvisatory element to Nordgren's music, too, a feeling of ideas suggesting other ideas and dictating their own form. The *Kwaidan Ballades*, each prompted by one of Lafcadio Hearn's Japanese ghost stories, often give the impression of a tale told not in words but in formidably pianistic gestures. Izumi Tateno plays them with great eloquence and resource; indeed all the performances here, by artists long and closely associated with the composer, are vividly communicative. Finely recorded.

Vítezslav Novák Bohemian 1870-1949

GROVE *Novák studied with Jiránek and Dvořák at the Prague Conservatory (1889-92) and was powerfully influenced by the folk music of Moravia and Slovakia, which he began to collect and study in 1896. The result was an outpouring of symphonic poems and songs, culminating in the dramatic cantata The Storm (1910) and the large-scale tone poem Pan for piano (1910). In 1909 he began teaching at the Prague Conservatory, and this occupied him more than composition in his later years, though he wrote several operas, much choral music and a few late instrumental scores, of which the Autumn Symphony (1934) and the South Bohemian Suite are representative. A skilled melodist and contrapuntist, he retained an essentially late Romantic style, which was supported by a meticulous technique.*

De profundis

Toman and the Wood Nymph, Op 40. Lady Godiva, Op 41. De profundis, Op 67
BBC Philharmonic Orchestra / Libor Pešek
Chandos CHAN9821 (66 minutes: DDD). Ⓕ
Recorded 1999

Vítězslav Novák was a keen walker and each piece on this absorbing CD testifies to his vivid sense of outdoors. He was also fascinated by the female psyche and two of the works programmed bring rival viragos to mind: Smetana's 'Šárka' (in the opening pages of *Lady Godiva*) and Strauss's *Salome* (the close of *Toman and the Wood Nymph*). Mid-way through *Lady Godiva*, sumptuous string writing takes the lead, though Novák's liking for sudden key shifts fires the atmosphere from 8'02", where Godiva's womanly virtue (in this case etched on strings and harp) faces minor-key confrontations from her feudal husband Leofric, savagely depicted by the brass. *Toman and the Wood Nymph* recalls the troubled world of Dvořák's Erben tone-poems. The storyline tells of a faithless lover kissed to death by a congregation of forest nymphs, and Novák pulls out the orchestral stops much as Strauss was doing for alternative narratives at around the same time.

Yet for all their lustre, excitement and charm, even *Godiva* and *Toman* cannot rival the oppressive power of Novák's wartime masterpiece *De profundis*, a work that surely levels with Martinů's *Lidice* as being among the most poignant musical memorials of the period. Composed during the Nazi occupation of Czechoslovakia, *De profundis* finds Novák employing a significantly darkened palette (try the Bergian descent from 3'59" into the *Largo lugubre* opening), though the exultant closing section (track 7) bears little resemblance to the various politically motivated 'happy endings' that were surfacing elsewhere. Novák's use of the organ runs parallel with Scriabin's in *The Poem of Ecstasy* (albeit to very different effect): indeed, the two works would pair wonderfully well in concert.

Libor Pešek shows obvious sympathy for this repertoire and the playing of the BBC Philharmonic reaches formidable heights of passion, notably at the close of *De profundis*. Alternative discs of Novák's music are few and far between, the best of them hailing, in the main, from Brno – and not all of those are currently available. Back in 1986, the late František Jílek made a fine digital version of *Toman* for Supraphon (nla), more rhythmically supple than Pešek's though not as well played. Also, by broadening the pace at the very end of the piece, Jílek minimises the *Salome* parallels. But Pešek still provides the better option overall.

Happily, Jaroslav Vogel's inspirational 1960-62 recordings of *Lady Godiva* and *De profundis* – which, like Jílek's, are with the Brno State Philharmonic – are still listed. Soundwise, there's no comparison: Ultraphon's bright-toned recording, though perfectly acceptable, lacks body, especially at the lower end of the spectrum. But Vogel's credentials as a fiery Novákian tell unmistakably at the dramatic opening of *Lady Godiva* (gutsy accents, particularly from the strings) and at 10'35" into *De profundis* (10'28" on the Chandos CD) where Novák's fugal writing is more clearly focused. Vogel's performance has an air of desperation about it, which is what you would expect from someone who had lived through the whole ghastly era. Pešek's is perhaps one step removed from all that, but it's still an extremely fine performance, one that suggests that a follow-up CD of Novák's *The Storm* should figure prominently among Chandos's future recording plans.

Piano Quintet, Op 12

Piano Quintet in A minor, Op 12. 13 Slovak Folksongs
Songs of a Winter Night, Op 30
Magdalena Kožená *mez* **Radoslav Kvapil** *pf*
Kocian Quartet (Pavel Hůla, Jan Odstrčil *vns* Zbynek Padourek *va* Václav Bernášek *vc*)
ASV CDDCA998 (67 minutes: DDD). Texts and translations included. Recorded 1996 Ⓕ

Novák's A minor Piano Quintet of 1896 was composed in the wake of his first fruitful study of the folk-song traditions of both Moravia and Slovakia. It is an accomplished creation, comprising a finely sustained *Allegro molto moderato*, an effective central theme and variations (based on a 15th-century Czech love-song) and a joyous, swaggering finale. Seven years later, Novák produced his piano suite, *Songs of a Winter Night*. Its four movements make a charming set, ranging in mood from the wistful intimacy of the opening 'Song of a moonlight night' to the gleeful merry-making of the last in the series ('Song of a carnival night'). Even during the ecstatic pealing that marks the climax of the memorable 'Song of a Christmas night', Novák's piano writing always remains wonderfully pellucid, a factor that also adds to the listener's enjoyment of his six volumes of Slovak songs, 13 of which are heard here. Gems include the plaintive *Sedla mucha* ('A fly sat on a cornflower') with its bewitching piano traceries, the harmonically searching *Svic, mila, mas komu* ('Light the lamp, my love') and the haunting, tragic tale of *Chodzila Mariska* ('Mariska's walking along the bank'). Radoslav Kvapil and the Kocian Quartet form a thoroughly convincing alliance in the early Piano Quintet. The excellent Kvapil also shines in the solo suite (although the balance is slightly too close for comfort), and in the song sequence he provides some tenderly idiomatic support to the characterful mezzo, Magdalena Kožená.

Further Listening
Suk Piano Quintet
Coupling: Piano Trio. Elegie. Piano Quartet
Štěpán *pf* **Suk Quartet; Suk Trio**
Supraphon 11 1532-2 (74 minutes: ADD: 2/94) Ⓜ
A collection of some of Suk's youthful works, offering enjoyable if undemanding listening. Fine performances

Michael Nyman

British 1944

GROVE *Nyman studied at the Royal Academy of Music with Alan Bush and with Thurston Dart at King's College, London. He wrote the seminal book Experimental Music: Cage and Beyond (1974). In his compositions he aims to break down the barrier between popular culture and 'serious' composition. He is best known for his film scores, including The Draughtsman's Contract (1982), The Cook, the Thief, his Wife and her Lover (1989), Prospero's Books (1991) and The Piano (1993). He has also written five operas, among which The Man who Mistook his Wife for a Hat (1986) amply demonstrates his musical style in its use of variation and modular form, lyrical vocal lines over restless, repetitive phrases and repeated harmonic blocks.*

The Piano Concerto

The Piano Concerto. MGV (Musique à Grande Vitesse)
Kathryn Stott *pf*
Royal Liverpool Philharmonic Orchestra; Michael Nyman Band; orchestra / Michael Nyman
Argo 443 382-2ZH (59 minutes: DDD). Recorded 1994 Ⓕ

Considering the international success of Jane Campion's film *The Piano*, it seems quite logical that Nyman should adapt his celebrated score into a concert piece. Though performed uninterrupted, the 32-minute concerto is divided into four clear-cut sections. The Scottish folksongs on which much of the score is based imbue the piece with a yearning, heartfelt quality not usually associated with this composer. Indeed, the whole concerto, as so convincingly advocated by Kathryn Stott and the RLPO, throbs with an unbridled romantic fervency (the second movement and the end of the third almost Rózsa-like in their ardour) that may come as something of a shock to hardened Nymanites or those who appreciate the less grandiose scoring for the film. More recognizably Nymanesque is *MGV*, a sort of *Pacific 231* for the 1990s, composed for the inauguration of the TGV North-European line in France. Here the composer's abstract style is eminently suited to describing a non-stop, imaginary railway journey through five regions between Paris and Lille; his repeated phrases and chugging, insistently propulsive rhythms create an effect that is totally spellbinding, with the strings adding an especially effective sense of speed and visual sweep. A rewarding disc that will appeal to Nyman fans old and new.

String Quartets

String Quartet No 4. Three Quartets
Camilli Quartet (Elisabeth Perry, Rachel Browne *vns* Prunella Pacey *va* Melissa Phelps *vc*) **Michael Nyman Band / Michael Nyman**
EMI CDC5 56574-2 (56 minutes: DDD). Recorded 1997 Ⓕ

Those who admire and enjoy Nyman's first three string quartets (available on Argo), will find much to enjoy in this, his Fourth. The Quartet derives from a piece called *Yamamoto perpetuo* which was especially composed for Yohji Yamamoto's autumn fashion show in Paris, and also makes use of material from Nyman's score to Christopher Hampton's film *Carrington*, and a Scottish melody that was noted down for *The Piano* but in the event wasn't used. The Camilli Quartet gives an invigorating and sensitive performance. *Three Quartets* dates from 1994 and is so named because it is scored for a string quartet, saxophone quartet and brass quartet. It's an interesting textural mix, allowing the opportunity to explore and develop nicely contrasting passages in Nyman's typically kaleidoscopic, frenetic manner, and is superbly performed here by the Michael Nyman Band. The recorded sound is good.

Johannes Ockeghem

Flanders c1410-1497

GROVE *The earliest reference to Ockeghem as a singer shows that he was a vicaire-chanteur at Notre Dame, Antwerp, for a year from June 24, 1443. His déploration on Binchois' death (1460) suggests a connection with the Burgundian ducal chapel where Busnois and Dufay worked. He entered the service of Charles I, Duke of Bourbon, in Moulins in the mid-1440s and was a member of the chapel in 1446-48. In the year ending September 30, 1453 he is cited in the French court archives 'nouveau en 1451'. This service continued during Louis XI's reign, though he held other offices, including a canonry at Notre Dame, Paris (1463-70). In 1470 he visited Spain, in 1484 Bruges and Dammes. After Louis death he remained premier chapelain and was still on the payroll in 1488. He enjoyed an enviable personal and professional reputation.*

His most imposing works are his mass settings. Several are based on pre-existing material, sacred or secular. One of the earliest is probably the Missa Caput which states the cantus firmus in the lowest voice, but in other (probably later) works, such as the Missa De plus en plus, he varied the treatment of the cantus firmus, assimilating it increasingly to the rhythmic and melodic character of the other voices; his two incomplete mass cycles are based on late chansons of his own, and his polyphonic Requiem is the earliest known setting. Others of his masses, including the Missa prolationum and the Missa Mi-mi, are freely composed. The former is perhaps the most extraordinary contrapuntal achievement of the 15th century, while the other clearly shows his own characteristic style, with its variations in mensuration, texture and sonority. His motets display even greater inventiveness, combining homophonic textures, skilful cantus firmus treatments, sweeping melodic lines, energetic rhythmic figures and frequent imitation. Most of his chansons use traditional formes fixes and feature treble-dominated textures, though some are canonic and occasionally anticipate early 16th-century chanson style. The level of contrapuntal skill and artistic excellence of his music laid a foundation for the achievements of Josquin's generation.

Missa prolationum

Ockeghem Missa prolationum.
Obrecht (attrib) Humilium decus. **Busnois** Gaude coelestis Domina. In hydraulis. **Pullois** Flos de spina.
Josquin Desprez Illibata Dei Virgo nutrix
The Clerks' Group / Edward Wickham
ASV Gaudeamus CDGAU143 (65 minutes: DDD). Ⓕ
Recorded 1995

This recording focuses on one of the most astonishing compositional feats of the second half of the 15th century: Ockeghem's *Missa prolationum*. The successive movements of the Ordinary of the Mass are based on double canons that progress from the unison to the octave, while at the same time the composer also exploits the inherent ambiguity of the mensural system (and hence the work's title) of the later Middle Ages so that the rhythmic relationships between the voices are constantly being transformed. The astonishing thing is how effortlessly Ockeghem weaves his complex polyphonic web, and this is reinforced here by the unfettered, direct way in which The Clerks' Group approaches the music. Although there are only eight singers in the group (so a maximum of two voices to a part), they bring a very satisfactory mix of the vocal agility one might expect from a small ensemble and the ability to sing through the long-breathed lines favoured by Ockeghem, without ever sounding strained or thin. The overall sound is immediate, crystal clear and closely recorded, but it never lacks for richness or blend – much credit to the ASV production team, too, in this respect.

Although at first sight the five motets on the disc seem only loosely related to each other and to the Mass (the works date variously from the 1460s through to the 1490s), there are potentially illuminating links: several of the composers appear to pay homage, whether directly or indirectly, to one another's pieces and in general they all opt for quite self-consciously complex structures yet create a musical idiom that is lucid and full of emotional responses to the texts (mostly Marian) they chose to set. There is no one who could seriously doubt that is the Franco-Netherlandish school at its best.

Missa 'l'homme armé'

Ockeghem Missa 'l'homme armé'. Ave Maria. Alma redemptoris mater
Josquin Desprez Memor esto verbi tui **Plainchant** Alma redemptoris mater. Immittet angelus Domini
Anonymous L'homme armé
Oxford Camerata / Jeremy Summerly
Naxos 8 554297 (57 minutes: DDD). Texts and translations included Ⓢ ●

The centrepiece of this recording is Ockeghem's *L'homme armé* Mass. It may be one of Ockeghem's earliest Masses, dating perhaps from the early 1450s. It is also one of his most curious. For the most part it lies in a relatively high register, belying the composer's usual predilection for low bass ranges; but every now and again the basses descend in spectacular fashion. In the third *Agnus*, they hold down the tune in very long notes, with the other voices seeming to float above them. Seldom before in the history of music can the articulation of time have been so clear a feature of a piece's design: it seems almost to have been suspended altogether. It is an extraordinary moment, and extraordinarily difficult to pull off in performance, but here the singers seem to have got it right. Elsewhere, Summerly's approach is nicely varied, but on the whole more meditative than emphatic; one might say that the performance grows in stature with each movement, as though keeping pace with the cycle's ambition. In its details the reading is not without the odd glitch, but taken as a whole it is a fine achievement. The accompanying motets work very well but it is a shame that the choir's richness of sound is not quite matched by the acoustic. They deserve a more inspiring venue. But the overall impression is resoundingly positive: those new to Ockeghem should find this super-budget disc too good an opportunity to pass up.

Missa 'De plus en plus'

Missa 'De plus en plus'. Presque transi. Prenez sur moi vostre exemple. O rosa bella o dolce anima mia. Aultre Venus estés. Petite camusette. Tant fuz gentement. Mort tu as navré
Orlando Consort (Robert Harre-Jones *counterten* Charles Daniels, Angus Smith *tens* Donald Greig *bar*)
Archiv Produktion 453 419-2AH (73 minutes: DDD). Texts and translations included. Ⓕ
Recorded 1996

This is a superb recording of Ockeghem's Mass, *De plus en plus*, by the Orlando Consort. The Orlandos' mixed programme of sacred and secular music offers a good, rounded picture of Ockeghem's art. In the Mass, the Orlandos are obvious first choice for those who prefer a soloistic approach, or for whom anything other than countertenors on top lines smacks of heresy. They are experienced singers with logical phrasing and breathing in solo passages, great interpretative acuteness, and a quality of ensemble that is of itself expressive. The Orlandos seem to achieve more with less: that is part of the magic of hearing Ockeghem sung this way. The accompanying songs certainly makes the case for Ockeghem's versatility as a song composer, a point emphasized by the differences of scoring to which they are especially sensitive. If this recording demonstrates anything, then it is that the sacred and the secular are very different worlds. If the Orlandos seem to experience trouble shifting gears between the two they are certainly not alone, either in England or abroad.

Requiem

Awards 1997

Ockeghem Requiem. Fors seulement. Missa 'Fors seulement'
Brumel Du tout plongiet/Fors seulement
La Rue Fors seulement
The Clerks' Group / Edward Wickham
ASV Gaudeamus CDGAU168 Ⓕ
(71 minutes: DDD). Texts and translations included. Recorded 1996 **ooo**

Top billing goes to the Requiem, Ockeghem's most widely recorded work and perhaps his most enigmatic piece, stylistically very wide-ranging and diverse. Aesthetic judgement is hard to pass, since it may well be incomplete; but the surviving movements contain some of his most arresting inspirations. This is the first version of any quality to feature sopranos on the top lines. Incidentally, no recording of the Requiem is uniformly excellent; on the other hand, the words of the Mass for the dead conjure up many associations, and The Clerks deserve praise for the verve and imagination with which they respond to the work's interpretative challenges. The fillers are the works built on Ockeghem's song *Fors seulement* (which includes Antoine Brumel's *Du tout plongiet*). It is difficult to decide which to praise more highly: the pieces themselves, which are incomparable, or the singing, which represents The Clerks' finest achievement to date. *Fors seulement* inspired a flowering of astonishing pieces scored for very low voices (initiated, it appears, by the composer himself): in both the Mass and in *Du tout plongiet*, the basses descendto written low Cs. In addition, these pieces are exceptionally richly scored (the Mass and the La Rue song are five-voice works), creating polyphony as dense and as dark as a strong Trappist ale. The Clerks achieve almost miraculous linear definition here, without losing an iota of the music's sensuous appeal: that's quite a feat, given the low pitch and awesome contrapuntal complexity involved. This must be counted as a major achievement.

Jacques Offenbach

German/French 1819-1880

GROVE *Offenbach's career began with a year's study at the Paris Conservatoire and several years experience as a solo and orchestral cellist; he became a theatre conductor in 1850, finally getting his own stage works performed in 1855. Writing mainly for the Bouffes Parisiens, he reached the peak of his international success in the 1860s; revivals and tours, as well as the score of his serious opera Les contes d'Hoffmann (unfinished, completed by Guiraud), dominated the 1870s.*

With Johann Strauss II, Offenbach was one of the two outstanding composers in popular music of the 19th century and writer of some of the most exhilaratingly gay, tuneful music ever written. Les contes d'Hoffmann has retained a place in the international repertory for its fantasy and its strongly appealing music; but his most significant achievements lie in operetta: Orphée aux enfers (1858), La belle Hélène (1864), La vie parisienne (1866), La Grande-Duchesse de Gérolstein (1867) and La Périchole (1868) are striking examples. Moreover, it was through the success of Offenbach's works abroad that operetta became an established international genre, producing major national exponents in Strauss, Sullivan and Léhar and evolving into the 20th-century musical.

Offenbach's comic subjects, usually satirical treatments of familiar stories with a sharp glance at contemporary society and politics, are enhanced by none-too-subtle musical devices, including the quotation of well-known operatic music in incongruous settings: his tunes are often built upon a rising phrase in a major key and his finales are made exciting by gradual tempo acceleration and the use of brass at climaxes. He had a rare gift for catchy tunes, usually in dance rhythms, and telling harmonic touches. Through its famous overture (in fact composed by Carl Binder) and can-can, Orphée aux enfers has remained his best-known operetta.

Gaîté parisienne

Offenbach Gaite parisienne (arr M Rosenthal) H
Rossini (arr/orch Respighi) La boutique fantasque
Boston Pops Orchestra / Arthur Fiedler
RCA Victor Living Stereo 09026 61847-2 Ⓜ
(64 minutes: ADD). Recorded 1954-56

Arthur Fiedler and the Boston Pops, for so long the guardians of traditional concert-hall light music in America, never made a better stereo recording than the amazing early (1954) complete Offenbach/Rosenthal *Gaîté parisienne* ballet score. It scintillates with effervescence and vitality, has just the right degree of brash vulgarity, yet the richly embracing acoustics of Symphony Hall ensure that the entry of the great 'Barcarolle' has warmth as well as allure. This transfer makes the very most of the outstanding mastertape. The coupling comprises some 27 minutes from the hardly less delectable Rossini/Respighi *La boutique fantasque* also brightly and atmospherically played and again given first-class sound from two years later. This release is a real collector's item, and not to be missed by anyone who cares about the history of stereo reproduction and also for the sheer *joie de vivre* of the music.

Gaite Parisienne (arr Rosenthal). Offenbachiana (arr Rosenthal)
Monte Carlo Philharmonic Orchestra / Manuel Rosenthal Ⓢ
Naxos 8 554005 (68 minutes: DDD)

Manuel Rosenthal was 92 when he made this recording – his third – of *Gaite Parisienne*, his ballet for Massine that had produced such a storm of applause in Monte Carlo back in 1938. He made very clear why he was anxious to do so: not only had there been poor recordings, cut versions and mauled arrangements of his score by others, but in his own previous recordings he had felt obliged to accommodate the dancers' wishes as regards tempos, and now he wanted to treat his work symphonically, with more spacious speeds that would enable details of the orchestration to emerge fully for the first time. So we can now accept this 45-minute version as authentic, and the more deliberate pace adopted in some places (beautifully and expressively so in the Barcarolle) in no way diminishes the brilliant impact of his treatment of Offenbach's heady tunes. The Monte Carlo orchestra, long familiar with the work, give their all to the aged maestro, with voluptuous string playing in lyrical sections; and the recording is exceptionally vivid, with the widest of dynamic ranges (somewhat blatant in *fortissimos*).

But the real joy of this disc is *Offenbachiana*, music drawn from a handful of the stage works arranged by Rosenthal while forced to kick his heels in Berlin for a fortnight owing to a breakdown in the equipment when he was about to record Gaite in 1953. This is a subtler, wittier and, if anything, even more scintillating score (which reminds us that for 11 years Rosenthal had been a pupil of that master-orchestrator Ravel). Absolutely not to be missed!

Les contes d'Hoffmann

Raoul Jobin *ten* Hoffmann; **Renée Doria** *sop* Olympia; **Vina Bovy** *sop* Giulietta; **Géori Boué** *sop* Antonia; **Fanély Revoil** *mez* Nicklausse; **Louis Musy** *bar* Lindorf; **André Pernet** *bass* Coppélius; **Charles Soix** *bass* Dapertutto; **Roger Bourdin** *bar* Dr Miracle; **René Lapelletrie** *ten* Spalanzani; **Camille Maurane** *bar* Hermann H
Chorus and Orchestra of the Opéra-Comique, Paris / André Cluytens
EMI mono ② CMS5 65260-2 (130 minutes: ADD). Ⓜ
Notes and text included. Recorded 1948

In the 1930s in Paris, Raoul Jobin and José Luccioni were the two great opera matinée-idols. Jobin was a French Canadian, made his début in 1930 and was soon singing at both the Opéra, as Faust, Lohengrin and Raoul in *Les Huguenots*, and at the Opéra-Comique, where he was a favourite Hoffmann and Don José. This recording may perhaps find him just a little late in his career. His years at the Metropolitan (throughout the German occupation) obviously took their toll, when he sang roles that were too heavy for him in such a huge theatre. However, the splendour of this set is the authenticity of the vocal style and the diction of such stalwarts of the Opéra-Comique ensemble as Louis Musy, Roger Bourdin, Fanély Revoil (better known as an operetta singer) and, luxurious casting, Camille Maurane in the small part of Hermann.

The three heroines are well inside their roles, but they are afflicted with a little strain in the higher-lying passages. Renée Doria sang all these parts later in her career – when this recording was made she was just at the outset, having made her début in Paris in 1944. Her Olympia is strong on the *staccato* notes but a bit fragile in the long phrases – this doll broke quite easily, one imagines. In the same act, André Pernet, a great figure from pre-war Paris is a superb Coppélius. In the Venice act, Vina Bovy is dramatically convincing as Giulietta, but hasn't much vocal sheen left (she made her début in 1919). Géori Boué, the Antonia, is one of the great figures from French post-war opera, but one feels that Giulietta would have been her role ideally. As for Jobin, despite some strain, he makes a convincing poet. Although there is such strong competition on CD where *Hoffmann* is concerned, this historic version is without doubt essential listening for a sense of style if the work absorbs you.

Les contes d'Hoffmann

Plácido Domingo *ten* Hoffmann; **Dame Joan Sutherland** *sop* Olympia, Giulietta, Antonia, Stella; **Gabriel Bacquier** *bar* Lindorf, Coppélius, Dapertutto, Dr Miracle; **Huguette Tourangeau** *mez* La Muse, Nicklausse; **Jacques Charon** *ten* Spalanzani; **Hugues Cuénod** *ten* Andrès, Cochenille, Pitichinaccio, Frantz; **André Neury** *bar* Schlemil; **Paul Plishka** *bass* Crespel; **Margarita Lilowa** *mez* Voice of Antonia's Mother; **Roland Jacques** *bar* Luther **Lausanne Pro Arte Chorus; Du Brassus Chorus; Suisse Romande Chorus and Orchestra / Richard Bonynge**

Decca ② 417 363-2DH2 (143 minutes: ADD). Notes, Ⓕ text and translation included. Recorded 1968 ●●

This is a wonderfully refreshing set, made the more sparkling in the CD transfer. The story emerges crystal-clear, even the black ending to the Giulietta scene in Venice, which in Bonynge's text restores the original idea of the heroine dying from a draught of poison, while the dwarf, Pitichinaccio shrieks in delight. One also has to applaud his rather more controversial decision to put the Giulietta scene in the middle and leave the dramatically weighty Antonia scene till last. That also makes the role of Stella the more significant, giving extra point to the decision to have the same singer take all four heroine roles. With Dame Joan available it was a natural decision, and though in spoken dialogue she is less comfortable in the Giulietta scene than the rest, the contrasting portraits in each scene are all very convincing, with the voice brilliant in the doll scene, warmly sensuous in the Giulietta scene and powerfully dramatic as well as tender in the Antonia scene. Gabriel Bacquier gives sharply intense performances, firm and dark vocally, in the four villain roles, Hugues Cuénod contributes delightful vignettes in the four *comprimario* tenor roles, while Domingo establishes at the very start the distinctive bite in his portrait of Hoffmann; a powerful and a perceptive interpretation. The recording is vivid, and the listener is treated to some first-class playing from the Suisse Romande Orchestra.

Additional recommendation

Les contes d'Hoffmann

Schicoff Hoffmann **Murray** Nicklausse **Serra** Olympia **Norman** Giulietta **Plowright** Antonia **van Dam** Lindorf, Coppélius, Dapertutto, Dr Miracle

Brussels National Opera Orchestra / Cambreling

EMI ③ CDS7 49641-2 (214 minutes: DDD: 12/88) Ⓕ

This is the version for Hoffmann completists – by far the longest edition reaching almost Wagernian proportions. And to match such scholarly pretentions, the casting is suitably luxurious. One of the highlights are the beautifully drawn characters portrayed by José van Dam.

Orphée aux enfers

(ed Minkowski/Pelly)

Yann Beuron *ten* Orphée; **Natalie Dessay** *sop* Eurydice; **Jean-Paul Fouchécourt** *ten* Aristée-Pluton; **Laurent Naouri** *bar* Jupiter; **Lydie Pruvot** *sop* Juno; **Ewa Podles** *mez* Public Opinion; **Steven Cole** *ten* John Styx; **Véronique Gens** *sop* Vénus; **Patricia Petibon** *sop* Cupid; **Jennifer Smith** *sop* Diane; **Etienne Lescroart** *ten* Mercury; **Virginie Pochon** *sop* Minerva **Grenoble Chamber Orchestra; Chorus and Orchestra of the Opéra National de Lyon / Marc Minkowski**

EMI ② CDS5 56725-2 (110 minutes: DDD). Notes, Ⓕ text and translation included. Recorded 1997 ●

Orphée aux enfers may be Offenbach's best-known operetta, but it has had limited attention on disc. The lightly scored original 1858 version was in two acts and four scenes. The spectacular 1874 version had lots of extra songs and ballet numbers. Since this latter demands huge forces, it is scarcely viable on stage today. The usual solution in the theatre is thus to add selected numbers from the 1874 version to the 1858 text, and this is what was done for the performances at Geneva, Lyons and Grenoble that formed the basis of this recording. Home listeners may prefer to make their own selections of numbers, and musicologically questionable decisions such as the rescoring of 1874 pieces for 1858 orchestral resources become more exposed. What matters most, though, is the quality of performance, and the pleasures of this one are formidable.

Above all, Natalie Dessay's exchanges in the First Act with her despised violinist husband (the admirable Yann Beuron) are superbly done. So is her sighing over Jean-Paul Fouchécourt's Aristeus, whose two big solos show equal elegance. Later come Laurent Naouri's formidable Jupiter and cameos such as Etienne Lescroart's agile performance of Mercury's song and Patricia Petibon's deliciously winning account of Cupid's 'Couplets des baisers'. Ensemble numbers are extremely well done and throughout, Marc Minkowski provides thoughtful, lively direction.

What causes doubt is the tendency towards overstatement, from the opening monologue of Eva Podles's Public Opinion, where almost every word seems to be given exaggerated emphasis, through Aristeus's crude falsetto in his opening solo, to a curiously mechanical version of John Styx's 'Quand j'étais roi de Béotie' and some gratuitous vocal gymnastics in the 'Hymne à Bacchus'. Ultimately, however, those doubts are banished by the positive virtues. Whereas those who want virtually every note Offenbach composed for *Orphée aux enfers* must stick with the 1978 Plasson/EMI recording, Minkowski offers a more faithful impression of Offenbach's original compact creation, with selected 1874 additions as a bonus. It is a consistently imaginative performance, altogether livelier than its predecessor, and at its best a superbly musical version of Offenbach's sparkling creation.

Carl Orff

German 1895-1982

GROVE *Orff studied at the Munich Academy and later, in 1920, with Kaminski. In 1924, with Dorothee Günther, he founded a school for gymnastics, music and dance, and out of this came his later activity in providing materials for young children to make music, using their voices and simple percussion instruments. His adult works also seek to make contact with primitive kinds of musical behaviour, as represented by ostinato, pulsation and direct vocal expression of emotion; in this he was influenced by Stravinsky (Oedipus rex, The Wedding), though the models are coarsened to produce music of a powerful pagan sensual appeal and physical excitement. All his major works, including the phenomenally successful Carmina burana (1937), were designed as pageants for the stage; they include several versions of Greek tragedies and Bavarian comedies.*

Carmina Burana

Gundula Janowitz *sop* **Gerhard Stolze** *ten* **Dietrich Fischer-Dieskau** *bar* **Schönberg Boys' Choir; Chorus and Orchestra of the Deutsche Oper, Berlin / Eugen Jochum**

DG The Originals 447 437-2GOR (56 minutes: ADD). Ⓜ
Text and translation included. Recorded 1967 ●●●

Since its original release, Jochum's performance has consistently been a prime recommendation for this much-recorded piece. Listening to it again in the superbly remastered sound, one can easily hear why. He pays great attention to detail – particularly with regard to tempo and articulation – yet the performance as a whole has a tremendous cogent sweep and the choruses have terrific power. The more reflective sections are not neglected, however, and movements such as 'Stetit Puella', with Janowitz sounding alluring and fey, have surely never been more sensitively handled. Stolze is ideal as the roasted swan and Fischer-Dieskau encompasses the very varied requirements of the baritone's music with ease. This distinguished performance, authorized by the composer and here sounding better than ever, retains its place at the head of the queue.

Carmina Burana

Beverly Hoch *sop* **Stanford Olsen** *ten* **Mark Oswald** *bar* **F A C E Treble Choir; Montreal Symphony Chorus and Orchestra / Charles Dutoit**

Decca 455 290-2DH (59 minutes: DDD). Ⓕ
Texts and translations included. Recorded 1996

Dutoit's is the most satisfying and enjoyable modern performance of *Carmina Burana* to have appeared for some time. He is scrupulous in his attention to the many markings found in the score and ensures that details of articulation and orchestration are audible, without obtruding from the overall texture. His tempos feel just right, and he has conveyed his evident enthusiasm for the music to his performers, who respond accordingly. Stanford Olsen's roasted swan song is appropriately weird – helped by Orff's strange accompaniment being superbly pointed, whilst Beverly Hoch compensates for some thinness of tone with expressive phrasing, including a sensuous *portamento* in her 'In trutina' solo. Apart from his ponderous first number, Mark Oswald delivers the baritone's music with sensitivity and gusto. The choral singing is exceptionally fine. The recording, clear and full-bodied, makes this the most recommendable of digital versions.

Carmina Burana

Christiane Oelze *sop* **David Kuebler** *ten* **Simon Keenlyside** *bar* **Knabenchor Berlin; Chorus and Orchestra of the Deutsche Oper, Berlin / Christian Thielemann**

DG 453 587-2GH (63 minutes: DDD). Text and Ⓕ
translation included. Recorded 1998 ●●

Over the years there have been some impressive recordings of *Carmina Burana* from DG, starting with Jochum's electrifying version, recorded in 1967. Thielemann's harks directly back to that classic account, and not just because, like Jochum's, it has the chorus and orchestra of the Deutsche Oper, Berlin. His overall timing is much longer than Jochum's urgent and incisive account – 63 minutes rather than 56 – but the difference lies predominantly in the slow, lyrical sections. So, although with Thielemann the opening movement of the 'Primo vere' section is much longer, he loses nothing in tension, simply following the score's marking *molto flessibile*. Thielemann's speeds in fast sections come very close to those of Jochum and there is a similarly bright incisiveness, with rhythms clipped and well sprung, and with a comparably high voltage generated. Although Thielemann's version has impressively full and brilliant sound, with fine inner clarity and wonderfully sharp definition of the many antiphonal contrasts, not only the chorus but more particularly the semi-chorus sound distant. The *pianissimos* are magical, but closer recording would have made the results even more involving. The choral singing is superb, warm and dramatic, reflecting the work of singers from the opera house, and the Knabenchor Berlin in the penultimate movement of the 'Court of Love' section adds an aptly earthy tang, well caught by the recording.

The soloists too, like Jochum's, are as near ideal as could be. David Kuebler is totally unfazed by the high tessitura of so much of the tenor writing: not just clean and precise and characterizing superbly in the 'roast swan' sequence, but singing most beautifully in his equally taxing solo in the 'Court of Love' section ('Dies, nox et omnia'). Christiane Oelze even matches the lovely Gundula Janowitz (for Jochum) in the soprano sections, ravishingly pure and true both in 'In trutina' and 'Dulcissime'. But it is Simon Keenlyside's singing which crowns this brilliant performance, at once clear, fresh and characterful. It is good to have this much-recorded work sounding as fresh as it did in that historic model.

Additional recommendation

Carmina burana

Soloists; London Symphony Chorus and Orchestra / Previn

EMI Great Recordings of the Century CDM5 66899-2 Ⓜ
(63 minutes: ADD: 10/86[R])

This is a classic reading, with a wonderful swagger and seductive rhythmic pointing. The soloists, too are splendid.

Catulli Carmina / Trionfo di Afrodite

Trionfi – Carmina Burana[a]; Catulli Carmina[b]; Trionfo di Afrodite[c]

[a]**Barbara Hendricks**, [bc]**Dagmar Schellenberger**, [c]**Lisa Larson**, [c]**Eva Maria Nobauer** *sops* [c]**Barbara Reiter** *contr* [a]**Michael Chance** *counterten* [bc]**Lothar Odinius**, [c]**Robert Swensen** *tens* [c]**Klaus Kuttler**, [a]**Jeffrey Black** *bars* [c]**Alfred Reiter** *bass*
[a]**St Albans Abbey Choir**; a**London Philharmonic Choir**; [bc]**Linz Mozart Choir**; [a]**London Philharmonic Orchestra**; [bc]**Munich Radio Orchestra / Franz Welser-Möst**

EMI ② CDS5 55519-2 (137 minutes: DDD). Texts and translations included. Recorded 1989 Ⓕ

Catulli Carmina and *Trionfo di Afrodite* with Welser-Möst are also available on HMV Classics HMV5 74367-2 Ⓑ

Catulli Carmina and *Trionfo di Afrodite* are under-represented in the current catalogue, unlike *Carmina Burana*, and it is here given a lithe and vigorous reading with spectacular playing from the LPO and fine singing from the choruses. Barbara Hendricks's vibrato may not be to all tastes and Jeffrey Black is too genial, lacking the requisite *slancio* quality his part demands, whilst Michael Chance's beautiful tone is not what was intended by the composer since a tenor singing in his highest register is specified. Nevertheless, this performance is more than the sum of its parts and Welser-Möst's attention to detail is evidence of his careful and considered approach. In the central section of *Catulli Carmina*, the unaccompanied settings of Catullus are well realized with secure intonation and variety of expression and the prologue, with its insistent ostinatos for four pianos and percussion, is quite electrifying.

Trionfo di Afrodite receives a thrilling and compelling performance and the final, orgiastic shouts of the chorus greeting the appearance of the goddess, make it the climax of the whole triptych. As bride and bridegroom, Dagmar Schellenberger and Lothar Odinius rise to the challenges of their parts with their wide-ranging and melismatic melodic lines. The other soloists and chorus sing with conviction and enthusiasm, supported by colourful and confident orchestral playing. Just occasionally, Welser-Möst presses ahead when Orff directs otherwise, but he draws out the dramatic qualities inherent in these works which were conceived for the theatre and despite blemishes, this set is now the preferred version of *Trionfo*.

Johann Pachelbel German 1653-1706

GROVE *Pachelbel was taught by two local musicians, Heinrich Schwemmer and GC Wecker. In 1669 he entered the university at Altdorf and was organist of the Lorenzkirche there, but left after less than a year for lack of money and in 1670 enrolled in the Gymnasium Poeticum at Regensburg, where he continued musical studies with Kaspar Prentz.*

After about five years as deputy organist at St Stephen's Cathedral, Vienna (1673-77), and a year as court organist at Eisenach, Pachelbel was appointed organist of the Predigerkirche at Erfurt in June 1678, where he remained for 12 years. During this time he was outstandingly successful as organist, composer and teacher (his pupils included JS Bach's elder brother, Johann Christoph) and was twice married. He left Erfurt in 1690 and, after short periods as organist in Stuttgart and Gotha, returned to Nuremberg, where he was organist at St Sebald until his death.

Pachelbel was a prolific composer. His organ music includes c70 chorales (mostly written at Erfurt), 95 Magnificat fugues (for Vespers at St Sebald) and non-liturgical works such as toccatas, preludes, fugues and fantasias. His preference for a lucid, uncomplicated style found fullest expression in his vocal music, which includes two masses and some important Vespers music as well as arias and sacred concertos. His modest contributions to chamber music include a canon that is now his best-known work.

Hexachordum Apollinis

Hexachordum Apollinis. Ciacconas—D; F minor
John Butt *org*
Harmonia Mundi HMU90 7029 (65 minutes: DDD) Ⓕ
Recorded on the Greg Harrold organ, Hertz Hall, University of California, Berkeley, USA

Hexachordum Apollinis is considered Pachelbel's finest composition in variation form. It consists of six Arias each comprising a theme and variations. The first five encompass the span of a perfect fifth but the sixth is something of an enigma; its home key deviates from the expected sequence forming the hexachord, it is in triple time while the others are in quadruple and it contains eight variations as against the five or six of the previous Arias. This final Aria, sub-titled 'Aria Sebaldina' after the patron saint of the church in Nuremberg where Pachelbel was organist, has long intrigued scholars. John Butt is a highly respected scholar, although his energies have been concentrated more towards the performance practices current in Bach's time. He certainly practises what he preaches. His playing on this disc has complete self-assurance and a startling directness which brings it all very much alive. It would be hard to argue against such convincing playing.

Like much non-liturgical keyboard music of the time, *Hexachordum Apollinis* was not specifically intended for a particular instrument; indeed, the title-page of the original 1699 manuscript, reproduced in the accompanying booklet, depicts both an organ and a harpsichord. Butt's choice would seem to be particularly sensible. This organ dates only from 1982, but is built in the style of organs made around 1700 in Ostfriesland, on the Dutch/German border, and produces the kind of clear, intimate sound more associated with a domestic instrument than with an ecclesiastical one. He uses its resources very sparingly and with unerringly sound judgement.

Keyboard Suites

Keyboard Suites – C, S25; D minor, S26; E minor, S28; E minor, S29; F, S32; G minor, S33; G minor, S33b; G, S34; A, S36
Joseph Payne *hpd*
BIS CD809 (74 minutes: DDD) Ⓕ

First-class recordings of fine organ music and motets by Pachelbel seem to have been unable to plant his name in the minds of the general musical public other than as the composer of that attractive but over recorded canon. The present suites (definitely for harpsichord, not organ) are all printed in the *Denkmaler der Tonkunst in Bayern* series, but except for Nos 29, 32 and 33b their authorship is very questionable. Whoever wrote them, however, they contain some very impressive movements – for example the gigues in Nos 36 and 29 and the allemands in Nos 28, 29 and 26 – and Pachelbel displays some intriguing rhythmic quirks on occasion.

Each of the suites consists of an allemand, courant and saraband, plus a 'gyque' [sic] in all but two cases; No 33 includes a lively 'ballett', Nos. 25, 36 and 28 a gavotte (that in A major a very jolly one); there are doubles in Nos 29 and 36. Playing on a copy of a bright-toned early Flemish instrument, Joseph Payne offers clean and vital performances, with neat ornaments (less profuse, except for No 33b and the sarabands of No 28); now and then, in his desire for expressiveness or to draw attention to a point, he is a bit mannered, but in general his playing is most appealing and he is recorded with total fidelity.

Giovanni Pacini

Italian 1796-1867

GROVE *Pacini studied singing with Marchesi in Bologna, then turned to composition. Between 1813 and 1867 he wrote nearly 90 operas, first modelling them on Rossini and later, after contact with Bellini's works, giving more attention to harmonic and instrumental colour. He was gifted with melodic invention, used to effect in a variety of cabaletta types; his accompaniments and ensemble writing are weak by comparison. Among the earlier works, Alessandro nelle Indie (1824), L'ultimo giorno di Pompei (1825), Gli arabi nelle Gallie (1827) and Ivanhoe (1832) were notable successes. In 1833 increased competition from Bellini and Donizetti caused his five-year withdrawal from the stage and he established a music school at his home in Viareggio and composed sacred works for the ducal chapel in Lucca, of which he was director from 1837. But with the immensely successful Saffo (1840), considered his masterpiece, he entered a period of more mature opera composition, producing La fidanzata corsa (1842), Maria, regina d'Inghilterra and Medea (1843). Though his success and reputation outside Italy were limited, his musical weaknesses can be attributed chiefly to the circumstances in which he worked. In the face of formidable competition within Italy, he satisfied a sophisticated public for half a century.*

Maria, Regina d'Inghilterra

Nelly Miricioiu *sop* Mary Tudor; **Bruce Ford** *ten* Riccardo Fenimoore; **José Fardilha** *bass* Ernesto Malcolm; **Mary Plazas** *sop* Clotilde Talbot; **Alastair Miles** *bass* Gualtiero Churchill; **Susan Bickley** *mez* Page; **Benjamin Bland** *bass* Raoul
Geoffrey Mitchell Choir; Philharmonia Orchestra / David Parry
Opera Rara ③ ORC15 (172 minutes: DDD). Notes, text and translation included. Recorded 1995-96 Ⓕ

Pacini wrote happily within the formal conventions of Italian opera in his time. Opening chorus, aria and cabaletta, duet likewise in two 'movements', big ensemble as finale of the middle act, 'brilliant' solo for prima donna just before the final curtain. The form (like sonata form or sonnet) is a good one, perhaps the best for opera to be itself in, rather than a play set to music; and for the most part Pacini exploits the form well. The plot is adapted from the play by Victor Hugo, and tells of Mary I's love for a scheming courtier, an Italian in Hugo, the Scotsman Fenimoore in Pacini. This Fenimoore, being the tenor, is loved by two ladies and is deceiving both. The other woman, Clotilde, is protected and loved by the baritone Ernesto, who finds out about Fenimoore, to accomplish the downfall of whom he puts himself at the disposal of Fenimoore's enemy, the Lord Chancellor (bass).

A great point about such a set-up is the scope it provides for duets, and these are both plentiful and good. There are choruses of merrymakers, soldiers and Londoners out for blood. The ensemble, an excellent example of its kind, comes at the point when Fenimoore is cornered and feelings run high. So do the voices. We are lucky to have Bruce Ford. At a *fortissimo* he may sound underpowered, and he does not play imaginatively with *mezza voce* effects, but he much more than copes: in florid passages he moves swiftly and gracefully, he appears to be comfortable with the tessitura, and in the Prison scene, which provided Ivanov with his greatest success, he sings with feeling and a sense of style.

The women have suitably contrasting voices, Mary Plazas's fresh and high, Nelly Miricioiu's older in tone, more dramatic in timbre. Both are expressive singers, and though Miricioiu too habitually resorts to the imperious glottal emphasis associated with Callas and Caballé, she brings conviction to all she does. The baritone, José Fardilha, has a touch of the flicker-vibrato that can give distinctive character, and Alastair Miles confers nobility of utterance upon the vindictive Chancellor. The cast, in fact, is worthy of the opera, which in this recording has probably its most important performance since the première of 1843. There is fine work from the Geoffrey Mitchell Choir and the Philharmonia under David Parry. Recorded sound is clear and well balanced, and the production handles the drama well. You are likely to play it straight through from start to finish, chafing at any interruption; and that says something for both the music and the drama.

Ignacy Paderewski Polish 1860-1941

GROVE *Pianist, composer and statesman Paderewski studied at the Warsaw Music Institute, in Berlin and with Leschetizky in Vienna, his career as a pianist beginning in 1888 with an exhausting international concert schedule; as a performer he was noted for his individual treatment of rubato. Meanwhile he composed during the summers, producing the opera Manru (1892-1901), the Symphony Op 24 and the Fantaisie polonaise Op 19 for piano and orchestra, typical products of the late Romantic Polish national school; perhaps better known are his programmatic piano miniatures and the Piano Concerto (1888). Between 1910 and 1921 he was active on behalf of Poland, making speeches, assisting victims of oppression and eventually becoming prime minister (1919). He also supported young Polish composers and worked on a new Chopin edition. He received numerous musical and national honours including a state burial in Arlington National Cemetery.*

Polonia Symphony

Symphony in B minor, Op 24, 'Polonia'
BBC Scottish Symphony Orchestra / Jerzy Maksymiuk
Hyperion CDA67056 (74 minutes: DDD). Ⓕ
Recorded 1998

Best-known as a legendary concert pianist and appointed first Prime Minister of Poland in 1919, Ignacy Jan Paderewski also found time to compose. In 1903 he embarked on his vast *Polonia* Symphony, which cost him some five years of labour and was to be his final major creation. First heard privately in Lausanne on Boxing Day, 1908, the symphony received its public première in Boston some eight weeks later under Max Fiedler and was soon taken up by both Hans Richter and André Messager. In its unashamedly epic countenance and theatrical sense of rhetoric, *Polonia* most closely resembles the two symphonies of Liszt as well as Tchaikovsky's *Manfred*, though it perhaps lacks the distinctive thematic profile of those masterworks. That said, the mighty opening movement (some half-an-hour in duration) is an impressive achievement, its stately introductory material sowing the seeds for much of what is to follow as well as acting as a most effective foil to the rousingly patriotic, defiant *Allegro vivace* proper. At first, the central *Andante con moto* meanders along moodily in an introspective, Rachmaninovian manner, but, about half-way through, the skies darken further and the music acquires a troubled, sombre flavour that cannot be dispelled (the bleak coda offers no consolation). The finale's truculent battle-cries (which manage to incorporate a cleverly disguised motif based on the first two bars of the Polish national anthem) are temporarily assuaged by two tranquil episodes. The BBC Scottish SO and its longstanding Polish chief Jerzy Maksymiuk mastermind a performance of eloquence and dashing commitment (only in the closing minutes does any hint of raggedness creep into the violins' bustling – and, by the sound of it, none-too-rewarding passagework). The recording, too, is pretty resplendent, and collectors with a sweet tooth for this sort of heady, late-romantic 'spectacular' shouldn't hesitate for a moment.

Annibale Padovano Italian 1527-65

GROVE *Padovano was organist at St Mark's, Venice (1552-65), then at the Graz court (from 1566, director of music 1567). Though important chiefly for his distinctive ricercares and improvisatory toccatas for organ (1556, 1604), he also published sacred works (1567, 1573) and madrigals (1561, 1564).*

Mass for 24 voices – Versions 1 and 2

Huelgas Ensemble / Paul van Nevel
Harmonia Mundi HMC90 1727 (54 minutes: DDD).
Text and translation included. Ⓕ
Recorded 2000

Among other things, the Huelgas Ensemble do a nice line in lavishly scored renaissance behemoths: think of the *Utopia triumphans* collection for Sony Classical, which included several such pieces from the 15th and 16th centuries, and Brumel's 12-voice Mass *Et ecce terre motus* which appeared nearly a decade ago. That number is doubled on this disc, which presents two performances of a Mass by Annibale Padovano, a prolific composer most often represented on disc by his instrumental music.

Padovano spent his career in Venice and in Graz, where he died in 1575 soon after the publication of a book of Masses. This wasn't one of them (perhaps unsurprisingly given the logistics involved); it survives instead in three choirbooks, now housed in the National Library in Vienna, from which Paul van Nevel made his transcription. In many ways it is a typical example of polychoral writing, although the disposition of the forces into three choirs of eight voices is rather unusual. Van Nevel underscores this by presenting the Mass first with a predominance of instruments and three voices in different ranges, one from each choir. The second reading is a mirror-image of the first, with about two dozen singers and three instruments: two cornets for the texture's higher reaches (a bit too high for singers' comfort) and a contrabass sackbut for reinforcement. (Incidentally, the insert-booklet gives the two versions in the wrong order.) Which of the two you prefer is a matter of taste, but you may find the choral one more involving: the individual lines receive much clearer definition, and aside from providing further touches of colour, the cornets are freer to ornament their lines imaginatively. As to the work itself, it may be pointless to introduce notions of 'quality' here: it is perhaps best considered as the support for an exceptional performance.

The sound is what mattered to the composer and the congregation, and presumably also to van Nevel and Harmonia Mundi. So there is no need to expect tours de force of contrapuntal brilliance à la Tallis (although for what it's worth there is an apparent reference to Josquin's *Pange lingua* Mass at the words 'per quem omnia facta sunt. Qui propter nos homines…'); similarly, the performances are as workmanlike as one might expect from these musicians, and not without charm, but they don't truly catch fire. Still, aficionados of renaissance instruments will want to experience those two dozen massed sackbuts and cornets; and one wouldn't want to argue with them.

Nicolò Paganini

Italian 1782-1840

GROVE *Through his technique and extreme personal magnetism Paganini was not only the most famous violin virtuoso but drew attention to the significance of virtuosity as an element in art. He studied with his father, Antonio Cervetto and Giacomo Costa and composition with Ghiretti and Paer in Parma. From 1810 to 1828 he developed a career as a 'free artist' throughout Italy, mesmerising audiences and critics with his showmanship; notable compositions were the bravura variations Le streghe (1813), the imaginative 24 Caprices Op 1 and the second and third violin concertos, surpassing in brilliance any that had been written before. After conquering Vienna in 1828 he was equally successful in Germany (Goethe, Heine and Schumann admired him), Paris and London (1831-4). His hectic international career finally shattered his health in 1834, when he returned to Parma. Apart from his unparalleled technical wizardry on the instrument, including the use of left-hand pizzicato, double-stop harmonics, 'ricochet' bowings and a generally daredevil approach to performance – all of which influenced successive violinists – he is most important for his artistic impact on Liszt, Chopin, Schumann and Berlioz, who took up his technical challenge in the search for greater expression in their own works.*

Violin Concertos

No 1 in E flat, Op 6; **No 2** in B minor, Op 7, 'La campanella'

Violin Concertos Nos 1 and 2
Salvatore Accardo *vn*
London Philharmonic Orchestra / Charles Dutoit
DG 415 378-2GH (69 minutes: ADD). Ⓕ
Recorded 1975

Paganini's violin music was at one time thought quite inaccessible to lesser mortals among the violin-playing fraternity, but as standards of technique have improved master technicians are now able to do justice to such works as these concertos. Salvatore Accardo is certainly among them, and we can judge his skill as early as the opening violin solo of the First Concerto. This is typical of the style, with its authoritative and rhetorical gestures and use of the whole instrumental compass, but so is the second theme which in its refinement and songlike nature demands (and here receives) another kind of virtuosity expressed through a command of tone, texture and articulation. Dutoit and the London Philharmonic Orchestra have a mainly subordinate role, certainly when the soloist is playing, but they fulfil it well and follow Accardo through the rhythmic flexibilities which are accepted performing style in this music and which for all we know were used by the virtuoso performer-composer himself. The recording is faithful and does justice to the all-important soloist.

Violin Concertos Nos 1 and 2
Ilya Kaler *vn*
Polish National Radio Symphony Orchestra / Stephen Gunzenhauser
Naxos 8 550649 (67 minutes: DDD). Ⓢ
Recorded 1992

Ilya Kaler is a Russian virtuoso, a pupil of Leonid Kogan. He is a first-rate fiddler and an excellent musician. Paganini's once fiendish pyrotechnics hold no terrors for him, not even the whistling harmonics, and how nicely he can turn an Italianate lyrical phrase, as in the secondary theme of the first movement of the First Concerto. Then he can set off with panache into a flying *staccato*, bouncing his bow neatly on the strings when articulating the delicious *spiccato* finales of both works. Stephen Gunzenhauser launches into the opening movements with plenty of energy and aplomb and is a sympathetic accompanist throughout – he is never heavy in orchestral writing that can easily sound vapid or stodgy. How nicely the violins shape the lyrical ritornello introducing the first movement of the Second, and there is some sensitive horn playing in the *Adagio*. Kaler's intonation is above suspicion and he is naturally balanced: there is none of the scratchiness that can ruin one's pleasure in Paganinian pyrotechnics. With excellent notes, this is a superior product at super-bargain price. The recordings were made in the Concert Hall of Polish Radio in Katowice. It has an ideal ambience for this music: nicely warm, not clouded. Great value on all counts.

Paganini Violin Concerto No 1
Saint-Saëns Havanaise in E, Op 83. Introduction and Rondo capriccioso in A minor, Op 28
Sarah Chang *vn*
Philadelphia Orchestra / Wolfgang Sawallisch
EMI CDC5 55026-2 (55 minutes: DDD). Ⓕ
Recorded 1993-94

Paganini would surely have been astonished at Sarah Chang's version of his No 1. She made her début with the piece in the Avery Fisher Hall at the age of eight(!), but had reached more advanced years (12) when she recorded it in Philadelphia for EMI. The performance is dazzling, particularly the finale where her light rhythmic touch and deliciously pert sliding 'harmonized harmonics' are a wonder of technical assurance. Note too, in the first movement, the relaxed ease of the decorated bouncing bow passages and the gently tender reprise of the second subject. The slow movement is not overtly romantic, but the freshness is never in doubt. One does not expect her to sound maturely sophisticated like Perlman and she understates the sultry atmosphere of the Saint-Saëns *Havanaise* to pleasing effect, yet manages the coda with spruce flexibility of phrase and the most subtle graduations of timbre. The *Introduction and Rondo capriccioso* has plenty of dash and she catches the Spanish sunlight in the *Introduction* without an overtly sensuous response. She is not flattered by the recording, which is balanced close. Sawallisch directs with verve and supports his soloist admirably.

Cantabile in D, Op 17[a]. Violin Concerto Nos 1[b] and 2 (arr vn/pf)[a]. Introduction and Variations on 'Nel cor più non mi sento' from Paisiello's 'La Molinara', Op 38. Moses-Fantasie[a]

Ilya Gringolts *vn* [a]**Irina Ryumina** *pf* [b]**Lahti Symphony Orchestra / Osmo Vänskä** Ⓕ

BIS CD999 (72 minutes: DDD). Recorded 1999

Ilya Gringolts (*b*1982 in St Petersburg) is an outstanding young Russian violinist; with this Paganini programme he began his recording career at the deep end. He's able to surmount the ferocious technical demands, and has, too, a notably rich, beautiful, unforced tone. In the unaccompanied *Nel cor più non mi sento* Variations, he seems rather careful – missing the passionate directness that Leila Josefowicz brings to this piece. But Gringolts's more expansive and delicate account is equally valid, the theme, with its freely expressive ornamentation, especially appealing. The other shorter items work well, too, in particular the elegant *Cantabile* – originally for violin and guitar. Only *La campanella* is a bit disappointing: one feels the need for a more vigorous approach, and despite the finesse of the playing it's difficult not to regret the absence of the orchestra. The First Concerto benefits from a truly outstanding accompaniment, performed (and recorded) with a wonderful sense of space and balance. Even the bass drum and cymbal parts are played with sensitivity – what can sound like a crudely overloaded score emerges here full of colour and grandeur. With such fine orchestral sonority, one might wonder what the concerto would sound like in its original key. Paganini played it in E flat, by tuning his strings a semitone higher, and wrote the orchestral parts in the higher key; his aim was to produce a more brilliant, penetrating sound. Present-day soloists, understandably, prefer the standard tuning for such a demanding work.

Gringolts plays with sweetness or brilliance as required, though one might wish the first movement hadn't had so many or such extreme tempo changes and that he had managed to give the *Adagio* a more dramatic tone, to match the darkly romantic orchestration. But the finale is terrific, with all the verve and high spirits one could want.

Centone di sonate

Centone di sonate Nos 7-12

Moshe Hammer *vn* **Norbert Kraft** *gtr* Ⓢ

Naxos 8 553142 (72 minutes: DDD). Recorded 1994

The *Centone di sonate* (a 'hotchpotch of sonatas') consists of 18 'sonatas' which are really salon works with a variety of movements – none of them in sonata form. Whether Paganini, who wrote them sometime after 1828, intended these pieces for public performance or merely for the use of the then abundant amateur musicians is not known. As usual in his works of this genre, it is the violin which hogs the limelight while the guitar remains a humble bag-carrier. The guitar parts are indeed so simple that they would have been within the reach of any amateur who was capable of keeping his end up with another musician; Segovia considered them beneath his dignity and refused many invitations to play them with famous partners! Nothing is harder than to be 'simple': Mozart managed it whilst at the same time being deceptively complex; Paganini did it at a far less sublime level, with sentimental, cheerful and pert tunes. Truth to tell, they are not the kind of works which impel one to listen to them at one sitting except for the most devoted *aficionado* of Paganini's violinistic voice or of hearing the guitar in an unremittingly subservient but genuinely complementary role.

These splendid performances on modern instruments make no claim to 'authentic' status, but they are no less appealing for that. They squeeze every last drop from the music with (inauthentically) full sound, and a Siamese-twin tightness of ensemble that was probably rare amongst those who played these works in Paganini's own time. In the end, these works have a charm that is hard for any but the most straitlaced to resist. It is unlikely that the *Centone* will ever be better played and/or recorded.

Violin and Guitar Duos

Six Sonatas for Guitar and Violin, Op 3. Sonata concertata in A, Op 61. 60 Variations on 'Barucabà', Op 14. Cantabile in D, Op 17

Scott St John *vn* **Simon Wynberg** *gtr* Ⓢ

Naxos 8 550690 (54 minutes: DDD). Recorded 1993

Six Sonatas for Guitar and Violin, Op 2. Cantabile e Valtz, Op 19. Variazioni di bravura on Caprice No 24. Duetto amoroso. Sonata per le gran viola e chitarra

Scott St John *vn* **Simon Wynberg** *gtr* Ⓢ

Naxos 8 550759 (59 minutes: DDD). Recorded 1993

Several of the violin/guitar duos testify to Paganini's amorous inclinations: the sections of the *Duetto amoroso* spell out the course of an affair, from beginning to separation, and may have been aimed (unsuccessfully, one imagines) at the Princess Elisa Baciocchi in Lucca. His conservative harmonic vocabulary springs few surprises and his melodies sometimes verge on banality, but by dint of sheer charm and technical ingenuity he somehow gets away with it; only the po-faced could resist an admiring smile at his effrontery. Collectively, these works present the full range of Paganini's technical armoury – the left-hand pizzicatos, high harmonics, double-stopping, 'sneaky' chromatic runs and the rest, and Scott St John betrays no difficulty in dealing with every googly that comes his way. More than that, in the daunting *Sonata per le gran viola e chitarra* (celebrating Paganini's acquisition of a Stradivarius instrument) cocks a snook at every viola joke that ever was. The guitar's role in the action varies from purely supportive subservience to more equal (though at a lower acrobatic level) partnership, as in the *Sonata concertata* and from time to time in the Op 3 Sonatas. Wynberg proves as well matched a partner as St John could have wished for. Violinists, guitarists and lovers of winsomeness for its own sake should revel in these very well recorded discs and will find much information in the booklet.

24 Caprices, Op 1

Itzhak Perlman *vn*
EMI Great Recordings of the Century Ⓜ
CDM5 67237-2 (72 minutes: ADD) ◉

This electrifying music with its dare-devil virtuosity has long remained the pinnacle of violin technique, and the *Caprices* encapsulate the essence of the composer's style. For a long time it was considered virtually unthinkable that a violinist should be able to play the complete set; even in recent years only a handful have produced truly successful results. Itzhak Perlman has one strength in this music that is all-important, other than a sovereign technique – he is incapable of playing with an ugly tone. He has such variety in his bowing that the timbre of the instrument is never monotonous. The notes of the music are dispatched with a forthright confidence and fearless abandon. The frequent double-stopping passages hold no fear for him. Listen to the fire of No 5 in A minor and the way in which Perlman copes with the extremely difficult turns in No 14 in E flat; this is a master at work. The set rounds off with the famous A minor Caprice, which inspired Liszt, Brahms and Rachmaninov, amongst others, to adapt it in various guises for the piano.

---

24 Caprices
Leonidas Kavacos *vn*
Dynamic CDS66 (77 minutes: DDD). Ⓕ
Recorded 1989-90 ◉

The Greek Leonidas Kavacos, who won first prize at the 1988 Paganini Competition in Genoa, as well as taking the 1991 *Gramophone* Concerto Award for the Sibelius Violin Concerto, is given a recorded sound that favours the lower strings of the violin, so much so that the sonority resembles a viola. He takes a truly intelligent view of the musical potential of Paganini's frequently tortuous-sounding Caprices. He also has a pretty formidable playing equipment and captures the mysterious and obsessive side of the music. The acoustic is spacious and affords an objective and balanced view of the music. He does not treat the *Caprices* as if they were merely *études*, but follows the composer's tempo markings with fidelity, notably in the Sixth Caprice. Kavacos saves his best playing for last: the final, and best-known, Caprice is quite superb.

---

24 Caprices [H]
Michael Rabin *vn*
EMI CDM7 64560-2 (69 minutes: ADD). Ⓜ
Recorded 1958. ◉◉

The almost legendary American, Michael Rabin, who died in 1972 at the age of 35 after slipping on a parquet floor, was a stupendous technician not greatly concerned with stylistic considerations. He is so close to the microphone that one hears every detail with razor-sharp clarity. This closeness has the undesirable effect of ironing-out virtually all the dynamic shadings of his bowing, so that the playing has an unnatural evenness. The Eighth Caprice, in E flat, is excruciating on an aural level. For technical finesse and sheer dexterity, however, Rabin is utterly brilliant, and in the immense number of passages where double-stopping raises its ugly head, his control of pitch is stunning. In the final Caprice, Rabin is notable for his wonderful singing quality in the highest register, where his controlled use of vibrato reigns supreme.

Giovanni Palestrina

Italian c1525/6-1594

GROVE *Palestrina was a pupil of Mallapert and Firmin Lebel at S Maria Maggiore, Rome, where he was a choirboy from at least 1537. He became organist of S Agapito, Palestrina, in 1544 and in 1547 married Lucrezia Gori there; they had three children. After the Bishop of Palestrina's election as pope (Julius III) he was appointed maestro di cappella of the Cappella Giulia in Rome (1551), where he issued his first works (masses, 1554); during 1555 he also sang in the Cappella Sistina. Two of Rome's greatest churches then procured him as maestro di cappella, St John Lateran (1555-60) and S Maria Maggiore (1561-6), and in 1564 Cardinal Ippolito d'Este engaged him to oversee the music at his Tivoli estate. From 1566 he also taught music at the Seminario Romano, before returning to the Cappella Giulia as maestro in 1571.*

During the 1560s and 1570s Palestrina's fame and influence rapidly increased through the wide diffusion of his published works. So great was his reputation that in 1577 he was asked to rewrite the church's main plainchant books, following the Council of Trent's guidelines. His most famous mass, Missa Papae Marcelli, may have been composed to satisfy the council's requirements for musical cogency and textual intelligibility. He was always in tune with the Counter-Reformation spirit; after his wife's death in 1580 he considered taking holy orders, but instead he remarried (1581). His wife, Virginia Dormoli, was a wealthy fur merchant's widow; his investments in her business eased his financial strains, and his last years at St Peter's were among his most productive.

Palestrina ranks with Lassus and Byrd as one of the greatest Renaissance masters. A prolific composer of masses, motets and other sacred works, as well as madrigals, he was (unlike Lassus) basically conservative. In his sacred music he assimilated and refined his predecessors' polyphonic techniques to produce a 'seamless' texture, with all voices perfectly balanced. The nobility and restraint of his most expressive works established the almost legendary reverence that has surrounded his name and helped set him up as the classic model of Renaissance polyphony.

Motets

Ave Maria. Alma Redemptoris mater a IV. Veni sponsa Christi. Surge, propera amica mea. Quae est ista. Magnificat IV toni. Hodie beata virgo. Ave regina coelorum a IV. Magnificat VII toni. Ave Maria a V. Ave maris stella
Camerata Nova / Luigi Taglioni
Stradivarius STR33375 (59 minutes: DDD). Texts and Ⓕ translations included. Recorded 1996

This is the new Italian sound of renaissance church music: a gentle vibrato, but a wonderfully loose and relaxed sound with a kind of breathy production. In the normal four-voice Palestrina texture both the two top voices are taken by women; but the sopranos are extremely light in their sound so they never dominate the texture, and the altos are of that wonderful variety that one usually only hears from Italians, with a firm and infinitely attractive chest register that goes confidently down to a low F. If the texture here is quite unlike what we are used to hearing from the best British ensembles, that is partly because there is an emphasis on line rather than on sonority. It's a sound of tremendous restraint. If one can say with confidence that this was not the sound Palestrina was expecting (any more than he was expecting the sound of The Tallis Scholars and their like), one can say with equal confidence that the Camerata Nova brings across the spirit and the polyphonic vitality of his music with astonishing power. Much credit must go to Luigi Taglioni for producing such a gentle and controlled ensemble. The music is also nicely chosen: a group of Marian motets, two Magnificat settings and a Marian hymn to form a neatly contrasted programme, with several pieces gloriously sung by four solo women's voices. If you thought that Palestrina was a composer of seamless and immaculate textures with just a touch too much surface gloss for comfort, this may be a record to help you to hear one of the world's most influential composers in a different light.

Masses

Missa Viri Galilaei. Missa O Rex gloriae. Motets – Viri Galilaei; O Rex gloriae
Westminster Cathedral Choir / James O'Donnell
Hyperion CDA66316 (68 minutes: DDD). Texts and Ⓕ translations included. Recorded 1988 ●

This is music in which Westminster Cathedral Choir excels: its response to the richly reverberant acoustic is warm and generous; it performs with the ease and freedom of kinship – a far cry from the studied perfection of many other choirs. Each motet is heard before its reworking as a Mass. The six-part scoring of *Viri Galilaei* (two trebles, alto, two tenors and bass) invites a variety of combinations and textures, culminating in the joyful cascading Alleluias at the end of Part I and the jubilant ascending series in Part II. In the Mass the mood changes from triumph to quiet pleading – a change partly due to revised scoring: the two alto parts beneath the single treble produce a more subdued sound.

The Choir clearly relishes this exploration of the deeper sonorities: in the *Creed* one entire section is entrusted to the four lowest voices. The four-part motet *O Rex gloriae* is lithe and fast-moving. The corresponding Mass, largely syllabic in style, gives the Choir the chance to show its superb command of phrasing and accentuation: the Latin comes over with intelligibility and subtlety. Listen, also, to the wonderful solo boys' trio in the 'Crucifixus', and for the carefully crafted canons in the *Benedictus* and *Agnus Dei*.

Missa ecce ego Johannes. Cantantibus organis. Laudate pueri. Magnificat IV toni. Peccantem me quotidie. Tribulationes civitatum. Tu es Petrus
Westminster Cathedral Choir / James O'Donnell
Hyperion CDA67099 (65 minutes: DDD). Texts and Ⓕ translations included. Recorded 1999 ●

For sheer beauty of sound, this recording is unsurpassed. The choice of a programme of music by Palestrina, the one composer ever to have been honoured by official ecclesiastical recognition, was inspired. This CD represents several high points of solemn liturgy; a six-part polyphonic Mass, *Ecce ego Johannes*, and two groups of motets, including a festal psalm, two penitential pieces, antiphons for the feasts of St Peter and St Cecilia and a solemn *alternatim Magnificat*. What is very admirable about the whole performance is the excellent integration of the choir. Ivan Moody underlines in his notes Palestrina's skill in the seamless interweaving of homophony and flowing counterpoint; the choir, in its turn, moves from one to the other with the utmost ease and art. In particular, the give-and-take of dovetailing produces a perfect balance. In this respect, top praise for the trebles, with a firm, mature tone and assured flexibility.

Missa Assumpta est Maria. Missa Sicut lilium inter spinas. Motets – Assumpta est Maria a 6; Sicut lilium inter spinas I. Plainchant: Assumpta est Maria
The Tallis Scholars / Peter Phillips
Gimell CDGIM020 (72 minutes: DDD) Ⓕ
Recorded 1989

In this recording of Palestrina's *Missa Assumpta est Maria* Peter Phillips has included the motet on which this work is based, together with another parody mass, the *Sicut lilium* with its corresponding motet. It is illuminating to hear how the larger-scale compositions unfold with reference to the original motets: close study, of course, would reveal much about the compositional processes of the High Renaissance, but any listener will be able to appreciate the organic relationship between motet and Mass.

In addition, Peter Phillips has deliberately paired two sharply contrasted parody Masses: *Assumpta est Maria*, the better known, is thought to be one of Palestrina's last masses, while *Sicut lilium* dates from relatively early in his career. The former, with its major tonality and divisi high voices, is marvellously bright and open and is given an outgoing performance, while the latter, inflected with chromaticism and melodic intervals that constantly fall back on themselves, is darker-hued and more plaintive, a mood well captured here in the intensity of the singing.

However, what is perhaps most striking is the difference in compositional technique between the two works: *Sicut lilium* relies largely on imitative textures for the unfolding of its structure (though there are the customary block chords on phrases such as 'et homo factus est', performed here with magical effect), while *Assumpta est Maria* makes far greater use of vocal scoring as a formal device and thus looks forward to the contrast principle of the baroque.

The Tallis Scholars make the most of the contrasted blocks of sound here, achieving an impressive vocal blend and balance. The phrasing, particularly in the Kyrie, is perhaps a little too mannered and the very beautiful Agnus Dei verges on the narcissistic and therefore becomes too static. The flow in the *Missa Sicut lilium*, though, is excellent throughout.

Giovanni Antonio Pandolfi

Italian fl1660-1669

Italian composer and violinist Pandolfi is a shadowy figure known only for handful of violin sonatas. He was among the instrumentalists of Archduke Ferdinand of Austria at Innsbruck when his opp 3 and 4 violin sonatas were published in 1660 and there is little doubt a 1669 volume of sonatas attributed to 'D. Gio. Antonio Pandolfi' is by the same composer.

Violin Sonatas

Awards 2000

Six Sonatas per chiesa e camera, Op 3. P
Six Sonatas for Violin and Continuo, Op 4
Andrew Manze *vn* **Richard Egarr** *hpd*
Harmonia Mundi HMU907241 Ⓕ
(80 minutes: DDD). ⚫⚫⚫

It would seem almost as if Andrew Manze had acquired proprietorial rights over the violin sonatas of Giovanni Antonio Pandolfi, or Antonio Pandolfi Mealli, as he called himself in the earlier of the two collections presented here. Incidentally it is not correct to describe the contents of the disc as Pandolfi's 'Complete Violin Sonatas' since there are four more for solo violin and continuo in a third collection issued in Rome in 1669. These are virtuoso performances of some quite extraordinary music.

Each sonata has its own descriptive subtitle and a movement layout which seems reluctant to conform to any set pattern. Presumably the sections have their own tempo indications, though these are not disclosed either in the booklet or in the listing on the reverse side of the box. A pity, since there are lots of interesting and unusual juxtapositions of a strikingly non-conformist nature. Much of the writing is characterized by virtuoso figurations which, especially in faster movements, might become a little wearisome in the hands of a lesser player. But Manze seems to sense this danger and averts it with panache and a highly developed sense of fantasy. Slow movements, on balance, are more interesting and there is an especially memorable one in *La Clemente*, the Fifth Sonata of Op 3, whose aria-like character is pathos-laden. Manze plays it sensitively and the result is touching. Several movements have a strong ostinato element and, in *La Monella Romanesca*, the third piece from Op 4, we have a set of variations on a melody contained in the bass. Harpsichordist Richard Egarr is a lively and an imaginative accompanist throughout. In short, an exhilarating recital of music whose exoticism, melancholy and wild, passionate outbursts resist categorization and convenient definition. Strongly recommended.

Sir Hubert Parry

British 1848-1918

GROVE *Parry studied at Oxford and with Pierson and Dannreuther, publishing songs, church music and piano works from the 1860s. He taught at the Royal College of Music from 1883 (succeeding Grove as director in 1894), also becoming professor at Oxford (1900-08) and president of the Musical Association (1901-8). Among his scholarly interests were Bach and the history of musical style, on which he wrote perceptively. His cantatas Scenes from Prometheus Unbound (1880), Blest Pair of Sirens (1887) and L'allegro ed il penseroso (1890) made a decisive impact for their poetic merit and advanced (Wagnerian) idiom. The anthem I was glad (1902), the choral Songs of Farewell (1916) and many of the unison songs including The Lover's Garland and Jerusalem show a similar regard for text and a fresh lyricism. His forceful personality and social position, together with his ethical views and intellectual vigour, enabled him to exercise a revitalising influence on English musical life in the late 19th century.*

Complete Organ Works

Fantasia and Fugue in G (1882 and 1913 vers)[a]. Three Chorale Fantasias[a]. Chorale Preludes, Sets 1[a] and 2[b]. Elegy in A flat[a]. Toccata and Fugue in G[a]. Elégie[b]
Various A Little Organ Book in Memory of Sir Hubert Parry[b]
James Lancelot *org*
Priory ② PRCD682AB (135 minutes: DDD). Ⓕ
Recorded [a]1997 and [b]2000 ⚫⚫⚫

British music has been well served by the independent labels, and Chandos and Hyperion have released CDs of music by Bantock, Dyson, Lambert, Stanford and many others. Priory has also made a significant contribution with its surveys of the organ works of Harwood, Howells, Ireland and Whitlock, and this two-CD set is a worthy addition to this collection.

It's all too easy to dismiss Parry's music as being workmanlike and living in the shadow of Bach and Brahms. Yet there is real beauty and passion here, and at his best Parry can match the intensity of his contemporary Max Reger. The appeal of this recording is enhanced by the inclusion of both the published and unpublished versions of the C major Fantasia and Fugue, and also by *A Little Organ Book*. This latter collection is an intensely moving tribute to Parry by 13 of his friends, colleagues and pupils (including Stanford, Bridge and Thalben-Ball).

This recording presents the best possible advocacy for Parry, and the combination of Lancelot and the Durham Willis/Harrison organ is, to coin a phrase, a 'dream ticket'. The greatness of Lancelot's playing lies in the perfect fusion of meticulously honed detail with an effortless flow to the whole performance. He fully exploits the beauty and grandeur of Durham's magical organ, and of all the available CDs, this one is the finest showcase for this most charismatic of cathedral instruments. The excellence of the playing is matched by the recording, and Jeremy Dibble has written an extremely comprehensive booklet – a model of its type. Quite simply, this is a definitive, outstanding, glorious recording.

Songs

Parry English Lyrics: Set 2 – O mistress mine; Take, O take those lips away; No longer mourn for me; Blow, blow, thou winter wind; When icicles hang by the wall. Set 4 – Thine eyes still shine for me; When lovers meet again; When we two parted; Weep you no more; There be none of beauty's daughters; Bright star. Set 5 – A Welsh lullaby. Set 6 – When comes my Gwen; And yet I love her till I die; Love is a bable. Set 7 – On a time the amorous Silvy. Set 8 – Marian; Looking backward. Set 9 – There. Set 10 – From a city window
Vaughan Williams Songs of Travel. Linden Lea
Robert Tear *ten* **Philip Ledger** *pf*
Belart 461 493-2 (77 minutes: ADD). Ⓑ
Recorded *c*1979

This selection of Parry's songs is very welcome in these fine and intelligent performances by Robert Tear and Philip Ledger. Parry does not always measure up to his texts (in the sonnets of Keats and Shakespeare especially), and is best when renouncing his teatime-Brahms style in favour of a more personal and imaginative idiom, as in 'When icicles hang by the wall' and 'From a city window'.

Vaughan Williams's great song-cycle, *Songs of Travel*, has a freshness partly deriving from the comparative rarity of hearing it in higher keys for the tenor voice. Both artists give the impression of having studied the songs as it were 'from scratch'. Tear's phrasing is a delight, showing exceptional sensitivity to the words, and Ledger's playing, with very sparing use of pedal, is scrupulously clean and careful over detail. The recorded sound is fine. No texts are included but it hardly matters: the diction is so clear you are unlikely to miss a word.

I was glad ... / Jerusalem

I was glad when they said unto me. Evening Service in D, 'Great'. Songs of Farewell. Hear my words, ye people. Jerusalem
Timothy Woodford, Richard Murray-Bruce *trebs* **Andrew Wickens, Colin Cartwright** *countertens* **David Lowe, Martin Pickering** *tens* **Bruce Russell, Paul Rickard** *bars* **John Heighway** *bass* **Roger Judd** *org* **Choir of St George's Chapel, Windsor / Christopher Robinson**
Hyperion CDA66273 (58 minutes: DDD). Texts included. Recorded 1987 Ⓕ

The more of Parry's music one comes to know, the more apparent it becomes that the 'received opinion' of him is askew. Take the 1882 settings of the *Magnificat* and *Nunc dimittis*, for instance. These, amazingly, were not published until 1982. This recording – another example of Hyperion's courageous policy – shows how un-Victorian in the accepted sense they are. In other words, they are bold, unconventional and unsanctimonious – like quite a lot of Victorian church music, one may add. Perhaps the big anthem, *Hear my words* (1894) shows more signs of conventionality, but it has an attractive part for solo soprano (treble here) and ends with the hymn 'O praise ye the Lord'. The St George's Chapel Choir, conducted by Christopher Robinson, sings these works with more ease than it can muster for the famous and magnificent Coronation anthem *I was glad*, ceremonial music that not even Elgar surpassed. A sense of strain among the trebles is always evident. Although a wholly adult choir in the *Songs of Farewell* might be preferable, these are assured and often beautiful performances – excellent diction – of these extraordinarily affecting motets. English music does not possess much that is more perfect in the matching of words and music than the settings of 'There is an old belief' and 'Lord, let me know mine end', invidious as it is to select only two for mention. A stirring *Jerusalem* completes this enterprising recording, which brings the sound of a great building into our homes with absolute fidelity.

Arvo Pärt

Estonian 1935

GROVE *Pärt was a pupil of Eller at the Tallinn Conservatory until 1963 while working as a sound producer for Estonian radio (1957-67); in 1962 he won a prize for a children's cantata (Our Garden) and an oratorio (Stride of the World).*

Early works followed standard Soviet models, but later he turned to strict serial writing, in rhythm as well as pitch (Perpetuum mobile,1963) and then collage techniques (Symphony no.2, 1966; Pro et contra for cello and orchestra,1966). In the 1970s he came into contact with plainchant and the music of the Orthodox Church, which affected his music both technically and spiritually. This is seen in, for example, Symphony no.3 (1971) and the cantata Song for the Beloved (1973) as well as Tabula rasa for three violins, strings and prepared piano (1977). The music of other composers is evoked, drawing on minimalist techniques of repetition, in such works as Arbos for chamber ensemble (1977, Janácek), Summa for tenor, baritone and ensemble (1980, Stravinsky), Cantus in Memory of Benjamin Britten for bell and strings (1980, Britten). Of more recent works, Pari intervalli echoes Bach chorale preludes, An den Wassern zu Babylon calls on 13th-century music and the St John Passion (1981) uses choral and instrumental heterophony recalling ancient incantation, always intense yet pure and ritualistic in effect.

Symphony No 3

Symphony No 3. Tabula rasa[a]. Fratres[b]
[ab]**Gil Shaham,** [a]**Adele Anthony** *vns* [a]**Erik Risberg** *prepared pf* [b]**Roger Carlsson** *perc* **Gothenburg Symphony Orchestra / Neeme Järvi** Ⓕ
DG 20/21 457 647-2GH (59 minutes: DDD).

Pärt's panoramic, occasionally fragmented Third Symphony of 1971 contrasts with his gaunt but entrancing tintinnabulation works of the late 1970s. There are beautiful things in the symphony – ancient modes imaginatively redeployed, sensitive orchestration (especially for strings and tuned percussion), striking musical development and a fair quota of aural drama. There are occasional anticipations of the *Cantus in memory of Benjamin Britten*, and the 'breathing' spaces between episodes are characteristic of Pärt's later work. It's the voice of someone stretching his musical wings, edging into areas of harmonic invention that would help inform his future style – a youthful late-romantic poised on the brink of greater things.

One might wonder how Gil Shaham might tackle a style of music in which, in terms of overt expression, 'less' most definitely means 'more'. In the event, his firm, silvery tone is ideal and his pin-sharp arpeggios at the beginning of *Fratres* are extraordinarily exciting. When Pärt drops the pace and switches to a slow, gradual *crescendo*, Shaham plays with a mesmerizing combination of control and reserved expressiveness. The more expansive *Tabula rasa* is given a full-bodied and unexpectedly dynamic performance, especially in the opening movement, which sounds like a cross between a jig and a quick march. The long second movement conjures up immeasurable spaces (a reference that Shaham himself alludes to in the booklet-note) and the spasmodic interjections of a prepared piano – an incredible effect, musically – is balanced virtually to perfection by the engineers. Kremer's ECM disc (with Schnittke, no less, on prepared piano) is sparer and marginally more ethereal, but the sheer sense of presence on this DG release adds a new perspective to our experience of the piece. Strongly recommended, even if you own alternative versions of this repertoire.

Symphony No 3. Collage on B-A-C-H. Tabula rasa[a]
[a]**Lesley Hatfield,** [a]**Rebecca Hirsch** *vns* **Ulster Orchestra / Takuo Yuasa**
Naxos 8 554591 (52 minutes: DDD). Ⓢ
Recorded 1999

The most interesting comparison here is between Takuo Yuasa and Neeme Järvi in Pärt's granitic Third Symphony. The piece was dedicated to Järvi, whose recent, daringly broad DG version shares disc space with Gil Shaham's fine recording of *Tabula rasa*. Pärt Three is a transitional work that draws heavily on Orthodox and Gregorian influences. It serves as a bridge to the composer's tintinnabulatory compositions, though there's one passage – it occurs in this context at 4'54" on track 6 – where battling brass and strings sound more like an off-cut from Nielsen's Fifth Symphony.

Takuo Yuasa's reading is somewhat akin to Järvi's first (BIS) recording, certainly for tempo (20'22" compared to Järvi's 20'58"; the DG version stretches to an epic 25'17"). The Ulster brass are excellent and if the Orchestra's strings aren't quite on a par with those in Bamberg and Gothenburg, they're still pretty good.

The shocking centrepiece of *Collage* alternates quotations from Bach's Sixth *English* Suite (the 'Sarabande') with dissonant commentary on the same material and, again, the performance works very well. The first movement of Yuasa's *Tabula rasa* doesn't quite match Kremer's second version for driving energy, and the prepared piano in 'Silentium' hasn't the eerie, disembodied quality that Alfred Schnittke brought to his pioneering ECM recording with Sondeckis. Leslie Hatfield and Rebecca Hirsch are a fair match for Shaham and Adele Anthony, though Järvi's Gothenburg orchestra is marginally more refined. But it's a good deal better than some CD rivals, and the recording is carefully balanced.

Tabula rasa, in particular, is a humbling masterpiece – its sense of space and atmosphere is unique – and if you do not yet know the work, here's your chance to test new waters. Quality samplings of Pärt's work don't come any cheaper.

Fratres

Fratres (seven versions). Festina Lente. Cantus in Memory of Benjamin Britten. Summa
Peter Manning *vn* **France Springuel** *vc* **Mireille Gleizes** *pf* **I Fiamminghi**
Telarc CD80387 (79 minutes: DDD). Ⓕ
Recorded 1994

Telarc's *Fratres-Fest* proves beyond doubt that good basic material can be reworked almost *ad infinitum* – if the manner of its arrangement is sufficiently colourful. This sequence is particularly imaginative in that it alternates two varied pairs of *Fratres* with atmospheric original string pieces, then separates the last two versions with the sombre pealing of *Festina Lente*. The first *Fratres* opens to a low bass drone and chaste, ethereal strings: the suggested image is of a slow oncoming processional – mourners, perhaps, or members of some ancient religious sect – with drum and xylophone gradually intensifying until the percussive element is so loud that it resembles Copland's *Fanfare for the Common Man*. One envisages aged protagonists who have been treading the same ground since time immemorial, whereas the frantically propelled, arpeggiated opening to the version for violin, strings and percussion leaves a quite different impression. Still, even here the music does eventually calm and Peter Manning provides an expressive solo commentary. All six arrangements share a common 'approach-and-retreat' formula, with ideas that arrive from – and subsequently retreat to – some distant horizon.

Next comes the gentle cascading of Pärt's *Cantus in Memory of Benjamin Britten*, with its weeping sequences and lone, tolling bell. The eight-cello *Fratres* uses eerie harmonics (as does the cello and piano version that ends the programme), whereas *Fratres* for wind octet and percussion is cold, baleful, notably Slavonic-sounding and occasionally reminiscent of Stravinsky. The alternation of *Summa* (for strings) and the quartet version of *Fratres* works nicely, the former more animated than anything else on the disc; the latter, more intimate. The performances are consistently sympathetic, and the recordings are excellent.

Berliner Messe

Berliner Messe. The Beatitudes. Annum per Annum. Magnificat. Seven Magnificat Antiphons. De profundis
Polyphony / Stephen Layton with **Andrew Lucas** *org*
Hyperion CDA66960 (74 minutes: DDD). Texts and translations included. Recorded 1997 Ⓕ

Pärt's music is about equilibrium and balance – balance between consonance and dissonance, between converging voices and, in the context of a CD such as this, between the individual works programmed. Stephen Layton has chosen well, starting with the variegated *Berliner Messe* and closing with the starkly ritualistic *De profundis*, a memorable and ultimately dramatic setting of Psalm 130 for male voices, organ, bass drum and tam-tam, dedicated to Gottfried von Einem. The Mass features two of Pärt's most powerful individual movements, a gently rocking 'Veni Sancte Spiritus' and a *Credo* which, as Meurig Bowen's unusually perceptive notes remind us, is in essence a major-key transformation of the better-known – and more frequently recorded – *Summa*. Everything here chimes to Pärt's tintinnabulation style, even the brief but fetching organ suite *Annum per Annum*, where the opening movement thunders an alarm then tapers to a gradual *diminuendo*, while the closing coda shoulders an equally well-calculated *crescendo*. The five movements in between are mostly quiet, whereas *The Beatitudes* flies back to its opening tonality on 'a flurry of quintuplet broken chords'. It is also the one place that witnesses a momentary – and minor – blemish on the vocal line, but otherwise Layton directs a fine sequence of warmly blended performances. If you are new to Pärt's music, then this disc would provide an excellent starting-point. We would suggest playing the individually shaded *Seven Magnificat Antiphons* first, then tackling the *Berliner Messe*, followed, perhaps, by the *Magnificat*. Polyphony employs what one might roughly term an 'early music' singing style, being remarkably even in tone, largely free of vibrato and alive to phrasal inflexions. As to rival discs, none is significantly better performed; but as each Pärt programme is, in a sense, a concept in itself, we would recommend listening as widely as possible. We would also suggest experimenting with playing sequences: by so doing you will maximize the subtle differences between individual pieces.

De profundis

Statuit et Dominus. Missa Sillabica. Beatus Petronius. Seven Magnificat Antiphons. De profundis. Memento mori. Cantate Domino Solfeggio
Estonian Philharmonic Chamber Choir / Tõnu Kaljuste with **Christopher Bowers-Broadbent** *org*
Virgin Classics VC5 45276-2 (61 minutes: DDD). Ⓕ
Texts and translations included. Recorded 1995-96

Pärt's demands on the organ as an accompaniment to voices are neither particularly complex nor technically demanding but do require exceptional sensitivity from the player. It is largely through skilful use of registration that Bowers-Broadbent displays his profound understanding of the music. He balances his role admirably, keeping a discreet distance from the singers for the most part and measuring the long drawn-out *crescendo* of *De profundis* to perfection. However, this is, of course, a disc devoted to Pärt's choral music and it is the choir, rather than the organist, who are the real heroes. The Estonian Philharmonic Choir doesn't sound as if it's studied the music long and hard, but these performances feel as if they come from the heart; there is a tangible sense of spiritual empathy. Listen to the magical, ethereal quality of the singing in the *Gloria* from the *Missa Sillabica* which Tõnu Kaljuste draws from his singers. And in the magical *Magnificat Antiphons* the Estonian choir reveal an even greater depth of feeling. The recording is gloriously atmospheric.

I am the True Vine

Bogoróditse Djévo. I am the True Vine. Kanon pokajanen – Ode IX. The Woman with the Alabaster Box. Tribute to Caesar. Berliner Messe[a]
Pro Arte Singers, [a]Theatre of Voices / Paul Hillier *bar* with **[a]Christopher Bowers-Broadbent** *org*
Harmonia Mundi HMU90 7242 (58 minutes: DDD). Ⓕ
Texts and translations included. Recorded 1998 ⭘

I am the True Vine was composed in 1996 for the 900th anniversary of Norwich Cathedral, whereas *Tribute to Caesar* and *The Woman with the Alabaster Box* were, as the booklet tells us, commissioned in 1997 for the 350th Anniversary of the Karlstad Diocese in Sweden. Both works bear witness to a widened expressive vocabulary and, like *I am the True Vine*, take their creative nourishment from the power of words. Note, in *The Woman with the Alabaster Box*, the mysterious harmonic computations of 'an alabaster box of very precious ointment', and the humbling impact of Jesus's critical response to his uncomprehending disciples. In *Tribute to Caesar* Pärt's setting of the question 'is it lawful to give tribute unto Caesar, or not?' faces a stark parallel when the chorus identifies the superscription on the penny as Caesar's. The remaining items can also be heard, in one form or another, on alternative recordings. Hillier's reading of the beautiful Ninth Ode from *Kanon pokajanen* is slower by some two minutes than Tõnu Kaljuste's première recording of the parent work on ECM (an absolute must for Pärt devotees), which is surprising given the less reverberant acoustic on the new CD. Both here and in the *Berliner Messe*, ECM's sound-frame suggests greater space and tonal weight, though this latest production is equally effective in its own quite different way. Pärt's 'revision' of the *Messe* is an update of his original score (which is warmly represented in its full-choir guise on Hyperion). In a second version (the one featured on ECM), the organ part was replaced by a string orchestra, whereas a third version (the one offered here) features an organ revision of the string score. Comparing Hillier's vocal quartet recording with Kaljuste's string version with choir inclines one towards the silvery organ registrations in the *Credo* and depth of organ tone in the *Agnus Dei*. As for the rest, there's sufficient contrast between the two to warrant owning – or at least hearing – both. With fine sound quality, first-rate singing and concisely worded annotation (by Paul Hillier) this should prove a popular, indeed an essential, addition to Pärt's ever-growing discography.

Te Deum

Te Deum. Silouans Song, 'My soul yearns after the Lord … . Magnificat. Berliner Messe
Estonian Philharmonic Chamber Choir; Tallinn Chamber Orchestra / Tõnu Kaljuste
ECM New Series 439 162-2 (66 minutes: DDD). Ⓕ
Texts and translations included. Recorded 1993 OO

Pärt's *Te Deum* sets the standard liturgical text to a wide range of nuances, shades and dynamics; brief string interludes provide heart-rending wordless commentaries, and the work's closing pages provide a serenely moving affirmation of holiness. Although relatively static in its musical narrative, Pärt's *Te Deum* is both mesmerizing and enriching. *Silouans Song* (1991), an eloquent study for strings, is as reliant on silence as on sonority. It is again austere and chant-like, although its dramatic interpolations approximate a sort of sacral protest. The brief *Magnificat* for *a cappella* choir (1989) positively showers multi-coloured resonances. However, the *Te Deum*'s closest rival – in terms of substance and appeal – is surely the 25-minute *Berliner Messe* (1990-92). Here again Pärt employs the simplest means to achieve the most magical ends: 'Veni Sancte Spiritus' weaves a luminous thread of melodic activity either side of a constant, mid-voice drone, while the weighted phrases of the 'Sanctus' take breath among seraphic string chords. And how wonderful the gradual darkening of the closing 'Agnus Dei', where tenors initially answer sopranos and an almost imperceptible mellowing softens the work's final moments. Beautiful sounds, these – gripping yet remote, communicative yet deeply personal in their contemplative aura, while the all-round standard of presentation – performance, engineering, documentation – serves Pärt as devotedly as Pärt serves the Divine Image.

Krzysztof Penderecki Polish 1933

GROVE *Penderecki was a pupil of Malawski at the Kraków Conservatory (1955-58), where he has also taught. He gained international fame with such works as Threnody for the Victims of Hiroshima for 52 strings (1960), exploiting the fierce expressive effects of new sonorities, but in the mid-1970s there came a change to large symphonic forms based on rudimentary chromatic motifs. Central to his work is the St Luke Passion (1965), with its combination of intense expressive force with a severe style with archaic elements alluding to Bach, and its sequel Utrenia, in which Orthodox chant provides musical material and at the same time a sense of mystery. His operas have been admired for their dynamic expression even if their discrete vignettes offer more opportunity for characterisation than development.*

St Luke Passion

Franziska Hirzel *sop* **François Le Roux** *bar*
Jean-Philippe Courtis *bass* **Manfred Jung** *narr*
West German Radio Chorus; North German Radio Chorus; Mainz Cathedral Choir; Orchestra of the Beethovenhalle, Bonn / Marc Soustrot
Dabringhaus und Grimm MDG337 0981-2 Ⓕ
(70 minutes: DDD). Text and German translation included. Recorded 1999

The West German Radio Chorus, a powerful presence in this performance, were also involved in one of two recordings of Penderecki's *St Luke Passion* made in 1967, a year after its completion. That Harmonia Mundi LP wasn't released until 12 years later, probably because the solo singers and conductor were identical to those on the Philips LP. More recently, the composer himself conducted a well-received account, resonantly recorded in Katowice Cathedral (Argo). Since then, Penderecki's blend of concentrated melodrama and expansive lamentation has lost ground to the more restrained, intimate spirituality of Pärt's *Passio* (*St John Passion*). But Penderecki's earlier style still has its advocates, as certain works by James MacMillan prove, and this new recording makes a strong case for it.

While Marc Soustrot can't erase the disparity between the brief Passion narrative and the drifting choral meditations, he maintains plenty of ongoing tension: as a result, the performance is about six minutes shorter than Penderecki's.

Not inappropriately, the sound has a raw edge with a touch of glare at climaxes. The booklet presentation is less than ideal, though, offering only a German translation alongside the Latin text. It also follows the Preface to the score of the work in failing to match the text Penderecki set: for example, the phrase 'et haec dicans exspiravit' in the narrator's final statement was actually omitted by the composer. But it's the performance which matters most, and this one is consistently excellent – a genuine team effort.

St Luke Passion (Passio et mors Domini nostri Jesu Christi secundam Lucam)
Sigune von Osten *sop* **Stephen Roberts** *bar*
Kurt Rydl *bass* **Edward Lubaszenko** *narr*
Cracow Boys' Choir; Warsaw National Philharmonic Chorus; Polish Radio National Symphony Orchestra / Krzysztof Penderecki
Argo 430 328-2ZH (76 minutes: DDD). Text and translation included. Recorded 1989 Ⓕ

The first performance in Münster Cathedral in 1966 of Penderecki's *Passio et mors Domini nostri Jesu Christi secundum Lucam* brought overnight fame and world recognition to the then 33-year-old composer, and succeeded, where many others had failed, in bringing the methods and language of the avant-garde to a much wider audience. Part of its immediate success must surely lie in his skilful fusion of past musical techniques (renaissance-like polyphony, Gregorian melismata and Venetian *cori spezzati*) with the colouristic avant-garde devices that he had been developing in the years preceding its composition.

Mind you, it was not without its detractors. Some critics, for the very reasons stated above, accused Penderecki of 'courting the masses' and of 'pure sensation-seeking', not to mention the fact that here was a young composer who had the audacity to court comparison with the sublime creations of Bach. Time, however, has proved some justification for the initial enthusiasm as the many hundreds (yes, hundreds!) of performances since its première testify.

It unfailingly creates an impressive impact on the listener with its dramatic energy and waves of tension, even if some of its language does sound a little dated. The performance, under the guiding hand of the composer, is all one could wish for with splendid performances from orchestra, chorus and soloists alike, while the recording, made in the Cathedral of Christ the King, Katowice, has a beautifully spacious and resonant sound that gives the work a somewhat timeless quality.

St Luke Passion – Stabat mater; Miserere; In pulverem mortis. Magnificat – Sicut locutus est. Agnus Dei. Song of Cherubim. Veni creator. Benedicamus Domino. Benedictus
Tapiola Chamber Choir / Juha Kuivanen
Finlandia 4509-98999-2 (52 minutes: DDD). Texts and translations included. Recorded 1993 Ⓕ

There is a neat correspondence in the way the earliest and most recent pieces included here – *Stabat mater* (1962) and *Benedictus* (1992) – both move to resolutions on simple major triads. The difference is in the extent to which the triads in the later work govern the musical fabric throughout. In the 1960s such common chords had to be fought for, and could even seem tacked on arbitrarily. In general, however, it is another kind of consistency that makes this disc musically worthwhile. Although all the works tend to be reflective and devotional, the contrapuntal medium of the unaccompanied chorus inspires the composer to an economical intensity all too often absent from his later instrumental works. Indeed, it is as part of that intensity that elements of his early, much more dissonant style, so powerfully represented in the three extracts from the *St Luke Passion* and the fragment from the *Magnificat*, re-emerge in the more traditional harmonic world of the later pieces – especially the *Veni creator*. Yet it should also be said that Penderecki's austere response to this celebratory text seems more than a little strange. Of the later works *Song of Cherubim* is the most powerful, ending with remarkably rapt 'Alleluias'. A note tells us that the composer regards the *Benedictus* as a draft to be reworked at a later stage. These performances are on the whole models of pure-toned clarity. Recordings are full of atmosphere but well balanced.

Further Listening
Pärt Passio Domini nostri Jesu Christi secundam Johannem
Lehtipuu *ten* **Hynninen** *bass* **Candomino Choir / Satomaa**
Finlandia 8573 87182-2 (62 minutes: DDD: 7/01) Ⓕ

Not as satisfying a performance of Pärt's *St John Passion* as the Hilliard Ensemble's (ECM) but it is more anguished and emphatic, though part of that is perhaps due to the more blatent sound. An interesting alternative none the less

Hiroshima Threnody

Anaklasisa. Threnody for the victims of Hiroshima. Fonogrammi. De natura sonoris I. Capriccio. Canticum canticorum Salomonis. De natura sonoris II. Dream of Jacob
Wanda Wilkomirska *vn* **Cracow Philharmonic Chorus; Polish National Radio Symphony Orchestra; aLondon Symphony Orchestra / Krzysztof Penderecki**
EMI Matrix CDM5 65077-2 (75 minutes: ADD). Recorded 1972-75 Ⓜ

Works such as the *Threnody for the victims of Hiroshima* delve deep within the recesses of collective memory, often triggering disturbing images. Even that master musical psychologist Alban Berg could hardly have approximated the

Threnody's chamber of horror – the blinding light of its opening bars, the aural swerve as trees bend and houses shatter, the jittery aftermath as fall-out spreads its poisonous message, and the myriad gestures and effects that amount to a terrifying experience. No other 20th-century instrumental work quite equals the *Threnody* for graphic impact and no other composer has provided the victims of Hiroshima and Nagasaki with such a dramatic or telling memorial.

What of the rest? Penderecki's invariable preference for slow motion, dense tonal clusters, roaring sonorities (*De natura sonoris II* rises to a deafening primeval groan), wailing vocalizations and sundry instrumental effects (tapping and screeching), not to mention a virtual absence of melody and definable rhythm, make for a pretty draining listening session. Yet it is a fascinating sound world for all that, and the *Threnody* is surely its most profound justification. The recordings report all with merciless clarity.

Giovanni Pergolesi Italian 1710-1736

GROVE *While studying with Durante in Naples Pergolesi worked as a violinist, and in 1731 he presented his first stage work, a dramma sacro. He became maestro di cappella to the Prince of Stigliano in 1732 and to the Duke of Maddaloni in 1734. Several more stage works followed for Naples and an opera seria, L'Olimpiade (1735), for Rome.*

Though only moderately popular in his lifetime, Pergolesi posthumously attained international fame as a leading figure in the rise of Italian comic opera. He wrote two commedie musicali, with both buffo and seria elements, and three comic intermezzos, each staged with an opera seria by him. The intermezzo La serva padrona (1733, Naples) is a miniature masterpiece of buffo style, spirited, with touches of sentiment and with clear, lively characterisation; it was widely performed and in 1752 initiated the Parisian Querelle des Bouffons. Livietta e Tracollo, also known as La contadina astuta (1734, Naples), became popular too. His other works include sacred music (notably a Stabat mater of1736), chamber cantatas and duets, and a few instrumental pieces.

Stabat mater

Stabat mater. Salve regina in C minor Ⓟ
Emma Kirkby *sop* **James Bowman** *counterten*
Academy of Ancient Music / Christopher Hogwood
L'Oiseau-Lyre Florilegium 425 692-2OH
(52 minutes: DDD). Texts and translations included. Ⓕ
Recorded 1988

Pergolesi's *Stabat mater*, written in the last few months of his brief life, enjoyed a huge popularity throughout the 18th century. But modern performances often misrepresent its nature, either through over-romanticizing it or by transforming it into a choral work. None of these are qualities overlooked in this affecting performance, for Emma Kirkby and James Bowman are well versed in the stylistic conventions of baroque and early classical music – and their voices afford a pleasing partnership. Both revel in Pergolesi's sensuous vocal writing, phrasing the music effectively and executing the ornaments with an easy grace. Singers and instrumentalists alike attach importance to sonority, discovering a wealth of beguiling effects in Pergolesi's part writing. In the *Salve regina* in C minor Emma Kirkby gives a compelling performance, pure in tone, expressive and poignant, and she is sympathetically supported by the string ensemble. The recording is pleasantly resonant.

Pergolesi Stabat mater
A Scarlatti Stabat mater
Gemma Bertagnolli *sop* **Sara Mingardo** *contr*
Concerto Italiano / Rinaldo Alessandrini *org*
Opus 111 OPS30-160 (70 minutes: DDD). Text Ⓕ
and translation included. Recorded 1998 ●

One thing which commends this recording of Pergolesi's *Stabat mater* above others seems to lie in the imaginative and stylistically assured direction of Rinaldo Alessandrini. He lays emphasis on the relationship between words and music, and he has come up with some ideas which probe deeper than many, in his aim to bring the piece to life with expressive fervour. And it was an inspired move to pair the work with another, earlier *Stabat mater* by Alessandro Scarlatti. Both settings were commissioned by the same Neapolitan brotherhood, Pergolesi's to replace the other which the brethren reckoned a little old-fashioned. It isn't really, for though it does not breathe the theatrical atmosphere of Pergolesi's iridescent music, it is far from being archaic and overall, perhaps, makes a stronger appeal to the contemplative spirit. Both settings are similarly scored for soprano and alto soloists with strings and continuo. Gemma Bertagnolli's secure technique – which allows her to indulge in virtuosic vocal athletics – and her clear, forceful delivery, are immediately appealing. It is Sara Mingardo, though, who makes the stronger impression with her slightly more disciplined approach and her fervent declamation. Both singers make much of the vivid word-painting – present in each of the settings – but wholeheartedly revelling in the melodic allure of the Pergolesi.

La serva padrona

Livietta e Tracollo[a]. La serva padrona[b] Ⓟ
[a]**Nancy Argenta** *sop* Livietta; [a]**Werner van Mechelen** *bass* Tracollo; [b]**Patricia Biccire** *sop* Serpina; [b]**Donato di Stefano** *bass* Uberto
La Petite Bande / Sigiswald Kuijken *vn*
Accent ACC96123D (80 minutes: DDD). Notes and Ⓕ
texts included. Recorded live in 1996

La serva padrona, most famous of *intermezzi*, is given here with a rare but comparable companion-piece. *Livietta e Tracollo* is also for two characters, light soprano and *buffo* bass, with two sections, originally to be played in the intervals of the evening's *opera seria*. Rather more complicated and improbable than *La serva padrona*, it tells of a girl disguised as a French peasant (male) seeking vengeance on a robber who in turn appears disguised as a pregnant Pole. She succeeds in the first half, while in the second the man, now disguised as an astrologer, has more luck and they agree to get married. Musically it is not so very inferior to the *Serva*. Both have more wit in the music than in the libretto, with deft parodies of *opera seria* and a popular appeal in the repeated phrases of their arias.

The performance here is a lively one with Nancy Argenta as a resourceful and not too pertly soubrettish Livietta. Kuijken's Petite Bande plays with a distinctively 'period' tone; the speeds are sprightly and the rhythms light-footed. In both works, the women are better than the men, who lack the comic touch. Patricia Biccire sings attractively, especially in her 'sincere' aria, 'A Serpina penserate', and she paces her recitatives artfully. A lower baroque pitch is used and the final number is the short duet, 'Per te io ho nel core', as in the original score.

Pérotin French *c*1155/60-*c*1225

GROVE *Pérotin was the most celebrated musician involved in the revision and re-notation of the Magnus liber (attributed to Léonin). Two decrees by the Bishop of Paris concerning the 'feast of the fools' and the performance of quadruple (four-voice) organum, from 1198 and 1199, have been associated with Pérotin since the theorist known as Anonymous IV stated that he composed four-voice settings of both the relevant texts. Attempts to identify him at Notre Dame have proved inconclusive. He may have been born c1155-60, revised the Magnus liber 1180-90 subsequently composed his three- and four-voice works and died in the first years of the 13th century; or he wrote the four-voice works early in his career, revised the Magnus liber in the first decade of the 13th century and died c1225. He was not necessarily attached to Notre Dame. As regards his Magnus liber revisions, Anonymous IV refers to his abbreviations and improvement of the work by substituting succinct passages in discant style for the more florid organum; this would seem to be confirmed by one source of the Magnus liber, although the substitute sections are not attributed there to a specific composer. The creation of three- and four-voice organum c1200 is an important step in the development of polyphony which until then had been conceived in terms of two voices, and Pérotin's compositions show great awareness of the implications for structure and tonality. The confusion over dating derives from unresolved problems of notation.*

Viderunt omnes / Sederunt principes

Pérotin Viderunt omnes. Alleluia, Posui Adiutorium. Dum sigillum summi Patris. Alleluia, Nativitas. Beata viscera. Sederunt principes
Anonymous Veni creator spiritus. O Maria virginei. Isias cecinit
Hilliard Ensemble (David James *counterten* John Potter, Rogers Covey-Crump, Mark Padmore, Charles Daniels *tens* Gordon Jones *bar*) **/ Paul Hillier** *bar*
ECM New Series 837 751-2 (68 minutes: DDD). Ⓕ
Texts included

This is a superb and original recording. It gives musical individuality to a group of works that have hitherto tended to sound much the same. Moreover, as a special attraction for those wanting to see artistic individuality in early composers, it includes all but one of the identifiable works of Pérotin. Inevitably his two grand four-voice organa take up much of the record. At nearly 12 minutes each they may have been the most ambitious polyphonic works composed up to the end of the 12th century. The Hilliard Ensemble adopts a suave and supple approach to both *Viderunt* and *Sederunt*, softening the pervasive rhythms that can make them a shade oppressive and showing a clear view of the entire architecture of each piece. They surge irrepressibly from one section to another, creating a musical momentum that belies the admirably slow speeds they generally adopt. They also beautifully underline the musical differences between the two works, producing a sound which seems a credible reflection of what one might have heard at Notre Dame in the late 12th century. What is particularly exciting is the way in which the musicians grasp at the individual dynamic of each work: the huge open spaces they create to project the text of the magical *O Maria virginei*; the breakneck virtuosity in their swirling performance of *Dum sigillum*, the gently modulated rhythms in the strophic *Veni creator*; the harder edge in their tone for *Alleluia Nativitas*; and so on. With a splendidly judged note by Paul Hillier, this is a recording of the highest distinction.

Allan Pettersson Swedish 1911-1980

GROVE *Pettersson, a pupil of Olsson and Blomdahl at the Stockholm Conservatory (1930-39), played the viola in the Stockholm PO (1939-51), then went to Paris for further study with Honegger and Leibowitz. Back in Sweden he concentrated on composition, in particular on large-scale, single-movement symphonies in an impassioned diatonic style (there were eventually 15, c1950-78); he also wrote concertos, songs and chamber pieces.*

Symphonies

Symphonies Nos 5 and 16
John-Edward Kelly *sax* **Saarbrücken Radio Symphony Orchestra / Alun Francis**
CPO CPO999 284-2 (65 minutes: DDD). Ⓑ
Recorded 1995

The orchestral playing is full of commitment, the account of the 40-minute Fifth (1960-62) sounding tremendously vivid; Francis has the edge over rival versions where it counts, in his overall view of this magnificent work. Yet the coupling – the last symphony the Swede completed – is better still. No 16 was written in 1979 for the American saxophonist Frederik Hemke. Here Kelly, who has made some minor modifications to the solo part for reasons explained in the booklet (the ailing composer appears to have been uncertain of the instrument's range), glides through the hair-raising virtuosity with breathtaking ease. This is the kind of advocacy Pettersson, who never heard the work, can only have dreamed of. An excellent disc.

Symphonies Nos 7 and 11
Norrköping Symphony Orchestra / Leif Segerstam Ⓕ
BIS CD580 (70 minutes: DDD). Recorded 1992

Most of Pettersson's major works are constructed as large, unified movements (although he was an accomplished miniaturist) and Nos 7 and 11, respectively 46 and 24 minutes in length, are no exceptions. The former in some ways is unrepresentative of the composer; the obsessiveness of mood and hectoring tone are present, especially in the *Angst*-ridden first and third spans, but the range of expression is much wider than in most of his other works. Composed in 1967-68, it has a unique atmosphere, both haunting and haunted, which will stay with you for a long time. His melodic genius is confirmed in the long and heartfelt central threnody, as well as by the beautiful quiet coda, truly music to 'soften the crying of a child'; its delivery by the Norrköping players has just the right amount of detachment. Segerstam's tempos permit the work to breathe and resonate not unlike Mahler. The 11th Symphony (1974) is less combative in tone, although it has its moments, and is not on the same elevated plane as the Seventh. The recording quality is first-rate, allowing both the devastating power and delicate fine detail of these scores to emerge equally well.

Hans Pfitzner German 1869-1949

GROVE *Pfitzner, a pupil of Knorr and Kwast at the Hoch Conservatory, Frankfurt, was a teacher in Berlin, Strasbourg and Munich until 1934, when he was relieved of his post. His earlier works, including the operas Der arme Heinrich (1895) and Die Rose vom Liebesgarten (1901), are Wagnerian, but in Palestrina (1917) he produced a remarkable piece of operatic spiritual autobiography, contrasting the pressures of the everyday world with the inner certainties of artistic genius. One of his certainties was of the supremacy of the German Romantic tradition - he was a powerful patriot - which he supported in polemical exchanges with Berg and implicitly in the cantatas (Von deutscher Seele, 1921; Das dunkle Reich, 1929) which were his main works after Palestrina. He also wrote three symphonies (1932, 1939, 1940), concertos for the piano (1922), the violin (1923) and two for the cello (1935, 1944), chamber music (including three string quartets) and c100 songs.*

Overtures and Preludes

Pfitzner Palestrina – Preludes, Acts 1, 2 and 3. Das Herz – Liebesmelodie. Das Käthchen von Heilbronn, Op 17 – Overture **R Strauss** Guntram – Overture. Capriccio – Prelude. Feuersnot – Liebesszene
Orchestra of the Deutsche Oper, Berlin / Christian Thielemann
DG 449 571-2GH (75 minutes: DDD). Ⓕ
Recorded 1995 ●

Christian Thielemann shows a marked fondness for broad tempos: even more obviously he loves big gestures and sumptuously rich sound. You can hear both tendencies in Pfitzner's *Käthchen von Heilbronn* Overture. On the face of it this is a problematic piece: very long (16 minutes) and with especially leisured transitions between its sections. After the big, bold, martial music of the opening you might expect a conductor to be a little nervous of the fact that Pfitzner allows a particularly lengthy transition to ensue before he even begins to prepare for his 'second subject', in fact the superbly romantic melody that represents Käthchen herself. Quite admirably, Thielemann does not hurry nor does he overstate the Käthchen theme: full, impassioned eloquence is reserved for its grandiose return. Although he allows the overture's big moments ample space to expand, there is no sense of mere waiting between them: he shows great care and sensitivity in Pfitzner's quieter pages. He obviously loves this music, and that is still more obvious in the *Palestrina* preludes, where the luminously pure textures of the first Prelude receive no less scrupulous attention than the nobly baying brass in the second or the velvety denseness of string sonority in some pages of the last. Thielemann's Strauss is no less effective. He finds a genuine Straussian line and ardour even in the not yet wholly mature *Guntram* Overture, builds a huge climax from the exquisite string sounds that begin the *Feuersnot* love scene and only falters just a little in the *Capriccio* Sextet; here he allows his solo strings to play just a little too forcefully. A distinguished début marked by ravishing orchestral playing. The recording is richly ample.

Piano Trio

Violin Sonata in E minor, Op 27. Piano Trio in F, Op 8[a]
Benjamin Schmid *vn* [a]**Clemens Hagen** *vc* **Claudius Tanski** *pf*
Dabringhaus und Grimm MDG312 0934-2 Ⓕ
(70 minutes: DDD). Recorded 1999 ●●

The Sonata is a fine piece from Pfitzner's maturity, while the much earlier Piano Trio is one of the most extraordinary works for the medium that you're likely to have ever heard. To be sure, enterprising chamber players hunting for neglected repertory may well have come across early critical reactions to both these pieces, and references to (for example, in the case of the Trio) Pfitzner's 'sick imagination' and the work's 'monstrous length' might put anyone off. When he wrote it Pfitzner was in despair at his financial and other problems; he told a friend that after finishing it all he wanted was to die. It does at times suggest a man at the end of his tether, but also a composer chronicling such a state when at the height of his powers.

It is long, extremely tense, at times weirdly obsessive, even hysterical, but all this takes place within a cunningly plotted ground plan. After the strange and powerful contrasts of the first movement, with its wild coda, the noble but perilously assaulted main theme of the slow movement, the dance-like but fraught and nervous *Scherzo*, Pfitzner begins his finale with a choleric gesture which soon fades to pathos and pallor. After 10 minutes of desperate attempts to climb out of this pit, a positive coda seems possible, but when the music turns instead to utterly euphonious calm the listener is likely to be moved by what seems in context heroic as well as wonderfully beautiful.

The Sonata, from 1918 (more than 20 years later), sounds like a demonstration – with various modernisms in the ascendancy all round – that Pfitzner's late romantic style and prodigious craft still had abundant life in them. Its inexhaustible inventiveness and the beauty of its themes are accompanied by a considerable enjoyment of virtuosity (hair-raising demands are made of both players) and, in the finale especially, by an infectious, impulsive warmth: Pfitzner, you realise, is having a high old time.

Both works are vastly welcome, in short, but that they should be so superbly played goes beyond all reasonable expectations. As the final pinnacle on a quite exceptional coupling, Claudius Tanski plays a Blüthner piano of 1925 whose beautiful warmth and the very slight 'ping' at the top of its register are simply ideal for this wonderful, inexplicably neglected music.

Lieder

Complete Lieder, Volume 2

Four Lieder, Op 4[c]. Three Lieder, Op 5[a]. Six Lieder, Op 6[b]. Five Lieder, Op 7[b]. Five Lieder, Op 9[c]. Three Lieder, Op 10[c]. Tiefe Sehnsucht[c]

[a]**Julie Kaufmann** *sop* [b]**Christoph Prégardien** *ten* [c]**Andreas Schmidt** *bar* [a]**Donald Sulzen,** [b]**Michael Gees,** c**Rudolf Jansen** *pfs*

CPO CPO999 364-2 (68 minutes: DDD). Texts and translations included. Ⓜ

Few of these songs are well known, and several appear on CD for the first time, but almost all of them are impressive, many quite memorably so. They are all relatively youthful – the latest set in this volume was written in 1901, when Pfitzner was 32 – but if he had written no more songs, these alone would prove him a major composer of Lieder. Try Op 6 No 3, in which a fine vocal line over darkly rolling keyboard figuration conjures up a powerful image of an exhausted migrant bird struggling to reach the shore. A magnificent blaze of sonority depicts a brilliant sunrise but also bleakly implies that it will be the bird's last. Op 6 No 5 is just as remarkable, an almost monotonic accompaniment and a slowly intensifying vocal line describing a couple walking through woods as love slowly dawns upon them: the phrase 'I love you' emerges to extraordinarily long note values (prodigious breath control from Christoph Prégardien) as though everything had implied it all along, but the poet is none the less rapt with amazement at it. If you've ever thought of him as off-puttingly learned rather than melodiously fresh, then almost every single song here will change your mind. German-speakers, by the way, will find a few mistranslations in the booklet, of which 'the man upstairs' for 'der Herr' ('the Lord') is the most entertaining. Schmidt and Prégardien share most of the material; both are excellent, though in the big gestures of Op 4 Schmidt forces his tone once or twice. Kaufmann's rather fragile soprano is confined to Op 5, where a pretty love-song and a tender lullaby suit her well. All three pianists are admirable and the recordings are exemplary. Anyone interested in Lieder who has so far not investigated Pfitzner will certainly find this collection a revelation.

Complete Lieder, Volume 3

An den Mond, Op 18[d]. Fünf Lieder, Op 11[acd]. Vier Lieder, Op 15[abd]. Zwei Lieder, Op 19[d]. Zwei Lieder, Op 21[c]. Untreu und Trost[d]

[a]**Julie Kaufmann** *sop* [b]**Iris Vermillion** *mez* [c]**Christoph Prégardien** *ten* [d]**Andreas Schmidt** *bar* [a]**Donald Sulzen,** [b]**Axel Bauni,** [c]**Michael Gees,** [d]**Rudolf Jansen** *pfs*

CPO CPO999 461-2 (58 minutes: DDD). Texts and translations included. Recorded 1996-98 Ⓜ

Volume 3 of Pfitzner's complete Lieder on CPO is quite extraordinary. Pfitzner was a 'literary composer' in the best sense – the libretto of his opera *Palestrina* is masterly – and in these songs his sensitivity to words often leads his music in strange yet impressive directions. Op 19 No 1, for example, sets a poem about obsessive longing, in a troubled state between waking and dreaming, day and night. Pfitzner's music is as strong and compelling as the longing it evokes, but also as unstable. In several of these songs a firm sense of key is denied (but the music never becomes 'atonal', never directionless), either by intense chromaticism or by a strikingly original use of the whole-tone scale, as in the big, vehement, almost cantata-like setting of Goethe's *An den Mond*. At the other end of the expressive scale is Op 11 No 1, Hebbel's *Ich und Du*, where extreme simplicity – lyrical phrases over bare diatonic chords – expresses two lovers' union with solemn grandeur.

But why imply that Pfitzner's expressive range has only two ends? Setting a naive anonymous poem for a competition to find 'new German folk-songs', he combines artless and artful to unexpectedly touching ends, while in Op 15 No 4, to a whimsical mock-rococo text by Eichendorff, he deftly provides not-quite-serious fake Haydn and a charming evocation (wittily underlined by the pianist Donald Sulzen) of a mechanical clock. The text of 'Michaelskirchplatz' (Op 19 No 2) is filled with images of young love but 'we smiled and were silent as St Michael's bells rang', and the whole song is memorably contained within bell sounds. No less impressively, in Op 15 No 1 Pfitzner approaches Schubert on his own ground (the song is called 'The hurdy-gurdy man') as he in effect sketches the earlier career of the strange old man that the wanderer approaches at the end of *Winterreise*. Hinting at the hurdy-gurdy's music also brings Pfitzner close to the world of Nielsen's 'Jens Vejmand', to moving and gripping effect. The performances are admirable throughout, as indeed are the recordings.

Complete Lieder, Volume 4

Fünf Lieder, Op 22[ad]. Vier Lieder, Op 24 [abcd]. Fünf Lieder, Op 26[acd]. Vier Lieder, Op 29[be]

[a]**Julie Kaufmann** *sop* [b]**Iris Vermillion** *mez* [c]**Christoph Prégardien** *ten* [d]**Andreas Schmidt** *bar* [e]**Robert Holl** *bass* [a]**Donald Sulzen,** [b]**Axel Bauni,** [c]**Michael Gees,** [de]**Rudolf Jansen** *pfs*

CPO CPO999 490-2 (62 minutes: DDD). Texts and translations included. Recorded 1996-1998 Ⓜ

These are the songs of Pfitzner's high maturity (his great opera *Palestrina* was written between Op 24 and Op 26) and they maintain a remarkable standard. Although the vocal lines are sometimes so expressively inflected that they are no longer conventionally 'tuneful', and although Pfitzner's harmonic language has by now become very daring, his fidelity to the often simple, strophic texts saves him from abstruseness. Op 22 No 3, for example, *Schön' Suschen*, has a folk-like poem by Bürger about someone falling deeply in love but then falling out again. The simplicity of Pfitzner's setting becomes much less straight-forward as the lover's emotion intensifies, but of course he is not unchanged by the experience, and the music reflects that. In the same poet's *Gegenliebe* (Op 22 No 4), a simple form almost burst asunder by the tempestuous keyboard writing very closely reflects the passion the text describes (if his love were to be returned, the poet says, 'Oh! Then my breast would no longer be able to contain its flames'). By now Pfitzner's piano writing has become very rich, sometimes virtuosic. To describe Op 24 No 3 (a setting of Petrarch's Sonnet No 92, in German translation) as a complex polyphonic study in which one of the keyboard's lines is intermittently taken over by the voice would be off-putting (though accurate), but it would quite understate the song's magical beauty and its extraordinary responsiveness to a far from easy text. Likewise, Op 26 No 2 (*Nachts*, to a poem by Eichendorff) could be defined as a piece in which a bell-like ostinato is rhythmically transformed and then reverts to its original form. But the precision with which this device parallels the poem's image is very moving. As to the singing, Kaufmann is once or twice taxed by a high-lying passage, and in his single song Holl is not in his best voice but beyond that it is all excellent, as are all four pianists. The recordings are very good, though for some reason Prégardien is rather more closely balanced than his colleagues.

Complete Lieder, Volume 5

Vier Lieder, Op 30[a]. Vier Lieder, Op 32[b]. Acht Lieder, Op 33[c]. Sechs Liebeslieder, Op 35[c]. Sechs Lieder, Op 40[a]. Drei Sonnette, Op 41[b]

[c]**Julie Kaufmann** *sop* [a]**Iris Vermillion** *mez* [b]**Robert Holl** *bass* a**Axel Bauni,** b**Rudolf Jansen,** c**Donald Sulzen** *pfs*

CPO CPO999 491-2 (74 minutes: DDD). Texts and translations included. Recorded 1996-98 Ⓜ

Alas, Pfitzner stopped writing songs in 1931, so this is the last volume in CPO's absorbing survey. But he could hardly have ended better, nor with more of a sense of farewell. Op 41 No 3, a setting of an Eichendorff sonnet about the long-awaited serenity of old age, ends with the arrival of an unexpected messenger, knocking cheerfully at the window. 'Astonished, you step out and do not return. Then at last comes the spring that never ends.' The messenger is death? Perhaps, but at this point a melody hinted at earlier finally flowers in calm D major. It is an extremely beautiful leave-taking, and Robert Holl sings it with deep but restrained feeling; but we have heard that melody before, in the fifth song of Op 40, a setting of Goethe's *Wanderers Nachtlied I* written only a week or so earlier. For such a short text (eight brief lines) it is a very big song, solemnly grave, and it is difficult to say what is more moving, the song itself or Iris Vermillion's passionate conviction that it is a masterpiece. Robert Holl is very fine throughout, perhaps acting a little too intensely in Dehmel's *The working man*, who has all that he wants from life save the time to enjoy it (Op 30), but in the bright vision experienced in the oppressive darkness of *Huss's Dungeon* (Op 32 – the vision is, again, of 'endless spring') and the dark grief of *To dawn* (Op 41) he is outstanding. Vermillion, however, is even finer, her firm mezzo capable both of quiet intimacy and the bold, grand gestures of Eichendorff's *The call to awake* (Op 40). The often epigrammatic Keller settings of Op 33 call for a lighter voice; so do the love songs, Op 35. Julie Kaufmann is a little too bright in earlier volumes, but she is alert to the quirkiness as well as the high lyrical lines of the Keller settings, and in the last song of Op 35, a stormily vehement vision of love destroying like fire, she takes brave risks. As before, nothing but praise for the three pianists and the sensitive recording balance.

Palestrina

Nicolai Gedda *ten* Palestrina; **Dietrich Fischer-Dieskau** *bar* Borromeo; **Gerd Nienstedt** *bass* Master of Ceremonies; **Karl Ridderbusch** *bass* Christoph Madruscht, Pope Pius IV; **Bernd Weikl** *bar* Morone; **Herbert Steinbach** *ten* Novagerio; **Helen Donath** *sop* Ighino; **Brigitte Fassbaender** *mez* Silla; **Renate**

Freyer *contr* Lukrezia; **Victor von Halem** *bass* Cardinal of Lorraine; **John van Kesteren** *ten* Abdisu; **Peter Meven** *bass* Anton Brus; **Hermann Prey** *bar* Count Luna; **Friedrich Lenz** *ten* Bishop of Budoja; **Adalbert Kraus** *ten* Theophilus; **Franz Mazura** *bass* Avosmediano
Tölz Boys' Choir; Bavarian Radio Chorus and **Symphony Orchestra / Rafael Kubelík**
DG 20th Century Classics ③ 427 417-2GC3 (206 minutes: ADD). Notes, text and translation included. Ⓜ
Recorded 1970s

Rafael Kubelík's magnificent, sumptuously cast DG recording of *Palestrina* is an almost impossible act to follow, indeed it's hard to imagine such an extravagance of vocal riches being encountered in a German opera recording nowadays: Brigitte Fassbaender ardently impulsive in the brief role of Palestrina's pupil Silla, Helen Donath pure-voiced and touching as his son Ighino, and an absolute constellation of superb basses and baritones, often doubling quite small parts: Karl Ridderbusch, Bernd Weikl, Hermann Prey, Franz Mazura, with at their head Dietrich Fischer-Dieskau as a surely unsurpassable Borromeo: dangerously powerful, intensely concerned and in magnificent voice. And those are just the 'secondary' roles! Pfitzner's text is one of the finest librettos ever written, and Gedda's singing gives the impression that the beauty of the words and their portrayal of Palestrina's dignity and suffering are more important to him than concern for his own voice. Kubelík's urgent conducting shows a visionary quality, and he clearly has a marvellous ear for the radiance of this wonderful score.

Astor Piazzolla Argentinian 1921-1992

Tangos

Piazzolla Libertango (arr Calandrelli). Tango Suite (arr S Assad) – Andante; Allegro. Le Grand Tango (arr Calandrelli). Sur – Regreso al amor. Fugata. Mumuki. Tres minutos con la realidad. Milonga del ángel. Histoire du Tango – Café 1930 (all arr Calandrelli)
Calandrelli Tango Remembrances
Yo-Yo Ma *vc* **Antonio Agri** *vn* **Nestor Marconi, Astor Piazzolla** *bandoneón* **Horacio Malvicino, Odair Assad, Sérgio Assad, Oscar Castro-Neves** *gtrs* **Edwin Barker, Héctor Console** *db* **Kathryn Stott, Gerardo Gandini, Leonardo Marconi, Frank Corliss** *pfs*
Sony Classical SK63122 (64 minutes: DDD). Ⓕ
Recorded 1987-97

Yo-Yo Ma is the latest international artist to surrender to the spell of the Argentinian dance: he can also be heard on the soundtrack of the film, *The Tango Lesson*. Here, surrounded by a brilliant group of experts in the genre, he presents with wholehearted commitment a well-varied programme of Piazzolla pieces. They range from the melancholy or sultry to the energetic or fiery. Among the latter, *Fugata* is ingenious, *Mumuki* richly eloquent, and *Tres minutos con la realidad* nervily edgy: in this last, Kathryn Stott understandably earned the admiration of her Argentinian colleagues. She also shines with Yo-Yo Ma in an exciting performance of *Le Grand Tango*: his playing in the *Milonga del ángel* is outstandingly beautiful. Special mention must also be made of some spectacular virtuosity by the Assad brothers in the *Tango Suite*. The characteristic bandoneón is featured with the cellist in *Café 1930*; and by technological trickery Yo-Yo Ma partners Piazzolla himself (recorded in 1987) in a confection called *Tango Remembrances*. Those who are already fans of this genre will be in no need of encouragement to procure this disc.

Aconcagua. Adiós Nonino (arr Morera)[a]. Oblivión (arr Morera). Tres tangos
Mika Väyrynen *accordion* [a]**Esko Hilander** *vn* [a]**Petteri Karttunen** *pf* **Kuopio Symphony Orchestra / Atso Almila**
Finlandia 3984-29723-2 (54 minutes: DDD). Ⓕ
Recorded 1999

The accordion, when handled as virtuosically as by Mika Väyrynen and in music which fits it like a glove – as in Piazzolla's *Tres tangos* and *Aconcagua* Concerto – is an irresistible instrument. The *Tres tangos* are an excellent set, more suite than concerto, and more intimate in scale than *Aconcagua* which, in keeping with its subject (Argentina's highest peak), possesses a greater massiveness of sound. Both were written for the bandoneon, a variant of the accordion, but Väyrynen uses a Russian Jupiter instrument, the sound of which 'is much akin to that of the bandoneon', so why not use the latter? Well, power and depth mainly; and questions of authenticity are not so acute here as they are in, say, Bach or Scarlatti. The result is most satisfactory and, if nothing else, proves that for Piazzolla tango could be a means to an expressive end as much as a vehicle for enjoyment. And enjoyment is the watchword for the whole of this brilliantly played and recorded disc

María de Buenos Aires

(arr Desyatnikov)
Julia Zenko, Jairo *vocs* **Horacio Ferrer** *narr*
Buenos Aires Coral Lírico; Kremerata Musica / Gidon Kremer *vn*
Teldec ② 3984-20632-2 (94 minutes: DDD). Notes, text and translation included. Recorded 1997-98 Ⓜ

María de Buenos Aires is victim, lover, heroine and *femme fatale*, a powerful illusion given substance and pathos by the approachable surrealism of the opera's librettist, Horacio Ferrer. Piazzolla's music harbours a Weill-like sense of foreboding; minor-key heartache invades almost everywhere, even when the dancing starts, the air thickens and the drink starts to flow. If you want to sample prior to purchasing, then try disc 1, track 4, 'I am María', potentially the set's hit number; the saucy 'Fugue and Mystery' (track 6 – an 'instrumental' where María walks the city streets), the aromatic 'Waltz-poem' (track 7) or the gorgeous, rambling bandoneón solo that opens the next track but which soon gives way to a rhythmically ferocious but heavily sentimental 'Accusation Toccata'. María is a textile-worker whose spirit is conjured from an asphalt-covered grave for various fresh encounters – not least with a gaggle of psychoanalysts who, in real life (Argentina around 1960) helped cope with a national neurosis caused by severe economic problems. Piazzolla's madcap 'Aria of the Analysts' (disc 2, track 4) recalls Bernstein's 'Gee, Officer Krupky' from *West Side Story*, but elsewhere the musical style has that air of ineffable sadness, melancholy and 'tragedy bravely borne' that is so typical of Piazzolla's music in general. Then again, *María de Buenos Aires* is a 'Tango Operita' and this remarkable performance keeps the dance element very much to the fore.

Leonid Desyatnikov's arrangement takes heed of various recorded predecessors (the most famous being a two-LP release that was issued not long after the piece was completed), but centres mainly on 'the graphically stark style of the Astor Quartet, a style that struck me [Desyatnikov] as the most natural one to adopt in a modern re-working of the music'. This latest set is fresher in tone, texturally more inventive and tellingly astringent than any rival. Julia Zenko is a sensually alluring singer and Jairo recalls the passionate, jazz-inflected delivery of that great tango past-master, Carlos Gardel. And then there's Kremer himself, agile, personable, tonally changeable, a template in sound for the tragic but elusive main protagonist, 'María tango, slum María, María night, María fatal, María of love'. Through him, you learn to love her.

Walter Piston

American 1894-1976

GROVE *Piston trained as a draughtsman before studying composition at Harvard (1919-24) and with Dukas and Boulanger in Paris; he then returned to Harvard (1926-60), becoming a renowned theory teacher. His textbook Harmony (1941) has been widely used. His music is in a clear, tonal style suggesting the neo-classical Stravinsky, Fauré and Roussel: the main works include eight symphonies (1937-65), five string quartets (1933-62) and the ballet The Incredible Flutist (1938).*

Violin Concertos

Violin Concertos Nos 1 and 2. Fantasia for Violin and Orchestra

James Buswell *vn* **National Symphony Orchestra of Ukraine / Theodore Kuchar** Ⓢ

Naxos 8 559003 (61 minutes: DDD). ●

Piston's First Violin Concerto, written in 1939, has much in common with the Barber, including a similar abundance of individual melody. Indeed the first movement's simple but immediately memorable second subject persists in the memory until, most engagingly, it is rhythmically transformed into the secondary theme of the deliciously rhythmic and later riotous Rondo finale. However, the heart of the work is in the moving, pensive central *Andantino molto tranquillo*. With just a hint of Gershwin in its bluesy opening, the movement is essentially searching and ruminative. This is a masterpiece, as will be confirmed when other violinists take it up.

The Second Concerto, written two decades later, is less obviously 'popular', its atmosphere more elusive. But its opening is similarly haunting and the more one hears it the more one is drawn by its depth of inner feeling. The first movement develops two ideas, one sinuously expressive (later passionate), the other pungently rhythmic and angular. The extended, pensive *Adagio* introduces a serene and very beautiful theme, which later forms a canonic duet with the flute. The finale is another sparkling, jaunty rondo. The *Fantasia* is a late work, first performed in 1973. In five intricately related sections, its language more dissonant with almost feverish, bravura *allegros* framed by troubled, lonely *adagio* passages, dominated by the soloist, which have been described as 'painfully aware and transcendentally serene'. The closing section is profoundly gentle. It may seem remarkable that these works should make their CD début played by a Russian orchestra, but it plays the music with splendid commitment, much subtlety of expression and fine ensemble too. The sure idiomatic feeling is explained by the fact its conductor, Theodore Kuchar, moved to the Ukraine from Cleveland, Ohio. James Buswell, who studied at the Juilliard (and made his solo début with the NYPO at the age of seven) is a superbly accomplished, dedicated and spontaneous soloist with a full timbre, and the recording is first-class.

Fantasy

The Incredible Flutist – Suite. Fantasy for English Horn, Harp and Strings. Suite for Orchestra. Concerto for String Quartet, Wind Instruments and Percussion. Psalm and Prayer of David

Scott Goff *fl* **Glen Danielson** *hn* **Theresa Elder Wunrow** *hp* **Juilliard Quartet** (Robert Mann, Joel Smirnoff *vns* Samuel Rhodes *va* Joel Krosnick *vc*);
Seattle Symphony Chorale and Orchestra / Gerard Schwarz

Delos DE3126 (68 minutes: DDD). Ⓕ
Recorded 1991-92

Gerard Schwarz's flutist fixes you with his limpid tone. However, it will always be known as the score with the Tango. Schwarz goes with the flow, the sway of the melody, but it can never linger long enough. The *Fantasy* enters darkened Elysian fields – Piston's lyricism sits well with this distinctive voice of sorrow and regret. We can trace their kinship right back to the composer's first published work – the orchestral *Suite* of 1929. At its heart is a long and intense pastorale: the cor anglais is there at the inception. Framing it, motoric syncopations carry us first to a kind of drive-by the blues with bar-room piano and Grappelli violin. The finale is essentially a fugal work-out: high-tech Hindemith. Piston's very last work, the *Concerto*, is 10 eventful minutes where the imperative is once again pitted against the contemplative. The mixing of timbres is masterly, a fleck of woodwind or a brush of tambourine or antique cymbal speaking volumes. But at the centre of gravity is the Juilliard Quartet, moving in mysterious ways, leading on to a closing viola solo – another dark voice posing both unanswered question and valediction. In fact, the last words uttered here are those of the *Psalm and Prayer of David* – a rare vocal setting for Piston, and as such, refreshingly open, unhackneyed, unhieratical. Performance and recording are superb.

Amilcare Ponchielli Italian 1834-1886

GROVE *After studying at the Milan Conservatory Ponchielli settled in the provinces as an organist and municipal band conductor, repeatedly attempting to establish himself as an opera composer. He finally won success in 1872 with the much-revised I promessi sposi, in 1874 with the Ricordi commission I lituani and above all in 1876 with La Gioconda. As professor of composition at the Milan Conservatory (from 1880) he taught Puccini and, briefly, Mascagni. He also composed much sacred music for S Maria Maggiore, Bergamo. Of his works, only La Gioconda, on a text drawn by Boito from Hugo, is in the modern repertory. An inspired stylisation of grand opera, it contains music that is alive, varied and sensitive, notably the tenor romanza 'Cielo e mar' and the famous 'Suicidio', and that foreshadows aspects of late Verdi and of verismo opera. Elsewhere Ponchielli's atmospheric colouring and symphonic treatment show remarkable imagination and workmanship, despite his lack of a strong personality.*

La Gioconda

La Gioconda[a] H
Bellini Norma – Casta diva[d]; Mira, o Norma[b]
Donizetti Lucrezia Borgia – Com'è bello!; M'odi, ah m'odi[d] **Rossini** Guglielmo Tell – Selva opaca[d]
Verdi Ernani – Fa che a me venga[c]. La forza del destino[d] – Madre, pietosa Vergine; La Vergine degli angeli. I lombardi[d] – Te, Vergin santa; O madre dal cielo
Giannina Arangi-Lombardi *sop* La gioconda; [a]**Alessandro Granda** *ten* Enzo Grimaldi; [a]**Gaetano Viviani** *bar* Barnaba; [a]**Camilla Rota** *mez* La Cieca; [a]**Corrado Zambelli** *bass* Alvise Badoero; [ab]**Ebe Stignani** *mez* Laura Adorno; [a]**Aristide Baracchi** *bar* Zuàne; [a]**Giuseppe Nessi** *ten* Isèpo; [c]**Enrico Molinari** *bar*; [a]**Chorus and Orchestra of La Scala, Milan;** [bcd]**Orchestra / Lorenzo Molajoli**
Naxos Historical mono ③ 8 110112/4 Ⓢ
(169 minutes: ADD). Recorded 1926-33 ●

Outstanding among Italian operatic sets of the interwar years, this was also the first complete recording of Ponchielli's masterpiece. Inevitably the sound quality of 1931 is at some disadvantage in comparison to later versions; the carefully orchestrated score, large-scale ensembles and off-stage effects need more space and clarity to do them full justice. Yet, to compensate, the voices have the vivid immediacy of their period and the transfers are excellent.

The work of chorus and orchestra is certainly among the strengths of the performance. That in turn reflects on the conductor, Lorenzo Molajoli, of whom Paul Campion in his appreciative notes for the booklet is tempted to guess that he may have been 'the *nom de disque* of another celebrated conductor who could not, for contractual reasons, be named'. It's an intriguing notion and one can quite see why his results here and the scarcity of information about him elsewhere encourage it; but Molajoli was real enough, a répétiteur for Toscanini in the early years of the century at La Scala, and later artistic director of Columbia Records in Italy. Anyway, he clearly has a sure grip on his forces and a strong feeling for the opera itself, which had been given at La Scala, under Toscanini, as recently as 1927 with Arangi-Lombardi and Stignani heading the cast in their present roles.

The three male principals were also Scala singers, though not in this opera. Alessandro Granda, a Peruvian who made his Italian début in 1927, was also Columbia's Pinkerton and Cavaradossi; as Enzo in *La Gioconda* he is perhaps a little too slender and lacking in heroic potential, yet the tone is incisive and the characterisation convincing. The baritone Gaetano Viviani (who for a season was La Scala's Telramund and Jokanaan) is most exciting, a Ruffo-imitator perhaps and a bit throaty, but rich, vibrant, grandly sinister and not unsubtle (his 'Pescator' is a model of suave robustness). These are not qualities shared by the Alvise, Corrado Zambelli, who sings with dull authority and unimpressive low notes: a pity they did not have Tancredi Pasero for the part. Mind, if they had, that would have meant the addition to the cast of one more singer with a fast vibrato (Camilla Rota's La Cieca being another), which might have proved all too much for listeners of more modern times. Stignani, whose young voice was ideal for the part of Laura, is free of it, and Arangi-Lombardi relatively so. But she, the heroine of the recording, is one of the main reasons for acquiring this set, which also includes a selection of her solo recordings, giving a fuller portrait of a highly distinguished artist.

Regarded by her contemporaries as a singer of the old school, she presents a Gioconda more appealing to modern tastes than the overcharged *verismo*-style of predecessors such as Eugenia Burzio. She brought to the role the refinements heard in her arias from *Lucrezia Borgia*, *I lombardi* and *La forza del destino*. There is also a thrilling intensity about her singing, so that, although Lauri-Volpi in his book *Voci parallele* (Garzanti: 1955) recalls that as an actress she was never quite able to liberate the impulses of her personality, one would be most unlikely to guess as much from these records.

La Gioconda
Maria Callas *sop* La Gioconda; **Fiorenza Cossotto** *mez* Laura Adorno; **Pier Miranda Ferraro** *ten* Enzo Grimaldo; **Piero Cappuccilli** *bar* Barnaba; **Ivo Vinco** *bass* Alvise Badoero; **Irene Companeez** *contr* La Cieca; **Leonardo Monreale** *bass* Zuàne; **Carlo Forte** *bass* A Singer, Pilot; **Renato Ercolani** *ten* Isepo, First Distant Voice; **Aldo Biffi** *bass* Second Distant Voice; **Bonaldo Giaiotti** *bass* Barnabotto
Chorus and Orchestra of La Scala, Milan / Antonio Votto
EMI mono ③ CDS5 56291-2 (167 minutes: DDD). Notes, text and translation included. Recorded 1959

Ponchielli's old warhorse has had a bad press in recent times, which seems strange in view of its melodic profusion, his unerring adumbration of Gioconda's unhappy predicament and of the sensual relationship between Enzo and Laura. But it does need large-scale and involved singing – just what it receives here on this now historic set. Nobody could fail to be caught up in its conviction. Callas was in good and fearless voice when it was made, with the role's emotions perhaps enhanced by the traumas of her own life at the time. Here her strengths in declaiming recitative, her moulding of line, her response to the text are all at their most arresting. Indeed she turns what can be a maudlin act into true tragedy. Ferraro's stentorian ebullience is most welcome. Cossotto is a vital, seductive Laura. Cappuccilli gives the odious spy and lecher Barnaba a threatening, sinister profile, whilst Vinco is a suitably implacable Alvise. Votto did nothing better than this set, bringing out the subtlety of the Verdi-inspired scoring and the charm of the 'Dance of the Hours' ballet. The recording sounds excellent for its age.

La Gioconda
Maria Callas *sop* La Gioconda; **Gianni Poggi** *ten* Enzo Grimaldi; **Paolo Silveri** *bar* Barnaba; **Maria Amadini** *mez* La Cieca; **Giulio Neri** *bass* Alvise Badoero; **Fedora Barbieri** *mez* Laura Adorno; **Piero Poldi** *ten* Zuàne; **Armando Benzi** *ten* Isèpo
RAI Chorus and Orchestra, Turin / Antonino Votto
Warner Fonit Cetra ③ 3984-29355-2 (165 minutes: ADD). Notes and text included. Live broadcast 1952

Callas recorded *La Gioconda* twice, here in 1952 and then, for EMI, in 1959. The choice between these versions is finely balanced. What is beyond doubt is that you must hear her in this part if you want to understand why she was such a great interpreter. Listening to her as Ponchielli's tragic heroine Gioconda must run Violetta pretty close for her best role, even though it wasn't as central to her career on stage; in the final, inspired act of Ponchielli's melodrama, all the tragedy of the wronged woman rising above her jealousy to allow her lover Enzo to escape with Laura, and then commit suicide, is expressed quite indelibly in words and music.

In her EMI recording she refined her interpretation; indeed she declared that anyone who wanted to understand what she was about should listen to the final act. If you take the role as a whole, here she is in stronger, in fact in overwhelming voice throughout, mixing love, fury, pathos, desperation in equal measure as she imprints on our minds the woman at the end of her tether so marvellously described in the score. Above all it is what she does in melding text and notes, and her complete emotional identification with the part that makes Callas's Gioconda the most emotion-laden in the work's history. Barbieri is a fit antagonist in the famous Act 2 duet and on her own a magnificent Laura.

As evil incarnate, Silveri is a powerful if unsubtle Barnaba. Neri, as the forceful Alvise, shows what Italian basses used to sound like, rich and firm in tone, imposing in manner: sad that he died so young. The drawback of the set is the ungainly, raw singing of Poggi, a fine voice ill-used by its owner. Apart from his penchant for cutting the score, Votto – as in the 1959 version – makes the most of the work's many strong points and overlooks its weak ones. The refurbished sound is admirable. Don't miss it.

Francis Poulenc French 1899-1963

GROVE *Poulenc's background gave him a musical and literary sophistication from boyhood, and he was already a publicly noted composer by the time he took lessons with Koechlin (1921-4): such works as his Apollinaire song cycle Le bestiaire (1919) and Sonata for two clarinets (1918) had shown the Stravinsky-Satie inclinations that assure him a place among Les Six. His ballet Les biches (1924), written for Dyagilev, established his mastery of the emotions and musical tastes of the smart set, opening a world of suavity and irony that he went on to explore in a sequence of concertante pieces: the Concert champêtre for harpsichord, the Aubade with solo piano and the Concerto for two pianos.*

Around 1935 there came a change in his personal and spiritual life, reflected in a sizable output of religious music, a much greater productivity and an important contribution to French song. Yet the basis of his style was unchanged: Stravinsky, Fauré and contemporary popular music continued to be his sources, even in the devotional music and the larger sacred works. The songs include four cycles. But his output of instrumental music, apart from the many piano pieces of a private character, continued to be modest: his most important later orchestral piece is the G minor organ concerto with strings and timpani (1938), which journeys between Bach and the fairground, while his main chamber works were the sonatas for flute, oboe and clarinet.

Music for the stage also continued to occupy him. There was another ballet, Les animaux modèles (1942), scores for plays and films, and a new departure into opera, begun with the absurd Apollinaire piece Les mamelles de Tirésias and pursued with more seriousness in his deeply felt tragedy of martyrdom, Dialogues des Carmélites (1957), as well as a setting of Cocteau's telephone monologue La voix humaine (1959).

Organ Concerto

Concerto for Organ, Strings and Timpani in G minor. Suite française, d'après Claude Gervaise. Concert champêtre
Elisabeth Chojnacka *hpd* **Philippe Lefebvre** *org*
Lille Symphony Orchestra / Jean-Claude Casadesus
Naxos 8 554241 (59 minutes: DDD). Ⓢ
Recorded 1997

Elisabeth Chojnacka gets off to a head start against most others who have recorded the *Concert champêtre* by using the right kind of instrument: she understands that it is much sillier to play newish music on a period instrument than old music on a modern one. The effective proportions secured here between her deft playing and the orchestra also owe much to Jean-Claude Casadesus's nice sense of judgement and to the work of an excellent recording team. It was particularly perverse of Poulenc to ask a harpsichord to contend with large brass and percussion sections and then, a decade later, employ only strings and timpani in his concerto for the intrinsically far more powerful organ; and that perversity is underlined here by using the massive organ of Notre Dame, Paris (whose imposing specification is supplied for the satisfaction of organ buffs) – though once again the recording technicians have skilfully succeeded in producing a string sonority that does not suffer beside the organ's awesome thunders. You can't help wondering whether Poulenc really had such a giant sound in mind, but it is undeniably thrilling; and the quieter moments are captured with commendable clarity and calm. From the interpretative point of view, it's quite a performance. The wind and percussion of the Lille orchestra get a chance to demonstrate their quality in accomplished playing of the spry dances of the *Suite française*. This is an eminently recommendable disc.

Concerto for Organ, Strings and Timpani in G minor. Piano Concerto[a]. Double Piano Concerto in D minor
[a]**Pascal Rogé, Sylviane Deferne** *pfs* **Peter Hurford** *org* **Philharmonia Orchestra / Charles Dutoit**
Decca 436 546-2DH (60 minutes: DDD). Ⓕ
Recorded 1992

The Piano Concerto has the right blend of melodic and textural richness, wit and warmth in the hands of these performers. The mood of its expansive first movement is more tender than usual here, with its incisive wit and spiky Stravinskian instrumentation being less in evidence. But the music can take this approach, and the ecstatically chorale-like music near the end of the movement is done to perfection. In the gentle *Andante con moto*, Rogé and Dutoit are in their element, but here again the powerful passages also make their impact, while the romp of a finale has the right *joie de vivre*. The Double Piano Concerto comes over with great vivacity, with Deferne and Rogé (playing second piano) skilfully unanimous and crisply recorded. The Organ Concerto, recorded in St Alban's Cathedral, is also successful; Peter Hurford's mastery in Bach serves him well in its more darkly baroque aspects, but he is equally idiomatic in the uninhibitedly bouncy passages.

Les biches

Poulenc Les biches – suite. Les animaux modèles. Matelote provençale. Pastourelle. Valse. Les mariés de la Tour Eiffel – Discours du Général; La baigneuse de Trouville. Aubade[a] **Satie** (orch Poulenc) Fête donnée par les Chevaliers Normands en l'honneur d'une jeune demoiselle. Prélude du Nazaréen No 1. Gnossienne No 3
[a]**Pascal Rogé** *pf* **French National Orchestra / Charles Dutoit**
Decca 452 937-2DH (79 minutes: DDD). Ⓕ
Recorded 1996

The disc's three main pillars owe their origin to the world of ballet, *Les biches* (written aged 20 for Diaghilev) being the work that, with its *joie de vivre*, first put Poulenc in the public eye. Aided by the clearest sound ever produced from the Salle Wagram, Dutoit gives a vivid performance of this Bright Young Things score, less slinky than others in the 'Adagietto' but light-footed in the 'Rag-Mazurka' and spikily brash in the outer movements. There was more maturity of feeling by the time *Aubade* was composed six years later: with its mood veering between harshly dramatic, gently melancholy and madcap-gay and its stylistic inconsistency, it has never been as popular as his other works, and recordings have often been dogged by problems of balance. The present performance manages to get this right, however, and this is the most satisfactory version currently available.

But for sheer lyrical beauty there is little in Poulenc to match the luscious outer movements of the splendid score for Lifar's 1940 *Animaux modèles*. The orchestral imagination in its 'Two roosters' movement is to be found again in Poulenc's arrangement of two of his mentor Satie's starkly hieratic Rosicrucian pieces – a clear case of making a silk purse out of a sow's ear. Rounding off an exceptionally well-filled and desirable disc is a handful of Poulenc miniatures, ranging from the vulgarity of his early *Valse* via the farcical *Mariés de la Tour Eiffel* pieces to the rumbustiously jolly *Matelote provençale*.

Concert champêtre

Sinfonietta. Concert champêtre. Pièce brève sur le nom d'Albert Roussel. Bucolique. Fanfare. Deux Marches et un Intermède. Suite française
Pascal Rogé *hpd*
French National Orchestra / Charles Dutoit
Decca 452 665-2DH (78 minutes: DDD). Ⓕ
Recorded 1994 ●

The *Concert champêtre* is a difficult work to bring off, and Poulenc is largely to blame: owing to his unfamiliarity with the then little-known harpsichord he miscalculated the balance, employing too large an orchestra, and his many delays in completing the work make themselves manifest in the bitty structure, with abrupt changes of pace in the outer movements that few performances make convincing. On record the concerto has suffered from too puny a harpsichord sound, and even here the instrument could with advantage have been more closely recorded.

Poulenc was equally dilatory in finishing the *Sinfonietta*. Though the work is more substantial than its title suggests, it does not outstay its welcome, at least in this engaging reading, which Dutoit shapes with vitality and sensitive phrasing, though even he cannot make the finale sound other than a patchwork. This is a vigorous, alert interpretation. The neat, characterful performances of the *Suite française* for wind, percussion and harpsichord, based on themes by the 16th century Claude Gervaise of the three-movement *musique de table* for a banquet at the 1937 Exposition Universelle, and of the tributes for the 60th birthday of Roussel and the 75th of Marguerite Long add to the disc's attractions.

Chamber works

Complete Chamber Works
Sextet for Piano and Wind Quintet[a]. Trio for Oboe, Bassoon and Piano[b]. Flute Sonata[c]. Oboe Sonata[d]. Clarinet Sonata[e]. Violin Sonata[f]. Cello Sonata[g]. Sonata for Two Clarinets[h]. Sonata for Clarinet and Bassoon[i]. Sonata for Horn, Trumpet and Trombone[j]. Villanelle[k]. Elégie[l]. Sarabande[m]
The Nash Ensemble (Philippa Davies [ac]*fl/kpicc* [abd]Gareth Hulse *ob* [aehi]Richard Hosford, [h]Michael Harris *cls* [abi]Ursula Leveaux *bn* [ajl]Richard Watkins *hn* [j]John Wallace *tpt* [j]David Purser *tbn* [f]Leo Phillips *vn* [g]Paul Watkins *vc* [m]Craig Ogden *gtr*) [a-g/kl]Ian Brown *pf*
Hyperion ② CDA672556 (146 minutes: DDD). Ⓕ
Recorded 1998

Invidious as it may seem to pick out just one of these excellent artists, special mention must be made of Ian Brown, who plays in nine of the 13 works included and confirms his standing as one of the most admired and musicianly chamber pianists of our day. He knows, for example, how to control Poulenc's boisterous piano writing in the Sextet without sacrificing the sparkle, and as a result the work coheres better than ever before. Like the Trio (whose opening reveals Stravinskian influence), it is a mixture of the composer's madcap *gamin* mood and his predominantly melancholy bittersweet lyricism. The latter characteristic is most in evidence in his most enduring chamber works: the solo wind sonatas with piano, all three of which were in the nature of *tombeaux* , the Flute Sonata for the American patron Mrs Sprague Coolidge, that for clarinet for Honegger, and that for oboe for Prokofiev. All are given idiomatic, sensitive and satisfying performances by the Nash artists.

The *Elégie* for Dennis Brain was a not altogether convincing experiment in dodecaphony: Poulenc had earlier dabbled in atonality and polytonality in the little sonatas (really sonatinas) for, respectively, two clarinets and for clarinet and bassoon. There is a touching reading of the little *Sarabande* for guitar. A hint of the guitar's tuning at the start of the second movement is almost the only Spanish reference in the Violin Sonata, which was composed *in memoriam* the poet Lorca, whose loss is bitterly suggested in the angry finale. In this work Poulenc allotted to the piano (his own instrument) rather more than equal status in the duo – a situation rather paralleled in the lighthearted Cello Sonata, over which the composer dallied longer than any other of his works – but balance in both is finely judged by the performers and the recording team. The whole issue wins enthusiastic recommendation: it bids fair to become the undisputed yardstick for the future.

Capriccio[a]. Sonata for Two Pianos[a]. Elégie[a]. Sonata for Piano Duet[a]. L'embarquement pour Cythère[a]. Violin Sonata. Elégie
Chantal Juillet *vn* **André Cazalet** *hn* **Pascal Rogé,** [a]**Jean-Philippe Collard** *pfs*
Decca 443 968-2DH (70 minutes: DDD). Ⓕ
Recorded 1989-94

Few records could be more haunting or thought-provoking than this. For the lasting and predominant impression is of how Poulenc's music is so frequently clouded by a sense of elegy, by an uneasy if richly fruitful truce between levity and despair. The presence of two *Elégies*, and by implication, a third, is therefore hardly insignificant. Yet how typical of Poulenc, given so sombre a setting, to ring the changes with infinite elegance and poetry. The *Elégie* for horn and piano, composed in memory of Dennis Brain's tragic death in 1957, sounds the darkest note, the *Elégie* for two pianos, on the other hand, is intended to evoke the aroma of cognac and Gauloises, while the Violin and Piano Sonata's central 'Intermezzo' and 'Presto tragico' luxuriantly and tersely recall the death of Federico Garcia Lorca, murdered by Franco's minions in 1936 for his combined liberalism and homosexuality. Elsewhere the light shines through. *L'embarquement pour Cythère* is classic Poulenc, mischievously linking Watteau's painting of idealized love and the comforting world of seaside chips, accordions and cheap perfume (both Watteau and Poulenc were frequent holiday visitors to Nogent-sur-Marne). Here is witty and dazzling relief indeed. Both the performances and the recording are quite superb. Pascal Rogé, who has the lion's share of the proceedings, could hardly sound more authentically Gallic, more stylishly aware of the composer's tears and laughter. Jean-Philippe Collard, Chantal Juillet and André Cazalet are distinguished partners.

Poulenc Oboe Sonata. Trio for Oboe, Bassoon and Piano **Britten** Temporal Variations. Six Metamorphoses after Ovid, Op 49. Two Insect Pieces. Phantasy, Op 2
François Leleux *ob* **Jean-François Duquesnoy** *bn* **Guillaume Sutre** *vn* **Miguel da Silva** *va* **Marc Coppey** *vc* **Emmanuel Strosser** *pf*
Harmonia Mundi Les Nouveaux Interprètes Ⓑ
HMN91 1556 (76 minutes: DDD). Recorded 1995

The pairing of these composers is apt, for they were friends and their musical high spirits often have a darker side. The oboist here possesses an excellent technique and is a deeply sensitive artist. Both qualities quickly become evident in the flowing and quietly poignant opening melody of Poulenc's Sonata, where Leleux's tone is not only beautiful but also admirably responsive to the subtle dynamic shading and rhythmic flexibility. However, this is far from the whole story, and the *grotesquerie* of the passage starting at 2'16" shows that there is more to his playing than gentleness – as does the mercurial *Scherzo*, delivered with delightful point and relish. The final *Déploration* of this sonata, as played here, is infinitely moving and nothing less than superb.

Fortunately Leleux and his pianist partner, who is equally attuned to Poulenc's world, have been extremely well recorded. This performance and that of the bouncy Trio both give keen pleasure. So do the Britten pieces, three of them early (the characterful *Six Metamorphoses* being the exception) and edgy. Performed as vividly as this, they are undoubtedly worth having. A fine and generously filled disc.

Solo piano works

Awards 1988/89

Les soirées de Nazelles. Deux Novelettes – No 1 in C; No 2 in B flat minor. Novelette 'sur un thème de M de Falla'. Pastourelle (arr pf). Trois mouvements perpétuels. Valse. 15 Improvisations – No 1 in B minor; No 2 in A flat; No 3 in B minor; No 6 in B flat; No 7 in C; No 8 in A minor; No 12 in E flat, 'Hommage à Schubert'; No 13 in A minor; No 15 in C minor, 'Hommage à Edith Piaf'. Trois Pièces

Pascal Rogé *pf*

Decca 417 438-2DH (67 minutes: DDD) Ⓕ
Recorded 1986

Humoresque. Nocturnes. Suite in C. Thème varié. 15 Improvisations – No 4 in A flat; No 5 in A minor; No 9 in D; No 10 in F, 'Eloge des gammes'; No 11 in G minor; No 14 in D flat. Two Intermezzos. Intermezzo in A flat. Villageoises. Presto in B flat

Pascal Rogé *pf*

Decca 425 862-2DH (63 minutes: DDD).
Recorded 1989 Ⓕ

These beautifully recorded and generously filled discs offer a rich diversity of Poulenc's output. On the first disc, the masterly *Soirées de Nazelles* were improvised during the early 1930s at a country house in Nazelles as a memento of convivial evenings spent together with friends. It paints a series of charming portraits – elegant, witty and refined. The *Trois mouvements perpétuels* are, like so many of the works represented here, lighthearted and brief, improvisatory in flavour and executed with a rippling vitality. The *Improvisations* constantly offer up echoes of the piano concertos with their infectious rhythmic drive – the 'Hommage à Schubert' is a tartly classical miniature in three-time played with just the right amount of nonchalant ease by Pascal Rogé. The 'Hommage à Edith Piaf' is a lyrical and touching tribute – obviously deeply felt. The *Humoresque* which opens the second recital is open-air and open-hearted in style, yet songlike too in its melodic richness. The simplicity of this music is deceptive, as is that of the warmly caressing C major Nocturne that follows, for both pieces need subtle phrasing, rubato and the kind of textures only obtainable through the most refined use of the sustaining pedal.

Rogé has these skills, and he is also fortunate in having an excellent piano at his disposal as well as a location (the Salle Wagram in Paris) that gives the sound the right amount of reverberation. There are many delights in this music and the way it is played here: to mention just one, listen to the masterly way that the composer and pianist together gradually bring around the flowing freshness of the C major Nocturne towards the deeply poignant feeling of the close. They should especially delight, and to some extent reassure, anyone who deplores the absence of charm and sheer romantic feeling in much of our century's music.

Figure humaine

Un soir de neige. Chansons françaises. Sept chansons. Chanson à boire. Petites voix. Figure humaine

New London Chamber Choir / James Wood

Hyperion CDA66798 (67 minutes: DDD). Texts and translations included. Recorded 1995 Ⓕ

Poulenc's unaccompanied secular choral works, which demand virtuoso choirs, evidently hold no terrors for James Wood and his choir. The major work here is the wartime *Figure humaine*, whose finale, 'Liberté', became an inspiration to the Resistance movement. The choir at once impresses by the vividness with which it treats words and by its intelligent verbal phrasing (though some vowels, especially nasal ones, are not entirely native-sounding): it commands a wide dynamic range, thrilling at climaxes, with perceptive tonal nuances; and the chording of the difficult chromaticisms is commendably assured. The most characteristic movement of the cantata, 'Toi ma patiente', is beautifully shaped, and the final cadence of 'En chantant' is perfectly 'placed', thanks to the bright-voiced sopranos. The accelerating passion in 'Liberté' is scarifying, and the final cry (complete with a blood-curdling top E) is overwhelming.

The other wartime work, *Un soir de neige*, is finely moulded throughout, with a movingly deep appreciation of its mood of melancholy contemplation. These all illustrate Poulenc's serious side. In the earlier *Sept chansons* there is a mixture of moods, which are well caught, though the nimble 'Marie' could have been better defined. There is a real sense of energy and an obvious enjoyment in the performance of the eight folk-song arrangements, especially 'Les tisserands', but also quiet pathos in 'La belle se sied au pied de la tour'.

Mélodies

Banalités. Bleuet. Chansons gaillardes. Chansons villageoises. Dernier poème. Quatre poèmes. Métamorphoses – C'est ainsi que tu es. Montparnasse. Poèmes – C. Priez pour paix. Rosemonde. Tel jour, telle nuit – Bonne journée; Une ruine coquille vide; Une herbe pauvre; Je n'ai envie que de t'aimer;Nous avons fait la nuit

Michel Piquemal *bar* **Christine Lajarrige** *pf*

Naxos 8 553642 (67 minutes: DDD). Ⓢ
Recorded 1996 OO

The first time Michel Piquemal met Pierre Bernac, for whom most of these songs were written, Piquemal recalls that Bernac said: 'I am very moved, because what you're doing is exactly what Francis Poulenc was hoping for. He would have been happy.' Afterwards Piquemal studied both with Bernac and Denise Duval, the two singers who were closest to the composer, so this recital is part of a real, authentic tradition.

The greatest challenge for a singer comes in the best-known songs, for instance *Montparnasse* and 'C'. Piquemal doesn't disappoint. He hasn't got the luxurious voice for the lyrical climax of the first, at the words 'Vous êtes en réalité un poète lyrique d'Allemagne / Qui voulez connaître Paris,' but he delivers all the complicated Apollinaire verse in this and the cycle *Banalités* with a complete understanding of the necessary balance between stressing the irony and maintaining the strict forward-moving musical line. In 'C', with Louis Aragon's extraordinary line – one of the most wonderful moments in all of Poulenc's songs – 'Et les armes désamorcées / Et les larmes mal éffacées', Piquemal achieves exactly the slight *rallentando* before the *pp* attack on the word 'délaissé' in the final line, and just as Bernac insisted, it's 'full of feeling'.

The one group that wasn't composed for a light baritone is *Chansons villageoises*, which, although sung and recorded by Bernac, was intended for a Verdi baritone; 'Un tour de chant symphonique' Poulenc called it. Like Bernac, Piquemal doesn't have the opulent vocal quality here that Poulenc was looking for, but instead he has an actor's way with the words that brings personality and humour to a text such as the opening 'Chanson du clair tamis' – *très gai et très vite* in Poulenc's marking. All the brilliance of Maurice Fombeure's poetry gains clarity from Piquemal's diction and sense of fun, while the ensuing sadness of 'C'est le joli printemps' and the macabre parable of 'Le mendiant' are sharply contrasted.

If you want to sample this disc, try *Bleuet*, and the 'sensitive lyricism' that Bernac wrote of. It's one of the saddest songs Poulenc composed, with its image of the young soldier, the blue referring to the uniform of the conscript who has seen such terrible things while he is still almost a child. It has to be sung 'intimately', wrote Poulenc; Bernac, however, thought that it should also be 'virile and serious'. The penultimate line in which the boy faces the reality – he knows death better than life – is sung by Piquemal with a natural feel for the simplicity of the poem, never overdoing the emphasis, and never becoming arch.

At Naxos's low price this is a first-rate introduction to Poulenc's songs, but more than that it is an example of the best kind of French singing. Christine Lajarrige is a sensitive accompanist, for Poulenc always acknowledged that his songs are duets, for voice and piano.

Le bestiaire ou Cortège d'Orphée. Cocardes. Trois poèmes de Louise Lalanne. A sa guitare. Tel jour, telle nuit. Miroirs brûlants – Tu vois le feu du soir. Banalités. Métamorphoses. Voyage. Le souris. La dame de Monte-Carlo

Dame Felicity Lott *sop* **Graham Johnson** *pf*

Forlane UCD16730 (64 minutes: DDD). Texts and translations included. Recorded 1994 Ⓕ

This programme of *mélodies* is perfectly chosen and balanced. Juxtaposing song cycles and single numbers from the whole of Poulenc's career, putting them in chronological order, it highlights the extreme modernity of Poulenc's choice of poetry with his universal appeal as a songwriter. *Le Bestiaire* from 1918, to Apollinaire's verses, is his earliest substantial group and it is remarkable how vivid and strong the Poulenc sound already was, when he was just 19. Of the three early Cocteau settings, *Cocardes*, Poulenc said he wanted 'the smell of French fries, the accordion, Piver perfume' – once one has that in mind, both pianist and singer do splendidly, with lines such as 'Lionoléum en trompe-l'oeil. Merci. Cinéma, nouvelle muse'. *Tel jour, telle nuit* was, of course, one of the great cycles composed for Pierre Bernac but the brighter colours of Lott's voice make it more romantic than, for instance, Souzay's interpretation. Graham Johnson as accompanist is the worthy successor to Dalton Baldwin and the composer himself as the perfect interpreter of these *mélodies*.

Tel jour, telle nuit[b]. Cocardes[b]. Une chanson de porcelaine[b]. Calligrammes[b]. Le bestiaire ou Cortège d'Orphée[b] – La colombe; Le serpent; La puce. Le travail du peintre[b]. A sa guitare[b]. Cinq poèmes de Ronsard[b]. Deux poèmes[b]. Vive Nadia[b]. Nuage[c]. Dans le jardin d'Anna[c]. Rosemonde[c]. Chansons villageoises[c]. Dernier poème[c]. Mais mourir[c]. Le disparu[c]. Hymne[c]. Quatre poèmes[c]. La fraîcheur et le feu[c]. Cinq poèmes[b]. Parisiana[c]. Huit chansons polonaises[a]. Paul et Virginie[b]. Trois chansons[b]. Pierrot[b]. Epitaphe[b]. Mazurka[b]

[a]**Urszula Kryger** *mez* [b]**François Le Roux,** [c]**Gilles Cachemaille** *bar* **Pascal Rogé** *pf*

Decca ② 460 326-2DH2 (139 minutes: DDD). Also available as part of a four-disc, mid-price set of the complete *mélodies* (460 599-2DM4). Texts and translations included. Recorded 1998 Ⓕ O

During the final years of his life, Poulenc described his own personality, 'What has often been praised as my charming modesty is fundamentally nothing more than an inferiority complex.' This sometimes seems to be reflected in his music, especially in the way that the little bursts of melody which are so haunting often burn themselves out before one can catch hold of them. It was Poulenc's opinion that his music could be divided between those pieces that evoked his childhood beside the Marne, the works that were inspired by the countryside of the Touraine and third, the Parisian-inspired pieces. With the poets Eluard, Cocteau and Apollinaire prominent, it's natural that Poulenc's *mélodies* are mostly Paris-bound affairs. In this two-disc set the lion's share of the singing goes to François Le Roux. With Gilles Cachemaille and Urszula Kryger joining in on the second disc, this completes Decca's project to record all of Poulenc's songs. Le Roux does these three Cocteau settings with wonderful timing and diction here. He occasionally sounds taxed by the high-lying phrases Poulenc composed for Pierre Bernac in *Tel jour, telle nuit* and *Calligrammes*. He is one of the few singers of today who really knows how to employ head-tones without sounding false but *A sa guitare*, composed for Yvonne Printemps, really is soprano territory. He's absolutely superb in the three extra songs for *Le bestiaire*, only recently published (taking the snake, the dove and the flea as their subjects).

The second disc begins with Cachemaille singing one of Poulenc's latest and most beautiful songs, *Nuage*, to a poem by Laurence de Beylié. This is followed by two other songs from the 1930s and 1950s, both to Apollinaire poems, *Dans le jardin d'Anna* and *Rosemonde*. These make a neat group, as do the two contrasting poems by Robert Desnos, *Dernier poème* and *Le disparu* with an Eluard setting, *Mais mourir* in between – evocations of the occupation, of the poet's friend and then his own transportation to the death camps. Cachemaille's voice is more sensual than Le Roux's but he doesn't have such a range of expression at his command. Cachemaille sings the *Chansons villageoises* with plenty of firm tone – Poulenc asked for a Verdi baritone of the Iago type for these. They really benefit from being heard with orchestra, but Pascal Rogé certainly plays them with splendid verve. His contribution to the arrangements of Polish folk-songs – Poulenc's homage to Chopin – is also crucial. *La fraîcheur et le feu*, seven songs composed from one long Eluard poem, is a big challenge and Cachemaille doesn't altogether avoid a sense of strain. In general both Cachemaille and Le Roux are more at home in the lighter songs. The more you listen to Poulenc's *mélodies*, the more fascinating they become.

Gloria and Stabat mater

Gloria[a]. Stabat mater[a]. Litanies à la vierge noire[b]
[a]Françoise Pollet *sop* **[a]French Radio Choir; [b]Maîtrise de Radio France; French National Orchestra / Charles Dutoit**
Decca 448 139-2DH (62 minutes: DDD). Texts and translations included. Recorded 1994 Ⓕ

Dutoit, with his sensitivity, vitality and insight, outdoes his recorded rivals in two of these works. The finest performance here is undoubtedly of the *Litanies*, whose orchestral introduction immediately impresses by its wonderfully hushed sense of reverence. Dutoit respects the composer's desire for the work to be performed with simplicity: this is an intimate, not an exteriorized, plea (occasioned by the death in a horrible accident of Poulenc's friend Ferroud, a composer who is now largely forgotten), and the refrain 'Ayez pitié de nous' is uttered with true intensity by a chorus of unmistakably French timbre.

There is thoughtful phrasing too in the *Gloria*, again and again marked by Dutoit's vision and care over detail. He accents the deliberately-paced initial movement strongly, is light-footed in the Stravinskian 'Laudamus te', is not too slow and avoids sentimentality in 'Domine Deus Agnus Dei', and gives grandeur to the start of the final movement. Françoise Pollet, warm and sweet-voiced in the repeated 'Qui tollis peccata mundi', is radiant in the final Amens. The *Stabat mater* presents difficulties of balance which here are satisfactorily solved (the basses' first entry is, for once, not too obscure, and the orchestra does not overwhelm everyone in the fury of 'Quis est homo'). And again Dutoit is illuminating in the vigour of 'Cujus animam' and the well-judged restraint of 'Quae moerabat' (which in Yan Pascal Tortelier's reading sounds inappropriately cheerful). But in this work the chorus, though good in the unaccompanied sections of 'O quam tristis', too often sings on the underside of notes. Ah well, it was perhaps too much to hope that all three works would reach the same level of excellence.

Gloria. Stabat mater
Janice Watson *sop* **BBC Singers; BBC Philharmonic Orchestra / Yan Pascal Tortelier**
Chandos CHAN9341 (56 minutes: DDD). Texts and translations included. Recorded 1994 Ⓕ ⦿

We are immediately struck, at the start of the *Gloria*, by the radiantly warm but clean orchestral sonority: only later does an uneasy suspicion arise that, apparently seduced by the sound, the recording engineers may be favouring it at the expense of the chorus, especially at orchestral *fortes*. But it is committed and thoroughly secure choral singing, perhaps most easily appreciated in some of the unaccompanied passages – tender in the almost mystic 'O quam tristis' and firm-toned at 'Fac ut ardeat' (both in the *Stabat mater*); it gives real attack at 'Quis est homo' (just holding its own against the orchestra); the sopranos can produce a bright, ringing tone; and only the very first line of the *Stabat mater*, lying low in the basses, needed to be a bit stronger (as in most performances). Janice Watson is a sweet-voiced soloist with very pure intonation; but she could with advantage have strengthened her consonants throughout. Tortelier gives intensely felt readings of both works – the murmurous ending of the *Stabat mater* and the thrilling *fortissimo* chords at 'Quoniam' in the *Gloria* spring to mind – and fortunately he keeps the vocal 'Domine Deus' entry moving at the same pace as at its introduction. He takes the

Stravinskian 'Laudamus te' fast and lightly; the only questionable speed is of 'Quae moerebat', which sounds too cheerful for the words ('mourning and lamenting'). Taken all in all, these are performances of undoubted quality.

Motets

Mass in G. Quatre motets pour un temps de pénitence. Quatre motets pour le temps de Noël. Exultate Deo. Salve regina

Berlin RIAS Chamber Choir / Marcus Creed

Harmonia Mundi HMC90 1588 (52 minutes: DDD). Ⓕ
Texts and translations included. Recorded 1995

There has never been a more beautiful performance of the *Salve regina*. And elsewhere this virtuoso choir displays, beyond impeccably pure intonation and chording (chorus-masters everywhere will note with envy the sopranos' clean, dead-sure attacks on high notes), a sensitivity to verbal meaning, dynamics and vocal colour that argues not only skilful direction but a complete ease and absorption into the music's often chromatic nature by all the singers. They bring a bright-eyed tone to the *Exultate Deo*, awe to 'O magnum mysterium' (in the Christmas motets), and a striking diversity of timbre to 'Tristis est anima mea' (in the penitential motets); in the Mass they interpret to perfection the *doucement joyeux* indication of the *Sanctus*. They appear to have been recorded in some large church, but without any problems of resonance and the words are extremely clear throughout. In all, this is a first-class disc.

Complete stage works

Dialogues des Carmélites[a]

Denise Duval *sop* Blanche de La Force; **Régine Crespin** *sop* Madame Lidoine; **Denise Scharley** *mez* Madame de Croissy; **Liliane Berton** *sop* Soeur Constance; **Rita Gorr** *mez* Mère Marie; **Xavier Depraz** *bass* Marquis de La Force; **Paul Finel** *ten* Chevalier de La Force; **Janine Fourrier** *sop* Mère Jeanne; **Gisèle Desmoutiers** *sop* Soeur Mathilde; **Louis Rialland** *ten* L'Aumônier; **René Bianco** *bar* Le Geôlier; **Jacques Mars** *bar* L'Officier; **Raphael Romagnoni** *ten* First Commissaire; **Charles Paul** *bar* Second Commissaire; **Michel Forel** *ten* Thierry; **Max Conti** *bar* Javelinot

Chorus and Orchestra of the Opera, Paris / Pierre Dervaux

Le gendarme incompris[b]

Nicolas Rivenq *bar* Monsieur Médor; **Jean-Paul Fouchécourt** *ten* Marquise de Montonson; **Jean-Christoph Benoit** *bar* Pénultième

Soloists Ensemble of the Garde Républicaine / François Boulanger

Les mamelles de Tirésias[c]

Duval *sop* Thérèse, Fortune-teller; **Marguérite Legouhy** *mez* Marchande de journaux, Grosse Dame; **Jean Giraudeau** *ten* Husband; **Emile Rousseau** *bar* Policeman; **Robert Jeantet** *bar* Director; **Julien Thirache** *bar* Presto; **Frédéric Leprin** *ten* Lacouf; **Serge Rallier** *ten* Journalist; **Jacques Hivert** *sngr* Son; **Gabriel Jullia** *sngr* Monsieur barbu

Chorus and Orchestra of the Opéra-Comique / André Cluytens

Les chemins de l'amour[d]

Yvonne Printemps *sop* **orchestra / Marcel Cariven**

Fanfare[e]

Toulouse Capitole Orchestra / Stéphane Cardon

L'histoire de Babar[f]

Sir Peter Ustinov *narr* **Paris Conservatoire Orchestra / Georges Prêtre**

La dame de Monte Carlo[g]

Mady Mesplé *sop* **Monte Carlo Philharmonic Orchestra / Prêtre**

La voix humaine[h]

Duval *sop* La Femme; **Orchestra of the Opéra-Comique, Paris / Prêtre**

Le bal masqué[i]

Benoit *bar* **Maryse Charpentier** *pf* **Soloists of the Paris Conservatoire Orchestra / Prêtre**

L'invitation au château[j]

David Grimal *vn* **Romain Guyot** *cl* **Emmanuel Strosser** *pf*

Sécheresses[k]

French Radio Choir; French New Philharmonic Orchestra / Prêtre

Figure humaine[l]. Un soir de neige[m]

The Sixteen / Harry Christophers

EMI Poulenc Edition acdmono/stereo ⑤
CMS5 66843-2 (380 minutes: [acdfhi]ADD/DDD). Texts included. Recorded [a]1958, [b]1998, [c]1953, [d]1941, [e]1998, [f]1965, [g]1985, [h]1959, [i]1965, [j]1998, [lm]1989 Ⓜ **OO**

Poulenc's stage works might seem to be divided between those that hark back to his youth as a member of Les Six, and the more pessimistic mood that overtook him after the Second World War. It doesn't really work like that, however, since it was after composing *Dialogues des Carmélites* that he returned to the work of Jean Cocteau to produce two contrasting monologues – *La voix humaine* and *La dame de Monte Carlo* in which the frivolous and the tragic are mixed with exquisite irony. It must have been quite a long-term investment when *Les mamelles de Tirésias* was recorded in 1953. This classic version under André Cluytens can never be surpassed as a souvenir of the earliest performances of what is still Poulenc's most successful opera, but the orchestral detail is much more vivid on the modern Ozawa set. Denise Duval was Poulenc's favourite soprano and although her voice has that slightly astringent quality in the upper reaches so typical of French female singers, her performances are so complete, musically and dramatically, that they ought to be studied by any aspiring soprano who wants to sing in French. Cocteau wanted Poulenc to compose *La voix humaine* for Callas but he would only consider Duval. It's a very difficult role to act and sing and again, although many famous divas have tackled it – Olivero, Scotto, Norman and Söderström among them – Duval's 'Elle' is sublime. Public and critics have always been somewhat divided by *Dialogues de Carmélites*. The *Gramophone* Award-winning Nagano version boasts as strong a cast as you could imagine for the time, but again, Duval, Crespin, Berton and the others have an intensity that it's difficult to imagine ever being equalled.

EMI has provided texts but no translations. Monsieur Poulenc would not have been amused. He insisted that *Carmélites* should be performed in translation outside France. The other items that make up the set include Poulenc's humorous and really beautiful incidental music for Anouilh's play *L'invitation au château*. As in so many other instances this finds Poulenc using little quotations and self-quotations. The fourth number 'Mouvement de valse hésitation' is a delicate variation on the Berger-De Féraudy waltz *Amoureuse* and elsewhere there is a hint of his 15th *Improvisation*. Similarly in *Le bal masqué*, there is a little five-note phrase which is a pre-echo of the husband's demand 'Donnez-moi du lard' in *Mamelles*. At the end of the fourth CD we do get to hear Mme Fresnay, the delectable Yvonne Printemps, in her waltz-song from Anouilh's *Léocadia*, 'Les chemins de l'amour'. It was Poulenc himself who called her singing 'literally divine'.

La dame de Monte Carlo, composed as a concert number for Denise Duval, is beautifully sung by Mady Mesplé. It's a bit like an opera-composer's take on the 'Let's face the music and dance' scene from the Astaire-Rogers movie *Follow the Fleet*, the gambler facing ruin outside the casino. The secular cantatas that end the last CD, two of them newly recorded by The Sixteen, provide yet more scope for contrasting Poulenc's shifts of mood between the cabaret and the chapel. Poulenc himself wrote: 'The vocal style of the *Stabat* or that of *Dialogues des Carmélites* is in fact as far removed from the song as the string quartet is from the string orchestra.'

Dialogues des Carmélites

Awards 1993

Catherine Dubosc *sop* Blanche de la Force; **Rachel Yakar** *sop* Madame Lidoine; **Rita Gorr** *mez* Madame de Croissy; **Brigitte Fournier** *sop* Soeur Constance; **Martine Dupuy** *mez* Mère Marie; **José van Dam** *bass-bar* Marquis de la Force; **Jean-Luc Viala** *ten* Chevalier de la Force; **Michel Sénéchal** *ten* L'Aumônier; **François Le Roux** *bar* Le Geôlier
Lyon Opéra Chorus and Orchestra / Kent Nagano
Virgin Classics ② VCD7 59227-2 Ⓕ
(152 minutes: DDD). Notes, text and translation included

Poulenc's *chef d'oeuvre* is one of the few operas written since *Wozzeck* that has survived in the repertory – and deservedly so. It is written from, and goes to, the heart, not in any extrovert or openly histrionic way but by virtue of its ability to explore the world of a troubled band of Carmelite nuns at the height of the terrors caused by the French Revolution, and do so in an utterly individual manner. Poulenc unerringly enters into their psyches as they face their fatal destiny. Nagano responds with perceptible keenness to the sombre, elevated mood and intensity of Poulenc's writing and unfailingly delineates the characters of the principals as they face their everyday martyrdom. The magisterial authority of Martine Dupuy's Mère Marie, the agony of Rita Gorr's Old Prioress, the inner torment of Catherine Dubosc's Sister Blanche, the restraint of Rachel Yakar's Madame Lidoine, the eager charm of Brigitte Fournier's Sister Constance are only the leading players in a distribution that is without any doubt admirable in almost every respect. The score is for once given complete. The recording for Virgin Classics is atmospheric and suggests stage action without exaggeration.

Les mamelles de Tirésias

Les mamelles de Tirésias
Barbara Bonney *sop* Thérèse; **Jean-Philippe Lafont** *bar* Director; **Jean-Paul Fouchécourt** *ten* Husband; **Wolfgang Holzmair** *bar* Policeman; **Gordon Gietz** *ten* Journalist; **Graham Clark** *ten* Lacouf; **Akemi Sakamoto** *mez* Marchande de journaux; **Mark Oswald** *bar* Presto; **Anthony Dean Griffey** *ten* Son
Tokyo Opera Singers; Saito Kinen Orchestra / Seiji Ozawa

Le bal masqué
Wolfgang Holzmair *bar*
members of the **Saito Kinen Orchestra / Seiji Ozawa**
Philips 456 504-2PH (72 minutes: DDD).
Notes, texts and translations included. Ⓕ
Recorded 1996

Les mamelles de Tirésias is Poulenc's *Così fan tutte*. On the surface it can easily be construed as little more than an absurd romp. Poulenc, though, has used Apollinaire's *sur-réaliste* drama – in 1917 it was the play that gave the word to the language – as a starting-point for a work that is full of emotion – regrets, nostalgia and longing, then finally at the end the rebirth of hope. Poulenc worked sporadically on the piece in the early 1940s, but eventually finished it in a great burst of creative energy after the end of the Second World War. During the German occupation of France, Poulenc mostly being away from Paris, much as the characters in the play are stranded in a mythical Zanzibar, he amused himself with details about the city and its *arrondissements* – the score is full of little musical references that match Apollinaire's untranslatable puns. This recording is the first to have been made since the classic André Cluytens version, which included several members of the original cast, including Poulenc's favourite soprano, Denise Duval; after she created the part of Thérèse, Poulenc described her as 'stunning Paris with her beauty, her acting talent and her voice'. It's a hard act to follow, but Barbara Bonney succeeds in creating a vivid character without trying to imitate Duval.

Seiji Ozawa has always possessed a special feeling for French opera of this period. The biggest advantage of this recording is the clarity of the orchestral sound – in the 1953 version the voices are so prominent that one loses all the beautiful detail in those heart-catching Poulenc juxtapositions, as the composer put it, 'in the midst of the worst buffoonery a phrase can effect a change in the lyric tone'. The vocal coach, Pierre Valet, deserves considerable recognition for the way in which he has succeeded in getting the Tokyo Opera Singers to articulate the French. As Presto and Lacouf, Mark Oswald and Graham Clark get to sing the wonderful duet about their gambling debts, 'Monsieur Presto, je n'ai rien gagné'. Wolfgang Holzmair is luxury casting as the Gendarme, and in the crucial role of Thérèse's husband, Jean-Paul Fouchécourt is splendidly clear, whether looking after the babies or discussing Picasso's art. Those who already know this opera will delight in this performance, and if you have not yet become acquainted with the taste of the banana leaf and the strawberry together – the symbol Apollinaire offers his lovers at the end – you have a real treat in store. *Les mamelles* is such a jewel on its own, but *Le bal masqué* makes a good fill-up.

Michael Praetorius

German 1571-1621

GROVE *The son of a strict Lutheran, Praetorius was educated at Torgau, Frankfurt an der Oder (1582) and Zerbst (1584). He was organist of St Marien, Frankfurt (1587-90), before moving to Wolfenbüttel, where he was court organist from 1595 and Kapellmeister from 1604. He temporarily served the Saxon court (1613-16), chiefly at Dresden, where he met Schütz and got to know the latest Italian music, and he worked in many other German cities. The most versatile German composer of his day, he was also one of the most prolific. His 21 extant sacred vocal publications include over 1000 Protestant hymn-based works, many for multiple choirs, as well as Latin music for the Lutheran service, motets, psalms and instrumental dances (Terpsichore, 1612). His encyclopedic treatise Syntagma musicum (published 1614-20), with detailed information on instruments and performing practice, is of immense documentary value.*

Dances from Terpsichore

Dances from Terpsichore – excerpts
New London Consort / Philip Pickett
L'Oiseau-Lyre Florilegium 414 633-2OH Ⓕ
(51 minutes: DDD).

This is pure sizzle and great fun from beginning to end. The massive collection of French court dances that Praetorius collected and arranged for his volume entitled Terpsichore in 1612 was just one in the extraordinary series of publications he issued within only 15 years. In terms of pure compositional achievement it may be the least interesting of those volumes, but it has always worked well in performance because it is unquestionably the best medium for exploiting the vast range of apparently current instruments that Praetorius later described in the second book of his musical encyclopaedia *Syntagma musicum*. Rackets, shawms, Rauschpfeifen, many kinds of stringed instruments and much else are all chronicled here. And the music in Terpsichore is tailor-made for an imaginative and rich display showing the varied sounds of one of music's most colourful eras. In all, there is a massive cast of nearly 40 musicians taking part, among them some of the most admired early-instrument names in London. There is any number of absolutely delicious sounds; and the groups are juxtaposed with quick-silver elegance.

The performances include some imaginative departures from the sketchy details of Praetorius's harmonizations, although it is rather odd that so little embellishment was used. There is an avoiding of the kind of individual showing-off that made some of the earlier Terpsichore recordings so exciting; the excitement is in the vitality and cleanness of the ensemble sound. The CD gives a stunning presence to the dazzling range of instruments too.

Lutheran Christmas Mass

Roskilde Cathedral Boys' Choir and Congregation; Gabrieli Consort; Gabrieli Players / Paul McCreesh P
Archiv Produktion 439 250-2AH (79 minutes: DDD).
Text and translation included. Ⓕ
Recorded 1993 ●

The aesthetic of contrast, so central to early baroque spectacle (sacred or profane), is inspired here by the traditional part played by the congregation in Lutheran worship. Praetorius's music for the *figuraliter* (the vocal/instrumental choirs) is greatly influenced by fashionable Venetian techniques. But what is striking is the way the old *alternatim* practices of the Protestant church blend so naturally with the intricate textures and scorings of a colourful Italian-style canvas, ranging from intimate dialogues to full grandiloquent sonority. What is more, the centrality of the chorale is never compromised. Despite all these ingredients, it is McCreesh's research and imagination that make this service such a powerful testament to the faith expressed by Lutherans of Praetorius's generation, and indeed by subsequent generations to which Bach was so indebted.

The service follows, to all intents and purposes, the Mass of the Roman rite (sung with distinction by the Gabrieli Consort though the sopranos seem a little unsure in the *Kyrie*) interspersed with a versatile array of motets, hymns, prayers, intoned readings, a superbly conceived and suitably mysterious Pavan by Schein for the approach to Communion and several rhetorically positioned organ preludes. For a congregation, the Gabrieli Consort and players are joined by the boys of Roskilde Cathedral, Denmark and a some local amateur choirs. The effect is remarkable for its fervour in the hymns; now one can see why *Von Himmel hoch da komm ich her* inspired so many settings in the 17th century. Other familiar tunes include *Quem pastores*, *Wie schön leuchtet der Morgenstern* in a shimmering prelude by Scheidt followed by a delicately nuanced motet on the same tune. *In dulci jubilo* is treated to a flamboyant setting by Praetorius featuring six trumpets. The spacious acoustic of the cathedral exhibits McCreesh's acute timbral sense; definition is not ideally sharp but this is a small price to pay for a natural perspective which embraces the sense of community worship essential for this project.

Zbigniew Preisner Polish 1955

A self-taught musician, he studied history of art at Kraków University. From 1978 he worked with the legendary Kraków cabaret Piwnica pod Baranami ('The cellar beneath the sign of the ram'). He made his début as a film composer in 1982 with Prognoza pogody ('Weather Forecast'), and from 1985 collaborated regularly with the film director Krzysztof Kieślowski until the latter's death in 1996. The success of Kieślowski's films, particularly La double vie de Véronique and the trilogy 'Three Colours' led to Preisner's flourishing career in Europe and the USA.

Requiem For My Friend

Elzbieta Towarnicka *sop* **Varsov Chamber Choir; Sinfonia Varsovia / Jacek Kaspszyk**
Erato 3984-24146-2 (74 minutes: DDD). Text and translation included. Recorded 1998 Ⓕ

As the success of his film scores shows, Zbigniew Preisner knows exactly how to compose effective and immediately impressive music with an acute sense of timing. *Requiem For My Friend*, his first work written specifically for concert performance, also shows this ability, but placed in a new context. Scored for five voices, organ, string quintet and percussion, the first part, 'Requiem', employs words from the Latin *Missa pro defunctis*, and one feels that the ghosts of chant and the polyphonic tradition are often not far away (particularly in the opening 'Officium' and the *Kyrie*). A good deal of other music is suggested during the course of the work: one occasionally thinks of the Górecki of the Third Symphony or *O Domina nostra*, or Pärt, and also other composers of film music such as Vangelis or Jerry Goldsmith. This said, however, the work has its own sense of direction and cohesion and the relatively limited resources are put to very effective use: the only section that does not work is the *Agnus Dei*, which relies too heavily on sentiment and whose Wurlitzerish combination of organ and strings is very saccharine. The most effective movement is the unaccompanied 'Lux aeterna', simple and folk-like, but there are memorable things particularly in the 'Lacrimosa', which attains a real dramatic power with its repetitive melodic tag, and the 'Offertory', whose character is defined by the subtle use of recitative-like vocal writing.

The second part of the work, 'Life', for much larger forces and also in nine movements, is generally less successful in that it has less sense of unity and relies not so much on distinctive musical material as on the kind of symphonic film music gestures which work excellently in context but which fail to sustain interest or to cohere as a concert work (try the Orff-Jerry Goldsmith sounds of 'Veni et vidi' for an example of this). There are nevertheless some fine things, such as the saxophone writing (and playing) in 'The beginning', or the hushed, valedictory 'Prayer'. This is music which wears its heart on its sleeve, and as a personal memorial to a friend (the film director, Krzysztof Kieslowski) that is entirely appropriate.

André Previn German/American 1929

GROVE *American conductor, pianist and composer of German birth, Previn studied in Berlin and at the Paris Conservatoire and moved to Los Angeles in 1939. His early career was in the film industry and as a jazz pianist. He made his conducting début in 1963 and was conductor-in-chief of the Houston SO, 1967-70. From 1965 he has been heard with the LSO (principal conductor, 1969-79), notably in strongly coloured late Romantic or early 20th-century music. He conducted the Pittsburgh SO, 1976-86, and became music director of the Los Angeles PO in 1986. He has composed musicals and orchestral and chamber works.*

Songs

Diversions[a]. Three Dickinson Songs[b].
The Giraffes go to Hamburg[c]. Sallie Chisum remembers Billy the Kid[d]. Vocalise[e]
[bc]**Renée Fleming,** [de]**Barbara Bonney** *sops* [c]**Renée Siebert** afl [e]**Moray Welsh** *vc* [a]**Vienna Philharmonic Orchestra;** [de]**London Symphony Orchestra / André Previn** [bcpf]
DG 471 028-2GH (57 minutes: DDD) Ⓕ
[a]Recorded live in 2000

The Prologue of Previn's *Diversions* for orchestra suggests that he'd been listening to Shostakovich's Eighth Symphony – certainly the motoric *allegro non troppo*, with its wailing high clarinet like a mortar shell in flight. It's an arresting start, less malignant than the Shostakovich but shot through with the same level of cynicism. The sweetly contrasted second idea, with the odd harmony straight out of Strauss, speaks with an American accent. Britten is in there too: the second-movement Passacaglia is very much in the tradition of Britten and Shostakovich, deeply rooted but searching, with solo riffs for clarinet, piccolo and cello exploring Previn's natural aptitude for the songful line. There's even a fleeting *film noir* moment where upper strings take up the principal idea as if suddenly drenched in Hollywood twilight. And in the final movement the emergence of a solo string trio hints at the Tippett Triple Concerto.

Many influences, then, but there are bound to be for such a busy and experienced international conductor. More at issue is how successfully Previn turns these influences into something uniquely his own. He's an elegant and technically adept craftsman; he knows exactly what he's doing with an orchestra. The music is varied and eventful. But it's also a little sporadic. You long for him to let go, to really run with an idea. A satisfying climax would be nice (and heaven knows, Shostakovich or Britten were not shy of those). But it's almost as if he's a little wary of slipping back into the overkill of those bad old Hollywood days. This is the antidote – just a tad precious.

Not so his word-setting. Previn is up there with the best of them – Barber, Bernstein, Copland. The three Emily Dickinson settings (personalised for Renée Fleming, his radiant Blanche in *Streetcar*) are special. His understanding of the poetry is reflected in the directness. Previn doesn't get in the way, nor does he inhibit the words. The amazing thing about Dickinson is the imperceptible way she slips from homespun to visionary. In the settings 'As imperceptively as grief' and 'Good morning midnight' the reflectiveness is tempered with an ever-present ecstasy.

Previn knows Dickinson, just as he knows Isak Dinesen (aka Karen Blixen). Her descriptive text 'Giraffes go to Hamburg' (from *Out of Africa*) is here a heartfelt *parlando* occasionally overcome in an expressive melodic flush: 'the high sweet air over the plains'. The alto flute (what a clever touch) is a subtle and constant reminder of the lush homeland these proud animals have been torn from; the sudden (and almost shocking) burst of bar-room piano points to the sideshow they'll become.

Previn's piano original of *Sallie Chisum remembers Billy the Kid* (also recorded by Barbara Bonney, for Decca) is preferable if only because it concentrates the mind and the imagination on the vocal nuances. Indeed, it's a tribute to Previn's word-setting that the orchestral colour adds so little and even, you might think, distracts so much. The poem's the thing. The voice is enough. More than enough in *Vocalise*, written in less than two hours when a previous attempt proved too clever for its own good. This, too, is the orchestral version (the piano and cello original has again been previously recorded by Bonney), but with no words to care for, Previn's answer to Rachmaninov can be as plush as it likes. Bonney's voice sinks back into the luxuriant texture, clearly enjoying the extra support. Maybe Previn should always set himself impossible deadlines.

A Streetcar Named Desire

Renée Fleming *sop* Blanche DuBois; **Rodney Gilfry** *bar* Stanley Kowalski; **Elizabeth Futral** *sop* Stella Kowalski; **Anthony Dean Griffey** *ten* Harold Mitchell; **Judith Forst** *mez* Eunice Hubbell; **Matthew Lord** *ten* Steve Hubbell; **Jeffrey Lentz** *ten* Young Collector; **Josepha Gayer** *mez* Flower Woman
San Francisco Opera Orchestra / André Previn
DG ③ 20/21 459 366-2GX3 (163 minutes: DDD). Ⓜ
Notes and text included. Recorded live in 1998

Tennessee Williams always resisted the operatic stage. Requests to turn *Streetcar* into an opera (and there were, not surprisingly, a good many) were always denied. His plays – and *Streetcar* in particular – were quite operatic enough without being sung. The music of Williams's poetry was always implicit. And yet … In 1964, as a gesture to composer Lee Hoiby, who underscored his ill-fated *Slapstick Tragedy*, Williams gave Hoiby the option to adapt any of his plays (including *Streetcar*) as an opera. Hoiby chose *Summer and Smoke*. But the door was finally open. André Previn came to it only in 1998. The offer, from Lotfi Mansouri of the San Francisco Opera, was nothing if not timely. After almost half-a-century of writing dramatic music for the movies, for the stage, to say nothing of his recent developments as a songsmith, opera was impatient for his touch. But *Streetcar*? It's perfect and yet not. The greater part of Previn's success has to do with his respect for, and understanding of, the music of Williams's text. Librettist Philip Littell has done an excellent job of adapting it, condensing it, mindful of how opera, by its very nature, seeks to elaborate and intensify the nodal points of any drama. In *Streetcar* those are easy enough to identify, but the real challenge (and accomplishment) here has been to preserve the play's narrative strength whilst losing more than an hour of its duration. You don't feel as if you've lost anything. All your favourite lines are just where you last left them.

Or seem to be. Previn's word-setting is now well practised and very skilled. His acute awareness of Williams's speech rhythms means that you hear every word. The jokes all land (you can hear the audience testify to that). The poetry takes wing. The tone of the play rings true. Previn's *Streetcar* begins with the ominous lowing of a tuba and a sleezy, twice-sounded, trumpet-laden chord slurred through too much heat and booze. There is no jazz in Previn's score – just the allusion to it, the smell of it, the flavour of it. The sound world is late, late, romantic. Berg crossed with Barber and suffused with Britten. The threat of violence restlessly, spikily, agitates just below the surface. Previn's score is rich in atmospherics. But richer yet is the way it takes Williams's lead in aspiring to a heady, ready lyricism where the play and players dare to dream of enchantment, tenderness, hope.

This is especially true of Blanche whose vain belief that 'soft people have got to shimmer and glow' is reflected in music almost as sweet as it is extinct. Previn is sparing with this music, but when it comes, it floats, unsullied by the grubbiness, the brutality, of the real world below. And just as Blanche retreats more and more into her imagined world, so Previn's music for her grows more fragrant, more voluptuous, transporting her and us to flightier regions. 'I want magic' is everything – and more – that she craves.

Renée Fleming must have been such an inspiration for Previn. She is currently at the peak of her powers. Indeed, you cannot imagine another singer of this stature who sounds and looks, in operatic terms, as one might imagine Blanche to sound and look. But then, you've only got to glance at the production photographs in the booklet to see just how carefully, and effectively, the opera has been cast. Fleming may have been a given for Blanche, but Rodney Gilfry's Stanley (big on baritonal bluster as well as biceps), Elizabeth Futral's Stella, and Anthony Dean Griffey's Mitch (whose idealism – not least the one brief, shining moment in Act 2 where he is able to articulate something of his belief in love – is so touching) are each outstanding.

All in all, then, a considerable piece of work. Not everything sits quite as you would like it to sit, not everything comes off the page with quite the force you may have envisaged (Blanche's rape music, for instance, is very much Previn in B-movie mode). The play, of course, remains something else altogether. A masterpiece. But Previn and Littell and their cast have gone further than you would have thought possible towards effecting a theatrically viable transition from page to musical stage. It is probably a score that will knit together in the mind, though at first the ideas may seem too fragmented. Operagoers have their own streetcar, which they board fearfully yet hopefully whenever a new opera comes along; it sounds at that moment very much as though they have stopped at a setting-down point they might actually recognize as Desire.

Sergey Prokofiev Russian 1891-1953

GROVE *Prokofiev showed precocious talent as a pianist and composer and had lessons from Glier from 1902. In 1904 he entered the St Petersburg Conservatory, where Rimsky-Korsakov, Lyadov and Tcherepnin were among his teachers; Tcherepnin and Myaskovsky, who gave him valuable support, encouraged his interest in Skryabin, Debussy and Strauss. He had made his début as a pianist in 1908, quickly creating something of a sensation as an enfant terrible, unintelligible and ultra-modern – an image he was happy to cultivate. His intemperateness in his early piano pieces, and later in such works as the extravagantly Romantic Piano Concerto No 1 and the ominous No 2, attracted attention. Then in 1914 he left the conservatory and travelled to London, where he heard Stravinsky's works and gained a commission from Diaghilev: the resulting score was, however, rejected (the music was used to make the Scythian Suite); a second attempt, Chout, was not staged until 1921.*

Meanwhile his gifts had exploded in several different directions. In 1917 he finished an opera on Dostoyevsky's Gambler, a violently involved study of obsession far removed from the fantasy of his nearly contemporary Chicago opera The Love for Three Oranges, written in1919 and performed in 1921. Nor does either of these scores have much to do with his Classical Symphony, selfconsciously 18th-century in manner, and again quite distinct from his lyrical Violin Concerto No 1, written at the same period and in the same key. There were also piano sonatas based on old notebooks alongside the more adventurous Visions fugitives, all dating from 1915-19.

Towards the end of this rich period, in 1918, he left for the USA; then from 1920 France became his base. His productivity slowed while he worked at his opera The Fiery Angel, an intense, symbolist fable of good and evil (it had no complete performance until after his death, and he used much of its music in Symphony No 3). After this he brought the harsh, heavy and mechanistic elements in his music to a climax in Symphony No 2 and in the ballet Le pas d'acier, while his next ballet, L'enfant prodigue, is in a much gentler style: the barbaric and the lyrical were still alternatives in his music and not fused until the 1930s, when he began a process of reconciliation with the Soviet Union.

The renewed relationship was at first tentative on both sides. Romeo and Juliet, the full-length ballet commissioned for the Bolshoi, had its première at Brno in 1938, and only later became a staple of the Soviet repertory: its themes of aggression and romantic love provided, as also did the Eisenstein film Alexander Nevsky, a receptacle for Prokofiev's divergent impulses. Meanwhile his own impulse to remain a Westerner was gradually eroded and in 1936 he settled in Moscow, where initially his concern was with the relatively modest genres of song, incidental music, patriotic cantata and children's entertainment (Peter and the Wolf, 1936). He had, indeed, arrived at a peculiarly unfortunate time, when the drive towards socialist realism was at its most intense; and his first work of a more ambitious sort, the opera Semyon Kotko, was not liked.

With the outbreak of war, however, he perhaps found the motivation to respond to the required patriotism: implicitly in a cycle of three piano sonatas (Nos 6-8) and Symphony No 5, more openly in his operatic setting of scenes from Tolstoy's War and Peace, which again offered opportunities for the two extremes of his musical genius to be expressed. He also worked at a new full-length ballet, Cinderella. In 1946 he retired to the country and though he went on composing, the works of his last years have been regarded as a quiet coda to his output. Even his death was overshadowed by that of Stalin on the same day.

Piano Concertos

No 1 in D flat, Op 10; **No 2** in G minor, Op 16; **No 3** in C, Op 26; **No 4** in B flat, Op 53 (left-hand); **No 5** in G, Op 55

Piano Concertos Nos 1-5
Vladimir Ashkenazy *pf*
London Symphony Orchestra / André Previn
Decca ② 452 588-2DF2 (126 minutes: ADD). Ⓜ
Recorded 1974-75 ●●

While it's true that the Prokofiev piano concertos are an uneven body of work, there's enough imaginative fire and pianistic brilliance to hold the attention even in the weakest of them; the best, by common consent Nos 1, 3 and 4, have stood the test of time very well. As indeed have these Decca recordings. The set first appeared in 1975, but the sound is fresher than many contemporary digital issues, and Ashkenazy has rarely played better. Other pianists have matched his brilliance and energy in, say, the Third Concerto, but very few have kept up such a sure balance of fire and poetry. The astonishingly inflated bravura of the Second Concerto's opening movement is kept shapely and purposeful and even the out-of-tune piano doesn't spoil the effect too much. And the youthful First has the insouciance and zest its 22-year-old composer plainly intended. Newcomers to the concertos should start with No 3: so many facets of Prokofiev's genius are here, and Ashkenazy shows how they all take their place as part of a kind of fantastic story. But there are rewards everywhere, and the effort involved in finding them is small. Why hesitate?

Piano Concertos Nos 1-5
Vladimir Krainev *pf*
Frankfurt Radio Symphony Orchestra / Dmitri Kitaienko
Teldec Ultima ② 3984 21038-2 (123 minutes: DDD). Ⓜ
Recorded 1991

Far too little heard of in the West, Vladimir Krainev shows how sheerly exciting these concertos can be in the hands of a virtuoso on top form. Here are the dash and flamboyance, the spacious and rhythmic grasp, the balletic poise and acrobatic daredevilry which announce a born Prokofiev player. Only in the Third Concerto, far and away the most popular of the five, does Krainev succumb to the temptations of smash-and-grab overstatement. In this case the first movement pushes forward in a crude, attention-grabbing manner, the second is laboured in places, and the finale is again rather roughly handled. Not that pussy-footing is what Prokofiev needs, but here the impression is of a foreground-only portrait of the music.

The finest performances are of the First, Fourth and Fifth Concertos, all of which have a splendid cut and thrust. Krainev revels in their extravagance and physicality, and he is backed up by beautifully prepared, sensitive orchestral playing. The massive Second Concerto is also fine, though here the recorded balance tends to swallow up important woodwind solo lines in a generalized warmth of ambience (elsewhere, for the most part, this warmth is a definite advantage). This set can hold its own against most of the competition.

Piano Concertos Nos 1 and 3[a]
Evgeni Kissin *pf*
Berlin Philharmonic Orchestra / Claudio Abbado
DG 439 898-2GH (42 minutes: DDD). Item marked [a] Ⓕ
recorded live in 1993 ●

Kissin always seems to have time to acknowledge the implications of Prokofiev's harmony, to allow the left hand to converse with the right (always naturally, never tricksily), and to gauge the relationship of his part to the orchestra. He is also scrupulous with dynamics. At the first entry in the C major Concerto he manages, as few pianists do, the *piano* contrast after the first three notes without losing soloistic presence. And he resists the temptation to shout out *forte* passages, so that Prokofiev's *fortissimos* stand in proper relief, as do his carefully placed accents (hear the opening theme of the same concerto's finale). Perhaps none of that strikes you as exceptional, but it is so in Prokofiev, where the sheer athletic demands are extreme and refinement seems like too much to ask. With a technique like his and an orchestra as responsive as the Berlin Philharmonic there are just a few places in the C major Concerto, such as the final pages, where Kissin might have allowed himself to be a bit more carried away. But there is no shortage of exhilaration in the youthful D flat Concerto, which is a model blend of attack, wit, poetry and drive. In fact there is little discernible difference between this studio recording and the live C major, either in accuracy or in excitement. It would be wrong to say that Kissin surpasses Ashkenazy (reviewed above). Bronfman on Sony Classical is virtually a match for him and offers the Fifth Concerto in addition. But DG's recording is clearer than the 20-year-old Decca set, and Abbado and the Berliners are far superior to Mehta and the Israel Philharmonic. Full price for 42 minutes of music may seem a bit steep; but what Kissin and Abbado have to offer is certainly in the luxury class.

Prokofiev Piano Concertos Nos 1 and 3
Bartók Piano Concerto No 3, Sz119
Martha Argerich *pf*
Montreal Symphony Orchestra / Charles Dutoit
EMI CDC5 56654-2 (70 minutes: DDD). Ⓕ
Recorded 1998 ●●

Martha Argerich's return to the studios in two concertos she has not previously recorded is an uplifting moment. As always with this most mercurial of virtuosos, her playing is generated very much by the mood of the moment, and those who heard her in Prokofiev's First Concerto with Riccardo Muti at London's Royal Festival Hall some years ago – a firestorm of a performance – may well be surprised at her relative geniality with Dutoit. Her entire reading is less hard-driven, her opening arguably more authentically *brioso* than ferocious, her overall view a refreshingly fanciful view of Prokofiev's youthful iconoclasm. The central *Andante assai* is inflected with an improvisatory freedom she would probably not have risked earlier in her career and in the *Allegro scherzando* she trips the light fantastic, reserving a suitably tigerish attack for the final octave bravura display. Again, while her performance of the Third Concerto is less fleet or nimble-fingered than in her early legendary disc for DG with Abbado (reviewed below); it is more delectably alive to passing caprice. Part-writing and expressive detail interest her more than in the past and there is no lack of virtuoso *frisson* in the first movement's concluding quasi-fugal *più mosso* chase. Once more Argerich is unusually sensitive in the central *Andantino*, to the fourth variation's plunge into Slavic melancholy and introspection. Personal and vivacious throughout, she always allows the composer his own voice.

This is true to an even greater extent in Bartók's Third Concerto where her rich experience in chamber music makes her often *primus inter pares*, a virtuoso who listens to her partners with the greatest care. In the *Adagio religioso* she achieves a poise that has sometimes eluded her in the past and her finale is specially characterful, her stealthy start to the concluding *Presto* allowing the final pages their full glory. Dutoit and the Montreal Symphony achieve a fine unity throughout. The recordings are clear and naturally balanced and only those in search of metallic thrills and rushes of blood to the head will feel disappointed.

Piano Concerto No 3[a]. Violin Concerto No 1 in D, Op 19[b]. Lieutenant Kijé – Suite, Op 60[c]
[a]**Martha Argerich** *pf* [b]**Shlomo Mintz** *vn*
[a]**Berlin Philharmonic Orchestra;** [bc]**Chicago Symphony Orchestra / Claudio Abbado**
DG Classikon 439 413-2GCL (69 minutes: ADD). Ⓑ
Recorded [a]1967, [b]1983, [c]1977

There have been others to match the bustle and brilliance of Argerich's Prokofiev, her coloristic range, her drive, her flashiness, her straining at the leash; but none who has so satisfyingly combined all those qualities, who has given us such a rocket-launched recapitulation in the first movement, such circus-routine vividness in the following variations, or such monstrous, hyperbolic fairy-tale imagery in the finale, and all done with the most engaging reckless abandon. Claudio Abbado has a highly-developed feeling for Prokofiev's sound world. Rarely has the fairy-tale atmosphere of the First Violin Concerto been more keenly evoked. He distills a sense of wonder and enchantment that is quite special. Textures are delicately coloured, dynamic nuances scrupulously observed and there are feather-light string sonorities.

Shlomo Mintz phrases with imagination and individuality; you need only hear the way he shapes the first bars for that to register. He plays with great polish and beauty of tone. Occasionally he colours a phrase by playing on the flat side of the note though his intonation is fine throughout. Abbado's otherwise excellent *Lieutenant Kijé* is marred by strange lapses of concentration from the Chicago Symphony Orchestra – split horn notes, a misread in the 'Troïka' (which is probably the movement you would most often want to play for friends) and some dicey solos besides. But mostly it's fine. The slightly grubby double-bass and saxophone solos in the 'Romance' are most characterful. The engineers produce a beautifully refined and homogeneous balance and it is very impressive indeed. There is plenty of space round the instruments and the sound is truthful.

Prokofiev Piano Concerto No 5[a] **Rachmaninov** 🄷
Piano Concerto No 2 in C minor, Op 18[b]
Sviatoslav Richter *pf*
Warsaw Philharmonic Orchestra / [a]**Witold Rowicki,** [b]**Stanislaw Wislocki**
DG 415 119-2GH (58 minutes: ADD). Ⓕ
Recorded 1959 **OO**

Prokofiev was to find no more dedicated an advocate for his keyboard works than Sviatoslav Richter. So how good that this artist's now legendary account of the Fifth Piano Concerto has been granted a new lease of life on CD. Although it has never really enjoyed the popularity of Prokofiev's Nos 1 and 3, here, however, attention is riveted from the very first note to the last. Richter delights in the music's rhythmic vitality and bite, its melodic and harmonic unpredictability. Both piano and orchestra are so clearly and vividly reproduced that it is difficult to believe the recording is actually 35 years old. Though betraying its age slightly more, notably in the sound of the keyboard itself, Rachmaninov's No 2 is certainly no less gripping. Not all of Richter's tempos conform to the score's suggested metronome markings, but his intensity is rivalled only by his breathtaking virtuosity. Never could the work's opening theme sound more laden, more deeply and darkly Russian.

Violin Concertos

No 1 in D, Op 19; **No 2** in G minor, Op 63

Violin Concertos Nos 1 and 2.
Solo Violin Sonata in D, Op 115
Gil Shaham *vn*
London Symphony Orchestra / André Previn
DG 447 758-2GH (60 minutes: DDD). Ⓕ
Recorded 1995

Rarely, if ever, have there been performances where soloist, orchestra and conductor all connect with such unerring intuition, where the music is treated so naturally. Previn ushers in the First Concerto's crystalline opening with gentle intensity, thereby raising the curtain for Gil Shaham's warmly tended first entry. Both make great play with the march theme that follows. The effect is almost like spicy gossip being shared between friends; the *Scherzo*, meanwhile, is equally rich in dialogue. Shaham's tone is at its most expressive at the beginning of the third movement, and at its most delicate just prior to the last big climax. This natural exegesis extends to the darker Second Concerto, even where Shaham or Previn linger about a particular phrase. The recording, too, is very impressive, with well defined string lines and a fine body of winds, brass and percussion (the all-important bass drum especially). Note how, beyond the raucous happenings of the second movement's central episode, the violins waft back with the principal theme (at 6'56"). Similar felicities occur regularly throughout both concertos, while the Second's finale – a riotous and slightly tongue-in-cheek *danse macabre* – is here sensibly paced and very well articulated. As if all that weren't enough, Shaham treats us to a substantial encore in the lively Solo Sonata that Prokofiev intended to be performed in unison by a group of young players.

Violin Concertos Nos 1 and 2
Itzhak Perlman *vn* **BBC Symphony Orchestra / Gennedy Rozhdestvensky** Ⓕ
EMI CDC7 47025-2. (49 minutes: DDD/ADD).

The catalogue contains enough recommendable rival versions of these technically demanding, astringent, yet warmly romantic concertos to suit all tastes (including Shaham, Mintz, Vengerov – in a *Gramophone* Award-winning performance, reviewed under Shostakovich – as well as Perlman). The mastery of Perlman's technique and feeling for these two works makes this a strong recommendation. The soloist is too far forward in the musical balance; yet one soon accepts this degree of prominence and very little of the fine orchestral detail is lost as a result. And so the final choice may well come down to Perlman's authority against the imagination and individuality of other interpreters. He is splendidly accompanied by Gennedy Rozhdestvensky and the BBC Symphony Orchestra.

Cinderella

Cinderella, Op 87. Summer Night – Suite, Op 123
Russian National Orchestra / Mikhail Pletnev Ⓕ
DG ② 445 830-2GH2 (138 minutes: DDD) **OO**

This is an outstanding release. There's simply no other way to describe it. If Mikhail Pletnev launches *Summer Night* somewhat brusquely, what follows is completely beyond reproach. Most striking of all is the radical clarity of texture which makes Prokofiev's modest suite seem at once unprecedentedly modern and that much more shrewdly realized in terms of colour. The score was extrapolated from the opera *The Duenna* (or *Betrothal in a Monastery*) in 1950 and its neglect, as Pletnev shows, is unaccountable. It is curious that a ballet as familiar as *Cinderella* should be so seldom heard in its entirety. Like *Romeo and Juliet*, *Cinderella* gives an impression of immense assurance, belying the hazards of cultural production under Stalin. It is strong without being daring, colourful without being extravagant, and again exhibits an emotional involvement often hidden in the past. This may sound reassuringly Tchaikovskian and yet there is also something pale and elusive in its make-up, something perhaps designed to reflect the character of its main protagonist.

The motif of Cinderella repressed, first heard at the very start of the ballet, is given a heavy tread, the Russian National Orchestra dragging its metaphorical feet to intensify the pensive mood. As for the second motto theme, anticipating her eventual happiness with her dream prince, it is not so much broad and impassioned as achingly beautiful. Nor is Pletnev's conducting without humour. The sisters' 'dancing lesson' has never been more vividly evoked than here, their unruly behaviour and slow learning curve precisely delineated in the truculent attack of the two solo violins. 'The Prince's first galop' (thrice he rushes off in search of his beloved) is as light as a feather, and is executed with matchless finesse by the Russian strings. The sound is good, the orchestral playing superb.

Cinderella[a]. Symphony No 1[b]
London Symphony Orchestra / André Previn
EMI Forte ② CZS5 68604-2
127 minutes: [a]DDD/[b]ADD). Synopsis included. Ⓜ
Recorded [a]1983, [b]1977

Previn's admirable *Cinderella* appeared originally on LP in 1983 but was never transferred to CD in its entirety, EMI opting for a single-disc 'highlights' compilation. It has come up quite beautifully in this transfer, the Abbey Road production (Grubb/Parker) possessing a most appealing warmth and lustre. Previn's imaginative, highly sympathetic direction combines warm-hearted affection as well as a most seductive theatrical flair (the whole of Act 2 is particularly memorable in this regard). Throughout, the LSO responds with considerable dash and character: occasionally, the strings are wanting in the last ounce of finesse and absolute technical security, but the woodwind contribution is especially felicitous. Comparing it with the immaculately honed but comparatively chilly Pletnev set, many may prefer this keenly priced reissue. Unfortunately, the 'bonus' item – an enthusiastic, but distractingly scrappy *Classical* Symphony is far from ideal. No matter, a bargain all the same.

Peter and the Wolf

Prokofiev Peter and the Wolf, Op 67[a]
Saint-Saëns Le carnaval des animaux[b]
[a]**Sir John Gielgud** *narr* **Academy of London / Richard Stamp**
Virgin Classics Ultraviolet CUV5 61137-2 Ⓜ
(51 minutes: DDD).

Gielgud matches Sir Ralph Richardson's actor's feeling for the words and relishes their sound as well as their meaning. He immediately sets his personal stamp in the introduction by the use of the older pronunciation of the word clarinet – here it is 'clarionet' – and he also savours the sound of the bassoon. The portrayal of the wolf by the horns makes an ominously bold contrast and the volley of gunfire from the hunters is spectacular. The story begins in an agreeably relaxed fashion, with delightful orchestral detail from the Academy players under the sympathetic direction of Stamp. The entry of the cat is a delicious moment with Sir John clearly involved with the creature's slinky cunning. High drama arrives at the moment of danger for the bird and later the superb climax where the wolf catches the duck has never been more tellingly brought off on record. The echo of the duck's theme on the plaintive oboe, when it is all too quickly a *fait accompli*, is wonderfully pathetic. The final jaunty processional is a joy. The account of *Le carnaval des animaux* is equally successful. The whole performance has the breezy spontaneity of a live occasion and, again, the warmly resonant acoustics of the recording add to the feeling of atmosphere and sense of occasion. There are many touches of individuality: the 'Tortoises' move their way through Saint-Saëns's geriatric version of Offenbach's can-can with a dignified serenity; the 'Elephant', represented by a solo double-bass, has an air almost of melancholy, while the 'Kangaroos' hop jauntily and the 'Fossils' dance with a percussive skeletonic clatter. There is a splendid clarinet solo here from Angela Malsbury and she also echoes the cuckoo's notes engagingly. The 'Pianists' are suitably ponderous in their own self-parody, although perhaps they could have stumbled more convincingly. Their playing elsewhere has fine virtuosity and their bravura helps to make the final parade really exhilarating. Some might feel that the famous 'Swan' cello solo is a shade too recessed but it makes the contrast with the finale which bursts in on the listener – the more effective. This realease comes highly recommended.

Romeo and Juliet

Cleveland Orchestra / Lorin Maazel
Decca Double ② 452 970-2DF2 (141 minutes: ADD). Ⓜ
Synopsis included. Recorded 1973 **OO**

It was George Szell who made the Cleveland Orchestra into a highly responsive virtuoso body, and when he died in 1970 he was in due course succeeded by Lorin Maazel, himself a renowned orchestral trainer. Here is Maazel's first Cleveland recording of Prokofiev's masterpiece, *Romeo and Juliet*, notable for a quite outstanding quality of orchestral playing. The strings in particular have a remarkable depth of tone, though they play with great delicacy when it is needed; but then the orchestra as a whole plays with extraordinary virtuosity, tonal weight and exactness of ensemble. If the woodwind have a somewhat piquant blend this suits the music, which is admirably served by Maazel's highly rhythmic, dramatic conducting. This vibrant complete recording, reissued yet again on CD, has the added advantage of being at mid-price and there is a useful synopsis in the notes. If the orchestral playing is a notable feature, so is the high-quality recording, which is well balanced and wide in range. It suffers little beside the best of today and is indeed a tribute to the excellent standards which Decca engineers achieved in the early 1970s. There are many fine versions in the catalogue but none surpasses this for passionate feeling, extraordinary orchestral virtuosity and colour. The Cleveland never made a finer recording than this.

Romeo and Juliet, Op 64
London Symphony Orchestra / André Previn
EMI Forte ② CZS5 68607-2 (149 minutes: ADD). Ⓜ
Notes included. Recorded 1973

It is good to have André Previn's set of *Romeo and Juliet* restored to circulation at such a reasonable price. The EMI recording (masterminded by Christopher Parker) still sounds pretty sumptuous and the legendary Kingsway bloom remains mercifully intact on CD. Compared with Maazel's dazzlingly assured Clevelanders, Previn's hard-working London Symphony Orchestra can sound just a touch cautious and technically fallible. Yet Previn's affectionate, wittily pointed reading has its place too: many will rightly respond to its sense of easy spontaneity, tender restraint and unaffected honesty. It is, in sum, a more relaxed, less relentlessly high-powered affair than his distinguished transatlantic rivals, but no less compelling for all of that.

Romeo and Juliet, Op 64
Kirov Theatre Orchestra / Valery Gergiev
Philips 50 Great Recordings ② 464 726-2PM2 Ⓜ
(144 minutes: DDD). Recorded 1990

This great ballet score has been very lucky on records. Both Previn's EMI set and the Decca Maazel recording, are very distinguished and make a powerful impression on the listener. This Russian recording could not be more different. It was made in the Kirov Theatre in Leningrad and has the fullness and amplitude characteristic of the finest western recordings, not surprising, as the recording team was from Philips. The orchestral playing, too, is superb by any international standard and has none of the sharp edges or raucousness we used to associate with Soviet *fortissimos*. Indeed, if there were a criticism of the playing it would be to suggest it is at times almost over-cultivated. The Introduction has a striking grace and flexibility, a sophistication of light and shade that some listeners might not expect. The action of the opening street scene and the sequence of events which follows is delineated with much delicacy of effect, crisp clear rhythms, great energy when called for, in the 'Morning dance', for instance and the most stylish instrumental response from all departments of the orchestra.

Perhaps it is all a shade mellow (Maazel demonstrated how pungent Prokofiev's scoring could sound) and the mood of the 'Balcony scene' is pure romanticism, relaxed and without sexual ardour: the strings float ethereally, there is a beautifully played violin solo, and at the climax the listener is quite carried away. The great climax of 'Juliet's funeral' (track 20) generates richly intense string playing and resoundingly powerful brass. But there is no sense of utter despair. So this is a performance to enjoy for the lyric feeling of Prokofiev's score and for the marvellous orchestral playing, but the starkness of the tragedy is more heart-rendingly conveyed elsewhere.

Complete symphonies

No 1 in D, Op 25, 'Classical'; **No 2** in D minor, Op 40; **No 3** in C minor, Op 44; **No 4** in C, Op 47 **(original 1930 version)**; **No 4** in C, Op 112 **(revised 1947 version)**; **No 5** in B flat, Op 100; **No 6** in E flat minor, Op 111; **No 7** in C sharp minor, Op 131

Awards 1985

Symphonies Nos 1-7
Royal Scottish National Orchestra / Neeme Järvi
Chandos ④ CHAN8931/4 Ⓕ
(260 minutes: DDD) ○○○

Prokofiev was not a natural symphonist. Albeit successful in emulating Haydn in the *Classical* Symphony, the Sixth Symphony is his only undisputed integrated symphonic structure (and an epic-tragic utterance as intense as any by Shostakovich). It has been suggested that his symphonies all have a sense of some unstaged scenario, and the Third and Fourth (and to a lesser extent, the Seventh) Symphonies actually rework material from his music for the stage. The Fourth (in both versions) in particular fails to convince as a symphony owing to the profusion and individuality of its often strikingly beautiful thematic ideas – it's a real patchwork quilt of a piece. Enter Neeme Järvi, nothing if not a man of the theatre, to give maximum dramatic intensity and character to all Prokofiev's ideas, whether they add up symphonically or not; capable of overawing his Scottish forces into playing of aerial lightness and easeful lyricism in the *Classical* Symphony, and pulling no punches where Prokofiev's inspiration (as in the Second and Third Symphonies) is at its most strident, violent and hysterical. Make no mistake, though, these are also readings of real stature: where there is symphonic 'line', Järvi unerringly finds it. Drawbacks? Some may feel the need for a deeper pile of string sound, particularly in the Fifth Symphony; and these typically spacious Chandos productions do not always ensure adequate projection for the woodwind, but more often than not one cannot fail to be impressed by the coherence and co-ordination, both musically and technically, of some of this century's most fabulous and fraught orchestral essays. As a cycle, this is unlikely to be challenged for some time.

Symphonies Nos 1 and 5

Symphony No 1. Peter and the Wolf[a]. March in B flat minor, Op 99. Overture on Hebrew Themes, Op 34*bis*[b]
[a]**Sting** *narr* [b]**Stefan Vladar** *pf*
Chamber Orchestra of Europe / Claudio Abbado
DG 429 396-2GH (50 minutes: DDD). Ⓕ
Recorded 1986-90 ○

Abbado's elegant and graceful reading of the *Classical* Symphony is one of the finest in the catalogue, and is particularly notable for its beautifully shaped phrasing, clarity of inner detail and crisp articulation. He seems to make all the right choices at all the right tempos. His first movement, the right side of measured, is dapper in the best sense and marked by keen detailing in the fugal development: note the clinching flourish in the timpani line – an exciting touch. Everywhere is elegance and rhythmic grace. Abbado's strings tread air through the *Larghetto*, the finale is indeed *molto vivace* with quicksilver articulation from the COE woodwinds, chortling and darting in and around the bar-lines. Abbado and the multi-talented Sting offer a lively and beautifully crafted account of Prokofiev's ever popular *Peter and the Wolf*. Any fears that the original freshness of Prokofiev's creation may be lost in favour of a less formal approach are soon dispelled – Sting is an effective and intelligent storyteller capable of capturing the imagination of adults and children alike, and there is never a feeling of contrivance or mere gimmickry. The orchestral playing is a real delight too; sharply characterized and performed with great affection. The *Overture on Hebrew Themes* is more commonly heard in its drier, more acerbic version for clarinet, piano and string quartet, but makes a welcome and refreshing appearance on this disc in Prokofiev's own arrangement for small orchestra. The spry *March* in B flat is a wartime novelty which seems to scent victory: it's a little like *Kijé*'s Wedding march with a twist from a certain *Three Oranges* – this version of it will do very nicely.

Symphonies Nos 1 and 5
Berlin Philharmonic Orchestra / Herbert von Karajan Ⓜ
DG Galleria 437 253-2GGA (71 minutes: ADD). ○○○

The playing throughout the First Symphony is beautifully cultured and there is wonderful lightness and delicacy. The first movement could sparkle more and the same could be said of the finale, yet the slow movement is very beautiful indeed. The sound has marvellous clarity and definition as well as exemplary range. Even more than 30 years after its first release, Karajan's Fifth Symphony still remains incomparable. The playing has wonderful tonal sophistication and Karajan judges tempos to perfection so that the proportions seem quite perfect. The recording, too, is extremely well balanced and has excellent ambience, and this reissue strikes you as smoother and more refined than both the original LP and any previous reissue. No other available version of this symphony begins to match this in distinction and stature. Even at full price this would still sweep the board and at its mid-price level it is a clear first choice.

Symphony No 5. Scythian Suite, Op 20
City of Birmingham Symphony Orchestra / Sir Simon Rattle
EMI CDC7 54577-2 (64 minutes: DDD). Ⓕ
Recorded 1992

Here is a Prokofiev Fifth as vibrant, intelligent and meticulously prepared as you'd expect from this partnership. In the mighty opening movement, there's real mystery about those fairy-tale slumberings at the start of the development, and how naturally Rattle quickens the pulse during the pages which follow, the sense of expectancy and adventure palpably conveyed. Enter the coda, and Rattle's expertly graduated dynamics ensure a riveting succession of spectacular climaxes. Here, too, EMI's impressive recording opens out magnificently. Rattle's scherzo is a marvellously quick-witted conception, the slow movement etched with genuine tenderness and bustling good humour reigns supreme in the spirited finale. The coupling is a stunning *Scythian Suite*, combining foundation-threatening pagan spectacle and heart-stopping beauty in ideal equilibrium. Brilliant!

Prokofiev Symphony No 5[a]
Stravinsky The Rite of Spring[b]
Berlin Philharmonic Orchestra / Herbert von Karajan
DG The Originals 463 613-2GOR (78 minutes: ADD). Ⓜ
Recorded [a]1968 and [b]1977 ●●●

Karajan's 1968 Prokofiev Fifth is a great performance. Whenever one compares it with later versions inevitably the DG account holds its place at the top of the list. The analogue recording was uncommonly good for its time. With the advantage of the Jesus-Christus Kirche acoustics, the sound is full and spacious, naturally defined and balanced; there is a slightly leonine quality to the strings and a natural bloom on woodwind and brass. Karajan lived with the work for a decade before he recorded it and this is immediately apparent in the way the first movement unfolds so inevitably. The ironic opening of the *Scherzo* with its flawless BPO articulation brings a splendid but unexaggerated bite, and in the more lyrical central section every subtle detail of colour comes over. The passionate string threnody of the *Adagio* (what playing, what intensity!) is superbly underpinned by darker wind murmurings; the tangibly hushed close leads naturally to the mellower opening of the essentially upbeat finale with its throbbing horns and instant echoes of *Romeo and Juliet*.

Karajan's *Rite of Spring* came a decade later and is more controversial. Stravinsky had been sarcastically scathing about the conductor's earlier 1964 account, even describing one section as 'tempo di hoochie-koochie'. So, Karajan let the work rest, and when he re-recorded it in January 1977 it was done in one single uninterrupted take. The result has less visceral excitement than the composer's own version and is without the brutally barbaric precision of Muti's Philadelphia account (HMV Classics), or the unrelenting thrust and tautness of Solti. But it is still very rewarding, combining both the symphonic and balletic aspects of this extraordinary score, with the BPO providing much sheer beauty of sound, as in the ravishing melancholy of the opening of Part II and the haunting 'Evocation des ancêtres', although other versions find more pungent drama when the horns enter later (track 17, 1'51"). The Philharmonie sound is excellent and both CD transfers are expertly managed to retain the full character of the originals.

Symphonies Nos 1 and 7

Symphonies Nos 1 and 7. The Love for Three Oranges – Suite, Op 33*a* **H**
Philharmonia Orchestra / Nicolai Malko Ⓑ
Classics for Pleasure CD-CFP4523. Recorded 1955 ●

A good record is always a good record and this one is a very good one indeed. Considering the date of the recording, its quality is astonishing. The balance is excellent and the actual sound seems hardly dated. It is bright and vivid without being artificial and the natural resonance of the hall never clouds detail. The playing of the Philhamonia at its peak is marvellous: try the deliciously elegant string line in the *Larghetto* of the *Classical* Symphony, or the chortling humour of both strings and wind in the finale of the Seventh. What attractive works these are in Malko's hands, with delicacy and a warm but not cloying romanticism and with everything part of the overall picture. The suite from *The Love for Three Oranges* is no less tellingly characterized, the 'March' crisply buoyant, the romantic interlude touchingly lyrical. Highly recommended.

Violin Sonatas

Violin Sonatas – No 1 in F minor, Op 80; No 2 in D, Op 94*a*. Five Melodies, Op 35*b*
Vadim Repin *vn* **Boris Berezovsky** *pf*
Erato 0630-10698-2 (63 minutes: DDD). Ⓕ
Recorded 1995

A clear first choice in this repertoire and heartening confirmation of the young Vadim Repin's considerable violinistic skills. Tension sets in right from the First Sonata's opening bars: the tone is bright, sweet, tremulous and warmly expressive, while the music's sombre mood is precisely gauged. Repin phrases with considerable sensitivity and his attack in the work's faster episodes – the *Allegro brusco*'s outer sections and most of the finale – has a Heifetzian 'edge'. Nervous energy is also much in evidence, while the *Andante* – one of Prokofiev's most haunting creations – has a wistfully distracted air that Boris Berezovsky matches with some notably perceptive piano playing. The *Allegrissimo* finale, too, is arresting: deftly fingered, percussively insistent and with a truly heartfelt projection of the work's tender closing phrase. One of Repin's leading qualities is his obvious interpretative sincerity; nowhere does one sense the suave affectation that afflicts some of his contemporaries, a fact that registers with particular force in the Second Sonata's opening *Moderato*. Here lesser artists often sound either matter-of-fact or uninterested, and even superior ones opt for relative coolness. Repin and Berezovsky, on the other hand, are both tender and relaxed; phrasal 'crossfire' and keen inflexion keep sparks flying in the *Scherzo*, the *Allegretto leggiero e scherzando* is appropriately limpid, and although the finale could have swaggered more freely, there are magical moments to spare. Both players achieve an impressive range of colour throughout and the five delightful *Melodies* make for a welcome sequence of encores. Very well recorded.

Prokofiev Violin Sonata in D, Op 94*a* H
K Khachaturian Violin Sonata, Op 1
Szymanowski Violin Sonata in D minor, Op 9
David Oistrakh *vn* **Vladimir Yampolsky** *pf*
Testament mono SBT1113 (65 minutes: ADD). Ⓕ
Recorded 1955

David Oistrakh's playing is, at its best, a calming force in an agitated world – intelligent, considered (just occasionally overcalculated), invariably poised, big-toned and confident. You know what to expect and are rarely disappointed, and these excellent refurbishments of key Oistrakh performances from the 1950s lend a characteristic narrative quality to a wide variety of repertoire. Best perhaps is the Prokofiev sonata, which Oistrakh himself instigated in reaction to hearing the flute-and-piano original. The playing is quietly confidential in the first and third movements, pert in the *Scherzo* and exuberant in the closing *Allegro con brio*. Oistrakh's phrasing is incisive without sounding aggressive (most notes retain their full measure of tone, even at speed), while his handling of rhythm is both supple and muscular. Szymanowski's post-romantic Op 9 is lusciously full-toned and expertly negotiated by Yampolsky, while the reading of Karen Khachaturian's Op 1 – a pleasant piece that is reminiscent of Kabalevsky, the lighter Shostakovich and, very occasionally, Gershwin – proves to be another masterly performance, especially in the delightful *Andante*. All in all, this is a quite superb disc, expertly annotated and very well presented. The Prokofiev Second Sonata is as near 'definitive' as anyone has a right to expect, while the remainder is typical of a violinist whose aristocratic playing and artistic diplomacy were – and remain – an inspiration to us all.

Piano Sonatas

No 1 in F minor, Op 1; **No 2** in D minor, Op 14; **No 3** in A minor, Op 28; **No 4** in C minor, Op 29; **No 5** in C, Opp 38/135; **No 6** in A, Op 82; **No 7** in B flat, Op 83; **No 8** in B flat, Op 84; **No 9** in C, Op 103; **No 10** in E minor, Op 137

Piano Sonatas Nos 2 and 7. The Love for Three Oranges, Op 33*ter* – March. 10 Pieces from Cinderella, Op 97 – No 10, Waltz. Six Pieces from Cinderella, Op 102 – No 4, Amoroso. Three Pieces, Op 96 – No 1, War and Peace – Waltz, Op 96 No 1
Barry Douglas *pf*
RCA Victor Red Seal RD60779 (56 minutes: DDD). Ⓕ
Recorded 1991

There has often been a tendency with Prokofiev's piano music for pianists to overplay the percussive, steely qualities of the piano writing at the expense of the lyrical aspects. Barry Douglas, however, attains the perfect blend – muscular and athletic where power and agility are called for, but ever alert to the lyricism which lies beneath the surface. The Second Sonata is a prime example. Douglas has the full measure of this youthful, energetic masterpiece, and one feels that he has fully assimilated this piece before committing it to disc. The first movement with its restless oscillation between expressive melody and ruminative figuration is thoughtfully fashioned, and the knockabout scherzo and fleet-footed energetic finale are delivered with much vigour and flair. The Seventh Sonata (the central work of Prokofiev's 'War Trilogy') is impressive too, with Douglas fully in command of its bristling difficulties. As for the rest of the disc, Douglas offers some of the less frequently heard piano transcriptions, of which the delirious 'love' Waltz from *Cinderella* and the March from *The Love for Three Oranges* crave particular attention. The recording is beautifully engineered and balanced.

Prokofiev Piano Sonata No 8. Visions fugitives, Op 22 – Nos 3, 6 and 9
Debussy Estampes. Préludes, Book 1 – Voiles; Le vent dans la plaine; Les collines d'Anacapri
Scriabin Piano Sonata No 5 in F sharp, Op 53
Sviatoslav Richter *pf*
DG Dokumente 423 573-2GDO (67 minutes: ADD). Ⓜ
Recorded 1963 ●●●

Sviatoslav Richter has long been one of the most dedicated champions of Prokofiev's keyboard music, with the Eighth Sonata always particularly close to his heart. It would certainly be hard to imagine a more profoundly and intensely experienced performance than that to which we are treated here, or indeed one that demonstrates a greater degree of keyboard mastery. After the yearning introspection of the temperamental opening movement and the *Andante*'s evocation of a more gracious past, the rhythmic tension and sheer might of sonority he conjures in the finale make it is not difficult to understand why the composer's biographer, I V Nestyev, suspected some underlying programme culminating in 'heroic troops resolutely marching ahead, ready to crush anything in their path'. In the uniquely Prokofievian fantasy of the three brief *Visions fugitives* he is wholly bewitching. As for the Fifth Sonata of Scriabin, his impetuous start at once reveals his understanding of its manic extremities of mood. For just these Russian performances alone, this excellently refurbished disc can without any doubt be hailed as a collector's piece. And as a bonus there is Debussy too, with infinite subtleties of tonal shading to heighten atmospheric evocation.

Alexander Nevsky

Alexander Nevsky, Op 78. Scythian Suite, Op 20
Linda Finnie *sop* **Scottish National Chorus and Orchestra / Neeme Järvi**
Chandos CHAN8584 (60 minutes: DDD). Text and translation included. Ⓕ

At the chill opening of Järvi's fine version of *Alexander Nevsky* one can really feel the bitter wind of the Russian winter. The acoustics of the Caird Hall in Dundee where these Chandos recordings were made adds an extra atmospheric dimension to this splendidly recorded performance. The choral entry has an affecting poised melancholy, yet their geniality in the call to 'Arise ye Russian people' has a ring of peasantry. The 'Battle on the Ice' is the enormously spectacular climax, with the bizarre dissonance of the orchestral *scherzando* effects given tremendous pungency capped by the exhilarating shouts of fervour from the singers. Linda Finnie's contribution is most eloquent too and Järvi's apotheosis very moving. The *fortissimo* force of Chandos's recording is especially telling. As a coupling, Järvi chooses the ballet *Ala and Lolly*, originally written for Diaghilev which, when rejected by him, became the *Scythian Suite*. Its aggressive motoric rhythms are as powerful as anything Prokofiev wrote (indeed, their primitive force has an element of almost brutal ugliness to which you may not wholly respond) but the lyrical music is top-quality Prokofiev. 'It remains one of his most richly imaginative, harmonically sophisticated and wonderfully atmospheric scores', suggests Robert Layton in the notes. Certainly Järvi has its measure and so do the Chandos engineers, but it's not music for a small flat.

Ivan the Terrible, Op 116

Liubov Sokolova *mez* **Nikolai Putilin** *bar*
Chorus of the Kirov Opera; Rotterdam Philharmonic Orchestra / Valery Gergiev
Philips 456 645-2PH (65 minutes: DDD). Text and translation included. Recorded 1996 Ⓕ

This studio account of *Ivan* ranks with the best of Gergiev's opera recordings. Of course, recommending just one version for the collection is not easy when the work, rather like the film itself, does not exist in a definitive form. Part 1 of Eisenstein's masterpiece was released in 1946 to worldwide acclaim, although Stravinsky for one did not care for its mix of iconography and melodrama. Prokofiev's health was so poor that he recommended that Gavriil Popov take over as composer for Part 2. Later he was able to resume work on the project – only to find it withheld from distribution. Soviet officials found its portrayal of Ivan's psychological decline too negative and, no doubt, too close to home. Which is not to say that Prokofiev intended to encode any criticism of Stalin in the notes. The film was released in the USSR in 1958 by which time plans to complete the trilogy had been abandoned, its prime movers long dead. Prokofiev thought highly enough of the score to reuse sections of it, but he left no guidelines for presenting it in the concert hall. Reshaping the music to fit a chronological narrative, Abram Stasevich fabricated an overlong oratorio. Gergiev's version is based on Stasevich; only here the music is left to fend for itself without the interpolated Russian texts. The Russian choir and some notably forward timpani help Gergiev to build the right atmosphere. The wide vibrato of his young mezzo is nothing if not authentic and there will be no complaints about the robust singing of Nikolai Putilin. James Agee acclaimed the film as 'A visual opera, with all of opera's proper disregard of prose-level reality' but if you want to experience the music divorced from the images, then Gergiev's account is among the most sheerly dramatic.

Ivan the Terrible – complete film music
Irina Chistyakova *contr* **Dmitry Stepanovich** *bass*
Vesna Children's Choir; Yurlov State Capella; Tchaikovsky Symphony Orchestra / Vladimir Fedoseyev
Nimbus ② NI5662/3 (99 minutes: DDD). Ⓕ
Recorded 1998 ⭘

The present issue is a must for completists in that it is produced in association with a new edition of the score (1997), collating all that survives of the composer's contribution to the project. Indeed, Fedoseyev goes so far as to include music from the Russian Orthodox Liturgy that occurs in the completed films but is not actually by Prokofiev.

Confused? Let's recap. Part 1 of Eisenstein's masterpiece was released in 1946 to worldwide acclaim, though Stravinsky for one did not care for its mix of iconography and melodrama. In poor health, Prokofiev recommended that Gavriil Popov take over as composer for Part 2. Later he did after all resume work – only to find the film withheld from distribution. Soviet officials found its portrayal of Ivan's psychological decline too negative and, no doubt, too close to home. Which is not to say that Prokofiev intended to encode any criticism of Stalin in the notes. The film was released in the USSR in 1958, by which time plans to complete the trilogy had been abandoned, its prime movers long dead.

We know Prokofiev thought highly enough of the score to re-use sections of it, but he left no guidelines for presenting it in the concert hall. The oratorio we always used to hear was fashioned in 1962 by Abram Stasevich; it provided the missing element of continuity by reshaping the cues to fit a chronological narrative. Muti recorded this to superb effect. Christopher Palmer's solution for Järvi was to dispense with Stasevich's interpolated speaker, whereas Rostropovich revived the melodramatic element in an edition by Michael Lankester with English-language narration (Sony Classical – nla). Gergiev's forceful version left the music to fend for itself, but was still based on Stasevich.

By cutting out the middleman, Fedoseyev now goes to the top of the heap as the most scholarly option. Launching the endeavour with an encouraging groan, he produces a more convincing, well-prepared performance than many that have come out of Russia of late. Not all of what he presents is familiar even from the films, and there is a certain amount of crudely illustrative material. His orchestra, the present-day manifestation of the USSR broadcasting band with which Rozhdestvensky was associated in the 1960s and 1970s, acquits itself well: crude primary colours predominate, and the brass players avoid inauthentic finesse. Gergiev has only the mock-Soviets of the Rotterdam Philharmonic, though his Kirov chorus are not outclassed by the Yurlov State Capella deployed here. Admittedly, Fedoseyev's contralto is extremely Russian, which you may find difficult in 'The song of the beaver'. Nor does he race in with quite Gergiev's irresistible flair. That said, Nimbus's Moscow-made recording is technically much better than you might expect.

The two-disc package includes a helpful account of the working methods of Prokofiev and Eisenstein, while key episodes are discussed in more depth and cross-referenced to the relevant tracks. Eisenstein's fraught relationship with the authorities and the suppression of *Ivan* Part 3 are also discussed, an attempt being made to disentangle the score from its inescapably propagandist aspect. True, the project's public role as a glorification of Soviet tyranny need not be as dominant as it can seem to be in Stasevich's oratorio. Whether it is better served here may depend on your attitude to listening to music in short, sharp (albeit authenticated) bursts.

Betrothal in a Monastery

Nikolai Gassiev *ten* Don Jerome; **Alexander Gergalov** *bar* Ferdinand; **Anna Netrebko** *sop* Louisa; **Larissa Diadkova** *contr* Duenna; **Evgeny Akimov** *ten* Antonio; **Marianna Tarassova** *mez* Clara; **Sergei Alexashkin** *bass* Mendoza; **Yuri Shkliar** *bass* Don Carlos
Kirov Opera Chorus and Orchestra / Valery Gergiev
Philips ③ 462 107-2PH3 (153 minutes: DDD).
Notes, text and translation included. Ⓕ
Recorded live in 1997

Betrothal in a Monastery.
Alexei Maslennikov *ten* Don Jerome; **Vladimir Redkin** *bar* Ferdinand; **Lyudmilla Sergienko** *sop* Louisa; **Galina Borisova** *mez* Duenna; **Arkady Mishenkin** *ten* Antonio; **Marina Shutova** *mez* Clara; **Mikhail Krutikov** *bass* Mendoza; **Vladislav Verestnikov** *bass* Don Carlos
Bolshoi Theatre Chorus and Orchestra / Alexander Lazarev
Melodiya ② 74321 60318-2 (154 minutes: DDD). Ⓜ
Notes included. Recorded 1990

Prokofiev's genial *Betrothal in a Monastery* may not be his most consistently inspired score, but it is immensely likeable, so it's very welcome to have two first-rate recordings to fill what was a gap in the catalogue. Collectors following the Philips Kirov series will probably look forward to adding another handsome-looking light-blue box set to their shelves. But three full-price discs? With almost identical timings the Bolshoi performance fits comfortably on to two, and at mid-price the Melodiya issue works out (presumably) at roughly half the cost. Furthermore, Lazarev and his cast and orchestra are not a whit inferior to Gergiev and company, and the two conductors have very similar approaches to pacing and characterization. If anything the slightly saltier Bolshoi style is more appropriate than the smoother Kirov, and Melodiya's richer, more resonant studio recording is in many ways preferable to Philips's dry-throated theatre acoustic.

And yet, go for the Melodiya set and you have to do without the libretto. Who these days is prepared to forgo the text, especially given that the score, itself by no means easily obtainable, has the words in Russian only? Melodiya does admittedly supply a detailed synopsis (as does Philips, of course), and if you want to keep abreast of the three couples who finally plight their troths after a double elopement and a variety of disguises and mistaken identities, it's the synopsis rather than the text that you need. But for closer acquaintance, you need the words.

Though there's precious little to choose between the two casts, generally speaking the male roles are slightly more successful at the Bolshoi (in particular Alexei Maslennikov's Don Jerome is superior to the initially rather hoarse Nikolai Gassiev), while the female ones are better at the Kirov (this goes especially for Anna Netrebko's mellifluous Louisa). Both Duennas are appropriately fruity. The Moscow chorus savours its chance to cavort as drunken monks in Act 4 even more than do its St Petersburg counterparts. So faced with an either/or choice you may find yourself having to go for the Philips set for the sake of having the text and translation, but you will probably find it hard not to resent the unnecessary expense of the extra disc.

The Fiery Angel

Awards 1996

Galina Gorchakova *sop* Renata; **Sergei Leiferkus** *bar* Ruprecht; **Vladimir Galusin** *ten* Agrippa; **Konstantin Pluzhnikov** *ten* Mephistopheles; **Sergei Alexashkin** *bass* Faust; **Vladimir Ognovanko** *bass* Inquisitor; **Evgeni Boitsov** *ten* Jakob Glock; **Valery Lebed** *bass* Doctor; **Yuri Laptev** *ten* Mathias; **Mikhail Kit** *bar* Servant; **Evgenia Perlasova** *mez* Landlady; **Larissa Diadkova** *mez* Fortune teller; **Olga Markova-Mikhailenko** *contr* Mother Superior; **Yevgeny Fedotov** *bass* Innkeeper; **Mikhail Chernozhukov** *bass* First Neighbour; **Andrei Karabanov** *bar* Second Neighbour; **Gennadi Bezzubenkov** *bass* Third Neighbour; **Tatiana Kravtsova** *sop* First Nun; **Tatiana Filimoniva** *sop* Second Nun
Chorus and Orchestra of the Kirov Opera / Valery Gergiev
Philips ② 446 078-2PH2 (119 minutes: DDD) Ⓕ
Notes, text and translation included
Recorded live in1993 **ooo**

The opera is no blameless masterpiece – Prokofiev's indulgence in lurid sensationalism sometimes gets the better of his artistic judgement. But that sounds a pretty po-faced judgement in the face of the overwhelming power which so much of this score exudes. This Maryinsky performance comes live from what is clearly a highly-charged occasion in one of the world's great opera houses. That brings with it the disadvantage of a constrained opera-pit acoustic, which makes some of Prokofiev's over-the-top scoring seem pretty congested. But the immediacy and clarity of the sound, plus the orchestra's rhythmic grasp, ensures that the effect is still blood-curdling. If Leiferkus's distinctive rich baritone at first sounds a touch microphoney, the ear can soon adjust to that too, and Gorchakova brings intense beauty as well as intensity to Renata's hysterics, taking us right inside the psychological drama. The supporting roles are filled with distinction and this makes a huge difference to the sustaining of dramatic tension, the *crescendo* which Prokofiev aimed to build through his five acts. Considering the extent of the stage goings-on there is remarkably little audience distraction on the recording.

The Gambler

Sergei Alexashkin *bass* General; **Ljuba Kazarnovskaya** *sop* Pauline; **Vladimir Galuzin** *ten* Alexis; **Elena Obraztsova** *mez* Babulenka; **Nikolai Gassiev** *ten* Marquis; **Valery Lebed** *bass* Mr Astley; **Marianna Tarassova** *mez* Blanche; **Victor Vikhrov** *ten* Prince Nilsky, Croupier II; **Andrei Khramtsov** *bass* Baron, Tall Englishman; **Yuri Laptev** *ten* Potapych; **Grigory Karassev** *bass* Casino Director; **Vladimir Zhivopistsev** *ten* Croupier I; **Gennadi Bezzubenkov** *bass* Fat Englishman
Chorus and Orchestra of the Kirov Opera / Valery Gergiev
Philips ② 454 559-2PH2 (115 minutes: DDD). Notes, text and translation included. Ⓕ
Recorded 1996

Prokofiev's second opera is his most extreme, in its musical language if not in its story-line. Alexey, the eponymous Gambler, is a noble-born teacher in the service of Babulenka's nephew (the retired General); he has a love-hate relationship with the General's step-daughter Pauline, who makes him gamble with her money and humiliates him by forcing him to insult others for her amusement. She in turn has a love-hate relationship with the Marquis, who has a hold over her via the General's debts. Thinking to rid her of that hold, Alexis wins a colossal fortune and offers it to her. Seeing only further humiliation, however, she scorns the offer, leaving Alexey in despair. Prokofiev set Dostoyevsky's story using the peculiar Russian branch of Dialogue Opera that abandons all set pieces and rounded forms for the sake of supposed Realism and truthfulness to the text. None of the characters steps outside the unfolding events into lyrical self-declaration, and it's left to the orchestra to offer psychological commentary on the goings-on, in the most modernist language Prokofiev could conceive around 1916.

So *The Gambler* demands a double act of empathy on the part of the western listener: one to engage with a little-known musical tradition where 'normal' operatic expectations are deliberately not gratified; and further, to sense the powerful affinity of the Russian soul with the act of gambling, which it looks on not judgmentally but as symbolic of self-destructive obsession, the workings of Fate, and more. For anyone willing and able to make those leaps, this new recording should be a compelling experience. Gergiev's orchestra play like beings possessed, which is the only way to do justice to a piece like this. The sense of impending doom is powerfully conveyed, and in the big gambling scene of Act 4 the tension is screwed up to an extraordinary pitch. Vladimir Galuzin shows himself as having real stamina and fine dramatic presence as Alexey, and Sergei Alexashkin is appropriately solid as the General. Ljuba Kazarnovskaya is rather ordinary as Pauline, but when Elena Obraztsova enters as Babulenka, with a voice that would curdle milk at a hundred paces, there's a genuine *frisson* of theatrical presence at work, and the rest of the performance never looks back from that point. The recording quality is superior to the patched-together live recordings which are the norm for this valuable Russian opera series.

The Love for Three Oranges

Mikhail Kit *bass* King of Clubs; **Evgeny Akimov** *ten* Prince; **Larissa Diadkova** *mez* Princess Clarissa; **Alexander Morozov** *bass* Leandro; **Konstantin Pluzhnikov** *ten* Truffaldino; **Vassily Gerello** *bar* Pantaloon; **Vladimir Vaneev** *bass* Tchelio; **Larissa Shevchenko** *sop* Fata Morgana; **Zlata Bulycheva** *mez* Linetta; **Lia Shevtsova** *mez* Nicoletta; **Anna Netrebko** *sop* Ninetta; **Grigory Karasev** *bar* Cook; **Feodor Kuznetsov** *bass* Farfarello; Herald; **Olga Korzhenskaya** *mez* Smeraldina; **Yuri Zhikalov** *bar* Master of Ceremonies; **Kirov Opera Chorus and Orchestra / Valery Gergiev**
Philips ② 462 913-2PH2 (102 minutes: DDD. Ⓕ
Texts and translations included). Recorded live in 1997 and 1998 ●

Goldoni's play of 1761, adapted by Meyerhold in 1914 and set by Prokofiev four years later, was in many respects way ahead of its time. As Lionel Salter pointed out in his review of the Lyon Opera recording under Kent Nagano, it prefigured not only Brecht but also the Theatre of Cruelty and the Theatre of the Absurd. Prokofiev fell with relish on the scenario, seeing in it an opportunity to puncture the pretensions of the opera house, rather as Stephen Sondheim's *Into the Woods*, working from the opposite direction and with more meagre compositional resources, has more recently used fairy-tale to try to add pretensions to the musical theatre.

Musically *The Love for Three Oranges* builds on Rimsky-Korsakov's *The Golden Cockerel*; and in turn Shostakovich's *The Nose* seeks to build on Prokofiev. It's a fabulously imaginative score, never reliant on cliché, always light on its feet and gloriously orchestrated. All credit to Gergiev and his Kirov players for provoking these observations. This is the fifth of their Prokofiev opera series, and it more than lives up to the high standards already set.

Among the evil conspirators at the court of the King of Clubs there are admittedly some dryish-sounding voices. But the main roles are superbly taken, most notably by tenor Evgeny Akimov as the whining, hypochondriac Prince. Other outstanding contributions come from Grigory Karasev as the giant cook who guards the Three Oranges, Feodor Kuznetsov as the demon Farfarello, and Anna Netrebko as the last of the three Princesses eventually released from the Oranges.

The only current rival complete recording is Kent Nagano's. Like Gergiev he conducts a meticulously prepared account and one that is equally sharp in its etching of Prokofiev's caustic wit. Though his cast displays less vocal distinction in the principal roles, there is more consistency in the minor ones. They sing in French, which was the language of the opera's first performances in Chicago in 1920 (the composer himself collaborated on the translation). Given the nature of the story, the original Russian is perhaps less vital than with most of Prokofiev's operas, and in many ways the very best way to experience the work is in the vernacular. But it's wonderful to have the choice between the Russian and French versions, each magnificently served; serious opera-collectors will ideally need to have both.

The Kirov recording was made live in Amstersdam in sessions spaced 10 months apart. There are no obvious joins, and the warmer ambience of the Concertgebouw amply compensates for the Maryinsky Theatre's more concentrated atmosphere. Though there is a certain amount of variance in the miking of the voices, this is never more than the action itself invites. Inevitably the audience misses out on the visual element, which is more than usually crucial with this opera. Even so, some of theverbal and situational humour clearly gets across, and the applause is understandably tumultuous

Awards 1990

(sung in French)
Gabriel Bacquier *bar* King of Clubs; **Jean-Luc Viala** *ten* Prince; **Hélène Perraguin** *mez* Princess Clarissa; **Vincent Le Texier** *bass-bar* Leandro; **Georges Gautier** *ten* Truffaldino; **Didier Henry** *bar* Pantaloon, Farfarello, Master of Ceremonies; **Gregory Reinhart** *bass* Tchelio; **Michèle Lagrange** *sop* Fata Morgana; **Consuelo Caroli** *mez* Linetta; **Brigitte Fournier** *sop* Nicoletta; **Catherine Dubosc** *sop* Ninetta; **Jules Bastin** *bass* Cook; **Béatrice Uria Monzon** *mez* Smeraldina
Chorus and Orchestra of Lyon Opéra / Kent Nagano
Virgin Classics ② VCD7 59566-2 Ⓕ
(102 minutes: DDD). Notes, text and translation included. OOO

This is a zany story about a prince whose hypochondriac melancholy is lifted only at the sight of a malevolent witch tumbling over, in revenge for which she casts on him a love-spell for three oranges: in the ensuing complications he encounters an ogre's gigantic cook who goes gooey at the sight of a pretty ribbon, princesses inside two of the oranges die of oppressive desert heat, and the third is saved only by the intervention of various groups of 'spectators' who argue with each other on the stage. The music's brittle vivacity matches that of the plot, and though there are no set-pieces for the singers and there is practically no thematic development – the famous orchestral March and Scherzo are the only passages that reappear – the effervescent score is engaging.

The performance is full of zest, with lively orchestral playing and a cast that contains several outstanding members and not a single weak one; and the recording is extremely good. Those desirous of so doing can delve into the work's symbolism and identify the objects of its satire – principally Stanislavsky's naturalistic Moscow Arts Theatre: others can simply accept this as a thoroughly enjoyable romp.

Semyon Kotko

Tatiana Pavlovskaya *sop* Sofya; **Ekaterina Solovieva** *sop* Lyubka; **Lyudmila Filatova** *mez* Semyon's mother; **Olga Markova-Mikhailenko** *mez* Khivrya; **Olga Savova** *mez* Frosya; **Evgeny Akimov** *ten* Mikola; **Nikolai Gassiev** *ten* Klembovsky, Workman; **Viktor Lutsiuk** *ten* Semyon Kotko; **Vladimir Zhivopistev** *ten* German interpreter; **Viktor Chernomortsev** *bar* Tsaryov; **Yuri Laptev** *bar* Von Wierhof; **Gennady Bezzubenkov** *bass* Tkachenko; **Grigory Karasev** *bass* Ivasenko; **Andrei Khramtsov** *bass* German NCO, German sergeant; **Yevgeny Nikitin** *bass* Remeniuk
Kirov Opera Chorus and Orchestra / Valery Gergiev
Philips ② 464 605-2PH2 (137 minutes: DDD).
Text and translations included. Ⓕ
Live recording

Valentin Katayev's tale of a local hero getting his girl despite strife with a prospective in-law is the kind of thing an opera-lover would normally take in their stride. What makes *Semyon Kotko* hard to live with is not the fact that the soldier-boy returning to his village in the Ukraine at the end of the First World War is so unimpeachably virtuous, nor even that the Germans who break up the wedding preparations and lay waste to the village are so one-dimensionally villainous – it's rather that the reactionary-collaborator father-in-law-to-be, Tkachenko, is so obviously a token of Soviet propaganda.

Prokofiev would probably never have considered such subject-matter at all had it not been for the political climate of the late 1930s and he did his best to make a working compromise between the order of the day and the kind of melodious simplicity he wanted to cultivate. He took Katayev's prose-draft as it stood and sought to minimise its schematic and propagandist elements. In Act 3 he came up with two of his most effective 'dramatic *crescendos*', first for the arrival of the reactionary Ukrainian cavalry, then for the burning of Semyon's cottage.

There are more fine moments in Act 4, where the oppositional writing for Soviets and Germans has something of the power of *Alexander Nevsky*, composed just before the opera. There's also some attractively pungent folk-imitation writing in the second tableau of Act 1. Some less distinguished scenes suggest a rummaging through Prokofiev's cast-off ideas for all-purpose filler material, but such passages are not so extensive or so deadly as to destroy all enjoyment.

This splendid recording plugs another major gap in the discography of opera. Gergiev's interpretation is ardent and well paced, his orchestra is in fine fettle, and his soloists are of high quality. Prokofiev gives little or no opportunity for star turns, but Viktor Lutsiuk's Semyon is passionate and youthful-sounding, and Tatiana Pavlovskaya as his beloved Sofya is radiant. The recording is free from the dryness and sudden shifts of perspective that have dogged some previous issues in this Mariinsky series.

War and Peace

Lajos Miller *bar* Prince Andrei Bolkonsky; **Galina Vishnevskaya** *sop* Natasha Rostova; **Katherine Ciesinski** *mez* Sonya; **Maria Paunova** *mez* Maria Akhrosimova; **Dimiter Petkov** *bass* Count Ilya Rostov; **Wieslaw Ochman** *ten* Count Pytor Bezukhov; **Stefania Toczyska** *mez* Helena Bezukhova; **Nicolai Gedda** *ten* Anatol Kuragin; **Vladimir de Kanel** *bass-bar* Dolokhov; **Mira Zakai** *contr* Princess Maria Bolkonsky; **Malcolm Smith** *bass* Colonel Vasska Denisov; **Nicola Ghiuselev** *bass* Marshal Mikhail Kutuzov; **Eduard Tumagian** *bar* Napoleon Bonaparte
Radio France Chorus; French National Orchestra / Mstislav Rostropovich

Erato Libretto ④ 2292-45331-2 (247 minutes: DDD). Notes, text and translation included.
Recorded 1986 Ⓜ

Over four hours long, 72 characters, 13 scene changes: is it any wonder that Prokofiev's *War and Peace*, adapted from Tolstoy's famously epic novel, has had few performances and even fewer forays into the recording studio? At the front of the booklet Rostropovich recalls how, as Prokofiev lay dying, he reiterated one wish, that Rostropovich should make this opera known to the world. It comes as no surprise, then, to find a deeply committed performance from both soloists (only 45 of them due to some adroit doubling), chorus and orchestra. Prokofiev adapted the novel into seven 'peace' and six 'war' tableaux, thus sustaining drama through contrast throughout its Wagnerian length. With few exceptions the multinational cast sings in good Russian and among them Lajos Miller is particularly affecting as Prince Andrei, pleasingly ardent in his opening moonlit aria. The central female role of Natasha is taken by Galina Vishnevskaya. She sang the role in the 1959 première and inevitably no longer sounds like an innocent 16 year old. Unfortunately, problems are compounded by a hardness in her tone and a lack of attention to detail in some of the quieter sections. Stefania Toczyska as the treacherous Helena makes a great impression, as does Katherine Ciesinski as Natasha's confidante, Sonya. Of the men, Nicolai Gedda as Prince Anatol sings with character and great style and Eduard Tumagian is an heroic and steadfast Napoleon. An added attraction of the recording are the sound effects, particularly in the war scenes, convincing but never too obtrusive. Good translations are provided in three languages, crowning a laudable achievement.

Francesco Provenzale

Italian 1624-1704

GROVE *Active in Naples, Provenzale had operas staged between 1654 and 1674 and became city maestro di cappella in 1665; he was later maestro di capella to the treasury of S Gennaro (1686-99) and served for two periods at the viceregal court. An important teacher, he worked as chief maestro at the conservatories S Maria di Loreto (1663-75) and the Turchini (1675-1701). He was the first prominent Neapolitan musician to compose opera and forerunner of the Neapolitan school of the 18th century. Il schiavo di sua moglie (1671) and La Stellidaura vendicata (1674), which survive complete, are largely modelled on the style of Venetians such as Cesti, but also include melodies of a dance-like, popular character. Provenzale wrote at least six other operas (two may have been adaptations of Cavalli's), secular cantatas and sacred music.*

Motets

Provenzale Cantemus, psallamus. O Jesu mea spes. Audite caeli. Angelicae mentes **P**
Avitrano Sonate a Quattro, Op 3 – No 2 in D, 'L'Aragona'; No 10 in C, 'La Maddaloni'
Marchitelli Sonata II
Roberta Invernizzi, Emanuela Galli *sops* **Giuseppe de Vittorio** *ten* **Cappella de' Turchini / Antonio Florio** *vc*

Opus 111 OPS30-211 (62 minutes: DDD). Ⓕ
Texts and translations included. Recorded 1998 ●

Antonio Florio and Cappella de' Turchini's ambitious survey of the finest baroque Neapolitan music turns to the well-nigh accepted father of the so-called Neapolitan School, Francesco Provenzale. Whilst scholars have argued that much of what is deemed 'Neapolitan' is really just 'Italian', this series has proved that such a view shows a limited knowledge of both the sources and the sheer range of musical idioms and 'dialects' which became established in the second half of the 17th century. Provenzale's three motets for two sopranos, published in 1689 (*Audite caeli* is for soprano and tenor) are hardly masterpieces but they are still good.

The bold challenges to the singer's techniques are often thrilling, but the flavour is less one of operatic transplantation than an indigenous sacred virtuosity which Provenzale jealously guarded; both the extensive *O Jesu mea spes* and *Angelicae mentes* see both Roberta Invernizzi and Emanuela Galli put through their paces, but they both sail through with well-matched timbres and nonchalant Mediterranean breeziness; only occasionally does their instinct for spontaneous moulding lead to questionable intonation. For the most part, the easy, imitative dialogue of

Provenzale's motets are revitalized by textually alert and finely projected singing. Of the instrumental interludes, Marchitelli's Sonata II for three violins is a real winner.

Giacomo Puccini Italian 1858-1924

GROVE *Puccini was fifth in a line of composers from Lucca. After studying music with his uncle, Fortunato Magi, and with the director of the Istituto Musicale Pacini, Carlo Angeloni, he started his career at the age of 14 as an organist at S Martino and S Michele, Lucca, and at other local churches. However, a performance of Verdi's Aida at Pisa in 1876 made such an impact on him that he decided to follow his instinct for operatic composition. With a scholarship and financial support from an uncle, he was able to enter the Milan Conservatory in 1880, where his chief teachers were Bazzini and Ponchielli.*

While still a student, Puccini entered a competition for a one-act opera. He failed to win, but the opera Le villi came to the attention of the publisher Giulio Ricordi, who arranged a successful production at the Teatro del Verme in Milan and commissioned a second opera. The libretto, Edgar, was unsuited to Puccini's dramatic talent and the opera was coolly received at La Scala in April 1889. It did, however, set the seal on what was to be Puccini's lifelong association with the house of Ricordi.

Manon Lescaut. produced at Turin in 1893, achieved a success such as Puccini was never to repeat and made him known outside Italy. Among the writers who worked on its libretto were Luigi Illica and Giuseppe Giacosa, who provided the librettos for Puccini's next three operas. The first of these, La bohème, widely considered Puccini's masterpiece, but with its mixture of lighthearted and sentimental scenes and its largely conversational style was not a success when produced at Turin in 1896. Tosca, Puccini's first excursion into verismo, was more enthusiastically received by the Roman audience at the Teatro Costanzi in 1900.

Later that year Puccini visited London and saw David Belasco's one-act play Madam Butterfly. This he took as the basis for his next collaboration and he considered it the best and technically most advanced opera he had written. He was unprepared for the fiasco attending its first performance in February 1904, when the La Scala audience was urged into hostility, even pandemonium, by the composer's jealous rivals; in a revised version it was given to great acclaim at Brescia the following May. By then Puccini had married Elvira Gemignani, the widow of a Lucca merchant, who had borne him a son as long ago as 1896. The family lived until 1921 in the house at Torre del Lago which Puccini had acquired in 1891. Scandal was unleashed in 1909 when a servant girl of the Puccinis, whom Elvira had accused of an intimate relationship with her husband, committed suicide. A court case established the girl's innocence, but the publicity affected Puccini deeply and was the main reason for the long period before his next opera.

This was La fanciulla del West, based on another Belasco drama it was given its première at the Metropolitan Opera, New York, in December 1910. In all technical respects, notably its Debussian harmony and Straussian orchestration, it was a masterly reply to the criticism that Puccini repeated himself in every new opera. What it lacks is the incandescent phrase, and this is probably why it has not entered the normal repertory outside Italy.

Differences with Tito Ricordi, head of the firm since 1912, led Puccini to accept a commission for an operetta from the directors of the Vienna Karltheater. The result, La rondine, though warmly received at Monte Carlo in 1917, is among Puccini's weakest works, hovering between opera and operetta and devoid of striking lyrical melody. While working on it Puccini began the composition of Il tabarro, the first of three one-act operas (Il trittico) which follow the scheme of the Parisian Grand Guignol - a horrific episode, a sentimental tragedy (Suor Angelica) and a comedy or farce (Gianni Schicchi). This last has proved to be the most enduring part of the triptych and is often done without the others, usually in a double bill.

In his early 60s Puccini was determined to 'strike out on new paths' and started work on Turandot, based on a Gozzi play which satisfied his desire for a subject with a fantastic, fairy-tale atmosphere, but flesh-and-blood characters. During its composition he moved to Viareggio and in 1923 developed cancer of the throat. Treatment at a Brussels clinic seemed successful, but his heart could not stand the strain and he died, leaving Turandot unfinished. After his wife's death in 1930, his house at Torre del Lago was turned into a museum.

Puccini's choral, orchestral and instrumental works, dating mainly from his early years, are unimportant, though the Mass in A flat (1880) is still performed occasionally. His operas may not engage us on as many different levels as do those of Mozart, Wagner, Verdi or Strauss, but on his own most characteristic level, where erotic passion, sensuality, tenderness, pathos and despair meet and fuse, he was an unrivalled master. His melodic gift and harmonic sensibility, his consummate skill in orchestration and unerring sense of theatre combined to create a style that was wholly original, homogeneous and compelling. He was fully aware of his limitations and rarely ventured beyond them. He represents Verdi's only true successor, and his greatest masterpiece and swansong, Turandot, belongs among the last 20th-century stage works to remain in the regular repertory of the world's opera houses.

Opera arias

La rondine – Chi il bel sogno di Doretta. La bohème – Sì, mi chiamano Mimì; Donde lieta uscì. Gianni Schicchi – O mio babbino caro. Manon Lescaut – In quelle trine morbide; Sola, perduta, abbandonata. Suor Angelica – Senza mamma, O bimbo. Tosca – Vissi d'arte. Madama Butterfly – Un bel dì vedremo; Che tua madre; Tu, tu, piccolo iddio. Turandot – Signore, ascolta!; In questa reggia; Tu, che di gel sei cinta

Julia Varady *sop*

Berlin Radio Symphony Orchestra / Marcello Viotti

Orfeo C323941A (52 minutes: DDD). Ⓕ

Recorded 1993 **oo**

A lovely and somewhat surprising record by the most fascinating and patrician lyric soprano of the present age: 'surprising' because, though Varady is associated closely enough with Verdi, the Puccini connection is less readily made, 'lovely' because the voice is still so pure, the style so musical and the response so intelligent, immediate and full-hearted. She adjusts wonderfully well to the Italian idiom, lightening the vowels, freeing the upper range, allowing more *portamento* than she would probably do in other music, yet employing in its use the finest technical skill and artistic judgement.

Her singing of Magda's song in *La rondine* opens the record and introduces a singer who sounds (give or take a little) half her actual age: Varady's début dates back to 1962. In Mimì's narrative she sings with so fine a perception of the character – the hesitancies, the joy in 'mi piaccion quelle cose' – that Schwarzkopf's exquisite recording comes to mind, just as, from time to time, and especially in the *Madama Butterfly* excerpts, the finely concentrated, tragic restraint of Meta Seinemeyer is recalled. It is good to hear, too, how sensitively Varady differentiates between characters, Manon Lescaut having that essential degree of additional sophistication in tone and manner. What runs as a thread through all of these characterizations is a feeling for their dignity. Mimì does not simper. Sister Angelica does not sob. Lauretta has resolution in her pleading. Butterfly, Liù and Tosca are what they should be: women whose pathos lies not in their weakness but in a passionate, single-minded fidelity. That leaves Turandot which is a mistake. That is, she is outside the singer's scope and should remain so: it is not merely a matter of vocal thrust, weight and stamina, but also of voice-character, although the performance of her aria has clear merits. None of which should deter purchase; overall this is singing to treasure.

Turandot – Non piangere, Liù!; Nessun dorma!. Gianni Schicchi – Avete torto! Firenze è come un albero fiorito. Il Tabarro – Hai ben ragione; Io voglio la tua bocca … Folle di gelosia!. La rondine – Parigi! è la citta dei desideri … Forse, come la rondine; Dimmi che vuoi seguirmi. La fanciulla del West – Una parola sola! … Or son sei mesi; Risparmiate lo scherno … Ch'ella mi creda libero. Madama Butterfly – Dipende dal grado di cottura … Amore o grillo; Addio, fiorito asil. Tosca – Recondita armonia; E lucevan le stelle. La bohème – Che gelida manina. Manon Lescaut – Tra voi, belle; Donna non vidi mai; Ah! Manon, mi tradisce; Ah! non v'avvicinate!; Manon … senti, amor mio … Vedi, son io che piango. Edgar – Orgia, chimera dall'occhio vitreo. Le villi – Ecco la casa … Torna ai felici dì

José Cura *ten*

Philharmonia Orchestra / Plácido Domingo

Erato 0630-18838-2 (71 minutes: DDD). Texts and translations included. Recorded 1997 Ⓕ

For those of us who can feast on a good tenor voice as if there were no tomorrow, this is (to put it crudely) the goods. First, however, a peculiarity of this programme is that it goes backwards. It starts with *Turandot* and recedes along a strict chronological line to *Le villi*. That of itself is an attractive idea, but it means that the terminus is a long and somewhat inconclusive excerpt, while the starting-point is 'Nessun dorma!'. We all know what that means these days, and it looks suspiciously like making a bid for the market if not for the kingdom. A dark, rather throaty, big and uncharming voice reiterates the famous command. As it takes the high As we realize that this is special, rising easily and thrillingly out of the baritonal middle register; Cura holds his high B ('vincerò') for the maximum length compatible with holding on to the succeeding A for even longer. But he is a man with surprises in store. 'Non piangere, Liù!' begins quietly and is thoughtfully phrased. Similarly he shows his unpredictability in the *Tosca* arias: 'Recondita armonia' is stolid, almost routine, but then 'E lucevan le stelle' becomes the real expression of a man facing up to the prospect of imminent execution, and writing a poem. Throughout, Cura displays a thrilling voice with an individual timbre. His 'face' wears too much of a scowl and he does not give the impression of thinking about the person he is nominally addressing, but this is a solo recital and perhaps it would be different in a complete opera. He is accompanied here with uncommon sympathy by a conductor who has a good deal more experience of singing than has the singer himself.

La bohème

Victoria de los Angeles *sop* Mimì; **Jussi Björling** *ten* Rodolfo; **Lucine Amara** *sop* Musetta; **Robert Merrill** *bar* Marcello; **John Reardon** *bar* Schaunard; **Giorgio Tozzi** *bass* Colline; **Fernando Corena** *bass* Benoit, Alcindoro; **William Nahr** *ten* Parpignol; **Thomas Powell** *bar* Customs Official; **George del Monte** *bar* Sergeant H

Columbus Boychoir; RCA Victor Chorus and Orchestra / Sir Thomas Beecham

EMI mono ② CDS5 56236-2 (108 minutes: ADD). Notes, text and translation included. Ⓕ

Recorded 1956 ○○○

The disadvantages of this famous Beecham *Bohème* are obvious. It is a mono recording and restricted in dynamic range. The sense of space for the complex crowd scene of Act 2 is to emerge with the maximum impact is inevitably lacking; the climaxes here and elsewhere are somewhat constricted; no less important, it is sometimes harder to focus on the subtleties of Puccini's orchestration. It was also made in a great hurry, and this shows in a number of patches of slightly insecure ensemble, even a couple of wrong entries. But there is no other important respect in which it does not stand at least half a head (often head and shoulders) above its more recent rivals. Nobody has ever been so predestinately right for the role of Mimì than Victoria de los Angeles: right both in vocal quality and in sheer involvement with every word and every musical phrase that Mimì utters. Beyond a certain point (usually a certain dynamic level) most sopranos stop being Mimì and simply produce the same sound that they would if they were singing Aida or Tosca. De los Angeles rarely does this; even under pressure (and Beecham's unhurried tempos do put her under pressure at times), the very difficulties themselves are used as an expressive and interpretative resource. Hers is the most moving and involving Mimì ever recorded. And Björling's is the most musical Rodolfo. He has the reputation of having been a bit of a dry stick, dramatically (on stage he looked like the other Bohemians' elderly, portly uncle), but on record he is the one exponent of the role to be credible both as a lover and as a poet. His voice is fine silver rather than brass, it can caress as well as weep, and his love for Mimì is more often confided than it is bellowed for all Paris to hear. This, indeed, is one of the most conspicuous differences between Beecham's account and most others: its simple belief that when Puccini wrote *pp* he meant it. Beecham (whose spell over his entire cast – in which there is no weak link – extends as far as teaching his Schaunard, John Reardon, an irresistibly funny, cut-glass English accent for the parrot-fancying milord) makes one realize what an intimate opera this is, how much of it is quiet, how many of its exchanges are *sotto voce*, and he thus enables his singers to use the full range of their voices and to employ subtleties of colour, phrasing and diction that are simply not available to a voice at full stretch (and in the process he largely cancels out the disadvantage of his recording's restricted dynamic range). It is the same with his handling of the orchestra: one would expect Beecham to seem understated, but again and again one turns back to his reading and discovers nothing missing – he has achieved as much or more with less. This is as complete a distillation of Puccini's drama as you are likely to hear.

La bohème
Mirella Freni *sop* Mimì; **Luciano Pavarotti** *ten* Rodolfo; **Elizabeth Harwood** *sop* Musetta; **Rolando Panerai** *bar* Marcello; **Gianni Maffeo** *bar* Schaunard; **Nicolai Ghiaurov** *bass* Colline; **Michel Sénéchal** *bass* Benoit, Alcindoro; **Gernot Pietsch** *ten* Parpignol
Schoenberg Boys' Choir; Berlin German Opera Chorus; Berlin Philharmonic Orchestra / Herbert von Karajan
Decca ② 421 049-2DH2 (110 minutes: ADD). Notes, text and translation included. Recorded 1972 Ⓕ

Pavarotti's Rodolfo is perhaps the best thing he has ever done: not only the finest recorded account of the role since Björling's on the Beecham set, but adding the honeyed Italianate warmth that even Björling lacked. He cannot quite match Björling's poetic refinement, and he is less willing to sing really quietly, but Pavarotti's sincerity counts for a great deal: his pride as he declares his vocation as a poet, the desperate feigning of his 'Mimì è una civetta' are points that most tenors miss or treat as mere opportunities for a big sing. His latter-day image may tend to hide it, but this recording is a reminder that Pavarotti is an artist of intelligence and delicacy as well as splendour of voice. His Mimì, Freni, sings beautifully and sensitively. Panerai is a strong, vividly acted Marcello. Harwood is an interesting Musetta: her tiny narration, in Act 4, of her meeting with the stricken Mimì is a gripping moment, and her waltz-song in Act 2 is a passionate (and irresistible) avowal to Marcello. Karajan is a great Puccini conductor who can linger over the beauties of orchestration without losing his grip on the drama or relaxing his support of the singers. There are not many operas of which a better case can be made for having more than one account in one's collection. For a modern *La bohème* to supplement the Beecham this Karajan set must go to the top of the list.

La bohème (sung in English)
Cynthia Haymon *sop* Mimì; **Dennis O'Neill** *ten* Rodolfo; **Marie McLaughlin** *sop* Musetta; **Alan Opie** *bar* Marcello; **William Dazeley** *bar* Schaunard; **Alastair Miles** *bass* Colline; **Andrew Shore** *bar* Benoit, Alcindoro; **Mark Milhofer** *ten* Parpignol; **Simon Preece** *bar* Customs Official; **Paul Parfitt** *bass-bar* Sergeant
Peter Kay Children's Choir; Geoffrey Mitchell Choir; Philharmonia Orchestra / David Parry
Chandos Opera in English ② CHAN3008 (111 minutes: DDD). Notes and text included. Ⓕ
Recorded 1997

The text (Grist and Pinkerton amended by David Parry) is a very acceptable rendering of a libretto which was, after all, first known in England, in English. However well sung, that first performance, at Manchester in 1897, is unlikely to have offered orchestral playing as fine as the Philharmonia's here, and Parry's well-controlled tempo is another strong factor in making this a special recording of the opera irrespective of language.

The singers have that first requisite of a good *Bohème* cast: they work as a team. Cynthia Haymon is a gentle Mimì, perfectly lovely in the middle register of her voice, just a little worn on top. Dennis O'Neill provides a rare pleasure in this music, singing softly at the right moments; he also produces such a very good top C in his aria that he has no need to give us another at the end of the Act instead of obliging with the composer's harmonies. Marie McLaughlin's Musetta is not quite the sparkler one had in mind, but the fellow Bohemians are capital, in voice as in spirits. The ensemble in Act 2 is first-rate, the contribution of the Peter Kay Children's Choir even better than that. The recording is superb.

Additional recommendation
La bohème
Carreras Rodolfo **Ricciarelli** Mimì **Putnam** Musetta **Wixell** Marcello
Royal Opera House Chorus and Orchestra / C Davis
Philips ② 442 260-2PM2 (106 minutes: ADD: 10/94) Ⓜ
Carreras and Ricciarelli make a wonderful pair of young lovers – totally credible, their fresh, supple totally suited to the roles. Davis conducts somwhat cooly for one of opera's most heartrending works

La Fanciulla del West

Awards 1978

Carol Neblett *sop* Minnie; **Plácido Domingo** *ten* Dick Johnson; **Sherrill Milnes** *bar* Jack Rance; **Francis Egerton** *ten* Nick; **Robert Lloyd** *bass* Ashby; **Gwynne Howell** *bass* Jake Wallace; **Paul Hudson** *bass* Billy Jackrabbit; **Anne Wilkens** *sop* Wowkle

Chorus and Orchestra of the Royal Opera House, Covent Garden / Zubin Mehta

DG ② 419 640-2GH2 (130 minutes: ADD) Ⓕ

Notes, text and translation included

Recorded 1977

This opera depicts the triangular relationship between Minnie, the saloon owner and 'mother' to the entire town of gold miners, Jack Rance, the sheriff and Dick Johnson (alias Ramerrez), a bandit leader. The music is highly developed in Puccini's seamless lyrical style, the arias for the main characters emerge from the texture and return to it effortlessly. The vocal colours are strongly polarized with the cast being all male except for one travesti role and Minnie herself. The score bristles with robust melody as well as delicate scoring, betraying a masterly hand at work. Carol Neblett is a strong Minnie, vocally distinctive and well characterized, whilst Plácido Domingo and Sherrill Milnes make a good pair of suitors for the spunky little lady. Zubin Mehta conducts with real sympathy for the idiom and the orchestra responds well.

Madama Butterfly

Renata Scotto *sop* Madama Butterfly; **Carlo Bergonzi** *ten* Pinkerton; **Rolando Panerai** *bar* Sharpless; **Anna di Stasio** *mez* Suzuki; **Piero De Palma** *ten* Goro; **Giuseppe Morresi** *ten* Prince Yamadori; **Silvana Padoan** *mez* Kate Pinkerton; **Paolo Montarsolo** *bass* The Bonze; **Mario Rinaudo** *bass* Commissioner

Rome Opera House Chorus and Orchestra / Sir John Barbirolli

HMV Classics ② HMVD5 72886-2 (142 minutes: ADD).

Notes, text and translation included. Ⓑ

Recorded 1966

This is Barbirolli's *Butterfly*; despite Scotto's expressiveness and Bergonzi's elegance it is the conductor's contribution that gives this set its durability and its hold on the affections. The Rome Opera Orchestra is not the equal of the Vienna Philharmonic for Karajan. However, the rapport between conductor and orchestra and their mutual affection for Puccini are evident throughout, and they make this the most Italianate of all readings. It is hugely enjoyable, not just in the big emotional outpourings (like the Act 2 interlude, where Barbirolli's passionate gasps and groans spur the orchestra to great eloquence) but in many tiny moments where you can almost see the conductor and his players lovingly and absorbedly concentrating on subtleties of phrasing and texture.

There is a lot of good singing, too. Scotto's voice will not always take the pressure she puts on it, but her portrayal is a touching and finely detailed one. The ever stylish Bergonzi sings with immaculate phrasing and perfect taste, Panerai is an outstanding Sharpless (beautifully sung, the embodiment of anxious, pitying concern) and di Stasio's Suzuki is attractively light-voiced and young-sounding.

The recording, however, is a bit narrow in perspective, rather close (really quiet singing and playing rarely register as such) and some of the voices are edged or slightly tarnished in loud passages. Barbirolli's set is perhaps for those who find the meticulously refined detail of Karajan studied (also ravishing and stunningly recorded); those, in short, for whom Latin warmth and impulsive open-heartedness are indispensable in this opera. They will find those qualities here, with singing to match, and will not mind the occasional patch of stridency.

Madama Butterfly

Mirella Freni *sop* Madama Butterfly; **Luciano Pavarotti** *ten* Pinkerton; **Robert Kerns** *bar* Sharpless; **Christa Ludwig** *mez* Suzuki; **Michel Sénéchal** *ten* Goro; **Giorgio Stendoro** *bar* Prince Yamadori; **Elke Schary** mez Kate Pinkerton; **Marius Rintzler** *bass* The Bonze; **Hans Helm** *bass* Commissioner

Vienna State Opera Chorus; Vienna Philharmonic Orchestra / Herbert von Karajan

Decca ③ 417 577-2DH3 (145 minutes: ADD).

Notes, text and translation included. Ⓕ

Recorded 1974

In every way except one the transfer of Karajan's radiant Vienna recording for Decca could hardly provide a firmer recommendation. The reservation is one of price – this Karajan is on three discs, not two, at full price. However it does allow each act to be self-contained on a single disc, and for such a performance as this no extravagance is too much. Movingly dramatic as Renata Scotto is on the Barbirolli set, Mirella Freni is even more compelling. The voice is fresher, firmer and more girlish, with more light and shade at such points as 'Un bel dì', and there is an element of vulnerability that intensifies the communication. In that, one imagines Karajan played a big part, just as he must have done in presenting Pavarotti – not quite the super-star he is today but already with a will of his own in the recording studio – as a Pinkerton of exceptional subtlety, not just a roistering cad but in his way an endearing figure in the First Act.

Significantly CD brings out the delicacy of the vocal balances in Act 1 with the voices deliberately distanced for much of the time, making such passages as 'Vienna la sera' and 'Bimba dagli occhi' the more magical in their delicacy. Karajan, in that duet and later in the Flower duet of Act 2, draws ravishing playing from the Vienna Philharmonic strings, getting them to imitate the *portamento* of the singers in an *echt-Viennes* manner, which is ravishing to the ear. Christa Ludwig is by far the richest and most compelling of Suzukis.

Madama Butterfly

Miriam Gauci *sop* Madama Butterfly; **Yordi Ramiro** *ten* Pinkerton; **Georg Tichy** *bar* Sharpless, **Nelly Boschková** *mez* Suzuki; **Josef Abel** *ten* Goro; **Robert Szücs** *bar* Prince Yamadori; **Alzbeta Michalková** *mez* Kate Pinkerton; **Jozef Opaček** *bass* The Bonze; **Vladimir Kubovčik** *bass* Commissioner, Registrar
Slovak Philharmonic Chorus; Bratislava Radio Symphony Orchestra / Alexander Rahbari
Naxos ② 8 660015/6 (141 minutes: DDD). Notes and Ⓢ text included. Recorded 1991

Though this would never be a first-choice *Butterfly*, it might serve quite happily as a *Butterfly* first-choice. That is, coming upon the opera fresh, never having heard it before, one could well find it a good introduction. It is consistently musical, avoids cheapness or exaggerated sentiment, and, while presenting worthily the enchanting and infinitely poignant score, it leaves plenty to be discovered with a widening knowledge of other and greater performances. An attractive feature is the youthfulness of the Butterfly and Pinkerton. The Pinkerton, a Mexican lyric tenor, Yordi Ramiro, gives as likeable, sincere a version of the character as any. And this is not a falsification of the part, at the very heart of which is the painful truth that likeable people may do very unlikeable things. It is a good voice: limited, but well defined and with a youthful freshness in its tone. The Butterfly is also young-sounding: Miriam Gauci, born in Malta. She sings uncompromisingly as a light lyric soprano, with an especially lovely quality in the upper range. The lightness brings limitations in this colossal role, and they are compounded by the immaturity of her acting-portrayal: she does many of 'the right things' but it is rare to find in her the flash of expressiveness that illuminates a character from within. A newcomer to the opera is not likely to be troubled by this, but will on the contrary be delighted by the quality of the voice and touched by the general appeal of the character. Alexander Rahbari conducts a performance that captures both the opera's charm and seriousness, not, however, its intensity.

Manon Lescaut

Mirella Freni *sop* Manon Lescaut; **Luciano Pavarotti** *ten* Des Grieux; **Dwayne Croft** *bar* Lescaut; **Giuseppe Taddei** *bar* Geronte; **Ramon Vargas** *ten* Edmondo; **Cecilia Bartoli** *mez* Singer; **Federico Davia** *bass* Innkeeper, Captain; **Anthony Laciura** *ten* Dancing Master; **Paul Groves** *ten* Lamplighter; **James Courtney** *bass* Sergeant
Chorus and Orchestra of the Metropolitan Opera / James Levine
Decca ② 440 200-2DHO2 (120 minutes: DDD). Notes, text and translation included. Ⓕ
Recorded 1992

With Luciano Pavarotti as a powerful Des Grieux, James Levine conducts a comparably big-boned performance of *Manon Lescaut*, bringing out the red-blooded drama of Puccini's first big success, while not ignoring its warmth and tender poetry in exceptionally full, vivid sound with the voices well in front of the orchestra. In the title-role Freni's performance culminates in an account of the big Act 4 aria, more involving and passionate than any of the others on rival versions, with the voice showing no signs of wear, and with her sudden change of face at the words 'terra di pace' ('a land of peace') bringing a magical lightening of tone. That aria makes a thrilling climax, when too often this act can seem a letdown. In this as in so much else, Levine conveys the tensions and atmosphere of a stage performance in a way that owes much to his experience at the Metropolitan. More completely than other versions, it avoids the feeling of a studio performance. Reactions to Pavarotti as Des Grieux will differ widely. The closeness of balance means that in volume his singing rarely drops below *mezzo forte*, but there is little harm in having so passionate a portrait of Des Grieux as Pavarotti's. Needless to say, the hero's big emotional climaxes in each of the first three acts come over at full force. The rest of the cast is strong too, with Dwayne Croft a magnificent Lescaut who, as well as singing with rich, firm tone, brings out the character's wry humour. Many collectors will count this a clear first choice among current versions.

Manon Lescaut **H**

Maria Callas *sop* Manon Lescaut; **Giuseppe di Stefano** *ten* Des Grieux; **Giulio Fioravanti** *bar* Lescaut; **Franco Calabrese** *bass* Geronte; **Dino Formichini** *ten* Edmondo; **Fiorenza Cossotto** *mez* Singer; **Carlo Forti** *bass* Innkeeper; **Vito Tatone** *ten* Dancing master; **Giuseppe Morresi** *bass* Sergeant; **Franco Ricciardi** *ten* Lamplighter; **Franco Ventrigilia** *bass* Captain
Chorus and Orchestra of La Scala, Milan / Tullio Serafin
EMI ② CDS5 56301-2 (120 minutes: ADD). Notes, Ⓕ text and translation included. Recorded 1957 **OO**

This performance is unique, with Act 4 for once a culmination in Callas's supreme account of the death scene. She may present a rather formidable portrait of a young girl in Act 1, but here the final act with its long duet and the big aria, 'Sola, perduta, abbandonata', is far more than an epilogue to the rest, rather a culmination, with Callas at her very peak. Di Stefano, too, is on superb form and Serafin's pacing of the score is masterly. Di Stefano wipes the floor with most of his rivals past and present: in Act 4 he has a concerned tenderness for Manon that others can only sketch, his debonair charm in 'Tra voi belle' is incomparable and (rarest of virtues among tenors) he never sings past the limits of his voice. Fioravanti as Lescaut and Calabrese as Geronte sing well if not very characterfully.

However, digital CD remastering in this instance loses out. A break has to be made in Act 2 – in a fairly innocuous place before the duet 'Tu, tu, amore tu'. The first two acts make up a total timing only a few seconds over the 75-minute limit, but evidently it was enough to prevent them going on to a single CD. That said, the CD brings the same advantages in refining the original boxy sound without glamorizing it in false stereo, plus the usual advantages of absence of background and ease of finding places. For an account of *Manon Lescaut* which comes fully to terms with the opera's huge contrasts of colour and mood you will also have to have a modern recording, for with all its improvements the sound here remains very dry.

La rondine

La rondine. Le Villi – Prelude; L'Abbandono; La Tregenda; Ecco la casa ... Torna ai felice dì. Morire!
Angela Gheorghiu *sop* Magda; **Roberto Alagna** *ten* Ruggero; **Inva Mula-Tchako** *sop* Lisetta; **William Matteuzzi** *ten* Prunier; **Alberto Rinaldi** *bar* Rambaldo; **Patricia Biccire** *sop* Yvette; **Patrizia Ciofi** *sop* Bianca; **Monica Bacelli** *mez* Suzy; **Riccardo Simonetti** *bar* Périchaud; **Toby Spence** *ten* Gobin; **Enrico Fissore** *bar* Crébillon
London Voices; London Symphony Orchestra / Antonio Pappano *pf*
EMI ② CDS5 56338-2 (131 minutes: DDD) Ⓕ
Texts and translations included
Recorded 1996 ●●●

It could not be more welcome when a recording transforms a work, as this one does, setting it on a new plane. *La rondine* ('The Swallow'), Puccini's ill-timed attempt to emulate Lehár in the world of operetta, completed during the First World War, has long been counted his most serious failure. Puccini's cunning has never been in doubt either, for he and his librettists interweave elements not just of *La traviata* but of *The Merry Widow* and *Die Fledermaus*, not to mention earlier Puccini operas. His melodic style may be simpler than before, but one striking theme follows another with a profusion that any other composer might envy. What Pappano reveals far more than before is the subtlety with which Puccini interweaves his themes and motifs, with conversational passages made spontaneous-sounding in their flexibility. Above all, Pappano brings out the poetry, drawing on emotions far deeper than are suggested by this operetta-like subject, thanks also to Gheorghiu's superb performance, translating her mastery as Violetta to this comparable character. Magda's first big solo, 'Che il bel sogno di Doretta', finds Gheorghiu at her most ravishing, tenderly expressive in her soaring phrases, opening out only at the final climax. From first to last, often with a throb in the voice, her vocal acting convinces you that Magda's are genuine, deep emotions, painful at the end, intensified by the ravishing beauty of her voice.

As Ruggero, Alagna has a far less complex role, winningly characterizing the ardent young student. What will specially delight Puccinians in this set is that he is given an entrance aria about Paris, 'Parigi e un citta', which transforms his otherwise minimal contribution to Act 1. The partnership of Gheorghiu and Alagna highlights the way that Puccini in the melodic lines for each of his central characters makes Ruggero's more forthright, Magda's more complex. Among much else, the role of the poet, Prunier, is transformed by the clear-toned William Matteuzzi in what is normally a *comprimario* role. Not only is his relationship with Magda beautifully drawn, his improbable affair with the skittish maid, Lisetta, is made totally convincing too, mirroring Magda's affair. For the fill-ups, the excerpts from *Le Villi*, warm and dramatic, make one wish that Pappano could go on to record that first of Puccini's operas, with Alagna giving a ringing account of Roberto's aria, as he does of the song, *Morire!* – with Pappano at the piano. Originally an album-piece written for a wartime charity, Puccini used it, transposed up a semitone, with different words, as the entrance aria for Ruggero. Altogether a set to treasure.

Il trittico

Il tabarro
Carlo Guelfi *bar* Michele; **Maria Guleghina** *sop* Giorgetta; **Neil Shicoff** *ten* Luigi; **Riccardo Cassinelli** *ten* Tinca; **Enrico Fissore** *bass* Talpa; **Elena Zilio** *mez* Frugola; **Barry Banks** *ten* Ballad-seller; **Angela Gheorghiu** *sop* Lover; **Roberto Alagna** *ten* Lover
London Voices; London Symphony Orchestra / Antonio PappaNo

Suor Angelica
Cristina Gallardo-Domâs *sop* Suor Angelica; **Bernadette Manca di Nissa** *contr* Princess; **Felicity Palmer** *mez* Abbess; **Elena Zilio** *mez* Monitoress; **Sara Fulgoni** *mez* Mistress of the Novices; **Dorothea Röschmann** *sop* Sister Genovieffa; **Judith Rees** *sop* Sister Osmina; **Rachele Stanisci** *sop* Sister Dolcina; **Francesca Pedaci** *sop* Nursing Sister; **Anna Maria Panzarella** *sop* First Almoner Sister, First Lay Sister; **Susan Mackenzie-Park** *sop* Second Almoner Sister; **Deborah Miles-Johnson** *contr* Second Lay Sister; **Rosalind Waters** *sop* Novice
London Voices; Tiffin Boys' School Choir; Philharmonia Orchestra / Antonio Pappano

Gianni Schicchi
José van Dam *bass-bar* Gianni Schicchi; **Angela Gheorghiu** *sop* Lauretta; **Roberto Alagna** *ten* Rinuccio; **Felicity Palmer** *mez* Zita; **Paolo Barbacini** *ten* Gherardo; **Patrizia Ciofi** *sop* Nella; **James Savage-Hanford** *treb* Gherardino; **Carlos Chausson** *bass* Betto di Signa; **Luigi Roni** *bass* Simone; **Roberto Scaltriti** *bar* Marco; **Elena Zilio** *mez* La Ciesca; **Enrico Fissore** *bass* Spinelloccio; **Simon Preece** *bar* Pinellino; **Noel Mann** *bass* Guccio
London Symphony Orchestra / Antonio Pappano
EMI ③ CDS5 56587-2 (162 minutes: DDD). Notes, texts and translations included. Ⓕ
Recorded 1997

No previous recordings bring such warmth or beauty or so powerful a drawing of the contrasts between each of the three one-acters in Puccini's triptych as these. It is Pappano above all, with his gift for pacing Puccini subtly, who draws the set together. In each opera he heightens emotions fearlessly to produce unerringly at key moments the authentic gulp-in-throat, whether for the cuckolded bargemaster, Michele, for Sister Angelica in her agonized suicide and heavenly absolution, or for the resolution of young love at the end of *Gianni Schicchi*. It will disappoint some that the starry couple of Angela Gheorghiu and Roberto Alagna do not take centre-stage, but quite apart from their radiant singing as Lauretta and Rinuccio in *Gianni Schicchi* – not least in that happy ending, most tenderly done – they make a tiny cameo appearance in *Il tabarro* as the off-stage departing lovers, a heady 45 seconds. It is the sort of luxury touch that Walter Legge would have relished. No doubt Gheorghiu would have been just as persuasive as Giorgetta in *Il tabarro* and as Sister Angelica, but having different sopranos in each opera sharpens the contrasts. Maria Guleghina makes a warm, vibrant Giorgetta, and the touch of acid at the top of the voice adds character, pointing to the frustration of the bargemaster's wife.

Even more remarkable is the singing of the young Chilean soprano, Cristina Gallardo-Domâs as Sister Angelica. Hers is a younger, more vulnerable Angelica than usual. Her vocal subtlety and commanding technique go with a fully mature portrayal of the nun's agony, her defiance of the implacable Princess as well as her grief over her dead son. As with Gheorghiu, the dynamic shading brings *pianissimos* of breathtaking delicacy. The Princess is powerfully sung by Bernadette Manca di Nissa, her tone firm and even throughout. Felicity Palmer, with her tangy mezzo tone, is well contrasted as the Abbess, and she is just as characterful as the crabby Zita in *Gianni Schicchi*. The casting in *Suor Angelica* is as near flawless as could be, with Elena Zilio and Dorothea Röschmann outstanding in smaller roles. Zilio is the only singer who appears in all three operas, just as effective as Frugola in *Il tabarro*, though there her full, clear voice is not always distinguishable from Guleghina as Giorgetta. Among the men Carlo Guelfi makes a superb Michele, incisive, dark and virile. He brings out not just the anger but the poignancy of the bargemaster's emotions, as in the duet with Giorgetta, when they lament what might have been. Neil Shicoff makes a fine Luigi, the nerviness in his tenor tone aptly bringing out a hysterical quality in the character. The male *comprimarios* are vocally more variable, if always characterful, as they are too in *Gianni Schicchi*. As Schicchi himself José van Dam's voice perfectly conveys the sardonic side of the character, and the top Gs he has to negotiate are wonderfully strong and steady. Maybe the full voice he uses for the name 'Gianni Schicchi', when in impersonation of old Buoso he is dictating the new will, makes too obvious a contrast with the quavering old man imitation, but it is what Puccini asked for.

Also worthy of praise is the comfortingly sumptuous and atmospheric sound, very wide in its dynamic range. Off-stage effects are magical, and always thanks to Pappano and fine playing from both the LSO and Philharmonia, the beauty and originality of the carefully textured instrumentation can be appreciated with new vividness. Thanks to Pappano and his well-chosen team, this is a set to renew one's appreciation of operas that represent Puccini still at his peak. He may have had doubts over the length of his triptych, but on disc in performances such as these they are utterly magnetic.

Il tabarro[a] **H**

Tito Gobbi *bar* Michele; **Margaret Mas** *sop* Giorgetta; **Giacinto Prandelli** *ten* Luigi; **Piero De Palma** *ten* Tinca; **Plinio Clabassi** *bass* Talpa; **Miriam Pirazzini** *mez* Frugola

Suor Angelica[b]

Victoria de los Angeles *sop* Suor Angelica; **Fedora Barbieri** *mez* Princess; **Mina Doro** *mez* Abbess, Mistress of the Novices; **Corinna Vozza** *mez* Monitoress; **Lidia Marimpietri** *sop* Sister Genovieffa, First Almoner Sister; **Santa Chissari** *sop* Sister Osmina, Second Almoner Sister, Novice; **Anna Marcangeli** *sop* Sister Dolcina; **Teresa Cantarini** *mez* Nursing Sister; **Silvia Bertona** *sop* First Lay Sister; **Maria Huder** *mez* Second Lay Sister

Gianni Schicchi[c]

Tito Gobbi *bar* Gianni Schicchi; **Victoria de los Angeles** *sop* Lauretta; **Carlo del Monte** *ten* Rinuccio; **Anna Maria Canali** *mez* Zita; **Adelio Zagonara** *ten* Gherardo; **Lidia Marimpietri** *sop* Nella; **Claudio Cornoldi** *ten* Gherardino; **Saturno Meletti** *bass* Betto di Signa; **Paolo Montarsolo** *bass* Simone; **Fernando Valentini** *bar* Marco; **Giuliana Raymondi** *sop* La Ciesca

Rome Opera Chorus; Rome Opera Orchestra / [a]Vincenzo Bellezza, [b]Tullio Serafin, [c]Gabriele Santini

EMI mono/stereo ③ CMS7 64165-2
(161 minutes: ADD). Texts and translations included. Ⓜ
Recorded [a]1955, [b]1957, [c]1958 **OO**

Unless you insist on the most up-to-date recorded sound, or on buying the individual operas of Puccini's trilogy separately, this is the classic *Trittico*. Gobbi's blackly authoritative but pitiful Michele in *Il tabarro* and his genially authoritative Schicchi (the two outer panels of the triptych *do* match, in an odd sort of way) have seldom been equalled, let alone surpassed. De los Angeles's Angelica is more purely and movingly sung than any other on record, and her Lauretta in *Gianni Schicchi* is enchanting.

Could it be said, even so, that *Il tabarro* is the weak link in this trilogy? It is a three-hander, surely, and neither the soprano nor the tenor are quite in Gobbi's league. Mas is a bit plummy and mezzoish, true, but the slight implication this gives that Giorgetta's liaison with the young stevedore Luigi is her last chance at escape from a hateful life and a marriage that has soured adds an extra twinge of pain to a plot in which all three principals are victims. And in this context Prandelli's slightly strenuous rawness of tone characterizes Luigi rather well. In *Gianni Schicchi*, Carlo del Monte as Rinuccio also looks like under-casting but in fact he's one of the few tenors who've recorded the part who sounds convincingly young, and his ardent praise of Florence and the 'new men' who are reinvigorating the city is proudly sung. Here, too, Gobbi is surrounded by a constellation of pungent character actors, and de los Angeles in *Suor Angelica* is teamed with a charmingly girlish, impulsive Genovieffa and with Fedora Barbieri's rigidly implacable Princess. With generally very stylish conducting throughout (only Belezza in *Il tabarro* is a touch staid, and he omits nearly all of Puccini's off-stage sound effects) only the rather elderly recordings might be seen as a drawback. EMI boldly labels the whole set 'stereo', but both *Il tabarro* and *Suor Angelica* sound like minimally 'processed' mono: a touch congested in fuller pasages, a hint of fizzy brightness here and there, but all well worth putting up with for such performances as these.

Tosca

Montserrat Caballé *sop* Tosca; **José Carreras** *ten* Cavaradossi; **Ingvar Wixell** *bar* Scarpia; **Samuel Ramey** *bass* Angelotti; **Piero De Palma** *ten* Spoletta; **Domenico Trimarchi** *bar* Sacristan; **William Elvin** *bar* Sciarrone, Gaoler; **Ann Murray** *mez* Shepherd Boy
Chorus and Orchestra of the Royal Opera House, Covent Garden / Sir Colin Davis
Philips Duo ② 438 359-2PM2 (118 minutes: ADD). Ⓜ
Recorded 1976

Caballé's Tosca is one of the most ravishingly sung on record, with scarcely a less than beautiful note throughout, save where an occasional phrase lies a touch low for her. She doesn't quite have the 'prima donna' (in quotes, mind) temperament for the part (the coquettish malice of 'but make her eyes black!', as Tosca forgives Cavaradossi for using a blonde stranger as model for his altarpiece of the Magdalen, is not in Caballé's armoury; either that or she knows that her voice would sound arch attempting it), but her portrayal is much more than a display of lovely sounds. She is precise with words, takes minute care over phrasing, and she knows to a split second where dead-centre precise pitching becomes crucial. Carreras's Cavaradossi is one of his best recorded performances: the voice untarnished, the line ample, and if he's tempted at times to over-sing one forgives the fault for the sake of his poetic ardour.

Wixell is the fly in the ointment: a capable actor and an intelligent artist, but his gritty timbre lacks centre and thus the necessary dangerous suavity. Davis's direction is flexible but dramatic and finely detailed; the secondary singers (Murray a convincingly boy-like Shepherd, Trimarchi an uncaricatured Sacristan, Ramey an aristocratic Angelotti) are all very good. The recording, despite some rather unconvincing sound effects, still sounds very well, with space around the voices and a natural balance between them and the orchestra. It's pity Philips, in its otherwise praiseworthy decision to pack two CDs into a jewel-case no thicker than those normally holding just one, should have saved space by omitting the libretto.

Tosca
Leontyne Price *sop* Tosca; **Giuseppe di Stefano** *ten* Cavaradossi; **Giuseppe Taddei** *bar* Scarpia; **Carlo Cava** *bass* Angelotti; **Piero De Palma** *ten* Spoletta; **Fernando Corena** *bass* Sacristan; **Leonardo Monreale** *bass* Sciarrone; **Alfredo Mariotti** *bass* Gaoler; **Herbert Weiss** *treb* Shepherd Boy
Vienna State Opera Chorus; Vienna Philharmonic Orchestra / Herbert von Karajan
Decca Legends ② 466 384-2DMO2 Ⓜ
(114 minutes: ADD). Text and translation included.
Recorded 1962 ●

Karajan's classic version of *Tosca* was originally issued on the RCA label, but produced by John Culshaw of Decca at a vintage period. The first surprise is to find the sound satisfying in almost every way, with a firm sense of presence and with each voice and each section of the orchestra cleanly focused within the stereo spectrum. What is less surprising is the superiority of this version as an interpretation. Karajan was always a master Puccinian, and this set was a prime example. A typical instance comes at the end of Act 1, where Scarpia's *Te Deum* is taken daringly slowly, and conveys a quiver of menace that no other version begins to match. An extra nicety is the way that in the instrumental introduction to Cavaradossi's first aria, 'Recondita armonia', he treats it as the musical equivalent of a painter mixing his colours, the very point Puccini no doubt had in mind. Karajan, though individual, and regularly challenging his singers is most solicitous in following the voices. It is fascinating to note what expressive freedom he allows his tenor, di Stefano, and he makes Leontyne Price relax, giving a superb assumption of the role, big and rich of tone; the voice is the more beautiful for not being recorded too closely.

Tosca 🄷
Maria Callas *sop* Tosca; **Giuseppe di Stefano** *ten* Cavaradossi; **Tito Gobbi** *bar* Scarpia; **Franco Calabrese** *bass* Angelotti; **Angelo Mercuriali** *ten* Spoletta; **Melchiorre Luise** *bass* Sacristan; **Dario Caselli** *bass* Sciarrone, Gaoler; **Alvaro Cordova** *treb* Shepherd Boy
Chorus and Orchestra of La Scala, Milan / Victor de Sabata
EMI mono ② CDS5 56304-2 (108 minutes: ADD).
Notes, text and translation included. Ⓕ
Recorded 1953 ●●●

The producer Walter Legge used often to question the necessity of stereo. Now more strikingly than ever in this remastering of one of the great classic performances of the gramophone, one of his own masterpieces as a creative recording producer, it is easy to see what he meant. With off-stage effects, for example – so important in Puccini – precisely placed, there is a sense of presence normally reserved for two-channel reproduction. In the long duet between Tosca and Cavaradossi in Act 3 you can even detect a difference of placing between the two singers. The immediacy is astonishing, and the great moment of the execution with trombones rasping and the fusillade reproduced at a true *fortissimo* has never been represented on record with greater impact. What is especially delightful is that where on most previous CD transfers of mono originals the results have emphasized the single-channel flatness, this is full and weighty. The slightly jangling brightness on some percussion instruments gives a hint of the age of the recording, but with mono of this vintage it is amazing what bloom there is even on the violins, and when it comes to the voices, one simply forgets the years, and drinks in the glory of one of the really great recorded opera performances as never before. The contrasts of timbre are beautifully brought out – amazingly wide with Gobbi as with Callas and with di Stefano producing his most honeyed tones. Wonderful as Gobbi's and di Stefano's performances are, and superbly dramatic as de Sabata's conducting is, it is Callas in the title-role that provides the greatest marvel, and here more than ever one registers the facial changes implied in each phrase, with occasional hints of a chuckle (usually ironic) apparent.

Tosca (sung in English)
Jane Eaglen *sop* Tosca; **Dennis O'Neill** *ten* Cavaradossi; **Gregory Yurisich** *bar* Scarpia; **Peter Rose** *bass* Angelotti; **John Daszak** *ten* Spoletta; **Andrew Shore** *bass* Sacristan; **Christopher Booth-Jones** *bass* Sciarrone; **Ashley Holland** *bass* Gaoler;**Charbel Michael** *mez* Shepherd Boy
Peter Kay Children's Choir; Geoffrey Mitchell Choir; Philharmonia Orchestra / David Parry
Chandos Opera in English ② CHAN3000 (18 minutes: DDD). Notes and text included. Ⓕ
Recorded 1995

This is an issue to delight far more than devotees of opera in English, a gripping account of Puccini's red-blooded drama. Above all, it offers the first major recording to demonstrate the powers of Jane Eaglen at full stretch in one of the most formidable, vocally satisfying portrayals of the role of Tosca in years. Parry here demonstrates his full understanding of Puccini and the bite and energy in the playing of the Philharmonia, not to mention the expressive warmth in the love music, will have you riveted as though hearing the music for the first time. The opulent Chandos sound, cleanly focused with plenty of atmosphere and presence, adds to the impact, whether in the power of the big tuttis or in the subtlety of whispered string *pianissimos*. Offstage effects are nicely evocative, though the sequence of bell-sounds at the start of Act 3 is so clear it suggests an orchestra rather than a Roman landscape. Otherwise, the slightly forward balance of voices against orchestra is very well judged. Eaglen is well matched by Dennis O'Neill as Cavaradossi, aptly Italianate in every register, and betraying only a slight unevenness occasionally on high notes under pressure. Gregory Yurisich makes a powerful Scarpia, younger-sounding than most, and therefore a more plausible lover. The others are well cast as well, notably Peter Rose who is as an outstanding, fresh-voiced Angelotti.

Turandot

Dame Joan Sutherland *sop* Princess Turandot; **Luciano Pavarotti** *ten* Calaf; **Montserrat Caballé** *sop* Liù; **Tom Krause** *bar* Ping; **Pier Francesco Poli** *ten* Pang, Prince of Persia; **Piero De Palma** *ten* Pong; **Nicolai Ghiaurov** *bass* Timur; **Sir Peter Pears** *ten* Emperor Altoum; **Sabin Markov** *bar* Mandarin
Wandsworth School Boys' Choir; John Alldis Choir; London Philharmonic Orchestra / Zubin Mehta
Decca ② 414 274-2DH2 (117 minutes: ADD). Notes, Ⓕ text and translation included. Recorded 1972

Turandot is a psychologically complex work fusing appalling sadism with self-sacrificing devotion. The icy Princess of China has agreed to marry any man of royal blood who can solve three riddles she has posed. If he fails his head will roll. Calaf, the son of the exiled Tartar king Timur, answers all the questions easily and when Turandot hesitates to accept him, magnanimously offers her a riddle in return – 'What is his name?'. Liù, Calaf's faithful slave-girl, is tortured but rather than reveal his identity kills herself. Turandot finally capitulates, announcing that his name is Love. Dame Joan Sutherland's assumption of the title role is statuesque, combining regal poise with a more human warmth, whilst Montserrat Caballé is a touchingly sympathetic Liù, skilfully steering the character away from any hint of the mawkish. Pavarotti's Calaf is a heroic figure in splendid voice and the chorus is handled with great power, baying for blood at one minute, enraptured with Liù's nobility at the next. Mehta conducts with great passion and a natural feel for Puccini's wonderfully tempestuous drama. Well recorded.

Turandot **H**
Maria Callas *sop* Princess Turandot; **Eugenio Fernandi** *ten* Calaf; **Dame Elisabeth Schwarzkopf** *sop* Liù; **Mario Borriello** *bar* Ping; **Renato Ercolani** *ten* Pang; **Piero De Palma** *ten* Pong; **Nicola Zaccaria** *bass* Timur; **Giuseppe Nessi** *ten* Emperor Altoum; **Giulio Mauri** *bass* Mandarin
Chorus and Orchestra of La Scala, Milan / Tullio Serafin
EMI mono ② CDS5 56307-2 (118 minutes: ADD). Notes, text and translation included. Ⓜ
Recorded 1957

To have Callas, the most flashing-eyed of all sopranos as Turandot, is – on record at least – the most natural piece of casting. Other sopranos may be comparably icy in their command, but Callas with her totally distinctive tonal range was able to give the fullest possible characterization. With her, Turandot was not just an implacable man-hater but a highly provocative female. One quickly reads something of Callas's own underlying vulnerability into such a portrait, its tensions, the element of brittleness. With her the character seems so much more believably complex than with others. It was sad that, except at the very beginning of her career, she felt unable to sing the role in the opera house, but this recording is far more valuable than any memory of the past, one of the most thrillingly magnetic of all her recorded performances, the more so when Schwarzkopf as Liù provides a comparably characterful and distinctive portrait, far more than a Puccinian 'little woman', sweet and wilting.

Next to such supreme singers it was perhaps cruel of Walter Legge to choose so relatively uncharacterful a tenor as Eugenio Fernandi as Calaf, but at least his timbre is pleasingly distinctive. What fully matches the singing of Callas and Schwarzkopf in its positive character is the conducting of Serafin, which is sometimes surprisingly free, but in its pacing invariably capturing rare colour, atmosphere and mood as well as dramatic point. The Ping, Pang and Pong episode of Act 2 has rarely sparkled so naturally, the work of a conductor who has known and loved the music in the theatre over a long career. The conducting is so vivid that the limitations of the mono sound hardly seem to matter. As the very opening will reveal, the CD transfer makes it satisfyingly full-bodied. Though with its rich, atmospheric stereo the Mehta set remains the best general recommendation, it is thrilling to have this historic document so vividly restored.

Henry Purcell

British 1659-1695

GROVE *Purcell was a chorister in the Chapel Royal until his voice broke in 1673. He was then made assistant to John Hingeston, whom he succeeded as organ maker and keeper of the king's instruments in 1683. In 1677 he was appointed composer-in-ordinary for the king's violins and in 1679 succeeded his teacher, Blow, as organist of Westminster Abbey. From 1680 he began writing music for the theatre. In 1682 he was appointed an organist of the Chapel Royal. His court appointments were renewed by James II in 1685 and by William III in 1689, and on each occasion he had the duty of providing a second organ for the coronation. The last royal occasion for which he provided music was Queen Mary's funeral in 1695.*

Purcell was one of the greatest composers of the Baroque period and one of the greatest of all English composers. His works include the fantasias for viols (masterpieces of contrapuntal writing in the old style) and some of the more modern sonatas for violins which reveal an acquaintance with Italian models. In time Purcell became increasingly in demand as a composer, and his theatre music in particular made his name familiar to many who knew nothing of his church music or the odes and welcome songs he wrote for the court. During the last five years of his life Purcell collaborated on five semi-operas in which the music has a large share, with divertissements, songs, choral numbers and dances. His only true opera (ie with music throughout) was Dido and Aeneas, written for a girls school at Chelsea; despite the limitations of Nahum Tate's libretto it is among the finest of 17th-century operas.

Complete Ayres for the Theatre

The History of Dioclesian, or The Prophetess, Z627[b]. King Arthur, Z628[b]. The Fairy Queen, Z629[b]. The Indian Queen, Z630[b]. The Married Beau, Z603[a]. The Old Bachelor, Z607[b]. Amphitryon, Z572[a]. The Double Dealer, Z592[a]. Distressed Innocence, Z577[a]. The Gordian Knot Unty'd, Z597[a]. Abdelazer, Z570[a]. Bonduca, Z574[a]. The Virtuous Wife, Z611[a]. Sonata While the Sun Rises in 'The Indian Queen'[b]. Overture in G minora. Sir Anthony Love, Z588 – Overture[a]. Timon of Athens, Z632[a]. The Indian Queen, Z630 – Symphony[b]

[a]The Parley of Instruments; [b]The Parley of Instruments Baroque Orchestra / Roy Goodman

Hyperion ③ CDA67001/3 (209 minutes: DDD). Ⓕ

Recorded 1994

All these works were published within 18 months of Purcell's death. The 13 suites of choice movements from plays and semi-operas, entitled *A Collection of Ayres, compos'd for the Theatre, and upon other occasions*, may well have been the editing work of Purcell's brother, Daniel. Whoever it was had a rare combination of musical integrity and commercial flair: the pieces lifted from Purcell's interpolations to plays are often reordered and arranged with a deftness and charm which conveys the spirit of the theatre as well as heightening the loss and poignancy of Purcell's passing. How moving the Rondeau Minuet from *The Gordian Knot Unty'd* must have seemed to those who knew and loved Purcell.

As a major retrospective of Purcell's life in the theatre, the *Ayres for the Theatre* mainly comprise instrumental dances from their original sources, though there are several movements readapted from sung airs, such as 'Fairest isle' from *King Arthur* and 'If love's a sweet passion' from *The Fairy Queen*. The tunes are wonderful and varied, the inner part-writing skilful and the rhythmic imagination knows no bounds. Even so, this is not music where more than a suite at a time can be recommended for ultimate satisfaction: stop while you still want more. And more you will most certainly want with Roy Goodman's alert and distinctive direction. If a few of the movements sound a touch mundane and lack dynamism as one follows on from another, the positive side is that the performances are never forced and rarely mannered. For the semi-opera 'suites', Goodman employs a full orchestra. What The Parley of Instruments has in abundance is a cordiality of expression which seems so absolutely right, especially in the slower airs.

Fantasias

Fantasia in F, Z745, 'Upon one note'. P

Fantasias – three part, Z732-34; four part, Z735-43. In Nomines – G minor Z746; G minor, Z747, 'Dorian'

Hespèrion XX (Sophie Watillon, Eunice Brandao, Sergi Casademunt, Wieland Kuijken, Marianne Müller, Philippe Pierlot *viols*) **/ Jordi Savall** *treb viol*

Auvidis Astrée ES9922 (54 minutes: DDD). Ⓜ

Recorded 1994 ●

Purcell's music for viols represents the final flowering of the English consort tradition. Viol consorts had been out of fashion for at least 20 years, ousted by the Italian violin sonatas and French ballet music. Purcell's polished essays in this antique form were neither published nor, apparently, widely circulated. Nevertheless, we cherish them today for their sublime expressiveness and craftsmanship. Jordi Savall and his group have achieved a state of abstraction seldom experienced in music. It almost goes without saying that Hespèrion's playing is always extremely beautiful: the music demands it. But any need to be rhetorical, to lean on a dissonance or pronounce a cadence, has been outgrown and discarded. The scale within which these features and more are articulated is so minimal, so subtle and yet ultimately so compelling, that from the first track the listener is transported into a rarefied aural dimension usually reserved for single movements or even phrases. Don't miss it.

Awards 1997

Fantasias – three part, Z732-4; four part, Z735-43; five part, 'upon one note', Z745. In Nomines – G minor, Z746; G minor, 'Dorian', Z747 P

Joanna Levine, Susanna Pell, Catherine Finnis *viols* **Phantasm** (Laurence Dreyfus, Wendy Gillespie, Jonathan Manson, Markku Luolajan-Mikkola *viols*)

Simax PSC1124 (51 minutes: DDD) Ⓕ

Recorded 1994 ○○○

Purcell's contrapuntal mastery is dazzling, with the points of imitation in the various sections of each fantasia treated in double or triple counterpoint, inversion, augmentation and all other technical devices – for instance, the initial subjects of fantasias Z739, 742 and 743 at once appear in mirror images of themselves – but the music's deep expressiveness and the dramatic tension created by its chromaticisms and unpredictable harmonies make it clear that he certainly had performance in mind (a matter of some dispute), even if, because of the king's dislike of such intellectual pursuits, only privately by conservative-minded music-lovers. It is this expressiveness which Phantasm emphasizes in this recording, both in their varied dynamics and in their use of vibrato. Speeds here are in general fast and there is great variety of bowing and hence of articulation.

Anthems and Services

Complete Anthems and Services, Volume 7 P

I was glad when they said unto me[b]. I was glad when they said unto me, Z19[a]. O consider my adversity, Z32[b]. Beati omnes qui timent Dominum, Z131. In the black dismal dungeon of despair, Z190. Save me, O God, Z51[b]. Morning and Evening Service in B flat, Z230 – Te Deum; Jubilate. Thy Way, O God, is Holy, Z60. Funeral Sentences for the death of Queen Mary II[b] – Drum Processional; March and Canzona in C minor, Z860; Man that is born of Woman, Z27; In the midst of Life, Z17[b]; Thou know'st Lord, Z58*b*; Thou know'st Lord, Z58*c*

Mark Kennedy, Eamonn O'Dwyer, James Goodman *trebs* **Susan Gritton** *sop* **James Bowman, Nigel Short** *countertens* **Rogers Covey-Crump, Charles Daniels, Mark Milhofer** *tens* **Michael George, Robert Evans** *basses* **[a]New College Choir, Oxford; [b]The King's Consort Choir; The King's Consort / Robert King**

Hyperion CDA66677 (70 minutes: DDD). Ⓕ

Recorded 1993

This recording is made up predominantly of anthems, devotional songs and a morning service (a functional, though not perfunctory, setting of the *Te Deum* and *Jubilate*) most of which disclose the range and quality of the composer's sacred *oeuvre* near its best. Of the two settings of *I was glad*, the first was, until not long ago, thought to be the work of John Blow. This full anthem more than whets our appetite with its agreeable tonal and melodic twists; when the *Gloria* arrives, we are assured that this is vintage Purcell by the sensitive pacing as much as an exquisite contrapuntal denouement. The earlier setting is more poignant. Opening with a string symphony in the spirit of a Locke consort, the music blossoms into a deliciously Elysian melodic fabric. Good sense is made of the overall shape and the soloists are, as ever, excellent. *Beati omnes* is a positive gem; this may well have been written for the composer's wedding. Of the small-scale pieces, *In the black dismal dungeon* is the real masterpiece and it is delivered astutely by the secure and musicianly voice of Susan Gritton. Finally to the funeral pieces. Here we have an ominous procession from the Guild of Ancient Fifes and Drums and the first appearance of four 'flatt' trumpets – as opposed to two plus two sackbuts; the effect of this subtle timbral change makes extraordinary sense of the music, engendering a new grandeur and uncompromising clarity as would have befitted such an occasion. The vocal performances are earthy and impassioned.

Funeral Music

Music for the Funeral of Queen Mary – March and Canzona in C minor, Z860. Funeral Sentences for the death of Queen Mary II. The Bell Anthem, Z49, 'Rejoice in the Lord alway'. Remember not, Lord, our offences, Z50. Give sentence with me, O Lord, Z12. Jehova, quam multi sunt hostes mei, Z135. O, I'm sick of life, Z140. My beloved spake, Z28. Hear my prayer, O Lord, Z15. O God, thou art my God, Z35. Voluntaries[a] – No 1 in C, Z717; No 4 in G, Z720 P

Winchester Cathedral Choir; Hilary Brooks *vc* **Baroque Brass of London; The Brandenburg Consort / David Hill** [a]*org* with **David Dunnett** *org*

Argo 436 833-2ZH (66 minutes: DDD). Texts included. Ⓕ

Recorded 1992

David Hill is a master of long-breathed melody and sustained intensity and he brings to Purcell's anthems a breadth of vision inspired by the time-span of earlier genres. Indeed, it is the range of anthems skilfully chosen from amongst Purcell's finest church music which distinguishes this disc as much as the funeral pieces.

Jehova, quam multi sunt hostes mei is particularly effective, exemplifying not only Hill's astute pacing but also his vigorous sense of the dramatic declamatory style which Purcell must have gleaned from continental sources. The open-throated treble sound is equally appropriate and characterizes the vocal colouring of almost all the works. The soloists for the verse anthems are drawn both from the ranks of the choir and a pool of professional soloists. Between them they shape the music with spirit and eloquence as can be relished in the abundant fruits of *My beloved spake*. The strings of The Brandenburg Consort balance the buoyant vocal style with sparkling rhythmic exchanges. Winchester benefits from that fragility and loneliness which a solo treble can give to 'In the midst of life', especially in a gothic acoustic. The Baroque Brass of London captures the doleful strains with finesse and makes wonderful musical sense of the Canzona.

Odes for St Cecilia's Day

1692, **Hail, bright Cecilia**, Z328; 1683, **Welcome to all the pleasures**, Z339

Hail, bright Cecilia; Welcome to all the pleasures
Susan Hamilton, Siri Thornhill *sops* **Robin Blaze, Martin van der Zeijst** *countertens* **Mark Padmore** *ten* **Jonathan Arnold, Peter Harvey, Jonathan Brown** *basses* **Collegium Vocale / Philippe Herreweghe**
Harmonia Mundi HMC90 1643 (73 minutes: DDD). Ⓕ
Texts included. Recorded 1997

The two famous St Cecilian Odes reflect a remarkable polarity in the composer's creative priorities: the shorter of the two, *Welcome to all the pleasures*, is a supreme amalgamation of Fishburn's words and Purcell's music, bursting with contained subtlety and enchantment. There is also a unique sense of conveying something novel, in this case an inaugural tribute on November 22, 1683, to the patron saint of music, henceforth annually celebrating 'this divine Science'. *Hail, bright Cecilia* from 1692 is three times longer and explores all the startling orchestral sounds which changed English music towards something approaching a Handelian palette. It is also truly *fin de siècle* (some might say Newtonian) in ambition and the imagery is as breathtakingly splendid now as it was when the Victorians first revered it for its boldness and scale. Such qualities clearly animate Herreweghe and he shapes this music with rapture and precision. The whole is infectiously fresh and never rushed. If not as brilliant or as full as McCreesh, Herreweghe is rather more sensitive to the nuances which irradiate from Purcell's colouring of words. He largely uses English voices. 'Hark! hark! each tree' boasts the versatile and effortless alto of Robin Blaze who, with the assured Peter Harvey, achieves a delightfully naturalistic lilt. This version certainly rivals McCreesh (for whom Peter Harvey also sings 'Wondrous machine' splendidly) for elevated characterization. One blip here is the piping soprano in 'Thou tun'st this world' (Susan Hamilton) where the voice seems technically and expressively limited. For beauty of sound, then, Herreweghe is your man. For dramatic immediacy and excitement, McCreesh.

Welcome to all the pleasures. Funeral Sentences for the death of Queen Mary. Birthday Ode, Z323, 'Come ye sons of art away'. March and Canzona in C minor, Z860. Hail, bright Cecilia
Emily Van Evera *sop* **Timothy Wilson** *counterten* **John Mark Ainsley, Charles Daniels** *tens* **David Thomas** *bass* **Taverner Consort, Choir and Players / Andrew Parrott**
Virgin Classics Veritas Double ② VBD5 61582-2 Ⓑ
(111 minutes: DDD). Recorded 1998

While McCreesh makes the score sparkle with his energetic view of tempos, Andrew Parrott parades his smooth and integrated forces with less instant theatricality. Instead we have a typically homogeneous and unfolding scenario which complements McCreesh's more effervescent and lush reading. The reappearance of Parrott's recordings of Purcell's earlier Cecilian ode, *Welcome to all the pleasures* and the time-honoured and particularly accessible *Come ye sons of art away* is also received with open arms. Some may distrust the low pitch (A=392) but the high tenor of Charles Daniels and the satisfying registral blend of Timothy Wilson and John Mark Ainsley in 'Sound the trumpet' are more than adequate recompense and the former's mellifluous rendering of 'Here the deities approve' is a real gem to be savoured.

Songs

She loves, and she confesses, Z413. Amintas, to my grief I see, Z356. Corinna is divinely fair, Z365. Amintor, heedless of his flocks, Z357. He himself courts his own ruin, Z372. No, to what purpose, Z468. Sylvia, 'tis true you're fair, Z512. Lovely Albina's come ashore, Z394. Spite of the godhead, pow'rful love, Z417. If music be the food of love, Z379/3. Phyllis, I can ne'er forgive it, Z408. Bacchus is a pow'r divine, Z360. Bess of Bedlam, Z370, 'From silent shades'. Let formal lovers still pursue, Z391. I came, I saw, and was undone, Z375. Who can behold Florella's charms?, Z441. Cupid, the slyest rogue alive, Z367. If prayers and tears, Z380. In Chloris all soft charms agree, Z384. Let us, kind Lesbia, give away, Z466. Love is now become a trade, Z393. Ask me to love no more, Z358. O Solitude! my sweetest choice, Z406. Olinda in the shades unseen, Z404. Pious Celinda goes to prayers, Z410. When Strephon found his passion vain, Z435. The fatal hour comes on apace, Z421. Sawney is a bonny lad, Z412. Young Thirsis' fate, ye hills and groves, deplore, Z473 Ⓟ
Barbara Bonney, Susan Gritton *sops* **James Bowman** *counterten* **Rogers Covey-Crump, Charles Daniels** *tens* **Michael George** *bass* **Mark Caudle, Susanna Pell** *vas da gamba* **David Miller** *lte/theorbo* **/ Robert King** *org/hpd*
Hyperion CDA66730 (76 minutes: DDD). Ⓕ
Texts included. Recorded 1993-94

This third and last volume of Purcell's non-theatrical secular songs consummates a most rewarding survey of 87 songs with more of the same: a vocal palette of six singers who are by now so steeped in the nuances of Purcell's strains that even the slightest offering sparkles with something memorable. The treasure is shared between Barbara Bonney and Susan Gritton who complement each other superbly. Gritton, becoming more refined in characterization and tonal colour by the day, is allotted the free-style and dramatic pieces whilst to Bonney's fluid and sensual melisma is designated the more strophic or *cantabile* settings. *Lovely Albina's come ashore* is one of the composer's most mature creations, tantalizingly hinting at a new, tautly designed and classically balanced type of song. This work, *If music be the food of love* (the best of the three versions) and *I came, I saw* are striking examples of how exceptionally Bonney negotiates Purcell's skipping and curling contours and makes these songs sound even finer creations than we previously thought. *From silent shades* ('Bess of Bedlam') is Purcell's quintessential mad-song and Gritton has the measure of it all the way; packed full of incident, imagery and musical detail, her narration is clear and finely judged, reporting the tale with irony and change of colour. The CD is beautifully and throughly documented.

Odes and Welcome Songs, Volumes 6-8

Gillian Fisher, Mary Seers, Susan Hamilton, Tessa Bonner *sops* **James Bowman, Nigel Short, Michael Chance** *countertens* **Mark Padmore, Andrew Tusa, Rogers Covey-Crump, Charles Daniels, John Mark Ainsley** *tens* **Michael George, Robert Evans** *basses* **New College Choir, Oxford; The King's Consort / Robert King**

Love's goddess sure was blind, Z331. Raise, raise the voice, Z334. Laudate Ceciliam, Z329. From those serene and rapturous joys, Z326 **P**
Hyperion CDA66494 (68 minutes: DDD). Ⓕ
Texts included. Recorded 1991

Of old, when heroes thought it base, Z333. Swifter, Isis, swifter flow, Z336. What, what shall be done on behalf of the man?, Z341 **P**
Hyperion CDA66587 (66 minutes: DDD). Ⓕ
Texts included. Recorded 1991

Come ye sons of art, away, Z323. Welcome, viceregent of the mighty king, Z340. Why, why are all the Muses mute?, Z343 **P**
Hyperion CDA66598 (68 minutes: DDD). Ⓕ
Texts included. Recorded 1991

These three CDs represent the final instalments in Hyperion's complete recording of Purcell's Odes and Welcome Songs. Purcell composed a number of these celebratory works between 1680 and 1695, and 24 survive. They were written for a wide range of events: most for royal birthdays, of King James II and Queen Mary, but also for a royal wedding, educational celebrations, and the 'Yorkshire Feast' of 1689. Hyperion's edition is to be warmly welcomed, not only for bringing to the catalogue such magnificent music, but also for the extremely sympathetic and musical performances by the The King's Consort under the direction of Robert King. Of all the works on these discs, probably the most well known is *Come ye sons of art, away* written for Queen Mary in 1694 (Volume 8). This joyous work contains some of Purcell's most ebullient music, typified by the duet for two countertenors, 'Sound the trumpet'. Like all of the works in the set this is surrounded by a well contrasted group of solos and duets for individual voices, instrumental interludes, and the occasional chorus. Less famous, but equally full of Restoration pomp and ceremony is the Yorkshire Feast song (Volume 7). Like many of the odes, the text for this is second-rate, ostensibly telling the story of York from the Roman occupation to the 17th century. However, this is merely the pretext for a splendidly varied set of vocal and instrumental items, the climax of which might be more fitting for a coronation than for a dinner of Yorkshire worthies!

Volume 6 contains four of the least well known if no less rich and varied odes, two of which are dedicated to the patron saint of music, St Cecilia. While composed for slightly smaller forces than the more ceremonial odes, these contain music which is equally jaunty and exhilarating. Throughout all three volumes the most striking fact is Purcell's extraordinary inventiveness, and his incredible facility at word setting: even the most lame texts come alive in his hands, and the variety of expression throughout is astonishing. Robert King's direction is always sensitive to both the broad span and individual nuances of Purcell's kaleidoscopic writing for voice and instruments. The King's Consort plays with great understanding throughout and has clearly absorbed the often elusive style of this music, in which many influences are combined. The vocal soloists are uniformly excellent, but special mention must be made of the soprano Gillian Fisher, and the countertenor James Bowman. The recordings are without fault, achieving both excellent internal balance and appropriate atmosphere and perspective.

O Solitude! my sweetest choice, Z406. Not all my torments can your pity move, Z400. Stript of their green our groves appear, Z444. The Blessed Virgin's Expostulation – Tell me, some pitying Angel, Z196. If music be the food of love, Z379/1. The fatal hour comes on apace, Z421. The Queen's Epicedium, 'Incassum, Lesbia, rogas', Z383. Cupid, the slyest rogue alive, Z367. Bess of Bedlam, 'From silent shades', Z370. An Evening Hymn on a Ground – Now that the sun hath veiled his light, Z193. O Solitude! my sweetest choice, Z406. Tyrannic Love – Ah! how sweet it is to love. The Fairy Queen – Hark! the echoing air. Pausanias – Sweeter than roses. The Tempest – Dear pretty youth. The Comical History of Don Quixote – From rosy bow'rs. Sophonisba – Beneath the poplar's shadow. The Indian Queen – I attempt from love's sickness. The History of Dioclesian **P**

– Let us dance, let us sing. King Arthur – Fairest isle
Nancy Argenta *sop* **Nigel North** *lte/gtr* **Richard Boothby** *va da gamba* **Paul Nicholson** *hpd/org*
Virgin Classics Veritas VC7 59324-2 Ⓕ
(74 minutes: DDD).Texts included. Recorded 1992 ●

Here we can delight in one of the best recordings of Purcell's songs (mainly taken from *Orpheus Britannicus*) to have emerged in recent times and arguably the most literary-sensitive accounts since Alfred Deller. Nancy Argenta proves that declamatory and strophic songs (and many sub-genres in between) can be negotiated in the same recital with supreme technical finesse, profound understanding of the texts and the type of inventive nuances which enhance the implied conceits of an extraordinary range of songs. Moreover, she has the technical and temperamental control to explore the expressive gamut, from impish and deliberately impersonal no-nonsense texts (such as 'Stript of their green', where the singer's rolling spontaneity is just what is called for) to the impulsive gestures and psychological tensions in 'Tell me, some pitying Angel' and 'From rosy bow'rs'. The former is an especially fine portrayal with its sustained organ continuo commentating alongside sundry plucks (always astutely gauged by Nigel North, Richard Boothby and Paul Nicholson) whilst Argenta delivers the Virgin's touching and anxious expostulation with a rare understanding and empathy. Sheer technical bravura, however, is what performances of these songs too frequently lack and the quality of pitching (notoriously awkward leaps abound) and tuning sets this disc in a class of its own; only very occasionally does shrillness or a rather lifeless vibrato detract from an otherwise exquisite release.

Dioclesian

Dioclesian, Acts 1-4 Ⓟ
Catherine Pierard *sop* **James Bowman** *counterten* **John Mark Ainsley, Mark Padmore** *tens* **Michael George** *bass* **Collegium Musicum 90 Chorus; Collegium Musicum 90 / Richard Hickox**
Chandos Chaconne CHAN0568 (54 minutes: DDD). Ⓕ
Text included. Recorded 1994

It was *Dioclesian*, the least known of the four semi-opera masterpieces of Purcell, for which the composer initially earned a reputation for writing stage music. The 'opera' was by all accounts a roaring success, though music played a less important part in the stage works of the 1690s than it did in the masque-related works of the previous decades – ironically just at the time when England could at last boast a dramatic master who could stand tall amongst the 'greats' of France and Italy. If the paucity of tableaux means a less atmospheric scenic context, such as we experience in *The Fairy Queen* or *King Arthur*, there is still much fine music which deserves to be highly regarded. Hickox is evidently committed to this score: the instrumental movements are all disciplined and yet display the buoyancy and variety of expression of one who senses the freshness of Purcell's first foray into the theatre. His soloists are authoritative Purcellians and they never disappoint and he manages to sustain the tension and climate he sets from the start.

Dido and Aeneas

Stephen Wallace *counterten* Second Witch; Ⓟ
Gerald Finley *bar* Aeneas; **Rosemary Joshua** *sop* Belinda; **Lynne Dawson** *sop* Dido; **John Bowen** *ten* First Sailor; **Dominique Visse** *counterten* First Witch; **Maria Cristina Kiehr** *sop* Second Woman; **Susan Bickley** *mez* Sorceress; **Robin Blaze** *counterten* Spirit; **Clare College Choir, Cambridge; Orchestra of the Age of Enlightenment / René Jacobs**
Harmonia Mundi HMC90 1683 (60 minutes: DDD). Ⓕ
Text and translation included. Recorded 1998 ●

Dido is a conveniently short piece and arguably one whose concentrated musical language and quicksilver dramatic juxtapositions are especially well suited to the recorded medium, giving full rein to Purcell's imagination and raising it out of its habitually stilted stage conventions. This is where Charles Mackerras's 1967 Archiv recording (nla) succeeded, especially in Tatiana Troyanos's exquisite pacing of Dido's noble and tragic demise; also successful in bringing out the work's full imaginative impact were the recent smaller-scale but atmospheric accounts from Andrew Parrott (Emma Kirkby as Dido) and Ivor Bolton (Della Jones on Teldec – nla) and – the pick of the crop until now – Christopher Hogwood, with the sensual immediacy of Catherine Bott as Dido.

René Jacobs is one of the very few luminaries of the current baroque dramatic scene not to have tackled this singular masterpiece until now, and he does so, like Hogwood, with a gaggle of top-class singers; when you can casually call on Maria Cristina Kiehr to sing her tuppenceworth of Second Woman, not to mention Robin Blaze as Spirit and Dominique Visse as First Witch, it augurs well for a new benchmark recording. Rosemary Joshua's Belinda is a straightforward, dramatically unobtrusive but essential presence, never manipulated to be more of an influence in Dido's life than Purcell clearly relates in the lady-in-waiting's gut offerings of advice, revealed in 'Pursue thy conquest love'. Of course, Act 2 is where things really get going, after the fairly perfunctory introduction to the solid hunk that is Aeneas. Whether you choose to cast your Sorceress as male (Hogwood plumps for David Thomas) or as a crooning hag, he or she has a crucial part in the overall 'temperament' of a performance, neither to be camped up unduly nor, similarly, made too earnest in delivery. Susan Bickley is a fine Sorceress of the old school, precise and yet retaining an authority through quality of tone rather than mere pantomime. This whole section is slowed down by Jacobs, who elasticates the chorus, 'Harm's our delight', around the witches. It is a brilliantly conceived, decidedly continental approach to dramatic gesture (Visse is terrifying), yet it adds something original to an opera whose odd mixtures have rarely been understood by foreign groups.

Jacobs' richly paletted, pacey and boldly theatrical reading will prove to be a breath of fresh air to those who feel that Purcell's music in general can withstand being 'un-Englished' for want of new approaches to colour, characterisation and the composer's inimitable lyrical undercurrent. The odd instrumental dance seems a touch lacking in native roughage (and 'Destruction's our delight' seeks too much attention), but the finely proportioned Orchestra of the Age of Enlightenment bound through the Grove's Dance are even more purposeful in the First Sailor's song which opens Act 3. Then we have the great music, set up acutely in distant foreboding after Dido's initial air, way back in Act 1. Lynne Dawson will disappoint few in her devastated, long-breathed and honest 'Lament', elegantly turned (if not vocally peerless) and, crucially, consequential of so much that has passed before. The last chorus is more beautifully sung than you've ever heard: a true funeral rite. These are the elusive ingredients of a compelling and truly involved reading. Imaginative and invigorating, Jacobs has revitalised *Dido*, taking it further away from the banks of Chelsea to a more universal world where this masterpiece surely belongs.

Dido and Aeneas **P**

Catherine Bott *sop* Dido; **John Mark Ainsley** *ten* Aeneas; **Emma Kirkby** *sop* Belinda; **David Thomas** *bass* Sorceress; **Elizabeth Priday** *sop* First Witch; **Sara Stowe** *sop* Second Witch; **Julianne Baird** *sop* Second Woman; **Daniel Lochmann** *treb* First Sailor; **Michael Chance** *counterten* Spirit; **Academy of Ancient Music Chorus and Orchestra / Christopher Hogwood**

L'Oiseau-Lyre 436 992-2OHO (52 minutes: DDD) Ⓕ
Notes and text included. Recorded 1992 **OO**

Emma Kirkby (whose Dido, for Parrott on Chandos, remains one of the finest on record) sings Belinda for Hogwood; David Thomas (whose Aeneas, on the same recording, was outstanding) sings the Sorceress; Michael Chance takes the tiny part of the Spirit, thereby putting its moment into centre stage as the gloriously conceived turning-point of the story. A few innovations, too. Following the arguments that the Sorceress could be a man, Hogwood's choice of Thomas has offered us perhaps the most eloquent version on disc so far.

Thomas gives full value to the words and the music. Less convincing is the use of a boy for the sailor's song; despite direct and spirited singing, its text is quite inappropriate for a boy. Much more successful is the use of the Drottningholm wind-machines to interpret the various stage-instructions and give the entire performance a real sense of verisimilitude. Catherine Bott is a fine Dido, even-voiced across the range and powerfully expressive if occasionally a touch free with the rhythms. John Mark Ainsley easily stands as the finest Aeneas since David Thomas. This is a very difficult role to handle dramatically, because its moods change so fast; and Ainsley handles all this with heartbreaking ease. This is a classic interpretation. So too is Hogwood's reading of the score, with his faultless sense of the right speed and the right rhythm as well as his ability to see the moment when everything must be interrupted in order to give the required space to the drama.

Dido and Aeneas **P**

Véronique Gens *sop* Dido; **Nathan Berg** *bass-bar* Aeneas; **Sophie Marin-Degor** *sop* Belinda; **Claire Brua** *sop* Sorceress; **Sophie Daneman** *sop* Second Woman, First Witch; **Gaëlle Mechaly** *sop* Second Witch; **Jean-Paul Fouchécourt** *ten* Spirit, Sailor; **Les Arts Florissants / William Christie**

Erato 4509-98477-2 (52 minutes: DDD). Notes and Ⓕ text included. Recorded 1994

William Christie's reading of *Dido* is very much in terms of the reputed French influence on Purcell. Overdotting, reverse dotting and *inégalité* are used throughout; the lines are often heavily embellished in the manner of Lully. This is a perfectly justifiable approach to the music, since there is little direct evidence to say exactly how much the French style dominated in England. This version – with single strings, an excellent small choir and a slightly obtrusive harpsichord – stands well alongside what is otherwise available: if you prefer *Dido* in the French manner this is the record you will want; if not, you will probably still want it as a very different view of a major work. Apart from a few moments' inattention in Belinda's 'Haste, haste to town', you would hardly notice that most of the cast are Francophone, except in that Nathan Berg's imposing bass-baritone finds it slightly easier to exploit the colour and the meaning of Aeneas's words. Véronique Gens is a lucid and sensible Dido, partnered by a sprightly Belinda from Sophie Marin-Degor and a good Second Woman from Sophie Daneman. Claire Brua's Sorceress is a splendidly insinuating conception, with a slithering melodic style.

Perhaps the main musical distinction of this version is the way Christie presents the final paragraphs. Up to this point he has taken generally quick speeds, and he runs the final confrontation of Dido and Aeneas at a headlong tempo, which works very well. Then he comes almost to a standstill at the moment when Aeneas leaves the stage, choosing an unusually slow speed for the chorus 'Great minds against themselves conspire'. This makes way for a dangerously slow Lament, which is heart-stopping, and the final chorus, which is not.

Additional recommendation

Dido and Aeneas

Baker *Dido* **Herincx** *Aeneas* **Clark** *Belinda*
English Chamber Orchestra / A Lewis

Decca 466 387-2DM Ⓜ
(53 minutes: ADD: 5/00)

A very early recording (1961) by Janet Baker in a role she was to make very much her own. Lewis directs a traditional but sensitive account of the score.

The Indian Queen

Emma Kirkby, Catherine Bott *sops* **John Mark Ainsley** *ten* **Gerald Finley** *bar* **David Thomas** *bass* **Tommy Williams** *sngr* **Chorus and Orchestra of the Academy of Ancient Music / Christopher Hogwood** Ⓟ
Also includes additional Act by Daniel Purcell
L'Oiseau-Lyre 444 339-2OHO (73 minutes: DDD) Ⓕ
Notes and text included. Recorded 1994

Christopher Hogwood makes us realise that for all the constraints, this score is not inherently small-scale and that it warrants all the subtlety of colour that can be achieved using 12 soloists and a decent sized choir and orchestra. Needless to say, Hogwood conveys a consistent, logical and meticulous understanding of the score. The orchestral playing is crisp and transparent, the AAM's articulation allowing the integrity of the inner parts to be heard to the full without compromising blend. Among a distinguished line-up of singers, John Mark Ainsley gets the lion's share and is perhaps marginally more effective as the Indian Boy than as Fame, but such gloriously mellifluous and controlled singing can only enhance the reputation of this work.

Emma Kirkby is in fine fettle and she executes the justly celebrated song 'I attempt from love's sickness' with her usual communicative panache. Then comes the pleasurably contrasted voice of Catherine Bott: 'They tell us that your mighty powers' could not be in better hands. David Thomas as Envy, with his two followers in the Act 2 masque, highlights this brilliant scene as the work of a true connoisseur of the theatre. Mature Purcell is most strongly felt in the deftly ironic invocation by the conjurer, Ismeron, whose 'Ye twice 10,000 deities' is delivered authoritatively by Gerald Finley, though the lulling to sleep, before the God of Dream's gloomy non-prediction, is unconvincing. On the whole, the quality of music shines very brightly in this reading, though the performance is perhaps a touch calculated in places. Recommended.

The Indian Queen
Tessa Bonner, Catherine Bott *sops* **Rogers Covey-Crump** *ten* **Peter Harvey** *bass* **Purcell Simfony Voices; Purcell Simfony / Catherine Mackintosh** *vn*
Linn Records CKD035 (60 minutes: DDD) Ⓕ
Recorded 1994

If *The Indian Queen* is less ambitious than the other three 'operas' there is the sure touch here of the composer at his most mature and adept. The Prologue, in which he had the rare opportunity to set an extended dialogue, is beautifully balanced, the humour in Act 2 delicate and inimitably charming, and the music in Act 3 – when Zempoalla's ill-fated love is prophesied by Ismeron the magician in 'Ye twice 10,000 deities' – ranks alongside the finest moments in Purcell's output. The small-scale character of the work, compared to its siblings, is taken a stage further by the Purcell Simfony, which employs a minute chamber-size group of four strings, doubling oboe and recorder, single trumpet and drums. The soloists sing with airy restraint but each responds to these Hilliardesque proportions with a rhythmic buoyancy and direct intimacy which projects a finely gauged overall conception of the work.

If the expressive power of the music is at times rather glazed, there is a sure atmosphere which is captured by a delightful perspective on the recorded sound, ensuring the light puff-pastry of 'I come to sing great Zempoalla's story' and 'I attempt from love's sickness' is both warm and yet never imposing. The ensemble is not always first-rate but there is nothing too worrisome and the instrumental numbers are elegantly shaped. Tessa Bonner gets the lion's share of the solo soprano numbers, ahead of the more colourful Catherine Bott, though the former's comparatively brittle sound has a crystalline quality which suits director Catherine Mackintosh's consistent, if austere strategy. To sum up, this release is consistently touching, one which in a paradoxical way gets under the skin despite the recessed emotional climate it conveys.

King Arthur

Awards 1995

Véronique Gens, Claron McFadden, Sandrine Piau, Susannah Waters *sops* **Mark Padmore, Iain Paton** *tens* **Jonathan Best, Petteri Salomaa, François Bazola-Minori** *basses* **Les Arts Florissants Chorus and Orchestra / William Christie** Ⓟ
Erato ② 4509-98535-2 Ⓕ
(90 minutes: DDD). Notes and text included
Recorded 1995 OOO

If the co-operation with John Dryden led to a unity of vision in terms of music's expressive role in the overall drama, Purcell was limited to a historical patriotic fantasy with little room for the magic and pathos of, say, the superior *Fairy Queen*. Yet in the context of a stage presentation, Purcell's music shines through strongly. On disc though, with just the music, not even the dramatic powers of William Christie can restore its place in the overall scheme. But never mind, this is a score with some magnificent creations and Christie is evidently enchanted by it. The choral singing is richly textured, sensual and long-breathed, yet always alert to a nuance which can irradiate a passage at a stroke, as Christie does in the bittersweet close of 'Honour prizing' – easily the best moment in Act 1. The instrumental movements are finely moulded so that sinewy counterpoint and rhythmic profile are always strongly relayed. The songs, too, have been acutely prepared and are keenly characterised without resorting to excess. All the basses deliver their fine music with aplomb. If there is one drawback to extracting the musical numbers from the 'opera' when they have so clearly been delivered within a theatrical context, it is that the contextual characterizations lend themselves less well to the musical continuity of a CD. But *King Arthur* without the play is dramatically a nonsense so why try to pretend? Christie does not but makes the strongest case yet for this music.

The Tempest

The Tempest[a]. Suite in G minor, Z770 – Overture[b]. Chaconne for Strings in G minor, Z730[c]. Sonata for Trumpet and Strings No 2 in D, Z850[d]. If ever I more riches did desire, Z544[e]. The Indian Queen – Trumpet Overture[f] **P**

[a]**Michael Colvin** *ten* Aeolus; [ae]**Meredith Hall** *sop* Amphitrite; [a]**Rosemarie van der Hooft** *mez* Ariel; [ae]**Gillian Keith** *sop* Dorinda; [a]**Brett Polegato** *bar* Neptune, First Devil; [ae]**Paul Grindlay** *bass-bar* Second Devil; [a]**Robert Stewart** *voc* Third Devil; [e]**Nils Brown** *ten* [df]**Norman Engel** *tpt*
Aradia Baroque Ensemble / Kevin Mallon *vn*
Naxos 8 554262 (76 minutes: DDD) Ⓢ
Texts included. Recorded 1997

There is so much pleasure to be had from Purcell's semi-operas that it is easy to wish we had more of them. Much of *The Tempest* is thought to have been written by other hands, but that is no reason for refusing to give it shelf-room. The score is cast in the same mould as Purcell's fully accredited dramatic works and offers a similar range of music. The Aradia Baroque Ensemble have taken as their source an 18th-century copy held by the University of Toronto, which involves a few minor changes to the accepted score. The Overture, Z770, remains at the beginning, but the chorus 'The Nereids and Tritons' is omitted from Act 5 and the Chaconne, Z730, has been placed at the end.

This Canadian early music group have received good reviews for their previous discs of Caldara and Lully on Naxos, and their Purcell is just as appealing. Director Kevin Mallon does not fuss over shaping the slower music, and the fast numbers go with plenty of zest. The ensemble includes oboes, recorders and bassoons, quite sparingly used, and bells for the setting of Ariel's 'Full fathom five' (naughtily ringing in the rests between the words 'Ding dong bell'). The line-up of solo singers has no weak links and a few real strengths. Brett Polegato may lack authority in the role of Neptune, but sings with a fine, warm, well-rounded tone. Meredith Hall brings a winning sensitivity to the long solo 'Halcyon days' and finds an ideal soprano partner in the young Gillian Keith. Purcell's setting of 'If ever I more riches did desire' and his Trumpet Sonata No 2 are substantial makeweights. The recording acoustic is more church than theatre, but lively enough. Recommended.

Sergey Rachmaninov

USSR/American 1873-1943

GROVE *Rachmaninov studied at the Moscow Conservatory (1885-92) under Zverev (where Scriabin was a fellow pupil) and his cousin Ziloti for piano and Taneyev and Arensky for composition, graduating with distinction as both pianist and composer (the opera Aleko, given at the Bolshoi in 1893, was his diploma piece). During the ensuing years he composed piano pieces (including his famous C sharp minor Prelude), songs and orchestral works, but the disastrous première in 1897 of his Symphony No 1 brought about a creative despair that was not dispelled until he sought medical help in 1900: then he quickly composed his Second Piano Concerto. Meanwhile he had set out on a new career as a conductor, appearing in Moscow and London; he later was conductor at the Bolshoi, 1904-6.*

By this stage, and most particularly in the Piano Concerto No 2, the essentials of his art had been assembled: the command of the emotional gesture conceived as lyrical melody extended from small motifs, the concealment behind this of subtleties in orchestration and structure, the broad sweep of his lines and forms and loyalty to the finer Russian Romanticism inherited from Tchaikovsky and his teachers. During the remaining years to the Revolution these provided him with the materials for a sizable output of operas, liturgical music, orchestral works, piano pieces and songs. In 1909 he made his first American tour as a pianist, for which he wrote the Piano Concerto No 3.

Soon after the October Revolution he left Russia with his family for Scandinavia; in 1918 they arrived in New York, where he mainly lived thereafter, though he spent time in Paris, Dresden and Switzerland. There was a period of creative silence until 1926 when he wrote the Piano Concerto No 4, followed by only a handful of works over the next 15 years, even though all are on a large scale. During this period, he was active as a pianist on both sides of the Atlantic (though never again in Russia). As a pianist he was famous for his precision, rhythmic drive, legato and clarity of texture.

Complete Piano Concertos

No 1 in F sharp minor, Op 1; **No 2** in C minor, Op 18; **No 3** in D minor, Op 30; **No 4** in G minor, Op 40. **Rhapsody on a Theme of Paganini**, Op 43

Piano Concertos Nos 1-4. Paganini Rhapsody
Earl Wild *pf* **Royal Philharmonic Orchestra / Jascha Horenstein**
Chandos ② CHAN7114 (134 minutes: ADD) Ⓕ
Recorded 1965 ●

Such is the luxuriance of sound revealed in these remasterings, it is difficult to believe the recording date; and such is the quality of the piano playing that it is easy to understand why Chandos should have wanted to go to such trouble. There are not so many Rachmaninov pianists who dare to throw caution to the wind to the extent that Earl Wild does in the outer movements of the First Concerto, fewer still who can keep their technical poise in the process. The improvisatory feel to the lyricism of the slow movement is no less remarkable. Wild's panache is every bit as seductive in No 4, and the *Paganini Rhapsody* is a rare example of a performance faster than the composer's own – devilishly driven in the early variations and with tension maintained through the following slower ones so that the famous eighteenth can register as a release from a suffocating grip, rather than an overblown, out-of-context exercise in grandiosity. Because of his lightness and touch Wild's tempos never seem excessive. Undoubtedly he shifts the balance from languishing pathos and overwhelming grandeur towards straightforward exuberance; but that may be no bad thing for refreshing our view of the composer. It keeps us in touch with an earlier tradition. The RPO appears to be revelling in the whole affair, in a way one would not have immediately associated with Horenstein. To pick on the very few weaknesses, the very relaxed clarinet tone in the slow movement of Concerto No 2 rather misses the character, and elsewhere in this work the balance engineers rather crudely stick a microphone under the cello section's nostrils. But then the solo playing in this concerto is generally a little disappointing too, as though Wild had actually played the piece rather too often. In No 3 there are the hateful cuts to contend with, and one senses that the performance has been rather thoughtlessly modelled on the composer's own, idiosyncracies and all. None the less, for the sake of the outstanding performances of Nos 1 and 4 and the *Rhapsody*, and for the unique combination of old-style bravura and modern sound, this issue earns a strong recommendation.

Piano Concertos Nos 1-4
Vladimir Ashkenazy *pf* **London Symphony Orchestra / André Previn**
Double Decca ② 444 839-2DF2 (135 minutes: ADD) Ⓜ
Recorded 1970-72 **oo**

Despite the recording dates, the sound and balance are superb and there is nothing to cloud or impede one's sense of Ashkenazy's greatness in all these works. From him every page declares Rachmaninov's nationality, his indelibly Russian nature. What nobility of feeling and what dark regions of the imagination he relishes and explores in page after page of the Third Concerto. Significantly his opening is a very moderate *Allegro ma non tanto*, later allowing him an expansiveness and imaginative scope hard to find in other more 'driven' or hectic performances. His rubato is as natural as it is distinctive and his way of easing from one idea to another shows him at his most intimately and romantically responsive. There are no cuts, and his choice of the bigger of the two cadenzas is entirely apt, given the breadth of his conception. Even the skittering figurations and volleys of repeated notes just before the close of the central *Intermezzo* cannot tempt Ashkenazy into display and he is quicker than any other pianist to find a touch of wistfulness beneath Rachmaninov's occasional outer playfulness (the *scherzando* episode in the finale).

Such imaginative fervour and delicacy are just as central to Ashkenazy's other performances. His steep unmarked *decrescendo* at the close of the First Concerto's opening rhetorical gesture is symptomatic of his romantic bias, his love of the music's interior glow. And despite his prodigious command in, say, the final pages of both the First and Fourth Concertos, there is never a hint of bombast or a more superficial brand of fire-and-brimstone virtuosity. Previn works hand in glove with his soloist. Clearly, this is no one-night partnership but the product of the greatest musical sympathy, of a mutual skill and affection. The opening of the Third Concerto's *Intermezzo* could hardly be given with a more idiomatic, brooding melancholy, a perfect introduction for all that is to follow. If you want playing which captures Rachmaninov's always elusive, opalescent centre then Ashkenazy is hard to beat. (The Second Concerto, our first choice in this work, is available on a single disc and is reviewed below.)

Piano Concertos Nos 1 and 4. Paganini Rhapsody
Zoltán Kocsis *pf* **San Francisco Symphony Orchestra / Edo de Waart**
Philips Solo 446 582-2PM (72 minutes: DDD) Ⓜ
Recorded 1982 **o**

Piano Concertos Nos 2 and 3. Vocalise (arr Kocsis)
Zoltán Kocsis *pf* **San Francisco Symphony Orchestra / Edo de Waart**
Philips Solo 446 199-2PM (75 minutes: DDD) Ⓜ
Recorded 1978-84 **o**

Few if any readings of the piano concertos and the *Paganini* Rhapsody spark or scintillate with such daredevilry, are of such unapologetic virtuoso voltage, as these. True, Kocsis can sometimes be more voluble than poised, breezing through the Third Concerto's haunting opening theme at the fastest flowing tempo and – for lovers of the ever-romantic Var 18 from the *Paganini* Rhapsody, in particular – sometimes sacrificing heart's-ease for high-octane bravura. Again, you may question his near *allegretto* spin through the Second Concerto's central *Adagio*, eagerly glimpsing so many dazzling athletic opportunities ahead. Even so, try him in the Third Concerto's cadenza (the slimmer and better of the two) and you will hear it topped and tailed with a ferocious and almost palpable aplomb. Listen to him snapping off phrase ends in the intricate reel of the *Paganini* Rhapsody's Var 15 or flashing fire in the *Allegro leggiero* from the First Concerto's finale and you may well wonder when you last encountered such fearless brilliance, pace and relish. Even those attuned to the darker, more introspective Rachmaninov of Ashkenazy will surely pause to wonder. Edo de Waart and the San Francisco Symphony Orchestra are no match for the LSO for Previn; yet, overall, this is the most propulsive and exciting set of the complete concertos. Kocsis's whirlwind tempos even allow him time for an encore – his own ardent elaboration of the *Vocalise*, a performance sufficiently ecstatic to set even the least susceptible heart a-flutter.

Piano Concerto No 1

Piano Concerto No 1[a]. Paganini Rhapsody[b]
Vladimir Ashkenazy *pf* [a]**Concertgebouw Orchestra;** [b]**Philharmonia Orchestra / Bernard Haitink**
Decca 417 613-2DH (52 minutes: DDD) Ⓕ

Showpiece that it is, with its lush romantic harmonies and contrasting vigorous panache, the First Concerto has much to commend it in purely musical terms and although its debts are clear enough (most notably perhaps to Rimsky-Korsakov), it stands on its own two feet as far as invention, overall design and musical construction are concerned. The *Paganini* Rhapsody is one of the composer's finest works and arguably the most purely inventive set of variations to be based on Paganini's catchy tune ever written. The wealth of musical invention it suggested to Rachmaninov is truly bewildering and his control over what can in lesser hands become a rather laboured formal scheme is masterly indeed. Ashkenazy gives superb performances of both works and the Concertgebouw and the Philharmonia are in every way the perfect foils under Bernard Haitink's sympathetic direction. There is weight, delicacy, colour, energy and repose in equal measure here and it is all conveyed by a full-bodied and detailed recording.

Piano Concerto No 2

Piano Concerto No 2. Paganini Rhapsody
Vladimir Ashkenazy *pf* **London Symphony Orchestra / André Previn**
Decca Ovation 417 702-2DM (58 minutes: ADD) Ⓜ
Recorded 1970-72 **OO**

What emerges most obviously here is the keen poetic individuality of Ashkenazy as a Rachmaninov interpreter. The composer himself is far rougher with his music than Ashkenazy ever is. Those who like Rachmaninov concertos to sound forceful above all will no doubt have reservations, but rarely has this work sounded so magically poetic. That is not just Ashkenazy's doing – his rubato is consistently natural – but the work of Previn and his players. Orchestral detail emerges more clearly than on other recordings, but thanks to finely balanced orchestral recording (no exaggeration of big violin tone) there are no gimmicks. The flute and clarinet *staccatos* for example after fig 39 in the finale are clear but unexaggerated, where too often engineers are tempted to bring those instruments unnaturally forward.

The playing of both Ashkenazy and the LSO continually conveys the impression not of a warhorse but of a completely new work; even such a favourite passage as the return of the slow-movement main theme just before fig 26 is pure and completely unhackneyed. But the performance which clinches the success of this delightful venture is that of the *Paganini Rhapsody*, magical from beginning to end in its concentrated sense of continuity, with the varying moods over the 24 variations leading inevitably from one to another. There is no great splurge of emotion on the great eighteenth variation, but instead there is a ripe sense of fulfilment, which is utterly tasteful. Although the final surprising quiet cadence could be pointed with more wit, the rest has so much delicacy that it is a marginal reservation.

Piano Concerto No 3

Piano Concerto No 3 in D minor, Op 30[a]. Cello Sonata in G minor, Op 19 – Andante (arr Volodos). Morceaux de fantaisie, Op 3 – No 5, Sérénade in B flat minor. Morceaux de salon, Op 10 – No 6, Romance in F minor. Preludes – F minor, Op 32 No 6. Prelude in D minor. Etudes-tableaux, Op 33 – No 9 in C sharp minor
Arcadi Volodos *pf* [a]**Berlin Philharmonic Orchestra / James Levine**
Sony Classical SK64384 (61 minutes: DDD) Ⓕ
Recorded 2000 and [a]live in 1999 **OO**

Straight into the top flight of Rachmaninov Thirds goes Arcadi Volodos's recording, live from the Berlin Philharmonie last year. No doubt about that. To the top of the top flight? Not quite. And no doubt about that either.

So many things about it are distinguished and thrilling. The flowing tempo of the opening bars and the subtle assertion of soloistic presence augur well. The way Volodos slows the end of the first mini-cadenza (towards 2'40") won't appeal to everyone, but at least Levine ensures that the following orchestral transition keeps moving. Otherwise Volodos's phrasing is consummately tasteful, all the way through to the cadenza. His textures are superbly graded, his tone never glaring, even under the pressure of torrents of notes. So what if he doesn't feel obliged to follow the tempos the composer chose for his 1939-40 recording? Why should he, when he has such a fine grasp of the structure? There is the feeling of a deep intake of breath as the development starts, and the cadenza (the 'big' original one) opens with a darkly idiomatic frown, suggesting limitless strength.

All is well, in fact, until mid-way in the cadenza, where Volodos inserts a hiatus before the *Allegro molto* (at 11'08"). It sounds terribly calculated, as does the way he steers the cadenza towards its main climax. Of course, a couple of mannerisms in a performance are neither here nor there. And if Volodos takes the end of the first-movement *subito più mosso*, rather than *poco accelerando al fine*, that's no more cavalier than many of the great exponents of the past. What is bothersome – and this is increasingly noticeable in the slow movement and the finale – is that such initiatives don't always feel part of an organically conceived interpretation (the composer himself remains the touchstone here). Nor do they register as spontaneous expressions of temperament or inspiration. Just a whiff of self-consciousness can be enough to cancel out a host of poetic or virtuosic touches. So while as a listener you may be amazed, and as a pianist envious, at the clarity and velocity Volodos can bring to the toccata from 7'20" in the finale, in the overall context it feels like a gratuitous display. That's just the most conspicuous example. In some ways it is surprising to hear applause at the end, since the performance, fine though it is, has the feel of the studio rather than a live occasion, not least because it is so fantastically clean.

Overall then this is not a world-beater, but certainly one to assess at the highest level.

Nothing but praise can be showered upon the BPO for their wonderfully cushioned but never complacent accompaniment and upon Levine for his avoidance of all the usual pitfalls. The piano is quite forwardly balanced, so that every tiniest note emerges bright as a new pin; and given how wonderfully Volodos shapes everything, it's fine, although you do occasionally feel that you aren't hearing the orchestra in its full glory. One or two woodwind solos sound artificially spotlit, but not outrageously so.

As for the solo pieces, the Cello Sonata arrangement is a marvel. It floats ecstatically, with air seemingly blowing through the textures as if through a Chekhovian country house on a cool summer evening. The final flourishes – Volodos's addition – have a touch of genius. This is heavenly, and the other solos are little short of that.

Rachmaninov Piano Concerto No 3[a]
Tchaikovsky Piano Concerto No 1 in B flat minor, Op 23[b]
Martha Argerich *pf* [a]**Berlin Radio Symphony Orchestra / Riccardo Chailly;** [b]**Bavarian Radio Symphony Orchestra / Kyrill Kondrashin**
Philips 446 673-2PH (73 minutes: DDD) Ⓕ
Recorded live in [a]1982 and [b]1980 ●●●

To describe both performances as 'live' is to deal in understatement, for rarely in her entire and extraordinary career has Argerich sounded more exhaustingly restless and quixotic, her mind and fingers flashing with reflexes merely dreamt of by other less phenomenally endowed pianists. Yet her Rachmaninov is full of surprises, her opening *Allegro* almost convivial until she meets directions such as *più vivo* or *veloce*, where the tigress in her shows her claws and the music is made to seethe and boil. The cadenza (the finer and more transparent of the two) rises to the sort of climax that will make all pianists' hearts beat faster and her first entry in the 'Intermezzo' interrupts the orchestra's musing with the impatience of a hurricane. But throughout these pages it is almost as if she is searching for music that will allow her virtuosity its fullest scope. In the finale she finds it, accelerating out of the second movement with a sky-rocketing propulsion. Here the music races like wildfire, with a truly death-defying turn of speed at 7'21" and an explosive energy throughout that must have left audience, conductor and orchestra feeling as if hit by some seismic shock-wave.

The Tchaikovsky, too, finds Argerich at her most inflammatory. Those who like their Tchaikovsky to be more magisterial and composed will look elsewhere but who would miss volleys of octave spun off like single notes, or a second movement central *Prestissimo* dispatched at a scarcely credible tempo? A performance, then, for those who like life in the fast lane, though it has to be said that such incandescence is hardly flaunted, more a 'spontaneous overflow of powerful feelings' of emotion recollected not so much in tranquillity as in fire and fury.
The recordings, given the tricky circumstances, are remarkably successful.

Rachmaninov Piano Concerto No 3 🅗
Tchaikovsky Piano Concerto No 1 in B flat minor, Op 23
Vladimir Horowitz *pf* **New York Philharmonic Symphony Orchestra / Sir John Barbirolli**
APR mono APR5519 (66 minutes: ADD) Ⓕ
Recorded live in 1940-41 ●●●

This is the Rachmaninov Third to end all Rachmaninov Thirds, a performance of such super-human pianistic aplomb, pace and virtuosity that it makes all comparisons, save with Horowitz himself, a study in irrelevance. It was Horowitz's 1930 recording with Albert Coates that made Artur Rubinstein pale with envy; goodness knows how he would have reacted had he heard Horowitz and Barbirolli! Taken from a 1941 New York broadcast (with apologies from the producer for snaps, crackles, pops and the like) Horowitz's tumultuous, near-apocalyptic brilliance includes all his unique and tirelessly debated attributes; his swooning rubato, thundering bass and splintering treble, his explosive attack, his super-erotic inflexions and turns of phrase. Try the skittering *scherzando* variation just before the close of the central *Intermezzo* and note how the pianist's velocity eclipses even his legendary recording with Fritz Reiner. This ultimate wizard of the keyboard is in expansive mood in the Tchaikovsky. There are ample rewards, too, for those who rejoice in Horowitz at his most clamorous, for the thunder and lightning of this 'Tornado from the Steppes'. The performance ends in what can only be described as a scream of octaves and an outburst by an audience driven near to hysteria. Barbirolli and the New York Philharmonic Symphony Orchestra are equal to just about every twist and turn of their volatile soloist's argument and so these performances (and most notably the finale of the Rachmaninov) are simply beyond price.

Piano Concerto No 4

Rachmaninov Piano Concerto No 4 🅗
Ravel Piano Concerto in G
Arturo Benedetti Michelangeli *pf* **Philharmonia Orchestra / Ettore Gracis**
EMI Great Recordings of the Century CDM5 67238-2 Ⓜ
(47 minutes: ADD). Recorded 1957 ●●●

In crude and subjective terms Michelangeli makes the spine tingle in a way no others can approach. How does he do it? Of course this is the secret every pianist would love to know, and which no writer can ever pin down. But it is possible to give some general indications. It is not a question of technique, at least not directly, because Ashkenazy, for example (on Decca) can match their most virtuosic feats; indirectly, yes, it is relevant, in that there are dimensions in Michelangeli's pianism which allow musical conceptions to materialise which might not dawn on others. It is not a question of structure, in the narrow sense of the awareness of overall proportions, judicious shaping of paragraphs, continuity of thought; but the way structure is projected and the way it is transmuted into emotional drama; of course these things are critical.

In one way or another most of the recordings in this section respond vividly to the excitement of Rachmaninov's dramatic climaxes; but with Michelangeli these climaxes seem to burst through the music of their own volition, as though an irresistible force of nature has been released. It is this crowning of a structure by release, rather than by extra pressure, which gives the performance a sense of exaltation and which more than anything else sets it on a different level. It enables him to be freer in many details (some of which may not be universally approved) yet seem more inevitable as a whole.

The impact of all this would be negligible without a sympathetically attuned conductor and orchestra. Fortunately that is exactly what Michelangeli has. Michelangeli's Ravel is open to criticism, partly because many listeners feel uncomfortable with his persistent left-before-right mannerism in the slow movement and with his unwarranted textual tinkerings (like changing the last note). But he is as finely attuned to this aloof idiom as to its temperamental opposite in the Rachmaninov. And although the recording cannot entirely belie its vintage, it does justice to one of the finest concerto records ever made.

'The Complete Recordings'

Awards 1993

Piano Concertos – Nos 1[b], 2[a], 3[b] and 4[b]. Paganini Rhapsody[a]. The isle of the dead, Op 29[c]. Vocalise, Op 34 No 14[c]. Symphony No 3 in A minor, Op 44[c]. Daisies. Nine Etudes tableaux, Op 33 – No 2 in C; No 7 in E flat. Etude tableau in A minor, Op 39 No 6. Lilacs (two versions, recorded in 1923 and 1942). Six Moments musicaux, Op 16 – Allegretto. Sérénade in B flat minor, Op 3 No 5. Humoresque in G, Op 10 No 5. Oriental Sketch in B flat. Polka de W R (three versions, recorded in 1919, 1921 and 1928). Preludes – C sharp minor, Op 3 No 2 (three versions, recorded in 1919, 1921 and 1928); G minor, Op 23 No 5; G flat, Op 23 No 10; E, Op 32 No 3; G, Op 32 No 5; F minor, Op 32 No 6; G sharp minor, Op 32 No 12 (H)

Beethoven Violin Sonata No 8 in G, Op 30 No 3. 32 Variations on an original theme in C minor, WoO80. **Schubert** Violin Sonata in A (Duo), D574. **Grieg** Violin Sonata No 3 in C minor, Op 45. **Schumann** Carnaval, Op 9. **Chopin** Piano Sonata No 2 in B flat minor, Op 35. Also includes solo piano works by other composers

Fritz Kreisler *vn* **Sergey Rachmaninov** *pf*
Philadelphia Orchestra / [a]Leopold Stokowski, [b]Eugene Ormandy, [c]Sergey Rachmaninov
RCA Victor Gold Seal mono ⑩ 09026 61265-2 (640 minutes: ADD). Recorded 1919-42 Ⓜ OOO

Here, on RCA's superbly remastered 10-disc set, is awe-inspiring and scintillating confirmation of Rachmaninov's greatness; as composer, pianist, chamber musician and conductor. Controversy over his stature as a composer may live on in the dustier corners of academia, but today once confident assertions that his music would never last, that it lacked the regenerative force of true tragedy or that it was, in essence, little more than a precursor of Hollywood, have been triumphantly erased. Works such as the Second Symphony, the Third Piano Concerto and the Second Piano Sonata are played without the once acceptable and debilitating cuts so sadly sanctioned by the composer, and innovative as well as traditional elements in Rachmaninov's writing are celebrated. What is indisputable, however, is Rachmaninov's quality as a pianist. Alternatively teasing and granitic in other composer's music (his way with Schumann's *Carnaval* and Chopin's Second Sonata, to name but two, will always incite argument) his performances of his own works are, quite simply, inimitable, imbued with a brio and aristocracy entirely his own. The most immediately appealing include all four concertos and the Paganini *Rhapsody*, Handel's *Harmonious Blacksmith* Variations (pure pianistic sorcery) and Rachmaninov's own second *Moment musical* and *Mélodie*, Op 3 No 2; the former of a mind-bending virtuosity, the latter aglow with the *cantabile* and rubato of another, far-off age. But everything is absorbing, nothing without interest. These recordings blazen out Rachmaninov's stature both as creator and re-creator in every golden bar.

Complete Symphonies

No 1 in D minor, Op 13; **No 2** in E minor, Op 27; **No 3** in A minor, Op 44. **Symphonic Dances**, Op 45

Symphonies Nos 1, 2[a] and 3[b]. Symphonic Dances, Op 45[b]. The isle of the dead, Op 29. Vocalise (arr cpsr). Aleko – Intermezzo; Gipsy Girls' Dance
London Symphony Orchestra / André Previn
EMI ③ CMS7 64530-2 (227 minutes: ADD) Ⓜ
Recorded 1974-76 OO

Items marked [ab] are also available on HMV Classics [a]HMV5 72833-2 and [b]HMV5 73475-2 Ⓑ

Rachmaninov's three symphonies reflect three very different phases in his creative development: the first (1895) is a stormy synthesis of contemporary trends in Russian symphonic music, the Second (1906-07), an epic study in Tchaikovskian opulence, and the third (1935-36) a seemingly unstoppable stream of original ideas and impressions. The Second was the first to gain wide acceptance, and with good reason. It shares both the key and general mood of Tchaikovsky's Fifth. Cast in E minor, its initial gloom ultimately turns to triumph, and the symphony includes enough glorious melodies to keep Hollywood happy for decades.

The First Symphony had a difficult birth, largely through the incompetent musical midwifery of Alexander Glazunov whose conducting of the work's première apparently left much to be desired. It is, however, an immensely promising piece and although undeniably the product of its times, prophetic not only of the mature Rachmaninov, but of other Northern voices, including – occasionally – the mature Sibelius. Both the Third Symphony and its near-contemporary, the *Symphonic Dances* find Rachmaninov indulging a fruitful stream of musical consciousness, recalling motives and ideas from earlier compositions, yet allowing gusts of fresh air to enliven and rejuvenate his style. Both works have yet to receive their full due in the concert hall, although the strongly evocative *Isle of the dead* is more securely embedded in the repertory.

What with these and a trio of warming shorter pieces, André Previn's mid-1970s LSO package is an excellent bargain. The performances are entirely sympathetic, avoiding familiar interpretative extremes such as slickness, bombast and emotional indulgence. Previn shows particular understanding of the Third Symphony, the *Symphonic Dances* and *The isle of the dead*, works that represent Rachmaninov at his most innovative and assured. The Second Symphony is played without cuts (not invariably the case, even today) and the recordings are generous in tone and revealing of detail.

Symphonies Nos 1-3
Concertgebouw Orchestra / Vladimir Ashkenazy
Double Decca ② 448 116-2DF2 (140 minutes: DDD) Ⓜ
Recorded 1980-82 ●●

Ashkenazy has made few more distinguished discs as conductor than his Rachmaninov symphony recordings of the early 1980s. They are to that decade what Ormandy's were to the 1960s or Previn's to the 1970s and their appearance in this two-disc format has the obvious attraction of economy. The downside of the repackaging is that you have to put up with a change of disc half-way through the Second Symphony and lose the shorter orchestral works included in the Previn set. Previn is the most natural but not always the most electrifying of Rachmaninov interpreters and many will find Ashkenazy preferable, particularly in No 1. Although some of Ashkenazy's speeds seem unnaturally pressed – he fairly tips us into the first movement reprise having declined to cap the climax with unvalidated bells – the excitement is infectious. Previn's LSO is not at its best in the *Larghetto* (placed third), but in the corresponding movement of the Second Symphony the boot is on the other foot. Not that Ashkenazy isn't convincing too – so long as you can forget the Previn. Ashkenazy's volatile approach is at its most extreme in the Third, the mood much less autumnal than it usually is, with the fruity Concertgebouw brass unconstrained. Such an unashamedly episodic rendering of the score has its drawbacks, but the virtuosic energy and romantic gush are hard to resist. Throughout the cycle, the players are unfailingly alert and the recordings sound very well indeed.

Symphony No 2

Symphony No 2. The Rock, Op 7
Russian National Orchestra / Mikhail Pletnev
DG 439 888-2GH (64 minutes: DDD) Ⓕ
Recorded 1993 ●●

Mikhail Pletnev's achievement is to make us hear the music afresh: a performance characterised by relatively discreet emotionalism, strong forward momentum and a fanatical preoccupation with clarity of articulation. When there is no Slavic wobble, it scarcely matters that his winds display an individuality which once or twice fails to transcend mere rawness – so much the better in this music! The strings, forceful and husky (with separated violin desks) are beyond reproach. The most remarkable playing comes in the finale. The lyrical effusions are superbly characterised without undermining the sense of inexorability, the climaxes not just powerful but affecting too. The closing pages bring a rush of adrenalin of the kind rarely experienced live, let alone in the studio. This is great music-making, the rubato always there when required, the long phrases immaculately tailored yet always sounding spontaneous. DG's unexpected coupling is *The Rock*, an early, rather bitty piece which is however very deftly scored and intriguingly Scriabinesque in places. In Pletnev's hands, the central climax is surprisingly powerful, with just a hint of the buzz-saw in the brass playing. The fabulous delicacy elsewhere is alone worth the price of admission.

Symphony No 3

Symphony No 3. Symphonic Dances
St Petersburg Philharmonic Orchestra / Mariss Jansons
EMI CDC7 54877-2 (72 minutes: DDD) Ⓕ
Recorded 1992 ●

This is one of the more distinguished Rachmaninov issues of recent years. While no Rachmaninov Third unfolds as inexorably as Previn's (reviewed above), it is refreshing to hear the opening 'motto' theme played perfectly in tune by an orchestra on even more dazzling form than the LSO, and Jansons unearths such exquisite details of sonority and texture that criticism is all but silenced. There have been more haunting, more fundamentally pessimistic accounts, but none with such an ear for Rachmaninov's sometimes risky orchestral effects. The *Symphonic Dances* are even more impressive. The insinuating waltz movement is irresistible, very free with idiomatic-sounding rubato, while the dynamic outer portions of the finale are superbly articulated, dazzling in the closing stages. EMI's close-miking of instrumental lines may inhibit the sort of tonal blend implied by Rachmaninov's scoring, but the distinctive heft and huskiness of Mravinsky's string section is not betrayed. In its lush, extrovert way, this disc is unbeatable.

Symphony No 3. Morceaux de fantaisie, Op 3 – No 3, Mélodie in E; No 4, Polichinelle in F sharp minor (both orch anon)
National Symphony Orchestra of Ireland / Alexander Anissimov
Naxos 8 550808 (52 minutes: DDD) Ⓢ
Recorded 1996

Can Anissimov hope to compete in a field that includes Ashkenazy's high-octane digital accounts in sundry bargain formats, not least a Double Decca two-pack offering all three symphonies? Perhaps surprisingly the answer is yes, for the conductor produces a highly distinctive performance of the Third, inspiring his orchestra to playing of considerable warmth and flair. Sound quality is excellent too. String tone is crucially important with this composer, and here again any worries prove unfounded. Not for Anissimov the 'neurotic' Russian-ness of Ashkenazy's Rachmaninov. Like Jansons, he disregards the first-movement exposition repeat, but he makes the orchestral voices speak with a gentler tone. There are shattering climaxes when the music calls for them, and the symphony ends in rousing style; elsewhere the sophisticated languor and careful phrasing recall André Previn's famous recording. Although some will be disappointed with the generally slow tempos, there is an unusual wholeness of musical vision and pacing which never sacrifices the needs of the larger structure to the lure of momentary thrills. The couplings are somewhat mysterious as no arranger is cited. Despite the short measure, this is thoroughly recommendable at the price.

Symphonic Dances

Symphonic Dances. The bells, Op 35
Elizaveta Shumskaya *sop* **Mikhail Dovenman** *ten* **Alexei Bolshakov** *bar* **Russian Republican Chamber Choir; Moscow Philharmonic Orchestra / Kyrill Kondrashin**
Melodiya 74321 32046-2 (69 minutes: ADD) Ⓜ
Recorded 1964 ●●

The *Symphonic Dances* receive a terrific, no-holds-barred performance. As you might expect, Kondrashin ignores the curious *Non allegro* tempo direction for the first movement and, unlike so many conductors, he is unfazed by Rachmaninov's unexpected reprise of the Orthodox chant, *Blagosloven esi, Gospodi*, towards the end of the last. Ploughing on with no loss of tension he finds additional adrenalin for the final bars. The concluding gong stroke, not taken literally as a dotted crotchet, is allowed to resonate a while. The transfers are not particularly distinguished. The picture is inclined to break up at climaxes, something odd has happened to the dynamic range and the tone is raw. Nevertheless, collectors will want this disc.

Neither work was at all familiar in the 1960s – fashionable opinion having all but silenced *The bells* in the UK – so Kondrashin's LPs were an important step towards the rehabilitation of a major composer. The performance of the choral work may strike some as unsophisticated but the music-making is hugely exciting in the classic Kondrashin manner. It is sung in Russian, of course, and it is extraordinary how this, together with the very Russian solo voices, turns it into a completely Russian work. Even if the soprano and baritone have a pretty wide vibrato and even sometimes tend to scoop, their singing is extremely exciting. The chorus is excellent. In both works, Kondrashin offers maximum impact, minimum fuss.

Trios élégiaques

Trio elegiaques in G minor; D minor, Op 9
Copenhagen Trio (Søren Elbaek *vn* Troels Svane Hermansen *vc* Morten Mogensen *pf*)
Kontrapunkt 32187 (65 minutes: DDD) Ⓕ
Recorded 1994 ●

The shade of Tchaikovsky haunts both these works. In the first, there are turns of phrase from his Trio, and much of the style and the textural approach to the problems derive from his example – not always a very good one, when it came to dealing with a virtuoso piano part against the weaker sound of the strings. Rachmaninov is ingenious, and handles his material expertly in a long, shapely movement. Tchaikovsky is more consciously the exemplar of the second Trio. Deeply impressed by the younger composer's *The Rock*, he had agreed to conduct the first performance in January 1894, a rare gesture of appreciation. On Tchaikovsky's death in October, the shocked Rachmaninov wrote his Trio 'in memory of a great artist', just as Tchaikovsky had once written a Trio in memory of another great artist, Nikolay Rubinstein. And here, too, there is a substantial variation movement, on a theme from *The Rock*. It is lyrically varied, not with conscious allusions after the manner of Tchaikovsky's elegy but with a sense of indebtedness that is unmistakable. Rachmaninov initially intended to have the opening statement of the theme played on the harmonium; he later revised the work, removing this appalling idea, and it is the second version which is recorded here – and well, in a fine performance that does full justice to a lengthy but affecting piece.

Complete Piano Music

Variations on a Theme of Chopin, Op 22. Variations on a Theme of Corelli, Op 42. Mélodie in E, Op 3 No 3. Piano Sonatas – No 1 in D minor, Op 28; No 2 in B flat minor, Op 36 (orig version); No 2 in B flat minor, Op 36 (rev version). 10 Preludes, Op 23. 13 Preludes, Op 32. Prelude in D minor. Prelude in F. Morceaux de fantaisie, Op 3. Morceau de fantaisie in G minor. Song without words in D minor. Pièce in D minor. Fughetta in F. Moments musicaux, Op 16. Fragments in A flat. Oriental Sketch in B flat. Three Nocturnes – No 1 in F sharp minor; No 2 in F; No 3 in C minor. Quatre Pièces – Romance in F sharp minor; Prélude in E flat minor; Mélodie in E; Gavotte in D. 17 Etudes-tableaux, Opp 33 and 39.
Transcriptions – **Bach** Solo Violin Partita No 3 in E, BWV1006 – Preludio, Gavotte, Gigue **Behr** Lachtäubchen, Op 303 (pubd as Polka de VR) **Bizet** L'Arlésienne Suite No 1 – Menuet **Kreisler** Liebesleid. Liebesfreud **Mendelssohn** A Midsummer Night's Dream, Op 61 – Scherzo **Mussorgsky** Sorochinsky Fuir – Gopak **Rachmaninov** Daisies, Op 38 No 3. Lilacs, Op 21 No 5. Vocalise, Op 34 No 14 (arr Kocsis) **Rimsky-Korsakov** The Tale of Tsar Saltan – The Flight

Rachmaninov Instrumental

of the Bumble-bee **Schubert** Die schöne Müllerin, D957 – Wohin? **Tchaikovsky** Cradle Song, Op 16 No 1
Howard Shelley pf
Hyperion ⑧ CDS44041/8 (449 minutes: DDD) Ⓜ
Recorded 1978-91 ●

This Hyperion set is a significant testament to Howard Shelley's artistry. Pianistically impeccable, he understands what Rachmaninov was about. The original piano works span 45 years of the composer's life. The earliest pieces here, the *Nocturnes*, strangely owe allegiance neither to Field nor Chopin, but are very much in the mid- to late 19th-century Russian salon style. The Third, in C minor, has nothing whatever to do with its title. Nicely written too, but still uncharacteristic, are four pieces from 1888, which amply demonstrate that from his early teens the composer had something individual to say. The *Mélodie* in E major is memorable for its hypnotic use of piano tone. Hyperion's recording quality can be heard at its very best here; there is real bloom and colour. Written shortly after his First Piano Concerto in the early 1890s, the *Morceaux de fantaisie*, Op 3 bring us to familiar Rachmaninov. The ubiquitous Prelude in C sharp minor is the second number but Shelley tries to do too much with it; he is more effective in the *Sérénade* with its Spanish overtones. In the E flat minor *Moment musical*, Op 16 one feels that he is able to master Rachmaninov's swirling accompaniments idiomatically. In Variation No 15 of the *Variations on a Theme of Chopin* he succeeds in bringing the notes to life, getting his fingers around the fleet *scherzando* writing.

The first set of Preludes is, of course, mainstream repertoire. In the warmly expressive D major Prelude he lends the piece a strong Brahmsian feel and it emerges as very well focused. He transforms the C minor into a restless mood picture. The First Sonata is often dismissed as being unwieldy but Shelley gives it a symphonic stature and allows it to be seen in conjunction more with the composer's orchestral writing. Shortly after the Third Concerto Rachmaninov wrote the Op 32 Preludes. Shelley conjures up an exquisite moonlit scene for the G major, but he is not as impressive in the B minor. However, with him it is always the music that dictates the course of the interpretation. In the two sets of *Etudes-tableaux* he excels, as he does too in the Second Sonata. He draws together the disparate elements of the finale with terrific mastery and is the equal of the 'Horowitz clones' for technique. In the *Corelli* Variations he is not quite in tune with the scope of the work but is outstanding in the transcriptions, if a little straight-faced. The recorded sound is never less than serviceable and is sometimes excellent.

Piano Sonata No 1

Rachmaninov Piano Sonata No 1 **Scriabin** Piano Sonatas – No 1 in F minor, Op 6; No 4 in F sharp, Op 30
Sergio Fiorentino pf
APR APR5556 (72 minutes: DDD) Ⓜ
Recorded 1995 ●

Sergio Fiorentino's reading of Scriabin's Fourth Piano Sonata is more intense and focused than most recent recordings. The delineation between melody and accompaniment in the opening movement is brilliantly accomplished and the winged *Prestissimo volando* which follows is exhilarating and superbly controlled. The First Sonata is no less impressive. His reading has youthful impetuosity in the first movement coupled with a powerful, tragic undertone in the second and fourth, and there is an imperious authority in his interpretation. Rachmaninov's First Piano Sonata has immense authority too, especially in the opening movement which is given a forceful, yet finely controlled, reading. Fiorentino strides through its formidable demands with consummate ease, and in the *Lento* there is much to be admired in his *cantabile* and beautiful phrasing. A very rewarding disc from a pianist of tremendous stature.

Piano Sonata No 2

Piano Sonata No 2 (original version). Preludes – Op 23: No 1 in F sharp minor; No 7 in C minor; Op 32: No 2 in B flat minor; No 6 in F minor; No 9 in A; No 10 in B minor. Etudes-tableaux – Op 39: No 2 in B minor; No 7 in C minor; F minor, Op 33 No 1. Morceaux de fantaisie, Op 3 – No 3 in E, 'Mélodie'; No 5 in B flat minor, 'Sérénade'
Zoltán Kocsis pf
Philips 446 220-2PH Ⓕ
(61 minutes: DDD). Recorded 1994 ●●

This richly exploratory recital – far removed from a popular or commercial programme – contradicts at every turn stale, still prevailing notions concerning Rachmaninov. For not only is the Second Sonata played in its original 1913 version rather than the stitched-together 1931 revision, but the shorter items include many of the composer's finest works. The seventh rather than the first C minor *Etude-tableau*, Op 39, for example, is an elegy of the most startling modernity with its *lamentoso* outcries, its memory of the Russian liturgy and its massive central carillon. How refreshing, too, to open with the Brahmsian syncopation and expressive richness of the A major Prelude, Op 32 No 9 and to mix mood and key to such kaleidoscopic and dazzling effect. Throughout, Kocsis's performances are as bold and stimulating as his choice of works, gloriously free-spirited and of an immense pianistic brio and command. Indeed his performance of the Second Sonata is as fulminating and rhapsodic as any on record. Action-packed in an exhausting and enthralling way, his reading never sounds arch or contrived. Kocsis possesses a stupendous technique, stepping out in dazzling style in the ultra-Russian *Etude-tableau*, Op 33 No 1 and clarifying the Siberian whirlwind of the F minor Prelude, Op 32 No 6 with a breathtaking clarity and focus. Kocsis's accompanying essay is no less stimulating and astringent than his playing (he is unsparing over the 1931 revision of the Sonata) and he has been magnificently recorded.

Piano Sonata No 2 in B flat minor, Op 36. Etudes-tableaux, Op 39
Freddy Kempf *pf* Ⓕ
BIS CD1042 (67 minutes: DDD). Recorded 1999 ⭘

Freddy Kempf's second disc in his series for BIS offers an enthralling example of that moment when early talent blossoms into fullness and individuality. Even if he lacks the concentrated intensity and force of more seasoned Rachmaninov pianists in the Second Sonata (played in the 1913 version rather than the brutally truncated 1931 revision), his youthful play of light and shade, his innate musical grace and fluency are rich compensation for an occasional diffidence (the opening of the second and, more surprisingly, third movements show him at his least engaged). But in the Op 39 *Etudes* he comes entirely and superbly into his own. He paces No 2 more generously than on a previous occasion in New York, showing a nice sense of Rachmaninov's volatility (*poco più vivo*) beneath his despondent *Dies irae* surface. His rhythmic poise and vivacity in the reluctantly festive No 4 show an authentic feel for its bustle and urgency, and his deeply welling – rather than merely hectoring – start to No 5 leads to an inclusive sense of its *appassionata* rhetoric and declamation. In No 6 the wolf seemingly swallows Red Riding Hood whole at 1'47" (part of an acute and poetic virtuosity that so enthralled Russian audiences at the disgraced 1998 Tchaikovsky Competition) while in No 7, an elegy that gives the lie to Rachmaninov's supposed conservatism), he achieves the sort of expressive freedom and elasticity that usually come to pianists far beyond his years. No 8 finds hims clarifying Rachmaninov's ornate polyphony with rare artistry and, finally, his way with the *Liebesleid*, quite without preening idiosyncrasy or mannerism, recreates a magical and touching sense of Rachmaninov's affection for Kreisler. BIS's sound is superb, fully capturing Freddy Kempf's dynamic range from whispering *pianissimos* to sonorous *fortissimos*. This is a very special record.

Preludes

24 Preludes, Opp 23 and 32. Prelude in D minor. Morceaux de fantaisie, Op 3. Lilacs. Daisies. Mélodie in E. Oriental Sketch in B flat. Moments musicaux, Op 16
Dmitri Alexeev *pf*
Virgin Classics ② VBD5 61624-2 Ⓑ
(138 minutes: DDD). Recorded 1987-89 ⭘

Alexeev's all-Russian mastery has seldom been heard to such advantage and his technical force and authority throughout are unarguable. True, he hardly wears his heart on his sleeve in the quixotic Minuet of Op 23 No 3, is less than poetically yielding in the Chopinesque tracery of Op 23 No 4. He does, however, capture the Slavonic malaise of No 1 with rare insight and his punishing weight and rhetoric in Op 23 Nos 2 or 7 will make even the most sanguine listener's pulse beat faster. He unleashes the central build-up of Op 32 No 7 with the impact of a Siberian whirlwind and time and again his icy, determinedly unsentimental approach gives added strength and focus to the composer's brilliant fury. Alexeev is more convincing in the more vertiginous numbers from the *Moments musicaux*, in Nos 2, 4 and 6 rather than in the opening rhythmic play of No 1 where he sounds altogether too literal and austere. Yet you only have to hear his way of making even *Polichinelle*'s well-worn phrases come up as fresh as paint or his trenchancy in *Oriental Sketch* to realise that you are in the presence of a master pianist. The recordings are of demonstration quality and the accompanying essay mirrors the rare toughness and integrity of these performances; the essential nobility of Rachmaninov's genius.

Etudes-tableaux

Etudes-tableaux – Op 33[a]:No 5 in D minor; No 6 in E flat minor; No 9 in C sharp minor; Op 39: No 1 in C minor; No 2 in A minor; No 3 in F sharp minor; No 4 in B minor; No 7 in C minor; No 9 in D. Preludes – Op 23: No 1 in F sharp minor; No 2 in B flat; No 4 in D; No 5 in G minor; No 7 in C minor; No 8 in A flat; Op 32: No 1 in C; No 2 in B flat minor; No 6 in F minor; No 7 in F; No 9 in A; No 10 in B minor; No12 in G sharp minor
Sviatoslav Richter *pf*
Olympia OCD337 (74 minutes: DDD/ADD) Ⓕ
Items marked [a] recorded 1983, others 1971

As in previous volumes in this valuable series, sound quality is on the dry side. But Richter's is the sort of playing which positively benefits from close analytical scrutiny, and serious collectors of piano recordings should need no further encouragement. Recorded in 1971 and 1983 they show a Richter in transition. Still in evidence is the prime-of-life virtuoso who burst on to the Western scene in the 1960s; but increasingly taking over is the uncompromising, ascetic philosopher-pianist of the 1980s. Metaphysics in Rachmaninov? Certainly. And not just the apparently superhuman fingerwork in the E flat minor *Etude-tableau* or the first C minor of Op 39. What comes across is something beyond expression. It is an overriding fatalism, a sense of the immense sadness of Russia, broken only by moments of heroic resistance. The Preludes are more resonantly recorded, with a rather disappointing tubby bass. If you can live with that there is a quite unique Rachmaninov to be heard here – a brave, noble spirit, expressed in writing of an unquenchable fervour and orchestral solidity.

Etudes-tableaux, Opp 33 and 39
John Lill *pf*
Nimbus NI5439 (64 minutes: DDD) Ⓕ
Recorded 1995

The *Etudes-tableaux* are known to be musical evocations of various pictorial or perhaps narrative ideas, though quite rightly Rachmaninov did not let on where the stimuli came from; there is certainly no sign that John Lill is much preoccupied with such matters. He is a powerful keyboard technician, which is the first necessity in approaching these virtuoso studies, and this puts him in a strong position for dealing with the bold assertiveness of some of them, for instance the first piece of all. He also has a very vivid sense of tempo (balancing speed and texture sympathetically), and equally a sense for the slight lifting of pressure as well as slowing up, or the reverse, which is the essence of true romantic rubato. Where he can seem less responsive than some of his colleagues is with the more delicate pieces, whose fantasy he perhaps underrates. But if he also loses something in introspection, he can command admiration with his magisterial delivery. In sum, a very strong set of performances of some fascinating music.

Etudes-tableaux – Op 33: No 2 in C; No 8 in G minor; Op 39: No 3 in F sharp minor; No 4 in B minor; No 5 in E flat minor. Preludes – Op 23: No 1 in F sharp minor; No 3 in D minor; No 5 in G minor; No 7 in C minor; No 10 in G flat; Op 32: No 6 in F minor; No 8 in A minor; No 10 in B minor; No 12 in G sharp minor. Five Morceaux de fantaisie, Op 3
Nikolai Demidenko *pf*
Hyperion CDA66713 (70 minutes: DDD) Ⓕ
Recorded 1994

Nikolai Demidenko's performances couple immense pianistic tact and skill, though the rushes of adrenalin, when they come (the searing central climax of the Op 3 'Elégie' or the A minor Prelude, Op 32 where a tiny motif is tempest-tossed seemingly in all directions at the same time)are almost palpable. The C major *Etude-tableau*, Op 23 No 2 rises and falls with supreme naturalness and impetus and the absence of all lushness or luxuriance in the G minor *Etude-tableau*, Op 32 No 8 is a pointed reminder of Rachmaninov's serious, religious inspiration. He creates a magnificent carillon of Moscow bells in the great B minor Prelude (the one Moiseiwitsch made so peculiarly his own) and his E flat minor *Etude-tableau*, Op 39 is arrestingly sombre and dry-eyed, its conclusion articulated with a rare sense of ebbing drama, of all passion spent. If you prefer Rachmaninov's emotional storms viewed acutely but from a distance then Demidenko is your man. The recordings faithfully mirror this pianist's very distinctive sound world.

The Bells

Rachmaninov The bells[a] **Prokofiev** Alexander Nevsky, Op 78[b]. Ivan the Terrible (arr Stasevich) – film music, Op 116[c]
[a]**Sheila Armstrong** *sop* [b]**Anna Reynolds,** [c]**Irina Arkhipova** *mez* [a]**Robert Tear** *ten* [a]**John Shirley-Quirk,** [c]**Anatoly Mokrenko** *bar* [c]**Boris Morgunov** *narr* [ab]**London Symphony Chorus** and **Orchestra /** [ab]**André Previn;** [c]**Ambrosian Chorus;** [c]**Philharmonia Orchestra /** [c]**Riccardo Muti**
EMI Double Forte ② CZS5 73353-2
(78 minutes: ADD) Ⓜ
Recorded [b]1971, [a]1975 and [c]1977 ⚭

The previous EMI Studio reissue of these fine André Previn accounts of *The bells* and *Alexander Nevsky* has now been superseded by this EMI Double Forte release with *Ivan the Terrible* – one of Riccardo Muti's finest recordings. Made in the Indian summer of London's Kingsway Hall it is a performance not to be missed. Of course, the fragmentary nature of the music – much more evidently a collection of film score links than *Alexander Nevsky* – is, to a degree, frustrating, but such is the fervour of the performance, the fulsome theatricality of Boris Morgunov's narration, that one is simply carried along by the 'visual' excitement of it all. The Ambrosian Chorus contribute an impressive imitation of the genuine Russian article, summoning up the requisite ballast for the big numbers, amply filling out one of the greatest of all Prokofiev 'tunes' in the 'Storming of Kazan' sequence: this is the noble *cantilena* that would later feature so prominently in *War and Peace*. If you would rather sample this re-release before buying, try the raucous 'Dance of the Oprichniki' and the finale. Was there ever a more resplendant final chord? All 28 seconds of it!

As for *The bells* and *Alexander Nevsky*, the soloists are first-rate. Sheila Armstrong is especially fine in *The bells* and Anna Reynolds provides genuine Slavonic intensity in her contribution to the Prokofiev. The chorals singing too, if without the special vocal timbre and enunciation of a Russian group, has undoubted fervour, while in the famous 'The Battle on the Ice' sequence in *Alexander Nevsky*, the orchestral playing has thrilling pungency and bite. The original analogue recordings were exceptionally well balanced and on LP the combination of ambient effect and sharpness of detail was ideally judged. The remastering increases the clarity and projection of the sound with, perhaps, a slight loss of warmth and atmosphere. However, the overall effect is vividly spectacular and compulsively dramatic. This disc is a real bargain for all three performances are very fine indeed.

Vespers, Op 37

Olga Borodina *mez* **Vladimir Mostowoy** *ten* **St Petersburg Chamber Choir / Nikolai Korniev**
Philips 442 344-2PH (56 minutes: DDD). Texts and translations included. Recorded 1993 Ⓕ

The St Petersburg Chamber Choir sing the *Vespers*, or *All-Night Vigil*, dramatically. Korniev follows the composer's markings carefully, but he is evidently concerned to give a concert performance endowed with vivid immediacy, and there are places where this departs from the reflective or celebratory nature of music that is so strongly grounded in Orthodox tradition. This is most marked with Olga Borodina, who is not the first fine singer to bring too operatic a note to her solo in 'Blagoslovi, dushe moya' ('Bless the Lord, O my soul'); Vladimir Mostowoy is more discreet in 'Blagosloven esi' ('Blessed art Thou').

The choir itself is excellent, with particularly

fine sopranos who can chant high above the others in beautifully pitched thirds; while there is, as ever in Russian church choirs, a splendid bass section that can underpin the textures with effortlessly rich low Cs, and find no difficulty with the famous descending scale down to a sonorous bottom B flat at the end of 'Nyne otpushchayeshi' (the *Nunc dimittis*). The recording is not always as clear as it could be with the textures and especially the words. A strength of the issue, which distinguishes it from almost all others available, is the booklet, which includes not only the full text in transliteration (with English, German and French translations), but also excellent essays.

Songs

12 Songs, Op 21. 15 Songs, Op 26. Were you hiccoughing?. Night

Joan Rodgers *sop* **Maria Popescu** *mez* **Alexandre Naoumenko** *ten* **Sergei Leiferkus** *bar* **Howard Shelley** *pf*

Chandos CHAN9451 (72 minutes: DDD). Texts and Ⓕ translations included. Recorded 1994-95

Two figures in particular haunt this second volume of Chandos's survey of Rachmaninov's songs – Feodor Chaliapin and Rachmaninov himself. They had become friends in the years when they worked together in an opera company and when Rachmaninov was concentrating on developing his piano virtuosity. As a result the Op 21 songs are dominated by an almost operatic declamatory manner coupled with formidably difficult accompaniments. Leiferkus rises splendidly to the occasion, above all in 'Fate' (Op 21 No 1), and so throughout the songs does Howard Shelley. He is unbowed by the technical problems and he understands the novel proportions of songs in which the piano's participation has an unprecedented role. He also enjoys himself in the roisterous exchanges with Leiferkus in what is really Rachmaninov's only lighthearted song, *Were you hiccoughing?*

The songs for the other voices are less powerful, in general more lyrical and intimate. Alexandre Naoumenko only has five songs, and they are not, on the whole, among the more striking examples, but he responds elegantly to 'The fountain' (Op 26 No 11). Maria Popescu gives a beautiful account of one of the most deservedly popular of them all, 'To the children' (Op 26 No 7), and of the remarkable Merezhkovsky setting, 'Christ is risen' (Op 26 No 6), no outburst of Orthodox jubilation but a grieving for the sorry state of the world into which a reborn Christ would now come. Joan Rodgers is enchanting in 'The Lilacs' (Op 21 No 5) and moving in the song acknowledging that love is slipping away, 'Again I am alone' (Op 26 No 9). She has complete mastery of the style, and nothing here is finer than her arching phrase ending 'How peaceful' (Op 21 No 7) – 'da ty, mechta moya' (and you, my dream) – with Shelley gently articulating Rachmaninov's reflective piano postlude from the world of Schumann.

Letter to K S Stanislavsky. 14 Songs, Op 34. From the Gospel of St John. Six Songs, Op 38. A prayer. All wish to sing

Joan Rodgers *sop* **Maria Popescu** *mez* **Alexandre Naoumenko** *ten* **Sergei Leiferkus** *bar* **Howard Shelley** *pf*

Chandos CHAN9477 (68 minutes: DDD) Texts and Ⓕ translations included. Recorded 1994-95

This set opens with a powerful dramatic outpouring. It is in fact a formal letter of apology, for unavoidable absence from a gathering, which Rachmaninov sent for Chaliapin to sing to Stanislavsky; and one of the most touchingly elegant phrases is simply the date on the letter, October 14, 1908. Perhaps he was showing a rare touch of irony in using his full lyrical powers in such a context; but at any rate, the piece nicely prefaces the two collections of his last phase of song-writing, before he left Russia for exile.

Some of his greatest songs are here, coloured in their invention by the four great singers whose hovering presence makes the disposition of this recital between four similar voices a highly successful idea. The Chaliapin songs go to Sergei Leiferkus, occasionally a little overshadowed by this mighty example (as in 'The raising of Lazarus', Op 34 No 6) but more often his own man, responding to the subtly dramatic, sometimes even laconic melodic lines with great sympathy for how they interact with the words, as with the Afanasy Fet poem 'The peasant' (Op 34 No 11). Alexandre Naoumenko inherits the mantle of Leonid Sobinov, and though he sometimes resorts to a near-falsetto for soft high notes, he appears to have listened to that fine tenor's elegance of line and no less subtle feeling for poetry. Pushkin's 'The muse' (Op 34 No 1) is most tenderly sung, and there is a sensitive response to line with 'I remember this day'. Maria Popescu has only two songs, 'It cannot be' and 'Music' (Op 34 Nos 7 and 8), but she has a light tone and bright manner. Joan Rodgers is exquisite in the most rapturous and inward of the songs (the great Felia Litvinne was the original here). Of the Op 38 set, Rachmaninov was particularly fond of 'The rat-catcher' (No 4), and especially of 'Daisies' (No 3), which she sings charmingly, but it is hard to understand why he did not add 'Sleep'. He might have done had he heard Rodgers's rapt performance with Howard Shelley, the music delicately balanced in the exact way he must have intended between voice and piano as if between sleep and waking.

Operas

Aleko

Sergei Leiferkus *bar* Aleko; **Maria Gulegina** *sop* Zemfira; **Anatoly Kocherga** *bass* Old Gipsy; **Ilya Levinsky** *ten* Young Gipsy; **Anne Sofie von Otter** *mez* Old Gipsy Woman

The Miserly Knight

Anatoly Kocherga *bass* Servant; **Sergei Aleksashkin** *bass* Baron; **Sergei Larin** *ten* Albert; **Ian Caley** *ten* Jew; **Vladimir Chernov** *bar* Duke

Francesca da Rimini
Sergei Leiferkus *bar* Lanciotto Malatesta; **Maria Gulegina** *sop* Francesca; **Ilya Levinsky** *ten* Dante; **Sergei Aleksashkin** *bass* Virgil; **Sergei Larin** *ten* Paolo

Gothenburg Opera Chorus and Orchestra / Neeme Järvi
DG ③ 453 452-2GH3 (174 minutes: DDD). Notes, texts and translations included. Recorded 1996 Ⓕ ●

Rachmaninov's three one-act operas that survive give evidence of real dramatic talent. Who else has written so accomplished a graduation exercise as *Aleko*? Tchaikovsky was dazzled, no doubt also flattered, by some suggestions of imitation. It is a number opera, based on Pushkin's dramatic poem *The Gipsies*, warning that the urban sophisticate cannot recapture pristine wildness, and has at its centre a superb soliloquy of lost love. Leiferkus takes a lyrical approach; this is a beautiful, tragic performance, ironically set against Ilya Levinsky's carelessly superficial charm as the Young Gipsy. Zemfira is sung with fierce spirit by Maria Gulegina, especially in her cruel 'Old husband' song, and at the end with a lingering caress that seems to be for neither man but for Death itself. The other operas are different matters, both tinged with Bayreuth experiences that Rachmaninov had absorbed more thoroughly than is sometimes allowed. *The Miserly Knight* is one of the 'little tragedies' in which Pushkin presents a moral issue but does not offer a solution. Here, it is the contrast between the old knight, claiming that his devotion to gold has taken him beyond passion into a realm of serenity, and his son, who merely needs the ready. The long central soliloquy, perhaps Rachmaninov's finest piece of dramatic writing, is superbly delivered by Sergei Aleksashkin, with the wide range of his eloquence drawing sympathy to the miser. Sergei Larin portrays his son Albert as a selfish extrovert; and Ian Caley does what he can to make the Jewish moneylender more human than an unpleasant caricature.

Francesca da Rimini requires Rachmaninov to triumph over an inept libretto by Modest Tchaikovsky. This he does to a remarkable degree, using Modest's inability to produce a text for the chorus of the damned to good advantage with wordless wails, and filling out the sketchy love duet with some 50 bars of a sensuous orchestral kiss. However, he should have rejected the banal placing of the final line, about the lovers reading no more that day, in favour of its breathtaking place in Dante, when their poring over Lancelot and Guinevere reveals their own love to them. Ilya Levinsky brings a more intensely lyrical line and manner to this than in *Aleko*, and Maria Gulegina ranges from docility before Lanciotto (Leiferkus again a jealous husband) to rapture in the love duet. Neeme Järvi leads all three operas, as the orchestra should do for much of the time, and the beautiful playing he draws from the Gothenburg orchestra helps to make these three records a set extolling Rachmaninov's operatic talent. An excellent 'trilogy', excellently presented.

Jean-Philippe Rameau

French 1683-1764

GROVE *Rameau's early training came from his father, a professional organist; he went to a Jesuit school, then had a short period of music study in Italy. In 1702 he was appointed maître de musique at Avignon Cathedral, and spent the next 20 years in various organist posts in France.*

By 1722 he was in Paris, where he was to remain; he had left his organist post at Clermont Cathedral to supervise the publication of his Traité de l'harmonie, *a substantial and controversial work about the relationship of bass to harmony. The* Traité *brought him to wide attention. As a composer, he was known only for his keyboard music (a second collection appeared in 1729-30) and his cantatas, though he had written some church music.*

His ambitions, however, lay in opera and at the age of 50 he had his first opera, Hippolyte et Aricie, *given at the Opéra. It aroused great excitement, admiration, bewilderment and (among the conservative part of the audience) disgust. It was fairly successful, as were the operas that followed, including the opéra-ballet* Les Indes galantes.

In 1745 Rameau was appointed a royal chamber music composer; thereafter several of his works had their premières at court theatres. Nine new theatre works followed in the mid-late 1740s, beginning with La princesse de Navarre *and the comedy* Platée; *but from 1750 onwards only two major works were written, for Rameau was increasingly involved with theory and a number of disputes, with Rousseau, Grimm and even former friends, pupils and collaborators such as Diderot and D'Alembert. When Rameau died he was widely respected and admired, though he was seen too as unsociable and avaricious.*

Rameau's harpsichord music is notable for its variety of texture, originality of line and boldness of harmony. But his chief contribution lies in his operas, especially those in the tragédie lyrique genre. He anticipated Gluckian reform by relating the overture to the ensuing drama. He brought to the numerous dances a wide range of moods using a richly varied orchestral palette and bold melodic lines. He wrote many fine pathetic monologues, usually at the beginnings of acts, with intense, slow-moving vocal lines and rich, sombre accompaniments. His recitative, while following the Lullian model, is more flexible in rhythms and more expressive in its declamation. Such tragédies as Hippolyte et Aricie *and* Castor et Pollux *stand among the great creations of French musical drama.*

Ouvertures

Awards 1998

Les fêtes de Polymnie; Les indes galantes; Zaïs; Castor et Pollux; Naïs; Platée; Les fêtes d'Hébé; Zoroastre; Dardanus; Les paladins; Hippolyte et Aricie; Le temple de la gloire; Pygmalion; Les surprises de l'Amour; Les fêtes de l'Hymen et de l'Amour; Acante et Céphise P
Les Talens Lyriques / Christophe Rousset
L'Oiseau-Lyre 455 293-2OH (70 minutes: DDD). Recorded 1996 Ⓕ ●●●

Rameau was an orchestrator of rare and individual genius and his operas, ballets and smaller entertainments are generously provided with some of the most original and alluring dance music to emerge from the 18th century. Roughly speaking, the music on this disc was written between 1733, the date of Rameau's first opera *Hippolyte et Aricie*, and 1761, when he produced his *comédie-lyrique*, *Les Paladins*.

Lovers of Rameau's music will be thoroughly familiar with most of the music played on the disc but will be delighted to find some rarities, too. The most remarkable of these is the overture to the *pastorale-héroïque*, *Acante et Céphise*. It was commissioned to celebrate the birth of the Duke of Burgundy in 1751. Adulatory prologues were out of fashion by the 1750s but instead Rameau attempted something entirely new – a portrayal in music of the good wishes of the nation, and the public rejoicing at the news of the Prince's birth. Rameau experimented with programmatic elements and vivid tone-painting elsewhere in his overtures, notably in those of *Platée* (1745), and *Zaïs* (1748).

The overture to *Acante et Céphise* is different again, with its inclusion of specific 'occasional' references. Its three sections are marked 'Voeux de la Nation', 'Feu d'Artifice' (whose bass-line is punctuated by cannon-fire) and 'Fanfare'. Les Talens Lyriques responds admirably to this music, relishing every bar of it in performances which are refined in ensemble and articulate in speech. Rousset proves himself a fine exponent of this rewarding repertoire.

Suites

Les fêtes d'Hébé; Acante et Céphise **P**
Orchestra of the Eighteenth Century / Frans Brüggen
Glossa GCD921103 (67 minutes: DDD) ●
Recorded live in 1996-97 Ⓕ

Frans Brüggen's affection for Rameau's orchestral music is confirmed by the many previous issues of dances from his operas. Those are on the Philips label but, for this programme of suites from Rameau's *opéra-ballet*, *Les fêtes d'Hébé* and the *pastorale-héroïque*, *Acante et Céphise*, Brüggen has defected to the Spanish label, Glossa. In respect both of presentation and sound, this recently established label has, as they say, done him proud, for this is certainly the most satisfying issue so far in Brüggen's occasional series. While the music of *Les fêtes d'Hébé*, one of Rameau's most successful operas, is comparatively well known, that of *Acante et Céphise* is not. It is an unjustly neglected piece, making Brüggen's suite of the overture and 15 dances all the more welcome.

The Orchestra of the 18th century responds atmospherically if not always unanimously to Brüggen's sensitive direction. He is a wonderfully rhythmic musician whose imagination is clearly and understandably fired by some of the most innovative and evocative orchestration to have emerged from the first half of the 18th century. *Acante et Céphise* was one of the earliest pieces in which Rameau introduced clarinets and these are at once heard to great effect in the brilliant overture, whose horn writing sometimes foreshadows Gluck. It is a splendid *pièce d'occasion* which many readers will find sufficient enticement to explore further. A captivating programme.

Pièces de clavecin

Premier Livre de pièces de clavecin (1706) – Suite in A minor. Pièces de clavecin (1724, rev 1731) – Suite in E minor, Suite in D **P**
Sophie Yates *hpd*
Chandos Chaconne CHAN0659 (71 minutes: DDD) Ⓕ
Recorded 1999 ●●

The release of a CD devoted to Rameau's harpsichord music is relatively rare. But it is less Rameau, and much more French keyboard music in general, that suffers neglect from an over-cultivated image. However, if Rameau's music is highly allusive, it is also possessed of an immediacy that makes it approachable today. Sophie Yates's firmly grounded yet sensitive and spirited playing will quickly dispel any lingering reservations, and she writes with authority and charm in the accompanying booklet (and plays here a copy of a 1749 Goujon harpsichord made by Andrew Garlick).

Yates's astute selection from Rameau's output is bound to please. The first suite, in A minor, is from the book of *Pièces de clavecin* published shortly after Rameau arrived in Paris in 1706, and displays a youthful brilliance that relies heavily on ornamentation (as, for example, in the Allemande 1 and the Courante) and, delightfully, occasionally reveals a certain provincialism – although Rameau never travelled to Italy, he clearly made certain assumptions about life there: his 'La Vénitienne' makes particular allusion to the beggars' bagpipe and hurdy-gurdy.

The second and third suites, from his later book of 1724 (rev 1731), are altogether more stylish and sophisticated. The E minor Suite begins sedately and with the gravitas befitting an Allemande, but is otherwise shot through with fashionable, pastoral *rondeaux*, and includes two of Rameau's best-known party pieces, 'Le rappel des oiseaux' and 'Tambourin'. The D minor Suite amuses with *pièces de caractère* (the flirtatious 'La follette', the devious 'Le lardon' and the pathetic 'La boiteuse') and amazes with the virtuosity of 'Les tourbillons' and 'Les Cyclopes'. But only a player of Yates's calibre can address the musical subtleties of 'Les soupirs', the deceptive 'Les niais de Sologne' and the sensuous 'L'entretien des muses'. A tour de force in every sense.

Awards 1992

Premier livre de pièces de clavecin. Pièces de clavecin en concerts. Nouvelles suites de pièces de clavecin. Les petits marteaux de M Rameau. La Dauphine **P**
Christophe Rousset *hpds*
L'Oiseau-Lyre ② 425 886-2OH2 Ⓕ
(129 minutes: DDD). Recorded 1989 ●●●

This recording of Rameau's solo harpsichord music outdistances most of the competition. Rousset does not include everything that Rameau wrote for the instrument but he does play all the music contained in the principal collections of 1706, 1724 and *c*1728 as well as *La Dauphine*. Rousset's phrasing is graceful and clearly articulated, the inflexions gently spoken and the rhythmic pulse all that one might wish for. Tempos are, for the most part, well judged and the playing admirably attentive to detail and delightfully animated. Only occasionally does Rousset perhaps just miss the mark with speeds that are uncomfortably brisk and lacking that choreographic poise which is such a vital ingredient in French baroque music.

However, when he is at his strongest he is irresistible and this is how we find him in 'Les niais de Sologne' and its variations, the reflective 'L'entretien des Muses', the animated 'Les cyclopes', 'La poule', 'L'enharmonique' and the dazzling A minor Gavotte and variations. In these and in many other of the pieces, too, Rousset's impeccable taste and seemingly effortless virtuosity provide the listener with constant and intense delight. The quality of the recording is ideal as are the two instruments which Rousset has chosen to play.

Motets

Deus noster refugium. In convertendo. Quam dilecta **P**

Awards 1995

Sophie Daneman, Noémi Rime *sops* **Paul Agnew** *ten* **Nicolas Rivenq** *bar* **Nicolas Cavallier** *bass* **Les Arts Florissants / William Christie**

Erato 4509-96967-2 (70 minutes: DDD) Ⓕ

Texts and translations included. Recorded 1994 ●●●

All three motets date from relatively early in Rameau's career, before he had really made a name for himself, yet all show to a certain extent some of the characteristics that 20 years or so later would so thrillingly illuminate his operas. *Deus noster refugium*, for instance, features impressive depictions of nature in turmoil that would not sound out of place in *Hippolyte et Aricie*, and all three begin with long, expressive solos not unlike the opening of an act from a *tragédie-lyrique*. *Quam dilecta* does sound a little more 'churchy' than the others, with its impressive, rather Handelian double fugue, but *In convertendo* – a work which Rameau heavily revised well into his operatic Indian summer in 1751 – absolutely reeks of the theatre.

Drop anyone familiar with the composer's operas into the middle of this piece, and surely only its Latin text would give away that this is church music. It comes as no surprise to find Christie going to town on this dramatic element. The slightly dry acoustic of the Radio France studio is a help, as are the forceful, penetrating qualities of the solo and choral singers. But it is Christie's command of gesture, pacing and contrast which really gives these performances such an invigorating character.

Castor et Pollux

Howard Crook *ten* Castor; **Jérôme Corréas** *bass* Pollux; **Agnès Mellon** *sop* Télaïre; **Véronique Gens** *sop* Phebe; **René Schirrer** *bar* Mars, Jupiter; - **Sandrine Piau** *sop* Venus, Happy Spirit, Planet; **Mark Padmore** *ten* Love, High Priest; **Claire Brua** *sop* Minerve; **Sophie Daneman** *sop* Follower of Hebe, Celestial Pleasure; **Adrian Brand** *ten* First Athlete; **Jean-Claude Sarragosse** *bass* Second Athlete; **Les Arts Florissants / William Christie** **P**

Harmonia Mundi ③ HMC90 1435/7

(173 minutes: DDD). Notes, text and translation included. Recorded 1992 Ⓕ ●

Castor et Pollux was Rameau's second *tragédie en musique*. Its first performance took place in October 1737 but the opera was greeted with only moderate enthusiasm. It was only with the composer's thoroughly revised version of 1754 that the opera enjoyed the popularity that it deserved. The revision tautened a drama which had never been weak but it dispensed with a very beautiful Prologue. Christie and Les Arts Florissants perform Rameau's first version complete with its Prologue. The librettist, Pierre-Joseph Bernard, was one of the ablest writers with whom Rameau collaborated and his text for *Castor et Pollux* has been regarded by some as the best of 18th-century French opera. Bernard focuses on the fraternal love of the 'heavenly twins' and specifically on the generosity with which Pollux renounces his immortality so that Castor may be restored to life. Christie's production was staged at Aix-en-Provence in the summer of 1991 and recorded by Harmonia Mundi a year later. This performance realises the element of tragedy, above all in the First Act, and Christie's singers sound very much at home with French declamation. A very beautiful score, affectionately and perceptively interpreted.

Dardanus

John Mark Ainsley *ten* Dardanus; **Véronique Gens** *sop* Iphise; **Mireille Delunsch** *sop* Venus; **Françoise Masset** *sop* Cupid; Pleasure; Phrygian Woman; **Magdalena Kožená** *mez* Shepherdess; Phrygian Woman; A Dream; **Jean-François Lombard** *counterten* A Dream; **Russell Smythe** *bar* Teucer; **Jean-Louis Bindi** *bass* Phrygian; **Jean-Philippe Courtis** *bass* Isménor; **Laurent Naouri** *bass* Anténor; **Marcos Pujol** *bass* A Dream; **Choeur des Musiciens du Louvre; Les Musiciens du Louvre / Marc Minkowski**

Archiv Produktion ② 463 476-2AH2

(156 minutes: DDD). Text and translation included. Recorded live in1998 Ⓕ ●

Between the Paris première of *Dardanus* in 1739 and its first revival in 1744, Rameau and his librettist revised the work so much, wrenching the plot in a different direction from Act 3 onwards, that to combine its two versions is near impossible. Though the dramatic problems in the score perhaps remain insurmountable, for a recording a conductor can choose whichever version has the best music. For Minkowski, that is the 1739 original, but he cannot resist importing a few numbers from 1744, even if they are mainly relatively unimportant. The exception is the superbly intense monologue 'Lieux funestes' for Dardanus in chains, which here resurfaces at the opening of Act 4. Minkowski describes it as 'the finest *haute-contre* aria ever written', and it has to be said it suits its new place very well.

Dardanus, son of Jupiter, is in love with Iphise, the daughter of his enemy Teucer – a love which, though forbidden, is reciprocated. Iphise is in fact promised to Teucer's ally Anténor, and much of the action concerns his and Dardanus's rivalry and Iphise's anguish. There is much use of the supernatural, something for which the opera was criticised in its day and which indeed prompted its revision. There is also a sea-monster, and the scene in which Anténor and Dardanus fight with the monster provides one of the more convincingly performed passages of dialogue on this recording, a significant point because ensemble acting is actually one of the least successful areas. This is a recording of a concert performance, and as so often the vital spark of dramatic continuity and urgency which can result from the performers having lived their parts on stage is not quite there. Laurent Naouri turns in a vivid performance as the hapless Anténor, Véronique Gens is noble and moving as the love-torn Iphise, and Mireille Delunsch is a powerful Venus, but the remaining singers, though vocally strong enough (especially John Mark Ainsley and Magdalena Kožená), often struggle to bring their characters to life. What we get instead is more like a series of highlights, but what highlights they are. They include two ravishing monologues for the troubled Iphise; the already mentioned monologue for Dardanus, sung with beauty and poise by Ainsley; a solar eclipse (no less); and a truly lovely sleep divertissement in Act 4, full of feathery lightness and drowsy tranquillity. And then there are the dances, always such an enjoyable feature of Rameau's scores. Minkowski conducts with an appropriate mixture of drive and tenderness, and is rewarded by responsive and sound playing and singing from his orchestra and chorus. A major release for Rameau fans certainly, well loaded with superb dramatic music.

Les fêtes d'Hébé

Awards 1998

Sophie Daneman *sop* Hébé, Une Naïde, Eglé; **Gaëlle Méchaly** *sop* L'amour; **Paul Agnew** *ten* Momus, Le ruisseau, Lycurgue; **Sarah Connolly** *mez* Sapho, Iphise; **Jean-Paul Fouchécourt** *ten* Thélème, L'oracle, Mercure; **Luc Coadou** *bass* Alcée; **Laurent Slaars** *bar* Hymas; **Matthieu Lécroart** *bar* Le fleuve; **Maryseult Wieczorek** *mez* Une Lacédémonienne, Une bergère; **Thierry Félix** *bar* Tirtée, Eurilas;
Les Arts Florissants / William Christie
Erato ② 3984-21064-2 (148 minutes: DDD) Ⓕ
Notes, text and translation included.
Recorded 1997

Rameau produced one of his most engaging scores for *Les fêtes d'Hébé*. The entertainment comprises a prologue and three *entrées*. All is prefaced with a captivating two-movement Overture whose playful second section has much more in common with a Neapolitan *sinfonia* than a traditional opera overture in the French mould. The dances belong to one of the composer's fruitiest vintages and Christie has capitalised upon this with a sizeable band which includes, where appropriate, a section of musettes, pipes and drums. The singers are carefully chosen for their contrasting vocal timbres and the line-up, by and large, is strong.

The leading roles in each of the opera's four sections are fairly evenly distributed between Sophie Daneman, Sarah Connolly, Jean-Paul Fouchécourt, Paul Agnew and Thierry Félix. The first three of this group are consistently engaging; their feeling for theatre, and their intuitive ability to seek out those aspects of Rameau's vocal writing which enliven it, seldom fail, and they bring considerable charm to their performances. Agnew, too, is on strong form though in the lower end of his vocal tessitura, required for the role of Momus in the Prologue, he sounds less secure than in his more accustomed *haute-contre* range. That can be heard to wonderful effect elsewhere and, above all, in a duet for a Stream and a Naiad (first *Entrée*) in which he is joined by Daneman. This beguiling little love-song is proclaimed with innocent fervour and tenderness. Félix has a rounded warmth and resonance and his occasional weakness of poorly focused tone has here been largely overcome. *Les fêtes d'Hébé* contains a wealth of inventive, instrumentally colourful and evocative dances. Small wonder that audiences loved it so much in the 1720s: with music of such vital originality, how could it be otherwise? Christie and Les Arts Florissants have possibly never been on crisper, more disciplined form than here, revelling in Rameau's beguiling pastoral images, tender and high-spirited in turn. A ravishing entertainment, from start to finish.

Hippolyte et Aricie

Awards 1997

Mark Padmore *ten* Hippolyte; **Anne-Maria Panzarella** *sop* Aricie; **Lorraine Hunt** *sop* Phèdre; **Laurent Naouri** *bass* Thésée; **Eirian James** *mez* Diane; **Gaëlle Mechaly** *sop* L'Amour, Female Sailor; **Nathan Berg** *bass* Jupiter, Pluton, Neptune; **Katalin Károlyi** *mez* Oenone; **Yann Beuron** *ten* Arcas Mercure; **François Piolino** *ten* Tisiphone; **Christopher Josey** *ten* Fate I; **Matthieu Lécroart** *bar* Fate II; **Bertrand Bontoux** *bass* Fate III; **Mireille Delunsch** *sop* High Priestess; **Patricia Petibon** *sop* Priestess, Shepherdess;
Les Arts Florissants / William Christie
Erato ③ 0630-15517-2 (182 minutes: DDD) Ⓕ
Notes, text and translation included
Recorded 1996

William Christie adheres throughout to the 1733 original (Rameau revised the start of Act 2 in 1757), in so doing opening up some passages previously omitted. He uses an orchestra with a good string weight and it plays with security both of ensemble and intonation, and with splendidly crisp rhythms. Despite the opera's title, the main protagonists are Theseus and his queen Phaedra, whose guilty passion for his son Hippolytus precipitates the tragedy. Phaedra is strongly cast with a passionate Lorraine Hunt who is particularly impressive in the superb aria, 'Cruelle mère des amours', which begins Act 3. Throughout the opera, one is also struck by the profusion of invention, the unobtrusive contrapuntal skill, the charm and colour of the instrumentation and the freedom allotted to the orchestra. The work's final scene, for example, set in a woodland, is filled with a truly enchanting atmosphere, ending, after the customary chaconne, with 'Rossignols amoureux' (delightfully sung by Patricia Petibon). Anna-Maria Panzarella makes an appealingly youthful Aricia, and Mark Padmore is easily the best Hippolytus on record, making the most of his despairing Act 4 aria, 'Ah, faut-il, en ce jour, perdre tout ce que j'aime?'. Pains have been taken with the whole cast over the expressive delivery of words and over neatness of ornamentation; and production values such as the proper perspective for the entry of the crowd rejoicing at Theseus's return have been well considered. All told, this is one of William Christie's best achievements.

Opéra-ballets

Les Indes galantes – Prologue **P**
Claron McFadden *sop* Hébé; **Jérôme Corréas** *bar* Bellone; **Isabelle Poulenard** *sop* L'Amour

Le Turc généreux
Nicolas Rivenq *bass* Osman; **Miriam Ruggieri** *sop* Emilie; **Howard Crook** *ten* Valère

Les Incas du Pérou
Bernard Deletré *bass* Huascar; **Isabelle Poulenard** Phanie; **Jean-Paul Fouchécourt** *ten* Carlos

Les fleurs
Fouchécourt Tacmas; **Corréas** Ali; **Sandrine Piau** *sop* Zaïre; **Noémi Rime** *sop* Fatime

Les sauvages
Rivenq Adario; **Crook** Damon; **Deletré** Don Alvar; **McFadden** Zima

Les Arts Florissants / William Christie
Harmonia Mundi ③ HMC90 1367/9 Ⓕ
(203 minutes: DDD)
Notes, text and translation included ●

Les Indes galantes was Rameau's first *opéra-ballet*. He completed it in 1735 when it was performed at the Académie Royale in Paris. *Opéra-ballet* usually consisted of a prologue and anything between three and five *entrées* or acts. There was no continuously developing plot but instead various sections might be linked by a general theme, often hinted at in the title. Such is the case with *Les Indes galantes* whose linking theme derives from a contemporary taste for the exotic and the unknown. Following a prologue come four *entrées*, 'Le Turc généreux', 'Les Incas du Pérou', 'Les fleurs' and 'Les sauvages'. William Christie and Les Arts Florissants give a characteristically warm-blooded performance of one of Rameau's most approachable and endearing stage works. Christie's control of diverse forces – his orchestra consists of some 46 players – his dramatic pacing of the music, his recognition of Rameau's uniquely distinctive instrumental palette and his feeling for gesture and rhythm contribute towards making this a lively and satisfying performance. The choir is alert and the orchestra a worthy partner in respect of clear textures and technical finesse; this can be readily appreciated in the spaciously laid out and tautly constructed orchestral Chaconne which concludes the work. The booklet contains full texts in French, English and German and the music is recorded in a sympathetic acoustic.

Einojuhani Rautavaara Finnish 1928

GROVE *Rautavaara studied with Merikanto at the Helsinki Academy (1948-52), where from 1966 he taught, and with Persichetti at the Julliard School (1955-56). His large output shows a variety of stylistic resource (Russian nationalists, Hindemith and advanced serialism) and he has written in many genres; notable is The True and False Unicorn (1971) for chorus, orchestra and tape.*

Piano Concerto No 3

Piano Concerto No 3, 'Gift of Dreams'[a]. Autumn Gardens
Helsinki Philharmonic Orchestra / Vladimir Ashkenazy [a]*pf*
Ondine ODE950-2 (68 minutes: DDD). Recorded 1999
Includes a conversation between Einojuhani Rautavaara and Vladimir Ashkenazy Ⓕ ●

Thinking back to seminal orchestral works from the turn of the 20th century – Strauss tone-poems, early Scriabin and Mahler symphonies, Debussy's *Nocturnes* – then leaping forwards a 100 years to Rautavaara's mellifluous *Autumn Gardens* (1999) underlines perennial musical values that the mid-20th century tended to sell short. There's a danger of mistaking Rautavaara's new-found consistency for complacency, but *Autumn Gardens* extends the Rautavaarian experience at least one step beyond the Seventh Symphony. You sense it especially in the animated finale, which begins *giocoso e leggiero* before a baroque-style, four-note figure slowly makes its presence felt. The figure is first heard on the bassoon, then shifts timbre and focus (timpani and bells play a crucial role later on), inspiring the strings to lyrical heights. The piquantly scored first movement conjures a gentle beating of wings, with glowing modulations that sometimes darken, though they never cloud the issue. The reflective central movement follows without a break.

The Piano Concerto (1998), Rautavaara's Third and an Ashkenazy commission, is stronger meat. More meditative than its predecessors though visited by some cluster-like dissonances, it seems to take its principal stylistic cue from the middle movement of Bartók's Second Piano Concerto. The opening string chord motive is simple, austere, the piano writing bold or decorative rather than overtly pianistic. Viewed as a whole, it is cast vaguely in the manner of Delius or Debussy, more an orchestral tone-poem with piano than a display piece. The most striking movement is the second, which incorporates some fairly harsh brass writing and memorably beautiful closing pages. The *Energico* finale calls in the big guns and is well served by Ondine's recording team, but one could imagine a more forceful performance. Otherwise, things go well. Rautavaara's annotation explains the thematic geneses of both works and offers some poetic guidelines for listeners. The disc closes with an interview, a disarmingly natural slice of dialogue where the composer relates to Ashkenazy how he views his works as received phenomena. That, for the most part, is precisely how his music sounds – like audible episodes drawn from nature, messages that, in a world seduced by banal artifice, are all-too-easily ignored.

Cantus arcticus, Op 61

Cantus arcticus, Op 61 (Concerto for Birds and Orchestra) with taped birdsong. Piano Concerto No 1, Op 45[a]. Symphony No 3, Op 20
[a]**Laura Mikkola** *pf* **Royal Scottish National Orchestra / Hannu Lintu**
Naxos 8 554147 (74 minutes: DDD) Ⓢ
Recorded 1997 ●

No other new music stands to benefit more from extensive exposure, not so much because of its quality (which is beyond question), as because of an almost tangible connection with nature, than that by Rautavaara. One constantly senses the joy of a man alone with the elements: awe-struck, contented, inspired. Bird-song comes from all directions, literally in the 'Concerto for birds and orchestra' or *Cantus arcticus*, which sets taped bird-song against a rustic orchestral backdrop. The piece ends with the reassuring cacophony of 'Swans Migrating', excellently recorded here. The young Finnish conductor, Hannu Lintu, directs a fine performance, though the flutes at the beginning of 'The Bog' (*Cantus*'s first movement) are rather over-accentuated. The bird-song tape blends well with the music and is very atmospheric. The First Piano Concerto and Third Symphony (out of seven) receive good performances, most notably the Brucknerian Symphony, an impressive and often dramatic work that begins and ends in the key of D minor. Rautavaara's orchestration incorporates four Wagner tubas, though some of the finest material is also the quietest. The slow movement is sullen but haunting, the *Scherzo* occasionally suggestive of Nielsen or Martinů and the finale brings the parallels with Bruckner fully within earshot.

The First Piano Concerto has a brilliance and immediacy that should please orchestral adventurers and piano *aficionados*. The solo writing employs clusters and much filigree fingerwork, but it is the noble, chorale-like second movement that leaves the strongest impression. Laura Mikkola gives a good performance. Naxos gives a full sound picture and overall, this is an excellent CD, concisely annotated by the composer.

Flute Concerto, Op 63

Flute Concerto, Op 63, 'Dances with the Winds'[a]. Anadyomene. On the Last Frontier[b]
[a]**Patrick Gallois** *fl* [b]**Finnish Philharmonic Choir; Helsinki Philharmonic Orchestra / Leif Segerstam**
Ondine ODE921-2 (59 minutes: DDD) Ⓕ
Recorded 1998 ●

Anadyomene (1968) suggests a Turner canvas recast in sound. It opens restlessly among undulating pastels, the tone darkens further, there are brief comments from flute and bass clarinet, the brass prompts a swelling climax, then the mood gradually becomes more animated before we are ferried back whence we came. It is 'a homage to Aphrodite, born of the sea foam, the goddess of love', and a very appealing one at that. The colourful Flute Concerto *Dances with the Winds* is a more extrovert piece with Nielsen as a fairly certain forebear. It shares its material between ordinary flute, bass flute, alto flute and piccolo. The action-packed opening movement withstands some fairly aggressive interjections from the brass, the brief second movement recalls the shrill sound world of fifes and drums; the elegiac *Andante moderato* offers plenty of jam for the alto flute, and the finale's striking mood-swings have just a hint of Bernsteinian exuberance. Rautavaara's prompt for *On the Last Frontier* (1997) was an early encounter with *The Narrative of Arthur Gordon Pym* by Edgar Allan Poe. He calls it 'a seafaring yarn in the typical boys' reading mould' and responds accordingly with a 24-minute slice of descriptive musical reportage, not of Poe's exact 'narrative', but of an imagined *Last Frontier* based on ideas from the story's closing section. It is an eventful, majestic, slow-burning tone-poem, nourished further by some distinctive instrumental solos and with telling use of a full-blown chorus. No texts are provided, and yet the aura of unexplored maritime depths and a sense of mystery associated with them carry their own wordless narrative. All three works are expertly performed and exceptionally well recorded.

Symphony No 7, 'Angel of Light'

Symphony No 7, 'Angel of Light'. Annunciations
Kari Jussila *org* **Helsinki Philharmonic Orchestra / Leif Segerstam**
Ondine ODE869-2 (65 minutes: DDD) Ⓕ
Recorded 1995 ●

The Seventh Symphony's opening *Tranquillo* evokes a calm though powerful atmosphere, with many Sibelian points of reference – most especially in recognizable echoes of the *Largo* fourth movement from Sibelius's Fourth Symphony, whereas the closing *Pesante-cantabile* is more in line with the symphonic world of Alan Hovhaness. The Angel idea originates in a series that already includes a number of other works (*Angels and Visitations* and *Angel of Dusk*, for instance), the reference being (as the composer himself explains) to 'an archetype, one of mankind's oldest traditions and perennial companions'. This Jungian axis is reflected in monolithic chords, ethereal harmonic computations (invariably broad and high-reaching) and an unselfconscious mode of musical development. Readers schooled in the more contemplative works of Górecki, Pärt and Tavener will likely respond to this spatially generous essay, though Rautavaara's language is more a celebration of nature than any specific religious ritual.

Comparisons with the *Annunciations* (for organ, brass quintet, wind orchestra and percussion) find the earlier work far harsher in tone, much more demanding technically (it calls for a formidable organ virtuoso) and more radical in its musical language. Here the style ranges from the primeval drone that opens the work through canon, 'bird forest' activity and the novel effect of having the 'notes of a dense chord weirdly circulating in the room' when the organ motor is switched off. Kari Jussila rises to the various challenges with what sounds like genuine enthusiasm (his fast fingerwork is amazing) while Leif Segerstam and the Helsinki Philharmonic fully exploit the tonal drama of both works. The recordings are warm and spacious.

String Quartets

String Quartets Nos 1 and 2. String Quintet, 'Unknown Heavens'
Jan-Erik Gustafsson *vc* **Jean Sibelius Quartet** (Yoshiko Arai-Kimanen, Jukka Pohjola *vns* Matti Hirvikangas *va* Seppo Kimanen *vc*)
Ondine ODE909-2 (62 minutes: DDD) Ⓕ
Recorded 1997

Here we encounter not one Rautavaara, but three: the fledgling student captivated by folklore; the dodecaphonic zealot stretching the expressive potential of 'the system'; and the triumphant melodist basking in his own unique brand of harmonic complexity. The stylistic leap from Rautavaara's Second Quartet to his Quintet, or *Unknown Heavens* is more a matter of tone than temperament. All three works are ceaselessly active, the First (1952) being perhaps the leanest, and the last (1997) the richest in texture.

Unknown Heavens takes its name from an earlier work for male chorus, which Rautavaara quotes, initially in the second bar of the first movement ('when the second violin answers the question opposed by the first,' as Rautavaara writes), many times thereafter, and then significantly revised ('in inverted intervals') at the start of the fourth movement. The third begins as a cello duet, sure justification of why – and how – five players are employed where the Kuhmo Music Festival originally commissioned a piece for four. 'The work seemed to acquire a will of its own,' writes Rautavaara.

The equally well-performed string quartets are stylistically rather more challenging. The First Quartet plays for just over 11 minutes and inhabits a mildly rustic world roughly akin to Kodály. Best here is the *Andante*'s haunting coda, whereas the 1958 Second Quartet is at its most inventive for the faster second and fourth movements. The current Rautavaara is more relaxed, more contemplative, wiser and softer-grained than his former self. He seems happier reflecting nature than organizing abstract patterns: you sense that the Quintet is authentically self-expressive, whereas the quartets speak interestingly about nothing in particular. The recordings are full-bodied and well balanced.

Piano Works

Etudes, Op 42. Icons, Op 6. Partita, Op 34. Piano Sonatas – No 1, 'Christus und die Fischer', Op 50; No 2, 'The Fire Sermon', Op 64. Seven Preludes, Op 7
Laura Mikkola *pf*
Naxos 8 554292 (61 minutes: DDD) Ⓕ
Recorded 1999

The most interesting aspect of hearing piano music by a composer known primarily for his orchestral work is in spotting those inimitable harmonic fingerprints that help define his musical personality. Rautavaara's piano music is full of tell-tale signs, even in an early work like the Op 7 *Preludes*, where the composer indulged a sort of clandestine protest against the 'neo-classical' confines he experienced both in Helsinki and America. Rautavaara was studying with Copland at the time but chose to keep his *Preludes* to himself. And yet it is Copland's Piano Sonata that spontaneously comes to mind during the austere opening of his 'The Black Madonna of Blakernaya' from *Icons*, perhaps the most striking of all Rautavaara's solo piano works. The translucent colours in 'The Baptism of Christ' make a profound effect, and so does the serenity of 'The Holy Women at the Sepulchre'. Aspects of 'angels' seem prophetically prevalent – whether consciously or not – in the *Etudes* of 1969. Each piece tackles a different interval: thirds in the first, sevenths in the second, then tritones, fourths, seconds and fifths. The third is reminiscent of Messiaen, and the fifth of Bartók, but Rautavaara's guiding hand is everywhere in evidence. Spirituality is an invariable presence, especially in the two piano sonatas, though the Second ends with an unexpected bout of contrapuntal brutality. Perhaps the most instantly appealing track is the brief but touching central movement of the three-and-a-half minute *Partita*, Op 34, with its gentle whiffs of Bartók. Laura Mikkola plays all 28 movements with obvious conviction, and Naxos's recorded sound is excellent.

A Requiem in Our Time

A Requiem in Our Time, Op 3[a]. Playgrounds for Angels[b]. Tarantará[c]. Independence Fanfare[d]. A Soldier's Mass[e]. Octet for Winds[f]. Hymnus[g]
[f]Petri Alanko *fl* **[f]Jussi Jaatinen** *ob* **[f]Harri Mäki** *cl* **[f]Otto Virtanen** *bn* **[f]Esa Tapani, [f]Mika Paajanen** *hns* **[d]Jouko Harjanne, [cg]Pasi Pirinen, [d]Jorma Rautakoski, [df]Aki Välimäki** *tpts* **[df]Valtteri Malmivirta** *tbn* **[g]Seppo Murto** *org* **[abe]Finnish Brass Symphony / Hannu Lintu**
Ondine ODE957-2 (62 minutes: DDD) Ⓕ
Recorded 1999-2000 ●

There's little hint here of the escapist aura that frames most of Rautavaara's recent orchestral work. Latest to arrive is the atmospheric *Hymnus* for trumpet and organ, composed in 1998 for Barry Millington's Hampstead and Highgate Festival. *Hymnus* opens and closes in darkness, courting sunlight for a faster central section and couched in a language that is at once florid and austere. Six years earlier Rautavaara had produced a cantata in celebration of the 75th Anniversary of Finland's independence, and his unusually expressive, half-minute *Independence Fanfare* is fashioned from the same work's concluding hymn. Solo trumpet is represented by the ruminative but technically demanding *Tarantará*, superbly played – as is *Hymnus* – by Pasi Pirinen.

Rautavaara calls *A Requiem in Our Time* for brass and percussion his 'breakthrough work' in that it won him an international composition competition in Cincinnati. That was back in 1953, prior to his studies with Copland, and the musical language seems to give at least half a wink in Vaughan Williams's direction. Dedicated to Rautavaara's mother (who had died during the war), it's a rather beautiful piece, more sorrowful than mournful and with some ingeniously crafted faster music.

A Soldier's Mass (1968) is the *Requiem*'s nearest musical relation. Rautavaara thinks of it as a 'companion work', though the forces called for are more generous and the overall spirit is far more extrovert. The 1962 *Octet* subscribes to an expressively varied dodecaphony, and the superb 12-minute *Playground for Angels* (1981) is a sort of musical hide-and-seek with lurking low brass and much quick-witted instrumental interplay. It reminds one at times of Janáček's *Capriccio*. It's a brilliant piece, fun to hear and probably just as much fun to play. The Finnish Brass Symphony does Rautavaara proud and Ondine's sound quality is spectacularly fine.

Vigilia

Pia Freund *sop* **Lilli Paasikivi** *mez* **Topi Lehtipuu** *ten* **Petteri Salomaa** *bar* **Jyrki Korhonen** *bass* **Finnish Radio Chamber Choir / Tino Nuoranne**
Ondine ODE910-2 (64 minutes: DDD). Text and translation included. Recorded 1997 Ⓕ ●

Although grounded in the faith of the Finnish Orthodox Church, *Vigilia* somehow manages to excavate a spiritual path beyond the confines of denominational dogma. Rautavaara's delicious blend of ancient and modern modes is pointedly exemplified in the 'First Katisma', where soprano and contralto, then tenor and baritone, proclaim 'Blessed is the man that walketh not in the counsel of the ungodly'. There, the harmonic drift is decidedly 'post-renaissance', whereas the 'Alleluias' that follow update to 'post-romantic' and the subsequent assurance that 'the Lord knoweth the way of the righteous' brings us on line with the wistful, nature-loving Rautavaara of the Seventh Symphony and *Cantus arcticus*. The *a cappella Vigilia* was a joint commission from the Helsinki Festival and the Finnish Orthodox Church; the original Evening and Morning Services date from 1971 and 1972, respectively, with this concert version following on later. Possible influences include Bartók, Stravinsky and Messiaen, though early music is a more palpable prompt and Rautavaara himself is always the leading voice. Rautavaara's employment, or rather absorption, of ancient modes runs roughly parallel with Steve Reich's in works such as *Tehillim* and *Proverb*, though by contrast with Reich, harmonic colouring takes its lead from poetic imagery rather than from the sounds of specific words. *Vigilia* uses variation technique to impressive effect; it is a refreshingly open-hearted piece, one that – whether sombre or celebratory, traditional or innovative – grants ritual narrative a vibrant voice and should earn its composer wide-scale recognition. The performance is beautifully sung and the recording bold and realistic.

Maurice Ravel French 1875-1937

GROVE *Ravel's father's background was Swiss and his mother's Basque, but he was brought up in Paris, where he studied at the Conservatoire, 1889-95, returning in 1897 for further study with Fauré and Gédalge. In 1893 he met Chabrier and Satie, both of whom were influential. A decade later he was an established composer, at least of songs and piano pieces, working with luminous precision in a style that could imitate Lisztian bravura (Jeux d'eau) or Renaissance calm (Pavane pour une infante défunte); there was also the String Quartet, somewhat in the modal style of Debussy's but more ornately instrumented. However, he five times failed to win the Prix de Rome (1900-05) and left the Conservatoire to continue as a freelance musician.*

During the next decade he was at his most productive. There was a rivalry with Debussy but Ravel's taste for sharply defined ideas and closed formal units was entirely his own, as was the grand virtuosity of much of his piano music from this period, notably the cycles Miroirs and Gaspard de la nuit. Many works show his fascination with things temporally or geographically distant, with moods sufficiently alien to be objectively drawn: these might be historical musical styles, as in the post-Schubertian Valses nobles et sentimentales, or the imagination of childhood, as in Ma mère l'oye, the

East (Shéhérazade) or on Spain (Rapsodie espagnole, the comic opera L'heure espagnole) or even ancient Greece in the languorous ballet Daphnis et Chloé, written for Diaghilev.

Diaghilev's Ballets Russes were also important in introducing him to Stravinsky, with whom he collaborated on a version of Mussorgsky's Khovanshchina, and whose musical development he somewhat paralleled during the decade or so after The Rite of Spring. The set of three Mallarmé songs with nonet accompaniment were written partly under the influence of Stravinsky's Japanese Lyrics and Schoenberg's Pierrot lunaire, and the two sonatas of the 1920s can be compared with Stravinsky's abstract works of the period in their harmonic astringency and selfconscious use of established forms.

However, Ravel's Le tombeau de Couperin predates Stravinsky's neo-classicism, and the pressure of musical history is perhaps felt most intensely in the ballet La valse where 3/4 rhythm develops into a dance macabre: both these works, like many others, exist in both orchestral and piano versions, testifying to Ravel's superb technique in both media (in 1922 he applied his orchestral skills tellingly to Mussorgsky's Pictures at an Exhibition). Other postwar works return to some of the composer's obsessions: with the delights and dangers of the child's world (the sophisticated fantasy opera L'enfant et les sortilèges), Spanishness (Boléro and the songs for a projected Don Quixote film), and the exotic (Chansons madécasses). His last major effort was a pair of piano concertos, one exuberant and cosmopolitan (in G), the other (for left hand only) more darkly and sturdily single-minded. Ravel died after a long illness.

Piano Concertos

Piano Concerto in G[ab]. Piano Concerto for the Left Hand[ac]. Valses nobles et sentimentales (orch cpsr)[b]

[a]**Krystian Zimerman** *pf* [b]**Cleveland Orchestra,** [c]**London Symphony Orchestra / Pierre Boulez**

Awards 1999

DG 449 213-2GH (56 minutes: DDD) Ⓕ

Recorded 1994 ●●●

Zimerman's pianism is self-recommending. His trills in the first movement of the G major Concerto are to die for, his passagework in the finale crystal-clear, never hectic, always stylish. For their part Boulez and the Clevelanders are immaculate and responsive; they relish Ravel's neon-lit artificiality and moments of deliberate gaudiness. That goes equally for the *Valses nobles*, which have just about every nuance you would want to be there, and none that you wouldn't. The recording is generous with ambience, to the point where some orchestral entries after big climaxes are blurred. Otherwise detail is razor-sharp and one of the biggest selling-points of the disc. Zimerman's humming may be a slight distraction for some listeners, especially in the Left-Hand Concerto, where you may not be always convinced that the LSO knew quite what it was supposed to do with the long notes of the main theme, and where there is a slight lack of tension in exchanges between piano and orchestra. There again, had the G major Concerto not been so wonderful those points might not have registered at all, for this is playing of no mean distinction. In the Left-Hand Concerto, Zimerman's phenomenal pianism sets its own agenda and brings its own rich rewards.

Orchestral Works

Le tombeau de Couperin. Pavane pour une infante défunte. Ma mère l'oye. Une barque sur l'océan. Alborada del gracioso

Orchestra of the Opéra National de Lyon / Kent Nagano

Erato 0630-14331-2 (69 minutes: DDD) Ⓕ

Recorded 1994 ●

The fairytale wonders and crystalline textures of *Ma mère l'oye* rarely fail to bring out the best in performers and sound engineers. And Nagano joins the score's other master magicians of the past decade, namely, Dutoit, Rattle and Boulez. But no consideration would be complete without putting into the frame Monteux's 1964 recording – it takes but a few seconds to hear 'through' a moderate degree of tape hiss to a group of crack musicians gathered around the revered *maître* and producing sublime chamber music, with the most finely gauged seeking out and savouring of expressive colour, character and period *charme*. Nagano enjoys perhaps the most present and tactile recorded sound of all available versions, with a fine bloom, if not quite the depth of the Dutoit or Boulez, or the focus for detail of the Rattle. Interpretatively, Nagano shares most with Rattle, preferring a wide variety of tempo; not as slow as him in Beauty's 'Pavane', though one might complain that 'Tom Thumb' suggests more movement than Nagano's tempo allows (he turns it into a dreamy woodland interlude). 'Pagodaland', by contrast, is more lively than usual, with the opening piccolo solo nicely inflected.

Both the Boulez and Nagano discs offer *Une barque sur l'océan*, and Nagano's account is one of the most most gripping ever heard. It is a piece whose transcription tends to find more apology than advocacy among Ravel commentators, and is a less frequent inclusion among Ravel anthologies on disc. A pity, as its alternating gentle sunlit sway (and what enchantment lies in the dappled detailing) and the huge waves of sound that arise from it are a gift to conductors who fancy themselves as Poseidon for eight minutes. The 'Prelude' of *Le tombeau de Couperin* is reminiscent of water music (an enchanted babbling brook?). Here Nagano eschews Dutoit's gentle rapids (and the score's challengingly fast metronome mark), facilitating more precise articulation and lovely colouring (wonderfully liquid woodwinds, so well caught by the recording). And in the 'Forlane', precise accentuation and articulation give the main theme a real lift. Questions of balance in *Le tombeau* between baroque manners and romantic warmth tend to find different answers from different interpreters, and different expectations from listeners. And some may feel that Nagano's 'expressive' haltings in the central sections of the 'Forlane' and 'Rigaudon' are more affectation than affection. Still, it would be wrong to end with a complaint. This is a distinguished Ravel collection.

Debussy Images – Ibéria **Ravel** Rapsodie espagnole. Pavane pour une infante défunte. Valses nobles et sentimentales. Alborada del gracioso **H**
Chicago Symphony Orchestra / Fritz Reiner
RCA Victor Gold Seal GD60179 (68 minutes: ADD) Ⓜ
Recorded 1956-57 **OO**

These performances are seldom less than mesmeric. The extremes of tempo and dynamics are exploited to the full in the Spanish night/day pieces: has any other conductor managed the gradual transition from *Ibéria*'s 'perfumes of the night' to the gathering brilliance of the succeeding morning's holiday festivities, with such a delicate, yet precisely focused tracery of sounds? This is the very stuff of a waking dream. And the disc opens with what has to be the slowest, most languid account of the 'Prélude' from the *Rapsodie espagnole* ever recorded; the resulting total concentration of the players on their conductor for control of rhythm and dynamics can be felt in every bar, creating a unique tension and atmosphere. Just listen to the finesse of the playing throughout, particularly the percussion, and marvel at how Reiner balances the textures in even the most riotous outbursts of the *Rapsodie*'s explosive 'Feria'. And the sound? It is difficult to think of any modern recording that renders the spectacle, colour and refinement of these scores with more clarity and atmosphere.

Boléro. Ma mère l'oye. Rapsodie espagnole. Une barque sur l'océan. Alborada del gracioso
Berlin Philharmonic Orchestra / Pierre Boulez
DG 439 859-2GH (76 minutes: DDD) Ⓕ
Recorded 1993 **OO**

You would hardly recognise Boulez's Ravel here from its previous chilly, chiselled self. Those early 1970s collaborations with the Cleveland and New York orchestras on Sony Classical are superseded on all grounds, not least on account of their close, contrived balances. But most striking of all is the clear superiority of the Berlin Philharmonic Orchestra's playing, which says more about Boulez's development as a podium technician than any relative deficiency in either of the American orchestras.

If Boulez's earlier manner might have been likened to that of an investigative pathologist at a post-mortem, his 1990s role could be described as a layer on of hands (with the occasional hint of the micro-surgeon; no bad thing in Ravel). In *Ma mère l'oye*, he is among the master magicians: subtleties of nuance and timing (previously in short supply) now abound; here is playing of a wholly different order of grace and beauty. A sense of drama and proportion are held in perfect equilibrium, with a moderate range of tempos for the set pieces, but slower tempos than before for the scene-setting 'Prélude' and linking interludes in order to realise their atmosphere and sheer sorcery. In the Spanish items, some may find the Berlin woodwinds too cultured in tone and artful in phrasing for their various improvisatory solos: it is rare to hear the first few minutes' solos in *Boléro* quite as strongly contoured as this (they are, too, predictably *legato*; do these players ever draw breath?). You may find yourself craving a hint of abandon from the brass, particularly in the 'Féria' from the *Rapsodie*; and here and in the *Alborada*, as before, tempos remain slower than average (the 'Habanera' is utterly hypnotic), strikingly so in the 'Féria' which now, aptly, sounds as much like Chabrier as Ravel: festive as opposed to driven and explosive. The sound is both present and resonant in the right degrees. Boulez's Ravel was always provocative; it is now evocative.

Fanfare pour 'L'éventail de Jeanne'. Shéhérazade. Alborada del gracioso. Miroirs – La vallée des cloches (arr Grainger). Ma mère l'oye. La valse
Maria Ewing *mez* **City of Birmingham Symphony Orchestra / Sir Simon Rattle**
EMI CDC7 54204-2 (75 minutes: DDD). Text and translation included. Recorded 1989 Ⓕ **O**

In the past there have been instances of Rattle's intensive preparation for setting down a much loved masterpiece precluding spontaneity in the end result. Not here. Along with the customary refinement and revelation of texture, there is a sense of Rattle gauging the very individual fantasy worlds of this varied programme with uncanny precision: an aptly childlike wonder for *Ma mère l'oye*'s fairy tale illustrations; the decadence and decay that drive *La valse* to its inevitable doom; and the sensual allure of the Orient in *Shéhérazade* providing a vibrant backdrop for Maria Ewing's intimate confessions. The three shorter items that make up this indispensable (and generously filled) disc are equally successful, all recorded with stunning realism.

Rapsodie espagnole. Menuet antique. Ma mère l'oye. La valse
Boston Symphony Orchestra / Bernard Haitink
Philips 454 452-2PH (63 minutes: DDD) Ⓕ
Recorded 1995

Alborada del gracioso. Le tombeau de Couperin. Valses nobles et sentimentales. Boléro
Boston Symphony Orchestra / Bernard Haitink
Philips 456 569-2PH (63 minutes: DDD) Ⓕ
Recorded 1996

Haitink returns here to Ravel pieces he recorded two-and-a-half decades ago (Haitink's 1970s Amsterdam Concertgebouw Ravel is still available on a Philips Duo). Are there good reasons for preferring Haitink's newer recordings to the old? The answer has to be 'yes'. Haitink's regular Philips producer and balance engineer, Volker Straus, reproduces this in, by today's standards, quite a close balance, but one that captures enough of Boston Symphony Hall's very open acoustic. That said, there isn't quite the spatial dimension and ambient warmth of Haitink's previous Concertgebouw recordings (where one has to tolerate a degree of analogue tape hiss). Also, some listeners may be alarmed by the vivid presence for both Boston's principal flute – generously phrased playing requiring 'generous' intakes of breath – and the very high incidence of platform noise (sample track 10 of *Ma mère l'oye* from 4'32"). As to Haitink's own contribution, the differences are small, but taken as a whole, justify the venture. Here or there you will find a rubato more easefully achieved, or a passage pointed or shaded with more imagination or emotion (the accentuation of the woodwind at the start of the 'Danse de rouet' from *Ma mère l'oye* and the rapt string playing at the start of its 'Le jardin féerique'); and here or there, a marginally faster or slower tempo, mainly to the music's benefit. The newer *La valse* avoids most of the stretchings and slowings, except the marked ones, of the old, its sights more firmly set on the final climax. And the tempo is more successfully maintained in *Boléro* – definitely 'a class act' with a veiled, silky blend of muted trumpet and flute tone from 4'13" and wonderfully suave but streetwise solos from the saxophones and trombone.

In short, other interpreters might live a little more dangerously, might sometimes 'hear' the music in more interesting ways, might evoke more period charm. But for a modern collection, these discs deserve to be taken very seriously. Haitink's new-look Ravel is central. And it is Ravel of great conviction and composure.

Daphnis et Chloé

Daphnis et Chloé. Rapsodie espagnole. Pavane pour une infante défunte **H**
Chorus of the Royal Opera House, Covent Garden; London Symphony Orchestra / Pierre Monteux
Decca The Classic Sound 448 603-2DCS (74 minutes: ADD). Recorded 1959-61 Ⓜ **OO**

Diaghilev's ballet *Daphnis et Chloé*, based on a pastoral romance by the ancient Greek poet Longus, was first produced in June 1912, with Nijinsky and Karsavina in the title roles and choreography by Mikhail Fokine. Pierre Monteux conducted the first performance, and 47 years later he recorded his peerless interpretation for Decca. Though the Second Suite from the ballet is familiar to concert-goers and makes an effective piece in its own right, the full score, with wordless chorus, conveys still greater atmosphere and magic. No work of more sheer sensual beauty exists in the entire orchestral repertoire, and Monteux was its perfect interpreter. He conducts with wonderful clarity and balance: every important detail tells, and there is refinement of expression, yet inner strength too. The LSO plays with superlative poetry and skill, and the chorus is magnificent in its tonal blend and colour. The *Rapsodie espagnole* and *Pavane* are also given ideal performances, and the recordings show off Decca's exceedingly high standards during the late 1950s and early 1960s.

Debussy Khamma **Ravel** Daphnis et Chloé
Het Groot Omroepkoor; Royal Concertgebouw Orchestra / Riccardo Chailly
Decca 443 934-2DH (74 minutes: DDD) Ⓕ
Recorded 1994 **O**

You would expect this *Daphnis* to sound superb, and it does. In the Concertgebouw acoustic the full flood of choral tone at the climax of Chailly's 'Daybreak' has to be heard to be believed (Chailly's timing of this sunburst is masterly), and this disc's ability to astonish with decibels at climaxes is greater than Decca's previous Dutoit or Monteux recordings of works by Ravel. Possibly the wind machine is cranked with excessive enthusiasm, and the strange lights scenes of *Daphnis* do not seem to be enjoyed or exploited for the strangeness that can result from even the ordinary (ie musical) instruments being asked to play or phrase in unusual ways. Chailly is faster, too, in the dance scenes where, if you are Rattle (on EMI), lingering leads to marvels of characterization, which isn't to say Chailly is bland.

Blandness is the last word to use in describing Chailly's way with Debussy's *Khamma*. This immediately pre-*Jeux* (conceptually speaking) ballet is a sort of Egyptian *Salome*-cum-*Rite of Spring*, in as much as Khamma dances herself to death for the Sun God Amun-Ra that he might be persuaded to save the city from siege. The ominous opening pages here are immediately gripping: a Nibelheim-like family of lower woodwind slithering around, marvellously focused drum, and trumpet fanfares that genuinely do 'give one the shivers' as Debussy once asserted. In general, Chailly, Decca and these superb musicians realise more of the score's 'discoveries of harmonic chemistry' and sheer theatre than one dared imagine possible.

Daphnis et Chloé. La valse
Berlin Radio Chorus; Berlin Philharmonic Orchestra / Pierre Boulez
DG 447 057-2GH (71minutes: DDD) Ⓕ
Recorded 1993-94 **O**

Increasingly, for considering modern recordings of *Daphnis*, it seems you must banish memories of 1959 Monteux; put behind you the most playful, mobile, texturally diaphanous, rhythmically supple account of the score ever recorded; one that is uniquely informed by history and selfless conductorial wisdom. For some, Monteux's view may remain a rather moderate one – certainly in terms of basic tempo and basic dynamic range; and Ravel's score suggests tempos and dynamics which modern performances, and especially recordings, have more faithfully reproduced.

Boulez has, of course, acquired a vast wealth of experience of conductorial wisdom (not least in subtle accommodations of pace and general phrasing) since his first New York recording of *Daphnis*. And here he has the Berlin Philharmonic Orchestra – on top form – to sustain and shape melody within some of his strikingly slow tempos (such as the opening, and Part 3's famous 'Daybreak'), and who remain 'composed' in his daringly fast ones (the 'Dance of the young girls around Daphnis' and the 'Danse guerrière' – one of the most exciting on disc). Just occasionally, you feel that there are parts of the work that interest him less than others (Chloé's 'Danse suppliante', and the 'amours' of the 'Pantomime'). But anyone who doubts Boulez's ability to achieve, first, a sense of ecstasy should hear this 'Daybreak'; secondly, a refined radiance (rather than ripe refulgence), should try the first embrace (track 5, 2'49"; at this point, this is also one of the very few recordings where you can hear the chorus); or, thirdly, to characterise properly the supernatural, listen to the 'flickering' accents he gives the string *tremolo* chords in the 'Nocturne'.

The chorus work, not least in the so-called 'Interlude', is outstanding; the harmonic boldness of this passage was just as startling in New York, but the Berlin chorus, unlike the New York one, is here properly set back. Vowel sounds are varied; the dynamics are just as powerfully graded and the passage builds superbly to the 'Danse guerrière', with off-stage brass perfectly placed and timed. In general, DG's recording – a sumptuous Jesus-Christus Kirche production – strikes exactly the right compromise between clarity and spaciousness, much as Decca's did for Dutoit. With the added lure of an expansive and often massively powerful *La valse* (spectacular timpani), this is now the most recommendable modern *Daphnis* available.

Daphnis et Chloé **H**
New England Conservatory Choir; Boston Symphony Orchestra / Charles Munch
RCA Victor Living Stereo 09026 61846-2 Ⓜ
(54 minutes: ADD). Recorded 1955 ●

This landmark *Daphnis*, made in stereo, sounds quite astonishing in this transfer. Robert Layton, writing in *Gramophone*, and comparing Monteux with Munch 'succumbed more readily to the heady intoxication, the dazzling richness of colour and virtuosity' of the Munch. Both Monteux and Munch understood the dangers of extremes and excessive lingering in this score; of sentiment turning into syrup and Ravel's 'Choreographic Symphony' (his own term) falling apart. It should be noted that, though their recordings balance Ravel's complex score more skilfully and imaginatively than most modern contenders, the score's huge range of dynamics could not be fully realised by the technology of the time.

String Quartet in F

String Quartet in F[a]. Violin Sonata in G[b]. Piano Trio in A minor[c]
[a]**Quartetto Italiano** (Paolo Borciani, Elisa Pegreffi *vns* Piero Farulli *va* Franco Rossi *vc*); [b]**Arthur Grumiaux** *vn* [b]**István Hajdu** *pf*; [c]**Beaux Arts Trio** (Daniel Guilet *vn* Bernard Greenhouse *vc* Menahem Pressler *pf*)
Philips Solo 454 134-2PM (ADD) Ⓜ
Recorded [a]1968, [bc]1965 ●

The playing by the Quartetto Italiano in the String Quartet is superb. The first movement is very languorous and though there is not quite enough contrast in the *Scherzo* between the loud pizzicato at the start and the soft bowed music a few seconds later – it sounds more like *mf* than Ravel's *pp* and *ppp* – the movement goes well and the slow music in the middle is most sensitively managed. In the slow movement, the main tune on the viola (it comes 14 bars from the start) is covered by the second violin, and this happens later on as well whenever the tune recurs. Yet here again most of the movement is beautifully played. The balance of the recorded sound is splendid. (Incidentally, this same recording is also reviewed with the Debussy String Quartet – see the review under Debussy).

The Beaux Arts Trio is very much at home in Ravel. The account of the Trio is a fine one, sensitively paced and perceptive of the music's volatile ebb and flow, of its refined textures. The recording has the wide dynamic range this work needs and there is a good stereo balance between the three instruments, at least in the first three movements. The sombre dignity of the *Passacaille* is particularly moving.

It is still one of the best performances of this work in the catalogue. Grumiaux is very communicative in the Violin Sonata, maintaining a beautifully long line in the first movement, although here he could have sometimes employed a little more of a sense of fantasy. Both he and Hajdu make a convincing job of this work's central Blues section.

Violin Sonatas

Awards 1997

Violin Sonatas – 1897; 1927. Tzigane. Pièce en forme de Habanera. Berceuse sur le nom de Gabriel Fauré. Sonata for Violin and Cello. Kaddisch (trans Garban)
Chantal Juillet *vn* **Truls Mørk** *vc* **Pascal Rogé** *pf/pf luthéal*
Decca 448 612-2DH (78 minutes: DDD) Ⓕ
Recorded 1995 ●●●

The piano luthéal, used at the Paris première of *Tzigane*, is an instrument modified to sound like a cimbalom. Its timbre isn't quite the same, but Pascal Rogé produces a wonderful range of sparkling metallic sounds, lending an exciting and exotic atmosphere to the performance. The violin playing in *Tzigane* is special too – Chantal Juillet's gipsy style is absolutely convincing, the opening solo passage delivered with brilliantly characterised rhythms and a fine sense of timing.

If *Tzigane* is the most striking item on the disc, the other performances aren't far behind. The short pieces are especially enjoyable – the velvety tone Juillet produces for *Kaddisch*, the elegant variations of tone in the *Pièce en forme de Habanera*, and the delicate textures and gentle phrasing of the *Berceuse*. In the two Violin Sonatas with piano the playing is fastidious and very well balanced. Rogé never dominates – in the loudest passages he produces a clear sound, with resonance carefully controlled. In the 'big' passages of the 1927 Sonata there's no attempt to rival the barnstorming excitement or the romantic warmth and urgency of some of the many other recommendable versions. Juillet's and Rogé's playing is cooler, but always expressive, with imaginative and beautiful variations of tone colour. Juillet and Mørk match each other excellently in the Sonata for Violin and Cello. Again, there's a wide range of sonorities, including some suitably grotesque sounds in the second movement, and infectious rhythmic *élan* in the finale. The recording is clear and bright.

Gaspard de la nuit

Ravel Sonatine[b]. Gaspard de la nuit[a]
Schumann Fantasiestücke, Op 12[a]
Martha Argerich *pf*
EMI CDC5 57101-2 (52 minutes: ADD) Ⓕ
Recorded live in [a]1978 and [b]1979 ●●

From the first note of 'Des abends' we are floating, thanks partly to Argerich's finely graded singing tone and partly to her taking the score's extraordinary pedal markings at something close to their face value. Once airborne, it seems all the worlds of Schumann's fantastical imagination are open to us. 'Aufschwung' is the epitome of ardour – a note of desperation never far beneath the surface. 'In der Nacht' skirts even closer to the borders of insanity, its post-*Appassionata* swirlings founded on staggeringly articulate fingerwork. Yet there is still room for an extra touch of dazzlement in the dartings of 'Traumes-Wirren'. Perhaps 'Ende vom Lied' might have relaxed a little more and offered a measure of consolation rather than more of the same kind of intensity; but the Coda is perfection.

The element of Latin American caprice in Argerich's Ravel *Sonatine* may not be everyone's idea of appropriate style; what it does, though, is take us close to the heart, if not of Ravel, then of the art of musical recreation itself. Everything here seems dictated by the feeling of the moment; yet the sheer beauty of sound, with textures once again bathed in fabulously imaginative pedalling, is no less overpowering. At the opening of the finale, Argerich's enthusiasm momentarily gets the better of her fingerwork, and around 0'50" to 0'55" her memory falters for an instant, an extra beat being added to put things back on course (in the parallel passage from 2'37" almost the opposite happens, and two beats are lost).

All this sits oddly with Bryce Morrison's perfectly reasonable description of the *Sonatine* in his essay as 'classically based, the epitome of distilled grace and Gallic understatement'. Yet he surely hits the nail on the head when he describes these performances as complementary to Argerich's studio accounts. For one thing her *Gaspard* is an astonishing four minutes faster than her by no means sedate DG recording from three years earlier (18'09"as against 22'21"). In expression it is polarised towards demonic flair and abandon, in a way scarcely imaginable under studio conditions. 'Ondine' flickers ravishingly and improvisatorily, but the later stages feel more like white-water rafting than the contemplation of a seductive water-nymph, and the big climax at 3'18" won't stand close scrutiny. On the other hand 'Le gibet' is as effective in its restraint as in its hallucinatory colourings – the passage from 2'23" is truly '*pp* sans expression'. Unsurprisingly, there is no shortage of horripilating malevolence in 'Scarbo'; the final stages have to be heard to be believed.

The sound picture may not be to all tastes, combining as it does a close-up image with a generous amount of ambience. This gives us simultaneously the clamorous impact of a super-pianist projecting to the back of a big hall and the atmosphere of a spellbound auditorium.

Gaspard de la nuit. Valses nobles et sentimentales. Jeux d'eau. Miroirs. Sonatine. Le tombeau de Couperin. Prélude. Menuet sur le nom de Haydn. A la manière de Borodine. Menuet antique. Pavane pour une infante défunte. A la manière de Chabrier. Ma mère l'oye[a]
Pascal Rogé, [a]Denise-Françoise Rogé *pfs*
Double Decca ② 440 836-2DF2 (142 minutes: ADD) Ⓜ
Recorded 1973-1994 ●●

Everything is expressed with a classic restraint, elegance and economy, an ideal absence of artifice or idiosyncrasy. Rogé knows precisely where to allow asperity to relax into lyricism and vice versa, and time and again he finds that elusive, cool centre at the heart of Ravel's teeming and luxuriant vision. True, those used to more Lisztian but less authentic Ravel may occasionally find Rogé diffident or *laissez-faire*. But lovers of subtlety will see him as illuminating and enchanting. How often do you hear *Ma mère l'oye* given without a trace of brittleness or archness, or find *Jeux d'eau* presented with such stylish ease and tonal radiance? Rogé may lack something of Thibaudet's menace and high-flying virtuosity in 'Scarbo' (also on Decca) but how memorably he re-creates Ravel's nocturnal mystery. Even if one misses a touch of cruelty behind Ondine's entreaty, few pianists can have evoked her watery realm with greater transparency. Arguably one of the finest Ravel recordings available.

Songs

Shéhérazade[bl]. Vocalise en forme de habanera[dj]. Chants populaires[abdefj]. Sur l'herbe[ej]. Histoires naturelles[ej]. Cinq mélodies populaires grécques[bj]. Tripatos[bj]. Ballade de la reine morte d'aimer[bj]. Manteau de fleurs[bj]. Rêves[bj]. Don Quichotte à Dulciné[efj]. Ronsard à son âme[fj]. Sainte[fj]. Les grands vents venus d'outre-mer[fj]. Un grand sommeil noir[fj]. Deux mélodies hébraïques[fj]. Trois poèmes de Stéphane Mallarmé[al]. Noël des jouets[aj]. Deux épigrammes de Clément Marot[aj]. Chansons madécasses[cgh]. Chanson du rouet[cj]. Si morne[cj]
[a]Dame Felicity Lott, [b]Mady Mesplé, [c]Jessye Norman *sops* **[d]Teresa Berganza** *mez* **[e]Gabriel Bacquier** *bar* **[f]José van Dam** *bass* **[g]Michel Debost** *fl* **[h]Renaud Fontanarosa** *vc* **[j]Dalton Baldwin** *pf* **[k]Toulouse Capitole Orchestra, [l]Orchestre de Paris Chamber Ensemble / Michel Plasson**

EMI Rouge et Noir ② CZS5 69299-2
(136 minutes: DDD) French texts included. Ⓜ
Recorded c1982

Despite the enormous popularity of Ravel's music, many of his songs remain comparatively little known and seldom recorded. This collection was the last in the series of editions of French song that Dalton Baldwin recorded for EMI. The first CD opens with Berganza's performance of *Shéhérazade*. Very accomplished, beautifully accompanied by Plasson and the Toulouse orchestra, it makes an interesting contrast to some of the versions done by sopranos. Berganza follows it with a splendid rendition of the *Vocalise en forme de habanera*, and the 'Chanson espagnole' from the *Chants populaires*. These last are divided among four singers – Gabriel Bacquier sings the 'Chanson française', José van Dam the Italian and Hebrew songs, while Dame Felicity Lott sings the least known, the Scottish.

Bacquier and van Dam really steal the show on this set. This is the most enjoyable performance ever recorded of *Histoires naturelles*. The smile in Bacquier's voice, his exquisite diction and timing make this the highlight of the first CD. Mady Mesplé's performance of the five Greek songs are splendid, and the four songs that follow – *Tripatos*, *Ballade de la reine morte d'aimer*, *Manteau de fleurs* and *Rêves* – are all rarities.

The second CD has van Dam's celebrated performance of the three *Don Quichotte* songs. His version with piano is very characterful. Norman contributes the *Chansons madecasses*; she has so often included this cycle in her recital programmes that it is now closely associated with her voice and personality. Dame Felicity Lott's group includes the *Mallarmé* songs, the early *Clémont Marot* songs (very good) and the charming *Noël des jouets*, and then the 'Chanson écossaise' – the fifth popular song, reconstructed by Arbie Orenstein in the 1970s.

This set is well worth acquiring for the sake of near completeness (it does not include *Fascination*, the slow waltz-song Ravel composed for Paulette Darty) and above all for the contributions from Gabriel Bacquier and José van Dam and, of course, Dalton Baldwin himself, sensitive, eloquent as always.

Alan Rawsthorne British 1905-1971

GROVE *Rawsthorne studied as a pianist at the Royal College of Music and abroad with Petri; only at the end of the 1930s did he begin to make a name as a composer. Influenced by Hindemith, he developed a highly crafted and abstract style, chiefly in concertos and other orchestral works. His inclination towards motivic thinking and variation structures brought some approximation to 12-note techniques, but tonal centres remained important. He wrote three symphonies (1950, 1959, 1964), two piano concertos (1939, 1951), two violin concertos (1948, 1956), three string quartets (1939, 1954, 1964) and sonatas for viola, cello and violin.*

Concerto for String Orchestra

Concertante pastorale[a]. Concerto for String Orchestra. Divertimento. Elegiac Rhapsody. Light Music. Suite for Recorder and String Orchestra[b] (orch McCabe)
[a]**Conrad Marshall** *fl* [a]**Rebecca Goldberg** *hn* [b]**John Turner** *rec* **Northern Chamber Orchestra / David Lloyd-Jones**
Naxos 8 553567 (64 minutes: DDD) Ⓢ
Recorded 1996

The most substantial offering here – the resourceful and magnificently crafted *Concerto for String Orchestra* – dates from 1949, and David Lloyd-Jones and his admirably prepared group give a performance which, in its emotional scope and keen vigour, outshines Sir Adrian Boult's (now-deleted) 1966 radio recording with the BBC Symphony Orchestra. Not only does Lloyd-Jones achieve a more thrusting urgency in the outer movements, he also locates an extra sense of slumbering tragedy in the *Lento e mesto*. He gives a sparkling account of the immensely engaging *Divertimento*, written for Harry Blech and the London Mozart Players in 1962; the rumbustious concluding 'Jig' (track 13) is as good a place as any to sample the spick-and span response of the Northern Chamber Orchestra. The *Concertante pastorale*, written for the Hampton Court Orangery Concerts, is an atmospheric, beautifully wrought 10-minute essay for solo flute, horn and strings. It's succeeded by the perky *Light Music* for strings, composed in 1938 for the Workers' Music Association and based on Catalan folk-tunes.

Then there's McCabe's expert orchestration of the miniature Suite for recorder and strings, the second of whose four linked movements is a reworking of a ballad from the *Fitzwilliam Virginal Book*. But the most exciting discovery has to be the 1963-4 *Elegiac Rhapsody*, a deeply felt threnody for string orchestra written in memory of Rawsthorne's friend, the poet Louis MacNeice. Not only does it pack a wealth of first-rate invention and incident into its 10-minute duration, it attains a pitch of anguished expression possibly unrivalled in this figure's entire output. Excellent notes and cleanly engineered.

Further listening
Honegger Symphony No 2
Couplings: Pacific 231. Rugby. Mouvement Symphonique No 3. Pastorale d'ete. Monopartita
Zurich Tonhalle Orchestra / Zinman
Decca 455 352-2DH (70 minutes: DDD: 5/99) Ⓕ
If you like Rawsthorne's *Concerto for string Orchestra* then try Honegger's Symphony No 2. Karajan's and Janson's accounts may be finer but these couplings persuade.

Violin Concertos

Violin Concertos Nos 1 and 2.
Cortèges – fantasy overture
Rebecca Hirsch *vn* **BBC Scottish Symphony Orchestra / Lionel Friend**
Naxos 8 554240 (64 minutes: DDD) Ⓢ
Recorded 1996

Rawsthorne enthusiasts should waste no time in snapping up this disc, containing as it does music-making of perceptive dedication and impressive polish. He completed his First Violin Concerto in 1947, dedicating the score to Walton (listen for the tongue-in-cheek quotation from *Belshazzar's Feast* just before the end). Cast in just two movements, it is a lyrically affecting creation that weaves quite a spell, especially in a performance as dignified and consistently purposeful as this. However, the revelation comes with the Second Concerto of 1956. Rebecca Hirsch and Lionel Friend locate a deceptive urgency and symphonic thrust in the opening *Allegretto* that genuinely compel. If anything, the succeeding *Poco lento* wears an even more anguished, nervy demeanour, the music's questing mood very well conveyed. By contrast, the finale (a theme and variations) proceeds in serene, almost carefree fashion, its witty coda forming a delightfully unbuttoned conclusion to a genuinely striking, much-underrated work.

As a curtain-raiser, Naxos gives us the fantasy overture, *Cortèges*. Commissioned by the BBC and premièred at the 1945 Proms by the LSO under Basil Cameron, it is a well-wrought essay, pitting an eloquent *Adagio* processional ('wistfully expressive rather than tragic in tone', as annotator Sebastian Forbes astutely observes) against an irrepressible *Allegro molto vivace* tarantella. The composer develops his material with customary skill, and Friend draws a committed and alert response from the BBC Scottish SO. Boasting a spacious, bright and admirably balanced sound picture (no attempt to spotlight the soloist), here is an enormously rewarding issue and a bargain of the first order.

Further listening

Piston Violin Concerto Nos 1 and 2

Coupling: Fantasia for Violin and Orchestra

Buswell *vn* **National Symphony Orch of Ukraine / Kuchar**

Naxos 8 559003 (61 minutes: DDD: 10/99) Ⓢ

The First Concerto has much in common with Barber's, including a similar abundance of individual melody, and it should be better known. Fine readings: a must buy disc.

Cello Concerto

Symphonic Studies. Oboe Concerto[a]. Cello Concerto[b]

[a]Stéphane Rancourt *ob* **[b]Alexander Baillie** *vc* **Royal Scottish National Orchestra / David Lloyd-Jones**

Naxos 8 554763 (72 minutes: DDD) Ⓢ

Recorded 1999 ●●

David Lloyd-Jones directs a swaggering, affectionate and ideally clear-headed account of Rawsthorne's masterly *Symphonic Studies* (1939), one of the most stylish and exuberantly inventive products of British music from the first half of the last century. The work displays a formal elegance, impeccable craftsmanship and healthy concision that are mightily exhilarating. It is indeed, as John Belcher observes in his thoughtful booklet-essay, an impressively assured orchestral début, its tightly knit 20-minute span evincing a remarkable emotional scope. The present performance must be deemed a great success – a worthy successor, certainly, to both Constant Lambert's classic 1946 Philharmonia version (now happily restored on Pearl) and Sir John Pritchard's admirable 1975 Lyrita recording with the LPO (nla).

First heard at the 1947 Cheltenham Festival, the Concerto for Oboe and String Orchestra was composed for Evelyn Rothwell. Brimful of gentle melancholy, it's another delectably clean-cut creation, whose touchingly eloquent first movement is succeeded by a wistfully swaying, at times cryptic *Allegretto con morbidezza* and a spirited, though never entirely untroubled *Vivace* finale. Impeccable solo work from RSNO principal oboe Stéphane Rancourt and a spick-and-span accompaniment to match.

There's another first recording in the guise of the Cello Concerto, a Royal Philharmonic Society commission from 1965. This is a major achievement, a work to rank beside Rawsthorne's superb Third Symphony and Third String Quartet of the previous year in its unremitting concentration and nobility of expression. A strongly lyrical vein runs through the notably eventful, ever-evolving opening movement (subtitled 'Quasi Variazioni'), whereas the central *Mesto* mixes dark introspection with outbursts of real anguish. The clouds lift, however, for the energetic, even rumbustious finale. A substantial, deeply felt utterance, in short, which will surely repay closer study. Suffice it to say, soloist Alexander Baillie gives a stunningly idiomatic rendering; Lloyd-Jones and the RSNO offer big-hearted, confident support.

Apart from a hint of harshness in the very loudest *tutti*s of the *Symphonic Studies*, Tim Handley's engineering is immensely vivid and always most musically balanced. Overall, a wonderfully enterprising triptych and astonishing value.

Film Music

The Captive Heart – Suite. Lease of Life – Main Titles and Emergency. Burma Victory – Suite. Saraband for Dead Lovers – Saraband and Carnival (all arr Schurmann). West of Zanzibar – Main Titles. The Cruel Sea – Main Titles and Nocturne. Where No Vultures Fly – Suite. Uncle Silas – Suite. The Dancing Fleece – Three Dances (all arr and orch Lane)

BBC Philharmonic Orchestra / Rumon Gamba

Chandos CHAN9749 (73 minutes: DDD) Ⓕ

Recorded 1999 ●

Incapable of shoddy craftsmanship and truly a 'composer's composer', Alan Rawsthorne brought a professional integrity, great clarity of expression and unerring economy of thought to every field of music in which he worked, not least the 27 film scores he penned between 1937 and 1964. Here there are selections from nine scores in all, the arranging and orchestrating duties being shared by the indefatigable Philip Lane and Gerard Schurmann (who worked closely with the composer on many of the original ventures). *The Cruel Sea* (1953) remains the best-known offering, its evocative, slumbering power and noble defiance as eloquent as ever. Bernard Herrmann, who knew a thing or two about the genre, rated *Uncle Silas* (1947) one of the greatest film scores he had ever encountered: try the delightfully flirtatious 'Valse caprice'. The charming 'Three Dances' from *The Dancing Fleece* (a Crown Film Unit production promoting British wool) can almost be viewed as a 'trial run' for *Madame Chrysanthème*, the one-act ballet Rawsthorne wrote in 1955for Sadlers Wells. The first track is an extended (18-minute) suite from the 1946 POW drama, *The Captive eart*, and there are also generous excerpts from *Where No Vultures Fly* and the documentary *Burma Victory* (full of decidedly superior, stirring invention). Keller was especially complimentary about *Lease of Life* (1954), a Robert Donat vehicle for which Rawsthorne supplied a 'rich miniature score' lasting about 13-and-a-half minutes, and the collection concludes with a flourish in the shape of the superbly swaggering 'Prelude and Carnival' from *Saraband for Dead Lovers* (1948). Gamba draws playing of panache and infectious enthusiasm from the BBC Philharmonic, with spectacularly wide-ranging Chandos sound. Not to be missed!

Further listening

Walton Film Music, Volume 1 – Hamlet. As you like it.
Gielgud *narr* **Bott** *sop* **Academy of St Martin in the Fields / Marriner**
Chandos CHAN8842 (52 minutes: DDD: 6/90) Ⓕ

All four of Chandos's Walton film music releases are worth exploring. *Henry V* (volume 3) is his most famous score but the Hamlet Suite is as good a place as any to begin to appreciate Walton's gift for evocative orchestration.

Chamber Works

Piano Quintet[a]. Concertante for Violin and Piano[b]. Piano Trio[c]. Viola Sonata[d]. Cello Sonata[e]
[abc]**Nadia Myerscough,** [a]**Mark Messenger** *vns* [a]**Helen Roberts,** [d]**Martin Outram** *vas* [ace]**Peter Adams** *vc* [a]**John McCabe,** [bce]**Yoshiko Endo,** [d]**Julian Rolton** *pfs*
Naxos 8 554352 (70 minutes: DDD) Ⓢ
Recorded 1997

Here's a disc brimming with high-quality music and superlative performances. The Piano Quintet, from 1968, is cast in a single continuous movement divided into four contrasting sections. Although only 15 minutes long, the quintet abounds with musical ideas and interest. Much of the material is vigorous, powerful and concisely presented, but there is much poetry, too, particularly in the *Lento non troppo* section and the brief epilogue that closes the energetic opening section. The *Concertante* for violin and piano is a much earlier work dating from the mid-1930s and, although early influences such as Shostakovich and even Busoni in 'Faustian' mood can be detected, it is perhaps among the earliest of Rawsthorne's works in which his own voice begins to emerge. First performed by the distinguished Menuhin-Cassadó-Kentner Trio, the Piano Trio of 1963 contains much impressive and finely crafted material, as well as a good deal of colourful soloistic writing. The Viola Sonata dates from 1937, but the score was lost shortly after its première only to be rediscovered in a Hampstead bookshop and revised in 1954. The Sonata is something of a watershed in Rawsthorne's early output, and shows a considerable advance in style and technique from the *Concertante* of only a few years earlier, and both this and the equally fine Cello Sonata of 1948 are particularly valuable additions to the catalogue.

Performances throughout are first-class, although John McCabe's commanding reading of the Piano Quintet stands out as exceptionally authoritative and compelling.

Jean-Féry Rebel French 1661-1747

GROVE *After serving the Count of Ayen in Spain, 1700-5, Rebel became a leading member of the French king's 24 Violons and the Académie Royale de Musique orchestra. He later held court posts including that of chamber composer (from 1726) and was active as a harpsichordist and conductor. An innovatory and esteemed composer, he wrote various vocal works, string sonatas, 'symphonies' for the Académie Royale dancers including Les caractères de la danse (1715), Terpsichore (1720) and the much admired Les élémens (1737), which begins with a famously alarming dissonance to represent chaos.*

Violin Sonatas

No 1 in A; No 3 in A minor; No 4 in E minor; No 5 in D; No 6 in B minor; No 7 in G minor; No 8 in D minor; No 9 in F
Andrew Manze *vn* **Jaap ter Linden** *va da gamba* **Richard Egarr** *hpd*
Harmonia Mundi HMU90 7221 (78 minutes: DDD) Ⓕ
Recorded 1998

This is Andrew Manze's first foray into the French baroque repertory with eight of Rebel's 12 seldom-heard violin sonatas of 1713. Manze, never short of genius or fire in the Italian and Austrian repertory, here relaxes his sound, making gentle and subtle use of tempo and dynamics and only occasionally breaking out into impassioned lyricism. But that does not mean to say that he has simply plugged into the fashionable French baroque sound with its easy grace and polite twiddles; one can easily imagine these sonatas being played in just such a pretty manner, but Manze has instead looked deep into the music and extracted from it a great variety of expression, including in many places an unexpected darkness, a brooding restraint immediately apparent in the *Grave* movements with which some of these sonatas open, but seldom far away even in the apparently carefree musettes, rondeaux or allemandes. It brings to the music an unexpected emotional edge, even a touch of menace. It would be a mean spirit who could not admire the intelligence and imagination which is so lovingly brought to this neglected music. Combined with the sympathetic contributions of Richard Egarr and Jaap ter Linden, this is baroque chamber music-making of the highest order.

Max Reger German 1873-1916

GROVE *Reger studied with Riemann (1890-95) in Munich and Wiesbaden (where his drinking habits began); in 1901 he settled in Munich and in 1907 moved to Leipzig to take a post as professor of composition at the university, though he was also active internationally as a conductor and pianist. He was appointed conductor of the court orchestra at Meiningen in 1911 and in 1915 moved to Jena.*

During a composing life of little more than 20 years, he produced a large output in all genres, nearly always in abstract forms. He was a firm supporter of 'absolute' music and saw himself in a tradition going back to Bach, through Beethoven, Schumann and Brahms; his organ music, though also affected by Liszt, was provoked by that tradition. Of his orchestral pieces, his symphonic and richly elaborate Hiller Variations and Mozart Variations are justly remembered; of his chamber music the lighter-textured trios have retained a place in the repertory, along with some of the works for solo string instruments. His late piano and two-piano music places him as a successor to Brahms in the central German tradition. He pursued intensively, and to its limits, Brahms's continuous development and free modulation, often also invoking the aid of Bachian counterpoint. Many of his works are in variation and fugue forms; equally characteristic is a great energy and complexity of thematic growth.

Symphonic Rhapsody, Op 147

Eine Lustspielouvertüre, Op 120. Symphonic Rhapsody, Op 147. Suite in A minor, Op 103*a*. Scherzino in C
Marie Luise Neunecker *hn* **Walter Forchert** *vn*
Bamberg Symphony Orchestra / Horst Stein
Koch Schwann 31498-2 (60 minutes: DDD) Ⓕ
Recorded 1994

The American violinist Florizel von Reuter concocted the so-called *Symphonic Rhapsody* for violin and orchestra from a mere 130 bars of Max Reger's manuscript. Reger had been preparing an *Andante and Rondo capriccioso* for violin and small orchestra at the time of his death, and von Reuter courted wide-scale controversy by working a modicum of material into a 25-minute epic that does not even approximate the form that Reger himself had in mind. Reger left precious few clues as to how he might have proceeded. Von Reuter's continuous structure falls into four distinct sections, with a perky little fugue at 16'22" and a fairly elaborate cadenza at 19'11". Fans of the expansive Violin Concerto will delight in this lyrical hybrid, a genuine meeting of like-minds though its principal composer would no doubt have produced something finer still. Walter Forchert gives an excellent performance, much as he does of the delightful A minor Suite, most of which was orchestrated from a violin-and-piano original by Adalbert Baranski. Here the tone is unashamedly Bachian, with a droning Trio to the 'Gavotte' and a most beautiful 'Aria' – the only movement that Reger himself refashioned – that takes its cue from Bach's Third Orchestral Suite. Horst Stein's programme opens and closes with winning examples of Reger in extrovert mode: the once-popular *Lustspiel* Overture, full of contrapuntal mischief, and the brief but fetching *Scherzino* in C major for horn and orchestra, composed in Weiden for the local music society. Stein's advocacy is all that one could wish for; the orchestral playing is quietly characterful and the recordings are good.

Serenade in G, Op 95

Suite im alten Stil, Op 93. Serenade in G, Op 95
Bamberg Symphony Orchestra / Horst Stein
Koch Schwann 315662 (66 minutes: DDD) Ⓕ
Recorded 1993

There are few orchestral works composed during the past 100 years that have been more unfairly neglected than Reger's delightful *Serenade*, Op 95. And what a beauty it is! The opening theme is unalloyed delight, while the first movement's expansive workings are eventful, affectionately discursive and formally well crafted. The second subject is one of Reger's loveliest melodies and the harp chimes that signal the melting return of the opening idea spell genuine magic. The contrapuntal finale is full of fun and the work ends – in thematic terms – whence it began, in a mood of pastoral reverie. As to the orchestra, Reger employs winds, brass and timpani framed by two separate string groups, one playing with mutes (the one placed on the right-hand side of the stage), the other without, so that antiphonal interplay between them is underlined. Lovers of mainstream romantic repertory cannot fail to respond and Stein's performance is, viewed overall, the most polished so far.

The *Suite in the Olden Style* started life as a duo for violin and piano but the orchestral version dates from the very end of Reger's tragically short career. The rumbustious first movement opens in the manner of Bach's Third *Brandenburg Concerto*; the *Largo* hints at Bruckner and the fugal finale is built on a puckish theme that seems to wind on into infinity. Here, then, is an excellent CD to counter all those unfounded rumours about Reger's 'dry, dull, academic' composing style. If you love Bach, Brahms, Bruckner or Dvořák, you have the potential to love at least Reger's *Serenade* virtually as much.

Four Symphonic Poems, Op 128

Four Symphonic Poems after Arnold Böcklin, Op 128. Variations and Fugue on a Theme of J A Hiller, Op 100
Royal Concertgebouw Orchestra / Neeme Järvi
Chandos CHAN8794 (67 minutes: DDD) Ⓕ
Recorded 1989

Mention of Reger's name in 'informed' circles is likely to produce a conditioned reflex: 'Fugue!'. In his day he was the central figure of the 'Back to Bach' movement, but he was also a romantic who relished all the expressive potential of the enormous post-Wagnerian orchestra. Chandos exploits the open spaces of the Concertgebouw, forsaking some healthy transparency for an extra spatial dimension; a more sumptuous glow. With Järvi's instinct for pacing in late romantic music, and his great orchestra's evident delight in the copious riches of the discovery, for the *Hiller* Variations, this disc is very tempting.

Anyone who warms to Vaughan Williams's *Tallis Fantasia* will immediately respond to the 'Hermit playing the violin', the first of the four *Böcklin* tone-poems; Debussy's 'Jeux de vagues' from *La mer* was obviously in Reger's mind for the second poem 'At play in the waves'; and the 'Isle of the dead' is Reger's no less doom- and gloom-laden response to the painting that so captured Rachmaninov's imagination. The final painting, 'Bacchanal', was described as a Munich beer festival in Roman costume – an entirely fitting description for Reger's setting of it!

Variations and Fugue on a Theme of Beethoven, Op 86. Eine Ballettsuite in D, Op 130. Four Symphonic Poems after Arnold Böcklin, Op 128
Norrköping Symphony Orchestra / Leif Segerstam
BIS CD601 (72 minutes: DDD) Recorded 1993 Ⓕ

This disc is well programmed to show off the contrasting sides of orchestral Reger: firstly, the familiar champion of absolute music and the German tradition in the Variations; secondly, in *Eine Ballettsuite*, the unlikely purveyor of a relatively lightly scored *divertissement* of six dance or character portraits 'for musical epicures'; and finally, in the *Böcklin* Poems, one who succumbed to the lure of programme music and 'impressionist' colour and timbre. In both the first and third *Böcklin* Poems Segerstam is closer to Reger's metronome markings than the faster, more freewheeling Järvi. Segerstam is also, throughout the Poems, more acutely responsive to the extremes – and the minutest gradations in between – of both pace and dynamics. For the first and third poems this means that you are now aware just how much of this music dwells in the regions of *pianissimo* and beyond, and also how fine an impressionist Reger was. In the Poems, Järvi, it has to be said, has the advantage of a great orchestra, rather than a very good one, and a more accommodating acoustic. BIS gives Segerstam another of its textbook recordings, that is to say: an ears only, halfway back in an average size, modern concert-hall experience.

Clarinet Quintet

String Quartet in E flat, Op 109.
Clarinet Quintet in A, Op 146[a]
[a]**Karl Leister** *cl* **Vogler Quartet** (Tim Vogler, Frank Reinecke *vns* Stefan Fehlandt *va* Stephan Forck *vc*)
Nimbus NI5644 (72 minutes: DDD) Ⓕ
Recorded 1999

For many the mere mention of the palindrome Reger incites a silent chorus of yawns. Yet who could fail to smile at the winding lyricism that opens both these works, or to the self-possessed fugue that potters gleefully at the end of the Op 109 String Quartet. This is music that simply had to be written, complex music maybe, but with so much to say at so many levels that once you enter its world, you're hooked. Previous recordings of the gorgeous Clarinet Quintet have included two with Karl Leister, though for sheer naturalness, musicality and team spirit, this new production will be hard to beat.

Reger's frequent allusions to early musical modes inspire playing of rare sensitivity. Humour surfaces in the *scherzo*'s rough and tumble, a downward scale idea backed by lively *pizzicatos*, teasingly discursive and with a sunny, song-like *Trio*. The slow movement recalls Brahms's Quintet but without the gipsy element, while the theme-and-variation finale reminds us that Reger's homage to Mozart extends beyond the chosen key of A major. The String Quartet, one of five that Reger wrote during his all-too-brief maturity, is more openly argumentative than the Quintet, especially in the first movement. Hints of Taranto inform the tarantella-like *scherzo* (with its powerful muted viola writing, at 1'56"), whereas the slow movement combines hymn-like nobility (3'16") with more echoes of Brahms. The closing fugue is the work of a joyful creator drunk on counterpoint, though there's plenty to engage the heart as well as the mind. The Vogler commands a wider range of tonal colour than the Berne Quartet (in their complete Reger quartet cycle) but the present coupling is ideal for all Doubting Thomases who would have you believe that Reger is a bore.

Piano Trios

Piano Trios – B minor, Op 2; E minor, Op 102
Gunter Teuffel *va* **Parnassus Trio** (Wolfgang Schröder *vn* Michael Gross *vc* Chia Chou *pf*)
Dabringhaus und Grimm MDG303 0751-2 Ⓕ
(67 minutes: DDD) ●

It was very wise to programme the masterly E minor Trio before its B minor predecessor. Unsuspecting listeners who jump straight in at Op 2 will discover a pleasing if discursive piece, forged in the shadow of Brahms, with an opening *Allegro appassionato* which, although half the length of its disc-companion's first movement, seems twice as long. The *Scherzo* is frumpish, the closing *Adagio con variazioni* sombre and somewhat long-winded. And yet the use of viola in place of a cello has its attractions, and there are numerous telling glimpses of the mature Reger.

The E minor Trio is something else again, a rugged masterpiece, with a finely structured opening *Allegro moderato, ma con passione* (the three stages of its argument are divided equally within a 15-minute framework), a mysterious *Allegretto* that opens in the manner of later Brahms then suddenly lets in the sunlight, and a noble, hymn-like *Largo* that recalls 'The Hermit with the Violin' from the *Böcklin* Portraits. Reger's Second Trio is full of audacious modulations and striking dramatic gestures; it *is* long (something in excess of 40 minutes), but never outstays its welcome. No one could reasonably ask for more than the Parnassus Trio offers, either in terms of drama or of interpretative subtlety. If you love Brahms and fancy diving in among a plethora of stimulating musical complexities, invest without delay.

Organ Works

Chorale Fantasias, Op 52 – Wachet auf, ruft uns die Stimme. Pieces, Op 145 – Weihnachten. Organ Sonata No 2 in D minor, Op 60. Symphonic Fantasia and Fugue, Op 57

Franz Hauk *org*

Guild GMCD7192 (73 minutes: DDD) Ⓕ

Played on the Klais organ of Ingolstadt Minster.

Recorded 1996 ●

Opinions about Reger's music tend to be polarised between admirers and detractors. The latter group would say of him, as Emperor Joseph II famously said of Mozart, that he wrote too many notes. Even in this new century the complexity of his scores still presents an awesome challenge to performers and listeners alike. Yet the rewards are immense; Reger is arguably even as great a composer as Liszt. His radical, eclectic approach took organ music to new dimensions, and he fully deserves a whole CD to himself. He's well served here by an inspired choice of player, instrument and venue.

Hauk's performances are amazingly virtuosic; he brings clarity of rhythm and articulation to the faster passages and a serene poetry to the quieter moments. He plays the spectacular Klais organ of Ingolstadt Minster, which must be one of the best instruments in Europe. Its brilliant tutti, combined with a 12-second reverberation, does full justice to Reger's epic climaxes, and there are some ravishing colours in the softer sections. As resident organist, Hauk knows this instrument intimately, and he exploits all the available colours and dynamics with mastery.

Guild's fine recording stops the reverberation from becoming excessive, and at the same time it captures the organ's full dynamic range. The CD comes with an excellent booklet from Hauk himself, and whatever your views on Reger, this disc can be unreservedly recommended as an overwhelming and uplifting experience.

Piano Works

Six Morceaux, Op 24. Silhouetten, Op 53. Blätter und Blüten, Op 58

Jean Martin *pf*

Naxos 8 550932 (79 minutes: DDD) Ⓢ

Recorded 1994

A valuable treat for all inquisitive piano buffs and dedicated Regerians, even if some of the music is of variable quality. Least impressive, perhaps, are the *Six Morceaux*, Op 24 (1898) – all of them fairly derivative, especially of Chopin (No 2), Schubert (No 4) and Brahms (No 5). Whether they quite repay their taxing demands is open to some doubt, whereas the *Silhouetten* Op 53 (1900) and *Blätter und Blüten* Op 58 (1900-02) are quite another matter. Both sets are rich in playful modulations and lyrical ideas. Op 53's opening 'Ausserst lebhaft' anticipates the mischievous Reger of the *Hiller* Variations; the Ninth recalls the Grieg of the *Lyric Pieces*, the 10th, Reger's own *Ballettsuite* (of some 13 years later), and the 12th, Brahms's late *Intermezzos*. All could enrich any programme of late-romantic piano music, while the more aphoristic (and technically simpler) *Blätter und Blüten* are lighter in tone, their high-points being (at least on first acquaintance) a charming 'Frühlingslied' and a thoughtful pair of 'Romanzen', the second of which recalls Smetana's piano music at its finest.

Seventy-nine minutes constitute a fair chunk out of anyone's leisure timetable but, with the present context, 44 of them (that is, Op 53 and 58) could be happily spent listening. Certainly Jean Martin plays well and is realistically recorded.

Violin Works

Six Preludes and Fugues, Op 131*a*. Preludes and Fugues, Op 117 – No 1 in B minor; No 2 in G minor; No 3 in E minor; No 5 in G; No 6 in D minor; No 7 in A minor; No 8 in E minor

Mateja Marinkovič *vn*

ASV ② CDDCA876 (82 minutes: DDD) Ⓜ

Recorded 1993 ●

Reger's knowledge of, and feeling for, the violin were all-embracing, and although his winding melodic lines can sometimes prove maddeningly discursive, there is much beauty in the writing – the A minor Prelude, or the E minor Prelude, Op 131*a* providing particularly good sampling points. Bach is of course an overwhelming presence: quite apart from direct quotations there is the all-pervasive influence of the unaccompanied Sonatas and Partitas, especially with regard to Reger's fugues, which invariably start with a hint of Bachian *déjà-vu* before modulating way beyond the baroque's customary orbit. All 13 works here are surprisingly varied in theme and tone, although even the most enthusiastic listener is advised not to take in more than a few at a time. The prize-winning violinist Mateja Marinkovič is professor at both the Royal Academy of Music and the Guildhall School of Music, and his warm-centred, tonally true performances serve Reger handsomely. A major addition to the solo violin repertory on CD, and a must for all Regerians.

Choral Works

Drei geistliche Gesänge, Op 110. Drei Gesänge, Op 39

Danish National Radio Choir / Stefan Parkman

Chandos CHAN9298 (56 minutes: DDD) Ⓕ

Texts and translations included

Recorded 1993-94

Visions of myriad notes covering the page would frighten most choirs away, but these singers are made of sterner stuff. For them complex contrapuntal structures, devious chromatic harmonies and textures so thick you need a forage knife to get through them, hold no terrors. Rather they not only weave their way through Reger's characteristically tangled scores without a moment's doubt, but illuminate the paths so clearly one hardly notices the dense musical undergrowth all around. Parkman has a clear-sighted view of what is wanted and, aided by singers whose pure, perfectly blended tone is in itself a joy to hear, he follows his vision unfalteringly: everything falls neatly into place making real musical sense. The hefty Op 110 Motets (ostensibly in five, but often diverging into as many as nine independent parts) can, and usually do, sound oppressively heavy, but here offer some of the most sublimely beautiful moments yet captured on CD. A triumph of skill over adversity.

Steve Reich

American 1936

GROVE *Reich studied drumming when he was 14 with the New York Philharmonic Orchestra timpanist; later he took a degree in philosophy at Cornell (1953-57) and studied composition at the Juilliard School (1958-61) and at Mills College (1962-63) with Milhaud and Berio, also becoming interested in Balinese and African music. In 1966 he began performing with his own ensemble, chiefly of percussionists, developing a music of gradually changing ostinato patterns that move out of phase, creating an effect of shimmering surfaces; this culminated in Drumming (1971), a 90-minute elaboration of a single rhythmic cell. From c1972 he added harmonic change to his music, and later (Tehillim, 1981) melody. He has also worked with larger orchestral and choral forces (The Desert Music, 1983). Different Trains (1988), for string quartet and tape, won a Grammy for best new composition.*

Music for 18 Musicians

Anonymous Ensemble / Steve Reich *pf*
ECM New Series 821 417-2 (57 minutes: ADD) Ⓕ
Recorded 1978

Steve Reich's first recording of *Music for 18 Musicians* was a landmark release in the history of new music on record and confirmed what a towering masterpiece it is. The recording was actually produced by Rudolf Werner for DG, following the release of a three-LP set of *Drumming*, *Six Pianos* and *Music for Mallet Instruments, Voice and Organ*. Legend has it that Roland Kommerell, at that time head of German PolyGram, foresaw the commercial potential of Reich's piece but realised that DG was not the best vehicle to market the recording. Kommerell therefore offered the recording instead to Manfred Eicher of ECM, a company which had hitherto only released jazz and rock. The ECM release sold well over 100,000 copies, around 10 times higher than might be expected of a new music disc. This episode changed the nature of ECM and signalled a new approach to marketing new music that has since been taken up by other companies. The 1978 recording still sounds beguilingly fresh. When Steve Reich and Musicians came to re-record *Music for 18 Musicians* for Nonesuch's 10-CD box set in 1996, their performance was amazingly 11 minutes longer than the ECM version. Normally, you would expect such a big difference to come from a slower tempo, but in fact the underlying pulse of both recordings is virtually identical. This is because of the unusual structure of *Music for 18 Musicians*, where the gradual fading-in and fading-out of different elements are not given a fixed number of repetitions but are played simply as long as it takes for this process to happen. In the 1996 version, these fade-ins and fade-outs are more finely graded and require more repetitions than in the 1978 version.

City life

Proverb. Nagoya marimbas. City life
Bob Becker, **James Preiss** *marimbas*
Theatre of Voices (Andrea Fullington, Sonja Rasmussen, Allison Zelles *sops* Alan Bennett, Paul Elliott *tens*); **Steve Reich Ensemble / Paul Hillier; Bradley Lubman**
Nonesuch 7559-79430-2 (42 minutes: DDD) Ⓕ
Recorded 1996

The Wittgenstein quotation 'How small a thought it takes to fill a whole life' serves as the basis of *Proverb* for three sopranos, two tenors, vibraphones and two electric organs, a composition that was premièred as a partial work 'in progress' at a 1995 Prom. The complete piece (it plays for some 14 minutes) holds together very well. Three sopranos 'sing the original melody of the text in canons that gradually augment, or get longer', whereas Perotin's influence can be heard in the tenor parts. Reich's skill at inverting, augmenting and generally transforming his material has rarely sounded with such immediacy. After a virtuosic, pleasantly up-beat *Nagoya marimbas* lasting four-and-a-half minutes comes *City life*, probably Reich's best piece since *Different Trains*. The sound-frame includes air brakes, pile drivers, car alarms, boat horns and police sirens, all of which are loaded into a pair of sampling keyboards and played alongside the instrumental parts (two each of flutes, oboes, clarinets and pianos, plus string quartet and bass).

The first movement opens with what sounds like a distant relation of Stravinsky's *Symphonies of Wind Instruments* then kicks into action on the back of a Manhattan street vendor shouting 'Check it out'. The second and fourth movements witness gradual acceleration – the second to a pile driver, the fourth to a heartbeat – and the third has the two sampling keyboards engaging in top-speed crossfire based on speech samples. The last and most dissonant movement utilises material taped when the World Trade

Centre was bombed in 1993. *City life* is a tightly crafted montage, formed like an arch (A-B-C-B-A), lean, clever, catchy and consistently gripping. In fact the whole disc should thrill dyed-in-the-wool Reichians and preach convincingly to the as-yet unconverted. The sound is excellent.

Ottorino Respighi Italian 1879-1936

GROVE *Respighi studied with Torchi and Martucci at the Liceo Musicale in Bologna (1891-1901), then had lessons with Rimsky-Korsakov during visits to Russia (1900-03). In 1913 he settled in Rome, teaching and composing. He is best known as the composer of highly coloured orchestral pieces, capitalising on the most brilliant aspects of Rimsky-Korsakov, Ravel and Strauss: Fontane di Roma (1916), Pini di Roma (1924), Vetrate di chiesa (1925), Trittico botticelliano (1927), Gli uccelli (arrangements of pieces by earlier composers, 1927) and Feste romane (1928). His interest in the past is to be heard not only in his arrangements of Arie antiche for orchestra but in the use of plainchant and the church modes in such pieces as the Concerto gregoriano (for violin, 1921) and the Quartetto dorico (1924). He also wrote operas (La bella dormente nel bosco, 1921) and vocal works. He was greatly helped by his wife, Elsa (b 1894), herself a composer.*

Piano Concerto in A minor

Piano Concerto in A minor. Toccata. Fantasia slava
Konstantin Scherbakov *pf* **Slovak Radio Symphony Orchestra / Howard Griffiths**
Naxos 8 553207 (51 minutes: DDD) Ⓢ
Recorded 1994

All these pieces are otherwise available in decent performances, but at this price how could anyone with the slightest weakness for Respighi hesitate? Scherbakov and Griffiths do a good deal more than dutifully go through the motions, the soloist in particular playing with delicacy and affection, grateful for the opportunities to demonstrate how well he would play Liszt or Rachmaninov, but in the *Toccata* he is interested as well in Respighi's more characteristic modal vein; as a Russian, he demonstrates that this too, like so much in Respighi, was influenced by the time he spent in Russia.

Russian soloist, English conductor and Slovak orchestra all enjoy the moment in the *Fantasia slava* where Respighi presents a morsel of Smetana in the evident belief that it's a Russian folk-dance, but the Concerto and the *Fantasia*, both very early Respighi, are not patronised in the slightest. The central slow section of the Concerto, indeed, achieves something like nobility, and although there is a risk of the pianism in this work seeming overblown and rhetorical, Scherbakov's fondness for Respighi's more fleet-footed manner doesn't let this happen often.

The *Toccata* is not so much an exercise in the neo-baroque, often though its dotted and florid figures promise it, more of an essay on how far one can be neo-baroque without giving up a post-Lisztian keyboard style and comfortable orchestral upholstery. But in a slow and florid central section, a rather melancholy aria that passes from the soloist to the oboe, to the strings and back again, there is a real quality of Bachian utterance translated not unrecognizably into a late romantic language. Scherbakov sounds touched by it, and obviously wants us to like it. The recordings are more than serviceable, but each work is given only a single track.

Roman Trilogy

Pines of Rome; Fountains of Rome; Roman Festivals

Roman Trilogy
Orchestra dell'Accademia di Santa Cecilia / Daniele Gatti
Conifer Classics 75605 51292-2 (66 minutes: DDD) Ⓕ
Recorded 1996 ●

This was Daniele Gatti's début as an orchestral conductor and it is an auspicious one. Although Respighi's trilogy might not seem ideal repertory for the purpose, nor perhaps the Santa Cecilia the ideal orchestra, both orchestra and repertoire have in fact been rather shrewdly chosen. The recording documents the results of a five-year, obviously happy, relationship with the orchestra and it plays quite beautifully for him in music that they must know backwards – it gave the first performances of *Pines* and *Fountains* and the European première of *Festivals*.

The reputation of these works as orchestral showpieces means that there are quite precise expectations of every performance, and Gatti fulfils these expectations admirably. But there are many signs that he has his own ideas about this music, and they are convincing as well as refreshing. 'The fountain of Valle Giulia at dawn', for example, is slower than usual, making for an attractively gentle pastoral. The breathless hush at the end of 'The Medici fountain at sunset' is very beautiful, too, and in the pitfall-ridden 'Pines of the Janiculum' pretty well everything is right: the appearance of the recorded nightingale magically timed and placed, against a softly warm string background (but with ardent solo playing), the rubato and phrasing finely judged, the piano and clarinet poetically evoking moonlight. At the other end of the dynamic spectrum there is a huge and satisfying *crescendo* to conclude 'Epiphany' (No 4 of *Festivals*) and a magnificent blare of extra brass at the end of 'Pines of the Appian Way'. First-class recording.

Roman Trilogy
Pittsburgh Symphony Orchestra / Lorin Maazel
Sony Classical SK66843 (64 minutes: DDD) Ⓕ
Recorded 1994-96 ●●

In ripely committed performances like Maazel's, there are few works to match Respighi's trilogy in showing off the glories of a modern orchestra in full cry. Maazel's is an exceptionally fine recording. The orchestral sound is perfectly natural and perfectly believable; the acoustic is perceptible and credible; Respighi's textures are satisfyingly rich but always comprehensible; instruments are in the right perspective, and when a solo line is prominent there is no sense that it has been artificially spotlit or moved for ward. Once you've got over the pleasurable relief of hearing such a sound again, you notice what a splendid orchestra this is: in *Pines* alone, what wonderfully velvety strings to evoke the shadows of the pines near a catacomb, what sensitive woodwind soloists as companions to the nightingale (poetically distant but beautifully clear) on the moonlit Janiculum! And then you enjoy not only the fine control of Maazel's big *crescendos* in the second and fourth movements, but the fact that you don't have to fiddle with the volume controls to appreciate both the quiet and the loud ends of those *crescendos*.

Roman Trilogy
Royal Philharmonic Orchestra / Enrique Bátiz
Naxos 8 550539 (61 minutes: DDD) Ⓢ
Recorded 1991

This Naxos disc is an extraordinary bargain. It has such excitement and verve that one can accept an extra degree of brazen extroversion, indeed revel in it. In *Roman Festivals* the opening 'Circuses' is immensely spectacular, its character very much in the unfettered gladiatorial tradition of the Coliseum: the trumpets and drums are quite thrilling. The gossamer opening of 'The Jubilee' leads to the most dramatic climax. In the 'October Festival' the strings play their Latin soliloquy very exotically for Bátiz. The closing section brings a gentle mandolin serenade. The great clamour of the Epiphany celebrations which follow unleashes a riotous *mêlée* from the RPO, which sounds as if it is enjoying itself hugely, and the obvious affinity with the final fairground scene of Petrushka is all the more striking when the strings have that bit more bite.

The *Pines* and *Fountains* are also very fine. When the unison horns signal the turning on of the Triton Fountain, and the cascade splashes through the orchestra, the RPO unleashes a real flood. Yet the lovely, radiant gentle evocation of the central movements of *The Pines*, and the sensuous Italian light of the sunset at the Villa Medici, are most sensitively realised by the RPO, and at the very beginning of the finale, 'The Pines of the Appian Way', the ever present sound, with its growling bass clarinet, gives a sinister implication of the advancing Roman might.

Church Windows

Church Windows. Brazilian Impressions. Roman Festivals
Cincinnati Symphony Orchestra / Jesús López-Cobos
Telarc CD80356 (71 minutes: DDD) Ⓕ
Recorded 1993

One could easily argue that neither *Church Windows* nor *Brazilian Impressions* is quite as successful as the 'essential' Respighi of *Pines, Fountains* and *Festivals*. The only answer to that, López-Cobos seems to suggest, is to take the music perfectly seriously and pay scrupulous attention not just to its potential for sonorous spectacle but to its wealth of beautifully crafted detail. The gong at the end of the second movement of *Church Windows* is magnificently resonant, as is the organ in the finale, and the work is given an extra inch or two of stature by sensitive handling of those moments that need but don't always get delicacy. He pays such care to character and detail in 'Butantan', that creepy depiction of a snake-farm in *Brazilian Impressions*, that you can not only recapture the real, crawling horror that Respighi experienced there, but discover in the music also a queer sort of Debussian grace as well. And as for *Roman Festivals*, well, what's wrong with 20-odd minutes of wide-screen spectacular once in a while? But if every colour is precisely rendered, the quiet passages as affectionately turned as they are here, what skill there is to be found in it, what a gift for immaculately precise instrumental detail. With that sort of handling all three pieces sound quite worthy of sharing shelf space with *Pines* and *Fountains*. The recording is spectacular.

String Quartet in D

String Quartet in D. Quartetto dorico. Il tramonto[a]
[a]**Anne Sofie von Otter** *mez* **Brodsky Quartet**
(Andrew Haveron, Ian Belton *vns* Paul Cassidy *va* Jacqueline Thomas *vc*)
Vanguard Classics 99216 (65 minutes: DDD) Ⓜ

An excellent coupling. For a start the one moderately popular work here, *Il tramonto*, receives a pretty well ideal performance in its chamber version. And Anne Sofie von Otter is as responsible for its presentation as chamber music as her colleagues are. She sings intimately, yet with both drama and pathos, and never makes an ugly sound. In the quartet version the piece has a sort of pre-Raphaelite quality that is most appealing.

Respighi's quartets are rarely played, though he wrote several and loved and understood the form: he was a member of a professional string quartet for several years. That group gave the first performance of the fairly early D major Quartet, which is warmly romantic, expertly written for the medium and often scrumptiously rich harmonically. Especially likeable is the so-called 'Intermezzo', in fact a gentle *Scherzo* that begins with charming hesitancy and has a rather yearning trio section. The themes of the other movements are very agreeable, but not yet very individual. The only movement that sounds particularly Italian is the finale, a forceful tarantella.

The *Quartetto dorico* is much stronger and more personal, one of the more striking fruits of Respighi's interest in the modes and early music. It is in a single, multi-section movement, starting with bold, unison rhetoric, but often striking a hushed, sometimes poignant, folk-like lyrical vein. This quite often features the viola, and Paul Cassidy audibly loves both this side of Respighi and the beautiful instrument that he plays (it was Britten's viola, and before that Frank Bridge's). Indeed the performances throughout are eloquent, rich-toned and full of colour and the recording is clean but warm.

Songs

Cinque canti all'antica. Sei liriche. Deità silvane. Ballata alla luna. Stornello. Stornellatrice. Contrasto. Tanto bella. Invito alla danza. L'ultima ebbrezza. Notturno. Luce
Leonardo de Lisi *ten* **Reinild Mees** *pf*
Channel Classics CCS9396 (60 minutes: DDD) Ⓕ
Texts and translations included. Recorded 1996

Leonardo de Lisi is a lyric tenor of real quality with a Lieder singer's subtlety, taste and responsiveness to words. In fact by the colour of the voice you might not take him to be an Italian and his French diction is almost impeccable in the two settings by Respighi (among the *Sei liriche*) of French texts, the quite magical 'Le repos en Egypte' and the striking 'Noël ancien'. If you have not so far thought of Respighi as a song composer you are in for a surprise. Sopranos quite often programme his charming *Stornellatrice* as an encore but it has equals and indeed superiors here. *Tanto bella*, for example: ample grateful melody over a lilting accompaniment, with a haunting middle section. The *Canti all'antica* are fresh and very simple. But with the *Sei liriche* of 1912 we reach audible French influence as well as French texts and by 1917 and *Deità silvane* Respighi's smooth lines have become flexible and his idiomatic keyboard writing is now filled with vivid imagery. Reinild Mees is obviously as fond of *Deità silvane* as de Lisi is. Both are excellently recorded.

La sensitiva

Deità silvane[a]. Nebbie[b]. Aretusa[b]. La sensitiva[b]
[a]**Ingrid Attrot** *sop* [b]**Linda Finnie** *mez*
BBC Philharmonic Orchestra / Richard Hickox
Chandos CHAN9453 (60 minutes: DDD). Texts and translations included. Recorded 1995 Ⓕ

In some of Respighi's comparatively neglected pieces, his accustomed richness and subtlety of orchestral colour go with a certain lack of melodic individuality. Once or twice in *Deità silvane* ('Woodland gods'), for example, one wishes that the poems' classical imagery would lead him towards an evocation or even a direct quotation from Italian music's 'classical' past of the kind that so often renders his better-known music so memorable. In *La sensitiva* ('The sensitive plant'), however, his care for the imagery and especially the prosody of Shelley's poem (in Italian translation) was so responsive that striking melodic invention was the result. The orchestral colour of the piece is exquisite, the succession of ideas (the sensitive plant is image both of unhappy lover and spurned artist) a good deal more than merely picturesque. In a performance as expressive as this it seems one of Respighi's best works, and a good deal more sophisticated than he is generally given credit for. *Aretusa* is fine, too, with bigger dramatic gestures, even richer colour and some magnificent sea music. The much better-known *Nebbie* is another example of Respighi finding a genuinely sustained melodic line in response to a text which obviously meant a great deal to him. Everything here is played with a real care for Respighi's line as well as his sumptuous but never muddy colours. First-class recording.

Nicolay Rimsky-Korsakov

Russian 1844-1908

GROVE *Apart from piano lessons, a love for the music of Glinka and a fascination with opera orchestras, Rimsky-Korsakov had little preparation for a musical career – he trained as a naval officer – until he met Balakirev (1861), who captivated him, encouraging his attempts at composition, performing his works and introducing him to Borodin, Dargomïzhsky, Cui and Mussorgsky. He wrote songs, orchestral works and an opera (The Maid of Pskov, 1873) before becoming professor at the St Petersburg Conservatory (1871) and inspector of naval bands (1873-84), teaching himself harmony and counterpoint, conducting at Balakirev's Free School and collecting folksongs. His next opera, May Night (1880), engaged his full creative powers with its blend of the fantastic and the comic (the realm in which he was to score most of his greatest successes), while Snow Maiden (1882) evoked a deeper world of nature-mysticism. Official duties at the imperial chapel (1883-91), work on the deceased Mussorgsky's and Borodin's manuscripts and advising for the publisher Belyayev interrupted composition, but he did produce the three colourful orchestral works by which he is best known, Sheherazade, the Spanish Capriccio and the Russian Easter Festival Overture, during 1887-88, after which he devoted himself to opera. Of the 12 dramatic works from Mlada (1892) to The Golden Cockerel (1909), Kitezh (1907) stands out for its mystical and psychological depths. Rimsky-Korsakov's operas far out-weigh in importance his other compositions, for both their brilliant scoring and fine vocal writing. If they lack dramatic power and strong characterisation, they nevertheless set delightful fantastic puppets in the context of musico-scenic fairy tales, using a dual musical language to delineate 'real' from 'unreal'. He transmitted his pellucid style to two generations of Russian composers, from Lyadov and Glazunov to Stravinsky and Prokofiev, all of whom were his pupils.*

Scheherazade, Op 35

Scheherazade[a]. Capriccio espagnol[b]. Russian Easter Festival Overture[c]
Herman Krebbers *vn* [ac]**Concertgebouw Orchestra /** [a]**Kyrill Kondrashin;** [b]**London Symphony Orchestra /** [bc]**Igor Markevitch**
Philips Solo 442 643-2PM (74 minutes: ADD) Ⓜ
Recorded [a]1980, [b]1963, [c]1965

Kondrashin's performance of *Scheherazade* is one of the very finest made of Russian music in the Concertgebouw; it has glamour and brilliance, and the resonance brings a wonderful feeling of spaciousness in the first movement and adds a thrill to the spectacle of the finale. Kondrashin has the full measure of this colourful score, while the finale builds up to a feeling of excitement which leads to a riveting climax at 'The Shipwreck'. Of course, any performance of this masterpiece stands or falls by the portrayal of Scheherazade herself by the solo violin, and here the Concertgebouw's leader, Herman Krebbers dominates the action from the gentle, beguiling opening to his exquisite closing solo, suggesting that all is well at last between the Sultan and his bewitching Sultana.

A brilliant performance of Rimsky's *Capriccio espagnole* follows, very well played by the London Symphony Orchestra under Igor Markevitch; indeed, the 1963 recording sounds far more lustrous than it did on LP. It is upstaged, however, by Markevitch's performance of the composer's *Russian Easter Festival Overture*, made two years later, when again the aura of the Concertgebouw ambience adds a glow to more remarkable playing from this great orchestra. Altogether a superb disc, and generously full.

Scheherazade. Capriccio espagnol
London Symphony Orchestra / Sir Charles Mackerras Ⓕ
Telarc CD80208 (60 minutes: DDD). Recorded 1990 ●

Sir Charles Mackerras throws himself into this music with expressive abandon, but allies it to control so that every effect is realised and the London Symphony Orchestra plays these familiar works as if it was discovering them afresh. Together they produce performances that are both vivid and thoughtful, while the solo violin in *Scheherazade* is seductively and elegantly played by Kees Hulsmann, not least at the wonderfully peaceful end to the whole work. The finale featuring a storm and shipwreck is superbly done, the wind and brass bringing one to the edge of one's seat.

This sensuous and thrilling work needs spectacular yet detailed sound, and that is what it gets here, the 1990 recording in Walthamstow Town Hall being highly successful and giving us a CD that many collectors will choose to use as a demonstration disc to impress their friends. The performance and recording of the *Capriccio espagnol* is no less of a success.

Scheherazade. Capriccio espagnol
London Philharmonic Orchestra / Mariss Jansons
EMI CDC5 55227-2 (62 minutes: DDD) Ⓕ
Recorded 1994 ●

This has got to be one of EMI's finest recordings, not as analytically transparent as some but vivid and immediate with a thrillingly wide dynamic range. As to Jansons's interpretation of the main work, he follows up the big bold, brassy opening with a surprisingly restrained account of the main theme as it develops, keeping power in reserve, building up more slowly than usual. What then is consistently striking in all four movements is Jansons's pointing of rhythm, lilting, bouncy and affectionate in a way that distinguishes this from most other versions. This is a *Scheherazade* that dances winningly, less earnest than usual, often suggesting a smile on the face. That is very welcome in a work that, for all its exotic colour and memorable themes, needs persuasive handling if it is not to seem like a lot of introductions leading to introductions, and codas leading to codas, with little meat in the middle. Jansons's control of structure leads to a masterly sense of resolution at the great climax towards the end of the finale, as the main theme returns *fortissimo*. Nowhere does this seem like a virtuoso exercise, brilliant as the playing of the LPO is, not least that of the warmly expressive violin soloist, Joakim Svenheden. Rather, emotionally involved, Jansons finds a rare exuberance in Rimsky-Korsakov's stream of ideas and colours, leading compellingly from one to another. The *Capriccio espagnol* brings a similar combination of expressive warmth and exuberance. In the brilliant 'Alborada' at the beginning of the *Capriccio* Jansons's speed is less hectic than some, and with springy rhythms it is made to sound relaxed, jolly rather than fierce. Not that in either work is there any shortage of biting excitement.

Scheherazade. Russian Easter Festival Overture
Vienna Philharmonic Orchestra / Seiji Ozawa
Philips 438 941-2PH (58 minutes: DDD) Ⓕ
Recorded live in 1993

Scheherazade is a work which brings the very best out of Seiji Ozawa, a colourist who likes to mould the music and make it dance. Instead of his own Boston Symphony, here he conducts the even richer-toned Vienna Philharmonic, with strings all the more sensuous in a live recording. It was made during a concert in the orchestra's home, the Musikvereinsaal in Vienna, and the tensions of a live performance consistently add compulsion to a work which can seem disconcertingly episodic. The violin solo of the leader, Rainer Honeck, from the start gives one a sense of firm purpose in the unfolding of these musical fairy-tales. Except in the love-scene of the third movement, 'The Young Prince and Princess', Ozawa's speeds tend to be on the slow side, but he readily sustains them, building up the climaxes with satisfying weight and concentration. The performance surprisingly tends to fall short in the dance-rhythms of the second movement, the 'Kalender Prince', with the oboe and bassoon solos sounding self-conscious and rather jerky. But the Viennese strings are also at their most sumptuous. The recording, forward balanced, is satisfyingly warm and full. Not everyone will relish the inclusion of applause at the end of the fourth movement. The welcome fill-up, though recorded in the same venue during a studio session, has similar characteristics.

Scheherazade. The Tale of Tsar Saltan, Op 57 – Tsar's farewell and departure; Tsarina in a barrel at sea; The three wonders
Philharmonia Orchestra / Enrique Bátiz
Naxos 8 550726 (61 minutes: DDD) Ⓢ
Recorded 1992

Bátiz proves an impulsive, purposeful interpreter. In the second movement, his performance is more lilting Ozawa's, with rubato more persuasive, helped by superb Philharmonia wind-playing. The fanfares which interrupt in echelon (track 2) are brisk rather than weighty, confirming a more volatile approach than Ozawa's. In the third movement the Philharmonia strings may not be quite as rich as the Viennese, but with the excellent, well-balanced recording revealing more inner detail the result is more refined, with a delectably lilting clarinet entry on the *grazioso* dance-rhythm (track 3). David Nolan's violin solos are more individually rhapsodic, if not always as immaculate tonally as the Viennese. In short, this budget issue is at least as compelling and just as exciting as its full-priced rival, and rather better recorded. The fill-up can be warmly recommended too, three movements from the five which Rimsky included in the orchestral suite of musical pictures from *Tsar Saltan*, starting with the delectable march entitled the 'Tsar's farewell and departure'. The other movements are 'Tsarina in a barrel at sea' and 'The three wonders', with the over-played 'Flight of the Bumble-Bee' hardly missed.

Kashchey the Immortal

Konstantin Pluzhnikov *ten* Kashchey; **Marina Shaguch** *sop* Princess; **Larissa Diadkova** *mez* Kashcheyevna; **Alexander Gergalov** *bar* Ivan Korolevitch; **Alexander Morozov** *bass* Storm Knight; **Kirov Opera Chorus and Orchestra / Valery Gergiev**
Philips 446 704-2PH (64 minutes: DDD). Notes, text Ⓕ and translation included. Recorded 1995

Rimsky-Korsakov's 'autumnal parable' is a strange and fascinating work. Cast in one act (three linked scenes), it tells of the evil sorcerer Kashchey who has imprisoned the Princess, eventually rescued by her lover Prince Ivan; the secret of Kashchey's immortality is discovered to lie held in the frozen tears of his daughter Kashcheyevna, and these flow when her failure to seduce the Prince touches the heart of the Princess, who embraces her. Human warmth can destroy even the fiercest sorcery. There was clearly an opportunity here for a contrast which had served Russian composers ever since Glinka's *Ruslan and Lyudmila*: that of the weirdly sinister and chromatic versus the comfortingly human diatonic. By 1902, the pattern might have come to seem a little threadbare, were it not for the fact that Rimsky-Korsakov had been impressed by what some aspects of Wagner's harmony might hold for him. The outcome was his own most advanced harmony, astonishing and terrifying in the portrayal of Kashchey, a powerful role sung here with magnificent villainy by Konstantin Pluzhnikov: this is a real *tour de force*. The human diatonics cannot help but be weaker, though Larissa Diadkova manages very affectingly the Kundry-like transition from seductress to suppliant under the Princess's compassionate embrace: she has considerably the more interesting part, and makes more of it than does Marina Shaguch of hers. Alexander Gergalov, too, is at his best in the seduction duet with Kashcheyevna. Perversely, the opera was a success in the 1905 uprising as a metaphor of humanity overcoming frigid authority, and retained some of that popularity in Communist times. A splendid version, well worth hearing.

The Legend of the Invisible City...

Nicolai Ohotnikov *bass* Prince Yury Vsevolodovich; **Yuri Marusin** *ten* Prince Vsevolod Yur'yevich; **Galina Gorchakova** *sop* Fevroniya; **Vladimir Galusin** *ten* Grishka Kuter'ma; **Nikolai Putilin** *bar* Fyodor Poyarok; **Olga Korzhenskaya** *mez* Page; **Evgeni Boitsov** *ten* First Upright Citizen; **Evgeny Fedorov** *bass* Second Upright Citizen; **Mikhail Kit** *bass* Bard; **Nikolai Gassiev** *ten* Bear Trainer; **Grigory Karasev** *bar* Beggar; **Bulat Minzhilkiev** *bass* Bedyay; **Vladimir Ognovienko** *bass* Burunday; **Tatiana Kravtsova** *sop* Sirin; **Larissa Diadkova** *mez* Alkonost; **Kirov Opera Chorus and Orchestra / Valery Gergiev**
Philips ③ 462 225-2PH3 (181 minutes: DDD) Ⓕ
Notes, text and translation included.
Recorded live in 1994

Rimsky-Korsakov's penultimate opera was never popular at home in Soviet times, partly because of unease about its religious nature and perhaps also because of its Wagnerian elements. Yet it is not the Russian *Parsifal*, as it has been foolishly described; rather, it draws upon the magical, the fantastic, the legendary and the religious, finding exciting and sometimes moving contact between them.

The plot has at its centre the woodland maiden Fevroniya and her betrothal to Prince Vsevolod. There are ceremonies, a Tartar abduction, and a final transfiguration when the mysterious city of Kitezh welcomes the lovers to eternal life. It is a beautiful score, and one of Rimsky-Korsakov's subtlest. Fevroniya is not an easy role. The original producer, Vassily Shkafer, was puzzled as to why the composer had written the central part 'for a dramatic soprano whereas the figure of Fevroniya is actually ... designed to be ... light, ethereal, disembodied.' Galina Gorchakova has the dramatic power, but, skilfully as she phrases the music, she lacks the simplicity first revealed in the forest and sustained throughout Fevroniya's trials. She has steady support from her tenor, Yuri Marusin who is a strong and lyrical Vsevolod, while Vladimir Galusin gives a hectic performance of the drunkard Grishka Kuter'ma. The live recorded sound occasionally seems to biff the microphones – the chorus, which sings excellently, is not always clear, and there is a great deal of clumping. However, the orchestra, which matters a great deal, is lucid.

Sadko

Vladimir Galusin *ten* Sadko; **Valentina Tsidipova** *sop* Volkhova; **Sergei Alexashkin** *bass* Okean-More; **Marianna Tarassova** *mez* Lyubava Buslayevna; **Larissa Diadkova** *contr* Nezhata; **Bulat Minjelkiev** *bass* Viking Merchant; **Gegam Grigorian** *ten* Indian Merchant; **Alexander Gergalov** *bar* Venetian Merchant; **Vladimir Ognovenko** *bass* Duda; **Nikolai Gassiev** *ten* Sopel; **Nikolai Putilin** *bar* Apparition; **Yevgeny Boitsov** *ten* Foma Nazarich; **Gennadi Bezzubenkov** *bass* Luka Zinovich; **Kirov Opera Orchestra / Valery Gergiev**

Philips ③ 442 138-2PH3 (173 minutes: DDD) Ⓕ
Notes, text and translation included.
Recorded live in 1993

For all its drawbacks, this complete version of *Sadko* from the Maryinsky company is a welcome addition to the catalogue. *Sadko* is a panoramic work, packed with numbers, rather less packed with event or with character. The various characters delivering themselves of a song or a ballad or an address are reasonably well contrasted, partly because of Rimsky-Korsakov's skills in drawing on different Russian influences and in differentiating between a simple tonal language for the real world and a more chromatic idiom for the seductive realm of the Sea King (Okean-More) and his daughter Volkhova. It needs a numerous and strong cast who can make the most of its opportunities.

Sadko is sung by Vladimir Galusin pretty steadily at full volume. He settles down a little as the opera proceeds, and by Act 3 is finding a more pacific manner. Valentina Tsidipova returns his advances, and makes her own, with a good feeling for line, if one can overcome resistance to the steady vibrato. The Sea King is strongly sung by Sergei Alexashkin, truculent at first but warming his tone as he comes to accept Sadko. But it is a pity that the best-known number from the opera, the song of the Indian Merchant, should be sung as half-heartedly as it is by Gegam Grigorian. Valery Gergiev leads his forces well, and draws some vigorous, colourful singing from the choruses. There is, however, a good deal of noise from the many stage comings and goings, with clumpings and hoarse whisperings as well as tunings-up and applause. The recording has difficulty in catching all the singers equally, but for the most part this is a fair representation of a colourful score.

The Tsar's Bride

Gennadi Bezzubenkov *bass* Vasily Sobakin; **Marina Shaguch** *sop* Marfa; **Dmitri Hvorostovsky** *bar* Grigory Gryaznoy; **Sergei Alexashkin** *bass* Grigory Malyuta-Skuratov; **Evgeny Akimov** *ten* Ivan Likov; **Olga Borodina** *mez* Lyubasha; **Nikolai Gassiev** *ten* Bomelius; **Irina Loskutova** *sop* Saburova; **Olga Markova-Mikhailenko** *mez* Dunyasha; **Liubov Sokolova** *mez* Petrovna; **Yuri Shkliar** *bass* Stoker; **Lyudmila Kasjanenko** *sop* Servant; **Victor Vikhrov** *ten* Young lad; **Kirov Opera Chorus and Orchestra / Valery Gergiev**

Philips ② 462 618-2PH2 (148 minutes: DDD) Ⓕ
Notes, text and translation included.
Recorded 1998 ●

The plot of *The Tsar's Bride* is awkward, turning on the search by Tsar Ivan the Terrible for a wife. His eye lights on Marfa, betrothed to Ivan Likov but also desired by Grigory Gryaznoy, who is trying to discard his lover Lyubasha in her favour. There is a sinister German, Bomelius, who deals in poisons and love potions: confusion and substitution here lead to Marfa's madness. The Tsar does not sing, but is represented, motivically, by the folk-tune familiar from *Boris Godunov* and Beethoven's Second *Razumovsky* Quartet. Tchaikovsky is the most potent influence on the work, not least since his death in 1893 seems to have freed Rimsky-Korsakov, though grieving personally, from a creative block; but the influence does not extend to subtle characterization. Particularly on record, however, there is much to relish, drawing as the work does on the kind of elegant, song-like melodic line of which Tchaikovsky was a supreme master.

Olga Borodina makes a Lyubasha both touching and commanding, eloquent in her response to the subtle melodic inflexions of her first, virtually unaccompanied, song, proud in her confrontation with the slimy Bomelius (a clever sketch by Nikolai Gassiev), then allowing her line and her rich tone to weaken as resolve collapses. Marina Shaguch is more of a problem as her rival Marfa. Initially her tone is oddly strident, and she does herself no favours by forcing it when she is supposedly anxious or in distress rather than enraged. She comes into her own in the eerie final aria, lost in her madness.

Hvorostovsky is a superb Gryaznoy, not an easy part: he must open the whole opera (no choral scene-setting here), and in a long monologue establish a villainous character who is given a remarkably sympathetic melodic line. He does this skilfully, phrasing starkly and with a kind of compacted passion. Nor is Marfa's rather anonymous lover Likov an easy role: Evgeny Akimov settles for delivering a lyrical line with elegance. Gergiev paces the score intelligently, allowing the singers to make the most of the set numbers and relishing the colour and energy of the dramatic confrontations.

Joaquin Rodrigo — Spanish 1901-1999

GROVE *Rodrigo, blind from the age of three, studied with Antich in Valencia and Dukas in Paris (from 1927), also receiving encouragement from Falla. His Concierto de Aranjuez for guitar and orchestra (1939) made his name and established his style of tuneful and smoothly colourful Hispanicism: his later works include similar concertos for violin, piano, cello, harp and flute as well as songs and small instrumental pieces, several for guitar.*

Concierto de Aranjuez

Concierto de Aranjuez[a]. Three Piezas españolas[b]. Invocacíon y danza[c]. Fantasía para un gentilhombre[d]
Julian Bream *gtr* **[a]Chamber Orchestra of Europe / Sir John Eliot Gardiner; [d]RCA Victor Chamber Orchestra / Leo Brouwer**
RCA Victor 09026 61611-2 (69 minutes: DDD) Ⓜ
Recorded [abc]1982-83, [d]1987 ●●●

In the early 1980s Bream had entered a phase in which both his musical and technical powers were at their height, which he too recognised and celebrated in this remarkable album. With it he confirmed that he is Segovia's truest and best successor, though in no sense his imitator, and established a benchmark in the history of the guitar on record. Everything he touched turns to music and is here recorded with the utmost reality. If anyone is wondering why he should here have taken his third bite at Aranjuez's cherry, it was in order to 'go digital' but in the event this proved a subsidiary *raison-d'être*. At the time the COE was no casual band assembled for a session but a newly-formed orchestra of young players from several countries, greeting the concerto as a fresh experience and playing it with splendid precision and vitality. John Eliot Gardiner's conducting is unfailingly idiomatic. Who catalyzed whom is hard to say but Bream certainly responded with the *Aranjuez* of his life, clean as a whistle, eloquently phrased and passionate; nothing is lost in the recording and the guitar is 'prestidigitalised' into unfailing audibility. *Aranjuezs* come and go but this one must remain as the touchstone for a very long time, reaffirming the thoroughbred character of a warhorse that so often sounds tired through overworking.

The concerto may be very familiar territory but the other items are not. Prior to this recording only Eric Hill on Saga Records had previously resisted the temptation to sever the 'Fandango' from the other two *Piezas españolas*; Bream too reassembles the triptych by restoring the exciting 'Zapateado' and the un-Rodrigo-like 'Passacaglia'. This triptych is a strongly atmospheric work whose difficulty has helped to keep it out of the concert halls until relatively recently. Bream's interpretation of *Invocación y danza* is equally masterly – one cannot imagine who else could have made it.

Leo Brouwer is a man of so many musical parts that the loss of one of them – his role as a virtuoso guitarist – has passed almost unnoticed; here he plays one of the others – that of conductor. What better than to provide the ammunition for others to fire, and to direct the campaign yourself? *Fantasía para un gentihombre* has its own merits and demerits, with Bream stressing the musical rather than the virtuosic elements, adopting somewhat slower tempos than other interpreters in most of the movements – that of the final 'Canarios' is more in keeping with the character of the dance itself. Brouwer's splendid control of the orchestra reflects his experience of both sides of the concerto 'fence'. This disc is a 'must'.

Rodrigo Concierto de Aranjuez
Castelnuovo-Tedesco Guitar Concerto No 1 in D, Op 99 **Villa-Lobos** Guitar Concerto
Norbert Kraft *gtr* **Northern Chamber Orchestra / Nicholas Ward**
Naxos 8 550729 (60 minutes: DDD) Ⓢ
Recorded 1992 ●

The time has long passed when it was possible to point to any one recording of any of these concertos (the Rodrigo in particular) as 'The Best'; as with players, one can only discern a 'top bracket' within which choice depends finally on personal preference – or allegiance to one's favourite performer, or indeed with the other works on the disc. Norbert Kraft's accounts of these concertos takes its place therein. In this recording Kraft is placed forwardly enough for every detail to be heard, but not to create an impression of artificiality. The Northern Chamber Orchestra plays with freshness and is alert to every detail and the beautifully clear recording catches it faithfully. At super-budget price this disc is an exceptional bargain.

Concierto de Aranjuez[ac]. Fantasía para un gentilhombre[ac]. Cançoneta[bc]. Invocacíon y danza[a]. Tres Pequeñas piezas[a]
[a]Pepe Romero *gtr* **[b]Augustín Léo Ara** *vn* **[c]Academy of St Martin in the Fields / Sir Neville Marriner**
Philips 438 016-2PH (64 minutes: DDD) Ⓕ
Recorded 1992 ●●

What we have here is simply one of the best: Pepe Romero, a close friend of Rodrigo, has the technique to do whatever he pleases, though his capacity for high speed does not tempt him to display it for its own sake. There is elegance and a certain nobility in his interpretations, though he lacks the warmth of Bream, for instance, and the 'flamenco steeliness' of his *rasgueados* does perhaps stand in uncomfortable contrast with the rest. The ASMF must know these scores by heart but, perhaps stimulated by the presence of a soloist who is so completely in command of his material, its immaculate support bears no trace of staleness. The *Cançoneta* (1923) is one of Rodrigo's earliest works, a small (just under three minutes) island of peaceful romantic dreams in a sea of guitar music, sweetly played by Ara (Rodrigo's son-in-law) and ignored in the annotation. There is no better recording of the *Invocacíon y danza*, and only one other (also by Romero) of the *Tres Pequeñas piezas*, in the last of which the steely *rasgueados* are entirely in character. If you are not already liberally provided with recordings of the two main items you may rightly be tempted by this outstanding recording.

Concierto de Aranjuez. Fantasía para un gentilhombre. Un tiempo fue Itálica famosa. Zarabanda lejana. Adela. Villancicos – Pastorcito Santo; Coplillas de Belén. Coplas del pastor enamorado
Manuel Barrueco *gtr* **Philharmonia Orchestra / Plácido Domingo** *ten*
EMI CDC5 56175-2 (67 minutes: DDD). Texts and translation included. Recorded 1995-97 Ⓕ

Concierto de Aranjuez. Fantasía para un gentilhombre.
Concierto para una fiesta
David Russell gtr **Naples Philharmonic Orchestra
(Florida) / Erich Kunzel**
Telarc CD80459 (72 minutes: DDD)   Ⓕ
Recorded 1997   ○○

Both of these discs are amongst the best recordings of the *Concierto de Aranjuez* and *Fantasía
para un gentilhombre*. Barrueco and Russell are
members of the guitar's top-drawer élite –
giving performances of crystalline clarity –
and they are both excellently supported by
their orchestras. In both these recordings the
guitar is foregrounded to the extent that it
achieves greater dominance than it ever does
in the concert hall. One might regard this as a
distortion, but as it more faithfully represents
what was/is in the composer's inner ear it
should be enjoyed in its own right. Neither do
these comments apply only to the guitar and
orchestra works of Rodrigo. If you already have
top-rated versions of either or both of these
pieces you may rest content with them, but if
you decide to add one of these new recordings to
your collection then your choice may depend
on the other items they contain. In Russell's
case it is the *Concierto para una fiesta*. The
thought 'where have I heard this before?' may
cross your mind – in relation to both musical
elements and the mode of orchestration. But
you may find these familiar echoes lovably
welcome. Barrueco adds two solos, neither one
yet dulled by overfamiliarity.

The *Zarabanda lejana* is given with the utmost
expressivity, and *Un tiempo fue Itálica famosa* is
delivered with panache. Barrueco has one more
trump card to play – his partnership with Plácido Domingo in four songs, selected from those
for which Rodrigo himself has made adaptations
for the guitar of the original piano accompaniments (the texts are given in four languages).
Both are longstanding devotees of Rodrigo's
music, and it shows. Domingo also conducts the
orchestra, an exercise in which both parties
demonstrate their happy meeting of minds.

Philippe Rogier   Flemish 1561-1596

📧 *Rogier was a chorister at Philip II of Spain's*
GROVE *chapel from 1572; he was ordained,
becoming vice-maestro in 1584 and maestro de capilla
in 1586. Of his large output (at least 250 works),
only 16 motets (1595), five masses (1598) and a few
chansons and other sacred works survive.*

Missa 'Ego sum qui sum'

Rogier Missa 'Ego sum qui sum'. Laboravi in gemitu
meo. Heu mihi Domine. Vias tuas. Taedet animam
meam. Peccavi quid faciam tibi. Dominus regit me
Gombert Ego sum qui sum
Magnificat / Philip Cave
Linn Records CKD109 (75 minutes: DDD) Texts and Ⓕ
translations included. Recorded 1999   ○

Philippe Rogier's death at the age of 35 in 1596
cut short a prolific stream of music. Worse was to
come. In 1734, a fire destroyed the library of the
Spanish royal chapel, which must have held a
large number of his compositions (at the time of
his death he was chief court musician to Philip II).
How large a number can be gauged from the
terrible earthquake that struck Lisbon in 1755,
swallowing up the royal library along with 243
works. Today we are left with only 51, of which
the present recital represents a sizeable proportion.

Rogier's music has Palestrina's imposing solidity
and classical feel, but is more florid, and freer in its
use of dissonance. In this sense it looks forward to
later Iberian music of the 17th century, achieving
a sustained intensity in the motets. The Mass is a
consummate demonstration, the skilful working
out of a motet by Gombert, whose influence is
very audible. The booklet-note rightly points out
how Rogier develops his model in very different
directions: the sequences that conclude most
movements are persuasively managed, but sound
utterly unlike Gombert. Rogier's Mass *Domine
Dominus noster* appears in a fine recording on
Ricercar. But Magnificat's interpretation is of a
different order. This is singing in the English
tradition, but with greater warmth and richness
than one is used to from mixed choirs of this
kind. Given Rogier's predilection for fully
scored writing, that richness pays dividends, as
does the relatively large cast of 18 singers. Interpretation and music are well matched in more
ways than one. Neither are strikingly original,
but both make a striking impression.

Ned Rorem   American 1923

📧 *Rorem studied with Sowerby in Chicago*
GROVE *(1938-39) and with Thomson (1944) and
Diamond in New York, also attending the Curtis
Institute (1943) and the Juilliard School. From
1949 to 1958 he was based in Paris, though spent
two of those years in Morocco: his published diaries of
this and later periods are flamboyantly candid. His
large output includes symphonies, instrumental
pieces and choral music, though he has been most
productive and successful as a composer of songs.*

More Than a Day

More Than a Day[a]. From an Unknown Past.
Water Music[b]
[a]**Brian Asawa** counterten [b]**Gary Gray** cl [b]**Margaret
Batjer** vn **Los Angeles Chamber Orchestra /
Jeffrey Kahane**
RCA Red Seal 09026 63512 2 (49 minutes: DDD)   Ⓕ
Text and translations included.   ○

Sun[a]. String Quartet No 3[b]
[a]**Lauren Flanigan** sop [b]**Mendelssohn Quartet**
(Nicholas Eanet, Nicholas Mann vns Ulrich Eichenauer
va Marcy Rosen vc) [a]**Manhattan School of Music
Symphony / Glen Barton Cortese**
Newport Classic NPD85657 (52 minutes: DDD)   Ⓕ
Texts included.   ○

After years of neglect by the big record companies, close on the heels of Susan Graham's recital of Ned Rorem's songs with piano accompaniment (Erato) come these two CDs exploring his works for voice and orchestra. *More Than a Day* is a cycle of nine songs to poems by Jack Larson, divided into three sections. The first part consists of seven octets each beginning with the question, 'Do I love you?'. The opening is joyful, with a soaring accompaniment as the poet affirms his love to be 'more than a look', but then as the sequence continues the mood gets darker as the orchestral colours become more complex. There is a piano adding a jazzy, disturbing element, but then an orchestral postlude seems to reaffirm the optimistic tone of the beginning.

The piano comes back in with whip-crack percussion in the second section, 'My brain is littered', where poet and composer contemplate the paraphernalia of illness and death. At the words, 'Still I recall their flowered graves', a tense *tremolo* in the strings leads to an almost operatic close that brings to mind one of Rorem's best-known orchestral works, *Eagles*. But then the piano returns and leads the players away to a gentler mood, with flute and clarinet solos for the last song, 'Oh love, see how the flowers mate'. Brian Asawa sings it all with courageous attack and full tone, displaying an impressive range for a countertenor.

The brief cycle *From an Unknown Past* is one of Rorem's earliest works, originally written for unaccompanied choir, then adapted for a solo voice and now orchestrated specially for Asawa. Scored for six winds and strings, the style is that of troubadour songs, appropriate for the mostly anonymous texts that lead to an extract from Dowland's *Third and Last Book of Songs* – 'Weep You No More, Sad Fountains', and then Shakespeare's 'Crabbed Age and Youth'. Despite the European texts and the fact that, as Rorem reveals in his introduction, the songs were composed in Hyères, the sound is unmistakably American. Why? It has something to do with that innocent optimism which, as Rorem once wrote, you only encounter in Americans.

Between the two song-cycles comes Rorem's *Water Music*, a concerto grosso from 1966 composed for violin and clarinet, with a brilliant accompaniment designed to show off the talents of the youth orchestra for which it was commissioned. It's a set of variations on a theme called 'Tune' and subtitled *Calm and sad*. When the tune appears, it's as lush as a Korngold film score, but only for a fleeting moment. The ensuing variations seem like a catalogue of bizarre encounters and experiences in which police sirens are evoked and storm clouds threaten. These three pieces, all played by the Los Angeles Chamber Orchestra with virtuosic panache, make for a satisfyingly varied programme.

Like the concerto grosso, *Sun* was composed in 1966, and this cycle for soprano and orchestra was intended by Rorem as a companion piece to his earlier *Poems of Love and the Rain*. 'The indicated need now seemed for songs of hate and the sun,' he quips in the introductory note. The opening song, based on an ancient Egyptian text credited to King Ikhnaton (*c*1360 BC) gives way to more modern musings on sunrises and sleepless nights, and copious sounds of ticking clocks. Rorem seems to have been going through a Russian phase when he composed this, the sonorities and rhythms suggest Stravinsky and Prokofiev. In his book *The Final Diary* (now re-titled *The Later Diaries*, because there have been others since), Rorem writes that the orchestra for *Sun* should be 'like gossamer' while the soprano soars to 'unnatural stratospheres'. It is a magnificent, large-scale enterprise to which those high sopranos who for years have made do with Strauss's *Four Last Songs* should look. Lauren Flanigan, who is fast becoming America's new prima donna, delivers it all with considerable aplomb.

Rorem's Third String Quartet completes the CD. This is a much later work (1990) in five movements and, unusually for Rorem, who often refers to the 'serial killers', it opens with a movement based on a 12-note row. But, he insists, it's a motive and not a row in the Schoenbergian sense. From this teasingly dissonant opening develops a luxuriously tuneful second movement called 'Scherzo-Sarabande-Scherzo'. This is the most obviously 'difficult' music on either of these discs, and Rorem seems aware of that as he provides a detailed programme for it, writing about torrents and whirling dervishes. The two CDs give a portrait of one of the most consistently surprising and individual composers of our time. Rorem cannot be bracketed with any school; he's just himself, with a breadth of vision and imagination that transcends labels.

Songs

Santa Fé – No 2, Opus 101; No 4, Sonnet; No 8, The wintry mind; No 12, The sowers. Clouds. Early in the morning. The serpent. Now sleeps the crimson petal. I strolled across an open field. To a young girl. Jeanie with the light brown hair. Ode. For Poulenc. Little elegy. Alleluia. Look down, fair moon. O you whom I often and silently come. I will always love you. The tulip tree. I am rose. The Lordly Hudson. O do not love too long. Far far away. For Susan. A journey. Sometimes with one I love. Love. Orchids. Stopping by woods on a snowy evening. Do I love you more than a day? Ferry me across the water. That shadow, my likeness
Susan Graham *sop* **Malcolm Martineau** *pf* with **Ensemble Oriol** (Christiane Plath *vn* Sebastian Gottschick *va* Friedeman Ludwig *vc*)
Erato 8573-80222-2 (61 minutes: DDD) Ⓕ
Texts included. Recorded 1999 ●●

If Rorem's songs are not as well known as those of Copland or Cole Porter it's probably because they're more difficult to sing. The earliest here is from 1947 (*The Lordly Hudson*, on a poem by Paul Goodman), the latest from 1983 (*That shadow, my likeness*, one of several Walt Whitman settings). Most of the others, though, were composed in the 1950s when Rorem was living in France. One could look for obvious French influences – Rorem was a close friend of

Auric and Poulenc – but strangely it is the later songs, from the cycle *Santa Fé* on poems by Witter Bynner, that have a more Gallic sound, the piano and string trio accompaniment having that aching, nostalgic mood which Rorem himself describes as 'a period removed from Time and, like the act of love, [it] has no limits, no beginning nor end.' The only song in French is a poem by Ronsard, an ode to peace, but two songs are about Paris. *Early in the morning*, a poem by Robert Hillyer, is an evocation of a young poet in love in and with Paris, its accompaniment a homage to all the sad waltzes that murmur their recollections of the city from Satie to Kosma. *For Poulenc*, written especially by Frank O'Hara for Rorem to set as part of an album of songs in memory of Poulenc, describes all the city in mourning.

Rorem called his autobiography *Knowing when to stop*, and it is a wonderful description of his own songs. The strength and beauty of Rorem's settings lies in their directness and candour. He doesn't linger, the poem and song are one, the melody growing from the accompaniment into the vocal line, but just as one seems able to grasp it, it's gone. Martineau plays with an unfailing sensitivity, giving the tiny shifts of mood from exuberance to elegiac melancholy their exact weight. In their conversation (see the booklet), Rorem says that he would like to compose a cycle for Susan Graham and another singer, perhaps a baritone, but adds, he would need a little encouragement. The triumphant success of this recital ought to be enough.

Further Listening

Piano Concerto for the Left Hand[a]. Eleven Studies for Eleven Players[b]

[a]Gary Graffman *pf* **[b]various artists / [b]Milanov; [a]Curtis Institute Student Orchestra / Previn**

New World NW80445-2 (62 minutes: DDD) Ⓕ

In the Piano Concerto Rorem's inspiration impresses by dint of its appealing lyrical fervour and colourful, assured instrumentation. The *Eleven Studies* is a charming suite, full of sparkling invention. Enthusiastic performances.

Johann Rosenmüller

German 1619-1684

GROVE *Rosenmüller first worked as an organist and teacher in Leipzig, but was imprisoned (on suspicion of homosexuality) in 1655. From 1658 he was a trombonist at St Mark's, Venice, and in 1678-82 also composer at the Ospedale della Pietà. Finally he returned to Germany as court Kapellmeister at Wolfenbüttel. A prolific composer, he was important in transmitting Italian styles to Germany, where his music was especially popular. He published four instrumental collections (1645-82), which move from simple dance suites to Italianate ensemble sonatas; the 12 sonatas of 1682 include much fugal writing. His sacred works number c200. The earliest are mainly small German concertos (many were published in two books, Kern-Sprüche, 1648 and 1652-53), but the later are mostly Latin, including psalms, solo cantatas and music for the Mass; these too show strong Italian features, and are notable for their expressiveness, clarity of form and idiomatic vocal writing.*

Vespro della beata Vergine

Canticum; Cantus Cölln; Concerto Palatino / Konrad Junghänel

Harmonia Mundi ② HMC90 1611/2 Ⓕ

(131 minutes: DDD). Texts and translations included

Recorded 1996 ⓞ

This release continues Cantus Cölln's important mission of illuminating Germany's finest 17th-century offerings, and this is a magnificent vindication of their efforts. His style is something of a godsend to Cantus Cölln, and vice versa. As a fluent and brilliant colourist of the most grandiloquent styles, he also never forsakes Teutonic contrapuntal discipline; the combination, at its best, produces a meticulously voiced control of texture and tautness of conception. These are also attributes long admired in the performances of this vocal ensemble, and they are heard with concentrated fervour in five Psalms and a Magnificat, interspersed with plainsong, motets (with texts expertly reworked to fit the Vespers) and two fine instrumental sonatas.

While 'Dixit Dominus', in terms of scale (it is over 600 bars long), is a memorable compendium of glistening scoring, rhythmic vitality, snappy declamation and textual characterization, there are other works where the totality of Rosenmüller's invention flatters rather more. 'Laudate pueri' evolves mesmerizingly, capped by a thrilling extended 'Sicut erat' (so too in the C minor Magnificat, whose opening chords resemble an early romantic opera overture).

Cantus Cölln gives a virtuoso performance of this work. 'He raiseth the poor out of the dust' is punctuated wonderfully by the instrumental commentary – and also 'Laetatus sum', where the singers' invigorating dialogue distracts the listener from D major overkill. 'Laude Jerusalem' is in the same vein, yet with a rolling sarabande momentum and an unusual *obbligato* combination of trumpet and cornetto. Cantus Cölln and Concerto Palatino demonstrate how a fairly small consort can sound majestic through extreme care in all matters of ensemble and intonation.

Further Listening

Rosenmüller Various vocal works. Ⓟ

Sonatas Nos 3, 4, 7, 10 and 11

The King's Noyse / Douglass *vn*

Harmonia Mundi HMU90 7179 (65 minutes: DDD: 12/96) Ⓕ

Rosenmüller's set of 12 sonates contain his most startlingly original instrumental music. Worth investigating.

Gioachino Rossini

Italian 1792-1868

GROVE *Rossini's parents were musicians, his father a horn player, his mother a singer. He learnt the horn and singing, and as a boy sang in at least one opera in Bologna, where the family lived.*

He studied there and began his operatic career when, at 18, he wrote a one-act comedy for Venice. Further commissions followed, from Bologna, Ferrara, Venice again and Milan, where La pietra del paragone was a success at La Scala in 1812. This was one of seven operas written in 16 months, all but one being comic.

This level of activity continued in the ensuing years. His first operas to win international acclaim come from 1813, written for different Venetian theatres: the serious Tancredi and the farcically comic L'italiana in Algeri, the one showing a fusion of lyrical expression and dramatic needs, the other moving easily between the sentimental, the patriotic, the absurd and the sheer lunatic. Two operas for Milan were less successful. In 1815 Rossini went to Naples as musical and artistic director of the Teatro San Carlo, which led to a concentration on serious opera. But he was allowed to compose for other theatres, and from this time date two of his supreme comedies, written for Rome, Il barbiere di Siviglia and La Cenerentola. The former has claims to be considered the greatest of all Italian comic operas, eternally fresh in its wit and its inventiveness. It dates from 1816; initially it was a failure, but quickly became the most loved of his comic works. The next year saw La Cenerentola, a charmingly sentimental tale in which the heroine moves from a touching folksy ditty as the scullery maid to brilliant coloratura apt to a royal maiden.

Rossini's most important operas in the period that followed were for Naples. The third act of his Otello (1816), with its strong unitary structure, marks his maturity as a musical dramatist. The Neapolitan operas, even though much dependent on solo singing of a highly florid kind, show an enormous expansion of musical means, with more and longer ensembles and the chorus an active participant; the accompanied recitative is more dramatic and the orchestra is given greater prominence. Rossini abandoned traditional overtures as well. In 1822 he married Naples' leading soprano Isabella Colbran, but it proved an ill match.

Among the masterpieces from this period are Maometto II (1820) and Semiramide (1823). In 1823 Rossini left for London and Paris where he took on the directorship of the Théâtre-ltalien, composing for that theatre and the Opéra. Some of his Paris works are adaptations (Le siège de Corinthe and Moïse et Pharaon); the opéra comique Le Comte Ory is part-new, Guillaume Tell wholly. This last, widely regarded as his chef d'oeuvre, is a rich tapestry of his most inspired music, with elaborate orchestration, many ensembles, spectacular ballets and processions in the French tradition, opulent orchestral writing and a new harmonic boldness.

At 37, he retired from opera composition. He left Paris in 1837 to live in Italy, but suffered prolonged and painful illness there. Isabella died in 1845 and the next year he married Olympe Pélissier, with whom he had lived for 15 years. He composed hardly at all during this period (the Stabat mater belongs to his Paris years); but he went back to Paris in 1855, and his health, humour and urge to compose returned. He wrote a quantity of pieces for piano and voices, with wit and refinement, that he called Péchés de vieillesse ('Sins of Old Age'), including the graceful and economical Petite messe solennelle (1863). He died, universally honoured, in 1868.

Overtures

Overtures – Guillaume Tell; La scala di seta; Il Signor Bruschino; Il barbiere di Siviglia; La gazza ladra; La Cenerentola **H**

Chicago Symphony Orchestra / Fritz Reiner

RCA Victor Gold Seal GD60387 (47 minutes: ADD) Ⓜ

Recorded 1958 **OOO**

This is one of the most famous of all collections featuring this sparkling repertoire. By the time of this recording, Fritz Reiner had built the Chicago Symphony into one of the world's greatest ensembles, and their swaggering yet supremely flexible virtuosity is heard to superb effect on this survey. Not that these accounts are in any sense overdriven or that Rossini's music is used merely as an excuse for high-powered orchestral display; far from it: Reiner's direction possesses elegance, genial high-spirits and (at times) an almost Beechamesque wit – sample, say, the pointed woodwind dialogue in the scintillating reading of *La Cenerentola* to hear this. In fact, the only regret one could possibly have about this simply marvellous music-making is that, with a total duration of just under 47 minutes there isn't more of it! Despite some (inevitable) residual hiss, the RCA transfer engineers have worked wonders with these elderly tapes, producing a far more full-blooded, transparent sound picture than one would have thought possible. At mid-price, this is unmissable. Buy it!

String Sonatas

Rossini Sonate a quattro – No 1 in G; No 2 in A; No 3 in C; No 4 in B flat; No 5 in E flat; No 6 in D **Bellini** Oboe Concerto in E flat **Cherubini** Horn Sonata in F **Donizetti** String Quartet in D (1828)

Roger Lord *ob* **Barry Tuckwell** *hn* **Academy of St Martin in the Fields / Sir Neville Marriner**

Double Decca ② 443 838-2DF2 (112 minutes: ADD) Ⓜ

Recorded 1964-68 **O**

Rossini's six string sonatas are usually heard performed by a string orchestra, although they were in fact composed for a quartet of two violins, cello and double bass. The sonatas, which display amazing musical dexterity and assurance, may date from as early as 1804. The world of 18th-century opera is never far away, with the first violin frequently taking the role of soprano soloist, particularly in the slow movements. Written for Rossini's friend Agostino Triosso, who was a keen double bass player, the sonata's bass parts are full of wit and suavity. There are other thoroughly recommendable modern digital versions, yet there is something very special about Marriner's Academy set, made for Argo in the late 1960s. The playing has an elegance and finesse, a sparkle and touch of humour that catches the full character and charm of these miraculous examples of the precocity of the 12-year-old composer. Among the substantial bonuses here are Donizetti's String Quartet, sounding elegant in its string-orchestra version, Bellini's Oboe Concerto, played stylishly by

Roger Lord and Cherubini's mini-concerto for horn and strings is dispatched with aplomb by by Barry Tuckwell. Highly recommendable.

Le nozze di Teti, e di Peleo

Le nozze di Teti, e di Peleo[a]. Il pianto d'Armonia sulla morte di Orfeo[b]

[a]Elisabetta Scano *sop* **[a]Cecilia Bartoli** *mez* **[a]Daniela Barcellona** *contr* **[a]Juan Diego Flórez, [a]Luigi Petroni, [b]Paul Austin Kelly** *tens* **La Scala Philharmonic Orchestra and Chorus, Milan / Riccardo Chailly**

Decca 466 328-2DH (69 minutes: DDD) Ⓕ

Recorded 1997 ●

The wedding cantata was Rossini's first formal court commission after his arrival in Naples in the autumn of 1815. It was an astonishing year: *Il barbiere* in February, the cantata in April, *La gazzetta* in September, and after that *Otello* and *La Cenerentola*. The cantata was written to celebrate the marriage of Princess Maria Carolina, Ferdinand IV's granddaughter, and the Duc de Berry, the second son of the future Charles X of France for whose coronation in 1825 Rossini would write *Il viaggio a Reims*.

The librettist based his pageant on the legend of Peleus and the sea-nymph, Thetis, fated to bear a son (Achilles) mightier than his father. The work includes a love duet and several symbolic tableaux in which the gods bless the nuptials and speculate about events which might flow from them. The Neapolitan court would have noted a decided lack of action here. Scenic splendour and lots of gorgeous music, superbly sung by the stellar talents of the Naples company, were the order of the day.

None of the music Rossini used in the cantata was new to him. But it was new to the Neapolitans and much of it will be new to present-day audiences. Rossini aficionados may fancy spending an evening eating foie gras, quaffing d'Yquem, and spotting the borrowings, but it is not a particularly productive game. The fact is, Rossini was a dab hand at expertly reassembling old music. *Le nozze di Teti, e di Peleo* works wonderfully well as *Le nozze di Teti, e di Peleo*. Game, set and second bottle of d'Yquem to Rossini.

Decca has assembled a mixture of stellar and sub-stellar talent for their recording. Cecilia Bartoli's Ceres (Isabella Colbran's role in Naples) will be the principal selling point. She appears in a sensuous duet with the goddess Juno (Daniela Barcellona), as well as the cantata's big showpiece aria (an astonishing reworking of the Count's Act 2 aria from *Il barbiere*, partly redeployed as 'Non più mesta' in *La Cenerentola*) and in the grand finale. Her singing is formidably, ferociously fine. The other star, a Rossini tenor of real pedigree, is Juan Diego Flórez; he sings Peleo, Giovanni David's role. Less successful is the Teti, the somewhat soubrettish Elisabetta Scano. Teti may seem to play a secondary role but this is no reason to economise; Rossini wrote the part for Margarita Chabrand, a great favourite with Neapolitan audiences.

Chailly's conducting is exemplary, and more besides. His way with something like the chorus 'Liete danze' has an irresistible lift and lilt, with Rossini spinning us into orbits of delight known hitherto only to him.

Rossini was 16 when he wrote *The Lament of Harmony on the Death of Orpheus*. It is a charming work, a fraction under 20 minutes in length, with a bustling overture, one chorus, an aria, and a final *aria con coro*. Paul Austin Kelly sings the role of Harmony with exemplary taste and technique. It is also pleasing to see booklet credits for the horn and cello soloists, Danilo Stagni and Giuseppe Laffranchini. The beguilingly beautiful cello writing in the recitative 'Ma tu che desti' looks all the way forward to *Guillaume Tell*. Astonishing!

All in all, then, this is a richly entertaining anthology of not-entirely-minor Rossini. The orchestra and chorus of the La Scala Philharmonic play and sing like angels and both recordings are, without question, superb.

Petite messe solennelle

Daniella Dessì *sop* **Gloria Scalchi** *mez* **Giuseppe Sabbatini** *ten* **Michele Pertusi** *bass* **Chorus and Orchestra of the Teatro Comunale, Bologna / Riccardo Chailly**

Decca ② 444 134-2DX2 (82 minutes: DDD) Ⓜ

Text and translation included. Recorded 1993 ●

A proper representative of the orchestrated version has been long overdue. Chailly's performance is a glorious heart-warming affair. Not that you are likely to be convinced right away. To ears accustomed to the *Kyrie* in its original form, the texturing here is pure suet. Nor does the sound of the largish and here rather distantly placed choir seem especially well focused in the *Christe eleison*. Gradually, though, the ear adjusts, the musicians warm to their task, the performance gets into its stride. The Bologna Chorus sings the *Gloria* and *Credo* with passion, clarity and love. The tenor is adequate, the bass superb, the two girls absolutely fabulous. (The *Qui tollis* is sung with near-shameless allure.) If the *Crucifixus* can never be as painful as it is in the sparer original version, this is amply offset by the sheer beauty of Daniella Dessì's singing and by the hair-raising force of the 'Et resurrexit' (superbly recorded) as Chailly and his choir realise it. By the end, after Gloria Scalchi's deeply affecting account of the *Agnus Dei*, you begin to wonder whether the orchestral version wasn't more than a match for the original. It isn't, but it is an indication of the cumulative eloquence of this utterly inspired performance that it comes to seem so.

Stabat mater

Luba Orgonasova *sop* **Cecilia Bartoli** *mez* **Raúl Giménez** *ten* **Roberto Scandiuzzi** *bass* **Vienna State Opera Concert Choir; Vienna Philharmonic Orchestra / Myung-Whun Chung**

DG 449 178-2GH (59 minutes: DDD). Text and translation included. Recorded 1995 Ⓕ ●

Chung's conducting of this work is somewhat Karajanesque: extremely beautiful orchestral playing; a choir which sings expressively but who yields something in focus and clarity of sound to the best rival English choirs; a strong dramatic sense with some unusual tempos that lead to the performance occasionally seeming mannered; and much fine solo singing, the singers encouraged to sing with great inwardness, with a special kind of *quiet* beauty. This is where the performance differs markedly from Richard Hickox's account. There the soloists sing their solo numbers in far more open and extrovert manner. Between Della Jones (Hickox) and Cecilia Bartoli there is simply no comparison; for Jones and Hickox 'Fac ut portem' is a dramatic oration, for Bartoli and Chung it is a private meditation. You pay your money and you take your choice.

The integration of singers, orchestra and acoustic is not quite as well managed as on the Chandos recording, where we have a church acoustic as opposed to the more secular sounding Golden Hall of the Vienna Musikverein. Nor is Chung's reading as straightforward, as right-sounding as Hickox's. Nevertheless this recording can be regarded as first among equals.

Stabat mater Ⓟ

Krassimira Stoyanova *sop* **Petra Lang** *mez* **Bruce Fowler** *ten* **Daniel Borowski** *bass* **RIAS Chamber Choir, Berlin; Academy for Ancient Music, Berlin / Marcus Creed**

Harmonia Mundi HMC90 1693 (57 minutes: DDD) Ⓕ
Text and translation included. Recorded 1999

One of the first, and best, recordings of this splendid but interpretatively elusive work was made in Berlin in 1954 under the direction of Ferenc Fricsay. Like the present recording, it featured the RIAS (Berlin Radio) Chamber Choir, though in those days the fledgling choir was supplemented in the full choruses by the famous St Hedwig's Cathedral Choir. Now on its own, it acquits itself superbly in all movements and dimensions with its own conductor, the English-born Marcus Creed. That this recording uses period instruments might seem in so obviously 'vocal' a piece to be of no particular moment. In practice, the work's prevailingly dark orchestral colours are memorably realised by the instrumentalists of Berlin's Academy for Ancient Music. In the grand opening movement, the four soloists are recorded uncomfortably far forward; but if you can establish an agreeable level for this movement, the rest of the performance sounds very well indeed. Choir and orchestra are themselves unfailingly well balanced. Creed's reading is full of character: immensely strong but always sensitively paced. Rossini might have raised an eyebrow at Creed's fondness for romantically protracted codas; equally, he would have applauded his sensitive moulding of the accompaniments, matched shrewdly but never indulgently to the singers' (and the music's) needs. The soloists themselves, young and highly talented, are excellent, more than a match for most rival teams.

Opera Arias

Cecilia Bartoli

Zelmira – Riedi al soglio. Le nozze di Teti e di Peleo – Ah, non potrian reistere. Maometto II – Ah! che invan su questo ciglio; Giusto ciel, in tal periglio. La donna del lago – Tanti affetti in tal momento. Elisabetta, Regina d'Inghilterra – Quant' è grato all'alma mia; Fellon, la penna avrai. Semiramide – Serenai vaghirai ... Bel raggio lusinghier

Cecilia Bartoli *mez* **Chorus and Orchestra of the Teatro La Fenice, Venice / Ion Marin**

Decca 436 075-2DH (59 minutes: DDD). Texts and translations included. Recorded 1991 Ⓕ

This sparkling disc brings together a collection of arias composed by Rossini for one of the great prima donnas of the 19th century, who was also his wife, Isabella Colbran. It is tempting to wonder whether even she had a voice to match that of Cecilia Bartoli, one of the most luscious, most exciting voices in opera. All those dazzling chromatic runs, leaps, cadenzas and cascading coloraturas are handled with consummate ease. Throughout, Bartoli sounds as if she's enjoying the music; there is always an engaging smile in the voice, although she is properly imperious in the extracts from *Elisabetta* and disarmingly simple in the prayerful 'Giusto ciel, in tal periglio' ('Righteous heaven in such danger') from *Maometto II*. The orchestral and choral forces provide a delightful intimacy, with some cheeky woodwind solos and fruity brass passages. The recording, produced at the Teatro La Fenice by Decca veteran Christopher Raeburn, favours the voices but gives it just enough distance to accommodate high Cs and astounding A flats at the bottom of the range. The orchestral perspective is changeable but satisfactory. For Rossini and Bartoli fans, this disc is a must.

Nelly Miricioiu

Elisabetta, Regina d'Inghilterra – Qant'è grato all'alma mia[a]. Aureliano in Palmira – Se tu m'ami, o mia regina[b]. Bianca e Falliero – Cielo, il mio labbro ispira[c]. Zelmira – Riedi al soglio[d]. Mosè in Egitto – Mi manca la voce[e]; Porgi la destra amata[h]. Semiramide – Se la vita[f]. Armida – Dove son io![g]. Vallace – Viva Vallace! Vallace Viva[i]

Nelly Miricioiu with [ehi]**Patrizia Biccire** *sops* [bc]**Enkelejda Shkosa** *mez* [i]**Antonia Sotgiù** *voc* [ceg]**Bruce Ford,** [dehi]**Barry Banks,** [h]**Dominic Natoli** *tens* [cdhi]**Gary Magee,** [hi]**Dean Robinson** *bars* [f]**Alastair Miles** *bass* [i]**Simon Bailey** *voc* [acdhi]**Geoffrey Mitchell Choir; Academy of St Martin in the Fields / David Parry**

Opera Rara ORR211 (67 minutes: DDD) Ⓕ
Texts and translations included. Recorded 1999

Rossini is a difficult composer to anthologise. I have no doubt that Callas and Walter Legge or Sutherland and Bonynge could have come up with something fascinating and fabulous had they been so minded. Caballé did, of course: the eminently collectable Rossini Rarities disc she produced for the Rossini bicentenary in 1968 (RCA, 11/92). For the rest, successful recitals have been few and far between, indifferent singing or poor planning principally to blame.

Not so Opera Rara's Rossini Gala. Patric Schmid's inventive programme focuses on Rossini's Naples period and the extraordinary array of roles he created for the great Spanish soprano, Isabella Colbran. What distinguishes this recital is that it doesn't only anthologise set-piece arias. Rossini gave Colbran some grand entrances and some even grander exits, and there are examples of both here: Queen Elizabeth's arrival and Zelmira's final florid song of thanksgiving. But we are also given two wonderful quartets, two exquisite duets, a famous *coup de théâtre* (the Act 2 finale of *Mosè in Egitto* with its terrific lightning-strike), and one of Rossini's finest pieces of music-theatre: the scene near the start of Act 2 of *Semiramide* where the Queen and her lover, the adulterous regicide Assur, have rows worthy of the Macbeths over events which are beginning to overshadow them.

Subscribers to the Chelsea Opera Group will remember Nelly Miricioiu's powerful portrayal of Semiramide in concert in London in 1998. Miricioiu is not a *bel canto* specialist; Santuzza (Chandos's 'Opera in English' *Cavalleria rusticana*, 8/98) is as much her territory as Semiramide. In neither role is the technique perfectly honed, but the effect is rarely less than compelling. Every one of the heroines presented here is vividly depicted, with a distinguished supporting cast (Enkeledja Shkosa, Bruce Ford and Alastair Miles's Assur all being outstanding) helping to etch each scene into the imagination.

The gala ends with an intriguing rarity which has nothing to do with Colbran or Miricioiu. *Vallace*, in case you are wondering, is a shortened, revised and relocated version of *Guillaume Tell* prepared for La Scala, Milan, in 1836-37. Austrian tyranny being an uncongenial subject to Milan's Austrian rulers, the libretto was recast to show English tyranny instead: Edward I's bloody crusade against the Scots, with William Wallace as a Scottish Tell. Rossini was not much involved in the adaptation, though he did agree to recast the finale scene so that the opera could end with a reprise of the overture's famous *pas redoublé*. It is that revised finale which we have here, a travesty of Schiller (and Rossini), but great fun.

Playing, choral work and conducting for this Rossini Gala are all of a high order of excellence. As is the engineering (the lightning strike in *Mosè in Egitto* is not for the faint-hearted). As always with Opera Rara, the accompanying 116-page booklet is superlatively informative. At the price of a single full-price CD, the disc is a terrific bargain, not least for the splendid hawk's-eye view the programme provides of 'serious' Rossini.

Il barbiere di Siviglia

Roberto Servile *bar* Figaro; **Sonia Ganassi** *mez* Rosina; **Ramon Vargas** *ten* Count Almaviva; **Angelo Romero** *bar* Bartolo; **Franco de Grandis** *bass* Don Basilio; **Ingrid Kertesi** *sop* Berta; **Kázmér Sarkany** *bass* Fiorello; **Hungarian Radio Chorus; Failoni Chamber Orchestra, Budapest / Will Humburg**

Naxos ③ 8 660027/9 (158 minutes: DDD) Ⓢ

Notes and text included. Recorded 1992

Not everyone will approve, but there are ways in which this super-budget set of *Il barbiere di Siviglia* puts to shame just about every other version of the opera there has yet been. Those it may not please are specialist vocal collectors for whom *Il barbiere* is primarily a repository of vocal test pieces. If, however, you regard *Il barbiere* (Rossini, ex-Beaumarchais) as a gloriously subversive music drama – vibrant, scurrilous, unstoppably vital – then this recording is guaranteed to give a great deal of pleasure.

'Performance' is the key word here. Humburg is described in the Naxos booklet as 'Conductor and Recitative Director'; and for once the recitatives really are part of the larger drama. The result is a meticulously produced, often very funny, brilliantly integrated performance that you will almost certainly find yourself listening to as a stage play. With a virtually all-Italian cast, the results are a revelation. The erotic allure of the duet 'Dunque io son' is striking. Similarly, Don Basilio's Calumny aria, superbly sung by Franco de Grandis, a black-browed bass from Turin who was singing for Karajan, Muti and Abbado while still in his twenties. This takes on added character and colour from the massive sense of panic created by de Grandis and the admirable Dr Bartolo of Angelo Romero when Basilio comes in with news of Almaviva's arrival in town.

The Overture is done with evident relish, the playing of the Failoni Chamber Orchestra (a group from within the Hungarian State Opera Orchestra) is nothing if not articulate. Aided by a clear, forward recording, a *sine qua non* with musical comedy, the cast communicates the Rossini/Sterbini text – solo arias, ensembles, recitatives – with tremendous relish. They are never hustled by Humburg, nor are they spared: the *stretta* of the Act 1 finale is a model of hyper-tension and clarity. It would have been nice to have an English version of the libretto, but you can't have everything at rock-bottom prices and Naxos provides an excellent track-by-track synopsis. This *Il barbiere* jumps to the top of the pile.

Il barbiere di Siviglia

Thomas Allen *bar* Figaro; **Agnes Baltsa** *mez* Rosina; **Francisco Araiza** *ten* Count Almaviva; **Domenico Trimarchi** *bar* Dr Bartolo; **Robert Lloyd** *bass* Don Basilio; **Matthew Best** *bass* Fiorello; **Sally Burgess** *mez* Berta; **John Noble** *bar* Official; **Ambrosian Opera Chorus; Academy of St Martin in the Fields / Sir Neville Marriner**

Philips ② 446 448-2PH2 (147 minutes: ADD). Notes, Ⓕ text and translation included. Recorded 1982

This was the most stylish and engaging account of *Il barbiere* to have appeared on record since the famous de los Angeles/Bruscantini set recorded by EMI with Glyndebourne forces in 1962. Here, making a rare but welcome appearance in an opera recording, is the stylish Academy of St Martin in the Fields. It is as pointed and sure-footed an account of the score as you could hope to hear, a reading which entirely belies the fact that this was Neville

Marriner's operatic début on record. Quite how the producer, in duets, ensembles and recitatives, created so live a sense of theatre in so essentially unconvivial a place as Watford Town Hall, north west of London, must for ever remain a mystery; there is here a real and rare sense of the delighted interplay of character: a tribute, in the first place, to the degree to which Thomas Allen, Francisco Araiza, Domenico Trimarchi, Agnes Baltsa, Robert Lloyd and their fellows are inside their roles musically and dramatically. There is no vulgar horseplay in the recording; but equally there is nothing slavish or literal about the way in which Rossini's, and Beaumarchais's comic felicities have been realised. The text is Zedda, more or less. Robert Lloyd takes the Calumny aria in C (D is the 'authentic' key), rightly so, for his is a magnificent bass voice. It's a grand characterization, very much in the Chaliapin style. Thomas Allen's Figaro and Francisco Araiza's Count bring out the opera's virility, its peculiarly masculine strength. Allen has a vivid sense of character and a brilliant technique. He also has a ripe sense of comedy.

Araiza is similarly compelling. Technically he is first-rate. His divisions are unusually bright and clean (though rapid triplets tend to go unshaded), the top (including some flashy cadences) true, shaped in a way which is both musically vivid and dramatically right, rounding out Araiza's portrait of an aristocrat distinguished by his ability to dominate and dispel mere domestic imbroglio. Equally, Araiza can be confiding, and funny. His whining music-master is a delight, right down to an unscripted attempt at a reprise of 'Pace e gioia' at the end of the scene, cut off by a petulant 'Basta!' from the excellent Bartolo, Domenico Trimarchi. Baltsa's Rosina, too, is infected by the set's general liveliness: witness the delighted gurgle of joy which escapes from her at the news of the Count's intentions. Recitatives, edited down here and there, are very alert, theatrically pointed; and Nicholas Kraemer's accompaniments on a sweet-sounding fortepiano are an added pleasure. Philips preferred a dryish, intimate acoustic; the small-theatre atmosphere this confers is very likeable, the more so as it allows Marriner the opportunity to conduct with a tautness and vigour which a boomier, more open acoustic would disallow. With excellent choral work in the all important ensembles, and with a delightful Berta from Sally Burgess, this is undoubtedly one of the very best *Barbers* the gramophone has given us.

Il barbiere di Siviglia

Sesto Bruscantini *bar* Figaro; **Victoria de los Angeles** *sop* Rosina; **Luigi Alva** *ten* Count Almaviva; **Ian Wallace** *bass* Dr Bartolo; **Carlo Cava** *bass* Don Basilio; **Duncan Robertson** *ten* Fiorello; **Laura Sarti** *mez* Berta; **Glyndebourne Festival Chorus; Royal Philharmonic Orchestra / Vittorio Gui**

EMI Rossini Edition ② CMS7 64162-2 (141 minutes: ADD). Notes, text and translation included. Recorded 1962 Ⓜ ●●●

Perhaps it is a shade misleading to refer to this classic EMI recording as a 'Glyndebourne' set. It has all the ingredients of a Glyndebourne production: notably the cast, the orchestra and chorus, and that doyen of Rossini conductors, Vittorio Gui. But as far as can be ascertained, there was no actual stage production of *Il barbiere* in 1962. Nor was the recording, for all its dryness and sharp-edged immediacy, actually made in Glyndebourne. It is a well-honed, conservatively staged stereophonic studio recording made by EMI in its Abbey Road Studio No 1 at the conclusion of the 1962 Glyndebourne season. Gui's performance is so astutely paced that whilst the music bubbles and boils every word is crystal-clear. This is a wonderfully declaimed reading of the score, but also a beautifully timed one. Gui's steady tempos also allow the music to show its underlying toughness. He also secures characterful playing from the RPO, from the wind players in particular. Where Victoria de los Angeles is so memorable is in the beauty of her singing and the originality of the reading. There has never been a Rosina who manages to be both as guileful and as charming as de los Angeles. Team her up with the incomparable Sesto Bruscantini and, in something like the nodal Act 1 duet, 'Dunque io son', you have musical and dramatic perfection. Gui's Dr Bartolo, Ian Wallace, is a fine character actor, given plenty of space by Gui, allowing his portrait of Dr Bartolo to emerge as a classic compromise between the letter and the spirit of the part.

La Cenerentola

Teresa Berganza *mez* Angelina; **Luigi Alva** *ten* Don Ramiro; **Renato Capecchi** *bar* Dandini; **Paolo Montarsolo** *bar* Don Magnifico; **Margherita Guglielmi** *sop* Clorinda; **Laura Zannini** *contr* Tisbe; **Ugo Trama** *bass* Alidoro; **Scottish Opera Chorus; London Symphony Orchestra / Claudio Abbado**

DG Double ② 459 448-2GTA2 (144 minutes: ADD) Notes, text and translation included. Ⓜ Recorded 1971 ●

Rossini's Cinderella is a fairy-tale without a fairy, but no less bewitching for that. In fact the replacement of the winged godmother with the philanthropic Alidoro, a close friend and adviser of our prince, Don Ramiro, plus the lack of any glass slippers and the presence of a particularly unsympathetic father character, makes the whole story more plausible. *La Cenerentola*, Angelina, is more spunky than the average pantomime Cinders. She herself gives Don Ramiro one of her pair of bracelets, charging him to find the owner of the matching ornament and thus taking control of her own destiny. Along the way, Don Ramiro and his valet Dandini change places, leading to plenty of satisfyingly operatic confusion and difficult situations.

This recording, when originally transferred to CD, was spread across three discs, but it has now been comfortably fitted into two, now at mid-price as well. It gives a sparkling rendition of the score with a lovely light touch and well-judged tempos from Abbado and the LSO and virtuoso vocal requirements are fully met by the cast. The chief delight is Teresa Berganza's Angelina, creamy in tone and as warm as she is precise. The supporting cast is full of character, with Luigi Alva a princely Don Ramiro, Margherita Guglielmi and Laura Zannini an affected and fussy pair of sisters, and Renato Capecchi as Dandini, gleeful and mischievous as he takes on being prince for a day. The recording sounds more than usually well for its age.

Additional recommendation

La cenerentola

Bartoli Angelina **Matteuzzi** Don Ramiro **Corbelli** Dandini **Bologna Teatro Comunale Chorus and Orchestra / Chailly**

Decca ② 436 902-2DH2 (148 minutes: DDD: 11/93) Ⓕ

For Bartoli fans, a cherishable set that doesn't quite match the sparkle of the Abbado. Matteuzzi sings well and there are some nicely drawn characters. Chailly directs with spirit

Le comte Ory

Juan Oncina *ten* Comte Ory; **Sari Barabas** *sop* Comtesse Adèle; **Cora Canne-Meijer** *mez* Isolier; **Michel Roux** *bar* Raimbaud; **Ian Wallace** *bass* La Gouverneur; **Jeannette Sinclair** *sop* Alice; **Monica Sinclair** *contr* Ragonde; **Dermot Troy** *ten* Chevalier; **Glyndebourne Festival Chorus and Orchestra / Vittorio Gui** H

EMI Rossini Edition mono ② CMS7 64180-2 (113 minutes: ADD). Notes, text and translation included. Recorded 1956 Ⓜ ●●

This now legendary production of *Le comte Ory* was one of Glyndebourne's principal glories in the 1950s. It was seen there over 30 times between 1954 and 1958; it also visited Paris (coals to Newcastle) and the Edinburgh Festival. Like Jane Austen's *Emma* it could be said to be faultless despite its faults. There are cuts. The French is not consistently good. The singing is variable, yet the Glyndebourne recording has several trump cards. Juan Oncina as the philandering Comte Ory has a matchless presence and charm. He is occasionally taxed by the tessitura of the role; but his diction is superb, and, with Gui in attendance, there is a flawless ease of emission where Rossini's melodies are at their most beguiling. Oncina and Gui do the supremely Rossinian thing of cultivating elegance of line and sweetness of sound above all else. Gui is also flawless in his pacing of the score, never regimenting the music.

This recording is one of the last masterpieces of the mono era. As soon as the voices come into play it is clear how astutely the recording has been staged for the gramophone by Gui and the engineers. It is occasionally quite remarkable in terms of clarity and guileful pointing of dramatic perspectives. And in Rossini's big ensembles that is a huge plus. Put on track 19 of the first disc, the Act 1 finale, and see if you don't agree. At moments like this you feel that God and Rossini are in their respective heavens and everything is right with the world.

Guglielmo Tell

Sherrill Milnes *bar* Guglielmo Tell; **Luciano Pavarotti** *ten* Arnoldo; **Mirella Freni** *sop* Matilde; **Della Jones** *mez* Jemmy; **Elizabeth Connell** *mez* Edwige; **Ferruccio Mazzoli** *bass* Gessler; **Nicolai Ghiaurov** *bass* Gualtiero; **John Tomlinson** *bass* Melchthal; **Cesar Antonio Suarez** *ten* Un pescatore; **Piero De Palma** *ten* Rodolfo; **Richard Van Allan** *bass* Leutoldo; **Ambrosian Opera Chorus; National Philharmonic Orchestra / Riccardo Chailly**

Decca ④ 417 154-2DH4 (235 minutes: ADD). Notes, Ⓕ text and translation included. Recorded 1980 ●

If ever there was a case for armchair opera – and on CD at that – it is Rossini's *Guglielmo Tell*. The very limitations which have made it, so far, a non-repertory work, give space for the imagination to redress the balance: the short, Rousseau-esque scenes of life by Lake Lucerne, the distant entrances and exits of shepherds and huntsmen, the leisurely but perfectly balanced side-vignettes of fisherman, hunter, child.

Thanks to the clarity and liveliness of the recording itself and, above all, the shrewd casting, this set creates a vivid *charivari* of fathers, sons, lovers and patriots, all played out against some of Rossini's most delicately painted pastoral cameos. Riccardo Chailly keeps up the undercurrent of tension between private love and public loyalty, as well as working hard the rustic jollity of the score. Tell himself could hardly have a better advocate than Sherrill Milnes, who portrays the moral rectitude of a man who casts himself in the role of his brother's keeper, while managing to glow with true ardour and integrity in the cause for which he is fighting. Arnoldo and Matilde, too, are cleverly cast. Pavarotti contains the coarse, direct impulsiveness of Arnoldo's shepherd stock with the tenderness of love, in his characteristic charcoal *cantabile* and the numbness of his remorse. Freni, singing opposite him as the forbidden Princess Matilde, phrases with aristocratic poise, folding into every fragment of embryonic *bel canto* the fragile ardour of a young girl's love. The vocal chemistry between them in their Act 2 declaration of love is a lively incarnation of their roles. A similarly interesting patterning of vocal timbres is produced by the casting of Elizabeth Connell as Edwige, Tell's wife, and of Della Jones as Jemmy, their son. Their last-act Trio with Matilde is matched by the contrasting colours of the basses of Ghiaurov, Tomlinson and Van Allan: their roles may be small, but their characters are vividly stamped on what is an excellent ensemble performance.

L'inganno felice

Annick Massis *sop* Isabella; **Raúl Giménez** *ten* Bertrando; **Rodney Gilfry** *bar* Batone; **Pietro Spagnoli** *bass* Tarabotto; **Lorenzo Regazzo** *bar* Ormondo; **Le Concert des Tuileries / Marc Minkowski**

Erato 0630-17579-2 (78 minutes: DDD). Notes, text Ⓕ and translation included. Recorded live in 1996 ●

This is a fine and tremendously enjoyable recording of an exquisite early Rossini one-acter. The plot resembles that of a late Shakespearian comedy. Set in a seaside mining community, it is concerned with the discovery and rehabilitation of Isabella, Duke Bertrando's wronged and, so he thinks, long-dead wife. It is a work that is comic and serious, witty and sentimental; and there, perhaps, lies the rub. Rossini, especially early Rossini, is meant to be all teeth and smiles, yet *L'inganno felice* is not quite like that. The very *mise-en-scène* is odd: 'seaside' and 'mining' being, in such a context, strangely contradictory concepts. This is a splendid performance, using a chamber ensemble of about 30 players. It is recorded with pleasing immediacy, which begins bullishly but settles to intimacy when the drama requires. The score is full of vocal pitfalls, not least for the tenor and for the baritone Batone. But Giménez and Gilfry cope more than adequately, with enough in reserve to produce moments of genuine ease and beauty. Annick Massis is a charming Isabella, good in her first aria, ravishing in her second. The final scene the work's finest sequence, is set at night amid the mining galleys and is beautifully performed here.

L'italiana in Algeri

Jennifer Larmore *mez* Isabella; **Raúl Giménez** *ten* Lindoro; **Alessandro Corbelli** *bar* Taddeo; **John del Carlo** *bass* Mustafà; **Darina Takova** *sop* Elvira; **Laura Polverelli** *mez* Zulma; **Carlos Chausson** *bass-bar* Haly; **Geneva Grand Theatre Chorus; Lausanne Chamber Orchestra / Jésus López-Cobos**

Teldec ② 0630-17130-2 (147 minutes: DDD). Notes, Ⓕ text and translation included. Recorded 1997 ⭘

This recording is hard to fault on any count. López-Cobos revels in all aspects of this dotty comedy, timing everything to perfection, enthusing his accomplished orchestra and cast to enjoy their collective self. First there's a magic moment as Isabella and Lindoro espy each other for the first time, and comment on the joy of reunion; then the main section gets under way to a perfectly sprung rhythm from the conductor, with all the passage's detail made manifest; finally the *stretta* is released with the kind of vitality that sets the feet tapping. Larmore obviously thoroughly enjoys the role and conveys that enjoyment in singing that matches warm, smiling tone to bravura execution of her *fioriture*. She is a mettlesome Isabella, who knows how to tease, then defy her would-be lover, Mustafà, and charm her real amour, Lindoro, her 'Per lui che adoro' sung with an immaculate line and sensuous tone, its repetition deftly embellished. Finally 'Pensa alla patria' evinces a touch of true *élan*. Lindoro is taken by that paragon among Rossini tenors, Raúl Giménez, who presents his credentials in 'Languir per una bella', honeyed tone succeeded by fleet runs. He is no less successful in his more heroic Cavatina in Act 2. Corbelli, another master-Rossinian, is witty as the put-upon Taddeo, his textual facility a marvel. The American bass-baritone, John del Carlo, is a characterful Mustafà, managing to suggest, as Rossini surely intended, a paradox of lovesick tyrant and ludicrous posturing without ever overstepping the mark into farce, and rolling Italian and his rotund roulades off his tongue with idiomatic assurance. The recording is up to Teldec's impeccably high standard.

L'italiana in Algeri

Marilyn Horne *mez* Isabella; **Ernesto Palacio** *ten* Lindoro; **Domenico Trimarchi** *bar* Taddeo; **Samuel Ramey** *bass* Mustafà; **Kathleen Battle** *sop* Elvira; **Clara Foti** *mez* Zulma; **Nicola Zaccaria** *bass* Haly; **Prague Philharmonic Chorus; I Solisti Veneti / Claudio Scimone**

Erato Libretto ② 2292-45404-2 (140 minutes: ADD) Ⓜ Notes and text included. Recorded 1980

Written within the space of a month during the spring of 1813, and with help from another anonymous hand, Rossini's *L'italiana in Algeri* was an early success, and one which went on to receive many performances during the 19th century, with an increasingly corrupt text. A complete reconstruction was undertaken by Azio Corghi and published in 1981; this recording uses this edition which corresponds most closely to what was actually performed in Venice in 1813. *L'italiana* is one of Rossini's wittiest operas, featuring as did a number of his most successful works a bewitching central character, in this case Isabella, who makes fun of her various suitors, with the opera ending with a happy escape with her beloved, Lindoro, a typical *tenorino* role. This fine recording has plenty of vocal polish. Scimone's biggest asset is Marilyn Horne as Isabella: possibly the finest Rossini singer of her generation and a veteran in this role, she sings Rossini's demanding music with great virtuosity and polish. Her liquid tone and artful phrasing ensure that she is a continuous pleasure to listen to. She is strongly supported by the rest of the cast: Kathleen Battle is a beguiling Elvira, Domenico Trimarchi a most humorous Taddeo, and Samuel Ramey a sonorous Bey of Algiers. Ernesto Palacio's Lindoro, however, has patches of white tone and is correct rather than inspiring. Scimone's conducting is guaranteed to give considerable pleasure.

Semiramide

Dame Joan Sutherland *sop* Semiramide; **Marilyn Horne** *mez* Arsace; **Joseph Rouleau** *bass* Assur; **John Serge** *ten* Idreno; **Patricia Clark** *sop* Azema; **Spiro Malas** *bass* Oroe; **Michael Langdon** *bass* Ghost of Nino; **Leslie Fryson** *ten* Mitrane; **Ambrosian Opera Chorus; London Symphony Orchestra / Richard Bonynge**

Decca ③ 425 481-2DM3 (168 minutes: ADD). Notes, Ⓜ text and translation included. Recorded 1966 ⭘⭘

Wagner thought it represented all that was bad about Italian opera and Kobbe's *Complete Opera Book* proclaimed that it had had its day – but then added that 'were a soprano and contralto to appear in conjunction in the firmament the opera might be successfully revived'. That was exactly what happened in the 1960s, when both Sutherland and Horne were in superlative voice and, with Richard Bonynge, were prominent in the reintroduction of so many 19th-century operas which the world thought it had outgrown. This recording brought a good deal of enlightenment in its time. For one thing, here was vocal music of such 'impossible' difficulty being sung with brilliance by the two principal women and with considerable skill by the men. Then it brought to many listeners the discovery that, so far from being a mere show piece, the opera contained ensembles of quite compelling dramatic intensity. People who had heard of the duet 'Giorno d'orrore' were surprised to find it remarkably unshowy and even expressive of the ambiguous feelings of mother and son in their extraordinary predicament. It will probably be a long time before this recording is superseded.

Il Signor Bruschino

Samuel Ramey *bass* Gaudenzio; **Claudio Desderi** *bar* Bruschino padre; **Kathleen Battle** *sop* Sofia; **Frank Lopardo** *ten* Florville; **Michele Pertusi** *bass* Filiberto; **Jennifer Larmore** *mez* Marianna; **Octavio Arévalo** *ten* Bruschino figlio, Commissario; **English Chamber Orchestra / Ion Marin**

DG 435 865-2GH (76 minutes: DDD). Notes, text and Ⓕ translation included. Recorded 1991

Witty and sentimental but also at times cruel, *Il Signor Bruschino* is the last, and arguably the best, of the one-acters Rossini wrote for the tiny Teatro San Moisè in Venice between 1810 and January 1813. These early *farse* can get by on tolerably good singing. What they can't do without is first-rate conducting – and on record clear, sharply defined orchestral sound. Choosing between the conducting of DG's Ion Marin and Claves's Marcello Viotti isn't all that difficult. Marin is far more vital; and what a cast there is on DG – a cast so expert and experienced they can't fail to bring the score wonderfully to life. Central to the whole enterprise is the Bruschino of Desderi, a superbly rounded portrait of a man who, despite the sweltering heat and the machinations of everyone around him, finally gives as good as he gets. Ramey's portrait of Gaudenzio is masterly, acted with relish and richly sung. Battle gives a ravishing account of Sofia's aria 'Ah!, donate il caro sposo' with its cor anglais colourings. This *Bruschino* is probably the one to have. One may occasionally have reservations about the conducting and the focus of the recording, but it's hard to imagine a better-cast account.

Tancredi

Ewa Podles *contr* Tancredi; **Sumi Jo** *sop* Amenaide; **Stanford Olsen** *ten* Argirio; **Pietro Spagnoli** *bar* Orbazzano; **Anna Maria di Micco** *sop* Isaura; **Lucretia Lendi** *mez* Roggiero; **Capella Brugensis; Collegium Instrumentale Brugense / Alberto Zedda**

Naxos ② 8 660037/8 (147 minutes: DDD). Notes Ⓢ and Italian text included. Recorded 1994 ○

Tancredi is a seminal work in the Rossini canon, a work which mingles a new-found reach in the musical architecture with vocal and instrumental writing of rare wonderment and beauty. The singing is splendid throughout, with a cast that is unusually starry. Podles has sung the role of Tancredi (to acclaim) at La Scala, Milan; the Amenaide, Sumi Jo, is a touch cool at first, too much the pert coloratura but this is not an impression that persists. Hers is a performance of wonderful vocal control and flowering sensibility. Podles, a smoky-voiced Pole, likes to go her own way at times. In the event, though, she and Sumi Jo work well together, and they sound marvellous. Podles also manages, chameleon-like, to adjust to the purer, more obviously stylish Rossini manner of a singer who is very unlike herself, the American tenor Stanford Olsen. His portrait of the conscience-stricken father Argirio matches singing of grace and impetus with great fineness of dramatic sensibility. As a result, something like the scene of the signing of his daughter's death-warrant emerges here as the remarkable thing it is. Zedda is lucky to have at his disposal another of those wonderfully stylish chamber orchestras and chamber choirs that Naxos seem able to conjure at will. The aqueously lovely preface to Tancredi's first entrance is a fairly representative example of the players' ear for Rossini's delicately-limned tone-painting. And the recording itself is beautifully scaled. As usual with Naxos, you get a multilingual synopsis plus an original-language libretto without translation. All in all, then, this is a fine set.

Il turco in Italia

Awards 1998

Michele Pertusi *bass* Selim; **Cecilia Bartoli** *mez* Fiorilla; **Alessandro Corbelli** *bar* Don Geronio; **Ramón Vargas** *ten* Don Narciso; **Laura Polverelli** *mez* Zaida; **Francesco Piccoli** *ten* Albazar; **Roberto de Candia** *bar* Prosdocimo; **Chorus and Orchestra of La Scala, Milan / Riccardo Chailly**

Decca ② 458 924-2DHO2 (142 minutes: DDD) Ⓕ Notes, text and translation included. Recorded 1997 ○○○

Add a star mezzo of Cecilia Bartoli's stature to a conductor of Riccardo Chailly's sympathies and *Il turco in Italia* was asking to be recorded. Chailly, of course, has recorded the work before – for CBS back in 1981 – but in the years since, he has matured as a Rossini conductor and the Scala orchestra has this music under its collective fingers; indeed there is an energy and vitality to this playing that is wholly infectious. For Chailly's earlier recording, Montserrat Caballé was a very underpowered Fiorilla; Bartoli is full of fire and mettle (her 'Sqallido veste bruna' is sensational). Michele Pertusi is a fine Selim and his performance seems to breathe stage experience – it is a characterization that is as vocally fine as it is theatrically adept. Alessandro Corbelli, reinforcing his credentials as a Rossini singer of flair and panache, is a strongly characterised

Geronio. This is a recording that smacks of the theatre, and unlike so many so-called comic operas, has lost nothing in its transfer to disc. Under Chailly's baton it fizzes and crackles like few other sets – recitatives are dispatched with the assurance of native Italian speakers and with a genuine feeling for the meaning of the text. Decca's recording is beautifully judged and the set makes a fine modern alternative to the now classic (but cut) 1954 recording under Gavazzeni with Maria Callas.

Nino Rota

Italian 1911-1979

GROVE *Rota studied at the Milan Conservatory, privately with Pizzetti (1925-6), with Casella in Rome, and at the Curtis Institute (1931-2). In 1939 he joined the staff at the Bari Conservatory (director from 1950). He wrote fluently in a cool, direct style: his output includes operas (notably The Italian Straw Hat, 1955), three symphonies, concertos and instrumental pieces, besides numerous film scores (many for Fellini, Visconti and Zeffirelli).*

Symphonies

No 1 in G; No 2 in F, 'Tarantina – Anni di pellegrinaggio'
Norrköping Symphony Orchestra / Ole Kristian Ruud Ⓕ
BIS CD970 (63 minutes: DDD). Recorded 1998

It is fascinating to encounter these early works by Nino Rota, written when he was in his twenties, after a period of study in the USA. Rota's early career was as a church musician, something to which he returned late in life, after decades composing for the screen and the theatre. The influences in the First Symphony (1935-39) include Sibelius and Stravinsky but perhaps more significantly Copland and Hindemith. It is clearly a youthful work, a bit long-winded, but showing Rota's already firm grasp of complicated and sophisticated orchestration. The last, fourth, movement especially seems to have a maturity that points towards future greatness.

The Second Symphony, which he began while still at work on the First, in 1937, is even more Coplandesque. What would this have sounded like to an audience in the 1930s (it wasn't performed until 1970)? In one way it would have seemed conservative in the extreme, showing no tendency towards atonality or any influence of jazz. The score carries a subtitle, 'Tarantina – Anni di pellegrinaggio', referring to the period Rota spent in the extreme south of Italy, teaching in Taranto. It could be dismissed as 'light music' and the style wouldn't have offended the most sensitive ears, yet each movement is full of beautiful instrumental detail and constructed in a pleasing way. Rota had yet to find his unmistakable voice, one infused with irony and humour, which would make him the perfect match for Federico Fellini. Devotees of his film music may find these symphonies bland, but anyone who enjoys the contemporary style of Alwyn or Coates in England will find these works worthwhile. The orchestra plays both symphonies with a good sense of period manner, never overdoing the lush sound. Recommended for the adventurous.

Piano Concertos

Piano Concertos – E minor; C
Massimo Palumbo *pf* **I Virtuosi Italiani / Marco Boni**
Chandos CHAN9681 (64 minutes: DDD) Ⓕ
Recorded 1998 ⊙

Both of these works are unashamedly romantic and nostalgic in style. The E minor Piano Concerto was composed in 1960 – at the same time as Rota's music for Fellini's film *La dolce vita*. As if in answer to the latter's extreme cynicism, the concerto seems to be a questioning exploration of the remaining possibilities in a modern, romantic form. The opening *Allegro-tranquillo* movement begins with a dreamlike theme on the piano which is then taken up by the orchestra and developed as a sort of conversation – the orchestra insisting on a heroic, almost martial sound, while the piano and woodwind reiterate the original soft mood. The first movement is over 16 minutes: away from the rule of the film-editor's stop-watch Rota felt free to indulge himself. The same four-note figure that runs through the opening is taken up in the second movement, a quiet, slow section with a haunting intensity. The finale continues the awake-in-a-dream contrasts. Rota composed four piano concertos, but the date of that in C major seems to be in doubt. It is earlier than 1960, and is a sparer, jauntier work, more redolent in mood of the 1920s. It, too, presents a dialogue between the quest-like piano part and the orchestra asserting a darker mood. Both concertos are played by Massimo Palumbo with brilliant technique, the recorded sound is excellent.

Film Music

The Godfather. Il gattopardo. Prova d'orchestra. La dolce vita. Otto e mezzo. Rocco e i suoi fratelli
La Scala Philharmonic Orchestra / Riccardo Muti
Sony Classical SK63359 (71 minutes: DDD) Ⓕ
Recorded 1979 ⊙

The influences on Nino Rota's music for *The Godfather* aren't hard to identify – Stravinsky, Ravel, Puccini. It's an ironic commentary on the sordid story to back it with surging neo-romantic symphonic music. Coppola's two-part epic of Italian immigrants in the USA and the drift into mob rule was probably the biggest assignment of Rota's long career. The score made a huge contribution to the film's success – so much so that after his death the studio returned to his music for *Godfather III*. Its mixture of Neapolitan folk-song spattered with jazzy honky-tonk makes for a pleasant opening to this second CD of Rota's music by Riccardo Muti and the Scala Philharmonic. Rota's career was inextricably bound up with those of the two most influential Italian film-makers of the 1950s and 1960s –

Fellini and Visconti. Fellini's two big successes of the early 1960s, *La dolce vita* and *Otto e mezzo* are represented by brief extracts – the open-air circus-parade finale of the latter score still has a mysterious, exuberant feel. The sources Rota drew on for this are similar to those in *The Godfather* but his use of them is surer and more original. The last collaboration with Fellini was the comedy about a rehearsal – *Prova d'orchestra*. Time is not being kind to a lot of Fellini's work which now seems self-indulgent, but conversely Visconti's films have a massive grandeur that is overwhelming. Muti's first volume of Rota had the ballroom sequence; here there is a brief suite of themes from the film. *Rocco e i suoi fratelli* caused a scandal in Italy in 1960 with its depiction of organised crime and corruption and it led to Visconti's rift with La Scala because of government interference. He would surely have smiled to think, nearly 40 years later, of the orchestra playing Rota's score for the film.

Albert Roussel

French 1869-1937

GROVE *After embarking on a naval career, in 1894 Roussel began studies with Gigout, moving on to train with d'Indy and others at the Schola Cantorum (1898-1908) where in 1902 he began teaching. In 1909 he made a tour of India and Indo-China, and he drew on that experience in writing his Hindu opera-ballet Padmâvatî; (1923), though other works, like the vocal-orchestral Evocations (1911) and ballet Le festin de l'araignée (1913), had already shown his ability to leaven d'Indyism with exotic material and Ravellian brilliance. In the Symphony No 2 (1921), he moved on to an almost polytonal density, but in the 1920s his music (like Ravel's) became more spare and astringent, though still with a rhythmic vigour and motivic intensity that can be seen as a highly personal extension of Schola thinking. His later, neo-classical works, marked by wide-ranging regular themes and motoric rhythms, include the Symphonies Nos 3 and 4, the orchestral Suite in F, the Piano Concerto, the String Quartet and two ballets, Bacchus et Ariane and Aenéas*

Bacchus et Ariane

Bacchus et Ariane, Op 43. Le festin de l'araignée, Op 17
BBC Philharmonic Orchestra / Yan Pascal Tortelier
Chandos CHAN9494 (68 minutes: DDD) Ⓕ
Recorded 1995

As compared to his contemporary Dukas, Roussel has been somewhat sidelined as a 'connoisseur's composer'. That presumably means that he did not write fat, lush tunes that could be exploited in television commercials, but produced works of vigorous ideas and more subtle quality. Record companies used to fight shy of his music – the Third and Fourth Symphonies have indeed maintained a foothold, but with the ballet *Bacchus et Ariane*, which is closely linked with the Third, we have mostly been given only its second half. Here are alert, rhythmically vital performances of Roussel's two most famous ballets, which even at the most exuberantly excited moments (like the 'Bacchanale' in *Bacchus*) preserve a truly Gallic lucidity, and which Tortelier marks by a captivating lightness of touch; and when it comes to quiet passages one could not ask for greater tenderness than in the beautiful end of Act 1 of *Bacchus* (shame on those conductors who neglect this for the more extrovert Act 2), when Bacchus puts Ariadne to sleep.

Le festin de l'araignée, written 18 years earlier, is in a quite different style. Where *Bacchus*'s trenchant idiom at times makes one think of Stravinsky's *Apollon Musagète*, *Le festin* (which had the misfortune to be overshadowed by the *Rite of Spring*, produced only eight weeks later) is atmospheric and more impressionistic (in the same vein as Roussel's First Symphony). It is a score full of delicate invention, whose one weakness is that for its full appreciation a knowledge of its detailed programme is needed – and that is provided here in the booklet. The BBC Philharmonic play it beautifully. If this is 'connoisseur's music', then be happy to be called a connoisseur: you will find it delectable.

Symphony No 3

Roussel Symphony No 3 in G minor, Op 42
Franck Symphony in D minor
French National Orchestra / Leonard Bernstein
DG Masters 445 512-2GMA (69 minutes: DDD) Ⓜ
Recorded live in 1981

This 1981 Roussel Third is recognizably via Bernstein, and is more kaleidoscopic and meaningful than you are likely to have heard it, unless you possess his first New York account. The *Rite of Spring*-cum-*Age of Steel* stamping rhythms of the first movement are now a little slower, the effect possibly a little relaxed until you arrive at the central climax (astonishing 'whooping' horns and crashing metal) and the coda (now superbly emphatic with ringing trumpets and lots more crashing metal). The slow movement's songful yearning is, as it was before, slow, sublime and intensely searching in the manner of its counterpart in Mahler's Sixth, though the contrasting *più mosso* is not now fast enough and has its limp moments. That said, the general control is superior, particularly at and around the movement's now awesome final climax. Bernstein's New Yorkers were uninhibitedly rowdy and brash in the finale; the finale's moments of brashness are now offset by rather more sophistication (at, again, a slower tempo).

The recording, which has a less than ideally focused bass drum, is both spacious and present, with an appropriate touch of astringency on top. Bernstein's Franck is atmospheric, big on rhetoric, extreme in its range of tempo and dynamics and typically intense. On the grand return in the finale of the slow movement's theme, Bernstein broadens massively. Vulgar? Perhaps, depending on your viewpoint. His control is again superb, with the orchestra's winds mellifluous in tone.

Miklós Rózsa

Hungarian/American 1907-1995

Raised in Budapest and on his father's rural estate, Rósza was exposed to Hungarian folk music from an early age. He studied piano with his mother (who was at the Budapest Academy with Bartók) and violin and viola with his uncle, a musician with the Royal Hungrian Opera. By the age of seven he was composing. In 1926 he was a student at the Leipzig Conservatory; by 1929 his chamber works were being performed and promoted throughout Europe. In 1931 moved to Paris where he finished his Theme, Variations and Finale, a work that soon gained international recognition. He was introduced to the film music genre through Honegger and from 1935-39 composed for London Films under Hungarian-born producer Alexander Korda. In 1940 he travelled with Korda to Hollywood to complete the score of The Thief of Baghdad and was soon in great demand as a freelance film composer and conductor. As a staff member at MGM (1948-62), he became one of the most highly regarded composers in the industry, writing music for over 100 films. The essence of his musical style springs from his early experiences with Hungarian peasant music. His works are also infused with the sentimental lyricism of the gypsy tradition.

Cello Concerto, Op 32

Piano Concerto, Op 31. Cello Concerto, Op 32
Brinton Smith *vc* **Evelyn Chen** *pf* **New Zealand Symphony Orchestra / James Sedares**
Koch International Classics 37402-2 Ⓕ
(62 minutes: DDD). Recorded 1997

The uncomfortably cavernous, slightly synthetic sound picture doesn't really do full justice to the soloists' sterling efforts, we would therefore recommend newcomers to the Rejto/Williams version ahead of this admittedly altogether more commanding recording. Enthusiasts, on the other hand, will be delighted to learn that the two performances on this disc complement each other beautifully: the sheer bravura of Smith's reading is infectious, whereas Rejto is a degree more reticent. The Piano Concerto (1966) is big-boned, virtuosic in the extreme and full of the most engaging local colour; it is cast in traditional three-movement form, the finale being an especially eventful creation. What's more, Rózsa's unerring sense of proportion ensures that the work never threatens to outstay its welcome. Chen is a dazzlingly secure, sympathetic exponent, and she builds a fine rapport with Sedares and the NZSO. Happily, the resonant acoustic is noticeably better controlled here, and the balance is excellent.

Violin Concerto, Op 24[a]. Cello Concerto, Op 32[b]. Tema con variazioni, Op 29*a*[c]
[ac]**Robert McDuffie** *vn* [bc]**Lynn Harrell** *vc* **Atlanta Symphony Orchestra / Yoel Levi**
Telarc CD80518 (72 minutes: DDD) Ⓕ
Recorded 1999 ●

Miklós Rózsa completed his dashingly eloquent Cello Concerto in 1968 for János Starker. Not only is Telarc's engineering incomparably more vivid and realistic than that of its predecessors, the actual performance is the most irreproachably stylish and urgently impassioned of the bunch. Lynn Harrell brings all his commanding presence, customary swagger and cast-iron technique to Rózsa's strikingly idiomatic solo writing. Add a polished and enthusiastic response from the Atlanta Symphony under Yoel Levi's eagle-eyed direction, and the results are exhilarating. Written in 1953-54 for Jascha Heifetz, the irresistibly colourful and sublimely lyrical Violin Concerto remains perhaps the most popular of all Rózsa's 'serious' compositions. While Heifetz's inimitable 1956 recording (see under Korngold) enshrines one of the most treasurable specimens of his jaw-dropping virtuosity, this newcomer possesses many sterling strengths of its own. Robert McDuffie makes a dauntingly accurate, sweet-toned soloist, producing the most radiant sonorities in the ravishing, Kodály-esque slow movement, while Levi and his Atlanta band once again prove model partners. Last but not least, McDuffie joins forces with Harrell for the engaging and eventful *Tema con variazioni* which originally began life as the centrepiece of the Op 29 *Sinfonia concertante* penned in 1958 for Heifetz and cellist Gregor Piatigorsky. Again, the performance is utterly sympathetic and stands up perfectly well to that legendary 1963 Heifetz/Piatigorsky collaboration.

Works for Violin and Piano

Variations on a Hungarian Peasant Song, Op 4. North Hungarian Peasant Songs and Dances, Op 5. Duo, Op 7. Solo Violin Sonata, Op 40
Isabella Lippi *vn* **John Novacek** *pf*
Koch International Classics 37256-2 Ⓕ
(62 minutes: DDD). Recorded 1994 ●

In his autobiography, *A Double Life* (Midas Books: 1982) Rózsa proudly declares that 'the music of Hungary is stamped indelibly…on virtually every bar I have ever put on paper', and nowhere are the fervent, rustic rhythms of the composer's beloved homeland more vividly assimilated than in his music for solo violin.

This is especially true of Opp 4 and 5, two early successes from 1929, both of which blaze with potent memories of the Magyar peasant music that Rózsa felt was all around him, and which he would jot down 'in a kind of delirium' during his youth on the family estate. Op 7 was written two years later and marked the end of his term as a student in Leipzig. Though evoking once again the gipsy fiddlers of his boyhood, the themes here are actually Rózsa's own and reveal some of the surging romanticism that would later characterise his film scores.

Following his memorable career in Hollywood, Rózsa made a satisfying return to 'pure' music with the Solo Violin Sonata of 1986. This passionate, energetic piece pays another loving tribute to the mother country that provided Rózsa with a 'living source of inspiration'. Isabella Lippi is a highly expressive soloist. She tackles the fiendishly animated passages with great panache but also displays a keen understanding of the music's pastoral colouring and darkly romantic fervour. Sympathetic support from her accompanist and clear, warm sound.

Edmund Rubbra British 1901-1986

GROVE *Rubbra, a pupil of Scott and of Holst and Morris at the Royal College of Music (1921-25), worked as a pianist, teacher and critic before his appointment as lecturer at Oxford (1947-68). His music took some while to develop independence from Ireland, Bax and Holst, but his First Symphony (1937) begins to show a characteristic style of rhapsodic growth tautened by thematic working and almost incessant polyphonic activity. His later works include 10 more symphonies, of which No 9 is an oratorio-like work (Sinfonia sacra, 1972), besides concertos for viola, piano and violin, four string quartets (1933-77), masses and motets (he became a Roman Catholic in 1948).*

Symphonies Nos 3 and 7

Symphony No 3, Op 49. Symphony No 7 in C, Op 88
BBC National Orchestra of Wales / Richard Hickox
Chandos CHAN9634 (71 minutes: DDD) Ⓕ
Recorded 1997 **OO**

For some years the Third Symphony was a repertory piece, at least on BBC programmes, but it fell completely out of favour in the late 1950s. Commentators have noticed a certain Sibelian cut to its opening idea (with woodwind in thirds) but everything else strikes you as being completely personal. There is a whiff of Elgarian fantasy in the fourth variation of the finale. It has been called the most genial and relaxed of Rubbra's symphonies but there is a pastoral feel to many of the ideas, bucolic even, in the same way that there is about the Brahms Second Symphony. Brahms springs to mind in the masterly variations and fugue of the finale, for not long before, Rubbra had orchestrated the Brahms *Handel* Variations.

Richard Hickox and his fine players give a very persuasive and totally convincing account of the symphony. Anyone coming to the Seventh for the first time, particularly in this performance, will surely not fail to sense the elevated – indeed exalted – quality of its musical thought. Its opening paragraphs are among the most beautiful Rubbra ever penned and it is evident throughout that this is music that speaks of deep and serious things. This performance speaks with great directness and power. The horn playing in the opening is eloquent and the orchestral playing throughout is of a uniformly high standard. To sum up, these are magnificent and impressive accounts and the recording is truthful and splendidly balanced.

Symphonies Nos 4, 10 and 11

Symphony No 4, Op 53. Symphony No 10, 'Sinfonia da camera', Op 145. Symphony No 11, Op 153
BBC National Orchestra of Wales / Richard Hickox
Chandos CHAN9401 (58 minutes: DDD) Ⓕ
Recorded 1993-94 **O**

Rubbra's music lacks the kind of surface allure that captivates the ear at first acquaintance, but he does have a sense of organic continuity that is both highly developed and immediately evident to the listener. Wilfrid Mellers put it in a nutshell when he said of the symphonies, there is 'nothing abstruse about their tonality and harmony', but they are difficult because 'the continuity of their melodic and polyphonic growth is logical and unremitting. The orchestration shows scarcely any concern for the possibilities of colour, nothing on which the senses can linger and the nerves relax. Second subjects are hardly ever contrasting ideas but rather evolutions from or transfigurations of the old.' The opening of the Fourth Symphony is one of the most beautiful things in the English music of our time. These pages are free from any artifice, and their serenity remains with the listener for a long time. The Fourth (1940-42) was a wartime work, though no one would ever guess so. The 10th and 11th Symphonies are from 1974 and 1979 respectively. Both are concentrated one-movement affairs that unfold with seeming inevitability and naturalness. To sum up, this is music made to last. Richard Hickox has the measure of its breadth and serenity, and secures total commitment from his excellent players. The Chandos recording is in the best traditions of the house.

Additional recommendations

Symphonies Nos 3 and 4
Couplings. A Tribute for Ralph Vaughan Williams on his 70th Birthday. Resurgam Overture
Philharmonia Orchestra / Del Mar
Lyrita SRCD202 (73 minutes: DDD: 11/90) Ⓕ

Dedicated performances of these superb symphonies under Normal Del Mar. The coupling *Resurgam*, a late work of great beauty, is particularly welcome.

Symphonies Nos 2 and 7
Coupling: Festival Overture
London Philharmonic Orchestra / Boult; New Philharmonia Orchestra / Handley
Lyrita SRCD235 (78 minutes: ADD: 12/92) Ⓕ

Rubbra possessed a keen sense of nature's power and you can certainly feel it in the haunting opening of the Seventh Symphony. Fine performances, excellently transferred.

Symphonies Nos 5 and 8

Symphony No 5 in B flat, Op 63. Symphony No 8, 'Hommage à Teilhard de Chardin', Op 132. Ode to the Queen, Op 83[a]
[a]**Susan Bickley** *mez* **BBC National Orchestra of Wales / Richard Hickox**
Chandos CHAN9714 (64 minutes: DDD) Ⓕ
Text included. Recorded 1998

In the early 1950s Rubbra's Fifth Symphony was a repertory piece and broadcast frequently. Ten years later it had all but disappeared from programmes, and although a second recording was made by the late Hans-Hubert Schönzeler, this is its first digital recording, and the finest account of the Fifth Symphony ever recorded. Part of the success of Richard Hickox's series is his instinctive feeling for the tempo at which this music best comes to life and his scrupulous adherence to dynamic markings. Find the right tempo and everything falls into place; observe every dynamic nuance and the textures achieve the right degree of transparency. Of course the quality of the recording also plays an important part: there is great detail, presence and warmth.

The Eighth Symphony (1966-8), subtitled *Hommage à Teilhard de Chardin*, was composed in a very different climate, for by the late 1960s Rubbra's music was out of fashion. The new symphony had to wait three years for its first performance in Liverpool. Teilhard de Chardin was a French Jesuit priest, a philosopher and palaeontologist, whose thought had a great influence on Rubbra. The music's mystical feel and luminous texture are at times reminiscent of Holst. The Eighth speaks of deep and serious things and in this performance proves a powerful musical experience. *The Ode to the Queen*, is something of a discovery. Commissioned by the BBC to celebrate the Coronation of the Queen, it is Rubbra's only song-cycle with full orchestra. The songs are highly inspired and beautifully sung here by Susan Bickley. A triumphant conclusion, then, to Richard Hickox's Rubbra cycle.

Additional recommendation

Symphony No 5

Couplings: Farnaby Improvisations. **Britten** Violin Concerto. **Heming** Threnody for a Soldier killed in Action

Olof *vn* **Hallé Orchestra / Barbirolli**

EMI British Composers CDM5 66053-2 Ⓕ

(71 minutes: ADD: 5/97)

A fascinating and rewarding release. Barbirolli's pioneering 1950 recording of Rubbra's Fifth is a delight from start to finish, and his Heming *Threnody* is hauntingly beautiful.

Further listening

Piston Symphony No 4. Couplings: Capriccio. Serenata. Three New England Sketches

Wunrow *hp* **Seattle Symphony Orchestra; New York Chamber Symphony Orchestra / Schwarz**

Delos DE3106 (64 minutes: DDD: 7/92) Ⓕ

If you like Rubbra's Fifth then try Piston's Fourth. Schwarz makes a strong case for this undeservedly under-recorded score, with its soul-searching, near atonal third movement.

Symphony No 9

Symphony No 9, 'Sinfonia sacra', Op 140. The Morning Watch, Op 55

Lynne Dawson *sop* **Della Jones** *mez* **Stephen Roberts** *bar* **BBC National Chorus and Orchestra of Wales / Richard Hickox**

Chandos CHAN9441 (57 minutes: DDD) Ⓕ

Texts included. Recorded 1993 ●

The Ninth (1973) is Rubbra's most visionary utterance and its stature has so far gone unrecognised (this is its only recording). Its subtitle, *Sinfonia sacra*, gives a good idea of its character. It tells the story of the Resurrection very much as do the Bach Passions. There are three soloists: the contralto narrates from the New Testament while the soprano takes the part of Mary Magdalen and the baritone that of Jesus. Other parts – those of disciples and angels – are taken by the chorus which also functions outside the action, in four settings of meditative Latin texts from the Roman liturgy or in Lutheran chorales to which Rubbra has put verses by Bernard de Nevers. The symphonic dimension is reinforced by the opening motive, which pretty well dominates the work. Its argument unfolds with a seeming inevitability and naturalness that is the hallmark of a great symphony.

Its depth and beauty call to mind only the most exalted of comparisons and it should be heard as often as *Gerontius* or the *War Requiem*. This is music of an inspired breadth and serenity and everyone connected with this magnificent performance conveys a sense of profound conviction. *The Morning Watch* is one of Rubbra's most eloquent choral pieces. It dates from 1946, and so comes roughly half-way between the Fourth and Fifth Symphonies. A setting of the 17th-century metaphysical poet, Henry Vaughan, it too is music of substance and its long and moving orchestral introduction is of the highest order of inspiration. Hickox and his fine team of singers and players deserve thanks and congratulations, as indeed does Chandos.

Piano Trios

Piano Trios – No 1 'in one movement', Op 68[a]; No 2, Op 138[f]. Meditazioni sopra 'Coeurs désolés', Op 67[b]. Phantasy, Op 16[c]. Sonata for Oboe and Piano in C, Op 100[d]. The Buddah – Suite (arr Cruft)[e]. Duo, Op 156[g]

Endymion Ensemble ([e]Helen Keen *fl* [bdeg]Melinda Maxwell *ob* [acef]Krysia Osostowicz, [c]Catherine Manson *vns* [e]Catherine Manson *va* [aef]Jane Salmon *vc* [abcdfg]Michael Dussek *pf*)

Dutton Laboratories Epoch CDLX7106 Ⓜ

(77 minutes: DDD). Recorded 2000 ●

How wise to kick off with the Piano Trio No 1 of 1950 – a magnificent beast, brimful of doughty integrity and always evincing a breathtaking contrapuntal scope. It is cast in a single movement, comprising an initial *Andante moderato* of glorious, long-breathed eloquence, a perky central *Episodio scherzando* and a concluding theme and three variations (labelled 'Meditazioni').

Like all of Rubbra's finest music, the score unfolds with an intuitive purpose and questing spirituality as awesome as it is rewarding, an observation that extends to its scarcely less imposing two-movement successor of 20 years later. The mood here is darker, more rarefied, the opening *Tempo moderato e deliberato* distilling a lofty austerity that not even the jaunty, syncopated rhythms of the *Allegro scherzando* second movement can quite dispel.

The remaining five items span virtually the whole of Rubbra's career. Even in the early *Phantasy* for two violins and piano (1927) Rubbra's burgeoning mastery of the flowing line and capacity for organic thought are already very much in evidence, the music's rapt, at times distinctly pastoral lyricism engagingly reminiscent of the young Herbert Howells's sublimely assured chamber offerings. It's a lovely work, as is the Suite for flute, oboe and string trio that Adrian Cruft prepared from Rubbra's incidental music to Clifford Bax's 1947 radio play, *The Buddha*. Of the two works for oboe, the appealing Sonata of 1958 (written for Evelyn Rothwell, later Lady Barbirolli) impresses by dint of its quiet cogency, while the 1949 *Meditazioni sopra 'Coeurs désolés'* (whose theme derives from Josquin's eponymous chanson) inhabits much the same gently ruminative landscape found in the last section of the Piano Trio No 1. That just leaves the deeply felt Duo for cor anglais and piano (Rubbra's very last chamber work, completed six years before his death in 1986).

Performances throughout are laudably poised and unstintingly dedicated; truthful sound and balance, too. A peach of a disc, not to be missed.

Further listening

Leighton Fantasy on an American Hymn Tune. Alleluia Pascha Nostrum. Variations. Piano Sonata
Hilton *cl* **R Wallfisch** *vc* **P Wallfisch** *pf*
Chandos CHAN9132 (70 minutes: DDD: 5/93) Ⓕ

Committed performances of some of Kenneth Leighton's imaginative and instrumentally challenging chamber music.

Violin Sonatas

Violin Sonatas[a] – No 1, Op 11; No 2, Op 31; No 3, Op 133. Four Pieces, Op 29[a]. Variations on a Phrygian Theme, Op 105
Krysia Osostowicz *vn* [a]**Michael Dussek** *pf*
Dutton Laboratories Epoch Series CDLX7101 Ⓜ
(59 minutes: DDD). Recorded 1999

A fine pianist and proficient violinist, Edmund Rubbra composed his First Violin Sonata in 1925 shortly after leaving the Royal College of Music. It's a notable achievement all round: its first two movements exhibit a bittersweet lyricism that will strike a chord with anyone who has ever responded to, say, John Ireland's glorious Second Violin Sonata or the chamber music of Howells. By contrast, the 'Fugal Rondo' finale intriguingly pursues an altogether more sturdy, determinedly neo-classical mode of expression. Written six years later in 1931, the Second Sonata already reveals a wider emotional scope, as well as a striking use of progressive tonality that at least one contemporary critic found 'disturbing and unnecessary'. Championed by the great Albert Sammons, it will come as a substantial discovery to many: comprising an eventful, ever-evolving first movement, a strong, but never sentimental 'Lament' centrepiece, and a quasi-Bartókian finale, its wild exuberance seems to look forward across the decades to the last movement of this same figure's Violin Concerto of 1959.

Framing that are the 1926 *Four Pieces* for beginners and the unaccompanied *Variations on a Phrygian Theme* that Rubbra composed in 1961 as a 50th birthday tribute for Frederick Grinke – a work of miracle compact resourcefulness. But even finer is the Third Sonata. It's a simply wondrous piece, its sense of purpose, rapt intuition and profound serenity irresistibly calling to mind Rubbra's Eighth Symphony, and it fully deserves the exalted advocacy it receives on this enterprising anthology. Indeed, Osostowicz and Dussek form an outstandingly sympathetic partnership.

Further listening

Ireland Violin Sonatas – No 1 in D minor; No 2 in A minor
Couplings: Bagatelle. Berceuse. Cavatina. The Holy Boy (arr cpsr) **Barritt** *vn* **Edwards** *pf*
Hyperion CDA66853 (66 minutes: DDD: 11/96) Ⓕ

A passionate, superbly disciplined reading of John Ireland's glorious Second Violin Sonata – the work that virtually established his reputation overnight.

Vocal Works

Missa Cantuariensis, Op 59[ab]. Magnificat and Nunc dimittis in A flat, Op 65[ab]. Missa in honorem Sancti Dominici, Op 66[a]. Prelude and Fugue on a Theme of Cyril Scott, Op 69 (arr Rose)[b]. Tenebrae, Op 72[a]. Meditation, Op 79[b]
[a]**St John's College Choir, Cambridge / Christopher Robinson** [b]*org*
Naxos 8 555255 (71 minutes: DDD) Ⓢ
Texts and translations included. Recorded 2000

With this valuable new Rubbra anthology Christopher Robinson and his St John's College Choir reinforces the favourable impression left by previous instalments in their English Choral Music series for Naxos. They prove especially eloquent, humane advocates of the eight-part *Missa Cantuariensis* (composed, as its name suggests, for Canterbury Cathedral and first sung there in July 1946). We've long needed a top-notch digital recording of this, the first of Rubbra's five Mass settings. Fortunately Robinson and company rise to the challenge admirably, not least in the exuberant concluding *Gloria* with its lung-burstingly high tessitura. We also get a thoroughly idiomatic rendering of the taut and imposing *Magnificat* and *Nunc dimittis* in A flat that Rubbra wrote two years later.

In the glorious *Missa in honorem Sancti Dominici* from 1949 (inspired by Rubbra's own conversion to Roman Catholicism the previous year, on the feast day of St Dominic) our Cambridge group doesn't quite match the sumptuous blend, miraculous unanimity or spine-tingling fervour displayed by James O'Donnell's Westminster Cathedral Choir (to quote the composer: '...this is not austere music: it may seem emaciated in its printed appearance, but red blood runs through its veins!'). On the other hand, these newcomers sound wholly captivated by the nine motets that make up the remarkable Op 72 *Tenebrae* (the first three dating from 1951, the remainder a decade later). Boasting an infinitely subtle harmonic and contrapuntal resource, these timeless, wonderfully compassionate settings of the responsories used during Matins on Maundy Thursday show Rubbra very much at the height of his powers, encompassing an extraordinarily wide dramatic and expressive range (witness the anguished 'Judas mercator pessimus' with its jagged tritones, or those jaw-droppingly potent triadic harmonies in the central portion of 'Una hora non potuistis').

Robinson also gives us two instrumental bonuses in the rapt *Meditation* for organ, Op 79, and Bernard Rose's transcription of the more substantial *Prelude and Fugue on a Theme of Cyril Scott* (originally written for piano in 1950 to celebrate Scott's 70th birthday). Throw in Naxos's praiseworthy production and helpful presentation, and you have a bargain of the first order.

Rubbra A Hymn to the Virgin, Op 13[ab]. Rosa mundi, Op 2[ab]. Fukagawa[b]. Pezzo ostinato, Op 102[b]. Songs, Op 4 – The Mystery[a]; Jesukin[ab]. Orpheus with his Lute, Op 8[ab]. Transformations, Op 141[b]. The Jade Mountain, Op 116[ab]. Improvisation, Op 124[c]. Discourse, Op 127[bc] **L Berkeley** Nocturne[b] **Howells** Prelude[b]
[a]**Tracey Chadwell** *sop* [b]**Danielle Perrett** *hp*
[c]**Tim Gill** *vc*
ASV CDDCA1036 (67 minutes: DDD) Ⓕ
Texts included. Recorded 1995

All but 10 minutes of this CD is devoted to Rubbra and several works here are first recordings, including the impressive *Transformations* for harp, Op 141, and the early miniatures that open the disc, the *Hymn to the Virgin* and *Rosa mundi*. Both reflect the world of Holst and Scott. Many of the pieces also reflect the strong attraction Rubbra felt for the Orient, from the early *Fukagawa* arrangement (1929), to *The Jade Mountain* (1962), as well as the inspiring harp pieces: the *Pezzo ostinato* and the *Transformations*, the most extended (and perhaps the most exalted) piece on the disc. Both derive inspiration from the Indian *raga*. Perrett plays with finesse and sensitivity and her free, imaginative handling of the *Pezzo ostinato* is admirable. She brings authority to the *Improvisation*, Op 124 (1964). Chadwell proves an intelligent interpreter of the songs, although she appears more backwardly balanced and there is just a shade too much echo round her voice. Generally speaking, though, the recording is first-rate. The overall character of this music is meditative and readers should select a few pieces at a time. Both the Lennox Berkeley *Nocturne* and the Howells *Prelude* are attractive pieces. This is a must for Rubbra *aficionados*.

Additional recommendation

Rubbra Advent Cantata, 'Natum Maria Virgine'. Inscape. Four Medieval Latin Lyrics. Song of the Soul. Veni, creator Spiritus.
Varcoe *bar* **Academy of St Martin in the Fields Chorus; City of London Sinfonia / Hickox**
Chandos CHAN9847 (56 minutes: DDD: 01/01) Ⓕ

A valuable contribution to the Rubbra centenary. *Inscape* is a particularly impressive work. Fine performances, too.

Poul Ruders

Danish 1949

Ruders studied piano and organ at the Odense Conservatory and graduated from the Royal Danish Conservatory in 1975. He worked initially as a church organist and freelance keyboard player. Although he had some lessons from Nørholm and orchestration from Kar Rasmussen, he describes himself as an essentially self-taught composer.

Ruders is widely recognised as the leading Danish composer of his generation. The large proportion of his works are for orchestra or large chamber ensemble; some of his scores use electronic keyboards and samplers. Ruders has developed a flexible musical language, organised only by his own 'homespun' systems; freely atonal but able to incorporate tonal references. His command of idiomatic instrumental and vocal writing, his strong sense of drama and his readiness to explore extremes of experience enable him to communicate directly and powerfully with audiences.

Violin Concerto No 1

Violin Concerto No 1[a]. Etude and Ricercare[b]. The Bells[c]. The Christmas Gospel[d]
[c]**Lucy Shelton** *sop* [ab]**Rolf Schulte** *vn* [c]**Speculum Musicae / David Starobin** *gtr* [a]**Riverside Symphony Orchestra / George Rothman;** [d]**Malmö Symphony Orchestra / Ola Rudner**
Bridge BCD9057 (62 minutes: DDD) Texts included. Ⓕ
Recorded 1994-95 ●

Ruders's First Violin Concerto (from 1981) begins as routine minimalist auto-hypnosis. But it develops some wonderfully inventive ways of disrupting and reassembling itself. Admittedly the last movement, with its chaconne based on Vivaldi and Schubert, tiptoes on the border of sensationalism. Otherwise the work could join Schnittke's Fourth as one of the few contemporary violin concertos with a strong claim to standard-repertoire status. Schulte gives an intense account of the solo part; the Riverside orchestra is tight in discipline, the recording close. All these factors help to make the overall musical impression extremely vivid. Less persuasive is Ruders's vocal writing in *The Bells* (the same Edgar Allen Poe texts as set by Rachmaninov), and there is something not quite convincing about the instrumental setting too – perhaps too uniform an intensity, too much frantic heterophony. *The Christmas Gospel*, tossed off in two weeks for a mixed animation and live-action film, is darkly impressive – necessarily simple and direct, but still rewarding, even when divorced from the visual images.

Corpus cum figuris

Four Dances in One Movement. Dramaphonia. Corpus cum figuris
Erik Kaltoft *pf* **Aarhus Sinfonietta / Søren Kinch Hansen**
BIS CD720 (70 minutes: DDD) Ⓕ
Recorded 1995-96

The name *Corpus cum figuris* ('body with figurations') comes from Thomas Mann's novel about a fictional German composer, *Dr Faustus*. There's no programmatic significance, says Poul Ruders; it was the title itself that set his imagination working. At times the piece does sound like a grotesque, terrifying break-dance, full of jagged, joint-dismembering syncopations. But something of Mann's apocalyptic conception seems to have got into Ruders's music too – the smell of sulphur, the sense of prevailing desolation. It comes over well in this moody but very precise performance. So too does *Dramaphonia*, a one-movement piano concerto with an 'orchestra' of 11 instruments. This is more sombre still than *Corpus cum figuris*, the pace prevailingly slow and brooding. But Ruders knows how to hold the attention, even when very little seems to be happening. *Four Dances in One Movement* makes an excellent contrast. The darkness of the other two works isn't entirely absent from *Four Dances*, but the sweetly parodistic waltz tune of the second dance is delicious. Perhaps the performance could be a little more satirically stylish.

The Handmaid's Tale

Marianne Rørholm *mez* Offred; **Hanne Fischer** *mez* Double; **Poul Elming** *ten* Luke; **Ulla Kudsk Jensen** *mez* Offred's Mother; **Anne Margrethe Dahl** *sop* Aunt Lydia; **Dijna Mai-Mai** *sop* Moira; **Lise-Lotte Nielsen** *sop* Janine; **Annita Wadsholt** *contr* Moira's Aunt; **Susanne Resmark** *contr* Serena Joy; **Kari Hamnøy** *contr* Rita; **Aage Haugland** *bass* Commander; **Gert Henning-Jensen** *ten* Nick; **Elsebeth Lund** *sop* Ofglen; **Pia Hansen** *mez* New Ofglen; **Bengl-Ola Morgny** *ten* Doctor; **Elisabeth Halling** *mez* Warren's Wife; **John Laursen** *ten* Commander X; **Uffe Henriksen** *bass* First Eye and Guard; **Morten Kramp** *bass* Second Eye and Guard
Royal Danish Opera Chorus and Orchestra / Michael Schønwandt
Da Capo ② 8 224165/6 (144 minutes: DDD) Ⓕ
Notes, text and translation included
Recorded live in 2000 **OO**

Poul Ruders says of his vividly imaginative opera that he composed it 'as though I were directing a film'. Precisely: it is divided into 44 scenes, some very short, several incorporating flashbacks in which present and past sometimes appear simultaneously. The opera's 'present' is the not too distant future, a hideous fundamentalist autocracy in which women have no rights, not even to read and write, and those of them convicted of 'gender-treachery' (adultery, second marriage, contraception, abortion) are compelled to become 'Handmaids', ritually impregnated by the husbands of childless women. The central character, Offred (Of Fred – the name of the man whose property she now is), is portrayed by two singers: her present, brainwashed and imperfectly remembering self, and Offred as she was in 'Time Before', happily married (though as her husband's second wife a 'gender traitor' to the new order) with a five-year-old daughter. The opera, based on Margaret Atwood's novel, depicts the brutal totalitarianism of 'Time Now', Offred's relationship with the Commander (Fred) and his alarming wife, her longing for her dimly remembered husband and child and her enlistment in a sort of resistance group. But it is in the very nature of the plot that we never learn her ultimate fate.

It is also in the plot's nature that it needs a great variety of types of music, as we move from past to present, from the grim rituals of Time Now to Offred's memories of Time Before. Ambiguous music, too, since in this shadowy, threatening world things are often not what they seem. Ruder's great achievement is to provide that variety and ambiguity from within the resources of his own style, in particular, he balances on the tightrope from tonality to atonality with great skill. The rituals of the Handmaids are accompanied by simple, chorale-like chants with 'minimalist' accompaniment, but any suspicion that Ruders is equating tonality with evil and atonality or extended tonality with good is soon contradicted by a quite different use of quasi-minimalism in the scenes from Offred's past. There are similarly several types of lyricism: one heard, for example, in an aria for Offred, another in the menacing instructions of the Handmaid's supervisor Lydia. But neither can be simply classified as 'tonal' or 'atonal'; to call them respectively 'warm' and 'cold' would be closer to the mark. In the same way references to the hymn *Amazing Grace*, associated with the Commander's wife Serena Joy (formerly a Gospel singer), can be in context either nostalgic or deeply sinister. The most striking passage to emerge from the score is a duet for the two Offreds in which both voices seem to be yearning for a tonal resolution – probably in D – but can no more achieve it than two people 20 years apart in time can meet.

Ruders has been best known hitherto for his prodigiously resourceful orchestral writing, and he surpasses himself here: electronic keyboards, samplers and additional percussion are added to the large orchestra, but many of the strangest, most nightmarish or most radiant sounds are produced by normal instruments used with brilliant originality. Some of the more monstrous inhabitants of this nightmare world are portrayed in vocal lines that go to extremes, but far more often the writing for voices is idiomatically singable. The cast, among whom there is not one single weak link, sing their hearts out, and Schønwandt conveys the kaleidoscopic colours of Ruder's score with a remarkable degree of clarity; the recording is first-class. On second thoughts perhaps Ruders' finest achievement is to evoke dazzling and frightening stage pictures with sound alone; it cries out for a production in English, the language in which Ruders set it.

John Rutter
British 1945

One of the most popular and widely performed composers of his generation, Rutter studied at Clare College, Cambridge then taught at

Southampton University, returning to Clare College as director of music in 1975. He left in 1979 to devote himself to composition and founded the Cambridge Singers with whom he has made many recordings of both his own and others' music. His works are predominately vocal; his musical style draws upon the British choral tradition – Holst, Vaughan Williams, Howells, Britten and Tippett – but also late 19th- early 20th-century European music, especially Fauré and Duruflé.

Requiem

Requiem[a]. Hymn to the Creator of Light. God be in my head. A Gaelic Blessing. Psalmfest – No 5, Cantate Domino. Open thou mine eyes[b]. A Prayer of St Patrick. A Choral Fanfare. Birthday Madrigals – No 2, Draw on, sweet night; No 4, My true love hath my heart. The Lord bless you and keep you
[a]Rosa Mannion, [b]Libby Crabtree *sops* **Polyphony; Bournemouth Sinfonietta / Stephen Layton**
Hyperion CDA66947 (69 minutes: DDD) Ⓕ
Texts and translations included. Recorded 1997 ⭘

Here is music finely crafted, written with love for the art and an especial care for choral sound. It is melodious without being commonplace, harmonically rich without being sticky, modern in the graceful way of a child who grows up responsive to newness but not wanting to kick his elders in the teeth. He gives us the heart's desire: we listen saying 'Ah yes!' and with a half-foreseen satisfaction 'Yes, of course! Lovely!' But he's on too familiar terms with our heart's desires, doesn't extend them, or surprise us into realizing that they were deeper and subtler than we thought. This is by way of cautiously savouring a remembered taste, which could readily be indulged without perceived need for an interval: one item leads to another and before we know it the pleasurable hour is over. The Requiem is the longest work; the other pieces vary from two to just over six minutes. Most are unaccompanied and show the choir of 25 voices as another of those expert groups of assured and gifted professionals that are among the principal adornments of modern musical life. Their capacity as a virtuoso choir is tested in the *Cantate Domino* and *Choral Fanfare*, but Rutter writes for real singers (not just singer-musicians) and their tone is unfailingly beautiful. The two soloists are excellent.

Five Traditional Songs

Rutter Five Traditional Songs
Vaughan Williams Five English Folksongs
Traditional (arr Rutter) I know where I'm going. Down by the sally gardens. The bold grenadier. The keel row. The cuckoo. She's like the swallow. Willow song. The willow tree. The miller of Dee. O can ye sew cushions? Afton water. The sprig of thyme. She moved through the fair (arr Runswick). The lark in the clear air (arr Carter)
Cambridge Singers; City of London Sinfonia / John Rutter
Collegium COLCD120 (66 minutes: DDD) Ⓕ
Texts included. Recorded 1992 ⭘

Pleasure in singing is almost the *raison d'être* of this disc. Rutter not only provides us with a healthy dollop of nostalgia, but gives these songs a whole new lease of life in some characteristically scrumptuous arrangements. For some, though, there is always the danger that the superficial charms of Rutter's arrangements can smother the fundamental beauty of the original melody. But then one would argue that he is not attempting to follow in the footsteps of the great folksong arrangers (he pays tribute to this tradition by including Vaughan Williams's *Five English Folksongs*). His arrangements belong more to the light music tradition; what Messrs Binge, Coates and Tomlinson achieved with orchestral colours Rutter finds primarily through vocal ones – and it's significant that the very finest arrangements here (including a ravishing 'Golden Slumbers') are unaccompanied. The singers are outstanding.

Camille Saint-Saëns

French 1835-1921

GROVE *Saint-Saëns was a child prodigy and his dazzling gifts early won him the admiration of Gounod, Rossini, Berlioz and especially Liszt, who hailed him as the world's greatest organist. He was organist at the Madeleine, 1857-75, and a teacher at the Ecole Niedermeyer, 1861-65, where Fauré was among his devoted pupils. He also pursued a range of other activities, organising concerts of Liszt's symphonic poems (then a novelty), reviving interest in older music, writing on musical, scientific and historical topics, travelling often and widely and composing prolifically; on behalf of new French music he co-founded the Société Nationale de Musique (1871). A virtuoso pianist, he excelled in Mozart and was praised for the purity and grace of his playing. Similarly French characteristics of his conservative musical style – neat proportions, clarity, polished expression, elegant line – reside in his best compositions, the classically orientated sonatas (especially the first each for violin and cello), symphonies (No 3, the Organ) and concertos (No 4 for piano, No 3 for violin. He also wrote 'exotic', descriptive or dramatic works, including four symphonic poems, in a style influenced by Liszt, using thematic transformation, and 13 operas, of which only Samson et Dalila (1877), with its sound structures, clear declamation and strongly appealing scenes, has held the stage. Le carnaval des animaux (1886) is a witty frolic; he forbade performances in his lifetime, Le cygne apart. From the mid-1890s he adopted a more austere style, emphasising the classical aspect of his aesthetic which, perhaps more than the music itself, influenced Fauré and Ravel.*

Violin Concertos

No 1 in A, Op 20; No 2 in C, Op 58; No 3 in B minor, Op 61
Philippe Graffin *vn* **BBC Scottish Symphony Orchestra / Martyn Brabbins**
Hyperion CDA67074 (76 minutes: DDD) Ⓕ
Recorded 1998 ⭘

The first two violin concertos of Saint-Saëns were composed in reverse order. The Second is the longer and lesser-known of the two, but the First Concerto more resembles the thematic charm and concise design of the First Cello Concerto. Cast in a single short movement that falls into three distinct sections, it launches the soloist on his way right from the start (six emphatic chords) and features a delightful central section with some felicitous woodwind writing. Hyperion holds a trump card in Philippe Graffin, whose elegant, emotionally charged playing is strongly reminiscent of the young Menuhin (he has a similar sort of sound) and whose understanding of the idiom is second to none – certainly among modern players.

Saint-Saëns's First Violin Concerto was composed in 1859, whereas his Second preceded it by a year. Unexpectedly, the first movement's thematic material has an almost Weberian slant. The orchestration is heavier than in the First, and the musical arguments are both more formal and more forcefully stated. It is a more overtly virtuoso work than the First Concerto, and perhaps rather less memorable, but again Graffin weaves a winsome solo line and Martyn Brabbins directs a strong account of the orchestral score, with prominently projected woodwinds. The relatively well-known Third Concerto (1880) is roughly the same length as the Second (around half-an-hour), but is more consistently interesting. The basic material is of higher quality, the key relations more telling and orchestration infinitely more delicate. No other recording liberates so much of the score's instrumental detail, probably because most of Graffin's predecessors have been balanced way in front of the orchestra.

Cello Concertos

No 1 in A minor, Op 33; **No 2** in D minor, Op 119

Cello Concerto No 2 in D minor, Op 119[c]. La muse et le poète, Op 132[ac]. Romance in E flat, Op 67[c] (orch cpsr). Cello Sonata No 2 in F, Op 123[b]
Steven Isserlis *vc* [a]**Joshua Bell** *vn* [b]**Pascal Devoyon** *pf* [c]**North German Radio Symphony Orchestra / Christoph Eschenbach**
RCA Red Seal 09026 63518-2 (76 minutes: DDD) Ⓕ
Recorded 1999

Steven Isserlis here follows up his earlier outstanding release of Saint-Saëns' cello music with another that's even more revelatory. This disc concentrates on the more neglected cello works that Saint-Saëns wrote towards the end of his long career. Just as the earlier Concerto and Sonata were written in the same year, 1872, so Saint-Saëns followed up the Second Concerto of 1902 with a sonata three years later.

It is true that neither Concerto nor Sonata quite matches its predecessor in memorable melody, but Isserlis, in powerful, imaginative performances, brings out other qualities to show how unjust their neglect is. That is particularly true of the Sonata, which, with Isserlis as passionate advocate, vividly supported by Pascal Devoyon, rivals Brahms's magnificent Second Cello Sonata in heroic power and scale.

At 33 minutes, this is easily the longest of Saint-Saëns' cello works, its ambitious tone of voice instantly established (as it is in the Brahms) and then masterfully sustained throughout the first movement. The second-movement *scherzo*, almost as long and far more than just an interlude, is a sharply original set of variations, leading to a songful slow movement which in turn leads up to a passionate climax. Then in the surgingly energetic finale, both Isserlis and Devoyon articulate the rapid passagework with thrilling clarity.

The cello writing in the Second Concerto is rather less grateful with its thorny passages of double-stopping, but the two-movement structure characteristic of Saint-Saëns works well, with each divided clearly in two, *Allegro* into *Andante*, *Scherzo* into cadenza and reprise of *Allegro*. Making light of technical problems, Isserlis is persuasive both in the bravura *Allegros* and in the hushed meditation of the slow section. Yet neither he, nor Eschenbach, can quite overcome the truncated feeling at the end, when the reprise of the opening material is so short.

The *Romance* is an adaptation of the slow fourth movement of the Cello Suite, Op 16, a charming piece which Saint-Saëns reworked several times. Yet best of all is the lyrical dialogue of *La muse et le poète*. Inspired by Alfred de Musset's poem, *La nuit de mai*, it opens with Saint-Saëns at his most luscious, reflecting de Musset's role as a hothouse romantic among French poets. It then moves seamlessly through contrasted episodes, with the violin (superbly played by Joshua Bell) representing the muse and the cello as the poet himself. A generous collection, warmly recorded.

Cello Concerto No 1. Le carnaval des animaux – The swan[a]. Romance in F, Op 36[b]. Romance in D, Op 51[b]. Cello Sonata No 1 in C minor, Op 32[b]. Chant saphique in D, Op 91[b]. Gavotte in G minor, Op posth[b]. Allegro appassionato in B minor, Op 43[b]. Prière, Op 158
Steven Isserlis *vc* [a]**Dudley Moore,** [b]**Pascal Devoyon** *pfs* [c]**Francis Grier** *org* **London Symphony Orchestra / Michael Tilson Thomas**
RCA Victor Red Seal 09026 61678-2 Ⓕ
(67 minutes: DDD). Recorded 1992

'Concerto!' was a Channel Four TV series that showed participating soloists in rehearsal, in conversation with Dudley Moore and Michael Tilson Thomas and, ultimately, in performance, which resulted in several recordings, of which this is one. This disc is recommendable not so much for Steven Isserlis's Cello Concerto – smooth and intelligent as that is – as for the additional fill-ups. *The swan* has Moore and Tilson Thomas as joint accompanists, elegantly executed, but the items with Pascal Devoyon are especially valuable, the First Cello Sonata full of elegantly tailored drama, the two *Romances*, *Chant saphique* and *Gavotte* palpable charmers, tastefully played; and the headstrong, thematically memorable *Allegro appassionato*, one of the finest shorter pieces in the cellist's repertory.

The disc is enhanced by the opportunity of hearing the rather affecting but relatively unfamiliar *Prière*, composed for André Hekking just two years before Saint-Saëns's death.

Additional recommendations

Cello Concerto No 1

Couplings: Suite, Op 16 (arr cpsr). Cello Sonata No 1. Romance, Op 36. Allegro appassionato. Le carnaval des animaux – The swan

Maisky *vc* **Hovora** *pf* **Orpheus Chamber Orchestra**
DG 457 599-2GH (70 minutes: DDD: 2/99)   Ⓕ
  Mischa Maisky's rich, velvety tone and brilliant
  technique give all the works here an arresting,
  memorable quality, and in the concerto, the Orpheus
  players sound as passionately involved as the soloist.

Cello Concertos Nos 1 and 2

Couplings: Suite, Op 16 (arr vc/orch). Allegro appassionato in B minor, Op 43. Le carnaval des animaux – The swan

Kliegel *vc* **Bournemouth Sinfonietta / Monnard**
Naxos 8 553039 (62 minutes: DDD: 11/97)   Ⓢ
  Maria Kliegel performs the Second Cello Concerto
  with impressive panache and precision. The First, too,
  is well played, though not a first choice for the work.

Piano Concertos

No 1 in D, Op 17; **No 2** in G minor, Op 22;
No 3 in E flat Op 29; **No 4** in C minor, Op 44;
No 5 in F, Op 103, 'Egyptian'

Piano Concertos – Nos 1[a]; 2[b]; 3[c]; 4[a] and 5[b]
Pascal Rogé *pf* [a]**Philharmonia Orchestra;** [b]**Royal Philharmonic Orchestra;** [c]**London Philharmonic Orchestra / Charles Dutoit**
Double Decca ② 443 865-2DF2 (140 minutes: ADD)   Ⓜ
Recorded 1978-79   ●

Saint-Saëns's First Concerto was written when the composer was 23 years old, and it is a sunny, youthful, happy work conventionally cast in the traditional three-movement form. A decade later he wrote the Second Concerto in a period of only three weeks. This concerto begins in a mood of high seriousness rather in the style of a Bach organ prelude; then this stern mood gives way to a jolly fleet-footed *Scherzo* and a *presto* finale: it is an uneven work, though the most popular of the five concertos and this is its most recommendable version.

The Third Concerto is perhaps the least interesting work, whilst the Fourth is the best of the five. It is in effect a one-movement work cast in three ingeniously crafted sections. Saint-Saëns wrote his last, the *Egyptian*, in 1896 to mark his 50 years as a concert artist. Mirroring the sights and sounds of a country that he loved, this is another brilliant work. Pascal Rogé displays a very secure, exuberant sense of rhythm, which is vital in these works, as is his immaculate, pearly technique. Dutoit is a particularly sensitive accompanist and persuades all three orchestras to play with that lean brilliance which the concertos demand. The recordings are true and well balanced.

Saint-Saëns Piano Concerto No 2   Ⓗ
Rachmaninov Piano Concerto No 3 in D minor, Op 30
Shostakovich Prelude and Fugue in D, Op 87 No 5
Emil Gilels *pf* **Paris Conservatoire Orchestra / André Cluytens**
Testament mono SBT1029 (65 minutes: ADD)   Ⓕ
Recorded 1954-56   ●●

Gilels was a true king of pianists and these Paris and New York based recordings only strengthen and confirm his legendary status. Here, again, is that superlative musicianship, that magisterial technique and, above all, that unforgettable sonority; rich and sumptuous at every level. What breadth and distinction he brings to the first movement of the Saint-Saëns, from his fulmination in the central octave uproar to his uncanny stillness in the final pages. High jinks are reserved for the second and third movements, the former tossed off with a teasing lightness, the latter's whirling measures with infinite brio. An approximate swipe at the *Scherzo*'s flashing double-note flourish, a false entry and a wrong turning five minutes into the finale offer amusing evidence of Gilels's high-wire act. No performance of this concerto is more 'live', and it's small wonder that Claudio Arrau included it among his desert island favourites.

Gilels's Rachmaninov is altogether more temperate yet, once more, this is among the few truly great performances of this work. His tempo is cool and rapid, and maintained with scintillating ease through even the most formidable intricacy. The cadenza – the finer and more transparent of the two – billows and recedes in superbly musical style and the climax is of awe-inspiring grandeur and the central *scherzando* in the finale is as luminous as it is vivacious. The finale's *meno mosso* variation is excluded and, it has to be said, Cluytens's partnership is distant and run of the mill. But the recordings hardly show their age in such admirably smooth transfers. Gilels's 'encore', Shostakovich's Prelude and Fugue No 5 is like a brilliant shaft of light after the Rachmaninov. The performance is perfection, entirely justifying Artur Rubinstein's comment after hearing him play in Russia: 'If that boy comes to the West, I shall have to shut up shop'.

Saint-Saëns Piano Concerto No 4 in C minor,   Ⓗ Ⓢ
Op 44[c]. Etude en forme de valse, Op 52 No 6[d] **Franck** Symphonic Variations[a] **Ravel** Piano Concerto in D[b]
Alfred Cortot *pf* [a]**London Philharmonic Orchestra / Landon Ronald;** [b]**orchestra,** [c]**Paris Conservatoire Orchestra /** [bc]**Charles Munch**
Naxos Historical 8 110613 (60 minutes: ADD)   Ⓢ
        ●●

Here are performances of a timeless vitality and validity. The exception is the Ravel Concerto, which is wildly approximate and confused. Whether played with one hand or two (Cortot rewrote the concerto for two hands, for which he was roundly castigated by Clifford Curzon), the final cadenza, in particular, is so battle-scarred that it's barely recognisable; though even here you can sense the spirit of this powerful and malignant score struggling to emerge through so many muddles and confusions.

Elsewhere, there is a super-abundance of wit and charm – of Cortot at his most beguiling. How typical is that holding back at the start of the Franck, that *espressivo ad libitum* rather than a mundane emphasis on the principal beat. How difficult to imagine a greater freedom at 3'48", one that so precisely captures the composer's *con fantasia* direction. Cortot's entry to the final *Allegro* is like a ray of scintillating light after the central meditation and, throughout, everything seems airborne and as if improvised on the spot. Cortot may have mischievously referred to Franck's '*cote artisan d'église*' (his church-worker style), but no pianist has played him with such romantic fervour and brilliance.

Cortot's capacity to be free and ecstatic yet bracingly unsentimental was one of his most exhilarating qualities, and his *rubato* at the start of the Saint-Saëns makes modern rivals such as Rogé (Decca) and Collard (EMI) pale in comparison. At 8'12" (*dolce tranquillo legato*) you will hear a classic instance of the *cantabile* for which Cortot was celebrated, and in the final pages of the same movement an inimitably limpid and delicate poetry. Again, in the central *Allegro vivace*, Cortot's famous or infamous scrambles and skirmishes are never at the expense of the music's innate elegance and style, and who else has spun off the Concerto's closing cascades with such glitter and aplomb? Cortot's playing may not have been note-perfect but there is no doubt that he was every inch the virtuoso.

As an encore, there is Saint-Saëns' *Etude en forme de valse*, and while the 1931 recording is by no means the equal of the legendary 1919 disc, a performance that prompted Horowitz's envy, it is gloriously alive with Cortot's verve and magic. Mark Obert-Thorn's transfers are exceptional (the Franck is in the 1934 rather than the 1927 performance with Landon Ronald) and all lovers of past but ever-present greatness will want this second and final Naxos volume of Cortot's sadly few concerto recordings.

Orchestral Works

Danse macabre in G minor, Op 40. Phaéton in C, Op 39. Le rouet d'Omphale in A, Op 31. La Jeunesse d'Hercule in E flat, Op 50. Marche héroïque in E flat, Op 34. Introduction and Rondo capriccioso in A minor, Op 28[a]. Havanaise in E, Op 83[a]

[a]Kyung-Wha Chung *vn* **[a]Royal Philharmonic Orchestra; Philharmonia Orchestra / Charles Dutoit**

Decca 425 021-2DM Ⓜ

(66 minutes: ADD) ●

It's enough to make you weep – at the age of three, Saint-Saëns wrote his first tune, analysed Mozart's *Don Giovanni* from the full score when he was five, and at 10 claimed he could play all of Beethoven's 32 piano sonatas from memory. There is some consolation that, according to a contemporary, physically 'he strangely resembled a parrot', and perhaps even his early brilliance was a curse rather than a blessing, as he regressed from being a bold innovator to a dusty reactionary. In his thirties (in the 1870s) he was at the forefront of the Lisztian avant-garde. To Liszt's invention, the 'symphonic poem' (Saint-Saëns was the first Frenchman to attempt the genre), he brought a typically French concision, elegance and grace. Charles Dutoit has few peers in this kind of music; here is playing of dramatic flair and classical refinement that exactly matches Saint-Saëns intention and invention. Decca's sound has depth, brilliance and richness.

Complete Symphonies

No 1 in E flat, Op 2; **No 2** in A minor, Op 55; **No 3** in C minor, Op 78, 'Organ'

Symphonies – A; F, 'Urbs Roma'; Nos 1-3

Bernard Gavoty *org* **French Radio National Orchestra / Jean Martinon**

EMI ② CZS5 69683-2 (156 minutes: ADD) Ⓜ

Recorded 1972-75 ●

Saint-Saëns's four early symphonies have rather tended to be eclipsed by the popularity of his much later *Organ* Symphony. It's easy to see why the latter, with its rich invention, its colour and its immediate melodic appeal has managed to cast an enduring spell over its audiences, but there is much to be enjoyed in the earlier symphonies too. The A major dates from 1850 when Saint-Saëns was just 15 years old and is a particularly attractive and charming work despite its debt to Mendelssohn and Mozart.

The Symphony in F major of 1856 was the winning entry in a competition organised by the Societé Sainte-Cécile of Bordeaux but was immediately suppressed by the composer after its second performance. The pressures of writing for a competition no doubt contribute to its more mannered style but it nevertheless contains some impressive moments, not least the enjoyable set of variations that form the final movement. The Symphony No 1 proper was in fact written three years before the *Urbs Roma* and shares the same youthful freshness of the A major, only here the influences are closer to Schumann and Berlioz. The Second Symphony reveals the fully mature voice of Saint-Saëns and in recent years has achieved a certain amount of popularity which is almost certainly due in part to this particularly fine recording. Inevitably we arrive at the *Organ* Symphony, and if you don't already have a recording then you could do a lot worse than this marvellously colourful and flamboyant performance. Indeed, the performances on this generous set are persuasive and exemplary. A real bargain, well worth investigating.

Symphony No 3

Symphony No 3[a]. Samson et Dalila – Bacchanale[b]. Le déluge – Prélude[b]. Danse macabre[b]

[a]Gaston Litaize *org* **[a]Chicago Symphony Orchestra, [b]Orchestre de Paris / Daniel Barenboim**

DG Galleria 415 847-2GGA (56 minutes: ADD) Ⓜ

Recorded 1976

Daniel Barenboim's recording of the Third Symphony has dominated the catalogue since it first appeared on LP. In fact it is one of the most exciting, physically involving recordings ever made of this work. Barenboim secures not only fine ensemble from his Chicago players but conveys supremely well the mounting excitement of a live performance, without ever falling into hysteria. The organ part has been superimposed on to the Chicago tape. It has Gaston Litaize at the organ of Chartres Cathedral, and though there may be objections in principle, the result is more sharply defined than on most rival recordings. The reissue is generous in offering an exhilarating 'Bacchanale' from *Samson et Dalila*, a sparkling *Danse macabre* in which Luben Yordanoff plays his violin solo beautifully, if not especially diabolically, and the rather engaging and not too sentimental Prélude from *Le déluge*. The remastering has brought a brighter overall sound picture, with the bass response drier, and a very slight loss of bloom on the upper strings. At the famous organ entry in the finale the ear notices that the top is harder, but the spectacle remains and retains its thrill.

Symphony No 3[a]. Le carnaval des animaux[b]
Peter Hurford *org* **Pascal Rogé, Christina Ortiz** *pfs* [a]**Montreal Symphony Orchestra;** [b]**London Sinfonietta / Charles Dutoit**
Decca Ovation 430 720-2DM (58 minutes: DDD) Ⓜ
Recorded 1980-82

In 1886 Saint-Saëns poured his considerable experience as an unequalled virtuoso of the organ, piano and practitioner of Lisztian unifying techniques into his *Organ* Symphony; it instantly put the French Symphony on the map, and provided a model for Franck and others. With its capacity for grand spectacle (aside from the organ and a large orchestra, its scoring includes two pianos) it has suffered inflationary tendencies from both conductors and recording engineers. Dutoit's (and Decca's) achievement is the restoration of its energy and vitality. The affectionate portraits in the 'zoological fantasy', *The carnival of the animals*, benefit from more intimate though no less spectacular sound, and a direct approach that avoids obvious clowning.

Saint-Saëns Symphony No 3 **Debussy** La mer **Ibert** Escales 🄷
Berj Zamkochian *org* **Boston Symphony Orchestra / Charles Munch**
RCA Living Stereo 09026 61500-2 (73 minutes: ADD) Ⓜ
Recorded 1956-59 **OO**

This famous recording was made in Symphony Hall, Boston. To combat the hall resonance the RCA engineers moved many of the seats from the body of the hall so that the orchestra could spread out, while the organ (situated behind the stage) was miked separately. The result was a wonderfully rich, sumptuous sound which also achieved internal clarity – one notices that in the *Scherzo* and the filigree passages for piano in the introduction to the finale. However, it is the spectacular moments that one remembrs: the rich bonding of organ and strings in the *Poco adagio* and the full-blooded organ entry from Berj Zamkochian in the finale. Munch's superb reading moves forward with a powerful lyrical impulse in a single sweep from the first note to the last. To make this issue even more enticing Munch's 1956 versions of Debussy's *La mer* and Ibert's *Escales* ('Port of call') have been included. There is some marvellous playing in both, especially from the lustrous Boston violins. Here, however, the original recordings were more closely balanced and the effect is less rich, the dynamic range less wide. The adrenalin runs high in both performances.

Le carnaval des animaux

Saint-Saëns Le carnaval des animaux
Poulenc Double Piano Concerto in D minor
Güher Perkinel, Süher Pekinel *pfs* **French Radio Philharmonic Orchestra / Marek Janowski**
Teldec 4509-97445-2 (38 minutes: DDD) Ⓜ
Recorded 1990

Güher and Süher Pekinel, highly talented twins of Turkish-Spanish parentage, playing together on a single piano, set off vivaciously into the Introduction of *Le carnaval des animaux*, tripping along with irresistible charm. Throughout, there is such an engaging lightness of touch beneath the surface sparkle that they dominate the performance. Yet the balance is well managed, and the partnership with Janowski and the French orchestra works admirably, so that time and again the ear is delighted, whether by the squawking hens and cockerels, the gentle, unhurried Offenbachian tortoises, the elephantine sylph, the galumphing kangaroos, the fragile, watery aquarium and the dainty fluttering within the aviary. The 'Pianists', for once, are deftly purposeful and sure of themselves; then the fossils dance past with perky insouciance. Perhaps the finest orchestral solo of all is 'The swan' (Eric Levionnais), who swims by with natural grace and simple dignity. The finale is as spirited as the opening and it is doubtful if there is a finer account of the Saint-Saëns.

This personable and perceptive duo then turn to the scintillating wit of Poulenc's Concerto for two pianos. They perform this work equally persuasively, and with plenty of dash and dazzle. Yet the secondary theme of the first movement is given a special haunting nostalgia, half-way between Satie and Ravel, and the delicious Mozartian pastiche of the *Larghetto* is equally relished. How nicely they make the melody sing, while the orchestral backing has the appropriate veiled sensuality and the docile coda is exquisite. Then the finale erupts with bouncing pianistic articulation and rather more strident comments from the orchestra, but again there is an exotic lyrical secondary tune that blossoms nicely before the brief closing burst of pianistic fireworks. The only drawback is the short playing time: 38 minutes; but it may be counted fair value at mid-price.

Saint-Saëns Le carnaval des animaux
Ravel Ma mère l'oye
Joseph Villa, Patricia Prattis Jennings *pfs*
Pittsburgh Symphony Orchestra / André Previn Ⓕ
Philips 400 016-2PH (49 minutes: DDD)

With the transfer to CD of the Ravel work, the mellowness of the original LP, atmospheric but finely transparent, is further enhanced. The same qualities are a great asset in *Le carnaval des animaux*, notably so in the beautifully transparent account of 'Aquarium' and in the finely judged, not-too-close balance of the solo cello in 'The swan', played with exquisite tenderness by Anne Martindale Williams. The piano tone is extremely faithful too, bright but never aggressive, with the piano chords rightly kept as a pulsing background against the string melody of 'Tortoises', and though the double-basses sound rather distant in 'The elephant', the sepulchral quality in their timbre is very realistic. The full ensemble used in the opening and closing movements is not so transparent, but that is mostly a question of instrumentation. There has rarely, if ever, been a more exuberant account of the final procession of the animals. This is one of the finest versions of this work. The one reservation is a purely technical one. There is no banding except between the two works.

String Quartets

Saint-Saëns String Quartets – No 1 in E minor, Op 112; No 2 in G, Op 153 **Fauré** String Quartet in E minor, Op 121
Miami Quartet (Ivan Chan, Cathy Meng Robinson *vns* Chauncey Patterson *va* Keith Robinson *vc*)
Conifer Classics 75605 51291-2 (75 minutes: DDD) Ⓕ
Recorded 1997

Saint-Saëns was 64 when he wrote the First Quartet, a closely argued, intense piece, and didn't follow it up for another 20 years; the Second Quartet is not dissimilar in style to those far more popular fruits of his old age, the three woodwind and piano sonatas. Though neither quartet has the melodic memorability of his best-known music, the neglect is hard to understand – there's an effortless mastery of string textures, inventive use of counterpoints, and a delightfully fresh approach to form, with continual surprises enlivening the overall unity.

The Miami Quartet is a brilliant ensemble. Exceptionally well balanced, there's an uncomplicated, unexaggerated *élan* to their playing, which seems just right for this music, in which intellectual playfulness is an important ingredient. The contrapuntal fun and games of No 2's finale has a stunning light-fingered virtuosity, yet the more serious moments are just as effective – the sweet serenity of the opening of No 1's *Adagio*, for instance. The Miami are highly recommended, even without taking into account their beautiful performance of the Fauré; the subtle harmonic and emotional shifts of this unique piece are captured most convincingly, with wonderfully affecting changes of tone colour. All round, an outstanding disc. The recording is admirably realistic; its clarity highlights the exceptional precision of the playing.

Piano Trios

No 1 in F, Op 18; No 2 in E minor, Op 92
Joachim Trio (Rebecca Hirsch *vn* Caroline Dearnley *vc* John Lenehan *pf*)
Naxos 8 550935 (65 minutes: DDD) Ⓢ
Recorded 1993

1863 and 1892 are the dates of these trios, of which No 1 was written by a composer not yet 30 but already a confident master of his craft. Bland his voice may be, but it is intelligent and agreeable: a French Brahms without genius, one dares suggest, although Mendelssohn also comes to mind. At the same time, there are passages unlike either of these composers, such as the bare and angular main theme of the A minor slow movement in No 1, though Grieg might have written it. Such music needs sympathetic, unfussy interpretation and the skilful and sensitive Joachim Trio gives it just that; as for the First Trio as a whole, the work is charming (try the fleet *Scherzo*) and the booklet-essay rightly notes the 'delicate brilliance' of the piano writing by a composer who was also an expert player. The E minor Trio, a more dramatic five-movement piece, is played here with fine judgement, being warmly expressive without sentimentality or mannerism. The recording is excellent.

Mélodies

Chanson (Nouvelle chanson sur un vieil air). Guitare. Rêverie. L'attente. Le chant de ceux qui s'en vont sur la mer. Le pas d'armes du Roi Jean. La coccinelle. A quoi bon entendre. Si vous n'avez rien à me dire. Dans ton coeur. Danse macabre. Mélodies persanes, Op 26 – La brise; Sabre en main; Au cimetière; Tournoiement. Marquise, vous souvenez-vous?. La Cigale et la Fourmi. Chanson à boire du vieux temps. Nocturne. Violons dans le soir. Guitares et mandolines. Une flûte invisible. Suzette et Suzon. Aimons-nous. Temps nouveau. Le vent dans la plaine. Grasselette et Maigrelette
François Le Roux *bar* **Krysia Osostowicz** *vn*
Philippa Davies *fl* **Graham Johnson** *pf*
Hyperion CDA66856 (78 minutes: DDD) Ⓕ
Texts and translations included. Recorded 1996

This is the most resounding blow yet to be struck for the *mélodies* of Saint-Saëns. François Le Roux with his incisive diction and ability to characterise each song, is a real champion for the man, once so successful, who became, as Graham Johnson puts it in the booklet, 'a footnote' rather than a chapter in the history of French music. Many of the poems that Saint-Saëns set were used by other composers, for instance *Dans ton coeur*, which became Duparc's *Chanson triste*, by 'Jean Lahor' (Henri Cazalis). Graham Johnson playfully suggests what a fortune Saint-Saëns might have made if he had survived long enough to write for the movies a bit more. The first song of the *Mélodies persanes*,

'La brise', is full of eastern promise, the second, 'Sabre en main' a rollicking bit of toy-soldier galloping away, but just as one is beginning to think that Johnson is shooting himself in the foot by being so ironic about the music they're performing comes the hauntingly beautiful fifth song, 'Au cimetière', with its quietly rippling accompaniment and the languorous poem about the lovers sitting on a marble tomb and picking the flowers. Le Roux sings this with controlled, quiet intensity. Johnson makes the point that it is of little importance from which part of the composer's life the songs come, he embodies that totally French 19th-century style, sometimes anticipating Hahn and Massenet, sometimes harking back to Boieldieu. If a setting of La Fontaine's fable about the cicada and the ant is pure salon charm, then the final 'Grasselette et Maigrelette' Ronsard *chanson*, composed when Saint-Saëns was 85 in 1920, is a vivacious *café-concert*-style evocation of old Paris.

Samson et Dalila

Plácido Domingo *ten* Samson; **Waltraud Meier** *mez* Dalila; **Alain Fondary** bar Priest; **Jean-Philippe Courtis** *bass* Abimelech; **Samuel Ramey** *bass* Old Hebrew; **Christian Papis** *ten* Messenger; **Daniel Galvez-Vallejo** *ten* First Philistine; **François Harismendy** *bass* Second Philistine; **Chorus and Orchestra of the Bastille Opera, Paris / Myung-Whun Chung**
EMI ② CDS7 54470-2 (124 minutes: DDD). Notes, Ⓕ text and translation included. Recorded 1991 **OO**

This is the most subtly and expertly conducted performance of this work to appear on CD, excellent as others have been in this respect, and also the best played and sung. Chung's achievement is to have welded the elements of pagan ruthlessness, erotic stimulation and Wagnerian harmony that comprise Saint-Saëns's masterpiece into a convincing whole. His success is based on the essentials of a firm sense of rhythm and timing allied to a realization of the sensuousness and delicacy of the scoring. Whether in the lamenting of the Hebrews, the forceful music written for the High Priest, the heroics of Samson, the sensual outpourings of Dalila, or the empty rejoicing of the Bacchanale, he and his orchestra strike to the heart of the matter – and that orchestra plays with Gallic finesse, augmented by a dedicated discipline.

The choral singing, though too distantly recorded, is no less alert and refined, with a full range of dynamic contrast. Meier's Dalila is a fascinating portrayal of this equivocal anti-heroine, seductive, wheedling, exerting her female wiles with the twin objects of sexual dominance and political command. All her sense of purpose comes out in her early greeting to the High Priest, 'Salut à mon père'; then she's meditative and expectant as Dalila ponders on her power at 'Se pourrait-il'. The set numbers are all sung with the vocal ease and long phrase of a singer at the zenith of her powers. She makes more of the text than Domingo who sings in his familiar, all-purpose style, admirable in itself, somewhat missing the particular accents brought to this music by the great French tenors of the past. They exist no more and one must salute the sterling and often eloquent tones of Domingo.

Fondary is superb as the High Priest, firm and rich in tone, commanding and vengeful in delivery: the most compelling interpreter of the part on disc, *tout court*. Ramey is luxury casting as the Old Hebrew, but as this is a part once sung by Pinza, Ramey probably felt he wasn't slumming it. After an unsteady start, he sings the small but important role with breadth and dignity. As Abimelech, Courtis makes much of little. Apart from the two reservations already made, the recording is admirable, with a wide and spacious sound, and the soloists forward, but well integrated into the whole. This must now be the outright recommendation for this work.

Samson et Dalila
Carlo Cossutta *ten* Samson; **Marjana Lipovšek** *mez* Dalila; **Alain Fondary** *bar* Priest; **Yves Bisson** *bar* Abimelech; **Harald Stamm** *bass* Old Hebrew; **Constantin Zaharia** *ten* Messenger; **Jerôme Engramer** *ten* First Philistine; **Ionel Pantea** *bass* Second Philistine; **Sofia Chamber Choir; Bregenz Festival Chorus; Vienna Volksoper Chorus; Vienna Symphony Orchestra / Sylvain Cambreling**
Koch Schwann ② 31774-2 (127 minutes: DDD) Ⓕ
Notes, text and translation included.
Recorded live in 1988

Cambreling draws as much sensuousness and delicacy from the score as any, and also attends to its pagan element with suitable brio. Though like some of his predecessors, he is inclined to linger unduly against the composer's express wishes, as in the marginally too slow tempo for 'Mon coeur s'ouvre à ta voix', he uses the gained time to underline the refinement of the scoring, helped by some lovely orchestral playing, which is in true theatrical balance with the singers.

Although by rights the polyglot cast should tell against the set, the French is in fact as idiomatic as any. While Lipovšek sometimes, like Meier for Chung, indulges in dramatic gestures strictly outside the realm of style appropriate to the piece, she sings for the most part with a luscious tone and is as pleasing to listen to as Meier and instils the whole role, by vocal means alone, with a sense of Dalila's dangerous powers of seduction. Working in a live performance she has an advantage over all her rivals in creating theatrical intensity. She is matched in that by Cossutta. The then 56-year-old tenor has just the *élan* in his attack that sometimes eludes Domingo (Chung). Some may find the vibrato that is part and parcel of Cossutta's timbre disturbing. Once that is taken on board, Cossutta's is as vigorous, pliable and musically attentive a Samson as any. Fondary was Chung's High Priest, and here he repeats his formidable assumption. The smaller roles are adequately taken and the choral singing is excellent. Stage noises are minimally distracting even during the dances; applause is confined to ends of acts.

Additional recommendation

Samson et Dalila

Vickers Samson **Gorr** Dalila

René Duclos Choir; Paris Opera Orchestra / Prêtre

EMI ② CDS7 47895-8 (121 minutes: ADD: 7/88) Ⓕ

A classic recording with Rita Gorr's magnificent Dalila towering over the performance. Vickers too is superb. The sound is not perfect but don't let that sway you.

Aulis Sallinen

Finnish 1935

GROVE *Sallinen was a pupil of Merikanto and Kokkonen at the Helsinki Academy (1955-60), where he returned to teach in 1970. In the late 1960s he began melding triads with avant-garde techniques; then in the 1970s he turned to opera, drawing on sources as diverse as Shostakovich, Janácek and Orff in The Horseman (1975), The Red Line (1978), The King Goes forth to France (1984) and Kullervo (1992). His concert works include four symphonies, five string quartets and concertos for violin and for cello.*

Orchestral Works

Variations for Orchestra, Op 8.
Violin Concerto, Op 18. Some aspects of Peltoniemi Hintrik's funeral march, Op 19. The nocturnal dances of Don Juanquixote, Op 58

Eeva Koskinen *vn* **Torleif Thedéen** *vc*

Tapiola Sinfonietta / Osmo Vänskä Ⓕ

BIS CD560 (63 minutes: DDD). Recorded 1992

Sallinen's operas and symphonies have stolen the limelight in recent years at the expense of other works fully worthy of attention, as this well-played and well-recorded disc proves. Whereas the Variations (1963) are somewhat anonymous if deftly written, the Violin Concerto (1968) is an altogether maturer work, unusually sombre for so bright a solo instrument, and perhaps the first piece to point to his later stature. His next published work was the Third String Quartet (1969), subtitled *Some aspects of Peltoniemi Hintrik's funeral march*, which, thanks to the Kronos Quartet's advocacy has become one of Sallinen's most heard works This arrangement for string orchestra dates from 1981. *The nocturnal dances of Don Juanquixote* is an extended fantasia for cello and strings, the title being the only parody of Strauss (although a solo violin enters late as Sancho Panza-leporello!). Sallinen is fond of playing games and all is never as it seems: one can almost hear the collective thud of critics' jaws falling open at this Arnold-like spoof.

Songs of Life and Death, Op 69

Songs of Life and Death, Op 69.
The Iron Age – Suite, Op 55*b*[a]

Margit Papunen *sop* **Jorma Hynninen** *bar* **Opera Festival Chorus; [a]East Helsinki Music Institute Choir; Helsinki Philharmonic Orchestra / Okko Kamu**

Ondine ODE844-2 (75 minutes: DDD) Ⓕ

Texts and translations included. Recorded 1995 ●

Listening to these two works by Aulis Sallinen is a bit like looking at two different photographs of the composer: the face is undeniably the same but not the perspective. *Songs of Life and Death* (1993-94) arose, rather by mischance, from a failed effort to compose a Requiem on verses by Lassi Nummi. Although title and outward form suggest Mahlerian associations, the conservative musical language brings Verdi to mind, and in a very real sense this cycle is a 20th-century equivalent of the latter's Requiem: both are symphonic in construction and operatic in idiom, composed from spiritual rather than religious standpoints, and make use of secular elements. There are differences, of course, not least in scale and conception. And while Sallinen's songs are also very much songs of *life*, death is not here perceived as a grim or tragic end, and this imparts to the whole a peculiarly late 20th-century aspect. Here at last is the choral-and-orchestral masterpiece Sibelius should have written, Finnish to the core yet international in appeal. It is one of the very finest compositions Sallinen has yet produced. Where in the *Songs of Life and Death* voices are the principal element, in the *Iron Age* Suite (1978-82) the focus is on the orchestra, the chorus being an important but more colouristic extra. The suite originated in music written for a series of prize-winning Finnish TV documentaries and in it the more familiar Sallinen of the symphonies and early operas is on display. Both works receive terrific performances.

Giuseppe Sammartini

Italian 1695-1750

Giovanni Battista Sammartini

Italian 1700-1775

GROVE *Oboist and composer Giuseppe Sammartini settled in London c1728 and soon won recognition as a brilliant performer, playing in concerts and operas (including Handel's). From 1736 he was music master to the Princess of Wales and her children. Noted for his fine tone, he transformed oboe playing in England. He was also a leading composer of solo flute and oboe sonatas, trio sonatas, concerti grossi, solo concertos etc; these are mainly conservative in style but have galant features of form and idiom. His other works include cantatas, arias and an English pastoral (c1740).*

Giovanni Battista, brother of Giuseppe, held posts as maestro di cappella of Milan churches from 1728, and (from 1768) the ducal chapel; he was an excellent organist and teacher. By the 1740s he was the city's most famous composer and his music was gaining popularity abroad. Later he had contact in Milan with JC Bach, Boccherini, Mozart and others.

Sammartini was a leading figure in the development of the Classical style. His music is notable for its strong continuity, rhythmic drive and variety of structure and texture. The first master of the symphony, he wrote over 60 such works; while the earliest combine Baroque and Classical traits, the middle-period ones (c1740-58) have an early Classical idiom, many using wind instruments as well as strings. The last symphonies point towards later styles (eg Mozart's). He also wrote concertos, other orchestral pieces and over 200 chamber works, including many trio sonatas. His late chamber works (notably six string quintets, 1773) are the most complex. Serious moods and expressive writing often appear in his three operas (1732-43) and his religious music, which includes oratorios, cantatas and psalms.

Recorder Concerto

G Sammartini Recorder Concerto in F. P
Concerti grossi – No 6 in E minor; No 8 in G minor
G B Sammartini Symphonies – G; D.
String Quintet in E
Conrad Steinmann *rec* **Ensemble 415 / Chiara Banchini** *vn*
Harmonia Mundi Musique d'abord HMA190 1245 Ⓑ
(63 minutes: DDD). Recorded 1986

Giuseppe Sammartini, the elder brother and virtuoso oboist, here contributes a recorder concerto and two concerti grossi sandwiched between two symphonies and a quintet for strings by the more progressive Giovanni Battista. The differences in style are unmistakable. Giuseppe's restless E minor 'Spiritoso' from the Sixth Concerto Grosso, the G minor *French Overture* and graceful minuets belong to a different musical world from that of G B's brash symphonies. Under the capable and lively direction of Chiara Banchini, Ensemble 415 presents these works at their best: lightly textured with brisk tempos, articulated with unusual precision (which the resonant church acoustic only slightly blunts) and sympathetically read; for though the quality of the music varies – the Symphony in G major is especially appealing, that in D major embarrassingly thin with its empty Vivaldian *arpeggios* – the performance never falters. Giuseppe's recorder concerto, rescued from a manuscript in Sweden, is nicely played by Conrad Steinmann. Banchini's solo in the *Largo* of GB's late String Quintet is most affecting, showing herself to be equally at home on the platform and in the front desk.

Erik Satie

French 1866-1925

GROVE *Satie entered the Paris Conservatoire in 1879, but his record was undistinguished. After leaving he wrote the triptychs of Sarabandes (1887), Gymnopédies (1888) and Gnossiennes (1890), of which the latter two sets are modal and almost eventless. In the 1890s he began to frequent Montmartre, to play at the café Chat Noir and to involve himself with fringe Christian sects. He also made the acquaintance of Debussy.*

From 1905-8 he was a student again, at the Schola Cantorum. At last in 1911 his music began to be noticed, and this seems to have stimulated a large output of small pieces, mostly for solo piano and mostly perpetuating his earlier simplicity in pieces with ironic titles. Sports et divertissements (1914), published with illustrations by Charles Martin, contains 20 miniatures eccentrically and beautifully annotated by Satie. In 1915 he came to the attention of Cocteau, who seized on him as the ideal of the anti-Romantic composer and who facilitated the more ambitious works of his last years: the ballets Parade (1917), Mercure (1924) and Relâche (1924), and the cantata Socrate (1918). These have the same flatness as the smaller pieces and songs, achieved by means of directionless modal harmony, simple rhythm and structures made up through repetition or inconsequential dissimilarity. In different ways the style had an effect on French composers from Debussy and Ravel to Poulenc and Sauguet, as later on Cage.

Parade

Parade. Trois Gymnopédies – Nos 1 and 3 (orch Debussy); No 2 (orch Corp). Mercure. Three Gnossiennes (orch Corp). Rêlache
New London Orchestra / Ronald Corp
Hyperion CDA66365 (66 minutes: DDD) Ⓕ
Recorded 1989

In 1918, the year after Diaghilev's Russian Ballet staged Satie's *Parade* in Paris, Poulenc wrote that 'to me, Satie's *Parade* is to Paris what *Petrushka* is to St Petersburg'. Satie was thenceforth adopted as the spiritual father of 'Les Six', whose ideal was the marriage of serious music with jazz, vaudeville, and the circus. Those who only know Satie from his early *Gymnopédies* and *Gnossiennes* – take heed: *Parade* shuffles along its apparently aimless, deadpan and wicked way with interjections from typewriters, lottery wheels, pistols and sirens.

What does it all mean? Ronald Corp could be accused of retaining a slightly stiff upper lip, but there may well be a seriousness of purpose behind Satie's balletic miniatures. Certainly, there is little sign here of the uproarious debunking of some of 'Les Six'. His orchestrations of the *Gnossiennes* and the remaining *Gymnopédie* are idiomatic, and his performances of all six have the requisite cool beauty. Hyperion's sound is spacious and natural.

Piano Works

Six Gnossiennes. Ogives. Petite ouverture à danser. Sarabandes. Trois Gymnopédies
Reinbert de Leeuw *pf*
Philips 446 672-2PH (67 minutes: DDD) Ⓕ
Recorded 1992

Tender, solemn, droll, silly and occasionally plain boring, Satie's piano music has certainly proved its appeal for performers and record collectors, judging from the number of recitals devoted to it. But this one is out of the ordinary, for unlike the majority of artists, who offer a mixed bag of pieces, Reinbert de Leeuw has chosen music that is entirely solemn and even hieratic in utterance. He begins with the archaically beautiful *Gnossiennes*, taking the first of them unusually slowly but with compelling concentration. The composer's devotees will be thrilled, though you have to surrender completely to get the message of this repetitive, proto-minimalist music. The four *Ogives* derive their name from church architecture and their unbarred, diatonically simple music has clear affinities with plainchant although unlike chant it is richly harmonised. Monotonous it may be, but that is part of its charm, if that term can apply to such a contemplative style. The very brief *Petite ouverture à danser* is a mere meandering sketch in lazy waltz-time, but all Satie is sacred to the converted and the writer of the booklet-essay accords it four lines, finding in it (as translated here) 'a suggestion of indifference, vacillating between a melancholy melody and indecisive harmony'. (Not exactly Beethoven, one might say.) The two pensively sad triptychs of *Sarabandes* and *Gymnopédies* – here very slow yet tonally most refined – complete this finely played and recorded disc, which offers nothing whatsoever of the bouncier *café-concert* Satie.

Sports et divertissements. Enfantillages pittoresques. Valse-ballet. Fantaisie-valse. Le piège de Méduse. Petite musique de clown triste. Première pensée Rose + Croix. Le fils des étoiles – La vocation; L'initiation. Carnet d'esquisses et de croquis. Petit prélude de 'La Mort de Monsieur Mouche'. Gambades. Caresse. Trois Peccadilles importunes. La diva de l'Empire. Les pantins dansent. Danse de travers. Petite ouverture à danser. Rêverie du pauvre

Pascal Rogé *pf*

Decca 455 370-2DH (61 minutes: DDD) Ⓕ
Recorded 1996

This unusual collection displays a broader diversity of style and expression than we expect from Satie. It contains the rarely heard *Sports et divertissements*, comprising 20 snap-shots, none lasting more than a minute or so, each evoking a sport or recreational activity. This is surely one of Satie's finest works, and it ought to be better known. Also recorded are early pieces, including the *Valse-ballet* and *Fantaisie-valse*, published in 1885. Much of this music displays a childlike innocence and simplicity, but here we also find wit, pastiche and evocation. Pascal Rogé has already consolidated his reputation as a performer of French repertoire. His responses are generally cool and reserved; this undoubtedly suits the ethereal timelessness of much of Satie's output, but occasionally one wishes, if only for contrast in the context of the disc as a whole, that Rogé would let himself go a bit more (the 'Esquisses et Sketch montmartrois' from the *Carnet d'esquisses et de croquis*, for example). That said, his playing is wholly idiomatic and vividly captures the spirit of Satie's idiosyncratic imagination. This collection of miniatures (the disc has 60 tracks) allows for selective listening, although each work, especially the *Sports et divertissements*, should be heard in its entirety. All are recorded with a wonderfully natural, if very close, piano sound.

Alessandro Scarlatti

Italian 1660-1725

GROVE *When he was 12 Alessandro Scarlatti was sent to Rome, where he may have studied with Carissimi. He married in 1678 and later that year was appointed maestro di cappella of S Giacomo degli Incurabili (now 'in Augusta'). By then he had already composed at least one opera and a second, Gli equivoci nel sembiante, was a resounding success in 1679. It confirmed Scarlatti in his chosen career as an opera composer and attracted the attention of Queen Christina of Sweden, who made him her maestro di cappella.*

In 1684 Scarlatti was appointed maestro di cappella at the vice-regal court of Naples, at the same time as his brother Francesco was made first violinist. It was alleged that they owed their appointments to the intrigues of one of their sisters (apparently Melchiorra) with two court officials, who were dismissed. For the next two decades over half the new operas given at Naples were by Scarlatti. Two of them, Il Pirro e Demetrio (1694) and La caduta dei Decemviri (1697), were especially successful, but by 1700 the War of the Spanish Succession was beginning to undermine the privileged status of the Neapolitan nobility, rendering Scarlatti's position insecure. In 1702 he left with his family for Florence, where he hoped to find employment for himself and his son Domenico with Prince Ferdinando de' Medici.

When these hopes failed, Scarlatti accepted the inferior position in Rome of assistant music director at S Maria Maggiore. With a papal ban imposed on public opera, he found an outlet for his talents in oratorio and in writing cantatas for his Roman patrons. In 1706 he was elected to the Arcadian Academy, along with Pasquini and Corelli. The following year he attempted to conquer Venice, the citadel of Italian opera, with Mitridate Eupatore and Il trionfo della libertà, but they both failed and Scarlatti was subsequently forced to return to Rome, where he was promoted to the senior post at S Maria Maggiore.

Scarlatti found little satisfaction in the life of a church musician, and towards the end of 1708 he accepted an invitation from the new Austrian viceroy to resume his position at Naples, where he remained for the rest of his life, though he maintained close contacts with his Roman patrons. It was probably in 1715 that he received a patent of nobility from Pope Clement XI. His final opera, La Griselda, was written for Rome in 1721, and he seems to have spent the final years of his life in Naples in semi-retirement.

Scarlatti's reputation as the founder of the Neapolitan school of 18th-century opera has been somewhat exaggerated. He was not influential or even very active as a teacher, nor was he the sole originator of the musical structures (da capo aria, Italian overture, accompanied recitative) with which his name is associated, although he did bring to these structures a level of skill and originality which surpassed those of his contemporaries. Some of his best music is in the chamber cantatas, too few of which are known today.

Cantatas

Già lusingato appieno da Zeffiri. Arianna. Poi che riseppe Orfeo. Bella madre de'fiori P

Christine Brandes *sop* **Arcadian Academy / Nicholas McGegan**

Conifer Classics 75605 51293-2 (72 minutes: DDD) Ⓕ

Texts and translations included. Recorded 1996 ●

Alessandro Scarlatti wrote some 700 cantatas: so it's four down, around 690-odd to go. Not that there'll be any complaint if they are all as delectable as this. Scarlatti's range of invention is as wide as his technical diversity, which even in this one genre is astonishing. Introductory sinfonias can be, as here, in one, two or three movements or absent altogether (*Orfeo*); arias can be in *da capo* form (his favourite) or *devisen* ('motto') or strophic, with midway and final ritornellos, as in *Bella madre de'fiori*, or without, accompanied only by continuo (as throughout in *Orfeo*) or with imitative or independent violin lines; recitatives are either accompanied or *secco*, but always expressive, often dramatic.

Possessed of an Emma Kirkby-like light and pure-toned voice, Christine Brandes invests all her words with meaning, colouring her tone and dynamics in accordance with the mood, and conveying fury as well as heartache. Technically, too, she is ideally suited to this repertoire: she is at ease with florid writing, shows a finely controlled *messa di voce* at the words 'Al trono' in *Già lusingato* and elsewhere, and is stylish in ornamenting repeat sections. The vitality, freshness and character of the Arcadian Academy's playing earns this disc an enthusiastic recommendation.

Il rosignolo (first version). Perchè tacete, regolati concenti?. Infirmata, vulnerata. Ombre tacite e sole. Il genio di Mitilde mente non vè. O pace del mio cor P

David Daniels *counterten* **Arcadian Academy / Nicholas McGegan**

Conifer Classics 75605 51319-2 (74 minutes: DDD) Ⓕ

Texts and translations included. Recorded 1998

The American countertenor, David Daniels has a fine, firmly produced voice, even throughout its range; both his intonation and his enunciation are impeccable; he is exact in his handling of florid passages; and his ornamentations are very stylish. If there is one reservation, it is that for too much of the time (except in *Infirmata, vulnerata*) he sings at one constant level of dynamics – though he produces an arresting *messa di voce* on the first word of *Ombre tacite*. It is possible the recording contributes to this: it is certainly responsible for the harpsichord sounding much weaker in some cantatas than in others.

By far the most substantial work here is the earliest, *Perchè tacete*, probably dating from the mid-1690s. It is the only one with a Venetian opera-type overture (three movements, the outer ones with Corellian suspensions, enclosing an intermittent *fugato*), and the numerous movements include four arias, three of which are of two strophes. At the other extreme is *Il rosignolo*, scored only for continuo and consisting of just two *da capo* arias joined by a recitative: the nightingale's song, it emerges, is a lament for love. Love is also the subject of *O pace del mio cor* (the lover vainly seeking peace of mind) and the 1716 *Ombre tacite*, the despairing lament of a deceived lover. In the recitatives of both of these, Scarlatti underlines emotive words with extraordinary harmonic progressions. A contrast to all of these is provided by *Il genio di Mitilde* (for continuo alone), where the flightiness and capricious moods of the loved ones are reflected in an ultra-busy, athletic cello part.

The one remaining work is something of an enigma: though in Latin and printed as a 'sacred concerto', the words could be interpreted as referring either to divine love or to human (which is presumably why McGegan includes it here). The style is plainer than in the others except for the vigorous ending: there are chromatic harmonies in the first aria, and a later aria is unusual in being constructed on a seven-bar ground bass. The disc as a whole demonstrates Scarlatti's range of styles and the diversity of his scoring, even within a single work.

Nel silenzio comune. Fermate, omai fermate. Clori vezzosa e bella. Piango, sospiro, e peno. Non sò qual più m'ingombra P

Brian Asawa *counterten* **Arcadian Academy / Nicholas McGegan** *hpd*

Conifer Classics 75605 51325-2 (64 minutes: DDD) Ⓕ

Texts and translations included. Recorded 1997

The virtually untapped gold mine of Alessandro Scarlatti's cantatas yields some further nuggets in this third volume. Of these five, only *Clori vezzosa e bella* has been recorded before (on a delightful disc – reissued on Belart – from that underrated artist, Helen Watts). That particular cantata is a miniature, just two arias with a recitative preceding each. The longest cantata here, *Nel silenzio comune*, has a brief three-movement overture followed by four arias, each with its introductory recitative. Brian Asawa makes much of the long first aria in particular, with the unexpected twists of its almost voluptuous lines; the delightful second has a charming interplay of dialogue and echoes between voice and violin; while the concluding aria happily represents the words ('trombe d'amante desio') with its trumpety triad figures in the violins and the voice. The violin playing has some subtly sensuous touches of timing, too, especially in the second aria. *Fermate omai* (a late work, from 1724) is shorter, just two arias enfolding a recitative, to a text about a heartless shepherdess denying her lover his pleasure. But the music is vivacious enough, depicting the amorous games with a lot of charm, and even hints of wit when Thyrsis – in his long, winding lines and sharp, 'agonised' breaks – sings of his torment and her cruelty.

Much more intense is *Piango, sospire, e peno*, a setting with two violins and continuo that begins with a rich *arioso*, full of expressive suspensions, and ends with an aria representing the lover's despair (short, broken phrases, with echoes on the violins), then a recitative and, lastly, another brief *arioso*. Finally, *Non sò qual più m'ingombra*, from 1716, which is a Christmas piece, with two arias, the second a flowing *siciliano*.

To all this Asawa brings a clear, ringing countertenor, often rising quite high, an unaffected expressive manner, a real feeling for Italian words and their place as part of the music and a welcome precision over detail. Even if some may feel that the countertenor isn't quite ideal for Scarlatti's cantatas, Asawa's understanding and artistry are persuasive. McGegan's interesting but not obtrusive harpsichord accompaniments are another positive feature of this pleasing CD.

Cain, overo il primo omicidio

Graciela Oddone, Dorothea Röschmann *sops* **Bernarda Fink** *contr* **Richard Croft** *ten* **Antonio Abete** *bass* **Academy for Ancient Music, Berlin / René Jacobs** *counterten* Ⓟ

Awards 1999

Harmonia Mundi ② HMC90 1649/50 (138 minutes: DDD). Text and translation included. Recorded 1997 Ⓕ ●●●

This is a remarkable work, startling from the very outset (where the vigorous overture is preceded by a solo violin), and this performance is stunning. The work was classified at the time not as an oratorio but as a *trattenimento sacro* ('sacred entertainment'), which suggests that its first performance, in 1707 in Venice, took place in a private palace rather than a church. But Scarlatti brought to the work, besides his seemingly inexhaustible invention, all the dramatic instinct that had made him famous as a composer of operas (of which he had already written about 40). Anyone charged with extracting a 'highlights' selection from this would find themselves in a quandary, since almost every number could be considered a highlight. How could he omit, for example, the brilliant opening aria (with violin interpolations) for Adam, two remorseful arias, with affecting chromaticisms, for Eve, two contrasting D minor arias in succession for the brothers out in the fields, one feeling Nature sinister, the other peaceful, the jealous Cain floridly swearing vengeance at being slighted or movingly bidding farewell to his parents, Lucifer (with excited violins) tempting Cain, Adam and Eve grieving over the absence of their sons, Abel in Heaven sending consolation, and so on and so on?

René Jacobs has assembled an absolutely outstanding cast whose technical accomplishment, dramatic commitment and stylish ornamentation could scarcely be bettered. Furthermore, the instrumental playing is first-class.

Humanità e Lucifero

A Scarlatti Humanità e Lucifero **Corelli** Trio Sonatas – B flat, Op 3 No 3; C, Op 4 No 1 **Rossana Bertini** *sop* **Massimo Crispi** *ten* **Europa Galante / Fabio Biondi** *vn* Ⓟ

Opus 111 OPS30-129 (61 minutes: DDD) Text and translation included. Recorded 1990s Ⓕ ●

Alessandro Scarlatti's oratorio, *Humanità e Lucifero*, here receives its first recording. It dates from 1704 when it was first performed at the Collegio Nazareno in Rome on the Feast of the Blessed Virgin Mary. The text is written in the Italian vernacular, more widely understood than Latin. It takes the form of a dispute between Humanity – who celebrates the birth of the Virgin – and Lucifer, who struggles with her for supremacy. Eventually, Lucifer recognises that in Humanity he has more than met his match and he returns to Lake Avernus and the nether regions 'neither prince nor king'. The imagery evoked by the unidentified librettist is charmingly naive and sometimes colourful, both aspects of which are characteristically capitalised upon by Scarlatti.

This is a vibrant score of instant melodic and harmonic appeal, very well sung by Rossana Bertini (Humanity) and marginally less so by Massimo Crispi (Lucifer). Bertini has a particularly bright vocal timbre which suits her role admirably. Her intonation is deadly accurate and her performance radiates light throughout. Crispi is more variable in the success with which he negotiates some of Scarlatti's exacting passagework. The voice is less refined in tone quality than Bertini's and, while this is appropriate to his Stygian role, there is a tendency towards bluster which adversely affects tonal focus. The music itself holds the attention throughout and, as so often with Scarlatti, there are moments of outstanding beauty, enhanced by delicate scoring perhaps for solo violin, cello or sopranino recorder. In contrast with these delicate touches are passages of resonant scoring for solo trumpet. The insertion of two trio sonatas by Scarlatti's contemporary, Corelli, from Opp 3 and 4 are also very affecting in context. They are sensitively played by Biondi and his instrumentalists who bring a rare sense of poetry to the slow movements. In summary, this is a rewarding issue and one which readers so far unacquainted with Scarlatti's vocal music are likely to find a very enjoyable introduction. Recorded sound is excellent and full texts with translations are included.

Domenico Scarlatti Italian 1685-1757

GROVE *In 1701 Domenico Scarlatti was appointed organist and composer of the vice-regal court at Naples, where his father Alessandro was maestro di cappella. In 1705 his father sent him to find employment in Venice where he may have first met Handel, with whom he formed a strong attachment. By 1707, however, he was in Rome, assisting his father at S Maria Maggiore, and he remained in Rome for over 12 years, occupying posts as maestro to the dowager Queen of Poland from 1711, to the Marquis de Fontes from 1714, and at St Peter's (assistant maestro of the Cappella Giulia from November 1713, maestro from December 1714).*

In 1719 Scarlatti resigned his positions in Rome and apparently spent some years in Palermo before taking up his next post, as mestre of the Portuguese court in Lisbon. The Lisbon earthquake of 1755 destroyed documents about his career there, but his duties included giving keyboard lessons to John V's daughter, Maria Barbara, and his younger brother, Don Antonio. When Maria Barbara married the Spanish crown prince in 1729 Scarlatti followed her to Seville and then, in 1733, to Madrid, where he spent the rest of his life. Although he continued to write vocal music, sacred and secular, the main works of his Iberian years are the remarkable series of keyboard sonatas, copied out in his last years and taken to Italy by his colleague, the castrato Farinelli.

Scarlatti married twice: in 1728 a Roman, Maria Catarina Gentili, and in 1739 a Spaniard, Anastasia Maxarti Ximenes. None of his nine children became a musician. In 1738 King John V of Portugal knighted him: he responded by dedicating to the king a volume of Essercizi per gravicembalo, the only music published during his lifetime under his supervision.

The seven operas Scarlatti wrote in Rome for Queen Maria Casimira were by no means failures, and his church music and secular cantatas contain much admirable music. But his fame rightly rests on the hundreds of keyboard sonatas, nearly all in the same binary form, in which he gave free rein to his imagination, stimulated by the new sounds, sights and customs of Iberia and by the astonishing gifts of his royal pupil and patron. In these he explored new worlds of virtuoso technique, putting to new musical ends such devices as hand-crossing, rapidly repeated notes, wide leaps in both hands and countless other means of achieving a devastating brilliance of effect.

Keyboard Sonatas

Kk1; Kk3; Kk8; Kk9; Kk11; Kk17; Kk24; Kk25; B minor, Kk27; Kk29; Kk87; Kk96; Kk113; Kk141; Kk146; Kk173; Kk213; Kk214; Kk247; Kk259; Kk268; Kk283; Kk284; Kk380; Kk386; Kk387; Kk404; Kk443; Kk519; Kk520; Kk523

Awards 1996

Mikhail Pletnev *pf*

Virgin Classics ② VBD5 61961-2 Ⓑ (140 minutes: DDD). Recorded 1994 ○○○

Every so often a major pianist reclaims Scarlatti for the piano with an outstanding recording and this is such an occasion. As Ralph Kirkpatrick put it, Scarlatti's harpsichord, while supremely itself, is continually menacing a transformation into something else. True, the relation of the music to harpsichord sound could hardly be closer – you can't argue on that point! – and of course it wouldn't have been composed the way it is for a different instrument. Scarlatti is marvellous at suggesting imaginary orchestrations and stimulating our own imagination. He makes us aware of the different vantage points as the music passes before us, of the different tones of voice and rhetorical inflexions – as various in these sonatas as the events in them are unpredictable. There are dances, fiestas and processions here, serenades, laments, and evocations of everything from the rudest folk music to courtly entertainments and churchly polyphony; and as the kaleidoscope turns you marvel at the composer who could embrace such diversity, shape it and put it all on to the keyboard.

This is strongly individual playing, be warned. Pletnev's free-ranging poetic licence may not be to your taste. Not that his spectacular virtuosity is likely to be controversial: this really is *hors de catégorie* and enormously enjoyable. And the evocations of the harpsichord are often very witty, but Pletnev doesn't shrink from using the full resources of the piano, sustaining pedal included, and if you baulk at the prospect of that as the means to an end he may not be for you.

The sustaining pedal is indeed dangerous in music which is almost wholly to do with lines, not washes of colour; its effect is to make us see Scarlatti as if through Mendelssohn's eyes. Yet moments of such falsification are rare. As often as not when Pletnev appears to be on the verge of stepping outside Scarlatti's world, or reinventing a little bit of it, it's because of some shaft of insight vouchsafed to his extraordinary musical mind that is well worth having. Characterization is everything, and though he can be a mite coy in the reflective sonatas he generally goes straight to the heart of the matter. The vigorous, full tone in the quick numbers is a joy, and most admirable is the way he makes sound immediately command character. That is something only the best artists are able to do. Superb recorded sound.

Keyboard Sonatas – C (manuscript – Yale University); G; D; C (all three ed Henle); G (ed Sociedad Española de Musicología, Madrid); D minor; A; G (all ed Unión Musical Española, Madrid); A (ed Musica Antiqua, Lisbon); A; E (both MS – Biblioteca de Catalunya, Barcelona); A (MS – British Library, London); A (MS – Real Conservatorio de Música, Madrid). Fandango in D minor P

Mayako Soné *hpd*

Erato 4509-94806-2 (51 minutes: DDD) Ⓕ

Recorded 1993 ○

It's a bit silly of Erato to label this disc 'Unpublished sonatas' when the publishers of eight of the present 14 are actually listed: if they meant 'recently discovered sonatas', why not say so? Apart from this, however, a certain scepticism is called for by the claim that these are by Scarlatti. A few may well be by him; the majority, to differing extents, are of doubtful authenticity. The most convincing 'possibles' are the exuberant Yale C major and three sonatas (two of them longer than usual) found in Valladolid and published by UME in Madrid. The *Fandango* has been worked up by the player here from a sketch (an impression of Scarlatti's improvisation?) in a private collection in Tenerife: shorter than the famous example attributed to Soler but closely resembling it in style. It is played with tremendous gusto – like everything else here – on a Blanchet copy by Mayako Soné, a young harpsichordist who is making quite a name for herself. Her experience as a continuo player has doubtless been a contributory factor in her strong rhythmic sense; and her crisp articulation is a pleasure to hear. Regardless of the authenticity of these pieces, this is a very attractive disc.

Keyboard Sonatas, Volume 2 – A minor, Kk3, G, Kk14; E, Kk20; B minor, Kk27; D minor, Kk32; D, Kk33, A, Kk39; E minor, Kk98; A minor, Kk109; D minor, Kk141; G, Kk146; A, Kk208; A, Kk209; D minor, Kk213; A, Kk322; D, Kk436; F minor, Kk481; D, Kk492. D minor, Kk517
Michael Lewin *pf*
Naxos 8 553067 (76 minutes: DDD) Ⓢ
Recorded 1995

Michael Lewin is an American pianist as dexterous and assured as he is audacious. Here there is no sense of 'studio' caution but only of liberating and dazzling music-making, live and on the wing. Kk492 in D could hardly provide a more brilliant curtain raiser, and in Kk3 in A minor (the one where Scarlatti's impish humour offers the musical equivalent of someone slipping on a banana skin) Lewin's playing positively brims over with high spirits. The D major Sonata, Kk33, is all thrumbing guitars and bursts of sunlight and in Kk141, with its cascades of repeated notes, Lewin even gives Martha Argerich a run for her money. There is a no less appealing balm and musical quality in the more restrained numbers such as Kk32 in D minor and Kk208 in A, though the recital comes to a suitably ebullient conclusion with Kk517 in D minor which is here like a river in full spate. The New York-based recordings are suitably lively (more successful than in Vol 1) and not even the most persistent lover of Scarlatti on the harpsichord could accuse Michael Lewin of an absence of the necessary glitter, panache and stylistic awareness.

Giacinto Scelsi Italian 1905-88

GROVE *Scelsi, of aristocratic birth, had no formal training and ranged over many styles in his earlier works while remaining constant to an ideal of music as a link with the transcendental. That remained his conviction in works after the 1950s, in which he often used microtones, thin textures and extremely slow movement.*

Kya

Kya[b]. Ixor. Maknongan. Tre Pezzi. Rucke di Guck[a]. Yamaon[b]
[b]**Johannes Schmidt** *bass* **Marcus Weiss** *sax*
[a]**Philippe Racine** *picc* [b]**Contrechamps Ensemble / Jürg Wyttenbach**
Hat-Hut Hat Now Series HATN117 Ⓕ
(56 minutes: DDD). Recorded 1997-98

This substantial cross-section of Scelsi's later works is very welcome, providing the chance to hear some of his most characteristic chant-like music. It is usually chant with an expressionistic edge, any hints of the rapt serenity of 'holy minimalism' (as in the second of the *Three Pieces*) emerging relatively rarely from the shadow of an altogether fiercer, wilder set of musical obsessions than those of Pärt or Tavener. These obsessions are most apparent here in the extraordinary three-movement *Yamaon* for bass singer and (mainly bass) instruments, the raw vocal rhetoric and gravelly instrumental counterpoints of which echo Xenakis at his most extreme. Otherwise the works are purely instrumental, and all performed in versions involving Marcus Weiss's saxophones (soprano, alto or bass). This is not always a good idea: in the case of *Rucke di Guck* (the original version for oboe with piccolo can be heard on CPO or Attacca) and in *Kya* (the version for clarinet and ensemble available on CPO), the relatively earthy, dense timbre of the saxophone sometimes cuts across the essential purity of the musical thought. It must also be said that CPO's documentation, sometimes including substantial extracts from the score, is far superior to that of this Hat-Hut issue, which among other things leaves us completely in the dark about the nature of the text sung in *Yamaon*. But whichever version you choose, this remarkable music will have a hypnotic effect on you, and the Hat-Hut recordings are technically first-rate.

Samuel Scheidt German 1587-1654

GROVE *Scheidt was organist of the Moritzkirche, Halle, for several years, and studied with Sweelinck in Amsterdam before becoming Halle court organist in 1609. From 1619-20 he was also court Kapellmeister, but the musical establishment almost disbanded (because of the Thirty Years War) in 1625. In 1627-30 he was director of music in Halle, also composing for the Marktkirche. His duties as court Kapellmeister resumed in 1638. Scheidt was active as an organ expert and a teacher and knew both Schutz and Schein.*

Scheidt distinguished himself in both keyboard and sacred vocal music, in which he combined traditional counterpoint with the new Italian concerto style. Contrapuntal chorale settings are important among his c150 keyboard pieces. Some appear in his three-volume Tabulatura nova (1624), the first German publication of keyboard music to be in open score rather than in German organ tablature or in two-staff format; the collection also contains variations and liturgical pieces. Scheidt left some 160 sacred vocal works. His first book, Cantiones sacrae (1620), consists of polychoral motets, some of them based on chorales, and his second (1620) of large concertos with obbligato instrumental parts. Small concertos for few voices make up the four volumes of Geistliche Concerte (1631 -40). Scheidt also composed dances, canzonas, sinfonias etc and canons.

Ludi Musici

Ludi Musici – Alamande a 4; Canzon ad imitationem Bergamas angl a 5; Canzon super Cantionem Gallicam a 5; Canzon super O Nachbar Roland a 5; Five Courants a 4; Courant dolorosa a 4; Two Galliards a 4; Galliard a 5; Galliard battaglia a 5; Three Paduanas a 4 **P**
Hespèrion XX / Jordi Savall *viol*
Auvidis Fontalis ES8559 (62 minutes: DDD) Ⓕ
Recorded 1995

Scheidt's *Ludi Musici* reflects the fusion of English and German traditions in the emergent world of instrumental music in early 17th-century Germany and is a mouth-wateringly diverse and inventive mixture of dance, canzona and variation. These are works which brim over with character and nonchalantly brilliant craftsmanship. Scheidt has that rare knack, for the 1620s and 1630s, of sustaining an instrumental piece for more than two minutes without bombarding us with a new idea every 10 bars; the longer pieces such as the Paduanas and the brilliant Canzon a 5 *ad imitationem Bergamas angl*, with its thrilling close, convey admirable long-term direction amid a concentrated love of ephemeral effect. This is a cocktail which Hespèrion XX relishes. The Pavans are, as you would expect from Jordi Savall, eventful. There are moments when an indulgence from Savall's treble viol stifles the potential for a more reflective allusion, but the overriding effect is of a performer striving to find a meaningful discourse, not content just to 'let the music play itself'; the colour and shape he brings to line and texture is often beguiling (disarmingly poignant in the stillness of the final Paduana), at times too much of a good thing but always engaging.

Johann Hermann Schein

German 1586-1630

GROVE *Schein trained as a soprano in the Dresden court chapel, studied at Schulpforta and Leipzig and later worked as music director and tutor to the children of Gottfried von Wolffersdorff, 1613-15. After a year as Kapellmeister at the Weimar court, he became Kantor of St Thomas's, Leipzig in 1616. He knew both Schütz, a close friend, and Scheidt. Primarily a composer for the voice, Schein was significant as one of the first composers to graft the modern Italian style on to the traditional elements of Lutheran church music. Much of his large sacred vocal output (nearly 400 works) is in five published volumes. The first part of Opella nova (1618) contains sacred concertos with continuo, clearly influenced by Viadana's but based (in most cases) on chorale melodies; the second part (1626), which uses fewer chorales, includes obbligato instrumental parts. His other sacred publications are a motet collection (1615), a book of sacred madrigals (1623) and the Cantional (1627), a hymnbook. Schein left some 90 secular vocal pieces, all to his own texts. Especially Italianate are the three-part settings in Musica boscareccia (1621-28) and his German continuo madrigals (1624 – the first such works to be published). He also composed songs and occasional works. His main instrumental work is the Banchetto musicale (1617), containing 20 variation suites.*

Israelis Brünnlein

Ensemble Vocal Européen / Philippe Herreweghe
Harmonia Mundi HMC90 1574 (79 minutes: DDD) Ⓕ
Texts and translations included
Recorded 1995

Anyone who hears this sympathetic account of *Israelis Brünnlein* ('The Fountains of Israel' – 26 sacred madrigals in five and six parts with a *basso seguente*) from Ensemble Vocal Européen will be convinced that this is one of the great pillars of German baroque music. It is fascinating not only as a demonstration of how the best German music incorporates foreign styles within indigenous techniques but also for Schein's discovery of his own unique expressive horizons, in ways which cannot directly be attributed to either Mantua or Leipzig. As in the *Lagrime di San Pietro* of Lassus (a composer whose poised contrapuntal craft is transmuted with profound respect by Schein), secular idioms successfully serve the sacred vision. Herreweghe, whose cool and collected reading of the Lassus masterpiece (see review under Lassus; refer to the Index) is vocally peerless, finds fresh priorities here. The exposed solo context draws out a greater sense of quasi-spontaneous attention, particularly in upbeat examples like 'Freue dich des Weibes' and the brilliance of 'Ist nicht Ephraim?'. Emotional intensity can, however, sound over-measured in works like 'Die mit Tränen säen' and 'Was betrübst', where dramatic urgency is required above the restrained shapeliness that is Herreweghe's hallmark. There are some fine singers (underpinned by the splendid Peter Kooy), even if the tenor tuning is not always beyond reproach; as an almost comprehensive – five pieces are left out – volume of 80-odd minutes, this further assures Schein's reputation as a master of exquisite characterization.

Johann Heinrich Schmelzer

Austrian c1620/23-1680

GROVE *Schmelzer was trained in Vienna and served in the court chapel from the mid-1630s, becoming a member of the orchestra in 1649 and vice-Kapellmeister in 1671. In 1679 he was made Kapellmeister. The leading Austrian composer of instrumental music before Biber, he wrote 150 ballet suites for court dramatic productions and over 100 sonatas. The former each have between two and nine dances, sometimes thematically related; some include elements of folk music. Notable among the sonatas are the six Sonatae unarum fidium (1664), the earliest published set for solo violin and continuo. Schmelzer's prolific output also includes sepolcri and other dramatic pieces, nearly 200 sacred works and some secular vocal music.*

Sonatae unarum fidium

Schmelzer Sonatae unarum fidium – Nos 1-6. P
Sonata for Violin and Continuo in A minor, 'Il cucù'
Biber (arr A Schmelzer) Sonata for Violin and Continuo, 'Victori der Christen'
Romanesca (Andrew Manze *vn* Nigel North *theorbo* John Toll *hpd/org*)
Harmonia Mundi HMU90 7143 (67 minutes: DDD)
Also includes a free sampler disc of Biber violin sonatas. Recorded 1995 Ⓕ ⦿

Performances of works from the indigenous Austrian 17th-century 'school' have made a significant impact on the *status quo* of mainstream baroque instrumental music of late. This is not to say that the more formalised Italian traditions, which dominated in Vienna until Schmelzer's gradual and unspectacular rise to Kappelmeister of the imperial court in 1679, have been in any way shown up; rather that the distinctive rhetorical flavour of *Mittel Europa* has both broadened our horizons and encouraged players and listeners to think more flexibly about the unique language of composers such as Biber and Schmelzer. These are men who have left a remarkable amount to the imagination: and yet, a step of faith, technical brilliance and a commitment to find the dramatic and emotional heart of these solo works reaps untold rewards. Whilst Biber has enjoyed the most marked renaissance of those in the employ of the imperial court, Schmelzer is the spiritual father of this colourful native expression.

Coming to these recordings from Biber's extravagant and incomparably theatrical sonatas, one is immediately struck by common stylistic threads but also by Schmelzer's studied lyricism, a searing and disarming feel for melodic progression (heard in the close of the *Cucù* Sonata) and the sense of a man who, when he is not following his tail with ostinato basses, has mastered the canzona-sonata mentality and takes full advantage of its freedom. All Biberian features certainly, but as Andrew Manze both explains in his note and demonstrates in his playing, there is less overall ostentation here; whilst the extraordinary Sonata No 4 latterly contains gloriously extended and potent outbursts, it is the patient arching direction of Schmelzer's melodic frame which draws one in. Manze and his accomplished continuo players (the theorbo is exquisite and distinctive) are wonderful exponents in this mesmerizing baroque byway.

Schmelzer Sonatae unarum fidium[b] **Anonymous** Ⓟ
Scordatura Violin Sonata[a] **Bertali** Chiaconna
John Holloway *vn* [ab]**Aloysia Assenbaum** *org*
[a]**Lars Ulrik Mortensen** *hpd/org*
ECM New Series 465 066-2 (63 minutes: DDD) Ⓕ
Recorded 1997 OO

Johann Heinrich Schmelzer was the first homegrown Kapellmeister to be appointed at the Hapsburg Court in Vienna in 1679, following generations of Italians hired for their *oltremontani* flair and easy command of prevailing fashion. Schmelzer's six sonatas from 1664 are certainly Italianate, and not without freewheeling virtuosity, but they also contain a type of extended lyricism, and, as in the opening of the Fourth Sonata, a sense of no-nonsense progression of comforting expectation. In fact, this work, and that by his dynamic forebear, Antonio Bertali (whose own *Chiaconna* is quite a partypiece) are typical 17th-century showcases for the violin where intricate and fantastical divisions unfold above a recurring bass pattern. The playing in this technically demanding repertoire is dazzling, and the intonation faultless. Yet equally impressive is the measured classicism and subtle poetical restraint of the protagonist, John Holloway. Not every bar of Schmelzer's set is compelling and Holloway opts for a consistent clarity of sound rather than milking every note as if it is of earth-shattering importance; he uses *rubato* discerningly, as in the introspective musings in the Fifth Sonata where the narrative is beautifully and elegantly articulated. The idea of a double continuo of organ and harpsichord is highly effective throughout.

The first recording of *Sonatae unarum* was made by Romanesca (see above), and they too opt for a counterpoint of continuos with organ and theorbo. The sense of a rich consort-like texture can only bring a much-needed breadth to music which might otherwise test the concentration over the course of an hour. To choose between these two fine recordings is not easy without significant qualification, save to say that Romanesca is more consistently adventurous and theatrical. Holloway and his excellent keyboardists are less extrovert, softer-grained and more inclined to hover with sweet and restrained decorum. Both recordings are exceptional in their way, revealing how much interpretative leeway Schmelzer gives his players.

Franz Schmidt

Czechoslovakian/Austrian 1874-1939

GROVE *Schmidt, a pupil of Bruckner and Fuchs at the Vienna Conservatory, was cellist in the Vienna Hofoper orchestra (1896-1911, for much of the time under Mahler), then taught at the Staatsakademie (1914-27) and the Musikhochschule (1927-31). In his music he continued the grand tradition, with peripheral influence from Schoenberg, Debussy and Hindemith: his works include four symphonies (1899, 1913, 1928, 1933), by which he made his name, the orchestral Variationen über ein Husarenlied (1931), chamber music (two string quartets, a piano quintet and two quintets for clarinet, piano and strings), organ pieces, the oratorio Das Buch mit sieben Siegeln (1937) and two operas (Notre Dame, 1904; Fredigundis, 1921).*

Symphony No 4

Awards 1996

Symphony No 4 in C. Variations on a Hussar's Song
London Philharmonic Orchestra / Franz Welser-Möst
EMI CDC5 55518-2 (72 minutes: DDD) Ⓕ
Recorded 1994 OOO

Writing in *The Symphony* (ed Robert Simpson, Penguin Books: 1967) the late Harold Truscott made a strong case for Franz Schmidt. He robustly dismissed the notion that his music does not travel. 'It "travels" very well, when allowed to do so, and I will go so far as to say that anyone who claims a love and understanding of

Beethoven, Brahms or Sibelius, should have no difficulty with Schmidt. There could,' he went on, 'scarcely be a more positive work than No 4, whose confidence is complete and without bombast' and it is obvious that Schmidt's mastery of the art of symphonic thinking and of the orchestra is everywhere in evidence. The symphony is in one unbroken span whose material derives from the haunting opening 21-bar theme on solo trumpet – in itself an idea of remarkable originality. Unlike Reger, whose influence can at times be clearly heard, Schmidt was a late developer and far from prolific. Indeed apart from the four symphonies, there is only one other orchestral work, the *Variations on a Hussar's Song* recorded here. For those who have never encountered his music, it is perhaps best if loosely described as rich in palette, in much the same way as Elgar, chromatic in its harmonic language yet never cloying, and above all it has an innate nobility, an elegiac dignity of utterance and a sense of vision. Not without reason did Truscott call Schmidt the 'only real successor to Bruckner – in so far as there is one at all'. Welser-Möst shows great feeling for this music and carries his fine players with him. Theirs is playing of eloquence and dedication.

Additional recommendation

Complete Symphonies

Chanteaux *vc* **Detroit Symphony Orchestra; Chicago Symphony Orchestra / Järvi**

Chandos CHAN9568 ④ (175 minutes: DDD: 3/90[R]; 3/92[R]; 4/96[R]) Ⓕ

Schmidt's four symphonies make for rewarding listening, especially in these colourful readings from Neeme Järvi.

Das Buch mit sieben Siegeln

Christiane Oelze *sop* **Cornelia Kallisch** *contr* **Stig Andersen, Lothar Odinius** *tens* **René Pape, Alfred Reiter** *basses* **Friedemann Winklhofer** *org* **Bavarian Radio Chorus and Symphony Orchestra / Franz Welser-Möst**

EMI ② CDS5 56660-2 (107 minutes: DDD) Ⓕ

Text and translation included. Recorded live in 1997 ●

Franz Welser-Möst shows complete sympathy with Schmidt's world and sensibility in what many admirers consider Schmidt's masterpiece, *Das Buch mit sieben Siegeln* ('The Book with Seven Seals'). Schmidt turned to the last book of the New Testament, the Revelation of St John the Divine, for his text. Nobility shines through almost every bar of the score. The recording offers fine sound, and a performance of great commitment and grandeur. Schmidt portrays John as a young man and apparently wished to have a Heldentenor rather than a lyric tenor sing the role, and this is observed here. The singing throughout is impressive from all concerned – and in particular Stig Andersen – and the sensitive orchestral response leaves no doubt of all the artists' belief in this visionary and often inspired work. On almost every count this Bavarian performance does justice to Schmidt's masterpiece. The technical balance of the recording has been expertly and musically done.

Additional recommendation

Das Buch mit sieben Siegeln

Röschmann *sop* **Lipovšek** *mez* **Lippert** *ten* **Hawlata** *bass* **Tachezi** *org* **Vienna Singverein; Vienna Philharmonic Orchestra / Harnoncourt**

Teldec 8573-81040-2 (117 minutes: DDD: 6/01) Ⓕ

A distinguished, live performance, though it doesn't quite beat Welser-Möst's: despite the Singverein's big sound they lack urgency and sheer pace at some crucial moments.

Further listening

Hindemith Das Unaufhörliche

Sonntag *sop* **Wörle** *ten* **Lorenz** *bar* **Korn** *bass* **Berlin Radio Children's Choir, Chorus and Symphony Orchestra / Zagrosek**

Wergo WER6603-2 ② (95 minutes: DDD: 10/97) Ⓕ

Hindemith's oratorio *The One Perpetual* is a setting of a poem by Gottfried Benn – celebrated literary adversary of Bertolt Brecht. A fascinating work to investigate.

Alfred Schnittke USSR 1934-1998

GROVE *Schnittke was a pupil of Rakov and Golubev at the Moscow Conservatory (1953-61), where he taught until 1972. His works often use quotations, parodies and stylistic imitations in a highly charged manner, though some are more unified in expression. Textures are rich and complexly varied and string instruments feature prominently in his output, which, apart from four symphonies and various stage works, includes five concerti grossi, four violin concertos, two violin sonatas and chamber music. He was a prolific writer on Russian music.*

Concerto grosso No 1

Concerto grosso No 1[a]. Quasi una sonata[b]. Moz-Art à la Haydn[c]

Tatiana Grindenko *vn* **Yuri Smirnov** *hpd/prep pf/pf* **Chamber Orchestra of Europe / [a]Heinrich Schiff, [bc]Gidon Kremer** [a]*vn*

DG Masters 445 520-2GMA (75 minutes: DDD) Ⓜ

Recorded live in 1988 ●

For a single representative of Alfred Schnittke's work you could choose nothing better than the first *Concerto grosso* of 1977. Here are the psychedelic mélanges of baroque and modern, the drastic juxtapositions of pseudo-Vivaldi with pseudo-Berg, producing an effect at once aurally exciting and spiritually disturbing. The piece has had many recordings, but never with the panache of Kremer and friends and never with the vivid immediacy of this live DG recording (in fact the solo violins are rather too closely miked for comfort, but that's only a tiny drawback). *Quasi una sonata* was originally composed in 1968 for violin and piano and it was something of a breakthrough piece for Schnittke as he emerged from what he called 'the puberty rites of serialism', letting his imagination run riot for the first time. No one could call it a disciplined piece, but if that worries you, you should leave Schnittke alone anyway. The transcription for solo violin and string orchestra is an ingenious one and Kremer again supplies all the requisite agonised intensity. *Moz-Art à la Haydn* is a very slight piece of work, and it really depends on visual theatricality to make its effect. Still, it complements the other two pieces, and this disc is an excellent introduction to this composer.

Concerto grosso No 6

Schnittke Concerto grosso No 6[a]. Violin Sonata **Takemitsu** Nostalgia **Weill** Concerto for Violin and Wind Orchestra, Op 12
Daniel Hope *vn* [a]**Simon Mulligan** *pf/hpd* **English Symphony Orchestra / William Boughton**
Nimbus NI5582 (73 minutes: DDD) Ⓕ
Recorded 1990

Full marks to Nimbus for variety. The danger is that three such different composers, combined in a way you would never expect in a concert, will cancel each other out. Fortunately, the performances are strong enough – even when heard in close succession – to justify the enterprise, and the recordings are no less successful in the way they capture the intimacy of tone characteristic of all four compositions. With the earlier of the Schnittke works, the Sonata, a textual point of some interest emerges. Usually, the harpsichord functions as the violinist's *alter ego* throughout, but Hope, with Schnittke's agreement, has the keyboardist move from harpsichord to piano from the final stages of the second movement onwards. The change is certainly justified in the finale, and adds an extra dimension to a commendably unexaggerated account of this turbulent score. There is room for a degree of detachment in the fraught *Concerto grosso* No 6 and this the Nimbus team provides.

The early Weill Violin Concerto can easily sprawl, and sound too earnest for its own good. Here there is an appropriate fluency, and excessive gravity is avoided. Daniel Hope is able to project the required authority, especially in the cadenza, and although some might prefer a more forward placement for the soloist, the excellent qualities of Hope's playing are no less appealing. As for Takemitsu's song of farewell for the film-maker Andrei Tarkovsky, the music is a model of how to balance emotional restraint and expressive warmth, and the performance does it justice.

Piano Quintet

Piano Quintet[a]. String Trio[b]. Fuga[c]. Klingende Buchstaben[d]. Stille Musik[e]
[a]**Dimity Hall,** [abce]**Mark Lubotsky** *vns* [a]**Irina Morozova,** [b]**Theodore Kuchar** *vas* [bde]**Alexander Ivashkin,** [a]**Julian Smiles** *vcs* [a]**Irina Schnittke** *pf*
Naxos 8 554728 (69 minutes: DDD) Ⓢ
Recorded 1999

Naxos here achieves the coup of employing both Alexander Ivashkin, the composer's champion and biographer, and his widow Irina. Recorded in 1999, the performances derive from concerts given at that year's Australian Festival of Chamber Music. Apart from the early, student piece *Fuga*, for solo violin, the works chosen represent a period of stylistic consolidation for Schnittke. Lacking the flash theatricality most readily associated with him, they none the less contain some of his most profound music.

The key work is the Piano Quintet (1972 to 1976), a memorial to the composer's mother and the piece in which he seems most clearly to have taken on Shostakovich's mantle. In the bitter waltzes of the second and fifth movements it is as if that composer is refracted through frosted glass (or seen through tears). Irina's piano is rightly prominent, the engine driving the other players' heightened expressivity, exposing the vulnerability and raw pain behind the Technicolor masks. There is something more than authenticity involved in hearing the ideas of a dead composer, writing in memory of his dead mother, brought to life by his widow.

The other substantial work is the String Trio written for Alban Berg's centenary, a less eerie, less angst-ridden utterance with its echoes of Schubert. The performance is less strongly projected than that of the Quintet, but is evocative enough. The typically intangible *Stille Musik* and the short *Klingende Buchstaben*, a tribute to Ivashkin, benefit from the latter's committed playing. *Fuga*, recorded here for the first time, becomes more Schnittke-like as it progresses from the Bach-Shostakovich of its opening.

The whole programme is well thought out, and if not everyone seems equally comfortable (the veteran Lubotsky's playing is not always ideally clean), it is rare to find the more demanding sort of contemporary music at this price. What of the alternatives? While direct competitors don't entirely avoid blandness, it is Kremer, Bashmet and friends, differently coupled and recorded on both sides of the Iron Curtain, who most effectively plumb the depths of Schnittke's expressive world. Also recommended: the Trio Sonata, Bashmet's arrangement of the Trio for string ensemble (RCA), and *In memoriam*, the composer's own, more radical orchestral reworking of the Quintet (Sony). With the advantage of economy, the present disc offers decent, unspectacular sound and comes with helpful notes by Richard Whitehouse (it's only the back inlay that muddles chronology). All hail to Naxos for issuing it.

Schnittke String Quartet No 3. Piano Quintet
Mahler/Schnittke Piano Quartet
Borodin Quartet (Mikhail Kopelman, Andrei Abramenkov *vns* Dmitri Shebalin *va* Valentin Berlinsky *vc*); **Ludmilla Berlinsky** *pf*
Virgin Classics VC7 59040-2 (66 minutes: DDD) Ⓕ
Recorded 1990 ●

Schnittke's chamber music does not have the high public profile of some of his symphonies and concertos, but in many ways it is more fastidiously composed and it certainly makes for equally rewarding listening at home. The Piano Quintet is the outstanding feature of this disc. Predominantly slow and mournful (it is dedicated to the memory of the composer's mother) and with a haunting waltz on the notes of the BACH monogram, it is here played with compelling intensity, especially by the pianist Ludmilla Berlinsky, daughter of the Borodin Quartet's cellist. The Piano Quartet is a conflation of the 16-year-old Mahler's first movement with his incomplete second movement in Schnittke's own paraphrase – another haunting experience, beautifully played and recorded. Less satisfying as a performance, because slightly glossed over, is the Third Quartet; but this is perhaps the finest and undoubtedly the most often performed of Schnittke's chamber works. As a whole the disc can be warmly recommended.

String Trio

String Trio. Violin Sonatas – No 1; No 2, 'Quasi una sonata'
Mateja Marinkovic´ *vn* **Paul Silverthorne** *va* **Timothy Hugh** *vc* **Linn Hendry** *pf* Ⓕ
ASV CDDCA868 (65 minutes: DDD)

This performance is extremely satisfying. It is atmospherically recorded, and convincingly reinforces the Trio's claims to be considered one of Schnittke's major works. The music is surely to be preferred in this original version, rather than as the 'Trio Sonata' of Yuri Bashmet's orchestral arrangement. Dating from 1985, and written in response to a commission from the Alban Berg Society of Vienna, the Trio is notable for the extent to which its reminiscences and re-creations are far less contrived and self-indulgent than is often the case with this composer. They are not merely backward-looking, nostalgic gestures, but suggest a blueprint for a new, romantically tinged post-modernism. Whether or not you go along with this analysis, it is difficult to deny that the Trio puts the pair of early violin sonatas into the shade. They are not negligible pieces, even so, and these performances have much to commend them. Mateja Marinković and Linn Hendry make a first-rate duo: even the most piano-bashing bits of the Second Sonata are not deprived of all musical sense, and the urgent interplay between the instruments is authentically intense.

Suite in the Old Style

Suite in the Old Style. Moz-Art à la Haydn. Praeludium in memoriam Dmitri Shostakovich. A Paganini. Stille Musik. Stille Nacht. Madrigal in Memoriam Oleg Kagan. Gratulations rondo
Mateja Marinkovič, Thomas Bowes *vns* **Timothy Hugh** *vc* **Linn Hendry** *pf*
ASV CDDCA877 (68 minutes: DDD) Ⓕ
Recorded 1993

At first glance, this disc presents a rather scrappy impression. It contains no large-scale pieces, and the largest work – the early *Suite in the Old Style* – is for the most part an uneventful exercise in dutiful imitation. It is what the *Suite* only hints at that the other works realise more fully. In the *Gratulations rondo* Schnittke again wears the mask of conformity to an old, easygoing classicism. When the mask begins to slip, we wonder what to think. Is this a serious lesson about the potential banality of classicism's familiar formulas? Are the distortions of those formulas expressive of affection or hostility?

These issues come most fully into focus in *Stille Nacht*, as Gruber's sweet little tune, with its obediently basic harmony, is subjected to quiet but ruthlessly dissonant deconstruction. 'Silent Night' acquires the connotations of Rachel Carson's *Silent Spring*, suggesting an environmental disaster rather than a cosy spirituality. Schnittke's ability to create memorable musical laments is well displayed here, in the Shostakovich and Kagan memorial pieces, in *Stille Musik* and even in *A Paganini*, which traces an absorbing contest between an apparent distaste for virtuosity and a celebration of it. The impact of these compositions is the greater for their relative concentration and Mateja Marinković is a player of admirable technical refinement. The recording is first-class, and the disc can serve as an ideal introduction to Schnittke for listeners who may have doubts about his larger-scale works.

Further listening
Gubaidulina String Quartets Nos 1-3
Coupling: String Trio
Danish Quartet
CPO CPO999 064-2 (70 minutes: DDD) Ⓕ

Intellectually and emotionally challenging, Gubaidulina's string quartets make for compelling listening. Anyone with an ear for 'tough' music should give them a try.

12 Penitential Psalms

Swedish Radio Choir / Tõnu Kaljuste
ECM New Series 453 513-2 (53 minutes: DDD) Ⓕ
Text and translation included. Recorded 1996 ●

Schnittke's 12 *Penitential Psalms* (1988) are not biblical: Nos 1-11 use 16th-century Russian texts and No 12 is a wordless meditation which encapsulates the spirit and style of what precedes it. Though at times dark and despairing in tone, this is in no sense liturgical music. It is too expansive, and reaches towards the ecstatic too consistently, to qualify as ascetic or austere. Indeed, the warmly euphonious chorale-like textures with which several of the movements end are sumptuous enough for one to imagine a soulful saxophone weaving its way through them. As this suggests, the recording is extremely, and not inappropriately, resonant, and the performance is polished to a fault, the individual lines superbly controlled and the textures balanced with a fine feeling for their weight and diversity. Although some may find this issue a little too refined, it realises the work's expressive world with imposing and irresistible authenticity. In these works, Schnittke seems to be doing penance for the extravagant indulgences of works such as *Stille Nacht* and the Viola Concerto, abandoning modernism in general and expressionism in particular. The music nevertheless retains strong links with the images of lament and spiritual aspiration, and there is nothing in the least artificial or contrived about its emotional aura. It is difficult to imagine a more convincing or better recorded account of it than this one.

Othmar Schoeck Swiss 1886-1957

GROVE *Schoeck studied at the Zürich Conservatory and with Reger in Leipzig (1907-8), then worked in Zürich and St Gall as a conductor. He was one of the leading Swiss composers of his time. His numerous songs, usually setting German Romantic poetry, establish him among the foremost lieder composers, but he also wrote important operas: the dense and richly scored Penthesilea (1927) and Vom Fischer und syner Fru (1930), which like other works is more folklike. The rest of his output includes choral and orchestral scores and a few chamber pieces*

Lieder

Unter Sternen, Op 55[a] – Frühgesicht; Ein Tagewerk I und II. Das Stille Leuchten, Op 60[a] – Reisephantasie; Das Ende des Festes; Jetzt rede du! Lieder, Op 20[a] – Auf ein kind; Nachruf. Lieder, Op 24*b* – Jugendgedenken[a]; Keine Rast[b]; Das Ziel[b]; Ravenna[b]. Lieder, Op 17[a] – Peregrina II. Lieder, Op. 19*a*[a] – Dämmerung senkte sich von oben. Hafis-Lieder, Op 33[a] – Ach, wie schön ist Nacht und Dämmerschein. Lieder, Op 19*b*[a] – Nachklang; Höre den Rath den die Leyer tönt; Diese Gondel vergleich ich. Lieder, Op 8[b] – Aus zwei Tälern; Auskunkt. Lieder, Op 31[b] – Kindheit; Im Kreuzgang von Santo Stefano. Zehn Lieder, Op 44[b]
Dietrich Fischer-Dieskau *bar* [a]**Margrit Weber,** [b]**Karl Engel** *pfs*
DG 463 513-2GFD (78 minutes: ADD) (M)
Recorded [a]1958 and [b]1977

No one has done more for the superb but persistently underrated songs of Schoeck than Fischer-Dieskau, and the 33 here are sung with outstanding subtlety and are very shrewdly chosen. 'Subtlety' includes a remarkable palette of vocal colour and at times extremes of dynamic. 'Shrewdness' involves not only selection but juxtaposition. *Nachruf*, a poignant song of old age and lament over lost companions, is followed by *Jugendgedenken*, a nostalgic summoning up of happy memories; both gain by the conjunction, and Fischer-Dieskau's beautiful phrasing of 'nur noch einmal' ('just once more I will look back') movingly links them as a diptych. Those who have yet to discover Schoeck need only sample the haunting *Im Kreuzgang von Santo Stefano* or the darkly quiet *Ravenna*, both evocations of the poignancy of transitoriness, to be immediately captured. This is the only available recording of the recondite but masterly Op 44 cycle.

Elegie, Op 36

Andreas Schmidt *bar* **Musikkollegium Winterthur / Werner Andreas Albert**
CPO CPO999 472-2 (58 minutes: DDD) (M)
Text and translation included. Recorded 1997

This is a wonderful disc. The *Elegie* was the first of Schoeck's song-cycles and among his most haunting. Its emotional origins are to be found in the turbulent affair he had with the pianist Mary de Senger, whose course Dr Chris Walton charts in his authoritative notes. They first met when de Senger auditioned for him in 1918 and their relationship survived various quarrels and reconciliations until 1923. The previous year Schoeck had begun composing a series of songs that in time came to form the present cycle. It can be said to portray 'the narrative of a dying love' and though the impulse was primarily autobiographical, his relationship with de Senger was not to disintegrate finally until after its completion and first performance. He began in the summer of 1922 by setting Eichendorff's poem, *Der Einsielder* – whose title he subsequently changed to *Der Einsame* ('The lonely one') – which he placed at the very end of the cycle.

The cycle comprises two dozen settings for baritone and chamber orchestra of poems by Lenau and Eichendorff. From the first notes the listener is drawn into Schoeck's world and remains under his spell for the remaining hour. What imaginative miniatures these are, powerful in atmosphere, full of inventive resource and sensitive colouring. Take, for example, the third song, 'Stille Sicherheit' ('Quiet certainty'), which takes one-and-a-half minutes but is so concentrated in feeling and heady in atmosphere that it conveys as much as a miniature tone-poem. The same may be said of No 11, 'Vesper', with its evocative tolling bells and powerful scents – and practically any of the later songs in this cycle. Not only is Schoeck's harmonic and orchestral palette subtle, but the vocal line is beautifully drawn and given the distinction of this artist, beautifully sung. This is one of the outstanding song-cycles of its period, very naturally recorded: its beauties resonate in the mind long after you have played it.

Penthesilea

Helga Dernesch *sop* Penthesilea; **Jane Marsh** *sop* Prothoe; **Mechtild Gessendorf** *sop* Meroe; **Marjana Lipovšek** *mez* High Priestess; **Gabriele Sima** *sop* Priestess; **Theo Adam** *bass-bar* Achilles; **Horst Hiestermann** *ten* Diomede; **Peter Weber** *bass* Herold **Austrian Radio Chorus and Symphony Orchestra / Gerd Albrecht**
Orfeo C364941B (80 minutes: ADD). Notes and text (F) included. Recorded live in 1982

Schoeck's one-act opera, *Penthesilea* is an astonishing and masterly score. It seems barely credible that a work so gripping in its dramatic intensity, and so powerful in atmosphere, should be so little known. It has the listener on the edge of the seat throughout its 80 short minutes and, like any great opera, it continues to cast a spell long after the music has ended. In the *Grove Dictionary of Opera*, Ronald Crichton wrote that 'at its most intense, the language of *Penthesilea* surpasses in ferocity Strauss's *Elektra*, a work with which it invites comparison'. In so far as it is a one-act work, set in the Ancient World, highly concentrated in feeling and with strongly delineated characters, it is difficult not to think of Strauss's masterpiece. Yet its sound world is quite distinctive. Though he is a lesser figure, Schoeck similarly renders the familiar language of Straussian opera entirely his own. The vocabulary is not dissimilar yet the world is different. We are immediately plunged into a vivid and completely individual world, packed with dramatic incident: off-stage war cries and exciting, dissonant trumpet calls. There is an almost symphonic handling of pace, but the sonorities are unusual: for example, there is a strong wind section, some 10 clarinets at various pitches, while there are only a handful of violins; much use is made of two pianos in a way that at times almost anticipates Britten. This performance emanates from the 1982 Salzburg Festival; Helga Dernesch in the title-role commands the appropriate range of emotions as Penthesilea and the remainder of the cast, including the Achilles of Theo Adam, rise to the occasion. The important choral role and the orchestral playing under Gerd Albrecht are eminently committed and the recording is good. There is a useful essay and libretto, though in German, not English.

Arnold Schoenberg

Austro/Hungarian 1874-1951

GROVE *Schoenberg began violin lessons when he was eight and almost immediately started composing, though he had no formal training until he was in his late teens, when Zemlinsky became his teacher and friend (in 1910 he married Zemlinsky's sister). His first acknowledged works date from the turn of the century and include the string sextet Verklärte Nacht as well as some songs, all showing influences from Brahms, Wagner and Wolf. In 1901-3 he was in Berlin as a cabaret musician and teacher, and wrote the symphonic poem Pelleas und Melisande, pressing the Straussian model towards denser thematic argument and contrapuntal richness.*

He then returned to Vienna and began taking private pupils, Berg and Webern being among the first. He also moved rapidly forwards in his musical style. The large orchestra of Pelleas and the Gurrelieder was replaced by an ensemble of 15 in Chamber Symphony No 1, but with greater harmonic strangeness, formal complexity and contrapuntal density. When atonality arrived in 1908, it was the inevitable outcome of a doomed attempt to accommodate ever more disruptive material. However, he found it possible a quarter-century later to return to something like his tonal style, as in the Suite in G for strings.

That, however, was not possible immediately. The sense of key was left behind as Schoenberg set poems by George in the last two movements of String Quartet No 2 and in the cycle Das Buch der hängenden Gärten, and for the next few years he lived in the new, rarefied musical air. With tonality had gone thematicism and rhythmic constraint; works tended to be short statements of a single extreme musical state, justifying the term 'expressionist' (Five Orchestral Pieces; Three Pieces and Six Little Pieces for piano). The larger pieces of this period have some appropriate dramatic content: the rage and despair of a woman seaching for her lover (Erwartung), the bizarre stories, melancholia and jokes of a distintegrating personality (Pierrot lunaire, for reciter in Sprechgesang with mixed quintet), or the progress of the soul towards union with God (Die Jakobsleiter).

Gradually Schoenberg came to find the means for writing longer instrumental structures, in the 12-note serial method, and in the 1920s he returned to standard forms and genres, notably in the Suite for piano, String Quartet No 3, Orchestral Variations and several choral pieces. He also founded the Society for Private Musical Performances (1919-21), involving his pupils in the presentation of new music under favourable conditions. In 1923 his wife died (he remarried the next year), and in 1925 he moved to Berlin to take a master class at the Prussian Academy of Arts. While there he wrote much of his unfinished opera Moses und Aron which is concerned with the impossibility of communicating truth without some distortion in the telling.

In 1933 he was obliged as a Jew to leave Berlin: he went to Paris, and formally returned to the faith which he had deserted for Lutheranism in 1898. Later the same year he arrived in the USA, and he settled in Los Angeles in 1934. It was there that he returned to tonal composition, while developing serialism to make possible the more complex structures of the Violin Concerto and the String Quartet No 4. In 1936 he began teaching at UCLA and his output dwindled. After a heart attack in 1945, however, he gave up teaching and made some return to expressionism (A Survivor from Warsaw, String Trio), as well as writing religious choruses.

Piano Concerto

Schoenberg Piano Concerto, Op 42[a]. Drei Klavierstücke, Op 11. Sechs Klavierstücke, Op 19.
Berg Sonata for Piano, Op 1. **Webern** Variations, Op 27
Mitsuko Uchida *pf* [a]**Cleveland Orchestra / Pierre Boulez**
Philips 468 033-2PH (63 minutes: DDD) Ⓕ
Recorded 2000 **OO**

Uchida's distinctive musical personality and outstanding technique make her Schoenberg, Berg and Webern well worth hearing however many other version of these works you have in your collection. Uchida brings a marvellous spontaneity and sense of drama to the more overtly romantic compositions here – Berg's Sonata and Schoenberg's Op 11 *Pieces*. This is certainly not one of those accounts of the Berg where you question the composer's wisdom in marking the first section for repeat. As for the Schoenberg, never has one been more aware of this music's closeness in time and spirit to the cataclysmic world of the monodrama *Erwartung*. Uchida's earlier recording of Op 11 was warmly praised, and this one is no less accomplished. Elsewhere, her relish for strongly juxtaposed contrast risks occasional overemphasis, as in the third of the Op 19 pieces, and the virtues of more sharply articulated playing in this repertory are demonstrated on Peter Hill's admirable super-bargain-price Naxos disc. His account of Webern's *Variations* is exemplary in its clarity and feeling for line; yet Uchida manages to suggest deeper links with more romantic perspectives without in any way traducing the music's inherent radicalism.

Links with romanticism are even more explicit in the texture and thematic character of Schoenberg's Concerto, and this performance places the work firmly in the tradition of Liszt and Brahms. Not even Pierre Boulez can bring ideal lucidity to the occasionally lumpy orchestral writing, but the performance as a whole, with excellent sound, has an attractive sweep and directness of utterance. Alfred Brendel's second recording (Philips) remains a fine achievment, but the orchestral playing is less refined than on the new disc, the recording drier, with a flatter perspective. Nor are Michael Gielen's readings of Schoenberg's two chamber symphonies as competitive as Uchidas's of the solo piano works.

Verklärte Nacht, Op 4

Verklärte Nacht. Pelleas und Melisande, Op 5
Berlin Philharmonic Orchestra / Herbert von Karajan
DG The Originals 457 721-2GOR (74 minutes: ADD) Ⓜ
Recorded 1973-74 **ooo**

This is a very distinguished coupling, superbly played by the BPO – a truly 'legendary' reissue, quite unsurpassed on record. Karajan never approached contemporary music with the innate radicalism and inside knowledge of a composer-conductor like Boulez; yet he cannot be accused of distorting reality by casting a pall of late-romantic opulence and languor over these works. He is understandably most at home in the expansive and often openly tragic atmosphere of Schoenberg's early tone-poems *Verklärte Nacht* and *Pelleas und Melisande*. The richly blended playing of the BPO provides the ideal medium for Karajan's seamless projection of structure and expression. He remains especially sensitive to the music's lyricism, to the connections that to his ears override the contrasts. Although *Verklärte Nacht* has certainly been heard in performances less redolent of 19th-century tradition, as well as less calculated in its recorded acoustic, this remains a powerfully dramatic reading. One man's view, then: but, given the man, a notably fascinating one.

Verklärte Nacht. Five Orchestral Pieces, Op 16. Three Piano Pieces, Op 11. Six Piano Pieces, Op 19. Piano Piece, Op 11 No 2 (arr Busoni)
Chicago Symphony Orchestra / Daniel Barenboim *pf*
Teldec 4509-98256-2 (77 minutes: DDD) Ⓕ
Recorded 1995

Barenboim's version begins with the evident belief that Schoenberg's initial marking of *Sehr langsam* is not an invitation to linger lovingly over every last semiquaver. The expressive trajectory of the whole is magnificently natural and persuasive. Only at the very end does Barenboim risk too weighty an articulation and too broad a tempo, a tendency confirming that his reading is stronger in passion than it is in tenderness. The recorded sound is also spacious in the extreme. Barenboim's superbly played account is a superior example of the 'wide screen' approach to Schoenberg's early masterwork favoured by conductors like Karajan and Sinopoli.

The appeal of this disc is greatly enhanced by the other items. There is a marvellously vivid performance of the Op 16 *Pieces* which, for clarity of texture and depth of expression, counts – along with Robert Craft's – as one of the most convincing of current versions. And we also hear Barenboim as pianist in the Op 11 and Op 19 *Pieces*. There are minor idiosyncracies in Op 19 – for example, a rather brisk tempo for No 6 – but Op 11 is excellent. As a bonus Barenboim also plays Busoni's 'amplification' (perhaps 'dilution' is a better term) of Op 11 No 2. This is one of the more pointless attempts by one talent to render another, very different talent more 'comprehensible', but it provides a distinctive and far from insignificant footnote to a Schoenberg disc of unusual substance and distinction.

Schoenberg Verklärte Nacht **Schubert** (arr Mahler) String Quartet No 14 in D minor, D810, 'Death and the Maiden'
Norwegian Chamber Orchestra / Iona Brown
Chandos CHAN9616 (69 minutes: DDD) Ⓕ
Recorded 1994

Given the wrong sort of performance, *Verklärte Nacht* can drag on interminably – but not here. Iona Brown's reading with the Norwegian Chamber Orchestra lends every instrumental exchange the immediacy of live theatre: her lovers are voluble, unstinting and spontaneously communicative. There is colour in every bar: Schoenberg's ceaseless shifts in tone and tempo seem freshly credible, and the sum effect is extraordinarily compelling. The up-front recording further compounds a sense of urgency; only the closing pages seem a trifle uncomfortable with such close scrutiny.

Rivals, however, are plentiful. Among older alternatives, Karajan and the BPO are the most tonally alluring; but Brown runs it close, and her young Norwegian players are with her virtually every bar of the way. No digital rival is quite as good. The Schubert-Mahler also offers further confirmation of a genuine artistic alliance. Mahler's bolstered textures work least well in the second movement, something that even Brown's advocacy doesn't quite compensate for; but the rest is shot through with genuine passion and vitality. A memorable disc.

Awards 1994

Schoenberg Verklärte Nacht, Op 4 (orig version) **H**
Schubert String Quintet in C, D956
Alvin Dinkin *va* **Kurt Reher** *vc* **Hollywood Quartet** (Felix Slatkin, Paul Shure *vns* Paul Robyn *va* Eleanor Aller *vc*)
Testament mono SBT1031 (73 minutes: ADD). Recorded 1950-51 Ⓕ **ooo**

This was the first ever recording of *Verklärte Nacht* in its original sextet form and it remains unsurpassed. When it was first reviewed in *Gramophone*, Lionel Salter wrote of it as being 'beautifully played with the most careful attention to details of dynamics and phrasing, with unfailing finesse, with consistently sympathetic tone, and, most important, with a firm sense of the basic structure'. The Schubert too fully deserves its classic status. The tranquillity of the slow movement has never been conveyed with greater nobility or more perfect control. The Hollywood Quartet made music for the sheer love of it and as a relaxation from their duties in the film-studio orchestras, for which they were conspicuously overqualified. They have incomparable ensemble and blend; and their impeccable technical address and consummate tonal refinement silence criticism. To add to the pleasure, the transfers could not be better.

Variations for Orchestra

Variations for Orchestra, Op 31. Pelleas und Melisande
Chicago Symphony Orchestra / Pierre Boulez
Erato 2292-45827-2 (62 minutes: DDD) Ⓕ
Recorded 1991 ●●

The two faces of Schoenberg could scarcely be more starkly juxtaposed than they are on this superbly performed and magnificently recorded disc – Boulez and the CSO at their formidable best. *Pelleas und Melisande* can be taken not only as Schoenberg's 'answer' to Debussy's opera (also based on Maeterlinck's play) but as his challenge to Richard Strauss's supremacy as a composer of symphonic poems. It is indeed an intensely symphonic score in Schoenberg's early, late-romantic vein, with an elaborate single-movement structure and a subtle network of thematic cross-references. Yet none of this is an end in itself, and the music is as gripping and immediate a representation of a tragic love story as anything in the German romantic tradition. To move from this to the abstraction of the 12-note Variations, Op 31 may threaten extreme anticlimax. Yet from the delicate introduction of the work's shapely theme to the turbulent good humour of the extended finale Schoenberg proves that his new compositional method did not drain his musical language of expressive vitality. The elaborate counterpoint may not make for easy listening, but the combination of exuberance and emotion is irresistible – at least in a performance like this.

Further Listening
Zemlinsky Die Seejungfrau
Couplings: Psalm XIII. Psalm XXIII.
Ernest Senff Chamber Chorus; Berlin Radio Symphony Orchestra / Chailly
Decca Entartete Musik 444 969-2DH Ⓕ
(65 minutes: DDD: 6/87[R])

Zemlinsky's *The mermaid*, a three-movement symphonic fantasy based on the Hans Andersen story, is a sumptuous and imaginative sea symphony. Don't miss it.

Awards 1995

Chamber Symphony No 1, Op 9[a]. Erwartung[b]. Variations for Orchestra, Op 31[c]
Phyllis Bryn-Julson *sop* **[a]Birmingham Contemporary Music Group; [bc]City of Birmingham Symphony Orchestra / Sir Simon Rattle**
EMI CDC5 55212-2 (75 minutes: DDD) Ⓢ
Text and translation included. Recorded 1993 ●●●

This well-filled disc offers an unusually comprehensive survey of the essential Schoenberg – the irascible late-romantic of the *Chamber Symphony* (1906), the radical expressionist of *Erwartung* (1909) and, in the *Variations* (1928), the synthesizer of expressionist moods with techniques that set up neo-classical associations. Rattle's account of the *Chamber Symphony* may well surpass that of the Orpheus Chamber Orchestra in the demonstration quality of the sound, which has remarkable depth and realism. Rattle ensures a superbly well characterised and integrated performance, which only veers towards over-emphasis at the very end. There is also ample refinement where that is called for, and this quality is no less abundant in *Erwartung*. Here the almost impressionistic sheen of the orchestral sound fits well with Phyllis Bryn-Julson's generally restrained approach to the vocal line. When it comes to the *Variations for Orchestra*, Rattle and the CBSO are supreme. This recording may well be the first to convey the full, astonishing range of the work's textures, from the most delicate chamber music to dense tuttis, without a hint of artificiality. But it is the interpretation which counts for most. Rattle brings all these textures to rhythmic and expressive life, avoiding the lumpiness and stridency which occasionally afflict other conductors. He has taken enormous care to follow Schoenberg's detailed markings, yet the result has a sovereign spontaneity. Despite strong competition from Boulez this performance is a triumph.

Five Orchestral Pieces, Op 16

Five Orchestral Pieces, Op 16. A Survivor from Warsaw, Op 46[cd]. Begleitmusik zu einer Lichtspielszene, Op 34. Herzgewächse, Op 20[a]. Serenade, Op 24[be]
[a]Eileen Hulse *sop* **[b]Stephen Varcoe** *bar* **[c]Simon Callow** *narr* **[d]London Voices; [e]Twentieth Century Classics Ensemble; London Symphony Orchestra / Robert Craft**
Koch International Classics 37263-2 Ⓕ
(69 minutes: DDD). Recorded 1994

This is an absorbing issue, not least for the sheer variety of works that it contains. The two largest compositions, Op 16 and Op 24, define the disc's range. The *Five Orchestral Pieces*, in which expressionism can be heard emerging from the chrysalis of late romanticism, are played with supreme finesse by the LSO, and Robert Craft probes the richly diverse textures with exemplary concentration and precision. The downside is some loss of immediacy. There are also slight reservations about the balance in *A Survivor from Warsaw*, where Simon Callow is, one imagines, placed behind the orchestra, depriving this harrowing work of its visceral impact. A closer focus would have been preferable. *Herzgewächse* and *Begleitmusik zu einer Lichtspielszene* are both well performed, the latter with a recessed perspective, similar to that in Op 16, which ensures an extremely well-blended texture without loss of detail. Nevertheless, the finest performance here is that of the *Serenade*, Op 24, where the sound (recorded in New York, not in London) is cleaner, and the characterization is superb from beginning to end. Stephen Varcoe is a rather breathy singer in the dauntingly angular and wide-ranging 'Sonnet', but the performance as a whole makes a convincing case for the work's high level of musical thought and purely technical mastery.

String Quartets

String Quartets – No 1, Op 7; No 2 in F sharp minor, Op 10[a]; No 3, Op 30; No 4, Op 37
[a]**Dawn Upshaw** *sop* **Arditti Quartet** (Irvine Arditti, David Alberman *vns* Garth Knox *va* Rohan de Saram *vc*)
Auvidis Montaigne ② MO782135 Ⓜ
(139 minutes: DDD). Recorded 1993 ○

These recordings were made in London, in collaboration with the BBC, and the sound is consistently spacious, with a natural clarity and an even balance; the details of Schoenberg's complex counterpoint, as evident in No 1 as in No 4, can be heard with a minimum of stress and strain. Though one occasionally gets the impression that the Arditti is relatively cool in its response to this often fervent music, the overall mood they create is far from anti-romantic, and they call on a very wide range of dynamics and tone colours. Even if every nuance in Schoenberg's markings is not followed, this is warmly expressive playing. Dawn Upshaw's contribution to the Second Quartet also helps to heighten the drama although she misses some of that mysterious, ecstatic quality which makes this music so haunting. It is in the Third and Fourth Quartets that the superior sound quality of the Auvidis Montaigne issue pays greatest dividends. Textural clarity is vital here, and although even the Arditti struggles to sustain the necessary lightness in the long second movement of No 4, their wider dynamic range brings you close to the toughly argued, emotionally expansive essence of this music. Yet the performance of No 3 is the finest achievement of the set: clarity of form and emotional conviction combine to create an absorbing account of a modern masterwork. It sets the seal on a most distinguished enterprise.

Schoenberg String Quartet in D. String Trio, Op 45[a]
Zemlinsky Two Movements for String Quintet. Two Movements for String Quartet
Andrea Wennberg *va* **Corda Quartet** ([a]Olga Nodel, Christiane Plath *vns* [a]Frauke Tometten-Molino *va* [a]Edith Salzmann *vc*)
Stradivarius STR33438 (79 minutes: DDD) Ⓕ
Recorded 1996 ○

While it is no longer necessary to introduce Zemlinsky as Schoenberg's brother-in-law and musical mentor, rather than as a composer in his own right, it is still interesting to hear programmes which compare and contrast their compositional developments. This well-performed disc confirms that, although after a similar start the two grew ever further apart, Zemlinsky's later music was much more than the unadventurous outpouring of a lesser talent. Written in the mid-1890s, Zemlinsky's Two Movements for string quintet are accomplished and personable studies whose obvious echoes of various late-romantic masters enhance rather than diminish their appeal. Much the same can be said (though the influences are slightly different) of Schoenberg's D major Quartet of 1897, even more impressive as a student piece in avoiding any hint of that diffuseness in which Zemlinsky occasionally indulged. By 1929, the date of the Two Movements for string quartet, Zemlinsky was still a late-romantic, though with an intensity suggesting familiarity with Berg's more recent pieces, like the *Lyric Suite* (dedicated to Zemlinsky). At that time, Schoenberg was already well on the road that would lead to the fragmented, atonal expressionism of the String Trio, exceptional though that work is in its impatience with the kind of links to classical and romantic traditions that Schoenberg usually admitted. The Corda Quartet conveys the full emotional range of these works.

Additional recommendation
Zemlinsky String Quartets Nos 3 and 4
Coupling: Müller-Hermann String Quartet in E flat
Artis Quartet
Nimbus NI5604 (68 minutes: DDD: 7/99) Ⓕ
Zemlinsky's string quartets, music swirling with impressive ideas, are the perfect introduction to the Second Viennese School. Strongly recommendable performances.

Further listening
Weigl String Quartets Nos 1 and 5
Artis Quartet
Nimbus NI5646 (70 minutes: DDD: 8/00) Ⓕ
Karl Weigl's music (an assistant to Mahler and a pupil of Zemlinsky) was admired by, among others, Strauss and Schoenberg. He was a late romantic but his nostalgia is both amiable and ultra-discreet. A very rewarding release.

Songs

Cabaret Songs – No 1, Galathea; No 2, Gigerlette; No 3, Der genügsame Liebhaber. Drüben geht die Sonne scheiden. Vier Lieder, Op 2. Die Aufgeregten, Op 3 No 2. Lieder, Op 6 – No 1, Traumleben; No 4, Verlassen; No 8, Der Wanderer. Gedenken. Jane Grey, Op 12 No 1. Zwei Lieder, Op 14. Folksong arrangements – Der Mai tritt ein mit Freuden; Es gingen zwei Gespielen gut; Mein Herz ist mir gemenget; Mein Herz in steten Treuen
Mitsuko Shirai *mez* **Hartmut Höll** *pf*
Capriccio 10 514 (63 minutes: DDD). Texts and translations included. Recorded 1993 Ⓜ

Mitsuko Shirai has pretty well the ideal voice for these songs. It's not large, but her subtle control of dynamics allows her to encompass surprisingly big gestures. Her intimacy and deft way with words bring great rewards, too. Most of these songs are early Schoenberg, still within hailing distance of Brahms or Wolf. Even in Op 14, where atonality is in sight, close motivic working and, in 'In diesen Wintertagen', a graceful vocal line, retain a kinship to the 19th-century Lied, and Shirai's easy negotiation of awkward intervals prevents them from ever sounding ungrateful. The strangest pieces here, but oddly attractive, are Schoenberg's folk-song arrangements. Much later than any of the original songs in this collection, in their close and sometimes busy counterpoint they are a touching homage to Brahms (who loved, collected and arranged such songs himself) and even to Bach: they are 'chorale preludes' in all but name. Shirai, very properly, sings them beautifully but plainly. Her husband is an ideally responsive partner; the recording is satisfactory, if a bit too close.

Choral Works

Friede auf Erden, Op 13. Kol nidre, Op 39. Drei Volkslieder, Op 49. Zwei Kanons – Wenn der schwer Gedrückte klagt; O dass der Sinnen doch so viele sind!. Drei Volkslieder (1929) – Es gingen zwei Gespielen gut; Herzlieblich Lieb, durch Scheiden; Schein uns, du liebe Sonne. Vier Stücke, Op 27. Drei Satiren, Op 28. Sechs Stücke, Op 35. Dreimal tausen Jahre, Op 50. De profundis (Psalm 130), Op 50*b*. Modern Psalm (Der erste Psalm), Op 50*c*. A Survivor from Warsaw, Op 46

John Shirley-Quirk, Günter Reich *narrs* **BBC Singers; BBC Chorus and Symphony Orchestra; London Sinfonietta / Pierre Boulez**

Sony Classical ② SM2K44571

(105 minutes: DDD/ADD). Texts and translations included. Recorded 1976-86 Ⓑ ●

Pierre Boulez's recordings of Schoenberg have been appearing at irregular intervals over many years. This two-disc compilation of choral works includes performances recorded on three separate occasions in 1982, 1984 and 1986, as well as transferring the 1976 recording of *A Survivor from Warsaw*, originally coupled on LP with three purely orchestral works. There s no lack of interpretative consistency in what we hear, however. By 1976 Boulez was a seasoned Wagner conductor, and while it may be simplistic to ascribe the weightiness and spaciousness of these Schoenberg performances to his experiences at Bayreuth, the generally recessed sound-perspective strongly suggests a desire to turn the BBC's Maida Vale studios into a much larger and more resonant hall. This distancing is especially evident in John Shirley-Quirk's declamation of the text of *Kol nidre*, one of Schoenberg's later and more substantial sacred compositions. Once you adjust to the balance, the performance itself has an appropriately fervent atmosphere, as do the accounts of the other works involving narrator, chorus and orchestra, the unfinished *Modern Psalm* and *A Survivor from Warsaw*. Both are characteristically intense and exultant, the *Psalm* with some particularly telling orchestral interjections, *A Survivor from Warsaw* with its climactic choral hymn (sung in Hebrew, though the booklet fails to provide transliterations of the Hebrew text both for this and for Psalm 130). Günter Reich's memorably dramatic (but not melodramatic) narration in *A Survivor from Warsaw* benefits from his relatively forward placing.

Most of the music on the discs is for chamber choir, usually unaccompanied. Boulez's expressiveness tends to be fairly generalised, creating and sustaining an overall mood rather than responding to every nuance of the text. The BBC Singers are technically excellent, but the recording magnifies the collective vibrato, the tonal fruitiness which can blur textural definition, especially in the close-knit part-writing of the six pieces for male choir, Op 35. Where the late-romantic sheen Boulez casts over Schoenberg's harmony works best is in such beautifully turned exercises in nostalgia as the German folk-song arrangements, especially the ravishingly beautiful 'Schein uns, du liebe Sonne'. Fortunately the singers find the necessary incisiveness for the Op 27 and Op 28 collections, even if a drier acoustic might have helped to clarify the convoluted lines of the problematic Op 27 No 4, 'Der Wunsch der Liebhabers'. It is a pity that Sony didn't take a little more care with the booklet; still, a firm recommendation.

Erwartung

Verklärte Nacht, Op 4. Erwartung, Op 17[a]

[a]**Anja Silja** *sop* **Philharmonia Orchestra / Robert Craft**

Koch International Classics 3-7473-2 Ⓕ

(58 minutes: DDD). Notes, text and translation included. Recorded 2000 ●●

An entirely apposite coupling, with night reflecting the darkness of the soul in both instances. In *Verklärte Nacht*, emotional turmoil is dispelled in Schoenberg's only 'happy ending'. The Dehmel poem which inspired it is not printed, though this accords with Craft's essentially abstract conception: no lingering in the brooding opening pages, the powerfully shaped central climax (track 3, 0'43") being fatalistic rather than impassioned. The D major response (track 5, the index points are not especially helpful) is heartfelt, and the moonlight sequence (track 5, 1'24") gently evocative. Craft applies canny restraint in the final climax (track 7, 0'52"), its reiteration (track 8, 1'49") registering afresh, before the radiant close (a shame those pulsating arpeggios are obscured). A fine account, if not the equal of Karajan or Mitropoulos.

What makes this disc indispensable is *Erwartung*. Anja Silja has no peer in the projection of its emotional extremes, and the plangency of her response outweighs any loss of vocal refinement since her 1980 account, with its superb but over-sensitised orchestral playing. She appreciates the text as the direct projection of emotion, and Craft is alive to the music's myriad subtleties; whether the rhythmic ostinato which menacingly curtails Scene 3 (track 11, 1'24"), or the exquisite poignancy throughout the first half of Scene 4 – a far cry from Levine's inappropriately romanticised approach or Sinopoli's analytic narcissism. Only Rattle, among modern recordings, finds the balance between pain and pathos, but Phyllis Bryn-Julson's contribution is sadly wanting.

The eerie tranquillity of the final moments, with their spellbinding 'Ich suchte' and eerily tapered close, sets the seal on what ranks as a great interpretation, spaciously but not diffusely recorded. A pity the divisions of the text are not reflected in the index points, but it hardly inhibits an urgent recommendation.

Gurrelieder

Susan Dunn *sop* **Brigitte Fassbaender** *mez* **Siegfried Jerusalem, Peter Haage** *tens* **Hermann Becht** *bass* **Hans Hotter** *narr* **St Hedwig's Cathedral Choir, Berlin; Dusseldorf Musikverin Chorus; Berlin Radio Symphony Orchestra / Riccardo Chailly**

Decca ② 430 321-2DH2 (101 minutes: DDD). Text Ⓕ and translation included. Recorded 1985 ●●

'Every morning after sunrise, King Waldemar would have a realization of the renewing power of nature, and would feel the love of Tove within the outward beauty of Nature's colour and form' (thus said Leopold Stokowski, who made the first-ever recording of *Gurrelieder*). This vast cantata, a direct descendant of Wagnerian music-drama, was for the turn-of-the-century musical scene in general, more the ultimate gorgeous sunset. Schoenberg started work on it in 1899, the same year as his *Verklärte Nacht*, but delayed its completion for over a decade, by which time some of his more innovatory masterpieces were already behind him. Schoenberg's forces are, to put it mildly, extravagant.

As well as the six soloists and two choruses, the orchestra sports such luxuries as four piccolos, ten horns and a percussion battery that includes iron chains; and so complex are some of the textures that, to achieve a satisfactory balance, a near miracle is required of conductor and recording engineers. Decca has never been mean with miracles where large-scale forces are concerned and this set is no exception. Chailly gives us a superbly theatrical presentation of the score.

The casting of the soloists is near ideal. Susan Dunn's Tove has youth, freshness and purity on her side. So exquisitely does she float her lines that you readily sympathise with King Waldemar's rage at her demise. Siegfried Jerusalem has the occasional rough moment but few previous Waldemars on disc have possessed his heroic ringing tones and range of expression. And Decca makes sure that its trump card, the inimitable Hans Hotter as the speaker in 'The wild hunt of the summer wind', is so tangibly projected that we miss not one single vowel or consonant of his increasing animation and excitement at that final approaching sunrise.

Gurrelieder

Deborah Voigt *sop* **Jennifer Larmore** *mez* **Thomas Moser, Kenneth Riegel** *tens* **Bernd Weikl** *bar* **Klaus Maria Brandauer** *spkr* **Dresden State Opera Chorus; Leipzig Radio Chorus; Prague Men's Chorus; Staatskapelle Dresden / Giuseppe Sinopoli**

Teldec ② 4509-98424-2 (113 minutes: DDD) Texts Ⓕ and translations included. Recorded live in 1995 ●

Sinopoli's account is more luxurious, he is more likely than Chailly to let his orchestra rip (the Staatskapelle Dresden letting rip is an awesome sound) and he is more generous with ample rubato. These qualities, together with Teldec's sumptuous live recording count for a great deal in this piece, and for their sake you might be prepared to put up with one or two less than ideal soloists. Deborah Voigt's voice is bright, vibrant, fearless in ff and in the upper register, but needing hard work to fine it down to really expressive, quiet singing. But when she does work hard she is impressive. So is Thomas Moser, sometimes a stalwartly baritonal Waldemar, once or twice a little unsteady, but with ringing, heroic top notes. Larmore is even brighter than Voigt, with a penetrating fast vibrato: strongly dramatic, but not as gravely moving as the best Waldtaube ever, Chailly's Brigitte Fassbaender. No actor in the Speaker's role, not even one as distinguished as Brandauer, will ever surpass Chailly's Hans Hotter, much richer of voice and rising to a splendidly full-throated (and sung!) final word, but Brandauer has wit and character on his side. The choral singing in the later scenes is opulent. Sinopoli takes 12 minutes longer over the piece than Chailly. Yes, his speeds are generally slower, and the long sequence of love-songs in Part 1 occasionally loses urgency as a result, but a good deal of the difference of timing is accounted for by flexible rubato, which will strike anti-Sinopolists as fussy but others as voluptuous.

Pierrot lunaire

Pierrot lunaire, Op 21. Herzgewächse, Op 20. Ode to Napoleon, Op 41

Christine Schäfer *sop* **David Pittman-Jennings** *narr* **Ensemble InterContemporain / Pierre Boulez**

DG 457 630-2GH (53 minutes: DDD) Ⓕ
Texts and translations included. Recorded 1997 ●

Pierre Boulez's third recording of *Pierrot lunaire* is an intense yet intimate reading, recorded in a way that is positively anti-resonant, and which veers, like the music itself, between harshness and reticence. Boulez's second recording (for Sony Classical), with Yvonne Minton, has long been notorious as the 'sung' *Pierrot*, flouting the composer's specific instructions about recitation. This time Christine Schäfer is more speech-orientated, the few fully sung notes perfectly pitched, and although slidings-away from sustained sounds are on the whole avoided, the effect is superbly dramatic in the work's more expressionistic movements. The work's existence in a strange world half-way between cabaret and concert hall is admirably caught. Boulez's first recording of the *Ode to Napoleon* was with David Wilson-Johnson and the Ensemble InterContemporain (also Sony Classical), and this one is a more than adequate replacement. David Pittman-Jennings has a heavy voice, but he skilfully inflects the sketchily notated dynamics of the vocal part, and the instrumental backing is forceful and well nuanced. The sound may be clinically dry, but when the performance has such expressive immediacy, this is scarcely a serious drawback. The disc is completed by the brief, exotic Maeterlinck setting from 1911, whose hugely demanding vocal line deters all but the hardiest. Christine Schäfer copes, while the accompaniment for celesta, harmonium and harp weaves its usual spell. A memorable disc.

Moses und Aron

David Pittman-Jennings *narr* Moses; **Chris Merritt** *ten* Aron; **László Polgár** *bass* Priest; **Gabriele Fontana** *sop* Young Girl, First Naked Woman; **Yvonne Naef** *mez* Invalid Woman; **John Graham Hall** *ten* Young Man, Naked Youth; **Per Lindskog** *ten* Youth; **Henk de Vries** *bar* Young Man; **Siegfried Lorenz** *bar* Another Young Man; **Chorus of the Netherlands Opera; Royal Concertgebouw Orchestra / Pierre Boulez**

DG ② 449 174-2GH2 (106 minutes: DDD). Notes, text and translation included. Recorded 1995 Ⓕ ●

Moses und Aron is respected rather than loved, with the reputation of being a tough assignment for all concerned. One of the essays in the booklet accompanying this recording calls it a didactic opera. Pierre Boulez, however, is a conductor in whom didacticism is close to a passion, and he is obviously passionate about this opera. We take it for granted that in any work to which he feels close, every detail will be both accurate and audible. But for Schoenberg *Moses und Aron* was a warning as well as a homily, and as much a confession of faith as either. Boulez, often himself a Moses preaching against anti-modern backsliding, is at one with Schoenberg here.

Some such reason, surely, has led to this being not only a performance of immaculate clarity, but of intense and eloquent beauty and powerful drama too. The recording was made during a run of stage performances, but in the Concertgebouw in Amsterdam, not in the theatre. In the beautiful acoustic of their own hall, the orchestra plays with ample richness and precision, and the sometimes complex textures benefit enormously from a perceptible space around them.

The choral singing matches the orchestral playing in quality: beautiful in tone, eloquently urgent, vividly precise in the difficult spoken passages. The soloists are all admirable, with no weak links. Merritt in particular seems to have all that the hugely taxing role of Aron demands: a fine control of long line, intelligently expressive use of words, where necessary the dangerous demagogue's glamour. Pittman-Jennings is a properly prophetic Moses, grand of voice. But the set is Boulez's achievement above all: he is as good at dramatic excitement as at soberly or poignantly expressive melody, and the long, orgiastic worship of the Golden Calf has all that one hopes for from it: power, menace, hysteria, the grotesque, but also a queerly impressive sensuous lyricism which is disturbingly alluring. This is one of Boulez's finest achievements, a compelling argument for *Moses und Aron* as an anything but coldly didactic opera.

Franz Schreker Austrian 1878-1934

GROVE *Schreker studied with Fuchs at the Vienna Conservatory (1892-1900) and won success with his ballet Der Geburtstag der Infantin (1908) and still more with his opera Der ferne Klang (1912), which established his mastery of a harmonically rich, luxuriantly eventful orchestral style, used to suggest the surreal power of music over the characters. In 1908 he established the Philharmonic Choir, which performed many new works, and in 1912 was invited to teach at the Music Academy in Vienna, from where he moved in 1920 to the directorship of the Berlin Musikhochschule: for the next 10 years his fame was at its peak. Meanwhile the operas Die Gezeichneten (1918) and Der Schatzgräber (1920) had shown a more Wagnerian manner, though he returned to his earlier style, influenced by the more expressionist Strauss, in Irrelohe (1924). Der singende Teufel (1928) and Der Schmied von Gent (1932) are more neo-classical, but continue his abiding concern with the metaphysics of artistic creation (he wrote all his own librettos). Christophorus (1927), unperformed in his lifetime and dedicated to Schoenberg, is the most extraordinary expression of his existential anguish and vision of voluptuousness. His few non-operatic works include a Chamber Symphony (1916) and songs.*

Overtures and Preludes

Prelude to a Drama. Valse lente. Ekkehard, Op 12. Symphonic Interlude. Nachtstück. Fantastic Overture, Op 15

BBC Philharmonic Orchestra / Vassily Sinaisky

Chandos CHAN9797 (78 minutes: DDD) Ⓕ
Recorded 1999 ●

Sumptuously performed and unflinchingly recorded, this collection will be seized on by Schreker enthusiasts, and they will enjoy every massively scored climax, every gorgeously coloured, embroidered and encrusted texture. Those who are only Schreker enthusiasts north-north-west may need to be warned that the climaxes are pretty frequent and that the textures are in constant flux. Listening to this programme uninterrupted is recommended only to addicts; others may wonder whether Schreker isn't repeating himself. All are operatic preludes or entr'actes (from *Die Gezeichneten, Der Schatzgräber* and *Der ferne Klang* respectively), and all serve similar functions: to represent in a darkened auditorium erotic acts or emotions that could scarcely be represented on a stage. To hear all three in rapid succession is rather like listening to repeated performances of the Prelude to *Der Rosenkavalier* (much shorter than any of Schreker's pieces, but Strauss had only two climaxes to depict). At least those pieces are punctuated by earlier, less heady things. The *Valse lente* is balletic light music, softly and delicately scored. *Ekkehard* is a tone-poem about a monk who falls in love with a Duchess and goes to war to defend her: each of these aspects has its own theme, and they are turbulently developed before a peaceful conclusion on Ekkehard's 'monastic' melody over a wonderfully palpable organ pedal. No programme is stated for the *Fantastic Overture*, but it approaches the three big dramatic pieces in richness. Not many composers demand quite so much of a vast orchestra as Schreker, and Sinaisky and his orchestra amply fulfil those demands and sound as if they are enjoying it enormously.

Die Gezeichneten

Heinz Kruse *ten* Alviano Salvago; **Elizabeth Connell** *sop* Carlotta; **Monte Pederson** *bar* Count Vitelozzo Tamare; **Alfred Muff** *bass* Duke Adorno/Capitaneo di Giustizia; **Lászlo Polgar** *bass* Lodovico Nardi, Podesta; **Christiane Berggold** *mez* Martuccia; **Martin Petzold** *ten* Pietro; **Robert Wörle** *ten* Guidobald Usodimare; **Endrik Wottrich** *ten* Menaldo Negroni; **Oliver Widmer** *bar* Michelotto Cibo; **Matthias Goerne** *bass-bar* Gonsalvo Fieschi; **Kristin Sigmundsson** *bass* Julian Pinelli; **Petteri Salomaa** *bass* Paolo Calvi; **Marita Posselt** *sop* Ginevra Scotti; **Reinhard Ginzel** *ten* First Senator; **Jörg Gottschick** *bass* Second Senator; **Friedrich Molsberger** *bass* Third Senator; **Herbert Lippert** *ten* A youth; **Berlin Radio Chorus; Deutsches Symphony Orchestra, Berlin / Lothar Zagrosek**

Decca Entartete Musik ③ 444 442-2DHO3 Ⓕ
(171 minutes: DDD). Notes, text and translation included. Recorded 1993-94 **OO**

The mingling in *Die Gezeichneten* of post-*Salome* opulence with post-*Salome* gaminess of subject matter is indeed strong stuff. Carlotta, a beautiful but gravely ill painter knows that her health would never withstand physical love. She is loved, he believes hopelessly, by the monstrously ugly nobleman Alviano; she is desired by the licentious Count Tamare. Drawn by the beauty of Alviano's soul she at first declares her love for him, but then deserts him for Tamare. On learning that she gave herself to Tamare voluntarily, knowing the fatal consequences, Alviano first kills his rival, then goes mad. Schreker's sheer resourcefulness is breathtaking. Each character seems to have not merely an identifying theme but a whole sound world. Scenes of extreme complexity are handled with total assurance. The score is melodious, fabulously multi-coloured and has great cumulative power. One reservation was hinted at by Alban Berg's reaction to the libretto: he found it superb but 'a bit kitschy'. It is, and this quality is intensified in the music by a curious impassivity. Carlotta's 'conversion' from spiritual to physical love is not accompanied by much change in her alluringly mysterious music; her characterization is fantastically detailed but has no depth. She, Alviano and Tamare are ideas, not people. It is an opera in which richness of detail, complexity of texture and sheer glamour replace humanity. The end is 'effective' but not tragic. Nevertheless, as a document of its time (1918) and as a score of unprecedented richness it abundantly deserves recording.

Zagrosek's reading is superb, his cast almost without flaw. Connell has all Carlotta's glamour, together with a purity of tone and a subtle response to words and phrasing that come close to giving her a soul. Kruse is less imaginative, one or two of Alviano's high notes give him trouble, but he sings strongly and lyrically; Pederson makes a grippingly formidable, physical opponent. The precision and detail of the subsidiary characters are praiseworthy throughout. The recording is remarkably fine.

Franz Schubert

Austrian 1797-1828

GROVE *Schubert, son of a schoolmaster, showed an extraordinary childhood aptitude for music, studying the piano, violin, organ, singing and harmony and, while a chorister in the imperial court chapel, composition with Salieri (1808-13). By 1814 he had produced piano pieces, settings of Schiller and Metastasio, string quartets, his first symphony and a three-act opera. Although family pressure dictated that he teach in his father's school, he continued to compose prolifically; his huge output of 1814-15 includes Gretchen am Spinnrade and Erlkönig (both famous for their text-painting) among numerous songs, besides two more symphonies, three masses and four stage works. From this time he enjoyed the companionship of several friends: frequently gathering for domestic evenings of Schubert's music (later called 'Schubertiads'), this group more than represented the new phenomenon of an educated, musically aware middle class, it gave him an appreciative audience and influential contacts as well as the confidence, in 1818, to break with schoolteaching. More songs poured out, including Der Wanderer and Die Forelle, and instrumental pieces – inventive piano sonatas, some tuneful, Rossinian overtures, the Fifth and Sixth Symphonies – began to show increased harmonic subtlety.*

In 1820-21 aristocratic patronage, further introductions and new friendships augured well. Schubert's admirers issued 20 of his songs by private subscription, and he and Schober collaborated on Alfonso und Estrella. Though full of outstanding music, it was rejected. Strained friendships, pressing financial need and serious illness – Schubert almost certainly contracted syphilis in late 1822 – made this a dark period, which however encompassed some remarkable creative work: the epic Wandererfantasie for piano, the passionate, two-movement Eighth Symphony (Unfinished), the exquisite Schöne Müllerin song cycle, Die Verschworenen and the opera Fierabras. In 1824 he turned to instrumental forms, producing the A minor and D minor (Death and the Maiden) string quartets and the lyrically expansive Octet for wind and strings; around this time he at least sketched the Great C major Symphony. With his reputation in Vienna now steadily growing Schubert entered a more assured phase. He wrote mature piano sonatas, notably the one in A minor, some magnificent songs and his last, highly characteristic String Quartet, in G. 1827-28 saw not only the production of Winterreise and two piano trios but a marked increase in press coverage of his music; and he was elected to the Vienna Gesellschaft der Musikfreunde. But though he gave a full-scale public concert in March 1828 and worked diligently to satisfy publishers – composing some of his greatest music in his last year, despite failing health – appreciation remained limited. At his death, aged 31, he was mourned not only for his achievement but for 'still fairer hopes'.

Schubert's fame was long limited to that of a songwriter, since the bulk of his large output was not even published, and some not even performed, until the late 19th century. Yet, beginning with the Fifth Symphony and the 'Trout' Quintet, he produced major instrumental masterpieces. These are marked by an intense lyricism, a spontaneous chromatic modulation that is surprising to the ear yet clearly purposeful and often beguilingly expressive, and, not least, an imagination that creates its own formal structures. His way with sonata form, whether in an unorthodox choice of key for secondary material (Symphony in B minor, 'Trout' Quintet) or of subsidiary ideas for the development, makes clear his maturity and individuality. The greatest of his chamber works is acknowledged to be the String Quintet in C, with its rich sonorities, intensity and lyricism, and in the slow movement depth of feeling engendered by the sustained outer sections embracing a central impassioned section in F minor. Among the piano sonatas, the last three represent another summit of achievement. His greatest orchestral masterpiece is the Great C major Symphony, with its remarkable formal synthesis, rhythmic vitality, felicitous orchestration and lyric beauty. Among the choral works, the partsongs and masses rely on homophonic texture and bold harmonic shifts for their effect; the masses in A flat and E flat are particularly successful.

Schubert effectively established the German Lied as a new art form in the 19th century. He was helped by the late 18th-century outburst of lyric poetry and the new possibilities for picturesque accompaniment offered by the piano, but his own genius is by far the most important factor. Reasons for their abiding popularity rest not only in the direct appeal of Schubert's melody and the general attractiveness of his idiom but also in his unfailing ability to capture musically both the spirit of a poem and much of its external detail. He uses harmony to represent emotional change (for example, magically shifting to a 3rd related key) and accompaniment figuration to illustrate poetic images (moving water, a church bell).

Schubert's discovery of Wilhelm Müller's narrative lyrics gave rise to his further development of the Lied by means of the song cycle. Again, his two masterpieces were almost without precedent and are unsurpassed. Both identify nature with human suffering, Die schöne Müllerin evoking a pastoral sound-language, and Winterreise a more intensely Romantic, universal, profoundly tragic quality.

Overtures

Der Teufel als Hydraulicus; Der Spiegelritter; Des Teufels Lustschloss; Der vierjährige Posten; Claudine von Villa Bella; Die Freunde von Salamanka; Die Zwillingsbrüder; Alfonso und Estrella; Die Verschworenen; Fierrabras P

Haydn Sinfonietta, Vienna / Manfred Huss

Koch Schwann 31121-2 (68 minutes: DDD) Ⓕ

Recorded 1997

The works here cover a span of some dozen years, ranging from the jaunty, bustling *Der Teufel als Hydraulicus* and the more ambitious *Der Spiegelritter*, both composed around the time of Schubert's 15th birthday, to the overtures to his richest and grandest stage works, *Alfonso und Estrella* (1821) and *Fierrabras* (1823). The teenage overtures, while giving few hints of Schubert's melodic genius, are full of striking dramatic gestures. There are intermittent echoes of Mozart and affinities between two effervescent operetta overtures of 1815, *Der vierjährige Posten* and *Claudine von Villa Bella*, and the contemporary Second Symphony. The boldest and most colourful of these early overtures is that to Schubert's first completed opera, *Des Teufels Lustschloss*, a grisly Gothic horror tale whose hero undergoes blood-curdling ordeals worthy of Indiana Jones. Schubert evidently relished the opportunity for orchestral grotesquerie, whether in the eerie chorale for horns and trombones in the development or the screeching, cackling coda, with its piercing woodwind and high trumpets. Of the later overtures, those to the one-act *Singspiels*, *Die Zwillingsbrüder* and *Die Verschworenen*, are delightfully conspiratorial, with a nod to Mozart's *Figaro* in the former and a strong dash of Rossini in the latter. *Alfonso und Estrella* and *Fierrabras* are altogether more imposing affairs. Each opens with a brooding, atmospherically scored slow introduction, while the main *Allegro* of *Alfonso* has a tremendous cumulative rhythmic force that points ahead to the *Great* C major Symphony. With his Viennese-based orchestra Manfred Huss does ample justice to Schubert's exhilarating invention. Tempos are lively, rhythms strong and propulsive and textures sharply etched, with Huss making the most of the composer's theatrical contrasts. The recording has admirable clarity and impact.

Symphonies

No 1 in D, D82; **No 2** in B flat, D125; **No 3** in D, D200; **No 4** in C minor, D417, 'Tragic'; **No 5** in B flat, D485; **No 6** in C, D589; **No 8** in B minor, D759, 'Unfinished'; **No 9** in C, D944, 'Great'

Awards 1989

Symphonies Nos 1-6, 8 and 9. Grand Duo in C, D812 (orch J Joachim). Rosamunde, D644 – Overture, 'Die Zauberharfe'

Chamber Orchestra of Europe / Claudio Abbado

DG ⑤ 423 651-2GH5 (320 minutes: DDD) Ⓕ

Recorded 1986-87 ○○○

Even from a conductor who had actively encouraged the Chamber Orchestra of Europe from the start, it is a remarkable tribute that Claudio Abbado chose this superb band of young musicians, founded by former members of the European Community Youth Orchestra, for this major Schubert project. A more obvious choice would have been the Vienna Philharmonic, or for that matter either of the other great orchestras with which he had been closely associated, the Chicago Symphony or the London Symphony Orchestra. But Abbado's confidence in his young players was repaid with compound interest. For all their fine qualities, his previous recordings of the central Viennese classics have never been remarkable for their warmth. With the COE in Schubert it is different. These are performances, recorded in three different venues, mainly in the Konzerthaus in Vienna, but also at Watford Town Hall, which have an authentic Schubertian glow. Anyone worried that a band with the words 'Chamber Orchestra' in the title might sound too puny for the later symphonies, need have no worries at all. The playing here is as satisfyingly powerful as it is polished, Abbado bringing an extra imaginative dimension without losing anything in freshness. Added to that, he uses specially edited texts for the six symphonies not included in the Neue Schubert-Ausgabe, with important and at times striking results. As Abbado says in a note, it was surprising, when so much scholarship had gone into reconstructing unfinished works, that 'symphonies which existed complete in autograph had not yet been edited from the original version'. He asked Stefano Mollo, a member of the orchestra, to do research on the original source material in Vienna, a task of detective work and collation that took him two years, and the results are included here.

So the middle section of the first subject in the Great C major Symphony has a semiquaver figure in the oboe melody quite different from what we have become used to, and four bars which Brahms cut from the *Scherzo* when he was editing the old Schubert-Ausgabe have been restored. Conversely the additional bars that Brahms added to the Fourth and Sixth Symphonies have been omitted. Abbado admits: 'There was some soul-searching on my part about the desirability of reversing some of Brahms's quite sensitive editorial decisions: the four bars he cut in the *Scherzo* of the Great C major, for example, are not Schubert's strongest'. No, not the strongest, one has to admit, but very striking none the less in their brassiness. On any count Schubertians will find refreshment here not just in the performances but in the texts too, and though any idea that the *Grand Duo* for piano duet was the missing 'Symphony No 7' has long been exploded, it is good to have that as a supplement to the authentic cycle in the arrangement made – at Brahms's suggestion – by Joseph Joachim. In principle the lovely slow movement of the *Tragic* Symphony may be too romantic as Abbado presents it, but with yearningly tender oboe playing (a mark of the whole set, from, we assume, Douglas Boyd the regular principal), it is the most winning account of all on record. The only place where Abbado's subtle pointing dangerously draws attention to itself is in the *Unfinished* Symphony. There in the first movement, the second subject has Abbado starting each phrase with a slight agogic hesitation, very beautiful and very refined, but not really so effective as the simpler, folk-like treatment favoured by others. Yet his slowing for the ominous opening of the development section in that movement adds superbly to the tremendous power of the climax as it builds up, a totally justified freedom of expression, the mark of a master interpreter.

In the Great C major, too, the hand of a master, the touches of individuality, the moments of freedom, give Abbado's reading an extra weight lacking in other interpretations. Much is owed to the crispness of the COE ensemble, not least in the enunciation of dotted rhythms or – in the finale – the scurrying triplets, where this is as clean in texture as a performance on period instruments. Though in conventional style Abbado allows a momentary easing into the second subject of the first movement of that symphony, and draws out the cello melody after the big climax of the slow movement, his choice of basic speeds makes those modifications seem naturally expressive and not at all self-indulgent. Abbado's extra items are generous too, not just the *Rosamunde* Overture but the Joachim arrangement of the *Grand Duo*, not likely to be confused with an original Schubert symphony but bringing illumination to a work which in the very forces involved – piano duet – gets unjustly neglected. With its fresh look at the texts, with its refined and imaginative performances, sunnily expressive, powerful and intense, this Abbado set has to be the first recommendation, guaranteed to bring joy and illumination.

Symphonies Nos 1-6, 8 and 9
Royal Concertgebouw Orchestra / Nikolaus Harnoncourt
Teldec ④ 4509-91184-2 (284 minutes: DDD) Ⓜ
Recorded live in 1992 ⊙

Harnoncourt, like Abbado on DG, has researched Schubert's own manuscripts, and corrected many unauthentic amendments that found their way into the printed editions of the symphonies, such as the eight bars later added to the Fourth Symphony's first movement exposition; but the differences between Harnoncourt's interpretative Schubert and Abbado's are startling. The Ninth's finale, unlike Abbado's, a whirling, spinning *vivace* – is borne aloft on astonishingly precise articulation of its rhythms and accents, and a springy delivery of the triplets. Characteristics, of course, one has come to expect from a Harnoncourt performance. Still, what a joy to hear this *Allegro*, and those of most of the earlier symphonies, seized with such bright and light-toned enthusiasm. Here is urgent, virile and vehement playing, never overforceful, over-emphatic or burdened with excessive weight. What came as a surprise was the consistent drawing out of these scores' potential for sadness and restlessness. Harnoncourt does not set apart the first six symphonies as merely diverting, unlike Abbado (out-and-out charm is seldom part of Harnoncourt's Schubertian vocabulary): their bittersweet ambiguities and apparent affectations of anxiety here acquire a greater significance, and the cycle, as a whole, a greater continuity.

Up to a point, the darker, more serious Schubert that emerges here, derives from the type of sound Harnoncourt fashions from his orchestra; not least, the lean string tone and incisive brass. And maybe, up to a point, from the corrections: Harnoncourt refers to the manuscripts as often being 'harsher and more abrupt in tone [than the printed editions], juxtaposing extreme dynamic contrasts', though you can't help feeling that contrasts in general have been given a helping hand. Trios are mostly much slower than the urgent minuets/scherzos that frame them (with pauses in between the two). And Schubert's less vigorous moments are very noticeable as such, and are inflected with varying degrees of melancholy – it is uncanny how the string playing, in particular, often suggests a feeling of isolation (along with the sparing vibrato is an equally sparing use of that enlivening facility: *staccato*). The *Unfinished* Symphony's first movement is a stark, harrowing experience (yet it remains a well-tempered musical one: gestures are never exaggerated); the opening is as cold as the grave itself; the second subject knows its song is short-lived. In both movements, the elucidation and balance of texture can only be described as masterly: just listen to the trombones casting shadows in both codas. This, then, is as seriously pondered, coherent and penetrating a view of the complete cycle as we have had. Whether or not you feel Harnoncourt focuses too much on Schubert's darker side, you have to marvel at his ability to realise his vision. The recorded sound offers that inimitable Concertgebouw blend of the utmost clarity and wide open spaces.

Symphonies Nos 1-6, 8 and 9
Staatskapelle Dresden / Sir Colin Davis
RCA Victor Red Seal ④ 09026 62673-2 Ⓕ
(269 minutes: DDD). Recorded 1994 ⭘

Back in 1981, Davis was the first to give us a Ninth with 'all' the repeats, as he does here. Since 1981, we've had Ninths that have also given us the repeats in the *da capo* of the *Scherzo* (which Davis didn't then, and doesn't now). But, with repeat-extended recordings of the Ninth, there is a fine line between being borne along by it, and, to be frank, becoming bored by it. Drive and energy play their part, but there are many other influencing factors – contrasts of tempo and dynamics, consistently spirited and incisive accentuation and articulation, and weight of orchestral sound, to which you might feel Davis has not quite enough of the first two, and maybe a touch too much of the third. Perhaps the jury needs further deliberation on the Davis Ninth; sample it extensively and you will continue to be impressed by the general magnificence of playing (trombones are never blatant), and by the beauty and airy articulacy of the sound. The cumulative effect of Davis's maintained tempos is heard to greater advantage in his *Unfinished*, among the finest of recent recordings, as are the Abbado and Harnoncourt. In Davis's first movement, there is none of their hastening for the dramatic and energetic moments and the benefit is heard in the coda's 'incomparable song of sorrow' (Einstein). There must be no doubt that Davis's achievement in the first six symphonies will have collectors cherishing this set. The delights are far too numerous to mention, and if reservations in the Ninth Symphony have caused alarm, not one of them applies here. His instincts never desert him: for the general pacing and weighting of the music (slow introductions with an old-world patience but no false grandeur); for knowing when to charm with a small slowing; and for knowing when to leave well alone (the serene and steady progress of the Fifth's *Andante*) and when to intervene (the gradual increase of tempo in the Sixth's finale). And where Abbado is scrupulous about dynamics, Davis is more selective; the Fourth's *Andante* is sublime and shapely, and the wind-down from the agitated second idea, with those dying falls, has never been more affectingly done.

The First Symphony's first movement immediately announces a satisfyingly rich and varied spectrum of tone colour allied to a lightness of touch, and then a beautifully sung second subject, the whole informed with a blithe Mozartian grace. What more could one ask for? Well, perhaps for the small adjustments in balance and dynamics that Davis makes in the movement's coda that speak volumes about the kind of preparation (study or experience; probably both) that has obviously gone into the majority of these realizations. And then there is the orchestra itself, retaining a few features of its former self. The horns have lost the old Eastern European vibrato, but it is still a warm sound; one, in the balance here, always clearly in the picture. The clarinets remain an acquired taste; their characteristic 'hoot' is very likeable (a joy in the yodelling which opens the *Allegro con brio* of the Third Symphony's first movement); their tone always individual enough to remain a distinct feature of the woodwind choir, indeed of tuttis in general. String tone is not full-bodied in the Berlin manner, but sweet, the playing always possessed of grace of movement (and when called on, power), their famed articulation rarely deserting them. Much is made of the spacious Lukaskirche acoustic; there are only a few places where it prevents an ideally focused image (the same could be said of the Harnoncourt Concertgebouw set) and one can't imagine many collectors forgoing the bloom for something more clinical. It must be said, though, that Abbado's cycle set new standards of textural clarity which are unlikely ever to be equalled on either modern or period instruments.

Symphony No 3

Symphonies Nos 3, 5 and 6 **H**
Royal Philharmonic Orchestra / Sir Thomas Beecham
EMI Great Recordings of the Century CDM5 66984-? Ⓜ
(78 minutes: ADD) Recorded 1955-59 ●●●

Beecham was well into his seventies when he made these recordings with the Royal Philharmonic, the orchestra he had founded in 1946. His lightness of touch, his delight in the beauty of the sound he was summoning, the directness of his approach to melody, and his general high spirits will all dominate our memory of these performances. But listening again, we may be reminded that Beecham could equally well dig deep into the darker moments of these works. Schubert's elation was rarely untroubled and the joy is often compounded by its contrast with pathos – Beecham had that balance off to a tee. It should be noted that he does not take all the marked repeats and he doctored some passages he considered over-repetitive. However, these recordings may also serve as a reminder of the wonderful heights of musicianship that his players achieved, as in the trio of the Third Symphony's Minuet, where a simple waltz-like duet between oboe and bassoon attains greatness by the shapeliness, ease and poignancy of its execution. Despite some signs of age, these recordings still preserve the brilliance of their readings and the tonal quality of this orchestra. Altogether, a disc to lift the heaviest of spirits.

Symphonies Nos 3 and 4. Overture in D, D590, 'In the Italian style'
Stockholm Sinfonietta / Neeme Järvi
BIS CD453 (62 minutes: DDD) Ⓕ

The Overture is a delight, even if the Stockholm woodwinds lack that last ounce of agility for their perky Rossinian imitations. About the Abbado DG set of the symphonies (Nos 3 and 4 are available separately but without the Overture), we have extolled the wonderfully spontaneous sounding playing. But alongside Järvi, Abbado can sound positively calculating. As remarked about Järvi's set reviewed below (Symphonies Nos 5 and 6), it is the 'freshness' of Järvi's approach that is so infectious, and that quality is here in abundance as well. The Stockholm Sinfonietta, though, lacks the corporate virtuosity of the Chamber Orchestra of Europe; in the finale of the Third Symphony both conductors set similarly brisk speeds, but the Swedes simply don't have the muscle to leap for joy like their COE counterparts, and in the finale of the Fourth you miss the clean articulation of those accompanying quavers on the strings that run through most of this movement and give it so much of its excitement and tension.

Neither is the engineering free of fault. The recording location is the same as for Nos 5 and 6 (the Stockholm Concert Hall), but you sense that the microphones have been moved back. The overall balance is uncannily natural, but a little more mellow than before. Timpani and brass are vivid (wonderful horns!), but in the tuttis and faster passages there ought to be a clearer profile of the strings. The Third Symphony is less afflicted than the Fourth, perhaps because it is more lucidly scored. So, Järvi for warmth, grace and the occasional impression of a rushed job, Abbado for drama rhythmic stability and sound of striking clarity.

Symphony No 5

Symphonies Nos 5 and 6. Overture in D in the Italian style, D591
Stockholm Sinfonietta / Neeme Järvi
BIS CD387 (72 minutes: DDD) Ⓕ

This Järvi disc abounds in freshness. As so often with Järvi, one notices an unusual degree of light and shade, while the phrasing always sounds spontaneous. He makes the music breathe, and the textures always sound deliciously airy without an accompanying loss of tonal weight in louder passages; a bright, well-focused BIS recording helps. In the Trio of the Sixth Symphony *Scherzo*, his balance of *forte-piano* accents, and *legato* continuation, is convincing but he does tend to come down on each accent so decisively that one hardly has time to recover before the next one – the intervening woodwind phrases leave little impression. Nevertheless, this is a recommendable coupling, with the Overture, D591, a generous filler.

Symphonies Nos 5 and 8
Concertgebouw Orchestra / Leonard Bernstein
DG 427 645-2GH (57 minutes: DDD) Ⓕ
Recorded live in 1987

Bernstein is surprisingly brisk in the first movement of the *Unfinished*, making it more clearly a sonata-form *Allegro*, with the semiquavers of the main theme given an almost Mendelssohnian quality in their lightness. Perhaps even more surprisingly he refuses to linger over the haunting melody of the second subject, keeping it very fresh, hardly at all moulding it in the way that Abbado does, for example, with the Chamber Orchestra of Europe. In the slow movement Bernstein opts for a rather heavily moulded treatment at an unusually slow tempo. However, with the *fortissimo* interjections all the weightier at Bernstein's speed, it is a strong and convincing reading. The sound in both No 5 and the *Unfinished* is comparably full and atmospheric to that for the *Great* C major (reviewed below).

In the Fifth some may similarly have reservations over Bernstein's relatively slow tempo for the second movement *Andante con moto*. Yet the refinement of the playing and the detailed imagination puts it in a league of its own. In all three fast movements of No 5, not least the finale, he adopts a dashing speed; light as well as brisk. Whatever detailed reservations there may be, Bernstein is consistently at his most magnetic, justifying his latter-day technique of having live recordings edited together and tidied up after.

Symphony No 8

Symphonies Nos 8 and 9
Berlin Philharmonic Orchestra / Günter Wand
RCA Victor Red Seal ② 09026 68314-2 Ⓜ
(85 minutes: DDD). Recorded live in 1995 ○○

The advantages of these Berlin readings over Wand's 1991 Hamburg Musikhalle/North German RSO recordings (also live) are, often, as you might expect: greater facility (in, say, the infamous string triplets in the Ninth's last movement), generally richer string sonority (a proper 'heft' for those stamping C major chords also in the Ninth's finale), sweeter, more vibrant and more focused woodwind (wonderful solos in the Eighth's second movement second subject), a mostly wider (though far from excessive) range of dynamics in the Eighth, more expansive phrasing, and accents more consistently placed (and recorded sound with marginally greater presence). The ground-plans remain the same, in other words, the basic tempo and its modification (and what ingenious and effective plans they are, and how marvellous it has been to re-encounter Wand's sublimely wrought rubato); as does the conductor's views on repeats (taken in the Eighth's first movement, but not in the Ninth's outer movements).

It is pointless to speculate whether the small details that *have* changed (for example, the now truly *pianissimo* second subject of the Eighth's first movement) are due to Wand's further four years' thought on the works, or changes brought about by the Berlin orchestra's own musical collective, or just 'another time, another place'. Maybe a bit of all three. If you already own the Hamburg recordings, there is no need to rush out to buy this (and, of course, you will also be the proud owner of the finest Schumann Fourth of the last two decades – the Hamburg Schubert Eighth's coupling). If you don't, this set is an obvious choice. Wand's Schubert is informed by a very special devotion, wisdom and insight, and a very individual spirit of adventure.

Schubert Symphony No 8
Mendelssohn Symphony No 4
Philharmonia Orchestra / Giuseppe Sinopoli
DG Masters 445 514-2GMA (62 minutes: DDD) Ⓕ
Recorded 1983 ○

Giuseppe Sinopoli made an auspicious choice of repertory for this, his first recording as Principal Conductor with the Philharmonia. It was this coupling which Guido Cantelli chose for one of his last recordings, made with the Philharmonia in the palmy days of the mid-fifties. Enough to say that Sinopoli could hardly have provided a sharper contrast in everything except the quality of the playing of the Philharmonia: this recording shines out as a superb example of Philharmonia refinement, responsiveness and virtuosity, a tribute not just to Sinopoli's own intensive work but to the standards he had built up largely with the help of his compatriot predecessor, Riccardo Muti.

In a sense with readings of both works so sharply individual as Sinopoli's no comparisons are strictly relevant. Where Cantelli for example made a glowing impact by his simple, natural way with every single movement, Sinopoli directs readings which in almost every bar call attention to unexpected points. Undoubtedly they will be controversial, both in the interpretative style and often in the very choice of speeds. What makes both performances intensely revealing, exhilarating and refreshing is the extraordinary intensity which compels attention from the very first note. Some may find the moulding of the great second subject theme on the cellos in the *Unfinished* too calculated. Others may feel that he moulds too much in the very slow account of the third movement of the *Italian*. Elsewhere the glow of commitment alongside such playing is intense.

Sinopoli's view of the *Unfinished*, from the menacing *pianissimo* of the opening motif onwards, makes the point strongly that this is a progress from darkness to light. The tragedy of the B minor first movement could hardly be contrasted more strongly against the ethereal glow of fulfilment in the second. The contrasting moods of the *Italian* Symphony are sharply etched too. In the first movement Sinopoli sets a dangerously fast speed, but unlike most rivals he sacrifices neither clarity, precision nor detail with delectable pointing in the rapid triplets and with subtle phrasing and shading of dynamic to match even Karajan (DG) at his slower speed. Both the middle two movements find Sinopoli adopting slow speeds and moulded phrasing, with the Pilgrims' March made weighty and melancholy in its beauty, the third movement bringing fairyland horn calls in the Trio. The final *Saltarello* is bitingly brilliant with Sinopoli at the end emphasizing in a final thrust Mendelssohn's refusal to allow the minor key to resolve into the major, leaving a bitter tang.

Symphony No 9

Symphony No 9[a]. **Wagner** Siegfried Idyll[b]
Vienna Philharmonic Orchestra / Sir Georg Solti
Decca Legends 460 311-2DM (74 minutes: DDD) Ⓜ
Recorded [b]1965 and [a]1981 ○○○

Solti's Ninth is likely to bowl you over when you first hear it – you somehow don't expect him to be such a mellow and smiling Schubertian, and of course the VPO playing has great vitality too. As a performance it is quite glorious and can hold its own with any of its rivals, and in terms of recorded sound it is amazing (one of Decca's very best, and in the demonstration class, still). In its LP format, it was notable for its wide-ranging dynamics, its warmth and real 'presence'. The sound is, indeed, full-bodied and well-defined. Yet the CD remaster is undoubtedly superior: the instruments seem positively tangible. Initially, you may wonder whether the higher transfer level of the CD is responsible for the greater sense of immediacy but adjusting the controls still leaves the CD sounding firmer, more 'present' and richer. Altogether a most impressive disc and though one might quibble about the balance (one is placed very forward in the concert hall), there is no doubt that this is a winner among the many recordings of this heavenly symphony.

Symphony No 9. Gesang der Geister über den Wassern, D714
Monteverdi Choir; Vienna Philharmonic Orchestra / Sir John Eliot Gardiner
DG 457 648-2GH (64 minutes: DDD). Text and translation included. Recorded live in 1997 Ⓕ

An outstanding example of the programmer's art. From the close of the choral song's watery passage of the soul, the common key of C allows the symphony's opening horn call then to ease us magically on to firmer ground for its own world of more confident journeying. Schubert might almost have intended it! An outstanding *performance* of the song, too; heard in the supremely evocative version for male voice and lower strings. These days, it is more difficult for new versions of the symphony to be 'outstanding'. Outstanding versions have fallen into two categories. Old masters, like Giulini and Wand, revisiting a score barnacled by traditional speedings and slowings, and bringing their own lifetimes' gained insights and affection to it (barnacles and all); and those who have thrown late 19th- and 20th-century traditions and instruments out of the window and started afresh, such as Norrington and Mackerras.

Gardiner, despite the generally lively tempos and light touch, is happy to embrace most of the barnacles. Obviously, you won't find Gardiner making cuts and halving the tempo for the finale's famous unison stamping Cs (which, in any case, is less of a barnacle than a massive holing below the water-line); but neither is there any incidence of Norrington's 'historical' phrasing vocabulary. Whether all this is how Gardiner feels the symphony should sound, or is born out of respect for a Viennese tradition, is hard to say. Whatever the case, in general, they play magnificently for him; the Vienna strings – with all the violins on the left – their familiar sweet-toned selves (showing little inhibition in their use of vibrato); and the special colours of their woodwinds' voices are always heard where they should be (memorably rustic, rueful oboes in the second movement, and a joyous 'singing out' of the entire section in the *Scherzo*'s Trio). As for the recorded sound, DG manages a satisfying compromise between spaciousness and presence. Of an audience there is not a hint.

Symphony No 10

Symphony No 10 in D, D936*a* (realised Newbould). Symphonic fragments – D, D615; D, D708*a* (orch Newbould)
Scottish Chamber Orchestra / Sir Charles Mackerras
Hyperion CDA67000 (54 minutes: DDD) Ⓕ
Recorded 1997

Someone will have to find another name for Schubert's *Unfinished* Symphony (the B minor) before too long. In fact there are six unfinished Schubert symphonies: there are two whole movement expositions for D615, torsos of three movements and a nearly complete *Scherzo* for D708*a*, and enough sketch material for Brian Newbould to attempt a complete conjectural reconstruction of D936*a*, the symphony Schubert began writing in the last weeks of his life. Inevitably some will ask, why bother?

Well, apart from the increase in the sense of wonder at Schubert's sheer productivity, there is some wonderful music here, especially the slow movement of D936*a*, desolate and warmly consoling by turns. As a whole, D936*a* suggests that, even at this late stage, Schubert was still thinking in terms of new developments. The concluding third movement, contrapuntally fusing elements of scherzo and finale, is like nothing else in Schubert – or in any other composer of the classical period. Of course, Newbould has had to do some guessing here, but the results are on the whole strikingly authoritative. The performances carry plenty of conviction and the recordings are atmospheric while allowing one to hear all significant detail. Altogether this is a fascinating disc – and not just for musicologists.

Octet in F, D803

Academy of St Martin in the Fields Chamber Ensemble (Kenneth Sillito, Malcolm Latchem *vns* Stephen Shingles *va* Denis Vigay *vc* Raymund Koster *chbr bass* Andrew Marriner *cl* Timothy Brown *hn* Graham Sheen *bn*)
Chandos CHAN8585 (60 minutes: DDD) Ⓕ
Recorded 1987

This recording offers wonderful sound, not just in the quality itself, which is superlative, but in the impression of an unartificial balance – for although the strings are quite clearly in the picture, they don't seem to be given quite such a helping hand as in most other recordings. A thoughtful, measured first-movement introduction sets the tone for the performance. A good, moderate basic tempo is chosen for the movement's main *allegro* section, but within that framework there is also some flexibility of phrase and pulse, so that the music breathes naturally and spontaneously.

There is indeed something of a relaxed, intimate Viennese flavour in the music-making which is immensely enjoyable, though some listeners might well prefer a stronger, more outgoing approach. In the *Adagio* Andrew Marriner floats his clarinet solo exquisitely, and the whole movement is most sensitively realised: each phrase seems to be pregnant with meaning. In the third movement *Allegro vivace* the players find an attractive, dancing rhythm, and the variations which follow are deliciously inflected. After a Minuet shaped with a good deal of subtlety and affection the performance is well rounded off with a strong, purposeful finale.

Octet. Minuet and Finale in F, D72
Vienna Octet; Vienna Wind Soloists
Decca Eclipse 448 715-2DEC (72 minutes: DDD) Ⓑ
Recorded 1990 OO

Over the years Decca has made a speciality of recording the Schubert Octet in Vienna, and this budget-priced reissue by the Vienna Octet, captured within the glowing acoustics of the Mozartsaal of the Vienna Konzerthaus, and ideally balanced by Christopher Raeburn, is most winning. The enticing warmth of the opening *Adagio* catches the listener's attention at once, and the central movements – the *Scherzo* bustling with vitality and the deliciously played *Andante con variazioni* – are unforgettable. Then comes the lovingly Schubertian *Menuetto*, and after an arresting *tremolando* introduction, the joyfully bucolic finale rounds things off in sparkling fashion. At its price, this Vienna version is now in a class of its own. As a bonus we are offered the *Minuet and Finale*, D72, two engaging miniatures from the composer's youth, nicely elegant in the hands of the Vienna Wind Soloists. The demonstration-standard recording makes this a bargain not to be passed by.

Trout Quintet

Piano Quintet in A, 'Trout', D667[a]. Quartet in G, D96[b]
[b]**Wolfgang Schulz** *fl* [a]**Gerhard Hetzel** *vn* **Wolfram Christ** *va* **Georg Faust** *vc* [a]**Alois Posch** *db* [b]**Göran Söllscher** *gtr* [a]**James Levine** *pf*
DG 431 783-2GH (65 minutes: DDD) Ⓕ
Recorded 1990 O

Schubert composed the *Trout* Quintet in his early twenties for a group of amateur musicians in the town of Steyr in Upper Austria, which lies upon the River Enns which was then noted for its fine fishing and keen fishermen. The Quintet, like all great occasional music, stands as strongly as ever today, with its freshly bubbling invention and sunny melodiousness. In the present version by James Levine and members of the Vienna Philharmonic, the unity of ensemble and common sense of purpose are most compelling. Both acoustically and musically, their performance has an affecting intimacy. Particularly noticeable are the warmth of Faust's cello playing within the texture and the heavenly phrasing of the Vienna Philharmonic's leader, Gerhard Hetzel, who was tragically killed in a walking accident in 1993. The piano is attractively balanced as a member of the ensemble, rather than as a soloist, which makes the variation fourth movement unusually appealing. Like most of their rivals, this group does not repeat the exposition in the finale.

A rarity has been included which ensures that any Schubertian will want this issue in their collection. The so-called Guitar Quartet, D96, is an arrangement of a trio by Wenzel Matiegka which Schubert made in 1814. It is a charming work, presumably intended for domestic use, whose grace and elegance are highly infectious in this delightful performance.

Piano Quintet in A, 'Trout', D667[a]. String Trios – B flat, D581; B flat, D111*a*
Members of the **Leipzig Quartet** (Andreas Seidel *vn* Ivo Bauer *va* Matthias Moosdorf *vc*); [a]**Christian Zacharias** *pf* [a]**Christian Ockert** *db*
Dabringhaus und Grimm MDG307 0625-2 Ⓕ
(66 minutes: DDD). Recorded 1998 OO

This *Trout* must surely be one of the very best versions of this much-recorded work – the sound is wonderfully natural, and so is the performance. You get the impression that here was an occasion when everything 'clicked', giving the playing a friendly, relaxed feeling that's just right for this carefree piece. Zacharias has the knack of making even the simplest phrase sound expressive, and the strings, without any exaggeration, produce the most beautiful tonal shadings. All five players, too, have an impressive sense of line; the phrasing and points of emphasis are balanced so that Schubert's expansive designs are projected compellingly. If the *Trout* shows a Schubertian spaciousness, his one completed String Trio is unusually compact. Another distinguished feature is the florid, Spohr-like elegance of much of the violin writing – Andreas Seidel is splendidly stylish and confident. This is another very fine performance, emphasizing the predominating gentle lyricism, but with plenty of vigour and panache when required. The String Trio fragment, less than two minutes, continues the same, 'let's hear everything' approach; it's a sketch for what subsequently became the comparatively familiar B flat Quartet, D112.

Schubert Piano Quintet in A, 'Trout', D667[a]
Mozart Piano Quartet in G minor, K478
Thomas Zehetmair *vn* **Tabea Zimmermann** *va* **Richard Duven** *vc* [a]**Peter Riegelbauer** *db* **Alfred Brendel** *pf*
Philips 446 001-2PH (75 minutes: DDD) Ⓕ
Recorded 1994 OO

Brendel is of course the lynchpin here and, as ever, balances heart and mind with innate good taste. Time and again you find yourself overhearing detail that might otherwise have passed for nothing: every modulation tells; every phrase of dialogue has been polished, pondered and carefully considered. And yet it *is* a dialogue, with the loose-limbed Thomas Zehetmair leading his supremely accomplished colleagues through Schubert's delightful five-tier structure. The *Scherzo* and *Allegro giusto* frolic within the bounds of propriety (some will favour an extra shot of animal vigour), whereas the first, second and fourth movements are rich in subtle – as opposed to fussy – observations. The recording, too, is exceedingly warm, with only the occasional want of inner detail to bar unqualified enthusiasm. Philips, as ever, achieves a well-rounded, almost tangible piano tone.

Mozart's G minor Quartet makes for an unexpected, though instructive, coupling, following the *Trout*. Here again there is much to learn and enjoy, especially in terms of phrasal dovetailing and elegant articulation (Brendel's opening flourish is a model of Mozartian phrase-shaping). Still, you may sometimes crave rather more in the way of *Sturm und Drang* – a fiercer, more muscular attack, most especially in the first movement. Yet there will be times when the conceptual unity and executive refinement of this performance – its articulate musicality – will more than fit the bill. Both works include their respective first movement repeats.

Piano Quintet in A, 'Trout', D667[a]. Adagio and Rondo concertante in F, D487
Kodály Quartet (Attila Falvay, Tamás Szabo *vns* Gábor Fias *va* János Devich *vc*) [a]**IstvánTóth** *db*
Jenö Jandó *pf*
Naxos 8 550658 (53 minutes: DDD) Ⓢ ●

This disc is further proof of Naxos's impressive ability to produce outstanding recordings at an astonishingly low price. Jenö Jandó's recording of the *Trout* Quintet, in a version which is based on the first edition of 1829, is buoyant and vigorous. The string support from members of the Kodály Quartet and István Tóth, despite some rough edges, is generally sonorous and appropriate. Balance is good, with the piano agreeably highlighted. The result is a performance which is a most desirable acquisition. Although Schubert wrote no concertos, he did write a *concertante* work for piano and strings which is also included here. Notwithstanding limitations of thematic invention, the *Adagio and Rondo* makes an attractive coupling. Jandó's sheer enthusiasm for this music provides a compelling alternative to other full-price accounts.

Piano Quintet in A, 'Trout', D667[a]. String Quartet No 14 in D minor, 'Death and the Maiden', D810[b] H
[a]**Sir Clifford Curzon** *pf* [a]members of the **Vienna Octet** (Willi Boskovsky *vn* Gunther Breitenbach *va* Nikolaus Hübner *vc* Johann Krump *db*); [b]**Vienna Philharmonic Quartet** (Willi Boskovsky, Otto Strasser *vns* Rudolf Streng *va* Robert Scheiwein *vc*)
Decca 417 459-2DM (71 minutes: ADD) Ⓜ
Recorded [a]1957, [b]1963 ●

Willi Boskovsky's gentle and cultured mind is very much responsible for the success of these performances of Schubert's two best-known chamber works. In the delectable *Trout* Quintet there is real unanimity of vision between the players, as well as an immaculate attention to the details of the scoring. Clifford Curzon's part in the performance is memorable especially for his quiet playing – the atmosphere is magical in such moments. Everywhere there is a great awareness of the delicacy and refinement of Schubert's inventiveness. The *Death and the Maiden* Quartet is no less successful. Schubert's strikingly powerful harmonies, together with a sustained feeling of intensity, all go to heighten the urgency of the first movement. Despite this, string textures are generally kept light and feathery. In the *Andante* all is subtly understated and although a mood of tragedy is always lurking in the background, never is it thrown at the listener. Boskovsky's understanding of the music is very acute and the performance cannot fail to satisfy even the most demanding. These are two vintage recordings and in the quartet the quality of sound is quite remarkable.

String Quintet in C, D956

Douglas Cummings *vc* **The Lindsays** (Peter Cropper, Ronald Birks *vns* Roger Bigley *va* Bernard Gregor-Smith *vc*)
ASV CDDCA537 (58 minutes: DDD) Ⓕ
Recorded 1985

Schubert's sublime C major Quintet is eminently well served on disc. With this version one is immediately struck by its naturalness. You are left with the impression that you are eavesdropping on music-making in the intimacy of a private home. Although there is plenty of vigour and power, there is nothing of the glamourised and beautified sonority that some great quartets give us. (The two cellos, incidentally, are both by the same maker, Francesco Rugeri of Cremona.) They observe the first-movement exposition repeat, and the effortlessness of their approach does not preclude intellectual strength. The first movement surely refutes the notion that Schubert possessed an incomplete grasp of sonata form, an idea prompted by the alleged discursiveness of some of the sonatas. This is surely an amazing achievement even by the exalted standards of his day, and The Lindsays do it justice, as indeed they do the ethereal *Adagio*. Here they effectively convey the sense of it appearing motionless, suspended as it were, between reality and dream, yet at the same time never allowing it to become static. The quartet sound is not so full-bodied or richly burnished as that produced by many rivals, lacking quite the splendour or richness given to the best sound-recordings, but they have what can only be called a compelling wisdom. Their reading must be placed at the top of the list and for many readers will be an obvious first choice.

Schubert String Quintet
Boccherini String Quintet in E, G275
Isaac Stern, Cho-Liang Lin *vns* **Jaime Laredo** *va* **Yo-Yo Ma, Sharon Robinson** *vcs*
Sony Classical SK53983 (76 minutes: DDD) Ⓕ
Recorded 1993 ●

A glamorous line-up of soloists is, of course, far from a guaranteed recipe for success in chamber music, especially in a work as democratic as the Schubert Quintet. But at the 1952 Prades Festival, Stern, Casals and colleagues achieved the miraculous in their now legendary recording, reissued by Sony with Casals's hitherto unpublished 1953 Schubert Fifth Symphony (reviewed below). Over 40 years on, Stern teamed up with an equally starry first cellist, Yo-Yo Ma, and three distinguished colleagues in a reading that often recalls the Prades performance in style and spirit. The quality of the string playing is fabulous, the communion between the five players close and intent, and the music-making marries keen intellectual and structural command with a generosity and spontaneity of impulse. The manner in which the players realise all the disturbing power of Schubert's muscular, rebarbative counterpoint is wholly admirable. Like Stern, Casals *et al* in 1952, the players bring to the *Scherzo* tigerish attack and demonic drive, suggesting an edge of desperation to the rollicking dance; the Trio, by contrast, is uncommonly slow and searching, evoking the haunted world of the *Heine* songs composed a few months earlier. The finale, too, has a desperate, almost manic energy. With the successive quickenings of the pace in the coda, here sounding absolutely inevitable, the gaiety becomes increasingly hysterical, even nightmarish; and the massive accent on the final D flat makes the close even more ominously ambivalent than usual.

The one real reservation about this powerful and disquieting performance is the lack of true *pianissimo* quality, partly, though one suspects not wholly, a consequence of close microphone placing. This, of course, affects the slow movement above all. On the other hand, the players go for broke in the central F minor catastrophe, Stern and Ma singing their great despairing melody with an abandon that rivals (and a purity of intonation that surpasses) Stern and Casals in the 1952 recording. So while the outer sections of the *Adagio* lack the last degree of inwardness and spirituality, this is an intensely compelling reading of the Quintet that realises to the full the unease and terror that shadow the music. It certainly ranks among the finest available.

The disc's attractions are enhanced by the inclusion of all marked repeats and by the presence of the Boccherini E major Quintet, the one with the world's most famous minuet. The other three movements prove no less delightful, with their characteristic mixture of sensuality and leisurely grace enlivened in the finale by touches of exotic Spanish colour; Stern and his colleagues give a highly appealing performance, full subtle timing and colour and savouring alike Boccherini's delicate detail and his often luscious textures.

String Quintet[a]. Symphony No 5[b] H
[a]**Isaac Stern,** [a]**Alexander Schneider** *vns* [a]**Milton Katims** *va* [a]**Paul Tortelier** *vc* [b]**Prades Festival Orchestra / Pablo Casals** [a]*vc*
Sony Classical Casals Edition mono SMK58992 Ⓜ
(76 minutes: ADD). Recorded 1952-53 ●●●

This should have an in-built fail-safe against hasty consumption, in that their interpretative ingredients are so rich, varied and unpredictable that to experience it all at once is to invite mental and emotional exhaustion. Casals is, of course, the lynchpin. A charismatic presence, he embraces everything with the passion of a devoted horticulturist tending his most precious flowers, and that his love extended beyond the realms of music to mankind itself surely enriched his art even further. The most celebrated Prades recording ever is still the Stern/Casals/Tortelier reading of the C major Quintet, a masterful traversal graced with elastic tempos, songful phrasing, appropriate rhetorical emphases (especially in the first and second movements) and fabulous string playing. The coupling here is a 'first release' of Schubert's Fifth Symphony, recorded in 1953 – a warm, keenly inflected performance, jaunty in the outer movements and with an adoring, broadly paced *Adagio*. One presumes that it has been held from previous view only because of a few minor executant mishaps. It is certainly well worth hearing. The transfer of the Quintet reveals itself as marginally warmer but occasionally less well-focused than previous incarnations. Still, the original was no sonic blockbuster to start with but this shouldn't deter you from hearing this disc.

Schubert String Quintet in C, D956[a]
Beethoven Grosse Fuge in B flat, Op 133[b]
Hagen Quartet (Lukas Hagen, Rainer Schmidt *vns*; Veronika Hagen *va*; Clemens Hagen *vc*);
[a]**Heinrich Schiff** *vc*
DG 439 774-2GH (68 minutes: DDD) Ⓕ
Recorded 1991[a] and 1993[b] ●●

By following Boccherini in using two cellos instead of two violas for his String Quintet, Schubert increased the potential for greater textural contrast. Moreover, the dichotomy between the tragic perspective and Viennese gaiety in the Quintet, so evident in much of Schubert's greatest music, generates an especially potent dramatic force.

The Hagen Quartet's performance of the first movement, which presents remarkably clear textural detail, is broad and expansive. The Hagen, unlike the Alban Berg Quartet, include the exposition repeat in a movement that lasts almost 20 minutes. Perhaps as a consequence, they play the *Adagio* second movement at an unusually fast tempo. However, through breathtaking dynamic control in the first section, passionate intensity in the second, and engaging spontaneity of the ornamentation in the final section, the Hagen achieve an expression that is powerfully compelling.

The second half of the Quintet is often treated as a period of emotional relief from the profound concentration of the first two movements. Startlingly, the Hagen maintain the tension with violent textural and dynamic contrast in the *Scherzo*, and distinctively varied registral sonority in the Trio. The finale, in which the Hagen effectively balance the music's charming Hungarian flavour with its more sinister touches, provides an arresting conclusion

The Hagen's account of Beethoven's *Grosse Fuge* is polished and sensitive and, though it may lack the raw excitement of the Alban Berg's live version, it vividly conveys the difference between Beethoven's and Schubert's compositional means. The Hagen's is an outstanding disc, in which exceptional performances, that challenge the finest alternatives, are complemented by superb recording.

Additional recommendations
String Quintet in C, D956
Alban Berg Quartet with **Heinrich Schiff** *vc*
EMI Great Recordings of the Century
CDM5 66890-2 (48 minutes: ADD: 10/83[R]) Ⓜ

A classic recording that still takes some beating. The music floats effortlessly in the outside sections, and the effect is mesmeric, and in the finale the players find just the right combination of understatement and swagger.

Coupling: **Schoenberg** Verklärte Nacht, Op 4 (orig version)
Hollywood Quartet (Felix Slatkin, Paul Shure vns; Paul Robyn va; Eleanor Aller vc) **Alvin Dinkin** *va* **Kurt Reher** *vc*
Testament mono SBT1031 (73 minutes: ADD: 4/94). Ⓕ

In the 1950s the authors of *The Record Guide* spoke of the Schubert as 'one of the best [LPs] in the discography of chamber music'; and so it remains. The Schoenberg, too, is superb. See the review of this disc under *Verklärte Nacht*.

String Quartets

No 10 in E flat, D87; **No 12** in C minor, **'Quartettsatz'**, D703; **No 13** in A minor, D804; **No 14** in D minor, **'Death and the Maiden'**, D810; **No 15** in G, D887

String Quartets Nos 10 and 13 **P**
Quatuor Mosaïques (Erich Höbarth, Andrea Bischof *vns* Anita Mitterer *va* Christophe Coin *vc*)
Auvidis Astrée E8580 (68 minutes: DDD) Ⓕ
Recorded 1995 ●

This recording of the A minor Quartet was the first ever on period instruments. With unusually broad tempos, the Mosaïques consistently stresses the music's pathos, loneliness and fatalism. The Hungarian-flavoured finale is normally seen as a stoically cheerful reaction to the pain that has gone before. But here it steals in as if in a dream from the spectral close of the Minuet, the opening melody delicately floated, its off-beat accents barely flicked; where the Alban Berg brings a faintly military strut to the C sharp minor melody (2'11"), the Mosaïques, suppressing any hint of swagger in the dotted rhythms, distils a doleful balletic grace.

In the *Andante* of the *Rosamunde* the Mosaïques, while slower than its rivals, never loses sight of the *gehende Bewegung*, the walking motion that underlies so many of Schubert's *andantes*. It matches its rivals in its tender, sentient phrasing, subtly flexing the pulse in response to harmonic movement. The Minuet, with its glassy, vibratoless *pianissimos*, is more eerily remote, less human in its desolation, than from the Alban Berg.

For the coupling the Mosaïques offers the early E flat Quartet, written when Schubert was just 16. Not even this affectionate, considered advocacy can do much for the dull, harmonically stagnant opening movement. But the players relish the raw energy of the *Scherzo*, with its braying donkey evocations, and bring a delicious demure wit to the Rossinian second theme of the finale (0'58"). And, as in the absorbing, moving reading of the A minor Quartet, the delicacy of nuance and clarity of texture, easier to obtain from the sparer-toned period instruments, is often revelatory. The recording is clean, vivid and immediate. In sum, an outstanding disc in every way.

String Quartets Nos 10[b] and 14[a]
Alban Berg Quartet (Günther Pichler, Gerhard Schulz *vns* Thomas Kakuska *va* Valentin Erben *vc*)
EMI CDC5 56470-2 (57 minutes: DDD) Ⓕ
Recorded live in [a]1994, [b]1997

String Quartets Nos 12 and 15
Alban Berg Quartet (Günther Pichler, Gerhard Schulz *vns* Thomas Kakuska *va* Valentin Erben *vc*)
EMI CDC5 56471-2 (60 minutes: DDD) Ⓕ
Recorded live in 1997 ●●

The Alban Berg Quartet's policy of making recordings at concert performances certainly produces impressive results: interpretations that avoid any feeling of routine or of being overcareful. What impresses above all is the flexibility and sensitivity of these performances. In the first movement of D887 the Alban Berg, by subtly drawing our attention to the precise emotional colour of all Schubert's magical harmonic shifts, finds a touching, intimate quality within the grand design. And it's certainly an advantage for any group performing this quartet to be able to produce such a magnificent *tremolando* – whether it's the forest murmurs of the first movement or the Gothic shuddering of the *Andante*'s middle section.

The G major Quartet is the outstanding performance on these discs, but *Death and the Maiden* isn't far behind, particularly the *con fuoco Scherzo* and finale. There are a few places, where Schubert is straightforwardly tuneful (in D703 and in the outer movements of D87, especially) where one wishes Günther Pichler would play in a simpler, more direct manner. The Busch Quartet's 1930s recordings of D810 and D887 are smoother, less emphatic than that of modern groups, and this enables it to convey the emotional nuances, particularly of the D minor Quartet, in a more inward and profound way. And the two quartets are available (with some repeats missing) on a single CD. But it's a measure of the Alban Berg Quartet's exceptional quality to realise that it is in the same league, with the same sense of players totally absorbed in the music. The recorded sound is immeasurably more vivid and lifelike.

String Quartets Nos 12[a], 13[b], 14[a] and 15[b]
Quartetto Italiano (Paolo Borciani, Elisa Pegreffi *vns* Piero Farulli *va* Franco Rossi *vc*)
Philips Duo ② 446 163-2PM2 (142 minutes: ADD) Ⓜ
Recorded [a]1965, [b]1976-77

The Italians' playing has freshness, affection, firm control and above all authority to a degree that no relative newcomer can match. It is notable not only for the highest standards of ensemble, intonation and blend, but also for its imaginative insights; these attributes readily apply to the music-making on this Duo reissue, particularly in the slow movements. Indeed, the players' progress through the wonderful set of variations in the *Andante con moto*, which reveals the *Death and the Maiden* Quartet's association with the famous Schubert song of that name, has unforgettable intensity (it is a grand conception packed with memorable detail – the evocation of terror in the early stages of the first movement coda has never been bettered).

The comparable *Andante* of No 13, with its lovely *Rosamunde* theme – which is approached here in a relaxed, leisurely manner – is held together with a similar (almost imperceptible) sureness of touch. When this work was originally issued, the first-movement exposition repeat was cut in order to get the quartet complete on to a single LP side. Here it has been restored.

Finest of all is the great No 15, a work of epic scale. The first movement alone runs to nearly 23 minutes, and the players' masterly grip over the many incidents that make up the *Allegro molto moderato* is effortless. For an encore we are given No 12, a piece on a smaller scale, but here presented with a comparable hushed intensity of feeling. This, like No 14, was recorded in 1965 and the textures are leaner than on the others, with a fractional edge on *fortissimos*. Nevertheless, the ear soon adjusts when the playing is as remarkable as this. The other recordings have more body, and a fine presence. The CD transfers throughout are excellent.

String Quartets Nos 14 and 15 H
Busch Quartet (Adolph Busch, Gösta Andreasson *vns* Karl Doktor *va* Hermann Busch *vc*)
EMI Références mono CDH7 69795-2 Ⓜ
(73 minutes: ADD). Recorded 1936-38 **OO**

Death and the Maiden is the best served of Schubert's quartets on CD. The Busch Quartet's account is now well over 60 years old but it still brings us closer to the heart of this work than any other. The slow movement, in particular, has an unmatched and marvellous eloquence. The same must also be said of the G major Quartet, a performance of surpassing beauty which reveals more of the depth and humanity of the score than any subsequent recording. Such are these performances that the music is quick to engross your thoughts to the exclusion of any consideration of the age of the recordings. The recording is, on the whole, good: exceptionally so in the quieter passages.

Piano Trios

Piano Trios[a] – B flat, D28 (Sonata in one movement); No 1 in B flat, D898; No 2 in E flat, D929. Notturno in E flat, D897[b]. String Trios[b] – B flat, D471; B flat, D581
[a]**Beaux Arts Trio** (Menahem Pressler *pf* Daniel Guilet *vn* Bernard Greenhouse *vc*); [b]**Grumiaux Trio** (Arthur Grumiaux *vn* Georges Janzer *va* Eva Czako *vc*)
Philips Duo ② 438 700-2PM2 (127 minutes: ADD) Ⓜ
Recorded 1966-69 **O**

These performances are polished, yet the many solo contributions from each of the players emerge with a strong personality. The Beaux Arts cellist brings lovely phrasing and a true simplicity of line, so right for Schubert – memorably in the lovely slow movement melody of the Trio No 2 in E flat.

In addition to the great piano trios (B flat, D898 and E flat, D929) the set includes the extremely personable, very early Sonata in B flat, D28, where the lyrical line already has the unmistakable character of its young composer. Also included is the *Notturno*, D897, a raptly emotive short piece played here with a remarkable depth of feeling that recalls the gentle intensity of the glorious slow movement of the String Quintet.

The recording is naturally balanced, although a little dry in the treble. Of the two rarer string trios, also early works, the four-movement Trio, D581 is totally infectious, with that quality of innocence that makes Schubert's music stand apart. Given such persuasive advocacy, and vivid recording, both pieces cannot fail to give the listener great pleasure.

Piano Trios Nos 1 and 2. Sonata in A minor, D821, 'Arpeggione'. Notturno in E flat, D897
Yuuko Shiokawa *vn* **Miklos Perényi** *vc*
András Schiff *pf*
Teldec ② 0630-13151-2 (127 minutes: DDD) Ⓕ
Recorded 1995 **OO**

This set begins with an outstanding performance of the *Arpeggione* Sonata. The recording is clear and spacious, and the outer movements have an effortless sense of momentum that is not too inflexible to allow for some expressive rubato and pointing of the phrases. There's no hint in Perényi's playing that this is a difficult work for the cello, and he produces a most beautiful, warm, serene tone for the *Adagio*. Schiff's special feeling for Schubert is apparent even in the most subsidiary details of the piano part and particularly in the more dominating roles of the trios and the *Notturno*.

These three well-matched players find exactly the right tone and feeling. In the first *Allegro* of the B flat Trio the superior recording helps them to convey the music's grandeur and the following *Andante* is played with a flowing, evocative style. Shiokawa's clear-toned, elegant violin playing is certainly a great asset here. In the *Notturno*, too, a flowing tempo doesn't spoil the tranquillity of the opening melody, but allows the contrasting episode to emerge triumphantly.

In the monumental E flat Trio Schiff, Shiokawa and Perényi seem sometimes to be a little polite and decorous, but their interpretation is certainly not lacking in vitality or variety. The finale in this performance lasts nearly 20 minutes: the players have gone back to the original version of the movement – Schubert made cuts when preparing the trio for publication. If you are an admirer of Schubert's 'heavenly length' then you will hear it as the true culmination of one of his greatest instrumental works.

Works for Piano Duet

Divertissements – à la hongroise, D818; sur des ℗
motifs originaux français, D823
Andreas Staier, Alexei Lubimov fp duet
Teldec 0630-17113-2 (66 minutes: DDD) Ⓕ
Recorded 1997 ○○

Schubert's *Divertissement à la hongroise*, his most
flamboyant essay in the Hungarian vernacular
style, has always overshadowed the *Divertissement* on French themes. Yet the less favoured
work is in some ways the more compelling. Its
profoundly un-divertimento-like first movement has a haunting, quintessentially
Schubertian second theme and one of the composer's most turbulent and tonally audacious
developments. The *Andantino*, a set of variations
on a glum little theme that sounds more plausibly French than anything else in the work, is
transfigured by its ravishing final variation in the
major; and the finale is a sprawling, colourful
rondo, built on a theme that equivocates
between G major and E minor.

Using a fine copy by Christopher Clarke of an
1826 Graf instrument, Staier and Lubimov give
performances which, in poetry, *élan* and sheer
relish have never been surpassed. One immediate advantage of a fortepiano in this music is the
way it clarifies the textures, especially in the bass
regions. Then there is the unique array of
colours available through the use of no fewer
than five pedals – the harp-like sonorities of the
una corda pedal, for instance, or the 'bassoon'
pedal, with its buzzing lower strings. The
instrument's *coup de grâce* is its so-called Turkish
pedal, attached to bass drum, bells and cymbals,
which the players unleash at with swashbuckling
effect. If you're a sceptic about period performance, then these hugely enjoyable performances
should convert you.

Sonata for Piano Duet in C, D812, 'Grand Duo'. Eight
Variations in A flat, D813. Trois marches militaires, D733
Daniel Barenboim, Radu Lupu pf duet
Teldec 0630-17146-2 (77 minutes: DDD) Ⓕ
Recorded 1993 ○

One might expect this combination of artists
playing Schubert to produce winning results,
and so it does. Rarely will you hear duet playing
of such refined elegance and multicoloured animation. Here, the playing is vivid and
glamorous; the dynamic and colouristic range of
Barenboim's and Lupu's performances suggests
a public environment. After the spirited brio of
the familiar *Marches militaires*, the remainder of
the disc contains music of greater seriousness
and architectural breadth. The Variations in
A flat are beautifully played, with subtle and discerning pianism. The largest work on this disc is
the C major Sonata: here it runs to 43 minutes,
longer than any of Schubert's solo sonatas. It can
reasonably be classed alongside Schubert's two
other late masterpieces in C, the *Great* Symphony and the String Quintet. The *Grand Duo* is
symphonic in scope and expression, although the

writing is innately pianistic. The fine detail of
Barenboim's and Lupu's account, their diversity
of colour and attack and their voicing of melodic
and inner lines, suggests an image of suitably
orchestral depth and variety. Furthermore, the
surface gloss of these performances is under
pinned by the most crystalline lucidity and
poetry. The recording is excellent.

Violin Sonatas

Violin Sonatas – D004; D385; D408
Gidon Kremer vn **Oleg Maisenberg** pf
DG 437 092-2GH (62 minutes: DDD) Ⓕ
Recorded 1991

The front cover of the booklet here refers to
these works as sonatinas, while the notes and
back cover have sonatas. In fact they have been
called both and, as the notes explain, the
diminutive designation was bestowed on them
by their publisher. The writer makes a case for
the grander title, and indeed they are hardly
slight, with the A minor and G minor lasting
over 20 minutes and only the popular D major
having something of the miniature about it. Furthermore, the minor mode of D385 and D408
(which here precede the D major) adds to one's
feeling that these are not lightweight pieces.

Clearly this is also the view of Gidon Kremer
and Oleg Maisenberg, who invest the first
movement of the A minor work with a lilting
melancholy, taking it slowly even for *Allegro
moderato* and often lingering over expressive
details longer than might be thought desirable;
however, this is better than applying pressure to
the music and they mostly maintain momentum.
Yet in their playing as a whole you feel that
they aim to give these works a depth and drama
that they do not altogether bear. Indeed, it is a
touch mannered, and whether you find it excessively so must be a matter of taste. The same is
true of this violinist's characteristic tone: it has a
certain thinness along with vibrant sweetness,
although it is undoubtedly touching. This said,
the two artists are very well attuned, and
Maisenberg is an admirable pianist. The recording is well balanced and very natural.

Additional recommendation
Violin Sonatas
D, D384; A minor, D385; G minor, D408
Dubeau vn **Kuerti** pf
Analekta fleurs de lys FL2 3042 (55 minutes: DDD) Ⓜ
No longer available in the UK, but try the internet

These performances are really impressive. Angèle Dubeau
and Anton Kuerti are at one in maintaining the intimate
tone of these works; they manage to make each detail
expressive, yet keep to a natural, unforced utterance.

Wandererfantasie, D760

Fantasie in C, D934[a]. Fantasy in C,
'Wandererfantasie', D760
[a]**Yuuko Shiokawa** vn **András Schiff** pf
ECM New Series 464 320-2 (50 minutes: DDD) Ⓕ
Recorded 1999 ○

Nearly all Schubert's great instrumental works maintain the classical four-movement layout: by the 1820s his mastery in handling and extending these designs was only shared by Beethoven. But he did turn occasionally to the fashionable, looser, fantasia-style forms – in the case of the *Wandererfantasie*, one of his most disturbing works, he seems to be using his structural know-how in order to subvert the expectations of classical form. András Schiff vividly brings out the switches between classical poise, intensely romantic mood-painting and near-expressionistic disruption; the key lies in the way he doesn't exaggerate any contrast, but makes each detail tell, so that the full range of the piece can be heard. One shouldn't underestimate the technical achievement – the lead-in to the *adagio* section is a perfect demonstration of a gradual *diminuendo*, of energy falling away, and when the *Adagio* arrives the chordal playing is superb – the melodic line perfectly balanced by the dark, melancholic colours in the bass.

Balance and lack of exaggeration inform the D934 *Fantasie*, too. From the start, when Shiokawa steals in above the piano *tremolando*, there's an air of magic. Her fine, silvery tone only rarely expands to a richer or more dramatic utterance, but her care not to overplay actually adds to the rich impression the performance gives. Whereas Kremer and Afanassiev present the central variation set as a brilliant showpiece, Schiff and Shiokawa paint a noticeably more varied picture – drama and virtuosity alternating with delicacy and touches of lyrical tenderness. In short, these are interpretations of rare penetration and individuality: a must for the Schubert section in your collection.

Schubert Fantasy in C, 'Wandererfantasie' D760
Schumann Fantasie in C, Op 17
Maurizio Pollini *pf*
DG The Originals 447 451-2GOR (52 minutes: ADD) Ⓜ
Recorded 1973 ●●●

The cover shows Caspar David Friedrich's familiar *The Wanderer above the Sea of Fog*. Pollini, on the other hand, is a wanderer in a transparent ether or crystalline light and both of these legendary performances, recorded in 1973 and beautifully remastered, are of a transcendental vision and integrity. In the Schubert his magisterial, resolutely un-virtuoso approach allows everything its time and place. Listen to his flawlessly graded triple *piano* approach to the central *Adagio*, to his rock-steady octaves at 5'23" (where Schubert's merciless demand is so often the cause of confusion) or to the way the decorations in the *Adagio* are spun off with such rare finesse, and you may well wonder when you have heard playing of such an unadorned, unalloyed glory. Pollini's Schumann is no less memorable. Doubting Thomases on the alert for alternating touches of imperiousness and sobriety will be disappointed, for, again, Pollini's poise is unfaltering. The opening *Moderato* is *sempre energico*, indeed, its central *Etwas langsamer* is so sensitively and precisely gauged that all possible criticism is silenced. The coda of the central march (that *locus classicus* of the wrong note) is immaculate and in what someone once called the finale's 'shifting sunset vapour' Pollini takes us gently but firmly to the shores of Elysium. Here is a record that should grace every musician's shelf.

Hüttenbrenner Variations

Andante in C, D29. Minuet in A minor, D277*a*. Minuet in A, D334. 13 Variations in A minor on a theme by Anselm Hüttenbrenner, D576. Andante in A, D604. Fantasy in C, 'Grazer Fantasie', D605*a*. Three Impromptus, D946
James Lisney *pf*
Olympia OCD479 (65 minutes: DDD) Ⓕ
Recorded 1995

James Lisney's unusual Schubert recital offers an illuminating programme of lesser-known works, demonstrating the composer's exploitation of tonal colour and keyboard sonority. After a sensitive performance of the enchanting C major *Andante*, D29, Lisney plays a group of pieces that exploit the expressive potential of A major/minor tonality. Two minuets establish the emotional contrast between these tonal colours: the A minor one is bold and defiant, with a tranquil F major trio, while the carefree, amiable A major work is balanced by a poignantly lyrical trio in E major. The *Variations on a theme by Anselm Hüttenbrenner* demonstrates a more complex and dramatic A major/minor dichotomy, which Lisney here presents beautifully with subtle control of the theme's different transformations and telling modal shifts. In addition, Lisney offers a thoroughly absorbing, searching account of the brooding, introspective A major *Andante* and a poetically romantic, finely conceived performance of the *Grazer Fantasie*.

To conclude, carefully observed interpretations of the three *Impromptus*, D946, whilst perhaps lacking the spontaneity of Brendel's reissued versions (on a two-disc set), nevertheless confirm Lisney as a thoughtful and perceptive Schubertian. This fascinating concert, which benefits from satisfyingly faithful recorded sound, should attract a wide audience.

Impromptus

Impromptus – D899; D935. Drei Klavierstücke, D946. Allegretto in C minor, D915
Maria João Pires *pf*
DG ② 457 550-2GH2 (108 minutes: DDD) Ⓕ
Recorded 1997 ●●●

This is something very special indeed. Maria João Pires's two-disc set of Schubert's *Impromptus*, significantly dedicated to Sviatoslav Richter, contains a booklet in which standard notes are replaced by carefully chosen extracts from Pires's own reading: reflections on time, space and wilderness from Yves Simon's *Le voyageur magnifique*; meditations on Schubert as

Wanderer; and thoughts from a neuroscientist on the 'physiology' of great music. Like so many prefaces, these words are best read afterwards, when certain fragments, different for each listener, may well close-focus in the mind elements still resonating in the ear. Pires's characteristic impassioned absorption in all she plays – that concentration which makes the listener appear to be eavesdropping on secrets shared between friends – could hardly find a truer soul mate than in the sensibility of Schubert. Each *Impromptu* has a rare sense of integrity and entirety, born of acute observation and long-pondered responses.

Pires's instinct for tempo and pacing brings a sense of constant restraint, a true *molto moderato* to the *Allegro* of the C minor work from D899, created by a fusion of right-hand *tenuto* here with momentary left-hand rubato there. Then there is the clarity of contour within the most subtly graded undertones of the G flat major of D899 which re-creates it as a seemingly endless song. Or an *Andante* just slow, just nonchalant enough for the *Rosamunde* theme of the D935 B flat major to give each variation space and breath enough to sing out its own sharply defined character.

The *Allegretto*, D915 acts as a *Pause* between the two discs, a resting place, as it were, for reflection and inner assessment on this long journey. Its end – which could as well be its beginning – is in the *Drei Klavierstücke*, D946 of 1828. The first draws back from the fiery impetuousness within the *Allegro assai*'s tautly controlled rhythms, to an inner world with its own time scale; the second, more transpired than played, has an almost unbearable poignancy of simplicity. The paradox of these unselfregarding performances is how unmistakably they speak and sing out Pires and her unique musicianship. To draw comparisons here would be not so much odious as to miss the point.

12 Waltzes, D969

12 Waltzes, D969. Six Moments musicaux, D780. Drei Klavierstücke, D946. **P**
Peter Katin *fp* Ⓕ
Athene ATHCD7 (74 minutes: DDD)
Recorded 1995

One of the most attractive features of Katin's Schubert disc is its comfortable intimacy, conjuring images of the composer's own domestic music-making. The Clementi square piano sounds wholly appropriate in the *Waltzes*, highlighting Schubert's magical blend of Viennese gaiety and warmer harmonic shades. In the *Drei Klavierstücke*, Katin further underlines his relaxed approach with some beautifully atmospheric effects and the inclusion of all repeats. Witness the timeless quality in the slower sections of the first piece; the menacing tremolos of the C minor music and the ethereal upper register of the A flat minor music in the second piece, and the subtly coloured textures and boldly projected voice-leading in the third one.

Complete Piano Sonatas

No 1 in E, D157; **No 2** in C, D279; **No 3** in E, D459; **No 4** in A minor, D537; **No 5** in A flat, D557; **No 6** in E minor, D566; **No 7** in E flat, D568; **No 8** in F sharp minor, D571; **No 9** in B, D575; **No 11** in C, D613; **No 12** in F minor, D625; **No 13** in A, D664; **No 14** in A minor, D784; **No 15** in C, 'Relique', D840; **No 16** in A minor, D845; **No 17** in D, D850; **No 18** in G, D894; **No 19** in C minor, D958; **No 20** in A, D959; **No 21** in B flat, D960

Piano Sonatas Nos 1-21
András Schiff *pf*
Decca ⑦ 448 390-2DM7 (498 minutes: DDD) Ⓜ
Recorded 1992-93

András Schiff's Schubert sonatas, of course, come into direct competition with the masterly set from Wilhelm Kempff, which is very special indeed (these were recorded in the mid- to late 1960s and are available on a seven-disc DG set). Kempff's unsurpassed performance of the last great B flat Sonata (No 21), for instance, is ravishingly beautiful, full of the insights of his long experience. But throughout his series Schiff's freshness of approach is spring-like in its appeal, and his response to these 19 works (he includes the fragments of the Eighth Sonata, which Kempff omits) – which he describes as 'among the most sublime contributions written for the piano' – is no less individual and certainly not short of poetic feeling or a sense of the music's overall design. Anyone who wants modern recordings of these great sonatas should be well content with Schiff's survey, even though the catalogue also includes many individual performances of great distinction. The excellent recordings were made in the Brahms-Saal of the Vienna Musikverein. Schiff's sonatas, incidentally, are all available separately and many of these individual issues are reviewed below.

Piano Sonatas No 1-14

Piano Sonatas Nos 1, 3 and 13
András Schiff *pf* Decca 440 311-2DH Ⓕ
(71 minutes: DDD). Recorded 1992-93 ●

This seventh volume in Schiff's Schubert sonata cycle spotlights the young composer, starting with the E major work (D157) which, at the age of 18, he chose as his official No 1. Schiff plays it with a delectable, springlike freshness and tonal charm – banishing every vestige of the 'impersonality' the insert-note writer warns us to expect in the opening *Allegro ma non troppo*. His delicate keyboard 'orchestration' is no less a delight in the slow movement, with its plaintive reminders of Mozart's Barbarina and her lost pin.

It is easy to understand why the E major Sonata (D459) of the following year first appeared in print, posthumously, as *Fünf Klavierstücke*. Each of the five movements inhabits a world of its own. And each is as unpredictable in sequence of ideas and modulation as in actual keyboard texture. Schiff himself revels in the music's romantic pre-echoes, not least in the demonstrative finale unusually headed *Allegro patetico*. The disc is completed by the A major Sonata of 1819, the last of Schubert's youthful essays in the genre before a four-year break, but the first of these early works to find a regular place in the repertory. Its gracious, lyrical charm is caught by Schiff in a reading of winning simplicity. No detail is overlooked (there are endless subtleties to enjoy just from his left hand) but never does his point-making intrude. Even in the spirited final *Allegro* his relaxed approach suggests not a hard-working concert pianist but a Schubert playing at home for the delectation of his friends.

Piano Sonatas Nos 2, 12 and 21
András Schiff *pf*
Decca 440 310-2DH (78 minutes: DDD) Ⓕ
Recorded 1992 ●

In his own contribution to the insert-notes, Schiff writes, '[Schubert's] music is most sensitive to tonal quality, especially in soft and softest dynamics. He's also a quintessentially Viennese composer, and for this reason a Bösendorfer Imperial has been chosen.' The C major Sonata, D279, eloquently reinforces Schiff's argument. Despite its strong Beethovenian flavour, most notably in the first two movements, Schiff is undemonstrative with the music's overt virtuosity, preferring to allow his sensitive *cantabile*, attractively enhanced by the Bösendorfer's delicate edge, to express Schubert's radiant lyricism.

Schubert left the first movement of the F minor Sonata, D625, incomplete and Schiff poignantly breaks off where the composer did. His graceful, elegant playing charmingly conveys the music's Biedermeier character in the second movement, and he shows a profound sympathy for Schubert's musical and expressive language through effective opposition of the finale's dramatic forces in a performance that matches Richter's affectionately attentive account.

In the B flat major Sonata, D960, Schiff's inclusion of the exposition repeat emphasises the music's discontinuities for a potent expression of the underlying unease, first apparent in the bass trills. Subtle shifts of key and colour are powerfully effective in both the slow movement and the finale, and deft control in the *Scherzo* yields much revelatory detail – further evidence of the appropriateness of the Bösendorfer sound.

Piano Sonatas Nos 4 and 20 **P**
Malcolm Bilson *fp*
Hungaroton HCD31587 (59 minutes: DDD) Ⓕ
Recorded 1995

Bilson's is not the first disc to highlight the close affinity between Schubert's A minor Piano Sonata, composed in March 1817, and the great A major Sonata from the composer's final year. In a recording of the same two works, Schiff – aided by the modern Bösendorfer piano's capacity for sustained serene tone – perceptively reveals the A minor Sonata's voice-leading threads in a compelling blend of romantic, dance-like grace and lyrical warmth. With judicious use of the moderator pedal, Bilson here effectively exploits the 1815 Lagrassa fortepiano's robust tone in a reading which, though less dramatic than Schiff's, atmospherically opposes different tonal regions. Schubert miraculously transformed the duple-metre theme of the A minor Sonata's slow movement into the flowing lines of the A major Sonata's rondo finale. Schiff's concentration on detail throughout this later work could be seen to be impeding the music's natural impetus. However, the spaciousness of his account does successfully convey the music's broad landscape. Bilson's blend of spontaneity and distinctive contrasts of tonal colour in all movements winningly conveys both the music's potently dramatic use of motivic material and its large-scale psychological spans.

Piano Sonatas Nos 5, 9 and 18
András Schiff *pf*
Decca 440 307-2DH (76 minutes: DDD) Ⓕ
Recorded 1992 ●●

Schubert's piano music from András Schiff always lifts the spirits, and this time quite a bit higher than most comparable available versions. Typically, he chooses his favourite Bösendorfer Imperial with its Viennese accent and writes in an introduction to the notes of its Schubertian sensitivity to tone-quality, particularly in the softest dynamics. Schiff cites the opening of the G major Sonata, D894 as an example and, indeed, this movement, which the composer originally called a Fantasy, has a gentle luminosity about it. Schiff's approach to the vast first movement more closely resembles Lupu's in its meditative, long-sighted qualities; but Schiff again triumphs, in coaxing both a wider and a more finely controlled tone palette out of his instrument. Schiff's greatest achievement here, though, is his organic view of the inner and outer worlds of this sonata. As in the song, 'Der Lindenbaum' (from *Winterreise*), images of both tender dream and harsh reality seem to shape the piece. Schiff makes them seem simply different sides of the same persona. One flows into and out of another, with the dark concentration of rhythm in the eye of the storm. In the last movement, Schiff outdoes Lupu in the dance of constantly shifting weights and measures, lights and half-lights which dapple the rondo's returns. Schiff seems to play through the childlike ears and eyes of Schubert himself.

This outstanding performance of D894 is nicely balanced by a deliciously understated D557, the most classically conceived of all Schubert's sonatas, and by the more adventurous D575. Here, Schiff continues to exploit the qualifying *ma non troppo* of the opening *Allegro* to create a sense of ideas and energies being held back within an unquiet serenity. If the slow movement is a little over-deliberate, the finale again seems to be constantly surprising itself with the new ideas which sing out as if they had only just been imagined.

Piano Sonatas Nos 7 and 19
András Schiff *pf*
Decca 440 308-2DH (61 minutes: DDD) Ⓕ
Recorded 1992

Those who like their C minor Sonata bulging with Byronic sentiment or exploding with theatrical sparks will no doubt find Schiff's unshowy approach intolerably ascetic though the absorption, the inner penetration of his playing here is worth the loss of a few histrionic thrills. His understanding is revealed in tiny, delicate touches – the way the C minor's first movement eases gently into the second subject, or the nicely timed silences in the Menuetto, with the *Allegro* finale arising after another short but pregnant pause. At the same time there's a profound grasp of the Schubertian pulse: the tension between subtle rubato and what Theodor Adorno called the 'somnambulistic' forward tread. It's beautifully judged, whether in minute details (the slight holding back in the running quavers near the start of the E flat Sonata is a perfect example) or in the longer term – the way D568's Minuet resumes the first movement's basic pulse. Schiff is emphatically not one of those pianists that wants to show you at every stage what a fabulously rich palette he possesses, but the sound he coaxes from his Bösendorfer is hauntingly lovely, and the Decca recording captures it, and the Vienna Musikverein Brahms-Saal's intimate warmth, superbly.

Piano Sonatas Nos 9, 12 and 13.
Moment musical in C, D780 No 1
Sviatoslav Richter *pf*
BBC Legends BBCL4010-2 (78 minutes: ADD) Ⓜ
Recorded live in 1979

Richter's Schubert is simply in a class of its own. No pianist did more to overturn the traditional view of the composer as a blithe, unreflecting child of nature. And in this Festival Hall recital three sonatas from 1817-19 unfold with a grandeur of conception, a spirituality and a stoical timelessness that were unique to Richter. The first two movements of the A major Sonata are, on the face of it, implausibly slow: but with his mesmeric, self-communing intensity Richter convinces you for the duration of the performance that no other way is admissable. Phrases, paragraphs are shaped with calm inevitability, underpinned by the sublime, luminous simplicity of Richter's *cantabile*; and no pianist is more sensitive to Schubert's magical harmonic strokes or understands more surely their place in the larger scheme. As Richter conceives them, the first two movements of the A major foreshadow the rapt, philosophical contemplation of the late G major and B flat Sonatas; and even the finale, projected with Richter's characteristic mastery and subtlety of rhythm, has something rarefied in its playfulness. Richter is equally lofty and far-sighted in the two lesser-known sonatas.

The BBC recording, while perhaps a shade bass-light, is warm, and does ample justice to Richter's vast dynamic and tonal palette. A bronchial March audience can intrude at the start of tracks, especially in finales. But no matter. All but those terminally resistant to Richter's uniquely introspective, long-spanned view of the composer should acquire as a matter of urgency these visionary performances by one of the greatest Schubertians of the century.

Piano Sonatas Nos 14-18

Piano Sonatas No 9, 15 and 18
Sviatoslav Richter *pf*
Philips ② 438 483-2PH2 (117 minutes: ADD) Ⓕ
Recorded live in 1979

Facts first. The G major Sonata, D894 takes up an entire CD, in comparison with the average 16 or 17 minutes. Richter's first movement is no less than 26'51" long. Then the C major, D840 appears not *unvollendet* at all, but with its little unfinished Menuetto and Rondo taking their own eye- and ear-opening place. Behind these facts lie the concepts which set these performances apart. The heavenly length of the first movement of D894 is created out of Richter's relationship with time itself. The more one listens to his late Schubert, the more one realises that movement and momentum are not conceived as linear. Rather they are cyclical, very much in the spirit of the final song of *Winterreise* in which the Leiermann's turning melody could be eternal. No wonder that it is to Richter that singers like Peter Schreier turn when working out the when and the how of their Schubert.

The opening *Molto moderato* is read as extremely slow: the ear begins by being on tenterhooks for what might come next – then shocked by the sudden, harsh brightening of tone as the first temporary modulation is prepared. As the movement progresses, the opening motif becomes like a mantra in an extended meditation in which the listener must go through the same discipline of private pacing as the performer. At a practical level, Richter's tempo allows the mood of *Molto moderato e cantabile* to be unbroken by busy-ness even as the theme metamorphoses into quaver figuration. The *Andante*, when at last it arrives, moves with a contrastingly lithe, blithe ease, more songlike, more forceful at its centre. The simplicity and clarity of movement created by Richter's fingers in the bright dance of weight and measure which is the final *Allegretto* (and which makes for an archaic, hymn-like *Andante* in D575) is Schubert's sweetness and light.

His dark side, in both these sonatas, is explored uncompromisingly by Richter in modulations of key and dynamics abrupt enough to hurt. Richter's complete incomplete Sonata, D840 is another extraordinary journey. Another endless *Moderato* (22 minutes) is this time relentless in the bare, unbeautiful resonance of its repeated figures which, all the more miraculously, become song accompaniment. It is followed by a strange, minimalist Menuetto and an almost surreal sense of bleakness as the pirouetting Rondo melts into thin air.

Piano Sonatas Nos 14 and 17
Mitsuko Uchida *pf*
Philips 464 480-2PH (62 minutes: DDD) Ⓕ
Recorded 1999

Mitsuko Uchida's Schubert is never less than wonderfully finished in pianistic terms, and as an interpretation it is only occasionally a little disappointing. In these two latest sonatas she is close to her best. The D major, a product of the composer's extended summer tour in Austria in 1825, is, as Misha Donat's essay notes, 'among Schubert's sonatas ... the most brilliant and extrovert'. With her exceptional finger technique Uchida takes its technical demands in her stride (there are several renowned Schubertians of whom this much cannot be said), yet she never allows physical excitement to become the be-all-and-end-all. She finds playfulness in the contrasting themes of the first movement, and handles the song-like writing of the second and fourth with the expertise of a great Lieder accompanist, each phrase being subtly inflected yet never to the detriment of the long line. However, the horn-call-based second theme in the slow movement sounds a little over-excited and more than a little over-pedalled. But when it and the main theme of the movement are superimposed on the final page, Uchida's tone is fabulously well graded. Most memorable of all are the half tones she deploys in the third movement *Trio* and the exceptional delicacy and refinement of her passagework in the finale.

In the A minor Sonata she brings out the world-weariness of the first movement, the fragile hopefulness of the *Andante*, and the finale's seething energy. The contrasting martial theme in the first movement again finds her a fraction over-excitable. Nor does the finale coda sweep all before it in the exultant way of a Richter.

Richter is on peak form in the D major sonata from Moscow in 1956 (Melodyia), and the A minor from Tokyo in 1979 (Olympia). Everything he does seems to have deeper roots and to be carried forward by an even stronger artistic imperative than Uchida's, so that he does not need to resort to her occasionally rather calculated-seeming hesitations in order to convince. (These are also among the better-recorded items in the hugely variable Richter legacy.)

But for an alternative in rich modern sound, Uchida remains a good bet. As before she uses a 1962 Steinway, which is just about ideal for Schubert. Once again the recordings, from the Vienna Musikverein, verge on the over-resonant; but in this instance they detract hardly at all from the music or the playing.

Piano Sonatas Nos 11, 14 and 21
Stephen Hough *pf*
Hyperion CDA67027 (76 minutes: DDD) Ⓕ
Recorded 1998

Stephen Hough's moving performance of Sonata No 21 is marked throughout by refined, discerning pianism and an uncommonly subtle ear for texture. In all four movements, he seeks out the music's inwardness and fragility, its ethereal, self-communing remoteness. The opening *Molto moderato*, unfolding in vast, calm spans, has a hypnotic inevitability; there are countless felicities of timing and colour, but always a vital sense of forward motion. Hough adopts a dangerously slow tempo in the *Andante* but sustains it through the breadth and concentration of his line, the subtlety of his tonal palette and his pointing of rhythmic detail. His rarefied grace and delicacy, his gentle probing of the music's vulnerability, are of a piece with his conception of the sonata as a whole.

As usual, Hyperion does not stint over playing time, offering another complete sonata in addition to the two-movement fragment, No 11. No 14, perhaps Schubert's most depressive instrumental work, is magnificently done. Hough distils an immense weight of suffering from the pervasive two-note motif that dominates the first movement like some massive, Wagnerian pendulum; but, typically, the lyrical music is limpidly coloured and poignantly inflected, with an unusually precise observation of Schubert's accents. The *Andante* is flowing and long-arched, with some ravishing soft playing, and he a brings a superb rhythmic impulse to the eerily scudding counterpoint of the main subject and a piercing tenderness to the contrasting F major theme (0'51"). The fragmentary C major Sonata, one of numerous Schubert torsos from the years 1817-22, is no great shakes: two pleasant but uneventful movements, both incomplete. It's unsurprising that Schubert lost interest in mid-flight. But Schubertians will be happy to have the fragment as a bonus to Hough's individual and searching readings of the two great sonatas, which take their place alongside the most recommendable in the catalogue. The pleasure is enhanced by the exemplary clarity, warmth and truthfulness of the recording.

Piano Sonatas Nos 14 and 17
Alfred Brendel *pf*
Philips 422 063-2PH (63 minutes: DDD) Ⓕ
Recorded 1987

There is an extraordinary amount of highly experimental writing in Schubert's piano sonatas. The essence of their structure is the contrasting of big heroic ideas with tender and inner thoughts; the first impresses the listener, the second woos him. The two works on this CD are in some ways on a varying scale. The D major lasts for 40 minutes, the A minor for around 23. However, it is the latter that contains the most symphonically inspired writing – it sounds as if it could easily be transposed for orchestra. Alfred Brendel presents the composer not so much as the master of Lieder-writing, but more as a man thinking in large forms. Although there are wonderful quiet moments when intimate asides are conveyed with an imaginative sensitivity one remembers more the urgency and the power behind the notes. The A minor, with its frequently recurring themes, is almost obsessive in character whilst the big

D major Sonata is rather lighter in its mood, especially in the outer movements. The recorded sound is very faithful to the pianist's tone, whilst generally avoiding that insistent quality that can mar his loudest playing.

Piano Sonatas Nos 15 and 18
Mitsuko Uchida *pf*
Philips 454 453-2PH (70 minutes: DDD) Ⓕ
Recorded 1996

Schubert's G major Sonata, D894, is the ultimate *Frühlingstraum*. Pervading the entire work is that oscillation between light-filled dream and stark waking reality. These may be juxtaposed in dramatic motivic contrast, but they are, quintessentially, twin sides of a single consciousness; and it is Mitsuko Uchida's supreme achievement to understand and re-create precisely this quality. She creates a true opening *molto moderato* of profound stillness and long distances. Chords really resonate and breathe out, yet her quick intakes of breath as the second subject steps into dance are tempered with the more flexible, whimsical intimacy of a Schiff. Uchida's gentleness of touch is ballasted by a firmly delineated bass and a weight of rhythmic articulation. She finds an easy, instinctive pace for the *Andante*, creating compacted shocks in the ringing chords of its minor-key episodes. These chords announce a Menuetto in which the Trio slinks in as the merest spectre of a Ländler, and leads to a finale in which Uchida creates a dance of the spirit within a deep inner stillness. The *Relique* Sonata, D840, one of Schubert's great and tantalizingly unfinished works, sounds entire, fully achieved in Uchida's hands. She shares with Schiff a leisured playing-out of the first movement. And her *Andante* is no less intimate in its *bel canto* of minute nuance and inflexion, starker and bleaker still than Schiff's masterpiece.

Piano Sonata No 16. Impromptus, D946
Alfred Brendel *p*
Philips 422 075-2PH Ⓕ
(61 minutes: DDD) ●

Though love of the music alone, as pianists know, is not enough to master these pieces, it is essential, and in this big A minor Sonata Brendel presents us with a drama that is no less tense for being predominantly expressed in terms of shapely melody. There is a flexibility in this playing that reminds us of the pianist's own comment that in such music 'we feel not masters but victims of the situation': he allows us plenty of time to savour detail without ever losing sight of the overall shape of the music, and the long first movement and finale carry us compellingly forwards, as does the *Scherzo* with its urgent energy, while the *Andante* second movement, too, has the right kind of spaciousness. In the *Impromptus* which date from the composer's last months, Brendel is no less responsive or imaginative. Richly sonorous digital recording in a German location complements the distinction of the playing on this fine disc.

Piano Sonata No 16. Impromptus, D946 **P**
Andreas Staier *fp*
Teldec Das Alte Werk 0630-11084-2 Ⓕ
(62 minutes: DDD). Recorded 1995 ●

Once again, it is Andreas Staier's imagination and insight as a musician, rather than Staier-as-fortepianist, which comes to the fore in this rich recital. In the Sonata, for instance, Staier sets up a wide gulf between the two poles of Schubert's musical material – the sustained and lyrical, and the percussive and propulsive – in metaphysical terms, if you like, between the inner and outer, the contemplative and active life of this movement. Then he starts to paint with the pedal: there is a choice of four on this 1825 Viennese Johann Fritz fortepiano, and his changing use of them as the hands wander through the development creates a wide landscape for the journey, reminiscent of some of the piano writing in *Winterreise*. Here, and in the even more far-reaching expressive palette of the E flat major *Impromptu*, Staier really does realise the truth of his own statement that this – unlike the multi-purpose modern concert grand – is truly a 'specifically Romantic instrument'. In the slow movement's variations, the shifting balance between the hands are uniquely tailored to the resonating scale of the instrument, to uniquely revelatory effect. None of this could happen without Staier's own exceptionally sensitive imagination. At the start of the E flat minor *Impromptu* he creates a wide area of open space for the *Andante*, with the little, high, cadenza-like scalic figure appearing, as a sudden and wonderful bright light, as time is momentarily suspended.

Piano Sonatas Nos 19-21

Piano Sonata No 19. Impromptus, D899.
Deutsche Tänze, D783
Imogen Cooper *pf*
Ottavo OTRC78923 (70 minutes: DDD) Ⓕ
Recorded 1989 ●

This is in fact the last of Imogen Cooper's six-disc cycle of the piano music of Schubert's last six years, a cycle launched in 1988 hard on the heels of similar cycles given on the concert platform in both London and Amsterdam. Like its predecessors, it confirms her as a Schubert player of exceptional style and finesse. Intuitively perceptive phrasing and a willingness to let the music sing within a wholly Schubertian sound world are prime virtues. And though (like her erstwhile mentor, Alfred Brendel) she is no slave to the metronome when contrasting first and second subjects in sonata expositions, she still makes the music her own without the self-consciously mannered kind of interpretation heard from one or two more recent rivals in this strongly competitive field. Her urgent yet poised performance of the late C minor Sonata certainly confirms her admission (in a 1988 *Gramophone* interview) that the comparatively clinical atmosphere of an audience-less recording venue worries her not at all. In

London's Henry Wood Hall her Yamaha is as clearly and truthfully reproduced (save for a slight suspicion of pedal-haze in the sonata's finale) as most else in the series. The *Impromptus* reveal an acutely sensitive response to Schubert's dynamic subtleties and surprises of key, while the 16 *German Dances* tell their own simple Viennese tale.

Piano Sonatas Nos 19 and 21
Sviatoslav Richter *pf*
Olympia OCD335 (78 minutes: ADD) Ⓕ
Recorded 1972

As any follower of Richter's Schubert knows, you have to allow his sense of time to take over. Resist it and you will draw a blank. Submit and you will pass through an unsuspected doorway into an inner world of timeless inevitability. The C minor first movement is all fierce concentration and bleakness, the second all intense inner singing, the third deceptive simplicity with silences weighted as if hovering over the music's own demise, and the finale has a hellish drive to it – an utterly compelling experience. Monumental as ever, the first movement of the B flat Sonata is immensely slow, the tempo chosen not with the opening theme in mind but with a view to the G flat trill and thc following silence, reminders of the chasm beneath. Don't expect any consolation from the slow movement or Grecian lightness from the *Scherzo*; all is directed towards the controlled desperation of the finale. Any duffer (to paraphrase Goethe) can make this sonata touching; but with Richter it becomes (to risk malicious misunderstanding) appalling. It bores into the soul.

Piano Sonatas Nos 19-21 **P**
Andreas Staier *fp*
Teldec Das Alte Werk ② 0630-13143-2 Ⓕ
(119 minutes: DDD). Recorded 1996

The harpsichord has all but replaced the concert grand in baroque keyboard music. But resistance to the fortepiano is still strong; that clattery tone, the lack of sustaining power in high registers – it just doesn't sing like a modern piano. However, there are many instances where the sound of the 1825 Johann Fritz piano, and especially Andreas Staier's handling of it, are simply revelatory. Staier uses the fortepiano's moderator pedals and the *una corda* pedal, which shifts the hammers so that they strike only one string each, to great effect. Staier's use of these tools never seem excessive or misplaced, and it's hard to believe that Schubert wouldn't have made similar use of them. It isn't only in the special effects department that the fortepiano scores. In the middle of the slow movement of D959 there's a remarkable, violent cadenza-like passage which is rarely effective on modern concert pianos. On the fortepiano you can strain and pound for all you're worth, and yet the *scale* of the sound feels absolutely right. The later recitative-like contrast of the *ffz* chords and short, pleading *piano* phrases at the climax of the second movement of D959 works wonderfully here. Similarly, Staier can play the *fzp* and *ffzp* accents in the trio section of D960's *Scherzo* with due emphasis without destroying the music's lightweight character. But it is Staier's handling of the instrument, not the instrument itself, that makes these recordings so exceptional. In tempo, phrasing and so on, his approach is thoroughly modern; in fact his performances would probably translate very effectively to a modern piano without any – or much – sense of incongruity.

Piano Sonata No 20. Moments musicaux, D780
Stephen Kovacevich *pf*
EMI CDC5 55219-2 (66 minutes: DDD) Ⓕ
Recorded 1994

Here is Schubert playing as compulsive and single-minded as any on record. Formidably serious and concentrated this is not for lovers of 'lilac time' or of softly focused, lyrical options. Indeed, it is often as if the Grim Reaper himself had cut a swathe through Schubert, forbidding at a glance even a touch of solace, let alone *Gemütlichkeit*. Yet the force and authenticity of such an outwardly controversial view is made unarguable and few pianists have penetrated more deeply to the dark, restlessly beating heart beneath Schubert's outwardly genial surface. The ferocity of Kovacevich's *fortissimo* chording in the development section of the sonata's first movement is typical of his refusal of all polite circumspection, and rarely can the *Andantino*, with its central elemental uproar, have sounded more spare or disconsolate. Even the *Scherzo* becomes both a memory of Beethoven's fierce whimsy and a presage of Chopin's irony, and more than touch of unease erases much chance of a conventionally meandering or leisurely view of the finale.

For Kovacevich, then, this is surely Schubert's sonata equivalent of *Winterreise*; a savage journey into oblivion. Many will look for light relief in the *Moments musicaux*, but again Kovacevich refuses all obvious sentiment or enticement. His tone remains lean and acidulous, and he possesses a rare ability to drain his sonority of all colour substance, accentuating the hectic flush of No 5 and achieving an extreme sense of desolation in No 6.

This record, then, is for those who concede that Schubert could be 'full of sorrow/And leaden eyed despair', a composer who had more than his share of life's vicissitudes. Competition from other great Schubertians (Schnabel, Brendel, Pollini, Lupu and Imogen Cooper, to name but five!) is intense, yet Kovacevich's Schubert inhabits a world of its own; an extraordinary achievement. The recordings are spectacularly bold.

Piano Sonata No 21. Allegretto in C minor, D915.
12 Ländler, D790
Stephen Kovacevich *pf*
EMI CDC5 55359-2 (58 minutes: DDD) Ⓕ
Recorded 1994

Kovacevich creates his own ambience with such force and fidelity that he achieves an ultimate musical illusion: a definitive and unarguable statement indelibly and disturbingly true to Schubert's always ambiguous genius. Of course, those wedded to a less savage sense of experience, to a lightness and civility that are part of Schubert's appeal, will look elsewhere. For even in his selection of encores, Kovacevich retreats at every opportunity into a crepuscular, near hallucinatory world, his sense of elegy all pervasive. In the sonata's first-movement repeat (the nine bars despised by Brendel but, clearly, relished by Kovacevich) the distant thunder of the opening erupts in a violent upheaval. The outwardly innocent quaver flourish at 4'03" flashes with sudden anger, a startling gesture, yet one wholly in keeping with a work where desperation so easily surfaces through autumnal sadness and resignation.

The *Andante*, too, is a marvel of the most concentrated musical thinking, there are some swingeing *sforzandos* in the finale to remind us, once more, of underlying menace and even the *Scherzo*'s brightly tripping outer sections are shadowed by an unusually dark-hued way with the central trio.

Throughout, the effort of interpretation is immense and so although you will doubtless return to other deeply cherished recordings you will probably find a special place for Kovacevich. No more darkly questing performance exists. The recordings faithfully capture Kovacevich's awe-inspiring dynamic range, from the merest whisper to an elemental uproar.

Piano Sonata No 21. Drei Klavierstücke, D946
Mitsuko Uchida *pf*
Philips 456 572-2PH (71 minutes: DDD) Ⓕ
Recorded 1997 ●●

Uchida's concentration and inwardness are of a rare order in her absorbed, deeply poetic reading of the B flat Sonata. No pianist makes you so aware how much of the first two movements is marked *pp* or even *ppp*; and none conjures such subtlety of colour in the softest dynamics: listen, for instance, to her playing of the three unearthly C sharp minor chords that usher in the first-movement development, or her timing and colouring of the breathtaking sideslip from C sharp minor to C major in the *Andante*. Other pianists may find a stronger undercurrent of foreboding or desperation in these two movements – though Uchida builds the development of the initial *Molto moderato* superbly to its dramatic climax. But none probes more hauntingly the music's mysterious contemplative ecstasy or creates such a sense of inspired improvisation. And her limpid *cantabile* sonorities are always ravishing on the ear. She is equally attuned to the less rarefied world of the *Scherzo* and finale, the former a glistening, mercurial dance, *con delicatezza* indeed, the latter graceful and quixotic, with a hint of emotional ambiguity even in its ostensibly cheerful main theme and a tigerish ferocity in its sudden Beethovenian eruptions.

The coupling is generous: the three *Klavierstücke*, D946, composed, like the sonata, in Schubert's final year, 1828, and assembled by Brahms for publication. She brings a wonderfully impassioned sweep, with razor-sharp rhythms, to the opening of the E flat minor, No 1, and mesmerically floats its slow B major episode. She also restores the beguiling barcarolle-like episode in A flat that Schubert excised from his autograph manuscript. The recording finely captures Uchida's subtle, pellucid sound world. A revealing disc from a Schubertian of rare insight and spirituality.

Complete Masses

No 1 in F, D105; **No 2** in G, D167; **No 3** in B flat, D324; **No 4** in C, D452; **No 5** in A flat, D678; **No 6** in E flat, D950. **Stabat mater**, D383

Masses – No 1; No 2; No 3; No 4[a]; No 5[a]; No 6[a]. Stabat mater. Also contains six other short works
Lucia Popp, Helen Donath, Maria Venuti *sops*
Brigitte Fassbaender *mez* **Adolf Dallapozza, Peter Schreier, Francisco Araiza, Josef Protschka** *tens*
Dietrich Fischer-Dieskau *bar* **Bavarian Radio Chorus and Symphony Orchestra / Wolfgang Sawallisch**
EMI Sawallisch Edition ④ CMS7 64778-2
(297 minutes: ADD/DDD). Texts and translations Ⓜ
included. Recorded 1980s ●●

Items marked [a] are also available on EMI Double Forte ② CDZ5 73365-2 together with Tantum ergo, D962, Ⓜ and Offertorium, D963

The rather meagre representation this music has always received in the catalogue would seem to suggest that much of what is included in these discs is of little more than academic interest. Certainly not even Schubert's greatest advocates would describe everything he wrote for the Church as a masterpiece; his use of counterpoint, most notably in the Sixth Mass, is often dismissed as rudimentary. But there can never be any doubting the sincerity of Schubert's intentions and given sensitive, well-conceived performances, his unquenchable gift for melodic invention and ability to write instantly attractive music overrides any technical shortcomings. Such are Sawallisch's performances. His clear sense of direction, his natural feel for the line and his unpretentious approach never fail to reveal the inherent beauty in almost everything Schubert wrote.

The Bavarian Radio Chorus, with its rich, vibrant tone, won't be to everyone's liking, but it shows a consistent level of technical accomplishment, following Sawallisch's naturally shaped lines and beautifully moulded hairpin dynamics with a wholly natural flow. Similarly, with such accomplished Schubertians as Lucia Popp and Fischer-Dieskau one can expect some memorable performances. The highlight of these discs is the deliciously delicate trio between Popp, Adolf Dallapozza and Dietrich Fischer-Dieskau, supported by some extraordinarily elegant orchestral playing, in the *Benedictus* of the Second Mass: if you had to take just one recording of Schubert to a desert island, this would be a strong contender. Sawallisch's is an impressive achievement for maintaining so consistent an approach and producing performances of exemplary musicianship. The recordings are first-rate, with the older analogue transfers coming up unusually well.

Mass No 5

Mass No 5. Deutsche Messe, D872 **P**
Stefan Preyer *treb* **Thomas Weinhappel** *counterten* **Jörg Hering** *ten* **Harry van der Kamp** *bass* **Arno Hartmann** *org* **Vienna Boys' Choir; Chorus Viennensis; Orchestra of the Age of Enlightenment / Bruno Weil**
Sony Classical Vivarte SK53984 (60 minutes: DDD) Ⓕ
Texts and translations included. Recorded 1993

In the *Deutsche Messe* Bruno Weil makes no attempt to impose interpretative individuality on music designed purely for liturgical use: he is content merely to oversee neat ensemble and balance. The orchestra, consisting mainly of wind instruments, doubles the chorus parts and while its role might seem largely superfluous it does provide a comfortable cushion on which the choir can relax while making its way effortlessly through such unchallenging music. It's a different story with the sparkling A flat major Mass, but again Bruno Weil's understated direction results in an immensely satisfying performance. There is a youthful vigour and infectious enthusiasm here. Of course, much of that comes from the superb singing of the Vienna Boys' Choir. Their exuberant 'Hosanna's in the *Sanctus* and *Benedictus* are more unashamedly joyful than such music has a right to be. The two boy soloists sing with a musical maturity way beyond their years. That is not to belittle the splendid contribution from the adult voices nor the exquisite playing of the Orchestra of the Age of Enlightenment. Weil achieves the perfect tonal blend: nothing disturbs the open-hearted honesty of this genuinely sincere performance.

Mass No 5[a]. Hymnus an den heiligen Geist, D948[b]. Psalm 92, D953[c]. Stabat mater in G minor, D175[d]
[c]**Mhairi Lawson,** [a]**Deborah York** *sops* [c]**Lynette Alcantara,** [a]**Sally Bruce Payne** *mezzos* [ab]**Neill Archer,** [bc]**Robert Burt** *tens* [bc]**Colin Campbell** *bar* [a]**Michael George,** [bc]**Robert McDonald** *basses* **Monteverdi Choir;** [abd]**Orchestre Révolutionnaire et Romantique / Sir John Eliot Gardiner**
Philips 456 578-2PH (73 minutes: DDD) Texts and translations included. Ⓕ

Gardiner's interpretation of Schubert's great, often visionary A flat Mass stands somewhere between the generously moulded, romantically inclined Sawallisch and the fresh, guileless reading from Bruno Weil using an all-male choir and boy soloists. Where Gardiner immediately scores is in the sheer poise and refinement of his performance: neither of the other choirs sing with such effortless blend, such perfect dynamic control or such precise intonation – a crucial advantage in, say, the tortuous chromaticism of the 'Crucifixus'. The orchestral playing too is superb, with a ravishing contribution from the woodwind who throughout the Mass are favoured with some of Schubert's most poetic writing.

Gardiner is straighter, more abstemious with *rubato*, than Sawallisch, though he usually allows the music more breathing space than the brisk, exuberant Weil. His minute care for Schubert's phrasing and dynamic marks and the fabulous control of his singers and players often make for deeply satisfying results – as in the gentle, luminous *Kyrie*, where Gardiner shows a typically acute feel for harmonic flux and the curve of the Schubertian line. The opening of the *Gloria* has a torrential energy, and Gardiner is not one to miss a trick in, say, the cataclysmic drama of the 'Crucifixus' or the long, smouldering *crescendos* and awesome modulations of the *Sanctus*. Occasionally, though, the very polish and precision of the music-making can seem a shade studied: the opening of the *Credo*, for instance, sounds almost like an elocution lesson; and Gardiner favours a smart pace and emphatic, martial accents in the Dona nobis pacem, where Sawallisch, at a slower tempo, finds altogether more breadth and nobility. Gardiner's soloists, led by the plangent, boyish tones of Deborah York, use their relatively limited opportunities well: the 'Gratias' trio, sung with chamber-musical delicacy, is one of the highlights. He opts for the original and less gargantuan version of the 'Cum sancto spiritu' fugue, and as an appendix he gives us the original draft of the 'Et incarnatus est', with several significant differences, including lighter scoring from the final version.

The additional items, none of them overfamiliar, are well contrasted. Two are late works: the rapt *Hymn to the Holy Ghost* and the solemn, declamatory Psalm 92, set to the Hebrew text for the famous Jewish cantor Salomon Sulzer and sung here in German translation. Even less well known is Schubert's 1815 setting of the first four verses of the *Stabat mater*, a poignant and, at times, intensely dramatic little piece. Performances of all three are first-rate, with Colin Campbell firm and resonant in the cantor's role in Psalm 92. The recorded sound is perfectly acceptable, though the balance favours the orchestra, especially the violins, over the chorus and even at times the soloists. Sawallisch, a Schubertian of vast experience and innate sympathy, is still top choice for a single version of the A flat Mass. But quite apart from the very considerable merits of Gardiner's version, his enterprisingly chosen extra items could make this a first choice for many.

Part-songs

Psalm 23, D706. Im Gegenwärtigen Vergangenes, D710. Gesang der Geister über den Wassern, D714. Gondelfahrer, D809. Coronach, D836. Nachthelle, D892. Grab und Mond, D893. Nachtgesang im Walde, D913. Ständchen, D920. Die Nacht, D983*c*.

Gott im Ungewitter, D985
Birgit Remmert *contr* **Werner Güra** *ten* **Philip Mayers** *pf* **Scharoun Ensemble; RIAS Chamber Choir, Berlin / Marcus Creed**
Harmonia Mundi HMC90 1669 (59 minutes: DDD) Ⓕ
Texts and translations included. Recorded 1998

Most of the part-songs here evoke some aspect of night, whether benevolent, romantic, transfigured or sinister. Between them they give a fair conspectus of Schubert's achievement in the part-song genre, ranging from the mellifluous, Biedermeier *Die Nacht*, forerunner of many a Victorian glee, and the gently sensuous *Gondelfahrer* to the eerie, harmonically visionary *Grab und Mond* and the brooding *Gesang der Geister über den Wassern*. Other highlights here include the alfresco *Nachtgesang*, with its quartet of echoing horns, *Ständchen*, a delicious nocturnal serenade, the austere, bardic Scott setting *Coronach* and the serenely luminous *Nachthelle*. The RIAS Chamber Choir confirms its credentials as one of Europe's finest, most virtuosic ensembles. It sings with rounded, homogeneous tone, wellnigh perfect intonation and an excitingly wide dynamic range. Characterisation tends to be very vivid, whether in the ecstatic central climax in *Nachthelle*, sharp contrasts in *Gesang der Geister über den Wassern* or the great sense of awe – and palpable feeling for Schubert's strange modulations – in *Grab und Mond*.

Birgit Remmert, the alto soloist in *Ständchen* (sung, incidentally, in the version with women's voices), sings well enough but with insufficient lightness and sense of fun. But Werner Güra negotiates what one of Schubert's friends called 'the damnably high' tenor solo in *Nachthelle* gracefully and with no sense of strain. Philip Mayers is a serviceable rather than specially imaginative pianist, though the delicate, silvery treble of the early 19th-century instrument is enchantingly heard in *Psalm 23* and the shimmering high repeated notes of *Nachthelle*; and the other instrumentalists make their mark – splendid rotund horns in *Nachtgesang im Walde*, sombrely intense strings in *Gesang der Geister*. The recorded sound is clear and warm, with a well-judged vocal-instrumental balance.

Stabat mater

Stabat mater. Magnificat in C, D486.
Offertorium in B flat, D963
Sheila Armstrong *sop* **Hanna Schaer** *mez* **Alejandro Ramirez** *ten* **Philippe Huttenlocher** *bar* **Lausanne Vocal Ensemble; Lausanne Chamber Orchestra / Michel Corboz**
Erato 4509-96961-2 (59 minutes: ADD) Ⓜ
Recorded 1979

Schubert's strikingly fresh setting of the *Stabat mater* (in a German translation) was written in the composer's 19th year, yet it displays clear anticipations of his later music, especially in the terzetto (No 11) for soprano, tenor, baritone and chorus and the striking chorus 'Wer wird Zähren sanflen Mitleids' (No 5) with its superb horn writing. There is a beautiful tenor aria with oboe obbligato, in which Alejandro Ramirez is very stylish, while the bass aria 'Sohn des Vaters' is dark and strong. Here Philippe Huttenlocher may not be quite sombre enough, yet his contribution is still most enjoyable. The singing of the Lausanne Vocal Ensemble, with the Lausanne CO under Corboz, combines clarity of focus with a firm sonority, and Schubert's lively fugues have plenty of vigour. The two shorter pieces, the Magnificat (again with a fine contribution from Ramirez) and the Offertorium, are also given strong performances. The recording, though not crystal clear, has transferred vividly.

Complete Secular Choral Works

Elisabeth Flechl, Ruth Ziesak *sops* **Martina Steffl, Angelika Kirchschlager** *mezzos* **Birgit Remmert** *contr* **Franz Leitner, Thomas Künne, Christoph Prégardien, Herbert Lippert** *tens* **Oliver Widmer** *bar* **Karl Heinz Lehner, Hiroyuki Ijichi, Edgard Loibl, Robert Holl** *basses* **Barbara Moser, András Schiff, Andreas Staier, Werner Schröckmayr** *pfs* **Arnold Schoenberg Choir; Vienna Concert-Verein / Erwin Ortner**
Teldec ⑦ 4509-94546-2 (480 minutes: DDD) Ⓕ
Texts and translations included. Recorded 1995-96

The scheme of presentation here is both sensible and imaginative. Each of the discs has a subject-heading and each has its share of the treasures. The first, 'Transience', opens with the setting of Goethe's *Gesang der Geister über den Wassern* for men's voices and string quartet (without violins), probably the supreme masterpiece of the whole collection. The fascinating contrapuntal treatment of Schiller's *Dreifach ist der Schritt der Zeit* in its male-voice setting, and the gentle melancholy of Scott's *Coronach* are also memorable. The love-songs on the second disc begin and end with the *Ständchen*, '*Zögernd leise*', its second version, with male-voice chorus, being the more attractive in these performances.

Under the heading of 'Eternity' (third disc) comes much that has perhaps a questionable place in a secular anthology: good to have, never the less, the anthem known to British choristers as *Where Thou reignest* as *Schiksalslenker, blicke nieder*. The fourth disc has 'Heroism' as its theme, with *Mirjams Siegesgesang* as its lengthiest work. 'Nature' (fifth disc) produces several masterpieces, including Kleist's *Gott in der Natur* and the magical *Nachthelle*. The sixth, devoted to 'Celebration', has some longer occasional pieces, none so delightful as the brief cantata written for his father's birthday in 1813, with guitar accompaniment. The last disc, 'Circle of Friends', begins, beguilingly, with *Der Tanz* and ends with *Zur guten Nacht*. Ortner's soloists do well, but it is in the choral singing that the great merit of these performances lies. The Arnold Schoenberg Choir is a fine body of musicians and here they show a virtually unflawed beauty and opulence of tone. The pianists, headed by András Schiff, are excellent.

Lieder

Elly Ameling

Lieder[a] – Im Abendrot, D799. Die Sterne, D939. Nacht und Träume, D827. Der liebliche Stern, D861. Der Vollmond strahlt, D797 No 3*b*. Der Einsame, D800. Schlaflied, D527. An Silvia, D891. Das Mädchen, D652. Minnelied, D429. Die Liebe hat gelogen, D751. Du liebst mich nicht, D756. An die Laute, D905. Der Blumenbrief, D622. Die Männer sind méchant, D866 No 3. Seligkeit, D433. Nachtviolen, D752. Du bist die Ruh, D776. Das Lied im Grünen, D917. Der Schmetterling, D633. An die Nachtigall, D497. An die Nachtigall, D196. Der Wachtelschlag, D742. Im Freien, D880. Die Vögel, D691. Fischerweise, D881. Die Gebüsche, D646. Im Haine, D738. Kennst du das Land, D321. Nur wer die Sehnsucht kennt, D877 No 4. Heiss mich nicht reden, D877 No 2. So lasst mich scheinen, D877 No 3. Die Liebende schreibt, D673. Nähe des Geliebten, D162. Heidenröslein, D257. Liebhaber in allen Gestalten, D558. Die junge Nonne, D828. Der König in Thule, D367. Gretchen am Spinnrade, D118. Gretchens Bitte, D564. Szene aus Goethes Faust, D126 (with Meinard Kraak *ten, chorus* and *org*). Suleika I, D720. Suleika II, D717. Raste Krieger!, D837. Jäger, ruhe von der Jagd, D838. Ave Maria, D839. An die Musik, D547. Schwestergrüss, D762. Sei mir gegrüsst, D741. Die Blumensprache, D519. An den Mond, D296. Abendbilder, D650. Frühlingssehnsucht, D957 No 3. Erster Verlust, D226. Nachthymne, D687. Die Sterne, D684. Der Knabe, D692. Wiegenlied, D498. Berthas Lied in der Nacht, D653 Lieder[b] – Ganymed, D544. Die Götter Griechenlands, D677. Der Musensohn, D764. Fülle der Liebe, D854. Sprache der Liebe, D410. Schwanengesang, D744. An den Tod, D518. Die Forelle, D550. Am Bach im Frühling, D361. Auf dem Wasser zu singen, D774. Der Schiffer, D694. An die Entfernte, D765. Sehnsucht, D516. An die untergehende Sonne, D457. Abendröte, D690

Elly Ameling *sop* [a]**Dalton Baldwin,**
[b]**Rudolf Jansen** *pfs*

Philips The Early Years ④ 438 528-2PM4
(260 minutes: ADD/DDD). Texts included. Ⓜ
Recorded 1972-84 ●●

The first *Im Abendrot* (the Lappe setting) introduces the smiling Ameling of 1973, her voice basking in the images of golden shafts of light, and rapt in an easeful *legato*. In the shorter vowels and pulsing pianistic light of *Die Sterne*, she still finds serenity, just as in *Der Einsame* the poet's solitude is sensed at the heart of a tingling, sentient world. The expressive subtlety of these performances comes from an unique fusion of response between Ameling and Baldwin during this period. In the second disc, their creative empathy is turned to Schubert's settings of Goethe. Ameling focuses on the vulnerability and childlike eagerness of Mignon, missing, perhaps, the nervous feverishness which lies just below the surface of these songs, and which Wolf was to exploit to the full. After one of the most perfectly-scaled performances of *Heidenröslein* on disc, Ameling and Baldwin turn to Goethe's Gretchen and Suleika, and to Scott's Ellen. Gretchen's searing vision at the spinning-wheel is answered by the rarely heard *Szene aus Goethes Faust* in which Ameling finds herself in the company of an anonymous and very spooky *Böser Geist*, as well as a ghostly choir who seem piped in from another planet. Seven years later, Ameling turns to a still stranger spirit world. The third disc, recorded in 1982, includes the lunar beauty of Schubert's Bruchmann setting, *Schwestergrüss*, articulated by a voice bleached of any colour. It is almost impossible to detect any sense of ageing in the voice here. Characterised by songs which search out the most elusive of soul moods, this third recital reveals Ameling's soprano at its most finely nuanced, in songs such as *Abendbilder* and the Novalis *Nachthymne*. In the final disc, at the age of 50, Ameling took on the challenge of some of Schubert's most visionary songs: facing Schiller's Greek gods, Goethe's *Ganymed*, Schlegel's *Der Schiffer* and moving through Mayrhofer's longing to Schlegel's final sunset. These songs stretch the voice and the mind to its very limits, yet Ameling's artistry seems to grow with the music itself. The set includes full texts but no translations. In the end, though, Ameling's singing renders them all but redundant.

Janet Baker

Lieder[a] – Gretchen am Spinnrade, D118. Was bedeutet die Bewegung?, D720. Ach, um deine feuchten Schwingen, D717. Schwestergruss, D762. Schlummerlied, D527. An die untergehende Sonne, D457. Heiss' mich nicht reden, D877 No 2. So lasst mich scheinen, D877 No 3. Nur wer die Sehnsucht kennt, D877 No 4. Kennst du das Land, D321. Berthas Lied in der Nacht, D653. Epistel an Herrn Josef Spaun, D749. Raste, Krieger, D837. Jäger, ruhe von der Jagd, D838. Ave Maria, D837. Hin und wieder, D239. Lieber schwärmt, D239 No 6. An die Nachtigall, D497. Schlafe, schlafe, D498. Delphine, D857. Wiegenlied, D867. Die Männer sind méchant, D886 No 3. Iphigenia, D573. Das Mädchen, D652. Die junge Nonne, D828. Am Grabe Anselmos, D504. Abendstern, D806. Die Götter Greichenlands, D677. Gondelfahrer, D808. Auflösung, D807. Lieder[b] – Die Forelle, D550. Rastlose Liebe, D138. Auf dem Wasser zu singen, D774. Der Tod und das Mädchen, D531. An die Musik, D547. Frühlingsglaube, D686. Der Musensohn, D764. An Sylvia, D891. Litanei, D343. Heidenröslein, D257. Nacht und Träume, D827. Du bist die Ruh', D776

Dame Janet Baker *mez* [a]**Gerald Moore,**
[b]**Geoffrey Parsons** *pf*

EMI Forte ② CZS5 69389-2 Ⓜ
(155 minutes: ADD). Recorded 1970-80 ●●

When the major part of this issue, the first 25 songs, appeared in 1971 under the title 'A Schubert Evening', the reviewer gave it a glowing review in *Gramophone*. EMI provided a lavish booklet with annotations on each song, texts and translations, and illustrations of the artists and of Schubert. Virtually nothing of that remains. The briefest summary of the notes, no pictures (just fancy and irrelevant artwork), no words. In a spectacular piece of mis-marketing, EMI seems to be setting out to frighten away those at whom this mid-price issue is aimed – among them many newcomers to Lieder.

That is a great shame as this set has some of the most glorious Schubert singing you can imagine. 'A Schubert Evening' was in part instigated as a complementary issue to Fischer-Dieskau's contemporaneous recording of all Schubert's songs suited to a male interpreter. Dame Janet chose those he had abjured, ones specifically written for a female protagonist. She fulfils almost every aspect of her riveting selection in terms of vibrant tone, immaculate line, control of dynamics, insights into the poems' meaning and lively storytelling, where that's called for.

EMI, in its documentation, seems to have overlooked the fact that five of the songs, Nos 7-11 on the second CD, come from an earlier recital. They are five of the songs that Baker often sang at recitals from the start of her career and to which she was particularly attached; *Am Grabe Anselmos* and *Gondelfahrer*, two superb pieces, are perhaps the most telling of a wonderful group. The remainder of the recordings from a 1980 recital with Parsons, showing no deterioration in the mezzo's singing, offer several of the composer's most popular pieces, all sung *con amore*. This is an issue to treasure.

Barbara Bonney

Ave Maria, D839. Ganymed, D544. Kennst du das Land, D321. Heiss mich nicht reden, D877 No 2. So lasst mich scheinen, D877 No 3. Nur wer die Sehnsucht kennt, D877 No 4. Liebhaber in allen Gestalten, D558. Heidenröslein, D257. Nahe des Geliebten, D162. Die Forelle, D550. Auf dem Wasser zu singen, D774. Im Abendrot, D799. Ständchen, D889. Du bist die Ruh, D776. Gretchen am Spinnrade, D118. Gretchens Bitte, D564. Der Hirt auf dem Felsen, D965

Barbara Bonney *sop* **Sharon Kam** *cl* **Geoffrey Parsons** *pf*

Teldec 4509-90873-2 (73 minutes: DDD). Texts and translations included. Recorded 1994 Ⓕ OO

Bonney's programme is most carefully planned. She begins with a substantial selection of Goethe settings, going to the heart of the matter in all the Mignon songs, singing *Ganymed* with exemplary *legato* and breath control. Then she makes a well-varied selection from many of the better-known pieces. She crosses paths with Blochwitz only in *Die Forelle* and *Auf dem Wasser zu singen*. Both take the same time over each, but it is worth noting that Jansen, for Blochwitz, finds more variety and lift in the barcarolle-like accompaniment of the latter song than does Parsons. Vocally speaking, both versions are enjoyable in their natural accomplishments.

Bonney's line and breath are again remarkable in *Du bist die Ruh*, which also demonstrates, as do all the other offerings, the purity of her tone – more North American clear-aired than Viennese creamy – yet that is never allowed to exclude depth of feeling. Indeed when she returns to the Goethe settings with *Gretchen am Spinnrade* she shows particular eloquence in the way that, at a deliberate pace, she builds the song unerringly to its climaxes and also catches the inwardness of Gretchen's state of mind. The recording is faultless.

Ian Bostridge

An den Mond, D193. Wandrers Nachtlied I, D224. Der Fischer, D225. Erster Verlust, D226. Heidenröslein, D257. Erlkönig, D328. Litanei auf das Fest Allerseelen, D343. Seligkeit, D433. Ganymed, D544. An die Musik, D547. Die Forelle, D550. Frühlingsglaube, D686. Im Haine, D738. Der Musensohn, D764. Wandrers Nachtlied II, D768. Der Zwerg, D771. Auf dem Wasser zu singen, D774. Du bist die Ruh, D776. Nacht und Träume, D827. Fischerweise, D881. Im Frühling, D882. An Silvia, D891

Ian Bostridge *ten* **Julius Drake** *pf*

EMI CDC5 56347-2 (69 minutes: DDD). Texts and translations included. Recorded 1996 Ⓕ OO

Bostridge's growing band of devoted admirers are sure to be satisfied by this selection from Schubert's most popular songs. They will once more wonder at his famed engagement with the text in hand and his innate ability both to sing each piece in an entirely natural manner and at the same time to search out its inner meaning, everything achieved without a vocal or technical mishap within hearing. His gift for finding the right manner for each song is exemplified in the contrast between the easy simplicity he brings to such apparently artless pieces as *Fischerweise*, *Frühlingsglaube* and the less familiar *Im Haine* (this a wondrous performance of a song that is the very epitome of Schubert the melodist) and the depth of feeling found in *Erster Verlust* (a properly intense reading), *Nacht und Traüme*, *Wandrers Nachtlied* I and II, *Du bist die Ruh* (so elevated in tone and style) and *Litanei*.

Bostridge also characterises spine-chillingly the intense, immediate drama of *Erlkönig* and *Der Zwerg*, though here some may prefer the weight of a baritone. In the latter piece Drake is particularly successful at bringing out the originality of the piano part, and in a much simpler song, *An Sylvia*, he gives to the accompaniment a specific lift and lilt that usually goes unheard. *An die Musik* might have benefited from a slightly simpler treatment and the piano in *Fischerweise* is a touch heavy, but the faults are marginal, and in these songs, as in everything else, the ear responds eagerly to the tenor's fresh, silvery tone and his ever-eager response to words. The recording and notes are faultless.

Ian Bostridge

Lied eines Schiffers an die Dioskuren, D360. Nachtstück, D672. Auf der Donau, D553. Abendstern, D806. Auflösung, D807. Geheimes, D719. Versunken, D715. Schäfers Klagelied, D121. An die Entfernte, D765. Am Flusse, D766. Willkommen und Abschied, D767. Die Götter Griechenlands, D677. An die Leier, D737. Am See, D746. Alinde, D904. Wehmut, D772. Über Wildemann, D884. Auf der Riesenkoppe, D611. Sei mir gegrüsst, D741. Dass sie hier gewesen, D775. Der Geistertanz, D116

Ian Bostridge *ten* **Julius Drake** *pf*

EMI CDC5 57141-2 (68 minutes: DDD) Recorded 2000 Ⓕ OO

Schubert, his poets, and his present interpreters Bostridge and Drake – all on top form – combine for a truly memorable experience. The first half of the programme is divided between settings of Mayrhofer and Goethe, two poets who drew the very best out of Schubert. Bostridge responds to this inspiration with singing that is worthy of the pieces both in terms of silvery, poised tone and inflection of the text. Such musing songs as *Nachtstück*, *Abendstern*, *Geheimes*, *Versunken* and *An die Entfernte* are delivered in that peculiarly plangent tone of the tenor's which causes his audiences to tremble in admiration.

Using vibrato, verbal emphases, *pianissimo*s and floated touches to quite magical yet seemingly spontaneous effect, these songs, and many others receive near-ideal performances. Only in the rough-hewn *Willkommen und Abschied* is a baritone rather than a tenor perhaps preferable, but even here the slight sense of strain is not inappropriate, and Drake's exuberant yet sensitive playing is here at its most potent. Elsewhere he is as subtle as his partner.

The second half of the programme, where the choice of poets is more eclectic, is no less pleasurable. Such outright masterpieces as the well-known *Die Götter Griechenlands*, that song of longing to a Schiller text, the delectable *Alinde*, the charming *Sei mir gegrüsst* and the Wolf-like and emotionally overwhelming *Dass sie hier gewesen* rub shoulders with slightly less familiar pieces, all given the benefit of these interpreters' unanimity of outlook and eloquence. Bostridge enthusiasts will lap up this wonderful issue; so ought all lovers of Schubert Lieder. Other singers such as Janet Baker (in, say, *Auflösung*), Fischer-Dieskau (in *An die Leier*) and Schreier have brought their own insights to bear on many of these songs but Bostridge need fear no comparison. The admirable recording catches voice and piano in ideal balance.

Dietrich Fischer-Dieskau

Lieder, Volumes 1-3 DG (21 discs) 437 214-2GX21 (1463 minutes: ADD). Volumes also available separately, as detailed below. Ⓑ
Recorded 1966-72

234 Lieder, written between 1811 and 1817
Dietrich Fischer-Dieskau *bar* **Gerald Moore** *pf*
DG ⑨ 437 215-2GX9 (404 minutes: ADD)
Recorded 1966-68 Ⓑ

171 Lieder, written between 1817 and 1828
Dietrich Fischer-Dieskau *bar* **Gerald Moore** *pf*
DG ⑨ 437 225-2GX9 (395 minutes: ADD)
Recorded 1969 Ⓑ

Die schöne Müllerin, D795. Winterreise, D911. Schwanengesang, D957
Dietrich Fischer-Dieskau *bar* **Gerald Moore** *pf*
DG ③ 437 235-2GX3 (184 minutes: ADD)
Recorded 1971-72 Ⓑ

Twenty-one discs at under £100 bringing together two of this century's greatest Lieder interpreters – it sounds like a recipe for success, as indeed it is, fulfilling the highest expectations. The recordings were made when Dietrich Fischer-Dieskau was at his peak and Gerald Moore could draw on a lifetime's experience and love of this repertoire. Though the set makes no claims to completeness, most of the songs for male voice are included here. The use of a single singer and pianist gives the set a unity that allows the listener to gasp anew at the composer's wide-ranging inspiration and imagination.

Fischer-Dieskau brings a unique understanding, an elegant line and a diction that renders the text clear without resort to the written texts. If occasionally he imparts an unnecessary weightiness to the lighter songs, this quibble is as nothing when his historic achievement is taken as a whole. And though he made many recordings of the song cycles these are perhaps the finest, with Moore the ideal partner. Try for example, the bleakness of 'Ihr Bild' from *Schwanengesang* or the hallucinatory happiness of 'Der Lindenbaum' from *Winterreise*. The songs themselves are basically in chronological order (but with the three song cycles collected together in the final box). It is unfortunate there is no index – trying to find individual songs can be frustrating. Also, the translations are distinctly quirky in places; better to use Richard Wigmore's excellent book *Schubert: The Complete Song Texts* (Gollancz: 1988) if you have a copy to hand.

Renée Fleming

Heidenröslein, D257. Die Forelle, D550. An die Nachtigall, D497. Im Frühling, D882. Die junge Nonne, D828. Nacht und Träume, D827. Auf dem Wasser zu singen, D774. Ave Maria, D839. Frühlingsglaube, D686. Gretchen am Spinnrade, D118. Du bist die Ruh, D776. Der Tod und das Mädchen, D531. Viola, D786. Die Männer sind méchant, D866 No 3
Renée Fleming *sop* **Christoph Eschenbach** *pf*
Decca 455 294-2DH (66 minutes: DDD). Texts and translations included. Recorded 1996 Ⓕ

When yet another recital of Schubert Lieder appears, composed in the main of well-known songs, one looks for some special attributes to set it off from what has gone before in such profusion. Renée Fleming frequently supplies just those touches of individual response and high art which the ear is seeking. Like Dame Margaret Price she brings considerable stage experience to bear on her readings in terms of dramatic immediacy. That is particularly true of *Die junge Nonne* and *Gretchen am Spinnrade*, both of which carry the charge of emotions made manifest at the moment of recording. There is almost as much to enjoy and appreciate in the more reflective, inward pieces. *Im Frühling*, in both voice and piano, catches very precisely the sense of longing evoked by the spring, with Eschenbach pointing up the poignancy of alternating major-minor. In *An die Nachtigall*, Fleming's tone is poised, finely controlled, even more so in the more difficult *Du bist die Ruh*, where she shades the end of the final two couplets with a ravishing *piano*. *Nacht und Träume*, still harder to sustain, is as time-stopping as it should be. In the sadly neglected flower-ballad *Viola* the pair suggest a true partnership of thought and execution. At least three other songs, *Auf dem Wasser zu singen*, *Ave Maria* and *Frühlingsglaube* seem marginally too slow. Here, and sometimes elsewhere, a shade more rhythmic verve, a greater attention to consonants, would improve on what is already a formidable array of virtues, and Eschenbach's habit of indulging in *ritenutos* sometimes becomes a distraction. These small points apart, this is a Liederabend to savour and faultlessly recorded too.

Matthias Goerne and Christine Schäfer

Lieder, Volume 27 – Lob der Tränen, D711. Lebensmelodien, D395. Sprache der Liebe, D410. Wiedersehn, D855. Sonett I, D628. Sonett II, D629. Sonett III, D630. Abendröte, D690. Die Berge, D634. Die Vögel, D691. Der Fluss, D693. Der Knabe, D692. Die Rose, D745. Der Schmetterling, D633. Der Wanderer, D649. Das Mädchen, D652. Die Sterne, D684. Die Gebüsche, D646. Blanka, D631. Der Schiffer, D694. Fülle der Liebe, D854. Im Walde, D708
Matthias Goerne *bar* **Christine Schäfer** *sop*
Graham Johnson *pf*
Hyperion CDJ33027 (78 minutes: DDD). Texts and translations included. Recorded 1995-96 Ⓕ

Goerne's brief is Schubert's settings of the brothers Schlegel, whose volatile character and life are amply and fascinatingly described in Johnson's introduction to the booklet. As ever in this series, there are songs that we should curse ourselves for neglecting for so long. Among the few settings of August von Schlegel is the interesting *Lebensmelodien*, where the Swan and the Eagle engage in a colloquy – the one all tranquil, the other all disturbed – and are observed by doves on whom Schubert lavishes his most beautiful music. In the formal *Wiedersehn*, as Johnson avers, Schubert imitates the style of a Handelian aria. The second of three Petrarch translations prefigures, arrestingly, the mood of *Winterreise*.

When we come to brother Friedrich and the quasi-cycle *Abendröte* we are in an even more exalted world where *Der Fluss*, another of Schubert's miraculous water songs, *Der Knabe*, above all *Die Rose*, where the fading of the rose is a metaphor for lost virginity (this, movingly done by Schäfer), and *Der Wanderer* show just how willingly Schubert responded to Schlegel's imagery. About Goerne's singing as such, ably assisted by Johnson's playing, there are no reservations, particularly in the visionary *Die Sterne*, but as the CD progresses his interpretations can seem a shade soporific; one wonders if he has lived long enough with these songs to penetrate to their heart. His easily produced, slightly vibrant and mellifluous baritone and sense of Schubertian style make him a largely rewarding interpreter. The recording is superb.

Christoph Prégardien

Lieder, Volume 23 – Der Tod Oscars, D375. Das Grab, D377[a]. Der Entfernten, D350. Pflügerlied, D392. Abschied von der Harfe, D406. Der Jüngling an der Quelle, D300. Abendlied, D382. Stimme der Liebe, D412. Romanze, D144. Geist der Liebe, D414. Klage, D415. Julius an Theone, D419. Der Leidende, D432. Der Leidende (second version), D432*b*. Die frühe Liebe, D430. Die Knabenzeit, D400. Edone, D445. Die Liebes-götter, D446. An Chloen, D363. Freude der Kinderjahre, D455. Wer sich der Einsamkeit ergibt, D478. Wer nie sein Brot mit Tränen ass, D480. An die Türen, D479. Der Hirt, D490. Am ersten Maimorgen, D344. Bei dem Grabe meines Vaters, D496. Mailied, D503. Zufriedenheit, D362. Skolie, D507
Christoph Prégardien *ten* [a]**London Schubert Chorale; Graham Johnson** *pf*
Hyperion CDJ33023 (78 minutes: DDD). Texts and translations included. Recorded 1994 Ⓕ

When the Hyperion Schubert Edition is completed, this latest wondrous offering will rank among its most precious jewels. Prégardien is a prince among tenor interpreters of Lieder at present, on a par with Blochwitz in instinctive, natural and inevitably phrased readings. Johnson, besides, of course, finding exactly the right performers for these songs, surpasses even his own high standard of playing in this series. Then there is Schubert himself, the Schubert of 1816 by and large, who was, Johnson tentatively suggests in his notes, going through a phase of 'bringing himself under control'. That means, largely but far from entirely, writing gently lyrical strophic songs, most of them of ineffable beauty and simplicity, starkly contrasting with the Harfenspieler settings from *Wilhelm Meister*, two of which were written in 1816, the other in 1822.

In such an outright masterpiece as *Der Jüngling an der Quelle*, Prégardien and Johnson confirm the latter's view that this piece 'makes time stand still'. They emphasise, in *Stimme der Liebe*, how Schubert uses shifting harmonies to indicate romantic obsession. They show in the two similar but subtly different versions of *Der Leidende* ('The suffering one') what Johnson calls 'two sides of the same coin', with the tenor's plangent, tender singing, line and text held in perfect balance. The two Hölty songs that follow, *Die frühe Liebe* and *Die Knabenzeit*, evince a wonderful affinity with thoughts of childhood on the part of poet and composer, again ideally captured here. So is the 'chaste and wistful' mood of Klopstock's *Edone*. The recording is ideally balanced .

Christine Schäfer

Im Frühling, D882. Die Blumensprache, D519. Die gefangenen Sänger, D712. Der Schmetterling, D633. An den Mond, D259. An den Mond, D296. Die Gebüsche, D646. Der Fluss, D693. Der Knabe, D692. Nacht und Träume, D827. Im Abendrot, D799. Glaube, Hoffnung und Liebe, D955. Vom Mitleiden Mariä, D632. Beim Winde, D669. Des Mädchens Klage, D6. Blanka, D631. Das Mädchen, D652. Die Rose, D745. Die junge Nonne, D828. Nähe des Geliebten, D162
Christine Schäfer *sop* **Irwin Gage** *pf*
Orfeo C450971A (79 minutes: DDD). Texts and translations included. Recorded 1997 Ⓕ

What makes Schäfer such a special artist is the candid, plaintive, natural quality of her tone and her simplicity of phrasing. These are combined with clear, unaffected diction, and a sense of vulnerability in the timbre, to evoke the pure spirit of each song. Some, used to more vibrant, luscious voices, may find Schäfer's tone too narrow or they may be troubled by moments when she is deliberately on the flat side of a note but they are part of her vocal personality and perhaps nearer to what was heard in Schubert's day. Her attributes as a Schubertian are confirmed by her discerning choice of songs in this generously filled programme. Whether the pieces are grave or cheerful, Schäfer finds the right expression. The simplicity at the start of *An den Mond* (D296) is succeeded by heightened intensity at just the appropriate moment, in the fifth stanza. In that underrated Schlegel setting, *Der Fluss*, she adds special urgency to the last line. In better-known songs, such as *Nacht und Träume* and *Im Abendrot* the soprano refreshes the familiar through a new draught of feeling, simple yet inward, and that is the epithet that comes most readily to mind in those two melancholic songs, *Das Mädchen* and *Die Rose*, the one about an unloved girl, the other about a flower speaking of its mortality. To end she catches the perfect Schubert/Goethe accord of *Nähe des Geliebten*, where 'Ich denke dein' and 'Ich bin bei dir' are affirmations of a deep love. Irwin Gage partners his singer with many touches of subtle, finely shaded phrasing. Add a surely balanced recording and Lieder lovers are in for a generous treat.

Elisabeth Schwarzkopf

An die Musik, D547. Im Frühling, D882. Wehmut, D772. Ganymed, D544. Das Lied im Grünen, D917. Gretchen am Spinnrade, D118. Nähe des Geliebten, D162. Die junge Nonne, D828. An Silvia, D891. Auf dem Wasser zu singen, D774. Nachtviolen, D752. Der Musensohn, D764. Six moments musicaux, D780[a]

Elisabeth Schwarzkopf *sop* [a]**Edwin Fischer** *pf*

EMI Références mono CDH5 67494-2 Ⓜ
(67 minutes: ADD). Recorded [a]1950 and 1952 ●

Many young and not-so-young singers can't abide Schwarkopf's interpretative style, which is strikingly at odds with the straightforward readings so often heard today. Playing devil's advocate, one can understand the nature of the complaints about her interventionist approach, her occasional distortion of vowel sounds and a general approach that William Mann once described to me as 'verschmuckt' (bejewelled). You may judge such views, for instance, in a song like *Auf dem Wasser*, where not a phrase is left to speak for itself; compare it with the natural and simple reading of her contemporary Irmgard Seefried (Testament), which is so much more appropriate to the song.

That said, the doubters should listen to this recital with Edwin Fischer, one of the greatest ever discs of Schubert singing. As so often in her recitals dating back to Oxford days in 1950, annoyance with the occasional mannerism soon gives way to wonder at such an amazingly eager response to every facet of a song and its setting. And truly inspired by Fischer, she throws caution utterly to the wind and astonishes us in accounts of *Die junge Nonne*, *Ganymed* and *Gretchen am Spinnrade* that have seldom if ever been surpassed for vocal consistency and concentration – though it is a pity the singer makes a break in the final, long phrase of *Ganymed*.

Fischer, one of the noblest Schubert interpreters of his or any time, is obviously a partner in a thousand and on his own confirms his stature in the legendary 1950 recording of the *Moments musicaux* better transferred here than ever before – as are the Lieder. So this is a CD no Schubertian can do without.

Awards 1995

Bryn Terfel

Lieder – Gruppe aus dem Tartarus, D583. Litanei auf das Fest Allerseelen, D343. Die Forelle, D550. An die Leier, D737. Lachen und Weinen, D777. Schwanengesang, D957 – Ständchen; Das Fischermädchen; Die Taubenpost. Meerestille, D216. Der Wanderer, D489 (formerly D493). Erlkönig, D328. Der Tod und das Mädchen, D531. Heidenröslein, D257. Wandrers Nachtlied II, D768. An die Musik, D547. Auf der Bruck, D853. Schäfers Klagelied, D121. An Silvia, D891. Du bist die Ruh', D776. An die Laute, D905. Rastlose Liebe, D138. Ganymed, D544. Der Musensohn, D764

Bryn Terfel *bass-bar* **Malcolm Martineau** *pf*

DG 445 294-2GH (69 minutes: DDD). Texts and Ⓕ
translations included. Recorded 1994. ●●●

Terfel's gift, now well known, is a generous, individual voice, a natural feeling for German and an inborn ability to go to the heart of what he attempts. His singing here is grand in scale – listen to any of the dramatic songs and the point is made – but like Hotter, whom he so often resembles, he is able to reduce his large voice to the needs of a sustained, quiet line, as in *Meerestille*. When the two come together as in *Der Wanderer*, the effect can be truly electrifying, even more so, perhaps, in *Erlkönig* where the four participants are superbly contrasted. Yet this is a voice that can also smile, as in *An die Laute* and 'Die Taubenpost' or express wonder, as in *Ganymed*, a most exhilarating interpretation, or again explode in sheer anger as in the very first song, the strenuous *Gruppe aus dem Tartarus*. Terfel is not afraid to employ rubato and vibrato to make his points and above all to take us right into his interpretations rather than leave us admiring them, as it were, from afar. Throughout, Martineau's at once vigorous and subtle playing is an apt support: his accompaniment in *Erlkönig* is arrestingly clear and precise.

Various singers

Lieder, Volume 24 – Schäfers Klagelied, D121. An Mignon, D161. Geistes-Gruss, D142 (two versions). Rastlose Liebe, D138. Der Gott und die Bajadere, D254. Tischlied, D234. Der Schatzgräber, D256. Der Rattenfänger, D255. Bundeslied, D258. Erlkönig, D328. Jägers Abendlied, D215. Jägers Abendlied, D368. Wer nie sein Brot mit Tränen ass, D480 (two versions). Nur wer die Sehnsucht kennt, D359. So lasst mich scheinen, D469*a* and D469*b* (two

fragments). Nur wer die Sehnsucht kennt, D481. Nur wer die Sehnsucht kennt, D656. An Schwager Kronos, D369. Hoffnung, D295. Mahomets Gesang, D549 (cptd R. Van Hoorickx). Ganymed, D544. Der Goldschmiedsgesell, D560. Gesang der Geister über den Wassern, D484 (cptd R Van Hoorickx). Gesang der Geister über den Wassern, D705 (cptd E Asti).
Christine Schäfer *sop* **John Mark Ainsley** *ten* **Simon Keenlyside** *bar* **Michael George** *bass* **Graham Johnson** *pf* **London Schubert Chorale / Stephen Layton**
Hyperion CDJ33024 (79 minutes: DDD). Texts and translations included. Recorded 1993-94 Ⓕ

Renewed praise first of all for Graham Johnson. This volume is as cogent an example as any of his method, a masterly exposition, in written words and musical performance, of the crucial relationship between Goethe and Schubert upon which Johnson throws a good deal of new light. Not all here is notable Schubert, but the lesser songs serve to place in perspective the greater ones.

The CD begins with one of the latter, *Schäfers Klagelied*, in a finely honed, dramatic performance by Ainsley, who is heard later on the disc always to advantage. Good as Christine Schäfer is in the first version of *An Mignon*, she is better in the sadly neglected *Der Gott und die Bajadere*, as Johnson avers. This is the only song in the genre about prostitution, and a haunting one too, even though, throughout its appreciable length, it relies on just one melody, and Schäfer precisely catches its haunting atmosphere. But the climax of her contribution comes in *Ganymed* – with Johnson providing exactly the right rhythmic lilt at the piano, her voice conveys all the elation of poem and music.

Schäfer is the child in a three-voice rendering of *Erlkönig*, a manner of performing the piece that has the composer's blessing. Johnson has surely never surpassed his account here of the hair-raisingly difficult piano part. Then he is just as accomplished with Keenlyside in a thrilling account of another masterpiece engendered by response to Goethe's genius, *An Schwager Kronos*. George, who perhaps has the least ingratiating songs to perform, sings with feeling and style but sometimes an excess of vibrato. An invaluable addition to this series.

Various singers

Lieder, Volume 26 – Der Einsame, D800. Des Sängers Habe, D832. Lied der Delphine, D857 No 1. Lied des Florio, D857 No 2. Mondenschein, D875. Nur wer die Sehnsucht kennt, D877 No 1. Heiss mich nicht reden, D877 No 2. So lasst mich scheinen, D877 No 3. Nur wer die Sehnsucht kennt, D877 No 4. Totengräberweise, D869. Das Echo, D990C. An Silvia, D891. Horch, horch! die Lerch', D889. Trinklied, D888. Wiegenlied, D867. Widerspruch, D865. Der Wanderer an den Mond, D870. Grab und Mond, D893. Nachthelle, D892. Abschied von der Erde, D829
Christine Schäfer *sop* **John Mark Ainsley** *ten* **Richard Jackson** *bar* **London Schubert Chorale; Graham Johnson** *pf*
Hyperion CDJ33026 (76 minutes: DDD). Texts and translations included. Recorded 1995 Ⓕ ●●

It is hard to know where to begin in praise of this disc. It has several centres of excellence, the first being Schäfer's beseeching, urgent account of the Mignon settings from Goethe's *Wilhelm Meister* that make plain her pre-eminence today among sopranos in Lieder. Next comes Ainsley's winningly fresh account of *An Silvia*. You may be surprised at how wholly new-minted Ainsley's ardent tones and Johnson's elating piano manage to make of such a hackneyed song. Schäfer and Johnson do the same service for *Horch, horch! die Lerch'*. Then comes the extraordinary discovery of this volume. As a rule, Johnson has excluded unaccompanied vocal pieces from his project; happily, he has made an exception in the case of the astonishingly original Seidl setting *Grab und Mond*, which touches on eternal matters, or rather the permanence of death, a message starkly expressed in typically daring harmony. The London Schubert Chorale gives it a spellbinding interpretation and also contributes positively to a performance of another Seidl setting, the better-known *Nachthelle*, where the high-lying tenor lead provides no problems for Ainsley. There have to be reservations over the work of Richard Jackson. No amount of creative intelligence can mask the fact that his dried-out tone is inadequate to the demands of *Der Einsame*, the unjustly neglected *Totengräberweise* and *Der Wanderer an den Mond*, which call for a richer palette of sound. Throughout, Johnson's playing and, of course, his admirable notes are their customary sources of pleasure and enlightenment. The recording is well-nigh faultless.

Various singers

Lieder, Volume 32 – An die Sonne, D439. Beitrag zur fünfzigjährigen Jubelfeier des Herrn von Salieri, D407. Das war ich, D174*a*/D450*a*. Didone Abbandonata, D510*a* (both cptd Hoorickx). Der Entfernten, D331. Entzückung, D413. Der Geistertanz, D494. Gott der Weltschöpfer, D986. Gott im Ungewitter, D985. Grablied auf einen Soldaten, D454. Das Grosse Halleluja, D442. Des Mädchens Klage, D389. Licht und Liebe, D352. Naturgenuss, D422. Ritter Toggenburg, D397. Schlachtgesang, D443. Die verfehlte Stunde, D409. Der Wanderer, D489. Zufriedenheit, D501. Zum Punsche, D492
Lynne Dawson, Patricia Rozario, Christine Schäfer *sops* **Ann Murray, Catherine Wyn-Rogers** *mezzos* **Paul Agnew, John Mark Ainsley, Philip Langridge, Jamie MacDougall, Daniel Norman, Christoph Prégardien, Michael Schade, Toby Spence** *tens* **Simon Keenlyside, Maarten Koningsberger, Stephan Loges, Christopher Maltman, Stephen Varcoe** *bars* **Neal Davies, Michael George** *basses* **Graham Johnson** *pf* **London Schubert Chorale / Stephen Layton**
Hyperion CDJ33032 (78 minutes: DDD). Notes, texts and translations included Ⓕ ●

Like the previous Schubertiads in the Edition, this disc mixes solo songs and partsongs, the familiar and the unfamiliar. The only really famous work here is *Der Wanderer*, that archetypal expression of romantic alienation whose popularity in Schubert's lifetime was eclipsed only by that of *Erlkönig*. Some of the partsongs – *Zum Punsche*, *Naturgenuss* and *Schlachtgesang* – cultivate a vein of Biedermeier heartiness that wears a bit thin today. Nor will Schubert's consciously archaic tribute to his teacher Salieri have you itching for the repeat button – though, like several other numbers, it shows the 19-year-old composer rivalling Mozart in his gift for musical mimicry. In compensation, though, are partsongs like the sensual *Der Entfernten*, with its delicious languid chromaticisms (relished here by the London Schubert Chorale), and the colourful setting of *Gott im Ungewitter*. The slight but charming setting of *Das war ich* is appealingly done by the light-voiced Daniel Norman, and Ann Murray brings her usual charisma and dramatic conviction to the pathetic Italian scena *Didone Abbandonata*.

Christine Schäfer is equally charismatic in the unjustly neglected *Die verfehlte Stunde* (recorded here for the first time), catching perfectly the song's mingled yearning and ecstasy and negotiating the mercilessly high tessitura with ease. Other happy discoveries include Schubert's virtually unknown third setting of *Des Mädchens Klage*, with its soaring lines, a melancholy tale of courtly love, sung by Christoph Prégardien with as much drama and variety as the music allows, and the surging *Entzückung* ('music for an infant Lohengrin,' as Graham Johnson puts it), for which Toby Spence has both the flexibility and the necessary touch of metal in the tone. Doubts were fleetingly raised by Lynne Dawson's slight tremulousness in *Des Mädchens Klage*, and by Christopher Maltman's prominent vibrato at *forte* and above in an otherwise involving performance of *Der Wanderer*. But, these cavils apart, no complaints about the singing or Graham Johnson's vivid accompaniments.

Various singers

Lieder, Volume 34 – La pastorella al prato, D513[fjpt]. Frohsinn, D520[q]. Der Alpenjäger, D524[r]. Die Einsiedelei, D563[j]. Das Grab, D569[u]. Atys, D585[o]. Der Kampf, D594[s]. Das Dörfchen, D598[fjpt]. Die Geselligkeit, D609[cdgt]. Sing-Übungen, D619[ac] (ed Roblou). Das Abendrot, D627[s]. Abend, D645[h] (ed Brown). Das Mädchen, D652[e]. Cantate zum Geburtstag des Sängers Michael Vogl, D666[blm]. Prometheus, D674[p]. Über allen Zauber Liebe, D682[k] (ed Hoorickx). Die gefangenen Sänger, D712[n]. Grenzen der Menschheit, D716[s]. Wandrers Nachtlied II, D768[r]

[a]Lorna Anderson, [b]Lynne Dawson, [c]Patricia Rozario *sops* **[d]Catherine Denley, [e]Marjana Lipovšek** *mezzos* **[f]John Mark Ainsley, [g]Ian Bostridge, [h]Martyn Hill, [i]Philip Langridge, [j]Jamie MacDougall, [k]Daniel Norman, [l]Michael Schade** *tens*; **[m]Gerald Finley, [n]Matthias Goerne, [o]Thomas Hampson, [p]Simon Keenlyside, [q]Stephan Loges, [r]Christopher Maltman** *bars* **[s]Neal Davies** *bass-bar* **[t]Michael George** *bass* **[u]London Schubert Chorale / Stephen Layton; Graham Johnson** *pf*

Hyperion Schubert Edition CDJ33034
(79 minutes: DDD). Texts and translations included. Ⓕ
Recorded 1991-99 ●

In his guise as a wizard of an impresario, Graham Johnson has gathered together four baritones and one bass-baritone (Neil Davies) to give us a feast of finely wrought, intelligent interpretations. Hampson's rendering of that outsider's lament, *Atys*, is at once an object-lesson in refined singing and a deeply felt outpouring of sorrow. Keenlyside, singing with as much firm, mellow tone and feeling as his American coeval, gives a properly intense, agonised account of the great, Zeus-defying *Prometheus*, magnificently supported by Johnson. Goerne is assigned the seldom-heard Schlegel setting, *Die gefangenen Sänger*, and brings his gently vibrant tone, reminiscent of his noted predecessor Herbert Janssen, and his natural gift for phrasing to bear on this strange but captivating piece. Maltman, growing in stature as a Lieder artist, begins the programme with the extrovert *Der Alpenjäger* and ends it with the introverted *Wandrers Nachtlied* on which he lavishes the hushed concentration due to a page of rapt utterance, a suitable conclusion to the performance of Goethe settings in the whole edition.

Neil Davies erupts into the series with three absorbing interpretations: the declamatory Schiller setting *Der Kampf*, the flowing, glowing *Das Abendrot* and the awe-inspiring *Grenzen der Menschheit*. All three evince his real affinity for the German language and the world of Schubert. He also has the low notes the pieces call for. The one female solo brings back Lipovšek at her most beguiling in the poignant and unforgettable Schlegel setting *Das Mädchen*, already performed just as movingly by Christine Schäfer in Vol 27. This wonderful fare is interspersed with lighter, less demanding material, all done with pleasure by varying groups of singers, plus three tenor solos. Langridge is predictably charming in *Die Einsiedelei*. Hill is not quite at his best and Norman's style is etiolated in their offerings. Piano playing both maintain Hyperion's usual high standard.

Various singers

Lieder, Volume 37 – Auf dem Strom, D943[cd]. Herbst, D945[a]. Bei dir allein, D866/2[c]. Irdisches Glück, D866/4[c]. Lebensmut, D937[c]. Schwanengesang, D957 – No 1, Liebesbotschaft[a]; No 2, Kriegers Ahnung[a]; No 3, Frühlingssehnsucht[a]; No 4, Ständchen[a]; No 5, Aufenthalt[a]; No 6, In der Ferne[a]; No 7, Abschied[a]; No 8, Der Atlas[b]; No 9, Ihr Bild[b]; No 10, Das Fischermädchen[b]; No 11, Die Stadt[b]; No 12, Am Meer[b]; No 13, Der Doppelgänger[b]. Die Taubenpost, D965A[b]. Glaube, Hoffnung und Liebe, D955[abc]

[a]John Mark Ainsley, [b]Anthony Rolfe Johnson, [c]Michael Schade *tens* **[d]David Pyatt** *hn* **Graham Johnson** *pf*

Hyperion Schubert Edition CDJ33037 Ⓕ
(80 minutes: DDD). Texts and translations included
Recorded 1998 ●

This disc, the last in Hyperion's Schubert Edition, is in large part devoted to the performance of the non-cycle *Schwanengesang*, that extraordinary collection in which Schubert seems more original and more inclined even than in earlier Lieder to peer into the future.

We usually encounter the work transposed for a baritone, though Schreier and Schiff have recorded it memorably for Decca. Johnson has astutely divided the songs between two voices. Ainsley is given the Rellstab settings, Rolfe Johnson the Heine, plus Seidl's *Die Taubenpost*, which so poignantly and airily closes the set. Ainsley interprets his songs with the tonal beauty, fine-grained phrasing and care for words (excellent German, of course) that are the hallmarks of his appreciable art, even if his voice sometimes lacks a difficult-to-define individuality of timbre. The over-exposed *Ständchen* is given a new spontaneity of utterance by both the singer and Graham Johnson. Anthony Rolfe Johnson brings all the appropriate intensity one would expect from him to the tremendous Heine settings. Sometimes his tone hardens when he is depicting the deserted lover present in so many of these pieces, but that is hardly inappropriate to the depth of feeling being expressed.

Most of the other songs of 1828, which open the recital, are assigned to Schade, who sings them with refined tone and an innate feeling for sharing his enjoyment in performing them, nowhere more so than in the opening *Auf dem Strom*, where David Pyatt's horn is a notable asset. Ainsley reads his sole offering here, *Bei dir allein*, with just the fiery passion it calls for.

In sum, this is a worthy, often inspired conclusion to the series, once more enhanced by Johnson's copious notes. It also has a complete index to the Edition. The recording is faultless.

Various singers

Lieder on Record, Volumes 1 and 2 **H**

Sopranos – **Pauline Cramer, Ursula van Diemen, Elise Elizza, Kirsten Flagstad, Marta Fuchs, Dusolina Giannini, Ria Ginster, Frieda Hempel, Lilli Lehmann, Lotte Lehmann, Frida Leider, Minnie Nast, Flora Nielsen, Aaltje Noordewier-Reddingius, Margaret Ritchie, Lotte Schöne, Elisabeth Schumann, Elisabeth Schwarzkopf, Irmgard Seefried, Meta Seinemeyer, Susan Strong** *Mezzo-sopranos* – **Therese Behr-Schnabel, Julia Culp, Elena Gerhardt, Marie Götze, Susan Metcalfe-Casals, Edyth Walker** *Contraltos* – **Edith Clegg, Ottilie Metzger, Maria Olszewska, Sigrid Onegin** *Tenors* – **Friedrich Brodersen, Karl Erb, Heinrich Hensel, John McCormack, Franz Naval, Julius Patzak, Sir Peter Pears, Aksel Schiøtz, Leo Slezak, Richard Tauber, Georges Thill, Gustav Walter** *Baritones* – **David Bispham, Leopold Demuth, Hans Duhan, Dietrich Fischer-Dieskau, Sir George Henschel, Gerhard Hüsch, Herbert Janssen, Charles Panzéra, Bernhard Sonnerstedt, Harold Williams** *Bass-baritones* – **Harry Plunkett Greene, Hans Hotter, Friedrich Schorr** *Basses* – **Feodor Chaliapin, Wilhelm Hesch, Alexander Kipnis, Paul Knüpfer, Endré Koréh, Lev Sibiriakov, Vanni-Marcoux, Ernst Wachter**

Various artists EMI mono 2x③ CHS5 66150-2/154-2 (205 and 202 minutes: ADD). Texts and translations Ⓜ included. Recorded 1898-1952

Much has happened to the interpretation of Lieder since 1952 and quite a bit since 1982 when this issue first appeared on LP. Yet there is still much to be learnt from listening to these 93 songs interpreted by 64 singers in a total of 129 performances. Styles have changed radically since the early decades of the century. Nowadays we insist on accuracy over every aspect of interpretation; in these older performances the text and its meaning takes precedence over almost everything else: nearly all these singers are keen to tell an urgent message and never mind if that involves excessive rubato, *ritardandos*, playing about with note values. Practically every singer is an individualist, the voice and style immediately recognizable. Today the manner is more uniform, the personal, eccentric approach often frowned upon.

The transfers are almost identical with those made by Keith Hardwick for the LP set, very many taken off vinyl, giving you the singers in very present form, no scratch intervening. The oldest discs – many rarities – are intractable: 1990s technology might has not improved on what we encounter here. These are fascinating and rewarding issues that no lover of Schubert and/or Lieder should be without.

Anne Sofie von Otter

Heidenröslein, D257. Wonne der Wehmut, D260. Der Jüngling an der Quelle, D300. Erntelied, D434. Im Walde, D708. Geheimes, D719. Suleika I, D720. Dass sie hier gewesen, D775. Viola, D786. Im Abendrot, D799. Abendstern, D806. Ave Maria, D839. Totengräbers Heimweh, D842. Bei dir allein, D866 No 2. Der Wanderer an den Mond, D870. Im Frühling, D882. An Silvia, D891. Ständchen, D920

Anne Sofie von Otter *mez* **Bengt Forsberg** *pf* with **Swedish Radio Chorus**

DG 453 481-2GH (69 minutes: DDD). Texts and Ⓕ translations included. Recorded 1996 ⭘

This is a recital alive with the delight of long-awaited encounter and the vocal security of choices well made. In songs such as *An Silvia* and *Geheimes* the wide-eyed wonder of her own discovery incarnates that of the songs' own subjects. Tiny moments of gentle emphasis, and a little spring on each note of its rising sequences adds to the wondering incredulity of *An Silvia*'s questionings. There are many epiphanies along the way for even the most experienced Schubertian. *Heidenroslein*, for example, is re-created as a sudden, elusive *Augenblick*, a passing moment in time in which pique and piquancy fuse without a hint of mere coyness. And listen to the way in which von Otter and the ever perceptive Bengt Forsberg bring a sense of wry self-awareness to *Der Wanderer an den Mond*.

The recital grows gradually darker, moving, by way of *Standchen*, D920 to the twilight of *Im Abendrot*. Here, long, firmly-grounded vowels are backlit by the afterglow of Forsberg's piano line before some deep, passionate digging into the *Angst* of *Totengrabers Heimweh*, and a wonderfully breathless, intimately urgent imprecation of an *Ave Maria*.

Song Cycles

Die schöne Müllerin, D795. **Schwanengesang**, D957. **Winterreise**, D911

Winterreise
Dietrich Fischer-Dieskau *bar* **Daniel Barenboim** *pf*
DG 463 501-2GFD (73 minutes: ADD) Ⓜ
Recorded 1979 ○○

Die schöne Müllerin[a]. Nacht und Träume, D827b. Ständchen, D889[b]. Du bist die Ruh, D776[b]. Erlkönig, D328[c]
Dietrich Fischer-Dieskau *bar*
[a]**Jörg Demus,** [bc]**Gerald Moore** *pfs*
DG 463 502-2GFD (75 minutes: ADD). Recorded [a]1968 (previously unreleased), [bc]1970 Ⓜ ○○

Schwanengesang. Vollendung, D579. Die Erde, D579b. An die Musik, D547. An Silvia, D891. Heidenröslein, D257. Im Abendrot, D799. Der Musensohn, D764. Die Forelle, D550. Der Tod und das Mädchen, D531
Dietrich Fischer-Dieskau *bar* **Gerald Moore** *pf* Ⓜ
DG 463 503-2GFD (73 minutes: ADD) ○○○

You wouldn't think that a recording by Fischer-Dieskau, given his huge Schubert discography, could still offer an exciting revelation – but that's what the 'new' *Die schöne Müllerin* recording offers. Explanations for its suppression vary. The singer seems to think it has something to do with its technical quality: the booklet-note, slightly more credibly, tells us that it was planned before DG decided to include the cycle in its 'complete' Schubert with the baritone and Gerald Moore, which caused this performance to be put on the back-burner. Now we can enjoy a reading that is absolutely spontaneous, daring in its dramatic effects – bold extremes of dynamics, for instance – and full of even more subtle detail than in Fischer-Dieskau's other recordings.

This approach owes not a little to Demus's piano. As Alan Newcombe says in his booklet-notes: 'Aided by Demus's lightly pedalled, often almost brusque *staccato* articulation, the result is starker, more elemental, less comfortable [than the reading with Moore], conceived on a larger scale.' To that one should add that the singer is at the absolute height of his powers; tone, line, breath control and intuitive imagination are most remarkable in the strophic songs that, in lesser hands, can seem over-long. Another feature of this is the significant underlining he gives to pertinent words. For instance, in *Pause* note how 'gehängt', 'durchschauert' and 'Nachklang' receive this treatment. It is this unique vision of the German language in music that still marks out this baritone from his many successors. Immediate, unvarnished sound heightens the value of this extraordinary performance.

There's hardly one of Fischer-Dieskau's eight and more recordings of *Winterreise* that one would want to be without, but the 1979 reading seems to represent his interpretative thoughts on the cycle at their most mature, while his voice was still in a pristine state, and the partnership with Barenboim, an artist the singer has lavished with praise, is one of close rapport allied with bold imagination on both sides, a large-scale interpretation that seems to have a whole world of sorrow and anguish in its projection. *Wasserflut* is as good a template as any of both artists' keen rapport throughout the entire performance. The singer's partnership with Gerald Moore in Schubert is well represented by their second, 1972 recording of *Schwanengesang*. It was one of the most rewarding fruits of their long collaboration and crowned their joint labours on the composer's oeuvre. Here, in the mostly cheerful Rellstab settings, as in the predominantly searing Heine ones, the singer is at the height of his powers, bringing to these late songs the benefit of his vast range of tone and expression. The extra nine, mostly popular songs only confirm the impression left by the quasi-cycle: who could resist this pair in *Die Forelle* and *An Silvia*?

Die schöne Müllerin, D975

Werner Güra *ten* **Jan Schultsz** *pf*
Harmonia Mundi HMC90 1708 (63 minutes: DDD) Ⓕ
Text and translation included. Recorded 1999 ○○○

An absolutely enthralling account of the cycle on virtually every count that seriously challenges the hegemony of the many desirable versions already available. In the first place Güra must have about the most beautiful voice ever to have recorded the work in the original keys (and that's not to overlook Wunderlich, a far less perceptive interpreter). Its owner has a technique second to none, able to vary his tone, sing a lovely *pianissimo* and/or a long-breathed phrase with perfect control. Then no musical or verbal subtlety seems to escape him at any stage of the young man's disillusioning journey from happiness to misery and death.

The plaintive quality of his voice and its youthful sap are precisely right for conveying the protagonist's vulnerability and, where needed, his self-pity. That great song 'Der Neugierige' encapsulates these virtues, with the final couplet of questioning the brook immaculately done, just as the *pp* at the close of the previous song is given a curious sense of uncertainty on the boy's part. The three strophic songs are finely varied: here, as throughout, the use of *rubato* is natural and inevitable and the integration of singer and pianist, who is happily playing a Bechstein, are at their most compelling.

'Mein' is properly eager, expectant, 'Pause' as plangent as it should be, especially at its end. The frenetic anger of the 14th and 15th songs is as over-heated as it should be, 'Die liebe Farbe' rightly hypnotic. In those great songs, 'Trockne Blumen' and 'Der Müller und der Bach', both artists go to the heart of the matter, and the final lullaby is soft-grained and consoling. Schultsz's contributions are sometimes controversial, always challenging.

Güra surpasses even the *Gramophone* Award-winning Bostridge, simply because his voice is under even better control and because his German is obviously more idiomatic. The Prégardien/Staier version, using a fortepiano, is almost austere – more reticent, more inward, than the new one and far from being outclassed by it. Güra and his pianist now share honours with that DHM recording among tenor recordings. Were it available, the CfP performance by the Partridges, at bargain price, would also be a worthy rival to the newcomers, enjoying as it does similar assets. The Harmonia Mundi sound, in spite of some reverberance, catches voice and piano in ideal balance.

Die schöne Müllerin, with a reading of six poems not set by Schubert
Ian Bostridge *ten* **Dietrich Fischer-Dieskau** *narr* **Graham Johnson** *pf*
Hyperion CDJ33025 (73 minutes: DDD) Ⓕ
Text and translation included.
Recorded 1994-95.

Awards 1996

The 20 songs of *Die schöne Müllerin* portray a Wordsworthian world of heightened emotion in the pantheistic riverside setting of the miller. The poet, Wilhelm Müller, tells of solitary longings, jealousies, fears and hopes as the river rushes by, driving the mill-wheel and refreshing the natural world. Ian Bostridge and Graham Johnson go to the heart of the matter, the young tenor in his aching tones and naturally affecting interpretation, the pianist in his perceptive, wholly apposite playing – and, of course, in his extensive notes. The sum of their joint efforts is a deeply satisfying experience. Bostridge has the right timbre for the protagonist and a straightforward approach, with an instinctive rightness of phrasing. His peculiarly beseeching voice enshrines the vulnerability, tender feeling and obsessive love of the youthful miller, projecting in turn the young lover's thwarted passions, self-delusions and, finally, inner tragedy. Nowhere does he stretch beyond the bounds of the possible, everything expressed in eager then doleful tones. Johnson suggests that 'Ungeduld' mustn't be 'masterful and insistent' or the youth would have won the girl, so that even in this superficially buoyant song the sense of a sensitive, sad, introverted youth is maintained. The daydreaming strophic songs have the smiling, innocent, intimate sound that suits them to perfection, the angry ones the touch of stronger metal that Bostridge can now add to his silver, the tragic ones, before the neutral 'Baches Wiegenlied', an inner intensity that rends the heart as it should. An occasional moment of faulty German accenting matters not at all when the sense of every word is perceived.

As a bonus we have here a recitation of the Prologue and Epilogue and of the Müller poems not set by Schubert: Fischer-Dieskau graces it with his speaking voice. The ideal Hyperion recording catches everything in very present terms. In all musical matters, everything Johnson writes only enhances one's enjoyment, if that is the right word, of a soul-searching interpretation.

Die schöne Müllerin
Dietrich Fischer-Dieskau *bar* **Gerald Moore** *pf*
EMI Great Recordings of the Century CDM5 66907-2 Ⓜ
(59 minutes: ADD). Text and translation included.
Recorded 1961

This reissue is the best of Fischer-Dieskau's three recordings of this work, made at the height of his – and Moore's – powers. Fischer-Dieskau's interpretation is simply more idiomatic and more natural. He and Moore are here more spontaneous than in 1951 (for EMI), less affected than in 1972 (reissued on a DG CD in 1985). The conglomeration of Fischer-Dieskau's subtleties and insights are almost overwhelming but here they are mostly subsumed in the immediacy of a highly individual, always alerting performance. But the difference between conscious interpretation and interior restraint can be felt if you compare Fischer-Dieskau and Patzak in the phrase 'sie mir gab' in 'Trockne Blumen'. Moore throughout offers a discerning and musically valid characterization of the participating stream: nothing is overplayed yet all is made manifest. So the intending purchaser is embarrassed with riches in a work that almost always brings the best out of its interpreters. Whichever other interpretation you opt for, you will certainly want Fischer-Dieskau for complete command and understanding of this glorious work.

Die schöne Müllerin
Julius Patzak *ten* **Michael Raucheisen** *pf*
Preiser mono 93128 (61 minutes: AAD) Ⓕ
Recorded 1943

Der Mensch hat so eine Stimme' ('The man has a tone of voice') says Rocco of Florestan, and it's always a phrase that seems particularly apt for the voice of the great Viennese tenor, Julius Patzak, who was, of course, an unsurpassed Florestan himself. The same plangent utterance that was so affecting in his portrayal of Beethoven's suffering hero informs his famous interpretation of Schubert's cycle about the lovelorn miller-hand. Indeed, his account of 'Die liebe Farbe' is so subjectively intense as to be hardly bearable, and the whole reading, with its poignant diction and lambent tone, places it quite in a class of its own. None reaches to the heart of the matter with quite Patzak's unerring skill. The range of his tone colour and methods of expression are evident not only in 'Die liebe Farbe' but also in the two great songs that succeed it.

In 'Die liebe Farbe', such phrases as 'grüne Rasen' and 'hat's jagen so gern' carry an enormous weight of grief as does the piercing enunciation of 'tote liebe' in 'Trockne Blumen'. The end of this song is taken very fast, as if in a fever of unjustified hope. But in earlier, happier moments, Patzak is no less eloquent – try the third verse of 'Des Müllers Blumen' or the whole of 'Morgengruss', where he creates the illusion of actually talking to the girl, or hear the intimate articulation in 'Der Neugierige' while, by contrast, the words tumble out abruptly in the fierce hatred of 'Der Jäger' and the following song. This is an interpretation that is *hors concours*, and not perhaps an interpretation one would wish to hear every day – it is too despairing. It is immensely detailed and subjective, free and spontaneous seeming, never calculated and sophisticated. Raucheisen is at times revelatory at the piano, at times wayward. The recording, though immediate, has the occasional distortion, and the piano is backward. But the greatness of the reading overrides any drawbacks, although listening to it does require a degree of faith.

Schwanengesang, D957

Awards 1990

Schwanengesang. Herbst, D945. Der Wanderer an den Mond, D870. Am Fenster, D878. Bei dir allein, D866 No 2
Peter Schreier *ten* **András Schiff** *pf*
Decca 425 612-2DH (63 minutes: DDD) Ⓕ
Texts and translations included.
Recorded 1989. **ooo**

Though *Schwanengesang* is not a song-cycle but a collection of Schubert's last (or 'swan') songs by their first publisher, it is generally felt to form a satisfying sequence, with a unity of style if not of theme or mood. This is certainly not weakened by the addition on the Decca disc of the four last songs which were originally omitted, all of them settings of poems by Johann Seidl. Seidl is one of the three poets whose work Schubert used in these frequently sombre songs and it is strange to think that all concerned in their creation were young men, none of the poets being older than Schubert. The listener can scarcely be unaware of a shadow or sometimes an almost unearthly radiance over even the happiest (such as 'Die Taubenpost', the last of all) and that is particularly true when the performers themselves have such sensitive awareness as here. Peter Schreier is responsive to every shade of meaning in music and text while András Schiff's playing is a miracle of combined strength and delicacy, specific insight and general rightness.

Awards 1992

Schwanengesang. Sehnsucht, D879. Der Wanderer an den Mond, D870. Wiegenlied, D867. Am Fenster, D878. Herbst, D945
Brigitte Fassbaender *mez* **Aribert Reimann** *pf*
DG 429 766-2GH (68 minutes: DDD) Ⓕ
Texts and translations included.
Recorded 1989-91. **ooo**

Fassbaender and Reimann offer something equally compelling but rather different in their account of *Schwanengesang*. Fassbaender's interpretation, idiosyncratic in every respect, pierces to the heart of the bleak songs with performances as daring and challenging as the playing of her partner. More than anyone, these two artists catch the fleeting moods of these mini-dramas, and their searing originality of concept. Even the lighter songs have a special individuality of utterance. This is a starkly immediate interpretation that leaves the listener shattered. The extra Seidl settings, rarely performed, are all worth hearing. Both of these notable partnerships are superb in their own ways.

Additional recommendations

Schwanengesang, D957

Couplings: Die schöne Müllerin. Winterreise. Einsamkeit
Fischer-Dieskau *bar* **Moore** *pf*
EMI ③ CMS5 66146-2 (203 minutes: ADD) Ⓜ

Dietrich Fischer-Dieskau's 1962 *Schwanengesang* is, for some, the most all-embracing interpretation of the 'cycle' ever given. Here his voice is a little fresher than in 1972 (DG). In sum, an essential purchase for any Schubertian

Couplings: 10 Lieder
Hotter *bar* **Moore** *pf* **H**
EMI Références CDH5 65196-2 (78 minutes: ADD) Ⓜ

Hans Hotter's pioneering 1954 recording is a deeply satisfying reading The nobility and softness of voice, the refinement of diction and the profound understanding of the text remain touchstones in interpreting this 'cycle'.

Winterreise, D911

Peter Schreier *ten* **András Schiff** *pf*
Decca 436 122-2DH (72 minutes: DDD). Text and translation included. Recorded 1991 Ⓕ **o**

Schreier, in his note in the accompanying booklet, refers to the unique density and spiritual concentration of the *Winterreise* songs; that, and their hallucinatory nature, inform this riveting performance from start to finish, nowhere more so than in 'Wasserflut' and 'Einsamkeit'. The latter is a paradigm of the whole searing, almost unbearable experience. If you can tolerate it you will be engaged and surely moved by the whole. In this song, Schreier leans into the words and notes of 'Ach, das die Luft so ruhig!' suggesting the cry of a desperate, tormented soul – as does the emphatic enunciation of the single word 'Bergstroms' earlier, in 'Irricht'. Also arresting is the curiously daring way Schreier asks the question at the end of 'Die Post', as if it were a spontaneous afterthought. These make the moments of calm and repose all the more eerie. The sad delicacy of Schiff's playing at the start of 'Frühlingstraum' sets the scene of the imagined May to perfection, and the flowing lift of his left hand in 'Täuschung' is as deceptively friendly as the light described by the singer. 'Das Wirtshaus' is all false resignation: voice and piano tell us of the man's tired emptiness. Anger and defiance are registered in raw, chilling tone and phraseology. The final songs taken simply, speak beautifully of acceptance. The recording is warm yet clear.

Winterreise
Bernd Weikl *bar* **Helmut Deutsch** *pf*
Nightingale Classics NC070960-2 (70 minutes: DDD) Ⓕ
Text and translation included. Recorded 1993

For those who prefer a baritone, Weikl seriously challenges the hegemony, among lower-voiced singers, of the many available versions. Indeed it is the absolute vocal security and evenness of Weikl's actual singing that so impresses even before one considers his view of the work. Nowhere is there any sign of strain, over-emphasis, faltering in pitch, or failure of nerve in executing a phrase with a long breath, and as the singer has such a strong voice one feels throughout that there is always something held in reserve.

As a reading the Weikl unerringly keeps that balance between detachment and subjectivity. Tempos are perfectly judged – and here Deutsch's well-observed, well-balanced playing makes a real contribution – a wonderful frozen feeling in 'Auf dem Flusse', for instance. Weikl displays many gradations of tone to enhance his thought-through reading – 'Gefrorne Tränen' is a good example – but he uses vocal emphases more sparingly, reserving his most pointed verbal accents for such things as 'Gras' in 'Erstarrung', 'Hähne' in 'Frühlingstraum' and 'Hunde' in 'Im Dorfe', but even these never upset the verities of line and firm tone, and the sheer beauty of the singing, as in 'Der Lindenbaum', is balm to the ear. For those who find Fischer-Dieskau's more agonised readings too much to bear, or find his style too interventionist, Weikl is the obvious choice. A superb recording.

Winterreise
Dietrich Fischer-Dieskau *bar* **Jörg Demus** *pf*
DG The Originals 447 421-2GOR (71 minutes: ADD) Ⓜ
Text and translation included. Recorded 1965 ●●

On the verge of his fifth decade, the singer was in his absolute prime – and it shows. Indeed listening to his interpretation is like coming home to base after many interesting encounters away from the familiar. Indeed, it is possibly the finest of all in terms of beauty of tone and ease of technique – and how beautiful, how smooth and velvety was the baritone's voice at that time. That this is the most interior, unadorned and undemonstrative of Fischer-Dieskau's readings perhaps arises from the fact that Demus, a discerning musician and sure accompanist, is the most reflective of all the singer's many partners in the cycle. Demus never strikes out on his own, is always there unobtrusively and subtly supportive, with the right colour and phrasing, literally in hand. Given an intimate, slightly dry recording, finely remastered, the whole effect is of a pair communing with each other and stating the sad, distraught message of Schubert's bleak work in terms of a personal message to the listener in the home. A deeply rewarding performance. Certainly if you want Fischer-Dieskau in the cycle you need look no further.

Winterreise **P**
Christoph Prégardien *ten* **Andreas Staier** *fp*
Teldec Das Alte Werk 0630-18824-2 Ⓜ
(74 minutes: DDD). Texts and translations included.
Recorded 1996 ●●

Prégardien and Staier have something new and important to offer. From the very first song, we are in the presence of a sensitive, inward man in fear of his fate. Something is actually happening to this sufferer's soul at the second 'des ganzen Winters Eis'; indeed the whole final verse of the second song expresses the youth's anguish. Just as memorable are the stab of pain in the repeated final line 'Da ist meiner Liebstens Haus' at the end of 'Wasserflut', the introverted misery of the ice-carving of the loved one's name in 'Auf dem Flusse' and the almost mesmeric feeling in the final verse as the torrent rages in the protagonist's heart. This is what the singing of this cycle is about: the exposing of raw nerves.

Staier is just as revelatory. Using his fortepiano to maximum effect, he finds so many fresh perceptions in his part, as in the precise weighting at the start of 'Einsamkeit' and, as important, ones that accord perfectly with those of his regular partner. Here you have the sense of performers who have lived together with the cycle and conceived a unified, thought-through vision. For example, listen to the way the pair mesh together to searing effect at the end of 'Irrlicht'. The ineffable sadness of 'Frühlingstraum' (the text ideally articulated, the close properly trance-like), the raw blast of winter in 'Der stürmische Morgen', the tense weariness of 'Der Wegweiser', the weary half-voice of 'Das Wirtshaus' – these and so much else contribute to the impression of a truly great performance. The recording is very finely balanced.

Additional recommendations
Winterreise, D911
Holzmair *bar* **Cooper** *pf*
Philips 446 407-2PH (70 minutes: DDD: 5/96) Ⓕ
A reading at the opposite extreme from Fischer-Dieskau's big-scale approach. Wolfgang Holzmair's and Imogen Cooper's natural, unvarnished view of this great work, earns them a strong recommendation.

Bär *bar* **Parsons** *pf*
EMI CDC7 49334-2 (75 minutes: DDD) Ⓕ
A wonderfully vivid performance from Olaf Bär; his use of the text is nothing short of masterly, with not a hint of overemphasis. One of the best *Winterreises* you can buy.

Die Verschworenen

Die Verschworenen, oder Der häusliche Krieg **P**
Soile Isokoski *sop* Countess Ludmilla; **Peter Lika** *bass* Count Heribert von Lüdenstein; **Rodrigo Orrego** *ten* Astolf von Reisenberg; **Andreas Fischer** *ten* Garold von Nummen; **Christian Dahm** *bass* Friedrich von Trausdorf; **Thomas Pfützner** *bass* Knight; **Mechthild Georg** *mez* Udolin; **Anke Hoffmann** *sop* Isella; **Lisa Larsson** *sop* Helene; **Susanne Behnes** *sop* Luitgarde; **Marion Steingötter** *sop* Camilla; **Iris Kupke** *sop* Woman; **Chorus Musicus; Das Neue Orchester / Christoph Spering**
Opus 111 OPS30-167 (64 minutes: DDD) Ⓕ
Notes, text and translation included
Recorded 1996

Ignaz Castelli's neatly wrought text, loosely based on Aristophanes' *Lysistrata*, prompted, early in 1823, Schubert's most dramatically viable stage-work, a one-act *Singspiel.* Aristophanes' story of aggrieved womenfolk withholding their favours until their husbands abandoned their warmongering is transposed here to Vienna during the Crusades and softened with a liberal injection of Biedermeier sentiment. Schubert's parodistic martial music for the macho warriors can occasionally grow wearisome, especially in the finale. Otherwise he scarcely puts a foot wrong. His dramatic pacing is sure and lively, his invention witty, touching and colourful, with its intermittent echoes of Mozart. The opera's gem is Helene's bittersweet F minor *Romanze*, with its sinuous clarinet obbligato (beautifully played) and haunting modulation to the major in the very last bars.

With his polished orchestra and fresh-toned chorus Christoph Spering gives a sympathetic, shrewdly paced account of the score, allowing the lyrical numbers plenty of breathing space and revealing a light, pointed touch in the comic ensembles. Of the singers, Peter Lika's Count has plenty of 'face', though his bass can become coarse under pressure. Rodrigo Orrego, as the knight Astolf, displays an agreeable, soft-grained tenor; and all four principal female roles are well taken, with Lisa Larsson showing a bright, pure tone and a shapely sense of phrase as Helene, and Soile Isokoski bringing real distinction to the role of the Countess, her warm, vibrant soprano, with its hint of mezzo richness and depth, reminiscent of Schwarzkopf.

The recording is vivid and well balanced, giving ample presence to the voices while allowing Schubert's felicitous scoring its due.

Ervin Schulhoff Bohemian 1894-1942

GROVE *Schulhoff was a pupil of Reger in Leipzig (1908-10) and later in Germany (1919-23) he associated with Klee and the dadaists; back in Prague he was active as a pianist, in jazz and as an exponent of Hába's quarter-tone music. His works include stage pieces, six symphonies and two piano sonatas, displaying diverse styles. He died in a concentration camp.*

Symphony No 3

Symphonies Nos 3 and 5
Prague Radio Symphony Orchestra / Vladimír Válek
Supraphon 11 2161-2 (53 minutes: DDD) Ⓕ
Recorded 1994

Posthumous premières of these works in the 1950s aroused little interest, but Schulhoff has acquired quite a following in recent years and this latest addition to his discography should not be overlooked. As always in music where there is no performance tradition to speak of, the range of interpretative possibilities is wide. On this showing, Vladimír Válek is the most deft and neo-classical of Schulhoff conductors, offering well-prepared, notably fluent accounts of both pieces; his aim seems to be to reconcile their blatant Communistic idiom with the lighter, Roaring Twenties manner of the composer's previous creative period.

In Israel Yinon's recording of the Third Symphony, you sense that the music is not just being given room to breathe; it can only be considered in the light of the composer's death in a Nazi concentration camp. Accordingly, Yinon adopts a much weightier tempo in the first movement, its ostinato unrelenting, its drums militantly thwacked.

Albrecht's idea of *moderato* is yet more funereal, suggesting that it is the Czech conductor who is out of line. Nevertheless, Válek's account is arguably the most persuasive of the three, executed with commendable crispness. In the Fifth Symphony, risking some loss of *gravitas*, Válek is again nothing if not urgent. The music makes better sense in his hands and any lack of clarity in the orchestral textures would seem to derive from deficiencies in the writing. Even the lack of a clinching melodic idea is made to appear less important. This is a valuable disc, well annotated.

Sextet

Sextet. String Quartet in G, Op 25. Duo[a]. Solo Violin Sonata[b]
Rainer Johannes Kimstedt *va* **Michael Sanderling** *vc* **Petersen Quartet** ([b]Conrad Muck, [a]Gernot Sussmuth *vns* Friedemann Weigle *va* [a]Hans-Jakob Eschenburg *vc*)
Capriccio 10 539 (77 minutes: DDD) Ⓕ
Recorded 1994 ●

As Schulhoff enthusiasts will have come to expect, the works represented are not at all uniform in style. The early quartet is prematurely neo-classical. It was conceived in 1918 when the composer was still serving in the Austrian Army. The German group certainly gives it their all. Taut and tough, they seem intent on radicalizing the discourse whether through a heightened response to its finer points or a profound understanding of the Beethovenian models that lurk beneath the surface invention. As a result, the Quartet emerges as a witty, substantial piece.

The string Sextet was completed six years later but sounds quite different, its Schoenbergian first movement well integrated with the more eclectic idiom of the rest. Whatever the outward manner, Schulhoff's rhythmic phraseology is metrically conceived. Even if you already know the Sextet the Petersen makes a plausible first choice. The aggressive communication of their playing is emphasised by the bright, not quite top-heavy sound balance.

The Janáček-Bartók-Ravel axis of the *Duo* is equally well served. The Sonata for solo violin (1927) is at least as interesting as similar works by Hindemith, less emotionally wrenching than the Bartók. That work was composed a couple of years after Schulhoff's premature death. A thoroughly distinguished issue by an ensemble seemingly incapable of giving a dull performance.

String Quartet No 1

Schulhoff String Quartet No 1 **Hindemith** String Quartet No 3, Op 22 **Weill** String Quartet
Brandis Quartet (Thomas Brandis, Peter Brem *vns* Wilfried Strehle *va* Wolfgang Boettcher *vc*)
Nimbus NI5410 (60 minutes: DDD) Ⓕ
Recorded 1992

All three works bear witness to a culture that, in terms of tempo and sensation, was in the process of excited transformation. The period covered is 1923-24, the time of rocketing German inflation, the establishment of the USSR, Rilke's *Duino Elegies* as well as major Kafka (who died in 1924), Mann, Musil, Cocteau and Bréton (his Surrealist manifesto). This music is full of it all. Hindemith's bold Third Quartet launches its explorations within a relatively formal framework, certainly in comparison with Schulhoff and Weill. Rich invention is tempered by a sense of outward propriety. Weill's Quartet opens with real expressive warmth, although it soon busies itself with a whole range of interesting ideas (the finale is particularly rich in incident), with a hoot of a *Scherzo* that suddenly swerves to a Reger-like March, then waltzes gently forth in a manner that suggests Shostakovich before embarking on further discursive episodes and scurrying off to a cheeky *diminuendo*. Granted, one feels that Weill is in search of something he never quite finds, but the very act of searching makes for an absorbing adventure.

Even more compelling, however, is Schulhoff's dazzling First Quartet, the last piece in the programme and a highly dramatic musical mystery tour. Urgency rules right from the opening bars, while Schulhoff's tonal palette is both wide-ranging and ingeniously employed: pizzicato, *col legno*, *sul ponticello*, harmonics (wonderfully effective in the finale), dense harmonic computations and a rhythmic vitality that recalls Bartók at full cry. The work's pale, equivocal coda recalls the parallel quartet mysteries of Schulhoff's fellow Holocaust victims Krása and Haas, while the work as a whole is far more than the sum of its restless and endlessly fascinating parts. A fine programme, lustrously recorded.

Robert Schumann German 1810-1856

GROVE *The son of a bookseller, Schumann early showed ability as a pianist and an interest in composing as well as literary leanings. He was also enthusiastic over the writings of 'Jean Paul' (JPF Richter), girl friends and drinking champagne, tastes he retained. In 1821 he went to Leipzig to study law but instead spent his time in musical, social and literary activities. He wrote some piano music and took lessons from Friedrich Wieck. After a spell in Heidelberg, ostensibly studying law but actually music, he persuaded his family that he should give up law in favour of a pianist's career, and in 1830 he went to live with Wieck at Leipzig. But he soon had trouble with his hands (allegedly due to a machine to strengthen his fingers, but more likely through remedies for a syphilitic sore). Composition, however, continued; several piano works date from this period.*

In 1834 Schumann founded a music journal, the Neue Zeitschrift für Musik; he was its editor and leading writer for ten years. He was a brilliant and perceptive critic: his writings embody the most progressive aspects of musical thinking in his time, and he drew attention to many promising young composers. Sometimes he wrote under pseudonyms, Eusebius (representing his lyrical, contemplative side) and Florestan (his fiery, impetuous one); he used these in his music, too. His compositions at this time were mainly for piano: they include variations on the name of one on his lady friends, Abegg (the musical notes A-B-E-G-G), the character-pieces Davidsbündlertänze ('Dances of the league of David', an imaginary association of those fighting the Philistines), Carnaval (pieces with literary or other allusive meanings, including one on the notes A-S-C-H after the place another girl friend came from), Phantasiestücke (a collection of poetic pieces depicting moods), Kreisleriana (fantasy pieces around the character of a mad Kapellmeister) and Kinderszenen ('Scenes from Childhood'). Affairs of the heart played a large part in his life. By 1835 he was in love with Wieck's young daughter Clara, but Wieck did his best to separate them. They pledged themselves in 1837 but were much apart and Schumann went through deep depressions. In 1839 they took legal steps to make Wieck's consent unnecessary, and after many further trials they were able to marry in 1840.

Schumann, understandably, turned in that year to song; he wrote c150 songs, including most of his finest, at this time, among them several groups and cycles, the latter including Frauenliebe und -leben ('A Woman's Love and Life') and Dichterliebe ('A Poet's Love'), which tells (to verse by Heine) a tragic Romantic story of the flowering of love, its failure and poet's exclusion from joy and his longing for death. Schumann, as a pianist composer, made the piano partake fully in the expression of emotion in such songs, often giving it the most telling music when the voice had finished.

In 1841, however, Schumann turned to orchestral music: he wrote symphonies and a beautiful, poetic piece for piano and orchestra for Clara that he later reworked as the first movement of his Piano Concerto. Then in 1842, when Clara was away on a concert tour (he disliked being in her shadow and remained at home), he turned to chamber music, and wrote his three string quartets and three works with piano, of which the Piano Quintet has always been a favourite for the freshness and Romantic warmth of its ideas. After that, in 1843, he turned to choral music, working at a secular oratorio and at setting part of Goethe's Faust. He also took up a teaching post at the new conservatory in Leipzig of which Mendelssohn was director. But he was an ineffectual teacher; and he had limited success as a conductor too. He and Clara moved to Dresden in 1844, but his deep depressions continued, hampering his creativity. Not until 1847-48 was he again productive, writing his opera Genoveva (given in Leipzig in 1850 with moderate success), chamber music and songs. In 1850 he took up a post in Düsseldorf as town musical director. He was at first happy and prolific, writing the eloquent Cello Concerto and the Rhenish Symphony (no.3: one movement depicts his impressions in Cologne Cathedral). But the post worked out badly because of his indifferent conducting. In 1852-53 his health and spirits deteriorated and he realised that he could not continue in his post. In 1854 he began to suffer hallucinations; he attempted suicide (he had always dreaded the possibility of madness) and entered an asylum, where he died in 1856, almost certainly of the effects of syphilis, cared for at the end by Clara and the young Brahms.

Cello Concerto in A minor, Op 129

Schumann Cello Concerto. Adagio and Allegro in A flat, Op 70. Fantasiestücke, Op 73. Fünf Stücke im Volkston, Op 102. Mass in C minor, Op 147 – Offertorium **Bargiel** Adagio in G, Op 38 **P**
Steven Isserlis *vc* **Dame Felicity Lott** *sop*
David King *org* **Deutsche Kammerphilharmonie / Christoph Eschenbach** *pf*
RCA Red Seal 09026 68800-2 (75 minutes: DDD) Ⓕ
Recorded 1996

Only two of the works in this forwardly recorded anthology – the *Fünf Stücke im Volkston* of 1840 and the Cello Concerto of a year later – were originally inspired by the cello. But in closely attuned, super-sensitive partnership with Eschenbach as both conductor and pianist, Steven Isserlis somehow persuades us that no instrument better revealed 'the beloved dreamer whom we know as Schumann', as Tovey once put it. Helped by unhurried tempos and a lovely-voiced *c*1745 Guadagnini cello, Isserlis draws out the rich, nostalgic poetry of the concerto's first two movements with the eloquence of speech. And with his buoyancy of heart and bow he silences all criticism of the finale – even its low-lying cadenza (this he subsequently plays again with the composer's surely less effective flourish for the soloist in the closing bars). The five engaging *Volkston* pieces with piano are vividly characterised and contrasted in mood. And the Op 73 and Op 70 miniatures lose nothing through transfer from clarinet and horn respectively to one of the composer's two optional alternatives. The *Adagio and Allegro* for horn surely gains in expressive intimacy and vitality when bowed rather than blown. The *Offertorium* (with its telling accompanying cello thread) is sung by Felicity Lott with heart-easing beauty. The inclusion of a hitherto unrecorded, noble *Adagio* by Clara Schumann's gifted half-brother, Woldemar Bargiel, also helps to make this disc a collector's piece.

Cello Concerto[a]. Adagio and Allegro in A flat, Op 70[b]. Fantasiestücke, Op 73[b]. Funf Stücke im Volkston, Op 102[b]
Heinrich Schiff *vc* **Gerhard Oppitz** *pf* **Berlin Philharmonic Orchestra / Bernard Haitink**
Philips 422 414-2PH (60 minutes: DDD). Recorded [a]1988, [b]1991(arr Grützmacher) Ⓕ ●

Schumann's Cello Concerto is a fairly dark, troubled work, and sometimes cellists are tempted to adopt a somewhat overwrought approach when playing it. In fact, it responds best to a more balanced approach, as exemplified in the performance by Heinrich Schiff. His playing is very eloquent, and quite strong, but there is also a feeling of dignity and refinement in his response to the music. Everything is perfectly in scale, and the work's essential nobility is allowed to emerge in a most moving fashion. Schiff's technique is faultless, and his tonal quality is very beautiful. Haitink and the BPO seem totally in sympathy with the soloist, and the recording is warm and well detailed. The three items with piano accompaniment comprise a series of short pieces which are for the most part sunnier in outlook than the Concerto, and they make an effective contrast to the larger-scale work. Again Schiff's playing is expressive, but his phrasing is full of subtlety and poetry, and Oppitz is a highly responsive partner.

Cello Concerto[a]. Piano Trio No 1 in D minor, Op 63[b]. Funf Stücke im Volkston, Op 102[c] **H**
Pablo Casals *vc* [b]**Alexander Schneider** *vn*
[b]**Mieczyslaw Horszowski,** [c]**Leopold Mannes** *pfs*
[a]**Prades Festival Orchestra / Eugene Ormandy**
Sony Classical Casals Edition mono SMK58993 (74 minutes: ADD). Recorded 1952-53 Ⓜ ●●

This disc provides a prime sampling of the Casals manner at its most inspired. His 1953 recording of Schumann's Cello Concerto is a startlingly demonstrative affair with heavily thrashed accents, savage entries and a general proneness to exaggeration that makes a meal out of Schumann's already heightened psycho-musical pathology. And yet Casals's unique brand of poetry is always heart-rending: try from 11'25" into the first movement and follow through to the next, and you'll hear palpable premonitions of the Elgar Concerto as well as some exquisite cello playing. Prior to an enjoyable (but, again, rather bullishly projected) set of *Stücke im Volkston*, we are offered an extremely fine reading of Schumann's sombre D minor Trio – this is undoubtedly a near-contender for 'best ever' status of this work.

Piano Concerto in A minor, Op 54

Piano Concerto in A minor, Op 54[a]. Carnaval, Op 9[b]. Waldszenen, Op 82[c] – Vogel als Prophet **H**
Dame Myra Hess *pf* [a]**orchestra / Walter Goehr**
Naxos Historical mono 8 110604 (62 minutes: ADD) Ⓢ
Recorded [a]1937, [b]1938 and [c]1931 ●

Unimpeachably honest, Hess's *Carnaval* may be less volatile or idiosyncratic than, say, Rachmaninov's but its special sensitivity and deep affection give it classic status. Hess was indeed 'a virtuoso in sound' (Stephen Kovacevich, her one-time student) with a capacity to play with a simplicity and poise that accentuated Schumann's free-ranging character and magic. Her opening is truly *quasi maestoso* (that swaggering air of assertion and importance) before bounding away truly *più moto* and *brillante*. How good to hear 'Papillons' touched off with such lightness and vivacity rather than trumpeted with a more familiar insensitivity. The central section of 'Chiarina' is hauntingly lost in reflection and, had he heard Hess's inwardness in Chopin, Schumann might well have changed his *agitato* direction. Again, Hess is a virtuoso in so many senses, more than capable of sweeping all before her in *Carnaval*'s exultant close.

Her 'Vogel als Prophet' is flexible and expressive in a style rarely encountered today; and who else has played the A flat episode in the Concerto's first movement or spun off the central Intermezzo with such rapt engagement? Some may find her finale a trifle sober-suited, but it is intensely musical, a performance which Nalen Anthoni suggests in his excellent accompanying essay stems from a tradition which emphasised Schumann's gentleness rather than his wildness or schizophrenia. The recordings may show their age but the transfers have come up outstandingly, allowing one to savour Hess's past but ever-present glory to the full.

Piano Concerto[a]. Introduction and Allegro appassionato in D minor (Concertstück), Op 92[a]. Violin Concerto in D minor, Op posth[b]. Cello Concerto[c]. Konzertstück in F, Op 86[d]
Daniel Barenboim *pf* **Gidon Kremer** *vn* **Paul Tortelier** *vc* **Gerd Seifert, Norbert Hauptmann, Christopher Kohler, Manfred Klier** *hns* **[a]London Philharmonic Orchestra / Dietrich Fischer-Dieskau; [b]Philharmonia Orchestra / Riccardo Muti; [c]Royal Philharmonic Orchestra / Yan Pascal Tortelier; [d]Berlin Philharmonic Orchestra / Klaus Tennstedt**
EMI Rouge et Noir ② CZS5 69692-2 (121 minutes: ADD). Recorded [a]1974, [b]1982, [cd]1978 Ⓜ ●

If ever a performance of Schumann's Piano Concerto stressed the principle of dialogue between soloist and conductor, then this is it. True, the Philharmonia's string ensemble isn't as water-tight under Fischer-Dieskau as it might have been under some other conductors; and poetry is invested at the premium of relatively low-level drama. Orchestral textures are absolutely right for Schumann – warm yet transparent, full-bodied yet never stodgy – and poetry is a major priority. Add Barenboim's compatible vision and keyboard finesse, and you indeed have a memorable reading. Despite the extensive competition, Stephen Kovacevich's memorable recording with Colin Davis remains the top recommendation for this work (reviewed under Grieg) though.

The more discursive *Introduction and Allegro appassionato* has plenty of interest, but remembering that this isn't exactly top-drawer Schumann, the performance could be more arresting. Conversely, the *Konzertstücke* has as much forthrightness as it could possibly take, certainly in terms of engineering: the four magnificent horns ring out with Olympian force, keenly supported by an animated BPO. The Cello Concerto is more smoothly recorded, but although Tortelier *père* had the measure of this fragile masterpiece's troubled spirit, his son was, at least at this stage in his career, less comprehensively perceptive.

As for the Violin Concerto, one finds oneself frequently moved by Kremer's solo playing – his handling of the slow movement has a tonal richness – but less than happy with Muti's indulgent accompaniment. The repetitions in this work are frequently misunderstood as symptoms of creative decline rather than as the trenchant rhetorical devices that they in fact are, and Muti gives the impression of being unconvinced by them. Nevertheless, Kremer and Muti are, within the useful context of this competitively-priced set, certainly up to the task of communicating what is still a scandalously underrated work. They also have the benefit of good engineering.

Piano Concerto[a]. Piano Quintet in E flat, Op 44[b]
Maria João Pires *pf* **[b]Augustin Dumay, [b]Renaud Capuçon** *vns* **[b]Gérard Caussé** *va* **[b]Jian Wang** *vc* **[a]Chamber Orchestra of Europe / Claudio Abbado**
DG 463 179-2GH (62 minutes: DDD) Ⓕ
Recorded [a]1997 and [b]1999 ●●

It makes an unusual and apt coupling to have the Schumann Piano Concerto alongside the most powerful of his chamber works. In both, Pires is inspired to give freely spontaneous performances, at once powerfully persuasive and poetic. In the Quintet it is a delight to get the feeling of interplay between musicians, distinguished individually, who plainly enjoy working together. So after the warmly dramatic contrasts of the first movement, the funeral march of the slow movement brings the keenest concentration, with the detached chords of the opening theme conveying deep mystery. The warmth of the whole performance is reflected in the way that Pires leads the team to play with natural, unselfconscious *rubato* in all four movements, the speeds perfectly chosen and the structure firmly held together. The rhythmic spring of the playing is a constant delight, too.

In the Concerto Pires is also at her most persuasive. Claudio Abbado has conducted in several previous recordings of the work, notably for Perahia on Sony and for Pollini on DG, yet here with the Chamber Orchestra of Europe instead of the Berlin Philharmonic he is able to match the volatile quality in Pires's performance with beautifully transparent accompaniment. So the hushed *Andante espressivo* section in the first movement (track 1, 4'42") finds the COE flute and clarinet fully matching their soloist in expressiveness. The central *Intermezzo* is light and fresh at a flowing *Andante grazioso*, free *rubato* making it sound like an improvisation. It leads to a sparkling account of the finale, which lightly emphasises the *scherzando* quality of the writing at a relatively relaxed speed.

Two beautifully judged performances, both very well recorded, make this an original and welcome coupling.

Schumann Piano Concerto
R Strauss Burleske in D minor, AV85
Hélène Grimaud *pf* **Deutsches Symphony Orchestra, Berlin / David Zinman**
Erato 0630-11727-2 (52 minutes: DDD) Ⓕ
Recorded 1995 ●

Such is Grimaud's immediacy of response to every change of mood in the opening *Allegro affettuoso* of Schumann's concerto that some listeners may think it a little too excitable – at the expense of maturer composure and poise. But never in this movement, nor in a finale of unflagging vitality and *joie de vivre*, is there any hint of mere keyboard display. You could certainly never hope to hear the first movement's nostalgic main theme played with a more eloquent simplicity. Piano and orchestra are in exceptionally close accord throughout, and not least in the intimate conversational exchanges of the *Andantino grazioso*.

Written when Strauss was a mere 22, the *Burleske* cries out for youthful virtuosity, volatility, caprice and charm – which we're given here with effortless fluency by all concerned. In what could vaguely be described as lyrical 'second subject' territory (from the start of track 5, *tranquillo*) who could fail to enjoy those amazing pre-echoes of irresistibly seductive, smiling (*con amore*) things-to-come a quarter of a century later in *Der Rosenkavalier*? The Erato sound is clear-cut rather than lusciously cushioned, but never hard-edged: it falls agreeably on the ear.

Piano Concerto. Introduction and Allegro appassionato in G, Op 92. Introduction and Allegro in D minor, Op 134
Murray Perahia *pf* **Berlin Philharmonic Orchestra / Claudio Abbado**
Sony Classical SK64577 (57 minutes: DDD) Ⓕ
Recorded 1994 ●●

From Perahia and Abbado the Piano Concerto comes across with refreshing eagerness, as if Schumann could scarcely pause for breath in an uprush of inspiration. But unflagging strength of direction by no means excludes the personal. The first movement, in particular, brings intimately revealing nuances of phrasing from Perahia, with a finely shaped, richly expressive cadenza before a delectably light-fingered, effervescent coda. Free of coy cosseting the *Andante* has a natural, gracious flow. However, a more expansive melodic glow in the middle section would not have gone amiss, not least when the violins soar into the upper reaches (a masterstroke of orchestration) near its end. Piquantly crunched acciaccaturas at the start inject the finale with inexhaustible rhythmic buoyancy. Recorded in Berlin's Philharmonie, the sound quality is vibrantly full and forward.

Perahia adds Schumann's two later works for piano and orchestra as couplings, of which the sorely neglected last in D minor was part of his birthday present for Clara barely six months before his breakdown. Though less immediately ear-catching than the Mendelssohnian G major work (where Perahia's exhilarating homecoming silences often heard accusations of protraction), Schumann's farewell to the genre – as played here – is striking as by far the more intense and laden of the two, with eventual major-key victory won after deeper internal struggle.

Violin Concerto

Schumann Violin Concerto in D minor, Op posth
Wieniawski Légende, Op 17.
Violin Concerto No 2 in D minor, Op 22
Juliette Kang *vn* **Vancouver Symphony Orchestra / Sergiu Comissiona**
CBC Records SMCD5197 (63 minutes: DDD) Ⓕ
Recorded 1996-98 ●

Juliette Kang here plays with quicksilver brilliance not only in the virtuosic Wieniawski concerto but in the rugged Schumann work, less grateful for the player. Yet, though she plays brilliantly, with dazzlingly clean articulation in bravura passages, these are comparatively small-scale readings. Where those virtuosos in the grand romantic tradition are balanced relatively close, Kang is more naturally balanced in a slightly recessed acoustic. The impression is of a sweet, silvery violin tone that cannot expand so fully; the orchestral strings, too, sound relatively small-scale. What matters is that the performances are all very persuasive. The Schumann, with its bravura double-stopping at the start, finds Kang fiery and impetuous, making up for barnstorming power, and when it comes to lyrical passages the poetry is beautifully caught. So too in the slow movement – introduced in a tender account of the brief opening cello solo – while the finale is taken at a speed which allows a delicious lilt in the dance-rhythms, yet not eccentrically slow as in the Kremer/Harnoncourt.

Similarly, in the Wieniawski Concerto, Kang is light and volatile in the rapid passagework, and relaxes sweetly into the songful beauty of the motto theme (track 5, 6'10"), playing with a natural, unexaggerated lyricism, unselfconscious in her expressiveness. Both the slow movement and the outer sections of the *Légende* have a similar natural and unaffected flow, while the finale again has Kang and Comissiona choosing a speed that is fast and brilliant, while allowing the dance-rhythms to spring infectiously.

Those who insist on display as the first essential may not be completely satisfied, but deeper qualities amply make up for that. For those who want this unique coupling, this is a first-class recommendation.

Complete Symphonies

No 1 in B flat, Op 38, 'Spring'; **No 2** in C, Op 61; **No 3** in E flat, Op 97, 'Rhenish'; **No 4** in D minor, Op 120

Symphonies Nos 1-4.
Overture, Scherzo and Finale, Op 52
Staatskapelle Dresden / Wolfgang Sawallisch
EMI Sawallisch Edition ② CMS7 64815-2 Ⓜ
(148 minutes: ADD). Recorded 1972 ●●

Schumann's symphonies come in for criticism because of his supposed cloudy textures and unsubtle scoring, but in the hands of a conductor who is both skilful and sympathetic they are most engaging works. Sawallisch's recordings, brightly transferred, are a much admired set. His style, fresh and unforced, is not as high powered as some other conductors but it is sensible, alert and very pleasing. He achieves great lightness in the First and Fourth Symphonies – there's always a sense of classical poise and control but never at the expense of the overall architecture of the pieces. The Second and Third Symphonies, larger and more far-reaching in their scope, again benefit from Sawallisch's approach. The playing of the Staatskapelle Dresden is superlative in every department, with a lovely veiled string sound and a real sense of ensemble. With the *Overture, Scherzo and Finale* thrown in for good measure, this is not to be missed.

Symphonies Nos 1 and 2
Bavarian Radio Symphony Orchestra / Rafael Kubelík
Sony Classical Essential Classics SBK48269 Ⓑ
(74 minutes: ADD). Recorded 1978-79 ●

Symphonies Nos 3 and 4. Manfred, Op 115 – Overture
Bavarian Radio Symphony Orchestra / Rafael Kubelík
Sony Classical Essential Classics SBK48270 Ⓑ
(76 minutes: ADD). Recorded 1978-79

It is hard to understand why Kubelík's wonderful cycle failed to make an impact when it was first issued. His sensitivity to detail, his refusal to bully Schumann's vulnerable structures and his ability to penetrate occasional thickets of orchestration, make these especially memorable. Just listen to the cheeky bassoon backing clarinet, 1'44" into the *Spring* Symphony's fourth movement or the to-ing and fro-ing between first and second violins (usefully separated, as virtually always with Kubelík) in the last movement of the Second. Only the first movement of the Fourth seems a little heavy-handed, but then the poetry of the *Romanze* and the exuberance of the finale more than make amends. First movement repeats are observed and the playing throughout is rich in felicitous turns of phrase. The sound, though, is a minor stumbling block: violins are thin, brass a little fuzzy and the whole production less focused than Sawallisch's set. But Kubelík's insights are too varied and meaningful to miss, and there is much pleasure to be derived from them. What with a stirring *Manfred* Overture added for good measure, they also constitute exceptional value for money.

Symphonies Nos 1-3; No 4 (1841 and 1851 G minor versions); WoO29, 'Zwickauer'. Overture, Scherzo and Finale, Op 52. Konzertstück in F, Op 86 **P**
Roger Montgomery, Gavin Edwards, Susan Dent, Robert Maskell *hns* **Orchestre Révolutionnaire et Romantique / Sir John Eliot Gardiner**
Archiv Produktion ③ 457 591-2AH3 Ⓕ
(202 minutes: DDD). Recorded 1996 ●

The first point to note is how much more comprehensive this is than previous cycles, even the outstanding RCA set of period performances from Roy Goodman and the Hanover Band. That offers the *Overture, Scherzo and Finale* in addition to the four numbered symphonies, but No 4 comes in the rare first version of 1841. Gardiner offers both versions, 1841 and 1851, and his performances of them are very well geared to bringing out the contrasts. Still more fascinating is the inclusion of both the early, incomplete Symphony in G minor, and the *Konzertstück* of 1849 for four horns, with the ORR soloists breathtaking in their virtuosity in the outer movements, using horns with rotary valves crooked in F. Otherwise, except in three specified movements, natural horns are used, braying clearly through orchestration which always used to be condemned as too thick. In his note, Gardiner fairly points out the merits of the 1841 version in transparency and other qualities, suggesting, as others have, that the doublings in the later version make it safer and more commonplace. Paradoxically in performance, Gardiner is if anything even more electrifying in the later, more thickly upholstered version, as ever clarifying textures and building up to a thrilling conclusion. Even the *Zwickauer* Symphony of 1832 emerges as very distinctive of Schumann.

The contrasts between Gardiner and Goodman in their approach to the numbered works are not as marked as expected, often as much a question of scale and recording quality as of interpretative differences, with Goodman's orchestra more intimate, and with the RCA sound a degree less brightly analytical. Both prefer fast speeds, with Goodman a shade more relaxed and Gardiner more incisive, pressing ahead harder, with syncopations – so important in Schumann – more sharply dramatic. One advantage that Gardiner has in his slightly bigger scale is that he brings out more light and shade, offering a wider dynamic range. Hence the solemn fourth movement of the *Rhenish* Symphony inspired by Cologne Cathedral – as with Goodman taken at a flowing speed – builds up more gradually in a bigger, far longer *crescendo*, in the end the more powerful for being held back at the start. Though the Goodman set still holds its place, Gardiner offers a conspectus of Schumann as symphonist that is all the richer and more illuminating for the inclusion of the extra rarities.

Symphonies Nos 1-4. Manfred, Op 115 – Overture **H**
Cleveland Orchestra / George Szell
Sony Classical Masterworks Heritage ② MH2K62349 Ⓜ
(135 minutes: ADD). Recorded 1958-60 ●

This famous set gives us the heart of George Szell, his feeling for style, for line and for Schumann's warming but fragile symphonic structures. Szell loved the Schumann symphonies (his eloquent booklet annotation makes that abundantly clear), but readers should be warned that he attempts to correct – and here we quote the Szell himself – 'minor lapses [in orchestration] due to inexperience' with 'remedies' that range from 'subtle adjustments of dynamic marks to the radical surgery of re-orchestrating whole stretches'. More often than not, the musical results serve Schumann handsomely. Szell sometimes takes *crescendo* to imply *accelerando*, but his insistence on watertight exchanges facilitates a snug fit between various instrumental choirs, the strings especially. Markings such as *Animato* (in the First Symphony's *Allegro molto vivace*) or *piano dolce* (in the same movement) are scrupulously observed, and so are most of Schumann's metronome markings. Playing standards are very high, but the close-set recordings occasionally undermine Szell's painstaking efforts to clarify Schumann's orchestration, the *Rhenish* being the worst offender.

The *Rhenish* again yields high musical dividends, with sensitively shaped central movements, but were we to single out just one track on the whole set, it would have to be the Second Symphony's *Adagio espressivo*, a performance of such warmth, nobility and elasticity (the latter not a quality normally associated with Szell) that it is tempting to grant it the accolade of 'best ever'. The *Manfred* Overture is given a wildly spontaneous performance (Szell's rostrum footwork is dramatically audible), with extreme tempos and some brilliant playing. Sometimes you may feel that Szell was being overprotective towards the music and that the same interpretations played live might have thrown caution to the wind. Still, Szell should certainly be granted equal status with his bargain stablemates Kubelík and Sawallisch. Both are perhaps marginally more spontaneous in the First and Third Symphonies, but Szell's loving exegeses underline details in the music that you won't have heard on many other recordings. Transfers and presentation are superb.

Symphony No 2

Symphony No 2. Konzertstück in F, Op 86. Manfred, Op 115 – Overture

Philharmonia Orchestra / Christian Thielemann

DG 453 482-2GH (76 minutes: DDD) Ⓕ

Recorded 1996 ○○

This programme is brilliantly designed for continuous listening. Thielemann is his own man, making no stylistic concessions to 'historically informed' performance. The disc begins with the *Manfred* Overture: its opening three chords are very smoothly delivered (they are usually incisive and strong), but they are justified by the spacious gravity and dignity of what follows. You may find this *Manfred* too ready to yield to introspective slower motion (a feature of the performance of the Second Symphony). Then *Manfred*'s interior world is blown away by 'something quite curious' as Schumann described his *Konzertstück* for four horns and orchestra. Replace 'curious' with 'dazzling', even 'reckless', and you might gain a better idea of the piece. Here is playing of great brilliance and bravado.

We've not had a performance of the Second Symphony as satisfying since Karajan's and Sawallisch's from the early 1970s. On first hearing, one occasionally feels that Thielemann had lost his sense of proportion, principally in the *Scherzo*, whose much slower Trios can sound self-conscious. But, more often than not, a few bars further on, and the nature of the expression released by that slower tempo makes clear the reason for its choice. And in the Symphony's outer *Allegros* Thielemann always ensures enough urgent propulsion and springing energy to make workable his many slowings. Never do you feel the tension sagging as a result of a slowing; on the contrary, the contrasts invariably intensify the drama. The Symphony's *Adagio* (over 12 minutes of it; 10 minutes is the average) is the disc's principal glory: a wondrously sustained and shaped *cantabile*, with the essential bass-line well defined. It might be thought a risky business recording Schumann in a church, but the microphones are close and this ample sound offers a convincing focus and proportion.

Symphony No 3

Symphony No 3. Overture, Scherzo and Finale, Op 52. Genoveva Overture

Philharmonia Orchestra / Christian Thielemann

DG 459 680-2GH (65 minutes: DDD) Ⓕ

Recorded 1998 ●

Thielemann's *Rhenish* is less controversial than his recording of the Second Symphony; less prone, as his incensed detractors would put it, to being 'pulled about'. The Third Symphony is, after all, a less troubled piece, and here the degree of tempo modification is more traditional than radical. But this *Rhenish* is broadly conceived, with the kind of depth of tone and loving attention to detail that any fine orchestra would give willingly to Giulini. Parallels with Giulini extend to the surprisingly swiftly delivered 'cathedral polyphony' of the fourth movement. It is taken (like Norrington!) almost at Schumann's metronome marking – considerably quicker than Karajan and Sawallisch – and has, in context, the feeling of a prelude to the finale. But its grandeur is far from compromised. There is a marvellous depth of tone, attack and wonderful resonant glow to the playing, with the antiphonally divided first and second violins filling the spectrum and illuminating the counterpoint. Nowadays it is rare to encounter Schumann playing and recording that, to this degree, seeks out and illuminates the lyricism, the majesty, the poetry and the joy of the *Rhenish*, and always expands magnificently for its moments of arrival. It is also unusual to hear this kind of bloom on the playing. Some of it comes courtesy of DG's spacious Watford Colosseum setting (with its skilfully contrived perspectives), but the majority of it is enabled by Thielemann from his players.

The Overture to *Genoveva* is almost equally fine, if without the drama one might have expected. Rather, the texture and workings here are integrated into an immensely satisfying, euphonious whole. Only in the *Overture, Scherzo and Finale* does Thielemann's broad manner work against the music: maybe the playing is less consistently resolute because the 'interpretation' is less settled in Thielemann's mind, or perhaps all it needed was another complete take. After Sawallisch or Goodman, most of it will come across as an overly serious, if amiable chug, with moments of fussiness (Schumann's *Vivo* and *Vivace* markings are largely ignored). Yet, even here, the *Meistersingerisch* gait may appeal, and the rich and splendid *maestoso* realization of the finale's main idea from 6'47" a form of justification for the broad manner, though the indulged lyrical response to it half a minute later is dangerously close to parody. But Thielemann's *Rhenish* is very special.

Symphony No 4

Schumann Symphony No 4
Schubert Symphony No 4 in C minor, D417, 'Tragic'
Mendelssohn Die schöne Melusine, Op 32
Berlin Philharmonic Orchestra / Nikolaus Harnoncourt
Teldec 4509-94543-2 (77 minutes: DDD) Ⓜ
Recorded live in 1995

'I think of it as one of the greatest symphonic poems' Harnoncourt has said of *Die schöne Melusine*. A bold claim, but here indeed is a bold and beauteous performance. Beauty first, 'the beauty of calm waters' as Tovey described the opening: upwardly curling mother-of-pearl Berlin winds and strings. Then boldness: and here the strongly rhythmic second theme is subjected to such a dramatic *animato* that its definition may strike you as initially blurred (a momentary impression though, and the Overture as a whole benefits from Harnoncourt's tempo contrasts).

The Berliners' musical collective would appear to have had a profound (and positive) effect on Harnoncourt in the Schubert. Compare, for instance, the slow movement with his Concertgebouw recording (part of a cycle: see the review under Schubert; refer to the Index to Reviews): there, the *Andante*'s relatively detached period manners are here (at a slower tempo, though still an *Andante*) transformed into a very real beauty and eloquence of phrase and expression. Very startling, if you don't know Harnoncourt's Amsterdam recording, is the removal of eight bars (from the printed editions) in the first movement's exposition, and Harnoncourt's fateful ('Tragic'?) half-tempo delivery of the finale's closing unison C chords.

Dramatic delaying tactics – whether tiny hesitations or huge fermatas – have always been a feature of Harnoncourt's conducting. Together with his insistent accentuation, sudden contrasts of dynamics, texture and tempo (for example, *Scherzo*/Trio tempos), you may feel that this Schumann Fourth (the familiar revision) sets out to contradict the symphony's apparent continuity, certainly compared to a performance like Wand's on RCA. But then, this is a performance that can catch fire spectacularly in a way that few others do, especially in the symphony's closing stages. The Berliners' playing is magnificent, the sound present and spacious.

Piano Quintet in E flat major, Op 44

Piano Quintet in E flat, Op 44. Andante and Variations, Op 46. Piano Quartet in E flat, Op 47. Fantasiestücke, Op 73. Adagio and Allegro in A flat, Op 70. Märchenbilder, Op 113. Violin Sonata No 2 in D minor, Op 121a **Marie-Luise Neunecker** *hn* a**Dora Schwarzberg, Lucy Hall** *vns* **Nobuko Imai** *va* **Natalia Gutman, Mischa Maisky** *vcs* a**Martha Argerich, Alexandre Rabinovitch** *pf*
EMI ② CDS5 55484-2 (146 minutes: DDD) Ⓕ
Recorded live in 1994

After 'one memorable day of rehearsal', as the introductory note puts it, Martha Argerich and a group of friends recorded this generously long programme at a public concert in Holland 'with the enthusiasm and intimate inspiration of a house-party'. The rarity is the *Andante and Variations*, Op 46, here brought up with all the spontaneous freshness of new discovery in a performance as enjoyable for its self-generating continuity as its diversity. Argerich and her fellow pianist, Rabinovitch divide keyboard responsibilities in the remainder of the programme. Her own major triumph comes in the Quintet (with truly inspirational help from Maisky's cello). Every note tingles with life and colour in an arrestingly imaginative reading of exemplary textural transparency. In none of the more familiar works in the concert is that little extra stimulus of live as opposed to studio recording combined with more finesse and finish than here.

In the Quartet Rabinovitch is a little less successful in concealing Schumann's inclination to entrust too much to his own instrument, with some aggressive accentuation *en route*. The finale is breathlessly, albeit excitably, fast. Rabinovitch is joined by Marie-Luise Neunecker in a hearty performance on the second disc of the *Adagio and Allegro* for horn and piano.

In the smaller pieces Argerich reaffirms herself as an artist of 'temperament', much given to the impulse of the moment. In place of clarinet, the Op 73 *Fantasiestücke* are played here with cello (Natalia Gutman), one of Schumann's two sanctioned alternatives despite its low-lying voice. However, in the *Märchenbilder* she partners the prescribed viola (Nobuko Imai). The recording itself is pleasingly natural. And there is heartening audience applause, judiciously unprotracted, as a further reminder that we are at a live performance.

String Quartets, Op 41

String Quartets, Op 41 – No 1 in A minor; No 3 in A
St Lawrence Quartet (Geoff Nuttall, Barry Shiffman *vns* Lesley Robertson *va* Marina Hoover *vc*)
EMI CDC5 56797-2 (59 minutes: DDD) Ⓕ
Recorded 1998

String Quartets, Op 41 – No 1 in A minor; No 2 in F; No 3 in A **P**

Eroica Quartet (Peter Hanson, Lucy Howard *vns* Gustav Clarkson *va* David Watkin *vc*)

Harmonia Mundi HMU90 7270 (79 minutes: DDD) Ⓕ

Recorded 1999

Schumann's relief and joy on Clara's return after her first extended concert tour since their recent marriage resulted in a great upsurge of creative activity in the summer of 1842. First to emerge were his only three string quartets, all completed within a couple of months not long after his 32nd birthday.

After occasional music-making together, Canadian artists the St Lawrence Quartet formed a permanent group in 1989, and are now established as ensemble-in-residence at California's Stanford University. 'I don't think I've heard them play a single phrase with anything less than life-and-death urgency' is perhaps the most pertinent critical comment in EMI's introductory note. Here, in their début recording, studio discipline – plus respect for Schumann's own veering from wayward romanticism towards a new classical control – brings its rewards in performances of irresistible youthful immediacy and intensity while at the same time, through the individuality of each strand in the argument, opening your ears anew to the sheer skill of the craftsmanship. The full, forward succulence of the recorded tone will also play a large part in winning these works new admirers.

Whereas the St Lawrence's EMI coupling plays for just on an hour, the Eroica's Harmonia Mundi issue, lasting for some 80 minutes, offers all three works at the same full price. The recorded tone here is a little less voluptuous, a little more astringent. But the main difference lies in this group's avowed pursuit of 'period style'. This neither robs their playing of emotion in slow tempo, nor of vitality elsewhere. But the end result could be summarised as more objectively classical than that of the fervently committed, open-hearted, vibrato-full Canadians.

Their recourse to the autograph scores reveals a structural change of outstanding interest: that what we now know as the four-bar *stringendo* leading from the First Quartet's slow A minor introduction into the main *Allegro* (surprisingly in F major) was in fact originally conceived as an arresting start to the second F major Quartet itself. Other small changes of prime interest to this group would seem to lie in details of fingering and bowing possibly suggested by Ferdinand David (leader of Leipzig's Gewandhaus Orchestra) when the Quartets were first tried out at Clara's 23rd birthday party that September.

In the First Quartet's opening 6/8 *Allegro* one wonders if the Eroica's insistent second-main-beat accentuation slightly disrupts continuity of line (as again in the *Scherzo*'s central Intermezzo). Nor do they dispel the feeling that Schumann's intricate syncopation in the course of the Second Quartet's variation movement defeats its own ends as the average ear so soon translates compound triple rhythm into simple duple. But both these new arrivals are more than welcome companions for the Melos Quartet's trilogy (DG – nla) of so many years ago.

Piano Trios

Awards 1999

Piano Trios – No 1 in D minor, Op 63; No 2 in F, Op 80

Florestan Trio (Anthony Marwood *vn* Richard Lester *vc* Susan Tomes *pf*)

Hyperion CDA67063 (57 minutes: DDD) Ⓕ

Recorded 1998 ●●●

For those who have always thought of Schumann's First Piano Trio as his finest chamber work after the Piano Quintet, the Florestan Trio may encourage you to think again about the Second Trio – a wonderful piece, full of poetic ideas. The artists make vigorous work of the first movement's urgent thematic interrelations but the real surprise is the third movement, a lilting barcarolle awash with significant counterpoint, although the heart of the Trio is its slow second movement – deeply personal music. The differences in the trios are more marked than their similarities. The Second Trio is mellow, loving and conversational, but the First is troubled, tense, even tragic – save, perhaps, for its Mendelssohnian finale. The Florestan Trio realises the music's myriad perspectives, coaxing its arguments rather than confusing them. Marwood employs some subtle *portamento* and varies his use of vibrato, whereas Susan Tomes never forces her tone. Real teamwork, equally in evidence for the gently cantering *Scherzo* and the fine, elegiac slow movement.

Piano Trio No 3 in G minor, Op 110. Fantasiestücke, Op 88. Piano Quartet in E flat, Op 47[a]

[a]**Thomas Riebl** *va* **Florestan Trio** (Anthony Marwood *vn* Richard Lester *vc* Susan Tomes *pf*)

Hyperion CDA67175 (71 minutes: DDD) Ⓕ

Recorded 1999 ●

It's scarcely surprising that a group with the name of Florestan should have an extra-special feeling for the composer who chose it as one of his own two youthful pseudonyms. After their 1999 *Gramophone* Award-winning disc of the first two piano trios, these players now champion three works which are less frequently encountered in concert, proving once again how a revelatory interpretation can make all of us think again.

The G minor Piano Trio (No 3) of 1851 suffers from over-repetitive, at times perfunctory, rhythmic patterning. But thanks to the mercurial vitality and the spontaneous response to every passing innuendo from all three interwoven voices, not a note here sounds unmotivated.

The three fanciful 1842 miniatures for piano trio (revised under the title of *Fantasiestücke* in 1849) have long, and rightly, been criticised for the dominance of the keyboard in all but the third, entitled 'Duet'. Susan Tomes makes no attempt to disguise this.

Last but not least, the Piano Quartet of 1842, long overshadowed by its much-loved romantic forerunner, the Piano Quintet. Misha Donat's appreciative note reminds us that even the loyal Clara waited some seven years before taking it into her repertory. In this work the rarely silent piano must not be allowed to dominate, which is why first praise goes to Susan Tomes for so keen an ear for balance. The *Scherzo* has a Mendelssohnian, elfin fleetness, and the finale (surely Schumann's *ne plus ultra* in exhilarating contrapuntal ingenuity) an exemplary textural clarity. The slow movement, played with a touching simplicity, speaks as eloquently as any of the composer's Clara-inspired love-songs. Excellently recorded, this welcome disc should win all three works a new lease of life.

Violin Sonatas

Violin Sonatas – No 1 in A minor, Op 105; No 2 in D minor, Op 121
Gidon Kremer *vn* **Martha Argerich** *pf*
DG 419 235-2GH (49 minutes: DDD) Ⓕ ●

Schumann's two violin sonatas are late works, dating from 1851, and both were written quickly, apparently in four and six days respectively. This rapidity of composition is nowhere evident except perhaps in the vigour and enthusiasm of the music. Argerich and Kremer, both mercurial and emotionally charged performers, subtly balance the ardent Florestan and dreamily melancholic Eusebius elements of Schumann's creativity. This is even more striking in the Second Sonata, a greater work than its twin, thematically vigorous with a richness and scope that make it a striking as well as ideally structured work. Kremer and Argerich have established a close and exciting duo partnership and this fine recording shows what like minds can achieve in music so profoundly expressive as this.

Violin Sonatas Nos 1 and 2; No 3 in A minor – Intermezzo
Ilya Kaler *vn* **Boris Slutsky** *pf*
Naxos 8 550870 (51 minutes: DDD) Ⓢ
Recorded 1993

These performances, powerfully recorded in Indiana by these two young Russian artists, are most enjoyable. The passion of their playing is perhaps not wholly Germanic, but every artist legitimately brings something of himself to the music he performs, and nothing here takes us out of touch with Schumann's world. There is an impressive intensity to this playing, although refinement and tenderness are rightly also present. Kaler and Slutsky mould these melodies well; it's a matter of timing as well as tone and dynamics, as the *Allegretto* of the A minor Sonata shows. The same movement also demonstrates how they follow Schumann naturally through his characteristically rapid changes of mood, while the finale that follows has power and purpose. The single movement from the composite 'FAE Sonata' dedicated to Joseph Joachim, in which Schumann collaborated with the young Brahms and Albert Dietrich, makes a useful bonus in a disc which would otherwise last under 50 minutes. The Naxos disc at super-bargain price represents fine value.

Davidsbündlertänze, Op 6

Etudes symphoniques, Op 13 (1852 version). Arabeske in C, Op 18. Davidsbündlertänze, Op 6. Blumenstück in D flat, Op 19
András Schiff *pf*
Teldec 4509-90176 2 (76 minutes: DDD) Ⓜ
Recorded 1995

Schumann was a great re-thinker, in Schiff's opinion not always for the better in later life – hence his choice of Schumann's original (1837) conception of the *Davidsbündlertänze* rather than its more usually heard 1851 revision. Except for a touch of mischief (subsequently removed) at the end of No 9, textual differences are slight. But Schiff prefers the fewer repeat markings in the first edition, so that ideas never lose their freshness. More importantly, the exceptional immediacy and vividness of his characterization reminds us that initially Schumann signed nearly all of these 18 'bridal thoughts' with an F (the impetuous Florestan) or an E (the introspective, visionary Eusebius) – or sometimes both – as well as including literary inscriptions (and one or two more colourful expression marks) as a clue to the mood of the moment.

Schiff laughs and teases, storms and yearns, as if the hopes and dreams of the youthful Robert, forbidden all contact with his distant beloved, were wholly his own – there and then. The impatient Florestan fares particularly well. For the much metamorphosed *Etudes symphoniques* Schiff chooses the generally used late version of 1852 with its admirably tautened finale. Here, his bold, firmly contoured approach reaffirms it as the most magisterially 'classical' work the young Schumann ever wrote. Schiff emphasises its continuity and unity as a whole. Even the five so-called supplementary variations emerge as more purposeful, less ruminative, than often heard. These Schiff wisely offers as an independent group at the end. The recital is completed by the *Arabeske* and *Blumenstück*, again played with a very strong sense of direction, even if Schiff is not yet Richter's equal in disguising the repetitiveness of the latter. Nothing but praise for the naturalness of the reproduction.

Etudes symphoniques, Op 13. Carnaval, Op 9. Kreisleriana, Op 16. Papillons, Op 2. Kinderszenen, Op 15. Davidsbündlertänze, Op 6. Fantasiestücke, Op 12 – No 1, Des Abends. Waldszenen, Op 82 – No 7, Vogel als Prophet Ⓗ
Alfred Cortot *pf*
Music & Arts mono ② CD-858 (131 minutes: ADD) Ⓜ
Recorded 1928-48 ●

It is good to have this Music & Arts sharply focused issue of Cortot's evergreen, ever-fresh performances on a well-presented two-CD set. These recordings have been reissued many times before. How many artists, today, one wonders, could hope to garner such tribute? So here, again, is that magically floated *cantabile* tugging at the heart-strings in 'Des Abends' (how one longs for the rest of the cycle) yet maintained with the flawless line and impetus of a great singer. In the *Davidsbündlertänze*, one of Cortot's most poetically potent if battle-scarred recordings, his confusion in Florestan's *schneller* in No 3 or in the vaulting leaps of No 12 is, perhaps, not quite what the composer had in mind in his instruction, *Mit Humor*. Yet who can resist his *dolce cantando* in No 14, the gem of his Schumann, alive with a rich polyphonic pianistic tradition that Alfred Brendel so sadly claims has virtually vanished from the music scene.

In *Kinderszenen* the 'poet' of the epilogue is at once Schumann and Cortot, creator and re-creator, and in the *Etudes symphoniques* the gold-dust scattering of the posthumous studies throughout the main work is done with such passion and inwardness that only a Beckmesser could possibly object. Playing like this seems light years away from today's style or standard. But *pace* Cortot, his idiosyncrasy, his pell-mell virtuosity and poetic ecstasy may strike a foreign and even alien note in our more puritan times yet, as Yvonne Lefebure so eloquently put it, 'even his wrong notes were those of a god'.

Davidsbündlertänze, Op 6. Fantasiestücke, Op 12
Benjamin Frith *pf*
Naxos 8 550493 (63 minutes: DDD) Ⓢ
Recorded 1991

The prize-winning British pianist Benjamin Frith indulges the *Davidsbündlertänze*'s caprice, highlighting the contrasts between fast and slower pieces, and summoning his excellent technique for some exciting pianism. But then contrast lies at the very heart of Schumann's inspiration. Frith favours impulse over refinement, and isn't afraid to throw caution to the winds, if the mood dictates. His *Fantasiestücke*, too, are forthright and outspoken, although 'Des Abends', 'Warum' and 'Ende vom Lied' each contain plenty of poetry. Naxos's recording is excellent. Certainly recommended, not only for the budget-conscious collector, but for those who enjoy youthful pianistic exuberance.

Fantasie in C, Op 17

Fantasie in C, Op 17
Piano Sonata No 1 in F sharp minor, Op 11.
Maurizio Pollini *pf*
DG 423 134-2GH (63 minutes: ADD) Ⓕ
OO

These works grew from Schumann's love and longing for his future wife Clara. Pollini's performances are superb, not least because they are so truthful to the letter of the score. By eschewing all unspecified rubato in the *Fantasie*, he reminds us that the young Schumann never wrote a more finely proportioned large-scale work; this feeling for structure, coupled with exceptional emotional intensity, confirms it as one of the greatest love-poems ever written for the piano. His richly characterised account of the Sonata is refreshingly unmannered. Certainly the familiar charges of protracted patterning in the faster flanking movements are at once dispelled by his rhythmic *élan*, his crystalline texture and his ear for colour. The CD transfer is most successful.

Fantasie in C, Op 17. Faschingsschwank aus Wien, Op 26. Papillons, Op 2 H
Sviatoslav Richter *pf*
EMI Studio CDM7 64625-2 (67 minutes: ADD/DDD) Ⓜ
Recorded 1961-62 OOO

There can surely be no doubt as to Richter's current status as elder statesman of the piano world. And collectors now have a bewildering array of his recent, mainly live performances and reissues to choose from. Richter's Schumann is unequalled. The *Fantasia* is arguably Schumann's keyboard masterpiece. And Richter plays it better than other pianists. Nobody can phrase as beautifully as he can, or produce those marvellously soft accompaniments beneath quietly singing tunes or toss off the middle movement with such speed and brilliance. There is astonishing poetry in his playing. It almost amounts to a rediscovery of the work.

And the same could be said of *Faschingsschwank aus Wien* and *Papillons*. (The way he plays the main theme of the latter should make you buy this disc if nothing else does – he seems to add stature to the work.) His assets in all of these works are, first, an unusually musical sense of phrasing. Secondly, he can reduce an accompaniment to a mere murmur without any loss of evenness so that a tune above it can sing even when it is soft. Thirdly, he uses a great deal of rubato, but always with impeccable taste; his rubato in slow passages has a mesmeric quality only partly due to the fact that he usually plays such passages much slower than other pianists. Fourthly, he has faultless technique. His superiority is apparent throughout. The recording is magnificent for its date. Classic performances which no pianophile should be without.

Fantasie in C, Op 17. Piano Sonata No 1
Leif Ove Andsnes *pf*
EMI CDC5 56414-2 (64 minutes: DDD) Ⓕ
Recorded 1996 O

Leif Ove Andsnes never lets us forget that Schumann was a mere 25 when writing his First Piano Sonata. His recording, with its youthful lightness of heart, is most refreshing. With fastish tempo and delectably light, scintillating fingerwork he dances through the first movement's sometimes all-too-persistent fandango rhythm, and though adopting an unspecified slower tempo for the smoother second subject maintains an unbroken continuity of flow from first note to last. The Aria sings with a spring-like wonderment and grace. And even if the tongue-in-cheek pomposity at the start of the

'Intermezzo' section is not fully relished, his lightness and clarity of texture and his rhythmic buoyancy win the day in the *Scherzo*, and yet again in the finale, which in heavier hands can so easily sound protracted.

The *Fantasie* comes across with arrestingly impulsive immediacy. Andsnes's extreme contrasts of urgency and poetic musing in the first movement might be thought over-episodic, but the requested fantasy and passion are all there. The central movement is brilliantly excitable and his acute response to every passing innuendo makes the finale a truly moving human confession – albeit in a different world from Pollini's trance-like, superhuman inner calm. Apart from brief loss of refinement in the *Fantasie*'s moments of heightened fervour, the tone-quality of the recording matches the distinction of the playing.

Schumann Fantasie. March in G minor, Op 76 No 2. Concert Studies on Caprices by Paganini, Op 10 – No 4 in C minor; No 5 in B minor; No 6 in E minor. Novellette in F, Op 21 No 1. Blumenstück in D flat, Op 19. Vier Nachtstücke, Op 23 **Brahms** Piano Sonatas – No 1 in C, Op 1; No 2 in F sharp minor, Op 2. Variations on a Theme by Paganini, Op 35. Capriccio in C, Op 76 No 8. Intermezzo in E minor, Op 116 No 5. Ballade in G minor, Op 118 No 3. Rhapsody in E flat, Op 119 No 4
Sviatoslav Richter *pf*
Philips ③ 438 477-2PH3 (184 minutes: DDD) Ⓕ
●●

Variable reproduction, coupled with this highly-strung artist's own unpredictability, inevitably results in ups and downs. But for the one-and-a-half discs of Schumann alone, this album can be cherished as a collector's piece. There is surely no one more finely attuned to Schumann's secret inner world. The miniatures give particular pleasure and how keenly he responds to that element of 'strangeness blended with the beautiful' (as romanticism was once defined) in the four *Nachtstücke* written with a supernatural premonition of his brother's death. All technical challenges are dissolved into the purest poetry in the three all-too-rarely heard *Concert Studies on Caprices by Paganini* and in the major work, the great Op 17 *Fantasie*, his own emotional warmth is fortunately matched by some of the ripest sonority that we're given in this album. It's a performance which obviously comes from the deepest places of his heart.

There are memorable things too in the two early Brahms sonatas, not least the strain of nostalgic lyricism so beautifully drawn from the first movement of No 1 in C major. The two sets of *Paganini* Variations in their turn bring bewitchingly light and delicate prestidigitation and seductively sung melody. But in burlier bravura, and notably in both excitable homecomings, there are some gaucheries and inaccuracies that would certainly not have got through in a studio recording. Of the miniatures, the intimate, elusive E minor *Intermezzo* is exquisitely phrased and shaded.

Fantasiestücke, Op 12a – No 1, Des Abends; No 2, Aufschwung; No 3, Warum?; No 5, In der Nacht; No 7, Traumes Wirren; No 8, Ende von Lied. Humoreske in B flat, Op 20a. Novelletten, Op 21b – No 1 in F; No 2 in D; No 8 in F sharp minor
Sviatoslav Richter *pf*
Melodiya mono 74321 29464-2 (71 minutes: ADD) Ⓜ
Recorded [a]1956 and [b]1960 ●

The booklet contains an anecdote about Arthur Rubinstein hearing Richter for the first time, 'It really wasn't anything out of the ordinary. Then at some point I noticed my eyes growing moist: tears began rolling down my cheeks ...'. What produces such a reaction cannot be put into words, but it probably has to do with Richter's uncanny ability to convey a sense of inevitability. In Schumann, for instance, Richter takes characterization and virtuosity in his stride and aims at the emotional truth beyond. Impetuosity and fantasy are there, but at the structural level rather than in the detail. The simplicity of his *Humoreske* gets to the heart of the matter as unerringly as the *élan* of his *Fantasiestücke* and the tensed steel of his *Novelettes*. Decent mono sound.

Kreisleriana, Op 16

Humoreske in B flat, Op 20. Kinderszenen, Op 15. Kreisleriana, Op 16
Radu Lupu *pf*
Decca 440 496-2DH (75 minutes: DDD) Ⓕ
Recorded 1993 ●●

As piano playing this disc has an aristocratic distinction reminiscent of Lipatti. As music-making it is underpinned by unselfconscious intuition, making you feel you are discovering the truth of the matter for the first time. It is difficult to recall a more revealing performance of Schumann's *Humoreske*. Lupu captures all the unpredictability of its swift-changing moods while at the same time imparting a sense of inevitability to the sequence as a whole. Florestan's caprice is as piquant as Eusebius's tenderness is melting. Yet there is an underlying unity in the diversity from Lupu, enhanced by most beautifully timed and shaded 'links'. Goodness knows how long this work has been in his repertory. But here it emerges with the keen edge of new love. Next, *Kinderszenen*: simplicity is its keynote. To begin with (as notably in the opening 'Von fremden Ländern und Menschen') you wonder if, in rejection of sentimentality, he might not be allowing himself enough time for wide-eyed wonderment. But you are soon won over by his limpid tonal palette and the sheer purity of his phrasing. Each piece tells its own magical little tale without the slightest trace of special pleading. Such pristine grace will never pall, however often heard. *Kreisleriana* in its turn offers rich contrasts of desperation, dedication and Hoffmannesque drollery. And except, perhaps, in the impetuous No 7 (taken dangerously fast), it brings further reminders that we are in the presence of a master pianist – among so much else able to rejoice in this work's endless dialogues between left hand and right with his opulent bass and gleaming treble. Reproduction is totally faithful throughout.

Kinderszenen, Op 15. Kreisleriana, Op 16
Martha Argerich *pf*
DG 410 653-2GH (52 minutes: DDD) Ⓕ
Recorded 1984

'A positively wild love is in some of the movements' so Schumann wrote to *Kreisleriana*'s only begetter, Clara Wieck. Martha Argerich's pianistically brilliant, highly charged recording makes that fact very clear. She is also at pains to emphasise the vein of caprice, even eccentricity, stemming from ETA Hoffmann, whose Kapellmeister Kreisler gave Schumann his title. Also, she is deeply appreciative of the searching introspective intensity of the slow numbers.

There's an enormous amount to admire and enjoy from this uncommonly individual artist, who always makes you listen to everything with new ears. Argerich's fast tempo is very fast – provocatively so in No 1 (especially the central episode in the major) and dangerously so in No 7 (where the fugal episode scarcely makes sense because it is so gabbled). As for the Hoffmannesque caprice, her No 8 is wholly winning. In the slow numbers the intensity of her involvement now and again finds outlet in impulsive little surges, alike of pace and dynamics, that can only be described as *echt* Argerich.

Argerich's *Kinderszenen* is a performance all children will love because of the vividness of the story-telling – not least in the whirlwind 'Catch me if you can', the dare-devil 'Knight of the Hobby-Horse', the eerie 'Frightening' and the deep drowsiness of 'Child falling asleep'. Adults, on the other hand, might find the reading over impressionable. Some may certainly prefer a rubato that draws less attention to itself.

Additional recommendation
Kreisleriana, Op 16
Kissin *pf*
Couplings: **Bach/Busoni** Chaconne. **Beethoven** Rondo Op 51 No2 and Rondo capriccio Op 129
RCA Victor Red Seal 09026 68911-2 (63 minutes: DDD) Ⓕ
The fantastic side of *Kreisleriana* is not always in focus here. That said, this is still a very enjoyable performance

Novelletten, Op 21

Allegro in B minor, Op 8. Novelletten, Op 21. Drei Fantasiestücke, Op 111. Gesänge der Frühe, Op 133
Ronald Brautigam *pf*
Olympia OCD436 (79 minutes: DDD) Ⓕ
Recorded 1993

The note reminds us that even the eight *Novelletten* chosen as the centrepiece here are not often heard in sequence as a set. Brautigam prefaces them with the early (1831-32) B minor *Allegro* originally intended as the first movement of a sonata. They are followed by the last two suites Schumann ever wrote for the piano – the *Gesänge der Frühe* only a year before his final breakdown. Most enjoyable is Brautigam's vitality – of imagination no less than of fingers. You are immediately gripped by his plunge into the Op 8 *Allegro*, with its arresting octave 'motto'. His mercurial fancy and ear for hidden melodic strands in the ensuing stream makes nonsense of hasty dismissal of this work as mere old-style virtuoso note-spinning. Moreover, such is his unflagging impulse in the eight *Novelletten* that you are never tempted to accuse Schumann of over-repetitively patterned figuration. Potently characterised and contrasted as are the three *Fantasiestücke*, Op 111 of 1851, Brautigam leaves no doubt as to their unity as a set – as he does again in the more elusive spiritual world of the five *Gesänge der Frühe*. The bright, clear tonal reproduction is acceptable enough.

Duets

Duets – Ländliches Lied, Op 29 No 1[bc]. Die Lotusblume, Op 33 No 3[bc]. Vier Duette, Op 34[ac]. Gedichte aus 'Liebesfrühling', Op 37[ac] – No 7, Schön ist das Fest des Lenzes; No 12, So wahr die Sonne scheinet. Drei Lieder, Op 43[bc]. Spanisches Liederspiel, Op 74 – No 2, Intermezzo[bc]; No 3, Liebesgram[bc]; In der Nacht[ac]. Vier Duette, Op 78[ac]. Lieder-Album für die Jugend, Op 79[bc] – No 10, Das Käuzlein; No 16, Weihnachtslied; No 19, Frühlings Ankunft; No 21, Kinderwacht. Minnespiel, Op 101[ac] – No 3, Ich bin dein Baum; No 7, Die tausend Grüsse. Spanische Liebeslieder, Op 138[bc] – No 4, Bedeckt mich mit Blumen; No 9, Blaue Augen hat das Mädchen. Sommerruh[bc]
[a]**Julia Varady** *sop* [b]**Peter Schreier** *ten* [c]**Dietrich Fischer-Dieskau** *bar* **Christoph Eschenbach** *pf*
DG Galleria 457 915-2GGA (61 minutes: ADD). Ⓜ
Texts and translations included. Recorded 1977

This is a model of a mid-price reissue – interesting, neglected material performed to perfection with texts and translations provided. Although Schumann's duets were primarily intended for home performance around the piano, they benefit enormously from readings by such fine artists as the three taking part in this recital – recorded in 1977, but sounding as if committed to disc yesterday, so excellent is the sound, so spontaneous the singing. Fischer-Dieskau claims the lion's share of the programme, duetting in turn with his wife Varady and with Schreier. Just occasionally, as in the delightful serenade, 'Unterm Fenster' from the Op 34 Duets, one wishes he had given place to his tenor colleague, who is in most ingratiating, mellifluous voice. The young Varady, with her vibrant tone and intense manner, is just as winning as her partners, nowhere more so than for 'In der Nacht', a setting that goes deeper than any of the other duets. Over a sinuous, chromatic obbligato on the piano, Schumann weaves a long, elegiac line for the voices. Wolf also set this text memorably and it's interesting to hear what Schumann does with another poem, *Bedeckt mich mit Blumen*, set so unforgettably by Wolf: the writing here has little of Wolf's intensity but has its own validity when sung with such romantic passion by the two men. That's followed by the pair hugely enjoying themselves in the paean to the beloved, 'Blaue Augen hat das Mädchen'. Finally there's a fascinating alternative version for two voices of the Heine poem *Die Lotusblume*, one of the composer's most popular pieces in his solo setting. Eschenbach's vivid, positive playing is another notable asset of this highly recommendable issue.

Frauenliebe und -leben, Op 42

Frauenliebe und -leben, Op 42. Gesänge, Op 31 – No 1, Die Löwenbraut; No 2, Die Kartenlegerin. Gedichte, Op 35 – No 1, Lust der Sturmnacht; No 8, Stille Liebe. Rose, Meer und Sonne, Op 37 No 9. Fünf Lieder, Op 40. Der Schatzgräber, Op 45 No 1. Volksliedchen, Op 51 No 2. Die Soldatenbraut, Op 64 No 1. Lieder-Album für die Jugend, Op 79 – No 5, Vom Schlaraffenland; No 22, Des Sennen Abscheid; No 26, Schneeglöcken. Mein schöner Stern!, Op 101 No 4. Abendlied, Op 107 No 6. Die Meerfee, Op 125 No 1. Dein Angesicht, Op 127 No 2
Anne Sofie von Otter *mez* **Bengt Forsberg** *pf*
DG 445 881-2GH (79 minutes: DDD). Texts and translations included. Recorded 1993 Ⓕ

This is one of those records where the promise of something exceptional in the first phrases is fully borne out by all that follows. The *Frauenliebe* cycle is sung by a character, as vividly defined as any Fiordiligi, Senta or Mimì in opera. Von Otter is one of those rare artists who can adapt the voice and yet be true to its natural identity. In these songs of Schumann (not only in the *Frauenliebe*) she seems, unselfconsciously, to find a new voice-personality for each and still to confine herself to what lies naturally within her scope, forcing nothing and falsifying nothing. The woman of the 'life and love' starts out as a girl. 'Seit ich ihn gesehen' has a shy, private rapture which then grows bold for 'Er, der Herrlichste von allen', frank in its enthusiasm, buoyant in the spirit of its rhythm, radiant as the voice rises to its highest notes. 'Ich kann's nicht fassen, nicht glauben' is fully outgoing, an expression of utter commitment, and the smile is always in the voice. The engagement-ring induces maturity, the girl now a woman. The wedding- day preparations, confiding of motherhood, dandling the baby, and then the emptiness of life at the husband's death: all are caught as in reality and in character. It is a completely absorbed and absorbing performance.

The generous selection of songs which follows works its spell partly by contrasts. The pastoral sweetness of 'Des Sennen Abschied' gives way to a grim, predatory ferocity of utterance in 'Der Schatzgräber', and the big Brahmsy sweep of 'Lust der Sturmnacht' throws into relief the wistfully tender mood of 'Dein Angesicht'. In these and in all else von Otter lights upon the right tone, and the right shades of that tone. The programme is well planned, too, rounded off with 'Rose, Meer und Sonne', sketching the melodies of *Frauenliebe und -leben* with which the recital began. Occasionally the piano is recorded too heavily or too prominently for the voice. But generally the sympathy and unanimity of singer and pianist are all that could be desired – as is the recital *in toto*. It doesn't matter how much of Schumann you already have on the shelves, this will still be a prized addition.

Frauenliebe und -leben, Op 42. Sieben Lieder, Op 104. Gedichte der Königen Maria Stuart, Op 135. Lieder und Gesänge – I, Op 27: No 1, Sag an, o lieber Vogel; No 4, Jasminenstrauch; III, Op 77: No 3, Geisternähe; No 4, Stiller Vorwurf; IV, Op 96: No 4, Gesungen!; No 5, Himmel und Erde. Romanzen und Balladen – III, Op 53: No 1, Blondels Lied; No 2, Loreley; IV, Op 64: No 1, Die Soldatenbraut. Die Kartenlegerin, Op 31 No 2
Juliane Banse *sop* **Graham Johnson** *pf*
Hyperion CDJ33103 (74 minutes: DDD) Texts and translations included. Includes readings of 'Traum der eignen Tage' and 'Nachschrift'. Ⓕ
Recorded 1997/8

This offering places Banse and Johnson among the most thoughtful and convincing of Schumann interpreters in the history of recording the composer's Lieder. From start to finish, in well-loved pieces and in others that will be new discoveries to many, the pair at once work in close concord and get to the heart of Schumann's very particular genius. The pair wholly dispel the oft-repeated view that Schumann's later songs are by and large failures: it is simply that the older man wrote differently from his younger, romantically exuberant self. Thus the 1852 settings of Mary Stuart unerringly capture the soul of the troubled Queen's predicaments through the most concise means. Not a florid or untoward gesture is allowed to destroy the mood of sustained concentration and intimate musings. Banse brings to the songs just the right sense of a person sharing her innermost thoughts with us, the mezzo-like warmth of her lower voice gainfully employed, Johnson's piano communing in consort with the voice.

Schumann showed himself equally in sympathy with the poems of Elisabeth Kulmann (Op 104), a susceptible girl who died at the age of 17, his writing here simple and apparently artless. The composer, amazingly, thinks himself into the thoughts of the imaginative, fanciful young poetess; so does his interpreter, Banse, here using a lighter, more palpitating tone. She is just as discriminating when preceding each song with Schumann's spoken introductions. She also recites the last poem of Chamisso's *Frauenliebe*, which Schumann declined to set. In the cycle itself she sings with consistent warmth and understanding; indeed comparisons seem beside the point, so satisfying is their interpretation, keenly paced, finely etched in terms of verbal emphasis, above all conveying the kaleidoscope of a woman's feelings depicted within. Johnson's commentary on the cycle is predictably enlightening, as – of course – are his detailed observations on the rest of the programme. The faultless recording completes one's pleasure in a very special issue.

Liederkreis, Op 39. Frauenliebe und leben, Op 42
Soile Isokoski *sop* **Marita Viitasalo** *pf*
Finlandia 0630-10924-2 (49 minutes: DDD). Texts and translations included. Recorded 1993-95 Ⓕ

This interpretation from this young Finnish soprano can stand comparison with the best. In her wonderfully straightforward and musical performance, she marries a sincere spontaneity with a warming sense of line and phrase, a style well learnt yet put to her own, positive purpose. Before you is the rapturous bride-to-be in all her moods, then the young woman struck almost dumb by unexpected grief. Nothing in her portrayal is forced or in the least contrived yet everything, felt from the heart, goes to it. And the voice itself? Well, reminders of Flagstad's richness, Ameling's naturalness and Price's precision are here to be heard and enjoyed. She is just as imaginative in Op 39 as in Op 42, giving a very central, unaffected account of the *Liederkreis* encompassing all its varied moods and one that makes its points unobtrusively and, as with Op 42, with the emphasis on long-breathed phrasing and rock-steady tone. The partnership with Viitasalo is obviously a fruitful one. The two artists think and 'breathe' alike though in Op 42 he is just occasionally too prominent, at least as recorded.

Liederkreis, Op 24 / Dichterliebe, Op 48

Liederkreis, Op. 24. Dichterliebe, Op. 48. Gesange, Op. 142 – Lehn deine Wang; Mein Wagen rollet langsam. Myrthen, Op. 25 – Die Lotosblume; Was will die einsame Tranen?; Du bist wie eine Blume. Der arme Peter, Op. 53 No. 3. Tragodie, Op. 64 No. 3.
Wolfgang Holzmair *bar* **Imogen Cooper** *pf*
Philips 446 086-2PH (67 minutes: DDD) Ⓕ
Texts and translations included

Here we have an ideal partnership in a thoughtfully conceived programme perfectly suited to its extraordinary talents. Holzmair's plangent, tenorish, gently vibrating voice, just right for Schumann, is beautifully supported and encouraged by Cooper's discerning, subtly arched playing, both wholly responsive to the love and longing expressed in Heine's wonderful poetry. The interpretations abound in verbal and musical perceptions yet nothing is ever in the least exaggerated. From the very first notes of the very first song, 'Mein Wagen rollet langsam', you know you are in for a special experience as you sense the rapport between the two artists, notice the flow and freedom of Cooper's playing, the feeling for the text in Holzmair's singing. Even when a word is emphasised, as at 'verdorben' at the end of 'Tragodie II' it is not done simply for effect, but because the underlining is wholly appropriate. In 'Die Lotusblume', the song's perfection untouched by familiarity, the plaintive quality in Holzmair's singing is wonderfully seconded by Cooper's soft-grained piano.

In Op 24, revelations come apace. Witness the lovely playing in the postlude to the third song, the unanimity of thought in the fourth, the dramatic impetus of the sixth, the sense of finality in the last. *Dichterliebe* is if anything even more satisfying, tempos, phrasing, inner feeling all confidently welded into a convincing whole, so much so that to single out any song, any detail would be out of place. Just listen – and be moved and delighted by a superb interpretation. To complete one's pleasure, the recording, made in the Esterhaza Palace at Eisenstadt, is faultlessly balanced, voice and instrument forward yet never obtrusively so. This is a 'must' for all Lieder enthusiasts. Those who aren't in that category ought to be converted if they try this disc.

Liederkreis, Op 24. Dichterliebe, Op 48. Belsatzar, Op 57. Abends am Strand, Op 45 No 3. Die beiden Grenadiere, Op 49 No 1. Lieder und Gesänge, Op 127 – No 2, Dein Angesicht; No 3, Es leuchtet meine Liebe. Vier Gesänge, Op 142 – No 2, Lehn deine Wang; No 4, Mein Wagen rollet langsam
Ian Bostridge *ten* **Julius Drake** *pf*
EMI CDC5 56575-2 (69 minutes: DDD) Ⓕ
Texts and translations included. Recorded 1997

Bostridge makes one think anew about the music in hand, interpreting all these songs as much through the mind of the poet as that of the composer and, being youthful himself, getting inside the head of the vulnerable poet in his many moods. That, quite apart from his obvious gifts as a singer and musician, is what raises Bostridge above most of his contemporaries who so often fail to live the words they are singing. Every one of the magnificent Op 24 songs has some moment of illumination, whether it's the terror conveyed so immediately – and immediacy of reaction is of the essence allround here – in 'Schöne Wiege', the breathtaking beauty and sorrow of 'Anfang wollt ich' or the breadth and intensity of 'Mit Myrten und Rosen'. In between the two cycles comes a group of the 1840 Leipzig settings that adumbrates every aspect of Bostridge's – and his equally perceptive partner's – attributes.

The vivid word-painting in *Belsatzar* brings the Old Testament scene arrestingly before us. The inward fantasy of *Abends am Strand* is keenly evoked with an appropriately raw touch on the word 'Schrein' ('howl'). Then there's the unexpected heroic touch the tenor brings to *Die beiden Grenadiere*, where Drake's imaginative contribution helps to paint the patriotic picture. Perhaps best of all is the unjustly neglected *Es leuchtet meine Liebe*, a melodrama here perfectly enacted by both performers. *Mein Wagen rollet langsam* forms a perfect introduction, in its lyrical freedom, to *Dichterliebe*, an interpretation to rank with the best available in terms of the sheer beauty of the singing and acute response to its sustained inspiration. Listen to the wonder brought to the discovery of the flowers and angels in 'Im Rhein', the contained anger of 'Ich grolle nicht', the sense of bereavement in 'Hör ist das Liedchen' and you'll judge this is an interpretation of profundity and emotional identification, the whole cycle crowned by the sensitivity of

Drake's playing of the summarizing postlude. To complete one's pleasure EMI has provided an exemplary and forward recording balance.

Liederkreis, Op 24. Dichterliebe, Op 48
Matthias Goerne *bar* **Vladimir Ashkenazy** *pf*
Decca 458 265-2DH (50 minutes: DDD). Texts and translations included. Recorded 1997 Ⓕ OO

Matthias Goerne is with little doubt the most probing male Lieder singer to emerge from Germany in recent years, an artist of extraordinary magnetism both in his live performances and on disc. With his dark, velvet timbre, intense *legato* line and searching response to the fluctuating shades of Heine's bittersweet verses, Goerne gives mesmeric readings of both *Dichterliebe* and the Op 24 *Liederkreis*. Partly because of the colour of his voice, partly because of some unusually broad tempos, both cycles emerge as more sombre and haunted than in the comparably fine recordings by Wolfgang Holzmair and Ian Bostridge. The fourth song of the *Liederkreis*, 'Lieb Liebchen', seems suffused with genuine death-weariness – barely a hint here of wryness or irony. In the following 'Schöne Wiege meiner Leiden', Goerne captures the feverishness of Heine's original which Schumann's lulling, nostalgic melody tends to mitigate; later in the song the lover's tottering reason and death-longing are chillingly realised.

In the first two songs of *Dichterliebe* Goerne underlines the sense of sorrow and regret with which Schumann shadows Heine's limpid love lyrics. And this sets the tone for a brooding, intensely inward reading, flaring into self-lacerating bitterness in 'Ich grolle nicht' and 'Das ist ein Flöten und Geigen', hardening into an iron stoicism in the closing song, before the overwhelming sense of longing and loss in the last line. Throughout, Ashkenazy is a positive, sympathetic partner, though here and there his sharply etched playing can be overassertive. If some may understandably prefer a higher, lighter voice in these cycles, Goerne is the equal of both Holzmair and Bostridge in interpretative insight and tonal beauty, and ventures a more daring range of expression than either.

Dichterliebe, Op 48. Die Lotosblume, Op 25 No 7. Die Minnesänger, Op 33 No 2. Romanzen und Balladen – II, Op 49: No 1, Die beiden Grenadiere; III, Op 53: No 3, Der arme Peter; IV, Op 64: No 3, Tragödie. Belsatzar, Op 57. Lieder und Gesänge – Op 127: No 2, Dein Angesicht; No 3, Es leuchtet meine Liebe. Gesänge, Op 142 – No 2, Lehn deine Wang; No 4, Mein Wagen rollet langsam **C Schumann** Lieder, Op 13 – No 1, Ich stand in dunklen Träumen; No 2, Sie liebten sich beide. Loreley. Volkslied
Christopher Maltman *bar* **Graham Johnson** *pf*
Hyperion CDJ33105 (77 minutes: DDD) Ⓕ
Texts and translations included. Recorded 2000 OO

With this superbly executed recital, Maltman leaps in a single bound into the front rank of Lieder interpreters today. Seemingly inspired by the wonderful programme assigned him by Johnson, he executes it with bitingly intense tone and an innate feeling for the German language, his high baritone easily encompassing every test placed on it by the lengthy programme. There are so many deeply satisfying performances here of mostly familiar songs that it is difficult to know which to alight on for special praise, but the last two groups – the sad, frightening tale of the near-deranged Peter and the great *Dichterliebe* cycle – undoubtedly and rightly form the climax of the recital.

Maltman's and Johnson's account of the cycle reminds one of the underrated version made long ago by Waechter and Brendel (Decca – nla): it has the same immediacy, the same perceptions, with the singer's voice on each occasion being of the ideal weight and tessitura, and in its absolute prime. All the inner melancholy of words and notes, all their variety of texture are adumbrated. And here we have the added advantage of Johnson's inspired exegesis of the work in his accompanying notes.

Johnson also points out the foretaste of Mahler in the third of the Peter songs, a piece Maltman sings with just the right touch of vulnerability. He is just as sensitive in such well-known pieces as *Die Lotusblume* and *Dein Angesicht*, and brings tremendous impulse of drama to the familiar *Die beiden Grenadiere*, here sounding new-minted. The songs by Clara are a pleasing bonus, but the difference between talent and genius is apparent in comparing her setting of 'Es fiel ein Reif' (from Heine's *Volkslied*) with Schumann's. A perfectly balanced recording adds to one's pleasure in listening to this generously filled CD, which is up to the high standard of this series to date.

Liederkreis, Op 24. Myrthen, Op 25 – No 7, Die Lotosblume; No 21, Was will die einsame Träne?; No 24, Du bist wie eine Blume. Romanzen und Balladen – Op 45: No 3, Abends am Strand; Op 49: No 1, Die beiden Grenadiere; No 2, Die feindlichen Brüder; Op 53: No 3, Der arme Peter; Op 64: No 3, Tragödie. Belsatzar, Op 57. Lieder und Gesänge, Op 127 – No 2, Dein Angesicht; No 3, Es leuchtet meine Liebe. Gesänge, Op 142 – No 2, Lehn deine Wang; No 4, Mein Wagen rollet langsam
Stephan Genz *bar* **Christoph Genz** *ten*
Claar ter Horst *pf*
Claves CD50-9708 (59 minutes: DDD). Texts and translations included. Recorded 1996-97 Ⓕ O

This is a recital of promise and fulfilment. Stephan Genz's voice and style are as wide-ranging as his mode of expression. He lives every moment of Op 24, entering into all aspects of Schumann's settings and Heine's originals yet never overstepping the mark in his verbal painting. The other Heine settings receive no less than their due. The sensuous and plaintive qualities in Genz's tone are well suited to the three Heine poems in *Myrthen*. In contrast he rises to the histrionic challenges of *Die beiden Grenadiere*, *Belsatzar* and the rarely encountered *Die feindlichen Brüder*, performances that are felt as immediately as if at the moment of composition. In *Abends am Strand* the voice follows to the full the song's romantic import. In the third song of Op 64, *Tragödie*, the baritone is joined by his talented tenor brother: their voices naturally blend well. Finally, Genz is inspired by that amazingly original song, *Mein Wagen rollet langsam*, to give of his absolute best. Here, as throughout, Claar ter Horst matches the perceptions of her partner, and both are caught in an amenable acoustic.

Liederkreis[a]
Vier Husarenlieder, Op 117. Myrthen, Op 25 – No 1, Widmung; No 3, Der Nussbaum; No 8, Talismane; No 15, Aus den hebraischen Gesangen; No 17, Venetianisches Lied I; No 18, Venetianisches Lied II; No 24, Du bist wie eine Blume. Romanzen und Balladen – Der Schatzgraber, Op 45 No 1; Op 49 – No 1, Die beiden Grenadiere; No 2, Die feindlichen Bruder; Tragodie, Op 64 No 3[b]. Spanisches Liederspiel, Op 74 – No 6, Melancholie; No 7, Gestandnis; No 10, Der Kontrabandiste. Dein Angesicht, Op 127 No 2. Mein Wagen rollet langsam, Op 142 No 4. Auftrage, Op 77 No 5
Bryn Terfel *bass-bar* **Malcolm Martineau** *pf* with [b]**Lorna Anderson** *sop* [b]**Timothy Robinson** *ten*
DG 447 042-2GH (78 minutes: DDD) Ⓕ
Texts and translations included
Recorded [a]1997 and 1999

A characteristically direct collection of Schumann songs from Bryn Terfel which, as always, sails close to the wind.

Terfel launches his very generous selection of Schumann's most noted Lieder with tremendous panache, just the quality called for by the late Lenau settings that comprise the *Husarenlieder*. The larger-than-life enthusiasm that these songs call for are typical of Terfel's very personal, word-for-word approach to everything in this recital. Pieces of story-telling, such as *Die beiden Grenadiere* and *Der Kontrabandiste*, and ballads such as *Der Schatzgraber* and *Die feindlichen Bruder* come vigorously to life given Terfel's gifts for word- and mood-painting. The method is highly individual and spontaneous.

At other times his very anxiety to make as much as he can of every word and note leads to an uncomfortable feeling that his own interventionist means are emphasising the singer rather than the song. Particularly in the *Liederkreis* cycle, tempos are often pulled about wilfully, rubato is carried to excess, *mezza voce* becomes a kind of whispered *Sprechgesang*, individual words are given little bursts of explosive tone (if you thought Fischer-Dieskau erred in that direction, Terfel carries the method much further). A little less would mean so much more. Put it down to youthful enthusiasm and a wish to communicate arrestingly, and the faults may be excused. For better and worse the style is overt and operatic.

Evidence that Terfel can penetrate to the heart of a song's meaning without overdoing his effects is there in a deeply felt reading of the Byron setting, *Mein Herz ist schwer*, and an impassioned account of that equivocal song, *Mein Wagen rollet langsam*. One misses the lighter touch of a soprano or tenor in purely lyrical pieces, such as *Der Nussbaum* (though in this his tone has a nice vibrant expectancy), *Auftrage*, *Dein Angesicht* and the two Venetian songs of Op 25. Throughout, but especially in the lute-like accompaniment to *Mein Herz ist schwer* and the postlude to *Mein Wagen rollet langsam*, Martineau's willingness to follow his singer wherever he goes and his understanding of Schumann's idiom is beyond praise.

Lieder Recitals

Olaf Bär

Drei Gedichte, Op 30. Sechs Gedichte, Op 36. Fünf Lieder, Op 40. Romanzen und Balladen, Opp 45, 49 and 53. Belsatzar, Op 57. Der Handschuh, Op 87
Olaf Bär *bar* **Helmut Deutsch** *pf*
EMI CDC5 56199-2 (72 minutes: DDD). Texts and translations included. Recorded 1996 Ⓕ

'Die beiden Grenadiere' apart, Schumann's ballads crop up too rarely in recital and on disc. All the more welcome, then, are Olaf Bär's bold and perceptive readings of some of the finest of them. In Op 45 he graphically realises the *grand guignol* of 'Der Schatzgräber' ('The treasure-seeker'), with Helmut Deutsch relishing the onomatopoeic keyboard part. Equally compelling is the neglected chivalric ballad, *Der Handschuh* ('The glove'): making vivid use, as ever, of his consonants, Bär slyly mocks the pomposity of the royal retinue in the opening recitative, savours Schumann's lion and tiger imitations (gleefully abetted by Deutsch) and catches to perfection the simpering, wheedling Lady Kunigunde. Scarcely better known than these ballads are the three Geibel settings, Op 30, and the six songs, Op 36 to homely, faded verses by Robert Reinick. Bär is both virile and incisive in the alfresco cheerfulness of 'Der Knabe mit dem Wunderhorn' and the macho bravado of 'Der Hidalgo', with its swaggering bolero rhythms.

Bär's freshness and unsentimental tenderness are well suited to the relatively modest songs of Op 36. And he and Deutsch respond sharply to the character sketches of Op 40, from the shy delicacy of 'Märzveilchen' ('March violets') through the sinister, twilit 'Muttertraum' to the aching intensity of 'Der Soldat' and the desperation behind the wedding merriment in 'Der Spielmann'. These days Bär's softer singing can sometimes be a shade breathy and unfocused, with high notes not quite integrated into the line; nor is his *legato* always seamless. Random comparison with Fischer-Dieskau also finds the older baritone predictably wider in his emotional and coloristic range, freer and more fluid in his phrasing and often more subtle in his individual insights. But the more open, direct Bär is invariably a sympathetic singer and an involving and, in the ballads, vividly dramatic interpreter. He and the ever-attentive Deutsch certainly make a persuasive case for these less favoured products of the great song year of 1840.

Simon Keenlyside

Complete Lieder, Volume 2

Drei Gedichte, Op 30. Die Löwenbraut, Op 31 No 1. 12 Gedichte, Op 35. Lieder und Gesänge aus Wilhelm Meister, Op 98*a* – No 2, Ballade des Harfners; No 4, Wer nie sein Brot mit Tränen ass; No 6, Wer sich der Einsamkeit ergibt; No 8, An die Türen will ich schleichen. Vier Husarenlieder, Op 117

Simon Keenlyside *bar* **Graham Johnson** *pf*

Hyperion CDJ33102 (70 minutes: DDD). Texts and translations included. Recorded 1997 Ⓕ ●●

In his notes Graham Johnson says that what we have always lacked is a convincing way of performing late Schumann songs, often spare in texture and elusive in style. Well, he and Keenlyside seem to have found one here in their wholly admirable versions of the very different Opp 98*a* and 117. The Op 98*a* settings of the Harper's outpourings from *Wilhelm Meister* have always stood in the shade of those by Schubert and Wolf. This pair show incontrovertibly that there's much to be said for Schumann's versions, capturing the essence of the old man's sad musings, as set by the composer in an imaginative, free way, alert to every nuance in the texts.

The extroverted Lenau *Husarenlieder* could hardly be more different. Keenlyside identifies in turn with the bravado of the first, the cynicism of the second, and the eerie, death-dominated mood of the fourth. The third, as Johnson avers, is a bit of a dud. Then it's back to the miracle year of 1840 for three seldom-heard Geibel *Knabenhorn* settings, Op 30. The pair enter into the open-hearted mood called for by these songs, most of all in the irresistible 'Der Hidalgo'. Keenlyside is just as forthright in *Die Löwenbraut* and in those of Op 35, the well-known Kerner settings, and he brings impressive control to the Eusebius ones, not least the all-enveloping 'Stille Tränen'. The interpretation of this quasi-cycle is convincing and unerringly paced. The recording and Johnson's persuasive playing are of the highest standard.

Awards 1997

Christine Schäfer

Complete Lieder, Volume 1

Das verlassene Mägdlein, Op 64 No 2. Melancholie, Op 74 No 6. Aufträge, Op 77 No 5. Op 79 – No 7*a*, Zigeunerliedchen I; No 7*b*, Zigeunerliedchen II; No 23, Er ist's!. Die Blume der Ergebung, Op 83 No 2. Röslein, Röslein!, Op 89 No 6. Sechs Gedichte und Requiem, Op 90. Op 96 – No 1, Nachtlied; No 3 Ihre Stimme. Lieder und Gesänge aus Wilhelm Meister, Op 98*a* – No 1, Kennst du das Land?; No 3, Nur wer die Sehnsucht kennt; No 5, Heiss' mich nicht reden; No 7, Singet nicht in Trauertönen; No 9, So lasst mich scheinen. Sechs Gesänge, Op 107. Warnung, Op 119 No 2. Die Meerfee, Op 125 No 1. Sängers Trost, Op 127 No 1. Mädchen-Schwermut, Op 142 No 3

Christine Schäfer *sop* **Graham Johnson** *pf*

Hyperion CDJ33101 (75 minutes: DDD) Ⓕ

Texts and translations included. Recorded 1995. ●●●

This disc launches Hyperion's Schumann Lieder project as auspiciously as Dame Janet Baker's recital opened their Complete Schubert Edition. As ever, Graham Johnson shows an unerring gift for matching singer and song. These are almost all late pieces, written between 1849 and 1852 under the shadow of depression and sickness; and their intense chromaticism can all too easily seem tortuous. However, imaginatively supported by Johnson, Christine Schäfer illuminates each of these songs with her pure, lucent timbre, her grace and breadth of phrase and her unselfconscious feeling for verbal meaning and nuance. The voice is an expressive, flexible lyric-coloratura; she can spin a scrupulously even *legato*, integrates the high notes of, say, 'Er ist's' perfectly within the melodic line, and has the breath control to sustain the long phrases of 'Requiem' with apparent ease. Aided by Johnson's lucid textures and uncommonly subtle feel for rubato and harmonic direction, Schäfer avoids any hint of mawkishness in songs like 'Meine Rose', Op 90 No 2, 'Mädchen-Schwermut' and 'Abendlied. Several songs here have been overshadowed or eclipsed by the settings by Schubert, Wolf or Brahms, and Schäfer and Johnson do much to rehabilitate them.

Schäfer brings an exquisite wondering stillness to the Goethe 'Nachtlied', more disturbed and earthbound than Schubert's sublime setting, but here, at least, scarcely less poignant. She also has the dramatic flair to bring off the difficult Mignon songs, especially the volatile, quasi-operatic 'Heiss' mich nicht reden' and 'Kennst du das Land', where the final verse, evoking Mignon's terrifying passage across the Alps, builds to a climax of desperate, almost demented yearning. At the other end of the emotional spectrum, Schäfer brings a guileful, knowing touch to the first of the *Zigeunerliedchen*; the Mendelssohnian 'Die Meerfee' glistens and glances and 'Aufträge' has a winning eagerness and charm, with a delicious sense of flirtation between voice and keyboard. In sum, a delectable, often revelatory recital. The recording is natural and well balanced, while Graham Johnson's typically searching commentaries complement the performances perfectly.

Der Rose Pilgerfahrt, Op 112

Inga Nielsen, Helle Hinz *sops* **Annemarie Møller, Elizabeth Halling** *mezzos* **Deon van der Walt** *ten* **Guido Päevatalu** *bar* **Christian Christiansen** *bass* **Danish National Radio Choir and Symphony Orchestra / Gustav Kuhn**

Chandos CHAN9350 (62 minutes: DDD) Ⓕ

Text included. Recorded 1993 ●

Amidst today's great upsurgence of interest in Schumann's later choral undertakings, the work's long neglect is no doubt due to its all-too-naive tale of a rose who, after an eagerly sought transformation into a maiden to experience human love, chooses to sacrifice herself for her baby. Schumann's own ready response to Moritz Horn's poem can best be explained by its underlying moral message together with a strain of German rusticity then equally close to the composer's heart. Having said that, how grateful Schumann lovers should be to Chandos for at last introducing the work to the English catalogue in so sympathetic yet discreet a performance from this predominantly Danish cast. All credit to the conductor, Gustav Kuhn, for revealing so much fancy in fairyland, so much brio in peasant merriment, and so much charm in more tender lyricism without ever making heavy weather of this essentially *gemütlich* little score. No praise can be too high for the Danish National Radio Choir: such immediacy of response leaves no doubt as to their professional status. Nor do the soloists or orchestra disappoint. Tonal reproduction is agreeably natural.

Der Rose Pilgerfahrt. Nachtlied, Op 108 **P**
Camilla Nylund, Anke Hoffmann, Simone Kermes *sops* **Claudia Schubert** *contr* **Rainer Trost** *ten* **Jochen Kupfer, Andreas Schmidt** *bars* **Chorus Musicus; Das Neue Orchester / Christoph Spering**
Opus 111 OPS30-190 (69 minutes: DDD) Ⓕ
Text and translation included. Recorded 1996 ●

This charming choral work is best described as a musical fairy-tale for the young at heart. Spering's version has the special interest of using chamber-like forces, with 'period' wind and brass, to reveal new subtleties of balance and colour in this composer's often unjustly criticised orchestration. The pleasing solo voices are tellingly contrasted and the lyrical eloquence of the narrator, Rainer Trost, deserves special mention; likewise the sensitive response, whether as elves, peasants or angels, of the chorus. The overriding reason for recommending this disc rather than the Chandos set (above) is its inclusion of the rarely heard *Nachtlied*. Inspired by a Hebbel poem, Schumann conveys the onset of night and the wonder of the nocturnal sky in a magnificent arch of arrestingly scored sound, before subsiding into sleep that 'comes softly as a nurse towards a child'. Lasting barely nine minutes, it surely ranks among Schumann's masterpieces – or so this finely shaped and deeply felt, mellow-toned performance persuades you.

Szenen aus Goethes Faust

Karita Mattila, Barbara Bonney, Brigitte Poschner-Klebel, Susan Graham *sops* **Iris Vermillion** *mez* **Endrik Wottrich, Hans-Peter Blochwitz** *tens* **Bryn Terfel** *bass-bar* **Jan-Hendrik Rootering, Harry Peeters** *basses* **Tölz Boys' Choir; Swedish Radio Chorus; Berlin Philharmonic Orchestra / Claudio Abbado**
Sony Classical ② S2K66308 (115 minutes: DDD)
Notes, text and translation included. Ⓕ
Recorded live in 1994 ●●

No one before Schumann had ever attempted to set Goethe's mystical closing scene, which he finished in time for the Goethe centenary in 1849. What eventually emerged as his own Parts 1 and 2 (in turn portraits of Gretchen and the by now repentant Faust) followed later, after his move from a Mendelssohn-dominated Leipzig to a Wagner-ruled Dresden, hence the striking difference in style. Nothing Schumann ever wrote is more dramatic than Faust's blinding and death in the course of Part 2. The Berlin Philharmonic is very forwardly recorded – occasionally perhaps a little too much so for certain voices. But never in the case of Bryn Terfel in the title-role. Any advance fears that he might disappoint were immediately banished not only by the generosity and flow of his warm, round tone but also the total commitment and conviction of his characterization. Moreover as Dr Marianus in Part 3 he offers some wonderfully sustained *mezza* and *sotto voce*. Karita Mattila's Gretchen is always sympathetically pure-toned, clean-lined and assured. At times, as positioned, the other male soloists seem a little outweighed by the orchestra. No praise can be too high for the Four Grey Sisters (so tellingly contrasted in vocal colour) led by Barbara Bonney: their midnight encounter with Faust and his eventual blinding is brilliantly done. And there is splendidly characterful choral singing thoughout from both adult and youthful choirs. In the more operatically conceived Parts 1 and 2 and the visionary Part 3, Abbado himself takes the music to heart and what he draws from his orchestra makes nonesense of the charge that Schumann was an inept scorer. This is worth every penny of its full-price.

Genoveva

Ruth Ziesak *sop* Genoveva; **Deon van der Walt** *ten* Golo; **Rodney Gilfry** *bar* Hidulfus; **Oliver Widmer** *bar* Siegfried; **Marjana Lipovšek** *mez* Margaretha; **Thomas Quasthoff** *bar* Drago; **Hiroyuki Ijichi** *bass* Balthasar; **Josef Krenmair** *bar* Caspar
Arnold Schoenberg Choir; Chamber Orchestra of Europe / Nikolaus Harnoncourt
Teldec ② 0630-13144-2 (129 minutes: DDD) Notes, Ⓕ
text and translation included. Recorded live in 1996 ●

For most listeners, Schumann's only opera is still a relatively unknown quantity but lovers of Schumann will celebrate a work that is at once intimate, thought-provoking and gloriously melodious. The libretto (by Schumann himself, after Tieck and Hebbel) deals with secret passion and suspected adultery, while the music mirrors emotional turmoil with great subtlety, and sometimes with astonishing imagination. Copious foretastes are provided in the familiar overture, and thereafter, discoveries abound. Sample, for example, the jagged counter-motif that shudders as Genoveva's husband Siegfried entreats Golo (his own *alter ego*) to guard his wife while he is away at war (disc 1, track 5, at 1'58"); or the off-stage forces representing drunken servants at 2'22" into track 9; or the almost Expressionist writing at 4'00" into track 10 where Golo responds – with seething hatred – to Genoveva's vengeance. You might also try track 2 on disc 2, at 3'37", where Golo brings Siegfried news of Genoveva's supposed adultery, music that is both pained and equivocal. The entreaties of Drago's ghost aren't too far removed from Siegmund's 'Nothung!' in

Act 1 of *Die Walküre* (track 4, at 6'10"), and Genoveva's singing from 'a desolate, rocky place' (track 5, first minute or so), sounds fairly prophetic of Isolde (who was as yet unborn, so to speak). Harnoncourt suspects that Genoveva was a 'counterblast' to Wagner, and although Wagner apparently thought the opera 'bizarre', there remains a vague suspicion of sneaking regard, even a smidgen of influence. Teldec's balancing is mostly judicious and the musical direction suggestive of burning conviction. The worthy though relatively conventional Gerd Albrecht (in Orfeo's mellow 1992 recording) only serves to underline the leaner, more inflected and more urgently voiced profile of Harnoncourt's interpretation. As to the two sets of singers, most preferences rest with the latter's line-up. Stage effects are well handled and the sum effect is of a top-drawer Schumann set within an unexpected structural context.

Heinrich Schütz German 1585-1672

GROVE *In 1590 Schütz moved with his family to Weissenfels. In 1598 Landgrave Moritz, impressed by his musical accomplishments, took him to Kassel, where he served as a choirboy and studied music with the court Kapellmeister, Georg Otto. In 1609 Schütz proceeded to the University of Marburg to study law, but Landgrave Moritz advised him to abandon his university studies and to go to Venice as a pupil of G Gabrieli; moreover, the landgrave provided the financial means to do this. Schütz remained in Venice for over three years, returning to Moritz's court at Kassel in 1613. The following year he was seconded to serve for two months at the electoral court in Dresden, and in 1615 the Elector Johann Georg I requested his services for a further two years. Moritz reluctantly agreed, and was obliged, for political reasons, to comply when the elector insisted on retaining Schütz in his permanent employ.*

As Kapellmeister at Dresden, Schütz was responsible for providing music for major court ceremonies, whether religious or political. He also had to keep the Kapelle adequately staffed and supervise the musical education of the choirboys. His pupils during the following decades included the composers Bernhard, Theile and Weckmann. In 1619 Schütz published his first collection of sacred music, the Psalmen Davids, dedicated to the elector, and later that year he married Magdalena Wildeck. She died in 1625, leaving Schütz with two daughters whom he placed in the care of their maternal grandmother; he never remarried.

Schütz was often absent from Dresden on his own or the elector's business, and in 1627 he was at Torgau, where his Dafne (the first German opera) was performed for the wedding of the elector's daughter Sophia Eleonora. Visits to Mühlhausen and possibly Gera were undertaken later in the year. Towards the end of the 1620s economic pressures of the Thirty Years War began to affect the electoral court. Musicians wages fell into arrears, and in 1628 Schütz decided on a second visit to Venice, where he was able to study developments in dramatic music under Monteverdi's guidance. He returned to Dresden in 1629, but two years later Saxony entered the war and musical activities at court soon came to a virtual halt. Schütz then accepted an invitation to direct the music at the wedding of Crown Prince Christian of Denmark. He arrived in Copenhagen in December 1633 and was paid a salary as Kapellmeister by King Christian IV until his return to Dresden in May 1635.

From Michaelmas 1639 Schütz was again absent from Dresden, this time for about 15 months in the service of Georg of Calenberg. On his return he found the Kapelle further depleted and its members living in penury, and for most of 1642-44 he was again employed at the Danish court. After a year in and around Brunswick he went into semi-retirement, spending much of his time in Weissenfels, though he retained the title and responsibilities of Kapellmeister at Dresden. The end of the Thirty Years War had little immediate effect on musical conditions and in 1651 Schütz renewed an earlier plea for release from his duties and the granting of a pension. This and later petitions were ignored and Schütz obtained his release only on the elector's death in 1656. He was far from inactive during his remaining 15 years. He continued to supply music for occasions at Dresden, frequently travelled and worked on the masterpieces of his last years – the Christmas History, the three Passions and the settings of Psalms cxix and c.

Schütz was the greatest German composer of the 17th century and the first of international stature. His output was almost exclusively sacred; he set mainly biblical texts and wrote little chorale-based music. His early works explore a variety of styles and genres: the polychoral Psalmen Davids (1619) are notable for their contrasting textures and sonorities, while the Cantiones sacrae (1625) present a wide range of motet settings, from the polyphonic to the concertato. Later, he exploited the Italian concertato idiom to the full, notably in the three books of Symphoniae sacrae (1629, 1647, 1650), which give equal weight to voices and instruments. His two sets of Kleine geistliche Concerte (1636, 1639), written after the Thirty Years War and for limited forces, emphasise the meaning of the text, combining principles of monody and counterpoint to create powerful and expressive declamation. Schütz's late works are dominated by the oratorical pieces and by the three unaccompanied 'dramatic' Passions, said to be the last great examples of the genre. His music, largely to German texts, constitutes the ultimate realisation of Luther's endeavours to establish the vernacular as a literary and liturgical language, and embodies the Protestant and humanistic concept of musica poetica in perhaps its most perfect form.

Secular Works

Freue dich des Weibes deiner Jugend, SWV453. Liebster, sagt in süssem Schmerzen, SWV441. Nachdem ich lag in meinem öder Bette, SWV451. Glück zu dem Helikon, SWV96. Haus und Güter erbat man von Eltern, SWV21. Tugend ist der beste Freund, SWV442. Teutoniam dudum belli atra pericla, SWV338. Wie wenn der Adler, SWV434. Siehe, wie

fein und lieblich ists, SWV48. Vier Hirtinnen, gleich jung, gleich schön, SWVAnh1. Lässt Salomon sein Bette nicht umgeben, SWV452. Die Erde trinkt für sich, SWV438. Wohl dem, der ein Tugendsam Weib hat, SWV20. Itzt blicken durch des Himmels Saal, SWV460. Syncharma musicum, SWV49
Weser-Renaissance Bremen / Manfred Cordes
CPO CPO999 518-2 (71 minutes: DDD) Ⓑ
Texts and translations included. Recorded 1997 ⓞ

Here is a discovery of several unrecorded byways of Schütz's miscellaneous secular *oeuvre*. Of course, the 17th century being what it is, secular and sacred are deliberately dovetailed into a cultural pea soup: these works are embedded in the literary morality of the age and are not entirely profane. There is a pleasing lightness of touch from the soloists (especially the soprano) and the instrumental consort does not attempt, as is so mistakenly regarded these days as the ideal, to ape the vocal lines at every turn in a wash of homogeneity; there are many distinctive virtuosic commentaries, as in *Tugend ist der beste Freund*, which Cordes (enhanced by the excellent recorded sound) allows to breathe naturally. Noble intensity and harmonious accord are the order of the day in the splendidly uplifting concerto *Teutoniam dudum*, which through its extraordinary structural clarity immediately delights the listener with a celebration of the cessation of hostilities after the miserable Thirty Years War. Most impressive, though, is the sympathetic and gentle treatment of the words from Weser-Renaissance, beautifully complemented by the soft articulation of the winds, especially in *Siehe, wie fein* and the domestic charm of *Wohl dem, der ein Tugendsam*. This is chamber music-making from the heart, tempered convincingly by the intellect and affectionately delivered.

Symphoniae sacrae, SWV341-67

Emma Kirkby, Suzie Le Blanc *sops* **James Bowman** *counterten* **Nigel Rogers, Charles Daniels** *tens* **Stephen Varcoe, Richard Wistreich** *basses* **Jeremy West, Nicholas Perry** *cornets* **Purcell Quartet** (Catherine Mackintosh, Catherine Weiss *vns* Richard Boothby *va da gamba* Robert Woolley *hpd*) Ⓟ
Chandos Chaconne ② CHAN0566/7
(139 minutes: DDD). Text and translation included. Ⓕ
Recorded 1993-94 ⓞ

These discs are in various ways revelatory. Schütz's collection is difficult to get through in one sitting, but each item in the collection is a jewel, albeit not ostentatiously displayed. This is church music on a small scale in terms of physical resources, but of enormous invention and beauty. Sometimes the Purcell Quartet do not push the music along quite enough. In general, however, the instrumentalists respond with enthusiasm and great understanding of the style of these rather recondite works. It takes considerable sensitivity to bring out the rich textures of *Meine Seele erhebt den Herren* or *Der Herr ist meine Stärke* without enjoying such moments at the expense of the vocal soloist. The relatively well-known bass solo *Herr, nun lässest du deinen Diener* is another example of a perfect match between voice and instruments.

Emma Kirkby brings all her customary charm and precision to her two solo arias. Both tenors are in their element, if sometimes a little understated, and Stephen Varcoe and Richard Wistreich really understand and communicate the glowing black and gold colours of Schütz's writing for the bass voice. Schütz's debt to Monteverdi is very much evident in *Der Herr ist mein Licht* and even more so in *Es steh Gott auf*, but Schütz's natural reluctance to 'deck out my work with foreign plumage' means that his own voice as a composer is always in evidence. This reconciliation of Italian *stile concertato* with Schütz's northern reticence is one of the challenges in performing his music, and one to which this recording rises magnificently.

Motets

Ich hab mein Sach Gott heimgestellt, SWV305. Ich will dem Herren loben allezeit, SWV306. Was hast du verwirket, SWV307. O Jesu, nomen dulce, SWV308. O misericordissime Jesu, SWV309. Ich leige und schlafe, SWV310. Habe deine Lust an dem Herren, SWV311. Herr, ich hoffe darauf, SWV312. Bone Jesu, verbum Patris, SWV313. Verbum caro factum est, SWV314. Hodie Christus natus est, SWV315. Wann unsre Augen schlafen ein, SWV316. Meister, wir haben die ganze Nacht gearbeitet, SWV317. Die Furcht des Herren, SWV318. Ich beuge meine Knie, SWV319. Ich bin jung gewesen, SWV320. Herr, wann ich nur dich habe, SWV321. Rorate coeli desuper, SWV322. Joseph, du Sohn David, SWV323. Ich bin die Auferstehung, SWV324 Ⓟ
Tölz Boys' Choir / Gerhard Schmidt-Gaden with **Roman Summereder** *org*
Capriccio 10 388 (77 minutes: DDD). Texts and translations included. Recorded 1989-90 Ⓕ

Getting music published evidently encountered economic difficulties during the Thirty Years' War, for Heinrich Schütz had to issue his *Kleiner geistlichen Concerten* ('Little Sacred Concertos') – short motets for vocal soloists and continuo – in two parts in, respectively, 1636 and 1639. The voices of the soloists here are typically very individual and characterful, and all are remarkably adroit and stylish, so the personal witness that is so pronounced in the text is particularly well portrayed. These are performers well used to the subtleties of baroque word-setting and they highlight all the ingenuity that Schütz lavished on these seemingly simple texts. There is an evident delight in the way the composer deployed his limited resources, constantly ringing the changes on traditional formulas to produce a richness of ideas that it took a Bach or Handel to emulate. The rather close recording allows all these intricacies to emerge undiminished and although the resonance of the acoustic seems restrained, this is no bad thing for repertoire that, despite its title, has the feel of chamber music.

Weinachtshistorie, SWV435

Herr, nun lässest du deinen Diener in Friede fahren, SWV352. Auf dem Gebirge, SWV396. Siehe, es erschien der Engel des Herren, SWV403. Weinachtshistorie, SWV435[a]. Magnificat anima mea, SWV468. Deutsches Magnificat, SWV494
[a]**Stephan Genz** *bar* **La Petite Bande / Sigiswald Kuijken** *vn*
Deutsche Harmonia Mundi 05472 77511-2
(68 minutes: DDD). Texts and translations included Ⓕ
Recorded live in 1998

Sigiswald Kuijken's reading of the passion-like *Christmas Story* scores not so much through overt dramaticism as through its neatly balanced blend of highly competent singing and playing and its consistently well-chosen tempos. These not only have a gentle momentum of their own, but also work well in relation to each other, so that the alternation of recitative-like solo narration and more colourful and elaborate interludes never loses coherence.

In Stephan Genz, furthermore, Kuijken has an excellent narrator – more lyrical than declamatory, but with a Lieder singer's ability to highlight the odd significant word through a subtle change in vocal colour – while there are other enjoyable contributions from Elisabeth Scholl (clear and penetrating as the Angel), Harry van der Kamp (stoic as ever as Herod), and (the opening bars apart) some fine cornett players.

The Christmas theme is continued with the late choral *Magnificat* in German; an earlier, imposing German *Nunc dimittis* for continuo and solo bass (van der Kamp again); a rather grand *Magnificat* in Latin; and two concerted settings of Gospel texts paralleled in the *Christmas Story*, one telling joyfully of Joseph's dream, the other featuring two plangent altos weeping at the slaughter of the innocents. All are performed with the same unassuming expertise and tasteful musicianship, with only an occasional insecurity among the sopranos to cause concern. The recording is full-bodied yet clear, and remarkably free from obtrusive edits.

Psalms of David

Psalmen Davids sampt etlichen Moteten und Concerten, SWV22-47
Cantus Cölln (Elisabeth Scholl, Annette Labusch *sops* Elisabeth Popien *mez* Stratton Bull *counterten* Gerd Türk, Wilfried Jochens, Jörn Lindemann *tens* Stephan Schreckenberger, Stephan MacLeod *basses*)
Concerto Palatino / Konrad Junghänel
Harmonia Mundi ② HMC90 1652/3
(143 minutes: DDD). Texts and translations included Ⓕ
Recorded 1997

Here is something to get excited about: a new recording, at last, of Schütz's first monumental publication of sacred music. Whether anything can be worth waiting for that long is a moot point, but Cantus Cölln and Concerto Palatino give us an interpretation that is unlikely to be surpassed. With eight singers and no fewer than two dozen instrumentalists, the scale is little short of symphonic. For sheer splendour, who can top *Danket dem Herren* (SWV45) or the next piece in the collection, *Zion spricht*? It is easy enough to single out the most opulent pieces, but as Peter Wollny remarks in his admirable booklet-notes, the whole point of the *Psalmen Davids* is its variety in the treatment of a medium whose potential for cliché is very great. The musicians respond to Schütz's demands with verve and perception and the sort of confidence that would carry any music aloft in triumph. The sound-recording does them full justice. You will almost certainly listen, enthralled, to the entire collection – nearly two-and-a-half hours – in one sitting.

Alexander Scriabin Russian 1872-1915

GROVE *Scriabin was a fellow pupil of Rachmaninov's in Zverev's class from 1884 and at the Moscow Conservatory (1888-92), where his teachers were Taneyev, Arensky and Safonov. From 1894 his career as a pianist was managed by Belyayev, who arranged his European tours and also published his works: at this stage they were almost exclusively for solo piano, and deeply influenced by Chopin (most are preludes and mazurkas), though in the late 1890s he began to write for orchestra. In 1903 he left Russia and his family to live in western Europe for six years with a young female admirer, and his musical style became more intensely personal, developing a profusion of decoration in harmony becalmed by unresolved dominant chords or whole-tone elements. The major works of this period include the Divine Poem and again numerous piano pieces.*

In 1905 he encountered Madame Blavatsky's theosophy, which soon ousted the enthusiasm for Nietschean superhumanism that had underlain the immediately preceding works. The static and ecstatic tendencies in his music were encouraged, being expressed notably in the Poem of Ecstasy and Prometheus, the latter intended to be performed with a play of coloured light. Still more ambitious were the plans for the Mysterium, a quasi-religious act which would have united all the arts, and for the composition of which the exclusively piano works of 1910-15 were intended to be preparatory, this journey into mystical hysteria going along with a voyage beyond tonality to a floating dissonance often based on the 'mystic chord' (C-F sharp-B flat-E-A-D).

Piano Concerto

Scriabin Piano Concerto in F sharp minor, Op 20
Tchaikovsky Piano Concerto No 1 in B flat minor, Op 23
Nikolai Demidenko *pf* **BBC Symphony Orchestra / Alexander Lazarev**
Hyperion CDA66680 (65 minutes: DDD) Ⓕ
Recorded 1993

The chief attraction here is the unusual coupling which pairs two sharply opposed examples of

Russian romanticism, and although the reasons for the neglect of Scriabin's Piano Concerto are not hard to fathom (its lyrical and decorative flights are essentially inward-looking), its haunting, bittersweet beauty, particularly in the central *Andante*, is hard to resist. Demidenko's own comments, quoted in the accompanying booklet, are scarcely less intense and individual than his performance: 'in the ambience, phrasing and cadence of his music we meet with a world almost without skin, a world of nerve-ends where the slightest contact can bring pain.' His playing soars quickly to meet the music's early passion head on, and in the first *più mosso scherzando* he accelerates to produce a brilliant lightening of mood. His flashing *fortes* in the *Andante*'s second variation are as volatile as his *pianissimos* are starry and refined in the finale's period reminiscence, and although he might seem more tight-lipped, less expansive than Ashkenazy on Decca, he is arguably more dramatic and characterful. Demidenko's

Tchaikovsky, too, finds him ferreting out and sifting through every texture, forever aiming at optimum clarity. While this is hardly among the greatest Tchaikovsky Firsts on record, it is often gripping and mesmeric. The orchestra responds admirably to its mercurial soloist and certainly comes alight at key moments in both concertos. The recorded balance is not always ideal and the piano sound is sometimes uncomfortably taut.

Piano Concerto in F sharp minor, Op 20[a]. Prometheus, Op 60, 'Le poème du feu'[b]. Le poème de l'extase, Op 54[c]
Vladimir Ashkenazy *pf* **Ambrosian Singers;** [ab]**London Philharmonic Orchestra;** [c]**Cleveland Orchestra / Lorin Maazel**
Decca 417 252-2DH (66 minutes: ADD) Ⓕ
Recorded [ab]1971, [c]1978

This CD gives us the essential Scriabin. The Piano Concerto has great pianistic refinement and melodic grace as well as a restraint not encountered in his later music. With *Le poème de l'extase* and *Prometheus* we are in the world of art nouveau and Scriabin in the grip of the mysticism (and megalomania) that consumed his later years. They are both single-movement symphonies for a huge orchestra: *Prometheus* ('The Poem of Fire') calls for quadruple wind, eight horns, five trumpets, strings, organ and chorus as well as an important part for solo piano in which Ashkenazy shines. The sensuous, luminous textures are beautifully conveyed in these performances by the LPO and the Decca engineers produce a most natural perspective, as well as an appropriately overheated sound in the sensuous world of *Le poème de l'extase*.

Symphonies

Symphonies – No 1 in E, Op 26[a]; No 2 in C minor, Op 29; No 3 in C minor, Op 43, 'Divin poème'. Le poème de l'extase, Op 54[b]. Prometheus, Op 60, 'Le poème du feu'[c]
[a]**Stefania Toczyska** *mez* [a]**Michael Myers** *ten* [c]**Dmitri Alexeev** *pf* [b]**Frank Kaderabek** *tpt* [a]**Westminster Choir;** [c]**Philadelphia Choral Arts Society; Philadelphia Orchestra / Riccardo Muti**
EMI ③ CDS7 54251-2 (188 minutes: DDD) Text and Ⓕ translation included. Recorded 1985-90

There can be few more thrilling sounds on disc (and no more compelling reason for a totally sound-proofed listening room) than the climax to Muti's *Poème de l'extase*. The clamour of bells here (both literal and imitative) reveals an essentially Russian heart at the core of this most cosmopolitan of Russian composers, and the *maestoso* proclamation of the theme of self assertion has the raised Philadelphia horns in crucially sharp focus. As in the corresponding climax in *Prometheus* (at 18'21"), this 'éclat sublime' is filled out with a floor-shaking contribution from the organ. Like the organ, the wordless chorus at this point in *Prometheus* registers more as a device for enriching and exalting the texture, rather than as a striking new presence.

Muti's *Prometheus* is, arguably, the most complete realization of the mind-boggling demands of this score ever to have been recorded. The inert opening ('Original chaos' – lovely *pp* bass drum!) and mysterious awakening have rarely sounded so atmospheric. Alexeev's first entry is not as strong willed as some, but he seems to be saving a more imperious attack for the same point in the recapitulation. Muti builds the work superbly: the imposing clash of states in the development (and the changes of tempo) charted with mighty assurance (beware of the *ff* dissonance at fig. 21, 10'23"!). And thereafter *Prometheus* is airborne, with Alexeev both agile and articulate in the 'Dance of Life' (16'44").

Throughout the cycle, the tonal allure of the Philadelphia Orchestra is fully in evidence. Only in the Third Symphony, *Divin poème*, do Muti and the EMI team seem to be on less than their indomitable form. Compared with some versions, the tempo relationships in the first movement don't fully convince. However, this cycle is unlikely to be seriously challenged for many a year. As a whole it immeasurably enhances Scriabin's stature as a symphonist and offers the kind of playing and recording which, as recently as two decades ago, Scriabin enthusiasts could only have imagined in their dreams.

Prometheus

Scriabin Prometheus **Stravinsky** The Firebird
Alexander Toradze *pf* **Kirov Opera Chorus and Orchestra / Valery Gergiev**
Philips 446 715-2PH (72 minutes: DDD) Ⓕ
Recorded 1997

Stravinsky and the short-lived Scriabin were almost contemporaries; of these two exactly contemporary works (1909-10), *Prometheus*, as Oliver Knussen has put it, is 'so much more than a period piece; pregnant with possibilities for the future', whereas *The Firebird*, aside from its 'Infernal Dance', rarely does anything more startling than pick up from where Rimsky-Korsakov left off – indeed, in certain sections, it shows that Stravinsky also knew his Scriabin rather well (for example, the Firebird's 'Dance of Supplication'). Gergiev's *Firebird* is certainly a startling performance. All manner of things contribute to the impression of distinction, among them the fact that this is that rare thing on record, an all-Russian complete *Firebird*.

The music-making seems alive with a special presence: the orchestra is fairly close, though there is a real sense of the hall, never more so than when a heart-stopping crack is let loose from the drums on Kashchey's appearance. But the primary presence here (obvious enough, but it needs saying) is of a man of the theatre, maybe too audibly (for some) breathing life into the proceedings, moving from one section of the ballet to the next with the transitional mastery of a Furtwängler, and taking risks with tempo (do hear the end of the 'Infernal Dance'). The darkness to light of the ballet's last few minutes is nothing less than mesmeric.

Prometheus is equally compelling. Toradze's solo contribution is slightly less the centre of the piece's universe than Argerich in the sensational Abbado recording, in terms of both imaginative daring and recorded scale, though it never lacks character. The only reservation about the Abbado is the relatively fined down impression of Scriabin's huge orchestra. Yet with the more imposing-sounding Russian team you really know about it. Gergiev's is also a much broader view of the piece, but it never sounds overly languid, indeed it enables him and Toradze, unlike Argerich and Abbado, to achieve a dizzying *accelerando prestissimo* in the final bars that is faster than anything that has preceded it.

Etudes

Etude in C sharp minor, Op 2 No 1. 12 Etudes, Op 8. Etudes, Op 42. Etude in E flat, Op 49 No 1. Etude, Op 56 No 4. Three Etudes, Op 65
Piers Lane *pf* Hyperion CDA66607 Ⓕ
(56 minutes: DDD). Recorded 1992 ○

Although Scriabin's *études* do not fall into two neatly packaged sets in the same way as Chopin's celebrated contributions, there is nevertheless a strong feeling of continuity and development running throughout the 26 examples produced between the years 1887 and 1912. This is admirably demonstrated in this excellent issue from Hyperion, which, far from being an indigestible anthology proves to be an intriguing and pleasurable hour's worth of listening charting Scriabin's progression from late-romantic adolescence to harmonically advanced mystical poet. Indeed, although these studies can be counted as amongst the most digitally taxing and hazardous of their kind, Scriabin also saw them as important sketches and studies for his larger works, and as experiments in his gradually evolving harmonic language and mystical vision.

Piers Lane attains the perfect balance of virtuoso display and poetic interpretation. Expressive detail and subtle nuance are finely brought out, and he is more than receptive to Scriabin's sometimes highly idiosyncratic sound world; rarely, for instance, has the famous 'Mosquito' *Etude* (Op 42 No 3) been captured with such delicate fragility as here, and in No 1 of the three fiendishly difficult *Etudes*, Op 65 the tremulous, ghostly flutterings are tellingly delivered with a gossamer-light touch and a sense of eerie mystery. The clear, spacious recording is exemplary.

Scriabin Etudes – C sharp minor, Op 2 No 1; Op 8: No 5 in E; No 11 in B flat minor; Op 42: No 2 in F sharp minor; No 3 in F sharp; No 4 in F sharp; No 5 in C sharp minor; No 6 in D flat; No 8 in E flat; Trois Etudes, Op 65. Piano Sonata No 6 in G, Op 62 **H**
Miaskovsky Piano Sonata No 3 in C minor, Op 19
Prokofiev Piano Sonata No 7 in B flat, Op 83
Sviatoslav Richter *pf*
Melodiya mono 74321 29470-2 (68 minutes: ADD) Ⓜ
Recorded 1952-58

Richter's interpretations in the 1950s had an elemental power and unselfconscious abandon that was refined and tempered in later life; the problem is the unreliable 1950s Soviet recording quality, compounded, presumably, by some decay in the master-tapes over the years, and not entirely redeemed by the NoNoise remastering technique. Nevertheless, here is an otherworldly Scriabin, cataclysmic and elevated, culminating in a vaporous, explosive, ultimately clamorous account of the Sixth Sonata. The Miaskovsky – formulaic Scriabin with an academic safety net – is probably better heard on other versions; from the amount of background noise on Melodiya you might think a *babushka* with her vacuum cleaner was competing for attention. Finally comes a muscular and emotionally searing Prokofiev Seventh which presents the only serious alternative to Pollini.

Mazurkas

10 Mazurkas, Op 3. Nine Mazurkas, Op 25. Two Mazurkas, Op 40
Gordon Fergus-Thompson *pf* Ⓕ
ASV CDDCA1086 (80 minutes: DDD) ○

Volume 4 of Gordon Fergus-Thompson's Scriabin series for ASV is of the complete *Mazurkas*. The *Mazurka* remains an intransigently indigenous dance genre, and Chopin's incomparable example is more than a hard act to follow. However, Scriabin was among the few who accepted such a challenge wholeheartedly and, while his gratitude to his beloved Polish master is obvious, so too is the skill with which he takes Chopin's Slavonicism on a journey through bittersweet nostalgia into a more convoluted idiom and, finally, into a pensive and hallucinatory shadowland. The elusive character of these fascinating and neglected works could hardly be presented more vividly and insinuatingly than by Fergus-Thompson. How well he understands the way Scriabin's momentary high spirits (in, say, No 4) collapse into morbid introspection in No 5 – into a close-knit chromaticism later refined still further by dark and obsessive intervals and patterning. The balletic leaps of No 6 are deftly contrasted with its sinuous central melody, and, however circuitous the route, Fergus-Thompson travels it with a special clarity and romantic fervour. The two confidential Op 40 *Mazurkas* are a notable success, and the recordings are crystalline and immediate.

Preludes

Complete Preludes – Op 2 No 2; Op 9 No 1; Opp 11, 13, 15-17, 22, 27, 31, 33, 35, 37, 39; Op 45 No 3; Op 48; Op 49 No 2; Op 51 No 2; Op 56 No 1; Op 59 No 2; Opp 67 and 74
Piers Lane *pf*
Hyperion ② CDA67057/8 (127 minutes: DDD) Ⓕ
Recorded 2000 ●●

Everything about this two-disc set is ideal. Beautifully packaged and recorded, and superbly played, there is the added bonus of an outstanding essay by Simon Nicholls, in which acute musical analysis is presented within the wider context of Scriabin's bewildering genius. Nicholls sees Scriabin as 'a musical Fabergé', a composer who contrasted his love of the ambitious epic with an even greater love of miniatures that could be 'short as a sparrow's beak or a bear's tail'. And throughout the extraordinary journey from Op 2 No 2 to Op 74, where the memories of Chopin are subdued by 'scarifying documents of individual and social catastrophe', you are tossed abruptly from a serene or bitter introspection to a crazed violence and exuberance, encouraged by idiosyncratic directions such as *patetico*, *con stravaganza*, *vagamente*, *irato impetuoso*, *sauvage belliqueux*. Well may Stravinsky have asked, 'Scriabin, where does he come from and who are his followers?'

The demands on the pianist are fierce, but it would be hard to imagine a more focused or immaculate reading than that offered by Piers Lane. Few pianists could show more sympathy and affection for such volatile romanticism, or display greater stylistic consistency. He underlines the despondency of the left-hand Prelude, Op 9 No 1 (here separated from its celebrated Nocturne companion); and in, for example, Op 11 No 3 the fleeting melodic outline is always kept intact amid so much whirling activity. The turbulence of No 14 is caught just as surely, and as an instance of how his scrupulousness is combined with the most vivid imagination, he gives us No 16 in an agitated and freely expressive style rather than opting for a more conventional, stricter tempo, creating a novel and nightmarish dimension. He takes No 2 at a true *Allegro* (as marked) and is never tempted into the sort of virtuoso skirmish offered by lesser players. Indeed, his gift for clarifying even the most tortuous utterances with an exemplary poise and assurance is among his finest qualities. The machine-gun fire of Op 31 No 3 and the menacing tread of Op 33 No 4 are fully realised, and Lane ably taps the darkest regions of the imagination in the final Op 74 Preludes.

These discs complement Piers Lane's earlier Hyperion recording of the complete Scriabin Etudes, and although competition is strong in this repertoire, especially from Evgeny Zarafiants and from Gordon Fergus-Thompson in his ongoing series, this new set of the Preludes should be in any serious record collection.

Preludes – Op 22; Op 27; Op 31; Op 33; Op 35; Op 37; Op 39; Op 48; Op 67; Op 74. Prelude in E flat, Op 45 No 3. Prelude in F, Op 49 No 2. Prelude in A minor, Op 51 No 2. Prelude in E flat minor, Op 56 No 1. Prelude, Op 59 No 2 **J Scriabin** Prelude in C, Op 2. Preludes, Op 3 – No 1 in B; No 2. Prelude in D flat
Evgeny Zarafiants *pf*
Naxos 8 554145 (65 minutes: DDD) Ⓢ
Recorded 1996 ●

With this second volume Evgeny Zarafiants completes his superb survey of Scriabin's 86 Preludes, adding four Preludes by Julian Scriabin, the composer's precociously gifted son, as encores. Listening to music of such morbid and refined intricacy played with the finest musical poise and commitment returns us to Stravinsky's bemused question, 'Scriabin, where does he come from, and who are his followers?' Is the angst and angry convolution of, say, Op 27 No 1 a slavonic memory of Brahms's Op 118 No 1? Does the explosive whimsy of Op 35 No 3 take its cue from the *Scherzo* of Beethoven's Op 26 Sonata? The hair-raising *presto* of Op 67 No 2 recalls the menace and enigma of the finale from Chopin's Op 35 Sonata, while the terse and belligerant Op 33 No 3 looks ahead to Stravinsky's sharpest modernist utterances. Yet if there are countless examples of reflection and prophecy, there are still more of the most startling originality. Scriabin is always Scriabin, and as he journeys from Op 22 to Op 74 into the darkest reaches of the imagination you are reminded that this is hardly music for the faint-hearted.

Once again, Zarafiants is equal to each and every vivid occasion. Whether in the fragrant *grazioso* of Op 22 No 2, where the line twists and turns like so much honeysuckle, in the toppling argument of Op 31 No 3, or in the *sauvage belliqueux* of Op 59 No 2, he is richly responsive, his playing alive with a rare pianistic skill and imaginative brio. The Brandon Hill recordings are resonant and full-blooded.

Complete Piano Sonatas

No 1 in F minor, Op 6; **No 2** in G sharp minor, Op 19, **'Sonata-fantasy'**; **No 3** in F sharp minor, Op 23; **No 4** in F sharp, Op 30; **No 5** in F sharp, Op 53; **No 6** in G, Op 62; **No 7** in F sharp, Op 64, **'White Mass'; No 8** in A, Op 66; **No 9** in F, Op 68, **'Black Mass'**; **No 10** in C, Op 70

Piano Sonatas Nos 1-10. Fantasie in B minor, Op 28. Sonata-fantaisie in G sharp minor
Marc-André Hamelin *pf*
Hyperion ② CDA67131/2 (146 minutes: DDD) Ⓕ
Recorded 1989-90 ●●

Scriabin was an ambitious composer. A romantic alchemist, he saw his music as a transmuting agent. Through its influence pain would become happiness and hate become love, culminating in a phoenix-like rebirth of the universe. With Shakespearian agility he would change the world's dross into 'something rich and strange'. Not surprisingly, given Scriabin's early prowess as a pianist, the 10 sonatas resonate with exoticism, ranging through the First Sonata's cries of despair, to the Second Sonata's Baltic Sea inspiration, the Third Sonata's 'states of being', the 'flight to a distant star' (No 4) and 'the emergence of mysterious forces' (No 5). Nos 7 and 9 are *White* and *Black Mass* Sonatas respectively, and the final sonatas blaze with trills symbolising an extra-terrestrial joy and incandescence.

Such music makes ferocious demands on the pianist's physical stamina and imaginative resource. However, Marc-André Hamelin takes everything in his stride. Blessed with rapier reflexes he nonchalantly resolves even the most outlandish difficulties. He launches the First Sonata's opening outcry like some gleaming trajectory and, throughout, his whistle-stop virtuosity is seemingly infallible. You might, however, miss a greater sense of the music's Slavonic intensity, its colour and character; a finer awareness, for example, of the delirious poetry at the heart of the Second Sonata's whirling finale. Hamelin's sonority is most elegantly and precisely gauged but time and again his fluency (admittedly breathtaking) erases too much of the work's originality and regenerative force. However, he shows a greater sense of freedom in the Fifth Sonata, and in the opalescent fantasy of the later sonatas, he responds with more evocative skill to subjective terms, as well as to moments where Scriabin's brooding introspection is lit by sudden flashes of summer lightning. The recordings are a little tight and airless in the bass and middle register, but the set does includes a superb essay on Scriabin.

Peter Sculthorpe Australian 1929

GROVE *Sculthorpe studied at Melbourne University and with Rubbra and Wellesz at Oxford (1958-61) and in 1963 he began teaching at Sydney University. His music features an expressive brilliance of colour and vigorous use of ostinato, sometimes reflecting his interest in Balinese music. His works include the opera Rites of Passage (1974), orchestral and vocal pieces (including the series Sun Music) and a sequence of nine string quartets.*

Piano Concerto

Piano Concerto. Little Nourlangie. Music for Japan. The song of Tailitnama

Kirsti Harms *mez* **Mark Atkins** *didjeridu* **Tamara Anna Cislowska** *pf* **David Drury** *org* **Sydney Symphony Orchestra / Edo de Waart**

ABC Classics 8 770030 (53 minutes: DDD) Ⓔ

Text included. Recorded 1996

Little Nourlangie dates from 1990. It takes its name from a small outcrop of rocks in Australia's Kakadu National Park on which can be found the Aboriginal Blue Paintings, depicting fish, boats and ancestral figures and which inspired the composer. *Little Nourlangie* is a characteristically striking creation, scored with much imaginative flair. It shares its diatonic main theme with that of Sculthorpe's 1989 guitar concerto, *Nourlangie*, and comprises four-and-a-half minutes of 'straightforward, joyful music' (to quote the composer). By contrast, *Music for Japan* exhibits a much more uncompromising demeanour. It was written in response to the Expo '70 exhibition in Osaka and according to annotator Graeme Skinner, is at once 'his most abstract and modernist orchestral score'. The work's title should be carefully heeded: the piece remains very much 'about' Australia, an impression doubly confirmed by the incorporation of a tape featuring a didjeridu played by Mark Atkins.

Sculthorpe has long been preoccupied with the music from other countries situated in and around the Pacific – and Japanese music in particular, elements of which he has incorporated into other works such as the present Piano Concerto of 1983. Sculthorpe's Piano Concerto is an imposing creation, less indigenous-sounding and 'pictorial' than many of his other compositions, including *The song of Tailitnama* (1974). Conceived for high voice, six cellos and percussion, this haunting piece was in fact written for a TV documentary. Edo de Waart presides over a set of performances that exhibit great commitment and exemplary finish. The recording and presentation are excellent too.

String Quartets

String Quartets – No 8; No 11, 'Jaribu Dreaming'; No 13, 'Island Dreaming'[a]. Little Serenade. From Nourlangie. Maranoa Lullaby[a]

[a]**Anne Sofie von Otter** *mez* **Brodsky Quartet**

Vanguard Classics 99215 (48 minutes: DDD) Ⓜ

It's been heartening to see the Peter Sculthorpe discography expanding so steadily in recent years. Discs of the superior quality of this enterprising new Vanguard anthology can only enhance the composer's reputation.

The Brodsky's lucid, raptly expressive accounts of the Eighth and Eleventh Quartets (dating from 1968 and 1990 respectively) easily withstand comparison with those admirable existing performances from both the Kronos (for whom No 11 was originally conceived) and Goldner Quartets. Naturally, the greatest interest here centres on the 13th Quartet of 1996. Written for mezzo Anne Sofie von Otter and the Brodsky, *Island Dreaming* (to give the piece its proper title) is another in a series of Sculthorpe's works (stretching back to the 1988 orchestral essay, *Kakadu*) inspired by the native music of the Australian far north as well as the islands in and around the Torres Strait. The quartet's ritualistic, almost trance-like demeanour and 'bird-call' string harmonics are entirely characteristic of its creator. Needless to say, in the safe hands of the present distinguished team Sculthorpe's inspiration exerts a hypnotic spell from start to finish. Anne Sofie von Otter's is also a haunting presence in the sweetly touching *Maranoa Lullaby* (based on an Aboriginal melody from Queensland). That just leaves the winsome *Little Serenade* (ideal encore material) and the 1994 miniature *From Nourlangie*, whose pentatonic melody will be familiar from both Sculthorpe's 1989 guitar concerto, *Nourlangie* (Sony Classical) and 1990's *Little Nourlangie* for orchestra and organ (ABC Classics). (In case you were wondering, *Nourlangie* is the name given to a small outcrop in Australia's Kakadu National Park, under the base of which there are a number of Aboriginal rock paintings.)

Boasting sound and balance of pleasing realism, this makes a most rewarding mid-price release.

John Sheppard British c1515-1559/60

He was at Magdalen College, Oxford, 1543-48, and by 1552 was a Gentleman of the Chapel Royal. Most of his extant music for the Latin rite probably dates from Mary's reign. The six-voice Magnificat, for example with its florid counterpoint and lack of imitation, belongs to the tradition of the Eton Choirbook composers. Among his more modern works are the four-voice Magnificat, the Missa 'Cantate' and the Mass 'The Western Wynde'. He was at his best when writing vigorous counterpoint around a plainchant. The English works, which include 15 anthems and service music, seem to date from Edward's reign.

Mass 'The Western Wynde'

Aeterne Rex altissime. Dum transisset Sabbatum II. Hostis Hérodes impie. In manus tuas III. Te Deum laudamus. Mass 'The Western Wynde'. The Second Service: Magnificat; Nunc dimitti

The Sixteen / Harry Christophers

Hyperion CDA66603 (63 minutes: DDD). Texts and Ⓕ translations included. Recorded 1992 ⊙

This disc centres round one of Sheppard's best-known four-part Masses, *The Western Wynde*. Though largely syllabic in style, in accordance with liturgical prescriptions at a time when taste in church music was turning towards ever greater emphasis on the text, this Mass still has moments that recapture the earlier visionary style in all its wonder. The section 'Et incarnatus est', coming after an amazing cadence at 'descendit de coelis' in the *Credo*, is a case in point. 'Pleni sunt coeli' is another, and also the opening of the *Benedictus*, where the melody unfolds unhurriedly over the delicate counterpoint of the mean and the bass. In such passages The Sixteen is in its element, each singer relating to the others with the intimacy and mutual understanding of performers of chamber music.

The supporting programme includes *alternatim* hymn settings, responsories and a *Te Deum*. In all of these the chant is sung with excellent phrasing and a smooth *legato*. Some subtle repercussions in the intonation to *Dum transisset Sabbatum* are particularly pleasing. In all five pieces, though, the tempo of the chant sections bore little relationship to the polyphony – the least far removed being that of the hymn *Aeterne Rex altissime*, where the individual chant notes had roughly the duration of a half-beat of the polyphony. The English *Magnificat and Nunc dimittis* reveal Sheppard fully conforming to the later syllabic style in a rich and joyful texture. Here, and in the Latin *Te Deum* The Sixteen display to the full their glowing vocal qualities. This is wonderful singing, with a sense of freedom and flow that is almost overpowering.

Missa Cantate

Missa Cantate[a]. Verbum caro factum est

[a]**Robert Evans** *celebrant* [a]**Donald Greig** *sub-deacon* [a]**Michael McCarthy** *deacon* [a]**Julian Podger** *lesson clerk* **Salisbury Cathedral Boy Choristers; Gabrieli Consort / Paul McCreesh**

Archiv Produktion 457 658-2AH (81 minutes: DDD) Ⓕ
Recorded 1998 ⊙

Something close to this reconstruction of the Third Mass of Christmas might have been heard in Salisbury Cathedral during the last years of the famous rite to which the Cathedral gave its name, the rite practised there since the 13th century. A reconstruction for the ears only, though. Even so, we can follow the slow peregrinations of the opening procession, 'Descendit de coelis', and visualise the highest point in the service, when the great bell tolls for the Consecration.

Hearing Sheppard's magnificent six-part Mass in its full musical context is a remarkable experience. The polyphonic singing is superb. The drama and strength, in particular of the *Sanctus* and the *Agnus*, are profoundly moving. Sheppard controls his material with exceptional skills of melody and structure, and the singers are able to match these at every point. Listeners may be astonished by the attempt to reproduce the Latin pronunciation of English clerics during this period – it was said by foreign ambassadors to be incomprehensible! The attempt to recover the style of the chant sections was courageous, though more flexibility in the longer stretches was needed. One surprising slip was the singing of only the cue of a collect ending; it could easily have been completed, since contemporary sources clearly indicate two more words for the collect in question. That said, these are in general excellent performances.

The Second Service

The Lord's Prayer. The Second Service – Magnificat; Nunc dimittis. Gaude, gaude, gaude Maria. Filie Ierusalem. Reges Tharsis et insulae. Spiritus sanctus procedens. Laudem dicite Deo nostro. Hec dies. Impetum fecerunt unanimes. Libera nos, salva nos

Choir of Christ Church Cathedral, Oxford / Stephen Darlington
Nimbus NI5480 (67 minutes: DDD). Texts and translations included. Recorded 1995 Ⓕ

This enjoyable recording opens with two works in English which were probably written within days of John Sheppard's early death, as Roger Bowers's introductory essay explains. The hypothesis is an intriguing one, for *The Lord's Prayer* and the Second Service largely lack the wayward dissonances that play an integral (and controversial) part in this composer's style. Whether the difference is due to the switch to the vernacular is a moot point, for the Latin Responds that make up most of the disc show off the older style more conspicuously. The most impressive of these is undoubtedly the elaborate *Gaude, gaude, gaude Maria*, but the piece that most clearly enunciates its composer's idiosyncrasies has to be the concluding *Libera nos* (Sheppard wrote two identically scored settings of this text, but neither the programme details nor Bowers's essay makes clear which one is performed here). Sheppard's special predilection for high voices makes the participation of boy trebles here particularly appropriate. In such traditional choral establishments, unanimity of ensemble is crucial. From that standpoint this choir is difficult to fault, although towards the end of the recital a certain tiredness is just perceptible. If anything, the sound is a shade top-heavy at times (as in *Filie Ierusalem*), but a couple of the Responds dispense with trebles altogether, providing a welcome contrast.

Dmitry Shostakovich

Russian/USSR 1906-1975

GROVE *He studied with his mother, a professional pianist, and then with Shteynberg at the Petrograd Conservatory (1919-25): his graduation piece was his Symphony no.1, which brought him early international attention. His creative development, however, was determined more by events at home. Like many Soviet composers of his generation, he tried to reconcile the musical revolutions of his time with the urge to give a voice to revolutionary socialism, most conspicuously in his next two symphonies, no.2 ('To October') and no.3 ('The First of May'), both with choral finales. At the same time he used what he knew of contemporary Western music (perhaps Prokofiev and Krenek mostly) to give a sharp grotesqueness and mechanical movement to his operatic satire The Nose, while expressing a similar keen irony in major works for the ballet (The Age of Gold, The Bolt) and the cinema (New Babylon). But the culminating achievement of these quick-witted, nervy years was his second opera The Lady Macbeth of the Mtsensk District, where high emotion and acid parody are brought together in a score of immense brilliance.*

Lady Macbeth was received with acclaim in Russia, western Europe and the USA, and might have seemed to confirm Shostakovich as essentially a dramatic composer: by the time he was 30, in 1936, he was known for two operas and three full-length ballets, besides numerous scores for the theatre and films, whereas only one purely orchestral symphony had been performed, and one string quartet. However, in that same year Lady Macbeth was fiercely attacked in Pravda, and he set aside his completed Symphony no.4 (it was not performed until 1961), no doubt fearing that its Mahlerian intensity and complexity would spur further criticism. Instead he began a new symphony, no.5, much more conventional in its form and tunefulness – though there is a case for hearing the finale as an internal send-up of the heroic style. This was received favourably, by the state and indeed by Shostakovich's international public, and seems to have turned him from the theatre to the concert hall. There were to be no more operas or ballets, excepting a comedy and a revision of Lady Macbeth; instead he devoted himself to symphonies, concertos, quartets and songs (as well as heroic, exhortatory cantatas during the war years).

Of the next four symphonies, no.7 is an epic with an uplifting war-victory programme (it was begun in besieged Leningrad), while the others display more openly a dichotomy between optimism and introspective doubt, expressed with varying shades of irony. It has been easy to explain this in terms of Shostakovich's position as a public artist in the USSR during the age of socialist realism, but the divisions and ironies in his music go back to his earliest works and seem inseparable from the very nature of his harmony, characterised by a severely weakened sense of key. Even so, his position in official Soviet music certainly was difficult. In 1948 he was condemned again, and for five years he wrote little besides patriotic cantatas and private music (quartets, the 24 Preludes and Fugues which constitute his outstanding piano work).

Stalin's death in 1953 opened the way to a less rigid aesthetic, and Shostakovich returned to the symphony triumphantly with no.10. Nos. 11 and 12 are both programme works on crucial years in revolutionary history (1905 and 1917), but then no.13 was his most outspokenly critical work, incorporating a setting of words that attack anti-semitism. The last two symphonies and the last four quartets, as well as other chamber pieces and songs, belong to a late period of spare texture, slowness and gravity, often used explicitly in images of death: Symphony no.14 is a song cycle on mortality, though no.15 remains more enigmatic in its open quotations from Rossini and Wagner.

Complete Cello Concertos

No 1 in E flat, Op 107; **No 2** in G, Op 126

Cello Concertos Nos 1 and 2
Mischa Maisky *vc* **London Symphony Orchestra / Michael Tilson Thomas**
DG 445 821-2GH (65 minutes: DDD) Ⓕ
Recorded 1993 ●

The Second Cello Concerto is one of the major concertos of the post-war period – as potent a representative of the composer's later style as the last three symphonies, be it through irony (second movement), poetry (first and third) or anger (beginning of the third). Few cellists have tended the *piano espressivo* of the *Largo*'s opening bars as lovingly as Mischa Maisky does, while the rapt quality of his soft playing and the expressive eloquence of his double-stopping wring the most from Shostakovich's extended soliloquy. Michael Tilson Thomas points and articulates with his usual skill. Only the opening of that movement (with its furious whoop horns) seems marginally underprojected, although the main climax later on is both immensely powerful and extraordinarily clear. The First Concerto harbours fewer mysteries than the Second and yet remains a pivotal work. Maisky phrases beautifully, while Tilson Thomas and the LSO again come up trumps, even though 1'33" into the finale the dramatic switch to 6/8 sounds less spontaneous than it does under, say, Maxim Shostakovich. In other respects, however, this is a forceful and fairly outgoing interpretation, beautifully recorded and a suitable coupling for the disc's star act – the finest available studio recording of the Second Concerto. In fact, this CD is now the prime recommendation for the two concertos coupled together.

Cello Concertos Nos 1 and 2
Heinrich Schiff *vc* **Bavarian Radio Symphony Orchestra / Maxim Shostakovich**
Philips 412 526-2PH Ⓕ
(61 minutes: DDD)

In the First Concerto, Heinrich Schiff's excellent version with the Bavarian Radio Symphony Orchestra under Shostakovich *fils* can hold its own against all opposition. The first movement is taut and well held together and the second is beautifully shaped, the passion and poignancy of the climax being particularly well conveyed. Schiff makes one listen to every nuance and wait upon every rest.

The Second Concerto comes between the 13th and 14th Symphonies, neither of which endeared Shostakovich to the Soviet Establishment. The concerto did not meet with the enthusiastic acclaim that had greeted No 1 and has not established itself in the repertory to anywhere near the same extent, perhaps because it offers fewer overt opportunities for display. It is a work of eloquence and beauty, inward in feeling and spare in its textures. The opening *Largo* could hardly be in stronger contrast to the corresponding movement of No 1. It seems rhapsodic and fugitive, and it takes time before one realises how purposeful is the soloist's course through the shadowy landscape. Yet the sonorities have the asperity so characteristic of Shostakovich. It is a haunting piece, lyrical in feeling, and gently discursive, sadly whimsical at times and tinged with a smiling melancholy that hides deeper troubles. The balance is generally excellent: the soloist is perhaps marginally forward, but the result is still very natural yet very clear and there is outstanding definition and realism. Recommended with enthusiasm.

Complete Piano Concertos

No 1 C minor for Piano, Trumpet and Strings, Op 35;
No 2 in F, Op 102

Piano Concertos Nos 1 and 2. The Unforgettable Year 1919, Op 89 – The assault on beautiful Gorky
Dmitri Alexeev *pf* **Philip Jones** *tpt* **English Chamber Orchestra / Jerzy Maksymiuk**
Classics for Pleasure CD-CFP4547 Ⓑ
(48 minutes: DDD)

Shostakovich's piano concertos were written under very different circumstances, yet together they contain some of the composer's most cheerful and enlivening music. The First, with its wealth of perky, memorable tunes, has the addition of a brilliantly-conceived solo trumpet part (delightfully done here by Philip Jones) that also contributes to the work's characteristic stamp. The Second Concerto was written not long after Shostakovich had released a number of the intense works he had concealed during the depths of the Stalin era. It came as a sharp contrast, reflecting as it did the optimism and sense of freedom that followed the death of the Russian dictator. The beauty of the slow movement is ideally balanced by the vigour of the first, and the madcap high spirits of the last. The poignant movement for piano and orchestra from the Suite from the 1951 film *The Unforgettable Year 1919*, 'The assault on beautiful Gorky', provides an excellent addition to this disc of perceptive and zestful performances by Alexeev. He is most capably supported by the ECO under Maksymiuk, and the engineers have done them proud with a recording of great clarity and finesse. A joyous issue.

Piano Concertos. Three Fantastic Dances, Op 5. 24 Preludes and Fugues, Op 87 – No 1 in C; No 4 in E minor; No 5 in D; No 23 in F; No 24 in D minor
Dmitri Shostakovich *pf* **Ludovic Vaillant** *tpt* **French Radio National Orchestra / André Cluytens**
EMI Composers in Person mono
CDC7 54606-2 (76 minutes: ADD) Ⓕ
Recorded 1958-59

Before devoting himself entirely to composition Shostakovich pursued a successful parallel career as a concert pianist, playing mostly romantic repertoire. These recordings were made at a time when he still played his own works in public, and they show him to have been a highly skilled player. His performances of both concertos are quite brilliant, and have a particularly vivacious, outgoing quality. In the First Concerto Ludovic Vaillant plays the trumpet part with character and great virtuosity, and the orchestral playing under Cluytens matches that of the composer in its joyous high spirits.

The three little *Fantastic Dances* are wittily brought to life. A different, far more serious, academic world is evoked by Shostakovich in his Preludes and Fugues. Here the composer shapes his own long contrapuntal lines with great skill, and these are very compelling, highly concentrated performances. The mono recordings are all very acceptable, save that of the last Prelude and Fugue, where a certain rustiness creeps into the sound. All these items have historical importance, but they also offer many rewards to the listener who is primarily interested in the music.

Complete Violin Concertos

No 1 in A minor, Op 99; **No 2** in C sharp minor, Op 129

Awards 1990

Violin Concertos Nos 1 and 2
Lydia Mordkovitch *vn* **Scottish National Orchestra / Neeme Järvi**
Chandos CHAN8820 (69 minutes: DDD) Ⓕ
Recorded 1989. **OOO**

This coupling completely explodes the idea of the Second Violin Concerto being a disappointment after the dramatic originality of No 1. Certainly No 2, completed in 1967, a year after the very comparable Cello Concerto No 2, has never won the allegiance of violin virtuosos as the earlier work has done, but here Lydia Mordkovitch confirms what has become increasingly clear, that the spareness of late Shostakovich marks no diminution of his creative spark, maybe even the opposite. In that she is greatly helped by the equal commitment of Neeme Järvi in drawing such purposeful, warmly expressive playing from the Scottish National Orchestra. With such spare textures the first two movements can be difficult to hold together, but here from the start, where Mordkovitch plays the lyrical first theme in a hushed, beautifully withdrawn way, the concentration is consistent.

The première recording of the work from David Oistrakh (on Chant du Monde but currently out of the catalogue), dedicatee of No 2 as of No 1, has remained unchallenged for a generation, and Mordkovitch does not always quite match her mentor in the commanding incisiveness of the playing in bravura passages. But there is no lack of power, and the more vital element in this work is the dark reflectiveness of the lyrical themes of the first two movements.

It is not just that Mordkovitch has the benefit of far fuller recording and a less close recording balance, but that her playing has an even wider range of colouring and dynamic than Oistrakh's. She conveys more of the mystery of the work and is perfectly matched by the orchestra. As in the First Concerto the principal horn has a vital role, here crowning each of the first two movements with a solo of ecstatic beauty in the coda. The Russian player on the Chant du Monde version is first-rate, no Slavonic whiner, but the SNO principal is far richer still, with his expressiveness enhanced by the wider dynamic and tonal range of the recording. The range of the recording helps too in the finale, where the *Allegro* has a satisfyingly barbaric bite, while the *scherzando* element is delectably pointed, as it is in the first movement too.

In the First Concerto Mordkovitch is hardly less impressive. As in Concerto No 2 one of her strengths lies in the meditative intensity which she brings to the darkly lyrical writing of the first and third movements. Here, too, she has never sounded quite so full and warm of tone on record before. In the brilliant second and fourth movements she may not play with quite the demonic bravura of Oistrakh, but again there is no lack of power, and in place of demonry she gives rustic jollity to the dance rhythms, faithfully reflecting the title of the finale, *Burlesque*. She is helped by recorded sound far fuller than Oistrakh's. This is a superb disc.

Violin Concerto No 1

Awards 1995

Shostakovich Violin Concerto No 1
Prokofiev Violin Concerto No 1 in D, Op 19
Maxim Vengerov *vn* **London Symphony Orchestra / Mstislav Rostropovich**
Teldec 4509-92256-2 (62 minutes: DDD) Ⓕ
Recorded 1994. Includes bonus disc **OOO**

There is an astonishing emotional maturity in Vengerov's Shostakovich. He uses Heifetz's bow but it is to David Oistrakh that he is often compared. His vibrato is wider, his manners less consistently refined, and yet the comparison is well founded. Oistrakh made three commercial recordings of the Shostakovich and one can guess that Vengerov has been listening to those earlier Oistrakh renditions as there is nothing radically novel about his interpretation. Some may find Vengerov's impassioned climaxes a shade forced by comparison. Yet he achieves a nobility and poise worlds away from the superficial accomplishment of most modern rivals. He can fine down his tone to the barest whisper; nor is he afraid to make a scorching, ugly sound. While his sometimes slashing quality of articulation is particularly appropriate to the faster movements, the brooding, silver-grey 'Nocturne' comes off superbly too, though it seems perverse that the engineers mute the low tam-tam strokes. Rostropovich has the lower strings dig into the third movement's passacaglia theme with his usual enthusiasm. Indeed the orchestral playing is very nearly beyond reproach.

Vengerov and Rostropovich take an unashamedly epic view of the Prokofiev concerto and it works well. Closely observed digital recording uncovers a wealth of detail, most of it welcome, with the conductor's erstwhile clumsy tendency barely noticeable. Towards the end of the first movement, the approach to the reprise of the opening melody on solo flute with harp, muted strings and lightly running tracery from the soloist is very deliberately taken, and the long-breathed finale builds to a passionate, proto-Soviet climax. The central *Scherzo* is breathtaking in its virtuosity.

Need one go on? If you're looking for a recording of the Shostakovich, Vengerov's coupling may be less logical than Mordkovitch's (above) but don't be deterred from investigating this extraordinary disc.

Shostakovich Violin Concerto No 1
Prokofiev Violin Concerto No 2 in G minor, Op 63
Vadim Repin *vn* **Hallé Orchestra / Kent Nagano**
Erato 0630-10696-2 (59 minutes: DDD) Ⓕ
Recorded 1995 ∞

Vadim Repin's interpretation of the Shostakovich comes across as less quintessentially Russian than Maxim Vengerov's in its avoidance of rhetorical overkill. Without in any way underplaying the bravura passages (the *Scherzo* is taken at an incredible speed), he stresses rather the chamber-like intimacy of Shostakovich's score. Rather surprising, perhaps, is the flowing tempo for the slow third movement, but, thanks also to Nagano and the Hallé, we do actually hear the music as a passacaglia. With Vengerov and Rostropovich intent on heightening strong emotions rather than clarifying textures, the LSO's contribution is comparatively impenetrable on Teldec. In the 'Nocturne' the tam-tam, inaudible in Abbey Road, is perfectly caught in Manchester.

Given Repin's dazzling achievement in the Shostakovich concerto, his Prokofiev is a shade disappointing. The violin is less sweetly caught and Repin sometimes makes the kind of uningratiating noises which imply some impatience with the straightforward *Romeo and Juliet*-style lyricism of the work. The finale sounds spontaneous but the lovely slow movement could do with more space to indulge its sweetly singing lines. However, if the coupling appeals, Repin represents a clear first choice – and anyone who cares about the Shostakovich will want to hear this disc.

Shostakovich Violin Concerto No 1
Tchaikovsky Violin Concerto in D, Op 35
Midori *vn* **Berlin Philharmonic Orchestra / Claudio Abbado**
Sony Classical SK68338 (73 minutes: DDD) Ⓕ
Recorded live in 1997

It makes an original and attractive coupling having the Tchaikovsky concerto together with this 20th-century Russian masterpiece. The implication is that Shostakovich in this darkly introspective work is less a modernist than a successor to the romantic Tchaikovsky, and Midori's readings, recorded live, do bring out the likenesses quite as much as the obvious contrasts. With the solo instrument naturally balanced, the most striking point about both performances is the way that Midori, never lacking in virtuoso bravura, makes an even more distinctive impression in the many passages where she plays in a hushed, intimate half-tone. At the beginning of the *Moderato* first movement of the Shostakovich her tone is so withdrawn that one must listen hard to detect precisely when she starts playing. In the passacaglia third movement she conveys an ethereal poignancy in her *pianissimo* playing. Even in the Tchaikovsky the degree to which Midori brings out a meditative quality in passages normally treated merely as sweet and songful is striking, a point established at the very start in her first ruminative solo.

As these are live recordings, it is not surprising that in both works Midori is often rhythmically free, always sounding spontaneous, though the central *Canzonetta* of the Tchaikovsky, at a markedly slow tempo, does run the risk of sounding a little sticky, with marked agogic hesitations. Even so the hushed intensity is most compelling, sparkling and volatile in the flourishes at the beginning of the finale of the Tchaikovsky. She adopts the tiny traditional cuts in the finale, arguably the preferable course. In both works Abbado is a powerful and sympathetic, yet discreet accompanist, with tuttis designed to support the soloist, rarely drawing attention to himself. In the finale of the Shostakovich it is striking how even before Midori enters Abbado finds an element of jollity in a movement which more often is treated as thrustful and demonic. Not that there is ever any lack of weight in the Berlin Philharmonic's playing, with a recording that is both warm and well detailed.

Violin Concerto No 2

Shostakovich Violin Concerto No 2
Prokofiev Violin Concerto No 2 in G minor, Op 63
Maxim Vengerov *vn* **London Symphony Orchestra / Mstislav Rostropovich**
Teldec 0630-13150-2 (62 minutes: DDD) Ⓕ
Recorded 1996 ○

This is an exceptionally fine peformance of the Shostakovich, the desperate bleakness perfectly realised. There has been no finer account since that of the dedicatee, David Oistrakh (Chant du Monde). With Rostropovich rather than Kondrashin on the podium, tempos are comparatively deliberate in the first two movements, but there is no lack of intensity in the solo playing and rather more in the way of light and shade. In the stratospheric writing of the *Adagio*, Vengerov is technically superb, while the all-pervading atmosphere of desolation has never been more potently conveyed. The finale is more extrovert than some will like, the fireworks irresistible, and yet you do not lose the disquieting sense of a composer at the end of his tether, seemingly contemptuous of his own material.

The Prokofiev is rather less successful, however. The balance there is partly to blame – the orchestra a remote presence, the soloist rather too closely scrutinised – but also there is a lack of intimacy in the interpretation itself. Vengerov self-consciously scales down his tone for the first movement's exquisite second subject, but the second movement, very slow and grand, is plagued by Rostropovich's over-insistent nuancing. Even if the finale has its impressive passages, there isn't quite enough light-hearted Spanishry in a piece written not to Soviet order but for Robert Soëtans to play in Madrid. Vengerov's sometimes 'overwrought' manner fits this music like a glove.

Film and light music

'The Film Album'

The Counterplan, Op 33 – Presto; Andante (with **Alexander Kerr** *vn*); The Song of the Counterplan. Alone, Op 26 – March; Galop; Barrel Organ; March, Altai; In Kuzmina's hut; School children; Storm Scene. The Tale of the Silly Little Mouse, Op 56 (arr Cornall). Hamlet, Op 116 – Introduction; Palace Music; Ball at the Castle; Ball; In the Garden; Military Music; Scene of the Poisoning. The Great Citizen, Op 55 – Funeral March. Sofia Perovskaya, Op 132 – Waltz. Pirogov, Op 76*a* (arr Atovmian) – Scherzo; Finale. The Gadfly, Op 97 – Romance (Kerr)

Royal Concertgebouw Orchestra / Riccardo Chailly

Decca 460 792-2DH (78 minutes: DDD) Ⓕ

Recorded 1998 ⭘

Only ardent film buffs and die-hard Shostakovich completists will cavil at this selection of Riccardo Chailly's rather offbeat collection, cutting across as it does several more serious-minded projects. He gives us some genuine novelties too. 'The Song of the Counterplan' (track 3) was transmogrified into an MGM production number in the 1940s for the film *Thousands Cheer*. Producer Andrew Cornall's new (non-vocal) suite from the *Tom and Jerry*-like *Tale of the Silly Little Mouse* was sanctioned by the composer's estate and makes its début here. The 'Funeral March' from *The Great Citizen* turns up again in the 11th Symphony (track 22). And the much later 'Waltz' from *Sofia Perovskaya* is also unfamiliar. Less committed listeners should perhaps sample track 11 for Shostakovich's take on the spooky weirdness of the theremin, and track 25 for the ubiquitous 'Romance' from *The Gadfly*. There may be no great music here – some of the darker numbers from *Hamlet* come closest with their echoes of *Stepan Razin* and the 13th Symphony – but with music-making of this quality it scarcely matters. For once you probably won't miss the raw primary colours and fish-glue pungency of an older interpretative tradition. Chailly has rarely sounded so unbuttoned in the studio and the selection is generous, if random. Only the final chord of the 'Finale' from *Pirogov* is a bit of a puzzle. Given the top-notch Decca production values on display, what sounds here like a drop-out or similar technical fault could be either the conductor executing a tricksy hairpin *diminuendo* or Shostakovich perpetrating a Mahler 7-type joke. Warmly recommended in any event.

'The Dance Album'

Moscow-Cheryomushki, Op 105 – concert suite (ed Cornall). The Bolt – ballet suite, Op 27*a* (1934 version). The Gadfly, Op 97 – Overture; The Cliff; Youth; Box on the Ear; Barrel Organ; Contredanse; Galop; At the Market Place; The Rout; The Passage of Montanelli; Finale; The Austrians; Gemma's Room

Philadelphia Orchestra / Riccardo Chailly

Decca 452 597-2DH (73 minutes: DDD) Ⓕ

Recorded 1995 ⭘

Although entitled 'The Dance Album', interestingly only one of the items on this disc (*The Bolt*) is actually derived from music conceived specifically for dance. However, what the disc reveals is that Shostakovich's fondness for dance forms frequently found expression in his other theatrical/film projects. The world première recording of a suite of four episodes from the 1959 operetta *Moscow-Cheryomushki* will be of particular interest to Shostakovich devotees. Despite the somewhat mundane plot, the score produces some surprisingly attractive and entertaining numbers, most notably perhaps the invigorating 'A spin through Moscow' and the 'Waltz'. For the suite from the ballet *The Bolt* Chailly brings us the less frequently heard 1934 version in which the composer dropped two of the eight numbers and changed some of the titles in order to deflect from the story-line of the ballet. Lots of parody and plenty of Shostakovich with his tongue planted firmly in his cheek is what we get, and if this aspect of the composer's output appeals then you will certainly enjoy Chailly's and his players' spirited and colourfully buoyant performances of this energetic score. Less familiar light is also shed on the music from the film *The Gadfly* which is heard here in a version which brings together 13 of the score's episodes and preserves Shostakovich's original orchestration, as opposed to the suite prepared and re-orchestrated by Levin Atovmyan. All the performances on the disc are superbly delivered and the recorded sound is excellent.

'The Jazz Album'

Jazz Suites Nos 1 and 2. Taiti trot, Op 16 Concerto for Piano, Trumpet and Strings in C minor, Op 35

[a]**Peter Masseurs** *tpt* [a]**Ronald Brautigam** *pf*

Royal Concertgebouw Orchestra / Riccardo Chailly

Decca 433 702-2DH (59 minutes: DDD) Ⓕ

⭘⭘

Shostakovich's lively and endearing forays into the popular music of his time were just that, and light years away from the work of real jazz masters such as, say Jelly Roll Morton or Duke Ellington And yet they do say something significant about Shostakovich's experience of jazz, as a comparison of these colourful, Chaplinesque *Jazz* Suites with roughly contemporaneous music by Gershwin, Milhaud, Martinu, Roussel and others will prove. Shostakovich engaged in a particularly brittle almost Mahlerian form of parody – his concert works are full of it – and that is what comes across most powerfully here. Besides, and as annotator Elizabeth Wilson rightly observes, 'real' jazz was treated with suspicion in Soviet Russia and Shostakovich's exposure to it was therefore limited.

The two *Jazz* Suites were composed in the 1930s, the First in response to a competition to 'raise the level of Soviet jazz from popular cafe music to music with a professional status', the Second at the request of the then-newly formed State Orchestra for Jazz (!). The First will make you chuckle, but it is the Second (subtitled

'Suite for Promenade Orchestra') that contains the best music, especially its achingly nostalgic Second *Waltz*. The instrumentation is light (the saxophone and accordion add a touch of spice to a generally bland recipe), while the playing here is quite superb. In fact, there's little to be said about Chailly's direction other than that it is good-humoured, affectionate and utterly professional, his Royal Concertgebouw players sound at home in every bar and the recording (Grotezaal, Concertgebouw) is both clean and ambient.

Taiti trot came to life when Nikolai Malko challenged Shostakovich to score Vincent Youmans's *Tea for Two* in an hour, or less – which he did, as a sort of mini-concerto for orchestra, each refrain being dealt to different instrumental forces. Fun that it is, its charm is terminal. Which leaves the Piano Concerto, music that for sophistication and inventive ingenuity is actually closer to what we now think of as jazz than the *Jazz* Suites (sample the free-wheeling, improvisatory opening to the last movement, on track 7).

Ronald Brautigam's instrument is twangy at the bass end, which mightn't seem too inappropriate, but as it was recorded two years before the other items on the disc (1988), I doubt that that was the intention. Still, it's a lively and fairly intense reading, neatly supported by Chailly and trumpeter Peter Masseurs, but ultimately less memorable than Alexeev (HMV Classics) or Jablonski or the composer himself (both nla).

The Golden Age

Royal Stockholm Philharmonic Orchestra / Gennadi Rozhdestvensky
Chandos ② CHAN9251/2 (134 minutes: DDD) Ⓕ
Recorded 1993

The Golden Age (1930) is an industrial exhibition organised in a capitalist country, at which a group of Soviet sportsmen have been invited to compete. The general idea of Shostakovich's characterization is to differentiate between goodies and baddies by assigning them respectively healthy-folk and decadent-bourgeois idioms. But then the trouble was, he couldn't stop himself enjoying being decadent. Not all of the 37 movements stand up independently of the stage-action. But the finales and the whole of Act 3 are top-notch stuff, at times surprisingly threatening in tone and symphonic in continuity; and there are several movements which could undoubtedly be promoted alongside the four in the familiar concert suite (the Tap Dance of Act 2 is especially appealing, for instance). Those who know their Shostakovich will be constantly intrigued by foretastes of *Lady Macbeth*, the Fourth Symphony and the *Hamlet* music, and by the appearance of Shostakovich's 'Tea for Two' arrangement as an Interlude in Act 2. This first complete recording is a major coup for Chandos. Admittedly not even their flattering engineering can disguise a certain lack of confidence and idiomatic flair on the part of the Royal Stockholm Philharmonic Orchestra. But let that not deter anyone with the least interest in Shostakovich, or ballet music, or Soviet music, or indeed Soviet culture as a whole, from investigating this weird and intermittently wonderful score.

Complete Symphonies

No 1 in F minor, Op 10; **No 2** in B, Op 14, 'To October'; **No 3** in E flat, Op 20, 'The first of May'; **No 4** in C minor, Op 43; **No 5** in D minor, Op 47; **No 6** in B minor, Op 54; **No 7** in C, Op 60, 'Leningrad'; **No 8** in C minor, Op 65; **No 9** in E flat, Op 70; **No 10** in E minor, Op 93; **No 11** in G minor, Op 103, 'The year 1905'; **No 12** in D minor, Op 112, 'The year 1917'; **No 13** in B flat minor, Op 113, 'Babiy Yar'; **No 14**, Op 135; **No 15** in A, Op 141

Symphonies Nos 1 and 3[a]
London Philharmonic [a]Choir and Orchestra / Bernard Haitink
Decca London 425 063-2DM (65 minutes: ADD/DDD)
Texts and translations included. Ⓜ
Recorded 1980-81
The cycle is also available as an 11-disc set:
444 430-2LC11 Ⓑ

Symphonies Nos 2[a] and 10
London Philharmonic [a]Choir and Orchestra / Bernard Haitink
Decca London 425 064-2DM (76 minutes: ADD/DDD)
Texts and translations included. Ⓜ
Recorded 1981

Symphony No 4
London Philharmonic Orchestra / Bernard Haitink
Decca London 425 065-2DM (68 minutes: ADD/DDD)
Texts and translations included. Recorded 1979 Ⓜ

Awards 1982/3

Symphony Nos 5[a] and 9[b]
[a]Concertgebouw Orchestra; [b]London Philharmonic Orchestra / Bernard Haitink
Decca London 425 066-2DM Ⓜ
(76 minutes: ADD/DDD). Texts and translations included. Recorded 1981 **ooo**

Symphony Nos 6 and 12
Concertgebouw Orchestra / Bernard Haitink
Decca London 425 067-2DM (74 minutes: ADD/DDD)
Texts and translations included. Recorded 1983 Ⓜ

Symphony No 7
London Philharmonic Orchestra / Bernard Haitink
Decca London 425 068-2DM (79 minutes: ADD/DDD)
Texts and translations included. Recorded 1979 Ⓜ

Symphony No 8
Concertgebouw Orchestra / Bernard Haitink
Decca London 425 071-2DM (62 minutes: ADD/DDD)
Texts and translations included. Recorded 1982 Ⓜ

Symphony No 11
Concertgebouw Orchestra / Bernard Haitink
Decca London 425 072-2DM (61 minutes: ADD/DDD)

Texts and translations included Ⓜ
Recorded 1983 ○

Symphony No 13
Marius Rintzler *bass* **Concertgebouw Choir and Orchestra / Bernard Haitink**
Decca London 425 073-2DM (64 minutes: ADD/DDD) Texts and translations included Ⓜ
Recorded 1982 ○

Symphony No 14. Six Marina Tsvetaeva Poems, Op 143
Julia Varady *sop* **Ortrun Wenkel** *contr* **Dietrich Fischer-Dieskau** *bar* **Concertgebouw Orchestra / Bernard Haitink**
Decca London 425 074-2DM
(72 minutes: ADD/DDD). Texts and translations included. Recorded 1980 Ⓜ ○

Symphony No 15[a]. From Jewish Folk Poetry, Op 79[b]
Elisabeth Söderström *sop* **Ortrun Wenkel** *contr* **Ryszard Karczykowski** *ten* **[a]London Philharmonic Orchestra; [b]Concertgebouw Orchestra / Bernard Haitink**
Decca London 425 069-2DM (73 minutes: ADD/DDD)
Texts and translations included. Recorded 1978 Ⓜ

This, the first complete Western cycle of the symphonies, conducted by Bernard Haitink, returns to the catalogue at mid price, Decca having jettisoned a few minor works and decoupled several major ones. It is hard to argue with this presentation when it includes modern annotations and full recording data. Concerned for tradition, and with the need to challenge it, the young Shostakovich could be classical and modern, polemical and prankish by turns. Haitink, not entirely po-faced, turns in a thoroughly decent account of the First Symphony, missing just a little of the element of pastiche. The recoupling with the Third does strike sparks, the language of the later music variously foreshadowed in divergent contexts. In the Fourth, Haitink offers no stupendous revelations, content to bring out the dignity of the writing in a piece where we have come to expect something more sensational, less perfectly controlled. His outer movements are helpfully split, by additional cues – but his literalness and sobriety fall short of the ideal, as, marginally, does the playing.

Haitink's Fifth, deeply considered and almost indecently well upholstered, is not easy to assess. Originally greeted with extreme reverence, it is an earnest attempt to make structural sense of the music's grand symphonic aspirations. It is only because the orchestral playing is generally so immaculate that one registers the curious glitch 2'13" into the *Largo*. That movement is less affecting than it can be, yet the preceding *Allegretto* is triumphantly brought off as a heavy-footed Mahlerian ländler. Then again, the first movement's long-limbed second subject chugs along reluctantly, dourly unphrased, with none of the easeful balm found in other interpretations. Haitink's Fifth is now generously paired with his solid, untrivial but scarcely earth-shattering Ninth. His Sixth and 12th are characterised by playing of *gravitas* and tonal splendour. This 12th could be seen as the 'best' modern version.

The *Leningrad* is another matter. It has rightly been praised for its symphonic integrity and splendid sound. Haitink's stoical view of the Eighth is highly impressive, though not very varied in mood. Curiously, the finale is mis-cued. Kurt Sanderling's reading (Berlin Classics) is also highly impressive. The 10th has always seemed less dependent on a conductor steeped in the Russian tradition, and the only drawback of Haitink's well-played, well-recorded account is his unsubtle, over-confident tone in the enigmatic third movement *Allegretto*. There is real demonic abandon in the *Scherzo*. Karajan's 10th (DG) is very desirable but he offers no makeweight. Haitink offers a well-prepared account of No 2, where the choral contribution has the odd awkward moment but the overall effect is very arresting. His 11th too has such weight and precision that his customary detachment is mostly less noticeable than his phenomenal control. Haitink's 13th boasts another of Decca's huge, reverberant recordings, of such 'cinematic' brilliance and range that it threatens to dwarf the music-making. The chorus and orchestra are on terrific form and the soloist, Marius Rintzler, would seem to be at one with Haitink's brooding approach (this is reviewed in greater depth further on).

As one of the first of Shostakovich's late scores to be taken seriously in the West, it is odd that the 14th should have been so poorly represented in the CD catalogue. Haitink's polyglot reading does not really represent a viable solution – too much vital and specific tone colour is lost along with the original note-values. To make matters worse, Fischer-Dieskau is in hectoring mode and both soloists' proximity to the microphones makes for uncomfortable listening, though the orchestral contribution is excellent. Barshai (Russian Disc) can lay claim to *absolute* authenticity. It is a fascinating document, as he and Vishnevskaya rage against the dying of the light in every song, slicing seconds (sometimes minutes) off the timings of the Western account. Generally speaking the sound is close and crude, by no means intolerable but sufficiently prone to distortion to inhibit a general recommendation. In its way, however, this disc is indispensable.

Haitink's 15th has always been highly regarded, despite some less than needle-sharp contributions from the percussion where it matters most. At medium price, and with a rather high-level transfer of its coupling (whose historical significance is ably outlined in the insert-note), this merits a place at or near the top of anyone's list. To sum up: Haitink's set, superbly engineered, is nothing if not reliable. For those who prize technical finesse over raw passion, Haitink remains a plausible first choice.

Symnphony No 1

Symphonies Nos 1 and 6
Scottish National Orchestra / Neeme Järvi
Chandos CHAN8411 (64 minutes: DDD) Ⓕ
Recorded 1984-85

The First Symphony, the 19-year-old composer's graduation piece from the then Leningrad Conservatory in 1925, may be indebted to Stravinsky, Prokofiev, Tchaikovsky and even Scriabin. But it rarely sounds like anything other than pure Shostakovich. The sophisticated mask of its first movement is drawn aside for a slow movement of Slav melancholy and foreboding, and the finale brilliantly stage-manages a way out. The Sixth (1939) takes the familiar Shostakovichian extremes of explosive activity and uneasy contemplation (that the composer reconciles in the finale of the First) and separates them into individual movements. Two swift movements (a mercurial but menacing *Scherzo*, and a real knees-up of a finale) follow on from an opening *Largo* whose slow lyrical declamations eventually all but freeze into immobility. Järvi has a will (and Chandos, the engineering) to explore the extremes of pace, mood and dynamics of both symphonies; his account of the First Symphony convinces precisely because those extremes intensify as the work progresses. Some may crave a fuller, firmer string sound, but the passionate intensity of the playing (in all departments) is never in doubt.

Symphony No4

Shostakovich Symphony No 4
Britten Russian Funeral
City of Birmingham Symphony Orchestra / Sir Simon Rattle
EMI CDC5 55476-2 (68 minutes: DDD) Ⓕ
Recorded 1994 ⦿

This could just be the most important Western recording of the Fourth since the long-deleted Ormandy and Previn versions. Naturally, it complements rather than replaces Kondrashin's reading (Chant du Monde), taped shortly after the work's belated unveiling in December 1961: papery strings and lurid brass cannot disguise that conductor's unique authority even when Shostakovich's colouristic effects are muted by rudimentary Soviet sound engineering. In his recording, Rattle's approach is more obviously calculated, supremely brilliant but just a little cold. A certain firmness and self-confidence is obvious from the first. The restrained Hindemithian episode is relatively square, the first climax superbly built. The second group unfolds seamlessly with the glorious *espressivo* of the strings not much threatened by the not very mysterious intrusions of harp and bass clarinet. Tension builds again, some way into the development, with the lacerating intensity of the strings' *moto perpetuo fugato* passage.

Six miraculously terraced discords herald the two-faced recapitulation. Kondrashin and Järvi (Chandos) find more emotional inevitability in Shostakovich's destabilizing tactics hereabouts. Rattle doesn't quite locate a compensating irony, although his closing bars are convincingly icy, with nicely audible gong. Even in Rattle's experienced hands, the finale is not all plain sailing. The initial quasi-Mahlerian march is underpinned by disappointingly fuzzy timpani strokes which lose the point of their own lopsidedness. But then the section's mock-solemn climax is simply tremendous (and tremendously loud). The incisive *Allegro* is launched with (deliberate?) abruptness at an unbelievably fast tempo and, even if the music doesn't always make sense at this pace, the results are breathtaking. The denouement is approached with real flair. A superbly characterised trombone solo, hushed expectant strings and the most ambiguous of all Shostakovich perorations is unleashed with devastating force. The coda is mightily impressive too. After this, the Britten encore risks seeming beside the point; this really is emotional play-acting. In sum, neither Kondrashin's nor Järvi's more direct emotional involvement are easily passed over. On the other hand, Rattle does give us a thrilling example of what a relatively objective, thoroughly 'modern' approach has to offer today. With its huge dynamic range and uncompromising, analytical style, EMI's recording pulls no punches, and the awesome precision of the CBSO's playing makes for an unforgettable experience.

Symphony No 5

Symphony No 5. Ballet Suite No 5, Op 27*a*
Scottish National Orchestra / Neeme Järvi
Chandos CHAN8650 (76 minutes: DDD) Ⓕ
Recorded 1988

There are more Shostakovich Fifths than you can shake a stick at in the catalogue, and several of them are very good. Järvi's makes perhaps the safest recommendation of them all: it has a generous coupling (which cannot be said of many of its rivals), it has no drawbacks (save, for some tastes, a slight touch of heart-on-sleeve in the slow movement) and a number of distinct advantages. A profound seriousness, for one thing, and an absolute sureness about the nature of the finale, which many conductors feel the need to exaggerate, either as brassy optimism or as bitter irony. Järvi takes it perfectly straight, denying neither option, and the progression from slow movement (the overtness of its emotion finely justified) to finale seems more natural, less of a jolt than usual. The SNO cannot rival the sheer massiveness of sound of some of the continental orchestras who have recorded this work, but while listening one hardly notices the lack, so urgent and polished is the playing. A very natural recording, too, and the lengthy Suite (eight movements from Shostakovich's early ballet *The Bolt*, forming an exuberantly entertaining essay on the various modes that his sense of humour could take) makes much more than a mere fill-up.

Symphony No 5[a]. Chamber Symphony, Op. 110*a*.
Vienna Philharmonic Orchestra / Mariss Jansons
EMI CDC5 56442-2 (71 minutes: DDD) Ⓕ
[a]Recorded live in 1997

Setting a course somewhere between Sanderling's grey-faced stoicism and Bernstein's relentless exposure of nerve-endings, Jansons exercises tight technical control, imparting rather less in the way of inner character. As usual he goes for maximal rhythmic clarity, smooth legato lines and extreme dynamic contrasts. Inevitably, some will feel that the luscious string sound only gets in the way and there are a few agogic touches. Isn't there something unnatural about the shift up a gear in the first-movement development (around 8'00"), the cliff-edge dynamics of the slow movement, the self-conscious pacing of the start of the finale?

More positively, there are some wonderfully sustained *pianissimos* from both strings and winds – try the return of the first movement's second subject (from 12'26"). EMI's recording is not quite ideal, cavernous and a little occluded in the bass; the presence of an audience is never betrayed and does not seem to have influenced the character of the music-making. The Chamber Symphony is distinguished by its unique atmosphere. If the magnificent Vienna strings are arguably too suave, it is also the conductor's coolly calculated conception that lacks the last ounce of brutality.

Symphonies Nos 5[a] and 6[b] **H**
Philadelphia Orchestra / Leopold Stokowski
Dutton Laboratories mono CDAX8017 Ⓜ
(79 minutes: ADD). Recorded [b]1940 and [a]1942

Edward Johnson's useful notes seek to portray Stokowski as 'one of the foremost interpreters of a great 20th-century composer', but what will strike many younger listeners at first is the 'period' quality of these performances. While the playing as such is enormously impressive, the interpretations even relatively 'straight', Stokowski's use of (carefully rehearsed) portamento to create a languorous *legato* line at emotional peaks is wholly out of step with current thinking. And contemporary recordings of this repertoire from published scores are much less prone to copyist's error.

Stokowski sets a sensible speed for the first movement of the Fifth and at once one is aware of the lustrous quality of the Philadelphia strings. The long-limbed second subject is indescribably luscious, taken at a deliberate tempo not exactly signalled by the preceding bars. The effect is repeated in the recapitulation. The *Scherzo* is rather uncomfortable, almost a gabble with details smudged, but the slow movement – huge portamentos at the start of course – is marvellous and has great depth of feeling.

Stokowski's reading of the Sixth is if anything even finer, the recording rather firmer too. A surprisingly deliberate tempo for the first movement is effortlessly sustained throughout. The second movement is here sometimes more piercingly loud than you feel the conductor would have wanted, but the *Presto* finale is the surprise, relatively steady to bring parallels with the Prokofiev of the *Classical* Symphony. There is an odd break 3'28" into the movement.

Stokowski gave the Sixth its Western première and this was its first recording. He remade both symphonies in the LP era but these earlier versions are preferable, glamorised only at the most superficial level: the warmth and intensity are real. Michael Dutton's transfers are, as ever, technically adroit, removing all trace of swish to present the musical information in its purest form even if this means uprooting and remaking the sound too radically for some ears. There are of course excellent recordings of both symphonies in stereo, but Stokowski's pioneering efforts should not be overlooked.

Symphony No 5
Berlin Symphony Orchestra / Kurt Sanderling
Berlin Classics Eterna BC2063 2 (51 minutes: ADD) Ⓕ
Recorded 1982

Kurt Sanderling's epic interpretation of the Fifth should appeal to those who responded positively to his Eighth (also on Berlin Classics). Recorded in East Berlin in 1982, it is again overwhelmingly 'pessimistic' in tone, while the recorded sound (analogue) is rather more refined. As before, the conductor sets out his ideas about the work, 'one of the towering masterpieces of the 20th century', in an accompanying interview. 'In the performances which I have directed I tried to avoid misunderstandings, driving home the message that the finale was not a rousing tribute to a party congress.' Despite the warning, you might not be quite prepared for the bleak immobility of Sanderling's closing pages. The movement sets out at quite a lick and its pacing is otherwise relatively traditional. This is post-Testimony Shostakovich with a vengeance. The first movement, though scarcely ardent in the Bernstein manner, so that passages like the start of the development seem strangely literal, is always carefully calculated. The baldness never turns into drabness. Perhaps the Berlin SO cannot match the glorious sonority of the Concertgebouw strings for Haitink, but with Sanderling the serene second subject never becomes a perfunctory trudge even when its return highlights deficiencies in the Berlin horn department. There is a potent sense of desolation as the music winds down.

The *Allegretto* is less convincing, deliberately prosaic in a Teutonic sort of way. In the notes, Sanderling refers to this music as 'a grim and biting parody', yet in his anxiety to avoid any hint of boisterousness he comes close to mere heaviness. The *Largo* is deeply felt, albeit curiously un-Slav in feeling. It's not simply a matter of pace – even in the 1960s Previn was taking it slower than this (RCA) – but rather of manner. Sanderling's glacial stoicism is easy to respect, harder to love. Nevertheless, if such uncompromising rigour strikes any sort of chord, don't hesitate. Sanderling fled Nazi Germany for Stalin's Utopia in 1936: as he sees it the issues are too grave for easy point-making. This is music with the emotional power to weld an audience together, sweeping aside all intellectual reservations and needing no embellishment from him.

Additional recommendation
Symphony No 5
London Symphony Orchestra / Previn
RCA 74321 24212-2 (76 minutes: ADD: 5/66R) Ⓢ

André Previn's classic 1960s recording of the Fifth still figures among the very finest accounts, but at fantastic super-bargain price it is the top recommendation.

Symphony No 7

Symphonies Nos 1 and 7
Chicago Symphony Orchestra / Leonard Bernstein
DG ② 427 632-2GH2 (120 minutes: DDD) Ⓕ
Recorded live in 1988 ⓞⓞ

The *Leningrad* Symphony was composed in haste as the Nazis sieged and bombarded the city (in 1941). It caused an immediate sensation, but posterity has been less enthusiastic. What business has the first movement's unrelated long central 'invasion' episode doing in a symphonic movement? Is the material of the finale really distinctive enough for its protracted treatment? Michael Oliver, in his original *Gramophone* review, wrote that in this performance 'the symphony sounds most convincingly like a symphony, and one needing no programme to justify it'. Added to which the work's epic and cinematic manner has surely never been more powerfully realised. These are live recordings, with occasional noise from the audience (and the conductor), but the Chicago Orchestra has rarely sounded more polished or committed. The strings are superb in the First Symphony, full and weightily present, and Bernstein's manner here is comparably bold and theatrical of gesture. A word of caution: set your volume control carefully for the *Leningrad* Symphony's start; it is scored for six of both trumpets and trombones and no other recording has reproduced them so clearly, and to such devastating effect.

Symphony No 7
Scottish National Orchestra / Neeme Jarvi
Chandos CHAN8623 (69 minutes: DDD) Ⓕ
Recorded 1988

Jarvi doesn't quite convince you that the symphony isn't overlong, nor do you yet feel that the leap from varied repetition (the infamous 'war-machine' section) to conventional development in the first movement can be made to sound entirely plausible, but he finds more moments of poetry in this score than do Haitink (Decca) or Berglund (EMI Double Forte), and he responds with great feeling to the post-cataclysmic desolation towards the end of the first movement.

Unlike Rozhdestvensky (Olympia – nla), Jarvi is more given to expressive generosity, whether in impassioned outpourings or moments of tenderness. Jarvi's enthusiasm in the opening *allegretto* is compelling, but he hurries certain details beyond the point where they can speak clearly. Rozhdestvensky has both clarity and drive here – but he doesn't quite find the warmth Jarvi releases in the music that follows. Looking over the remainder of the work, Jarvi is more telling in the *Scherzo* (lovely bass clarinet and low flutes in the recap) and Rozhdestvensky more stirring in the third movement, the sharp edges he brings to the opening wind chorale and violin recitatives heighten the intensity and emphasise the consolatory role of the long flute theme that follows. Again, in the finale, honours are fairly evenly distributed: the early stages are unusually exciting under Jarvi the closing pages gritty and determined in Rozhlestvensky's hands. As to recorded sound, Jarvi has the advantage; the Rozhdestvensky sounds slightly constricted and hard after the warm spaciousness of the Chandos issue, but the ear soon adjusts.

In sum, Rozhdestvensky's version presents a more consistently compelling sense of narrative, but as it is now deleted the Jarvi remains the leading competitor. Though it doesn't convince you that the *Leningrad* is one of Shostakovich's supreme masterpieces, it shows how much is lost by writing it off as a wartime morale-booster.

Symphony No 8

London Symphony Orchestra / André Previn
HMV Classics HMV5 74370-2 (61 minutes: ADD) Ⓑ
Recorded 1973 ⓞⓞ

The Eighth Symphony, written in 1943, two years after the *Leningrad*, offers a wiser, more bitterly disillusioned Shostakovich. The heroic peroration of the Seventh's finale is here replaced by numbed whimsy and eventual uneasy calm. André Previn has since re-recorded the Eighth (DG) but this youthful account serves to remind us that the music is the product of a young man's imagination. The remake has greater breadth in every sense and, note for note, the orchestral playing is often finer. Even so the urgency of this earlier version is to be preferred. At that time, Previn seemed content to add a patina of mid-Atlantic gloss, and a good deal of subtlety, to the raw expressivity of the earlier Soviet recordings; he had not yet adopted the self-consciously epic manner thought appropriate today. With Sanderling among the few who know how to bring off the symphony as a gloomy and spiritless *in memoriam*, the lithe freshness of the Previn remains a compelling alternative. EMI's transfer is punchy and focused, but the orchestra seems smaller than before, drier and cleaner in the bass.

Shostakovich Symphony No 8
Mozart Symphony No 33 in B flat, K319
Leningrad Philharmonic Orchestra / Evgeny Mravinsky
BBC Legends/IMG Artists ② BBCL4002-2 Ⓜ
(82 minutes: ADD). Recorded live in 1960 ⓞ

There was a time when Mravinsky's greatness had to be taken on trust, such was the paucity of his representation in the record catalogues. The situation has been transformed in recent years; hence this version of the Shostakovich has to find its niche in a market-place documenting the orchestra's prowess in the piece from the 1940s to the 1980s. In a variety of different transfers (and at a variety of different pitches) Mravinsky's March 1982 concert performance is widely known. But in 1960, when the orchestra made an epochal visit to these shores with Rostropovich, Rozhdestvensky and Shostakovich himself in tow, the work had never been heard here and was unavailable on disc. Small wonder the event was such a sensation, with the November 1960 *Gramophone* leading the call for new recordings of the Soviet repertoire played on the tour. Instead, the orchestra stayed on to tape a famous set of the last three Tchaikovsky symphonies for DG. It was memories of this Royal Festival Hall rendition, the Eighth's UK première, together with an intermittently available low-fi MK recording, that kept its reputation alive.

Mravinsky was a conductor in the Karajan mould both in his undemonstrative, albeit politically ratified, exercise of authority and the way in which his interpretations remained broadly consistent from one decade to the next. The sinews had stiffened just a little by 1982, but the differences are slight when set beside the transforming zeal of a Furtwängler or a Bernstein. The authentic timbre of the Leningrad Philharmonic is there in both – the winds tearing into their phrases like scalded cats, the string sound huge and inimitable, dominating the soundstage and yet never fat or complacent.

In almost every respect, Mravinsky's London performance lives up to its legendary status, and the sound has been reprocessed to yield excellent results in compartmentalised stereo. Unfortunately, the listeners in the hall are surprisingly restless. The first movement is patiently built, stoic, even bleaker than usual from this source and with only minor technical imperfections: the problem is the veritable barrage of coughing. The power and control of the second and third movements is awesome by any standards and here the audience is less intrusive. In the finale, Mravinsky keeps a tight rein on his players, adopting marginally slower tempos and securing finer results than he did in 1982. This is the conductor at his peak. The climax is cataclysmic with the paying public at last stunned into silence during the magical coda.

Shostakovich dedicated the symphony to Mravinsky, and it is for this work that most people will want to acquire the set.

Additional recommendation

Symphony No 8

Berlin Symphony Orchestra / Kurt Sanderling

Berlin Classics Eterna BC2064-2 (67 minutes: ADD: 7/94) Ⓕ

Massively slow and studied, Sanderling's powerfully arresting 1976 performance is recommended to anyone prepared to try a radical alternative to the forward thrust of more familiar Soviet recordings.

Symphony No 9

Symphonies Nos 9 and 15

Moscow Philharmonic Orchestra / Kyrill Kondrashin

Melodiya 74321 19846-2 (54 minutes: ADD) Ⓜ

Recorded 1965 and 1974 ○○

After Mravinsky's politically motivated refusal to undertake the première of the 13th in 1962, Shostakovich found a stalwart interpreter in Kyrill Kondrashin. Shostakovich recordings don't come any more authentic than this. Objectively speaking, the playing of the Moscow Philharmonic is not uniformly distinguished. Kondrashin can be startlingly brisk, the panache and brilliance hardening into mannerism. The transfers are no more than serviceable and the badly translated accompanying notes are untrustworthy at best. That said, here is unbeatable music-making, and these are arguably among Kondrashin's greatest recordings. The classic Ninth (from 1965) is conveniently paired with a superbly vivid 15th (from 1974), generally hard-driven *à la* Mravinsky but far more convincingly poised. The first movement goes at a frightening lick, deserting the toy shop for the asylum, the slow movement lacks only the very last ounce of desolation and the finale, always intelligently conceived, is suitably emotive at the close. The sound has immediacy and just enough depth. Though of earlier vintage, the Ninth enjoys a more generous acoustic, the tape a little prone to distortion at moments of stress (which for Kondrashin come more often than usual). Both interpretations have a tonal weight and sarcastic intent which cannot fail to shock the uninitiated. To sum up: he finds in these scores an unrivalled dramatic tension, bringing to the surface raw emotions that more smoothly executed Western accounts play down. We may be impressed by the diligent literalness and sobriety of Haitink, but to what extent should we worry if he illuminates aspects of the music the composer himself thought unimportant? It isn't simply a matter of 'authentic' orchestral timbre. Kondrashin's versions document a very special kind of insight.

Symphony No 10

Shostakovich Symphony No 10 **Mussorgsky** (orch Shostakovich) Songs and Dances of Death

Robert Lloyd *bass* **Philadelphia Orchestra / Mariss Jansons**

EMI CDC5 55232-2 (72 minutes: DDD) Ⓕ

Recorded 1994

Stalin died on March 5, 1953, the same day as Prokofiev. In the summer of that year Shostakovich produced a symphony which can be taken as his own return to life after the dark night of dictatorship – the last two movements included, for the first time in his output, his personal DSCH signature (the notes D, E flat, C, B natural, in the German spelling). In the West the 10th Symphony is now widely regarded as the finest of the cycle of 15, not just for its sheer depth of personal feeling, but because it finds the purest and subtlest musical representation of that feeling. Perhaps this is why it is less dependent than some of Shostakovich's major works on a conductor steeped in the Russian idiom. Anyone expecting a welter of hairpin *diminuendos* and expressive nudges will be disappointed by Jansons's Shostakovich – solid, sturdy and rhythmically taut rather than overly individualistic for the most part. Jansons's first movement is basically brisk, with thrustful strings and conscientiously Soviet-style woodwind. It is a cogent enough view and yet the sense of underlying desolation is lacking, despite the conductor's vocal exhortations. The *Scherzo* is brilliantly articulated – even if the relatively leisurely pace robs the music of its potential to intimidate. The 'difficult' third movement is more convincing, though again unusually confident in tone. It would be churlish not to single out the superb horn playing. The main body of the finale (the introduction is separately tracked by the way) is launched with precise rhythmic clarity rather than irrepressible enthusiasm. In short, this is an excellent, sometimes dazzling choice among modern versions but it may strike seasoned listeners as slightly sterile, at once tightly controlled and spiritually disengaged. There is more passion in the coupling. Robert Lloyd is curiously under-represented on CD in the Russian repertoire that suits him so well. His admirers are bound to want this performance, which is very impressive as sheer singing. Throughout the disc, the close focus of the recording exposes a few instances of less than perfect synchronization but with playing so spectacularly accomplished, if not recognizably Philadelphian, this must be counted an outstanding achievement in its way.

Symphony No 10
Berlin Philharmonic Orchestra / Herbert von Karajan
DG 439 036-2GHS (52 minutes: DDD) Ⓕ
Recorded 1981 ●

Few works give a deeper insight into the interior landscape of the Russian soul than the 10th Symphony of Shostakovich, and this is a powerful and gripping account of what is, by general consent, Shostakovich's masterpiece. Karajan has the measure of its dramatic sweep and brooding atmosphere, as well as its desolation and sense of tragedy. Haitink's is nowhere near so intense or for that matter so well played, though the recording has impressive transparency of detail. There are many things here (the opening of the finale, for example) which are even more succesful than in Karajan's 1966 recording (DG Galleria), though the main body of the finale still feels too fast – however, it is (at crochet=176) what the composer asked for. His earlier account of the first movement is for some more moving – particularly the poignant coda. However, the differences are not significant and this is hardly less impressive. The CD enjoys the usual advantages of greater range and presence, and deserves a strong recommendation.

Additional recommendation
Symphony No 10
Berlin Philharmonic Orchestra / Karajan
DG Galleria 429 713-2GGA (51 minutes: ADD) Ⓜ
Karajan's powerful 1966 recording is a steal at mid price.

Symphony No 13

Marius Rintzler *bass* **Concertgebouw Orchestra Choir** (male voices); **Concertgebouw Orchestra / Bernard Haitink**
Decca 425 073-2DM (64 minutes: DDD). Notes, texts and translations included. Recorded 1984 Ⓜ ●●

With one single reservation Haitink's account of *Babiy Yar* is superb. The reservation is that Marius Rintzler, although he has all the necessary blackness and gravity and is in amply sonforous voice, responds to the anger and the irony and the flaming denunciations of Yevtushenko's text with scarcely a trace of the histrionic fervour they cry out for. The excellent chorus, though, is very expressive and it makes up for a lot, as does the powerful and sustained drama of Haitink's direction. He has solved the difficult problems of pacing a symphony with three slow movements (one is gripped throughout) and the atmosphere of each movement is vividly evoked, with a particular care for the subtleties of Shostakovich's orchestration. The orchestral sound, indeed, is magnificent: one can readily believe that the huge forces called for in the score were actually provided, but this does not necessitate any unnatural focusing on (say) the celcste in order that it shall register. The perspective is very natural throughout, and there is an excellent sense of the performance taking place in a believable space.

Symphony No 14

Symphony No 14. Two Pieces for String Quartet (arr Sikorski)
Margareta Haverinen *sop* **Petteri Salomaa** *bass* **Tapiola Sinfonietta / Joseph Swensen**
Ondine ODE845-2 (59 minutes: DDD). Text and translation included. Recorded 1994-95 Ⓕ ●

The multilingual version of the 14th Symphony was sanctioned by the composer but it remains a rarity on disc; some vital and specific tone colour is lost along with the original note values, and the 'three lilies' adorn the grave of 'The Suicide' more elegantly in the Russian. Haitink may not agree. He elected to use the multilingual text in his 1980 recording and now Joseph Swensen presents this compelling alternative. We tend to take sonic excellence for granted these days but this is a true state-of-the-art recording with the soloists more naturally placed than in the rival Decca issue and an orchestral sound combining great clarity with just enough hall resonance. The performance has character too, if lacking the pervasive chill of the earliest Soviet accounts. The conductor secures excellent results from the Tapiola Sinfonietta.

Of the soloists, the bass-baritone Petteri Salomaa is particularly impressive: his is a voice of rare tonal beauty, a Billy Budd rather than a Boris. His pronunciation is a little odd at times, but you may not see this as a problem. Tempos are perceptibly more 'extreme' than Haitink's, with the opening 'De profundis' dangerously slow in the modern manner and a strikingly well-characterised instrumental contribution to 'A la Santé' ('In the Santé Prison'). The fillers, larger than life, brilliantly dispatched and curiously inappropriate, are based on original quartet pieces which only came to light in the mid-1980s. The first shares material with *Lady Macbeth of Mtsensk*; the second appears as the polka from *The Age of Gold*! This is nevertheless a more rewarding, more probingly conducted disc than most of the current Shostakovich crop.

Complete String Quartets

No 1 in C, Op 49; **No 2** in A, Op 68; **No 3** in F, Op 73; **No 4** in D, Op 83; **No 5** in B flat, Op 92; **No 6** in G, Op 101; **No 7** in F sharp minor, Op 108; **No 8** in C minor, Op 110; **No 9** in E flat, Op 117; **No 10** in A flat, Op 118; **No 11** in F minor, Op 122; **No 12** in D flat, Op 133; **No 13** in B flat minor, Op 138; **No 14** in F sharp minor, Op 142; **No 15** in E flat minor, Op 144

Awards 1977

String Quartets Nos 1-15
Fitzwilliam Quartet (Christopher Rowland, Jonathan Sparey *vns* Alan George *va* Ioan Davies *vc*) Decca ⑥ 455 776-2LC6 Ⓑ
(377 minutes: ADD)
Recorded 1975-77 ooo

If Shostakovich's cycle of 15 symphonies can be said to represent a musical thread passing through the whole of the composer's public life, then it can be argued that his cycle of 15 string quartets represents the private persona of the man behind the mask, from the beginning of his personal anguish in the late 1930s, until his death in 1975. At the time of his First Quartet, composed in 1938, he was already an experienced and respected composer with five symphonies to his credit as well as much music for stage and film. Thenceforth his symphonic music inscrutably presented the emotions – albeit largely ironically – that the State expected from its leading composer, while the quartets provided an outlet for the emotions within and for his personal responses to the events taking place in the world around him. If the music is rich in irony, then the language the composer uses is straightforward, with a defined tonality, simple melodies, uncluttered rhythms and clear textures. There is only one possible composer, so recognizably individual is the voice.

The Fitzwilliam Quartet originally recorded its cycle in the mid-1970s, shortly after a concentrated period of study with the composer. Despite being recorded in analogue, the sound quality is still remarkably good. The group has a remarkable understanding of the idiom and of the music's underlying motivation. In the First Quartet it captures the uneasy mood (reminiscent of the contemporary Fifth Symphony) behind the seemingly placid surface. In the Fourth Quartet, it gives the Jewish idioms – a metaphor for the oppressed artist and never far away in Shostakovich's music – a more deliberate, and thus more natural-sounding, tempo. Probably the best known of the quartets is No 8, composed in Dresden in 1960 and dedicated to the victims of Fascism and of the War, and in view of the constant use of the DSCH motif and the quotations from several of his own pieces, there can be little doubt that Shostakovich considered himself among their number. It's a grim, often macabre, work and once again the Fitzwilliam captures the loneliness of the composer. So often, his solo melodies, set against a stark and sombre accompaniment, sound like a voice crying in the wilderness. The quartets are well worth getting to know and the performances by the Fitzwilliam Quartet, despite their age, still seem to reach the heart of the composer's intentions.

Awards 2000

String Quartets – Nos 1-5[c]; 6-10[b]; 11-15[a]. Two Pieces[b]
Emerson Quartet (Eugene Drucker, Philip Setzer vns Lawrence Dutton va David Finckel vc)
DG ⑤ 463 284-2GH5 Ⓕ
(360 minutes: DDD). Recorded live in [a]1994, [b]1998 and [c]1999 ooo

The Emerson Quartet have played Shostakovich all over the world, and this long-pondered *intégrale* sets the seal on a process that has brought the quartets to the very centre of the repertoire – the ensemble's and ours. Operating here out of Aspen, Colorado, several geopolitical worlds away from the old Soviet Union, the Americans outpace the classic Borodin recordings in almost every movement, their virtuosity powerfully evident in the many *scherzos* and toccata-like passages. While some listeners will miss the intangible element of emotional specificity and sheer Russianness that once lurked behind the notes, the playing is undeniably committed in its coolness, exposing nerve endings with cruel clarity. The hard, diamond-like timbre of the two violins (the leader's role is shared democratically) is far removed from the breadth of tone one might associate with a David Oistrakh, just as cellist David Finckel is no Rostropovich. But these recordings reveal surprising new facets of a body of work that is not going to stand still. The Fourth Quartet is a case in point, more delicate than most rivals with the finale relatively pressed, less insistently Jewish. The Fifth sometimes seems closer to Ustvolskaya or American minimalism than the mid-century Soviet symphonic utterance we are used to; the Emerson's almost hectoring mode of address and unfluctuating tempo are maintained for as long as (in)humanly possible. The very vehemence of, say, the finale of the Ninth tends to blunt the harmonic sense of the music, leaving something more visceral and rosiny than the argument can stand. To get the unique feel of this set, sample one of the encore pieces, the 'Polka' from *The Age of Gold*. Humanity and wit are in short supply, but can you resist the sheer explosive brilliance of the technique?

DG's recording is exceptionally vivid if somewhat airless, the separation of the instruments being achieved at the expense of tonal blend.

Given that all the quartets were taped live with only remedial patching, the audience is commendably silent: their enthusiastic applause is retained for Nos 1, 2, 9 and 12 only. This, surely, is a Shostakovich cycle for the 21st century.

String Quartets Nos 1, 3 and 4. Two Pieces for String Quartet (1931)
Shostakovich Quartet (Andrei Shishlov, Sergei Pishchugin *vns* Alexander Galkovsky *va* Alexander Korchagin *vc*)
Olympia OCD531 (77 minutes: ADD) Ⓕ
Recorded 1978-85 ●

String Quartets Nos 2, 5 and 7
Shostakovich Quartet
Olympia OCD532 (78 minutes: ADD) Ⓕ
Recorded 1978-85 ●

String Quartets Nos 6, 8 and 9
Shostakovich Quartet
Olympia OCD533 (74 minutes: ADD) Ⓕ
Recorded 1978-85

String Quartets Nos 10, 11 and 15
Shostakovich Quartet
Olympia OCD534 (78 minutes: ADD) Ⓕ
Recorded 1978-85 ●●

String Quartets Nos 12-14
Shostakovich Quartet
Olympia OCD535 (73 minutes: ADD) Ⓕ
Recorded 1978-85 ●

Any attempt to rank these players in relation to their more widely acclaimed opposite numbers in the Borodin Quartet seems pointless at this level of dedication; both teams have lived through this most extraordinary of 20th-century quartet-cycles many times. If any general observation about the two can be made, it is that the Borodin finds more corporate subtleties and passing shades in some of the earlier quartets, while the individual members of the Shostakovich Quartet make even stronger, more vibrant soloists. In the context of Shostakovich's many, very vocal solos and recitatives, it hardly seems invidious to single out the first violinist, Andrei Shishlov – dark, powerful and flawless of intonation throughout. Listen to his sleight-of-hand freedom in the unaccompanied melody of No 6's finale: the Borodin's Mikhail Kopelman doesn't begin to touch imagination like that.

These players also teach us to hold in equal awe the more classically contained quartets – No 6 and the outer movements of No 10 have a special grace – and all the slow movements are impressively unfolded with a steady fluency (notable in the passacaglias). As for the last rites of No 15, not even the Borodin finds such implicit human warmth in the still *fugato* of the Elegy. In tandem with the impassioned solos of the later movements, it's an impressive summing-up of this team's best intentions. Balances in the earlier recordings are less than kind to second fiddle and cellist and are uncomfortably boxy. You'll also have to adjust the volume-level for consecutive listening. If you seek only a single-disc token of the achievement, that with Nos 10, 11 and 15 is the one to have.

String Quartets No 14

String Quartets Nos 4, 11 and 14
Hagen Quartet (Lukas Hagen, Rainer Schmidt *vns* Veronika Hagen *va* Clemens Hagen *vc*)
DG 445 864-2GH (71 minutes: DDD) Ⓕ
Recorded 1993-94

The Hagen has chosen a fascinating journey to the unusual at-one-with-the-world radiance that ends the 14th. Already in this interpretation of the Fourth we hear those voices from beyond the grave that trouble the later quartets. The introspective shading of the *Andantino*'s earlier stages, climax included, sounds as if the mutes are already on. And when in fact the players do take them up – for the rest of the movement and the whole of the ensuing *Allegretto* – the sound becomes even more refined; note how first violin Lukas Hagen sings out his solo at fig. 29 (track 2, 3'31") with a frail, unearthly beauty which sounds as if it emanates from a viola d'amore.

Corporate work is faultlessly and subtly in sympathy with the essence of the piece; the only individual weakness occurs when Shostakovich asks the cellist to come to the fore in the finale's build-up of tension – Clemens Hagen's tone doesn't really make itself felt here – though the collective *fortissimo* cry from the heart shortly afterwards makes amends with even more intensity than some of the Hagen's senior counterparts (including the Shostakovich Quartet on Olympia) have previously found there.

Clemens lacks the presence to take the lead in Quartet No 14, dedicated to the cellist of the Beethoven Quartet, and emphasising his role accordingly; the sound can be lovely, but right at the start he has the misfortune to be echoed by his more characterful brother. Still, the F sharp major ending is as implicitly moving as it can be, and joint string power in crises comes very close to the genuine Russian article. Indeed, in the fifth-movement *Humoresque* of the 11th the limelighted second violin – Rainer Schmidt, the quartet's febrile and ever-impressive outside influence – brings so much forceful tone to the swelling of his two repeated notes that it sounds as if two violins are playing in unison, not just the one. Again, the joint approach to chants and combats, not to mention Lukas's extraordinary handling of the *glissandos* in the second movement, bring an urgently vocal quality to the work.

Piano Quintet in G minor, Op 57

Piano Quintet in G minor, Op 57[a].
Piano Trio No 2 in E minor, Op 67
Elisabeth Leonskaja *pf* **Borodin Quartet** (Mikhail Kopelman, [a]Andrei Abramenkov *vns* [a]Dmitri Shebalin *va* Valentin Berlinsky *vc*)
Teldec 4509-98414-2 (63 minutes: DDD) Ⓕ
Recorded 1995 ●

The Piano Quintet is almost symphonic in its proportions, lasting some 35 minutes, and has been popular with audiences ever since its first performance in 1940. Much of its popularity stems from Shostakovich's highly memorable material, particularly in the boisterous and genial *Scherzo* and finale movements. Because of the presence of a piano and of the powerful emotions expressed in them, the Quintet and Trio are commonly given very big performances. Those on this recording are by no means small, but they are chamber music, and that seems to be the view of the pianist as well as the string players. The finale of the Piano Trio actually gains in power from this, the greatest weight of tone being reserved for the true climax, and half the intensity of the Quintet, in this reading, comes from a remarkably wide and masterfully controlled range of sonority and dynamic. Leonskaja is a superb partner in both works. The recordings are very fine, with the balance just right.

Piano Trios

Shostakovich Piano Trios – No 1 in C minor, Op 8; No 2 in E minor, Op 67 **Schnittke** Trio
Vienna Piano Trio (Wolfgang Redik *vn* Marcus Trefny Stefan Mendl *pf*)
Nimbus NI5572 (69 minutes: DDD) Ⓕ
Recorded 1998 ●

Shostakovich's adolescent First Trio's ramshackle structure seems to matter less than its surprisingly Gallic-sounding, passionately late-romantic invention. The Vienna Piano Trio offers a rich-toned and meticulously prepared account. The tricky cello opening to the Second Trio is wonderfully ethereal here, and the even more tricky accumulating tempo over the entire movement is steady and logical, though this and the main tempo for the *Scherzo* are both more reined in than in the composer's own account (once available on Supraphon). The passacaglia and finale are properly intense and none the worse for being kept within the bounds of euphony, though the ideal performance, yet to be realised on CD, would be one which drained bitterer dregs of sorrow and took excitement closer to the point of hyperventilation.

Schnittke's Trio is more than an interesting makeweight. The String Trio original dates from 1985, the fateful year of the composer's first stroke and a period when he seemed to have a direct line to a kind of other-worldly inspiration (far more so than in later years when he claimed that more or less explicitly). True, the two longish movements occasionally seem at a loss, and at such times the gaucheness curiously echoes that of the teenage Shostakovich. Overall though this is one of Schnittke's most economical and restrained scores, and one of his finest. At every turn the Vienna Piano Trio is sensitive to the character and flow of this haunting music. A fine disc, then – imaginative programming, accomplished performances, and rich, well-balanced recording.

24 Preludes and Fugues, Op 87

No 1 in C; **No 2** in A minor; **No 3** in G; **No 4** in E minor; **No 5** in D; **No 6** in B minor; **No 7** in A; **No 8** in F sharp minor; **No 9** in E; **No 10** in C sharp minor; **No 11** in B; **No 12** in G sharp minor; **No 13** in F sharp; **No 14** in E flat minor; **No 15** in D flat; **No 16** in B flat minor; **No 17** in A flat; **No 18** in F minor; **No 19** in F flat; **No 20** in C minor; **No 21** in B flat; **No 22** in G minor; **No 23** in F; **No 24** in D minor

Shostakovich Preludes and Fugues Nos 4, 12, 14, 15, 17 and 23 **Scriabin** Poème-nocturne, Op 61. Two Danses, Op 73. Vers la flamme, Op 72. Fantasie in B minor, Op 28 **Prokofiev** Piano Sonatas – No 4 in C minor, Op 29; No 6 in A, Op 82. Pieces, Op 12 – Legend. Visions fugitives, Op 22 – Allegretto; Animato; Molto giocoso; Con eleganza; Commodo; Allegretto tranquillo; Con vivacita; Feroce; Inquieto; Con una dolce lentezza. Pieces, Op 32 – Danse; Waltz. Three Pieces from Cinderella, Op 95 – Gavotte. 10 Pieces from Cinderella, Op 97 – Autumn fairy; Oriental dance. Six Pieces from Cinderella, Op 102 – Grand waltz; Quarrel
Sviatoslav Richter *pf*
Philips ② 438 627-2PH2 (152 minutes: DDD) Ⓕ ●

Richter's greatest triumphs are in the Shostakovich Preludes and Fugues. From the glacial spaces of the E flat Prelude to the benediction of the F major, each is placed in its own world, each projected as a long, steady accumulation of musical thought. No recorded performances, not even the composer's own, are as compelling. This two-disc set is a mixture of live and studio recordings. At times the piano tone lacks lustre (particularly in the Prokofiev Sixth Sonata, one of the studio recordings), but overall the quality is fine. Which is to say that while this may not be exactly a voluptuous sonic experience at least there are no barriers between the listener and Richter's elevated music-making. The compilation begins with four of the most vaporous and highly charged of Scriabin's late pieces. Disdaining their invitations to lurid nuance and indulgent phrasing, Richter brings to them an intensity and concentration which dispel any thoughts of decadence. In its place are purity and idealism, and the apparent restriction of tone colour conceals a myriad of precisely chiselled lines and weighted chords. So without making any obvious show of it he releases the inner power of the music – the menace in the galloping triplets of 'Flammes sombres' (second of the two *Danses*, Op 73), the fierce ecstasy of *Vers la flamme*, for instance.

Less successful, however, is the earlier *Fantasie*, which runs out of steam rather seriously in the culminating stages. But this is virtually the only sign of any decline in Richter's virtuoso powers. If any work puts those powers to the test it is Prokofiev's Sixth Sonata, and here the finale goes at a tremendous lick, as irresistible as a river in full spate. Both middle movements are also fast-flowing streams, but again it is structural inevitability rather than surface excitement which makes the pulse race, the more so for the fact that the opening *Allegro* is deliberately held back – obstinately insistent in rhythm and dry in tone. As the Sonata's first performer back in his student days Richter speaks with obvious authority in this work. And over the years he has made the smaller-scale Fourth Sonata very much his own property too, investing every moment of it with meaning. In the shorter Prokofiev pieces it is good to hear him in more mellow mood. The Op 12 *Legend* is dreamy and seductive, the *Visions fugitives* full of fantasy and grace, and he clearly loves every tiniest corner of the *Cinderella* pieces, the more secretive the better.

Preludes and Fugues Nos 1-24
Tatyana Nikolaieva *pf*
Melodiya ③ 74321 19849-2 (168 minutes: DDD) Ⓕ
Recorded 1987 ⭘

Tatyana Nikolaieva was in at the birth of Shostakovich's Preludes and Fugues, and she made them one of the cornerstones of her repertoire. But you don't need to know those facts in order to sense the authority and insight of her interpretations. She gives the three-hour cycle a wonderful over-arching sense of unity, of an unbroken voyage of exploration. That may not have been the composer's intention (he actually spoke out specifically against such a view of the work), but there are plenty of indications in the structure and character of his music to justify Nikolaieva's approach. Her recordings of the complete Preludes and Fugues are the finest monuments to a much lamented artist. It is truly sad that her playing was not fully appreciated in the West until so late in her career. Not that her performances are seriously flawed; and if the acoustic is a fraction too close and dry, better this than an over-resonant sound. It gives space for the music to breathe rather than suffocating it with unwanted stage-mist; and it enables many more of Nikolaieva's nuances to register.

Preludes and Fugues Nos 1-24
Vladimir Ashkenazy *pf*
Decca ② 466 066-2DH2 (142 minutes: DDD) Ⓕ
Recorded 1995 ⭘

Here is a Shostakovich Preludes and Fugues cycle to be reckoned with. Admittedly, it starts none too promisingly with, by the highest standards, a rhythmically stiff, tonally lumpy C major Prelude and some overpedalling in the fugue. The neo-baroque figuration of the A minor Prelude and its spiky Fugue, on the other hand, presents his true credentials. On form and well prepared, as here, Ashkenazy remains a formidably fluent pianist, and the clarity and energy he brings to the faster, denser pieces is surpassed only by Richter (Philips). The sound itself is quite 'pingy', with a generous ambience behind it. That serves to heighten the impact of the more demonstrative pieces, but makes it difficult for Ashkenazy to sustain the atmosphere of the more meditative ones. Or maybe he simply doesn't feel the music that way. In the final D minor Fugue (No 24), where you can almost hear Shostakovich's 10th Symphony being born, Ashkenazy fails to build the texture as mightily as the early stages lead you to expect. Nikolaieva surpasses him here, and in general she reveals both subtler and grander perspectives, especially in her tauter, more drily recorded 1987 Melodiya set. Even so the balance-sheet for Ashkenazy comes out comfortably in the black. For consistency of pianism, straightforward integrity of interpretation and high quality of recording, his set can be warmly recommended.

From Jewish Folk Poetry, Op 79

From Jewish Folk Poetry, Op 79. The New Babylon – suite (arr Rozhdestvensky)
Tatyana Sharova *sop* **Ludmila Kuznetsova** *mez* **Alexei Martynov** *ten* **Russian State Symphony Orchestra / Valéry Polyansky**
Chandos CHAN9600 (70 minutes: DDD). Text and translation included. Recorded 1995-96 Ⓕ ⭘

This recording of Shostakovich's song-cycle *From Jewish Folk Poetry* is first-rate. For a start Polyansky's three vocal soloists are uncommonly well chosen: the light, youthful, slightly vulnerable soprano, the rich, world-weary mezzo and the ardent but unheroic tenor are ideally suited to the texts Shostakovich cunningly chose to convey his solidarity with mass suffering. Polyansky sets spacious tempos which allow every nuance of that suffering to register, and his orchestra is responsive and idiomatic in colouring. The recording, by Russian engineers, feels almost too good to be true in its excessive warmth; otherwise this version is preferable to the rival Rozhdestvensky on RCA. Polyansky's choice of the first of Shostakovich's 35 or so film scores makes for a more than welcome coupling. Polyansky offers an admirably idiomatic version of the Suite. He is especially adept at choosing timbres to reflect mood and situation. Even if you don't know the story-line the music was designed to accompany, this performance is so vividly characterised it can hardly fail to engage you.

Lady Macbeth of the Mtsensk District

Galina Vishnevskaya *sop* Katerina Izmailova; **Nicolai Gedda** *ten* Sergey Dubrovin; **Dimiter Petkov** *bass* Boris Izmailov; **Werner Krenn** *ten* Zinovy Borisovich Izmailov; **Robert Tear** *ten* Russian peasant; **Taru Valjakka** *sop* Aksinya; **Martyn Hill** *ten* Teacher; **Leonard Mroz** *bass* Priest; **Aage Haugland** *bass* Police Sergeant; **Birgit Finnila** *mez* Sonyetka; **Alexander Malta** *bass* Old convict; **Leslie Fyson** *ten* Milhand, Officer; **Steven Emmerson** *bass* Porter; **John Noble** *bar* Steward; **Colin Appleton** *ten* Coachman, First foreman; **Alan Byers** *bar* Second foreman; **James Lewington** *ten* Third foreman; **Oliver Broome** *bass* Policeman; **Edgar Fleet** *ten* Drunken Guest; **David Beaven** *bass* Sentry; **Lynda Richardson** *mez* Female convict
Ambrosian Opera Chorus; London Philharmonic Orchestra / Mstislav Rostropovich
EMI ② CDS7 49955-2 (155 minutes: ADD) Ⓕ
Notes text and translation included ⭘

Rostropovich's cast has no weak links to it. More importantly, he gives a full-blooded projection of the poignant lyricism that underlies the opera's brutality. Vishnevskaya's portrayal of Katerina is at times a bit too three-dimensional, you might think, especially when the recording, which favours the singers in any case, seems (because of her bright and forceful tone) to place her rather closer to you than the rest of the cast. But there is no doubt in her performance that Katerina is the opera's heroine, not just its focal character, and in any case Gedda's genially rapacious Sergey, Petkov's grippingly acted Boris, Krenn's weedy Zinovy, Mroz's sonorous Priest, and even Valjakka in the tiny role of Aksinya, all refuse to be upstaged.

The 'minor' parts are luxuriously cast from artists who may not have had the advantage of singing their roles on stage but have clearly relished building them into vivid portraits. The close focusing on the voices and the relative distancing of the orchestra into a warmer, more ample acoustic is a bit more noticeable on CD than it was on LP.

Lady Macbeth of the Mtsensk District
Maria Ewing *sop* Katerina Izmailova; **Sergei Larin** *ten* Sergey; **Aage Haugland** *bass* Boris Izmailov; **Philip Langridge** *ten* Zinovi Izmailov; **Heinz Zednik** *ten* Shabby Peasant; **Kristine Ciesinski** *sop* Aksinya; **Ilya Levinsky** *ten* Teacher; **Romuald Tesarowicz** *bass* Priest; **Anatoly Kotcherga** *bass* Police Sergeant; **Elena Zaremba** *mez* Sonyetka; **Kurt Moll** *bass* Old Convict; **Grigory Gritziuk** *bar* Millhand; **Carlos Alvarez** *bass* Officer; **Guillaume Petitot** *bass* Porter; **Jean-Pierre Mazaloubaud** *bass* Steward; **Alan Woodrow** *ten* Coachman; **Jean-Claude Costa, Jean Savignol, Jose Ochagavia** *tens* First, Second and Third Foremen; **Philippe Duminy** *bass* Policeman; **Mario Agnetti** *ten* Drunken Guest; **Johann Tilli** *bass* Sentry; **Margaret Jane Wray** *sop* Woman Convict **Chorus and Orchestra of the Opera-Bastille, Paris / Myung-Whun Chung**
DG ② 437 511-2GH2 (156 minutes: DDD) Ⓕ
Notes, text and translation included.

The main flaws in Rostropovich's historic recording of this opera with Galina Vishnevskaya in the title-role (and by 'historic' I don't mean 'old' but that soprano and conductor, both close friends of the composer, were obviously fired by the importance of recording the work in its unexpurgated form for the first time, and communicated that fire to their colleagues) are its very close focus on the solo voices and the at times distracting use of dramatizing effects: even when the chorus aren't singing they can often be heard muttering. Both are corrected in this new account, which has a very natural balance between voices and orchestra, and allows a cast of pungent singer-actors to do their own dramatizing. Rostropovich's version, for all that this is an opera that stands or falls by the performance of the principal soprano, is luxuriously cast, from Nicolai Gedda as Katerina's lover Sergey down to Aage Haugland (the new set's Boris) as the Sergeant. Although some of the names in the new cast are perhaps less familiar, they are no less distinguished: Larin is less characterful than Gedda but a real Russian tenor with impressive line and care for words, Haugland is a formidable bully of a Boris, Tesarowicz and Kotcherga are vivid in their roles, Zaremba a Carmen-like bitch of a Sonyetka while Kurt Moll as the Old Convict contributes much more than a cameo: he adds a whole tragic dimension to Act 3 that Alexander Malta, for Rostropovich, cannot approach.

Maria Ewing's voice is nowhere near as commanding as Vishnevskaya's, and the recorded focus emphasises this. There are times when you can hardly hear her above the orchestra; others indeed where you certainly cannot, and she is an unequal partner in the duet scenes with Larin and Haugland. This goes with such an intensely dramatic utterance, swooping up to and away from notes, that her singing and her *parlando* (her *Sprechstimme*, indeed) are sometimes hard to distinguish. The crucial test of her style of interpretation is the tragic 'aria' in Act 3 where Katerina realises the worthlessness of the man for whom she has murdered and suffered both humiliation and a destruction of all hope. Ewing is graphically expressive, every word placed in poignant relief, but at times you have to guess at what notes she's sketching and the whole passage is taken at about half its marked speed. Time standing still at such a moment is effective and not inappropriate, but you only have to turn to Vishnevskaya and Rostropovich to realise than the passage can be lyrically sung and given a sense of forward movement without any loss of pathos; rather the reverse, indeed.

Chung is a first-rate Shostakovich conductor, and he gets a warmer, fuller sound from his spaciously recorded Paris players than the no doubt intentionally leaner quality that Rostropovich asks of the LPO. Oddly enough the extra brass players that the score calls for make more impact in the slightly drier older recording, and there are sufficient pages on which Rostropovich finds a touch more hysterical energy or lurid colour to prefer his account even if Ewing had been a closer match for the imperious but for that very reason more moving Vishnevskaya. Katerina is the *Lady* Macbeth of the Mtsensk District and her fall, which begins with her descent to the vulgar Sergey, is great. Ewing is a slighter character: fascinating but not tragic.

The Nose and The Gamblers

The Nose
Edvard Akimov *bar* Kovalyov; **Valery Belykh** *bass* Ivan Yakolevich; **Nina Sasulova** *sop* Praskovya Osipovna; **Boris Tarkhov** *ten* District Inspector; **Boris Druzhinin** *ten* Ivan; **Aleksandr Lomonosov** *ten* Nose; **Igor Paramonov** *bass* Footman; **Valery Solovyanov** *bass* Clerk; **Lyudmila Sokolenko** *sop* Bread-roll seller; **Ashot Sarkisov** *sop* Doctor; **Alexander Braim** *ten* Yaryzhkin; **Lyudmila Sapegina** *mez* Alexandra Grigoryevna Podtochina; **Lyudmila Ukolova** *sop* Daughter; **Moscow Chamber Theatre Chorus and Orchestra / Gennadi Rozhdestvensky**

The Gamblers
Vladimir Rybasenko *bass* Alexei; **Vladimir Tarkhov** *ten* Ikharyov; **Valery Belykh** *bass* Gavryushka; **Nicolai Kurpe** *ten* Krugel; **Ashot Sarkisov** *bass* Shvokhnyev; **Yaroslav Radivonik** *bar* Utyeshitelny; **Leningrad Philharmonic Orchestra / Gennadi Rozhdestvensky**
Melodiya ② 74321 60319-2 (150 minutes: DDD) Ⓜ
Recorded 1974 and 1978 ○

With upwards of 70 solo roles and a repertoire of grotesqueries apparently designed to put *Wozzeck* in the shade, *The Nose* was always calculated to be provocative. No wonder its first production in 1930 was reviewed (not unsympathetically) as The Hand-bomb of an Anarchist; and no wonder it soon fell foul of the increasingly vicious dumbing-down of the Soviet arts, not to be heard again in Russia until 1974 when Boris Prokovsky and Gennadi Rozhdestvensky mounted it at the Moscow Chamber Theatre.

That production was immortalised in this classic recording, whose belated appearance on CD ought to be cause for unqualified celebration. So it would be if artistic grounds were all. Goodness knows how much rehearsal it took to master the manic complexities of the score, but the sheer clarity and confidence in characterization achieved is little short of miraculous. Edvard Akimov scores a personal triumph as the physiognomically challenged Kovalyov, and Rozhdestvensky is on the ball throughout. Even the recording quality has by and large stood the test of time.

This was the biggest remaining gap in the Shostakovich CD discography, and we'll be lucky to have anything to rival it in the foreseeable future. More's the pity then that we get no libretto or translation. Without one or other of these it's hard to see how you can ever get more than a surface impression of the piece. Even the otherwise helpful synopsis is silent about the insertion of a couple of minutes of text from the original story near the end, which Shostakovich only agreed to at the time of the 1974 production and which isn't given in the (Russian-only) Complete Edition score.

Shostakovich's other Gogol opera, the unfinished *The Gamblers*, also receives a wonderful performance, full-blooded and idiomatic. It makes a generous and appropriate filler.

Jean Sibelius

Finnish 1865-1957

GROVE *Sibelius studied in Helsinki from 1886 with Wegelius, also gaining stimulus there from Busoni, though at the same time he fostered ambitions as a violinist. In 1889 he went to Berlin to continue his composition studies with Becker, then after a year to Vienna under Goldmark and Fuchs. He returned to Helsinki in 1891 and immediately made a mark with his choral symphony Kullervo, though it took him another decade to establish a wholly consistent style and to emerge from the powerful influence of Tchaikovsky: important stages on the journey were marked by the Karelia suite, the set of four tone poems on the legendary hero Lemminkäinen (including The Swan of Tuonela), the grandiose Finlandia and the first two symphonies.*

As these titles suggest, he was encouraged by the Finnish nationalist movement (until 1917 Finland was a grand duchy in the Russian empire), by his readings of Finnish mythology (Kullervo and Lemminkäinen are both characters from the Kalevala, which was to be the source also for subjects of later symphonic poems) and in some degree by the folk music of Karelia. But the most important stimulus would seem to have been purely musical: a drive towards continuous growth achieved by means of steady thematic transformation, and facilitated by supporting the main line very often with highly diversified ostinato textures instead of counterpoints. The singleness of purpose also has to do with the frequently modal character of Sibelius's harmony.

The Violin Concerto of 1903 was effectively a farewell to 19th-century Romanticism, followed by a pure, classical expression of the new style in the Symphony no.3. This was also a period of change in his personal life. In 1904 he bought a plot of land outside Helsinki and built a house where he spent the rest of his life with his wife and daughters, removed from the city where he had been prone to bouts of heavy drinking. Also, his music gained a large international following, and he visited England (four times in 1905-12) and the USA (1914). Symphony no.4, with its conspicuous use of the tritone and its austere textures, took his music into its darkest areas; No 5 brought a return to the heroic mould, developing the process of continuous change to the extent that the first movement evolves into the scherzo.

But that work took him some time to get right (written in 1915, it was revised in 1916 and again in 1919), and after World War I he produced only four major works: the brilliant and elusive Symphony No 6; No 7, which takes continuity to the ultimate in its unbroken unfolding of symphonic development; the incidental music for The Tempest; and the bleak symphonic poem Tapiola. He lived for another three decades, but published only a few minor pieces; an eighth symphony may possibly have been completed and destroyed. His reputation, however, continued to grow, and his influence has been profound, especially on Scandinavian, English and American composers, reflecting both the traditionalism and the radical elements in his symphonic thinking.

Violin Concerto in D minor, Op 47

Sibelius Violin Concerto
Tchaikovsky Violin Concerto in D, Op 35
Kyung-Wha Chung *vn* **London Symphony Orchestra / André Previn**
Decca The Classic Sound 425 080-2DCS Ⓜ
(66 minutes: ADD). Recorded 1970 ○

If the vital test for a recording is that a performance should establish itself as a genuine one, not a mere studio run-through, Chung's remains a disc where both works leap out at you for their concentration and vitality, not just through the soloist's weight and gravity, expressed as though spontaneously, but through the playing of the LSO under Previn at a vintage period. The great melodies of the first two movements of the Sibelius are given an inner heartfelt intensity rarely matched, and with the finale skirting danger with thrilling abandon. Chung's later Montreal version of the Tchaikovsky (also Decca) is rather fuller-toned with the tiny statutory cuts restored in the finale. Yet the very hint of vulnerability amid daring, a key element in Chung's magnetic, volatile personality, here adds an extra sense of spontaneity. This remains breathtaking playing, and the central slow movement, made to flow without a hint of sentimentality, has an extra poignancy. The Kingsway Hall sound, full and sharply focused, gives a sense of presence to match or outshine today's digital recordings.

Violin Concerto[a]. Symphony No 2 in D, Op 43[b] **H**
[a]Ginette Neveu *vn* **[a]Philharmonia Orchestra / Walter Susskind; [b]New York Philharmonic Symphony Orchestra / Sir John Barbirolli**
Dutton Laboratories Essential Archive mono
CDEA5016 (71 minutes: ADD) Ⓑ
Recorded 1940-46 **oo**

In Ginette Neveu's fêted account of Sibelius's Violin Concerto, the strength, passion and stamina of the solo playing is particularly admirable, though Walter Susskind's Philharmonia accompaniment is rather foursquare, especially in the finale. Heifetz and Beecham triumph every time. Still, EMI's famous recording is a fine memento of a fiery interpretation, and the solo line comes across with miraculous immediacy in Mike Dutton's transfer – better, in fact, than the orchestra, which tends to retreat under a veil whenever the music quietens. Barbirolli's impulsive New York recording of the Second Symphony burns bright and fast, but there are countless minor imprecisions that may irritate on repetition. A handful of slow but distant swishes suggests that Dutton's generally excellent refurbishment might have been based on an early LP transfer.

Awards 1991

Violin Concerto (original 1903-04 version and final 1905 version)
Leonidas Kavakos *vn* **Lahti Symphony Orchestra / Osmo Vänskä**
BIS BISCD500 (75 minutes: DDD) Ⓕ
Recorded 199 **ooo**

It is difficult to conceive of a masterpiece in any other form than it is. The impression the listener receives from Sibelius's Fifth Symphony – or *The Rite of Spring* or *La mer* – must convey what Schoenberg called the illusion of spontaneous vision. It is as if the artist had caught a glimpse of something that has been going on all the time and that he has stretched out and effortlessly captured it. One of Sibelius's letters written to his friend Axel Carpelan in the autumn of 1914 puts it perfectly: 'God opens his door for a moment, and his orchestra is playing Sym 5'. But of course it is not like that and Sibelius worked for seven years (1912-19) before the Fifth Symphony reached its final form. Sibelius was nothing if not self-critical and a number of his works underwent their birthpangs in public. The main theme came to him much earlier than 1903 and he recognised it for what it was, an inspired idea which remained unchanged. After its first performance in Helsinki in 1904 Sibelius decided to overhaul it. He realised the necessity to purify it, to remove unnecessary detail that impedes the realization of a cogent structure. In its finished form, it was given in Berlin with Karl Halir as soloist and Richard Strauss conducting.

Listening to Sibelius's first thoughts played with great virtuosity and excellent taste by Leonidas Kavakos and the superb Lahti orchestra is an absorbing experience. One is first brought up with a start by an incisive orchestral rhythmic figure at what would be fig. 1 of the 1905 score (track 1, 1'23") from whereon the orchestra plays a more assertive role in the proceedings. In the unaccompanied cadenza 21 bars later (2'11") there is some rhythmic support while to the next idea on cellos and bassoon (fig. 2), the soloist contributes decoration. And then at seven bars before fig. 3 (3'41") a delightful new idea appears which almost looks forward to the light colourings of the later *Humoresques*. Although it is a great pity that it had to go, there is no doubt that the structural coherence of the movement gains by its loss both here and on its reappearance (14'03"). It is the ability to sacrifice good ideas in the interest of structural coherence that is the hallmark of a good composer. There are other changes Sibelius must have regretted though not, one suspects, the second long and unaccompanied cadenza whose removal greatly improves the overall shape of the movement. There are some hair-raising difficulties early on in the finale and one rather regrets the disappearance of the delightful idea starting at about 1'30". The fewest changes are in the slow movement which remains at the same length. As in the case of the Fifth Symphony, where the revision is far more extensive than it is here, the finished work tells us a great deal about the quality of Sibelius's artistic judgement, and that, of course, is what makes him such a great composer.

This disc offers an invaluable insight into the workings of Sibelius's mind. Kavakos and the Lahti orchestra play splendidly throughout and the familiar concerto which was struggling to get out of the 1903–04 version emerges equally safely in their hands. The BIS team have put us greatly in their debt by making the two versions available for study side by side.

Additional recommendations

Violin Concerto
Couplings: Tchaikovsky and Glazunov Violin Concertos **H**
Heifetz *vn* **London Philharmonic Orchestra / Beecham; Barbirolli**
EMI References mono CDH7 64030-2 Ⓜ
(80 minutes: AAD: 10/92)
A masterly interpretation from 1935 – Heifetz's virtuosic, cool approach matched by Beecham, an ideal Sibelian.

Coupling: Nielsen Violin Concerto
Lin *vn* **Philharmonia; Swedish Radio Symphony Orchestra / Salonen**
Sony Classical SK44548 (69 minutes: DDD: 1/89) Ⓕ
A *Gramophone* Award-winning coupling. Beautiful playing from the ever-sensitive Cho-Liang Lin.

Coupling: Tchaikovsky Violin Concerto
Mullova *vn* **Boston Symphony Orchestra / Ozawa**
Philips 416 821-2PH (67 minutes: DDD: 5/87) Ⓕ
Viktoria Mullova's début disc captured two powerful, high-octane readings – fire and ice combined!

Couplings: Tchaikovsky Violin Concerto
Repin *vn* **London Symphony Orchestra / Krivine**
Erato 4509 98537-2 (67 minutes: DDD: 5/96) Ⓜ
Another fine coupling of this popular pair. Vadim Repin shows great imagination and technical flair.

Couplings: Karelia Suite. Belshazzer's Feast.
Kuusisto *vn* **Helsinki Philharmonic Orchestra / Segerstam**
Ondine ODE878-2 (65 minutes: DDD: 5/96) Ⓕ
There's nothing like the Helsinki orchestra in Sibelius. This is a performance with great character.

Finlandia, Op 26

Finlandia, Op 26. Karelia Suite, Op 11.
Tapiola, Op 112. En saga
Philharmonia Orchestra / Vladimir Ashkenazy
Decca Ovation 417 762-2DM (63 minutes: DDD) Ⓜ
Recorded 1980-85 ⓞ

More than 30 years separate *En saga* and *Tapiola*, yet both works are quintessential Sibelius. The latter is often praised for the way Sibelius avoided 'exotic' instruments, preferring instead to draw new and inhuman sounds from the more standard ones; and the former is, in many ways, just as striking in the way the orchestration evokes wind, strange lights, vast expanses and solitude. Both works suggest a dream-like journey: *En saga* non-specific though derived from Nordic legend; *Tapiola* more of an airborne nightmare in, above and around the mighty giants of the Northern forests inhabited by the Green Man of the Kalevala, the forest god Tapio (the final amen of slow, bright major chords brings a blessed release!). Ashkenazy's judgement of long term pacing is very acute; the silences and shadows are as potent here as the wildest hurricane. And Decca's sound allows you to visualise both the wood and the trees: every detail of Sibelius's sound world is caught with uncanny presence, yet the overall orchestral image is coherent and natural. In addition, his *Finlandia* boasts some of the most vibrant, powerful brass sounds on disc.

Additional recommendation
Tapiola and En Saga
Couplings: Spring Song. Scenes with Cranes. Canzonetta. Valse romantique. The Bard. Valse triste
Claesson *cl* **Gothenburg Symphony Orchestra / Järvi**
DG 457 654-2GH (71 minutes: DDD: 12/00) Ⓕ
You are always in safe musical hands with Neeme Järvi and his Sibelius never fails to please. The Gothenburgers plays these short pieces with great charm and panache.

Six Humoresques, Opp 87 and 89

Six Humoresques, Opp 87 and 89. Two Serenades, Op 69. Two Pieces, Op 77. Overture in E. Ballet scene
Dong-Suk Kang *vn* **Gothenburg Symphony Orchestra / Neeme Järvi** Ⓕ
BIS CD472 (62 minutes: DDD). Recorded 1989 ⓞ

The music for violin and orchestra here is marvellously rewarding and gloriously played. The six *Humoresques*, Opp 87 and 89 come from the same period as the Fifth Symphony, at a time when Sibelius was toying with the idea of a second violin concerto, and some of the material of the *Humoresques* was possibly conceived with a concerto in mind. Sibelius wrote that these radiant pieces convey something of 'the anguish of existence, fitfully lit up by the sun', and behind their outward elegance and charm, there is an all-pervasive sadness. This is even more intense in the *Serenades*, which are glorious pieces and quintessential Sibelius. Dong-Suk Kang is an outstanding player. His impeccable technique and natural musical instinct serve this repertoire well and he seems to have established an excellent rapport with Järvi and the Gothenburg orchestra. The two fill-ups are juvenilia and are only intermittently characteristic. The Overture is very much in his *Karelia* idiom, though they are of undoubted interest to all Sibelians. The recording up to BIS's usual high quality.

Karelia Suite

Karelia Suite. Incidental music – King Christian II; Pelleas and Melisande (all original versions)
Anna-Lisa Jakobsson *mez* **Raimo Laukka** *bar*
Lahti Symphony Orchestra / Osmo Vänskä
BIS CD918 (78 minutes: DDD). Texts and translations included. Recorded 1997-98 Ⓕ

Sibelius supplied four numbers for the February 1898 Helsinki première of Adolf Paul's historical drama *King Christian II* – the 'Minuet', 'The Fool's Song', 'Elegy' and 'Musette' – and these eventually took their place in the five-movement concert suite alongside the 'Nocturne', 'Serenade' and 'Ballade' which the composer completed the same summer. The street music of the 'Musette' is simply delightful in its original garb without added strings, and in both the 'Serenade' and 'Ballade' Vänskä uncovers strong thematic and stylistic links with the almost exactly contemporaneous First Symphony. The defiant quality these fine artists bring to 'The Fool's Song' (eloquently delivered by Raimo Laukka) is also very likeable. Music-making of refreshing perception and meticulous sensitivity similarly illuminates this first complete recording of Sibelius's original incidental music for a 1905 production of Maeterlinck's symbolist play (the venue was again Helsinki's Swedish Theatre). There are 10 numbers in all.

The performance of the *Karelia Suite* in its original scoring (which acts as a splendid curtain-raiser here) has been compiled from Vänskä's complete recording of the original

Karelia music. Both outer movements have a real sense of pageantry about them (Vänskä directs with exhilaratingly clean-limbed swagger), though there are certain reservations about his occasional predilection for exaggerated and affected *pianopianissimos*. Thus, at around 3'30" in the central 'Ballade' (track 2), the dynamic level drops almost below the threshold of audibility and has you rushing to boost the volume control (Vänskä repeats this trick twice in the *King Christian II* 'Elegy', and towards the end of the final number in *Pelléas*). For optimum results, therefore, playback needs to be higher than many listeners may think reasonable. That said, the engineering is quite spectacularly truthful throughout and there is no doubt that this is an unusually absorbing collection.

Kullervo, Op 7

Lilli Paasikivi *mez* **Raimo Laukka** *bar* **Helsinki University Chorus; Lahti Symphony Orchestra / Osmo Vänskä**
BIS CD1215 (81 minutes: DDD) Ⓕ
Text and translation included. Recorded 2000 **OO**

Over the past decade or so, *Kullervo* has deservedly come in from the cold, and this imposing BIS newcomer swells the current crop of contenders to a healthy nine. Vänskä is undoubtedly a Sibelian of strong instinct, and his *Kullervo* enshrines an interpretation of extraordinary grandeur and slumbering, runic mystery. After an ideally paced opening *Allegro moderato* (the Lahti strings lacking just a touch in sheer muscle and breadth of tone), 'Kullervo's Youth' lasts an eyebrow-raising 19'18", well over three minutes longer than any predecessor. Courageously, Vänskä sticks to his guns, the music's unnervingly tragic portents distilled with mournful gravity. It's in the big central *scena* that BIS's sumptuously realistic, excitingly wide-ranging production really comes into its own. Vänskä directs with keen observation and tingling narrative flair, not missing the wondrous poetry of the nature music accompanying the lament of Kullervo's sister. What's more, his soloists and chorus are first-rate, though baritone Raimo Laukka is not quite as fresh-voiced here as he was for Segerstam's in 1994. Following a splendidly lusty 'Kullervo goes to War', Vänskä crowns proceedings with a thrillingly grim and inevitable 'Kullervo's Death', with eloquent contributions from the men of the Helsinki University Chorus.

As should be clear by now, this recording must feature high on any short list. The recent reappearance on EMI Double Forte of Berglund's pioneering, superlatively engineered Bournemouth version is certainly welcome, though the deletion of that conductor's Helsinki digital remake (also for EMI) is disappointing.

Despite one or two eccentricities, both Segerstam and Paavo Järvi quarry the staggering originality of Sibelius's youthful vision to often riveting effect. The fleeter Saraste, too, gives a humane, thoroughly likeable performance, whereas Salonen's stunningly articulate realisation with the Los Angeles PO perhaps is marginally too slick for comfort. Only Sir Colin Davis adopts as daringly expansive a view as Vänskä, but his hard-working LSO forces simply don't sound as wholly attuned to the idiom as their Finnish rivals. Whether Vänskä's epic conception as a whole 'stacks up' with quite the same cumulative majesty as, say, the digital Berglund is debatable, but its insights are legion and for many it will be a natural first choice.

Kullervo, Op 7
Marianne Rørholm *contr* **Jorma Hynninen** *bar* **Helsinki University Chorus; Los Angeles Philharmonic Orchestra / Esa-Pekka Salonen**
Sony Classical SK52563 (70 minutes: DDD). Text Ⓕ
and translation included. Recorded 1992 **O**

Sibelius's *Kullervo* was the symphonic poem-cum-symphony with which he made his breakthrough in Finland in 1892. Common to all recordings, including Salonen's, is the magisterial presence of Jorma Hynninen. Salonen keeps a firm grip on the proceedings and maintains a real sense of momentum throughout. Moreover, temptations to dwell on beauty of incident or to indulge in expressive emphasis are resisted, and this extraordinary piece is all the more telling as a result. The drama of the central scena is vividly realised and both Marianne Rørholm and Jorma Hynninen are impressive – as are the male voices of the Finnish chorus. An impressive performance, and the orchestral playing and recording are absolutely first-class.

Legends, 'Lemminkäinen Suite', Op 22

Legends, 'Lemminkäinen Suite', Op 22. En Saga, Op 9
Swedish Radio Symphony Orchestra / Mikko Franck
Ondine ODE953-2 (74 minutes: DDD) Ⓕ
Recorded 1999 **OO**

Still only in his early twenties, a private pupil of Jorma Panula and yet another outstanding product of the Sibelius Academy's conducting class, Mikko Franck presides over the most intrepidly individual and pungently characterful performance of the *Lemminkäinen Legends* since Leif Segerstam's 1995 Helsinki PO account for this same Finnish label. Clocking in at an eyebrow-raising 53'48" overall, Franck's conception evinces an unhurried authority, a generous expressive scope and a richly stocked imagination remarkable in one so young.

'Lemminkäinen and the Maidens of the Island' unfolds in especially gripping fashion here. Even more than Segerstam, Franck takes an extraordinarily long-breathed, flexible view of this heady tableau, imparting an unashamedly sensual voluptuousness to the secondary material in particular. It's a risky, impulsive approach, but one that pays high dividends in terms of intoxicating sweep, brazen ardour and, well, sheer daring. Both 'The Swan of Tuonela' (which, in a refreshing change from the norm these days, Franck places second, according to Sibelius's final wishes) and 'Lemminkäinen in Tuonela' combine dark-hued grandeur with tingling atmosphere, the latter's haunting A minor central episode handled with particular perception. True, 'Lemminkäinen's Return' lacks something in animal excitement, but its unruffled sense of purpose, rhythmic spring and sinewy, clean-cut textures serve up plenty of food for thought none the less.

The *Legends* are preceded by an uncommonly fresh *En Saga*, brimming with watchful sensitivity and interpretative flair, and once again studded with revelatory detail (the strings' momentary dissonance at 5'32" in the score, bar 29 after fig H – to cite just one example from many – really makes you sit up). Throughout, the Swedish RSO responds with heartwarming application and genuine enthusiasm, audibly galvanised by Franck's fervent, always invigorating direction. The engineering, too, is very good, without perhaps being absolutely in the top flight.

An auspicious recording début, then, from a young artist of clearly prodigious potential.

Legends, 'Lemminkäinen Suite', Op 22.
Finlandia, Op 26. Karelia Suite, Op 11
Iceland Symphony Orchestra / Petri Sakari
Naxos 8 554265 (73 minutes: DDD) Ⓢ
Recorded 1997

Most impressive. In its keen intelligence, fiery snap and thrust, Petri Sakari's account of the four *Legends* proves more than a match for the finest. The Iceland SO may not be world-beaters, but they respond to their thoughtful young Finnish maestro's illuminating direction with clean-limbed zest and commitment to the cause (their winds are an especially personable bunch).

Perhaps the highlight of the new set is 'Lemminkäinen in Tuonela', which, like Segerstam and Salonen before him, Sakari places second (reverting to the composer's original scheme), and where he distils a relentless concentration and pin-sharp focus (only Segerstam is more gripping in this brooding essay). Of course, no one should miss out on the heady opulence of Ormandy's magnificent Philadelphia strings in those glorious singing lines of 'Lemminkäinen and the maidens of the island', but the Icelanders play their hearts out and anyway Sakari gives a dramatic reading of bold contrasts and strong symphonic cohesion. No grumbles, either, about 'The Swan of Tuonela' or 'Lemminkäinen's Homeward Journey' which is firmly controlled, dashingly detailed and genuinely exciting (as opposed to merely excitable).

Sakari's rewarding *Legends* comes very near the top of the heap alongside (though, ultimately, not ahead of) Segerstam, Saraste and Ormandy. In the popular couplings, Sakari's unhackneyed approach once again pays dividends, though his unusually brisk (and ever-so-slightly hectic) tempo for the main portion of the *Karelia* Suite's opening 'Intermezzo' isn't always convincing . None the less, this is quite a bargain. Eminently pleasing sound, too: free of gimmickry and tonally very true.

Legends, 'Lemminkäinen Suite', Op 22. Tapiola
Helsinki Philharmonic Orchestra / Leif Segerstam
Ondine ODE852-2 (70 minutes: DDD) Ⓕ
Recorded 1995

The four *Legends* first began to surface in Sibelius's mind in 1893, at the same time as he was working on his *Kalevala* opera, *The Building of the Boat*, the prelude to which became 'The swan of Tuonela'. (It is not the only thing from the opera that found its way into the *Legends*. The lovely A minor idea for muted strings in the middle section of 'Lemminkäinen in Tuonela' is also among the sketches, where Sibelius scribbled over it the words, 'the Maiden of Death'. In the opera she would have rowed Väinämöinen across the river to Tuonela. In the tone-poem she symbolises the very opposite, the loving mother whose ministrations return Lemminkäinen to life.) In 1954 Sibelius reversed the order of the inner movements so that 'The swan' preceded 'Lemminkäinen in Tuonela'. Perversely Segerstam disregards the composer's wishes and places them in the old order. To be fair, there is a case for this order in that you otherwise have two highly dramatic pieces ('Lemminkäinen in Tuonela' and 'Lemminkäinen's Homeward Journey') placed alongside each other; most CD players are programmable anyway. Segerstam gets very good results from the Helsinki orchestra which responds with a keen enthusiasm that is inspiriting. The performance is free from excessive mannerisms and his account of *Tapiola* is very impressive. He tellingly evokes the chilling terrors and awesome majesty of the Nordic forest.

Luonnotar, Op 70

Luonnotar, Op 70. Karelia Suite. Andante festivo.
The Oceanides, Op 73. King Christian II, Op 27 – Suite. Finlandia
Soile Isokoski *sop* **Gothenburg Symphony Orchestra / Neeme Järvi**
DG 447 760-2GH (72 minutes: DDD). Text and translation included. Recorded 1992-95 Ⓕ

This CD offers the *Karelia* and *King Christian II* suites, both from the 1890s, together with outstanding accounts of two of the strangest and most haunting masterpieces of Sibelius's maturity, *Luonnotar* and *The Oceanides*. Of special interest is *Luonnotar*, which tells of the creation of the world as related in Finnish mythology and was written for the legendary Aino Ackté. Not surprisingly, perhaps, it places cruel demands on the soloist both in terms of tessitura and dynamics. Soile Isokoski is magnificent and possesses an impressive accuracy both in intonation and dynamics above the stave. Järvi gets an excellent response from his fine Gothenburg players and tellingly conveys the atmosphere and mystery of this extraordinary score. The excellent note speaks of it as 'unlike anything else in the entire repertoire' – which indeed it is! What a wonderfully evocative score *The Oceanides* is, and what an atmospheric, magical account, we have here. The performances of the *Karelia* and *King Christian II* suites are not quite in this class but they are enjoyable, and the recording is quite exemplary.

Pelleas and Melisande

Cassazione, Op 6. Pelleas and Melisande, Op 46. Suite mignonne, Op 98a. Suite champêtre, Op 98b. Suite caractéristique, Op 100. Presto
Tapiola Sinfonietta / Tuomas Ollila
Ondine ODE952-2 (56 minutes: DDD) Ⓕ
Recorded 1999-2000

Don't let the low opus number hoodwink you: *Cassazione* dates from 1904 and was first given under Sibelius's baton at the same Helsinki concert as the première of the first version of the Violin Concerto. Revised the following year but never published, it's well worth hearing, containing as it does echoes of both *Pelleas and Melisande* (the clarinets' tune in sixths from 1'19" presages the theme for 'The Three Blind Sisters') and the Second Symphony's finale (the treading *pizzicato* bass a little later on at 7'01"). The dashing *Presto* began life as the third movement of Sibelius's Op 4 String Quartet in B flat of 1889-90, and was subsequently transcribed for string orchestra in 1894. The three suites date from 1921-22. True, the *Suite caractéristique* serves up a pretty thin brew, but both the *Suite mignonne* and *Suite champêtre* contain their fair share of felicities and are delightfully scored.

These performances from Tuomas Ollila and the Tapiola Sinfonietta evince a bracing, unsentimental thrust and high degree of technical finish, though some will crave more in the way of affectionate charm and tingling atmosphere. However, it's in the *Pelleas and Melisande* incidental music that these newcomers truly throw down the gauntlet. There's no hint of the customary portentous grandeur in Ollila's 'At the Castle Gate', a nervy urgency that resurfaces with a vengeance in 'Melisande at the Spinning Wheel' and the ensuing 'Entr'acte'. Elsewhere, those screaming winds and *sul ponticello* strings at the heart of 'At the Seashore' set one's teeth on edge, while textures throughout are uncommonly transparent (sample the pure arctic air of the 'Pastorale'). What's missing is any real sense of poignancy or pathos: 'The Death of Melisande' is very cool, the characteristically bleached string timbre emphasising the disconcertingly pristine, self-conscious mood. An intriguing and intelligent re-think, then, but not to all tastes (anyone brought up on, say, Beecham will be in for a shock). Crystal-clear, slightly clinical sound.

Swanwhite, Op 54

Pelleas and Melisande – Incidental Music, Op 46. Swanwhite, Op 54 – The Harp; The Maiden with the Roses; The Prince Alone; Swanwhite and the Prince; Song of Praise. King Christian II – Incidental Music, Op 27
Sauli Tiilikainen *bar* **Iceland Symphony Orchestra / Petri Sakari**
Chandos CHAN9158 (79 minutes: DDD). Text and translation included. Recorded 1992 Ⓕ

These performances are natural and unaffected and radiate immense care and pleasure in music-making. The *King Christian II* music includes 'The Fool's Song', complete with soloist, and very good he is too, and a short 'Minuet'. Petri Sakari's performance is totally unaffected and full of enthusiasm; the players sound as if they are enjoying this score and communicate their pleasure. Phrasing is attentive, musical through and through but never fussy. The *Pelleas and Melisande* is a version many collectors would want to have. It is imaginative, totally musical, strong on atmosphere and observant of dynamic subtleties. There may be readers who might find some of the tempos on the slow side; they are unhurried, but in context they feel right. Unfortunately there is only room for five movements from the *Swanwhite* music. All are beautifully played, though; every detail is allowed to take its time and the phrasing, although attentive, is free of the slightest taint of narcissism. Let 'Swanwhite and the Prince' serve as an example of how well thought out and natural in feeling the phrasing is! Added to this, the Chandos recording is beautifully transparent, warm and well detailed.

The Wood Nymph, Op 15

The Wood Nymph, Op 15. The Wood Nymph (melodrama). A lonely ski-trail. Swanwhite, Op 54 – incidental music (original version)
Lasse Pöysti *narr*
Lahti Symphony Orchestra / Osmo Vänskä Ⓕ
BIS CD815 (62 minutes: DDD). Recorded 1996 ⭘

Although most Sibelians will know of the tone-poem, *The Wood-Nymph*, they will not have heard it, as the score has remained in Helsinki University Library. It opens very much in *Karelia* mode, and as one might expect, inhabits much the same world as the Lemminkäinen *Legends*. Though it is less developed than the 1892 *En saga*, let alone the *Legends* in their definitive form, it still bears the characteristic Sibelian hallmarks. The present disc gives us an opportunity to put it alongside the melodrama of the same name, scored for speaker, horn, strings and piano. This is a setting of the mainland-Swedish poet, Viktor Rydberg, best known in the Sibelius context for *Autumn Evening* ('Höstkväll'). The tone-poem which was given a month after the première of the melodrama follows much the same basic layout, though the chamber music-like texture offers numerous felicities.

Not content with these interesting novelties, the CD also gives us two other works new to the catalogue, another short melodrama, *A lonely ski-trail* to words by Bertel Gripenberg, which in its piano form dates from 1925 and which Sibelius scored for harp and strings as late as 1948, a short, slight and atmospheric piece; and above all, the complete incidental music to Strindberg's *Swanwhite*. The score runs to some 30 minutes and is full of that special light and sense of space characteristic of *Pelleas and Melisande*. The playing of the Lahti orchestra under Osmo Vänskä is excellent and the recording, too, is very fine: spacious, well detailed and refined. Obviously a self-recommending issue which no Sibelian should miss.

Complete Symphonies

No 1 in E minor, Op 39; **No 2** in D, Op 43; **No 3** in C, Op 52; **No 4** in A minor, Op 63; **No 5** in E flat, Op 82; **No 6** in D minor, Op 104; **No 7** in C, Op 105

Symphonies Nos 1-7. The Oceanides. Kuolema – Scene with cranes. Nightride and Sunrise[a]
City of Birmingham Symphony Orchestra, [a]Philharmonia Orchestra / Sir Simon Rattle
EMI ④ CMS7 64118-2 (267 minutes: DDD) Ⓜ
●

Symphonies Nos 1-4 and 6 are also available on HMV Classics: HMV5 740602; HMV5 72319-2; HMV5 73048-2 Ⓑ

Simon Rattle's reissued Sibelius cycle is now accommodated on four mid- (as opposed to five full) price CDs, losing among the fill-ups only Kennedy's well-played account of the concerto. The first movement of Symphony No 1 is impressive and its epic quality is splendidly conveyed. You may be less taken with the slow movement: the rather mannered closing bars, not particularly acceptable in the concert hall, are distinctly worrying on disc. The measured tempo of the *Scherzo* is also a problem: it is slower than the metronome marking and the movement lacks fire. However, *The Oceanides* is the finest on disc. In the Second Symphony, Rattle's first movement is again on the slow side and the Trio section of the *Scherzo* is pulled about. The Fourth and Seventh find him at his finest and the magnificent EMI recording is very richly detailed and well defined. The Fourth distils a powerful atmosphere in its opening pages; one is completely transported to its dark landscape with its seemingly limitless horizons. Only Beecham has surpassed Rattle in the slow movement. Rattle's version of the Sixth is still among the best around, with tremendous grip and concentration. In both the Third and the Fifth he is equally impressive, although his handling of the celebrated transition in the first movement of the Fifth in his Philharmonia version is preferable (reviewed further on). However, the inducement of *The Oceanides*, *Nightride and Sunrise* and an evocative account of the 'Scene with cranes' from *Kuolema* tips the scales in Rattle's favour.

Symphonies Nos 1-7
Philharmonia Orchestra / Vladimir Ashkenazy
Decca Double 2x② 455 402-2DF2 and 455 405-2DF2 (144 and 150 minutes: ADD/DDD) Ⓜ
Recorded 1980-96 ●●

Of all the cycles of Sibelius's symphonies recorded during recent years this is one of the most consistently successful. Ashkenazy so well understands the thought processes that lie behind Sibelius's symphonic composition just as he is aware, and makes us aware, of the development between the Second and Third Symphonies. His attention to tempo is particularly acute and invariably he strikes just the right balance between romantic languor and urgency. The Philharmonia plays for all it's worth and possesses a fine body of sound. The recordings are remarkably consistent in quality and effectively complement the composer's original sound world.

Symphony No 1

Symphony No 1. Karelia Suite. Finlandia
Oslo Philharmonic Orchestra / Mariss Jansons
EMI CDC7 54273-2 (62 minutes: DDD) Ⓕ
Recorded 1990

Jansons's account of the First Symphony is thrilling. It has excitement and brilliance without exaggerations. Tempos throughout are just right, the phrasing breathes naturally and the sonority is excellently focused. Jansons never presses on too quickly but allows each phrase, each musical sentence to register so the listener feels borne along on a natural currrent. Moreover, excitement is not whipped up but arises naturally from the music's forward momentum. The Oslo Philharmonic is a highly responsive orchestra of no mean virtuosity and it plays with a splendid intensity and fire not only in the symphony but also the *Karelia Suite* and *Finlandia* which sound very fresh. All the artistic decisions here seem to be right and the orchestral playing further enhances the high renown this ensemble now enjoys. Very good recording too.

Additional recommendation
Symphony No 1
Couplings: Symphonies Nos 2 and 4. Finlandia. Karelia Suite
Philharmonia / Ashkenazy
Decca Double ② 455 402-2DF2
(144 minutes: DDD: 5/86[R]) Ⓜ
Symphony No 1 is one of the finest recordings in Ashkenazy's Philharmonia Sibelius cycle. See above

Symphony No 2

Symphonies Nos 2 and 6
London Symphony Orchestra / Sir Colin Davis
RCA Victor Red Seal 09026 68218-2 Ⓕ
(73 minutes: DDD). Recorded 1994 ●●

The eloquent polyphony, purity of utterance and harmony of spirit give the Sixth Symphony a special place in the canon. Sibelius's mastery enables him to move with a freedom so complete that the musical events are dictated by their own inner necessity. And in Davis's hands this music unfolds with a freedom and naturalness that are totally convincing. As Sibelius said of the Fourth Symphony, this is music 'with nothing of the circus about it', and in this reading there is no playing to the gallery. There is no playing to the gallery either in Sir Colin's account of the Second. He views the work as a whole and does not invest detail with undue expressive vehemence at its expense, but strikes just the right balance between the nationalist-romantic inheritance on the one side and the classical power of Sibelius's thinking on the other. The first movement has dignity and breadth, and as with Karajan (EMI), the pacing of climaxes is magisterial. The recording has splendid presence and space.

Symphony No 2. Pohjola's Daughter, Op 49. **H**
Legends – No 2, The Swan of Tuonela; No 4, Lemminkäinen's return. Finlandia
NBC Symphony Orchestra / Arturo Toscanini
Naxos Historical mono 8 110810 (76 minutes: ADD) Ⓢ
Recorded live in 1940

As the symphony's finale builds to its apotheosis, you'll have to contend with trumpets that sound as if they more usually play at wedding parties for *The Godfather*. This is presumably how Toscanini liked his trumpets (and woodwinds and strings) to sound when singing, just as he liked them to deliver more forceful, rhythmical figures with a vengeance – the 'vengeance' perhaps a result of close microphones and/or little evidence of a hall acoustic. All of which means that if your notions of Nordic nobility in the symphony are gathered across the decades from recordings by Kajanus, Collins, Koussevitzky and Karajan, you should probably give Toscanini a wide berth. If you did, however, you would be depriving yourself of perhaps the most dramatically intense and physically exciting performances of the symphony and *Pohjola's Daughter* ever recorded. The present Naxos accounts of the symphony and *Pohjola's Daughter* are already available (at twice the price) in RCA's Toscanini Edition. The only audible difference lies in the more 'filtered' (and arguably smoother) sound of the Naxos transfer. The same could be said of *Pohjola's Daughter*, but here Naxos has used a different source, with a noisier surface, though less flutter. By way of shorter items, the Naxos release offers, as does RCA's, 'The Swan of Tuonela' and *Finlandia*, but the RCA performances are later ones with cleaner, clearer and more boldly projected sound. Which leaves Naxos's extra carrot (apart from the price) – a 'Lemminkäinen's return' electric with energy.

Symphonies Nos 2 and 3
Lahti Symphony Orchestra / Osmo Vänskä
BIS BISCD862 (76 minutes: DDD) Ⓕ
Recorded 1996-97

The first issue in the Sibelius cycle by Osmo Vänskä and the Lahti orchestra (Symphonies Nos 1 and 4) made a strong impression. Indeed it holds its own against the most exalted competition, including the coupling by the LSO and Sir Colin Davis. The present set does not disappoint either: these artists are right inside this music.

First, the Second Symphony where competition is stiffest, with Karajan, Barbirolli and Colin Davis leading a field that includes Szell (Philips – nla), Kletzki (EMI – nla) and Ormandy (Sony). Admittedly it would have been preferable if Vänskä had set a slightly brisker tempo at the very opening, though he is not alone in the pace he adopts. Karajan and Sir Colin are equally measured. Kajanus took 8'14" over this movement and Sibelius's first biographer, the scholar-critic Erik Furuhjhelm, records that the composer took it even faster! Perhaps the briskest of all modern performances is Neeme Järvi and the Gothenburg Symphony Orchestra. Vänskä's reading is both powerfully wrought and well thought-out though there are some self-conscious touches. He pulls back a little too much at the *tranquillo* marking in the first movement (track 1, 4'31"), of which one becomes too aware. Elsewhere he makes one think afresh about the score. The F sharp major tune on the strings in the slow movement marked *ppp* is played as a barely audible whisper (track 2, 4'40") and so exaggerated does it seem that the wind four bars later sound (and are) much louder than the marked *pianissimo*. But these are minor matters in a performance marked by feeling and eloquence.

It is good to see the Third Symphony doing so well on record. Vänskä sets the right tempo for the first movement and gets the right atmosphere. The opening bars do not build up as powerfully as they do in the hands of the LSO and Sir Colin, and it is possible to feel a certain want of momentum in the slow movement by their side and in comparison with Kajanus's pioneering set. On the whole, however, this is a very good performance, well paced and full of perceptive touches. The sound is excellent and, exceptionally wide-ranging.

Additional recommendations
Symphony No 2
Coupling: Romance for Strings
Gothenburg Symphony Orchestra / Järvi
BIS CD252 (DDD: 10/84) Ⓕ
This is a performance full of sinew and fire. Fast and vigorous in the first movement, the orchestra play with tremendous commitment

Couplings: Legends, 'Lemminkaïnen Suite', Op 22. Valse Triste. Andante festivo.
Oslo Philharmonic Orchestra / Jansons
EMI CDC7 54804-2 (61 minutes: DDD: 7/93) Ⓕ
This is a beautiful performance of the Second Symphony, full of incidental detail and given a majestic, aristocratic sweep. This is a version with no playing to the gallery.

Symphony No 3

Symphony No 3. Pohjola's Daughter, Op 49. **H**
Pelleas and Melisande – No 2, Melisande; No 6, Pastorale; No 7, At the spinning wheel; No 8, Intermezzo; No 9, Death of Melisande.
Nightride and Sunrise
London Symphony Orchestra / Anthony Collins
Beulah mono 3PD8 (68 minutes: ADD) Ⓕ
Recorded 1954-55 ●

The name Anthony Collins (1893-1963) probably doesn't mean a great deal to the majority of younger readers, but for quite a few serious Sibelius *aficionados* his 1950s Decca recordings hold cult status. In these transfers the original recordings are revealed for the fine achievements they were: beautifully balanced, clear and vivid, allowing us to hear these performances in intimate detail – which is how they deserve to be heard. Collins is a first-rate musical landscape-painter. He doesn't just give us the bold sweeping brush-strokes; he shows how the landscapes team with minute life. Rustling string textures aren't blandly homogenised – tiny details catch the ear, and then vanish again. Woodwind bird calls or horn calls can be acutely expressive – some passages remind one of Sibelius's comments about quasi-human voices in the nature sounds around his forest-home. But exaggeration is alien to the Collins approach. Nothing is forced, almost everything is fresh and vital.

Symphonies Nos 3 and 5
London Symphony Orchestra / Sir Colin Davis
RCA Red Seal 09026 61963-2 (61 minutes: DDD) Ⓕ
Recorded 1992 ●

Some 20 years have passed since Davis's last Sibelius cycle, with the Boston Symphony Orchestra for Philips. Generally speaking Sir Colin's version of the Third has greater breadth and sense of scale than his previous account or any other. His first movement has a majestic stride and great power; and he has the measure of the slow movement's pantheistic musings. The Fifth is more tautly held together than before; the first movement moves forward and onwards with a powerful feeling of inevitability and purpose. The transition in the first movement to the *Scherzo* section is masterly. Listening to this disc, one wonders anew at the sheer originality of this piece, and that is, of course, the touchstone of a great performance. Sir Colin Davis understands Sibelius as do few others and senses the vital currents that flow through these symphonies, and the London Symphony Orchestra know this and respond accordingly with playing of distinction. The recording is in every way first-class, vivid in detail and truthful in perspective.

Symphonies[a] Nos 3 and 5. March of the Finnish Jaeger Battalion, Op 91 No 1[b] 🅗
[a]London Symphony Orchestra; [b]Helsinki Philharmonic Orchestra / Robert Kajanus
Koch Historic mono 37133-2 (62 minutes: ADD) Ⓜ
Recorded 1928-1933 ●

Finlandia has already reissued all Kajanus's London recordings on a three-disc set. That edition contains transfers made by Anthony Griffith for World Records, issued in the 1970s, and they still sound very good indeed. Griffith had the advantage of working from original masters: Koch's Mark Obert-Thorn has been obliged to use commercial pressings and while he has obtained good sound, there is inevitably more background noise and an unevenness in the quality which is not present in Finlandia's transfers. However, Koch has scored an important point by including Kajanus's only Sibelius recording with his own Helsinki orchestra. The piece itself is perhaps the composer's weakest, but the performance has great historical importance, for it is played by an orchestra with which Sibelius had close links, and under a conductor who was his chosen interpreter. We can hear clearly just why Sibelius admired Kajanus so much in the two symphonies here. At the age of 76 he was still able to generate a good deal of tension and energy in the London Symphony Orchestra's playing, yet there is a particular sense of balanced, logical music-making, a seemingly natural authority in the phrasing and an apparent inevitability in the way he unfolds the composer's symphonic argument. Everything seems perfectly in place, and the music speaks to us in a very direct and compelling fashion.

Additional recommendations

Symphony No 3
Coupling: Symphony No 1
Iceland Symphony Orchestra/Sakari
Naxos 8 554102 (68 minutes: DDD: 1/99) Ⓢ

A worth well worth considering for those on a budget. Good, committed playing from the Iceland SO.

Symphonies Nos 3 and 4
Couplings: Symphonies Nos 1 and 2
Helsinki Philharmonic Orchestra / Berglund
EMI Double Forte ② CZS5 68643-2 Ⓜ
(140 minutes: DDD: 5/96)

Berglund's Sibelius is always listening to; few conductors have such experience in this music. Quite a bargain!

Symphony No 4

Awards 1997

Symphonies Nos 1 and 4
London Symphony Orchestra / Sir Colin Davis
RCA Red Seal 09026 68183-2 Ⓕ
(78 minutes: DDD). Recorded 1994 ●●●

Sir Colin Davis takes us completely inside the Fourth Symphony – we become part of it and feel we inhabit it. It is arguably the finest and most powerful reading of the work to have emerged since the days of Karajan. It was always one of the triumphs of his Boston survey on Philips. Along with the 1937 Beecham and the 1966 Berlin Philharmonic Karajan sets the Colin Davis was one of the most inward and searching readings committed to disc. We are not long – indeed barely a few bars – into the first movement before we realise that we are in a totally different world from most other interpretations. There is a far greater sense of breadth but it is in terms of imaginative insight that Davis scores. What is there to say of his First save that it, too, has an excitement, a sense of immediacy and authenticity of feeling that is equally convincing. This is Sibelius conducting of real stature and the LSO responds with total commitment. RCA provides a first-rate recording.

Symphonies Nos 4 and 7. Kuolema – Valse triste
Berlin Philharmonic Orchestra / Herbert von Karajan
DG Galleria 439 527-2GGA (66 minutes: ADD) Ⓜ
Recorded 1965-67 ○○

Karajan recorded the Fourth Symphony three times, once in the 1950s with the Philharmonia and twice with the Berlin Philharmonic. The work obviously meant a great deal to him. He insisted on its inclusion in his very first concert on his appointment at the Berlin Philharmonic in the early 1960s at a time when Sibelius's cause had few champions in Germany, so keen was he to stake its claim as one of the great symphonies of the day. Karajan's account has withstood the test of time as one of the most searching, profound and concentrated performances of this masterpiece, and its reappearance at mid price was very welcome. The Seventh is finer than his earlier Philharmonia version but does not enjoy quite the same classic status. Karajan's *Valse triste* is wonderfully seductive. Indispensable!

Symphonies – Nos 4 and 7[a]. Pelléas et Mélisande, Op 46. Swanwhite, Op 54. The Tempest – Dance of the Nymphs. Tapiola, Op 112 **H**
Royal Philharmonic Orchestra / Sir Thomas Beecham
BBC Legends/IMG Artists ② BBCL4041-2 (139 minutes: ADD)
Recorded live in [a]1954 and 1955. Includes Beecham on Sibelius, broadcast 1955 Ⓜ ○

In a broadcast concert to mark Sibelius's 90th birthday on December 8, 1955, the RPO under Sir Thomas Beecham (friend of the composer for nearly 50 years and one of his doughtiest champions) played to a capacity Royal Festival Hall. The inclusion here of the British and Finnish national anthems, both stirringly done, recreates the necessary sense of occasion. In the delightful, too rarely encountered *Swanwhite* suite, from which Beecham omits the powerfully sombre fifth movement ('The Prince alone'), one may at first miss his characteristic concentration and charisma, but his leisurely, affectionate rendering grows on one. Orchestral discipline takes a dip with the Fourth Symphony, but far more disconcerting is the all pervading air of loose-limbed impatience: the opening *Tempo molto moderato, quasi adagio* is wayward and fussy. There are glimpses of greatness in the third movement (the strings at the climax have a refulgent warmth about them), as well as some effective dynamic emendations in the finale, but overall it's a curiously uninvolving display.

Only in the concert's second half does this legendary partnership really begin to show what it's capable of. The *Pelléas* suite distils a poetic enchantment (try the ineffably touching 'Mélisande') and tingling sense of atmosphere that not only make you forget about the maddeningly bronchial audience, but also act as a timely reminder that these artists' glorious studio recording dates from exactly the same period (EMI – unavailable at present). *Tapiola* is even finer, a performance of giant authority, devastating emotional candour and towering humanity – indeed Beecham's most powerful *Tapiola* currently available. As an encore, the fetching 'Dance of the Nymphs' from *The Tempest* is delectably done. As a substantial bonus there's a radiantly moving Sibelius Seventh from the 1954 Proms, and a personable, at times entertainingly scatty talk on Sibelius and his music by the inimitable maestro recorded for the BBC's Third Programme two weeks before that 90th-birthday concert. A mandatory purchase for the frequently spellbinding contents of disc 2 alone.

Additional recommendations

Symphonies Nos 1 and 4
Vienna Philharmonic Orchestra / Maazel
Belart 461 325-2 (69 minutes: ADD: 2/97) Ⓢ
Maazel's early 1960s Sibelius cycle still sounds good and his interpretations have aged very well. A real bargain

Lahti Symphony Orchestra / Vänskä
BIS BISCD861 (76 minutes: DDD) Ⓕ
Osmo Vänskä is one of today's leading Sibelians and this fine coupling shows us his strengths

Symphonies Nos 1, 2 and 4
Coupling: Symphony No 5
Boston Symphony Orchestra / Davis, C
Philips Duo 446 157-2PM2 ② (154 minutes: ADD: 3/77[R]) Ⓜ
Sir Colin Davis's late-1970s Boston Sibelius cycle has a lot of admirers and well so competitively reissued, should entrance a new generation of music-lovers.

Symphony No 5

Awards 1996

Symphony No 5 (original 1915 version). En saga (original 1892 version)
Lahti Symphony Orchestra / Osmo Vänskä
BIS BISCD800 (58 minutes: DDD) Ⓕ
Recorded 1995 ○○○

Every so often a CD appears which, by means of some interpretative insight, changes our view of a piece of music. This disc changes our whole perspective in a wholly different sense, for it gives us a glimpse of two familiar masterpieces in the making. Sibelius struggled with the Fifth Symphony for almost seven years from about 1912 until it reached its definitive form in 1919. Although the finished score of the first version does not survive, the orchestral material does, so it was not difficult to reconstruct the score.

To study how the two scores differ is to learn something important about the creative process and it is this mystery that makes this disc imperative listening – and not just for Sibelians. The four-movement 1915 score has a more complex harmonic language than the final score and so it provides a missing link, as it were, between the Fourth Symphony and the definitive Fifth. The opening horn motive has yet to emerge, and the finale's coda has yet to acquire its hammer-blow chords. And in between you will find that the various themes, some distinctly recognizable, others taking off in totally unexpected directions and charting unknown regions.

The version of *En saga* with which we are familiar does not come between the *Kullervo* Symphony and the *Karelia* music but from 1901 between the First and Second Symphonies and was made for Busoni. The original offers fascinating material for comparison: there is a brief glimpse of Bruckner, whose work he had encountered in Vienna a year or two earlier, and the orchestral writing, though not always as polished as in the later version, still has flair. Praise to the Lahti orchestra and their fine conductor, and the excellent and natural balance.

Sibelius Symphony No 5[a] **Nielsen** Symphony No 4, 'The inextinguishable', FS76[b]. Pan and Syrinx FS87[b]
[a]Philharmonia Orchestra, [b]City of Birmingham Symphony Orchestra / Sir Simon Rattle
EMI CDM7 64737-2 (78 minutes: DDD) Ⓜ
Recorded 1981-84 ∞

Symphony No 5 is also available on
HMV Classics HMV5 72158-2 Ⓑ

Rattle's 1982 recording of the Sibelius Fifth is a remarkable achievement for a young man; it was (and remains) one of the very best in the catalogue. He handles the transition between the first movement and the *Scherzo* section in masterly fashion – more convincingly than in his later CBSO performance, good though that is. It received (and more to the point, deserved) numerous accolades at the time and it is a pleasure to have it reissued at mid and recently bargain price. Rattle's version of *Pan and Syrinx*, is one of the most poetic interpretations of this little masterpiece ever committed to disc, while his account of Nielsen's Fourth is perceptive and well shaped, though it lacks some of the fire and abandon recalled from a broadcast he made with the Philharmonia Orchestra in the late 1970s. Strongly recommended.

Additional recommendations

Symphony No 5

Couplings: Symphony No 1. Romance for strings.
New York Philharmonic Orchestra / Bernstein; various artists
Sony Classical SBK63060 (77 minutes: ADD: 2/66[R]) Ⓑ

Leonard Bernstein's Sibelius always occupied a place outside the mainstream, but he had plenty to say.

Couplings: Symphony No 3
Oslo Philharmonic Orchestra / Jansons
EMI CDC5 55533-2 (58 minutes: DDD: 5/96) Ⓕ

Another Sibelius disc from Oslo with masses of detail and some superb playing under Jansons's watchful gaze.

(The original and definitive 1919 versions)
Lahti Symphony Orchestra / Vänskä
BIS BISCD863 (68 minutes: DDD: 12/97) Ⓕ

This is a disc for Sibelius addicts. It offers a fascinating view of the composer's musical processes, and since the original No 5 will never be performed, a unique chance

Further listening

Simpson Symphony No 3
Coupling: Symphony No 5
Royal Philharmonic Orchestra / Handley
Hyperion CDA66728 (71 minutes: DDD: 2/95) Ⓢ

Robert Simpson's Third Symphony has a strength and structural integrity that should appeal to Sibelians.

Symphony No 6

Symphonies Nos 6 and 7. Tapiola, Op 112
Lahti Symphony Orchestra / Osmo Vänskä
BIS BISCD864 (68 minutes: DDD) Ⓕ
Recorded 1997 ∞

The Lahti orchestra bring total dedication to these great scores and Osmo Vänskä, as we have observed in his remarkable accounts of the First and Fourth Symphonies, is a Sibelian of substance. With this account of the Sixth and Seventh he brings his survey to a triumphant conclusion. Indeed this is every bit as impressive as the First and Fourth. To the Sixth Symphony he brings total concentration: a serene slow movement but a very fast Scherzo and tautly held-together finale. The Seventh is finely conceived and paced and though the Lahti orchestra are not the equal of the Finnish RSO for Saraste or the Helsinki PO for Berglund (both conductors fine Sibelians), directed by Vänksä they give the more compelling and convincing performances.

The *Tapiola* is thrilling: atmospheric and powerfully built up and though it does not displaces Karajan, Koussevitzky, Beecham and so on, it is a measure of its splendour and power – and the terror it evokes – that it invites only the most exalted comparisons. Of course, in the Sixth Symphony one would not want to be without either Sir Colin Davis, the Beecham or any of the Karajan versions – least of all his 1981 reading – and for the Seventh the roll-call must certainly include Koussevitzky's seminal account as well as both Sir Colin's Boston and LSO accounts (the latter recently deleted).

However, this impressive issue should, without a shadow of a doubt, be heard by all Sibelians.The recorded sound is in the first flight and there are excellent notes by Andrew Barnett, too.

Symphonies Nos 6 and 7. The Tempest – Suite No 2, Op 109
Iceland Symphony Orchestra / Petri Sakari
Naxos 8 554387 (71 minutes: DDD) Ⓢ
Recorded 2000

A most enjoyable conclusion to Petri Sakari's Sibelius symphony cycle. Sakari's Sixth impresses by dint of its unpretentious honesty and quiet cogency. As on previous instalments within this series, the Icelanders respond with a keen fervour as contagious as it is heartwarming. Their woodwind roster comprises an especially personable bunch, and if the strings inevitably lack that very last ounce of tonal clout and sheer composure provided by, say, Karajan's Berlin Philharmonic or the San Francisco Symphony under Blomstedt – to name but two of the strongest rivals – there's no missing the touching expressive warmth they bring to the work's transcendental closing pages. In Sakari's hands both outer movements develop real fire and purpose, and he uncovers plenty of happy detail along the way – the distinctive colouring of the bass clarinet being one of this performance's chief pleasures.

Sakari's Seventh, too, is very good indeed, patient and imaginative in the manner of Vänskä, or Sanderling's much underrated, irresistibly sinewy 1974 recording with the Berlin Symphony Orchestra. Perhaps the Iceland Symphony's principal trombonist could have been just a touch more assertive for that heroic initial solo six bars after fig C, and the timpanist appears to enter a bar late just before fig E, but the only sizeable niggle concerns Sakari's not-quite-seamless handling of that tricky *Poco a poco affrettando* transition passage into the *Vivacissimo* section beginning at fig J, itself not entirely free of a certain breathless fluster. All of which means, of course, that Sakari's conception as a whole is not as thrillingly inevitable an experience as Koussevitzky's, Maazel's (a magnificent reading, sounding fresher than ever on a new Decca Legends compilation) or Boult's masterly 1963 concert relay with the RPO. That said, Sakari builds the shattering *Largamente* climax at fig Z superbly, and the closing bars are exceptionally fine. Not a front-runner, perhaps, but no mean achievement all the same. Well worth investigating at Naxos price.

Additional recommendations

Symphonies Nos 5 and 6

Couplings: Legends, 'Lemminkaïnen Suite', Op 22

Berlin Philharmonic Orchestra / Karajan

DG Galleria 439 982-2GGA (69 minutes: ADD: 1/95) Ⓜ

DG The Originals ② 457 748-2GOR2 (ADD) Ⓜ

Couplings: Symphonies 4-7. The Swan of Tuonela. Tapiola

Karajan's glorious account of the Sixth remains, for some, unsurpassed. His DG Berlin Fifth is also very fine and indisputably the best of his four accounts.

Symphony No 6

Couplings: Symphony No 4. The Tempest – incidental music, Op 109: Prelude. Legends, 'Lemminkaïnen Suite', Op 22 – Lemminkaïnen's return. The Bard

Royal Philharmonic Orchestra; London Philharmonic Orchestra / Beecham

EMI Beecham Edition CDM7 64027-2 Ⓜ

(79 minutes: ADD: 3/92)

A disc to prove why Beecham was among Sibelius's favoured interpreters: he really understands every note.

Symphony No 7

Symphony No 7[a] Ⓗ

Pelleas and Melisande[a] – Melisande; Spring in the park; Intermezzo; The death of Melisande.

The Tempest[b] – incidental music, Op 109: Prelude; The oak-tree; Humoresque; Caliban's Song; Berceuse; Prospero; Miranda. Scenes historiques, Op 25[b] – Festivo. In memoriam, Op 59[b]. Legends, Op 22[b] – Lemminkäinen's return

[a]**New York Philharmonic Orchestra;** [b]**London Philharmonic Orchestra / Beecham**

Dutton Laboratories CDAX8013 (76 minutes: ADD) Ⓜ

Recorded 1936-42 OO

One of the special things about Beecham's Sibelius is its sheer sonority: the strings have a fresh, vernal sheen quite different from the opulence of Koussevitzky or Karajan, though Sir Thomas had all their flexibility and plasticity of phrasing, perhaps even more, together with the ability to create an atmosphere easier to discern than define. This still comes across despite the more limited frequency range of these early recordings, in which the strings easily lose their bloom. In all, Beecham recorded the Seventh Symphony three times – his last version was in 1955 with the RPO (HMV Classics), but this 1942 account is easily his best: it has a powerful thrust and an intensity altogether missing from his RPO reading. Although Sir Thomas never passed the records, possibly due to 'the rather hollow sound' of the acoustic or some minor blemishes of execution, they were released in America and, as Lyndon Jenkins reminds us, fortunately for us, he lost the subsequent lawsuit. Mind you, the sound at the opening of the 1942 'Melisande' is undoubtedly hollow and not the equal of Beecham's pre-war Sibelius Society version (EMI). The performance of the symphony is quite magisterial and is altogether tougher and stronger in profile than either of his later ones. The transfer is pretty magisterial too.

Some of the remaining material on this disc has not been available since the days of shellac. Of particular interest are the items from Beecham's first *Pelleas and Melisande* and his earlier recordings of the pieces from *The Tempest*. The Prelude is undoubtedly the most terrifying so far put on disc, his account of 'The oak-tree' is more atmospheric and chilling than his 1955 reading, and the same goes for the 'Berceuse'. In short, strongly recommended.

Symphonies Nos 2[a], 5[a] and 7[b]. Swanwhite[c] – Ⓗ

The maidens with roses. Tapiola[d]. Pohjola's Daughter[c]

[acd]**Boston Symphony Orchestra;** [b]**BBC Symphony Orchestra / Koussevitzky**

Pearl ② GEMMCDS9408 (125 minutes: ADD) Ⓕ

Recorded [b]1933 (live), [a]1935, [c]1936 and [d]1939 OOO

Among the great conductors closely identified in the public mind with Sibelius (Kajanus, Beecham and Karajan), Koussevitzky is the one whose star has faded. Not among serious collectors, of course, but as far as the wider musical public is concerned. But if he has not acquired cult status, his claims on our allegiance is every bit as strong. In the 1930s and 1940s, Koussevitzky's reputation as a great Sibelius conductor was second to none. Less well known is the fact that he was a relatively late convert to his cause: not until the mid 1920s was his enthusiasm really fired. In 1926, two years after he had come to Boston, he presented the Seventh Symphony, and his celebrated recording was made seven years later during his guest appearances with the BBC Symphony Orchestra. It remains the most electrifying performance ever committed to disc, an account of extraordinary intensity and concentration, and the new transfer gives it a body and presence that are exhilarating.

Koussevitzky recorded the Second Symphony in Boston two years later, in 1935, and then again in 1950. The present version of the work was the second to appear – Kajanus's pioneering account had been made in 1930 for Columbia. Koussevitzky's, however, is very different: the opening *allegretto* is far more measured and has the greater breadth, though one suspects that Kajanus was closer to Sibelius's intentions. Of course, the orchestral playing of the Boston Symphony is vastly superior, particularly the strings, which positively glow. The anonymous 1930 London orchestra (it was in fact the LSO) was at that time no match for 'the aristocrat of orchestras'. Throughout this Boston performance there is a sustained feeling for line, a tenuto of remarkable quality and a sense of direction and power that are altogether exceptional. Koussevitzky's account of the Fifth Symphony has been surpassed in dramatic fire only by Toscanini, and *Pohjola's daughter* has the same wonderful sense of line Koussevitzky achieved in the Symphonies Nos 2 and 7.

The wonderfully concentrated and thrilling account of *Tapiola* is among the pantheon of great performances on record; such is its intensity that one wonders whether it has ever been surpassed, even by Beecham and Karajan. In Koussevitzky's hands the forests seem to howl in some kind of primaeval agony. His performance of 'The Maidens with roses' from *Swanwhite* is a seductive performance. A marvellous set, excellently transferred.

Additional recommendations

Symphonies Nos 6 and 7 Coupling: Nightride and Sunrise
Berlin Symphony Orchestra / Sanderling
Berlin Classics 0092 812BC (70 minutes: DDD) Ⓜ

A coupling that enjoys quite a following among informed Sibelians. By no means mainstream but worth exploring.

Couplings: Symphony No 5. The Oceanides. Finlandia. Tapiola
Helsinki Philharmonic Orchestra / Berglund
EMI Double Forte ② CZS5 68646-2 (112 minutes: DDD) Ⓜ

The other half of Berglund's 1980s Sibelius cycle. Notable for its rugged intensity.

Symphonies Nos 3, 6 and 7
Couplings: Violin Concerto. Finlandia. Tapiola. Legends, 'Lemminkaïnen Suite', Op 22
Accardo *vn* **Boston Symphony Orchestra; London Symphony Orchestra / Davis, C**
Philips Duo 446 160-2PM2 ② (146 minutes: ADD:11/75R) Ⓜ

Another 'second half' of a cycle. The symphonies have a wonderful sheen and the couplings are particularly generous. Another classy budget-price compilation.

Symphony No 7
Couplings: **Schubert** Symphony No 8. **Bizet** Jeux d'enfants – excerpts. Ravel Daphnis et Chloé
Royal Philharmonic Orchestra / Boult
BBC Music Legends/IMG Artists BBCL4039-2 Ⓜ
(75 minutes: ADD: 12/00)

Boult was not a conductor you'd immediately associated with Sibelius but this honest, well-conceived reading forms part of a highly enticing concert.

Further listening
Simpson Symphony No 5
Coupling: Symphony No 3
Royal Philharmonic Orchestra / Handley
Hyperion CDA66728 (71 minutes: DDD: 2/95) Ⓢ

A powerful symphonic vision forged from fierce emotions and vivid imaginings. An overwhelming experience.

Works for Violin and Piano

Five Pieces, Op 81. Novelette, Op 102. Five Danses champêtres, Op 106. Four Pieces, Op 115. Three Pieces, Op 116
Nils-Erik Sparf *vn* **Bengt Forsberg** *pf*
BIS CD625 (57 minutes: DDD) Ⓕ
Recorded 1993 ⦿

No one listening to this music would doubt that Sibelius had a special feeling for the violin. Whether he is composing lighter music such as the captivating 'Rondino' from the Op 81 set or the more substantial later pieces, such as the first of the *Danses champêtres*, which comes close to the world of *The Tempest*. Neither the Op 115 nor the Op 116 set contains great music but they are much finer than they have been given credit for. Both 'On the heath' and the 'Ballade', Nos 1 and 2 of Op 115, have an innocence that calls to mind the wonderful *Humoresques* for violin and orchestra. In particular 'The Bells', Op 115 No 4 is a rather cryptic miniature and the 'Scène de danse' of Op 116, with its striking tonal juxtapositions, is a kind of Finnish equivalent of the Bartók *Romanian Dances*. Nils-Erik Sparf and Bengt Forsberg are dedicated and sensitive exponents who make the most of the opportunities this repertoire provides. One small reservation: the piano tone sounds a little thick at the bottom end, and the violin is by no means the dominant partner. Enthusiastically recommended.

Songs

King Christian II, Op 27 – Fool's Song of the Spider. Five Christmas Songs, Op 1. Eight Songs, Op 57. Hymn to Thaïs. Six Songs, Op 72 – No 3, The kiss; No 4, The echo nymph; No 5, Der Wanderer und der Bach; No 6, A hundred ways. Six Songs, Op 86. The small girls
Monica Groop *mez* **Love Derwinger** *pf*
BIS CD657 (66 minutes: DDD). Texts and translations Ⓕ included. Recorded 1994

Monica Groop, following her success in the Cardiff Singer of the World Competition, has built up a busy career. Communication is her strength, and unevenness of line a relative weakness. Sibelius's songs are a rich and still undervalued part of the song repertoire. Still only four or five are really well known, and none of those is included here. Not all are of very special quality: the title is probably the best thing about the 'Fool's Song of the Spider' (from *King Christian II*), and the *Hymn to Thaïs* gains interest through being Sibelius's only song in English rather than through intrinsic merit. Yet there are many delights here, including the closing waltz-song, *The small girls*. The acoustic is perhaps somewhat too reverberant but has plenty of presence.

Songs, Volume 3. Seven Songs, Op 13. Six Songs, Op 50. Six Songs, Op 90. The Wood Nymph. Belshazzar's Feast – The Jewish Girl's Song. Resemblance. A Song. Serenade. The Thought[a]
Anne Sofie von Otter, [a]Monica Groop *mezzos*
Bengt Forsberg *pf*
BIS CD757 (67 minutes: DDD). Texts and translations Ⓕ included. Recorded 1994-95

The vast majority of Sibelius's songs are in Swedish, the language with which he grew up as a child, and here they are given by a distinguished native Swedish partnership. The *Seven Songs*, Op 13, are all Runeberg settings and come from the composer's early years (1891-2). Best known, perhaps, are 'Spring is flying' and 'The dream', but there are others, such as 'The young hunter', that are no less delightful and characterful. The other Runeberg settings here, the *Six Songs*, Op 90, come towards the end of Sibelius's career as a song composer (1917-18). 'The north', as in all the nature poetry of Runeberg, touches a very special vein of inspiration. Along with 'Die stille Nacht', Op 50 No 5, which is equally affectingly given by these two artists – it is among his finest songs. Interest naturally focuses on the rarities.

The Wood Nymph, not to be confused with the melodrama or the tone-poem, is recorded here for the first time. As well as *A Song*, there are two other early Runeberg settings, the 1888 *Serenade* and *Resemblance*, both of them also première recordings. 'The Jewish Girl's Song' will be familiar from the incidental music to *Belshazzar's Feast*, and is affecting in this form – particularly sung as it is here. Given the artistry and insight of this splendid partnership, and the interest and beauty of the repertoire, this is a self-recommending issue.

Arioso, Op 3. Seven Songs, Op 17. Row, row duck. Six Songs, Op 36. Five Songs, Op 37. Pelleas and Melisande, Op 46 – The three blind sisters. Six Songs, Op 88. Narcissus
Anne Sofie von Otter *mez* **Bengt Forsberg** *pf*
BIS CD457 (67 minutes: DDD). Texts and translations included. Recorded 1989 Ⓕ

In all, Sibelius composed about 100 songs, mostly to Swedish texts but his achievement in this field has, naturally enough, been overshadowed by the symphonies. Most music lovers know only a handful like 'Black roses', Op 36 No 1, and 'The Tryst' and the most popular are not always the best. Sibelius's output for the voice has much greater range, diversity and depth than many people suppose. For collectors used to hearing them sung by a baritone, the idea of a soprano will seem strange but a lot of them were written for the soprano Ida Ekman. Anne Sofie von Otter not only makes a beautiful sound and has a feeling for line, but also brings many interpretative insights to this repertoire. The very first song from the Op 17 set is a marvellous Runeberg setting, 'Since then I have questioned no further' and it was this that Ida Ekman sang for Brahms. Von Otter captures its mood perfectly and has the measure of its companions too. Her account of 'Black roses' is particularly thrilling and she is very persuasive in the weaker Op 88 set. She sings throughout with great feeling for character and her account of 'Astray', Op 17 No 6, has great lightness of touch and charm. The Opp 36 and 37 sets are among the finest lyrical collections in the whole of Sibelius's song output, and they completely engage this artist's sensibilities. These are performances of elegance and finesse.

Everyman, Op 83

Incidental Music – Everyman, Op 83; Belshazzar's Feast, Op 51. The Countess's Portrait, Op posth
Lilli Paasikivi *mez* **Petri Lehto** *ten* **Sauli Tiilikainen** *bar* **Pauli Pietiläinen** *org* **Leena Saarenpaä** *pf*
Lahti Chamber Choir; Lahti Symphony Orchestra / Osmo Vänskä
BIS CD735 (65 minutes: DDD). Texts and translations Ⓕ included. Recorded 1995

These are all first recordings and interest centres on the score Sibelius wrote for Hofmannsthal's morality play, *Jedermann* ('Everyman') in 1916. The final score comprises 16 numbers and runs to some 40 minutes. Some of the music is fragmentary and hardly makes sense out of context, though most of it is atmospheric and all of it is characteristic. The sustained *Largo* section for muted, divided strings (track 11), is among the most searching music Sibelius ever wrote for theatre and, artistically, is fit to keep company with *The Tempest* music. Overall the material does not lend itself to being turned into a suite in the same way as *Belshazzar's Feast* but this recording rescues from obscurity some strangely haunting and at times really inspired music – the last 25 minutes are very powerful.

By all accounts Hjalmar Procopé's *Belshazzar's Feast* was a feeble play and when it first appeared, one newspaper cartoon showed the playwright being borne aloft in the composer's arms. There seems little doubt that his name would not be alive were it not for Sibelius's music. The latter certainly makes an expert job of creating an effective and (in the case of the 'Notturno') a moving concert suite. *The Countess's Portrait* (1906) is a wistful, pensive and charming piece for strings, which was only published two years ago. Obviously this is a self-recommending issue of exceptional interest.

Karelia

Incidental Music – Karelia; Kuolema. Valse triste, Op 44 No 1 (1904 versions)
Heikki Laitinen, Taito Hoffren *sngrs* **Kirsi Tiihonen** *sop* **Raimo Laukka** *bar* **Lahti Symphony Orchestra / Osmo Vänskä**
BIS CD915 (76 minutes: DDD). Texts and translations Ⓕ included. Recorded 1997

This is a disc which will be of great interest to Sibelians. The original score of the *Karelia* music was discovered in the conductor Kajanus's library after his death in 1933 and his widow returned it to Sibelius three years later. The music extended to eight tableaux which portrayed various episodes in Karelian history. In the 1940s Sibelius destroyed the score, about which he had had second thoughts since its première in 1893, sparing only the overture, the movements familiar from the suite and the first number, 'A Karelian Home – News of War'. Fortunately for posterity, a set of orchestral parts came to light, albeit incomplete, and were put into shape by Kalevi Kuoso. It was these that the composer Kalevi Aho used in preparing the edition on which this recording is based.

In all there are some 40 minutes of music, over half of which is new. Those familiar with the 'Ballade' from the Op 11 Suite will no doubt be slightly disconcerted to hear the familiar cor anglais melody taken by a baritone and will find the piece too long in its original form. The opening of the fifth tableau, 'Pontus de la Gardie at the gates of Käkisalmi [Kexholm Castle] in 1580', is highly effective and leads into the famous 'Alla marcia'. It is fascinating to hear what the piece is like, and what Sibelius was prepared to lose. Listening to this reaffirms and illumines both the sureness of his artistic judgement and the vitality of his creative imagination. Sibelius's incidental music to *Kuolema*, the play by his brother-in-law, Arvid Järnefelt, dates from 1903. The most familiar music from it is the *Valse triste*, which Sibelius revised the following year, adding flute, clarinet, horns and timpani and making it altogether more sophisticated harmonically and melodically. Osmo Vänskä and his Lahti players prove reliable and responsive guides in this atmospheric music and it is hard to imagine their performances being improved on. Wide-ranging and expertly balanced recorded sound.

The Tempest, Incidental Music

The Tempest – Incidental Music, Op 109
Kirsi Tiihonen *sop* **Lilli Paasikivi** *mez* **Anssi Hirvonen, Paavo Kerola** *tens* **Heikki Keinonen** *bar* **Lahti Opera Chorus and Symphony Orchestra / Osmo Vänskä**
BIS CD581 (68 minutes: DDD). Text and translation included. Recorded 1992 Ⓕ ●

A first recording of the full score! Sibelius's music for *The Tempest*, his last and greatest work in its genre, was the result of a commission for a particularly lavish production at the Royal Theatre, Copenhagen in 1926. The score is far more extensive than the two suites and consists of 34 musical numbers for soloists, mixed choir, harmonium and large orchestra. Readers will be brought up with a start by the music for the 'Berceuse', the second item, which uses a harmonium rather than the strings with which we are familiar from the two suites and although it is still more magical in the familiar orchestral suite, the original has an other-worldly quality all its own. The music is played in the order in which it was used in the 1927 production of the play and there are ample and excellent explanatory notes. The 'Chorus of the Winds' is also different but no less magical in effect. Of course, taken out of the theatrical context, not everything comes off – but even if the invention is not consistent in quality, at its best it is quite wonderful. The singers and chorus all rise to the occasion and Osmo Vänskä succeeds in casting a powerful spell in the 'Intermezzo', which opens Act 4. The recording is marvellously atmospheric though it needs to be played at a higher than usual level setting as it is a little recessed. For Sibelians this is a self-recommending issue.

Additional recommendation
The Tempest
Viljakainen *sop* **Groop** *mez* **Silvasti** *ten* **Hynninen, Tilikainen** *bars* **Finnish Opera Festival Chorus; Finnish Radio Symphony Orchestra/Saraste**
Ondine ODE813-2 (60 minutes: DDD) Ⓕ

A fine alternative version with idiomatic singing and playing frpom these Finnish performers.

Choral Songs

Partsongs, Op 18[a] – No 1, The Broken Voice; No 3, The Boat Journey of Väinämöinen; No 4, Fire on the Island; No 6, The Song of my Heart. Busy as a Thrush[a]. Play, Beautiful Girl[a]. Rakastava, Op 14[a]. The Thrush's Toiling[a]. Festive March[a]. Cantata for the Helsinki University Ceremonies of 1897, Op 23[a]. To Thérèse Hahl[a]. Nostalgia[c]. Not with Grief[a]. Wonderful Gifts[c]. March of the Finnish Jaeger Battalion, Op 91 No 1. Three Runeberg Songs[a]. Awaken![a]. Choir of the Winds. Ballad[a]. The Son's Bride. Men from Plain and Sea, Op 65*a*[a]. Dreams[a]. Christmas Song[a]. Give Me No Splendour, Op 1 No 4[a]. Bell Melody of Berghaill Church, Op 65*b*[a]. Three Introductory Antiphons, Op 107*b*. Ode, Op 113 No 11[a]. Carminalia[bc]. Primary School Children's March[c]. In the Morning Mist[c]. Hail, O Princess[a]. The Landscape Breathes, Op 30[a]. Three American School Songs. The Way to School[a]. School Song[a]. March of the Labourers[a]. The World Song, Op 91*b*. Song of the Athenians, Op 31 No 3[bc]. To the Fatherland[a]. Song for the People of Uusimaa[a]. Finlandia[a]
[a]**Tapiola Chamber Choir;** [b]**Friends of Sibelius / Hannu Norjanen;** [c]**Tapiola Choir / Kari Ala-Pöllänen** with **Ilmo Ranta** *pf* **Johanna Torikka** *org/harm*
Finlandia 0630-19054 2 ② (147 minutes: DDD) Ⓕ
Texts and translations included. Recorded 1996-97

This survey of Sibelius's complete choral songs is important – and irresistible – for both its consistently fine performance and its historical context. The two-disc set begins where – in the mythology of Finnish oral tradition – all music began: with the life-giving song of Väinämöinen from the *Kalevala*'s compilation of folk poetry; the verse which tuned Sibelius's ear to the musicality of the Finnish language (at a time when he and his social class still spoke Swedish) also inspired his first distinctive song settings. Here, excellent production most sensitively captures the division and shifting of the finely blended voices of the

Tapiola Chamber Choir, as solo and ensemble voices trace the asymmetrical metres and modal cadences of works such as 'The Boat Journey' from Op 18 and 'The Lover'. References to the *Kalevala* return in the group of songs for ceremonies and festivities in which solo exhortations are pitted against shifting choral harmonies, as images of journey, hope and freedom are expressed in the supple melodies of 10 songs for a university degree ceremony from 1897 (Op 23).

A fervent and optimistic tribute to Finland's great romantic painter Albert Edelfelt sets works by Sibelius's beloved Swedish-language poet, Rüneberg: and his 'Autumn Evening' could be an aural re-creation of one of the painter's own canvases. Sibelius's music pierces dark, close harmonies with high lines of anguish, presaging the imaginative virtuosity of later masterpieces such as 'Men from Plain and Sea' and 'Dreams' with their sense of the wandering and yearning of the human spirit. The second disc follows three simple Christmas carols with the composer's sacred and liturgical pieces. Among these early prentice works, the bells of Helsinki's great Kallio Church ring out: the peal which Sibelius wrote for the fine 1912 Nordic Jugendstil building still rings out twice a day, and here we are treated to the words as well. The songs for children range from uninspired English-language commissions for American schools, to a tiny and perfect setting of 'The Landscape Breathes', in which the girls' voices slowly and chromatically thaw from their unison freeze. Finland's and Sibelius's unjingoistic patriotism returns at the end with gently yet distinctively harmonised hymns to specific regions of the motherland and, finally, with the great *Finlandia* hymn.

Robert Simpson British 1921-1997

GROVE *Simpson, a pupil of Howells (1942-6), worked for the BBC (1951-80). His main achievement was his cycles of nine symphonies and eight string quartets, both begun in 1951 and both displaying a dynamic tonality quite individual in its energy and purposefulness, encouraged more than influenced by his admiration for Beethoven, Bruckner and Nielsen (on whom he published studies).*

Symphonies Nos 1 and 8

Royal Philharmonic Orchestra / Vernon Handley
Hyperion CDA66890 (73 minutes: DDD) Ⓕ
Recorded 1996

Here is an inspiring encounter with music whose surface affinities (the dynamism of Beethoven, the registral awareness of Berlioz, the obsessional drive of Bartók and so on) fade from the mind as its unique blend of unquenchable energy and alert meditation takes you over. Like a number composers, Simpson seems to have responded to the power of late Beethoven and thought, 'I can do that'; like very few, he can.

The First's construction on the basis of proportionally related tempos enables it to be simultaneously part of the world of conflict and feeling and yet at the same time somehow soaring above it. The Eighth, by contrast, seems to embody some colossal inner rage. Each partial untying of its knotted psyche unleashes apocalyptic fury, and the quietus of harmonic resolution is denied until the very last moment.

The Eighth had an unhappy première performance in 1982. For this recording Vernon Handley hasclearly devoted a labour of love to it, and he seems to have persuaded the Royal Philharmonic to do the same.

Symphonies Nos 2 and 4
Bournemouth Symphony Orchestra / Vernon Handley
Hyperion CDA66505 (75 minutes: DDD) Ⓕ
Recorded 1992

The opening of the Second Symphony is breathtaking – an 'active but mysterious' idea, utterly distinctive in its silvery harmonic colouring, it holds the key to a world where wistfulness can transmute into energy and where energy itself occasionally has to be rescued from the obsessional corners it drives itself into. The slow movement is no less characteristic of its composer in its gentle restorative quality, probing unfamiliar areas of the mind and conjuring them to life. For the finale it is doubtful if there is any parallel in Simpson's output; the rhythmic drive and grittiness of Beethoven's Seventh Symphony is there in the background, but there is an almost irresponsible rollicking character similar to the Hindemith of the *Symphonic Metamorphoses*.

The Fourth Symphony contains perhaps the most remarkable and certainly the most instantly communicative of Simpson's Beethoven paraphrases. The model here is the scherzo of the *Choral* Symphony, with a Haydn quotation supplying material for the Trio section. To stay so close to the structure of the original and yet to create such an entirely new and individual experience is a feat of genuine compositional virtuosity. It is like Icarus and the sun all over again, except that Simpson gets away with it.

Some may find the following slow movement featureless. But experience suggests that a mind-stretching power will eventually disclose itself. In the meantime there are the constantly renewing horizons of the first movement to savour, with that special combination of transparent texture, blunt rhythms and polytonal shadings that gives Simpson's musical paragraphs their forward-looking momentum. And finally there are the massively energizing shouts which crown the work. All this gives the Bournemouth Symphony Orchestra and Vernon Handley plenty to get their teeth into, and their response is as splendid as in their *Gramophone* Award-winning account of Simpson's Ninth Symphony.

Symphonies Nos 3 and 5
Royal Philharmonic Orchestra / Vernon Handley
Hyperion CDA66728 (71 minutes: DDD) Ⓕ
Recorded 1994 **OO**

The Third Symphony is Simpson's best-known work and Vernon Handley play the symphony like the repertoire piece it deserves to be, and Hyperion's recording reveals a wealth of unsuspected detail and beauty. The Beethovenian impulse still comes across, and the abrasive edge is only slightly softened. But what has been gained is clarity, blend and perspective, plus a sense of dialogue (Simpson's polyphony never ceases to amaze) and an altogether subtler realisation of the luminosity of Simpson's scoring. The long accumulating second movement is absorbingly poetic, witty in its dialogue, and inevitable in its conclusion.

The Fifth Symphony is surely one of Simpson's most vivid pieces. Moods of terror, anger, anxious probing and fierce determination are right on the surface, and there is a feeling of terrific will-power being exerted to transmute those moods into a symphonic experience. Perhaps one could hear more of the cutting edge of Simpson's scoring more piccolo trumpet and timpani in the first panic-stricken outburst, for example. But it is a fearsomely demanding score. What one should be saying is that this is one of the great symphonies of the post-war era, magnificently realised by all concerned.

Symphonies Nos 6 and 7
Royal Liverpool Philharmonic Orchestra / Vernon Handley
Hyperion CDA66280 (60 minutes: DDD) Ⓕ
Recorded 1987

The first performances of these symphonies had shown many characteristic and admirable qualities, but there was a suspicion of some tentativeness a lowering of sights even, after the explosive Fifth Symphony. One should have guessed that closer acquaintance and more expert performance would show this to be more a matter of concentration of ideas and of conscious change of direction. The Royal Liverpool Philharmonic Orchestra and Vernon Handley show the Sixth to be a work of immense inner power, and if the Seventh is a more cryptic statement this recording certainly brings it into a clearer focus than previously.

Whereas Tippett (in the same year, curiously) wrote a birth-to-death symphony (his Fourth) Simpson's Sixth shifts the process one stage back – from conception to prime of life. Intense expectancy gives way to a memorable downward-stalking unison figure, the fertilised seed which becomes the most active force in the early stages of the work. From here to the irresistible energy of the final pages Simpson's control of musical momentum can only be marvelled at; and if you don't marvel at it, that may be because you are worrying about the apparent restriction on colour and lyricism, and thus missing the point.

As yet the final D major outcome still refuses to register as a natural outcome, although presumably there is any amount of logical justification for it. The neutral, non-triadic conclusion to the Seventh rings truer, though in this work the processes before it are more inscrutable—not in the technical sense, but simply in terms of what the techniques are driving at. But anyone who has puzzled over, and then clicked with, say, Sibelius's Fourth or Shostakovich's 15th, will know how dangerous it is to jump to conclusions. And even if the click never happens, one probable masterpiece is surely enough to be getting on with.

Awards 1989

Symphony No 9
Bournemouth Symphony Orchestra / Vernon Handley
Hyperion CDA66299 (68 minutes: DDD) Ⓕ
Recorded 1988. Also includes an illustrated talk on the work by the composer

If you know that feeling of expectancy, of vast potential energy, at the outset of a great symphony, you will surely respond to the opening of Simpson's Ninth – and be wholly engrossed. You will be led through shifting pedal-points and wedge-shaped themes encompassing a specific harmonic universe; through waves of energy pulsating fit to burst, until burst they do into a titanic scherzo ('Beethoven would probably have thought that some lunatic had got hold of one of his scherzos' as Simpson puts it); through slow, disembodied traceries of string lines, through awe-inspiring climaxes to a no less awe-inspiring hushed coda. And as rising scales pass through the coda's pedal-points into the final glacial sonority you will know that you have heard one of the finest symphonies of the post-war era.

The composer adds an explanatory 18-minute talk. Here are laid bare some of the salient constructional features of the work – the opening's basis in chorale prelude procedures (a fairly cosmic rethinking thereof!), the single underlying pulse of the entire work (a recurrent feature in Simpson's output, but never before applied on this scale), the palindromic variations in the second half, the debts to Bach, Beethoven and Bruckner. To which one might add that the rigorous processes described in this talk suggest a somewhat unlikely kinship with Bartók at his most abstract (as in the first movement of the *Music for strings, percussion and celesta*).

Bartók, it is safe to say, has as little to do with this work's symphonic instincts as any other 'big name' of the last 50 years or so. Simpson stands not at any fixed pole of today's music, but rather at a kind of magnetic north, free from attempts of musical cartographers to pin down his position, spiritually allied to composers of any age and style who have penetrated to the essence of music's motion in time. A totally absorbing symphony and the performance and recording are surely the best possible tribute to all concerned.

String Quartets

String Quartets Nos 7 and 8
Hyperion CDA66117 (51 minutes: AAD) Ⓕ
Delme Quartet (Galina Solodchin, Jeremy Williams vns John Underwood va Stephen Orton, vc)
Recorded 1983

String Quartet No 9
Hyperion CDA66127 (58 minutes: AAD) Ⓕ
Recorded
Delme Quartet (Galina Solodchin, Jeremy Williams *vns* John Underwood *va* Stephen Orton, *vc*)
Recorded 1984

Quiet music with a sense of purpose and forward-looking destiny; slow music which bears the promise of a controlled release of energy, these are rare and treasurable qualities in music of our time, and they make their presence felt at the beginnings of Simpson's Seventh and Eighth Quartets. How he progresses through subdued scherzo to vehement climax is something to reflect on at length, and with further acquaintance comes the Beethovenian thrill of hearing the music think. But at first these things just steal up on you and take the breath away.

The Seventh Quartet is dedicated to Susi Jeans, widow of astronomer and mathematidan Sir James Jeans, the Eighth is dedicated to entomologist David Gillett and his wife. Both works draw on the kind of motion suggested by those areas of sdentific enquiry. On the other hand the Ninth calls up what would seem to be the bitterest enemy of forward movement – the palindrome; 32 variations and a fugue, in fact, on the minuet from Haydn's Symphony No 47 and all of them, like the original theme, palindromic. If Simpson's powers of invention falter at any stage in this hour-long tour de force you would be hard pushed to discover where. But then this music so completely absorbing that the necessary critical detachment is difficult to achieve. The only reservation that did register was over recording quality, which for the Ninth Quartet is disappointingly boxy – sensuous appeal is not what this music is about, but a more ingratiating acoustic would not do it any harm – and to hear the Seventh without the distraction, however faint, of traffic noise would be preferable.

The Delme Quartet's performances are outstandingly dedicated. The Ninth Quartet was composed for their 20th anniversary and they prove themselves entirely worthy of the honour.

String Quartet No 13. String Quintet No 2. Clarinet Quintet
Thea King *cl* **Christopher van Kampen** *vc* **Delmé Quartet** (Galina Solodchin, John Trusler *vns* John Underwood *va* Jonathan Williams *vc*)
Hyperion CDA66905 (64 minutes: DDD) Ⓕ
Recorded 1997 ⭘

An invigorating and thought-provoking disc. In the Clarinet Quintet of 1968 the wind partner is treated as an equal of the strings, which makes the linear and contrapuntal inventiveness all the more remarkable and absorbing, though for some it may make the music seem no more than monochrome. Like late Beethoven, Simpson seems to begin by charting a realm just out of emotional reach yet somehow crucial to one's psychic well-being. The mental energy gained then spills over into actual fast music, even into an engaging jigginess. The Quintet feels as though it could go on much longer than its actual 31 minutes without the inventive resources drying up. The rarefied conclusion is all the more moving for its steadiness of gaze. The 13th Quartet (1989) retains many familiar Simpson hallmarks. It opens with a sinewy, deceptively triadic theme which soon gives way to spidery, triplety counterpoint. It is all very ascetic and self-denying and the second and fourth movements go into an interior, attenuated world in which it is difficult to feel entirely at home.

The even more recent String Quintet No 2 keeps its cards just as close to its chest. Again the design alternates austere, lyrical music with a knotty *Allegro*, initially short-lived but gradually expanding, while the slower sections are more or less constant in duration. The impression is less of conflict and resolution than of a stand-off between the two tempo-types, eyeing one another in mutual suspicion; the conclusion is bleak-Sibelian. The Delmé is a longstanding Simpson advocate and it seems to have the ideal sound for him – crystalline, alert and focused, as though beyond obvious human expressiveness in a realm of higher wisdom. The same goes for their admirable partners, Thea King and Christopher van Kampen. This may be one of the less immediately accessible Simpson programmes, but it is still richly rewarding.

Vocal Works

Canzona[a]. Media morte in vita sumus[b]. Tempi[c]. Eppur si muove[d]
[d]**Iain Quinn** *org* [ab]**Corydon Brass Ensemble;** [bc]**Corydon Singers / Matthew Best**
Hyperion CDA67016 (68 minutes: DDD) Ⓕ
Texts included. Recorded 1997 ⭘

Simpson would never have claimed that choral music was his *métier*. Yet for lovers of his music there is something especially revealing about the two pieces recorded here. In *Media morte in vita sumus* ('In the midst of death we are in life') he deliberately reverses the scriptural motto in order to articulate his personal 'anti-pessimist' creed. The musical setting for chorus, brass and timpani is appropriately austere, and Simpson's words are translated into Latin for the sake of universality. *Tempi* for *a cappella* chorus is a *jeu d'esprit*, the text consisting entirely of Italian tempo and character markings. The Corydon Singers offers superbly confident performances, as does the Corydon Brass Ensemble which also shines in the comparatively well-known *Canzona*. It's impossible to avoid comparisons with Nielsen when it comes to the 31-minute *Eppur si muove* ('But it does move') for organ. This 12-minute *ricercare* followed by a 19-minute passacaglia sets its jaw squarely against conventional organ-loft grandiosity. Its intellectual monumentality is clearly in the *Commotio* mould, though it's considerably tougher going than Nielsen's late masterpiece. Iain Quinn joins the long line of dedicated performers who have made Hyperion's Simpson series such a consistent triumph. Recording quality leaves nothing to be desired.

Nikos Skalkottas Greek 1904-1949

GROVE *Skalkottas studied as a violinist at the Athens Conservatory and as a composer in Berlin with Juon, Kahn, Jarnach (1925-7), Weill (1928-9) and Schoenberg (1927-31). In 1933 he returned to Athens, where he worked as a back-desk violinist. His Berlin works are relatively compact and high-spirited, being almost exclusively instrumental and following the neo-classicism of his teachers (in 1927 his music became atonal, but not yet serial). But the bulk of his music dates from 1935-45, when the genres remained traditional but the forms were greatly expanded to contain a deep complexity of serial thematic working: major works of this period include the Third Piano Concerto (1939), the Fourth Quartet (1940) and the overture The Return of Odysseus (1943); he wrote several concertos, chamber and vocal music. He also produced tonal works, including a collection of 36 Greek Dances for orchestra (1936).*

Piano Concerto No 1, AK16

Piano Concerto No 1, AK16[a]. The Maiden and Death – Ballet Suite, AK12. Ouvertüre concertante, AK46
[a]**Geoffrey Douglas Madge** *pf* **Iceland Symphony Orchestra / Nikos Christodoulou** Ⓕ
BIS CD1014 (56 minutes: DDD). Recorded 1998 ●

BIS's Skalkottas cycle started very well and gets better with each release. The First Piano Concerto's characteristic use of a family of note-rows, rather than just one, may have ignited the rift between the apprentice composer and his teacher, Schoenberg. The neo-classical elements cannot have been to the latter's liking, either. Geoffrey Douglas Madge gives a barnstorming performance and the accompaniment is electrifying. The orchestra is heard at its best and in its own right in the suite from the folk-ballet *The Maiden and Death* (1938). Here Skalkottas's brilliant orchestration shines through in what is much more than a pre-run of *The Mayday Spell*. The idiom is less fragmentary than the latter; indeed, it suggests a Greek *Miraculous Mandarin*, if less overtly spectacular in sound or scandalous in plot.

The disc concludes with a further movement from the unfinished Second Symphonic Suite (1944-5; compare the *Largo sinfonico* on the first disc). This *Ouvertüre concertante* is pretty much what the title leads you to expect it to be, a superbly scored sonata-derivative, employing the composer's note-row-complex manner in a most attractive fashion.

Violin Concerto, AK22

Violin Concerto, AK22[a]. Largo Sinfonico, AK4*a*. Greek Dances, AK11 – Epirotikos; Kretikos; Tsamikos; Thessalikos; Mariori mou-Mariori mou; Arkadikos; Kleftikos (arr cpsr)
[a]**Georgios Demertzis** *vn* **Malmö Symphony Orchestra / Nikos Christodoulou** Ⓕ
BIS CD904 (78 minutes: DDD). Recorded 1997 ●

From Nikos Skalkottas's earliest works, a personal idiom was clearly in evidence, combining European modernism with the rhythmic dynamism of Greek traditional music, and characterised by a tensile strength and translucency of sound. Like Bartók, Skalkottas wrote 'popular' music without compromise. The *Greek Dances* are ideal encore pieces, not least in these suave arrangements for strings.

The Violin Concerto of 1937 is among his major works, with a solo part that is demanding yet integral to the symphonic nature of the score – something that Georgios Demertzis's vital account readily conveys here. The close of the *Andante* possesses true lyrical repose, before the finale provides fireworks as well as clinching the musical design.

The *Largo Sinfonico*, completed in 1944, embodies some of Skalkottas's most personal music; its span of 26 minutes is a seamless fusion of variation and sonata forms, and it is as satisfying formally as it is emotionally. Nikos Christodoulou's accompanying notes speak of a private musical universe, yet the plangency of the cello theme and the remorseless tread of the central climaxes betray an unease that must surely be inseparable from the time of composition. The final bars, with the thematic material recast as a series of unearthly chords, feel as much a stoic acceptance of reality as they are a 'harmony of the spheres'. With the Malmö orchestra fully attuned to the idiom, Christodoulou's powerfully shaped reading makes for a compelling experience.

String Quartet No 3, AK34

String Quartets – No 3, AK34; No 4, AK35
New Hellenic Quartet (Georgios Demertzis, Dimitris Chandrakis *vns* Paris Anastasiades *va* Apostolos Chandrakis *vc*)
BIS CD1074 (58 minutes: DDD) Ⓕ
Recorded 1999

Make no mistake about it, BIS's Skalkottas cycle is among the most stimulating recording projects of recent years, and the present disc further enhances its status. The Third Quartet (1935) marked his full return to composition after four years of depression and likely stylistic uncertainty, and the contrasts in idiom evident from his Berlin years are replaced by a tight integration of form and content. The alternate harmonic and melodic presentation of material throughout the opening movement is paralleled by the modal cadential idea which increasingly pervades the *Andante*, in turn governing the tonal outcome of the finale. What appears an overtly classical structure takes on a unity akin to Bartók's Third Quartet.

Quartet No 3 is one of the few Skalkottas pieces to have featured in the UK catalogue. The Dartington Quartet recorded the piece back in 1965 (HMV – nla), while the Greek Quartet's account surfaced briefly during the early 1980s (EMI Greece – nla). In terms of musicianship, the New Hellenic are significantly superior to either, while their dedication establishes the previously unrecorded Fourth Quartet as the missing masterwork in the 'golden age' of inter-war quartet writing.

In his booklet-note, Kostis Demertzis speculates that the work may have been originally planned as a symphony for strings, but the rhythmic velocity of the first movement and *Scherzo* is such that few larger ensembles would be able to do it justice. Formally, the work has intriguing parallels with Beethoven's Op 127 quartet, not least the variation sequence comprising the lengthy second movement; and the fantasia-like third variation seems almost a thematic nucleus for the whole work. Quartet No 4 needs repeated listening for its myriad subtleties to come through, but the New Hellenic ensure that this is as pleasurable as it is enthralling. Natural recorded sound, with a realistic dynamic range, sets the seal on this most rewarding disc.

Violin Sonatinas

Violin Sonatinas[a] – No 1, AK46; No 2, AK47; No 3, AK48; No 4, AK49. March of the Little Soldiers, AK53[a]. Rondo, AK54[a]. Nocturne, AK55[a]. Little Chorale and Fugue, AK56[a]. Gavotte, AK57[a]. Scherzo and Menuetto Cantato, AK58[a]. Solo Violin Sonata, AK69

Georgios Demertzis *vn* [a]**Maria Asteriadou** *pf* Ⓕ
BIS CD1024 (66 minutes: DDD)
Recorded 1998

Here's a window onto Skalkottas's music for his own instrument, itself a microcosm of his development. There is nothing stylistically tentative about the early Solo Violin Sonata (1925). Written with a Bachian economy of manner, the composer draws in references to jazz and popular music; the finale serves notice of his technical skill with an arching four-part fugue, reaching maximum intensity at the point where it returns to the prelude. The sense of a still-emerging personality is reinforced by the first two *Sonatinas* (both 1929, the *Andantino* is all that survives from No 1). Skalkottas's rhythmic incisiveness owes something to Stravinsky and even Bartók, but the tang of the harmonic writing is his alone. With the Third and Fourth *Sonatinas* (both 1935), the Skalkottas idiom, sinuous and expressive, is in place. The thematic integration of No 3 is breathtaking, as is the variety of tone with which the violin sustains continuity in the *Andante*. If the Fourth *Sonatina* is almost too diverse in mood, its *Adagio* is one of Skalkottas's finest: a threnody unfolding in three waves of mounting intensity, it looks forward to the expansive slow movements of the composer's last decade.

The miniatures are anything but trifles. *March of the Little Soldiers* is a savage take on militarism, while *Nocturne* reinterprets the expressive vocabulary of the 'song without words' for the 20th century. There could be no more sympathetic advocate than Georgios Demertzis. As in his recording of the Violin Concerto (BIS), he gets to the heart of Skalkottas's demanding but deeply felt music, with Maria Asteriadou an attentive partner. Inquiring performers and listeners alike should not hesitate to acquire this disc.

Bedřich Smetana Bohemian 1824-1884

GROVE *Smetana took music lessons from his father, a keen violinist, and from several local teachers. In his teens he attended the Academic Gymnasium in Prague, but neglected school work to attend concerts (including some by Liszt, with whom he became friendly) and to write string quartets for friends, until his father sent him to the Premonstratensian Gymnasium at Plzen. At first he earned a precarious living as a teacher in Prague until, in January 1884, he was appointed resident piano teacher to Count Leopold Thun's family, which provided him with the means to study harmony, counterpoint and composition with Josef Proksch. When he failed in an attempt to launch a career as a concert pianist in 1847, Smetana decided to found a school of music in Prague. This showed little profit, but he was able to earn something by teaching privately and by playing regularly to the deposed Emperor Ferdinand, and in 1849 he was able to marry Katerina Kolárová, whom he had known since his Plzen days.*

Smetana's financial situation improved little in the years that followed, and political uncertainty and domestic tragedy only added to his unrest: three of his four daughters died between 1854 and 1856. When he heard there was an opening for a piano teacher at Göteborg he jumped at the chance. In Sweden his prospects improved, and he was in demand as a pianist, teacher and conductor. Inspired by Liszt's example, he composed his first symphonic poems. His wife's health forced him to return to Bohemia with her in 1859, but she died at Dresden on the way home. After two further summers in Göteborg, between which he found a second wife in Bettina Ferdinandová, Smetana felt the need to return permanently to Prague in order to play an active role in the reawakening of Czech culture that followed the Austrian defeat by Napoleon III at Magenta and Soferino.

He was disappointed to find himself no more successful in Prague than he had been before. It was not until his first opera, The Brandenburgers in Bohemia, was enthusiastically received in January 1866 that his prospects there improved. His second, The Bartered Bride, was speedily put into production and soon found favour, though (as with his other operas) foreign performances long remained rarities. As principal conductor of the Provisional Theatre, 1866-74, Smetana added 42 operas to the repertory, including his own Dalibor (on a heroic national theme) and The Two Widows. Dalibor and Libus˘e (performed at the opening of the National Theatre in Prague in 1881) are Smetana's two most nationalistic operas; when completing the latter he also planned a vast orchestral monument to his nation which became the cycle of symphonic poems entitled Má vlast ('My fatherland'), including the evocative and stirring Vltava, a picture of the river that flows through Prague.

In 1874 there appeared the first signs of the syphilis that was to result in Smetana's deafness. The String Quartet From my Life (1876) suggests in its last movement the piercing whistling that haunted his every evening, making work almost impossible. He somehow managed to complete two more operas, a second string quartet and several other works, but by 1883 his mental equilibrium was seriously disturbed. In April 1884 he was taken to the Prague lunatic asylum, where he died the following month.

Smetana was the first major nationalist composer of Bohemia. He gave his people a new musical identity and self-confidence by his technical assurance and originality in handling national subjects. In his operas and symphonic poems he drew on his country's legends, history, characters, scenery and ideas, presenting them with a freshness and colour which owe little to indigenous folksong but much to a highly original and essentially dramatic musical style.

Má vlast

Czech Philharmonic Orchestra / Rafael Kubelík
Supraphon 11 1208-2 (78 minutes: DDD) Ⓕ
Recorded live in 1990 ⚪⚪

Smetana's great cycle of six tone-poems, *Má vlast*, celebrates the countryside and legendary heroes and heroines of Bohemia. It is a work of immense national significance encapsulating many of the ideals and hopes of that country. What a triumphant occasion it was when Rafael Kubelík returned to his native Czechoslovakia and to his old orchestra after an absence of 42 years and conducted *Má vlast* at the 1990 Prague Spring Festival. Supraphon's disc captures that live performance – not perfectly, since the sound is efficient rather than opulent – but well enough to show off what is arguably the finest performance on record since Talich's early LP set.

You'd never imagine that Kubelík had emerged from five years of retirement and a recent serious illness, such is the power and eloquence of his conducting. He takes a lyrical rather than a dramatic view of the cycle, and if there is strength enough in more heroic sections there is also a refreshing lack of bombast. Kubelík's intimate knowledge of the score shows time and time again in the most subtle touches. Even the weakest parts of the work are most artfully brought to life, and seem of much greater stature than is usually the case. 'Vltava' flows beautifully, with the most imaginative flecks of detail, and in 'From Bohemia's Woods and Fields' there are vivid visions of wide, open spaces. The orchestra rewards its former director with superb playing.

Má vlast
Concertgebouw Orchestra / Antál Dorati
Philips Solo 442 641-2PM (79 minutes: DDD)
Recorded 1987 ⚪

The Concertgebouw Orchestra, vividly directed by Antál Dorati, gives a strongly characterised performance of this epic cycle. The romantic opening of 'Vyšehrad' benefits from the glowing hall ambience, while 'Vltava' builds impressively from the gentle trickling streams to the river's powerful course through the St John's rapids – and how beautifully the Concertgebouw strings sing the main theme. 'Sárka', for all its bloodthirsty scenario, never descends into melodrama, 'From Bohemia's woods and fields' is gloriously diverse, and the darkly sombre opening of 'Tábor' contrasts with the hammered forcefulness of 'Blaník', which never becomes bombastic because of the crisply pointed orchestral articulation, while the performance is enhanced by the lovely playing in its enchanting pastoral interlude. Dorati's imaginative grip on this last, wayward piece holds the listener throughout all its episodes to the grandiloquent final peroration. The recording is out of Philips's top-drawer.

Má vlast Ⓗ
Czech Philharmonic Orchestra / Václav Talich
Supraphon mono 11 1896-2 (74 minutes: AAD). Ⓕ
Recorded 1954 ⚪⚪⚪

Try listening from just before six minutes into 'From Bohemia's Woods and Fields' and you reach the very heart of this great performance. The CPO brass lunges towards the main melody with unconstrained eagerness, their impact much aided by smiling *glissandos*. And as Talich and his players climb aboard Smetana's homespun melody, everything assumes a sunny glow: it's almost as if the entire work thus far had prepared for that one magical moment. But there are countless additional splendours: the luminous mobility of 'Vltava', the grimness of 'Sárka' (so different here to the excitable Kubelík), the sense of foreboding in 'Tábor' and the chest-swelling patriotism of 'Blaník'. The strings retain more than a hint of the *portamentos* that were such a distinctive feature of Talich's 1929 recording, but the woodwinds are notably superior and the basically excellent sound releases more of the music's dynamism than was easily audible on 78s.

The transfer makes a warmer case for the original tapes than did the old LPs, and generally serves Talich well – except in one maddening respect. A couple of bars have dropped from 'Tábor', thus utterly ruining the contour of a major climax. The offending cut was not present on the original recording. If you can write off the missing bars as 'historical wear and tear', then expect a *Má vlast* that's way above average, an inspired affirmation of national pride by a wonderful people who had only recently escaped one form of tyranny, and would subsequently fall prey to another.

Additional recommendation
Má vlast
Czech Philharmonic Orchestra / Mackerras
Supraphon SU3465-2 (76 minutes: DDD: A/00)
A live recording from the Rudolfinum in Prague as part of the Prague Spring Festival finds the West's leading Czech music specialists very much at home with the music and the orchestra. The sound beats most other contenders.

Libuše – Prelude

Má vlast – Vltava. The bartered bride – Overture; Polka; Furiant; Dance of the Comedians. The Kiss – Overture. Libuše – Prelude. The two widows – Overture
Cleveland Orchestra Chorus; Cleveland Orchestra / Christoph von Dohnányi
Decca 444 867-2DH (57 minutes: DDD). Text and translation included. Recorded 1993-94 Ⓕ ●

Pride of place must go to the magnificent Overture to *Libuše*, a work that was completed in 1872 but not actually premièred until 1881, two years before Dvořák composed his *Hussite* Overture along vaguely similar lines. The opening brass-and-timpani fanfare anticipates Janáček's *Sinfonietta*, although ensuing incident is more reminiscent of Smetana's own *Má vlast* and, especially, Wagner. Dohnányi effects ideal pacing and tapers a beautifully graded *diminuendo* away from the bold opening, but the strings are occasionally less than precise. *The two widows* opens somewhat in the manner of late Verdi though the overall flavour is unmistakable. Then there is the delightful 'Polka' and the lively Overture to *The Kiss*, both prime-cut samplings of Smetana's mature style. *The bartered bride* suite is very nicely done, although don't expect Dohnányi's 'Dance of the Comedians' to match Szell's Cleveland recording of 30 years earlier for precision, especially among the strings. In the 'Polka', vivid stereophony lends considerable presence to the chorus, which makes a very bold entrance: You may feel you have been gatecrashed by a crowd of unannounced guests! 'Vltava' is equally effective, what with its stylishly phrased opening, sensitive transitions (especially into the 'Peasant's Wedding' episode) and powerful current later on. The sound is resonant and full-bodied.

Piano Works

Three Poetic Polkas, B95. Three Salon Polkas, B94. Polkas – E; G minor; A; F minor. Two Souvenirs of Bohemia in the form of Polkas, B115. Two Souvenirs of Bohemia in the form of Polkas, B116
András Schiff *pf*
Teldec 3984-21261-2 (57 minutes: DDD) Ⓕ
Recorded 1998 ●

The E flat *Allegro, tempo rubato* from the *Souvenirs of Bohemia in the form of Polkas*, Op 13 presents a blend of yearning chromaticism typical of the composer, with additional elements drawn from Chopin. The work was composed during Smetana's Swedish sojourn and suggests aching homesickness expressed in musical terms. Op 12 is also Chopinesque, though the expansive *moderato* second movement (the longest piece on the programme) has a folk-like melodic slant, harmonic richness and sense of narrative that are entirely Smetana's own. The three *Salon* (or 'Drawing Room') *Polkas*, Op 7, dedicated to Smetana's first wife, are among the most charming, especially the first piece. Much of this music was written in the wake of great loss (annotator Graham Melville-Mason suggests the second of the three *Poetic Polkas* could reflect the illness and death of Smetana's second daughter), but its cheerful demeanour spells courage and optimism.

Perhaps the most immediately appealing piece on the disc is the delightful A major *Polka* that in some bizarre way anticipates the Waltz from Bernstein's 1980 *Divertimento*. Schiff's programme is of varying levels of technical difficulty but the same interpretative virtues are common throughout: a marked liking for inner voices, a lilt to the rhythms (notably in the second Op 13 piece), crisp fingerwork and a natural approach to rubato. Comparing Schiff to the excellent Jan Novotný on Supraphon (which programmes the majority of pieces included here) shows that while the Hungarian is more prone to employ colouristic effects, the Czech more likely to lay equal stresses on all voices (which is useful for underlining Smetana's often sombre harmonies). Both players are undeniably masterful, although Schiff's delicious brand of pianistic sorcery will probably win this music the largest audiences, and Teldec's recording is marginally the better of the two.

The Bartered Bride

Gabriela Beňačková *sop* Mařenka; **Peter Dvorský** *ten* Jeník; **Miroslav Kopp** *ten* Vašek; **Richard Novák** *bass* Kecal; **Jindřich Jindrák** *bar* Krušina; **Marie Mrázová** *contr* Háta; **Jaroslav Horáček** *bass* Mícha; **Marie Veselá** *sop* Ludmila; **Jana Jonášová** *sop* Esmeralda; **Alfréd Hampel** *ten* Circus master; **Karel Hanuš** *bass* Indian; **Czech Philharmonic Chorus and Orchestra / Zdeněk Košler**
Supraphon ③ 10 3511-2 (137 minutes: DDD). Notes, text and translation included. Recorded 1980-81 Ⓕ ●

There is something special about a Czech performance of *The bartered bride* and this one is no exception. The hint of melancholy which runs through the work is wonderfully evoked, as well as its marvellous gaiety. Zdeněk Košler has the rhythm and lilt of the music in his bones, like any Czech conductor worth his salt. The Czech Philharmonic has long had one of the finest of all woodwind sections, and especially in this music they play with a sense of their instruments' folk background, with phrasing that springs from deep in Czech folk-music.

This sets the musical scene for some moving performances. The warm, lyrical quality of Gabriela Beňačková's voice can lighten easily to encompass her character's tenderness in the first duet, 'Věrné milováni', or 'Faithful love', the considerable show of spirit she makes when Jeník appears to have gone off the rails. Her Act 1 lament is most beautifully sung. Peter Dvorský as Jeník plays lightly with the score, as indeed he should, or the character's maintaining of the deception can come to seem merely cruel. Even old Kecal comes to new life, not as the conventional village bumbler, but as a human character in his own right as Richard Novák portrays him – quite put out, the old boy is, to find his plans gone astray. In fact, all of the soloists are excellent. The chorus enjoys itself hugely, never more so than in the Beer chorus. Altogether this is a delightful, touching and warming performance.

Libuše

Gabriela Beňačková *sop* Libuše; **Václav Zítek** *ten* Přemysl; **Antonín Svorc** *bass* Chrudoš; **Leo Marian Vodička** *ten* Stáhlav; **Karel Průša** *bass* Lubtor; **René Tuček** *bar* Radovan; **Eva Děpoltová** *sop* Krasava; **Věra Soukupová** *mez* Radmila; **Prague National Theatre Chorus and Orchestra / Zdeněk Košler**
Supraphon ③ 11 1276-2 (166 minutes: DDD)
Notes, text and translation included. Ⓕ
Recorded live in 1983

Libuše is a patriotic pageant, static and celebratory, with such plot as there is concerning the mythical founder of Prague, Libuše, and her marriage to the peasant Přemysl, founder of the first Czech dynasty. Václav Zítek makes a fine, heroic Přemysl; but the triumphant performance comes, as it must, from Gabriela Beňačková. The opera concludes with a series of tableaux in which Libuše prophesies the future kings and heroes who will assure the stability and greatness of the nation. At the end of a long performance her voice is undimmed in its ringing splendour; and earlier, as near the very start, the beauty of her tone and line seeks out all the warmth, character and humanity which she proves to be latent in Smetana's spacious but seemingly plain vocal writing. *Libuše* is scarcely Smetana's greatest opera, as he liked to claim, but especially in so splendid a performance from Beňačková, and under the grave but impassioned direction of Zdeněk Košler, it makes compelling listening. The live recording does include some applause, but there is little else in the way of distraction.

Fernando Sor

Spanish 1778-1839

GROVE *After leaving Spain, Spanish composer and guitarist Fernando Sor lived in Paris (1813-15 and from 1826) and London (1815-26) and visited Russia (1823). He was a famous concert performer and wrote over 60 guitar works (sonatas, studies, variations etc) and an important method (1830). His guitar music is notable for its part-writing. He was also admired for his songs and eight ballets (1821-28); other works include an opera (1797) and chamber and keyboard pieces.*

Guitar Works

Fantaisies – No 12, Op 58; No 13, Op 59, 'Fantaisie élégiaque'. Studies, Op 60
Nicholas Goluses *gtr*
Naxos 8 553342 (65 minutes: DDD) Ⓢ
Recorded 1994

Sor's guitar works is an *oeuvre* that is perhaps the most consistent in quality, and most manageable in quantity of any major guitar composer of the period. Whilst Sor was born and died later than Beethoven his language was closer to that of Mozart, barely on the edge of romanticism. He was a polished, elegant composer, whose works have more quiet emotional content and expressiveness than those of his contemporaries, and though he often calls for technical virtuosity he doesn't lean too heavily on it. The *Fantaisie*, Op 58 is not one of Sor's more riveting works. Goluses plays it in a somewhat matter-of-fact way. The *Fantaisie élégiaque*, arguably Sor's finest single work, elicits a very different response, a deeply sensitive and dignified reading in which the moments of silent grief are given the breathing-space they call for. Sor devoted five opus numbers to his 97 studies, of which Op 60 was the last. Each has a clear technical and/or musical purpose and even the simplest is lovingly crafted music – which is how Goluses treats it, with lots of care lavished on it. The guitar of Sor's time differed from today's in construction, stringing and sound, and Sor played without using the right-hand nails. Goluses uses a modern instrument and plays with nails, which inevitably leads to differences in sound and, to some extent, interpretation. Accepting the differences, Goluses sets a benchmark for present-day guitarists.

Grand Sonatas – C, Op 22; C, Op 25. Divertissement, Op 23. Eight Short Pieces, Op 24
Adam Holzman *gtr*
Naxos 8 553340 (75 minutes: DDD) Ⓢ
Recorded 1994

The major works in Holzman's programme are the two sonatas, each with four movements. Of these Op 25 is by far the finer – and the best work of its kind from the period; the last movement is a Minuet, a final lightening of atmosphere that was not then uncommon. The *Divertissement*, Op 23 contains 10 pieces – *Valses*, *Allegrettos*, *Andantes*, a *Minuetto* and an *Allemande*. With a few exceptions they are more likely to be of interest to guitarists than to the general listener. Holzman plays very well, with a softer sound than Goluses (see above), and in a tighter acoustic. At slower tempos he exercises a pleasing degree of rubato and commendable dynamic shading; one wishes he had done likewise in the quicker ones, which incline to the metronomic. These are two discs that should, both in their own right and at super-budget price, be irresistible to guitarists.

Introduction and Variations on 'Que ne suis-je la fougère!', Op 26. Introduction and Variations on 'Gentil Housard', Op 27. Introduction and Variations on 'Malbroug', Op 28. 12 Studies, Op 29. Fantaisie et Variations brillantes, Op 30
Jeffrey McFadden *gtr*
Naxos 8 553451 (62 minutes: DDD) Ⓢ
Recorded 1995

This contribution to Naxos's integral archive of Sor's guitar music consists neatly of the last works he published with Meissonnier, before transferring to Pacini. Sets of variations, whether *per se* or framed in the *Fantaisie*, Op 30, abound. The *12 Studies*, Op 29 are described as 'Book 2', those of Op 6 being 'Book 1', and are here given as Nos 13-24, as they were in the original edition of 1827. Jeffrey McFadden is a very musical player, with the clear and three-dimensional tone for which his fingers are admirably suited. No composer for the guitar of the time wrote studies that were more truly expressive than those of Sor; McFadden plays them, and everything else here, with humanity and respect. An outstanding disc.

Louis Spohr German 1784-1859

GROVE *Spohr gained his first important experience as a chamber musician at the Brunswick court, soon becoming a virtuoso violinist and touring throughout Germany; his playing was influenced particularly by his admiration for Rode. As Konzertmeister in Gotha (1805-12) he took up conducting (with a baton) and had some of his own works performed but was most successful as a touring artist (1807-21) with his wife, the harpist Dorette Scheidler. Operatic conducting posts at Vienna (1813-15) and Frankfurt (1817-19) coincided with significant bursts of composing activity, yielding chamber music and the successful operas Faust (1813) and Zemire und Azor (1819). He settled down as Kapellmeister at Kassel in 1822, where the premières of Jessonda (1823; his greatest operatic success), the oratorio Die letzten Dinge (1826) and the Symphony No 4 (1832) were major achievements; here too he contributed to the cultivation of interest in both Bach and Wagner. A favourite in England, he received international honours and became Generalmusikdirektor at Kassel (1847), but by the 1850s he was an aging, middle-class representative of a rather sober tradition, and after his death his works were largely forgotten.*

Spohr's early Romantic origins and his devotion to Mozart largely determined his style, with its careful craftsmanship and adherence to classical forms but also its freely expressive elements (much chromaticism and a fondness for the elegiac). Among his instrumental works (15 violin and 10 other concertos, ten symphonies, virtuoso solo works, scores of chamber works, including a series of double quartets), the four clarinet concertos, the string quartets, the Violin Concerto No 8 ('In the form of a vocal scene') and the Octet and Nonet for wind and strings are noteworthy. His operas anticipate Wagner in being through-composed and in their use of leitmotif.

Violin Concertos

Violin Concertos – No 1 in A, Op 1; No 14 in A minor, Op 110, 'Sonst und Jetzt'; No 15 in E minor, Op 128
Ulf Hoelscher *vn* **Berlin Radio Symphony Orchestra / Christian Fröhlich**
CPO CPO999 403-2 (66 minutes: DDD) Ⓑ
Recorded 1995

Hoelscher has the elegance and almost vocal quality with which Spohr's violin writing is associated, but he can also master the virtuosity which is needed for the oddest work here, entitled *Sonst und Jetzt*, or 'Then and Now'. There is something of an in-joke for violinists here. Irritated by the playing of the Norwegian virtuoso, Ole Bull, whom Schumann regarded as the equal of Paganini, Spohr wrote this piece contrasting the lyrical qualities of the violin (in an expansive re-creation of the Minuet) with a hectic *Tarantella* embodying all he disliked in the showy 'modern' style. The idea falls flat as a piece of music criticism, simply because Spohr produces rather a good *Tarantella* and integrates it ingeniously and not contentiously with his more lyrical music. Hoelscher could have made the point by playing the two kinds of music in more extreme fashion; but, if it is true that nothing is colder than the ashes of dead controversies, the more musical course is to play the work as he does, warmly and without *parti-pris*. The Concerto No 15 is a rather more weary piece, in which Spohr goes through the motions expertly but without his full creative attention. Op 1 is a juvenile work (he was 18), obviously close to his beloved Mozart in spirit but also heavily influenced by Kreutzer, Rode and especially Viotti. The best movement is the delightful *Siciliano*, which Spohr embellishes lovingly.

Piano Trios

Piano Trios – No 3 in A minor, Op 124; No 4 in B flat, Op 133
Borodin Trio (Rostislav Dubinsky *vn* Laszlo Varga *vc* Luba Edlina *pf*)
Chandos CHAN9372 (66 minutes: DDD) Ⓕ
Recorded 1994

Spohr's late piano trios are virtuoso works, in every sense. They are ingeniously composed and are difficult to balance with true effect; above all they demand great technical dexterity, and the dexterity to allow many extremely difficult passages to play a secondary or supporting role. In particular No 3 in A minor places demands on the players who need virtuosity of the kind which the Borodin Trio are well able to provide. Their skills need no recommendation; here, they also have a subtlety and quickness of response that come from a proper sympathy with Spohr's idiom. They rise to the occasion with, for instance, the racing piano fingerwork in the Variations of No 3; they also respond with the flexibility of tempo the music needs for its full expressive effect. Moreover, in places where Spohr seems to have lost concentration for a moment – his capacity to meander down beguiling but distracting chromatic paths, his habit of striking a cliché chord like a dramatic attitude, his gear-changing modulations – the Borodin hold faith and make the music come off effectively. The A minor Trio is the more worthwhile piece, and deserves all this interpretative concentration; but the rather less well invented work in B flat, apparently here receiving a first recording, is worth having for some recreational music. The recording team can't always have had an easy task with balance; it all works excellently.

Sir John Stainer British 1840-1901

GROVE *English organist, scholar and composer Stainer, after appointments at St Michael's College, Tenbury, and Oxford University, became organist at St Paul's Cathedral (1872-88), reforming the musical service there, increasing the number of musicians and expanding the repertory. He soon became a pre-eminent church musician, scholar and composer, helping found the Musical Association, and becoming professor at Oxford University. He was knighted in 1888. As a scholar he made valuable editions of music before Palestrina and Tallis (Early Bodleian Music, 1901). His services and anthems were fashionable during his lifetime and his hymn tunes are still used; his oratorio The Crucifixion (1887) is one of his best-known works.*

The Crucifixion

Martyn Hill *ten* **Michael George** *bass*
BBC Singers; Leith Hill Festival Singers / Brian Kay
with **Margaret Phillips** *org*
Chandos CHAN9551 (71 minutes: DDD) Ⓕ
Text included. Recorded 1997

Stainer's *Crucifixion* unfolds with a seamless ease, never jolting the listener with gratuitous theatricality or the type of rhetorical intensity which the English find mildly embarrassing. The emotional engagement here is about an unintrusive sobriety, affected by a glowing sentimental identification with the Saviour's plight. One has to admire Stainer for writing a challenging work of sensible length which, without an orchestra, is achievable and satisfying for a capable parish choir: Stainer's *Crucifixion* is a celebration of amateurism, that cherished English virtue. Brian Kay has worked a great deal with committed amateurs, in this case the Leith Hill Festival Singers, the festival of which he is director. There is indeed an underlying freshness of expression here, of singers with eyes and ears on stalks and a real sense of purpose. They are fortified by the excellent BBC Singers. Margaret Phillips's imaginative, genial registrations, not to mention her skilful accompaniment, provide notable support to the fine contributions of the solosits. An unselfregarding and genuine performance.

Sir Charles Villiers Stanford Irish/British 1852-1924

GROVE *Stanford was educated at Cambridge (1880-84), where he was appointed organist of Trinity College in 1873 and professor in 1887; from 1883 he also taught at the RCM (his own education had been completed under Reinecke in Leipzig, 1874-5, and Kiel in Berlin, 1876). A demanding and highly influential teacher, he also demanded much of himself in living up to the great tradition, though the weight of academic responsibility could be leavened by his Irish heritage of folksong and mysticism and by his keen feeling for English words. Yet, apart from his Anglican cathedral music, little of his large output (nearly 200 opus numbers) has remained in performance. His works include ten operas (notably Shamus O'Brien, 1896; Much Ado about Nothing, 1901; and The Travelling Companion, given posthumously,1926), a quantity of choral music and songs (his B flat Service of 1879 is still used, and some of his sensitive partsongs are remembered, particularly The Blue Bird), seven symphonies and other orchestral scores (Clarinet Concerto, 1902, and a series of Irish Rhapsodies), eight string quartets, and organ and piano music.*

Violin Concerto

Violin Concerto in D, Op 74. Suite for Violin and Orchestra, Op 32
Anthony Marwood *vn* **BBC Scottish Symphony Orchestra / Martyn Brabbins**
Hyperion CDA67208 (67 minutes: DDD) Ⓕ
Recorded 2000

This is a discovery of major importance. Hubert Parry (no mean critic) regarded Stanford's Violin Concerto as one of his finest works, yet it has been played rarely, if at all, since his death in 1924. One preliminary word of warning though: despite Stanford's reputation as a disciple of Brahms, don't listen to this concerto expecting it to sound Brahmsian. Often enough it does, but when it doesn't it isn't because Stanford has failed to match the quality of his 'model'; far more often it's because he is going his own way, speaking with his own and not a derivative voice.

The very opening of the concerto is a case in point: the soloist's melody is accompanied by a beautifully delicate texture of plucked strings and rippling woodwind. There's nothing quite like it in Brahms; nor is Brahms always so generous with his thematic material as Stanford is in this movement. After that 'first subject' and an extensive and varied 'second subject group', a big and dramatic orchestral *tutti* leads not to the expected development but to a new and quite splendid theme. There's plenty of room for virtuosity, but very often the display is modified by a pensive quality, a reticence, that is seemingly Stanford's own, and most attractive.

The slow movement is also notable for its individual scoring (very spare at the outset; a magical return of the melancholy opening melody at the end over murmuring *tremolando* strings) and for its melodic distinction. The sadness of the first theme is again reticent, adding greatly to the eloquence of the heartfelt *tutti* that leads to the finest theme in the entire work, upon which Stanford lavishes rhapsodic figuration of great beauty. The finale is lighter and quite short – an economical rondo on a jovial Irish theme – but its exuberance is finely and subtly crafted.

There's not a player better suited to bringing this concerto back to life than Anthony Marwood. He easily surmounts its technical demands, but his distinction as a chamber musician enables him to seek out all its quieter subtleties and pensive asides. The Suite is a lesser but still highly entertaining work, an exercise in neo-baroque designed as a warmly affectionate tribute to Joseph Joachim. Its sheer ingenuity (the first movement, for example, is a combination of sonata form and two sets of interlocked variations) saves it from being a mere exercise, and its melodic freshness from being a mere makeweight to the masterly concerto. First-class orchestral playing, sympathetically conducted, and a recording that is both clean and spacious.

Symphony No 3 in F minor, 'Irish'

Stanford Symphony No 3 in F minor, 'Irish', Op 28
Elgar Scenes from the Bavarian Highlands, Op 27
Bournemouth Symphony Chorus; Bournemouth Sinfonietta / Norman Del Mar
EMI British Composers CDM5 65129-2 (70 minutes: ADD). Text included. Recorded 1981-82 Ⓜ ●

A valuable addition to the catalogue on its initial appearance, Norman Del Mar's characteristically enterprising 1982 recording of Stanford's *Irish* Symphony re-emerges in splendidly vital fashion on this beautifully presented release. Compared with Vernon Handley and the excellent Ulster Orchestra on Chandos, Del Mar is perhaps just a touch lacking in charm and it is undoubtedly the former who more effectively minimises the element of dutiful convention which occasionally afflicts both outer movements (Handley is nearly three minutes quicker in the opening *Allegro moderato*, yet there is no feeling of undue haste). However, Del Mar draws the threads together most satisfyingly for the symphony's ample peroration, and his Bournemouth band responds with commendable vigour throughout. Preceding the Stanford here is a rare outing for the orchestral version of Elgar's *Scenes from the Bavarian Highlands*. This six-movement choral suite shows Elgar at his most carefree and joyous, qualities savoured to the full in Del Mar's exuberant performance.

Requiem, Op 63

Requiem, Op 63[a]. The Veiled Prophet of Khorassan[b] – Overture; Ballet music: No 1; No 2; There's a Bower of Roses
Frances Lucey, Virginia Kerr *sops* **Colette McGahon** *mez* **Peter Kerr** *ten* **Nigel Leeson-Williams** *bass*; **RTE Philharmonic Choir; National Symphony Orchestra of Ireland / [a]Adrian Leaper, [b]Colman Pearce**
Marco Polo ② 8 223580/1 (104 minutes: DDD) Texts and translations included. Recorded 1994 Ⓕ ●

It is most moving to hear this *Requiem* and to reflect that for the best part of a century a work so rich in feeling and craftsmanship has lain largely silent and unregarded. The opening *Requiem aeternam* ought of itself, one would think, to have ensured at least the occasional revival: a warm, lyrical composition, firmly structured and with something unmistakably personal about it, rather as with Dvořák. The *Kyrie* seems to express affection, though 'For what?' one wonders – perhaps for the sheer beauty of sound. The 'Gradual' allows interest to slip, recaptured by the 'Sequence', plentiful in ideas and rising to a generous climax in the 'Lacrimosa'. The 'Offertorium' brings a touch of 19th-century Grand Manner, tightening up later with a robust, fugal 'Quam olim Abrahae'. The *Sanctus* ends vigorously with its 'Pleni sunt caeli', and a sweet, well-sustained orchestral passage (perhaps with Beethoven in mind) leads into the 'Benedictus'. A Funeral March introduces the *Agnus Dei*, and the whole work, not all that much shorter than the Verdi Requiem, ends with a spacious, steadily developed 'Lux aeterna'. Soloists and chorus are used with relish for the capabilities of the human voice, and in listening one thinks quite as much of opera as of oratorio.

As a fill-up on the second disc we are given further rarities, the Overture and other excerpts from *The Veiled Prophet of Khorassan*, the first of Stanford's operas. The Overture, which is more Brahms than Mendelssohn and has a genial suggestion of the Irish jig, is a thoroughly likeable piece, so once more we are left feeling that here is still another area of Stanford's output that might well reward attention. The performances are able and enthusiastic. Recorded sound might be sharper, but at least it falls more kindly on the ears than do many of more vaunted origin. In any case, we are deeply in Marco Polo's debt for this revival.

Stabat mater, Op 96

Stabat mater, Op 96. Te Deum, Op 10 No 1. Six Bible Songs, Op 113
Ingrid Attrot *sop* **Pamela Helen Stephen** *mez* **Nigel Robson** *ten* **Stephen Varcoe** *bar* **Ian Watson** *org* **Leeds Philharmonic Chorus; BBC Philharmonic Orchestra / Richard Hickox**
Chandos CHAN9548 (74 minutes: DDD). Texts and translations included. Recorded 1995 Ⓕ ●

Writing of his old teacher in 1952, Vaughan Williams foretold that his time would come round again: 'With the next generation the inevitable reaction will set in and Stanford will come into his own.' It has taken more than a generation, but at last it does begin to look as though he was right. This recording of a 'symphonic cantata', the *Stabat mater*, strong in ideas, deeply felt and structurally assured, will certainly strengthen the steadily growing appreciation of his worth. The Prelude, impressive as it is, is almost *too* soundly constructed, and the first choral movement, rich in its Verdi-like foreground of soloists, signs off with a slightly self-conscious repetition of the opening words by the soprano. Stanford is never abashed by the prospect of melodic commitment, and the orchestral Intermezzo comes out boldly with what promises to be a good, old-fashioned Grand Tune; but then he seems to remember where he is, and the piece ends with murky explorations that seem not quite to find what they may be seeking. The work itself ends, as

Stanford Vocal

Lewis Foreman suggests in his useful notes, in *Eternity*: 'we seem to reach the crest of a hill only to find the path stretching onward and upward to another.' The performance carries conviction, with Hickox exercising that natural rightness of his so that in a work such as this, without predecessors on record, a listener will feel that this is how it should 'go'.

Fine orchestral playing and choral singing give pleasure throughout. The solo quartet is led by Ingrid Attrot's colourful but none too evenly produced soprano, and in the *Bible Songs* Stephen Varcoe sings sensitively to the judiciously registered organ accompaniment of Ian Watson. The most tuneful of *Te Deum*s follows, blithe and buoyant in its orchestrated version.

Morning and Evening Services

Morning and Evening Services in B flat, Op 10[a].
Evening Services – A, Op 12[a]; F, Op 36[a]; E flat[b].
Two Anthems, Op 37[b]. Three Motets, Op 38. Pater noster. The Lord is my Shepherd[a]
Winchester Cathedral Choir / David Hill with
[a]**Stephen Farr,** [b]**Christopher Monks** org
Hyperion CDA66964 (78 minutes: DDD)　　　Ⓕ
Texts included. Recorded 1997　　　　　　　　◯

The Evening canticles settings in A major, B flat major, C major, F major and G major are familiar to us already, but here Hyperion comes up with E flat major; and this is but Vol 1. The *Magnificat and Nunc dimittis* in E flat major dates back to 1873 and, according to the valuable notes by Dr Jeremy Dibble, is not with any certainty known even to have been performed. Perhaps this is because both settings are almost indecently tuneful: an apocalyptic 'scattered the proud', a broadly melodious 'to be a light' and a 'Gloria' as catchy as a comic opera. As for the B flat major settings written six years later, these (both Morning and Evening services) have long owed their popularity to a melodic gift that is almost Schubertian and a correspondingly deft mastery of construction.

Winchester Cathedral Choir is surely one of the best in the UK. Under David Hill, the trebles have some of the bright, distinctive tone of the Westminster Cathedral boys. The men are excellent, and all of them sound as though they are singing for the joy of it. Several of these works involve more than the customary four parts, and the eight-part *Pater noster*, recorded for the first time, has splendid richness, with the choir forming massive pillars of sound in the powerful climax. Stanford's writing for the organ is also a delight, and at times we might wish that the fine playing of both organists had been brought into sharper focus. The choir we hear with rare clarity, and to do so is an unmixed pleasure.

Evening Service in G, Op 81. Morning Service in C, Op 115. Six Bible Songs and Hymns, Op 113
Winchester Cathedral Choir / David Hill org with
Stephen Farr, Christopher Monks orgs
Hyperion CDA66965 (67 minutes: DDD)　　　Ⓕ
Texts included. Recorded 1997　　　　　　　　◯

Stanford's *Bible Songs* are occasionally introduced into programmes one or two at a time, but it is rare to have all six. Four of the songs take their text from the Psalms, the others from Isaiah and Ecclesiasticus, but each has a generic title: 'A Song of Freedom', 'A Song of Wisdom' and so forth. They are written for baritone with organ accompaniment, and here we hear what is a rarity indeed, namely the alternation of songs and hymns as Stanford intended. The songs were published in 1909, the hymns a year later, but they are designed to slot in so that the cycle takes the form of a cantata. This bare description gives no idea of the enriched effect. The hymns are mostly well known (*Let us with a gladsome mind* is the first), and there is always a strong emotional effect to be gained from such a process. Stanford had no formulated design, as upon an audience, but if he had he could hardly have achieved it with a surer touch.

The great revelation of this disc is afforded by the performance of the songs and hymns as an entity. Only four of the six songs fall to William Kendall, who sings them well though the tessitura is occasionally a little low for him. The baritone Plunket Greene was the dedicatee and first performer, but one of the songs (No 4) had a separate dedication to the soprano Agnes Nicholls. It was presumably with this in mind that 'A Song for Peace' is allocated to the choir's fine treble soloist, Kenan Burrows. The corresponding allocation of 'A Song of Wisdom', however, seems not entirely an *act* of wisdom: the visionary text and broad, powerful setting call for a different kind of timbre. The choral singing is excellent, as are the organists. In particular, it is good to find the changes of tempo in the *Te Deum* so effectively carried through. Indeed, the whole of the C major Service – is surely the masterpiece.

Evening Service in C, Op 115. Ye Choirs of New Jerusalem, Op 123. Gloria in B flat, Op 128.
St Patrick's Breastplate. Motets, Op 135 – No 2, Eternal Father; No 3, Glorious and Powerful God. For lo, I raise up, Op 145. Magnificat in B flat, Op 164. Lighten our Darkness. How beauteous are their feet
Winchester Cathedral Choir / David Hill with
Stephen Farr, Christopher Monks orgs
Hyperion CDA66974 (64 minutes: DDD)　　　Ⓕ
Texts included. Recorded 1997　　　　　　　◯◯

This disc includes some of Stanford's best work, starting with the Evening Service in C. At Winchester they take a broad view of this, bringing out a meditative grandeur rather than the more pressing enthusiasm in favour elsewhere. In general, the tempo is brisk, matched with verbal and rhythmic life in abundance. *For lo, I raise up* is particularly exciting. Written in 1914, this marvellous setting of Habakkuk's vision of a war-torn world that is eventually to 'be filled with the knowledge of the glory of the Lord' needs a choir that can forget it is 'in church'. The narrative must be eager-eyed, crisp on the words and intense in drive and attack; and that is just about how it is here. In the eight-part *Magnificat* the speed is risky, and may indeed be a little too headlong at the expense of clarity; but again it is rhythmically exhilarating. The anthem *Lighten our Darkness* is recorded here for the first time (Stanford wrote it in 1918 for St George's, Windsor, but the manuscript got lost, and having been found in 1935 was neglected till the present day). The prayer is lovingly treated, and the performance is worthy of the honour bestowed.

Songs

Tragödie, Op 14 No 5. Op 19 – No 2, A Lullaby; No 5, To the Rose. Windy Nights, Op 30 No 4. Clown's Songs from 'Twelfth Night', Op 65. The Fairy Lough, Op 77 No 2. Songs of the Sea, Op 91. Songs of Faith, Op 97 – No 4, 'To the Soul'; No 6, 'Joy, Shipmate, Joy'. Phoebe, Op 125. A Fire of Turf, Op 139. The Pibroch, Op 157 No 1. For Ever Mine. Tom Lemminn
Stephen Varcoe *bar* **Clifford Benson** *pf*
Hyperion CDA67124 (77 minutes: DDD) Ⓕ
Texts and translations included. Recorded 1999 ●

Stanford's *Songs of the Sea* have kept the British baritone afloat for the best part of a century. Drake's hammock and the barnacles of The Old Superb used to be familiar in parlours and drawing-rooms throughout the land. The cries of Captain Keats and his crew ('"Ship ahoy!" a hundred times a day'), the alliterative mysteries of 'Fetter and Faith ... Faggot and Father' and the assurance that Drake even now was 'ware and waking' were assimilated almost as the words of folksongs, while the music seemed part of our flesh and blood. They are splendid songs, and the set of five constitutes a small masterpiece. Sceptical readers should try them again in this new recording. Stephen Varcoe and Clifford Benson give a most sensitive performance, not emasculated but treating them thoughtfully. The two quieter songs, 'Outward Bound' and 'Homeward Bound', become more central, better integrated, than usual, and the very fact that this is the solo version, without the male-voice chorus added later, makes it easier to hear them (the whole set) as a personal utterance. With 'Drake's Drum', for instance, Varcoe is very intent upon seeing sense, where others have often sought for little beyond a generalised patriotic earnestness. These, perhaps, are *The Songs of the Sea* as Captain Edward Fairfax Vere might have sung them.

In reviewing the first volume, Michael Oliver wrote of the difficulty of reconciling the Irishman and the Brahmsian in Stanford: the melodic vein of the one seemed at odds with the harmonic language of the other. The problem is real enough, but arises less urgently in the present selection; indeed, sometimes (as in 'Devon, O Devon', the third of the sea songs) the elements support each other very happily. The occasions here when a dichotomy of style does cause trouble are found in the *Songs of Faith*. Whitman's auto-intoxication incites Stanford to indulge in grandiose gestures that are not natural to him at all. He is much more at home with Shakespeare and Dekker, or, for that matter, with Quiller-Couch and Winifred M Letts, whose *A Fire of Turf* provides him with poems for some congenial and masterly settings. All are beautifully performed by these excellent artists, and the programme is annotated with expertise by Jeremy Dibble.

Wilhelm Stenhammar

Swedish 1871-1927

GROVE *Stenhammer was brought up in a cultivated and musical family; he composed from childhood and had little formal training. His earlier music is in a late Romantic style showing influences from Wagner, Liszt and Brahms, but from 1910 he moved towards a more classical manner, stimulated by contrapuntal studies and a profound concern with Beethoven. Much of his music has a Nordic colour, though he did not use folk material. His works include two symphonies (1903, 1915), two piano concertos, a Serenade (1913), cantatas (Sången, 1921), six string quartets (1894-1916) and songs. An admired pianist, he was also conductor of the Göteborgs Orkesterförening (1906-22), making the city a musical rival to Stockholm.*

Piano Concertos

Piano Concerto No 1 in B flat minor, Op 1. Symphony No 3 in C – fragment
Mats Widlund *pf* **Stockholm Philharmonic Orchestra / Gennadi Rozhdestvensky**
Chandos CHAN9074 (51 minutes: DDD) Ⓕ
Recorded 1992 ●

Piano Concerto No 2 in D minor, Op 23[a]. Serenade in F, Op 31[b]. Florez och Blanzeflor, Op 3[b]
Ingvár Wixell *bar* **Janos Solyom** *pf* [a]**Munich Philharmonic Orchestra;** [b]**Swedish Radio Symphony Orchestra / Stig Westerberg**
EMI Matrix CDM5 65081-2 (73 minutes: ADD) Ⓜ
Text and translation included. Recorded 1970-74

The First Piano Concerto comes from 1893, when Stenhammar was 22, and such was its success during the 1890s that he was invited to play it with the Berlin Philharmonic under Richard Strauss. In time, however, he grew tired of it and became careless as to its fate. Both the autograph and the orchestral parts were destroyed when Breslau was bombed during the Second World War. But recently a copy probably made for the American première came to light in the Library of Congress. Chandos also offers a short fragment from the Symphony No 3 in C major, on which Stenhammar embarked in 1918-19. At not much under 50 minutes it is perhaps overlong, but still has much charm, and Widlund and Rozhdestvensky make a most persuasive case for it. The recording has great depth and warmth and the strings of the Stockholm orchestra have great richness of sonority.

Symphony No 2 in G minor, Op 34

Symphony No 2 in G minor, Op 34. Excelsior!, Op 13. Two Songs, Op 4 (orch cpsr). Reverenza
Anne Sofie von Otter *mez* **Royal Stockholm Philharmonic Orchestra / Paavo Järvi**
Virgin Classics VC5 45244-2 (76 minutes: DDD) Ⓕ
Text and translation included. Recorded 1996

This account of the G minor Symphony has a lot going for it. Järvi is eminently straightforward and sensitive, the architecture of the piece is well shaped and detail attentively handled. He hardly puts a foot wrong and has great feeling for the piece. It is a distinguished performance – and what a wonderful score! The fill-ups are generous: the *Reverenza* movement which Stenhammar included in the original version of the *Serenade* for orchestra but subsequently excised, comes off well. The two Op 4 Songs – 'The girl came from meeting her lover' is a subtle and refined song and its companion, 'The girl on Midsummer's Eve', is even lovelier – have never been recorded before in their orchestral form.

Von Otter is on home ground and in radiant voice. The exhilarating *Excelsior!* overture, which comes from the mid-1890s, is the standard coupling, and is given here with great panache. The only caveat is that the recording is not in the top flight. There is insufficient transparency in climaxes and the sound is two-dimensional with little front-to-back depth. *Reverenza* fares much better and so do the songs. In any event these performances score strongly on artistic grounds and will give pleasure and delight.

Alessandro Stradella

Italian 1644-1682

GROVE *Stradella spent most of his career in Rome, where he lived independently but composed many works to commissions from Queen Christina of Sweden, the Colonna family and others. Most of his stage works there were prologues and intermezzos, notably for operas by Cavalli and Cesti revived at the new Tordinona Theatre in 1671-2. His life included many scandals and amorous adventures. He left Rome in 1677 after a dispute, and went by way of Venice and Turin (escaping an attempt on his life) to Genoa (1678). His only comic opera, Il Trespolo tutore, was given there in c 1677; later he presented several other operas, including Il Corispero. He was killed there in 1682, again a consequence of an amorous intrigue.*

Stradella was one of the leading composers in Italy in his day and one of the most versatile. His music was widely admired, even as far afield as England. Most of it is clearly tonal, and counterpoint features prominently. His vocal output includes c 30 stage works, several oratorios and Latin church works and some 200 cantatas (most for solo voice). In his operas the orchestra consists of two violin parts and continuo, but some other works, such as the oratorio S Giovanni Battista (1675, Rome), follow the Roman principal of concerto grosso instrumentation. There is a clear differentiation between aria and recitative (which sometimes includes arioso writing), but their succession is still fluid; various aria forms are used. Stradella's 27 surviving instrumental works are mostly of the sonata da chiesa type. The scoring and textures of a Sonata di viole of his make it the earliest known concerto grosso; it was apparently a model for Corelli's concertos Op 6.

Cantatas

Ah! troppo è ver. Si apra al riso ogni labro. Sonata di viole
Lavinia Bertotti, Emanuela Galli, Barbara Zanichelli *sops* **Roberto Balconi** *counterten* **Maurizio Sciuto** *ten* **Carlo Lepore** *bass* **Orchestra Barocca della Civica Scuola di Musica di Milano / Enrico Gatti**
Arcana A79 (67 minutes: DDD). Texts included Ⓕ
Recorded 1997

Ferma, ferma il corso. Frena o filli il fiero orgoglio. Fuor della Stigia sponda. Non avea il sole ancora. Si salvi chi può. Sinfonias – No 12; No 22 Ⓟ
Christine Brandes *sop* **Paul O'Dette** *lte* **Ingrid Matthews** *vn* **Mary Springfels** *va da gamba* **Barbara Weiss** *hpd/org*
Harmonia Mundi HMU90 7192 (69 minutes: DDD) Ⓕ
Recorded 1997

These two releases represent different aspects of Stradella's work. The Arcana issue features two Christmas cantatas, *Si apra al riso* for three mixed solo voices, two violins and continuo, and the larger *Ah! troppo è ver* for mixed solo voices, with a concertino of violin, cello and continuo, and ripieno strings supplying the concerto grosso. The disc also contains a Sonata consisting of concertino and ripieno elements, a *concerto grosso*, in fact, of which form Stradella was a pioneer. The other disc contains five chamber cantatas for solo voice – here, a soprano – and continuo, whose sequence is interrupted by two interesting and lively instrumental *Sinfonias*. The movements of the first are strikingly varied, while the second is a set of variations on a moderately extended 'ground'. Gatti and his almost all-Italian ensemble of singers and instrumentalists enliven this music, his imagination responding unfailingly to Stradella's often individual, at times, quirky style, and his feeling for texture and declamation most impressive. These and other qualities may be sensed at once in the splendid, larger-than-life account of *Ah! troppo è ver*. The performances have rough patches, but they convey with fervour the spirit and occasional atmosphere of the music.

The chamber cantatas disc is technically accomplished, maintaining a level of finesse and attention to detail not always present in the other. Christine Brandes has a lightly coloured, ingenuous voice, just a little pinched in her uppermost register and strained to its limits in the ferociously demanding cantata *Ferma, ferma il corso*. Her diction is clear and her inflexions pay close attention to the meaning and mood of the texts. As in the Christmas cantatas, so too in these more intimate pieces Stradella often surprises us with melodies that strike off in unexpected directions. Stradella's cantatas will handsomely reward ears that savour expressive subtlety.

San Giovanni Battista

Catherine Bott, Christine Batty *sops* **Gérard Lesne** *counterten* **Richard Edgar-Wilson** *ten* **Philippe Huttenlocher** *bar* **Les Musiciens du Louvre / Marc Minkowski** P

Awards 1993

Erato 2292-45739-2 (61 minutes: DDD) Ⓜ
Notes, text and translation included
Recorded live in 1991 ooo

Although an outstanding oratorio composer, Stradella was considered in his time foremost as a composer for the theatre, and he treated the New Testament story of the imprisonment and murder of John the Baptist with real dramatic force. *San Giovanni Battista* was first performed in Rome in 1657. The librettist, a Sicilian priest, Girardo Ansaldi, dispensed with a *testo* or narrator, concerning himself more directly with the exchanges between Herod and John the Baptist. Stradella portrays this relationship with great subtlety, as he does equally that between Herod, his wife Herodias and their daughter Salome.

The work is in two parts. Events in Part 1 are presented in three stages. After a *Sinfonia* there follows a pastoral scene in which John bids farewell to the countryside as he prepares to travel to Herod's court. In the second stage the scene moves to the court where the king's birthday festivities are in full swing. Stage three is marked by the arrival of John who interrupts proceedings with a command that Herod give up his brother's wife. Herod is enraged and orders John to be thrown into prison. Part 2 contains the well-known events leading to the beheading of John and concludes with a masterly duet in which the contrasting emotions of foreboding and joy are expressed by Herod and Salome, respectively.

Marc Minkowski has assembled a strong team of soloists with Gérard Lesne in the title-role. Additionally there are three brief sections allotted to a chorus fulfilling various functions in the first part of the oratorio. Minkowski paces the music well, making the most of Stradella's admirably effective contrasts of texture and mood. Lesne's portrayal of John the Baptist is affecting, and his warm tone and subdued vocal colour suit the music in Part 2 especially well. Herodias and Salome both come over well though neither singer succeeds in concealing the difficulties presented by Stradella's wide tessitura. Catherine Bott gives a virtuoso performance of her aria 'Sù, coronatemi' and Huttenlocher's Herod is splendid.

To conclude, this animated and imaginative approach to a masterly score does the work justice. Minkowski realises the inherent richness of invention and the sheer beauty of the music with insight, affection and a lively awareness of its dramatic intent. The recording is excellent.

Eduard Strauss Austrian 1835-1916
Johann Strauss I Austrian 1804-1849
Josef Strauss Austrian 1827-1870
Johann Strauss II Austrian 1825-1899

GROVE *This Austrian family of dance musicians and composers gave the Viennese waltz its classic expression. Johann senior, a violinist in Josef Lanner's dance orchestra, formed a band in 1825 which became famous for its open-air concerts with his original dance music and paraphrases on the symphonic and operatic music of the day, all performed with exquisite precision. He took the band on European tours from 1833, creating a sensation with the fire and finesse of his conducting, violin in hand. His music, its Austrian folk flavour refined by a characteristic rhythmic piquancy (cross-rhythms, syncopations, pauses and rests), includes over 150 sets of waltzes, besides galops, quadrilles (which he introduced to Vienna), marches (notably the Radetzky-Marsch Op 228), polkas and potpourris.*

Johann had three sons who were composer-conductors. Johann II, also a violinist and the most eminent member of the family, directed his own orchestra, 1844-49, in rivalry with his father's; after 1849 the two Strauss bands were merged into one. Vienna's imperial-royal music director for balls, 1863-71, and Austria's beat-known ambassador (the 'king of the waltz'), he was acclaimed by swarms of admirers, especially on European tours, 1856-86, and in the USA (1872). In form, his waltzes resemble his father's – slow introduction, five waltzes and coda – but the sections are longer and more organic; the melodies, often inspired, are wide and sweeping, the harmonic and orchestral details richer and more subtle, even Wagnerian in places. Among his most celebrated waltz masterpieces, dating from the 1860s and early 1870s, are Accellerationen Op 234, Wiener Bonbons Op 307, An die schönen, blauen Donau ('The Blue Danube') Op 314, Wein, Weib und Gesang Op 333 and Wiener Blut Op 354. Of his 17 operettas, the sparkling Die Fledermaus (1874) and the colourfulDie Zigeunerbaron (1885) deservedly claim a central place in the repertory.

His brother Josef was a melancholy introvert, shared the direction of the family orchestra in the 1850s and 1860s, and composed waltzes in a more serious, Romantic vein, as well as polkas, quadrilles and marches. The younger brother Eduard, Vienna's imperial-royal music director for balls, 1872-1901, became the best conductor of the family and was much sought after by orchestras throughout Europe.

'Ein Straussfest II'

E Strauss Ohne Aufenthalt, Op 112
Josef Strauss Plappermäulchen, Op 245. Sphären-Klänge, Op 235. Jockey, Op 278
J Strauss I Chinese Galop, Op 20
J Strauss II Ägyptischer Marsch, Op 335a. Künstler-Quadrille, Op 71. Kaiser-Walzer, Op 437. Freikugeln, Op 326. Jubelfest-Marsch, Op 396.

Tritsch-Tratsch-Polka, Op 214. Geisselhiebe, Op 60. Klipp Klapp, Op 466. Wein, Weib und Gesang, Op 333. Perpetuum mobile, Op 257

Cincinnati Pops Chorale and Orchestra / Erich Kunzel
Telarc CD80314 (68 minutes: DDD) Ⓕ
Recorded 1991-92

This collection sets out to adorn popular Strauss pieces with sound effects to outdo anything one hears at a Vienna New Year Concert. It starts with Eduard Strauss's *Ohne Aufenthalt*, which is accompanied by steam railway effects, has bullets flying mercilessly in the *Freikugeln* Polka, and includes neighing nags and swishing whips in the *Jockey* Polka. The fun is increased by the inclusion of the *Künstler-Quadrille*, a sort of 1850s 'Hooked on Classics' that begins with Mendelssohn's 'Wedding March' and continues through the likes of Mozart's Symphony No 40 and Chopin's 'Funeral March' Sonata to Beethoven's *Ruins of Athens* and *Kreutzer* Sonata. If the Viennese lilt is just a shade lacking in the waltzes, the playing is nevertheless excellent throughout. The Strausses themselves would have approved.

New Year's Day Concerts

'New Year's Day Concert, 1999'
J Strauss I Furioso-Galopp, Op 114. Radetzky March, Op 228. Walzer à la Paganini, Op 11[a] (arr Rot) **J Strauss II** Scherz-Polka, Op 72 (arr Rot)[a]. Sinngedichte, Op 1. G'schichten aus dem Wienerwald, Op 325. Tritsch-Tratsch-Polka, Op 214. Donauweibchen, Op 427. Hopser-Polka, Op 28. Künstlerleben, Op 316. Banditen-Galopp, Op 378. Unter Donner und Blitz, Op 324. Perpetuum mobile, Op 257. An der schönen, blauen Donau, Op 314
Vienna Philharmonic Orchestra / Lorin Maazel [a]*vn*
RCA Red Seal 74321 61687-2 (77 minutes: DDD) Ⓕ
Recorded live in 1999

This is the 10th time that Maazel has conducted the New Year's Concert in Vienna, more often than anyone since Willi Boskovsky. What is always endearing is that Maazel, unlike any maestro since that former concert-master, boldly takes up his solo violin. He sets the right atmosphere with his two *concertante* items, the *Scherz-Polka* of Johann Strauss II and the *Walzer à la Paganini* of Strauss I, both arranged for him by Michael Rot, and what does it matter if most of the violin section of the Vienna Philharmonic could play them just as well? The distinctive point about the 1999 concert is that it marked the centenary of the death of the younger Johann and the 150th of his father.

Aptly the programme starts with the very first of his hundreds of opuses, the 'Epigram Waltz', *Sinngedichte*, precisely setting out the pattern he always favoured in waltzes, just as winningly lyrical as the many later favourites. Some New Year's Concerts take you by storm with their bite and energy. This one makes its points above all by charming. The seductive languor of the introduction to *G'schichten aus dem Wienerwald* ('Tales from the Vienna Woods'), with its haunting zither solo, sets the pattern, followed by such rarities as the late *Donauweibchen Waltz* ('Little Woman of the Danube') on themes from the operetta, *Simplicius*, and the *Hopser-Polka*, insinuating rather than thrusting. The uproarious *Banditen-Galopp*, with its police-whistles and gunshots, then raises the temperature, and the sequence of favourites at the end sparkles as brightly as ever. A winning disc.

'New Year's Day Concert 2000'
E Strauss Mit Extrapost, Op 259. Gruss an Prag, Op 144 **J Strauss I** Radetzky March, Op 228 **J Strauss II** Lagunen-Walzer, Op 411. Hellenen-Polka, Op 203. Albion-Polka, Op 102. Liebeslieder, Op 114. Ritter Pasman – Csárdás. Wein, Weib und Gesang, Op 333. Persischer Marsch, Op 289. Process, Op 294. Eljen a Magyar!, Op 332. Vom Donaustrande, Op 356. An der schönen, blauen Donau, Op 314 **Josef Strauss** Die Libelle, Op 204. Künstlergruss, Op 274. Marien-Klänge, Op 214 **Suppé** Ein Morgen, ein Mittag, ein Abend in Wien – Overture
Vienna Philharmonic Orchestra / Riccardo Muti
EMI ② CMS5 67323-2 (92 minutes: DDD) Ⓜ
Recorded live in 2000

The title *Mit Extrapost* ('By Special Post') of the final item in the first half of this New Year's Concert might just as readily apply to the remarkable way in which record companies these days get out the finished article within 10 days or so of the actual performance. The only trace of corners being cut is in the absence of track timings. Otherwise the result is perfection itself – a polished presentation of a concert that seemed exhilarating and stylish on television on New Year's Day and does so no less now. The balance between familiar and unfamiliar in the programme is as well judged as ever. The latter includes a fair homage to various nationalities – to the Greeks in the *Hellenen-Polka*, the British in the *Albion-Polka*, the Czechs in *Gruss an Prag* – to complement the more familiar *Persischer-Marsch* and *Eljen a Magyar!* Utterly delightful is another piece that is, surprisingly, receiving its first performance at these concerts – Josef's *Marien-Klänge* Waltz, which confirms the second brother's unique sensitivity and refinement. Among the more familiar items, Muti also takes the right option in giving the full version of the *Wein, Weib und Gesang* Waltz, which is too often played with its introduction abridged. Most importantly, the music throughout flows along as naturally and beguilingly as the Danube itself. Nobody who has enjoyed any previous Vienna New Year Concert should be disappointed with this new one.

Orchestral Works

J Strauss II Complete Works, Volume 34
Russischer Marsch, Op 426. Slaven-Potpourri, Op 39. Fünf Paragraphe, Op 105. La favorite, Op 217. Nikolai-Quadrille, Op 65. Abschied von St Petersburg, Op 210. Der Kobold, Op 226. Im russischen Dorfe, Op 355 (orch Schönherr). Dolci pianti (with Jozef Sikora *vc*). Niko-Polka, Op 228

Bratislava Radio Symphony Orchestra / Michael Dittrich
Marco Polo 8 223234 (69 minutes: DDD) Ⓕ
Recorded 1991

J Strauss II Complete Works, Volume 35
Zivio!, Op 456 (orch Fischer). Architecten-Ball-Tänze, Op 36. Jäger, Op 229. Accelerationen, Op 234. Der Liebesbrunnen, Op 10 (orch Kulling). Die Zeitlose, Op 302. Königslieder, Op 334. Im Sturmschritt, Op 348. Der Blitz, Op 59 (orch Babinski). Heut' ist heut', Op 471 (orch Babinski). Die Wahrsagerin, Op 420
Košice State Philharmonic Orchestra / Johannes Wildner
Marco Polo 8 223235 (74 minutes: DDD) Ⓕ
Recorded 1991

J Strauss II Complete Works, Volume 36
Matador-Marsch, Op 406 (orch Fischer). Kreuzfidel, Op 301. D'Woaldbuama (Die Waldbuben), Op 66 (orch Babinski). Process, Op 294. Elfen-Quadrille, Op 16 (orch Kulling). Mephistos Höllenrufe, Op 101. Bitte schön!, Op 372. Die Extravaganten, Op 205. Fledermaus-Quadrille, Op 363. Der Klügere gibt nach, Op 401. Neu-Wien, Op 342. Diplomaten-Polka, Op 448
Košice State Philharmonic Orchestra / Alfred Walter
Marco Polo 8 223236 (68 minutes: DDD) Ⓕ
Recorded 1989-91 ●

Volume 34 offers a distinct Russian flavour. The most obviously familiar item is the opening *Russischer Marsch*, while the waltz *Abschied von St Petersburg* will also be familiar to some. It's a fine swinging waltz, with an attractive cello solo in the introduction. *Dolci pianti*, one of three romances surviving from Strauss's Russian visits, provides further material for a cello soloist, while the piquant *Niko-Polka* offers as good an example as any of the delights to be found among the unfamiliar works of the Waltz King. Not the least attraction of Vol 34 is the conductor Michael Dittrich and his alert, *echt-Wienerisch* performances here. On Vol 35 Johannes Wildner's conducting shows up to much better effect than has often been the case. Marches have always been his strong point, and the collection thus gets off to a good start with *Zivio!* from the operetta *Jabuka*. There are other attractive pieces on offer, too, from the perpetual favourite *Accelerationen*, through the delicate polka-mazurka *Die Zeitlose* to the magisterial *Königslieder* (a waltz from Strauss's most successful period) and the polka-mazurka *Die Wahrsagerin* on melodies from *The Gipsy Baron*.

Volume 36 offers perhaps the most attractive music of the three volumes. Again the performance of the haunting waltz *Mephistos Höllenrufe* may not erase memories of some previous versions, but such pieces as the *Neu-Wien* waltz and the excellently played *Fledermaus-Quadrille* are among the composer's most agreeable creations. Perhaps the most pleasant surprise of all comes from the waltz *Die Extravaganten* which, with its endearing themes and richly inventive harmonic and orchestral touches, shows above all the merits of Marco Polo's voyage of Straussian rediscovery.

J Strauss II Complete Works, Vol 43
Reitermarsch, Op 428. Walzer-Bouquet No 1. Postillon d'amour, Op 317. Simplicius Quadrille, Op 429. Wilde Rosen, Op 42 (arr Babinski/Kulling). Die Tauben von San Marco, Op 414. Auf dem Tanzboden, Op 454 (arr Pollack). Des Teufels Antheil (arr Pollack). Trifolien (comp with Josef and Eduard Strauss). Herrjemineh, Op 464
Slovak State Philharmonic Orchestra, Košice / Christian Pollack
Marco Polo 8 223243 (58 minutes: DDD) Ⓕ
Recorded 1992

J Strauss II Complete Works, Vol 44
Maskenfest-Quadrille, Op 92. Aschenbrödel-Walzer. Von der Börse, Op 337. Monstre-Quadrille (with Josef Strauss). Autograph Waltzes (arr Cohen). Auf freiem Fusse, Op 345. Schützen-Quadrille (with Josef and Eduard Strauss). Altdeutscher Walzer (arr Pollack). Nur nicht mucken, Op 472 (arr Peak). Hinter den Coulissen (comp with Josef Strauss)
Slovak State Philharmonic Orchestra, Košice / Christian Pollack
Marco Polo 8 223244 (56 minutes: DDD) Ⓕ
Recorded 1992

J Strauss II Complete Works, Vol 45
Fest-Marsch, Op 452. Zigeunerbaron-Quadrille, Op 422. Ischler Walzer. Ritter Pasman – ballet music. Pasman-Quadrille (arr Pollack). Eva-Walzer. Potpourri-Quadrille. Der Carneval in Rom – ballet music (arr Schönherr)
Slovak State Philharmonic Orchestra, Košice / Alfred Walter
Marco Polo 8 223245 (59 minutes: DDD) Ⓕ
Recorded 1993

Volumes 43 and 44 explore the more remote corners of the Waltz King's output. They include as many as four collaborations between Johann and his two brothers, of which the *Trifolien* waltz and *Schützen-Quadrille* most engagingly permit a comparison of all three brothers' strengths. Both volumes also include a waltz from the composer's 1876 visit to the USA. The *Walzer- Bouquet* No 1 (originally the *Manhattan Waltzes*) is a convincingly authentic Strauss arrangement of themes from his earlier waltzes, but it is difficult to feel as sure of the worth or authenticity of the *Autograph Waltzes*, which may merely comprise themes thrown off by Strauss and worked up by an eager US publisher. The other particular curiosities here are *Auf dem Tanzboden*, a musical evocation of a painting, and the *Altdeutscher Walzer*, which is really no more than an *entr'acte* from the operetta, *Simplicius*. The attractive early waltz *Wilde Rosen* receives a compelling performance from Christian Pollack, without the somewhat heavy beat he imparts to the *Walzer-Bouquet*. Generally Pollack seems better in the polkas and quadrilles, which he gives genuine 'lift' and sparkle, as here in several delightful polkas and the *Maskenfest-Quadrille*.

By contrast, Vol 45 is relatively free of the polkas and polka-mazurkas that tend to sound somewhat leaden in the hands of Alfred Walter. Over half this CD is devoted to items from Strauss's only opera *Ritter Pasman* – not just the ballet music (played in a fuller version than on some occasions), but also the *Pasman-Quadrille* and *Eva-Walzer* arranged by other hands from the score. The posthumous *Ischler Walzer* proves a piece of genuine charm, and the *Potpourri-Quadrille* compiled by Strauss for his visit to London in 1867 provides fun value with its quotations from earlier Strauss quadrilles interspersed with a selection of Scottish airs. The inclusion of the *Carneval in Rom* ballet music in a modern arrangement seems unfortunate in a collection such as this with an accent on authenticity. In sum, all three CDs rank among the more interesting and enjoyable in this adventurous series.

Additional recommendation
Waltzes
Vienna Philharmonic Orchestra / Boskovsky
Eloquence 467 413-2 (77 minutes: DDD) Ⓢ
There have been no finer recordings of Johann Strauss than those by Willi Boskovsky and the VPO. If you've no waltzes in your collection this bargain disc is surely a must.

Arrangements

J Strauss I (arr Weinmann) Wiener Gemüths, Op 116. Beliebte Annen, Op 137. Eisele und Beisele Sprünge, Op 202 **J Strauss II** Schatz, Op 418 (arr Webern). Wein, Weib und Gesang, Op 333 (arr Berg). Kaiser-Walzer, Op 437 (arr Schoenberg) **Lanner** (arr Weinmann) Marien-Walzer, Op 143. Steyrische-Tänze, Op 165. Die Werber, Op 103
Wolfgang Schulz *fl* **Ernst Ottensamer** *cl* **Alois Posch** *db* **Heinz Medjimorec** *pf* **Alfred Mitterhofer** *harm* **Alban Berg Quartet** (Günter Pichler, Gerhard Schulz *vns* Thomas Kakuska *va* Valentin Erben *vc*)
EMI CDC7 54881-2 (62 minutes: DDD) Ⓕ
Recorded 1992

In the Alexander Weinmann arrangements of Lanner and the elder Johann Strauss, one is able to appreciate to the full the clear lyrical lines of works whose full orchestration is very much built upon the foundation of the string quartet. Likewise, in the large-scale waltzes of the younger Strauss one cannot but admire the skill and affection with which Webern, Berg and Schoenberg used the limited resources available to their Society for Private Musical Performances. Indeed, if string quartet, piano, flute and clarinet inevitably struggle to capture the full splendour of the march introduction to the *Kaiser-Walzer*, the imaginative way in which Schoenberg finds a chamber ensemble substitute for Strauss's full orchestral sound is perhaps the most impressive aspect of the various arrangements here. On its own terms, the collection is extremely impressive. The Alban Berg Quartet has made a fine selection of some of the most melodic works from over half a century of prodigious invention, and it plays them with affection and relish. From Lanner's tender *Marien-Walzer*, through to Strauss Junior's most magisterial waltz, the clarity and refinement of the playing is tempered with a sense of lightheartedness and fun. If you fancy a Viennese dance collection with a different slant, don't hesitate to go for this admirable release.

'A Tribute to Johann Strauss'

J Strauss II Schwipslied[a]. Die Fledermaus – Overture; Spiel' ich die Unschuld[a]. Frühlingsstimmen, Op 410[a]. Im Krapfenwald'l, Op 336. Liebeslieder, Op 114[a]. Eine Nacht in Venedig – Frutti di mare!...Seht, oh seht![a]. Pesther Csárdás, Op 23. Pizzicato Polka. Die Tänzerin Fanny Elssler – Draussen in Sievering[a] (arr Stalla). Wiener Blut – Wiener Blut[a] (arr Müller). Wienerwald Lerchen[a] (arr Schönherr). Wo die Zitronen blüh'n, Op 364[a] (arr Genée)
[a]**Sumi Jo** *sop* **Vienna Volksoper Orchestra / Rudolf Bibl**
Erato 3984-25500-2 (58 minutes: DDD). Texts and translations included. Recorded 1998 Ⓕ

Here is an imaginatively conceived and brilliantly executed collection of vocal Johann Strauss numbers. In an exciting performance of the original soprano solo version of *Frühlingsstimmen*, Sumi Jo's luxurious coloratura soars gloriously over the orchestra. The vocal arrangement of the *Liebeslieder-Walzer* and Richard Genée's show-piece adaptation of *Wo die Zitronen blüh'n* are no less thrilling. But it is by no means just the coloratura pieces in which Sumi Jo excels. The characterisation she gives to the contrasted parts of the audition song from *Die Fledermaus* makes it as compelling an interpretation as any. The fish-selling song from *Eine Nacht in Venedig* comes up with equal freshness. Add the way she skips from note to note in 'Draussen in Sievering' and the gentle hiccup at the end of the 'Tipsy Song' (an adaptation of the *Annen-Polka*), and one has an uncommonly well-thought-out and superbly varied collection. The participation of the Vienna Volksoper players under veteran conductor Rudolf Bibl ensures the authentic style not only in the vocal items but also in the short linking orchestral pieces. There was no need, though, for yet another *Fledermaus* Overture. It's a pity, too, that Erato claims 10 minutes' more playing time than there actually is, and that Michael Rot's excellently scholarly notes are sadly mangled in their English translation. Nothing, though, can diminish the exquisite quality of Sumi Jo's singing.

Die Fledermaus

Julia Varady *sop* Rosalinde; **Lucia Popp** *sop* Adele; **Hermann Prey** *ten* Eisenstein; **René Kollo** *ten* Alfred; **Bernd Weikl** *bar* Doctor Falke; **Ivan Rebroff** *bass/mez* Prince Orlofsky; **Benno Kusche** *bar* Frank; **Ferry Gruber** *ten* Blind; **Evi List** *sop* Ida; **Franz Muzeneder** *bass* Frosch; **Bavarian State Opera Chorus and Orchestra / Carlos Kleiber**
DG The Originals ② 457 765-2GOR2 (107 minutes: ADD). Notes, text and translation included. Recorded 1975 Ⓜ

Twenty-five years after its original release there is still no recording of *Die Fledermaus* that, for many collectors, matches this one for the compelling freshness of its conductor's interpretation – the attention to every nuance of the score and the ability to bring out some new detail, all allied to extreme precision of vocal and instrumental ensemble. The ladies, too, as so often seems to be the case in recordings of *Die Fledermaus*, are quite superlatively good, with ideally characterised and projected singing. If the men are generally less outstandingly good, one can have no more than minor quibbles with the Eisenstein of Hermann Prey or the Alfred of René Kollo. But it is less easy to accept Ivan Rebroff singing the role of Orlofsky falsetto. Some collectors find that his contribution quite ruins the whole set, but most will find it tolerable enough for the glories to be found elsewhere on the recording. DG remastered the set to make it sound as though it were recorded only yesterday; but it continues to provoke puzzlement by the break between discs, which occurs during the Act 2 finale. If a split into such uneven lengths is to be made, why not have it between Acts 1 and 2? Enough of minor quibbles – this set is a 'must buy'.

Die Fledermaus H

Elisabeth Schwarzkopf *sop* Rosalinde; **Rita Streich** *sop* Adele; **Nicolai Gedda** *ten* Eisenstein; **Helmut Krebs** *ten* Alfred; **Erich Kunz** *bar* Doctor Falke; **Rudolf Christ** *ten* Prince Orlofsky; **Karl Dönch** *bar* Frank; **Erich Majkut** *ten* Doctor Blind; **Luise Martini** *sop* Ida; **Franz Böheim** buffo Frosch; **Philharmonia Chorus and Orchestra / Herbert von Karajan**

EMI Great Recordings of the Century mono ② CMS5 67074-2 (110 minutes: ADD). Notes, texts and Ⓜ translation included. Recorded 1955 OO

This classic set is the aptest of candidates for EMI's Great Recordings of the Century. Such is the CD transfer that one completely forgets that this is in mono, not stereo, and the extra sense of presence and space makes for a clearer separation of the voices, well-forward in the manner of EMI's recordings in the mid-1950s. In his note, Richard Osborne quotes Schwarzkopf on what Karajan (and her husband, Walter Legge, as producer) were seeking to bring out: 'grit, dash, pep'. That may sound as though the result is serious rather than comic, but not at all so. What is striking above all is the animation of the production. The dialogue is so strongly characterised and so brilliantly acted, with each character so sharply defined, that even the most determined non-German-speaker will not only follow but be charmed by it. Legge's editing down of the dialogue was very much part of his concept, alongside the immaculate, inspired casting of soloists. The very first confrontation between Streich as the parlourmaid, Adele, and Schwarzkopf as Rosalinde, her mistress, is delicious, with the characters so vividly heightened. So it is throughout the set.

One may question the choice of a tenor Orlofsky, but Karajan and Legge were following the example of Max Reinhardt in his famous Berlin production of 1929, and Rudolf Christ in cabaret style presents a wonderfully convincing portrait of an effete, slightly tipsy nobleman. As for the others, it would be hard to imagine more compelling portraits than these, consistently reflecting Legge's genius in assembling his team. The musical performance, like the deft speaking of the dialogue, is both polished and exuberant. It is astonishing what precision Karajan achieves in his moulding of Viennese rubato, not only from his singers but from the Philharmonia players. Unlike the previous CD incarnation (also at mid-price) this one offers a complete libretto and translation. The dialogue is tracked separately, but few will want to omit it when it adds so much – very economically in time – to the total joy of the experience.

Der Zigeunerbaron

Pamela Coburn *sop* Saffi; **Herbert Lippert** *ten* Barinkay; **Wolfgang Holzmair** *bar* Homonay; **Rudolf Schasching** *ten* Zsupán; **Christiane Oelze** *sop* Arsena; **Júlia Hamari** *mez* Czipra; **Elisabeth von Magnus** *contr* Mirabella; **Jürgen Flimm** *bar* Carnero; **Robert Florianschutz** *bass* Pali; **Hans-Jürgen Lazar** *ten* Ottokar; **Arnold Schoenberg Choir; Vienna Symphony Orchestra / Nikolaus Harnoncourt**

Teldec ② 4509-94555-2 (150 minutes: DDD). Notes, Ⓕ text and translation included. Recorded live in 1994 O

This set comes with a sticker proclaiming the inclusion of 40 minutes of unpublished music. Well, 14 perhaps – certainly no more than 15. False claims aside, though, this is an uncommonly interesting and enjoyable release. The extra music comes becauseHarnoncourt and Johann Strauss specialist Norbert Linke have sought to restore *Der Zigeunerbaron* to the form it had before Strauss made various cuts. The real merits of the set lie elsewhere. Not least, Harnoncourt has stripped away generations of Viennese schmaltz and performing tradition.

This is the first recording to include every number of the published score, and for once the music is sung at its original pitch, without the usual downward transpositions for Zsupán and Homonay. Most particularly Harnoncourt has completely rethought the style of the performance. *Der Zigeunerbaron* is a long work, described as 'Komische Oper' rather than 'Operette', and much of its music is unusually solid for Strauss. Harnoncourt gives the major numbers their full weight, phrasing them beautifully, and drawing refined singing from the soloists, among whom Herbert Lippert and Pamela Coburn combine beautifully in the duet 'Wer uns getraut?', and Christiane Oelze is a delectably sweet Arsena.

The necessary light relief comes not only from Zsupán (Rudolf Schasching in fine voice) but from usually omitted subsidiary numbers. Elisabeth von Magnus sings Mirabella's 'Just sind es vierundzwanzig Jahre' with exhilarating comic zest, and joins with Jürgen Flimm (more actor than singer) to make the trio 'Nur keusch und rein' an irresistible delight. The live recording comes with some audience laughter and coughs but with the applause suppressed. This deserves to win new admirers both for Harnoncourt and for Strauss's masterly score.

Richard Strauss German 1864-1949

GROVE *Strauss's father, a professional horn player, gave him a musical grounding exclusively in the classics, and he composed copiously from the age of six. He went briefly to university, but had no formal tuition in composition. He had several works given in Munich, including a symphony, when he was 17, and the next year a wind serenade in Dresden and a violin concerto in Vienna. At 20, a second symphony was given in New York and he conducted the Meiningen Orchestra in a suite for wind. In 1885 he became conductor of that orchestra, but soon left and visited Italy. He had been influenced by Lisztian and Wagnerian thinking; one result was Aus Italien, which caused controversy on its première in 1887. By then Strauss was a junior conductor at the Munich Opera.*

Other tone poems followed: Macbeth, Don Juan and Tod und Verklärung come from the late 1880s. It is Don Juan that, with its orchestral brilliance, its formal command and its vivid evocation of passionate ardour (he was in love with the singer Pauline von Ahna, his future wife), shows his maturity and indeed virtuosity as a composer. With its première, at Weimar (he had moved to a post at the opera house there), he was recognized as the leading progressive composer in Germany. He was ill during 1891-3 but wrote his first opera, Guntram, which was a modest success but a failure later in Munich. His conducting career developed; he directed many major operas, including Wagner at Bayreuth, and returned to Munich in 1896 as chief conductor at the opera. To the late 1890s belong the witty and colourful Till Eulenspiegel, a portrait of a disrespectful rogue with whom Strauss clearly had a good deal of sympathy, the graphic yet also poetic and psychologically subtle Don Quixote (cast respectively in rondo and variation forms) and Ein Heldenleben, 'a hero's life', where Strauss himself is the hero and his adversaries the music critics. There is more autobiography in the Symphonia domestica of 1903; he conducted its première during his first visit to the USA, in 1904.

Strauss was now moving towards opera. His Feuersnot was given in 1901; in 1904 Salome was begun, after Wilde's play. It was given at Dresden in 1905. Regarded as blasphemous and salacious, it ran into censorship trouble but was given at 50 opera houses in the next two years. This and Elektra (given in 1909) follow up the tone poems in their evocation of atmosphere and their thematic structure; both deal with female obsessions of a disordered, macabre kind, with violent climaxes involving gruesome deaths and impassioned dancing, with elements of abnormal sexuality and corruption, exploiting the female voice pressed to dramatic extremes.

Strauss did not pursue that path. After the violence and dissonance of the previous operas, and their harsh psychological realism, Strauss and his librettist Hofmannsthal turned to period comedy, set in the Vienna of Maria Theresa, for Der Rosenkavalier; the score is no less rich in inner detail, but it is applied to the evocation of tenderness, nostalgia and humour, helped by sentimental Viennese waltzes. Again the female voice – but this time its radiance and warmth – is exploited, in the three great roles of the Marschallin, Octavian and Sophie. It was given at Dresden in 1911 with huge success and was soon produced in numerous other opera houses. Strauss followed it with Ariadne auf Naxos, at first linked with a Molière play, later revised as prologue (behind the scenes at a private theatre) and opera, mixing commedia dell'arte and classical tragedy to a delicate, chamber orchestral accompaniment. The two versions were given in 1912 and (in Vienna) 1916. Strauss had been conducting in Berlin, the court and opera orchestras, since 1908; in 1919 he took up a post as joint director of the Vienna Staatsoper, where his latest collaboration with Hofmannsthal, Die Frau ohne Schatten, was given that year: a work embodying much symbolism and psychology, opulently but finely scored, and regarded by some as one of Strauss's noblest achievements. His busy, international conducting career continued in the inter-war years; there were visits to North and South America as well as to most parts of Europe in the 1920s, which also saw the premières of two more operas, both at Dresden, the autobiographical, domestic comedy Intermezzo and Die ägyptische Helena. His last Hofmannsthal opera, Arabella, an appealing re-creation of some of the atmosphere of Rosenkavalier, followed in 1933. Of his remaining operas, Capriccio (1942), a 'conversation-piece' in a single act set in the 18th century and dealing with the amorous and artistic rivalries of a poet and a musician, is the most successful, with its witty, graceful, serene score.

During the 1930s Strauss, seeking a smooth and quiet life, had allowed himself to accept – without facing up to their full import – the circumstances created in Germany by the Nazis. For a time he was head of the State Music Bureau and he once obligingly conducted at Bayreuth when Toscanini had withdrawn. But he was frustrated at being unable to work with his Jewish librettist, Stefan Zweig (Hofmannsthal had been part-Jewish), and he protected his Jewish daughter-in-law; during the war years, when he mainly lived in Vienna, he and the Nazi authorities lived in no more than mutual toleration. When Germany was defeated, and her opera houses destroyed, Strauss wrote an intense lament, Metamorphosen, for 23 solo strings; this is one of several products of a golden 'Indian summer', which include an oboe concerto and the Four Last Songs, works in a ripe, mellow idiom, executed with a grace worthy of his beloved Mozart.

Concertos

Awards 1996

Horn Concertos Nos 1 and 2. Duett-Concertino, AV147. Serenade, Op 7
David Pyatt *hn* **Joy Farrall** *cl* **Julie Andrews** *bn* **Britten Sinfonia / Nicholas Cleobury**
Classics for Pleasure 573 513-2 (B)
(66 minutes: DDD). Recorded 1994 ○○○

David Pyatt won the BBC's 'Young Musician of the Year' Competition back in 1988. Since then the fledgling has well and truly flown. This is sensationally good horn playing. Primarily, there's his noble *legato*: the heart of the matter, a beautiful sound, full, even and unclouded. He is sparing with the brassy timbres, holding them in reserve for dramatic effect, for such times as the instrument's well-rounded jocularity must take on a brazen, huntsmen-like air, or rise to shining heroics – like the challenging motto theme of the First Concerto. His shaping of the big phrases rolls off the page with ease and authority, but equally, so much of his personality is conveyed in the rhythmic articulation: a dashing, Jack-be-nimble mischievousness (even a touch of impudence?) in Strauss's athletic *allegros*. Most of all, though – and this is rare – he loves to play quietly, really quietly. He is a master of those dreamy, far-away departures – twilit forest-murmurings: mysterious, unreal.

The recording helps here, with a beautifully integrated balance. The sound of the early *Serenade*, Op 7, is particularly fine with ripe, euphonious *tuttis* and room enough for individual personalities to open up. And that is the most remarkable aspect of the piece, the utterly natural way it blends and contrasts across the whole spectrum of wind voices. Two of them take centre-stage in the delightful *Duett-Concertino*. Joy Farrall's clarinet and Julie Andrews's bassoon are like Octavian and the Baron Ochs in this gentle but spirited opus. This is a spendid disc, then, and sympathetically directed, too.

Horn Concertos Nos 1 and 2. Oboe Concerto, AV144. Duet Concertino. Burleske in D minor, AV85. Parergon, Op 73. Panathenäenzug: Symphonic Study in the form of a Passacaglia, Op 74. Till Eulenspiegels lustige Streiche, Op 28. Don Juan, Op 20. Ein Heldenleben, Op 40
Peter Damm *hn* **Manfred Clement** *ob* **Manfred Weise** *cl* **Wolfgang Liebscher** *bn* **Malcolm Frager, Peter Rösel** *pfs* **Dresden Staatskapelle / Rudolf Kempe**
EMI ③ CMS7 64342-2 (224 minutes: ADD) Ⓜ
Recorded 1970-75 ●

Violin Concerto in D minor, Op 8. Symphonia domestica, Op 53. Also sprach Zarathustra, Op 30. Tod und Verklärung, Op 24. Der Rosenkavalier – Waltzes. Salome – Dance of the Seven Veils. Le bourgeois gentilhomme – Suite, Op 60. Schlagobers – Waltz. Josephslegende – Suite
Ulf Hoelscher *vn* **Dresden Staatskapelle / Rudolf Kempe**
EMI ③ CMS7 64346-2 (222 minutes: ADD) Ⓜ
Recorded 1970-75 ●

Metamorphosen for 23 Solo Strings, AV142. Eine Alpensinfonie, Op 64. Aus Italien, Op 16. Macbeth, Op 23. Don Quixote, Op 35. Dance Suite on Keyboard Pieces by François Couperin, AV107
Paul Tortelier *vc* **Max Rostal** *va* **Dresden Staatskapelle / Rudolf Kempe**
EMI ③ CMS7 64350-2 (208 minutes: ADD) Ⓜ
Recorded 1970-75 ●●

'From the store of glorious memories of my artistic career, the tones of this master orchestra ever evoke feelings of deepest gratitude and admiration' (thus spoke Strauss when greeting the Dresden orchestra in 1948 on its 400th Anniversary). You get the feeling that this orchestra is justifiably proud of its tones, and its Straussian associations. Kempe, it seems, was the man to draw that pride out, and give it purpose. Some may find Kempe an occasionally circumspect Straussian, one who preferred decorum to decibels in the protracted cacophony that concludes the *Symphonia domestica*, and who ensures that the famous '2001' opening to *Also sprach Zarathustra* isn't so awesome that the rest of the piece is an anti-climax.

It is difficult, though, to think of many other Straussians with the imagination and understanding to bring these scores to life from within. For Kempe, like Reiner, clarity of texture and a natural flexibility of pacing were prerequisites for the characterful animation and interaction of orchestral soloists or instrumental groups, but never at the expense of the long-term direction of the music. His technique, too, ensured the kind of feats of ensemble and precision that you might have expected from the Chicago Symphony Orchestra under Reiner, but Kempe's orchestra, of course, retains its warmer and cherishably Old World tones.

There are many self-evidently great Strauss performances here, including perhaps the most vital and communicative *Don Quixote* ever recorded. The recordings vary in perspective from an ideally distanced, natural layout to the closer and slightly 'contained' and the vividly present. Clear, light-toned timpani with very little bass resonance further enhance Kempe's precise rhythmic control, and soloists are invariably up-front, but rarely at the expense of orchestral detail. The recordings benefit from the warm acoustics of Dresden's Lukaskirche.

Also sprach Zarathustra

Also sprach Zarathustra. Ein Heldenleben Ⓗ
Chicago Symphony Orchestra / Fritz Reiner
RCA Living Stereo 09026 61494-2 (76 minutes: ADD) Ⓜ
Recorded 1954 ●●

It is astonishing to reflect that this recording of *Also sprach Zarathustra* was made on March 8, 1954, in stereo when Toscanini was still (just) recording in low-fi in New York's Carnegie Hall. The sound may be tonally fierce by current standards (less so than many oft-praised Mercury reissues) but the balance is fully acceptable, with the first and second violins set close to the listener (and the microphones) on either side of the podium, and the basses hard left.

Reiner's *Also sprach* is intense and extrovert. In his second year with the Chicago Symphony Orchestra, the conductor was already getting a thrilling response from the strings, although woodwind intonation could be a problem. Confident and well played as it is, the spectacular opening sunrise inevitably lacks the impact of modern recordings. What we have instead is a measure of raw passion and forward thrust unequalled on disc. In the reflective passages, conductor and/or engineers display some reluctance to achieve a real *pianissimo*, but as the tempo builds Reiner invariably creates great excitement and the orchestral playing is marvellous. Reiner's reading of *Ein Heldenleben* has humanity as well as virtuosity – the touching closing section is memorable.

Also sprach Zarathustra, Op 30. Don Juan, Op 20
Berlin Philharmonic Orchestra / Herbert von Karajan
DG 439 016-2GHS (54 minutes: DDD) Ⓕ
Recorded 1983

The playing of the Berlin Philharmonic Orchestra is as glorious as ever; its virtuosity can be taken for granted along with its sumptuous tonal refinement, and in Strauss, of course, Karajan has no peer. As a recording it is very good indeed though it does not offer the spectacular definition and transparency of detail of the Dorati, but the playing, it goes without saying, is in a totally different league. The famous opening has greater intensity in his 1974 version and it is possible to prefer the marginally greater warmth and glow of the strings in the early account – the DG engineers adopt a slightly closer balance on this newcomer – while recognising the greater range and impressive detail, particularly in the bass, of this 1983 recording. The *Don Juan* coupling is a fine performance too. To sum up, this issue is a strong first recommendation at full price, but taken overall the earlier 1973 account – now reissued at mid price on DG Originals – holds sway.

Additional recommendation
Also sprach Zarathustra, Op 30
Couplings: Don Juan, Op 20. Till Eulenspiegels lustige Streiche. Salome – Dance of the Seven Veils
Berlin Philharmonic Orchestra / Karajan
DG The Originals 447 441-2GOR (79 minutes: ADD) Ⓜ
Herbert von Karajan's classic 1974 account of Strauss's popular tone poem is unsurpassed, even by himself. Now at mid price, it's the first choice for collectors.

Don Juan and Ein Heldenleben

Don Juan[a]. Till Eulenspiegels lustige Streiche[a]. Ein Heldenleben[b]
[a]**Cleveland Orchestra / George Szell;** [b]**Philadelphia Orchestra / Eugene Ormandy**
Sony Classical Essential Classics SBK48272 Ⓑ
(75 minutes: ADD). Recorded 1957-60

In *Heldenleben* Ormandy's hero is a transatlantic with a fat cigar in his mouth, and that he's out to impress is obvious from the start. He employs glamorous representatives, too: slick brass and percussion, smartly ordered winds and a plush, generous army of strings. Yet, he is not without soul, as his 'Works of Peace' and 'Retirement from the World and the Fulfilment of his Life' ably illustrate. In fact, his having *been* fulfilled earlier on in the score only goes to underline his profound change of heart. And with solo violinist Ansel Brusilow an eloquent commentator, and truthful if rather opaque sound, the hero's 'Indian summer' is most eloquently portrayed. Turn then to Szell, and the contrast is quite startling. Szell used to play his own piano-solo arrangement of *Till Eulenspiegel* to Strauss, and his recording of the work reveals the depth of his perception. No hint of brashness here, just wit, myriad detail and astonishing orchestral virtuosity. There can't be many better *Don Juans* on CD. The transfers from fair-to-middling originals are absolutely first-rate.

R Strauss Don Juan[a]. Ein Heldenleben[b]
Wagenaar Cyrano de Bergerac, Op 23[a]
[a]**Concertgebouw Orchestra;** [b]**New York Philharmonic Symphony Orchestra / Willem Mengelberg**
Pearl mono GEM0008 (71 minutes: ADD). Ⓜ
Recorded 1928-42

Mengelberg's changes to *Ein Heldenleben* were designed to emphasise the score's brilliance. So the opening triplets are bowed separately rather than slurred, and *Luftpausen* are inserted to articulate the phrasing. Later in the work, Mengelberg's famous *portamentos* are worked on and the melodic lines put together gradually to perfect intonation and ensemble. Illicit emendations are clearly audible in this 72-year-old recording. You might expect such interventionist conducting to sound artificial or calculated, as it almost invariably does in the forays made by present-day period orchestras into early 20th-century repertoire, but nothing could be further from the truth. Whatever Mengelberg's methods, there is nothing artificial about this glorious, ardent account of Strauss's score. The hero can seldom have sounded more ebullient, whether in love or war. The critics' mixture of incomprehension and petty spite is realised to perfection, and those string *portamentos* (sounding utterly natural) are well to the fore as the hero retreats from worldly concerns.

The secret of all this has to lie in Mengelberg's familiarity with the score, although it may help that the American orchestra's style of playing was markedly more 'modern' than that of Mengelberg's Concertgebouw. As Pearl's excellent documentation states, by the time this recording was made Mengelberg had 'nearly three decades' worth of *Heldenlebens* under his belt'. Only hours after these sessions were completed, the orchestra gave the first performance of *An American in Paris*. In Mark Obert-Thorn's transfer, the recording seems little short of miraculous given its age; apart from the restricted dynamic range, it sounds better than many made 20 years later, combining deep, solid bass with astonishing clarity – including, alas, perfect reproduction of the subway trains passing underneath Carnegie Hall!

So what if there is a whiff of contrivance about the 1938 Concertgebouw performance of *Don Juan*. The main work remains indispensable for anyone remotely interested in Strauss or in the history of recording. Perhaps, as the booklet says, this is the definitive *Heldenleben*. The bonus item, Wagenaar's *Cyrano de Bergerac* Overture, makes little odds; it is *Don Juan* crossed with *Die Meistersinger* and here we have the real thing.

R Strauss Ein Heldenleben, Op 40
Mozart Symphony No 36 in C, 'Linz', K425
London Symphony Orchestra / Sir John Barbirolli
BBC Legends/IMG Artists BBCL4055-2 Ⓜ
(73 minutes: ADD). Recorded live in 1969 ●

Because Sir John Barbirolli's studio recording of *Ein Heldenleben* appeared posthumously, as Sir Thomas Beecham's stereo remake had done, it seemed to sum up a lifetime's achievement – 'a hero's life' for the conductor as much as the composer. It can be argued that this live performance is even more remarkable than the familiar studio version. It is a degree faster certainly and a shade tougher, too, although this impression has something to do with the vivid but shrill acoustics of the venue. There is more electricity in the playing, less subtlety and richness in the sound. No doubt the actual remastering has been carefully done, and the accompanying documentation is excellent.

Like Bernstein in his last years, Barbirolli could be an uninhibited re-shaper of the music he loved. The opening passage is grand to be sure, even a bit loose in places, but then the interpretation doesn't offer too much too soon. Things are tauter in the Royal Festival Hall. The leader, John Georgiadis, copes heroically with the beloved's (and the conductor's) demands. Michael Kennedy's authoritative note explains that they looked through the part together in exhaustive detail. The battle scene has breadth and dignity, by no means slower than Karajan was wont to take it in his last days. For once there is no sense of disappointment when the ringing climax gives way to the hero's works of peace. As in the studio, so here, the pot-pourri of motifs from the composer's back-catalogue has a particularly emotive quality: Barbirolli, painfully aware of his mortality, lavishes every ounce of affection and sensibility on these allusions to music he would not live to conduct again. The Elgarian nobility of the closing stages is again striking.

How to sum up? Sir John's is a *Heldenleben* like no other, deeply moving, albeit less 'authentic' than the wonderfully lithe accounts we have from Willem Mengelberg (1928) and Arturo Toscanini (1941). Strauss himself was yet more restrained and aristocratic. The bugbear of 'authenticity' is more threatening in the *Linz*. Michael Kennedy, as you might expect, warms to the performance. Barbirolli, he tells us, conducted Mozart 'throughout his career, giving it not only elegance but strength and vigour'. Younger listeners might not put it quite the same way. Such big-hearted music-making remains enjoyable, but 'elegance' signifies something different these days. That, you may well think, is our loss. Certainly, the finale has all the vigour that one could wish for, and we are told that the conductor was particularly happy with the rendition as a whole. This release is warmly recommended.

Eine Alpensinfonie

Eine Alpensinfonie, Op 64.
Der Rosenkavalier – Suite for Orchestra
Vienna Philharmonic Orchestra / Christian Thielemann
DG 469 519-2GH (77 minutes: DDD) Ⓕ
Recorded live in 2000 ●●

'I will call my *Alpine Symphony* the *Anti-Christian*, because in it there is moral purification by means of one's own strength, liberation through work, worship of glorious, eternal nature.' In the end, of course, Strauss shied away from the inflammatory subtitle, yet the quotation is instructive. With more on his mind than a day's hike, Strauss had originally intended the work to convey a Nietzschean vitalism (is it coincidence that the trombones announce the summit in grandiloquent Zarathustrian fifths?).

Thielemann's is, by a considerable margin, the finest account we have had since Karajan's (and is rather better played): the performers' emotional commitment is stamped on every bar. Having the VPO on top form is a decided advantage: the brass-playing throughout is electrifying, no mean achievement since this disc was recorded live. It becomes clear very early on that we're in for something special, but anyone wishing to sample the performance at its formidable best might start 'on the glacier' (track 9) – the perilously high trumpet writing more confidently negotiated than for Karajan – and continue until they are 'on the summit'. On the way up, 'Dangerous moments' (track 10) is simply superb, Thielemann and the orchestra alive to every flickering nuance of accent and dynamic. And I've never heard the oboe's awe-struck contemplation of the surrounding vistas better done, the *rubato* exactly conveying the climber's physical breathlessness and spiritual exaltation. Thereafter, Strauss's ecstatic tumult is given full rein. This is a *real* performance: no-one holding back, no-one playing safe.

Which isn't to imply anything unsubtle: you really hear the close kinship between 'Rising mists' (track 13) and the passage in which the Captain and Doctor contemplate the lake in which Berg's Wozzeck has just drowned himself, so clearly does Thielemann articulate the disparate strands. Only when manoeuvring 'On the wrong track through thickets and undergrowth' does he seem unsure how best to clarify Strauss's knotted textures (tellingly, Karajan gets through this section a touch faster). It is difficult to resist singling out the violins' *glissando* down to the very last note, so otherworldly that it's almost frightening, and surely one of the weirdest sounds ever conjured from the Vienna Phil. In principle, one might object to some of Thielemann's bizarrely slow tempos (as at fig 31 – track 4, 3'10"ff) and his tendency to linger over phrase endings (especially noticeable as night falls again), but here at least is someone who believes in the music and has something to say about it.

The various *Rosenkavalier* 'suites' usually seem insubstantial, but this one, at nearly 25 minutes, is both a generous filler and an effective wind-down after the main work. Thielemann seems keen to defend the pot-pourri from any charge of vulgarity, which means that such moments as Sophie and Octavian's final duet – ravishingly done here – make more of an impact than the very opening. The protracted pause before the great Trio is also a feature of Thielemann's performances of the complete opera.

Captured in a recording at once lushly upholstered and thrillingly visceral, divided violins and all, this is unquestionably Thielemann's finest release to date. Occasional audience noises in both works never amount to a serious distraction. Ozawa and even Previn with the same orchestra are effectively superseded, though Karajan's narrower range of tempos and absolute sense of where the music is going will still be preferred by some.

Eine Alpensinfonie, Op 64

Berlin Philharmonic Orchestra / Herbert von Karajan

DG Karajan Gold 439 017-2GHS (51 minutes: DDD) Ⓕ
Recorded 1980 ●●

The *Alpensinfonie* is no longer a rarity on disc, but there are still grounds for preferring the famous Karajan version to subsequent digital rivals, especially in this successful remastering. Karajan's sureness of line is always impressive in Strauss and, while the Berlin Philharmonic Orchestra is not at its immaculate best, there is some magnificent playing here. The sound remains rather fierce, but a number of passages have been substantially remixed and the effect is certainly less constricted overall. Perhaps it doesn't matter that the horn theme which floats in with the (still blinding) 'Sonnenaufgang' is not quite aligned with the strings. More worrying is the subtle transformation of the opening phrase of 'Der Ansteig': whereas we used to experience it 'from the bottom up' with the balance favouring the basses, we hear more cellos now—and most of them fluff the B flat! That said, the breadth and majesty of Karajan's conception is indisputable.

Eine Alpensinfonie. Don Juan

San Francisco Symphony Orchestra / Herbert Blomstedt

Decca Ovation 466 423-2DM (70 minutes: DDD) Ⓜ
Recorded 1988 ●●

The *Alpine Symphony* is the last of Richard Strauss's great tone-poems and is in many ways the most spectacular. The score is an evocation of the changing moods of an alpine landscape and the huge orchestral apparatus of over 150 players encompasses quadruple wind, 20 horns, organ, wind machine, cowbells, thunder machine, two harps and enhanced string forces. Its pictorialism may be all too graphic, but what virtuosity and inspiration Strauss commands. Herbert Blomstedt's reading penetrates beyond the pictorialism into the work's deeper elements. It emerges as a gigantic hymn to nature on a Mahlerian scale.

Tempos are slower, but these are justified by the noble expansiveness of the final pages, towards which the whole performance moves with impressive inevitability. The playing of the San Francisco Symphony is magnificent, with subtle use of vibrato by the strings and superb performances, individual and corporate, by the wind sections. The *Don Juan* performance is fine too. The recording is excellent, the big climaxes thrilling and the whole well balanced.

Till Eulenspiegels lustige streiche[a]. Also sprach Zarathustra[a]. Don Juan[a]. Ein Heldenleben[b]. Eine Alpensinfonie[c]

[a]Chicago Symphony Orchestra, [b]Vienna Philharmonic Orchestra;[c]Bavarian Radio Symphony Orchestra / Sir Georg Solti

Decca Double ② 440 618-2DF2 (152 minutes: ADD) Ⓜ
Recorded 1970s ●

This set is remarkable value. The formidable power of Sir Georg Solti's personality dominates all these brilliantly played performances. The intensity is never in doubt; one cannot but be continually gripped by this kind of music-making, for the great Hungarian conductor is never daunted by the recording studio. *Eine Alpensinfonie*, with the Bavarian Radio Symphony Orchestra, has the most glorious tone (especially the brass). Such is the amplitude of the sound – and the warm commitment of the playing – that it counteracts the conductor's tendency to press forward, almost as if he is driven by some remorseless spirit.

Till Eulenspiegel, *Also sprach Zarathustra*, *Ein Heldenleben* and *Don Juan* were recorded at the peak of Solti's reign as Music Director of the Chicago Symphony in the early and mid-1970s. The playing is magnificently opulent, even Germanic in feeling, and the bravura is tremendously assured. *Till Eulenspiegel* brings a particularly vivid start with the sound most clearly placed in its natural setting and atmosphere. Solti's version is excellent on very count. It is simply impossible to resist the sweep and intoxicating power of this great orchestra unleashed, yet at the same time held by the conductor in an absolutely firm grip.

Even if other performances of Strauss's music have more subtlety of feeling, Solti's admirers will count this anthology a great bargain. The CD transfers of these brilliant Decca analogue recordings of 1975 are certainly impressive.

Don Quixote

Don Quixote. Lieder – Morgen, Op 27 No 4; Der Rosenband, Op 36 No 1; Wiegenlied, Op 41 No 1; Freundliche Vision, Op 48 No 1; Waldseligkeit, Op 49 No 1; Die heiligen drei Könige, Op 56 No 6

Dame Felicity Lott *sop* **André Vauquet** *va*
François Guye *vc* **Suisse Romande Orchestra / Armin Jordan**
Mediaphon MED72 165 (69 minutes: DDD) Ⓜ
Recorded 1996

Above all, this disc is notable for taking advantage of the superlative acoustic of the Victoria Hall in Geneva, home of the Suisse Romande Orchestra, thus giving us the most impressively recorded *Don Quixote* yet, in sound terms. The detail of the brilliant scoring is clearly delineated while at the same time the whole picture is one of amazing warmth and resplendence. The spread of sound and its wonderful luminosity are things to marvel at and, of course, they are ideal for this inspired score.

Happily Jordan and his orchestra offer a performance worthy of both the place and the production – no aspect of the score missed. François Guye brings out all Quixote's endearing and aggravating qualities without a hint of exaggeration, his tone always full and poised. His viola partner makes a suitable companion, and the individual soloists from the orchestra also distinguish themselves.

The songs are more than a makeweight. Lott, the leading Straussian soprano of the day, knows just how to make the most of six of the composer's best-loved songs with ethereal, fine-grained tone and line. As with the tone-poem, Jordan presents the music without any excess of sentiment. So what a great pity, then, that texts and translations are not provided, the only blot on a disc that is certain to give much pleasure and satisfaction.

Symphonia domestica

Symphonia domestica. Tod und Verklärung
Bavarian Radio Symphony Orchestra / Lorin Maazel
RCA Red Seal 09026 68221-2 (74 minutes: DDD) Ⓕ
Recorded 1995

Symphonia domestica contains some exquisitely tender and beguiling invention, something of which Lorin Maazel must be acutely conscious because this is his second digital recording of the work. The conductor's quest for technical perfection can on occasion produce an alienating effect, but only those who demand Karajan's saturated sonorities in this repertoire will be dissatisfied with the chamber-like results that are achieved here. Maazel keeps a sophisticated yet altogether less ostentatious grip on the proceedings, being concerned to let individual lines register without strain.

This *Tod und Verklärung* is his fourth rendition on disc and, again, with the rhetoric pared down, the awkward corners seem to disappear. These are refreshing, thoughtful, superbly prepared performances which will inevitably strike some listeners as being understated. The orchestral playing is remarkably fine, and the recordings are faithful and true, with just a hint of artificiality in the placing of instrumental solos: the sound of the solo violin in Tod's evocation of childhood is not ideally pure, for instance. In the *Symphonia domestica*, Maazel's approach is decidedly subtler, belying the glitzy packaging favoured by RCA.

Symphony in F minor, Op 12

Symphonies – D minor, AV69[a]; F minor, Op 12[b]
[a]**Bavarian Radio Symphony Orchestra;**
[b]**Berlin Radio Symphony Orchestra / Karl Anton Rickenbacher**
Koch Schwann 365322 (74 minutes: DDD) Ⓕ
Recorded 1996-97

The D minor Symphony is a piece of purely specialist interest, it being the work of a well-schooled 16-year-old rather than a Mendelssohnian prodigy. No less a conductor than Hermann Levi conducted its first performance, but Strauss soon became anxious to suppress it altogether and he would no doubt have been quite horrified to read of its resuscitation today. The beautiful acoustic of the Herkulessaal flatters the orchestra and its not inappropriately 'provincial' horns.

The more familiar work in F minor was admired by several distinguished contemporaries. Brahms nevertheless thought it no more than 'quite pretty'. The piece gets under way with a descending scale that seems to anticipate the *Alpensinfonie*, but the dutiful academicism of what follows provides little foretaste of the mature Strauss. While the inner movements are possessed of greater individuality, *Don Juan* is worlds away. Rickenbacher's performance is commendably fresh and alert.

Metamorphosen

Awards 1982/3

Tod und Verklärung. Metamorphosen
Berlin Philharmonic Orchestra / Herbert von Karajan
DG 410 892-2GH (52 minutes: DDD) Ⓕ
Recorded 1982. ○○○

These are a clear first-choice in both works. Karajan's *Metamorphosen* has almost unbearable intensity and great emotional urgency – it is a very gripping and involving account. The sound is marginally more forward and cleaner than is ideal, though the rich ambience is very appealing. *Tod und Verklärung* is not so spectacularly recorded as some more modern versions, but it is a greater performance that just about any other, and finer than any of Karajan's earlier versions. Indeed, it is quite electrifying, with superb playing and a life-and-death intensity to the climaxes. It is more vividly recorded than his most recent previous version, and the performance is tauter (25'23" against 27'00" in 1974) and more powerful.

In both works, it would be difficult to improve on these performances by the greatest Richard Strauss conductor of his day and the glorious BPO, and the quality of the recording gives no cause for reproach.

Violin Sonata in E flat, Op 18

R Strauss Violin Sonata in E flat, Op 18
Bartók (arr Székely) Six Romanian Folkdances, Sz56
Stravinsky (arr Stravinsky/Dushkin) Divertimento
Vadim Repin *vn* **Boris Berezovsky** *pf*
Erato 8573-85769-2 (53 minutes: DDD) Ⓕ
Recorded 2000

Stylistically, Strauss's lyrical Op 18 (1887) sits poised somewhere between Brahms's chivalrous song-cycle *Die schöne Magelone* and Strauss's own *Don Juan* of the following year. The finale is rich in heroics though not before a seductive 'Improvisation' and the appearance of one of Strauss's loveliest melodies. Anyone familiar with Heifetz's three recordings – his second, the first of two with the late Brooks Smith, is probably the most comprehensively expressive – will have a job adapting to anyone else. No one draws a sweeter, more tender opening phrase, though Vadim Repin, like Gidon Kremer, more or less matches Heifetz in terms of repose.

Repin's feline violin faces leonine support from Boris Berezovsky, almost to excess at around 5'20" into the first movement and for the stormy centre of the second (2'39"), where the piano threatens to take over. Berezovsky's outsize musical personality draws maximum mileage from Strauss's virtuoso piano writing, though he too is capable of relaxing, as in the tranquil passage from 3'40" into the first movement. Berezovsky's elegant fingerwork is nicely demonstrated in the decorative figurations that dominate the third section of the second movement (from around 3'44"). Kremer and Oleg Maisenberg are also excellent, but Repin's engagement with the music's lyrical element just about gives him the edge . Heifetz is more 'accompanied' by Brooks Smith than partnered by him.

Echoes of Strauss return for the *Adagio* from Stravinsky's *Fairy's Kiss* re-run, a witty *Divertimento* prepared in collaboration with violinist Samuel Dushkin. Repin's strongest current rival is Perlman, though his reading is perhaps less subtly characterised and, again, Berezovsky's strong-arm pianism strengthens the frame.

Bartók's ubiquitous *Romanian Folkdances* are rather less spicy here than you would expect from someone who has fiddled in gypsy style with Lakatos, but Repin's harmonics in the 'Pe loc' third movement are admirably clean and the final dances are suitably dashing. The sound is very well balanced.

Choral Works

Deutsche Motette, Op 62[a]. Gesänge, Op 34. An den Baum Daphne (epilogue to 'Daphne'), AV137[b].
Die Göttin im Putzzimmer, AV120
[a]**Tina Kiberg,** [b]**Marianne Lund** *sops* [b]**Christian Lisdorf** *treb* [a]**Randi Stene** *contr* [a]**Gert Henning-Jensen** *ten* [a]**Ulrik Cold** *bass*; [b]**Copenhagen Boys' Choir; Danish National Radio Choir / Stefan Parkman**
Chandos CHAN9223 (57 minutes: DDD). Texts and translations included. Recorded 1993 Ⓕ

Under Stefan Parkman the Danish National Radio Choir has established a reputation second to none. Parkman handles his singers as if they were a fully fledged symphony orchestra; which is not at all inappropriate in this programme by the supreme master of orchestral colour. From the heart of the 16 chorus parts of the *Deutsche Motette* a further seven are projected by solo voices emerging imperceptibly from the midst of a dense, luxuriant texture. The depth of colour and range of emotions are every bit as extensive in these works as in the great orchestral tone-poems; indeed few orchestral tone-poems evoke dusk and sunset so vividly as 'Der Abend', the first of the 1897 *Zwei Gesänge*. There is a wonderfully luminous soundscape here; a combination of superb compositional skill, sensitive musical direction, superlative choral singing and a warm, full-bodied recording.

Four Last Songs, AV150 (Op posth)

Four Last Songs[a]. Capriccio – Morgen mittag um elf! ... Kein andres[b]. Tod und Verklärung[c]
[ab]**Gundula Janowitz** *sop* [a]**Berlin Philharmonic Orchestra / Herbert von Karajan;** [b]**Bavarian Radio Symphony Orchestra,** [c]**Staatskapelle Dresden / Karl Böhm**
DG Classikon 439 467-2GCL (65 minutes: ADD) Ⓜ
Recorded 1971-72

Here is a feast of glorious Strauss at bargain price, though the performances are anything but bargain in quality. In spite of strong challenges from far and wide, the singing of them by Gundula Janowitz has, arguably, still not been surpassed for Straussian opulence and tenderness – we emphasise 'arguably', for people feel passionately about interpretations of this work! – and Karajan conducts a near-ideal account of the orchestral score. Janowitz, in glorious voice, sings the *Four Last Songs* flowingly. The recording is more hazy than on the other two exemplary performances. The fashion of the moment to denigrate Böhm is incomprehensible when you encounter readings as splendid as his two contributions here, in which he again proves himself an ideal Straussian.

The live account of *Tod und Verklärung* caught at the 1972 Salzburg Festival but not released until 1988 (in memoriam) builds naturally to its various incandescent climaxes, and the music is never allowed to drag or descend into sentimentality. The playing of the Dresden orchestra is lithe and warm. The final scene of *Capriccio* comes from the complete set recorded in Munich in 1971. Once more Böhm judges tempos and texture to a nicety, the music always moving forward in perfect balance to its end.

R Strauss Four Last Songs **Wagner** Wesendonk Lieder. Tristan und Isolde – Prelude and Liebestod
Cheryl Studer *sop* **Dresden Staatskapelle / Giuseppe Sinopoli**
DG 439 865-2GH (61 minutes: DDD) Ⓕ
Notes, texts and translations included

In the Strauss, Cheryl Studer's voice, lyrical yet with dramatic overtones, seems near-ideal for Strauss and for this work in particular, quite apart from the sheer beauty and technical accomplishment of her singing. In the first two songs there is the necessary ecstasy and longing in her singing as Strauss reviews, elegiacally, his musical credo. For example, one could cite the loving treatment in 'September' of the phrases beginning 'Langsam tut er', the singer's tone poised, the shading of the line perfectly natural. It is the seamless *legato* and lovely voice that again make 'Beim Schlafengehen' so rewarding, while in the final song Studer is suitably hushed and reflective. Sinopoli and the Staatskapelle Dresden provide ideal support for their singer with the playing in all these works as lyrically expressive as the singing above it.

Similar praise can be given to the reading of the *Wesendonk Lieder*. Here, once again, one notes Studer's amazing combination of vocal mastery and interpretative insight. Every dynamic and expressive mark is scrupulously followed (listen to the *piano* at 'Luft' and 'Duft' in the second song) in the pursuit of seamless phrasing and a due attention to the text. The richness of her singing, the thorough mastery of German diction and phraseology, make this another special performance. Sinopoli's reading of the Prelude to *Tristan* is flowing, intense and spontaneous and the playing is predictably superb, all adding to the disc's worth. The recordings are for the most part happily spacious and well focused.

Four Last Songs[a]. Arabella – Er ist der Richtige nicht[b]; Der Richtige so hab ich stets zu mir gesagt[c]; Das war sehr gut, Mandryka[b]. Ariadne auf Naxos – Es gibt ein Reich[b]. Capriccio – Closing scene[c] **H**
Lisa della Casa, Hilde Gueden *sops* **Alfred Poell** *bar* **Paul Schoeffler** *bass-bar* **Franz Bierbach** *bass* **Vienna Philharmonic Orchestra / [a]Karl Böhm, [b]Rudolf Moralt, [c]Heinrich Hollreiser**
Decca Historic mono 425 959-2DM (67 minutes: ADD). Texts and translations included Ⓜ
Recorded 1953-54 ●

Four Last Songs, AV 150[a]. Capriccio – Morgen mittag um Elf[a]. Arabella[b] – Ich danke, Fräulein…Aber der Richtige; Mein Elemer; Sie wollen mich heiraten; Das war sehr gut **H**
Dame Elisabeth Schwarzkopf, Anny Felbermeyer *sops* **Josef Metternich** *bar* **Philharmonia Orchestra / [a]Otto Ackermann, [b]Lovro von Matačic**
EMI Références mono CDH7 61001-2 Ⓜ
(68 minutes: ADD). Recorded 1953-54 ●●

Strauss's *Four Last Songs* are a perfect summation of the composer's lifelong love-affair with the soprano voice deriving from the fact that he married a soprano, Pauline Ahna. They are also an appropriate and deeply moving farewell to his career as a composer and to the whole romantic tradition, and they have inspired many glorious performances. In recent times there has been a tendency to linger unnecessarily over what are already eloquent enough pieces. Lisa della Casa, in her naturally and lovingly sung performance under Karl Böhm (the first-ever studio recording of the pieces back in 1953) makes no such mistake. In this incarnation this is a wonderful offering at medium price backed by other invaluable Strauss interpretations from the Swiss diva. Her particular gift is to sing the pieces in a natural, unforced manner with gloriously unfettered tone. Her and Böhm's tempos tend to be faster than those employed by most of her successors.

The *Four Last Songs* are sung with equal beauty by Elisabeth Schwarzkopf. She sings 'Im Abendrot' even more beautifully than della Casa, and with an even more serene feeling of the coming of Death. Her interpretation is extraordinarily moving. The songs gain a great deal also, by being sung in the published order. It is good to have these outstanding performances on CD, especially as they also allow us to hear Schwarzkopf in two Strauss operatic roles she never sang on stage. The voice is at its best and there are moments of rare insight, such as the lovely *pp* 'Du kennst mich wieder' in 'Frühling'. Also the Philharmonia of 1953 was something special, and the excellent balance of the recording brings out Straussian subtleties galore.

The *Capriccio* finale was recorded before Schwarzkopf made the complete recording. It is a more forceful, less lovable performance. The *Arabella* excerpts, on the other hand, exacerbate regret that she didn't record the whole opera. She brings just the right mixture of hauteur and impulsiveness to the enigmatic heroine.

Additional recommendation
Four Last Songs, Op posth
Coupling: Wagner Wesendonk Lieder
Norman *sop* **Leipzig Gewandhaus Orchestra / Masur**
Philips 50 Great Recordings 464 742-2PM Ⓜ
(48 minutes: DDD)
Jessye Norman's glorious performance of Strauss's deeply poignant swansong lifed the *Gramophone* solo vocal award in 1984. If you're a Janowitz or Schwarzkopf advocate you'll find it too langorous. For anyone else it's surely unmissable, even with the short running time.

Opera Arias

Jane Eaglen
Salome – Ach, du wolltest mich nicht deinen Mund küssen lassen. Guntram – Fass'ich sie bang. Ariadne auf Naxos – Es gibt ein Reich. Arabella – Mein Elemer!. Die ägyptische Helena – Zweite Brautnacht! **Mozart** Lucio Silla – Ah, corri, vola...Quest'improvviso tremito. Don Giovanni – Or sai chi l'onore; Crudele! Ah no, mio bene...Non mi dir. Idomeneo – Idol mio, se ritroso; Oh smania! oh furie!…D'Oreste, d'Aiace
Jane Eaglen *sop* **Israel Philharmonic Orchestra / Zubin Mehta**
Sony Classical SK60042 (65 minutes: DDD) Ⓕ
Texts and translation included. Recorded 1997 ●

The partnership of Eaglen and the Israel Philharmonic under Zubin Mehta is at its strongest in the Richard Strauss tracks of this

Mozart and Strauss compilation. The orchestra's superbly balanced wind soloists create dark shadows for *Guntram*'s Freihild, as she reflects within them, at first perplexed and then, in unflaggingly focused voice, thankful for her love for the Minnesinger – and for the glory of her top B. If Ariadne's distraction is captured rather less convincingly, then the sustained rapture of *Die ägyptische Helena*'s 'Zweite Brautnacht!' draws the full effulgence from Eaglen's golden soprano in what seems to be one breathless sentence. The five Mozart arias here remind us just what a formidable Mozartian Eaglen is, though one longs for a livelier orchestral presence. Eaglen's own skills at pacing and charging with emotion Elektra's passages of accompanied recitative make for real momentum, lit by a bright platinum gleam in the voice in 'Oh smania! ... D'Oreste, d'Aiace'; and her instinctive phrasing gives eloquent voice to Elektra's more demure moments in 'Idol mio'.

Renée Fleming

Der Rosenkavalier[a] – Da geht er hin; Ach, du bist wieder da!; Die Zeit, die ist ein sonderbar Ding; Ich hab ihn nicht einmal geküsst; Marie Theres!...Hab' mir's gelobt; Ist ein Traum. Arabella[b] – Ich danke, Fräulein. Capriccio[c] – Interlude; Wo ist mein Bruder?

Renée Fleming *sop* with [ab]**Barbara Bonney** *sop* [a]**Susan Graham** *mez* [a]**Johannes Chum** *ten* [ac]**Walter Berry** *bass-bar* **Vienna Philharmonic Orchestra / Christoph Eschenbach**

Decca 466 314-2DH (78 minutes: DDD). Texts and translations included. Recorded 1998 Ⓕ OO

This is a happily chosen Strauss showcase for Fleming. Her creamy, full-toned, vibrant voice is about the ideal instrument not only for the Marschallin but also for the other parts she attempts here. She has mastered the phraseology and verbal inflexions needed for all three roles, and imparts to them a quick intelligence to second the vocal glories. Sometimes her performance as the Marschallin or Countess Madeleine recalls, almost uncannily, those of Schwarzkopf, leaving one in no doubt that she has studied the readings of her distinguished predecessor. If Schwarzkopf with a slightly slimmer tone has the finer line and quicker responses, her successor provides the richer tone. Fleming need fear no comparisons with more recent interpreters such as Te Kanawa, Tomowa-Sintow and, as Madeleine only, Janowitz. Indeed, Fleming's account of the closing scene of *Capriccio* is just about ideal. Her deluxe team of co-stars includes Susan Graham, who makes an ardent suitor in *Rosenkavalier*'s Act 1 duets; her timbre is so similar to Fleming's that it's hard to tell them apart, though she is not as verbally acute as her partner. And Barbara Bonney finally commits an extract of her enchanting Sophie, the best since Lucia Popp's; she also joins Fleming in the Arabella-Zdenka duet. Even the cameo appearances of a lackey at the close of Act 1 of *Der Rosenkavalier*, of Faninal after the Act 3 trio, and the major-domo in the closing scene from *Capriccio*, are filled by the veteran Walter Berry. Under Eschenbach, the VPO plays immaculately – the horn solo in the Moonlight music is pure magic – and the sound quality is outstandingly life-like, a typically first-class Michael Haas production. A treat for Straussians.

Elisabeth Meyer-Topsøe

Ariadne auf Naxos – Ein schönes war; Es gibt ein Reich. Arabella – Mein Elemer! **Wagner** Die Walküre – Der Männer Sippe; Du bist der Lenz. Lohengrin – Einsam in trüben Tagen. Tannhäuser – Dich teure Halle; Allmächt'ge Jungfrau. Der fliegende Holländer – Joho hoe!...Traft ihr das Schiff. Tristan und Isolde – Mild und leise

Elisabeth Meyer-Topsøe *sop* **Copenhagen Philharmonic Orchestra / Hans Norbert Bihlmaier**

Kontrapunkt 32249 (60 minutes: DDD) Ⓕ
Texts included. Recorded 1996 OO

There are few, if any, sopranos today who can sing this repertory more securely than Meyer-Topsøe. A pupil of Nilsson, she sings with her teacher's ringing confidence, tone and technique solid and unblemished. It is heartening to hear once more a Scandinavian interpreter of Wagner with such a thrilling sound, one for whom the challenge of Senta, Elsa, Elisabeth and Isolde are as nothing. All that said, there is as yet room in some items for more dramatic involvement. Studio restrictions and/or a somewhat careful conductor may not be a help in that respect. An exception to this stricture is the Liebestod, where Meyer-Topsøe sounds a Nilsson-like touch of transfiguration.

Her Straussian credentials have already been revealed in the *Four Last Songs* . They are amply confirmed here in her Ariadne and Arabella. Here's evidence, most of all in a gloriously outgoing 'Es gibt ein Reich', of identification with a given role. Her Arabella is hardly less engrossing as she ponders on her 'Fremde Mann', the soprano's even, youthful timbre exactly right for the eager yet thoughtful girl. Bihlmaier seems happier in Strauss than in Wagner.

The recording rightly has the singer centre-stage, the exciting voice caught in a natural acoustic. Only German texts are provided, no translations, and it's slight pity that the tracks have not been arranged in chronological order. But, that shouldn't deter connoisseurs of the voice heroic from acquiring this CD.

Julia Varady

Salome – Ach! du wolltest mich nicht deinen Mund küssen lassen. Ariadne auf Naxos – Overture; Ein Schönes war; Es gibt ein Reich. Die Liebe der Danae – Wie umgibst du mich mit Frieden; Interlude, Act 3. Capriccio – Interlude; Wo ist mein Bruder?; Kein andres, das mir so im Herzen loht[a]

Julia Varady *sop* **Bamberg Symphony Orchestra / Dietrich Fischer-Dieskau** [a]*bar*

Orfeo C511991A (62 minutes: DDD) Ⓕ
Recorded 1999 O

After giving choice recitals of Verdi and Wagner, Varady turned her attention to Strauss, and once again the results are for the most part rewarding. The final scene of *Salome*, under the watchful eye of Varady's husband, Fischer-Dieskau, has the perfection of pitch and phrase one expects of this singer, as well as an expected acuity for the meaning of the text. Perhaps, away from the theatre in a part she never undertook on stage, the absolute conviction of such great interpreters as Cebotari, Welitsch and Rysanek is absent, but not by much. The two almost consecutive solos of Ariadne benefit from shapely, poised singing, ever obedient to the score, although occasionally one misses the creamier tones that Lisa della Casa (DG) and Gundula Janowitz (DG video, and EMI) brought to the part. As Danae, Varady seems a shade tentative and vocally out of sorts. There need be no reservations about the final scene of *Capriccio*, in which she catches ideally Countess Madeleine's emotional perplexity as she tries (unsuccessfully) to choose between her poet and musician admirers. Both her identification with the role and her execution of Strauss's operatic farewell to his beloved soprano voice are near-ideal. Fischer-Dieskau, endearingly, sings the short part of the Haushofmeister. However, his conducting, although sensibly paced, sometimes errs on the side of caution. As a whole, this CD nicely complements Fleming's Strauss concert on Decca, the two discs offering a compendium of the composer's writing for the soprano voice he loved so much.

Various Artists

Der Rosenkavalier – Wie du warst! Wie du bist; Da geht er hin ... Ach, du bist wieder da! ... Die Zeit, die ist ein sonderbar Ding; Mir ist die Ehre; Mein Gott, es war nicht mehr ... Heut oder morgen ... Marie Theres'... Hab' mir's gelobt ... Ist ein Traum

Régine Crespin, Elisabeth Söderström, Hilde Gueden *sops* **Heinz Holecek** *bar* **Vienna State Opera Concert Choir; Vienna Philharmonic Orchestra / Silvio Varviso**

Decca 452 730-2DC (62 minutes: ADD) Ⓑ
Recorded 1964 ●●

This, one of the most desirable discs in the whole recorded history of the opera, has led a Cinderella existence since it first appeared 33 years ago. Now invited to the ball, it ought to be accorded status as a princess. Crespin, quite heart-rending as the Marschallin, is in pristine voice. She fills her music with silvery, sensuous tone and at the same time judges every note, every phrase to perfection, whether in the monologue, or the final scenes of Acts 1 and 3. These extracts benefit from having, as Strauss intended, a soprano Octavian – and what a soprano! Söderström's vibrant, impassioned singing is just what the role calls for. Together she and Crespin make the close of Act 1 a thing to savour. Then in the Silver Rose Presentation she is joined by Gueden still able in her late-forties to float Sophie's high-lying phrases as to the manner born, while in the last act Gueden finds just the right sense of embarrassment in the presence of the Marschallin. It is a thousand pitics the opera was not recorded complete, not least because Varviso, as at those Covent Garden performances, is in his absolute element, elegant and ardent, finding an idiomatic Straussian ebb and flow with the VPO on rapturous form, all recorded with Decca's 1960s skill. Christopher Raeburn provides the notes, filling in the plot as best he can in the absence of texts and translations. This is a must.

Arabella

Julia Varady *sop* Arabella; **Helen Donath** *sop* Zdenka; **Dietrich Fischer-Dieskau** *bar* Mandryka; **Walter Berry** *bass* Waldner; **Helga Schmidt** *mez* Adelaide; **Elfriede Höbarth** *sop* Fiakermilli; **Adolf Dallapozza** *ten* Matteo; **Hermann Winkler** *ten* Elemer; **Klaus-Jürgen Küper** *bar* Dominik; **Hermann Becht** *bar* Lamoral; **Doris Soffel** *mez* Fortune Teller; **Arno Lemberg** *spkr* Welko; **Bavarian State Opera Chorus; Bavarian State Orchestra / Wolfgang Sawallisch**

Orfeo ② C169882H (144 minutes: DDD). Notes, text and translation included. Recorded 1981 Ⓕ ●

Complete except for a brief cut in Matteo's part in Act 3, Sawallisch's 1981 Orfeo recording of *Arabella* has been easily fitted on to two CDs. Sawallisch is the most experienced conductor of Strauss's operas alive today and at his best in this one, his tempos exactly right, his appreciation of its flavour (sometimes sentimental, at others gently ironic and detached) unequalled. Helen Donath's delightful Zdenka is a perfect foil for Varady's Arabella. Varady's singing of the title-role is characterful and intelligent. One should be left with ambivalent feelings about this heroine; is she lovable or a chilling opportunist? Or both? And while Fischer-Dieskau's singing of Mandryka has not the total security of his earlier DG recording of the role with Keilberth, he remains the best Mandryka heard since the war.

Ariadne auf Naxos

Dame Elisabeth Schwarzkopf *sop* Ariadne; **Irmgard Seefried** *sop* Composer; **Rita Streich** *sop* Zerbinetta; **Rudolf Schock** *ten* Bacchus; **Karl Dönch** *bar* Music-Master; **Hermann Prey** *bar* Harlequin; **Fritz Ollendorff** *bass* Truffaldino; **Helmut Krebs** *ten* Brighella; **Gerhard Unger** *ten* Scaramuccio; **Lisa Otto** *sop* Naiad; **Grace Hoffman** *mez* Dryad; **Anny Felbermayer** *sop* Echo; **Hugues Cuénod** *ten* Dancing Master; **Alfred Neugebauer** *spkr* Major-Domo; **Philharmonia Orchestra / Herbert von Karajan** **H**

EMI Great Recordings of the Century mono ② CMS5 67077-2 (128 minutes: ADD/mono) Ⓜ
Recorded 1954 ●●●

Karajan's *Ariadne* is perfectly cast, magnificently performed, and very well recorded. The scoring, for a small orchestra, demands virtuoso playing from what, in effect, is a group of soloists: and the members of the Philharmonia Orchestra rise brilliantly to the occasion. There is a warmth and beauty of tone, a sweep of phrase, that gives lively promise of the wonderful playing we hear throughout the opera. Karajan's genius has never been more apparent than in his treatment of the Bacchus-Ariadne scene, in which he makes the score glow with a Dionysiac ardour and in which, at the tremendous climax when Bacchus enters and is greeted by Ariadne as the herald of Death, he gets an ample volume of tone from his players.

Every character is vividly brought to life – Karl Dönch's harassed music master is offset by the cynical dancing master of Hugues Cuénod, and Alfred Neugebauer, in his speaking role, conveys with a superbly calm pomposity his contempt for both sets of artists. The way he enunciates his words is superb. The other small parts, all sung by experienced artists, are wholly in the picture. Rita Streich sings the lyrical phrases of Zerbinetta beautifully. Technical difficulties do not appear to exist for her and all she does is musical. Irmgard Seefried, as the Composer, has less beauty of tone but more variety. The ineffably lovely trio for the Naiad, Dryad and Echo is exquisitely sung by Lisa Otto, Grace Hoffman and Anny Felbermayer, paralleled by the equally beautiful singing of the other trios. They are simply ravishing and, like all the concerted music, have a perfect ensemble. The *commedia dell'arte* characters are all very good, especially Hermann Prey: and their ensembles between themselves and with Zerbinetta are a great delight. After an awkward start, Elisabeth Schwarzkopf, as Ariadne, brings the dark tone that is needed, to Ariadne's sorrows, and gives us much lovely singing thereafter, and also all the rapture called for at the end of her great address to the herald of Death and in her greeting to Bacchus. Rudolf Schock sings the latter with heroic tone and sufficient nuance to make one believe in the youthful god.

The general impression is of a truly magnificent performance and recording in which all concerned have, under Karajan's superb direction, been inspired to give of their best.

Ariadne auf Naxos

Gundula Janowitz *sop* Ariadne; **Teresa Zylis-Gara** *sop* Composer; **Sylvia Geszty** *sop* Zerbinetta; **James King** *ten* Bacchus; **Theo Adam** *bass-bar* Music Master; **Hermann Prey** *bar* Harlequin; **Siegfried Vogel** *bass* Truffaldino; **Hans Joachim Rotzsch** *ten* Brighella; **Peter Schreier** *ten* Scaramuccio, Dancing Master; **Erika Wustmann** *sop* Naiad; **Annelies Burmeister** *mez* Dryad; **Adele Stolte** *sop* Echo; **Erich-Alexander Winds** *spkr* Major-Domo;
Staatskapelle Dresden / Rudolf Kempe
EMI Opera ② CMS7 64159-2 (118 minutes: ADD) Ⓜ
Notes, text and translation included
Recorded 1968 ●●

At mid-price this classic set cannot be recommended too highly. Nobody knew more about how to pace Strauss's operas than Kempe, and he was at his best when working with the Staatskapelle Dresden, a group of players who have Strauss in their veins. This reading brings out all the sentiment and high spirits of this delightful work, and the results are beautifully recorded. Janowitz's golden tones were ideal for the title-role, which she sings with poise and inner feeling, though she makes little of the text. Zylis-Gara is a suitably impetuous Composer in the engaging Prologue where 'he' meets and has a gently erotic encounter with the charming but flighty Zerbinetta, a role here taken with brilliant accomplishment by Sylvia Geszty, who made it her own in the 1960s. James King is a forthright though none too flexible Bacchus. The smaller parts are also well taken.

Capriccio

Elisabeth Schwarzkopf *sop* The Countess; **Eberhard Waechter** *bar* The Count; **Nicolai Gedda** *ten* Flamand; **Dietrich Fischer-Dieskau** *bar* Olivier; **Hans Hotter** *bass-bar* La Roche; **Christa Ludwig** *mez* Clairon; **Ruldolf Christ** *ten* Monsieur Taupe; **Anna Moffo** *sop* Italian Soprano; **Dermot Troy** *ten* Italian Tenor; **Karl Schmitt-Walter** *bar* Major-domo
Philharmonia Orchestra / Wolfgang Sawallisch
EMI Great Recordings of the Century mono
② CMS5 67394-2 (135 minutes: ADD). Notes, Ⓜ
text and translation included. Recorded 1957 ●●●

Not only is *Capriccio* a source of constant and none-too-demanding delight but its performance and recording, especially in this CD reincarnation, are well-nigh faultless. Walter Legge assembled for the recording in 1957 what was almost his house cast, each singer virtually ideal for his or her part. Some might say that no role she recorded suited Schwarzkopf's particular talents more snugly than Countess Madeleine. Her ability to mould words and music into one can be heard here to absolute advantage. Then the charming, flirtatious, sophisticated, slightly artificial character, with the surface attraction hiding deeper feelings revealed in the closing scene (quite beautifully sung), suit her to the life. She, like her colleagues, is superbly adept at the quick repartee so important an element in this work.

As her brother, the light-hearted, libidinous Count, the young Eberhard Waechter is in his element. So are the equally young Nicolai Gedda as the composer Flamand, the Sonnet so gently yet ardently delivered, and Fischer-Dieskau as the more fiery poet Olivier. Christa Ludwig is nicely intimate, conversational and cynical as the actress Clairon, handling her affairs, waning with Olivier, waxing with the Count, expertly. Above all towers the dominating presence of Hotter as the theatre director La Roche, impassioned in his defence of the theatre's conventions, dismissive of new and untried methods, yet himself not above a trivial flirtation – and how delicately Hotter manages his remarks about his latest protegee as she dances for the assembled company.

Even with so many distinguished singers gathered together, it is the closeness of the ensemble, the sense of a real as distinct from a manufactured performance that is so strongly conveyed. And Legge did not neglect the smaller roles: Rudolf Christ makes an endearingly eccentric Monsieur Taupe, the veteran Schmitt-Walter a concerned Major-domo. Anna Moffo and Dermot Troy sing the music of the Italian soprano and tenor with almost too much sensitivity.

Crowning the performance is the musical direction of Wolfgang Sawallisch, always keeping the score on the move, yet fully aware of its sensuous and its witty qualities: Krauss's amusing libretto has much to do with the work's fascination. Both the extended Prelude and the interludes are gloriously played by the vintage Philharmonia Orchestra, who are throughout alert to the old wizard's deft scoring, as refined here as in any of his earlier operas. The recording might possibly have given a little more prominence to the instruments; in every other respect, although it is in mono, it hardly shows its age. This is a jewel in the industry's crown and it will be a source of enduring pleasure to those familiar or unfamiliar with Strauss's inspired swansong. Bravo!

Additional recommendation

Capriccio

Janowitz The Countess; **Fischer-Dieskau** The Count; **Schreier** Flamand; **Prey** Olivier

Bavarian Radio Symphony Orchestra / Bohm

DG ② 445 347-2GX2 (142 minutes: ADD: 11/94) Ⓜ

Karl Böhm's 1971 *Capriccio* stands on a par with the Sawallisch, but is better recorded. It captures the glorious Janowitz voice in its prime. Her lovely Countess Madeleine is supported by portrayals of a comparative stature.

Elektra

Astrid Varnay *sop* Elektra; **Res Fischer** *contr* Klytemnestra; **Leonie Rysanek** *sop* Chrysothemis; **Helmut Melchert** *ten* Aegisthus; **Hans Hotter** *bass-bar* Orestes; **Heiner Horn** *bass* Tutor; **Gertie Charlent** *sop* Confidante; **Helene Petrich** *sop* Trainbearer; **Hasso Eschert** *ten* Young Servant; **Arno Reinhardt** *bass* Old Servant; **Käthe Retzmann** *sop* Overseer; **Ilsa Ihme-Sabisch** *contr* First Maidservant; **Trude Roesler** *mez* Second Maidservant; **Marianne Schröder** *mez* Third Maidservant; **Marlies Siemling** *sop* Fourth Maidservant; **Käthe Möller-Siepermann** *sop* Fifth Maidservant; **Cologne Radio Chorus and Symphony Orchestra / Richard Kraus** Ⓗ

Koch Schwann mono ② 31643-2 (100 minutes: ADD). Notes included Ⓕ

Recorded live in 1953 ●

Hard to realise that in 1953, when this *Elektra* was broadcast from Cologne, no recording of the work existed, probably because it was considered too daring for the public to buy in the required numbers. This version, appearing officially for the first time, would have caused quite a stir had it been issued at the time. Obviously rehearsed with care, it fulfils all the work's exigent demands. It features Varnay at the peak of her career in an *annus mirabilis* for her, when she had been acclaimed at Bayreuth for her Brünnhilde and Isolde. As with those roles, she brings to her interpretation a response perfectly suited to it, adapting her tone to its special needs in terms of nuance and phrase. Her voice, in far better fettle than when she sang the part at the 1964 Salzburg Festival under Karajan, is fully equal to Strauss's inordinate demands: she is a true *Hochdramatische* of a kind hard to find today, even if her tone hardens a little under pressure at the top.

Rysanek, who sang Chrysothemis in London in the early 1950s to arresting effect, was the leading interpreter of the part over many years. Here, in her early prime, her truly Straussian voice soars easily over the orchestra, seeming to take on further sheen the higher she goes. As in all her parts, she gives her whole self to projecting the emotions of the moment. Res Fischer's Klytemnestra is a securely sung, clearly declaimed reading which eschews the histrionics often heard in the part. In a radio studio, she and Varnay turn the mother-daughter confrontation into an intimate conversation with all sorts of undertones. Then there's Hotter, as Orestes, in a heroic role that might have been written for him: his noble utterance and (on this occasion) wholly steady voice impart true stature to this small but important part, his enunciation of the text, as ever, having a Lieder-singer's acuity. Melchert brings variety and an appropriately sharp-edged tone to Aegisthus.

Kraus, who did much sterling work for Cologne Opera and Radio, conducts a precise, finely shaped and well-timed reading, avoiding all excess except that which is implicit in the score. Of course, in this of all operas one misses a more sumptuous recording of the score, but by and large this is a performance that affords the listener with real satisfaction.

Elektra

Birgit Nilsson *sop* Elektra; **Regina Resnik** *mez* Klytemnestra; **Marie Collier** *sop* Chrysothemis; **Gerhard Stolze** *ten* Aegisthus; **Tom Krause** *bar* Orestes; **Pauline Tinsley** *sop* Overseer; **Helen Watts** *contr* **Maureen Lehane, Yvonne Minton** *mezzos* **Jane Cook, Felicia Weathers** *sops* First, Second, Third, Fourth and Fifth Maidservants; **Tugomir Franc** *bass* Tutor; **Vienna Philharmonic Orchestra / Sir Georg Solti**

Decca ② 417 345-2DH2 (108 minutes: ADD). Notes, text and translation included. Recorded 1966-67 Ⓕ ●●●

Elektra is the most consistently inspired of all Strauss's operas and derives from Greek mythology, with the ghost of Agamemnon, so unerringly delineated in the opening bars, hovering over the whole work. The invention and the intensity of mood are sustained throughout the opera's one act length, and the characterisation is both subtle and pointed. It is a work peculiarly well suited to Solti's gifts and it is his best recording in the studios. He successfully maintains the nervous tension throughout the unbroken drama and conveys all the power and tension in Strauss's enormously complex score which is, for once, given complete. The recording captures the excellent singers and the Vienna Philharmonic in a warm, spacious acoustic marred only by some questionable electronic effects. Notwithstanding the latter, this is undoubtedly one of the greatest performances on record and sounds even more terrifyingly realistic on this magnificent transfer.

Elektra H

Inge Borkh *sop* Elektra; **Jean Madeira** *mez* Klytemnestra; **Lisa della Casa** *sop* Chrysothemis; **Max Lorenz** *ten* Aegisthus; **Kurt Böhme** *bass* Orestes; **Alois Pernerstorfer** *bass-bar* Tutor; **Anny Felbermayer** *sop* Confidante; **Karol Loraine** *mez* Trainbearer; **Erich Majkut** *ten* Young Servant; **György Littasy** *bass* Old Servant; **Audrey Gerber** *sop* Overseer; **Kerstin Meyer, Sonja Draksler, Sieglinde Wagner, Marilyn Horne** *mezzos* **Lisa Otto** *sop* First, Second, Third, Fourth and Fifth Maidservants; **Vienna State Opera Chorus; Vienna Philharmonic Orchestra / Dimitri Mitropoulos**

Orfeo mono ② C456972I (107 minutes: ADD) Ⓜ

Recorded live in 1957 **oo**

This is an enthralling performance. Mitropoulos made a speciality of the score, his most important contribution to opera interpretation. Souvenirs exist of his performances at the Met in 1949 and at the Maggio Musicale in Florence in 1950, but his Salzburg reading is the one to have. No other conductor, not even Böhm or Solti in the studio, quite matches the *frisson* of this literally overwhelming account. And it confirms that Inge Borkh is indeed the most comprehensively equipped soprano for the title-role, vocally secure – high C apart – and emotionally capable of fulfilling every demand of the strenuous part. In the great scene with Orestes she first expresses ineffably the sorrow at his supposed death, the 'tausendmal' and 'nie wiederkommt' passage done with such a searing sense of loss; then comes the great release of recognition – sung with immense warmth – followed by another almost silvery voice as Elektra recalls her lost beauty. It is a passage of singing to return to repeatedly for its many insights.

Borkh is hardly less impressive in her psychologically tense tussle with her mother, in her wheedling flattery of her sister when she wants Chrysothemis's aid in killing Klytemnestra, or in the charm offensive to fool Aegisthus where her command of textual detail is so sure. Chrysothemis finds in della Casa an unusual interpreter, wonderfully ecstatic and pure of voice if not as emotionally involving as some. Madeira is a formidable Klytemnestra, her nightmarish thoughts expressed in a firm voice, accurately deployed. Böhme, a real bass, presents an implacable, angry Orestes, not as subtle or as sympathetic as Krause for Solti. Lorenz's fading *Heldentenor* is ideal to express Aegisthus's fatuity. And the maids have never, surely, been cast with such secure voices. Inevitably, cuts are made as is almost always the case in the theatre where, otherwise, Elektra might be left voiceless by the end. If you want the complete score, the famous Solti set will do very nicely. If you want Borkh, you must choose between the Böhm in stereo (DG) or this unique experience.

Die Frau ohne Schatten

Awards 1992

Julia Varady *sop* Empress; **Plácido Domingo** *ten* Emperor; **Hildegard Behrens** *sop* Dyer's Wife; **José van Dam** *bar* Barak the Dyer; **Reinhild Runkel** *contr* Nurse; **Albert Dohmen** *bar* Spirit-Messenger; **Sumi Jo** *sop* Voice of the Falcon; **Robert Gambill** *ten* Apparition of a Young Man; **Elzbieta Ardam** *mez* Voice from above; **Eva Lind** *sop* Guardian of the Threshold; **Gottfried Hornik** *bar* One-eyed Brother; **Hans Franzen** *bass* One-armed Brother; **Wilfried Gahmlich** *ten* Hunchback Brother; **Vienna Boys' Choir; Vienna State Opera Chorus; Vienna Philharmonic Orchestra / Sir Georg Solti**

Decca ③ 436 243-2DHO3 (195 minutes: DDD) Ⓕ

Notes, text and translation included

Recorded 1989-91 **ooo**

This was the most ambitious project on which Strauss and his librettist Hugo von Hofmannsthal collaborated. It is both fairy tale and allegory with a score that is Wagnerian in its scale and breadth. This Solti version presents the score absolutely complete in an opulent recording that encompasses every detail of the work's multi-faceted orchestration. Nothing escapes his keen eye and ear or that of the Decca engineers. The cast boasts splendid exponents of the two soprano roles. Behrens's vocal acting suggests complete identification with the unsatisfied plight of the Dyer's Wife and her singing has a depth of character to compensate for some tonal wear. Varady gives an intense, poignant account of the Empress's taxing music. The others, though never less than adequate, leave something to be desired. Domingo sings the Emperor with vigour and strength but evinces little sense of the music's idiom. José van Dam is likewise a vocally impeccable Barak but never penetrates the Dyer's soul. Runkel is a mean, malign Nurse as she should be, though she could be a little more interesting in this part. It benefits from glorious, dedicated playing by the VPO.

Guntram

Alan Woodrow *ten* Guntram; **Andrea Martin** *bar* The Old Duke; **Elisabeth Wachutka** *sop* Freihild; **Ivan Konsulov** *bar* Robert; **Hans-Peter Scheidegger** *bar* Freihold; **Enrico Facini** *ten* The Duke's Fool; **Thomas Kaluzny** *bar* Messenger, Young Man, Minnesinger; **Jin-Ho Choi** *bar* Old Man, Minnesinger; **Ute Trekel-Burkhardt** *mez* Old Woman; **Manfred Bittner** *ten* Young Man, Minnesinger; **Matthias Heubusch** *voc* Minnesinger; **Werdenfelser Male Chorus; Marchigiana Philharmonic Orchestra / Gustav Kuhn**

Arte Nova Classics ② 74321 61339-2 Ⓢ

(100 minutes: DDD). Text included

Recorded live in 1998

However much influenced by Wagner this, Strauss's first opera, may have been, it already shows Strauss moving off strikingly in his own melodic and harmonic direction. The work contains much attractive, well-crafted music, but from the start it was lamed by the composer's own prolix libretto and by his (at this stage) hesitant dramaturgy. The story of the brave, libertarian knight Guntram's adventures in 13th-century Germany and his love for the heroine Freihild, daughter of the local ruler, whose husband Duke Robert is a sort of villain and opponent of peace, is really one about individual responsibility being more important than religious orthodoxy, something that offended Strauss's strict Catholic mentor, Alexander Ritter. This performance, a live one under the experienced Straussian Gustav Kuhn, gives a very fair idea of its virtues and defects. His direction is vigorous, forward moving, strongly limned with a proper advocacy of the score's more original features, with resplendent playing from his orchestra. Even so, it remains unlikely the piece will be regularly staged when there are so many of Strauss's mature operas waiting to be revived.

The performance is well served by its two principals. In the title-role, the ENO tenor Alan Woodrow, under-used at home, here makes a more-than-passable Heldentenor in the first of many roles for that voice calling for strong, virile, penetrative tone. Woodrow produces just that, plus much of the romantic fervour Guntram's role calls for. Elisabeth Wachutka is reasonably successful as the object of Guntram's desires. Though her tone can be edgy, she rises finely to the challenge of her extended monologue in Act 2. The rest, who don't have much to do, are no more than so-so. The recording is clear and well balanced. At the price, this is worth sampling to hear Strauss's apprentice effort in the operatic field he was so soon to grace with many masterpieces.

Der Rosenkavalier

Der Rosenkavalier (sung in English) – Prelude; Wie du warst! Wie du bist; Da geht er hin…Ach, du bist wieder da!…Die Zeit, die ist ein sonderbar Ding; Ein ernster Tag, ein grosser Tag!; In dieser feierlichen Stunde der Prüfung; Mir ist die Ehre; Da lieg' ich!; Herr Kavalier!; Ist halt vorbei; Mein Gott, es war nicht mehr; Heut oder morgen oder den übernächsten Tag; Marie Theres'…Hab' mir's gelobt; Ist ein Traum
Yvonne Kenny *sop* Marschallin; **Diana Montague** *mez* Octavian; **John Tomlinson** *bass* Baron Ochs; **Rosemary Joshua** *sop* Sophie; **Andrew Shore** *bar* Faninal; **Jennifer Rhys-Davies** *sop* Marianne; **Elizabeth Vaughan** *mez* Annina **Peter Kay Children's Choir; Geoffrey Mitchell Choir; London Philharmonic Orchestra / David Parry**
Chandos Opera in English CHAN3022 Ⓕ
(80 minutes: DDD). Recorded 1998 ○

This is a delightful disc, with a cast of principals that need fear little from comparison with international singers on original-language recordings. One can only regret that Chandos and the Peter Moores Foundation, which so faithfully underwrites this admirable venture, haven't been bold enough to record the whole work. In particular one would like much more of Tomlinson's Ochs, well known from the ENO production. In the close of Act 2 he shows us just how much can be made of the text, using a translation he has sensibly tailored to his own needs, and projects with enormous relish in a role that suits his vocal acting to perfection.

Yvonne Kenny, ENO's much loved Marschallin, sings of the joys and sorrows of love with beautiful tone and shapely phrasing, her voice of an ideal weight for the part. Like Tomlinson she is keen with her words. By her side is Diana Montague's eager, ardent Octavian, the two singers matching each other in evincing strong emotions. With Rosemary Joshua – another singer repeating her ENO role – as a mettlesome Sophie, easing naturally into her high lines, the trio is the climax of Act 3 that it should be. Andrew Shore makes much of little as Faninal. Only Elizabeth Vaughan's harsh, overdone Annina is a drawback. David Parry nicely catches both the serious and comic sides of things, and his pacing of everything but the final scene, which is a shade too hesitant, is admirable. He persuades the LPO to play at the top of its bent for him, so that the score sounds as warm and rich-hued as it should in a typically spacious Chandos recording.

Der Rosenkavalier **H**
Dame Elisabeth Schwarzkopf *sop* Die Feldmarschallin; **Christa Ludwig** *mez* Octavian; **Otto Edelmann** *bass* Baron Ochs; **Teresa Stich-Randall** *sop* Sophie; **Eberhard Waechter** *bar* Faninal; **Nicolai Gedda** *ten* Italian Tenor; **Kerstin Meyer** *contr* Annina; **Paul Kuen** *ten* Valzacchi; **Ljuba Welitsch** *sop* Duenna; **Anny Felbermayer** *sop* Milliner; **Harald Pröghlöf** *bar* Notary; **Franz Bierbach** *bass* Police Commissioner; **Erich Majkut** *ten* Feldmarschallin's Major-domo; **Gerhard Unger** *ten* Faninal's Major-domo, Animal Seller; **Karl Friedrich** *ten* Landlord **Loughton High School for Girls and Bancroft's School Choirs; Philharmonia Chorus and Orchestra / Herbert von Karajan**
EMI ③ CDS5 56242-2 (191 minutes: ADD) Ⓕ
Notes, text and translation included
Recorded 1956 ○○○

Also available on EMI mono ③ CDS5 56113-2 (182 minutes: ADD) Ⓕ

Der Rosenkavalier concerns the transferring of love of the young headstrong aristocrat Octavian from the older Marschallin (with whom he is having an affair) to the young Sophie, a girl of *nouveau riche* origins who is of his generation. The portrayal of the different levels of passion is masterly and the Marschallin's resigned surrender of her ardent young lover gives opera one of its most cherishable scenes. The comic side of the plot concerns the vulgar machinations of the rustic Baron Ochs and his attempts to seduce the disguised Octavian (girl playing boy playing girl!). The musical richness of the score is almost indescribable with stream after stream of endless melody, and the final trio which brings the three soprano roles together is the crowning glory of a masterpiece of the 20th century.

This magnificent recording, conducted with genius by Karajan and with a cast such as dreams are made of, has a status unparalleled and is unlikely to be challenged for many a year. The Philharmonia play like angels and Schwarzkopf as the Marschallin gives one of her greatest performances. The recording, lovingly remastered, is outstanding. In 1956 stereo was new to the commercial recording world and, unwilling to gamble everything on the new medium, producer Water Legge arranged for the sessions to be captured in both mono and stereo, using separate microphone layouts and separate balance engineers. This is the mono recording's first issue on CD and one is immediately struck by the mono recording's warmer, closer balance: Schwarzkopf, for example, a significantly more rounded, fuller and essentially dominant presence, never in danger of being overwhelmed by the orchestra. The detail and transparency of the overall canvas on the stereo recording is more naturally convincing, but the mono will make a special appeal to those who prefer intimate access to these great singers. The dilemma is that each recording is impressive in its way and yet so very different. Students of the voice will almost certainly favour the mono set; devotees of the opera itself may well prefer the stereo.

Der Rosenkavalier

Maria Reining *sop* Die Feldmarschallin; **Sena Jurinac** *sop* Octavian; **Ludwig Weber** *bass* Baron Ochs; **Hilde Gueden** *sop* Sophie; **Alfred Poell** *bar* Faninal; **Anton Dermota** *ten* Italian Tenor; **Hilde Rössl-Majdan** *mez* Annina; **Peter Klein** *ten* Valzacchi; **Judith Hellweg** *sop* Leitmetzerin; **Berta Seidl** *sop* Milliner; **Walter Berry** *bass* Police Commissioner; **Harald Pröglhöf** *bass* Feldmarschallin's Major-domo; **August Jaresch** *ten* Faninal's Major-domo; **Erich Majkut** *ten* Animal Seller, Landlord; **Franz Bierbach** *bass* Notary; **Vienna State Opera Chorus; Vienna Philharmonic Orchestra / Erich Kleiber**

Decca Legends ③ 467 111-2DMO3 Ⓜ

(197 minutes: ADD). Notes, text and translation included. Recorded 1954 **OO**

Decca has done wonders in cleaning the sound on this reissued classic recording. It seems warmer and more spacious than in any of its LP guises. The bloom on the playing of the Vienna Philharmonic is grateful to the ear, and the voices stand ideally in relation to the instruments. That is doubly heartening given the fact that Kleiber's interpretation still stands above that of any of his successors. His innate and deep understanding of the score and his instinctive feeling for this area of the Viennese idiom remain unsurpassed; so does his convincing treatment of the score's weaker pages (it is here given complete). Above all, Kleiber never makes the mistake of lingering too long over the work's purple passage, nor does he overheat its more active ones: the key to his reading is a combination of lightness, line and incandescence – try the opening of Act 2.

The vocal glory of the set remains Sena Jurinac's Octavian. Here in more refulgent voice perhaps than anywhere else on disc, she gives the performance of one's dreams. How gleaming yet how warm is her voice, how naturally impetuous and intense her colloquies with her elders. Jurinac carefully denotes Octavian's growing fascination with Sophie. Then, as the maudlin Mariandl of Act 3, she changes her tone subtly, never exaggerating. Finally, her voice soars gloriously in the trio and duet that crown the work. It is without question a definitive interpretation, and will surely remain so.

Maria Reining's Marschallin has been badly underrated. Her approach is natural, stylish and very moving in its simplicity – and its obedience to the score. Not a trace of self-consciousness or arch phrasing spoils the patent honesty of her portrayal. The voice itself sounds a little tremulous at the start, and it never quite gains the warmth other Marschallins achieve, but the unmannered yet absolutely idiomatic enunciation of the text is compensation enough, and her partnership with Jurinac's Octavian is often memorable. Hilde Gueden's singing may be a shade sophisticated for Sophie (and she shouldn't show dislike for Ochs before she has met him), but the accuracy and firm focus of her singing count for much. Ludwig Weber's Ochs is a ripe, assured assumption sung with total command of the text and in an authentic Viennese accent. All the singers are versed in that essential command of Strauss's *parlando* style, so that Hofmannsthal's racy, keenly fashioned libretto is given wit and point. Although the admiration for Karajan remains undiminished, Kleiber is the performance to take to your desert island.

Additional recommendation

Der Rosenkavalier

Crespin Marschallin **Minton** Octavian **Jungwirth** Ochs **Donath** Sophie **Vienna Philharmonic Orchestra / Solti**

Decca 417 493-2DH3 (200 minutes: DDD: 3/87) Ⓕ

For those craving good sound and a reading of great charm – Crespin's rather Gallic Marschallin is wondrously sung – Solti's 1968 set is worth considering. Many collectors rate this even more highly than the classic Karajan set.

Salome

Cheryl Studer *sop* Salome; **Bryn Terfel** *bar* Jokanaan; **Horst Hiestermann** *ten* Herod; **Leonie Rysanek** *sop* Herodias; **Clemens Bieber** *ten* Narraboth; **Marianne Rørholm** *contr* Page; **Friedrich Molsberger** *bass* First Nazarene; **Ralf Lukas** *bass* Second Nazarene; **William Murray** *bass* First Soldier; **Bengt Rundgren** *bass* Second Soldier; **Klaus Lang** *bar* Cappadocian; **Orchestra of the Deutsche Oper, Berlin / Giuseppe Sinopoli**

DG ② 431 810-2GH2 (102 minutes: DDD). Notes, text and translation included. Recorded 1990 Ⓕ **OO**

Strauss's setting of a German translation of Oscar Wilde's play is original and erotically explicit. It caused a sensation in its day and even now stimulates controversy. Sinopoli's recording is a magnificent achievement, mainly because of Cheryl Studer's representation of the spoilt Princess who demands and eventually gets the head of Jokanaan (John the Baptist) on a platter as a reward for her striptease ('Dance of the Seven Veils'). Studer, her voice fresh, vibrant and sensuous, conveys exactly Salome's growing fascination, infatuation and eventual obsession with Jokanaan, which ends in the arresting necrophilia of the final scene. She expresses Salome's wheedling, spoilt nature, strong will and ecstasy in tones that are apt for every aspect of the strenuous role.

She is supported to the hilt by Sinopoli's incandescent conducting and by Bryn Terfel's convincing Jokanaan, unflaggingly delivered, by Hiestermann's neurotic Herod, who makes a suitably fevered, unhinged sound as the near-crazed Herod, and Rysanek's wilful Herodias. The playing is excellent and the recording has breadth and warmth. This is eminently recommendable. For a newcomer to the work, Studer's superb portrayal may just tip the balance in favour of Sinopoli, though Sir Georg Solti's famous version is in a class of its own, with a gloriously sung Salome and the ravishingly beautiful playing of the Vienna Philharmonic.

Salome
Leonie Rysanek sop Salome; **Eberhard Waechter** bar Jokanaan; **Hans Hopf** ten Herod; **Grace Hoffman** mez Herodias; **Waldemar Kmentt** ten Narraboth; **Rohangiz Yachmi** mez Page; **Peter Wimberger** bass-bar First Nazarene; **Siegfried Rudolf Frese** bass Second Nazarene; **Tugomir Franc** bass First Soldier; **Frederick Guthrie** bass Second Soldier; **Reid Bunger** bar Cappadocian; **Ewald Aichberger** ten Slave; **Vienna State Opera Orchestra / Karl Böhm**
RCA Red Seal ② 74321 69430-2 (98 minutes: ADD) Ⓜ Recorded live 1972 ●

Recordings released from Austrian Radio archives of performances in the period after the State Opera's re-opening in 1955 confirm what a golden era it was. The most arresting, indeed utterly thrilling, set is the 1972 *Salome*, lauded to the skies at the time for its musical virtues and, for the most part, for its Klimt-inspired staging. Rysanek, in pristine voice, sings the Salome of one's dreams. With a Wagner-sized voice but also one capable of refined *pianissimos*, she rises to every vocal challenge with ease, confidence and consummate intelligence. Her interpretation catches both the wilfulness and lasciviousness of the teenage princess, reaching a climax in every sense for the opera's final scene, which Rysanek sings as a sustained, rapturous love song in that intense, sensual, sensuous manner that was her trademark. At the same time she treats the text as to the manner born. Inspired by the live occasion and by her conductor (one of her greatest admirers), she gives her all in an account of the role that puts just about everyone else, Ljuba Welitsch apart, in the shade.

Underlining and supporting Rysanek's reading, drawing at once chamber-music refinement and ecstatic colours from the Vienna Philharmonic, Böhm fulfils every aspect of the score, making it sound as revolutionary in style as it must have seemed at its première. All this is caught in a much more natural acoustic than the larger-than-life sound on Decca's two recordings and the Chandos. Waechter repeats his Jokanaan from the Decca/Solti version, but here he is in more electrifying form. So is Kmentt as Narraboth. Hopf has all the notes for Herod, even though his singing is sometimes clumsy, and Hoffman is a rough-hewn Herodias, but notwithstanding their relative inadequacies this recording is urgently recommended to anyone who likes real music-theatre.

Salome
Birgit Nilsson sop Salome; **Eberhard Waechter** bar Jokanaan; **Gerhard Stolze** ten Herod; **Grace Hoffman** mez Herodias; **Waldemar Kmentt** ten Narraboth; **Josephine Veasey** mez Page; **Tom Krause** bar First Nazarene; **Nigel Douglas** ten Second Nazarene; **Zenon Koznowski** bass First Soldier; **Heinz Holecek** bass Second Soldier; **Theodore Kirschbichler** bass Cappadocian; **Vienna Philharmonic Orchestra / Sir Georg Solti**
Decca ② 414 414-2DH2 (99 minutes: ADD). Notes, text and translation included. Recorded 1961 Ⓕ ●●●

Solti's *Salome* was one of Decca's notable Sonic-stage successes and still beats most of its competitors in terms of sound alone. There is a real sense here of a theatrical performance, as directed by John Culshaw, with an imaginative use of movement. Of course, the vivid, nervous energy of Strauss has always been Solti's territory, and this is an overwhelming account of Strauss's sensual piece, sometimes a little too hard-hitting for its or our good: there are places where the tension might be relaxed just a shade, but throughout, the VPO answers Solti's extreme demands with its most aristocratic playing. With only a single break, the sense of mounting fever is felt all the more. Birgit Nilsson's account of the title-role is another towering monument to her tireless singing. Here, more even than as Brünnhilde, one notices just how she could fine away her tone to a sweet and fully supported *pianissimo*, and her whole interpretation wants nothing of the erotic suggestiveness of sopranos more familiar with the role on stage.

Gerhard Stolze's Herod is properly wheedling, worried and, in the final resort, crazed, but there are times, particularly towards the end of his contribution, when exaggeration takes over from characterisation. Other interpretations show how effects can be created without distortion of the vocal line. Eberhard Waechter is an aggressive rather than a visionary Jokanaan. Grace Hoffman is a suitably gloating Herodias. Much better than any of these, Nilsson apart, is Waldemar Kmentt's wonderfully ardent Narraboth. Hardly any of the rivals since 1961 has managed a true challenge to this simply outstanding recording.

Salome

Inga Nielsen *sop* Salome; **Robert Hale** *bass-bar* Jokanaan; **Reiner Goldberg** *ten* Herod; **Anja Silja** *sop* Herodias; **Deon van der Walt** *ten* Narraboth; **Marianne Rørholm** *contr* Page; **Bent Norup** *bar* First Nazarene; **Morten Frank Larsen** *bar* Second Nazarene; **Per Høyer** *bar* First Soldier; **Stephen Milling** *bass* Second Soldier; **Anders Jokobsson** *bass* Cappadocian; **Henriette Bonde Hansen** *sop* Slave; **Danish National Radio Symphony Orchestra / Michael Schønwandt**

Chandos ② CHAN9611 (99 minutes: DDD) Ⓕ
Notes, text and translation included
Recorded 1998

Inga Nielsen is a Salome of quite exceptional talent, even inspiration. Better than any of her predecessors she creates a princess who sounds credibly teenaged with surely just the pearl-like yet needle-sharp tone Strauss intended. Nobody has so convincingly conveyed the impression of a spoilt, petulant innocent with the will and determination to get her way – and then exploited her manipulative character to frightening effect as, sexually awakened, Salome becomes obsessed with the body of Jokanaan. In a performance that is vocally stunning from Salome's first entrance, Nielsen fashions her reading with supreme intelligence in her response to words and notes. Throughout she sings keenly, even maliciously off the text. While still having nothing but praise for Studer's beautifully sung portrayal on the Sinopoli set – her tone is more refulgent, less narrow than Nielsen's but she is not so much inside the role – or for Nilsson's vocally overwhelming portrayal for Solti, Nielsen simply seems a Salome by nature, made for the part.

Happily Nielsen's riveting interpretation receives suitable support. Schønwandt yields to none of his illustrious predecessors in impressing on us the still-extraordinary originality, fascination and tense horror of Strauss's score. From start to finish, including an electrifying account of the Dance, his is a fierily direct, highly charged yet never vulgar reading. Hale, who has partnered Nielsen in this work at the Brussels Opera, is a noble-sounding, resolute Jokanaan of long experience. Although he doesn't attempt the larger-than-life, tremendous performance of Terfel for Sinopoli, and his tone is not as steady, his reading is surely more of a piece with the opera as a whole. Goldberg is just right as the degraded, superstitious, lecherous Herod, vocally astute and characterful. Silja is a well-routined, if sometimes over-the-top Herodias. The smaller roles are particularly well sung too.

Chandos provides a recording of extraordinary range and breadth, yet one that makes sure that the singers take stage front. Anyone who already has the highly regarded Sinopoli version will probably not feel the need to invest in this new set, but we would urge newcomers to hear it. Even though other elements are well taken care of on earlier versions, Nielsen is really unmissable.

Die schweigsame Frau

Kurt Böhme *bass* Sir Morosus; **Martha Mödl** *mez* Housekeeper; **Barry McDaniel** *bar* Barber; **Donald Grobe** *ten* Henry Morosus; **Reri Grist** *sop* Aminta; **Lotte Schädle** *sop* Isotta; **Glenys Loulis** *mez* Carlotta; **Albrecht Peter** *bar* Morbio; **Benno Kusche** *bar* Vanuzzi; **Max Proebstl** *bass* Farfallo; **Bavarian State Opera Chorus and Orchestra / Wolfgang Sawallisch**

Orfeo d'or ② C516992I (126 minutes: ADD) Ⓕ
Recorded at a broadcast performance in 1971

That ardent and devoted Straussian, William Mann, slated this production (in *Opera*) when he saw it at its première in Munich in 1971 because the score was 'cut to ribbons', declaring that it was therefore, in Strauss's home city, 'a national disgrace'. Notwithstanding this objection, all the liveliness and spirit of the Munich event is conveyed in this recording from the archives of Bavarian Radio to the extent that you hear a lot of stage noises. Sawallisch wholly enters into the spirit of the Ben Jonson comedy as adapted for his libretto by Stefan Zweig. The cast, excellent all round, easily get their collective tongues around the profusion of words. Kurt Böhme, near the end of his long career, is, as he was in the flesh, a magnificently rotund Morosus, with real 'face' in his singing and possessing all the bass notes that Hotter (DG) and Adam (on the absolutely complete EMI version) don't quite possess, being bass-baritones. The then-young American singers, all of whom spent most of their careers in Germany, cast as Aminta, Henry and the Barber, all possess good German. Grist is a delightfully fresh and pleasing Aminta and Barry McDaniel an inventive Barber, though his rivals on the other sets are even better. As Henry, Grobe isn't quite the equal of Wunderlich – who can be? Mödl enjoys herself hugely as the Housekeeper.

Sawallisch, in 1971 newly appointed Music Director in Munich and destined to do so much there for the cause of Strauss, manages to keep clear all the many strands in Strauss's score; so do Böhm and Janowski. This version, in stereo, has that advantage over the DG, but the singing on the latter is, by a small margin, superior. If you want every note you must have Janowski – three CDs, but at mid-price.

Further listening

Daphne

Gueden Daphne **King** Apollo **Schoeffler** Peneios **Wunderlich** Leukippos
Vienna State Opera Chorus; Vienna Symphony Orchestra / Bohm

DG ② 445 322-2GX2 (94 minutes: ADD: 11/94) Ⓜ
Live recording

Daphne is not perhaps as involving as Strauss's later operas, but it contains some typically beautiful writing for the soprano voice in the title-role. A fine performance.

Die Liebe der Danae

Kupper Danae **Schöffler** Jupiter **Traxel** Mercury Ⓗ
Vienna State Opera Chorus, Vienna Philharmonic Orchestra / Clemens Krauss

Orfeo mono ③ C292923D (164 minutes: ADD: 5/00). Ⓕ
Live recording from the Salzburg Festival

Despite a number of pages in Strauss's most appealing, late autumnal vein, this is a deeply flawed work, not least because of the wordy and rather empty libretto. For Strauss completists, though, this 1952 recording is the one to have.

Friedenstag
Weikl Commandant **Hass** Maria **Ryhänen** Sergeant
Bavarian State Opera Chorus and Orchestra / Sawallisch
EMI CDC5 56850-2 (77 minutes: DDD: 9/99) Ⓕ

Friedenstag may not be one of Strauss's most inspired creations but this splendidly committed performance – recorded live in 1988 – offers excellent advocacy for it.

Igor Stravinsky

Russian/French/American 1882-1971

GROVE *Stravinsky was the son of a leading bass at the Mariinsky Theatre in St Petersburg, he studied with Rimsky-Korsakov (1902-8), who was an influence on his early music, though so were Tchaikovsky, Borodin, Glazunov and (from 1907-8) Debussy and Dukas. This colourful mixture of sources lies behind The Firebird (1910), commissioned by Dyagilev for his Ballets Russes. Stravinsky went with the company to Paris in 1910 and spent much of his time in France from then onwards, continuing his association with Dyagilev in Petrushka (1911) and The Rite of Spring (1913).*

These scores show an extraordinary development. Both use folktunes, but not in any symphonic manner: Stravinsky's forms are additive rather than symphonic, created from placing blocks of material together without disguising the joins. The binding energy is much more rhythmic than harmonic, and the driving pulsations of The Rite marked a crucial change in the nature of Western music. Stravinsky, however, left it to others to use that change in the most obvious manner. He himself, after completing his Chinese opera The Nightingale, turned aside from large resources to concentrate on chamber forces and the piano.

Partly this was a result of World War I, which disrupted the activities of the Ballets Russes and caused Stravinsky to seek refuge in Switzerland. He was not to return to Russia until 1962, though his works of 1914-18 are almost exclusively concerned with Russian folk tales and songs: they include the choral ballet Les noces ('The Wedding'), the smaller sung and danced fable Renard, a short play doubly formalized with spoken narration and instrumental music (The Soldier's Tale) and several groups of songs. In The Wedding, where block form is geared to highly mechanical rhythm to give an objective ceremonial effect, it took him some while to find an appropriately objective instrumentation; he eventually set it with pianos and percussion. Meanwhile, for the revived Ballets Russes, he produced a startling transformation of 18th-century Italian music (ascribed to Pergolesi) in Pulcinella (1920), which opened the way to a long period of 'neo-classicism', or re-exploring past forms, styles and gestures with the irony of non-developmental material being placed in developmental moulds. The Symphonies of Wind Instruments, an apotheosis of the wartime 'Russian' style, was thus followed by the short number-opera Mavra, the Octet for wind, and three works he wrote to help him earn his living as a pianist: the Piano Concerto, the Sonata and the Serenade in A.

During this period of the early 1920s he avoided string instruments because of their expressive nuances, preferring the clear articulation of wind, percussion, piano and even pianola. But he returned to the full orchestra to achieve the starkly presented Handel-Verdi imagery of the opera-oratorio Oedipus rex, and then wrote for strings alone in Apollon musagète (1928), the last of his works to be presented by Dyagilev. All this while he was living in France, and Apollon, with its Lullian echoes, suggests an identification with French classicism which also marks the Duo concertant for violin and piano and the stage work on which he collaborated with Gide: Perséphone, a classical rite of spring. However, his Russianness remained deep. He orchestrated pieces by Tchaikovsky, now established as his chosen ancestor, to make the ballet Le baiser de la fée, and in 1926 he rejoined the Orthodox Church. The Symphony of Psalms was the first major work in which his ritual music engaged with the Christian tradition.

The other important works of the 1930s, apart from Perséphone, are all instrumental, and include the Violin Concerto, the Concerto for two pianos, the post-Brandenburg 'Dumbarton Oaks' Concerto and the Symphony in C, which disrupts diatonic normality on its home ground. It was during the composition of this work, in 1939, that Stravinsky moved to the USA, followed by Vera Sudeikina, whom he had loved since 1921 and who was to be his second wife (his first wife and his mother had both died earlier the same year). In 1940 they settled in Hollywood, which was henceforth their home. Various film projects ensued, though all foundered, perhaps inevitably: the Hollywood cinema of the period demanded grand continuity; Stravinsky's patterned discontinuities were much better suited to dancing. He had a more suitable collaborator in Balanchine, with whom he had worked since Apollon, and for whom in America he composed Orpheus and Agon. Meanwhile music intended for films went into orchestral pieces, including the Symphony in Three Movements (1945).

The later 1940s were devoted to The Rake's Progress, a parable using the conventions of Mozart's mature comedies and composed to a libretto by Auden and Kallman. Early in its composition, in 1948, Stravinsky met Robert Craft, who soon became a member of his household and whose enthusiasm for Schoenberg and Webern (as well as Stravinsky) probably helped make possible the gradual achievement of a highly personal serial style after The Rake. The process was completed in 1953 during the composition of the brilliant, tightly patterned Agon, though most of the serial works are religious or commemorative, being sacred cantatas (Canticum sacrum, Threni, Requiem Canticles) or elegies (In memoriam Dylan Thomas, Elegy for J. F. K.). All these were written after Stravinsky's 70th birthday, and he continued to compose into his mid-80s, also conducting concerts and making many gramophone records of his music. During this period, too, he and Craft published several volumes of conversations.

The Complete Stravinsky Edition

The Complete Edition, Volume 1 **H**
The Firebird[a]. Scherzo à la russe[a]. Scherzo fantastique[b]. Fireworks[a]. Petrushka[a]. The Rite of Spring[a]. Renard[c]. L'histoire du soldat – Suite[c]. Les noces[d]
Mildred Allen *sop* **Regina Sarfaty** *mez* **Loren Driscoll, George Shirley** *tens* **William Murphy** *bar* **Richard Oliver, Donald Gramm** *basses* **Toni Koves** *cimbalom* **Samuel Barber, Aaron Copland, Lukas Foss, Roger Sessions** *pfs* **[d]American Concert Choir; [d]Columbia Percussion Ensemble; [a]Columbia Symphony Orchestra; [b]CBC Symphony Orchestra; [c]Columbia Chamber Ensemble / Igor Stravinsky**
Sony Classical ③ SM3K46291 (194 minutes: ADD) Ⓜ
Recorded 1959-63

This set contains virtually all the music from Stravinsky's 'Russian' period, including the three great ballets. It is fascinating to chart his development from the 1908 *Scherzo fantastique* with its orchestral colours scintillating in the best Rimsky-Korsakovian manner, to the wholly original language of *Les noces* with its almost exclusively metrical patterns and monochrome scoring (soloists, chorus, pianos and percussion) begun only six years later. The links are there: witness the Rimskian bumble-bee that flies through the *Scherzo* to find its winged counterpart two years on in *The Firebird*; and the primitive rhythmic force of Kastchei's 'Infernal dance' in *The Firebird* finding its fullest expression, another three years later, in *The Rite of Spring*; and so on. Each work is a logical, if time-lapse progression from the previous one. Like *Les noces*, the animal rites of the farmyard opera-cum-burlesque *Renard* (1916) and *L'histoire du soldat* (1918), a morality play designed for a small touring theatre company (the Suite included here omits the speaking roles) leave behind the lavish orchestra of *The Rite* for small and unusual instrumental and vocal combinations.

To have the composer at the helm, and a consistent approach to the way the music is recorded, ensures that those links are clearly established. The orchestra that takes the lion's share of the task, the Columbia Symphony, was assembled by CBS to include many of the finest players in America. One could criticise the recordings for close balances and spotlighting, but many modern contenders will more often than not deprive you of adequate articulation of the music's linear and rhythmic ingenuity. On the whole these recordings reproduce with good tone, range, openness and presence. As to Stravinsky the conductor, only *Les noces* finds him at less than his usual rhythmically incisive self. This *Petrushka* is more representative: it pulsates with inner life and vitality – incidentally, he uses his leaner, clearer 1947 revision, not the original 1911 score as the booklet claims.

The Complete Edition, Volume 2
Apollo[a]. Agon[b]. Jeu de cartes[c]. Scènes de ballet[d]. Bluebird – Pas de deux[a]. Le baiser de la fée[a]. Pulcinella[a]. Orpheus[e]
Irene Jordan *sop* **George Shirley** *ten* **Donald Gramm** *bass* **[a]Columbia Symphony Orchestra; [b]Los Angeles Festival Symphony Orchestra; [c]Cleveland Orchestra; [d]CBC Symphony Orchestra; [e]Chicago Symphony Orchestra / Igor Stravinsky**
Sony Classical ③ SM3K46292 (210 minutes: ADD) Ⓜ
Recorded 1963-65

Volume 2 comprises ballets written between 1919 and 1957. *Pulcinella* was based on music originally thought to have been written by Pergolesi, but now known to be the work of various 18th-century composers. In 1919 Stravinsky had not long embraced neo-classical style, but here was a brilliant example of old wine in new bottles, with the melodies sounding as if they come from the pen of Stravinsky himself. The composer conducts a lively, sharply-accented account of the score. 1928 saw the production of two Stravinsky ballets. *Apollo*, a mainly quiet, contemplative score, written for string orchestra, has many passages of great beauty. Stravinsky the conductor does not linger over these but allows the work's cool classical elegance to speak for itself. In *Le baiser de la fée* Stravinsky used themes by Tchaikovsky as the basis for his score. Once again, the music seems quite transformed, and the result is a most captivating work. Stravinsky's watchful, affectionate performance is perfectly proportioned. His arrangement of the 'Pas de deux' from Tchaikovsky's *Sleeping Beauty* is no more than a reduction for small pit orchestra, however, and a mere curiosity. In *Jeu de cartes*, which dates from 1936, Stravinsky used music by Rossini and others, but here the references are only fleeting and merely enhance the humour of this robust, outgoing score. His performance brings out all the work's vigour and personality very effectively, but here and there rhythms become slightly unstuck, and a slightly hectic quality manifests itself.

Scènes de ballet was written in 1944 and possesses a slightly terse quality in the main, though there are some more lyrical passages. Stravinsky does nothing to soften the work's edges in his performance, and it emerges as a strong, highly impressive piece. *Orpheus* was completed in 1947 and shows Stravinsky's neo-classical style at its most highly developed. Much of the music is quiet, after the manner of *Apollo*, but then the orchestra suddenly erupts into a passage of quite savage violence. Stravinsky conducts this passage with amazing energy for a man in his eighties, and elsewhere his performance has characteristic clarity and a very direct means of expression typical of a composer performance. Finally *Agon*, written in 1957, attracts the listener with its colourful opening fanfares and then pursues an increasingly complex serial path in such a brilliant and highly rhythmical fashion that one is hardly aware that the technique is being used. This work, brilliantly conducted by Stravinsky, is an ideal introduction to his late style and to the serial technique itself. Remastering has been carried out with the greatest skill, and all the recordings in this set sound very well indeed for their age.

The Complete Edition, Volume 4
Symphonies – No 1 in E flat[a]. Stravinsky in rehearsal. Stravinsky in his own words. Symphony in Three Movements[b]. Symphony in C[c]. Symphony of Psalms[d]
Toronto Festival Singers; [ad]Columbia Symphony Orchestra; [b]Columbia Symphony Orchestra; [c]CBC Symphony Orchestra / Igor Stravinsky
Sony Classical ② SM2K46294 (143 minutes: ADD) Ⓜ
Recorded 1961-66

The word 'symphony' appears in the title of each work on these two discs, but this term covers some very diverse material. Stravinsky was in his mid-twenties when he wrote his Symphony in E flat, and the score is very much in the style of his teacher Rimsky-Korsakov. It has genuine colour and flair, however, and the octogenarian conductor brings paternalistic affection and a good deal of vigour to his performance. The *Symphony in C* dates from 1940, when Stravinsky was in his neo-classical phase. The work has many beautiful pages, as well as much pungent wit. In this performance Stravinsky drives the music much harder than he did in his 1952 mono recording with the Cleveland Orchestra, and although there are some exciting moments the music does tend to lose its elements of grace and charm.

The performance of the *Symphony in Three Movements* is also characterised by the use of fastish tempos. But this violent work, written in 1945, and inspired by events in the Second World War, responds more readily to a strongly driven interpretation. Stravinsky wrote his *Symphony of Psalms* in 1930, and this composition reflects his deep religious convictions in varied settings from the Book of Psalms. His use of a chorus is interestingly combined with an orchestra which lacks upper strings. Stravinsky conducts a fervent, serious, beautifully balanced performance.

All the 1960s recordings in this set sound very well in their CD transfers. In some quarters the elderly Stravinsky has been wrongly portrayed as a frail, inadequate figure who only took over performances when works had been thoroughly rehearsed for him. Nothing could prove more clearly that this was not true than the rehearsal excerpts in this set, which show a vigorous, alert octogenarian very much in control of proceedings, and rehearsing passages in some detail.

Violin Concerto

Stravinsky Violin Concerto in D[a] **Lutosławski** Partita for Violin, Orchestra and Obbligato Solo Piano (1985)[b]. Chain 2 (1984)[b]
Anne-Sophie Mutter *vn* **Phillip Moll** *pf*
[a]Philharmonia Orchestra / Paul Sacher; [b]BBC Symphony Orchestra / Witold Lutosławski
DG 423 696-2GH) Ⓕ
(56 minutes: DDD ●●

This disc contains some spellbinding violin playing in a splendidly lifelike recording, and it's a bonus that the music, while unquestionably 'modern', needs no special pleading: its appeal is instantaneous and long-lasting. Mutter demonstrates that she can equal the best in a modern classic – the Stravinsky Concerto – and also act as an ideal, committed advocate for newer works not previously recorded. The Stravinsky is one of his liveliest neo-classical pieces, though to employ that label is, as usual, to underline its rough-and-ready relevance to a style that uses Bach as a springboard for an entirely individual and unambiguously modern idiom. Nor is it all 'sewing-machine' rhythms and pungently orchestrated dissonances. There is lyricism, charm and above all humour: and no change of mood is too fleeting to escape the razor-sharp responses of this soloist and her alert accompanists, authoritatively guided by the veteran Paul Sacher. Lutosławski's music has strongly individual qualities that have made him perhaps one of the most approachable of all contemporary composers. This is an enthralling collaboration between senior composer and youthful virtuoso and should not be missed.

Agon

Stravinsky Circus Polka. Ode. Scherzo à la Russe. Scènes de ballet. Concertino. Agon. Greeting Prelude 'Happy Birthday to You'. Canon on a Russian Popular Tune. Variations 'Aldous Huxley in memoriam'
Stafford Smith/Key (arr Stravinsky)
The Star-Spangled Banner
London Symphony Orchestra / Michael Tilson Thomas
RCA Red Seal 09026 68865-2 (76 minutes: DDD) Ⓕ
Recorded 1996 ●●

This CD has been absorbingly programmed to chart the progress from Stravinsky's early years in America, awkwardly coming to terms with a new language, a new and rather harsh economic climate and a musical public that welcomed him warmly enough but was at the same time welcoming scores of other refugee musicians. Acutely conscious of money and the absence of it, he attempted in vain to obtain film music commissions from Hollywood and tried to write pop songs and to make money in the relatively prosperous world of jazz. But the *Scherzo à la Russe*, originally for jazz band (played here in its orchestral version), sounds like a rejected movement from *Petrushka*. Rather more shrewdly he wrote the *Scènes de ballet* for a Broadway revue and was rewarded with a respectable run of performances. The *Concertino*, written for string quartet long before Stravinsky's arrival in America, arranged there for a chamber orchestra of 12 instruments, is a neat demonstration of how much of his late style was already present in his earlier work. The proto-serial *Agon* and the super-serial *Variations* both represent Stravinsky's relief and sheer exuberance, not so much at finding serialism as at realising that he had been writing quasi-serially all his life and that he could exploit its techniques while remaining himself.

What makes this hugely entertaining as well as instructive is the infectious zest of the performances. The enjoyable racket of the *Circus Polka*, the gorgeous trumpet tune in *Scènes de ballet*, the delight in inventing entrancing new sonorities that is central to *Agon*, the more arcane but none the less obvious pleasure in the *Aldous Huxley* Variations of constructing perfect, crystalline mechanisms – all these are conveyed with exemplary precision. The recordings are brilliant.

Apollon musagète

Apollon musagète (1947 version). The Firebird – Suite. Scherzo fantastique, Op 3
**Royal Concertgebouw Orchestra /
Riccardo Chailly**
Decca 458 142-2DH (71 minutes: DDD)   Ⓕ
Recorded 1994-95

The fact that Stravinsky's revision dispensed with 'half the woodwind, two of the three harps, glockenspiel and celesta from the original scoring' (to quote the excellent insert-note) hardly constitutes the bleaching process that a less colour-sensitive performance might have allowed. Part of the effect is due to a remarkably fine recording where clarity and tonal bloom are complementary, but Chailly must take the credit for laying *all* Stravinsky's cards on the table rather than holding this or that detail to his chest. Everything tells, much as it does in the *Scherzo fantastique* – whether the euphonious winds and brass at 3'52", the motorised repeated notes later on (at 8'31") or the ornamental swirlings that, in stylistic terms, dance us all the way from Rimsky's Arabian Nights to the unmistakably Russian world of *The Firebird*. *Apollon musagète* is of course something else again, and Chailly takes the lyrical line, pointing without punching and allowing his excellent strings their head. The coda is jaunty, the 'Apothéose' suitably mysterious, and 'Variation d'Apollon' features fine solo work from the orchestra's leader, Jaap van Zweden. Viable alternatives include leaner, more ascetic readings, but Chailly balances gracefulness with tonal substance and the sound is glorious.

Le baiser de la fée

Le baiser de la fée. Faun and Shepherdess, Op 2. Ode
Lucy Shelton *sop* **Cleveland Orchestra /
Oliver Knussen**
DG 449 205-2GH (64 minutes: DDD). Text and   Ⓕ
translation included. Recorded 1995-96   ○○

Oliver Knussen offers us the best-played, best-recorded and most sensitively interpreted account of *Le baiser de la fée* that we have had so far on CD, with meticulous attention to Stravinsky's dynamic markings and delicate instrumental pointing. Stravinsky's subtle Tchaikovsky orchestrations (the musical 'grid' of *Le baiser*) inspire a reading that exhibits delicate sensibilities and quick reflexes, and

Knussen's fill-ups respond equally well to those same qualities. The mildly erotic *Faun and Shepherdess* is seductively played, with soprano Lucy Shelton sounding agile and vocally appealing. The tripartite *Ode* is a quietly eventful memorial for Natalie Koussevitzky. Even Stravinsky's own 1965 Columbia Symphony Orchestra recording, although full of lovely things and of great historical interest, is outclassed here.

Le baiser de la fée[a]. Symphony in C[b]. Pulcinella[c].   Ⓗ
L'histoire du soldat – Suite[d]. Octet[e]
[c]**Mary Simmons** *mez* [c]**Glenn Schnittke** *ten* [c]**Philip
MacGregor** *bass* [abc]**Cleveland Orchestra,**
[de]**Chamber Ensemble / Igor Stravinsky**
Sony Classical Masterworks Heritage mono ②
MH2K63325 (155 minutes: ADD)   Ⓜ
Recorded 1952-55   ○

This two-CD set calls itself 'The Mono Years 1952-55' to distinguish the recordings from those Stravinsky made in the following decade, of the same repertoire – in stereo – gathered together by Sony Classical for its 22-disc Stravinsky Edition and subsequent reissues. The four orchestral works here benefit from a refinement of tone and elegance of manner not equalled by the Columbia and CBC Symphony Orchestras in the stereo remakes. To be fair, the more closely miked strings and woodwinds of the stereo recordings, though undeniably vivid, and occasionally better at profiling leading thematic lines, could be unkind to string tone. And given the effortlessness with which many orchestras nowadays handle the difficulties of a Stravinsky score, it must be said that not everything in these Cleveland sessions speaks with the poetry of precision. Here or there in Cleveland, you will find slightly faster or slower tempos, some of the slower ones allowing more expressive shaping of song (*Le baiser de la fée*) or clearer exposition of intricate ingenuity (the first movement of the *Symphony in C*). There is a graceless (even grotesque) plod for the fiancée's short solo variation in the *Baiser de la fée* 'Pas de deux' (track 6), but the more flowing tempo for the ballet's haunting final 'Berceuse' is a definite plus; as are the chamber items, recorded with the cream of New York's players, and sounding like Stravinsky's happiest studio sessions. Quite apart from the expertise of the playing, the pleasure these musicians took in two of Stravinsky's wittiest scores is communicated so vividly that one completely forgets the source is mono.

Danses concertantes

Danses concertantes. Orpheus
Orpheus Chamber Orchestra
DG 459 644-2GH (50 minutes: DDD)   Ⓕ
Recorded 1995-96   ○

As recorded 'blueprints' of these neo-classical ballet scores, the Orpheus Chamber Orchestra's conductorless performances are more accomplished than the composer's own. Stravinsky the conductor rarely enjoyed this degree of evenly matched and 'finished' instrumental tone and apparently effortless accuracy of pitch and ensemble – qualities which, along with a compact sonic presentation respecting the different intensities of each instrument, expose a hitherto unattained degree of detail. There is poetry in all this precision too; a precision of character that emerges as a result of so much properly achieved and from an abundance of imaginative phrasing and nuances of rhythm from players at one with each other and at one with the idiom; for example, the delicacy, tenderness and 'controlled freedom' of the exchanges in the opening 'Theme' of the central movement of *Danses concertantes*, or the wonderfully skittish flute incursions in its succeeding 'Pas de deux'.

The acoustic of the Orpheus Chamber Orchestra's regular recording haunt, the Recital Hall at New York State University's Performing Arts Center in Purchase, is ideally matched to the scale and intention of these performances and presumably allows these conductorless players to interact as the most subtly responsive of chamber groups. Perhaps the acoustic's compactness does bring a little 'tightening' of tone above *mezzo-forte* in the *Danses concertantes*, but this is not troublesome. Strongly recommended.

<hr>

The Firebird

The Firebird – Suite (1945). Jeu de cartes
Granada City Orchestra / Josep Pons
Harmonia Mundi HMC90 1728 (58 minutes: DDD) Ⓕ
Recorded 2000 ●

Stravinsky does not specify the number of strings to be used for the 1945 *Firebird* suite, but the wind forces are exactly the same as in *Jeu de cartes*, where he asks for strings in the proportion 12, 10, 8, 6, 6. The Granada City Orchestra provide 11, 10, 7, 6, 4, which seems a better balance.

In *Firebird*, Pons and his players quite convince you that we are missing something when it is played by a full-size symphony orchestra. Real quiet and delicacy of detail are easier for a 'large chamber' group, especially when the conductor seems to be urging them to play like chamber musicians, listening intently to each other and giving real character to solo passages. Solo strings are allowed *portamento* from time to time, and one reason why Pons chose a magically slow speed for the outset of the finale was surely that he knew his first horn would sound wonderful at that tempo. Speeds are often a touch on the slow side, not to make life easier for the players but because they and their conductor have obviously enjoyed working on subtle phrasings and *rubato*. Yet they can play fast too and with a big tone without congestion. But above all one is reminded how full this score is of quiet, delicate colour.

There are some slowish tempos in *Jeu de cartes* too, but not at the expense of crispness of detail and lightness of touch. No, this is not a coupling in which we marvel that the Granada City Orchestra can put up a respectable showing, but one in which you salute with respect an ensemble of pronounced and attractive character and a

conductor who understands that moderately small can be very beautiful.

<hr>

Stravinsky The Firebird (Original version 1910). 💰
Symphonies of Wind Instruments
London Symphony Orchestra / Kent Nagano
Virgin Classics The Classics VM5 61848-2 Ⓑ
(59 minutes: DDD). Recorded 1991-92 ●●

The reissue of Kent Nagano's vividly detailed new LSO recording of the original Stravinsky *Firebird* score must go right to the top of the recommended list. From the very opening the clearly delineated kaleidoscope of orchestral colour reminds one of Dorati's famous Mercury recording, but the new Virgin sound balance produced by Andrew Keener is even finer, slightly softer-grained, richer, but with hardly less impact. At the opening, the playing generates slightly less tension than with Dorati, but the concentration steadily increases, the orchestral colour glows radiantly, and the big set pieces – the spectacular 'Danse infernale' of Kashchei, the lovely 'Princesses' Round Dance' and the 'Berceuse' – are all superbly played. The final climax expands gloriously. Nagano also uses the original 1920 score of the *Symphonies of Wind Instruments* and the result is ear-tickling in the best sense, with sonorities juxtaposed most skilfully, textures keenly balanced, and a well-maintained onward flow.

<hr>

The Firebird. The Rite of Spring. Perséphone
Stephanie Cosserat *narr* **Stuart Neill** *ten* **Ragazzi,**
The Peninsula Boys Chorus; San Francisco Girl's
Chorus; San Francisco Symphony Chorus and
Orchestra / Michael Tilson Thomas
RCA Red Seal (special price) ③ 09026 68898-2 Ⓕ
(119 minutes: DDD). Text and translation included
Recorded live in 1996-98 ●

On the face of it, an odd compilation. Why issue one of Stravinsky's least-known ballets in harness with two of his most popular? The answer lies partly in *Perséphone*'s revisiting, 20 years on, of the theme of *The Rite* (earth and rebirth) with Homer's Greece replacing pagan Russia in a neo-classical piece described by Elliott Carter as 'a humanist *Rite of Spring*'. Rather more difficult to explain is the presence of *The Firebird* (the complete 1910 score plus a piano), but a performance as good as this is its own justification. And if three discs – avoiding a mid-ballet disc change – appears extravagant, RCA obligingly prices them as two. We have no idea how much post-concert 'patching' there was after the two live recordings (*The Firebird* and *The Rite*), but the playing is superbly 'finished'. Possibly, the ballet's ending was better on that particular night than any of the others; certainly, Tilson Thomas's timing and shading of the last minutes' darkness-to-light is spellbinding, the management of the *crescendo* on the final chord, even more so. Perfumes are distinctly French, with the *Firebird*'s 'supplication' as seductive as any on disc. The general exuberance of the playing in *The Rite* might also be thought French, though the virtuoso delivery and flamboyance are recognisably American. It isn't a *Rite* that investigates the score's radicalism; rather it is one to send you home from the concert hall exhilarated.

You would be lucky to catch *Perséphone* in the concert hall. Rather baffling given the quality of a piece which shares with *Oedipus Rex* an inspired blend of distancing and direct appeal, and with *Apollo* and *Orpheus*, an archaic beauty and limpidity. The singers rise to that challenge (and others) with superb choral work. Stravinsky called *Perséphone* a 'melodrama', referring to the spoken title-role. And as Persephone *is* Spring, RCA has cast an aptly youthful-sounding actress in the part, very good at eagerness, passion and compassion. It may be that the voice is too young for *gravitas*; it may equally be that, as recorded there was no need to project in the same way, and stage projection might have helped create an element of *gravitas*. It is a small point, and her relative immediacy is always appealing. In all other respects, RCA's balance can't be criticised.

L'histoire du soldat

L'histoire du soldat (in English)[a]. Concerto in E flat, 'Dumbarton Oaks'

[a]**David Timson,** [a]**Benjamin Soames,** [a]**Jonathan Keeble** *spkrs* **Northern Chamber Orchestra / Nicholas Ward**

Naxos 8 553662 (76 minutes: DDD). Ⓢ
Recorded 1995-96

In this full-length *The Soldier's Tale* (the English translation by Michael Flanders and Kitty Black), the actors have the full measure of their parts, and the musicians, taken as a group, about two-thirds the measure of theirs. The notes are there, but not always the will to make something of them. Perhaps one shouldn't expect violin- and trumpet-playing of the flair and feature of Manoug Parikian and Maurice André in the classic 1962 Markevitch recording (now part of a two-disc set on Philips, and spoken in the original French). On the other hand Nicholas Cox's always fully responsive clarinet-playing on the Naxos recording is a vast improvement on Markevitch's narrow-toned and quavery clarinettist. If Nicholas Cox seems to do a little better out of the Naxos balance than some of his musical colleagues, it is probably because of his more consistent projection of character.

In general, it is a very natural balance that welds the years and miles between the separately recorded actors and musicians into a reasonably convincing illusion of a single-stage whole (with the actors placed in front of the musicians), though it is less convincing than the Markevitch, where the same acoustic was used by both actors and musicians (and where Jean Cocteau's narrator can become almost submerged). The generous bonus here is Stravinsky's modernised 'Brandenburg Concerto', *Dumbarton Oaks*, marginally more presently recorded than the musical contributions to the main work, but with the same mixture of determination to put it across (a wonderful strutting *marcato* at the start of the finale) and lapses into a competent neutral. So, should you be interested at the price? If you only know *The Soldier's Tale* through the Concert Suite (most of the music; none of the words), and can sample before purchasing this complete recording, try two 'low points' – the very opening ('The soldier's march'), and the close ('The devil's triumphal dance') – and if the proceedings don't strike you as tame and lacking vitality, this could be a very rewarding use of a fiver.

Petrushka

Petrushka (1947 version). Pulcinella

Peter Donohoe *pf* **City of Birmingham Symphony Orchestra / Sir Simon Rattle**

HMV Classics HMV5 73551-2 (74 minutes: DDD) Ⓑ
Recorded 1986 ●

Simon Rattle's performance of *Petrushka* is most notable for its fresh look at details of scoring and balance, with pianist Peter Donohoe making a strong impression. The results are robust and persuasive, though one sometimes has the impression that the characters are being left to fend for themselves. The atmospheric sound with its generous middle and bass is certainly very natural. The symphony too is eminently recommendable, sounding more high-spirited than it sometimes has, with Rattle particularly relishing the jazzy bits.

Petrushka (1947 version). Pulcinella

Anna Caterina Antonacci *sop* **Pietro Ballo** *ten* **William Shimell** *bar* **Royal Concertgebouw Orchestra / Riccardo Chailly**

Decca 443 774-2DH (73 minutes: DDD). Text and translation included. Recorded 1993 Ⓕ ●

In *Petrushka* Chailly has his players characterise even the smallest detail. Note the tongue-in-cheek lead-in to the 'Russian Dance' and the carefree 'squeeze-box' character of the dance itself (with dynamic crossfire between wind and brass and some excellent piano playing). 'Petrushka' (second tableau) is played *con amore*, with much humanity and not entirely without malice: perhaps the anger and frustration aren't as blatant as they might be; but the pain and humiliation certainly are. It's a performance that breathes, that sings and neither rushes its fences nor loses sight of the score's very specific rhythmic profile. As for the recording, given top-ranking engineers – who could rightly expect anything less than exceptional?

The coupling, too, is equally colourful: a pert, sweet-centred *Pulcinella*, with an expressive *concertino* in the 'Ouverture', winsome phrasing elsewhere and extremely brilliant accounts of the two *Allegro assais* (tracks 23 and 35). Here there is an incisiveness, attack and buoyancy to the rhythms. The singing is vividly characterised and, again, the recording is spectacular.

Pulcinella

Pulcinella. Renard. Two Suites. Rag-Time
Jennifer Larmore *mez* **John Aler, Frank Kelly** *tens* **Jan Opalach, John Cheek** *basses* **Saint Paul Chamber Orchestra / Hugh Wolff**
Teldec 4509-94548-2 (73 minutes: DDD). Texts and translations included. Recorded 1994 Ⓕ

Hugh Wolff's *Pulcinella* is a witty, incisive alternative. Just try the *Vivo* with its frolicking trombone and wilting double-bass solo and note how stylishly they phrase their closing duet. His singers are generally above par, Jennifer Larmore especially. Wolff offers for couplings the best *Rag-Time* for 11 instruments on disc – gently swinging and with no hint of self-consciousness – plus keenly focused accounts of the two Suites for small orchestra and an exceedingly enjoyable *Renard*. Here the singing is again excellent and there's a novelty in that Wolff has tweaked the published translation and in so doing has effected a more natural flow to the comedy. Again, there is a plethora of detail – subtle underlinings, useful clarifications and felicitous turns of phrase – and the recording is excellent.

The Rite of Spring

The Rite of Spring (two versions) **H**
Philharmonia Orchestra / Igor Markevitch
Testament mono/stereo SBT1076 (67 minutes: ADD) Ⓕ
Mono version recorded 1951, stereo 1959 **OO**

Markevitch's 1959 stereo *Rite* is in a league of its own. This is a model of how to balance the score (and of how to create the illusion of a wide dynamic range within more restricted parameters). Markevitch would have been totally familiar with every note of the piece (in 1949 he sent Stravinsky a list of mistakes he had noticed in the recently revised edition), and by 1959 he clearly knew what it needed in performance, including how to keep its shock-value alive. There are 'improprieties' here, such as the slowing for the 'Evocation of the Ancestors' (making the most of those timpani volleys), but nothing serious. As it happens, Markevitch's 'Introduction' to Part 2 is unusually fast, but he is able to take in the following small marked variations of tempo, providing valuable contrasts. And in any case, the playing is so alive, alert and reactive, whatever the dynamic levels: listen to the incisive clarinets' entry in the 'Mystic Circles' and the *frisson* imparted to the following *pianissimo tremolando* from the strings (track 4 after 4'06").

We could fill the rest of the page with similar highlights and other features unique to the performance, but that would be to spoil the fun of discovery (or rediscovery – and what a transfer of the original!). This is a great *Rite* for lots of reasons, not the least of which is that the sessions were obviously electric. As a fascinating bonus, Testament also offers a 1951 mono recording of a great *Rite* in the making. The differences are not radical, but enough to justify the idea.

The Rite of Spring[a]. Apollon musagète[b]
City of Birmingham Symphony Orchestra / Sir Simon Rattle
EMI CDC7 49636-2 (65 minutes: DDD) Ⓕ
Recorded [a]1987 and [b]1988 **OO**

Recordings of *The Rite of Spring* are legion, but it is rare to find Stravinsky's most explosive ballet score coupled with *Apollon musagète*, his most serene. The result is a lesson in creative versatility, confirming that Stravinsky could be equally convincing as expressionist and neo-classicist. Yet talk of lessons might suggest that sheer enjoyment is of lesser importance, and it is perfectly possible to relish this disc simply for that personal blend of the authoritative and the enlivening that Simon Rattle's CBSO recordings for EMI so consistently achieve. Rattle never rushes things, and the apparent deliberation of *The Rite*'s concluding 'Sacrificial Dance' may initially surprise, but in this context it proves an entirely appropriate, absolutely convincing conclusion. Rattle sees the work as a whole, without striving for a spurious symphonic integration, and there is never for a moment any hint of a routine reading of what is by now a classic of the modern orchestral repertoire. The account of *Apollon* has comparable depth, with elegance transformed into eloquence and the CBSO strings confirming that they have nothing to fear from comparison with the best in Europe or America. The recordings are faithful to the intensity and expressiveness of Rattle's Stravinsky, interpretations fit to set beside those of the composer himself.

The Rite of Spring. Pulcinella[a]
[a]**Olga Borodina** *mez* [a]**John Mark Ainsley** *ten* [a]**Ildebrando d'Arcangelo** *bass* **Berlin Philharmonic Orchestra / Bernard Haitink**
Philips 446 698-2PH (71 minutes: DDD). Text and translation included. Recorded 1995 Ⓕ **O**

The booklet's interior artwork – a jagged cubist pattern of white print on a black background and vice-versa – will strike you as either inventive or deeply irritating, but its contrasts are mirrored in the success and failure of the two performances. Despite occasional instances of affectionate pointing, and finely done solos from the tenor and bass, conditions for this *Pulcinella* – among them, a possible unfamiliarity with the notes – do not lend themselves to buoyancy, fun and quick wittedness, and a wonderfully effervescent score is rendered, for the most part, four-square and flat. But how different is this *Rite*; and if the opening bassoon solo – a very melancholy air, beautifully eased into – hints at a performance more ear-caressing than earth-cracking, what emerges is as comprehensive a realisation of the many elements of this score as any on record. The light-toned recording combines vividly present and analytical clarity with a mostly audible sense of space; its sophistication only slipping in those moments where the parts don't relate to the whole. Opinions will differ about whether those 'moments' are few or many, but the balance allows a very high yield of the score's intricacies and radicalism, and provides a clear window on the wonderful expressive variety of the playing. But what of Haitink's parameters? As it happens, they are mainly Stravinsky's, with tempos that keep the work on its feet, an avoidance of inflexions alien to the score, and an appreciation of how much more radical *The Rite* can sound if not turned into a percussion concerto. When all is said and done, you have to ask yourself with any performance of *The Rite*, are you left shaken by it? You will be by this one.

The Rite of Spring. Canticum sacrum[a]. Requiem Canticles. Choral Variations on 'Vom Himmel hoch'
Irène Friedli *mez* **Frieder Lang** *ten* **Michel Brodard** *bar* [a]**Lausanne Pro Arte Choir; Suisse Romande Chamber Choir and Orchestra / Neeme Järvi**
Chandos CHAN9408 (75 minutes: DDD). Texts and translations included. Recorded 1994 Ⓕ ●

Järvi's is a weighty account of *The Rite* and it packs a massive punch. He does not opt for showily fast tempos (save towards the end of the 'Sacrificial Dance', where a combination of high speed and rather heavy sonority garbles a little of the detail) and at times – in the 'Mystical Circles', for instance – he leans on the accents, diminishing the springiness of the rhythm. Elsewhere, though, the articulation tingles appropriately, and the orchestral sound is often beautiful, often cleanly detailed. One would not, even so, put it among the top half-dozen current recordings of *The Rite of Spring* were it not for the quite splendid couplings, where the very qualities that are a slight disadvantage in *The Rite* give urgency and eloquence to a couple of scores that are still regarded as among Stravinsky's most difficult. Both soloists are good, especially the elegantly lyrical tenor, and the chorus sing with wonderfully jubilant confidence. A slight tendency to overmark dynamics, noticeable in *The Rite*, is evident at the beginning of the *Requiem Canticles*, where Stravinsky firmly instructs that the strings are not to play loudly and Järvi just as firmly begs to differ. But he has obviously been moved by the fervour of the piece, and he demonstrates that a sonorous, full-voiced account can be just as effective as the more usual reading of the score as a quiet chamber ritual.

After that there is no doubting how much fun Stravinsky had in so industriously outdoing Bach's contrapuntal ingenuity in the *Choral Variations*. Järvi obviously loves all those extra twiddly bits too, and is more successful than any other conductor at demonstrating what a Christmassy work it is. These are decent recordings throughout but a little lacking in resonance in the *Canticum sacrum* (its pauses very precisely tailored to the reverberation time of St Mark's in Venice, after all), and the organ-blower motor of the Victoria Hall in Geneva sounds as though it needs servicing. Otherwise a highly recommendable coupling, especially to those who love *The Rite*.

Octet

Rag-Time. Octet. Three Pieces. L'histoire du soldat – Suite. Pastorale. Concertino Septet. Epitaphium
Lorna McGhee *fl* **Dmitri Ashkenazy** *cl* **Alan Brind** *vn* **Cristina Bianchi** *hp* **European Soloists Ensemble / Vladimir Ashkenazy** *pf*
Decca 448 177-2DH (59 minutes: DDD) Ⓕ
Recorded 1994 ●

This is probably Ashkenazy's finest Stravinsky CD. The catchy but immensely clever Septet scores a double bulls-eye by employing formal ingenuity (the closing Gigue features four separate fugues on four versions of an eight-note row) without 'losing' the untutored listener. Written for violin, viola, cello, clarinet, horn, bassoon and piano, it is followed by the disc's closing selection, a 1'29" *Epitaphium* that offers brief confirmation of the older Stravinsky's serial leanings. The journey started with *Rag-Time*, composed in 1918 and peppered with the metallic twang of a cimbalom. Ashkenazy's performance of this is very well played, as is the Octet, with its scampering variations and gentle, *bossa-nova* style final bars (did Stravinsky ever write anything more charming than this?). Again, the performance is confident and unfussy, while Dmitri Ashkenazy blows plenty of spirit into the *Three Pieces* for solo clarinet (the third especially) and Ashkenazy *père* joins him – together with violinist Alan Brind – for a no-nonsense account of a trio arrangement of *The Soldier's Tale* Suite. Here Brind favours light bowing and bland characterisation, whereas the elegant *Pastorale* and lively *Concertino* are, by turns, colourful and punchy. Decca's recordings are uniformly good throughout; so is the standard of playing, and although one might maintain other preferences in this or that individual piece, the programme is both stimulating and entertaining.

Songs

Pastorale. Deux poèmes de Paul Verlaine. Two Poems of Konstantin Bal'mont. Three Japanese Lyrics. Three Little Songs, 'Recollections of my Childhood'. Pribaoutki. Cat's Cradle Songs. Four Songs. Mavra – Chanson de Paracha. Three Songs from William Shakespeare. In memoriam Dylan Thomas. Elegy for J F K. Two Sacred Songs (after Wolf)
Phyllis Bryn-Julson *sop* **Ann Murray** *mez* **Robert Tear** *ten* **John Shirley-Quirk** *bar* **Ensemble InterContemporain / Pierre Boulez**
DG 20th Century Classics 431 751-2GC Ⓜ
(58 minutes: ADD). Texts and translations included
Recorded 1980

It may be true that this disc lacks the focus of a single major work, but it is also much more than a random compilation of unrelated miniatures. Principally, it offers an aurally fascinating contrast between two groups of pieces: Stravinsky's relatively early Russian settings, as he worked through his own brand of nationalism, reaching from the salon style of *Pastorale* to the folk-like vigour of a work like *Pribaoutki*; then the late serial compositions, written in America, which prove that the rhythmic vitality and melodic distinctiveness of the early works survived undimmed into his final years. Stravinsky may have regarded texts as collections of sounds whose natural rhythms had no role to play in their musical setting, but the essential meaning still comes through unerringly, whether it is that of the plaintive Paracha's song from the opera *Mavra* or the sombre *Elegy for JFK* (to an Auden text). The disc is rounded off by the very late Wolf arrangements, and while one might quibble here and there about Boulez's choice of tempo, or the balance of voice and instruments, the disc as a whole is immensely satisfying.

Les noces

Les noces[a]. Mass[b]
Anny Mory *sop* **Patricia Parker** *mez* **John Mitchinson** *ten* **Paul Hudson** *bass* **English Bach Festival Chorus; Trinity Boys' Choir; Martha Argerich, Krystian Zimerman, Cyprien Katsaris, Homero Francesch** *pfs* [a]**English Bach Festival Percussion Ensemble;** [b]members of the **English Bach Festival Orchestra / Leonard Bernstein**
DG 20th Century Classics 423 251-2GC Ⓜ
(44 minutes: ADD). Texts and translations included ●

Les noces
Traditional Russian Village Wedding Songs Play, Skomoroshek. River. Trumpet. Cosmas and Demian. The Drinker. Green Forest. God bless, Jesus. My White Peas. Steambath. Berry. Black Beaver. In the House. Bunny with Short Legs. The Bed. Birch Tree
Pokrovsky Ensemble / Dmitri Pokrovsky
Nonesuch 7559-79335-2 (54 minutes: DDD) Ⓕ
English texts included

Many readers will probably look askance at the short timing here? However, never mind the width, feel the quality – these are top-drawer Bernstein performances, excellently recorded. *Les noces* sports an impressive array of pianists; but that need not be a decisive factor, since rhythmic precision and good balance are far more at a premium than individual flair or power – fortunately these individuals are equally fine ensemble players. It is even more important that the choir should be meticulously prepared (which they are), that the vocal soloists should be precise and full-blooded (which they are) and that the conductor should impart a sense of the profundity of the whole conception (which Bernstein emphatically does). The Mass is an ideal coupling for *Les noces*, not just because of the shared importance of the chorus, but because it, too, displays a fundamental ritual experience, in this case the sacrament of worship rather than marriage, with archetypal clarity. Bernstein's reading has all the calm devotion of the composer's own, even if the soloists are rather variable. Highly recommended.

For the Nonesuch recording Dmitri Pokrovsky and the singers in his ensemble travelled to southern and western Russia in search of melodics and texts related to *Les noces*; and they found rich pickings. True, the melodic similarities are not as tangible as the folk sources for *Petrushka* but the 15 songs, here recorded with immense flair and enjoyment to a variety of instrumental accompaniments, will be a revelation to all listeners. Be prepared for some acerbic sounds. Authentic Russian folk polyphony is an extraordinarily modern-sounding experience, as is authentic open-throated singing. The value of the disc is multiplied by the fact that the singers have carried over the style and expressive content of the folksongs into their performance of *Les noces* itself, bringing it to life in a way that must surely be unprecedented and uniquely illuminating. Not only that, but Pokrovsky had the inspired idea of recreating the instrumental parts on an Apple Macintosh computer, thus continuing Stravinsky's search for the ideal mechanical realisation.

Oedipus Rex

Symphony of Psalms. Oedipus Rex
Ivo Zídek *ten* Oedipus; **Věra Soukupová** *mez* Jocasta; **Karel Berman** *bass* Créon; **Eduard Haken** 🄷 *bass* Tiresias; **Antonin Zlesák** *ten* Shepherd; **Zdeněk Kroupa** *bar* Messenger; **Jean Desailly** *narr* **Czech Philharmonic Chorus and Orchestra / Karel Ančerl**
Supraphon Historical 11 1947-2 (73 minutes: AAD) Ⓕ
Recorded 1964-66 ●●

Oedipus Rex is one of Stravinsky's most compelling theatre pieces, a powerful drama that re-enacts the full force of a glorious highspot in ancient culture. The text is by Jean Cocteau, who once said, pertaining to his work on *Oedipus*, that 'any serious work, be it of poetry or music, of theatre or of film, demands a ceremonial, lengthy calculation, an architecture in which the slightest mistake would unbalance the pyramid' (quoted from *Diary of an Unknown*, pub. Paragon House). The fusion of words and music in *Oedipus*, indeed its very 'architecture', is masterly and arrests the attention consistently, from the animated severity of the opening narration, through the calculated tension of its musical argument, to the tragic restraint of its closing pages.

Karel Ančerl was one of Stravinsky's most committed exponents. This particular recording of *Oedipus Rex* was taped in the Dvořák Hall of the House of Artists, Prague, and earned itself at least three major awards. Ančerl traces and intensifies salient points in the tragedy yet maintains a precise, sensitive touch; his vocal collaborators include the noble Karel Berman (Créon) who, like Ančerl himself, suffered considerably during the Nazi occupation of Czechoslovakia; then there's a fine Jocasta in Věra Soukupová and the convincing but occasionally unsteady Ivo Zídek singing the part of Oedipus. Both here and in the *Symphony of Psalms* – one of the most serenely perceptive recorded performances of the work – the Czech Philharmonic Chorus excel, while Supraphon's 1960s engineering (not the DDD suggested on the box) has an appealing brightness.

The Nightingale

The Nightingale. Renard[a]
Natalie Dessay *sop* Nightingale; [a]**Vsevolod Grivnov** *ten* Fisherman; **Marie McLaughlin** *sop* Cook; [a]**Laurent Naouri** *bass* Chamberlain; **Albert Schagidullin** *bar* Emperor; [a]**Maxim Mikhailov** *bass* Bonze; **Violeta Urmana** *mez* Death; **Olivier Berg** *ten* **Wassyl Slipak** *ten* **Grzegorz Staskiewicz** *bass* Japanese Envoys; [a]**Ian Caley** *ten*
Paris National Opera Chorus and Orchestra / James Conlon
EMI CDC5 56874-2 (63 minutes: DDD). Notes, texts Ⓕ and translations included. Recorded 1999 ●

The Nightingale is an awkward piece, begun before *The Firebird* but finished, unwillingly, only after Stravinsky had decisively changed his own direction and that of Western music with *The Rite of Spring*. He tried to hide the join, he said, but it sticks out like a sore thumb, and one great quality of Conlon's performance is that if anything he emphasises the miniature opera's straddling of two expressive worlds. In the beautiful Prelude he makes it quite clear that even pre-*Firebird* Stravinsky already owed almost as much to Debussy as to Rimsky-Korsakov, and with the arrival of the exceptionally beautiful tenor voice of Vsevolod Grivnov as the Fisherman you strongly suspect that this is the recording *The Nightingale* has been waiting for.

Natalie Dessay is lovely in the title-role: no mere twittering air-head coloratura but touchingly expressive in her two songs (a pity, though, that she is placed so close to the microphone: the score says she should be in the orchestra pit, not on stage). But then Act 2 arrives, at its outset sounding, as Stravinsky said, like the newly installed St Petersburg telephones shrilling, and Conlon is no less responsive to the dissonances and the abrupt motif-juggling of Stravinsky's post-*Rite* manner. In the music of the Japanese envoys, even, a link between Orthodox chant and the austere rituals of Stravinsky's very late works is obvious. The rest of the cast is fully up to Dessay's and Grivnov's standard; Marie McLaughlin's Russian diction being particularly commendable.

Though entertaining, *Renard* is, alas, not quite so successful. Grivnov is part of the problem: he just sings beautifully, seemingly unaware of the music's low humour and peasant pungency, but even Conlon doesn't match the composer's own robust vividness. *Renard*, however, is the fill-up, 17 minutes out of 63, and *The Nightingale* is pleasure unalloyed.

The Rake's Progress

Jerry Hadley *ten* Tom Rakewell; **Dawn Upshaw** *sop* Anne; **Samuel Ramey** *bass* Nick Shadow; **Grace Bumbry** *mez* Baba the Turk; **Steven Cole** *ten* Sellem; **Anne Collins** *contr* Mother Goose; **Robert Lloyd** *bass* Trulove; **Roderick Earle** *bass* Keeper; **Chorus and Orchestra of Opéra de Lyon / Kent Nagano**
Erato ② 0630-12715-2 (138 minutes: DDD) Ⓜ
Recorded 1995 ●

Any number of the world's opera houses would have given their eye teeth for the privilege of presenting the première of Stravinsky's only true opera, but he, intensely money-conscious though he was (and he had worked on the piece for three years without a commission fee), insisted on La Fenice in Venice – because he was fond of the city, of course, but also because *The Rake's Progress* is a chamber opera. And this is a chamber performance of it, with a fairly small orchestra, much singing of almost *parlando* quality and crystal-clear words. It is also intimate, with a strong sense of the stage, of characters reacting to each other. With Nagano's on the whole brisk tempos, it gives the impression of a real performance, and a gripping one. Upshaw's is not the purest soprano voice to have attempted the role of Anne, and there have been more spectacular high Cs than hers, but she is movingly vulnerable, totally believable.

So is Hadley, acting at times almost too vividly for the music's line: as he occasionally demonstrates he has a wonderfully beautiful head voice. He is not, therefore, quite the touchingly likeable 'shuttle-headed lad' that Alexander Young portrayed so unforgettably in the composer's own recording, but no other Tom Rakewell surpasses him. Ramey's is a bigger voice than most of the others here – firm and superbly produced. Collins and Lloyd are both first-class as Mother Goose and Trulove, Cole an unusually light-voiced, confidingly conspiratorial Sellem. If any, Bumbry is the disappointment of the cast, somewhat over-loud and baritonal almost throughout, but the French chorus sing nimbly and in admirable English. Stravinsky's own recording is still to be cherished, but of modern recordings of *The Rake's Progress* this is a hugely, if not the most, enjoyable one.

The Rake's Progress
Ian Bostridge *ten* Tom Rakewell; **Deborah York** *sop* Anne; **Bryn Terfel** *bass-bar* Nick Shadow; **Anne Sofie von Otter** *mez* Baba the Turk; **Peter Bronder** *ten* Sellem; **Anne Howells** *mez* Mother Goose; **Martin Robson** *bass* Trulove; **Julian Clarkson** *bass* Keeper of the Madhouse; **Monteverdi Choir; London Symphony Orchestra / Sir John Eliot Gardiner**
DG ② 459 648-2GH2 (134 minutes: DDD). Notes, Ⓕ text and translation included. Recorded 1997 ●●

Gardiner's *Rake's Progress*, in all but one respect, easily withstands comparison with its five rivals, and in several it surpasses them; if you are happy with Terfel's Nick Shadow, it can be set alongside Stravinsky's own 1964 recording as the finest available. Gardiner is conscious throughout that this is a chamber opera, and the orchestral textures are outstandingly clean and transparent, the rhythmic pointing crisp but airy. This enables his cast to give a fast-moving, conversational account of the text, with every word crystal-clear (including those from the chorus) and no need for any voice to force.

This benefits the soprano and tenor especially. Deborah York, in her first operatic recording, sounds a very young and touchingly vulnerable

Anne; her voice may seem a little pale, but there is pathos as well as brilliance in her Act 1 aria, and the desolation of her reaction to Tom's marriage to Baba the Turk ('I see, then: it was I who was unworthy') is moving; her Act 3 lullaby has an affecting, child-like quality. Ian Bostridge is the best Tom Rakewell since Alexander Young in Stravinsky's recording: he too sounds likeably youthful, sings with intelligence and sweetness of tone and acts very well.

Howells is an unexaggerated Mother Goose, and von Otter's economy of comic gesture is a marvel. 'Finish, if you please, whatever business is detaining you with this person' receives the full Lady Bracknell treatment from most mezzos; von Otter gives it the vocal equivalent of a nose wrinkled in well-bred disdain. Terfel often demonstrates that he can fine his big voice down to the subtlety of the other principals, and when he does he is a formidably dangerous, insinuating Shadow. But almost as often he not only lets the voice rip but indulges in histrionics quite uncharacteristic of the performance as a whole. You may not mind: why after all should the Devil restrainedly under-act? At times, though, he sounds bigger than the orchestra. The recording is close but theatrically atmospheric. There are a few sound effects, though some may find the raucous owl in the graveyard scene distracting.

Josef Suk

Bohemian 1874-1935

GROVE *Suk studied at the Prague Conservatory, 1885-92, where he was Dvořák's favourite pupil, and in 1898 married his daughter. Dvorák was, too, the dominant influence on his early music, as in the Serenade for strings (1892) and the Fairy Tale suite (1900); later, most notably in the vast symphony Asrael (1906) – written under the impact of the deaths of his wife and his father-in-law – he developed a more personal style comparable with Mahler's in structural mastery and emotional force. He drew little on folk music. Other works include two published quartets (he was second violinist in the Czech Quartet for most of his life and played in over 4000 concerts), piano pieces (Things lived and Dreamed, 1909) and a group of symphonic poems, A Summer's Tale (1909), The Ripening (1917) and the choral-orchestral Epilog (1929). From 1922 he directed a master class in composition at the Prague Conservatory.*

Asrael, Op 27

Bavarian Radio Symphony Orchestra / Rafael Kubelík
Panton 81 1101-2 (64 minutes: ADD) Ⓕ
Recorded 1981

To use large-scale symphonic form for the purging of deep personal grief carries the danger that the result will seriously lack discipline. In 1904-05 Suk's world was shattered by two visits from Asrael (the Angel of Death in Muslim mythology): he lost his father-in-law (and revered teacher) Dvořák, and his beloved wife, Otylka. Forgivably, Suk does perhaps linger a little too long in the fourth movement's gentle, mainly lyrical portrait of Otylka, but elsewhere the progress is as satisfying psychologically as it is symphonically. Much of the music has a concentrated dream-like quality; at the extremes, spectral nightmare visions merge with compensatory surges of lyrical ardour. Set Kubelík's reading alongside any of the other modern versions and one is immediately aware of a wholly compelling imaginative intensity and interpretative flair that betoken a true poet of the rostrum. Kubelík's control throughout is awesome and he conjures up playing of enormous expressive subtlety from his fine Munich orchestra. No other recorded performance – not even Václav Talich's legendary 1952 Supraphon account – succeeds in conveying the intensely personal nature of this music with such devastating emotional candour. Technically, too, one need have no qualms about this Panton disc – the Bavarian Radio engineers secure most truthful results.

Epilogue, Op 37

Epilogue, Op 37. A Fairy Tale, Op 16
Luba Orgonasova *sop* **Iván Kusnjer** *bar* **Peter Mikuláš** *bass* **Royal Liverpool Philharmonic Choir and Orchestra / Libor Pešek**
Virgin Classics VC5 45245-2 (70 minutes: DDD). Text Ⓕ and translation included. Recorded 1997

Scored for soprano, baritone, bass, large and small mixed choruses and orchestra, and running for 40 minutes without a break, *Epilogue* was described by its creator as 'the last part of a cycle, the spirit of which manifested itself for the first time in *Asrael*: it goes through the whole of human life, into reflection on death and the dread of it, before the appearance of the song of earthly love – all this leading up to the exhilarating song of liberated mankind.' Pešek's massed forces bring genuine enthusiasm, vigour and dedication to Suk's extraordinarily ambitious, subtly clothed creation, the music's kaleidoscopic range of colour and mood conveyed with commendable sensitivity and unerring perception. Pešek's ever-involving conception is extremely satisfying in its clear-headed rigour and cumulative thrust. The lucidly balanced, spectacularly full and wide-ranging engineering handles those positively seismic *tuttis* in the last section with some aplomb. John Tyrell's notes carry the requisite authority, but there are, however, some irritating discrepancies in the booklet presentation.

Pešek's account of *A Fairy Tale* (into which we are plunged after a gap of a mere four seconds) faces formidable competition from his own 1981 recording with the Czech PO (available on Supraphon). In the gorgeous opening tableau the excellent violin soloist (surprisingly uncredited, although it is in fact the RLPO Principal Malcolm Stewart) plays with a poignant restraint and unaffected purity that is extremely moving. Again, Pešek directs with considerable imagination and flair (the arresting start of the last movement certainly generates a heady sense of spectacle here). If that earlier account continues to have the edge in terms of tangy local colour and dramatic cutting edge, Suk's radiant score is imbued with an extra human warmth and wistful intimacy on Merseyside that provide ample compensation. A most welcome issue.

Ripening, Op 34

Ripening, Op 34. Praga, Op 26
Royal Liverpool Philharmonic Choir and Orchestra / Libor Pešek
Virgin Classics VC7 59318-2 (67 minutes: DDD) Ⓕ
Recorded 1992 ●

Completed in 1917, *Ripening* shows Suk at his peak. This vast yet tightly organised tone-poem shares many of the autobiographical concerns of its large-scale orchestral predecessors (*Asrael* and *A Summer's Tale*). Throughout, Suk handles his outsize forces with a truly Straussian confidence and virtuosity, nowhere more strikingly than in the extended Fugue which attains a climax of truly devastating proportions; the profound serenity of the ensuing coda (where a wordless female chorus is used to magical effect) could not have been harder won. The coupling, *Praga*, is an affectionate, enjoyably grandiloquent portrait-in-sound of that fair city dating from 1904. Pešek and the RLPO are accomplished and communicative. The engineering, too, is first-class.

A Summer's Tale, Op 29

A Summer's Tale, Op 29. Fantastic Scherzo, Op 25
Czech Philharmonic Orchestra / Sir Charles Mackerras
Decca 466 443-2DH (66 minutes: DDD) Ⓕ
Recorded 1997 ●

A Summer's Tale, cast in five movements, contains some of Suk's most entrancingly original inspiration, not least the shimmering, heat-haze evocation that is 'Noon' and the succeeding Intermezzo entitled 'Blind musicians' (featuring a doleful, spare-textured dialogue between first a pair of cors anglais and then solo violin and viola). Certain commentators have criticised the piece's lack of cohesion, yet, in a towering performance its slumbering organic power, sense of spectacle and visionary beauty can take the breath away. The dramatic fervour of Mackerras's performance is tremendously compelling, and his magnificent Czech orchestra responds with commitment and poise throughout. A direct comparison with Libor Pešek's RLPO version perhaps reveals an added humanity and emotional clout. But it's doubtful whether the Czech Philharmonic has ever been captured by the microphones with greater richness and depth (bass-drum fanciers are in for a field day); the lustrous results are achieved by Decca's Hazell/Lock production team, and provided the seismically wide dynamic range doesn't prove an obstacle to domestic harmony (best warn the neighbours in advance!), a sonic feast is guaranteed. Mackerras offers a delectable bonus in the shape of the *Fantastic Scherzo*, with its indelible, lilting second subject – once heard, forever etched in the memory. Truth to tell, Mackerras conducts with greater fire and temperament here than in the main offering (the music's *danse macabre*, at times positively Mahlerian, characteristics brought out most perceptively). Despite minor qualms, then, this remains a classy, thrillingly accomplished coupling.

Chamber Works

Chamber works, Volumes 1-3
Supraphon ③ 11 1874-2 Ⓜ
(aas: 208 minutes: ADD/DDD). Recorded 1966-92

String Quartets – No 1 in B flat, Op 11[a]; No 2, Op 31[b]. Tempo di menuetto[b]. Meditation on an Old Czech Hymn, Op 35*a*[b]. Quartet movement in B flat[a]
Suk Quartet ([a]Antonín Novák, [b]Ivan Straus, Vojtěch Jouza *vns* Karel Rehák *va* Jan Stros *vc*)
Supraphon 11 1531-2 (71 minutes: ADD/DDD) Ⓜ
Recorded 1966-92 ●

Piano Trio in C minor, Op 2. Elégie, Op 23. Piano Quartet in A minor, Op 1. Piano Quintet in G minor, Op 8
Josef Suk *vn* **Jan Talich** *va* **Michaela Fukačová** *vc* **Pavel Stěpán** *pf* **Suk Trio** (Josef Suk *vn* Josef Chuchro *vc* Josef Hála, Jan Panenka *pfs*); **Suk Quartet** (Antonín Novák, Vojtěch Jouza *vns* Karel Rehák *va* Jan Stros *vc*)
Supraphon 11 1532-2 (74 minutes: ADD/DDD) Ⓜ
Recorded 1966-92

Mélodie. Minuet. Balada in D minor. Four Pieces, Op 17. Ballade in D minor, Op 3 No 1. Serenade in A, Op 3 No 2. Bagatelle, 'Carrying a Bouquet'. Barcarolle in B flat. Balada in D minor. Elégie, Op 23. Sousedská
Jiří Válek *fl* **Josef Suk, Jitka Nováková, Ludmila Vybíralová, Miroslav Kosina, Jaroslav Krištůfek, Zdeněk Mann** *vns* **Marek Jerie, František Host, Ivo Laniar** *vcs* **Tomáš Josífko** *db* **Renata Kodadová** *hp* **Josef Hála** *pf/harm* **Jan Panenka, Iván Klánský** *pfs* **Josef Fousek, Libor Kubánek** *perc* **Suk Quartet**
Supraphon 11 1533-2 (63 minutes: ADD/DDD) Ⓜ
Recorded 1966-92

A treasure-trove of heartfelt music performed with refinement and flair. Volume 1 concentrates on Suk's string quartet output (Suk himself was the second violinist in the great Czech Quartet for 40 years). If the First Quartet (1896) doesn't quite show the same freshness or entrancing melodic vein of the String Serenade of four years earlier, it remains a delightfully unassuming creation with the genial presence of Suk's teacher Dvořák looming large over the proceedings. It is followed by a rare hearing for the alternative finale Suk composed some 19 years later in 1915. By this time, of course, the composer had already found his own strongly personal voice. Both the resourceful Second Quartet of 1911 (an ambitious one-movement essay of nearly 28 minutes' duration and considerable emotional variety) and the deeply-felt *Meditation on an Old Czech Hymn* (1914) are works of some substance well worth exploring, and these passionate accounts enjoy excellent sound. The remaining two volumes perhaps contain more to interest Suk aficionados than newcomers, though the adorable *Four Pieces* for violin and piano, Op 17, have always remained great favourites.

Volume 2 features youthful offerings: the Piano Trio, the Piano Quartet, the likeable, if rather garrulous, Piano Quintet of 1893 and the touching *Elégie* for piano, violin and cello from 1902, written to celebrate the anniversary of the death of the poet and dramatist, Julius Zeyer. Apart from the *Four Pieces* already mentioned, the third and final volume also contains, amongst much else, the *Elégie* in its original guise for violin, cello, string quartet, harmonium and harp, no fewer than three different *Ballades* in D minor conceived for various instrumental combinations during Suk's days at the Conservatory, the 'Barcarolle' slow movement of a very early String Quartet from 1888, as well as the composer's last completed piece from 1935, the engaging *Sousedská* for five violins, double-bass, cymbals and triangle. Recording dates range from 1966 to 1992 (most of the material is designated as AAD), but the quality is consistently praiseworthy and the volumes are available either separately or gathered together within an attractive slipcase.

Sir Arthur Sullivan British 1842-1900

GROVE *Sullivan, a Chapel Royal chorister, became a pupil of Sterndale Bennett at the Royal Academy of Music (1856) and studied at the Leipzig Conservatory (1858-61). The promise shown by his incidental music for The Tempest (1861) and other early concert works led to festival commissions and conducting posts, which he complemented with work as organist, teacher and song and hymn tune writer; from 1866, he also dabbled in comic opera. His increasing success in this last field – with CF Burnand in Cox and Box and then WS Gilbert in Trial by Jury – culminated in the formation by Richard D'Oyly Carte of a company expressly for the performance of Gilbert and Sullivan works. With HMS Pinafore the collaborators became an institution. Their works, produced at the Savoy Theatre from 1881 (the most popular 'Savoy Operas' were The Mikado and The Gondoliers), won a favour with English-speaking audiences that has never waned. Sullivan was knighted in 1883 and continued to conduct, notably the Leeds Festival and the Philharmonic Society concerts, but his serious ouput dwindled. A breach with Gilbert (1890), recurring ill-health and the relative failure of his last works clouded his final years.*

Sullivan was essentially an eclectic, drawing on elements from opera, ballads, choral and church music, by composers from Hander to Bizet. Some lack of emotional depth and an unsure grasp of large-scale structure have limited the success of his more serious music (Golden Legend, Ivanhoe). It was in Gilbert's satirical subjects and witty verses that his talents found their happiest, most graceful and consistent inspiration, underpinned as they are by a highly professional compositional technique. Here his inventive melodies fit perfectly the sense and accentuation of the words, while lively choruses underscore traits of particular groups (male and female) and deft instrumentation points up character. His clever parodies of serious music and use of 'tune combination' increase the fun.

Symphony in E, 'Irish'

Symphony in E, 'Irish'. The Tempest – Suite. Overture in C, 'In Memoriam'
BBC Philharmonic Orchestra / Richard Hickox
Chandos CHAN9859 (75 minutes: DDD) Ⓕ
Recorded 2000 ●

Plaudits all round to Richard Hickox and his excellent Manchester band (and the Chandos production team) for at last granting Sullivan's *Irish* symphony the first wholly recommendable digital recording it so richly deserves. And what a charmer of a work it is! Mendelssohn (and his *Reformation* Symphony above all) provides the dominant stylistic template, but the work is soundly constructed, effectively scored, and the *scherzo*'s irresistibly perky oboe tune, in particular, already reveals a very real melodic gift. Like Owain Arwell Hughes (CPO – nla) before him, Hickox observes the first-movement repeat, but his direction is infinitely more imaginative (at the hushed heart of the development section, sample the tingling atmosphere he conjures during those magical bars beginning at 9'13") and he never allows tensions to sag. What's more, the playing of the BBC Philharmonic ideally combines bright-eyed affection, keen vigour and nimble polish.

Following the symphony's successful March 1866 première under August Manns, Sullivan was asked to provide a work for that same year's Norwich Festival. The sudden death of his father just a few weeks before the festival proper jolted Sullivan into penning the likeable overture, *In Memoriam*. Written within 10 days and first given in Norwich on October 30 under Julius Benedict, the work soon won great popularity, though in terms of inventive freshness and orchestral scope it is rather trumped by the astonishingly confident incidental music for Shakespeare's *The Tempest* that Sullivan had written nearly six years earlier while still a student at the Leipzig Conservatory. Indeed, it comes as no surprise to learn that the British première of *The Tempest* in April 1862 made the 19-year-old a celebrity overnight, and the present suite draws upon seven of the original 12 numbers. Again, Hickox and company do plentiful justice to Sullivan's precocious inspiration, not least the powerfully moody 'Introduction', delectable 'Overture to Act IV' and the exquisite skip of the 'Dance of Nymphs and Reapers' (appealing echoes in the last-named of Schumann's *Spring* Symphony). A thoroughly enjoyable collection, then, accorded sound of glowing realism in the finest Chandos tradition.

Sullivan Cello Concerto in D[a] (reconstr Mackerras and Mackie). Symphony in E, 'Irish'[b]. Overture di ballo[b]
Elgar Romance, Op 62[a] (arr vc)
[a]**Julian Lloyd Webber** *vc* [a]**London Symphony Orchestra / Sir Charles Mackerras;** [b]**Royal Liverpool Philharmonic Orchestra / Sir Charles Groves**
EMI British Composers CDM7 64726-2 (71 minutes: ADD/DDD). Recorded [a]1986 and [b]1968 Ⓜ

Sir Charles Groves's sturdy yet affectionate reading of Arthur Sullivan's wholly charming *Irish* Symphony was always one of the best of his EMI offerings with the RLPO, and the 1968 recording remains vivid. In the sparkling *Overture di ballo*, again, Groves conducts with plenty of character. There are also first-rate performances of Sullivan's undemanding Cello Concerto from 1866 (in a fine reconstruction by Sir Charles Mackerras – the manuscript was destroyed in Chappell's fire of 1964) as well as Elgar's wistful little *Romance* (originally for bassoon). This is a thoroughly attractive and rewarding mid-price reissue.

Overtures

Overtures – Cox and Box; The Sorcerer; HMS Pinafore; The Pirates of Penzance; Patience; Iolanthe; Princess Ida; The Mikado; Ruddigore (arr Toye); The Yeomen of the Guard; The Gondoliers; The Grand Duke
Royal Ballet Sinfonia / Andrew Penny
Naxos 8 554165 (70 minutes: DDD) Ⓢ
Recorded 1997

The first thing that sets this apart from other collections of Sullivan overtures is that – for the first time – it covers the entire Gilbert and Sullivan output. The only works that are missing are *Thespis*, *Trial by Jury* and *Utopia Limited*, none of which had overtures as such. The sensible addition of the overture to *Cox and Box* means that all the Sullivan comic operas likely to be of interest to the general collector are here. An even more intelligent feature is that they are presented in chronological order, so that one can chart the progression of Sullivan's comic opera style from the very French-sounding ending of *Cox and Box* and the equally French-sounding opening of *The Sorcerer* through to more distinctively Sullivanesque sounds of the later pieces.

Of course, none of this would count for much if the performances were not up to scratch. Happily they are models of their kind. Andrew Penny has an agreeably light touch, alternatively reflective and sparkling, and gets graceful phrasing from the Royal Ballet Sinfonia – ideal performers of light music. Nobody wanting a collection of Sullivan's comic opera overtures should need to look elsewhere.

Victoria and Merrie England

RTE Sinfonietta / Andrew Penny
Marco Polo 8 223677 (78 minutes: DDD) Ⓕ
Recorded 1993

Five years before Edward German's comic opera *Merrie England*, this Sullivan ballet score was staged at the Alhambra Theatre as part of the celebrations of Queen Victoria's Diamond Jubilee. The original full score appears not to have survived. However, a complete piano reduction was published, along with an orchestral suite, and in addition Sullivan reused earlier material such as his *Imperial March* and music from his early ballet *L'île enchantée*. From all these sources Roderick Spencer has made this very convincing re-creation of the full score. And very worthwhile it proves too. As the notes explain, British ballet in those days was not classical ballet as we know it today but mime-drama. Spectacle was what it was all about, and Sullivan rose to the occasion admirably.

There are some most attractive passages – not only in the recycled material but also, for instance, the Solo Variation for the May Queen and perhaps above all the Waltz of Wood Nymphs, which would well repay taking over into the light music repertory. In addition Sullivan skilfully weaves in various patriotic British melodies as well as traditional dances such as a morris dance and a sailors' hornpipe. Such pastiche is the sort of thing that Sullivan did particularly well, and Andrew Penny and the RTE Sinfonietta do the whole score proud. This is as rewarding as any of the CDs of Sullivan without Gilbert that Marco Polo have issued.

The Gondoliers

The Gondoliers. Overture di ballo (1870 version)
Richard Suart *bar* Duke of Plaza-Toro; **Philip Creasey** *ten* Luiz; **John Rath** *bass* Don Alhambra; **David Fieldsend** *ten* Marco; **Alan Oke** *bar* Giuseppe; **Tim Morgan** *bar* Antonio; **David Cavendish** *ten* Francesco; **Toby Barrett** *bass* Giorgio; **Jill Pert** *contr* Duchess of Plaza-Toro; **Elizabeth Woollett** *sop* Casilda; **Lesley Echo Ross** *sop* Gianetta; **Regina Hanley** *mez* Tessa; **Yvonne Patrick** *sop* Fiametta; **Pamela Baxter** *mez* Vittoria; **Elizabeth Elliott** *sop* Giulia; **Claire Kelly** *contr* Inez; **D'Oyly Carte Opera Chorus and Orchestra / John Pryce-Jones**
TER ② CDTER2 1187 (109 minutes: DDD) Ⓕ
Recorded 1991

This is one of a series of recordings by the new D'Oyly Carte Opera Company that offers a vastly better quality of sound than any of its ageing competitors. Orchestral detail is the most immediate beneficiary, and the overture serves to demonstrate John Pryce-Jones's lively tempos and lightness of touch. Outstanding among the singers are perhaps John Rath, who gives Don Alhambra's 'I stole the prince' and 'There lived a king' real presence, and Jill Pert, a formidable Duchess of Plaza-Toro. Richard Suart not only provides the leading comedy roles with exceptionally clear articulation and musicality, but also adds considerable character to his portrayals. David Fieldsend and Alan Oke provide attractive portrayals of the two gondoliers, and Lesley Echo Ross and Regina Hanley are also most agreeable.

Seasoned listeners may note numerous changes of detail as a result of the purging of the performance material of changes made to the parts around the time of the 1920s Savoy Theatre revivals. There is no dialogue, but added value is provided by Sullivan's sunniest comic opera score being accompanied by the sparkling *Overture di ballo*, played in its original version with some traditional cuts opened up.

Additional recommendation

The Gondoliers

Coupling: Cello Concerto in D[a]

Evans Duke of Plaza-Toro **Young** Luiz **Brannigan** Don Alhambra **Lewis** Marco **Cameron** Giuseppe **Glyndebourne Festival Chorus; Pro Arte Orchestra / Sargent; [a]Lloyd Webber** *vc* **[a]London Symphony Orchestra / [a]Mackerras**

HMV Classics ② HMVD5 73672-2 (114 minutes: ADD/DDD) Ⓑ

A really beautiful 'Pair of sparkling eyes' from Lewis.

HMS Pinafore

Richard Suart *bass* Sir Joseph Porter; **Felicity Palmer** *mez* Little Buttercup; **Rebecca Evans** *sop* Josephine; **Thomas Allen** *bar* Captain Corcoran; **Michael Schade** *ten* Ralph Rackstraw; **Donald Adams** *bass* Dick Deadeye; **Valerie Seymour** *sop* Hebe; **Richard Van Allan** *bass* Bill Bobstay; **John King, Philip Lloyd-Evans** *bars* Bob Becket; **Welsh National Opera Chorus and Orchestra / Sir Charles Mackerras**

Telarc CD80374 (74 minutes: DDD). Notes and text included. Recorded 1994 Ⓕ OO

As always, Mackerras keeps the livelier numbers moving along comfortably without ever a hint of rushing, while giving full weight to the tender moments and, above all, caressing all the details of Sullivan's delicious orchestration. Right from the overture, with its beautifully shaped *Andante* section, this is music-making to perfection. Of the singers, Felicity Palmer's Buttercup truly oozes plumpness and pleasure, while Thomas Allen's Captain does not just the crew of the *Pinafore*, but all of us, proud. If Rebecca Evans's Josephine is a shade lacking in colour, Mackerras has found in Michael Schade's Ralph Rackstraw a most elegant addition to his G&S team. As for Richard Suart's Sir Joseph Porter, this is surely as stylish a demonstration of patter singing as one can find anywhere on disc, while Donald Adams's Dick Deadeye is no worse for his 40-odd years singing the role. Add orchestral playing of refinement, choral work whose perfection extends from the formal numbers to the varied inflexions of 'What nevers?', plus a recording that brings out the instrumental detail to perfection, and one has a *Pinafore* that is unadulterated delight from first note to last.

Additional recommendation

HMS Pinafore

Coupling: Trial by Jury

Baker Sir Joseph Porter **Cameron** Captain Corcoran **Lewis** Ralph Rackstraw **Brannigan** Dick Deadeye **Sinclair** Little Buttercup **Milligan** Bill Bobstay **Glyndebourne Festival Chorus; Pro Arte Orchestra / Sargent**

HMV Classics ② HMVD5 73056-2 (101 minutes: ADD) Ⓑ

A sensitive reading of *HMS Pinafore* and a super coupling: George Baker is superb as the judge in *Trial by Jury*.

The Mikado

John Holmes *bass* The Mikado; **John Wakefield** *ten* Nanki-Poo; **Clive Revill** *bar* Ko-Ko; **Denis Dowling** *bar* Pooh-Bah; **John Heddle Nash** *bar* Pish-Tush; **Marion Studholme** *sop* Yum-Yum; **Patricia Kern** *mez* Pitti-Sing; **Dorothy Nash** *sop* Peep-Bo; **Jean Allister** *mez* Katisha. Iolanthe – excerpts **Elizabeth Harwood, Elizabeth Robson, Cynthia Morey** *sops* **Heather Begg, Patricia Kern** *mezzos* **Stanley Bevan** *ten* **Eric Shilling, Denis Dowling, Julian Moyle** *bars* **Leon Greene** *bass* **Sadler's Wells Opera Chorus and Orchestra / Alexander Faris**

Classics for Pleasure ② CD-CFPD4730 (135 minutes: ADD). Recorded 1962 Ⓑ OO

At the core of these performances are some of the finest British singers of 30 years ago, all of whom were chosen not just for their singing but for their sense of the theatricality and humour of Gilbert and Sullivan. Just listen, for instance, to how John Heddle Nash gives full expression to every word of Pish-Tush's 'Our great Mikado'. Here, too, is Marion Studholme's delicious Yum-Yum and Elizabeth Harwood's joyous Phyllis. If one singles out Clive Revill for special mention, it is because his Ko-Ko is uniquely well judged and imaginative, combining superb comic timing, verbal clarity and vocal dexterity. His 'little list' is hilarious, and one can almost feel one's hand gripped at the words 'shake hands with you *like that*'. At the helm in both works is Alexander Faris who knew supremely well how to capture the lightness and sparkle of operetta. The new Overture put together for *The Mikado* by Stephen Dodgson may come as a surprise, but it is apt and cleverly done. The sound is inevitably dated when compared with more recent recordings, but it scarcely mars the enjoyment.

Additional recommendation

The Mikado

Adams The Mikado **Rolfe Johnson** Nanki-Poo **Suart** Ko-Ko **Van Allen** Pooh-Bah **McLaughlin** Yum-Yum **Howells** Pitti-Sing **Palmer** Katisha **Welsh National Opera Chorus and Orchestra / Mackerras**

Telarc CD80284 (79 minutes: ADD) Ⓕ

A delicious Nanki-Poo and a magnificent Katisha.

The Pirates of Penzance

Eric Roberts *bar* Major-General Stanley; **Malcolm Rivers** *bar* Pirate King; **Gareth Jones** *bar* Samuel; **Philip Creasy** *ten* Frederic; **Simon Masterton-Smith** *bass* Sargeant of Police;

Marilyn Hill Smith *sop* Mabel; **Patricia Cameron** *sop* Edith; **Pauline Birchall** *mez* Kate; **Susan Gorton** *contr* Ruth; **D'Oyly Carte Opera Chorus and Orchestra / John Pryce-Jones**
TER ② CDTER2 1177 (85 minutes: DDD) Ⓕ
Recorded 1990

The revival of the D'Oyly Carte Opera Company produced the first digital recordings of complete Gilbert and Sullivan scores, and this TER set is a very happy example. Philip Creasy is an engaging and vocally secure Frederic, and Marilyn Hill Smith trips through 'Poor wandering one' with a delectable display of vocal ability and agility. The couple's interplay with the chorus in 'How beautifully blue the sky' is quite enchanting, and their exchanges in 'Stay, Frederic, stay' splendidly convincing. Eric Roberts makes the Major-General a thoroughly engaging personality, and the dotty exchanges between Simon Masterson-Smith's Sargeant of Police and his police force are sheer joy. Even such details as the girls' screams at the appearance of the pirates in Act 1 have a rare effectiveness. John Pryce-Jones keeps the score dancing along. Those who want the dialogue as well as the music must look elsewhere, but this is certainly to be recommended.

Additional recommendation
Pirates of Penzance
Couplings: Overture In C, 'In Memoriam'. The Sorcerer. Cox & Box. Princess Ida
Baker Major-General Stanley **Milligan** Pirate King **Lewis** Frederic **Brannigan** Sergeant of Police **Morison** Mabel **Glyndebourne Festival Chorus; Pro Arte Orchestra / Sargent**
HMV Classics ② HMVD5 730622 (113 minutes: ADD) Ⓑ
A glorious 'Paradox' trio, and the lovely duet for Mabel and Frederic beautifully sung by Morison and Lewis.

The Yeomen of the Guard

Peter Savidge *bar* Sir Richard Cholmondeley; **Neill Archer** *ten* Colonel Fairfax; **Donald Adams** *bass* Sergeant Meryll; **Peter Hoare** *ten* Leonard; **Richard Suart** *bar* Jack Point; **Donald Maxwell** *bar* Shadbolt; **Alwyn Mellor** *sop* Elsie; **Pamela Helen Stephen** *mez* Phoebe; **Felicity Palmer** *mez* Dame Carruthers; **Clare O'Neill** *sop* Kate; **Ralph Mason** *ten* First Yeoman **Peter Lloyd Evans** *bar* Second Yeoman

Trial by Jury
Rebecca Evans *sop* Plaintiff; **Barry Banks** *ten* Defendant; **Richard Suart** *bar* Judge; **Peter Savidge** *bar* Counsel; **Donald Adams** *bass* Usher; **Gareth Rhys-Davies** *bar* Foreman; **Welsh National Opera Chorus and Orchestra / Sir Charles Mackerras**
Telarc ② CD80404 (121 minutes: DDD). Notes and texts included. Recorded 1995 Ⓕ ●

Between them, *The Yeomen of the Guard* and *Trial by Jury* contain all that is best in Sullivan's music for the theatre. In the former there is some of his more serious and ambitious writing, in the latter some of his most consistently light-hearted and engaging. All of this is brought out in Telarc's series of recordings with Welsh National Opera. As always, Sir Charles Mackerras paces the music impeccably, and he has assured contributions from such stalwarts as Donald Adams, Felicity Palmer and Richard Suart. The last-named may be a shade light-voiced compared with some of the more comic performers of Jack Point and the Learned Judge; but in *The Yeomen* it is surely his performance that stands out. His handling of the dialogue after 'Here's a man of jollity' is masterly, and his 'Oh, a private buffoon' is as winning as any, with impeccable clarity of diction and a perfectly judged French accent for 'jests ... imported from France'. Neill Archer and Alwyn Mellor are admirable as Fairfax and Elsie; but Pamela Helen Stephen could have displayed more of the minx in Phoebe Meryll's personality, while in *Trial by Jury* Barry Banks has too small a voice to convince as the Defendant. Recommended, especially if you want both works on the same set.

Further listening
Iolanthe
Coupling: Overture di Ballo[a]
Baker The Lord Chancellor **Wallace** Earl of Mountararat **Young** Earl Tolloller **Brannigan** Private Willis
Glyndebourne Festival Chorus; Pro Arte Orchestra; [a]BBC Symphony Orchestra / Sargent
HMV Classics ② HMVD5 73675-2 (106 minutes: ADD) Ⓑ
Sir Malcolm Sargent's affectionate handling of the score contributes to the great success of this issue.

Ruddigore
Coupling: The Merchant of Venice – Suite[a]
Baker Sir Ruthven Murgatroyd **Lewis** Dauntless **Brannigan** Sir Despard Murgatroyd
Glyndebourne Festival Chorus; Pro Arte Orchestra / Sargent; [a]City of Birmingham Symphony Orchestra / [a]Dunn
HMV Classics ② HMVD5 73681-2 (97 minutes: ADD) Ⓑ
Lacking nothing in the way of humour and drama, this is above all a musical performance.

Franz von Suppé Austrian 1819-1895

GROVE *In Vienna Suppé became Kapellmeister at the Theater in der Josefstadt (1840), Theater an der Wien (1845), Kaitheater (1862) and Carltheater (1865). He wrote a string of effective stage scores, from overtures (Poet and Peasant, Light Cavalry) and incidental music to genuine Viennese operettas, opera parodies and even operas, some of which survive as viable theatre works. Among the most popular were the farce Gervinus (1849) and the operettas Flotte Bursche (1863), Fatinitza (1876) and above all Boccaccio (1879). At its best his music is light and fluent, elegant and immediately appealing.*

Overtures

Overtures – Leichte Kavallerie; Tricoche und Cacolet; Boccaccio. Afrikareise – Titania Waltz. Fatinitza. Humorous Variations on the Popular Song, 'What comes there from on high?' Die Heimkehr von der

Hochzeit. Herzenseintracht – Polka. Franz Schubert. Triumph Overture
Slovak State Philharmonic Orchestra, Košice / Alfred Walter
Marco Polo 8 223683 (62 minutes: DDD) Ⓕ
Recorded 1994

This is another fascinating insight from Marco Polo into the wider output of a composer unjustly typecast through the brilliance of his rousing overtures. Here the familiar *Leichte Kavallerie* and *Fatinitza* overtures serve to demonstrate the thoroughly reliable conducting and playing of Alfred Walter and the Košice orchestra, without quite offering a challenge to the most rousing interpretations available elsewhere. What are of interest are the rarities. Of the unfamiliar overtures, that to *Tricoche und Cacolet*, a Viennese adaptation of a Meilhac and Halévy play, is perceptibly in the French style of Offenbach, with some attractive themes and a marvellous passage for bassoon, while the *Triumph Overture* has a typically exciting ending. The overture to *Die Heimkehr von der Hochzeit* is perhaps less striking, while that to *Franz Schubert* (a one-act operetta portraying the composer on stage) is mainly notable for its use of Schubertian themes – *Der Erlkönig*, *Der Wanderer*, the German Dance No 7 (also used later in *Lilac Time*), *Der Schäfer und der Reiter* and *Die Taubenpost*. Among the other pieces, the *Afrikareise* waltz finds Suppé very much in Straussian territory, while *Herzenseintracht* proves that he could also produce a polka with the best. Perhaps the most intriguing item is Suppé's set of humorous variations on the *Fuchslied*, a popular Viennese student song which we would recognise as *A-hunting we will go*. It all provides further proof that Suppé's entertaining writing extended way beyond his overtures.

Requiem in D minor

Aleksandra Baranska *sop* **Katarzyna Suska** *contr* **Jerzy Knetig** *ten* **Andrzej Hiolski** *bass* **Cracow Philharmonic Chorus and Orchestra / Roland Bader**
Koch Schwann 312482 (71 minutes: DDD). Text and translation included. Recorded 1989 Ⓕ

Suppé composed his Requiem in 1855 in memory of Franz Pokorny, the theatre manager to whom he owed much of his early conducting and compositional experience. The demands of a large-scale religious work held no terrors for Suppé and the work is powerfully and imaginatively written, with much of the operatic flavour of Verdi's Requiem of 19 years later. The chorus has the major vocal contribution, with the bulk of the solo opportunities going to the two lower voices. Anyone wishing to sample the riches of the work should try the hauntingly beautiful 'Hostias', with its eerie brass and woodwind and stirring bass solo, or the *Agnus Dei*, with its plaintive funeral march developing into a typically expansive Suppé theme. This disc offers a spacious reading of an impressive and moving work that offers much more than mere curiosity value.

Jan Pieterszoon Sweelinck

Dutch 1562-1621

GROVE *Sweelinck studied with his father, organist of the Oude Kerk, Amsterdam, succeeding him in or before 1580. He remained in this post all his life, with a few excursions to inspect new organs in other cities. Among the most influential and sought-after teachers of his time, he included Germans among his pupils, notably Scheidt, Jacob Praetorius and Scheidemann. He wrote over 250 vocal works, including a complete French psalter (1604-21), motets (1619), chansons (1594, 1612) and Italian madrigals (1612). But he is best known for his c70 keyboard works, which include monumental fugal fantasias, concise toccatas and well-ordered variation sets. He perfected forms derived from, among others, the English virginalists and greatly influenced 17th-century north German keyboard music, becoming one of the leading composers of his day. His son Dirck (1591-1652), who succeeded him at the Oude Kerk in 1621, edited a popular song collection (1644) and also composed songs and keyboard music.*

Organ Works

Toccata in C. Ballo del granduca. Ricercar.Malle Sijmen. Mein junges Leben hat ein End'. Aeolian Echo Fantasia. Onder een linde groen. Toccata in A minor I. Erbarm dich mein, o Herre Gott. Poolsche dans
James David Christie *org*
Naxos 8 550904 (64 minutes: DDD) Ⓢ
Played on the C B Fisk Organ, Houghton Chapel, Wellesley College, USA. Recorded 1993

The Houghton Chapel is nowhere near as resonantly spacious as the Oude Kerk in Amsterdam, but its relative intimacy does not rob the organ of its natural resonance and tonal beauty. James David Christie presents what is, in effect, a most satisfactory re-creation of one of Sweelinck's organ recitals, given daily between 1580 and 1621, for the burghers of Amsterdam. One hopes they were appreciative of the most consistently witty and generous-spirited keyboard music before the era of Buxtehude, Couperin and Bach.

While Christie may not possess the lyricism of a Leonhardt, the humane warmth of a Piet Kee or the mercurial whimsy of a Koopman, he is, in his own right, a bold, stylish, unhasty player, clearly thoroughly versed in early performance practice, with an incisive technique disclosing musical intelligence and common sense. He is particularly successful in the five major variation sets here, relishing the variety of decorative motifs but still conveying an impression of structural coherence and unity. Just occasionally his articulation might have worked better in a somewhat larger acoustic: at times a more obviously singing touch might have suggested greater tenderness in quieter moments and more ample majesty in louder ones. Nevertheless, with appealing registrations, an almost ideal choice of programme, good notes and undistractingly natural recording this is recommended.

Choral Works

Ab Oriente. Angelus ad pastores ait. Beati omnes. Beati pauperes. Cantate Domino. De profundis. Diligam te Domine. Domine Deus meus. Ecce nunc benedicite. Ecce prandium. Ecce virgo concipiet. Euge serve bone. Gaudeate omnes. Gaude et laetare. Hodie beata Virgo Mariae. Hodie Christus natus est. In illo tempore. In te Domine speravi. Iusti autem. Laudate Dominum. Magnificat. Non omnis. O Domine Jesu Christe. O quam beata lancea. O sacrum convivium. Paraclectus autem. Petite et accipietis. Qui vult venire post me. Regina coeli. Tanto tempore. Te Deum laudamus. Timor Domini. Ubi duo vel tres. Venite, exultemus Domino. Vide homo. Videte manus meas. Viri Galilaei

Clare College Choir, Cambridge / Timothy Brown with **James Grossmith, Andrew Henderson** *org*
Etcetera ② KTC2025 (141 minutes: DDD). Ⓕ
Notes,texts and translations included
Recorded 1998 ○

Lurking suspicion that Jan Pieterszoon Sweelinck is a true doyen of sacred vocal music is emphatically confirmed in an important and invigorating world première recording of the complete 1619 *Cantiones sacrae*. This collection of 37 motets in five-voices demonstrates, above all, the quality of his aesthetic, one in which textual representation and pure contrapuntal pleasure converge with effortless mastery; you only have to hear the first minute of the first track, a quasi-introit, 'Gaudete', of infectious energy, to dance to its affirmative and buoyant rhythms and bask in the clarity of the harmonic conception. *Cantiones sacrae* projects a distinctive containment, both in scale and emotional judgement, which should appeal to choirs of all shapes and sizes – and listeners too; drawing close parallels with William Byrd can be a hazardous exercise, though there is some common territory, borne out by biography, that Sweelinck survived as a Catholic in a Protestant working environment. By turning to the Roman vulgate in later years for his texts, as he does here, Sweelinck mirrors Byrd's own practice in the *Gradualia*, if far less methodically. As these pieces would not, therefore, have adorned the liturgy, their use was most likely limited to domestic situations and to the Collegium Musicum in Amsterdam, an institute founded especially to promote Sweelinck's compositions.

These performances by the young voices of Clare College Choir are impressive. Brown expertly circumnavigates his disciplined larger forces of about 26 voices around an oeuvre which is both introspective and ecstatic. The smaller-scale consort is perhaps less polished, the tuning of the sopranos has a tendency to 'dip' intermittently, and there is an occasional 'piping kettle' quality to the timbre. Generally, too, the lack of colorific range and resonance betrays the youthful membership of the choir; this can be telling in some of the slower music. These are small gripes in a project which stands out for a pioneering place in the catalogue and its fine advocacy of Sweelinck's seemingly unlimited resource.

Karol Szymanowski

Polish 1882-1937

GROVE *Szymanowski was born into an artistic family of the Polish landed gentry and began his musical education with his father. At 13, in Vienna, he was powerfully impressed by hearing Wagner for the first time. He then had formal tuition from Zawirski and Noskowski in Warsaw (1901-4), and during the next decade began to make an international reputation for music in the German tradition, relating to Wagner, Strauss and Reger: the main works of this period include the Symphony No 2 (1910), Piano Sonata No 2 (1911) and the opera Hagith (1913).*

During these years he visited Italy, Sicily and north Africa he also encountered Pelléas, The Firebird and Petrushka, and all these enriching influences were remembered in his abundant output of 1914-17, when he was confined by the war to Russia. Works of this period are typically classical or oriental in inspiration, and ornately figured in a manner relating to Skryabin or Debussy. They include the choral Symphony No 3 (1916), Violin Concerto No 1 (1916), Myths for violin and piano (1915) and the piano triptychs Metopes (1915) and Masques (1916). He then used this new, highly sensuous language to tackle the theme of The Bacchae in his opera King Roger (1926), set in the orientalized Norman kingdom of Sicily.

In 1919 he settled in Warsaw, now the capital of an independent Poland; and he began while completing King Roger to compose in a nationalist style, drawing on folk music in his choral orchestral Stabat mater (1926), ballet Harnasie (1935) and other works. He accepted the directorship of the Warsaw Conservatory (1927-32), but his last years were dogged by ill health, and he wrote nothing after his Violin Concerto No 2 (1933) and a pair of piano mazurkas, adding to a set of 20 dating from 1924-5. Other works include two quartets, songs, folksong arrangements and cantatas.

Violin Concertos

Awards 1997

Violin Concertos – No 1, Op 35; No 2, Op 61. Three Paganini Caprices, Op 40. Romance in D, Op 23
Thomas Zehetmair *vn* **Silke Avenhaus** *pf*
City of Birmingham Symphony Orchestra / Sir Simon Rattle
EMI CDC5 55607-2 (65 minutes: DDD) Ⓕ
Recorded 1996 ○○○

They make an admirable coupling, the two Szymanowski violin concertos, but a demanding one for the soloist. They are both so beautiful that it must be tempting to embellish both with a similarly glowing tone. They inhabit quite different worlds (they were written 16 years apart) and Zehetmair shows how well they respond to quite different approaches.

In the First, after a rapt solo entry, he uses for the most part a lovely but delicate tone, expanding to athletic incisiveness but not often to lushness. It all fits very well with Sir Simon

Rattle's handling of the orchestra: occasionally full and rich but mostly a sequence of exquisitely balanced chamber ensembles. Generous but finely controlled rubato from both the soloist and the conductor allows the concerto's improvisatory fantasy to flower; and the quiet close even has a touch of wit to it.

Zehetmair's sound is immediately less ethereal, more robust, for the opening melody of the Second Concerto. This is the sort of tone, you suspect, that he would use in Bartók's Second Concerto, and it points up a vein of indeed Bartókian strength to this work's longer and firmer lines. Rattle, too, seeks out bolder and more dense colours. It is characteristic that even the more musing lyrical pages here are given a warmer colour than superficially similar moments in the First Concerto.

The *Paganini Caprices* were equipped by Szymanowski not with deferential accompaniments but with independent and quite freely composed piano parts. They change Paganini, even where the violin part is unmodified (most of the time but not quite all), into a late romantic virtuoso, with a hint of Lisztian poetry alongside the expertly pointed-up fireworks of the Twenty-Fourth *Caprice*; even here Zehetmair is a listening violinist, not one to upstage his excellent pianist. The *Romance*, the warmest and most luscious piece here, is beautifully done but with a touch of restraint to prevent it cloying. A first-class coupling, and a recording that makes the most of the superb acoustic of Symphony Hall in Birmingham.

Symphony No 2

Symphony No 2 in B flat, Op 19. Concert Overture in E, Op 12. Wordsong, Op 46[a]. Songs of the Infatuated Muezzin, Op 42[a]

[a]**Zofia Kilanowicz** *sop* **London Philharmonic Orchestra / Leon Botstein**

Telarc CD80567 (68 minutes: DDD) Ⓕ

Recorded 2000 ⭘

The *Concert Overture* is a hugely gifted young composer's homage to Richard Strauss, and fully worthy of its model in impetuousness, rich sonority and close-woven polyphony. The Second Symphony is no less rich but more disciplined, with Reger's influence added to (and modifying) that of Strauss and with Szymanowski's own high colouring, sinuous melody and tonal adventurousness now in their first maturity. The *Infatuated Muezzin* songs are a high point of his middle period, Debussyan harmony and florid orientalising arabesques fusing to an aching voluptuousness, colour now applied with the refinement of a miniaturist. Leon Botstein is fully aware of the quite different palettes these pieces use, and the London Philharmonic Orchestra play splendidly.

Wordsong (Telarc's translation for *Słopiewnie*) is the key to Szymanowski's final phase, a setting of five poems in an artificial language, using Slavonic roots to suggest a sort of 'pre Polish'. Szymanowski responded to the poems' assonances, rhythms and alliterations (he couldn't resist 'słodzik słowi słowisienkie'), finding for them a fusion of folk elements, archaisms and melodies that retain something of the discarded middle period's exoticism. You sense the influence of Stravinsky (*Les noces* in particular) and hear already both the folk vigour and the ritual purity of Szymanowski's late style (in the third song, too, there is a startling pre-echo of the slow movement of Górecki's Third Symphony).

There is a slight, attractive tremor to Kilanowicz's voice, but she has both the almost white purity and the flexible coloratura the songs need. It is very hard to make a single adverse comment about this important addition to the Szymanowski discography. If you insist, some of the dates on the jewel-case are wrong.

Symphony No 3

Symphony No 3, 'The Song of the Night', Op 27[a]. Violin Concertos[b] – No 1, Op 35; No 2, Op 61

[a]**Wiesław Ochman** *ten* [b]**Konstanty Andrzej Kulka** *vn* [a]**Polish Radio Chorus of Krakow; Polish National Radio Symphony Orchestra / [a]Jerzy Semkow, [b]Jerzy Maksymiuk**

HMV Classics HMV5 73860-2 (73 minutes: ADD) Ⓑ

Recorded [b]1979 and [a]1982 ⭘

The opening of the First Violin Concerto makes an extraordinary introduction to Szymanowski's soundworld (with Kulka the gleamingly rich-timbred, idiomatically committed soloist). The Polish orchestra's glitteringly atmospheric textures remind one of early Stravinsky, yet there is also a sensuous exoticism that gives the music a luminosity of colour all its own, and when the solo violin enters rapturously and the orchestra coalesces into vibrant intensity, Maksymiuk's concentration is wholy inexorable. The Concerto is structured in a single movement, but the music constantly changes mood and colour until an ecstatic cadenza leads into the final overwhelmingly passionate *Lento assai*, and the work ends mysteriously with a touchingly ethereal solo soliloquy.

The cyclic Second Concerto initiates a more nostalgic lyricism, but not for long, for the later *tuttis* are awesome in their astringent passion. Here the vibrant cadenza (more extended than its predecessor) is the centrepiece, leading into an energetic *Rondo-Scherzo* drawing on Góral folk music, although a semi-tranquillity is re-established before the vigorous close, which quotes the main theme of the work's opening section. The Third Symphony (*Song of the Night*) is a similarly ecstatic setting of an exotic Persian poem for tenor, chorus and large orchestra, and under Semkow's baton is even more powerful, with its headily luxuriant obsessional intensity, the wordless chorus contributing to the rich sensuality of texture, but eventually leading to a more subdued closing epilogue (where the tenor soloist is excellent). In such brilliantly evocative performances all this music communicates very powerfully, richly projected by the vividly full-blooded yet atmospheric recording.

Symphony No 4

Harnasie, Op 46[a]. Symphony No 4, 'Symphonie concertante', Op 60[b]. Mazurkas, Op 50 – No 1 in C; No 2 in A. Theme and Variations in B flat minor, Op 3
Andrzej Bachleda *ten* **Wiesław Kwasny** *vn* **Felicja Blumental** *pf* [a]**Cracow Radio Chorus and Symphony Orchestra / Antoni Wit;** [b]**Polish National Radio Symphony Orchestra / Jerzy Semkow**
EMI Matrix CDM5 65307-2 (75 minutes: ADD) Ⓜ
Recorded 1974-79

With the exception of the early and unashamedly Brahmsian *Theme and Variations*, this is all late Szymanowski, Szymanowski giving up just a little of the colour and opulence of his middle period to respond with delight to the fresh and invigorating rawness of the folk music of the Tatra region. He responds most obviously, of course, in the folk ballet *Harnasie*, with its frequent imitations of raucous folk fiddling and the fervour of choral folk-song and its heartfelt evocations of Poland's mountain country. But surely the wonderfully poised opening theme of the *Symphonie concertante* owes something to this influence too (a theme so beautiful that Szymanowski cannot resist returning to it as the true destination of all the previous beauties of his slow movement)? The last movement might almost be a supplement to *Harnasie*, but the use throughout of wind and string solos sounds very much like a 'refinement' of the peasant fiddle and trumpet in the ballet.

Since the performances are very good indeed, and the recordings clean and decent, the coupling is a very recommendable one. All the more so since Western pianists still seem reluctant to programme the *Symphonie concertante*, and *Harnasie*, which calls for tenor and violin soloists and a chorus as well as orchestra, is unlikely ever to prove popular in the concert hall. Both are full of delights. The *Theme and Variations* and the two Mazurkas are well played; the latter will undoubtedly whet your appetite for the more intimate and subtle aspects of 'late Szymanowski' – and will send you off hunting for the other 18 Mazurkas.

Complete Piano Music

Piano Sonatas – No 1 in C minor, Op 8; No 2 in A, Op 21; No 3, Op 36. Four Etudes, Op 4. 12 Etudes, Op 33. Fantasy in C, Op 14. Masques, Op 34. Two Mazurkas, Op 62. 20 Mazurkas, Op 50. Métopes, Op 29. Four Polish Dances, Op 47. Nine Preludes, Op 1. Prelude and Fugue in C sharp minor. Romantic Waltz. Variations in B flat minor, Op 3. Variations on a Polish Folk Theme, Op 10
Martin Jones *pf*
Nimbus ④ NI1750 (269 minutes: DDD) Ⓢ
Recorded 1992-93

Szymanowski was in every sense a 'perturbed spirit', his life stricken by poverty, ill-health, belated recognition (despite Artur Rubinstein's dazzling championship), alcoholism and a furtive and psychologically corrosive homosexuality. Yet such was his genius that he could transcend and transmute such elements to create some of the most exotic and multi-dimensional music of the century. Already, the Op 1 *Preludes*, despite their bias towards Chopin and Scriabin, exude a heady and intense fragrance; and who could call the wildly thrusting and propulsive Var 7 or the ricocheting double-note finale of Op 3 the work of a languid composer lacking both zeal and the 'hard, gem-like flame' of a tirelessly questing vision? The First Sonata's *Tempo di menuetto* delights with its delectable Christmas-tree sparkle, and if the Op 14 *Fantasy* looks back to an essentially Lisztian theatricality, *Métopes* and *Masques* lead us into a mythology memorably described by Anthony Payne as a world where 'opulent, luxuriant textures are constructed from tiny flickering motives, the harmonies often bi-tonally complex. The sonorities shimmer and oscillate … and melodic lines, usually simple in essence, are coloured by elaborate melismata.' The *Mazurkas*, too, may take their cue from Chopin, yet they speak with a different Tatra voice and accent. But the greatest work is the Second Sonata, composed for Rubinstein and premièred by him in 1912.

This gargantuan gift is surely a truer successor to Beethoven's *Hammerklavier* than Boulez's Second Sonata, and it would be hard to overestimate the quality of Jones's performance. His lucidity and assurance in page after page of Szymanowski's intricacy and effulgence are awe-inspiring. To play and record Szymanowski's complete piano works requires a technical brio, facility and emotional empathy given to few; Nimbus's sound is not first-class, and its presentation is unimaginative, but no lover of works of rare musical genius performed with exemplary skill should miss this set.

Piano Sonata No 1

Piano Sonata No 1 in C minor, Op 8. Mazurkas, Op 50 – No 13, Moderato; No 14, Animato; No 15, Allegretto dolce; No 16, Allegramente – vigoroso. Etudes, Op 33. Four Polish Dances, Op 47. Prelude and Fugue in C sharp minor
Martin Roscoe *pf*
Naxos 8 553867 (69 minutes: DDD) Ⓢ
Recorded 1996

This volume three concludes Martin Roscoe's cycle of Szymanowski's piano music (a pity, then, that we will not get to hear his account of the Third Sonata and the remaining six *Mazurkas*). It offers a cross-section of Szymanowski's styles as a composer for the keyboard, from the early First Sonata (always described as post-Chopin and post-Scriabin but, Roscoe convincingly demonstrates, no less importantly post-Liszt as well) to the pungent *Mazurkas*, with their flavour of Bartók as well as of late Grieg.

The *Prelude and Fugue* is an interesting link between that early Sonata (the Lisztian fugue was written shortly after it, the harmonically more adventurous prelude four years later) and the Op 33 *Etudes* which are usually referred to as representing Szymanowski's 'impressionist' phase. Again, Roscoe makes you question this conventional description: yes, the harmonies look rather Debussyan but they don't often sound that way. These very brief pieces (just over a minute on average) are studies in the conventional sense, written by one fine pianist for another, Alfred Cortot, but they are also exercises in harmonic subtlety and rich in Szymanowski's personal fantasy. The *Four Polish Dances* inhabit the same world as the *Mazurkas*, and it's obvious that Roscoe enjoys open fifths and flat sevenths as much as Szymanowski did.

A warm recommendation, then, although one tinged with regret. For a complete edition of Szymanowski's piano music Martin Jones's survey on Nimbus is admirable but Naxos's piano sound is much preferable. Given the omission of the Third Sonata and the remaining *Mazurkas* one could supplement Roscoe's three volumes with Pavel Kamasa's superb recording of the complete *Mazurkas* (Koch Schwann) and Raymond Clarke's of the Third Sonata (Athene).

Stabat mater, Op 53

Awards 1995

Stabat mater, Op 53. Litany to the Virgin Mary, Op 59. Symphony No 3, Op 27, 'The song of the night'
Elzbieta Szmytka *sop* **Florence Quivar** *contr* **Jon Garrison** *ten* **John Connell** *bass* **City of Birmingham Symphony Orchestra and Chorus / Sir Simon Rattle**
EMI CDC5 55121-2 (56 minutes: DDD) Ⓕ
Texts and translations included. Recorded 1994 ❍❍❍

The first impression here is that Rattle is relatively new to Szymanowski. There's a huge enthusiasm here, a missionary quality that bespeaks the recent convert. On the other hand the care over matters of balance, the knowledge of just those points where Szymanowski's complexity needs very careful handling if it's not simply to blur into opacity, suggest a conductor who has been there before and knows the dangers. You get the feeling that a conscious decision was made to delay recording this music until the circumstances were right.

The CBSO Chorus sound thoroughly at home not only in the music but in the language too. The clincher on the decision to go ahead with this recording might well have been Rattle's realisation that in Elzbieta Szmytka he had a soprano who might have been born to sing Szymanowski's pure, floated and very high-lying soprano lines (in the *Stabat mater* and the *Litany*; in the symphony he uses a tenor, which was Szymanowski's own first choice). The result is very fine: one of the most beautiful Szymanowski recordings ever made. And yet 'beautiful Szymanowski' isn't all that hard if the orchestra's good enough and the conductor capable. Rattle's insistence that all of the music be heard, its bones and sinews as well as its flesh, its urgency and passion as well as its deliquescent loveliness, makes for uncommonly gripping Szymanowski as well. He reminds one of how much more there is to the Third Symphony than voluptuous yearning: solemnity, for one thing, and a fierce ardour that can indeed knock you sideways.

The choice of soloists for the *Stabat mater* is interesting: alongside Szmytka's radiant purity are Quivar's throaty vibrancy and Connell's weighty darkness. Not a matching trio, but the contrast is appealing; it adds to the rich differentiation of sonority that Rattle draws from his chorus and orchestra. Garrison in the symphony is a touch hard and strenuous, less enraptured than one or two of the Polish tenors (and sopranos) who've recorded it, but he's a musicianly and likeable singer. The recording is outstanding: lucid, rich and spacious, with tremendous and perfectly focused climaxes.

King Roger

Awards 2000

Thomas Hampson *bar* Roger II; **Elzbieta Szmytka** *sop* Roxana; **Ryszard Minkiewicz** *ten* Shepherd; **Robert Gierlach** *bar* Archbishop; **Jadwiga Rappé** *contr* Deaconess; **Philip Langridge** *ten* Edrisi **City of Birmingham Symphony Youth Chorus; City of Birmingham Symphony Chorus**
Symphony No 4, 'Symphonie concertante', Op 60
Leif Ove Andsnes *pf* **City of Birmingham Symphony Orchestra / Sir Simon Rattle**
EMI ② CDS5 56823-2 (112 minutes: DDD). Notes Ⓕ
text and translation included. Recorded 1996-98 ❍❍❍

King Roger is a ravishingly beautiful opera, but a very fragile one. With a shrill soprano or a less than ideally cast tenor it would be fatally flawed. Minkiewicz's Dionysiac Shepherd betrays a slight hardness and a touch of stress in full voice, but he has both the allure and the mystery that the role imperatively demands. Almost his first words are 'My God is as beautiful as I', and he should vocally suggest that he is indeed radiantly beautiful. His voice shades to a croon at times, but he never sounds epicene.

Szmytka is a wonderful Roxana, with beautifully pure high notes and bell-like coloratura. At the end of Act 2 her florid aria is repeated (in Szymanowski's concert version), at just the point where you might well have replayed the earlier track for the pleasure of listening to her again. The use of distinguished singers in the smaller roles is no extravagance: Langridge evokes the exotic strangeness of the Arab sage Edrisi, while Rappé and Gierlach add to the hieratic gravity of the opening scene. Hampson in the central role is in fine voice, easily conveying Roger's authority, his angry but bewildered rejection of the Shepherd's new religion. He is even finer, however, in Act 5, where the King is painfully torn between Dionysus and Apollo. The ambiguity of the final scene remains, as it must. Is Roger accepting the Shepherd in place of Roxana? Or, since Roxana herself immediately succumbs to the Shepherd's glamour, is Roger achieving wholeness by at last acknowledging feminine intuitions within himself?

That these questions remain resonant and provoking at the end of the performance is a tribute both to the work itself, and also to Rattle's handling of it. The orchestral textures are voluptuously rich and subtly coloured, aided by a spacious recording (the vast Byzantine basilica of the opening scene is magnificently evoked) and orchestral playing of a very high order indeed. But the score has sombre and austere colours as well as exotically rich ones, and the dramatic urgency of the performance makes Szymanowski's opera seem even shorter than it is. This is the finest recording of *King Roger* that has so far appeared. The Fourth Symphony, in Szymanowski's later, folk-derived and harder-edged style, is a huge contrast: quite a shock after the opera's radiant conclusion. Andsnes's powerfully athletic playing points up the music's affinities with Prokofiev, and both he and Rattle emphasise the new vigour that Szymanowski was drawing from the fiddle music of the Tatra region, but in the lovely slow movement Roxana's world still seems within reach.

Toru Takemitsu Japanese 1930-1996

GROVE *Takemitsu was a pupil of Kiyose from 1948. Influenced by Webern, Debussy and Messiaen, he has reflected what is most oriental in these composers: a concern with timbre and elegant sound and with the precision of the moment rather than with pattern and development. His music often gives the impression of spatial experience and of materials evolving freely of their own accord; silence is fully organized. Some of his works use Japanese instruments, but most are for Western orchestral and chamber media. Among the best known are Requiem for strings (1957), November Steps for biwa, shakuhachi and orchestra (1967), A Flock Descends into the Pentagonal Garden (1977) and From me flows what you call Time (1990) for percussion quintet and orchestra.*

'Quotation of Dream'

Day Signal. From Heaven. Quotation of Dream[a]. How Slow the Wind. Twill by Twilight. Archipelago S. Dream/Window. Night Signal

[a]Paul Crossley, [a]Peter Serkin *pfs*
London Sinfonietta / Oliver Knussen
DG 20/21 453 495-2GH Ⓕ
(71 minutes: DDD). Recorded 1996 ●●●

'Dream', 'Slow', 'Twilight': these are the kind of words that give the key to Takemitsu's later style, and all the works on this disc were written between 1985 and 1993. The Debussy connection is easy to hear, but, simply because of that, Takemitsu's own personal blend of the flowing and the disjunctive, against a harmonic background consistently more dense than Debussy's, stands out as one of the most significant late 20th-century responses to an early 20th century master. Second-hand impressionism it is not.

Oliver Knussen's performances are models of balance and clarity, with the music's purely colouristic qualities not excessively indulged. Also crucial here is the excellent quality of the DG recording, extremely well-designed for the way most of these pieces alternate so subtly between soloistic writing and fuller yet no less richly imagined textures. *Dream/Window* sets the tone for the kind of restrained yet eloquent ceremonies that can also be heard in the tribute to Feldman, *Twill by Twilight* and the two beautifully constructed works, *How Slow the Wind*, and *Quotation of Dream*. It is extremely tempting to say that this is the best single CD of Takemitsu's music so far issued.

To the Edge of Dream

To the Edge of Dream. Folios – I, II and III. Toward the Sea III. Here, There and Everywhere. What a Friend. Amours perdues. Summertime. Vers, l'Arc-en-ciel, Palma

John Williams *gtr* **Sebastian Bell** *alto fl*
Gareth Hulse *ob d'amore* **London Sinfonietta / Esa-Pekka Salonen**
Sony Classical SK46720 (60 minutes: DDD) Ⓕ
Recorded 1989

Toru Takemitsu is an original, refined composer and something of a latter-day impressionist, as titles like *To the Edge of Dream* suggest. It may therefore come as a surprise to find him arranging songs by Lennon and McCartney, Gershwin and others for solo guitar. Yet these prove to have attractive touches of the subtlety found in Takemitsu's own compositions, and they also provide useful contrast to the more substantial works on this beguiling disc. *Folios*, the earliest composition included, already reveals Takemitsu's musical catholicity in its reference to a Bach chorale. *Toward the Sea* and *Vers, l'Arc-en-ciel, Palma* are both more expansive mood pieces, the former (for guitar and alto flute) almost too reticent and hesitant beside the richer textures of the latter, which is enhanced by the additional solo role given to the oboe d'amore as well as its beautifully laid out orchestral accompaniment. *To the Edge of Dream* is in effect a guitar concerto, with a wider range of mood and an even more developed role for the orchestra than *Vers, l'Arc-en-ciel, Palma*. It provides a particularly satisfying focus for a sensitively performed and well recorded disc. Even if we hear rather more of the guitar relative to the orchestra than we would in the concert hall, this is not unreasonably artificial.

I Hear the Water Dreaming

I Hear the Water Dreaming[d]. Toward the Sea I[a]. Le fils des étoiles[b]. Toward the Sea II[bd]. And then I knew 'twas Wind[bc]. Toward the Sea III[b]. Air

Patrick Gallois *fl* **[a]Göran Söllscher** *gtr* **[b]Fabrice Pierre** *hp* **[c]Pierre-Henri Xuereb** *va* **[d]BBC Symphony Orchestra / Sir Andrew Davis**
DG 20/21 453 459-2GH (67 minutes: DDD) Ⓕ
Recorded 1996 ●●

This disc is a follow-up to Oliver Knussen's selection of orchestral works on the *Gramophone* Award-winning 'Quotation of Dream', and is in one sense at least a far bolder concept, risking the inclusion of three different versions of the same work, *Toward the Sea*, which in duration amount to about half of the total playing time.

Yet the risk is justified. The three short but beautifully fashioned movements of *Toward the Sea*, inspired by Melville's great novel *Moby Dick*, are vintage Takemitsu in their spell-binding evocativeness and economy, and throughout these performances Patrick Gallois' range of tone colour and sensitivity to line are of exceptional quality. Even if you finally conclude that the original version with guitar is, after all, the best, the variations of texture and atmosphere which the different instrumentations provide make for absorbing listening.

The rest of the programme easily sustains this level, although *And then I knew 'twas Wind* (citing a poem by Emily Dickinson) is rather more loosely constructed than its companions, underlining just how rarely the pejorative term 'improvisatory' can be applied to Takemitsu's refined and understated art. Gallois and his colleagues don't have the field to themselves in this repertory, and some listeners will rightly value Aurèle Nicolet's accounts for Philips of *And then I knew 'twas Wind*, *Toward the Sea III* (nla) and *Air*. But the superb technical quality of the recording and the subtle yet alert responsiveness of the interpretations make this an outstanding release. It's a dream of a disc.

Thomas Tallis

British c1505-1585

GROVE *Tallis was organist of the Benedictine Priory of Dover in 1532, then probably organist at St Mary-at-Hill, London (1537-38). About 1538 he moved to Waltham Abbey where, at the dissolution (1540), he was a senior lay clerk. In 1541-2 he was a lay clerk at Canterbury Cathedral, and in 1543 became a Gentleman of the Chapel Royal; he remained in the royal household until his death acting as organist, though he was not so designated until after 1570. In 1575 Elizabeth I granted him a licence, with Byrd, to print and publish music, as a result of which the Cantiones sacrae, an anthology of Latin motets by both composers, appeared later that year.*

His earliest surviving works are probably three votive antiphons (Salve intemerata virgo, Ave rosa sine spinis and Ave Dei patris filia) in the traditional structure common up to c1530: division into two halves, with sections in reduced and full textures. Other early works include the Magnificat and another votive antiphon, Sancte Deus, both for men's voices. Two of his most sumptuous works, the six-voice antiphon Gaude gloriosa Dei mater and the seven-voice Mass ' Puer natus est nobis ', date from Mary Tudor's brief reign (1553-8), the former featuring musical imagery and melismatic writing, the latter expert handling of current techniques of structural imitation and choral antiphony. He also composed six Latin responsories and seven Office hymns for the Sarum rite and large-scale Latin psalm motets early in Elizabeth's reign. The 40-voice motet, Spem in alium, an astonishing technical achievement, may have been composed in 1573.

Tallis was one of the first to write for the new Anglican liturgy of 1547-53. Much of this music, including If ye love me and Hear the voice and prayer, is in four parts with clear syllabic word-setting and represents the prototype of the early English anthem. His Dorian Service is in a similar style. Among his Elizabethan vernacular music are nine four-voice psalm tunes (1567) and various English adaptations of Latin motets (e.g. Absterge Domine); the Latin Lamentations and the paired five-voice Magnificat and Nunc dimittis also date from this period. His instrumental works include keyboard arrangements of four partsongs and many cantus firmus settings and a small but distinguished contribution to the repertory of consort music which includes two fine In Nomines. Tallis's early music is relatively undistinguished, with neither Taverner's mastery of the festal style nor Tye's modernisms. But much of his later work is among the finest in Europe, ranging from the artless perfection of his short anthems to the restrained pathos of the Lamentations.

Beati immaculati

Beati immaculati. Puer natus est nobis. Mass 'Puer natus est nobis'. Viderunt omnes. Dies sanctificatus. Celeste organum. Viderunt omnes. Suscipe quaeso Dominus. Gaude gloriosa Dei mater
Chapelle du Roi / Alistair Dixon
Signum Records SIGCD003 (65 minutes: DDD) Ⓕ
Texts and translations included. Recorded 1997

The illuminating insert-notes by Nick Sandon place Mary's short reign within the bewilderingly stormy context of the 16th century with a calm understanding that enables the listener to see how this Latin music came to be written. Incidentally, the first piece was originally an English setting of *Beatus vir*. Sandon says it falls naturally into place with its Latin text. But the verses in the booklet don't exactly correspond to what is being sung, which raises an unnecessary question mark. Sandon's edition of the Proper Salisbury chants for the Third Mass of Christmas are performed between the polyphonic items. Meticulously researched, they serve as a foil to the sumptuous settings of the Ordinary.

If only they had been sung with more solemnity and gusto, omitting those irritating little bursts of volume on the high notes! All these chants would have sounded more authentic at a slower tempo with the occasional semi-metrical dactyl: as it is, they comes across rather as a poor relation beside the magnificence of Tallis's seven-part polyphony. The polyphonic singing is exemplary, the clarity of the individual parts and the rhythmic interplay well under control. The singers enter into the spirit of the liturgical texts, in particular in the third section of the *Agnus Dei*. In the final motet, *Gaude gloriosa*, which presents major difficulties because of its structure and length, their interpretation at times almost touches the visionary.

Lamentations of Jeremiah

Lamentations of Jeremiah. Motets – Absterge Domine; Derelinquat impius; Mihi autem nimis; O sacrum convivium; In jejunio et fletu; O salutaris hostia; In manus tuas; O nata lux de lumine. Salve intemerata virgo
The Tallis Scholars / Peter Phillips
Gimell CDGIM025 (68 minutes: DDD) Ⓕ
Texts and translations included ●

This, the third volume of the survey by The Tallis Scholars of the music of the Tudor composer, Thomas Tallis, contains the well-known *Lamentations*, eight motets, and the extended motet *Salve intemerata virgo*. The *Lamentations* and motets are typical of the style of late Renaissance English composers. The overall mood is one of considerable austerity and their simplicity is indicative of the probability of their having been written for the private use of loyal Catholics rather than for formal ritual. *Salve intemerata virgo*, on the other hand, looks back to the glories of the late 15th century. In particular, Tallis's use of the phrygian mode gives the work as a whole a strong sense of the medieval. Despite this disparity of styles the Tallis Scholars acquit themselves, as always, with great distinction. In the *Lamentations* and motets they achieve an appropriate sense of intimacy, while in *Salve intermerata virgo* they rise fully to the challenges of one of the more extended and demanding examples of Tudor choral composition. In addition the formidable challenges which this latter work sets for the conductor, such as the sense of pace, variation of dynamics, and overall architecture of the work, are all extremely well handled by Peter Phillips. The recording is very fine.

Lamentations of Jeremiah[a]. Absterge Domine[b]. In jejunio et fletu[a]. If ye love me[a]. O sacrum convivium[b]. Audivi vocem de caelo[a]. Derelinquat impius[a]. Salvator mundi, salva nos I[a]. Solfa-ing Song a 5[b]. In Nomine a 4 No 1[b]. Benedictus[a]. Fond youth is a bubble[b]. Psalm Tunes for Archbishop Parker's Psalter[a] – No 3, Why fum'th in sight; No 8, Tallis's Canon. Like as the doleful dove[b]. When shall my sorrowful sighing slake[b]. Te lucis ante terminum I[a]
[a]Theatre of Voices / Paul Hillier; [b]The King's Noyse / David Douglass
Harmonia Mundi HMU90 7154 (71 minutes: DDD) Ⓕ
Recorded 1995 ●

This is imaginative programme planning – atmospheric renaissance music performed by choral and instrumental forces in amiable juxtaposition rather than combination. The 16-strong Theatre of Voices, who are based at the University of California at Davis, sing throughout with a dark-browed *gravitas* and warmth of feeling that are thoroughly appropriate and give considerable pleasure. The secular music plus (surprisingly perhaps, but interestingly) *Absterge Domine* and *O sacrum convivium* are done by The King's Noyse, an expert renaissance violin consort, though they realise the sombre harmonic undertow so characteristic of Tallis less successfully than the singers. It ends with the tranquil evening office hymn, *Te lucis ante terminum* (complete with its alternating plainchant). Unlike most English groups in this repertoire, the Theatre of Voices do not use falsettists (authenticity may be on their side). Compared with The Tallis Scholars, the high-lying tenor parts here – often assigned by other groups to male altos – are perhaps not always impeccably blended, and the female voices sometimes have a slight flatward colouring. But, in compensation, this American group certainly taps a rich vein of pathos in this affecting music while remaining stylistically convincing, and Tallis's two most famous psalm-tunes are done with much relish. A distinctive, and on the whole, commendable issue, warmly recorded, and with a sumptuously produced CD booklet.

Additional recommendation
Lamentations of Jeremiah
'Lamenta': Brumel Lamentations **A Ferrabosco I** De lamentatione Ieremiae prophetae **Palestrina** Lamentations for Holy Saturday **Tallis** Lamentations of Jeremiah **R White** Lamentations of Jeremiah
The Tallis Scholars / Peter Phillips
Gimell CDGIM996 (73 minutes: DDD: 6/98). Ⓕ
Texts and translations included

A reissue compilation of 16th-century Tenebrae music for Holy Week. The Lamentations texts set are quite different, but all show an intensity and a devotional power that work cumulatively to produce a remarkably satisfying disc.

Spem in alium

Te lucis ante terminum. Salvator mundi. Spem in alium. In jejunio et fletu. O salutaris hostia. Lamentations I and II. Miserere. Mass for four voices
Magnificat / Philip Cave
Linn Records CKD075 (67 minutes: DDD) Ⓕ
Texts and translations included. Recorded 1999 ●●●

This is quite simply the best performance of Tallis's 40-part *Spem in alium* to date. Sung by a constellation of singers, many of them familiar names from other well-established choral groups, it is a gripping realisation. The effect of the slowly moving harmonies is enhanced by a well-conceived and very positive use of dynamics. Precise entries, gently undulating rhythms that are wonderfully supple, and then those firm antiphonal phrases – one group of choirs answered by another at 'Creator coeli et terra' – raise the tension, until we twice almost miss a heart-beat at the well-placed rest before 'Respice …'. Philip Cave's note on Tallis's recusancy background, his coded use of numbers and his acquaintance with influential members of the Catholic nobility (in particular the Duke of Norfolk, soon to be executed), gives the listener valuable insights into the whole corpus of Tallis's Latin compositions, particularly those of a penitential nature like the *Lamentations* or the Lenten responsory *In jejunio et fletu*, and further heightens their poignancy.

That great motet, so central to the whole programme, is well supported by the four-part Mass and the delightful group of other pieces for various combinations of voices. The hymn *Te lucis* with its alternating chant strophes sounding so very English (almost too perfect for what was, after all, just run-of-the-mill everyday chant!) has the tempo relationship of the chant to the polyphony just right, which is a tremendous plus, rarely achieved.

Spem in alium. Salvator mundi (I, II). Sancte Deus, sancte fortis. Gaude gloriosa Dei mater. Miserere nostri. Loquebantur variis linguis
The Tallis Scholars / Peter Phillips
Gimell CDGIM006 (43 minutes: DDD) Ⓕ
Recorded 1984 **OO**

For the 1985 quatercentenary of Tallis's death, Peter Phillips and The Tallis Scholars produced this version of *Spem in alium*; in many respects it is clearly the most successful ever recorded. Not only is the choir superb and the interpretation an intelligent one; this is also the only recording in which the eight choir choirs seem genuinely to sing from different positions in the stereo spread, a technical achievement that leads to some thrilling antiphonal exchanges. Above all, Phillips's reading is a confident and assertive one. The effect is more that of a plea than a prayer, and the overall shaping is most characterful. Inevitably there are problems of balance, both at the top of the texture (several of the trebles are given rather too much prominence) and in the middle, where in full sections the music of the inner voices sometimes blends too readily into rich chords rather than emerging as a complex web of counterpoint.

But these are relatively small complaints to be made against what is frankly an outstanding achievement. This is a *Spem in alium* to be cherished. Phillips has paired *Spem in alium* with another of Tallis's largest and most celebrated works, *Gaude gloriosa Dei mater*. Here the texture is absolutely crystal, with verse sections sung by solo voices, and again the music has been paced with great care. It is certainly highly accomplished; and the same must be said of the readings of the five shorter pieces that complete the disc. What a fitting tribute to Tallis in his centenary year. No one who cares for Tudor choral music should be without it.

Tan Dun

Chinese/America 1957

Growing up during the Cutural Revolution, Tan Dun received no early musical training. After working as a violinist, at the age of 19 he entered the composition department of Beijing's reopened Central Conservatory of Music. There he encountered Western music and was stimulated by visits of guest composers Goehr, Crumb and Takemitsu. He moved to New York in 1986.

Yi2

Tan Dun Yi2 **Rouse** Concert de Gaudí
Sharon Isbin *gtr* **Gulbenkian Orchestra / Mu Hai Tang**
Teldec 8573-81830-2 (57 minutes: DDD) Ⓕ
Recorded 2000 **OOO**

These two concertos will come as a shock to anyone who believes that guitar music is about Spanishry and tunes to carry away in memory's pocket, but if approached with open ears the shock should benefit both them and the guitar. Chrisopher Rouse's tribute to Gaudí is as spectacular and unconventional as its eponym's cathedral in Barcelona – and it is at least finished! The strummed opening seems to herald another *Concierto de Aranjuez* but it is utterly deceptive; any connection with traditional Spanish music is soon submerged in a polychromatic and eclectic succession of episodes.

Tan Dun's *Yi2* recalls the shamanistic rituals that accompanied burials near his childhood home, but 'does not relate to the death of any one person'. Intense orchestral passages represent 'the weeping and wailing by everyone present – a part of the ritual'. The Chinese lute, the pipa, was in the composer's mind but here he fuses Chinese traditions with elements of flamenco. The music has been described as 'flamenco meets Stravinsky in the Hard Rock Café', which leaves out only the Chinese element that pervades the whole of this astonishing fabric of strange sounds and fluctuating emotions. It is perhaps the most remarkable work yet written for guitar and orchestra. No superlative would be excessive in describing Sharon Isbin's performances in this vivid recording. Her work on behalf of the guitar's present and future remains unparalleled, a continuation of that of Segovia and Julian Bream in earlier decades, supported by skill, musicality, dedication and seemingly boundless energy.

Symphony 1997

Yo-Yo Ma *vc* **Imperial Bells Ensemble of China; Yip's Children's Choir; Hong Kong Philharmonic Orchestra / Tan Dun**
Sony Classical SK63368 (72 minutes: DDD) Ⓕ
Text and translation included. Recorded 1997 **O**

Writing history into music is nothing new. The reunification of Hong Kong with China has inspired numerous commissions of one sort or another, Dun's *Symphony 1997* being among them. However, few will have utilised musical instruments that date back 2,400 years. The bianzhong is a family of tuned bells that, collectively, spans a five-octave range. They were discovered in an ancient tomb that was excavated as recently as 1978, and Dun's symphony gives them pride of place. In 'Heaven' (the symphony's first main episode), the bianzhong's grandeur 'rises from the earth's grave', though its presence is scarcely less imposing elsewhere. *Symphony 1997* opens and closes with a simple, touching 'Song of Peace'. It is cast in three sections ('Heaven', 'Earth' and

'Mankind'), the solo cello taking the role of commentator through wordless song. 'Water' (track 8) is a sub-division of 'Earth' and includes a demonstrative solo cadenza reminiscent of the finale from Kodály's Op 8 Solo Sonata, whereas the following track has the orchestra slowly re-enter like some huge, sonorous community.

Needless to say, Yo-Yo Ma's playing has great panache and intensity. 'Earth' represents Dun at his most characteristically inventive, but elsewhere dominant influences include Chinese popular music, various European late-romantics, Hindemith, Stravinsky and Varèse. There are also reminiscences of Beethoven and Puccini. *Symphony 1997* is a highly theatrical, lavishly scored montage, which is frequently rhythmic, richly atmospheric and with merging styles that reflect both China and the neighbour that has once again become family.

Marco Polo

Thomas Young *ten* Polo; **Alexandra Montano** *mez* Marco; **Dong-Jian Gong** *bass* Kublai Khan; **Susan Botti** *sop* Water; **Shi-Zheng Chen** *sngr* Rustichello, Li Po; **Nina Warren** *sop* Sheherazada, Mahler, Queen; **Stephen Bryant** *bar* Dante, Shakespeare; **Cappella Amsterdam; Netherlands Radio Chamber Orchestra / Tan Dun**

Sony Classical ② S2K62912 (100 minutes: DDD) Ⓕ
Notes and text included. Recorded live in 1996

Mobility and re-creation are key concepts in Tan Dun's 'opera within an opera', although readers expecting gravy-train minimalism will be disappointed. Tan uses rhythm in the old-fashioned way, at key dramatic moments or in support of internal and external action. The 're-creative' element concerns opera directors and their potential responses 'to different elements of these tales [concerning Marco Polo] in creating the dramatic world of the opera'. The 'plot', which has been skilfully rendered verbal by Paul Griffiths (although words in this context have a strongly allusive function), concerns three journeys: one physical, one spiritual and one musical. The components of the name 'Marco'/'Polo' are initially polarised to represent 'Marco the traveller' and 'Polo the memory' (their words are similarly divided), although the two do eventually join forces for a duet.

Musically, *Marco Polo* is based on the interconnection of two very separate currents – Eastern operatic and instrumental traditions ('Opera 1'), and Western opera traditions with a blend of Eastern and Western instruments ('Opera 2'). The forceful opening (a recurring idea) is shared among Chinese percussion, whereas much of the string writing that follows curves in the style of Chinese popular music. The 'physical' aspect of the journey calls on medieval, Middle Eastern, Indian, Tibetan, Mongolian and Chinese influences. Mahler counts among the 'Western' components (Shakespeare and Dante are two others), quite literally on track 14 of the second disc where 'Der Trunkene im Frühling' from *Das Lied von der Erde* makes a cameo appearance. Tan Dun's instrumentalists and vocal team give virtuoso performances, but special mention should be made of Susan Botti and Thomas Young, although the most astonishing vocal contribution of all comes from Shi-Zheng Chen, whose range and agility are remarkable. *Marco Polo*'s instrumentation includes a substantial battery of percussion, various national instruments (pipa, sitar, Tibetan bells and so on), 'optional' old instruments, plus woodwind, brass and strings.

Documentation is intriguing, albeit occasionally cryptic. The recording is excellent.

Giuseppe Tartini Italian 1692-1770

GROVE *After abandoning plans for a monastic career Tartini studied in Assisi (probably with Cernohorsk‡) and by 1714 had joined the orchestra at Ancona. He later spent time in Venice and Padua, where he settled in 1721 as principal violinist at the basilica of S Antonio. He worked there until 1765 except for a period in Prague (1723-6). Besides performing with success, he founded in 1727-8 a 'school' of violin instruction; his many pupils included JG Graun, Nardini and Naumann.*

Tartini was one of the foremost Italian instrumental composers, writing over 400 works: these include violin concertos and sonatas (many with virtuoso solo parts), trio sonatas and sonatas for string ensemble. Most have three movements, ordered slow-fast-fast (sonatas) or fast-slow-fast (concertos). His later works in particular approach Classical structures and display galant features, including regular four-bar melodic phrases. Elaborate cadence formulae are especially characteristic. He also composed some sacred music. Noteworthy among his writings are a work on violin playing and ornamentation, Traité des agréments de la musique – published only in1771 but thought to have been written earlier (L Mozart, in 1756, is thought to have borrowed from it, but it may be the other way round) – and two treatises on the acoustical foundations of harmony (1754, 1767), in which his discovery of the Difference tone phenomenon is discussed.

Violin Concertos

Violin Concertos – D, D15; G, D78; B flat, D123; G, D80; A minor, D115
Gordan Nikolitch *vn* **Auvergne Orchestra / Arie van Beek**

Olympia OCD475 (76 minutes: DDD) Ⓜ
Recorded 1996

The Auvergne Orchestra is not a period instrument ensemble but it demonstrates a lively and playful rapport with late baroque music. The performances are full of vitality and caprice. Nikolitch is a sensitive player who is constantly aware of the underlying poetry in Tartini's music, above all in slow movements. In these Tartini sometimes appended poetic mottoes, often in secret code, mainly drawn from Tasso and Metastasio. These established the mood of the movement in question and, more and more, became the focal point of the work. Sometimes, too, Tartini would provide a concerto with an alternative slow movement, one of which he might regard as definitive. One such instance is included in this programme (in the G major Concerto, D80) where, happily, Nikolitch gives us both slow movements. The dance-like character of many of the outer movements is an attractive feature of Tartini's concertos. Bright and clear recorded sound.

Violin Concertos – C, D4[a]; E minor, D56[b]; F, D63[c]; G, D75[d] **P**
[ad]**Federico Guglielmo,** [c]**Carlo Lazari** *vns* **L'Arte dell'Arco /** [b]**Giovanni Guglielmo** *vn*
Dynamic CDS220 (64 minutes: DDD) Ⓕ
Recorded 1998

The works in this fourth volume of Tartini's violin concertos all supposedly belong to the composer's earliest period, that is to say the years between *c*1720 and 1735. One of them, in E minor, has long been popular with soloists and has often been recorded. The remaining three, however, are less familiar and, it is claimed, here make their first appearance on disc. The C major piece sounds as if it might be the earliest concerto here, though many of the distinctive hallmarks of Tartini's style are firmly in place – little chromaticisms and short-lived, playful melodic patterns in the outer movements, and wistfully lyrical solo cantilenas in the tenderly expressive slow one. The author of the accompanying note erroneously claims the tonal plan is more imaginative than in Vivaldi's concertos. Tartini simply avails himself of a more advanced pool of stylistic knowledge, in no sense improving on the art of his forebears – especially Vivaldi.

An enjoyable programme with engaging solo contributions from Federico Guglielmo. Listeners will notice the acid quality of the *tutti* playing, and by a recorded sound that does little to ameliorate it, though having acknowledged them, they may quickly adjust to them.

Violin Sonatas

Violin Sonatas – G minor, 'Devil's Trill', B:g5; A minor, B:a3. Variations on a Gavotte by Corelli, B:F11 – excerpts. Pastorale in A, B:A16 (all arr Manze) **P**
Andrew Manze *vn*
Harmonia Mundi HMU90 7213 (69 minutes: DDD) Ⓕ
Recorded 1997 ●

The romantic connotations of Tartini's Violin Sonata in G minor, the *Devil's Trill*, deriving from the composer's own account of an appearance by the devil in a dream, have contributed towards making it one of the great *morceaux favoris* of the 19th and 20th centuries. It is, furthermore, just about the only remaining piece of baroque music where a piano accompaniment can still be countenanced without uniformly raised eyebrows. Some traditions do, indeed, die hard. But, of course, Tartini never intended anything of the kind; in fact, he probably never envisaged a keyboard continuo part at all, since none of his surviving autographs contains a figured bass for keyboard realisation. They do, however, mostly include unfigured bass parts though, as Tartini himself remarked, he provided them, often as an afterthought, and more for reasons of convention than any other.

Andrew Manze sees this as a justification for playing all the pieces in his programme without bass accompaniment. On the whole the experiment works well, since the expressive content and structural *puissance* of the music lies foremost in Tartini's melodic line. There are moments, however, where harmonic support from the bass is required, and at such times, above all in the *Devil's Trill* Sonata, Manze has had to introduce chords in the violin part to compensate for the absence of a cello. Manze's athletic technique, his musical sensibility and perhaps, too, his engaging sense of fun, ensure fascination and entertainment in equal measure. The 'diabolical' finale of the G minor Sonata has rhythmic poise, expressive delicacy and commendable virtuosity, and few admirers of this challenging piece will feel compromised by the absence of a string bass. None will regret the passing of the piano in this context. A stimulating release, beautifully recorded, and rich in fantasy.

Sir John Tavener British 1944-

GROVE *Tavener studied with Berkeley and Lumsdaine at the Royal Academy of Music (1961-5). Most of his music is explicitly religious, influenced by late Stravinsky but containing strong, bold images from a variety of other sources; his biblical cantata The Whale (1966) enjoyed a vogue. An early leaning towards Catholic devotion reached a consummation in the Crucifixion meditation Ultimos ritos (1972) and the opera Thérèse (1979). In 1976 he converted to the Russian Orthodox faith, composing in a simpler, luminous style (Liturgy of St John Chrysostom for unaccompanied chorus, 1978; Protecting Veil for cello and orchestra, 1989).*

The Protecting Veil

Awards 1992

Tavener The Protecting Veil. Thrinos
Britten Solo Cello Suite No 3
Steven Isserlis *vc* **London Symphony Orchestra / Gennadi Rozhdestvensky**
Virgin Classics VM5 61849-2 Ⓑ
(74 minutes: DDD). Recorded 1991 ●●●

First impressions of *The Protecting Veil* are of a consonant, major-key sweetness that could portend a pastoral after the style of Samuel Barber. Yet it soon becomes evident that this is not neo-romantic music. The religious aura of this Hymn to the Mother of God explains its style – moving between simple contemplativeness and heartfelt lament – but not the enthusiasm with which audiences have greeted it. One suspects that its most telling effect – the return of the opening idea with heightened eloquence at the end, which then dissolves into potent images of grief – is one major reason for its impact. Many listeners will also welcome Tavener's total rejection of contemporary complexity, though there is a price to pay for this in occasional passages where the musical thought grows dangerously desultory. But this performance, well recorded, is ideal in every way, with a soloist who shapes the long, simple lines effortlessly, and a conductor who is never tempted to push the music on beyond its natural pace.

Steven Isserlis also plays Britten's Third Suite with free expression and fine control. After the Tavener this is the music of a troubled, doubting mind, and a feeling of dramatic tension replaces his meditative ritual. There is nevertheless a touching sense of humanity in Tavener's short, unaccompanied *Thrinos*, a lament for a close friend, whose simple chant is clouded by the colours of a vivid sorrow. As with *The Protecting Veil*, the recordings of the Britten and *Thrinos* are superbly natural and immediate.

...Depart in Peace

...Depart in Peace. My Gaze Is Ever Upon You. Tears of the Angels
Patricia Rozario *sop* **Matthew Rooke** *tambura* **BT Scottish Ensemble / Clio Gould** *vn*
Linn Records CKD085 (59 minutes: DDD) Ⓕ
Recorded 1998 ●●

The most immediately striking work on this disc is the meditative, extremely beautiful ... *Depart in Peace*, for soprano, violin, tambura and strings. Dedicated to the memory of Tavener's father, it is a setting of the *Nunc dimittis*, interspersed with Alliuatic antiphons. The work follows a hypnotic sequence of repeating segments – an ecstatic string sequence with soprano (the first Alliuatic antiphon); the Song of Simeon (soprano, solo violin, tambura and cellos); an exquisitely beautiful, hymn-like sequence (the second Alliuatic antiphon) and finally an ecstatic Middle-Eastern sounding chant (the third Alliuatic antiphon). As the work progresses the antiphons lengthen on each repetition – the effect, over 25 minutes, is spellbinding and stunning.

Tavener describes *My Gaze Is Ever Upon You* as 'a series of sixteen gazes, moments and ecstatic breaths, written in Trinitarian guise' for solo violin, with taped violin and string bass drone. Although less obviously immediate to the ear than ... *Depart in Peace*, it nevertheless weaves a magical spell, as does *Tears of the Angels* for solo violin and strings, which Tavener asks to be played 'at the extreme breaking point of tenderness'. All is performed with great authority, conviction and beauty, and Patricia Rozario's singing in ... *Depart in Peace* is extraordinarily fine. A beautiful disc.

Akathist of Thanksgiving

James Bowman, Timothy Wilson *countertens* **Martin Baker** *org* **Westminster Abbey Choir; BBC Singers; BBC Symphony Orchestra / Martin Neary**
Arc of Light SK64446 (78 minutes: DDD). Text and translation included. Recorded live in 1994 Ⓕ

With the success of the ecstatic *Protecting Veil* (reviewed above) it has perhaps been easy to forget how rigorous and austere Tavener's music was only a few years previously. In 1986, his music had reached an extreme of 'inner silence'. *Eis Thanaton* was the work which broke through the barrier, moving painfully from darkness to light, but nevertheless the blaze of light of pieces such as the *Akathist* was hardly to be predicted. An *akathistos* is a long hymn used in the Orthodox rite, prescribed liturgically in the modern Russian use to be sung at Matins on the Saturday in the fifth week of Great Lent. The prototype *akathist* (others were written later) is addressed to the Mother of God and was written during the seventh century. The text Tavener sets is not liturgical, but was written strictly according to liturgical structure by Archpriest Gregory Petrov in a Siberian prison camp shortly before his death in the 1940s. The poetry is remarkable, for the quality and variety of its life-affirming imagery as much as for the fact that it was written at all in circumstances of such adversity.

The danger in setting such poetry of course is that the music will be correspondingly diverse and lack structure. To an extent Tavener has avoided this by founding each section on a pedal note which furnishes the mode, though to claim this as a Byzantine procedure is extremely misleading since no Byzantine composer would ever use all eight tones of the *oktoechos* in a single work. The undeniable musical richness of each of the sections is therefore contained within each modal 'frame', but somehow this does not generate a real harmonic structure for the work.

Having said that, the score is a catalogue of riches. The dark-hued, quasi Bulgarian male-voice sections, the sparkling countertenor duets, the variety of the scoring and the deeply moving recurring 'Amin', and the unexpected quiet climax in the ninth *kontakion* sung by a solo countertenor, are all extraordinarily powerful. They are very well sung indeed on this live recording (though the tenors have trouble maintaining control when in the higher registers); in particular the trebles are beyond reproach, and the duets by Bowman and Wilson wonderfully sensitive.

Akhmatova Songs

Akhmatova Songs[a]. Diódia[b]. Many Years[c]. The World[d]
[acd]**Patricia Rozario** *sop* **Vanbrugh Quartet** (Gregory Ellis, Elizabeth Charleson *vns* Simon Aspell *va* Christopher Marwood *vc*)
Hyperion CDA67217 Ⓕ
(63 minutes: DDD) ●●

The centrepiece of this disc devoted to works by John Tavener is *Diódia*, the third and latest of his string quartets. Tavener appears to have reserved the string quartet medium almost exclusively as a vessel into which to pour the distillations of some of his largest and most important compositions. Just as Tavener's first quartet, *The Hidden Treasure* (1989), drew material from the large-scale choral piece *The Resurrection*, and the second, *The Last Sleep of the Virgin* (1991), from the choral work *The Apocalypse*, so similarly *Diódia* (1995) grew out of material drawn from *The Toll Houses*.

Based on a book by a Californian Orthodox monk, the large-scale choral work *The Toll Houses* deals with the concept that symbolises 'the posthumous states of being of the soul, where it is decided whether the soul spends a certain amount of time in hell and a certain time in heaven [sic]'. Tavener describes *Diódia* as 'liquid metaphysics', and that is an excellent description of this wonderfully meditative and haunting music. As with all of Tavener's work, it eschews traditional form and instead unfolds as a series of musical episodes that alternate with each other in almost mantric fashion. The overall atmosphere is contemplative, with passages of luminous beauty, but these are interrupted at various points by some more energetic, worldly episodes. A particularly haunting passage featuring a repeated rhythmic figure played on bandir (drum) makes several appearances throughout and also brings this extraordinary work to a close. The Vanbrugh Quartet's intense and committed performance here is of the highest calibre.

The remaining items on the disc all feature music for soprano and string quartet, beautifully performed in these recordings by Patricia Rozario, for whom Tavener has composed many pieces. *The World* is a movingly intense setting of an equally astonishing and moving poem by Kathleen Raine, and its inclusion, together with the austerely beautiful *Akhmatova Songs*, originally composed for soprano and cello but heard here in an arrangement for soprano and string quartet, make a welcome addition to the catalogue. In sum, then, an indispensable and thoroughly recommendable disc.

Eternity's Sunrise

Eternity's Sunrise[a]. Funeral Canticle[b]. Petra: A Ritual Dream[c]. Sappho: Lyrical Fragments[d]. Song of the Angel[e]

[ade]**Patricia Rozario,** [d]**Julia Gooding** *sops* [bc]**George Mosley** *bar* [e]**Andrew Manze** *vn* **Academy of Ancient Music** [bc]**Chorus and Orchestra / Paul Goodwin**

Harmonia Mundi HMU90 7231 (65 minutes: DDD) Ⓕ
Notes, texts and translations included
Recorded 1998

Once upon a time we dreamt of breaking down musical barriers, but nowadays we can happily recount how many have been broken. This particular venture reconciles genres and generations on various fronts – between father and son, religious denominations, old and new musical modes, poetry and liturgy, and old instruments newly employed. The title-piece, *Eternity's Sunrise*, was born in the wake of loss. Tavener's late father was its prompting inspiration, and Diana, Princess of Wales its dedicatee. The tonal structure is simple: earth is represented by the solo soprano, angels by hand bells and heaven by a modest instrumental ensemble. It is a deceptively simple work, and rendered especially appealing in this context by Harmonia Mundi's vivid recording. Tavener devotees will love it.

The brief and warmly harmonised *Song of the Angel* for soprano and solo violin is set at a further distance but works well. *Petra: A Ritual Dream* calls on the Greek poet Giorgios Seferis to help reinvent the transcendent (represented, in terms of music, by violin harmonics). George Mosley intones the text, backed by a small chorus. Some of Tavener's word setting is fairly dramatic, and there is a folkloric slant to selected melodic lines. Tavener's *Sappho: Lyrical Fragments* (1981), the earliest work on the programme, is set for two sopranos with brief instrumental interludes between sections. Mysterious yet gripping, the *Fragments* owe something to Stravinsky (of, say, *Apollo*) whereas the last and longest piece on the disc – the *Funeral Canticle* for Tavener's father – cradles its texts between disparate styles, from plainchant to a reassuring variation on the Bach-style chorale. Could this be the son holding the father's hand, or vice versa? Whatever the unconscious subtext, *Funeral Canticle* is probably the most durable piece here.

Innocence

Innocence. The Lamb. The Tiger. The Annunciation. Hymn to the Mother of God. Hymn for the Dormition of the Mother of God. Little Requiem for Father Malachy Lynch. Song for Athene

Patricia Rozario *sop* **Leigh Nixon** *ten* **Graham Titus** *bass* **Alice Neary** *vc* **Charles Fullbrook** *bells* **Martin Baker** *org* **Westminster Abbey Choir; English Chamber Orchestra / Martin Neary**

Sony Classical SK66613 (64 minutes: DDD) Ⓕ
Texts included. Recorded 1994-95 ●

This is recommended as a single disc to convince anyone of the mastery of John Tavener. As well as the superb new work, *Innocence*, specially written for Westminster Abbey – encapsulating in 25 minutes what many of his more expansive pieces have told us – we have a rich and rewarding selection of other shorter choral pieces. They include not just the established favourites like the two intense Blake settings, *The Lamb* and *The Tiger*, and the two hymns for the Mother of God – here more openly passionate than in previous recordings – but the bald and direct *Little Requiem for Father Malachy Lynch*, the sharply terraced *Annunciation* and the *Song for Athene*, all among Tavener's most beautiful and touching inspirations. The theme of *Innocents* is Innocent Victims, which prompted Tavener to compose a ritual built on texts from varied sources, Christian, Jewish, Islamic and Hindu. This involves a range of elements, set physically apart from each other.

So the main choir, soprano (representing Holy Wisdom) and cello are at the centre, with the baritone soloist on one side intoning prayers for mercy in the language of the Orthodox church, and with the tenor soloist entering behind with Islamic prayers, and far away the pure sounds of a boys' choir. The result is both moving and atmospheric, with the climax introducing one element after another in rich *crescendo*, to provide a resolution very comparable to Britten's in the *War Requiem*.

Neary draws intensely committed singing from his choir, with the principal soloists, Patricia Rozario and Graham Titus, both excellent, as well as the tenor, Leigh Nixon, with Alice Neary an expressive cellist. All the performances have a warmth of expressiveness which defies any idea of ecclesiastical detachment. The discs of shorter Tavener works from both The Sixteen (Collins – nla) and St George's Chapel Choir (Hyperion) offer excellent performances of the four shortest and best-known works, but they seem relatively cool next to Neary's, whose reading of the *Hymn to the Mother of God* is overwhelmingly powerful within its three-minute span.

The recording vividly captures Westminster Abbey's acoustic with extreme dynamics used impressively to convey space and distance.

Svyati

God is With Us. Song for Athene. The Lamb. The Tiger. Magnificat and Nunc dimittis. Funeral Ikos. Two Hymns to the Mother of God. Love Bade Me Welcome. As One Who Has Slept. The Lord's Prayer. Svyati[a]

[a]**Tim Hugh** *vc* **St John's College Choir, Cambridge / Christopher Robinson**

Naxos 8 555256 (70 minutes: DDD) Ⓢ

Recorded 2000

To be sure, if John Tavener's reputation were to rest solely on his unaccompanied choral music and nothing else, then his stature as one of the most striking and original composers working today would be little diminished. Much of Tavener's creativity is founded on the traditions of his Orthodox faith and of Orthodox chant, and yet curiously, intentionally or unintentionally, he has also, through works such as those presented here, extended the tradition of English choral music. Through their popularity *The Lamb*, *The Tiger* and *Song for Athene* have become immovably imbedded in our choral tradition, but one need only listen to the splendid *Magnificat and Nunc dimittis*, for instance, to find a unique symbiosis of Eastern and Western traditions at work.

Many of the works presented on this CD have enjoyed wide circulation on numerous Tavener-only and compilation discs, but the performances here from the Choir of St John's College, Cambridge, under the direction of Christopher Robinson, have much to recommend them and, of course, Naxos's super-budget price makes this issue all the more desirable, especially for those seeking a survey of Tavener's choral music for the first time.

The inclusion of *Svyati* for solo cello and choir, with its echoes of *The Protecting Veil*, enhances the disc's desirability even more, and opens a window on to Tavener's more overtly Eastern/Orthodox-inspired music. Tim Hugh's serenely beautiful account of the solo cello part is worth the price of the disc alone, but it's a winner from beginning to end, and there is no hesitation in recommending it to devotees and newcomers alike. The recording, made in St John's College Chapel, is resplendently atmospheric.

Svyati. Eternal Memory. Akhmatova Songs. The Hidden Treasure. Chant

Patricia Rozario *sop* **Daniel Phillips, Krista Bennion Feeney** *vns* **Todd Phillips** *va* **Steven Isserlis** *vc* **Kiev Chamber Choir / Mykola Gobdych; Moscow Virtuosi / Vladimir Spivakov**

RCA Victor Red Seal 09026 68761-2 Ⓕ

(70 minutes: DDD). Text included

Recorded 1995

'O Holy One', or 'Svyatiy', to quote its correct transliteration, sets a religious text as a backdrop to Isserlis's warm, soaring solo oration. *Eternal Memory* recalls the 1992 *Gramophone* Award-winning *The Protecting Veil*, albeit with its own very individual structure: it opens with a paradisiacal passage in the style of Byzantine chant (think of the *1812* Overture's first few minutes), then turns restless for a middle section that suggests Biber's 'Drunken Revellers' (in *Battalia*) gate-crashing a Shostakovich string quartet. The revellers eventually hobble off, the Byzantine mood returns and 'Paradise persists'. And if proof were needed that not all Tavener sounds the same, then the six stark but startling *Akhmatova Songs* would surely provide it. All are utterly unalike, varying in style from the wailing declamations of 'Dante', through the more comforting tones of 'Pushkin and Lermontov' to the concise mini-drama of 'The Muse'. Soprano Patricia Rozario is a vivid vocal actress who commands an astonishingly wide range.

The Hidden Treasure Quartet is, in a sense, a cello solo with string trio accompaniment. The work follows a sort of bridge from the Paradise 'from which we have fallen' to the 'Paradise which Christ promised to the repentant thief'. The CD ends with palindromic *Chant* for unaccompanied cello, a four-minute encore from the eloquent soloist who more-or-less predominates throughout 70 arresting minutes.

One hesitates to offer a blanket recommendation in an area where critical reaction is frequently polarised, but do at least try the *Akhmatova Songs*, music that could profitably sit alongside similarly compelling song-cycles by Mussorgsky and Shostakovich. RCA's sound quality is excellent throughout.

Total Eclipse

Agraphon[a]. Total Eclipse[b]

[a]**Patricia Rozario** *sop* [b]**Max Jones** *treb* [b]**Christopher Robson** *counterten* [b]**James Gilchrist** *ten* [b]**John Harle** *sax* [b]**New College Choir, Oxford;**

Academy of Ancient Music / Paul Goodwin
Harmonia Mundi HMU90 7271 (62 minutes: DDD) Ⓕ
Texts and translations included. Recorded 2000 ○○

John Tavener's ability to arrest the listener's ear is nowhere more apparent than in the extraordinary opening pages of *Total Eclipse*. The work, Tavener tells us, is an esoteric contemplation on the word *metanoia* – meaning 'change of mind' or 'conversion' – and Tavener uses the conversion of St Paul on the road to Damascus to give the work structure and meaning. Ideally, *Total Eclipse*, premièred in 2000, needs to be experienced *in situ*: the spatial separation of instrumental groups and the space in which the work should be performed are essential components combined to create a transcendental, metaphysical experience. A high, sustained ison (drone) on strings, the rolling of multiple antiphonal timpani and the anarchic, terrifying 'alarm' calls of the solo soprano saxophone (a symbolic representation of St Paul) create a visceral effect on the listener, and the subsequent descending choral sequences on the word *Stavroménos* (Crucified) and Christ's calling of Saul are equally striking.

The recording can only hint at the spatial effects that Tavener envisaged, but it has nevertheless been exceptionally well committed to disc. Paul Goodwin and his team have no problems coping with Tavener's demands, and John Harle's stunning account of the solo saxophone part, together with Christopher Robson's and James Gilchrist's vocal contributions, make this extraordinary work a must for all Tavener fans.

Agraphon, for soprano, timpani and strings (1995), is no less extraordinary. Here Tavener chooses as his text a powerful set of verses by the Greek poet Angelos Sikelianos that were penned during the German occupation of Athens in 1941. The work places extraordinary intonational and stylistic demands upon the soprano: indeed Patricia Rozario, whose voice the work is specifically written for, spent several months in India studying and perfecting the techniques that Tavener calls for. The effort must have been worthwhile, for Rozario produces a compelling performance of exceptional intensity. A very fine and compelling disc indeed.

John Taverner

British c1490-1545

GROVE *The earliest unequivocal references to Taverner occur in 1524-25, when he was a lay clerk at the collegiate church of Tatershall. In 1526 he accepted the post of instructor of the choristers at Cardinal College (now Christ Church), Oxford, and c1530 became a lay clerk (and probably instructor of the choristers) at the parish church of St Botolph, Boston. By 1537 he had retired from full-time employment as a church musician. Although he was embroiled in an outbreak of Lutheran heresy at Cardinal College (in 1528) there is no evidence, contrary to popular opinion, that his views were seriously in conflict with Catholicism or that he ceased composing on leaving Oxford.*

Most of his extant works, which include eight masses, three Magnificats, numerous motets and votive antiphons and a few consort pieces and fragmentary secular partsongs, probably date from the 1520s. The three six-voice masses use cantus firmi, sectional structure, huge spans of melisma and skilful counterpoint; of the smaller-scale masses ' Western Wynde ' is based on a secular tune and in a less expansive, more Lutheran style. Characteristic of his writing is the development of a melodic or rhythmic fragment in imitation or canon or as an ostinato figure. The Magnificats are large-scale, florid works in the English tradition, also using cantus firmi. Two of his antiphons, however, Mater Christi sanctissima and Christe Jesu, pastor bone, clearly show Josquin's influence. His four-voice In Nomine, the prototype of this English genre, is simply a transcription of the 'In nomine Domine' section of his Missa 'Gloria tibi Trinitas'.

Taverner was pre-eminent among English musicians of his day: he enriched and transformed the English florid style by drawing on its best qualities, as well as on some continental techniques, and produced simpler works of great poise and refinement.

Missa Mater Christi sanctissima

Hodie nobis caelorum Rex. Mater Christi sanctissima. Magnificat sexti toni. Nesciens mater. Quemadmodum a 6. Missa Mater Christi sanctissima. In nomine a 4 Ⓟ
Fretwork (Wendy Gillespie, Richard Campbell *treble viols* Susanna Pell, Julia Hodgson, Richard Boothby *bass viols* William Hunt *great bass viol*) **The Sixteen / Harry Christophers**
Hyperion Helios CDH55053 (65 minutes: DDD) Ⓑ
Texts and translations included
Recorded 1992 ○

The Sixteen offer an impressive account of the composer's five-part *Missa Mater Christi sanctissima*, based on his votive anthem of the same name. It is a lively and vigorous work, beautifully crafted, and this performance amply matches that craftsmanship. Harry Christophers attempts no liturgical reconstruction, concentrating instead upon sheer musical quality. Three female sopranos replace the boy trebles. The music is pitched up a tone, which has the effect of adding brilliance to every climax. He demonstrates the good acoustic of St Jude's in Hampstead – an acoustic of space and definition, ideal for the interweaving of the strands of early Tudor polyphony; indeed, clarity and a sense of space are hallmarks of the recording. The supporting programme of the Christmas responsory, *Hodie*, the votive anthem *Mater Christi* and a four-part *Magnificat* is completed – unexpectedly but most delightfully – by two pieces for viols.

Missa Sancti Wilhelmi

Missa Sancti Wilhelmi. Motets – O Wilhelme, pastor bone; Dum transisset Sabbatum; Ex eius tumba Ⓟ
The Sixteen / Harry Christophers
Hyperion Helios CDH55055 (52 minutes: DDD) Ⓑ
Texts and translations included. Recorded 1990

The *Missa Sancti Wilhelmi* is not one of Taverner's best known works, but there is no reason why this should be the case. Though it does not have the sometimes rather wild melodic beauty of the six-voice Masses, it is nevertheless an impressive work in a more modern imitative style, in keeping with its model *O Wilhelme, pastor bone*. The Sixteen perform with their customary clarity and precision, and convey enthusiasm even in the somewhat syllabic *Gloria* and *Credo* movements of the Mass, something which is not always easy to do. While both the 'Wilhelm' works and *Dum transisset Sabbatum* are among Taverner's later works, there is no doubt at all that *Ex eius tumba* is one of the earliest. It is firmly late medieval in style, and the intricate tracery of its construction makes a thought-provoking contrast to the pieces in a more 'continental' imitative style. At 15 minutes this is a substantial composition, and one can only be surprised that it is so little-known. *Dum transisset Sabbatum* is, however, the high point of the disc, and if The Sixteen do not quite attain the ecstatic heights achieved in the recording by The Tallis Scholars, neither do they fail to rise to Taverner's inspiration.

Pyotr Ill'yich Tchaikovsky

Russian 1840-1893

GROVE *Tchaikovsky began piano studies at five and soon showed remarkable gifts; his childhood was also affected by an abnormal sensitivity. At 10 he was sent to the School of Jurisprudence at St Petersburg, where the family lived for some time. His parting from his mother was painful; further, she died when he was 14 – an event that may have stimulated him to compose. At 19 he took a post at the Ministry of Justice, where he remained for four years despite a long journey to western Europe and increasing involvement in music. In 1863 he entered the Conservatory, also undertaking private teaching. Three years later he moved to Moscow with a professorship of harmony at the new conservatory. Little of his music so far had pleased the conservative musical establishment or the more nationalist group, but his First Symphony had a good public reception when heard in Moscow in 1868.*

Rather less successful was his first opera, The Voyevoda, given at the Bol'shoy in Moscow in1869; Tchaikovsky later abandoned it and re-used material from it in his next, The Oprichnik. A severe critic was Balakirev, who suggested that he wrote a work on Romeo and Juliet: this was the Fantasy-Overture, several times rewritten to meet Balakirev's criticisms; Tchaikovsky's tendency to juxtapose blocks of material rather than provide organic transitions serves better in this programmatic piece than in a symphony as each theme stands for a character in the drama. Its expressive, well-defined themes and their vigorous treatment produced the first of his works in the regular repertory.

The Oprichnik won some success at St Petersburg in 1874, by when Tchaikovsky had won acclaim with his Second Symphony (which incorporates Ukrainian folktunes); he had also composed two string quartets (the first the source of the famous Andante cantabile), most of his next opera, Vakula the Smith, and of his First Piano Concerto, where contrasts of the heroic and the lyrical, between soloist and orchestra, clearly fired him. Originally intended for Nikolay Rubinstein, the head of Moscow Conservatory, who had much encouraged Tchaikovsky, it was dedicated to Hans von Bülow (who gave its première, in Boston) when Rubinstein rejected it as ill-composed and unplayable (he later recanted and became a distinguished interpreter of it). In 1875 came the carefully written Third Symphony and Swan Lake, commissioned by Moscow Opera. The next year a journey west took in Carmen in Paris, a cure at Vichy and the first complete Ring at Bayreuth; although deeply depressed when he reached home – he could not accept his homosexuality – he wrote the fantasia Francesca da Rimini and (an escape into the 18th century) the Rococo Variations for cello and orchestra. Vakula, which had won a competition, had its première that autumn. At the end of the year he was contacted by a wealthy widow, Nadezhda von Meck, who admired his music and was eager to give him financial security; they corresponded intimately for 14 years but never met.

Tchaikovsky, however, saw marriage as a possible solution to his sexual problems; and when contacted by a young woman who admired his music he offered (after first rejecting her) immediate marriage. It was a disaster: he escaped from her almost at once, in a state of nervous collapse, attempted suicide and went abroad. This was however the time of two of his greatest works, the Fourth Symphony and Eugene Onegin. The symphony embodies a 'fate' motif that recurs at various points, clarifying the structure; the first movement is one of Tchaikovsky's most individual with its hesitant, melancholy waltz-like main theme and its ingenious and appealing combination of this with the secondary ideas; there is a lyrical, intermezzo-like second movement and an ingenious third in which pizzicato strings play a main role, while the finale is impassioned if loose and melodramatic, with a folk theme pressed into service as second subject. Eugene Onegin, after Pushkin, tells of a girl's rejected approach to a man who fascinates her (the parallel with Tchaikovsky's situation is obvious) and his later remorse: the heroine Tatyana is warmly and appealingly drawn, and Onegin's hauteur is deftly conveyed too, all against a rural Russian setting which incorporates spectacular ball scenes, an ironic background to the private tragedies. The brilliant Violin Concerto also comes from the late 1870s.

The period 1878-84, however, represents a creative trough. He resigned from the conservatory and, tortured by his sexuality, could produce no music of real emotional force (the Piano Trio, written on Rubinstein's death, is a single exception). He spent some time abroad. But in 1884, stimulated by Balakirev, he produced his Manfred symphony, after Byron. He continued to travel widely, and conduct; and he was much honoured. In 1888 the Fifth Symphony, similar in plan to the Fourth (though the motto theme is heard in each movement), was finished; a note of hysteria in the finale was recognized by Tchaikovsky himself. The next three years saw the composition of two ballets, the finely characterized Sleeping Beauty and the more decorative Nutcracker, and the opera The Queen of Spades, with its ingenious atmospheric use of Rococo music (it is set in Catherine the Great's Russia) within a work of high emotional tension. Its theatrical qualities ensured its success when given at St Petersburg in late 1890. The next year Tchaikovsky visited the USA; in 1892 he heard Mahler conduct Eugene Onegin at Hamburg. In 1893 he worked on his Sixth Symphony, to a plan – the first movement was to be concerned with activity and passion; the second, love; the third, disappointment; and the finale, death. It is a profoundly pessimistic work, formally unorthodox, with the finale haunted by descending melodic ideas clothed in anguished harmonies. It was performed on October 28. He died nine days later: traditionally, and officially, of cholera, but recently verbal evidence has been put forward that he underwent a 'trial' from a court of honour from his old school regarding his sexual behaviour and it was decreed that he commit suicide. Which is true must remain uncertain.

Piano Concertos

No 1 in B flat minor; **No 2** in G, Op 44; **No 3** in E flat, Op 75

Piano Concerto No 1[a]. The Nutcracker – Suite, Op 71*a* (arr Economou)[b]
Martha Argerich, [b]Nicolas Economou *pfs*
[a]Berlin Philharmonic Orchestra / Claudio Abbado
DG 449 816-2GH (53 minutes: DDD) Ⓕ
Recorded [b]1983 live in [a]1994

Tchaikovsky's First Concerto has already appeared twice on disc from Martha Argerich in complementary performances: live and helter-skelter on Philips with Kondrashin (reviewed under Rachmaninov), studio and magisterial with Dutoit on DG. Now, finely recorded, here is a third, live recording with the BPO and Claudio Abbado surpassing even those earlier and legendary performances. Argerich has never sounded on better terms with the piano, more virtuoso yet engagingly human. Lyrical and insinuating, to a degree her performance seems to be made of the tumultuous elements themselves, of fire and ice, rain and sunshine. The Russians may claim this concerto for themselves, but even they will surely listen in disbelief, awed and – dare one say it – a trifle piqued. Listen to Argerich's *Allegro con spirito*, as the concerto gets under way, where her darting *crescendos* and *diminuendos* make the triplet rhythm speak with the rarest vitality and caprice. Her nervous reaching out towards further pianistic frays in the heart-casing second subject is pure Argerich and so are the octave storms in both the first and third movements that will have everyone, particularly her partners, tightening their seat belts. The cadenza is spun off with a hypnotic brilliance, the central *Prestissimo* from the *Andantino* becomes a true 'scherzo of fireflies', and the finale seems to dance off the page, a far cry from more emphatic Ukranian point-making and brutality. For encores DG has reissued Argerich's 1983 performance of *The Nutcracker* where she is partnered by Nicolas Economou in his own arrangement, a marvel of scintillating pianistic prowess, imagination and finesse.

Violin Concerto in D, Op 35

Piano Concertos[a] Nos 1-3. Violin Concerto[b]
Kyung-Wha Chung *vn* **Victoria Postnikova** *pf*
[a]Vienna Symphony Orchestra / Gennadi Rozhdestvensky; [b]Montreal Symphony Orchestra / Charles Dutoit
Double Decca ② 448 107-2DF2 (142 minutes: DDD) Ⓜ
Recorded 1981-82

Our top recommendation in this work is Kyung-Wha Chung's 1970 version on Decca with André Previn (reviewed under Sibelius). If your main priorities in Tchaikovsky concertos are visceral excitement, barnstorming virtuosity and nifty tempos, Chung's later version is probaby not the set for you. Tempos here are generally broad, and although there is no lack of pianistic thunder – Victoria Postnikova commands a handsome tone – the interpretative accent falls securely beneath the music's surface. The First Concerto is revealing in the sense that dialogue between soloist and orchestra is particularly sensitive; listen, for example, to the delicately voiced woodwinds at 6'38" (in the first movement), to Postnikova's subsequent response and, most especially, to the pianist's free yet nimble handling of the second movement's treacherous *valse-prestissimo* (4'05"). As Tchaikovsky Firsts go, this is among the most searching, personal and individual available, though one can already hear a loud opposition: '*too* slow, *too* mannered, *too* indulgent, *too* soft-grained, orchestrally'.

Again, in the Second and Third Concertos Postnikova plumbs the depths. Her handling of Tchaikovsky's epic cadenzas is second to none – starting at 1'55" into the Second Concerto's first movement, then between 13'26" and 19'13", where the solo writing is so massive in scale that you temporarily forget the mute presence of an orchestra. Rozhdestvensky views Tchaikovsky's orchestral architecture with a fine sense of perspective. This is *real* interpretation and presents a powerful case for a much maligned work (torso though it is). True, there is still room for critical controversy (the Second Concerto's first movement is hardly *Allegro brillante*), but Postnikova and Rozhdestvensky have so much to say about the music. Decca also offers a poised and elegantly phrased account of the Tchaikovsky Violin Concerto, where a rather edgy-sounding Kyung-Wha Chung is offered blandly 'regular' support by the Montreal Symphony Orchestra under Dutoit. Not a world-beater by any means, but a sensible makeweight, very well recorded. As indeed is the rest of the set, although the Vienna Symphony strings will strike some as rather thin in tone. An altogether riveting reissue and a genuine bargain as well.

Tchaikovsky Violin Concerto **Brahms** (arr Joachim) Hungarian Dances – No 1 in G minor; No 2 in D minor; No 4 in B minor; No 7 in A
Sarah Chang *vn* **Jonathan Feldman** *pf* **London Symphony Orchestra / Sir Colin Davis**
EMI CDC7 54753-2 (49 minutes: DDD)   (F)
Recorded 1992-93   ●

The range of dynamic truthfulness conveyed in Sarah Chang's performance, helped by a clear, full, naturally-balanced recording, brings not just momentary delight in individual phrases but cumulative gain, in this reading which so strongly hangs together. Not only does Chang play with exceptionally pure tone, avoiding heavy coloration, but her individual artistry does not demand the wayward pulling-about often found in this work. In that she is enormously helped by the fresh, bright and dramatic accompaniment provided by the LSO under Sir Colin Davis. In the outer movements Chang conveys wit along with the power and poetry, and the intonation is immaculate. Brahms's *Hungarian Dances* are delectable, marked by the sort of naughty pointing of phrase and rhythm that tickles one's musical funny-bone just as the playing of Kreisler always did. Here is a young artist who really does live up to the claims of the publicists. (See also the review in the Collections section – 'Sir Georg Solti – A Celebration' which includes Maxim Vengerov's stunning live performance of the Violin Concerto, with the LPO under Mstislav Rostropovich.)

1812 Overture, Op 49

Tchaikovsky 1812 Overture, Op 49[a]. Capriccio   [H]
italien, Op 45[b] **Beethoven** Wellingtons Sieg, 'Die Schlacht bei Vittoria', Op 91[c]
[a]**University of Minnesota Brass Band;**
[ab]**Minneapolis Symphony Orchestra;** [c]**London Symphony Orchestra / Antál Dorati**
Mercury Living Presence 434 360-2MM   (M)
(66 minutes: ADD). Also includes commentary by Deems Taylor on the making of the recordings
Recorded 1955-60   ●●

Both battle pieces incorporate cannon fire recorded at West Point, with *Wellington's Victory* adding antiphonal muskets and *1812*, the University of Minnesota Brass Band and the bells of the Laura Spelman Rockefeller carillon. In a recorded commentary on the *1812* sessions, Deems Taylor explains how, prior to 'battle', roads were blocked and an ambulance crew put on standby. The actual weapons used were chosen both for their historical authenticity (period instruments of destruction) and their sonic impact, the latter proving formidable even today. In fact, the crackle and thunder of *Wellington's Victory* could easily carry a DDD endorsement; perhaps we should, for the occasion, invent a legend of Daring, Deafening and potentially Deadly. Dorati's conducting is brisk, incisive and dramatic. *1812* in particular suggests a rare spontaneity, with a fiery account of the main 'conflict' and a tub-thumping

peroration where bells, band, guns and orchestra conspire to produce one of the most riotous key-clashes in gramophone history. *Capriccio italien* was recorded some three years earlier (1955, would you believe) and sounds virtually as impressive. Again, the approach is crisp and balletic, whereas the 1960 LSO Beethoven recording triumphs by dint of its energy and orchestral discipline. As 'fun' CDs go, this must be one of the best – provided you can divorce Mercury's aural militia from the terrifying spectre of real conflict. Wilma Cozart Fine has masterminded an astonishingly effective refurbishment, while the documentation – both written and recorded – is very comprehensive.

1812 Overture. Romeo and Juliet – Fantasy Overture. Marche slave, Op 31. Francesca da Rimini, Op 32
Royal Liverpool Philharmonic Orchestra / Sian Edwards
EMI Eminence CD-EMX2152   (M)
(66 minutes: DDD)   ●●

It is an extraordinary achievement that the young British conductor, Sian Edwards, should have made her recording début with a Tchaikovsky programme of such distinction. She immediately achieves a splendid artistic partnership with the RLPO, whose playing is so full of vitality, and whether in *1812* with its vigour and flair, its cluster of lyrical folk melodies and a spectacular finale with thundering canon, or in *Marche slave*, resplendently patriotic, in a uniquely Russian way, together they bring the music tingling to life in every bar. *Romeo and Juliet*, on the other hand, needs a finely judged balance between the ardour and moonlight of the love music, the vibrant conflict of the battle, and the tragedy of the final denouement, which is uncannily well managed.

Most intractable interpretatively is *Francesca da Rimini*, with its spectacularly horrifying picture of Dante's inferno which the composer uses to frame the central sequence depicting the lovers, Francesca and Paolo, and the doom-laden atmosphere which surrounds their intense mutual passion. Edwards's grip on this powerfully evocative sequence of events is unerringly sure, and she takes the orchestra through the narrative as only an instinctive Tchaikovskian could. The work opens with an unforgettable sense of nemesis and ends with a truly thrilling picture of the whirlwinds of Hell, into which the lovers are cast, still in their final passionate embrace. In sum, this is one of the best mid-price Tchaikovsky discs. The recording is excellent.

Hamlet – Fantasy Overture, Op 67

Francesca da Rimini, Op 32. Hamlet – Fantasy   [H]
Overture, Op 67
New York Stadium Orchestra / Leopold Stokowski
dell'Arte CDDA9006 (43 minutes: ADD)   (F)
Recorded 1958

Stokowski's inspired performance of *Hamlet* is still far, far superior to any other recorded version. *Francesca* is nearly as fine and generates enormous tension at the sequence just before the lovers are discovered where their passion is encompassed in polyphonic string textures of the greatest intensity. Then, after the dramatic moment of their death, they are consigned to the whirlwinds of Dante's Inferno, which rage frenziedly until the riveting final climax, where the gong is not allowed to drown the nemesis of bold orchestral dissonances at the last few bars. Stokowski's reading is equally memorable for the beguiling wind solos in the romantic middle section – depicting the idyll of the lovers – shaped with characteristic magic.

Hamlet is sensational. It is also even better recorded than *Francesca*, and the sonority of the lower strings is particularly telling at the electrifying opening, while at the big climax the weight of the trombones and tuba is splendidly caught. But perhaps the most spectacular moment is the foreboding march-like sequence, dominated by the side-drum, which is sinisterly dramatic each time it appears: this device anticipates Shostakovich at the climax of the first movement of the Fifth Symphony, and the emotional character of the playing is very Russian in its fervour. The desolation of mood of the coda is intensely moving, with a power of melancholy to equal that at the close of the *Pathétique* Symphony.

Hamlet does not have a love theme to match *Romeo and Juliet*, but its equivalent possesses a unique colour when it appears in the woodwind. Ophelia's melody on the oboe is utterly poignant, and when it returns there is a rustling in the strings which subtly creates a sense of uneasiness. If you are wondering about the identity of the New York Stadium Orchestra, Bert Whyte, the brilliant engineer of this recording and also one of the founders of the Everest label, has affirmed that it is the New York Philharmonic under a pseudonym. This was the pre-Bernstein era and the ensemble isn't always immaculate, but the tremendous commitment of the playing more than compensates. It is unclear whether Bryan Crimp's remastered version (which del-l'Arte issued on a 12-inch 45rpm disc) is used for the CD, but certainly the sound is cleaner than originally. During the closing years of his life Stokowski said, 'When I get to Heaven I shall shake Tchaikovsky by the hand and thank him for all the wonderful music he has given us'.

The Nutcracker, Op 71

The Nutcracker[a]. Queen of Spades – Duet of Daphnis and Chloë[b]

[b]**Cathryn Pope** *sop* [b]**Sarah Walker** *mez* [a]**Tiffin Boys' School Choir; London Symphony Orchestra / Sir Charles Mackerras**

Telarc ② CD80137 (88 minutes) Ⓕ

Recorded 1986 ●

This is Tchaikovsky's most rewarding ballet score, and for those who like a clear decision in such matters, this must be first choice, if only just. Indeed, it is the marvellous sound of the Telarc CDs that clinches the matter. The recording engineer is the illustrious Jack Renner who masterminded all the early digital Cleveland CDs. Here he has the advantage of the acoustics of Watford Town Hall, and his microphone placing is very perceptive. The set has the subtle extra resonance of a concert hall, which adds a little glamour to the violins and a glowing extra warmth to the middle and lower range. Yet there is no blurring and no 'empty-hall' feeling – the reverberation sounds just right. Now to the performance. Mackerras is renowned for the vitality of his conducting and he takes the 'Miniature Overture' quite fast. But the playing is deliciously neat and the sweetness of the recorded violin timbre adds a little mellowness.

Throughout the party scene Mackerras presses, yet he is never inflexible and has a fine flair for detail. From scene 5 onwards the action becomes quite riveting; the recording opens up its spectacularly wide dynamic range, and we have a taste of what is to come when 'The magic spell begins', the Christmas tree grows to a great orchestral climax and we are made aware of how Tchaikovsky adds to the depth and sonority with his writing for the tuba (this is especially striking again in the gloriously sumptuous sound for the climax of the great Act 2 'Pas de deux'). Mackerras creates an *1812*-like excitement in 'The Battle between the Nutcracker and the Mouse King' and Jack Renner interpolates some real canon and gunshots to add to the spectacle. But it is done judiciously and good-humouredly, for this is a battle and the effect stays in perspective.

One of the key moments in the ballet is Tchaikovsky's thrilling climbing melody when Clara and Prince travel through the pine forest to the Prince's fairy kingdom, and Mackerras gives this a glorious serenity helped by the glowing sound and the fine LSO playing. The LSO is on top form in the 'Divertissement' that forms the main part of Act 2. Mackerras's approach is sparkling rather than elegant. Yet in the choral 'Waltz of the Snowflakes' Mackerras's spry lightness is very pleasurable, the chorus timbre is warm and the *accelerando* at the end is convincing. The gorgeously expansive recording is most impressive when Tchaikovsky lets himself go, and no other 19th-century composer could score a romantic orchestral climax better than he. As an appendix we are offered the 'Duet of Daphnis and Chloë', a charming vignette from *The Queen of Spades*. It is nicely sung and the recording is distanced. The Telarc notes are splendid.

The Nutcracker

Kirov Opera Chorus and Orchestra / Valery Gergiev

Philips 462 114-2PH (81 minutes: DDD) Ⓕ

Recorded 1998 ●

This is *The Nutcracker* as a short ride in a fast machine. You may find that your most positive responses to this *Nutcracker* will come after a higher than usual intake of caffeine. Obviously, a fair measure of Tchaikovsky's score is meant to be continuous, but the Kirov's animated action never lets up for a moment. It may have something to do with squeezing it on to a single disc (no pauses for breath, even between the First and Second Acts); and under the circumstances, it is not surprising that Gergiev doesn't want to relax the momentum with the usual repeat of the leisurely 'Grandfather Dance'. But this is probably how he conducts *The Nutcracker* at the Kirov, and the elegance with which he moves from loud or fast sections of the score to quieter or slower ones – for example, the Arabian dance starting with a *diminuendo* – speak of ease gained from experience.

What we don't have here is a *Nutcracker* to enhance the ambience of a room lit by Christmas tree lights and a log fire. What we do have, however, is a realisation that makes it clear why Stravinsky so loved the Tchaikovsky ballets. If there is an ostinato working away in the accompaniment, Gergiev gives it prominence and energy (the swift tempos help, of course). And credit for the very high yield of unusual features of this most inventively scored of all the ballets should probably be evenly divided between Gergiev, the specific timbres of the orchestra and the very immediate sound. When not caught up in the colourful exuberance of it all, one may notice that the image lacks depth, the violins are a little thin in upper regions, and the brass occasionally play-out with the familiar Russian welly, wobble and weather. Equally, the ear may be briefly diverted by minor imprecisions and the odd extraneous noise. But has there ever been a *Nutcracker* so captured apparently 'on the wing', or, for that matter, so exciting?

The Nutcracker. The Sleeping Beauty – Aurora's Wedding

Montreal Symphony Orchestra / Charles Dutoit

Decca ② 440 477-2DH2 (135 minutes: DDD) Ⓕ

Recorded 1992

Many of the favourite characteristic dances seem freshly minted, notably the 'Dance of the Sugar-plum Fairy', with its deliciously liquid celesta, and the perky 'Chinese Dance'. The 'Waltz of the Snowflakes' (Act 1) with the children's chorus also has great charm. The transparency of the recorded sound, which helps to make all this possible, is immediately noticeable in the delightful gossamer string textures of the 'Miniature Overture'. But the big Act 2 *Adagio*, too, is exceptionally satisfying, its histrionics conveyed with passionate flair, yet without hysterical rhetoric at the excitingly grand climax. The recording is very vivid: bright but without glare, and the balance between detail, weight and hall resonance seems exactly right. 'Aurora's Wedding' is the truncated version of *The Sleeping Beauty* which Diaghilev adopted in repertory after his extravagant London production of the complete ballet in 1921 nearly bankrupted him. The music, after introducing both Carabosse and the Lilac Fairy, passes on to the christening, includes the hunting scene in Act 2, where the Prince has a vision of his sleeping princess, then moves on to the happy ending and the dances which form the highlight of the last act.

Serenade in C, Op 48

Serenade in C, Op 48. Souvenir de Florence, Op 70

Vienna Chamber Orchestra / Philippe Entremont

Naxos 8 550404 (65 minutes: DDD) Ⓢ

Recorded 1990

This is one of the many CDs now on the market that dispel the myth once and for all that only full-price recordings contain really outstanding performances. The Naxos label is just about as 'bargain' as you can get, and here they have given us superlative performances of two of Tchaikovsky's most endearing works. The Serenade in C contains a wealth of memorable and haunting music, beautifully and inventively scored and guaranteed to bring immense pleasure and delight to those dipping their toes in to the world of classical music for the first time. Philippe Entremont and the Vienna Chamber Orchestra give a marvellously polished and finely poised performance full of warmth, affection and high spirits, and the famous second movement Waltz in particular is played with much elegance and grace. The *Souvenir de Florence*, originally written for string sextet, makes a welcome appearance here in Tchaikovsky's own arrangement for string orchestra. This is a delightfully sunny performance, full of suavity, exuberance and romantic dash, but always alert to the subtleties of Tchaikovsky's skilful, intricate part-writing. The *Adagio cantabile* is particularly notable for some extremely fine and poetic solo playing from the violin and cello principals of the VPO. The beautifully spacious recording does ample justice to the performances.

The Sleeping Beauty, Op 66

Czecho-Slovak State Philharmonic Orchestra / Andrew Mongrelia

Naxos ③ 8 550490/92 (174 minutes: DDD) Ⓢ

Recorded 1991

Andrew Mongrelia is clearly a ballet conductor to his fingertips. His account of *The Sleeping Beauty* is not only dramatic, when called for, but graceful and full of that affectionate warmth and detail which readily conjure up the stage imagery. Moreover, the House of Arts in Košice seems to have just the right acoustics for this work. If the sound is too brilliant the louder passages of Tchaikovsky's score can easily hector the ear; if the effect is too mellow, the result can become bland. Neither happens here – the ear is seduced throughout and Mongrelia leads the listener on from number to number with an easy spontaneity. The woodwind playing is delightful (try track 9 with its 'singing canaries' – so like Delibes in its scoring). At the end of Act 1 the Lilac Fairy's tune is given a spacious, *frisson*-creating apotheosis. The alert Introduction to Acts 2 and 3 brings crisp brass and busy strings on the one hand, arresting hunting horns on the other, and what sparkling zest there is in the strings for the following 'Blind-man's buff' sequence, while the famous Act 2 Waltz has splendid rhythmic lift. Act 3 is essentially a great extended *Divertissement*, with Tchaikovsky's imagination at full stretch through some two dozen characterful dance numbers of every balletic flavour, are all played here with fine style. Irrespective of price, this vies with Gergiev as a first choice among current recordings of the score, and you get two-and-a-half hours of music. The value is even more remarkable when the excellent notes clearly relate the ballet's action to each of the 65 separate cues.

The Sleeping Beauty
Russian National Orchestra / Mikhail Pletnev
DG ② 457 634-2GH2 (159 minutes: DDD Ⓕ
Recorded 1997 **OO**

Given the total engagement in every bar of this recording, especially the vivid and varied characterisation, one is left wondering why there appeared to be less of it in this team's DG cycle of the Tchaikovsky symphonies. That Pletnev knows and loves this score was already obvious from his own piano arrangements of parts of it, and their recordings (Virgin Classics and in Philips's Great Pianists series). And if ever proof was needed of the pianist's ability to transfer completely intact to the orchestra his own special brand of fantasy and superfine articulacy, this is it. Hardly a minute passes without one's ear being enchanted by an affective gesture of the utmost precision, poise and sensitivity (all the various solos are superbly done); and significantly, the now-familiar Pletnev ideal of the tactfully and revealingly balanced *tutti* does not result in anticlimax, as it did in some of the symphonies.

If you need convincing, try the last 10 minutes of Act 2 – a symphonic impression of the 100-year sleep, owing not a little to Wagner in its methods and to something of the magical workings of Tchaikovsky's own sea music for *The Tempest* – and ask yourself if you have ever heard it as atmospherically shaded, the subtle glints of Tchaikovsky's wonderful orchestration as well caught, or the transition from static contemplation, through the kiss, to genuinely joyful activity as well gauged.

A very special combination of all the right choices is made as regards dynamics, tempo and differentiation of mood and, like so much else in this performance, a scene whose potential is rarely as fully realised as it is here. The DG sound is as vibrant as you could wish, with deeper perspectives and a superbly managed ambience, with the 'magical' scenes bathed in the appropriate enchanted halo, yet the textures kept clear in the active, louder sections of the score. It is a fractionally more brilliant sound than DG supplied in the symphonies (at last, the timpani are fully in focus!) and if the cellos are occasionally obviously spotlit and the violins inclined to a very slight steeliness in their upper reaches, there is no denying the expert matching of tone and body of these divided fiddles. Good to hear the formidable partnership once again firing on all cylinders.

The Sleeping Beauty
Kirov Theatre Orchestra / Valery Gergiev
Philips ② 434 922-2PH3 (164 minutes: DDD) Ⓕ
Recorded 1992 **O**

Many authorities regard this as Tchaikovsky's finest ballet score and, indeed, one of the greatest ballet scores of all time. It contains many wonderful things: the Waltz from Act 1 includes some wonderfully arching phrasing that soars with tremendous passion, while the 'Panorama' of Act 2 is one of the composer's finest melodic ideas. The 'Pas de six' of Act 1 and the contrasted Fairy dances of Act 3 bring the same almost Mozartian grace (combined with Tchaikovsky's own very special feeling for orchestral colour) that he displays in the *Nutcracker* characteristic dances, which turn simple ballet vignettes into great art. Valery Gergiev is at home in this score. He secures splendidly alive and sympathetic playing from his orchestra and the Philips recording is full and sumptuous. Tchaikovsky's big climaxes expand properly, the strings are full and natural and the woodwind colours glow.

Suite No 2, Op 53

Suite No 2, Op 53. The Tempest
Detroit Symphony Orchestra / Neeme Järvi
Chandos CHAN9454 (64 minutes: DDD) Ⓕ
Recorded 1994-95

Tchaikovsky's elusive blend of instrumental precision and free-flowing thematic fantasy in the Second Suite meets its match in the Detroit/Järvi partnership: the conductor's imagination works alongside the lean, clean Detroit sound with interesting results. The strings are not always the ideal: the lush chordings and central fugal energy of the opening movement, 'Jeu de sons', cry out for a richer, Russian tone. But the semiquaver patter is beautifully done, the lower lines clear and personable. Keen articulation and driving force go hand-in-glove as Järvi prepares for the entry of the four accordions in the virile 'Rondo-Burlesque', sweeping on to the folk-song of the central section with characteristic aplomb. It is in the Schumannesque phrases and the subtly shifting moods of the most poetic movement, 'Rêves d'enfant', that Järvi really comes into his own; the short-lived, other-worldly radiance at the heart of the movement seems more than ever like a preliminary study for the transformation scenes of *The Nutcracker*, just as the woodwind choruses look forward to that and *Sleeping Beauty*.

The magical haze surrounding Prospero's island in *The Tempest* doesn't quite come off; here it's Pletnev (reviewed above) who surprises us with the true magician's touch, but then his Russian horns, and later his trumpeter, cast their incantations more impressively. Järvi is no more successful than any other conductor in stitching together Tchaikovsky's strong impressions of the play, though a little more forward movement in the love-music might have helped.

Swan Lake, Op 20

Montreal Symphony Orchestra / Charles Dutoit
Decca ② 436 212-2DH2 (154 minutes: DDD)　　Ⓕ
Recorded 1991　　●

No one wrote more beautiful and danceable ballet music than Tchaikovsky, and this account of *Swan Lake* is a delight throughout. This is not only because of the quality of the music, which is here played including additions the composer made after the première, but also thanks to the richly idiomatic playing of Charles Dutoit and his Montreal orchestra in the superb and celebrated location of St Eustache's Church in that city. Maybe some conductors have made the music even more earthily Russian, but the Russian ballet tradition in Tchaikovsky's time was chiefly French and the most influential early production of this ballet, in 1895, was choreographed by the Frenchman Marius Petipa. Indeed, the symbiosis of French and Russian elements in this music (and story) is one of its great strengths, the refinement of the one being superbly allied to the vigour of the other, notably in such music as the 'Russian Dance' with its expressive violin solo. This is a profoundly romantic reading of the score, and the great set pieces such as the Waltz in Act 1 and the marvellous scene of the swans on a moonlit lake that opens Act 2 are wonderfully evocative; yet they do not overshadow the other music, which supports and strengthens them as gentler hills and valleys might surround and enhance magnificent, awe-inspiring peaks, the one being indispensable to the other. You do not have to be a ballet aficionado to fall under the spell of this wonderful music, which here receives a performance that blends passion with an aristocratic refinement and is glowingly recorded.

Manfred Symphony, Op 58

Manfred Symphony, Op 58. The Tempest, Op 18
Russian National Orchestra / Mikhail Pletnev
DG 439 891-2GH (76 minutes: DDD)　　Ⓕ
Recorded 1993　　●

There are no cheap thrills in Pletnev's *Manfred*. Percussion and brass are very carefully modulated, their brilliance and power reserved quite noticeably for what Pletnev sees as the few crucial climactic passages in the outer movements. Timpani in particular provide support rather than make a show – it is the lower strings that course through Manfred's outburst in the second movement (from 5'50"), not the almost standard spurious timpani swells. It is the strong, dark woodwind, not the more usual stuttering horns, that you initially hear in the first movement's concluding *Andante con duolo* (from 13'09"). The deep satisfaction to be had from this account comes from the superlative strings, and from Pletnev's pacing which, more often than any of the listed additional recommendations, takes notice of Tchaikovsky's tempo indications, most obviously in the properly

flowing third movement's pastoral, and in the successful bonding of the finale's episodic structure (the magniloquent Muti's Achilles' heel).

More eccentric is Pletnev's drop in tempo for those rising unison scales on strings at the start of the bacchanale, but it is less troubling than Toscanini's and Jansons's speeding up for those hammering chords before Astarte returns; and, mercifully, there are none of the cuts made by Toscanini. *The Tempest*, a generous coupling, brings much the same priorities and equal rewards – no more need be said, except to observe that the horns receive a better deal from the balance than in the symphony. As to the recording generally, the timpani are probably less focused than Pletnev would have wanted; in other respects, the sound does justice to the riches of his orchestra and seriousness of his intent.

Complete Symphonies

No 1 in G minor, 'Winter Daydreams', Op 13; No 2 in C minor, 'Little Russian', Op 17; No 3 in D, 'Polish', Op 29; No 4 in F minor, Op 36; No 5 in E minor, Op 64; No 6 in B minor, 'Pathétique', Op 74

Symphonies Nos 1-6. Violin Concerto in D, Op 35[a]. Piano Concerto No 1 in B flat minor, Op 23de. 1812 Overture, Op 49. Capriccio italien, Op 45. Eugene Onegin – Polonaise; Waltz. Marche slave, Op 31. The Nutcracker – Suite, Op 71[a]. Romeo and Juliet Fantasy Overture. Serenade in C, Op 48. The Sleeping Beauty – Suite. Swan Lake – Suite. Variations on a Rococo Theme, Op 33[c]
[a]**Christian Ferras**, [b]**Michel Schwalbé** *vns* [c]**Mstislav Rostropovich** *vc* [d]**Sviatoslav Richter** *pf*
Berlin Philharmonic Orchestra, [e]**Vienna Symphony Orchestra / Herbert von Karajan**
DG ⑧ 463 774-2GB8 (531 minutes: ADD/DDD)　　Ⓑ
Recorded 1962-80　　●●

Karajan was unquestionably a great Tchaikovsky conductor. Yet although he recorded the last three symphonies many times, he did not turn to the first three until the end of the 1970s and then proved an outstanding advocate. In the Mendelssohnian opening movement of the First, the tempo may be brisk, but the music's full charm is displayed and the melancholy of the *Andante* is touchingly caught. Again at the opening of the *Little Russian* (No 2), horn and bassoon capture that special Russian colouring, as they do in the engaging *Andantino marziale*, and the crisp articulation in the first movement *allegro* is bracing. The sheer refinement of the orchestral playing in the *scherzos* of all three symphonies is a delight, and finales have great zest with splendid bite and precision in the *fugato* passages and a convincing closing peroration.

The so-called *Polish* Symphony (No 3) is the least tractable of the canon, but again Karajan's apt tempos and the precision of ensemble makes the first movement a resounding success. The *Alla tedesca* brings a hint of Brahms, but the Slavic dolour of the *Andante elegiaco* is unmistakeable and its climax blooms rapturously. No doubt the reason these early symphonies sound so fresh is because the Berlin orchestra was not over-familiar with them, and clearly enjoyed playing them. The sound throughout is excellent. It gets noticeably fiercer in the Fourth Symphony, recorded a decade earlier, but is still well balanced. The first movement has a compulsive forward thrust, and the breakneck finale is viscerally thrilling. The slow movement is beautifully played but just a trifle bland. Overall, though, this is impressive and satisfying, especially the riveting close.

DG has chosen the 1965 recording of the Fifth, rather than the mid-'70s version, and they were right to do so. It is marvellously recorded (in the Jesus-Christus Kirche): the sound has all the richness and depth one could ask and the performance too is one of Karajan's very finest. There is some indulgence of the second-subject string melody of the first movement. But the slow movement is gloriously played from the horn solo onwards, and the second re-entry of the Fate theme is so dramatic that it almost makes one jump. The delightful Waltz brings the kind of elegant warmth and detail from the violins that is a BPO speciality, and the finale, while not rushed Mravinsky fashion, still carries all before it and has power and dignity at the close.

The *Pathétique* was a very special work for Karajan (as it was for the Berlin Philharmonic) and his 1964 performance is one of his greatest recordings. The reading as a whole avoids hysteria, yet the resolution of the passionate climax of the first movement sends shivers down the spine, while the finale has a comparable eloquence, and the March/*Scherzo*, with ensemble wonderfully crisp and biting, brings an almost demonic power to the coda. Again the sound is excellent, full-bodied in the strings and with plenty of sonority for the trombones.

The *String Serenade* is digital, brightly recorded in the Philharmonie in 1980, but naturally balanced. Marvellous playing, of course. The Waltz, with a most felicitous control of *rubato*, is the highlight, and the *Elégie* is certainly ardent; and if the first movement could have been more neatly articulated, the finale has tremendous bustle and energy. As for the *concertante* works, the account of the glorious *Rococo* Variations with Rostropovich is another classic of the gramophone, even though it uses the truncated score. The First Piano Concerto is a disappointment, with Richter and Karajan failing to strike sparks as a partnership. In spite of brilliant solo playing, the first movement lacks supporting tension in the orchestra, and in the finale one can sense Richter wanting to press forward, while Karajan seems to hold back: the coda itself hangs fire in the orchestra.

Similarly Ferras was not an ideal choice for the Violin Concerto. Not all will take to his somewhat febrile timbre, with its touches of near-schmaltz. But the performance as a whole works better than the Piano Concerto.

Romeo and Juliet is finely done, passionate and dramatic, if not quite so spontaneously inspired as Karajan's early VPO version for Decca, especially at the opening. But *Marche slave*, ideally paced, is very successful, sombre and exciting by turns. *Capriccio italien* and *1812* are both brilliantly played, and the triptych of ballet suites can be recommended almost without reservation, with the *Sleeping Beauty* suite memorable for some very exciting climaxes.

Even with the reservations about the two concertos, this bargain box is a fine investment, and certainly value for money. The documentation is excellent.

Symphonies Nos 1-6
Berlin Philharmonic Orchestra / Herbert von Karajan
DG Symphony Edition ④ 429 675-2GSE4 Ⓜ
(264 minutes: ADD). Recorded 1975-79

Those who are looking for an outstanding bargain, need go no further than this Karajan set (one of the most enticing we can think of). All six numbered symphonies are squeezed on to only four CDs, selling at mid-price. The minor snag is that Nos 2 and 5 are broken between discs, but even there one is no worse off than with an ordinary LP. Karajan's discography reveals no fewer than seven versions of the *Pathétique* and six each of Nos 4 and 5, but the ones here, dating from 1975 and 1976, are in almost every way, both for sound and as interpretations, the finest he has done, and far preferable to his more recent DG series made with the Vienna Philharmonic.

Symphonies Nos 1, 2 and 3, dating from 1979 are Karajan's only recordings of those earlier works, but ones which saw him at his very finest, combining high polish with freshness and lyrical spontaneity. There are points where he is clearly preferable even to Jansons, as in the superb building of the final climax on the horn theme in the slow movement of No 1. Many will also prefer Karajan's faster speed in the first movement of No 2, where for once Jansons takes an unusually measured, if finely pointed, view.

Though in the opening of No 4 with Karajan, the digital transfer makes the brassy motto theme a little too fierce, generally these are among the best of his 1970s recordings from Berlin, fuller and more detailed than the digital sound on his Vienna versions of Nos 4-6.

Symphonies – Nos 1-6. Manfred Symphony, Op 58. Capriccio Italien, Op 45. Serenade in C, Op 48. The Tempest, Op 18. Romeo and Juliet. Eugene Onegin – Polonaise
Bournemouth Symphony Orchestra / Andrew Litton
Virgin Classics ⑥ VB5 61893-2 Ⓢ
(420 minutes: DDD). Recorded 1989-93

Here is another of those extraordinary Virgin bargain boxes, offered at an astonishingly low price (six well-filled CDs for well under £20) and, as with the previous collection of Mozart concertos, serenades and symphonies, these Tchaikovsky performances would be highly recommendable if they cost twice as much, while the recordings – realistically set back in a concert hall acoustic – are superb, full-bodied, and wide ranging and brilliant.

The playing of the Bournemouth Orchestra may not always be quite as polished as say, the Berlin Philharmonic for Karajan, but it is still very, very good indeed: ensemble is as keen as it is passionately responsive. Moreover Litton has a natural ear for Tchaikovskian detail – time and again he draws the listener to revel in those delightful orchestral touches with which Tchaikovsky decorates and embroiders his melodies (witness the close of the slow movements of both the Second and Fourth Symphonies).

Litton gets off to an outstanding start with Nos 1 and 2 where the atmosphere is imbued with bonhomie and high spirits. The Mendelssohnian opening of *Winter Daydreams* is full of charm, the *scherzo*s sparkle, slow movements are touching; and the finale of the *Little Russian* is winningly zestful, with a contrasting catchy lilt for the second subject.

Litton readily disguises the structural flaws of the *Polish* Symphony with his geniality and a clever ebb and flow of tempos: the changing lyrical atmosphere of the inner movements is caught with evocative colouring and subtle rubato. 'Superbly articulated playing', commented Edward Greenfield in his original review of the outer movements, and this especially applies to the *fugatos*, never more so than in the finale, where the grandiose coda is also played for all its worth, and more.

In No 4 one is more aware of the slight distancing of the sound, and Litton matches it by his spacious tempo in the first movement and the slow but steady build up of tension which reaches its zenith at the end of the development. The woodwind of the second subject is full of balletic charm, and that rocking string figure is seductively silky.

That same broad approach to No 5 – the one comparative disappointment – works less well: one needs more impetus in the outer movements, yet there is massive weight in the coda. But Litton is back on form in No 6, and Edward Greefield thought it 'arguably the finest of the cycle... full of temperament, not just fiery but tender too' (5/93). The phrasing of the first movement's secondary theme is ravishing, and the climax is as powerful as the cumulative peak of the *scherzo*/march, where the steady tempo does not detract from the *scherzo* element. The Finale is most eloquent and beautifully played.

In *Manfred* Litton's emphasis is on its programmatic basis. He depicts Astarte exquisitely, the 'Alpine Fairy' *scherzo* is equally delightful, as is the tenderly delicate oboe solo which opens the pastoral scene of the *Andante*; yet the thrilling close of the first movement (with powerful, thrusting horns) and the organ entry at the close of the finale are both splendidly dramatic.

The extra items are all enjoyably spontaneous, the *Capriccio italien* has visceral thrills and panache, the *String Serenade* is warmly romantic; and both *Romeo and Juliet*, matching romantic pathos with passion, and the underrated but masterly Shakespearean *Tempest* are among the highlights. Even if you have much of this repertoire already, this set remains very enticing.

Symphonies Nos 1-6. Manfred Symphony, Op 58. Romeo and Juliet – Fantasy Overture. Capriccio italien, Op 45. 1812 Overture, Op 49. Marche slave, Op 31. Francesca da Rimini, Op 32. The Storm, Op 76
Concertgebouw Orchestra / Bernard Haitink
Philips Bernard Haitink Symphony Edition ⑥
442 061-2PB6 (423 minutes: ADD) Ⓜ
Recorded 1961-79

It is clear that Haitink is more at home with symphonic substance than with the shorter colourful showpieces. This set documents his development as a conductor (and a Tchaikovskian) – the shorter pieces being recorded between 1961 and 1972, the symphonies between 1974 and 1979. The exception is the student Tchaikovsky's overture, *The Storm*, recorded with the symphonies, and the performance of which is so masterful, colourful and exciting that you might think it a more mature work (though exactly *whose* 'more mature' work it might be isn't always easy to say). As the symphonies comprise eighty per cent of the contents of this package, let us deal briefly with the rest. You might wonder if Haitink had ever heard an Italian singing an Italian song, as anything less capricious or Italian would be hard to imagine. There are moments in the feud music of *Romeo and Juliet* that suggest Haitink's resolve, and his communication of that resolve, was not what it was shortly to become. From eight years later, we have the brilliantly realised (and recorded) letter of the score in *Francesca*, the *1812* Overture and *Marche slave*.

On to the symphonies: as a symphonic cycle, it remains temperate, considered and patient, living mostly at a fair distance from the edge, with rarely a hint of exaggeration or overemphasis – sterling qualities indeed. Haitink's grand and dignified manner is immensely stirring and satisfying. Throughout the symphonies, tempos and dynamics are chosen to guarantee impeccable articulation, beauty of tone production, flawless instrumental balances and a typical awareness of the important climactic moment. These recordings of the symphonies have all been available on CD before, with the exception of *Manfred* which was long overdue for reissue. Its pastoral and orgy (third and fourth movements) encapsulate what is both most frustrating and most formidable in Haitink's Tchaikovsky. Philips's Concertgebouw engineering broke new ground with the symphonies. The *tuttis* here reproduce with a clarity and epic splendour that have rarely, if ever, been bettered.

Symphonies Nos 1-6
Russian National Orchestra / Mikhail Pletnev
DG ⑤ 449 967-2GH5 (263 minutes: DDD) Ⓕ
Recorded 1995

First things first, and the very opening of the First Symphony's first movement, subtitled 'Daydreams on a Wintry Road', is initially very dreamy at a tempo a lot slower than you might be used to (and Tchaikovsky's marking). One wonders, though, if the shape of the first theme is best served by a tempo this slow (and even if subsequent developments are impressively grand, do the proceedings have sufficient momentum?). The spirit of the dance also seems loath to visit the finale: very impressive indeed is the holding back of the heavies so that *tutti* force is more evenly balanced than usual with ensuing fugal vigour, but might not the wind band have been persuaded to kick a little higher in the second subject (or the coda be sent on its way with a touch more forward motion and flamboyance)?

It may be that one has to try and forget the various familiar Russian ways with these symphonies (say, of Svetlanov, Markevitch or Temirkanov), as Pletnev seems keener to focus attention on Tchaikovsky's other cosmopolitan, classical self. It is surely significant that he avoids the time-honoured unmarked dynamic and tempo adjustments felt to be essential props (for varying repetitions and building climaxes) by virtually all other interpreters. And his orchestra's cultured tones seem ever more fitted for the job: there is a choir-like blend and evenness of tone from the top to the bottom of the orchestra (brass contributions, in particular, are rounded and sonorous); and it's a very Russian-sounding 'choir' in that, time after time, your attention is caught by the colour, richness and definition of the orchestra's basses, whether bass trombone, tuba, bassoon or string basses (and the cavernous bell-like boom of the gong must rate a mention). All of this is heard to great effect in the Second Symphony's finale, lightly dispatched with (wicked?) relish as outsize Haydn (turn to, say, Maazel or even Markevitch to hear how blatancy and overemphasis cheapen this movement).

In the Second Symphony's finale, ideals and actual performance come together (a point confirmed by the final uproarious cannon-fire *crescendo* from the timpani). On other occasions though, the seriousness of intention can preclude real performance tensions. One listens with a certain detached fascination to the Fourth's first movement, admiring such things as the steady continuity rather than contrast between the two subject groups (they are, after all, both *moderatos*) and the tamed 'fate' fanfares in the brass. But will it ever deliver? Perhaps it does in the coda, where these magnificent strings give out the last statement of the first moderato theme – but only perhaps.

A refusal to overstate the case again ennobles much of the Fifth Symphony, but for Pletnev, the *Pathétique*, one suspects, stands apart from the other symphonies, as this account remains an interpretation that throws moderation to the winds. Compared with his 1991 debut recording on Virgin Classics, the first movement *Allegro* is a degree more moderate, but the *Scherzo*/March is not a whit less immoderate (a warning to those who don't like death-defying speed in this movement). Here the finale is broader tragedy with darker colourings; the strings sing with greater intensity and there is no stinting on blistering trumpet tone at the top of the climactic scale. The trumpets' *fff* outburst in the first movement's development is equally powerful, though you can now hear more of the surrounding activity. And that is a tribute to the DG recording; more open, clearer and more present than the Virgin recording, and one that perhaps conveys a greater sense of occasion.

The layout is ungenerous but it avoids splitting the symphonies between discs – and the five discs are priced as four.

Symphonies Nos 1 and 2

Symphony No 1
Oslo Philharmonic Orchestra / Mariss Jansons Ⓕ
Chandos CHAN8402 (44 minutes: DDD)

Symphony No 2. Capriccio italien, Op 45
Oslo Philharmonic Orchestra / Mariss Jansons
Chandos CHAN8460 (48 minutes: DDD) Ⓕ
Recorded 1985

The composer gave the work the title *Winter Daydreams*, and also gave descriptive titles to the first two movements. The opening *Allegro tranquillo* he subtitled 'Dreams of a winter journey', while the *Adagio* bears the inscription 'Land of desolation, land of mists'. A *Scherzo* and finale round off a conventional four-movement symphonic structure. In the slow movement Jansons inspires a performance of expressive warmth and tenderness, while the *Scherzo* is managed with great delicacy and sensitivity. Both the opening movement and finale are invested with vigour and passion, and everywhere the orchestral playing is marvellously confident and disciplined. The recording has not only impact and immediacy but also warmth and refinement.

Jansons also has the full measure of the Second Symphony. It is a direct performance – the first movement *allegro* is relatively steady, but never sounds too slow, because of crisp rhythmic pointing – and the second movement goes for charm and felicity of colour. The finale is properly exuberant, with the secondary theme full of character, and there is a fine surge of adrenalin at the end. The *Capriccio italien*, a holiday piece in which the composer set out to be entertaining, is also played with great flair and the hint of vulgarity in the Neapolitan tune is not shirked. Again the closing pages produce a sudden spurt of excitement which is particularly satisfying. The recording here is just short of Chandos's finest – the massed violins could be sweeter on top, but the hall resonance is right for this music and there is a proper feeling of spectacle.

Symphonies Nos 4-6

Leningrad Philharmonic Orchestra / Evgeny Mravinsky
DG ② 419 745-2GH2 (129 minutes: ADD) Ⓕ
Recorded 1960

These recordings are landmarks not just of Tchaikovsky interpretation but of recorded orchestral performances in general. The

Leningrad Philharmonic plays like a wild stallion, only just held in check by the willpower of its master. Every smallest movement is placed with fierce pride; at any moment it may break into such a frenzied gallop that you hardly know whether to feel exhilarated or terrified.

The whipping up of excitement towards the fateful outbursts in Symphony No 4 is astonishing – not just for the discipline of the *stringendos* themselves, but for the pull of psychological forces within them. Symphony No 5 is also mercilessly driven, and pre-echoes of Shostakovichian hysteria are particularly strong in the coda's knife-edge of triumph and despair. No less powerfully evoked is the stricken tragedy of the *Pathétique*. Rarely, if ever, can the prodigious rhythmical inventiveness of these scores have been so brilliantly demonstrated.

The fanatical discipline is not something one would want to see casually emulated but it is applied in a way which sees far into the soul of the music and never violates its spirit. Strictly speaking there is no real comparison with Mariss Jansons's Chandos issues, despite the fact that Jansons had for long been Mravinsky's assistant in Leningrad. His approach is warmer, less detailed, more classical, and in its way very satisfying. Not surprisingly there are deeper perspectives in the Chandos recordings, but DG's refurbishing has been most successful, enhancing the immediacy of sound so appropriate to the lacerating intensity of the interpretations.

Symphony No 4

Oslo Philharmonic Orchestra / Mariss Jansons
Chandos CHAN8361 Ⓕ
(42 minutes: DDD) ●

A high emotional charge runs through Jansons's performance of the Fourth, yet this rarely seems to be an end in itself. There is always a balancing concern for the superb craftsmanship of Tchaikovsky's writing: the shapeliness of the phrasing; the superb orchestration, scintillating and subtle by turns; and most of all Tchaikovsky's marvellous sense of dramatic pace. Rarely has the first movement possessed such a strong sense of tragic inevitability, or the return of the 'fate' theme in the finale sounded so logical. The playing of the Oslo Philharmonic Orchestra is first rate: there are some gorgeous woodwind solos and the brass achieve a truly Tchaikovskian intensity. Recordings are excellent.

Symphony No 5

Oslo Philharmonic Orchestra / Mariss Jansons
Chandos CHAN8351 (43 minutes: DDD) Ⓕ
Recorded 1984 ●

With speeds which are fast but never breathless and with the most vivid recording imaginable, this is as exciting an account as we have had of this symphony. In no way does this performance suggest anything but a metropolitan orchestra, and Jansons keeps reminding one of his background in Leningrad in the great years of Mravinsky and the Philharmonic. Nowhere does the link with Mravinsky emerge more clearly than in the finale, where he adopts a tempo very nearly as hectic as Mravinsky's on his classic DG recording. In the first movement he resists any temptation to linger, prefering to press the music on, and the result sounds totally idiomatic. In the slow movement Jansons again prefers a steady tempo, but treats the second theme with delicate rubato and builds the climaxes steadily, not rushing his fences, building the final one even bigger than the first. In the finale it is striking that he follows Tchaikovsky's notated slowings rather than allowing extra *rallentandos* – the bravura of the performance finds its natural culmination.

The Oslo string ensemble is fresh, bright and superbly disciplined, while the wind soloists are generally excellent. The Chandos sound is very specific and well focused despite a warm reverberation, real-sounding and three-dimensional with more clarity in *tuttis* than the rivals provide.

Symphony No 5
Vienna Philharmonic Orchestra / Valery Gergiev
Philips 462 905-2PH (46 minutes: DDD). Ⓕ
Recorded live in 1998

This is the genuine article – live and alive – an unpatched one-off performance bursting at the seams with passion, presence, theatre and vitality. But make no mistake, this is *not* lofty Tchaikovsky. Only you can decide, however, whether Gergiev's very physical bursts of tone and tempo manoeuvres, particularly in the first two movements, are what you want in a recording of this symphony. Reactions may differ from one hearing to the next, always admiring such things as the dramatic effectiveness of the strong bass pedal link between the end of the finale's opening *Andante* and the start of its ensuing *Allegro vivace*, but occasionally being left uneasy by some of the tempo contrasts.

'Love at first sight', as Gergiev's collaboration with the orchestra has been described, translates here into body-and-soul compliance with the conductor's expressive intentions. For its own part the orchestra does what it does best: strings lacing the lyricism with their famed vibrato-rich playing, and bouncing the outer sections of the third movement *Waltz* as only they know how. The slight compression of the Austrian Radio recording for Gergiev is not troublesome; on the contrary, it enables a higher than usual transfer level, and thus greater immediacy for the feel and the features of what was clearly an 'event'.

Symphony No 6

Symphony No 6[b]. Marche slave, Op 31. The Seasons, Op 37*b*[a]. Six morceaux composés sur un seul thème, Op 21[c]. The Sleeping Beauty (arr Pletnev) – excerpts
Russian National Orchestra / Mikhail Pletnev *pf*
Virgin Classics ② VBD5 61636-2 (138 minutes: DDD) Ⓑ
Recorded [a]1989, [b]1991 and [c]1994 ●●●

There's no denying that Russian orchestras bring a special intensity to Tchaikovsky, and to this Symphony in particular. But, in the past, we have had to contend with lethal, vibrato-laden brass and variable Soviet engineering. Not any more. Pianist Mikhail Pletnev formed this orchestra in 1990 from the front ranks of the major Soviet orchestras, and the result here has all the makings of a classic. The brass still retain their penetrating power, and an extraordinary richness and solemnity before the Symphony's coda; the woodwind (soft, veiled flute tone, dark-hued bassoons) make a very melancholy choir; and the strings possess not only the agility to cope with Pletnev's aptly death-defying speed for the third movement march, but beauty of tone for Tchaikovsky's yearning *cantabiles*, and their lower voices add thunderous black density to the first movement's development's shattering intrusion. Pletnev exerts the same control over his players as he does over his fingers, to superb effect. The dynamic range is huge and comfortably reproduced with clarity, natural perspectives, a sense of instruments playing in a believable acoustic space, and a necessarily higher volume setting than usual. *Marche slave*'s final blaze of triumph, in the circumstances, seems apt.

Pletnev finds colours and depths in *The Seasons* that few others have found even intermittently. Schumann is revealed as a major influence, not only on the outward features of the style but on the whole expressive mood and manner. The opening of 'May' is straight from the contemplative Schumann – his Eusebius persona – while the mercurial *staccato-legato* exchanges near the start of 'January' are intrusions from the lighter Florestan. That alternation of civilised soulfulness and delicious, faintly wicked humour recurs again and again in this performance. Even the melancholy song of 'October' has its tiny touches of Pletnevian naughtiness, but how beautifully the tune itself sings. And as a display of pianism the whole set is outstanding, all the more so because Pletnev's brilliance isn't purely egoistic. Even when he does something unmarked – like attaching the hunting fanfares of 'September' to the final unison of 'August' – he's so persuasive that you could believe that this is somehow inherent, if not actually explicit, in the material. The six *Morceaux*, Op 21, emerge here as fascinating, richly enjoyable works. This is all exceptional playing, and the recording – bright in the treble, but also warm in tone – is ideally attuned to all its moods and colours.

Symphony No 6 **H**
Piano Concerto No 1 in B flat minor, Op 23
Vladimir Horowitz *pf* **NBC Symphony Orchestra / Arturo Toscanini**
Naxos Historical mono 8 110807 (71 minutes: ADD) Ⓢ
Recorded live in 1941

Every home should probably have one. After all, Horowitz, that ultimate wizard of the keyboard, was preserved for posterity in the concerto on five different occasions. This performance from Carnegie Hall was taped the month before Horowitz and his father-in-law Toscanini made their better-known studio recording for RCA. Both performances marshal an old war-horse into a thoroughbred racer (past the finishing-post, mane flying in the wind, minutes before most of the competition), and the differences between them owe as much to the sound as the performances. RCA's bursts more vibrantly into the living-room, but the orchestral bass booms, throwing into unfortunate relief a comparatively narrow-range, shallow piano sound with an unhelpful 'ring' in the instrument's middle register. In the end, despite its dazzle, the impression the performance leaves is one of antics, aggression and impatience. The live performance has a less uniform presence and body, but there is a parity of sound between orchestra and piano, and a less confused picture of Horowitz's playing, which allows you to register a greater variety of touch, colour, maybe even timing. Toscanini's *Pathétique* always was 'the real thing', in the sense of expression being honestly and directly communicated. But here, there is no mistaking Toscanini pushing the boundaries in, say, a more brilliant *Scherzo*/March; and a broader finale where the extra playing-out in the finale's second theme contrasts effectively with the quiet sobbing from high cellos with the same theme just before the end. The latter might seem a cliché, but it convinces in the context of a reading that holds all the elements of this symphony in perfect poise.

Variations on a Rococo Theme

Variations on a Rococo Theme, Op 33. Nocturne No 4, Op 19. (arr Tchaikovsky). Pezzo capriccioso, Op 62. When Jesus Christ was but a child No 5, Op 54. Was I not a little blade of grass? No 7, Op 47 (both orch Tchaikovsky). Andante cantabile, Op 11 (arr Tchaikovsky)
Raphael Wallfisch *vc* **English Chamber Orchestra / Geoffrey Simon**
Chandos CHAN8347 (48 minutes: DDD) Ⓢ
Recorded 1984 ●

This account of the *Rococo* Variations is the one to have: it presents Tchaikovsky's variations as he wrote them, in the order that he devised and including the *allegretto moderato con anima* that the work's first interpreter, 'loathsome Fitzenhagen', so high-handedly jettisoned. (See also the review under Dvořák where Mstislav Rostropovich uses the published score rather than the original version.) The first advantage is as great as the second: how necessary the brief cadenza and the *andante* that it introduces now seem, as an up-beat to the central sequence of quick variations (Fitzenhagen moved both cadenza and *andante* to the end). And the other, shorter cadenza now makes a satisfying transition from that sequence to the balancing *andante sostenuto*, from which the long-suppressed eighth variation is an obvious build-up to the coda – why, the piece has a form, after all!

Raphael Wallfisch's fine performance keeps

the qualifying adjective 'rococo' in mind – it is not indulgently over-romantic – but it has warmth and beauty of tone in abundance. The shorter pieces are well worth having: the baritone voice of the cello suits the *Andante cantabile* and the Tatyana-like melody of the *Nocturne* surprisingly aptly. The sound is first-class.

String Quartets

String Quartets – No 1 in D, Op 11; No 2 in F, Op 22; No 3 in E flat minor, Op 30. Quartet Movement in B flat. Souvenir de Florence, Op 70
Yuri Yurov *va* **Mikhail Milman** *vc*
Borodin Quartet (Mikhail Kopelman, Andrei Abramenkov *vns* Dmitri Shebalin *va* Valentin Berlinsky *vc*)
Teldec ② 4509-90422-2 (151 minutes: DDD) Ⓕ
Recorded 1993 ○○○

Who could fail to recognise the highly characteristic urgency and thematic strength of the F major Quartet's first movement development section, or miss premonitions of later masterpieces in the Third Quartet's *Andante funèbre*. None of these works is 'late' (the last of them pre-dates the Fourth Symphony by a couple of years), yet their rigorous arguments and sweeping melodies anticipate the orchestral masterpieces of Tchaikovsky's full maturity. So why the neglect – that is, of all but the First Quartet? The most likely reason is our habitual expectation of orchestral colour in Tchaikovsky, a situation that doesn't really affect our appreciation of the early, almost Schubertian D major Quartet (the one with the *Andante cantabile* that moved Tolstoy to tears). The Second and Third Quartets are noticeably more symphonic and particularly rich in the kinds of harmonic clashes and sequences that Tchaikovsky normally dressed for the orchestral arena. Even minor details, like the quick-fire exchanges near the beginning of No 3's *Allegretto*, instantly suggest 'woodwinds' (you can almost hear oboes, flutes and clarinets jostle in play), while both finales could quite easily have been transposed among the pages of the early symphonies. But if these and other parallels are to register with any conviction, then performers need to locate them, and that's a challenge the Borodins meet with the ease of seasoned Tchaikovskians.

They are natural and spontaneous, most noticeably in the first movement of the exuberant *Souvenir de Florence* sextet, and in that wonderful passage from the Second Quartet's first movement where the lead violin calms from agitated virtuosity to a magical recapitulation of the principal theme – an unforgettable moment, superbly paced here. Additionally we get a 15-minute B flat Quartet movement – an appealing torso imbued with the spirit of Russian folksong.

Solo Piano Works

Morceaux – Op 10; Op 19 – No 1, Rêverie du soir, No 5, Capriccioso; Op 40 – No 2, Chanson triste, No 8, Valse; Op 51 – No 1, Valse de salon, No 3, Menuetto scherzoso, No 5, Romance; Op 72 – No 5, Méditation, No 12, L'espiègle, No 15, Un poco di Chopin. Romance in F minor, Op 5. Valse-scherzo in A, Op 7. The Seasons, Op 37*b* – No 1, January; No 5, May; No 6, June; No 11, November
Sviatoslav Richter *pf*
Olympia OCD334 (80 minutes: DDD/ADD) Ⓕ
Recorded 1983 ○

Richter elevates Tchaikovsky's miniatures far beyond the salon. No interpretative frills, just trenchant fingerwork and perfectly sculpted sound, so that slight unbendings become immensely touching. The effect is to convey not so much the surface melancholy of these pieces as their underlying strength of character. A curious sense of permanence comes through, as if the music is being contemplated rather than felt. Not for imitation, perhaps (who could imitate such perfect harmonic and structural weighting?), but this is breathtaking, inspiring artistry, and it sets its own terms. Sound quality is on the dry side. But Richter's is the sort of playing which positively benefits from close analytical scrutiny, and serious collectors of piano recordings should need no further encouragement.

Liturgy of St John Chrysostom

Liturgy of St John Chrysostom, Op 41. Nine Sacred Pieces. An Angel Crying
Corydon Singers / Matthew Best
Hyperion CDA66948 (75 minutes: DDD). Texts and translations included. Recorded 1997 Ⓕ ○

Tchaikovsky's liturgical settings have never quite caught the popular imagination which has followed Rachmaninov's (his All-Night Vigil, at any rate). They are generally more inward, less concerned with the drama that marks Orthodox celebration than with the reflective centre which is another aspect. Rachmaninov can invite worship with a blaze of delight, setting 'Pridite'; Tchaikovsky approaches the mystery more quietly. Yet there is a range of emotion which emerges vividly in this admirable record of the Liturgy together with a group of the minor liturgical settings which he made at various times in his life. His ear for timbre never fails him. It is at its most appealing, perhaps, in the lovely 'Da ispravitsya' for female trio and answering choir, beautifully sung here; he can also respond to the Orthodox tradition of rapid vocalisation, as in the Liturgy's Creed and in the final 'Blagosloven grady' (in the West, the Benedictus). Anyone who still supposes that irregular, rapidly shifting rhythms were invented by Stravinsky should give an ear to his Russian sources, in folk poetry and music but also in the music of the Church.

Matthew Best's Corydon Singers are old hands at Orthodox music and present these beautiful settings with a keen ear for their texture and their 'orchestration'. The recording was made in an (unnamed) ecclesiastical acoustic of suitable resonance, and sounds well. Transliterated texts and translations are provided in a booklet that includes an outstandingly good essay on the tradition and the music by Ivan Moody.

Songs

Songs, Op 6 – No 1, Do not believe, my friend; No 2, Not a word, o my friend; No 4, A tear trembles; No 5, Why?; No 6, None but the lonely heart. Cradle Song, Op 16 No 1. Op 38 – No 2, It was in the early Spring; No 3, At the ball. Reconciliation, Op 25 No 1. Op 47 – No 1, If only I had known; No 5, I bless you, forests; No 6, Does the day reign?; No 7, Was I not a little blade of grass?. Do not ask, Op 57 No 3. Op 60 – No 4, The Nightingale; No 7, Gipsy's Song; No 11, Exploit. I opened the window, Op 63 No 2. Op 73 – No 2, Night; No 6, Again, as before, alone. To forget so soon. I should like in a single word

Lina Mkrtchyan *contr* **Evgeny Talisman** *pf*

Opus 111 OPS30-219 (74 minutes: DDD) Ⓕ

Texts and translations included. Recorded 1998

Deep purple velvet is the best way to describe this Armenian contralto's voice. The timbre is rich, the quality unflawed. No less remarkable is the lady's art, strikingly personal and in tune with Tchaikovsky's inward-looking mind and feeling for inner drama. With ample resources of volume, she nevertheless chooses to sing quietly for much of the time in these essentially private utterances, so that when the full voice is used it is as though the powerful emotions are breaking through and will brook no further restraint. And yet they are, quite speedily, brought again under the control of a mind preoccupied with its own thoughts. In *Not a word, o my friend* Mkrtchyan is mindful that this is a song (partly) about silence: the 'droog' in question is as though at her side and she murmurs her confidences. In *It was in the early Spring* she sings all first three-and-a-half verses in a unified tone of musing reminiscence till exclamations in the lyric prompt a *crescendo*, and then a light caress of rhythm and melody restores the gentle affection. The pianist, Evgeny Talisman, is less than ideally clear; yet this seems to provide added insight, more sense of the piano's function in so many of these songs.

The Snow Maiden

Irina Mishura-Lekhtman *mez* **Vladimir Grishko** *ten* **Michigan University Musical Society Choral Union; Detroit Symphony Orchestra / Neeme Järvi**

Chandos CHAN9324 (79 minutes: ADD). Text and translation included. Recorded 1994 Ⓕ

Tchaikovsky wrote his incidental music for Ostrovsky's *Snow Maiden* in 1873, and though he accepted it was not his best, he retained an affection for it and was upset when Rimsky-Korsakov came along with his full-length opera on the subject. The tale of love frustrated had its appeal for Tchaikovsky, even though he was not to make as much as Rimsky did of the failed marriage between Man and Nature. But though he did not normally interest himself much in descriptions of the natural world, there are charming pieces that any lover of Tchaikovsky's music will surely be delighted to encounter. A strong sense of a Russian folk celebration, and of the interaction of the natural and supernatural worlds, also comes through, especially in the earlier part of the work. There is a delightful dance and chorus for the birds, and a powerful monologue for Winter; Vladimir Grishko, placed further back, sounds magical.

Natalia Erassova (for Chistiakov's recording on CdM) gets round the rapid enunciation of Lel's second song without much difficulty, but does not quite bring the character to life; Mishura-Lekhtman has a brighter sparkle. Chistiakov's Shrove Tuesday procession goes at a much steadier pace than Järvi's, and is thus the more celebratory and ritual where the other is a straightforward piece of merriment. Both performances have much to recommend them, and it is not by a great deal that Järvi's is preferable. But the balance is tilted by CdM providing only an English (and French) translation of the text and no Russian transliteration; Chandos provides transliteration and an English translation.

'The Tchaikovsky Experience'

Iolanta – Who can compare with my Mathilde; Iolanta and Vaudémont duet. Oprichnik – Natalya's arioso. Mazeppa – The old man's gone, how my heart beats; Sleep my baby, my pretty. The Maid of Orleans – Farewell, Forests. The Queen of Spades – Stay, I beg of you!; I love you beyond all measure. Undina – Undina's song. The Voyevoda – Bastryukov's aria. Vakula the Smith – Oksana's aria. Eugene Onegin – Let me perish, but first let me summon (Letter Scene). The Enchantress – Kuma's arioso

Inessa Galante, Marina Shaguch *sops* **Alexander Fedin** *ten* **Sergei Leiferkus** *bar* **Royal Opera House Orchestra, Covent Garden / Neeme Järvi**

Royal Opera House Records 75605 55022-2 (79 minutes: DDD). Recorded 1997 Ⓕ

There can scarcely be a more beautiful or subtle account of the Letter scene from *Eugene Onegin* than that given here by Inessa Galante. She makes us believe that these are the inner thoughts of an obsessed young girl as she moulds her phrases with a sense of spontaneous feeling. The voice itself shows that it has blossomed into a warm, vibrant, evenly produced instrument, and its owner uses it with unfailing musicality, aided by Järvi's sympathetic support. This is the glorious centrepiece of 'The Tchaikovsky Experience', with excerpts from all his operas.

Galante is possibly even more moving as vulnerable Iolanta learning of her blindness from her admirer Vaudémont in the composer's last opera. This, one of the most touching duets in Tchaikovsky, is compellingly sung here by Galante and the tenor Alexander Fedin. Marina Shaguch deserves almost as much praise. Her voice isn't as easily produced as Galante's but is more dramatic in character. She has some of the rarer material to interpret, such as the haunting solo from *Undina* and as poor, demented Maria at the end of *Mazeppa*, singing a lullaby to her sweetheart dying in her arms. Sergei Leiferkus sings with his customary conviction in Robert's soliloquy from *Iolanta*. Though his account of Yeletsky's solo from *The Queen of Spades* isn't as ingratiating as some, it is delivered with compensating intelligence. Järvi conducts all the music with command of idiom, drawing refined playing from the ROH Orchestra. Texts and translations aren't included but you can write off for them. Even so, this is an important disc, well recorded and generously filled.

Opera Arias

Tchaikovsky Eugene Onegin – Let me perish, but first let me summon. The Queen of Spades – What am I crying for, what is it?. The Enchantress – Where are you, beloved?…Hurry to my side. Oprichnik – I heard voices and footsteps **Verdi** La forza del destino – Son giunta!…Madre, pietosa Vergine; Pace, pace, mio Dio. Otello – Mia madre aveva ... Piangea cantando…Ave Maria. Aida – Qui Radames verrà?… O patria mia. Il trovatore – Tacea la notte placida...Di tale amor

Galina Gorchakova *sop* **Chorus and Orchestra of the Kirov Opera / Valery Gergiev**

Philips 446 405-2PH (60 minutes: DDD). Texts and translations included. Recorded 1995 Ⓕ

Gorchakova promises to be one of the vocal giants of her generation. This recital programme marks her first steps into the Italian repertoire on disc. For a star of the Kirov, Verdi's St Petersburg opera – *La forza del destino* – makes an apt choice. Arriving at the monastery gate, her Leonora immediately announces herself as a Verdi soprano of tragic stature, shaping 'Madre, pietosa Vergine' with the dark colouring of a troubled soul. The Willow song from *Otello* is predictably doom-laden, for Gorchakova is no simple, creamy, lyrical Desdemona. The Aida is less successful and sounds as if it is not yet fully in her voice. It might have been better to offer 'Ritorna vincitor', as she seems uncomfortable with long, slow phrases around the top of the stave. The top C is very loud and the conclusion, broken off sharply in full voice, is not what Verdi asks for. After that, the *Trovatore* goes much better: the aria has splendid vocal depth and the cabaletta is surprisingly nimble, especially at Gergiev's brilliant pace. Elsewhere his conducting of the Verdi needs more pace.

As an interpreter of Tchaikovsky, Gorchakova has already won her laurels on the stage. Despite the size and dark colour of the voice, her soprano is still youthful enough for her to play a plausible Tatyana and the Letter scene will be one of the major reasons for acquiring this disc. The heart of the scene is sung with the kind of *pianissimo* that one would use to carry to the back of the theatre, rather than an inward *pianissimo* intended for the microphone. The *Queen of Spades* aria (Lisa's short solo from Act 1, that is) is so full of beautiful, soaring tone that one resents being cut off just at the point where Herman enters for their duet. The brief aria from *The Enchantress* includes an exciting high B. Elsewhere there is one worrying sign to be mentioned. That is a tendency to go flat when the music is soft and slow (both the *Otello* and the *Aida* suffer from passages of sinking pitch) and one has to hope that difficulties like this are not allowed to defeat her. Gorchakova is no highly polished automaton as a singer. Her artistry is about letting this voice out of its cage and harnessing its formidable energy. The Philips recording team has done well to capture it so truthfully in the studio.

Eugene Onegin

Dmitri Hvorostovsky *bar* Eugene Onegin; **Nuccia Focile** *sop* Tatyana; **Neil Shicoff** *ten* Lensky; **Olga Borodina** *mez* Olga; **Alexander Anisimov** *bass* Prince Gremin; **Sarah Walker** *mez* Larina; **Irina Arkhipova** *mez* Filipievna; **Francis Egerton** *ten* Triquet; **Hervé Hennequin** *bass-bar* Captain; **Sergei Zadvorny** *bass* Zaretsky; **St Petersburg Chamber Choir; Orchestre de Paris / Semyon Bychkov**

Philips ② 438 235-2PH2 (141 minutes: DDD). Notes, text and translation included. Recorded 1992 Ⓕ ●

Entirely at the service of Tchaikovsky's marvellous invention, Semyon Bychkov illuminates every detail of the composer's wondrous scoring with pointed delicacy and draws playing of the utmost acuity and beauty from his own Paris orchestra – enhanced by the clear, open recording – and the St Petersburg Choir are superbly disciplined and alert with their words. Focile offers keen-edged yet warm tone and total immersion in Tatyana's character. Aware of the part's dynamic demands, she phrases with complete confidence, eagerly catching the girl's dreamy vulnerability and heightened imagination in the Letter scene, which has that sense of awakened love so essential to it. Hvorostovsky is in his element. His singing has at once the warmth, elegance and refinement Tchaikovsky demands from his anti-hero. Together he, Focile and Bychkov make the finale the tragic climax it should be; indeed the reading of this passage is almost unbearably moving. Shicoff has refined and expanded his Lensky since he recorded it for Levine, and Anisimov is a model Gremin, singing his aria with generous tone and phrasing while not making a meal of it. Olga Borodina is a perfect Olga, spirited, a touch sensual, wholly idiomatic with the text – as, of course, is the revered Russian mezzo Arkhipova as Filipyevna, an inspired piece of casting.

Eugene Onegin Ⓗ

Evgeny Belov *bar* Eugene Onegin; **Galina Vishnevskaya** *sop* Tatyana; **Sergei Lemeshev** *ten* Lensky; **Larissa Adyeva** *mez* Olga; **Ivan Petrov** *bass* Prince Gremin; **Valentina Petrova** *sop* Larina; **Evgenya Verbitskaya** *mez* Filipyevna; **Andrei Sokolov** *ten* Triquet; **Igor Mikhailov** *bass* Zaretsky; **Georgi Pankov** *bass* Captain; **Bolshoi Theatre Chorus and Orchestra / Boris Khaikin**

Melodiya mono ② 74321 17090-2 (140 minutes: ADD) Recorded 1955 Ⓜ ●

The classic Khaikin version, generally accepted as the most convincing and knowledgeable performance the work has yet received, wears its 45 years lightly: indeed, the recording of the voices and even the orchestra, albeit in mono, has a great deal to teach producers today in terms of a natural sound. The reading's virtues are, above all, Khaikin's unforced, unexaggerated, wholly integrated direction, with players and singers who know the score from the inside giving an entirely idiomatic reading (if you can forgive the watery horns). From the very first scene you feel the impetus of the performance and are drawn into its truly Russian ambience. Khaikin brings into perfect balance the dramatic and yearning aspects of the score in a lyrical, delicate reading. With his incisive but sympathetic beat, he clearly characterises those many passages of intimate feeling without which any account of the piece crucially fails. The young Vishnevskaya is a near-ideal Tatyana, having exactly the right voice for the part and totally convincing us that she *is* Tatyana. She is incomparable. What a genuine, unsophisticated outpouring of passion the Letter scene becomes as she interprets it and how superbly she sings it!

Few tenors before or since Lemeshev have offered precisely the right tone and character for Lensky. From his first entry we hear a plaintive timbre and easy way with the language that proclaim a true poet. Belov's Onegin, though not quite in that class, is a resolute member of a real ensemble and rises to the challenge of the final scenes. All that disappoints is the presentation: numerous spelling mistakes and no libretto.

Iolanta

Galina Gorchakova *sop* Iolanta; **Gegam Grigorian** *ten* Vaudémont; **Dmitri Hvorostovsky** *bar* Robert; **Sergei Alexashkin** *bass* King René; **Nikolai Putilin** *bar* Ibn-Hakia; **Larissa Diadkova** *mez* Martha; **Nikolai Gassiev** *ten* Alméric; **Tatiana Kravtsova** *sop* Brigitta; **Olga Korzhenskaya** *mez* Laura; **Gennadi Bezzubenkov** *bar* Bertrand; **Chorus and Orchestra of the Kirov Opera, St Petersburg / Valery Gergiev**

Philips ② 442 796-2PH2 (96 minutes: DDD). Notes, Ⓕ text and translation included. Recorded 1994

Iolanta, the touching little princess, blind and virginal, into whose darkness and isolation there eventually shines the 'bright angel' of Duke Robert, is delightfully sung by Galina Gorchakova. There is a freshness and sense of vulnerability here, especially in the opening scenes with Martha in the garden as she sings wistfully of something that appears to be lacking in her life: the *Arioso* is done charmingly and without sentimentality. Gegam Grigorian sometimes sounds pinched and under strain, even in the Romance. He is also overshadowed by Hvorostovsky who is here at his best: warm and with a somewhat dusky tone. The King, Provence's 'bon roi René', is benignly if a little throatily sung by Sergei Alexashkin, and he has at hand a sturdy-voiced Ibn-Hakia in Nikolai Putilin. Valery Gergiev conducts a sensitive performance, responding constructively to the unusual scoring, and not overplaying the more demonstrative elements in a score that gains most through some understatement. The booklet very sensibly prints in parallel columns a transliteration of the Russian, then English, German and French; the text in the original Cyrillic is printed separately at the end.

Mazeppa

Nikolai Putilin *bar* Mazeppa; **Irina Loskutova** *sop* Maria; **Sergei Alexashkin** *bass* Kochubey; **Larissa Dyadkova** *mez* Lyubov; **Viktor Lutsiuk** *ten* Andrei; **Viacheslav Luhanin** *bass* Orlik; **Vladimir Zhivopistsev** *ten* Iskra; **Nikolai Gassiev** *ten* Drunken Cossack; **Kirov Opera Chorus and Orchestra / Valery Gergiev**

Philips ③ 462 206-2PH3 (170 minutes: DDD). Notes, text and translation included Ⓕ Recorded live in 1996

This Kirov recording is extremely telling at all the crucial moments, without emerging as consistently superior to Järvi on DG. Nikolai Putilin's Mazeppa has a heavier voice than his DG counterpart, and he shows more strain (Tchaikovsky takes his baritone to a high A flat at one point). But his dramatic range is greater and he is more believable both as ruthless tyrant and love-struck old man. So honours are fairly even here. Similarly Irina Loskutova's Maria cannot compete with DG's Galina Gorchakova for beauty of tone and purity of line, and in anything above a *mezzo piano* her voice spreads quite alarmingly. Yet it is Loskutova who is the more moving at the opera's quiet conclusion. It's the same story but in reverse with the two Kochubeys. For Philips Sergei Alexashkin is heftier of voice in Act 1, but it's DG's Anatoly Kocherga, initially rather dry and underpowered, who grows in dramatic stature in the Prison and Execution scenes, darkening the timbre and timing his delivery to perfection, where Alexashkin can only add stagey sobs and routine barks of defiance. The balance-sheet is fairly even with the smaller roles too.

Scientific measurement would probably show little difference between the Kirov Orchestra's instinctive *sostenuto* and the plausible copy of it manufactured by the Gothenburgers, or between the full-throated Russian of a native chorus and the Stockholm Royal Opera's more than passable imitation. However, the extra sense of dramatic immediacy here is unmistakable. Järvi was swift in the 'Gopak', stomach-churning in the Prison and Execution scenes, and vivid in the 'Battle of Poltava'; Gergiev is even more so. Incidentally, Gergiev departs from the score in the Battle, bolstering it with a forceful return of the famous *Slava!* folk-song and omitting Tchaikovsky's transition to the following scene (though the booklet makes no mention of it).

The orchestra-pit sound is dryish, with little or no bloom on the strings and indifferently balanced woodwind. The *frisson* of curtain going up, audience presence, applause between scenes, and movement of voices on stage, offers some compensation, and you soon adapt. But the results of editing together more than one live performance are not entirely satisfactory. There are some bumpy edits on held vocal notes and voices sometimes jump to different positions on stage. Musically both sets are distinguished, but if forced to choose we would take the Gergiev, for an extra sense of the drama being lived out. However, the DG set has better sound quality and marginally more consistent singing.

The Queen of Spades

Gegam Grigorian *ten* Herman; **Maria Gulegina** *sop* Lisa; **Irina Arkhipova** *mez* Countess; **Nikolai Putilin** *bar* Count Tomsky; **Vladimir Chernov** *bar* Prince Yeletsky; **Olga Borodina** *mez* Pauline; **Vladimir Solodovnikov** *ten* Chekalinsky; **Sergei Alexashkin** *bass* Surin; **Evgeni Boitsov** *ten* Chaplitsky; **Nikolai Gassiev** *ten* Major-domo; **Gennadi Bezzubenkov** *bass* Narumov; **Ludmila Filatova** *mez* Governess; **Tatiana Filimonova** *sop* Masha; **Kirov Theatre Chorus and Orchestra / Valery Gergiev**

Philips ③ 438 141-2PH3 (166 minutes: DDD). Notes, text and translation included. Recorded 1992 Ⓕ

There are major problems with all the current sets of *The Queen of Spades*, but Valery Gergiev, one of the outstanding Tchaikovskians of the day, here coaxes from a thoroughly Western-sounding Kirov Theatre Orchestra what is surely the most refined account of the score yet recorded, and one that is never lacking energy or full-blooded attack. His is not so much a compromise approach as one which stresses fatalism and underlying sadness. The recording was made in the Kirov Theatre itself, and there is admittedly some constriction to the orchestral sound picture; but for many the atmosphere of a real stage-venue will be a plus, and the all-important balance between voices and orchestra is just right. If the spine still fails to tingle as often as it should, that is mainly a reflection of the respectable but unexciting singing, though it would be folly to expect greater thrills from any of the three rival sets, and in many ways Gergiev's conducting elevates his above them all.

Alexander Tcherepnin

USSR/French/American 1899-1977

GROVE *An American composer of Russian origin, Tcherepnin's father Nikolay Nikolayevich (1873-1945) was a pupil of Rimsky-Korsakov who wrote ballets for Dyagilev (Le pavillon d'Armide, 1908) and settled in Paris in 1921. Alexander completed his studies there and became associated with Martinu and Beck, experimenting with new scales in a Franco-Russian neo-classical style (including one sometimes known by his name: C-D flat-E flat-E-F-G-A flat-A-B-C). In 1934-7 he travelled in the Far East, which brought about additions to his range of materials. In 1950 he settled in the USA. His large output, spirited in style and cosmopolitan in manner, includes ballets, four symphonies (1927-57), six piano concertos (1919-65), chamber and keyboard music.*

Piano Concertos

Piano Concertos – No 1, Op 12; No 4, 'Fantaisie', Op 78; No 5, Op 96

Murray McLachlan *pf* **Chetham's Symphony Orchestra / Julian Clayton**

Olympia OCD440 (71 minutes: DDD). Recorded 1995 Ⓕ

The Tcherepnin piano concertos are in their various ways cast in the same exuberant, heartfelt romantic manner. However, there is real variety within this general approach. The First, written in Paris in 1920, takes not the slightest interest in what was beginning to occupy French musicians and most other Parisian expatriates at the beginning of that exciting decade: it looks east, to a Georgia which Tcherepnin had known before exile, and north to an influence from, of all composers, Sibelius. The result is inventive but, predictably, less original than the later concertos. The Fourth, written in 1947, looks further east to China, a country which Tcherepnin had toured in the 1930s and where he met his future wife. It is more a set of three tone-poems, lightly accommodating Chinese musical gestures into the familiar romantic language, than a symphonic concerto. The Fifth belongs to 1963, and is a much more enigmatic work, and also by some way the most original of the entire set of six. Murray McLachlan is a fine advocate of this music, which is technically demanding and, in the Fifth Concerto, also demanding of a subtle understanding if the most is to be made of its laconic gestures and rather greyer lyricism. The Chetham's Symphony Orchestra reaffirms its ability to cope with technically testing scores and, guided by Julian Clayton, to make musical sense of them with the command of more experienced musicians.

Narcisse et Echo, Op 40

The Hague Chamber Choir; The Hague Residentie Orchestra / Gennadi Rozhdestvensky

Chandos CHAN9670 (53 minutes: DDD) Recorded 1998 Ⓕ

Tcherepnin's *Narcisse et Echo* was one of the first of Diaghilev's Paris ballets, produced in 1911 and hence anticipating Ravel's *Daphnis et Chloé* by a year. Tcherepnin's ear is a match for Ravel's in orchestral subtlety, and his skill in scoring for his large orchestra decorates the ballet with some ravishing sounds. The work was reproached at the time for being static, which it could hardly help being when Narcissus spends the last quarter of an hour gazing adoringly at his reflection in a pool. Not even Nijinsky could do much with that, even with Tcherepnin's most sensuous music twining itself lovingly around him. There is also a dance for Narcissus with the hapless Echo, and some set pieces for a group of Boeotians. Neither of these generates much musical exhilaration, nor, despite a flurry of rhythmic complexity, does the arrival of a troop of depressingly sober Bacchantes. Tcherepnin gives them all lovely sounds, but there is nothing of Ravel's intoxicating energy, let alone his exquisite melodic invention. But as aural sensation it is captivating, especially when played as beautifully as it is here.

Georg Philipp Telemann

German 1681-1767

GROVE *Telemann was one of the most prolific composers ever. At 10 he could play four instruments and had written arias, motets and instrumental works. His parents discouraged musical studies, but he gravitated back to them. At Leipzig University he founded a collegium musicum; at 21 he became musical director of the Leipzig Opera at 23 he took on a post as church organist. The next year he moved to Z̆ary, as court Kapellmeister, where he wrote French-style dance suites, sometimes tinged by local Polish and Moravian folk music, and cantatas. In 1708 he went in the same capacity to the Eisenach court and in 1712 to Frankfurt as city music director. As Kapellmeister of a church there, he wrote at least five cantata cycles and works for civic occasions, while his duties as director of a collegium musicum drew from him instrumental works and oratorios.*

He was offered various other positions, but moved only in 1721, when he was invited to Hamburg as director of music at the five main churches and Kantor at the Johanneum. Here he had to write two cantatas each Sunday, with extra ones for special church and civic occasions, as well as an annual Passion, oratorio and serenata. In his spare time he directed a collegium musicum and wrote for the opera house; the city councillors waived their objections to the latter when he indicated that he would otherwise accept an invitation to Leipzig. He directed the Hamburg Opera from 1722 until its closure in 1738. In 1737 he paid a visit to Paris, appearing at court and the Concert Spirituel. From 1740 he devoted more time to musical theory, but from 1755 he turned to the oratorio. He published much of his music, notably a set of 72 cantatas and the three sets of Musique de table (1733), his best-known works, each including a concerto, a suite and several chamber pieces. He was eager to foster the spread of music and active in publishing several didactic works, for example on figured bass and ornamentation. He was by far the most famous composer in Germany; in a contemporary dictionary he is assigned four times as much space as J. S. Bach.

Telemann composed in all the forms and styles current in his day; he wrote Italian-style concertos and sonatas, French-style overture-suites and quartets, German fugues, cantatas, Passions and songs. Some of his chamber works, for example the quartets in the Musique de table, are in a conversational, dialogue-like manner that is lucid in texture and elegant in diction. Whatever style he used, Telemann's music is easily recognizable as his own, with its clear periodic structure, its clarity and its ready fluency. Though four years senior to Bach and Handel, he used an idiom more forward-looking than theirs and in several genres can be seen as a forerunner of the Classical style.

Concertos

Concerto for Three Horns, Violin and Orchestra in D major. Overture-Suites – C, TWV55:C5, 'La bouffonne'; F, TWV55:F11, 'Alster Echo'. Concerto in G, 'Grillen-Symphonie' P

Anthony Halstead, Christian Rutherford, Raul Diaz *hns* **Collegium Musicum 90 / Simon Standage** *vn*

Chandos Chaconne CHAN0547 (70 minutes: DDD) (F)

Recorded 1993

This release shows Telemann at his most irrepressibly good-humoured and imaginative. There's a concerto for three rattling horns and a solo violin (a splendid sound, with the horns recorded at what seems like the ideal distance), and an elegant suite for strings which sounds like Handel, Bach and a few French composers all thrown in together. More striking, though, is the most substantial piece on the disc, the *Alster Echo* Overture-Suite, a nine-movement work for strings, oboes and horns full of tricks and surprises occasioned by a host of representative titles. Thus 'Hamburg Carillons' brings us horns imitating bells, 'Concerto of Frogs and Crows' has some mischievously scrunchy wrong notes, and in 'Alster Echo' there's a complex network of echoes between oboes and horns. But the show-stealer is the *Grillen-Symphonie* ('Cricket Symphony'). This is a work for the gloriously silly scoring of piccolo, alto chalumeau, oboe, violins, viola, and two double-basses, a somewhat Stravinskian combination that you're unlikely to encounter every day. But it's not just the instrumentation that's irresistibly odd. There is a slow movement with curious, melancholy woodwind interventions a little reminiscent of *Harold in Italy*, and a finale which is quite a hoot.

Overture-Suites

Overture-Suite in A minor[a]. Concerto in E minor for Recorder and Flute[b]. Viola Concerto No 1 in G[c]. Ouverture des nations anciennes et modernes for Strings and Continuo, TWV55 P

[b]**Franz Verster** *fl* **Paul Doctor** *va* [a]**South-West German Chamber Orchestra / Friedrich Tilegant;** [b]**Amsterdam Chamber Orchestra / André Rieu;** [c]**Concerto Amsterdam / Frans Brüggen** *rec*

Teldec Das Alte Werk 9031-77620-2 (M)

(69 minutes: ADD). Recorded 1967-68

Four performances of the highest calibre, marvellously recorded in the 1960s and now sounding as fresh as the day they were made. Two of them feature the distinguished recorder player Frans Brüggen. He is at his inimitable finest, and this is very fine indeed, in the masterly Suite in A minor for recorder and strings (every bit as fine a work as the Bach B minor Suite for the same instrumentation) and the

E minor Concerto for recorder, transverse flute and strings with its attractive interplay of solo texture. Here he is joined by Franz Verster. Brüggen then moves to the conductor's podium to direct the Concerto Amsterdam, joined by a superb viola player, Paul Doctor, in the famous G major Viola Concerto. The *Ouverture des nations anciennes et modernes* is another suite, full of the composer's most felicitious invention. The music is played with great character and the CD transfer is exemplary.

Overture-Suite in G, 'La changeante'. Ouverture des nations anciennes et modernes. Suite in D
Northern Chamber Orchestra / Nicholas Ward
Naxos 8 553791 (58 minutes: DDD) Ⓢ
Recorded 1996

These are three particularly attractive orchestral suites from an almost daunting legacy of some 130 such pieces by Telemann. Ward directs the modern-instrument band from his position as first violin, securing tidy ensemble and maintaining buoyant rhythms. The least performed of the Suites is *La changeante*, framed by the key of G minor. Ward brings plenty of charm and some graceful gesture to the dances, yet too often underplays their character. Better this, by far, than those occasionally encountered mannerisms which exaggerate the importance of Telemann's sometimes elusive subtitles; but some of this playing may strike you as just a little too serious. The *Ouverture des nations anciennes et modernes*, like *La changeante*, is scored for strings and continuo. This is a delicious piece, full of witty contrasts, and prefaced by one of Telemann's most supple French overtures. The performance fails either to convey fully its nobility or to capitalise upon the radiance of Telemann's affable harmonies; but the playing is anything but lifeless, and repeats are scrupulously observed. While these two Suites probably date from Telemann's early years in Hamburg or even, in the case of *Les Nations*, slightly earlier, the remaining Suite in D major belongs to the very last years of his life. Scored for woodwind, two horns and strings it possesses some of the hallmarks of early classicism, demonstrating not only the octogenarian Telemann's fluency with a newly emerging idiom but also a certain flair for it. As before, the playing is rhythmic and sympathetic. In summary, an attractive release which does not, however, realise the music's full potential to entertain. But the playing is so good that it deserves inclusion in this guide.

Overture-Suites – G minor, TWV55:g4; A minor, TWV55:a2; C, TWV55:C6; D, TWV55:D15; D minor, TWV55:d3; F minor, TWV55:f1 **Vienna Concentus Musicus / Nikolaus Harnoncourt** 🅿
Teldec Das Alte Werk ② 4509-93772-2 Ⓜ
(148 minutes: ADD). Recorded 1978 ●

Harnoncourt is nowhere more at home than in the aesthetic world of this music. The Overtures of the ravishing G minor Suite and the bolder C major work show him to be a master of noble gesture and purposeful articulation. There is a robust, biting energy about Harnoncourt which is infectious; often, as in the Bourée *en trompette* of the C major work, one imagines that the exaggerated contrasts and deliberate accentuations would appear mannered if executed by anyone other than Harnoncourt. Throughout, he conjures up subtle rhythmic deviations, each paragraph flexibly shaped but still controlled and naturally breathed. If pliancy of this kind is an answer to making sense of baroque phrasing, then texture speaks volumes too: Telemann's oboe writing in particular, and its place within a string body, is exceptionally skilled; his scoring of three oboes is especially effective and the oboists play with irresistible *esprit*. The D major Suite is full of instances where their performances brim with personality, contributing greatly to that fruity and ever so musty nose which characterises Concentus Musicus on vintage form. The recorded sound is full of presence. With Harnoncourt one can imagine few exponents better suited to this colourful repertoire. This release is full of many unique delights.

Additional Recommendation
Overture-Suites
F, 'Alster Echo', TWV55: F11; G, 'Burlesque de Don Quichotte', TWV55: G10. B flat, 'La Bourse' 🅿
Tafelmusik Baroque Orchestra / Lamon *vn*
Analekta fleurs de lys FL2 3138 (68 minutes: DDD) Ⓕ
No longer available in the UK, but try the internet

Music of sparkling invention, guaranteed to bring amusement and agreeable entertainment to listeners and performers alike. The performances from this top baroque orchestra are exemplary. A perfect Telemann release.

Musique de Table

Musique de Table, 'Tafelmusik', Part 3 – Concerto for Two Horns and Strings in E flat; Overture in B flat; Quartet in E minor; Sonata for Oboe and Continuo in G minor; Trio in D; Conclusion in B flat
Orchestra of the Golden Age
Naxos 8 553732 (73 minutes: DDD) Ⓢ
Recorded 1995

The Orchestra of the Golden Age bring expressive warmth to this evergreen repertoire. The present disc contains the third of the three 'Productions' that make up Telemann's most comprehensive orchestral/instrumental publication. It's the shortest of the three and so can be accommodated comfortably on a single disc. Like its predecessors, the Third consists of an orchestral Suite, Quartet, Concerto, Trio, Sonata for melody instrument with figured bass and an orchestral 'Conclusion'. Telemann had already generously provided for transverse flute, trumpet and solo violins in the previous 'Productions' while maintaining the flute profile (Quartet and Trio) in the third anthology; he gives pride of place to oboe(s) in the Suite, Sonata and Conclusion, and a pair of horns in the Concerto.

One might feel that a slightly augmented string section would have been justified for the orchestral suites and concertos. But, in this instance the players realise the innate nobility of the French overture character with a justly 'occasional' tempo. In the Concerto, which comes over well, if perhaps a shade rigidly in its rhythm, the horn players Roger Montgomery and Gavin Edwards sustain an evenly balanced and tonally secure partnership. That also goes for the lightly articulated flute partnership of Edwina Smith and Felicity Bryson in the Trio. The lovely G minor Oboe Sonata is played with warmth and expressive intimacy by Heather Foxwell. Telemann brings all to a vigorous close with a little three-section orchestral coda, marked *Furioso*. This is a set which makes rather more of Telemann's inflective *délicatesse* than others at twice or even three times the price.

Chamber Works

Sonates Corellisantes – No 1 in F, TWV42:F2. Paris Quartets, 'Nouveaux quatuors en Six Suites' – No 6 in E minor, TWV43:e4. Essercizii Musici – Trio No 8 in B flat, TWV42:B4. Quartets – A minor, TWV43:a3; G minor, TWV43:g4 **P**
Florilegium Ensemble
Channel Classics CCS5093 (53 minutes: DDD) Ⓕ
Recorded 1992 **OO**

The rarity here is the *Sonata Corellisante* for two violins and continuo in which Telemann pays tribute to Corelli. The remaining works are the sixth and perhaps finest of the 1738 *Nouveaux Quatuors* or *Paris Quartets* as they have become known, a little *Quartet* (or *Quadro*) in G minor, a B flat Trio from the *Essercizii Musici* collection (*c*1739) and a fine Concerto da camera (Quartet) in A minor, very much along the lines of Vivaldi's pieces of the same kind in which each instrument other than the continuo has an obbligato role. The finest work here is the *Paris Quartet*, which consists of a Prelude, a sequence of dance-orientated movements and an elegiac Chaconne that lingers long in the memory. The performance is full of vitality and probes beneath the music's superficialities. There is, throughout the programme here, an intensity and a youthful spontaneity about this playing which has considerable appeal.

Kleine Cammer-Music – Partita No 2 in G, TWV41:G2. Essercizii Musici – Solo No 5 in B flat, TWV41:B6; Solo No 11 in E minor, TWV41:e6; Trio No 12 in E flat, TWV42:Es3. Der getreue Music-Meister – Sonata in A minor, TWV41:a3. Der Harmonische Gottesdienst – No 26, Am Sonntage Jubilate in C minor, TWV1:356[a]; No 31, Am ersten Pfingstfeiertage in G, TWV1:1732[a] **P**
Paul Goodwin *ob* **Nigel North** *lte/theorbo* **Susan Sheppard, [a]Lynden Cranham** *vcs* **John Toll** *hpd*
Harmonia Mundi HMU90 7152 (65 minutes: DDD) Ⓕ
Recorded 1995 **O**

Paul Goodwin is surely one of the finest baroque oboists of the moment, so when he turns his mind to such a master of agreeable and skilfully composed chamber music as Telemann, it must be worth our while listening in. Every piece has its own character and charms: here is a seven-movement Partita from the *Kleine Cammer-Music* of 1716, then a couple of Solos and a quirky Trio involving an obbligato harpsichord from the *Essercizii Musici* of 1739, while a Lesson from the giant 1720s part-work, *Der getreue Music-Meister*, sits alongside movements with oboe obbligato from the slightly earlier sacred cantata collection *Der harmonische Gottesdienst*. The variety of form and nomenclature is more than matched on this disc by that of accompaniments which, as so many of the best continuo teams do these days, make an indispensable creative contribution to the success of the performance as a whole.

With the boisterous and inspired Romanesca pair of Nigel North and John Toll on board this is no surprise. A cello also takes the original vocal line in the cantata movements, though the identity of the player (Susan Sheppard) is not made clear in the booklet. As for Goodwin himself, his playing is bold and bright with solid, versatile technique and fluid phrasing, and his interpretations are detailed and intelligent while losing nothing in spontaneity. The recorded sound for all instruments is perhaps rather aggressive over the space of an hour's listening, but then these are performances which by their very refusal to be timid demand full attention from the listener.

Trio Sonatas – F, TWV42:F10; G minor, TWV42:g7. Quartets – C, TWV43:C2; B minor, TWV43:b3; G, TWV43:G12 **P**
Limoges Baroque Ensemble (Maria-Tecla Andreotti *fl* Sergio Azzolini *bn* Gilles Colliard *vn* Vittorio Ghielmi *va da gamba* Bruno Cocset *vc/violone* Willem Jansen *hpd*) **/ Christophe Coin** *va da gamba*
Auvidis Astrée E8632 (56 minutes: DDD) Ⓕ
Recorded 1997 **OO**

This discerningly assembled programme of chamber music with viola da gamba shows off the composer in some of his finest and most varied colours. Each piece is of sustained musical interest and expressive charm. Christophe Coin, who plays viola da gamba and directs the ensemble, is one of the most interesting minds at work in this period, and his performances are full of rhythmic energy, expressive fervour and technical expertise. Coin has always been keen to highlight Telemann's sensibility towards colour and texture, a feature that becomes strikingly apparent in the Quartet in B minor. It is scored for flute, viola da gamba, bassoon and continuo and, like its companion in C major, conforms with an Italian *concerto a quattro*. The two slow movements of the B minor work are enormously expressive, the one tinged with melancholy, the other more conventionally lyrical. More startling than either of these, though, is the exotic finale with its central European folk-dance rhythmic inflexions, so beloved by the composer. The remaining pieces are all delightful, especially the Quartet in G major, scored for flute, two violas da gamba and harpsichord. Why is the companion piece always ignored? It is on a comparable inspirational level.

This is a first-rate release and one of the most invigorating discs of Telemann's chamber music available. The recorded sound is outstanding.

12 Fantaisies for Violin without Continuo, TWV40: 14-25. Der getreue Music-Meister – 'Gulliver' Suite in D, TWV40:108 **P**

Andrew Manze, Caroline Balding *vns*

Harmonia Mundi HMU90 7137 (78 minutes: DDD) Ⓕ

Recorded 1994

Andrew Manze brings a very distinctive angle to the 12 *Fantaisies*. We have learnt to take virtuosity for granted with Manze – his remarkable feats allow the most prejudiced to forget that he is playing a baroque fiddle. But without such an instrument he could barely create such a biting astringency in the more self-effacing and tortured moments (*Fantaisie* No 6) or a cultivated assurance and definition in articulation to the recognisably regular sections, such as *Fantaisie* No 10, where Telemann is working in established forms – particularly in the latter works in the set where dance forms predominate.

If characterisation is the key, Manze is arguably more persuasive than any of his rivals. He grows through phrases in the Gigue of the Fourth *Fantaisie* in a fashion which gives the work a peculiarly stoical strength, purrs through the contrapuntally conceived *Fantaisies* with nonchalant disdain for their extreme technical demands and leaves sighs and pauses hanging with supreme eloquence. With sheer lucidity, imagination and colour, he most acutely captures the sense of a famous public figure ensconced in a private world against the backdrop of a musical world in a state of flux. To add spice to an already outstanding release, we have the short and delightful *Gulliver* Suite for two violins.

12 Sonate metodiche **P**

Barthold Kuijken *fl* **Wieland Kuijken** *va da gamba* **Robert Kohnen** *hpd*

Accent ② ACC94104/5D (140 minutes: DDD) Ⓕ

Recorded 1994 **OO**

No, the title is hardly an incentive to part with one's pocket-money. But with Telemann we should know better than to be taken in by such packaging details. These are, in fact, 12 skilfully written and entertaining sonatas, published in two sets of six and issued in 1728 and 1732. Telemann seems, right from the start, to have had two instruments in mind: flute or violin, and though Barthold Kuijken has elected to play all of them on a baroque flute, he does so with such technical mastery that there is little cause for regret. He savours the many playful ideas contained in the faster movements and realises a touching sense of melancholy in several of the slow ones. Among the most impressive of the sonatas is that in B minor, which Kuijken plays with sensitivity and technical panache. The interpretation is on a sufficiently elevated level to warrant unqualified praise. The recorded sound is first-rate.

Hamburger Admiralitätsmusik

Hamburger Admiralitätsmusik, TWV24:1. Overture-Suite in C, TWV55:C3, 'Hamburger Ebb und Fluth' **P**

Mieke van der Sluis *sop* **Graham Pushee** *counterten* **Rufus Müller** *ten* **Klaus Mertens, David Thomas, Michael Schopper** *basses* **Alsfeld Vocal Ensemble; Bremen Baroque Orchestra / Wolfgang Helbich**

CPO ② CPO999 373-2 (119 minutes: DDD) Ⓑ

Text and translation included. Recorded live in 1995

The orchestral suite *Hamburger Ebb und Fluth* has been recorded many times and is one of the most engaging examples from Telemann's pen of a form at which he excelled. The Bremen Baroque Orchestra give a lively and elegantly shaped performance of the work, introducing to its French overture a degree of *gravitas* appropriate to the occasion. Following the orchestral suite comes the *Admiralitätsmusik* serenade itself whose own introductory French overture's opening gestures call to mind the overture to Handel's *Music for the Royal Fireworks* written a quarter of a century later. Richey's poem is a paean to Hamburg, its institutions, its government and, not least, its prosperity.

Each of the soloists assumes a role. Hamburg (Harmonia) is assigned to the soprano, judicial wisdom (Themis) to a countertenor, prosperity (Mercurius) to a tenor, the Elbe (Albis), North Sea (Neptunus) and republican liberty (Mars) to three basses. Recitatives and arias for these dramatis personae make up the greater part of Richey's text, lightly seasoned with occasional choruses for nymphs, tritons and the like. While it is more than likely that the audience in whose honour the serenade was written responded more readily to the topical and topographical allusions in Richey's text than to Telemann's music, quite the reverse applies today. Richey's platitudinous, at times flatulent sentiments are not likely to fire the imagination of late 20th-century landlubbers.

The solo team is strong, but the Alsfeld Vocal Ensemble does not always match them in tonal precision. The string playing is clean but would have better served the music if it had been more rhythmically incisive. In sum, this is a fascinating issue. Clear sound from a live recording.

Die Donner-Ode, TWV6:3

Der Herr ist König, TWV8:6. Die Donner-Ode, TWV6:3

Ann Monoyios, Barbara Schlick *sops* **Axel Köhler** *counterten* **Wilfried Jochens** *ten* **Harry van der Kamp, Hans-Georg Wimmer, Stephan Schreckenberger** *basses* **Rheinische Kantorei; Das Kleine Konzert / Hermann Max**

Capriccio 10 556 (65 minutes: DDD). Texts and translations included. Recorded 1990-92 Ⓕ

The *Donner-Ode* was one of Telemann's biggest public successes during his lifetime and is a striking piece in its own right, a vivid reaction to the Lisbon earthquake of 1755. The shock caused to the international community by this dreadful event (in which some 60,000 people were killed) was enormous, and in Hamburg a special day of penitence was the occasion for this 'Thunder Ode', though it does perhaps suggest a rather smug satisfaction that such a disaster didn't befall northern Germany. 'The voice of God makes the proud mountains collapse', the text proclaims, 'Give thanks to Him in His temple!' The music, too, both in its mood and in that extraordinarily up-to-date style of Telemann's later years, frequently conjures the benign, entertainingly song-like pictorial mood of a Haydn Mass or oratorio. Entertaining is the word, though, especially in this energetic performance under Hermann Max. He is fleet-footed and buoyantly athletic, benefiting from what is becoming his customary excellent team of German soloists.

For the coupling Max chooses another German work, the cheerful cantata *Der Herr ist König*, written much earlier in the composer's life and more Bach-like in character and form (though it is worth pointing out that since it survives partly in Bach's hand, we ought perhaps to conclude that Telemann was the one wielding the influence here). As in the *Ode*, choir, soloists and orchestra are bright, tight-knit and well recorded, making this release an enjoyable one.

Die Hirten an der Krippe ...

Die Hirten an der Krippe zu Bethlehem, TWV1:797. **P**
Siehe, ich verkündige Euch, TWV1:1334. Der Herr hat offenbaret, TWV1:262

Constanze Backes *sop* **Mechthild Georg** *contr* **Andreas Post** *ten* **Klaus Mertens** *bass* **Michaelstein Chamber Choir; Telemann Chamber Orchestra / Ludger Rémy**

CPO CPO999 419-2 (65 minutes: DDD). Texts and translations included. Recorded 1996 Ⓕ

The tenderly expressive and ingenuous character of German Protestant Christmas music of the baroque seldom fails to exert its magic. Though the greatest achievements in this tradition greatly diminished after Bach, there were exceptions. One of them is Telemann's intimate and imaginative oratorio *Die Hirten an der Krippe zu Bethlehem* ('The Shepherds at the Crib in Bethlehem'). The text is by the Berlin poet, Ramler and though Ramler's taste for classical forms sometimes makes his work stiff and austere, nothing could be further removed from this than his intimate account and celebration of Christ's birth. Certainly, it touched a chord in Telemann, who responded with music of expressive warmth and irresistible charm.

This is not at all the world of Bach's *Christmas Oratorio*, indeed it is only approximately a sixth of the length of Bach's masterpiece. Telemann's concept is one rather of noble simplicity, a sought-after goal in post-Bach church music which, in this respect, at least, provided a perfect foil to Ramler's text. Every reader will recognise the melody of the opening number as belonging to the Latin carol *In dulci jubilo*. Telemann's harmonisation of the 16th-century tune sets the scene concisely and intimately. Thereafter, follows one delight after another. Of outstanding beauty are the 'Shepherd's Song' and the bass aria, 'Hirten aus den goldnen Zeiten'. This is an extremely pleasurable, well-filled, disc with a pervasive charm. The remaining two items are both Christmas cantatas, of 1761 and 1762 respectively, and contain music of enormous appeal. Performances are excellent, with outstanding singing by Klaus Mertens and Mechthild Georg. Both choir and orchestra rise to the occasion under the sensitive and stylish direction of Ludger Rémy. Three hitherto unrecorded pieces in performances of such vitality make this comfortably a very strong issue.

Cantatas

Lobet den Herrn, alle seine Heerscharen, TWV1:061. Wer nur den lieben Gott lässt walten, TWV1:593. Der Tod ist verschlungen in den Sieg, TWV1:320

Dorothee Fries *sop* **Mechthild Georg** *contr* **Andreas Post** *ten* **Albert Pöhl** *bass* **Friedemann Immer Trumpet Consort** (Friedemann Immer, Klaus Osterloh, Ute Hübner *tpts* Stefan Gawlik *timp*) **Bach Collegium Vocale, Siegen; Hanover Hofkapelle / Ulrich Stötzel**

Hänssler Classic CD98 179 (56 minutes: DDD). Texts and translations included. Recorded 1997 Ⓕ

While Telemann's concertos, suites, instrumental chamber music and oratorios have been well explored by performers, his large-scale cantatas, comparatively speaking, have not. Part of the problem is that there is a truly daunting number of them. And, it need hardly be said, the quality is variable. But few are utterly devoid of inspiration and the three pieces contained in this programme rise well beyond that category. Until now they have remained very possibly unperformed, but certainly unrecorded. These are not domestic pieces of the kind which characterise his well-known Hamburg anthology, *Der harmonische Gottesdienst*, but generously, sometimes colourfully orchestrated works with choruses, recitatives, arias and chorales. The format, in short, is Bach-like, though with nothing remotely comparable to the great opening choral fantasies of which Bach was the master. Telemann usually treats his hymn melodies simply, this approach lending them a distinctive, ingenuous charm.

The three cantatas offer strong contrasts of colour and of mood. The New Year piece, *Lobet den Herrn* has glittering trumpet parts with timpani and Telemann's deployment of them is deft and effective. The Neumeister setting, on the other hand, with an orchestra confined to strings and woodwind, is quietly spoken and more reflective. Performances are stylish, and the director, Ulrich Stötzel, has a lively feeling for Telemann's frequent use of dance rhythms. The soloists are expressive, notably Mechthild Georg, who offers a lyrical account of her aria with oboe in the Easter cantata, *Der Tod ist verschlungen in den Sieg*. In short, this is a release which should interest and delight all readers with a taste for the music of this imaginative, prolific and seemingly indefatigable composer, whose fecundity too often prompts generalisations that are as unwelcome as they are unjustified.

Orpheus

Roman Trekel *bar* Orpheus; **Ruth Ziesak** *sop* Eurydice; **Dorothea Röschmann** *sop* Orasia; **Werner Güra** *ten* Eurimedes; **Maria Cristina Kiehr** *sop* Ismene; **Hanno Müller-Brachmann** *bar* Pluto; **Isabelle Poulenard** *sop* Cephisa, Priestess; **Axel Köhler** *counterten* Ascalax; **RIAS Chamber Choir, Berlin; Academy for Ancient Music, Berlin / René Jacobs**
Harmonia Mundi ② HMC90 1618/9
(159 minutes: DDD). Notes, text and translation included. Recorded 1996 Ⓕ

This is the first performance on disc of an opera that was recognised as being the product of Telemann's pen only some 20 years ago. The original libretto was by a Frenchman, Michel du Boullay. Telemann seems to have adapted the text to suit Hamburg taste, but though the libretto has survived virtually complete, a small part of the score is lost. For the edition used here, Peter Huth – who has also contributed a useful essay – Jakob Peters-Messer and René Jacobs have filled the lacunae with music from other Telemann sources. Telemann's *Orpheus* has an additional dimension to the standard version of the legend in the person of Orasia, widowed Queen of Thrace. She occupies a key position in the drama, first as murderess of Eurydice of whose love for Orpheus she is jealous, then of Orpheus himself, since he, understandably, rejects her advances. The plot develops effectively, contributing greatly to the dramatic coherence and overall satisfaction provided by text and music alike. In common with a great many operas for the Hamburg stage, *Orpheus* contains arias sung in languages other than the German vernacular. Italian was the usual alternative, but here there are airs in French, too, and Telemann, on these occasions, lends emphasis to the 'mixed style' aesthetic, in which he was an ardent believer, by retaining the distinctive stylistic character of each country. But the German arias are often both the most interesting and the most varied, since it is the Lied and the *arioso*, as developed in the Passion-Oratorio settings, that provide those additional ingredients which vitalise, refresh and give distinction to his music.

The cast is first-rate. Dorothea Röschmann projects a passionate and temperamental Orasia for whom Telemann has provided several strongly characterised arias. Orpheus is sung by Roman Trekel, Eurydice by Ruth Ziesak. Telemann adorns both roles with an affecting blend of lyricism and pathos. Eurydice's part in the drama is, perforce, relatively small but her music is often alluring and nowhere more so, perhaps, than when she welcomes the shades, who gather to prevent an opportunity for the lovers to look upon one another during the rescue scene. There are some forward-looking harmonies here which foreshadow later developments in opera. Orpheus's music is, appropriately, captivating more often than not; and it is strikingly varied in character.

The other major beneficiary of Telemann's musical largesse is Orpheus's friend, Eurimedes, a tenor role expressively sung by Werner Güra. Pluto, a bass-baritone role sung with resonance and authority by Hanno Müller-Brachmann, appears in Act 1 only; but he has some splendid music. The remaining roles are small, but, of these, Ismene, one of Orasia's ladies-in-waiting, deserves mention for the aria, 'Bitter und süss sind Rachgier und Liebe'. This double-edged piece is ravishingly sung by Maria Cristina Kiehr. And another, for Pluto's servant Ascalax, contains moments of vivid word-painting fluently if, perhaps, tamely handled by Axel Köhler. In choosing a soprano of the calibre of Isabelle Poulenard to sing the minor role of Cephisa, a nymph, Jacobs showed shrewd judgement, since Telemann wrote a virtuoso aria for her which Poulenard sings with brilliance and technical skill. Cephisa also shares some delightful music with a chorus of nymphs.

There are several fine choruses, lightly and articulately sung by the RIAS Chamber Choir and a handful of invigorating instrumental numbers. Jacobs and his musicians deserve congratulations, and so does Harmonia Mundi for the first-rate recording. This is an important and hugely enjoyable release.

Sir Michael Tippett British 1905-1998

GROVE *Tippett studied with C Wood and Kitson at the RCM (1923-8), then settled in Oxted, Surrey, where he taught, conducted a choir and began to compose. However, dissatisfaction with his technique led him to take further lessons with Morris (1930-32), and he published nothing until he was into his mid-30s. By then he was conducting at Morley College, of which he became music director in 1940; there he performed his oratorio A Child of our Time (1941), which uses a story of Nazi atrocity but draws no simple moral from it, concluding rather that we must recognize within ourselves both good and evil. Earlier works, like the String Quartet No 1 and the Concerto for double string orchestra, had married Stravinskian neo-classicism with a bounding rhythm that came from the English madrigal, but the oratorio added to these a Baroque concept of form and black spirituals to replace the chorales of a Protestant Passion. It also made clear Tippett's willingness to exert himself in the public world, which he did again as a conscientious objector in 1943 in accepting imprisonment rather than conscription.*

A Child of our Time seems further to have released creative energy that went into a series of works – two more quartets, the cantata for tenor and piano Boyhood's End and the Symphony No 1 – leading to the composition of the opera The Midsummer Marriage in the years1946-52. This, at once a pastoral, a modern morality and a mystery play of psychic growth, called for a further extension of resources: luminous static harmony, orchestral brilliance, a bold command of large spans of time, and a lively variety of rhythm in the largely danced middle act. The message is again that of the oratorio: before marriage the central characters must each accept the wedding within their personalities of intellect and carnality. The theme relates to The Magic Flute, and Tippett's sources for his own libretto also include Shaw, Yeats and Eliot.

The opera's musical exuberance spilt over into succeeding works, including the Fantasia concertante on a Theme of Corelli for strings and the Piano Concerto, but then through the Symphony No 2 (1957) came a clearing and hardening of style towards the vivid block forms and declamatory vocal style of the opera King Priam, composed in 1958-61, which concerns the problem of free will. Once more an opera had its offshoots; notably in the Piano Sonata No 2 and the Concerto for Orchestra, with its distinct gestures and circular formal schemes, but followed by a new, ecstatic continuity in the cantata The Vision of St Augustine (1965). Here the baritone's central narrative is subverted by huge choral parentheses, representing the density of thought and feeling embracing the simple account of the circumstances leading up to the vision. In his opera The Knot Garden (1970) he concentrates on the emotional substance of clashes of personality and their outcome. His unusually candid if stylized presentation of raw human relationships and of the need to make a success of the seemingly incompatible ones produce a score of lapidary compression, notable for its metallic sonorities, its use of a 12-note theme (though not serial technique) to represent fractured relationships and its revival of blues and boogie-woogie in a manner analogous to his use of spirituals in A Child of our Time.

Symphony No 3 continues to explore the seemingly inexhaustible flow of invention stimulated by the 'light' and the 'shadow'; the abstract musical argument of the first part is answered by the overtly human involvement of the second, where blues again express a basic human predicament and Beethoven's music provides archetypal gestures. The range of reference is wider in the opera The Ice Break, where again the blues stand for human warmth in a time of uncertainty but where the composer alludes to diverse strands of high and popular culture in a work that depicts and transfigures clashes of age, race and milieu. Again, the opera is composed of fragmentary scenes in which archetypal characters confront one another, but now in a context of global discord; the musical style is even more jaggedly kaleidoscopic, as it is also in Symphony No 4, which abandons the vocal solution of the Third but finds in purely musical development a metaphor of physical birth, growth and dissolution. Other late works include the oratorio The Mask of Time (1982), a grand restatement of Tippett's musical and philosophical concerns, as well as a Concerto for string trio and orchestra.

Concerto for Double String Orchestra

Concerto for Double String Orchestra. Fantasia concertante on a Theme of Corelli. The Midsummer Marriage – Ritual Dances

BBC Symphony Chorus and Orchestra / Sir Andrew Davis

Teldec British Line 4509-94542-2 (64 minutes: DDD) Ⓕ
Text and translation included
Recorded 1993

Sir Andrew Davis's formidable Tippettian credentials shine through in every bar of this outstanding anthology. Aided by realistic, firmly focused sound, the *Concerto for Double String Orchestra* sounds glorious here. What's more, Davis directs a performance of enormous humanity, intelligence and dedication – even Sir Neville Marriner's excellent EMI remake now seems a little matter-of-fact by comparison. In the slow movement Davis secures a rapt response from his BBC strings (the exquisite closing bars are drawn with ineffable tenderness), while the finale bounds along with irrepressible vigour and fine rhythmic panache. Davis's *Fantasia concertante* is an even more remarkable achievement. This is another inspirational display: sensitive and fervent, yet marvellously lucid and concentrated too. Once again, the BBC strings are on radiant form, and the lyrical intensity of their playing during the central climax has to be heard to be believed. Davis's identification with this sublime music is total. Much the same applies, for that matter, to the committed and incisive account of the 'Ritual Dances' from *The Midsummer Marriage*, a veritable tour de force to which the BBC Symphony Chorus contributes thrillingly in the final dance.

Divertimento on Sellinger's Round. Little Music for Strings. The Heart's Assurance (orch Bowen). Concerto for Double String Orchestra

John Mark Ainsley *ten* **City of London Sinfonia / Richard Hickox**

Chandos CHAN9409 (71 minutes: DDD). Text included. Recorded 1995 Ⓕ

Chandos has here secured the first recording of the orchestral version of Tippett's major song-cycle, *The Heart's Assurance*. The *Concerto for Double String Orchestra* is Tippett's first masterwork, and it's marvellous to have a recording that does justice to all those antiphonal textural subtleties. One might wish for a touch more brio in the first movement and a richer, stronger tone in places: for example, the slow movement's sublime outer sections. But this is still a very satisfying performance, not least because the finale comes across with such a winning blend of vitality and eloquence. Meirion Bowen's orchestration of *The Heart's Assurance* had Tippett's approval, and it is undoubtedly a resourceful piece of work. What makes the effect so different from the voice and piano original is that the all-important doublings of voice and instrument seem so much more prominent when the instrument in question can sustain the sound for as long as the voice itself. For this reason the original may be preferable, and in addition, despite John Mark Ainsley's excellent contribution to this recording, the final song doesn't build to its overwhelming climax as inexorably as it should. However, this is a valuable Tippett disc, and the recording is satisfyingly rich in detail.

The Rose Lake

The Rose Lake[a]. The Vision of St Augustine[b] Ⓕ
[b]**John Shirley-Quirk** *bar* **London Symphony Chorus and Orchestra / [a]Sir Colin Davis, [b]Sir Michael Tippett**
Conifer Classics 75605 51304-2
(68 minutes: [b]ADD/[a]DDD). Text and translation included. Recorded [a]1997, [b]1971 ●●

Although Tippett let it be known that *The Rose Lake* would be his last orchestral work, it does not sound valedictory. It is based on the profound impression made on him, during a holiday in Senegal, of a small lake which at midday was transformed from whitish green to translucent pink. Tippett imagines the lake singing and frames the five verses of its song with glittering ostinatos and bright toccatas, with much tuned percussion including three octaves of the rototoms of which he made such effective use in *Byzantium*. It is a simple, rondo-like structure but a satisfying one, with the lake first awakening (calm, woodland horns), its song then echoing from the sky (woodwind and string counterpoint) and reaching 'full song' (a long, eloquent string line underpinned by drums) at the centre. The latter half of the work is not a literal mirror-image of the first, but a series of poetic and ingenious 'doubles' of what went before, ending with magical horn calls recalling those in *The Midsummer Marriage*, a quiet rattle of xylophone and rototoms and, as a surprising coda, an abrupt sequence of *staccato* wind chords.

It is a lovely and a moving piece, brimming with characteristically Tippettian melody. Almost as important, it is of just the right length to couple with the composer's own recording of one of his greatest but also one of his least often performed masterpieces. *The Vision of St Augustine* is hideously difficult to perform, but the choral singing here is quite heroic, and John Shirley-Quirk's account of the taxing solo part nothing short of superb. On further acquaintance it reveals itself as truly visionary and profoundly moving. In short, an essential coupling for all admirers of Tippett's music. Davis's account of *The Rose Lake* is as urgently communicative as Tippett's own of the cantata, and the older recording is by no means put in the shade by the newer: both are excellent.

Symphony No 1

Symphony No 1. Piano Concerto
Howard Shelley *pf* **Bournemouth Symphony Orchestra / Richard Hickox**
Chandos CHAN9333 (72 minutes: DDD) Ⓕ
Recorded 1994 ●

The riot of proliferating counterpoint that is Tippett's Symphony No 1 presents enough problems of orchestral balance to give recording teams (not to mention conductors) nightmares. Chandos has managed highly creditable degrees of containment and clarity, without loss of realism, and the impact, when the last movement finally settles on to its long-prepared harmonic goal, is powerful and convincing. As with other Hickox performances in this Tippett series, doubts as to whether initial impetus is sufficient to keep the complex structures on course prove groundless. This is a fine account, well balanced between lively rhythmic articulation and broad melodic sweep. The performance of the Piano Concerto is no less notable for the inexorable way in which its mighty design unfolds. There may be too much decorum, too little passion, in certain episodes, yet Howard Shelley makes persuasive sense of the *con bravura* marking in the finale, and his shaping of the first movement's long, dreamingly decorative lines is as alert and sensitive as his control of the second movement's more dynamic discourse. This is a truly symphonic concerto, with a wealth of invention, remarkable textural ingenuity and a particularly imaginative use of the orchestra to complement the bright colours of the solo instrument. The recording is faultless.

Symphony No 2

Symphony No 2. New Year – Suite
Bournemouth Symphony Orchestra / Richard Hickox
Chandos CHAN9299 (65 minutes: DDD) Ⓕ
Recorded 1994

The balance Hickox achieves between attention to detail and large-scale symphonic sweep is exemplary, and especially impressive in the tricky finale, where he conveys the essential ambiguity of an ending which strives to recapture the optimistic *élan* of the work's opening without ever quite managing it. The Chandos recording, too, gives us much more of the symphony's contrapuntal detail. The first recording of music from Tippett's latest opera *New Year*, première d in 1989, is thoroughly welcome. The music of this suite may seem over-emphatic to anyone who hasn't experienced the opera in the theatre, and the recording relishes the booming electric guitars and wailing saxophones, as well as the taped spaceship effects. Yet there are many imaginative moments, like the use of the 'paradise garden' sarabande borrowed from *The Mask of Time*, and the exotic arrangement of *Auld Lang Syne* near the end. This is Tippett firing on all cylinders, with a performance and recording to match.

Symphony No 3

Praeludium. Symphony No 3
Faye Robinson *sop* **Bournemouth Symphony Orchestra / Richard Hickox**
Chandos CHAN9276 (64 minutes: DDD). Text included. Recorded 1993 Ⓕ ●●

The Third Symphony, first heard in 1972, is one of Tippett's most complex and highly charged attempts to create a convincing structure from the collision between strongly contrasted musical characteristics. The work evolves from a purely orchestral drama – fast first movement, slow second movement, both large-scale, followed by a shorter *Scherzo* – to a less extended but also tripartite sequence of blues settings, the whole capped by a huge, climactic coda in which the soprano voice finally yields the last word to the orchestra. The first two movements (Part 1, as Tippett calls it) remain a considerable technical challenge, especially to the strings, but this performance manages to sustain an appropriate level of tension without sounding merely effortful, and without skimping on the opportunities for eloquence of phrasing. It could well be that Tippett has over-indulged the percussion in the slow movement, but this vivid and well-balanced recording lets us hear ample detail without exaggerating the bright colours and hyper-resonant textures. The later stages have the advantage of a superbly characterful singer in Faye Robinson. She has the power, the edge, and also the radiance, to make Tippett's progression from idiosyncratic blues to Beethoven-quoting peroration utterly convincing. The work ends, famously, on a question-mark, dismissing the unrestrained affirmation of Beethoven's *Choral* finale in favour of the unresolved opposition of loud brass and soft strings. Will that 'new compassionate power/To heal, to love' which the text 'senses' actually be achieved? Nearly thirty years on, the jury is still out on Tippett's great humanist challenge. Meanwhile, there can be no questioning the achievement of this performance and recording, coupled strikingly with the highly characteristic *Praeludium* for brass, bells and percussion of 1962.

String Quartets

String Quartets – No 1[a]; No 2 in F[a]; No 3[a]; No 4[b]; No 5[c]
The Lindsays (Peter Cropper, Ronald Birks *vns* [a]Roger Bigley, [bc]Robin Ireland *vas* Bernard Gregor-Smith *vc*)
ASV ② CDDCS231 (123 minutes: ADD/DDD) Ⓕ
Recorded 1975-92 ⭘

Tippett coached the The Lindsays for these recordings of his first three quartets, and the other two were written for it. In a note written for the quartet's twenty-fifth anniversary in 1992 he said that in these recordings they were 'concerned to establish good precedents in matters of style, so that succeeding generations of interpreters start at an advantage'. In fact one of the most enjoyable things about these readings is that they are so very characteristic of the The Lindsays. Of course a number of the qualities that one might call 'characteristic' are uncommonly well suited to Tippett's earlier quartets: big tone, sheer vigour of attack and an infectious enjoyment of his lithe sprung rhythms.

These performances are indeed excellent precedents for later interpreters. They do establish a style – big-scaled, urgently communicative – that is presumably 'authentic' and yet they challenge listeners as well as other performers to imagine how else they might be done. They also affirm the aching absence of a quartet between the Third and the Fourth (Tippett intended to write one in the late 1940s or early 1950s but got side-tracked by *The Midsummer Marriage* and did not write another for over 20 years) and make one wonder what the rejected two movements of the First Quartet might be like. It is wonderful, though, to hear the five as a sequence in such authoritative readings. The recordings sound very well, but have been transferred at an exceptionally high level.

Tippett String Quartet No 5 **Brown** Fanfare to welcome Sir Michael Tippett **Purcell** Fantasias – F, Z737; E minor, Z741; G, Z742 **Morris** Canzoni Ricertati – No 1, Risoluto; No 6, Lento sostenuto **C Wood** String Quartet in A minor
The Lindsays (Peter Cropper, Ronald Birks *vns* Robin Ireland *va* Bernard Gregor-Smith *vc*)
ASV CDDCA879 (76 minutes: DDD) Ⓕ
Recorded 1992 ⭘

This curious mixture of a programme is a precise re-creation of the concert at which Tippett's Fifth String Quartet had its first performance. Music by two of his teachers and one of his great inspirers is preceded by a greeting prelude that quotes both Purcell and Tippett himself. Tippett's Quartet is quite typical of him, both in its exquisitely singing lyricism and in the fact that it is by no means a mere looking back towards his earlier lyrical phases. Here intensification of expression is often achieved by distillation, towards such a simplicity of utterance that at crucial moments the music thins sometimes to one, often to no more than two, of the quartet's voices. RO Morris's *Canzoni Ricertati* subject faintly folk-like melodies to ingenious fugal and canonic treatment. In Charles Wood's quartet, the ingenious interplay of short motives in his *Scherzo* is something that might have caught the young Tippett's ear, and his finale dresses up the Irish folk-song *The lark in the clear air* in its best Sunday clothes. The Purcell *Fantasias* point up Tippett's Purcell-ancestry rather touchingly as does Christopher Brown's miniature *Fanfare*. The Lindsays' beautiful performances are cleanly but not clinically recorded.

Piano Sonatas

Piano Sonatas Nos 1-3
Nicholas Unwin *pf*
Chandos CHAN9468 (55 minutes: DDD) Ⓕ
Recorded 1995 ⭘

These are very big performances indeed, giving a clear and infectious impression of how satisfying these sonatas must be when you have a technique as commanding as Nicholas Unwin's. The tireless toccata vein in Tippett's piano writing, the abrupt grandeur of some of his juxtapositions, what one might call the 'Beethoven-plus' element (angular dotted figures not far from the *Grosse Fuge*, a buoyant humour closely related to the late *Bagatelles*) – all these are finely conveyed. Possibly missing is the blithely springy lightness of touch that some other pianists have found, especially in the First Sonata. Unwin is capable of light, transparent textures and of fluid lyricism, so he provides pretty well 90 per cent or more of what these sonatas require. No one has supplied more, though it might have been a different 90 per cent: these are works that can take a variety of interpretations and gain from them. The recordings match the performances well, offering a commandingly big piano sound, but there is also no lack of more sober colour.

Choral Works

The Windhover. The Source. Magnificat and Nunc dimittis, 'Collegium Sancti Johannis Cantabrigiense'. Lullaby. Four Songs from the British Isles. Dance, Clarion Air. A Child of Our Time – Five Negro Spirituals. Plebs angelica. The Weeping Babe
Finzi Singers / Paul Spicer with **Andrew Lumsden** *org*
Chandos CHAN9265 (55 minutes: DDD) Ⓕ
Texts included. Recorded 1994 ⭘

The Finzi Singers are eloquent in the Spirituals, and polished in the *British Songs* (especially the beguiling 'Early One Morning'). However, it is especially good to have the works which represent early sightings of Tippett's later, less lusciously lyrical style – the *Lullaby* (with countertenor, reminding us that it was written for the Deller Consort) and the *Magnificat* and *Nunc dimittis*: here not only are the intonation and phrasing of the tricky lines supremely confident, but the accompanying organ is recorded with exemplary naturalness. The vocal sound throughout is generally no less successful. There may be almost too full and rich a texture for the linear intricacies of *Plebs angelica* and *The Weeping Babe* to make their maximum effect, but there is no lack of exuberance in *Dance*, *Clarion Air* and the other secular pieces.

The Heart's Assurance

Tippett Music. Songs for Ariel. Songs for Achilles. Boyhood's End. The Heart's Assurance
Purcell If music be the food of love, Z379/2. The Fairy Queen – Thrice happy lovers. The Fatal hour comes on apace, Z421. Bess of Bedlam, Z370. Pausanias – Sweeter than roses
Martyn Hill *ten* **Craig Ogden** *gtr* **Andrew Ball** *pf*
Hyperion CDA66749 (70 minutes: DDD) Ⓕ
Texts included. Recorded 1994 ⭘

The two longest works – the cantata *Boyhood's End* and song-cycle *The Heart's Assurance* – challenge the musicianship and sensitivity of both singer and pianist alike. *Boyhood's End* (1943), a setting of prose that is never prosaic, shows the ecstasy of *Midsummer Marriage* to be already within the system, and the profusion of notes has to be mastered so that the dance shall seem as delicate and natural as graceful improvisation. In *The Heart's Assurance* (1951) the spirit is similar, although the technical accomplishment of all concerned, composer and performers, is heightened.

For the singer, in addition to the quite fearsome difficulties of pitch and rhythm, there is also likely to be some problem of tessitura, particularly in the third of the songs, 'Compassion'. For the pianist, concentration has to be divided between the virtuosic writing of his own part and responsiveness to the singer, his notes, words and expression.

Martyn Hill and Andrew Ball are wonderfully at one in all this, and the balancing of voice and piano has been finely achieved. The *Songs for Achilles*, with guitar, also convey a real sense of ardent improvisation, and the voice rings out freely. The *Songs for Ariel* here work their natural magic. Tippett's affinities with Purcell are felt at one time or another in most of these compositions, starting with the opening of the programme, the setting of Shelley's *Sleep*. It is good also to have the Purcell 'realisations' included on this release. The disc was issued to mark the composer's 90th birthday, and it serves as a most touching and eloquent tribute.

Thomas Tomkins British 1572-1656

GROVE *Tomkins, from a musical family, claimed Byrd as his teacher. He divided his time between Worcester Cathedral (organist from 1596) and London, becoming a Gentleman in Ordinary of the Chapel Royal by 1620, assistant organist from 1621 and senior organist from 1625; that year he wrote music for Charles I's coronation. He left Worcester in 1654. A prolific and respected successor of Byrd, he composed church music, including over 100 anthems (Musica Deo sacra, 1668), madrigals (1622, among them When David heard, a moving, polyphonic setting of a powerful text), over 50 keyboard pieces and a few highly original fantasias, pavans and galliards for viol consort. His half-brothers John, Giles and Robert and his son Nathaniel were also musicians.*

Keyboard Works

Barafostus' Dream. Fantasia. Fancy. Fancy for two to play. Fortune my foe. A Ground. A Grounde. In Nomine, 'Gloria tibi Trinitas'. The Lady Folliott's Galliard. Miserere. Pavan. Pavan and Galliard, 'Earl Strafford'. Pavan and Galliard of Three Parts. A sad pavan for these distracted times. Toy, 'Made at Poole Court'. What if a day. Worster Braules
Carole Cerasi *hpd* **James Johnstone** *virg/bhpd*
Metronome METCD1049 (74 minutes: DDD) Ⓕ
Recorded 2000 ⭘⭘

Forming a mental picture of Thomas Tomkins is not difficult. Most of the pieces here were composed in the 1640s and '50s, yet adopt the style of three or four decades earlier, when composers like Gibbons, Bull and Tomkins's own teacher Byrd were alive. A contemporary of these men, Tomkins had survived them through the execution of Charles I and the destruction during the Civil War of the organ at Worcester Cathedral, where he had presided since 1596. Now, in later life, he had retired to live with his family and quietly compose plainsong settings, variation sets, fancies, grounds and pavans 'for these distracted times'. But though about as fashionable as a 'Welcome home, Walter Raleigh' hat, these pieces have a quality to them – showing by turns something of the exuberance of Bull and the eloquence of Byrd – that is more than enough to maintain their currency today. This disillusioned early version of a *Daily Telegraph* reader was nothing less than the last representative of that great school of keyboard composers known as the English virginalists, and more than 350 years on, it matters not a bean to the listener which decade he was writing in.

Carole Cerasi's selection of about a third of Tomkins's extant keyboard pieces showcases all of the genres in which he composed, as well as demonstrating the excellence and range of her own technique. Few listeners will fail to be impressed by the fearless accuracy and panache with which she throws off Tomkins's torrential passagework and finger-breaking double thirds, but she is sensitive, too, in the slower pavans and fancies. Like Leonhardt, she achieves a supreme eloquence in such pieces by the sheer precision and control with which she places each note, and it is a pleasure just to hear her playing.

Copies of two different instruments are used – a feisty Italian harpsichord for the more outgoing pieces, a melancholy virginal for the gentler ones – while Cerasi is joined by her husband for the fulsome *Fancy for two to play*. An outstanding disc from this fine young harpsichordist.

Prelude. Fancy. Three In Nomines. Voluntary. Pavan and Galliard of Three Parts. Fancy (arr cpsr). Toy, 'Made at Poole Court'. Pavan. Robin Hood. Two Pavans. Ground **P**

Bernhard Klapprott *hpd/virg*

Dabringhaus und Grimm MDG607 0704-2 (72 minutes: DDD). Recorded 1995 Ⓕ

Tomkins is perhaps best known as a later representative of the school of English madrigalists, and one of Byrd's most talented pupils; yet he composed in all the genres available to him, and left a substantial quantity of keyboard music. Tomkins is at his best when unfettered by preordained conceits, and while he cannot match his great mentor's grasp of form or his knack for writing instantly memorable tunes, the best pieces here are not without charm (the little *Toy*, for example). Bernhard Klapprott plays mostly on a harpsichord, and more rarely on a much softer virginal, which seems the more effective instrument for conveying the music's unaffected delicacy. He strives to find the right expression for each piece; rubato is applied differently from one work to the next according to each piece's character, rather than exclusively by genre. Tempos could have been equally varied: they are uniformly on the slow side, even where greater agility would at least be warranted (as in the Galliard). The choice of instrument may have something to do with this: the virginal's softer sound encourages more rapid runs, whereas the harpsichord's seems to do the opposite. Still, a pleasing disc: Klapprott's advocacy of Tomkins reminds us how much of this first golden age of the keyboard remains unexplored.

Choral Works

Third Service. O Lord, let me know mine end. O that the salvation were given. Know you not. In Nomine (1648). In Nomine (1652). Voluntaries – G; C; A minor

New College Choir, Oxford / Edward Higginbottom with **David Burchell** *org*

CRD CRD3467 (62 minutes: DDD). Texts included Ⓕ
Recorded 1990

This is a well-balanced programme of sacred music by Thomas Tomkins. The four movements of the Third, or Great Service, together with the three anthems are spaced out with five organ pieces – two *In Nomines* and three voluntaries – chosen and arranged in such a way that the resulting key sequence has a satisfying natural flow. After an unassuming intonation, the truly royal *Te Deum* of the Great Service takes off with great verve and vigour, the rich 10-part texture of the full sections contrasting well with the lighter scoring of the verses. This energy and these contrasts are characteristic of the performances as a whole. There is some delightful solo singing in the verse anthems, in particular the alto solo in *O Lord, let me know mine end.* The two solo trebles are kept busy: they have a rather distinctive but complementary tone-quality, which makes up for a slight imbalance in volume. In general, however, the balance is good and the ensemble excellent. The trebles are a confident group with good articulation; they soar up to their top B flats with ease.

Michael Torke American 1961

At first influenced by Stravinsky and Bartók, Torke wrote his earliest orchestral work, Statement (1979), for the Milwaukee Music for Youth ensemble, in which he played principal bassoon. He entered the Eastman School in 1980 and studied composition with Schwantner and Rouse among others. At this time he began to incorporate pop and jazz elements into his music. After graduating from the Eastman School he studied at Yale, where his teachers included Rzewski. He gained notoriety in 1985 for the pop-tinged Ecstatic Orange.

Book of Proverbs

Book of Proverbs[a]. Four Proverbs[b]

[a]**Valdine Anderson,** [b]**Catherine Bott** *sops*
[a]**Kurt Ollmann** *bar* [a]**Netherlands Radio Choir and Philharmonic Orchestra / Edo de Waart;**
[b]**Argo Band / Michael Torke**

Decca 466 721-2DH (52 minutes: DDD). Texts and translations included. Recorded [a]1996 and [b]1993 Ⓕ **OO**

You would have to go a long way to find music as communicative and as uplifting as Michael Torke's. What's more, his compositions are uniquely individual and full of integrity. Listen to this disc, and you will find an essentially traditional harmonic language at work, but the result is most definitely music of today. Furthermore, for all Torke's ingenious construction techniques, this is music straight from the heart; it's also full of optimism.

The opening track of this disc, the orchestral prelude to his *Book of Proverbs*, is a perfect example of Torke's style: lucid, invigorating and wonderfully orchestrated. His settings of texts from the Bible's *Book of Proverbs* abound in skilful musical device, but the meaning and power of the texts is never lost, and is quite frequently heightened and brought into sharper focus. A sense of momentum towards a climax is beautifully achieved throughout the work's eight movements by Torke's decision to expand the use of the chorus in each setting, until, in the final proverb 'Boast not of Tomorrow', the entire chorus sing together. Movement 6, 'Drink our Fill of Love', for baritone and men's chorus, is one of the highlights: a veritable mini-drama, beautifully structured with a harmonic tension building to an impressive climax. Just the sort of sophisticated musical treatment of a text that one would find in a song by Stephen Sondheim.

To complete the disc, Decca has included the recording of Torke's *Four Proverbs* which first appeared on the Argo label. Smaller in both duration and scoring (just solo soprano and small ensemble), it nevertheless possesses the same ingenuity, melodic inventiveness and immediate appeal of the larger work. Performances throughout the disc are uniformly excellent, and the recorded sound is clean, bright and atmospheric. This is a must for all enthusiasts of Torke's music.

Tomás de Torrejón y Velasco

Spanish 1644-1728

GROVE *Torrejón y Velasco went to Peru in 1667 when his employer was appointed viceroy there. He held administrative (non-musical) posts until 1676 when he became maestro de capilla of Lima Cathedral. He was admired for his villancicos, some of them polychoral; he also wrote liturgical music (notably vespers for Charles II) and an opera La púrpura de la rosa (after Calderón) celebrating Philip V's 18th birthday in 1701; it is the earliest surviving opera from the New World.*

La púrpura de la rosa

Isabel Alvarez *sop* Amor; **Alicia Borges** *mez* Belona; **Graciela Oddone** *sop* Adonis; **Adriana Fernández** *sop* Celfa; **Marcello Lippi** *bar* Chato; **Elisabetta Riatsch** *mez* Cintia; **Nadia Ortega** *sop* Clori; **Furio Zanasi** *bar* Desengaño; **Susanna Moncayo** *mez* Dragón; **Fabián Schofrin** *counterten* Envidia; **Sandrah Silvio** *sop* Flora; **Sandra Galiano** *sop* Ira; **Eliana Bayón** *sop* Libia; **Mariana Rewerski** *sop* Sospecha; **Isabel Monar** *mez* Venus; **Cecilia Diáz** *mez* Marte; **Madrid Zarzuela Theatre Orchestra and Chorus; Elyma Ensemble / Gabriel Garrido**

K617 ② K6171082 (129 minutes: DDD) Ⓕ

Texts and English notes included. Recorded 1999 ⭘

The first-ever recording of Tomás Torrejón y Velasco's opera *La púrpura de la rosa* was produced by Andrew Lawrence-King's Harp Consort for DHM; now we are presented with another version, based on a production mounted in opera houses in Geneva and Madrid under the musical direction of Gabriel Garrido.

The opera was originally first performed in Lima, Peru, in 1701: a homage by the newly-appointed viceroy, the Count of Monclava, to King Philip V of Spain on his 18th birthday. The libretto, which retells the story of Venus and Adonis, was written by the great Spanish playwright Pedro Calderón de la Barca, and had previously been set to music by the court composer Juan Hidalgo and performed in Madrid in 1660. Hidalgo's opera has sadly been lost, and it is impossible to know how much Torrejón y Velasco's setting owes to it, if anything. It is a great shame that South American musicologist Bernardo Illari's detailed essay on the decisions he had to take in the making of his edition of *La púrpura de la rosa* are presented only in French and Spanish in the booklet: his summary is both frank and illuminating, so that the listener knows exactly which parts have been reconstructed (in effect, composed by Illari) and what has been the intention behind each decision.

The textual problems (in terms of both text and music) of the source result in some marked differences between this version and that by the Harp Consort, but this is not the place to explore these in any detail. The listener should be aware, however, that both versions have introduced additional items, and both show considerable ingenuity, based on years of experience in techniques of improvisation and early music performance, in the realisation of the score. The only quibble with the Garrido/Illari version is their determination to use a much broader palette of instrumental colour, to the extent of involving wind instruments such as oboes, shawms, recorders and dulcians in a quasi-obbligato manner at times: a lack of instrumental colour, Illari believes, would be contrary to the spirit of the work. There are times, however, when the instrumentation is very effective, as in the cave scene where Mars encounters the allegorical figures of Anger, Suspicion, Envy, Fear and, finally, Disillusion, in a confrontation with his own emotions: here organ continuo and low winds enhance the spookiness already inherent in the disembodied vocal writing for these initially mysterious characters. The Harp Consort, for all its richly sensual sound world, is less evocative here.

The great strength of the new recording by Garrido in terms of performance is the way in which it conveys the dramatic nature of the piece. The fact that it was performed on stage before being taken into the recording studio helped, but there is also a fundamental difference in approach: not only is Garrido's dramatic pacing more revealing, but also his interpretation is far more text-based. And what a text! This is powerful, evocative writing, full of poetry, universal resonances and deep human emotions.

Garrido's singers, more operatically trained than most of those on the Harp Consort version, and more at home with the language, use the music to enhance the text, singing the dialogues and soliloquies with real meaning so that the tragic tale of Venus and her beautiful but doomed Adonis unfolds with great immediacy. If the Harp Consort's roses – the symbol of Adonis's blood and the flower into which he is finally transformed – are of red satin, sensual and enveloping, Garrido's have the scent – and the thorns – of the real thing.

Given that the recordings are so different, one can only recommend that you have both. Torrejón y Velasco is not Monteverdi or Cavalli, not Lully or Purcell, but with this one work he shows himself to have been an instinctive opera composer writing in a highly distinctive idiom with its roots in Spanish tradition: a few more commissions from the viceroy and he could well have made his mark on operatic history.

La púrpura de la rosa (ed Stein/Lawrence-King)
Ellen Hargis *sop* Caliope, Adonis; **Judith Malafronte** *mez* Terpsicore, Venus; **María del Mar Fernández Doval** *sop* Urania, Marte; **Josep Cabré** *bar* El Tiempo, Desengaño; **Gloria Banditelli** *mez* España, Dragón; **Päivi Järviö** *mez* Belona; **Douglas Nasrawi** *ten* Chato; **Nancy Mayer** *mez* Celfa; **Johanna Almark** *sop* Amor; **Santina Tomasello** *sop* Flora, Envidia; **Gabriela de Geanx** *sop* Cintia, Temor; **Catríona O'Leary** *sop* Clori, Sospecha; **Jennie Cassidy** *mez* Libia, Ira; **chorus; The Harp Consort / Andrew Lawrence-King** *hp/hpd/org*
Deutsche Harmonia Mundi ② 05472 77355-2 Ⓕ
(137 minutes: DDD). Text and translation included
Recorded 1997

Tomás de Torrejón y Velasco was one of the most important musical figures in late 17th-century Peru. Born and educated in Spain, he became a page to the future viceroy of Peru and at the age of 23 accompanied him to Lima (the administrative and cultural centre of Spain's colonial empire). There for more than half a century he was *maestro de capilla* at the cathedral, writing polychoral works that achieved considerable fame. In 1701 he was commissioned to compose an opera to honour the new king, Philip V, on his 18th birthday: it was the first opera produced in the New World whose music is extant. Preceded by a *loa* in which allegorical figures hail the arrival of a new star, *La púrpura de la rosa* ('The blood of the rose') is a one-act opera on a text by Calderón. It deals with the myth of Venus and the initially hesitant Adonis and the jealousy of Mars, who is goaded on by his sister Bellona; inserted into it are popular dances, low-life characters – a peasant, his wife and a soldier (providing what may charitably be called comic relief) – and some personifications of human emotions. The work's quite individual style differs markedly from contemporary Italian baroque opera: recitatives are absent, replaced by strophic *ariosos*; all the characters but two are allotted to actresses, so the tessitura throughout is high; and the three main characters are each provided with a theme that serves to identify them at the start of a scene.

The music, which incorporates South American dance rhythms, has been edited by the American scholar Louise Stein, who has colourfully filled out the original's single continuo line with an instrumental ensemble typical of the period and reconstructed choruses and *diferencias* in the dances. The prevalence of women's voices makes it almost impossible to know who everyone is, and what is going on, unless one keeps a firm eye on the libretto; and it is somewhat bewildering that Mars is the most feminine-sounding; but all the singers are good, particularly Ellen Hargis in the demanding part of Adonis.

Concerted voices tend to be overloud (abetted by the acoustics of the recording venue); and not until well into the second half is much attempt made to underline the work's dramatic course – for example, off-stage placing, frequently called for, is totally ignored – and this often results in long, repetitious strophic sequences. But the dramatic high spot – the battle between Mars, who seeks to wreak revenge on Adonis, and Venus, who implores Jupiter to intervene with his thunderbolts – is stirring and occurs to the rhythm of a *xácara*. Predictably, the most moving music is at the death of Adonis and Venus's lament for him. After the play itself, the mournful mood is rudely dispelled with a rowdy kind of *vaudeville* on a peasant's lot. All of the performers, and DHM's enterprise in making this rare work known, are to be warmly applauded. There is much here to enjoy.

Charles Tournemire

French 1870-1939

Tournemire was a pupil of Widor at the Paris Conservatoire and of Franck, whose place as organist at Ste Clotilde he inherited in 1898; from 1919 he also taught at the Conservatoire. His works include operas, oratorios and eight symphonies (1900-24), often on religious and esoteric subjects. But he is remembered for the monumental L'orgue mystique (1932), 51 organ masses using plainsong melodies appropriate to a particular Sunday, for the liturgical year, in a mystical style between Franck and Messiaen.

Symphony No 8

Symphonies – No 5 in F minor, Op 47; No 8 in G minor, 'Le triomphe de la mort', Op 51
Liège Philharmonic Orchestra / Pierre Bartholomée
Auvidis Valois V4793 (69 minutes: DDD) Ⓕ
Recorded 1997

The Liège Philharmonic may not be a world-class orchestra, but it plays with wholehearted commitment and sensitive dynamics, and is directed by a conductor who is clearly in sympathy with the Franckian school, so that these performances offer a very satisfactory presentation of this deeply felt, passionate music. Tournemire (who was one of Franck's successors at Ste Clotilde) could best be described as a romantic mystic: unlike some other enormously prolific composers, his ideas have quality and his treatment of them is both original and extremely effective. Those wishing to sample his style are recommended to start with the beatific *Pastorale* of the Fifth Symphony, a work written in 1913-14 and inspired by Alpine scenery which produced in him a poetic mood of exaltation.

The Eighth Symphony of a decade later, which employs a gigantic orchestra in virtuoso and varied fashion and is somewhat bolder in harmonic idiom, is subtitled *Triumph over Death* and was written on the death of the composer's dearly loved wife (to whom the Fifth Symphony had been dedicated).

Both works are most unorthodox in terms of their form. The Fifth consists of a first movement in which a chorale appears three times, each time followed by an *Allegro* section: the second movement is the tender *Pastorale* that then leads into a joyous finale that is headed 'Towards the light'. The Eighth is still more unusual in that a single theme ingeniously runs throughout its two movements, the first a sorrowing *Lento* that is followed by a luminous more light-hearted section. The second continues for a while in similar vein but, with more brilliant scoring, gives way to an intimate meditation and ends in a transport of radiance. Without doubt, a remarkably individual and gripping work that demands to be heard.

Suite évocatrice, Op 74

Tournemire Suite évocatrice, Op 74
Vierne Symphony No 3, Op 28
Widor Symphonie Gothique, Op 70
Jeremy Filsell *org*
Herald HAVPCD145 (71 minutes: DDD)
Recorded in 1991 on the Harrison and Harrison organ of Ely Cathedral Ⓕ OO

Compared with, say, the symphonies of Tchaikovsky or Sibelius the organ symphonies of Widor and his pupil Vierne are not particularly long. But in terms of organ music they are among the longest single works in the repertory. Within their five-movement form the composers set out to exploit the full expressive range of the organ, and it was no coincidence that the organ symphony developed in turn of the century France. The great French organ builder Aristide Cavaillé-Coll was then producing instruments capable of hitherto undreamt-of colour and expression. Both Widor (at St Sulpice) and Vierne (at Notre Dame) had at their disposal the finest instruments in Paris and they indulged themselves fully in their symphonies. The subtitle of Widor's Ninth (*Gothic*) says it all. The structure is vast, intricately detailed, and almost forbidding in its grandness. Vierne's Third also presents an awesome spectacle, full of complex music and technically demanding writing, while Tournemire's neo-classical Suite gives a moment almost of light relief in such heavyweight company. Jeremy Filsell is an outstanding virtuoso player with a gift for musical communication, and the Ely Cathedral organ produces the range of the great French instruments, but within an altogether clearer acoustic. These are performances and recordings of exceptional quality.

Mark-Anthony Turnage

British 1960

Turnage studied at the Royal College of Music, with Oliver Knussen and John Lambert. He gained wide attention with his first orchestral score Night Dances (1981) which won the Guinness Prize and revealed the eclectic nature of his style, drawing on a wide range of early 20th-century sources and the inflections of jazz and blues harmonies. An even wider stylistic net informs On All Fours for 13 instruments (1986), in which Baroque dance forms, refracted through the model of Stravinsky's Agon, provide the rhythmic impulsion. He attracted wide attention with his opera Greek (1988, Munich).

Blood on the Floor

Martin Robertson *sax/bass cl* **John Scofield** *elec gtr*
Peter Erskine *drum kit* **Ensemble Modern / Peter Rundel**
Argo 455 292-2ZH (69 minutes: DDD) Ⓕ
Recorded live in 1996 OO

Blood on the Floor is an impressive demonstration of the composer's ability to straddle the worlds of jazz, rock and art music without descending to the modish doodling of his crossover peers. The overall title comes from a painting by Francis Bacon, while the music ranges widely in its references and allusions. The disc's packaging plays upon the theme of urban alienation and, of course, *Blood on the Floor* has its harrowing aspects. A younger brother of the composer died as a consequence of drug addiction, and several of its nine movements could scarcely be more explicitly titled. At the same time, the punchy, amplified, vernacular element should not disguise the fact that this is also an elegantly crafted suite, ingeniously laid out for the 30-odd musicians of Ensemble Modern plus a solo trio of electric guitar, drum kit and saxophone.

The participation of John Scofield puts flesh on the bones of Turnage's longstanding idiomatic involvement with Miles Davis, and the 'classical' influences include the usual culprits – Stravinsky, Britten and, conceptually at least, Hans Werner Henze. Somehow, the contradictions don't jar as you'd expect. Operating in an age in which the acquisition of a unified and personal voice is no longer considered top priority, Turnage's eclecticism does not lead to the usual anonymity. His bluesy, shell-shocked lyricism is very much his own. The abrasive opening movement spews out key thematic material in a series of angry, violent climaxes, and yet this is not the dominant mood. 'Junior Addict', inspired by a poem by Langston Hughes, is powerfully melodic with its bleak soprano saxophone solo weaving through woodwinds above a subterranean bass. Get this far and you should be hooked.

Elsewhere the symphonic Turnage is in the ascendant, seeming to aim for the clinching quasi-Mahlerian expression of hope tempered by fatalism, dispelling the fears. The recording is edited together from live performances given in a variety of venues and the immediate style of miking, pop-influenced track-listings and (trilingual) annotations will not be to everyone's taste. That said, the playing is undeniably superb and, for the moment, this feels like a major release.

An Invention on Solitude

Two Memorials[a]. An Invention on Solitude[b]. Sleep on[c]. Cortège for Chris[d]. Two Elegies Framing a Shout[e]. Three Farewells[f]. Tune for Toru[g]

Nash Ensemble ([f]Philippa Davies *fl* [bdf]Richard Hosford *cl* [bf]Marianne Thorsen, [bf]Elizabeth Wexler *vns* [bf]Lawrence Power *va* [bcdf]Paul Watkins *vc* [f]Skaila Kanga *hp* [cdeg]Ian Brown *pf* [ce]Richard Hosford *cl* [ae]Martin Robertson *sop sax*)

Black Box BBM1065 (58 minutes: DDD) Ⓕ

An effective showcase for the composer's small-ensemble music of the 1990s, this album might have been entitled 'Another Side of...Mark-Anthony Turnage'. Where, in some of his major orchestral works, Turnage's idiom has seemed quintessentially urban, indebted (via Tippett and Britten) to Stravinsky and Berg, here we come surprisingly close to the much-derided English pastoral tradition. The jazz element is evident too, as you might expect, but there is little trace of the composer's penchant for rock and raunch; the mood is more wistful than confrontational. Anyone who thinks that contemporary music and memorable melodic writing are somehow incompatible should audition this disc without delay. From the plangent solo sax of the *Two Memorials* to the intensely evocative solo piano version of *Tune for Toru*, there is little to frighten the horses and much that touches the heart. The biggest utterance is the clarinet quintet, *An Invention on Solitude*, composed, like much of this music, during Turnage's work on the score of his most recent opera, *The Silver Tassie*.

The Nash Ensemble are no strangers to the composer's sound world and their firmly focused, unsentimental playing is well served by the boldly immediate recording. This is one of a series of Black Box issues which promises exclusive access to a special website containing additional notes, audio tracks and other info.

Additional recommendation

Blood on the Floor. Dispelling the Fears. Night Dances. Some Days. Your Rockaby.

Various artists, orchestras and conductors

Decca British Music Collection 468 814-2DM (139 minutes: DDD: 8/01) Ⓜ

An excellent mid-price collection for newcomers to Turnage. Performances and recording are superb.

Erkki-Sven Tüür

Estonia 1959

Drawing on both his immediate classical heritage and aspects of jazz and rock, Tüür came to prominence with the Architectonic series of nine ensemble pieces (1990-93), each with an atmospheric and open-minded approach to instrumental writing. This timbrel sensitivity has been continued in such recent works as the Third Symphony (1997), whose formal subtlety and thematic resource is a promising continuation of the Nordic tradition.

Crystallisatio

Architectonics VI. Passion. Illusion. Crystallisatio. Requiem

Estonian Philharmonic Chamber Choir; Tallinn Chamber Orchestra / Tõnu Kaljuste

ECM New Series 449 459-2 (64 minutes: DDD) Ⓕ

Text and translation included

Recorded 1994-95

Architectonics VI sounds like one of those titles that are too good to resist, and it is to the credit of Erkki-Sven Tüür that he admits as much in the brief interview in the booklet to this beguiling disc (the sumptuous annotation in English is translated in reduced form in German and French). Tüür's piece – written in 1992 – isn't architectonic in construction (well, any more than the music of a hundred other composers), but it is well put together and effective on its own terms. *Passion* and *Illusion*, both for string orchestra and composed in 1993, are closer in spirit to the prevailing 'New Simplicity' of current East Baltic composition. *Passion*, indeed, is occasionally reminiscent of Tüür's better-known compatriot, Arvo Pärt, although the brief *Illusion* has a curiously English feel to it. The title track, *Crystallisatio* (1995), is scored for three flutes, bells, string orchestra and live electronics and is somewhat more demanding in scope. It is here that Tüür's synthesis of minimalism with serial techniques is heard most eloquently; not wholly achieved, perhaps, but fascinating in application.

By far the biggest piece is the Requiem (1992-93; in memory of the conductor Peeter Lilje). It is a deeply felt, half-hour-long setting of the Mass for the dead, and is of markedly different character to the other pieces here. This is a handsomely produced, thought-provoking release. Anyone wanting to hear up-to-the-minute new music that will not sear the ears off his or her head should try it.

Symphony No 3

Symphony No 3. Cello Concerto[a]. Lighthouse
[a]**David Geringas** *vc* **Vienna Radio Symphony Orchestra / Dennis Russell Davies**
ECM New Series 465 134-2 (64 minutes: DDD) Ⓕ
Recorded 1998

It looks as though news of the death of the symphony has been greatly exaggerated. Symphonies are appearing at a startling rate today, and their composers often talk enthusiastically about finding new ways of engaging with traditional Western symphonic thought. Among the younger generation of would-be symphonists, Erkki-Sven Tüür is one of the most hope-inspiring. The first movement of his Third Symphony builds impressive momentum from the contrast of two types of music: one dogged and metronomic, the other free and apparently tempo-less. These eventually collide, producing an electrifying climax. The second movement has wildly diffuse elements – from Lutosławskian modernism to quasi-Bachian chorale tune and lush tonal romanticism. This is clearly music of strong personality, integrity and confidence, with warmth as well as acerbity, directness as well as ingenuity. The same could equally be said for the string fantasy *Lighthouse*, and still more for the Cello Concerto, though here the transition from modernism to romantic lyricism is easier to follow and harder to resist. Also appealing is the vigour of much of the writing, especially for the strings – occasionally recalling the great string works of Tippett.

Like his Finnish near-neighbour and fellow symphonist Kalevi Aho, Tüür is plainly worth taking very seriously, and it's good to report that the performers on this disc do just that; everything sounds authoritative and full of seasoned intensity. Excellent recordings too. A must for the curious, and for those who care about the future of the symphony.

Marco Uccellini Italian c1603-1680

GROVE *Uccellini became head of instrumental musica at the Modena court in 1641 and maestro di cappella at Modena Cathedral in 1647. From 1665 he was court maestro di cappella at Parma. He composed instrumental music, stage works and vocal pieces; his solo and ensemble sonatas (1639-49) are notable for their thematic unity, chromaticism and advanced violin technique.*

Sonatas

Sonatas – Op 4 No 2; Op 5 Nos 3, 4, 9 and 12; Op 7 Nos 1, 3 and 11; Op 9 No 1. Arias, Op 4 – Nos 2, 3 and 9. Sonata over Toccata No 5. Correntes – Nos 4, 9 and 20
Romanesca (Andrew Manze *vn* Nigel North *archlte/baroque gtr/theorbo* John Toll *hpd/org*)
Harmonia Mundi HMU90 7196 (65 minutes: DDD) Ⓕ
Recorded 1996

This companion recital to Romanesca's disc of Biagio Marini's violin music features violin sonatas, instrumental arias and *correntes* by Marini's contemporary Marco Uccellini. Uccellini, along with Marini, Fontana, Turini and several others, developed an idiomatic, virtuosic approach to violin writing which aspires to emulate the expressive range of the human voice. With their imaginative exploration of the violin's technical potential and in the pioneering spirit of the time, these composers made significant and lasting contributions both to technique and form. Thus in Uccellini's music we are made aware of a distinctively exploratory, improvisatory idiom in which there is a highly developed sense of fantasy.

It is one of Andrew Manze's many strengths that he unfailingly responds to the technical and interpretative challenges of this repertoire with curiosity, stylistic propriety and playful imagination. Expressive delicacy, engaging inflexions and a discerning love of detail are all of the greatest assistance in bringing these pieces to life. In each department Romanesca succeeds admirably, enlivening Uccellini's extravagant gestures with demonstrative panache and rhythmic vigour, the more introspective ones with affectionate warmth. The gamut of Uccellini's expressive range, and Romanesca's realisation of it, are vividly displayed in the fine Sonata No 1 from the composer's Op 7 (1660). The instrumental sonorities are rewarding, and this aspect of the performance has been very well captured by the sympathetic recorded sound.

Edgard Varèse French/American 1883-1965

GROVE *Varèse studied with d'Indy at the Schola Cantorum (1903-5) and Widor at the Paris Conservatoire (1905-7), then moved to Berlin, where he met Strauss and Busoni. In 1913 he returned to Paris, but in 1915 he emigrated to New York; nearly all his compositions disappeared at this stage, with the exception of a single published song and an orchestral score, Bourgogne (1908), which he took with him but destroyed towards the end of his life. His creative output therefore effectively begins with Amériques for large orchestra (1921), which, for all its echoes of Debussy and of Stravinsky's early ballets, sets out to discover new worlds of sound: fiercely dissonant chords, rhythmically complex polyphonies for percussion and/or wind, forms in continuous evolution with no large-scale recurrence.*

In 1921 he and Carlos Salzedo founded the International Composers Guild, who gave the first performances of several of his works for small ensemble, these prominently featuring wind and percussion, and presenting the innovations of Amériques in pure, compact form: Hyperprism (1923), Octandre (1923) and Intégrales (1925). Arcana (1927), which returns to the large orchestra and extended form with perfected technique, brought this most productive period to an end.

There followed a long stay in Paris (1928-33), during which he wrote Ionisation for percussion orchestra (1931), the first European work to dispense almost entirely with pitched sounds, which enter only in the coda. He also took an interest in the electronic instruments being developed (he had been calling for electronic means since his arrival in the US [illegible]1), and wrote for two theremins or ondes martenot in Ecuatorial for bass, brass, keyboards and percussion (1934). The flute solo Density 21. 5 (1936) was then his last completed work for nearly two decades.

During this time he taught sporadically and also made plans for Espace, which was to have involved simultaneous radio broadcasts from around the globe; an Etude pour Espace for chorus, pianos and percussion was performed in 1947. Then, with electronic music at last a real possibility owing to the development of the tape recorder, he produced Déserts for wind, percussion and tape (1954) and a Poème électronique (1957-8), devised to be diffused in the Philips pavilion at the Brussels Exposition of 1958. His last years were devoted to projects on themes of night and death, including the unfinished Nocturnal for voices and chamber orchestra (1961).

The Complete Works

Awards 1999

Tuning Up. Amériques. Poème électronique. Arcana. Nocturnal. Un grand sommeil noir (orig version/orch Beaumont). Offrandes. Hyperprism. Octandre. Intégrales. Ecuatorial. Ionisation. Densité 21.5. Déserts. Dance for Burgess

Sarah Leonard, Mireille Delunsch *sops* **Kevin Deas** *bass* **Jacques Zoon** *fl* **François Kerdoncuff** *pf* **Edgard Varèse** *electronics* **Prague Philharmonic Choir; ASKO Ensemble; Royal Concertgebouw Orchestra / Riccardo Chailly**

Decca ② 460 208-2DH2 (151 minutes: DDD). Texts and translations included. Recorded 1992-98 Ⓕ ●●●

This set is announced as 'The Complete Works' of Edgar Varèse. 'Complete' requires clarification. Excluded are the electronic interlude, *La procession du Vergès*, from the 1955 film *Around and About Joan Mirò* (is this still extant?) and the 1947 *Etude* Varèse wrote as preparation for his unrealised *Espace* project – material from which, according to Chou Wen-Chung, found its way into later works.

Successively Varèse's pupil, amanuensis and executor, Professor Chou would appear ideally placed to advise on a project of this nature. Yet it does seem surprising to omit the *Etude*, completed, performed and apparently extant, while including *Tuning Up*, which Varèse never realised as such, and *Dance for Burgess*, which does not exist in a definitive score. That said, the former is an ingenious skit on the orchestral machine, while the latter is an unlikely take on the Broadway dance number: the light they shed on Varèse's preoccupations in the late 1940s makes their inclusion worth while.

Works such as *Octandre* and *Intégrales* require scrupulous attention to balance if they are to sound more than crudely aggressive: Chailly secures this without sacrificing physical impact – witness the explosive *Hyperprism*. He brings out some exquisite harmonic subtleties in *Offrandes*, Sarah Leonard projecting the texts' surreal imagery with admirable poise. The fugitive opening bars of *Ionisation* sound slightly muted in the recorded ambience, though not the cascading tuned percussion towards the close.

The instrumentational problems of *Ecuatorial* are at last vindicated, allowing Varèse's inspired mix of brass and electronic keyboards to register with awesome power. Chailly opts for the solo bass, but a unison chorus would have heightened the dramatic impact still further. *Amériques*, the true intersection of romanticism and modernism, is performed in the original 1921 version, with its even more extravagant orchestral demands and bizarre reminiscences of *The Rite of Spring* and Schoenberg's *Five Orchestral Pieces*, understandably replaced in the revision. *Arcana* was recorded in 1992, Chailly probing beyond the work's vast dynamic contours more deeply than any other rival on disc.

No one but Varèse has drawn such sustained eloquence from an ensemble of wind and percussion, or invested such emotional power in the primitive electronic medium of the early 1950s. *Déserts* juxtaposes them in a score which marks the culmination of his search for new means of expression. The opening now seems a poignant evocation of humanity in the atomic age, the ending is resigned but not bitter. The tape interludes in Chailly's performance have a startling clarity, as does the *Poème électronique*, Varèse's untypical but exhilarating contribution to the 1958 Brussels World Fair. The unfinished *Nocturnal*, with its vocal stylisations and belated return of string timbre, demonstrates a continuing vitality that only time could extinguish. Varèse has had a significant impact on post-war musical culture, with figures as diverse as Stockhausen, Charlie Parker and Frank Zappa acknowledging his influence. Chailly's recordings demonstrate, in unequivocal terms, why this music will continue to provoke and inspire future generations.

Arcana / Amériques

Ionisation[a]. Amériques[a]. Arcana[a]. Density 21.5. Offrandes[b]. Octandre[b]. Intégrales[b]

Rachel Yakar *sop* **Lawrence Beauregard** *fl* [a]**New York Philharmonic Orchestra;** [b]**Ensemble InterContemporain / Pierre Boulez**

Sony Classical SMK45844 (77 minutes: ADD/DDD) Ⓜ
Texts and translations included ●●

Edgard Varèse has become one of those composers whose music is more talked about than performed. His music and ideas have had a considerable influence on the development of 20th-century music, and yet even today his works are rarely heard in the concert hall. Varèse was a pioneer, a quester and above all a liberator. Music for him was a form of 20th-century alchemy – the transmutation of the ordinary into the extraordinary, an alchemical wedding of intellectual thought with intuitive imagination. The remarkable thing about his music is that there is not a single weak work in his output; every piece has something new and unique to offer, and has the unmistakable fingerprint of his highly individual style. It was the writings of the 14th-century cosmologist and alchemist Paracelsus that formed the inspiration behind his orchestral work *Arcana*, a vast canvas of sound built entirely out of one melodic motive. Echoes of Stravinsky and others are discernible, but the totality of *Arcana* is pure Varèse.

The same is true of *Amériques*, a title that Varèse emphasised was not to be taken as 'purely geographical but as symbolic of discoveries – new worlds on earth, in the sky or in the minds of men'. Here romanticism and modernism seem to coexist side by side, where allusions from works such as *La mer* and *The Firebird* seem like memories carried into his brave new world. The remaining items consist of smaller chamber works which display Varèse's most radical, though equally rewarding, styles. Boulez and his players give committed, virtuosic performances of these challenging and intriguing works.

Additional recommendation

Amériques. Arcana. Ionisation. Déserts – Episodes I-IV

Chicago Symphony Orchestra / Boulez

DG 471 137-2GH (68 minutes: DDD) Ⓕ

Boulez's new Chicago remakes are not all gain; that said, the *Amériques* shows the conductor at his interpretative best and the non-electronic *Déserts* is also very fine.

Ralph Vaughan Williams

British 1872-1958

Vaughan Williams studied with Parry, Wood and Stanford at the Royal College of Music and Cambridge, then had further lessons with Bruch in Berlin (1897) and Ravel in Paris (1908). It was only after this that he began to write with sureness in larger forms, even though some songs had had success in the early years of the century. That success, and the ensuing maturity, depended very much on his work with folksong, which he had begun to collect in 1903; this opened the way to the lyrical freshness of the Housman cycle On Wenlock Edge and to the modally inflected tonality of the symphonic cycle that began with A Sea Symphony. But he learnt the same lessons in studying earlier English music in his task as editor of the English Hymnal (1906) – work which bore fruit in his Fantasia on a Theme by Tallis for strings, whose majestic unrelated consonances provided a new sound and a new way into large-scale form. The sound, with its sense of natural objects seen in a transfigured light, placed Vaughan Williams in a powerfully English visionary tradition, and made very plausible his association of his music with Blake (in the ballet Job) and Bunyan (in the opera The Pilgrim's Progress). Meanwhile the new command of form made possible a first symphony, A London Symphony), where characterful detail is worked into the scheme. A first opera, Hugh the Drover, made direct use of folksongs, which Vaughan Williams normally did not do in orchestral works.

His study of folksong, however, certainly facilitated the pastoral tone of The Lark Ascending, for violin and orchestra, and then of the Pastoral Symphony. At the beginning of the 1920s there followed a group of religious works continuing the visionary manner: the unaccompanied Mass in G minor, the Revelation oratorio Sancta civitas and the 'pastoral episode' The Shepherds of the Delectable Mountains, later incorporated in The Pilgrim's Progress. But if the glowing serenity of pastoral and vision were to remain central during the decades of work on that magnum opus, works of the later 1920s show a widening of scope, towards the comedy of the operas Sir John in Love (after The Merry Wives of Windsor) and The Poisoned Kiss, and towards the angularity of Satan's music in Job and of the Fourth Symphony. The quite different Fifth Symphony has more connection with The Pilgrim's Progress, and was the central work of a period that also included the cantata Dona nobis pacem, the opulent Serenade to Music for 16 singers and orchestra, and the A minor string quartet, the finest of Vaughan Williams's rather few chamber works.

A final period opened with the desolate, pessimistic Sixth Symphony, after which Vaughan Williams found a focus in the natural world for such bleakness when he was asked to write the music for the film Scott of the Antarctic : out of that world came his Seventh Symphony, the Sinfonia antartica, whose pitched percussion colouring he used more ebulliently in the Eighth Symphony, the Ninth returning to the contemplative world of The Pilgrim's Progress.

Complete Symphonies

No 1, 'A Sea Symphony'; **No 2**, 'A London Symphony'; **No 3**, 'A Pastoral Symphony'; **No 4** in F minor; **No 5** in D; **No 6** in E minor; **No 7**, 'Sinfonia antartica'; **No 8** in D minor; **No 9** in E minor

Symphonies – No 1[a]; No 2; No 3[b]; Nos 4-6; No 7[c]; Nos 8-9. Flos campi. Serenade to Music

[a]Joan Rodgers, [b]Alison Barlow, [c]Alison Hargan *sops* **William Shimell** *bar* **Christopher Balmer** *va* **Liverpool Philharmonic Choir; Royal Liverpool Philharmonic Orchestra / Vernon Handley**

EMI Eminence ⑥ CDBOX-VW1 (396 minutes: DDD) Ⓜ

No 2; Nos 2 and 8

Handley's performances can withstand comparison with the very best. The first to appear was the Fifth Symphony. Rightly acclaimed on its initial release, this remains a gloriously rapt, yet formidably lucid realisation. The coupling, a supremely dedicated rendering of the exquisite *Flos campi*, is just as distinguished. Handley's masterly pacing is a compelling feature of both the *Sea Symphony* and *Sinfonia antartica*, but, whilst it is difficult to fault either performance on artistic grounds, here more than elsewhere one notes the limitations of the slightly cramped acoustic of Liverpool's Philharmonic Hall.

There are no technical shortcomings about the intense Third or the Fourth, with its unbridled ferocity and orchestral virtuosity. The Second and Eighth bring outstandingly perceptive, marvellously communicative music-making, with both scores emerging as fresh as the day they were conceived. Handley's interpretation of the Sixth Symphony is a model of cogency and long-term control. Don't be deceived by the element of slight reserve in the opening movement. It soon transpires that Handley already has his eyes firmly set on the work's terrifying apex, namely the baleful climax of the succeeding *Moderato*. Handley's *Scherzo* teems with busy detail, its feverish contrapuntal workings laid out before us with maximum clarity and force. So many performances have come to grief in the finale; Handley's is a triumphant exception. In this desolate, inconsolable landscape (with not an *espressivo* marking in sight), Handley achieves a truly awesome hush and concentration.

And what of the Ninth, VW's other 'E minor'? Few interpreters on disc have probed much beneath the surface of this elusive, craggy masterpiece. Handley captures the music's mordant wit, while allowing the listener to revel afresh in the astonishing vitality and startlingly original sonorities of VW's ever-imaginative inspiration. The overriding impression left is one of supreme sensitivity and utter dedication to the cause. In the visionary finale, whose monumental, block-like structure gradually takes shape before our eyes like Stonehenge itself, Handley's conception just has the edge over his rivals in terms of elemental power and effortless inevitability. The recordings are admirably natural.

Additional recommendations

Symphonies Nos 1-8
Coupling: Partita for Double String Orchestra.
Baillie, Ritchie *sops* **Cameron** *bar* **Gielgud** *narr* **London Philharmonic Choir and Orchestra / Boult**
Belart 461 442-2 ⑤ (353 minutes: ADD: 6/97) Ⓢ

Music-making of the highest calibre throughout. The mono engineering is always vivid, often stunningly so – especially in *A Sea Symphony* and *Sinfonia antartica*. If you don't already know these magnificent recordings, don't hesitate for a moment.

Symphonies Nos 1-9
Couplings: Fantasia on a Theme by Thomas Tallis. The Wasps. Serenade to Music. In the Fen Country. Norfolk Rhapsody No 1. The Lark Ascending. English Folk Song Suite. Fantasia on 'Greensleeves'. Concerto for Two Pianos and Orchestra. Job
Armstrong, Burrowes, Price *sops* **Case** *bar* **London Philharmonic Choir and Orchestra; New Philharmonia / Boult; various artists**
EMI ⑧ CZS5 73924-2 (534 minutes: ADD: 1/01) Ⓕ

Enticing value and an ideal supplement to Belart's super-bargain box of Boult's mono VW cycle for Decca.

Symphonies Nos 1-9
Coupling: Norfolk Rhapsody No 1. Fantasia on a Theme by Thomas Tallis. Fantasia on 'Greensleeves'. Five Variants of 'Dives and Lazarus'.
Hohenfeld, Valente *sop* **Allen** *bar* **Philharmonia Choir and Orchestra / Slatkin**
RCA Red Seal ⑥ 09026 61460-2 (minutes: DDD) Ⓜ

Slatkin draws playing of incomparable refinement from a superbly co-ordinated Philharmonia throughout.

Symphony No 1

Dame Felicity Lott *sop* **Jonathan Summers** *bar* **Cantilena; London Philharmonic Choir and Orchestra / Bernard Haitink**
EMI CDC7 49911-2 (71 minutes: DDD) Ⓕ
Text included. Recorded 1989 ○○

A firm hand on the tiller is needed to steer a safe course through this, Vaughan Williams's first and most formally diffuse symphony, completed in 1909. Haitink is clearly an ideal choice of helmsman, and he is helped by a remarkably lucid recording that resolves details that would rarely be revealed in live performance. What might be more unexpected here is the obvious affinity he shows for this music: while never transgressing the bounds of Vaughan Williams's characteristically English idiom, he manages to place the work in the European mainstream, revealing a whole range of resonances, from Bruckner and Mahler to the Impressionists. Not all the glory should go to the conductor, of course. Both soloists are particularly fine, the vulnerability behind the spine-tingling power of Felicity Lott's voice providing excellent contrast to the staunch solidity of Jonathan Summers. The LPO Chorus, aided by Cantilena, is on top form and the whole enterprise is underpinned by the LPO's total commitment and expertise.

Symphony No 1 🄷 $
Dame Isobel Baillie *sop* **John Cameron** *bar* **London Philharmonic Choir and Orchestra / Sir Adrian Boult**
Belart mono 450 144-2 (68 minutes: ADD) Ⓢ
Recorded 1952 ○○○

'Classic recording of Symphony No 1' proclaims the sleeve of this super-budget Belart CD. That assessment is absolutely spot-on. Fine as is Boult's own 1968 stereo remake (available on an EMI reissue), this Decca performance surpasses it for sheer fervour and concentration: no one before or since has held the finale together with quite such effortless mastery. Vaughan Williams himself lent his supervision to the sessions, and the mono sound remains remarkably full-blooded, if inevitably rather lacking in range. No Vaughan Williams enthusiast can afford to overlook the present reissue. The singular lack of texts is, however, an irritating oversight.

Symphony No 2

Vaughan Williams Symphony No 2, 'A London Symphony' (original version, 1913)
Butterworth The Banks of Green Willow
London Symphony Orchestra / Richard Hickox
Chandos CHAN9902 (68 minutes: DDD) Ⓕ
Recorded 2001 ○○

It was during the summer of 1911 that George Butterworth (a victim of The Great War, and whose enchanting 1913 idyll, *The Banks of Green Willow*, comprises the achingly poignant curtain-raiser here) first suggested to Vaughan Williams that he should write a purely orchestral symphony. VW dug out some sketches he had made for a symphonic poem about London, while at the same time deriving fruitful inspiration from HG Wells's 1908 novel, *Tono-Bungay* (and its visionary final chapter in particular). Geoffrey Toye gave the successful Queen's Hall première in March 1914, and VW subsequently dedicated the score to Butterworth's memory. Over the next two decades or so, the work underwent three revisions (including much judicious pruning) and was published twice (in 1920 and 1936). In his compelling 1941 recording with the Cincinnati SO, Eugene Goossens employed the 1920 version, which adds about three minutes of music to that definitive 1936 'revised edition'. Now Richard Hickox at long last gives us the chance to hear VW's original, hour-long canvas – and riveting listening it makes too!

Whereas the opening movement is as we know it today, the ensuing, expanded *Lento* acquires an intriguingly mournful, even world-weary demeanour. Unnervingly, the ecstatic full flowering of that glorious E major *Largamente* idea, first heard at fig F in the final revision, never materialises, and the skies glower menacingly thereafter. Towards the end of the *Scherzo* (at 5'44") comes a haunting episode that Arnold Bax was particularly sad to see cut ('a mysterious passage of strange and fascinating cacophony' was how he described it in his autobiography, *Farewell, My Youth* [Scholar Press; 1992]). The finale, too, contains a wealth of additional material, most strikingly a liturgical theme of wondrous lyrical beauty (try from 6'42") and, in the epilogue, a gripping paragraph (beginning at 15'47") which looks back to the work's introduction as well as forward to the first movement of *A Pastoral Symphony*. Sprawling it may be, but VW's epic conception evinces a prodigal inventiveness, poetry, mystery and vitality that do not pall with repeated hearings.

Hickox and the LSO respond with an unquenchable spirit, generous flexibility and tender affection that suit VW's ambitious inspiration to a T, and Chandos's sound is big and bold to match. An essential purchase for anyone remotely interested in British music.

Symphony No 3

Symphonies Nos 3 and 4
Amanda Roocroft *sop* **London Philharmonic Orchestra / Bernard Haitink**
EMI CDC5 56564-2 (72 minutes: DDD) Ⓕ
Recorded 1996 ●

These are thought-provoking interpretations of great dedication and intelligence. If Haitink's deeply felt conception of *A Pastoral Symphony* is the most daringly broad we've yet had on disc, its concentration and abundant character grip from first measure to last. Aided by orchestral playing of the highest quality, the opening movement unfolds with a luminous serenity, its climaxes unerringly 'placed', yet Haitink is also acutely aware of the ominous stirrings just beneath the surface. Most distinctive of all is the *Moderato pesante* third movement which, as Haitink views it, is a monumentally sombre, even intimidating affair. This is an interpretation of compelling individuality and tragic intensity which all Vaughan Williams aficionados should investigate forthwith.

The same holds true for the Fourth. Again, Haitink presides over a performance of immense integrity and long-term rigour. Speeds here are less controversial. By not driving the first movement too hard, Haitink allows us to savour the full expressive eloquence of the strings' *appassionato sostenuto* secondary idea. What's more, the *Scherzo* possesses fine rhythmic point, and the transition into the finale generates a tremendous expectancy. In this last movement Haitink keeps a firm hand on the tiller and steadfastly refuses to whip up any artificial excitement, but its rugged symphonic strength must surely command enormous respect.

Symphony No 4

Symphonies Nos 4[a] and 5[b] H
[a]**BBC Symphony Orchestra / Ralph Vaughan Williams;** [b]**Hallé Orchestra / Sir John Barbirolli**
Dutton Laboratories mono CDAX8011 Ⓜ
(66 minutes: ADD)
Recorded [a]1937 and [b]1944 ●●●

No performance on record of Vaughan Williams's Fourth Symphony has ever quite matched this very first one, recorded under the composer's baton in October 1937. As Michael Kennedy says in his highly illuminating note for the Dutton Laboratories reissue, it is 'taken at a daredevil pace', and more importantly has a bite and energy beyond any rival. If early listeners to this violent work were shocked by the composer's new boldness, here his conducting demonstrates the passionate emotion behind the piece. The remastered sound is so vivid and immediate, so full of presence, that in places one almost has the illusion of stereo before its time.

Sir John Barbirolli's première recording of the Fifth Symphony, made in February 1944 eight months after the first performance, is hardly less remarkable. This, too, has never been matched since for the stirring passion of the great climaxes in the first and third movements, with Barbirolli in each carefully grading the intensity between exposition and recapitulation. It is also a revelation to find him taking the triple-time of the Passacaglia finale much faster than latter-day rivals, relating it more closely than usual to the great example of the finale of Brahms's Fourth Symphony, making it no pastoral amble but a searing argument. Here again hiss has been virtually eliminated, but that has left the high violins sounding rather papery. Even so, there's no lack of weight in the big climaxes, with brass and wind atmospherically caught. An outstanding issue for all lovers of this composer's music, not just those who specialise in historic recordings.

Additional recommendations

Symphony No 4

Couplings: The Wasps Overture. Fantasia on a Theme by Thomas Tallis. Oboe Concerto.

Royal Philharmonic Orchestra / Berglund; various artists

EMI British Composers CDM5 66539-2 Ⓜ

(75 minutes: ADD: 1/98)

Berglund's view is thrusting and propulsive in the manner of VW's own legendary 1937 recording with the BBC SO.

Couplings : Violin Concerto, 'Concerto accademico'.

Sillito *vn* **London Symphony Orchestra / Thomson**

Chandos CHAN8633 (50 minutes: DDD: 1/89) Ⓕ

Thomson approaches the work as a magnificent piece of symphonic argument – exuberant, full of rumbustious humour and spiced with exquisite passages of lyricism.

Symphony No 5

Symphony No 5[a]. Valiant-for-truth[b]. The Pilgrim Pavement[c]. Psalm 23 (arr Churchill)[b]. Hymn-tune Prelude on 'Song 13' by Orlando Gibbons (arr Glatz)[a]. Prelude and Fugue in C minor[a]

[c]**Ian Watson** *org* [bc]**Richard Hickox Singers;** [a]**London Symphony Orchestra / Richard Hickox**

Chandos CHAN9666 (71 minutes: DDD). Texts included. Recorded 1997 Ⓕ **OO**

This is an exceptionally powerful yet deeply moving account of the Fifth. Aided by glowing, wide-ranging engineering, Hickox's is an urgently communicative reading. The first and third movements in particular emerge with an effortless architectural splendour and rapt authority, the climaxes built and resolved with mastery. The *Scherzo* is as good a place as any to sample the lustrous refinement of the LSO's response. Hickox ensures that the symphony's concluding bars positively glow with gentle ecstasy: here is a Fifth that can surely hold its own in the most exalted company. Material from *The Pilgrim's Progress* made its way into the Fifth Symphony and two of the five enterprising couplings here provide further links with John Bunyan's timeless allegory: the 1940 motet for mixed voices with organ, *Valiant-for-truth* and John Churchill's 1953 arrangement for soprano and mixed chorus of Psalm 23 (originally sung by The Voice of a Bird in Act 4 of *The Pilgrim's Progress*). The latter receives its finely prepared recorded début on this occasion, as do both *The Pilgrim Pavement* (a 1934 processional for soprano, chorus and organ) and Helen Glatz's string-orchestra arrangement of the solo-piano *Hymn-tune Prelude on 'Song 13'* by Gibbons. Which just leaves the Prelude and Fugue, originally written for organ in 1921, but heard here in a sumptuous orchestration.

Additional recommendations

Symphony No 5

Coupling: **Bax** Tintagel

Philharmonia; London Symphony Orchestra / Barbirolli

EMI British Composers CDM5 65110-2 Ⓜ

(54 minutes: ADD: 3/95)

Barbirolli's much-loved 1962 Philharmonia account of VW's No 5 superbly transferred by John Hadden.

Couplings: The Lark Ascending. Norfolk Rhapsody No 1

Chang *vn* **London Philharmonic Orchestra / Haitink**

EMI CDC5 55487-2 (68 minutes: DDD: 12/95) Ⓕ

Haitink directs a reading of enormous integrity and lucidity with the London Philharmonic on radiant form.

Further listening

Tubin Symphony No 4, 'Sinfonia lirica'

Coupling: Symphony No 9[a]. Toccata[a]

Bergen Symphony Orchestra; [a]**Gothenburg Symphony Orchestra / Jarvi**

BIS CD227 (64 minutes) Ⓕ

If you wish to explore the 20th-century symphony beyond the standard repertoire don't miss Estonian composer Eduard Tubin's music. The atmosphere of his Fourth Symphony (1944) is predominantly pastoral, a mixture of the Slavonic and the Nordic.

Symphony No 6

Symphony No 6 in E minor[a]. The Lark Ascending[b]. A Song of Thanksgiving[c]

[c]**Betty Dolemore** *sop* [c]**Robert Speaight** *narr* [c]**Harry Grab** *org* [b]**Jean Pougnet** *vn* [c]**Luton Choral Society;** [a]**London Symphony Orchestra,** [bc]**London Philharmonic Orchestra / Sir Adrian Boult**

Dutton Laboratories mono CDBP9703 Ⓑ

(69 minutes: ADD). Recorded 1949-52 **OO**

Although it was Boult who premièred VW's awesome Sixth Symphony, his white-hot February 1949 account with the LSO was not in fact the work's début recording – that singular honour falling to Stokowski and the New York Philharmonic (who pipped their British counterparts to the post by just two days). The return to the catalogue of Boult's legendary version – last available on an identically programmed Great Recordings of the Century anthology (EMI – nla) – is a cause for celebration, especially in such a vivid transfer (if fractionally hollow in the bass) and so modestly priced to boot. Like Stokowski's scarcely less thrilling realisation, the performance offers us the opportunity to hear VW's original *Scherzo*. This has been allotted a separate track at the end of the symphony, its place taken by the same team's February 1950 recording of the composer's revision (not an ideal arrangement, perhaps). Whether the performance as a whole entirely displaces Sir Adrian's marvellous 1953 Decca version with the LPO (available in a disappointingly rough transfer on Belart) is open to debate, but both interpretations comprehensively outflank Sir Adrian's New Philharmonia stereo remake for EMI in terms of fiery concentration and sheer guts.

Written in response to a commission from the BBC in 1943 for a work to celebrate the defeat of Hitler's Germany, *A Song of Thanksgiving* was first broadcast shortly after VE Day. This commercial recording followed in December 1951. The work (which is scored for soprano, narrator, chorus and orchestra) has a smattering of decent invention (including, from around 4'30", fleeting echoes of the Sixth's second movement), but overall it's hardly representative of VW at his most inspired.

Last, and certainly not least, comes a wholly cherishable account (from October 1952) of *The Lark Ascending*, with Jean Pougnet a wonderfully silky toned, humane soloist. Boult's accompaniment, too, is a model of selfless dedication and intuitive rapture. For some, it remains, quite simply, the most tenderly unaffected and profoundly moving *Lark* on disc, though the string timbre on that earlier EMI restoration is much preferable to this over-processed newcomer. None the less, a most valuable VW reissue.

Symphony No 6. Fantasia on a Theme by Thomas Tallis. The Lark Ascending
Tasmin Little *vn* **BBC Symphony Orchestra / Sir Andrew Davis**
Teldec British Line 9031-73127-2 (62 minutes: DDD) Ⓕ
Recorded 1990 ○

Sir Andrew Davis clearly thought long and hard before committing this enigmatic and tragic symphony to disc, and the result is one of the most spontaneous and electrifying accounts of the Sixth Symphony available. The urgency and vigour of the first and third movements is astonishing, leaving one with the impression that the work might have been recorded in one take. His treatment of the second subject's reprise in the closing pages of the first movement is more underplayed and remote than the beautifully sheened approach of some recordings, but is arguably more nostalgic for being so. The feverish, nightmare world of the *Scherzo* is a real tour de force in the hands of an inspired BBC Symphony Orchestra, and the desolate wasteland of the eerie final movement has rarely achieved such quiescence and nadir as here. Davis's searchingly intense *Tallis Fantasia* is finely poised with a beautifully spacious acoustic. The disc concludes on a quietly elevated note with Tasmin Little's serene and gently introspective reading of *The Lark Ascending*. The recording is excellent.

Symphony No 6. In the Fen Country. On Wenlock Edge
Ian Bostridge *ten* **London Philharmonic Orchestra / Bernard Haitink**
EMI CDC5 56762-2 (69 minutes: DDD). Text and translation included. Recorded 1998 Ⓕ ○○

This is a noble, rewarding and profoundly musical account of the Sixth. Drawing some magnificently clean and sonorous playing from the LPO (and aided by a ripe and wide-ranging recording), Haitink steers a characteristically purposeful course through the first movement, alighting on precisely the right tempo for the second subject's final ecstatic metamorphosis. Right from the outset, one notes how the supreme articulation of the orchestral playing helps to make so much sense of the composer's trenchant counterpoint. However, it's in the succeeding *Moderato* that Haitink really pulls ahead of most of his rivals, his eloquent conception displaying a riveting long-term rigour. No complaints, either, about the implacable

mystery and tingling concentration of Haitink's epilogue. Altogether a distinguished Sixth, and one which deserves to rank alongside the finest currently available. It's also difficult to imagine a more refined, sympathetic rendering of *In the Fen Country* than Haitink's. It unfolds with melting beauty and tender grace. A cherishable display indeed, and the delights continue with *On Wenlock Edge*. Ian Bostridge sings with moving ardour and intelligence (his 'Is my team ploughing?' is an especially compulsive interpretation), whilst Haitink's support is a model of scrupulous sensitivity and delicate nuance. All in all, a release to savour.

Symphony No 7

Sheila Armstrong *sop* **London Philharmonic Choir and Orchestra / Bernard Haitink**
EMI CDC7 47516-2 (42 minutes: DDD) Ⓕ
Recorded 1984 ○○

Scored for wordless soprano solo and chorus plus a large orchestra, this Seventh Symphony was based on the composer's music for the film *Scott of the Antarctic*. It comprises five movements; the Prelude, which conveys mankind's struggle in overcoming hostile natural forces; a *Scherzo*, which depicts the whales and penguins in their natural habitat; 'Landscape', which portrays vast frozen wastes; Intermezzo, a reflection of the actions and thoughts of two members of the party; and 'Epilogue', describing the final tragic assault on the South Pole. Bernard Haitink's conducting is highly imaginative, very concentrated and very committed, and the LPO responds to him with some wonderfully atmospheric playing, full of personality and colour. Armstrong's eerie disembodied soprano voice and the remote chorus heighten the atmosphere, so that the score emerges as a powerful, coherent essay in symphonic form. The recording is magnificently sonorous and spacious.

Additional recommendations
Symphony No 7
Couplings: Oboe Concerto. Tuba Concerto. The Wasps Overture. Fantasia on 'Greensleeves'. Five Variants of 'Dives and Lazarus'. Elgar Introduction and Allegro. Serenade. *Cockaigne*.
Ritchie *sop* **Hallé Choir and Orchestra / Barbirolli** various artists
EMI British Composers ② CMS5 66543-2 Ⓜ
(138 minutes: ADD: 11/98)
Sir John Barbirolli's première recording has an imposing grandeur and a marvellous humanity. Equally sympathetic performances of VW's concertos for oboe and tuba.

Symphony No 9

Symphonies Nos 8 and 9
London Philharmonic Orchestra / Bernard Haitink
EMI CDC5 57086-2 (67 minutes: DDD) Ⓕ
Recorded 2000 ○○○

A friendly word of warning to VW fans everywhere: Haitink will make you think again. No 'little' Eighth, this, rather an unapologetically big-scale conception, full of doughty integrity and always seeking out the intuitive logic that binds VW's symphonic thinking. If the *Scherzo alla marcia* falls short in terms of twinkling good humour here, the preceding, inimitably subtitled *Variazioni senza tema* unfolds with a revelatory sweep and purposefulness.

Likewise, the finale by and large forfeits celebratory pomp and glitter in favour of a sinewy, intriguingly defiant strength entirely consistent with Haitink's patient view as a whole. Most distinctive of all is the sublime *Cavatina* for strings: very measured, raptly concentrated and imbued with a lofty serenity to relate it all the more movingly to the great *Romanza* of VW's Fifth Symphony. Some may find the emotional temperature set just a few notches too low for comfort, but, as a thought-provoking alternative to Barbirolli (Pye – nla), Handley and Slatkin, Haitink's Eighth certainly earns its spurs.

Turning to the craggy, questing Ninth, both Slatkin and Handley have given of their considerable best in this fascinating, wonderfully vital utterance. On balance, Haitink's resplendent new version can be rated as the finest yet, a thrillingly convinced and convincing demonstration of the timeless universality of VW's masterpiece. Witness the clear-sighted dedication and stoic grandeur of the opening *Moderato maestoso*. Not only is Haitink meticulously faithful to the letter and spirit of the score, VW's argument evolves with a nobility and wholeness that grip from first measure to last. Those *ff tenuto* strings at Fig 2 (1'02") in the second movement have just the right 'mud on boots' feel to them, and, like Handley before him, Haitink doesn't overplay his hand in the central lyrical episode (its chaste beauty all the more affecting as a consequence). The hobgoblins of the *Scherzo* cackle with malevolent glee, yet Haitink proves just as tenderly responsive to the strings' ravishing *cantabile e sostenuto* dialogue between Figs 30 and 34 (from 4'06" to 4'42").

It's in the awesome final movement, though, where Haitink really surpasses himself: VW's monolithic vision is surveyed with an organic power and cumulative impact that leaves one dumb struck with admiration and gratitude.

Throughout, the LPO play marvellously for their former chief, and EMI's Abbey Road sound is excellent, truthful in timbre and expertly balanced (listen out for some handsomely extended bass sonorities). A distinguished achievement and absolutely not to be missed.

Symphony No 9. Piano Concerto in C
Howard Shelley *pf* **London Symphony Orchestra / Bryden Thomson**
Chandos CHAN8941 (57 minutes: DDD) Ⓕ
Recorded 1990

Alongside the scorching account of the apocalyptic Fourth Symphony, this clear-headed, perceptive traversal of the enigmatic Ninth has fair claims to be regarded as the best thing in Bryden Thomson's underrated VW cycle for Chandos. Thomson's urgent conception of the opening *Moderato maestoso* in particular has a sweep and momentum one might not have previously associated with this movement, yet the gain in terms of sheer concentration and symphonic stature is irrefutable. Granted, some may find the outer sections of the succeeding *Andante sostenuto* just a little too lacking in evocative magic, but there's no gainsaying the effectiveness of gallumphing woodwind in the oafish *Scherzo*; certainly, the LSO's saxophone trio seems to be enjoying its day out hugely. In the finale, too, Thomson's approach is more boldly assertive than usual – not the way one would always want to hear this music, perhaps, but a thoroughly valid and convincing performance all the same. The coupling, Howard Shelley's distinguished remake of the same composer's craggily elusive Piano Concerto, is both imaginative and desirable. All in all, a highly recommendable disc: the LSO is in fine fettle, whilst the glowing sound is close to ideal.

Additional recommendations

Piano Concerto

Coupling: **Foulds** Dynamic Triptych
Shelley *pf* **Royal Philharmonic Orchestra / Handley**
Lyrita SRCD211 (57 minutes: DDD: 3/93) Ⓕ

A vital reading of the one-piano version by Howard Shelley, aided by one of the most searching of Vaughan Williams conductors.

Coupling: Finzi Eclogue. **Delius** Piano Concerto
Lane *pf* **Royal Liverpool Philharmonic Orchestra / Handley**
EMI Eminence CD-EMX2239 (61 minutes: DDD: 11/95) Ⓜ

Piers Lane brings an exhilarating dash and bravura to Vaughan Williams's craggy concerto, aided by Vernon Handley's characteristically lucid, watchful direction.

String Quartets

String Quartets – No 1 in G minor; No 2 in A minor. Phantasy Quintet[a]
[a]**Garfield Jackson** *va* **Maggini Quartet**
Naxos 8 555300 (66 minutes: DDD) Ⓢ
Recorded 2000

Why is Vaughan Williams's Second Quartet not part of the international chamber repertory? Played as eloquently as this it seems unarguably a masterpiece, and a masterpiece specifically of its time: 1942/43. Its first movement and deeply fraught *Scherzo* are as troubled as Shostakovich (whose music at moments, like a sudden stab of violence in that first *allegro*, it passingly resembles), while the misleadingly titled slow 'Romance' is haunted and haunting. It is tranquil but not at peace. It achieves an impassioned nobility and approaches serenity at the end, but something ghostly (it walks again in the Epilogue to the Sixth Symphony) refuses to be exorcised until the beautiful calm finale.

What these players do with the two much earlier pieces is no less remarkable. In them Vaughan Williams's style is audibly emerging from the influences (notably Ravel, briefly his teacher) that helped form it. In the First Quartet's opening movement an arching, lyrical melody that sounds like Vaughan Williams speaking with a French accent (and is it a French lark that ascends a little later?) has shed the accent by its return; something similar happens in the finale. But it was not an immature composer (he was 36, after all) who in the slow movement recognised a kinship with Fauré. And the *Phantasy Quintet* is audibly by the composer of the *Tallis* Fantasia, grateful to Ravel for giving him access to a deft rhythmic flexibility, but exploring his own unmistakable territory in the serenity tinged with poignancy of the slow movement. The Maggini Quartet and Garfield Jackson clearly love this music deeply; they play it with great beauty of tone and variety of colour and with passionate expressiveness. The ample recording allows both grand gestures and quiet intimacy. A coupling to confirm that Vaughan Williams was a great composer.

Dona nobis pacem

Dona nobis pacem[a]. Sancta civitas[b]
[a]**Yvonne Kenny** *sop* [b]**Philip Langridge** *ten* **Bryn Terfel** *bass-bar* [b]**St Paul's Cathedral Choir; London Symphony Chorus and Orchestra / Richard Hickox**
EMI British Composers CDC7 54788-2
(63 minutes: DDD). Texts included Ⓕ
Recorded 1992 **OO**

This is a generous and inspiring coupling of two of Vaughan Williams's most important choral utterances. Hickox coaxes magnificent sounds from the LSO throughout: in *Dona nobis pacem*, for example, the sense of orchestral spectacle during 'Beat! Beat! drums!' is riveting in its physical impact. The London Symphony Chorus combines full-throated discipline and sensitivity to nuance, and Hickox's trio of soloists is excellent, with Terfel outstandingly eloquent. *Sancta civitas* is a work whose multi-layered scoring places great demands on both conductor and production team alike: suffice it to report, it is difficult to see Hickox's inspirational account of this still-underrated score being surpassed for years to come. EMI's clean, wide-ranging sound is admirable.

Additional recommendations

Dona nobis pacem
Coupling: Five Mystical Songs
Wiens *sop* **Rayner Cook** *bar* **London Philharmonic Choir and Orchestra / Thomson**
Chandos CHAN8590 (57 minutes: DDD: 3/89) Ⓕ
A strong, convincing and well-paced interpretation. Brian Rayner Cook could scarcely be bettered.

Couplings: Four Hymns. Toward the Unknown Region. O clap your hands. Lord, thou hast been our Refuge
Howarth *sop* **Ainsley** *ten* **Allen** *bar* **Corydon Singers and Orchestra / Best**
Hyperion CDA66655 (76 minutes: DDD: 5/94) Ⓕ
An enticing VW collection enhanced by the late Christopher Palmer's typically illuminating booklet-notes.

Further listening

Magnificat
Coupling: Song of Thanksgiving, Choral Hymns, Shepherds of the Delectable Mountains, Old 100th
Dawson *sop* **Wyn-Rogers** *contr* **Ainsley** *ten* **Terfel** *bar* **Corydon Singers, CLS / Best**
Hyperion CDA66655 (73 minutes: DDD: 8/92) Ⓕ
The only version available of the sensuous *Magnificat*.

Mass in G minor

Vaughan Williams Mass in G minor. Te Deum in G
Howells Requiem. Take him, earth, for cherishing
Mary Seers *sop* **Michael Chance** *counterten* **Philip Salmon** *ten* **Jonathan Best** *bass* **Corydon Singers / Matthew Best** with **Thomas Trotter** *org*
Hyperion CDA66076 (60 minutes: ADD) Ⓕ
Texts included **OO**

Vaughan Williams's unaccompanied Mass in G minor manages to combine the common manner of Elizabethan liturgical music with those elements of his own folk-music heritage that make his music so distinctive, and in so doing arrives at something individual and new. The work falls into five movements and its mood is one of heartfelt, if restrained, rejoicing. Howells's Requiem dates from 1936, a year after the death of his only son. The work was not released in his lifetime but was reconstructed and published in 1980 from his manuscripts. It is a most hauntingly beautiful work of an intensely personal nature. *Take him, earth, for cherishing* was composed to commemorate the assassination of J F Kennedy. The text is an English translation of Prudentius's 4th-century poem, *Hymnus circa Exsequias Defuncti*. Again it shows the great strength of Howells's choral writing, with a clear outline and affecting yet unimposing harmonic twists. The Corydon Singers give marvellous performances and the sound is very fine.

A Cotswold Romance

A Cotswold Romance. Death of Tintagiles
Rosa Mannion *sop* **Thomas Randle** *ten* **Matthew Brook** *bar* **London Philharmonic Choir; London Symphony Orchestra / Richard Hickox**
Chandos CHAN9646 (54 minutes: DDD) Ⓕ
Text included. Recorded 1997

A Cotswold Romance is a gift from Vaughan Williams to those who hold the music of *Hugh the Drover* in deep affection but who, under torture, would probably have to admit that the opera itself is less than perfect. *Hugh*, first produced in 1924, enjoyed sufficient immediate success for a set of records to be produced with the original cast. It then had to wait till 1979 for a complete recording on LP (reissued on EMI), and till 1994 for a new one on CD. The adaptation as a dramatic cantata came out in 1951, reducing the two-act opera to 10 numbers and rescoring some of the music to allow a (still) larger part for the chorus. The addition of wordless chorus is delightful, not least when the chorus sings the first part of Hugh's song of the road and re-enters with delicious harmonies at 'All the scented night'. Thomas Randle, who has the voice of a man of the road and a lover, is admirably cast. Rosa Mannion, with a slight hint of turning tremulous under pressure, is otherwise an ideal Mary, and the chorus is excellent. Hickox conducts with brio and with due feeling for the romance.

Death of Tintagiles (14'46" to the *Cotswold Romance*'s 39'30") comprises incidental music written for a play by Maeterlinck, performed without much success in 1913. In his interesting notes, Stephen Connock associates it with *Riders to the Sea* and the *Sinfonia antartica*; and it is true that there are sternly impressive moments, of menace and darkness. It hardly seems viable as an orchestral suite, but is never the less good to have on this disc.

On Wenlock Edge

Merciless Beauty. Two English Folksongs. Ten Blake Songs. Along the Field. On Wenlock Edge
John Mark Ainsley *ten* **The Nash Ensemble** (Gareth Hulse *ob* Leo Phillips, Elizabeth Wexler *vns* Roger Chase *va* Paul Watkins *vc* Ian Brown *pf*)
Hyperion CDA67168 (69 minutes: DDD) Ⓕ
Texts included. Recorded 1999 ●

The programme here has an identity of its own and as such is without competitors. Its 'theme' is to collect those of Vaughan Williams's songs which have something other than piano accompaniment. *On Wenlock Edge* (1909) is for voice, piano and string quartet, *Merciless Beauty* (1921) with string trio, *Along the Field* (1927) and *Two English Folksongs* (published 1935 but of earlier date) voice and violin, and the Blake songs (1957) with oboe. Eligible for inclusion might have been *Four Hymns* (1914) with piano and viola, and perhaps *The Willow Whistle* (1939) for voice and pipe. The *Three Vocalises* of 1958, with clarinet, are specifically for soprano, but show the composer's continuing taste for such combinations right into the last year of his life.

And there *is* a taste, a feel, to them. Whereas a piano accompanies almost in the literal sense of keeping the voice company, supporting it, even suggesting the home comforts of which the instrument has been normally part, the solo violin or oboe isolates it. The absence of chordal comforts disquiets; the instrument has its independent being, and between it and the voice intervenes a sometimes chilling sense of space. This is particularly so in the Blake settings and the Housman of *Along the Field*: these are not comfortable poems, and the strange fusion of interdependence and alienation between voice and instrument is entirely apt. All are memorable and deeply affecting compositions, and the disc makes a valuable contribution simply by associating them.

It also does much more, for the performances come very close to the heart's desire. John Mark Ainsley's tenor is wonderfully true in pitch and adaptability. He sings with the right sense of a civilised personal utterance, refined and restrained, yet capable of full-bodied tone and a ringing *forte* when needed: the cry 'O noisy bells, be dumb' is as emotional as an operatic climax and all the more effective for the exceptional frankness of its release.

It seems that he has rarely done better on record; these are highly demanding pieces, the voice unremittingly exposed, and he brings to them a fine poise, in breathing, phrasing, expression and the even emission of quite beautiful tone. He has also the considerable advantage of exceptional players to work with. Individually admirable, they combine in *On Wenlock Edge* to give an unusually imaginative performance. The attack of the opening phrase and the clarity of detail in what sometimes can sound like an impressionist smudge alert their listeners from the start; and probably never has the haze of summertime on Bredon been as potently evoked. A somewhat austere delight, perhaps, but a great one.

Songs of Travel

Vaughan Williams Songs of Travel
Butterworth Bredon Hill and other songs.
A Shropshire Lad **Finzi** Let us garlands bring, Op 18
Ireland Sea Fever. The Vagabond. The Bells of San Marie
Bryn Terfel *bass-bar* **Malcolm Martineau** *pf*
DG 445 946-2GH (77 minutes: DDD) Ⓕ
Texts included. Recorded 1995 ●●

There is a touch of genius about this man. To those who have known most of these songs since childhood and heard them well performed innumerable times, it will come not quite as a revelation but more as the fulfilment of a deeply felt wish, instinctive rather than consciously formed. As in all the best Lieder singing, everything is specific: 'Fly away, breath' we recite, thinking nothing of it, but with this singer it is visual – we see it in flight, just as in *Sea Fever* we know in the very tiniest of gaps that in that second he has *heard* 'the seagulls crying'. As in all the best singing of songs, whatever the nationality, there is strong, vivid communication: he will sometimes sing so softly that if he had secured anything less than total involvement he would lose us. There is breadth of phrase, variety of tone, alertness of rhythm, all the musical virtues are there; and yet that seems to go only a little way towards accounting for what is special.

In more detail then. *Bredon Hill*: 'a happy noise to hear' is the robust observation of a fulfilled and carefree man, 'and come to church in time' is exultant hubris, 'I hear you' has anger in it, 'I will come' resentful submission. Finzi's 'O mistress mine': 'in delay there lies no plenty' is the free, open-throated call of lovers to make time run (since we can't make it stand still), and 'Youth's a stuff will not endure' is a lightly intimated memento mori, half seriousness, half joke. 'When I was one-and-twenty' (*A Shropshire Lad*): the 'wise man' who pedalled his tuppeny-ha'penny thought-for-the-day is a pompous loud-mouth, 'but oh tis true' has the groan of acknowledgement, and the repeated 'tis true' comes from the private recesses of the soul, which knows it is!

One after another, these songs are brought to a full life. There is a boldness about Terfel's art that could be perilous, but which, as exercised here, is marvellously well guided by musicianship, intelligence and the genuine flash of inspiration. Malcolm Martineau's playing is also a delight: his touch, in its way, is as sure and illuminating as the singer's.

Vaughan Williams On Wenlock Edge[a]. Songs of Travel[a] **Butterworth** Love blows as the wind blows[b] **Elgar** Pleading, Op 48 No 1[b]. Song Cycle, Op 59[b]. Two Songs, Op 60[b]

Robert Tear *ten* **Thomas Allen** *bar* **City of Birmingham Symphony Orchestra / [a]Sir Simon Rattle, [b]Vernon Handley**

EMI British Composers CDM7 64731-2
(69 minutes: DDD/ADD). Texts included Ⓕ
Recorded 1979-83 ●

Neither of Vaughan Williams's song cycles was originally written with orchestral accompaniment. *On Wenlock Edge* was scored for accompaniment of piano and string quartet, while the *Songs of Travel* were written with piano. Both lose a little when sung with orchestra but the gain seems to considerably outweigh any loss, especially when three such superb artists are involved. Tear's singing is notable for some wonderfully long phrases (as also is Allen's in the other cycle) together with the other Tear qualities, of clarity of words and such matters. The CBSO plays especially well for Rattle – all in all, superb performances that do real justice to Vaughan Williams's imagination, his care for words and his orchestration. The Tear/Handley Elgar and Butterworth items are rarities and were all première recordings. Throughout, Tear sings with sensitivity and the CBSO under Handley gives irreproachably alert imaginative support. The recording is vivid and well balanced.

Serenade to Music

Serenade to Music[cd]. The Poisoned Kiss – Overture. Old King Cole[cd]. Five Mystical Songs[ad]. Prelude on an Old Carol Tune. The Running Set. 49th Parallel – Prelude. Sea Songs. The Lark Ascending[c]. Two Hymn-Tune Preludes. Oboe Concerto in A minor[b]. Fantasia on 'Greensleeves'. Preludes on Welsh Hymn-Tunes – No 2, Rhosymedre; No 3, Hyfrydol (orch Foster). Violin Concerto in D minor, 'Concerto accademico'[c]. Five Variants of 'Dives and Lazarus'

[a]Stephen Roberts *bar* **[b]Roger Winfield** *ob* **[c]Bradley Creswick** *vn* **[d]Northern Sinfonia Chorus; Northern Sinfonia / Richard Hickox**

EMI British Composers ② CZS5 73986-2 Ⓜ
(157 minutes: DDD)
Recorded 1983, 1984 and 1987 ●●

This release comprises the contents of nearly three exemplary VW collections from the 1980s (the only casualty being a fine *Flos campi* – a work that Hickox has anyway since re-recorded with violist Philip Dukes and these same Tyneside forces on Chandos). Outstanding items include swaggeringly affectionate performances of the lovely 1929 overture to *The Poisoned Kiss* and that delightful 1923 ballet *Old King Cole* (the latter featuring a splendidly lusty contribution from the Sinfonia Chorus). Hickox also directs a most sensitive account of the glorious *Five Mystical Songs* (though baritone Stephen Roberts's timbre lacks something in bloom). Bradley Creswick surpasses himself in the Violin Concerto and *The Lark Ascending* (irreproachably poised and sensitive realisations, both), and if Roger Winfield isn't quite as agile or quick-witted a protagonist of the Oboe Concerto as some of his rivals, his is a supremely touching presence all the same, and Hickox's typically warm-hearted, pliant accompaniment strikes one as quite masterly. Even old chestnuts like the *Fantasia on 'Greensleeves'* and *Five Variants of 'Dives and Lazarus'* come up as fresh as the day they were created, and there's also an agreeable clutch of relatively unfamiliar offerings to enjoy, not least the stirring prelude to the 1941 film *49th Parallel* (VW's first effort for the big screen) and those two generously sung *Hymn-Tune Preludes* (listen to 'Hyfrydol' for a pungent example of VW's penetrating modality). All in all, cracking value for money.

Serenade to Music. Flos campi. Five mystical songs[a]. Fantasia on Christmas carols[a]

Elizabeth Connell, Linda Kitchen, Anne Dawson, Amanda Roocroft *sops* **Sarah Walker, Jean Rigby, Diana Montague** *mezzos* **Catherine Wyn-Rogers** *contr* **John Mark Ainsley, Martyn Hill, Arthur Davies, Maldwyn Davies** *tens* **[a]Thomas Allen, Alan Opie** *bars* **Gwynne Howell, John Connell** *basses* **Nobuko Imai** *va* **Corydon Singers; English Chamber Orchestra / Matthew Best**

Hyperion CDA66420 (68 minutes: DDD) Ⓕ
Texts included. Recorded 1990 ●

In 1938 Sir Henry Wood celebrated his 50 years as a professional conductor with a concert. Vaughan Williams composed a work for the occasion, the *Serenade to Music*, in which he set words by Shakespeare from Act 5 of *The Merchant of Venice*. Sixteen star vocalists of the age were gathered together for the performance and Vaughan Williams customized the vocal parts to show off the best qualities of the singers. The work turned out to be one of the composer's most sybaritic creations, turning each of its subsequent performances into a special event. Hyperion has gathered stars of our own age for this outstanding issue and Best has perceptively managed to give each their head whilst melding them into a cohesive ensemble. A mellow, spacious recording has allowed the work to emerge on disc with a veracity never achieved before.

The coupled vocal pieces are given to equal effect and the disc is completed by Nobuko Imai's tautly poignant account of *Flos campi*, in which the disturbing tension between solo viola and wordless chorus heighten the work's crypticism.

Additional recommendations

Serenade to Music

Coupling: The Wasps Overture. Symphony No 2. Fantasia on 'Greensleeves'

Sols inc Baillie, Suddaby *sops* **Nash** *ten* **Henderson** *bar* **BBC Symphony Orchestra; Queen's Hall Orchestra / Wood**

Dutton Laboratories CDAX8004 (63 minutes: ADD: 10/93) Ⓜ

This performance with the 16 original soloists possesses a very special beauty and atmosphere.

Couplings: English Folk Song Suite. Fantasia on a theme by Thomas Tallis. Fantasia on 'Greensleeves'. The Lark Ascending. Wasps (excerpts)

Sols inc Burrowes *sop* **Partridge** *ten* **Noble** *bass* **London Philharmonic Orchestra / Boult; various artists**

HMV5 72162-2 Ⓑ

(66 minutes: ADD)

A well-matched group of soloists, with a passionate commitment in the climaxes unmatched since Wood.

Five Tudor Portraits

Five Tudor Portraits. Five Variants of 'Dives and Lazarus'

Jean Rigby *mez* **John Shirley-Quirk** *bar* **London Symphony Chorus and Orchestra / Richard Hickox**

Chandos CHAN9593 (55 minutes: DDD) Ⓕ

Text included. Recorded 1997

First heard at the 1936 Norwich Festival, Vaughan Williams's *Five Tudor Portraits* find the composer at his most dazzlingly inventive, the resourceful and witty writing fitting Skelton's words like a glove. Moreover, an irresistible humanity illuminates the most ambitious of the settings, 'Jane Scroop (Her Lament for Philip Sparrow)', which contains music as compassionate as Vaughan Williams ever conceived. It is a life-enhancing creation and well deserving of this first-rate recording. Aided by disciplined, ever-willing orchestral support, the London Symphony Chorus launches itself in lusty fashion into the ale-soaked narrative of 'The Tunning of Elinor Rumming', though the resonant acoustic rather precludes ideal clarity of diction. Hickox is exuberant in this sparkling tableau, while Jean Rigby's characterful contribution should raise a smile. John Shirley-Quirk's is a touching presence in 'My Pretty Bess', and the mordant, black humour of 'Epitaph of John Jayberd of Diss' is effectively captured. Jane Scroop's lament in the fourth (and surely best) movement finds these fine artists at their most perceptive. How ravishingly Hickox moulds his strings in the hushed passage following 'It was proper and prest!' where the music movingly anticipates the poignancy of the closing section. Listen out, too, for the wealth of exquisitely observed woodwind detail in the enchanting funeral processional. The concluding 'Jolly Rutterkin' goes with a swing, though Shirley-Quirk is a mite unsteady at the top of his range. The coupling is a heart-warming *Dives and Lazarus*, with the LSO strings producing their most lustrous tone.

The Pilgrim's Progress

Gerald Finley *bar* Pilgrim; **Peter Coleman-Wright** *bar* John Bunyan; **Jeremy White** *bass* Evangelist, Envy, Third Shepherd; **Donaldson Bell** *bar* Pontius Pilate; **Gidon Saks** *bass* Apollyon, Lord Hate-Good, Mistrust; **Richard Coxon** *ten* Pliable, Mister By-Ends; **Francis Egerton** *ten* Timorous, Usher; **Roderick Williams** *bar* Obstinate, Watchful, First Shepherd; **Adrian Thompson** *ten* Lord Lechery, Celestial Messenger; **Rebecca Evans** *sop* Madam Wanton, Shining One; **Pamela Helen Stephen** *mez* Madam Bubble, Shining One, Heavenly Being II; **Anne-Marie Owens** *mez* Madam By-Ends, Pickthank; **Christopher Keyte** *bass* Simon Magus; **John Kerr** *bass* Judas Iscariot; **Susan Gritton** *sop* Malice, Bird, Shining One, Heavenly Being I; **Neil Gillespie** *ten* Worldly Glory; **Jonathan Fisher** *bar* Demas; **Mark Padmore** *ten* Interpreter, Superstition, Second Shepherd; **Robert Hayward** *bar* Herald; **Mica Penniman** *sop* Woodcutter's Boy; **Chorus and Orchestra of the Royal Opera House, Covent Garden / Richard Hickox**

Chandos ② CHAN9625 (130 minutes: DDD) Ⓕ

Notes and text included. Recorded 1997

The Royal Northern College of Music mounted a highly successful production in 1992, serving for a new generation to bring the kind of understanding and enjoyment fostered by the famous performances at Cambridge 40 years earlier. It was the recollection of those that made Christopher Bishop (producer of the Boult recording) say that 'perhaps the future of *Pilgrim* lies not in the opera house but with amateurs, and Vaughan Williams would be the last composer to be dismayed at that'. There is nothing amateur*ish* about the RNCM (available on the company's own label), where of course the students are in a sense already professional; but the performance, especially in the Vanity Fair scene and other concerted passages, comes through with the energy and well-rehearsed precision of the best amateur productions.

Otherwise it is a matter of choice between Hickox's excellent version and the classic Boult. Both have more forward recorded sound than the RNCM, and are inevitably stronger in soloists, voice for voice. Voice for voice, Boult does better than Hickox, though with an exception that is crucial. John Noble was a fine Pilgrim on the earlier recording, but Gerald Finley brings not only a voice that is as good and well suited but also a dramatic quality that is more colourful and intense. But Boult's cast is very strong, with several of the short parts, such as the Herald (Terence Sharpe) better sung than as here (Robert Hayward). In the Valley of Humiliation the voice of Apollyon comes as an amplified sound from off-stage, but on record the trick is to catch an overpowering terror, and this they manage better on EMI, partly by virtue of having Robert Lloyd to strike it, and also by the producer's decision to bring it closer. Nor, in the comparison, is there any sense of a confrontation of 'bright young feller' and 'grand old fuddy-duddy'. Boult does not *sound* like an old man, any more than Hickox sounds like a youngster. The Boult recording, finely remastered, is a strong survivor. Hickox has a bigger canvas for the recorded sound, and achieves a clearer texture. The newer version also has Gerald Finley, and is a fine performance anyway.

The Pilgrim's Progress

John Noble *bar* Pilgrim; **Raimund Herincx** *bass* John Bunyan, Lord Hate-Good; **John Carol Case** *bar* Evangelist; **Wynford Evans** *ten* Pliable; **Christopher Keyte** *bass* Obstinate, Judas Escariot, Pontius Pilate; **Geoffrey Shaw** *bass* Mistrust, Demas; **Bernard Dickerson** *ten* Timorous, Usher; **Sheila Armstrong** *sop* Shining One 1; **Marie Hayward Segal** *sop* Shining One 2, Madam Wanton; **Gloria Jennings** *mez* Shining One 3, Madam By-Ends; **Ian Partridge** *ten* Interpreter, Superstition; **John Shirley-Quirk** *bar* Watchful; **Terence Sharpe** *bar* Herald; **Robert Lloyd** *bass* Apollyon; **Norma Burrowes** *sop* Branchbearer, Malice; **Alfreda Hodgson** *contr* Cupbearer, Pickthank; **Joseph Ward** *bar* Lord Lechery; **Richard Angas** *bass* Simon Magus, Envy; **John Elwes** *ten* Worldly Glory; **Delia Wallis** *mez* Madam Bubble; **Wendy Eathorne** *sop* Woodcutter's Boy; **Gerald English** *ten* Mister By-Ends; **London Philharmonic Choir and Orchestra / Sir Adrian Boult**

EMI British Composers ② CMS7 64212-2

(153 mintues: ADD). Notes and texts included Ⓜ

Recorded 1970-71 ⦿

When this glowing performance of one of Vaughan Williams's most raptly beautiful works first appeared in 1972 as a centenary offering to the composer, it was hoped that the record would lead to more stage performances on both sides of the Atlantic. That hope, alas, was not fulfilled. That Vaughan Williams drew from a whole series of Bunyan inspirations over 30 years has made for meatiness of material and little or no inconsistency of style. 'They won't like it,' predicted the composer after the first performance at Covent Garden. 'They don't want an opera with no heroine and no love duets – and I don't care. It's what I meant, and there it is.' Though he described the work as a 'morality', he was aggressively concerned that it should be treated as an opera, not as an oratorio. One can see what he meant. He wanted the work's strength and cohesion brought out, not just its piety, but in truth precious little is lost from not having it staged, and the format of recording might well be counted as ideal, allowing the listener to picture his own staging.

Sir Adrian's portrait, marvellously characterful, stands as one of the very finest of his many records of Vaughan Williams's music, beautifully paced and textured with the fascinating references to the symphonies – not just No 5 which took material from the previously written Act 1 but (at least by implication) Nos 3, 4 and 7 as well, not to mention the *Serenade to Music*. In every way Vaughan Williams's Bunyan inspirations permeated his music, and this opera stands as their centre-point. John Noble, who as a very young singer scored a great success in the 1954 Cambridge production, may not have the richest or most characterful baritone, but his dedication and understanding make for compelling results. Outstanding among the others are such singers as Sheila Armstrong, Ian Partridge, Norma Burrowes and John Shirley-Quirk. The chorus – subject of rather tough treatment from Boult (this set has the bonus of Boult's sharp-tongued rehearsals: to the chorus: 'You talk ... you talk like market-women') sings with fervour, and the sound – using the always helpful London Kingsway Hall – remains first-rate.

Riders to the Sea

Riders to the Sea[a]

Norma Burrowes *sop* Nora; **Dame Margaret Price** *sop* Cathleen; **Helen Watts** *contr* Maurya; **Benjamin Luxon** *bar* Bartley; **Pauline Stevens** *mez* Woman **Ambrosian Singers; Orchestra Nova of London / Meredith Davies**

Epithalamion[b]

Stephen Roberts *bar* **Jonathan Snowden** *fl* **Howard Shelley** *pf* **Bach Choir; London Philharmonic Orchestra / Sir David Willcocks**

Merciless Beauty[b]

Philip Langridge *ten* members of the **Endellion Quartet** (Andrew Watkinson, James Clark *vns* David Waterman vc)

EMI British Composers CDM7 64730-2

(75 minutes: ADD/DDD). Texts included Ⓜ

Recorded [a]1970 and [b]1986 ⦿

Vaughan Williams completed his masterly setting of J M Synge's one-act drama, *Riders to the Sea*, in 1932. Although it has enjoyed the occasional revival, it remains one of the least-known and most under-appreciated of VW's major works. Indeed, with scoring that is both economical and intensely evocative, it can be a gripping experience, especially when presented as sympathetically as here. The cast is uniformly strong, and Meredith Davies inspires everyone to give of their very best. The 1970 sound has come up superbly, creating a rather more vivid impression, in fact, than its modern partners from 1986. These are also both considerable rarities. *Epithalamion* is a large-scale cantata from 1957 based on Edmund Spenser's love-poem of the same name: musically, it draws extensively on material used in VW's 1938 masque, *The Bridal Day*, and its emotional centrepiece, 'The Lover's Song', boasts a viola solo of exquisite beauty. Finally, there is *Merciless Beauty*, three pithy Chaucer settings for tenor and string trio from 1921. Performances are all one could wish.

Additional recommendation

Riders to the Sea

Couplings: Household Music. Flos Campi

Attrot, Dawson *sops* **Finnie, Stephen** *mezs* **Daymond** *bar* **Dukes** *va* **Northern Sinfonia and Chorus / Hickox**

Chandos CHAN9392 (79 minutes: DDD: 11/95) Ⓕ

Less congested, freer orchestral texture than the above recording offers, capturing a feeling of timelessness.

Giuseppe Verdi

Italian 1813-1901

GROVE *Born into a family of small landowners and taverners, at 12 Verdi was studying with the local church organist at the main church in nearby Busseto, whose assistant he became in 1829. In 1832 he was sent to Milan, but was refused a place at the conservatory and studied with Vincenzo Lavigna, composer and former La Scala musician. He returned to Busseto where he was passed over as maestro di cappella but became town music master in 1836 and married Margherita Barezzi, his patron's daughter (their two children died in infancy).*

Verdi had begun an opera, and tried to arrange a performance in Parma or Milan; he was unsuccessful but had some songs published and decided to settle in Milan in 1839 where his Oberto was accepted at La Scala and further operas commissioned. It was well received but his next, Un giorno di regno, failed totally; and his wife died during its composition. Verdi nearly gave up, but was fired by the libretto of Nabucco and in 1842 saw its successful production, which carried his reputation across Italy, Europe and the New World over the next five years. It was followed by another opera also with marked political overtones, I lombardi alla prima crociata, again well received. Verdi's gift for stirring melody and tragic and heroic situations struck a chord in an Italy struggling for freedom and unity, causes with which he was sympathetic; but much opera of this period has political themes and the involvement of Verdi's operas in politics is easily exaggerated.

The period Verdi later called his 'years in the galleys' now began, with a long and demanding series of operas to compose and (usually) direct, in the main Italian centres and abroad: they include Ernani, Macbeth, Luisa Miller and eight others in 1844-50, in Paris and London as well as Rome, Milan, Naples, Venice, Florence and Trieste (with a pause in 1846 when his health gave way). Features of these works include strong, sombre stories, a vigorous, almost crude orchestral style that gradually grew fuller and richer forceful vocal writing including broad lines in 9/8 and 12/8 metre and above all a seriousness in his determination to convey the full force of the drama. His models included late Rossini, Mercadante and Donizetti. He took great care over the choice of topics and about the detailed planning of his librettos. He established his basic vocal types early, in Ernani: the vigorous, determined baritone, the ardent, courageous but sometimes despairing tenor, the severe bass; among the women there is more variation.

The 'galley years' have their climax in the three great, popular operas of 1851-53. Rigoletto, produced in Venice (after trouble with the censors, a recurring theme in Verdi), was a huge success, as its richly varied and unprecedentedly dramatic music amply justifies. No less successful, in Rome, was the more direct Il trovatore, at the beginning of 1853; but six weeks later La traviata, the most personal and intimate of Verdi's operas, was a failure in Venice – though with some revisions it was favourably received in 1854 at a different Venetian theatre. With the dark drama of the one, the heroics of the second and the grace and pathos of the third, Verdi had shown how extraordinarily wide was his expressive range.

Later in 1853 he went with Giuseppina Strepponi, the soprano with whom he had been living for several years, and whom he married in 1859 – to Paris, to prepare Les vêpres siciliennes for the Opéra, where it was given in 1855 with modest success. Verdi remained there for a time to defend his rights in face of the piracies of the Théâtre des Italiens and to deal with translations of some of his operas. The next new one was the sombre Simon Boccanegra, a drama about love and politics in medieval Genoa, given in Venice. Plans for Un ballo in maschera, about the assassination of a Swedish king, in Naples were called off because of the censors and it was given instead in Rome (1859). Verdi was involved himself in political activity at this time, as representative of Busseto (where he lived) in the provincial parliament; later, pressed by Cavour, he was elected to the national parliament, and ultimately he was a senator. In 1862 La forza del destino had its première at St Petersburg. A revised Macbeth was given in Paris in 1865, but his most important work for the French capital was Don Carlos, a grand opera after Schiller in which personal dramas of love, comradeship and liberty are set against the persecutions of the Inquisition and the Spanish monarchy. It was given in 1867 and several times revised for Italian revivals.

Verdi returned to Italy, to live at Genoa. In 1870 he began work on Aida, given at Cairo Opera House at the end of 1871 to mark the opening of the Suez Canal: again in the grand opera tradition, and more taut in structure than Don Carlos. Verdi was ready to give up opera; his works of 1873 are a string quartet and the vivid, appealing Requiem in honour of the poet Manzoni, given in 1874-75, in Milan, Paris, London and Vienna. In 1879 composer-poet Boito and publisher Ricordi prevailed upon Verdi to write another opera, Otello; Verdi, working slowly and much occupied with revisions of earlier operas, completed it only in 1886. This, his most powerful tragic work, a study in evil and jealousy, had its première in Milan in 1887; it is notable for the increasing richness of allusive detail in the orchestral writing and the approach to a more continuous musical texture, though Verdi, with his faith in the expressive force of the human voice, did not abandon the 'set piece' (aria, duet etc) even if he integrated it more fully into its context – above all in his last opera. This was another Shakespeare work, Falstaff, on which he embarked two years later – his first comedy since the beginning of his career, with a score whose wit and lightness betray the hand of a serene master, was given in 1893. His final work was a set of Quattro pezzi sacri (although he was a non-believer). He spent his last years in Milan, rich, authoritarian but charitable, much visited, revered and honoured. For his funeral 28,000 people lined the streets.

Overtures and Preludes

Overtures and Preludes – Oberto; Un giorno di regno; Nabucco; Ernani; Giovanna d'Arco; Alzira; Attila; I masnadieri; Macbeth; Il corsaro; La battaglia di Legnano; Luisa Miller; Rigoletto; La traviata; I vespri siciliani; Un ballo in maschera; La forza del destino; Aida
Berlin Philharmonic Orchestra / Herbert von Karajan
DG ② 453 058-2GTA2 (113 minutes: ADD) Ⓜ
Recorded 1975

Karajan was one of the most adaptable and sensitive of dramatic conductors. His repertoire in the theatre is extraordinarily wide, and he is at home equally in Verdi, Wagner, Richard Strauss and Puccini. In this celebrated 1975 collection of all of Verdi's overtures, he gives us some fine insights into the composer's skill as an orchestrator, dramatist and poet. Though Karajan had only recorded *Aida* complete his dramatic instincts bring some fine performances of the lesser-known preludes. The earliest, *Nabucco* from 1842 (the collection is arranged chronologically), already shows a mastercraftsman at work, with a slow introduction promising much. *La traviata* shows a quite different skill – the delicate creation of a sensitive poet working in filigree. The final four preludes are great works fully worthy of this individual presentation. Even the lesser-known preludes are enhanced by Karajan's dramatic instincts. Good recordings, though less than outstanding.

Overtures and Preludes – Oberto; Nabucco; Giovanna d'Arco; Alzira; La battaglia di Legnano; Attila; I masnadieri; Il corsaro; Un giorno di regno; Ernani; I due Foscari; Macbeth. Ballet Music – Macbeth
BBC Philharmonic Orchestra / Sir Edward Downes
Chandos CHAN9510 (76 minutes: DDD) Ⓕ
Recorded 1996

These performances from an experienced British operatic stalwart have dignity (witness the brass in *Nabucco*), panache and splendidly colourful orchestral playing, including real string virtuosity, using the widest dynamic range. The *crescendo* at the opening of *Giovanna d'Arco* is most compelling. Some of the shorter preludes are full of atmosphere. The brief *Macbeth* Prelude is particularly potent, and the ballet music is both dramatic and rumbustious while *I masnadieri* closes with a swooning cello solo. *La battaglia di Legnano* which ends the programme has plenty of full-blooded brass at the opening and close. The recording is spectacular.

Messa da Requiem

Verdi Messa da Requiem[b]. Overture 'I vespri siciliani'[c]
Schubert Mass No 6 in E flat, D950[a]
[a]**Anne Pashley,** [b]**Amy Shuard** *sops* [a]**Sybil Michelow,** [b]**Anna Reynolds** *mezzos* [a]**David Hughes,** [b]**Richard Lewis,** [a]**Duncan Robertson** *tens* [a]**William McCue,** [b]**David Ward** *basses*
[a]**Scottish Festival Chorus,** [a]**New Philharmonia Orchestra; Philharmonia** [b]**Chorus and** [bc]**Orchestra / Carlo Maria Giulini**
BBC Legends/IMG Artists BBCL4029-2 Ⓜ
(153 minutes: ADD). Recorded live [bc]1963 and [a]1968

In Great Britain in the 1960s, the art of large-scale choral singing reached what was arguably its apogee with the work of the two choruses featured here: the Philharmonia Chorus, directed by Wilhelm Pitz, and the Edinburgh Festival Chorus, directed by Arthur Oldham (neither man gets a credit in the BBC Legends booklet, though Alan Blyth mentions both in his note). Even allowing for the fact that this Prom performance of the Verdi *Requiem* was given around the time of an intensive period of rehearsal during which the EMI studio recording was also being made, the Philharmonia Chorus's singing is stunningly good: first-rate diction, impeccable intonation, fine dynamic control and absolute involvement in the music as Giulini relays it to them.

In the Schubert Mass the Edinburgh Festival Chorus acquits itself magnificently. Giulini's reading is powerful and reverential, one in which the chorus comes to speak with the single voice of an individual believer.

The Verdi is superbly recorded. Where EMI's engineers, working within the narrower confines of the Kingsway Hall on Giulini's 1964 account, ended up with an unduly close and overloaded sound in the 'Dies irae' and *Sanctus*, the unnamed BBC team working live in the Royal Albert Hall produce sound that is focused yet open, clear but warm. In the more intimate solo numbers, there is little to choose between the recordings, though the live performance inevitably has more atmosphere.

Giulini's reading of the *Requiem*, thrilling yet humane, is precisely the one we hear on the EMI recording, with the Philharmonia Chorus and Orchestra as expert live as they are on record (the orchestral playing is well-nigh flawless; only Karajan's Berliners or Szell's Cleveland Orchestra could have matched what the Philharmonia achieve here).

Of the solo singers, the youngest, Anna Reynolds, could have gone straight into the EMI recording, so well does she sing. Richard Lewis, nearing the end of his career, is less gorgeous of voice than EMI's Nicolai Gedda, but the bass, David Ward, here at the height of his powers, is more than a match for the younger Nicolai Ghiaurov.

As for Amy Shuard and EMI's Elisabeth Schwarzkopf, they are complementary. Giulini had originally wanted Callas for the recording; like Shuard, she had the Aida-voice the soprano part (the 'Libera me', in particular) is generally believed to need. Schwarzkopf, the nominated stand-in, sings throughout with astonishing skill and sensibility – an object-lesson in how the part should be handled vocally. Shuard is also technically fine; not as fine as Schwarzkopf but very much the real thing dramatically and absolutely right for the live performance. In short, an indispensable set.

Messa da Requiem
Cheryl Studer *sop*; **Dolora Zajick** *mez*; **Luciano Pavarotti** *ten*; **Samuel Ramey** *bass*
Chorus and Orchestra of La Scala, Milan / Riccardo Muti
EMI digital ② CDS7 49390-2 (88 minutes: DDD) Ⓕ
Text and translation included. Recorded live in 1987

Muti's tempos, both in his 1979 EMI version and here are substantially faster (*Sanctus*) or slower (opening *Kyrie*, 'Rex tremendae', 'Lacrymosa') than Verdi indicates and permits far more *rallentandos* than are marked. Nobody wants slavish adherence to what may be accounted only as suggestions on the composer's part, but Muti does sometimes lose the overall view of a movement by overplaying his hand as an interpreter. That is the main criticism of a performance that is certainly positive in terms of its dramatic strength, deriving from Muti's close rapport with his Scala forces, who perform with great dedication in carrying out his meticulous attention both to instrumental and to rhythmic detail.

Here he has a very different chorus from the much smaller professional British group on his earlier set (on EMI Double Forte). That has advantages and disadvantages. The sound here is grander, more specifically operatic in scale as one would expect, with some arrestingly histrionic effects such as the bold, black-browed singing at 'Rex tremendae' and the awed *senza misura* incantation at the start of the 'Libera me'. But there is not quite the bright, incisive quality found on the former recording. The *Sanctus*, a few seconds slower than in 1979, is still unwontedly quick, but the Scala singers seem to revel in coping with the speed, as they do with the hard-driving 'Dies irae'. Similar detailed effects inform the fine playing of the Scala orchestra, not least the beseeching strings right at the start of the whole work and the plangent wind in the 'Ingemisco'.

Recording live, or mostly so, always helps to catch the frisson of a real occasion, but it has a certain drawback here in that the performance starts hesitantly, particularly where the soloists are concerned. Cheryl Studer seems at the beginning a shade tentative and over-awed, but as the evening develops she confirms what a fine *lirico-spinto* soprano she is. The final phrase of the 'Offertorio' is perfectly accomplished and the whole of the 'Libera me' is delivered with strong, firm tone and a deal of passion. Her slightly resinous tone blends very well with Zajick's in the 'Recordare' and the *Agnus Dei*, one of the set's most successful movements. On her own Zajick also improves from an anonymous start to reach heights of eloquence at the start of the 'Lux aeterna'. The dark grain of her chest register contrasts with a degree of brilliance at the top.

Many will probably buy the recording for Pavarotti. He is in his best, most persuasive form, more individual and subtle in utterance (listen to his many shades of colour in the 'Ingemisco') than for Solti (Decca), even if the voice has lost a little of its old opulence. He is also more considerate of his colleagues in the unaccompanied passages, which here are as carefully blended as on any recording, much helped by Ramey's solid bottom line. Ramey trumps even Pavarotti at 'Hostias' in the 'Domine Jesu', his *dolcissimo* singing here full of inward feeling. 'Oro supplex', taken up to Verdi's tempo rather than being dragged as it can be by heavier basses, is firmly and securely phrased. Others have sung the bass part with more character, few – except Pinza – with such security and musicality.

The recording is rather recessed with the character of the soloists' voices hard to discern. However, where the chorus and orchestra are concerned, the new Muti certainly achieves a theatrical perspective, catching the atmosphere of La Scala, and the choral recording obviously has a bigger range than on his old set.

Messa da Requiem[a]. Te Deum[b]. Aida – Sinfonia[c]. La forza del destino – Sinfonia[d]. Luisa Miller Sinfonia[e]. La traviata – Preludes: Act I and II[f]. I vespri siciliani – Sinfonia[g]

[a]**Renata Tebaldi** *sop* [a]**Cloe Elmo** *mez* [a]**Giacinto Prandelli** *ten* [a]**Cesare Siepi** *bass* [b]**Westminster Choir;** [a]**Chorus and Orchestra of La Scala, Milan;** [bcdefg]**NBC Symphony Orchestra / Arturo Toscanini**

Istituto Discografico Italiano mono ② IDIS345/46 Ⓜ (135 minutes: ADD). Recorded 1940-43, 1945 and live in 1950

Most Toscanini aficionados are familiar with his 1938 London and/or 1940 and 1953 New York performances, which are all available at present in varying incarnations, but fewer may know this 1950 version of the *Requiem* from La Scala. Lucky Milanese at the time, having the luxury of hearing Toscanini conduct the work one year, de Sabata the next (*that* recording has been available from time to time on Italian labels) . What this Toscanini and the de Sabata have in common, a very positive asset, is the presence of the young Tebaldi, who never appeared on later sets. Not many soprano soloists in the long history of the work on disc have come so close to fulfilling all its demands. At the time her tone had the ethereal beauty the part calls for while also having the Italianate weight to carry easily and firmly over the orchestra in the 'Libera me' (although in the slow section she makes one uncomfortable break in the line). She may not have the subtlety of Milanov in the 1938 and 1940 performances but she is the more reliable singer, one who feels the music instinctively.

The other soloists are good if not outstanding. Elmo has all the notes well within her compass and Tebaldi's refulgence of tone, but she is not always as sensitive to Verdi's markings as she ought to be. Prandelli, who also sings for de Sabata, is an admirable tenor, his plangent tone and innate sense of style always to the fore (although Björling in 1940 is his superior). Siepi, also heard in 1953, is a secure and idiomatic bass.

Toscanini, according to Harvey Sachs's biography, expressed himself dissatisfied with the performance. Perhaps he found the chorus a shade unruly: certainly the readings of the choirs in 1938 and 1953 are preferable, but the singing tone, always a requisite with this conductor, is there in the playing of La Scala's orchestra. As for Toscanini, he seems at his best, combining – in equal parts – dramatic force with lyrical warmth, as he does in the other recordings. The sound is reasonable although it is also rather confined.

The NBC performances that comprise the remainder of CD 2 are in more faithful sound. The *Te Deum* is little different from the RCA issue of the work. The overtures all show Toscanini's wonderful rapport with Verdi, making one regret he recorded so few of the master's operas. The overture to *Forza*, so urgent and involving, so acutely executed, is a template of the rest and therefore unmissable – as indeed is most of this rewarding set, but the notes are poor, giving no information on the provenance of the material.

Messa da Requiem[a]. Quattro pezzi sacri[b] **P**
[a]**Luba Orgonasova,** [b]**Donna Brown** *sops* **Anne Sofie von Otter** *mez* **Luca Canonici** *ten* **Alastair Miles** *bass* **Monteverdi Choir; Orchestre Révolutionnaire et Romantique / Sir John Eliot Gardiner**
Philips ② 442 142-2PH2 (120 minutes: DDD) Ⓕ
Notes, texts and translations included
Recorded 1992

Gardiner's Verdi *Requiem* is in a class of its own. His are readings that combine a positive view and interpretative integrity from start to finish, something possible only in the context of the superb professionalism of the (augmented) Monteverdi Choir, which sings with a burnished and steady tone throughout and suggests, rightly, a corporate act of worship. Its contribution is beyond praise.

He might also have been surprised and delighted to hear the soloists' contribution sung with such precision by such a finely integrated quartet, who perform the important unaccompanied passages with special grace and sensitivity. Instead of hearing the usual jostle of vibratos, here the four voices are firm and true. Individually they are also distinguished. Pride of place must go to Orgonasova who gives the performance of her life. The exactly placed high B in the 'Quid sum miser' section of the 'Dies irae', the perfect blending with von Otter at 'Dominum', the whole of the *Andante* section of the 'Libera me', sung with ethereal tone and a long breath, make the heart stop in amazement.

In 'Oro supplex' Gardiner follows Verdi's tempo marking. More often he follows tradition, with slower speeds than those suggested, and he allows more licence than the score, or conductors like Toscanini. But as his liberties all seem so convincing in the context of the whole, who should complain? In the *Pezzi sacri*, Gardiner gives the most thrilling account yet to appear.

The recording, made in Westminster Cathedral, has a huge range which may cause problems in confined spaces. You are liable to be overwhelmed, for instance, by the 'Dies irae'.

Messa da Requiem. Quattro pezzi sacri
Elena Filipova *sop* **Gloria Scalchi** *mez* **César Hernández** *ten* **Carlo Colombara** *bass* **Hungarian State Opera Choir and Orchestra / Pier Giorgio Morandi**
Naxos ② 8 550944/5 (126 minutes: DDD) Ⓢ
Texts and translations included. Recorded 1996

Morandi brings to his interpretation a youthful, Italian energy and generosity of expression. Given a judicious choice of young soloists, all up to their exigent tasks, an excellent chorus (a shattering 'Dies irae', an alert, not too drilled *Sanctus*, a disciplined 'Libera me' fugue) and a well-fashioned recording, this set makes a compelling case for recommendation as an alternative to Gardiner's period-performance set. Try track 7, the 'Rex tremendae', where you can hear how Morandi builds a movement unerringly to an appropriately tremendous climax.

The soloists show how involved they are in the work, form a good ensemble and individually exhibit the intelligence to sing quietly as needed. Filipova and Scalchi combine into a rich-toned duo in 'Liber scriptus', spoilt a little by moments of indeterminate pitch from the soprano (later the two contrast well in the *Agnus Dei*). Hernández, with his warm, baritonal, Spanish-style tenor, sings a sensitive 'Ingemisco' (a touch of insecurity at the start excepted), succeeded by Colombara's truly magisterial conjuring of the flames of hell at 'Confutatis maledictis'. Filipova's floated entry at 'huic ergo' in the succeeding trio and the sheer intensity of the whole 'Lacrymosa' bring the 'Dies irae' to a fitting close.

The rest of the work's performance is on an equivalent level of achievement, Morandi always judging speeds to a nicety. The fill-up to this large-scale reading is a fine performance of the *Quattro pezzi sacri*.

Additional recommendation
Messa da Requiem
Caniglia *sop* **Stignani** *mez* **Gigli** *ten* **Pinza** *bass* **H**
Rome Opera Chorus and Orchestra / Serafin
EMI Références mono CDH5 67486-2 Ⓜ
(72 minutes: ADD: 5/90[R]). Text and translation included

Tullio Serafin's 1939 *Requiem* recording is something of a classic, with Ebe Stignani and Ezio Pinza ideal proponents of their parts and Maria Caniglia and Beniamino Gigli almost as good. Note, there are small cuts.

Messa solenne in E flat

Messa solenne in E flat. Qui tollis in F. Tantum ergo in F. Tantum ergo in G. Laudate pueri in D. Pater noster in G. Ave Maria in D. Messa per Rossini – Libera me
Elisabetta Scano, Cristina Gallardo-Domâs *sops* **Sonia Prina** *mez* **Juan Diego Flórez, Kenneth Tarver** *tens* **Eldar Aliev** *bass* **Giuseppe Verdi Symphony Chorus and Orchestra, Milan / Riccardo Chailly**
Decca 467 280-2DH (69 minutes: DDD) Ⓕ
Texts and translations included. Recorded 2000

The *Pater noster* and *Ave Maria* of 1880 and the 'Libera me' from the composite *Messa per Rossini* (later the bases from which Verdi developed the full *Requiem*) are clearly enough established in the canon, if rarely performed or recorded. The remaining five works, notably the *Messa solenne*, are all pieces dating from his late teens and twenties. Though in these youthful pieces there are few, if any, indications of the mature opera-composer to come, they provide a fascinating view of the young Verdi's development. As the pupil of Busseto choirmaster Ferdinando Provesi, untraditional and anti-clerical in that role, he was led towards operatic models, with choral writing echoing Rossini ensembles.

The *Messa solenne*, sketched out in 1833 when Verdi was 20, but revised and performed only two years later, is, sadly, incomplete. The aim was to write a *Missa brevis*, setting only a *Kyrie* and a *Gloria*, but two sections are missing from the *Gloria*, the 'Qui sedes' and 'Quoniam', leaving only the opening 'Gloria in excelsis', the 'Qui tollis' and the final 'Cum sancto spirito'.

The very opening of the first *Kyrie* sounds transition-like, a clearing of the throat before the main argument is put in an almost Beethovenian style. That brief movement is very square, and the lyrical setting of the 'Christe' in compound time is conventional too, but then in the second *Kyrie*, even briefer than the first, the natural vigour of the young Verdi emerges positively in sharply rhythmic choral writing.

The three movements of the *Gloria* are similarly variable in their inspiration, with chirpy woodwind writing in the 'Laudamus te' of the opening section (a baritone prominent), and echoes of Bellini and Mozart in the 'Qui tollis' (with soprano solo). That last, like the 'Christe', was newly written for the 1835 performance, reflecting Verdi's studies in Milan. Generally throughout these student pieces – including the two early *Tantum ergo* settings and the separate 'Qui tollis' – *allegros* are more striking than slow passages. Most Rossinian of all is the *Laudate pueri*, an ensemble piece with two tenor soloists and a bass joining the chorus, in which, after a jaunty flute solo, there is a full Rossini-like *crescendo*.

If none of this music brings the sort of insights that, say, Berlioz's youthful inspirations so often do, it is consistently enjoyable, and warmly and incisively performed under Chailly by the Milan choir and orchestra as well as a splendid line-up of soloists, all fresh and clear. The soprano, Cristina Gallardo-Domâs (best remembered for her moving Sister Angelica in Antonio Pappano's EMI set of Puccini's *Trittico*), is the lovely soloist in the *Ave Maria*, written in 1880, heightening its anticipations of Desdemona's Willow song and 'Ave Maria' in *Otello*. Equally, the *a cappella* setting of the *Pater noster*, which precedes it, anticipates the last act of *Otello*. It makes one wonder why these two pieces for contrasted forces, designed to go together, are so neglected.

Less surprising is the neglect of the 'Libera me', when in fact it is a draft for the great 'Libera me' in the *Requiem*. It is true that most of the ideas are already fully worked out, but the changes in detail make all the difference, notably the striking *fortissimo* chords with bass drum which introduce the 'Dies irae' in the later version. Here, too, the beautiful, sensitive singing of Gallardo-Domâs enhances an apt and welcome supplement to a rare collection. Excellent Decca sound, though the unaccompanied chorus in the *Pater noster* is rather distant.

Opera Choruses

Opera choruses: Nabucco – Gli arredi festivi giù cadano infranti; Va, pensiero, sull'ali dorate. I Lombardi – Gerusalem!; O Signore, dal tetto natio. Macbeth – Tre volte miagola; Patria oppressa. I masnadieri – Le rube, gli stupri. Rigoletto – Zitti zitti. Il trovatore – Vedi! Le fosche notturne spoglie; Squilli, echeggi la tromba guerriera. La traviata[a] – Noi siamo zingarelle ... Di Madride nio siam mattadori. Un ballo in maschera – Posa in pace. Don Carlos – Spuntato ecco il dì. Aida – Gloria all'Egitto. Otello – Fuoco di gioia. Requiem – Sanctus

[a]Marsha Waxman *mez* **[a]David Huneryager, [a]Richard Cohn** *basses* **Chicago Symphony Chorus and Orchestra / Sir Georg Solti**

Decca 430 226-2DH (70 minutes: DDD) Ⓕ

Texts and translations included. Recorded 1989 ●

Verdi's choruses occupy a special place in his operas. They are invariably red-blooded and usually make a simple dramatic statement with great impact. The arresting 'Chorus of the Hebrew Slaves' ('Va, pensiero') from *Nabucco* is probably the best-known and most popular chorus in the entire operatic repertoire, immediately tugging at the heart-strings with its gentle opening cantilena, soon swelling out to a great climax. Solti shows just how to shape the noble melodic line which soars with firm control, yet retaining the urgency and electricity in every bar. The dramatic contrasts at the opening of 'Gerusalem!' from *I Lombardi* are equally powerfully projected, and the brass again makes a riveting effect in 'Patria oppressa' from *Macbeth*. But, of course, not all Verdi choruses offer blood and thunder: the volatile 'Fire chorus' from *Otello* flickers with an almost visual fantasy, while the wicked robbers in *I masnadieri* celebrate their excesses (plunder, rape, arson and murder) gleefully, and with such rhythmic jauntiness that one cannot quite take them seriously. The 'Gipsies' chorus' from *La traviata* has a nice touch of elegance, and the *scherzo*-like 'Sanctus', from the *Requiem*, which ends the concert, is full of joy. But it is the impact of the dramatic moments which is most memorable, not least the big triumphal scene from *Aida*, complete with the ballet music, to provide a diverse interlude in the middle. The recording is in the demonstration class.

Opera Duets

Otello – Gia nella notte densa; Venga la morte!. Aida[a] – La fatale pietra; Morir si pura e bella; O terra addio[b]. Il trovatore[a] – Miserere...Ah, che la morte ognora. Simon Boccanegra – Cielo di stelle orbato; Vieni a mirar la cerula. I vespri siciliani – Pensando a me! I Lombardi alla prima crociata[a] – Oh belle, a questa misera; All'armi! La traviata[a] – Libiamo, ne'lieti calici. Rigoletto – Ah! veglia, o donna; Signor ne principe; T'amo! T'amo; E il sol dell'anima; Addio, addio[c]. Don Carlo – E dessa!...Un detto, un sol; Vago sogno m'arrise; Ma lassù ci vedremo. I masnadieri – Qual mare, qual terra; Qui nel bosco?; Lassù risplendere.

Angela Gheorghiu *sop* **Roberto Alagna** *ten* [bc]**Sara Mingardo** *mez* [c]**Brian Parsons,** [c]**Rodney Gibson** *tens* [ab]**London Voices; Berlin Philharmonic Orchestra / Claudio Abbado**
EMI CDC5 56656-2 (70 minutes: DDD) Ⓕ
Texts and translations included. Recorded 1998

This long, fascinating, highly ambitious recital, nothing less than a conspectus of Verdi's soprano-tenor duets, is executed with distinction on all sides. Gheorghiu deserves particular plaudits. It seems that nothing in Verdi (and indeed in much else) is beyond her capabilities. Her singing here, especially as Gilda, Aida and Desdemona, is so exquisite, the tone so warm and limpid, the phrasing so shapely as surely to melt any heart. Take, for example, Gilda's touching exchanges with Giovanna, herself sung by the superb mezzo, Sara Mingardo (also heard as a grieving Amneris), the whole of Aida's solo beginning 'Presago il core', with the soprano's warm lower register coming into play, and that ultimate test, Desdemona's poised 'Amen'. Throughout, both musically and interpretatively, she simply cannot be faulted.

Neither she nor her husband is backward in coming forward with less hackneyed pieces, those from the early operas – try the section starting 'Ma un'iri di pace' in the *Masnadieri* duet, the two voices in ideal blend, phrases and tone sweetly shaded with the following cabaletta all light eagerness on both sides. Then there's plangent singing on both sides in the sad little piece from *Vespri*, though it's a pity they did not attempt this in the original French. Here and throughout Alagna is his customary self, assured (a few over-pressed high notes, some unwritten, apart), impassioned, thoughtful and accurate in his phraseology, nowhere more so than in the parts he is unlikely as yet to take on stage – Radames and Otello. Even more important in so many passages, Alagna finds the right *mezzo-piano*, where heavier tenors have to sing *forte*, notably in the closing phrases where Otello wafts his love of Desdemona on to the night air – a moment of sheer magic.

Abbado and the Berlin Philharmonic Orchestra are at their peak of achievement and the recording catches these voices in their full glory, making this a most desirable issue, possibly the best the pair has yet made.

Opera Arias

Roberto Alagna
Luisa Miller – Oh! fede negar potessi...Quando le sere al placido. I Lombardi alla prima crociata – La mia letizia infondere. Aida – Se quel guerrier...Celeste Aida. Ernani[f] – Mercè, dilette amici...Come rugiada al cespite...O tu che l'alma adora. Un ballo in maschera – Forse la soglia...Ma se m'è forza perderti. Otello[bcde] – Dio! mi potevi; Niun mi tema. La forza del destino – Prelude, Act 3; La vita è inferno...O, tu che in seno. Macbeth – O figli, o figli miei!...Ah, la paterna mano. Jérusalem – L'Emir auprès de lui...Je veux encore entendre. Il trovatore[af] – Ah! si, ben mio...Di quella pira
Roberto Alagna *ten* with [a]**Angela Gheorghiu** *sop* [b]**Andrew Busher** *ten* [c]**James Bobby** *bar* [d]**Richard Fallas,** [e]**Noel Mann** *basses* [f]**London Voices; Berlin Philharmonic Orchestra / Claudio Abbado**
EMI CDC5 56567-2 (64 minutes: DDD) Ⓕ
Texts and translations included. Recorded 1997

Alagna here shows, in the most demanding programme imaginable, that there is little if anything wrong with his technique and a great deal right with his sense of Verdian style. Indeed, he takes the score as his bible. That is evident, for instance, in his treatment of Otello. In the great Act 3 Monologue, besides thinking himself into the Moor's deep well of despondency at this juncture of the tragedy, evinced in a slightly juddering tone, he sings the opening passage as written, staying on the A flat and E flat, not going for unwanted melodrama. Then the cantilena is sung with the appropriate touch of pained nobility. In the Death scene he finds the right pent-up voice for 'Come sei pallida' and the repeated 'Desdemona', then sings 'Or morendo' with a *pp* on the high G, as Verdi enjoins.

So much else in the recital is just as thoughtfully interpreted. He solves the problem of the high B flat at the end of 'Celeste Aida' by starting it *mezzo-forte* and shading it away affectingly in a well-executed *diminuendo*, having sung the whole aria in a suitably poetic manner. Alagna is the brigand to the life in Ernani's introductory aria. Riccardo's (or if you like Gustaf's) Act 3 aria is charged with emotion, the tone properly plaintive and darkened for the middle section. Then there's perhaps the most taxing aria for tenor in all Verdi: Alvaro's 'O, tu che in seno' from *Forza*. Following the most eloquent playing by the Berlin Philharmonic's clarinet in the long introduction, Alagna catches the Inca's sense of longing in the recitative and then rises to the challenge of the aria's relentless tessitura with fine-grained, almost heroic tone. Nor does he shirk the high Cs in 'Di quella pira'.

The rarity here is the item from *Jérusalem*, sung in Alagna's other tongue. The BPO's contribution, under Abbado's distinguished direction, is as accomplished as you might expect.

The recording allows us to hear the full bloom of Alagna's voice, but occasionally the sound of the voice appears to stray or float around the sound spectrum, a disconcerting effect, but that's not enough of a distraction to prevent a strong recommendation.

Andrea Bocelli
Il trovatore – Ah! sì, ben mio; Di quella pira. Rigoletto – Ella mi fu rapita!; Possente amor mi chiama; La donna è mobile. Un ballo in maschera – Di' tu se fedele; Ma se m'è forza perderti. Aida – Celeste Aida. La traviata – De' miei bollenti spiriti; O mio romorso!. I Lombardi alla prima crociata – La mia letizia infondere. Ernani – Mercè, dilette amiche. Don Carlo – Io la vidi. Luisa Miller – Quando le sere al placido. La forza del destino – La vita è inferno
Andrea Bocelli *ten* **Israel Philharmonic Orchestra / Zubin Mehta**
Philips 464 600-2PH (61 minutes: DDD) Ⓕ
Texts and translations included. Recorded 2000

The *lirico-spinto* repertoire of the tenor in Verdi is well represented here, the *lirico* part by arias from *La traviata* and *Rigoletto*, the *spinto* by (for instance) Manrico's call to arms and the recitatives before 'Quando le sere' in *Luisa Miller* and 'Io la vidi' in *Don Carlo*. They are oddly ordered – the *stretta* in *Il trovatore* preceding its aria, the Duke's famous song in *Rigoletto* separated from his aria and cabaletta by items from *Un ballo in maschera*, with no attention to chronology throughout – but it doesn't greatly matter. The point is that we have some of the best singing within this repertoire recorded in recent years. Actually, the order does matter in so far as it probably supposes the tenor to be shown to best advantage in the opening number (which is the 'Di quella pira'), whereas that is far from being so. In fact, the last item, the solo from *La forza del destino*, would have done that job far better. This shows well the individuality of timbre, the cleanness of style and the attentiveness to words and feeling, all of these qualities being present in a degree which clearly establishes the singer as an artist, one with a particular affinity for the Verdi line and its intensity of emotion.

To be sure, there are limits. In *La forza* he hardly makes a real and truly addressed prayer out of the 'Leonora mia, soccorrimi'. His recitative, expressive as it is, doesn't quite put the words to work ('O rimembranza'). In *La traviata* it takes time before affection enters his voice, and when it does it hardly brings a smile with it. He sometimes gives the impression of having learnt a lesson too well, or of applying it too rigidly (the unvarying quavers in 'Di tu se fedele'). But he has learnt. He lightens gracefully in both the *Traviata* and *Ballo*. He phrases well and often with remarkable breadth (as in 'Celeste Aida'). Remarkably, too, his voice remains flexible ('Celeste Aida' again), although the characteristic tone is of that concentrated kind which can become rigid. The quality, timbre and power are still something of a puzzle and will probably remain so until one has had the experience of his singing live and unamplified. But the individuality of tone is welcome, as is its fine, unwavering definition.

Orchestra and chorus perform well under Mehta, who quite probably strikes just the right balance of sympathy and authority to help Bocelli in this extension of his repertoire.

Angela Gheorghiu

Aida – Qui Radames verrà; O patria mia. Un ballo in maschera – Morrò, ma prima in grazia. Don Carlo – Tu che le vanità. La forza del destino – Pace, pace, mio Dio. Otello[a] – Era più calmo?; Mia madre aveva; Piangea cantando; Ave Maria. Rigoletto – Gualtier Maldè...Caro nome. Simon Boccanegra – Come in quest'ora bruna. Il trovatore[b] – Che più t'arresti?... Tacea la notte placida...Di tale amor. I vespri siciliani – Mercè, dilette amiche

Angela Gheorghiu *sop* [a]**Laura Polverelli,** [b]**Tiziana Tramonti** *mezzos* **Giuseppe Verdi Symphony Orchestra, Milan / Riccardo Chailly**

Decca 460 952-2DH (67 minutes: DDD). Texts and translations included. Recorded 1998-99 Ⓕ

So much is enthralling in this superbly executed recital that it is hard to know where to begin. In some respects Elisabetta's long scene from *Don Carlo* is a template for everything. There you hear the *spinto* sound that is just about ideal for the long breathed phrases at the start; the floated tone and *voce portando* in the remembrances of happier days in France; finally, in the agitated section, comes the glottal attack so reminiscent of great Verdi sopranos from the past. As important as any of these attributes is Gheorghiu's ability to think herself from nowhere into a new character. All Elisabetta's torment of the soul is there. Callas is an obvious influence at certain key moments, and the reading need fear nothing by comparison. Montserrat Caballé in the complete *Don Carlo* (EMI) is another great singer recollected, but Gheorghiu, as sensitive as the Spanish soprano, has the more appropriate voice.

'O patria mia' is again just about ideal, with the difficult close nicely encompassed. One notices here, too, the acuity with words, the wonderful control of breath, the poise of line. Throughout the programme, Chailly gives not only considerate support but also helps by establishing tempos that never drag. Each aria flows easily and naturally, effects all the better for being made within a firmly set context. Gheorghiu's warmth of feeling and tone informs the *Boccanegra* Amelia's sea-influenced thoughts, but here, and possibly for Gilda (a poor note near the end of 'Caro nome' should have been re-taken), a slightly brighter timbre would be preferable. The prayer of that other Amelia, the erring wife of King Gustavus in *Ballo*, adumbrates all her desperation. Better still are the even more desperate thoughts of the *Forza* Leonora *in extremis*, an interpretation to rank with the most compelling on disc.

At last, sated with so much sure artistry, we reach Desdemona. The Willow song flows beautifully in voice and orchestra, and with so many shades and colourings used the 'Ave Maria' has a beseeching, inward quality. Scotto or de los Angeles find even more pathos in the scena, but none sings with quite the same degree of security and natural ease.

The Milan recordings, at two sessions and venues, are excellent.

Thomas Hampson

Macbeth – Perfidi! All'anglo contro me; Ove son oi?...Vada in flamme. Ernani – Oh, dei verd'anni miei. I due Foscari – Eccomi solo alfine...O vecchio cor, che batti. Il corsaro – Alfin questo corsaro è mio prigione!... Cento leggiarde vergini. Le trouvère – Tout est désert... Son regard. Les vêpres siciliennes – Oui, je fus bien coupable...Au sein de la puissance. I masnadieri – Tradimento! Pareami che sorto. Stiffelio – Ei fugge!... Lina, pensai che un angelo. La traviata – Di Provenza il mar; Ne rispondi. Giovanna d'Arco – Ecco il luogo... Speme al vecchio era una figlia

Thomas Hampson *bar* **Orchestra of the Age of Enlightenment / Richard Armstrong**

EMI CDC5 57113-2 (65 minutes: DDD) Ⓕ

Texts and translations included

Despite distinguished appearances as Germont in *La traviata* and the Marquess of Posa in *Don Carlos*, Thomas Hampson does not slot readily into the mind under the heading of Verdi-baritone. Perhaps because his operatic repertoire is so varied, or possibly because of his close association with song, we tend to 'hear' him inwardly in languages other than Italian. If so, this recital-disc should go far to redress the balance. His warm, well-rounded voice with its extensive range and fine evenness of production suits the lyric Verdi admirably. If we sample first the *Traviata* excerpt, all of these qualities are evident, and so is his tasteful way with the music, the phrasing, the feeling for the verses' shape, the generous supply of voice without show or exaggeration. Moreover, in the second verse particularly, the song becomes a genuine appeal, steadily growing in urgency.

Macbeth is a different proposition. He has sung the role on stage, but the two excerpts heard here hardly present him to the mind's eye in character. His voice cannot take on the hard, ruthless edge, nor has it the colours for the bitterness or deadness of spirit implicit in the 'Pietà, rispetto', the counterpart of 'the sear, the yellow leaf' speech in Shakespeare. Compare Sherrill Milnes in the set under Muti (EMI): first with bite to the vocal tone ('Perfidi!'), then with a tone drained of hope, confronting the future with woeful realism. Hampson's singing is not without character, but the character is not Macbeth's.

We rarely hear the baritone arias from *Stiffelio*, *Il corsaro* and *Giovanna d'Arco* as concert-pieces, and it is interesting also to have 'Il balèn' from *Trovatore* as 'Son regard, son doux sourire' from the French version. Hampson sings most beautifully in that, not least in the ornamentation and cadenza where (as with others in the recital) he shows the thoroughness of his well-schooled technique. Throughout, he is expressively accompanied, and the recorded sound catches his voice very faithfully.

Julia Varady

Nabucco – Ben io t'avenni...Anch'io dischiuso un giorno. Il trovatore – Tacea la notte placida...Di tale amor; Timor di me?...D'amor sull'ali rosee. La traviata – E strano!...Ah, fors'è lui...Follie! Sempre libera[a]; Teneste la promessa...Addio del passato. Un ballo in maschera – Ecco l'orrido campo...Ma dall'arido stelo divulsa...Morro, ma prima in grazia. La forza del destino – Pace, pace, mio Dio

Julia Varady *sop* [a]**Lothar Odinius** *ten* **Bavarian State Orchestra / Dietrich Fischer-Dieskau**

Orfeo C186951 (51 minutes: DDD) Ⓕ

Recorded 1995

Varady endows these arias we have heard hundreds of times, and of which we all have our favourite memories and recordings, with renewed life through an art which is fully responsive, highly fastidious, lovely in the quality of its sound and individual in its timbre and inflection. The beauty of tone is evident first of all in its well-preserved purity (and Varady, born in 1941, is of an age when normally allowances have to be made). Hers is not a full-bodied, rich Ponselle-like voice, but she makes wonderfully effective use of her resources, which include a surprisingly strong lower register and an upward range that (as we hear) easily encompasses the high D flat and has an E flat available. She is dramatic in style yet also thoroughly accomplished in her scales, trills and other *fioriture*. Her first *Trovatore* aria, for instance, includes the cabaletta with its full complement of technical brilliances. The musical instinct seems almost infallible – a 'wrong' *portamento* or rubato always irritates and here everything seems just right. A remarkable sensitivity is at work throughout.

The orchestra is conducted by Fischer-Dieskau, Varady's husband, and here too is a fine example of a positive, non-routine collaboration, the pacing and shading of the orchestral parts so frequently having something specific to offer (for example, in the letter passage from *La traviata*). The recording is well balanced.

Aida

Birgit Nilsson *sop* Aida; **Grace Bumbry** *mez* Amneris; **Franco Corelli** *ten* Radames; **Mario Sereni** *bar* Amonasro; **Bonaldo Giaiotti** *bass* Ramfis; **Ferruccio Mazzoli** *bass* King; **Piero de Palma** *ten* Messenger; **Mirella Fiorentini** *mez* Priestess; **Chorus and Orchestra of Rome Opera / Zubin Mehta**

HMV Classics ② HMVD5 73410-2 Ⓑ

(141 minutes: ADD). Recorded 1966

Il trovatore

Franco Corelli *ten* Manrico; **Gabriella Tucci** *sop* Leonora; **Robert Merrill** *bar* Count di Luna; **Giulietta Simionato** *mez* Azucena; **Ferruccio Mazzoli** *bass* Ferrando; **Luciana Moneta** *mez* Ines; **Angelo Mercuriali** *ten* Ruiz, Messenger; **Mario Rinaudo** *bass* Old Gipsy; **Chorus and Orchestra of Rome Opera / Thomas Schippers**

HMV Classics ② HMVD5 73413-2 Ⓑ

(123 minutes: ADD). Recorded 1964

In the 1950s and 1960s EMI made a series of what have become classics with Rome Opera forces that have Verdi in their blood. These two recordings greeted with reservations then, now seem like manna from heaven in aworld starved of true Verdian voices. Above all there is Corelli's truly *spinto* tenor, a thrilling sound in itself, and used, both as Radames (one of the most exciting on disc) and as Manrico, with far more sensitivity than is usually allowed for. Tucci is a Leonora in the Tebaldi mould, with a strong voice and natural phrasing. Simionato, a shade past her best, remains an affecting, idiomatic Azucena. Robert Merrill is a Verdi baritone of poise and style. Schippers conducts with verve.

In *Aida*, Nilsson matches Corelli in vocal bite and gets inside the character, even if she is a touch unwieldy at times. As on stage, Bumbry is an imposing, spirited Amneris, Sereni makes an above-average Amonasro and Giaiotti sounds like Pinza as Ramfis – praise cannot be higher. Mehta conducts with a deal of dramatic verve. The recording is excellent in both cases.

Aida H

Maria Callas *sop* Aida; **Richard Tucker** *ten* Radames; **Fedora Barbieri** *mez* Amneris; **Tito Gobbi** *bar* Amonasro; **Giuseppe Modesti** *bass* Ramphis; **Nicola Zaccaria** *bass* King of Egypt; **Elvira Galassi** *sop* Priestess; **Franco Ricciardi** *ten* Messenger; **Chorus and Orchestra of La Scala, Milan / Tullio Serafin**

EMI Callas Edition mono ② CDS5 56316-2 (F) (144 minutes: ADD). Notes, text and translation included. Recorded 1955 OO

Aida, the daughter of the Ethiopian king, is a prisoner at the Egyptian court where she falls in love with Radames, an Egyptian captain of the guard; Amneris, the Egyptian princess, also loves him. The tensions between these characters are rivetingly portrayed and explored, and the gradual build-up to Aida's and Radames's union in death is paced with the sureness of a master composer.

Callas's Aida is an assumption of total understanding and conviction; the growth from a slave-girl torn between love for her homeland and Radames, to a woman whose feelings transcend life itself represents one of the greatest operatic undertakings ever committed to disc. Alongside her is Fedora Barbieri, an Amneris palpable in her agonised mixture of love and jealousy – proud yet human. Tucker's Radames is powerful and Gobbi's Amonasro quite superb – a portrayal of comparable understanding to stand alongside Callas's Aida.

Tullio Serafin is quite simply ideal, and though the recording cannot compete with modern versions (it was never, in fact, a model of clarity), nowhere can it dim the brilliance of the creations conjured up by this classic cast.

Additional recommendations

Aida

Price Aida **Vickers** Radames **Gorr** Amneris

Orchestra e coro del Teatro dell'Opera di Roma / Solti

Decca 417 416-2DH3 (152 minutes: ADD: 9/87) (F)

A set that's hard to resist for its great line-up of singers: Leontyne Price's performance really catches fire in Act 3. Solti's conducting, albeit exciting, is rather wilful, though.

Milanov Aida **Björling** Radames **Barbieri** Amneris H

Rome Opera Chorus and Orchestra / Perlea

RCA Victor mono GD86652 (149 minutes: ADD: 8/88) (M)

Notes, text and translation included

Zinka Milanov's, Jussi Björling's and Fedora Barbieri's performances are superb. Add Leonard Warren as a fiery Amonasro and Boris Christoff as an imperious Ramfis, and this recording has one of the most vocally distinguished casts ever assembled for this opera.

Caballé Aida **Domingo** Radames **Cossotto** Amneris

Chorus of the Royal Opera House, Covent Garden; New Philharmonia Orchestra; Trumpeters of the Royal Military School of Music, Kneller Hall / Muti

EMI ③ CDS5 56246-2 (148 minutes: ADD: 1/87R) (M)

Montserrat Caballé gives her most successful Verdi performance on record, full of those vocal subtleties and beauties that inform her best singing, while Riccardo Muti gives an impassioned and subjective account of the score.

Un ballo in maschera

Giuseppe di Stefano *ten* Riccardo; **Tito Gobbi** *bar* Renato; **Maria Callas** *sop* Amelia; **Fedora Barbieri** *mez* Ulrica; **Eugenia Ratti** *sop* Oscar; **Ezio Giordano** *bass* Silvano; **Silvio Maionica** *bass* Samuel; **Nicola Zaccaria** *bass* Tom; **Renato Ercolani** *bar* Judge; **Chorus and Orchestra of La Scala, Milan / Antonino Votto** H

EMI Callas Edition mono ② CDS5 56320-2 (F) (130 minutes: ADD). Notes, text and translation included. Recorded in 1956 OO

Ballo manages to encompass a vein of light-hearted frivolity (represented by the page, Oscar) within the confines of a serious drama of love, infidelity, noble and ignoble sentiments. None of the more recent recordings has quite caught the opera's true spirit so truly as this one under Votto's unerring direction. Callas has not been surpassed in delineating Amelia's conflict of feelings and loyalties, nor has di Stefano been equalled in the sheer ardour of his singing as Riccardo. Add to that no less a singer than Tito Gobbi as Renato, at first eloquent in his friendship to his ruler, then implacable in his revenge when he thinks Riccardo has stolen his wife. Fedora Barbieri is full of character as the soothsayer Ulrica, Eugenia Ratti a sparky Oscar. It is an unbeatable line-up.

Un ballo in maschera

Plácido Domingo *ten* Riccardo; **Piero Cappuccilli** *bar* Renato; **Martina Arroyo** *sop* Amelia; **Fiorenza Cossotto** *mez* Ulrica; **Reri Grist** *sop* Oscar; **Giorgio Giorgetti** *bass* Silvano; **Gwynne Howell** *bass* Samuel; **Richard Van Allan** *bass* Tom; **Kenneth Collins** *ten* Judge; **David Barrett** *bar* Servant; **Haberdashers' Aske's School Girls Choir; New Philharmonia Orchestra; Chorus of the Royal Opera House, Covent Garden / Riccardo Muti**

EMI CMS5 66510-2 (127 minutes: ADD) (M) Notes, text and translation included. Recorded 1975 O

This is the *Ballo* which, above all else, glories in Muti as an exuberant man of the theatre. The impetus with which he whips up the constituent parts of an ensemble into the vortex, and the juxtaposition of blasting *tutti* with slim, sweetly phrased woodwind detail, so typical of this opera, hits the ear more thrillingly than ever. So does the equally characteristic tugging undercurrent of the *ballo* against the intrigue of the *maschera*, activated by Muti with such acute perception and élan.

He provides pliant, springing support for all his singers too: Domingo, a warm, generous Riccardo, is every bit as happy with Muti as with Abbado. The same cannot be said of Martina Arroyo, the weak link on this recording. Dramatically forceful, but curiously cool and detached from the expressive nuancing of her part, she has little of the vulnerability of a Ricciarelli (Abbado), or the individuality of a Price (Solti). But, although this mid-price recording may not offer the most consistently luxurious vocal banquet, none the less, with Cossotto's stentorian Ulrica and Cappuccilli's staunch, resilient Renato, its strong sense of theatrical presence and its dramatic integrity will make it the chosen version for many new collectors.

Additional recommendation

Un ballo in maschera

Ricciarelli Amelia **Domingo** Riccardo **Bruson** Renato
Chorus and Orchestra of La Scala, Milan / Abbado
DG ② 453 148-2GTA2 (127 minutes: ADD) Ⓜ
Notes included

A wholly satisfying and unified performance, largely because Abbado and his La Scala forces give us a total sense of a theatrical experience. Ricciarelli and Domingo give involved and expressive performances.

Don Carlo

Plácido Domingo *ten* Don Carlo; **Montserrat Caballé** *sop* Elisabetta di Valois; **Shirley Verrett** *mez* Eboli; **Sherrill Milnes** *bar* Rodrigo; **Ruggero Raimondi** *bass* Filippo II; **Giovanni Foiani** *bass* Grand Inquisitor; **Simon Estes** *bass-bar* Monk; **Delia Wallis** *mez* Tebaldo; **Ryland Davies** *ten* Conte di Lerma; **John Noble** *bar* Herald; **Maria-Rosa del Campo** *sop* Voice from Heaven; **Ambrosian Opera Chorus; Royal Opera House Orchestra, Covent Garden / Carlo Maria Giulini**
EMI Great Recordings of the Century ③
CMS5 67401-2 (209 minutes: ADD) Ⓜ
Text and translation included. Recorded 1970 ●●●

From the day that Giulini conducted the now legendary production of *Don Carlo* at Covent Garden in 1958, a recording of the opera by him looked a must. In fact, it was to be 12 years before EMI took the plunge, but the set was worth waiting for: it's the five-act version in Italian, without the cuts made at the Royal Opera, and well recorded and handsomely cast. Giulini himself had slowed down since the live performances, but the blend of majesty and lyric beauty that he brings to the opera is hard to resist. The music glows warmly in his hands, as befits one of Verdi's most human dramas.

His cast gathers together five of the leading singers of the 1970s. In particular, the trio of Caballé, Domingo and Milnes seemed to be rather predictably the names on almost every Italian opera recording at the time, but how glad we would be to have young singers like them today. Caballé, though occasionally sounding blowsy, is exquisite whenever quiet singing is called for, and Domingo is at his golden best throughout. Their murmured farewells at the monastery of San Giusto in Act 5 have never been surpassed. Verrett is a fiery Eboli (although it is a shame Giulini did not give her more pace in 'O don fatale'), and Milnes provides generous-hearted singing as Rodrigo. It is good to have an Italian bass as Philip II, but Raimondi lacks the black tone and fearsome presence of his notable predecessor in the role, Boris Christoff. Lovers of the opera will want to investigate the four-act version under Santini and also the five-act version in French under Pappano, both on EMI (which has more or less cornered the market for this opera). Otherwise, 30 years on, Giulini's splendid performance is as satisfying as any, probably still the number one recommendation.

Don Carlos

Roberto Alagna *ten* Don Carlos; **Karita Mattila** *sop* Elisabeth; **Waltraud Meier** *mez* Eboli; **Thomas Hampson** *bar* Rodrigue; **José van Dam** *bass-bar* Philippe II; **Eric Halfvarson** *bass* Grand Inquisitor; **Csaba Airizer** *bass* Monk; **Anat Efraty** *sop* Thibault; **Scot Weir** *ten* Comte de Lerme, Herald; **Donna Brown** *sop* Voice from Heaven; **Chorus of the Théâtre du Châtelet; Orchestre de Paris / Antonio Pappano**
EMI ③ CDS5 56152-2 (206 minutes: DDD) Ⓕ
Notes, text and translation included.
Recorded live in 1996 ●●

This is an eloquent and inspiriting performance of Verdi's singular music-drama depicting private tragedy within public conflict, and a recording of the French version. With regard to the text, Pappano excludes the opening scene for the chorus at Fontainebleau, cut by the composer before the first night; he includes the important dress-changing scene at the start of Act 3 (which explains Carlos's ardour towards the 'wrong' woman), a snippet of the Elisabeth-Eboli duet in Act 4, and the whole of the Carlos-Philippe duet after Posa's death (the theme of which was reused in the *Requiem*). Pappano also chooses some of the alternative settings, notably in the Rodrigue-Philippe duet in Act 2 and the farewell encounter of Elisabeth and Carlos in Act 5, amendments that Verdi made for the neglected 1872 Naples revision. Neither seems an improvement.

Pappano's is a subtly shaped, superbly paced and vital interpretation from start to finish. He is as able to encompass the delicacies of the Veil song and the succeeding exchanges as he is to purvey the grand, tragic passion of Elisabeth and Carlos in Act 2, the intricacies and changes of feeling in the colloquy between Rodrigue and Philippe, the terrible menace of the Grand Inquisitor. The Orchestre de Paris supports him with playing of dedication and sensitivity. Giulini's noble conducting of the Italian version (reviewed above) comes to mind when listening to Pappano and his players. Praise cannot be higher.

By and large he has singers who can sustain his vision. Mattila sings a lovely Elisabeth. Her soft-grained yet strong tone and exquisite phrasing in all her solos and duets are balm to the ear. By Mattila's side Alagna offers an equally involving Carlos, presenting a more vulnerable picture of the unbalanced infante. His is a fully rounded portrayal that will please his many admirers, the difficult tessitura seldom troubling him and his French, of course, is impeccable. As Rodrigue, Marquis de Posa, Hampson also has idiomatic French. His mellifluous baritone well suits this French version and he provides many moments of vocal beauty. Arguably, the death needs a more imposing voice but the added decibels can easily be borne to appreciate Hampson's intelligence. Van Dam nicely balances the exterior authority and interior agony of Philippe, everywhere in command of line, language, phrase.

The recording catches the *frisson* of the theatrical experience. The positioning of the singers on stage never causes problems; everything is clear and in its place, and the balance with the pit sounds natural. This is a landmark in the *Don Carlos* discography.

Additional recommendation

Don Carlos

Domingo Don Carlos **Ricciarelli** Elisabeth de Valois **Nucci** Rodrigue **Chorus and Orchestra of La Scala, Milan / Abbado**

DG ④ 415 316-2GH4 (233 minutes: DDD: 12/85) Ⓕ

Notes, text and translation included

Abbado's trail-blazing account of the French *Don Carlos* has been underrated in some quarters. True, it has now been surpassed by Antonio Pappano's recording, but it is still worth consideration for those who want more of the work's alternative music (tracked separately).

Ernani

Mario Del Monaco *ten* Ernani; **Anita Cerquetti** *sop* Elvira; **Ettore Bastianini** *bar* Don Carlo; **Boris Christoff** *bass* De Silva; **Luciana Boni** *sop* Giovanna; **Athos Cesarini** *ten* Don Riccardo; **Aurelian Neagu** *bass* Jago; **Maggio Musicale Fiorentino Chorus and Orchestra / Dimitri Mitropoulos** Ⓗ

Bel Canto mono ② BCS5011 (118 minutes: ADD) Ⓜ

Notes included. Recorded live in 1957

This is a performance to delight Verdians, Florence seriously challenging its La Scala rival on EMI. The calibre and strength of the singing here reminds one how often today we put up with third-best. Each of the four principals not only has a voice of essential power but also has Verdian style as part of their interpretative make-up. Furthermore they are led by the legendary Mitropoulos, such a force for good at the Maggio Musicale until his untimely death. He easily encompasses the cut and thrust, the rudimentary fervour of one of Verdi's earliest successes, combining at once rude rhythms with lyrical breadth of phrase in supporting his admirable cast and firmly controlling the many ensembles, and his orchestra responds with eagerness to his positive beat.

Cerquetti, whose brief but distinguished career came to an abrupt end not long after this performance took place, had an evenly projected *spinto* soprano and used it with such command that she was at the time spoken of as Tebaldi's equal. She encompasses with confidence her taxing aria and cabaletta at the beginning of the work, and makes the most of what little the composer offers his soprano thereafter, shining particularly in the final trio, where Verdi is at his most inspired. As the eponymous hero, Del Monaco shows conclusively that he was more than the stentorian tenor he was often portrayed as being in his day, combining, in the lovers' brief moment of repose in Act 2, with Cerquetti's Elvira in a quietly reflective way. Of course, where the supposed bandit breathes fire, Del Monaco is there with the appropriately flashing tone that made him so popular.

Verdi gives his baritone, Don Carlo, the meatiest music. Bastianini, then at the height of his appreciable powers, sings all his solos with resplendent and keen tone. Although he doesn't provide all the subtleties of line and colour Bruson achieves for Muti, Bastianini touches a real note of eloquence at 'O sommo Carlo' in Act 3. As old Silva, Christoff is his imposing self, rivalling his younger Bulgarian colleague, Ghiaurov, on the version from La Scala: both are excellent, but Christoff makes more of the text.

Mitropoulos sanctions a few regrettable cuts not tolerated by Muti. In other respects there's little to choose between these two live performances. For its age the sound on this 'new' version is remarkably good and well worth investigating at mid-price.

Ernani

Plácido Domingo *ten* Ernani; **Mirella Freni** *sop* Elvira; **Renato Bruson** *bar* Don Carlo; **Nicolai Ghiaurov** *bass* Don Ruy, Gomez de Silva; **Jolanda Michieli** *sop* Giovanna; **Gianfranco Manganotti** *ten* Don Riccardo; **Alfredo Giacomotti** *bass* Iago; **Chorus and Orchestra of La Scala, Milan / Riccardo Muti**

EMI ③ CDS7 47083-8 (128 minutes: DDD) Ⓕ

Notes, text and translation included.

Recorded live in 1982

Renato Bruson's Don Carlo is an assumption that is as gripping dramatically as it is vocally. In his portrayal more than anywhere, the musical tension of *Ernani* becomes manifest, and everywhere Bruson offers superb Verdi singing. Domingo's Ernani is hardly less impressive and he benefits from being caught live on stage. His opening aria and cabaletta are full of delicate touches and obedience to the dynamic marks. In the last act, his recitative, 'Tutto ora tace d'intorno' has great pathos, and his contributions to the final trio an overwhelming eloquence. Here, too, Freni achieves most, the etching in of 'Il riso del tuo volto fa ch'io veda', a brief utterance of happiness, most affecting, and her desperate appeals to Silva for mercy sung with brio.

In her opening aria and cabaletta, the famous 'Ernani, Ernani', too much is asked of a voice not really meant by nature for this kind of heavy duty, but none can quite match the sorrow and heartbreak of Elvira's predicament that Freni manages in the theatre. Ghiaurov, rusty as his voice had become, creates a great impression of dignity and implacable strength, and many of those qualities are carried over into his singing. 'Infelice' is delivered with mature nobility, 'Ah, io l'amo' is intensely moving. Ghiaurov is denied Silva's probably spurious cabaletta. Otherwise the work is given complete.

Muti conducts the score in exemplary manner. He has learnt when to allow his singers licence to phrase with meaning and when to press on.

The La Scala chorus gives us the genuine sound of Italian voices in full flight, sounding much more inside their various assumptions than their rivals. The audience is occasionally in evidence, as are the on-stage effects, but the atmosphere of being in an opera house and taking part, as it were, in a real occasion has all the advantages over the aseptic feeling of a studio.

Falstaff

Tito Gobbi *bar* Falstaff; **Rolando Panerai** *bar* Ford; **Dame Elisabeth Schwarzkopf** *sop* Alice Ford; **Anna Moffo** *sop* Nannetta; **Luigi Alva** *ten* Fenton; **Fedora Barbieri** *mez* Mistress Quickly; **Nan Merriman** *mez* Meg Page; **Tomaso Spatoro** *ten* Dr Caius; **Renato Ercolani** *ten* Bardolph; **Nicola Zaccaria** *bass* Pistol; **Philharmonia Chorus and Orchestra / Herbert von Karajan** H
EMI Great Recordings of the Century
② CMS5 67083-2 (120 minutes: ADD). Notes, text and translation included. Recorded 1956 Ⓜ ●●●

This *Falstaff* still stands (with Toscanini) peerless in the catalogue. At its centre stands Tito Gobbi, and his is a presence large enough to encompass both the lord and the jester, the sensuous and the sensual, and the deep seriousness as well as the deep absurdity of his vision. Few Falstaffs have such a measure of the simplicity of his first monosyllables in the bustle around him; few find the poise as well as the confusion within his music. Karajan's recording is incomparable in its quartet of merry wives. Schwarzkopf's Alice radiates both the 'gioia nell'aria' and the 'gioia nel'cor' of Verdi's writing, Fedora Barbieri's redoubtable Mistress Quickly, with her stentorian cries of 'Povera donna!', puts other readings in the shade; Anna Moffo's Nannetta, perfectly matched in timbre and agility with Luigi Alva's Fenton, is a constant delight. It is, above all, their corporate presence which works at such a distinctively higher level. Rolando Panerai is a magnificent Ford; his 'E sogno? o realtà?' is a high point of the performance.

This 1956 recording has been discreetly and skilfully doctored, but a little background hiss does remain. But one doesn't actually end up hearing it. This great recording is a-flutter with pungent solo detail, realising, with Nannetta, that the world is 'tutto deliro, sospiro e riso'. The episodes of the opera, its exits and entrances, its subjects and counter-subjects, pass with the unique sensibility of Verdi's final great exuberant fugue of life.

Falstaff
Domenico Trimarchi *bar* Falstaff; **Roberto Servile** *bar* Ford; **Julia Faulkner** *sop* Alice Ford; **Dilbèr** *sop* Nannetta; **Maurizio Comencini** *ten* Fenton; **Anna Maria di Micco** *sop* Mistress Quickly; **Anna Bonitatibus** *mez* Meg Page; **Enrico Facini** *ten* Doctor Caius; **Alessandro Cosentino** *ten* Bardolph; **Franco de Grandis** *bass* Pistol; **Chorus and Orchestra of Hungarian State Opera / Will Humburg**
Naxos ② 8 660050/1 (120 minutes: DDD) Ⓢ
Notes and synopsis included. Recorded 1996

This set from Naxos does a good job in challenging the best in the field. Humburg, responsible for the well-liked *Barbiere* from the same stable, strikes just the right balance between the high spirits and the delicacy in Verdi's last and most miraculous score, and secures a sympathetic response from his singers and players. He has sensibly chosen a predominantly Italian cast for a work that depends, more than any other in Verdi, on pinpoint enunciation of the text, Boito's delightful refashioning of Shakespeare. Nobody is better at this than Trimarchi, a veteran of many stage performances and recordings of the comic roles in Italian opera, and a Falstaff of wit and resource. He, like the rest, adopts the conversational, intimate style needed, nowhere more so than in the interview with 'Fontana' where, in the *sotto voce* Verdi wants, he tells how Ford is about to be cuckolded. It is just one point in a reading full of ripe understanding, the characterisation nicely held between comedy and autumn melancholy. Another advantage is that his voice lies, as the role requires, ideally poised between baritone and bass. It is true that his vibrato has loosened, and when he places pressure on his tone it becomes unsteady – but that is true of a number of other interpreters on CD and hardly detracts from a lovable portrait all-round.

Servile, Humburg's expert Figaro, proves a formidable Ford: quick to anger, truly anguished in his monologue of jealousy, always secure in voice, adept with his words. Around their men are gathered a lively group of merry wives, most notably the lightly scheming, even-voiced, soul-of-the-party Alice of Julia Faulkner, whose Italian is so idiomatic that you would be hard-pressed to tell that she wasn't native-born, and the vocally smiling, irrepressible Quickly of di Micco, who sensibly avoids the exaggerations often imposed on the part but follows Verdi's markings to the letter. The Meg is more than adequate.

Although the Nannetta and Fenton sing well, they miss the ethereal beauty and steadiness of tone to be found elsewhere, but they, like the Caius, Bardolph and Pistol, enter into the spirit of a well-produced set that employs just enough devices to suggest a stage performance. The sound is sensibly balanced, although once or twice the voices seemed disconcertingly either closer or further away from the microphones. However, this is a *Falstaff* to savour and one that surely bears repetition.

Falstaff H
Giuseppe Valdengo *bar* Falstaff; **Frank Guarrera** *bar* Ford; **Herva Nelli** *sop* Alice Ford; **Teresa Stich-Randall** *sop* Nannetta; **Antonio Madasi** *ten* Fenton; **Cloe Elmo** *contr* Mistress Quickly; **Nan Merriman** *mez* Meg Page; **Gabor Carelli** *ten* Dr Caius; **John Carmen Rossi** *ten* Bardolph; **Norman Scott** *bass* Pistol; **Robert Shaw Chorale; NBC Symphony Orchestra / Arturo Toscanini**
RCA Gold Seal mono ② 74321 72372-2 (117 minutes: ADD). Notes, text and translation included. Recorded 1950 Ⓜ ●●●

This *Falstaff* remains, as it always has been, one of the half a dozen greatest opera sets ever recorded. It is a miracle in every respect. How Toscanini loved Verdi and how he strained every sinew to fulfil this amazing score's variety in line, feeling and colour. Whether it is the clarity and discipline of the ensembles, the extraordinary care taken over orchestral detail or the alert control of dynamics, Toscanini is supreme, yet nothing is done for effect's sake; everything seems natural, inevitable, unforced, as though the score was being created anew before us with chamber-music finesse – and the atmosphere of a live performance adds to the feeling of immediacy. Nobody dares, or seems to want to interrupt the magic being laid before them. Toscanini in his old age is matching the subtlety and vitality of the composer's own Indian summer – or one might be tempted to say spring, so delicate and effervescent does the scoring sound.

If, vocally, the main glory is the wonderful sense of ensemble gained through hours of hard rehearsals, individual contributions are almost all rewarding. Indeed, Valdengo's Falstaff, under Toscanini's tutelage, has not been surpassed on disc even by Gobbi. Flexibility, charm, exactness, refinement inform his beautifully and wisely sung portrayal. He is no less pointed and subtle in his encounter with Frank Guarrera's imposing Ford. Another great joy of the set is the women's ensemble, their contribution the very epitome of smiling chatter. The Alice, Meg and Nannetta (Stich-Randall – none better), all sound, as they were, fresh and youthful. Herva Nelli is a lively and delightful Alice and Cloe Elmo's Quickly is as rich and ripe of voice and diction as any on disc, though a trifle coarse at times. The Fenton is sweet and Italianate in tone, but not as stylish as others. The smaller roles are all very much part of the team.

This set should certainly be a source of delightful revelation to a new generation of collectors who may have a wrong-headed view of what Toscanini was about. The remastering gives it clearer, more immediate sound than ever heard before from the originals.

La forza del destino

La forza del destino (1869 version)
Martina Arroyo *sop* Leonora; **Carlo Bergonzi** *ten* Don Alvaro; **Piero Cappuccilli** *bar* Don Carlos; **Ruggero Raimondi** *bass* Padre Guardiano; **Biancamaria Casoni** *mez* Preziosilla; **Sir Geraint Evans** *bar* Melitone; **Antonio Zerbini** *bass* Marchese; **Florindo Andreolli** *ten* Trabuco; **Mila Cova** *mez* Curra; **Virgilio Carbonari** *ten* Mayor; **Derek Hammond-Stroud** *bar* Surgeon; **Ambrosian Opera Chorus; Royal Philharmonic Orchestra / Lamberto Gardelli**
EMI Opera ③ CMS5 67124-2 (168 minutes: ADD) Ⓜ
Notes, text and translation included. Recorded 1969 ●

This wonderfully multifarious opera demands an array of principal singers who need to be skilled in an unusually wide range of vocal and dramatic skills. It is a 'chase' opera in which Carlos pursues Alvaro and Leonora through two countries, through cloister and convent, through scenes popular and martial, all treated on the most expansive scale. It is dominated by its series of magnificent duets that are composed so that the music marches with the development of situation and character.

Gardelli's reissue is an excellent mid-price buy. It features Bergonzi, that prince among Verdi tenors, as an exemplary and appealing Alvaro, and Piero Cappuccilli – like Bergonzi at the peak of his powers when this set was made – as a full-blooded and Italianate Carlos. In the three all-important duets, their voices blend ideally. Leonora was the most successful of Arroyo's recorded roles, and she sings here with a feeling and urgency appropriate to Leonora's desperate situation. Casoni's vital Preziosilla, Raimondi's grave but over-lugubrious Padre Guardiano and Sir Geraint's keenly characterised Melitone all complete a well-chosen cast. Over all presides Gardelli, a Verdi conductor with an instinctive feeling for the ebb and flow of his music.

La forza del destino (1862 version)
Galina Gorchakova *sop* Leonora; **Gegam Grigorian** *ten* Don Alvaro; **Nikolai Putilin** *bar* Don Carlos; **Mikhail Kit** *bass* Padre Guardiano; **Olga Borodina** *mez* Preziosilla; **Georgy Zastavny** *bar* Melitone; **Askar Abdrazakov** *bass* Marchese; **Nikolai Gassiev** *ten* Trabuco; **Lia Shevtzova** *mez* Curra; **Gennadi Bezzubenkov** *bass* Mayor; **Yuri Laptev** *ten* Surgeon; **Kirov Theatre Chorus and Orchestra / Valery Gergiev**
Philips ③ 446 951-2PH3 (158 minutes: DDD) Ⓕ
Notes, text and translation included. Recorded 1995

It is appropriate that the first recording of the first version of *Forza* should come from St Petersburg, where the work had its première in 1862. By and large the artists fare splendidly, four of the five principals enjoying the weight of voice and command of the appropriate style to make their roles tell. Gorchakova evinces the weight of voice, also the broad sweep of tone and line, that her solos demand. Added to that there is a feeling for dramatic situation. 'Pace, pace', for instance is suitably filled with foreboding, the lustrous, dark timbre recalling that of Ponselle – and there can be no higher praise. Just once or twice, at the top, the voice becomes a shade strident, and ideally one wants more pointed articulation of the text but it is an interpretation of formidable achievement.

Grigorian is an exciting Alvaro; no other tenor today, and few in the past, could fulfil the demands of the part as easily as he does: the confident *spinto* thrust in the voice is just right. He effortlessly rises to the generosity of phrase the role calls for and fills the many elegiac phrases with the feeling of melancholy they need. Only Bergonzi for Gardelli surpasses him by virtue of more idiomatic Italian and a finer line, but the superiority is slight and Bergonzi doesn't have to contend with the added music of 1862.

Grigorian finds a worthy adversary in Putilin's Carlos. Putilin need fear no comparisons even with the admirable Cappuccilli for Gardelli. Although, like his predecessors and coevals in the role, he is shy of following Verdi's dynamic markings, in other respects his refulgent baritone is just the instrument for Carlos and he breathes the right fire in his implacable hatred of his imagined enemy Alvaro. Borodina easily encompasses the high-lying (for a mezzo) demands of Preziosilla and sounds the right seductive and martial notes for her role.

The one disappointment is the singing of the veteran Kit, who sounds grey and woolly, with no real centre to his tone. As the humorous element in Verdi's mix, Zastavny seems at first a shade faceless, but as his part progresses, one begins to admire the fact that it is being sung truly, not guyed, which makes his sermon seem a proper successor to the monologues of Rigoletto and Macbeth, albeit in a comic vein. The minor parts are well done. Excellent recording.

La forza del destino **H**

Stella Roman *sop* Leonora; **Frederick Jagel** *ten* Don Alvaro; **Lawrence Tibbett** *bar* Don Carlos; **Ezio Pinza** *bass* Padre Guardiano; **Irra Petina** *mez* Preziosilla; **Salvatore Baccaloni** *bass* Melitone; **Louis d'Angelo** *bar* Marquese; **Thelma Votipka** *mez* Curra; **Alessio de Paolis** *ten* Trabuco; **Lorenzo Alvary** *bass* Mayor; **John Gurney** *bass* Surgeon; **Metropolitan Opera Chorus and Orchestra, New York / Bruno Walter**

Naxos Historical mono ③ 8 110038/40 Ⓢ

(168 minutes: AAD). Recorded live in 1943

There has never been quite so electrifying a *Forza* as Walter's vital, brilliantly executed reading, which encapsulates the essence of the forthcoming drama. It confirms what few may know today, that Walter was a superb interpreter of Verdi. Yet this was the first time he had conducted *Forza*, so his lithe, finely honed reading is all the more remarkable. The other revelation is the Leonora of Stella Roman, a greatly underrated soprano brought to the Met in 1941, who yields few points to such notable interpreters of the part as Ponselle, Milanov and Tebaldi. They apart, you would go far to hear a Leonora so well equipped for the role, and so committed to it, one who uses her warm, generous voice to unerring effect in projecting the woman's dire predicament.

Padre Guardiano appears in the guise of Pinza, none better, and sounding, one uncertain high E apart, secure, concerned and authoritative. Jagel as Don Alvaro passes easily the test of the taxing aria of sad recollection at the start of Act 3. Tibbett as Don Carlos compels attention at every entry with his distinctive timbre and faultless style, but truth to tell the glorious tone had dulled since his great days in the 1930s and at times he sounds stretched by the part. Both his arias suffer cuts. Carlos's second (of three) duets with Alvaro is also excised as was then the custom, and *strettas* throughout are foreshortened. Baccaloni enjoys himself hugely as Melitone and obviously relishes his encounters with his superior, the Padre Guardiano, the two Italians revelling in the text. Petina is a lively but lightweight Preziosilla.

The sound is a bit crackly and restricted but good enough to enjoy an absorbing account of the score. It is strange that Naxos did not see fit to exclude the Spanish introductions to the broadcast. This vivid version has much to commend it at the price.

Additional recommendations

La forza del destino

Price Leonora **Domingo** Don Alvaro **Milnes** Don Carlo **John Alldis Choir; London Symphony Orchestra / Levine**

RCA ③ 74321 39502-2 (171 minutes: DDD: 10/87). Ⓜ

Notes, text and translation included

A well-cast set and a strong recommendation. Leontyne Price followers will be no doubt tempted, but note she is past her prime here. The recording is uncut.

Callas Leonora **Tucker** Don Alvaro **Tagliabue** Don Carlo **Chorus and Orchestra of La Scala, Milan / Serafin**

EMI ③ CDS5 56323-2 (164 minutes: ADD: 10/87). Ⓕ

Notes, text and translation included

Callas is superb as Leonora and, Tagliabue aside, the rest of the cast turn in fine performances. Conductor Tullio Serafin does, however, make some cuts in the score.

I Lombardi alla prima crociata

June Anderson *sop* Giselda; **Luciano Pavarotti** *ten* Oronte; **Samuel Ramey** *bass* Pagano; **Richard Leech** *ten* Arvino; **Ildebrando d'Arcangelo** *bass* Pirro; **Yanni Yannissis** *bass* Acciano; **Jane Shaulis** *mez* Sofia; **Anthony Dean Griffey** *ten* Prior; **Patricia Racette** *mez* Viclinda; **Chorus and Orchestra of the Metropolitan Opera, New York / James Levine**

Decca ② 455 287-2DHO2 (129 minutes: DDD) Ⓕ

Notes, text and translation included

Recorded 1996

Pavarotti appeared in the Metropolitan Opera production of *I Lombardi* in 1993 and this recording is the delayed result. He is in good voice and sings Oronte's aria with fine *legato*, binding the decorative turns of the cabaletta beautifully into the vocal line and throwing in a respectable top C to show us he still can.

I Lombardi is a viscerally exciting opera. The first complete recording, conducted by Lamberto Gardelli (Philips), set a good benchmark in 1972, but that need not deter us from welcoming this lively newcomer. The Met Opera Orchestra plays with splendid precision and, as Turks and Crusaders, women of the harem and virgins, the Met Chorus has a high old time on both sides of *I Lombardi*'s war-zone. Levine himself has improved beyond recognition as a Verdian; this studio recording is well paced and has a good sense of theatre. Everything is swift and crisp on the surface.

The best role goes to the soprano Giselda, specially tailored for the delicate skills of Erminia Frezzolini. Among the current crop of Verdi sopranos, June Anderson is probably as plausible a modern Frezzolini as any. There is some lovely, pure-toned singing in her big scene at the end of Act 2 and her coloratura is shining bright, both in this cabaletta and later in 'In fondo all'alma'. Samuel Ramey makes a relatively lightweight Pagano, who alone decorates his second verses. In the second tenor role Richard Leech holds his own, although his voice does not take well to the microphone. Ildebrando d'Arcangelo proudly represents the younger generation of Italian singers in the small role of Pirro, and Patricia Racette sings brightly as Viclinda.

Gardelli's crusading first recording has a rough Italianate vigour that lovers of early Verdi will enjoy, but Levine and his forces more than hold their ground with pace and brilliance, and a bright, modern recording with on balance a better cast and the voices well forward.

Luisa Miller

Montserrat Caballé *sop* Luisa; **Luciano Pavarotti** *ten* Rodolfo; **Sherrill Milnes** *bar* Miller; **Bonaldo Gaiotti** *bass* Count Walter; **Anna Reynolds** *mez* Federica; **Richard van Allan** *bass* Wurm; **Annette Céline** *mez* Laura; **Fernando Pavarotti** *ten* Peasant; **London Opera Chorus; National Philharmonic Orchestra / Peter Maag**

Decca ② 417 420-2DH2 (144 minutes: ADD). Notes, text and translation included. Recorded 1970s Ⓕ ●

This transitional work shows Verdi enhancing his skills and refining his musical style. The plot, based on a Schiller drama, involves the tragedy and death of Luisa and her beloved Rodolfo brought about by the evil Wurm, apt predecessor of Verdi's Iago. The title-role could not find a more appealing interpreter than Caballé, who spins a fine line and is highly responsive to Luisa's sad situation. She is partnered by Pavarotti at the height of his powers as Rodolfo. He excels in 'Quando le sere al polacido', the work's most famous aria. As Luisa's equivocal father, Miller, Milnes gives one of his best performances on disc and van Allan is a properly snarling Wurm.

Maag, an underrated conductor, directs a strong, well-proportioned performance. He gives the impression of being in love with this opera and he goes right to the heart of the score, finding its seriousness as well as its fire. The last act is specially fine, containing what are regarded as among the gramophone classics, the two duets of Luisa, first with her father, then with Rodolfo. The production is unobtrusively effective in creation of atmosphere and is spaciously recorded.

Additional recommendation

Luisa Miller

Ricciarelli Luisa **Domingo** Rodolfo

Chorus and Orchestra of the Royal Opera House, Covent Garden / Maazel

DG ② 459 481-2GTA2 (133 minutes: ADD: 5/88R) Ⓜ

Notes, text and translation included

Finely sung performances, and a close rival to Decca's set, though compared with Maag, Lorin Maazel is a mere businessman in his handling of the score.

Macbeth

Piero Cappuccilli *bar* Macbeth; **Shirley Verrett** *mez* Lady Macbeth; **Nicolai Ghiaurov** *bass* Banquo; **Plácido Domingo** *ten* Macduff; **Antonio Savastano** *ten* Malcolm; **Carlo Zardo** *bass* Doctor; **Giovanni Foiani** *bass* Servant; **Sergio Fontana** *bass* Herald; **Alfredo Mariotti** *bass* Assassin; **Stefania Malagú** *mez* Lady-in-waiting; **Chorus and Orchestra of La Scala, Milan / Claudio Abbado**

DG The Originals ② 449 732-2GOR2 (154 minutes: ADD) Notes, text and translation included. Recorded 1976 Ⓜ ●

Verdi's lifelong admiration for Shakespeare resulted in only three operas based on his plays. *Macbeth*, the first, originally written in 1847, was extensively revised in 1865. Without losing the direct force of the original, Verdi added greater depth to his first ideas. Once derided as being un-Shakespearian, it is now recognised as a masterpiece for its psychological penetration as much as for its subtle melodic inspiration.

Abbado captures perfectly the atmosphere of dark deeds and personal ambition leading to tragedy, projected by Verdi, and his reading holds the opera's disparate elements in the score under firm control, catching its interior tensions. He is well supported by his Scala forces. Shirley Verrett may not be ideally incisive or Italianate in accent as Lady Macbeth, but she peers into the character's soul most convincingly. As ever, truly inspired by Abbado, Cappuccilli is a suitably haunted and introverted Macbeth who sings a secure and unwavering *legato*. Domingo's upright Macduff and Ghiaurov's doom-laden Banquo are both admirable in their respective roles.

Additional recommendation

Macbeth

Mascherini Macbeth **Callas** Lady Macbeth **Tajo** Banquo **Chorus and Orchestra of La Scala, Milan / de Sabata**

EMI mono ② CMS5 66447-2 (139 minutes: ADD: 1/94) Ⓜ

Notes, text and translation included. Live recording

Callas's portrayal of Lady Macbeth is definitive and Victor de Sabata's conducting is electrifying. However, the rest of the cast are not up to much, and the recorded sound is poor. A set for Callas fans only perhaps.

Nabucco

Tito Gobbi *bar* Nabucco; **Bruno Prevedi** *ten* Ismaele; **Carlo Cava** *bass* Zaccaria; **Elena Suliotis** *sop* Abigaille; **Dora Carral** *sop* Fenena; **Anna d'Auria** *sop* Anna; **Giovanni Foiani** *bass* High Priest of Baal; **Walter Krautler** *ten* Abdallo

Vienna Opera Orchestra; Vienna State Opera Chorus / Lamberto Gardelli

Decca ② 417 407-2DH2 (121 minutes: ADD) Notes, text and translation included. Recorded 1965. Ⓕ ●

The years have hardly lessened the excitement of listening to this vigorous, closely-knit performance. One realises why we were all amazed by Suliotis's account of the role of Abigaille. Her singing seizes you by the throat through its raw depiction of malice and through its youthful, uninhibited power. With the benefit of hindsight one can hear how a voice treated so carelessly and unstintingly could not last long, and so it was to be; but we should be glad for the brightness of the meteor while it flashed all too briefly through the operatic firmament. As an interpretation, her Abigaille seems a little coarse set beside the refinements shown by Scotto for Muti on EMI. However, Suliotis can manage by nature what Scotto has to conjure up by art, and she is certainly a subtler artist than Dimitrova on the wayward Sinopoli/DG version.

Gobbi, nearing the end of his illustrious career in 1965, remains the most convincing interpreter on record of the crazed king. The voice may have become a shade hard and uningratiating, but his use of Italian and his colouring of his tone, finally his pathos, are certainly not rivalled by Cappuccilli (Sinopoli). Carlo Cava exudes impacable fury as old Zaccaria, but he is inclined to go through his tone at *forte*. Prevedi is more than adequate as Ismaele, Carral less than adequate as Fenena (here DG score with Valentini Terrani).

One of the main assets of the Decca remains Gardelli's prompt, unfussy, and yet thrillingly delivered interpretation, clearly conveyed to his excellent Viennese forces. It is much more steadily and convincingly paced than Sinopoli's reading. The recording is forward and has plenty of presence, but it now sounds a little boxy beside the greater spaciousness of the DG. But the panache of the Decca enterprise silences criticism (except when the minute cuts in Nabucco's part are conceived). It is a pleasure to hear the bold inspiration of Verdi's first triumph conveyed with such conviction. Listen to the Act 1 finale and you are sure to be won over to the set as an entity.

Otello

Plácido Domingo *ten* Otello; **Cheryl Studer** *sop* Desdemona; **Sergei Leiferkus** *bar* Iago; **Ramon Vargas** *ten* Cassio; **Michael Schade** *ten* Roderigo; **Denyce Graves** *mez* Emilia; **Ildebrando d'Arcangelo** *bass* Lodovico; **Giacomo Prestia** *bass* Montano; **Philippe Duminy** *bass* Herald; **Hauts-de-Seine Maîtrise; Chorus and Orchestra of the Opéra-Bastille, Paris / Myung-Whun Chung**
DG ② 439 805-2GH2 (132 minutes: DDD) Ⓕ
Notes, text and translation included
Recorded 1993 ●●

Just as *Othello* is a difficult play to bring off in the theatre, so *Otello* is a difficult opera to bring off out of it. For some years now, Domingo has been, on stage, the greatest Otello of our age. On record, though, he has had less success. Leiferkus and Domingo have worked closely together in the theatre; and it shows in scene after scene – nowhere more so than in the crucial sequence in Act 2 where Otello so rapidly ingests Iago's lethal poison. By bringing into the recording studio the feel and experience of a stage performance – meticulous study subtly modified by the improvised charge of the moment – both singers help defy the jinx that so often afflicts *Otello* on record. The skill of Leiferkus's performance is rooted in voice and technique: clear diction, a very disciplined rhythmic sense and a mastery of all ornament down to the most mordant of mordents. Above all, he is always *there* (usually stage right in this recording), steely-voiced, rabbiting on obsessively. We even hear his crucial interventions in the great Act 3 *concertato*.

Domingo is in superb voice; the sound seems golden as never before. Yet at the same time, it is a voice that is being more astutely deployed. To take that cruellest of all challenges to a studio-bound Otello, the great Act 3 soliloquy 'Dio! mi potevi', Domingo's performance is now simpler, more inward, more intense. It helps that his voice has darkened, winning back some of its russet baritonal colourings.

Chung's conducting is almost disarmingly vital. Verdi's scoring is more Gallic than Germanic. The score sounds very brilliant in the hands of the excellent Opéra-Bastille orchestra, and, in Act 4, very beautiful. Maybe Chung is wary of the emotional depths and, occasionally, the rhythmic infrastructure is muddled and unclear. And yet, the freshness is all gain. He is already a master of the big ensemble and the line of an act. Tension rarely slackens. On the rare occasions when it does, the mixing and matching of takes is probably to blame.

Studer's is a carefully drawn portrait of a chaste and sober-suited lady. Perhaps Verdi had a sweeter-voiced singer in mind for this paragon of 'goodness, resignation, and self-sacrifice' (Verdi's words, not Shakespeare's). Studer's oboe tones keep us at a certain distance, yet you will look in vain for a better Desdemona. What's more, Studer is a singer who can single-mindedly focus the drama afresh, as she does more than once in Act 3. DG's recording is clear and unfussy and satisfyingly varied; Studer, in particular, is much helped by the beautifully open acoustic the engineers provide for the closing act. This is undoubtedly the best *Otello* on record since the early 1960s. It also happens to be the first time on disc that a great Otello at the height of his powers has been successfully caught in the context of a recording that can itself be generally considered worthy of the event, musically and technically.

Otello Ⓗ
Ramon Vinay *ten* Otello; **Herva Nelli** *sop* Desdemona; **Giuseppe Valdengo** *bar* Iago; **Virginio Assandri** *ten* Cassio; **Leslie Chabay** *ten* Roderigo; **Nan Merriman** *mez* Emilia; **Nicola Moscona** *bass* Lodovico; **Arthur Newman** *bass* Montano; **NBC Chorus and Symphony Orchestra / Arturo Toscanini**
RCA Gold Seal mono ② GD60302 Ⓜ
(125 minutes: ADD). Recorded 1947 ●●●

One of the century's legendary achievements on record confirms its reputation on this well-managed reissue. Here Toscanini's blazing intensity, his full comprehension of every facet of the score are evident throughout. The attack and dedication of chorus and orchestra are apparent throughout; so is the discipline and textural clarity on all sides. The sound remains dry, but somehow this very close, confined quality accords with the work's own claustrophobic quality – if only Otello had gone out into the open air and thought about the reality of the evidence before him, he might not have been so easily caught up in Iago's web of deceit.

Valdengo's Iago continues to put others in the shade. His light, almost elegant and seemingly cheerful tone, his mordant, sinister delivery of the *Credo*, his insinuating and perfectly accurate delivery of the imagined Dream all tell of his willingness to follow Toscanini's guidance, for he never sang so well for anyone else. This is a faultless performance. So, in terms of interpretation, is Vinay's Otello – the tormented, fearsomely commanding Moor to the life. Nelli's sincerity of purpose, her accuracy and her true tone compensate for a slightly pallid reading of Desdemona's thoughts and feelings. The smaller roles are all worthily taken. Any incidental drawback should not prevent anyone hearing this overwhelming interpretation. Toscanini identifies so sympathetically with the human condition, as did Verdi himself – and it is from Verdi, at whose feet he sat, that Toscanini learnt his trade.

Otello

Giuseppe Giacomini *ten* Otello; **Dame Margaret Price** *sop* Desdemona; **Matteo Manuguerra** *bar* Iago; **Dino di Domenico** *ten* Cassio; **Alain Gabriel** *ten* Roderigo; **Martine Mahé** *mez* Emilia; **Luigi Roni** *bass* Lodovico; **Vincent le Texier** *bass-bar* Montano; **Anton Kúrňava** *bass* Herald; **Slovak Philharmonic Chorus; Les Petits Chanteurs de Bordeaux; Orchestre National de Bordeaux Aquitaine / Alain Lombard**

Forlane ② UCD216774 (128 minutes: DDD) Ⓕ

Notes, text and translation included

Recorded live in 1991

On the evidence of this *Otello*, and much else, Giacomini is more viscerally exciting than any of the famous Three. Certainly no tenor in this role since Del Monaco in his prime had the elemental, almost frightening power evinced by Giacomini's reading, but his talents go well beyond the possession of a real *tenore robusto*. His dark, louring tone and agonised delivery of the text exactly match the passion and jealousy of the Moor, alternately achingly sorrowful as he imagines his wife's infidelities, and fierily tormented as he rants and raves at her supposed wrongdoing. There is much to study in this searing interpretation, which is on a par with Vinay's for Toscanini and sung in the same dark-grained, tormented fashion.

Giacomini's overwhelming portrayal is worthily supported. Dame Margaret Price provides rounded, cleanly produced tone, even if there are a few signs of wear, and her interpretation – in response to a real occasion – is emotionally compelling. In the Act 3 duet, she brings to the passage beginning 'Mi guarda!' and the line 'E son io l'innocente' the depth of Desdemona's heart-stricken soul as she tries to defend herself against Otello's accusations, and her Act 4 scene is shaped and executed with the expected sense of impending doom.

Matteo Manuguerra, an experienced and sympathetic Verdian, was already in his mid-sixties when this performance took place and there are times when his voice has to be husbanded, but he shows much intelligence in portraying the subtlety of Iago's evil. The smaller roles are decently if not exceptionally cast.

Alain Lombard keeps the performance consistently on the boil. He handles the public scenes, most notably the Act 3 ensemble (given uncut), with the urgency and large scale they call for. His chorus and orchestra, while not quite in the highest class, perform with keen awareness of the score's pithy quality. This set may not entirely challenge the hegemony of the 1947 Toscanini and Serafin sets, but it is histrionically exciting, largely because of the live ambience (the audience is remarkably quiet, clapping only at the end of acts) and there is a straightforward honesty about it that has eluded more glamorous recordings. Stage noise is seldom in evidence. The recording is at times over-resonant, but catches the excitement of the occasion. With Giacomini giving such an authentically vivid account of the title-role, most Verdians will want to own this set.

Additional recommendations

Otello

Domingo Otello **Scotto** Desdemona **Milnes** Iago **National Philharmonic Orchestra; Ambrosian Opera Chorus / Levine**

RCA ② 74321 39501-2 (134 minutes: ADD: 3/86R) Ⓜ

For some this is the finest of Plácido Domingo's several recorded portrayals of Otello. Also, Renata Scotto's Desdemona is one of the most moving on disc. At mid price this set is a real winner.

Vickers Otello **Rysanek** Desdemona **Gobbi** Iago **Rome Opera Chorus and Orchestra / Serafin**

RCA ② 09026 63180-2 (144 minutes: ADD: 11/88R) Ⓜ

Tito Gobbi's Iago remains irreplaceable (except possibly for Giuseppe Valdengo's for Toscanini), and Jon Vickers is a superb Otello, more metallic and heroic than Plácido Domingo's though not necessarily more sensitive.

Rigoletto

Leonard Warren *bar* Rigoletto; **Bidù Sayão** *sop* Gilda; **Jussi Björling** *ten* Duke; **Norman Cordon** *bass* Sparafucile; **Martha Lipton** *contr* Maddalena; **William Hargrave** *bass* Monterone; **Thelma Altman** *sop* Giovanna; **Richard Manning** *ten* Borsa; **George Cehanovsky** *bar* Marullo; **Maxine Stellman** *mez* Countess Ceprano; **John Baker** *bass* Count Ceprano; **Metropolitan Opera Chorus and Orchestra, New York / Cesare Sodero**

Naxos Historical ② 8 110051/2 (116 minutes: ADD) Ⓢ

Recorded live in 1945

This performance marked the return of Björling to the Met after a wartime break of four years spent mostly in his native Sweden. And what a return it was: at 34 he was at the absolute peak of his powers and sings a Duke of Mantua imbued with supreme confidence and tremendous brio – just try the start of the Quartet. He and the house clearly revel in his display of tenor strength, yet that power is always tempered by innate artistry. If not a subtle interpreter, he is always a thoughtful one, and never indulges himself or his audience.

Similarly, Warren was, at the time, at the zenith of his career. Vocally he is in total command of the role and the house. His reading, although slightly extroverted in some areas, evinces a firm tone, a secure line and many shades of colour. He is at his very best in his two duets with Gilda (sadly and heinously cut about) and no wonder, given the beautiful, plangent singing of Sayão, whose 'Care nome' is so delicately phrased, touching and keenly articulated. 'Tutte le feste' is still better, prompting Paul Jackson (who in general is unjustifiably hard on the performance in *Saturday Afternoons at the old Met*, Duckworth: 1992) to comment that Sayão's 'lovely, pliant, fully rounded tones are immediately affecting'. Indeed, in spite of the merits of the two male principals, it is her truly memorable interpretation that makes this set essential listening.

All round, there are few recordings that match this one for vocal distinction – perhaps only the Serafin-Callas-Gobbi on EMI and the Giulini-Cotrubas-Cappuccilli on DG. They are much more expensive but, of course, boast superior sound (there are moments of distortion here, though not too many). Björling and Warren both made later studio sets, but neither matches his live contribution here, off the stage.

The final virtue of this absorbing experience is the conducting of the little-known Sodero. His moderate – but never sluggish – tempos allow for almost ideal articulation on all sides, and his insistence on letting us hear the score so clearly makes one regret even more all those excisions then common in the opera house and the studios. This is a set worth £10 or so of any Verdian's money.

Rigoletto

Tito Gobbi *bar* Rigoletto; **Maria Callas** *sop* Gilda; **Giuseppe di Stefano** *ten* Duke; **Nicola Zaccaria** *bass* Sparafucile; **Adriana Lazzarini** *mez* Maddalena; **Plinio Clabassi** *bass* Monterone; **Giuse Gerbino** *mez* Giovanna; **Renato Ercolani** *ten* Borsa; **William Dickie** *bar* Marullo; **Elvira Galassi** *sop* Countess Ceprano; **Carlo Forti** *bar* Count Ceprano; **Chorus and Orchestra of La Scala, Milan / Tullio Serafin** H

EMI mono ② CDS5 56327-2 (118 minutes: ADD) Ⓕ

Notes, text and translation included

Recorded 1955 **oo**

That one recording should continue to hold sway over many other attractive comers after 45 years is simply a tribute to Callas, Gobbi, Serafin and Walter Legge. Whatever the merits of its successors, and they are many, no *Rigoletto* has surpassed Gobbi in tonal variety, line, projection of character and understanding of what Rigoletto is about; no Gilda has come anywhere near Callas in meaningful phrasing – listen to 'Caro nome' or 'Tutte le feste' on any other set if you are disbelieving – nor achieved such a careful differentiation of timbre before and after her seduction; no conductor matches Serafin in judging tempo and instrumental detail on a nicety; nor benefited from a chorus and orchestra bred in the tradition of La Scala; no producer has equalled Legge in recording voices rather than the space round them. And di Stefano? Well, he may not be so stylish a Duke as some others, but the 'face' he gives his singing, and the sheer physical presence he conveys, not to mention his forward diction, are also unique in this opera.

Nothing in this world is perfect, and so there are some small drawbacks here. Serafin sadly makes small cuts in the first Gilda-Rigoletto duet and omits entirely the Duke's cabaletta as used to be practice in the theatre. Gobbi could be said not to have quite the weight of voice ideally called for by a Verdi baritone role. Finally, the recording, although immeasurably improved from previous issues of the set, still has one or two places of distortion obviously present on the original tape. In every other way, this remains the classic performance on record, and one that should be on the shelf of every self-respecting Verdi collector.

Rigoletto

Renato Bruson *bar* Rigoletto; **Andrea Rost** *sop* Gilda; **Roberto Alagna** *ten* Duke; **Dimitri Kavrakos** *bass* Sparafucile; **Mariana Pentcheva** *contr* Maddalena; **Giorgio Giuseppini** *bass* Monterone; **Antonella Trevisan** *mez* Giovanna; **Ernesto Gavazzi** *ten* Borsa; **Silvestro Sammaritano** *bass* Marullo; **Nicoletta Zanini** *mez* Countess Ceprano; **Antonio de Gobbi** *bass* Count Ceprano; **Marilena Laurenza** *sop* Page; **Ernesto Panariello** *bass* Usher; **Chorus and Orchestra of La Scala, Milan / Riccardo Muti**

Sony Classical ② S2K66314 (121 minutes: DDD) Ⓕ

Notes, text and translation included

Recorded live in 1994

You immediately feel that added *frisson* of a 'real' occasion in this live recording, and that continues throughout a well-prepared and well-integrated performance, with applause restricted to ends of acts, and virtually no audience noise. As for Muti's interpretation, it is rewardingly vital, rhythmically speaking. Every moment is acutely and alertly sprung with speeds tending to be on the brisk side. It is a pleasure to hear how Muti observes the importance Verdi gives to oboe, clarinet and bassoon, how profitably he makes all his singers observe to the letter what Verdi wrote.

Ah, Roberto Alagna! Many will want this set for his participation alone. Listen to the Duke's aria and cabaletta at the start of Act 3 and you will hear this young tenor's tone perfectly suited and his phrasing immaculately turned. Both in 'La donna è mobile' and the opening of the Quartet one might like a shade more variation in dynamics and tonal colour, but then Alagna has the sappy, brilliant voice and, above all, the *slancio* the part demands, and his singing reflects the Duke's wilful, libidinous nature. His is a most attractive contribution to the set. At the end of the Duke-Gilda duet, Muti demands and gets the full cadenza written into the score. It is finely turned by Alagna, and by Rost, who offers an altogether lovely performance, ideal in almost every respect. With just the right weight of voice for the role, all her singing is full-toned and precisely articulated, and the tone itself is vibrant and tangy. Rost hasn't the specifically Italian sound but she is an accomplished technician, and dies heart-rendingly.

The years have been kind to Bruson's voice (he was 58 when this recording was made), but it has to be said that, especially in the first half of the opera, the vibrato is now disturbing when the tone comes under pressure. Perhaps because he is afraid he cannot sustain a line at a lower dynamic level, he seems unwilling to sing at less than *mezzo-forte*. His remains a considered, eloquent interpretation through which courses a father's concern and anguish. Only Gobbi for Serafin provides a range of colour and shades of meaning beyond all his rivals. Kavrakos is a suitably sturdy, dour Sparafucile. After a blowzy start Pentcheva proves a seductive-sounding Maddalena. Alagna's superbly vital Duke and Rost's greatly appealing Gilda may well sway you in favour of this set. However, as engineered here – the action seems somewhat distanced, as though you are sitting in the balcony rather than the stalls – you need a very high volume setting to get a satisfactory level from the singers; then the orchestra sounds too loud. Of course the Serafin will remain unrivalled for many, but its aged sound and the disfiguring cuts is a serious drawback for newcomers.

Simon Boccanegra

Piero Cappuccilli *bar* Simon Boccanegra; **Mirella Freni** *sop* Amelia; **José Carreras** *ten* Gabriele; **Nicolai Ghiaurov** *bass* Fiesco; **José van Dam** *bass-bar* Paolo; **Giovanni Foiani** *bass* Pietro; **Antonio Savastano** *ten* Captain; **Maria Fausta Gallamini** *sop* Maid; **Chorus and Orchestra of La Scala, Milan / Claudio Abbado**

DG The Originals ② 449 752-2GOR2 Ⓜ

(136 minutes: ADD). Notes, text and translation included. Recorded 1977 ●●

This famous recording has become a gramophone classic, a performance in the studio after a series of performances at La Scala in the Strehler staging. The close, slightly claustrophobic recording exactly mirrors the mood of nefarious activities and intrigues following Boccanegra's rise to be Doge of Genoa, he and his lovely daughter victims of the dark deeds round them. In his plebeian being, clement exercise of authority and warm, fatherly love, Simon Boccanegra is made for Cappuccilli who, under Abbado's tutelage, sings it not only *con amore* but with exemplary, delicately tinted tone and unbelievably long-breathed phrasing. As his daughter Amelia, Freni was just entering her quasi-*spinto* phase, and expands her lyric voice easily into the greater demands of this more dramatic role. Similarly heavier duties had not yet tarnished the youthful ardour and sap in the tone of the 30-year-old Carreras. As the implacable Fiesco, Ghiaurov exudes vengeful command, and van Dam evil machinations as the villain Paolo. Over all presides Abbado in what remains one of his greatest recordings, alert to every facet of the wondrous score, timing every scene, in an opera tricky to pace, to near-perfection, and in sum bringing theatrical drama into the home. This set should now be an essential adornment to any reputable collection of Verdi.

Simon Boccanegra

Tito Gobbi *bar* Simon Boccanegra; **Victoria de los Angeles** *sop* Amelia; **Giuseppe Campora** *ten* Gabriele; **Boris Christoff** *bass* Fiesco; **Walter Monachesi** *bar* Paolo; **Paolo Dari** *bar* Pietro; **Paolo Caroli** *bar* Captain; **Silvia Bertona** *mez* Maid; **Chorus and Orchestra of the Rome Opera House / Gabriele Santini**

EMI Références mono ② CHS5 67483-2 Ⓜ

(119 minutes: ADD). Notes, text and translations included. Recorded 1957

Although the sound of this version, even in its refurbished state, is indifferent, as it was even for the standards of its day, it simply cannot be overlooked because it preserves two interpretations that are now of historic importance – Gobbi's Boccanegra and Christoff's Fiesco, the brothers-in-law (in real life) rivalling each other in projecting dramatic conviction. Even with Cappuccilli's superb reading in mind (he recorded Boccanegra both for Gavazzeni and Abbado), Gobbi's still remains definitive. Through his sensitive diction and fine gradations of tone he portrays unforgettably the Doge's changes of character, so unerringly delineated by Verdi himself, from unruly pirate to commanding Doge to loving father and, after the poisoning, to tragic hero. The weary acceptance and sad accents of the final scene match those of Cappuccilli in his equally moving interpretations, especially that on the Abbado set. Gobbi at the time was at the height of his vocal powers so that the often high tessitura bothers him little, though it is certainly true that Cappuccilli has still greater resources to call on.

Christoff may not have quite the vocal amplitude of Ghiaurov (DG), but his reading has more vocal character. His pungent, crisply articulated singing is ideally suited to the proud, implacable patrician Fiesco. His singing shades into deeply felt remorse in the final, conciliatory meeting with Boccanegra. If you want to judge the calibre of both portrayals look no further than the close of the Prologue and listen to Christoff's relishing of Boccanegra's discomfiture at 'L'ora suono del tuo castigo' ('the hour of your punishment is at hand') as Boccanegra discovers his beloved Maria is dead, followed by Gobbi's cry 'Si; spaventoso, atroce sogno il mio!' ('Yes, a terrible and fearful dream is mine'), so eloquently accented.

Los Angeles is an Amelia very much in the mould of Ricciarelli (RCA), vulnerable in character, gentle and elegiac in voice with just a suggestion of strain in the highest register. Los Angeles's tone is actually clearer, more girlish than that of either of her rivals, and she is more adept than either of them at suggesting passion for Gabriele and a daughter's love for her father through her sensitive painting of words. She is quite exquisite in the downward runs in the final ensemble. Campora makes a likeable, fiery Gabriele more in the mould of Carrerras (DG) than Domingo (RCA). Monachesi is an imposing Paolo.

Neither Santini's conducting nor the playing of the Rome Opera Orchestra matches that of their La Scala counterparts (DG). Abbado's realisation of this work is unlikely to be surpassed, though Gavazzeni's reading has much to commend it. The voices in this mono recording are more fairly caught than the chorus and orchestra, but there is a persistent though hardly disturbing tape hiss.

EMI are to be castigated for their failure to give us any details about the performers or the recording: surely in reissuing a 33-year-old set that has such historic importance as this, they should blow their own trumpet a little. In sum, though, this is a set those interested in great recordings of Verdi operas must get (even if they may regret the needless cuts).

Stiffelio

José Carreras *ten* Stiffelio; **Sylvia Sass** *sop* Lina; **Matteo Manuguerra** *bar* Stankar; **Wladimiro Ganzarolli** *bass* Jorg; **Ezio di Cesare** *ten* Raffaele; **Maria Venuti** *mez* Dorotea; **Thomas Moser** *ten* Federico; **Austrian Radio Chorus and Symphony Orchestra / Lamberto Gardelli**

Philips ② 422 432-2PM2 (109 minutes: ADD). Notes, text and translation included. Recorded 1979 Ⓜ

Stiffelio's rediscovery in the late 1960s enabled this reassessment, fully discussed in Julian Budden's introduction to the set. The drama has greater unity. Stiffelio himself is almost a dry run for Otello, a man of generous instincts who is forced into a ruinous situation. As a whole the score is, as Budden suggests, the most unjustly neglected of Verdi's operas. Had it not been suppressed by the censors, and then unsatisfactorily revised, it would surely have a regular part in the repertory because the story and its handling are both far superior to what preceded them in the Verdi canon.

The title-role is a gift for an accomplished tenor: Carreras catches the moral fervour and uncertainties of the part with his open-hearted, spontaneous performance. As Lina, who is torn between steadfastness and vulnerability, Sylvia Sass also offers a rewarding performance, alternating delicacy with fiery strength, although technically she isn't always as secure as one might ideally wish. Manuguerra is appropriately venomous as Stankar but his voice hasn't any particular distinction, tending to sound nasal, nor has his reading much in the way of individuality, but he is never less than adequate. Gardelli here adds another vital performance to his long series of Verdi readings. But any reservations pale before the importance of the work in hand to all Verdians, and enough is achieved to prove its worth. Besides, it is an essential purchase for Carreras enthusiasts.

La traviata

Maria Callas *sop* Violetta Valery; **Alfredo Kraus** *ten* Alfredo Germont; **Mario Sereni** *bar* Giorgio Germont; **Laura Zanini** *mez* Flora Bervoix; **Piero De Palma** *ten* Gastone; **Alvaro Malta** *bar* Baron Douphol; **Maria Cristina de Castro** *sop* Annina; **Alessandro Maddalena** *bass* Doctor Grenvil; **Vito Susca** *bass* Marquis D'Obigny; **Manuel Leitao** *ten* Messenger; **Chorus and Orchestra of the Teatro Nacional de San Carlos, Lisbon / Franco Ghione**

EMI mono ② CDS5 56330-2 (123 minutes: ADD) Ⓜ
Recorded live in 1958 **OO**

Callas caught live is preferable to Callas recorded in the studio and Violetta was perhaps her supreme role. The former Covent Garden producer Ande Anderson pointedly commented that, whereas other sopranos made you cry in the final act of *Traviata*, Callas also made you cry in the second, and one hears here what he meant as Callas's Violetta comes to the stark realisation that she is going to have to give up her one and only true beloved seemingly for ever. The desperation that enters her voice at 'Non sapete' is surpassed only at the sorrow and emptiness in the lead-in to 'Dite alla giovine', then the fatalism of 'morro! la mia memoria', which John Steane in his note that accompanies this essential CD reissue, describes as being sung with such 'fullness of heart and voice'.

Then the final act is almost unbearable in its poignancy of expression: the reading of the letter so natural in its feeling of emptiness, the realisation that the doctor is lying so truthful, the sense of sheer hollowness at what is possibly the whole opera's most moving moment, 'Ma se tornando…': 'If in returning you have not saved my life, then nothing can save it'. All this and so much else suggests that Callas more than anyone understood what this role is truly about. Much of what she achieves here can be heard in embryo on the 1953 Cetra set (nla), made before she was quite such a mature artist. No doubt a studio recording by EMI would have been technically more perfect: the note at the end of 'Addio del passato' would have been remade when the singer was fresh, avoiding the frailty encountered here, but then we might have been deprived of this 'official' record of what she sounded like in this part in the theatre. Those of us who heard her at Covent Garden a few months after the performance enshrined here will know that it is a true likeness of those unforgettable readings.

But there is more to it even than that. Alfredo Kraus's Alfredo as heard here is as appealing as any on record. His Schipa-like tone at that stage in his career, his refinement of phrasing, especially in the duets with Callas, and his elegant yet ardent manner are exactly what the role requires. Mario Sereni may not quite be in the class of his colleagues but his Germont *père* is securely, sincerely and often perceptively sung and more acutely characterised than in his account of the part with de los Angeles. Almost as important, contrary to what you may read in some earlier reviews, Franco Ghione is an expert, knowledgeable conductor of this score, yielding to his singers yet prompt and dramatic when need be, and able to draw singing string tone from his excellent orchestra in the two preludes.

So are there any drawbacks? Yes indeed; the prompter is all too audible, the audience coughs intrusively, particularly during the recitative at the start of Act 3, and the score is extensively cut in the manner traditional to pre-authentic days. Nevertheless, if it's to be but one *Traviata* in your collection, it must be this one.

La traviata
Ileana Cotrubas *sop* Violetta; **Plácido Domingo** *ten* Alfredo; **Sherrill Milnes** *bar* Germont; **Stefania Malagù** *mez* Flora; **Helena Jungwirth** *sop* Annina; **Walter Gullino** *ten* Gastone; **Bruno Grella** *bar* Baron; **Alfredo Giacomotti** *bass* Marquis; **Giovanni Foiani** *bass* Doctor; **Walter Gullino** *ten* Giuseppe; **Bavarian State Opera Chorus and Orchestra / Carlos Kleiber**
DG ② 415 132-2GH2 (106 minutes: ADD). Notes, text and translation included. Recorded 1977 Ⓕ ⭘

This performance is so compelling dramatically – and as a recording much more natural than most of its rivals – that it really should be a newcomer's first choice. Cotrubas's peculiarly plaintive, vibrating timbre and highly individual nuances seem to be perfectly fitted to the part. To those she adds more of a sense of involvement and spontaneity than any other on disc. In Act 2, if she does not have you close to tears, you must have a hard heart indeed. At 'Più non esiste', this Violetta leaves no doubt that all previous experience has been erased from her mind in Alfredo's arms. Then, the very precise articulation and observance of note values, so typical of the set as a whole, at 'non sapete' emphasises the sudden realisation that all she now lives for is to be taken from her, just as at 'Così alla misera' she feels the blow has fallen as she communes to herself, the tears held back on the accentuated word 'implacabil'. At 'Amami, Alfredo' the whole bottled-up sense of mortality and lost happiness breaks forth uncontrollably. A superb interpretation.

That first scene of Act 2 is the clue to any great reading of the role of Violetta. It is not undermined by the rest of Cotrubas's performance. 'Sempre libera', at Kleiber's fast pace, is nervously exciting as it should be, with firm attack from the singer. The exchanges with Annina and the Doctor in Act 3 could not be more touching, the dots over the semiquavers at 'ogni speranza è morta!' properly observed and proving the dramatic effect Verdi intended for them. Kleiber gives the score a Toscanini-like sense of dramatic purpose and impending doom. You can hear that in the final *allegro* section of the Violetta-Germont duet, with note values, double dots and the like firmly observed. Much earlier in the score Kleiber and his excellent Munich players give the dance music *chez* Violetta a chilling emptiness.

Domingo gives Alfredo one of his best performances, singing with sensitivity and grace – note the real *pianissimo* at the end of the Act 1 duet with Violetta – and altogether following her and their conductor away from routine. Kleiber's volatile, incisive direction, sometimes in questionable tempos, has worn perhaps a little less well than the rest. But then you hear Cotrubas's heart-rending 'Amami, Alfredo' and inevitably lean towards this set.

La traviata (sung in English)
Valerie Masterson *sop* Violetta; **John Brecknock** *ten* Alfredo; **Christian du Plessis** *bar* Germont; **Della Jones** *mez* Flora; **Shelagh Squires** *mez* Annina; **Geoffrey Pogson** *ten* Gastone; **John Gibbs** *bar* Baron; **Denis Dowling** *bar* Marquis; **Roderick Earle** *bass* Doctor; **Edward Byles** *ten* Giuseppe; **John Kitchiner** *bar* Messenger; **Chorus and Orchestra of English National Opera / Sir Charles Mackerras**
Chandos Opera in English Series ② CHAN3023 (119 minutes: ADD). Text included. Recorded 1980 Ⓕ ⭘

Each new encounter with this increases both respect and affection – not just for the recording but for the opera itself. This is partly an effect of opera-in-English, at any rate in such a very human opera as *Traviata*, and Edmund Tracey's translation also improves on reacquaintance ('I wonder' used to seem a terrible substitute for 'E strano' but it now seems natural enough in context). It is also partly a testimony to the imaginative freshness with which all details of the performance have been approached. The choruses, which usually sound like so much well-rehearsed routine, are alive with intelligent responsiveness. Similarly, Mackerras does not allow the orchestra to take anything for granted.

Valerie Masterson's Violetta is infinitely touching, not only through her expressiveness but perhaps primarily because the music is so scrupulously sung. Her *staccatos*, triplets and arpeggios in the first duet are so cleanly placed; her gradations of tone in the great solo are so finely judged; her control of the soft high notes in the last Act's farewell is so clearly that of a singer who knows that, whatever the fashionable cant to the contrary, singing comes first. Sensitivity and study have added the rest, and the result is simply one of the most satisfying accounts of the role on record. If there is a limitation it lies in the want of richer tonal resources, and this is true also of the Alfredo, John Brecknock. Christian du Plessis as the father sounds not quite so firm and even in his production; good, however, in rounding off the two verses of his famous song. Della Jones and Denis Dowling bring their minor roles to life, and indeed there is not much by way of weakness in the whole of this heart-warming production.

La traviata

Tiziana Fabriccini *sop* Violetta; **Roberto Alagna** *ten* Alfredo; **Paolo Coni** *bar* Germont; **Nicoletta Curiel** *mez* Flora; **Antonella Trevisan** *mez* Annina; **Enrico Cossutta** *ten* Gastone; **Orazio Mori** *bass* Baron; **Enzo Capuano** *bass* Marquis; **Francesco Musinu** *bass* Doctor; **Ernesto Gavazzi** *ten* Giuseppe; **Ernesto Panariello** *bass* Servant; **Silvestro Sammaritano** *bass* Messenger; **Chorus and Orchestra of La Scala, Milan / Riccardo Muti**
Sony Classical ② S2K52486 (136 minutes: DDD)
Notes, text and translation included Ⓕ
Recorded live in 1992

An exciting and eloquent reading on all sides, this version must now be rated with the established frontrunners – but, as with some of those, most notably any of Callas's versions, it is not for the fainthearted, or for those who like their Violettas to have full, equally, produced voices. Fabriccini is evidently not an Act 1 Violetta. But even without assured coloratura and with problems at the *passagio*, she is one who is going to hold our attention and move us. In Act 2 so much bespeaks not only complete identification with Violetta's predicament but also vocal acumen of an exceptional kind, often based on the seemingly lost art of *portamento*. Because this is a live performance we are conscious that the singer's acting is part of the secret of the reading's success; that and the obvious youth of a soprano who is not yet a preening prima donna. The final tragedy is still better, very much modelled on Callas. The voice, more settled now than anywhere in the performance manages her role with long-breathed phrasing and pathetic accents, the result of a true understanding of Verdian style yet never self-conscious – this is great singing *and* interpretation.

The death is deeply moving. Alagna, in the role that brought him to attention, is just the Alfredo for this Violetta; youthfully ardent, with keen-edged tone, finely attuned to the *legato* essential in Verdi. The recording is taken from four performances, given at La Scala, and is a theatrical view full of electricity, vitally executed by the forces of La Scala, as vital as any in the recorded history of the work. Don't miss it.

La traviata

Angela Gheorghiu *sop* Violetta; **Frank Lopardo** *ten* Alfredo; **Leo Nucci** *bar* Germont; **Leah-Marian Jones** *mez* Flora; **Gillian Knight** *mez* Annina; **Robin Leggate** *ten* Gaston; **Richard Van Allan** *bass* Baron; **Roderick Earle** *bass* Marquis; **Mark Beesley** *bar* Doctor; **Neil Griffiths** *ten* Giuseppe; **Bryan Secombe** *bass* Messenger; **Rodney Gibson** *ten* Servant; **Chorus and Orchestra of the Royal Opera House, Covent Garden / Sir Georg Solti**
Decca ② 448 119-2DHO2 (127 minutes: DDD) Ⓕ
Notes, text and translation included
Recorded live in 1994

For Angela Gheorghiu, Violetta was the right role at the right time. The whole drama is there in her voice, every expression in the eyes and beat of the heart reflected in the way she shapes and colours Verdi's vocal lines. Her quiet singing is particularly lovely, affording subtle variations of tenderness and inner anxiety. When she does choose to make a point with force, as in her sudden warmth of feeling towards Giorgio Germont at 'Qual figlia m'abbracciate' or her chilling cry of 'Morro!', accompanied by a loud thump on the table, her ideas always hit home. A few moments of vocal weakness are accentuated by the microphone, mainly a tendency to go sharp and some hardness at the top of the voice that was not troublesome in the theatre. Otherwise, she is the most complete and moving Violetta we have had since her compatriot, Ileana Cotrubas.

These live performances were the first time that Sir Georg Solti, at the age of 82, had conducted a staged *La traviata* and he wanted two young singers who were also coming fresh to the opera. What was so spellbinding in the theatre was the touching intimacy they brought to their scenes together. Instead of the duets for Violetta and Alfredo turning into standard Italian operatic bawling, they became lovers' whispers. The effect comes across here in the cadenzas, where Gheorghiu and Frank Lopardo really seem to be listening to each other. Elsewhere, one is more aware than in the theatre that Lopardo's light tenor is far from being an idiomatic Italian voice. His idiosyncratic tone quality and un-Italian vowels can be problematical, as is some ungainly lifting up into notes. Leo Nucci, Decca's resident Verdi baritone at the time, makes a standard Giorgio Germont, not more, and apart from Leah-Marian Jones's energetic Flora, the smaller roles do not say a great deal for the Royal Opera's depth of casting.

Solti insisted that the opera be performed complete. But there is nothing studied about his conducting: the performance is fresh and alive from the first note to the last, the result of a lifetime's experience of how to pace a drama in the opera house. With the increasing number of live opera sets, a recommendation for *La traviata* is likely to be based on whether one is prepared to accept noises-off or not. Decca's recording is well balanced and vivid, dancing feet and banging doors included. Among the live sets, Giulini and Callas at La Scala in 1955 must be *hors concours*, but in rather awful sound. Muti's more recent La Scala set, in which he has to wrestle with Tiziana Fabbricini's wayward talents as Violetta, is the nearest comparison.

Additional recommendations

La traviata

Callas Violetta **di Stefano** Alfredo **Bastianini** Germont **Chorus and Orchestra of La Scala, Milan / Giulini**
EMI mono ② CMS5 66450-2 (124 minutes: ADD: 2/91) Ⓜ

Surely the most famous recording of *Traviata*, with Callas as an incomparable Violetta. The big let down, though, is Bastianini's Germont and the poor recorded sound.

De los Angeles Violetta **del Monte** Alfredo **Sereni** Germont **Rome Opera Chorus and Orchestra / Serafin**
EMI Double Forte ② CZS5 73824-2 Ⓜ
(119 minutes: ADD: 12/85R)

Also available on HMV Classics HMVD5 728082-2 Ⓑ

At bargain price, don't miss this version. The Alfredo and Germont are both well portrayed, but above all Victoria de los Angeles's Violetta is quite unforgettable.

Il trovatore

Il trovatore (sung in English)
Dennis O'Neill *ten* Manrico; **Sharon Sweet** *sop* Leonora; **Alan Opie** *bar* Count di Luna; **Anne Mason** *mez* Azucena; **Clive Bayley** *bass* Ferrando; **Helen Williams** *sop* Ines; **Mark Le Brocq** *ten* Ruiz; **Geoffrey Mitchell Choir, London Philharmonic Orchestra / David Parry**
Chandos Opera in English Series ② CHAN3036 Ⓕ
(135 minutes: DDD). Notes and English text included
Recorded 2000

One's own vernacular is the language of common sense, and *Il trovatore* is not of that realm. The extremes of passion and unreason flare amid confusion and night. In old days it was 'Arouse ye!', and at the end Azucena would cry 'Then hast thou slain thy brother!' and di Luna answer 'Oh day of horror'. Of course in one way it's progress to have sensible modern English instead, but is that way *Il trovatore*'s?

Whatever the language, it's an inspired score. Over the years, the tunes that once seemed so banal (the di-di-dum tune that brings down the curtain at the end of the Azucena-Manrico duet, for instance) have lost their music-hall associations, and though one still smiles at their appearance it is much more likely to be with affection and not a little wonder at the potency of their survival. David Parry's handling of the score and the LPO's playing bring out its full vigour and brilliance together with a large measure of the work's underlying depth – the tense and fateful passions at its heart. The scene of Azucena's capture in Act 3 is one which tests whether the performance is working: the very essence of the opera is there in the progression of the 'Giorni poveri' solo ('Though my life was poor') and the excited chromatics of the ensemble that follows. The sudden change to violence is most effectively achieved here, and the whole opera turns on this moment.

Its fate also depends on the singers. As a team, the cast is strong, though individually they have limitations. Sharon Sweet is a Leonora who sings her notes well (and in this opera that counts for much) but establishes surprisingly little vocal character. This is a nice girl but not a noble woman: her tone lacks the majesty and sumptuous quality the part needs, and her manner, though sympathetic, remains ordinary, not reflecting (except perhaps in the 'Miserere') the tense dramatic life of the opera. Anne Mason as Azucena sounds young, and her voice, a mezzo-soprano of quite beautiful quality, wants the contralto element which it is important for this part to have. She is, however, a constant pleasure to hear. Dennis O'Neill's Manrico commands respect. A veteran now, without the youthful thrill in his voice, he sings with fine fullness of tone in the heroic passages and with skill and scrupulous care in the gentler lyrical music: his 'Ah! sì, ben mio' (somewhat surprisingly Englished to start 'When holy church') would repay a singer's study. But the most completely satisfying performances come from the baritone and bass. The latter, Clive Bayley, calls to mind singers of earlier times such as Peter Dawson, Howell Glynne and more recently Stafford Dean: the vocal production has a kind of solidity we don't hear too often nowadays. Alan Opie is totally admirable, making a real character out of what can be a pasteboard villain and singing his highly demanding music in the best traditions of the Verdi baritone.

The Geoffrey Mitchell Choir sing almost too well. The Count's retainers in Act 1 sound like eager, intelligent students of history; the gypsies at the anvil and the soldiers looking forward to blood and plunder are models of refinement. The production also errs, if anything, on the side of reticence: the finale of Act 2 for instance (the rescue scene) needs, in a studio recording, to convey some sense of the clash of mighty opposites and general shimozzle on stage. Offstage voices and instruments are all well handled, and for the most part we are successfully drawn in. 'This is the story/Of *Il trovatore*' began the old rhyme: if we don't make sense of it this time round, we probably never will.

Il trovatore
Maria Callas *sop* Leonora; **Giuseppe di Stefano** *ten* 🄷 Manrico; **Rolando Panerai** *bar* Count di Luna; **Fedora Barbieri** *mez* Azucena; **Nicola Zaccaria** *bass* Ferrando; **Luisa Villa** *mez* Ines; **Renato Ercolani** *ten* Ruiz, Messenger; **Giulio Mauri** *bass* Old Gipsy; **Chorus and Orchestra of La Scala, Milan / Herbert von Karajan**
EMI ② CDS5 56333-2 (129 minutes: ADD). Notes, Ⓕ
text and translation included. Recorded 1956 OO

Callas and Karajan took the world by the ears in the 1950s with this *Il trovatore*. Leonora was one of Callas's finest stage roles, and this recording is wonderfully intense, with a dark concentrated loveliness of sound in the principal arias that puts one in mind of Muzio or Ponselle at their best. Walter Legge always managed to team Callas with the right conductor for the work in question. Often it was Serafin, but Karajan in *Il trovatore* is utterly compelling. This opera, like Beethoven's Seventh Symphony and Stravinsky's *The Rite of Spring*, is one of music's great essays in sustained rhythmic intensity; dramatically it deals powerfully in human archetypes. All this is realised by the young Karajan with that almost insolent mastery of score and orchestra which made him such a phenomenon at this period of his career. There are some cuts, but, equally, some welcome inclusions (such as the second verse of 'Di quella pira', sung by di Stefano with his own unique kind of *slancio*).

Although the EMI sound is very good, one or two climaxes suggest that in the heat of the moment, the engineer, Robert Beckett, let the needle run into the red and you might care to play the set in mono to restore that peculiar clarity and homogeneity of sound which are the mark of Legge's finest productions of the mono era. But whatever you do don't miss this set.

Il trovatore
Plácido Domingo *ten* Manrico; **Leontyne Price** *sop* Leonora; **Sherrill Milnes** *bar* Count di Luna; **Fiorenza Cossotto** *mez* Azucena; **Bonaldo Giaiotti** *bass* Ferrando; **Elizabeth Bainbridge** *mez* Ines; **Ryland Davies** *ten* Ruiz; **Stanley Riley** *bass* Old Gipsy; **Neilson Taylor** *bar* Messenger; **Ambrosian Opera Chorus; New Philharmonia Orchestra / Zubin Mehta**
RCA Red Seal ② 74321 39504-2 Ⓜ
(137 minutes: ADD) Notes, text and translation included. Recorded 1969

There are details here which fully justify its inclusion and will be enough to tempt any collector's palette. The Leonora of Leontyne Price is the high point of the Mehta recording: her velvety, sensuous articulation of what is certainly an 'immenso, eterno amor' is entirely distinctive and dramatically astute. The New Philharmonia is a no less ardent protagonist. Mehta's pacing may be uneven, his accompanying breathless, but he draws robust playing in bold primary colours to which the recording gives vivid presence. The acoustic serves Manrico less well: he seems to be singing in the bath when we first overhear him. This, though, is a younger, simpler Domingo than the one we encounter elsewhere, and there are passages of wonderfully sustained intensity. Cossotto's Azucena is disappointing. All the vocal tricks and techniques are there, but it is very much a concert performance in which she, and therefore we, are never entirely engaged.

Il trovatore
Plácido Domingo *ten* Manrico; **Aprile Millo** *sop* Leonora; **Vladimir Chernov** *bar* Count di Luna; **Dolora Zajick** *mez* Azucena; **James Morris** *bass* Ferrando; **Sondra Kelly** *contr* Ines; **Anthony Laciura** *ten* Ruiz; **Glenn Bater** *bass* Old Gipsy; **Tim Willson** *ten* Messenger; **New York Metropolitan Opera Chorus and Orchestra / James Levine**
Sony Classical ② S2K48070 (129 minutes: DDD) Ⓕ
Notes, text and translation included
Recorded 1991

This is the most recommendable among modern versions of *Trovatore*, with a reading all-round that finely balances the lyrical and melodramatic elements in the score. Once Leonora appears, the reading takes on true Verdian style. This is a reading to please the ear and move the heart. Immediately this Leonora is confronted with Count di Luna, we hear the firm, vibrant, implacable tones of Chernov. His voice is in its absolute prime and he sings everything with the confident panache that suggests as much. Our upright hero is Domingo, aged a little since his earlier recordings of Manrico for Mehta (listed overleaf) and Giulini. The artistry and management of the voice are as rewarding as of old, and Domingo reserves his best for the last and greatest scene when both his sovereign phrasing – 'Riposa, o madre' sung in a single breath – and his involvement take on the aura of active participation. Manrico's feelings of love for his mother, momentary contempt for Leonora and eventual tragic pathos are firmly targeted: we hear once more the noble tenor we know and can listen to in sappier voice for Giulini.

As Azucena, Zajick gives an effective and strong-willed performance, wanting only the last ounce of character: she is also at her best in the final act. The Met chorus is no more than adequate on this occasion, but as ever the house's orchestra plays with the virtuosity it reserves for its musical director. Levine's reading is well timed, properly earthy yet refined in the many delicate touches Verdi evinces in arias and duets. Pavarotti's predominantly lyrical tenor (for Mehta on Decca) is not ideal for Manrico but he sings it with such unfailing musicality and sense of line that Pavarotti enthusiasts need not hesitate to acquire this version, confident that their hero's portrayal is set in suitable surroundings. However, the whole reading is not as well integrated as the Levine, and by a hair's breadth that is probably the better sung. Mehta's earlier, much-lauded recording for RCA remains very much in the frame.

Additional recommendation
Il trovatore
Price Leonora **Corelli** Manrico **Simionato** Azucena
DG mono ② 447 659-2GX2 (139 minutes: ADD: 9/95) Ⓜ
Leontyne Price, at the height of her powers, gives a vital performance, living every moment of her part, and Franco Corelli is an exciting Manrico. The most compelling reason for hearing this set, though, is Giulietta Simionato's deeply felt, sovereignly sung Azucena.

I vespri siciliani

Cheryl Studer *sop* Elena; **Chris Merritt** *ten* Arrigo; **Giorgio Zancanaro** *bar* Montforte; **Ferruccio Furlanetto** *bass* Procida; **Gloria Banditelli** *contr* Ninetta; **Enzo Capuano** *bass* De Bethune; **Francesco Musinu** *bass* Vaudemont; **Ernesto Gavazzi** *ten* Danieli; **Paolo Barbacini** *ten* Tebaldo; **Marco Chingari** *bass* Roberto; **Ferrero Poggi** *ten* Manfredo; **Chorus and Orchestra of La Scala, Milan / Riccardo Muti**
EMI ③ CDS7 54043-2 (199 minutes: DDD) Ⓕ
Notes, text and translation included
Recorded live in 1989-90

Vespri is one of the most difficult of Verdi's operas to bring off. Scribe's libretto, true to Parisian taste nurtured on Auber and Meyerbeer, is a somewhat superficial, broken-backed affair (though Verdi accepted it with alterations); Verdi's attempt to fulfil Parisian tastes, long ballet and all, isn't at all times convincing, yet for the most part the composer rose above the demands for show and grandeur to disclose the real feelings of his characters, none of whom is a particularly lovable creature (in that they resemble those in *Attila*). Andrew Porter, when reviewing Levine's RCA set on LP back in 1974, commented that the opera 'is a structure involving large ensembles, elaborate spectacle...intricate and novel orchestral effects, a big ballet, and virtuoso singers pushed to the limits of their technique'.

Muti realises all these assets with unperturbed ease and easily overcomes any drawbacks, real or imagined. He rouses his forces, solo and concerted, with all his old gifts for energising rhythms and shaping a Verdian line. He yields where wanted to the needs of his singers, presses on when the drama or a dull page demands it, and draws the best out of what is generally considered Verdi's most telling ballet music. He is less impulsive, and more ready to take his time than Levine. La Scala's Orchestra and Chorus play and sing with the flair of authenticity – as indeed they should.

The set is graced by some superb singing – at least in the two most important and interesting roles, those of Elena and Monforte. Cheryl Studer confirmed her ebullient form in *Attila* as a *lirico-spinto* with full control of coloratura, thus placing her in the royal line of Ponselle, Callas, Sutherland and Caballé (the last two of whom encouraged Studer to undertake this kind of repertory). In her first appearance, as she instils the Sicilians with courage, 'Coraggio, su coraggio', she immediately shows her mettle with confident, inspiriting attack, the tone vibrant, the diction fiery. In the duet with Arrigo in Act 4, her long solo 'Arrigo! ah, parli ad un core', a passage made famous by Callas, she floats her tone most appealingly, the accents delicate, affecting. In the Bolero she rivals any of her predecessors in delicacy, a real smile in the voice, the phrasing long breathed, the coloratura, not quite perfect, but near it. Taken with her soaring contributions to the ensembles, this is great singing by any standards, past or present. Her characterisation catches Elena's combination of fire and softness.

To find Zancanaro in equally impressive form is an added blessing. Monforte is the work's most interesting character, the French governor of Sicily, father of the Sicilian Arrigo, who is his sworn enemy. In his great scene at the start of Act 3, Zancanaro finds deeper strains of feeling than we have heard from him in any other role, and then sings the subtle written aria 'In braccio alle dovizie' with a refinement of line and variety of dynamics that enhance the strength of voice and clarity of diction we have always admired in his singing.

He is just as eloquent in the ensuing duet with Arrigo, taken here by Chris Merritt, another singer inspired by the occasion or the work to surpass himself: Merritt delivers all his music with such conviction and such a belief in himself that past criticism of his voice is almost silenced. Which leaves, of the principals, Furlanetto. So accomplished and heard to such advantage in Mozart and Rossini, he here sounds overparted. 'O tu Palermo' lacks the weight and authority of a Pinza, Pasero or Christoff – or even Raimondi on RCA – but he improves immeasurably after that, pronoucing his anathemas on the French and stirring his supporters with a verve that compensates for any failings in vocal power. Small roles are taken with accomplishment.

Those who want their orchestras to be big and resonant may be disappointed by the confined sound heard here. However, the voices are, on the whole, caught well in a true theatre perspective. A few coughs and some applause will only worry those who must have complete silence.

The RCA set has much to commend it, most of all Domingo's full-flooded Arrigo, though he gives points to Merritt in Act 5. On balance this set is more convincingly cast and conducted. It won't please those who are longing to hear the piece in the original, but Verdi did approve of the Italian version and certainly would have approved of its vital execution here.

Tomás Luis de Victoria

Spanish 1548-1611

GROVE *Victoria was a choirboy at Avila Cathedral; when his voice broke he was sent to the Jesuit Collegio Germanico, Rome (c1565), where he may have studied under Palestrina. He was a singer and organist at S Maria di Monserrato (1569- at least 1574) and from 1571 to 1576-7 he taught at the Collegio Germanico (maestro from 1575). He became a priest and joined the Oratory of S Filippo Neri. In the 1580s he returned to Spain as chaplain to Philip II's sister the Dowager Empress Maria, at the Descalzas Reales convent, Madrid, from 1587 until her death in 1603; he remained there as organist until his death, apart from a visit to Rome (1592-5), when he attended Palestrina's funeral.*

The greatest Spanish Renaissance composer, and among the greatest in Europe in his day, he wrote exclusively Latin sacred music. Most was printed in his lifetime; in 1600 a sumptuous collection of 32 of his most popular masses, Magnificats, psalms and motets appeared in Madrid. Though his output ranged widely through the liturgy, he is chiefly remembered for his masses and motets, which include well-known pieces (Missa Ave regina caelorum, Missa pro victoria, O magnum mysterium, O quam gloriosum, O vos omnes). Like Palestrina, he wrote in a serious, devotional style, often responding emotionally to the texts with dramatic word-painting. Some of his more poignant pieces are characterised by a religious, almost mystical fervour.

Masses

Missa Gaudeamus. Missa pro Victoria (both ed Dixon). Motets – Cum beatus Ignatius; Descendit angelus Domini; Doctor bonus amicus Dei Andreas; Ecce sacerdos magnus; Estote fortes in bello; Hic vir despiciens mundum; O decus apostolicum; Tu es Petrus; Veni, sponsa Christi (all ed Skinner)

The Cardinall's Musick / Andrew Carwood

ASV Gaudeamus CDGAU198 (78 minutes: DDD) Ⓕ

Texts and translations included

Recorded 1998-99

There have been some fine recordings of Victoria's music in recent years, but none finer than this one at its best. The Cardinall's Musick has become known for its CDs of English renaissance polyphony, but its approach, which joint directors Andrew Carwood and David Skinner describe as 'open and soloistic', works extremely well here, too. The two contrasted Mass settings are given the same highly expressive treatment as the motets, which, sung one to a part, have a madrigalian quality bringing out beautifully the natural, unforced rhetoric of Victoria's idiom.

The *Missa Gaudeamus*, based on a Morales motet, is scored for six voices. Performed with only two singers on each part, it sounds as rich and dark as the strongest chocolate; the overall blend is superb, clear and strikingly well balanced. With only two female voices on the upper part, the polyphonic texture is not, as is so often the case, top-heavy; each strand carries equal weight, just as the densely contrapuntal writing demands. The final canonic *Agnus Dei* is sublime, and throughout – even in the longer movements – Carwood's sure-footed pacing allows the polyphony to ebb and flow like the swell of the sea.

The *Missa pro Victoria*, based on Janequin's *chanson*, *La guerre*, could hardly be more different in its forward-looking polychoral idiom. Here the writing is more condensed, more economical, but nevertheless highly dramatic. The ending of the *Gloria* is breath-taking, as is the magical opening of the *Sanctus* and the final 'dona nobis pacems' of the *Agnus Dei*. The clarion calls of the second *Kyrie* are equally striking.

The Cardinall's Musick is as responsive to the text as in motets such as *O decus apostolicum*, the final Alleluia of which is deliciously pointed, or *Descendit angelus Domini*, in which Victoria's subtle musical articulation of the text is perfectly matched by some appropriately ardent singing. There are so many high spots on this disc that it is simply impossible to mention them all, and this is perhaps still more to the group's credit given that, as explained in the notes, a bout of flu among the singers cannot have made for the easiest of recording sessions.

Officium defunctorum (1605)
Gabrieli Consort / Paul McCreesh
Archiv Produktion 447 095-2AH (60 minutes: DDD) Ⓕ
Text and translation included. Recorded 1994 **OO**

This is a remarkable recording. In some ways it is like a rediscovery, for here is an approach not too far from Pro Cantione Antiqua at its best and yet that group never recorded the work. The Gabrieli Consort adds chant to the Requiem Mass itself, thus creating more of a context for Victoria's magisterial work. We have therefore the Epistle and preceding prayer, the Tract, Sequence, Gospel, Preface, Lord's Prayer and Postcommunion in addition to the polyphony; this also means, for example, that the *Kyrie* is sung nine-fold with alternating chant instead of simply three-fold only in polyphony. One may presume that the chant was taken from a suitable Spanish source by Luis Lozano Virumbrales, who is an expert in this field and the author of the insert-notes together with Paul McCreesh.

The performance itself is stately and imposing, with a tremendous homogeneity of sound: the use of an all-male choir, together with the added chant, lends it a tangibly monastic feel, though it would have been a fortunate monastery indeed that had falsettists of this quality. About the performance of the chant there are two points of interest: firstly, that it is doubled, like the polyphony, by a bajón, common Spanish practice at this period, and secondly, that McCreesh is not afraid to have the falsettists singing the chant too. The pace of the polyphony often seems to be unhurried, but it never feels slow, and Westminster Cathedral Choir is of course faced with the hugely reverberant acoustics of its home building.

From the beginning the singing is involving and incarnate, but the real magic comes nearer the end: from the *Agnus Dei* onwards one feels that the Gabreli Consort have really got the measure of the music and is allowing it to speak through them. The final great responsory, the 'Libera me', is performed with heart stopping power and conviction. McCreesh's approach shows how the Mass would have fitted into and complemented the liturgical framework without ever losing its own internal power and drama. A revelatory disc.

Additional recommendation
Officium defunctorum
Westminster Cathedral Choir / Hill
Hyperion CDA66250 (58 minutes: DDD: 9/87) Ⓕ
A stunning and at times breathtaking performance. An absolute must for any lover of Victoria's music.

Awards 1985

Missa O quam gloriosum. Missa Ave maris stella. Motet – O quam gloriosum
Westminster Cathedral Choir / David Hill
Hyperion CDA66114 (57 minutes: DDD) Ⓕ
Recorded 1983 **OOO**

This is likely to become one of your most cherished discs. It is notable for its spacious depth of sound, volatile unpredictability of interpretation, and above all the soaring *sostenuto* of the boy trebles, with their forward and slightly nasal tone quality. With their magnificently controlled *legato* lines, the Westminster boys treat Victoria's music as though it were some vast plainchant, with a passion that excites and uplifts. The choir is recorded in the exceptionally resonant Westminster Cathedral, at a distance and with great atmosphere.

Ave maris stella is not one of Victoria's familiar Masses, quite simply because no music publisher has made it available to choirs in a good, cheap edition. To have it rescued from obscurity is laudable in itself, but to have it sung with such poise and sensitivity is an unexpected double treat. Unlike *O quam gloriosum*, this is a work that thrills with echoes of Victoria's Spanish upbringing, of Morales and his predecessors, even of Josquin Desprez, whose own *Ave maris stella* Mass was brought to the cathedrals of the Iberian peninsula earlier in the century. The plainchant melody, familiar to all of us through Monteverdi's setting in the 1610 Vespers, completely dominates Victoria's music, for it is placed most often in huge treble lines that wheel high above the general texture. Magnificent as the early parts of the work are, nothing quite matches the final five-part *Agnus Dei*, sung here with admirable support and breadth and exquisitely shaped by David Hill. Recommended without any reservation.

Veni Sancte Spiritus. Dum complerentur. Missa Dum complerentur. Popule meus. Vexilla Regis. Veni Creator Spiritus. Pange lingua gloriosi. Lauda Sion
Westminster Cathedral Choir / James O'Donnell with **Joseph Cullen** *org*
Hyperion CDA66886 (70 minutes: DDD). Texts and translations included. Recorded 1996 Ⓕ ●●

Westminster Cathedral Choir here makes a special contribution to the music of Tomás Luis de Victoria. The *Missa Dum complerentur*, for Pentecost, is based on Victoria's own motet; he adds an extra voice in the parody Mass setting and draws much on the opening material of the motet as well as its distinctive 'Alleluia' sections which ring out like a peal of bells – especially in this excellent performance. Indeed, the motet is finely conceived, with Victoria characteristically responding to the imagery of the text with changes of texture and pacing within the essentially contrapuntal idiom: a true master.

The choir, with its full-bodied sound and well-sustained vocal lines, has, over long years of tradition in singing this particular part of the repertory, achieved an almost intuitive feel for the flow of the music, which is perhaps as near as we'll ever get today to the authentic situation of professional church singers in Rome or the Spanish cathedrals in the 16th century. What we'll never know is whether the sonority – in particular the timbre of the boys' voices – resembles anything Victoria might have heard, that distinctive focus and intensity of tone well illustrated by the two Holy Week settings on the disc: the homophonic *Popule meus* and the hymn *Vexilla Regis*. This, and the two Pentecost hymns, are performed *in alternatim* with alternate verses in plainchant and polyphony. This is a superb and compelling disc that adds to our knowledge and appreciation of Victoria's art.

Heitor Villa-Lobos Brazilian 1887-1959

GROVE *Villa-Lobos was taught to play the cello by his father, and in his teens he performed with popular musicians in the city. He then travelled widely, returning to Rio in his mid-20s for a few formal lessons. From 1923 to 1930 he was in Paris, where he wrote several works in his Chôros series, giving Brazilian impressions a luxuriant scoring: Messiaen and others were impressed. He returned to Brazil, where he did valuable work in reforming musical education. In 1945 he founded the Brazilian Academy of Music in Rio de Janeiro. Also during this period he produced the cycle of nine Bachianas brasileiras for diverse combinations (1930-45), marrying the spirit of Brazilian folk music with that of Bach; the two for eight cellos (one with soprano) have been especially successful. His gigantic output includes operas, 12 symphonies (1916-57), 17 string quartets (1915-57), numerous songs and much piano music.*

Chôros No 11

Ralf Gothóni *pf* **Finnish Radio Symphony Orchestra / Sakari Oramo**
Ondine ODE916-2 (62 minutes: DDD) Ⓕ
Recorded 1998 ●

Villa-Lobos wrote five piano concertos as well as other works for piano and orchestra with less *concertante* titles, such as *Momoprecoce* and the third of the *Bachianas Brasileiras*: in fact *Chôros* No 11 is the largest-scale of them all, though despite its ferociously demanding solo part it has been described rather as a 'mammoth concerto grosso'. If that term conjures up for you an image of a neat neo-classical work, forget it: this is Villa-Lobos in his usual excitably coloured, hyper-exuberant style, writing in a grandiose loose form that – since few of its vast proliferation of themes are developed – defies analysis but whose overall effect is strangely riveting. Every so often lyrical passages occur among the manic busyness, and the linked second movement, profligately overscored as it is, is really romantic, with three related but not identical melodic ideas (and a big cadenza). The finale, which begins with a *fugato*, is thematically more integrated than the rest (for a time, at least) and consequently could be considered the most successful movement. The sound is vivid, Ralf Gothóni contributes prodigious feats of virtuosity and the Finnish orchestra displays total commitment to this quite extraordinary work.

Bachianas Brasileiras Nos 2, 4 & 8

Bachianas Brasileiras Nos 2, 4 and 8
Cincinnati Symphony Orchestra / Jesús López-Cobos
Telarc CD80393 (70 minutes: DDD) Ⓕ
Recorded 1995 ●

If any parallels existed between Bach and Brazilian idioms, they were largely in Villa-Lobos's mind – even the Fugue in No 8 of these *Bachianas Brasileiras* is totally un-Bach-like; so anyone coming fresh to these exotically coloured, rather sprawling works should not be misled by false expectations. But fascinating, indeed haunting, in a highly individual way, they are. In view of the composer's sublime indifference to instrumental practicalities (as, for instance, the feasible length of a trombone *glissando*), his carelessness over detail in his scores, his Micawber-like trust that problems of balance he had created would be sorted out in performance, the chaotic state of the printed scores and orchestral parts of his music (littered as they are with wrong notes and questionable points), and numerous misreadings in past performances, the only half-way reliable yardstick for conductors or critics is the composer's own recordings, made in the 1950s and now preserved in a six-CD box on EMI.

Compared to them, the present issue shows a number of differences. Chief of these is the warmer, more generalised sound, with less emphasis on clarity of detail. This works reasonably well in the Preludio of No 8, where concentration on the melodic line and the adoption of a slower tempo aid the movement's lyricism (likewise the more sentimental approach to the Aria of No 2). The Aria of No 8 is unquestionably more poetic and the Dansa of No 4 lighter; but in the most famous movement, the hilarious and ingenious 'Little train of the Caipira' of No 2, the rasps near the start and the clatter of wheels on the track (evoked by the fiendishly difficult piano part) are far too subdued in favour of the 'big tune'.

López-Cobos deals persuasively with knotty questions of balance, such as in the middle section of No 3's Toccata, and brings to the fore the bell-like araponga bird's cry in No 4's Coral, but makes less of that movement's jungle screeches. He makes clear the thematic link between the sections of No 4's Aria, and seeks to overcome the repetitious pattern of its Preludio by taking a faster speed rather than by the wealth of tonal nuance the composer himself introduced. Perhaps such detailed comparisons are superfluous: enjoy, enjoy!

Amazonas

Gênesis. Erosño (Origem do rio Amazonas). Amazonas. Dawn in a tropical forest

Czecho-Slovak Radio Symphony Orchestra, Bratislava / Roberto Duarte

Marco Polo 8 223357 (62 minutes: DDD) Ⓕ
Recorded 1990

Do not be deterred by the thought of an Eastern European orchestra playing unfamiliar Villa-Lobos. The Czecho-Slovak Radio Orchestra is clearly a very skilled and flexible body, and the conductor Roberto Duarte, a Brazilian authority on Villa-Lobos, has instilled South American colour and rhythmic vitality into his players quite brilliantly. The best of the four works is probably the earliest, *Amazonas*, which was written in 1917. Here, at the age of 30, Villa-Lobos's imagination was extraordinarily fertile, and this early evocation of Brazilian folklore, with its use of unusual instruments and strange orchestral timbres, is remarkably advanced for its date.

The short tone poem *Dawn in a tropical forest* is a late work dating from 1953, and this has a more lyrical, more classical style. The remaining two works also come from the last phase in Villa-Lobos's career, and have similar themes. *Gênesis*, written in 1954, is a large-scale symphonic poem and ballet which depicts its enormous subject with all the extravagant colour and use of complex rhythms that were the composer's trademark. *Erosño*, or *The Origin of the Amazon*, composed in 1950, is another ambitiously complex work. All four items are captured in faithful, wide-ranging sound.

Solo Piano Works

As três Marias. Prole do bebê, Books I and II. Rudepoêma

Marc-André Hamelin *pf*

Hyperion CDA67176 (64 minutes: DDD) Ⓕ
Recorded 1999

Music for Children

Carnaval das crianças. Guia pratico, Volumes 1-6

Caio Pagano *pf*

Glissando 779 009-2 (65 minutes: DDD) Ⓕ
Recorded 2000 ●

Here are two invaluable raids on Villa-Lobos's rich and exotic store of piano music. First and foremost is Marc-André Hamelin, whose transcendental sheen and facility bless everything he plays. He makes *As três Marias* ('The three stars') wink and scintillate with an inimitable verve before continuing with both books of *Prole do bebê*, registering the change from affection to savagery with an impeccable degree of mastery and insight. In Book 1 the tolling bells which are at the heart of the enchanting 'Caboclinha' ring out *fortissimo* and *ben marcato*, while the fleetness that Hamelin delivers in 'O Polichinello' leaves all others standing.

Yet such delectable charm is virtually erased by the increasingly astringent and percussive Book 2. Here the insect and animal world has graduated from innocence to experience with a vengeance. The 'Little Wooden Horse', eyes dilating and nostrils flaring, gallops away from danger and the paper cockroach sounds disillusioned with its lot. Red Riding Hood, too, would surely have fled in terror, not deceived for a moment, from Villa-Lobos's jaw-snapping, not-so-little 'Glass Wolf'. Finally, there is *Rudepoêma*, the composer's supposed masterpiece. Rubinstein was understandably disconcerted by a portrait of such roughness. Hoping for a more genial offering with which to delight his adoring public he quickly abandoned *Rudepoêma*. True, there are brief moments of bittersweet accessibility (the first at 8'41"), but elsewhere the assault is relentless, and even Hamelin's superb and unflagging brio hardly reconciles you to the music's length and bombast.

Hyperion's production is as immaculate as ever, and the uninformative accompanying notes, which tell us that the second *Prole do bebê* 'continues the charm of the first' are compensated for by a fine illustration of Helen Millard's glass wolf baying at the moon and stars.

Caio Pagano's brilliant and more amiable

recital is devoted to music for children and includes six of the 11 volumes entitled *Guia pratico*. Here one enters a magical world quite without the adult pain and nostalgia that colour Schumann's *Kinderszenen* and Debussy's *Children's Corner*, those masterpieces of childhood fantasy. A nun waltzes as she gives a child a necklace and Garibaldi goes to Mass with a real spring in his step. Two doves sing of their love, safe from all possible harm, while a wandering troubadour presses his claims on a countess with much vehemence. A widow looking for a husband is no less eagle eyed and determined, and virtually all these pieces, performed by Pagano with the liveliest of *engagement*, are so witty and touching that you are left longing for Volumes 7-11.

Carnaval das crianças is a more ornate celebration of colour and brio, and even when you miss the percussion and off-beat drum strokes from the finale of the piano and orchestra version (reissued by EMI in a performance by Cristina Ortiz and Vladimir Ashkenazy) you can only delight in Pagano's relish, his crisp and stylish playing. He is excellently recorded and the booklet includes several fine photographs of both composer and pianist and an apt front cover of Edivaldo's *Children with Kites*.

Prole do bebê No 1. Cirandas. Hommage à Chopin
Sonia Rubinsky *pf*
Naxos 8 554489 (65 minutes: DDD) Ⓢ
Recorded 1994 ⊙

Villa-Lobos's claim that his music was 'the fruit of an immense, ardent and generous land' at once disarms familiar criticism of extravagance and formlessness. To regard such largesse through the blinkered eyes of someone exclusively nurtured on a more restrained and economical diet is unacceptable. There may be tares among the wheat but such strictures hardly apply to the music in this Vol 1 which commences with the enchanting *Prole do bebê*, Book 1 (the Second Book is a tougher, altogether more astringent and percussive experience, while a Third Book is sadly lost, according to James Melo in his outstanding accompanying notes).

Intimately associated with Artur Rubinstein (who rearranged Villa-Lobos's miniatures, omitting some and ending 'O Polichinelo' with an unmarked rip-roaring *glissando*), *Prole do bebê* is here played complete. Sonia Rubinsky makes light of a teasing rhythmic mix in 'Morenhina' (No 2) and in 'Caboclinha' (No 3) she relishes Villa-Lobos's audacity; his way of making his seductive melody and rhythm surface through a peal of church bells.

Again, despite strong competition from Alma Petchersky on ASV in the no less delightful *Cirandas*, Rubinsky scores an unequivocal success, ideally attuned to the central and beguiling melody of 'Terezinha de Jesus' (No 1) with its *forte e canto* instruction, and allowing the fight between the carnation and the rose (No 4) to melt into a delicious love duet. Her way with the acrobatic flight of No 12 ('Otha o passarinho, Dominé') and the dark erotic undertow to 'Que lindos olhos' (No 15) is entirely sympathetic, and she makes a strong case for Villa-Lobos's idiosyncratic tribute to Chopin; one which presents him as a man of raging passion rather than more circumspect emotion. Much celebrated in her native Brazil and also in America, Sonia Rubinsky is excellently recorded – the path is surely set for a major series.

Bachianas Brasileiras No 5

Bachianas Brasileiras – Nos 4, 5, 7 and 9.
Chôros No 10, 'Rasga o coração'
Renée Fleming *sop* **BBC Singers; New World Symphony / Michael Tilson Thomas**
RCA Red Seal 09026 68538-2 (78 minutes: DDD) Ⓕ
Recorded 1996 ⊙

In his booklet-note, the commentator here calls *Chôros* No 10 the masterpiece of that quintessentially Brazilian series. It is certainly the most ambitious, with very large orchestral and choral forces in a complex mélange of urban street song (a popular *schottisch* by Medeiros), chattering native Indian chants and bird-song twitterings, of mysterious jungle atmosphere, compulsive ostinato rhythms and virtuoso orchestral effects.

The present performance is excellent. The couplings here are illuminating, consisting as they do of more Villa-Lobos – four of his highly individual tributes to Bach's influence. By far the best known of the *Bachianas Brasileiras* is, of course, No 5, whose Aria demonstrates the composer's ability to spin a haunting long-flowing melody. Renée Fleming is the sweet-toned soloist with the cello section of this accomplished orchestra of young graduates from American conservatoires: warmly lyrical as she is, however, and brilliantly exact in the dartings of the Dansa, her words are not very distinct even in the slow-moving Aria.

By his deeply expressive shaping of No 4's Preludio Tilson Thomas avoids any satiety with its extreme monothematicism, and in the second movement secures coherent continuity despite the (rather loud) insistent interventions of the araponga bird's repeated note. He produces a beautifully poetic tranquillity in the brief Prelude of No 9 and complete lucidity and rhythmic buoyancy in its Fugue. If that is the most Bachian of the series, the much more substantial No 7 also has its moments of homage: its first movement has a fine breadth, and its finale is an impressive and serious-minded large-scale fugue that begins quietly and culminates in a grandiose blaze of sound; but the busy Toccata is characteristically and challengingly Brazilian, and the first part of its Giga (before it goes all Hollywood) is delightfully fresh in this invigorating performance.

Bachianas Brasileiras – No 2: Toccata; No 4; No 5. 🅗
Miniaturas – No 2, A Viola. Modinhas e Canções, Series I – No 3, Cantilena. Mornoprecoce. Chôros No 10, 'Rasga o coração'
Victoria de los Angeles *sop* **Frederick Fuller** *bar*

Magda Tagliaferro *pf* **Chorale des Jeunesses Musicales de France; French Radio National Orchestra / Heitor Villa-Lobos** *pf*
EMI Composers in Person mono CDC5 55224-2 Ⓕ
(78 minutes: ADD). Recorded 1948-57 ⭘

For those encountering Villa-Lobos for the first time the simplest approach is via his purely lyrical side – the two songs so sympathetically sung by Frederick Fuller, *A Viola* with its gently insistent rumba rhythm and *Cantilena* wending its way above an unchanging pedal-note before repeating the melody wordlessly. The same wordless treatment is adopted in the haunting first movement of the *Bachianas Brasileiras* No 5 for soprano and eight cellos (which has become Villa-Lobos's best-known piece, partly because of commercial exploitation): the radiance of de los Angeles's voice more than compensates for the less than tidy ensemble in places that the composer achieves as conductor.

Moving to the non-vocal works, nobody could fail to enjoy the Toccata from the Second *Bachianas Brasileiras*, a brilliantly vivid sound picture of a little country train determinedly and happily chuffing along – as inventive as Honegger's earlier *Pacific 231* but more fun: the final exhausted long emission of steam cannot but make you laugh. The orchestral virtuosity which that piece demands reappears in the complex rhythms of the finale of *Bachianas Brasileiras* No 4, whose much more straightforward first three movements, however, provide some clue to the composer's avowed preoccupation with Bach. Villa-Lobos's lifelong interest in children is illustrated by the noisily high-spirited fantasy *Momoprecoce* (derived from the piano suite *Children's Carnival*): its dedicatee, Magda Tagliaferro, brings to it all the requisite energy and boisterousness. *Chôros* No 10 brings into play a chorus chanting against a hail of *staccato* syllables: the overall effect is totally unique and immensely exciting. The quality of transfer is bright and clear.

Choral Works

Missa São Sebastião. Bendita sabedoria. Praesepe[a]. Cor dulce, cor amabile. Panis angelicus. Sub tuum praesidium. Ave Maria a 5. Ave Maria a 6. Pater noster. Magnificat-alleluia[b]

[a]**Ansy Boothroyd**, [b]**Elizabeth McCormack** *mez*
Corydon Singers and Orchestra / Matthew Best
Hyperion CDA66638 (77 minutes: DDD). Texts and translations included. Recorded 1992-93 Ⓕ

Asked to identify the composer of all these religious works except the Mass one would be most unlikely to think of Villa-Lobos. That larger-than-life exotic, that extravagantly experimental and boisterous figure, the composer of such chastely restrained music, the sweetly gentle *Cor dulce*, the mellifluous imitative counterpoint of the first of the *Bendita sabedoria* (six brief choral pieces on biblical texts), the controlled fervour of the *Pater noster*? Even the impressive and grandiose *Magnificat-alleluia* gives no hint of its country of origin. The one clue here might be that, of the two *Ave Marias*, the (earlier) five-part setting is in Portuguese. It is only the Mass that reveals all. Amid its austere style and purely diatonic, contrapuntal idiom the *Sanctus* suddenly seems to come from a different background: then one remembers that Sebastian is the patron saint of Rio de Janeiro; and looking into the score one finds that the liturgical heading of each movement is followed by a local one, the final *Agnus Dei* bearing the subtitle 'Sebastian, protector of Brazil'.

This programme, all of unaccompanied music except for the *Magnificat-alleluia*, should not be listened to as a continuity if some feeling of sameness is to be avoided: the Corydon Singers are most efficient in all they do, but the outstanding performance is of the Mass.

Antonio Vivaldi

Italian 1678-1741

GROVE *Vivaldi was the son of a professional violinist who played at St Mark's and may have been involved in operatic management. Vivaldi was trained for the priesthood and ordained in 1703 but soon after his ordination ceased to say Mass; he claimed this was because of his unsure health (he is known to have suffered from chest complaints, possibly asthma or angina). In 1703 he was appointed maestro di violino at the Ospedale della Pietá, one of the Venetian girls orphanages; he remained there until 1709, and held the post again, 1711-16; he then became maestro de' concerti. Later, when he was away from Venice, he retained his connection with the Pietá (at one period he sent two concertos by post each month). He became maestro di capella, 1735-8; even after then he supplied concertos and directed performances on special occasions.*

Vivaldi's reputation had begun to grow with his first publications: trio sonatas (probably 1703-5), violin sonatas (1709) and especially his 12 concertos L'estro armonico op.3 (1711). These, containing some of his finest concertos, were issued in Amsterdam and widely circulated in northern Europe; this prompted visiting musicians to seek him out in Venice and in some cases commission works from him (notably for the Dresden court). Bach transcribed five op.3 concertos for keyboard, and many German composers imitated his style. He published two further sets of sonatas and seven more of concertos, including La stravaganza op.4 (c1712), Il cimento dell'armonia e dell'inventione (c1725, including 'The Four Seasons') and La cetra (1727). It is in the concerto that Vivaldi's chief importance lies. He was the first composer to use ritornello form regularly in fast movements, and his use of it became a model; the same is true of his three-movement plan (fast-slow-fast). His methods of securing greater thematic unity were widely copied, especially the integration of solo and ritornello material; his vigorous rhythmic patterns, his violinistic figuration and his use of sequence were also much imitated. Of his c550 concertos, c350 are for solo instrument (more than 230 for violin); there are c40 double concertos, more than 30 for multiple soloists and nearly 60 for orchestra without solo, while more than 20 are chamber concertos for a small group of solo instruments without orchestra (the 'tutti' element is provided by the instruments all playing together). Vivaldi was an enterprising orchestrator, writing several concertos for unusual combinations like viola d'amore and lute, or for ensembles including chalumeaux, clarinets, horns and other rarities. There are also many solo concertos for bassoon, cello, oboe and flute. Some of his concertos are programmatic, for example 'La tempesta di mare' (the title of three concertos). Into this category also fall 'The Four Seasons', with their representation of seasonal activities and conditions accommodated within a standard ritornello form these are described in the appended sonnets, which he may have written himself.

Vivaldi was also much engaged in vocal music. He wrote a quantity of sacred works, chiefly for the Pietà girls, using a vigorous style in which the influence of the concerto is often marked. He was also involved in opera and spent much time travelling to promote his works. His earliest known opera was given in Vicenza in 1713; later he worked at theatres in Venice, Mantua (1718-20), Rome (probably 1723-5), possibly Vienna and Prague (around 1730), Ferrara (1737), Amsterdam (1738) and possibly Vienna during his last visit. He was by most accounts a difficult man; in 1738 he was forbidden entry to Ferrara ostensibly because of his refusal to say Mass and his relationship with the singer Anna Giraud, a pupil of his with whom he travelled. More than 20 of his operas survive; those that have been revived include music of vitality and imagination as well as more routine items. But Vivaldi's importance lies above all in his concertos, for their boldness and originality and for their central place in the history of concerto form.

Wind Concertos

Bassoon Concertos – C, RV472; D minor, RV482; E minor, RV484; F, RV491; G, RV494; G minor, RV495; A minor, RV499
Klaus Thunemann *bn* **I Musici**
Philips 446 066-2PH (57 minutes: DDD) Ⓕ
Recorded 1994 ●

Vivaldi's distinctive individuality is in full flower in the rich invention which characterises the *tuttis* of the fast movements of his bassoon concertos; and in the slow movements, as so often elsewhere, he proves himself a poet with the most delicate of sensibilities. In all of them, he seems to have been inspired by the colour and range of the instrument itself, exploring almost every possibility available to him in the bassoon of his day and, like Rameau in France, writing especially rewardingly for it in the tenor register. Thunemann, of course, plays an instrument of present-day manufacture, in keeping with the modern string instruments of I Musici; but he makes a very beautiful sound indeed.

To all but the most committed Vivaldians only one of the seven concertos here may seem at all familiar. That is the atmospheric Concerto in E minor (RV484) with its undulating first movement *tuttis* inspired, one might suspect, by Venetian waters. Thunemann instils life into every bar of his interpretation, performing dazzling feats of athleticism apparently with the utmost of ease, while at the same time giving thought to ornamentation. Not a note is either out of tune or misplaced and, in slow movements, many of which possess beguiling lyrical charm, Thunemann reveals himself as a musician of great sensitivity. The *Largo* of the first concerto on the disc (RV491) is a striking example. Readers familiar with Vivaldi's sacred vocal music will recognise its derivation in part from a passage to be found both in his *Magnificat* (RV610) and his *Kyrie* (RV587). In the present context Vivaldi imbues an already arresting harmonic pattern with a drowsy, almost dreamlike fantasy in which the bassoon writing, treated here with an affecting improvisatory freedom, ranges widely with some striking intervals against sustained, softly modulating strings. It's a brief moment of magic.

Six Flute Concertos, Op 10
Patrick Gallois *fl* **Orpheus Chamber Orchestra**
DG 437 839-2GH (49 minutes: DDD) Ⓕ
Recorded 1992 ●

Patrick Gallois is a player of agility and sensitivity, an intelligent artist who can make his metal flute speak with all the subtlety of varied articulation and tone colour that some of us had come to assume was only possible on the wooden baroque instrument. These are deliciously light performances, in the best sense of the word; plenty of air allowed in, sparing and thoughtful use of vibrato, and above all an infectious bounce to the music-making in general. Gallois's sunny approach is matched by the excellent string players of the Orpheus Chamber Orchestra, whose stunning unanimity of ensemble, crispness of attack and sheer concentration-level once again make it hard to believe that they operate without a conductor. And both soloist and orchestra are equally responsive, too, to the uniquely tranquil beauties of the Vivaldian slow movement.

Flute Concertos, Op 10.
Flute Concerto in C minor, RV441
Nicolaus Esterházy Sinfonia / Béla Drahos *fl*
Naxos 8 553101 (59 minutes: DDD) Ⓢ
Recorded 1995 ●

Vivaldi's flute concertos have certainly not been neglected on disc, and there is a wide choice of 'authentic' and middle-of-the-road versions played on both tranverse flute and recorder; this present selection is in the MOR vein and faces numerous competitors. In the flute concertos Béla Drahos is a superb soloist, as smooth as silk and agile as a kitten, and whose flights of fanciful embellishment might have won Vivaldi's approval. The Esterházy Sinfonia sounds a little beefy at times in its opening statements, but in the presence of the soloist its touch is appropriately light, and the third *Largo* ('Il sonno'), of Op 10 No 2, 'La notte', is impressively hushed.

The outer movements of the bonus concerto, R441, dance on the lightest of feet; the work was originally written for the recorder, but on whichever instrument it is played, you wonder why it has no other currently listed recording. This present one would carry a warm recommendation even if it were not at bargain price.

Double Concerto for Two Oboes and Strings in D minor, RV535. Concertos for Multiple Instruments – A, RV552, 'per eco in lontano'; D, RV562; F, RV568; F, RV569; G minor, RV577, 'per l'orchestra di Dresda' **P**

Philharmonia Baroque Orchestra / Nicholas McGegan

Reference Recordings RRCD77 (72 minutes: DDD) Ⓕ
Recorded 1996 ●

Here is Vivaldi-playing with a commendably light, athletic touch. It is so easy to make a meal out of his orchestral *tutti*s yet these performances inspire the music with expressive delicacy and rhythmic vitality. The programme is a colourful one of concertos for a variety of instruments, wind and strings, in various combinations. Apart from occasional instances of predictable passagework, present above all in some of the wind writing, this music is engaging on many different levels. Slow movements such as the wonderfully free violin fantasy of RV562 reveal the exhilarating flights of fancy of which Vivaldi was capable, while the profusion of alluring inflexions present in fast and slow movements alike makes strong appeal to the senses. Vivaldi was no stranger to the art of parody and, in the opening movement of RV568, we find him introducing sensuous, sighing quaver motifs present in the finale of the *Concerto a due cori per la Santissima Assenzione di Maria Vergine* (RV535). This kind of approach to Vivaldi's music greatly enlivens and refreshes its innate character. The disc is superbly recorded, allowing us to revel in every sonorous detail of solo and continuo playing alike.

Oboe Concertos – C, RV447; C, RV450; D, RV453; A minor, RV461; A minor, RV463. Concerto for Violin and Oboe in B flat, RV548

Douglas Boyd *ob* **Marieke Blankestijn** *vn* **Chamber Orchestra of Europe**

DG 435 873-2GH (59 minutes: DDD) Ⓕ
Recorded 1991 ●

Vivaldi wrote 17 solo oboe concertos, three for two oboes and another for oboe and violin. In this virtuoso programme the oboist, Douglas Boyd, has chosen five of the solo oboe concertos together with the more modestly conceived but no less captivating Concerto in B flat for oboe and violin. The oboe concertos have been selected discerningly, not only for their musical interest but also, it would seem, with an eye to their rarity value on the concert platform. Boyd, playing a modern oboe, gives fluent, sensitively shaped performances and is supported in a lively manner by the strings of the COE. Boyd is expressive in slow movements – they almost invariably possess considerable lyrical appeal – and athletic in faster ones; and he needs to be, for Vivaldi seldom showed mercy on his soloists. From among the many beautiful movements here the *Larghetto* of the Concerto in A minor (RV461) stands out and may be ranked among Vivaldi's happiest creations for the oboe. Fine recorded sound.

Cello Concertos

Cello Concerto in A minor, RV422. Violin Concerto in D minor, Op 4 No 8. String Concertos – C, RV117; E minor, RV134; G, RV151, 'Alla rustica'. Amor, hai vinto, RV683. Cessate, omai cessate, RV684 **P**

Sara Mingardo *mez* **Francesca Vicari** *vn* **Luigi Piovano** *vc* **Concerto Italiano / Rinaldo Alessandrini** *hpd*

Opus 111 OPS30-181 (60 minutes: DDD). Texts and translations included. Recorded 1996 Ⓕ ●

This thoughtfully and attractively devised programme by Rinaldo Alessandrini and Concerto Italiano breaks up a sequence of five well contrasted concertos with two of Vivaldi's chamber cantatas. The two vocal pieces are both for alto with divided violins, viola and continuo; and their subject matter, dealt with in the customary pattern of two alternating recitatives and arias, concerns the efficacy of Cupid's arrows on those incredibly susceptible denizens of Arcadia.

Sara Mingardo enlivens this music at every turn. Her voice is warm in tone, evenly projected and, in a pastoral setting where the cruel pangs of loveare felt in almost every bar, appropriately anguished. The chamber cantatas are still among Vivaldi's better kept secrets and there is much that satisfies heart and mind alike. Of the five concertos three are *concerti a quattro*, or strings without soloist; in the solo concertos cellist Luigi Piovano and violinist Francesca Vicari, who also leads Concerto Italiano, are fluently stylish and technically assured. Like Alessandrini and his ensemble, they bring plenty of graceful gesture and effective articulation to the music.

A most satisfying recital, both interpretively and for the window it opens on to the composer's widely ranging expressive vocabulary.

Cello Concertos – C minor, RV402; D minor, RV406; G, RV414. Sonatas – A minor, RV44; E flat, RV39; G minor, RV42 **P**

Christophe Coin *vc* **Academy of Ancient Music / Christopher Hogwood** *hpd*

L'Oiseau-Lyre 433 052-2OH (67 minutes: DDD) Ⓕ
Recorded 1990 ●

Christophe Coin's feeling for dance rhythms, his clear articulation and musical phrasing and his sharp ear for detail bring the concertos and sonatas alive in an infectious way. He is both firmly and imaginatively supported in the sonatas by a fine continuo group, and in the concertos by the strings of the Academy of Ancient

Music. In the sonatas Christopher Hogwood varies the colour of the accompaniments by moving between harpsichord and organ, while cello and baroque guitar add further variety and support. In the concertos, fast movements are characterised by vigorous, idiomatic passage-work for the solo instrument punctuated by pulsating Vivaldian rhythms in the *tuttis*. In the slow movements, richly endowed with lyricism, the expressive intensity of the music is, on occasion, almost startling, revealing Vivaldi as a composer capable of far greater affective gestures than he is often given credit for. This music never fails to move the spirit.

Awards 1996

Double and Triple Concertos
Two Cellos and Strings in G minor, RV531; Violin, Cello and Strings in F, RV544, 'Il Proteo ò sia il mondo rovescio'; Three Violins and Strings in F, RV551; Two Violins and Strings in A, RV552, 'Per eco in lontano'; Violin, Two Cellos and Strings in C, RV561; Two Violins, Two Cellos and Strings in D, RV564
Christophe Coin *vc* **Il Giardino Armonico / Giovanni Antonini**
Teldec Das Alte Werk 4509-94552-2 Ⓕ
(64 minutes: DDD). Recorded 1994 ●●●

This is a strong programme which almost unfailingly presents the Venetian composer in his most colourful clothing. Though Vivaldi often wrote imaginatively for pairs of wind instruments, his musical ideas were of necessity confined by their technical limitations. With violins and cellos, on the other hand, he was better able to extend his creative faculties, which resulted in music of more sustained interest. This is certainly true of the two concertos which he wrote for two violins, two cellos and strings, one of them (RV564) included here. Making an even rarer appearance on disc is a Concerto in F major for violin and cello (RV544), the least well known of three such works from Vivaldi's pen. Two versions of this concerto exist, the other (RV572) containing additional parts for pairs of flutes and oboes. Both carry the engaging title *Il Proteo ò sia il mondo al rovescio*. Infrequently performed, too, is a C major piece for violin, two cellos and strings (RV561), though the characteristically Vivaldian ritornello of the opening movement may recall other contexts in the minds of listeners.

The three remaining works are fairly mainstream Vivaldi: the G minor Concerto for two cellos (RV531), the F major Concerto for three violins (RV551) and the A major Concerto for two violins, one of them functioning as an echo, the *violine per eco in lontano* (RV552). From this, readers will infer a pleasing variety of texture and, within the limits of a purely string programme, colour. Il Giardino Armonico has thought carefully about the latter, ringing the changes in the keyboard continuo between organ and harpsichord, and introducing a theorbo, too. But what makes this disc a real winner is the exhilarating character of the playing, both solo and ripieno. Playing of vitality and lyricism brings Vivaldi's music to life in a thrilling manner. Indeed, the integrity and musicianly character of these performances is in no small measure heightened by the presence of Christophe Coin. An outstanding issue.

Violin Concertos

Sinfonia for Strings in G, RV149. Concertos for Violin and Strings, Op 8 – No 5 in E flat, RV253, 'La tempesta di mare'; No 6 in C, RV108, 'Il piacere'. Double Concerto for Viola d'amore, Lute and Strings in D minor, RV540. Concertos for Multiple Instruments – A, RV552, 'Per eco in lontano'; C, RV558 **P**
Academy of Ancient Music / Andrew Manze *vn*
Harmonia Mundi HMU90 7230 (65 minutes: DDD) Ⓕ
Recorded 1996 ●

In one respect or another all the pieces here are vintage Vivaldi and, taken together, they offer a fair conspectus of his expressive range, his feeling for instrumental colour and his originality. Three of the four works performed have become firm favourites among 20th-century audiences: the Concertos for viola d'amore and lute (RV540), for violin, echo violins and strings (RV552) and *con molti istromenti* (RV558). The fourth item, a wonderfully spirited *Sinfonia* (RV149), Vivaldi wrote as an introduction to a serenata, now lost, by another composer.

The performances are splendid. Manze has a pleasing awareness of the inherent poesy and fantasy in Vivaldi's music and has the technique to make the most of it. *La tempesta di mare* is particularly enjoyable and the tenderly expressive Concerto for viola d'amore and lute – the gently swung rhythm of the sublime *Largo* is as pleasing as Manze's ornamented repeats.

The orchestra is generally on good form, responsive to Vivaldi and Manze alike. These aspects can be savoured above all in the C major Concerto with its treble recorders, tenor chalumeaux, mandolins, theorbos, violins, cello and string *tutti*. Vivaldi was clearly intent on showing off the diverse, multicoloured musical talents of his pupils in this rhythmically infectious piece. A delightful programme, executed with refinement.

Sinfonias – Bajazet, Dorilla in Tempe, Farnace, Il giustino, L'Olimpiade, Ottone in Villa, La verita' in Cimento. Violin Concertos[a] – C minor, 'Amato bene', RV761; F, RV571. Concerto for Strings in D minor, RV128. Sinfonia for Strings in G, RV149
[a]**Federico Guglielmo** *vn* **L'Arte dell'Arco / Christopher Hogwood**
Deutsche Harmonia Mundi 05472 77501-2 Ⓕ
68 minutes: DDD). Recorded 1998 ●

Federico Guglielmo, solo violinist, has assembled an engaging programme of Vivaldi's opera overtures, or sinfonias 'avanti l'opera'. Interspersed are three of the composer's concertos, one of them of the ripieno type, that is, without soloists, another an infrequently performed violin concerto, *Amato bene*, the third a colourful piece with pairs of oboes, horns and a bassoon, with a lyrically expressive slow movement for the solo violin. Under its guest director, Christopher Hogwood, the playing of L'Arte dell'Arco is spirited, with a textural transparency and stylistic discipline.

The music is almost unfailingly attractive. Most of the pieces are scored for strings but the invigorating Overture to *Bajazet*, he who was conquered by Tamerlano, fields a resonant pair of horns, while oboes feature prominently in that to Vivaldi's first opera, *Ottone in Villa*. Vivaldi was no stranger to the art of self-borrowing and there are instances of it in *Dorilla in Tempe*, which quotes the opening movement of 'Spring' from the *Four Seasons* and *L'Olimpiade* which, for its last movement, borrows from the 'Ut collocet' of a *Laudate pueri* (RV601) that Vivaldi had probably written a year or two earlier. Any occasional lack of finesse in this playing is amply compensated for by its convivial spirit and by the vitality and well-sustained interest of the music itself. In short, an entertaining programme, imaginatively brought to life by players whose revelry in its content is contagious.

Viola d'amore Concertos

Concerto for Viola d'amore, Lute and Strings in D minor, RV540. Chamber Concerto in G minor, RV107. Concerto for Cello and Strings in G, RV413. Concerto for Flute and Strings in G minor, 'La notte', RV439. Concerto for Oboe and Strings in D minor, RV454. Concerto for Two Horns and Strings in F, RV539. Concertos for Multiple Instruments – in D minor, RV566; in F, 'Il Proteo ò sia il mondo rovescio', RV572 **P**

Orchestra of the Age of Enlightenment

Linn Records CKD151 (74 minutes: DDD) Ⓕ

Recorded 2000

It is a nice idea for the Orchestra of the Age of Enlightenment to record a disc of such varied Vivaldian fare. The young women of the orchestra which Vivaldi directed at the Ospedale della Pietà in Venice were as renowned for the range of instruments they could wield as for their virtuosity; so it seems neatly apposite that the OAE, so full of capable soloists itself, should use this music to celebrate its members' own star qualities. And the mixture is a wide one: three solo concertos; a rare Concerto for two horns; the deservedly popular Concerto for lute and viola d'amore, two concertos for typically extravagant Vivaldian multiple line-ups; and one of those chamber concertos in which all the players are soloists.

The OAE play with great expertise and good taste throughout. Judging by the list in the booklet, they use a relatively large body of strings, but, although this is noticeable, there is no feeling of heaviness, and indeed the use of two double-basses gives the sound a substantial foundation which is at the same time deliciously light on its feet. There is a total of 16 soloists listed: among the highlights are David Watkin's habitually assured and intensely musical playing of the Cello Concerto; Lisa Beznosiuk, sensitive as ever in *La notte* (though struggling a bit against the string sound); Andrew Clark and Roger Montgomery, treading securely and confidently through the Concerto for two horns; Anthony Robson, a little under the note sometimes but showing good breath control and phrasing in the Oboe Concerto; and a fairy-light performance of the Concerto for lute and viola d'amore from Elizabeth Kenny and Catherine Mackintosh.

The performances are all directorless, and there was the odd place where a guiding hand might have pepped things up (or stopped the theorbo from twiddling so much in the slow movement of the Cello Concerto), but in general this is a relaxed and convivial Vivaldi programme that one can simply sit back and enjoy.

Viola d'amore Concertos – D, RV392; D minor, RV393; D minor, RV394; D minor, RV395; A, RV396; A minor, RV397 **P**

Orchestra of the Age of Enlightenment / Catherine Mackintosh *va d'amore*

Hyperion CDA66795 (67 minutes: DDD) Ⓕ

Recorded 1995

John Evelyn (1620-1706) was beguiled and surprised by the sound of the viola d'amore, but he should hardly have been so by the fact that it was on that occasion 'played ... by a *German*'; that was the nationality of most of the composers who wrote for it – Bach, Biber, Telemann and Mattheson. The instrument was distinguished by its wide compass, its use of sympathetic strings (not bowed but allowed to resonate), and the fact that it lent itself to playing 'the lyra way' (as with the bass viola da gamba), facilitating the use of multiple stopping and contrapuntal textures. Vivaldi was obviously no less attracted by it; six concertos are a lot for such an unusual instrument, and it is fair to say that they represent some of the most beguiling music he wrote. Mackintosh, on top form, acts her role with the utmost virtuosity, lovely tone, unimpeachable intonation, and fine style – with some elegant embroidery. The OAE is admirable, making this recording one to treasure.

String Concertos

Concertos for Strings – G minor, RV531; D, RV564. Concertos for Recorder and Strings – A minor, RV108; G, RV436. Trio Sonatas – D minor, 'La follia', RV63; C minor, RV83 **P**

Musica Alta Ripa

Dabringhaus und Grimm MDG309 0927-2 (56 minutes: DDD). Recorded 1999 Ⓕ

None of the pieces is new to the catalogue, but the playing is of a calibre that might entice readers to consider these alternative versions. The two largest works are the Concerto for two cellos and strings in G minor, and another, in D major, for two violins, two cellos and strings. Both fare well in the hands of sensitive performers such as these, and especially enjoyable is the beautifully inflected playing of the two solo cellists in the G minor work.

Albert Brüggen is an excellent cellist, and here (alongside partner Juris Teichmanis) he fulfils expectation raised by previous discs. Vivaldi wrote two concertos for pairs of solo violins and cellos; the other is RV575 – and both are satisfying pieces with beguiling slow movements. Melodically, this one gives pride of place to a solo violin in its centrally placed *Largo*, but one should nevertheless be allowed to hear more of the solo cello than is granted by this performance. The rhythmic élan of the finale is quite exhilarating.

The two remaining concertos feature a recorder. One, RV436, is scored for transverse flute with strings, though a descant recorder has been substituted here. The other, RV108, is a chamber concerto for treble recorder, two violins and continuo. The soloist in each is Danya Segal, who brings the music to life with fluency and unpretentious eloquence. An attractive menu is completed by two strongly contrasting sonatas which, in their quite different ways, demonstrate Vivaldi's craftsmanship and invention in the medium. The D minor Sonata is the concluding item in Vivaldi's first printed opus (1705), and consists of a set of 19 variations on the 'Follia' melody. The other, in C minor, is for violin and cello, and its strength of character and solo writing for a high and a low instrument invites comparison with the equally impressive, better known Sonata for treble recorder and bassoon (RV86). In this work, Vivaldi sustains a supple, at times brilliant dialogue between the protagonists.

This disc makes rewarding listening. The pieces have been chosen with real discernment and they are played with virtuosity and an effective understanding of style.

String Concertos – D minor, RV129, 'Concerto madrigalesco'; E flat, RV130, 'Sonata al santo sepolcro'; C minor, RV202; G minor, RV517; B flat, RV547; C minor, RV761. Sinfonia in B minor, RV169, 'Sinfonia al santo sepolcro' **P**
Adrian Chamorro *vn* **Maurizio Naddeo** *vc*
L'Europa Galante / Fabio Biondi *vn*
Opus 111 OPS2027 (52 minutes: DDD) Ⓕ
Recorded 1990 ●

This invigorating programme contains well-known and less well-known concertos by Vivaldi. The performances sparkle with life and possess an irresistible spontaneity. The Concertos for one and two violins (RV761 and RV202) are comparative rarities and are played with agility and insight by the soloist director Fabio Biondi and his alert and responsive ensemble. Biondi himself is capable of light and articulate bowing and has a natural feeling for graceful turns of phrase. Vivaldi's virtuoso writing occasionally finds chinks in his armour, but with enlightened music-making of this order it matters little. Everywhere Vivaldi's infectious rhythms are tautly controlled and the music interpreted with character and conviction.

Perhaps the highlight of the disc is the Concerto in B flat for violin and cello. Outer movements are crisply articulated and played with almost startling energy while the poignant lyricism of the *Andante* is touchingly captured. A refreshing and illuminating disc; the recorded sound is clear and ideally resonant.

Dresden Concertos – D, RV213; D, RV219; D, RV224; D minor, RV240; E flat, RV260; A, RV344; B minor, RV388
Cristiano Rossi *vn* **Accademia I Filarmonici / Alberto Martini**
Naxos 8 554310 (67 minutes: DDD) Ⓢ
Recorded 1998

The Dresden link was forged by Vivaldi's friend and one-time pupil, Johann Georg Pisendel. Pisendel visited Venice in 1716 when he appears to have struck up a warm friendship with Vivaldi, who dedicated several sonatas and concertos to him. The seven violin concertos on this disc have survived in manuscripts preserved in the Dresden Sächsische Landesbibliothek. Much of this music will be entirely new to most collectors. By and large these are pieces which do not wear their hearts on their sleeves. There are few extravagant flourishes and perhaps less than we might expect in the way of extrovert gesture. But there is no lack of brilliance in the solo violin writing – Pisendel's reputation as a virtuoso was hardly less than Vivaldi's – and, as ever, the music contains a profusion of effective rhythmic ideas. The solo violin parts are entrusted to Cristiano Rossi who often, though not always, discovers the fantasy in Vivaldi's solo writing. The bowing is graceful and relaxed even if intonation is occasionally awry. The A major Concerto, RV344 affords a good instance of soloist and orchestra at their most persuasive. But the lyrically expressive violin melody against a dotted rhythm continuo of the *Largo* of RV224 is unquestionably the most alluring. The more you hear this music, the more you are likely to be captivated by it. The recorded sound seems a little boxy and confined, but textures come through clearly all the same.

'L'estro armonico', Op 3

L'estro armonico **P**
Europa Galante / Fabio Biondi *vn*
Virgin Classics Veritas ② VMD5 45315-2 Ⓕ
(100 minutes: DDD). Recorded 1997-98 ●●

No other set of Vivaldi's concertos contains the sheer variety on display in *L'estro armonico*. The catalogue has seldom been without a decent recording of these ceaselessly fascinating concertos, though none begins to approach this version in respect of fantasy and exuberance. Fabio Biondi and his Italian ensemble, Europa Galante, bring something entirely fresh and vital to oft-performed repertoire, illuminating well-trodden paths with affective articulation and eloquently voiced inflexions. Not all of their extravagant, Mediterranean gestures, perhaps, will find favour with listeners; indeed, some of Biondi's own embellishments can be a little inapposite. Tempos are well chosen, by and large, and ensemble is clear-textured and evenly balanced. The continuo group, which includes harpsichord, organ, archlute and baroque guitar, makes an important contribution to the overall success. This music is wonderful stuff, rejuvenating and immensely satisfying.

'La stravaganza', Op 4

Concertos for Violin and Strings, 'La stravaganza', Op 4 – No 1 in B flat, RV383*a*; No 2 in E minor, RV279; No 3 in G, RV301; No 4 in A minor, RV357; No 5 in A, RV347; No 6 in G minor, RV316*a*
Andrew Watkinson *vn* **City of London Sinfonia / Nicholas Kraemer**
Naxos 8 553323 (52 minutes: DDD) Ⓢ
Recorded 1995

Violin Concertos, 'La stravaganza', Op 4 – No 7 in C, RV185; No 8 in D minor, RV249; No 9 in F, RV284; No 10 in C minor, RV196; No 11 in D minor, RV204; No 12 in G, RV298
Andrew Watkinson *vn* **City of London Sinfonia / Nicholas Kraemer**
Naxos 8 553324 (46 minutes: DDD) Ⓢ
Recorded 1995

La stravaganza is the second of the sets of concertos published during Vivaldi's lifetime. It was issued in about 1714 as the composer's Op 4 and, as with the greater number of his printed collections, contains 12 works. They are essentially violin concertos, although, to a much lesser extent than *L'estro armonico*, Vivaldi also provides on occasion solo parts for an additional violin or cello. These concertos have long been favourites, above all, perhaps, for the profusion of lyrically affecting slow movements, of which those belonging to Concertos Nos 1, 4, 5 and 12 are notably fine examples: in this music there is delicate nuance, poetic fantasy and sheer originality lying beneath the immediately recognisable hallmarks of the composer's outward style.

Nicholas Kraemer is no stranger to this repertory having already recorded two of Vivaldi's other printed sets, Opp 8 and 9. Those, however, were with his period-instrument Raglan Baroque Players, whereas *La stravaganza* is played on instruments tuned to today's standard pitch. This, paradoxically, may be closer to the pitch which Vivaldi himself used rather than the lower baroque pitch.

Listening to this music, so full of vitality, invention and expressive tenderness, leaves one feeling exhilarated and the better for so doing. Andrew Watkinson plays with virtuosic flair, but senses the highly developed fantasy present in every one of the concertos. His embellishments are tasteful and restrained and his melodic line always clearly articulated. Tempos, for the most part, are effectively judged, though the almost unbearably beautiful *Largo* of the First Concerto, with its emotionally highly charged modulation towards the close, is perhaps a shade too slow.

The strings of the City of London Sinfonia sound tonally bright and unfailingly alert. Only in the *Adagio* of No 8 does the balance of the recording falter; the harpsichord's arpeggios (cf the *Adagio molto* of 'Autumn') might have been allowed a little more prominence.

The Four Seasons, Op 8 Nos 1-4

Violin Concertos, Op 8 – Nos 1-4, 'The Four Seasons': No 1 in E, 'Spring', RV269; No 2 in G minor, 'Summer', RV315; No 3 in F, 'Autumn', RV293; No 4 in F minor, 'Winter', RV297; **No 5** in E flat, RV253, **'La tempesta di mare'; No 6** in C, RV180, **'Il piacere'; No 7** in D minor, RV242; **No 9** in D minor, RV236; **No 10** in B flat, RV362, **'La caccia'; No 11** in D, RV210; **No 12** in C (two versions, RV178 and RV449)

The Four Seasons, Op 8 Nos 1-4. Violin Concertos in E flat, RV257; in B flat, RV376; in D, RV211 🅿
Giuliano Carmignola *vn* **Venice Baroque Orchestra / Andrea Marcon**
Sony Classical SK51352 Ⓕ
(72 minutes: DDD) **OO**

Vivaldi's *Four Seasons*, like nature's, come and go in their various moods and meteorological vicissitudes. We've had ochre sunsets from Louis Kaufmann, Harnoncourt's Breughel-style rusticity and the provocative Nigel Kennedy, to mention but a scant few. Giuliano Carmignola's primary claim on our attentions (this is his second shot at the piece) is, aside from a delightfully woody-sounding baroque instrument, a keen narrative flair. Furthermore, he knows the musical period, understands principles of embellishment and doesn't hesitate to enrich his performances with added colour and with rhythmic thrust.

'Spring' arrives in rude high spirits, toying with birdsong (slowly at first then speeding up) and with thunder thrashing between violin desks. The violas' 'barking dog' is worryingly prominent (that is if you don't like dogs) and the finale contrasts a swelling *legato* against sparkly solo passagework. The 'impetuous weather' of 'Summer' has power enough to keep the National Grid up and running, and the diverse winds of the multi-faceted opening *Allegro* of 'Autumn' and the way the harpsichord holds its own in the second and third movements are wonderful. The cruel weathers of 'Winter' inspire the expected bursts of virtuosity while the *Largo*'s raindrops unexpectedly seep through to the busy bass line (most versions don't allow for the leak). Varieties of plucked continuo help fill out textures and Carmignola himself plays with immense brilliance.

The three additional violin concertos are all said to be first recordings and reveal a rather different aspect of Vivaldi's style. Generally speaking, they sound more formal than the *Four Seasons*, almost pre-classical in RV257's opening *Andante molto e quasi allegro* and with sideways glances at Rameau in the opening of RV211 (which also includes a brief first-movement cadenza). Dance rhythms again predominate.

Great sound, by the way, full and forward and with every instrumental strand given its proper due. Thinking in terms only of the *Four Seasons*, good rivals are so plentiful that comparative discussion becomes less a question of 'who gets it right' than how you like your birds and storms. There are countless period-instrument options and almost as many that use modern instruments but take heed of period performing practice. Up to now, the period favourites have been Il Giardino Armonico and Harnoncourt's Concentus Musicus Wien, but there's no reason why this new version shouldn't join their hallowed ranks. It certainly deserves to.

Violin Concertos, Op 8 – Nos 1-4, 8 and 9 🅿
Enrico Onofri *vn* **Paolo Grazzi** *ob*
Il Giardino Armonico / Giovanni Antonini
Teldec 4509-96158-2 (61 minutes: DDD) Ⓕ
Recorded 1993 ●●

Il Giardino Armonico doesn't do anything extraordinary; it is more a matter of its demonstration of what can be achieved with small forces – 5.1.2.1 plus soloist and continuo. Here, small is flexible and it highlights the differences in colour achieved by varying the continuo – bassoon, cello, organ, harpsichord and theorbo, unobscured by the ripieno, all have their moments. Numbers of 'chamber' dimensions also favour unanimity of attack and changes of dynamics and pace, all vividly accomplished by IGA. The dog barks harshly in 'Spring' but without disturbing the shepherd's peaceful dreams, and the chill of 'Autumn' in the *Adagio molto* is conveyed by the ethereal strings with the harpsichord firmly relegated to a supporting role. Onofri is as good a soloist as may be met in a long march, pitch-perfect, incisive but not 'edgy', and effortlessly alert to every nuance. All the foregoing good things are also to be found in the other two concertos from Op 8, together with Grazzi's liquid-toned and agile oboe playing in that in D minor, attractively supported in the *Largo* by theorbo and bassoon. A tasty addition to any collection.

Violin Concertos, Op 8[a] – Nos 1-5. Oboe Concerto in A minor, RV461[b]. Bassoon Concerto in D minor, RV481[c]
[b]**Robin Williams** *ob* [c]**Ursula Leveaux** *bn* [a]**Anthony Marwood** *vn* **Scottish Chamber Orchestra / Nicholas McGegan**
Classic fM The Full Works 75605 57045-2 Ⓜ
(67 minutes: DDD). Recorded 1998 ●

The aim of Classic fM's The Full Works series is to make classical music more accessible. Although modern instruments and pitch are used in these recordings, should any listener be persuaded to take the further step of trying and liking fully 'authentic' recordings, that would be the icing on very well-baked and tasty cakes. Anthony Marwood gets just about everything stylistically right, and shows an instinctive flair for embellishment in *The Four Seasons*. These performances (and that of the comparably programmatic *La tempesta di mare*), with sprucely pointed and sensitively controlled support, succeed in the difficult task of making these concertos sound fresh. Likewise, there is nothing but praise for Robin Williams's oboe playing (with some passages of remarkable 'snake's-tongued' articulation) and Ursula Leveaux's concealment of the difficulty of meeting Vivaldi's often near-outrageous demands on bassoon players, past and present. Both put their skills at the service of pure music-making. Authentic or not, all these beautifully balanced performances are some of the most enjoyable available.

Violin Concertos, Op 8 – Nos 1-4. Oboe Concertos, Op 7 – No 1 in B flat, RV465; No 5 in F, RV285*a* 🅿
Andrew Manze *vn* **Marcel Ponseele** *ob*
Amsterdam Baroque Orchestra / Ton Koopman
Erato 4509-94811-2 (56 minutes: DDD) Ⓕ
Recorded 1993-94 ●

This is a splendid set, valid for a lifetime of pleasure. Little differences in attention to detail soon begin to show, first at 0'17" of the first movement of 'Spring', where the chords that are usually hit hard are here given a happy little squeeze. Amsterdam Baroque (consisting here of 13 instrumentalists) plays with the unanimity of one mind and body, with extreme changes of volume that never sound theatrically contrived, as concerned with the fate of every note as with the shaping of each phrase. Manze's bow breathes vocal life into his strings; in the slow movements many notes whisper their way into being, and his *fortissimo* whiplashes have rasp-free edges. There are many delightful little personal touches – his slurred resolution of the sighing appoggiatura at 2'50" in the third movement of 'Spring', and the way he nudges his way up the ladder of trills in the first movement of 'Autumn' are just two. The remaining works come from Op 7, in the first of which (RV465) the oboe is the designated soloist; its transcribed role in No 5 (RV285*a*) accords with baroque practice. Both are charming works with a high level of inspiration, played with no less affection than the *Seasons*.

Violin Concertos, Op 8 – Nos 1-6
Mariana Sirbu *vn* **I Musici**
Philips 446 699-2PH (60 minutes: DDD) Ⓕ
Recorded 1995 ●

Mariana Sirbu here joins the company of the many artists who have recorded *The Four Seasons*. Sirbu is no less incisive than any of the others and, particularly in the slow movements which she plays with little added adornment, her lines are fine and imaginatively nuanced. I Musici remain crisp and responsive, and a novel touch is their addition of a lute to the continuo; it is from time to time audible, providing the little fill-ins usually the prerogative of the harpsichord, as for example in the final *Presto* of 'Summer' and the *Adagio molto* of 'Autumn', though in the latter its economical comments perhaps lack the icy edge of the harpsichord. The two other concertos from Op 8 (*La tempesta di mare* and *Il piacere*) are no less compellingly played.

This may be counted among the very best middle-of-the-road versions of *The Four Seasons*, strongly recommended to first-time buyers. The well-balanced recording has brightness and life.

Violin Concertos, Op 8 – Nos 5-7, 9-11 and 12 (two versions) Ⓟ
Enrico Onofri *vn* **Paolo Grazzi** *ob*
Il Giardino Armonico / Giovanni Antonini
Teldec Das Alte Werk 4509-94566-2 Ⓕ
(74 minutes: DDD). Recorded 1994-95 ●

In the completion disc of Il Giardino Armonico's Op 8, as two of the concertos exist in alternative forms, with oboe *vice* violin (RV236 = 454, RV178 = 449), they are given in both versions – with negligible differences in tempo. The virtues of Il Giardino Armonico are, if anything, even more vividly apparent in this recording. Onofri is once again spellbinding in his imaginative use of a varied continuo, here highlighted in the *Adagio* of RV362 (*La caccia*) played only by violin and theorbo. One complaint: if there is logic behind the order in which the concertos are presented, it is not apparent. The first volume has six concertos (61 minutes), Vol 2 has eight (74 minutes), whereas to place Nos 1-6 and RV454 on one disc, and Nos 7-12 and RV449 on the other would have created no apparent problem. One would, however, need a far more compelling reason not to make a beeline for the nearest CD store for these magical and finely recorded discs.

Concertos for Multiple Instruments

Concerto for Multiple Instruments in C, RV557. Ⓟ
Double Concertos – 2 Oboes in D minor, RV535; Oboe and Bassoon in G, RV545; 2 Trumpets in C, RV537; 2 Horns in F, RV538. Oboe Concerto in A minor, RV461. Bassoon Concerto in E minor, RV484
Ensemble Zefiro / Alfredo Bernardini
Astrée Naïve E8679 (64 minutes: DDD) Ⓕ
Recorded 1998 ●●

Ensemble Zefiro is one of the most remarkable baroque bands to emerge during the last decade or so, though we hear of it less often than it deserves. Its specialised front line is its battery of exceptionally gifted wind players, but the support troops of strings and continuo are no less worthy of commendation. In all technical and musical respects they think, breathe and act as one. Their dynamic range (from *sotto voce* whisper to as many *f*s as you regard as adding up to '*issimo*') is put to vivid and impressive use, whether terraced in *crescendos* or *diminuendos*, or in the finely judged squeezing of notes. The *Allegros* are crisp, animated, joyously propulsive and full of Italian sunshine, and the eloquent music-making of the oboe and bassoon soloists effortlessly conceals Vivaldi's severe technical demands.

It is perhaps the slow movements that make the deepest impression: how many times have we heard the same harmonic progressions but marvelled at Vivaldi's ability to invest them with constantly new charm and depth? There are appealing conversations in those of RV545 (oboe and bassoon), RV535 (two oboes), RV557 (two recorders, whose players are not among the declared personnel in the booklet!) and RV538 (two cellos). They are all marked by stylish embellishment, and the last was an irresistible reminder of the benchmark recording of the two-cello Concerto RV531 by Pleeth and Bylsma with the AAM (L'Oiseau Lyre).

Nicholas Anderson has rightly described Alberto Grazzi as 'the poet of the bassoon'; in this recording we have a veritable eisteddfod. This is a faultless and marvellous recording.

Concertos[a] – D, 'L'inquietudine', RV234; E, 'Il riposo, per il Santissimo Natale', RV270. Recorder Concerto No 2 in G minor, 'La notte', RV439[b]. Concerto for 2 Cellos in G minor, RV531[c]. Concertos for Multiple Instruments – A, 'Per eco in lontano', RV552; F, 'La tempesta di mare', RV570; B flat, 'Concerto funèbre', RV579 Ⓟ
[b]**Lorenzo Cavasanti** *rec* [c]**Maurizio Naddeo,** [c]**Antonio Fantinuoli** *vcs* **Europa Galante / Fabio Biondi** [a]*vn*
Virgin Veritas VC5 45424-2 (64 minutes: DDD) Ⓕ
Recorded 1999 ●

There's a real lickety-split opening to this colourful disc of Vivaldi concertos: the violin concerto *L'inquietudine*, not one of its composer's best-known, really earns its title with a restlessly virtuosic solo part, dispatched with taut, nervous energy by Fabio Biondi.

In truth there's some scintillating music here, as well as performances which mix suitable inspiration with scrupulous but unfussy attention to detail. The nearest we get to well-trodden ground here are the vigorous *La tempesta di mare* and the fantastical *La notte* (played here in their later 'flute' revisions, but on recorder), and both are performed with tightly controlled virtuosity, and with plenty of surprises – the giant off-beat accents in both concertos' finales, for instance. Elsewhere we get a creamy account of the charming (but perhaps slightly long) *Concerto per eco in lontano*, a strong-boned concerto for two violins, and an exquisite, muted-string Christmas concerto entitled *Il riposo*. If the sombre *Concerto funèbre* for multiple soloists is a slight disappointment, it is only because Concerto Italiano (for Erato) have recently taken it to another level of dark theatricality. Overall, though, this is another disc to add to the growing pile of wonderfully refreshing and enlightening Vivaldi recordings to have come out of Italy in recent years.

Concertos for Multiple Instruments – C, 'Per la Solennità di S Lorenzo', RV556[b]; C, RV554; B flat, 'Concerto funèbre', RV579[b]. Concerto for Strings in E flat, 'Sonata al Santo Sepolcro', RV130[b]. Clarae stellae, RV625[a]. Stabat mater in F minor, RV621[ab]
[a]**Sara Mingardo** *contr* **Concerto Italiano / Rinaldo Alessandrini** [b]*hpd*
Opus 111 OPS30-261 (71 minutes: DDD) Ⓕ
Texts and translations included. Recorded 1999 ●

'Rediscover the feminine vocal world of the Red Priest in Venice' state the cover notes to this release. In fact, only two of the six pieces offered here are vocal, of which the star work, the *Stabat mater*, is one of the few by Vivaldi thought to have been written for a male alto. In both the motet *Clarae stellae* and the *Stabat mater*, Mingardo's singing is firm and richly coloured, moving easily through a range that includes the kind of rock-solid low notes that few male altos seem able to produce. In the *Stabat mater*, furthermore, she demonstrates exemplary control in some notably slow tempos. Where well-regarded recordings of the piece from Andreas Scholl and Robin Blaze have scored through sheer vocal beauty, Mingardo and Alessandrini present a dejectedly emotional and drawn-out reading which, without resorting to hysterics, reaches several levels deeper into the text. This is something quite special, and it's only a pity that the voice is somewhat recessed in the balance.

The instrumental pieces on the disc make a fascinating selection, ranging from two of Vivaldi's kaleidoscopic 'multi-instrument' concertos to the tiny *Sonata al Santo Sepolcro*, and all are performed crisply and with plenty of thoughtful and original detail by Alessandrini and his band. Most striking is the *Concerto funèbre*, a consolatory piece full of unusual instrumental colours – including parts for a chalumeau and three viole all'inglese (a 'lost' instrument substituted here by violas d'amore) – which in its introductory slow movement even manages to take on a rather Beethovenian hue. Elsewhere, the *San Lorenzo* Concerto sees gaily bubbling outer movements framing a memorable slow one in which a typically serene solo violin line is accompanied by a gently prodding C clarinet. It is an extraordinary sound, but only one of the many delights and surprises of this inspiriting disc, which is in almost all respects a most satisfying Vivaldi release.

Chamber Concertos

Chamber Concertos – D, RV93; D, RV94; F, RV98, 'La tempesta di mare'; G minor, RV104, 'La notte'; G minor, RV107; A minor, RV108; F, RV442. Trio Sonata in D minor, RV63 **P**

Il Giardino Armonico

Teldec 4509-91852-2 (67 minutes: DDD) Ⓕ

Recorded 1990-92 ●

There are baroque groups that are frankly dull and there are others on whom stylistic felicity sits naturally and gracefully. Il Giardino Armonico, an 11-strong group of young Italians, is one of the best. Italy, the birthplace of the baroque, has been curiously slow in coming forward with a specialised unit such as this, but the wait has been worthwhile; Il Giardino Armonico is as Italian as the music itself – brightly coloured, individualistic, confident, stylish, arrestingly decorated, bubbling with enthusiasm and ... add your own adjectives. The only un-Italian thing about them is their collective unanimity! Set these performances against any others in the catalogue and, with no detriment to the others, the differences are likely to deal you a blow to the solar plexus. Any sneaking fear that such unbridled élan leads to a uniformly vigorous approach is unfounded; equally 'Italian' is their wide dynamic range, dramatically exploited in RV104 and RV63, and all calls for serenity are answered. The recording is bright and clear.

Trio Sonatas

Trio Sonatas for Two Violins and Continuo, Op 1 – No 7 in E flat, RV65; No 8 in D minor, RV64; No 9 in A flat, RV75; No 10 in B flat, RV78; No 11 in B minor, RV79; No 12 in D minor, RV63, 'Variations on La Follia' **P**

L'Arte dell'Arco / Christopher Hogwood *hpd/org*

Deutsche Harmonia Mundi 05472 77350-2 Ⓕ

(54 minutes: DDD). Recorded 1997 ●

The stronger works of Vivaldi's Op 1 are concentrated within the second half of the set, recorded here. Among them is the best known of the Trios from the collection, the 20 variations on the theme of Spanish origin, *La Follia*. The instruments are tuned fractionally higher than today's concert pitch, rather than the lower A=415, around which most current period-instrument groups prefer to hover. Recent research points to a Venetian tradition of a higher, therefore brighter, pitch in the 17th and 18th centuries. Another feature of the recording lies in the instruments themselves, which belong to the collection of the Ospedale della Pietà with which Vivaldi was associated, on and off, throughout his working life.

The performances are extremely appealing: great consideration is given to instrumental sonority and interplay, and careful thought has gone into the punctuation and phrasing of the music. In this way the listener is at once engaged both in the gesture and oratory of these beautifully crafted pieces. Vivaldi's layout of movements, in all but the last sonata of the set, loosely conforms with that of a typical *sonata da camera* and, within his chosen schemes, he injects all the expressive contrasts and rhythmic vitality which characterise his concertos. L'Arte dell'Arco sensibly, and to some effect, rings the changes of colour and texture in the basso continuo; cello, theorbo, harpsichord and chamber organ are all called upon, but, in one of the sonatas, the two violins are supported by cello, without either keyboard or plucked string. With Hogwood's exemplary playing and tasteful judgement, the pleasure in this disc is complete.

---

12 Trio Sonatas for Two Violins and Continuo, Op 1. Sonata for Cello and Continuo in A minor, RV43. Trio Sonatas for Two Violins and Continuo – C, RV60; F, RV70; G minor, RV72. Trio Sonata for Violin, Cello and Continuo in C minor, RV83

Sonnerie (Emilia Benjamin, Monica Huggett *vns* Alison McGillivray *vc* Gary Cooper *hpd*) with **William Carter** *gtr/lte/theorb*

CPO ② CPO999 511-2 (143 minutes: DDD) Ⓕ

Recorded 1997-98 ●

Good recordings of Vivaldi's Op 1 are hard to come by. The set lacks the distinctive imprint of what we understand and recognise as Vivaldian, yet the pieces have great charm if handled sensitively and imaginatively. These have long been virtuous features in Monica Huggett's playing: her gently inflected approach to the music, shared by the other members of Sonnerie, is a constant pleasure, and is heard to great advantage in the many beguiling slow movements.

In addition to the Op 1 Trio Sonatas, Sonnerie plays two further trios, a Sonata for two violins, a Sonata for violin, cello and continuo and one of Vivaldi's nine cello sonatas. These miscellaneous additions to Sonnerie's programme are in all but one instance more immediately identifiable as products of Vivaldi's pen than the Op 1 pieces. The G minor Sonata hints at other of Vivaldi's chamber works, while the Sonata in F major (RV70), in its two-violin writing, brings to mind Vivaldi's double concertos. The writing is essentially unaccompanied, but in this performance a discreet plucked string instrument is included. The Trio Sonata in C major (RV60) is the least Vivaldian of the appended group and its authenticity was questioned until fairly recently. Yet its spirited *Allegro* finale seems at times to foreshadow passages in the concertos of *L'estro armonico* (Op 3).

Alison McGillivray plays the Cello Sonata with a feeling for the music's declamatory content as well as for its lyrical properties. She ornaments freely but with restraint and her intonation is excellent. The remaining Sonata, for violin and cello (RV83), is a worthy companion piece to the better-known Sonata for treble recorder and bassoon (RV86). Even more than RV70, the supple, virtuoso dialogue for the treble and bass protagonists is concerto-like and is sustained with even balance and expressive sensibility by Huggett and McGillivray.

This is a first-rate release which comfortably outclasses any rival versions of Vivaldi's Op 1, as well as providing us with a rare opportunity of hearing several other uncommonly encountered pieces. Strongly recommended.

Cello Sonatas

Cello Sonatas – E flat, RV39; E minor, RV40; G minor, RV42; A minor, RV44; B flat, RV45; B flat, RV46 **P**

Pieter Wispelwey *vc* **Florilegium Ensemble** (Elizabeth Kenny, William Carter *ltes/theorboes/gtrs* Daniel Yeadon *vc* Neal Peres da Costa *hpd/org*)

Channel Classics CCS6294 (66 minutes: DDD) Ⓕ

Recorded 1994 ●

Vivaldi wrote with great imagination for the cello, and the sonatas, like the concertos, are plentifully endowed with affecting melodies – the third movement of the E minor Sonata is a superb example – and virtuoso gestures. It would seem, on the strength of these pieces, that Vivaldi possessed a rare sensibility to the expressive *cantabile* possibilities in writing for the cello. Certainly, few baroque composers other than Bach and perhaps Geminiani realised the instrument's solo potential better than he.

Wispelwey is a sensitive player who draws a warm if at times under-assertive sound from his instrument. Fast movements are clearly articulated, slow ones lyrically played with some feeling for the poetry of the music. The performances are thoughtful and enlightened, with a continuo group that includes organ, harpsichord, cello, archlutes, theorboes and guitars in a variety of combinations. The quality of the recorded sound is fine.

Violin Sonatas

12 Violin Sonatas, 'Manchester Sonatas' **P**

HMU90 7089: No 1 in C, RV3; No 2 in D minor, RV12; No 3 in G minor, RV757; No 4 in D, RV755; No 5 in B flat, RV759; No 6 in A, RV758

HMU90 7090: No 7 in C minor, RV6; No 8 in G, RV22; No 9 in E minor, RV17*a;* No 10 in B minor, RV760; No 11 in E flat; RV756; No 12 in C, RV754

Romanesca (Andrew Manze *vn* Nigel North *lte/theorbo/gtr* John Toll *hpd*)

Harmonia Mundi HMU90 7089/90 Ⓕ

(73 and 72 minutes: DDD). Recorded 1992 ●

Vivaldi is so well known for his concertos that we are apt to overlook his admittedly much smaller output of sonatas. This set of 12 for violin and continuo was discovered in Manchester's Central Music Library during the 1970s, though five of them exist in versions which have been known for much longer. It is probable that all of them date from the early- to mid-1720s when Vivaldi assembled them to present to Cardinal Ottoboni on the occasion of his visit to Venice, the city of his birth, in 1726.

The violinist Andrew Manze has an appealing rapport with this music and is expressive in his shaping of phrases. He reveals sensibility towards Vivaldi's pleasing melodic contours. Indeed, this is a quality in which these sonatas abound, not only in the varied Preludes with which each Sonata begins but also in the brisker, sometimes very brisk allemandes and correntes. He ornaments the music with an effective blend of fantasy and good taste and he dispenses with bowed continuo instruments, preferring the lighter textures provided by harpsichord, archlute, theorbo or guitar. This is music of great beauty and vitality which will delight most if not all lovers of the late baroque; and it is sympathetically interpreted and warmly recorded.

Stabat mater in F minor, RV621

Confitebor tibi Domine, RV596[a]. Deus tuorum militum, RV612[b]. Stabat mater in F minor, RV621[c]. In turbato mare, RV627[d]. O qui coeli terraeque serenitas, RV631[d]. Non in pratis aut in hortis, RV641[e] **P**

[d]**Susan Gritton** *sop* [abe]**Jean Rigby** *mez* [c]**Robin Blaze** *counterten* [ab]**Charles Daniels** *ten* [a]**Neal Davies** *bass* **The King's Consort / Robert King**

Hyperion CDA66799 (78 minutes: DDD). Texts and translations included. Recorded 1998 Ⓕ ●

This release in Robert King's complete cycle of Vivaldi's church music mainly features works unconnected with the Ospedale della Pietà, including a motet written in Rome and the famous *Stabat mater* composed for a church in Brescia. All are for solo voice or voices and orchestra, and for the most part they all carry the typical Vivaldi trademarks: boisterous energy alongside a tender if angular lyricism; a vivid and excitable responsiveness to verbal imagery; and what the insert-notes describe as 'a shocking radicalism: a willingness to strip music down to its core and reconstitute it from these simplest elements.'

The best works on this disc are the first three. *In turbato mare* is a rip-roaring 'simile' motet which makes use of the old operatic device of comparing a troubled soul to a storm-tossed ship finding peace in port. The noble *Non in pratis aut in hortis* is an *introduzione*, a short motet designed to precede a performance of a lost *Miserere*; since it ends on a half-close, it is followed here (with musical if not liturgical logic) by the *Stabat mater*.

All are excellently sung; few recordings exist of the first two, but it is hard to imagine the ebulliently virtuosic Susan Gritton and the movingly firm-voiced Jean Rigby being significantly bettered. By contrast, the *Stabat mater* is well-trodden territory, but the warmly mellifluous Robin Blaze easily matches his rivals on disc. The King's Consort is a little raw in the string department, but in general it shows bright and lively form and is well served by an acoustic perfectly suited to the occasion. Under King's direction, too, they capture splendidly the spirit of this uncomplicated but atmospheric music.

Domine ad adiuvandum me, RV593. Beatus vir, RV597. Stabat mater, RV621. Magnificat, RV610*a* **P**
Ex Cathedra Chamber Choir and Baroque Orchestra / Jeffrey Skidmore
ASV Gaudeamus CDGAU137 (70 minutes: DDD) Ⓕ
Texts and translations included. Recorded 1991

This is an interesting and mainly successful attempt to place a handful of Vivaldi's sacred pieces in a liturgical context. The most well-known work here is the *Stabat mater* for alto voice and strings, but the others deserve to be heard more often than they are.

Ex Cathedra Chamber Choir is a well-disciplined, youthful sounding ensemble whose contribution to the recording is first-rate. And it is from the choir that solo voices emerge as required, giving the performances a homogeneity of sound and intent. The instrumentalists, too, make a strong contribution and together with the voices project interpretations which are full of vitality. There are, of course, rival versions on disc of all the music sung here, but on the strength of the thoughtful way it has been presented by the director of Ex Cathedra, Geoffrey Skidmore, this is perhaps the most affecting of them. Few will be disappointed, for example, by the gently inflected, poignant account of the *Stabat mater* by the countertenor Nigel Short. Hardly a detail has been overlooked, even to the extent of allowing the listener to hear a distant bell during the opening Versicle. In short, only the painfully and unnecessarily small typeface of the accompanying texts fails to please.

Stabat mater, RV621. Cessate, omai cessate, RV684. Filiae mestae Jerusalem, RV638. String Concertos – C, RV114; E flat, RV130, 'Sonata al Santo Sepolcro' **P**
Andreas Scholl *counterten* **Ensemble 415 / Chiara Banchini** *vn*
Harmonia Mundi HMC90 1571 Ⓕ
(52 minutes: DDD). Texts and translations included
Recorded 1995 ●●●

Here is a very attractively prepared menu whose main course is the *Stabat mater* for countertenor and strings. Hors-d'oeuvres and side-dishes consist of a ripieno concerto (RV114), a chamber cantata for countertenor and strings (RV684), a string sonata in E flat (RV130) and an introductory motet to a lost *Miserere* (RV638).

Taken together, the pieces demonstrate something of Vivaldi's diverse style as a composer. The two instrumental works offer the strongest contrasts, the Concerto suggestive, above all in its opening movement, of an opera sinfonia, the Sonata redolent with poignant suspensions and darkly sonorous in its first movement, but yielding to a tautly constructed fugue in the second. The chamber cantata, if closely related to the two sacred vocal items on the disc in respect of tonal colour, differs from them in character. Conforming with the standard Italian cantata pattern at the time of two pairs of alternating recitative and *da capo* aria Vivaldi enlivens his pastoral idyll with two particularly affecting arias, the first with a palpitating *pizzicato* violin, the second a virtuoso vocal *tour de force* illustrating the plight of the forsaken lover. Andreas Scholl brings the whole thing off superbly with only a moment's faulty intonation at the close of the first aria. Unlike settings of the *Stabat mater* by Pergolesi and others, Vivaldi used only the first 10 of the 20 stanzas of the poem. His deeply expressive setting of the poem will be familiar to many readers, but few will have heard such an affecting performance as Scholl achieves here. The lyrical prayer of human yearning for faith contained in the 'Fac ut ardeat' movement is tenderly sung and here, as throughout the programme, sympathetically supported by Ensemble 415 under Chiara Banchini's experienced direction.

Dixit Dominus in D, RV594

Magnificat in G minor, RV610*a*[a]. Lauda Jerusalem in E minor, RV609[b]. Kyrie in G minor, RV587[c]. Credo in E minor, RV591[d]. Dixit Dominus in D, RV594[e] **P**
[abe]**Susan Gritton,** [abe]**Lisa Milne** *sops* [ae]**Catherine Denley** *mez* [ae]**Lynton Atkinson** *ten* [e]**David Wilson-Johnson** *bar* **The King's Consort Choristers and Choir; The King's Consort / Robert King**
Hyperion CDA66769 (63 minutes: DDD). Texts and translations included. Recorded 1994 Ⓕ

King's 'super-group' featuring choristers drawn from seven English cathedral and collegiate choirs sounds better than ever – technically reliable, with a good, full sound – and are a credit to King's vision in bringing them together. This volume has five typically uplifting works, three of which – *Lauda Jerusalem*, *Dixit Dominus* and the G minor *Kyrie* – offer the opulent sound of double choir and orchestra. *Dixit Dominus* is the most substantial, a colourful 23-minute sequence of varied solos and choruses, with trumpets, oboes and two organs all chipping in, most notably in an awe-inspiring depiction of the Day of Judgement. The other two are perhaps less striking, though *Lauda Jerusalem* is certainly charming in its two-soprano interchanges. Highlights of the single-chorus works include another exquisite soprano duet and a fiery 'Fecit potentiam' in the *Magnificat*, and an extraordinary 'Crucifixus' in the *Credo* which departs from the pain-wracked norm by seemingly depicting with lugubrious slow tread Christ's walk to Calvary.

King manages very well in capturing the essence of Vivaldi's bold, sometimes disarmingly straightforward style. These tidy performances are driven with just the right amount of springy energy – neither too much nor too little – and are well recorded in the warm resonance of St Jude's Church, Hampstead in London.

Beatus vir in C, RV597

Dixit Dominus in D, RV595[ab]. Domine ad adiuvandum me, RV593[a]. Credidi propter quod, RV605. Beatus vir in B flat, RV598[ab]. Beatus vir in C, RV597[abc] **P**

[a]**Susan Gritton,** [b]**Catrin Wyn-Davies** *sops* [b]**Catherine Denley** *mez* [c]**Charles Daniels** *ten* [c]**Neal Davies** *bar* [c]**Michael George** *bass* **Choir of The King's Consort; The King's Consort / Robert King**

Hyperion CDA66789 (70 minutes: DDD) Ⓕ
Texts and translations included. Recorded 1997

Here are two of Vivaldi's most extended and impressive psalm settings. These are the single-choir *Dixit Dominus*, RV595 (Psalm 110), and double-choir *Beatus vir*, RV597 (Psalm 112). Vivaldi set both psalms more than once, and King's programme also includes the single-movement *Beatus vir*, RV598, as well as the response, *Domine ad adiuvandum me*, RV593, and the conservatively styled Vesper psalm, *Credidi propter quod*, RV605.

The King's Consort Choir makes a lively and warm-textured contribution; the solo line-up is also quite strong; with Susan Gritton and Catrin Wyn-Davies providing an evenly matched, lightly articulated partnership in their two duets. Neal Davies and Michael George are splendidly robust in their vigorous 'Potens in terra' duet from *Beatus vir* (RV597). Catherine Denley gives an appropriately strongly inflected account of 'Judicabit in nationibus' but is intimate and tender in her beautiful 'De torrente in via bibet' (from *Dixit*). The remaining soloist, Charles Daniels, delivers the virtuoso 'Peccator videbit' (*Beatus vir*, RV597) with articulate lightness and comfortable agility. Although consisting of only three movements and of short duration, the G major *Domine ad adiuvandum me*, is easily on a level with the larger-scale pieces. Its expressive warmth is irresistible, its textual illustration effective and its structure taut, coherent and satisfying. This is a rewarding issue, spaciously recorded.

Gloria in D, RV589

Gloria in D, RV589. Magnificat in G minor, RV611. Concerto for Strings in D minor, RV243. Concerto for Oboe, Trumpet and Strings in D, RV563

Deborah York, Patrizia Biccire *sops* **Sara Mingardo** *contr* **Andrea Mioh** *ob* **Gabriele Cassone** *tpt* **Akademia; Concerto Italiano / Rinaldo Alessandrini**

Opus 111 OPS1951 (60 minutes: DDD). Texts and translations included. Recorded 1997 Ⓕ

Once you recover from the shock of hearing the opening chorus of Vivaldi's *Gloria* sung at what initially strikes you as a breakneck tempo, you will quickly begin to enter into the vital spirit of Rinaldo Alessandrini's performance. In fact it is not only this introductory movement that is thought-provoking but also the carefully considered tempos of several other sections of the work, some of them much slower than we have become used to. Alessandrini lays far greater emphasis than many of his rivals on the meaning of the Latin text. The two supplicatory sections, 'Domine Deus, Rex caelestis' and 'Domini Deus, Agnus Dei', are both sensitively handled with affective dynamic shading; in the first of them Alessandrini avails himself of Vivaldi's option for a violin solo rather than the more customarily heard oboe. The piece is lyrically sung by Deborah York with a beautifully sustained and imaginatively ornamented violin accompaniment played by Francesca Vicari. The soloist in the second of these movements, Sara Mingardo, also makes a favourable impression.

The other sacred vocal work in this release is the latest of several adaptations Vivaldi made of a *Magnificat* which he had originally written for the Pietà. One of the principal differences between this version and the earlier ones lies in five effectively contrasted arias for named singers among the *figlie di coro* of the Pietà. In this performance the solos are distributed among three rather than five artists, but it hardly matters since each is sung with distinctive character and accomplished technique.

Two concertos of contrasting aspect and instrumentation complete this very attractive programme. Both have been recorded previously, though, in the case of RV563 (sometimes encountered under the catalogue number RV781), not quite in the way it is performed here, with a natural trumpet and oboe as playful protagonists in the outer movements. In the slow movement the trumpet is tacet, the oboe assuming a solo role with scalewise passages of a somewhat vacuous character. Never mind, this is a rewarding issue above all, perhaps, for the expressive performance of the *Magnificat*.

Motets for Solo Voices & Strings

In furore gustissimae irae, RV626. Longo mala, umbrae, terrores, RV629. Clarae stellae, scintillate, RV625. Canta in prato, ride in monte, RV623. Filiae mestae Jerusalem, RV638. Nulla in mundo pax, RV630

Deborah York *sop* **Catherine Denley** *mez* **James Bowman** *counterten* **The King's Consort / Robert King**

Hyperion CDA66779 (60 minutes: DDD). Texts and translations included. Recorded 1996 Ⓕ

This volume in Robert King's exploration of Vivaldi's sacred music offers five of his motets for solo voice and strings, together with RV623, one of the *Introduzioni* he composed to precede his liturgical choral pieces. As ever with Vivaldi, they are utterly beguiling pieces of music, impossible to dislike and easy to be beguiled by. Their Latin texts – which usually allow for two arias separated by a recitative and followed by an 'Alleluia' – are about as profound as the sonnets which accompany *The Four Seasons*, but they inspire in Vivaldi just the same kind of charmingly uncomplicated reaction. Nightingales, scenes of general Arcadian bliss, the storms of God's wrath and the touching sorrow of the mournful daughters of Jerusalem before the Cross – all bring forth what you might be tempted to call stock responses were it not for the fact that the music is always so instantly recognisable as being by Vivaldi.

Vivaldi's singers must have been good to judge from these pieces, which show a brand of virtuosity more at home in the instrumental concerto than the aria. James Bowman and Catherine Denley are both on good form (the latter having a particularly taxing number to sing), but the star of the disc is Deborah York, yet another of the many outstanding young sopranos to have arrived on the scene in recent years. Her *In furore iustissimae irae* is a *tour de force* of vocal power and agility with a teasing little top C at the end of the first aria; while the deceptive beauties of *Nulla in mundo pax sincera* are artfully conjured by sly *portamentos*.

The string accompaniments throughout are buoyant but beefy, aided by an excellent recorded sound, and tempos seem well judged.

Salve regina in C minor, RV616

Salve regina in C minor, RV616. Introduzione al Miserere, RV641. Introduzione al Gloria, RV637. Salve regina in G minor, RV618. Concerto for Violin and Strings in C, RV581 ('Per la Santissima Assenzione di Maria Vergine')

Gérard Lesne *counterten* **Fabio Biondi** *vn* **Il Seminario Musicale**

Virgin Classics Veritas VC7 59232-2 (77 minutes: DDD). Texts and translations included Recorded 1991 Ⓕ

The principal works here are two settings of the Marian antiphon *Salve regina*, but the French countertenor Gérard Lesne follows this with an extended *Introduzione* to a *Miserere*, one of two by Vivaldi, and an *Introduzione* to a *Gloria*; and by way of making up a programme, he divides the four vocal pieces into two groups inserting a Violin Concerto between them. The main bias of this music is contemplative, often deeply so, as is the case with the darkly expressive, sorrowful introduction to the *Miserere non in pratis*. Lesne approaches the music with style. Indeed, a stronger advocate for these affecting compositions is hard to imagine since he is technically almost faultless.

Then there is the Concerto in C major (*in due cori*), a splendid example of Vivaldi's skill in this medium, admirably played by the violinist Fabio Biondi with Lesne's own group Il Seminario Musicale. Vivaldi enthusiasts will require no further proof of this disc's merit, but readers in general should also find much to enjoy here, both in the singing and playing.

The recorded sound is pleasantly resonant, serving the best interests of Lesne's voice and of the instruments too. A fine release.

Juditha triumphans, RV644

Maria Cristina Kiehr *sop* **Ann Murray, Susan Bickley, Sarah Connolly, Jean Rigby** *mezzos* **The King's Consort Choir; The King's Consort / Robert King**

Hyperion ② CDA67281/2 (148 minutes: DDD) Text and translation included. Recorded 1997 Ⓕ

All the solo roles in Vivaldi's only surviving oratorio, *Juditha triumphans*, were written for the female voices of the Ospedale della Pietà in Venice, where Vivaldi was, at the time, acting choirmaster. The work, with its Latin libretto by Giacomo Cassetti, dates from 1716. In his introduction, Michael Talbot surmises that the oratorio would have been introduced by a sinfonia. That seems likely, but none has survived, so two movements from one of Vivaldi's colourfully scored concertos *con molto stromenti* (RV555) serve as a preface to Robert King's recording.

The cast, with Ann Murray in the title-role, is a strong one, and the wonderfully diverse instrumental obbligatos are a constant delight; yet the sum of the parts does not always add up to an entirely rewarding whole. The powerful drama is understated, overall, but this is the most stylish if not always the most dramatically satisfying of the versions to have appeared on disc. Certainly, Maria Cristina Kiehr turns in a performance of constant pleasure as Holofernes's servant Vagaus and Sarah Connolly's fuller-textured voice, with its warmth of timbre, conveys a sympathetic picture of Abra, Judith's servant. There is more passion to the story of Judith and Holofernes and Vivaldi's setting of it than we are allowed to hear in this performance, but that said, King's reading, more than any other, allows us to revel in the sheer beauty and kaleidoscopic brilliance of Vivaldi's score.

Opera Arias and Sinfonias

Opera Arias and Sinfonias: Griselda – Sinfonia; Ombre vane, ingiusti orrori; Agitata da due venti. Tito Manlio – Non ti lusinghi la crudeltade. Ottone in Villa – Sinfonia; Gelosia, tu già rendi l'alma mia; L'ombre, l'aure, e ancora il rio[a]. L'Atenaide – Ferma, Teodosio. Bajazet – Sinfonia. L'Incoronazione di Dario – Non mi lusinga vana speranza. Catone in Utica – Se mai senti spirarti sul volto; Se in campo armato P

Emma Kirkby, [a]**Liliana Mazzarri** *sops*
The Brandenburg Consort / Roy Goodman
Hyperion CDA66745 (75 minutes: DDD). Texts and translations included. Recorded 1994 Ⓕ

This is an entertaining programme. The arias have been chosen with discernment, thoughtfully grouped and effectively interspersed with three of Vivaldi's opera *sinfonias*. The formula proves so successful that it even occurs to you that this was maybe the happiest solution to reviving at least the more problematic of Vivaldi's operas. Emma Kirkby's voice is still maturing, filling out, and she is able to achieve an ever increasing variety of colour. Her 'Ombre vane, ingiusti orrori', a ravishing piece from *Griselda* (1735), is beautifully and effortlessly controlled, delicately shaded and rhythmically vital; and her feeling for apposite embellishment comes across with pleasing spontaneity and stylistic assurance. The voice is supported and highlighted by the sympathetic partnership of The Brandenburg Consort conducted by Roy Goodman. This disc will delight Vivaldi enthusiasts. Excellent recorded sound.

Ottone in Villa

Monica Groop *mez* Ottone; **Nancy Argenta** *sop* Caio Silio; **Susan Gritton** *sop* Cleonilla; **Sophie Daneman** *sop* Tullia; **Mark Padmore** *ten* Decio; **Collegium Musicum 90 / Richard Hickox** P
Chandos Chaconne ② CHAN0614
(145 minutes: DDD). Notes, text and translation included. Recorded 1997 Ⓕ

This, Vivaldi's very first opera, was premièred in Vicenza in 1713 and was an instant hit. The story is a relatively uncomplicated one by the standards of baroque opera, of amatory pretences and misunderstandings: it has been admirably summarised by Eric Cross (who has edited the work) as a 'light-weight, amoral entertainment in which the flirtatious Cleonilla consistently has the upper hand, and gullible Emperor Ottone (a far from heroic figure) never discovers the truth about the way he has been deceived'. The score proceeds in a succession of *secco* recitatives (with just a very occasional *accompagnato*) and *da capo* arias – which the present cast ornament very stylishly. There are no duets or ensembles except for a perfunctory final chorus in which the characters merely sing in unison; but there is an abundance of tuneful arias, and when Vivaldi can be bothered to write proper accompaniments to them – he often merely has violins doubling the voice, plus a bass-line – he can provide interesting imitative counterpoint. Several arias employ only the upper strings without cello and bass except in ritornellos.

The small Vicenza theatre could not afford star singers, so only limited opportunities were provided for vocal virtuosity; but the present cast makes the most of its opportunities, both in display and in meditative mood. It is not always easy to tell the three sopranos apart, but Susan Gritton well suggests the scheming minx Cleonilla; Nancy Argenta with her bright voice has the castrato role that includes several fine arias, and displays a *messa di voce* in an echo aria; and Sophie Daneman, in a breeches role, produces a wide range of colour. Monica Groop slightly undercharacterises Ottone except when roused to dismiss Rome's anxiety at his dalliance. It is quite a relief to hear one male voice, and Mark Padmore is excellent. Richard Hickox keeps a firm rhythmic hand on everything and delivers quite the best and neatest Vivaldi operatic recording yet.

Richard Wagner German 1813-1883

GROVE *Wagner was the son either of the police actuary Friedrich Wagner, who died soon after his birth, or of his mother's friend the painter, actor and poet Ludwig Geyer, whom she married in August 1814. He went to school in Dresden and then Leipzig; at 15 he wrote a play, at 16 his first compositions. In 1831 he went to Leipzig University, also studying music with the Thomaskantor, CT Weinlig; a symphony was written and successfully performed in 1832. In 1833 he became chorus master at the Würzburg theatre and wrote the text and music of his first opera, Die Feen; this remained unheard, but his next, Das Liebesverbot, written in 1833, was staged in 1836. By then he had made his début as an opera conductor with a small company which however went bankrupt soon after performing his opera. He married the singer Minna Planer in 1836 and went with her to Königsberg where he became musical director at the theatre, but he soon left and took a similar post in Riga where he began his next opera, Rienzi, and did much conducting, especially of Beethoven.*

In 1839 they slipped away from creditors in Riga, by ship to London and then to Paris, where he was befriended by Meyerbeer and did hack-work for publishers and theatres. He also worked on the text and music of an opera on the 'Flying Dutchman' legend; but in 1842 Rienzi, a large-scale opera with a political theme set in imperial Rome, was accepted for Dresden and Wagner went there for its highly successful première. Its theme reflects something of Wagner's own politics (he was involved in the semi-revolutionary, intellectual 'Young Germany' movement). Die fliegende Holländer ('The Flying Dutchman'), given the next year, was less well received, though a much tauter musical drama, beginning to move away from the 'number opera' tradition and strong in its evocation of atmosphere, especially the supernatural and the raging seas (inspired by the stormy trip from Riga). Wagner was now appointed joint Kapellmeister at the Dresden court.

The theme of redemption through a woman's love, in the Dutchman, recurs in Wagner's operas (and perhaps his life). In 1845 Tannhäuser was completed and performed and Lohengrin begun. In both Wagner moves towards a more continuous texture with semi-melodic narrative and a supporting orchestral fabric helping convey its sense. In 1848 he was caught up in the revolutionary fervour and the next year fled to Weimar (where Liszt helped him) and then Switzerland (there was also a spell in France); politically suspect, he was unable to enter Germany for 11 years. In Zürich, he wrote in 1850-51 his ferociously anti-semitic Jewishness in Music (some of it an attack on Meyerbeer) and his basic statement on musical theatre, Opera and Drama; he also began sketching the text and music of a series of operas on the Nordic and Germanic sagas. By 1853 the text for this four-night cycle (to be The Nibelung's Ring) was written, printed and read to friends – who included a generous patron Otto Wesendonck, and his wife Mathilde, who loved him, wrote poems that he set, and inspired Tristan und Isolde – conceived in 1854 and completed five years later, by which time more than half of The Ring was written. In 1855 he conducted in London; tension with Minna led to his going to Paris in 1858-9. 1860 saw them both in Paris, where the next year he revived Tannhäuser in revised form for French taste, but it was literally shouted down, partly for political reasons. In 1862 he was allowed freely into Germany; that year he and the ill and childless Minna parted (she died in 1866). In 1863 he gave concerts in Vienna, Russia etc; the next year King Ludwig II invited him to settle in Bavaria, near Munich, discharging his debts and providing him with money.

Wagner did not stay long in Bavaria, because of opposition at Ludwig's court, especially when it was known that he was having an affair with Cosima, the wife of the conductor Hans van Bülow (she was Liszt's daughter); Bülow (who condoned it) directed the Tristan première in 1865. Here Wagner, in depicting every shade of sexual love, developed a style richer and more chromatic than anyone had previously attempted, using dissonance and its urge for resolution in a continuing pattern to build up tension and a sense of profound yearning; Act 2 is virtually a continuous love duet, touching every emotion from the tenderest to the most passionately erotic. Before returning to the Ring, Wagner wrote, during the mid-1860s, The Mastersingers of Nuremberg: this is in a quite different vein, a comedy set in 16th-century Nuremberg, in which a noble poet-musician wins, through his victory in a music contest – a victory over pedants who stick to the foolish old rules – the hand of his beloved, fame and riches. (The analogy with Wagner's view of himself is obvious.) The music is less chromatic than that of Tristan, warm and good-humoured, often contrapuntal; unlike the mythological figures of his other operas the characters here have real humanity.

The opera was given, under Bülow, in 1868; Wagner had been living at Tribschen, near Lucerne, since 1866, and that year Cosima formally joined him; they had two children when in 1870 they married. The first two Ring operas, Das Rheingold and Die Walküre, were given in Munich, on Ludwig's insistence, in 1869 and 1870; Wagner however was anxious to have a special festival opera house for the complete cycle and spent much energy trying to raise money for it. Eventually, when he had almost despaired, Ludwig came to the rescue and in 1874 – the year the fourth opera, Götterdämmerung, was finished – provided the necessary support. The house was built at Bayreuth, designed by Wagner as the home for his concept of the Gesamtkunstwerk ('total art work'- an alliance of music, poetry, the visual arts, dance etc). The first festival, an artistic triumph but a financial disaster – was held there in 1876, when the complete Ring was given. The Ring is about 18 hours music, held together by an immensely detailed network of themes, or leitmotifs, each of which has some allusive meaning: a character, a concept, an object etc. They change and develop as the ideas within the opera develop. They are heard in the orchestra, not merely as 'labels' but carrying the action, sometimes informing the listener of connections of ideas or the thoughts of those on the stage. There are no 'numbers' in the Ring; the musical texture is made up of narrative and dialogue, in which the orchestra partakes. The work is not merely a story about gods, humans and dwarfs but embodies reflections on every aspect of the human condition. It has been interpreted as socialist, fascist, Jungian, prophetic, as a parable about industrial society, and much more.

In 1877 Wagner conducted in London, hoping to recoup Bayreuth losses; later in the year he began a new opera, Parsifal. He continued his musical and polemic writings, concentrating on 'racial purity'. He spent most of 1880 in Italy. Parsifal, a sacred festival drama, again treating redemption but through the acts of communion and renunciation on the stage, was given at the Bayreuth Festival in 1882. He went to Venice for the winter, and died there in February of the heart trouble that had been with him for some years. His body was returned by gondola and train for burial at Bayreuth. Wagner did more than any other composer to change music, and indeed to change art and thinking about it. His life and his music arouse passions like no other composer s. His works are hated as much as they are worshipped; but no-one denies their greatness.

Orchestral Excerpts from Operas

Lohengrin – Prelude. Tannhäuser – Overture. Siegfried Idyll. Götterdämmerung – Siegfried's Rhine Journey; Siegfried's Funeral March **H**

Lucerne Festival Orchestra; Vienna Philharmonic Orchestra / Wilhelm Furtwängler

Testament mono SBT1141 (61 minutes: ADD) Ⓕ

Recorded late 1940s ●

This is, as they say, something else. The *Lohengrin* Act 1 Prelude opens the disc of studio recordings, the only item of five with the Lucerne Festival Orchestra. The way the Swiss brass *crescendos* on the upbeat to the climactic delivery of the hymn must rate as among the most elating of all Furtwängler moments. Why this and the *Tannhäuser* Overture have never been issued before remains a mystery, as probably do *all* the reasons why, in the latter piece, the Vienna Philharmonic sounds on fire for Furtwängler and on duty for, say, Knappertsbusch in 1953 (once available on a Decca LP). Siegfried's Rhine Journey evolves in one seamless sweep, barring the split-second but disconcerting rhythmic hiatus at the moment of take-off (4'51"). And mercifully, Furtwängler doesn't tag on the trite concert ending (as did Reiner and Toscanini), giving a chance to wonder at the uniquely resonant low brass sounds of the VPO. Then on to the Funeral March, every dark sound fully charting the depths, every phrase carrying special import, and, as in the *Siegfried Idyll*, the occasional passage reminding us of standards of tuning of the day. The latter account, Furtwängler's only recording of the piece, engages rather than diverts and charms, with Vienna string playing typically sweet and rapturous, and 'Siegfried, Hope of the World' tensely built to an almost delirious climax. Depth, presence and a naturally achieved clarity characterise all these recordings, and 78 sources only occasionally make their presence felt.

Tannhäuser – Overture and Venusberg Music.
Die Meistersinger von Nürnberg – Prelude, Act 3.
Tristan und Isolde – Prelude and Liebestod
Berlin Philharmonic Orchestra / Herbert von Karajan
DG Karajan Gold 439 022-2GHS (50 minutes: DDD) Ⓕ
Recorded 1984

What is so special about Karajan's digital recordings that they are reissued at full price and, ungenerously in this case, with only their original programme? The answer might be another question: when, in modern times, have you heard from Berlin (or anywhere else) such long-drawn, ripe, intense, characterful, perfectly formed and supremely controlled Wagner playing? Not from some other sources with the *Tannhäuser* Overture, whose Pilgrims are less solemn and grand and whose revellers produce less of Karajan's joyous *éclat*. Moving on a few minutes, and the passage where Karajan's Venus succeeds in quelling the riot finds Karajan effecting a spellbinding sudden *diminuendo* (from 4'41", track 2), leaving us with the enchanted eddying of the orchestra. It must surely qualify as one of Karajan's 'greatest moments', had not the seemingly unstoppable tidal wave that preceded it already done so. The true keeper of Berlin's 'Wagner on record' latterly has been Daniel Barenboim. His *Tristan* Prelude (taken from the complete set, reviewed below), is more conventionally paced (i.e. faster) than Karajan's, with the phrasing just as steeply raked, and the balance and control, in some respects, even more accomplished. But the breadth of Karajan's conception is matched by his concentration (it never feels too slow), the playing is achingly intense, the whole superbly built, and the reserves of tone he is able to draw on for the climax seem limitless.

Tristan und Isolde – Love Music (arr Stokowski). Die Walküre – Ride of the Valkyries; Wotan's Farewell and Magic Fire Music. Götterdämmerung – Siegfried's Death and Funeral March (both arr Gerhardt). Siegfried Idyll
National Philharmonic Orchestra / Charles Gerhardt
Chesky CD161 (78 minutes: DDD) Ⓕ
Recorded 1985-95

Charles Gerhardt opens with Stokowski's unashamedly indulgent synthesis of the themes from *Tristan und Isolde*, with the vocal parts seamlessly welded into the orchestration, beginning at the Introduction to Act 2, including the Love Music from the same act and the Liebestod. Gerhardt moves naturally from yearning and languishing to real passion, following Stokowski in using divided strings, employing 16 first violins, 10 second violins, 12 violas and 12 double-basses. The off-stage six-part hunting-horn episode (at 1'35") sounds glorious with the expansion to 10 horns weighted with a bass trombone, Wotan's infinitely touching Farewell to his daughter, Brünnhilde, in *Die Walküre*, and the following truly magical Fire Music.

Even without the voices the tremendously committed string playing is very moving indeed, and the recording is superb. The *Siegfried Idyll* is also beautifully played and makes a flowing, gentle interlude. Gerhardt lets the tension slip a little in the middle but gathers the themes together magnetically in the involving closing section. He then begins Siegfried's Death and Funeral March earlier than Stokowski, at the moment when Hagen kills Siegfried. The result is very direct and powerful with fine brass playing. The Valkyries then ride, or rather gallop in at breakneck speed to finish the concert exuberantly.

The recordings were made in Walthamstow (*Tristan*, 1985), All Saint's, Petersham (*Die Walküre*, 1994 – the best sound of all), Air Studios (*Siegfried Idyll*, 1995), and St John's, Smith Square (*Götterdämmerung*, 1990), and the Valkyries bring another clear, bright studio offering (1995). This is a record for hi-fi buffs, and on really discerning equipment it is fascinating to compare the ways in which the five different engineers have coped with the widely varying ambience effects here, with their positioning of the microphone.

Introduction to The Ring

Der Ring des Nibelungen – spoken introduction with 193 musical examples
Deryck Cooke *narr* **various singers; Vienna Philharmonic Orchestra / Sir Georg Solti**
Decca The Classic Sound ② 443 581-2DCS2 (141 minutes: ADD). Booklet of musical illustrations included. Recorded 1967 Ⓜ

Deryck Cooke died, prematurely, in 1976 before he completed his comprehensive study on *The Ring*. Fortunately, in 1967, Decca had had the foresight to invite him to record this introduction to the cycle. In this he developed at length his ideas on its leitmotifs using 193 examples, most of them taken from the Solti recording, and a few made specifically to illustrate a point Cooke was making. Wagner, as he avers, described the motifs as 'melodic moments of feeling', not signposts or tags. He also adds that their psychological significance and development are of the essence in comprehending *The Ring*, and divides them into four groups – character, objects, events, emotions – then proceeds to describe, in simple, pungent language, how they are deployed throughout the work. His straightforward, unfussy method and delivery, so typical of a man quite without egotistical pretension, enhances one's understanding and, more important, enjoyment of this mighty work. An essential adjunct to any cycle.

Wesendonk Lieder

Wesendonk Lieder. Tristan und Isolde – Prelude, Act 1; Mild und leise. Götterdämmerung – Dawn and Siegfried's Rhine Journey; Starke Scheite

Julia Varady *sop* **Deutsches Symphony Orchestra, Berlin / Dietrich Fischer-Dieskau**

Orfeo C467981A (71 minutes: DDD). Texts and translations included. Recorded 1997 Ⓕ ●●

This is a truly riveting recital of Wagner from Varady (magnificent singing) and Fischer-Dieskau. There have been few such warmly and intelligently sung versions of the Immolation. Maybe on stage Brünnhilde might have been beyond Varady; here there's not a sign of strain as she rides the orchestra, sympathetically supported by her husband. But what makes it stand out from performances by possibly better-endowed sopranos is her deep understanding of the text: again and again, nowhere more so than at 'Ruhe, ruhe, du Gott', where Varady's vibrating lower register is so effective, you feel the tingle factor coming to the fore. Earlier, the passage starting 'Wie Sonne lauter' benefits from the lyrical sound and faultless line Varady exhibits; then in the more heroic final sections, this Brünnhilde is like a woman transfigured. And transfiguration is, of course, a feature of Varady's concentrated, urgent Liebestod, her complete absorption with the text as much as with the music an object-lesson in great Wagner singing.

Her reading of the *Wesendonk Lieder* is no less remarkable, no less enthralling. Nothing here of the slow, wallowing approach often favoured today. The feeling of the words is one of very present emotions. Try the final section of 'Stehe still!' starting 'Die Lippe verstummt' or the emphasis on the single word 'Smaragd' in 'Im Treibhaus' or the whole of a most beautifully etched 'Träume'. She is helped here by Fischer-Dieskau's refusal to indulge the music. On his own the *Tristan* Prelude and the *Götterdämmerung* Dawn and Rhine Journey are keenly shaped. The players of his Berlin orchestra cover themselves in glory. The recording is exemplary.

Opera Duets

Love Duets

Siegfried – Act 3 scene 3. Tristan und Isolde[a] – Act 2 scene 2 (concert version from 'O sink hernieder')

Deborah Voigt *sop* [a]**Violeta Urmana** *mez* **Plácido Domingo** *ten* **Royal Opera House Orchestra, Covent Garden / Antonio Pappano**

EMI CDC5 57004-2 (57 minutes: DDD). Texts and translations included. Recorded 1999 and [a]2000 Ⓕ ●

It appears that in 1862, three years before *Tristan und Isolde*'s première, Wagner hoped that the Schnorrs, his original Tristan and Isolde, would give part of the Love duet in a concert performance. This never took place, and nothing was known about the musical preparations Wagner made for the event until 1950; even then it seems the material remained unexamined, and certainly unused, until very recently. Omitting the first 15 minutes or so, the duet was to start at 'O sink hernieder' and continue to the end, including in it the interpolations of Brangäne. The question which forms in the listener's mind as the end approaches is how that is to be managed. This supreme expression of eroticism in music culminates in erotic catastrophe. It is hard to imagine a concert performance ending with the rude abruptness of the score, but worse to think of its possible closure (as in some early recordings) on a glib and alien major chord. However, without giving the game away, the solution constitutes a stroke of genius; it has that kind of simplicity and rightness that evokes a cry of 'But of course!', almost as though one had thought of it oneself – which assuredly one had not. Unfortunately the booklet-notes provide no information on the genesis of this ending.

Amazing as it is to relate, Domingo's voice, after all these years and all this unsparing usage, is still the most beautiful – the most richly firm and even – that we have heard on recordings of this music. He is exact and lyrical in his reading of the music, and is largely if not invariably, imaginative and convincing in his dramatic commitment. Voigt impresses as being less successfully 'in character', especially as the *Siegfried* Brünnhilde, whose exaltation and wonder lack the majesty of her godly state as they do the excitement of her humanity. The fresh and vibrant tones are good to hear even so, as is the firm-voiced mezzo of Violeta Urmana's Brangäne.

The Covent Garden orchestra play for Pappano with fine attentiveness and exhilaration, and it seems that he brings a renewing spirit to everything he touches.

Tannhäuser – Dich teure Halle. Die Walküre – Der Männer Sippe. Der fliegende Holländer – Joho hoe! Traft ihr das Schiff. Götterdämmerung – Höre mit Sinn; Starke Scheite. Lohengrin – Einsam in trüben Tagen. Parsifal – Grausamer! Fühlst du im Herzen. Tristan und Isolde – Wie lachend sie

Waltraud Meier *mez* **Bavarian Radio Symphony Orchestra / Lorin Maazel**

RCA Red Seal 09026 68766-2 (72 minutes: DDD) Texts and translations included. Recorded 1996-97 Ⓕ ●

This is without question the most thrilling Wagner disc to appear in years. Bleeding chunks have had a bad press, but when they are performed like this, with utter conviction, verbal acuity and vocal control, producing results at once inspiriting and deeply moving, criticism is silenced. Meier and Maazel have reached, instinctively or not, an ideal rapport: together they create a unanimity of outlook based on urgency in conveying the sense of each passage, so that each heroine comes before us newly minted, at speeds in every case faster than what has become the custom today.

In Senta's Ballad, Meier and Maazel bring before us, so immediately, the distraught, possessed woman of Wagner's imagining. Then we hear an Elsa totally convinced of her saviour's arrival, as Meier, with her ever vivid word-painting, mentions 'Ein golden Horn', a more positive girl than usual. Waltraute's Narration, benefiting from Maazel's forward-moving tempo and Meier's deeply felt utterance, coheres into a symbol of Wagner's late mastery. Kundry is portrayed as truly trying to win back Parsifal. Isolde's irony is felt in every bar of her Narration and Curse: it's the ability to imprint the smallest phrase on the mind that so distinguishes all these readings and makes them special. You hear that again in Sieglinde's compelling description of Wotan's appearance, even more in Brünnhilde's Immolation. Meier is reaching towards the pinnacle of Wagner singing represented by this latter role; here are the strength of will and the pathos called for by the great finale.

The Bavarian Radio Symphony sounds truly committed to Maazel, who faithfully follows the ebb and flow of Meier's singing, and the recording, sympathetic to the voice, offers worthy support.

Tannhäuser – Overture. Siegfried Idyll. Tristan und Isolde – Prelude and Liebestod

Jessye Norman *sop* **Vienna Philharmonic Orchestra / Herbert von Karajan**

DG 423 613-2GH (54 minutes: DDD). Text and translation included. Recorded live in 1987 Ⓕ

For the Wagner specialist who has a complete *Tannhäuser* and *Tristan* on the shelves, this disc involves some duplication. Even so, it is not hard to make room for such performances as are heard here. For the non-specialist, the programme provides a good opportunity for a meeting halfway, the common ground between Master and general music-lover being the *Siegfried Idyll*. This offers 20 minutes of delight in the play of musical ideas, structured and yet impulsive, within a sustained mood of gentle affection. The orchestration is something of a miracle, and it can rarely have been heard to better advantage than in this recording, where the ever-changing textures are so clearly displayed and where from every section of the orchestra the sound is of such great loveliness. It comes as a welcome contrast to the *Tannhäuser* Overture, with its big tunes and *fortissimos*, the whole orchestra surging in a frank simulation of physical passion. A further contrast is to follow in the *Tristan* Prelude, where again Karajan and his players are at their best in their feeling for texture and their control of pulse. Jessye Norman, singing the Liebestod with tenderness and vibrant opulence of tone, brings the recital to an end. There is scarcely a single reminder that it was recorded live.

Der fliegende Holländer

Theo Adam *bar* Holländer; **Anja Silja** *sop* Senta; **Martti Talvela** *bass* Daland; **Ernst Kozub** *ten* Erik; **Annelies Burmeister** *mez* Mary; **Gerhard Unger** *ten* Steuermann; **BBC Chorus; New Philharmonia Orchestra / Otto Klemperer**

EMI Great Recordings of the Century

③ CMS5 67408-2 (152 minutes: ADD) Ⓜ

Notes, text and translation included. Recorded 1968 ⊙

Klemperer's magisterial interpretation of this work was unavailable in any form for far too long so that its reissue was most welcome. As ever, Klemperer by and large justifies some moderate tempos by the way in which he sustains line and emphasises detail. Only once or twice – in the Spinning and Sailors choruses – do you sense a lack of propulsion. Otherwise there is throughout a blazing intensity to the reading that brooks no denial. The storm and sea music in the Overture and thereafter is given stunning power, and the Dutchman's torture and passion is evoked in the orchestra. Indeed, the playing of the New Philharmonia is a bonus throughout. Klemperer catches as convincingly as anyone the elemental feeling of the work – the sense of the sea, basic passions and the interplay of character unerringly adumbrated.

There have been few baritones before or since Theo Adam who have sustained the line of the Dutchman so well and so intelligently reached the heart of the matter where the text is concerned. Silja's bright, sometimes piercing timbre isn't to everyone's taste, but hers is a most moving portrayal of trust and loyalty and love unto death, the interpretation of an outstanding singing-actress. Martti Talvela, singing magnificently and suggesting a formidable presence, is a bluff, burly Daland. Ernst Kozub's Erik has its clumsy moments, but one admires the shining tone. Gerhard Unger offers an ardent, cleanly articulated Sailor. Annelies Burmeister is a ripe Mary. The BBC Chorus is very much in the picture. The overall sound is a shade on the dry side.

Der fliegende Holländer

Robert Hale *bass-bar* Holländer; **Hildegard Behrens** *sop* Senta; **Kurt Rydl** *bass* Daland; **Josef Protschka** *ten* Erik; **Iris Vermillion** *mez* Mary; **Uwe Heilmann** *ten* Steuermann; **Vienna State Opera Concert Choir; Vienna Philharmonic Orchestra / Christoph von Dohnányi**

Decca ② 436 418-2DHO2 (145 minutes: DDD) Ⓕ

Notes, text and translation included.

Recorded 1991

Singers, conductor, chorus, orchestra and engineers combine to make Dohnányi's set the most successful modern recording of the work. With the Vienna Philharmonic responding to Dohnányi's precise and energising beat from start to finish the sea does really seem to course through the score as Wagner intended. Dohnányi emphasises the raw, even untutored sound of much of the orchestration, giving the wind and brass the prominence they deserve. Taut, springy rhythms abound from the Overture onwards. He opts for the three-act version and the full ending.

Hale is an exemplary Dutchman and sings with great depth and understanding. This is evident throughout a masterly traversal of his long monologue, where the required torment in the tone is revealed to the full. Behrens captures Senta's single-minded passion and infatuation, singing the quieter passages with refined sensitivity, the forceful ones with fearless attack; and satisfaction extends to the lesser roles. The chorus is superb as sailors, ghost crew and townspeople, singing with firm tone and exact attack. Nothing here is left unconsidered, yet, amazingly, for the most part a real sense of the theatre is achieved throughout. For that we have to thank the Decca team. Balance, depth, perspectives all seem blessedly natural; undoctored and inevitable, so that one is able to take the sound picture for granted.

Götterdämmerung

Awards 2000

Astrid Varnay *sop* Brünnhilde; **Bernd Aldenhoff** *ten* Siegfried; **Ludwig Weber** *bass* Hagen; **Heinrich Pflanzl** *bass* Alberich; **Hermann Uhde** *bar* Gunther; **Martha Mödl** *sop* Gutrune, Third Norn; **Elisabeth Höngen** *mez* Waltraute; **Elisabeth Schwarzkopf** *sop* Woglinde; **Hanna Ludwig** *sop* Wellgunde; **Hertha Töpper** *mez* Flosshilde; **Ruth Siewert** *mez* First Norn; **Ira Malaniuk** *mez* Second Norn; **Chorus and Orchestra of the Bayreuth Festival / Hans Knappertsbusch** H

Testament mono ⊙ ⑥ SBTLP6175; ④ SBT4175 Ⓕ (281 minutes: ADD). Notes, text and translation included. Recorded live in 1951 **ooo**

Testament awakened this sleeping Brünnhilde after half a century in Decca's vaults, held there because of an age-old dispute over rights between that company and EMI. This is a fitting memorial, alongside the exactly contemporaneous *Parsifal* (Teldec), to the phoenix-like reincarnation of Bayreuth post-war and to Wieland Wagner's genius as a producer and gatherer of all the talents to the Green Hill. The other hero of the occasion, as with *Parsifal*, is Knappertsbusch. From the first bars of the Prologue he takes us right into the work, as concerned as three notable Norns (Mödl the most arresting of the three when prophesying the conflagration to come) with the inevitability of the tragic events portrayed within. He then takes us from Stygian gloom to mountain-top ecstasy with a masterly touch few equal. There we meet Varnay's youthful, vibrant, womanly heroine. Beside her is Aldenhoff's not-so-lovely Siegfried, yet once you become accustomed to his aggrandising, extrovert moments you hear a Heldentenor in the old mould, alive to every word and communicating with his audience. Later, arriving at Gibichung Hall, you meet the most forthright, articulate Gunther in Uhde. His greeting to Siegfried, 'Begrüsse froh, O Held', makes one realise why Uhde is pre-eminent in this role. Beside him is Weber's louring, gloating, ambitious Hagen. What intelligence there is in every bar he sings (try 'Ein Weib weiss ich' or the whole of the Watch). As Gutrune, Mödl is not your usual sweet-toned milksop but a women not afraid to show her deep emotions. The great mezzo Höngen as Waltraute conveys with amazing immediacy Wotan's despair, and, with a shudder in her tone at 'Da brach sich sein Blick', the tenderness of his thoughts on his beloved Brünnhilde, making one feel it to be the most moving moment in the whole *Ring* and consoling us for occasionally grainy tone.

Throughout Act 2, Knappertsbusch is trenchant in characterising the tremendous conflicts depicted therein. Weber rouses the vassals with vigorous enthusiasm. Varnay is tremendous in her denunciations of Siegfried, Aldenhoff as vivid in his replies. Such immediacy can only be found in the opera house – damn the momentary lapses in ensemble, the few distractions when scenery is being moved or the audience coughs. In Act 3 the Rhine Maidens, led by Schwarzkopf, are too backwardly placed, the sole blot on the sound picture. In Siegfried's Narration, Aldenhoff captures the vitality of his earlier exploits, supported by gloriously rippling strings, and sings a fulsome death-song. Knappertsbusch, eagerly supported by Bayreuth's hand-picked orchestra (all individually named in the accompanying booklet), unleashes all the tremendous import of the Funeral March. Finally Varnay carries all before her, in better voice than later at Bayreuth, in a visionary account of the Immolation that rightly crowns a noble interpretation of her role and the whole work. The recording, transferred by Paul Baily, is superior even to that of the 1951 *Parsifal*, with only a few passages of uncertain balance to fault it, supporting an experience from the opera house nobody ought to miss.

Lohengrin

Jess Thomas *ten* Lohengrin; **Elisabeth Grümmer** *sop* Elsa; **Christa Ludwig** *mez* Ortrud; **Dietrich Fischer-Dieskau** *bar* Telramund; **Gottlob Frick** *bass* King Henry; **Otto Wiener** *bass* Herald; **Vienna State Opera Chorus; Vienna Philharmonic Orchestra / Rudolf Kempe**

EMI Great Recordings of the Century ③ Ⓜ CMS5 67415-2 (217 minutes: ADD). Text and translation included. Recorded 1963? 64? **oo**

For some years now it has seemed increasingly anomalous that the Kempe *Lohengrin* (remastered for CD reissue in 1988) should remain available at full price. Since 1995, collectors in search of a mid-price version with Jess Thomas in the title-role have been able to rely on the 1962 Bayreuth Festival recording, conducted by Wolfgang Sawallisch: and less than a year later came DG's mid-price reissue of their 1971 Kubelík performance, with James King as Lohengrin, a studio recording superior in sound quality to both Kempe and Sawallisch.

Not that the sound on EMI is ever less than adequate. It may have less presence, a narrower perspective than other versions, but neither the 'studio' ambience – the recording was made in the Theater an der Wien – nor the occasionally excessive prominence of the voices prevents Kempe's reading from projecting a strongly theatrical quality. But it is the all-round excellence of the cast, plus the bonus of an uncut Act 3, which makes this the leading mid-price recommendation. Thomas combines ardour and anguish as well as any, and with Fischer-Dieskau a formidable (but never over-emphatic) antagonist, and Gottlob Frick a majestic King Henry, the drama of the opera's central conflict remains supremely immediate and powerful.

As Elsa and Ortrud, Elisabeth Grümmer and Christa Ludwig are ideal opposites, the former radiant yet quite without the simpering overtones that afflict some Elsas, the latter as potent in seductive insinuation as in demonic ferocity. Not even Ludwig can surpass the visceral intensity of Astrid Varnay in the 1953 Bayreuth set under Keilberth, and Keilberth's Telramund and Elsa (Hermann Uhde and Eleanor Steber) are also outstanding: yet Wolfgang Windgassen's Lohengrin is not as distinguished, nor as distinctive, as Jess Thomas's here. Even more importantly, Keilberth's reading lacks the visionary quality that Kempe finds in the score. Ultimately, it is the power of that vision which raises this performance above its rivals.

Lohengrin

Paul Frey *ten* Lohengrin; **Cheryl Studer** *sop* Elsa; **Gabriele Schnaut** *sop* Ortrud; **Ekkehard Wlaschiha** *bar* Telramund; **Manfred Schenk** *bass* King Henry; **Eike Wilm Schulte** *bar* Herald; **Bayreuth Festival Chorus and Orchestra / Peter Schneider**

Philips ④ 434 602-2PH4 (212 minutes: DDD) Ⓜ
Notes, text and translation included. Recorded 1990

Schneider's is a splendidly absorbing performance of *Lohengrin*. This underrated conductor provides a straightforward, no-nonsense reading in the best *Kapellmeister* tradition, avoiding the extremes of tempo interpretation of some more highly-powered conductors. He obtains playing and singing of the highest calibre from the Bayreuth orchestra and chorus, sustains the long and sometimes tedious-seeming paragraphs of Acts 1 and 2 without ever allowing boredom to intervene, and brings extraordinary tension to such forward-looking scenes as Lohengrin's arrival, the Ortrud-Telramund dialogue and the psychologically intense duet for Elsa and Lohengrin in Act 3. Elsa was one of the roles with which Studer made her name on the international scene; she sings it here once more with refulgent tone, understanding of the text and comprehension of Elsa's dreamy then troubled personality. Particularly affecting is her desperate appeal to Lohengrin at the end of Act 2. Paul Frey is a sensitive, chivalrous Lohengrin, even if his voice hasn't quite the Heldentenor strength of some of his predecessors. Evil is reasonably well represented. Wlaschiha is a vital and nasty Telramund, keenly projecting the character's chip-on-the-shoulder malevolence of the words. Schnaut has an imposing, powerful soprano although more could have been made of the words than she achieves. Schenk is a well-routined King, Schulte a superb Herald. Incidentally, Schneider observes the traditional (Wagner's) cut just before Lohengrin's Farewell, although the passage is printed in full in the booklet. This set is well worth considering in a sparse recommendable field of available versions.

Lohengrin

James King *ten* Lohengrin; **Gundula Janowitz** *sop* Elsa; **Dame Gwyneth Jones** *sop* Ortrud; **Thomas Stewart** *bar* Telramund; **Karl Ridderbusch** *bass* King Henry; **Gerd Nienstedt** *bass* Herald; **Bavarian Radio Chorus and Symphony Orchestra / Rafael Kubelík**

DG ③ 449 591-2GX3 (222 minutes: ADD). Notes, Ⓜ
text and translation included. Recorded 1971 ●

The attributes of Kubelík's *Lohengrin* have been underestimated. It will hold your interest from first to last, not least thanks to Kubelík's masterly overview. Not only does he successfully hold together all the disparate strands of the sprawling work, he also imparts to them a sense of inner excitement through his close attention to the small notes and phrases that so often delineate character in this score and through his vital control of the large ensembles. He is helped inestimably by the Bavarian Radio forces – gloriously singing strings, characterful winds, trenchant, involving chorus – of which he was, in 1971, a beloved chief.

There's never a dull moment in his vivid, theatrical *Lohengrin*. The recording imparts a suitably spacious atmosphere to the piece but also places the principals up front where they should be except when distancing is required – as at Lohengrin's first appearance and at the moment when Elsa appears on the balcony to address the night breezes. Janowitz's Elsa is one of the set's major assets. Pure in tone, imaginative in phrasing, she catches the ear from her first entry, very much suggesting Elsa's vulnerability. Later she eloquently conveys her deep feelings in the love duet, followed by her voicing of all the doubts that beset her character.

King's Lohengrin is more ordinary; today we would be grateful for such solid, musical and well-judged singing. Few if any Lohengrins can sing the passage starting 'Höchstes Vertraun' (third disc, track 5) with anything like King's true tone and powerful conviction. Though not as detailed or subtle in his colouring of the text as some, Thomas Stewart sings a sturdy Telramund, managing the high tessitura with consummate ease. He is horribly plausible in his complaints against Elsa. This portrayal discloses him as a grossly undervalued singer.

Dame Gwyneth Jones's portrayal, taken all-round, is reasonably convincing despite turning a vibrato that might flatteringly be called opulent into something more objectionable. Her Ortrud registers high on the scale of vicious malevolence in the part. The difficulty, as it always has been with this intelligent artist, is that the subtlety evinced in quiet passages is vitiated when the tone comes under pressure – but some Ortruds today are far more guilty in that respect than Jones. As King Henry, Ridderbusch offers a judicious blend of sympathy and authority dispensed in fluent, warm tone. Nienstedt makes the Herald's pronouncements moments to savour. The chorus are nothing short of superb. So, this makes an irresistible bid for recommendation. It is well recorded, sounding wholly resplendent and as cogently conducted as any of its rivals.

Lohengrin

Peter Seiffert *ten* Lohengrin; **Emily Magee** *sop* Elsa; **Deborah Polaski** *sop* Ortrud; **Falk Struckmann** *bar* Telramund; **René Pape** *bass* King Henry; **Roman Trekel** *bar* Herald; **Chorus of the Deutsche Oper, Berlin; Staatskapelle Berlin / Daniel Barenboim**

Teldec ③ 3984-21484-2 (211 minutes: DDD). Notes, texts and translations included Ⓕ

Recorded 1997

This recording is based on the cast with which Barenboim performed the opera at the Berlin State Opera in 1996, although the tenor taking the title-role is different. The chorus, so important in this work, sings with refinement, discipline and enthusiasm in its many roles while all departments of the orchestra play the score to the hilt. Barenboim himself manages to give an overriding unity to a work that can, in lesser hands, sprawl. That's particularly true as regards Act 2, which can test a listener's concentration; not here when the conductor so unerringly weaves the disparate elements into a coherent, forward-moving whole. He is also to be commended for playing Act 3 complete, restoring not only the theatre cuts often made in recording but also the second verse of Lohengrin's Grail narration, cut by Wagner before the first night. In the opera house it is sensibly omitted because it lengthens the act unduly. The only reservation concerns the famous Prelude to Act 3 which seems too brash and too fast.

All the singers, with one exception, are regulars at the Berlin State Opera. The exception is Seiffert as Lohengrin, who in tone, phrasing and sheer lyrical ardour makes a near-ideal white knight. His Elsa is Emily Magee, her tone full and refulgent, her interpretation deeply felt. The one worry is that her voice is so much like that of Polaski that they are hard to tell apart in their long confrontation in Act 2. Polaski makes a splendidly forceful and articulate Ortrud, only very occasionally sounding taxed by heavier passages, most worryingly in her closing imprecations. Struckmann's Telramund isn't as tortured as Fischer-Dieskau's in Kempe's set, but these vital, involving interpretations have their own validity. Pape is a model King Henry, pouring out his concerns in golden tone. Trekel is a strong Herald. The set is enhanced by a perfectly balanced and warm recording.

Die Meistersinger von Nürnberg

Thomas Stewart *bar* Hans Sachs; **Sándor Kónya** *ten* Walther; **Gundula Janowitz** *sop* Eva; **Franz Crass** *bass* Pogner; **Thomas Hemsley** *bar* Beckmesser; **Gerhard Unger** *ten* David; **Brigitte Fassbaender** *mez* Magdalene; **Kieth Engen** *bass* Kothner; **Horst Wilhelm** *ten* Vogelgesang; **Richard Kogel** *bass* Nachtigall; **Manfred Schmidt** *ten* Zorn; **Friedrich Lenz** *ten* Eisslinger; **Peter Baille** *ten* Moser; **Anton Diakov** *bass* Ortel; **Karl Christian Kohn** *bass* Schwartz; **Dieter Slembeck** *bass* Foltz; **Raimund Grumbach** *bass* Nightwatchman; **Bavarian Radio Chorus and Symphony Orchestra / Rafael Kubelík**

Calig ④ CAL50971/4 (272 minutes: ADD) Ⓕ

Recorded 1967 **OO**

There could be no more fitting memorial to Kubelík than the appearance of this, probably the most all-round satisfying *Meistersinger* in the era of stereo. It was recorded in 1967 by Bavarian Radio to mark the work's centenary the following year. Kubelík conducts an unforced, loving interpretation, showing a gratifying grasp of overall structure. As a whole the reading has an unobtrusive cohesion achieved within flexible tempos and dynamics. Everything proceeds at an even, well-judged pace with just the right surge of emotion at the climaxes. All this is conveyed unerringly to his own Bavarian Radio Symphony forces.

Stewart's Sachs is certainly his most successful performance on disc. He offers a finely moulded, deeply considered reading that relies on firm, evenly produced, mostly warm tone to create a darkish, philosophical poet-cobbler. Kónya is simply the most winning Walther on any set, superseding Sawallisch's excellent Heppner by virtue of a greater ardour in his delivery. Kónya pours out consistently warm, clear tone, his tenor hovering ideally between the lyric and the heroic. Nor are there many better Evas than the young Janowitz, certainly none with a lovelier voice. Franz Crass, a less pompous Pogner than some, sings his part effortlessly, with noble feeling. Hemsley, though singing his first Beckmesser, evinces a close affinity with the Town Clerk's mean-mindedness, and his German is faultless. Unger is a paragon among Davids, so eager in his responses and finding just the right timbre for the role. His Magdalene, again perfect casting, is the young Fassbaender. With a characterful Kothner in Engen, the requirements for a near-ideal *Meistersinger* ensemble are in place. As the recording doesn't betray its age this would undoubtedly be the first choice among stereo versions.

Die Meistersinger von Nürnberg
Bernd Weikl *bar* Hans Sachs; **Ben Heppner** *ten* Walther; **Cheryl Studer** *sop* Eva; **Kurt Moll** *bass* Pogner; **Siegfried Lorenz** *bar* Beckmesser; **Deon van der Walt** *ten* David; **Cornelia Kallisch** *contr* Magdalene; **Hans-Joachim Ketelsen** *bar* Kothner; **Michael Schade** *ten* Vogelgesang; **Hans Wilbrink** *bar* Nachtigall; **Ulrich Ress** *ten* Zorn; **Hermann Sapell** *bar* Eisslinger; **Roland Wagenführer** *ten* Moser; **Rainer Büse** *bass* Ortel; **Guido Götzen** *bass* Schwarz; **Friedmann Kunder** *bass* Foltz; **René Pape** *bass* Nightwatchman; **Bavarian State Opera Chorus; Bavarian State Orchestra / Wolfgang Sawallisch**
EMI ④ CDS5 55142-2 (257 minutes: DDD). Notes, text and translation included. Recorded 1993 Ⓕ ●

Sawallisch's *Meistersinger* is very much a version for today – profoundly musical, as it was bound to be under him, sung with a consistent beauty of sound, and recorded truthfully and spaciously. Anybody coming to the work for the first time, and wanting a version backed by modern sound, will find it a sensible choice, a performance for the most part measuring up to the score's many demands on its interpreters.

Sawallisch obtains singing and playing on the highest level of achievement, observant of detail, rich in texture, sure in pacing and – very important in this score – anxious to move forward where there is any danger of the music seeming over-extended, as in the recital of the tones and the Act 2 episode of Beckmesser's courting. Sawallisch's reading also catches the warmth that pervades the whole opera, yet is also successful in deftly projecting its comedy. It must be said, however, that with Sawallisch the earth doesn't move, the spirit is seldom lifted as it should be. On the other hand, nobody is better than Sawallisch at characterising the disputes between the Masters in Act 1, or the pointed humour of the Act 2 Sachs-Beckmesser scene, and much else of that nature is unobtrusively right.

Where the recording itself is concerned, great care has been taken over the placing of the singers in relation to one another and the correct distancing of the voices where called for. The balance in relation to the orchestra seems just about ideal. In the modern manner the chorus is placed a little too far back. Even so, Sawallisch takes an honoured place in the illustrious company of interpreters. His reading is full of thoughtful *aperçus* and natural flow, and displays a sensible overview of the score. Vocally it will satisfy all but those with the most demanding tastes in, and/or, long experience in Wagnerian interpretation.

Parsifal

Jess Thomas *ten* Parsifal; **George London** *bass-bar* Amfortas; **Hans Hotter** *bass* Gurnemanz; **Irene Dalis** *mez* Kundry; **Gustav Neidlinger** *bass* Klingsor; **Martti Talvela** *bass* Titurel; **Niels Möller** *ten* First Knight; **Gerd Neinstedt** *bass* Second Knight; **Sona Cervená** *mez* **Ursula Boese** *contr* **Gerhard Stolze, Georg Paskuda** *tens* Squires; **Gundula Janowitz, Anja Silja, Else-Margrete Gardelli, Dorothea Siebert, Rita Bartos** *sops* **Sona Cervená** *mez* Flower Maidens; **Bayreuth Festival Chorus and Orchestra / Hans Knappertsbusch**
Philips ④ 416 390-2PH4 (250 minutes: ADD) Ⓕ
Notes, text and translation included
Recorded live in 1962 ●●●

There have been many fine recordings of this great Eastertide opera, but none have so magnificently managed to capture the power, the spiritual grandeur, the human frailty and the almost unbearable beauty of the work as Hans Knappertsbusch. This live recording has a cast that has few equals. Hotter is superb, fleshing out Gurnemanz with a depth of insight that has never been surpassed. London's Amfortas captures the frightening sense of impotence and anguish with painful directness whilst Thomas's Parsifal grows as the performance progresses and is no mean achievement. Dalis may lack that final degree of sensuousness but he provides a fine interpretation nevertheless. Throughout the work, Knappertsbusch exercises a quite unequalled control over the proceedings; it is a fine testament to a great conductor. The Bayreuth acoustic is well reproduced, and all in all this record is a profound and moving experience.

Awards 1981

Parsifal
Peter Hofmann *ten* Parsifal; **José van Dam** *bass-bar* Amfortas; **Kurt Moll** *bass* Gurnemanz; **Dunja Vejzovic** *mez* Kundry; **Siegmund Nimsgern** *bass* Klingsor; **Victor von Halem** *bass* Titurel; **Claes Hakon Ahnsjö** *ten* First Knight; **Kurt Rydl** *bass* Second Knight; **Marjon Lambriks, Anne Gjevang** *mezzos* **Heiner Hopfner** *ten* **Georg Tichy** *bass* Squires; **Barbara Hendricks, Janet Perry, Inga Nielsen** *sops* **Audrey Michael** *mez* **Doris Soffel, Rohângiz Yachmi Caucig** *contrs* Flower Maidens; **Hanna Schwarz** *mez* Voice from above; **Berlin Deutsch Opera Chorus; Berlin Philharmonic Orchestra / Herbert von Karajan**
DG ④ 413 347-2GH4 (256 minutes: ADD) Ⓕ
Notes, text and translation included
Recorded 1979-80 ●●●

Karajan's *Parsifal* seems to grow in stature as an interpretation on each rehearing; on its CD transfer it appears to have acquired a new depth, in terms of sound, because of the greater range of the recording and the greater presence of both singers and orchestra. As in practically all cases, CD offers a more immediate experience.

Karajan's reading, a trifle stodgy in Act 1, grows in intensity and feeling with the work itself, reaching an almost terrifying force in the Prelude to Act 3 which is sustained to the end of the opera. Moll's Gurnemanz is a deeply expressive, softly moulded performance of notable beauty. Vejzovic, carefully nurtured by Karajan, gives the performance of her life as Kundry. Hofmann's tone isn't at all times as steady as a Parsifal's should be, but he depicts the character's anguish and eventual serenity in his sincere, inward interpretation. Van Dam is a trifle too placid as Amfortas, but his singing exhibits admirable power and fine steadiness. Nimsgern is the epitome of malice as Klingsor. The choral singing doesn't have quite the confidence of the superb orchestral playing which has both qualities of Keats's imagining of beauty and truth in abundance.

Das Rheingold

Das Rheingold
John Tomlinson *bass* Wotan; **Linda Finnie** *mez* Fricka; **Graham Clark** *ten* Loge; **Helmut Pampuch** *ten* Mime; **Günter von Kannen** *bar* Alberich; **Eva Johansson** *sop* Freia; **Kurt Schreibmayer** *ten* Froh; **Bodo Brinkmann** *bar* Donner; **Birgitta Svendén** *mez* Erda; **Matthias Hölle** *bass* Fasolt; **Philip Kang** *bass* Fafner; **Hilde Leidland** *sop* Woglinde; **Annette Küttenbaum** *mez* Wellgunde; **Jane Turner** *mez* Flosshilde; **Bayreuth Festival Orchestra / Daniel Barenboim**
Teldec ② 4509-91185-2 (149 minutes: DDD) Ⓕ
Notes, text and translation included
Recorded live in 1991 ●●

Die Walküre
Poul Elming *ten* Siegmund; **Nadine Secunde** *sop* Sieglinde; **Anne Evans** *sop* Brünnhilde; **John Tomlinson** *bass* Wotan; **Linda Finnie** *mez* Fricka, Siegrune; **Matthias Hölle** *bass* Hunding; **Eva Johansson** *sop* Gerhilde; **Eva-Maria Bundschuh** *sop* Helmwige; **Ruth Floeren** *sop* Ortlinde; **Shirley Close** *mez* Waltraute; **Hebe Dijkstra** *mez* Rossweisse; **Birgitta Svendén** *mez* Grimgerde; **Hitomi Katagiri** *mez* Schwertleite; **Bayreuth Festival Orchestra / Daniel Barenboim**
Teldec ④ 4509-91186-2 (233 minutes: DDD) Ⓕ
Notes, text and translation included
Recorded live in 1992 ●●

These are enthralling performances. Tomlinson's volatile Wotan is the most potent reading here. He manages to sing every word with insistent meaning and forceful declamation while maintaining a firm *legato*. His German is so idiomatic that he might have been speaking the language his whole life and he brings breadth and distinction of phrase to his solos at the close of both operas. Anne Evans has a single, important advantage over other recent Brünnhildes in that her voice is wholly free from wobble and she never makes an ugly sound. Hers is a light, girlish, honest portrayal, sung with unfailing musicality if not with the ultimate insights. Linda Finnie is an articulate, sharp-edged Fricka, and Graham Clark a sparky, incisive Loge. Nadine Secunde's impassioned Sieglinde is matched by the vital, exciting Siegmund of Poul Elming, and Matthias Hölle as both Hunding and Fasolt is another of those black basses of which Germany seems to have an inexhaustible supply.

The whole of *Das Rheingold* is magnificently conducted by Barenboim, a more expansive Wagnerian than Böhm. By 1991 he had the full measure of its many facets, bringing immense authority and power to building its huge climaxes, yet finding all the lightness of touch for the mercurial and/or diaphanous aspects of this amazing score. He has the inestimable advantage of a Bayreuth orchestra at the peak of its form, surpassing – and this says much – even the Metropolitan orchestra for Levine, and his reading is more convincing as a whole than Levine's. Similar qualities inform his interpretation of *Die Walküre*. Barenboim has now learnt how to match the epic stature of Wagner's mature works, how to pace them with an overview of the whole, and there is an incandescent, metaphysical feeling of a Furwänglerian kind in his treatment of such passages as Wotan's anger and the Valkyrie ride. The orchestra is superb. It is backed by a recording of startling presence and depth, amply capturing the Bayreuth acoustic.

Rienzi

René Kollo *ten* Cola Rienzi; **Siv Wennberg** *sop* Irene; **Janis Martin** *sop* Adriano; **Theo Adam** *bass* Paolo Orsini; **Nikolaus Hillebrand** *bass* Steffano Colonna; **Siegfried Vogel** *bass* Raimondo; **Peter Schreier** *ten* Baroncelli; **Günther Leib** *bass* Cecco del Vecchio; **Ingeborg Springer** *sop* Messenger of Peace; **Leipzig Radio Chorus; Dresden State Opera Chorus; Staatskapelle Dresden / Heinrich Hollreiser**
EMI ③ CMS5 67131-2 (225 minutes: ADD) Ⓜ
Notes, text and translation included
Recorded 1974-76

Rienzi is grand opera with a vengeance. Political imperatives count for more than mere human feelings, and politics means ceremony as well as warfare: marches, ballet music and extended choruses are much in evidence in this work, while even the solo arias often have the rhetorical punch of political harangues. It could all be an enormous bore. Yet the young Wagner, basing his work on Bulwer Lytton's story of the tragic Roman tribune, did manage to move beyond mere tub-thumping into a degree of intensity that – for those with ears to hear – prefigures the mature genius to come. In the end, Rienzi himself is more than just a political animal, and the existential anguish of Tannhäuser, Tristan and even Amfortas can be found glimmering in the distance.

This performance is not ideal in every respect, either musically, or as a recording. But its virtues outweigh its weaknesses by a considerable margin. Siv Wennberg was not in best voice at the time, but the other principals, notably René Kollo and Janis Martin, bring commendable stamina and conviction to their demanding roles. Above all Heinrich Hollreiser prevents the more routine material from sounding merely mechanical, and ensures that *Rienzi* has a truly Wagnerian sweep and fervour.

The Complete Ring Cycle

Das Rheingold

George London *bass-bar* Wotan; **Kirsten Flagstad** *sop* Fricka; **Set Svanholm** *ten* Loge; **Paul Kuen** *ten* Mime; **Gustav Neidlinger** *bass* Alberich; **Claire Watson** *sop* Freia; **Waldemar Kmentt** *ten* Froh; **Eberhard Waechter** *bar* Donner; **Jean Madeira** *contr* Erda; **Walter Kreppel** *bass* Fasolt; **Kurt Böhme** *bass* Fafner; **Oda Balsborg** *sop* Woglinde; **Hetty Plümacher** *sop* Wellgunde; **Ira Malaniuk** *mez* Flosshilde

Die Walküre

James King *ten* Siegmund; **Régine Crespin** *sop* Sieglinde; **Birgit Nilsson** *sop* Brünnhilde; **Hans Hotter** *bass-bar* Wotan; **Christa Ludwig** *mez* Fricka; **Gottlob Frick** *bass* Hunding; **Vera Schlosser** *sop* Gerhilde; **Berit Lindholm** *sop* Helmwige; **Helga Dernesch** *sop* Ortlinde; **Brigitte Fassbaender** *mez* Waltraute; **Claudia Hellmann** *sop* Rossweisse; **Vera Little** *contr* Siegrune; **Marilyn Tyler** *sop* Grimgerde; **Helen Watts** *contr* Schwertleite

Siegfried

Wolfgang Windgassen *ten* Siegfried; **Hans Hotter** *bass-bar* Wanderer; **Birgit Nilsson** *sop* Brünnhilde; **Gerhard Stolze** *ten* Mime; **Gustav Neidlinger** *bass* Alberich; **Marga Höffgen** *contr* Erda; **Kurt Böhme** *bass* Fafner; **Dame Joan Sutherland** *sop* Woodbird

Götterdämmerung

Birgit Nilsson *sop* Brünnhilde; **Wolfgang Windgassen** *ten* Siegfried; **Gottlob Frick** *bass* Hagen; **Gustav Neidlinger** *bass* Alberich; **Dietrich Fischer-Dieskau** *bar* Gunther; **Claire Watson** *sop* Gutrune; **Christa Ludwig** *mez* Waltraute; **Dame Gwyneth Jones** *sop* Wellgunde; **Lucia Popp** *sop* Woglinde; **Maureen Guy** *mez* Flosshilde; **Helen Watts** *contr* First Norn; **Grace Hoffman** *mez* Second Norn; **Anita Välkki** *sop* Third Norn

Vienna State Opera Chorus; Vienna Philharmonic Orchestra / Sir Georg Solti

Decca ⑭ 455 555-2DMO14 (876 minutes: ADD) Ⓜ
Notes, texts and translations included
Recorded 1958-65. *Also available separately* ●●

As perspectives on the Solti/Culshaw enterprise lengthen, and critical reactions are kept alert by the regular appearance of new, or newly issued, and very different recordings, it may seem increasingly ironic that of all conductors the ultra-theatrical Solti should have been denied a live performance. There are indeed episodes in this recording that convey more of the mechanics of the studio than of the electricity of the opera house – the opening of *Die Walküre*, Act 2, and the closing scenes of *Siegfried* and *Götterdämmerung*, for example. Yet, in general, dramatic impetus and atmosphere are strongly established and well sustained, sometimes more powerfully than is usually managed in the theatre. As just one example one would instance the superb control with which the intensity of Donner's summoning up of the thunder in *Das Rheingold* is maintained across Froh's greeting to the rainbow bridge into Wotan's own great salutation. At the majestic climax of this scene the power of feeling conveyed by George London's fine performance counts for more than any 'artificiality' in the way the voice is balanced against the orchestra. Equally memorable in a totally different context is Solti's management of the long transition in *Götterdämmerung* between Hagen's Watch and the appearance of Waltraute. Nothing could be less mannered or unnatural than Solti's grasp of perspective and feeling for the life of each phrase in this music.

Even so, we are not proposing to offer a full-blown revisionist interpretation of Solti's *Ring*, arguing that he always prefers deliberation to impetuosity and that the recording itself has the ideal natural balance. On CD the clarity of instrumental detail is consistently remarkable, and while not all the singers sound as if they are constantly in danger of being overwhelmed there are some vital episodes, especially those involving Windgassen and Nilsson. Awareness of what these artists achieved in other recordings strengthens the suspicion that they may have been giving more than we actually get here. Windgassen is not allowed to dominate the sound picture in the way his part demands, and Nilsson can seem all-too relaxed within the comforting cocoon of the orchestral texture. Factors like these, coupled with those distinctive Soltian confrontations between the hard-driven and the hammily protracted, have prevented the cycle from decisively seeing off its rivals over the years.

It is nevertheless questionable whether any studio recording of *The Ring* could reasonably be expected to be more atmospheric, exciting or better performed than this one. The VPO is not merely prominent, but excellent, and such interpretations as Svanholm's Loge, Neidlinger's Alberich and Frick's Hagen remain very impressive. Above all, there is Hotter, whose incomparably authoritative, unfailingly alert and responsive Wotan stands up well when compared to his earlier Bayreuth accounts. Nowhere is he more commanding than in *Siegfried*, Act 1, where one even welcomes Stolze's mannerisms as Mime for the sparks they strike off the great bass-baritone.

Earlier in this act the interplay of equally balanced instruments and voices in relatively intimate conversational phrases displays the Culshaw concept at its most convincing. The care taken over the SonicStage production was graphically chronicled by Culshaw in *Ring Resounding* (Secker & Warburg: 1967). He would have been astonished to hear what his successors have achieved in renewing his production through digital remastering. One now realises how much of the original sound was lost on the old pressings. In comparison with the 1980 Janowski/RCA version, the approaches are so different they almost seem like different experiences. Culshaw was intent on creating a theatre on record with all the well-known stage effects; the rival version eschews all such manifestations. In general, Janowski presents a much more intimate view of the work than Solti's. However many other *Rings* you may have, though, you will need this one.

Das Rheingold
Theo Adam *bass-bar* Wotan; **Annelies Burmeister** *mez* Fricka; **Wolfgang Windgassen** *ten* Loge; **Erwin Wohlfahrt** *ten* Mime; **Gustav Neidlinger** *bass* Alberich; **Anja Silja** *sop* Freia; **Hermin Esser** *ten* Froh; **Gerd Nienstedt** *bass* Donner; **Vera Soukupova** *mez* Erda; **Martti Talvela** *bass* Fasolt; **Kurt Boehme** *bass* Fafner; **Dorothea Siebert** *sop* Woglinde; **Helga Dernesch** *sop* Wellgunde; **Ruth Hesse** *mez* Flosshilde
Bayreuth Festival Chorus and Orchestra / Karl Böhm
Philips ② 412 475-2PH2 (137 minutes: ADD) Ⓕ
Notes, text and translation included
Recorded live in 1967 ○○○

Die Walküre
James King *ten* Siegmund; **Leonie Rysanek** *sop* Sieglinde; **Birgit Nilsson** *sop* Brünnhilde; **Theo Adam** *bass* Wotan; **Annelies Burmeister** *mez* Fricka, Siegrune; **Gerd Nienstedt** *bass* Hunding; **Danica Mastilovic** *sop* Gerhilde; **Liane Synek** *sop* Helmwige; **Helga Dernesch** *sop* Ortlinde; **Gertraud Hopf** *mez* Waltraute; **Sona Cervená** *mez* Rossweisse; **Elisabeth Schärtel** *contr* Grimgerde; **Sieglinde Wagner** *contr* Schwertleite; **Bayreuth Festival Chorus and Orchestra / Karl Böhm**
Philips ④ 412 478-2PH4 (210 minutes: ADD) Ⓕ
Notes, text and translation included
Recorded live in 1967 ○○○

Siegfried
Wolfgang Windgassen *ten* Siegfried; **Theo Adam** *bass* Wanderer; **Birgit Nilsson** *sop* Brünnhilde; **Erwin Wohlfahrt** *ten* Mime; **Gustav Neidlinger** *bass* Alberich; **Vera Soukupova** *mez* Erda; **Kurt Boehme** *bass* Fafner; **Erika Köth** *sop* Woodbird
Bayreuth Festival Orchestra / Karl Böhm
Philips ④ 412 483-2PH4 (223 minutes: ADD) Ⓕ
Notes, text and translation included
Recorded live in 1967 ○○○

Götterdämmerung
Birgit Nilsson *sop* Brünnhilde; **Wolfgang Windgassen** *ten* Siegfried; **Josef Greindl** *bass* Hagen; **Gustav Neidlinger** *bass-bar* Alberich; **Thomas Stewart** *bar* Gunther; **Ludmila Dvořáková** *sop* Gutrune; **Martha Mödl** *mez* Waltraute; **Dorothea Siebert** *sop* Woglinde; **Helga Dernesch** *sop* Wellgunde; **Sieglinde Wagner** *contr* Flosshilde; **Marga Höffgen** *contr* First Norn; **Annelies Burmeister** *mez* Second Norn; **Anja Silja** *sop* Third Norn
Bayreuth Festival Chorus and Orchestra / Karl Böhm
Philips ④ 412 488-2PH4 (249 minutes: ADD) Ⓕ
Notes, text and translation included
Recorded live in 1967 ○○○

Wagner's *Der Ring des Nibelungen* is the greatest music-drama ever penned. It deals with the eternal questions of power, love, personal responsibility and moral behaviour, and has always been open to numerous interpretations. For every generation, it presents a new challenge, yet certain musical performances have stood the test of time. One would recommend the recording made at Bayreuth in 1967 since, above all others, it represents a true and living account of a huge work as it was performed in the opera house for which it was largely conceived. Every artist who appears at Bayreuth seems to find an extra dedication in their comportment there, and on this occasion many of the singers and the conductor surpassed what they achieved elsewhere. Böhm's reading is notable for its dramatic drive and inner tension. For the most part he also encompasses the metaphysical aspects of the score as well, and he procures playing of warmth and depth from the Bayreuth orchestra. Birgit Nilsson heads the cast as an unsurpassed Brünnhilde, wonderfully vivid in her characterisation and enunciation, tireless and gleaming in voice. Wolfgang Windgassen is equally committed and alert as her Siegfried and Theo Adam is an experienced, worldly-wise Wotan.

No *Ring* recording is perfect but this faithfully recorded version conveys the strength and force of the epic's meaning.

Das Rheingold[a]
Theo Adam *bass-bar* Wotan; **Yvonne Minton** *mez* Fricka; **Peter Schreier** *ten* Loge; **Christian Vogel** *ten* Mime; **Siegmund Nimsgern** *bass-bar* Alberich; **Marita Napier** *sop* Freia; **Eberhard Büchner** *ten* Froh; **Karl-Heinz Stryczek** *bass* Donner; **Ortrun Wenkel** *contr* Erda; **Roland Bracht** *bass* Fasolt; **Matti Salminen** *bass* Fafner; **Lucia Popp** *sop* Woglinde; **Uta Priew** *mez* Wellgunde; **Hanna Schwarz** *contr* Flosshild

Die Walküre[b]
Siegfried Jerusalem *ten* Siegmund; **Jessye Norman** *sop* Sieglinde; **Jeannine Altmeyer** *sop* Brünnhilde; **Theo Adam** *bass-bar* Wotan; **Yvonne Minton** *mez* Fricka; **Kurt Moll** *bass* Hunding; **Eva-Maria Bundschuh** *sop* Gerhilde; **Ruth Falcon** *sop* Helmwige; **Cheryl Studer** *sop* Ortlinde; **Ortrun Wenkel** *contr* Waltraute; **Uta Priew** *mez* Rossweisse; **Christel Borchers** *mez* Siegrune; **Kathleen Kuhlmann** *contr* Grimgarde; **Anne Gjevang** *contr* Schwertleite

Siegfried[c]
René Kollo *ten* Siegfried; **Theo Adam** *bass-bar* Wanderer; **Jeannine Altmeyer** *sop* Brünnhilde; **Peter Schreier** *ten* Mime; **Siegmund Nimsgern** *bass-bar* Alberich; **Ortrun Wenkel** *contr* Erda; **Norma Sharp** *sop* Woodbird

Götterdämmerung[d]
Jeannine Altmeyer *sop* Brünnhilde; **René Kollo** *ten* Siegfried; **Matti Salminen** *bass* Hagen; **Siegmund Nimsgern** *bass-bar* Alberich; **Hans Günter Nöcker** *bar* Gunther; **Norma Sharp** *sop* Gutrune; **Ortrun Wenkel** *contr* Waltraute; **Uta Priew** *mez* Wellgunde; **Lucia Popp** *sop* Woglinde; **Anne Gjevang** *contr* First Norn; **Daphne Evangelotos** *mez* Second Norn; **Ruth Falcon** *sop* Third Norn
Men's Voices of the Leipzig State Opera; Dresden State Opera Chorus; Staatskapelle Dresden / Marek Janowski
RCA Red Seal ⑭ 74321 45417-2 Ⓑ
(839 minutes: DDD). Notes, texts and translations included. Recorded [a]1980, [b]1981, [c]1982, [d]1983 ○○

Here's a true and desirable bargain. This, the first digitally recorded cycle to appear on CD, has always had a great deal to commend it, and at budget price it becomes even more attractive. One of its most telling assets is the actual recording, still the most natural, clear and most sensitively balanced available. Then it has the Dresden Staatskapelle playing with the utmost beauty from start to finish and with lean power when that's called for. Voices and players are in an ideal relationship. Which is not to say that such purple passages as the Magic Fire Music, Ride of the Valkyries, Rhine Journey and Funeral March want anything in visceral excitement. Janowski conducts a direct, dramatic interpretation, concerned throughout with forward movement. His clear-sighted conducting conveys theatrical excitement from start to finish without fuss or attempts at portentous readings. All this makes it an ideal introduction to the *Ring* for any young collector, who can later go on to more philosophically inclined interpretations.

The casts are by and large excellent. *Das Rheingold* is dominated by three central performances – Nimsgern's vibrant, articulate Alberich, Schreier's wonderfully vital, strikingly intelligent and articulate Loge and Adam's experienced Wotan. But Fricka, Giants and Rhinemaidens are all well cast, and the whole performance grips one's attention from start to finish as the kaleidoscopic drama unfolds.

Die Walküre introduces us to Norman's involving if not wholly idiomatic Sieglinde and, even better, the youthful Jerusalem's near-ideal Siegmund, forthright and sincere, not forgetting Moll's granite Hunding. Adam is so authoritative, so keen with the text, so inside his part that an occasional unsteadiness can be overlooked. With Altmeyer's Brünnhilde we come to the one drawback of the set. Though in this and the succeeding operas, we are thankful for such clear, clean and youthful tone, her reading is unformed and one-dimensional, lacking the essential insights of a Varnay or Behrens. In the title-role in *Siegfried* Kollo gives one of his most attractive portrayals on disc, full of thoughtful diction poised on clear-cut tone. Schreier misses nothing in his interpretation of the dissembling, wily Mime, Adam is at his very best as the wise, old Wanderer, and the smaller parts are well catered for. In *Götterdämmerung*, Salminen is a commanding, often subtle Hagen, though inclined to bark in his call, Nöcker a splendid Gunther.

This set is particularly recommended to anyone wanting a reasonably priced introduction to the cycle. Even at a higher level, it has much going for it in comparison with supposedly more prestigious recordings.

The Complete Ring Cycle in English

The Valkyrie (sung in English)
Alberto Remedios *ten* Siegmund; **Margaret Curphey** *sop* Sieglinde; **Rita Hunter** *sop* Brünnhilde; **Norman Bailey** *bar* Wotan; **Ann Howard** *contr* Fricka; **Clifford Grant** *bass* Hunding; **Katie Clarke** *sop* Gerhilde; **Anne Evans** *sop* Helmwige; **Ann Conoley** *sop* Ortlinde; **Elizabeth Connell** *sop* Waltraute; **Anne Collins** *contr* Rossweisse; **Sarah Walker** *mez* Siegrune; **Shelagh Squires** *mez* Grimgerde; **Helen Attfield** *sop* Schwertleite; **English National Opera Orchestra / Sir Reginald Goodall**
Chandos Opera in English Series ④ CHAN3038 Ⓕ
(249 minutes: ADD). Notes and English translation included. Recorded live in 1976 ●

Siegfried (sung in English)
Alberto Remedios *ten* Siegfried; **Norman Bailey** *bass-bar* Wanderer; **Rita Hunter** *sop* Brünnhilde; **Gregory Dempsey** *ten* Mime; **Derek Hammond-Stroud** *bar* Alberich; **Anne Collins** *contr* Erda; **Clifford Grant** *bass* Fafner; **Maurine London** *sop* Woodbird; **Sadler's Wells Opera Orchestra / Sir Reginald Goodall**
Chandos ④ CHAN3045 (279 minutes: ADD) Ⓕ
English text included. Recorded live in 1973 ●●

The Rhinegold (sung in English)
Norman Bailey *bar* Wotan; **Katherine Pring** *mez* Fricka; **Emile Belcourt** *ten* Loge; **Gregory Dempsey** *ten* Mime; **Derek Hammond-Stroud** *bar* Alberich; **Lois McDonall** *sop* Freia; **Robert Ferguson** *ten* Froh; **Norman Welsby** *bar* Donner; **Anne Collins** *contr* Erda; **Robert Lloyd** *bass* Fasolt; **Clifford Grant** *bass* Fafner; **Valerie Masterson** *sop* Woglinde; **Shelagh Squires** *mez* Wellgunde; **Helen Attfield** *sop* Flosshilde; **English National Opera Orchestra / Sir Reginald Goodall**
Chandos Opera in English Series ③ CHAN3054 Ⓕ
(174 minutes: ADD). Notes and English text included
Recorded live in 1975 ●

Twilight of the Gods (sung in English)
Alberto Remedios *ten* Siegfried; **Norman Welsby** *bar* Gunther; **Aage Haugland** *bass* Hagen; **Derek Hammond-Stroud** *bar* Alberich; **Rita Hunter** *sop* Brünnhilde; **Margaret Curphey** *sop* Gutrune; **Katherine Pring** *mez* Waltraute; **Anne Collins** *contr* First Norn; **Gillian Knight** *mez* Second Norn; **Anne Evans** *sop* Third Norn; **Valerie Masterson** *sop* Woglinde; **Shelagh Squires** *mez* Wellgunde; **Helen Attfield** *contr* Flosshilde; **English National Opera Orchestra and Chorus / Sir Reginald Goodall**
Chandos Opera in English ⑤ CHAN3060 Ⓕ
(312 minutes: ADD). Notes and English text included
Recorded live in 1977 ●

Valkyrie: There is something inevitable, even eternal about Goodall's long-breathed, full-toned, often ideally articulated reading. The ENO management's faith in him was handsomely repaid in his ability to convey his lifetime vision to his regular cast and eventually to his audiences. On paper, tempos may look unacceptably slow; in practice there are very few places – perhaps Siegmund's Spring song and Sieglinde's reply – where they seem too tardy. That is largely due to his ability to find the *Hauptstimme* for every paragraph of the music, indeed for a whole act and, perhaps even more, to his ability to persuade players and singers alike to sustain a long line. Listeners familiar only with the Solti cycle will hardly recognise this as the same work.

By 1976 all his singers were entirely inside their respective roles and so able to project a feeling of familiarity with their music that is evident in every bar. Like all the most satisfying sets of the *Ring*, it benefits enormously from being heard live in a theatre acoustic, and here no compromises have to be made, so superb are producer John Mordler's and his team's skills. You seem to be seated in centre stalls imbibing the performance.

Rita Hunter bestrides the role of Brünnhilde in a confident manner achieved in relatively modern times only by Birgit Nilsson, whose bright tone and effortless top Hunter's so much resembles. She is also a thoughtful, very human interpreter of the role, keen with her words and investing them with the right import. By her side Bailey confirms that he is as excellent a Wotan as any since Hans Hotter. His reading of the taxing part is virtually tireless and his interpretation combines authority with fatherly concern. The great monologue, finely articulated, is a pleasure from start to finish, his anger at the start of Act 3 fearsome, and his farewell moving.

Remedios's Siegmund remains one of the most sweetly sung and appealing on disc. If Curphey is not quite in his class vocally, she offers a deeply felt and sympathetic Sieglinde. Ann Howard is, rightly, a termagant of a Fricka, with a touch of asperity in her tone. Clifford Grant is a sonorous, towering Hunding. The Valkyries, comprised of many of the most promising female singers of the day (among them Elizabeth Connell and Anne Evans), acquit themselves very well. All the cast benefit from Andrew Porter's carefully wrought, very singable translation. Overall, then, a hearty welcome back to a great recording.

Siegfried: That Reginald Goodall idolised Klemperer and Knappertsbusch is evident in every aspect of this weighty, consistently thought-through interpretation; indeed it consoles us for the cycle Klemperer never recorded. The performance is also a reminder of what those then in charge of the ENO – Stephen Arlen, Lord Harewood and Edmund Tracey – had the sense to realise: that here was a unique opportunity to let a seasoned Wagnerian have his head in terms of the time and trouble to prepare a cycle in his own long time-scale.

The results are there for all to hear in the total involvement of every member of the orchestra, the lyrical lines of the singers, the superb enunciation of Andrew Porter's faultless translation. Remedios's fresh, lyrical singing is a joy from start to finish; nobody since has equalled him as Siegfried. Dempsey's Mime is at once subtle, funny yet menacing. Those who so praise Tomlinson as Wotan/Wanderer cannot have heard Bailey's better sung, articulate and eloquent assumption, another reading not since surpassed. The smaller roles are all of a piece with the rest. Then to crown the performance we have Rita Hunter's glorious Brünnhilde, so luminously and keenly sung, just about on a par with Nilsson in the role. All of them are wonderfully supported by Goodall and his players. Only in some of Siegfried's Act 1 forging and his struggle with Fafner might one ask for a shade more physical energy, but that's a small price to pay for such understanding of Wagnerian structure.

Rhinegold and *Twilight of the Gods*: After more than 25 years, these recordings remain gripping for reasons similar to those applying to the other sections of the English *Ring* reissued by Chandos. In spite of speeds that in other hands would seem often unreasonably slow, or to an extent because of them, Goodall's interpretation has an unerring sense of lyrical and dramatic concentration, every paragraph, phrase and bar carefully considered and executed with loving care by singers and players alike, all so closely coached by their veteran conductor. Above all there is the refined *legato* observed by all the singers. And the sense of real-life occasion, the theatre's acoustic clearly felt throughout.

Andrew Porter's wonderfully lucid translation is given its full due by all the soloists, who once more sound an utterly convincing team. In *Rhinegold* the main honours are carried off by Emile Belcourt's plausible, witty and articulate Loge, Hammond-Stroud's imposing, strongly sung Alberich, Robert Lloyd's sympathetic Fasolt and Bailey's ever-authoritative Wotan. With a pleasing trio of Rhinemaidens headed by Masterson's gleaming Woglinde, Clifford Grant's gloomy, louring Fafner and Anne Collins's deep-throated Erda, the strength of the ENO roster at the time is there for all to hear.

In *Twilight*, Hunter and Remedios excel themselves as a more heroic than tragic pair, their singing steady, keen with words and very much in character following so many performances, by 1977, of the complete cycle. The recently departed Aage Haugland offers a welcome souvenir of his career as a louring Hagen, though I seem to recall Clifford Grant used. Welsby uncovers the right touches of weak will for Gunther while Curphey is suitably alluring as sister Gutrune. Pring offers an appropriately urgent and strongly sung Waltraute. The Norns could hardly be more strongly cast.

By and large, the playing of the ENO Orchestra is of an equally consistent nature, responding to Goodall's long-breathed conducting with playing of beauty and strength adding up to a formidable traversal of the score. The recording, masterminded by John Mordler, need not fear comparison with anything more recent. Indeed the absence of unwanted reverberation and excessive sound effects is most welcome. What we get is the music unvarnished and truthful, for which many thanks again to the foresight of the ENO directors of the day and to Peter Moores for providing the wherewithal to execute it. Anyone wanting the work in the vernacular, who hasn't already acquired it in its previous incarnations, need not hesitate.

Der Ring des Nibelungen – abridged **H**

Sopranos – **Florence Austral, Noel Eadie, Florence Easton, Tilly de Garmo, Nora Gruhn, Genia Guszalewicz, Frida Leider, Göta Ljungberg, Elsie Suddaby, Louise Trenton**

Mezzos – **Evelyn Arden, Lydia Kindermann,**

Elfriede Marherr-Wagner, Maartje Offers, Maria Olczewska
Contraltos – **Emmi Leisner, Gladys Palmer, Nellie Walker**
Tenors – **Waldemar Henke, Rudolf Laubenthal, Kennedy McKenna, Lauritz Melchior, Albert Reiss, Heinrich Tessmer, Walter Widdop** *Baritones* – **Howard Fry, Emil Schipper, Deszö Zádor**
Bass-baritones – **Rudolf Bockelmann, Friedrich Schorr** *Basses* – **Ivar Andrésen, Frederick Collier, Arthur Fear, Eduard Habich, Emanuel List**
Orchestras – **Berlin State Opera, London Symphony, Vienna State Opera**
Conductors – **Karl Alwin, Sir John Barbirolli, Leo Blech, Albert Coates, Lawrance Collingwood, Robert Heger, Karl Muck**
Pearl mono ⑦ GEMMCDS9137 (500 minutes) Ⓜ
Recorded 1926-32

Here we have, in its entirety, what one might term the Old Testament of *The Ring* recordings, the discs made in the late 1920s and early 1930s in London and Berlin. The operas given the major share are *Die Walküre* and *Siegfried*. The four extracts from *Das Rheingold* are notable only for Friedrich Schorr's magisterial 'Abendlich strahlt'. *Götterdämmerung* suffers most from being reduced to brief extracts, although the passages have been well chosen to give a substantial flavour of the vast work.

Coates and the slightly less admirable Blech share the conducting with a few incursions from Heger, the young Barbirolli and others. The playing, mostly by the LSO of the day and the Berlin State Opera Orchestra, is remarkable for its sweep, also for its care over detail, much of which has astonishing clarity considering the dates of the recordings. Coates is particularly successful in projecting the ardour of the *Walküre* love duet and the forging of the sword in *Siegfried*. His speeds are always on the swift side.

Of course, the singing is the most treasurable aspect of the whole enterprise. Encountering Leider again one realises anew that few, if any, have equalled her combination of vocal security, close-knit line and phrasing, and that matching of feeling with a goddess's natural dignity. Her Brünnhilde is an assumption all aspiring heroic sopranos should closely study (but they don't!). Fledgling Heldentenors would be unwise to listen to Melchior for they might be inclined to suicide. The sheer élan, strength and verbal acuity of his singing are, and will surely remain, unique. For these reasons alone he is unsurpassable as Siegfried, a role that ideally suited his remarkable attributes. Schorr's Wotan is just as remarkable. Once again tone, technique and text are in perfect accord as his noble bass-baritone fills every passage grandly, movingly.

The sound is vivid throughout these seven (for the price of five), generously filled CDs. The voices are recorded more successfully than in most modern versions of these works, and their relationship with the orchestra is more natural than that favoured in studios today. This is a set no enquiring Wagnerian should be without.

Tannhäuser

Tannhäuser (Paris version)
Plácido Domingo *ten* Tannhäuser; **Cheryl Studer** *sop* Elisabeth; **Andreas Schmidt** *bar* Wolfram; **Agnes Baltsa** *mez* Venus; **Matti Salminen** *bass* Hermann; **William Pell** *ten* Walther; **Kurt Rydl** *bass* Biterolf; **Clemens Biber** *ten* Heinrich; **Oskar Hillebrandt** *bass* Reinmar; **Barbara Bonney** *sop* Shepherd Boy; **Chorus of the Royal Opera House, Covent Garden; Philharmonia Orchestra / Giuseppe Sinopoli**
DG ③ 427 625-2GH3 (176 minutes: DDD). Notes, text and translation included Ⓕ

Domingo's Tannhäuser is a success in almost every respect. He evokes the erotic passion of the Venusberg scene and brings to it just the right touch of nervous energy. This is boldly contrasted with the desperation and bitterness of the Rome Narration after the hero's fruitless visit to the Pope seeking forgiveness: Domingo's description of how Tannhäuser avoided every earthly delight on his pilgrimage is delivered with total conviction. In between he berates the slightly prissy attitude of his fellow knights on the Wartburg with the dangerous conceit of someone who knows a secret delight that they will never enjoy in their measured complacency. His tenor must be the steadiest and most resplendent ever to have tackled the part, although his German is far from idiomatic. Baltsa also has problems with her German, but she has the range and attack for an awkwardly lying part.

It is obviously Sinopoli's concern throughout to bring out every last ounce of the drama in the piece, both in terms of orchestral detail and in his awareness in this opera of the longer line, often sustained by the upper strings. The Philharmonia's violins respond with their most eloquent playing. The kind of *frisson* Sinopoli offers is evident in the anticipatory excitement at the start of Act 2 and the iron control he maintains in the big ensemble later in the same act. Cheryl Studer's secure, beautiful voice has no difficulty coping with Sinopoli's deliberate tempos. She takes her part with total conviction, both vocal and interpretative, phrasing with constant intelligence. Andreas Schmidt is a mellifluous, concerned Wolfram, Salminen a rugged, characterful Landgrave and Barbara Bonney an ideally fresh Shepherd Boy. The Covent Garden Chorus sings with consistent beauty of sound, and has been sensibly balanced with the orchestra. Domingo and Studer make this version a winner.

Tristan und Isolde

Lauritz Melchior *ten* Tristan; **Kirsten Flagstad** *sop* Isolde; **Sabine Kalter** *contr* Brangäne; **Emanuel List** *bass* King Marke; **Herbert Janssen** *bar* Kurwenal; **Frank Sale** *ten* Melot; **Octave Dua** *ten* Shepherd; **Leslie Horsman** *bar* Steersman; **Roy Devereux** *ten* Young Sailor; **Royal Opera House Chorus, Covent Garden; London Philharmonic Orchestra / Fritz Reiner** H
Naxos Historical mono ③ 8 110068/70 (209 minutes: ADD). Recorded live in 1936 Ⓢ

This is an improved remastering by Ward Marston of a VAI set which received a warm welcome for preserving the rewarding partnership of Flagstad and Melchior, some would say unsurpassed in their respective roles and here on great form. The soprano, though at the start of her career in the part, is already a fully formed Isolde, and one marvels at Melchior, confirming his stature as the greatest Wagner tenor of all time. The rest of the cast are nothing special. Reiner, after a slow start, provides the right breadth and vitality to the work even when the playing leaves a little to be desired. The then-customary cuts are made in Acts 2 and 3. At super-bargain price (the VAI was at full price) this is an essential purchase for Wagnerians.

Tristan und Isolde
Wolfgang Windgassen *ten* Tristan; **Birgit Nilsson** *sop* Isolde; **Christa Ludwig** *mez* Brangäne; **Martti Talvela** *bass* King Marke; **Eberhard Waechter** *bar* Kurwenal; **Claude Heater** *ten* Melot; **Erwin Wohlfahrt** *ten* Shepherd; **Gerd Nienstedt** *bass* Helmsman; **Peter Schreier** *ten* Sailor; **Bayreuth Festival Chorus and Orchestra / Karl Böhm**
DG The Originals ③ 449 772-2GOR3 Ⓜ
(219 minutes: ADD). Notes, text and translation included. Recorded live in 1966 ●●●

Tristan und Isolde
Siegfried Jerusalem *ten* Tristan; **Waltraud Meier** *mez* Isolde; **Marjana Lipovšek** *mez* Brangäne; **Matti Salminen** *bass* King Marke; **Falk Struckmann** *bar* Kurwenal; **Johan Botha** *ten* Melot; **Peter Maus** *ten* Shepherd; **Roman Trekel** *bar* Helmsman; **Uwe Heilmann** *ten* Sailor; **Berlin State Opera Chorus; Berlin Philharmonic Orchestra / Daniel Barenboim**
Teldec ④ 4509-94568-2 (235 minutes: DDD) Ⓕ
Notes, text and translation included. Recorded 1994 ●

Böhm's recording is a live Bayreuth performance of distinction, for on stage are the most admired Tristan and Isolde of their time, and in the pit the 72-year-old conductor directs a performance which is unflagging in its passion and energy. Böhm has a striking way in the Prelude and Liebestod of making the swell of passion seem like the movement of a great sea, sometimes with gentle motion, sometimes with the breaking of the mightiest of waves. Nilsson characterises strongly, and her voice with its cleaving-power can also soften beautifully. Windgassen's heroic performance in Act 3 is in some ways the crown of his achievements on record, even though the voice has dried and aged a little. Christa Ludwig is the ideal Brangäne, Waechter a suitably-forthright Kurwenal, and Talvela an expressive, noble-voiced Marke. Orchestra and chorus are at their finest.

Over several seasons of conducting the work at Bayreuth, Barenboim has by now thoroughly mastered the pacing and shaping of the score as a unified entity. Even more important, he has peered into the depths of both its construction and meaning, emerging with answers that satisfy on almost all counts, most tellingly so in the melancholic adumbration of Isolde's thoughts during her narration, in the sadly eloquent counterpoint of bass clarinet, lower strings and cor anglais underpinning King Marke's lament, and in the searingly tense support to Tristan's second hallucination. These are but the most salient moments in a reading that thoughtfully and unerringly reveals the inner parts of this astounding score.

The obverse of this caring manner is a certain want of spontaneity, and a tendency to become a shade self-regarding. You occasionally miss the overwhelming force of Furtwängler's metaphysical account or the immediacy and excitement of Böhm's famous live Bayreuth reading, but the very mention of those conductors suggests that Barenboim can live in their world and survive the comparisons with his own perfectly valid interpretation. Besides, he has the most gloriously spacious yet well-focused recording so far of this opera and an orchestra not only familiar with his ways but ready to execute them in a disciplined and sensitive manner. The recording also takes account of spatial questions, in particular the placing of the horns offstage at the start of Act 2.

Salminen delivers a classic account of Marke's anguished reproaches to Tristan, his singing at once sonorous, dignified and reaching to the heart, a reading on a par with that of his fellow-countryman Talvela for Böhm. Meier's Isolde is a vitally wrought, verbally alert reading, which catches much of the venom of Act 1, the visceral excitement of Act 2, the lambent utterance of the Liebestod. Nothing she does is unmusical; everything is keenly intelligent, yet possibly her tone is too narrow for the role. Lipovšek's Brangäne tends to slide and swim in an ungainly fashion, sounding at times definitely overparted. Listening to Ludwig (Böhm) only serves to emphasise Lipovšek's deficiencies. Then it is often hard on the newer set to tell Isolde and Brangäne apart, so alike can be their timbre. As with his partner, Jerusalem sings his role with immaculate musicality; indeed he may be the most accurate Tristan on disc where note values are concerned, one also consistently attentive to dynamics and long-breathed phrasing. On the other hand, although he puts a deal of feeling into his interpretation, he hasn't quite the intensity of utterance of either Windgassen (Böhm), or, even more, Suthaus (Furtwängler). His actual timbre is dry and occasionally rasping: in vocal terms alone Suthaus is in a class of his own. Yet, even with reservations about the Isolde and Tristan, this is a version that will undoubtedly hold a high place in any survey of this work, for which one performance can never hope to tell the whole story.

Die Walküre

Lauritz Melchior *ten* Siegmund; **Astrid Varnay** *sop* Sieglinde; **Helen Traubel** *sop* Brünnhilde; **Friedrich Schorr** *bass-bar* Wotan; **Kerstin Thorborg** *mez* Fricka; **Alexander Kipnis** *bass* Hunding; **Metropolitan Opera Orchestra and Chorus / Erich Leinsdorf** 🅗
Naxos Historical mono ③ 8 110058/60 Ⓢ
(176 minutes: DDD). Recorded live in 1941

This *Walküre* is an important document, never before available here. It marks the début of Traubel as Brünnhilde and, more important, the first Metropolitan appearance of Varnay in any role. She took over Sieglinde at a few hours' notice from an ailing Lehmann and caused something of a sensation. In her autobiography *55 Years in Five Acts* (Northeastern University Press), Varnay tells how frightened she was and how Melchior helped her overcome her nerves, guiding her through the sets and promising to support her. It is hardly surprising then that the pair give a truly wonderful account of their encounters in Acts 1 and 2. She seems totally involved in the role, conveying her ardour for Siegmund in fresh, warm and easy tones and rising superbly to the highly charged moment in Act 3 when she realises she is pregnant with Siegfried. Melchior, seemingly rejuvenated by Varnay's presence, sings with even more fervour and feeling than ever, at 53 showing no sign of the passing years.

Taking over a role previously associated with Flagstad, Traubel almost but not quite makes one forget her predecessor as Brünnhilde, singing with just as much ease and acutely projected tone, but one does sometimes miss Flagstad's warmer, more yielding sound. Still, there's much to admire in her vital and confident singing. Today, when no *Hochdramatische* comes anywhere near her security, she would be welcomed with open arms for such a rock-steady top and such a solid technique all-round. As her Wotan, Schorr is in sadly depleted voice. Although the same age as Melchior, the years had not been as kind to him. Some of the old warmth and authority is there, especially in the Farewell, but too often his lack-lustre tone is sad to hear. No wonder Wotan's long narrative is reduced almost to nothing. On the other hand Thorborg remains an imposing Fricka, and Kipnis purveys Hunding's nastiness in black-browed, rolling tones.

Leinsdorf drives hectically throughout perhaps taking his cue from the recently departed Bodanzky. At 55 minutes his Act 1 must be the fastest recorded. His later, RCA studio recording (now on Decca) shows greater maturity, but the excitement generated here has its own justification, not least since the playing is so resplendent. Few allowances have to be made for the good mono sound. At around £15 this is worth considering if only for Varnay and Melchior.

Sir William Walton British 1902-1983

GROVE *Walton was educated at Oxford, and was a member of the Sitwells circle from the beginning of the 1920s. His first important work was Façade, setting poems by Edith Sitwell for reciter and sextet and evidently modelled on Pierrot lunaire while looking more to Les Six in its wit and jazziness. The next works again showed Parisian connections: with Stravinsky and Honegger in the overture Portsmouth Point, with Prokofiev in the Viola Concerto. Then, without losing the vividness of his harmony and orchestration, he responded to the English Handelian tradition in Belshazzar's Feast and to Sibelius in his First Symphony, though here Elgar too is invoked, as in much of his later music. The Violin Concerto (1939) confirmed this homecoming.*

The next decade was comparatively unproductive, except in film music (Henry V, Hamlet). At the end of it he married and moved to Ischia, where all his later works were composed. These include the opera Troilus and Cressida, found theatrically effective if conservative in approach when given at Covent Garden in 1954, and his one-act opera The Bear, a parodistic Chekhovian extravaganza, given at Aldeburgh in 1967. Among the late orchestral works are a Cello Concerto, cooler and more serene than the earlier concertos, a Second Symphony and miscellaneous pieces including a finely-worked set of Hindemith Variations, which shows an improvisatory character typical of his late music.

Cello Concerto

Cello Concerto. Symphony No 1 in B minor
Lynn Harrell *vc* **City of Birmingham Symphony Orchestra / Sir Simon Rattle**
HMV Classics HMV5 74320-2 Ⓑ
(74 minutes: DDD). Recorded 1990-91

Simon Rattle's version of Walton's First Symphony is as intelligent and dynamic a traversal as one would expect from this talented figure. Texturally speaking, the inner workings of Walton's score are laid bare as never before, aided by what sounds like a meticulously prepared CBSO. Some may find a touch of contrivance about Rattle's control of dynamics in the scorching first movement, but there's absolutely no gainsaying the underlying tension or cumulative power of the whole. Under Rattle the *Scherzo* darts menacingly (the most convincing account of this music since the classic 1966 Previn account), while the slow movement is an unusually nervy, anxious affair. Certainly, the finale is superbly athletic and lithe, though by now one is beginning to register that EMI's sound is, for all its transparency and natural perspective, perhaps a little lightweight for such enormously red-blooded inspiration. Overall, though, Rattle's is a very strong account and his disc's claims are enhanced by the coupling, a wholly admirable performance of the same composer's luxuriant Cello Concerto. Here Rattle and Lynn Harrell form an inspired partnership, totally dedicated and achieving utter concentration throughout – no mean feat in this of all works which demand so much from both performers and listeners.

Belshazzar's Feast. Henry V. Crown Imperial
Bryn Terfel *bass-bar* **Waynflete Singers; L'Inviti; Bournemouth Symphony Chorus and Orchestra / Andrew Litton**
Decca London 448 134-2LH (60 minutes: DDD) Ⓕ
Text included. Recorded 1995

More than anyone since Previn, Litton thrillingly conveys the element of wildness in

Walton's finest inspirations, notably in the works of the pre-war period. It is partly a question of his treatment of the jazzy syncopations which are such a vital element in Walton. Litton is not alone in treating them with a degree of idiomatic freedom – the composer himself as interpreter set the pattern – but as with Previn, Litton's affinity with the jazz element comes from inside, clearly reflecting his American background. Consistently he makes the music crackle with high-voltage electricity, and again he echoes Previn in the way he can screw tension up to the limit and beyond, resolving grinding dissonances on heart-warming concords.

The exceptionally full and vivid recording brings out the opulence as well as the sensuousness of Walton's orchestration, regularly enhancing Litton's expressive warmth as a Waltonian in the great romantic melodies. Not only that, the bitingly dramatic contrasts of brass and percussion have never been more vivid, with the Bournemouth orchestra playing magnificently, not just with brilliance but with passionate commitment. *Belshazzar's Feast* was recorded in Winchester Cathedral and the problems for the engineers must have been daunting, for the reverberation time is formidably long. However, thanks to brilliant balancing there is ample detail and fine focus in exceptionally incisive choral and orchestral sound. The great benefit is that this emerges as a performance on a bigger scale than its rivals, with the contrasts between full chorus and semi-chorus the more sharply established. The vividly dramatic soloist is Bryn Terfel, spine-chilling in his narration describing the writing on the wall.

In *Crown Imperial* a cathedral acoustic does bring some lack of clarity, but it is a stirring performance. Litton's years as Principal Conductor of the Bournemouth Symphony Orchestra could hardly have had a richer culmination on disc.

Viola Concerto in A minor

Viola Concerto in A minor. Symphony No 2. Johannesburg Festival Overture
Lars Anders Tomter *va* **English Northern Philharmonia / Paul Daniel**
Naxos 8 553402 (61 minutes: DDD) Ⓢ
Recorded 1995

This disc opens with one of the wittiest, most exuberant performances of the *Johannesburg Festival Overture*: Daniel encourages the orchestra's virtuoso wind and brass soloists to point the jazz rhythms idiomatically, making the music sparkle. The Viola Concerto is just as delectably pointed, the whole performance magnetic. Tomter's tone, with its rapid flicker-vibrato, lacks the warmth of Kennedy's (reviewed below), but the vibrato is only obtrusive in that upper-middle register and his intonation is immaculate, his attack consistently clean, to match the crisp ensemble of the orchestra. Although he adopts relatively measured speeds both for the *Scherzo* and the jaunty opening theme of the finale, the rhythmic lift brings out the *scherzando* jollity of the latter all the more.

Daniel's keen observance of dynamic markings is again brought out in the stuttering fanfare theme of the *Scherzo*, with muted trumpets and trombones for once played *pianissimo* as marked. The close of the slow epilogue has never been recorded with such a profound hush as here, subsiding in darkness, and the recording team is to be complimented on getting such beautiful sound, clean with plenty of bloom. Paul Daniel adopts a relatively broad tempo in the Symphony's first movement, which makes less impact than in Andrew Litton's powerful Decca version, and the flowing tempo for the central slow movement makes for a lighter, less passionate result too. The finale, with its brassy first statement of the Passacaglia theme, brings fine dynamic contrasts, but again Litton and others produce a fatter, weightier sound, which on balance is preferable. Yet Daniel's view is a very valid one, to round off most convincingly an invaluable addition to the Walton discography.

Walton Viola Concerto[a] **Bruch** Violin and Viola Concerto in E minor, Op 88[b]. Romance, Op 85[c]. Kol Nidrei, Op 47[c]
Yuri Bashmet *va* [b]**Viktor Tretyakov** *vn* **London Symphony Orchestra /** [a]**André Previn,** [bc]**Neeme Järvi**
RCA Red Seal 09026 63292-2 (64 minutes: DDD) Ⓕ
Recorded 1994 and 1996 **OO**

Presumably, this outstanding version of the Walton Viola Concerto from Yuri Bashmet, warm and intense, recorded in 1994, was held up for lack of a suitable coupling. Having the three Bruch works may seem odd, but with the passionate Bashmet the mixture works well. After all, both composers are at their most richly lyrical, and though in style they are worlds apart, the Bruch Double Concerto and the Walton Concerto date from successive decades, written respectively in 1911 and 1929. In the Walton, Bashmet adopts a very slow speed for the opening *Andante*, but is fast and incisive in the vigorous third subject, and the central *Scherzo* brings a dazzling display of virtuosity. In the finale, Bashmet finds plenty of fun in Walton's *scherzando* writing, but then draws out the epilogue at a very slow speed, beautifully sustained, not just by him but by Previn and the orchestra, the ideal accompanists.

The rarely-played Bruch Double Concerto is better known in the version for clarinet and viola. As performed here by Bashmet with his pure-toned violinist colleague, Viktor Tretyakov, it gains in sensuousness from having the solo instruments closely allied rather than sharply contrasted. It is amazing what a fund of melodic invention Bruch kept into his seventies, not just in this concerto but in the glorious *Romance* for viola and orchestra of 1912. Bashmet again gives a heartfelt performance, as he does of *Kol Nidrei*. With Bashmet at his finest, and the LSO playing beautifully for both conductors, this is a disc to recommend to anyone with a taste for romantic viola music.

Violin Concerto

Violin Concerto[a]. Cello Concerto[b]
[a]**Dong-Suk Kang** *vn* [b]**Tim Hugh** *vc* **English Northern Philharmonia / Paul Daniel**
Naxos 8 554325 (60 minutes: DDD) Ⓢ
Recorded 1997 ●

The Walton Violin and Viola Concertos have been coupled several times previously, usually with the same soloist, but companies have shied away from this equally apt coupling of the two larger-scale string concertos. The cellist is Tim Hugh, outstanding in every way, whose reading is the most searching yet. More than direct rivals he finds a thoughtfulness, a sense of mystery, of inner meditation in Walton's great lyrical ideas – notably the main themes of the outer movements and the yearning melody of the central section of the second movement *Scherzo*. Most strikingly his *pianissimos* are more extreme. The openings of both the outer movements are more hushed than ever heard before on disc, with Hugh in inner intensity opting for broader speeds than usual. Not that he dawdles, as the overall timings of each movement make plain, and the bravura writing finds him equally concentrated, always sounding strong and spontaneous in the face of any technical challenges.

As in their previous Walton recordings, Paul Daniel and the English Northern Philharmonia play with equal flair and sympathy, so that the all-important syncopations always sound idiomatic. But though the recorded textures are commendably clear, the strings are too distantly balanced, lacking weight, so that moments where the violins are required to surge up warmly sound thin – hardly the fault of the players.

In the Violin Concerto, though, one welcomes the way that the brass raise the echoes of Leeds Town Hall, making Walton's orchestration sound even more sumptuous than usual, despite the lack of body in the strings. Dong-Suk Kang plays immaculately with fresh, clean-cut tone, pure and true above the stave. If this is not quite so warmly romantic an approach as that of Kyung-Wha Chung or Tasmin Little, there is nothing cold or unsympathetic about his reading, with the rubato in the Neapolitan second theme of the *Scherzo* delectably pointed. Many will also applaud the way that Kang opts for speeds rather faster and more flowing than have latterly been favoured. That follows the example of Heifetz as the original interpreter, and Kang similarly relishes the bravura writing, not least in diamond-sharp articulation in the *Scherzo*. An excellent coupling, with the Cello Concerto offering new depths of insight.

Violin Concerto. Viola Concerto
Kennedy *vn/va* **Royal Philharmonic Orchestra / André Previn**
EMI CDC7 49628-2 (57 minutes: DDD) Ⓕ
Recorded 1987 ●●

These concertos are among the most beautiful of the 20th century. Walton was in his late twenties when he composed the viola work, and in it he achieved a depth of emotion, a range of ideas and a technical assurance beyond anything he had so far written. Lacking in the brilliance of the violin, the viola has an inherently contemplative tonal quality, and Walton matches this to perfection in his score, complementing it rather than trying to compensate as other composers have done. There is a larger element of virtuosity in the Violin Concerto, but it is never allowed to dominate the musical argument. Kennedy gives wonderfully warm and characterful performances which are likely to stand unchallenged as a coupling for a long time. He produces a beautiful tone quality on both of his instruments, which penetrates to the heart of the aching melancholy of Walton's slow music, and he combines it with an innate, highly developed and spontaneous-sounding sense of rhythmic drive and bounce which propels the quick movements forward with great panache. Previn has long been a persuasive Waltonian and the RPO responds marvellously, with crisp and alert playing throughout. The recordings are very clear and naturally balanced with the solo instrument set in a believable perspective.

Sinfonia concertante

Walton Façade – Suites Nos 1-3[a]. Siesta[b]. Sinfonia concertante[a]. Portsmouth Point[a]
Arnold Popular Birthday[a]
Eric Parkin *pf* **London Philharmonic Orchestra /** [a]**Jan Latham-König,** [b]**Bryden Thomson**
Chandos CHAN9148 (59 minutes: DDD) Ⓕ
Recorded 1990-92

The *Sinfonia concertante* (1926-27) with its sharply memorable ideas in each movement and characteristically high voltage, has never had the attention it deserves, and that is all the more regrettable when there is such a dearth of attractive British piano concertos. The soloist, Eric Parkin, is perfectly attuned to the idiom, warmly melodic as well as jazzily syncopated. He points rhythms infectiously and shapes melodies persuasively, though the recording sets the piano a little backwardly, no doubt to reflect the idea that this is not a full concerto.

Jan Latham-König proves most understanding of the composer's 1920s idiom, giving the witty *Façade* movements just the degree of jazzy freedom they need. The Third Suite, devised and arranged by Christopher Palmer, draws on three apt movements from the *Façade* entertainment, ending riotously with the rag-music of 'Something lies beyond the scene'. That is a first recording, as is Constant Lambert's arrangement of the Overture, *Portsmouth Point*. *Siesta* is given an aptly cool performance under Thomson, and the *Popular Birthday* is Malcolm Arnold's fragmentary linking of *Happy Birthday to You* with the 'Popular Song' from *Façade*, originally written for Walton's seventieth birthday. The impact of some of the pieces, notably in *Façade*, would have been even sharper, had the recording placed the orchestra a fraction closer.

Short Orchestral Works

Overtures – Johannesburg Festival; Portsmouth Point; Scapino. Capriccio burlesco. The First Shoot (orch Palmer). Granada Prelude. Prologo e Fantasia. Music for Children. Galop final (orch Palmer)
London Philharmonic Orchestra / Bryden Thomson
Chandos CHAN8968 Ⓕ
(70 minutes: DDD)

While enthusiasts for Walton's music may justifiably complain that there is not enough of it, they usually concede that what there is is readily available in good recorded performances. However, thanks to the dedicated and skilful work of Christopher Palmer, still more of it is now coming to light. How many people, one wonders, have ever heard *The First Shoot*, a miniature ballet written for a C B Cochran show in 1935, the *Granada Prelude* devised for that television company in the 1960s, or the *Prologo e Fantasia*, which was the composer's last work, written for Rostropovich and his National Symphony Orchestra of Washington. Such fresh and welcome goodies as these appear along with familiar material such as the splendidly open-air, nautical overture *Portsmouth Point* that Walton wrote nearly 40 years earlier, at the very start of his career. The Cochran piece, as orchestrated by Palmer, has five little sections that are delightfully jazzy in a way that recalls *Façade*, and one's only regret is that there's not more of it. All this music is in the excellent hands of Bryden Thomson and the LPO, and Palmer's booklet essay is a model of stylish, informative writing. The recording is richly toned, taking some edge off the composer's characteristically sharp scoring.

Spitfire Prelude and Fugue. Sinfonia concertante[a]. Variations on a Theme by Hindemith. March – The History of the English Speaking Peoples
[a]**Peter Donohoe** *pf* **English Northern Philharmonia / Paul Daniel**
Naxos 8 553869 (53 minutes: DDD) Ⓢ
Recorded 1996

Naxos opts for the original version of the *Sinfonia concertante* rather than Walton's revision, with piano writing and orchestration slimmed down. Walton himself, before he died, suggested such a return. As soloist Peter Donohoe plays with power and flamboyance, brought home the more when the piano is very forwardly balanced, too much so for a work which does not aim to be a full concerto, leaving the orchestra a little pale behind. Even so, hopefully this account, broad in the first movement, flowing in the central *Andante*, will persuade others to take it up, young man's music built on striking, colourful ideas, used with crisp concision.

Paul Daniel is splendid at interpreting the jazzy syncopations with the right degree of freedom, and in the *Spitfire Prelude and Fugue* he adds to the impact by taking the big march tune faster than many, similarly demonstrating that *The History of the English Speaking Peoples* March, buried for rather too long, is a match for Walton's other ceremonial marches. Best of all is the performance of the *Hindemith* Variations, given here with winning panache. The strings of the English Northern Philharmonia may not be as weighty as in some rival versions, but the articulation is brilliant, and the complex textures are all the more transparent. The fire and energy of the performance has never been surpassed on disc.

Symphony No 1

Symphony No 1. Belshazzar's Feast
Thomas Hampson *bar* **Cleveland Orchestra Chorus; City of Birmingham Symphony Chorus and Orchestra / Sir Simon Rattle**
EMI CDC5 56592-2 (78 minutes: DDD) Ⓕ
Recorded 1990-97

This is a winning coupling, with Walton's two searing masterpieces from the 1930s given electrifying performances under Rattle. This recording of the symphony first appeared coupled with the Cello Concerto (reviewed above), but *Belshazzar's Feast* is more recent, recorded with a combination of atmospheric warmth and clarity unmatched in any other version, another tribute to the acoustic of Symphony Hall, Birmingham. Rattle, with players he knows so well, combines expressive freedom with knife-edged precision of ensemble, and it is the same in *Belshazzar's Feast*. It is true that compared with Previn in his vintage version – still sounding wonderfully well, with the transfer of the analogue recording full and forward – the opening sections are not quite so warmly expressive and have less elbow-room rhythmically. Also, with Previn the celebrations after the king's death have more jollity in them, where Rattle, with syncopations made exceptionally sharp and biting, conveys much more a manic intensity entirely in keeping with the subject. Rattle's total timing is over three minutes shorter than those of either Previn or Litton. That, incidentally, has made all the difference in allowing these two works to be fitted on a single CD. Not that there is any feeling of haste in Rattle's reading, just of extra tautness, with incisive playing and singing from both the orchestra and the massive chorus.

It was an inspired idea to bring in the Cleveland Orchestra Chorus alongside the Birmingham chorus. Though other versions have ample weight of choral sound, this one consistently scores in the terracing of sound, with dynamic shading wonderfully precise and with the semi-chorus magically distinct. As baritone soloist Thomas Hampson sings immaculately with warm tone and clear focus, and if the description of the writing on the wall is not quite as mysterious as it can be, that again reflects Rattle's tautness and urgency.

Symphony No 1. Partita
English Northern Philharmonia / Paul Daniel
Naxos 8 553180 (64 minutes: DDD) Ⓢ
Recorded 1994

Daniel demonstrates clearly here his natural affinity with Walton's music. In the sustained paragraphs of the First Symphony he knows unerringly how to build up tension to breaking point, before resolving it, and then building again – a quality vital above all in the first and third movements. He is freer than many in his use of rubato too, again often a question of building and resolving tension, as well as in the degree of elbow-room he allows for jazzy syncopations, always idiomatic. This symphony, with its heavy orchestration, would certainly have benefited from rather drier sound, but well-judged microphone balance allows ample detail through. Only occasionally do you feel a slight lack of body in high violin tone, a tiny reservation.

Daniel's reading of the *Partita*, originally written for Szell and the Cleveland Orchestra, brings out above all the work's joyfulness. It may not be quite as crisp in its ensemble as that of the dedicatees, but the degree of wildness, with dissonances underlined, proves a positive advantage in conveying enjoyment. In the slow movement Daniel at a relatively slow speed is markedly more expressive than those brilliant models, again a point which makes the performance more endearing, and if Daniel's speed for the finale is just a little cautious, the precision and rhythmic bounce readily justify his approach. Irrespective of price, this is a version of the much-recorded symphony that competes with the finest ever, and outshines most.

String Quartet in A minor

Piano Quartet in D minor[a]. String Quartet in A minor
[a]**Peter Donohoe** *pf* **Maggini Quartet** (Laurence Jackson, David Angel *vns* Martin Outram *va* Michal Kaznowski *vc*)
Naxos 8 554646 (58 minutes: DDD) Ⓢ
Recorded 1999 ●●

The Maggini Quartet give refined and powerful performances in this Naxos release. The opening of the 1947 String Quartet is presented in hushed intimacy, making the contrast all the greater when Walton's richly lyrical writing emerges in full power. There is a tender, wistful quality here, which culminates in a rapt, intense account of the slow movement, where the world of late Beethoven comes much closer than most interpreters have appreciated. The poignancy of those two longer movements is then set against the clean bite of the second movement *Scherzo* and the brief hectic finale, with their clear and transparent textures.

With Peter Donohoe a powerful and incisive presence, and the Maggini Quartet again playing most persuasively, the early Piano Quartet – an astonishing achievement for a teenage composer – is also given a performance of high contrasts, enhanced by a refined recording which conveys genuine *pianissimos* that are free from highlighting. If, in the first three movements, the pentatonic writing gives little idea of the mature Walton to come, some characteristic rhythmic and other devices are already apparent. Even the pentatonicry suggests that the boy had been looking at the Howells Piano Quartet rather than any Vaughan Williams. It is in the finale that one gets the strongest Waltonian flavour in vigorously purposeful argument, though there the echoes are different, and Stravinsky's *Petrushka* is an obvious influence. The only reservation is that, refined as the recording is, the piano is rather too forwardly balanced.

Belshazzar's Feast

Belshazzar's Feast. Overtures – Portsmouth Point; Scapino. Improvisation on an Impromptu of Benjamin Britten
John Shirley-Quirk *bar* **London Symphony Chorus and Orchestra / André Previn**
EMI CDM7 64723-2 (68 minutes: ADD). Text included Ⓜ
Recorded 1972 ●

Previn's 1972 version of *Belshazzar's Feast*, recorded at the time of the composer's 70th birthday, is preferable to his 1986 version for ASV. The bite of the choral sound and the closer focus make the result far sharper and more dramatic, even though some of the speeds are more spacious. John Shirley-Quirk as soloist is also preferable to the less firm Benjamin Luxon, having more subtlety and refinement as well as a firmer voice The transfer is outstandingly good with fine bloom and plenty of weight. EMI also provides most generous couplings.

Belshazzar's Feast[a]. Coronation Te Deum. Gloria[b]
[b]**Ameral Gunson** *contr* [b]**Neil Mackie** *ten* [a]**Gwynne Howell,** [b]**Stephen Roberts** *bars* **Bach Choir; Philharmonia Orchestra / Sir David Willcocks**
Chandos CHAN8760 (62 minutes: DDD). Texts included. Recorded 1989 Ⓕ ●

With Sir David Willcocks in charge of the choir which he has directed since 1960, one need have no fears that the composer's many near-impossible demands of the chorus in all three of these masterpieces will not be met with elegance and poise. There is as well, in *Belshazzar*, a predictably fine balance of the forces to ensure that as much detail as possible is heard from both chorus and orchestra, even when Walton is bombarding us from all corners of the universe with extra brass bands and all manner of clamorous percussion in praise of pagan gods. Such supremely musical concerns bring their own rewards in a work that can often seem vulgar. The revelation here is the sustained degree of dramatic thrust, exhilaration and what Herbert Howells called 'animal joy' in the proceedings. How marvellous, too, to hear the work paced and scaled to avoid the impression of reduced voltage after the big moments. Gwynne Howell is the magnificently steady, firm and dark toned baritone. The *Gloria* and *Coronation Te Deum* are informed with the same concerns: accuracy and professional polish are rarely allowed to hinder these vital contributions to the British choral tradition. The recording's cathedral-like acoustic is as ideal for the *Te Deum*'s ethereal antiphonal effects, as it is for *Belshazzar*'s glorious spectacle; and Chandos matches Willcocks's care for balance, bar by bar.

The Bear

Della Jones *mez* Madame Popova; **Alan Opie** *bar* Smirnov; **John Shirley-Quirk** *bar* Luka; **Northern Sinfonia / Richard Hickox**
Chandos CHAN9245 (53 minutes: DDD) Ⓕ
Text included. Recorded 1993 ●

If Walton's sense of humour was firmly established from the start in *Façade*, his one-acter, *The Bear*, among his later works brings out very clearly how strong that quality remained throughout his life. In this Chekhov tale, Walton times the melodramatic moments marvellously – notably the climactic duel between the mourning widow and her husband's creditor (the bear of the title) – and Hickox brings that out most effectively. Walton also deftly heightens the farcical element by introducing dozens of parodies and tongue-in-cheek musical references, starting cheekily with echoes of Britten's *Midsummer Night's Dream*. Hickox brings out the richness of the piece as well as its wit, helped by the opulent Chandos recording which still allows words to be heard clearly. The casting of the three characters is as near ideal as could be. Della Jones is commanding as the affronted widow, consistently relishing the melodrama like a young Edith Evans. Alan Opie as Smirnov, 'the bear' is clean-cut and incisive, powerfully bringing out the irate creditor's changing emotions, while John Shirley-Quirk, still rich and resonant, is very well cast as the old retainer, Luka.

Troilus and Cressida

Awards 1995

Judith Howarth *sop* Cressida; **Arthur Davies** *ten* Troilus; **Clive Bayley** *bass* Calkas; **Nigel Robson** *ten* Pandarus; **Alan Opie** *bar* Diomede; **James Thornton** *bar* Antenor; **David Owen-Lewis** *bass* Horaste; **Yvonne Howard** *mez* Evadne; **Peter Bodenham** *ten* Priest; **Keith Mills** *ten* Soldier; **Bruce Budd** *bass* First Watchman; **Stephen Dowson** *bass* Second Watchman; **Brian Cookson** *ten* Third Watchman; **Chorus of Opera North; English Northern Philharmonia / Richard Hickox**
Chandos ② CHAN9370/1 (133 minutes: DDD) Ⓕ
Notes and text included. Recorded 1995 ●●●

Troilus and Cressida is here powerfully presented as an opera for the central repertory, traditional in its red-blooded treatment of a big classical subject. Few if any operas since Puccini's have such a rich store of instantly memorable tunes as *Troilus and Cressida*. Walton wrote the piece in the wake of the first great operatic success of his rival, Benjamin Britten. What more natural than for Walton, by this time no longer an *enfant terrible* of British music but an Establishment figure, to turn his back on operas devoted like Britten's to offbeat subjects, and to go back to an older operatic tradition using a classical love story, based on Chaucer (not Shakespeare). Though he was much praised for this by early critics in 1954, he was quickly attacked for being old-fashioned. Even in the tautened version of the score he offered for the 1976 Covent Garden revival – with the role of the heroine adapted for the mezzo voice of Dame Janet Baker – the piece was described by one critic as a dodo. Yet as Richard Hickox suggests, fashion after 40 years matters little, and the success of the Opera North production in January 1995 indicated that at last the time had come for a big, warmly romantic, sharply dramatic work to be appreciated on its own terms. This recording was made under studio conditions during the run of the opera in Leeds in the UK. The discs amply confirm what the live performances suggested, that Walton's tautening of the score, coupled with a restoration of the original soprano register for Cressida, has proved entirely successful.

Hickox conducts a performance that is magnetic from beginning to end. The scene is atmospherically set in Act 1 by the chorus, initially off-stage, but then with the incisive Opera North chorus snapping out thrilling cries of 'We are accurs'd!'. The libretto is unashamedly archaic in its use of 'opera-speak' like that, with 'thee's and 'thou's and the occasional 'perchance'. Though the text may put some off, it is plainly apt for a traditional 'well-made opera' on a classical subject. The first soloist one hears is the High Priest, Calkas, Cressida's father, about to defect to the Greeks, and the role is superbly taken by the firm, dark-toned Clive Bayley. Troilus's entry and his declaration of love for Cressida bring Waltonian sensuousness and the first statements of the soaring Cressida theme. Arthur Davies is not afraid of using his head voice for *pianissimos*, so contrasting the more dramatically with the big outbursts and his ringing top notes. This is a young-sounding hero, Italianate of tone. Similarly, Judith Howarth's Cressida is quite girlish, and she brings out the vulnerability of the character along with sweetness and warmth. After Calkas has defected to the Greeks, her cry of 'He has deserted us and Troy!' conveys genuine fear, with her will undermined.

All told, although some fine music has been cut, the tautened version is far more effective both musically and dramatically, with no *longueurs* at all. The role of Diomede, Cressida's Greek suitor, can seem one-dimensional, but Alan Opie in one of his finest performances on record sharpens the focus, making him a genuine threat, with the element of nobility fully allowed. As Antenor, James Thornton sings strongly, but is less steady than the others, while Yvonne Howard is superb in the mezzo role of Evadne, Cressida's treacherous servant and confidante. Not just the chorus but the orchestra of Opera North, the English Northern Philharmonia, respond with fervour.

Naturally and idiomatically they observe the Waltonian rubato and the lifting of jazzily syncopated rhythms which Hickox as a dedicated Waltonian instils, echoing the composer's own example. As for the recorded sound the bloom of the acoustic enhances the score, helped by the wide dynamic range.

Peter Warlock

British 1894-1930

GROVE *Warlock was self-taught, though he was in contact with Delius from 1910, and was a friend of Van Dieren, Moeran and Lambert. Under his original name of Heseltine he wrote on music and edited English works of the Elizabethan era. As Warlock he produced a large output of songs, some dark, desolate and bleakly intense (The Curlew for tenor and sextet, 1922), others rumbustious, amorous or charming, but all informed by an exceptional sensitivity to words and high technical skill. He also wrote choral music and a few instrumental pieces (notably Capriol Suite for strings, 1926, based on 16th-century dances).*

Songs

The Wind from the West. To the Memory of a Great Singer. Take, o take those lips away. As ever I saw. The bayley berith the bell away. There is a lady. Lullaby. Sweet content. Late summer. The Singer. Rest sweet nymphs. Sleep. A Sad Song. In an arbour green. Autumn Twilight. I held love's head. Thou gav'st me leave to kiss. Yarmouth Fair. Pretty Ring Time. A Prayer to St Anthony. The Sick Heart. Robin Goodfellow. Jillian of Berry. Fair and True. Ha'nacker Mill. The Night. My Own Country. The First Mercy. The Lover's Maze. Cradle Song. Sigh no more ladies. Passing by. The Contented Lover. The Fox Ⓕ
John Mark Ainsley *ten* **Roger Vignoles** *pf*
Hyperion CDA66736 (69 minutes: DDD) Texts included. Recorded 1994 Ⓕ

Philip Heseltine, so strangely renamed, did not facilitate either the singing or the playing of his songs. For the voice they have a way of passing awkwardly between registers, and though the high notes are not very high they tend to be uncomfortably placed. The pianist, caught for long in a pool of chromatics, suddenly finds his hands flying in both directions. Yet for the singer with the control of breath and command of voice that John Mark Ainsley so splendidly employs here, and for a pianist with Roger Vignoles's sureness of touch and insight, they must be wonderfully satisfying to perform, for there is such a love of song implicit in them and such a personal voice speaks through them. The programme here is arranged chronologically, from 1911 to 1930. Early and Elizabethan poems are the favourite source, and then the poems of contemporaries such as Belloc, Symons and Bruce Blunt. Even the earliest of the songs, *The Wind from the West*, has the characteristic touch of a lyrical impulse, directly responsive to words, and a fastidious avoidance of strophic or harmonic banality. Often a private unease works within the chromaticism as in the *Cradle Song* ('Be still, my sweet sweeting'), yet nothing could be more wholehearted in gaiety when he is in the mood for it (viz. *In an arbour green*, *Robin Goodfellow*, *Jillian of Berry*). Ainsley sings with fine reserves of power as well as softness; he phrases beautifully, and all the nuance that is so essential for these songs (in *Sleep*, for instance) is most sensitively judged. Vignoles is entirely at one with singer and composer.

Choral Works

Warlock A Cornish Carol. I saw a fair maiden. Benedicamus Domino The Full Heart. The Rich Cavalcade. Corpus Christi. All the flowers of the spring. As Dewe in Aprylle. Bethlehem Down. Cornish Christmas Carol **Moeran** Songs of Springtime. Phyllida and Corydon
Finzi Singers / Paul Spicer
Chandos CHAN9182 (76 minutes: DDD) Ⓕ
Texts included. Recorded 1992

The Peter Warlock of the evergreen *Capriol Suite* and the boisterous songs seems a world away from the introverted and intense artist of these unaccompanied choral carols. Perhaps Warlock's real genius was an ability to create profound expression in short musical structures, but even the more outgoing pieces – the joyful *Benedicamus Domino* and the Cornish Christmas carol with its gentle hint at 'The First Nowell' – have an artistic integrity which raises them high above the level of the syrup of modern-day carol settings. Given performances as openly sincere and sensitive as these, few could be unmoved. In the two Moeran madrigal suites there is an indefinable Englishness – the result of a deep awareness of tradition and love of the countryside. The Finzi Singers' warm-toned, richly expressive voices capture the very essence of this uniquely lovely music.

Carl Maria von Weber

German 1786-1826

GROVE *Weber studied in Salzburg (with Michael Haydn), Munich (JN Kalcher) and Vienna (Abbé Vogler), becoming Kapellmeister at Breslau (1804) and working for a time at Württemberg (1806) and Stuttgart (1807). With help from Franz Danzi, intellectual stimulation from his friends Gänsbacher, Meyerbeer, Gottfried Weber and Alexander von Dusch and the encouragement of concert and operatic successes in Munich (especially Abu Hassan), Prague and Berlin, he settled down as opera director in Prague (1813-16). There he systematically reorganised the theatre's operations and built up the nucleus of a German company, concentrating on works, mostly French, that offered an example for the development of a German operatic tradition. But his searching reforms (extending to scenery, lighting, orchestral seating, rehearsal schedules and salaries) led to resentment. Not until his appointment as Royal Saxon Kapellmeister at Dresden (1817) and the unprecedented triumph of Der Freischütz (1821) in Berlin and throughout Germany did his championship of a true German opera win popular support. Official opposition continued, both from the Italian opera establishment in Dresden and from Spontini in Berlin; Weber answered critics with the grand heroic opera Euryanthe (1823, Vienna). His rapidly deteriorating health and his concern to provide for his family induced him to accept the invitation to write an English opera for London; he produced Oberon at Covent Garden in April 1826. Despite an enthusiastic English reception and every care for his health, this last journey hastened his decline; he died from tuberculosis, at 39.*

Weber's Romantic leanings can be seen in the novel emotional flavour of his music and its relevance to emergent German nationalism, his delicate receptivity to nature and to literary and pictorial impressions, his parallel activities as critic, virtuoso pianist and Kapellmeister, his dedication to the evolution of a new kind of opera uniting all the arts and above all his wish to communicate feeling. His role as a father-figure of musical Romanticism was acknowledged by those who succeeded him in the movement, from Berlioz and Wagner to Debussy and Mahler. His melodic and harmonic style is rooted in classical principles, but as he matured he experimented with chromaticism (the diminished 7th chord was a particular favourite). He also was among the subtlest of orchestrators, writing for unusual but dramatically apt and vivid instrumental combinations (clarinet and horn, muted and un-muted strings etc). All his most successful music, including the songs and concertos, is to some degree dramatically inspired.

Weber won his widest audience with Freischütz, outwardly a Singspiel celebrating German folklore and country life, using an idiom touched by German folksong. Through his skilful use of motifs and his careful harmonic, visual and instrumental designs notably for the Wolf's Glen scene, the outstanding example in music of the early Romantic treatment of the sinister and the supernatural – he gave this work a new creative status. Euryanthe, despite a weak libretto, further advances the unity of harmonic and formal structures, moving towards continuous, freely composed opera. In Oberon Weber reverted to separate numbers to suit English taste, yet the work retains his characteristically subtle motivic handling and depiction of both natural and supernatural elements. Of his other works, some of the German songs, the colouristic Konzertstück for piano and orchestra, the dramatic clarinet and bassoon concertos and the virtuoso Grand duo concertant for clarinet and piano deserve special mention.

Clarinet Concertos

Clarinet Concertos – No 1 in F minor, J114; No 2 in E flat, J118. Grand duo concertant, J204
Sharon Kam *cl* **Itamar Golan** *pf* **Leipzig Gewandhaus Orchestra / Kurt Masur**
Teldec 0630-15428-2 (64 minutes: DDD) Ⓕ
Recorded 1996

Teldec provides a good programme in having the two Weber clarinet concertos coupled with a work which is virtually another concerto but with piano accompaniment, the *Grand duo concertant*. Sharon Kam is a young Israeli whom Kurt Masur heard in her home country, immediately inviting her back to Leipzig to play concertos. She was contracted by Teldec in 1994, but this is the first disc entirely devoted to her playing, revealing her as a most imaginative and individual artist, using the widest tonal and dynamic range, and with a very sure technique, with every note cleanly in place. As the opening movement of the First Concerto demonstrates, she has the gift of magicking a phrase, and one mark of her magnetism and flair is the way she can hold tension over an exaggerated pause or *tenuto*. Most remarkable of all is the dark intensity of Kam's account of the slow minor-key *Romanza* of the Second Concerto, with the soloist clearly the one insisting on a very measured tempo, when Masur's preference is always towards flowing *Andantes*. She is similarly impressive in the *Grand duo concertant*, though there the piano tone of Itamar Golan is on the shallow side.

Clarinet Concertos – Nos 1 and 2. Clarinet Concertino in E flat, J109. Clarinet Quintet in B flat, J182
Kari Kriikku *cl* **New Helsinki Quartet** (Jan Söderblom, Petri Aarnio *vns* Ilari Angervo *va* Jan-Erik Gustafsson *vc*)
Finnish Radio Symphony Orchestra / Sakari Oramo
Ondine ODE895-2 (76 minutes: DDD) Ⓕ
Recorded 1996

Kari Kriikku's are brilliant performances of works that more or less reinvented the clarinet as an instrument of brilliance, at any rate in the hands and under the flashing fingers of Weber's friend Heinrich Baermann. The formidable difficulties hold no terrors for Kriikku; indeed, wonderfully fluent as his playing is in, for instance, the fireworks music that ends the Second Concerto and the Quintet, one almost wants there to be more sense of difficulties overcome as witness of the virtuoso as hero. But that would be to quibble, especially when Kriikku has such a wide range of expression and such an intelligent approach to the music. He plays the First Concerto as a slightly tense, witty work, giving the *Adagio* a long-breathed lyricism and the finale humour as well as wit. The only questionable element is his own over-long cadenza to the first movement. The Second Concerto is treated as a more lyrical and dramatic work, with an elegant *polacca* finale, and there is a beautiful length of phrasing in the *Andante*, as there is in the 'Fantasia' movement of the Quintet. Kriikku neatly touches off the mock-sinister intervention in the Quintet's finale, refusing to take it seriously. He is well accompanied throughout.

Piano Sonatas

Piano Sonatas – No 1 in C, J138; No 2 in A flat, J199. Rondo brillante in E flat, J252, 'La gaîté'. Invitation to the Dance, J260

Hamish Milne *pf*
CRD CRD3485 (76 minutes: DDD) Ⓜ
Recorded 1991 ⓞ

Weber's piano music, once played by most pianists, has since suffered neglect and even the famous *Invitation to the Dance* is now more often heard in its orchestral form. Since he was a renowned pianist as well as a major composer, the neglect seems odd, particularly when other pianist composers such as Chopin and Liszt are at the centre of the concert repertory; but part of the trouble may lie in the difficulty of the music, reflecting his own huge hands and his tendency to write what the booklet-essay calls 'chords unplayable by others'. Hamish Milne makes out a real case for this music, and his playing of the two sonatas is idiomatic and resourceful, even if one cannot banish the feeling that Weber all too readily used the melodic and harmonic formulae of 18th-century *galanterie* and simply dressed them up in 19th-century salon virtuosity. From this point of view, a comparison with Chopin's mature sonatas or Liszt's magnificent single essay in the form reveals Weber as a lightweight. A hearing of the first movement in the First Sonata will quickly tell you if this is how you may react, while in its *Presto* finale you may praise a Mendelssohnian lightness but also note a pomposity foreign to that composer. Leaving aside the musical quality of these sonatas, this is stylish playing which should win them friends. The *Rondo brillante* and *Invitation to the Dance* make no claim to be other than scintillating salon music, and are captivating in Milne's shapely and skilful performances. The recording is truthful and satisfying.

Lieder

Meine Lieder, meine Sänge, J73. Klage, J63. Der Kleine Fritz an seine jungen Freunde, J74. Was zieht zu deinem Zauberkreise, J86. Ich sah ein Röschen am Wege stehn, J67. Er an Sie, J57. Meine Farben, J62. Liebe-Glühen, J140. Über die Berge mit ungestüm, Op 25 No 2. Es stürmt auf der Flur, J161. Minnelied, J160. Reigen, J159. Sind es Schmerzen, J156. Mein Verlangen, J196. Wenn ich ein Vöglein war', J233. Mein Schatzerl ist hübsch, J234. Liebesgruss aus der Ferne, J257. Herzchen, mein Schätzchen, J258. Das Veilchen im Thale, J217. Ich denke dein, J48. Horch'!, Leise horch', Geliebte, J56. Elle était simple et gentilette, J292

Dietrich Fischer-Dieskau *bar* **Hartmut Höll** *pf*
Claves CD50-9118 (52 minutes: DDD). Texts and translations included. Recorded 1991 Ⓕ ⓞ

'In my opinion the first and most sacred duty of a song-writer is to observe the maximum of fidelity to the prosody of the text that he is setting.' Weber was writing in defence of a number he composed for an obscure play, but his words can stand as an apologia for his 90-odd songs. His contribution to German song has been underrated, for his ideas were different from those of his contemporaries. Fischer-Dieskau used to resist suggestions that he might take up Weber's songs, and it is good that he has now done so, even late in his career. Always sensitive to words, he now responds with the subtlety of understanding that comes from many years of closeness to German poetry. Only very occasionally is there the powerful emphasis on the single expressive word that sometimes used to mar his interpretations, keeping them too near the surface of the poetry. He can still use individual colour marvellously: the tonal painting of 'blue', 'white' and 'brown' in *Meine Farben* is exquisitely done. But more remarkable, here and in other songs, is the manner in which he follows the novel melodic lines which Weber has contrived out of the poetry.

Ein steter Kampf is a masterly example; so is *Was zieht zu deinem Zauberkreise*, one of the few songs in which Weber enters Schubertian territory; so are *Es stürmt auf der Flur* and *Liebesgruss aus der Ferne*. Not even Fischer-Dieskau can quite bring off the coy *Der Kleine Fritz* by slightly sending it up (the only hope), and there is something a bit hefty about *Reigen*, a very funny wedding song full of 'Heissa, lustig!' and 'Dudel, didel!', though Hartmut Höll does wonders with the clanking accompaniment. Höll varies his tone so much here from the warmth and depth of his touch elsewhere that one wonders if the engineers did not take a small hand: why not? These are charming, touching, witty, colourful verses, often by minor figures of Weber's circle, and they drew from him music that heightens their point. Fischer-Dieskau's intelligent artistry could not more eloquently support the praise for Weber from Wilhelm Müller, poet of *Die schöne Müllerin* and *Winterreise*, as 'master of German song'.

Der Freischütz

Peter Schreier *ten* Max (Hans Jörn Weber); **Gundula Janowitz** *sop* Agathe (Regina Jeske); **Edith Mathis** *sop* Aennchen (Ingrid Hille); **Theo Adam** *bass* Caspar (Gerhard Paul); **Bernd Weikl** *bar* Ottokar (Otto Mellies); **Siegfried Vogel** *bass* Cuno (Gerd Biewer); **Franz Crass** *bass* Hermit; **Gerhard Paul** *spkr* Samiel; **Günther Leib** *bar* Kilian (Peter Hölzel); **Leipzig Radio Chorus; Staatskapelle Dresden / Carlos Kleiber**
DG The Originals ② 457 736-2GOR2 Ⓕ
(130 minutes: ADD). Notes, text and translation included. Recorded 1973 ⓞⓞ

Carlos Kleiber's fine set of *Der Freischütz* earns reissue on CD for a number of reasons. One is the excellence of the actual recorded sound with a score that profits greatly from such attention. Weber's famous attention to details of orchestration is lovingly explored by a conductor who has taken the trouble to go back to the score in manuscript and observe that there are differences between that and most of the published versions. So not only do we hear the eerie sound of low flute thirds and the subtle contrast of unmuted viola with four-part muted violins in Agathe's 'Leise, leise', among much else, with a new freshness and point, but all the diabolical effects in the Wolf's Glen come up with a greater sense of depth, down to the grisliest detail. The beginning of the Overture, and the opening of the Wolf's Glen scene, steal upon us out of a primeval silence, as they should. All this would be of little point were the performance itself not of such interest. There is a good deal to argue about but this is because the performance is so interesting. Whatever one may feel about some of Kleiber's tempos, and one may feel some of them to be unwise in both directions, they spring from a careful, thoughtful and musical mind. The singing cast is excellent, with Gundula Janowitz an outstanding Agathe to a somewhat reflective Max from Peter Schreier, at his best when the hero is brought low by the devilish machinations; Edith Mathis is a pretty Aennchen, Theo Adam a fine, murky Caspar. The dialogue, spoken by actors, is slightly abbreviated and occasionally amended. Kleiber's reading produces much new insight to a magical old score.

Anton Webern

Austrian 1883-1945

GROVE *Webern studied at Vienna University under Adler (1902-6), taking the doctorate for work on Isaac; in composition he was one of Schoenberg's first pupils (1904-8), along with Berg. Like Berg, he developed rapidly under Schoenberg's guidance, achieving a fusion of Brahms, Reger and tonal Schoenberg in his orchestral Passacaglia, already highly characteristic in its modest dynamic level and its brevity. But he was closer than Berg in following Schoenberg into atonality, even choosing verses by the same poet, George, to take the step in songs of 1908-9. His other step was into a conducting career which he began with modest provincial engagements before World War I.*

After the war he settled close to Schoenberg in Mödling and took charge of the Vienna Workers Symphony Concerts (1922-34). Meanwhile he had continued his atonal style, mostly in songs: the relatively few instrumental pieces of 1909-14 had grown ever shorter, ostensibly because of the lack of any means of formal extension in a language without key or theme. However the songs of 1910-25 show a reintroduction of traditional formal patterns even before the arrival of serialism (especially canonic patterns, no doubt stimulated, as was the instrumentation of many of these songs, by Pierrot lunaire), to the extent that the eventual adoption of the 12-note method in the Three Traditional Rhymes (1925) seems almost incidental, making little change to a musical style that was already systematised by strict counterpoint.

However, Webern soon recognised that the 12-note principle sanctioned a severity and virtuosity of polyphony that he could compare with that of the Renaissance masters he had studied. Unlike Schoenberg, he never again sought to compose in any other way. Rather, the highly controlled, pure style of his Symphony appears to have represented an ideal which later works could only repeat, showing different facets. His use of the series as a source of similar motifs, especially in instrumental works, merely emphasises the almost geometrical perfection of this music, for which he found literary stimulus in Goethe and, more nearly, in the poetry of his friend and neighbour Hildegard Jone, whose words he set exclusively during his last dozen years. With Schoenberg gone, Berg dead and himself deprived of his posts, Webern saw Jone as one of his few allies during World War II. He was shot in error by a soldier after the end of hostilities, leaving a total acknowledged output of about three hours' duration.

Complete works, Opp 1-31

Awards 1978

Passacaglia, Op 1 (**London Symphony Orchestra / Pierre Boulez**). Entflieht auf leichten Kähnen, Op 2 (**John Alldis Choir / Boulez**). Five Songs from 'Der siebente Ring', Op 3. Five Songs, Op 4 (**Heather Harper** *sop* **Charles Rosen** *pf*). Five Movements, Op 5 (**Juilliard Quartet**). Six Pieces, Op 6 (**LSO / Boulez**). Four Pieces, Op 7 (**Isaac Stern** *vn* **Rosen** *pf*). Two Songs, Op 8 (**Harper** *sop* **chamber ensemble / Boulez**). Six Bagatelles, Op 9 (**Juilliard Qt**). Five Pieces, Op 10 (**LSO / Boulez**). Three Little Pieces, Op 11 (**Gregor Piatigorsky** *vc* **Rosen** *pf*). Four Songs, Op 12 (**Harper** *sop* **Rosen** *pf*). Four Songs, Op 13. Six Songs, Op 14 (**Harper** *sop* **chbr ens / Boulez**). Five Sacred Songs, Op 15. Five Canons on Latin Texts, Op 16 (**Halina Lukomska** *sop* **chbr ens / Boulez**). Three Songs, Op 18 (**Lukomska** *sop* **John Williams** *gtr* **Colin Bradbury** *cl* **/ Boulez**). Two Songs, Op 19 (**John Alldis Ch, mbrs LSO / Boulez**). String Trio, Op 20 (**mbrs Juilliard Qt**). Symphony, Op 21 (**LSO / Boulez**). Quartet, Op 22 (**Robert Marcellus** *cl* **Abraham Weinstein** *sax* **Daniel Majeske** *vn* **Rosen** *pf* **/ Boulez**). Three Songs from 'Viae inviae', Op 23 (**Lukomska** *sop* **Rosen** *pf*). Concerto, Op 24 (**mbrs LSO / Boulez**). Three Songs, Op 25 (**Lukomska** *sop* **Rosen** *pf*). Das Augenlicht, Op 26 (John **Alldis Ch, LSO / Boulez**). Piano Variations, Op 27 (**Rosen** *pf*). String Quartet, Op 28 (**Juilliard Qt**). Cantata No 1, Op 29 (**Lukomska** *sop* **John Alldis Ch; LSO / Boulez**). Variations, Op 30 (**LSO / Boulez**). Cantata No 2, Op 31 (**Lukomska** *sop* **Barry McDaniel** *bar* **John Alldis Ch; LSO / Boulez**). Five Movements, Op 5 – orchestral version (**LSO / Boulez**) **Bach** (orch Webern) Musikalischen Opfer, BWV1079 – Fuga (Ricercata) No 2 (**LSO / Boulez**) **Schubert** (orch Webern) Deutsche Tänze, D820 (**Frankfurt Radio Orchestra / Anton Webern**) (recorded live in 1932)

Various artists

Sony Classical ③ SM3K45845 Ⓜ

(223 minutes: ADD). Notes, texts and translations included. Recorded 1967-72 **ooo**

Webern is as 'classic' to Boulez as Mozart or Brahms are to most other conductors, and when he is able to persuade performers to share his view the results can be remarkable – lucid in texture, responsive in expression. Despite his well-nigh exclusive concern with miniature forms, there are many sides to Webern, and although this set is not equally successful in realising all of them, it leaves you in no doubt about the music's sheer variety, as well as its emotional power, whether the piece is an ingenious canon-by-inversion or a simple, folk-like *Lied*. From a long list of performers one could single out Heather Harper and the Juilliard Quartet for special commendation; and the smooth confidence of the John Alldis Choir is also notable. The recordings were made over a five-year period and have the typical CBS dryness of that time. Even so, in the finest performances which Boulez himself directs, that remarkable radiance of spirit so special to Webern is vividly conveyed. It is a fascinating bonus to hear Webern himself conducting his Schubert arrangements – music from another world, yet with an economy and emotional poise that Webern in his own way sought to emulate.

Passacaglia, Op 1

Webern Passacaglia, Op 1. Six Pieces, Op 6. Five Pieces, Op 10. Variations, Op 30 **Bach** (arr Webern) Musikalisches Opfer, BWV1079 – Ricercar a 6
Schoenberg A Survivor from Warsaw, Op 46
Gottfried Hornik *narr* **Vienna State Opera Chorus; Vienna Philharmonic Orchestra / Claudio Abbado**
DG 431 774-2GH (50 minutes: DDD). Text and translation included. Recorded 1989-92 Ⓕ ●

This is a fine reading of the rarely-heard and forcefully dramatic Variations, Op 30. Abbado and the VPO are responsive to the romantic intensity of the early *Passacaglia*, and the sets of expressionist miniatures are even more convincing in their blend of delicacy and power. The fourth piece from Op 6, the closest Webern came to concentrating the essence of a Mahlerian funeral march, and ending with an ear-splitting percussion *crescendo*, is all the more effective for Abbado's refusal to set a self-indulgently slow tempo. Technically, these recordings outshine the competition, though there are other memorable interpreters – Boulez especially in Op 30. Given the evident rapport between Webern and Abbado it seems odd that the disc doesn't include more of Webern's music. The Bach arrangement is nevertheless an ear-opening exercise in passing baroque counterpoint through a kaleidoscope of expressionist tone colours, and Schoenberg's *A Survivor from Warsaw* retains its special power to move and disturb.

Webern Passacaglia, Op 1. Five Pieces, Op 5. Six Pieces, Op 6. Im Sommerwind **Bach** (orch Webern) Musikalisches Opfer, BWV1079 – Ricercar a 6
Schubert (orch Webern) Deutsche Tänze, D820
Berlin Philharmonic Orchestra / Pierre Boulez
DG 447 099-2GH (67 minutes: DDD) Recorded 1993-94 Ⓕ ●

With the exception of the Bach and Schubert arrangements this is all relatively early, pre-serial Webern, yet Boulez devotes as much care and as much affection to the D minor *Passacaglia* and to the undeniably immature but irresistibly luscious *Im Sommerwind* as to the far more characteristic Op 5 and Op 6 pieces. Indeed, if the *Passacaglia* is anything to go by, a Brahms symphony cycle from Boulez would be a fascinating prospect, while his reading of the 'idyll for large orchestra' suggests that his Delius might be no less interesting. Boulez does not imply that the mature Webern is present here in embryo; but he does perhaps make us ask how much of that later music is, like this, inspired by nature.

To be reminded of Brahms by the *Passacaglia* is no less appropriate. This is a Janus of a piece, looking back not only to Brahms's Fourth Symphony but beyond (the presence of the Bach/Webern *Ricercar* points that up), and at the same time moving onwards from the delicate chamber passages in *Im Sommerwind* towards the 'orchestral chamber music' of Op 5 and Op 6. Boulez looks both ways too, with rich orchestral amplitude and expressive phrasing (very broad rubato) but he also notices Webern's already marked liking for transparent textures, quiet subtleties of string colour and the sound of the muted trumpet. And yes: heard in this context the shorter pieces are a logical progression. They are intensely expressive, with a wide range of emotion often within a few bars; no wonder Boulez prefers the earlier, richer scoring of Op 6. He obviously loves their Mahler-derived dissolution of the boundary between orchestral and chamber music, and encourages the orchestra to play with great tonal beauty, aware that a recurrent marking in mature Webern is 'tenderly'. Those qualities recur in the Bach and Schubert arrangements; the rubato in the Fourth Schubert Dance and the Viennese charm of the Fifth suggest that a Boulez *Fledermaus*, even, might be a gleam at the back of his mind. The recordings are warm and clean.

Symphony, Op 21

Symphony, Op 21. Das Augenlicht, Op 26. Cantatas – No 1, Op 29; No 2, Op 31. Variations, Op 30. Five Pieces, Op posth. Drei Lieder
Christiane Oelze *sop* **Gerald Finley** *bar*
BBC Singers; Berlin Philharmonic Orchestra / Pierre Boulez
DG 447 765-2GH (59 minutes: DDD). Texts and translations included. Recorded 1994 Ⓕ ●

Pierre Boulez has been conducting this music for 40 years, and his interpretations have evolved from the youthful Domaine Musical recordings, through the incisive CBS readings of 1967-72 (reviewed above), to this present 'late' style. Boulez encourages the Berlin Philharmonic to play with great tonal beauty, and the recordings are warm as well as clean. Tempos are generally broader than they were 30 years ago, and forms are outlined more expansively. There are moments of high drama – the sudden outburst from the solo horn in the second movement of Op 21, the representations of thunder and lightning in the first movement of Op 29 – but these are balanced by an eloquent spaciousness and refinement, as with the glowing canonic lines in the first movement of Op 21. Only in Boulez's account of the Op 30 *Variations* do you feel that the emphasis on lyric inwardness risks an excess of decorum, the raw contrasts of texture and mood so strong in the CBS version sacrificed to an overall blend that deprives Webern of some of his power to shock.

That power is explosively present in the *Five Pieces* from 1913, especially in the astonishing No 3, and also, less aggressively, in the whispered *Sprechgesang* of the *Drei Lieder*. But the other side of Webern, the sheer tenderness of his lyrical imagination, is conveyed with distinction by the solo singing and the beautifully integrated BBC Singers, superbly accurate in the cantatas and *Das Augenlicht*. A distinguished disc.

Kurt Weill German/American 1900-1950

GROVE *Weill was a pupil of Humperdinck, Busoni and Jarnach in Berlin (1918-23); their teaching informed his early music, including the choral Recordare (1923) and the Concerto for violin and wind (1924), the latter also influenced by Stravinsky. But the deeper influence of Stravinsky, coupled with an increased consciousness of music as a social force, led him to a rediscovery in the mid-1920s of tonal and vernacular elements, notably from jazz, in his cantata Der neue Orpheus and one-act stage piece Royal Palace, written between two collaborations with the expressionist playwright Georg Kaiser: Der Protagonist and Der Zar lässt sich photographieren. In 1926 he married the singer Lotte Lenya, who was to be the finest interpreter of his music.*

His next collaborator was Brecht, with whom he worked on The Threepenny Opera (1928), The Rise and Fall of the City of Mahagonny (1929) and Happy End (1929), all of which use the corrupted, enfeebled diatonicism of commercial music as a weapon of social criticism, though paradoxically they have beome the epitome of the pre-war culture they sought to despise. Yet this is done within the context of a new harmonic consistency and focus. These works have also drawn attention from the theatre works in which Weill developed without Brecht during the early 1930s, Die Bürgschaft and Der Silbersee (with Kaiser again).

In 1933 he left Germany for Paris, where he worked with Brecht again on the sung ballet The Seven Deadly Sins. Then in 1935 he moved to the USA, where he cut loose from the European art-music tradition and devoted himself wholeheartedly to composing for the Broadway stage, intentionally subordinating aesthetic criteria to pragmatic and populist ones. Yet these works are still informed by his cultivated sense of character and theatrical form.

'Ute Lemper sings Kurt Weill'

Der Silbersee – Ich bin eine arme Verwandte (Fennimores-Lied); Rom war eine Stadt (Cäsars Tod); Lied des Lotterieagenten. Die Dreigroschenoper – Die Moritat von Mackie Messer; Salomon-Song; Die Ballade von der sexuellen Hörigkeit. Das Berliner Requiem – Zu Potsdam unter den Eichen (arr Hazell). Nannas-Lied. Aufstieg und Fall der Stadt Mahagonny – Alabama Song; Wie man sich bettet. Je ne t'aime pas. One Touch of Venus – I'm a stranger here myself; Westwind; Speak low

Ute Lemper *sop* **Berlin Radio Ensemble / John Mauceri**
Decca New Line 425 204-2DNL (50 minutes: DDD) Ⓕ
Texts and translations included ●●

The songs in this collection are mostly from the major works Weill composed between 1928 and 1933, but also included are one from his years in France and three items from the 1943 Broadway musical *One Touch of Venus*. By comparison with the husky, growling delivery often accorded Weill's songs in the manner of his widow Lotte Lenya, Ute Lemper has a voice of clarity and warmth. What distinguishes her singing, though, is the way in which these attributes are allied to an irresistible dramatic intensity. Her 'Song of the Lottery Agent' is an absolute tour de force, apt to leave the listener emotionally drained, and her *Je ne t'aime pas* is almost equally overwhelming. Not least in the three numbers from *One Touch of Venus*, she displays a commanding musical theatre presence. This is, one feels, how Weill's songs were meant to be heard.

The Seven Deadly Sins

Die sieben Todsünden[a]. Symphony No 2[b]
Teresa Stratas, Nora Kimball *sops* **Frank Kelley, Howard Haskin** *tens* **Herbert Perry, Peter Rose** *basses* **Chorus and Orchestra of the Opéra National de Lyon / Kent Nagano**
Erato 0630-17068-2 (65 minutes: DDD). Text and translation included. Recorded [a]1993; [b]1996 Ⓕ ●

Weill and Brecht's *Seven Deadly Sins*, written in haste just after their flight from Hitler's Germany, was their last major collaboration. The question of its interpretation will always be bound up with the memory of Lotte Lenya, who created the role of Anna I. This performance of *Sins* was recorded at the same time that Stratas performed it for Peter Sellars's film of the work (available on video from Decca). There is a certain amount of stage noise in this recording, especially in 'Lust' – the heart of the work. Stratas's singing isn't pretty, but then it's not meant to be; she projects text and music in such a dramatic and heartfelt way that it puts this version immediately in the front rank. Nagano's conducting begins with a very slow introduction, which may sound off-putting to those familiar with the much sprightlier Rattle or Masur versions, which also have soprano soloists. As the performance progresses though, Nagano's control of the drama seems just right. The recorded sound of the symphony is noticeably better than that of *Sins*. As Weill's only major orchestral work, it has never really caught on, though the orchestral writing is as sophisticated as anything in his operas. With so many versions of *Die sieben Todsünden*, preferences for voice and coupling are important. Fassbaender and von Otter both have a selection of Weill songs and arias, Réaux with Masur has the *Lulu* suite, Ross with Rattle, Stravinsky's *Pulcinella*. For first-time Weill buyers, we are inclined to recommend this version over all the others.

Der Silbersee

Heinz Kruse *ten* Severin; **Juanita Lascarro** *sop* Fennimore; **Heinz Karl Gruber** *bar* Olim; **Helga Dernesch** *mez* Frau von Luber; **Heinz Zednik** *ten* Baron Laur; **Graham Clark** *ten* Lottery Agent; **Catrin Wyn-Davies** *sop* First Shop Assistant; **Katarina Karnéus** *mez* Second Shop Assistant; **Paul Whelan** *bar* First Fellow; **Gidon Saks** *bass* Second Fellow; **Stephen Alder** *bar* Third Fellow; **Andrew Weale** *sngr* Fourth Fellow; **London Sinfonietta Chorus; London Sinfonietta / Markus Stenz**
RCA Red Seal ② 09026 63447-2 (85 minutes: DDD) Ⓕ
Notes, text and translation included
Recorded 1996

Der Silbersee, the last work Weill composed in Germany before fleeing the Nazis in 1933, is in some ways the most ambitious of all his European theatre pieces. It isn't an opera, but an epic drama with large-scale orchestra and chorus to augment the singing actors. In it Weill found a new voice musically, one he would use immediately afterwards in the two works he wrote in Paris later in 1933, the Second Symphony and the *ballet-chanté*, *Die sieben Todsünden*.

This recording, easily the best, is based on a concert performance at the 1996 Proms in London. The problem with *Der Silbersee* in concert, and to a lesser extent on disc, is that once the lengthy scenes of dialogue have been removed, the impact of many of the musical points is lost. For instance, the two best-known songs, Fennimore's aria 'Ich bin eine arme Verwandte' and the Ballad of Caesar's Death occur in different scenes in Act 2, yet come next to each other here. Two London productions have shown that the work is dramatically viable, although Georg Kaiser's text, with its own brand of social expressionism, is hard to translate. Its story of homeless men, trigger-happy policemen, lottery tickets and swindling hypocrites has a topical appeal in each decade. What it lacks is that quality of sarcastic wit which brought out the best in Weill – in his works with Brecht in Europe and then with Ira Gershwin, Alan Jay Lerner and Ogden Nash in the USA. The music always gives way to the drama here, so that the ending, which on stage can be extraordinarily moving, just fades away. (The two men, who have been enemies but are united in despair, decide to drown themselves in the lake, but when they reach the shore, it's frozen over and a voice tells them that they must go on.)

The singing here is good, with HK Gruber characterful as Olim, and Heinz Kruse, in the part created in Magdeburg by Ernst Busch (who recorded two songs at the time), torn between love and revenge. Helga Dernesch is typically incisive in her one sung contribution, an all-too-brief duet. Those who know recordings of Fennimore's two songs by Lotte Lenya, Ute Lemper and others may find Juanita Lascarro a trifle restrained, but she is singing in character, whereas Lenya and all the other *chanteuses* are giving the songs a makeover in the tradition of cabaret.

Street Scene

Kristine Ciesinski *sop* Anna Maurrant; **Richard Van Allan** *bass* Frank Maurrant; **Janis Kelly** *sop* Rose Maurrant; **Bonaventura Bottone** *ten* Sam Kaplan; **Terry Jenkins** *ten* Abraham Kaplan; **Meriel Dickinson** *mez* Emma Jones; **Angela Hickey** *mez* Olga Olsen; **Claire Daniels** *sop* Jennie Hildebrand; **Fiametta Doria** *sop* First Nursemaid; **Judith Douglas** *mez* Second Nursemaid; **English National Opera Chorus and Orchestra / Carl Davis**
TER Classics ② CDTER21185 (146 minutes: DDD) Ⓕ
Recorded 1989

Street Scene is the most ambitious product of Weill's American years. It's something of a *Porgy and Bess* transferred from Catfish Row to the slum tenements of New York. Where *Porgy and Bess* is through-composed with recitatives, though, *Street Scene* offers a mixture of set musical numbers, straight dialogue, and dialogue over musical underscoring. The musical numbers themselves range from operatic arias and ensembles to rousing 1940s dance numbers. It is consistently well sung, particularly where style is concerned. Weill described the work as a 'Broadway opera', and it demands a vernacular rather than a classical operatic singing style. This it duly gets from Kristine Ciesinski as Anna Maurrant, while Janis Kelly's beautifully clear but natural enunciation and her sense of emotional involvement make daughter Rose's 'What good would the moon be?' a performance of real beauty. Praiseworthy too is Richard Van Allan as the murderous husband, his 'Let things be like they always was' creating a suitably sinister effect. Among the subsidiary attractions is the appearance of Catherine Zeta Jones, performing the swinging dance number 'Moon-faced, starry-eyed'.

Hugo Wolf

Austrian 1860-1903

GROVE *Wolf played the violin, piano and organ as a child and studied briefly at the Vienna Conservatory (1875-7, meeting his idol Wagner) but, lacking discipline and direction, he had to rely on friends and cultured benefactors for help and introductions. His first important works, the songs of 1877-8, arose from the effects of his sexual initiation and first romantic attachment. Some are bright, others agonised, reflecting his depression and illness from a syphilitic infection. Though in 1880 this cloud seemed to abate, a pattern of cyclic mood swing and sporadic creativity was already established. Holidays, studies of Wagner and radiant song settings alternated with personal estrangements and a dark, dramatic strain in his music. For three years (1884-6), he wrote trenchant musical criticism for the Wiener Salonblatt, siding with Wagner and against Brahms, meanwhile working on Penthesilea (1883-5) and the D minor Quartet (1878-84) and beginning a secret love affair with Melanie Köchert. Compositional mastery and a sense of purpose came only in the late 1880s,* when he turned from subjectivity to imaginative literature as a stimulus. In 1888 Eichendorff's poetry and in particular Mörike's inspired a sudden flowering of song music that in profusion and variety matched Schubert and Schumann. His acclaimed public performances won new converts, and in February 1889 he finished the 51 songs of the Goethe songbook, in April 1890 the 44 Spanish songs. Publication and critical recognition turned his thoughts to opera but from 1891 physical exhaustion and depressive phases stemmed the flow of original music. In 1895 he composed his only completed opera, Der Corregidor, but it was unsuccessful; in 1897 he composed his last songs and had the mental breakdown that led to his terminal illness.

Wolf's strength was the compression of large-scale forms and ideas – the essences of grand opera, tone poem and dramatic symphony – into song. Combining expressive techniques in the piano part with an independent vocal line, and using an array of rhythmic and harmonic devices to depict textual imagery, illustrate mood and create musical structure, he continued and extended the lied tradition of Schubert and Schumann. Yet he was original in his conception of the songbook as the larger dramatic form; each one seems to have been planned in advance to represent a poet or source. Folk music, nature studies, humorous songs and ballads peopled by soldiers, sailors, students or musicians recur in the German settings, while religious or erotic themes dominate the Spanish and Italian songbooks.

Lieder Recitals

Elly Ameling

Spanisches Liederbuch – Die ihr schwebet um diese Palmen; Ach, des Knaben Augen; Mühvoll komm' ich und beladen; In dem Schatten meiner Locken; Sagt, seid Ihr es, feiner Herr; Mögen alle bösen Zungen; Alle gingen, Herz, zur Ruh; Tief im Herzen trag' ich Pein; Komm, o Tod, von Nacht umgeben; Ob auch finstre Blicke glitten; Bedeckt mich mit Blumen; Sie blasen zum Abmarsch; Wer tat deinem Füsslein weh; Geh' Geliebter, geh' jetz. Mörike Lieder – Das verlassene Mägdlein; Nimmersatte Liebe; Verborgenheit; Im Frühling; Elfenlied; Auf ein altes Bild; Lied vom Winde
Elly Ameling sop **Rudolf Jansen** pf
Hyperion CDA66788 (59 minutes: DDD). Texts and ⓕ translations included. Recorded 1991 ●

This is a gratifying distillation of Ameling as a Wolf interpreter, a late flowering of her art in which we are consoled for some loss in the quality and quantity of tone by the insights offered. In so many of these readings, her performance represents Wolf singing of the most telling kind. The four central songs tell us all. To 'Ob auch finstre Blicke glitten' she brings a depth of verbal accent and inner expression that places it among Wolf's highest achievements. There follow a properly weary, care-ridden account of 'Alle gingen, Herz, zur Ruh', a languorous evocation of 'Bedeckt mich mit Blumen' and a tragic entry into the abasing world of 'Mühvoll komm' ich und beladen'. The two sacred songs are hardly less impressive. Her choice ends with

a reading of 'Geh' Geliebter', in which Ameling sheds the years to give us all the ardent thoughts of the girl reluctant at dawn to leave her lover. If you have hesitated before buying the complete EMI set, you might prefer to try this rewarding and distinguished selection. Ameling shows equal discernment in her choice from the Mörike settings, catching – as the best Wolf interpreters can do – the specific mood of each. If there is a favourite here it has to be 'Das verlassene Mägdlein', where the dreadful anguish of the abandoned girl, so unerringly caught by Wolf, is expressed in a mood of almost toneless lassitude – just right. Jansen is an ideal partner, nowhere more so than when he rightly underplays the rhythm of 'Sie blasen zum Abmarsch'.

Hans Hotter

Goethe Lieder – Harfenspieler: I, Wer sich der Einsamkeit ergibt; II, An die Türen; III, Wer nie sein Brot; Cophtisches Lied I and II; Anakreons Grab; Ob der Koran von Ewigkeit sei?; So lang man nüchtern ist; Prometheus; Grenzen der Menschheit. Italienisches Liederbuch – Ein Ständchen Euch zu bringen; Schon streckt' ich aus; Geselle, woll'n wir uns in Kutten hüllen. Drei Gedichte von Michelangelo. Eichendorff Lieder – Der Musikant. Mörike Lieder – Der Tambour; Nimmersatte Liebe; Fussreisedf; Verborgenheit
Hans Hotter bass-bar **Gerald Moore** pf
Testament mono SBT1197 (70 minutes: ADD) ⓕ
Texts and translations included
Recorded 1951, 1953 and 1957 ●●

At last: a reissue of Hotter's 1953 Hugo Wolf recital, which forms the centrepiece of this release, and it's in far better, more immediate sound than on the original LP. Hotter's interpretations of Prometheus, Grenzen der Menschheit, the gloomy Harfenspieler Lieder and resigned Michelangelo settings – Wolf at his greatest – remain virtually unsurpassed. They were surely written with a bass-baritone of Hotter's calibre in mind, and, quite apart from his vocal prowess, his verbal insights are once again remarkable, while the account of the naughty monks' exploits from the Italian Songbook remind us of Hotter the humorist. The earlier and later items that complete the CD disclose similar gifts, notably the delightful Der Tambour – and Anakreons Grab, which, both in 1951 and 1957, matches the Innigkeit of Goethe's poem and Wolf's setting. Moore is a masterly partner in music that severely taxes the pianist. This disc is a must for Wolf enthusiasts.

Peter Schreier

Mörike Lieder – Der Genesene an die Hoffnung; Ein Stündlein wohl vor Tag; Der Tambour; Nimmersatte Liebe; Fussreise; Verborgenheit; Im Frühling; Auf einer Wanderung; Der Gärtner; In der Frühe; Gebet; Neue Liebe; Wo find'ich Trost?; Frage und Antwort; Lebe wohl; Heimweh; Denk'es, o Seele!; Der Jäger; Storchenbotschaft; Bei einer Trauung; Selbstgeständis; Abschied
Peter Schreier ten **Karl Engel** pf
Orfeo C142981A (60 minutes: DDD). Texts and ⓕ translations included. Recorded 1996 ●

Peter Schreier's ever-supple tenor, honed by keen-eyed intelligence and a verbal palate sharp enough to taste and try every last word, makes him a Wolf interpreter of the highest order. In this meticulously shaped programme of 22 of Wolf's eager settings of Mörike, one wonder appears after another. Schreier and his ever-sentient pianist, Karl Engel, move from a gentle awakening of love, which grows in intensity towards the innermost core of songs of doubt and fear, and on through a gallery of wonderfully dry, wry tableaux to the final farewell and the kicking of the critic downstairs.

The first song here, *Im Frühling*, epitomises the equilibrium, security and entirety of performances which have grown from long-pondered consideration. The long, drowsy vowels, and Schreier's sensitivity to the high-register placing of crucial words of longing all fuse into the slow-walking movement of cloud, wing, river, breeze, as language becomes expanded and enriched by tone. Schreier's remarkable steadiness of line in *Verborgenheit* reveals the song's secrets only reluctantly: the fierce intensity of sudden illumination is all the more searing. Grotesquerie and poignancy coexist in *Bei einer Trauung*, and we feel every catch of the voice as Schreier turns weird and whimsical tale-teller in *Storchenbotschaft*.

Elisabeth Schwarzkopf

Mörike Lieder – Im Frühling; Auf eine Christblume I; Lied vom Winde. Goethe Lieder – Philine; Mignon; Der Schäfer; Blumengruss; Frühling übers Jahr; Anakreons Grab; Phänomen; Ganymed. Spanisches Liederbuch – Mühvoll komm' ich und beladen; In dem Schatten meiner Locken; Bedeckt mich mit Blumen; Wer tat deinem Füsslein weh; Wehe der, die mir verstrickte. Italienisches Liederbuch – Nun lass uns Frieden schliessen. Sechs Lieder für eine Frauenstimme – Mausfallen-Sprüchlein. Sechs alte Weisen H

Dame Elisabeth Schwarzkopf *sop* **Gerald Moore** *pf*

EMI Festspieldokumente mono CDH7 64905-2 (71 minutes: ADD). Texts included Ⓕ

Recorded live in 1958 ○○○

'A blissful experience of the purest lied art' reported the *Salzburger Nachrichten* on Schwarzkopf's recital. The recording derives from the Austrian Broadcasting Corporation's archive. It gives a marvellous sense of presence, recalling most vividly what it was that made the memory of Schwarzkopf's song recitals precious. First, the quality of voice, caught here at its purest and most radiant; then the full concentration of a total sensibility, emotion and intellect fused, upon the songs: every one of them lived a special life on each separate occasion. The riches of this recital are beyond the scope of a short review. Every song here deserves a paragraph to itself, and the appreciation of Gerald Moore's work would have a large share in each. The disc, for one who cares for Wolf's songs and the art of their performance, is beyond price.

Anne Sofie von Otter and Olaf Bär

Spanisches Liederbuch

Anne Sofie von Otter *mez* **Olaf Bär** *bar*

Geoffrey Parsons *pf*

EMI ② CDS5 55325-2 (109 minutes: DDD). Texts and translations included. Recorded 1992-94 Ⓕ ●

The songs are performed not in the published order but in one devised by Bär for several recitals of the set given by this trio, and now carried over into the recording studio. For the 10 religious songs the reordering works well. In any case here the two singers show a deep and rewarding comprehension of the agony and ecstasy of poems and music. Listen, too, to von Otter's sense of smiling wonder in 'Ach, des Knaben Augen' as the holy mother looks into her son's eyes. By contrast in 'Mühvoll komm' ich und beladen' she changes to a searing, soul-searching manner that captures completely the woman's remorse, magnificently so at the climactic 'Nimm mich an'. Bär is as tense and inward in the great 'Herr, was trägt der Boden hier', capturing the voices of penitent and Christ to perfection. Note, too, Parsons's deliberately heavy gait in 'Die du Gott gebarst'. There are problems, however, in the secular songs.

With von Otter, apart from downward transpositions that make the piano parts sound unduly dark and Parsons consequently a shade heavy-handed, there is little to quarrel with. She teases, flirts, falls in love with the best of them, alert with her words, but never overdoing the archness. Bär, though, is not only up against the perhaps more formidable challenge of Fischer-Dieskau (on DG) but also against his own reordering. He does not have the immense tonal range and emotional charge of the older baritone. 'Herz, verzage nicht geschwind' is broader, more biting in Fischer-Dieskau's reading, for instance, 'Ach im Maien' that much more mellifluous, but you could say that Bär's more contained, but by no means reticent approach has its own, Wolfian justification. But it is entirely Bär's fault that songs Nos 21 and 24, which should be sung as a group, lose some of their force when separated as here, thoughtfully as Bär sings each in its turn. However, the readings as a whole are worthy of the collection. There is more space around the voices than on the closer-miked DG set, where Fischer-Dieskau is very much a presence in the room with you. This newer version doesn't replace the old, but those who want another, fresh, valid view of the *Spanisches Liederbuch* or just want to hear von Otter in her element will wish to acquire these two absorbing discs.

Various Artists: Hugo Wolf Society Edition H

Mörike Lieder – excerpts. Spanisches Liederbuch – excerpts. Italienisches Liederbuch – excerpts. Eichendorff Lieder – excerpts. Goethe Lieder – excerpts. Drei Gedichte von Michelangelo. Gedichte von Scheffel, Mörike, Goethe und Kerner – excerpts. Gedichte von Richard Reinick – excerpts. Gedichte nach Heine, Shakespeare und Lord Byron – excerpts

Marta Fuchs, Ria Ginster, Tiana Lemnitz, Elisabeth Rethberg, Alexandra Trianti *sops* **Elena Gerhardt** *mez* **Karl Erb, John McCormack, Helge Rosawaenge** *tens* **Herbert Jansson, Gerhard Hüsch** *bars* **Friedrich Schorr** *bass-bar* **Alexander Kipnis, Ludwig Weber** basses with various pianists
EMI mono ⑤ CHS5 66640-2 (375 minutes: ADD) Ⓜ
Texts and translations included
Recorded 1931-38 ooo

The old Hugo Wolf Society recordings hold their place not only as regards the distinction of the readings but as evidence of the pioneering work done by Ernest Newman and Walter Legge in the promulgation of the composer's highly original style. Six volumes were issued on 78rpm discs between 1931 and 1938, but a planned seventh was not released as a set (because of the war intervening) until the LP reissue came out in 1981. Here a further six titles have been unearthed from the EMI archives. This is a cornucopia of delights for the Lieder lover. Gerhardt had the whole of the first volume to herself, and launches the project with a typical honesty of approach. Her slightly grand voice and inimitable style may not be to modern tastes but persist and you'll surely respond to the generosity of her singing. The next volumes are dominated by Hüsch, Janssen and Kipnis, to whom Legge assigned exactly the right pieces for their respective styles. All are deeply rewarding, but Hüsch in love-songs from the *Spanish Songbook* and Kipnis in the *Michelangelo* Songs and so much else make particularly memorable contributions. Among the women, the much underrated Greek soprano, Alexandra Trianti brings just the right lightness of touch to some of the teasing, airy pieces from the *Italian Songbook*. Ria Ginster is a fresh, pleasing soprano, but she slightly under-characterises her offerings. Not so Elisabeth Rethberg, who encompasses the grander passions of the *Italian Songbook* and is unsurpassed in the sorrowful abasement of 'Mühvoll komm' ich und beladen' from the *Spanish Songbook*. Legge perceptively brought in Schorr for a defiant 'Prometheus' (in Wolf's orchestral version) and McCormack for an elevating 'Ganymed'. In 1937, Roswaenge sings a hair-raising 'Feuerreiter'.

Other singers in the later volumes who bring their special individuality of utterance to bear on specific areas of Wolf's output are Fuchs (touching as Mignon and so eager in the great love-song, 'Geh, Geliebter, geh jetzt!'), the refined, sensitive Erb and the lovely Lemnitz, whose 'In der Frühe, Schlafendes Jesuskind' and 'Wiegenlied im Sommer' are unmissable. Janssen also returned in 1937 for deeply eloquent accounts of some of the most inspired pieces in the *Spanish Songbook*, including a 'Schlafendes Jesuskind' almost as rewarding as Lemnitz's reading. The gem among the previously unpublished items is Kipnis's sensual, intimate 'Verschwiegene Liebe'. Then to round things off Gerhardt is heard again in a newly issued version of a rarely heard, grief-laden song, 'Uber Nacht', on which she lavishes all her love for Wolf. The pianists from Bos to Moore are uniformly excellent, though not always as perceptive as their successors today. It is Wolf and the singers who make this one of the great enterprises of the pre-war gramophone.

Iannis Xenakis

Greek/French 1922

GROVE *Xenakis was a French composer of Greek parentage and Romanian birth. In 1932 his family returned to Greece, and he was educated on Spetsai and at the Athens Polytechnic, where he studied engineering. In 1947 he arrived in Paris, where he became a member of Le Corbusier's architectural team, producing his first musical work, Metastasis, only in 1954, based on the design for the surfaces of the Philips pavilion to be built for the Brussels Exposition of 1958. This, with its divided strings and mass effects, had an enormous influence; but in ensuing works he moved on to find mathematical and computer means of handling large numbers of events, drawing on (for example) Gaussian distribution (ST/10, Atrées), Markovian chains (Analogiques) and game theory (Duel, Stratégie). Other interests were in electronic music (Bohor, 1962), ancient Greek drama (used in several settings) and instrumental virtuosity (Herma for piano, 1964; Nomos alpha for cello, 1966). His later output, chiefly of orchestral and instrumental pieces, is large, many works from the mid-1970s onwards striking back from modernist complexity to ostinatos and modes suggestive of folk music.*

Knephas

A Colone. Nuits. Serment. Knephas. Medea
New London Chamber Choir; Critical Band / James Wood
Hyperion CDA66980 (58 minutes: DDD). Texts and translations included. Recorded 1997 Ⓕ ooo

This enterprising release is a great success, showing just how varied – and unintimidating – Xenakis's music can be. The performances are nothing short of phenomenal in their technical assurance and emotional power, and the recording is also something special, giving the singers just the right degree of space and resonance to project the often complex textures with all the necessary precision. The earliest works offer different angles on the composer's ultra-expressionist idiom, with *Nuits* (1967) adopting a very direct way of representing its anguished lament for the martyrs of Greece's struggle for freedom after 1945. *Medea* (also 1967) uses much more text, and its chant-like style has affinities with Stravinsky's *Les noces*, but the overall effect is much harsher, with abrasive yet imaginative instrumental writing. *A Colone* (1977) also has Stravinskian affinities, and the text (Sophocles's description of the delights of Colonus) prompts music which is uninhibitedly exuberant. This warmer, more celebratory side of Xenakis is carried over into *Serment* (1980), a short setting of a text derived from the Hippocratic Oath and not, one suspects, an entirely serious effort, though there is nothing trivial about it either. Finally, the superb *Knephas* ('Darkness') of 1990 begins in an appropriately unsparing manner, but ends with a hymnic apotheosis which recalls Messiaen in its harmonic character and warmth of atmosphere. Here is one of the 20th-century's most important musical voices, and this recording does it full justice.

Jan Dismas Zelenka

Bohemian 1679-1745

GROVE *After serving Count Hartig in Prague, Zelenka became a double bass player in the royal orchestra at Dresden in 1710. He studied with Fux in Vienna and Lotti in Venice, 1715-16; from 1719 he remained in Dresden, except for a visit to Prague in 1723. Having gradually taken over the duties of the ailing Kapellmeister, Heinichen, he was made only church music composer (1735); Hasse was the new Kapellmeister. He composed mainly sacred works, among them three oratorios, 12 masses, and many other pieces; his output also includes a festival opera (1723, Prague), six chamber sonatas for oboes (c 1715) and other instrumental pieces. His music, like that of Bach (whom he knew), is notable for its adventurousness, its contrapuntal mastery and its harmonic invention.*

Capriccios

Capriccios – No 2 in G; No 3 in F. P
Concerto a 8 in G. Hipocondrie a 7 in A
Das Neu-Eröffnete Orchestre / Jürgen Sonnentheil
CPO CPO999 458-2 (61 minutes: DDD) Ⓕ
Recorded 1996

This disc contains two of Zelenka's five *Capriccios*, a Concerto for eight instruments and the intriguingly titled *Hipocondrie*, which occupies ground somewhere between suite and concerto. Zelenka was skilled in the art of combining instruments of differing colours, ordering them about in a way that makes us wonder if he had a grudge against players. The horn-writing in the *Capriccios* is merciless, with uncommonly high parts often emerging in exposed moments in the texture. Zelenka's melodic facility, rhythmic imagination and instinctive feeling for effective instrumental ranges and colours are sufficient to sustain interest. There is an inventive freshness about his music which contains surprises at almost every turn. Sometimes, however, as in the finale of the Concerto in eight parts, sequential patterns are overworked, giving the movement a somewhat amorphous, unsatisfying shape. Initial rather good ideas, almost always arresting, are less well sustained than, say, Telemann's, even if they are sometimes bolder and more adventurous. Sonnentheil achieves spirited, amiable performances from Das Neu-Eröffnete Orchestre, an able body of period-instrumentalists. The two horns are excellent, and, if oboes and strings sound a shade unrefined occasionally, this does little to spoil enjoyment of an entertaining programme.

Trio Sonatas

Trio Sonatas – No 1 in F; No 3 in B flat; No 4 in G minor P
Ensemble Zefiro (Paolo Grazzi, Alfredo Bernardini *obs* Alberto Grazzi *bn* Manfred Kraemer *vn* Lorenz Duftschmid *violone* Gian Carlo Rado *theorbo* Rinaldo Alessandrini *hpd/org*)
Auvidis Astrée E8563 (52 minutes: DDD) Ⓕ
Recorded 1995 ●

Zelenka was one of a gifted group of composers associated with the Dresden court during the first half of the 18th century. The court orchestra, one of the best around at that time, boasted a particularly accomplished wind section, and it may have been for some of these players that Zelenka wrote his six trios. The sources have not survived complete in all cases, and the realisation, for example, of the bass parts in the First and Third Sonatas, both of them included here, must always be conjectural. Ensemble Zefiro has thought carefully about this and has arrived at a solution which is both idiomatic and, it seems, in keeping with the surviving material. The playing is spirited and plentifully endowed with virtuosity. The oboists Paolo Grazzi and Alfredo Bernardini are technically secure and tastefully imaginative in their ornamentation. Bassoonist Alberto Grazzi is also fluent and furthermore a sensitive ensemble player. Keyboard continuo is stylishly provided by Rinaldo Alessandrini, sometimes playing harpsichord, at other times organ; and additional continuo support includes violone and theorbo. Readers so far unacquainted with these sonatas are in for a treat, for this is music rich in fantasy, exciting for its virtuosic content, unusually extended in the working out of its ideas, and effectively constructed.

Trio Sonatas – No 2 in G minor, No 5 in F; No 6 in C minor P
Ensemble Zefiro (Paolo Grazzi, Alfredo Bernardini *obs* Alberto Grazzi *bn* Roberto Sensi *db* Rolf Lislevand *theorbo* Rinaldo Alessandrini *hpd/org*)
Auvidis Astrée E8511 (52 minutes: DDD) Ⓕ
Recorded 1993 ●

For sheer élan and spirit the baroque instrumental players on this disc take some beating. Zelenka's six sonatas for two oboes, bassoon and continuo are among the most rewarding and at times most difficult pieces of baroque chamber music in the oboe repertory. Indeed, pieces demanding such virtuosity from these instruments were probably without precedent at the time (1715). The writing is often such as to make us wonder if they were destined for friends or for enemies of the composer. Here, then, we are treated to some splendidly invigorating playing of music which offers a great deal beyond face value. The sounds of the solo instruments themselves, together with an effective continuo group of double-bass, harpsichord/organ and theorbo are admirably captured in the recording.

Six Trio Sonatas
Heinz Holliger, Maurice Bourgue *obs* **Klaus Thunemann** *bn* **Thomas Zehetmair** *vn* **Klaus Stoll** *db* **Jonathan Rubin** *lte* **Christiane Jaccottet** *hpd*
ECM New Series ② 462 542-2 (100 minutes: DDD) Ⓕ

Zelenka's sonatas for two oboes, bassoon and continuo extended the boundaries of baroque oboe writing in much the same way as Bach's flute sonatas did for the flute. Little or nothing as technically advanced had been seen before, and at times Zelenka's writing, often idiosyncratic, is such that we might mischievously wonder whether it was a love of the oboe or a vendetta against certain oboists that prompted him to write such demanding music. Heinz Holliger, Maurice Bourgue and Klaus Thunemann recorded these pieces for Archiv in 1972, but the new release is more rhythmically flexible and more sensitive in its use of dynamics and ornamentation. Again, the performers play modern instruments, but with a virtuosity and intuitive musicianship that compensate for the warmer, woodier sound of their baroque counterparts. Zelenka completed his set of six sonatas in about 1716. Five of them are laid out using the four-movement scheme of a *sonata da chiesa* while the remaining one (No 5) adopts the more up-to-date three-movement pattern. Alone among the six, the Third Sonata is written for violin and oboe rather than a pair of oboes.

The playing on these two discs is of a high order, although the continuo is a shade overbearing at times. But Holliger and Bourgue effortlessly seek out every nuance of this music that is so brimming with character. Quite simply, there is not a dull bar to be found throughout these warmly expressive pieces. Both players are able to sustain effortlessly the extended melodic contours which are such a feature of these sonatas, while at the same time never losing sight of the music's poetry. In Sonata No 3 Zehetmair proves himself a sympathetic partner to Holliger, in playing that is lively and clearly defined.

The Lamentations of Jeremiah

Michael Chance *counterten* **John Mark Ainsley** *ten* **Michael George** *bass* **Chandos Baroque Players**
Hyperion CDA66426 (73 minutes: DDD). Texts and translations included. Recorded 1990 Ⓕ

Between the incomparable settings by Thomas Tallis and the extremely austere one by Stravinsky (which he called *Threni*) the 'Lamentations of Jeremiah' have attracted surprisingly few composers. Perhaps the predominantly sombre tone, without even the dramatic opportunities presented by the *Dies irae* in a Requiem, is off-putting. Be that as it may, Zelenka showed remarkable resourcefulness in his 1722 setting for the electoral chapel at Dresden, where he was *Kapellmeister*. His musical language is in many ways similar to that of JS Bach but there are also daring turns of phrase which are entirely personal. The six *Lamentations* feature each singer twice; this performance is intimate, slightly spacious in tempo and with a resonant acoustic.

Alexander Zemlinsky

Austrian 1871-1942

GROVE *Zemlinsky was a pupil of Fuchs at the Vienna Conservatory (1890-92). In 1895 he became a close friend of Schoenberg's;he also had encouragement from Mahler, who presented his opera Es war einmal at the Hofoper in 1900. His orchestral fantasy Die Seejungfrau dates from these years. By this time he was working as a theatre conductor in Vienna his later appointments were at the German theatre in Prague (1911-27) and the Kroll Opera in Berlin (1927-31). In 1933 he fled to Vienna, and then in 1938 to the USA. From the same background as Schoenberg, and similarly influenced by Mahler and Strauss, he developed an impassioned style in such works as his Second Quartet (1914), one-act operas Eine florentinische Tragödie (1917) and Der Zwerg (1922), and Lyric Symphony (1923). Later works, including the opera Der Kreidekreis (1932), the Sinfonietta (1934) and the Fourth Quartet (1936), are influenced more by Weill and German neo-classicism.*

String Quartets

String Quartets – No 1 in A, Op 4; No 4, Op 25. Two Movements for String Quartet
Pražák Quartet (Vaclav Remes, Vlastimil Holek *vns* Josef Klusoň *va* Michal Kaňka *vc*)
Praga Digitals PRD250 107 (70 minutes: DDD) Ⓕ
Recorded 1997

String Quartets – No 1; No 2, Op 15
Artis Quartet (Peter Schuhmayer, Johannes Meissl *vns* Herbert Kefer *va* Othmar Muller *vc*) Ⓕ
Nimbus NI5563 (65 minutes: DDD). Recorded 1997

Zemlinsky's four quartets have never quite become part of the established chamber music repertory. That they deserve a place in that repertory is eloquently argued by both these couplings. In the richly post-Brahmsian First Quartet the Artis produces splendidly ample tone, warm intensity of expression and, in the demurely lilting *Scherzo*, a touch of humour. The Pražák does not have quite their Austrian colleagues' variety of colour (the Artis plays a Montagnana, an Andrea Guarneri, a Guadagnini and an Andrea Amati, which helps) and its slower tempos, though adding a touch of geniality to the first movement, also adds a hint of heavy-footedness to the *Scherzo*. On the other hand it is readier to play quietly, and reveals more shadow in the slow movement. The Artis's account of the Second Quartet is startlingly successful in conveying its abrupt, at times violent oscillations of mood and its extraordinary vehemence, while very properly finding the centre of its emotional world to be a poignant lyricism. The Pražák has the still harder task of the Fourth Quartet, one of the most demanding pieces for the medium ever written. If you unworthily suspect that its slowish *Scherzo* in the First Quartet is due to caution, its account of the Fourth's concluding double fugue convincingly demonstrates its hair-raising virtuosity. In the rest of this work its very slightly rougher, brighter sound is a positive advantage, though in the elaborately florid textures of the penultimate variation movement it shows that it can also produce sweet tone and a fine line.

Until both quartets complete their cycles you shouldn't part with either of these discs. If you insist on a recommendation at this stage it would have to be, but only by a whisker, for the Artis. But the Pražák adds a substantial bonus in the form of a pair of movements from an abandoned quartet of 1927, the first strangely based on an almost derisive fragment of *Yankee Doodle*, the second an apparent attempt to fuse a slow movement, at times mysterious, at times intense, with more aggressive music that eventually gives birth to an enigmatic Minuet. Both discs are well recorded, the Nimbus sound being a little warmer than the Praga.

Sechs Gesänge, Op 13

Zemlinsky Sechs Gesänge, Op 13 **Mahler** Lieder eines fahrenden Gesellen. Rückert-Lieder
Anne Sofie von Otter *mez* **North German Radio Symphony Orchestra / Sir John Eliot Gardiner**
DG 439 928-2GH (56 minutes: DDD). Texts and translations included. Recorded live in 1993 Ⓕ

This is another absolute winner for both von Otter and Gardiner. The three works make an ideal programme, the two Mahler pieces forming a sensible frame for the central Zemlinsky. In all three offerings von Otter offers that peculiar gift of hers consisting of utter conviction allied to wonderful musicianship. In terms of tempo, phrasing, balance and sheer interpretative know-how, the pair take no false steps and very many fruitful ones. You will look hard to find a version of *Lieder eines fahrenden Gesellen* filled with such sense of emotions being felt and expressed so immediately. Von Otter and Gardiner make the work live here and now for our time, Gardiner rewardingly alert to every nuance and subtlety in Mahler's orchestral writing, which the clear recording admirably seconds.

The Zemlinsky is the real revelation, though, far preferable to the piano version of these shadowy Maeterlinck settings. These songs of sexual liberation and *fin de siècle* decadence, which mirror precisely the world of *Jugendstil* as exemplified in Klimt's paintings – and are equally multi-mirrored, highly coloured and erotic – cry out for instrumental clothing. Gardiner revels in the dream-world orchestration while von Otter perfectly catches their hothouse atmosphere and underlines the texts' meaning without ever indulging in any overemphases. It's almost a relief to come up into the open air of Mahler's Rückert setting, 'Ich atmet' einen linden Duft', where von Otter lightens her timbre, bringing a gentle smile into her tone. In these settings, she once more finds the right 'face' for each song – even expanding grandly into the affirmations at the end of 'Um Mitternacht' – and then ends a compelling disc with just the other-worldly serenity predicated by 'Ich bin der Welt'. There's no need to seek out any other recording of these pieces.

Ein lyrische Symphonie, Op 18

Berg Lyric Suite (arr cpsr). Fünf Orchesterlieder nach Ansichtskartentexten von Peter Altenberg, Op 4[a] **Zemlinsky** Ein lyrische Symphonie, Op 18[b]
[ab]Vlatka Orsanic *sop* [b]**James Johnson** *bar* **South West German Radio Symphony Orchestra / Michael Gielen**
Arte Nova 74321 27768-2 (67 minutes: DDD) Ⓢ
Recorded 1994

A first-class bargain, let down only by inadequate notes, the fact that the words of the vocal pieces are not provided and a slightly but not disagreeably lean orchestral sound. Gielen has the reputation of a specialist in contemporary music, of 'advanced' contemporary music in particular, and that might imply that he will take a coolish view of Zemlinsky. In fact he responds with a beautiful sense of long, lyrical line, and although his orchestra lacks the last degree of sumptuousness, his accuracy and clarity of detail reveal more of the subtle beauties of the score than some more opulent readings, as well as bolder vehemence. His control of tempo and his readiness to slow the music to breathless stillness are both admirable.

These virtues would count for a lot less if the soloists were merely competent. Both are more than that. Orsanic is clean and accurate; although she does not hover as ecstatically as she might in the fourth song, she responds to the solo string writing at its opening with an imaginative fining-down of tone. Even so, she sounds rather more at home in the Berg *Altenberg* Lieder, where she reacts intelligently to the texts and opens out to lyrical vehemence at the end of the cycle. Johnson is still better, a fine lyric baritone with dignity, clear diction and admirable phrasing. The pieces from the *Lyric* Suite are exceptionally well done, richness of texture combining with excellent precision of attack, fine solo playing and warm expressiveness.

In sum, Gielen's reading of the Zemlinsky will not disappoint any admirer of the work, regardless of their bank balance.

Additional recommendation
Ein lyrische Symphonie, Op 18
Voigt *sop* **Terfel** *bass-bar* **Vienna Philharmonic Orchestra / Sinopoli**
DG 449 179-2GH (49 minutes: DDD) Ⓕ

A sumptuously rich performance from Sinopoli and the Vienna Phil, with both soloists on superb form. In the absence of Riccardo Chailly's *Gramophone* Award-winning account (nla), this is the top choice if price is not an issue.

Songs

Posthumous Songs – Sechs Lieder. Zwei Lieder. Zwei Preislieder. Wandl' ich im Wald des Abends. Vier Lieder. Zwei Brettl-Lieder. Drei Lieder. Zwei Balladen. Lieder auf Gedichte von Richard Dehmel – Ansturm; Vorspiel; Auf See. Vier Lieder. Und einmal gehst du
Ruth Ziesak *sop* **Iris Vermillion** *mez* **Hans-Peter Blochwitz** *ten* **Andreas Schmidt** *bar* **Cord Garben** *pf*
Sony Classical SK57960 (70 minutes: DDD). Texts Ⓕ and translations included. Recorded 1993

These are the songs Zemlinsky didn't publish; why not? When sung as they are here in chronological order the reason for a while seems obvious: they have little individuality until about a third of the way through the collection. From then on things get much more interesting. The three settings of Richard Dehmel have a concentrated, poignant intensity so impressive that one is tempted to speculate about hidden reasons for Zemlinsky's reticence. 'Jane Grey' (from *Zwei Balladen*), for example, was entered for a competition to which Schoenberg submitted a setting of exactly the same text. Is that why it almost out-Schoenbergs Schoenberg in its tenuous hold on tonality, its curiously gripping angularity? But in 'Der verlorene Haufen' (*Zwei Balladen*), also set by Schoenberg for the same competition, Zemlinsky seems to be out-Mahlering Mahler in the fearsome march-toccata that accompanies this grim tale of a front-line regiment contemplating death each morning. The manner of the Dehmel songs is recaptured in a haunting group of settings of Hofmannsthal (*Vier Lieder*); there are also two curious comic ballads (the *Brettl-Lieder*, one quite funny, the other – about a man who eats so much that he bursts – rather disgusting), a most beautiful cradle-song over a dead child ('Über eine Wiege', *Drei Lieder*) and a much later, nobly stoic contemplation of old age (*Und einmal gehst du*) that are in no way inferior to the best of Zemlinsky's published songs. Blochwitz, Schmidt and Garben are splendid, Vermillion matches them admirably, and Ziesak, if a little hard and bright at times, can fine her voice down to an effective intimacy. The recordings are excellent.

Eine florentinische Tragödie

Zemlinsky Eine florentinische Tragödie
Iris Vermillion *mez* Bianca; **Heinz Kruse** *ten* Guido Bardi; **Albert Dohmen** *bar* Simone
A Mahler (orch Colin and David Matthews) Die stille Stadt. Laue Sommernacht. Bei dir ist es traut. Licht in der Nacht. Waldeinsamkeit. Emtelied
Iris Vermillion *mez* **Royal Concertgebouw Orchestra / Riccardo Chailly**
Decca Entartete Musik 455 112-2DH
(71 minutes: DDD). Notes, texts and translations Ⓕ included. Recorded 1996 ●

Eine Florentine Tragedy is a disturbing, shocking piece, but to make its fullest impact it also needs to sound ravishingly beautiful. Zemlinsky's sumptuous scoring often demands an orchestra of the Royal Concertgebouw's stature, and in this reading it sounds quite magnificent. But the score also needs a conductor of subtlety and shrewdness to point up the two passages of constrasting serene lyricism, one where Simone's wife Bianca assures Count Bardi of her eternal love and another when husband and wife rediscover their love for each other. Vermillion is very fine at both these points, her mezzo timbre adding warmth to her line. Kruse is admirable too, fining down his ringing tenor in that duet scene, and, as Simone, Dohmen is forceful and dangerous. But Chailly is the real star, pacing the opera so well that it seems over in no time, drawing richly complex but never muddy textures from his remarkable orchestra. On hearing the Alma Mahler songs one is struck by the benefits of their orchestration. But here again, exquisitely though Vermillion sings these songs, Chailly must take at least half the credit. Each song is taken faster than in most recordings with piano, and every one of them gains from it in impulsive urgency. In Zemlinsky's opera and Alma Mahler's songs the recording leaves nothing to be desired: the colours are rich and clean.

Der König Kandaules

James O'Neal *ten* König Kandaules; **Monte Pederson** *bar* Gyges; **Nina Warren** *sop* Nyssia; **Klaus Häger** *bass* Phedros; **Peter Galliard** *ten* Syphax; **Mariusz Kwiecien** *bar* Nicomedes; **Kurt Gysen** *bass* Pharnaces; **Simon Yang** *bass* Philebos; **Ferdinand Seiler** *ten* Sebas; **Guido Jentjens** *bar* Archelaos; **Hamburg State Philharmonic Orchestra / Gerd Albrecht**
Capriccio ② 60 071/2 (128 minutes: DDD). Recorded Ⓕ live in 1996. Notes, text and translation included

Der König Kandaules, based on a play by André Gide, is Zemlinsky's last opera, written during the Nazis' rise to power and complete in short score when he fled to America in 1938. He showed it to his pupil Artur Bodanzky, then a principal conductor at the Met, who seems to have warned him that the libretto would not be acceptable – in one scene Kandaules tricks his wife into undressing in front of a fisherman he has recently befriended, then into sleeping with him. Zemlinsky never completed the orchestration of *Der König Kandaules* but left a large number of indications of scoring. Antony Beaumont's orchestration sounds perfectly convincing. When two excerpts from the score were performed and recorded in 1994 it already looked as though a major work by Zemlinsky was about to be revealed. And that is the case: a marvellous and quite characteristic score, but in some ways a dismaying one. All the orchestral richness and the voluptuously singing lines that one expects are there, but wedded to a plot that seems all too accurately to reflect the disorder and disillusion of the times in which it was written.

Nyssia, the wife so chaste and beautiful that until now no one but Kandaules has seen her unveiled, is portrayed in music of quite sumptuous allure, but her reaction to his betrayal is more Salome-like than tragic: she orders the fisherman Gyges to kill her husband and take his place, in her bed as well as on the throne. Gyges, the poor but honest peasant, is a murderer himself: he killed his own wife because, as Candaules would have agreed, she was his property. And Kandaules the seeming altruist, whose greatest pleasure is to share his wealth with others, is in fact simply boasting of his good fortune: even his wife's beauty is a sort of torment to him if other men are not jealous of it. And in Zemlinsky's musical portrayal the more his baseness becomes obvious the more glamorous and sympathetic he is.

The performance is a fine one, O'Neal lacking only the last touch of heroic vocal stature for Kandaules, Warren only a little stretched by the Ariadne-like role of Nyssia, Pederson first class (a moment or two of suspect intonation aside) as Gyges. Albrecht is perfectly at home in this sort of music, the orchestra's admirable richness of tone does not obscure detail, and the recording is atmospheric (stage business audible) but clear. Zemlinsky's reputation can only be enhanced by this ravishing, richly complex, disturbing opera.

Bernd Alois Zimmermann

German 1918-1970

GROVE *Zimmermann encountered the music of Stravinsky and Milhaud while serving in the army, and in 1942 was able to return to studies, with Lemacher and Jarnach; he also attended the courses given by Fortner and Leibowitz at Darmstadt, 1948-50, and most of his published works date from after this period. From 1957 he taught at the Cologne Musikhochschule. At first he brought together Stravinskian neo-classicism and 12-note technique, but in the mid-1950s he passed through extreme Webernism to a style rich in allusions and quotations, expressing an aesthetic of 'pluralism'. His main works of this kind include the opera Die Soldaten (1965) and the Requiem für einen jungen Dichter (1969); later his style became sparer. His output includes concertos (Dialoge for two pianos, 1960) and other orchestral scores and chamber music, these instrumental works often cast as imaginary ballets. His writings throw light on the state of composition in his day.*

Requiem für einen jungen Dichter

Vlatka Orsanic *sop* **James Johnson** *bar* **Michael Rotschopf, Bernhard Schir** *spkrs* **Christoph Grund** *org* **Alexander von Schlippenbach Jazz Band; Cologne Radio Chorus; Stuttgart Radio Chorus; Edinburgh Festival Chorus; Bratislava Slovak Chorus; Bratislava City Chorus; South-West German Radio Symphony Orchestra / Michael Gielen**

Sony Classical SK61995 (64 minutes: DDD) Ⓕ
Recorded 1995 ◎◎

Zimmermann's *Requiem for a young Poet* is a humbling polyphony of 20th-century misdeeds – riveting, provocative, uncompromising and as essential to our understanding of 1960s 'serious' music as The Beatles are to an informed perception of that decade's pop culture. In fact, the two momentarily converge when Zimmermann quotes The Beatles' song *Hey Jude* (something of a horrific pun, especially given the *Requiem*'s use of the German language and of Hitler's voice in particular). The work opens to a hollow drone, a sort of post-Holocaust *Zarathustra* framing a gallery of voices, three of them, like Zimmermann's own, being suicides: the poets Vladimir Mayakovsky, Konrad Bayer and (via Mayakovsky) Sergei Essenin. The spoken word is crucial throughout; in fact Bayer provided the *Requiem*'s chilling motto: 'What can we hope for? There is nothing that awaits us except death'.

The vast opening section consists of a 'Prolog', two 'Requiems' (each launched to an agonised choral cry) and a 'Ricercar'. Taped voices recall major post-war cultural, religious and political figures (sometimes in person): Wittgenstein, for example, who was associated with the Vienna Circle of which Bayer was a member. Recited extracts from his 'Philosophical Investigations' (relating specifically to the idea of 'language games') precede the voice of Pope John XXIII; then Hitler, Chamberlain, the former Greek Prime Minister Andras Papandreou, readings from Pound, Schwitters, Camus etc; musical fragments by Wagner, Milhaud and Messiaen – a tumbling stream of consciousness where thinkers and artists have the definite upper hand. Most texts are spoken in German and although there are no detailed texts or translations provided, one presumes that the point of quotation was more a matter of evoking memory and specific events than pondering the wisdom of those present. The work's brief later sections rely more on voices and instruments than on pre-recorded reportage (jazz is a strong presence), although the latter returns with a vengeance for a deeply pessimistic 'Dona nobis pacem', with Beethoven (the *Choral* Symphony), von Ribbentrop, Stalin, Goebbels, Churchill and Bayer himself in fateful attendance. The *Requiem* climaxes to the unsettling sound of massed demonstrations and ends with a forcefully punctuated choral declamation (or affirmation) of the words "Do... /na... /no... /bis... /pa... /cem"! Fans of Zimmermann's opera *Die Soldaten* will have already braced themselves.

'The piece is inscribed to all the catastrophes that the human race has brought down upon itself and addresses those aspects of human behaviour that have opened up the way to such a Day of Wrath or that threaten to do so.' Hiekel's words ring true but barely touch the aural scope and emotional impact of this incredible piece, its sustained tension, telling juxtapositions (voices that echo or mix in various perspectives), the devastating effect of those 'montage-like' chords and the rude (but rare) invasions of humour. Michael Gielen, with his impressive gallery of skills, is the ideal interpreter.

Collections

Orchestral

Cello Concertos

Boccherini (arr Grutzmacher) Cello Concerto in B flat, G48 **Bruch** Kol Nidrei, Op 47
Elgar Cello Concerto in E minor, Op 85
Haydn (arr Gevaërt) Cello Concerto No 2 in D, HobVII*b*/2 – Allegro moderato; Adagio
Pablo Casals *vc* **London Symphony Orchestra / Sir Landon Ronald; BBC Symphony Orchestra / Sir Adrian Boult**
Biddulph mono LAB144 (79 minutes: ADD) Ⓜ
Recorded 1936-46

The leonine growl that prefaces Elgar's most introspective orchestral masterpiece is played here with uncompromising defiance, whereas the weary solo ascent that follows can rarely – if ever – have conveyed a deeper sense of disorientation. Casals's handling of the solo line is wistful, sometimes wilful, profoundly personal and ideally accompanied by the ever-attentive Sir Adrian Boult. Just listen to the *Scherzo*'s cheeky banter (track 7, from 1'25"), to the pointing of wind phrases in particular – precise yet unforced and always musically responsive. The most affecting passage of all occurs at around 6'31" into the finale (track 9), at the moment where Elgar seems overwhelmed by feelings almost too painful to bear. No other performance is quite as successful in contrasting the 'brave front' of Elgar's bolder *tuttis* with the ineffable sadness of his solo writing. Occasional hiccups in the cello line (the odd spot of discoloration) go for nothing and Casals's distant groaning merely serves – like Glenn Gould's humming and Toscanini's singing – to compound an impression of total commitment.

Biddulph's annotation relates how a changing critical climate gradually became sympathetic to Casals's account of the Elgar Concerto (initial reactions were fairly hostile), and how Britain's handling of the Franco situation in Spain deeply offended Casals. Projected sessions never materialised, and the Haydn Concerto recording that is here issued for the first time (it was set down the day after the Elgar) remained incomplete. What we do have, however, is very well recorded, typically eloquent and full of interpretative incident, with sundry expressive subtleties and an especially memorable account of the *Adagio*. Of course purists will baulk at Gevaërt's arrangement, just as they will also lament Grützmacher's handiwork in a famous – and equally characterful – account of the Boccherini B flat Concerto.

Kol Nidrei, on the other hand, is given one of the slowest, purest and most deeply felt readings imaginable, perfectly reflecting the pain, resolution and quiet victory that mark the three stages of repentance (Kol Nidrei is the pivotal evening prayer for the Jewish Day of Atonement). Transfers are, again, excellent (Ward Marston was at the control desk), and if you are in search of 'The Essential Casals' – no, 'The Quintessential Casals' – then you need look no further than this.

Favourite Cello Concertos
Albinoni (arr Palmer) Adagio in G minor
Bach (arr Palmer) Cantata No 147 – Jesu, joy of man's desiring **Dvořák** Cello Concerto in B minor, B191 **Elgar** Cello Concerto in E minor, Op 85. Romance, Op 62. Une idylle in G, Op 4 No 1
Fauré Elégie, Op 24 **Gounod** Ave Maria
J Lloyd Webber Jackie's Song **Saint-Saëns** Cello Concerto No 1 in A minor, Op 33. Allegro appassionato in B minor, Op 43. Le carnaval des animaux – Le cygne **Schumann** (arr Palmer) Kinderszenen, Op 15*a* – Träumerei, Op 15 No 7 **Tchaikovsky** Variations on a Rococo Theme in A, Op 33
Julian Lloyd Webber *vc* **with various orchestras and conductors**
Philips ② 462 115-2PM2 (155 minutes: DDD) Ⓜ
Recorded 1984-98

A first-class package in every way. As we know from his live performances, Julian Lloyd Webber has a firm, richly coloured and full-focused tone; moreover it records well. His lyrical warmth projects tellingly over the entire range and his involvement in the music communicates consistently and tellingly. He has chosen his accompanists well too. His account of the great Dvořák Concerto is full of passionate feeling, with a tender *Adagio*, and Neumann and the Czech Philharmonic give him thoroughly persuasive backing, playing with plenty of bite in *tuttis*, the Slavonic exuberance always to the fore. His performance of the Elgar concerto has the huge advantage of Lord Menuhin as his partner, a true Elgarian if ever there was one. It is a performance of real understanding and rare intensity, which never oversteps the work's emotional boundaries and is imbued with innate nostalgia: the *Adagio* has a haunting Elysian stillness. The Saint-Saëns is played for the splendid bravura war-horse that it is, and we are also given a rare chance to hear the original, uncut version of Tchaikovsky's *Rococo* Variations. Lloyd Webber soon proves that it is superior to the truncated version used in most other recordings; moreover his spontaneous warmth in Tchaikovsky's long-drawn lyrical lines, which he makes sound very Russian in character, makes a perfect foil for the sparkling virtuosity elsewhere. Among the encores the lovely *Träumerei* stands out for its freely improvisational feeling and Lloyd Webber's own tribute to Jacqueline du Pré is played as an ardent, tuneful and timely postscript.

Les introuvables de Jacqueline du Pré
Bach Cello Suites – No 1 in G, BWV1007; No 2 in D minor, BWV1008 (rec live 1962) **Beethoven** 12 Variations on Handel's 'See the conqu'ring hero comes', WoO45[i]. Seven Variations in E flat on Mozart's 'Bei Männern, welche Liebe fühlen', WoO46[i]. 12 Variations in F on 'Ein Mädchen oder Weibchen', Op 66[i] (recorded live in 1970). Cello Sonatas[c] – No 3 in A,

Op 69; No 5 in D, Op 105 No 2 **Bruch** Kol Nidrei, Op 47[a] **Chopin** Cello Sonata, Op 65[i] **Delius** Cello Concerto[e] **Dvořák** Cello Concerto in B minor, B191[g]. Silent woods, B182[g] **Elgar** Cello Concerto in E minor, Op 85[d] **Fauré** Elégie, Op 24[a] **Franck** Violin Sonata in A[i] (arr *vc/pf*) **Handel** Oboe Concerto in G minor, HWV287[b] (arr *vc/pf* Slatter. rec live 1961)
Haydn Cello Concertos – No 1 in C[h]; No 2 in D[d]
Monn (arr Schoenberg) Cello Concerto in G minor[d]
Saint-Saëns Cello Concerto No 1 in A minor, Op 33[f]
Schumann Cello Concerto in A minor, Op 129[f]
Jacqueline du Pré *vc* [a]**Gerald Moore**, [b]**Ernest Lush**, [c]**Stephen Kovacevich** *pfs* [d]**London Symphony Orchestra / Sir John Barbirolli;** [e]**Royal Philharmonic Orchestra / Sir Malcolm Sargent;** [f]**New Philharmonia Orchestra,** [g]**Chicago Symphony Orchestra,** [h]**English Chamber Orchestra / Daniel Barenboim** [i]*pf*
EMI ⑥ CZS5 68132-2 (857 minutes: ADD) Ⓑ

As the title suggests, this fine six-disc retrospective of Jacqueline du Pré's recording career – a mere 10 years long – was masterminded by French EMI. Aptly the English commentary by Jeremy Siepmann quotes Sir John Barbirolli's memorable remark in Christopher Nupen's television film, *Jacqueline*: 'If you have no excesses in the full bloom of youth, what will there be to pare away on the long road to maturity?' The wonder was that Jacqueline du Pré was mature in her artistry from the start, and it is good that from the period even before the first official EMI sessions the collection includes three BBC recordings: Bach's Cello Suites Nos 1 and 2 and a Handel sonata arranged from the Oboe Concerto in G minor. Those early BBC recordings are inevitably flawed, but the sheer scale of the artistry is never in doubt. Of the handful of items recorded by EMI in July 1962 with Gerald Moore accompanying, only Bruch's *Kol Nidrei* is included.

The Delius was du Pré's first concerto recording, and she was not nearly as much at ease as she came to be later. The CD transfers do not minimise any of the flaws in the original recordings, notably the disappointing sound given to her Chicago recording of the Dvořák Concerto. Not only is the orchestral sound both coarse and thin with a high degree of background hiss, the cello is balanced far too close. Even with that balance one registers clearly the wide dynamic range of du Pré's playing, down to a whispered *pianissimo*. It was right to include it and also the cello sonata recordings of Chopin and Franck, the last recordings ever made by du Pré in December 1971. The tone may not have been quite so even as earlier, but the fire and warmth are undiminished. All the concerto recordings are welcome with the tear-laden quality in the slow movement of the Schumann matching that in the Elgar. It is good that the supreme Beethoven sonata recordings she made with Stephen Bishop (later Kovacevich) are included here, both sparkling and darkly intense. From the Beethoven series recorded at the 1970 Edinburgh Festival by the BBC only the three sets of variations are included. A must for anyone who was ever magnetised by du Pré's playing.

Miscellaneous Concertos

English Recorder Music
Arnold (orch Lane) Recorder Concertino, Op 41*a*[a] **Bullard** Recipes[a] **Gregson** Three Matisse Impressions[b] **Lane** Suite ancienne[a] **Lyon** Recorder Concertino[a] **Parrott** Prelude and Waltz[a] **Pitfield** Recorder Concerto[a]. Three Nautical Sketches[a]
John Turner *rec* **Royal Ballet Sinfonia /** [a]**Gavin Sutherland,** [b]**Edward Gregson**
Olympia OCD667 (74 minutes: DDD) Ⓕ
Recorded 1999

Sir Malcolm Arnold's harmony is never either predictable or bland, as the plangent opening of his *Concertino* immediately shows. It has a haunting central 'Chaconne' and a characteristic, gaily dancing finale. But the unforgettable finale here comes from Philip Lane's *Suite ancienne* (unashamed pastiche), with the irresistible closing exuberance of 'Beau Brummel's Bath Night' (whatever went on, or rather came off?). Thomas Pitfield, born in Bolton, was a much admired professor of composition at the Royal Manchester College, subsequently the Royal Northern College of Music, and his Recorder Concerto, which uses both treble and descant recorders, moves easily from English pastoralism to a southern 'Tarantella'. The same composer's *Nautical Sketches* draws on sea shanties with an equally light touch: the delectable opening 'Quodlibet' is highly suitable for a 'spot the tune' parlour game. Edward Gregson's evocative style is a kind of French/English impressionism, and he does well by Matisse. 'Luxe, calme et volupté' is all three, and the winsome closing 'Danse' suggests a shepherd piping. David Lyon's *Concertino* also has Gallic influences: its wry 'Badinage' neatly offsets the wan delicacy of the central waltz. Parrott's *Prelude* opens more astringently, then he relents for another delectably embroidered waltz. *Recipes* prepared by Bullard titillates the palette, with morning 'Coffee and Croissants', followed by a 'Barbecued' tango, a witty 'Prawn' habanera, and after a 'Special Chop Suey' takeaway ends with a circus galop enthusiastically relishing 'Fish and Chips'.

The invention of all these works is consistently diverting. With a brilliant soloist in John Turner and first-rate accompaniments from the Royal Ballet Sinfonia under Gavin Sutherland (or Gregson, conducting his own work), this disc is extremely enjoyable and highly recommendable.

Homage to Benny Goodman
Arnold Clarinet Concerto, Op 115 **Bernstein** Prelude, Fugue and Riffs **Copland** Clarinet Concerto
B Goodman Rachel's Dream **G Jenkins** Goodbye (arr Luis) **Paganini** Caprice in A minor, Op 24 No 1
Powell Clarinade **Prima** Sing, sing, sing
Sauter Clarinet à la King **Stravinsky** Ebony Concerto
Traditional Tiger Rag (all arr Walden)
Sabine Meyer, Wolfgang Meyer *cls*
Bamberg Symphony Orchestra and Big Band / Ingo Metzmacher
EMI CDC5 56652-2 (70 minutes: DDD) Ⓕ
Recorded 1997

Starting with a dazzling account of Sir Malcolm Arnold's Second Concerto, the one written for Benny Goodman, this is not just a tribute to the great polymath among clarinettists but a most attractive collection of music that is middle-of-the-road in the best sense, echoing the achievement of Goodman himself in crossing barriers. Not everything was composed for him but this is music which suited his style, as it does that of Wolfgang Meyer, even more than that of his celebrated sister, Sabine. One notes that only one of the longer works, the *Ebony Concerto*, and one of the shorter ones, the Paganini *Caprice* in jazzed-up form, feature Sabine Meyer, though four of the big band arrangements feature them both in duet. Sabine Meyer gives a slightly understated performance of the *Ebony Concerto*, subtle in phrasing and tonal shading but not quite sharp enough to bring out the full point of Stravinsky's angular cross-rhythms.

It remains a fine performance, crisply accompanied by the Bamberg Symphony Big Band under Metzmacher. Even so, Wolfgang Meyer and the Bambergers play at higher voltage and with sharper attack whether in the Arnold, the Copland or the Bernstein. In the big band arrangements, duetting alongside her brother, Sabine then loses all inhibitions, equally bringing out the fun in these jazz arrangements. In sum, an excellent, generous mixture, well played and well recorded.

Piano Concertos

Moura Lympany in recital H

Albéniz (arr Godowsky) Tango, Op 165 No 2
Chopin Fantaisie-impromptu in C sharp minor, Op 66 **Granados** Goyescas – No 4, Quejas o la maja y el ruiseñor **Mozart** Piano Concertos[a] – No 12 in A, K414/K385*p*; No 21 in C, K467
Turina Rapsodia sinfónica, Op 66[b]
Dame Moura Lympany *pf* [ab]**Philharmonia Orchestra /** [a]**Herbert Menges,** [b]**Walter Susskind**
Dutton Laboratories mono CDCLP4000 (77 minutes: ADD). Recorded 1949-54 Ⓕ

Now that Dame Moura Lympany has ended her performing career, this recorded tribute comes as a special blessing. For long associated with the romantic virtuoso repertoire which she played with an unalloyed polish and graciousness, Dame Moura possessed the most catholic of tastes and her 1955 disc of Mozart's Concertos, K414 and K467, is surely among her finest offerings. Every change of mood, every subtlety of modulation is registered without fuss, narcissism or the sort of self-consciousness so often taken for an authentic style; her performances are of superfine quality and in impeccable taste. There are distinguished contributions from individual members of the Philharmonia and although the orchestra under Herbert Menges occasionally moves with a heavier tread than their soloist, they are none the less satisfyingly robust with no scaling down of drama. In Turina's picture-postcard charmer there is less heat and dazzle than in some other readings, yet both here and in Granados's 'Maiden and the Nightingale' there is delicate rather than lurid colouring. The recordings are adequate.

Addinsell Warsaw Concerto **Gottschalk** (orch Hazell) Grande fantaisie triomphale sur l'hymne national brésilien, RO108 **Litolff** Concerto Symphonique No 4 in D minor, Op 102 – Scherzo **Rachmaninov** Piano Concerto No 2 in C minor, Op 18
Cristina Ortiz *pf* **Royal Philharmonic Orchestra / Moshe Atzmon**
Decca 414 348-2DH (58 minutes: DDD) Ⓕ
Recorded 1984

The C minor Concerto of Rachmaninov symbolises romanticism at its ripest. Its combination of poetry and sensuous warmth with languorously memorable melodic lines balanced by exhilarating pianistic brilliance avoids any suggestion of sentimentality. The simple chordal introduction from the soloist ushers in one of the composer's most luscious tunes, yet the slow movement develops even greater ardour in its melodic contour, and the composer holds back a further haunting expressive idea to bring a lyrical contrast to the scintillating finale.

The genuinely inspired pastiche *Warsaw Concerto* by Richard Addinsell has a principal theme worthy to stand alongside those of Rachmaninov and its layout shows satisfying craftsmanship. Ortiz plays this main theme with great affection and she is equally beguiling in the delicious Litolff *Scherzo*. The effect here is of elegance rather than extrovert brilliance: this is reserved for the Gottschalk *Grande fantaisie triomphale*, which is played with a splendid panache that almost covers its inherent vulgarity and certainly emphasises its ingenuous charm. Throughout the recording balance is realistic and the reverberation adds an attractive bloom.

Trumpet Concertos

Baroque Trumpet Concertos

Albinoni Concerto in B flat, Op 7 No 3[b]
Baldassare Sonata for Cornett, Strings and Continuo in F[b] **Corelli** Sonata for Trumpet and Strings in D
Franceschini Sonata for Two Trumpets, Strings and Continuo in D (Friedrich) **A Marcello** Oboe Concerto in D minor[b] **Torelli** Sonata a 5 con tromba, G7
Viviani Capricci armonici – Sonata prima
Vivaldi (rev Malipiero) Concerto for Two Trumpets and Strings in C, RV537[a]
Håkan Hardenberger, [a]**Reinhold Friedrich** *tpts*
I Musici
Philips 442 131-2PH (54 minutes: DDD) Ⓕ
Items marked [b] transcribed for trumpet
Recorded 1993

No trumpet player can make a career as a baroque player on a modern instrument without performing music originally written for other instruments; the domestic repertoire is simply not sustainable (it could be argued that the Torelli and Corelli works only sound truly colourful on a natural trumpet and tonally bland even with Hardenberger's modern playing). No complaints with transcriptions *per se*: a good one can leave the original looking to its laurels. Some disappointment must be registered, however, that Hardenberger has not investigated his own fare from the multifarious collections of fine 18th-century concertos.

Most listeners will enjoy this highly exacting playing and his silky articulation and rhythmic discipline – the Vivaldi is as high-tech and effortless as you will ever hear. I Musici are a curious choice of accompanists. Still sporting their timelessly vigorous and yet unashamedly Mediterranean approach to baroque chamber playing, there is quite a temperamental polarity here, one would suspect, between their style and Hardenberger's Nordic and less overtly emotional playing. The result, however, is not as marked as you might expect, since Hardenberger vocalises more in this recording than in the past (all slow movements are warmer and less 'worked out' than in previous discs of this nature) and he responds to I Musici's full-blooded playing in a similarly jaunty way. The Marcello D minor Concerto has some especially sweet moments.

Classical Trumpet Concertos

Fasch Concerto for Trumpet, Oboe d'amore, Violin and Strings in E **Haydn** Concerto in E flat, HobVIIe/1 **Hummel** Concerto in E flat **Neruda** Concerto in E flat **F Weber** Variations in F

John Wallace *tpt* **John Anderson** *ob d'amore* **Peter Thomas** *vn* **Philharmonia Orchestra / Christopher Warren-Green, Simon Wright**

Nimbus NI7016 (75 minutes: DDD) Ⓕ
Recorded 1983-88

The famous Haydn Concerto sounds bright and forthright with trumpeter and orchestra freshly caught in the spacious Church of All Saints, Tooting. Wallace's technical strength and impish articulation are characterised by crisp tonguing and a strident (if at times fairly uncompromising) trumpet sound in the outer movements. Peace is restored in a beautifully judged slow movement in which Wallace floats rather than imposes. Less refined than some other recordings of this work (track 2 at 3'43" has an extraordinary blemish in the lower register of the strings), there is a natural freshness here which one rarely hears in this old war-horse.

The Neruda Concerto, written originally for the corno da caccia, makes an attractive trumpet piece, flawed only by its unbalanced episodic structure. Hummel's Concerto is a persuasive work, by and large, and it is given a bold reading here by Wallace, full of incident, some examples of which trip out of the bell in a fairly conventional manner. Others are decidedly quirky, such as the mock antiquated tuning on the opening trill of the second movement. Rather more effective are the dazzling embellishments which look forward to the salon and the new virtuoso tradition of the 19th century which the trumpet inhabited once valves had been invented. Friedrich Dionysius Weber's Variations in F major are typical of this musically slight but entertaining world in which the cornet/trumpet was beginning to thrive. Wallace is utterly at home in this idiom, bringing to the music the swagger and facility upon which its characterisation depends. Finally we step back to the Indian summer of the trumpet, the early classical years and the stratospherically high trumpet range demanded by Carl Friedrich Christian Fasch. His Concerto for trumpet, oboe d'amore and violin is an exciting work, brilliantly played.

Haydn Trumpet Concerto in E flat, HobVIIe/1 **Hertel** Trumpet Concerto in D **Hummel** Trumpet Concerto in E flat **J Stamitz** (realised Boustead) Trumpet Concerto in D

Håkan Hardenberger *tpt* **Academy of St Martin in the Fields / Sir Neville Marriner**

Philips 420 203-2PH (59 minutes: DDD) Ⓕ
Recorded 1986

This recording made such a remarkable impression when it first appeared in 1987 that it created overnight a new star in the firmament of trumpeters. The two finest concertos for the trumpet are undoubtedly those of Haydn and Hummel, and Hardenberger plays them here with a combination of sparkling bravura and stylish elegance that are altogether irresistible. Marriner and his Academy accompany with characteristic finesse and warmth, with the lilting dotted rhythms of the first movement of the Hummel, seductively jaunty.

The lovely *Andante* of the Haydn is no less beguiling, and both finales display a high-spirited exuberance and an easy bravura which make the listener smile with pleasure. He is no less distinctive in the lesser concerto of Johann Hertel and the other D major work attributed to Johann Stamitz but probably written by someone with the unlikely name of JB Holzbogen. This takes the soloist up into the stratosphere of his range and provides him also with some awkward leaps. The Hertel work also taxes the soloist's technique to the extremities, but Hardenberger essays all these difficulties with an enviably easy aplomb and remains fluently entertaining throughout. The recording gives him the most vivid realism and presence, but it is a pity that the orchestral backcloth is so reverberant; otherwise the sound is very natural.

Violin Concertos

Heifetz the Supreme Ⓗ

Bach Violin Partita No 2 in D minor, BWV1004 – Chaconne **Brahms** Violin Concerto in D, Op 77[a] **Bruch** Scottish Fantasy, Op 46[b] **Gershwin** (arr Heifetz) Three Preludes[c] **Glazunov** Violin Concerto in A minor, Op 82[d] **Sibelius** Violin Concerto in D minor, Op 47[e] **Tchaikovsky** Violin Concerto in D, Op 35[f]

Jascha Heifetz *vn* [c]**Brooks Smith** *pf* [aef]**Chicago Symphony Orchestra /** [af]**Fritz Reiner;** [b]**New Symphony Orchestra /** [b]**Sir Malcolm Sargent;** [d]**RCA Victor Symphony Orchestra /** [de]**Walter Hendl**

RCA Red Seal ② 74321 63470-2 Ⓜ
(154 minutes: ADD). Recorded 1955-65

For once a record company's hype is totally justified. Heifetz was and is supreme. Witness how he plays the Bach 'Chaconne', with an extraordinary range of dynamic and feeling, and a total grip on the structure. The subtlety of his bowing is a thing to marvel at. This is a superb and indispensable anthology, excellently accompanied too. How persuasively Reiner shapes the opening of the Brahms, and Sargent the *Scottish Fantasy*; how tenderly Heifetz plays the 'Canzonetta' of the Tchaikovsky, and then astonishes us with his quicksilver brilliance in the finale. The violin's first entry in the Sibelius is quite Elysian, and Heifetz's tone in the slow movement sends shivers down the spine. He discovered all the romantic charm in the Glazunov concerto, and virtually made it his own. And how good that the selection ends with Gershwin, sparklingly syncopated and bluesy by turns: nothing else here better shows the flexibility of the Heifetz bow arm, even if the microphones are too close.

Mysliveček Violin Concerto No 4 in B flat
Schubert Rondo for Violin and Strings in A, D438
Spohr Violin Concerto No 8 in A minor, 'in modo di scena cantate', Op 47 **Viotti** Violin Concerto No 22 in A minor, G97
Elizabeth Wallfisch *vn* **Brandenburg Orchestra / Roy Goodman**
Hyperion CDA66840 (79 minutes: DDD) Ⓕ
Recorded 1995

The revival in the popularity of the violin concerto during the latter part of the 18th century is winningly celebrated in this delightful, superbly recorded programme. Mysliveček's Fourth Concerto sets the tone with music of graceful charm, in which Wallfisch engagingly deploys her fluent virtuosity to reveal the music's full expressive potential. With sensitive accompaniment from the Brandenburg Orchestra, she presents a satisfying feeling of orderly balance in the first movement, poignantly expresses the *Larghetto*'s affecting melodiousness with incisive phrasing, and negotiates the athletic leaps in the finale with compelling vitality. Wallfisch and the Brandenburg go on to give an enchanting account of Viotti's A minor Violin Concerto (No 22). Although Schubert never wrote a violin concerto, he left some impressive *concertante* violin music that attests to his own early training on the instrument. Finally, Spohr's A minor Concerto (No 8) gives a theatrical element to the programme, and Wallfisch and her forces vividly evoke the music's striking vocal character.

Brahms Violin Concerto in D, Op 77[b] **Hindemith** Violin Sonata in E flat, Op 11[a] **Schnittke** Quasi una Sonata[a]
Schumann Violin Concerto in D minor, Op posth[c]
Sibelius Violin Concerto in D minor, Op 47[c]
Weber Grand duo concertant, J204[a]
Gidon Kremer *vn* [a]**Andrei Gavrilov** *pf* [b]**Berlin Philharmonic Orchestra / Herbert von Karajan;** [c]**Philharmonia Orchestra / Riccardo Muti**
EMI Forte ② CZS5 69334-2 (151 minutes: ADD) Ⓜ
Recorded 1976-82

It would be hard to imagine a finer showcase for Kremer's talent. The Schumann has been a benchmark performance for some years, strong and purposeful in the outer movements, hushed and dedicated in the central slow movement. With Muti a challenging yet sympathetic partner, the Sibelius is also given a remarkable performance, notable not just for Kremer's expressive warmth, but for his inner intensity in the great opening melodies of the first two movements, each played as a hushed meditation, but with the first flowing freely, fanciful and poetic, not too slow for an *Allegro moderato*. The finale is then fast and volatile.

This recoupling for the two-disc format is also valuable for offering Kremer's glowing account of the Brahms Concerto, his first collaboration with Karajan, one which plainly inspired them both. The spaciousness of the first movement brings total concentration, to justify Kremer's freedom of expression. The slow movement possesses poise and purity, leading to a beautifully sprung account of the finale, with dance rhythms brought out. The analogue recording is comparably spacious. In the three new items Gavrilov proves a comparably inspired partner, with the Weber so winningly characterised – fiery in the first movement, dedicated in the *Andante* and exuberant in the finale – that one almost forgets the original clarinet version, so satisfying is the transformation. The early Hindemith Sonata can rarely have been played with such warmth and intensity, and the Schnittke work, full of extended, pregnant pauses, is superbly held together by the concentrated interplay of the performers, an astonishing 20-minute tapestry.

American Orchestral

American Dreams

Barber Adagio for Strings, Op 11 **Canning** Fantasy on a Hymn Tune **Carmichael** (arr Van Cleve/Dant): Johnny Appleseed Suite – Prayer and Cathedral Vision **Carpenter** Sea Drift **Chadwick** Symphonic Sketches – Noël **Foote** Suite in E, Op 63 – Pizzicato and Adagietto **Gershwin** (arr cpsr): Lullaby
Indianapolis Symphony Orchestra / Raymond Leppard
Decca 458 157-2DH (61 minutes: DDD) Ⓕ
Recorded 1997

A most appealing concert, featuring a healthy sprinkling of rare Americana which deserve to be much better known. George Whitefield Chadwick's Yuletide evocation, 'Noël', forms the enchanting curtain-raiser. Next comes Barber's ubiquitous *Adagio* in a decent enough, if hardly memorable rendering. The spirit of Tchaikovsky (and the *Scherzo* from his Fourth Symphony in particular) hovers benignly over the *pizzicato* outer portions of the second movement of Bostonian Arthur Foote's Op 63 Suite in E (1907-8); by contrast, the lyrical *Adagietto* at its core radiates a chaste and noble eloquence. Anyone who has ever responded to the likes of Griffes and Loeffler will also surely revel in the exquisitely wrought, thoroughly impressionistic progress of John Alden Carpenter's powerful 1933 tone-poem inspired by Whitman's *Sea Drift*, while lovers of VW's *Tallis* Fantasia will detect a kindred radiance and mastery of string sonority in Thomas Canning's *Fantasy on a Hymn Tune* (conceived during the Second World War when the composer was teaching mechanics at a Nebraska air-base). That just leaves Gershwin's lilting *Lullaby* for strings and the tuneful, touchingly sincere 'Prayer and Cathedral Vision' from Hoagy Carmichael's *Johnny Appleseed Suite* (which is, according to annotator Byron Adams, the best of the purely orchestral offerings written by this legendary, Indiana-born songsmith towards the end of his life). Throughout, Raymond Leppard draws a consistently alert and affectionate response from his Indianapolis band, and their efforts have been very well served by the Decca sound engineers (though the acoustic of Indianapolis's Hilbert Circle Theater is not, in all truthfulness, of the most flattering). All told, an admirably enterprising and rewarding issue.

American Light Music Classics
Anderson The Belle of the Ball. Plink, Plank, Plunk! **Arndt** (orch Zamecnik) Nola **Bratton** (orch Saddler) The Teddy Bears' Picnic **Friml** (orch Minot) Chanson, 'In Love' **Gershwin** (orch Berkowitz) Promenade **Gillis** Symphony No 5½, 'A Symphony for Fun' **Rodgers** (orch Walker) Carousel Waltz **Gould** American Symphonette No 3 – Pavanne **Guion** (orch Schmid) The Arkansas Traveller **Herbert** (orch Langey) March of the Toys **Holzmann** Blaze away **MacDowell** (orch Woodhouse) To a Wild Rose, Op 51 No 1 **Mills** (orch Crooke) Whistling Rufus **Nevin** (orch Myddleton) Narcissus, Op 13 No 4 **Pryor** The Whistler and His Dog **Rose** Holiday for Strings **Scott** (orch Lane) The Toy Trumpet **Sousa** (orch Winter) The Washington Post
New London Orchestra / Ronald Corp
Hyperion CDA67067 (73 minutes: DDD) Ⓕ
Recorded 1998

Leroy Anderson, John Philip Sousa and Rudolf Friml are all still household names (well, to many readers, at any rate), but no matter how well you know the tune, how many can remember the name of the composer of *The Teddy Bears' Picnic* – composed by John W. Bratton in 1907 decades before words were set to it – or *Narcissus*, a little masterpiece by Ethelbert Nevin from 1891? The latter had two English adaptations. In the 1890s it was used as the tune for one of Marie Lloyd's successes at the Palace in Cambridge Circus, *There they are, the two of them on their own*, and 50 years later Joyce Grenfell and Norman Wisdom used it for their 'Laughter' record. Anyone who grew up in the era of the BBC Light Programme will recognise many of the other pieces played on this CD. In his notes, Andrew Lamb fills us in, for instance, where Frederick Allen Mills is concerned. His *Whistling Rufus* sounds familiar, and surely Lehár knew it and took some inspiration from it when he composed the Cake-Walk in Act 3 of the *Merry Widow*. Mills's best-known work is the song, *Meet me in St Louis, Louis* revived 40 years after its composition for the Minelli film. The longest item on the disc is Don Gillis's Symphony No 5½ subtitled *A Symphony for Fun*. Originally a trombonist, Gillis went on to a radio career and became Toscanini's producer. Once the staple of bandstand and palm court orchestras, these lovely old tunes have a freshness and charm akin to the best light-hearted literature or illustration from the same period. Easy listening, yes, but produced with formidable skill. Ronald Corp and the New London Orchestra play the whole sequence with verve and dedication. Clear, good recording.

Koussevitzky conducts American Music Ⓗ
Copland El salón México **Foote** Suite in E minor, Op 63 **Harris** Symphonies – No 1; No 3 **McDonald** San Juan Capistrano
Boston Symphony Orchestra / Serge Koussevitzky
Pearl mono GEMMCD9492 (79 minutes: AAD) Ⓜ
Recorded 1934-40

Music lovers with a romantic hankering for the American desert and the Great Outdoors may well know Roy Harris's high, wide and handsome Third Symphony already, but the chances of having heard Serge Koussevitzky's 1939 recording of it are somewhat more remote. If you can accept and enjoy the soundtracks of classic Westerns, then you'll have no trouble with this CD: the playing of the Boston Symphony burns through a veil of surface hiss with the ease and accuracy of a blow-torch, and Koussevitzky's conducting tends to confirm the judgement of many, that this is indeed the greatest American symphony. It's a tremendous experience, and although the work is barely 17 minutes long, it none the less constitutes an epic journey. Koussevitzky was a great musical pioneer, and his recordings of Copland's saucy *El salón México* and Arthur Foote's delightful Suite (easily as appealing as, say, Grieg's *Holberg Suite*) are rightly regarded as classics. Add Harris's First Symphony and Harl McDonald's colourful essays, and you have the basis of an absorbing concert, one that is likely to give you a great deal of enjoyment.

American Tapestry
Griffes The White Peacock **Hovhaness** Symphony No 2, 'Mysterious Mountain', Op 132 **Ives** Orchestral Set No 1, 'Three Places in New England' **Piston** Suite, The Incredible Flutist **Schuman** New England Triptych
Dallas Symphony Orchestra / Andrew Litton
Dorian DOR90224 (73 minutes: DDD) Ⓕ
Recorded 1995

A dazzling calling-card for the formidable technical and interpretative skills of the Litton/Dallas Symphony partnership, featuring five American masters at their most approachable; an ideal introduction for anyone yet to dip a toe into the vast range of repertoire beyond Gershwin, Copland and Barber. We kick off in exhilarating style with William Schuman's marvellous *New England Triptych* of 1956. Taking its cue from hymn tunes by Schuman's countryman William Billings (1746-1800), the work comprises two bustling tableaux framing a central meditation ('When Jesus wept') of exalted beauty and compassion. Next comes Charles Griffes's gorgeous *The White Peacock* – a transatlantic cousin, if you will, to Debussy's *Prélude à l'après-midi d'un faune*. With the first of Ives's *Three Places in New England*, for all the fastidious refinement on show, Litton's direction remains oddly earthbound and short on atmosphere. Otherwise, all goes swimmingly, the giddy, increasingly hilarious din of the central 'Putnam's Camp' dashingly well conveyed. No grumbles, either, about Litton's clean-limbed, purposeful way with Alan Hovhaness's *Mysterious Mountain* (his Second Symphony, composed in 1955 for Stokowski and the Houston Symphony), a serene yet agreeably sturdy score. Lastly, there's the crowd-pleasing concert suite that Walter Piston fashioned from his 1938 ballet score, *The Incredible Flutist*. It's a delectably tuneful and witty confection, crammed with indelible invention (who could fail to be seduced by the languid charms of the 'Tango of the Merchant's Daughters' or 'Siciliana'?). Rest assured, Litton and his terrific band do Piston absolutely proud. The glorious acoustic of Dallas's Eugene McDermott Hall lends an enticing glow to a sound picture of bewitching tonal naturalness and stunning range (bass-drum fanciers will have a field-day in both outer movements of the Schuman). A classy collection indeed.

British Orchestral

The Beecham Collection – Delius H

An Arabesk[dfh]. A Mass of Life – Part 2 No 3: Prelude[h]. Songs of Sunset – Parts 1-7[bdfh]; Part 8[cegi]. I-Brasil[ah]. Le ciel est pardessus le toit[ej]. Cradle Song[ej]. Irmelin Rose[ej]. Klein Venevil[eh]. The Nightingale[ej]. Twilight Fancies[ej]. The Violet[eh]. The Violet[ej]. Whither[eh]

[a]**Dora Labbette** *sop* [b]**Olga Haley,** [c]**Nancy Evans** *mezzos* [d]**Roy Henderson,** [e]**Redvers Llewellyn** *bars* [f]**London Select Choir;** [g]**BBC Chorus;** [h]**London Philharmonic Orchestra;** [i]**Royal Philharmonic Orchestra / Sir Thomas Beecham** [j]*pf*

Somm Recordings mono SOMM-BEECHAM8 Ⓜ
(74 minutes: ADD). Recorded 1929-46

The Beecham Collection – Handel H

Piano Concerto in A (arr Beecham)[a]. The Gods Go a'Begging[b] – Introduction; Minuet; Hornpipe; Musette; Tambourine; Gavotte; Sarabande; Fugato. The Gods Go a'Begging[c] – Introduction; Larghetto; Gavotte; Allegro; Ensemble; Bourrée. The Origin of Design[d]

[a]**Lady Betty Humby Beecham** *pf* [abd]**London Philharmonic Orchestra;** [c]**Royal Philharmonic Orchestra / Sir Thomas Beecham**

Somm Recordings mono SOMM-BEECHAM7 Ⓜ
(75 minutes: ADD). Recorded 1932-49

Thanks to Shirley, Lady Beecham, we have here a splendid range of Beecham recordings from Sir Thomas's personal archive, most of them never issued before. The great treasure is the live recording of Delius's orchestral song-cycle to words by Ernest Dowson, *Songs of Sunset*. Rob Cowan has already described the performance as 'achingly beautiful', and that is no exaggeration. It was recorded at the Leeds Festival in 1934, and presents a strikingly different view of the work from that of other interpreters on disc.

Far more than any rival, Beecham conveys a virile thrust and energy in the writing, partly opting for faster speeds. Thanks to Beecham's magnetism arguments have a tautness that can otherwise seem to ramble. Both in this, with its seven linked sections, and in the single span of *An Arabesk*, a setting of Jens Peter Jacobsen in Philip Heseltine's translation, the line of the argument is clarified. Roy Henderson is the clean-cut, sensitive baritone soloist in both, sounding very English, with Olga Haley a fresh, bright mezzo soloist in the *Songs of Sunset*.

What has no doubt prevented this inspired reading of the *Songs of Sunset* from being issued before is that the test pressing of the final climactic section is missing. So, to have the work complete, that final ensemble for soloists and chorus together is included here in the studio recording which Beecham made for HMV in 1946, but which he rejected. With Nancy Evans and Redvers Llewellyn as soloists, it makes an excellent conclusion, with the chorus more clearly focused than its predeccessor in 1934. What matters is that the choral sound in both has ample weight. An apology is given for the noisy surfaces at the ends of 78 sides, but the full-bodied nature of the transfer makes that flaw exceptionally easy to ignore.

Dora Labbette is the enchanting soprano soloist in all the separate songs, bright and silvery, attacking even the most exposed high notes with astonishing purity and precision, producing magical *pianissimos*. Four of the 10 come in the beautiful orchestral versions, with the rest accompanied at the piano by Beecham himself. He may not have been the most accomplished pianist, but his natural magnetism still shines out, not least in the striking early song, longer than the rest, *Twilight Fancies*.

The disc of Beecham's arrangements of Handel is just as distinctive, always elegant and warmly expressive. He defies latterday taste if anything even more radically than Stokowski in his arrangements of Bach, yet is similarly winning. The 10 movements from the ballet, *The Origin of Design*, come from the very first recording sessions of Beecham's newly founded London Philharmonic in December 1932. The following month he re-recorded three of the movements (available on Dutton), but extraordinarily this far bigger selection of movements was never issued – brilliantly performed, with the players on their toes, not least the soloist Leon Goossens. Sadly the 78 side containing the 'Serenade' is so damaged that the opening of the movement has had to be omitted.

Seven of the movements from the later ballet, *The Gods Go a'Begging*, made between 1933 and 1938 did get published, but all the rest, including the six movements from the same ballet recorded with the RPO in 1949, have never appeared in any format, inexplicably so when Beecham is in sparkling form throughout.

The oddity is the four-movement Piano Concerto which Beecham cobbled together from various Handel movements (which are unidentified here) for his then-wife, the pianist Betty Humby. The result makes a curious confection, starting with a nine-minute 'Chaconne' in which grandly spacious sections punctuate energetic chaconne variations.

The result is energetic, sounding less like Handel than 20th-century pastiche, with keyboard figuration and pianistic tricks unashamedly reflecting the romantic concerto tradition. As in the Delius disc, transfers bring satisfyingly full-bodied sound, if with obvious limitations. What is clear throughout is the Beecham magic – wonderful control of phrasing and rhythm in performances that are light of touch and full of fun.

British Light Music Classics 3

Ancliffe Smiles, then Kisses **Binge** Miss Melanie **Caryll** The Pink Lady **Coates** Music Everywhere **Dexter** Siciliano **Duncan** Girl from Corsica **Ellis** Alpine Pastures **Evans** Lady of Spain **Farnon** Portrait of a Flirt **Godin** Valse septembre **Joyce** Songe d'automne **Ketèlbey** In a Persian Market[a] **Melachrino** Woodland Revel **Monckton** Soldiers in the Park **Richardson** Melody on the Move **Strachey** In Party Mood. Theatreland **Tomlinson** Little Serenade **Torch** On a Spring Note **Wood** Montmartre

[a]**New London Light Opera Chorus, New London Orchestra / Ronald Corp**

Hyperion CDA67148 (80 minutes: DDD) Ⓕ

Recorded 1999

This third Hyperion helping of British Light Music Classics proves no less rewarding than its predecessors. The almost obligatory pieces by Coates, Farnon and Ketèlbey are here, and so too are such favourites of the post-Second World War era as Haydn Wood's *Montmartre*, Trevor Duncan's *Girl from Corsica*, Ernest Tomlinson's *Little Serenade* and Sidney Torch's *On a Spring Note*. All have popped up from time to time in similar collections over the past few years; what makes these Hyperion collections especially rewarding is the way they introduce items not otherwise readily available. Examples include the two pieces by Jack Strachey – the bouncy *In Party Mood*, which served as the signature tune of *Housewives' Choice*, and the rousing march *Theatreland*. There is also a gratifying whiff of mountain air and cowbells in Vivian Ellis's *Alpine Pastures*, which was for many years the signature tune of *My Word*.

No less welcome are pieces from an earlier age that both LP and CD have tended to neglect. *Valse septembre* by Felix Godin was prominently featured in the film *Titanic*, but the elegant and shapely *Smiles, then Kisses* by that fine craftsman Charles Ancliffe has probably been neglected since the post-Second World War revival of 'Olde Tyme Dancing'. Ronald Corp and the New London Orchestra play with their familiar accomplishment and affection and, if anything, an even surer grasp of pace than before. The CD is gratifyingly full and excellently recorded.

Brian Kay's British Light Music Discoveries

Alwyn Suite of Scottish Dances **Arnold** The Roots of Heaven – Overture **Bennett** Little Suite **Jacob** The Barber of Seville Goes to the Devil **Johnstone** Tarn Hows **Langford** Two Worlds **Langley** The Coloured Counties **Lyon** Joie de vivre **Parker** The Glass Slipper – Overture **Sargent** Impression of a Windy Day, Op 9

Royal Ballet Sinfonia / Gavin Sutherland

ASV White Line CDWHL2113 (70 minutes: DDD) Ⓜ

Recorded 1998

Though Brian Kay's name and portrait are used to promote this splendid collection, one suspects the driving force may have been its producer and annotator, Philip Lane, who has done such a lot for British light music on CD. With so much of Malcolm Arnold's music available, it is astonishing that his typically ebullient and tuneful overture *The Roots of Heaven* is here receiving its first recording. The same goes for William Alwyn's attractive set of Scottish dances, which are largely based on traditional tunes. Gordon Jacob's witty take-off of Rossini's best-known overture is the best-known piece here, but all the rest are very well worth getting to know. Richard Rodney Bennett's utterly charming *Little Suite* includes a waltz in best *Murder on the Orient Express* style, and the ebullient overture by David Lyon is a splendid representation of his work. You may never have thought of Sir Malcolm Sargent as a composer, but his contribution proves as rewarding as any, being a most attractive tone-poem with some appropriately breezy melodies. Then there is Clifton Parker's dainty overture to the musical play *The Glass Slipper*, plus three tone-poems by sometime BBC producers – Alan Langford contrasting the old world and the new, and Maurice Johnstone and James Langley elegantly depicting some of England's loveliest countryside. This really is a most enterprising and enjoyable collection, with stylish playing from the Royal Ballet Sinfonia.

Summer Streams

G Bush Divertimento **Hedges** Divertimento **Langford** Four Pieces **Lyon** Intermezzo **Sumsion** A mountain tune **Wright** Two Pieces[a]

Royal Ballet Sinfonia / David Lloyd-Jones with [a]**Richard Friedman** *vn*

ASV White Line CDWHL2121 (72 minutes: DDD) Ⓜ

Recorded 1997-98

As Alan Langford's Waltz glides in on track 1, instinct tells you this CD is going to be pure delight to all lovers of English string music – and it doesn't disappoint. Langford was a pupil of Benjamin Frankel, and the four pieces gathered together here combine to make a perfect little suite and also display Langford's masterly writing for strings. The slightly more weighty sound world of the late Geoffrey Bush's *Divertimento* of 1943, a substantial three-movement work, can easily rub shoulders with the string music of Elgar, Finzi and Vaughan Williams. Where has it been hiding, and why is it not heard more often? Beautifully structured and brimming with memorable ideas, this will be an irresistible discovery to all who hear it. Geoffrey Wright's charming 'Summer Stream' (from which the disc takes it title) is one of two miniatures for strings and harp, the other being a slightly roguish Irish jig originally composed for Sean O'Casey's play *Cock-a-doodle Dandy*. As we progress to Herbert Sumsion's Graingeresque *A mountain tune* and David Lyon's *Intermezzo* (*My Fair Lady* meets a 'light' Brucknerian ländler) we realise that there isn't a weak piece to be heard on this disc. The programme closes with Anthony Hedges's substantial *Divertimento* for strings (1971), a work 'light' in spirit perhaps, but one that can surely hold its head high in the company of some of our finest string music. The performances are, like all the music here, a pure delight to the ear.

French Orchestral

Marches and Overtures à la Française
Adam Si j'étais roi – Overture **Boieldieu** La dame blanche – Overture **Gounod** Marche funèbre d'une marionnette **Meyerbeer** Coronation March
Offenbach La belle Hélène – Overture. Orphée aux enfers – Overture. Les contes d'Hoffmann – Prelude
Rossini Guillaume Tell – Overture[d]
Rouget de Lisle La marseillaise **Saint-Saëns** Suite algérienne in C, Op 60 – Marche militaire française. Marche héroïque in E flat, Op 34
Detroit Symphony Orchestra / Paul Paray
Mercury Living Presence 434 332-2MM Ⓜ
(66 minutes: ADD). Recorded 1959-60

They don't make collections like this any more! Or so it seems. Yet can musical tastes really have changed so radically from the days when people would patiently turn over a 78rpm record for the second half of Boieldieu's *La dame blanche* Overture? Unlikely, and there must surely be a welcome for such a collection of charmingly melodious, unpretentious and yet well-crafted pieces as on this CD. Paul Paray (1886–1979) was a genuine son of Normandy who in his seventies could still bring out the Gallic warmth, excitement and sparkle of these pieces. The recording sounds just a shade raw with the violins at the top of their range, but generally the warmth and richness of sound exhibited here make it quite unbelievable that these recordings are now 38-odd years old.

Tortelier's French Bonbons
Adam Si j'étais roi – Overture **Auber** Le cheval de bronze – Overture **Chabrier** Habanera. Joyeuse marche **Gounod** Marche funèbre d'une marionnette **Hérold** Zampa – Overture **Maillart** Les dragons de Villars – Overture **Massenet** Les Erinnyes – Tristesse du soir. Thaïs – Méditation[ac]. Mélodie – Elégie (arr Mouton)[b]. La Vierge – Le dernier sommeil de la Vierge **Offenbach** La belle Hélène – Overture (arr Haensch). Les contes d'Hoffmann – Entr'acte et Barcarolle[c].
Thomas Mignon – Overture; Me voici dans son boudoir
[a]**Yuri Torchinsky** *vn* [b]**Peter Dixon** *vc*
[c]**Royal Liverpool Philharmonic Choir;**
BBC Philharmonic Orchestra / Yan Pascal Tortelier
Chandos CHAN9765 (75 minutes: DDD) Ⓕ
Recorded 1999

This splendid collection is a worthy successor to many nostalgically remembered LPs by Paul Paray and others. The concert opens in the bandstand with gusto and style; and after Hérold's *Zampa* comes Gounod's whimsical little *Marche funèbre d'une marionnette*, beloved of Alfred Hitchcock. The succession of wind (and harp) solos at the opening of *Mignon* is beautifully played (there is plenty of warm romantic feeling throughout the disc) and Adam's *Si j'étais roi* is delectably pointed, as is the exhilarating closing galop of Auber's *Cheval de bronze*. Maillart's grandiose, very French military piece is vigorously projected, Chabrier lilts, and the gentler evocations by Massenet make seductive interludes. But it is the overall zest one remembers. Tortelier doesn't push anything too hard, yet gives the rhythms plenty of lift, and his codas fizz nicely. The BBC Philharmonic is on top form and the Chandos recording is top-drawer, vivid, resonant and glowing. All in all, a programme to cheer you up on a bleak winter's day. Just try *La belle Hélène* and you will be won over.

Miscellaneous Orchestral

Sir John Barbirolli
Haydn Symphony No 83 in G minor, 'La Poule'
Lehár Gold und Silber, Op 79 **J Strauss II** Die Fledermaus – Overture. Kaiser-Walzer, Op 437. Perpetuum mobile, Op 257. Tritsch-Tratsch-Polka, Op 214 **R Strauss** Der Rosenkavalier Suite
Hallé Orchestra / Sir John Barbirolli
BBC Legends/IMG Artists BBCL4038-2 Ⓜ
(76 minutes: ADD). Recorded live in 1969 **OO**

Among all the treasures rediscovered in the BBC archives, this disc of a Barbirolli Promenade Concert of 1969 is among the most enticing. He opens with one of his favourite Haydn symphonies, and only Beecham can match his delightful characterisation of *The Hen* (dainty violins, plus gently clucking oboe) which Haydn makes sure we hear several times in the course of a most appealing first movement. As shaped by JB the *Andante* combines an Elysian simplicity with classical beauty of line, and the *Minuet* and finale similarly match grace with exuberance. There is surely no finer performance on disc.

Then comes the Johann Strauss section, with Sir John himself vocalising in the Overture's glorious waltz theme. But the highlight is a richly contoured, magical account of the *Emperor Waltz*, with all the mellow nobility of line one associates with Bruno Walter, plus an added touch of Barbirolli's Italianate sunshine. The reprise is so lovely it would melt the hardest heart. Then follows a fun performance of the

Tritsch-Tratsch-Polka, with outrageous agogic tempo distortions and sudden pauses which bring a couple of great bursts of laughter from the Promenaders. But the best is yet to come.

With the *Rosenkavalier* suite the Hallé strings and horns surpass themselves. This musical patchwork may be no more than a comparatively inept pot-pourri, but Sir John invests each section of the score with such loving detail that one can only regret that he never recorded the whole opera. The Prelude, with its sexy, whooping horns, and a great passionate *tenuto* on the key moment of the lovers' passionate embrace (behind the curtain), then leads on to a wonderful feeling of tenderness as their ardour gently subsides. Later the Presentation of the Rose scene, with exquisite oboe playing, is meltingly beautiful. After the great surge of the Viennese waltz sequence, the closing section and the softly sensuous duet that sees Octavian and Sophie raptly departing together is wonderfully affectionate, rudely interrupted, of course, by the explosive coda (which is rather badly in need of some re-organisation).

The encore is Lehár's *Gold and Silver*, and Sir John encourages his Promenaders to hum along gently so as not to overwhelm its famous lyrical melody; and he even manages to entice them into a *pianississimo* when it is reprised. Prommers in the late 1960s were then just as appreciative but more self-disciplined than they are today, and there is no hint of vulgarity and much warmth in their response. Sir John cuts the coda to make time for his own witty little speech in appreciation of their contribution, continuing with a warmly expressed wish to return with his orchestra; and this alone is worth the price of an unforgettable disc, recorded with great warmth and atmosphere.

Sir Thomas Beecham: The RPO Legacy Volume 1 H

Bach Christmas Oratorio, BWV248 – Sinfonia **Berlioz** Le corsaire, Op 21 **Chabrier** Joyeuse marche **Debussy** Printemps **Mussorgsky** Khovanshchina – Dance of the Persian Slaves **Sibelius** Tapiola, Op 112 **Smetana** The Bartered Bride – Overture; Polka; Dance of the Comedians

Royal Philharmonic Orchestra / Sir Thomas Beecham

Dutton Laboratories mono CDLX7027 Ⓑ
(74 minutes: ADD). Recorded 1946-47

With astonishingly full mono sound, this first disc in the RPO Legacy series vividly captures the tense excitement of the months following Beecham's founding of the orchestra in 1946. It starts with the recording of the Berlioz *Corsaire* Overture which was the very first from the RPO to be issued. Beecham at hectic speed in the opening flourish challenges his violins to keep up, and the result has an apt element of wildness while offering fine ensemble. *Tapiola*, recorded a few weeks later in November 1946, similarly has a rugged intensity as well as polish, with the terracing of texture and dynamic beautifully brought out even in mono. Finest of all in the collection is the Debussy *Printemps* which Beecham conducted as early as 1913, but which he never recorded again. Though the sessions began on the very day that *Tapiola* was recorded, the contrast of mood is astonishing. Finnish ruggedness and severity give way to sensuousness and beauty in the first of the two sections and to energy and colour in the second. Bach, not a composer generally associated with Beecham, inspires him to a performance which suggests French rather than German music, sweet and elegant, and the Smetana and Chabrier are electrifying, not least the horn trills in the Chabrier. The Dutton transfers have a vivid sense of presence with contrasts of dynamic and texture more clearly established than is common in mono recordings of the 1940s.

Sir Thomas Beecham: The RPO Legacy, Volume 5 H

Berlioz King Lear, Op 4 – Overture **Delius** Summer Evening (ed & arr Beecham) **Dvořák** The Golden Spinning Wheel, Op 109 **Handel-Beecham** The Great Elopement (excerpts) **Haydn** Symphonies – No 40 in F; No 102 in B flat **Liszt** Symphonic Poem, Orpheus, S98 **Massenet** La Vierge – Le dernier sommeil de la Vierge **Méhul** Les deux aveugles de Tolède – Overture **Mendelssohn** Octet, Op 20 – Scherzo. Die schöne Melusine, Op 32 – Overture **Paisiello** Nina, o sia la pazza per amore – Overture **Saint-Saëns** Le rouet d'Omphale in A, Op 31

Royal Philharmonic Orchestra / Sir Thomas Beecham

Dutton Laboratories ② 2CDEA 5026 Ⓑ
(151 minutes: ADD). Recorded 1947-51 ●

Older readers who collected Beecham 78s in the late 1940s, will remember all these recordings. The two cherishable overtures by Méhul and Paisiello show the great maestro with a twinkle in his eye, but it is the Dvořák *Golden Spinning Wheel* that one never forgets and rightly remembers for its vividness. In this new Dutton transfer the sound is remarkably wide-ranging, delivering astonishingly crisp percussion and bright violins which offset the truly golden horns, and it comes up almost like a modern recording. The performance, too, of what is essentially an episodic piece, is wonderfully alive and spontaneous.

Fair Melusina was another favourite, and to end the first disc Dennis Brain leads the RPO horns with superb confidence in the spectacular *Trio* of the Minuet of Beecham's pioneering recording of Haydn's 40th, F major Symphony. The performance of No 102 is marvellous: what grace and vitality there is here. The Mendelssohn *Scherzo* is as light as thistledown, and only Martinon (Decca) approached Beecham's exquisite touch in *Le rouet d'Omphale*. *Orpheus*, too, sounds especially beautiful in Beecham's hands, while Handel-Beecham is like Bach-Stokowski: its unique qualities (here an affectionate elegance and a true feeling for baroque colour) certainly counter any charges of anachronism. This is altogether an unmissable collection; and the Dutton transfers are fresh, clear and full-bodied like the old 78s were (even on modest equipment). The notes, as usual, are by Lyndon Jenkins, and they are as informative as ever.

Sir Thomas Beecham Ⓗ
Favourite Overtures, Volume 2
Mozart Le nozze di Figaro. Don Giovanni. Die Zauberflöte[a] **Weber** Oberon. Der Freischütz **Brahms** Tragic Overture **Wagner** A Faust Overture **Berlioz** Le carnaval romain **Rossini** La scala di seta
London Philharmonic Orchestra, [a]Berlin Philharmonic Orchestra / Sir Thomas Beecham
Dutton Laboratories mono CDLX7009 Ⓑ
(75 minutes: ADD). Recorded 1933-40

The *Zauberflöte* Overture is taken from Beecham's complete recording of the opera, and he shows a measured, profound response to Mozart's inspiration. All his characteristic elegance is still there, but the 43 players of the Berlin Philharmonic are made to play in a concentrated, highly characterful fashion. He provides a strong, arrestingly dramatic account of the *Don Giovanni* Overture, yet his *Nozze di Figaro* bubbles over with charm and wit. He finds plenty of drama in the Wagner, and the Brahms has an appropriate and highly impressive strength and profundity of feeling. A reading such as this effectively gives the lie to Beecham's reputation in some quarters as a lightweight interpreter. Perhaps the best performance of all is the overture by his beloved Berlioz, for energy and excitement are matched by playing of the most affecting delicacy and poetry in the piece's more reflective passages. All the engineering is outstanding.

Han-Na Chang
The Swan – Classic Works for Cello and Orchestra
Bruch Ave Maria, Op 61 **Dvořák** Silent Woods, B182 **Fauré** (arr Hazell) Sicilienne, Op 78. Après un rêve, Op 7 No 1 **Glazunov** Chant du ménestrel, Op 71 **L J Kim** (orch R Panufnik) Korean Elegy **Rachmaninov** (arr Hazell) Vocalise, Op 34 No 14 **Respighi** Adagio con variazioni **Saint-Saëns** (arr Hazell) Le cygne **Tchaikovsky** Nocturne, Op 11
Han-Na Chang *vc* **Philharmonia Orchestra / Leonard Slatkin**
EMI CDC5 57052-2 (63 minutes: DDD Ⓕ
Recorded 2000 ○○

The phenomenally gifted Han-Na Chang's first CD (which included a glorious account of Tchaikovsky's *Rococo* Variations) to which Rostropovich – who also conducted it – gave his enthusiastic imprimatur – received the highest praise. She was 13 then; now she is 18, but that wonderfully spontaneous musicality which is hers by natural instinct (one thinks of the young Menuhin) has flowered with maturity. Her line is marginally firmer, and her ardour and sensibility bring phrasing which simply breathes with the music. The opening Fauré *Après un rêve* begins with winning delicacy – its ardour never over-emotes, while *Sicilienne* is utterly delightful. But it is perhaps in Rachmaninov's *Vocalise* that her singing line and subtle colouring touch the heartstrings most poignantly, although the much less familiar Respighi *Adagio*, Dvořák's *Klid* and the Kim *Elegy* all have a disarmingly simple eloquence. Saint-Saëns' famous *Swan* has never glided by more guilelessly (yet there is a subtle dynamic control) and, not surprisingly, the slavic dolour of Tchaikovsky's *Nocturne* is perfectly caught.

'You can see that I am in love with all these pieces,' Chang says in the notes, and her passionate advocacy of Bruch's *Ave Maria*, 'full of inner conflicts', makes for a splendid coda to a highly enjoyable disc, with Slatkin a warmly supportive accompanist. Chris Hazell's arrangements of about half the items are superb. As Chang notes in the booklet: 'I think they reflect in a very honest way what the composers had in mind.' The recording is beautiful, and has an 'old-fashioned' mellow EMI analogue-style ambience, but with the cello set forward and caught with total digital realism.

Antál Dorati
Les Ballets Russes Ⓗ
Boccherini (arr Françaix) Scuola di ballo **Chabrier** (arr cpsr, Mottl and Rieti) Cotillon **d'Erlanger** Les cent baisers **J Strauss II** (arr Desormière) Le beau Danube
London Philharmonic Orchestra, London Symphony Orchestra / Antál Dorati
Pearl mono GEM0036 (74 minutes: ADD) Ⓜ
Recorded 1937

The impact of Diaghilev's Ballets Russes on the artistic and musical world in the West was so widespread that when he died in 1929 it was assumed that his ballet company would go with him. In the 1930s, however, under the joint management of René Blum and Colonel Vassily de Basil, the Ballet Russe de Monte-Carlo emerged with a new generation of stars and soon the dynamic young Antál Dorati as Music Director. Apart from still photographs and stage designs, there is so little to help a modern audience imagine what those glittering seasons were like that this CD has an almost dreamlike quality. When the company danced at Covent Garden, the London Philharmonic was the orchestra in residence, so these performances are authentic – unlike so many concert readings of ballet scores, this is how the music would have sounded in the theatre.

The four ballets represented were all popular items on the programme for several seasons. Although the last to be recorded, in 1939, *Scuola di ballo*, Jean Françaix's arrangement of 10 pieces by Boccherini, was one of the first works presented by the company in 1933. It was choreographed by Léonide Massine and based on a play by Goldoni. Massine himself danced the central male role, with two of the most glamorous ballerinas as his partners – Irina Barnonova and Tatiana Riabouchinska. The sound is, as Françaix put it, 'full of Parisian modernisms'. Balanchine's ballet, *Cotillon*, was also one of the earliest post-Diaghilev efforts by the company. Chabrier's music was mostly orchestrated by Vittorio Rieti, and the ballet was designed by Christian Bérard. Unlike Balanchine's later, more abstract work, it had a narrative about guests at a formal dance in a private house, with the theme of 'The hands of fate'. Balanchine himself danced the First Guest at the première, with Tamara Toumanova as the Daughter of the House.

Le beau Danube, with Johann Strauss's music arranged by Roger Desormière, was one of the most enduringly popular of Massine's ballets. The sets were by Vladimir Polunine, based on the drawings of Constantin Guys. Alexandra Danilova had a great success as the Street Dancer, with Massine himself as the Hussar. The finale, with Baronova's solo culminating in 32 *fouettés* and then the rival Hussar and Dandy trying to outdo each other in pirouettes, can easily be imagined here in the ecstatic conducting of Dorati.

The rarest piece is Baron Frédéric d'Erlanger's *Les cent baisers*. Dorati conducted the world première at Covent Garden in July 1935 – the choreography was by Bronislava Nijinska with designs by Jean Hugo, and Baronova and Lichine in the main roles. The Hans Andersen tale of the Princess and the Swineherd is a story of romantic disillusion, and d'Erlanger's music, although evoking courtly traditions, has a swooning, almost Korngold-like mood. The sound of these recordings from the 1930s is very clear and free of distortion. Anyone with a curiosity about the great days of the Ballets Russes is likely to be utterly enthralled by this totally enchanting disc.

Julian Lloyd Webber
Cello Moods

Bach Orchestral Suite No 3 in D, BWV1068 – Air[b] **Borodin** String Quartet No 2 in D – Notturno[b] **Caccini** Ave Maria[b] **Chopin** Nocturne No 2 in E flat, Op 9 No 2[b] **Debussy** Rêverie[b] **Elgar** Chanson de matin, Op 15 No 2[b] Salut d'amour, Op 12[b] **Rheinberger** Organ Sonata No 11 in D minor, Op 148 – Cantilena (all arr Cullen)[b] **Boccherini** Cello Concerto No 9 in B flat, G482 – Adagio[b] **Bruch** Kol Nidrei, Op 47[b] **Franck** Panis angelicus[b] **Glazunov** Mélodie, Op 20 No 1[b] **J Lloyd Webber** Jackie's Song[c] **Massenet** Thaïs – Méditation[b] **Traditional** Sakura Sakura[a]

Julian Lloyd Webber *vc* [a]**Jayson Kouchak** *pf* [b]**Royal Philharmonic Orchestra / James Judd;** [c]**BBC Concert Orchestra / Barry Wordsworth**

Philips 462 588-2PH (74 minutes: DDD) Ⓕ

This collection of Julian Lloyd Webber's recordings is of popular encore pieces (mostly transcriptions). He opens with a tastefully 'vocal' rendering of Franck's *Panis angelicus* and ends with a noble *Cantilena* from Rheinberger; however, the highlight is a movingly warm, yet not over-the-top account of Bruch's *Kol Nidrei*. His own charming little tribute to Jacqueline du Pré, and the Massenet 'Méditation' on a cello rather than a violin are very appealing. Other highlights are Caccini's gently touching *Ave Maria*, which is the kind of half-familiar, nostalgic piece one can't put a name to. The Russian melodies are played romantically, but without swooning: the most enjoyable is the least-known, Glazunov's *Mélodie*, Op 20 No 1. However the Chopin *Nocturne* in E flat major stands out as an example of an untranscribable piano piece. Lloyd Webber has a firm, richly coloured and full-focused tone which records well. If you enjoy typical lollipops played on the cello with affectionate flair, then neither the warm recording, nor the quantity of music offered, can be faulted.

Sergei Nakariakov
No Limit

Bruch Canzone in B, Op 55[a] **Gershwin** (arr Dokshitser) Rhapsody in Blue[b] **Massenet** Thaïs – Méditation[a] **Saint-Saëns** Introduction and Rondo capriccioso in A minor, Op 28[b] **Tchaikovsky** Andante cantabile, Op 11[a]. Variations on a Rococo Theme in A, Op 33[a] (all arrangements by Mikhail Nakariakov unless otherwise indicated)

Sergei Nakariakov [a]*flugelhn*/[b]*tpt* **Philharmonia Orchestra / Vladimir Ashkenazy**

Teldec 8573-80651-2 (62 minutes: DDD) Ⓕ
Recorded 1999

What a wonderful trumpeter the young Sergei Nakariakov is! So beautiful is his tone, so naturally musical is his phrasing, so astonishing is his easy virtuosity, that he almost reconciles you to these arrangements. Certainly to the Saint-Saëns, which comes off with splendid panache – and that hair-raisingly fast tonguing at the end is extraordinary. (Is it single- or double-tonguing? It's so clean that it's impossible to decide.) The disc is worth considering for this piece alone.

But, oh dear, Tchaikovsky's *Andante cantabile* on the flugelhorn just does not work, for all the warmth of line and the tasteful vibrato. The *Rococo* Variations fare rather better, with the melodic line at times lying higher up. It really is a lyrical (Variation 3 is beautifully phrased) and bravura tour de force, but still sounds far better on a cello. Max Bruch's *Canzone* emerges unscathed, and Massenet's 'Méditation' is romantically stylish if inevitably carrying a whiff of the bandstand. Certainly flugelhorn playing of this calibre is rare.

Nakariakov is undoubtedly in his element in Gershwin, where he returns to the trumpet. He clearly enjoys himself and it is a sparkling performance, with a nice jazzy inflection, and here the trumpet's middle and lower range is used to good effect, with a touch of humour when the bassoon briefly takes over. The big tune is introduced delicately and beguilingly with a mute; but in the following string tutti the saxes fail to shine through.

Throughout, Ashkenazy provides good support; these are very much accompaniments, and the recording balance reflects that priority. But that Gershwin opening should have been left to the clarinet (it was apparently Benny Goodman's idea in the first place).

Itzhak Perlman
A la carte
Glazunov Mazurka-Oberek in D. Meditation, Op 32
Kreisler The Old Refrain. Schön Rosmarin
Massenet Thaïs – Méditation **Rachmaninov** Vocalise, Op 34 No 14 **Rimsky-Korsakov** (arr Kreisler) Fantasia on Two Russian Themes, Op 33
Sarasate Zigeunerweisen, Op 20. Introduction and Tarantella, Op 43 **Tchaikovsky** (orch Glazunov) Scherzo in C minor, Op 42 No 2
Wieniawski Légende, Op 17. Zigeunerweisen
Itzhak Perlman *vn* **Abbey Road Ensemble / Lawrence Foster**
EMI CDC5 55475-2 (63 minutes: DDD) Ⓕ
Recorded 1995

A most enjoyable programme. Perlman approximates the 'old school' with something of an actor's skill: he feels the period, not as a first-hand witness (even at 50, he is far too young for that), but as a respectful recipient of a great tradition. His 'Méditation' is an elevated 'easy listen', sensitively accompanied. The Glazunov *Mazurka-Oberek* should be at least as popular as Saint-Saëns's concert pieces for violin and orchestra, and Perlman does it proud. The initial pages of Rachmaninov's *Vocalise* are a little over-sweet (too many well-oiled slides), but its latter half achieves genuine expressive eloquence. Glazunov's *Meditation* is suitably honeyed, and the Kreisler-Rimsky *Fantasia* (where Goldmark's A minor Concerto hovers around the main theme) is given a truly splendid performance. Of the rest, the two Kreisler pieces are exceptional, *Schön Rosmarin* especially, while Lawrence Foster's expert Abbey Road Ensemble provides a discreet but flavoursome orchestral base.

Wolfgang Sawallisch
Stokowski Transcriptions
Bach Cantatas: No 208 – Schafe können sicher weiden; No 140 – Wachet auf!; No 80 – Ein' feste Burg. Toccata and Fugue in D minor, BWV565
Beethoven Piano Sonata No 14 in C sharp minor, 'Moonlight', Op 27 No 2 – Adagio sostenuto
Boccherini String Quintet in E, G275 – Minuet
Chopin Prelude in E minor, Op 28 No 4
Debussy Suite bergamasque – Clair de lune. Préludes, Book 1 – No 10, La cathédrale engloutie
Franck Panis angelicus **Rachmaninov** Prelude in C sharp minor, Op 3 No 2 **Tchaikovsky** String Quartet No 1 in D, Op 11 – Andante cantabile. At the ball, Op 38 No 3[a]
[a]**Marjana Lipovšek** *mez* **Philadelphia Orchestra / Wolfgang Sawallisch**
EMI CDC5 55592-2 (66 minutes: DDD) Ⓕ
Recorded 1995

Quite apart from the reissues of Stokowski's own recordings, there are several other discs of these highly coloured arrangements. Though Stokowski's own recordings, even those he made in extreme old age, generally have a degree more flair and dramatic bite than any others, the contrasts are not always what you would expect. So it is surprising to find that the BBC Philharmonic strings are more ripely resonant than those of the Philadelphia Orchestra in Franck's *Panis angelicus*, though that is an exception, and possibly Sawallisch simply wanted to minimise the piece's bold vulgarity. One of the items common to these discs is the *Adagio* from Beethoven's *Moonlight* Sonata, and there Sawallisch brings out far more of the mystery of what becomes an evocative, atmospheric piece, making the Bamert disc seem clinical. This collection also gains in glamour from having Marjana Lipovšek as an appropriately Slavonic-sounding soloist in the orchestration of the Tchaikovsky song, *At the ball*. This EMI disc provides a generous programme together with richly rounded recording, well defined in the bass. Yet Bamert's even more generous selection of 15 encore pieces overlaps on only three items, and includes more in which Stokowski has the greatest fun tweaking the ear provocatively, such as Mozart's *Turkish Rondo*: the advice to anyone with a sweet tooth is to get both discs for maximum indulgence.

Sir Georg Solti
Hungarian Connections
Bartók Hungarian Sketches, Sz97. Romanian folkdances, Sz68 **Kodály** Háry János, Op 15 – Suite[a]
Liszt Two Episodes from Lenau's Faust, S110 – Der Tanz in der Dorfschenke. Hungarian Rhapsody No 2 in D minor (orch Döppler) **L Weiner** Csongor és Tünde, Op 10*b* – Introduction; Scherzo
[a]**Laurence Kaptain** *cimb* **Chicago Symphony Orchestra / Sir Georg Solti**
Decca 443 444-2DH (72 minutes: DDD) Ⓕ
Recorded live in 1993

This is a terrific programme. The sequence is imaginative, the material extremely attractive, and the standard of performance high. The *Mephisto Waltz* swirls in heady abandon, with strings as delicate as thistledown, and some snappy work from the Chicago brass. The once-ubiquitous Second *Hungarian Rhapsody* is wittily turned, although Döppler's sundry added counterpoint and rather tame orchestration tend to mute the rustic edge of Liszt's original. The performance, though, has plenty of life, and the recording conjures up a realistic sense of aural perspective. Sir Georg's empathy for this idiom is everywhere in evidence, and never more so than in Bartók's *Romanian folkdances*, where lightness of touch and sensitive rubato re-create a crucial feeling of improvisation. The *Hungarian Sketches* are tellingly pointed, with fluid lines in 'Evening in the Village' and 'Melody', a hilarious *ff* trombone/tuba belch in 'A Little Tipsy' and cleanly differentiated percussion in the 'Bear Dance'. Solti's version is now perhaps the current front-runner, and makes for a most entertaining musical diversion. Nice, too, to hear music by the underrated Leó Weiner, his *Csongor és Tünde* ballet with its subtle reminiscences of Nicolai's *Merry Wives of Windsor* Overture and Liszt's *Dante* Symphony. The busy *Scherzo* is the sort of thing Bartók might have composed had he not outgrown the worlds of Strauss and Dohnányi, while the Introduction is reminiscent of Kodály in pastoral vein. Kodály himself is represented by a genial account of the *Háry János* Suite, superbly recorded and with some distinctive solo work.

Vytautas Sondeckis
Romantic Cello Works
Davïdov Ballade, Op 25. Pieces, Op 20 – By the Fountain **Dvarionas** By the Lake. Introduction and Rondino **Rachmaninov** Vocalise, Op 34 No 14 **Rimsky-Korsakov** Serenade, Op 37. Tale of Tsar Saltan – Flight of the Bumble-bee (arr Traubas) **Rubinstein** Melody in F, Op 3 No 1 **Shostakovich** (arr Atovmyan) Ballet Suite No 2 – Adagio **Taneyev** Canzona in F minor **Tchaikovsky** Mélodie in E flat, Op 42 No 3 (arr Meschan'inov). Nocturne in D minor, Op 19 No 4. Andante cantabile, Op 11
Vytautas Sondeckis *vc* **Lithuanian Chamber Orchestra / David Geringas**
Naxos 8 554381 (60 minutes: DDD) Ⓢ
Recorded 1999

This CD has a solid cellistic pedigree. Vytautas Sondeckis's father, Saulius Sondeckis, known as a conductor, is also a cellist and a pupil of Rostropovich. The conductor, David Geringas (another Rostropovich student), is Vytautas's teacher. Vytautas himself, born in 1972, is already a mature artist; he produces a classically fine cello tone. His playing gives the impression of being straightforward and unaffected, yet he allows himself the space for rhythmic flexibility and expressive freedom; the Tchaikovsky *Andante cantabile*, ending the disc, is an especially memorable interpretation.

The programme is well thought out, and has a good mixture of the familiar and the more recherché. Within the general romantic Russian theme there's plenty of variety, from the virtuosic, colourfully orchestrated Davïdov pieces to the more folksy style of the Lithuanian Dvarionas.

The Rachmaninov, another high point, sounds less dreamy, more passionate than usual, and it's good to hear the Taneyev, originally for clarinet and strings and then arranged for cello and piano, in this version for cello and strings – it's a beautiful, finely worked-out piece.

The only dissatisfaction is with the recording – adequate but slightly lacking in perspective and spaciousness. With fine, expressive orchestral playing and good arrangements, however, this adds up to a most attractive disc – yet another desirable Naxos release.

Michael Tilson Thomas
New World Jazz
J Adams Lollapalooza **Antheil** A Jazz Symphony **Bernstein** Prelude, Fugue and Riffs **Gershwin** Rhapsody in Blue **Hindemith** Ragtime **Milhaud** La création du monde **Raksin** The Bad and the Beautiful – main theme **Stravinsky** Ebony Concerto
Tad Calcara, Jerome Simas *cls*
New World Symphony / Michael Tilson Thomas *pf*
RCA Red Seal 09026 68798-2 (68 minutes: DDD) Ⓕ
Recorded 1997 ●●

The Ultimate Jazz Album, this, imaginatively programmed and impeccably realised by all involved. We kick off with the dazzling world première recording of John Adams's six-and-a-half-minute *Lollapalooza* (1995), whose infectiously rhythmic, post-modern cavortings are relished to the full by Tilson Thomas and his superb young band. This *Rhapsody in Blue* evinces an improvisatory fantasy and edge-of-seat, theatrical fervour to make one appreciate anew the extraordinary boldness, reckless danger even, of Gershwin's ground-breaking inspiration. Bernstein's exhilarating *Prelude, Fugue and Riffs* receives the outing of a lifetime, a gloriously idiomatic, stunningly assured display which, like the wonderfully poised reading of Stravinsky's *Ebony Concerto*, invites and fully withstands comparison with the best rivals. We also get a singularly deft and atmospheric performance of Milhaud's 1923 ballet masterpiece, *La création du monde*, whose striking pre-echoes of Gershwin have never seemed more potent. All of which leaves Hindemith's 'well-tempered' *Ragtime*, a mischievous reworking from 1921 of the C minor Fugue from Book 1 of the *48* (and dispatched on this occasion with a gleeful exuberance), George Antheil's endearingly outrageous *A Jazz Symphony* and David Raksin's gorgeous main title for Vincente Minnelli's *The Bad and the Beautiful* (1952). Thrillingly realistic sound throughout. Not to be missed!

Arturo Toscanini H
Martucci Song of Remembrance[a]
Schumann Symphony No 2 in C, Op 61 **Tommasini** Il carnevale a Venezia **Wagner** A Faust Overture
[a]**Bruna Castagna** *mez* **NBC Symphony Orchestra / Arturo Toscanini**
Naxos Historical ② 8 110836/7 (89 minutes: ADD) Ⓢ
Recorded 1941

Schubert Symphony No 2 in B flat, D125
Wagner Parsifal – Prelude; Good Friday music (concert version); Klingsor's Garden (concert version)
NBC Symphony Orchestra / Arturo Toscanini
Naxos Historical 8 110838 (73 minutes: ADD) Ⓢ
Recorded 1940 ●

The success of any Toscanini broadcast series depends largely on the quality of available source material, and on that count alone, Naxos's enterprise seems notably superior to most that have preceded it. With reference to the 1941 concert, disc 1 (46'51") features significant Wagner and Schumann, while disc 2 (42'21") is given over to works by Martucci and Tommasini that not everyone will want. Still, the performances are quite something and, as on previous CDs in this series, there are real gems.

Martucci's lyrical *La canzone dei ricordi* (or 'The Song of Remembrance') was orchestrated by the composer in 1900 and is vaguely reminiscent of Debussy's *La damoiselle élue* (composed two years earlier). Bruna Castagna's seamless mezzo is well employed, and so are the tender-toned NBC strings. Debussy's muse also haunts Tommasini's colourful *Carnival of Venice* Variations where

Toscanini's characteristic interpretative priorities are textural clarity, singing lines and driving rhythms. Neither work strikes one as especially memorable; perhaps the Martucci just edges it. Both sound adequate, though the opening bars of *La canzone* are prone to crumble.

The tension of the opening pages of the 1941 account of Wagner's *Faust* Overture, the swelling Brucknerian curve of the broadened principal theme and the finely tensed delivery of the main argument, all are exceptional. So is the playing, though it's not as demonstrably spectacular as the second movement of Schumann's Second Symphony. Aside from *staccato*-style phrasing at great speed, the switch between the main motive and two successive trios witnesses a degree of dynamic elasticity that any soloist would view as a severe challenge. Here, the entire band swings from one episode to the next like a single player. It's simply stunning.

The first movement is again visited by dynamic extremes. The *Adagio espressivo* responds to Toscanini's penchant for long-breathed, singing lines (not inappropriately, given Schumann's songful muse) and the finale is made flexible by tiny adjustments in tempo that are also evident in the better-known NBC/Toscanini broadcast of 1946. There, as here, tempos are generally swift (very similar in fact), but the string playing is less well drilled and inflections far less dramatic. In a word, the 1941 performance is tighter.

Turning to the 1940 concert, Schubert's Second is again up against a Toscanini rival, from 1938 this time. But while the 1946 Schumann Second does at least have a spot of extra clarity on its side, the 1938 Schubert Two (the two performances are usefully coupled together on Dell'Arte) sounds bad-tempered and relentless virtually for the duration. Two years later, Toscanini let the air in – and he also encouraged his players to sing. True, the mood is still high-octane and speeds are pretty nifty (a pitch rise in the second movement further intensifies a sense of haste). But those who know only the earlier broadcast will note how this second version accommodates added perspectives, as well as extra flexibility and countless tiny *crescendos* that were barely hinted at before. It's a far more musical reading, better balanced as sound though not as viscerally 'immediate'.

The *Parsifal* selection is fascinating, though the 'acid top' that grated on the old Music & Arts LPs is still sometimes in evidence. Generally, though, the sound is improved and the performances are, for the most part, extraordinarily gripping. The Prelude is the exception, which Toscanini played with greater intensity on other occasions, though here the closing pages are beautifully sustained. Naxos advises us that, in addition to the Prelude and Good Friday Music, we should expect 24 minutes of Klingsor's Garden. Not so. The general intention seems to have been to counter the static aura of the previous excerpts with a healthy quota of music drama. What we actually hear is the Prelude to Act 2, followed by the Third Act Prelude, the animated lead-up to Klingsor's Magic Garden, the Garden itself and then an orchestrated version of the opera's serene closing pages. Why Toscanini didn't insert the Good Friday Music between the Klingsor's Garden and the finale is anyone's guess, but as a makeshift 'synthesis' it works well, and most of the playing is fabulous. It offers a tantalising glimpse of what Toscanini's *Parsifal* might have sounded like in the theatre, though tempos are rather faster than we have been led to expect.

John Williams
The Guitarist
Anonymous Lamento di Tristan. Ductia. Saltarello
Domeniconi Koyunbaba **Houghton** Stélé
Satie Gnossiennes Nos 1 and 2. Gymnopédie No 3 (all arr Williams) **Theodorakis** Three Epitafios
J Williams Aeolian Suite
John Williams *gtr* **orchestra / William Goodchild**
Sony Classical SK60586 (63 minutes: DDD) Ⓕ
Recorded 1998

The seemingly polarised but reconcilable elements of protest and a yearning for space and time for contemplation appear to be buried in Williams's psyche. Here they find full expression. Turkish, Greek and Greek-influenced music are the backbone of the programme: Domeniconi's programmatic *Koyunbaba* speaks for itself, as does the music of Theodorakis ('love, loneliness and freedom of expression'), and Satie's is seen as an 'early reaction against 19th-century Romanticism'; Houghton's *Stélé* and Williams's own skilfully wrought *Aeolian Suite*, too, have declared connections with Greek music. Total technical mastery is something that has never been lacking in Williams's performances (barring the occasional slips that all artists make in concert), and to it he here adds a modest but unfailingly tasteful ability as an arranger. *Koyunbaba* is a work that can seem interminable – and in many hands it *does*, but Williams's performance of it is heartfelt, not contrived, and Houghton's *Stélé* reveals the longings that can dwell in the souls of composers who began with jazz, rock and media music. If you have to live with only one recording by Williams it should be this one. It is perhaps the most personal musical statement he has yet made, and it is in every sense immaculately recorded.

Viennese Orchestral

Lanner Jäger Lust, Op 82. Steyrische Tänze, Op 165. Die Schönbrunner, Op 200 **J Strauss I** Radetzky March, Op 228 **J Strauss II** Elektro-magnetische, Op 110. Der Kobold, Op 226. Luzifer, Op 266. Morgenblätter, Op 279. Vergnügungszug, Op 281. Elektrophor, Op 297. An der schönen, blauen Donau, Op 314. Seid umschlungen, Millionen, Op 443. Eine Nacht in Venedig – Overture **Josef Strauss** Harlekin-Polka, Op 48. Dorfschwalben aus Österreich, Op 164. Ohne Sorgen, Op 271
Vienna Philharmonic Orchestra / Nikolaus Harnoncourt
Teldec ② 8573 83563-2 (96 minutes: DDD) Ⓕ
Recorded live in 2000 and 2001 ●

Even if you were disappointed by Harnoncourt's recording of *Die Fledermaus* (Teldec) – purposeful rather than sparkling – you have little need to worry here. As one might expect from this conductor, the usual delight of a New Year concert goes with fresh insights and a fair sprinkling of novelties. First of those, insisted on by Harnoncourt himself, is the original version of the *Radetzky* March by Johann Strauss I, in its revised version always the final encore.

Plainer in its orchestration and with more repeats, the original proves no substitute for what we are used to. Though it is good to hear it for a change as a novel opening item, this is the only place in the whole concert where one feels a hint of the rhythmic stiffness that one fears from Harnoncourt, the period specialist. Happily at the end there is no lack of swagger in his traditional performance of the March.

As a bonus with this year's disc the notes offer a revealing history of the New Year Concerts, which developed from Strauss concerts at the summer festival in Salzburg between 1929 and 1933. After the Anschluss in 1938, when the Nazis threatened to disband this self-governing orchestra, a Strauss concert was given under Clemens Kraus on December 31, 1940, intended as a demonstration of Austrian individuality after the country's incorporation into the Third Reich. The first actual New Year's concert came 12 months later, silencing Kraus's doubts that a morning concert would find the audience hungover after celebrations the night before.

That note is written by the chairman of the orchestra, by tradition a player, Dr Clemens Hellsberg, who makes an illuminating comment on Harnoncourt, the first conductor of a New Year's concert to have once played in the orchestra. Dr Hellsberg says how fascinating it was to 're-examine the Philharmonic's Strauss tradition through the eyes of this analytical yet so impulsive conductor'.

The results certainly justify the choice. Particularly impressive is the way Harnoncourt finds fun and sparkle even in the military rhythms of the *Night in Venice* Overture, and how he differentiates the Joseph Lanner items from the rest, with three included to celebrate the composer's bicentenary. *Jägers Lust* ('Huntsman's delight'), new to the concerts, is a joy with its 'rifle shot' on the timpani and opulent horns. Other novelties include the *Elektro-magnetische* Polka and *Electrophor* Polka, nicely contrasted, and the Polka-Mazurka *Der Kobold* ('The Goblin') with charming *pizzicato* effects and another *pianissimo* coda, all by Johann Strauss II.

Apart from these items, the seductive account of the *Seid umschlungen, Millionen* Waltz with its silky introduction and strong contrasts between sections is especially enjoyable. Also the *Excursion Train* Polka, even without train noises, here given for the 16th time at a New Year Concert, one of the items most frequently included – apart from the *Blue Danube* and *Radetzky* March, which as encores here come on a second, bonus disc. A vintage year for the event, recorded with pinpoint brilliance.

Vienna Soirée

Heuberger Der Opernball – Overture
Lanner Die Schönbrunner, Op 200. Tourbillon-Galopp, Op 142 No 1 **Lehár** Ballsirenen. Gold und Silber, Op 79 **Suppé** Ein Morgen, ein Mittag, ein Abend in Wien – Overture **Ziehrer** Wiener Bürger, Op 419. Freiherr von Schönfeld, Op 442. Fächer, Op 525
Vienna Philharmonic Orchestra / Sir John Eliot Gardiner
DG 463 185-2GH (57 minutes: DDD) Ⓕ
Recorded 1999

Sir John Eliot Gardiner draws scintillating performances from the VPO in this delightful collection of overtures, waltzes and shorter pieces, including one item not otherwise available, Lanner's dashing *Tourbillon-Galopp*. Gardiner sets the pattern in a performance of the Suppé overture at once high-powered, highly polished and deliciously sprung. Compared with most other performances, this is a reading of fearless extremes, both in dynamics and tempos. It seems a bigger, stronger piece as a result, not just light and undemanding. Some may find the high tension and brisk manner of the openings of some items diminishes the cosy Viennese charm, but there is ample compensation not just in the pinpoint precision of ensemble but the glorious resonance of the VPO's playing, and Gardiner, as in his Vienna recording of Lehár's *The Merry Widow*, enters fully into the Viennese spirit. Lehár's *Ballsirenen* waltz is, in fact, a fantasy on themes from that operetta, refined and tender as well as ebullient. The other Lehár item, too, the *Gold and Silver* waltz, brings magical *pianissimos* when the main theme is repeated. It has sometimes been claimed that the Viennese lilt is just an excuse for imprecision, but with Gardiner, polish and lilt go together, as in the underlined hesitations in Ziehrer's *Wiener Bürger* waltz. Most winning of all are the rarer, shorter items, where Gardiner and the Viennese players uninhibitedly shrug off all thought of vulgarity, playing Ziehrer's *Fächer* Polonaise and *Schönfeld* March with irresistible zest and bounce. The DG recording, made in the Vienna Musikverein, has ideal freshness and clarity as well as warmth.

Chamber

String Ensembles

French Chamber Music

Debussy Sonata for Flute, Viola and Harp
Françaix Octet **Ibert** Trois pièces brèves
Jolivet Chant de Linos **Ravel** Introduction and Allegro
Rainer Kussmaul, Madeleine Carruzzo *vns* **Wolfram Christ** *va* **Georg Faust** *vc* **Alois Posch** *db* **Margit-Anna Süss** *hp* **Ensemble Wien-Berlin** (Wolfgang Schulz *fl* Hansjörg Schellenberger *ob* Karl Leister *cl* Milan Turkovič *bn* Günter Högner *hn*)
Sony Classical SK62666 (71 minutes: DDD) Ⓕ
Recorded 1996

This is a well-assembled programme, played by an expert ensemble and recorded with striking fidelity. The quality of the individual players can perhaps best be heard in the second of the Ibert pieces, the Debussy trio and the virtuoso flute threnody by Jolivet (originally a 1944 Conservatoire test-piece when Jean-Pierre Rampal was the winner), here performed in the later version when he rescored the piano part. The intensity and greater profundity of the latter two works particularly suit this group of rich-toned and serious-minded artists, whose ensemble is flawless; they excel in lyrical passages, such as the tender opening of the Françaix Octet's slow movement, but their extremely emotional reading of the first part of the Ravel (for which a leisurely pace is taken) is at variance with the Gallic spirit of understatement and limpidity. This is the only reservation about these interpretations: the waltz in the third Ibert piece could have been more playful and the *gamin* example in the finale of the entertaining Françaix Octet (a superbly crafted work) more carefree.

Musica Baltica P

Albrici Sinfonia in D minor. Sonata a 5
Anonymous Fantasia a 7 **Baltzar** Pavane a 3 in C
Becker Sonata a 5 in F **Fischer** Herzlich tut mich verlangen **Hasse** Suite in D minor **Kirchoff** Sonata in B flat **Luetkeman** Choralfantasie a 5, 'Innsbruck, ich muss dich lassen'. Fantasia a 5 **Meder** Sonata, 'Der Polnische Pracher'. Sonata di Battaglia in C
Vierdanck Capriccios – a 2 in D minor; a 4 in D minor
Musica Antiqua Köln / Reinhard Goebel
Archiv Produktion 459 619-2AH (81 minutes: DDD) Ⓕ
Recorded 1998

This is one of Musica Antiqua Köln's most diverting and original projects, tracing with illumination and alacrity the hidden treasures of the late Hanseatic age. As Reinhard Goebel eloquently describes in a richly-woven note, the Ostsee became a patriciate of merchants who disseminated German culture and manners to trade-route centres – such as Lübeck, Stockholm, Riga or Danzig – before local musicians transmitted the received wisdom in their own dialect. This programme is no mere journey through the Baltic ports but a riveting exposé of high-class instrumental music from the 17th century. Not many sources survive after the ravages of a war-torn region whose remaining collections faced the ultimate assault in the last war. Goebel has assembled a good deal of his astonishingly varied programme from the wonderful 'safe-haven' Duben Collection in Uppsala, Sweden. The heady mix of styles ranges from the fragrant chorale-fantasies of the North German contingent (Fischer's *Herzlich tut mich verlangen* is a little peach) to the Viennese-influenced works such as Andreas Kirchoff's taut and quixotic vignette; the unabashed regional swagger of Albrici's Sonata for two trumpets which, if less ostentatious than examples by Biber and Vejvanovsky, provides an uncompromisingly distinctive Nordic flourish. The English pavan, with its imploring contrapuntal grandeur, infuses the earlier *Fantasies* by Luetkeman and Anonymous and the Baltzar work; Vierdanck's Italianate extroversion and Meder's skilful progammatic pieces (though the *Sonata di Battaglia* is rather too much of a good thing) are only a soupçon of national taste and genre. Musica Antiqua Köln are alive to all of them. While the early-century works might generally benefit from viols (rather than the comparatively astringent mid-baroque, violin-dominated consort), the degree of focus and incandescence is only intermittently undermined by fluffy entries and the occasional suspect intonation. In the Baltzar Pavane a 3, each line is beautifully voiced and caressed. A first-rate undertaking, both revelatory and immensely pleasurable.

Neapolitan Chamber Works P

Durante Concerto for Two Violins, Viola and Continuo in G minor **Mancini** Sonata for Recorder, Two Violins and Continuo in D minor **Sarri** Concerto for Recorder, Two Violins, Viola and Continuo in A minor
A Scarlatti Sonata for Recorder, Two Violins and Continuo in A minor **D Scarlatti** Sonata for Mandolin and Continuo in D minor, Kk90
Il Giardino Armonico Ensemble / Giovanni Antonini *rec*
Teldec Das Alte Werk 4509-93157-2 Ⓕ
(54 minutes: DDD). Recorded 1993

The idea of a selection of music that might have been heard in early 18th-century Naples is not a new one but, in the area of chamber music, it has not been more vividly brought to life than on this disc. Domenico Scarlatti's Sonata is one of several believed to have been intended for a solo instrument with continuo, and here the soloist is as clean and quick-fingered a mandolinist as you could find, even if you hired a private detective (he is also the violist!) – a beguiling performance indeed. The remaining items lack any other recording, and all are to be welcomed. Sarri was a prolific composer of vocal music and the Concerto was his only instrumental work, with the recorder singing 'arias' that would tax any diva. There is something in each of the others to surprise and delight, such as the subtly tear-shedding chromatics of the opening *Affetuoso* of Durante's Concerto and the *Piano* of Alessandro Scarlatti's Sonata, a recorder/violin duo. Every item is illuminated by sensitivity to expressive nuance and dynamics, and the recording is close to perfection.

Sonatas from Dresden P

Furchheim Sonatas – E flat; D. Sonatella in A
Fux Rondeau **Thieme** Sonatas – E minor; D minor
Ziani Sonatas – No 11 in G minor; No 12 in D minor
Musica Antiqua Köln / Reinhard Goebel *vn*
Vanguard Classics 99199 (55 minutes: DDD) Ⓜ
Recorded 1999

The exuberantly baroque city of Dresden provides the peg on which to hang some well-contrasted string sonatas by composers associated at one time or another with its culturally sophisticated court. Venetian composer Pietro Andrea Ziani (1616-84), a contemporary of Cavalli, worked there for a couple of years in the mid-1660s. The music of the Austrian-born Johann Joseph Fux (1660-1741) was popular in Dresden (though he never actually worked there), and this programme features an attractive *Rondeau*. Clemens Thieme (1631-68) and Johann Wilhelm Furchheim (?1635-82) both hailed from Dresden or its neighbouring countryside and were associated with the court Kapelle. Their music is, both rhythmically and texturally, perhaps the most interesting on the disc. What a wealth of ideas is contained in these pieces and what a civilised court it must have been, artistically at least, under all those Johann Georgs (II-IV) to have fostered such diversity and profusion of talent following the 30 Years War.

Musica Antiqua Köln always seems to be at its very best when conveying the expressive variety and textural richness of 17th-century ensemble music. The string sound on this recital is first-rate throughout, disciplined, tonally clear with an intentional edge to it, and warmly communicative. Furchheim's Sonatas in E flat and A major bring us into close contact with the manner of Biber or Schmelzer, although in these instances without the former's virtuosity. To get the most out of this repertoire it is best to play two or three pieces at a time, rather than listen to the entire programme uninterrupted. Highlights include Furchheim's A major *Sonatella* and Fux's seven-part *Rondeau*, played with fantasy and verve by these splendid players under Reinhard Goebel's experienced direction.

Wind Ensembles

Beethoven Quintet for Piano and Wind in E flat, Op 16[a] **Brahms** Trio for Horn, Violin and Piano in E flat, Op 40[b] **Dukas** Villanelle[c] **Marais** Le Basque[d] (arr hn and pf) **Mozart** Quintet for Horn and Strings in E flat, K407/K386[e] **H**

Dennis Brain *hn* [b]**Max Salpeter** *vn* [cd]**Wilfrid Parry,** [b]**Cyril Preedy** *pfs* [a]**Dennis Brain Wind Ensemble;** [e]**English String Quartet**

BBC Legends/IMG Artists BBCL4048-2 Ⓜ
(72 minutes: ADD). Recorded 1957 ●●●

This is a marvellous record which does the fullest justice to the art of Dennis Brain, whom Boyd Neel called 'the finest Mozart player of his generation on any instrument'. This 1957 recording of the Mozart Horn Quintet surely bears that out. Brain has warm support from the English String Quartet, particularly in the lovely slow movement, but here his playing consistently dominates the ensemble lyrically, while the closing *Rondo* is sheer joy. So is Marais' delectable *Le Basque*. James Galway has subsequently made this piece his own on record, but Brain uses it as a witty encore, without showing off. Needless to say, the performance of the Brahms Horn Trio is very fine indeed. The infinitely sad, withdrawn atmosphere of the slow movement created by Brain's gentle soliloquy (track 11, 1'57") is unforgettable; and again the infectious hunting-horn whooping of the finale carries all before it. The recording is distanced in a resonant acoustic and is not ideally clear, but one soon forgets this.

The Dukas *Villanelle* is an arch-romantic piece which all horn players feature for the want of something better, and Dennis Brain's ardour all but convinces us that it is fine music. But the highlight of the programme is the Beethoven piano and wind quintet in which Brain shows himself the perfect chamber music partner. Without wishing to dominate, he can't help making his mark at every entry. And his colleagues join him to make a superb team. This recording was made at the 1957 Edinburgh Festival in front of a live audience, but they are mercifully quiet, and the balance is quite perfect. The recording, too, is astonishingly real. The very opening, not loud, nevertheless makes one sit up. The blending is so perfect, and Parry's pianism is not only the bedrock of the performance – the playing itself is very beautiful indeed.

The players echo each other in the development section of the first movement is sheer delight; and how splendidly they play the coda (with a superb flourish of triplets from Brain) too. The piano opening of the slow movement is wonderfully poised, and the first wind entry is gloriously full; the finale, not pressed too hard, is delightfully jaunty. In short, this is the performance against which all others must now be judged.

The Goossens Family

Bach Easter Oratorio – Sinfonia[d] **Boyce** Matelotte[c] **Dunhill** Three Short Pieces, Op 81 – Romance[c] **Elgar** (arr Jacob) Soliloquy[e] **Finzi** Interlude in A minor, Op 21[d] **Henschel** Shepherd's Lament[c] **Hughes** Bard of Armagh[c] **Krein** Serenade for Oboe and Two Harps[ab] **Nicholas** (trans M Goossens) Melody[ab] **Pitfield** Rondo lirico[c] **Richardson** Scherzino[c] **Saunders** A Cotswold Pastoral[d] **Somers-Cocks** Three Sketches – No 1[c] **Stanton** Two Pieces – Chanson pastorale[c]

Leon Goossens *ob* [a]**Marie Goossens,** [b]**Sidonie Goossens** *hps* [c]**David Lloyd** *pf* [d]**Fitzwilliam Quartet;** [e]**Bournemouth Sinfonietta / Norman Del Mar**

Chandos Enchant CHAN7132 Ⓜ
(61 minutes: DDD) ●

It is sad that this touching tribute to Leon Goossens, a superstar among oboists long before the term was invented, has had to wait so long to appear on CD. The disc is described as honouring the whole Goossens family, and the harpists Marie and Sidonie (now over 100) certainly deserve recognition, but their contribution here is peripheral. They simply accompany their brother in two of the most charming items, Michael Krein's songful *Serenade* and Morgan Nicholas's hymn-like *Melody*. Sir Eugene Goossens, conductor and composer, arguably the most prominent of all the family, is mentioned only incidentally in the note.

Melvin Harris's essay puts admirably in context the place of Leon Goossens' style and technique in the development of oboe-playing in Britain, emphasising how this collection of short oboe pieces, many originally written for Goossens, represents a personal triumph. In June 1962, just after he had recorded the Bach Double Concerto, BWV1060, with Yehudi Menuhin for EMI – a classic recording – he was injured in a car crash and suffered serious damage to the muscles around his mouth, vital for any wind-player.

It was both a medical marvel and a tribute to Goossens' will-power that he ever played again, and this collection bears formidable witness to that triumph. Though the technical facility may not be quite the same as earlier, the warmth of tone and the ability to charm are undiminished. That he was in his late seventies at the time only adds to the marvel.

No dates are given, but Brian Couzens made these recordings even before he founded his own Chandos label. All but the Elgar *Soliloquy* appeared on an RCA LP in the late '70s. The *Soliloquy* – the one movement Elgar completed (in short score) of an oboe suite for Goossens – was included both on LP and CD in a Chandos collection of shorter Elgar pieces.

This collection is especially welcome because so many of the items are unique recordings, most of the composers being seriously under-represented in the catalogue. One of the exceptions is Finzi, whose beautiful *Interlude* is the most extended piece here, superbly played by the Fitzwilliam Quartet, with contrasted sections covering a wide emotional range. All items earn their place, but it is particularly pleasing to have the carefree little *Rondo* by Thomas Pitfield with its witty pay-off. Teacher of John McCabe among others, Pitfield, who died recently, is a composer who deserves a disc to himself.

The performance of the Bach *Sinfonia* may seem old-fashioned played with such expressive warmth, and no source is given for the jaunty Boyce hornpipe, *Matelotte*, but those are niggling points. Charm is the key to the whole collection, and such an illuminating portrait of a great artist too little represented on disc is most welcome.

String Quartets

Black Angels

Crumb Black Angels **Tallis** (arr Kronos Qt) Spem in alium **Marta** Doom. A sigh **Ives** (arr Kronos Qt/Geist) They are there! **Shostakovich** String Quartet No 8 in C minor, Op 110
Kronos Quartet (David Harrington, John Sherba *vns* Hank Dutt *va* Joan Jeanrenaud *vc*)
Nonesuch 7559-79242-2 Ⓕ
(62 minutes: DDD) **OO**

This is very much the sort of imaginative programming we've come to expect from this talented young American quartet. With an overall theme of war and persecution the disc opens with George Crumb's *Black Angels*, for electric string quartet. This work was inspired by the Vietnam War and bears two inscriptions to that effect – *in tempore belli* (in time of war) and 'Finished on Friday the 13th of March, 1970', and it's described by Crumb as 'a kind of parable on our troubled contemporary world'. The work is divided into three sections which represent the three stages of the voyage of the soul – fall from grace, spiritual annihilation and redemption. As with most of his works he calls on his instrumentalists to perform on a variety of instruments other than their own – here that ranges from gongs, maracas and crystal glasses to vocal sounds such as whistling, chanting and whispering. *Doom. A sigh* is the young Hungarian composer István Marta's disturbing portrait of a Romanian village as they desperately fight to retain their sense of identity in the face of dictatorship and persecution. Marta's atmospheric blend of electronic sound, string quartet and recorded folk-songs leave one with a powerful and moving impression. At first sight Tallis's *Spem in alium* may seem oddly out of place considering the overall theme of this disc, but as the insert-notes point out the text was probably taken from the story of Judith, in which King Nebuchadnezzar's general Holofernes besieged the Jewish fortress of Bethulia. Kronos's own arrangement of this 40-part motet (involving some multi-tracking) certainly makes a fascinating alternative to the original. A particularly fine account of Shostakovich's Eighth String Quartet (dedicated to the victims of fascism and war) brings this thought-provoking and imaginative recital to a close. Performances throughout are outstanding, and the recording first-class.

Kronos Quartet – 25 Years

Adams John's Book of Alleged Dances **Ali-Zade** Mugam Sayagi **Benshoof** Traveling Music. Song of Twenty Shadows **Crumb** Black Angels **Feldman** Piano Quintet[a] **Glass** String Quartets – No 2, 'Company'; No 3, 'Mishima'; No 4, 'Buczak'; No 5 **Golijov** The Dreams and Prayers of Isaac the Blind[b] **Górecki** String Quartets – No 1, Op 62, 'Already it is Dusk'; No 2, Op 64, 'Quasi una fantasia' **Gubaidulina** String Quartet No 4 **Pärt** Fratres. Psalom (arr Höfer). Summa. Missa Sillabica[c] **Phan** Tragedy at the Opera **Piazzolla** Five Tango Sensations[d]. Four, for Tango **Reich** Different Trains **Riley** Cadenza on the Night Plain. G Song. Salome Dances for Peace – Echoes of Primordial Time; Good Medicine Dance **Schnittke** String Quartets – No 2; No 4. Collected Songs Where Every Verse is Filled with Grief (arr Kronos) **Sculthorpe** String Quartets – No 8; No 11, 'Jaribu Dreaming'. From Ubirr[e] **Volans** String Quartet No 1, 'White Man Sleeps'
Kronos Quartet (David Harrington, John Sherba *vns* Hank Dutt *va* Joan Jeanrenaud *vc*) [c]**Ellen Hargis** *sop* [c]**Suzanne Elder** *contr* [c]**Neal Rogers** *ten* [c]**Paul Hillier** *bass* [b]**David Krakauer** *cl/bass, cl/basset hn* [e]**Michael Brosnan,** [e]**Mark Nolan** *didjeridoos* [d]**Astor Piazzolla** *bandoncón* [a]**Aki Takahashi** *pf*
Nonesuch ⑩ 7559-79504-2 Ⓜ
(653 minutes: ADD/DDD). Recorded 1973-98

The string quartet is both the most exclusive and the most approachable of small instrumental combinations. On the one hand it has hosted some of the most profound and ethereal repertory in Western music, while on the other it is peculiarly responsive to popularisation. Perhaps having a head-count that approximates the average pop group helps, and there is plenty of scope for projected 'personality'. But there is also something intriguing about a good piece for string quartet, a sense of being a privileged fly on the wall, eavesdropping on conversations that were only really meant to be shared among four – a sort of cerebral or spiritual voyeurism. The Kronos Quartet has always known how to make audio theatre out of chamber music, what with its numerous commissions, imaginative programmes, flexible playing style and an openness to world music that is particularly apparent in this majestic 25th anniversary collection. Kronos knows the meaning of quality, but also has the common touch. Nonesuch offers us a generous helping of reissues, supplemented by around two hours' worth of new material. So *Summa* (which is among the most sensual of Pärt's tintinnabulatory works) and the concise *Missa Sillabica* appear here for the first time. John Adams is represented by the up-tempo delights of *John's Book of Alleged Dances* and Steve Reich by his durable – and partly autobiographical – *Different Trains*. Taxing as this is, it is hard to imagine that Gubaidulina's compelling Fourth Quartet – which also calls for multiple quartets – would have been much easier to realise. But if you put on the first movement of Kevin Volans's *White Man Sleeps* and sample its closing pages, you hear what must surely have been a thematic prompt for *Different Trains* (Volans's piece dates from 1984, Reich's from 1988). The similarity is striking.

George Crumb's terrifying *Black Angels* is a sort of anti-Vietnam War protest in sound that anticipates Schnittke in its juxtaposition of the old (in this case Schubert's *Death and the Maiden* Quartet) and the new. Both Schnittke and Górecki suggest profound inner conflicts laid bare, though the specific manners of their personal expression are highly contrasted: those who are rested by Górecki's ubiquitous Third Symphony (reviewed under Górecki) should brace themselves for his chamber music. Kronos back-packs across city, desert or plain, sighing deeply with Astor Piazzolla (on bandoneón) for his *Five Tango Sensations* and toughening up for his more aggressive *Four, for Tango* (another first release). Turn then to Osvaldo Golijov and you confront the Jewish world of klezmer, with clarinettist David Krakauer spicing up *The Dreams and Prayers of Isaac the Blind*. Franghiz Ali-Zadeh conjures folk motives from Azerbaijan, and Peter Sculthorpe (in *Jabiru Dreaming*, Quartet No 8, *From Ubirr*) reinvents the music of the Aborigines (offered here for the first time on CD). P.Q. Phan's tragi-comic *Tragedy at the Opera* recalls a Vietnamese singer who died in the line of stage duty (trying to sing a female role) and among the Americans, Ken Benshoof gives us his accessible, mostly upbeat *Traveling Music* (the Kronos's first commission) and the extraordinarily moving elegy *Song of Twenty Shadows* – again a first release. Morton Feldman is represented by his slow-breathing, delicately textured Piano Quartet (with Aki Takahashi), Philip Glass by four surprisingly variegated Quartets (Nos 2-5) and Terry Riley by excerpts from *Salome Dances for Peace* (the most minimalistic music on the set), the neo-baroque *G Song* (Riley's first piece for Kronos) and the colourful *Cadenza on the Night Plain*. The last two are first releases. Nonesuch's presentation is a minor work of art in itself here and the documentation an informed easy read, although there is precious little to indicate what is – or what is not – a first release. You would be hard pressed to find a more friendly, or more attractive, *entrée* to the world of new music.

Smetana Quartet

SBT1074 **Dvořák** String Quartet No 12 in F, 'American', B179. Piano Quintet in A, B155[a]
Janáček String Quartet No 1, 'The Kreutzer Sonata'
SBT1075 **Dvořák** Terzetto in C, B148. String Quartet No 14 in A flat, B193 **Janáček** String Quartet No 2, 'Intimate Letters'
Smetana Quartet (Jiří Novák, Lubomir Kostecký *vns* Milan Skampa *va* Antonín Kohout *vc*)
[a]**Pavel Stěpán** *pf*
Testament ② SBT1074/5 Ⓕ
(oas: 79 and 77 minutes: ADD). Recorded 1965-66 ●

Listening to these discs tempts one to think that in the 1960s the Smetana was the Berlin Philharmonic of quartets – just as in the 1950s the Hollywoods might have been fancifully called the Philadelphia Orchestra of quartets. Much of the playing here is in a class of its own, only later equalled by the Borodin and Alban Berg Quartets in terms of finesse and ensemble. The Dvořák performances must be numbered among the very best now in the catalogue: their phrasing has none of the artificiality that marks some professional quartets (that is to say that a phrasing once rehearsed becomes, as it were, mechanically reproduced so that while the line rises and falls it doesn't genuinely breathe) and it is an enormous relief to hear genuine *pianissimo* tone and so natural and unforced an ensemble. There are numerous recordings of each of the Janáček Quartets but in terms of tonal finesse, perfection of ensemble and depth of feeling the present issues would be difficult to beat.

The String Quartet in 18th-Century England Ⓟ

Abel String Quartet in A, Op 8 No 5 **Marsh** Quartetto in B flat in imitation of the Stile of Haydn's Opera Prima **Shield** String Quartet in C minor, Op 3 No 6
Webbe Variations in A on 'Adeste Fideles'
S Wesley String Quartet in E flat
Salomon Quartet (Simon Standage, Micaela Comberti *vns* Trevor Jones *va* Jennifer Ward-Clarke *vc*)
Hyperion CDA66780 (69 minutes: DDD) Ⓕ
Recorded 1995 ●

For various reasons connected with the patterns of its social life, the string quartet was slow to become established in England. The work that opens this CD, by the German-born Abel, comes from the first set of quartets to be published in London (in 1769); it is an amiable piece, graceful enough, harmonically rather static and texturally unenterprising. The few Englishmen who ventured into the string quartet genre did rather better. William Shield's work, the sixth of a set published in 1782, begins with a passionate C minor gesture and has some echoes of Haydn both in the ingenuity of its humour and in its seriousness, though not in his technique nor his sureness of taste; but the *Adagio* is very remarkable, quite individual in the tone of its expression and reaching an extraordinarily imaginative climax in each half with a sort of free-flying violin passage, in its way breathtaking. The finale too is sombre in quite an original way. John Marsh (a lawyer and a landowner, though music was his passion), wrote his quartet 'in imitation of the Stile of Haydn's Opera Prima' in the 1780s: it is a very fluent, polished piece, close in manner to Haydn's Op 1 No 1, with a spirited 6/8 opening movement, two minuets (the second particularly delightful) with an appealing *Largo* of charm and warmth, between them, and a witty finale with some lively invention.

Samuel Webbe, too, used Haydn as his model – the slow movement of the *Emperor* Quartet – for his variations on *Adeste Fideles*: it is a beautiful, highly ingenious piece, harmonically rich, exquisitely crafted. But the most unexpected work here is certainly the Samuel Wesley Quartet, usually supposed to date from the very beginning of the 19th century but surely more likely, as Peter Holman says in his note, to be 20 years later – the energetic, leaping lines, the complex figuration, the abrupt gestures, the free textures: all this speaks of a later, post-classical era. It is a substantial and powerful piece, wholly individual in tone. The Salomon brings a good deal of fire to this piece, and indeed, once past the Abel, it plays this music with splendid conviction, as it amply merits. This CD is something of a revelation.

Duos

Americana

Chaplin (arr Ogermann) Smile **Foster** Jeanie with the light brown hair. Old folks at home (both arr Heifetz) **Gershwin** Short Story (arr Dushkin). Three Preludes. Porgy and Bess – Summertime; A woman is a sometime thing; My man's gone now; Bess, you is my woman now; It ain't necessarily so; Tempo di Blues (arr Heifetz) **Joplin** The Ragtime Dance. The Easy Winners (both arr Perlman) **Novacek** Four Rags **Ponce** (arr Heifetz) Estrellita **Traditional** (arr Heifetz) Deep River **Vieuxtemps** Souvenir d'Amérique, Op 17
Leila Josefowicz *vn* **John Novacek** *pf*
Philips 462 948-2PH (64 minutes: DDD) Ⓕ
Recorded 1999 **OO**

Here's a major virtuoso not yet in her mid-twenties simply letting her hair down. Josefowicz has been acclaimed in the Sibelius and Tchaikovsky concertos under Neville Marriner (Philips – nla) and she's played with John Novacek since she was eight. Their rapport is stunning. Josefowicz's magical technique is based on total control with occasional *glissandos* and extremely subtle near-blue notes.

Novacek's own *Four Rags*, close to the novelty piano idiom, are wonderful vehicles for the duo; Vieuxtemps' variations on 'Yankee Doodle' (*Souvenir d'Amérique*) are hilarious in a way which Gottschalk pioneered; and in Joplin's *Ragtime Dance* the composer's request for foot-stamping effects (1'58") is followed, and the parallel thirds (at 2'17") go wonderfully on the violin in Perlman's transcription.

Josefowicz's melodic playing in Ponce's *Estrellita* ('Mexican Serenade') is irresistibly seductive, but the climax of the CD comes with a free approach to the Heifetz arrangements of six magnificent songs from *Porgy and Bess*. These two know much more about jazz than Heifetz ever did, and the Josefowicz/Novacek interpretations belong to the tradition of Fitzgerald/Nelson Riddle or Miles Davis/Gil Evans. Every song comes across as an eloquent portrayal of its character's predicament – baleful bereavement in 'My man's gone now', casual cynicism in 'It ain't necessarily so', and so on.

'Americana' is a rapturous delight which Josefowicz fans, Gershwin fans, violin aficionados and many others cannot afford to miss. Fine recording, too. In short a fantastic talent and a hugely enjoyable anthology.

Cello Song

Bach Cantata No 156, Ich steh mit einem Fuss im Grabe – Sinfonia **Brahms** Five Lieder, Op 105 – Wie Melodien zieht es mir **Castelnuovo-Tedesco** Sea Murmurs, Op 24a **Chopin** Cello Sonata in G minor, Op 65 – Largo **Debussy** Beau soir **Delius** Hassan – Serenade **Dvořák** Seven Gipsy Melodies, B104 (Op 55) – Songs my Mother Taught Me
Elgar Romance, Op 62 **Grieg** Lyric Pieces, Book 3, Op 43 – To the Spring **Messiaen** Quatuor pour la fin du temps – Louange à l'Eternité de Jésus
Rachmaninov Romance in F minor **Schumann** Fünf Stücke im Volkston, Op 102 – No 2, Langsam
Scriabin Etudes in B flat minor, Op 8 No 11
Traditional The Star of the County Down
Villa-Lobos O Canto do capadócio
Julian Lloyd Webber *vc* **John Lenehan** *pf*
Philips 434 917-2PH (53 minutes: DDD) Ⓕ
Recorded 1992

As the title of this disc implies, all the pieces contained therein are rather in the same slowish-paced, lyrical vein, but their sequence has been cleverly chosen so that there is still plenty of variety to keep the listener's attention. Some of the items are original cello and piano pieces, others are skilful arrangements, and there is a good mixture of well known and unusual offerings. Elgar's bassoon *Romance* translates particularly well to the cello, as do the Brahms, Debussy and Dvořák songs, and only in the arrangement of Grieg's piano piece *To the Spring* does one feel that a cello is a little out of place. The Messiaen excerpt is the longest and the most profound item, and it exists quite happily as an entity away from the rest of the *Quatuor*. Throughout, Julian Lloyd Webber plays with exceptional sensitivity, sympathy and tonal beauty – it would be difficult to find better performances of this kind of repertoire anywhere on records of today or yesterday. John Lenehan gives good support, and Philips have provided a mellow, roomy recording.

Devil's Dance

Bazzini La ronde des lutins, Op 25 **Bolcom** Graceful Ghost **Brahms** Walpurgisnacht, Op 75 No 4 **Grieg** (arr Achron) Puck, Op 71 No 3 **Korngold** (arr Révay) Caprice fantastique, 'Wichtelmännchen' **Mendelssohn** Hexenlied, Op 8 No 8 **Morris** Young Frankenstein – A Transylvanian Lullaby **Paganini** (arr Schumann) Caprice No 13 in B flat **Saint-Saëns** (arr cpsr) Danse macabre, Op 40 **Sarasate** Concert Fantasy on Gounod's 'Faust' **Tartini** (arr Kreisler) Violin Sonata in G minor, 'Devil's Trill' **Williams** (arr cpsr) The Witches of Eastwick – The Devil's Dance **Ysaÿe** Solo Violin Sonata in A minor, Op 27 No 2 – first movement
Gil Shaham *vn* **Jonathan Feldman** *pf*
DG 463 483-2GH (69 minutes: DDD) Ⓕ
Recorded 1998-99 ●

According to the prominent red caution notice provided, one approaches the opening track on this CD at one's peril. But as it happens John Williams's title-piece, ingenious as it is, is less devilish than the closing excerpt from Ysaÿe's Solo Violin Sonata, Op 27 No 2, which, after a whiff of unaccompanied Bach, offers the *Dies irae* as a demonic *cantus firmus* (always clear) for Gil Shaham's dazzlingly fiendish decorations. Tartini's *Devil's Trill* Sonata (supposedly inspired in a dream by the Prince of Darkness himself), heard in Kreisler's arrangement, opens with a disarmingly mellow warmth. Shaham makes light of the once much-feared trills and here totally civilises the satanic influence. If you need to be petrified by this piece, you have to turn to Andrew Manze's recording. Nevertheless, overall this is a most engaging collection, imaginatively devised, played with panache, and given demonstration sound quality – not a scratch can be heard.

There are quite a few 'finds' too, notably Grieg's delicious 'Puck', a sparkling *scherzando*, and Korngold's impish *Wichtelmännchen*, with its quirky coda, while Mendelssohn's *Hexenlied* has a 'sprite'-ly charm (and taxes the pianist too, as any accomplished goblin should). Bazzini's *La ronde des lutins* remains one of the most hair-raising of all violinistic showpieces, and is taken here at a fair old lick, and with much aplomb, while William Bolcom's elegantly *Graceful Ghost* brings a wraith-like halcyon interlude. Here Jonathan Feldman's stylish 'raggery' is affectionately debonair. Saint-Saëns' *Danse macabre* works well enough as a violin solo, and Feldman makes a strong 'orchestral' contribution, using the composer's own piano transcription; indeed he is so good that one doesn't greatly miss the orchestra. And it was an excellent idea to include in the documentation the whole Cazalis poem which inspired this piece, with its whistling winter wind and lascivious skeletons.

Presumably this is intended as a crossover record, and it is a very good one. Paganini himself could not have presented this programme with more diabolically easy bravura, and certainly not with such a consistent sense of style.

Devil's Trill

Gluck Orfeo ed Euridice – Dance of the Blessed Spirits **Leclair** Sonatas for Violin and Continuo – D, Op 8 No 2; C minor, Op 5 No 6 **Tartini** Sonata for Violin and Continuo in G minor, 'Devil's Trill' **Vivaldi** (arr Respighi) Sonata for Violin and Continuo in D, Op 2 No 11
Yuval Yaron *vn* **Jeremy Denk** *pf*
Naim Audio NAIMCD018 (48 minutes: DDD) Ⓕ
Recorded 1996 ●●

This is truly beautiful violin playing, elegant in the opening *Larghetto* of Tartini's *The Devil's Trill* Sonata and with the truest intonation later on. The cadenza, too, is extremely brilliant, though never 'showy'. Both sonatas by the 18th-century dancer-turned-composer Jean Leclair find Yaron in fine fettle, with a winsome tone and tastefully controlled vibrato. Respighi's naughty-but-nice reworking of a sonata that Vivaldi dedicated to Frederick IV of Norway and Denmark features some delicious piano harmonies beneath the solo line, and you would be hard put to find a more eloquent voicing of the Gluck/Kreisler 'Mélodie'. So who, you may ask, *is* Yuval Yaron? Violin *aficionados* may already have encountered him, but the more general reader might like to know that he won First Prize at the 1975 Sibelius Competition in Helsinki, studied with Gingold and at Heifetz's masterclasses and is currently Professor of Violin at the Indiana University School of Music in Bloomington, where his excellent pianist Jeremy Denk also serves and where Naim's recordings were. The timing is stingy but, as already suggested, Yaron's playing is an absolute joy to behold.

Duos for Violin and Cello

Bach Two-Part Invention No 6 in E, BWV777 **Handel/Halvorsen** (arr Press) Passacaglia **Kodály** Duo, Op 7 **Ravel** Sonata for Violin and Cello
Kennedy *vn* **Lynn Harrell** *vc*
EMI CDC5 56963-2 (58 minutes: ADD) Ⓕ
Recorded 1999

Here's a brilliant expiation for crusty old curmudgeons who would tell you that Kennedy's musical priorities are rather to shock than to please. Kennedy plays into Lynn Harrell's hands as if the two men had once shared a single umbilical chord. Ravel's rarely heard Sonata for Violin and Cello finds them locked in earnest dialogue (as in the first movement) or sparring furiously (in the second), alternating sundry dramatic effects, such as slammed cello *pizzicatos* and lacerating bowed *fortissimos* (a Kennedy speciality). They also alternate harmonics (2'40" into the *Très vif* second movement), then bring a veiled brand of poetry to the slow movement (marked *Lent* and a sure recollection of the Piano Trio's *Passacaille*, composed some six years earlier). It's an amazing piece, mostly characteristic but with fleeting suggestions of various contemporaries. One imagines that Kennedy's interest in various indigenous musics fuels his enthusiasm for Kodály's earthy Op 7. You can almost see him chuckle at the tipsy folk-tune at 4'32" into the last movement – even more so when it makes a humorous return at 7'31" – and Harrell's playing mirrors the mood exactly. As to the Handel-Halvorsen *Passacaglia*, Kennedy and Harrell employ a very individual brand of fire – teasing, grappling, racing or duetting as if they were playing jazz. Wonderful fun and an urgent candidate for the Replay button, that's if you reach it before the Bach Two-part Invention has started. If it has, you'll end the listening session with a mood of sublime simplicity. You can't really go wrong, either way.

Espana!

Albéniz Suite española, Op 47 – Sevilla; Cádiz; Aragon; Castilla. Pavana capricho, Op 12. Iberia – Triana. Navarra **Falla** La vida breve – Danses espagnoles. El amor brujo – Ritual Fire Dance
Infante Danses andalouses **Lecuona** Malagueña
Katia and Marielle Labèque *pf*
Philips 438 938-2PH (59 minutes: DDD) Ⓕ
Recorded 1993

The Labèque sisters give us the right Iberian mixture of vigour, brilliance, shadows and languor, and seem to be thoroughly enjoying themselves in music that they know well. There is no more exciting keyboard performance of Falla's 'Ritual Fire Dance'. This is actually a transcription by Mario Bragiotti. Indeed, save for the *Danses Andalouses* by Manuel Infante, every piece here is a transcription and the Labèques themselves have had a hand in that of Lecuona's exquisitely sultry *Malagueña*, which includes quietly plucked strings at the two-minute mark. But no one would know that this music was not originally written for two pianos, for everything is idiomatic. Indeed, the transcription of Albéniz's *Suite española* and *Pavana capricho* is by the composer, while that of his 'Triana' (music that beautifully blends vivacity and delicacy) is by his friend Granados. The recording is intimate yet atmospheric.

Fantaisie for Flute and Harp

L Boulanger Nocturne **Caplet** Rêverie
Fauré Fantaisie, Op 79. Après un rêve, Op 7 No 1. Sicilienne, Op 78. Pièce **Piazzolla** Histoire du Tango
Ravel Pavane pour une infante défunte
Saint-Saëns Romance, Op 37 **Traditional** El diablo suelto. La partida. Spanish Love Song (trans Galway). Urpila. Bailecito de procesión **Villa-Lobos** Modinha. Bachianas Brasileiras No 5
Anna Noakes *fl* **Gillian Tingay** *hp*
ASV White Line CDWHL2101 (76 minutes: DDD) Ⓜ
Recorded 1996

Here is a lightweight but entertaining collection, which happily juxtaposes French insouciance with Latin American sparkle. The pair of South American folksongs which opens the programme are real lollipops; then comes some lilting Villa-Lobos; first the sultry rhythmic *Modinha*, nudged with a nice rhythmic subtlety, and then the famous (soprano/cello) *Bachianas Brasileiras* No 5, which sounds seductive enough on the flute. The disc includes flowing, coolly beautiful Fauré and a gentle, haunting *Nocturne* by Lili Boulanger (meltingly phrased by Anna Noakes), followed by a romantic *morceau* by Saint-Saëns. One of the most enticing later pieces is the chimerical *Rêverie* of André Caplet and the recital ends with a highly individual and immediately arresting suite of four strongly flavoured miniatures by Astor Piazzolla called *Histoire du Tango*, bewitching in their combination of Latin rhythmic inflexions with a smoky Parisian night-club atmosphere. They are presented with much *élan* and sparkle and given added lift by various uninhibited percussive thwacks from both players. Although the harp sounds somewhat recessed, it always provides a glowing web of sound.

Fantasías Mediterráneas – Spanish Music for Clarinet and Piano

Brotons Sonata, Op 64 **C Cano** Vigilias
Guinjoan Fantasía **J Menéndez** Introducción, Andante y Danza. Contemplación
Montsalvatge Self-Paráfrasis
A Romero Fantasía, sobre temas de la ópera 'Lucrecia de Borgia' de Donizetti
Yuste Estudio melódico
Joan Enric Lluna *cl* **Jan Gruithuyzen** *pf*
Clarinet Classics CC0017 (72 minutes: DDD) Ⓕ
Recorded 1997

According to the artist featured here (the principal clarinet of the Bournemouth Sinfonietta), the clarinet is, after the guitar, one of the most popular instruments in Spain – largely as a result of the numerous wind bands, whose tradition goes back well over a century. Little of the extensive Spanish solo repertoire for the instrument has found its way outside the country, however; and this conspectus of a century-and-a-half of composers for it will be practically virgin territory for all but the best-informed.

The three earliest figures represented here were all primarily virtuosos who held posts in leading Spanish orchestras and, in two of the cases, as teachers at the Madrid Conservatory. The opening *Fantasía* by Antonio Romero is one of those old-fashioned competition or audition test-pieces which makes every kind of terrifying demand on a player – however, it is also one which Lluna sails through effortlessly and with a display of total assurance, also retaining quality in the highest register.

Born half a century and more later, Miguel Yuste and Julián Menéndez both produced music of more intrinsic value, although the latter's *Introducción, Andante y Danza* (the last section of which shows a nice turn of fantasy) again puts the emphasis on technical adroitness, but now with a command of colour: his *Contemplación* is a charming pastoral, and

Yuste's *Estudio melódico* has a long-breathed romantic lyricism. After these, Montsalvatge's dissonant grotesqueries in a brief paraphrase of a section of his 1958 Partita come like an invigorating splash of cold water, preparing the ground for the rhythmically vital, freely dodecaphonic *Fantasía* by the now 68-year-old Joan Guinjoan (which puts both players on their mettle) and for two major works on the disc by two much younger composers.

César Cano's (b.1960) *Vigilias* utilises some unorthodox instrumental techniques (not all of which are particularly rewarding musically) and presents formidable difficulties, which Lluna (the work's dedicatee) and his excellent pianist seem to take in their stride; but most impressive of all is the 1986 two-movement Sonata by Salvador Brotons (b.1959, once a pupil of Montsalvatge), an imaginative and mainly lyrical work with a vivacious angular finale – a sonata that richly deserves to be taken into virtuoso players' repertoire.

Impressions d'enfance

Bartók Violin Sonata No 2, Sz76
Enescu Impressions d'enfance, Op 28
Schulhoff Violin Sonata No 2
Plakidis Two Grasshopper Dances
Gidon Kremer *vn* **Oleg Maisenberg** *pf*
Teldec 0630-13597-2 (63 minutes: DDD) Ⓕ
Recorded 1996 ●●

This is a fabulous recital, the sort that suggests wet ink on the page and performances born more of impulse than of duty. The Enescu sequence is pure delight, from the gipsy-like cadences of the unaccompanied 'Minstrel' that opens the suite, through the virtual-reality chirruping of 'The bird in the cage and the cuckoo on the wall', to the ingenious 'linking' miniatures – half a minute apiece or less – that etch a cricket and 'Wind in the chimney'. *Impressions d'enfance* (1940) ends with an extraordinarily graphic 'Sunrise'. The idiom straddles late Debussy and mature Bartók, though Enescu's characteristically Romanian flavouring soon gives the game away. Kremer's performances are agile, lean and impetuous, with copious slides and numerous flushes of warmth.

Furthermore, he carries the camp-fire element into the Bartók, rhapsodising rapturously over the final climax and effecting a magical *diminuendo* towards the sonata's close. Maisenberg commands a multi-shaded tonal palette and it's a delight to encounter a work that can be – in unsympathetic hands – a listening trial transformed into a sort of cerebral Hungarian rhapsody. Again, agility is a keyword.

Which leaves Ervín Schulhoff's outspoken Second Violin Sonata, a product of 1927, touched by Hindemith's influence in the first movement, and by heated emotions in the second. Kremer and Maisenberg give it showcase treatment and the recording is, as elsewhere, first-rate. The encore is unaccompanied, a pair of folky, heavily double-stopped *Grasshopper Dances* by Peteris Plakidis.

Kremerata Musica

Berg Four Pieces, Op 5[ae]. Chamber Concerto – Adagio (arr cpsr)[abe] **Mahler** Quartet in A minor[bcde] **Schoenberg** Piece in D minor[be]. String Trio, Op 45[bcd]. Phantasy, Op 47[be] **Webern** Two Pieces for Cello and Piano[de]. Four Pieces, Op 7[bc]. Three Little Pieces, Op 11[de]. Cello Sonata[de]
[a]**Sabine Meyer** *cl* [b]**Gidon Kremer** *vn* [c]**Veronika Hagen** *va* [d]**Clemens Hagen** *vc* [e]**Oleg Maisenberg** *pf*
DG 447 112-2GH (76 minutes: DDD) Ⓕ
Recorded 1994

This is a Second Viennese School disc that revels in extremes: for example, there could hardly be a greater contrast than that between Schoenberg's very early, very anodyne piece for violin and piano (it could easily be mistaken for Schubert at his least poetic) and his last instrumental work, the forceful, economical *Phantasy*. Even so, the playing throughout is so refined and expressive that the later music's eroded but still potent links with the romantic tradition are unmistakable. The result is fascinating, and one of the best releases of its kind for some years. Mahler's honorary membership of the Schoenberg school – as early patron and model – is acknowledged in his own youthful movement for piano quartet, an evocative mixture of Brahmsian and Wagnerian elements that showed the way forward with exemplary clarity. As for Schoenberg's pupils, Webern's rapid progress from languid late romanticism (in the two cello pieces of 1899) to aphoristic expressionism is powerfully displayed, the close positioning of the cello in the Op 11 Pieces adding to the larger-than-life impression of these performances. Sabine Meyer's clarinet is also closely recorded in the Berg pieces, but music so rich in striking incident can stand such immediacy, as can Berg's arrangement of the *Chamber Concerto*'s slow movement for clarinet, violin and piano. Nevertheless, the finest music-making of all is heard in Schoenberg's Trio, an account in which technical mastery and expressive fantasy combine to brilliant effect.

Los bandidos

Bach Viola da gamba Sonata No 3 in G minor, BWV1029 **Lindberg** Los bandidos **Mussorgsky** Pictures at an Exhibition **Schumann** Drei Fantasiestücke, Op 73 **Stravinsky** The Firebird – Infernal dance of King Kashchei; Lullaby; Finale (all arr Lindberg)
Christian Lindberg *tbn* **Roland Pöntinen** *pf*
BIS CD988 (69 minutes: DDD) Ⓕ
Recorded 1998 ●

As Christian Lindberg continues his mischievous, iconoclastic, wild man act with his partner in crime Roland Pöntinen, we soon realise that they are actually pussy-cats, not bandits. How could a bandit caress Bach's G minor Viola da gamba Sonata with such controlled elegance and purring refinement, or turn a phrase with such seamless and conventional poise in Schumann's *Fantasiestücke* while shooting from the hip? So, we have a 1'51" piece by Lindberg called *Los bandidos*, referred to in a heavy-humoured note, but after these red herrings, enter two clean-shaven and responsible artists seriously redefining the parameters of trombone and piano chamber music. Clearly, either Lindberg or BIS feels that such badinage is going to sell more records (and they may well be right), but this great trombonist need make no apologies for playing arrangements in his quest for musical challenges beyond the confines of original trombone repertoire.

As it happens, the transcription of Mussorgsky's *Pictures at an Exhibition* does not quite convince; it has attracted transcribers galore, and none more influential to brass players than Elgar Howarth's brass ensemble version of 1977. This is indeed a tour de force, although as much for Lindberg's battling bravely against its unidiomatic gait as anything. He may perform extraordinary feats of dexterity in 'Goldenberg and Schmuyle' – and the characterisation is compelling – but one yearns for an 'orchestral' palette, which perhaps an organ could have given him? Anyway, a solo work cannot really be summoned from this score any more than a saxophone concerto can from Mahler's Fifth. The best transcriptions of *Pictures* are when the arranger exploits the relationship between melodic flair and evocative imagery through detailed colouring. It doesn't happen here with the piano harnessed to the relatively limited atonal possibilities of the trombone: a huge void without a symphonic canvas. Maybe it works wonderfully live, with Lindberg's all-singing all-dancing communicative flair. The rest of the programme reveals his remarkably natural feeling for line, rare in many brass soloists. The articulation and lip trills in the Bach are exquisite; there's no shortage of good taste here, or in the Schumann, though he could vary his vibrato rather more on the long notes.

The *Firebird* transcription is thrilling. A disc of two halves then, but as always with this duo something outstanding and memorable emerges.

Emmanuel Pahud

Paris French Flute Sonatas **Dutilleux** Sonatine
Ibert Jeux. Aria **Jolivet** Chant de Linos
Messiaen Le merle noir **Milhaud** Sonatina for Flute and Piano, Op 76 **Poulenc** Flute Sonata
Sancan Sonatine
Emmanuel Pahud *fl* **Eric Le Sage** *pf*
EMI CDC5 56488-2 (66 minutes: DDD) Ⓕ
Recorded 1997

Examinations are usually viewed with aversion and some suspicion, but the Paris Conservatoire's custom of commissioning new works for its final examinations has valuably enriched the repertoire for wind instruments: three of the works on this disc – the *Sonatinas* (of 1943 and 1946 respectively) of the exact contemporaries Dutilleux and Sancan, and Messiaen's *Le merle noir* – owe their origin to these competitive exams. By their nature they lay stress on technical virtuosity, as indeed do nearly all the works here, which though differing widely in idiom share a certain Gallic style recognisable by its 'clarity, refinement and lightness of touch', as the insert-note puts it. These qualities are also characteristic of the playing of the Swiss-born Emmanuel Pahud, Principal Flute of the Berlin Philharmonic, who has a lighter tone than some of his distinguished predecessors. All the items here have been recorded before, however. Excellent partnered by Eric Le Sage, Pahud's brilliant and sensitive performances are outstanding. Exhilaratingly skittish in the brief *scherzando* finale of the Sancan and that of the Poulenc, intense in the Jolivet, mysteriously atmospheric in the first movement of the Dutilleux (a work undervalued by its composer), tender in the Ibert *Aria* and powerfully athletic at the end of the Messiaen, this disc is a winner.

Pastoral

Bax Clarinet Sonata[a] **Bliss** Pastoral (posth)[a]. Two Nursery Rhymes[b] **Ireland** Fantasy-Sonata in E flat[a]
Stanford Clarinet Sonata, Op 129[a]
Vaughan Williams Six Studies in English folk song[a]. Three Vocalises for Soprano Voice and Clarinet[b]
Emma Johnson *cl* [b]**Judith Howarth** *sop*
[a]**Malcolm Martineau** *pf*
ASV CDDCA891 (74 minutes: DDD) Ⓕ

A lovely programme, radiantly performed and most judiciously chosen. Things get under way in fine style with John Ireland's marvellous *Fantasy-Sonata*: beautifully written, passionately argued and encompassing (for Ireland) a wide range of moods; it's certainly a work that shows this underrated figure at the height of his powers. The Clarinet Sonata by Ireland's teacher, Stanford, is one of that composer's most successful works: formally elegant and most idiomatically laid out, it boasts a central *Adagio* (entitled 'Caoine' – an Irish lament) of considerable eloquence. Johnson is a gloriously mellifluous exponent in both Vaughan Williams's *Six Studies* and the Bax Sonata, and in the first movement of the latter she manages to convey a slumbering mystery that is somehow almost orchestral in its imaginative scope. Judith Howarth joins Johnson for the haunting *Three Vocalises* (one of Vaughan Williams's very last utterances from his final year) and makes an equally agile showing in Bliss's delightful *Two Nursery Rhymes* and touching *Pastoral*. A real pleasure, then, from start to finish and Malcolm Martineau proffers superb accompaniments.

Portes Ouvertes –
The 20th-Century Cello, Volume 3

Britten Cello Sonata, Op 65[a]. Tema-Sacher
Debussy Cello Sonata in D minor[a] **Dutilleux** Trois Strophes sur le nom de Sacher **Reger** Suite in A minor, Op 131c No 3 **Webern** Three Little Pieces, Op 11[a]
Matt Haimovitz *vc* [a]**Philippe Cassard** *pf*
DG 457 584-2GH (64 minutes: DDD) Ⓕ
Recorded 1996

This recital of 20th-century cello compositions sustains the thesis that extreme contrast, not merely variety, has been the spice of

20th-century musical life. To juxtapose two works from 1914, Reger's Third Suite and Webern's *Three Little Pieces*, the former expansive and retrospective, the latter aphoristic and reaching nervously into an unknowable future, makes the point with admirable immediacy. The rest of the music here is more mainstream, the Britten Sonata showing that there was as much mileage left in the old classical genres in 1960 as Debussy had found in his Sonata more than 40 years before. With these works, of course, Haimovitz is competing against a long series of distinguished predecessors on disc, and his partnership with Cassard can't match their empathy in the Britten, or – it goes without saying – of Rostropovich and Britten himself in both sonatas. The recording as such is at its best in the unaccompanied works, its closeness and resonance reinforcing the powerful musical profile of Dutilleux's elegant yet forceful *Strophes*, and helping to ensure that Reger does not seriously outstay his welcome. In Webern, Debussy and Britten the piano sound has an abrasive aspect to it, as if the object were to underline the incompatibility of two such different instruments. But the playing is technically first-rate, and should certainly open doors (why the French title?) to anyone exploring this repertory for the first time.

Recital

Abbott Alla caccia **Beethoven** Horn Sonata in F, Op 17 **Damase** Pavane variée. Berceuse, Op 19 **Koechlin** Horn Sonata, Op 70 **Hindemith** Horn Sonata **Schumann** Adagio and Allegro in A flat, Op 70 **F Strauss** Nocturno, Op 7

David Pyatt *hn* **Martin Jones** *pf*

Erato 3984-21632-2 (66 minutes: DDD) Ⓕ

Recorded 1996

Beethoven's Horn Sonata – in its day successfully premièred by the famous Bohemian virtuoso and composer, Punto – is nevertheless written rather clumsily for the horn (the composer suggested the cello as a viable alternative), and even Dennis Brain had problems with it. David Pyatt – *Gramophone*'s Young Artist of the Year in 1996 – sails off into the work with aplomb and gives it one of the finest performances on or off record. He makes it seem to sit easily on the instrument and provides just the right kind of timbre and buoyant lyrical flow – indeed it sounds like a masterpiece, which it very nearly is. He is helped by a first-rate partnership with Martin Jones and an excellently balanced recording.

The second piece here is an attractive novelty by Franz Strauss, the father of Richard, and another famous player who advised Wagner on the format of Siegfried's horn call. Koechlin's Sonata, more fluent than Beethoven's, has a rather fine *Andante très tranquille*, and another Frenchman, Jean-Michel Damase, provides two short but memorable occasional pieces. The Hindemith Sonata is wayward: it never seems quite sure where it is progressing harmonically, but Pyatt and Jones are so naturally and spontaneously attuned to the work that it becomes readily assimilable. Allan Abbott's *Alla caccia* is an endearing lollipop while Schumann's *Adagio and Allegro* here emerges flowing almost as easily as if it had been written by Mozart – who knew just what a horn could manage without sounding effortful. Altogether this is a splendid recital that will give much pleasure to any lover of this intractable but highly rewarding instrument.

Recital 2000

Crumb Four Nocturnes **Prokofiev** Violin Sonata No 2 in D, Op 94a **Respighi** Violin Sonata in B minor **Webern** Four Pieces, Op 7

Anne-Sophie Mutter *vn* **Lambert Orkis** *pf*

DG 469 503-2GH (63 minutes: DDD) Ⓕ

Recorded live in 2000

This is a live recording, made at a pair of concerts in May, and 'live' is undoubtedly the word for it. All the performances have an improvisatory quality, interpretative decisions seemingly made before your very ears. At the beginning of the Prokofiev it is as though Mutter and Orkis, realising that the audience in the Beethovensaal are already uncommonly silent and attentive, had decided after a quick glance at each other to begin the Sonata almost confidingly, with quiet tenderness and muted colour. Once or twice they take risks: the third and most epigrammatic of the Webern pieces is played with a mere thread of tone; in the hall it must have approached the limits of audibility. But this approach powerfully distils the intimate but intense emotions of these pieces; there is something close to pain in the second of them.

Once in a while the risks show. Not long after the opening of the Prokofiev there is an abrupt, stabbed accent that you suspect Mutter would have had second thoughts about in a studio recording, and an equally sudden expressive scoop in the slow movement – hauntingly poignant as she phrases and colours it – robs her intonation of its purity for a moment. There are similar but less hazardous extremes in the big gestures and expansive palette of the Respighi; fewer in George Crumb's evocative, post-Bartókian *Nocturnes*, with their striking use of plucked, brushed or drummed piano strings. Throughout the recital Mutter's playing is nervously intense, emotionally searching, and you are bound to refer this to the fact that she dedicates the disc to the memory of her husband, who died five years ago. It is vulnerable music-making, not always comfortable, but deeply expressive and often moving. The recording is spacious, the audience hushed.

Romanze – The Romantic Viola

Bridge Allegro appassionato, H82. Pensiero, H53a **Bruch** Romance, Op 85 **Glazunov** Elégie in G minor, Op 44 **Glinka** Viola Sonata – Allegro moderato; Larghetto ma non troppo (Andante) **Kalliwoda** Nocturnes, Op 186 – Larghetto; Allegretto, ma un poco vivo; Allegro moderato **Schumann** Märchenbilder, Op 113

Yuko Inoue *va* **Kathron Sturrock** *pf*

Black Box BBM1034 (70 minutes: DDD) Ⓕ

Recorded 1999

An introductory note from the Japanese-born, England-domiciled violist, Yuko Inoue, explains that this disc was timed to commemorate the 20th anniversary of her Tokyo recital début. She also salutes Kathron Sturrock, her closely attuned keyboard partner as well as the writer of exemplary *multum in parvo* booklet-notes.

The programme is predominantly inspired by the viola's special gift of nostalgic, romantic reverie, and it makes ideal late-night fireside listening. It would certainly be hard to find any more heart-easing valedictory lullaby than the last of Schumann's four *Märchenbilder*, written three years before his own breakdown. Companion pieces by Glazunov and Bruch are less memorable, though the latter's *Romanze* would no doubt better justify its length in its original, orchestrally accompanied version. Twilight yields to sunshine in three irresistible miniatures by Kalliwoda. And for the more musicologically minded, the recital offers the intriguing comparison of Glinka and Frank Bridge when both were in their twenties. Glinka, surely wisely, abandoned his classically derivative Viola Sonata – its two movements are played here as completed by the Russian violinist Borisovsky. But the searchingly introspective *Allegro appassionato* and *Pensiero* that Bridge (himself a fine violist) wrote for Lionel Tertis are truly prophetic little masterpieces.

The playing throughout is plainly an unlaboured labour of love, warmed the more (with only a second or two's loss of textural clarity) by the mellow resonance of the recording venue at Potton Hall in Suffolk.

Souvenirs

Bach Orchestral Suite No 3, BWV1068 – Air (arr Windsperger) **Debussy** Beau soir (arr Heifetz) **Dvořák** Humoresque in G flat, B187 No 7 (arr Wilhelmj). Four Romantic Pieces, B150 **Ibert** Histoires – Le petit âne blanc **Kreisler** Caprice viennois, Op 2. Schön Rosmarin. Tambourin chinois, Op 3 **Massenet** Thaïs – Méditation (arr Marsick) **Rachmaninov** Two Morceaux de salon, Op 6 **Sarasate** Zigeunerweisen, Op 20 **Schubert** Ave Maria, D839 (arr Wilhelmj/Heifetz) **Stravinsky** Duo concertant – Dithyrambe **Szymanowski** Nocturne and Tarantella, Op 28

Kyung-Wha Chung *vn* **Itamar Golan** *pf*

EMI CDC5 56827-2 (77 minutes: DDD) Ⓕ

Recorded 1998

Chung dispatches her 19 souvenirs with endearing candour and a refreshing lack of affectation. Dvořák's *Humoresque* is served in Wilhemj's arrangement, which here sounds a good deal more capricious than the more familiar – and sweeter – Kreisler version (more like Dvořák's solo piano original, too). The *Four Romantic Pieces* are intimate and lightly brushed, though Chung sounds perhaps a little impatient with the last piece (a rapt *Larghetto*). Szymanowski's fragrant *Nocturne* sings to a shimmering accompaniment, recalling Roxana's exotic vocal lines in *King Roger*, though there's an upbeat, quasi-Spanish central section and a highly flammable *Tarantella* to follow that puts the excellent Itamar Golan through his paces. Stravinsky is represented by the wistful 'Dithyrambe' from his *Duo concertant*, played with an appropriate sense of stillness, and Bach by an expressive account of the ubiquitous 'Air' from the Third Orchestral Suite. The Kreisler group is memorable more for its wit than its warmth, and while Chung bows a smooth line in the Wilhelmj-Heifetz *Ave Maria* re-hash, Golan's rippling arpeggios are a little too prominent and the coda is surely one of the most tasteless moments in the violinist's 'encore' repertory.

It's nice to have Rachmaninov's Op 6 pieces, the first sounding like a near-relation of Schumann's D minor Piano Trio, the second – a racy 'Hungarian Dance' – performed here with genuine swagger. Chung's tone suddenly thins at 2'17" into the *Thaïs* 'Méditation' (a colouristic effect?); *Beau soir* is suitably smoky, *Le petit âne blanc* suavely charming and Golan's perky playing 4'06" into *Zigeunerweisen* confirms that he is no 'mere' accompanist. Chung herself makes an elegant gipsy fiddler, though when it comes to left-hand *pizzicatos*, she's no Vengerov. With excellent sound and a generous playing time, this disc makes for a relaxing – and at times extremely rewarding – listening experience.

Virtuoso Music for Trumpet

Arban Variations on a theme from Bellini's 'Norma'[a]. Variations on a Tyrolean Theme[a] **W Brandt** Concert Piece No 2 **Falla** La vida breve – Danse espagnole[b] **Fauré** Le réveil[b] **Paganini** Caprice in E flat, Op 1 No 17[b]. Moto perpetuo in C, Op 11[b] **Saint-Saëns** Le carnaval des animaux – The swan[b] **Sarasate** Zigeunerweisen, Op 20[c] **Tchaikovsky** Valse-scherzo in C, Op 34[b] **Waxman** Carmen Fantasia[a]

Sergei Nakariakov *tpt* **Alexander Markovich** *pf*

Teldec 4509-94554-2 (59 minutes: DDD) Ⓕ

Items marked [a] arr Markovich, [b]Nakariakov, [c]Dokshitzer. Recorded 1994 ●

Sergei Nakariakov is an extraordinary talent. It is one thing to be able to play the violin at the age of 17 with the technical aplomb of one's elders but a brass instrument – on a purely physical level – requires a strength and maturity which can be accelerated only so fast. His prowess as a trumpeter lies not only in the sphere of technical wizardry, which he has in super-abundance, but in a security of tone and interpretational vision: the subtle tuning in this selection of mainly transcribed violin pieces and the gypsy-ish *portamento*s are astute and accomplished. The Russian-ness of his playing is fascinating; he has that intensity of tone that Westerners find so hard to emulate without sounding corny or chastened. Nakariakov has a focused but fat, epic sound (though no doubt it will get even more wholesome with age) and a total security and command in all registers. His technique is particularly admirable in the lower reaches where he seems rarely to need the air at his disposal to progress through phrases. Nakariakov's slow playing is fluid, especially in *Le réveil*.

Virtuoso Works for Violin and Piano

Bazzini La ronde des lutins, Op 25 **Bloch** Baal shem – Nigun **Kreisler** Schön Rosmarin. Tambourin chinois. Caprice viennois **Messiaen** Thème et Variations **Paganini** I palpiti, Op 13 **Sarasate** Caprice basque, Op 24 **Tchaikovsky** Souvenir d'un lieu cher, Op 42 – No 2, Scherzo in C minor; No 3, Mélodie in E flat **Wieniawski** Polonaise No 1 in D, Op 4. Légende, Op 17

Maxim Vengerov *vn* **Itamar Golan** *pf*

Teldec 9031-77351-2 (67 minutes: DDD) Ⓜ

Recorded 1993

Maxim Vengerov is such a masterful musician that everything he touches turns to gold. Firstly, his intonation is impeccable. The purity and steadiness of Paganini's *I palpiti* is such that one never has the impression of his being under any strain. The double-stopping episodes in Wieniawski's *Légende* appear to come as naturally to him as single notes. He captures the mawkish Slavonic melancholy with real intensity. In the Kreisler selection Vengerov is gentle and generous-spirited, charmingly pure in *Schön Rosmarin* and idiomatic for the tongue-in-cheek *Tambourin chinois*. The Bazzini has terrific attack, though it might have been more impish. The piece is undeniably inconsequential, but one is left gawping at the phenomenal accuracy and confidence of the left-hand *pizzicato* section at the end. In conclusion it must be said that rarely if ever does one hear the Tchaikovsky *Mélodie* played with more eloquence or refined tone colour.

Miscellaneous Chamber Groups

Cello World

Beethoven Andante con Variazioni, WoO44 No 2 **Schumann** Violin Sonata No 3, WoO27 – Intermezzo. **Fauré** Morceau de concours **Léonard** L'âne et l'ânier, Op 61 No 4 **Dvořák** Romantic Piece, B150 No 4 **Seiber** Dance Suite (all arr Isserlis) **Debussy** Nocturne et Scherzo **Berlioz** La captive, Op 12 **Saint-Saëns** Le carnaval des animaux – The Swan **Villa-Lobos** O Canto do Cisne Negro **Martinů** Duo **Rachmaninov** Lied **Scriabin** Romance **Popper** Dance of the Elves, Op 39 **J Isserlis** Souvenir russe **Tavener** The Child Lived **Tsintsadze** Miniatures – Chonguri **Vine** Inner World

Steven Isserlis *vc* **Dame Felicity Lott** *sop* **Maggie Cole** *hpd* **Thomas Adès, Michael Tilson Thomas, Dudley Moore** *pfs*

RCA Red Seal 09026 68928-2 (74 minutes: DDD) Ⓕ

Recorded 1997

As one might expect from so characterful an artist as Steven Isserlis, this is a cello recital with a difference, attractive in a delightfully offbeat way. The last and longest item, *Inner World* by the Australian Carl Vine, for amplified cello with electronic support, could easily become a cult piece. Starting like a cadenza for some romantic cello concerto, it grows ever more elaborate, always tonal and lyrical, with the soloist in duet with himself at times, culminating in a wild, exciting coda. You might regard that as the most controversial item, but for a very wide audience it could be a winner. Otherwise, there are only two regular cello showpieces, Saint-Saëns's 'The Swan' exquisitely done with a final whispered half-tone (in a recording evidently taken from the television series with Michael Tilson Thomas and Dudley Moore) and Popper's *Dance of the Elves*, as flamboyant as you will ever hear it. It may seem gimmicky that the opening item, the Beethoven Variations, transcribed from a Sonatina for mandolin and piano (1796), should here have anachronistic harpsichord accompaniment. Yet as a performance it certainly works, with exhilarating pointing of the final syncopated variation. Most of Isserlis's transcriptions are from violin originals, including the comic Léonard piece, full of ever more exaggerated hee-haws, set against the carter's song in the middle. The Fauré *Morceau de concours* is an exception, transcribed from a flute piece.

In all those items Thomas Adès is an inspired accompanist, specially relishing the witty 1920s parodies in Mátyás Seiber's *Dance Suite*, including one delectable *glissando* near the end. The Cuban cross-rhythms of the jolly pizzicato piece by the Georgian, Sulkhan Tsintsadze, are also wittily pointed by both artists. Other oddities include the jolly little Martinů *Duo* (with Isserlis taking both parts), and the unlikely *Nocturne et Scherzo*, in fact a little waltz, which Debussy wrote in an anonymous style in Russia in 1882. It is good too to have Isserlis's tribute to his grandfather, the pianist Julius Isserlis, in a nostalgic folk-based Russian piece. The two items with Felicity Lott bring extra freshness and beauty, not just the Berlioz song but the Tavener piece with accompaniment for cello alone. With first-rate sound this is going to give great pleasure to Isserlis's many admirers.

Journey to the Amazon

L Almeida Historia do Luar[a] **Barrios** Waltz, Op 8 No 4. Julia Florida **Brouwer** Canción de cuna, 'Berceuse'[a] (arr Grenet) **Canonico** Aire de Joropo[a] (arr Lauro/Diaz) **Lauro** Seis por derecho[a]. El marabino. Valses venezolanos – No 3, Natalia[a] **Montaña** Porro[a] **Savio** Batucada[a] **Thiago de Mello** A Hug for Pixingha[a]. Chants for the Chief[ab] – No 1, A Chamada dos ventos/Canção Nocturna; No 2, Uirapurú do Amazonas (both arr cpsr). Lago de Janaucá. A Hug for Tiberio[a]. Cavaleiro sem Armadura[ab] (arr Wolff) **Vianna** Cochichando[a] (arr Barbosa-Lima)

Sharon Isbin *gtr* with [a]**Gaudencio Thiago de Mello** *perc* [b]**Paul Winter** *sax*

Teldec 0630-19899-2 (55 minutes: DDD) Ⓕ

Recorded 1997

No one is currently doing more to free the guitar from its rent-a-programme image than Sharon Isbin. She is not South American, nor does the Amazon flow through Cuba, Colombia, Venezuela or Paraguay, but none of this matters in the least. Others before her have hitched rides with specialists in particular areas and sounded like uncomfortable passengers, but Isbin has loved and felt this music for over a quarter of a century and in the company of

Thiago de Mello and Paul Winter is entirely at home. One might fear the addition of assorted percussive sounds and 'rain-forest' noises to be intrusive, especially in the familiar items, but they are atmospherically enhancing, handled with great discretion (delightfully in Grenet's arrangement of Brouwer's *Canción de cuna*) and often rhythmically uplifting. Lauro's setting of the traditional *Seis por derecho* has never sounded more full of vitality. The guitar has a wide range of tone colour, which Isbin exploits with skill and taste in traversing the gamut from tenderness to joyously rhythmic energy. The excellent annotation resides in a concertina-form booklet, which is user-friendly in that respect, but whose printing in white on a 'rain-forest' background is not equally so. Recording is beautifully clear and well balanced. Waste no time in getting your hands on this disc.

Mnemosyne

Anonymous Alleluia nativitatis. Eagle Dance. Fayrfax Africanus. Novus novus. Russian Psalm
Athenaeus Delphic Paean **Billings** When Jesus Wept
Brumel Agnus Dei **Dufay** Gloria **Garbarek** Loiterando. Strophe and Counter-Strophe
Guillaume le Rouge Se je fayz dueil
Hildegard of Bingen O ignis Spiritus Paracliti
Mesomedes Hymn to the Sun **Tallis** O Lord, in Thee is all my trust **Tormis** Estonian Lullaby
Traditional Mascarades. Quechua Song. Remember me, my dear (all arr Hilliard Ensemble)
Jan Garbarek *saxes* **The Hilliard Ensemble**
ECM New Series ② 465 122-2 (105 minutes: DDD) Ⓕ
Texts and translations included. Recorded 1998

'A sign we are, inexplicable without pain… .' The words are by the 19th-century German poet Friedrich Hölderlin, taken from *Mnemosyne*, one of the cryptic hymns that he wrote before descending into madness. ECM publishes the entire first strophe as a sort of legend, and the reference is telling. 'Mnemosyne' was the mother of the muses, and the word also means 'memory'. For Hölderlin, song was an 'abandoned, flowing nature', a description that fits this album beautifully. Memory, ecstasy, pain, joy, reconciliation: all are, at one time or another, signalled in the present programme.

Garbarek spices the English 13th-century *Alleluia nativitatis* that opens the second disc with some unexpectedly Eastern-sounding modulations. The *Delphic Paean* that follows dives headlong among some absorbing dissonances, whereas Garbarek's own *Strophe and Counter-Strophe* enjoys a more sophisticated harmonic climate. Add Basque folk-song fragments warmed by the breathy aural contours of Garbarek's saxophone, and you have a characteristic sampling of a sequence that lasts, in total, for one-and-three-quarter hours. Both discs feature twilit Estonian lullabies (placed third on disc 1, and sixth on disc 2). Dufay's *Gloria* (sung *sans* Garbarek) ends on a desolate, protracted Amen, with Fayrfax Africanus marking an exultant point of contrast. Brumel's *Agnus Dei* allows Garbarek to temporarily monopolise the main melody line, but perhaps the most striking collaboration of all is for Hildegard's *O ignis Spiritus* which reaches spine-tingling levels of ecstasy. The second CD includes a Russian Psalm where Garbarek adopts a resonant bass presence, an up tempo Iroquois and Pasllcimiut Eagle dance and, to close, works by William Billings and Mesomedes that complete the musical arch with something close to perfection. It is a difficult disc to categorise. Maybe we should view it as a collaborative original composition which balances ancient and modern, sacred and profane, body and soul.

Emmanuel Pahud

Debussy Syrinx[d]. Chansons de Bilitis (arr Lenski)[b]. La plus que lente[c] **Prokofiev** Flute Sonata in D, Op 94[b] **Ravel** Trois chansons madécasses[d]
[d]**Katarina Karnéus** *mez* [abd]**Emmanuel Pahud** *fl*
[d]**Truls Mørk** *vc* [bcd]**Stephen Kovacevich** *pf*
EMI CDC5 56982-2 (61 minutes: DDD) Ⓕ
Recorded 1999

Pahud's range of tone colour is amazing – no one listening to the Prokofiev Sonata is likely to feel short-changed by not hearing it in its familiar violin transcription, and in 'Aoua!', the central song of Ravel's *Chansons madécasses*, Pahud gets closer than most flautists to playing, as the composer directs, 'like a trumpet'. His dynamic range is still more startling, if anything, but there is never any sense of him extending the instrument beyond its nature, of forcing it to do un-flute-like things. Katarina Karnéus's clean French diction and wide range are well suited to the Ravel (the *Chansons madécasses* ideally demand a mezzo who is also a soprano, or vice versa). The *Chansons de Bilitis* recorded here are not Debussy's set of three songs nor, strictly speaking, his incidental music for a stage entertainment based on Pierre Louÿs's poems. It is the *Six épigraphes antiques* (for piano duet or two pianos) that Debussy based on that stage music which have been transcribed for flute and piano by Karl Lenski. The flute is either evoked or deliberately imitated throughout the *Epigraphes* and it seems, especially when played this beautifully, a permissible and appropriate addition to the flautist's repertoire. To which the Prokofiev Sonata is, of course, central, and Pahud gives it a big, bold and vivid reading, but with nothing overstated in the lyrical dialogues of the opening movement or the warmly expressive *Andante*. The recording is a little close but richly colourful.

Henry Purcell and his Time

Baltzar Divisions on 'John Come Kiss me Now'[b]
Jenkins Fantasia in three parts **W Lawes** Fantasia-Suite No 7 in D minor **Locke** The Broken Consort – Suites Nos 3[b] and 4 **Purcell** Pavans – B flat, Z750; G minor, Z752[a]. Fantasia upon a Ground, Z731[ab]
C Simpson Prelude. Divisions on a Ground[b]
Scaramouche (Andrew Manze, Caroline Balding *vns* Jaap ter Linden *bass viol* Ulrike Wild *hpd/org*)
[a]**Foskien Kooistra** *vn* [b]**Konrad Junghänel** *theorbo*
Channel Classics CCS4792 (60 minutes: DDD) Ⓕ
Recorded 1992

On this disc of English 17th-century chamber music, Scaramouche offers a homogeneous selection of music and instrumental combinations. (The disc advertises itself, by the way, as offering the music of 'Henry Purcell and His Time', a claim whose level of accuracy – Lawes, for one, died over a decade before Purcell was born – is eloquently symbolised by a portrait of an unmistakably Elizabethan lady on the front of the box!) Here the innocent charm of other selections of this nature is largely replaced by the weightier, more sober pronouncements of Lawes, Locke and Purcell, but also by a bold interpretative vigour which makes it just as lively a listen in its own way.

Jaap ter Linden's rendition of his Simpson piece is suitably poetic, while Andrew Manze's version of *John Come Kiss me Now* has a Turkey-in-the-Straw ending that will certainly make you chuckle. This may be a slightly less polished and fluent recording than some others, but in the end, moments such as these – as well as the fact that there is lastingly rewarding music to be heard here – will make you want to play this disc again and again.

Trios for 4 P

Handel Trio Sonatas, Op 2 – No 1 in B minor; No 4 in F
Leclair Ouverture in G, Op 13 No 1
Quantz Trio Sonata in C
Telemann Trio Sonatas – G minor, TWV42:g9; A minor, TWV42:a4
Palladian Ensemble (Pamela Thorby *recs* Rachel Podger *vn* Susanne Heinrich *va da gamba* William Carter *archlte/gtr*)
Linn Records CKD050 (63 minutes: DDD) Ⓕ

The programme has been artfully chosen to demonstrate the diversity of styles current at more or less the same period of time. The Handel sonatas, the earliest works here though not published until 1730, are fundamentally Italianate; Leclair, despite this overture in the French style, also displays *goûts réunis*; Telemann, catholic in his tastes, is happy to include robust folk influences; and Quantz, less contrapuntal and more *galant* than the others, looks ahead to pre-classical style. The present performances exude a sense of enjoyment in the verve the artists bring to the second and last movements of the Handel F major and the delicious lightness of the initial *Allegro* of the Quantz; and in the Telemann A minor (from the *Essercizii musici*) Pamela Thorby and Rachel Podger exhibit virtuoso tonguing and bowing (though the finale is too rushed).

Equally attractive, however, is the shaping of *affettuoso* movements, notably the *Grave* of the Telemann G minor. The *Largo* of Handel's Op 2 No 1 can often sound lumbering, but the ensemble's adoption of the *Andante* speed indicated in the C minor version is much more convincing and effective.

The only reservations about this disc – and they are very slight indeed – concern some of William Carter's contributions: his accents in the finale of Telemann's G minor Trio are rather too rumbustious, and in the lively first *Allegro* of Handel's Op 2 No 1 the archlute continuo will be too dry for most tastes.

Instrumental

Thomas Adès *pf*

20th Century Piano

Busoni Sonatina No 3, 'ad usum infantis' **Castiglioni** Come io passo l'estate **Grieg** Norwegian Peasant Dances, Op 72 – Knut Luråsens halling I; The Goblin's Bridal Procession; The Bride of Skudal **Janáček** Intimate Sketches – Cekám Tě! **Kurtág** Les Adieux in Janáčeks Manier. Egy igaz ember emlékére. Hommage à Csajkovszkij. Hommage à Nancy Sinatra. Keringó. A Megvadult lenhajó lång. Preludium e Korál. Tears **Nancarrow** 3 Canons for Ursula **Stanchinsky** Canon a 4 voci. Sonata No 2 in G **Stravinsky** Piano-Rag Music. Souvenir d'une marche boche. Valse pour les enfants
Thomas Adès *pf*
EMI CDC5 57051-2 (72 minutes: DDD) Ⓕ
Recorded 2000 ●

Given free rein to construct a recital programme a composer/pianist will almost always present an audience with a very different kind of recital from that of a concert pianist per se. Look not for standard repertoire and virtuosic display for it's unlikely to be on the agenda. Expect instead a programme of exploration and of unexpected juxtapositions, which is exactly what Thomas Adès delivers.

Adès opens this enterprising selection of 20th-century piano music with Niccolò Castiglioni's *How I Spent the Summer*, an incident-packed 'travel diary' suite telling of adventures during a vacation in the Italian Alps. Though partly aimed at aspiring young pianists it nevertheless contains some sophisticated pianistic invention and engages the listener's attention all the way. It's a particularly welcome gem too, considering the woeful dearth of Castiglioni in the catalogue at present. Next comes Grieg. Adès gives us beautifully crafted, sharply characterised readings of three pieces from *Slåtter*, Op 72, reminding us that Grieg was often harmonically adventurous and forward-looking as well as a master miniaturist.

Adès's genuine respect and admiration for the music on this disc shines through again and again, making the performances throughout not just fine, but special too. Busoni's Sonatina No 3 *ad usum infantis* is not only an excellent example of this but also of the subtlety of Adès's playing. Only in the Alexey Stanchinsky pieces is one aware of a degree of hesitancy and lack of focus.

However, Adès excels in his selection of pieces from György Kurtág's piano cycle *Playing Games*, and indeed takes real pleasure in the composer's mischievous sense of humour – check out the grotesque transformations of Debussy and Tchaikovsky in *The Mad Girl with*

Flaxen Hair and *Homage to Tchaikovsky*. There are more gems for the uncovering here too, not least an impressive account of Conlon Nancarrow's *Three Canons for Ursula*. In sum, a fascinating and rewarding disc. Recorded sound is warm and atmospheric.

Géza Anda *pf*

Bartók Concertos for Piano and Orchestra – No 1, Sz83[a]; No 2, Sz95[b]; No 3, Sz119[b] **Chopin** Waltzes[d] – No 1 in E flat, Op 18; No 2 in A flat, Op 34 No 1; No 3 in A minor, Op 34 No 2; No 4 in F, Op 34 No 3; No 5 in A flat, Op 42; No 6 in D flat, 'Minute', Op 64 No 1; No 7 in C sharp minor, Op 64 No 2; No 8 in A flat, Op 64 No 3; No 9 in A flat, Op 69 No 1; No 10 in B minor, Op 69 No 2; No 11 in G flat, Op 70 No 1; No 12 in F minor, Op 70 No 2; No 13 in D flat, Op 70 No 3 **Mozart** Concerto for Piano and Orchestra No 21 in C, K467[c]

Géza Anda *pf/[c]dir* [ab]**Berlin Radio Symphony Orchestra / Ferenc Fricsay;** [c]**Salzburg Camerata Academica**

Philips Great Pianists of the 20th Century ②
456 772-2PM2 (155 minutes: ADD) Ⓜ
Recorded 1959-75 ●

Philips's tribute to a great artist incomparable in Bartók and no less so in Schumann is marred by a selection of bewildering eccentricity. True, no pianist played the Bartók concertos with such matchless precision and elegance, but the accompanying choice of 13 of Chopin's waltzes (the omission of No 14 is unexplained), made when Anda was already ill and dispirited, and a Mozart concerto performance that hardly suggests his glory in its prime, is doubly inexplicable when you consider his rich and scintillating recorded legacy (the Brahms *Paganini* Variations, Schumann's *Etudes symphoniques*, *Kreisleriana* and *Carnaval*, the Liszt Sonata and, by way of *bonne-bouche*, the Delibes-Dohnányi *Valse lente* all, thankfully, available on Testament).

More positively, it is impossible to celebrate sufficiently Anda's and Fricsay's partnership in Bartók. Anda famously played all three concertos in one concert, presenting their spiral from savage iconoclasm through neo-baroque virtuosity to autumnal joy and reflection with unflagging brio and finesse, and his Edinburgh Festival performance of the Second Concerto quickly acquired legendary status. His matchless clarity and rhythmic verve colour every page, and in the slow movements of Concertos Nos 2 and 3 his timing, like that of a great actor, and unique tonal sheen lend a remarkable atmosphere to those evocations of the *Puszta*, the mysterious Hungarian plains, whose seemingly limitless expanse is contrasted by the hyperactivity of their 'night music'. Here, Anda's differentiation between, say, *piano*, *pianissimo* and *ppp* is uncannily precise, his articulation of the fugue from the Third Concerto not only razor-sharp but a wonder of dancing vivacity and refinement; a far cry from so many less subtle and bludgeoning alternatives. The first disc is indispensable, the second a missed opportunity.

Martha Argerich *pf*

Début Recital

Brahms Two Rhapsodies, Op 79 **Chopin** Scherzo No 3 in C sharp minor, Op 39. Barcarolle in F sharp, Op 60 **Liszt** Hungarian Rhapsody No 6 in D flat. Piano Sonata in B minor, S178 **Prokofiev** Toccata in D minor, Op 11 **Ravel** Jeux d'eau

Martha Argerich *pf*

DG The Originals 447 430-2GOR (71 minutes: ADD) Ⓜ
Recorded 1960-71 ●●●

Here, on this richly filled CD, is a positive cornucopia of musical genius. Martha Argerich's 1961 disc remains among the most spectacular of all recorded débuts, an impression reinforced by an outsize addition and encore: her 1972 Liszt Sonata. True, there are occasional reminders of her pianism at its most fraught and capricious (Chopin's *Barcarolle*) as well as tiny scatterings of inaccuracies, yet her playing always blazes with a unique incandescence and character.

The Brahms *Rhapsodies* are as glowingly interior as they are fleet. No more mercurial Chopin *Scherzo* exists on record and if its savagery becomes flighty and skittish (with the chorale's decorations sounding like manic bursts of laughter), Argerich's fine-toned fluency will make other, lesser pianists weep with envy. Ravel's *Jeux d'eau* is gloriously indolent and scintillating and the Prokofiev *Toccata* (a supreme example of his early iconoclasm) is spun off in a manner that understandably provoked Horowitz's awe and enthusiasm. Liszt's Sixth *Hungarian Rhapsody* is a marvel of wit and daring and the B minor Sonata is among the most dazzling ever perpetuated on disc. The recordings have worn remarkably well and the transfers have been expertly done.

Claudio Arrau *pf*

Albéniz Iberia, Book 1 **Bach** Chromatic Fantasia and Fugue in D minor, BWV903 **Balakirev** Islamey **Brahms** Variations on a Theme by Paganini, Op 35. Piano Concerto No 1 in D minor, Op 15[a] **Liszt** Rhapsodie espagnole, S254. Harmonies poétiques et réligieuses, S173 – No 3, Bénédiction de Dieu dans la solitude. Années de pèlerinage – Troisième année, S163 – Les jeux d'eau à la Villa d'Este. Etudes d'exécution transcendante, S139 – Chasse-neige

Claudio Arrau *pf* [a]**Concertgebouw Orchestra / Bernard Haitink**

Philips Great Pianists of the 20th Century ②
456 706-2PM2 (157 minutes: ADD) Ⓕ
Recorded 1927-76 ●

It will come as a big surprise to many admirers of Claudio Arrau, a thoughtful philosopher of the keyboard, to hear the first item on this issue. You could hardly imagine a more dazzling virtuoso display in Balakirev's spectacular showpiece, *Islamey*. It was recorded for Polydor in the late 1920s, when Arrau was in his mid-twenties, and the panache is irresistible. Not only are the brilliant outer sections breathtaking in the clarity of the scampering triplets, with the heaviest textures made clear – helped by a full-toned transfer – the tonal resonance and the velvety warmth of *legato* in the sensuous melodic writing of the central section are equally distinctive. That item alone is enough to make this a compelling issue, and the other items on the first of the two discs amplify that spectacular start, presenting Arrau in his earlier years as a dazzling virtuoso, evidently uninhibited in the recording studio. That is so, whether in the Bach *Chromatic Fantasia* (aptly improvisatory in tone and again with textures crystal-clear); in Liszt (the *Rhapsodie espagnole* given astonishing lightness and clarity in this 1936 performance) and Albéniz (with the mystery and keen originality of the piano-writing heightened).

Both the Bach and the Albéniz date from the mid-1940s, and one imagines the Philips compilers may have wondered how to cap all these free and intense studio performances. Overall, the present set does tend to confirm the impression that over the years Arrau grew increasingly self-conscious in the recording studio, not exactly inhibited but less able to indulge in flights of spontaneous imagination, as he had done earlier. The three Liszt performances which complete the programme on the first disc, recorded between 1969 and 1976, are among the finest he made for Philips, with the cello-like resonances of *Bénédiction* reminding one of Arrau's playing in the central section of *Islamey* and the shimmering at the start of 'Chasse-neige', the twelfth *Transcendental Study*, made magical in an impressionistic way. There is much to enjoy too in Arrau's 1974 reading of Brahms's *Paganini* Variations, when the relatively broad speeds never sound slack or lack tension. Rather the Brahmsian textures are clarified, and rhythms pointed the more persuasively, particularly in the flights of fantasy in the Second Book. In the performance of the 1969 version of the First Brahms Concerto with Haitink and the Concertgebouw, the first two movements are rather heavy-going, not helped by an expressive style which tends towards *rallentando*s in what are already broad basic speeds. The finale is sharper, clean and unrushed, strong and dramatic, yet it is a pity that in the single representation of Arrau in this wide-ranging series, this second of the two discs is devoted completely to Brahms, instead of developing the imaginative pattern of the first.

Jorge Bolet *pf*

Liszt Années de pèlerinage – Première année: Suisse, S160 – Au bord d'une source; Deuxième année: Italie, S161 – Sonetto 104 del Petrarca. Consolation in D flat, S172 No 2. Etudes d'exécution transcendante d'après Paganini, S140 – No 3 in A flat minor, 'La campanella'. Etudes d'exécution transcendante, S139 – No 9, Ricordanza; No 11, Harmonies du soir. Gnomenreigen, S145 No 2. Harmonies poétiques et religieuses, S173 – No 7, Funérailles. Hungarian Rhapsody No 12 in C sharp minor, S244. La leggierezza, S144 No 2. Liebesträume in A flat, S541. Mephisto Waltz No 1, S514. Réminiscences de Don Juan , S418. Réminiscences de Norma, S394. Rigoletto Paraphrase, S434. Venezia e Napoli, S162
Jorge Bolet *pf*
Philips Great Pianists of the 20th Century ②
456 814-2PM2 (53 minutes: DDD/ADD) Ⓜ
Recorded 1979-84

The second volume of Philips's tribute to Jorge Bolet, with one noble exception, is taken from his later Liszt recordings for Decca, dating from 1978-85 and a time when his quest for perfection led him to be more sober and circumspect. One is awed by a grandeur and regality that forbade all possible levity. Bolet's musical thunder, whether distant or unleashed, is virtually omnipresent, a constant reminder of how excellent it is 'To have a giant's strength, but it is tyrannous/To use it like a giant.'

The central build-up of *Funérailles*, a work superbly suited to Bolet's inherently sombre nature, is monumental, and who else has stormed the climax of the Third *Liebestraum* with such tonal magnificence, fleshing out the harmonies with added notes, which is an endearingly old-fashioned touch that also colours the summit of *Funérailles*?

La campanella may be more magisterial than scintillating, and others may have tripped the light fantastic more engagingly in *Gnomenreigen*, yet both are played with formidable finish and resource. In the opening pages of *La leggierezza* one hears 'the eternal note of sadness', a touch of elegy, and if in *Harmonies du soir* Bolet slides gratefully into his favourite mood, that of a troubled repose, he also offers a performance of a Himalayan range and grandeur.

Put simply, his *Réminiscences de Don Juan* is so musical, so superior to that of other more flashy players who turn its epic display into a mere potboiler, and how romantically yet precisely he paces *Ricordanza*, resisting all temptation in some of Liszt's most effusive and sumptuously decorated variations to hysteria or exaggeration.

Finally, that 'noble exception', the *Norma* paraphrase taken from a performance in Alabama in 1988, and an interpretation in which 'Bolet's divine slowness' takes on a truly extraordinary dimension. Such a performance erases memories of a less than joyful or sun-drenched *Venezia e Napoli* or a First *Mephisto Waltz* with stout and clamorous rather than *pianissimo* nightingales. The sound of Bolet's beloved and burnished Bechstein has come up admirably, and these records ensure Bolet a unique place in the pianist's Pantheon.

Kevin Bowyer *org*

Danish Organ Works
Gade Three Tone Pieces, Op 22 **Nielsen** Commotio, FS155 **Nørgård** Partita concertante, Op 23
Syberg Prelude, Intermezzo and Fugato
Kevin Bowyer *org*
Nimbus NI5468 (70 minutes: DDD) Ⓕ
Recorded on the Marcussen organ of Odense Cathedral, Denmark in 1995

This disc contains four large and little-known works, although with the exception of *Prelude, Intermezzo and Fugato* by Franz Syberg, all are currently represented in the catalogue. Gade's three pleasant but unexceptional pieces are decidedly Mendelssohnian. Per Nørgård presents a work crammed full of diverse stylistic allusions (including a remarkably Shostakovich-like slow movement which Bowyer clearly relishes), while Nielsen's powerful *Commotio*, undeniably one of the glories of 20th-century organ music, rules itself out of most organists' portfolios by being long and difficult. Bowyer's declared purpose in putting this programme together is to celebrate the Danish town of Odense – only Gade had no direct connection with the place. Bowyer himself has spent a considerable part of this decade there – winning the Odense international organ competition in 1990 and subsequently making most of his recordings there. He hardly needs an excuse for using the Marcussen in Odense Cathedral, however – it makes a simply lovely sound and he is clearly very much at ease with it.

Mandelion – 20th Century Organ Works

Burrell Arched Forms with Bells **Ferneyhough** Sieben Sterne **Gowers** Toccata and Fugue **Graham** Three Pieces **Iliff** Trio **Mellers** Opus Alchymicum **Pärt** Pari intervalli **Ridout** The Seven Last Words
Tavener Mandelion
Kevin Bowyer *org*
Nimbus ② NI5580/1 (138 minutes: DDD) Ⓕ
Recorded on the Marcussen organ, Tonbridge School Chapel, Kent in 1998

This is an extraordinary collection, another tribute to Bowyer's prodigious exploratory fervour. It is surprising to find how much such a diverse group of composers has in common in the period following Messiaen's stupendous innovations which redefined the personality of the organ. This is emphasised by the use of a single instrument throughout. But the religious shadow of Messiaen also falls on Tavener in *Mandelion*, an eloquent 1981 piece which has given the title to the whole collection. *Mandelion* is a meditation on icons and the various images of the face of Christ. Not Roman Catholic, of course, but by no means Tavener's spiritual minimalism of more recent times, and there is a blazing triadic climax at 16'10" and C major to end with. Nothing like that in the magisterially confident *Seven Stars* which Ferneyhough wrote in 1970. There are passages where the player has to improvise in the style set and no registration is specified. Bowyer takes it all in his capacious stride, as he does the half-hour *Opus Alchymicum* by Mellers where he had a special role in the work's final form. It seems over-extended but the final 'Illuminatio' makes a superb toccata on its own.

An even older work is probably the best part of the weaker second CD – *The Seven Last Words* by Alan Ridout (1934-96). Written for Alan Wicks in 1967, this is a vivid evocation of the chosen scenario, pertinent and concentrated, where every section has audible coherence. There's a striking elegy for two-part pedal solo. Of the other pieces Diana Burrell's *Arched Form with Bells* is genuinely inventive in both textures and continuity, and there really are church bells at the end; Pärt's 1976 memorial tribute is placidly minimal; and Patrick Gowers's *Toccata and Fugue*, already available on CD twice without its fugue (Priory and OxRecs), dwarfs its much later partner. There's plenty to explore in this imaginative anthology.

Marcelo Bratke *pf*

Le Groupe des Six

Auric Adieu New York **Durey** Trois Préludes a la mémoire de Juliette Méérowitch, Op 26
Honegger Sept Pièces brèves **Milhaud** Printemps – Volume 1, Op 25; Volume 2, Op 66 **Poulenc** Trois Mouvements perpétuels. Trois Pièces
Tailleferre Romance **Les Six** Album des Six
Marcelo Bratke *pf*
Olympia Explorer OCD487 (62 minutes: DDD) Ⓜ
Recorded 1996

With his clean-cut technique, tonal sensitivity and verve, Marcelo Bratke confirms the very favourable impression created by his previous discs. Contrary to the popular image, few of these pieces by Les Six are nose-thumbingly facetious: the only real exception, clearly intended to shock the *bourgeois*, is the much too long and rather bad foxtrot with 'wrong-note' harmonies by Auric, the youngest of the six. The oldest was the now almost completely forgotten Durey; the highly charged first, at least, of his sombre tributes to a friend, and his contribution to a 1920 album, suggest an original mind. Of the three composers born in 1892, the most traditionally diatonic music comes from Tailleferre, with an entirely Fauré-esque *Romance*; Milhaud is represented by a predominantly calm set of pastorals, polytonal in idiom but, except for the first, not altogether free from a charge of note-spinning; and the most interesting is Honegger, who besides a thoughtfully dreamy 'Sarabande' in the collective album contributes seven varied, tersely packed miniatures that experiment in polytonality and atonality. Poulenc's familiar *Mouvements perpétuels* are, however, trivia as compared with the *Trois Pièces*, the Scriabinesque harmonies and exotic arabesques of whose 'Pastorale' hint at mysterious depths, and whose improvisatory 'Hymne' furnished several ideas for the later *Concert champêtre*; the brittle final 'Toccata', with its rapid-fire note-repetitions, provides a scintillating vehicle for Bratke's brilliance of articulation. The recording quality matches his excellence.

Alfred Brendel pf

Beethoven Rondo for Piano and Orchestra in B flat, WoO6[a]. Quintet for Piano and Wind in E flat, Op 16[b]. Piano Sonatas – No 17 in D minor, 'Tempest', Op 31 No 2; No 26 in E flat, 'Les adieux', Op 81a;

No 30 in E, Op 109. 11 Bagatelles, Op 119. 15 Variations and Fugue on an Original Theme in E flat, 'Eroica', Op 35. Seven Variations in F on Winter's 'Kind, willst du ruhig schlafen', WoO75. Fantasia in G minor, Op 77. Rondo in G, Op 51 No 2 **Dvořák** Slavonic Dances[c] – B78: No 1 in C; No 2 in E minor; No 6 in A flat; No 8 in G minor; B145: No 1 in B; No 2 in E minor; No 4 in D flat; No 6 in B flat; No 7 in A **Haydn** Piano Concerto in D, HobXVIII/11[d] **Liszt** Années de pèlerinage – Deuxième année, Italie, S161: Sonetto 47 del Petrarca; Sonetto 104 del Petrarca. Harmonies poétiques et réligieuses, S173 – No 3, Bénédiction de Dieu dans la solitude; No 7, Funérailles; No 10, Cantique d'amour. Etudes d'exécution transcendante d'après Paganini, S140 – E flat; A flat minor. Hungarian Rhapsody in A minor, S244 No 11. Mephisto Waltz No 1, S514. Opera Transcriptions – Oberon, S574; Il trovatore, S433; Tristan und Isolde, S447 **Mozart** Piano Concerto No 27 in B flat, K595[e] Rondo for Piano and Orchestra in D, K382[e] **Prokofiev** Piano Concerto No 5 in G minor, Op 55[f] **Schoenberg** Piano Concerto, Op 42[g]. **Schubert** Fantasy in C, 'Wanderer', D760. Drei Klavierstücke, D946 **Stravinsky** Three Movements from Petrushka

Alfred Brendel *pf* with **[c]Walter Klien** *pf* **[b]members of the Hungarian Wind Quintet; [a]Vienna Volksoper Orchestra / Wilfried Boettcher; [d]Vienna Chamber Orchestra, [e]Vienna Pro Musica Orchestra / Paul Angerer; [f]Vienna State Opera Orchestra / Jonathan Sternberg; [g]South West German Radio Symphony Orchestra, Baden-Baden / Michael Gielen**

Vox ⑥ CD6X3601 (453 minutes: ADD) Ⓑ
Recorded 1955-66 ●

Writing with superb authority, Alfred Brendel once answered his own rhetorical question. 'What is piano playing of genius? Playing which is at once correct and bold. Its correctness tells us that is how it has to be. Its boldness presents us with a surprising and overwhelming realisation: what we had thought impossible becomes true.' Setting his penetrating eye on his own favourite pianists (Edwin Fischer, Cortot, Kempff etc.), Brendel provided a flawless verbal image of his own playing. Heard at his greatest, as in these Vox and Regis reissues of recordings dating from 1955-67, he makes criticism fall silent. Wherever you turn, you will not hear a dishonest note or phrase, anything less than profoundly considered. Even Prokofiev's Fifth Concerto, music Brendel despises and which he recorded when his career was still not fully launched, comes up fresh, its extravagance illuminated by a pin-point wit and delicacy rather than a more familiar aggression.

True, most great artists regard their early recordings with suspicion. Yet even Brendel, with his intimidating scrutiny, must have periodically delighted in his early candour and assurance, his effortless resolving of complexity into simplicity, in the absolute 'rightness' of his interpretations and their untrammelled virtuosity. His later work for Philips may be more speculative but his early freshness, even *sang-froid*, is something to marvel at. Here, he wears his profound insights with the lightest of touches. Thought-provoking and personal to the last, his performance of Mozart's final Concerto captures exactly music of a clouded radiance with a momentary burst of anger at 3'22" in the finale, a 'do not go gentle into that good night' reminder of Mozart's lack of resignation. The selection, too, of Beethoven's Sonatas abounds with unselfconscious slants and angles unknown to lesser artists. Brendel is grave but never ponderous in the central *adagio* of Op 31 No 2 (not Op 21 as the booklet declares), finds a dazzling reconciliation between seemingly unreconcilable elements (*dolce* and *vivace*) at the start of Op 109, and shows an uninhibited joy in every surprise the composer offers in Op 81*a*. On the other hand you will rarely hear a more internal or communing performance of Schubert's *Wanderer*, almost as if Brendel is telling us that such outwardly uncharacteristic music hardly goes against the grain but remains an organic part of Schubert's *oeuvre*. In Liszt's *Cantique d'amour* you can sense him caught in the breathless central elaboration, yet he never allows his playing to degenerate into either a salon, conversational elegance or flashy rhetoric. His inwardness, too, in the central blessing of the 'Bénédiction' is a marvel of poetic insight.

Brendel may be celebrated for his intellectual probity, yet, as this memorable album shows, his warmth and humanity are supported by an unfaultering virtuosity. Here, surely, is an incomparable marriage of heart and mind.

David Briggs *org*

Great European Organs, Volume 57

Brewer Marche héroïque **Bridge** Adagio in E, H63 No 3 **Faulkes** Grand choeur in D **Harris** Caprice **Macpherson** Fantasy-Prelude **Mendelssohn** (arr Best) Athalie – War March of the Priests **Parry** Chorale Preludes, Set 2 – Eventide **Stanford** Organ Sonata No 3 in D minor, 'Britannica', Op 152

Priory PRCD680 (68 minutes: DDD) Ⓕ
Played on the Lewis organ of St John the Evangelist, Upper Norwood, London. Recorded 1999 ●

Perhaps a more appropriate title would be 'Great British Organ', as this CD is a celebration of home-grown artistry: Victorian and Edwardian music played on a vintage late 19th-century instrument by one of Britain's finest organists. Although this Lewis organ may not be in a prestigious venue like a cathedral, city hall or concert hall, this doesn't mean it's an instrument of lesser quality. On the contrary, it has all the colour and brilliance one hears on the larger organs Lewis built for Southwark Cathedral and the Kelvingrove Art Gallery, Glasgow (these latter instruments can be heard on previous 'Great European Organs' CDs).

Briggs's programme is ideally suited to the organ, too, and he gives splendid performances. You can tell from the finely judged *rubato* and judicious choice of tempos that he is an experienced choral and orchestral conductor as well as a very fine soloist. This all makes for eminently satisfying music-making, and his imaginative use of the organ means that we hear all its available tone colours.

Priory's production is of the highest order – the recording is excellent and the insert-notes informative. Inevitably as the century progresses this organ will show signs of wear and tear, so it's good to have a recording made so soon after the recent restoration by Harrisons. Lovers of the late 19th-century British organ will certainly be indebted to Briggs and Priory for committing to CD the magnificent sound of this Lewis instrument.

Shura Cherkassky *pf*

Liadov A musical snuffbox, Op 32 **Liszt** Piano Concerto No 1 in E flat, S124[a]. Liebestraum in A flat, S541 No 3. Réminiscences de Don Juan (Mozart), S418. Hungarian Rhapsody No 13 in A minor, S244. Faust (Gounod) – Waltz, S407 Ⓗ
Saint-Saëns Le carnaval des animaux – Le cygne
Shura Cherkassky *pf* [a]**Philharmonia Orchestra / Anatole Fistoulari**
Testament mono SBT1033 (62 minutes: ADD) Ⓕ
Recorded 1952-58

Here, in excellent transfers of HMV recordings dating from the 1950s, is a vintage Cherkassky recital. Mercurial and hypnotic, his way with Liszt's E flat Concerto reminds us in every nook and cranny that he has always been able to enliven and transform even the most over-familiar score. True, there are moments – such as the start of the *Allegro vivace* – where he is less than ideally poised or balletic (one of those instances where his elfin caprice can seem close to uncertainty and where he leads Fistoulari and the Philharmonia a Puckish dance: now you hear me, now you don't), yet his sparkle and charm are inimitable. Again, in Variation 1 of the *Don Juan* Fantasy he is perhaps more flustered than *elegantamente*, but even when his virtuosity is less than watertight, his playing is infinitely more fascinating and imaginatively varied. Cherkassky can be garrulous or somnolent, his phrasing languorous or choppy, yet in the ecstatic, long-breathed descent just before the coda of the *Liebestraum* No 3 and in all of the *Hungarian Rhapsody* No 13 and the *Faust* Waltz, his mastery has seldom, if ever, sounded more effortless or unalloyed. Finally, an encore of *friandises*: Godowsky's fine-spun elaboration of Saint-Saëns's 'Le cygne'.

Margaret Fingerhut *pf*

Tchaikovsky and his Friends
Arensky Intermezzo in F minor, Op 36 No 12. Le ruisseau dans la forêt. Romance, Op 53 No 5
Glazunov Etudes, Op 31 – No 2 in C minor; No 3 in E minor. Prelude in D, Op 25 No 1 **Liadov** Two Bagatelles, Op 17. Prelude in B minor, Op 11 No 1. Prelude in F sharp minor, Op 39 No 4 **Rachmaninov** Canon in E minor. Morceaux de fantaisie, Op 3 – No 1, Elégie in E flat minor; No 3, Mélodie in E; No 4, Policinelle in F sharp minor **Taneyev** Scherzo in E flat minor. Andante semplice **Tchaikovsky** Humoresque in E minor, Op 10 No 2. Nocturne in C sharp minor, Op 19 No 4. Chant sans paroles in A minor, Op 40 No 7. Dumka, Op 59
Margaret Fingerhut *pf*
Chandos CHAN9218 (78 minutes: DDD) Ⓕ
Recorded 1992

The title is a reasonable one, for the younger five composers here were Tchaikovsky's musical friends as well as being known to him and greatly admiring of him. The Russian salon piano piece, owing a good deal to song and therefore to French example, was an immensely popular genre in Moscow and St Petersburg circles, and Tchaikovsky set examples both good and risky. The lively pieces, such as his wonderfully catchy Humoresque, not only put Russian folk idioms into currency, but could seize the sharpest of 20th-century Russian ears, Stravinsky's, and go into *The Fairy's Kiss* with his own rhythmic bounce. The tender ones could veer in the direction of sentimentality, and sometimes lurch over the margins of good taste. A good variety is represented here. Margaret Fingerhut has chosen intelligently. She has not spared herself, for there are one or two occasions where her technique is fully stretched. However, she has a real understanding of the genre, and can knock off the rapid fancy (such as Taneyev's *Scherzo*) and the sudden, almost manic burst of energy (uncharacteristically in the indolent Liadov's F sharp minor Prelude), as well as the dreamy meditation (Liadov's first Op 17 Bagatelle, 'La douleur' or Tchaikovsky's own Nocturne or Rachmaninov's Mélodie) and a genre piece such as Arensky's pretty little picture of a brook running through a forest. Her greatest talent is for a flexibility of phrasing that always sings. These are in the best sense sympathetic performances, and should give pleasure.

Annie Fischer *pf*

Bartók 15 Hungarian Peasant Songs, Sz71
Brahms Piano Sonata No 3 in F minor, Op 5
Dohnányi Rhapsody in C, No 3 Op 11 **Liszt** Three Concert Studies, S144 – No 3, Un sospiro. Grandes études de Paganini, S141 – No 6, Quasi Presto
BBC Legends/IMG Artists mono BBCL4054-2 Ⓜ
(64 minutes: ADD). Recorded live in 1961

Few pianists have found a more direct path to poetic truth than Annie Fischer. Blessedly free of all attitudinising or exaggeration, her finest performances (like all truly great artists she had her off-days) burned with a fierce clarity and vision, and her London appearances, both in recital and with Otto Klemperer during the 60s, became the stuff of musical legends. Like, say, Schnabel and Myra Hess, Annie Fischer felt inhibited in the studios, and the story of her endlessly protracted Hungaroton recording of the complete Beethoven Piano Sonatas testifies to her discomfort. So all credit to those who rescued this magnificent recital taken live from the 1961 Edinburgh Festival. How characteristic is that mix of brio and poetry in the Brahms F minor Sonata. Others, such as Radu Lupu, may be more romantically inclined but few have played this early masterpiece with such sweep and panache. Her assault on the notorious octave swirl commencing the first-movement development may be more fearless than impeccable, but the final pages of the *Andante* are truly *molto appassionato* and *fortissimo*, and how typical is that forthright – not merely vague or impressionistic – end to the Intermezzo, with its muffled timpani strokes. In such hands the finale is an epic waltz indeed, and she reveals the glory of one daunting rhetorical gesture after another.

Her Bartók is wonderfully free-wheeling and idiomatic, and in Liszt's *Un sospiro* the directness of her playing throughout suggests heroic rather than sentimental passion. Her way with the Dohnányi *Rhapsody*, too, reminds us of her versatility, her joy in unbounded virtuosity as well as her dedication to the great masterpieces of the repertoire. The recordings faithfully reflect a special sense of occasion, and the excellent notes offer an apt reminder that Annie Fischer lived before a time when 'genuine musical interest was often squeezed to the margins'.

Ignaz Friedman *pf*

Ignaz Friedman Plays Mendelssohn, Chopin and Liszt

Chopin Ballade No 3 in A flat, Op 53. Impromptu No 2 in F sharp, Op 36. Mazurkas – No 5 in B flat, Op 7 No 1; No 6 in A minor, Op 7 No 2; No 7 in F minor, Op 7 No 3; No 17 in B flat minor, Op 24 No 4; No 23 in D, Op 33 No 2; No 25 in B minor, Op 33 No 4; No 26 in C sharp minor, Op 41 No 1; No 31 in A flat, Op 50 No 2; No 41 in C sharp minor, Op 63 No 3; No 44 in C, Op 67 No 3; No 45 in A minor, Op 67 No 4; No 47 in A minor, Op 68 No 2. Nocturne No 16 in E flat, Op 55 No 2 **Liszt** Hungarian Rhapsody No 2 in C sharp minor, S244 No 2 **Mendelssohn** Songs without Words – A, 'Hunting Song', Op 19 No 3; G minor, 'Venetian Gondola Song', Op 19 No 6; F sharp minor, 'Venetian Gondola Song', Op 30 No 6; C minor, Op 38 No 2; A flat, 'Duetto', Op 38 No 6; E flat, Op 53 No 2; F, Op 53 No 4; F sharp minor, Op 67 No 2; A, 'Kinderstück', Op 102 No 5

Ignaz Friedman *pf*

Biddulph LHW044 (77 minutes: ADD) Ⓜ

Recorded 1930-36

If many modern pianists can be dismissed with damning brevity, Ignaz Friedman's elegance and aplomb demand a book rather than a review. In his tantalising selection of Chopin *Mazurkas* his inimitable brio allows for both a sense of peasant origins (that slight lift on the second beat, that light or emphatic – according to context – stress on the third) and the rarest sense of fantasy and idealisation. His rapid tempo in, say, Op 24 No 4 offers him, paradoxically, time for one enchanting felicity or passing piquancy after another, and an airborne lightness and freedom. His *legato* and *cantabile* make notes melt together rather than merely join or elide with another, and in Op 63 No 3 the attributes of such haunting sweetness combine with an authentic 'wood-note wild'. Who would have thought that Op 67 No 3, a relatively slight work, could be spun off with such vivacious idiosyncrasy or that the Third *Ballade* could emerge free from all constraint (why not plunge down the keyboard in a cascade of double rather than single notes and end with further reinforcements in a cloud of glory?) True, Friedman can play free and easy with the score. Taken at such a speed the Second *Impromptu*'s final *leggiero* scales turn into an unapologetic display, their innate beauty compromised by an extravagant flurry. But in the E flat *Nocturne*, Op 55 No 2, with its subtle prophecy of Fauréan radiance, Friedman spins the most magical of lines. Seemingly as natural as breathing, Friedman's artistry is quite without (disfiguring) archness, leaving younger pianists to wonder at such insouciance, at such effortless transcending of received wisdom. The transfers are admirable, and Allan Evans's notes are good enough to survive some careless proof-reading.

Great European Organ Collections

EMI Great Cathedral Organ Series, Volume 1

Gigout 10 Organ Pieces – No 4, Toccata[f] **Howells** Rhapsody, Op 17 No 1[e] **Karg-Elert** Pastel in F sharp, Op 92 No 3[d] **Parry** Choral Fantasy No 1, Old 100th[e] **Reubke** Sonata on the 94th Psalm in C minor[b] **Saint-Saëns** Fantaisie in D flat, Op 101[a] **Statham** Lament[d] **S S Wesley** Choral Song and Fugue[e] **Whitlock** Four Extemporizations – No 4, Fanfare[c]

[a]**Christopher Dearnley** *Salisbury Cathedral* [b]**Roger Fisher** *Chester Cathedral* [c]**Noel Rawsthorne** *Liverpool Anglican Cathedral* [d]**Heathcote Statham** *Norwich Cathedral* [e]**Herbert Sumsion** *Gloucester Cathedral* [f]**Arthur Wills** *Ely Cathedral*

Amphion Recordings PHICD160 (76 minutes: ADD) Ⓕ

Recorded 1963-70 ●

The 19 LPs of EMI's 'Great Cathedral Organs' series released between 1963 and 1971 constituted one of the most important recording projects in the history of the English organ. The brainchild of producer Brian Culverhouse (whose booklet-essay provides some fascinating anecdotes), it featured organs of impeccably English lineage and organists steeped in the centuries' old traditions of English cathedral music. Since most of these organs have long since been replaced or modified in an attempt to give them a more European flavour, and many modern-day English cathedral organists belong to a more cosmopolitan musical generation, these recordings have assumed particular historical significance. They recorded, quite literally, the end of an era. The CD transfers vary from the disappointing (Ely) to the outstanding – interestingly enough, the oldest recordings, those made on Liverpool's vast Willis organ, have come out with simply staggering presence – but all provide vivid aural pictures of these uniformly wonderful organs set within generous helpings of their respective cathedrals' gloriously atmospheric acoustics. The men who oversee the day-to-day running of the music in a great cathedral don't necessarily make the best solo performers on disc, and many of these performances would not bear close scrutiny beside other available versions. But while this disc does not set out to offer itself as a rival to other recorded performances, Roger Fisher's stunning and breathtakingly exciting account of the Reubke, despite the pervasive hiss, is a performance-in-a-million, and Noel Rawsthorne elicits awed admiration with his brilliantly communicative playing.

Great European Organs, Volume 26

Ravanello Theme and Variations in B minor
Reger Five Easy Preludes and Fugues, Op 56 – No 1 in E **Schmidt** Chaconne in C sharp minor
Shostakovich Lady Macbeth of the Mtsensk district – Passacaglia **Stanford** Fantasia and Toccata in D minor, Op 57
Keith John *org*
Priory PRCD370 (73 minutes: DDD Ⓕ
Recorded on the organ of Gloucester Cathedral, UK in 1991 ●●●

On the face of it this CD might look as if its appeal is purely for those with a specialist taste in large-scale post-romantic organ music. Certainly Schmidt's gargantuan *Chaconne* represents a daunting prospect both to player and listener, while Shostakovich's only organ solo begins with the kind of chilling dissonance which would certainly scare off those of a delicate disposition. Similarly, neither Stanford nor Reger usually attract a crowd when their organ music is played – and who has ever heard of Ravanello? But if ever a recording was made to shatter preconceptions, this is it.

For a start, the Gloucester organ makes a wondrous sound and Priory's recording is in a class of its own; in terms of sound alone this surely ranks as one of the best ever CDs of organ music. Then Keith John quite literally pulls out all the stops to produce an unparalleled display of virtuosity and musicianship. His technical prowess turns the Schmidt into a thrilling tour de force, while few could question, after hearing his performances, that the Stanford is one of the best works ever written by a British composer or that Ravanello's music doesn't deserve the neglect it currently suffers.

Great European Organs, Volume 48

Commette Scherzo **Dallier** Cinq Invocations
Guilmant Marche funèbre et chant séraphique, Op 17 No 3 **Ibert** Trois Pièces **Philip** Toccata and Fugue in A minor
Gerard Brooks *org*
Priory PRCD558 (79 minutes: DDD) Ⓕ
Recorded on the Cavaillé-Coll organ in the Abbey Church of St Ouen, Rouen in 1995

Here we have a magnificent recording of one of the truly Great European Organs. In Gerard Brooks, Priory has found a player as eager to reveal the glories and subtleties of one of Cavaillé-Coll's greatest creations as his own impressive virtuosity. Widor's description of this as a 'Michelangelo of an organ' seems singularly apt in the light of a disc which displays the instrument so vividly. A simple reading of the track list might imply that such opulent resources are being squandered on a collection of oddities drawn from the ample dark recesses of French organ literature. If Guilmant is the only familiar name (so far as organists are concerned, Ibert is an obscure figure), the music of the others is as familiar as a new Andrew Lloyd Webber score – we're sure we've heard it all before but can't quite remember where.

Edouard Commette's *Scherzo* is clearly first cousin to Henri Mulet's famous *Carillon sortie*, Achille Philip's Toccata comes from the same stable as that from Boëllman's *Suite gothique*, while Henri Dallier's *Invocations* inspired by Latin Marian texts could easily pass for Vierne, especially the glittering final Toccata. But if the idioms are familiar and the ideas derivative, the musical quality in both intellectual and emotional terms is undeniable. Simply put, this is a programme of immensely enjoyable music, all of which bears repeated listening and is certainly deserving of a place on the shelves of lovers of good organ music.

Great European Organs, Volume 51

Bach Pastorale in F, BWV590 **G Böhm** Vater unser im Himmelreich, WKii138 **Buxtehude** Prelude, Fugue and Chaconne in C, BuxWV137 **Eben** Homage to Dietrich Buxtehude **Guridi** Triptico del Buen Pastor. **Liszt** (trans Schaab) Orpheus, S98
Saint-Saëns Fantaisie in D flat, Op 101
Peter King *org*
Priory PRCD618 (78 minutes: DDD) Ⓕ
Recorded on the Klais organ of Bath Abbey in 1997 ●

This seems rather a peculiar programme with a focus on Buxtehude and the North German baroque and with a few other disparate pieces thrown in to spice up the menu. Peculiar or not, it works superbly. The new Bath Abbey instrument is adorable – a complete rejection of the argument often propounded that, on purely musical terms, an organ built outside the British Isles is inappropriate for a major English ecclesiastical building – and it makes everything here sound convincing and impressive. This sumptuous instrument is well served by a beautifully proportioned recording. For those interested in the music rather than the instrument, Peter King's performances range from the solid (Buxtehude's *Praeludium* in G minor) to the near-inspired (Bach's *Pastorale*). Eben's *Homage* is based on material from the two Buxtehude pieces on the disc and uses Buxtehudian structures and figurations in a typically astute Eben manner. The inclusion of the Liszt and Saint-Saëns is obviously inspired by King's deep fondness for these pieces – it shows in every bar of these lovingly nurtured performances – while the Guridi has moments which allow us to hear the organ's more atmospheric qualities. Not everybody will be immediately attracted to this disc by the music, but for the sheer pleasure of hearing a truly wonderful, modern instrument, this release cannot be recommended too highly.

Twelve Organs of Edinburgh

Bach Concerto in G, BWV592[be] **Bridge** Adagio in E, H63 No 2[df] **Bruhns** Praeludium in E minor[cg] **Buxtehude** Prelude, Fugue and Chaconne in C, BuxWV137[bh]. Praeludium in D minor, BuxWV140[di] **Couperin** Messe pour les paroisses – Tierce en taille[bh] **Handel** Il pastor fido – Overture[dj]. Ode for St Cecilia's Day, HWV76 – March[df] **Hesse** Variations on an original theme, Op 34[ck] **Hollins** Concert Overture No 3 in F minor[be] **Høvland** Toccata – Now thank we all our God[df] **Humperdinck** (arr Lemare) Hänsel und Gretel – Angel scene[bl] **Krebs** O König, dessen Majestät[cg] **Leighton** Prelude, Scherzo and Passacaglia, Op 41[cm] **Mendelssohn** Organ Sonata in B flat, Op 65 No 4[an] **Pachelbel** Alle Menschen müssen sterben[di] **Saint-Saëns** Fantaisie in E flat[ao] **Sweelinck** Ballo del granduca[ao] **Tomkins** Voluntary[ap] **Walond** Voluntary in D[ap]
[a]Peter Backhouse, [b]Timothy Byram-Wigfield, [c]Michael Harris, [d]John Kitchen *orgs*
Priory ② PRCD700AB (153 minutes: DDD) Ⓕ
Played on the organs of [e]St Cuthbert's Church, [f]McEwan Hall, [g]Canongate Kirk, [h]Greyfriars Kirk, [i]Reid Concert Hall, [j]St Cecilia's Hall, [k]St Andrew's and St George's Church, [l]St Mary's Episcopal Cathedral, [m]St Giles Cathedral, [n]Broughton St Mary's Church, [o]St Stephen's Church Centre, [p]Lodge Canongate, Kilwinning

On these CDs, the instruments span three centuries and originate in Britain, Northern Ireland, Denmark and Austria. From the 18th century, we hear two surviving British organs with an exquisite, singing tone. The 19th century brought greater power and variety of orchestral colour, well illustrated by Byram-Wigfield's performance of the Humperdinck at St Mary's Cathedral. The 20th century has seen a return to a clearer, more 'baroque' type of organ-building, together with the use of computer technology to improve playing aids and the design of the mechanism and casework. The Rieger organ at St Giles Cathedral is a supreme example of an outstanding contemporary instrument.

Together with its long history, the organ can boast an extensive repertoire, and the discs feature music from five centuries and five European countries. The pieces have been brilliantly chosen by the players to display the essential character of each organ, and this alone is a considerable achievement.

It's always interesting to see and hear an artistic partnership developing between the player and the organ, and all four performers strike up a fruitful and happy relationship with their respective instruments. Occasionally, the pairing might appear unexpected, such as playing Sweelinck on a 19th-century Willis, but with Backhouse it becomes a great success. Other pairings could be described as a match made in heaven, and into this category falls Byram-Wigfield's colourful performances of Hollins and Humperdinck, and Kitchen's spontaneous, stylish performances of Buxtehude, Handel and Pachelbel. Harris's playing of Leighton's masterpiece is quite stunning, and this track is an awesome monument to 20th-century organ-building and composition at the highest level.

Priory's recordings and production are, as always, truly excellent. Byram-Wigfield contributes informative booklet-notes and Backhouse a superb collection of photographs.

Marc-André Hamelin *pf*

The Composer-Pianists

Alkan Esquisses, Op 63 – No 46, Le premier billet-doux; No 47, Scherzetto **Bach/Feinberg** Kommst du nun, Jesu, vom Himmel herunter BWV650 **Busoni** Fantasia after J. S. Bach **Feinberg** Berceuse, Op 19a **Godowsky** Toccata in G flat, Op 13 **Hamelin** Etudes – No 9, 'd'après Rossini'; No 10, 'd'après Chopin'; No 12 (Prelude and Fugue) **Haydn/Alkan** Symphony No 94 in G, 'Surprise' – Andante **Medtner** Improvisation in B flat minor, Op 31 No 1 **Rachmaninov** Moment musical in E flat minor, Op 16 No 2. Etude-tableau in E flat, Op 33 No 4 **Scriabin** Poème tragique in B flat, Op 34. Deux Poèmes, Op 71 **Sorabji** Pastiche on Hindu Song from Rimsky-Korsakov's 'Sadko'
Marc-André Hamelin *pf*
Hyperion CDA67050 (68 minutes: DDD) Ⓕ
Recorded 1998

Here is a cunning and potent mix of every conceivable form of pianistic and musical intricacy (it excludes the merely decorative, salon or ephemeral). Everything is of the most absorbing interest; everything is impeccably performed. Hamelin's richly inclusive programme ranges from Godowsky's *Toccata*, music of the most wicked, labyrinthine complexity, to three of his own projected cycle of 12 *Etudes*, among them a ferociously witty and demanding Prelude and Fugue and a reworking of Chopin's Op 10 No 5, full of black thoughts as well as black notes. Then there is Alkan's sinister absorption of the *Andante* from Haydn's *Surprise* Symphony (loyal to Haydn, Alkan's teasing perversity also makes such music peculiarly his own); a *Berceuse* by Samuel Feinberg that prompts Francis Pott, in his brilliantly illuminating notes, to question what sort of child would be lulled by such strangeness; some superb Medtner and Scriabin and a cloudy, profoundly expressive *Fantasia after J. S. Bach* by Busoni. Clearly among the most remarkable pianists of our time, Hamelin makes light of every technical and musical difficulty, easing his way through Godowsky's intricacy with yards to spare, registering every sly modulation of Alkan's 'Le premier billet-doux' and generating a white-hot intensity in Rachmaninov's admirably revised version of his Second *Moment musical*. Here, Hamelin's maintenance of a 'line' set within a hectically whirling complexity is something to marvel at. Taut, sinewy and impassioned, this performance is a worthy successor to Rachmaninov's own legendary disc. Every phrase and note is coolly appraised within its overall context and the results are audacious and immaculate as required. Hyperion's sound is superb.

Christopher Herrick *org*

Organ Dreams, Volume 2

Barber (arr Strickland) Adagio, Op 11 **Dubois** In paradisum **Bridge** Adagio in E, H63 No 2 **Elgar** 11 Vesper Voluntaries, Op 14 **Guilmant** Sonata No 7 in F, Op 89 – Rêve **Howells** Siciliano for a High Ceremony **Liszt** Evocation à la Chapelle Sixtine, S658 **Schumann** Study in A flat, Op 56 No 4 **S Wesley** Short Pieces with Voluntary – No 5 in A minor; No 8 in F; No 9 in F; No 11 in D

Christopher Herrick *org*

Hyperion CDA67146 (73 minutes: DDD) Ⓕ
Recorded 1999

After eight highly acclaimed discs of 'Organ Fireworks' the winning combination of Christopher Herrick and Hyperion have turned their attention towards the calmer and more reflective repertory grouped under the title 'Organ Dreams'. Volume 2 consists mostly of original organ music spanning the period 1815-1952, all of which fits the instrument in Ripon Cathedral like a well-tailored glove.

Not every title reflects a dream-like state, though the disc's opening track – Dubois' *In paradisum* creates an aura of calm. Frank Bridge's oft-played *Adagio in E* is also smoothly shaped, with its grand climax carefully controlled. Guilmant's 'Rêve' of 1902 is delicious, its impressionistic perfume wafting effortlessly.

With a running time of 19 minutes, Elgar's rarely heard *Vesper Voluntaries* of 1889 form the centrepiece of Herrick's programme. What charmers they are: mostly *mezzo-piano* in dynamic, with occasional fuller-bodied outbursts, none of them outstays its welcome. They are followed by Howells' rambling *Siciliano* (the most recent piece on the disc), which Herrick keeps moving. However, he does allow himself plenty of time for William Strickland's convincing arrangement of Barber's *Adagio*.

The Liszt is a shameless piece of kitsch which borrows freely from Allegri's *Miserere* and Mozart's *Ave verum corpus*. More worthwhile are Schumann's *Study* and a quartet of miniatures by Samuel Wesley. The only fault with the whole package is that the portrait purporting to be that of Wesley senior is, in fact, that of his natural son, Samuel Sebastian.

In summary, this thoroughly enjoyable disc is sensitively and affectionately played, and it works well at a single hearing.

Organ Fireworks, Volume 6

Cocker Tuba tune **Elgar** Organ Sonata No 1 in G, Op 28 **Hollins** A Trumpet Minuet **CS Lang** Tuba tune **Lemare** Concertstück in the form of a Polonaise, Op 80 **Spicer** Kiwi Fireworks – Variations on 'God defend New Zealand' **Sumsion** Introduction and Theme **Wagner** (trans Lemare, arr Westbrook and Herrick) Die Meistersinger von Nürnberg – Prelude, Act 1

Christopher Herrick *org*

Hyperion CDA66778 (76 minutes: DDD) Ⓕ
Recorded on the Norman and Beard organ in the Town Hall, Wellington, New Zealand in 1995

This series turned into something of a world tour for Christopher Herrick and the 'Organ Fireworks' team, and here they travel to New Zealand. They have come up with one genuine piece of 'home-grown' music (although C.S. Lang left New Zealand for England almost before he could tell a nappy from a hazard) and a connection with Edwin Lemare; he played this organ three months after its completion in 1906. However, the starting-point for this programme is the tradition of civic organ concerts which was exported from the town halls of Edwardian England to such far-flung corners of the British Empire as Singapore, South Africa and, of course, New Zealand. The Wellington Town Hall organ is typical of a large turn-of-the-century English symphonic organ, and while it might seem a little extravagant to go half-way round the world to find one, it is, following its 1985-86 restoration, rare in being substantially unaltered and in excellent working condition. Full organ is gloriously meaty, the flue tone beautifully blended and the solo reeds a joy to behold – a silvery Tromba perfect for Hollins's elegant Minuet; a gutsy Tuba ideal for both Cocker and Lang. As ever, Herrick's performances have both musical integrity and great communicative flair: his is a matchless performance of the Elgar Sonata, in which the composer's strangely awkward use of the organ, in places treating it almost orchestrally, is immaculately managed.

Organ Fireworks, Volume 7

Bonnet In Memoriam – Titanic, Op 10 No 1 **Edmundson** Toccata, 'Vom Himmel hoch' **Guilmant** Deuxième Offertoire sur des Noëls, Op 33 **Johnson** Trumpet Tune in F **Lefébure-Wély** Noël varié **Litaize** Variations sur un Noël angevin **Karg-Elert** Improvisation, Op 81, 'Nearer my God to Thee' **Pachelbel** Prelude, 'Vom Himmel hoch' **Reubke** Sonata on the 94th Psalm in C minor

Christopher Herrick *org*

Hyperion CDA66917 (70 minutes: DDD) Ⓕ
Recorded on the Klais organ of the Hallgrímskirkja, Reykjavík in 1996

Iceland: Land of Volcanoes. What an appropriate place for Christopher Herrick to set off this batch of fireworks. But in keeping with the awesome, almost vengeful spectacle of an Icelandic volcano in full spate these are not all the cheerful, colourful sparklers of a British Guy Fawkes Night. Central to the disc is a stunning performance of Julius Reubke's massive Sonata on the 94th Psalm ('O God, to whom vengeance belongeth'). It must be said straight away that this performance surpasses any version yet to appear on CD. Herrick throws himself into the work with almost manic intensity, culminating in a breathtakingly virtuosic account of the fugue. Equally spectacular is this magnificent Klais; its *chamade* reeds punching into the air with primeval ferocity, its dark, full-throated chorus reeds seeping over the music like molten lava. And all this captured in a recording of exceptional clarity and presence. Maintaining the tradition of choosing music to match the recording's geographical location, Herrick has come up with two pieces (by Bonnet and Karg-Elert) linked in some respect to the sinking of the *Titanic*. (Of course, it actually sank off Greenland, but, in the scale of things, Iceland isn't *that* far away!) The rest of the programme (with the exception of a harmless *Trumpet Tune* by David Johnson) has a Christmassy flavour; reflecting, one supposes, the preponderance of snow in Iceland. There are splendid *Noëls* by Guilmant, Lefébure-Wély and Litaize, and the disc ends with a sizzling account of Edmundson's *Toccata* on the chorale *Vom Himmel hoch*. The recording is magnificent.

Myra Hess *pf*

1938-42 HMV Recordings H

Bach Cantata No 147, Herz und Mund und Tat und Leben – Jesu, bleibet meine Freude (arr Hess) **Brahms** Piano Pieces, Op 76 – No 2, Capriccio in B minor; No 3, Intermezzo in A flat. Capriccio in D minor, Op 116 No 7. Intermezzo in E flat, Op 117 No 1. Intermezzo in C, Op 119 No 3 **Ferguson** Piano Sonata in F minor, Op 8 **Matthay** Elves, Op 17. Stray Fancies, Op 22 **D Scarlatti** Keyboard Sonata in G, Kk14 **Schumann** Carnaval, Op 9

Dame Myra Hess *pf*

Biddulph mono LHW025 (76 minutes: ADD) Ⓜ

Recorded 1938-42 ●

Those who, sadly, retain an image of Dame Myra Hess as either a sober-suited pianist inclined towards severity or a 'graciousness' that excluded the toughest, most durable virtues, are in for a surprise. For here, on this truly glorious record, she ranges effortlessly from sheer wit and style (Schumann's *Carnaval*) to a dancing rhythmic magic (Scarlatti), from a glowing poetic inwardness (all the Brahms, with perhaps Op 76 No 3 as the distantly shining star of the set) to a matchless eloquence (Howard Ferguson's tragic masterpiece, his 1938-40 Piano Sonata). Yet all such qualities are seamlessly joined. Nothing is forced, and whether you consider her regal tonal resource (tirelessly celebrated by Stephen Kovacevich, her finest pupil) or a naturalness and candour easy to underestimate, everything is achieved with supreme authority; an illusion achieved by only the truest artists. What an object-lesson, then, for today's harassed young pianists, jostling for attention in an increasingly commercial market-place, a reminder of a poetic and speculative artistry beyond price. Finally, David Lennick's transfers are masterly, and Wayne Kiley's notes refer movingly to the legendary wartime National Gallery concerts held in London, where Hess's performances created an 'indelible image of hope and vision in adversity'.

Josef Hofmann *pf*

Grand Piano – The Polish Virtuoso H

Hofmann Impressions for Piano – No 3, The Sanctuary[a]. Kaleidoscope, Op 40 No 4[a] **Moszkowski** La jongleuse, Op 52 No 4[a]. Etincelles, Op 36 No 6[a]. Serenata, Op 15 No 1[b]. Guitarre, Op 45 No 2[a]. Caprice espagnol, Op 37[a] **Friedman** Viennese Waltzes on Themes from Gärtner – Nos 1-4[b]. Estampes, Op 22 – Nos 2 and 4[b]. Elle danse, Op 10 No 5[b] **Paderewski** Humoresques de concert, Op 14[c] – No 1, Minuet; No 3, Caprice; No 6, Cracovienne fantastique. Miscellanea, Op 16[c] – No 1, Légende in A flat; No 4, Nocturne in B flat. Mélodie, Op 8 No 3[c]

[a]**Josef Hofmann**, [b]**Ignaz Friedman**, [c]**Ignaz Jan Paderewski** *pf*

Nimbus NI8802 (71 minutes: DDD) Ⓜ

From piano rolls released between 1919 and 1932

Chopin Piano Sonata No 2 in B flat minor, Op 35. Nocturnes – D flat, Op 27 No 2; F minor, Op 55 No 1. Polonaises – A, Op 40 No 1; A flat, Op 53. Scherzos – No 1 in B minor, Op 20; No 3 in C sharp minor, Op 39. Waltz in A flat, Op 42. Berceuse in D flat, Op 57 H

Josef Hofmann *pf*

Nimbus NI8803 (76 minutes: DDD) Ⓜ

From piano rolls released between 1920 and 1927

These performances taken from Duo-Art rolls are played, via a 'robot' created in 1973, on a modern concert Steinway under the supervision of Gerald Stonehill, a world authority on the Duo-Art catalogue. As a result, they sound as vivid and sparkling as if they had been given yesterday – indeed, so vivid is the piano tone that it emphasises brightness at the expense of warmth. To some extent this may be because of the difference in tone-quality between the instruments on which the recordings were made and that used for the reproduction, but sneaking doubts still remain concerning the matching of the robot's responses, resulting in some lack of really soft passages.

Doubts about realism are lessened by a performance of Chopin's 'funeral march' Sonata by Hofmann (Cherkassky's teacher), revered by contemporaries such as Rachmaninov. Though the dynamic range in the piece is not large (the limitations being at the *ff* end), it sounds a convincingly natural reading. But better still are the A flat *Polonaise*, which boasts a fine crisp *élan*, the B minor *Scherzo*, which employs a very full dynamic range and, like the C sharp minor *Scherzo*, illustrates the real meaning of *Presto con fuoco*, and a delicately pearly A flat *Waltz*. The *Berceuse*, coolly played, slightly suffers from a weakness also found elsewhere in the series – too obtrusive a middle register in relation to the melody above, whether due to the voicing of the piano or to a miscalculation in the adjustment of Duo-Art's two dynamic systems ('accompaniment' and 'theme'). Hofmann is heard again, and at his stunning best, on the disc devoted to three Polish virtuosos. A group of five pieces by his teacher Moszkowski is notable for perfectly controlled *staccato* touch, vital rhythmicality, neat rapid repeated notes and some delectable lightness, while Hofmann's own *Kaleidoscope* shows his breath-taking mercurial virtuosity .

Ignaz Friedman is represented by Moszkowski's once popular *Serenata* and by a handful of his own pieces in which he can display the superb technique for which he was famous. There is undeniably an air of exhibitionism about *Elle danse* and the elaborate fantasias on waltz themes by a singer friend (No 3 particularly lavishly ornate); but with such coruscating playing who would want to complain? Paderewski did not have the natural facility of the others – he was a late starter – but attracted huge and adoring crowds everywhere and was the most highly paid. There is a sparkle about his lively 'Caprice' in the style of Scarlatti and a quite attractive, if conventional, nationalist feeling in the 'Cracovienne fantastique'. The series is provided with first-class notes and Nimbus is to be applauded for its courageous enterprise.

Vladimir Horowitz *pf*

The solo European recordings, 1930-36, Volumes 1 and 2 H

APR5516 – **Chopin** Etudes – C sharp minor, Op 10 No 4; G flat, 'Black Keys', Op 10 No 5; F, Op 10 No 8; F, Op 25 No 3 (recorded 1934). Mazurkas – F minor, Op 7 No 3; E minor, Op 41 No 2; C sharp minor, Op 50 No 3. Scherzo No 4 in E, Op 54. Piano Sonata No 2 in B flat minor, 'Funeral March', Op 35 – Grave ... doppio movimento (rec 1936)
Liszt Funérailles, S173 No 7. Piano Sonata in B minor, S178

APR5517 – **Bach/Busoni** Nun freut euch, lieben Christen gmein, BWV734 **Beethoven** 32 Variations on an Original Theme in C minor, WoO80 **Debussy** Etude No 11 'Pour les arpèges composés' **Haydn** Keyboard Sonata in E flat, HobXVI/52 **Poulenc** Pastourelle. Toccata **Prokofiev** Toccata in D minor, Op 11 (rec 1930) **Rachmaninov** Prelude in G minor, Op 23 No 5 **Rimsky-Korsakov/Rachmaninov** The tale of Tsar Saltan – Flight of the bumble-bee
D Scarlatti Keyboard Sonatas – B minor, Kk87; G, Kk125 **Schumann** Presto passionato in G minor (rec 1932). Arabeske in C, Op 18. Traumes Wirren, Op 12 No 7. Toccata in C, Op 7 **Stravinsky** Petrushka – Russian dance (rec 1932)
Vladimir Horowitz *pf*
APR mono ② APR5516/7 Ⓜ
(oas: 69 and 71 minutes: ADD)

Horowitz's 1930-36 European recordings are beyond price, and so it is more than gratifying to have them permanently enshrined on APR rather than fleetingly available elsewhere. This is notably true of Horowitz's legendary, forever spine-tingling 1932 recording of the Liszt Sonata. Here, once more, is that uniquely teasing and heroic sorcery with octaves and passagework that blaze and skitter with a manic force and projection; an open defiance of all known musical and pianistic convention. Horowitz's virtuosity, particularly in his early days, remains a phenomenon, and hearing, for example, the *vivamente* elaboration of the principal theme or the octave uproar preceding the glassy, retrospective coda is to be reminded of qualities above and beyond the explicable. His way with the Chopin *Mazurkas* unites their outer dance elements and interior poetry with a mercurial brilliance and idiosyncrasy, and who but Horowitz could use his transcendental pianism to conjure a *commedia dell'arte* vision of such wit and caprice in Debussy's *Etude, Pour les arpèges composés*? Schumann's *Traumes Wirren* is spun off with a delicacy and dancing magic and in the same composer's *Presto passionato* Horowitz's performance hints at the schizophrenic violence and darkness that finally engulfed Schumann. Of the previously unpublished recordings, the first movement from Chopin's Second Sonata is as macabre and tricky as ever, with a steady, oddly menacing tempo. Prokofiev's *Toccata*, on the other hand, is tossed off at a nail-biting speed, and not even a small but irritating cut, a wild, approximate flailing at the end and an added chord by way of compensation, can qualify the impact of such wizardry. In Rachmaninov's G minor Prelude, however, Horowitz's volatility gets the better of him. If Horowitz, in common with virtually every other pianist, was not equally convincing in every composer and was even 'a master of distortion' for some, he was a Merlin figure of an indelible, necromantic brio for all others. Bryan Crimp explains the origin of the recordings at admirable length and if they, though expertly transferred, do show their age somewhat, nothing can lessen the impact of Horowitz's early charisma.

The Last Recording

Chopin Mazurka in C minor, Op 56 No 3. Nocturnes – E flat, Op 55 No 2; B, Op 62 No 1. Fantaisie-impromptu in C sharp minor, Op 66. Etudes – A flat, Op 25 No 1; E minor, Op 25 No 5 **Haydn** Piano Sonata in E flat, HobXVI/49 **Liszt** 'Weinen, Klagen, Sorgen, Zagen', Präludium, S179 **Wagner/Liszt** Paraphrase on Isolde's Liebestod from 'Tristan und Isolde', S447
Vladimir Horowitz *pf*
Sony Classical SK45818 (58 minutes: DDD) Ⓕ
Recorded 1989

More than any other pianist of his generation, Vladimir Horowitz was a legend in his lifetime, not only for his staggering technique but also for the personality and authority of his playing. Other pianists such as Rubinstein and Arrau may have been finer all-rounders (there were gaps in his repertory even in the classical and romantic field), but none has left so many performances distinguished by a special individuality that is covered, though hardly explained, by the word magic. As Murray Perahia has written, from the point of view of a pianist over 40 years his junior, 'he was a man who gave himself completely through his music and who confided his deepest emotions through his playing'. The performances in this last of his recordings, made in New York in 1989 and with superlative piano sound, are wonderfully crystalline and beautifully articulated, yet there is warmth, too, in the Haydn sonata that begins his programme and nothing whatever to suggest that octogenarian fingers were feeling their age or that his fine ear had lost its judgement. The rest of the disc is devoted to Chopin and Liszt, two great romantic composers with whom he was always associated, the last piece being Liszt's mighty transcription of Wagner's *Liebestod*, in which the piano becomes a whole operatic orchestra topped by a soprano voice singing out her love for the last time. Apparently this was the last music Horowitz ever played, and no more suitable ending can be imagined for a great pianistic career informed by a consuming love of music that was expressed in playing of genius. A uniquely valuable record.

Stephen Hough *pf*

Stephen Hough's New Piano Album
Chaminade Autrefois, Op 87 No 4. Pierrette, Op 41
Godowsky Triakontameron – Alt Wien **Hough** Etude de Concert. Musical Jewellery Box **Kálmán** Was weiss ein nie geküsster Rosenmund (arr Hough)
Liszt Soirée de Vienne in A minor, S427 No 6
Moszkowski Etincelles, Op 36 No 6
Pabst Paraphrase on 'Sleeping Beauty' (arr Hough)
Paderewski Mélodie in G flat, Op 16 No 2
Rachmaninov Humoresque in G, Op 10 No 5. Mélodie in E, Op 3 No 3 (1940 vers)
Rodgers Carousel – The Carousel Waltz. The King and I – Hello, Young Lovers (all arr Hough)
Schubert Moment musical in F minor, D780 No 3. Die schöne Müllerin, D795 – No 8, Morgengruss (all arr Godowsky) **Tchaikovsky** Dumka, Op 59. Humoresque in E minor, Op 10 No 2. Swan Lake, Op 20 – Pas de quatre (arr Wild)
Traditional The Londonderry Air (arr Hough)
Stephen Hough *pf*
Hyperion CDA67043 (78 minutes: DDD) Ⓕ
Recorded 1997-98

Stephen Hough fashions a viable programme culled from a bottomless piano bench of transcriptions, encores and other sundry ear-ticklers. Indeed, Hough proves that one can make a well-balanced meal using only desserts. Modern pianists, to be sure, are more calorie conscious than their forebears, and Hough is no exception. It's not his way to emphasise inner voices or linger over juicy modulatory patterns, *à la* Hofmann, Moiseiwitsch, Horowitz, Cortot or Cherkassky. If Hough prefers to bind Godowsky's garish counterpoints with skimmed milk rather than double cream, he's cheeky (and smart!) enough to insert his own *ossias* into Moskowski's *Etincelles*, or to retool the Tchaikovsky/Pabst *Sleeping Beauty* Paraphrase to more brilliant pianistic effect. As in his previous 'Piano Albums', Hough serves up his own Rodgers & Hammerstein transcriptions. If the decorative note-spinning in 'Hello, Young Lovers' distracts from rather than enhances the eloquent original, the pianist's giddy romp through 'The Carousel Waltz' is a tour de force that brilliantly recaptures both the tender and tough-minded qualities inherent in the musical's book. Hough's own *Etude de Concert* gets plenty of finger-twisting mileage out of a rather unmemorable theme, harmonised, however, with clever Gershwinisms. The unadorned Rachmaninov and Tchaikovsky selections are played with heartfelt simplicity and a lean yet singing sonority.

Julius Katchen *pf*

Balakirev Islamey **Brahms** Piano Sonata No 3 in F minor, Op 5. Variations on an original theme in D, Op 21 No 1. Hungarian Dances **Chopin** Ballade No 3 in A flat, Op 47. Fantasie in F minor, Op 49
Franck Prélude, choral et fugue **Liszt** Hungarian Rhapsody No 12 in C sharp minor, S244
Mendelssohn Prelude and Fugue in E minor/E, Op 35. Introduction and rondo capriccioso, Op 14
Rorem Piano Sonata No 2
Julius Katchen *pf*
Philips Great Pianists of the 20th Century ②
456 856-2PM2 (157 minutes: ADD) Ⓜ
Recorded 1949-62 ●●

The booklet-essay claims that Katchen's 1949 Brahms F minor Sonata was the first ever piano LP. You are likely to be totally bowled over by it now. Katchen plays each of the five movements as to the manner born, calling to mind Schumann's eulogy: 'We heard the most genial playing, which made an orchestra out of the piano. There were sonatas, more like disguised symphonies...'. You begin to wonder if this colossal performance will spoil the rest of the programme. It all has immense character, but apart from the Brahms at the end nothing quite reaches the same heights.

Katchen certainly makes a good case for Ned Rorem's Sonata, a pastiche-Gallic affair which in less temperamental and skilful hands would almost certainly sound merely insipid. The Mendelssohn *Prelude and Fugue* eventually tips over into Wagnerian hyperbole, while the *Introduction and rondo capriccioso* is treated as a pretext for flash-fingered display, as is, more justifiably, the Liszt *Rhapsody*.

Not many pianists would dare to deliver *Islamey* with such delirious abandon, and the central section is fabulously atmospheric. Whether the last few pages come off depends on personal tolerance levels, however; at these tempos they're inevitably something of a smash and grab affair. The Franck *Prélude* is unfolded patiently and with marvellously natural rhetorical presence, and the two Chopin pieces have the feeling of one-off, showstopping encores designed to bring the house down, rather than considered interpretations for repeated listening.

In these particular instances the recording quality must be partly to blame, because the Brahms Variations sound immediately warmer and less concerned with effect. They are all the better for Katchen's letting the climaxes grow organically rather than screaming them out. And the *Hungarian Dances* are pure joy. Katchen played music on his own terms rather than the composer's. He was a big enough artist to get away with that most of the time, and when the temperamental affinity was particularly strong, as with early Brahms, the results were well-nigh incomparable.

Wilhelm Kempff *pf*

Bach Chromatic Fantasia and Fugue in D minor, BWV903 **Beethoven** Piano Sonata No 22 in F, Op 54 **Schubert** Piano Sonata No 12 in F minor, D625. Drei Klavierstücke, D946. Impromptus, D899 – No 3 in G flat; No 4 in A flat

BBC Legends/IMG Artists BBCL4045-2 Ⓜ
(77 minutes: ADD). Recorded live in 1969 ooo

Kempff's art was at its apogee at the time of his 70th birthday in the autumn of 1965; rigour and fantasy held in perfect poise. Bryce Morrison, who has provided the notes for this BBC Legends release, and who was present at this concert – and indeed many other legendary recitals, recalls: 'If I were to single out one musical experience that transcended all others, it would have to be Wilhelm Kempff's 1969 Queen Elizabeth Hall recital. At his greatest, as he undoubtedly was on this occasion, Kempff's playing seemed bathed in a numinous light or halo of sound, his choice of music by Bach, Beethoven, and Schubert seemingly improvised on the spot.'

The performance of Op 54 has a wonderful intellectual fluidity. BM writes in his note: 'One could say that Kempff dissolves the separation between the supposed Apollonian and Dionysian creations of Mozart and Beethoven. With Kempff you simply hear music of a timeless magic, graced, like all great art, with a touch of enigma.' As Alfred Brendel has remarked in a recent essay ('Beethoven's Musical Characters'; *New York Review of Books*: November 16, 2000), this little-loved, highly original work establishes two contrasting characters at the beginning, male and female, animus and anima, which the finale brilliantly synthesises. That is Kempff's understanding of it to a T.

Brendel has said of Kempff, 'he was an Aeolian harp, ever ready to respond to whatever interesting wind blew his way'. It is a remark that applies especially well to Kempff's Schubert. He has said that in his early years Schubert's music was a book with seven seals. He played Schubert Lieder, but it was not until much later, after the First World War, that he entered the private world of the piano sonatas. For him, Schubert's 'heavenly length' was never lengthy if seen in proportion to the larger experience. 'If length becomes evident as longueur,' Kempff has written, 'the fault lies with the interpreter (I speak from my own experience …).'

Not here. The reading is wonderfully taut yet touched with a rare ease of utterance. The enigmatic end is perfectly judged (and well 'heard' by an audience whose applause merely stutters into life). After the 'disconsolate lyricism' (BM's phrase) of the sonata, the *Drei Klavierstücke* offer more or less unalloyed pleasure, Kempff winging the music into life. The playing has charm, dash and magic. He once said of Schubert's piano music: 'It ought not to be subjected to the glaring lights of the concert halls, as it is the confession of an extremely vulnerable spirit. Schubert reveals his innermost secrets to us *piano-pianissimo*.' We hear this wonderfully well in Kempff's playing of the first of his two encores, the Impromptu in G flat, where his fabled *cantabile* comes even more mesmerisingly into its own. An Aeolian harp indeed!

At the start of the recital, Kempff provides a shrewdly voiced and somewhat Mendelssohnian account of Bach's *Chromatic Fantasia and Fugue*. It is a performance to free the fingers and light the way ahead, the great work assuming the role of warm-up man with as good a grace as can be expected.

Rare Recordings, 1936-1945 Ⓗ

Bach Chromatic Fantasia and Fugue in D minor, BWV903. Cantata No 147, Herz und Mund und Tat und Leben – Choral: Wohl mir, dass ich Jesum habe (arr Kempff) **Beethoven** Piano Concerto No 5 in E flat, 'Emperor', Op 73[a] **Chopin** Berceuse in D flat, Op 57. Mazurkas – No 7 in F minor, Op 7 No 3; No 34 in C, Op 56 No 2. Fantaisie-impromptu in C sharp minor, Op 66 **Fauré** Nocturne No 6 in D flat, Op 63 **Mozart** Piano Concerto No 21 in C, K467[b] **Liszt** Années de pèlerinage – Première année, S160: Au lac de Wallenstadt; Au bord d'une source; Eglogue; Deuxième année, S161: Il penseroso; Sonetto 123 del Petrarca. Venezia e Napoli, S162 – No 1, Gondoliera

Wilhelm Kempff *pf* [a]**Berlin Philharmonic Orchestra / Peter Raabe;** [b]**Leipzig Symphony Orchestra / Hans Weisbach**

Music & Arts ② CD1071 (134 minutes: AAD). Ⓕ
Recorded 1936-45 oo

Here is musical treasure confirming that Wilhelm Kempff was a unique artist, whose miraculous pianism expressed a poetry as deep as it was natural. His early teacher, Heinrich Barth, is quoted in the sleeve-note as saying, 'Boy, what I cannot give you must come from heaven,' to which one can only retort that Kempff's gifts were, indeed, heaven-sent. A more modest teacher, Marguerite Long, listened in astonishment to Kempff's performance of Fauré's Sixth Nocturne (a work she had played to the composer and taught to successive generations of French pianists), chastened and feeling that she was hearing this rapturous piece for the first time.

How to explain the start of the central section, with its idealised birdsong emerging in a *pianissimo* so delicate and luminous that it seems to come from another world? Above all, the playing has an improvisatory freedom that can never be taught; ironically, considering Kempff's nationality, this may well be the most magically recreative performance of a Fauré piano work ever to appear on record. Kempff's Chopin, too, is a marvel of poise and economy, a classic instance of his style and understatement, and his Liszt, taken from the gentler, more picturesque side of his genius, is evocative in a manner unthinkable from any other pianist. Who else could confide the opening of the 'Sonetto 123 del Petrarca' with such a sense of its *lento placido*, *dolcissimo* and *espressivo* or close with a more beatific or glowing memory of the poet's words, 'I saw on earth angelic grace.' Again, his Bach is light-years away from other more pedantic or 'correct' versions, freely and unapologetically romantic in the *Chromatic Fantasia*, light, buoyant and inimitably voiced in the *Fugue*.

Then there are two live performances of concertos where the supposed division between Mozart's Appollonian and Beethoven's Dionysian genius seems to melt at a touch. Here is the most radiant, least hectoring of *Emperor* Concertos with a rapt sense of poetry beneath the outer tumult that not even the dim 1936 recording can hide. The Mozart is introduced as played by 'Professor Kempff', but the performance is so filled with light and air, a spirit of adventure and, in the finale, a transcendental fleetness, that the title seems comically ponderous and inept. Kempff's cadenzas, which include a quote from the C minor Fantasia, K475, offer further instances of his inventiveness, his wit and solemnity. Most of the recordings, when you stop to consider them, have come up remarkably well and those who thirst for true musical genius should invest in this double album without delay. These are rare recordings in every sense.

Brahms Ballades, Op 10. Piano Pieces – Op 76; Op 116-19 **Schumann** Arabeske in C, Op 18. Kreisleriana, Op 16 **H**
Wilhelm Kempff *pf*
Philips Great Pianists of the 20th Century mono ② 456 862-2PM2 (153 minutes: ADD) Ⓜ
Recorded 1950-56

Many of Kempff's recordings, made in stereo, have been regularly reissued, but the mono recordings of Brahms and Schumann, like so many from that mono LP era, have been seriously neglected. Yet in many ways these were the high points of Kempff's work in the recording studio. They are masterly, notable for their utmost concentration and sense of spontaneity, the magnetic, improvisatory quality in the playing. The transfers are superb, full and firm, bringing out the resonance and warmth of Kempff's piano sound, often giving the illusion of full stereo. Indeed, comparing this recording of the four *Ballades*, Op 10 with the stereo one which Kempff made later in 1972 for DG, the Decca mono sound is preferable, and the interpretations here are more keenly concentrated, with a greater sense of repose at speeds generally a shade broader.

The beauty of Kempff's playing, his ability to produce a singing *legato*, while using the pedal lightly, plainly stems from Kempff's early training as an organist. So it is that even the densest passages in the Brahms pieces, involving much octave doubling, have a rare transparency, with the melodic line always brought out, as in the middle section of the *Capriccio*, Op 116 No 3.

The seven *Fantasies* of Op 116 mark a high point in their range of expression and the way that Kempff builds them as a sequence, three *Capriccios* and four *Intermezzos*. With his incisive articulation Kempff is as strong and positive as anyone, while finding extra clarity, and using the subtlest dynamic shading. And though his style is flexible in an improvisatory way, it is fascinating to find that he is much less inclined than other pianists to use agogic hesitations, preferring not to disturb his seamless melodic lines. The Schumann performances have similar qualities, with the *Arabeske* flowing easily, totally charming. *Kreisleriana* dates from a little later, 1956, again songful and flowing, with the fifth section sparkling and full of fantasy and the sixth, *Sehr langsam*, as rapt as you are ever likely to hear it.

Bach Nun komm' der Heiden Heiland, BWV659. Cantata No 147, 'Herz und Mund und Tat und Leben' – Jesu bleibet meine Freude. Cantata No 140, 'Wachet auf, ruft uns die Stimme' – Wachet auf, ruft uns die Stimme (all arr Kempff) **Beethoven** Piano Sonata No 27 in E minor, Op 90[a] **Liszt** Deux Légendes, S175. Années de pèlerinage – Première année Suisse, S160 – Au lac de Wallenstadt; Au bord d'une source; Eglogue. Deuxième année Italie, S161 – Il penseroso; Canzonetta del Salvatore Rosa; Sonetto 47 del Petrarca; Sonetto 104 del Petrarca; Sonetto 123 del Petrarca. Venezia e Napoli, S162 – No 1, Gondoliera **Mozart** Piano Concerto No 23 in A, K488[a] **Schubert** Piano Sonata No 16 in A minor, D845
Wilhelm Kempff *pf* [a]**Bamberg Symphony Orchestra / Ferdinand Leitner**
Philips Great Pianists of the 20th Century mono/[a]stereo ② 456 865-2PM2 (149 minutes: ADD) Ⓜ
Recorded 1950-60

As in the first Kempff volume in the Philips Great Pianists series, the items here have been chosen by Alfred Brendel who is quoted as saying that Kempff's Liszt recordings are 'the greatest we have', and one may agree with Steinberg that the two *Légendes*, inspired by St Francis of Assisi and St Francis of Paola, are the 'crown jewel' of the collection. Like the other Liszt recordings here, Kempff made them for Decca in 1950 during the brief period when he forsook DG; though there is a hint of clatter in the topmost register, Kempff's wonderfully clear and transparent re-creation of Liszt's bird-sounds in the first of the two has never been matched on disc. The composer's poetic side is consistently brought out, not just in the *Légendes*, but in the inspired selection from the *Années de pèlerinage*.

While DG has over the years kept most of its Kempff recordings in the catalogue, it is specially valuable that these and the other Decca recordings should be included here. It is fascinating to compare Kempff's 1953 Decca recording of the Schubert A minor Sonata, D845, with the one he recorded later for DG in his Schubert sonata cycle. Here in the earlier version, with speeds marginally broader, he is lighter and more transparent, bringing out the poetry more intensely, yet emphasising structural strength in his observance of the exposition repeat, ignored on DG. In that same year Kempff recorded the three Bach transcriptions, reflecting his early training as an organist in their warmth and weight, very freely romantic by latter-day standards but wonderfully persuasive in keyboard colourings. Both of the DG recordings have long been staples of the catalogue, with Kempff again at his freshest and most poetic in the elusive little Op 90 Sonata of Beethoven, making the music sing. He similarly gives a magical performance of Mozart's A major Concerto, always phrasing with winning individuality, but never in a wilful way to draw attention away from Mozart. In all this material transfers are clean and fresh.

Evgeni Kissin *pf*

Evgeni Kissin in Tokyo
Anonymous Natu – Wa Kinu. Todai – Mori. Usagi (all arr Caegusa) **Chopin** Nocturne in A flat, Op 32 No 2. Polonaise in F sharp minor, Op 44
Liszt Concert Studies, S144 – La leggierezza; Waldestrauschen **Prokofiev** Piano Sonata No 6 in A, Op 82 **Rachmaninov** Lilacs, Op 21 No 5. Etudes tableaux, Op 39 – No 1 in C minor; No 5 in E flat minor **Scriabin** Mazurka in E minor, Op 25 No 3. Etude in C sharp minor, Op 42 No 5
Evgeni Kissin *pf*
Sony Classical SK45931 (73 minutes: DDD) Ⓕ
Recorded live in 1987

One reason for buying this CD is that it contains dazzling piano playing by a 15-year-old Russian set fair for a career of the highest distinction. A better reason is that the recital contains as full a revelation of the genius of Prokofiev as any recording ever made in any medium. The Sixth Sonata is the first of a trilogy which sums up the appalling sufferings of Russia under Stalin in a way that is only otherwise found in Shostakovich's 'middle' symphonies. Kissin plays it with all the colour and force of a full orchestra and all the drama and structural integrity of a symphony, plus a kind of daredevilry that even he may find difficult to recapture.

As for the rest of the recital only the Rachmaninov pieces are as memorable as the Prokofiev, although everything else is immensely impressive (the Japanese encore-pieces are extremely trivial, however). Microphone placing is very close, presumably in order to minimise audience noise; but the playing can take it, and indeed it may even be said to benefit from it.

Zoltán Kocsis *pf*

Bartók Six Romanian Folkdances, Sz56
Debussy Deux arabesques. D'un cahier d'esquisses. L'isle joyeuse. Estampes. Fantaisie[a]
Dohnányi Variations on a Nursery Song, Op 25[a]
Grieg Lyric Pieces, Book 3, Op 43 **Liszt** Années de pèlerinage, troisième année, S163 – Les jeux d'eau à la Villa d'Este **Rachmaninov** Piano Concerto No 4 in G minor, Op 40[b]. Prelude in C sharp minor, Op 3 No 2. Vocalise, Op 34 No 14 (arr Kocsis)
Zoltán Kocsis *pf* [a]**Budapest Festival Orchestra / Ivan Fischer;** [b]**San Francisco Symphony Orchestra / Edo de Waart**
Philips Great Pianists of the 20th Century ②
456 874-2PM2 (153 minutes: DDD) Ⓜ
Recorded 1982-95 OO

As a pianist, Zoltán Kocsis (also a conductor, composer and musicologist) is at once fastidious, interpretatively innovative and profoundly respectful of the recorded legacies left by major artists of the past – most notably those of Bartók and Rachmaninov. His recording of Rachmaninov's Fourth Concerto reawakens memories of the composer's own.

Edo de Waart and his San Francisco players are with him every single bar of the way, heightening the drama of the outer movements, and tenderising the wistful *Largo*. The solo playing is agile and quick-witted, with amazing finger velocity and a distinctive brand of rubato. The sudden switches in mood betray lightning reflexes and the piano tone is never brittle or clangorous. One might imagine that Kocsis's arrangement of the *Vocalise* would subscribe to the same taut, trimly tailored pianistic aesthetic: but what we hear is malleable almost to excess and, towards the end of the piece, extravagantly decorated.

The C sharp minor Prelude is given a far more central reading, and a brilliant one at that. Memories of Rachmaninov also inform Kocsis's approach to Grieg's Op 43 *Lyric Pieces*, particularly the chirruping 'Vöglein' and of 'Erotik' which – unlike the *Vocalise* – allows for phrasal freedom while holding fast to the musical line. Control is a very Kocsisian attribute, and helps to forge aural sculpture out of Debussy's two early *Arabesques*. The *Suite bergamasque* is scarcely less accomplished while *Estampes* and *D'un cahier d'esquisses* balance sensuality and spontaneity. Kocsis brings a winning lilt to *L'isle joyeuse*, although his fingerwork remains extraordinarily clear throughout.

The *Fantaisie* for piano and orchestra is given a fine performance which centres more on clarity than atmosphere, while the *Nursery* Variations combines fun with pianistic finesse: both works are superbly accompanied by Fischer and the Budapest Festival Orchestra (which Fischer and Kocsis co-founded). Liszt's ochre-tinted fountain is viewed with the hindsight of Bartók (or so it seems): Kocsis's performance attends rather more to the music's harmonic constituents than to its virtuoso aspect. And then there are Bartók's *Romanian Folkdances*, idiomatic, characterful and musically satisfying. The recorded sound has great presence.

Fritz Kreisler *vn*

The Complete Victor Recordings Ⓗ
Works by Albéniz, Bach, Balogh, Bass, Beethoven, Berlin, Bizet, Boccherini, Braga, Brahms, Böhm, Cadman, Chaminade, Chopin, Cottenet, De Curtis, Dawes, Debussy, Dohnányi, Drdla, Dvořák, Earl, Falla, Foster, Friedberg, Friml, Gärtner, Gluck, Godard, Godowsky, Gounod, Grainger, Granados, Grieg, Handel, Haydn, Herbert, Heuberger, Hirsch, Hubbell, Jacobi, Johnson, Korngold, Koschat, Koželuch, Krakauer, Kramer, Kreisler, Lalo, Lehár, Lemare, Leroux, Liliuokalani, Logan, Mascagni, Massenet, Mendelssohn, Meyer-Helmund, Moszkowski, Nevin, Offenbach, Openshaw, Owen,

Paderewski, Paganini, Poldini, Rachmaninov, Raff, Rameau, Ravel, Rimsky-Korsakov, Romberg, Schubert, Schütt, Scott, Seitz, Smetana, Spencer, Tchaikovsky, Thomas, Tosti, Townsend, Valdez, White and Winternitz
Fritz Kreisler *vn* with various artists
RCA Gold Seal mono ⑪ 09026 61649-2 Ⓜ
(781 minutes: ADD). Recorded 1910-46

If Jascha Heifetz was the firebrand among virtuosos, Bronislaw Huberman the passionate intellectual and Joseph Szigeti the articulate thinker, Fritz Kreisler was the ultimate gentleman – an easygoing, genial and comforting old-world master whose large discography centres mainly on the many sweetmeats that are associated with his name.

This neatly packaged and beautifully transferred collection of 'The Complete Victor Recordings' is in many respects the ultimate tribute: over 200 tracks covering the period 1910-46 and tracing a subtle stylistic curve from the vibrant and quick-wristed performances of the teens to the wistful, elegant and slightly off-colour 1946 recording of Kreisler's Straussian *Viennese Rhapsodic Fantasietta*.

However, readers unable to stomach acoustic 78s are duly warned that primitive technology dominates the first six CDs, whereas the rest is made up of generally well-engineered electrical recordings. Still, such was Kreisler's sure projection and richness of tone that, like certain great singers of the period (with McCormack being a fair case in point), he triumphed over inadequacies of sound. High points of his early discography include revealing 'one off' recordings of the 'Canzonetta' from Tchaikovsky's Violin Concerto and the *Scherzando* from Lalo's *Symphonie espagnole* (both 'first commercial releases'), Kreisler's own arrangement of Chopin's A minor *Mazurka*, Op 67 No 4, a truncated Bach Double Concerto with Efrem Zimbalist and the various items with John McCormack.

Kreisler's electrical RCA recordings are dominated, at least in terms of repertoire, by the oft-reissued sonata performances with Rachmaninov, all of them combining violinistic poise with taut, muscular pianism. As to the rest, there are countless gems and a plethora of duplications: six of the *Thaïs* 'Méditation', five each of *Caprice viennois*, *Liebesleid* and *Liebesfreud*, four of Dvořák's *Humoresque*, etc. – so many subtle varieties of a single basic conception, whether in terms of colour, rubato or phrasing.

Some contrasts are fairly marked; one can think in particular of *Mighty Lak' a Rose*, where the electrical recording with pianist Carl Lamson is so much more stylish than Kreisler's acoustical duet with Geraldine Farrar. Then there are the previously unissued 1929 sessions with Lamson and poignant, reflective performances. 'The King of Violinists' (as he was sometimes known) was without any doubt an undisputed master of musical aperitifs and desserts: taken in moderation, these recordings will give boundless pleasure.

Morten Gunnar Larsen *pf*

Fingerbreaker
Blake Brittwood Rag. Dictys on Seventh Avenue
Joplin The Cascades. The Entertainer. Scott Joplin's New Rag. Solace **Lamb** American Beauty Rag. The Ragtime Nightingale. Sensation
Jelly Roll Morton Don't you leave me here. Fingerbreaker. Kansas City Stomp **Scott** Grace and Beauty. Kansas City Rag. The Ragtime Betty
Smith Echo of Spring. Finger Buster. Rippling Waters
Morten Gunnar Larsen *pf*
Decca 460 499-2DH (67 minutes: DDD) Ⓕ
Recorded 1998

Norwegian pianist Morten Gunnar Larsen's résumé as a specialist in ragtime and early jazz styles mirrors his considerable keyboard artistry in a recital that instructs as much as it delights. Larsen is able to point up the stylistic differences between the six composers here in purely pianistic terms. He revels as much in Jelly Roll Morton's blues roots and hard-edged chord voicings, for instance, as he does the New Orleans legend's brass-band tinged polyrhythms and eloquent melodic invention in *Kansas City Stomp* and *Don't you leave me here*. For all of the title cut's virtuosic ebullience, Larsen is not afraid to roughen up the sonority when needed, yet curiously misinterprets Morton's rhythmic intentions in the second chorus. The pianist is totally in sync, though, with Eubie Blake's extrovert, Tin Pan Alley-influenced brand of ragtime, and serves up the composer's trademark 'backward boogie woogie' effects with gusto. By contrast, Larsen's reserved decorum in the Joplin selections seems rather sober and prim. He sheds his inhibitions, though, in the James Scott and Joseph Lamb triumvirates, and imbues stride master Willie 'The Lion' Smith's decorative flourishes with a wistful, patrician quality: a convincing foil to the composer's own forthright playing style.

Simon Lindley *org*

French Organ Works
Boëllmann Suite gothique, Op 25 **Bonnet** Romance sans paroles **M-A Charpentier** Te Deum, H146 – Prelude **Guilmant** Grand Choeur in D, 'alla Handel'. Cantilene pastorale, Op 19 **Langlais** Trois méditations (1962) **De Maleingreau** Suite mariale
Vierne 24 Pièces en stile libre, Op 31 – Epitaphe; Berceuse. Stèle pour un enfant défunt **Widor** Symphony No 5 in F minor, Op 42 No 1 – Toccata
Simon Lindley *org*
Naxos 8 550581 (74 minutes: DDD) Ⓢ
Recorded on the organ of Leeds Parish Church in 1991

Two of the most popular organ showpieces are here – Widor's Toccata and the Toccata which comes as the last movement of Boëllmann's *Suite gothique*. In addition there is the majestic *Te Deum* Prelude by Charpentier (familiar to a wide audience as the Eurovision signature tune) and the gentle *Berceuse* which Vierne wrote for his baby daughter. Alongside these evergreens, mainstays of any organ-lover's CD collection, are some more unusual but no less enjoyable pieces: Guilmant's glorious *Grand Choeur 'alla Handel'*, Bonnet's delightful *Romance sans paroles* and Paul de Maleingreau's *Suite mariale*. In short, a real feast of some of the best French organ music. Simon Lindley, organist at the musically-renowned Leeds Parish Church, gives fine, no-nonsense performances which should appeal especially to those exploring this music for the first time. The organ makes a super noise, and the Naxos recording is highly commendable. It may not be an instrument of which the *cognoscenti* of French organ music would immediately approve, but there is enough sensitivity and interpretative insight in Lindley's performances to make this a worthwhile buy for casual listener and specialist alike.

Dinu Lipatti *pf*

The Last Recital H

Bach Partita in B flat, BWV825 **Chopin** Waltzes – Nos 1 and 3-14 **Mozart** Piano Sonata No 8 in A minor, K310/K300*d* **Schubert** Impromptus, D899 – No 2 in E flat; No 3 in G flat

Dinu Lipatti *pf*

EMI Références mono CDH5 65166-2 Ⓜ

(73 minutes: ADD). Recorded live in 1950 ○○○

Apart from the two Schubert *Impromptus*, the programme of Lipatti's last recital consisted of works he had recorded only some 10 weeks earlier for EMI, in a Geneva studio, while enjoying a miraculous cortisone-wrought new lease of life. However, when honouring this Besançon Festival engagement on September 16th, 1950, very much against the advice of his doctors, leukaemia had once more gained the upper hand. Less than three months later he was dead, aged only 33. As those of us who have long cherished the original LPs already know, the only evidence of weakness was the omission of the last of the concluding Chopin *Waltzes* (in his own favoured sequence, that in A flat major, Op 34 No 2). For the rest, the recital stands as 'one of the great musical and human statements, a testimony to his [Lipatti's] transcendental powers, an almost frightening assertion of mind over matter', as the sympathetic introductory note puts it in the insert-booklet. One has to marvel at the clarity of articulation and part-playing in the Bach Partita, at once so attentive to craftsmanly cunning yet so arrestingly unpedagogic and alive. For Mozart he finds a wonderfully translucent sound world, rich in subtleties of colouring – not least in the slow movement's laden song. And as in the two Schubert *Impromptus*, the musical message is all the more affecting for its totally selfless simplicity and purity of expression. Even if just one or two of the *Waltzes* might be thought too fast, with over-swift internal tempo changes for contrasting episodes, his gossamer lightness of touch and mercurial imaginative fancy explain why his way with them has now acquired legendary status. The only small regret is that this most excellently remastered medium-price CD deprives us of the endearingly spontaneous extended arpeggio with which Lipatti prefaced the opening Partita, as if in greeting to his instrument, and likewise the improvisatory modulation with which he carried his Besançon listeners from Bach's B flat major to Mozart's A minor.

Oleg Maisenberg *pf*

Maisenberg Live at the Konzerthaus

Beethoven Piano Sonata No 2 in A, Op 2 No 2 **Chopin** Fantasie in F minor, Op 49. Mazurkas – Op 63: No 2 in F minor; No 3 in C sharp minor; A minor, Op 67 No 4. Nocturnes, Op 15 – No 4 in F; No 5 in F sharp **Debussy** Suite bergamasque. Estampes. Images, Book 2. Préludes, Book 1 **Liszt** Variations on 'Weinen, Klagen, Sorgen, Zagen', S180. Années de pèlerinage: Italie, S161 – Sonetto 104 del Petrarca. **Schubert** transcriptions – Der Wanderer, S558 No 11; Am Meer, S560 No 4. Litanei, S562 No 1 **Mozart** Allegro in B flat, K400/K372a. Fantasia in C minor, K475. Adagio in B minor, K540 **Rachmaninov** Adagio sostenuto in D flat, Op 16 No 5 **Ravel** Pavane pour une infante défunte. Miroirs **Schubert** Impromptus, D899 – No 1 in C minor; No 3 in G flat **Scriabin** Five Preludes, Op 16. Deux Poèmes, Op 32. Three Pieces, Op 45 **Tchaikovsky** The Seasons, Op 37b. Méditation in D, Op 72 No 5

Oleg Maisenberg *pf*

Glissando ⑤ 779 027-2 (353 minutes: DDD) Ⓜ

Recorded live in 1994 and 1995

During the 1994-95 concert season in Vienna Oleg Maisenberg performed a cycle of 12 piano recitals. Each evening was devoted to a single composer and Glissando's five-CD compilation was taken live from this momentous occasion. Maisenberg is not only a pianist in the grandest Russian traditon but a wholly individual player free to explore his wide-ranging and, clearly, beloved repertoire with a transcendental imaginative resource. How one envies his Viennese audience as they listened rapt night after night to performances so fascincating and illuminating that, without a trace of narcissism or preening mannerism, every work, whether by Mozart or Debussy, Beethoven or Tchaikovsky, emerged in an unforgettable way, as vivid and alive as the day it was first created.

Like Gilels and Richter, two of his greatest compatriots, Maisenberg is a superlative interpreter of Debussy and Ravel, his imaginative scope far remote from the dryness that can afflict other jaded but supposedly expert or 'authentic' pianists. In Ravel's *Miroirs*, 'Noctuelles' is as luminous as it is fragile (listen to that final fluttering *pianissimo*) and there is an acute sense of a dangerous undertow beneath an idyllic sun-lit surface in 'Une barque sur l'océan'. What narcotic languor he achieves in Debussy's 'Les sons et les parfums tournent dans l'air du soir' (the title is taken from Baudelaire's *Fleurs du Mal*), what mix of stealth and aggression at the start of 'La sérénade interrompue', the quasi-*guitarre* strokes snapped off with sudden violence. 'La fille aux cheveux de lin' has seldom been sung more simply or beguilingly and in 'Cloches à travers les feuilles' the final spiralling descent captures a profound sadness, a timeless and archaic evocation of funeral bells tolling from All Saints to All Souls Day. Maisenberg's exceptionally slow tempos may make French pianists, in particular, recall Ravel's caustic reminder that he wrote a *Pavane for a Dead Infanta* and *not* a dead Pavane, or view his way with the pastoral delicacy of Debussy's *Suite bergamasque* as lacking in a more traditional elegance or understatement. Yet even they will surely admit that they have rarely heard a more generous, less hard-bitten response.

At the opposite extreme, Maisenberg rides the savage rhetorical storms of Liszt's *Weinen, Klagen* Variations as surely, evoking the composer's anguish and final religious solace after the death of two of his three children. On the other hand the way he allows the slow waltz of Tchaikovsky's 'December' from *The Seasons* to blossom and evolve would seduce a saint. In Chopin he is as audacious but convincing as ever. Hear him at 16'21" in the Fantasie or in his selection of three Mazurkas and you will note a deep-dyed romanticism and despondency that few would risk in the studio.

Maisenberg is scarcely less revelatory in the great masters of Vienna, his adopted city, and so his recitals are a triumph from start to finish. Here is a pianist who in Liszt's immortal words 'can make emotion weep and sing and sigh...and breathe the breath of life', a reminder of a musical stature that has sometimes seemed extinct. William Sinkovitz's notes are excellent, Glissando's presentation is both lavish and tasteful, the recordings are of a thrilling immediacy, and who is going to object to prolonged applause before, after and between each item when it is so richly deserved?

Wayne Marshall *org*

Symphony

Dupré Symphony No 2 in C sharp minor, Op 26. Evocation, Op 37 – Allegro deciso **Hakim** Vexilla Regis prodeunt **Roger-Ducasse** Pastorale in F
Widor Symphony No 6 in C minor, Op 42 No 2
Wayne Marshall *org*
Virgin Classics VC5 45320-2 (72 minutes: DDD) Ⓕ
Recorded on the Marcussen organ of Bridgewater Hall, Manchester in 1997

Although you may be torn between open-mouthed admiration for the sheer technical bravado of the playing and horror at Wayne Marshall's breathtaking speeds, the former sentiment will win the day. He plays at speeds beyond the ability of any normal human being. The first movement of Widor's Sixth Symphony is marked *Allegro*, a word musical dictionaries translate as 'lively'. There are plenty of markings implying a faster speed. Yet it just cannot be possible to play faster than this. Listening amazed at such incredibly athletic finger- and foot-work you won't know whether to laugh or cry. Surely Widor could never have expected his works to sound quite like this – yet if he wanted his music to amaze and excite he surely can have no cause for complaint here. For while Marshall's stunning virtuosity is certainly the main feature of this performance, he is also an astute musician who successfully treads that fine line between mere exhibitionism and musical respectability. Perhaps highest praise must go to the mighty Manchester Marcussen; certainly no Cavaillé-Coll could have supported playing of this agility with such clarity. Marshall displays the organ mostly in hefty, full-throated combinations of stops; even the tranquil opening of the lovely Roger-Ducasse *Pastorale* only gives passing glimpses of some of the gentler stops. Sadly, a somewhat violently waving swell pedal and a rather unfortunate piece of tuning mar the character of the lone reed stop featured in the fourth movement of the Widor. Yet this is a stunning recording of a magnificent organ and there is no denying that few organ discs on the market present quite such brilliant playing.

Yehudi Menuhin *vn*

Menuhin in Japan Ⓗ

Bach Solo Violin Sonatas – No 1 in G minor, BWV1001; No 2 in D minor, BWV1002 – Sarabande. Solo Violin Partita No 3 in E, BWV1006 **Bartók** Six Romanian Folkdances, Sz56[a] (arr Székely)
Beethoven Sonatas for Violin and Piano[a] – No 5 in F, 'Spring', Op 24; No 9 in A, 'Kreutzer', Op 47
Brahms Hungarian Dance No 1 in G minor[a] (arr Joachim) **Dvořák** (arr Kreisler) Slavonic Dance in E minor, B78 No 2[a]. Symphony No 9 in E minor, 'From the New World', B178[a] – Largo
Granados (arr Kreisler) 12 Danzas españolas, Op 37[a]
Kreisler Caprice viennois, Op 2[a] **Nováček** Perpetuum mobile, Op 5 No 4[a] **Ravel** (arr Catherine) Pièce en forme de habanera[a] **Sarasate** Danzas españolas[a] – Malagueña; Habanera; Romanza andaluza, Op 22 No 1 **Tartini** (arr Kreisler) Sonata for Violin and Continuo in G minor, 'Devil's Trill'[a]
Wieniawski Scherzo-tarantelle in G minor, Op 16[a]
Yehudi Menuhin *vn* with [a]Adolf Baller *pf*
Biddulph mono ② LAB162/3 (146 minutes: ADD) Ⓜ
Recorded 1951

Here's a fully fired-up Menuhin, high on adrenalin and relishing the thrill of the moment. The circumstances were a Japanese tour, a punishing concert schedule and a two-day sequence of sessions which, on the evidence of the manifest results, probably involved a minimum of 'takes'. There were technical audio problems, most of them concerning substandard shellac and a rough-sounding end product. Surface levels are unusually high for 1951 commercial releases, but the recorded balance is adequate. What really surprises is the raging intensity and burnished tone quality of Menuhin's playing, especially when considering that his commercial recordings from the same period were prone to roughness. Even close scrutiny, though, suggests it is not a question of those 'rough edges' being camouflaged by a blanket of surface noise. It seems that this playing really is as good as it sounds! The *Kreutzer* Sonata throws caution to the wind (a little too much perhaps in first movement's central section) with a compensating spontaneity that recalls Menuhin's audacious youth and those fabulous records from the 1930s. Adolf Baller is no mere accompanist, but an immensely strong player in his own right, with plenty of individual ideas. The Bach solo sonatas are truly home territory for Menuhin, and these particular readings show greater maturity than his pre-war recordings and a surer technical command than the two complete sets that he made a few years later. In his notes Erik Wen rightly suggests that the Japanese performances 'project an expressive, almost improvisatory, freedom while maintaining an eloquent pacing throughout', though the sound on the pre-war set is better. The heat remains full on for Tartini's *Devil's Trill*, again notably superior to Menuhin's earlier commercial recording. The 'encores' breathe fire and passion by the second: Brahms's First *Hungarian Dance* is super-fast and the Dvořák 'Negro Spiritual Melody' (ie the principal theme from the *New World* Symphony's *Largo*) witnesses a veritable flood of tone. Occasionally in these shorter pieces the tempo is pushed too far, but the excitement is almost tangible. A marvellous release.

Arturo Benedetti Michelangeli *pf*

Beethoven Piano Sonata No 4 in E flat, Op 7 **Brahms** Variations on a Theme by Paganini, Op 35[a]. Four Ballades, Op 10[b] **Chopin** Mazurkas – No 19 in B minor, Op 30 No 2; No 20 in D flat, Op 30 No 3; No 22 in G sharp minor, Op 33 No 1; No 25 in B minor, Op 33 No 4; No 34 in C, Op 56 No 2; No 43 in G minor, Op 67 No 2; No 45 in A minor, Op 67 No 4; No 46 in C, Op 68 No 1; No 47 in A minor, Op 68 No 2; No 49 in F minor, Op 68 No 4 **Mompou** Cançon i danza No 1[a] **Schumann** Album für die Jugend, Op 68 – No 36, Matrosenlied; No 38, Winterszeit I; No 39, Winterszeit II. Carnaval, Op 9[c]
Arturo Benedetti Michelangeli *pf*
Philips Great Pianists of the 20th Century
[a]mono/stereo ② 456 904-2PM2 Ⓜ
(149 minutes: [b]ADD/DDD). Recorded 1942-81 ●

No more imperious or mesmeric pianist has ever existed than Arturo Benedetti Michelangeli. His psychological complexity is evident at every turn, switching in a trice from a chill and intimidating perfection to a flickering romantic susceptibility. Above all, this is the playing of a unique master – at no point could you ever mistake Michelangeli for another pianist. That this provides a two-edged sword is part of the mystery and fascination. In what sense is Michelangeli's neutral and inhibited, if pianistically ultra-precise, Beethoven Op 7 Sonata *Allegro molto e con brio*? He conjures a near mystical stillness in the second movement *Largo*, but his freeze-dried pianism in the final Rondo is the reverse of *grazioso*. On the other hand he is hypnotic in the wintry declamation of his selection from Schumann's *Album for the Young* while in *Carnaval* his pianism is of a calibre that, even when heartless, holds his listeners in a vice-like grip. 'Arlequin' struts and spins with an incomparably teasing elegance and finesse. Even though he offers wildly trumpeting *Papillons*, and refuses to indulge the *piano* and *forte* jocular contrasts of 'Pierrot', there's breathlessly surging and *agitato* (as marked) 'Chopin' and a piquancy and drollery throughout, startling to those who consider Michelangeli's 'egotistical sublime' above such characterisation. Again, the *poco espressivo* of Var 13, Book 2 from Brahms's *Paganini* Variations is very *poco* indeed and the *molto dolce* of Var 12, Book 1 is coldly compromised, but the overall mastery is phenomenal. The *glissandos* of Var 13 in Book 1 become part of a wild stamping dance that makes a mockery of so many other more effortful alternatives. Michelangeli is crystalline and compelling in Brahms's Fourth *Ballade* in a manner far removed from gentler and more romantic received wisdom and in his selection of Chopin *Mazurkas* he strips away all decorative surface gestures, penetrating to their very essence, confiding their shifts of mood with the rarest sense of vision and darkness. Op 33 No 4 in B minor, which Michelangeli often played as an encore, reminds one of a patrician refinement that has remained unequalled. The transfers are excellent.

Chopin Fantasie in F minor, Op 49. Ballade No 1 in G minor, Op 23. Waltz in E flat, Op posth **Debussy** Images – Reflets dans l'eau; Hommage à Rameau; Cloches à travers les feuilles; Et la lune descend sur le temple qui fût **Schumann** Carnaval, Op 9. Faschingsschwank aus Wien, Op 26 **Mompou** Cançons i danses No 6 – Canción Ⓗ
Arturo Benedetti Michelangeli *pf*
Testament mono ② SBT2088 Ⓕ
(130 minutes: ADD). Includes a half-hour rehearsal sequence. Recorded live in 1957

Readers who are familiar with Michelangeli's 1971 DG recording of Debussy's *Images* will be astonished at this highly mobile 1957 concert performance of 'Cloches à travers les feuilles', which is almost a full minute faster than its stereo successor; or 'Reflets dans l'eau', which glides across the water's surface with such swiftness and ease that the more considered DG alternative – glorious though it is – sounds studied by comparison. 'Hommage à Rameau' is shaped with the utmost finesse and 'Et la lune descend sur le temple qui fût' coloured by exquisitely graded nuances. The performance of Schumann's *Carnaval* is a choice gallery of aural sculpture, whether in the minutely calculated responses of 'Pierrot', the teasing rubato of 'Coquette', the energy and attack of 'Papillons', the effortless flow of 'Chopin' or the ecstatic lingerings in 'Aveu'. Michelangeli's 'Eusebius' is tender but unsentimental, whereas his 'Florestan' has enough 'reflective' ingredients to suggest that the two characters are closer in spirit than we often think. *Faschingsschwank aus Wien* contrasts muscular assertiveness (the opening *Allegro*) with the most amazing control (in the 'Romanze'), while the 'Intermezzo' promotes a virtually orchestral range of dynamics. Michelangeli's

Chopin has a rare nobility, the *Fantasie* especially which, at a rather faster tempo than usual, holds together as a narrative entity. Then there is the imposing First *Ballade* and the encores – a sunny posthumous E flat *Waltz* (a regular extra on Michelangeli's concert programmes) and Mompou's sad but tender 'Canción'. This disc leaves you humbled by, and grateful for, some wonderful piano playing. Michelangeli's art is both rare and elusive, his expressive vocabulary finely distilled and unlikely to impress those who listen only for technical mastery. So it's ironic that those who criticise Michelangeli for 'coldness' or 'aloofness' are often the very commentators who are so dazzled by his virtuosity that they cannot hear beyond it. Testament's transfers are superb.

Mikhail Pletnev *pf*

Pletnev Live at Carnegie Hall

Bach (arr Busoni) Partita No 2 in D minor, BWV1004 – Chaconne **Balakirev** Islamey **Beethoven** Piano Sonata No 32 in C minor, Op 111 **Chopin** Four Scherzos, Opp 20, 31, 39, 54 **Moszkowski** Etude de virtuosité, Op 72 No 6 **Rachmaninov** Etude-tableau in E flat minor, Op 39 No 5 **D Scarlatti** Sonata in D minor, Kk9 **Scriabin** Deux Poèmes, Op 32 – No 1 in F sharp

Mikhail Pletnev *pf*

DG ② 471 157-2GH2 (102 minutes: DDD) Ⓕ

Recorded live in 2000 OO

The billed recital was the Bach-Busoni transcription, the Beethoven Sonata Op 111 and the Chopin Scherzos, and the rest – five items on a 'bonus' CD, finishing with Balakirev's *Islamey* – amount nearly to a half-programme on top. The recording comes with buckets of applause, linking every item, and by the end of *Islamey* the audience is in a state of near frenzy (and the piano beginning to complain). Some may blow hot and cold over Pletnev but he is not to be missed. As celebrity recitals go this must have been an exceptional spectacle. There is an old-time feel about it, as if Horowitz might have been about to walk out on stage. Bach, Beethoven, Chopin and a few others are of the party but it is the pianist people have come to hear, and they are expecting to be astonished.

When covering the ground in such thoroughbred style, Pletnev's athleticism has an allure which is a pleasure in itself. The tumultuous codas of Chopin's Scherzos are meat and drink to him, and in making a dash for home, over hedge and ditch, there is never a doubt about his stamina. It is a thrilling dash too, the mechanics of piano playing thrown off, the virtuosity transcendental – and the house brought down (four times). There has been grace along the way, many special moments, and always a faultless sense of timing. But with Pletnev in this mood the personality does seem disappointingly limited. It is the devil in his make-up who predominates, and you don't have to travel far in the first Scherzo to find yourself questioning the volatility and the exaggerated feverishness of it all. Is there nothing more to these wonderful pieces than tempests, and charm and coquettishness in the slower bits? Does the middle section of the first one – folk-like and remote – really have to be perfumed to high heaven? But that is his way: toy with the detail and then snatch it away, play with the line and texture to see what novelties one might come up with, hold up the flow, if fancy invites, or perhaps step on the gas. Add a gloss, in other words, as if this constantly performed music could not be interesting to modern listeners unless given a new slant, or a wholesale transcription. It's a point of view, but as Pletnev takes us with him through the flea-markets you ask yourself: if the operation has to be done, could there not be more authenticity of feeling and less vulgarity?

In Chopin he can strike you as a heartless fellow. The Beethoven is a traversal rather than a completely coherent interpretation of the last Sonata he offers, but it is full of striking things. The first movement alternates agitation with near-stasis, and the coda is floated away like something out of Medtner; but the spirit of inquiry and control of mass and sonority are of such an order that the ground is made fertile, the communication fresh. What Beethoven would have thought at having so many of his indications and inflections of expression stood on their heads we shan't know, but no doubt he would have considered it a futile endeavour for the performer to take delight in the physical challenges and to allow the sense to emerge from the sound. The *Arietta*, played very slowly, is ideally hymn-like and direct; and although some of the detailing in the variations strikes you as weird, the breath of the huge second movement as a lyrical span is impressively sustained, right through to the final trilling, which is wonderful. Not a monumental version of the Sonata entirely hewn from the rock, then, and that makes a nice change.

The Bach-Busoni at the beginning, an uncharacteristically misguided transcription and such a waste of time, will not disappoint admirers of it. The Scriabin, Moszkowski and Balakirev, though, are outstanding among the encores. Oh yes, a Carnegie Hall début with attitude and knobs on, and no, it is never dull. But best to have been there, perhaps.

The Rachmaninov Piano

Beethoven Piano Sonata No 26 in E flat, 'Les adieux', Op 81*a* **Chopin** Andante spianato and Grande Polonaise in E flat, Op 22

Mendelssohn Andante cantabile and Presto agitato in B. Rondo capriccioso in E, Op 14

Rachmaninov Etudes-tableaux – Op 33: No 6 in E flat minor; No 8 in G minor; No 9 in C sharp minor; Op 39: No 5 in E flat minor. Variations on a theme of Corelli, Op 42

Mikhail Pletnev *pf*

DG 459 634-2GH (74 minutes: DDD) Ⓕ

Recorded 1998

Gimmickry? Not a bit of it. This is a genuinely illuminating and thought-provoking issue. More than that, it's immensely enjoyable. The freedoms and avoidances of convention which

Pletnev often likes to allow himself here sound consistently inspired and true to the spirit of the music. The instrument is Rachmaninov's pre-war American Steinway. What you hear is a well-regulated tone, a little more uneven between the registers and a little thinner overall than its modern counterpart, but never measly or tinny, with the exception of the high treble, which sometimes gives an impression similar to excessive use of the soft pedal. Some of the glittering passagework in the Chopin does becomes rather glaring, especially when pushed beyond *mezzo-forte*. On the whole though, even this is easy to adapt to, because in Pletnev's hands the texture is so rich in nuance, his own eloquence apparently released from all inhibitions. There's also a significant gain in transparency. Indeed if anyone wanted to claim that this kind of instrument has all the advantages of the 'early' piano with none of the drawbacks it would be hard to disagree. Whether it would stand up to the demands of having to project to the back of a full-size concert hall is debatable, but heard in DG's close yet well-ventilated recording, it sounds marvellous. Rarely will you hear as involving an account of the Rachmaninov *Corelli* Variations, and only Richter has surpassed Pletnev in the *Etudes-tableaux*. Nor is it only Rachmaninov's own opulent textures which are thrillingly clarified. The *Les adieux* Sonata is wonderfully free, both in rubato and voicing, and never so at the expense of the longer lines of the structure. Pletnev's Mendelssohn is breathtakingly poetic and, in the *Rondo capriccioso*, stunningly articulate, every single phrase subtle yet unselfconscious. All in all, this is one of the very finest achievements in Pletnev's already imposing discography.

Maurizio Pollini *pf*

Boulez Piano Sonata No 2 **Prokofiev** Piano Sonata No 7 in B flat, Op 83 **Stravinsky** Petrushka – three movements **Webern** Piano Variations, Op 27
Maurizio Pollini *pf*
DG The Originals 447 431-2GOR (68 minutes: ADD) Ⓜ
Recorded 1971-76 ●●●

Perfection needs to be pursued so that you can forget about it. Pollini's *Petrushka* movements are almost inhumanly accurate and fast; but what comes across is an exhilarating sense of abandon, plus an extraordinary cumulative excitement. The Prokofiev Seventh Sonata remains a benchmark recording not only for the athleticism of its outer movements but for the epic remorselessness of the central *Andante*. The Webern Variations are a magical fusion of intellectual passion and poetry, and the Boulez Sonata vividly reminds us why the European avant-garde was such a powerful force in the 1950s. These recordings are a monument to what it is possible for two hands to achieve on one musical instrument. The 'original-image bit-processing' has given a bit more brilliance and presence, as claimed, and another gain is the retention of atmosphere between movements.

Sviatoslav Richter *pf*

Chopin Etude in E, Op 10 No 3 **Liszt** Valses oubliées, S215 – No 1; No 2. Etudes d'exécution transcendante, S139 – No 5, Feux follets; No 11, Harmonies du soir **Mussorgsky** Pictures at an Exhibition **Rachmaninov** Prelude in G sharp minor, Op 32 No 12 **Schubert** Moment musical No 1 in C, D780. Impromptus, D899 – No 2 in E flat; No 4 in A flat H
Sviatoslav Richter *pf*
Philips 50 Great Recordings 464 734-2PM Ⓜ
(74 minutes: ADD). Recorded live in 1958 ●●

Even at the height of his powers Richter could be an erratic player, but on this occasion the force was with him from first note until last. Not only did the recital help to spread the Richter 'legend' in the months leading up to his much-hyped London and New York débuts in 1960, his Mussorgsky *Pictures* made a decisive contribution to the rehabilitation of that piece as a staple of the piano repertoire. Here is virtuosity entirely at the service of the music, defying anyone to say a word against Mussorgsky's pianistic imagination or to want to hear Ravel's orchestral make-over ever again. The rest of the recital displays Richter's view of the romantic repertoire at its first mature flowering, after a period of occasionally experimental overstatement and before its rigidification. His Schubert, Chopin and Liszt share a common core of determined resistance to buffeting emotions. Yet on the surface his Schubert is as beautiful and refined as anyone's; the possibly disconcerting intensity of his Chopin is built strictly around the composer's expression markings; and as all collectors of recorded piano music already know, his Liszt *Feux follets* remains a benchmark performance to this day. It is impossible to say for sure if the Prokofiev sonatas presented here are the absolute best available, though one suspects they are. He was in at the birth, or nearly so, of all three pieces, and his identification with their expressive worlds is complete. Defiance and unstoppable momentum are at the heart of the matter, and virtuosity of the highest order is pressed into the service of those core values. It is doubtful whether anyone has taken the *Scherzo* of the Sixth Sonata more convincingly at this tempo (the fast end of *allegretto*), for instance, or found more wide-ranging yet integrated drama in all three movements of the Eighth. You could certainly wish for more refined recording quality on the first disc, though the Prokofiev sonatas are well enough recorded, especially the Eighth. Overall it's difficult to imagine a truer encapsulation of the Richter phenomenon. If by any chance you have missed these recordings in past incarnations you now have an opportunity not to be passed up.

Chopin Ballade No 3 in A flat, Op 47[a]. Barcarolle in F sharp, Op 60[a]. Etudes, Op 10 – No 1 in C[b]; No 3 in E[a]; No 4 in C sharp minor[b]; No 6 in E flat minor[b]; No 10 in A flat[b]; No 12 in C minor (2 versions)[ab]. Four Mazurkas, Op 24[a]. Scherzo No 4 in E, Op 54[a] **Debussy** Images, Set 2[a] – Cloches à travers les

feuilles. L'isle joyeuse[a]. Préludes – Book 1[a]: No 1, Danseuses de Delphes; No 2, Voiles; No 3, Le vent dans la plaine; No 4, Les sons et les parfums; No 5, Les collines d'Anacapri; No 6, Des pas sur la neige; No 7, Ce qu'a vu le vent d'Ouest; No 9, La sérénade interrompue (2 versions); No 10, La cathédrale engloutie; Book 2[c] **Prokofiev** Danse, Op 32 No 1[a]
Sviatoslav Richter *pf*
BBC Legends/IMG Artists mono/[c]stereo
② BBCL4021-2 (149 minutes: ADD) Ⓜ
From broadcast performances [a]1961, [b]1963 and [c]1967

Chopin and Debussy were, along with Wagner, the composers Richter always said meant the most to him. This remarkable compilation bears out that rather surprising confession. The opening of the Third *Ballade* hangs languorously in the air, every note perfectly weighted and intensely alive; the impetuosity to come is never predictable, always improvisatory in feel, with just a couple of insignificant fluffs as the price of abandon to the flow of inspiration. Similarly rapturous in their fantasy and onward momentum are the *Scherzo* No 4, *Mazurkas* and *Barcarolle*. Richter's Debussy radiates a hypnotic power quite beyond the routinely expressive and picturesque; it's elevated music-making, with every aspect of pianistic art, including wizardry with the sustaining pedal, at its most highly developed. One could single out the smouldering intensity of the 'Sérénade interrompue', initially all half-lights and heat haze, then explosive and sun-baked, and finally sexily insinuating in the serenade itself. You thought Richter was an unremittingly serious player? Try his matchlessly skittish 'Danse de Puck'. Only in 'La cathédrale engloutie' is he hoist by his own petard, when he sticks doggedly to an edition which has been shown to be inaccurate and scores an uncharacteristic number of mis-hits on the way. The 1961 Festival Hall recital concludes with Richter's controversially frenetic view of the Chopin E major Study. Though uncomfortable listening, it is based strictly on the markings in the score and follows the *Vivace* marking of the autograph rather than the *Lento* of the first publication. These recordings are all slightly too distantly miked, but the 1962 Snape Maltings recital sounds satisfyingly immediate. Here the C sharp minor Study is so fast it almost meets itself coming back; at the other extreme the hallucinatory pedalling of the slow E flat minor prepares the way for more of Richter's magical Debussy. However well stocked his discography may seem to be, this issue takes its place at or near the very top.

Aleksandar Serdar *pf*

Bach Partita in D minor, BWV1004 – Chaconne **Brahms** Waltzes, Op 39 **Chopin** Andante spianato and Grande Polonaise in E flat, Op 22 **Galuppi** Piano Sonata No 5 in C **Mendelssohn** Variations sérieuses in D minor, Op 54
Aleksandar Serdar *pf*
EMI Debut CDZ5 72821-2 (74 minutes: DDD) Ⓑ
Recorded 1997

This disc from EMI's Debut series presents a richly varied recital with playing of consistently high quality. It has been superbly recorded in the Abbey Road studios, giving this Belgrade-born pianist every opportunity to show his talent to best effect. Serdar gives a diverse and hugely enjoyable programme; he is clearly a thoughtful musician with imagination and personality. His Galuppi Sonata No 5 (which used to be a favourite of Michelangeli's) is exquisitely moulded, balancing tonal refinement with wonderful freshness and spirit. The same qualities of beauty and elegance abound in Chopin's *Andante spianato and Grande Polonaise*: there are many more crisp and muscular performances of the *Polonaise* on record, but few so concerned with colour, nuance and melodic shape. Maybe this piece should set the pulse racing a little more, but it is good to hear it treated so lovingly, rather than rushed off its feet merely to prove a pianist's virtuoso credentials. Less convincing is Serdar's Mendelssohn: while his sharp reflexes in the *Variations sérieuses* are impressive, it needs more warmth of tone and, towards the end, a more heroic sweep and greater expressive intensity. The Brahms *Waltzes* begin belligerently, but he goes on to delight and tease with his range of expressive resource. Busoni's pianistic amplification of Bach's great D minor *Chaconne* – a much maligned, but still much performed, transcription – sits slightly uncomfortably at the end of the recital (the shift of expressive weight following the Brahms *Waltzes* jolts at first). Serdar's individual imagination is still in evidence, but some passages lack poise and grandeur.

Solomon *pf*

Solomon in Berlin H
Bach Concerto in the Italian style, BWV971
Beethoven Piano Sonatas – No 3 in C, Op 2 No 3; No 14 in C sharp minor, 'Moonlight', Op 27 No 2
Chopin Fantasie in F minor, Op 49. Nocturne in B flat minor, Op 9 No 1. Scherzo No 2 in B flat minor, Op 31
Brahms Intermezzos – E, Op 116 No 4; E flat minor, Op 118 No 6. Rhapsody in B minor, Op 79 No 1
Solomon *pf*
APR mono ② APR7030 (92 minutes: ADD) Ⓜ
Recorded live in 1956 ●

This invaluable issue brings together on two short CDs recitals given by Solomon in 1956 for Berlin Radio. This was the time of Solomon's greatest success when, as Bryan Crimp puts it in his excellent notes, he had acquired a Midas touch, at long last reaping the rewards his artistry deserved. The recordings are clean but airless, yet they do little to dim one's sense of Solomon's quality, his masterly but unobtrusive virtuosity, his unsullied honesty and musicianship. How typical is his robust, pacy opening *Allegro* in the Bach, how impeccable his unfolding of the central *Andante*; a truly seamless aria in such hands. His rhythmic zest in the finale, too, is hard to resist. In Beethoven Solomon is, not surprisingly, no less remarkable. By 1956 he had modified his celebrated slow tempo for the first movement of Op 27 No 2, yet the playing remains sculpted and marmoreal, a statement mixing abstraction and elegy and wholly devoid of impressionism or 'moonlit' overtones. Solomon's Brahms is no less lucid and classic, though his B minor *Rhapsody* has a truly *agitato* sweep and propulsion. Here Solomon's poise and *sang-froid* are only just on the right side of detachment. The same might be said of his Chopin *Fantasie*. Solomon was hardly a pianist to wear his heart on his sleeve, and although there have been other, more richly idiosyncratic *Fantasies* on record, there are few more masterly or refined. Finally, criticism falls silent when you listen to Solomon in the B flat minor *Nocturne*, where his magically 'contained' eloquence re-creates a pearl beyond price. Here, heart and mind work in faultless harmony and alliance.

Andreas Staier *hpd*

Variaciones del Fandango español

Albero Recercata, Fuga and Sonata – G; D
Boccherini Guitar Quintet in D, G341 – Fandango (arr Staier/Schornsheim)[a] **Ferrer** Adagio and Andantino in G minor **Gallés** Keyboard Sonatas – No 9 in C minor; No 16 in F minor; No 17 in C minor
López Variaciones del Fandango español
Soler Fandango
Andreas Staier *hpd* with [a]**Christine Schornsheim** *hpd* [a]**Adela Gonzáles Cámpa** *castanets*
Teldec 3984-21468-2 (65 minutes: DDD) Ⓕ
Recorded 1998 ●

The heyday of the fandango dance was in the 18th century (Mozart introduced a form of it in *Figaro*, following Gluck's *Don Juan*). It was danced by a single couple who did not touch but whose movements were highly erotic; and there were several local varieties of it, including the malagueña, the granadina, the rondeña and the murciana. Andreas Staier does not, despite the disc's title, confine himself to the fandango rhythm or to the key of D minor which was so prevalent for it. He kicks off with stunning virtuosity with Soler's famous piece (if it really *was* by him), with its exciting build-up and fearsome hand-crossings. After the initial *tiento* (which he pulls about with violent changes of speed), he tears at a most un-fandango-like breakneck pace into the dance, whirling breathlessly to the end and employing a free range of registrations on his German-type instrument. He does not make the mistakes of spoiling the cumulative effect by rubatos and changes of speed or tacking on a reprise which wrongly ends the work on the tonic instead of the dominant. He adopts the same fast pace for the very similar but shorter variations on the fandango by López (which he discovered), who was an organist in the royal chapel in Madrid under Charles III and IV. It is a distinct relief to find a more authentic speed adopted in a free arrangement for two harpsichords of a fandango from a Boccherini quintet, which is enlivened by (obbligato) castanets. Albero's *recercatas* and gigantic fugues are every bit as astonishing in their chromaticisms and eccentric key-shifts as Bach's *Chromatic Fantasia and Fugue* – in fact, more outlandish. The *recercatas* resemble the older lute *préludes non-mesurés*; the lively sprawling fugues (that in D minor a gigue) call forth brilliantly virtuosic playing and splendidly rhythmic stamina; and each work closes with a binary sonata movement which contains Scarlattian chordal scrunches. Of the other non-fandango works here, the most interesting is an F minor Sonata by Josep Gallés, a Catalan whose other sonatas disclose a somewhat disorganised musical mind.

Fredrik Ullén *pf*

Got a Minute?

Brahms Study after Chopin's Etude, Op 25 No 2 **Chopin** Waltz in D flat, 'Minute', Op 64 No 1 **Cortot** Adagio after Chopin's Cello Sonata, Op 65 **Ferrata** Second Study after Chopin's Waltz, Op 64 No 1 **Furst** Showpan Boogie **Godowsky** Waltz after Chopin's Op 64 No 1 **Gruenberg** Jazz Masks, Op 30a **Joseffy** Two Concert Studies after Chopin **Michałowski** Paraphrase on Chopin's Waltz, Op 64 No 1 **Moszkowski** Waltz after Chopin's Op 64 No 1 **Philipp** Two Concert Studies after Chopin's Op 64 **Reger** Five Special Studies after Chopin **Rosenthal** Study after Chopin's Waltz, Op 64 No 1 **Sorabji** Pastiche on Chopin's Waltz, Op 64 No 1. Pasticcio capriccioso sopra l'op 64 no 1 del Chopin
BIS CD1083 (77 minutes: DDD) Ⓕ
Recorded 2000 ●

Now here's a treasure trove for those with a sweet tooth. Godowsky's infamous reworkings of Chopin's Etudes are, of course, familiar, but few are aware of the diversity of Chopin arrangements conjured by Godowsky's peers. This collection concentrates on the surprising range of treatments of the *Minute* Waltz, from virtuosic enhancements à la Moszkowski or Rosenthal to the wild and fantastical pastiches of Sorabji. True, the usual understanding of transcription – the idiomatic recasting of music from one medium to another – may be stretched by this sort of super-pianistic amplification, but the wit and invention of these ear-tickling fantasies have their own authentic rewards.

Musically, the most daring works are by Reger and Sorabji, who treat Chopin's structures as springboards for their own imaginative adventures. Try Reger's transformation of Chopin's Etude in thirds (Op 25 No 6), cruelly recast in sixths, or the wealth of subsidiary thematic embellishment in his elegant gloss on the C sharp minor Waltz (Op 64 No 2). The Polish Chopin specialist Aleksander Michałowski wrote numerous Chopin elaborations, and his version of the *Minute* Waltz is as dazzling as it is demanding. Rosenthal, Joseffy and Ferrata were all Liszt pupils, and their treatments, although varied, exhibit familiar traits: doubling in thirds, and a saturation of filigree embroidery and polyphonic enrichment. It's all good harmless fun, and Chopin – like Bach – can easily withstand the treatment without suffering irrevocable damage to the identity and purity of the originals.

As if to prove the point, Ullén ends his exploration with the original D flat Waltz, and makes the astute observation that 'our perception of a piece depends as much on our knowledge of its descendants as of its precursors'.

Ullén performs these treacherous pieces with astonishing clarity and dexterity, dispatching the torrents of notes and intricate detail with unruffled aplomb. Anyone who plays Ligeti's Etudes must have mental agility and a fearless technique, but Ullén also shows a refinement of nuance and musical shape, making music of even the most over-written material. The principal caveat is his tendency to keep the embellishing figuration too much in the foreground, at the expense of depth of sonority in the melodic line; there are also places that cry out for bolder primary colours, rather than Ullén's pastel shades. That said, this is a remarkable achievement, and should be snapped up by all piano enthusiasts. The recorded sound is rather glassy, but crystal clear.

Jason Vieaux *gtr*

Guitar Recital

Barrios Waltzes, Op 8 – Nos 3 and 4. Julia Florida – Barcarola **Bustamente** (arr Morel) Misionera **Krouse** Variations on a Moldavian Hora. Merlin Suite del recuerdo. Morel Chôro. Danza Brasileira. Danza in E minor **Orbón** Preludio y Danza **Pujol** Preludios – Nos 2, 3 and 5

Jason Vieaux *gtr*

Naxos 8 553449 (64 minutes: DDD) Ⓢ
Recorded 1995

This is the début recording by an artist of great talent. His technical prowess is impressive to say the least, as near flawless as one may get, and his tone is as clear and expressive as his musical thinking. There are now many finger-perfect guitarists on tap, but those of Vieaux's natural musicality are rare indeed; everything in the moulding of the phrases comes from within – you just can't *programme* sensitivity of this kind. The main thrust of the music is Latin-American, a nice juxtaposition of the well known (Morel, Barrios, Pujol and Bustamente) with some unfamiliar but substantial (of their kind) pieces by Merlin and Orbón. The apparent 'misfit' is the work by Krouse, far removed from Latin America, but why should music of this quality be excluded, for whatever reason? It is included for the best of reasons, because the performer loves it and is right to do so. The theme is Moldavian and the language of the imaginative and technically punishing variations convincingly matches it. Vieaux plays everything with chameleon-like felicity of style and feeling. Superb recording and excellent notes complete an issue of the greatest distinction.

Arcadi Volodos *pf*

Piano Transcriptions

Horowitz Variations on a Theme from Bizet's 'Carmen' **Rachmaninov** Morning, Op 4 No 2. Melody, Op 21 No 9 (all arr Volodos) **Liszt** Hungarian Rhapsody No 2 in C sharp minor, S244 (arr Horowitz). Litanei, S562 No 1. Schwanengesang, S560 – No 3, Aufenthalt; No 10, Liebesbotschaft
Rimsky-Korsakov The tale of Tsar Saltan – Flight of the bumble-bee (arr Cziffra) **Prokofiev** Pieces from Cinderella – Gavotte, Op 95 No 2; Oriental dance, Op 97 No 6; Grand waltz, Op 107 No 1
Tchaikovsky Symphony No 6 in B minor, Op 74, 'Pathétique' – Allegro molto vivace (arr Feinberg)
Bach Trio Sonata No 5 in C, BWV529 – Largo (arr Feinberg) **Volodos** Concert Paraphrase on Mozart's 'Turkish March'

Arcadi Volodos *pf*

Sony Classical SK62691 (61 minutes: DDD) Ⓕ
Recorded 1996 ●●

Arcadi Volodos, Russian-born but Spanish-based, here declares himself both as elegant lyricist and spectacular virtuoso; his playing is as tactful as it is audacious, the work, surely, of a romantic pianist for our times. His tributes to Horowitz (the ultimate Russian virtuoso icon) and Cziffra (the *ne plus ultra* of pianistic necromancy) are as coolly masterful as they are personally engaging and are wholly devoid of wilfulness or undue idiosyncrasy. Those anxious for Horowitz's splintering treble and thundering bass or for Cziffra's manic explosions and accelerations will listen in vain. Mercifully, Volodos remains his own man, tempering some heart-stopping octaves and *glissandos* at the close of Feinberg's transcription of the *Scherzo* from Tchaikovsky's *Pathétique* Symphony with a touch of nonchalance, and in Feinberg's other arrangement, guiding Bach gently but firmly into the 19th century. Volodos is no less beguiling in his own Rachmaninov song transcriptions; here is that dreamed-of vocal 'line', luscious *cantabile* and aristocratic rather than ostentatious voicing and texturing. Last but far from least, his elaboration of Mozart's 'Turkish March' seasons the most decadent and epicurean taste with a teasing wit and insouciance. Sony's sound is superlative and this delectable recital makes one long for more substantial as well as glittering fare from a pianist who, as his producer puts it, 'never loosens the reins of his guiding intellect'.

Arcadi Volodos at Carnegie Hall

Liszt Hungarian Rhapsody No 15 in A minor, S244, 'Rákóczy'. A Midsummer Night's Dream – Wedding March, S410 (both arr Horowitz)
Rachmaninov Fragment in A flat. Etudes-tableaux – No 8 in D minor, Op 39; C minor, Op posth
Schumann Bunte Blätter, Op 99 **Scriabin** Piano Sonata No 10 in C, Op 70. Enigma, Op 52 No 2. Caresse dansée, Op 57 No 2. Prelude in B, Op 2 No 2

Arcadi Volodos *pf*

Sony Classical SK60893 (72 minutes: DDD) Ⓕ
Recorded live in 1998 ●●

Taken live from his Carnegie Hall début recital at the age of 26, this recital confirms a daunting legend. Volodos is unquestionably among the world's master pianists, a virtuoso for whom even the most fiercely applied difficulties simply do not exist. At the same time, everything is given with an unfaltering sense of equilibrium; as fast as you marvel at one thing it is immediately counterpointed by another. His technique in, say, the Liszt *Rhapsody* and *Wedding March Variations* (the first of two encores) is stupendous but never at the expense of musical quality. His sonority can be as delicate as it is thunderous and full-blooded. His accuracy and taste are impeccable so that instead of celebrating something self-serving or rip-roaring you find yourself conscious of higher virtues, of rhythm that can be magically free or held in a vice-like grip, as well as an unequalled fluency and aplomb. In Scriabin's Tenth Sonata he is faithful to the composer's obsessive and opalescent vision at every point, more than equal to even the most decadent and esoteric directions. Volodos's Rachmaninov, in his brief but gloriously enterprising selection, is played with the same magical sense of flux and clarity, and never more so than in the D minor *Etude-tableau* with its yearning and disconsolate double-note flow or in the C minor, posthumously published *Etude-tableau*. Yet if one had to choose just one item from this recital for a desert island, it would have to be Schumann's *Bunte Blätter*, an audacious gathering with a graphic shift from the lighter to the darker side of romanticism (Nos 1-8 and 9-14 respectively). Sony's sound triumphs over difficult circumstances, and if a teasing touch of enigma remains, both in performance and choice of repertoire, with an artist of this calibre you can hardly say that the golden age of pianism is dead.

Gillian Weir *org*

Organ Master Series – Volume 1

Hindemith Organ Sonata No 1 **Jongen** Sonata Eroica, Op 94 **Reubke** Sonata on the 94th Psalm in C minor **Willan** Introduction, Passacaglia and Fugue, B149

Priory PRCD751 (74 minutes: DDD) Ⓕ

Played on the Aeolian-Skinner Organ of The First Church of Christ, Scientist, Boston, Massachusetts. Recorded 2000

A mouth-watering programme, containing four of the finest romantic works for organ. Hindemith is probably the only name widely known, but if anyone thinks of him as a rather dry composer they should listen to Weir's outstanding performance of his Sonata No 1. As Dame Gillian says in her programme notes, this is the most romantic of Hindemith's three sonatas, but it gives her the opportunity to bring to the fore the more classical sounds of the Aeolian-Skinner organ.

This instrument was designed by Dame Gillian's husband, Lawrence Phelps, and is one of the largest in the USA. It has a thrilling *tutti* and a huge range of lovely colours which Dame Gillian exploits with complete mastery. It receives a fine, natural recording from Priory, and organ buffs will be well satisfied with the detailed notes about the instrument.

Dame Gillian's virtuoso playing vividly communicates itself to the listener, and at all times she performs with clarity of articulation and flexibility of tempo. Perhaps there's a little too much rubato in the Willan, especially in the Passacaglia, and one may prefer the more natural flow of Francis Jackson's inspired 1964 recording. However the Jongen and Reubke sonatas receive strong, dramatic performances which are amongst the finest ever recorded. In comparison, Filsell's Reubke, although impeccably played, feels a little cool. In sum, an irresistible combination of great music, great playing and a spectacular instrument.

Sophie Yates *hpd*

French Baroque Harpsichord Works Ⓟ

D'Anglebert Pièces de Clavecin – Suite in G minor; Tombeau de M. de Chambonnières **F Couperin** L'Art de toucher le clavecin – Prélude in D minor. Livre de clavecin, Deuxième ordre – Seconde Courante; Sarabande, 'La Prude'; Les Idées heureuses; La Voluptueuse **Forqueray** La Rameau; La Boisson; La Sylva; Jupiter **Rameau** L'enharmonique. L'Egyptienne. La Dauphine

Sophie Yates *hpd*

Chandos Chaconne CHAN0545 (71 minutes: DDD) Ⓕ

Recorded 1993

Sophie Yates has a real understanding of the French style – so difficult to capture, with its special conventions and elaborate ornamentation. Her phrasing is subtle as well as musical; and she proves herself capable of the flexibility proper to this music without risk to the underlying pulse or to continuity. Her reading of *La Dauphine*, Rameau's last harpsichord piece, is justifiably free and improvisatory, since it is thought to be a transcription of Rameau's extemporisation at the wedding of the Dauphin in 1747. She savours Rameau's bold enharmonics, too, shows drive and energy in his *L'Egyptienne*, impressive dignity in Forqueray's tribute to his great contemporary and in a d'Anglebert sarabande, expressiveness in Forqueray's *La Sylva* and a sense of enjoyment in the trenchant drama of the flashing thunderbolts of his *Jupiter*. Yates also has the advantage of admirable recording of a particularly beautiful and rich-sounding instrument (a copy of a Goujon).

Choral

Ampleforth Schola Cantorum

'Carols from Ampleforth'

Traditional O come, all ye faithful. Once in Royal David's city. Unto us is born a son. The Sussex Carol. God rest you merry, gentlemen. Hark! the herald angels sing (all arr Willcocks). Personent hodie (arr Holst). Good King Wenceslas (arr Jacques). Adam lay y-bounden (arr Warlock). Angel tidings (arr Rutter). Past three o'clock. Ding dong! merrily on high (both arr Wood). It came upon a midnight clear. Come with torches.

Silent Night (all arr Little). Still, still, still (arr Ledger). The Infant King (arr Pettman). The First Nowell (arr Stainer/Willcocks) **H C Stewart** On this day earth shall ring **M Praetorius** A great and mighty wonder **Mathias** Sir Christemas
Ampleforth Schola Cantorum / Ian Little with **Simon Wright** *org*
Ampleforth Compact Discs AARCD1 Ⓕ
(58 minutes: DDD)

Here is a programme of carols as traditional as turkey and plum pudding, and as wholesome. You don't have to groan at the approach of *Have yourself a merry little Christmas* or any other feeble compromise with the changing times; there's not even a bleat from John Tavener and William Blake's unprofitably questioned little lamb. Musically, the programme is in the first place a triumph for Anon, and then for Sir David Willcocks whose arrangements are rich in seasonable splendour and knowledge of how to get the best out of choir and organ. Other arrangers have done good work too, including the choir's director, Ian Little, who provides inspired embellishments in the last verse of *It came upon a midnight clear* but may just possibly have gone a little over the top towards the end of Silent Night. He has also trained a splendid choir. Forthright tone from the trebles, ample tone from the men, combine to live up to the name of their foundation. The organist, Simon Wright, does an excellent job, varying the might of his invincible reeds and implacable pedals with a scattering of two-foot spangle-dust, light and bright as a Christmas-tree fairy. The building itself is aurally spacious, the harmonies of *Ding dong! merrily on high* engaging in merry argument with their echo. There will doubtless be homes in which a playing of this disc will constitute the Christmas Day reveille, and if the rest of the day goes as well they can count themselves lucky.

Cambridge Singers

'Hail, Gladdening Light'

J Amner Come, let's rejoice **Anonymous** Rejoice in the Lord **Bairstow** I sat down under his shadow **Dering** Factum est silentium **Elgar** They are at rest **J Goss** These are they that follow the lamb **W H Harris** Bring us, O Lord God **Howells** Nunc dimittis **Morley** Nolo mortem peccatoris **Philips** O beatum et sacrosanctum diem **Purcell** Remember not, Lord, our offences, Z50 **Rutter** Loving shepherd of Thy sheep **J Sheppard** In manus tuas **Stanford** Justorum animae, Op 38 No 1 **R Stone** The Lord's Prayer **Tallis** O nata lux **Tavener** A hymn to the mother of God. Hymn for the dormition of the mother of God **Taverner** Christe Jesu, pastor bone **Tomkins** When David heard **Vaughan Williams** O vos omnes **Walton** A litany **C Wood** Hail, gladdening light
Cambridge Singers / John Rutter
Collegium COLCD113 (72 minutes: DDD) Ⓕ
Texts and translations included ●

This has the subtitle 'Music of the English Church' and it is arranged under four main headings: anthems and introits (these count as one), Latin motets, settings of hymns and other poetry, and prayer-settings. Each of them is well represented in a programme that varies delightfully in period and style, and in performances which are remarkably consistent in quality. Some of the items will come as discoveries to most listeners: for example, the anthem *Come, let's rejoice*, a splendid, madrigal-like piece written by John Amner, organist from 1610 to 1641 at Ely Cathedral where these recordings were made. Others are equally impressive in their present performance: a deep quietness attends the opening of Richard Dering's *Factum est silentium*, which ends with rhythmic Alleluias set dancing with subdued excitement. Among the hymn-settings is one by a 16-year-old called William Walton. Included in the prayers is the choirmaster's own setting, characteristically made for pleasure, of *Loving shepherd of Thy sheep*. All are unaccompanied, and thus very exactingly test the choir's blend of voices, its precision, articulation and feeling for rhythm. In all respects it does exceptionally well; the tone is fresh, the attack unanimous, the expression clear and sensitive, the rhythm on its toes. These are young and gifted singers, formed with disciplined enthusiasm into a choir with a distinctive style – and, incidentally, recorded with admirable results by a family firm which operates from a studio built at the bottom of the garden.

Sing, ye Heavens

Anonymous Pange lingua. Veni Creator Spiritus. Vexilla Regis **Croft** (arr Rutter) O God, our help in ages past **Gibbons** Drop, drop slow tears **Luther** (arr Rutter) A mighty fortress **Miller** (arr Rutter) When I survey the wondrous Cross **Monk** (arr Rutter) All things bright and beautiful. Christ the Lord is risen today **R H Prichard** (arr Rutter) Love divine, all love excelling **Purcell** (arr Rutter) Christ is made the sure Foundation **Rutter** Eternal God **Scholefield** (arr Rutter) The day thou gavest, Lord, is ended **Schulz** (arr Rutter) We plough the fields and scatter **Tallis** Glory to thee, my God **Traditional** (arr Rutter) Amazing Grace. Be thou my vision. The King of love my Shepherd is. Let all mortal flesh keep silence. Lo! he comes with clouds descending. Morning has broken
Thelma Owen *hp* **John Scott** *org* **Cambridge Singers; City of London Sinfonia Brass / John Rutter**
Collegium COLCD126 (77 minutes: DDD) Ⓕ
Texts and translations included. Recorded 2000 ●

The Service was the Lord's; anthem, canticles, psalms and responsories were the choir's; and the hymns were anybody's. That (roughly) is one remembers it. Of course the best of hymns were acknowledged as having dignity, strength and other appeals to heart and head; and with descants and special harmonies by Vaughan Williams or David Willcocks they could join in musical character and interest. But it seems to be a relatively recent development that their performance has become something of an art form.

The art lies in knowing how much to arrange and how much to leave be. On the whole John Rutter has it right. In *Love divine*, for instance, the first verse has the voices in unison and the harmonies 'straight', verse 2 has the choir in standard four-part harmony, and verse 3 has a descant and new harmonies, both of which are emboldened to acquire a richer life towards the end. Most are accompanied by the organ, some by organ and brass, a few by harp. These include the group described as 'folk hymns' ending with *We plough the fields and scatter*, taken at a brisk pace and sounding almost Haydnesque. Gibbons's *Drop, drop slow tears* is sung unaccompanied throughout, with no 'improvements'. Tallis's *Glory to thee, my God* has verse 4 in double canon. And Rutter provides a hymn of his own, *Eternal God*, written in 1999 'with the aim of augmenting the meagre stock of hymns which make mention of music'.

Generally, the selection is fine, both words and music. In performance, the plainsong hymns are rather too 'barred', and the somewhat garish stained-glass ending of *Let all mortal flesh keep silence* will not be to everyone's taste. But this, as we know, is an excellent choir; they are fortified by some splendid players; and presentation and recorded sound (apart from recessing the choir too much in the hymns with brass) are admirable also.

Clare College, Cambridge

Blessed Spirit – Music of the soul's journey

Anonymous Requiem aeternam. Kontakion of the Dead. Domine Jesu Christe. O quanta qualia. In paradisum **Byrd** Iustorum animae **Harris** Faire is the Heaven **Hildegard of Bingen** O felix anima **Holst** The Evening Watch, H159 **Parry** Songs of Farewell – No 4, There is an old belief **Schütz** Selig sind die Toten **Sheppard** Audivi vocem de caelo **Tavener** Funeral Ikos **Tchaikovsky** Blessed are they **Traditional** Steal Away (arr Brown). Deep River (arr Luboff) **Victoria** O quam gloriosum **Walford-Davies** Psalm No 121 and Requiem aeternam

Clare College Choir, Cambridge / Timothy Brown

Collegium COLCD127 (71 minutes: DDD) Ⓕ

Texts and translations included. Recorded 2000 ⦿

There can be nothing but praise for the excellence of these performances, for the quality and choice of the music itself and, most of all, for the gorgeous sound quality of these recordings made in Ely Cathedral. Add to this some eminently readable booklet-notes and we have a real winner, even if the overall aural effect bears a striking resemblance to those ubiquitous inoffensive compilation discs played in hotel lobbies the world over.

Within the basic theme of death and the soul's subsequent journey to paradise the music juxtaposes chunks of plainsong and standard cathedral choir repertoire with some rather more esoteric choral pieces. Whether it's the ancient plainchant *In paradisum*, Psalm 121 sung to Walford Davies's fine Anglican chant, William Harris's richly textured anthem *Faire is the Heaven* or the almost erotically indulgent arrangement by Timothy Brown of *Steal Away*, Clare College Choir distinguish it all with finely crafted and beautifully shaped performances that are not just note-perfect but intensely perceptive as well. There's no hint of the sickliness we sometimes experience when church music is exposed to such slick professionalism on disc – rather a real sense of wonder and awe at the timeless beauty of the programme.

It is difficult to listen to the disc in its entirety without falling into some kind of soporific trance, but taken individually each piece is, in its own way, as dramatic and earth-shaking as the garish blue cover leads us to suspect.

Illumina

Anonymous Lumen ad revelationem **Byrd** O lux, beata Trinitas **Grechaninov** The seven Days of the Passion, Op 58 – O gladsome light **Harris** Bring us, O Lord God **Hildegard of Bingen** O choruscans stellarum **Holst** Nunc dimittis, H127 **Josquin Desprez** Nunc dimittis **Ligeti** Lux aeterna **Palestrina** Christe, qui lux es et dies. Lucis Creator optime **Rachmaninov** Vespers, Op 37 – Nunc dimittis **Rautavaara** Vigilia – Evening Hymn **Rutter** Hymn to the Creator of Light **Tallis** O nata lux de lumine. Te lucis ante terminum **Tchaikovsky** Vesper Service, Op 52 – Hail, gladdening Light **Whyte** Christe, qui lux es et dies **Wood** Hail, gladdening light

Clare College Choir, Cambridge / Timothy Brown

Collegium COLCD125 (76 minutes: DDD) Ⓕ

Texts and translations included. Recorded 1999 ⦿

Retrospectively the disc's final item, Ligeti's *Lux aeterna*, dominates the recital. Not only does it make an indelible impression, but it also casts its light over the entire programme and style of singing. To a listener who has not heard it before (a slightly smaller category than might be thought, as the piece was used in the film *2001: A Space Odyssey*) it may even come as the light on the road to Damascus, a blinding revelation of unknown choral sonorities. An extraordinary sound-world is opening up, with long, finely-ruled streams of light, a spectrum of colours wide as the distance from heaven to earth, and all mingling eventually within the cavern of a great bell. The challenge to singers (even when assisted by the reverberance of Ely Cathedral's Lady Chapel) is formidable indeed, and these young voices (with lungs and ears involved also) do marvellously well. And so they do throughout. The quality of choral tone here is remarkable: no thready sopranos, none of those bone-dry basses, but a sound that, though strictly disciplined in the matter of vibrato, is still fresh and natural. They achieve wonders of *crescendo*, as in William Harris's *Bring us, O Lord God*, and their opening chords (in Tallis's *O nata lux* for instance) are as if cut by the sharpest slicer ever made. Even so, this smooth, flawless beauty of sound is, in some contexts, like the modern beauty of the face of a heroine in some televised piece of period-drama. Josquin Desprez's *Nunc dimittis* is an example: the singing is extremely beautiful, but conceptually (and not just in the women's voices) seems anachronistic. It's as though they have worked on their programme with the precept 'All choral music aspires to the condition of Ligeti'. A wondrous record, all the same.

Dresden Kreuzchor

Musica Divina

Bach Der Geist hilft unsrer Schwachheit, BWV226 **Brahms** Motets, Op 29 – Schaffe in mir, Gott, ein reines Herz **Bruckner** Os justi **Draeseke** Psalm 93, Op 56 **Duda** Friede über Israel, Op 25 **Hessenberg** O Herr, mache mich zum Werkzeug deines Friedens, Op37 No 1 **Homilius** Domine, ad adiuvandum me. Herr, wenn Trübsal da ist **Mendelssohn** Jauchzet dem Herrn alle Welt **Reger** Nachtlied, Op 138 No 3 **Schein** Psalm 116 **Schütz** Die Himmel erzählen die Ehre Gottes, SWV386. Das ist je gewisslich wahr, SWV388

Dresden Kreuzchor / Roderich Kreile

DG 453 484-2GH (76 minutes: DDD) Ⓕ
Texts and translations included.
Recorded 1997

The choir is in quite splendid form here: fine in blend, balance and tone, scrupulously precise, alert and responsive to the direction of its still relatively new conductor, Roderich Kreile, appointed 28th Kantor in 1997. The very opening phrases tell us what we want to know in embarking on a recital of this kind: it's a choir that has the life of the music within it. The opening of Schütz's *Das ist je gewisslich wahr* ('This is a faithful saying ... that Christ Jesus came into the world to save sinners') is chorale-like in form, but has an underlying rhythmic vitality which a duller choir could easily miss but which here carries the rich promise of a wonderful piece of work about to unfold. And so it does, and still more so the Creation motet (*Die Himmel erzählen*) which follows.

And then comes the work which alone would give sufficient reason for drawing special attention to the recital. Johann Schein's 'Das ist mir lieb', one of a collection dating from 1616 when a certain Burchhard Grossmann thought to celebrate his return to health by commissioning 16 composers to set Psalm 116 to music (all can be heard on a three-disc set on CPO). Schein's contribution is vivid as a picture-book, with tears that flow and feet that slide to illustrate the text, sometimes also as effective in natural speech-rhythms as a good dramatic monologue. It is a magnificently resourceful piece of writing, and ends with a funfair of Hallelujas.

But everything here is worth hearing. Some of the motets are of recent composition, one of them, Kurt Hessenberg's prayer to 'make me an agent of your peace' a quietly intense plea for reconciliation, doubly moving in the context of this recital and coming from this place. Bach is, of course, the master at the centre of all – practically every later composer pays some implicit tribute. *Der Geist hilft unsrer Schwachheit* is the second of the Six Motets, inexhaustible in its development of ideas, harmonic and contrapuntal. It also seems to assume similar tirelessness in its singers; and as far as this choir is concerned, the confidence is well placed, for their vitality fully meets the challenge. It is an excellent record, and (to go a little further) an inspiring one.

Ely Cathedral

Magnificat and Nunc dimittis, Vol 14

Bairstow Evening Service in G **Blow** Evening Service in G **Bullock** Evening Service in D **Child** Evening Service in E minor **Cruft** Collegium Regale **Greene** Evening Service in C **Orr** Short Service **Rose** Evening Service in C minor **Wills** Evening Service on Plainsong tones **C Wood** Evening Service in G

Ely Cathedral Choir / Paul Trepte with **David Price** *org*

Priory PRCD592 (71 minutes: DDD) Ⓕ
Recorded 1996

All of the items here are worthy of the series, and each has its distinctive flavour. Ernest Bullock's *Magnificat*, which opens the recital, is a good example of Anglican unpredictability. Gentle and lyrical in mood and manner, it develops with what seems to be an almost rhapsodic freedom, the organ part moving with a fluent independence, and as intimate as a piano accompaniment. Bernard Rose, in his Service for trebles, approaches the canticle in similar mood but with entirely different results, making much of the resonance of boys' voices in thirds, and giving full rein to his invention in his writing for the organ. Robin Orr is another who puts much of his more creatively adventurous self into the organ part, and his settings are not made for comfort: the first *Gloria* for instance strikes an awed note, with its rather severe minor tonality. Adrian Cruft, most modern of these composers, in both date and style, writes boldly, with skill in the deployment of the voices in his men-only settings, which, the notes tell us, were originally for accompaniment by wind instruments as an alternative to accompaniment by the organ. From the 17th century there are masterly settings by John Blow and William Child; from the eighteenth, Maurice Greene; nothing from the nineteenth (unless it be said that Bullock, Wills, Wood and Bairstow were all children of the nineteenth). With fine work by the organist, David Price, and with the choir showing itself a confident, spirited master of its business, the performances are to be relished.

Hereford Cathedral

Magnificat and Nunc dimittis, Volume 7

Darke Evening Service in A minor **Davies** Evening Service in G (Festal)[a] **Dyson** Evening Service in F[a] **Harwood** Evening Service in A flat[a] **Lloyd** Hereford Service[a] **Shephard** Hereford Service[a] **Stanford** Services in F, Op 36 – Evening Service[a] **Sumsion** Evening Service in D[a] **Vann** Hereford Service[a]

Hereford Cathedral Choir / Roy Massey with [a]**Huw Williams** *org*

Priory PRCD535 (68 minutes: DDD) Ⓕ
Texts included. Recorded 1995

We follow these reliable generations of church musicians (which is what most of them are, the presence of Walton and Tippett being exceptions), and recall that composing was a part-time occupation, almost a luxury, in the daily round that normally comprised taking choir practice and playing the organ, giving lessons and conducting the choral society. The variety of the settings here is a striking feature – Harold Darke's for unaccompanied choir, Dyson's quietness. Almost invariably the individual finds something of his own to add – for example, Richard Lloyd reintroducing 'My soul doth magnify' at the end of his *Magnificat*. Hearing again the well-known favourites (Sumsion in D major, Harwood in A flat), one appreciates exactly why they have so established themselves, just as in Stanford in F major (not among his most familiar settings) we see the hand of the master. We also watch 'modernity' cautiously advancing – in Stanley Vann's fine Hereford Service, for instance. Hereford Cathedral Choir is admirable throughout and benefits from the clear recorded sound.

King's College, Cambridge

Best Loved Hymns

Bain Brother James's Air[a] (arr Johns) **Bourgeois** Praise to the Lord, the Almighty[b] **Gibbons** Drop, drop slow tears **Goss** Praise my soul, the King of Heaven[b] **Handel** Thine be the glory, risen, conquering Son[b] (arr Cleobury) **W Harris** O what their joy and their glory must be[b] **Howells** All my hope on God is founded[bc] **Ireland** My song is love unknown[b] **Luther** A mighty fortress is our God[bc] (arr Rutter) **Miller** When I survey the wondrous cross[b] **Parry** Dear Lord and Father of Mankind[b] **Rutter** Be thou my vision[a] **Scholefield** The day thou gavest, Lord, is ended[b] **Taylor** Glorious things of Thee are spoken[b] **Traditional** All people that on earth do dwell[bc] (arr Vaughan Williams). Morning has broken[a] (arr Rutter). Let all mortal flesh[b] (arr Jackson) **Vaughan Williams** Come down, O Love Divine[b]
[a]**Sioned Williams** *hp* [b]**Benjamin Bayl, Thomas Williamson** *orgs* **King's College Choir, Cambridge;** [c]**The Wallace Collection / Stephen Cleobury**
EMI Classics CDC5 57026-2 (69 minutes: DDD) Ⓕ
Recorded 2000 ●

Here is the high art of hymnody. No tentative playover on the stopped diapason while knee-joints crack and fingers fumble for collection money. No intrusive notes from the congregation with members who pride themselves on 'singing seconds' (presumably, as Harvey Grace remarked, because the interval almost exclusively used is that of a third). These are musical performances, as surely as if they were the canticles and anthems featured here, and in some instances the form is indeed that of the hymn-anthem. The hymns themselves, as the title proclaims, are 'best loved', but are presented with elaborations for brass, organ, harp and descanting trebles. Dressed up in Sunday best, they are thrilling in majesty, exquisite in contemplative piety, but very largely cordoned off amid notices that say 'Do not join in'.

The selection probably reflects modern, conservative good taste quite faithfully. At the popular end, *Brother James's Air* and *Morning has broken* are admitted; at the mystical other, *Let all mortal flesh keep silence* preserves the ancient tune but swathed in subtly abrasive harmonies. Of things grandly Victorian, *The day Thou gavest* is in, but *Lead, kindly light* and *Abide with me* are out. Some would have found a place among any 'top 10' chosen 50 years ago – *Dear Lord and Father of Mankind, When I survey the wondrous Cross* and *Praise, my soul, the King of Heaven* for example. Some such as *All my hope on God is founded* and *Be thou my vision* are relatively new to the lists. Two – *A mighty fortress* and the *Old Hundredth* – seem timeless.

The famous choir sing well (though their uncovered 'ee' sounds nag somewhat, as does an oddly unyielding element somewhere in the men's voices). The accompaniments are skilfully played, colourfully arranged and spaciously recorded. Excellent annotations are provided by Alan Luff, who comes up with a fund of information such as the identity of Brother James (a Christian Scientist, James Leith Macbeth Bain) and the origin of the tune *Abbot's Leigh*, which was composed in 1941 when BBC listeners were complaining that *Glorious Things of Thee are Spoken* was still being sung to the old German national anthem.

'Credo'

Panufnik Song to the Virgin Mary **Penderecki** The Cherubic Hymn. Agnus Dei **Plainchant** Stetit angelus (Offertory antiphon); Credo I[b]; Ave Maria (Offertory antiphon); Alleluia; Tota pulchra es, Maria (Alleluia with verse); Missa pro defunctis – Agnus Dei[bc]; Pater noster[b] **Rachmaninov** Vespers, Op 37[a] – Bless the Lord, O my soul; Blessed is the man. Liturgy of St John Chrysostom, Op 31 – Cherubic Hymn; The Lord's Prayer **Stravinsky** Ave Maria. Credo
[a]**Paul Nicholson** *counterten* [b]**Richard Eteson,** [c]**Edward Saklatvala** *cantors* **King's College Choir, Cambridge / Stephen Cleobury**
EMI CDC5 56439-2 (64 minutes: DDD) Ⓕ
Texts and translations included. Recorded 1997

The logic of this programme, juxtaposing two very different responses to religious texts, is not entirely apparent. The 20th-century works are not directly influenced by the plainchant of the Western Catholic church yet neither are they all rooted in the Eastern Orthodox tradition. It is the second (1949) version of Stravinsky's *Credo* that is performed here – setting the Catholic rather than the Orthodox text – while both Panufnik and Penderecki were practising Catholics. Indeed only Rachmaninov's gorgeous pieces give us the genuinely Orthodox view – and that from a man who was not himself a staunch follower of the faith. Frankly, though, with music as indescribably beautiful as this and performances which are of almost breathtaking artistry, who needs logic in programming? The climax of Penderecki's *Cherubic Hymn* is measured to absolute perfection, every last ounce of passion squeezed from the long-drawn-out build-up to this shattering moment: the chanted *Pater noster* has that timeless quality which seems to come from another world – enhanced, as is everything on this disc, by a deliciously atmospheric recording. If there is a niggling reservation it is in the lack of real bass resonance, especially in the Rachmaninov. By the very nature of its make-up an English collegiate choir will never possess men's voices with the kind of maturity you would hear in a Russian Orthodox choir. But with such committed, sensitive and musically perceptive singing, this is one of the very finest discs to have come from King's during Stephen Cleobury's tenure as Director.

'A Festival of Nine Lessons and Carols'

Adès The Fayrfax Carol **Bach** In dulci jubilo **Darke** In the bleak mid-winter **Goldschmidt** A tender Shoot **Ord** Adam lay ybounden **Rutter** Dormi, Jesu **Tavener** The Lamb **Traditional** Once in Royal David's city. Up! good Christen folk. The Truth from Above. Sussex Carol. In dulci jubilo. God rest you merry, gentlemen. Gabriel's Message. Joys Seven. Riu, riu, chiu. While Shepherd's watched. I saw three ships. O come, all ye faithful. Hark! the herald angels sing **Weir** Illuminare, Jerusalem

King's College Choir, Cambridge / Stephen Cleobury

EMI ② CZS5 73693-2; EL5 56891-4 (83 minutes: DDD) Recorded 1999 Ⓜ OO

Surprising as it may seem, this is the first complete commercial recording of this celebrated event. Happily, little has changed down the years to rob the service of its sense of serenity and quiet joy. On the present recording, the readings are all skilfully done, and the carols, in Stephen Cleobury's felicitous phrase, are 'the handmaid' of Milner-White's liturgy. Since 1918, the repertory has evolved, quietly, almost imperceptibly. Indeed, one of the pleasures of this 80th anniversary recording is its chronicling of the care and imagination with which successive organists and choirmasters have selected and arranged the music down the years. The choir's performance style, too, has changed at a pleasingly slow rate, though rather a lot has changed since the (abridged) service was last recorded. The present choir's music-making is lighter toned, the diction cleaner, the pacing altogether more urgent. This is a lustier, merrier style of carol singing. Their fresher, less consciously beautiful style both suits and reflects the performing preferences of our age; yet out there, amid the secularised mass markets toward which releases like this are unerringly aimed, there is a palpable hankering after mystery. Does this explain the recording itself? Unlike its analogue predecessors, this spectacularly engineered digital affair puts, not the choir, but the famous King's acoustic centre-stage. The choir as always is self-evidently 'there', the trebles very much so; and although the congregational version of *God rest you merry, gentlemen* is something of a muddle, the hymns generally sound well: the descants in great barnstorming perorations of *O come, all ye faithful* and *Hark! the herald angels sing* thrillingly caught. Above all is the thrill of having this great event complete on record for the first time. The philosopher George Santayana has said: 'Fixity of tradition, of custom, of language is perhaps a prerequisite to complete harmony in life and mind.' That may not be a fashionable view in *fin de siècle* Britain, but it is why, each Christmas, this Festival of Nine Lessons and Carols sends a beam out into the world of special luminescence and beauty.

Laudibus

'All in the April evening'

Bennet All creatures now **Byrd** Ave verum corpus **Campion** Never weather-beaten saile more willing bent to shore (arr Parry) **Elgar** As torrents in summer. My love dwelt in a northern land, Op 18 No 3. Grant Crimond (arr Ross) **Morley** Fyer, fyer **Roberton** All in the April evening **Stanford** The bluebird, Op 119 No 3 **Sullivan** The long day closes **Traditional** O can ye sew cushions? (arr Bantock). Ca' the Yowes. The turtle Dove (both arr Vaughan Williams). All through the night. The banks o' Doon. Dream Angus. Drink to me only with thine eyes. An Eriskay love lilt. Wee Cooper o'Fife (all arr Roberton) **Vaughan Williams** Three Shakespeare Songs **Warlock** Corpus Christi

Laudibus / Michael Brewer

Hyperion CDA67076 (69 minutes: DDD) Recorded 1998 Ⓕ O

How Sir Hugh Roberton would have loved these fresh young voices. '*Soo* gracious, *soo* musical', he used to murmur when the audience leant their uncertain voices to a rehearsal of *Crimond*. The new choir under Michael Brewer may not be quite so expert in the choral *portamento* as the Glasgow Orpheus used to be, but they sing in that tradition, the first requirement of which is beautiful sound, in tone and blend. Sir Hugh's arrangements of Scottish folk-songs find a natural home here, the melodies sweet and strong, the hummed accompaniments gentle and affectionate. Those by Vaughan Williams have a more distinctive flavour, and this, too, is well brought out, with feeling for the characteristic rise-and-fall, the sadness lurking close to the heart. The programme takes a natural half-time break after some more of Sir Hugh, and wakes us from an interval-nap with Morley's *Fyer, fyer* and John Bennet's *All creatures now*: they make us feel that, compared with the first Elizabethans, we're never really more than half-awake anyway. The effect of having a choir (even if a relatively small one), rather than single voices, is not what we are used to in these things, but Laudibus have the rhythm of them in their bones and the sense of the words in their heads. Then there are some of the masterpieces among our later part-songs: Elgar's *My love dwelt in a northern land* (lovely to hear that magical third verse so well done), Stanford's *The bluebird* (with the smoothest of textures and a charming soloist), Warlock's *Corpus Christi* and Vaughan Williams's *Tempest* settings. And then, in spirit if not in truth, back to Sir Hugh for *The long day closes*, Sullivan's patent eye-moistener. A delightful disc.

St Mary's Cathedral, Edinburgh

'Great Cathedral Anthems, Volume 8'

Brahms Ein deutsches Requiem, Op 45 – Wie lieblich sind deine Wohnungen (sung in English)[a]
Byrd Christe, qui lux es et dies. O Lord, make thy servant Elizabeth our Queen **Gibbons** O clap your hands **Harwood** O how glorious is the Kingdom[a]
Howells Salve regina **Ley** Prayer of King Charles I
Lotti Crucifixus a 8 **Stanford** Three Motets, Op 38
Taverner Quemadmodum desiderat cervus
Walton The Twelve[a]
Choir of St Mary's Cathedral, Edinburgh / Timothy Byram-Wigfield with [a]**Peter Backhouse** *org*
Priory PRCD557 (64 minutes: DDD) Ⓕ
Recorded 1996

If there are some to whom the choir of Edinburgh's Episcopal Cathedral are introducing themselves in this recital, they are likely to be impressed and want to hear more. This is a choir that can sustain long phrases (fine ones in the marvellous motet by Taverner), lengthy and concentrated works too (as with Walton's *The twelve*), finding plentiful resources of energy in matters of attack and rhythm. The trebles (14 plus four girls) are bright-toned and sing some formidably challenging music with well-founded confidence. The choir also possess useful soloists, most notably the baritone who so effectively opens *The twelve*. The organist proves his merit from the start with an exciting performance of the virtuosic solo which introduces *O how glorious is the Kingdom*, and skilfully manages the accompaniment (not as easy as it may sound) to 'How lovely are Thy dwellings'. It is an enterprising programme, finding room for cherished old acquaintances such as Charles I's evening prayer in its graceful setting by Henry Ley. The acoustic is helpful, neither dry nor excessively reverberant, and the balance between choir and organ is judiciously established.

Miscellaneous

Complete New English Hymnal 1
York Minster Choir / Philip Moore with **John Scott Whiteley** *org*
Priory PRCD701 (70 minutes: DDD) Ⓕ
Texts included. Recorded 2000 ●

Complete New English Hymnal 2
Marlborough College Chapel Choir / Robin Nelson with **Ian Crabbe** *org*
Priory PRCD702 (71 minutes: DDD) Ⓕ
Texts included. Recorded 2000 ●

Complete New English Hymnal 3
Ely Cathedral Choir / Paul Trepte with **Scott Farrell** *org*
Priory PRCD703 (77 minutes: DDD) Ⓕ
Texts included. Recorded 2000 ●

Jerusalem the Golden – The English Hymn, Volume 2
Wells Cathedral Choir / Malcolm Archer with **Rupert Gough** *org*
Hyperion CDP12102 (66 minutes: DDD) Ⓕ
Texts included. Recorded 2000 ●

As with its Psalms and English anthems series, Priory dodges around the country, a cathedral here, a chapel there, and each volume assigned to a different choir. Hyperion, for its first two issues at least, has stayed with Wells Cathedral, creating a strong impression that they could not have done it better. There is a fine sense of English well-being in these records – sunlight beaming in through the windows putting still more colour into cheeks that are as rosy as apples in the Dean's orchard. One can almost smell the Sunday roast.

This has something to do with the wholesomeness of the voices, and with it comes a sense of enjoyment. They sing 19th-century hymns – *Abide with me*, *Praise, my soul, the King of Heaven*, *The day thou gavest* and so forth – and bring out the best in them. *Jerusalem the Golden* gives its name to the collection, and about it we learn, from Alan Luff's deep-mined booklet-notes, no end of fascinating information (such as, the tune was written originally for different words and in triple time, the composer complaining that the editor of *Hymns Ancient and Modern* had turned his waltz into a polka).

Wells, it seems, has pretty well the ideal acoustics. York Minster, in Priory's Volume 1, is magnificent in its spacious opulence, but the listener feels a little like a television camera observing the impressive scene from above. The Chapel of Marlborough College is quite the opposite: here one is face-to-face with the singers, and the absence of reverberation incurs some lack of atmosphere. Ely Cathedral restores the sense of space, and, by association, holiness; and theirs is a fine record (as indeed, in their different ways, are all three), just very slightly limited in its appeal, for some, by a certain rigidity of tone somewhere among the men's voices. The boys are excellent (Ely is alone among the three choirs on Priory in not having any girls). Their programme is the most varied, with (for instance) two attractive carols among the hymns, the Easter *Alleluia* and *Now the green blade riseth*. Marlborough starts with *Morning has broken* and includes *Were you there?* and *Holy Night*. York has *Sing to the Lord glad hymns of praise* to the tune 'St Hugh of Lincoln' or 'Little Sir William'. Each choir has a share of favourites, so that *Glorious things of thee are spoken* (Austria) also goes to York, whose record ends with Parry's *Jerusalem*.

The standard of performance is high. All of the choirs take care over phrasing and appropriate variation of volume. Diction is good (though the Marlborough girls are inclined to shade the 'o' sound, as in 'to', to a French 'tu' or German 'tü'). The cathedral organists bring out the sumptuous resources of their instruments, and all are well recorded. As to the hymns themselves, they are remarkably good company: the prospect of 'those endless sabbaths' brightens considerably.

'Fairest Isle' – A New National Songbook
Anonymous The British Grenadiers[bc]. The Broom of Cowdenknowes[a]. Farewell to Lochabar (arr J C Bach)[b] **Arne** The Miller of Dee[b]. Rule Britannia[abc]. **Barsanti** Overture in G, Op 4 No 1 **Carey** Sally in our Alley[b] **Charke** Medley Overture **Dibdin** Tom Bowling[a] **Handel** The Melancholy Nymph[a] **Hook** The Lass of Richmond Hill[b] **Pepusch** Cease your Funning[a] **Purcell** Fairest Isle[a]. 'Twas within a Furlong[a] **Shield** The Ploughboy[a]. The Milkmaid[b] **Vernon** When that I was a Little Tiny Boy[b]
Catherine Bott *sop* [b]**Joseph Cornwell** *ten* [c]**Psalmody; The Parley of Instruments / Peter Holman**
Hyperion CDA67115 (63 minutes: DDD) Ⓕ
Texts included. Recorded 1999

Peter Holman puts the date at *c*1970 when, as a nation, we stopped singing our national songs. Certainly 'British Songs for British Boys' was the politically incorrect title of the songbook from which a whole generation sang while the Battle of Britain was in progress. *Fairest Isle*, *The British Grenadiers* and *Rule Britannia* were all shamelessly included, though, hardly surprisingly, not *The Melancholy Nymph*, *The Milkmaid* or *'Twas within a Furlong of Edinboro' Town* with Jenny's speculations about life 'when my maiden treasure's gone'. Each as performed here is a delight, whether *Sally in our Alley*, with its ingenious running bass on the cello or the elegant flutes with *pizzicato* that accompany *Farewell to Lochabar*. And these are all authentic 18th-century arrangements, with never a false touch. The performances are as delightful as the songs. Both singers have an attractive personal way with them. Catherine Bott is particularly good in *Tom Bowling*, with its strangely moving last verse, and her contributions to *Rule Britannia* ring out royally. Joseph Cornwell has a splendid natural vibrancy and cleanness of style, ideal in *The Ploughboy* and *The Miller of Dee*. The Parley plays as for the joy of it, and the two overtures are charming discoveries, especially Richard Charke's medley, which is rather like those games musical families inflict on each other where there pass in rapid succession some 30 tunes of which, with luck, you manage to get perhaps three.

New College Choir, Oxford

'Agnus Dei' I and II
Allegri Adagio in G minor[a]. Miserere mei **Bach** Cantata No 147, Herz und Mund und Tat und Leben – Jesu, bleibet meine Freude[a]. St John Passion, BWV245 – Ruht wohl **Barber** Agnus Dei, Op 11 **Bizet** Agnus Dei **Brahms** Geistliches Lied, Op 30[a] **Bruckner** Christus factus est[a] **Byrd** Ave verum corpus **Elgar** (arr Cameron) Variations on an original theme, 'Enigma', Op 36 – Lux aeterna **Fauré** Ave verum, Op 65 No 1 (both arr Higginbottom)[a]. Cantique de Jean Racine, Op 11 (arr Rutter)[a]. Requiem, Op 48[a] – In paradisum; Pie Jesu; Libera me **Górecki** Totus tuus, Op 60 **Lotti** Crucifixus a 8 **Martin** Mass for Double Choir – Agnus Dei **Mendelssohn** Hear my prayer **Monteverdi** Selva morale e spirituale – Beatus vir[a] **Mozart** Ave verum corpus, K618[a] **Palestrina** Missa Papae Marcelli – Kyrie **Purcell** Hear my prayer, O Lord, Z15 **Rachmaninov** Vespers, Op 37 – No 6, Ave Maria **Schubert** Psalm 23, D706 (all arr Cameron)[a] **Tavener** The Lamb
New College Choir, Oxford; [a]**Capricorn / Edward Higginbottom**
Erato 3984-29588-2 (139 minutes: DDD) Ⓜ
Recorded 1996-97 ●

This mid-price combines the two popular choral compilations 'Agnus Dei I' and 'Agnus Dei II'. From the original first disc the Allegri, Bach, Fauré and Mendelssohn are clear favourites. When we realise that Barber's *Agnus Dei* is an arrangement of his famous *Adagio* and that Elgar's *Lux aeterna* is 'Nimrod' with a halo, then those must be added too.

The performances are delightful, with the single exception of 'Jesu, bleibet meine Freude' ('Jesu, joy of man's desiring') where each of the choir's minims has its swell and *diminuendo* so that they bounce along before us like so many faintly ridiculous balloons. Thomas Herford is the excellent soloist in *Hear my prayer* and a capital exponent of the high C in the Allegri. The quality of choral sound is very fine: also the warmth of the acoustic, not usually associated with New College Chapel, is ideal.

From the original second disc, the performance of the famous *Adagio* ascribed to Albinoni, courtesy of Remo Giazotti, and set here by John Cameron to a text, in Latin, from the New Testament, is deserving of as much success as Barber's *Adagio*. The other items from that issue are taken at rather faster speeds than usual. Lotti's *Crucifixus*, Schubert's 23rd Psalm and Martin's *Agnus Dei* from the Mass for Double Choir are examples, and all of them benefit, especially in this context. The choir itself has long been one of the best in its normal repertoire of church music, and these excursions have emboldened it in coloration and expressive scope. Purcell's *Hear my prayer*, for instance, is sung with exceptional intensity. Some of the arrangements may be questionable. Albinoni is fair game, but Brahms's lovely Op 30 forfeits the spiritual quietness of church when deprived of its organ accompaniment, and Schubert is not really in need of strings and harp. For all that, though, it remains a delightful compilation, and not to be dismissed by 'serious' musicians on account of its wider appeal.

St Paul's Cathedral

'Advent at St Paul's'
Anonymous Laudes Regiae. Angelus ad Virginem (arr Willcocks)[a]. O come, O come, Emmanuel (arr Carter)[a]. Rejoice in the Lord alway **Britten** A Hymn of St Columba[a] **Bruckner** Virga Jesse floruit **Byrd** Laetentur coeli **A Carter** Toccata on Veni Emmanuel[b] **Gibbons** This is the record of John[a] **Handl** Ecce concipies[c] **R Lloyd** Drop down, ye heavens[a] **Palestrina** Matins Responsory. Vesper Responsory **Parsons** Ave Maria **Peerson** Blow out the trumpet[a] **Rutter** Hymn to the Creator of Light

Weelkes Hosanna to the Son of David **Wilby** Echo Carol[a]
St Paul's Cathedral Choir / John Scott [b]*org* with
[a]**Andrew Lucas** *org*
Hyperion CDA66994 (71 minutes: DDD) Ⓕ
Text and translations included. Recorded 1997

As in the seasonal calendar a single window opens first, so in this Advent recital a solo voice sings in the distance; and by the end, all windows alight, the great Cathedral is filled with the organ's *fortissimo* from deepest pedal sub-bass to brightest trumpet and topmost piccolo. The programme begins with some plainsong dating back to the first millennium of the era. The end, more plainsong but not so plain now, has *O come, O come, Emmanuel* decked in 20th-century garb, audaciously arranged, then to become the subject of an organ toccata with sufficient energy to propel the hymn, the Cathedral and all into the new age. In between comes a satisfying alternation of ancient and modern. Particularly splendid is Martin Peerson's *Blow out the trumpet*, an anthem strong in rhythm and colour. Robert Parsons's five-part *Ave Maria* is also a joy. The modern works include an interesting, deeply felt piece by John Rutter, *Hymn to the Creator of Light*: its first section, less ingratiating (but not therefore less good) than his more characteristic style, is followed by an angular refulgence of praise in preparation for a chorale-melody sung quietly in octaves amid an affectionate interweave of gentle polyphony – the effect is lovely. The choir is on top form. Britten's *Hymn of St Columba* is especially well performed, probably making the strongest impression of all. Andrew Lucas is the remorselessly exercised organist in this, and John Scott takes over for the Toccata: both are excellent.

'Hear my Prayer'
Allegri Miserere mei[abdij] **B Rose** Feast Song for St Cecilia[acf] **Brahms** Ein deutsches Requiem – Ich hab' nun Traurigkeit[aj] **Britten** Festival Te Deum, Op 32[aj] **Harvey** Come, Holy Ghost[aeg] **Mendelssohn** Hear my prayer[aj] **Stanford** Evening Canticles in G[aij] **Tavener** I will lift up mine eyes **Wise** The ways of Zion do mourn[ahj]
[a]**Jeremy Budd,** [b]**Nicholas Thompson** *trebs*
[c]**Simon Hill,** [d]**Wilfred Swansborough** *countertens*
[e]**Andrew Burden,** [f]**Alan Green** *tens* [g]**Nigel Beaven,**
[h]**Charles Gibbs,** [i]**Timothy Jones** *basses*
St Paul's Cathedral Choir / John Scott with
[j]**Andrew Lucas** *org*
Hyperion CDA66439 (76 minutes: DDD) Ⓕ
Texts and translations included. Recorded 1990

The special distinction of this disc is the work of the treble soloist, Jeremy Budd. He sings in a programme which is very much the choirboy's equivalent of an operatic soprano's 'Casta diva' and more of that sort. As it is, he crowns the Allegri *Miserere* with its five top Cs, spot-on, each of them (rather like Melba singing 'Amor' at the end of Act 1 in *La bohème* five times over). He commands the breath, the long line and the purity of tone necessary for the solo in Brahms's Requiem and copes with the difficult modern idiom of Jonathan Harvey's *Come, Holy Ghost* with an apparent ease that to an older generation may well seem uncanny. Other modern works are included. John Tavener's *I will lift up mine eyes*, written for St Paul's in 1990, has its characteristic compound of richness and austerity; and in this, the words penetrate the mist of echoes more successfully than do those of the *Feast Song for St Cecilia*, written by Gregory Rose and set to some very beautiful music by his father Bernard. It is good, as ever, to hear Stanford's Evening Service in G, with its almost Fauré-like accompaniment finely played by the excellent Andrew Lucas; and for a morning canticle there is Britten's *Te Deum* with its effective build-up to 'Lord God of Sabaoth' and its faint pre-echo of *The Turn of the Screw* at 'O Lord, save Thy people'. There is also a melancholy anthem by Michael Wise, whose fate it was to be knocked on the head and killed by the watchman to whom he was cheeky one night in 1687.

Psalms for St Paul's Volume 9
Bairstow Psalm 107 **Hurford** Psalm 108 **Jacobs** Psalm 112 **Ouseley** Psalm 105 **Stewart** Psalm 106 **Turle** Psalm 109. Psalm 110 **Vann** Psalm 113 **Woodward** Psalm 111
Huw Williams *org* **St Paul's Cathedral Choir / John Scott**
Hyperion CDP11009 (63 minutes: DDD) Ⓕ
Texts included. OO

Psalms for St Paul's Volume 12
Bertalot Psalm 141 **Camidge** Psalm 140 **Day** Psalm 139 **Hanforth** Psalm 145 **Hervey** Psalm 143 **Monk** Psalm 144. Psalm 146 **Rose** Psalm 121 **Scott** Easter Anthem **Stanford** Psalms 147, 149 and 150 **Stewart** Psalm 142 **Talbot** Psalm 150 **Willcocks** Psalm 148
Huw Williams *org* **St Paul's Cathedral Choir / John Scott**
Hyperion CDP11012 (64 minutes: DDD) Ⓕ
Texts included. Recorded 2000 OO

The phrase 'fearfully and wonderfully made', coined some 3000 years ago by the Psalmist for his 139th Psalm, perfectly describes these final releases in Hyperion's series, Psalms from St Paul's. Over the course of 12 discs all 150 Psalms have been presented in the traditional Anglican grouping covering Matins and Evensong for every day of a 30-day month. After weeks in which we have been subjected to wounds which 'stink and are corrupt through my foolishness' (8th morning), heathen who 'grin like a dog and run about through the city' (11th evening), 'all manner of flies and lice' (21st morning), not to mention the shedding of innocent blood, 'even the blood of their sons and of their daughters' (21st evening), the unrestrained joy of the 30th evening, especially Psalm 150, comes as a welcome relief. And to mark the end of the monthly cycle Psalm 150 is sung to an appropriately celebratory chant (unique in having its own built-in descant) by Stanford which also provides a fitting conclusion to an exceptionally inspiring and captivating – not to say enchanting – series.

The intense pleasure and satisfaction to be gleaned from these discs is hard to explain to the uninitiated, who will seek in vain for any intrinsically musical interest. But while the 20 simple chords of a typical Anglican chant might appear a preposterously miniscule structure to those weaned on Bach cantatas or Mahler symphonies, for the true aficionado the framework of a chant offers infinite scope for expressive creativity. James Turle (1802-82) conjured up real pathos in his lovely chant for Psalm 109 while the Revd Sir Frederick Arthur Ouseley (1825-89) achieved an air of total contentment for Psalm 105. In more recent times Barry Rose shamelessly milks the St Paul's acoustic with his delicious chant to Psalm 121 (included as an appendix to the final disc), John Bertalot gives us a tantalisingly bittersweet chant for Psalm 141 while Sir David Willcocks depicts true majesty for Psalm 148.

Huw Williams' accompaniments are models of sensitivity and discretion, although not without occasional touches of humour ('ye dragons and all deeps' seems to shake the very foundations in Psalm 148 while his 'right hand' certainly provides generous support for Psalm 139), and John Scott's relaxed direction, lovingly caressing these timeless words and phrases, ensures that the leisurely pace, which might from less inspired choral directors induce its hearers to a state of suspended animation, here creates an aura of mystery and sanctity; an aura fully enhanced by this spacious and warmly atmospheric recording. Here, surely, is the very apogee of English Psalm singing.

Portsmouth Cathedral

Magnificat and Nunc Dimittis, Volume 4
Andrews Evening Service in G **Bairstow** Evening Service in D **Brewer** Evening Service in E flat **Darke** Evening Service in F **Howells** Evening Service in E. Evening Service in B minor **Lassus** Magnificat quarto toni **R Shephard** Salisbury Service **Stanford** Evening Service in C, Op 115 **Victoria** Nunc dimittis **Weelkes** Evening Service for Trebles – Magnificat; Nunc dimittis
Portsmouth Cathedral Choir / Adrian Lucas with **David Thorne** *org*
Priory PRCD527 (79 minutes: DDD) Ⓕ
Texts included. Recorded 1995 ●

One good thing after another; it almost surprises that a succession of *Mags* and *Nuncs* can be so varied, satisfying and enjoyable. The programmes in this excellent series allow for a fair variety of styles and centuries, but in this instance a particularly generous share of the credit must go to the performances. Forthright and invigorating, they give rise to a distinct suspicion that the whole business may be a pleasure: that the choristers have some rhythm in their bones and at certain points might even have a smile on their faces. It is there right from the start, with Brewer in E flat (and how undeservedly stodgy that can sound in performance) bright with energy and encouraging a conviction that there genuinely is something in which to rejoice. This extends to Lassus, Victoria and Weelkes, where, instead of the more usual formal reading of notes, there is a common effort of understanding and imagination, lifting the notes off the page and sometimes, with a little judicious semi-*staccato*, setting them a-dance. Nor is there any lack of sensitive shading or of repose in the right places – a fine feeling for mood in the lovely and little-known B minor setting of Howells, for example. A splendid recital, with a fine choice of repertoire, and consistently admirable playing by the organist.

Robert Shaw Festival Singers

O Magnum Mysterium
Górecki Totus tuus, Op 60[a] **Lauridsen** O Magnum Mysterium[b] **Poulenc** Quatre motets de Noël – O magnum mysterium[a] **Rachmaninov** Vespers, Op 37 – Praise the name of the Lord[a] **Schubert** Der Entfernten, D331[b] **Tallis** If ye love me[ac]. A new commandment[ac] **Traditional** Amazing Grace[a]. Sometimes I feel like a moanin' dove[a]. Wondrous Love[a] **Victoria** O vos omnes, qui transitis per viam[ac]. O magnum mysterium[ac]
[a]**Robert Shaw Festival Singers,** [b]**Robert Shaw Chamber Singers / Robert Shaw**
Telarc CD80531 (57 minutes: DDD). Ⓕ
Recorded 1992, 1994, 1997 and live in [c]1989 ●●

This compilation of unaccompanied choral music is a tribute to Robert Shaw, one of the world's great choir trainers. He quickly established that reputation back in the 1940s, when Toscanini chose the Robert Shaw Chorale for major choral recordings with the NBC Symphony Orchestra. Later, over two decades as music director of the Atlanta Symphony, Shaw was diverted more towards the orchestral repertory, his choral recordings then usually involving the orchestra too.

After retiring from that post in 1988 he once again found time for unaccompanied choral music, establishing in 1989 a summer festival of choral concerts and workshops at Quercy in south-central France, using a choir of students from American universities chosen by competitive audition. Between then and 1994 he made a series of recordings for Telarc with that festival choir. They provide most of the items here, atmospherically recorded in St Pierre at Gramat.

The four opening items on the disc, the Tallis and Victoria motets, were recorded in that first year, 1989, with the intention of including them with similar repertory on a full disc. In the event, they now appear on disc for the first time, immaculate performances from a relatively large choir, which demonstrate the consistent refinement of matching and balance characteristic of Shaw's choral work.

The Poulenc and Rachmaninov items also date from 1989, the movement from the Rachmaninov *Vespers* demonstrating the fervour that Shaw could draw from his singers. The two American hymns and one spiritual item are from the 1992 Festival, with Shaw's own arrangements exploiting the sort of elaborate choral effects he relished in other music. The last and longest item on the disc, the Górecki motet, recorded in 1994, brings a performance which concentratedly sustains a very slow speed and extremes of *pianissimo* that are both rapt and dreamlike.

The Schubert part-song and the Lauridsen motet, recorded with Shaw's chamber singers back in the United States, readily match the rest of the programme in their refinement and beauty of sound – particularly the Lauridsen. It is a fine piece by a composer, born in 1943, who spices a traditional idiom with clashing intervals in a way that Purcell would certainly have enjoyed. At under an hour the compilation might have been more generous, but that is a tiny criticism to set against the outstanding quality of singing and recording.

Worcester Cathedral

Great Cathedral Anthems – XI

Beach Let this mind be in you **Dirksen** Songs of Isaiah – Arise, shine **Friedell** Draw us in the Spirit's tether **Hancock** Earthquake, Wind and Fire **Hoiby** The Lord is King **Macfarlane** Open our eyes **Neswick** Happy are they that fear the Lord **Parker** Jam sol recedit igneus **Rorem** Exaltabo te, Domine **Sowerby** I was glad

Judith Hancock *org* **Choir of Saint Thomas Church, Fifth Avenue / Gerre Hancock**

Priory PRCD629 (64 minutes: DDD) Ⓕ

Texts included. Recorded 1999

Great Cathedral Anthems – XII

Atkins Abide with me. If ye then be risen with Christ. There is none that can resist thy voice **Day** Turn back O Man. When I survey the wondrous cross **Elgar** Light out of darkness. O hearken thou **Guest** For the Fallen **Lucas** Sacerdotes Domini **Tomkins** O sing unto the Lord. When David heard that Absolom was slain **Willcocks** My heart is fixed, O God

Adrian Lucas *org* **Worcester Cathedral Choir / Sir David Willcocks**

Priory PRCD750 (61 minutes: DDD) Ⓕ

Recorded 2000

To conclude its series of Great Cathedral Anthems – a series which, at just 12 discs, merely scratches the surface of the available repertoire – Priory celebrates the work, not of a major church music composer, but of one of the best-known and most highly respected choral directors of our time. And, in taking Sir David Willcocks back to Worcester, where from 1950 to 1957 he was Master of the Choristers, we are also given an opportunity to celebrate the music of one of Britain's most musically influential cathedrals. Of course the Worcester choir under Willcocks in the 1950s would have been a very different-sounding body from their 21st-century successor, here singing (presumably after only a handful of rehearsals) under an awe-inspiring 'legend', and perhaps it is unfair to criticise the occasional raggedness of blend and ensemble while the over-bright boys' tone seems a world apart from the smooth 'coo' which became Willcocks' hallmark at King's College, Cambridge. But Willcocks never made recordings with his Worcester Choir and, given the chance to hear such Worcester gems as *When I survey* by Edgar Day, assistant under Willcocks, and *If ye then be risen* by Willcocks' predecessor at Worcester, not to mention rarely heard anthems by the greatest Worcesterian of them all, Elgar, the combination of a legendary choral director, a keen and enthusiastic choir and Adrian Lucas's resourceful and vivid organ accompaniments, makes this a fitting conclusion to an eminently rewarding series.

The penultimate disc in the series gives British church music aficionados a rare chance to sample American anthems. Few of those included here will be familiar to English ears and only Harold Friedell's charming *Draw us in the Spirit's tether* could be mistaken for the genuine English product. But the unfettered drama, vivid musical imagery and sheer Technicolor opulence of these anthems make a refreshing change from the restrained emotions and tight-lipped charm of their English counterparts. Under Gerre Hancock, himself something of a legend in church music circles, the choir of St Thomas's New York prove themselves to be one of the best cathedral choirs on either side of the Atlantic and Judith Hancock's polished and imaginative organ accompaniments add a fine touch of distinction. Priory's recording achieves the perfect balance between atmosphere (which in this location is most generous) and clarity.

Vocal

Roberto Alagna *ten*

French Arias

Bazin Maître Pathelin – Je pense à vous quand je m'éveille **Berlioz** La damnation de Faust – Nature immense **Bizet** Les pêcheurs de perles – A cette voix; Je crois entendre encore **Bruneau** L'attaque du Moulin – Le jour tombe **Cherubini** Les abencérages – Suspendez à ces murs; J'ai vu disparaître l'espoir **Gluck** Iphigénie en Tauride – Quel langage accablant; Unis dès la plus tendre enfance **Gounod** Mireille – Mon coeur est plein d'un noir souci; Anges du paradis **Grétry** Les fausses apparences ou L'amant jaloux – Tandis que tout sommeille **Halévy** La juive – Rachel, quand du Seigneur **Lalo** Le roi d'Ys – Puisqu'on ne peut fléchir; Vainement, ma bien-aimée **Massenet** Le Cid – Ah! tout est bien fini; O souverain, ô juge, ô père **Méhul** Joseph – Vainement Pharaon dans sa reconnaissance; Champs paternels **Meyerbeer** L'africaine – Pays merveilleux **Saint-Saëns** Samson et Dalila[a] – Vois ma misère **Thomas** Mignon – Elle ne croyait pas

Roberto Alagna *ten*

[a]**London Voices; Orchestra of the Royal Opera House, Covent Garden / Bertrand de Billy**

EMI CDC5 57012-2 (72 minutes: DDD). Texts and translations included. Recorded 1999-2000 Ⓕ

This is one of the best recitals Alagna has recorded. By juxtaposing familiar with somewhat lesser-known arias, he offers a survey of French operatic style from 1778 (Grétry's *L'amant jaloux*) to 1893 (Bruneau's *L'attaque du moulin*). As John Steane points out in his booklet, the French tenor, and what was expected of him, shifted from the *haute-contre* type of the late 18th century, through heroic antics of the 1830s and 40s, when Nourrit and Duprez launched the fashion for stentorian high notes, to the more modern elegance demanded by Massenet and his successors.

Of the operas that will be curiosities to all but the most travelled music-lovers, Cherubini's *Les abencérages* and Méhul's *Joseph* are both worthy of revival. Alagna deals with the climactic cry of 'Je te perds; mon âme flétrie t'adresse d'éternels adieux' from *Les abencérages* most effectively, the high notes taken softly, as the composer would have expected, while in *Joseph* he sounds suitably tormented.

Like *Joseph*, Bazin's *Maître Pathelin* from 1856 knew a lot of success in its time, mostly because of the aria sung here, 'Je pense à vous quand je m'éveille'. This used to be a favourite concert item with French tenors, and Alagna begins very well, establishing the ardent mood. A comparison with two singers of the past, Gaston Micheletti in a 1931 disc, and Gérard Friedmann in an abridged version from French Radio (Musidisc Gaieté Lyrique) finds the older singer more vehement, almost hectoring, and the sadly little-recorded Friedmann more gentle. Alagna falls somewhere between the two; more of a variation of tone in the reprise of the haunting melody would have been welcome.

Grétry's *L'amant jaloux* is a jolly little piece – there was a complete EMI recording of it in the 70s which had Charles Burles as the hero. In this mandolin-accompanied serenade, he is singing to the wrong woman as it turns out. These lovely songs from Grétry's operas whet the appetite, which is then rather let down when one hears them all the way through.

The final item is also one of the best, Dominique's farewell to the forests from *L'attaque du moulin*. This is based on Zola's tale (the author later provided Bruneau with original librettos). In this scene, the noble-hearted Flemish soldier has been captured by the Germans and accused of helping their French enemies. As he anticipates being shot at dawn, the young man sings this almost ecstatic song to the sky and the trees. It's a captivating moment, and Alagna gives it for all its worth, in the score the composer asks for a very full-out treatment of the climaxes.

In the better-known numbers, Alagna is predictably suave as Wilhelm Meister in *Mignon*, a delicate 'Elle ne croyait pas'. The Bizet, Lalo and Gounod all find him on form too. In the other pieces that are associated with more heroic voices, he sometimes uses a rather throaty sounding effect, especially noticeable in the aria from *Le Cid*, though as Vasco in *L'africaine* he rises to a really thrilling 'O paradis'. There has never been a satisfactory recording of this opera. On this evidence, perhaps it should be Alagna's next project.

Sergei Alexashkin *bass*

Russian Opera Arias, Volume 2
Borodin Prince Igor – I hate a dreary life; No sleep, no rest; How goes it Prince? **Mussorgsky** Boris Godunov – Once in the town of Kazan
Rimsky-Korsakov Sadko – O fearful crags (Song of the Viking Guest). The Tsar's Bride – Sleep has overcome her. Mozart and Salieri – Everyone says there's no justice; No, I can't oppose my fate; You will sleep for a long time, Mozart!
Rachmaninov Aleko – By the magical power of the singing; The entire encampment sleeps
Tchaikovsky Mazeppa – So this is my reward. Eugene Onegin – Everyone knows love on earth
Sergei Alexashkin *bass* **Ambrosian Opera Chorus; Philharmonia Orchestra / Gennadi Rozhdestvensky**
Chandos CHAN9629 (74 minutes: DDD) Ⓕ
Texts and translations included. Recorded 1997

Over this recital shines the steady light of Osip Petrov, the great artist who with the première of Glinka's *Life for the Tsar* in 1836 initiated a tradition of bass singing that was to colour the whole of Russian opera. It includes, as this admirably selected programme shows, a grave solemnity of voice, but also a baritonal elegance and a wide range of colour, a manner tragic, ruminative or seductive, together with the ferocious humour we encounter in Mussorgsky's Varlaam (another of Petrov's creations). The characteristics touch on much lying deep in Russia's life, and the line has included Stravinsky's father, Feodor, Mikhail Koryakin, Feodor Chaliapin and many others.

Sergei Alexashkin is a worthy inheritor of it, and this recital arouses hopes for more than just glimpses of some great roles. Alexashkin has the range to give subtle contrast to different roles in the same opera: the gloomy regret of Prince Igor's aria and also the brighter manliness which the Khan Konchak brings to their exchanges, the exhausted sorrowfulness of Rachmaninov's Old Gipsy and the more youthful acquaintance with the identical betrayal now encountered by Aleko. There is the dignity but also the coldness and the sudden glint of paranoia which possesses Salieri as he faces what he conceives to be his artistic duty in murdering Mozart, yet the jollity is only just this side of the maudlin in Mussorgsky's Varlaam and Borodin's Galitsky. Much depends on the subtle modifications of tone, still more on his ability to phrase with due care for meaning, whether in the free-ranging recitative of Salieri or, in Gremin's declaration of his devotion to Tatyana, the soaring melodic response to the warmth of the sun that has lit his life.

Rozhdestvensky and the Philharmonia are superb companions in these ventures into a great repertory; and Chandos backs it all very well with full texts and translations.

Victoria de los Angeles *sop*

Songs of Spain – traditional and early; medieval; renaissance; baroque. Medieval and renaissance songs of Andalusia. Renaissance songs. 19th- and 20th-century arrangements and art songs by Barrera/Calleja, Falla, Granados, Guridi, Halffter, Lorca, Mompou, Montsalvatge, Nin, Rodrigo, Toldrá, Vals and Valverde. Opera arias – Goyescas, La Tempranica (Giménez) and La vida breve
Victoria de los Angeles *sop* with various artists
EMI mono/stereo ④ CMS5 66937-2 Ⓜ
(301 minutes: ADD/DDD). Texts and translations included. Recorded 1950-92 ●

Nothing could be more appropriate in celebrating Victoria de los Angeles's 75th birthday than this extensive conspectus of her recordings of Spanish song over 40 years. We begin with her 1950 set of traditional songs arranged by Graciano Tarragó, evocative of an era and a style preserved amazingly in various collections. The singer here is not as outgoing or communicative as she was soon to become, perhaps a shade intimidated by this early encounter with the microphone. There is a certain sameness to her approach, but the voice of the young artist, so refulgent, is a delight in itself. The renaissance and baroque pieces that fill the rest of the first disc are another matter. Not only is the music more accessible but de los Angeles performs it with a winning charm. The second disc is devoted entirely to medieval and renaissance songs recorded in 1960 and 1967 with the Ars Musicae de Barcelona.

The last two discs bring us to 19th- and 20th-century arrangements of traditional material and original compositions. Among the former, Lorca's set, *Canciones populares españolas*, are absolutely irresistible both in themselves and as performed by the unflagging Victoria in 1970. These imaginative re-creations, full of sentiment, verve and fun, release every aspect of the singer's genius – eager, forward tone, vital enunciation of the texts and unfettered joy in the mere act of communication.

The remainder of the songs on this CD, all of which featured frequently in the soprano's recitals, maintain this high standard, including Mompou's touching 'Damunt de tu, només les flors', Montsalvatge's lullaby for a black baby, with which she always bewitched her audiences, and Rodrigo's 'De los álamos vengo' (which, incidentally, appears in its unadorned form earlier in the set). Then what was perhaps de los Angeles's signature-tune, Valverde's 'Clavelitos' – not the early 78rpm version, though, but the 1960 stereo remake – a sure-fire encore at most of her recitals.

The final CD includes her unrivalled recordings of Granados's *Tonadillas*, and his *Tres majas dolorosa*, suffering love epitomised in music and interpretation, as it is in Salud's arias from Falla's *La vida breve*. Then, dating from a live recital at Hunter College, NY, in 1971 with her close contemporary Alicia de Larrocha at the piano, we have Granados's *Canciones amatorias*, another favourite item of the singer's, and her dark-grained, intense account of Falla's *Seven Spanish Popular Songs*, with exuberant, subtly shaped support from Larrocha. Catching the bird on the wing, as it were, adds a further dimension of immediacy to our appreciation of this much loved artist. And we leave her at the end of that recital and this engrossing set, tapping our feet as she sings a Zapateado from a zarzuela, the vocal patter delivered with stunning verve, about a tarantula that has stung the precocious singer. Lionel Salter provides the predictably well-informed and amusing notes, but it is a pity he was not allowed space to describe in more detail the wide variety of material. Andrew Walter's transfers are impeccable.

Songs and Arias by Brahms 🄷
Falla, Fusté, Granados, Guridi, Handel, Nin, Respighi, Schumann, Toldrá, Turina, Valverde and Vives
Victoria de los Angeles *sop* with various artists
Testament mono SBT1087 (75 minutes: ADD) Ⓕ
Recorded 1942-53

The two Respighi songs are magical performances – *Stornellatrice*, with the golden voice at its richest and *E se un giorno tornasse*, a study in subtle shading of tone, a dialogue between a mother and her dying, jilted daughter. For those two brief items alone, superbly transferred, this collection is an essential for all admirers of this singer, but there is so much more. Having Handel's 'O had I Jubal's lyre' in German rather than English may be odd, but the performance sparkles and among the Lieder it is good to have not just 'Der Nussbaum' – the Schumann song which was always special to her – but two previously unpublished, 'Widmung' from the Myrthe songs and 'Ich grolle nicht' from *Dichterliebe*. Through the whole collection the superb transfers capture the full-throated glory of los Angeles's voice at the beginning of her career. The 1942 recordings of two Hungarian folk-songs, previously unpublished, may be rough and limited – made when the singer was only 18 – but they amply demonstrate that already the voice was fully developed in its beauty. No fewer than 18 of the 27 items are of Spanish songs, and though in one or two instances los Angeles was destined to make even more idiomatic readings later with a Spanish accompanist, these ones with Gerald Moore as her partner have a freshness and brilliance that has rarely been matched in this repertory. In particular it is good to have her first recording of the encore number which she made her own, *Clavelitos*.

Anthologies

Great Singers at the Maryinsky Theatre 🄷
Opera Arias with various accompaniments
Sopranos – **Olimpia Boronat** (Les Huguenots), **Eugenia Bronskaya** (Hamlet, A Life for the Tsar), **Elena Katulskaya** (Mireille, Thaïs), **Maria Kovalenko** (The Queen of Spades), **Lydia Lipkowska** (The Snow Maiden), **Antonina Nezhdanova** (Fra Diavolo, Lakmé,

La traviata, Die Zauberflöte); *Mezzo-soprano* – **Evgenia Popello-Davidova** (Lakmé); *Contralto* – **Evgenia Zbrueva** (The Queen of Spades); *Tenors* – **David Juzhin** (La Gioconda), **Andrei Labinsky** (Halka), **Dmitri Smirnov** (Mefistofele, La traviata), **Leonid Sobinov** (The Demon), **Eugene Vitting** (The Queen of Spades); *Baritone* – **Mikhail Karakash** (The Queen of Spades); *Basses* – **Vladimir Kastorsky** (Eugene Onegin), **Lev Sibiriakov** (Judith, Thaïs, Requiem – Verdi)
Nimbus Prima Voce mono NI7865 (78 minutes: ADD) Ⓢ
Notes and some synopses included. Recorded 1908-13

Here is a superb collection, 'courtesy [we are told] of the Director of Staff of the St Petersburg State Museum of Theatre and Music'. All of the originals are rare, and some must be practically unique. Among the soprano solos, particularly exciting is Boronat's account of the Queen's cabaletta in *Les Huguenots*, queenly indeed as far as the letter of the score is concerned but brilliant in technique and often exquisite in shading. Nezhdanova in both *Lakmé* excerpts (the Bell song and now even more famous 'flower' duet) sings with lovely purity and easy command. Lipkowska's *Snow Maiden* is an utter charmer, and also delightfully youthful in tone is Katulskaya's Mireille. Of the tenors, Labinsky's *Halka* solo has exemplary evenness of line, as has the baritone Karakash in Yeletsky's aria. Kastorsky's Gremin and Sibiriakov's admonition of the Israelites in *Judith* are among the finest of all; and how skilfully Sibiriakov subdues his mighty bass in the *Thaïs* duet with Katulskaya. The original copies used are all in pristine condition.

Greatest Voices of Bolshoi Ⓗ
Opera Arias
Sopranos – **Valeria Barsova** (Snow Maiden), **Xenia Derzhinskaya** (The Queen of Spades), **Vera Firssova** (Christmas Eve), **Tamara Milash-kina** (The Enchantress), **Antonina Nezhdanova** (A Life for the Tsar), **Bella Rudenko** (Lakmé), **Natalia Spieller** (Iolanta), **Galina Vishnevskaya** (La forza del destino); *Mezzo-sopranos* – **Irina Arkhipova** (Samson et Dalila), **Elena Obraztsova** (Boris Godunov), **Nadezhda Obukhova** (Prince Igor); *Tenors* – **Zurab Andzhaparidze** (The Queen of Spades), **Vladimir Atlantov** (Prince Igor), **Ivan Kozlovsky** (Boris Godunov, Snow Maiden), **Sergei Lemeshev** (Eugene Onegin, Sadko), **Georgi Nelepp** (Askold's Grave), **Leonid Sobinov** (Lohengrin); *Baritones* – **Pavel Lisitsian** (The Queen of Spades), **Yuri Mazurok** (Mazeppa), **Grigori Pirogov** (Askold's Grave); *Basses* – **Feodor Chaliapin** (Don Quichotte), **Maxim Mikhailov** (Prince Igor), **Evgeny Nesterenko** (A Life for the Tsar), **Ivan Petrov** (Iolanta), **Alexander Pirogov** (Prince Igor), **Mark Reizen** (Boris Godunov)
Melodiya mono/stereo ② 74321 39505-2 Ⓜ
(149 minutes: ADD). Recorded 1910-80

Here's richness. From Glinka onwards, standards were set for Russian singing which we can, for the great 19th-century artists, only deduce from their music but which we may fairly suppose founded the great tradition we can hear upheld on record for much of the twentieth. What did Osip Petrov, the bass who dominated Russian opera for half a century from 1826, really sound like? Probably less like Chaliapin – though the great dramatic bass is represented here in lyrical vein by his beautiful performance of Don Quichotte's death scene in 1927 (Massenet) – than his namesake Ivan Petrov as King René (1952), or than the powerful Maxim Mikhailov, superb in Khan Konchak's aria (1953), or than the cultivated Mark Reizen, whose début was as Pimen in 1921, singing wonderfully here in 1951 and who made his final appearance as Gremin in 1985, on his ninetieth birthday, to a devoted Bolshoi cast and audience. Alexander Pirogov's fine delivery of Galitsky's aria (1951) and Evgeny Nesterenko's of Susanin's farewell (1979) seem but younger branches of this great oak planted by Petrov.

The tenor tradition lies closer to French style than to anything more intrinsically Russian, let alone Italian. Here is the superlative Leonid Sobinov, in fine voice as Lohengrin (1910); but why not some of his Lensky, who here goes to the elegant Sergei Lemeshev (1953)? Here too is Ivan Kozlovsky, unforgettable as the Simpleton in *Boris* in 1927 and still in full command as Tsar Berendey in 1957. On the other hand, the powerful Slavonic line of dominating mezzos and contraltos has made a mark upon opera that has at times led to tradition becoming something of a prison. Nadezhda Obukhova exhibits some of these risks in the very strength of her singing of Konchakovna (1941); however, here are Elena Obraztsova (part of Marina's aria in 1968) and Irina Arkhipova (Dalila's 'Mon coeur' in 1980) showing how rich and diverse it can be.

The sopranos are the most varied group. Some exhibit the powerful vibrato which has been such a cause of complaint in the West, though Valeria Barsova (1951) shows how it can be lightly and expressively applied to the Snow Maiden. Bella Rudenko's chirpy coloratura sparkles in Lakmé's Bell Song (1967). Antonina Nezhdanova exhibits a warmer, stronger manner in Antonida's Romance (1914) that suggests her as a mother figure to Galina Vishnevskaya, at the height of her powers as Verdi's *Forza* Leonora in 1959. Much more could be mentioned, and Grigori Pirogov's remarkable baritone as the Unknown in *Askold's Grave* (1910) should certainly not be overlooked. The transfers are fine.

Legendary Baritones Ⓗ
Opera Arias and Songs with various accompaniments
Lucien Fugère (Le jongleur de Notre Dame); **Victor Maurel** (Tosti: Au temps du grand roi); **Antonio Magini-Coletti** (Falstaff); **Mattia Battistini** (La traviata); **Mario Ancona** (Un ballo in maschera); **Maurice Renaud** (Le roi de Lahore); **Eugenio Giraldoni** (Otello); **Riccardo Stracciari** (Tosca); **Giuseppe de Luca** (Ernani); **Titta Ruffo** (Falstaff); **Pasquale Amato** (I due Foscari); **Joseph Schwarz** (Tannhäuser); **Heinrich Schlusnus** (Hans Heiling); **Renato Zanelli** (Zazà); **Carlo Galeffi** (Rigoletto); **John Charles**

Thomas (Andrea Chenier); **Lawrence Tibbett** (Il barbiere di Siviglia); **Gerhard Hüsch** (Der Wildschütz); **Igor Gorin** (Attila)
Nimbus Prima Voce mono NI7867 Ⓢ
(77 minutes: ADD). Recorded 1905-41

Prizes for all here, except possibly John Charles Thomas. *Andrea Chenier* is not the subtlest of operas, and 'Nemico della patria' does not call for the fine nuance of a Fischer-Dieskau, but it does want more than the mouthing of words and *tutta forza* for the notes. The voice is magnificent, but in this 'legendary' company we look also for taste. And in its various guises we find it: in the 80-year-old Fugère with his immaculate definition and unmawkish tenderness; in Maurel with a charm of old-world manners in his courtly song to Madame la Marquise; Magini-Coletti with his humorous but gentlemanly Falstaff; Battistini wearing his elegant paternal suit, and Ancona bestowing upon the outraged husband the dignity of more-in-sorrow-than-in-anger. After that comes Maurice Renaud, about whom one might raise a complaint concerning emotional expression achieved at the expense of the vocal line; yet there is stylistic refinement too, and a richly imaginative care for the Massenet aria, phrase by phrase. With Stracciari one might wonder about the voice production, so free one moment, throat-laden in another; then there is Amato with his rapid vibrancy, Galeffi with his weakness for the emotional quiver. Yet all are artists, and their work will repay study. The Germans are a distinguished trio too, and the Russian-born Igor Gorin is superb in his *Attila* aria. Ruffo, rich in vocal colours, de Luca gracious in the exercise of traditional virtues... But there it is: a prize-giving here would have something for (almost) everybody, including those responsible for the transfers and booklet, for the choice of singers and their matching up with arias.

Singers of Imperial Russia, Volumes 1-4 H

Awards 1993

GEMMCDS9997/9: recorded 1900-11: *Soprano* – **Medea Mei-Figner;** *Tenors* – **Ivan Ershov, Nikolai Figner** and **Leonid Sobinov;** *Baritone* – **Ioakim Tartakov;** *Basses* – **Adamo Didur and Vasili Sharonov**
GEMMCDS9001/03: 1901-11: *Sopranos* – **Natalia Ermolenko-Juzhina** and **Maria Michailova;** *Mezzo-soprano* – **Antonina Panina;** *Tenors* – **David Juzhin, Andrei Labinsky** and **Gavril Morskoi;** *Baritones* – **Oskar Kamionsky** and **Polikarp Orlov;** *Basses* – **Dmitri Bukhtoyarov, Vladimir Kastorsky, Vasili Sharonov** and **Lev Sibiriakov**
GEMMCDS9004/06: 1901-24: *Sopranos* – **Irena Bohuss, Anna El-Tour, Janina Korolewicz-Wayda, Maria Kuznetsova, Lydia Lipkowska** and **Nadezhda Zabela-Vrubel;** *Contralto* – **Evgenia Zbrueva;** *Tenors* – **Dmitri Smirnov** and **Eugene Witting;** *Bass* – **K E Kaidanov**
GEMMCD9007/09: 1901-14: *Sopranos* – **Maria Michailova** and **Antonia Nezhdanova;** *Mezzo-soprano* – **Galina Nikitina;** *Contralto* – **Evgenia Zbrueva;** *Tenors* – **Alexandr Alexandrovich, Alexandr Bogdanovich, Alexandr Davidov, Andrei Labinsky** and **Eugene Witting;** *Baritone* – **Nikolai Shevelev. Basses – Vladimir Kastorsky** and **Lev Sibiriakov**
Pearl mono 4x③ GEMMCDS9997/9, 9001/3, 9004/6 and 9007/9 Ⓜ
(oas: 207, 209, 222 and 221 minutes: AAD) OOO

This is the equivalent of one of those exhibitions for which queues form long and deep and daily outside the Tate Gallery or the Royal Academy: in fact, if a similar exhibition of paintings, furniture and porcelain from the Tsar's palaces were mounted in London it would surely be a sell-out. Quite simply, there has never been a published collection to match this, both in the quality of the items and in its extensiveness. Of the singers of Imperial Russia, the world came to know Chaliapin, who eclipsed the rest. He is not among the artists presented here, but we have, among the basses, two who at least for vocal splendour are his equal: Adamo Didur, the Pole who was New York's first Boris Godunov (preceding Chaliapin there), and Lev Sibiriakov, another giant of a man with a magnificently produced voice to match. The tenors include Smirnov and Sobinov, a kind of collector's Tweedledum and Tweedledee, though in fact very unalike indeed. New to most listeners will be Ivan Ershov, heard in Siegfried's Forging Song from St Petersburg, 1903, with piano and anvil accompaniment: an astonishing voice and most accomplished in technique. Evgenia Zbrueva the contralto, sopranos Nezhdanova, Ermolenko-Jushina, Mei-Figner and the superbly recorded Korolewicz-Wayda are also plentifully represented. Most amazing of all, perhaps, is the vividness of sound. These are some of the world's rarest recordings and they are almost all in pristine condition.

Stars of English Opera, Volume 1 H

Opera Arias with various orchestras and conductors
Sopranos – **Gwen Catley** (Rigoletto), **Joan Cross** (Così fan tutte), **Dame Joan Hammond** (Gianni Schicchi, Tosca); *Mezzos* – **Janet Howe** (Samson et Dalila), **Gladys Ripley** (Don Carlo), **Marjorie Thomas** (Alcina); *Tenors* – **Webster Booth** (Esmeralda), **James Johnston** (The Bartered Bride), **David Lloyd** (Don Giovanni, Die Zauberflöte), **Heddle Nash** (La favorita, Les pêcheurs de perles); *Baritones* – **John Hargreaves** (Rigoletto), **Redvers Llewellyn** (Falstaff), **Dennis Noble** (Il barbiere di Siviglia); *Bass* – **Oscar Natzke** (Die lustigen Weiber von Windsor)
Dutton Laboratories mono CDLX7018 Ⓑ
(75 minutes: ADD). All items sung in English.
Recorded 1938-49

The discs chosen come from that fruitful period in British singing in the years before, during and just after the Second World War, when Columbia and HMV were busy recording a crop of native singers performing so eloquently in their native tongue. The group of tenors alone is a distinguished one, headed by Heddle Nash, whose dreamy, poised *mezza voce* is heard to perfection in Nadir's Romance from *Les pêcheurs de perles*, one of his most beguiling records. His ardent, refined singing of 'Spirit so fair' from *La favorita*, made during the same 1944 Liverpool session, is equally desirable. So is James Johnston's account of Jeník's aria from *The Bartered Bride*. Most welcome of all are Don Ottavio's second aria and Tamino's Portrait solo as sung by David Lloyd, whose forthright, mellifluous tone and persuasive performances offer Mozart singing of the highest calibre. Joan Cross's account of Fiordiligi's Act 2 aria, is another fine piece of Mozart singing – and isn't that Dennis Brain playing the horn solos? Marjorie Thomas's refined art is recalled in her pure Handelian *legato* while Llewellyn offers character but a rather attenuated tone in Ford's aria, Hargreaves much feeling but stilted diction as Rigoletto. If these two baritones were limited in appeal, Noble was one of great distinction regarding tone, line and diction. His 1939 HMV 'I'm the factotum' launches this disc in the most engaging way. Transfers, as usual from this source, are exemplary, surface noise wholly eliminated, voices clean and forward.

Stars of English Opera, Volume 3

Opera Arias and Ensembles with various orchestras and conductors

Sopranos – **Dame Isobel Baillie** (Alessandro), **Joyce Gartside** (Simon Boccanegra), **Dame Joan Hammond** (Faust), **Dora Labbette** (La bohème), **Miriam Licette** (Le nozze di Figaro), **Dame Maggie Teyte** (The Maid of Orleans); *Contraltos* – **Kathleen Ferrier** (Orfeo ed Euridice), **Jean Watson** (Un ballo in maschera); *Tenors* – **Gerald Davies** (La bohème), **Tano Ferendinos** (L'Arlesiana, Werther), **James Johnston** (Simon Boccanegra), **Heddle Nash** (L'elisir d'amore, Faust); *Baritones* – **Arnold Matters** (Simon Boccanegra), **Frederick Sharp** (Simon Boccanegra); *Basses* – **Norman Allin** (La reine de Saba), **Owen Brannigan** (Faust), **Howell Glynne** (Simon Boccanegra)

Dutton Laboratories mono CDLX7024 Ⓑ

(77 minutes: ADD). Recorded 1927-50

Norman Allin is perhaps the most striking revelation: sturdy and firm as a rock (but by no means hard-hearted), individual and memorable, and there is nothing to be found quite like him today. Somewhat like him a generation after was Howell Glynne, who is heard here in Fiesco's aria from *Simon Boccanegra*, one of the best of the old Sadlers Wells singers and later a very good Baron Ochs at Covent Garden. It is good also to hear Jean Watson: Canadian-born, she came to us after the war and sang a stunning Azucena. Her Ulrica solo is scrupulous but not very dramatic. 'Scrupulous' is the word for all these, including the Melboid sopranos, Licette, (Labbette) Perli and Teyte. If there is a disappointment it is with Arnold Matters's dull-toned Boccanegra, balanced, however, by the pleasure of hearing Joyce Gartside and James Johnston as the lovers. And shedding her light over all is Kathleen Ferrier, whose test-pressing of 'What is life?' suggests not so much a star of the British opera as a nearly full moon in the international firmament. It is a delightful collection, the sound vivid and compelling as ever.

Dame Isobel Baillie and Kathleen Ferrier

To Music H

Songs, Arias and Duets by [a]**Arne**, [ab]**Brahms**, [b]**Elgar**, [b]**Gluck**, [b]**Greene**, [a]**Grieg**, [b]**Handel**, [ab]**Mendelssohn**, [ab]**Purcell**, [a]**Schubert** and [a]**Scott**

[a]**Dame Isobel Baillie** *sop* [b]**Kathleen Ferrier** *contr*

Gerald Moore *pf*

APR mono APR5544 (69 minutes: ADD) Ⓜ

Recorded 1941-45. All items sung in English

This is a delightful disc, with a happily chosen programme and well-matched contributions from both singers. Even so, it has to be admitted that the first thought concerns date. The piano arrangements of Purcell duets and Handel arias are definitely of the period; nothing could be more remote from the modern style which was even then coming into vogue. But 'dated' in a much better way is the quality of the singing itself. Would you today find the runs in Purcell and Handel sung with at once such clear articulation and such smoothness? Dame Isobel is sometimes a little pipey but mostly charming. Ferrier is royal. The transfers are excellent.

Dame Janet Baker *mez*

Haydn Arianna a Naxos, HobXXVIb/2[a] **Schubert** Der Blinde Knabe, D833[b]. Totengräberweise, D869[b] **Schumann** Frauenliebe und -leben, Op 42[c]. Der Page, Op 30 No 2[b]. Meine Rose, Op 90 No 2[b] **R Strauss** Vier Lieder, Op 27[b] – No 3, Heimliche Aufforderung; No 4, Morgen. Befreit, Op 39 No 4[b] **Wolf** Spanisches Liederbuch[b] – Die ihr schwebet um diese Palmen; Geh' Geliebter

Dame Janet Baker *mez* [a]**John Constable,** [b]**Paul Hamburger,** [c]**Geoffrey Parsons** *pfs*

BBC Music Legends/IMG Artists BBCL4049-2 Ⓜ

(80 minutes: ADD)

Recorded live in [ab]1968 and [c]1971 ●●

Although recorded on three separate occasions, and with different accompanists, this programme is fairly typical of the recitals that Dame Janet gave in the late 1960s and early '70s when she was at the absolute peak of her form. She probably wouldn't have opened with the Haydn, reserving it usually as the final item in the first half, an operatic climax to work towards. She recorded it later with Raymond Leppard (for Philips – nla) but this live version has a wonderful sense of intimacy. The recording is first rate, with marvellous presence; Baker has that ability to invest a simple phrase in the first recitative such as 'la face splenda del nostro amor' with unforgettable poignancy. In the second part, as Ariadne rails against her fate, she allows herself an almost *verismo*-like outburst at 'ei qui lascia in abbandono'. This cantata can sometimes seem a bit heavyweight on a recital programme, but as Baker sings it seems to grows in beauty and intensity.

Frauenliebe und-leben was the work that brought Baker early fame as a recording artist, in her recital for Saga. Later she recorded it again for EMI with Barenboim. This recording from 1968, accompanied by Geoffrey Parsons, finds her in luxurious full voice, revelling in each successive melody. It isn't preferable to the earlier Saga version with Isepp, but here she lets herself go more at certain key moments such as 'O lass im Traüme' in the third song. This cycle belonged to Janet Baker, and with the single exception of Sena Jurinac, there just isn't a singer to equal her in it.

The songs recorded in the studio with Paul Hamburger include two by Wolf, not available anywhere else in Baker's discography. 'Geh' Geliebter' is sung with typical ardour. The two Schubert and Schumann songs are fresh and lively, but it is the Strauss group that has the highest voltage. *Heimliche Aufforderung* doesn't really suit her, with its intoxicated ardour, but *Morgen* is a superb example of that hushed, rapt quality that was one of the characteristic joys of Baker's art. The final song, *Befreit*, achieves a dramatic thrust that suggests the theatre in the best possible sense. Admirers who already possess Baker's other versions of this material should not be deterred – this is a splendid souvenir of her in the full glory of her prime. Newcomers to Baker's singing – there can't be many people under 30 who heard her live – are in for a treat.

Song Recital

Britten Corpus Christi carol **Busch** Rest
Fauré Automne, Op 18 No 3. Prison, Op 83 No 1. Soir, Op 83 No 2. Fleur jetée, Op 39 No 2. En sourdine, Op 58 No 2. Notre amour, Op 23 No 2. Mai, Op 1 No 2. La chanson du pêcheur, Op 4 No 1. Clair de lune, Op 46 No 2 **Gurney** The fields are full
Ireland The Salley Gardens **Parry** Proud Maisie. O Mistress Mine **Quilter** Love's Philosophy, Op 3 No 1
Schubert Am Grabe Anselmos, D504. Abendstern, D806. Die Vögel, D691. Die Götter Griechenlands, D677. Gondelfahrer, D808. Auflösung, D807
Stanford La belle dame sans merci
R Strauss Morgen, Op 27 No 4. Befreit, Op 39 No 4
Vaughan Williams Linden Lea
Warlock Pretty Ring-time
Dame Janet Baker *mez* **Gerald Moore** *pf*
EMI CDM5 65009-2 (75 minutes: ADD) Ⓜ
Texts and translations included. Recorded 1967-69

This CD is a timely reminder, a generous one too, of Baker in her prime. At the peak of her career at the end of the 1960s, the tone is at its most beautiful, the singing as secure as it is intelligent. One realises anew that here is one of the great singers of the century and one comfortable in so many idioms. It may be that some native singers of Fauré and Schubert capture the soul of these songs more unerringly, but few actually sing them so glowingly, so intensely. The typical Schubertian sadness brings out the very best in her. Nobody has sung *Am Grabe Anselmos* with so much sincere and deep feeling, nor have the lamenting echoes of *Die Götter Griechenlands* ever sounded more haunting. Technically the performances are also without fault. In her own language, Dame Janet is at home in every sense. The gems here are the Stanford ballad, the tensions of the tale sustained throughout by both artists, the tender sorrow of Britten's *Corpus Christi*, the fervent outpouring of Quilter's *Love's Philosophy*. Everywhere Moore is at one with his partner, always supportive, perceptive, with that soft and inimitable touch of his. The recordings, for their dates, are exemplary in balance and presence.

Song Recital

Brahms Vier ernste Gesänge, Op 121[d]. Lieder, Op 91[e]. Four Duets, Op 28[f] **Chausson** Poème de l'amour et de la mer, Op 19[b] **Duparc** Phidylé[b]. La vie antérieure[b]. Le manoir de Rosemonde[b]. Au pays où se fait la guerre[b]. L'Invitation au voyage[b] **Ravel** Shéhérazade[a]
Schumann Frauenliebe und-leben, Op 42[c]
Dame Janet Baker *mez* [f]**Dietrich Fischer-Dieskau** *bar* [e]**Cecil Aronowitz** *va* [cf]**Daniel Barenboim** *pf*
[a]**New Philharmonia Orchestra / Sir John Barbirolli;** [b]**London Symphony Orchestra /** [de]**André Previn** *pf*
EMI ② CZS5 68667-2 (134 minutes: ADD) Ⓜ
Recorded 1967-77

There comes a time in each great singer's career when they are at the peak of their form: artistry, voice, confidence, everything is at the maximum. Where Dame Janet Baker is concerned, that happy coincidence was in the years from 1967 to 1971. On the opera stage, her Dido in *Les troyens*, her Lucretia, Octavian, Dorabella and finally Diana in *Calisto* showed us her range of dramatic and comic skills. On the concert platform, working with Barbirolli, Szell, Giulini, Boult, Boulez and Barenboim, everything she did seemed well-nigh perfect. This two-CD selection from her EMI recordings opens with her famous performance of Ravel's *Shéhérazade* under Barbirolli, recorded in 1967. Of the song-cycles they recorded, this is perhaps the least regarded – Baker's voice never had quite the sensuous quality one is hoping for in this piece; but the security, the joy in the sound of her voice as she sings of Asia, and the right pace, all add up to a very fine recording. What is missing can be noted in the final line, about the beautiful boy walking past, with his feminine movements. One waits for a hint of irony, a slight smile of regret in the voice, but it isn't there. Baker was not given to innuendo; her humour was more robust. The succeeding Chausson *Poème de l'amour et de la mer* and then the group of songs by Duparc, recorded nearly 10 years later, show up a marked deterioration in her voice. Where once all had been steady, there is a beat that becomes intrusive, a sense of strain on some of the high notes, even here and there a slight worry over the pitch. *Le manoir de Rosemonde* is the best performance, the high drama bringing out the best in her.

The performance of Schumann's *Frauenliebe und -leben* dates from 1975. Although at the time many people thought this outshone if not eclipsed Baker's earlier, justly famous Saga disc, this is debatable. The sound is certainly better on EMI and in the mid-1960s she had the ability to convey both the hushed, girlish quality of the earlier songs and the mature, and then even tragic, tones for the last three. The extra verbal clarity of this later performance does not make up for the slight sense of strain. There are no reservations whatsoever about the Brahms songs, with Previn. The extra darkness in Baker's voice by 1977 makes these the highlight of the whole selection. In the *Vier ernste Gesänge*, and then the two Op 91 songs with piano and viola, Baker, Previn and Cecil Aronowitz achieve the perfect balance. As an encore we get four Brahms duets with Dietrich Fischer-Dieskau. Everything Dame Janet recorded is worth hearing, and this pair of discs gives an unusual cross-section of her repertory. There are no texts or translations, nor even synopses of the songs. Since these mid-price reissues are presumably aimed at the widest possible audience, all we can ask is 'Why not?'. As with every great Lieder singer, 50 per cent of Baker's art resides in her enunciation of the text; to be denied the chance to follow the words is infuriating.

Cecilia Bartoli *sop*

An Italian Songbook

Bellini Vaga luna che inargenti. L'abbandono. Malinconia, ninfa gentile. Il fervido desiderio. Torna, vezzosa Fillide. Vanne, o rosa fortunata. Dolente imagine di figlia mia. La farfalleta. Per pietà, bell'idol mio **Donizetti** Il barcaiolo. Ah, rammenta, o bella Irene. Amore e morte. La conocchia. Me voglio fa'na casa **Rossini** Péchés de vieillesse – Book 3: L'esule; Book 11: A ma belle mère; Aragonese. La passeggiata. Mi lagnerò tacendo – Boléro. Soirées musicales – La danza

Cecilia Bartoli *mez* **James Levine** *pf*

Decca 455 513-2DH (67 minutes: DDD) Ⓕ

Texts and translations included. Recorded 1996

The transforming power of imagination is rarely shown so clearly. On record and in recital these songs and their like have so often appeared as tepid little exercises, cautious investigations of the voice, the acoustic, the audience. But now, behold, they burgeon. Life abundant lies within the vocal line, and even the silly old accompaniments sound well. Such is the effect of the Bartoli-Levine combination. From the very first bars it feels that something special among Bartoli's many fine recordings have come into being here with these two distinguished artists in association. These are thoughtful, passionate and colourful performances, which outshine all previous versions of the more familiar songs. Among the less familiar items, Bellini's *Torna, vezzosa Fillide* may come as the most engaging discovery. Rossini's miniature Requiem for his mother-in-law seems not to be a joke, whereas the *Aragonese* (a setting in the style of Aragon of *Mi lagnerò tacendo*) surely must be. There might have been something to say here and now about intrusive 'h's and that other intrusion, a breathy quality sometimes cultivated in the interests of expression or intimacy, but they are not gross or prohibitive features of the singing here, and the lovely voice and lively art make ample amends.

Arie Antiche

Anonymous O leggiadri occhi belli **Caccini** Tu ch'hai le penne, amore. Amarilli **Caldara** Selve amiche. Sebben, crudele **Carissimi** Vittoria, vittoria! **Cavalli** Delizie contente **Cesti** Intorno all'idol mio **Giordani** Caro mio ben **Lotti** Pur dicesti, o bocca bella **Marcello** Quella fiamma che m'accende **Paisiello** Nel cor più non mi sento. Il mio ben quando verrà. Chi vuol la zingarella **Parisotti** Se tu m'ami **A Scarlatti** Già il sole dal Gange. Son tutta duolo. Se Florindo è fedele. O cessate di piagarmi. Spesso vibra per suo gioco **Vivaldi** Sposa son disprezzata

Cecilia Bartoli *mez* **György Fischer** *pf*

Decca 436 267-2DH (66 minutes: DDD) Ⓕ

Texts and translations included. Recorded 1990-91 ⦿

With Scarlatti and Vivaldi among the composers, these *arie antiche* are not necessarily very old. Italian singers have long been accustomed to lumping together all songs earlier than Mozart (or perhaps Haydn) under this heading, piously including them at the start of a recital so as to establish a classical tone and give them time to try out their voices before entering on the more strenuous and popular part of their programme. Bartoli here devotes a whole disc to them, as things delightful in themselves, varied in mood and style, and calling in turn on almost all the essential arts of a good singer. No one can come away with a feeling of having been short-changed at the end of this. Her voice is ideal, both silken and chaste, finely controlled, cleanly produced. With a simple, direct song such as the famous *Caro mio ben* she will never fuss or show off; with Vivaldi's *Sposa son disprezzata* she exploits the most deliciously languishing tone and sometimes one more frankly passionate and 'operatic'. Most of the items are gems, and to all of them György Fischer brings the touch of the expert jeweller, knowing exactly how best to set off the beauties of voice and melody.

Chant d'amour

Berlioz Tristia, Op 18 – La mort d'Ophélie. Zaïde, Op 19 No 1 **Bizet** Chant d'amour. Ouvre ton coeur. Adieux de l'hôtesse arabe. Tarantelle. La Coccinelle **Delibes** Les filles de Cadix **Ravel** Chants populaires – Chanson française; Chanson espagnole; Chanson italienne; Chanson hébraïque. Vocalise en forme de Habanera. Deux mélodies hébraïques. Tripatos **Viardot-Garcia** Hai luli!. Havanaise. Les filles de Cadix

Cecilia Bartoli *mez* **Myung-Whun Chung** *pf*

Decca 452 667-2DH (68 minutes: DDD) Ⓕ

Texts and translations included. Recorded 1996 ⦿

Cecilia Bartoli goes from strength to strength. Taking on the French repertory in this delightful disc, she also gives us some great rarities. The opening Bizet group includes two of his best-known songs, *Ouvre ton coeur* and *Adieux de l'hôtesse arabe*. In the first, one perhaps might ask for more of a smile in the voice. In the pessimistic Hugo poem about the Arab girl bidding farewell to the handsome traveller, Bartoli relishes the muezzin-like vocalise on 'Hélas, adieu, souviens-toi'. This is one of the best performances of this mini-drama since Conchita Supervia's orchestral-accompanied version. In this, and the succeeding *Tarantelle*, 'tra-la-la's and froth, one is prompted to wonder if there will one day be a Bartoli *Carmen*. *La Coccinelle* ('The ladybird') is a little salon gem, with a fast waltz motif. Bartoli uses a croaky little voice to act out the Ladybird.

Delibes's *Les filles de Cadix*, all trills and sunshine, is contrasted with an equally demanding setting of the same poem by Pauline Viardot. *Hai luli!* with words by Xavier de Maistre is a sad second-cousin to the Willow Song from Rossini's *Otello*. *Havanaise* is a real curiosity: the first and last stanzas, sung in Spanish, frame a middle section in French which breaks into a Rossinian flight of coloratura before returning to the swaying movements of the dance. Evenings *chez* Viardot must have been enlivened considerably by such songs. The narration of Ophelia's death, words by Ernest Legouvé, vaguely based on Shakespeare, ends with a wordless melody which Bartoli sings in a hushed, beautiful tone. In *Zaïde* she plays the castanets with skill; if this song is less interesting than the evocations of Spain by Bizet, Delibes and Viardot, that's Berlioz's fault, not Bartoli's. In the concluding Ravel group, an interesting contrast can be made between Viardot's *Havanaise* of the 1840s and Ravel's *Habanera* of 1907. In the four popular songs, Bartoli is especially effective in the Hebrew number as well as the two other *Mélodies hébraïques*, 'Kaddish' and 'L'énigme éternelle'. All these Ravel songs have often been recorded, so one cannot help wishing that Bartoli and Chung had stayed with the 19th-century French salon repertory to uncover more rarities. Still, this is one of the most satisfying recitals by one of the great singers of our time. First-rate recording and sensitive accompaniment throughout.

Italian Songs

Beethoven La Partenza, WoO124. Four Ariettas, Op 82. In questa tomba oscura, WoO133
Haydn Arianna a Naxos, HobXXVI*b*/2 **Mozart** Ridente la calma, K152/K210a **Schubert** Didone abbandonata, D510. Im Haine, D738. An die Leier, D737. La pastorella al Prato, D528. Vier Canzonen, D688. Pensa, che questo istante, D76. Willkommen und Abschied, D767
Cecilia Bartoli *mez* **András Schiff** *pf*
Decca 440 297-2DH (68 minutes: DDD) Ⓕ
Texts and translations included. Recorded 1992

It is good to be reminded of these composers' responses to the Italian muse in this particularly well-cast recital. Central Europe, in the person of András Schiff, meets Italy, in Cecilia Bartoli, to delightful, often revelatory effect. The simple form and undemanding vocal line of Beethoven's little *La Partenza* makes for a truthfulness of expression which Bartoli's clear, light-filled enunciation recreates to the full. With her warm breath gently supporting the voice's lively, supple inflexion, she reveals Beethoven's own skill in word-setting both here and in two fascinatingly contrasted settings of 'L'amante impaziente' in the *Ariettas*, Op 82. Schubert's 10 *Canzone* selected here show a wide range of treatment, from the compressed lyric drama of Dido's lament 'Vedi quanto adoro', in which Bartoli's lives intensely from second to second, to the honeyed Goldoni *pastorella* and the thrumming, pulsating serenade of 'Guarda, che bianca luna', D688 No 2. A gently, fragrantly shaped Mozart *Ridente la calma*, and a Haydn *Arianna a Naxos* of movingly immediate and youthful response complete this unexpectedly and unusually satisfying recital.

Live in Italy

Bellini Malinconia, ninfa gentile. Ma rendi pur contento **Berlioz** Zaïde, Op 19 No 1 **Bizet** Carmen – Près des remparts de Séville **Caccini** Nuove musiche e nuova maniera de scriverle – Al fonte al prato; Tu ch'hai le penne. Amarilli mia bella **Donizetti** La conocchia. Me voglio fa'na casa **T Giordani** Caro mio ben **Handel** Il trionfo del Tempo e del Disinganno – Lascia la spina **Montsalvatge** Canto negro
Mozart Oiseaux, si tous les ans, K307/K284*d*. Le nozze di Figaro – Voi che sapete **Rossini** Mi lagnerò tacendo, Book 1 – No 2 in D; No 3 in D minor, 'Sorzico'; No 4 in E, 'Il risentimento'. L'orpheline du Tyrola. Zelmira – Riedi al soglio. Canzonetta spagnuola
Schubert La pastorella al Prato, D528
Viardot Havanaise. Hai luli! **Vivaldi** Griselda – Agitata da due venti
Cecilia Bartoli *mez* **Jean-Yves Thibaudet** *pf*
Sonatori de la Gioiosa Marca
Decca 455 981-2DH (77 minutes: DDD) Ⓕ
Texts and translations included. Recorded live in 1998

Bartoli's voice is still in lovely, almost unflawed condition. With the assurance of a practised technique that she has made completely her own she is free to discover more in the music she sings and to realise the expressive resources open to her. If one wishes to take stock of her growth as an artist, the second item in her programme, Caccini's *Amarilli*, affords an opportunity. She recorded it first in 1990 in a touching performance, beautiful as sound and sensitive in mood (available on Decca). But the mood was set, and she was singing a song written and remembered. In the newer recording she is living and seemingly inventing it. Thus the development of feeling at 'Credilo pur' brings a fresh impulse, a more urgent appeal, and the repetitions of the beloved name acquire a musing, improvisatory quality. All of this (and much more of its kind) is sheer enrichment.

Nevertheless, if the vocal equivalent of a selective weedkiller could be employed, it might make short work of two other fast-growing products of this fair field. One, the persistent aspirating of runs, is probably too deep-rooted by now; the other, more insidious, is of comparatively recent cultivation, a breathy winsomeness, an exhalation of pretty pathos or girlish wide-eyed intimacy. If this were reserved for occasional use it might be acceptable and effective, but in the present recital it is habitual. As for the technique used in passagework such as abounds in the Vivaldi aria, it does facilitate rapid movement and helps to ensure clear articulation. Everything is heightened in these performances – the rich depth of contralto tone, languor and vivacity in the Viardot songs, the panache of the Berlioz, and smouldering promise and fiery fulfilment of Rossini's *Canzonetta spagnuola*. The variety of accompaniments is another attraction, all delightfully played. With the live atmosphere and the sense of freedom around the voice, this is surely the most faithful and revealing of all Bartoli's records to date.

Cecilia Bartoli & Bryn Terfel

Cecilia & Bryn – Duets

Donizetti L'elisir d'amore – Come sen va contento! ... Quanto amore! Ed io spietata! **Mozart** Le nozze di Figaro – Cinque dieci; Cosa stai misurando; Se a caso madama; Or bene, ascolta, e taci ... Se vuol balare signor Contino; Signor ... la vostra sposa ... Crudel! perchè finora; Un moto di gioia, K579. Così fan tutte – Passeggiamo anche noi ... Il core vi dono. Don Giovanni – Alfin siam liberati ... Là ci darem la mano. Die Zauberflöte – Pa-Pa-Pa-Papagena **Rossini** Il barbiere di Siviglia – Ebben, signor Figaro? ... Dunque io son? L'italiana in Algeri – Ai capricci della sorte

Cecilia Bartoli *mez* **Bryn Terfel** *bass-bar*
Orchestra dell'Accademia di Santa Cecilia / Myung-Whun Chung

Decca 458 928-2DH (54 minutes: DDD) Ⓕ
Texts and translations included. Recorded 1998

Splendidly well-matched duettists, Bartoli and Terfel (or are we on Christian-name terms even in review?) are as vivid a pair of vocal comedians-and-charmers as any in the business. The fatal thing would be if they tried to outdo each other, but, to all aural appearances, they do not: they spark naturally and nicely, and gain accordingly, both as individuals and as an act. They are also instinctively good at making records. Recitative can be light and quick-witted – listeners are following the libretto and don't need points underlined or played for laughs. Don Giovanni can whisper sweet nothings in Zerlina's ear, Adina can suggest a subtle compound of feelings in a shading of tone. Both singers know that their voice-faces must never go blank, the unseen movements inert, and in the Papagena-Papageno duet (for instance) the interplay is as clear to the mind's eye as any stage-action would be in the theatre. Sometimes there is a hair's-breadth misjudgement (in *Il barbiere* Rosina's 'Un biglietto?' should surely be all surprise and wonderment, and the 'Eccola quà' a businesswoman's *fait accompli*), but generally all goes well, the point being that there is nothing 'general' about it (when Figaro, in the other opera, starts on his room-measurements in the very opening moments of the disc he is actually counting, we 'see' him and know that this is what for the moment is on his mind). Of the singing as such, it is good to be able to report Terfel on graceful form and Bartoli in fine voice. There is much to be enjoyed in this recital, finely recorded and with such stylish accompaniment under Myung-Whun Chung.

Carlo Bergonzi *ten*

The Sublime Voice of Carlo Bergonzi 🄷

Excerpts from operas by Cilea, Leoncavallo, Mascagni, Ponchielli, Puccini and Verdi

Carlo Bergonzi *ten* with **Renata Scotto, Dame Joan Sutherland, Renata Tebaldi** *sops* and others

Decca ② 467 023-2DX2 (154 minutes: ADD) Ⓜ ●

The collection opens with one of the warmest *gelide manine* ever. Carlo Bergonzi's voice is at its freshest and most beautiful (the recording comes, with other excerpts, from the 1959 *Bohème* under Serafin), but impresses especially with the variety of its handling, the fertility of imagination. A year earlier, the *Butterfly* is similarly delightful, Bergonzi's Pinkerton being all confidence and energy. These are some of the best things, but the composer most closely associated with Bergonzi, and of whom we hear most, is not Puccini but Verdi. From the *Rigoletto* of 1964 (Kubelík) all of the Duke's solos find something very close to their ideal singer, the clean cut of the voice suiting their requirement for an elegance of manner. That is an immediate presence, too, in the items from *Un ballo in maschera* (Solti, 1962): Bergonzi's voice at the start of the second disc enters with magical lightness and grace in the opening phrases of 'La rivedrà nell' estasi'. Then, how the Karajan *Aida* (1959) challenges its singers with those (one would think) impossibly slow speeds – and how nobly Bergonzi meets the challenge in his 'Celeste Aida'. Not everything is as good as that: he unexpectedly turns his verse of 'Parigi, o cara' to mush, and one wouldn't choose his 'Di quella pira' to take into battle. Otello's monologue (1975) is not really in his voice or sensibility. Some of the excerpts end abruptly, and sometimes the sequence is disconcerting. Transfers are generally fine, but tracks from the 1958 recital under Gavazzeni have a rough surface on the voice.

Robin Blaze *counterten*

German 17th-Century Church Music

Bach Cantata No 53, Schlage doch, gewünschte Stunde[a] **H Bach** Sonatas – No 1 in C; No 2 in F **J Christoph Bach** Ach, dass ich Wassers g'nug hätte[a] **J M Bach** Auf, lasst uns den Herren loben[a] **Bernhard** Was betrübst du dich, meine Seele[a] **Buxtehude** Jesu, meine Freud und Lust, BuxWV59[a]. Jubilate Domino, omnis terra, BuxWV64[a] **Geist** Vater unser, der du bist im Himmel[a] **Krieger** O Jesu, du mein Leben[a] **Rosenmüller** Christum ducem, qui per crucem[a]. Sonata No 2 in E minor **Schütz** Erbarm dich mein, O Herre Gott, SWV447[a]

[a]**Robin Blaze** *counterten* **The Parley of Instruments / Peter Holman**

Hyperion CDA67079 (74 minutes: DDD) Ⓕ
Texts and translations included. Recorded 1998 ●

The principal pleasure of this programme is that Robin Blaze is so refreshingly natural and is no more singing to 'pip' a perceived rival than to force his personality on the listener. In fact, Blaze's musical instincts are ideal for this marvellous pre-Bach solo repertory which represents a supreme test for an alto singer of any description: the rhetorical language is often profoundly intense, the richly wrought string textures must be conversed with, since the instrumental writing is so suggestive in its close dialogue and, most critically, the voice must assume its *primus inter pares* with a glowing warmth of expression. In short, Blaze scores on all fronts. In Johann Christoph Bach's celebrated lament, *Ach, dass ich Wassers*, Blaze colours the dolorous text with much affection and peerless control, though The Parley of Instruments provides a fairly pedestrian accompaniment. The Parley's renaissance violin consort in the brighter numbers lends an incandescent and grainy immediacy, especially in the first of the two mesmerising Buxtehude cantatas, *Jesu, meine Freud und Lust*. Here and in the beguiling setting of the Lord's Prayer by Christian Geist, Blaze unassumingly traverses the quick-shifting moods with consummate ease, sailing sweetly and effortlessly above the consort with long-breathed chorale phrases and then in *Jubilate Domino*, elevating the text with an infectious rhythmic energy. Blaze has many distinctive qualities in the current firmament, not least his superb intonation (no current practitioner comes close), his capacity for listening as a true chamber musician (though The Parley doesn't listen enough to him) and a light, uncloying timbre, intelligently focused and exquisitely nuanced. Highly recommended.

Barbara Bonney *sop*

American Songs
Argento Six Elizabethan Songs **Barber** Ten Hermit Songs, Op 29 **Copland** 12 Poems of Emily Dickinson **Previn** Sallie Chisum remembers Billy the Kid. Vocalise[a]
Barbara Bonney *sop* [a]**Sato Knudsen** *vc*
André Previn *pf*
Decca 455 511-2DH (76 minutes: DDD) Ⓕ
Texts included. Recorded 1996 **oo**

Barbara Bonney is allegedly related to Billy the Kid. Allegedly. She herself is convinced, or rather was convinced, when she first saw the pictures. The resemblance to her own father was 'terrifying': the big searching eyes, the ears that stick out – the look. And then an American friend in London gave her a copy of *The Collected Works of Billy the Kid*, and that's where André Previn came in. *Sallie Chisum remembers Billy the Kid* – the spur of this all-American programme – takes its cues from Wild West history – or is that mythology? Sallie Chisum was a prostitute who went to bed with both Billy and Pat Garrett, and her words are starry-eyed. Previn sets them as she will have remembered them, touches of sweet sentiment in the voice played off against the dusty and gritty realities of the keyboard. There's more than a hint of the bar-room piano in that. And then up soars the voice recalling the 'flower in his lapel' and the fragrance of it lends a touch of naïvety. The Argento was a shrewd choice, not just on account of its rarity value (this is the world première recording), but because Bonney and Previn both have ties with England which adds something to our perception of the cycle's Anglo/American cross-breeding. Both are brilliantly articulate and quick of reflex, the mix of ancient and modern, the ornate and the reflective – indeed the somnambulant – is beautifully judged.

The Copland and Barber sets are splendid, too. In Copland's Emily Dickinson, Bonney of course has the wholesome, homespun qualities – the pure and simple gifts – this music demands. We know how raptly she will sustain 'Heart, we will forget him!', and she does. There is ecstasy and truth in this voice. But she can be feisty, too, deploying a determined and surprisingly resilient low register for 'There came a wind like a bugle' and the awesome plunge to 'East of eternity' in 'Sleep is supposed to be'. And where Dickinson is the playful child – as in 'Why do they shut me out of Heaven?' and 'Going to Heaven!' – there is a knowing coyness. In all this, Previn's contribution, his partnership, is invaluable. Listen to him sign off 'Going to Heaven!' Not so much the exclamation mark, more the wink. And listen to him, too, lending weight and masculinity to the bolder illuminations of Barber's *Hermit Songs*. His resoluteness undoubtedly helps Bonney darken and intensify her response to these songs. 'The Monk and his Cat' sounds all the more cosy and incongruous in consequence. We may have each other, it seems to say, but in the end we have only ourselves. To that end, the closing song is marvellous. A very real sense of isolation permeates the final stanza. Bonney and Previn may be two, but for the time being they are one.

Diamonds in the Snow
Awards 2000
Alfvén The Forest Sleeps, Op 28 No 6. So take my heart **Grieg** I love but thee, Op 5 No 3. Op 25 – No 2, A Swan; No 4, With a waterlily. Last Spring, Op 33 No 2. From Monte Pincio, Op 39 No 1. Six Songs, Op 48. Peer Gynt – Solveig's Song. The Princess **Sibelius** Astray, Op 17 No 4. Op 36 – No 4, Sigh, sedges, sigh, Op 36 No 4; No 6, The Diamond on the March Snow. Songs, Op 37 – No 4, Was it a dream?; No 5, The Maiden's Tryst **Sjöberg** Tonerna **Stenhammar** The Girl Came Home from her Tryst, Op 4b No 1. Fylgia, Op 16 No 4. Adagio, Op 20 No 5. I skogen. Sverige
Barbara Bonney *sop* **Antonio Pappano** *pf*
Decca 466 762-2DH (72 minutes: DDD) Ⓕ
Texts and translations included. Recorded 1999 **ooo**

Scandinavian songs have long had a special place in Barbara Bonney's repertoire, and it is perhaps surprising that she has waited so long to devote a whole recital on disc to those for voice and piano. But then, intelligent singers tend to know their own voices best. This lovely soprano still sounds very like springtime, though in fact summer is getting on. The pure, silvery tones remain to her, while opening out into full bloom is the rose garden; a few years ago it would not have been apparent that these richer colours, with their intimations of depth and maturity, were biding their time, steadily developing their potential. And the songs need such resources – not each singly, but if a whole programme is planned, then, as a sequence they call for more than the voice of innocence and sunshine. Bonney, at this stage of her career, has both the maidenly silver for Solveig's Song, *Die verschwiegene Nachtigall* (Op 48) and the Stenhammar songs, and the fuller emotional and vocal reserves for *Zur Rosenzeit* and *Ein Traum* (also Op 48) and the Sibelius group. Antonio Pappano is a first-rate accompanist and in combination these two artists have much to say – it is not necessary to go beyond the first song (Grieg's *Våren*) to recognise that. Those who feel they are already well stocked with this once-unfamiliar repertoire are urged that there is a great deal to discover and enjoy in these performances; for those who may think of starting, here is a golden opportunity.

Lucrezia Bori *sop*

Opera Arias H

Acis y Galatea, Amantes chasqueaos, L'amour mouillé, La bohème, Les contes d'Hoffmann, Don Giovanni, Don Quijote de la mancha, Louise, Madama Butterfly, Manon, Mignon, Le nozze di Figaro, La rondine, Il segreto di Susanna, La traviata and La vida breve; songs by **Arditi**, **Falla**, **Glazunov**, **Goetz**, **Götze**, **Joves**, **Nin**, **Pagans**, **Pestalozzi**, **Rumbold**, **Schumann**, **J Strauss II**, **A G Thomas** and **Valverde**

Lucrezia Bori *sop* with various artists

Romophone mono ② 81017-2 (147 minutes: ADD) Ⓕ

Recorded 1925-37

Until Romophone brought out the complete run of her Victor recordings, Bori looked like becoming the forgotten prima donna. Volume 1 was welcomed in *Gramophone* as reintroducing 'one of the most adorable and fascinating of singers on records', and its successor now follows her from the heyday of her career to the time of her last recordings, some 18 months after her official retirement at the age of 50. The originals were often issued on noisy shellac, and at 78rpm most played above the correct pitch. In these conditions the voice could sound thin, and the 'image' (if that overused word be permitted) suffered accordingly. The repertoire of songs may not have helped: perhaps in its time *Ciribiribin* and so forth were welcomed as a form of 'crossover', but even now, at this distance in time, from behind the sweetly tweet-a-tweeting singer, Groucho has only to lift an eyebrow or Harpo to turn down his nether lip, and the birdsong takes a perilously farcical flight. Fortunately we are just sufficiently far away to detach the records from impediments of this kind. The complete edition, which the two volumes comprise, returns the singer to us as new. Among the recordings said to be previously unpublished, best are two songs by Nin, dating from the singer's last session, at the end of 1937. There are also some alternative takes (all good), and the two 1925 duets with McCormack. A great pleasure lies in the discovery (or maybe confirmation) that the 1937 recordings show only slight deterioration of voice and have such vividness of character. Best remain well-known things such as Mimì's narrative, Musetta's waltz-song, the *Mignon* solos and some of the Spanish songs such as the *Malagueña* by Don Pagans. The most commonplace, trivial or exasperatingly 'pretty' banalities endear themselves if they provide an extra opportunity to hear this exquisite, highly individual, totally lovable artist.

Ian Bostridge *ten*

The English Songbook

Britten The Salley gardens[a] **W C D Brown** To Gratiana dancing and singing[a] **Delius** Twilight Fancies[a] **Dunhill** The Cloths of Heaven, Op 30 No 3[a] **Finzi** The dance continued, Op 14 No 10[a]. Since we loved, Op 13 No 7[a] **German** Orpheus with his lute[a] **Grainger** Bold William Taylor, BFMS43[a]. Brigg Fair, BFMS7[b] **Gurney** Sleep[a] **Parry** No longer mourn for me[a] **Quilter** Come away, death, Op 6 No 1[a]. I will go with my father a-ploughing[a]. Now sleeps the crimson petal, Op 3 No 2[a] **Somervell** To Lucasta, on going to the wars[a] **Stanford** La belle dame sans merci[a] **Traditional** The death of Queen Jane[a]. The little turtle dove[a]. My love's an arbutus (arr. Stanford)[a] **Vaughan Williams** Linden Lea[a]. Silent Noon[a] **Warlock** Cradle Song[a]. Jillian of Berry[a]. Rest, sweet nymphs[a]

Ian Bostridge *ten* [a]**Julius Drake** *pf* [b]**Polyphony / Stephen Layton**

EMI CDC5 56830-2 (69 minutes: DDD) Ⓕ

Texts included. Recorded 1999 ●

The recital begins with Keats and ends with Shakespeare: that can't be bad. But it also begins with Stanford and ends with Parry; what would the modernists of their time have thought about that? They would probably not have believed that those two pillars of the old musical establishment would still be standing by in 1999. And in fact how well very nearly all of these composers stand! Quilter's mild drawing-room manners might have been expected to doom him, but the three songs here – the affectionate, easy grace of his Tennyson setting, the restrained passion of his *Come away, death* and the infectious zest of *I will go with my father a-ploughing* – endear him afresh and demonstrate once again the wisdom of artists who recognise their own small area of 'personal truth' and refuse to betray it in exchange for a more fashionable 'originality'. Likewise Finzi, whose feeling for Hardy's poems is so modestly affirmed in *The dance continued*. Does that song, incidentally, make deliberate reference, at 'those songs we sang when we went gipsying', to *Jillian of Berry* by Warlock (whose originality speaks for itself)? *Jillian of Berry* itself perhaps calls for more full-bodied, less refined tones than

Bostridge's. One could do with a ruddier glow and more rotund fruitiness in the voice. Yet for most of the programme he is not merely a well-suited singer but an artist who brings complete responsiveness to words and music. The haunted desolation of Delius's *Twilight Fancies* is perfectly caught in the pale hue of the voice which can nevertheless give body and intensity to the frank cry of desire, calming then to *pianissimo* for the last phrase amid the dim echoes of hunting horns in the piano part. Julius Drake plays with strength of imagination and technical control to match Bostridge's own.

Maria Callas *sop*

Bellini Norma – Casta diva **Bizet** Carmen – L'amour est un oiseau rebelle; Près des remparts de Séville; Les tringles des sistres **Catalani** La Wally – Ebben? ... Ne andrò lontana **Donizetti** Lucia di Lammermoor – Spargi d'amaro pianto **Giordano** Andrea Chénier – La mamma morta **Gluck** Orphée et Eurydice – J'ai perdu mon Eurydice **Puccini** Gianni Schicchi – O mio babbino caro. La bohème – Sì, mi chiamano Mimì; Donde lieta uscì. Madama Butterfly – Un bel dì vedremo. Tosca – Vissi d'arte **Rossini** Il barbiere di Siviglia – Una voce poco fa **Saint-Saëns** Samson et Dalila – Mon coeur s'ouvre à ta voix **Verdi** La traviata – Ah, fors'è lui; Addio del passato H

Maria Callas *sop* with **various artists**

EMI Classics CDC5 57050-2 (74 minutes: ADD) Ⓕ

Texts and translations included ●●

Bellini Norma – Casta diva. La sonnambula – Ah! non credea mirarti **Bizet** Carmen – L'amour est un oiseau rebelle; Près des remparts de Séville; Les tringles des sistres **Catalani** La Wally – Ebben? ... Ne andrò lontana **G Charpentier** Louise – Depuis le jour **Cilea** Adriana Lecouvreur – Io son l'umile ancella **Donizetti** Anna Bolena – Al dolce guidami. Lucia di Lammermoor – Spargi d'amaro pianto **Giordano** Andrea Chénier – La mamma morta **Gluck** Orphée et Eurydice – J'ai perdu mon Eurydice **Gounod** Roméo et Juliette – Je veux vivre **Massenet** Le cid – De cet affreux combat; Pleurez, mes yeux. Manon – Adieu, notre petite table **Meyerbeer** Dinorah – Ombre légère **Mozart** Le nozze di Figaro – Porgi, amor **Puccini** La bohème – Sì, mi chiamano Mimì; Donde lieta uscì. Gianni Schicchi – O mio babbino caro. Madama Butterfly – Un bel dì vedremo. Manon Lescaut – In quelle trine morbide. Tosca – Vissi d'arte. Turandot – Signore, ascolta!; Tu, che di gel sei cinta **Rossini** Il barbiere di Siviglia – Una voce poco fa **Saint-Saëns** Samson et Dalila – Printemps qui commence; Mon coeur s'ouvre à ta voix **Spontini** La vestale – O Nume, tutelar degli infelici **Verdi** Otello – Ave Maria. Rigoletto – Gualtier Maldè; Caro nome. La traviata – Ah, fors'è lui; Addio del passato. Il trovatore – D'amor sull'ali rosee H

Maria Callas *sop* **with various artists**

EMI Classics ② CMS5 57062-2 (148 minutes: ADD) Ⓕ ●●

The single disc here would seem to come with the subtitle 'Callas sings film', as half the items have been chosen to link with film soundtracks. It may be interesting to learn that 'Vissi d'arte' was used in a film called *Copycat* or that the Habanera from *Carmen* now has three film credits to its name, but that is unlikely to sway the confirmed opera-lover. The more important factors will be the generous length of the CD at 74 minutes and its full-price tag, which is optimistic for what is in effect a sampler designed to encourage purchasers to investigate Callas's recordings further.

Of course, there is nothing cut-price about the performances. The 17 tracks on this disc are taken from recordings that made operatic history in the second half of the 20th century. It is particularly heartening to find items from the 1954 Puccini recital disc that Callas made with Serafin, where the singing is perfectly schooled in every detail. The two extracts from the live performance of *La traviata* in Lisbon are welcome for showing that Callas was as impressive live as on disc, though it is a shame that 'Ah, fors' è lui' is shorn of both its recitative and cabaletta.

Purchasers of the two-disc compilation get all these tracks and about the same number again. With Callas this also means double the range of experience, which would not be the case with every singer: the smouldering sexuality of Dalila's 'Printemps qui commence' is unlike anything on the single disc and so is the virginal purity of Gilda's 'Caro nome' from *Rigoletto*. Hearing early and late recordings mixed up sometimes means a jolt in the quality of voice we hear, as when the impeccable young Callas of Dinorah's 'Ombra leggiera' gives way to the unsteady Waltz song from Gounod's *Roméo et Juliette*. But whatever Callas sang, there were moments that she brought to life unlike anybody else. We may have technically less fallible singers today, but we do not have personalities like hers, and that is ultimately to the music's loss. To judge from the high percentage of French operas represented here and the Paris-centric notes, the set was planned primarily for French buyers. Any compilation of Callas, however, will appeal to everybody.

Emma Calvé *sop*

The Complete 1902 G&T, 1920 Pathé and 'Mapleson Cylinder' Recordings H

Opera arias – Amadis de Gaulle, Carmen, Cavalleria rusticana, Les contes d'Hoffmann, Le domino noir, Faust, Galathée, Hamlet, Manon, Mignon, Mireille, Norma, Le nozze di Figaro, Le pardon de Ploëmel, La perle du Brésil, La périchole, Philémon et Baucis, Pré aux clercs, Roméo et Juliette, Sapho and La vivandière; songs by **Beethoven**, **Bland**, **De Lara**, **Foster**, **Gounod**, **Hahn**, **Key**, **Massenet**, **Thomas** and **Traditional**

Emma Calvé, Cécille Merguillier *sops* with various artists

Marston mono ② 52013-2 (139 minutes: ADD) Ⓕ

Recorded 1902-20

In the alphabetical index of great singers, Calvé follows Callas, and the sequence is suggestive. Both were actress-singers who brought revelations of opera-as-theatre to the audiences of their time; both acted with the voice (as contemporary accounts of Calvé tell and as we know to be so with Callas); and both were strong personalities among the most famous women in the world. One sad and striking difference is that Callas's recordings testify amply to this, while Calvé's are inadequate in repertoire as well as technical conditions to do her justice. Yet much is caught, right from those extraordinary cylinders made at performances in the Metropolitan in 1902 where, among all that is lost, her high-notes can be heard ringing out well into the house above the orchestra, with a tone sufficiently distinctive for us to associate it with the studio recordings made later that same year. They in turn are reinforced by the amazingly vivid series made for Pathé in 1920, by which year the singer was in her early sixties. The quality of copies used and results obtained is fine. There is a second singer here and her presence adds greatly to its attractions. Cécile Merguillier recorded for Pathé and Edison in 1904 and 1905 when virtually in retirement though only in her early forties, and still singing with fresh voice, assured technique and captivating style. A light soprano, she was singing Philine in *Mignon* in 1887, the night the old Opéra-Comique burnt down. Her solos from *Mireille* and *Philémon et Baucis* are especially delightful, and as far as can be ascertained, this is the first time a full sequence of her records has been collected on disc. The issue is finely presented, with informative notes.

Enrico Caruso *ten*

Caruso 2000 H

Flotow Martha – M'appari tutt'amor **Halévy** La Juive – Rachel, quand du Seigneur **Leoncavallo** Pagliacci – Vesti la giubba **Massenet** Manon – Je suis seul; Ah! fuyez, douce image. Le Cid – Ah! Tout est bien fini!; O Souverain, O Juge, O Père! **Meyerbeer** L'Africaine – O Paradis **Ponchielli** La Gioconda – Cielo e mar! **Puccini** Tosca – Recondita armonia **Rossini** La danza – Tarantella neopolitana. Petite messe solennelle – Domine Deus **Verdi** Aida – Se quel guerrier io fossi; Celeste Aida. Un ballo in maschera – Forse la soglia attinse; Ma se m'è forza perderti. Macbeth – O figli, O figli miei; Ah, la paterna mano. Rigoletto – La donna è mobile. Il trovatore – Ah! sì, ben mio; Di quella pira

[a]**Enrico Caruso** *ten* [b]**Vienna Radio Symphony Orchestra / Gottfried Rabi**

BMG Classics 74321 69766-2 (64 minutes: AAD) Ⓕ

Recorded [a]1906-1920 and [b]1999

For me, from an early age onwards, the singing of Caruso has been one of life's riches, and it has needed nothing beyond good reproduction of the original recordings; but for many, their admiration for the voice is offset by the dim, unnatural sound of the orchestral accompaniments, and the pleasure of listening is lost. 'Caruso 2000' sets out to remedy this, re-recording and replacing the pre-electrical orchestra. Of course, this has been done before, in the 1930s, with results that were too variable for the series as a whole to be counted a success. This new attempt is better in every way. Most importantly, it preserves faithfully the beauty of Caruso's voice, and should reveal to a new generation the *soul* of his singing. This is an artist: the possessor of a magnificent voice and a fine technique to be sure, but also one who felt and believed in the music he sang, living it creatively and bringing a full, generous humanity to everything he touched.

The accompanying leaflet describes the process and the principles which guided selection of the 16 items. Most are of arias Caruso recorded only once, but here are dates of the versions where more than one recording exists: 'La donna è mobile' 1908, 'Celeste Aida' (with recitative) 1911, 'M'appari' 1906, 'Cielo e mar!' 1910, 'Vesti la giubba' 1907, 'Recondita armonia' 1909. All deserve their place except the 'Domine Deus' (1920), and this might be justified in as far as it shows the seriously degenerative forces at work in his singing during the last years. The CD ends with what is described as the 'original version' of the *Pagliacci* recording: one hopes most of us could get better results out of our 78s than that!

To sum up: the listener will not be beguiled into thinking that this is a record made yesterday of a new and up-and-coming tenor of our own time, but Caruso *is* brought within the listening-range of people who have had to exclude him in the past. Listeners who already know the records are quite likely to find pleasure too, as points here and there which seemed stylishly abrupt or flawed in some detail settle down in a natural orchestral context rather than suffering the unnatural exposure of pre-electrical recording. In fact, all is essentially great glory.

Caruso in Opera, Volume 2 H

Arias – L'Africaine, Andrea Chenier, La bohème (Leoncavallo and Puccini), Carmen, Cavalleria rusticana, Don Pasquale, Eugene Onegin, La favorita, Les Huguenots, Macbeth, Martha, Nero, La reine de Saba, Rigoletto, Tosca and Il trovatore

Enrico Caruso *ten* with various artists

Nimbus Prima Voce mono NI7866 (79 minutes: ADD) Ⓢ

Recorded 1905-20

The 1906 recording of 'M'apparì' from *Martha* comes first, and it introduces an aspect of Caruso's singing that rarely finds a place in the critical commentaries: his subtlety. Partly, it's rhythmic. The move-on and pull-back seems such an instinctive process that we hardly notice it (though no doubt a modern conductor would – and check it immediately). It makes all the difference to the emotional life of the piece, the feeling of involvement and spontaneous development. Then there is the phrasing, marvellously achieved at the melody's reprise. The play of louder and softer tones, too, has every delicacy of fine graduation; and just as masterly is the more technical covering and (rare) opening of notes at the *passaggio*. An edition of the score which brought out all these features of Caruso's singing would be a densely annotated document. It would, even so, be a simplification, for accompanying all this is the dramatic and musical feeling, which defies analysis – and, of course, the voice. That voice! You may feel you know all these records and hardly need to play them, yet there is scarcely an occasion when the beauty of it does not thrill with a sensation both old and new (the first 'Ah!' is one of recognition, the second of fresh wonder). So it is with nearly all of the items here: all, in fact, save the *Eugene Onegin* aria, which remains external, and the late *L'Africaine* recording with its saddening evidence of deterioration. The transfers are excellent.

Tracey Chadwell *sop*

Tracey Chadwell's Song Book
R R Bennett A Garland for Marjory Fleming[a]
Cresswell Words for Music[a] **Farquhar** Six Songs of Women[a] **Joubert** The Turning Wheel, Op 95[a]
Lefanu I am Bread[a]. A Penny for a Song[a]
Lilburn Three Songs[a] **Lumsdaine** A Norfolk Songbook[b] **Maconchy** Sun, Moon and Stars[a]. Three Songs[a] **Whitehead** Awa Herea[a]
Tracey Chadwell *sop* [a]**Pamela Lidiard** *pf* [b]**John Turner** *recs*
British Music Society ② BMS420/1CD Ⓕ
(141 minutes: ADD). Texts included. Recorded 1988-94

Tracey Chadwell, a soprano of exceptional gifts and intelligence, died in her mid-thirties early in 1996 after a long and courageous battle with leukaemia. Nicola Lefanu, who contributes an affectionate note to this anthology of recordings from the BBC archives, was at her last concert, three weeks before her death, and says that 'she looked and sounded ravishing'. She always did, and apart from its value as a memorial to a much loved and deeply missed artist and as a collection of fine songs (many of them written for her), this pair of discs could stand as a model to other singers in the expert management of a voice, in fearless vocal resource and joyful adventurousness in choice of repertory.

She had admirable taste: there is no music here that needs special pleading, and her advocacy of all of it is compelling. Most of it is unfamiliar, much of it not recorded before, so it is probably helpful to single out a few particular pleasures: Lefanu's haunting, intimate and subtle *I am Bread* easily sustaining its seven-minute duration, not least because of Chadwell's care over line and florid detail; the elegant talent of David Farquhar, making a simple but memorable thing of Sir Philip Sidney's 'My true love hath my heart and I have his'; the strong drama and toughly strong melody of Gillian Whitehead's *Awa Herea*, using texts in Maori and English, and making huge demands of the singer's technique as well as her imagination; Richard Rodney Bennett's beautiful settings of the poems of a child who died at eight years old (Chadwell's tender line in 'Sweet Isabell' is deeply moving here); the big, striking gestures of John Joubert's fine short cycle. She brings a wonderfully pure tone and limpid line to Elizabeth Maconchy's Thomas Traherne settings. Pamela Lidiard, her regular accompanist, is an ideally sensitive partner and the recordings are excellent.

Boris Christoff *bass*

Opera Arias 🄷
Don Carlo, Don Giovanni, Ernani, La forza del destino, Iphigénie en Aulide, Mefistofele, Nabucco, Norma, Simon Boccanegra, La sonnambula and I vespri siciliani
Boris Christoff *bass* with various artists
EMI Références mono CDH5 65500-2 Ⓜ
(80 minutes: ADD). Recorded 1949-55

The grieving king, the patriarchal priest, the smirking demon: these are all expected presences in Christoff's gallery of vivid characters, and one might well extend the list mentally by a dozen or so more before thinking of Leporello. Christoff sang very little Mozart but the Catalogue aria in *Don Giovanni* featured in his concert programmes. It is a marvellous performance, and alone provides a very good reason for buying this disc. Almost as unlooked for may be the Count's aria in *La sonnambula*, sung with affection and a nearly perfect *legato*. Warmth of tone perhaps is wanting, in both that and the 'Infelice' (*Ernani*), but there is certainly no lack of emotional warmth in the fine solos from *I vespri siciliani* and *Simon Boccanegra*.

Philip's great aria in *Don Carlo* ends with a too overt and prolonged tearfulness (avoided in later versions), but this recording is still among the supremely impressive mementos of its era. It comes from one of Christoff's first sessions in the studios, and is strikingly natural and lifelike, as are all the 78s heard here. In the 1955 recordings one is more aware of the microphone: for example, in his most authoritative vein, Christoff is splendidly represented by the Gluck aria (*Iphigénie en Aulide*) made in 1951, whereas the same magnificence is present in the excerpts from *Nabucco* (1955) but just slightly diminished by seeming to be made somewhat larger than life.

When all is over, however, the first item demands a replay: that Catalogue song of Leporello's. John Hughes's admirable notes concede that the performance 'may lack the necessary touch of humour' – but it surely does not! Gaiety, rhythm, even a chuckle, a swelling grandeur in the portrayal of the 'maiestosa', a daintiness in 'la piccina': it is all there, and with it a certain suavity of style, and, rarer still, the elegant phrases of 'Nella bionda' sung with scrupulous *legato*. This disc goes into the 'Essential Christoff Collection' forthwith.

Régine Crespin *sop*

Berlioz Les nuits d'été **Ravel** Shéhérazade[a]
Debussy Trois chansons de Bilitis[b]
Poulenc Banalités[b] – Chansons d'Orkenise; Hôtel. La courte paille[b] – Le carafon; La reine de coeur. Chansons villageoises[b] – Les gars qui vont à la fête. Deux poèmes de Louis Aragon[b]
Régine Crespin *sop* [b]**John Wustman** *pf* [a]**Suisse Romande Orchestra / Ernest Ansermet**
Decca Legends 460 973-2DM (68 minutes: ADD) Ⓕ
Texts and translations included. Recorded 1963-67

Some recordings withstand the test of time and become acknowledged classics. This is one of them. Régine Crespin's voluptuous tone, her naturally accented French and her feeling for the inner meaning of the songs in the Berlioz and Ravel cycles are everywhere evident. Better than most single interpreters of the Berlioz, she manages to fulfil the demands of the very different songs, always alive to verbal nuances. In the Ravel, she is gorgeously sensuous, not to say sensual, with the right timbre for Ravel's enigmatic writing. The Debussy and Poulenc songs on this disc enhance its worth. Crespin offers an extremely evocative, perfumed account of the Debussy pieces and is ideally suited to her choice of Poulenc, of which her interpretation of 'Hôtel' is a classic. Ansermet and his orchestra, though not quite note-perfect, are right in timbre and colour for these rewarding cycles. The sound is reasonable given the age of the recording.

Julia Culp *mez*

The Complete Victor and Electrola Recordings H

Bayly Long, long ago **Beethoven** The Cottage Maid, WoO155 No 3. Faithful Johnnie, Op 108 No 20 **Boulton** All Through the Night **Brahms** Volks-Kinderlieder – Wiegenlied. Immer leiser wird mein Schlummer. Feldeinsamkeit, Op 86 No 2 **Calcott** Drink to Me Only **Danks** Silver Threads Among the Gold **Debussy** Nuit d'étoiles **Gruber** Stille Nacht (2 recordings) **Horn** I've Been Roaming **Kreisler** Cradle Song. Cradle Song 1915. The Old Refrain **Lange** Dutch Serenade **Lieurance** Lullaby. By the Waters of Minnetonka **Liszt** Es muss ein Wunderbares sein, S314 **Marshall** There's a Bower of Roses by Bendemeer's Stream **Mendelssohn** Elijah – O rest in the Lord. Auf Flügeln des Gesanges, Op 34 No 2 **Molloy** Love's old sweet song **Ochs** Dank sei dir, Herr **Purcell-Cockrane** Passing By **Reger** Schlichte Weisen, Op 76 – Maria Wiegenlied **Rogers** At Parting **Romberg** Blue Paradise - Auf Wiedersehn **Saint-Saëns** Samson et Dalila – Printemps qui commence; Mon coeur s'ouvre à ta voix **Schubert** Heidenröslein, D257. Der Tod und das Mädchen, D531. Du bist die Ruh, D776. Im Abendrot, D799. Ave Maria, D839. Der Lindenbaum, D911 No 5. Ständchen, D957 No 4 **Schumann** Myrthen, Op 25 – No 3, Der Nussbaum; No 24, Du bist wie eine Blume. Mondnacht, Op 39 No 5 **Traditional** Auld Lang Syne. Gelukking Vaderland **Wagner** Wesendonk Lieder – Träume **Weckerlin** Mignonette **Wolf** Vorborgenheit
Julia Culp *mez* with **various artists**
Romophone ② 81035-2 (154 minutes: ADD) Ⓕ
Recorded 1914-26

'And to learn to sing Lieder,' said old-timers expatiating on the advantages of having lived in the early years of the 20th century, 'you went to Elena Gerhardt or Julia Culp.' We who listened with bated breath to such revelations knew all about the German mezzo, but little about the Dutch. Her records had long disappeared from the catalogue, and if any of them turned up in the secondhand shops it would be *Bendemeer's Stream* (a lugubrious variant of *The Mountains of Morne*) or *Auld Lang Syne*. Her *Frauenliebe und -leben* was spoken of with a reverence which, on hearing it, seemed to be justified only in part. That (in two versions) was recorded earlier on the Odeon label and is not included in the present collection, which brings the singer into clearer focus and has the virtue of completeness within its given field.

Whether completeness is not a questionable virtue in this instance may itself be a relevant question. The repertoire was not chosen with an eye to liveliness or variety. At first, or for six of the first seven tracks, she and the band between them make everything sound like a hymn. More of the same is to follow, but at this point (and how thankful one is!) come three songs in succession – *I've Been Roaming*, *Mignonette* and *Heidenröslein* – in which the contralto tone is lightened and the whole character brought to life. Even so, there is little on the first CD that specifically shows her to have been a great Lieder singer. On the second disc, Brahms's *Immer leiser wird mein Schlummer* is more persuasive, catching imaginatively the pallid tone and restless thoughts of the dying girl. But it is not really until the last group, the six Lieder recorded by the new electrical process in 1926, that we come face to face with the recitalist of reputation.

Previously we have been listening to a very good singer, but that is a rather different matter. All those other songs – *Auld Lang Syne* and the rest – have shown a beautiful voice, well captured on record, finely reproduced in these transfers, and exceptional in the evenness of its production. The 1926 recordings show a good deal more about her art, yet the Victors will repay any young singer's study if the interest is centred on *legato* and breath control. Listening to those on their own, one might think the old-timers should have refined that sentence of theirs with a difference in emphasis: to learn how to sing *Lieder* you might indeed go to Gerhardt, but to learn to *sing* Lieder you could not do better than with Culp.

David Daniels *counterten*

Sento amor

Gluck Telemaco – Se parentro alla nera foresta. Orfeo ed Euridice – Che puro ciel!; Ahimè! Dove trascorsi? ... Che farò senza Euridice? **Handel** Tolomeo – Inumano fratel ... Stille amare. Partenope – Rosmira, oh! Dio! ... Sento amor; ch'io parta?; Furibondo spira il vento **Mozart** Ascanio in Alba – Ah di sì nobil alma. Mitridate, re di Ponto – Venga pur, minacci; Vadasi ... oh ciel ...Già dagli occhi. Ombra felice! ... Io ti lascio, K255
David Daniels *counterten* **Orchestra of the Age of Enlightenment / Harry Bicket**
Virgin Classics Veritas VC5 45365-2 Ⓕ
(62 minutes: DDD). Texts and translations included.
Recorded 1999

Curiously, the music on this disc is presented in reverse chronological order. Any slight reservations that one might feel at the beginning or in the middle are swept away when it comes to the end, for David Daniels is a magnificent interpreter of Handel and sings these arias with a freedom, a passion and a beauty of tone that he does not quite achieve in the later music. The dramatic recitative 'Inumano fratel', from *Tolomeo*, is declaimed with great force; Daniels uses the words as well as the notes to produce a performance of due rhetorical power, and both here and in the lamenting aria that follows his tone is ringing and finely focused. In the first of the *Partenope* arias the detail of Handel's complex line is etched with exemplary clarity; the second, another song of despair (as the hero Arsace thinks himself abandoned by his beloved), is done softly, with much expressive intensity; and the third is a *tour de force*, an angry piece full of rapid semiquavers thrown off with vitality and precision. This is model Handel singing, at one with the idiom and its expressive language. Much of the continuo accompaniment is assigned, happily, to a lute. Gluck's 'Che farò' is finely sung, full and warm in tone, and with some very sweet *legato*, but is perhaps a shade objective and sober for a character allegedly in desperation. The wonderment of 'Che puro ciel!' is better caught by both Daniels and the orchestra. Of the Mozart pieces, the *Ascanio in Alba* aria is done with due vigour. In the concert aria one might wish for a rather sharper attack than a countertenor can readily provide, but something of the excitement of this piece is certainly caught. The two arias for Farnace from *Mitridate* that begin the disc are cleanly sung, with some happy touches of phrasing (particularly at the little ornamental figures in 'Venga pur', done with a nice hint of wit), delicate, warm tone and sensible, effective cadenzas, but the total result does seem slightly pallid for Mozart. But this is in sum a very enjoyable recital, of appealing music, done by one of the most distinguished countertenors.

Geraldine Farrar *sop*

Geraldine Farrar in French Opera H

Opera Arias and Duets – Carmen, Les contes d'Hoffmann, Manon, Mignon, Roméo et Juliette and Thaïs

Geraldine Farrar *sop* with various artists

Nimbus Prima Voce mono NI7872 (79 minutes: ADD) Ⓢ

Recorded 1908-21

This is a lovely addition to the Prima Voce series. Farrar's Carmen appears as a model of effectiveness within the restraints of good musical and dramatic behaviour. The 'Séguedille' is sheer enchantment (irresistible promise in that breathed 'je l'aimerai' and the dreamily provocative reprise of 'Près des remparts'), while in the 'Chanson bohème' we catch the energy of her personality as well as the carrying power of her by no means robust lyric soprano. These are all cherishable records, of the kind that on some pleasant desultory evening with the gramophone one will feel a prompting to take down from the shelves. Seasoned collectors should not necessarily assume that they already have everything on the disc: there is, for instance, the unpublished 'Je veux vivre' (*Roméo et Juliette*) from 1911, a performance of surprising delicacy and charm. The Prelude to Act 4 is there, too, in a recording from 1921 said to be by the orchestra of La Scala conducted by Toscanini, one of those legendary sessions which put him off the gramophone for a decade. If he had heard the results as cleanly defined as they are here, he might have thought again.

Renée Fleming *sop*

The Beautiful Voice

Dvořák Songs my mother taught me, B104 No 4
Cano Luna – Epilogo **Canteloube** Chants d'Auvergne – Baïlèro **Charpentier** Louise – Depuis le jour
Flotow Martha – 'Tis the last rose of summer
Gounod Faust – O Dieu! que de bijoux! ... Ah! je ris
Korngold Die tote Stadt – Glück, das mir verblieb
Lehár Die lustige Witwe – Es lebt eine Vilja
Massenet Manon – Obéissons quand leur voix appelle **Orff** Carmina Burana – In trutina
Puccini La rondine – Chi il bel sogno di Doretta
Rachmaninov Vocalise, Op 34 No 14 (arr Braden)
J Strauss II Die Fledermaus – Klänge der Heimat
R Strauss Morgen, Op 27 No 4

Renée Fleming *sop* **English Chamber Orchestra / Jeffrey Tate**

Decca 458 858-2DH (70 minutes: DDD) Ⓕ

Texts and translations included. Recorded 1997

Sweet tooth, prepare for action. What does Lamb say in his *Chapter on Ears*? Something about piling honey upon sugar and sugar upon honey. The programme capitulates in stages. It begins well, sharpening the palate with Marguerite's Jewel Song after Louise's erotic musings. Soon we are swaying dreamily with the 'Viljalied' and then reclining in the drowsy sunshine and languid trickle of Canteloube's 'Baïlèro'. Louise, in this performance, cares for words and feelings as well as tone, Marguerite relishes her new role of 'coquette', and Manon plays lovingly with the consciousness of her own beauty. Throughout, the singing provides pleasures that are *not* simply those of 'the beautiful voice', as the title has it. Occasionally, it is true, one wishes for a more athletic style (the creamy Caballé-Te Kanawa associations spiced with a dash of Ninon Vallin perhaps). But this *is* 'the beautiful voice', no doubt about that, exercised with skill and heard in what will appeal widely as a programme of captivatingly beautiful music.

Great Opera Scenes

Britten Peter Grimes – Embroidery in childhood[b]
Dvořák Rusalka – O silver moon **Mozart** Le nozze di Figaro – Porgi, amor; E Susanna non vien! ... Dove sono **R Strauss** Daphne – Ich komme, grünende Brüder **Tchaikovsky** Eugene Onegin – Letter scene[a]
Verdi Otello – Era più calmo? ... Mia madre aveva ... Piangea cantando ... Ave Maria[a]

Renée Fleming *sop* [a]**Larissa Diadkova** *mez* [b]**Jonathan Summers** *bar* **London Symphony Orchestra / Sir Georg Solti**

Decca 455 760-2DH (72 minutes: DDD) Ⓕ

Texts and translations included. Recorded 1996

Here's a singer who has reached complete maturity as an artist, revelling in her vocal and interpretative powers. To the warm and vibrant voice is added an imagination that places Fleming in the first rank among today's lyric sopranos. The eclectic, ambitious choice of programme allows us to hear every aspect of her art. She is exactly the impulsive Tatyana, the girl's unreasoned ardour pouring out here in a stream of richly varied tone and feeling. Desdemona's Willow song is full of foreboding, also full of lovely singing, the repeated 'Cantiamo' voiced with precision of tone and timing, notes fined away with the utmost sensitivity. Ellen Orford's Embroidery aria is sung beautifully, the high B flat and A flat on 'Now' taken perfectly *pianissimo* after the *forte* A. These scenes benefit enormously from being placed in context, allowing Fleming to fit into the relevant situation. Diadkova is an idiomatic, responsive Filipyevna, and she makes the most of Emilia's few phrases. Summers is a wise and experienced Balstrode. All in all, Fleming lays claim here to Te Kanawa territory, and proves a worthy successor. More than Dame Kiri, she identifies with each character and moulds her voice to the woman in question. For Sir Georg this is obviously a labour of love, nowhere more so than in the postlude to *Daphne*, most sensuously done; he and the LSO provide worthy support for their superb soloist. The recording is faultless, capturing voice and orchestra in ideal balance.

I Want Magic

Barber Vanessa – He has come…Do not utter a word, Anatol **Bernstein** Candide – Glitter and be gay **Floyd** Susannah – Ain't it a pretty night; The trees on the mountains **Gershwin** Porgy and Bess – Summertime; My man's gone now **Herrmann** Wuthering Heights – I have dreamt **Menotti** The Medium – Monica's Waltz **D Moore** The Ballad of Baby Doe – The Letter Song **Previn** A Streetcar Named Desire – I want magic! **Stravinsky** The Rake's Progress – No word from Tom…I go to him

Renée Fleming *sop* **Metropolitan Opera Orchestra, New York / James Levine**

Decca 460 567-2DH (58 minutes: DDD) Ⓕ

Texts and translations included. Recorded 1998 ●●●

This survey of operas old and new reinforces the feeling that the current generation of star singers in the USA is making an effort to explore home-grown repertory. Fleming's voice is sumptuous, her lower register especially sounds so warmly resonant that it is reminiscent of Leontyne Price in her glory days. Fleming shows herself equal to every mood; only at the end of 'Glitter and be gay' is there a false moment when she rather overdoes the brittle laughter. What beautiful tunes there are here, including the waltz song from *The Medium* and 'Ain't it a pretty night' from *Susannah*. This was recorded before Fleming took part in the world première of André Previn's *A Streetcar Named Desire* in San Francisco and her programme ends with a sneak preview of that. 'I want magic!' is Blanche's philosophy of life, justifying her flights of fancy. Among the other items, Fleming makes the extract from *Wuthering Heights* sound positively Mahleresque, and Anne's great aria from *The Rake's Progress* – 'officially' an American opera, Stravinsky, Auden and Kallman at least all being resident there when it was written – suits her surprisingly well. Levine and the Met Orchestra provide idiomatic accompaniment.

Bruce Ford *ten*

Three Rossini Tenors

Rossini La donna del lago – Alla ragion deh rieda; Qual pena in me. Otello – No, no temer, serena; Non m'inganno, al mio rivale; Ah! vieni, nel tuo sangue … Ahimè fermate … Che fiero punto è questo. Ricciardo e Zoraide – Donala a questo core. Armida – Come l'aurette placide; In quale aspetto imbelle

Nelly Miricioiu *sop* **Paul Austin Kelly, Bruce Ford, William Matteuzzi** *tens* **Geoffrey Mitchell Choir; Philharmonia Orchestra, Academy of St Martin in the Fields / David Parry**

Opera Rara ORR204 (70 minutes: DDD) Ⓕ

Texts and translations included. Recorded 1996

'Only *three*?' Rossini might have remarked. During the years 1815-22 which this recital so thrillingly celebrates, Rossini had four, possibly five, world-class tenors at his disposal. Still, it is a good marketing ploy, with Opera Rara's three tenors turning in bravura performances in repertoire which *the* three tenors have only occasionally flirted with. It says much for Rossini's guile, and the guile of the programming, that one comes away from this recital, not bored or sated, but thrilled and satisfied. Amusingly, there is no actual trio for tenors until the last track, the astonishingly beautiful scene in *Armida* where Carlo and Ubaldo hold the adamantine shield up to Rinaldo's gaze and, in so doing, confront him with an image of his own baseness. Rossini's leading heroic tenor was Andrea Nozzari. Bruce Ford sings the Nozzari roles here, with Paul Austin Kelly and William Matteuzzi taking turn and turn about with the more purely brilliant roles (Uberto, Rodrigo, Ricciardo) Rossini wrote for the celebrated *tenore contraltino* in the Naples company, Giovanni David. All three acquit themselves superbly. To have Nelly Miricioiu on hand to sing Elena and Desdemona is an added bonus. David Parry and the Philharmonia Orchestra give performances of great dash and beauty. The recording places the orchestra rather obviously to the rear of the singers, but that is no bad thing. Slightly more distracting is the fact that the Rossini tenor is clearly a difficult creature for the microphone to decipher and absorb, particularly *en masse*. Thus, while Matteuzzi and Kelly are allowed to coo into the microphones like a pair of sucking doves, Bruce Ford is cast more in the role of the blackguard outsider, never quite as well forward, the sound never quite as 'clean'. The insert-notes are altogether excellent.

Inessa Galante *sop*

Russian Recital at Wigmore Hall

Glinka The lark. The poor singer. To the lyre **Medtner** As soon as roses wither. The waltz **Rachmaninov** Oh never sing to me again. Songs – Op 14 No 11, Spring waters; Op 21 No 7, How fair this spot; Op 26 No 10, Before my window; Op 38 No 1, In my garden at night; Op 34 No 14, Vocalise **Rimsky-Korsakov** Songs – Op 56 No 1, The nymph; Op 2 No 2, The rose and the nightingale; Op 43 No 1, The lark sings louder **Tchaikovsky** Songs – Op 16 No 1, Cradle song; Op 38 No 3, At the ball; Op 47 No 7, Was I not a little blade of grass? Eugene Onegin – Tatyana's Letter scene. The Queen of Spades – Lisa's Aria

Inessa Galante *sop* **Roger Vignoles** *pf*

Campion RRCD1348 (59 minutes: DDD) Ⓕ

Recorded live in 1999

Ever since her highly praised 1995 début recital, for Campion, Inessa Galante has been winning golden opinions. She is indeed a remarkable artist, but also an uneven one. That first review noted a need to use words and especially consonants to enhance expression, and here, for all her sensitivity with phrasing in metrically uneven verse, she can still too often lose verbal clarity. Listeners are not helped by a booklet that finds seven pages for three-language blurbs about the artists and even about the Wigmore Hall, but none for the original texts. A further reservation is that, when under pressure on high notes, her voice falls prone to a fast vibrato, too regularly applied, which she loses in all registers with her softer singing.

This can be ravishing. The close of Glinka's pretty song about the lark, Tchaikovsky's 'Cradle song' and his touching piece about the girl plucked like a blade of grass and withering in the embrace of a horrible old man, as well as Medtner's setting of Pushkin's little elegy to the withered roses, are all beautifully handled, not least thanks to Roger Vignoles' sensitive piano playing. He has an intelligent feeling for these songs, and sympathetic musicianship in support of Galante's performances, but also the virtuosity demanded by Rachmaninov's 'Spring waters'. He makes the most of the two operatic excerpts, valuable only in that they kindle the wish to hear Galante in, especially, *The Queen of Spades*. The recording is very fair, though it cannot help picking up contributions from one or two bronchially challenged members of the audience.

Amelita Galli-Curci *sop*

Opera Arias and Songs Ⓗ

Arias from Il barbiere di Siviglia, Dinorah, Don Pasquale, Lakmé, Lucia di Lammermoor, Manon Lescaut (Auber), Martha, Le nozze di Figaro, I Puritani, Rigoletto, Roméo et Juliette, La sonnambula and La traviata; songs by **Alvarez**, **Benedict**, **Bishop**, **Buzzi-Peccia**, **David**, **Delibes**, **Giordani**, **Grieg**, **Massenet**, **Proch**, **Samuels** and **Seppilli**

Amelita Galli-Curci *sop* with various artists

Romophone mono ② 81003-2 (159 minutes: ADD) Ⓕ

Recorded 1916-20

In *Gramophone* in 1923 the Editor wrote: 'One of the most solid grounds I have for facing the coming of old age with equanimity is the reasonable hope that I shall spend it listening to as many records of *la diva* Galli-Curci's voice as there are of Caruso's'. The purity of her voice was certainly a delight; it was at that time firm and even throughout its wide compass; and her fluency in scalework, precision in *staccato*, and ability to swell and diminish on a long-held high note were exceptional. She was an artist who could phrase and nuance exquisitely and who, within the boundaries of a more or less pretty joy and sadness, could be quite poignantly expressive. In the years of her greatest fame and success, roughly the decade from 1916 to 1926, her operatic repertoire was the standard one for the 'coloratura' soprano, and it is well represented by her records. What they also have, making them treasurable beyond anything that such a summary might suggest, is a personal flavour, a caress, a way of making words sound like water purling gently on a summer's afternoon, a dreaminess that can awaken to fun and affection though she could also flatten rather sadly in pitch. The transfers on this release, which concentrates on her recordings up to 1920, are of fine quality and make for a most enjoyable disc.

Lesley Garrett *sop*

A Soprano Inspired

S Adams The Holy City **Brahe** Bless this house **Caccini** (arr Ingham) Ave Maria **Fauré** Requiem, Op 48 – Pie Jesu **Franck** Panis angelicus **Handel** Messiah – I know that my Redeemer liveth **d'Hardelot** Because **Humperdinck** Hänsel und Gretel – Abends will ich schlafen gehn (sung in English) **Malotte** The Lord's Prayer **Mascagni** Cavalleria rusticana – Regina coeli ... Inneggiamo, il Signor **Mozart** Exsultate, jubilate, K165/K158*a* – Alleluia. Vesperae solennes de confessore in C, K339 – Laudate Dominum. Mass No 18 in C minor, 'Great Mass' – Laudamus te **Rodgers** The Sound of Music – Climb ev'ry mountain[a] **Schubert** Ave Maria, D839 **R Strauss** Zueignung, Op 10 No 1 **Tippett** Five Negro Spirituals – By and By[a] **Verdi** La forza del destino – La Vergine degli angeli[a] **Vivaldi** Nulla in mundo pax, RV630 – Nulla in mundo pax

Lesley Garrett *sop* [a]**chorus; Britten Sinfonia / Ivor Bolton**

Conifer Classics 75605 51329-2 (73 minutes: DDD) Ⓕ

Recorded 1997

Lesley Garrett is such a 'conviction' singer. She has always caught the imagination by the way she sings every word as if she meant it – as here in *The Holy City*, turning dross almost into gold. The programme for this CD is typically eclectic, drawn from the baroque to the Broadway musical. She sings Vivaldi, Handel (a nicely decorated 'I know that my Redeemer liveth') and Mozart (the 'Laudamus te' from the C minor Mass and a joyous 'Alleluia' at the start) with straightforward vigour. In her opera selection, she phrases Leonora's Prayer from *Forza* with a fine feeling for Verdian line, follows the somewhat dubious tradition started by Elisabeth Schumann of singing the 'Abendgesang' from *Hänsel und Gretel* with herself, and gives the Easter Hymn, though she couldn't undertake Santuzza on stage, with the passion appropriate to its context. Of the two Lieder, an open-hearted *Zueignung* is preferable to a rather sentimental *Ave Maria*. The 'Pie Jesu' from Fauré's Requiem and Franck's *Panis angelicus*, both sung with the simple sincerity that is Garrett's hallmark, confirm that she has lost little or none of that fresh, forward, no-nonsense sound that is so appealing to her large audience. The unexpected choice of the Tippett item and the revival of d'Hardelot's *Because*, delivered with the security of technique that marks all these readings, is welcome. It is hard to resist her glorious account of 'Climb ev'ry mountain'. Ivor Bolton switches easily between idioms, though is obviously most at home in the baroque. The recording is brightly lit but not offensively so.

Soprano in Red

Chabrier L'étoile – O petite étoile; Je suis Lazuli! **Coward** Bitter Sweet – If love were all **Heuberger** Der Opernball – Im chambre séparée **Lehár** Zigeunerliebe – Hör' ich Cymbalklänge. Friederike – Warum hast du mich wachgeküsst? Die lustige Witwe – Es lebt eine Vilja, ein Waldmägdelein[a] **Novello** Perchance to dream – We'll gather lilacs. The Dancing Years – Waltz of my heart **Offenbach** La belle Hélène – On me nomme Hélène la Blonde. Orphée aux enfers – J'ai vu le Dieu Bacchus[a]; Ce bal est original[a] **Romberg** The New Moon – Softly, as in a morning sunrise; Lover, come back to me **J Strauss II** (arr Benatzky) Casanova – Nuns' Chorus and Laura's Song[a] **Sullivan** The Contrabandista – Only the night wind sighs alone

Lesley Garrett *sop* [a]**Crouch End Festival Chorus; Royal Philharmonic Concert Orchestra / James Holmes**

Silva Screen Classics SILKTVCD1 Ⓕ
(60 minutes: DDD). All items sung in English. Recorded 1995

Lesley Garrett has won herself a huge following of those who respond to her straightforward, unaffected vocalising, to the clarity and brightness of her voice and its ringing top notes. What also appeals about Garrett's recordings is the attention paid to less familiar material and the quest for authenticity of period style. Both facets are fully evident in this collection. The eager entreaties of Laura's Song from *Casanova*, the bright expressiveness of 'If love were all' and the sheer joyfulness of 'Waltz of my heart' (complete with piano contribution) are highlights. Especially gratifying, though, are the rarities. In the pedlar Lazuli's two numbers from Chabrier's *L'étoile*, Garrett's clarity of diction shows off Jeremy Sams's lyrics to fine effect and she should certainly win over the Sullivan faction with the first ever recording of an engaging little number from the pre-Gilbert operetta *The Contrabandista*. In Novello's 'We'll gather lilacs' double tracking permits Garrett to duet with herself. Ensemble and momentum go curiously adrift at the choral entries in Offenbach's 'Hymn to Bacchus', but this detracts only a little from another delightful Garrett collection.

Angela Gheorghiu *sop*

Casta Diva

Bellini Norma – Casta Diva[a]; Ah! bello, a me ritorna[a]. I puritani – Qui la voce sua soave… Ah! rendetemi la speme; Vien, diletto. La sonnambula – Ah! non credea mirarti **Donizetti** Anna Bolena – Piangete voi?[a]… Al dolce guidami castel natio. Lucia di Lammermoor – Regnava nel silenzio; Quando rapito in estasi **Rossini** Guglielmo Tell – S'allontanano alfine!…Selva opaca. Il barbiere di Siviglia – Una voce poco fa…Io sono docile. L'assedio di Corinto – L'ora fatal s'appressa…Giusto ciel! in tal periglio[a]

Angela Gheorghiu *sop* [a]**Chorus of the Royal Opera, Covent Garden; London Symphony Orchestra / Evelino Pidò**

EMI CDC5 57163-2 (61 minutes: DDD) Ⓕ
Texts and translations included **OO**

Once again we have to count our blessings. As with the recent recital by Karita Mattila (Erato – reviewed further on), we are a lucky generation, in this respect at least, that here we have sopranos with such purity of tone, evenness of production and scrupulous musicianship; and with Gheorghiu's recital it is rare that ghost-voices of singers from the past enter the listening mind clamouring to be brought out for comparison. If they do so at all it is in the solos from *Il barbiere di Siviglia* and *Lucia di Lammermoor*. Gheorghiu, one could say, is not a Rosina: in the famous cavatina she catches the determination of those 'lo giurai's and 'vincerò's but not the fun-loving trickster behind them. As Lucia, more surprisingly, she simply fails to make it clear that this is a ghost story with blood in it.

Otherwise we are in the land of heart's desire. In 'Casta diva' and the other Bellini solos, Gheorghiu finds (better than most) the right balance between purity of line and the inflections needful for expression. In the aria from *I puritani* the phrases are finely bound yet movingly 'inner'; and then, with 'Vien, diletto', comes a marvellously vivid change, the face lighting up with eagerness located in the bright vowels and pointed rhythms. The scales, trills and ornaments are also a delight, whether as sheer technical accomplishment or as heighteners of emotion.

Perhaps listeners should be warned that, although Lucia's cabaletta sports a high D and Elvira's an E flat, these are not (as they would be with Sutherland) crowning events: the 'event', so to speak, is the whole performance.

My World

Brediceanu Mult mă'ntreabă inima **Brodszky** Be my love **Cavadia** Umbra **Delibes** Les filles de Cadix **Dvořák** Songs my mother taught me, B104 No 4 **Falla** El paño moruno **Grieg** Solveig's Song **Hadjidakis** Pai efiye to treno **Leoncavallo** Mattinata **Liszt** Oh! quand je dors, S282 **J Martini** Plaisir d'amour **Mezzetti** Cântec se sirenă **Mitake** Kawa no Nagare no yô ni **Montsalvatge** Canto negro

Ovalle Azulão **Parisotti** Se tu m'ami, C xxii, 68 **Poulenc** Les chemins de l'amour **Respighi** Nebbie **Satie** Je te veux **Schubert** Ständchen, D957 No 4 **Schumann** Myrthen, Op 25 – No 1, Widmung; No 24, Du bist wie eine Blume **R Strauss** Zueignung, Op 10 No 1 **Sup** Guriwoon Guemgang San **Traditional** Durme, kerido hijico (arr Behar)
Angela Gheorghiu *sop* **Malcolm Martineau** *pf*
Decca 458 360-2DH (75 minutes: DDD) Ⓕ
Texts and translations included. Recorded 1997

This eclectic programme makes a welcome change from recorded recitals devoted to one composer, one genre. Gheorghiu avers, in a frank note, that she thrives on change, loves to be in different countries and experience different idioms so she 'wanted to create a unique recital programme that would reflect all these aspects of my interests'. She certainly has done that: her generous choice boxes the compass from classical through German, Spanish, Italian and French song to ethnic pieces. She also points out that many of the items exploit the warm qualities of her lower voice: the haunting pieces, semi-popular, from the far east, for instance; even more the Greek popular song. Still better are the three songs from her native Romania. Then there's Ovalle's insinuating *Azulão*, chosen apparently at the suggestion of Martineau, the singer's creative partner, and sung in that soft-grained manner peculiar to Gheorghiu. She ends with a bravura account of the Lanza favourite *Be my love*, the slight accent in the English almost an advantage. Similarly her indeterminate German makes her three Lieder sound unidiomatic, but each of these love-songs is given with such conviction that the customary criteria for judgement can for once be set aside. Her French is much better; in any case the erotic charge of the Satie and Poulenc pieces is amply felt. There's much else to commend: the elegiac quality in Respighi's infinitely sad *Nebbie* contrasting with the earthy high spirits of Montsalvatge's *Canto negro* and the Delibes song, and the wistful touch in the famous Dvořák. With an admirably faithful recording as a bonus, this ought to be a runaway success.

Angela Gheorghiu & Roberto Alagna

Opera Arias and Duets

Berlioz Les troyens – Nuit d'ivresse![ab]
Bernstein West Side Story – Only You ... Tonight, it all began tonight[ab] **G Charpentier** Louise – Depuis le jour[a] **Donizetti** Anna Bolena – Al dolce guidami[a]. Don Pasquale – Tornami a dir[ab] **Gounod** Faust – Il se fait tard! ... O nuit d'amour[ab] **Mascagni** L'amico Fritz – Suzel, buon di ... Tutto tace[ab] **Massenet** Manon – Je suis seul! ... Ah! fuyez, douce image[b]; Toi! Vous! ... N'est-ce plus ma main[ab] **Offenbach** La belle Hélène – Au mont Ida[b] **Puccini** La bohème – O soave fanciulla[ab]
[a]**Angela Gheorghiu** *sop* [b]**Roberto Alagna** *ten*
Orchestra of the Royal Opera House, Covent Garden / Richard Armstrong
EMI CDC5 56117-2 (61 minutes: DDD) Ⓕ
Texts and translations included. Recorded 1995

Ideally matched, the two young lyric artists of our day who have most taken the hearts and hopes of public and critics sing here in a programme that is both aptly and imaginatively selected. It ranges quite widely over the French and Italian repertoires, always combining instant satisfaction with a wish for more. The Cherry duet from *L'amico Fritz* comes first, and the voices have just the right freshness for it, the soprano warm-toned, the tenor elegant and cleanly defined; the style too is charming, natural and mutually responsive. Then with the excerpts from *Manon* they are not only well suited but show already a real dramatic impulse in their duet, again with its developments so well felt and understood. The Garden scene works unusual magic. The solos provide welcome opportunities: Gheorghiu, delightful in 'Depuis le jour', is even more so in the aria from *Anna Bolena*, exquisitely phrased and shaded as though it were the slow movement of a sonata by Mozart. 'Ah! fuyez, douce image' opens with the softness associated from long ago with Smirnov and Muratore; Alagna never forgets what he is singing about, is thrilling on his high B flats and finely controlled in the concluding *diminuendo*. His Mount Ida song from *La belle Hélène* has panache and humour, a deliciously promising *pianissimo* start to the last verse and a good robust C thrown in before he finishes. And then, inspiration on somebody's part, there is *West Side Story*. 'Tonight' has never been better sung, and it also brings us to the other element in this recital – the playing of the Covent Garden orchestra under Richard Armstrong. In this, they make us realise afresh how distinctively flavoured (in harmony and orchestration) is Bernstein's marvellous score: the duet is intensely moving, yet the rhythm is kept strong and there is no sugar-coating or melting into slush. Repeatedly, in Gounod and Bernstein as in Mascagni and Puccini, one reacts with an 'I'd never noticed that before' or simply a smile or sigh of pleasure in the sound.

Beniamino Gigli *ten*

The Complete HMV Recordings, 1918-32 Ⓗ

Opera arias and duets – L'amico Fritz, La bohème, Cavalleria rusticana, Faust, La favorita, Fedora, La Gioconda, Iris, Lodoletta, Mefistofele, Les pêcheurs de perles, Stabat mater (Rossini), Tosca; songs by **Cannio**, **de Curtis**, **Niedermeyer**, **Schubert**, **Sullivan** and **Tosti**
Beniamino Gigli *ten* with various artists
Romophone mono ② 82011-2 (139 minutes: ADD) Ⓜ
Recorded 1918-19 and 1931-2

The first of these two CDs enshrines the golden youth of Gigli, and therefore some of the most beautiful tenor sounds ever committed to disc. Listen to the three extracts from *La Gioconda* – the Act 1 encounter with Barnaba, 'Cielo e mar' and the love duet with Laura made at the first sessions in Milan in 1918 – and imagine yourself with the audiences when the singer had one of his earliest successes as Enzo; also enjoy the honeyed, mellifluous timbre, the homogeneous tone, the fluid delivery, the enthusiastic attack that must have enthralled Gigli's contemporaries. The ease and naturalness of the sound still have the power to amaze the ear, as they do in such a dreamy, sweet account of 'Apri la tua finestra' from Mascagni's *Iris*. Then in 'Spirto gentil' (*La favorita*), the subtle, suave way Gigli moves into the reprise has surely never been equalled, let alone surpassed. Pieces that he repeated later – the arias of Cavaradossi and *Faust*, the Act 1 duet from *La bohème*, for instance – are here done with fewer of the maddening if endearing traits that informed the later recordings. Faust was not yet in his repertory, but the aria and even more the Garden Duet with the estimable Maria Zamboni are filled with the kind of immediate, open-hearted passion that is the hallmark of all Gigli's records. A pity he has such an acid-toned partner in the Cherry Duet from *L'amico Fritz* because he is perfectly suited by the role of the shy Korbus.

Six tracks into the second disc we are carried forward 12 years to 1931, when Gigli returned to HMV from his fruitful spell with Victor, chronicled on Romophone. This is the fully-fledged Gigli with which collectors will be most familiar, the voice more mature, the style a deal coarsened. Yet who can resist Tosti's *Addio* or Sullivan's *The Lost Chord* (conducted by Barbirolli), both sung in delightfully accented English, or even his outrageously self-indulgent account of the Dream from *Manon*, in Italian? The 1931 coupling of the arias from *Faust* and *La bohème* must have been Gigli's best-selling operatic 78s: both pieces are sung in score pitch, the tenor's high C now firmly in place. Neither reading is a model of style, but both are emotionally overwhelming, the boyish charm, use of *portamento* and verbal detailing of his Rodolfo especially winning. In a famous account of the *Cavalleria* duet, he is partnered by an impassioned Giannini: both artists exhibit an authentic *spinto* style now severely in jeopardy. At the end come a wonderfully forthright account of 'Cujus animam' from Rossini's *Stabat mater* (though he abjures the high D flat) and two soulful Neapolitan songs by de Curtis, perfect Gigli territory. The transfers of the electrics are faultless; the sound of the acoustics, poor recordings in themselves, is less amenable.

Alma Gluck *sop*

Anonymous (words by Ben Jonson) Have you seen but a white lily grow? **Bellini** La sonnambula – Ah! non credea mirarti **Bishop** Lo, here the gentle lark **Bizet** Carmen – Je dis que rien ne m'épouvante **Charpentier** Louise – Depuis le jour **Godard** Jocelyn – Oh! ne t'éveille pas encore **Hahn** Chansons grises – L'heure exquise **Handel** Atalanta – Care selve, ombre beate. Theodora – Angels, ever bright and fair **Humperdinck** Hänsel und Gretel – Suse, liebe, Suse **Loewe** War schöner als der schönste Tag **Massenet** Elégie **Puccini** La bohème – Quando m'en vo' soletta; Donde lieta uscì **Rameau** Hippolyte et Aricie – Rossignols amoureux **Rimsky-Korsakov** Snow Maiden – Going berrying; Lel's Third Song. Sadko – Song of the Indian Guest. The Tsar's Bride – Haste thee, mother mine **Saint-Saëns** Le timbre d'argent – Le bonheur est chose légère **Smetana** The Kiss – Cradle song **Tosti** La serenata

Alma Gluck *sop* with various artists

Nimbus Prima Voce NI7904 (77 minutes: ADD) Ⓢ

Recorded 1911-17

In 1915 W J Henderson called Gluck 'the most beautiful lyric soprano before the public'. Her record of *Carry me back to old Virginy* was the first celebrity disc in America to sell over a million copies. Yet her career lasted little beyond a decade; less, if one counts time out for re-training. It was a delicate voice and, as she soon found, any sort of operatic hurly-burly endangered it. There still must have been something wrong in its training or usage. Her records remain a precious memento, and the best of her recorded art can be very happily sampled here. The Nimbus transfer process suits Gluck well. Otherwise it might be a foregone conclusion that with Marston's two-CD volume still available, readers would be referred back to the more comprehensive selection. As it is, Nimbus has three items not included by Marston, all good, and one of them, the famous solo from *Jocelyn*, surely quintessential. Gluck had the most lovely soft tones, perhaps of all, in the upper part of the voice; and in this lullaby ('Angels guard thee' in the English version) the precise take and pure quality of the upper notes are heavenly. In Musetta's song from *La bohème* (also absent from Marston) she gives a lesson to all screaming Musettas, singing (as Nigel Douglas observes in his booklet-note) *con molta grazia ed eleganza* as Puccini recommended. *Lo, here the gentle lark*, the third bonus item, matters less and is not one of the showier versions abounding in *alts*; resourcefully sung, even so. Included are most of the gems – the Rameau, Loewe's *canzonetta*, Hahn's *L'heure exquise* and *Have you seen but a white lily grow?* for instance.

Susan Graham *mez*

Il tenero momento

Gluck Paride ed Elena – O del mio dolce ardor. Iphigénie en Tauride – O toi qui prolongeas mes jours; O malheureuse Iphigénie!; Non, cet affreux devoir...Je t'implore et je tremble. Orphée et Eurydice – Qu'entends-je? Qu'a-t-il dit?; J'ai perdu mon Eurydice **Mozart** Le nozze di Figaro – Non so più cosa son; Voi che sapete. La clemenza di Tito – Parto, parto, ma tu, ben mio[a]; Deh per questo istante. Idomeneo – Non ho colpa, e mi codanni. Lucio Silla – Dunque sperar poss'io...Il tenero momento

Susan Graham *mez* [a]**Antony Pay** *bscl* **Orchestra of the Age of Enlightenment / Harry Bicket**

Erato 8573-85768-2 (63 minutes: DDD) Ⓕ

Recorded 2000 **OO**

It's a very long time since I heard an operatic recital by a modern singer that satisfied me as much as this one does. Graham, now at the apex of her career, displays her skills as singer and interpreter in a sensibly planned and executed programme, comprised of arias from roles she has sung on stage. In consequence, unlike her coeval and colleague Renée Fleming in her recent recital (Decca), Graham sounds entirely inside all her music and dispenses it with a confidence and attack that is truly amazing, but the refulgent, vibrant voice and faultless technique – except perhaps in a virtuoso cadenza at the end of Orfeo's Act 2 showpiece (from the Viardot 1869 edition of Gluck's work) – are wholly at the service of the music, the mezzo showing a sensitive empathy with the emotions of every character she portrays. Vulnerable Iphigénie, insecure Sesto, palpitating Cherubino, forlorn Orfeo (in 'J'ai perdu'), lovelorn Paris and Cecilio (*Lucio Silla*) all come before us in lifelike form by virtue of Graham's exemplary use of words, themselves enhanced by firm consonants. Beyond that there is her understanding of the baroque verities and her idiomatic command of Italian and French.

If you need to be convinced to buy this disc – and you can sample before buying – then listen to Sesto's two arias. They are templates of the rest in the ideal moulding of phrase, evenness of tone throughout a wide tessitura and exemplary coloratura allied to an identification with the youth's plight. The moment to savour most is the reprise, in the second piece, of the words 'Deh, per questo istante solo' where Graham employs a quite magical *mezza voce*.

To complete one's pleasure in a treasurable CD, there are the wholly stylish playing of the alert orchestra under the command of Harry Bicket, who is a specialist in this kind of music, and a perfect balance in the recording between voice and instruments.

Elisabeth Grümmer *sop*

Great Singers of the Century

Mendelssohn Lieder, Op 71 – No 2, Frühlingslied; No 6, Nachtlied. Auf Flügeln des Gesanges, Op 34 No 2. Scheidend, Op 9 No 6. Neue Liebe, Op 19*a* No 4
Schoeck Lieder, Op 10 – Erinnerung; Die Einsame. Lieder, Op 20 – Auf meines Kindes Tod; Nachruf. Ergebung, Op 30 No 6. Motto, Op 51 No 2. Das holde Bescheiden, Op 62 – Auf der Teck; Im Park; Nachts
Schumann Frauenliebe und -leben, Op 42 **Wolf** Spanisches Liederbuch – In dem Schatten meiner Locken; Mögen alle bösen Zungen; Bedeckt mich mit Blumen; Sie blasen zum Abmarsch
Elisabeth Grümmer *sop* **Aribert Reimann** *pf*
Orfeo C506001B (68 minutes: ADD) Ⓕ
Recorded 1963, 1966 and 1968 **OO**

The glorious Hänsel on the classic Karajan recording for EMI of Humperdinck's opera, a famed Donna Anna, Agathe, Elisabeth, Elsa and Eva, all of which she recorded to universal praise, Grümmer was none the less disgracefully under-recorded, in particular in relation to her recital repertory.

The central interpretation here, the Schumann cycle, discloses all this sincere, warm soprano's many virtues, above all her ability to sing the music in exemplary style with unaffected, straightforward feeling, entirely free from gloss and mannerisms and, where appropriate, a charming glint in her voice. In that sense she is a throwback to some of her great pre-war predecessors such as Lehmann and Lemnitz, but she is a better technician than either of those revered artists. She is the deferential, happy, wondering girl of the first songs to the life, then the eager bride and grateful mother, finally the desolate widow. Word and note are in perfect alliance; everything is clear, filled with meaning yet nothing is exaggerated or portentous, and the tone itself is amazingly fresh for a singer in her mid-fifties.

Mendelssohn's *Auf Flügeln des Gesanges* and *Neue Liebe* are sung with the same fresh spontaneity. So are some interesting settings of Eichendorff and Mörike by Schoeck. The four masterpieces from Wolf's *Spanish Songbook* are still better: *Bedeckt mich mit Blumen* has just the right erotic languour, *In dem Schatten meiner Locken* just the right sense of fun without any of the archness that can ruin its irresistibly loving message. Reimann, here and throughout, is a finely imaginative partner and the recording could not be bettered. This is a CD for all connoisseurs of Lieder singing at its very best.

Nathan Gunn *bar*

American Anthem – from Ragtime to Art Song

Barber Songs, Op 13 – No 3, Sure on this shining night; No 4, Nocturne **Bolcom** Cabaret Songs – Over the piano; Fur (Murray the Furrier); Song of Black Max
Copland Old American Songs, Set 1 – Long time ago. Old American Songs, Set 2 – At the river
Gorney Americana – Brother, Can You Spare a Dime?
Hoiby The lamb **Ives** General William Booth Enters into Heaven. Slugging a vampire. Two little flowers
Musto Recuerdo **Niles** The lass from the Low Countree **Rorem** Early in the morning. The lordly Hudson **Scheer** Lean Away (arr Thomas). American Anthem. At Howard Hanks' House. Holding each other (all arr Musiker) **Traditional** I wonder as I wander (arr Niles/Horton). Shenandoah (arr Musiker)
Nathan Gunn *bar* **Kevin Murphy** *pf*
EMI Debut CDZ5 73160-2 (68 minutes: DDD) Ⓑ
Recorded 1998

Nathan Gunn is a protégé of the Met in New York and this is an exceptional début. As the title of the collection implies, there is a wide range of styles united simply through being American music, and Gunn wanted to illustrate the rich diversity of his inheritance. He has plenty of classics at his disposal. Of the three by Ives, *Slugging a vampire* is swashbuckling; *General William Booth* is delivered with complete confidence; and *Two little flowers* is suitably charming. Copland's arrangements of *Long time ago* and *At the river* are dead right and particularly moving in Gunn's smooth and steady delivery. The two Barber songs show the same effortless command. When Gunn moves towards the vernacular he chooses three hilarious character sketches from William Bolcom's *Cabaret Songs*, which are done with perfect rhythmic control in partnership with Kevin Murphy at the piano. In the traditional tunes and the real pop songs by Scheer they are just as effective as a team. Gunn's flexible, lyrical baritone often resembles Thomas Hampson and he brings the same intelligence to a wide range of Americana. Well recorded, if slightly harsh at times, but negligible notes and you are referred to the EMI web site for the texts. But a real discovery.

Thomas Hampson *bar*

Operetta Arias

Kálmán Gräfin Mariza – Komm, Zigány. Die Csárdásfürstina – Die Mädis vom Chantant **Lehár** Das Land des Lächelns – Dein ist mein ganzes Herz! Paganini – Gern hab' ich die Frau'n geküsst. Der Zarewitsch – Wolgalied **Millöcker** Der Bettelstudent – Ach ich hab' sie ja nur auf die Schulter geküsst; Ich knüpfte manche zarte Bande **J Strauss II** Eine Nacht in Venedig – Treu sein, das liegt mir nicht. Der Zigeunerbaron[a] – Als flotter Geist **Stolz** Auf der Heide blüh'n die letzten Rosen. Mein Herz ruft nach dir – Ich sing' mein Lied. Wien wird schön erst bei Nacht. Trauminsel – Ich hab' mich tausendmal verliebt **Tauber** Der singende Traum – Du bist die Welt für mich **Zeller** Der Obersteiger[a] – Sei nicht bös

Thomas Hampson *bar* [a]**London Voices; London Philharmonic Orchestra / Franz Welser-Möst**

EMI CDC5 56758-2 (60 minutes: DDD) Ⓕ

Texts and translations included

Thomas Hampson's elegant baritone is one of the glories of today, and he brings seemingly effortless power and grace to this collection of Viennese operetta arias. The clarity of the words is exemplary, and the selection of items is of especial interest. Some of the numbers are more usually associated with tenors rather than baritones, and Hampson accommodates them partly through his own flexible range, partly with discreet transposition (a semitone in 'Dein ist mein ganzes Herz!', for instance). He does well, too, to remind us of Richard Tauber's skill as a composer, plus the fact that 'Sei nicht bös' (heard here in an unfamiliar orchestration) was written for a male singer. Reminders of Millöcker's classic *Bettelstudent* are welcome too, with Hampson rather more at home as the blustering Colonel Ollendorf than as the beggar student himself, where more of a 'devil may care' approach might have helped. In the Kálmán numbers, the opportunities for graceful phrasing of 'Komm, Zigány' perhaps suit Hampson better than the comedy of 'Die Mädis vom Chantant', though the latter is given an especially effective ending. It all makes a pleasant change from the usual operetta recital, with stylish accompaniments from the London Philharmonic and Welser-Möst. There is admirable documentation, too, from Miles Kreuger and operetta authority Michael Miller. If only this hadn't resulted in a booklet too thick for the jewel-case!

Ben Heppner *ten*

German Romantic Opera Arias

Beethoven Fidelio – Gott! Welch Dunkel hier! ... In des Lebens[a] **Korngold** Die tote Stadt[b] – O Freund, ich werde sie nicht wiedersehen **Wagner** Rienzi[b] – Allmächt'ger Vater. Der fliegende Holländer[b] – Willst jenes Tag's; Tristan und Isolde[b] – Dünkt dich das? Siegfried[b] – Selige Ode auf sonniger Höh! Götterdämmerung[b] – Brünnhilde, heilige Braut! Parsifal[b] – Nur eine Waffe taugt **Weber** Der Freischütz[b] – Nein! länger trag'ich nicht die Qualen ... Durch die Wälder. Euryanthe[b] – Wehen mir Lüfte Ruh

Ben Heppner *ten* [a]**Bavarian Radio Symphony Orchestra / Sir Colin Davis;** [b]**North German Radio Symphony Orchestra / Donald Runnicles**

RCA Red Seal 09026 63239-2 (70 minutes: DDD) Ⓕ

Texts and translations included. Recorded 1998

Heppner is among the most consistent of tenors in this kind of repertory, the only drawback to this excellent recital being the nonsensical chronological order chosen by RCA. How could it place Wagner (his items themselves out of chronology) before Beethoven and Weber and then suddenly follow Weber with Korngold? All of which cannot detract from the beauty, reliability and musicality of every item in this pot-pourri of German opera. Particularly welcome is Heppner's singing of Tristan's, Siegfried's and Parsifal's music: with his secure technique and sturdy frame these roles have surely found their ideal interpreter for the first decade of the new century. Much as you might dislike bleeding chunks and the way they end in mid-air, such firmly sung and intelligently phrased readings justify the practice on this occasion. Heppner would also be an ideal interpreter, on this evidence, of Max and Adolar in the Weber operas, the lyrical and dramatic nicely held in balance. In the items, other than the Beethoven, Heppner is admirably partnered by Donald Runnicles. The recording is exemplary.

Roy Henderson *bar*

Centenary Recital

Songs – **T Arne**, **Boyce**, **G Butterworth**, **Dale**, **Hatton**, **Purcell**, **Short**, **Stanford**, **Tchaikovsky**, **Vaughan Williams** and **Warlock**

Roy Henderson *bar* with various artists

Dutton Laboratories mono CDLX7038 Ⓑ

(72 minutes: ADD). Recorded 1925-45

Roy Henderson was one of the country's most distinguished baritones during the interwar years. He sang Count Almaviva at Glyndebourne's inaugural season in 1934, was an outstanding Elijah and for many years virtually monopolised the all-important baritone solo in Delius's *A Mass of Life* and *Sea Drift* until he retired in 1952. He was also a noted recitalist, and to celebrate his centenary Dutton has had the excellent idea of reissuing his most significant 78rpm discs of British song, very few previously available either on LP or CD. We start with his 1940s Decca recordings of

Butterworth's *A Shropshire Lad* and a tranche of Warlock, Vaughan Williams and Stanford songs. The transferred sound is clarity itself, matching the same attribute in Henderson's approach to words. Indeed he is quoted by Tully Potter in his notes as saying: 'It is the words that count, and determine the pace, the variations and the time'. He observes his dictum in his eloquently shaped and subtly inflected readings, notable for the true half-voice he employs on many occasions, especially in 'Is my team ploughing?' in the Butterworth cycle.

Other delights are his warm tone and fine *legato* in Vaughan Williams's lovely *Orpheus with his lute* and the sheer élan in Boyce's *Song of Momus to Mars*, a Dryden setting. The Vocalions and Columbias, dating from the 1920s, disclose a firmer, meatier tone, although the sensitivity is already there in Ireland's *Sea Fever*, a Henderson favourite – he re-recorded it for Decca. He also offers varied and amusing accounts of Hatton's *Simon the Cellarer* and the traditional *O no, John!* Finally, a 1929 account of Tchaikovsky's *To the forest* shows that Henderson was just as successful in non-British song. Gerald Moore, Ivor Newton and Eric Gritton provide excellent support in this generously filled, rewarding tribute.

Wolfgang Holzmair *bar*

An die ferne Geliebte

Beethoven Adelaide, Op 46. An die ferne Geliebte, Op 98 **Haydn** Songs, HobXXVIa – No 9, Trost unglücklicher Liebe; No 12, Du zu späte Ankunft der Mutter; No 16, Gegenlied; No 22, Lob der Faulheit; No 30, Fidelity; No 31, Sailor's Song; No 33, Sympathy; No 34, She Never Told her Love; No 35, Piercing Eyes; No 36, Content; No 41, The Spirit's Song; No 42, O Tuneful Voice **Mozart** Die Betrogene Welt, K474. Das Veilchen, K476. An Chloe, K524. Das Traumbild, K530. Eine kleine deutsche Kantate, K619

Wolfgang Holzmair *bar* **Imogen Cooper** *pf*

Philips 454 475-2PH (80 minutes: DDD) Ⓕ

Texts and translations included

There must be few more moving songs in the English language than Haydn's *The Spirit's Song*, *Content* and *She Never Told her Love*, wholly on a par with his work in other fields in terms of harmonic ingenuity and emotional feeling. Or so it seems when they are sung with the deep eloquence provided by Holzmair, seconded by Cooper's perceptive piano playing. Over and over again in this absorbing, generous recital, but particularly in the Haydn, Holzmair more than ever sounds like a baritone equivalent of his great fellow-countryman, Julius Patzak.

There's the same plangent tone, the same ability to conjure forth the inner meaning of a song in an almost reticent way. Yet Holzmair is no less successful in the extrovert jollity of the familiar *Sailor's Song*. The slight accent in his otherwise commendable English somehow adds to the attraction of these readings. The partnership is just as successful in its Mozart choices, Cooper displaying typical *jeux d'esprit*, and they give a properly solemn account of the Masonic cantata, K619, with its many echoes of *Die Zauberflöte*. Even such a familiar song as *Das Veilchen* is performed with such spontaneity that it might have been written yesterday.

In the two Beethoven offerings, the many available versions provide strong competition. *Adelaide*, perhaps, calls for a slightly more outgoing fervour as provided recently by the Award-winning Stephan Genz, who also offered on the same CD a wonderfully youthful *An die ferne Geliebte*, but Holzmair in his more retiring, gentle way presents another, equally valid view of the cycle, one that yields up subtleties few others have found in the work, not least because he and Cooper have such a rapport that they seem to think as one.

Hans Hotter *bass-bar*

Opera Monologues, 1957-62 Ⓗ

Mussorgsky Boris Godunov – I have attained the highest power; Your Majesty, I make obeisance; Farewell, my son, I am dying **Rossini** Il barbiere di Siviglia – La calunnia è un venticello **R Strauss** Die schweigsame Frau – Wie schön ist doch die Musik **Verdi** Don Carlo – Ella giammai m'amò **Wagner** Der fliegende Holländer – Die Frist ist um. Die Meistersinger von Nürnberg – Was duftet doch der Flieder; Wahn! Wahn! Uberall Wahn!

Hans Hotter *bass-bar* **Dorothea Siebert** *sop* **Lorenz Fehenberger** *ten* **Bavarian Radio Chorus and Symphony Orchestra / Meinhard von Zallinger, Rudolf Alberth, Eugen Jochum**

Orfeo d'Or C501991B (67 minutes: ADD) Ⓜ

Recorded 1957-62. All items sung in German

Too many young collectors today know Hotter only as a Wagnerian (then usually in the Solti *Ring* where he was past his best) and/or as a fine interpreter of Lieder. In fact he was also renowned in Austria and Germany in other repertory, and even as an accomplished comedian, singing his roles, as was then the custom, in the vernacular. These tracks, drawn from Bavarian Radio archives, tell us something of that other Hotter. In *Don Carlos*, he sang both King Philip and, more often, the Grand Inquisitor. He gives us a haunted yet commanding Philip, sung in a commendable *legato*. His amusing Don Basilio – the Slander Aria – couldn't be a greater contrast. A video exists showing Hotter's giant, scheming, faintly ridiculous prelate, commanding the scene, as he commands the aria here. He is equally in character in Sir Morosus's monologue – the old man at last contented and at peace. But the revelation here is Hotter's Boris.

He sang the role on stage just once, at Hamburg in 1937, but 20 years later Bavarian Radio mounted a studio production of Mussorgsky's opera under Jochum with Hotter in the title-role. In both Act 2 monologues, the scene with Shuisky (the subtle, wily Fehenberger) and Boris's death, Hotter presents a frightened, superstitious yet still authoritative and curiously sympathetic Tsar. All are sung with a wealth of inner meaning and fidelity to dynamic marks while avoiding histrionics that are not in the notes. Here, at the peak of his powers, Hotter is as superb as he is in his 1960 account of the Dutchman's monologue, a benchmark reading.

Equally setting standards for others to emulate are his versions of Sachs's monologues, so refined and thoughtful. As in all Hotter's performances, it is the interior meaning conveyed through a deep understanding of the text, allied to warmth and beauty of the voice, that remains so telling; here is the singing-actor *par excellence*.

Dmitri Hvorostovsky *bar*

Songs and Dances of Death

Borodin Prince Igor – No sleep, no rest
Mussorgsky Songs and Dances of Death
Rachmaninov Aleko – Aleko's cavatina
Rimsky-Korsakov Sadko – The paragon of cities; Beautiful city! Kashchey the Immortal – In this, night's darkest hour. Snow Maiden (second version) – Under the warm blue sea. The Tsar's Bride – Still the beauty haunts my mind **Rubinstein** The Demon – Do not weep, my child; On the airy ocean; I am he whom you called. Nero – Vindex's Epithalamium: I sing to you, Hymen divine!
Dmitri Hvorostovsky *bar* **Kirov Theatre Orchestra / Valery Gergiev**
Philips 438 872-2PH (62 minutes: DDD) Ⓕ
Texts and translations included. Recorded 1993

In the scenes from Rubinstein's *The Demon* Hvorostovsky, superbly supported by Valery Gergiev and his Kirov orchestra recorded in their own theatre, has done nothing better than his impersonation of the devil; in the the third extract he projects the gloating demon to the life. This is splendid stuff. So is Vindex's rollicking Epithalamium from the same composer's *Nero*, sung with wonderful breadth and confidence. Then he changes character again to bring before us the emotional torment of Rachmaninov's Aleko as he recalls the love Zemfira once had for him. The best of the Rimsky items as regards music and interpretation are Nizgir's aria from the *Snow Maiden* and Gryaznoy's musing on past triumphs in the field of love from *The Tsar's Bride*. Here Hvorostovsky varies his tone more successfully than in the other Rimsky items. Mussorgsky's *Songs and Dances of Death* need an imposing bass rather than a lyric baritone to make their true mark, yet these are more than acceptable performances, helped by the excellent recording. This is a fascinating disc.

Kalinka

Kalinka. Barinya. Ah! Do you hear, my dearest friend? On the Little Mountain. Round Dance. Why have you misted over, clear sunset? I met you. The Little Willow. How was I, a tender young maiden? Rhyming Song. Ah, you field. As never the white birch tree. The noise of the town cannot be heard. In the dark forest. Already the fog has descended. Ah, shady spot. Birch-broom. I set off alone down the road
Dmitri Hvorostovsky *bar* **St Petersburg Chamber Choir / Nikolai Korniev**
Philips 456 399-2PH (57 minutes: DDD) Ⓕ
Texts and translations included. Recorded 1996

These Russian folk-songs are all arrangements, by different hands, some hands as distinguished as those of Rimsky-Korsakov and Shostakovich. Mostly they are for solo voice with a chorus sometimes participating in the narrative or verbal sketch, sometimes humming, sometimes bearing the burden of the song. There is not, however, much attempt to imitate a folk manner. The arrangements are sometimes light and barely intervene, as with Shostakovich's, especially in some of the rapidly pattering numbers. Others are slow and suffused with melancholy, richly harmonised in a manner that would surprise any peasant but can, at best, make a beautiful new composition altogether. Among them is Paul Reade's version of *Ivushka*, or *The Little Willow*, sung with soaring intensity by Hvorostovsky over warmly shifting harmonies from the chorus. Some arrangements are quite elaborate, not always as effectively as this. It is a striking collection, with most of the songs rather closer to original composition than to what we normally think of as arrangement. The recording does justice not only to Hvorostovsky but to the choir's nimble sopranos and to basses who can move around the area below the bass stave without effort. An unusual, enjoyable anthology.

Maria Ivogün *sop*

Opera Arias and Songs Ⓗ

Anonymous O du liebs Angeli[a]. Z'Lauterbach han i'mein Strumpf verlor'n[a]. Gsätzli. Maria auf dem Berge[a] **Bishop** Lo, here the gentle lark[b]
Chopin Nocturne in E flat, Op 9 No 2[b] (arr *sop/orch*)
Handel L'allegro, il penseroso ed il moderato, HWV55 – Sweet bird[b] (recorded 1925) **Donizetti** Don Pasquale – Ah! un foco insolito[b] (rec 1924). Lucia di Lammermoor – Ardon gl'incensi[b] (rec 1917)
Kreisler Liebesfreud[b] **Meyerbeer** Les Huguenots – Une dame noble et sage[b] (German) **Nicolai** Die lustigen Weiber von Windsor – Nun eilt herbei[b] (all rec 1917) **Rossini** Il barbiere di Siviglia – Una voce poco fa[b] (rec 1925) **Schubert** Ständchen (Horch! Horch! die Lerch), D899[b]. Winterreise, D911 – Die Post[b] **J Strauss II** Frühlingsstimmen, Op 410[b] (rec 1924). G'schichten aus dem Wienerwald, Op 325[b]. An die schönen, blauen Donau, Op 314[c]. Die Fledermaus – Klänge der Heimat[c] **Verdi** La traviata – E strano ... Ah, fors'è lui ... Sempre libera[b] (sung in German, rec 1916)
Maria Ivogün *sop* [a]**Michael Raucheisen** *pf* [b]**orchestra;** [c]**Berlin State Opera Orchestra / Leo Blech**
Nimbus Prima Voce NI7832 (78 minutes: ADD) Ⓢ
Recorded 1916-32

Somewhere or other, after much searching of the memory, ransacking of the catalogues and phoning around among connoisseurs, it might be possible to discover a more delightful example of the coloratura's art than that of Maria Ivogün as displayed in her recording of Kreisler's *Liebesfreud*, made in 1924: if so, one such does not spring to mind now. With the most pure and delicate of tones, nothing shrill or piercing about them, she sings way above a normal mortal's reach, ease and accuracy in the purely technical feats going along with a lilt and feeling for the idiomatic give-and-take of waltz rhythm that are a joy musically. Turn to Handel, with the solo from *Il penseroso*, and the same art is put to lovely use in a different idiom. Her *Traviata* aria has warmth and spontaneity; her Frau Fluth in *Die lustigen Weiber von Windsor* is a woman of charm and energy; and the 1934 recording of the Czardas in *Die Fledermaus* shines as bright in spirit as in clarity of timbre. From the same period comes the set of four songs, Swiss and German, that show most touchingly her command of the art to be simple. This is an admirable introduction to a most lovely singer, and it represents the Prima Voce series at its best.

Sumi Jo *sop*

Prayers

Anonymous Sometimes I feel like a motherless child[a] **Bernstein** Take care of this house[b] **Caccini** Ave Maria (arr Mercurio) **Donizetti** Maria Stuarda – Deh! Tu di un umile preghiera[c] **Fauré** Requiem, Op 48 – Pie Jesu **Gounod** Messe solennelle de Sainte Cécile – Sanctus[c] **Loewe** Gigi – Say a Prayer for Me Tonight **Mozart** Laudate Dominum, K339[c] **Preisner** Requiem For My Friend – Lacrimosa[c] **Ravel** Kaddisch **Rossini** L'assedio di Corinto – L'ora fatal s'appressa...Giusto ciel![c] **Schubert** Der vierjährige Posten, D190 – Gott! Höre meine Stimme **J Strauss II** Casanova[c] – Nuns' Chorus; Laura's Song **R Strauss** Breit' über mein Haupt dein schwarzes Haar, Op 19 No 2[a] **Traditional** Amazing Grace

Sumi Jo *sop* [b]**Susan Graham** *mez* [c]**Cologne Philharmonic Choir; Gürzenich-Köln Orchester / James Conlon** [a]*pf*

Erato 8573 85772-2 (57 minutes: DDD) Ⓕ

Recorded 2000

The 'Prayers' theme is little more than a peg on which to hang this latest solo disc by favourite Korean soprano Sumi Jo. The 15 tracks range far and wide, embracing everything from the baroque era to the Broadway musical, taking in opera, oratorio, Singspiel, Lieder and even a spiritual along the way. Some passing amusement can be had from the essay in the booklet, which turns intellectual somersaults trying to persuade us that all these pieces are really prayers – even Richard Strauss's worldly love-song *Breit' über mein Haupt*.

None of this is likely to trouble the singer's admirers, who are the target audience. If anything, the far-flung musical styles play to Sumi Jo's advantage as they serve to disguise any lack of variety in the singing itself, sometimes a criticism of this soprano in the past. Here there is much to enjoy, as a beautiful voice goes hand in hand with mostly well-judged accompaniments from the Gürzenich-Köln Orchestra under James Conlon and a first-rate recording. Ravel's *Kaddisch*, performed in the orchestral version, comes across with haunting sensuality. The aria from Rossini's *L'assedio di Corinto* is an imaginative choice, expressively sung. There is no sentimental lingering over the 'Pie Jesu' from Fauré's Requiem, and any suspicion that the disc might lapse into soporific 'singing monks' mode is held at bay by the inclusion of lively tracks such as the Mozart *Laudate Dominum* and the extract from Schubert's *Der vierjahrige Posten*. It is probably inevitable that a selection of this sort will field a couple of dubious items – the sugary arrangement of Caccini's *Ave Maria* by Steven Mercurio will set some teeth on edge, and *Amazing Grace* feels as if it has washed up on the wrong continent – but the majority of these 'prayers' take wing. It is, on balance, an attractive collection.

La Promessa

Bellini Malinconia, ninfa gentile. Per pietà, bell'idol mio **Benedict** La capinera **Caldara** Alma del core **Cesti** Intorno all'idol mio **Donaudy** O del mio amato ben. Vaghissima sembianza **G Giordani** Caro mio ben **Gluck** Paride ed Elena – O del mio dolce ardor **Handel** Rinaldo – Lascia ch'io pianga. Giulio Cesare – V'adoro, pupille **Mozart** Ridente la calma, K152/K210*a* **Paisiello** L'amor contrastato – Nel cor più non mi sento **Rosa** Star vicino **Rossini** Soirées musicales – La promessa **Sarti** Giulio Sabino – Lungi dal caro ben (arr Parenti) **A Scarlatti** Se Florindo è fedele **D Scarlatti** Qual farfalletta amante **Tosti** Non t'amo più! **Verdi** Ad una stella

Sumi Jo *sop* **Vincenzo Scalera** *pf*

Erato 3984-23300-2 (68 minutes: DDD) Ⓕ

Texts and translations included. Recorded 1997

Here is one of the most delightful singers of our time heard in a programme that extends her repertoire on record and, being apt and congenial in itself, brings a double refreshment. There is a delicious coolness about the Korean soprano's singing: an 18th-century elegance. And not the slightest coldness about it; simply a humanity and a civilisation where the heart is not worn on the sleeve. Interestingly, this is so even in the songs which often excite a more overtly passionate style of performance, Tosti's *Non t'amo più!* and the two by Stefano Donaudy. Similarly, such light-hearted 19th-century pieces as Rossini's 'La promessa' and Benedict's *La capinera* carry their gaiety with poise and refinement.

It is partly that they benefit from the company of Handel and Mozart, partly that the clear voice and graceful style bring out the classicism in which their composers were educated rather than the thicker romanticism to which their age was tending. Voice and style here are as one, and the opening *Caro mio ben* is a fine example of both. The tone remains unequivocally that of a high lyric soprano but now with a mature and reassuring warmth in the lower notes. The phrases are beautifully sustained and are shaded with respect for the unity of line. The quickening pace of the middle section is well judged, as is the modestly decorated 'tanto rigor' leading back to the principal melody. Sumi Jo is responsive to the urgency of Bellini's *Malinconia* and the lightness of Domenico Scarlatti's *Farfalletta*. Vincenzo Scalera accompanies tastefully, and recorded sound is fine.

Sumi Jo at Carnegie Hall

Adam Le toréador – Ah, vous dirai-je, maman **Bellini** I Puritani – Son vergin vezzosa; Qui la voce ... Vien, diletto **Benedict** The Gipsy and the Bird **Bernstein** Candide – Glitter and be gay **Bishop** Lo, here the gentle lark **Cho** Seonguja **Herbert** Naughty Marietta – Italian Street Song **Hong** Springtime of home **Kim** I shall live in the Blue Mountains **Mozart** Vorre spiegarvi, oh Dio, K418 **Offenbach** Les contes d'Hoffmann – Les oiseaux dans la charmille **J Strauss II** Die Fledermaus – Mein Herr Marquis (arr Rauber)

Sumi Jo *sop* **Orchestra of St Luke's / Richard Bonynge**

Erato 3984-21630-2 (64 minutes: DDD) Ⓕ
Recorded live in 1996

This sounds like a good night out at Carnegie Hall, and not one whose memory is spoilt when heard again, transferred to disc. Apart from a little wear on the upper register at a *forte*, the voice remains pure, firm and lovely, its tone rather fuller than when we first knew it, the technique secure, its accomplishments impressively displayed. Expressiveness is perhaps not a prime requisite here, and indeed one might wish for a programme that did require a little more than a pretty smile shaded off now and again into a pretty pathos; but all goes well and the audience's evident enthusiasm is well justified. The only item which doesn't really succeed is Adam's variations on the nursery tune, *Ah, vous dirai-je, maman*, usually thought of simply as a display piece. The air is a wistful little thing, sung by a girl feeling the first torments of love and finding consolation in the tender, softly rocking melody of a song. That feeling is absent in Sumi Jo's technically admirable performance. Happily, in the very next item, 'Qui la voce' from *I Puritani*, Sumi Jo's singing has just the right degree of emotion for a concert performance, with Bonynge and his players responding sensitively to the quickening of pulse and its sad relaxation. This and the Polonaise, sung later in the programme, find the singer at her delightful best, as does the Mozart with which the recital so enchantingly opens. The three songs said to be of Korean origin sound thoroughly western, and application to the booklet-notes gains no further enlightenment. Still, this is not the kind of occasion for queries and complaints. Here is a delectable singer amidst an appreciative public, and we are fortunate to have the opportunity of sharing their enjoyment.

Virtuoso Arias

Bellini La sonnambula – Ah! non credea mirarti ... Ah! non giunge[a] **Bernstein** Candide – Glitter and be gay[a] **Delibes** Lakmé – Où va la jeune indoue ... Là-bas dans la forêt plus sombre[a] **Donizetti** Lucia di Lammermoor – Mad scene[a] **Meyerbeer** Dinorah – Ombre légère[a] **Mozart** Die Zauberflöte – Der Hölle Rache[b] **Rossini** Il barbiere di Siviglia – Una voce poco fa ... Io son docile[a] **R Strauss** Ariadne auf Naxos – Noch glaub' ich dem einen ganz ... So war es mit Pagliazzo ... Als ein Gott kam jeder gegangen[a] **Verdi** Rigoletto – Gualtier Maldè ... Caro nome[a] **Yoon** (arr. Constant) Barley Field[a]

Sumi Jo *sop*
[a]**Monte-Carlo Philharmonic Orchestra / Paolo Olmi;** [b]**Paris Orchestral Ensemble / Armin Jordan**

Erato 4509-97239-2 (74 minutes: DDD) Ⓕ
Texts included. Recorded 1994

Many listeners, well disposed towards most kinds of vocal recital, still tend to approach a new 'coloratura' programme with misgivings – all of which would seem to be obviated here. The emotional range of the music goes well beyond mere prettiness, whether of girlish glee or wilting pathos. The florid passages (commonly tagged 'display') are assumed by the singer to have an expressive purpose, which she then seeks out and fulfils. Her tone is bright but not piercing, her style clean but not cold; she understands perfectly well that, though these arias are famous for their high notes, far more of the singer's time is spent in the middle register, where a scrawny or breathy tone and flawed *legato* will not be excused on account of a few brilliances *in alt*. Intelligence is clearly at work from the start, in the enunciation of the words. 'Una voce poco fa qui nel cuor mi risuono': the 'qui' ('here') is the 'gesture-word', the one that makes it actual and individual. 'La vincerò' is determined, but not doubly-underlined or given that arch, over-confident touch which may gain a point but, in doing so, forfeits likeableness. In *La sonnambula* sympathy is actually *strengthened* by the cleaning-up of all those downward portamentos that have threatened to become inseparable from the music since Callas and Sutherland introduced them. Similarly, the Mad scene from *Lucia di Lammermoor* is enacted as a genuinely dramatic piece but with a fresh realisation, rather than from a mind loaded with memories of those illustrious predecessors. The only way in which Jo appears at a disadvantage is in the relative hardness of some high notes. Zerbinetta's aria, for instance, is a shade uncomfortable (clearly written with more of the German *Kopfstimme* in mind), while the Korean song, *Barley Field*, is entirely lovely in sound and does not rise above an A flat.

Yvonne Kenny *sop*

Great Operatic Arias, Volume 5

Bizet The Pearl Fishers – I'm all alone here...As once before; Leïla! Leïla!...Your heart was never tuned to mine[b] **Boughton** The Immortal Hour – How beautiful they are **Catalani** La Wally – I'll float into the distance **Donizetti** Linda di Chamounix – Linda! Linda![b] **Handel** Joshua – O had I Jubal's lyre. Rinaldo – Hear thou my weeping **Mozart** Idomeneo – Gentle zephyrs, soft caressing. Nehmt meinen Dank, ihr holden Gönner, K383 **Porter** Kiss Me, Kate – So in love am I **Puccini** Gianni Schicchi – Oh, my beloved father **Purcell** The Indian Queen – I attempt from love's sickness. King Arthur – Fairest isle **Rossini** Semiramide – Dark day of dread![a]. William Tell – Dark, sombre wood **Stravinsky** The Rake's Progress – Gently, little boat[c] **Sullivan** The Mikado – The sun, whose rays **Zeller** The Bird

Catcher' – When you're sent roses in this land
Yvonne Kenny *sop* [a]**Della Jones** *mez* [b]**Barry Banks** *ten* [c]**Geoffrey Mitchell Choir; Philharmonia Orchestra / David Parry**
Chandos Opera in English Series CHAN3035 (76 minutes: DDD). Texts included Ⓕ ●●

Lovely, lovely record, and that wretched, inevitable little word 'but' had better be admitted immediately and sent on its way. The 'but' concerns tone-quality when, at a certain volume and a certain height, a bright, metallic tinkle of wear or overtones obtrudes and momentarily compromises the purity of sound. It has long been a feature of Kenny's voice and makes only intermittent appearance here (in the *Pearl Fishers* duet, for example), but it has to be mentioned. That aside, delight is more or less continuous from start to finish.

Taking a look at the programme, one might at first think its order haphazard and likely to be too fragmentary and inconsequential: not so in practice. The disc opens with Lauretta's plea to her daddy ('daddy' surely, not 'father') and is quite happily followed by Ilia's invocation to the breezes, then back to Purcell and on to Handel and Donizetti and so forth. The jumps are not ones to break a leg over though. Perhaps this is because everything here, from Purcell to Cole Porter, is treated in a spirit of thinking the best – and finding it. All concerned seem united in this – the singer, the players and their admirable conductor. When a refined musical spirit is brought to it, the music responds. Handel's 'Jubal's lyre' responds as we no doubt expected it to, but when Rossini's 'Dark day of dread!' follows, instead of the heavyweight posturing suggested by the title, we find a blissfully scored duet, an idyll of love-birds in thirds with orchestral *pizzicatos*; and when this is followed by the famous solo from *La Wally*, that too is heard as an utterance almost refined in its passion, the song of a heartbroken girl rather than an aria for the spotlighted diva.

Delightful throughout is the cleanness of style: intervals, intonation, phrasing, the handling of words. Perhaps the characters need more differentiation, but then again perhaps not (this is not Mimì turning into Tosca, or Violetta into one of the Leonoras). As for the oddities – *The Mikado, Kiss me Kate* and so on – they all earn their welcome. And the odd notion of ending a lyric-soprano recital with what is properly a tenor solo (the Faery song from *The Immortal Hour*) proves to make for an inspired and magical coda.

Alfredo Kraus *ten*

Alfredo Kraus con el Corazón
Bonfa/Maria Canción de Orfeo[b] **Chapí** El milagro de la Virgen – Flores purísimas[a] **Chaplin** Eternally[a] **Fain** Love is a many splendored thing[a] **Guerrero** El huésped del sevillano – Mujer de los ojos negros[b] **Guridi** El caserío – Yo no sé que veo en Ana María[a]. La meiga – Yo te vi pasar[b] **Jiménez** Corazón, corazón[c] **Kosma** Les feuilles mortes[b] **Lara** Noche de Ronda[a] **Luna** La pícara molinera – Paxarín, tu que vuelas[a] **Maggio/Ferilli** Un amore così grande[a] **Monnot** Hymne à l'amour[a] **Esparza Oteo** Rondalla[c] **Porter** You do something to me[a] **Ramírez** Alfonsina y el mar[a] **Serrano** La dolorosa – La roca fría del Calvario[a]. Los claveles – Mujeres[a]. La alegría del batallón – Al mismo rey del moro[b]. Alma de Dios – Canción del vagabundo[b] **Sorozábal** La tabernera del puerto – No puede ser[b] **Pérez Soriano** El guitarrico – Jota[a] **Soutullo/Vert** El último romántico – Bella enamorada[b] **Moreno Torroba** Luisa Fernanda – De este apacible rincón de Madrid[b] **Trenet/Lasry** La mer[b] **Vives** Doña Francisquita – Por el humo se sabe[a]
Alfredo Kraus *ten* [a]**Tenerife Symphony Orchestra / Víctor Pablo Pérez;** [b]**Gran Canaria Philharmonic Orchestra / Carlos Riazuelo;** [c]**Madrid Complutense University Orchestra / Santiago López**
RCA Victor ② 74321 72246-2 (101 minutes: DDD) Ⓕ
Song arrangements by Peter Hope and Joan Albert Amargós ●

Released originally in Spain in 1991, these two CDs are reissued now as a tribute to the treasured tenor who died in 1999. Each CD derives from a separate concert – one in Tenerife, the other in Kraus's native Las Palmas. Both begin with five popular songs of varying nationalities, sung in their original language but with varying degrees of success: witness Charles Chaplin's *Eternally* or Sammy Fain's *Love is a many splendored thing are a required taste*, both pushed to the top of the voice and with overblown orchestral accompaniments. On the other hand, Charles Trenet's *La mer*, sung in more tender fashion, fares rather better.

The real glory of the two CDs lies in the seven zarzuela numbers that each contains. Some have been recorded by Kraus on previous occasions, but others (such as the two Guridi numbers and the Chapí rarity) probably have not. Either way, no tenor has ever created the frisson that Kraus does in this glorious music. Has anyone, for instance, shaped and caressed the phrases of 'Mujeres' from *Los claveles* as lovingly and sweetly as he does? Has anybody made the romance from *El caserío* such a tender realisation of affection for a woman who has too often been taken for granted? And, among the many performances of the aria from *Doña Francisquita*, has anyone balanced the passion, reflection and finely shaped line as he does?

The second CD ends with a further two songs performed to the accompaniment of an orchestra of mandolins, lutes and guitars. They make a glorious noise, and Kraus sounds thoroughly at home. But the zarzuela numbers are the real glory of this invaluable souvenir of a wonderful singer.

Erich Kunz *bar*

Opera Arias Ⓗ
Don Giovanni, Der lustige Krieg, Eine Nacht in Venedig, Le nozze di Figaro, Der Vogelhändler, Der Waffenschmied, Der Wildschütz, Zar und Zimmermann, Die Zauberflöte and Der Zigeunerbaron; Viennese songs by various composers
Erich Kunz *bar* with various artists
Testament mono SBT1059 (79 minutes: ADD) Ⓕ
Recorded 1947-53

Here is Kunz in his absolute prime, moving his agreeable voice around Figaro's, Leporello's and Papageno's music with the confidence derived from experience in the roles in Vienna, but without the slightest sense of routine. It should not be forgotten that he was one of the first German-speaking singers to learn his Da Ponte roles in Italian: his diction and accent in them, as we find here, are virtually perfect. Under Karajan, in Figaro's 'Non più andrai' he is disciplined by a fast tempo, while Ackermann is more yielding in Leporello's 'Madamina'. Karajan also conducts the Giovanni/Zerlina duet (with the incomparable Seefried). It is a wonderful souvenir of two artists, their voices blending ideally, who sang so often together in that notable ensemble in Vienna. Kunz was also loved in his home city for his assumption of *buffo* parts in Lortzing's operas, and he brings to their arias, again with Ackermann in sympathetic support, a rich vein of comic characterization without ever resorting to caricature – Kunz was, above all, a sensitive musician. The second half of this issue is devoted to operetta items and Viennese songs. In the former it may be complained that he was often adopting, and transposing down, music written originally for a tenor: four songs from *Ein Nacht in Venedig*, in the Korngold rescension, rather suffer in that respect, yet Kunz's wholly idiomatic approach almost makes us forget the anomaly. In what are mostly Heurigen songs, he is absolutely in his element; only his older, tenor colleague, Julius Patzak was his peer in these. The accompanying Schrammel Ensemble are wholly authentic. Try, if you can, *Da draussen in der Wachau*, so beguiling in tone and style, and you will not be able to resist the rest.

Vesselina Kasarova *mez*

A Portrait

Handel Rinaldo – Or la tromba in suon festante **Gluck** Orfeo ed Euridice – Che farò senza Euridice? **Mozart** Le nozze di Figaro – Voi che sapete. Don Giovanni – Batti, batti, o bel Masetto **Rossini** La Cenerentola – Nacqui all'affano[abdeg]. Il barbiere di Siviglia – Una voce poco fa. L'Italiana in Algeri – Pronti abbiamo e ferri e mani ... Amici in ogni evento ... Pensa alla patria[g] **Donizetti** Anna Bolena – Sposa a Percy ... Per questa fiamma indomita ... Ah! pensate che rivolti[cfg]. La favorita – Fia dunque vero ... O mio Fernando! **Bellini** I Capuleti e i Montecchi – Se Romeo t'uccise un figlio ... La tremenda ultrice spada[cfg]

Vesselina Kasarova *mez* [a]**Isolde Mitternacht-Geissendörfer** *sop* [b]**Barbara Müller** *contr* [c]**Andreas Schulist,** [d]**Dankwart Siegele** *ten* [e]**Tim Hennis** *bass* [f]**Leonid Savitzky** *bass* [g]**Bavarian Radio Chorus; Munich Radio Orchestra / Friedrich Haider**

RCA Red Seal 09026 68522-2 (64 minutes: DDD) Ⓕ

Texts and translations included. Recorded 1996

This is the stuff of legends: it is difficult to imagine a début opera recital that could give so much pleasure. The vibrant richness of Kasarova's tone allied to her totally uninhibited manner before the microphone allows her to bring to astonishing life each of the characters portrayed within. She begins as she continues, with tremendous panache as Rinaldo invokes trumpets to great deeds, and Kasarova proves the warrior-lover to the life, Handel's complex coloratura used as an engine to express youthful fire. Then immediately she becomes the tender, lamenting Orpheus, real grieving in the plush, well-controlled tone. The two Mozart pieces disclose different timbres in the voice – bright and palpitating as befits Cherubino, soft-grained and sensuous as suits Zerlina. Kasarova is a fabulous Rossinian. In the three pieces here she combines vitality, verbal acuity and dispatch of *fioriture*. It's wonderful how she starts in mild, forgiving manner, caressing the start of 'Non più mesta', then lets fly in viscerally exciting manner for the roulades.

Even the well-trodden path of 'Una voce' sounds newly-minted as you seem to hear Rosina's varied thoughts passing through her mind, the text freshly inflected. As Isabella inspires her followers in 'Pensa alla patria', one notes the subtle accents on 'il tenero amor' and 'Caro, ti parli in petto', evincing all Isabella's inner feelings for her beloved Lindoro. Then it's off on another invigorating display at 'Fra pochi istanti'. From here Kasarova moves on to so-called *bel canto* territory. With 'O mio Fernando!' it's again the judgement of tonal colour, here sensual, heartstopping, while Jane Seymour's resistance to Henry VIII (weakly impersonated here) shows yet another 'face', dignified and noble. But in both Leonora's and Romeo's cabaletta, 'La tremenda ultrice spada', a little less might mean so much more: there is too much emphasis, too many breaths. But that is part of the style of a singer who is making no concessions to the studio, rather living out every moment of the given dramas, admirably supported by Haider and his orchestra.

Solveig Kringelborn *sop*

Black Roses

Grieg Six Songs, Op 25 **Nielsen** Six Songs, FS18 **Rangström** The Girl under the New Moon. Pan. The Only Moment. Melody. Prayer to the Night. Villemo **Sibelius** Six Songs, Op 36

Solveig Kringelborn *sop* **Malcolm Martineau** *pf*

Virgin Classics VC5 45273-2 (55 minutes: DDD) Ⓕ

Texts and translations included. Recorded 1996

The Grieg and Sibelius sets are decently represented on CD, particularly the obvious songs like 'A Swan' and 'Black Roses', after which the whole disc is named. All the Rangström songs have been recorded at one time or another, though not all are currently available, and two of the six Nielsen, FS18 set are not easily come by. But any addition to the *romans* repertoire (the *romans*, incidentally, is the Scandinavian equivalent of the German Lied or the French *mélodie*) is welcome, and one with as much charm as this, doubly so. Kringelborn opens with the Rangström group – and with the haunting

Runeberg setting, 'The Only Moment' – and characterises all of them with real sensitivity. On home territory and Grieg, Kringelborn is very persuasive though the Sibelius set is not uniformly successful. She could have made more of the ending of 'But my bird is long in homing'. 'Black Roses' comes off very well indeed. So, for the most part, do the Nielsen songs, except 'Lake of memory', where Kringelborn sounds a shade tentative – and slightly under the note. Summing up, if there are any reservations, it is that Kringelborn tends to set greater store by a smooth *legato* and beauty of sound than dramatic character. Mind you, she has beauty of sound to set store by, and a pleasing vocal personality, and there is so much that gives delight. Malcolm Martineau's accompanying throughout is admirable. He is wonderfully supportive and responsive to every change of mood, and the recording is absolutely first-class.

Sergei Larin ten

Russian Arias, Volume 1

Borodin Prince Igor – Daylight is fading
Rachmaninov Boris Godunov – One last story
Rimsky-Korsakov May Night – Hey there! Boys!; How calm, how cool it is here. Sadko – Song of the Indian guest **Dargomïzhsky** Rusalka – Some unknown power **Glinka** Ruslan and Lyudmila – There is a desert country **Tchaikovsky** Eugene Onegin – I love you, Olga; Monsieur Triquet, favour us with a couplet[a]; Faint echo of my youth. Mazeppa – In bloody battle, on the field of honour ... Here days passed by in happy succession. Cherevichki – Does your heart, maiden, not hear. The Queen of Spades – I do not know her name; Forgive me, loveliest of creatures; What is our life? A game!
Sergei Larin *ten* [a]**Ambrosian Opera Chorus; Philharmonia Orchestra / Gennadi Rozhdestvensky**
Chandos CHAN9603. (75 minutes: DDD) Ⓕ
Texts and translations included

Since he has started making recital discs with Chandos, Sergei Larin has come into focus as a recording artist much more clearly than when his name tended to get lost among many others in the cast-list of Russian operas. His art has certainly deepened now, with more fully expressive delineation of phrases and, perhaps with Rozhdestvensky to help, a more complete responsiveness to mood and structure. But perhaps he has outgrown Lensky, the impetuous, ill-fated young poet in *Eugene Onegin*. The love-song in Act 1 hasn't the youthful ardour and impulse, and the great aria of the Duel scene is a fine piece of singing rather than the elegiac and then impassioned utterance of doomed youth. Larin now is much closer (vocally) to Hermann in *The Queen of Spades* than to Lensky, and the fire burns bright in Hermann's 'What is our life?'. The programme is full of plums: there's the Hindu Guest with his famous song, Vladimir of *Prince Igor* with that lovely nocturnal invocation, and Levko with his lullaby in *May Night*. Less expected presences are Monsieur Triquet from *Eugene Onegin* and Pimen, the old monk in *Boris Godunov*. At first one thinks that that must be a crazy misprint; but no, it is a setting by Rachmaninov, an imaginatively orchestrated piece of student-work. The orchestra here make a notable contribution to the recital's success, and it is a further sign of grace that the chorus are brought in for the Cossacks' 'Go get the Mayor' spree in *May Night*.

Jennifer Larmore mez

My Native Land

Aborn 'Tis Winter now. Shall I compare thee to a Summer's day. Make me an instrument of Thy peace **Abramson** Soldier, Soldier **Barber** Bessie Bobtail, Op 2 No 3. Songs, Op 10 – No 1, Rain has fallen; No 2, Sleep now; No 3, I hear an army. Sure on this shining night, Op 13 No 3 **Copland** Old American Songs, Set 2 – The little horses; Zion's walls; At the river; Ching-a-ring **J Duke** In the fields. 20th century. Heart! We will forget him! **Heggie** He's gone away. The leather-winged bat. Barb'ry Allen. To say before going to sleep. White in the moon **Hoiby** Winter Song. A letter **Hundley** The astronomers **Ives** My native land. The things our fathers loved. Memories **Naginski** Richard Cory **Niles** Black is the color of my true love's hair. Fee Simple
Jennifer Larmore *mez* **Antoine Palloc** *pf*
Teldec 0630-16069-2 (75 minutes: DDD) Ⓕ
Selected texts included. Recorded 1996

Jennifer Larmore has chosen this programme with care: it feels like a personal choice, sung with personal concern. Whether it's recast traditional, homegrown original or something altogether loftier, she seems to know where it's coming from. American song is nothing if not outspoken and this is a full, ripe, outspoken voice. *Black is the color of my true love's hair* gives you the measure of it – a handsome song, handsomely recast, the low-lying phrases of its glorious melody just as dark as dark can be. Occasionally the characterisation slips into the Bryn Terfel school of the overstated. But then again you wouldn't want to be without the broadness of her Southern Belle in Robert Abramson's setting of *Soldier, Soldier*. For the rest, the unfamilar are among the richest pickings. The directness of Jake Heggie's setting of the traditional text *He's gone away* is at once disarming. It's impossible to date and yet there is something longstanding and venerable about it. Four other Heggie songs are offered, and in each case it's amazing how he assumes the identity of his texts. Lee Hoiby's work is most appealing, not least his impassioned Wilfred Owen setting, *Winter Song*, and Emily Dickinson's *A letter*, which is as shy, sly and wry as its deliciously knowing text. But ultimately, there is Samuel Barber. His two James Joyce settings, *I hear an army* and *Rain has fallen*, are stunning, the former vivid, vehement, the latter defined by an inconsolable and very particular melancholy, culminating in a furious piano cadenza that says more about frustration and despair than even Joyce's text. Antoine Palloc plays it here with an awareness and strength of purpose that mark out his contributions throughout the disc. And, of course, there is *Sure on this shining night* – as fine a song about wonder and the infinite as any. James Agee's text is one of nine reproduced in the beautifully illustrated booklet. It is a pity all the texts have not been included. Good as Larmore's diction is, they are needed.

Lotte Lehmann *sop*

Songs – **Balogh**, **Beethoven**, **Brahms**, **Cimara**, **Franz**, **Gounod**, **Grechaninov**, **Hahn**, **Jensen**, **Marx**, **Mozart**, **Pfitzner**, **Sadero**, **Schubert**, **Schumann**, **Sjöberg**, **Wolf** and **Worth** Ⓗ
Lotte Lehmann *sop* with various artists
Romophone mono ② 81013-2 Ⓕ
(157 minutes: ADD). Recorded 1935-40

Lotte Lehmann was at the height of her powers as a song interpreter in the late 1930s: the bloom of youth is still in the tone, now enhanced by the experience of many years of stage interpretation. Thus, her characters *in extremis* become something of a talisman of suffering women. Her impassioned Gretchen in Schubert's great song is sister to, and inhabits the same world as, Lehmann's Leonore and Sieglinde. The searing intensity of 'Was hör ich alte Laute?' in Schumann's *Alte Laute* goes through you, becomes etched in the mind, just as do certain phrases in her operatic portrayals. Yet while the passions are felt on a large scale throughout these songs, the intimate mould of Lieder singing is never breached. The readings are generous and free, never dull, careful or limited, or by another token overladen with detailed word-painting in the Schwarzkopf manner. Unlike many of her contemporaries Lehmann ranged wide in her choice of repertory. She digs out Jensen's *Lehn' diene Wang' an meine Wange* and makes you believe this little sentimental song is a masterpiece. However, it is for the Schubert (including 12 songs from *Winterreise*, so immediate in effect, no holds barred), Schumann, Brahms and Wolf, that the myriad admirers of this artist will want these two lavishly filled CDs. The transfers are clean and clear, but at times impart a slight glare to Lehmann's tone. This offering is an essential addition to the Lehmann discography.

Dame Felicity Lott *sop*

My Garden

Barab One Perfect Rose **Berners** Red Roses and Red Noses **Chabrier** Lied. Toutes les fleurs
Chausson Le temps des lilas **Fauré** Green, Op 58 No 3. Les roses d'Ispahan, Op 39 No 4
Franck Le mariage des roses **Musto** Triolet. The Rose Family **Schumann** Mein Garten, Op 77 No 2. Jasminenstrauch, Op 27 No 4. Herzeleid, Op 107 No 1. Die Blume der Ergebung, Op 83 No 2. Erstes Grün, Op 35 No 4. Volksliedchen, Op 51 No 2
Stanford From the red rose
Stanley & Allen Cabbages, Cabeans and Carrots
Wolf Mörike Lieder – Er ist's; Im Frühling; Der Gärtner. Eichendorff Lieder – Nachtzauber. Goethe Lieder – Frühling übers Jahr; Anakreons Grab
Haydn Wood Roses of Picardy
Dame Felicity Lott *sop* **Graham Johnson** *pf*
Hyperion CDA66937 (65 minutes: DDD) Ⓕ
Texts and translations included. Recorded 1996

The green-fingered accompanist has cultivated another fine display. Graham Johnson's garden of song is a splendid place for finding not only the usual hardy annuals from Germany, but also rare flowerings of the repertoire from France, England and the United States. The first half of this disc is devoted to Schumann and Wolf in about equal measure. There are some unusual items among the Schumann, such as the opening 'Mein Garten' and Ophelia's 'Herzeleid'; for the Wolf selection, Johnson extends the frontiers of his garden rather drastically, so as to take in the green hill of 'Im Frühling' and the graveyard of 'Anakreons Grab'. No doubt he wanted to include a few major songs, but it is in these that Dame Felicity is most likely to be found wanting. Compared with the best rival performances, neither 'Im Frühling' nor 'Nachtzauber' reveals its hidden depths, though her warm and affectionate singing of 'Anakreons Grab' is on a higher level. The lighter Wolf songs, by contrast, are nicely turned. Once into the French and English half, there is no looking back, not least because the singer is twice as communicative in these languages as she is in German. The opening line of Chausson's *Le temps des lilas* is as idiomatic as one could wish, floating elegantly and sensuously over the long opening sentence and knowing just where to place the crucial change in vocal colour. The English-language group finds her lavishing a sensuality on Stanford's music that would probably have made the composer blush. There are two fine pithy songs by the American John Musto and another sarcastic one by Seymour Barab; then, in another rapid change of costume, she reappears in Eliza Doolittle's rags to end the disc with a delightfully upper-class fake Cockney rendering of *Cabbages, Cabeans and Carrots*. In the best Graham Johnson style, the disc is both instructive and fun at the same time.

Giovanni Martinelli *ten*

Complete Acoustic Recordings, 1912-24 Ⓗ
Arias and Duets – L'Africaine, Aida, Un ballo in maschera, La bohème, Carmen, Cavalleria rusticana, Don Pasquale, Ernani, Eugene Onegin, Faust, La Gioconda, Guillaume Tell, Iris, La Juive, Lucia di Lammermoor, Madama Butterfly, Manon Lescaut, Martha, Pagliacci, Rigoletto, Tosca, La traviata, Il trovatore, Werther and Zazà; songs by **Bizet**, **Castaldo**, **Leoncavallo**, **Mascagni**, **Roxas** and **Tosti**
Giovanni Martinelli *ten* with various artists
Romophone mono ③ 82012-2 (208 minutes: ADD) Ⓕ
Recorded 1912-24

As John Steane points out in his predictably perceptive notes to this reissue of all Martinelli's recordings by the acoustic process, he has always – and still – divides opinion, the believers admiring his distinctive voice and style, his amazing breath control, the disbelievers reviling his (to them) dry and strained tone. His acoustic recordings often serve to confirm the view of the detractors, his voice sounding drier and more nasal than is the case with the electrics, which suddenly reveal, like a picture cleaned, the strength of his tone and the power of its projection. So where titles here were remade after 1925, in every case the later versions to the pre-electrics are preferable, not least the items from *Trovatore*, but there is so much material not later repeated and so important to understanding Martinelli that this is a 'must' for collectors, especially in such faultless transfers.

Many tracks chronicle roles Martinelli essayed during the early part of his long career at the Metropolitan, when Caruso was still alive. The long list of Puccini arias, Edisons of 1912 and Victors of 1913-14, and two versions of 'Cielo e mar' reveal the tenor's peculiar gifts of keenly etched line, long breath and classic definition of the text. Then, among the Verdi items, we gain an intimation of what his Riccardo and Ernani must have been like on stage, the former's Barcarolle a model of Verdian style where the singing is concerned but a shade stiff in expression, the latter's aria evincing the fire and straightforward honesty of Martinelli's Verdi singing. The famous souvenirs of his Don José to Farrar's Carmen, wonderfully vivid on both sides, take us to the heart of a real performance, with the tenor almost too noble in feeling.

Other notable partnerships are remembered in the *Aida* duets with Ponselle (in even finer voice than on the electric remake) and the *Butterfly* love duet with Alda, Martinelli's *legato* ideal in all cases. Arias from *L'Africaine*, *Don Pasquale*, *Lucia di Lammermoor*, *Onegin* and *Zazà* are interesting but not essential Martinelli.

The main reason, however, for acquiring these three CDs is the irreplaceable recordings from *Guillaume Tell* – aria, duet with Journet, trio with de Luca and Mardones (including an unpublished take). Nobody before or since has conveyed Arnold's patriotic fervour with Martinelli's *élan*, or sustained the high-lying phrases with such technical control. And who, Caruso apart, has sung Eleazar's arias (both previously unpublished) with such dignity and feeling? And don't overlook, with de Luca, the gentle avowal of friendship from *Don Carlo*, notable for its unforced entwining of the two voices. No, by the end of three CDs, the disbelievers are surely put to flight.

Opera Arias and Duets H

Giordano Andrea Chenier – Un dì all'azzurro spazio[e]; Come un bel dì di maggio[f]. Fedora[e] – Amor ti vieta; Mia madre, la mia vecchia madre **Mascagni** Cavalleria rusticana[f] – O Lola; Mamma, quel vino è generoso **Leoncavallo** Pagliacci – Recitar!...Vesti la giubba[f]; Per la morte! smettiamo...No, Pagliaccio non sona[d]. Zazà – E un riso gentil[f] **Puccini** La bohème – Che gelida manina[e]. Tosca – E lucevan le stelle[e] **Verdi** Rigoletto – La donna è mobile. Il trovatore – Quale d'armi fragor...Di quella pira[ad]. La forza del destino[b] – Oh, tu che in seno; Invano Alvaro...Le minacciei fieri accenti. Aida – Se quel guerrier io fossi...Celeste Aida[e]; Nume, custode e vindici[c]
Giovanni Martinelli *ten* [a]**Grace Anthony** *sop* [b]**Giuseppe de Luca** *bar* [c]**Ezio Pinza** bass [d]**Metropolitan Opera Chorus and Orchestra / Giulio Setti,** [e]**Josef Pasternack,** [c]**Rosario Bourdon**
Preiser Lebendige Vergangenheit mono 89062 Ⓕ
(68 minutes: AAD). Recorded 1926-27

Here is one of the most fascinating of singers. He can also be one of the most thrilling, his voice having at its best a beauty unlike any other, his art noble in breadth of phrase and concentration of tone. It also has to be said that his records hardly make easy or restful listening, but what at first may even repel soon becomes compulsive, the intensity of expression and individuality of timbre impressing themselves upon the memory with extraordinary vividness. Martinelli's career was centred on the Metropolitan, New York, where he sang first at the height of the Caruso era, inheriting Caruso's more dramatic roles in 1921. This selection makes an unrepresentative start with 'La donna è mobile', but the excerpts from *Il trovatore* and *La forza del destino* have the very essence of the man, masterly in his shaping and shading of recitative, or in the long curves of his melodic line and the tension of his utterance. There are also superb performances of solos from *Andrea Chénier* and *Pagliacci*, the involvement of his 'No, Pagliaccio non son' unequalled before or since. These are recordings from 1926 and 1927, the period in which his vocal and artistic qualities were probably best matched. The transfers are fine apart from the song from Leoncavallo's *Zazà* which plays below pitch.

Karita Mattila *sop*

Arias and Scenes
Janáček Jenůfa – Jenůfa's Prayer **Lehár** Die lustige Witwe – Es lebt eine Vilja, ein Waldmägdelein **Puccini** Manon Lescaut – In quelle trine morbide **R Strauss** Elektra – Ich kann nicht sitzen und ins Dunkel starren **Tchaikovsky** The Queen of Spades – It is close on midnight already; What am I crying for? **Verdi** Simon Boccanegra – Come in quest'ora bruna **Wagner** Lohengrin – Einsam in trüben Tagen; Euch Lüften, die mein Klagen. Die Walküre – Der Männer Sippe; Du bist der Lenz
Karita Mattila *sop* **London Philharmonic Orchestra / Yutaka Sado**
Erato 8573 85785-2 (56 minutes: DDD) Ⓕ
Texts and translations included

We are surely a favoured generation that has three singers – Renée Fleming, Angela Gheorghiu and Karita Mattila (and perhaps more that don't come quite so easily to mind) – who satisfy so pre-eminently the taste for a soprano voice that has these sensuous virtues of richness, smoothness, firmness and purity.

On their own, and number by number, the performances are delightful. A lovelier voice one could not wish for, and it suits all of these operatic characters in turn, for all, whatever the nationality and present mood, presuppose a lyric soprano with powers of generous expansion, a warmth of tone in the essential middle register, and resources on high that can match the excitements of an emotional climax with a voice rich in its reserves of range and volume. Mattila has all of that, and the mastery to turn from Russian to Italian, German to Czech, Puccini to Janáček, Wagner to Lehár. She phrases well (hear the start of 'In quelle trine morbide'), commands a mature tone and manner (try Sieglinde's narrative) and is scrupulous over matters of detail (getting the climax of Lisa's 'midnight' aria right, for instance, where many don't).

If that is enough – and it is certainly a great deal – then this recital (well recorded and with admirable orchestral work) will give unspoilt pleasure. If something additional is wanting – and those who are accustomed to read between the lines will probably sense that there is – it is at least not so urgently wanting that its absence should spoil the pleasure of what is present.

John McCormack *ten*

Opera and Operetta Arias H

Il barbiere di Siviglia, Barry of Ballymore, La bohème, Carmen, L'elisir d'amore, Faust, La fille du régiment, La Gioconda, In a Persian garden, Lakmé, Lucia di Lammermoor, Naughty Marietta, Les pêcheurs de perles, Rigoletto and La traviata; songs by **Balfe**, **Barker**, **Blumenthal**, **Cherry**, **Claribel**, **Crouch**, **MacMurrough**, **Marshall**, **Parelli**, **Rossini** and **Traditional**

John McCormack *ten* with various artists

Romophone mono ② 82006-2 (155 minutes: ADD) Ⓕ

Recorded 1910-11

You think, at the start of this journey through the recordings of two years, that here is McCormack at his absolute best, in the first of the *Lucia di Lammermoor* solos; but no, for the second one ('Tu che a Dio spiegasti l'ali'), made two months later, is better still, a perfection of lyrical singing, the music lying ideally within his voice as it was at that time, and with the heart and imagination more evidently involved. A little later comes 'Una furtiva lagrima', where the modulation into D flat major ('m'ama') brings surely some of the most beautiful, most unflawed tenor singing ever recorded. This album, from 1910 and 1911, presents him in finest voice. He was only 25 at the outset: in the first flush of his operatic success and already the partner of Melba and Tetrazzini. His favourite baritone partner was Mario Sammarco, who turns up as a blustery Figaro to his elegant Almaviva, retiring to a more discreet distance behind the recording horn in the duet from *Les pêcheurs de perles* (the deservedly rare version included here along with the more familiar 10 inch). They also join in the *gondolieri*-like harmonies of Rossini's *Li marinari* (splendid high Bs from McCormack) and give each other a run for their money in a full-bodied, exciting account of the duet from *La Gioconda*. McCormack, it is true, had still to develop eloquence as a singer of songs, but his eventual mastery is clearly foretold in the old Irish song, *She is far from the land*, a haunting and heartfelt piece of tender nostalgia. The transfers are excellent.

Lauritz Melchior *ten*

Complete MGM Recordings 1946-7 H

F Andersen I det frie[b] **Bach/Gounod** Ave Maria **Bizet** Agnus Dei[b]; Cantique de Noël **Bond** I Love You Truly **De Curtis** Torna a Surriento **De Koven** O Promise Me **Geehl** For You Alone **Heuberger** The Kiss in Your Eyes **Hildach** Der Lenz **Kern** The Song is You **Lehár** You Are my Heart's Delight **Leoncavallo** Mattinata. Pagliacci[c] – Vesti la giubba; No, Pagliaccio non son **Nevin** The Rosary **Porter** Easy to Love[b] **Puccini** Tosca[c] – Recondita armonia; E lucevan le stelle **Rotter** Spring Came Back to Vienna **Schubert** Who is Silvia?, D891 **J Strauss** II Kaiser, Op 437 **Stravinsky** Summer Moon (arr Klenner) **Traditional** All mein Gedanken[a]; Helan går[b]; Silent Night **Youmans** Without a Song

Lauritz Melchior *ten* [a]**Lou Raderman** *vn* [a]**Albert Sendry** *org* **MGM Studio Orchestra and** [b]**Chorus / Georgie Stoll** [a]*pf*; [c]**Giocomo Spadoni**

Romophone mono ② 82019-2 (78 minutes: ADD) Ⓕ

Recorded 1946-7 ●

In the years just after the war, two of the 20th-century's greatest singers, Pinza and Melchior, moved from the opera house into a world of more popular music. They were castigated for their pains because it was considered they were lowering the standards of their art. Today we take a much more tolerant attitude to these things; indeed it is frequently encouraged, especially by record companies. Melchior's move into films and the like was successful with the general public, and MGM signed him up for a series of recordings, made in 1946-47, when he was 56. They are presented here in their entirety.

The legendary Danish Heldentenor, still at the time singing Wagner at the Metropolitan, tackles a good deal of dross but turns more or less everything into gold by dint of his dignified artistry. A few of the songs are beyond even him to save, but he sings Schubert's *Who is Sylvia?*, Italian songs (in the original), Viennese operetta (in English) and Christmas songs – Bizet's *Cantique de Noël* a particular success – with total conviction. In a Danish children's song (this item comes from a film soundtrack) and a Swedish drinking song, both introduced by his own speech, his disarming honesty of approach is its own justification. The latter is an absolutely delightful and jovial end to the whole project, with a cry of 'Skol' to round it off!

That his voice had lost virtually nothing of its operatic opulence is proved in Cavaradossi's two arias, not wholly idiomatic in style, and Canio's two jealous outbursts, all recorded at the final session on December 26, 1947, by which time he was 57. As Canio, his impassioned utterance is full of the requisite pathos and power, yet avoiding the extravagant effects of some Italian tenors, a fitting end to his distinguished career in the studio recording the heavier tenor repertory. The transfers, by Mark Obert-Thorn, are exemplary.

Miscellaneous

The Reopening of La Scala Concert

Boito Mefistofele[a] – Prologue **Puccini** Manon Lescaut – Intermezzo; Act 3[b] **Rossini** La gazza ladra – Overture. Guillaume Tell – Passo a sei; Wedding Chorus[c]; Soldier's Dance. Mosè in Egitto – Dal tuo stellato soglio[d] **Verdi** Nabucco – Overture; Va pensiero[e]. I vespri siciliani – Overture. Quattro pezzi sacri[f] – Te Deum

[bc]Mafalda Favero, [d]Renata Tebaldi *sops* **[cd]Jolanda Gardino** *mez* **[bcd]Giovanni Malipiero, [b]Giuseppe Nessi** *tens* **[b]Mariano Stabile** *bar* **[b]Carlo Forti, [acd]Tancredi Pasero** *basses* **[abcef]Chorus and Symphony Orchestra of La Scala, Milan / Arturo Toscanini**

Naxos Historical mono ② 8 110821/2 Ⓢ
(108 minutes: AAD). Recorded from a broadcast performance in 1946

The war over, the Milanese set about the immediate rebuilding of the bombed La Scala. By 1946 the work was complete in time for Toscanini to return – by public demand – to his old house to direct the opening concert. This legendary occasion features on CD in tolerable enough sound to enjoy its many virtues. Chief among them are the old maestro's inimitable, indeed unique way of inspiriting singers and orchestra to perform Rossini and Verdi as perhaps never before or since. Nobody else combines the ability to give these composers musical precision and make the music sing as does Toscanini (try the cello melody in the *Vespri* Overture, or, for his exactness of execution, the following *staccato* passage). Those attributes are evident in all the overtures presented here, giving the music that quality of *Italianità* of which Toscanini was an absolute master. Or try the three piercing chords just before the chorus enters in 'Va, pensiero' to judge the conductor's interpretative genius. Then, who (except perhaps Beecham) would be able to invest the dances from *William Tell* with such a light, exuberant touch? And, still on the first CD, there is the utterly heart-warming feeling in the Prayer from *Mosè in Egitto* with the very young Tebaldi glorious on the soprano line and the veteran Pasero intoning, as only an Italian bass can intone, the bass-line.

The Verdi *Te Deum* that opens the second disc displays that special quality found in Italian choral singing, and all the chorus members sing their hearts out for their old master, even when there are some less than steady moments which reveal that the war's exigencies haven't yet quite been overcome. Then we hear something of Toscanini's affection for two of his other operatic loves, Puccini and Boito. The Intermezzo to *Manon Lescaut* is a searing experience, followed by a performance of Act 3 given by three of La Scala's stars of the pre-war and wartime era, plus the inimitable *comprimario* Giuseppe Nessi as the Lamplighter. Favero and Malipiero, with their clear diction and ability to sing off the words with agility, show what Puccini interpretation has lost in authenticity in these days of international homogenised performance. Toscanini is again in his element, while in the Prologue to *Mefistofele* he shows an affinity with this eccentric score. Pasero has a high old time in the title-role. Only the inadequate notes, which keep on repeating the same information in different articles and say nothing whatsoever about the performances, mar a most important issue, surely a must for opera collectors.

Diana Montague *mez*

Great Operatic Arias, Volume 2

Berlioz La damnation de Faust, Op 24 – D'amour l'ardente flamme **Delibes** Lakmé – Viens Mallika; Dôme épais le jasmin ... Sous le dôme épais (Flower duet) **Donizetti** La favorite – Fia dunque vero? ... O mio Fernando **Gluck** Orfeo ed Euridice – Che farò senza Euridice? **Gounod** Faust – Faites-lui mes aveux **Offenbach** La périchole – O mon cher amant, je te jure; Ah! quel dîner je viens de faire!; Tu n'es pas beau, tu n'es pas riche **Rossini** Le comte Ory – A la faveur de cette nuit obscure **Saint-Saëns** Samson et Dalila – Printemps qui commence; Amour! viens aider ma faiblesse!; Mon coeur s'ouvre à ta voix **A Thomas** Mignon – Connais-tu le pays?; Me voici dans son boudoir

Diana Montague *mez* **Mary Plazas** *sop* **Bruce Ford** *ten* **Philharmonia Orchestra / David Parry**

Chandos Opera in English Series CHAN3010 Ⓕ
(76 minutes: DDD). English texts included. Recorded 1997

Montague, our leading interpreter of what the French call the *Falcon* repertory (after a singer of this special character), has been far too little celebrated, at least on disc, so this superbly executed programme of French opera arias, with one exception, sung in the vernacular with impeccable diction and full of dramatic import, must be reckoned the jewel so far in the Chandos Opera in English series. Above all it is Montague's distinctive timbre, sense of the correct style and complete identification with each character in turn that make the recital so thrilling, exciting and pleasing.

An account of Orfeo's 'What is life?' that equals if not surpasses Ferrier's, a Delilah to die for, each of her arias given a different character as required, a Marguerite (Berlioz's) who yearns with the best on disc (Montague's low tones here so eloquent, the climax given all its due before the intense reprise), a Mignon who is suitably mysterious ('Have you heard of the land?' so full of longing for a lost ideal with a marvellous lift at the words 'my home') and a Donizetti Léonore who 'speaks' so tenderly of her love for her Fernando, with a cabaletta, including repeat, to show off the singer's forceful attack, all these emotional states are contained within a line and tone that respect vocal verities.

Montague has often been called upon to take breeches roles on stage so it is good to be reminded of her lighter touch, not only as Siebel and Frédéric, but also as Isolier, a part she sang to critical approval at Glyndebourne in 1997: the trio from *Comte Ory* is graced by Bruce Ford's elegant Ory and Plazas as the Countess Adèle.

Plazas also partners Montague in a nicely flowing account of *that* duet from *Lakmé*. Finally we have Montague the witty comedienne in three deliciously articulated numbers of *Périchole*. Parry and the Philharmonia provide euphonious, Francophile accompaniments and, where needed, as in the Gluck and Berlioz, true passion. The recording keeps a nice balance between voice and orchestra. This is a triumph for Diana Montague.

Claudia Muzio *sop*

Opera Arias H

Aida, Un ballo in maschera, La bohème, Carmen, Cavalleria rusticana, Les contes d'Hoffmann, Ernani, La forza del destino, Gianni Schicchi, La Gioconda, Guillaume Tell, Louise, Madama Butterfly, Madame Sans-Gêne, Manon, Manon Lescaut, Mefistofele, Mignon, Otello, Pagliacci, Il segreto di Susanna, Suor Angelica, Tosca, La traviata, Il trovatore, I vespri siciliani and La Wally; songs by **Braga**, **Burleigh**, **Buzzi-Peccia**, **Delibes**, **Donaudy**, **Giordano**, **Mascheroni**, **Olivieri**, **Roxas** and **Sanderson**
Claudia Muzio *sop* with various artists
Romophone mono ② 81010-2 (140 minutes: ADD) Ⓕ
Recorded 1917-25

Romophone has put us in its debt by issuing the 1917-25 Pathés and adding four unpublished and fascinating Edison titles. Inevitably there is some overlapping with the first set (reviewed below) but it is surprising how many titles were not remade by the soprano. Here we have, on the first disc, an impassioned and nicely shaded 'Suicidio!' in a reading that is amazingly accomplished given that Muzio was just 28 at the time. 'O patria mia' and 'Un bel dì' adumbrate the sheer beauty of the voice of the young *spinto*: strength is there, but also refinement and feeling, although the technical command, as often with this singer, isn't always faultless. Above all, we catch an echo over the years of what Muzio must have been like: deeply affecting, in these roles, confirming contemporary comment.

The songs are irresistible. Buzzi-Peccia's *Baciarmi* is poised sensuously on a skein of gossamer tone. In another song, Burleigh's *Jean*, we can delight in Muzio's excellent and clear English and also in the better sound. Then come the four 'new' Edisons, which include Donaudy's *O del mio amato ben*, later repeated in 1935 for Columbia: the performance is just as plangent. Even more tenderly accented is a little-known and unattributed song, *Torna amore*, and the even more evocative traditional *Mon jardin*.

Opera Arias and Duets H

Adriana Lecouvreur, Andrea Chénier, L'Arlesiana, La bohème, Cavalleria rusticana, Cecilia, La forza del destino, Mefistofele, Norma, Otello, La sonnambula, Tosca, La traviata and Il trovatore; songs by **Buzzi-Peccia**, **Debussy**, **Delibes**, **Donaudy**, **Parisotti**, **Refice** and **Reger**. Also contains part of Tosca, Act 1, recorded live in 1932
Claudia Muzio *sop* with various artists
Romophone mono ② 81015-2 (155 minutes: ADD) Ⓕ
Recorded 1934-35

This set completes Romophone's comprehensive survey of all Muzio's records, masterminded by Ward Marston. Since their first release, Muzio's Columbias of 1934-5 have always been her most accessible discs, but they have never, even on previous CD reissues, sounded so present and clear as here. This most eloquent of divas seems to be in the room with us, and the music in hand is delivered with such sincere passion, such total conviction, that tears are brought to the eyes. Not for a moment can one be anything but enthralled by these readings. Since there is not enough material to fill two CDs, Romophone have added a substantial extract from Act 1 of a 1932 San Francisco *Tosca*, primitively recorded and so far known only to a few Muzio fanatics. However, this is an essential issue for anyone wanting to know about the art of one of the most lovable and vital interpreters.

Opera Arias and Songs H

Adriana Lecouvreur, L'Africaine, L'amico Fritz, Andrea Chénier, Bianca e Fernando, La bohème, Carmen, Les contes d'Hoffmann, Eugene Onegin, La forza del destino, Hérodiade, I Lombardi, Loreley, Madame Sans-Gêne, Mefistofele, Pagliacci, Paride e Elena, Rinaldo, Salvator Rosa, La traviata, Il trovatore, I vespri siciliani, La Wally and Zazà; songs by **Bachelet**, **Buzzi-Peccia**, **Chopin**, **Guagni-Benvenuti**, **Herbert**, **Mascheroni**, **Monahan**, **Pergolesi**, **Rossini** and **Sodero**
Claudia Muzio *sop* with various artists
Romophone mono ② 81005-2 (153 minutes: ADD) Ⓕ
Recorded 1911-25

The crackles and surface noise that usually afflict Edison reproduction have all but been eliminated, so that we can hear Muzio's voice in its absolute prime without, as it were, the effort of listening through a sea of interference. The sheer beauty of the soprano's voice and her wonderful intensity of expression can now be experienced with astonishing immediacy. All the Muzio gifts, including that of refined, exquisite phrasing combined with that peculiarly heart-rending intensity that was hers alone, are heard in that enchanting song by Bachelet, *Chère nuit* (first disc, track 8). If your dealer will let you hear that, even if you are sceptical about singers of the past, you are sure to make off home with this set, eager to hear the rest. A feast of captivating interpretations await the listener.

Heddle Nash *ten*

The Incomparable Heddle Nash H

Puccini La bohème – Act 4[a]
Opera Arias and Duets – Il barbiere di Siviglia, Così fan tutte, Don Giovanni, Die Fledermaus, La jolie fille de Perth and Rigoletto
Heddle Nash *ten* [a]Rodolfo with various artists including [a]**Lisa Perli** *sop* Mimì; [a]**Stella Andreva** *sop* Musetta; [a]**John Brownlee** *bar* Marcello; [a]**Robert Alva** *bass* Schaunard; [a]**Robert Easton** *bass* Colline **London Philharmonic Orchestra / Sir Thomas Beecham**
Dutton Laboratories mono CDLX7012 Ⓑ
(69 minutes: ADD). Recorded 1929-35

When he made this recording of Act 4 of *La bohème* in 1935 Nash was at the height of his powers and sings a spontaneous, quite Italianate Rodolfo. Perli makes a simple, heartfelt Mimì. The rest of the cast falls far short of the principals, but Beecham is at his most alert, and sensitive too. Nash's Mozart is most elegantly represented by the well-nigh faultless versions of Ottavio's arias, made at the time of his sensational Covent Garden début in 1929 in *Don Giovanni*. The phrasing is refined, the breath long, the big run in 'Il mio tesoro' encompassed in a single span. The Duke of Mantua's three arias tell us just why this was one of Nash's favourite roles early in his career. He makes the most of the execrable translation by singing it with total conviction, and his lyric tenor rings out with just the right *élan*, matched by subtle colourings. The Serenade from *La jolie fille de Perth* is justly renowned because it displays to perfection the elegiac, minstrel-like quality of Nash's tone and his impassioned delivery – and yet he is said to have had a cold on the day it was made! The transfers (including the solo items) are superior to any previous issues, bringing the voices into one's room without let or hindrance.

Anne Sofie von Otter *mez*

Lamenti

Bertali Lamento della Regina d'Inghilterra[abd]
Legrenzi Il ballo del Gran Duca, Op 16 – Corrente nona[de] **Monteverdi** Madrigals, Book 7 – Con che soavità[ade]. Lamento d'Arianna[ac] **Piccinini** Ciaccona[c] **Purcell** Incassum, Lesbia, rogas, Z383[ad]. O Solitude! my sweetest choice, Z406[ac] **Vivaldi** Cessate, omai cessate, RV684[ad]
[a]**Anne Sofie von Otter** *mez* [b]**Franz-Josef Selig** *bass* [c]**Jakob Lindberg** *theorbo* [d]**Musica Antiqua Köln / Reinhard Goebel** [e]*vn*
Archiv Produktion 457 617-2AH (60 minutes: DDD) Ⓕ
Texts and translations included. Recorded 1997

Anne Sofie von Otter adds to her laurels with this issue, which belies any doom and gloom suggested by its title with singing of an intensity of expression, subtlety of nuance and rich palette of vocal colour that leave one full of admiration. Whether lamenting a stony-hearted lover (*Cessate, omai cessate*) or a faithless one (in *Arianna*, all that remains of a lost Monteverdi opera), a queen of Arcadia (*Incassum, Lesbia, rogas*) or the husband of an English queen (presumably Charles I, in view of the frenzied cries for revenge), von Otter fills every word with vivid meaning while still preserving the musical line. Vengeance is also the passionate response of the lover in the Vivaldi cantata (no stranger to the record catalogue), superbly performed here, with full-blooded instrumental backing by Musica Antiqua Köln. At the opposite end of the emotional spectrum, another highlight of the disc is Purcell's sad, touching *Incassum, Lesbia*. His *O Solitude!* is built on a ground bass, as of course is the little piece for solo theorbo by Piccinini, as well as the Legrenzi *Corrente* – neither of which, in fact, suggests lamenting. The most varied instrumentation occurs in Monteverdi's sectional *Con che soavità*, with its changeable tempos and ornamental vocal line. The contribution by an admirable bass, Franz-Josef Selig, in two brief but low-lying narrations in the Bertali (a work largely in recitative, but with interludes for three violas) should not be overlooked. Altogether an outstanding disc

Wings in the night – Swedish Songs

Alfvén Songs, Op 28 – No 3, I kiss your hand; No 6, The forest sleeps **Sigurd von Koch** Exotic Songs No 1, In the month of Tjaitra; No 3, Of lotus scent and moonlight. The wild swans – spring night's rain; Mankind's lot; The wild swans
Peterson-Berger Nothing is like the time of waiting. Swedish folk ballads, Op 5 – No 1, When I go myself in the dark forest; No 3, Like Stars in the Heavens. Three Marit's Songs, Op 12. Böljeby Waltz. Return. Aspåkers Polka **Rangström** Poems by Bo Bergman – No 1, Wings in the night; No 3, Melody. The Dark Flower – No 2, Prayer to the night; No 4, Farewell. Pan. Old Swedish **Sjögren** Lieder from Wolff's 'Tannhäuser', Op 12 – No 4, Hab'ein Röslein dir gebrochen; No 6, Ich möchte schweben. Du schaust mich an mit stummen Fragen **Stenhammar** Songs and Moods, Op 26 – No 1, The Wanderer; No 4, Miss Blonde and Miss Brunette; No 5, A ship sails; No 9, Coastal song. Songs, Op 37 – No 1, Jutta comes to the Volkungs; No 2, In the maple's shade
Anne Sofie von Otter *mez* **Bengt Forsberg** *pf*
DG 449 189-2GH (74 minutes: DDD) Ⓕ
Texts and translations included. Recorded 1995

If von Otter's and Forsberg's intention in compiling this recital was to provide an introduction to the riches of Swedish song so compelling that purchasers of it will hunger for more, they have succeeded. There are very few songs here that could not be programmed without apology or fear of comparison alongside the best German Lieder of the same period (the 40 years between 1884 and 1924). They contain considerable variety of mood and musical style, and the recital has been cleverly programmed to demonstrate in particular the range and the development of the two finest song composers here, Wilhelm Peterson-Berger and Wilhelm Stenhammar. Both were greatly gifted melodists, Peterson-Berger holding to an almost folk-like vein of simple lyricism, while Stenhammar reached further and touched darker moods, and the other composers here are by no means cast into the shade by these two masters. The performances are superb, quiet shadings of colour and subtle phrasings under immaculate control, a mere thread of voice often used to draw you into the heart of a song quite magically. Forsberg is an ideally imaginative and positive partner. You will probably find yourself playing several of these songs over and over again (for von Otter's exquisite little flourish of coloratura at the end of von Koch's *Of lotus scent*, for example, or for her delightful touch of humour and affection describing little chicks 'who can hardly walk' stumbling into the first warm sun of summer in the first of Peterson-Berger's *Marit's Songs*).

Adelina Patti *sop*

Opera Arias and Songs H
Adelina Patti *sop* with Mario Ancona, Mattia Battistini, Emma Calvé, Fernando De Lucia, Edouard de Reszke, Emma Eames, Lucien Fugère, Wilhelm Hesch, Lilli Lehmann, Félia Litvinne, Francesco Marconi, Victor Maurel, Dame Nellie Melba, Lillian Nordica, Adelina Patti, Pol Plançon, Maurice Renaud, Sir Charles Santley, Marcella Sembrich, Francesco Tamagno and Francesco Viñas
Nimbus Prima Voce mono ② NI7840/1 Ⓜ
(120 minutes: ADD). Recorded 1902-28

This is a 'historical' issue for straightforward enjoyment. Although the originals were made in the very earliest years of recording, they are reproduced here with a vividness that calls for very little in the way of 'creative listening', making allowances and so forth. It starts in party mood with the first Falstaff of all, Victor Maurel, singing to a bunch of cronies in the studio of 1907 the 'Quand'ero paggio' which he sang at La Scala in the première of 1893. They cheer and call for an encore, which he gives them, then again (and best of all) this time in French. The record has been transferred many times to LP and CD, but never has it been so easy for the listener to 'see' it and feel part of it.

The magnificent bass Pol Plançon follows with King Philip's solo from *Don Carlos*, beautifully even in production and deeply absorbed in the character and his emotions. The hauntingly pure, well-rounded soprano of Emma Eames in Tosti's *Dopo* (a real passion there despite its restraint), and then the miraculously spry and elegant 80-year-old Lucien Fugère lead to the first of the Patti records: the one her husband thought unladylike and asked to be withdrawn from the catalogue, *La calesera*, and the most joyous she ever made. Tamagno, Melba, Nordica, Renaud: they are all here, and on thrillingly good form. The copies of these rarities have been selected with great care, and, while other transfers have, technically, got more 'off' the record, none has captured the beauty of the voices more convincingly.

Pavarotti *ten*

Luciano Pavarotti – Live Recital
Beethoven In questa tomba oscura, WoO133
Bellini Dolente imagine di figlia mia. Malinconia, ninfa gentile. Vanne, o rosa fortunata. Bella Nice, che d'amore. Ma rendi pur contento **Bononcini** Griselda – Per la gloria d'adorarvi **Cilea** L'arlesiana – E la solita storia **Donizetti** Me voglio fa'na casa. L'elisir d'amore – Una furtiva lagrima **Puccini** Tosca – Recondita armonia; E lucevan le stelle
A Scarlatti Gia il sole al Gange **Tosti** La serenata. Non t'amo più!. Luna d'estate. Malià. Chanson de l'adieu. L'ultima canzone. 'A Vucchella. L'alba separa dalla luce l'ombra. Marechiare
Verdi Rigoletto – La donna è mobile
Luciano Pavarotti *ten* **Leone Magiera** *pf*
Decca 466 350-2DH (68 minutes: DDD) Ⓕ
Recorded live 1997-99 ●

To sustain a career for 40 years is a remarkable achievement for any singer, exceptionally so for a tenor. Hugues Cuénod, who was still amazing audiences with 'things that it amuses my voice to sing' well into his eighties, is an exception to every rule; Tito Schipa stayed before the public for 46 years, but with a lighter voice and in a less demanding repertory than Pavarotti's. While Pavarotti can show off no high C in this collection, his upper register is still free enough for a full-voiced B natural or a triumphant B flat. He has lost little of his sense of long-spanned, finely sustained line, and it is surely not merely caution that leads him now to make extensive use of a crooning head voice and of intimate *mezza voce* shadings and to take such evident pleasure in the varieties of covered tone that can be drawn from the first syllable of the word 'luna' (in Tosti's *Luna d'estate*).

However the title of this collection is misleading; it is not so much a live recital as a selection of items recorded at a number of recitals. The voice is recorded very closely, perhaps to diminish the distraction of moving from one acoustic to another (it cannot disguise the fact that Leone Magiera plays at least three different pianos, not all of them of the highest quality) and listening to Pavarotti at a range of about three feet does reveal or even exaggerate the fact that here and there he does sound his age: a phrase cautiously approached, a high note prepared with a longer pause than heretofore and the vocal equivalent of crossed fingers, a hint of tarnish to the tone, of effort or strain hidden by charm and professionalism. All the more praiseworthy, then, that he should include the five Bellini songs (not so demanding as many of that composer's arias, but they insist on the most limpid *cantabile*); all the more engaging that he chooses no fewer than nine by Tosti because he so obviously enjoys them. *Marechiare* and after it the *Rigoletto* aria are obviously the encores, and in them one hears the old trouper delighted to be called back once again.

Ezio Pinza *bass*

Opera Arias H
Aida, Attila, La bohème, Le caïd, Don Carlo, Don Giovanni, Faust, La Juive, Lucia di Lammermoor, Mignon, Norma, I Puritani, Robert le diable, Il trovatore, I vespri siciliani and Die Zauberflöte
Ezio Pinza *bass* with various artists
Nimbus Prima Voce mono NI7875 (73 minutes: ADD) Ⓢ
Recorded 1923-30

There can surely be few dissenting voices where the quality of Pinza's singing is concerned. Play a record of his to a hardened old collector or a green newcomer and they will join in praising his golden, vibrant tone, seamless *legato*, the evenness of his vocal emission through a couple of octaves. It has been said that he seldom sings below *forte*: that is wholly negated here by a performance of the lullaby from Thomas's *Mignon*, sung almost entirely *mezza voce*, a lulling and soft-grained song that would send any child into blissful slumber. Another French item, the famous Tambour-major air from Thomas's lesser-known *Le caïd*, not only confirms Pinza's excellence in French enunciation, but also shows quite another side of his personality: jocular, a smile in the tone, exuberance in the delivery. The RCA Victors of Italian opera are well known, yet one marvels anew at the easy command of Pinza's Oroveso, Procida, King Philip and Ramphis, the character of each nicely etched in, even in extract. To complement these there is his grave Sarastro, his warmly sighing Colline. All the phrases where other basses either exaggerate or lose focus in reaching a high or low note are done quite effortlessly. His Giovanni suggests a formidable personality, and we end with him in the distinguished company of Rethberg and Gigli for their glorious account of the *Attila* trio.

All the electrics are transferred carefully from RCA Victors in good condition. Where the six 1923-24 HMV acoustics are concerned you hear Nimbus's much-discussed additional resonance, room or otherwise, come into play. It is an acceptable procedure if you understand that you are not hearing exactly what the original sound is like. The most persuasive title here is 'Cinta di fiori' from *I Puritani*, where the *cantabile* rolls out with fabulous ease.

Rosa Ponselle *sop*

Rosa Ponselle On the Air, Volume 1, 1934-36 H

Bartlett A Dream **Bizet** Carmen – Danse bohémienne; Habanera; Seguédille; Mêlons! Coupons!. Ouvre ton coeur **Bond** I Love You Truly **Brahms** Volks-Kinderlieder – Wiegenlied **Charles** When I Have Sung My Songs **Del Riego** Homing **Dvořák** Humoresques, B187 – No 7 in G flat **Eden** What's In The Air **Gluck** Alceste – Divinités du Styx **Grosvenor** I Carry You In My Pocket **Kountz** The Sleigh Kreisler The Old Refrain **Lehár** Die lustige Witwe – Waltz Song **Lockhart** In the Luxembourg Gardens **Mana-Zucca** The Big Brown Bear[a] **Mascagni** Cavalleria rusticana – Voi lo sapete; Ave Maria (arr from Intermezzo by Weatherly) **Mozart** Don Giovanni – Batti, batti **Nevin** The Rosary **Padilla** La violetera Ponce Estrellita **Reger** Schlichte Weisen, Op 76 – Maria Wiegenlied **Romani** Fedra – O divina Afrodite **Saint-Saëns** Samson et Dalila – Printemps qui commence **Sandoval** Ave Maria **Schaefer** The Cuckoo Clock **Schubert** Erlkönig, D328 **Serradell** La golondrina **Spross** Will-o-the-Wisp **J Strauss II** An der schönen, blauen Donau, Op 314 **O Straus** Der tapfere Soldat – Mein Held! **Tchaikovsky** Songs, Op 6 – Nun wer die Sehnsucht kennt **Tosti** Goodbye. L'ultima canzone **Traditional** The Last Rose of Summer. Danny Boy. Comin' thro' the Rye **Valverde** Clavelitos

Rosa Ponselle *sop* [a]**Charles Henderson** *pf* **orchestra / André Kostelanetz**

Marston ② 52012-2 (145 minutes: ADD) Ⓕ

Recorded 1934-36

In the 1930s, at the height of the Depression, the Americans weren't going to the opera very much – the Met was regularly half empty. Nor were they buying many records; they were, however, smoking. Chesterfield's, one of the leading tobacco manufacturers, sponsored a weekly radio programme, and a frequent guest on it was Rosa Ponselle. According to the late John Ardoin, who wrote the notes to accompany this set, Ponselle herself said these off-the-air recordings were a more accurate record of her singing than her studio-made discs.

The sound is variable, there is a good deal of hiss and some distortion, but the familiar Ponselle style comes across loud and clear. It seems quite extraordinary now, but Ponselle made no commercial discs between 1930 (when she was at the very peak of her career) and 1939, when, just after her marriage, she was about to retire. Her singing is generous, emotive, a bit over the top sometimes in slight songs such as Ponce's *Estrellita* or Serradell's *La golondrina*. She has no difficulty crossing over to operetta, with *Der tapfere Soldat* ('The Chocolate Soldier') and *The Merry Widow*, since her stage career had begun in vaudeville. The only opera extracts here from roles she sang on stage are from *Carmen*, *Cavalleria rusticana* and Romani's *Fedra*.

The strength of her voice posed problems for the engineers, but by moving the broadcast microphone away from the orchestra, they were able to capture something of the energy and power of Ponselle's singing that she felt was absent from her earlier 78s. A lot of the material is ephemeral, but in a trifle like *The Sleigh* by Kountz one gets a vivid glimpse of her agility – it was one of the thrills of Ponselle's singing that such a huge voice had such a facility with coloratura passages, and that she could fine down the tone to wonderful *pianissimos*.

The sentimentality of many of these songs, such as Bartlett's *A Dream* or Bond's *I Love You Truly* would be completely beyond the scope of most modern singers, but Ponselle's directness lifts them above kitsch. It is sad that she didn't include arias from some of the operas she was singing at the Met at the same time – *Don Giovanni* (she was Donna Anna, of course, but here sings Zerlina), *Luisa Miller* or *Andrea Chénier*. As it is, this collection offers a fascinating souvenir of this great singer in her prime.

Dame Margaret Price *sop*

The Romantic Lied

Cornelius Trauer und Trost, Op 3 **Liszt** Freudvoll und leidvoll, S280. Über allen Gipfeln ist Ruh, S306. Mignons Lied, S275. Der du von dem Himmel bist, S279 **Wagner** Wesendonk Lieder **Wolf** Mörike Lieder – Er ist's; Begegnung; Der Gärtner; In der Frühe; Lebe wohl; Heimweh; Gesang Weylas; Bei einer Trauung

Dame Margaret Price *sop* **Graham Johnson** *pf*

Forlane UCD16728 (71 minutes: DDD) Ⓕ

Texts and translations included. Recorded 1993

Price and Johnson have done it again. He has chosen a programme for her that exactly suits her talents and style, and she (with his inestimable help) has executed it with commitment and understanding. The programme in itself is fascinating, comparing and contrasting composers of roughly the same generation and period. The cross-fertilisation of musical ideas is apparent, yet each emerges as an artist with something highly individual to say. Wolf isn't a composer with whom Price has been very much associated until now, but in a group of the Mörike settings, she proves herself at one with the poems and their music, catching in particular the restless ardour of *Begegnung*, the timeless mystery of *Gesang Weylas*, and the peculiarly Wolfian charm of the lighter pieces. Liszt is even more to her liking. She and Johnson choose the later, longer version of *Freudvoll und leidvoll* and make a grand romantic statement of it that is just right. The interpretation of the *Wesendonk Lieder* is the crowning glory of this wonderful recital. A virtually faultless reading, speeds (no unwanted lingering), phrasing, line and tone ideally adapted to the words and music. Johnson places the piano part in perfect relationship with the voice, helped by the exemplary recording of both.

Rosa Raisa *sop*

The Complete Recordings, 1917-26 H

Opera arias and duets – L'Africaine, Aida, Andrea Chénier, Cavalleria rusticana, Don Giovanni, Ernani, La forza del destino, La Gioconda, Madama Butterfly, Mefistofele, Norma, Otello, Tosca, Il trovatore and I vespri siciliani; songs by **Tchaikovsky** and **Yradier**
Rosa Raisa *sop* with various artists
Marston mono ③ 53001-2 (227 minutes: ADD) Ⓜ
Recorded 1917-26 Ⓜ

'I would listen to them, and then break them into pieces' wrote Raisa in 1962, explaining why she possessed none of her own records. It is a pity she could not have heard them in these fine transfers and reproduced on modern equipment. Her objection was that they failed to show the volume of her voice, and that is very probably true. The impression they give is that of an ample lyric soprano with a dramatic style rather than a full dramatic voice. What they preserve is a sound of exceptional beauty and in several instances singing of equally exceptional skill. Outstanding is the single previously unpublished item, the cabaletta 'Ah! bello a me ritorna' from *Norma*, recorded for Brunswick in 1929. A superb demonstration of vocal mastery, it seems totally unaware of difficulties. The semiquaver passagework, the bold intervals, the matching of rhythmic energy with lyric grace, all are mastered with apparent ease. It is of course sad to think that this is all that remains of a Norma often reported as having been the finest of all in this century, at any rate up to Callas's time.

There are many other lovely things here. Raisa's chequered career as a recording artist began with the aria from *Andrea Chénier*, 'La mamma morta', on Pathé in 1917, and this was also the subject of her last recording, in 1933. Despite the difference in tempo (the later version being more expansive), they are very alike in style and affectionate in feeling. Similarly with the six (no less) versions of 'Voi lo sapete'. Her 'Un bel dì' is unexpectedly touching and intimate, the manner delicate and girlish, till the 'per non morir', when the girl becomes woman. The duets with her baritone husband, Giacomo Rimini, include one (clear-voiced and dramatic against a scrunchy background) from *Il trovatore* on a Vitaphone soundtrack. Then the third disc ends with an interview, not especially illuminating but nice to have, given in 1962 and in lively style, a year before her death. Raisa was one of the great singers of her time, and among them perhaps the most outstanding example of neglect by the major record companies. The Marston catalogue is enriched by this release.

Elisabeth Rethberg *sop*

Opera Arias H

Aida, Andrea Chénier, La bohème, Der Freischütz, Lohengrin, Madama Butterfly, Le nozze di Figaro, Otello, Serse, Sosarme, Tannhäuser, Tosca and Die Zauberflöte; songs by **Bishop**, **Braga**, **Cadman**, **Densmore**, **Flies**, **Gounod**, **Grieg**, **Griffes**, **Hildach**, **Jensen**, **Korschat**, **Lassen**, **Loewe**, **Massenet**, **Mendelssohn**, **Rubinstein**, **Schubert**, **Schumann**, **Taubert** and **Tchaikovsky**
Elisabeth Rethberg *sop* with various artists
Romophone mono ② 81012-2 (158 minutes: ADD) Ⓕ
Recorded 1924-29

They're very collectable, these Romophone complete editions. Up they go on the shelves, and you know that there is another small but quite important area in the history of singing on records properly covered, ready for reference at any time, and reference that will be a pleasure because the standard of transfer is so reliable. In this instance it is the Rethberg Brunswicks: records which capture the voice in its lovely prime. Purely as a singer, Rethberg was surely the most gifted and accomplished lyric soprano of her age. The essential gift was a voice of exquisite quality, and her upbringing contributed to the purity of intonation and a feeling for musical style. Her production was even and fluent; on all these records there is scarcely a note or a phrase that is not delightful purely as singing. Some of the later records show it also as a voice capable of considerable expansion in volume. In Aida's 'O patria mia' Rethberg is celestial, ample in volume, sensitive in feeling, phrasing beautifully, taking the C softly and in a broad single sweep. Equally lovely is her Mimì, and then in the *Andrea Chénier* aria there is such an unpressured beauty of utterance that it almost becomes a different composition. A previously unpublished delight is a blissful performance of Eugen Hildach's *Der Spielmann*, and among the less familiar songs is a charmer by Carl Taubert, *Es steht ein Baum in jenem Tal*.

Opera Arias and Duets H

L'Africaine, Andrea Chénier, The Bartered Bride, La bohème, Carmen, Madama Butterfly, Le nozze di Figaro, Tosca, Die Zauberflöte and Der Zigeunerbaron; songs by **Bizet**, **Mozart**, **Pataky** and **R Strauss**
Elisabeth Rethberg *sop* with various artists
Preiser Lebendige Vergangenheit mono 89051 Ⓕ
(71 minutes: AAD). Recorded 1920-25

Elisabeth Rethberg died in 1976, when little notice was taken of the passing of a singer once voted the world's most perfect. The year 1994 was the centenary of her birth, so this fine selection of her early recordings was well timed.The earliest catch her at the charming age of 26 (the voice settled, but still that of a young woman), and the last of them, made in 1925, find her just into her thirties, mature in timbre, feeling and artistry. It is doubtful whether a judicious listener would at any point cry 'Ah, it's an Aida voice!', but Aida was the part for which she became most famous. In Countess Almaviva's first aria, her *legato* is the next thing to perfection; in Pamina's 'Ach, ich fühl's' the head tones are beautifully in place, the portamentos finely judged, emotion always implicit in the singing. The duets with Richard Tauber include the music of Micaëla and Don José sung with unrivalled grace and intimacy, Rethberg shading off the end of her solo most elegantly, Tauber softening in his so as to welcome and not overwhelm the soprano's entry. As for the songs, they are equally delightful.

Opera Arias and Ensembles H

L'Africaine, Aida, Attila, Un ballo in maschera, Boccaccio, Carmen, Cavalleria rusticana, Don Giovanni, Faust, Die Fledermaus, Der fliegende Holländer, Lohengrin, I Lombardi, Madama Butterfly, Die Meistersinger von Nürnberg, Le nozze di Figaro, Otello, Il rè pastore, Tannhäuser and Der Zigeunerbaron; songs by **Brahms**, **Mendelssohn** and **Wolf**

Elisabeth Rethberg *sop* with various artists

Romophone mono ② 81014-2 (155 minutes: ADD) Ⓕ

Recorded 1927-34

To the older collector of vocal recordings it is to be feared that not many of these records will come as new. Attention can be directed, however, to the last three. These were made in 1932 in the Bell Telephone Laboratories as part of an experiment in improved recording methods. They were recorded at 33rpm, and they achieved startling results. The quality of the voice is captured to perfection, but most impressive is the freedom of emission, no longer confined within the studio but able to ring and expand, the contrasts of loud and soft tones being effective and often as exquisite as they would have been in the flesh. Most revealing is Elisabeth's Greeting from *Tannhäuser*, sung with piano accompaniment but with a dramatic conviction and enthusiasm far more vivid than that of the earlier orchestral version. Other new items are unpublished takes of the two Verdi trios with Gigli and Pinza, differing slightly in balance, but very little in style. The six electric Parlophones include the tender Micaëla's aria and the solo from *L'Africaine* with its haunting unaccompanied introduction. Supreme among the Victors is the second *Un ballo in maschera* aria, the *Meistersinger* duet with Schorr running it close. It is also good to have the complete Nile scene from *Aida*, with Lauri-Volpi in his prime, de Luca a bit past his. Transfers are of the usual high standard, and with the first volume, this is clearly the primary source of a comprehensive Rethberg collection on disc.

Bidù Sayão *sop*

Opera Arias H

Faust, Manon and Roméo et Juliette; songs by **Braga**, **Debussy**, **Duparc**, **Hahn**, **Koechlin**, **Moret**, **Ravel** and **Villa-Lobos**

Bidu Sayão *sop* with various artists

Sony Classical Masterworks Heritage mono

MHK62355 (73 minutes: ADD) Ⓕ

Recorded 1941-50 ○

Beauty, charm, exquisite voice, brilliant technique, personality, Bidù Sayão had them all. This recital opens with her most famous recording, *Bachianas Brasilieras* No 5 by Villa-Lobos, with the composer conducting. She recognised the opportunity for her particular soprano in the violin part that Villa-Lobos had written for this work and persuaded him to adapt it for soprano. Their famous recording was achieved in just one experimental take. In that her voice is used in a purely instrumental way, when she enters on the next track as Gounod's Juliette, one is struck by the presence the use of words adds to the voice. In the Jewel song from *Faust* she conveys a sense of joyous laughter to the 'Ah' in 'Ah, je ris de me voir si belle', without any sense of vulgarity, or playing to the (armchair) gallery. Massenet's *Manon* was the role of her Met début in 1937 and again her vocal acting immediately sketches in Manon's playful character in the Act 1 aria about the 'premier Voyage'. How can a voice suggest a pout? One would have to ask Brigitte Bardot, but Sayão can do it, when she starts to sing about the 'couvent' she's being sent to. Sayão's voice had none of the acid nasal quality of the typical French light soprano, so she can manage to do all sorts of little things with the language without making it sound harsh. Sayão studied with Jean de Reszke; she is the youngest of his pupils on disc, and perhaps the only one still around today, at least the only one who had a great career. The presentation is superb: there are splendid photographs and reproductions of the original LP sleeves.

Opera Arias – La bohème, Don Giovanni, Gianni Schicchi, Madama Butterfly, Le nozze di Figaro, Pagliacci, La sonnambula and La traviata. La damoiselle élue (**Debussy**)

Bidù Sayão *sop* with various artists

Sony Classical Masterworks Heritage mono

MHK63221 (73 minutes: ADD) Ⓜ

Recorded 1941-50

Charm is an elusive thing. Singers guilty of laying it on too thick might listen to Sayão and try to hear what she does, and just as important, what she doesn't do. Take the contrast between Violetta and Mimì. In the Act 1 aria from *La traviata*, there is no smile in the voice. It's all beautiful, limpid singing, but when she reaches that crucial 'Follie!' recitative, there is no joy in the cries of 'gioir!' but, as is surely correct, desperation. Then comes Mimì and the tone is at once warmer, full of the reticent hopefulness that is typical of the personality; when she gets to the climactic 'Ma quando ven lo sgelo' she really lets it all glow. Strange that these two Parisian coughers are so often bracketed together – in fact their basic characters are quite different, and in the subtlest way Sayão shows how a singer can differentiate without resorting to any distortion or method-acting tricks.

The revelation in this recital was Sayão's Cherubino. Lord Harewood in his notes says that she probably never sang it on the stage, but she makes of the two overfamiliar arias something totally delicious and new. Her Susanna was well known and one of her favourite parts (with Pinza as her Figaro), but although she has no difficulty in singing the Countess's aria, somehow one knows that the part isn't quite right for her. Both the Zerlina arias are done with just the right mixture of coquetry and toughness. Sayão sang Debussy's *La damoiselle élue* in New York with Toscanini, the year before her Met début in 1937.

This recording, made in 1947 with Ormandy and the Philadelphia Orchestra, is a remarkable instance of her ability to invest words and vocal line with character. In a recent interview, Sayão related how much she had wanted to sing Madam Butterfly but, although she felt she could have acted it, the orchestration was too heavy for her voice, and so she never dared take on the role. Her recording of 'Un bel dì' shows how she would have tackled it. Surprisingly, she did sing Nedda in *Pagliacci*, in her final season at San Francisco, and she must have made an unusually sympathetic impression.

With its companion volume this CD restores much of Sayão's recorded legacy to the catalogue. She is one of the most consistently fascinating singers of this era at the Met, in the two decades surrounding the Second World War. The booklet, as with all these beautifully produced Masterworks reissues, has colour reproductions of early record sleeves and nostalgic photographs, including two of Sayão modelling a hat fashioned from a copy of her first LP.

Aksel Schiøtz *ten*

The Complete Recordings 1933-46, Volume 1 Ⓗ
Opera and Oratorio Arias – Così fan tutte, Die Entführung aus dem Serail, Eugene Onegin, Don Giovanni, Faust and Die Zauberflöte; Acis and Galatea, Christmas Oratorio, Messiah, St Matthew Passion, Die Schöpfung and Solomon; songs by **Dowland** and Was mich auf dieser Welt betrübt (**Buxtehude**)
Aksel Schiøtz *ten* with various artists
Danacord mono DACOCD451 (75 minutes: ADD) Ⓕ
Recorded 1933-46

Schiøtz's singing was always the very epitome of silvery elegance. His attributes in Handel, Haydn and Mozart are amply confirmed in this, the first disc of Danacord's comprehensive 10-disc survey of all his recorded output. Sadly his career was cut short by a brain tumour in 1946, but for the 10 years of his prime, he was rightly fêted for his beautiful singing and masterly sense of style. Long before period-instrument performances were current, Schiøtz and Wöldike were seeking an authentic style of performing Handel and Bach, as exemplified here in the poised, unaffected account of the opening solos from *Messiah*, and arias from the *St Matthew Passion* and *Christmas Oratorio*. 'Frohe Hirten' from the latter and the lovely aria by Buxtehude sound even better now that they have been released from the scratch on the originals, the transfers expertly done by EMI's Andrew Walter. Also in the oratorio field the aria from *Die Schöpfung* demonstrates perfectly the singer's delicately etched line and pure tone.

There are few more fine-grained versions of Tamino's 'Portrait' aria, Ottavio's arias nor of Pedrillo's Serenade, but 'Un aur'amorosa' suffers from an uncomfortably fast speed. Schiøtz is also among the most elegiac of Lenskys in that character's lament (slightly cut), the most sweet-toned of Fausts, the top C taken in the head as is the case with other tenors of his ilk. It seems hardly to matter that these pieces are sung in Danish. The Dowland, like the Handel, is given authentically, though a guitar rather than a lute is used for the accompaniments.

As a bonus there are rehearsal performances of Acis's 'Love sounds the alarm', minus *da capo*, and 'Sacred raptures' from *Solomon*, the former impeccable, the latter showing an unaccustomed fallibility in the runs. The booklet is full of interesting photos and articles.

The Complete Recordings, 1933-46, Volume 2 Ⓗ
Grieg Melodies of the Heart, Op 5[b] – No 1, Two brown eyes; No 3, I love but thee. Songs, Op 33 – No 2, Last Spring[b]; No 9, At Rondane[c]. Songs and Ballads, Op 9 – No 4, Outward Bound[c]
Schubert Die schöne Müllerin, D795[a]
Aksel Schiøtz *ten*
[a]**Gerald Moore**, [bc]**Folmer Jensen** *pfs*
Danacord mono DACOCD452 (75 minutes: ADD) Ⓕ
Texts and translations included ●

The Complete Recordings, 1933-46, Volume 3 Ⓗ
Bellman Fredman's Epistles – Dearest brothers, sisters and friends; Old age is with me; Sit down around the spring here. Fredman's Songs – Hear bells give out a frightful boom; So tipsy we are taking leave; Joachim lived in Babylon **Brahms** Die Mainacht, Op 43 No 2. Sonntag, Op 47 No 3. Ständchen, Op 106 No 1 **Buxtehude** Aperite mihi portas justitiae, BuxWV7 **Grieg** Songs, Op 49 – No 3, Kind greetings, fair ladies; No 6, Spring showers. The Poet's farewell, Op 18 No 3 **Schumann** Dichterliebe, Op 48
Aksel Schiøtz *ten* with various artists
Danacord mono DACOCD453 (69 minutes: ADD) Ⓕ
Texts and translations included ●

The years 1945-46 were particularly fruitful ones for Schiøtz in relation to recording. With Walter Legge's eager support the Danish tenor could at last come to London to resume his recording career with *Die schöne Mullerin*, which takes up the lion's share of Vol 2. The Danacord transfer of this sensitive reading is now the one to go for: not only is the sound marginally superior to Preiser's earlier transfer but added to it are five wonderful readings of Grieg songs, these actually recorded for the composer's centenary in 1943. In particular the popular *I love but thee* and the gloriously ardent *Last Spring* find in Schiøtz an ideal interpreter, a singer whose style so effortlessly and unassumingly goes to the heart of the matter. He is just as convincing in the three lesser known songs by Grieg in Vol 3, devoted to six months of recording activity at the start of 1946.

Yet another facet of his art is revealed in the Bellman songs, aptly recorded in Sweden, Schiøtz disclosing his sense of humour in the bawdy songs of the 18th century, pleasure-loving Bellman. In *So tipsy we are taking leave*, he captures to perfection the devil-may-care, bawdy mood and in all these attractive pieces finds a willing partner in Ulrik Neumann's guitar. But this third volume is most valuable for giving us Schiøtz's marvellous *Dichterliebe*, perhaps his finest achievement of all on disc.

Then come three Brahms songs, never issued on 78s, that are also near ideal, especially the delicately floated line of *Die Mainacht*. Gerald Moore, as ever, fits his playing intuitively to the singer he's partnering. Then, after the Grieg and Bellman, comes more evidence of the tenor's and Wöldike's championship of Buxtehude, then a neglected figure, which again benefits from Schiøtz's innate sense of the right style for the music in hand. It also allows us to hear a pleasing mezzo (Elsa Sigfuss) and bass (Holger Nørgaard). Andrew Walter's remastering of all this disparate material at Abbey Road is faultless.

The Complete Recordings, 1933-46, Volume 4 H
Hartmann Tell me, star of night, Op 63. Little Christine – Sverkel's romance **Lange-Müller** Once Upon a Time – Serenade; Midsummer song **Mozart** Per pietà, non ricercate, K420 **Riisager** Mother Denmark
Schubert Die schöne Müllerin, D795 – No 1, Das Wandern; No 6, Der Neugierige; No 7, Ungeduld; No 8, Morgengruss; No 10, Tränenregen; No 11, Mein; No 15, Eifersucht und Stolz; No 17, Die böse Farbe; No 19, Der Müller und der Bach; No 20, Des Baches Wiegenlied **Schubert/Berté** Das Dreimäderlhaus – excerpts **Weyse** Angel of Light, go in splendour. In distant steeples. The Sleeping-Draught – Fair lady, open your window
Aksel Schiøtz *ten* with various artists
Danacord mono DACOCD454 (72 minutes: ADD) Ⓕ
Texts and translations included

'Hidden Treasure' is the appropriate subtitle for this volume of the complete Schiøtz recordings. It begins with the 10 songs from what ought to have been a complete *Schöne Müllerin*, two songs recorded in London in 1939, eight with Hermann D. Koppel, who took over from Moore, in Denmark in 1939-40. The cycle was never finished, because – it seems – Koppel as a Jew had to flee his country when the Nazis occupied it. Schiøtz's voice, when he was 33, was even fresher, his reading even more spontaneous in suggesting the vulnerable youth's love and its loss, most poignant in an account of 'Der Müller und der Bach' that surpasses in forlorn expression other famed tenor interpreters such as Patzak, Pears, Schreier and Bostridge, but the whole sequence is a pleasure to hear for the plangency of Schiøtz's singing. There follows part of the Mozart aria *Per pietà* that the tenor sang as test for EMI in 1938, interesting as a rarity but not special. By contrast all the Danish items are desirable, among them the two Hartmann offerings: *Tell me, star of night*, a haunting song, is given ideal voicing by Schiøtz as is 'Sverkel's romance' from a romantic work, *Little Christine*, based on an Andersen fable.

The two items by Lange-Müller, written as incidental music for a play called *Once Upon a Time*, are even better, in particular the magical 'Midsummer song'. The note-writer tells how wonderful was Schiøtz's singing of this item in an open-air performance in 1941. His recordings had made Schiøtz famous and he also appeared the same year playing the role of Schubert in *Lilac Time*, of which we hear an amusing pot-pourri (a photo in the booklet shows him in the part). That Schiøtz was not averse to popular items is confirmed by Riisager's *Mother Denmark*, which he brought to London for that first session in May 1939. It is a song written for a *diseuse* about the delights of the homeland, and Schiøtz delivers it with the intimacy it calls for. Again, the transfers are faultless and this example of Anglo-Danish co-operation is highly recommendable.

Tito Schipa *ten*

Opera Arias H
L'Arlesiana, Il barbiere di Siviglia, La bohème, Don Giovanni, Don Pasquale, L'elisir d'amore, La favorita, Lakmé, Luisa Miller, Manon, Martha, Pagliacci, Rigoletto, La traviata and Werther
Tito Schipa *ten* with various artists
Preiser Lebendige Vergangenheit mono 89160 Ⓕ
(77 minutes: AAD). Recorded 1925-28

The Master. And yes: he surely is, and never more so than in the recordings of this period. Schipa was then at the height of his fame and fortune, the voice approaching the end of its very best days (a thrill and a freshness which began to diminish in the early 1930s) and with the art having developed just about as far as it would go. Lovely examples are: 'Sogno soave' (*Don Pasquale*), 'Questa o quella' and 'E il sol dell'anima' (*Rigoletto*), the *Traviata* duets, the *Lakmé* and *Werther* solos, Harlequin's Serenade (*Pagliacci*), 'E la solita storia' (*L'Arlesiana*) and the finale of *La bohème* with the exquisite Bori. But if 'The Master', then one whose mastery was exercised within severe limitations. Today's tenors in the repertoire cultivate an extensive upper range, whereas Schipa sings here nothing above a B flat, transposing 'La donna è mobile', and even lowering 'M'appari' so that the B flat becomes an A. His modern successors attempt and often attain a brilliance of bravura which can make Schipa sound tame and cautious (his 'Ecco ridente' is fine but lacks the brilliance of true virtuosity, and his 'Il mio tesoro' is essentially a bit of artful dodging). There are other limitations too, but these are enough for the present: and enough remains to place him among the unforgettables and the irreplaceables. Any of the recommendations mentioned will show why, and there is the added, vital and elusive quality of voice-personality.

This collection comprises a complete run of Schipa's operatic records made electrically for the Victor company. Transfers are faithful, with the sound well defined. Among all the many CDs currently devoted to him this would be a very suitable first choice.

The Complete Victor Recordings, 1922-25 H

Opera arias and duets – L'africaine, Il barbiere di Siviglia, La bohème, La corte del amor (Padilla), Don Pasquale, L'elisir d'amore, Emigranyes (Barrera), Lakmé, Lucia di Lammermoor, Manon, Marta, Mignon, Pagliacci, Rigoletto, La sonnambula, La traviata and Werther; songs by **Barthélemy**, **Buzzi-Peccia**, **Costa**, **di Crescenzo**, **de Feuntes**, **di Capua**, **Huarte**, **Lakacios**, **Oteo**, **Paladilhe**, **Perez-Freire**, **Ponce**, **Roig**, **Schipa** and **Silvestri**

Tito Schipa *ten* with various artists.

Romophone mono ② 82014-2 (150 minutes: ADD) Ⓕ
Recorded 1922-25

Tito Schipa is utterly special. Whether by art or personality (not always readily separable) he is one of those singers who instantly establish themselves in mind, memory and affections. He had a voice that could ring out strongly as well as commanding the style and delicacy for which he was renowned. He also had the skill, taste and personal magnetism to make something magical out of some very third-rate music (a faculty that contributed to the restriction of his artistic growth), and there are plenty of examples here – such as one called *Quiéreme mucho*, which veterans will recognise as a wartime hit over here called *Yours*. Alan Blyth's introductory essay points out that the acoustic Victors have been the least commonly reissued of Schipa's recordings, and that, while this is perhaps understandable (because the most popular of the titles were remade electrically a year or two later), they also catch him at the peak of his career and in his prime. Sometimes, indeed, the earlier recordings are marginally preferable to the more familiar remakes: the Dream song from *Manon* is rather more elegant, the *Pagliacci* serenade a shade more charming, and in the *Traviata* duets his partner, Amelita Galli-Curci, enjoys better vocal health. More importantly, some of the best items were never re-recorded, including the delightful *Sonnambula* duet and *Mignon* arias. Some of the songs, too, are charming, *Pesca d'amore* for example and the tiny tarantella by Vicenzo di Crescenzo called *Ce steve 'na vota*. 1925 saw the advent of electrical recording, and roughly a dozen of Schipa's first electricals are included. These are more ingratiating in the quality of the singing than in that of the recorded sound: one sympathises with those who complained at the time that the microphone added an unnatural harshness; it is also true that the shellac used just then often produced a particularly high and gritty surface-noise. Whatever has been done to mitigate them, these are still features that limit pleasure in listening here to the recordings of that period. Better quality came in with some of the very latest, and among these are the solos from *Werther* and *Lakmé* and the Death scene from *La bohème* with Lucrezia Bori, all among Schipa's very best. All who love singing will value Schipa's art, and all who value his art will want these records.

Andreas Scholl *counterten*

German Baroque Cantatas

Albertini Sonata quarto in C minor
J Christoph Bach Ach, das ich Wassers g'nug hätte
Buxtehude Fried- und Freudenreiche Hinfahrt, BuxWV76 – Muss der Tod denn auch entbinden (Klag-Lied). Jubilate Domino, omnis terra, BuxWV64
Erlebach Wer sich dem Himmel übergeben
Legrenzi Libro quarto di sonate, La cetra' – Sonata quinta **Rovetta** Salve mi Jesu **Schütz** Kleiner geistlichen Concerten, SWV306-37 – Was hast du verwirket, SWV307; O Jesu, nomen dulcem, SWV308. Symphoniae sacrae, SWV341-67 – Herzlich lieb hab ich dich, o Herr, SWV348 **Tunder** Ach, Herr lass deine lieben Engelein

Andreas Scholl *counterten* **Concerto di Viole** (Brian Franklin, Friederike Heumann, Brigitte Gasser, Arno Jochem de la Rosée); **Basle Consort** (Pablo Valetti, Stephanie Pfister *vns* Karl Ernst Schröder *lte* Markus Märkl *hpd/org*)

Harmonia Mundi HMC90 1651 (72 minutes: DDD) Ⓕ
Texts and translations included. Recorded 1997

Expressively versatile though Scholl unquestionably can be, it is perhaps in the sphere of elegy and plaint that his art can be heard to strongest advantage. Two pieces of outstanding merit fall into this category and are sung here with tonal beauty, stylistic assurance and expressive *puissance*. One of them is Johann Christoph Bach's lament *Ach, das ich Wassers g'nug hätte*. This member of the family worked during the second half of the 17th century and was greatly admired by J S Bach, who described him as 'profound'. The lament, in *da capo* form, is scored for countertenor, violin, three violas da gamba, cello and organ. The other is the much better-known strophic 'Klag-Lied' from the longer *Fried- und Freudenreiche Hinfahrt* by Buxtehude, written in memory of his father who had died early in 1674. Scholl does great justice to each of these intimate pieces, attending as much to the spirit and utterance of the texts as to the sorrowful and at times searing inflections of the music.

These performances alone would be sufficient enticement to acquire the disc but, happily, there is much else in the programme to touch our sensibilities. Schütz is well represented with three tenderly expressive pieces, two of them from the *Kleiner geistlichen Concerten* and a third from the *Symphoniae sacrae* (1647); and Franz Tunder by a declamatory and rhythmically graceful setting of a verse of the hymn *Herzlich lieb hab ich dir, o Herr*. This piece is one of two whose composers have been wrongly exchanged on the track listing: the other is *Salve mi Jesu* which, though preserved in a Tunder manuscript, is probably the work of the Venetian, Giovanni Rovetta. Sensibly, the order of events is punctuated by two works for instrumental ensemble, one of them by Ignazio Albertini, the other by Legrenzi, whose position in the history of recording seems still to be that of occasional stand-in. He deserves better, and doubtless will come into his own one day. The playing of the two groups, Concerto di Viole and the Basle Consort, is accomplished and refined, both in ensemble and tuning, providing sensitive support in the vocal pieces and affecting insights to the instrumental ones. Despite the fanciful (if ingenious) packaging, which is brittle, inconvenient and impractical, this release is strongly recommended.

Heroes

Gluck Orfeo ed Euridice – Che farò senza Euridice. Telemaco – Ah non turbi **Handel** Serse – Fronde tenere…Ombra mai fù. Semele – Where'er you walk. Saul – O Lord, whose mercies; Such haughty beauties. Rodelinda – Con rauco mormorio; Vivi tiranno!. Giulio Cesare – Dall' ondoso periglio…Aure deh, per pietà **Hasse** Artaserse – Palido il sole **Mozart** Ascanio in Alba – Al mio ben. Mitridate, Re di Ponto – Venga pur, minacci

Andreas Scholl *counterten* **Orchestra of the Age of Enlightenment / Sir Roger Norrington**

Decca 466 196-2OH (58 minutes: DDD) Ⓕ

Texts and translations included. Recorded 1998 ●

Heroes indeed! This is some of the finest heroic singing around, and in a countertenor voice – often supposed to be weakly or effeminate. There is heroism here in both love and war. Andreas Scholl's countertenor is formidable in every sense and transmits sturdy, masculine emotion just as forcefully as the softer sorts called for in, for example, what are probably the two most famous of the arias here: 'Ombra mai fù' (Handel's 'Largo'), which opens the recital, and 'Che farò' from *Orfeo*. The first of these discloses a wonderfully ample, creamy voice, beautifully even and controlled, capable of a poignantly soft top F and firm in profile in the lower register; the latter elicits an outpouring, a passionate one, of lovely tone, with a line of the chastity and purity that exactly captures Gluck's vision of his semi-divine hero. In 'Where'er you walk' – a tenor piece, transposed – he seems tonally more constrained, yet it is an uncommonly smooth and flowing performance. Of the other Handel items, particular mention should be made of the *Saul* aria 'O Lord, whose mercies', one of the loveliest Handel ever wrote, sung with great intensity of tone; the *Rodelinda* arias, one of them full of rapid *fioritura*, riskily but faultlessly delivered, and a peaceful one about a murmuring stream which, if perhaps taken rather quickly, nevertheless is a fine, serene piece of singing. The Hasse item is strong and impassioned, giving scope to Scholl's full bottom register; and of the two Mozart arias the one from *Mitridate* is a noble, powerful statement of defiance, done strongly and directly. Norrington provides generally sympathetic accompaniments. This is an exceptional recital in which one of today's most beautiful and imaginatively used voices is heard at its finest.

A Musicall Banquet

Anonymous Go, my flock, go get you hence. O bella più. O dear life, when shall it be? Passava Amor su arco desarmado. Sta notte mi sognava. Vuestros ojos tienen d'Amor **Batchelar** To plead my faith **Caccini** Amarilli mia bella. Dovrò dunque morire? **Dowland** Far from triumphing court. In darkness let me dwell. Lady, if you so spite me. Sir Robert Sydney His Galliard **Guédron** Ce penser qui sans fin tirannise ma vie. Si le parler et le silence. Vous que le bonheur rappelle **Hales** O eyes, leave off your weeping **Holborne** My heavy sprite **Martin** Change thy mind since she doth change **Megli** Se di farmi morire? **Tessier** In a grove most rich of shade

Andreas Scholl *counterten* **Edin Karamazov** *ltes/gtr/orph* **Christophe Coin** *bass viol* **Markus Märkl** *hpd*

Decca 466 917-2DH (67 minutes: DDD) Ⓕ

Texts and translations included.

Like his *Varietie of Lute Lessons*, also published in 1610, Robert Dowland's *A Musicall Banquet* is an odd and interestingly innovative collection. It includes works by his famous father as well as by several otherwise unknown English composers alongside four pieces with French texts, two with Spanish texts, and four in Italian. There are timeless masterpieces like John Dowland's *In darkness let me dwell* and Caccini's *Amarilli mia bella*; but there is also a pioneering attempt to bring a truly international repertory to England.

The complete volume has been recorded twice before, in the late 1970s: Nigel Rogers did a splendid version with the inspired partnership of Anthony Bailes and Jordi Savall (EMI – nla); and the Consort of Musicke, as part of their complete John Dowland set, presented a version – with four excellent singers and Anthony Rooley on particularly eloquent form on the lute – coming a little closer to the source in the use of a voice on some of the generally texted bass-lines (this is currently available only on the 1997 L'Oiseau-Lyre complete reissue on 12 CDs). But it was high time for a new version; and, with music in four languages, there could hardly be a better collection to show the qualities of Andreas Scholl. He has that ability to float a line marvellously without compromising the clarity of the text; and if some listeners feel that greater variety of colour is possible, he more than compensates with his unwavering, faultless control.

Edin Karamazov carries the bulk of the accompaniment with a range of plucked instruments and performing styles: he shows particular success in the cruelly exposed and slow lines of

In darkness let me dwell and in the more jaunty Spanish songs. Markus Märkl is a spirited harpsichordist in five pieces, and the wonderful Christophe Coin shows an astonishing range of colours and techniques on the bass viol.

This recording may not supersede the two earlier versions, but it offers many interesting alternatives, including a good reconstruction of the thoroughly garbled Italian that Dowland printed for *Sta notte*. Nobody will be disappointed. (No sleeve material was submitted.)

Elisabeth Schwarzkopf *sop*

Unpublished Lieder and Songs 1957-64 H

Bizet Pastorale[a] **Brahms** Von ewiger Liebe, Op 43 No 1[a]. Deutsche Volkslieder – In stiller Nacht[a]. Volks-Kinderlieder – Sandmännchen[a]. Wiegenlied, Op 49 No 4[a] **Flies** Wiegenlied[a] **Mozart** Un moto di gioia, K579[b]. Warnung, K433a[a] **Parisotti** Se tu m'ami, C xxii, 68[a] **Schubert** Claudine von Villa Bella – Liebe schwärmt auf allen Wegen[a]. Lachen und Weinen, D777[a]. Die Vögel, D691[a]. Der Jüngling an der Quelle, D300[a]. Du bist die Ruh, D776[a]. Wiegenlied, D498[a]. Die Forelle, D550[a] **Schumann** Widmung, Op 25 No 1[a] **R Strauss** Ruhe, meine Seele, Op 27 No 1[a]. Zueignung, Op 10 No 1[a].Wiegenlied, Op 41 No 1[a] **Wagner** Wesendonk Lieder – Traüme[a] **Wolf** Eichendorff Lieder[a] – Die Zigeunerin; Nachtzauber. Alte Weisen[a] – Tretet ein, hoher Krieger; Das Köhlerweib ist trunken

Elisabeth Schwarzkopf *sop* [a]**Gerald Moore,** [b]**Walter Gieseking** *pfs*

Testament SBT1206 (72 minutes: ADD) Ⓜ

Recorded 1957-64 ●

'Unpublished' is a word to warm the hearts and imaginations of collectors, and many of these recordings, though originally passed for issue, aren't even listed in official discographies. The first track here is a case in point – the aria from Schubert's *Claudine von Villa Bella* was a favourite with Schwarzkopf, but if one compares this recording from 1961 with the one eventually issued, made four years later, the 1965 version is more relaxed, having more of a sense of the surging lover's declaration. Persevere, though, and there are gems to be found.

Wolf's 'Die Zigeunerin' was one of Schwarzkopf's standbys. Perhaps you recall her singing it at the end of the first half of her last Royal Festival Hall concert in 1975. This was often a great moment in a Schwarzkopf recital – all nerves by then banished, the voice under control, she would play with the acoustic of the hall, using little echo effects that are caught on this recording. Maybe the reason it wasn't used, as in several other cases on the CD, is that the voice is a little too far forward, the pianist seeming to be banished to halfway back in the studio; but this gives a lovely sense of presence.

In other cases the songs were discarded probably because there simply wasn't room on the LP. One of these is the single track which is not accompanied by Gerald Moore, *Un moto di gioia*, part of her famous Mozart programme accompanied by Walter Gieseking. It is a joy, as is *Warnung* with Moore. The other 'encore' pieces by Flies, Bizet and Parisotti must surely have been intended for the LP called *Songs You Love*, a Cook's Tour through song. In *Se tu m'ami* there is a slight fluff on one of the little laughs which perhaps led to its exclusion, but in every other way it is as charming and beguiling as any light-hearted song Schwarzkopf ever recorded.

The Brahms group is compelling. This was the beginning of a project to record a whole LP of Brahms songs with which she continued into the 1970s, though only a few songs were ever released (on the fourth and final 'Songbook' LP). Strauss's *Zueignung* seems awfully slow, and less involved than one would expect.

Wagner's 'Träume' is the one instance of the unpublished take being preferable to that issued. Again, one can see why the later recording is a more dramatic reading, but here the voice is poised with such lightness and it's so intimate – if you're in doubt about the prospect of this CD, listen to that followed by the Bizet *Pastorale* and then 'Die Zigeunerin'. At once one is in the presence of the great singer, a perfectionist in everything she did, as hard on herself when judging her records as she sometimes could be on her students. She would shake her head after some lovely piece of pure vocalism and murmur, 'Ah, but that's the easy part'.

The Unpublished EMI Recordings (1946-52) H

Opera arias – La bohème, La traviata and Die Zauberflöte (sung in English); songs and sacred works by Bach, Gounod, T Arne, Morley, Mozart, Schubert, R Strauss and Wolf

Elisabeth Schwarzkopf *sop* with various artists

Testament mono ② SBT2172 (134 minutes: ADD) Ⓕ

Texts and translations included. Recorded 1946-52 ●

Good heavens!, I hear you cry, what need for more Schwarzkopf when there's already a heap of her recordings available, including performances of much of the same repertory. Well, there's a very good reason why Testament – and Schwarzkopf herself – thought this unissued material worth unearthing from the copious EMI archive. It may be heretical in the record world to say so, but Walter Legge had an Achilles' heel: he demanded perfection, and it was just occasionally bought at the expense of spontaneity. In the case of the commercial recordings included here, he thought his wife could perform the pieces better on a later occasion, but now we may judge that these earlier interpretations have that much more eager freshness than the previously published versions.

That's particularly so in the case of Bach's *Jauchzet Gott* and Mozart's *Exsultate, jubilate*. With Schwarzkopf in pristine, youthful voice, her production at its easiest, her breath long, both works shine forth as joyful things to hear – tone, line, runs, all in perfect accord. The remainder of the first CD, bar the final track, is a conspectus of the work the soprano was doing at the time, in the late 1940s, at Covent Garden where she was for a while a member of the resident company. Her Violetta, in English, and her Mimì, in Italian, both show her care over the words, which are inflected with heartfelt meaning in both cases. But the gem here is Schwarzkopf's private recording of all Pamina's role sung at home in English to piano accompaniment in order that she might learn the role properly in the vernacular. So here we have an invaluable souvenir of a quite beautifully sung performance of 51 years ago. Schwarzkopf introduces this delightful oddity herself, a further bonus for posterity. The very last item on this CD brings a discovery of a very different kind. Legge apparently thought the Bach-Gounod *Ave Maria* wasn't musically worthy of the partnership, so the performance was never issued. How wrong he was: it turns out to be one of those occasions when a great artist can convert dross into gold.

On the second disc we have another addition to the singer's recorded legacy in a charming account of Morley's *It was a lover and his lass*. For the rest, it's all discarded takes of Lieder issued in later performances. None is as compelling as the 1948 *Gretchen am Spinnrade*, a performance of concentrated feeling urgently executed, and an irresistible account of *Der Musensohn* is preferable to issued versions because of its verve. Two versions of Wolf's *Storchenbotschaft* are included; the first from 1948 the simpler, more natural, the second from 1951 a shade over-elaborated. Of the remaining Wolf songs, all recorded in 1951, three songs demand mention: *Bedeckt mich mit Blumen*, always a favourite with the singer, for its dreamy eroticism ideally adumbrated and sung with just the vibrancy called for, a reading of *Im Frühling*, filled with spring's yearning, and *Wiegenlied im Sommer*, in which Schwarzkopf's soothing, tender tones would persuade any child to untroubled sleep. Throughout, Gerald Moore is the soprano's faithful, supportive partner, and EMI's clean recording adds to profound pleasure in an issue lovingly performed and lovingly prepared, with evocative photos and full texts and translations.

Irmgard Seefried *sop*

Lieder by Brahms, Flies, Mozart, Schubert and Wolf H
Irmgard Seefried *sop* with various artists
Testament mono SBT1026 (74 minutes: ADD) Ⓕ
Recorded 1946-53

Another 'must' for anyone who loves Seefried. In these wonderfully immediate and faithful transfers of performances made in Vienna and London, Seefried is heard at the peak of her powers, when her voice was at its freshest and easiest. In the Mozart, whether the mood is happy, reflective or tragic, Seefried goes unerringly to the core of the matter. Here we have the archness of *Die kleine Spinnerin*, the naughty exuberance of *Warnung*, the deep emotion of *Abendempfindung* and *Unglückliche Liebe*. We are offered five Schubert songs, including an unsurpassed *Auf dem Wasser zu singen*, so airy and natural; a pure, elevated *Du bist die Ruh* and a poised, ravishing *Nacht und Träume*. The lullabies of Flies, Schubert and Brahms are all vintage Seefried. The Wolf items are a real treasure trove: a sorrowful, plangent account of *Das verlassene Mägdelein* (perhaps the most compelling interpretation of all here; unutterably moving), an enchanting, spontaneous *Elfenlied* (with Gerald Moore marvellously delicate here). For the most part, Moore is in attendance to complete one's pleasure in an irresistible and generously filled disc.

Mitsuko Shirai *mez*

Songs with Viola
Brahms Zwei Lieder, Op 91 **A Busch** Nun die Schatten dunkeln. Wonne der Wehmut. Aus den Himmelsaugen **Dargomïzhsky** Elegy, 'She is coming' **Gounod** Evening song **Loeffler** Quatre poèmes, Op 5 **Marx** Durch Einsamkeiten **Reutter** Fünf antike Oden, Op 57 **R Strauss** Stiller Gang, Op 31 No 4
Mitsuko Shirai *mez* **Tabea Zimmermann** *va*
Hartmut Höll *pf*
Capriccio 10 462 (66 minutes: DDD) Ⓕ
Texts and translations included. Recorded 1993-94

Voice and viola, we think, form a soothing combination: the sound of the words suggests as much, and memories of Brahms's Op 91 confirm it. The Brahms songs come second in this present programme, and on either side are compositions by Richard Strauss and Adolf Busch that are very much in keeping, the mood generally peaceful, the style essentially lyrical. Then come the *Quatre poèmes* of Charles Martin Loeffler (1861-1935). These, like the songs by Busch and, later, Hermann Reutter, are recorded now for the first time and they form a welcome addition to the small catalogue of Loeffler's works on record. In this programme, they, together with Reutter's 'Sappho', provide a contrast, a more bracing and varied use of the combination. Mitsuko Shirai, now mezzo-soprano, sings with almost consistently firm and beautiful tone. She lightens the voice skilfully, as in Brahms's 'Gestillte Sehnsucht', and produces some beautifully sustained singing, as in the third of the Loeffler *Poèmes*, 'Le son du cor'. There is also an assured authority in this deeper voice with no less of the familiar charm. With fine playing by Tabea Zimmermann, especially in the Reutter cycle where the instrument is most imaginatively exploited, and with Hartmut Höll as sensitive as ever, this is a desirable disc.

Amy Shuard *sop*

Giordano Andrea Chénier – La mamma morta[a]
Mascagni Cavalleria rusticana – Voi lo sapete[a]
Puccini Turandot – In questa Reggia[a]. Gianni Schicchi – O mio babbino caro[a]. Tosca – Vissi d'arte[a]. La bohème – Quando m'en vo' soletta[a] **Tchaikovsky** Eugene Onegin – Tatyana's Letter Scene, Act 1[b]
Verdi Aida[a] – Ritorna vincitor; L'insana parola; Qui Radames verrà; O patria mia. Un ballo in maschera – Morrò, ma prima in grazia[a]
Amy Shuard *sop* [a]**Royal Opera House Orchestra, Covent Garden / Sir Edward Downes;** [b]**Royal Philharmonic Orchestra / George Weldon**
Dutton Laboratories CDCLP4006 Ⓜ
(56 minutes: DDD). Recorded 1961-62

'Where has this voice been all my life?' people will be saying as they come upon it for the first time in this disc. And indeed others, for whom the voice was for so many years just around the corner and a few tube stops away, will wonder whether they appreciated it properly when it was part of more or less day-to-day experience. The impression here is magnificent: a tone as beautiful as, say, mid-period Tebaldi and a volume comparable to that of Shuard's great teacher, Dame Eva Turner. The first phrase of all, the opening of 'Ritorna vincitor', could almost be mistaken for Dame Eva's, every 'r' so resolutely rolled, and an expression severely that of the princess rather than the slave-girl. She softens in manner and volume for 'Numi, pietà', but on the whole this is an Aida in the heroic mould, and even in 'O patria mia' the mood is firmly regulated, the nostalgia kept within bounds. Turandot is also Turneresque, formidable in vocal demeanour, indomitable on high.

Plenty of critical opinion – and Alan Blyth's notes quote Harold Rosenthal, Philip Hope-Wallace and Andrew Porter – can be adduced to confirm from live experience the superb impression created by these records, though some will not remember it quite so. Nevertheless, she was a genuinely distinguished operatic artist, and in international casts (as in *Un ballo in maschera*) clearly earned her place.

Of the negative elements, the record recalls her somewhat unvarying countenance and a sense of limited responsiveness (she knows when to soften, as she does, beautifully, in Tatyana's Letter scene, but doesn't enter into the development of feeling towards that point). However, it also revives a memory of her warm, moving and very accomplished singing of the *Ballo* aria, and it kindles a wish that we could have heard her in *Andrea Chénier*. The gift and accomplishment put on record here remain outstanding, as is the quality of transfer.

Giuseppe Di Stefano *ten*

Opera Arias H

L'amico Fritz, L'Arlesiana, L'elisir d'amore, La fanciulla del West, La forza del destino, Gianni Schicchi, Manon, Mignon, Tosca and Turandot; songs by **Bixio**, **Tagliaferri**; Sicilian folk-songs

Giuseppe Di Stefano *ten* with various artists

Testament mono SBT1096 (79 minutes: ADD) Ⓕ

Recorded 1944-56

Very moving it is to hear this voice again in its absolute prime. It is hardly possible to hear those Swiss recordings of 1944, with piano, and be untouched by the thought, as well as the sound, of this 22-year-old, singing his heart out, with so much voice and, already, with so much art. The 'Una furtiva lagrima' is perhaps not the fully polished article, but what Forster called the Italian 'instinct for beauty' is there, with lovely shading and phrasing. It is good to have the two Bixio songs (*Se vuoi goder la vita* and *Mamma*), previously unpublished, heartfelt, open-throated performances in the national tradition that used to get mocked and is now so missed. Indeed, thinking of that sequence of recordings, one could well wish this disc had given priority to reproducing them all: there is an amazingly good 'Pourquoi me réveiller?', for instance, and (till the end) a beautifully restrained *Musica proibita*. Still, what we have here fulfils exactly the promise of the label's name: it is a testament, and a testament of youth. The later operatic recordings, from 1955, find the tenor with some signs of wear and with a recklessly open way of taking his high As and B flats, but there is real passion, and imagination with it. In the latest recording, a commonplace song called *Passione* from 1956, one almost looks up at the speakers to see the face there: it seems so very clear and lifelike. Some of the sound (recording or transfer) seems overbright – the second *Manon* solo is a prime example – but it is always vivid and compelling. In the booklet-listing a translation of the song-titles would have been welcome. It would also have been useful if Peter Hutchinson's notes had related the excerpts to Di Stefano's career (did he for instance ever sing Dick Johnson, Rinuccio and Calaf on stage?).

Elsie Suddaby *sop*

Songs and Arias by **M Arne**, **T Arne**, **Bach**, **Besly**, **Carey**, **Denza**, **Ford**, **German**, **Handel**, **Haydn**, **Jackson**, **MacCunn**, **Mendelssohn**, **Morley**, **Mozart**, **Purcell**, **Schubert**, **Somervell**, **Stanford** and **Warlock** H

Elsie Suddaby *sop* with various artists

Amphion mono PHICD134 (80 minutes: ADD) Ⓜ

Recorded 1924-52

Elsie Suddaby (1893-1980) was a close contemporary of Isobel Baillie and Dora Labbette and in many ways she evinces the strongest personality of the three, and has a distinctive timbre very much her own. That can be heard in the first item, Michael Arne's *The lass with the delicate air*, a piece she virtually appropriated as her signature tune. She sings it with such variety of tone and, yes, such delicacy of accent, that one capitulates at once to so graceful an artist. In Dido's Lament, the singular quality of being able, simply and naturally, to move the listener is there: adding appoggiaturas to the recitative and discreetly employing *portamento* in the Lament itself she goes to the heart of the matter. There is also the joyfully affirmative side of her art, shown in a fresh account of 'Rejoice greatly' from *Messiah* and 'Endless pleasure', as Semele wallows in her conquest of Jupiter. Better still is a version of 'Let the bright Seraphim' (*Samson*) that rings the rafters with its zealous delivery. Runs in all these Handel pieces are keenly accomplished, though not quite with Baillie's assurance. These HMV recordings catch Suddaby in her prime, when she was in her thirties, yet on a Decca 10-inch of 1941 of Thomas Arne's *Where the bee sucks* and Morley's *It was a lover and his lass*, there is no diminution of her powers, and even the Warlock songs and Mozart's *Agnus Dei*, when Suddaby was in her late fifties, find the tone almost as fresh as ever and wholly free of wobble. The CD is a generous offering, the transfers mostly well done and the booklet obviously a labour of love.

Dame Joan Sutherland *sop*

The Art of the Prima Donna

Opera Arias – Artaxerxes, Die Entführung aus dem Serail, Faust, Hamlet, Les Huguenots, Lakmé, Norma[a], Otello, I Puritani, Rigoletto[a], Roméo et Juliette, Samson, Semiramide[a], La sonnambula and La traviata

Dame Joan Sutherland *sop* [a]**Chorus and Orchestra of the Royal Opera House, Covent Garden / Francesco Molinari-Pradelli**

Decca Legends ② 467 115 2DL2 Ⓜ

(109 minutes: ADD). Texts and translations included. Recorded 1960 ○○○

The occasion of Dame Joan Sutherland's 70th birthday in November 1996 prompted Decca to reissue numerous opera sets from the 1960s. The two-disc recital, 'The Art of the Prima Donna' has hardly been out of the catalogue since 1960 – now it's remastered for Classic Sound. There cannot be many admirers who haven't already got this, so for newcomers to Sutherland on disc one can only say – listen and wonder. Her voice, even throughout its range right up to the high E, always keeping its natural quality, is heard at its early fullness. Perhaps the best tracks of all are 'The soldier tir'd' from *Artaxerxes* and 'Let the bright seraphim' from *Samson*, but every track is beautiful. 'Casta Diva' – her earliest attempt at it – is her most limpid recording of this prayer, 'Bel raggio' from *Semiramide* has sparkling decorations, quite different from the ones she sang on the complete recording six years later, and the whole thing ends with the Jewel Song from *Faust*. It was a big voice and sounded at its best in larger theatres; listening to 'O beau pays' from *Les Huguenots*, one can see Sutherland in one's mind's eye, in pale blue silk, as Marguerite de Valois at the Royal Albert Hall in 1968. It is difficult to imagine anyone, coming to it for the first time, being disappointed.

Richard Tauber *ten*

Opera Arias and Duets 🄷

Aida, Il barbiere di Siviglia, The Bartered Bride, La bohème, Carmen, Don Giovanni, Eugene Onegin, Der Evangelimann, La forza del destino, Fra Diavolo, I gioielli della Madonna, Der Kuhreigen, Madama Butterfly, Martha, Mignon, Der Rosenkavalier, Tosca, Die tote Stadt, La traviata, Il trovatore, Die Walküre and Die Zauberflöte

Richard Tauber *ten* with various artists

Preiser Lebendige Vergangenheit mono ② 89219 Ⓕ

(143 minutes: AAD). Recorded 1919-26

Das Deutsche Volkslied 🄷

Opera Arias – Don Giovanni and Die tote Stadt; songs by **Heymann** and **R Strauss**

Richard Tauber *ten* with various artists

Claremont mono CDGSE78-50-64 Ⓜ

(67 minutes: ADD). Recorded 1924-39

These two issues present a neatly complementary view of Tauber's career. The Preiser set gives us a picture of the young tenor in his days almost exclusively as an opera artist in German-speaking lands singing his repertory in the vernacular. It evinces the golden, sappy, honeyed tone of Tauber in his prime. The style at this stage is wholly disciplined, but already we hear that outgoing, spontaneous exuberance that was soon to bring him world-wide fame in operetta. Few if any tenors have sung Mozart quite so beautifully as Tauber at this point in his career: the 1922 Bildnis aria is a model of its kind, preferable to his later version, and an object-lesson in phrasing for any aspiring tenor. His interpretations of Lensky's aria, the famous piece from *Der Evangelimann*, José's Flower Song, Jenik's aria (a glorious 1919 version) and Wilhelm Meister's farewell to Mignon show the plangent, almost melancholic timbre with which Tauber could invest such repertory. Then for pure singing his readings of the Italian Tenor's aria, Siegmund's Spring Song, Alfredo's aria and Pinkerton's outpouring of remorse are hard to beat. Add to this the many duets he never repeated in electric versions and you have a most desirable issue. In the company of regular colleagues of that time, such as Rethberg, Bettendorf, Sabine Kalter and, best of all perhaps, Lotte Lehmann (*Die tote Stadt* duets), his contributions reveal his generosity of both voice and manner. This is free-ranging, rich-hued singing marred only by most of the music being sung in the 'wrong' language. There are a few downward transpositions in the solos, but that was common practice at the time. Otherwise there's little to criticise here in the performances and none in the excellent transfers. The more intimate side of Tauber's art comes in the series of *Volkslieder* he recorded for Parlophone in 1926, nicely transferred by Claremont. Here one admires the very personal way in which he caresses these charmingly unassuming pieces. Four Strauss songs from 1932 sessions follow, notable for the passion in the tone. What a pity the CD wasn't completed with more Lieder rather than operatic items already available in numerous transfers, including the less-than-satisfactory Ottavio arias of 1939. But at the end there's a gem: 'Kennst du das kleine Haus am Michigansee?' where Tauber lavishes on a trifle all the magic of his incredible technique and heady tone, including those *pianissimos* conjured from nowhere. The transfers are excellent.

Bryn Terfel *bar*

We'll Keep a Welcome – The Welsh Album

T Gwynn Jones Diolch I'r Iôr[ef] **W S Gwynn Williams** My Little Welsh Home[f] **A Hughes** Tydi a Roddaist[ef] **J Hughes** Calon Lân[ef]. Cwm Rhondda[ef] **James** Hen Wlad fy Nhadau[ef] **M Jones** We'll Keep a Welcome[ef] **Lewis** Bugail Aberdyfi[a] **Parry** Myfanwy[ef] **Prichard** Hyfrydol[ef] **Richards** Cymru Fach[f] **Traditional** Ar Lan y Môr[f]. Dafydd y Garreg Wen[cdf]. Men of Harlech[ef]. Sosban Fach[ef]. Ar Hyd y Nos[ef]. Hiraeth[cef]. Suo Gân[f] **Troyte** Sunset Poem[b] **O Williams** Sul y Blodau[a]

Bryn Terfel *bar* **Bryan Davies** [a]*pf*/[b]*org* [c]**Meinir Heulyn,** [d]**Katherine Thomas** *hps* [e]**Black Mountain Chorus,** [e]**Risca Male Choir,** [f]**Welsh National Opera Orchestra / Gareth Jones**
DG 463 593-2GH (75 minutes: DDD) Ⓕ
Texts and translations included

If the Welsh people showed signs of caution when voting for a National Assembly, they might have been stirred into greater numbers at the ballot box by this finely sung and unashamedly patriotic collection of songs featuring their mastersinger Bryn Terfel.

The programme is indeed 'eclectic', as described by Terfel, ranging from the unfamiliar, such as *Cymru Fach* with its Schubertian modulations and Arwel Hughes's beautiful melody *Tydi a Roddaist*, to such well-known songs as *Ar Hyd y Nos* ('All Through the Night') and *We'll Keep a Welcome*, made popular not so long ago by Sir Harry Secombe.

Careful planning has evidently been given to the content of this CD, but with a diverse cast-list of two choirs, the Orchestra of the Welsh National Opera, harp, organ and piano, it is impossible to prevent the occasional jolt to the ear. The melancholy and introspective mood of the lullabies and songs expressing a longing for the Homeland followed by such robust fare as *Cwm Rhondda* and *Men of Harlech*, taken here at a jaunty tempo, would benefit from a longer pause between tracks.

Chris Hazell has written some attractive arrangements to enhance such songs as *Ar Lan y Môr* ('On the Seashore'), which has a grave oboe obbligato, and a sympathetic setting of *Suo-Gân* ('Lullaby') for solo voice and orchestra.

The simple *legato* line of *Dafydd y Garreg Wen* ('David of the White Rock'), accompanied by harp, shows off Terfel's vocal sensitivity, and is such a highlight that it is a pity he could not have opened his CD with the solo version (instead of a choral version) of *Hen Wlad fy Nhadau* ('Land of my Fathers'), which is reprised anyway for full choir as a finale.

This album offers a rare treat in hearing Bryn Terfel relishing the music of Wales sung in his native tongue, with two vigorous supporting choirs who also demonstrate a gentler side to their art in humming the introduction to *Ar Hyd y Nos* ('All Through the Night'). With the two distinguished harpists and keyboard players they provide the best possible advertisement for repertoire that has for too long been neglected by the major record companies.

Opera Arias

Borodin Prince Igor – No sleep, no rest
Donizetti Don Pasquale – Bella siccome un angelo
Gounod Faust – Vous qui faîtes l'endormie **Mozart** Le nozze di Figaro – Non più andrai. Don Giovanni – Madamina, il catalogo è questo; Deh! vieni alla finestra. Così fan tutte – Rivolgete a lui lo sguardo. Die Zauberflöte – Der Vogelfänger bin ich ja
Offenbach Les contes d'Hoffmann – Allez!...Pour te livrer combat...Scintille, diamant **Rossini** La Cenerentola – Miei rampolli femminini **Verdi** Macbeth – Perfidi! All'angelo contra me v'unite!...Pietà, rispetto, amore. Falstaff – Ehi! paggio! ...L'Onore! Ladri! **Wagner** Tannhäuser – Wie Todesahnung... O du mein holder Abendstern. Der fliegende Holländer – Die Frist ist um
Bryn Terfel *bass-bar* **Orchestra of the Metropolitan Opera, New York / James Levine**
DG 445 866-2GH (71 minutes: DDD) Ⓕ
Texts and translations included.
Recorded 1994-95

In a careless moment we might describe Bryn Terfel as a very physical singer, and it would be true up to a point. His physical presence is much in evidence when he sings, or for that matter when he talks or just breathes. Having seen him 'in the flesh', one seems to see him while hearing the sound of his voice on records. But the crowning distinction of Terfel's art (granted the voice, the technique and the general musicianship) is its intelligence. As with words, so with characters: each is a specific, sharp-minded creation, and none is a stereotype. This Leporello exhibits his master's catalogue with pride; it is the book of life and not to be taken lightly. This Don Magnifico recounts his dream in all good faith (he doesn't *know* that he's a complete idiot, and doesn't deliberately set himself up to sound like one). No less impressive, as an aspect of intelligence, is the linguistic command, and still more so the use he makes of it: the sheer mental concentration of his Dutchman carries intense conviction and an ever-specific understanding. In short, this is a magnificent recital with fine recorded sound.

Luisa Tetrazzini *sop*

Opera Arias H

Un ballo in maschera, Il barbiere di Siviglia, Carmen, Dinorah, La forza del destino, Las hijas del Zebedeo, Lakmé, Linda di Chamounix, Lucia di Lammermoor, Mignon, La perle du Brésil, Rigoletto, Roméo et Juliette, Rosalinda, La sonnambula, La traviata, Il trovatore, I vespri siciliani and Die Zauberflöte; songs by **Benedict**, **Brahms**, **Cowen**, **De Koven**, **Eckert**, **Gilbert**, **Grieg**, **Moore**, **Pergolesi**, **Proch** and **Venzano**
Luisa Tetrazzini *sop* with various artists
Romophone mono ② 81025-2 (150 minutes: ADD) Ⓕ
Recorded 1904-20

Though Tetrazzini was one of the most prized and assiduously collected of recording artists in her time, her career on record was not really very satisfactory. As was true of several others she repeated the same items in several versions, whereas, especially in those days of such restricted recording-time, an extension to the repertoire would have been so much more welcome. The repertoire itself relied heavily on the familiar *chevaux de bataille*, the Mad scenes, Bell song, Shadow song and so forth, and often when something out of the way comes along, either, like the 'Pastorale' from Veracini's *Rosalinda*, it is not well suited, or, as with Proch's vapid variations, it was not worth doing in the first place.

There must also have been difficulties in successfully catching a voice which combined such brilliance and power with what could all too often emerge on record as a colourless and even infantile quality. Of the Victors reproduced here the best and most essential Tetrazzini is the 1911 'Ah, non giunge' (*La sonnambula*). The cabaletta, 'Di tale amor', following 'Tacea la notte' (*Il trovatore*) is also a joy. The *Lucia di Lammermoor* sextet and *Rigoletto* quartet with Caruso, Amato and others are also prime attractions, fine performances in many (but not all) ways and remarkably clear and lifelike as recorded sound. The five Zonophones are interesting collector's pieces, and not the write-off they are sometimes said to be, but a mixed pleasure, with Tetrazzini cheerfully distributing pearls while her brother-in-law, Cleofonte Campanini, administers a remorselessly clonking piano accompaniment.

Maggie Teyte *sop*

Chansons by **Berlioz**, **Debussy**, **Duparc** and **Fauré** H
Dame Maggie Teyte *sop* with various artists
Pearl mono GEMMCD9134 (74 minutes: ADD) Ⓜ
Recorded 1936-41

There was some sort of magic in the air at the EMI Abbey Road Studios in London on March 12 and 13, 1936. Maggie Teyte, just short of her 48th birthday, and Alfred Cortot, both of whom had been well acquainted with Claude Debussy, recorded 14 of his *mélodies*. This is no studio-bound recital but a performance, the passion and beauty of tone matched stroke for stroke by pianist and singer. These records, and the later ones Teyte made with Gerald Moore, are among the jewels of Debussy singing and playing. No one with an interest in French song should hesitate to acquire them, for they provide a lesson, not just in pronunciation of the French language (though like her contemporary and supposed rival, Mary Garden, Teyte sang with a pronounced English accent – something which entranced the French in the *belle époque*, when all things English were *à la mode*).

The beauty of Teyte's tone, the freshness and girlish quality of her high notes – something which never deserted her, and she continued to sing for another 20 years after this recording – are constantly astonishing. So, too, is the passion she puts into phrases such as 'Qu'il était bleu, le ciel, et grand l'espoir!' in 'Colloque sentimental' from the second book of *Fêtes galantes*, or the decidedly dark-hued 'Il me dit: 'Les satyres sont morts,' in 'Le tombeau des Naïdes' from *Chansons de Bilitis*.

Those who already have some of the other reissues of Teyte's Debussy recordings will find that this Pearl disc has a rather higher surface noise, perhaps the price one has to pay for getting the voice more forward. One wonders why Pearl have called the disc 'Chansons', the correct term for these settings is *Mélodies* – or there is the good old English word 'song'.

Dawn Upshaw *sop*

Goethe Lieder
Mozart Das Veilchen, K476 **Schubert** Rastlose Liebe, D138. Gretchen am Spinnrade, D118. Mignons Gesang, D877 No 4. Suleika I, D720. Versunken, D715. Wanderers Nachtlied II, D768. Ganymed, D544. An den Mond, D296 **Schumann** Liebeslied, Op 51 No 5. Nachtlied, Op 96 No 1. Lieder und Gesänge aus Wilhelm Meister, Op 98*a* – No 1, Mignon; No 5, Heiss mich nicht reden; No 7, Singet nicht in Trauertönen **Wolf** Blumengruss. Die Bekehrte. Die Spröde. Frühling übers Jahr
Dawn Upshaw *sop* **Richard Goode** *pf*
Nonesuch 7559-79317-2 (53 minutes: DDD) Ⓕ
Texts and translations included. Recorded 1993

Upshaw and Goode are a musical marriage made in heaven, each a highly individual, probing and sincere artist prepared to challenge received views on a song. Thus their *Gretchen am Spinnrade* in this programme of all-Goethe settings is an outburst of a desperate and infinitely perturbed woman breaking conventional bonds. To emphasise the point Upshaw leans into the first syllable of 'nimmer' at each repetition with added feeling and times the climax of the great song at the word 'Kuss' in an overwhelming way, only such a similarly involving (although very different) interpreter as Lotte Lehmann could. Goode's playing simply underlines and reinforces the singer's intense utterance.

The Schumann settings are filled with just as much spontaneous emotion and direct imagination. The pair make as strong a case as is possible for Schumann's setting of Mignon's *Kennst du das Land* being superior even to Wolf's, the repeated 'Kennst du das wohl?' carrying an extraordinary charge. The singer's voice is also ideally fitted for Wolf's teasingly sensual *Die Spröde* and *Die Bekehrte* and the pair bring the lightest touch to *Blumengruss*. Finally they give Mozart's *Das Veilchen* a deeper meaning than almost any interpreters. An ideally balanced, forward yet spacious recording enhances the pleasure.

Awards 1995

I wish it so
Bernstein West Side Story – I feel pretty. Candide – Glitter and be gay. The Madwoman of Central Park West – My new friends **Blitzstein** Juno – I wish it so. No for an Answer – In the clear. Reuben, Reuben – Never get lost **Sondheim** Anyone Can Whistle – There won't be trumpets. Saturday Night – What more do I need? The Girls of Summer – The Girls of Summer. Merrily We Roll Along – Like it was. Evening Primrose – Take me to the world **Weill** One Touch of Venus – That's him. Lady in the Dark – The saga of Jenny; My ship. Lost in the Stars – Stay well
Dawn Upshaw *sop* **orchestra / Eric Stern**
Nonesuch 7559-79345-2 (45 minutes: DDD) Ⓜ
Texts included. Recorded 1993

Bernstein, Blitzstein, Sondheim and Weill are a good quartet to explore in a recital and Dawn Upshaw's clear soprano is well suited to nearly all these songs. The Blitzstein numbers will only be familiar to specialists. 'I wish it so' from Blitzstein's adaptation of O'Casey's *Juno* seems to herald the mood of the whole disc, songs of longing, some optimistic, some resigned. 'In the clear' is one of the songs from *No for an Answer*, Blitzstein's follow-up to *The Cradle Will Rock*; it was first given in 1940, the same week that saw the first night of Weill's *Lady in the Dark*. In the Blitzstein, Eric Stern's arrangement with a solo cello part played by Matthias Niegele turns the song into a melancholy lullaby. This and a brilliant performance of 'Glitter and be gay' from *Candide* show off Upshaw's impressive range – from the coloratura of the Bernstein to mezzo-ish moodiness for the Blitzstein. Of the Weill songs, 'Stay well' from *Lost in the Stars* is especially successful, and 'That's him' from *One Touch of Venus* is playful. The two numbers from *Lady in the Dark* are given the most extensive overhaul, the melody of 'The saga of Jenny' such as it is disappears beneath Larry Wilcox's rearrangement and although Upshaw sings 'My ship' quite beautifully, again Daniel Troob has made an arrangement that pulls it about. All in all, this is a very attractive foray into the Broadway territory.

Norman Walker *bass*

A Portrait of Norman Walker H

Opera and Oratorio Arias – Acis and Galatea, The Children of Don, The Creation, The Dream of Gerontius, Dylan, Die Entführung aus dem Serail, Faust, Judas Maccabaeus, Messiah, La morte d'Orfeo, Le quattro stagioni (**B Marcello**), Die Zauberflöte; songs by **Capel**, **Haynes**, **Lane Wilson**, **Purcell** and **Storace**

Norman Walker *bass* with various artists

Dutton Laboratories mono CDLX7021 Ⓑ

(71 minutes: ADD). Recorded 1928-54

Norman Walker was one of our leading basses for some 17 years from 1937 when he sang as the Commendatore and the Speaker at Glyndebourne and King Mark (with Dame Eva Turner as Isolde) at Covent Garden. From then on he balanced his career nicely between the stage and the concert hall. This welcome reissue opens resplendently with Walker singing Handel and Haydn in the classic manner: steady, burnished tone, every run in its place and diction exemplary. Then comes Walker's unsurpassed account of the Angel of the Agony's solo from *Gerontius*, so urgent, so sympathetic, here allowed to run on to let us hear Heddle Nash sing 'I go before my judge' so movingly. Of Walker's opera repertory we hear a student account of 'O Isis und Osiris', which gives some evidence of what was to follow, and a test made in 1944 for Walter Legge of Osmin's aria, which suggests he might have been a good interpreter of that role. The extracts indicate Walker's dramatic prowess (though his Italian is far from idiomatic) – as does his brief contribution to the closing trio from *Faust*, with Joan Cross a suitably distraught Marguerite. More valuable than these, however, because they display so unerringly Walker's gifts as a conviction-singer, are the four British songs made at one session in 1952 with Gerald Moore. They are exemplified in the bass's confident tone, unobtrusive word-painting and subtle use of rubato. Indeed the singer, in these faultless transfers, seems to be in the room with us. Malcolm Walker provides a warm, personal cameo of his father in his notes.

Dolora Zajick *mez*

The Dramatic Soprano Voice

Cilea Adriana Lecouvreur – Acerba voluttà **Gluck** Orphée et Eurydice – J'ai perdu mon Eurydice. Alceste – Divinités du Styx **Mascagni** Cavalleria rusticana – Voi lo sapete **Mussorgsky** Khovanshchina – Sily potalnye **Rossini** Semiramide – Ah! quel giorno ognor rammento **Saint-Saëns** Samson et Dalila – Mon coeur s'ouvre à ta voix **Tchaikovsky** The Maid of Orleans – Prostite vy kholhv **Verdi** Don Carlo – O don fatale. Macbeth – La luce langue; Una macchia è qui tuttora. Il trovatore – Condotta ell'era in ceppi

Dolora Zajick *mez* **Royal Philharmonic Orchestra / Charles Rosekrans**

Telarc CD80557 (69 minutes: DDD) Ⓕ

Zajick, widely known as one of the leading operatic mezzo-sopranos of the day, is introduced here as a soprano, though neither the voice nor repertoire seems greatly to have changed. The addition of Lady Macbeth to the list of roles is interesting but not surprising, for it has been sung quite often by mezzos (on records, for instance, by Cossotto, Höngen and Verrett). It is not clear what purpose is served by apportioning the voice and (presumably) the repertoire to a different vocal category; the case is perhaps made out in the booklet, which was not included in the review copy, but it would have to be remarkably strong to convince us that Gluck's Orpheus, Verdi's Azucena and Mussorgsky's Marfa are roles for a soprano, however dramatic.

The voice is certainly one of exceptional quality and power. In spite of some 20 years of hard usage (she had been singing professionally for some time before winning her Tchaikovsky prize in 1982), the surface remains to a large extent unworn, its high and low notes particularly thrilling in thrust and opulence. The limitation lies in something which, if not exactly Slavonic wobble (Zajick is American by birth), is 'operatic vibrato', a condition common to many powerful voices where sustained notes, especially at a *forte*, may be perfectly firm while losing evenness and definition elsewhere. This affects the pleasure of her 'J'ai perdu mon Eurydice' more than that of 'Divinités du Styx' and of her Rossini rather more than her Cilea. In Verdi her richness of tone and assurance of dramatic authority carry the day.

Best is probably the *Don Carlos*: a towering performance of Eboli's great solo, impresssive on record, overwhelming in the effect one can imagine it having in the theatre. The deep, baleful phrases of Azucena in *Il trovatore* have the authentic quality, too. In *Semiramide* it is good to hear her singing the runs without aspirates.

In *Khovanshchina* she catches well the awe of Marfa's invocation and the humanity of her prophetic utterance. As Lady Macbeth she is not imaginative in colouring or in verbal expressiveness but rises triumphantly to the climaxes, both the loud and the soft. With no other solo recital to her name in the current catalogue, Zajick is certainly welcome to the opportunities afforded by this one, in which she is well supported by the RPO and its sympathetic conductor.

Chant

Anonymous 4

1000: A Mass for the End of Time – Medieval Chant and Polyphony for the Ascension

Anonymous Judicii signum. Quem creditis super astra/Viri galilei. Celestis terrestrisque. Prudentia prudentium. Dominus in sina. Ascendens cristus. Salvator mundi/Rex omnipotens die hodierna. Elevatus est rex fortis/Viri galilei. Ante secula. Omnipotens eterne. Corpus quod nunc/Psallite domino. Apocalypse 21:1-5. Regnantem sempiterna. Cives celestis patrie

Anonymous 4 (Marsha Genensky, Susan Hellauer, Jacqueline Horner, Johanna Rose *sngrs*)

Harmonia Mundi HMU90 7224 (72 minutes: DDD) Ⓕ

Texts and translations included. Recorded 2000

For their tenth recording and their first of the new millennium, Anonymous 4 have decided to go apocalyptic. Not that it shows in the customary purity and calmness of their chanting, but for this CD they have taken as their theme the Last Judgment as evoked in a liturgical reconstruction of a Mass for Ascension Day from about the year 1000. The fears of what would happen at the end of the first millennium were genuine and widespread: Mankind would be judged and found wanting, Satan would appear and reap destruction. The apocalyptic visions of St John the Divine are echoed in the processional hymn with which Anonymous 4 begin their recording, *Judicii signum*, but otherwise the troped chants of the Proper and Ordinary of the Mass focus on Christ's Ascension, and refer to his coming to judge the quick and the dead in the more straightforward language of the liturgy.

Much of the music on this CD comes from manuscripts of chant and early polyphony from around 1000, mostly from the abbey of St Martial in Limoges, but with two pieces from the Winchester Troper. A lot of the chant, then, is Aquitanian in origin, and it can sound quite different to the now more familiar Gregorian tradition, with melodies that have a sweep and range not commonly encountered there. Indeed, Anonymous 4 make the most of these steeper melodic curves, notably in the troped Offertory *Elevatus est rex fortis/Viri galilei*, which gives them something to get their teeth into; elsewhere the chanting can sound a little tentative or even become rather static. Generally, though, the flow is good, and the different ways of embellishing the chant are convincingly done and provide welcome contrast. The embellishments range from the addition of other vocal lines which move in parallel or contrary motion to the chant, or simply serve as a sustained drone (a kind of harmonic trope of the melody), to the introduction of various types of ornament: repeated notes, simple turns, or Eastern-sounding slides. These are used sparingly and are executed with great precision.

The insert-notes make commendably clear which pieces have been elaborated polyphonically by the group, so alerting the listener to this further element of reconstruction. Leading chant scholars have been consulted about certain aspects of interpretation, and the recording is on the whole as exemplary in its thoughtful presentation as in the scrupulous performances they offer. If at times their singing is over-careful and unspontaneous, their fans will not be disappointed by this, the latest impressive contribution to little-known corners of the very early musical repertory by the 'fab four of medieval music' as *The New Yorker* has described them.

Ensemble Organum

Chants of the Church of Rome

Vespers for Easter Sunday

Ensemble Organum / Marcel Pérès *bar*

Harmonia Mundi HMC90 1604 (79 minutes: DDD) Ⓕ

Texts and translations included. Recorded 1996

Most scholars agree that a link exists between the Old Roman repertoire and the so-called Gregorian. The latter became official in Carolingian times, leading to the invention of Western notation. The main problem regarding this link is the absence of notated sources of Old Roman chant before the 12th to 13th centuries. These reconstructed Vespers are an attempt to demonstrate not only the magnificent service of Easter Vespers as sung in St John of the Lateran in the 12th century, but also a whole repertoire and performance style, carried through from at least six centuries previously. Marcel Pérès defends his theory that as late as the 12th century and beyond, the style of performance in a Roman basilica would have been similar to that practised today in Eastern rite Christianity. Indeed, many of the earliest neume shapes we strive to interpret spring to life in the light of such a style.

This performance is exhilarating, even convincing. An outline of the famous Gregorian *Alleluia, Pascha nostrum*, for example, which we sing today from sources dating from the late 9th and early 10th centuries, can be detected, buried beneath countless repetitions of typical phrases and a proliferation of ornament, elements that serve to build up a cumulative impression of strength. They are pruned away in the Gregorian revision, which is terser, more structured melodically and more coherent, according to a later understanding of modality. There can be no question that this is an important disc.

Canterbury Cathedral

Gregorian Chant
Mass for the Feast of St Thomas of Canterbury.
The Office of Matins for St Thomas of Canterbury.
St Dunstan's Kyrie
Lay Clerks of Canterbury Cathedral Choir / David Flood
Metronome METCD1003 (74 minutes: DDD) Ⓕ
Texts and translations included. Recorded 1994

A recording of music for the Feast of St Thomas à Becket by the Lay Clerks of Canterbury Cathedral is a delightful idea. The music for this feast in the Salisbury rite is rich and memorable, particularly that for the Offices. In this case the selection from Matins includes five magnificent responsories and two antiphons, as well as the hymn *Martyr Dei* and the Invitatory, *Assunt Thomas Martyris*. This last item is particularly valuable, since though the Invitatory has generally not found much favour in recordings and concerts (either as chant or set polyphonically), the cumulative effect of the form is, quite simply, extraordinary.

This anthology also includes the Mass for the Feast of St Thomas (in which the Sequence, *Solemne canticum*, is especially impressive) and the *Kyrie*, *Rex splendens*, attributed to St Dunstan. The singing is restrained and sober and somewhat lacking in colour. The problem seems to be that there is little response to the words on the part of the singers: the chant somehow does not sound 'organic', as though it were sung liturgically. This is a difficult problem to solve, but there is no doubt that the quality of the singing itself is very high. Certainly no one with an interest in Western chant should hesitate to buy this very worthwhile recording.

Sister Marie Keyrouz *sop*

Melchite Sacred Chant
Hymns to the Blessed Virgin
Sister Marie Keyrouz *sop* **L'Ensemble de la Paix**
Harmonia Mundi HMA195 1497 (63 minutes: DDD) Ⓕ
Recorded 1993

With very little hint of nasality or of singing from the throat, Sister Marie Keyrouz accomplishes the most florid ululations with the greatest of ease, the voice continuously and impressively set in relief by a reverberant acoustic and a drone bass provided by a small choir of male voices. The area touched on by this extremely rare repertory is a fascinating one, not much illuminated by the brief, and at times almost impenetrable, notes provided.

The Melchite churches of the Near East in the 4th and 5th centuries AD were those that remained, in a period of frequent schism, faithful to Byzantium ('Melchite' derives from a Syriac word meaning 'Emperor'). The liturgy of these churches was very influential: many of the most famous hymns of the Orthodox church, for example, were composed in the 6th century by Romanos the Melodist in Syriac style; like Sister Marie, Romanos was born in what is now the Lebanon. So some of these melodies, if authentic, may be part of a repertory more ancient than any other surviving Christian chant. For the earlier part of their history, of course, they would have had to rely on oral transmission for their survival. How far they were changed in that process, how far they were affected by an Islamic tradition growing up around them and by translation of their texts from Greek and Syriac into Arabic, only a specialist could really say; certainly the notes that accompany this collection do not. This would be only a quibble were not three of the longer chants attributed to Sister Marie herself, described either as 'in improvised style' or as 'written improvisation'; one of these is a setting of part of Romanos's most celebrated text, the Akathistos. The main difference between these and most of those whose origin is unattributed is their greater virtuosity: in them Sister Marie uses a wider vocal range, a rather more dramatic, declamatory utterance and still more florid melismata. It makes fascinating listening: a border territory between Christian and Islamic chant, at times revealing a modal simplicity beneath the flexible ornament, at others well-nigh hiding it in ecstatic wailings.

Russian Patriarchate Choir

Suprasl - Orthodox Mosaic
Victor Korolev *ten* **Oleg Kovalev** *bass*
Russian Patriarchate Choir / Anatoly Grindenko
Opus 111 OPS30-229 (79 minutes: DDD) Ⓕ
Texts and translations included. Recorded 1999 OO

The Russian Patriarchate Choir has yet again produced a magnificent recording of fascinating and unknown chant repertoire. This time, the music comes from a manuscript from the Monastery of Suprasl, Poland, showing, remarkably, the influence of a variety of chant traditions, including Greek, Slavic and Romanian. The work of reconstruction and transcription, by Anatoly Konotop, reveals a repertory of extraordinary richness and originality, mixing Balkan characteristics (the most obvious of which is the drone) with Slavic. There are two extended chants, one a Cherubic Hymn and the other a sublime chant for the veneration of the Epitaphios on Holy Friday, but all of the music, even the relatively short pieces such as the Demestvenny setting of verses from Psalm 140, has a long-breathed quality, a sense of the infinite, reflected in its huge melodic arches.

Listening to the Russian Patriarchate Choir, it is difficult to believe that any of the singers ever breathe, so naturally do they phrase these huge lines. It has always been the choir's aim to work with such early repertories in a liturgical context, however, and this shows quite clearly in their approach to this extraordinary music; musicology here is put to both practical and spiritual use. The overall result produces a recording of surpassing beauty.

Anonymous Vigil in Kiev
Russian Patriarchate Choir / Anatoly Grindenko
Opus 111 OPS30-223 (78 minutes: DDD) Ⓕ
Texts and translations included. Recorded 1997

Here is a revelatory exploration of unknown Russian riches, here monastic polyphony. This is a repertory that contains more or less familiar versions of harmonised chants and often some spectacularly startling variants: notable of mention are the Deacon's *Priidite* (invitatory, monophonic), the elaborate fourfold response 'Tebe Gospodi' in the insistent litany, and the astonishing chromatic 'slips' in the *Canticle of Simeon*, the *Megalynarion* and in the *Trisagion* at the end of the *Great Doxology*.

Another item worthy of note is the Vespers prayer in which the bass is given the lion's share, especially at cadences, while the upper voices move smoothly from chord to chord. Full texts are provided, although there are one or two oddities in the English translation. The singing is sublime. There can be few choirs in the world who are able to combine such richness of sound with such prayerful attention to text, always perfectly declaimed.

Singphoniker

Officium
Anonymous Officium Beatae Mariae Virginis. Ad Vesperas. In Conceptione Beatae Mariae Virginis
Singphoniker / Godehard Joppich
Glissando 779007-2 (75 minutes: DDD) Ⓕ
Texts and translations included. Recorded 1999 ⭘

Don't let the jokey name fool you: these gentlemen are serious about their plainchant. Directed by the scholar Godehard Joppich, these six German singers present an interpretation of plainchant very different from the more speculative attitudes of such ensembles as the French Organum and the Spanish Alia Musica. While they describe their approach as one of 'scholarly reinterpretation', they avoid the ornaments and embellishments favoured by their more experimental counterparts. Some may see it as a more conservative approach, but the result is very satisfying. That is partly to do with the sound quality and recording, both of which are full-bodied and solid. Clearly these are professional singers and not monks, but there is none of the 'churchy' tameness that too often bedevils the plainchant performances given by English ensembles.

Another positive aspect is the programming, which reveals aspects of liturgical structure in a way that makes musical sense to a modern listener: thus the main item here is the full Marian Vespers. Each of the five psalms is coupled with its antiphon, which both precedes and follows the psalm itself. In the source used here (a late 14th- or early 15th-century manuscript from Hamburg), all five antiphons are drawn from the *Song of Solomon*, which imparts a satisfying sense of coherence and of – dare one use the word? – logic.

The series also includes two of the most famous Marian pieces, the *Regina celi* and *Alma redemptoris mater*. Presented as an unbroken sequence of continuous music, the 'experience' of plainsong has an aesthetic impact which popular plainchant compilations simply cannot match. Following the full Vespers is a selection from the rhymed office of another Hamburg manuscript from the late 15th century. So many plain-chant interpretations inserted into liturgical reconstructions are simply bland, however these give unalloyed pleasure to the listener. It is a pity that Joppich's insert-notes do not spell out his conception of performance. To the knowledgeable audience which such a recording clearly deserves to attract, the continuing debate over plainchant interpretation would surely be worth pursuing. The booklet is quite beautifully illustrated.

Solesmes Abbey Choir

Gregorian Chant H
The complete 1930 HMV Recordings
Solesmes Abbey Choir / Dom Joseph Gajard
Pearl mono ② GEMMCDS9152 (96 minutes: ADD) Ⓜ
Recorded 1930

When Solesmes produced their album of 12 records of Gregorian chant, it was a historic moment. They were making the first major contribution to the documentation of an art having its roots well back in the first millennium, an art underlying much of the subsequent development of Western music. The remarkable unity and flow of the chant was surely due to the fact that they were all singing this music day in, day out, and an occasional *portamento*, or lack of ensemble was a normal, understandable part of the package.

This is a sound of youthful vigour, with all the hallmarks of the familiar Solesmes style already there, well in place: the soaring phrases with their softened peaks and quiet final syllables; the firm enunciation of first syllables; the lifted accents on short notes; the quaint interpretation of the salicus; but over it all, its own special, innate quality, which combines unmistakable spirituality with robust everyday living. That quality, and a certain quiet confidence, are present in this singing to a degree rarely attained by any other monastic choir. The remastering, naturally, has not succeeded in eliminating all the needle hiss. One hardly notices this, by the way, such is the selective power of the human ear!

This collection is really Everyman's basic anthology of Gregorian chant. It ranges from well-known hymns and pieces of the Ordinary, through gems from the Temporale and the Common of Saints, to some of the greatest masterpieces of the repertoire, including the Good Friday responsory *Tenebrae factae sunt* and the splendid first mode offertory *Jubilate Deo* for the second Sunday after Epiphany. It also contains some items one rarely hears nowadays, such as the powerfully moving *Media vita* – 'In the midst of life we are in death'.

Medieval-Mid Renaissance

Acantus

Italian sacred simple polyphony of the Middle Ages and after

Adoramus te Christe. Adoramus te Domine. Alleluia. Benedictus. Credo apostolorum. Cum autem venissem. De profundis. Gaude flore. O crux fructus. O Virgineta bella. Quasi cedrus. Qui nos fecit ex nichilo. Salva sponsa Dei. Salve, sancte Pater. Salve Virgo rubens rosa. Sanctus. Sicut pratum. Vergene madre pia. Verzene benedeta

Acantus

Gimell CDGIM516 (58 minutes: DDD) Ⓕ

Recorded 1997 ⚭

For those expert in medieval music, this disc offers a relatively unknown repertory hardly ever recorded; for music lovers who just want a new musical experience, it's here in trumps; and for those who are not particularly musical it offers a vivid, ethnic-sounding experience with earthy spirituality. There are some very odd things about the packaging. The only title for the disc seems to be the name of the group, Acantus, which includes Alessandra Fiori, Gloria Moretti, Stefano Pilati and Marco Ferrari, people who have been doing excellent work for years but who have never quite managed to find an ensemble or a record company that remains intact. As the first 'guest' group ever to be issued by Gimell (of The Tallis Scholars fame), it's a confidence-inspiring choice.

Another odd feature is that there is only the most indirect indication of what is recorded here, essentially just a list of titles (as given in the heading above) without mentioning that some pieces are from the 13th century, some from the 15th, one from the 19th and one from the contemporary folk tradition. Hints of that information appear in the Italian version of the insert-notes, rather less in the digest of it provided in other languages. This repertory of semi-popular sacred music – known to scholars as 'cantus planus binatim', 'primitive polyphony' (in the days when such language was allowable), 'polifonia semplice' and 'folk polyphony' – contains many glorious pieces, and Acantus gives a massively convincing account of them.

Alia Musica

El canto espiritual judeoespañol

Anonymous (arr Sánchez) Albinu malkenu. Yede rašim. Nostalgia y alabanza de Jerusalén. \`Et ša'aré rašón. Yirú \`enenu. Los siete hijos de Hana. Hodú l'Adonay. Yašen al teradam. El mélej. Noche de aljad. Ki ešmerá šabat. La fragua del estudio. Dodí yarad leganó. La ketubá de la ley

Alia Musica / Miguel Sánchez *voc*

Harmonia Mundi HMI98 7015 (62 minutes: DDD) Ⓕ

Texts and translations included

This is a recital of sacred music, liturgical and paraliturgical, from the Judeo-Spanish or Sephardic tradition, where ancient Jewish psalmody and cantillation have assimilated many of the musical characteristics and compositional techniques of Muslim Spain and the Ottoman empire. One doesn't listen for long before hearing the augmented second, the typical ornamentation, the voice-production with its Middle Eastern flavour, the interplay of free rhythm, Arabic metrical, and also what Solange Corbin has described as 'rythme unaire'. Then there are all those characteristic Turkish instruments: kanun, 'ud, ney, kaval and kamanya, each with its own delightfully unusual timbre. Alia Musica is an ensemble of eight singers and players, all male with one exception, three of them being both players and singers. The leader, Miguel Sánchez, sings his solos with remarkable ease and flexibility. The contralto, Albina Cuadrado, has a powerful, yet tender voice, well suited to her highly elaborate lament for the seven sons of Hannah, sung in 'ladino' (Jewish-Spanish); and also to the Sabbath evening *Noche de aljad* intercessions. One striking example of the interplay of styles is the 12th-century Hebrew poem by Yehudá aben Abbas, *\`Et ša'aré rašón*, with its abundant ornamentation in the dramatic slow-beat solo cantillation, contrasting with a measured chorus with drone, and a vigorously animated rhythmic finale. This is a splendid achievement.

Alla Francesca

Cantigas de Santa Maria

(collected by Alfonso X 'el Sabio')

Nembressete madre de Deus. Maravillosos et piadosos. Quen a omagen da Virgen. U alguen a Jhesucristo. Como Jhesucristo fezo a san Pedro. Nunca ja pod'aa virgen. O ffondo do mar. Nas mentes senpre tener. Quen bõa dona querra loar. Non pod' ome pela virgen. Pois que dos reis nostro Sennor. Como o nome da virgen. Gran piadad'e merce. Quen diz mal da Reynna espiritual. Santa Maria amar. Pero que seja a gente. Null ome per ren

Alla Francesca (Brigitte Lesne, Emmanuel Bonnardot, Pierre Hamon, Pierre Bourhis, Florence Jacquemart, Brigitte Le Baron, Katarina Livljanic, Catherine Sergent)

Opus 111 OPS30-308 (64 minutes: DDD) Ⓕ

Texts and translations included. Recorded 1999 ●

These Spanish canticles, assembled by King Alfonso the Wise to honour the Blessed Virgin Mary, contain some delightful stories of miracles attributed to her intercession. They are becoming increasingly popular with early-music ensembles. Like many other groups, Alla Francesca were faced when recording them with problems to which no ready answer can be found. For whom were they intended? Probably not the Court. How were they performed? We just do not have a clue, except that there are many illustrations in the manuscript that depict musical instruments. But were the *Cantigas* accompanied? Perhaps these instruments are merely symbolic: we just do not know. What can be done to fill in the gaps left by imperfect notational indications?

Alla Francesca's response to this last question is to rely on their own experience and musical instincts. More specific answers will depend upon the knowledge and taste of any present-day performers. Alla Francesca's singers and players have immersed themselves in 'the ancestral techniques of traditional music'. Compared with other groups, however, their approach is simple and natural. One often hears the forceful tones associated with the folk music of central Europe. But this performance is all gentleness and moderation: the singers avoid overdoing their vocal ornamentation; Brigitte Lesne's rippling tones lighten the horizon, the tempos are never forced; the instruments are subtly chosen and grouped. Some of the mantra-like refrains to the miracle ballads might have a mesmeric effect on the average listener, whereas the more developed chant-like melodies (for example, *Santa Maria amar*) are arresting in their beauty. To relish all the subtlety that lies under the mantle of simplicity actually takes time, for this is music for whoever truly has time to listen, not for modern man with all his rush and haste...except, perhaps, as a potent antidote? It's certainly well worth the effort, for the recording quality is first-class.

Armes, Amours – Songs of the 14th and 15th Centuries

Anonymous Ho, ho, ho. Man, assay. Or sus vous dormes trop. Helas, Olivier Basselin. Ecce quod natura. Bel fiore **Andrieu** Armes, amours/O flour des flours **Binchois** Tant plus ayme. Busnois Est-il merchy **Ghiselin** La spagna **Grimace** A l'arme, a l'arme **Joye** Ce qu'on fait a quatimini **Morton** Il sera/L'ome armé (two versions). N'aray je jamais mieulx **Paumann** Mit ganczem Willen

Alla Francesca (Emmanuel Bonnardot, Raphaël Boulay, Pierre Hamon, Marco Horvat, Brigitte Lesne); **Alta** (Michèle Vandenbrouque, Pierre Boragno, Gilles Rapin)

Opus 111 OPS30-221 (56 minutes: DDD) Ⓕ

Texts and translations included. Recorded 1997

This disc is an impressive vindication of the marriage of voices and instruments in secular music of this period. The case for all-vocal performance, very prevalent among English groups, has perhaps been greeted more cautiously elsewhere; but rarely has instrumental participation been so positively espoused. In any case, the performance of the songs by wind-bands alone is well attested, and Alta manages brilliantly on its own: those war-horses, *Or sus* and *A l'arme, a l'arme* are as exciting as if they had been sung. Oddly enough, it is the vocal selections that are more of a mixed bag: certain songs seem somehow under-interpreted, like Morton's *N'aray je jamais mieulx*, whose poignant melancholy is belied by a disconcertingly brisk tempo. And what of Busnois's *Est-il merchy*, here shorn of the repeats prescribed by the rondeau form? Ironically, this abridged version is admirable for its subtle handling of the tactus, and an impressive fluidity of exchange between the three singers: coming from musicians of this calibre, the formal solecism is all the more disconcerting. Yet in songs like *Ho, ho, ho*, *Ce qu'on fait a quatimini* and *Helas, Olivier Basselin* we find the group at its inventive and sure-footed best once again. And it certainly deserves credit for its adroit blend of well-known pieces with lesser-known finds. A few strange moments, then, but many more marvellous ones.

Beauté Parfaite – The Autumn of the Middle Ages

Anonymous Pour vous servir. Or sus, mon cuer, vers ma dame t'encline. Tousjours servir je veuil. Tant qu'en mon cuer/Sur l'erbette. Or sus, vous dormes trop Cheulz qui volent retourner. La belle et la gente rose. Quant la douce jouvencelle. Instrumental Piece **Anthonello de Caserta** Beauté parfaite **Binchois** Adieu, jusques je vous revoye. Ay douloureux disant helas **Dufay** J'ay mis mon cuer. Je vous pri/Ma tres douce amie/Tant que mon argent **Fontaine** Pastourelle en un vergier **Grenon** La plus belle **Legrant** Entre vous, nouviaux mariés **Libert** Se je me plains **Paullet** J'aim. Qui? **Raulin de Vaux** Savés pour quoy suy sy gay **Solage** Fumeux fume par fumee **Vaillant** Par maintes foys

Alla Francesca

Opus 111 OPS30-173 (68 minutes: DDD) Ⓕ

Texts and translations included. Recorded 1996

This is probably the most rounded and successfully varied anthology of late 14th- and early 15th-century songs available. There have been several fine recordings of secular music from this period – a relief to those who feel that this area has suffered relative neglect in comparison to sacred genres. This collection spans a range of styles – from Solage at his weirdest (the famous *Fumeux fume*, sung here at a very slow tempo that is surprisingly effective) to Binchois at his most melancholy (*Ay douloureux*) and Dufay in his sprightly, May Day mode – and includes a number of light pastoral or genre pieces, jocose or slightly scurrilous: *Pastourelle en un vergier* is an example of the ballade form at its liveliest and most direct. As a cross-section of expressive registers and attitudes, it is a very astute and intelligent piece of programming.

Equally impressive is the variety of interpretative approaches, and the polish with which each is carried off. There is great discrimination in the use of instruments. The astonishing artistry of the flautist and recorder player, Pierre Hamon is notable (*Par maintes foys*), but the individual singers are also given greater chance to shine individually and (most importantly) the two agendas no longer compete with each other.

This is the place to mention Brigitte Lesne, whose distinctive but perfectly controlled vibrato is a singing-lesson in itself; and the scarcely less individual timbre of Emmanuel Bonnardot, restrained yet intense. Both are heard in *Adieu, jusques je vous revoye*. Even as straightforward a piece as *Pastourelle en un vergier* is fastidiously shaped, yet without the least bit of fuss. This awareness of the importance of detail is evident in the treatment of the texts. In all cases, they are responded to imaginatively, with a clear understanding of the intention, and the structural integrity of the poetic form (both literary and musical) is respected. Thus, it is easier to engage with the music on the many levels present both between and within pieces. Yet nearly every piece is approached in a different way: no mean feat with 22 works on offer. The disc closes with the magical *Je vous pri*, on paper a slight enough piece, but here deeply intelligent and compellingly expressive – adjectives that apply to these interpretations as well.

Anonymous 4

A Star in the East
Medieval Hungarian Christmas Music
Anonymous 4 (Ruth Cunningham, Marsha Genensky, Susan Hellauer, Johanna Rose *sngrs*)
Harmonia Mundi HMU90 7139 (68 minutes: ADD) Ⓕ
Texts and translations included

This disc is a selection of liturgical and paraliturgical Christmas pieces, taken from medieval Hungarian sources. Most are monophonic, but there is a modest sprinkling of simple polyphonic pieces for two, three and four voices. The charm of the performance lies in its unpretentious, almost childlike simplicity – suggested, maybe, by the delightful extracts from the Christmas story as quoted in the notes. The classic liturgical pieces, which include the Introit *Dum medium silentium*, the splendid Gradual *Speciosa forma*, and others, are heard in a version which tends to use the pentatonic scale, thus avoiding both B natural and B flat. The sung readings are impressive with their polyphonic settings. The rich Genealogy (*Liber generationis*) with its beautifully constructed melody are most enjoyable. Some of the vernacular pieces, as well as the Latin song for New Year's Day, have a regular ternary rhythm. The Hungarian *Te Deum* offers an interesting alternative for the concluding verses: it simply transposes the original theme up a fourth. The booklet is a marvel.

Love's Illusion
Motets from the Montpellier Codex
Anonymous 4 (Ruth Cunningham, Marsha Genensky, Susan Hellauer, Johanna Rose *sngrs*)
Harmonia Mundi HMU90 7109 (64 minutes: DDD) Ⓕ
Texts and translations included. Recorded 1992-93

One could easily imagine that a programme such as this, of 29 13th-century motets, all composed around the same theme of *fin amours* and all sung unaccompanied by an all-female vocal ensemble, might end by becoming wearisome on the ear. Anonymous 4 have proved conclusively in this recording that this need not be so, that, in any case, there is already an infinite variety of mood and style among the songs and that it is possible further to vary them in performance, using no other means than the voices themselves. The directness of the group's approach is always refreshing: their tone is unaffected, their pitch secure. The songs are presented with simplicity in a clear acoustic. There is a total absence of any improvised doodling on reconstructed medieval instruments, which is rather a relief. One gets a sense of quiet satisfaction and enjoyment from the singers themselves, also the feeling that the singers are trying to teach us something about the music, the mechanics of the motet and how it works, almost as if they were demonstrating to a class of music students. They sometimes go out of their way to sing a single part and then to repeat it with another part added, and then finally to give us a polished rendering of the whole motet, complete with all its parts. Occasionally they add a drone – once with a doubling at the fifth above.

The Binchois Consort

Marriage of England and Burgundy
Anonymous O pulcherrima mulierum/Girum coeli circuivi. Incomprehensibilia firme/Praeter rerum ordinem **Busnois** Regina coeli I. Regina coeli II
Frye Missa Sine Nomine. Missa Summe trinitati
The Binchois Consort / Andrew Kirkman
Hyperion CDA67129 (75 minutes: DDD) Ⓕ
Recorded 1999-2000 **OO**

This is another disc to derive inspiration from the marriage in 1468 of Charles the Bold, Duke of Burgundy, and Margaret of York, sister of Edward IV and Richard III. The event fascinates performer-scholars because a manuscript of polyphony survives that can be very plausibly linked to these wedding celebrations (it is now kept in the Royal Library of Belgium in Brussels). After the Ferrara Ensemble's CD of mostly secular music came the Clerks' Group's mix of Masses from the manuscript (including Walter Frye's *Flos regalis* and Plummer's three-voice setting) and secular English songs. Now, with last year's Early Music Award-winners, the Binchois Consort, offering an all-sacred programme, four out of the five so-called 'Brussels' Masses (all of them in fact by English composers) are now available in fine performances.

It would be easy to insist on the fact that this programme is led by recent research. The attribution to Walter Frye of the anonymous three-voice Mass that opens this recording was made by Andrew Kirkman himself, and those of the two motets that conclude it to Busnois were proposed by Sean Gallagher (*O pulcherrima/Girum coeli*) and Rob Wegman (*Incomprehensibilia firme/Praeter rerum ordinem*), all of them young scholars with impeccable credentials. Kirkman's notes are informative and detailed, but he is as concerned as his singers to drive home the music's purely aesthetic, chamber-musical qualities. As to Kirkman's attribution there is no doubt: listen to the sustained duets of the *Sanctus* and *Agnus Dei*, and there can be no doubt that the Mass is by a composer of the first rank; one has to agree that Wegman's attribution of *Incomprehensibilia* cries 'Busnois' out of the speakers: it could hardly be by anyone else. Rightly Kirkman gently expresses doubts concerning *O pulcherrima/Girum coeli*, – in fact it puts one very firmly in mind of late Dufay, and of his motet *Ave regina coelorum* in particular.

In some these are faultlessly judged and engaging performances. The music's nuances and details are very sensitively rendered, but so is the sense of larger-scale architecture and pacing; and Kirkman's long-standing commitment to Frye is particularly evident. The performances of Busnois' motets (both conjecturally attributed and firmly ascribed) are, at their best, equally exciting; but just occasionally there is the hint of strain in the higher voices' upper reaches and in the intricate tracery of *O pulcherrima* and *Incomprehensibilia* (particularly the latter, whose many sections do not quite flow together), and of the singers bracing themselves for the cross-rhythms of *Regina coeli I.* But these are details, and it is difficult to imagine more lucid or elegant performances. In a very short time, the Binchois Consort have established themselves as one of the very finest ensembles in the field.

Capilla Flamenca

The A-La-Mi-Re Manuscripts

Anonymous Plus oultre. Salve Regina (on Myn Hert) **Alamire** Tandernaken op den Rijn **Gascogne** Missa Myn hert – Kyrie **Isaac** Maudit soyt **Josquin** Proch dolor/Pie Jhesu. Plaine de duel **Marbianus de Orto** Dulces exuviae **Moulu** Mater floreat **Mouton/Févin** Celeste beneficium/ Adiutorium nostrum **Newseider** Myn hert altyt heeft verlanghen **De la Rue** Autant en emporte. Jam sauche. Myn hert altyt heeft verlanghen. Soubz ce tumbel **Rigo** Celle que j'ay **Willaert** Missa super Benedicta es – Agnus Dei

Capilla Flamenca

Naxos 8 554744 (62 minutes: DDD) Ⓢ

Texts and translations included. Recorded 1999 ⭘

Petrus Alamire – without the curious hyphens of this disc's title – was the head of a thriving workshop of music-copyists connected with the Netherlands court in the early 16th century. His beautiful manuscripts were sent to princes, popes and the super-rich across Europe, and contained music by the greatest composers of the age.

The works recorded here are a minute sampling of what was produced, in some ways an unrepresentative one: the majority of these manuscripts contained not songs, but sacred music, especially masses. Yet in another way this recit beautifully captures the tone and ambience of the Netherlands court: grave, serious, sometimes cerebral music, but richly and densely involving. Josquin is represented by the songs of his old age, and de la Rue, the star composer of the court chapel, by pieces written for his patron, Margaret of Austria, aunt of Charles V. They are exactly suited to the rich, warm and expressive tone of Capilla Flamenca, which records on Naxos for the first time. The group is complemented here by the instrumental consort La Caccia which provides light relief and occasional accompaniment. This alliance is well judged and satisfying: it is not often one hears a crumhorn consort in full flood. Some decisions seem to make light of the music's potential (Josquin's *Plaine de duel*, for example, taken at somewhat too brisk a pace), but on the whole there is much fine music-making to savour: especially enjoyable is the countertenor Marnix de Cat's delivery of de la Rue's *Soubz ce tumbel* (a distant precursor of Telemann's *Canary Cantata*), a lament on Margaret's favourite pet. The accompanying notes give an informative account of Alamire's colourful life, and the value of his enterprise. As to a final recommendation, it would be silly to pretend that cost is irrelevant: this is excellent value for money.

Missa Alleluia – Music at the Burgundian Court

Works include **La Rue** Missa Alleluia **Obrecht** Salve regina **Josquin Desprez** Huc me sydereo

Capilla Flamenca

Eufoda CDEUF1232 (60 minutes: DDD) Ⓕ

Here is classically full-throated, rich Flemish singing. The motets are hardly new to the catalogue, but these readings more than hold their own. Worth noting is the use of choirboys, notably in Obrecht's six-voice *Salve regina*, and Josquin's *Huc me sydereo*, here in its six-voice version. But the centrepiece here is unquestionably the Mass by Pierre de la Rue. The singing is mostly very stylish, with a sound image to wallow in. Strongly recommended.

La Capella Reial de Catalunya

El Cançoner del Duc de Calabria

Almodar Ah, Pelayo que desmayo!

Anonymous Ay luna que reluzes. Dizen a mi que los amores he. Gózate, Virgen sagrada. Si de vos mi bien. Un niño nos es nacido. Con qué la lavaré. Ojos garços ha la niña. Si la noche haze escura (attrib. F. Guerrero). Estas noches à tan largas. Vella, de vós som amorós (attrib. M. Flechaa). Yo me soy la morenica. Falai, meus olhos **Carceres** Soleta so jo ací **Flecha** Que farem del pobre Joan! Teresica hermana **Morales** Si n'os hubiera mirado

La Capella Reial de Catalunya / Jordi Savall

Auvidis Astrée ES9960 (68 minutes: DDD) Ⓜ

Texts and translations included. Recorded 1995

This is vintage Capella Reial. The singing and playing are superb (as always), and the repertory – melodious and dancey by turn – of the Cançoner del Duc de Calabria is right up its alley. Amazingly, this is the first commercial recording dedicated to this songbook from the Valencian court of the Duke of Calabria – surprising because of the accessibility and quality of the music. Several items from the book have become well known (notably the ubiquitous *Riu, riu, chiu*, which, thankfully, is not included here), but up till now it has been difficult to gain an appreciation of the collection as a whole. Published in Venice in 1556, it records an earlier repertory, dating from the first decade of the 16th century through the 1530s and, possibly, 1540s. The Valencian court was one of the major cultural centres of the Iberian peninsula at this period, and the court culture was heavily influenced by the latest humanistic trends from Italy. In musical terms, the repertory of the *Cançoner* reflects this mix of imported and indigenous elements; most of the songs conform to the fixed-form *villancico* of the later 15th century, but within the essential refrain-and-verse structure much of the writing reveals a more madrigalian idiom. Indeed, popular-style refrains are often succeeded by madrigalian verses, and Capella Reial reinforce this through the scoring adopted; popular songs and refrains attract full-blown 'orchestrations' (the *tutti* ensemble of viols, winds, plucked instruments and percussion so characteristic of the Capella ensemble), or at least varied combinations of instruments, while the more imitative sections blend voices, viols and harp or vihuela. The songs are well chosen and nicely varied in poetic content and interpretation; it is particularly good to have the relatively few Catalan items from the songbook, which when sung by Jordi Savall's excellent team of native singers, are lent a distinctly dark flavour – thanks to the covered vowel sounds of the language. This is an outstanding disc which brings to light another unjustly neglected corner of the repertory in performances that reveal Capella Reial at its best.

La Columbina Ensemble

Canciones, Romances and Sonetos

Encina Triste España sin ventura! Antonilla es desposada. Tan buen ganadico. Mi libertad en sosiego. Pues que tú, Reina del cielo. Cucú, cucú, cucú **Guerrero** Niño Dios, d'amor herido. Prado verde y florido. Huyd, huyd. Si tu penas no pruevo. Todo quanto pudo dar **Romero** A quién contaré mis quejas. En Belén están mis amores. Como suele el blanco zisne. Soberana María. Las voces del fuego **Vásquez** A, hermosa, abrime cara de rosa. Con qué la lavaré. Torna, Mingo, a namorarte. Si no os uviera mirado. En la fuente del rosel. Soledad tengo de tí. Buscad buen amor. O dulce contemplación. De los álamos vengo

La Columbina Ensemble (Mariá Cristina Kiehr *sop* Claudio Cavina *counterten* Josep Benet *ten* Josep Cabré *bass*)

Accent ACC95111D (56 minutes: DDD) Ⓕ

Texts and translations included. Recorded 1995

In this survey of Spanish song in the 16th- and 17th-centuries the pieces chosen admirably reflect the consistency of idiom and quality during the period. Distinctive to the repertory is the blend of popular and *culto* elements, in both text and music. Madrigalian elements gradually infiltrate the simple, homophonic idiom cultivated by Encina and are thoroughly mastered by Juan Vásquez, the genius of Spanish song of the first half of the 16th century, and subsequently by Francisco Guerrero. All these developments are further consolidated by Romero, a near contemporary of Monteverdi, the two- and three-part songs selected here reflecting the 16th-century continuum that dominates the early Spanish baroque. Apart from some *stile concitato* effects in the battle-cry refrains to *En Belén están mis amores* and *Las voces del fuego*, these technically highly accomplished but effective pieces are still predominantly in the renaissance polyphonic idiom. None of the songs is more than about four minutes long, and most last around two, so that La Colombina's carefully chosen groupings of works by the same composer help to make a larger structure, and they very successfully juxtapose the more familiar (Guerrero's *Prado verde y florido* or Vásquez's *De los álamos vengo*) with the less well known while giving a good insight into the range of the repertory. Their interpretations are always expressive and sensitive to the imagery of the text, and the blend and accuracy of ensemble are exemplary. These are utterly convincing performances without any need whatsoever for the 'orchestrated' approach so familiar from, say, Hespèrion XX. Here the madrigalian writing so apparent within Spanish forms such as the *villancico*, *romance* and *soneto* finally comes into its own for about the first time on CD.

Discantus

Campus Stellae – 12th-Century Pilgrims' Songs

Tropes of 'Benedicamus domino' – Ad superni regis decus; Dies ista celebris; Congaudeant catholici; Dies ista gaudium; Gregis pastor; Mira dies oritur. Conductus motets – Plebs domini; Flore vernans gratie. Prosae – Alleluia ... Gratulemur et letemur; Res est admirabilis; Quam dilecta tabernacula; Clemens servulorum gemitus tuorum. Versi – Uterus hodie virginis floruit; Lilium floruit. Kyrie tropes – Rex immense; Cunctipotens genitor Deus. Judicii signum

Discantus / Brigitte Lesne

Opus 111 OPS30-102 (69 minutes: DDD) Ⓕ

Recorded 1994

All-female ensembles have hitherto been rather thin on the ground, but following on from Anonymous 4 and the high-voice section of Sequentia, here is Discantus, a 10-member group of sopranos and contraltos, dedicated to breathing new life into the performance of sacred monody and early polyphony. This is an attractive and varied selection of pieces illustrating different aspects of 12th-century French music, the main sources being two manuscripts from the school of St Martial de Limoges and the *Codex Calixtinus*, or *Liber Sancti Jacobi*, compiled in Burgundy, but relating to the famous pilgrimage to the shrine of St James of Compostela. The work which remains in the memory, after listening with delight to the whole of this absorbing programme, is undoubtedly a piece (from a rather later source) based on the Sibylline Oracles, *Judicii signum*, with its ominous, low-voiced announcement of the Last Judgement. Indeed, the alternation from piece to piece of high and low voices, of solo and choir, of monody and polyphony is adroitly and effectively managed throughout the recital, so that the musical interest of a well-balanced and well-planned programme is sustained. Brigitte Lesne and her singers have learnt how to make repercussion sound discreetly convincing. The cadential ornamentation, sometimes involving a kind of double polyphonic shake, might perhaps have gained from being allowed a little more panache. The vocal timbre is clear and fresh and the whole performance moves along with cheerful confidence.

Dame de Flors

Ecole Notre-Dame de Paris

Discantus (Anne Guidet, Claire Jéquier, Lucie Jolivet, Brigitte Le Baron, Anne Quentin, Catherine Schroeder, Catherine Sergent) **/ Brigitte Lesne**

Opus 111 OPS30-175 (59 minutes: DDD) Ⓕ

Texts and translations included. Recorded 1996 ⦿

One is struck by the overwhelming majority of pieces in honour of the Virgin Mary in the extant sources of the School of Notre-Dame. Indeed, the rich and many-faceted devotion to Our Lady, which characterised the Middle Ages and reached its peak in the 12th and 13th centuries, was itself paralleled by the secular devotion to the ideal Lady of chivalry sung by troubadour and trouvère alike. Such devotion may well have contributed in no small measure to the development of the art of music, in particular of the *ars antiqua* with its musical forms: organum, conductus and motet. This is a gentle, unaffected programme of such pieces, some of them of almost childlike simplicity, others of ingenious complexity. The theme that unites them is Mary, seen as Star, Fountain, Maidservant, but above all, as Lady of Flowers, herself the mystical Flower watered by celestial dew, Rose, Lily, Blossom without a thorn. Discantus present her with imagination and sensitivity. An all-female ensemble of eight singers – might that not be a recipe for a bland 'sameness' in an hour-long Marian programme? However, Discantus achieve an amazing degree of variety by the simplest of means: by opposing vocal registers, by alternating solo and *tutti*, by varying the tempos and by delicate phrasing. The mood of each piece is carefully studied. Despite one slight imperfection of pitch, the sheer beauty and purity of the music is absolutely captivating.

Doulce Mémoire

Messe de mariage 🅿

Anonymous Pavane fait au mariage de Mr de Vandosme. Pavane fite pour le mariage de Henri le Grand. Muse honorons de ta chanson **Bati** Elevatione **Bernardi** Sinfonia Prima – a 6; a 8. Sinfonia Seconda a 8 **Du Caurroy** Au Roy, victorieux guerrier. A la Royne, ninfe qui tient tant d'heur **Gagliano** Messe à double choeur **Guami** Offertoire **Lejeune** Epithalame à deux choeurs. Te Deum

Doulce Mémoire / Denis Raisin-Dadre

Astrée Naïve E8808 (63 minutes: DDD) Ⓕ

Texts and translations included. Recorded 2000 ⦿

Doulce Mémoire's account of the Funeral Mass for Henry IV of France (assassinated in 1610) is arguably the finest of several available recordings of that piece (Astrée Naïve). Here, Denis Raisin-Dadre evokes another great state occasion connected with that monarch, his wedding to Maria de' Medici in 1600, celebrated first in Florence in September (with the Duke of Tuscany standing proxy for the king), then in Lyon in December, this time with Henry in person. This is reflected in the programme's mix of Italian and French repertories. At the risk of sounding sectarian, The French get the better deal: Marco da Gagliano's Mass for double choir flatters the ear more than it does the intellect. It would have been just right for a wedding at which most participants' minds would (one presumes) have been on other things. But for sheer musical interest, listen to the celebratory songs by Du Caurroy, and Lejeune's magnificent *Epithalame* (all of them in *vers mesuré* style). In terms of scoring, the range on offer is naturally greater and more festive than was the case on the funeral disc, and the acoustic result is every bit as compelling (the opening *Pavane fait au mariage de Mr de Vandosme* sets the tone excellently).

An interesting programme, then, whose execution is generally on a par with its conception. Just occasionally, the voices are a touch tentative in the upper reaches (for example from 4'30" of the epithalamium, and elsewhere in details of ornamentation) and towards the end the pace flags somewhat (specifically in Le Jeune's *Te Deum*), but then there is much more to praise and enjoy. The changes of scoring in the lengthy epithalamium are nicely judged. The progress of these musicians reminds one of their compatriots the Clément Janequin Ensemble, for whom the ideal integration of voices and instrumentation – originally a matter of trial and error – has of late been fully vindicated. Midway between the somewhat dogmatic genre of liturgical reconstruction and more loosely themed programmes, this approach lightly evokes the occasion, leaving the listener's imagination free to roam and fill in those details which it alone can supply.

Viva Napoli – Canzoni Villanesche 🅿

Azzaiolo Il primo libro de villotte – Al di dolce ben mio; Chi passa per 'sta strada. Il secondo libro de villotte – Girometta senza te **Bendusi** Pass'e mezzo della paganina, gagliarda. Pass'e mezzo ditto il romano, Pass'mezzo ditto il compasso **Caroso** Il ballarino – Chiarenzana **Festa** Madonna io sono un medico perfetto **Lassus** Madonna mia pietà. La cortesia voi donne predicate. Tu sai, madonna mia, ch'io t'amo e voglio **Nasco** Il primo libro di canzone villanesche alla napolitana – Vorria che tu cantassi **Negri** Le gratie d'amore – Bizzarria d'amore **Nola** Chi la gagliarda **Valente** Intavolatura di cimbalo – Gaillarda Napolitana; Tenore grande alla Napolitana **Willaert** Vecchie letrose non valete niente. O bene mio. Madonna mia fa **Zanetti** Il scolaro – La bella Pedrina; Saltarello

Ensemble Doulce Mémoire / Denis Raisin-Dadre *fl*

Astrée Naïve E8648 (63 minutes: DDD) Ⓕ

Texts and translations included. Recorded 1998 ⦿

To date, Ensemble Doulce Mémoire's discography has been fairly evenly divided between French and Italian repertories. Here the group associates itself more firmly still with a specific location and repertory, that of Naples in the mid-16th century. One finds here the usual suspects of the popularising trend with which Naples is associated: Gian Domenico da Nola, Adrian Willaert (represented by his infamous *Vecchie letrose* and the delightful *Madonna mia fa*) and the young Lassus, on whom the city's popular musical culture clearly made a lasting impression. Indeed, the imaginative and entertaining programme notes invite us to imagine Lassus masterminding an evening's entertainment at the home of his Neapolitan employer, of which this is the programme. Some recent releases have shown that such recreations are by no means easy to carry off convincingly; but Denis Raisin-Dadre and his ensemble do just that.

Similarly, this disc's other theme, the villanella and its more learned polyphonic offshoots, has been generously treated by native Italian ensembles (notably on the Opus 111 label); it is a great compliment to these French musicians that they can hold their own in their Italian masquers' outfits. There is hardly a track that fails to convince; the diminutions in *Madonna mia pietà*, in common with the instrumental contributions in general, are skilfully done (even if they place more rhythmic constraints on the voices than one would like), and *Vecchie letrose* is as nasty as it ought to be. Even when the improvisatory licence is occasionally exceeded, the general tenor of this recital is strong enough to be convincing. The ensemble takes great care to present the booklet-notes as integral to the disc's conception; and after an hour's entertainment, a little unscripted surprise awaits. This repertory is slowly gaining decent representation on disc, but it is doubtful that there is a better-judged recital than this one.

Early Music Consort of London

The Art of the Netherlands

A Agricola De tous biens plaine (two versions). Fortuna desparata **Anonymous** Fortuna desperata. Mijn morken gaf mij een jonck wijff **Barbireau** Een wrolick wesen **Brumel** Du tout plongiet/Fors seulement. Missa 'Et ecce terrae motus'
Busnois Fortuna disperata **Compère** O bone Jesu
Ghiselin Ghy syt die wertste boven al
Hayne Van Ghizeghem De tous biens plaine. De tous biens plaine (arr Josquin) **Hofhaimer** Ein fröhlich wesen **Isaac** Donna di dentro dalla tua casa. Missa 'La bassadanza' **Josquin Desprez** Scaramella va alla guerra. Allégez moy, doulce plaisant brunette. Allégez moy, doulce plaisant brunette (anonymous arrangement for two lutes). El grillo è buon cantore. De profundis clamavi a 5. Benedicta es, caelorum regina. Credo 'De tous biens playne'. Guillaume se va chauffeur. Adieu mes amours. Adieu mes amours (16th-century anonymous arrangement for organ). Inviolata, integra et casta es, Maria **Mouton** Nesciens mater virgo virum **Obrecht** Ein fröhlich wesen. Haec Deum caeli. Laudemus nunc Dominum
Ockeghem Prenez sur moi vostre exemple. Ma bouche rit. Intemerata Dei mater **La Rue** Missa 'Ave sanctissima Maria'. Ave sanctissima Maria
Tinctoris Missa sine nomine

Early Music Consort of London / David Munrow
Virgin Classics Veritas ② VED5 61334-2 Ⓜ
(132 minutes: ADD). Texts and translations included.
Recorded 1975 ●●●

This is arguably Munrow's most consistent and most polished collection, devoted to the sacred and secular polyphony of the mid- to late-15th century. These recordings remain marvellously fresh and vital – even in the case of pieces that have since had more polished or more clearly recorded interpretations. That is especially true of the sacred music, recorded entirely vocally and (in most cases) one to a part. It would be a challenge to name a more tempestuous reading of Brumel's 'Earthquake Mass', a more sombre, self-absorbed *Intemerata Dei mater* (this is still the only recording at super-low pitch), or more luminously clear canons (in *Ave sanctissima Maria* and *Nesciens mater*). In the recordings of secular music, the passage of time is rather more obvious. But idiosyncratic though it may now appear, the choice of instruments always combines flair and verve. In the songs, tempos are rather more languorous than one is now used to, but Munrow's finest inspirations still strike very deep. The phrase 'essential listening' is often used (perhaps too often), but it surely applies to 'The Art of the Netherlands'. A word of warning: the contents of the three original LPs are not reproduced exactly. The entire instrumental portion, some 20 minutes of music, is cut. This is one of the most influential recordings of early music ever made.

Ensemble Cantilena Antiqua

Canticum Canticorum
The sacred symbol of love in the medieval musical tradition
Ensemble Cantilena Antiqua / Stefano Albarello *counterten*
Symphonia SY95135 (72 minutes: DDD) Ⓕ

This intriguing collection of music on the Song of Solomon includes not only 12th- and 13th-century Western monody and polyphony, but also Hebrew, Sephardic and Maronite melodies. The performances blend voices and instruments in a manner much favoured by Italian ensembles today; there is some fine singing, that of the countertenor Stefano Albarello being particularly striking. Text and documentation are intelligently and stylishly presented.

Ensemble Clément Janequin

Les Plaisirs du Palais

Anonymous C'est tout abus. Si vous n'avez madame. Triquedon daine **Appenzeller** Je pers espoir. Musae Jovis **Barbion** Pour quelque paine que j'endure **Baston** Ung souvenir me conforte **Certon** En languissant avoir secours j'attens. Que n'est-elle auprès de moy
Clemens non Papa Priere devant le repas, O souverain Pasteur **Dambert** Secouez moy **Decarella** En Tour la feste Saint Martin **Gombert** La chasse au lièvre
Hesdin Ung vray musicien **Le Heurteur** Mirelaridon

Mittantier Laissons amour **Le Roy** Alemande du pied de cheval. Bransle de Champaigne. Bransles de Poictou **Sermisy** Aupres de vous à 2 voix. Aupres de vous à 4 voix. Hau, hau, hau le boys! **Susato** Priere apres le repas, Pere esternel
Ensemble Clément Janequin / Dominique Visse
Harmonia Mundi HMC90 1729 Ⓕ
(61 minutes: DDD). Recorded 2000

This is a feast indeed. Ensemble Clément Janequin often hold their concerts seated round a table, and the theme of feasting recurs in their discography as well (remember their superb 'Une fête chez Rabelais'). Here the menu boasts a greater preponderance than usual of anonymous and lesser-known (indeed, obscure) *chanson* composers, alongside masters like Certon and Sermisy. But the programme's exoticism extends to the greatest composers of the time: Gombert's *La chasse au lièvre* could be described as a pastiche in the style of Janequin's representative songs (*La chasse* being the obvious model). In Gombert's narrative, however, the hunters end up round a table. Dominique Visse and his gang were bound to perform this piece sooner or later. Here it is the centrepiece of their recital, and like the whole, finds them at their best.

That said, one needs to be familiar with their discography to appreciate this new offering to the full. Around Gombert's hunt the disc is arranged palindromically, topped and tailed with prayers before and after the meal; but Clemens non Papa's exhortation to partake in moderation seemingly goes unheeded. There follows the familiar miscellany of love-songs, of ribaldry and drink, of voices and instruments. But there are new twists, and real gems, in the more out-of-the-way selections, like Mittantier's *Laissons amour*. Appenzeller's well-known deploration on Josquin is a fitting pendant to his *Je pers espoir*, itself modelled on Josquin's *Mille regretz*. Another new departure is the use of just one voice accompanied by viols (Bruno Boterf in Certon's *En languissant* and Visse in Sermisy's *Aupres de vous*).

One also needs to be familiar with the French *chanson* repertory in general; and certainly one must understand the texts, without which certain interpretative tricks may disconcert. (A pity, then, that some of the translations are wildly off base – a recurring problem with Harmonia Mundi, and crucial to put right with an idiom as exotic as this). So this is a connoisseur's feast, but it grows in stature with repeated hearing.

Canciones y Ensaladas P
Brudieu En los mon pus sou dotada del set goigs **Flecha** La bomba. La guerra **Mudarra** Fantasias – primer tono; quarto tono; quinto tono **Valderrábano** Contrapunto sobre el tenor del conde claros **Vásquez** Ojos morenos. Que yo, mi madre, yo. Mi mal de causa es. Gentil senora mia. Cavallero, queraysme dexar. Agora que sé de amor. El que sin ti bivir, ya no querrìa. Lágrimas de mi consuelo
Ensemble Clément Janequin / Dominique Visse *counterten*
Harmonia Mundi HMC90 1627 (58 minutes: DDD) Ⓕ
Texts and translations included. Recorded 1997

It is a real pleasure to hear some more of Vásquez's excellent songs on disc: usually it is the *villancicos* in popular vein that are featured, but here we have some of the more serious, madrigalian pieces. Try *Lágrimas de mi consuelo*, one of his most extended settings in which he comes closest to the motet style of the period, and savour those mournful suspensions. Mostly the songs are considerably shorter, lasting only two or three minutes, but Vásquez is a masterful songster and perfectly encapsulates the mood of each text. Brudieu's strophic setting, in Catalan, of the Seven Joys of the Virgin calls for sustained singing, around which the instrumentalists here weave increasingly elaborate extemporised divisions. All the songs, and also the *ensaladas*, are performed with one voice to a part and slightly varying combinations of organ, viol and plucked strings (lute, vihuela, guitar). Each member of the Ensemble Clément Janequin is closely miked, but the overall blend is superb, and the rich, translucent sonority achieved is utterly compelling.

What distinguishes this CD above all is the liveliness of the musical response to the words that are being sung: the pronunciation is not 100 per cent consistent, but every word is crystal-clear and the level of vocal energy and focus is always spot on, all of which is especially noticeable in the *ensaladas*. Here the interpretation is just right: theatrical and colourful, often funny, but never camp or ludicrously over the top, all this stemming from Visse's own instinctive and secure sense of the theatrical. Even if Flecha had not considered this plausible combination of voices and instruments when he composed the *ensaladas*, surely he would have appreciated these versions of *La bomba* and *La guerra* for their sensitivity to the texts and the real flair at the heart of the performance.

Ferrara Ensemble

Balades a III chans P
Anonymous Adieu vous di, tres doulce compaynie. Lamech Judith et Rachel de plourer. Le mont Aon de Thrace **Antonius de Civitate** lo vegio per stasone **Cordier** Tout par compas suy composés **Grimace** Se Zephirus, Phebus et leur lignie **Matteo da Perugia** Rondeau-refrain. Pres du soloil deduissant s'esbanoye **Trebor** Helas pitié envers moy dort si fort. Si Alexandre et Hector fussent en vie
Ferrara Ensemble / Crawford Young
Arcana A32 (59 minutes: DDD) Ⓕ
Texts and translations included. Recorded 1994

The *ballade*, that noblest form (in every sense) of 14th-century secular music, was meant to honour the dukes and counts who did so much to foster the fine arts while war, famine and plague raged round them. Their musical protégés were by all accounts a slightly surreal bunch, dedicated seekers-out of weirdness, addicted to the bottle – possibly even to hashish. Small wonder that so much of their music seems hopelessly capricious on the page. Crawford Young's special achievement is to demonstrate what many enthusiasts of *Ars subtilior* have felt all along. In performance, that wilful strangeness can suddenly come across with astonishing naturalness: all it takes is the right singers, and here they are. Or perhaps that last sentence should read: 'here she is'. It is no slight on the other members of the Ferrara Ensemble to say that the mezzo-soprano, Lena Susanne Norin, steals the show. Her singing can only be described as luscious. True, the quality of these performances is partly a matter of direction. Tempo is of the first importance because it determines the specific gravity of the dissonances. Beyond that, however, the sensitivity to these details is down to Norin herself. This fierce-looking music, once tamed, becomes almost unbelievably sensuous. The tone of the accompanying string instruments is perfectly judged, the sound-recording outstanding – warm and glowing. The presentation of *ballades* is a tricky business: to perform all three stanzas can take well over 10 minutes. In the past, singers have tended to confine themselves to just one or two stanzas. That has the advantage of fitting more music into a recital, but aesthetically it makes about as much sense as trimming the tail of a peacock. A glorious recital.

En doulz chastel de Pavie – Songs from the Visconti court around 1400

Anonymous Istanpitta Isabella. Chanconeta tedesca (two versions). Constantia **Ciconia** La fiamma del to amor. Le ray au soleyl. Sus une fontayne
Philippus de Caserta En remirant. De ma doulour. En attandant souffrir **Senleches** La harpe de mélodie
Ferrara Ensemble (Lena Susanne Norin *contr* Eric Mentzel *ten* Stephen Grant *bar* Randall Cook *va d'arco* Marion Fourquier *hp* Crawford Young *gtr*)
Harmonia Mundi HMC90 5241 (61 minutes: DDD) Ⓕ
Texts and translations included. Recorded 1997

This disc focuses on one of *Ars subtilior*'s most influential figures, Philippus de Caserta, three of whose songs are quoted in Johannes Ciconia's virelai, *Sus une fontayne* in an unusually comprehensive form of homage. All four works appear here, along with two canonic pieces by Ciconia and the admirable Jacob de Senleches. The latter deserves a disc all to himself, but here at least we have his incomparable *La harpe de mélodie*, one of *Ars subtilior*'s most perfect creations. Caserta's pieces are dense and labyrinthine, but once again the Ferrara Ensemble triumphs over all but the most intractable intricacies: only *En remirant* remains elusive. Several instrumental items are included to round off the disc and refresh the ear, incidentally giving violist, Randall Cook (an admirable accompanist) his place in the sun. The recorded sound is excellent.

The Whyte Rose

Anonymous Ballo de love (arr Young). Danse de Cleves. Fayre and discrete fresche wommanly figure. Love wolle I withoute eny variaunce/T'Andernacken al op den Rijn. My wofull hert of all gladnesse baryeyne. My herte ys so plungit yn greffe. Thus ye compleyne my grevous hevynesse **Busnois** Anima liquefacta est/Stirps Jesse. Je ne puis vivre ainsi **Frye** Alas, alas is my chief song. Salve virgo mater pya. Sospitati dedit **Molinet** Tart ara mon cuer sa plaisance
Morton Le souvenir de vous me tue
Ockeghem Quant de vous seul
Robertus d'Anglia El mal foco arda quella falsa lingua
Ferrara Ensemble / Crawford Young *lte*
Arcana A301 (66 minutes: DDD) Ⓕ
Texts and translations included. Recorded 1997 **OO**

The emphasis here is on secular music, but motets are represented as well. As for the repertory, it includes such prominent names as Busnois, Ockeghem, Morton and Frye (to whom one may attribute *Alas, alas, alas*, here listed as anonymous), but there is a fair sprinkling of first-rate songs by lesser-known or anonymous composers, and instrumental dances favoured as light relief on some of this ensemble's previous recordings. The sound is strikingly warm, vivid and clear, and captures the almost sensuous interplay of lines whatever the distribution.

In the English music the almost weightless approach to rhythm works wonderfully: Frye's music lays very little agogic stress on the strong beat. But in the pieces by Busnois, whose music draws so much more from rhythmic impetus, this approach is less effective and leads to the very few solecisms on the disc (such as the perceptible slowing of the pulse in the first phrase of *Je ne puis vivre*, or the occasional lack of direction in *Anima mea liquefacta est*). Yet even in these pieces there are moments that can only be described as gorgeous, and elsewhere the combination of sound-image and interpretative nous is as admirable as anything the group has achieved: one can mention, almost at random, *Alas, alas*, *Quant de vous seul*, *Le souvenir*, *Tart ara*.

Gothic Voices

The Earliest Songbook in England

Anonymous Verbum patris umanatur. In hoc ortus occidente. Regis cuius potentia. Ecce torpet probitas. Magno gaudens gaudio. Rerum deus conditor. Cantu miro. Vacillantis trutine. In natali novi regis. Diastematica. Divino maduit. Virgo mater salvatoris. Tronus regis instauratur. Benedicamus domino: Spiritus almi. Adulari nasciens. Agnus Dei: Qui pius est factus. Resonet, intonet. Ad honorem salvatoris I. Ad honorem salvatoris II. Argumenta faluntur fisice. Flos floriger. Licet eger cum egrotis. Ad cantus letitie
Gothic Voices (Catherine King *contr* Steven Harrold, Rogers Covey-Crump, Charles Daniels, Leigh Nixon *tens* Stephen Charlesworth *bar*)
Hyperion CDA67177 (65 minutes: DDD) Ⓕ
Texts and translations included. Recorded 1999

The eight leaves of the Cambridge University Library manuscript Ff. I. 17 are surely not in fact the earliest songbook in England; but this is nevertheless an astonishing and varied collection, copied around 1200, almost certainly in England. The texts are not in English but in Latin, and much of the music is likely to have originated elsewhere; moreover the songs are mostly what we now call sacred *conductus*, though they include the standard Goliardic fare of love-songs and songs of fierce political invective. Like so much from those years, the leaves survive only because they were used later for binding something else, and they must be just a tiny portion of something originally much bigger, but they make a splendidly contrasted collection of music. It is marvellous to have most of the music presented together on one disc.

And of course it is even more marvellous that Gothic Voices should have done it. Nothing is overstated yet nothing is allowed to pass without a burning musical conviction in the performances. Everything has a crystalline audibility. The two-voice pieces are done with the purity of intonation that we have come to expect from Gothic Voices; and the monophonic songs are all given with particular verve – especially in the four sung by Catherine King, who seems to become a more indispensable artist with each recording.

It should be mentioned that in the edition used by John Stevens the basically unrhythmed notes are read in a 'syllabic' interpretation, that is, with each syllable of the text sounding roughly the same length. This is now perhaps the most widely accepted approach, though some listeners may occasionally feel that the frequent Goliardic metres of the poetry demand something that dances more openly.

Jerusalem: Vision of Peace

Anonymous Plainchant – Te Deum; Mass of Easter Day in Jerusalem: Gradual, Hec dies quam fecit Dominus; Alleluia, Pascha nostrum; Gospel. Luto carens et latere. Jerusalem! grant damage me fais. Jerusalem accipitur. O levis aurula!. Hac in die Gedeonis. In salvatoris/Ce fu en tres douz tens/In veritate. Veri vitis germine. Luget Rachel iterum. Invocantes Dominum/Deus, qui venerunt. Congaudet hodie celestis curia **Guiot de Dijon** Chanterai por mon coraige **Hildegard of Bingen** O Jerusalem aure civitas **Huon de St Quentin** Jerusalem se plaint et li pais
Gothic Voices / Christopher Page
Hyperion CDA67039 (73 minutes: DDD) Ⓕ
Texts and translations included. Recorded 1998

This disc explores numerous aspects of the Crusades. The stirring three-part conductus *Luto carens* suggests a parallel between the crossing of the Red Sea and the journey undertaken by the Christian armies marching towards the Holy Land. Rachel weeping for her children, *Luget Rachel*, may refer to the fall of Jerusalem in 1187. Other aspects include the emotions of those left behind; chants and prayers for victories as well as losses; devotion to the Blessed Virgin, often chosen as patron of the military Orders, and, not surprisingly, a certain anti-Semitism. Broadly speaking, we hear three styles of performance. The polyphonic pieces, alert and rhythmic, have that delightfully rough-edged vocal quality the men singers exploit to perfection. If one slid a page of parchment between finger and thumb, theirs would undoubtedly be the hairy side. By contrast, Catherine King's would be the smooth. Her quiet, subtle phrasing graces her three solo pieces, including Hildegard's *O Jerusalem*. The third style is the men's quaint, peculiarly un-French singing of the chant: a Rogations antiphon, *Invocantes Dominum* for times of war, from the 13th-century Worcester MS F160 (or an identical source). Incidentally, the *Alleluia* cue should have led into the full version. Then a *Te Deum* (also from F160), sung triumphantly to the joyful accompaniment of bells; and the Easter *Hec dies*, *Alleluia* and *Gospel* from an exciting find, a 12th-century Sacramentary from the Holy Sepulchre itself. The whole programme is a truly fascinating compilation.

Lancaster and Valois – French and English Music, 1350-1420

Anonymous Puis qu'autrement ne puis avoir. Soit tart, tempre, main ou soir. Le ior. Avrai je ja de ma dame confort? Sanctus. Je vueil vivre au plaisir d'amours **Cesaris** Se vous scaviez, ma tres douce maistresse. Mon seul voloir/Certes m'amour **Cordier** Ce jur de l'an **Fonteyns** Regali ex progenie **Machaut** Donnez, signeurs. Quand je ne voy ma dame. Riches d'amour et mendians. Pas de tor en thies pais **Pycard** Credo **Solage** Tres gentil cue **Sturgeon** Salve mater domini/Salve templum domini
Gothic Voices / Christopher Page *Ite*
Hyperion CDA66588 (59 minutes: DDD) Ⓕ
Texts and translations included. Recorded 1991 ●

This is the 10th recording to come from Christopher Page's Gothic Voices and, the considerable success of their previous recordings notwithstanding, this is perhaps their best yet. In the space of 11 years, Page and his group have reinvented performance practice in medieval and 15th-century music, as powerful and popularising an influence as David Munrow and his Early Music Consort of London in the 1970s. 'Lancaster and Valois' takes its name from the chosen repertoire: French secular songs of the late 14th and early 15th centuries juxtaposed with sacred English pieces from around 1400.

Much thought has been given to the ordering of the pieces and the grouping of the voices, resulting in the greatest possible diversity. In *Tres gentil cuer* by Solage, Page sets an ideally lilting tempo, with the text finely enunciated by Margaret Philpot, the tenors (in this instance Charles Daniels and Leigh Nixon) adding definition but never threatening to engulf. This is followed by a *Credo* by the English composer Pycard, the longest and most stately piece on the disc, exploiting the richer timbres of tenors and baritones. With excellent sound and entertaining and scholarly notes by Christopher Page, this is an irresistible disc.

The Marriage of Heaven and Hell – 13th-Century French Motets and Songs

Anonymous Je ne chant pas. Talens m'est pris. Trois sereurs/Trois sereurs/Trois sereurs. Plus bele que flors/Quant revient/L'autrier jouer. Par un martinet/Hé, sire!/Hé, bergier! De la virge Katerine/Quant froidure/Agmina milicie. Ave parens/Ad gratie. Super te Jerusalem/Sed fulsit virginitas. A vous douce debonnaire. Mout souvent/Mout ai esté en doulour. Quant voi l'aloete/Dieux! je ne m'en

partiré ja. En non Dieu/Quant voi la rose. Je m'en vois/Tels a mout. Festa januaria
Bernart de Ventadorn Can vei la lauzeta mover
Blondel de Nesle En tous tans que vente bise
Colin Muset Trop volontiers chanteroie.
Gautier de Dargies Autre que je ne seuill fas
Gothic Voices / Christopher Page
Hyperion CDA66423 (46 minutes: DDD) Ⓕ
Texts and translations included ○○

The reasons for the dazzling success of Gothic Voices both in the recording studio and in the concert hall are once again evident in this collection. It is both an entertaining and well-planned recital and, if one chooses to take it that way, reading Christopher Page's insert-notes while listening, a detailed lecture-recital. The music, all French and dating from the 13th century, is that seemingly impenetrable repertoire of polytextual motets, unexpectedly compared and contrasted with monophonic trouvère songs. The comparison is illuminating, and the performances of both genres of music are up to Gothic Voices' usual high standards. The clever juxtaposition of the trouvère Bernart de Ventadorn's *Can vei la lauzeta mover* with the triple-texted motet *Quant voi l'aloete/Dieux! je ne m'en partiré ja/NEUMA* encapsulates the thinking behind this recording: a compelling musical experience and a provocative intellectual one.

Music for the Lion-Hearted King
Anonymous Twelfth Century Mundus vergens. Novus miles sequitur. Sol sub nube latuit. Hac in anni ianua. Anglia, planctus itera. Etras auri reditur. Vetus abit littera. In occasu sideris. Purgator criminum. Pange melos lacrimosum. Ver pacis apperit. Latex silice **Blondel de Nesle** L'amours dont sui espris. Ma joie me semont **Gace Brulé** A la doucour de la bele seson **Gui IV, 'Li chastelain de Couci'** Li nouviauz tanz
Gothic Voices / Christopher Page
Hyperion CDA66336 (60 minutes: DDD) Ⓕ
Texts and translations included ○

Christopher Page has a remarkable gift for creating enthralling programmes of early music bound together by a brilliantly-chosen central theme, or appellation. This collection is no less distinguished and every bit as fascinating, musically and historically. Whether or not Richard himself ever actually listened to any of these pieces is beside the point: they are all representative of the period of his lifetime and are gathered together here in his name for the 800th anniversary of his coronation (1189). Two types of 12th-century vocal music are represented: the *conductus* – which can be written for one, two, three or even four voices and the *chanson*, or noble, courtly love song. The singers cannot be applauded too highly for performances marked by an extraordinary insight into how this music should be tackled, that is, with a fair degree of restraint as well as know-how, given the sort of audience it might have had in Richard's day: the royal court or the household of some high-ranking ecclesiastical figure.

The Spirits of England and France, Volume 1 – The 14th and 15th centuries
Anonymous Quant la douce jouvencelle. En cest mois de May. Laus detur multipharia. Credo. La uitime estampie real[a] **J Cooke** Gloria **da Perugia** Belle sans per **Machaut** Ay mi! dame de valour **Pykini** Plaisance, or tost
The12th and 13th centuries
Anonymous Deduc, Syon, uberrimas. Je ne puis/Par un matin/Le premier jor/Iustus. Beata nobis gaudia. Virgo plena gratie/Virgo plena gratie/Virgo. Crucifigat omnes. Flos in monte cernitur. In Rama sonat gemitus. Ave Maria. La septime estampie real[a]. La quarte estampie real[a] **Pérotin** (attrib) Presul nostri temporis
Gothic Voices / Christopher Page;
[a]**Pavlo Beznosiuk** *medieval fiddle*
Hyperion CDA66739 (63 minutes: DDD) Ⓕ
Texts and translations included. Recorded 1994

From the beautifully swift and unsentimental reading of the opening song, *Quant la douce jouvencelle*, through to the magically perfumed close with what Page calls the 'irredeemably English style' of *Ave Maria*, each piece has its own musical excellence. In the works of around 1400 it is usually Rogers Covey-Crump who leads the singing, with a skilled and nuanced grasp of the style that seems to grow with each recording. For the earlier works the spoils are divided between Paul Agnew, Julian Podger, Andrew Tusa and Leigh Nixon, all tenors with spirit and individuality. Finally, as an innovation in Gothic Voices recordings, Pavlo Beznosiuk plays three *estampes* on the medieval fiddle, without percussion and without any embellishment or deviation from the notes of their single surviving manuscript. While not everybody will be happy about this literal attitude to the problem of early instrumental music, Beznosiuk's playing is so rhythmically alive and so irresistible as to justify the approach. A superb recording from Gothic Voices, again.

The Spirits of England and France, Volume 2 – Songs of the Trouvères
Adam de la Halle Assenés chi, Grievilier
Anonymous Domna pos vos ay chausida. Quant voi la fleur nouvele. Amors m'art con fuoc am flamma. Trois Estampies **Audefroi le Bastart** Au novel tens pascor **Ernoul li Vielle** Por conforter mon corage
Gace Brulé Desconfortez, plains de dolor. Quant define fueille et flor. De bien amer grant joie atent. Cil qui d'amours **Gautier de Dargies** La doce pensee
Gontier de Soignies Dolerousement commence
Guibert Kaukesel Un chant novel. Fins cuers enamourés **Richart de Semilli** Je chevauchai
Gothic Voices / Christopher Page *medieval lte* with **Robert White** *bagpipes* **Nick Bicat** *perc*
Pavlo Beznosiuk *fiddle*
Hyperion CDA66773 (62 minutes: DDD) Ⓕ
Texts and translations included. Recorded 1994 ○○

This is a disc devoted to monophonic song and one of startling power and originality. Essentially it explores two repertories: the serious *grand chant*, particularly in the work of Gace Brulé, whose four songs here are presented with tremendous conviction and in wonderfully spacious readings; and the lighter dance songs, where Page often includes instruments, played with robust good humour. As regards the rhythmic approach, this is neatly varied to match the needs of particular songs: sometimes an equalist interpretation, sometimes syllabic, and sometimes in strict metre roughly derived from the principles of modal rhythm. That seems a thoroughly judicious and musical solution, and it gives the disc considerable variety of pace.

Margaret Philpot shows her astonishing stylistic range in the five songs she sings, from Richart de Semilli's jovial *Je chevauchai* via Gace Brulé's wonderful *De bien amer* and concluding with *Au novel tens pascor*, the late *chanson de toile* by Audefroi le Bastart. Emma Kirkby makes a welcome return to Gothic Voices with two glorious performances: her success in later music has been so great over the last few years that it has been too easy to forget quite how expressive she can be in early monophony, especially with Page's rattling folk-style lute playing in *Domna pos vos ay chausida*. Once again Gothic Voices have produced a record that sets new standards.

The Spirits of England and France, Volume 3
Anonymous Abide, I hope it be the best. Exultavit cor in Domino **Binchois** Qui veut mesdire si mesdie. Amoureux suy et me vient toute joye. Adieu mon amoureuse joye. Ay douloureux disant helas. Magnificat secundi toni. Se la belle n'a le voloir **Bittering** En Katerina solennia/Virginalis concio/Sponsus amat sponsum **Cardot** Pour une fois et pour toute **Dunstable** Beata Dei genitrix **Fontaine** J'ayme bien celui **Johannes de Lymburga** Descendi in ortum meum **Legrant** Se liesse **Machaut** Il m'est avis qu'il n'est **Power** Gloria **Velut** Lassies ester vostres chans de liesse. Un petit oyselet chantant
Gothic Voices / Christopher Page
Hyperion CDA66783 (67 minutes: DDD) Ⓕ
Texts and translations included. Recorded 1995 ●

Gothic Voices continue their long-term exploration of early English and French polyphony with an offering devoted to the work of Binchois and his musical forebears of both 'nationalities'. Consistent with the ensemble's usual approach to this repertoire, voices and instruments are not mixed; instead, Christopher Page is joined by the lutenists Christopher Wilson and Shirley Rumsey in energetic renderings of several of the songs: light, and delightful, relief.

The songs of Binchois are relatively late territory for Gothic Voices. It has been 12 years or so – in 'The Castle of Fair Welcome' (on Hyperion) – since they covered this repertoire in any depth, and comparison with the present disc is instructive. Over the years there have been more, and deeper, men's voices; the hard-edged, polished chrome patina has perhaps mellowed and burnished with time. Perhaps, too, the almost obsessive concern with clarity and intonation has been allowed to ease a little, in favour of a heightened sensitivity to the affective projection of both text and music. Perhaps, but only just. The hard edge creeps back in when the programme strays from Binchois back on to earlier repertory, such as Power's marvellous five-voice *Gloria* – here portrayed as an exercise in risk-taking for composer and singers alike. Its brashness, though glorious to listen to, leads to an inevitable query, for there seem to be not one but two programmes here. Binchois's songs, characterized by their restraint and understatement, seem uneasy in the company of so many of his exuberant contemporaries and immediate predecessors (and the not-so-immediate – what is Machaut doing here?).

The singers do their utmost to reflect the difference in tone, but that only makes the discrepancy more telling. This is a pity, for the Binchois pieces are finely pitched, and deserved to have more space to themselves – more space also for the singers to acclimatise themselves to Binchois's languorous melancholy. Page knows a show-stopper when he hears one, and the haunted *Ay, douloureux*, clocking in at nearly nine minutes, stands out from other items in the collection like a hothouse plant. That is not meant to belittle the rest, but to suggest that, as a programme, this particular collection is perhaps not as well rounded as so many of its predecessors: the sum of its parts. Yet there is so much that is deeply moving and magical that anything less than a warm recommendation would be Scrooge-like.

The Spirits of England and France, Volume 4
Anonymous Missa Caput (ed Curtis). The story of the Salve regina. Salve regina. Jesu for thy mercy[a]. Clangat tuba. Alma redemptoris mater. Old Hall Manuscript – Agnus Dei **Smert** Jesu fili Dei[a] **Traditional** Make we merry[a]. Nowell, nowell, nowell
[a]**Shirley Rumsey,** [a]**Christopher Wilson** *ltes*
Gothic Voices / Christopher Page [a]*lte*
Hyperion CDA66857 (66 minutes: DDD) Ⓕ
Texts and translations included Recorded 1996

This recording breaks new ground for Gothic Voices in terms of repertory. For the first time, the group tackles a large-scale, multi-movement work. One could hardly imagine a more appropriate Mass for their début in the genre than the anonymous English *Caput* cycle. Composed *c*1440 and long thought to be by Dufay, it lays fair claim to being the single most influential work of the 15th century. Its most innovative technical features were widely copied by continental composers, but on this recording we can at last begin to appreciate what all the fuss was about: few on the continent at the time were capable of writing music of such breathtaking confidence. One can feel the impact, the delighted surprise of contemporary listeners on hearing that very first burst of four-note writing in the *Kyrie*. In that respect, it is sobering to think that the identity of this supremely influential composer may forever remain a mystery.

That phrase 'breathtaking confidence' aptly describes Gothic Voices, who are on the top of their form. Initially one could hardly fail to be surprised by the briskness of this performance, but there is little sign of hurry even in the most demandingly athletic places. Although the declamation of the text is kept fairly low-key, the sense of phrase and line, of the notes taking their place amid a kaleidoscope of changing sounds, is all beautifully judged. And with intonation and ensemble of this consistency, it is possible to revel in sheer sonority. What else? The accompanying items make for lighter listening and a nicely balanced programme. This, then, is a disc that grows in stature with each hearing.

The Spirits of England and France, Volume 5
Anonymous Missa, 'Veterem hominem'. Jesu, fili virginis. Doleo super te. Gaude Maria virgo. Deus creator omnium. Jesu salvator. A solis ortus. Salvator mundi. Christe, qui lux es. To many a well. Sancta Maria virgo. Mater ora filium. Ave maris stella. Pange lingua **Dunstable** Beata mater
Gothic Voices / Christopher Page
Hyperion CDA66919 (65 minutes: DDD) Ⓕ
Texts and translations included. Recorded 1996

Gothic Voices' peculiar brand of extrovert dynamism puts a new spin on the performance of 15th-century Mass music; more than just a Mass, what we have here is a glimpse into the very mind of a medieval composer. Music as contemplation, certainly, but active, not passive; music in which each single voice conveys weight, number, proportion. Thus, the recurring head-motif at the beginning of each movement of the *Veterem hominem* Mass cycle is experienced not so much as a structural device as a manifestation of divine immutability. In a similar spirit, the same tempos are retained in all the movements; this has not been attempted very often, but far from being unrelenting, the result suits both pieces very well. If Page and friends let rip in the Mass and in the carols (delivered with exhilarating brashness), they deliberately adopt a more placid approach for some of the smaller Marian pieces. As to the chants that intersperse the polyphony, they provide contrast; but can it be that the 15th-century singers who polished off their polyphony with such gusto, took their 'daily bread' of plainsong with so little salt?

The Study of Love – French Songs and Motets of the 14th Century
Anonymous Pour vous servir. Puis que l'aloe ne fine. Jour a jour la vie. Combien que j'aye (two versions). Marticius qui fu. Renouveler me feïst. Fist on dame. Il me convient guerpir. Le ior. En la maison Dedalus. La grant biaute. En esperent. Ay las! quant je pans **Machaut** Dame, je suis cilz/Fins cuer. Trop plus/Biauté paree/Je ne suis. Tres bonne et belle. Se mesdisans. Dame, je vueil endurer **Pycard** Gloria. **Solage** Le basile
Gothic Voices / Christopher Page
Hyperion CDA66619 (60 minutes: DDD) Ⓕ
Texts and translations included. Recorded 1992 **OO**

The title of the disc speaks of the ways in which the discourses of love (and 'love') in the late Middle Ages are partly, perhaps largely, derived from books – the Bible, classical poetry and myths, the earlier medieval literary tradition – rather than some expression of unmediated personal feeling. But music was a powerful means for the late medieval artist to try to transcend the bookish intertextualities of the literary texts. Rarely have Gothic Voices, both as individuals and as a group, sounded more alive and present. The accord of vowel colour between the singers in some of the fully texted pieces is marvellous, a feature pointed up the more by juxtaposition with those works in which Page continues his experiments with lower-voice vocalisation. Where some slight untidiness creeps in, the impression often given is the positive one of risk being happily taken in the recording sessions. A wonderful addition to the catalogue, and the recorded sound is superlative.

The Voice in the Garden – Spanish Songs and Motets, 1480-1550 **P**
Anonymous Pase el agoa, ma Julieta. Harto de tanta porfía. Dindirín, dindirín. Ave, Virgo, gratia plena. Dentro en el vergel. Entra Mayo y sale Abril **Encina** Mi libertad en sosiego. Los sospiros no sosiegan **Enrique** Mi querer tanto vos quiere **Mena** Yo creo que n'os dió Dios. La bella malmaridada **Peñalosa** Por las sierras de Madrid. Ne reminiscaris, Domine. Precor te, Domine. Sancta Maria
Instrumental works – **Anonymous** A la villa voy **Milán** Fantasías 10, 12 and 18 **Narváez** Fantasía II tono; Fantasía III tono. Paseávase el rey moro **Fernández Palero** Paseávase el rey moro **Segni** Tiento
Gothic Voices / Christopher Page with **Christopher Wilson** *vihuela*
Andrew Lawrence-King *hp*
Hyperion CDA66653 (52 minutes: DDD) Ⓕ
Texts and translations included. Recorded 1993 **OO**

As usual with Gothic Voices, there is a mixture of all-vocal and solo-instrument performances, never the twain meeting and a mixture of what used to be called sacred and secular: motets by Peñalosa sit cheek by jowl with love songs and instrumental fantasies, giving an unusual and intriguing picture of the repertory. In general the record has all the qualities that make anything by Gothic Voices a required purchase for collections that aim at serious coverage of early centuries; and the resourceful selection of music makes it an important contribution to the understanding of Spanish culture. A note of special praise for Christopher Wilson's performances of the vihuela solos which have a control and eloquence that are truly impressive. Andrew Lawrence-King characteristically throws new light on some of this repertory with his immaculate range of colours and textures on the harp.

The Harp Consort

The Play of Daniel
Douglas Nasrawi *ten* Daniel; **Jeremy Birchall** *bass* Habacuc; **Harry van der Kamp** *bass* King Baltassar; **Ian Honeyman** *ten* King Darius; **Barbara Borden** *sop* Queen; **Caitríona O'Leary** *voc* Child;
The Harp Consort / Andrew Lawrence-King *hp/psaltery/org*
Deutsche Harmonia Mundi 05472 77395-2 Ⓕ
(78 minutes: DDD). Notes, text and translation included. Recorded 1997

Andrew Lawrence-King has assembled a thoughtful and attractive rendering of *The Play of Daniel*. The rhythmic interpretation of the unmeasured pitches is sensitively varied. A single pitch-standard is retained throughout – which seems to be the best approach, though there are plenty of good reasons for thinking otherwise. And, most important of all, the drama works well because careful and original thought has been given to the meaning of the words: as one example among many, Daniel's final speech is prefaced with a grand organ introduction that actively frames it as a prophecy well apart from the story. In fact the entire flow of the closing scenes is particularly effectively caught. Douglas Nasrawi is an excellent Daniel, managing to encompass the wide range of musical styles in the role without losing the strong character; and he gives a wonderfully expressive reading of the great lament as Daniel enters the lions' den. Ian Honeyman may well be the first Darius on record to portray him fully as a thoroughly nice but weak man: somehow the music invites a bolder approach at the moment when Darius usurps Belshazzar, but plainly the present interpretation works better. Harry van der Kamp is a splendidly strong Belshazzar; and all the smaller roles are well characterised. Alongside this is a superbly skilled instrumental ensemble. There is a reasonable case for thinking instruments are unnecessary in *Daniel* and impede the musical flow; but here their performances are so good and so well judged that most listeners will welcome their contribution. There are many different ways of doing *The Play of Daniel*, but this one is thoroughly viable throughout.

Henry's Eight

Missa cum iucunditate
Clemens non Papa Pater peccavi. Ego flos campi **Josquin Desprez** Absolve, quaesumus, Domine **Ockeghem** Ave Maria **Pierre de la Rue** Missa cum iucunditate **Willaert** O crux splendidior
Henry's Eight / Jonathan Brown *bass*
Etcetera KTC1214 (60 minutes: DDD) Ⓕ
Texts and translations included. Recorded 1997 **OO**

The *Missa cum iucunditate* is one of Pierre de la Rue's most widely circulated settings, and hearing it sung as zestfully as it is here, one understands why. It is indeed pervaded by the 'jollity' of the title, and belies de la Rue's rather dour reputation. In a previous recording The Hilliard Ensemble sang it one-to-a-part and sounded as though they were nearing the end of a long recording session; Henry's Eight involves all its members, so that the addition of a second countertenor in the *Credo* is neither contrived nor artificial, but an extension of what precedes it. The ensemble seems also to have allowed itself time to locate the music's rhetorical peaks: each movement has something new and fresh to offer, but the 'Osanna' stands out especially, demonstrating their ability to 'sing out' in an unrestrained manner, while still sounding unmistakably English. The selection of motets complements the Mass handsomely, and shows off some of the Eight's other emotional registers. The gems here are the performances of Ockeghem's *Ave Maria* (perhaps the finest available, contemplative and tensile: witness the final descent of the top line) and of Josquin's funeral motet, *Absolve, quaesumus, Domine*. Musically less impressive are the motets by Clemens non Papa, a composer whose style too often flirts with blandness. Another, very minor, concern is that the booklet-notes are remarkably misinformed in places. Such points need to be made, but cannot overshadow a very impressive achievement.

Hespèrion XXI

Diáspora Sefardí
Alejandría Las estrellas de los cielos **Esmirna** El Rey de Francia[a]. Yo era niña de casa alta **Jerusalén** Hermoza muchachica **Marruecos** Nani, nani[a] **Rhodes** El moro de Antequera[a]. La guirnalda de rosas[a] **Salónica** Levantose el Conde Niño[a]. Axerico de quinze años **Sarajevo** Por que llorax blanca niña[a]. A la una yo nací. Paxarico tu te llamas **Sofía** El rey que tanto madruga[a]. En la santa Helena. Longe de mi tu estarás **Turquía** Por allí pasó un cavallero[a]. Two Improvisations
[a]**Montserrat Figueras** *sop* **Hespèrion XXI / Jordi Savall** *viol/lira/rebab*
Alia Vox ② AV9809 (130 minutes: DDD) Ⓕ
Texts and translations included. Recorded 1999 **OO**

It is perhaps ironic that the Inquisition should have helped to preserve and enrich the musical tradition of the Sephardic Jews. Inquisitorial records provide an important source of information on musical practice in the Jewish community that until the diaspora of 1492 resided in the Iberian peninsula. The *conversos* who remained in Spain regularly came under suspicion for singing their own songs – taken as evidence of reversion to their own faith – while those who were expelled fanned out through northern Africa, eastern Europe and the Middle East. Thus, although the Sephardic tradition had its roots in medieval Hispanic culture, it was subsequently open to and enriched by multiple and diverse musical influences. Hespèrion XXI's recreation of this repertory casts its net wide, drawing on material from late medieval Spain, but also adapting living ballad traditions in Greece and incorporating Balkan-Turkish elements. It is important to emphasise the *creativity* of the musical process at work here: the oral tradition of the Sephardic Jews is all but lost, and we know little enough about actual performance practice in previous centuries. No matter: the result is beautiful, exotic, fantastical and at times profoundly moving. Montserrat Figueras's distinctive voice seems ideally suited to the long-breathed, meandering melodies, punctuated by those sinuous, fluttering, Eastern-sounding ornaments at which she excels. And even if the mix of languages makes it impossible to follow the story-line without recourse to the booklet-notes, she conveys a strong narrative sense: try the extended ballad *Por que llorax blanca niña* or the strangely mesmeric lullaby *Nani, nani*. The instrumental accompaniment of plucked and bowed strings, recorders and percussion, comes across as genuinely improvisatory (although a good deal must surely have been worked out in advance), and this is also true of the purely instrumental creations on the second CD, some of which are simply called improvisations. The playing of the instrumentalists is superb, and it all makes for compelling listening.

The Hilliard Ensemble

Officium
Jan Garbarek *sax* **The Hilliard Ensemble**
(David James *counterten* Rogers Covey-Crump, John Potter *tens* Gordon Jones *bar*)
ECM New Series 445 369-2 (78 minutes: DDD) Ⓕ
Latin texts included. Recorded 1993. Also includes Plainchant, Notre Dame polyphony and motets by Dufay, de la Rue and Morales – with saxophone

The play between ancient chant and structured jazz-style improvisation creates a sort of spiritual time warp where past and present happily co-exist on the basis of shared musical goals. For no matter how one views so-called crossover (such a silly term), or the relative lack of wisdom in sticking to rigid musical boundaries, the evidence is conclusive: 'Officium' transcends any limitations imposed by time and style. If you have any doubts, then play either the opening or closing tracks, both of which find Jan Garbarek (a master of apposite extemporisation) easing around Christóbal de Morales's polyphonic 'Pace mihi domine' (from the *Officium defunctorum*) as if it were his own creation. The effect is enchanting and when, eight tracks later, the same piece is presented *sans* Garbarek's saxophone, we somehow miss the commentary. If the probable success of this album prompts certain jazz fans and early music specialists to commiserate over their invaded territories, or cynics to align Garbarek and the Hilliards with Górecki and the Monks, then take heart: we're still listening to Respighi's ancient masters, Stravinsky's 'Pergolesi', Tchaikovsky's Mozart and Loussier's Bach, not to mention Ellington's Tchaikovsky. Stylistic cross-pollination makes for a healthy creative environment, and this CD is one of its happiest symptoms. Recordings, documentation and presentation are exemplary.

Spain and the New World
Alba Stabat mater **Alonso** La tricotea
Anonymous Tierra içielos se quexavan. Di, por que mueres en cruz. Dindirin, dindirin. Si la noche haze escura **Encina** Triste España sin ventura!. Cucú, cucú, cucú. Hoy comamos y be bamos. Mas vale trocar **Escobar** Clamabat autem mulier. Pásame por Dios barquero. Salve regina **Franco** In ilhuicac cihuapille (attrib). Memento mei, Deus. Dios itlazo nantzine (attrib) **Guerrero** Ave Virgo sanctissima **Lienas** Salve regina **Lobo** O quam suavis est, Domine **Luchas** A la caça, sus, a caça **Millán** O dulce y triste memoria **Mondéjar** Ave rex noster **Morales** Pater noster. Parce mihi, Domine. Magnificat a 6 **Padilla** Transfige, dulcissime Domine **Peñalosa** Inter vestibulum et altare. Magnificat quarti toni **Rivafrecha** Vox dilecti mei **Urreda** Nunca fué pena ma yor
The Hilliard Ensemble (David James, Ashley Stafford *countertens* Rogers Covey-Crump, John Potter, Mark Padmore *tens* Gordon Jones *bar*)
Virgin Classics Veritas ② VED5 61394-2 Ⓑ
(126 minutes: DDD). Texts and translations included. Recorded 1990-91

Originally released in late-1991, this two-CD set was The Hilliard Ensemble's contribution to the Columbus commemorations of the following year. It was also their first recording after Paul Hillier's departure from the group. In keeping with the Columbus theme, the collection includes music composed both in the Old World and in the New. The languages used are Latin for the sacred music and Spanish for the secular – but in addition there are two small pieces in Nahuatl, the tongue of the Aztecs.

With well over two hours of music, there is time for The Hilliard to dwell on many composers and genres, most of whom have but a small representation on disc. Spanish polyphony has a marked tendency to asperity in its treatment of dissonance, and generally eschews the more complex forms of polyphony adopted by Franco-Flemish composers: that makes for sobriety in its sacred music, and directness in the secular. This is best heard in the music of Encina and Peñalosa in the early 16th century; the closest Spain comes to a home-grown exponent of the international style is Morales, one of whose splendid *Magnificat*s stands out as a high point.

The Hilliard Ensemble is more at ease with sacred music than with secular pieces. Those in the latter category come across either as forced, or as insufficiently defined. The collection as a whole, however, is a distinctive one, and offers a convincing picture of a country whose polyphonic tradition has often passed for a poor relation of the mainstream continental idiom.

Paul Hillier *voc*

Chansons de Trouvères
Anonymous Volez vous que je vous chant. Quant voi la flor nouvele **Colin Muset** En mai, quant li rossignolez **Gace Brulé** Les oxelés de mon païx. A la douçor de la bele seson **Moniot d'Arras** Ce fu en mai **Thibault de Champagne** Aussi conme unicorne sui. Deus est ensi conme li pellicanz. Chançon ferai, que talenz m'en est pris
Paul Hillier *voc*
Andrew Lawrence-King *psaltery/hp/org*
Harmonia Mundi Classical Express HCX3957184 (70 minutes: DDD). Texts and translations included Ⓢ
Recorded 1996 ●

The repertoire of *trouvère* songs is one 'we are only now beginning to explore', writes Margaret Switten. Here we have an enlightened and well-chosen selection, sensitively presented and delightfully sung by Paul Hillier with insight and feeling. The main object of the poets' attention is *fin'amor*, but other themes, including the return of spring, make their joyful appearance, and there is one piece in a completely different vein, a serious piece of religious polemics: *Deus est ensi conme li pelliçanz*. The melodies, simple and stanzaic, are of great beauty. Outstanding in this respect is Gace Brulé's *A la douçor de la bele seson*. Many are modal (Dorian) and a few share a well-known opening phrase with a Gregorian *melodie-type* that Andrew Lawrence-King has made much use of in his accompaniments. His own contribution is momentous: if the manner in which these songs were originally performed still remains a mystery for the singer, it is even more of an enigma for the accompanist. But Andrew Lawrence-King has taken the word *trouvère* to heart: he is a true 'finder'. His empathy with text, music and singer is total: he 'invents' with a sure touch, and it is not going too far to say it is a touch of genius.

Distant Love

Codax Cantigas de Amigo – Prelude[b]; Ondas do mar de vigo[a]; Mundad'ei comigo[a]; Mia jrmana fremosa treides comigo[a]; Aj deus se sab'ora meu amigo[a]; Quantas sabedes amar amigo[a]; Eno sagrado en vigo[a]; Aj ondas que eu vin veer[a]; Postlude[c]
Rudel Dansa[b]. Belhs m'es l'estius el temps floritz[ac]. Lanquan li jorn son lonc en may[a]. No sap chantar qui so non di[ac]. Pro ai del chan essenhadors[ab]. Quan lo rius de la fontana[ac]. Quan lo rossinhols el follos[ab]
[a]**Paul Hillier** *voc*
Andrew Lawrence-King [b]*hp*/[c]*psaltery*
Harmonia Mundi HMU90 7203 (68 minutes: DDD) Ⓕ
Texts and translations included. Recorded 1994-98 ⭘

This is a jewel, both for its music and in its performance. The title, 'Distant Love', is described by Margaret Switten in her note as a 'magic formula' that 'still haunts our imagination'. It was invented by the 12th-century troubadour Jaufre Rudel to evoke his own love, unattained and unattainable, for the fabulous Countess of Tripoli, in whose arms he is said to have died. A century later Martin Codax presents a woman singing of her desire for the absent lover she awaits in the port of Viga. Andrew Lawrence-King uses snatches of melody from both composers to create, with delicate subtlety, a preamble, a final *Dansa*, and various interludes. Very occasionally he adds a gentle accompaniment. Paul Hillier interprets each composer with intense sympathy and a remarkable command of the two languages – Galician-Portuguese and Old Occitan. He recites in a normal spoken voice the two Rudel poems lacking music, with Andrew Lawrence-King's added harp interludes for the first, and a quietly improvised accompaniment on the psaltery for the second. A great delight is Rudel's wonderful melody, composed for his most famous poem *Lanquan li jorn* and justly admired and imitated by the German Minnesinger Walther von der Vogelweide.

Micrologus

Cantico della Terra

Nicholay sollemnia[b]. Sonet vox ecclesie[b]. Passione di Diamante[a]. Miserere di Santu Lussurgiu[a]. O divina virgo flore[b]. Dammi conforto[b]. Passione di Giulianello[a]. Stava la Madre[a]. Iam lucis orto sidere[b]. Kyrie eleison[b]. Gloria[b]. Sanctus[b]. Miserere di Sessa Aurunca[a]. Gloria di Montedoro[a]. Chi vol lo mondo despreçcare[b]. Submersus jacet Pharao[b]. O Lylium convallium[b]. Madonna Santa Maria[b]
[a]**Quartetto Vocale Giovanna Marini** (Giovanna Marini, Patrizia Bovi, Francesca Breschi, Patrizia Nasini, *vocs*); [b]**Micrologus**
Opus 111 OPS30-277 (61 minutes: DDD) Ⓕ
Texts and translations included. Recorded 1999

This is an odd and intriguing mixture. The Quartetto Vocale Giovanna Marini and Micrologus have taken a special interest in the way existing devotional folk music has a certain amount in common with the earliest written music of Italy – primarily the 'simple polyphony' and the monophonic lauda. By adopting the vocal styles of today's folk musicians – in particular the throaty and reedy singing styles with a large quantity of vocal slides and glottal stops – they have come up with new and invigorating interpretations.

As a theoretical approach, this is very old indeed. For decades there has been a branch of research that seeks material in common between the traditional and the old. But that research has produced little in the way of solid results; and from the present recording you could well conclude that the two have little in common.

Even so, the juxtaposition is musically exciting. The Quartetto Vocale present some astonishing examples of traditional polyphony; tracks 7 and 13, in particular, leave the listener gasping at the boldness of the music and the courage of the singers. Alongside this, Micrologus give slightly more restrained performances of early Italian music, of which the most fascinating is the group of Mass movements (tracks 10-12) from sources written around 1400.

A special note of welcome, too, for the insert-notes, which provide excellent documentation so the listener is never confused about what is old and what is new. Everything is done with such spirit that any listener considering what can be gained from such an interchange will find plenty to think about.

The Newberry Consort

Il Solazzo 🄿

Anonymous 14th Century Italian La Badessa. Bel fiore danza. Nova stella. Cominciamento di gioia. Trotto. Principe di virtu **Bartolino da Padova** Alba columba **Ciconia** O rosa bella. Ligiadra donna **Jacopo da Bologna** Non al suo amante **Landini** La bionda treccia. Dolcie signorie. Donna, s'i, t'o fallito. El gran disio **Zacharo de Teramo** Rosetta. Un fior gentil
The Newberry Consort / Mary Springfels
Harmonia Mundi HMU90 7038 (62 minutes: DDD) Ⓕ
Texts and translation included. Recorded 1990

If medieval Italian music pales somewhat in comparison to the glories of opera from the 19th century onwards, there are still riches to be discovered in this collection of *trecento* vocal and instrumental works. The Chicago-based ensemble, The Newberry Consort, use a mere five performers to provide over an hour of entertainment. This was the era of writers such as Dante, Petrarch, Boccaccio, but also of Simone Prodenzani – the author of a cycle of sonnets entitled *Il Solazzo*, many of which were later set to music. While some of the *Solazzo* texts are presented here in musical form (the scurrilous *La Badessa* is one), Italian ballata from leading composers of the time are also represented – Ciconia's *O rosa bella* and Landini's *La bionda treccia*, for example. The vocal numbers are all taken by mezzo Judith Malafronte and countertenor Drew Minter who clear the hurdles of tricky pronunciation and flamboyantly complex vocal lines to give a thoroughly communicative performance of this wonderful music. Mary Springfels provides elegant and musical direction as well as that essential ingredient to a disc such as this – the informative booklet. If the prospect of an hour of early Italian song sounds daunting, fear not, for the instrumental dances on the disc (especially the anonymous *Cominciamento di gioia*) are played with a vitality that will make you want to jump up and join in! Explorers of the riches from Italian times long gone by need have no qualms when sampling from this lively, superbly performed disc.

Villon to Rabelais

Anonymous Amours m'ont fait. L'autrier quant je chevauchoys. La belle se siet. Belles tenés moy. Bon vin. En amours n'a si non bien. En douleur et tristesse. Faisons bonne chère. Héllas! Mon coeur n'est pas à moy. J'aimeray mon amy. My, my. Puis qu'autrement ne puis avoir. Petit fleur. Quant je suis seullecte. Réveillez-vous, Piccars. Rolet ara la tricoton. Suite of Bransles. Danse de Cleves (arr Duffin). La gelosia (arr Duffin). Petit vriens (arr Duffin)
Busnois Vostre beauté **Févin** Faulte d'argent. Il fait bon aimer l'oyselet. Soubz les branches
Marot Jouissance vous donneray **Stockhem** Je suis d'Alemagne. Marchez là dureau
The Newberry Consort (Drew Minter *counterten* William Hite *ten* Tom Zajac *bar/hp/recs/perc* David Douglass *vielle*) **/ Mary Springfels** *vielle/rebec*
Harmonia Mundi HMU90 7226 (72 minutes: DDD) Ⓕ
Texts and translations included. Recorded 1997

Rarely does an Anglo-Saxon early music ensemble declaim French quite so convincingly. This recital from The Newberry Consort takes in the huge variety of expressive registers in secular music from the late 15th and early 16th centuries, including dance music (which takes up a fairer proportion of the recital than is often the case). Part of the attraction is that most of these pieces have previously been neglected on disc because of their anonymous status: this includes works better known among scholars than by the general public, but whose musical worth transcends purely historical considerations. If the disc shows any bias, it is towards pieces of popular inspiration, often through the use of rustic texts, sometimes combined with more artful poems (as in *Puis qu'autrement/Marchez là dureau* or *Vostre beauté/Vous marchez du bout du pie*, or the settings of *La tricotée*). This is the only evident connection between Villon and Rabelais and the pieces recorded here (none of which set texts by either writer). The projection and enunciation of texts has been given careful thought, and is clearly executed so that recourse to the booklet is only necessary in those cases when several texts are declaimed at once. Drew Minter's contribution is worth mentioning in this regard, and the ensemble as a whole sings out even when the effect turns to slapstick (as in the drinking-song *Bon vin*).

It has become a truism that secular repertories are too often treated as also-rans in the discography of this period; a recital like this one helps to redress that imbalance very stylishly. Fittingly, it is dedicated to the memory of the scholar Howard Mayer Brown, who did so much to further the understanding of instruments and their participation in renaissance music. It is a worthy tribute.

New London Consort

The Pilgrimage to Santiago P
Including Cantigas de Santa María (coll/comp Alfonso el Sabio), the seven Cantigas de Amigo by Martin Codax; other medieval vocal and instrumental works from the Codices Las Huelgas and Calixtinus
New London Consort / Philip Pickett
L'Oiseau-Lyre ② 433 148-2OH2 (126 minutes: DDD) Ⓕ
Texts and translations included

In recent years a far higher standard of performance together with more rigorous scholarship has come to be expected from those who choose to perform this kind of repertoire. Philip Pickett has been in the forefront of this impressive rise in confidence (as much about what is not known as is definitely known) as this two-disc set amply demonstrates. What may perhaps be surprising to some is the quality of the music itself. The *Cantigas* remain some of the most enticing melodies ever written, and the New London Consort do them full justice with an array of instrumentalists and singers who are, however, used with discretion. Similarly the moving *Cantigas de Amigo* of Martin Codax are beautifully sung with a restraint that pays expressive dividends. The polyphonic music from the Las Huelgas and Calixtinus manuscripts completes, with a flourish, the survey tied together by the Santiago label. If there is early polyphony that sounds fresher than the four-part *Belial vocatur*, for example, it has yet to be recorded. In addition to polyphonic works of various genres, Pickett has also chosen to record the four *planctus* settings from the Las Huelgas Codex: moving in themselves, they are valuable pieces also for their historical associations.

Orlando Consort

Passion

Compère Crux triumphans **Dufay** Victimae paschali laudes. Vexilla regis prodeunt
Josquin Desprez Victimae paschali laudes
Isaac Easter Mass Proper **Obrecht** Salve cru **Tinctoris** Lamentationes Jeremiex
Orlando Consort (Robert Harre-Jones *counterten* Charles Daniels, Angus Smith *tens* Donald Greig, Robert Macdonald *basses*)
Metronome METCD1015 (62 minutes: DDD) Ⓕ
Texts and translations included. Recorded 1996

This is an attractive programme of Holy Week and Easter pieces, some by unlikely composers such as Tinctoris, the 15th-century musical theorist. It is centred around Isaac's four-part *Easter Mass*, with its polytextual structure. Isaac sets all the pieces of the Proper, with the exception of the Offertory, and he interweaves three popular Easter tunes. The end product is a wonderfully joyful and festive Mass, the nearest modern equivalent that comes to mind being Honegger's Christmas cantata with its carol sequence. Isaac's Mass is flanked by Tinctoris's moving *Lamentation*, two settings of the *Victimae paschali laudes*, and three fine pieces honouring the Cross.

The Orlando Consort do full justice to this splendid programme. The singing is superb, the individual parts easily identifiable yet marvellously blended. Listeners may be slightly foxed by the pronunciation of the Latin, particularly by the nasal French vowels. Much care has gone into this search for authenticity.

The Saracen and the Dove – Music from the Courts of Padua and Pavia around 1400

Anonymous O Maria, virgo davitica
Anthonello de Caserta Del glorioso titolo
Bartolino da Padova Imperial sedendo. La douce chiere **Ciconia** Doctorum principem. Per quella strada. O felix templum jubila. O Padua sidus praeclarum. Con lagreme bagnandome. Gloria, 'Spiritus et alme'. Sus une fontayne. Le ray au soleyl. Una panthera
Zachara da Teramo Un fior gentil. Sumite, karissimi. Dime, Fortuna. Gloria, 'Ad ogni vento'
Orlando Consort (Robert Harre-Jones *counterten* Charles Daniels, Angus Smith *tens* Donald Greig *bar*)
Archiv Produktion 459 620-2AH (74 minutes: DDD) Ⓕ
Texts and translations included. Recorded 1998 ●

This recording is really about Johannes Ciconia, that delicious and innovative composer who is now believed to have spent the late 1390s in the Visconti court at Pavia before moving to the different cultural centre of Padua in the next decade. But it ingeniously puts Ciconia into a wider musical context, most particularly that of Antonio Zachara da Teramo, who has in recent years begun to seem even more distinctive and almost as great. The juxtaposition of works here shows the deft hand of Margaret Bent, who also contributes an informative note.

The Orlando Consort does the music proud. Never before have the two most intricate works in the repertory – Ciconia's *Sus une fontayne* and Zachara's *Sumite, karissimi* – sounded so clear, so elegant and so easy. The hard edges in florid pieces such as *Per quella strada* and Anthonello's *Del glorioso titolo* positively glitter. And the grand motets, performed here with voices alone for the first time, make a stunningly powerful impression. Given that some recent recordings of Ciconia's music have been resolutely idiosyncratic, the very seriousness of these performances is to be saluted.

Even so, certain pieces fail to jump to the ear quite so readily as in some earlier performances: the sudden changes of mood and texture in *Una panthera* or *O felix templum* go past almost unnoticed, the words are rarely allowed to help the musical flow, and forms occasionally get flabby. Moreover there is a tendency to favour an unvarying *forte* in the motets: they are indeed grand pieces, but such resistance to delicacy seems at variance with the Ars Subtilior that Ciconia favoured in several of his works. But all said it's a major achievement.

Worcester Fragments

English Sacred Music of the Late Middle Ages
Orlando Consort (Robert Harre-Jones *counterten* Charles Daniels, Angus Smith *tens* Donald Grieg *bar*)
Amon Ra CD-SAR59 (58 minutes: DDD) Ⓕ
Texts and translations included. Recorded 1992

In this recording the Orlando Consort provides the listener with the chance to gain an overall impression of how music developed in England during the 13th and early 14th centuries – a development distinguished by its intriguing variety, creativity and undoubted beauty, its peculiar sweetness being marked by the constant harmonic use of the interval of a third. The Orlando Consort manage to achieve a balance between the type of buzzing vocal timbre, believed to have been that of the Middle Ages with its roughness of approach, and their own good solid modern standards of professional musicianship. The Consort also attempt to reproduce what scholars now believe to have been the way in which ecclesiastical Latin was pronounced in medieval England.

Piffaro

A Flemish Feast – Flemish Renaissance Wind Music

Agricola Crions Noel **Agricola/Ghiselin** Duo
Alamire T'andernaken **Anonymous** Flemish melodies. De tous biens playne. Wij sheyt edel vrouwe. Die winter is verganghen **Brassart** Fortis cum quevis actio
Clemens non Papa O Crux benedicta. Ave mundi spes Maria **Ghiselin** Je loe amours
Lapicida T'andernaken **La Rue** Ave regina caelorum. Pourquoy non Obrecht J'ay pris amours. Laet u ghenoughen, liever Johan **Pullois** Les larmes
Susato Passe et medio. Gaillardes. La Morisque. Entre du fol. Mon désir. La dona. Allemaigne. Bransles. Bergerette **Tyling** T'andernaken al op den Rijn
Piffaro / Joan Kimball, Robert Wiemken
Archiv Produktion 457 609-2AH (65 minutes: DDD) Ⓕ
Recorded 1999

Over the last 20 years the growing acceptance of all-vocal performance of medieval and early renaissance song has narrowed the repertory of latter-day instrumentalists. Whether or not one accepts the premises behind the shift, the result is an undeniable marginalisation of instruments on record. This seriously distorts one's perception of what must have been, for if voices and instruments were kept separate to some extent at least, plainly instruments were everywhere and played a crucial part in society. More recordings like this one are needed to redress the balance. Piffaro is not alone in presenting all-instrumental programmes – the Dufay Consort springs to mind – but one could hardly imagine a more attractive introduction to the medium. Piffaro gives an elegant, spirited recital, varied and fast-paced, which reflects instruments' many functions, from the private entertainment of the rich to those of the populace. Most are either straight transcriptions or arrangements of pre-existing pieces, though some were probably intended specifically for instrumental performances. But the bulk of such performances consisted in improvisations, by their very nature irrecoverable. One selection arranged by Grant Herreid takes a freer approach to the musical text, suggesting which embellishments might have been made to one of the best-known tunes of all, *J'ay pris amours*. More interpretative licence of this kind is surely the way forward for ensembles like Piffaro. There is a real breadth of musicianship here (the performers each play several instruments) and, in addition to polished performances and intelligent programming, listeners will find informative booklet-notes by the distinguished organologist Keith Polk and black-and-white photographs of the instruments concerned, making clear their division into families.

Pomerium

Carolus Maximus - Music in the life of Charles V

Crecquillon Carolus magnus erat. Quis te victorem **Josquin Desprez** Mille regretz **Gombert** Missa a la Incoronation, 'Sur tous regrets' – Kyrie; Gloria. Mille regretz. Qui colis Ausoniam **Lassus** Heroum soboles. Si qua tibi obtulerint **Morales** Missa, 'L'homme armé' – Credo. Jubilate Deo omnis terra. Missa, 'Mille regretz' – Sanctus. Missa pro defunctis – Agnus Dei. Circumdederunt me **Narváez** La canción del Emperador, 'Mille regres'[a]. Fantasia del octavo tono[a]

[a]**Dolores Costoyas** *vihuela* **Pomerium / Alexander Blachly**

Glissando 779008-2 (73 minutes: DDD) Ⓕ

Texts and translations included. Recorded 1999

This recording by Pomerium marks an auspicious start for a new label – Glissando – created by Peter Czornyj, formerly of DG Archiv. 'Music in the life of Charles V', produced to accompany a major exhibition on the 500th anniversary of his birth, brings together some of the many pieces dedicated to or closely associated with the Emperor. Charles was a great musical enthusiast, gaining his first music lessons at the age of seven, and, almost 50 years later, after his retreat to the Jeronymite monastery at Yuste, priding himself on his musical discernment when presented with a Mass by Guerrero.

His European profile is reflected in the selection of works offered here by French, Flemish and Spanish composers: only the northern composers served in his celebrated Flemish chapel, though the vihuelist Luys de Narváez was master of the choirboys in the chapel of his son Philip. Morales, the leading Spanish composer of his time, never found favour at the royal court even though he dedicated several works to Charles. An interesting programme, then, from favourites such as Josquin's chanson *Mille regretz* (known as the 'Song of the Emperor' and also presented in Narváez's version for vihuela) to less familiar repertory by Gombert and Crecquillon.

Gombert's *Missa 'Sur tous regrets'* is characteristically dense, but it nevertheless recreates something of the highly developed ceremonial of Charles's chapel. The motets by Crecquillon – an underrated composer – are very fine. Pomerium's performances, recorded in the resonant acoustic of the Ascension Roman Catholic Church in New York, are measured and generally well balanced, allowing the closely woven polyphonic textures to speak for themselves. Flow is mostly good, although parts of the *Credo* from Morales's *Missa 'L'homme armé'* sound rushed, as does Crecquillon's motet *Quis te victorem*.

While Alexander Blachly's direction is not insensitive to phrasing, more attention could be given to overall shaping and, especially in the motets, the musical rhetoric. For all the vocal energy behind these interpretations, they occasionally come across as bland. That said, the disc affords a fascinating insight into the repertory of Charles's chapel and, to a lesser extent, chamber: well worth adding to any self-respecting CD collection of renaissance polyphony.

La Reverdie

Legenda Aurea

Anonymous Facciam laude a tuc'ti i sancti. Sia laudato San Francesco. San Domenico beato. Ciascun ke fede sente. Santa Agnese da Dio amata. Novel canto/Sia laudato San Vito. Laudiam 'li gioriosi martiri. Pastor principe beato. Magdalena degna da laudare. Spiritu Sancto dolçe amore. Benedicti e llaudati

La Reverdie

Arcana A304 (70 minutes: DDD) Ⓕ

Texts and translations included. Recorded 1999 ⊙

La Reverdie has focused on *laude* in the past, specifically of the Marian variety. Here they concentrate on the praise of other saints. Some of them are well known such as *Sia laudato San Francesco*, but others are less so. This ensemble has always mixed voices and instruments in highly imaged and striking ways. In the case of the *laude* repertory, recent research by the American scholar Blake Wilson into the Laudesi societies that abounded in Italy (perhaps most obviously in Tuscany, from where the two manuscripts represented here originate) confirms a richly documented variety of approaches to performance of this intrinsically popular genre, ranging from voices alone to an array of hired instrumentalists of all sorts. In the longer pieces comprising many stanzas, La Reverdie improvises added counterpoints, both vocal and instrumental, and individual singers step into the limelight, sometimes declaiming the text without the benefit of music.

Regarding the relationship of text to music, La Reverdie advocates a metrical interpretation of the notation's unmeasured neumes. This makes intuitive sense, given the formal markers of a genre destined for a congregation singing in the vernacular. Just as the variety of performance options must have been welcome to congregations of the time, so it is on this CD: there is something to suit every taste. La Reverdie's core quartet of female vocalists have a pleasing quality, and are matched by an equal number of equally striking male singers. The unspecified soloist on the opening track, *Facciam laude a tuc'ti i sancti*, rings the changes most compellingly. There is now a considerable number of *laude* recordings in the discography. This is one of the finest, and also the most satisfying La Reverdie recording.

La Romanesca

Al alva venid – Spanish secular music of the 15th and 16th centuries **P**

Anonymous Al alva venid. L'amor, dona, ch'io te porto. Rodrigo Martines. A los maitines era. Nina y vina **Encina** Más vale trocar. Si abrá en este baldrés! Qu'es de ti, desconsolado? Hoy comamos y bevamos **Mudarra** Tres libros de musica – Si me llaman a mi; Ysabel, perdiste la tu faxa; Guárdame las vacas **Narváez** Paseavase el rey moro. Lós Seys libros del delphin – Diferencias de Guardame las vacas **D Ortiz** Trattado de glosas – Recercarda segunda sobre el passamezzo moderno; Recercada tercera para viola de gamba sola; Recercada quarta sobre la folia; Recercada quinta sobre el passamezzo antiguo; Recercada settima sobre la Romanesca **Pisador** Libro de música – En la fuente del rosel; La manana de Sant Juan **Vásquez** Orphenica lyra – De los álamos vengo; Con qué la lavaré; Glosa sobre Tan que vivray; De Antequera sale el moro

La Romanesca (Marta Almajano *sop* Paolo Pandolfo *va da gamba* Juan Carlos de Mulder *vihuela/gtr* Pedro Estevan *perc*) **/ José Miguel Moreno** *vihuela*

Glossa GCD920203 (60 minutes: DDD) Ⓕ

Texts and translations included. Recorded 1995 **OO**

Many of these pieces – songs and vihuela music from 16th-century Spain – have been recorded at least once, if not dozens of times before, but this CD takes pride of place in this repertory. La Romanesca performs with true *fantasía* but without any of the mannerisms – the excesses and the understatements – of many of its predecessors and rivals: it seem to hit it just right.

It has mostly selected songs with a strong popular flavour – precisely those songs that have attracted most attention because they are simply so attractive – but their realisations are restrained in terms of instrumental accompaniment (plucked strings, viol and a smattering of percussion), but full of musical vitality – in other words, the emphasis is, justly, on the music and not the 'orchestrated' arrangement of it. The players, led by José Miguel Moreno, are brilliant, and the singer, Marta Almajano shines in this repertory. She brings out perfectly the lyricism inherent in the popular-inspired court song tradition – take, for example, Vásquez's lovely *De los álamos vengo*: these songs demand an elusive blend of sophistication and simplicity. The instrumentalists make the most of the virtuoso element already making itself felt in the works of the vihuelists and Ortiz's *recercadas*. It's good to have a 'straight' version of Encina's *Más vale trocar*, which is often treated in an upbeat manner at odds with the text. The same applies to Vásquez's *Con qué la lavaré* although this is, arguably, just a touch too slow. Overall, it is a pleasurable experience to listen to this disc. Take it with you wherever you go, and especially to that desert island.

Sequentia

Edda – Myths from medieval Iceland

Baldur's Dreams. The End of the Gods. Havamal – Odin's Rune-verses. In Memory of Baldur. The Song of Fire and Ice. The Song of the Mill. The Tale of Thrym. Völuspa I-III, 'The Prophecy of the Sybil'

Sequentia (Barbara Thornton, Lena Susanne Norin *vocs* Elizabeth Gaver *vn* Benjamin Bagby *voc/lyre*)

Deutsche Harmonia Mundi 05472 77381-2 Ⓕ

(77 minutes: DDD). Recorded 1996 **O**

Sequentia has amazed and delighted even native Icelanders with the curiosity, imagination and dedication with which it has been bringing to life some of the island's earliest music. The Cologne-based Sequentia, specialists in the northern European oral song tradition, have worked painstakingly on Iceland's great store of *rímur* – the medieval sung poetry, possibly related to the early *chanson de geste*, and whose strains can still be detected in children's playground songs in Reykjavík today. Sequentia has applied its research into the performance of *rímur* to re-creating sung texts from the *Elder* or *Poetic Edda*. Of course we have no way of knowing how this music really did sound; but listening to Benjamin Bagby and his colleagues, you will find yourself compelled by the vigour, eloquence and integrity of their own re-created authenticity. Isolation has at least ensured that living Icelandic offers pretty good indications for the pronunciation of Old Norse – and Bagby has listened with a keen ear. The late Barbara Thornton's copper-bright soprano is heard alone and with her colleagues in three 'panels' from the apocalyptic *Prophecy of the Sybil*, 'Völuspá'. They form the real set-pieces of this recital. In between, spirited fiddle pieces are played by Elizabeth Gaver; Bagby gives a virtuoso 14-minute performance of *The Tale of Thrym*; and the voices entwine in the haunting *In Memory of Baldur*. It's a wonderful disc.

The Scholars of London

French Chansons
Arcadelt En ce mois délicieux; Margot, labourez les vignes; De temps que j'estois amoureux; Sa grand beauté **Bertrand** De nuit, le bien
Clemens Non Papa Prière devant le repas; Action des Graces **Costeley** Arrête un peu mon coeur
Gombert Aime qui vouldra; Quand je suis aupres
Janequin Le chant des oiseaux. Or vien ça, vien, m'amye **Josquin Desprez** Faulte d'argent. Mille regretz **Lassus** Beau le cristal. Bon jour mon coeur. Un jeune moine. La nuict froide et sombre. Si je suis brun **Le Jeune** Ce n'est que fiel. **Passereau** Il est bel et bon **Sandrin** Je ne le croy **Sermisy** Tant que vivray en eage florissant. Venez, regrets. La, la Maistre Pierre
Tabourot Belle qui tiens ma vie **Vassal** Vray Dieu
The Scholars of London
Naxos 8 550880 (60 minutes: DDD) Ⓢ
Texts and translations included. Recorded 1993

Listening to this carefully crafted selection, one is struck by the flexibility of a style that accommodates so many distinctive temperaments – the verve of Janequin, the suavity of Sermisy, the gravity of Gombert. It is a democratic genre in the truest sense, appealing to the great (Josquin and Lassus) while permitting lesser figures to shine as well. The term 'democratic' also describes the *chanson*'s appeal, then as now: here are some of the most beguiling tunes of any period. To call these performances unobtrusive is to do them no injustice. The Scholars of London capture the wistful elegance of the courtlier pieces – for example, Le Jeune's *Ce n'est que fiel*. In some of the more scurrilous songs there is a Gallic rambunctiousness but at times the tempos are a shade too brisk for comfort, and the choice of pitch-standard in Janequin's famous *Chant des oiseaux* (sung here in its through-composed version) sets a strain on the singers' accustomed agility. But such details merely affect the odd piece. This is a disc that gives great pleasure: like ephemera trapped in amber, the music in this collection bears modest yet touching testimony to a period that produced much 'great' music. Its smaller creations are no less admirable.

Sinfonye

The Courts of Love Ⓟ
– Music from the time of Eleanor of Aquitaine
Anonymous 12th Century L'on qui dit q'amors est dolce chose **Bernart de Ventadorn** Ara'm conseillatz seignor. Conartz, ara sai au be. Quan vei la lauzeta mover **Cadenet** S'anc fuy belha ni prezada (vocal and instrumental versions) **Gace Brulé** Quant je voi la noif remise. Quant voi le tens bel et cler. Quant flours et glais et verdues s'esloigne. Quant li tens reverdoie
Giraut de Bornelh S'ie'us queir conseil, bel' amig' Alamanda **Gui d'Ussel** Si be'm partetz, mala domna, de vos **Raimbaut de Vaqeiras** Calenda maya (vocal and instrumental versions)
Sinfonye (Mara Kiek *voc* Andrew Lawrence-King *medieval hp* Jim Denley *perc*) **/ Stevie Wishart**
Hyperion CDA66367 (64 minutes: DDD) Ⓕ
Texts and translations included ⭘

This recital consists of songs and instrumental pieces dating from the end of the 12th century and derived from the 'courts of love' of Aquitaine, Champagne, Flanders and elsewhere. These courts, created around aristocratic figures such as Marie of Champagne and Eleanor of Aquitaine, were essentially a charade of the medieval law courts, to which lovers could bring their complaints. Thus the texts of the songs are concerned with the dilemmas of infidelity, betrayal and unrequited love. All that survives of this music is melodies for singing: these have been sensitively arranged by Stevie Wishart for a small selection of medieval instruments, including the symphony, a sort of hurdy-gurdy, medieval fiddles, lutes and percussion.

All the players of Sinfonye are both expert and relaxed, projecting the music with great character. Six of the pieces are sung by Mara Kiek with considerable feeling: her unusual voice production and tone help to give a sense of 'distance' to the performances, and strike a suitably plaintive note. Hyperion's recording catches all the vocal and instrumental inflexions with great fidelity and a natural balance. All in all, a fascinating glimpse of music and manners from a remote if influential corner of medieval civilisation.

Red Iris – Instrumental music from 14th-century Italy Ⓟ
Istampite – Trotto; Tre Fontane; Principio di virtu; La manfredina and la rotta; Chominciamento di gioa; Palamento; Two Salterellos; Belicha
Sinfonye (Jim Denley, Pedro Estevan *perc*) **/ Stevie Wishart** *medieval fiddle/hurdy-gurdy/dir*
Glossa GCD920701 (53 minutes: DDD) Ⓕ
Interactive CD. Recorded 1996 ⭘

Many people have recorded the 14th-century instrumental dances that appear only in a single manuscript now in London. Apart from some pieces apparently for keyboard, they are almost the only known early works for a solo melody instrument. The nine pieces (out of a total of 15) presented here offer no repertorial novelty. What is new is the way Stevie Wishart plays them. She views the shorter pieces as dances, to be performed with percussion accompaniment.

This is common enough, though they are done extremely well, with Jim Denley and Pedro Estevan producing a stunning range of sounds from their various percussion instruments. But the longer ones are treated as elaborate and weaving instrumental solos, without any accompaniment. Stevie Wishart plays them on the vielle and, in one case, on the hurdy-gurdy, never rushing, never tempted to gloss over the many unexpected details in the lines. This kind of approach seems extremely productive: it stresses the sheer quality and inventiveness of the melodies, and it perhaps aligns them with their true historical context, the repertory of long monophonic *lais* from the 14th century.

That in its turn somehow makes the pieces far more than virtuoso showpieces. But it says much for the power of Stevie Wishart's playing that she keeps the music constantly interesting (one of the pieces lasts over 10 minutes) and is invariably persuasive. The disc comes with a CD-ROM track that portrays, among other things, frescoes of the time, the instruments and the manuscript. But even without that this is a superbly convincing performance, recorded with a nice full sound and giving relatively familiar music an added intellectual depth.

High Renaissance-baroque

Al Ayre Español

'Spanish Baroque, Volume 1'
Anonymous Canción a dos tiples. Two Pasacalles **C Galán** Al espejo que retrata. Humano ardor **F de Iribarren** Quién nos dira de una flor. Viendo que Jil, hizo raya **Literes** Ah del rustico pastor **J de Torres** Más no puedo ser. Al clamor **F Valls** En un noble, sagrado firmamento
Al Ayre Español / Eduardo López Banzo
Deutsche Harmonia Mundi 05472 77325-2 (70 minutes: DDD). Texts and translations included. Recorded 1994

López Banzo could well be set to achieve for the Spanish baroque what William Christie and Les Arts Florissants have done for French music of the 17th and 18th centuries. There are many parallels between English and Spanish musical cultures in the baroque: French and Italian stylistic and structural elements are incorporated into a musical language that is nevertheless as clearly Spanish as the Purcell idiom is English.

The melodiousness characteristic of the Spanish repertory and its rhythmic patterns are immediately apparent. The *villancicos* and *cantadas* by Torres, Literes, Iribarren and Valls are all sectional works that alternate recitative and arias in the manner of the Italian cantata, but they also introduce minuets, elegant slow movements, lively refrains and even Spanish dances of popular origin such as the *jácara*. Indeed, the disc ends with one of those foot-tapping pieces (performed in cathedrals and chapels on such joyous feasts as Christmas) by Iribarren who was chapelmaster at Malaga Cathedral.

The performances are very fine. The instrumentalists seem to be completely at home with the style and point up the idiomatic syncopations with just the right degree of emphasis. Under the secure direction of López Banzo, they generally serve the music extremely well. The singers are Spanish, which is probably essential, at least at this stage in our knowledge of the repertory. They, too, are excellent. The soprano Marta Almajano's voice is agile and well focused with a hint of that dark, enriching quality – like velvet-clad steel – that seems to characterise the Spanish voice (think of Victoria de los Angeles or even Plácido Domingo). She is, as the music demands, expressive or virtuoso, lyrical or brilliant, and always has a superb sense of line.

Brian Asawa *counterten*

The dark is my delight
Anonymous This merry pleasant spring. There were three ravens. The dark is my delight. Willow Song. Miserere my Maker. Where the bee sucks. O death, rock me asleep **Campion** How hath Flora robb'd her bower. Ayres – Come let us sound with melodie the praises; Turne backe you wanton flier. Author of light, revive my dying spright. Oft have I sigh'd for him that heares me not **Dowland** The First Booke of Songs or Ayres – Can she excuse my wrongs with vertues cloake; Now, O now I needs must part; Go, Cristall teares; Come againe, sweet loue doth now enuite; His goulden locks time hath to siluer turnd; Awaie with these selfe louing lads. The Second Booke of Songs or Ayres – Flow my teares fall from your springs; Sorrow sorrow stay, lend true repentant teares; A Sheperd in a shade his plaining made. The Third and Last Booke of Songs or Aires – Time stands still; It was a time when silly bees could speake
Brian Asawa *counterten* **David Tayler** *lte*
RCA Red Seal 09026 68818-2 (74 minutes: DDD) Ⓕ
Texts included. Recorded 1997

The singing here is most distinctive at a clear, forthright *forte*, most pleasing at a gentle *piano*. The impression is of a bright voice, unusually high-toned, quite unlike (say) Deller and Bowman. The programme is most welcome. Campion's melodic grace after Dowland's more complex utterance earns its place, and both find a happy follow-up in the mixed anonymous group. Asawa's mellower tones give pleasure in *Time stands still* and *Go, cristall teares*. He measures up to many of the challenges in *Sorrow sorrow stay* and is sensitive to the modulations in Campion's *Oft have I sigh'd*. In the first of the 'popular' songs, *This merry pleasant Spring*, he introduces an admirable trill. David Tayler accompanies tastefully. It is regretable that the recording is marred by little bumps and that the voice and lute have an unequal share in the balance.

Bell' Arte Antiqua

The Italian Connection
Corelli Trio Sonata in A minor, Op 3 No 12[ab] **Geminiani** Sonatas for 2 Violins and Continuo[ab] – in D 'Bush aboon Traquair'; in F 'The last time I came o'er the moor'. Sonata for Violin and Continuo in D minor, Op 1 No 2[ab] **Lonati** Sonata for Violin and Continuo in G minor[a] **Matteis** Divisions on a Ground in D minor[a] **Veracini** Sonata in A, Op 2 No 9[a] **Vivaldi** Trio Sonata for 2 Violins and Continuo in D minor, RV64[ab]
Bell' Arte Antiqua ([a]Lucy van Dael, [b]Jacqueline Ross *vns* William Hunt *va da gamba* Terence Charlston *hpd*)
ASV Gaudeamus CDGAU199 (60 minutes: DDD) Ⓕ
Recorded 1998

If the Bell' Arte Antiqua isn't yet a household name with baroque music lovers, it soon could be. Lucy van Dael and William Hunt, already members of more than one high-profile early music ensemble, join forces here with Jacqueline Ross and Terence Charlston to breathe fresh life into the Italian duo and trio sonata repertory.

Corelli is represented by a Roman sonata da chiesa of great vitality and breadth that demonstrates the high level of technical and musical rapport already established between van Dael and Ross. Van Dael performs a sonata by Corelli's lesser-known Neapolitan contemporary, Lonati, with equal amounts of verve and sensitivity, bringing to it a superb command of period ornamentation. She infuses Matteis's virtuoso variations on *La Folia* with the immediacy of an unfolding drama that will encourage listeners to make comparisons with Corelli's set.

Elements of the personal styles of Corelli and Lonati come together in the trio sonatas of their student, Geminiani, in the idiomatic ornamentation of the *Andante* of the D major Sonata, the seemingly demure opening *Grave* of the D minor Sonata (deftly characterised by van Dael and Ross with musical gestures akin to raised eyebrows and fluttering eyelashes) and the compelling dialogue between the violins and the bass viol in the *Grave* of the F major Sonata.

The D minor Trio Sonata of Vivaldi is nicely understated. The members of Bell' Arte Antiqua draw attention to the thematic links between the rhythmically contrasting Preludio and Corrente; then, in the succeeding *Grave*, stretch and sustain their individual lines while inviting listeners to luxuriate in the glorious suspensions that result.

Veracini's Sonata completes the picture. Like with his fellow expatriate, Geminiani, he used British folksongs as inspiration for instrumental pieces: Veracini's *Aria scozzese con variazione* would impress even the best Scottish folk fiddler and it may come as a happy surprise that the opening *Andante* of Geminiani's F major Sonata was inspired by *The last time I came o'er the moor*.

These are stylish performances. There are no gimmicks, just good music, beautifully played.

Robin Blaze *counterten*

English Lute Songs

Anonymous The Last of the Queenes Maskes **Banister** The Tempest[a] – Come unto these yellow sands; Where the bee sucks; Dry those eyes; Full fathom five. Give me my lute[a] **Blow** Lovely Selina, innocent and free[a] **Campion** Faire if you expect admiring[a] **Danyel** Can doleful notes[a] **Dowland** In darknesse let mee dwell[a]. The Third and Last Book of Songs or Aires[a] – Time stands still; Behold a wonder heere **R Johnson II** The Tempest[a] – Full fathom five; Where the bee sucks; Fantasia **W Lawes** Why soe pall and wan, fond lover[a]. He that will not love[a]. To the Sycamore[a]. Gather ye rosebuds while you may[a] **Locke** Psyche – The delights of the bottle[a] **Purcell** The Second Part of Musick's Hand-maid – Rigadoon in C, Z653; Song Tune in C, Z T694; A New Irish Tune in G, Z646; Sefauchi's Farewell in D minor, Z656. St Cecilia's Day Ode, Z328 – Tis Nature's voice[a]. Welcome Song, Z324 – Be welcome then, great Sir[a]. The History of Dioclesian – Still I'm wishing[a]. Birthday Ode, Z332 – By beauteous softness[a] **Reggio** Arise, ye subterranean winds[a]

[a]**Robin Blaze** *counterten* **Elizabeth Kenny** *lte*

Hyperion CDA67126 (71 minutes: DDD) Ⓕ

Texts included. Recorded 1999 ●●

Seventy minutes of countertenor may not be everyone's idea of fun, but Robin Blaze has the special ingredients to transcend any latent prejudice, especially in a recital as wide-ranging and intelligently programmed as this. Opening with Johnson's *Tempest* Songs, Blaze and his fine accompanist, Elizabeth Kenny, mellifluously shift from the melancholic Dowland to the less ubiquitous theatre songs of William Lawes, as they move inexorably to the great Orpheus, Henry Purcell – via several by-waters of English 17th-century song. Blaze has always had a natural and unforced instrument, but its hovering sweetness, which he employs to pretty effect throughout, can now ripen on cue, as in *In darknesse let mee dwell*. This is perhaps the most elusive quality in a countertenor and Blaze has the means to colour his texts, not just with superior diction, but timbral variation to keep the listener hearing each song afresh. In a recital of two halves – 15 so-called lute songs and 15 Restoration pieces – there are too many highlights to list. One is Danyel's *Can doleful notes*, a superb Jacobean example of pleasuring in a particular conceit (in this case, whether art can truly express grief). Blaze moves from embedded cynicism to tender faith in music's power. There is an impressive and buoyant security in the Banister songs – three from Shadwell's famous 1674 production of *The Tempest* – and around some exquisite solo lute numbers Blaze appears as ever the natural heir to James Bowman in *Be welcome then, great Sir*. It is wonderfully gauged, as is John Blow's delectable *Lovely Selina*, even if some may find him occasionally sitting a little high on the note. Another fine achievement from two of Britain's brightest and best.

Cambridge Taverner Choir

Music from Renaissance Portugal

Anonymous Si pie Domine **Carreira** Stabat mater **P de Cristo** Magnificat. Ave Maria. Sanctissimi quinque mar tires. De profundis. Lachrimans sitivit anima mea. Ave Regina caelorum **A Fernandez** Libera me Domine. Alma redemptoris mater **D Lôbo** Missa pro defunctis

Cambridge Taverner Choir / Owen Rees

Herald HAVPCD155 (69 minutes: DDD) Ⓕ

Texts and translations included. Recorded 1992 ●●

This is one of those rare examples of scholarship and musicianship combining to result in performances that are both impressive and immediately attractive to the listener in excellent music. There is a wonderful glow about this recording that reflects the skilful engineering on the part of Herald as well as the imagination of the sonority on Rees's part. The striking feature of his approach is the emphasis on the meaning of the words. This choir sings of the Day of Judgement or the rejoicing due to the Virgin as if it really means it: Rees is not afraid to shape phrases, to use dynamics, to vary the intensity of the sound in the service of the words which, though even more familiar to the monks and chapel singers who originally performed these pieces at the monastery of Santa Cruz in Colmbra, would have had an immediacy and a reality for them that it is hard to recapture today. How graphic those texts, in fact, are, and how well this choir brings them to life.

Cappella de'Turchini

'Vespers at the Oratorio dei Girolamini'
Anonymous Plainchant Antiphons and Responses
Caresana Vanitas vanitatum. Iste confessor
Giamberti Similabo eum viro sapienti
Provenzale Dixit Dominus. Confitebor. Beatus vir. Exulta, jubila. Laudate pueri. Magnus secundum nomen suum. Magnificat. Lauda Jerusalem
F Rossi Sinfonia a 5 **Tricarico** Accipite jucunditatem
Emanuela Galli, Roberta Andalò, Roberta Invernizzi *sops* **Daniela del Monaco** *contr* **Giuseppe de Vittorio, Rosario Totaro** *tens* **Giuseppe Naviglio** *bar* **Coro Mysterium Vocis; Cappella de'Turchini / Antonio Florio**
Opus 111 OPS30 210 (75 minutes: DDD) Ⓕ
Texts and translations included. Recorded 1998

Those who have collected any of the other volumes (this one is the fifth) of this enterprising series of Neapolitan baroque music will relish the unabashed and inimitable vocabulary of these forgotten composers; declamatory vocal concerto, operatic theatricality, as well as earthy allusions to vernacular dance and other distilled and aurally transmitted traditions – cocking a snook at the forbidding gaze of Vesuvius – leaven themselves with purely sacred traditions with delectable ease. Antonio Florio's exotic-sounding group, Cappella de'Turchini (Turchini means turquoise, which was the colour of the tunics of one of Naples's leading conservatories at the time) are just the fillip for those who need constantly reminding that the musical world revolved more around 17th-century Naples than it did the majority of centres that patronised the great composers. Neapolitans may not have enjoyed being lorded over by the Spanish but musically it often makes for a fascinating musical cocktail, and judging by Francesco Provenzale's Vespers, such a historical juxtaposition of styles contributes directly to the resourceful realisation of strong texts and responsive musical imagery.

This is a speculative reconstruction of a Vespers service for the Order of Girolamo, *c*1670, and much of the music displays impressive and inventive craftsmanship. With the majority of the music by Provenzale, Naples's most celebrated composer of the period, there is still an equally invigorating and spontaneous colouring of text. In the case of the *Beatus vir*, a solo soprano conveys this distinctly fulsome text with chromatic melodic inflexions as if they were still wet on the page. Such movements give us the most penetrating view of the composer's expressive powers, as Provenzale is forced to plan for over a quarter-of-an-hour, a long time in the stop-start, fashion-conscious mid-baroque. Here, and in the refined *Dixit Dominus* and *Confitebor*, the Cappella de'Turchini is more concerned with conveying originality and characterisation than the finer points of ensemble and intonation. If that sounds a little back-handed, there are enough reasons to feel that declaiming text, by the glorious exploitation of open throated Latin larynxes, is justifiably the ultimate priority. Even if some of the voices don't bear the closest scrutiny, this is musicianship that communicates where it matters.

Cologne Musica Fiata

The Feast of San Rocco, Venice, 1608 **P**
Barbarino Motets, Book 1, 'Il Primo libro de motetti' – O sacrum convivium[a] **Castaldi** Capricci a 2 stromenti – Capriccio detto svegliatoio[a] **Cima** Concerti ecclesiastici – Sonata per il violino, cornetto e violone; Sonata per il violino e violone **G Gabrieli** Toccata. Symphoniae sacrae, liber secundus – Benedictus es, Dominus[a]; Cantate Domino[a]; In ecclesiis[a]; Jubilate Deo[a]; Misericordia tua Domine. Canzoni et Sonate – Canzon V, a 7; Canzon X, a 8; Canzon XVII, a 12; Sonata XIX, a 15; Sonata per tre violini. Dulcis Jesu patris imago[a]. Sacrae symphoniae – Canzon primi toni, a 10; Canzon in echo duodecimi toni, a 12. Buccinate in neomenia tuba a 19. Timor et tremor[a]. Toccata primi toni. Magnificat[a]
Grandi Motets, Book 2[a] – Cantemus Domino; Heu mihi. O quam tu pulchra es[a]. Motets with sinfonie – Salvum me fac, Deus[a] **Monteverdi** Salve, O Regina[a]
[a]**La Capella Ducale; Cologne Musica Fiata / Roland Wilson** with **Christoph Lehmann** *org*
Sony Classical ② S2K66254 (126 minutes: DDD) Ⓕ
Texts and translations included. Recorded 1994

Wilson's starting-point is the famous description of the festivities that took place on the patronal feast-day in the Scuola di San Rocco, the most luxurious of the six Venetian *scuole grandi*, written by the English eccentric and traveller Thomas Coryate. Frustratingly, although Coryate provides a well-observed and detailed account of the various instrumental and vocal groupings used, the names of neither performers nor composers are revealed. To this extent 'The Feast of San Rocco' is something of a fiction; nevertheless, it is an intelligent one, a thoughtful and well-researched attempt to put flesh and blood on the bare bones of Coryate's anecdote. Three main repertories are drawn upon: Gabrieli's large-scale motets; canzonas and other purely instrumental works also mostly by him; and smaller-scale solo motets mostly by Alessandro Grandi. The latter are especially welcome. Evidence of Monteverdi's influence is everywhere in his music, but that doesn't detract from its freshness and charm. There are darker moments, too, as in the extraordinary four-voice dialogue *Heu mihi*, an essay in the affective, chromatic manner.

More typical of Grandi's work is the exquisite *O quam tu pulchra es*, an atmospherically erotic text from the Song of Songs, delivered here with urgent rhetorical force by David Cordier and underpinned by the lightest of continuo accompaniments. And one of the most virtuosic of all Grandi's motets, *Salvum me fac, Deus*, with its range of more than two octaves, is expertly negotiated by Harry van der Kamp in an engaged yet controlled performance.

As regards the interpretation of the larger-scale festive pieces, Wilson has adopted the Praetorius approach to the thorny problem of instrumentation and voice distribution. Just occasionally the solo voices are overwhelmed by the instrumental forces; both *Buccinate in neomenia tuba* and *Dulcis Jesu patris imago* suffer from such moments. But at its best, this recording is as compelling as any comparative version on offer.

The Consort of Musicke

Earth, Water, Air and Fire – A new look at John Dowland and friends

Dowland The First Book of Songs or Ayres – Sleepe wayward thoughts; Would my conceit; Come againe, sweet loue doth now enuite. The Second Booke of Songs or Ayres – Sorrow sorrow stay; Wofull heart with griefe opressed; Toss not my soule. A Pilgrimes Solace – Goe nightly cares the enemy to rest; From silent night; Thou mighty God. In darknesse let mee dwell. Shall I strive **Locke** Psyche – Break, distracted heart **Morley** Canzonets, or Little Short Songs to Three Voyces – Deep lamenting, grief betraying. The First Booke of Canzonets to Two Voyces – Leave now, mine eyes lamenting **Sermisy** Las, je m'y plains **Tomkins** O let me live for true love **Weelkes** Madrigals to Three, Four, Five and Six Voyces – Cease sorrowes now

The Consort of Musicke (Evelyn Tubb *sop* Lucy Ballard *contr* Andrew King *ten* Simon Grant *bass*) / **Anthony Rooley** *lte*

ASV Gaudeamus CDGAU187 (71 minutes: DDD) Ⓕ

Texts included. Recorded 1998

This is a fascinating recording, not least because one may very well be inclined to take against it from the start or even before. Its eye-catching title is not helpful: either too superficially or too profoundly relevant, and if the latter then requiring a more convincing justification than is given in Anthony Rooley's short and barely adequate introductory note. And then the first sounds of the first track: Dowland's *Come againe* has its first phrase sung in a low octave in a two-part arrangement (by whom?) till the other voices enter. They slow down and speed up, ending with a further *accelerando* ('by sighs and tears more hot than are thy shafts') and a defiant isolation of the last word ('while she for triumph – laughs!'). There is always something irritating about performances which draw attention to themselves *as* performances, and a lot of that may be found in this recital. The isolated 'laughs' makes its point (the monstrosity of it, the comic indignity, that after all this palaver – 'I sit, I weep, I faint, I die' – what does she do? 'Laughs'!). Then into more serious matters, as in *Would my conceit*; and this carefully studied text, so deliberately punctuated and insistently inflected, does yield rewards, while in Tomkins's *O let me live* the play of languishingly poignant harmonies against the light movement of the 'fa la's goes well beyond what one might have thought of as merely the conventions of madrigal. In *Shall I strive*, there is a thoughtful working-through of a dilemma. In the final item, *Thou mighty God*, a first reaction, noting the difference in timing (7'44" to this group's previous recording's 3'50", on L'Oiseau-Lyre), may be to think 'Well, they've surely overdone it this time'. But just you listen.

Alfred Deller *counterten*

Songs and Airs H

Anonymous, Bedyngham, Campion, Ciconia, Dowland, R Joynson, Morley, Purcell, Rosseter and J Wilson

Alfred Deller *counterten* with various artists

EMI Références mono CDH5 65501-2 Ⓜ

(77 minutes: ADD). Recorded 1949-54 ●

All but two of the pieces here are by English composers of the late 16th- and 17th-centuries; the odd ones out are Johannes Ciconia's *O rosa bella* and John Bedyngham's setting of the same text, which belong to the 14th and 15th centuries, respectively. Curiously, some of these recordings reveal Deller on rather less than top form. Dowland's *Slow my tears*, for instance, is marred by a persistent huskiness while certain others display a marked expressive restraint. But, almost needless to say, there is also plenty of vintage Deller here, in which category Morley's Shakespeare settings, *It was a lover and a lass* and *O Mistress mine*, certainly belong. Comparably affecting are Robert Johnson's *Full fathom five* and the celebrated anonymous setting of Desdemona's *Sing, willow, willow, willow*. Most touching of all, though, is the anonymous *Caleno custure me!* from *Henry V*, which Deller sings with exquisite sensibility. That and the popular *Greensleeves* would be quite sufficient on their own to make you go at once in search of this disc. Sadly, the Purcell songs seem rather dated, not so much for Deller's singing of them as for the archaic sound of the harpsichord, the tuning, and the playing of them, sometimes technically insecure and often with quaintly realised continuo lines. Notwithstanding these reservations, the anthology is a precious one, with moments of real magic. The transfers have been remastered skilfully too.

I Fagiolini

All the King's Horses

Anonymous Basses danses: Par fin despit; La volunté. Bransle gay: Mari je songerois. Der Hundt. Saltarello el francosin **Arcadelt** O felic'occhi miei **Cara** Mentre io vo per questi boschi **Certon** La, la, la, je ne l'ose dire **Finck** In Gottes Namen faren wir **Isaac** J'ay pris amours **Janequin** Frère Thibault. Le chant des oyseaulx **Othmayr** Der Winter kalt. Ich weiss mir ein Maidlein **Patavino** Dillà da l'aqua **Rore** Or che'l ciel e la terra **Ruffo** La gamba. El travagliato **Sandrin** Puisque vivre en servitude. La volunté **Senfl** Ach Elslein. Sich hat ein' neue Sach' aufdraht. Ich weiss nit. Wiewohl viel Herter Orden sind **Sermisy** Au pres de vous

I Fagiolini; Concordia / Mark Levy *viol*

Metronome METCD1013 (67 minutes: DDD) Ⓕ

Texts and translations included

We travel here to France, Germany and Italy, and the results are most appealing: these spirited performances articulate both text and music in a clear and attractive manner. In the French repertory I Fagiolini successfully takes up the challenge of emulating the Ensemble Clément Janequin's masterful approach to text-projection, and its softer sound and slightly more relaxed approach (try *Frère Thibault*) will please those who find the French ensemble too rough. Even in such a well-known piece as *Le chant des oyseaulx* it finds new, delightful inflexions. The German selections are rather less well known (or at any rate less often recorded) than the French, but just as convincingly dispatched: the pieces by Senfl, Othmayr and Isaac are well worth discovering. Isaac's arrangement of *J'ay pris amours* (performed here by Concordia) reminds us just how much of a virtuoso contrapuntalist he was. The disc aims to represent the sheer diversity of early 16th-century secular music: diversity of mood and content, and of possible relations between voices and instruments. This anthological ambition is the set's most conspicuous success, and carries the disc forward even when individual items or details appear to miss the mark (the concluding madrigal by Rore is too slow, and more generally the Italian selection is the least satisfying of the three). The sound-recording, immediate and close, is well up to Metronome's usual standard, and the booklet is well laid-out and presented.

Florilegium

In the Name of Bach

G C Bach Siehe, wie fein und lieblich (Geburtstagkantate)[a] **J E Bach** Violin Sonata in F minor. Sammlung auserlesener Fabeln I – Die ungleichen Freunde[b]; Die Unzufriedenheit[b]; Der Affe und die Schäferin[b]; Der Hund[b] **W F Bach** Adagio and Fugue in D minor, F65. Duetto for Two Flutes in E minor, F54 **J C Bach** Sonata for Keyboard, Violin and Cello in G, T313/1 (Op 2 No 2) **J B Bach** Overture in D – Passepieds Nos 1 and 2; La Joye

[b]**Catherine Bott** *sop* [a]**Julian Podger,** [a]**Robert Evans** *tens* [a]**Michael McCarthy** *bass* **Florilegium**

Channel Classics CCS9096 (75 minutes: DDD) Ⓕ

Notes and texts included. Recorded 1995

Here is a Bach family anthology featuring three members of the clan whose music seldom finds its way into record catalogues. The earliest representative is Georg Christoph, one of Sebastian Bach's uncles. He was, for a time, town Kantor at Schweinfurt in Franconia where in 1684 he received a visit on his birthday from his two brothers. Georg Christoph was so delighted that, shortly afterwards, he wrote a cantata to record the event, *Siehe, wie fein und lieblich* ('Behold, how good and how pleasant it is for brethren to dwell together in unity'). Tenors Julian Podger and Robert Evans, with bass Michael McCarthy, provide a well-focused and evenly balanced ensemble seemingly to savour the spirit in which the piece was written. Next in the family chronology comes Johann Bernhard Bach, a cousin of J.S.B. Not a great deal of his music survives, but among that which does are four orchestral suites which may well have resulted from his exposure to those of Telemann who was already a fluent master of the form. It is a pity that Florilegium saw fit to include only three short dances from the Fourth Suite in D major. The music is well worth performing without omission. The highly gifted but emotionally complex Wilhelm Friedemann is represented by the long-admired, poignant and oft-recorded *Adagio and Fugue* in D minor for two flutes and strings, and by one of his several *Duettos* for two flutes, this one in E minor. Florilegium, corporately and individually, plays the music with heartfelt expression and a sensibility that mirrors the stylistic idiom.

It is the music of J S Bach's nephew and pupil, Johann Ernst, which occupies the greater part of the programme. This member of the family seems wholeheartedly to have embraced the early classical idiom, further demonstrating, both in the Violin Sonata in F minor and in the four songs selected from his *Sammlung auserlesener Fabeln*, that he was a composer with a distinctive and affecting musical vocabulary at his disposal. Catherine Bott gives warmly expressive performances, savouring the considerable lyrical content of a little-known area of Bach family industry. The prodigious talent of this dynasty again reaches a peak in Florilegium's programme with a Quartet in G major by Johann Christian, the 'London Bach'. Musically speaking, the expansive opening movement is especially engaging but the entire work is played with elegance and charm by these artists. In summary, this is varied and enjoyable entertainment, well off the beaten track. Although the absence of any translation from the German of the texts of the four songs is regrettable, it does not prevent a warm recommendation.

Jean-Paul Fouchécourt *ten*

Air(s) de cour – French songs from the 16th to 18th centuries

Anonymous Ma belle si ton ame[a] **Attaingnant** Chansons et danses[a] – Tant que vivrai **Bataille** Airs de différents autheurs, mis en tablature de luth[a] – Un satire cornu; Ma bergère non légère **Brassens** Marquise[c] **Chabanceau de la Barre** Si c'est un bien que l'esperance[b] **Couperin** Doux liens de mon coeur[d]. Qu'on ne me dise[d]. Zéphire[b] **Du Buisson** Plainte sur la mort de M Lambert[e] **M Lambert** Airs de cour[b] – Trouver sur l'herbette; Par mes chants tristes et touchants; Ma bergère est tendre et fidelle; Pour jouir d'un bonheur; Vous ne sçauriez mes yeux; Vos mespris **Lully** Récit de la beauté[b] **Moulinié** Paisible et ténébreuse nuit[a]. Puisque Doris[a]. Amis enivrons nous[a] **Richard** Ruisseau qui cours apres toy-mesme

Jean-Paul Fouchécourt *ten* **Eric Bellocq** [a]*lte*/[b]*theo*/[c]*gtr* [b]**Nicolas Mazzoleni, Simon Heyerick** *vns* [bd]**Christine Plubeau** *va da gamba* **Olivier Baumont** [e]*org*/[bd]*hpd*

Glissando 779 013-2 (69 minutes: DDD) Ⓕ

Notes, texts and translations included

Recorded 2000 **OO**

This anthology traverses 150 years of the *air de cour* repertory, from its beginnings in the 'Parisian' chanson to the time of François Couperin. So it is probably the most comprehensive survey of the genre, and it certainly bids fair to be one of the finest. Fouchécourt chooses wisely and well: the earlier repertory has been fairly well served, but much of what he offers will be new to most. His light tenor is well known from the opera repertoire, but he manages just fine on his own. The opening 'Tant que vivray' seems rather low-pitched for his voice, but the following pieces allow him to stretch his vocal chords languorously, wittily or eloquently in turns.

His lyricism speaks for itself, but the drinking song *Amis environs nous* is robust and suitably breathless, and his portrayal of the hapless protagonist in 'Un satire cornu' has irony tinged with compassion. Is it that Fouchécourt is French? No disrespect intended to Nigel Rogers, Charles Daniels and other fine practitioners of the genre, but the Gallic ease with which Fouchécourt characterises these different situations is quite distinctive. And it could only occur to a Frenchman to connect this genre to the modern song-writer Georges Brassens, whose (slightly revised) setting of a text by Corneille nicely divides the programme into two halves. The later period is, if anything, more limited and conventionalised in its expressive scope (despite the increased instrumentation), but Fouchécourt's sense of line and ornamentation keep things moving along.

Fretwork

Celestiall Witchcraft – The Private Music of Henry and Charles, Princes of Wales
Coprario Chi può miravi. When pale famine. Fortune and Glory **Gibbons** Fantasias a 3 'for the great double bass' – No 2; No 3. Fantasias a 6 – No 5; No 6 **A Ferrabosco II** So beauty on the waters stood. Pavan. In Nomine a 6. So breake off this last lamenting kisse **W Lawes** Consort Sett a 5 in A minor. Pavin and Almain. Fantazia and Serabrand **Mico** Parte Seconda **Monteverdi** Madrigals, Book 3 – O come è gran martire (arr Lawes). Là tra'l sangue (arr Mico)
Fretwork with **Mark Padmore** *ten* **Paul Nicholson** *org* **Nigel North** *lte* **William Carter** *theorbo*
Virgin Classics Veritas VC5 45346-2 Ⓕ
(72 minutes: DDD). Texts included. Recorded 1998 ●

The title of this recording comes, appropriately, from Thomas Campion's *Elegie upon the untimely death of Prince Henry*: 'his carriage was full of celestiall witchcraft, winning all to admiration and love personall.' Henry's musical taste was equally so, and listeners to this CD are implicitly asked to consider whether, had he lived to become king instead of Charles, the course of English musical history (not to say non-musical history) might have been quite different. Coprario's two airs – one mourning the death of Henry, the other comforting Charles – must have provided the initial inspiration for the CD. Happily, Henry's music tutor, Alfonso Ferrabosco II, figures prominently here: two airs from his 1609 collection, sublimely sung and accompanied on the lute; a wistful pavan in three parts, delicately played with cadences that end with a whisper; and an *In Nomine* 'through all parts' of great subtlety. Thomas Lupo's polished six-part fantasia that opens the recording – offering a further example of the sort of music Henry is known to have enjoyed – Fretwork's performance doesn't disappoint: it captures the rhetoric of the beginning, bringing crystal clarity to the syncopations of the middle section while articulating the musical architecture. William Lawes is the composer most closely associated with the young Charles I, and his music is represented on this disc by a fantasia, three dances (a mournful Pavin followed by a wittily played Almain and a danceable Saraband), an affecting transcription he made of a Monteverdi madrigal, and one of the Royal Consorts in the richer, six-part version calling for two theorbos. The two Gibbons *Fantasias for the great double bass* allow William Hunt to shine on his wonderfully resonant larger viol. Fretwork produces polished, sophisticated performances complemented by those of Padmore and North, offering delightfully bewitching entertainment fit for a king.

Gabrieli Consort

Awards 1993

Venetian Vespers P
Gabrieli (ed Roberts) Intonazione[a]. Versicle and response: Deus in adiutorium; Domine ad adiuvandum **Rigatti** Dixit Dominus **Grandi** O intemerata. Antiphon: Beata es Maria **Monteverdi** Laudate pueri **Banchieri** Suonata prima[a]. Antiphon: Beatam me dicent **Monteverdi** Laetatus sum **Finetti** O Maria, quae rapis corda hominum. Antiphon: Haec est quae nescavit **Rigatti** Nisi Dominus **Banchieri** Dialogo secondo[a]. Antiphon: Ante thronum **Cavalli** Lauda Jerusalem **Grandi** O quam tu pulchra es **Anonymous** Praeambulum[a]. Chapter: Ecce virgo **Monteverdi** Deus qui mundum crimine iacentem. Versicle and response. Ave Maria; Dominus tecum. Antiphon. Spiritus Sanctus **Rigatti** Magnificat **Marini** Sonata con tre violini in eco. Collect: Dominus vobiscum – Deus, qui de beatae Mariae. Dismissal: Dominus vobiscum – Benedicamus Domino **Monteverdi** Laudate Dominum **Fasolo** (ed Roberts) Intonazione – excerpts[a] **Rigatti** Salve regina
Gabrieli Consort and Players / Paul McCreesh with [a]**Timothy Roberts** *org*
Archiv Produktion ② 459 457-2ATA2 Ⓑ
(96 minutes: DDD). Texts and translations included.
Recorded 1990 ●●●

Paul McCreesh's sense of adventure made quite an impact with his reconstruction of Doge Grimani's Coronation in 1595. This follow-up recording takes as its starting point a Vespers service 'as it might have been celebrated in St Mark's, Venice 1643', and it is no less striking a speculation. McCreesh is wisely not attempting to re-create a historical event but to provide a rejuvenating context for some more wonderful

Venetian church music. There can be little doubt that listening to psalm settings within a liturgical framework illuminates the theatricality and significance of the works in a unique way, barely possible in an ordinary format where one work simply follows another. Yet the quality of the music is what really counts, and this is where McCreesh deserves the greatest praise. He has skilfully blended a range of diverse concerted works with equally innovative and expressive solo motets, each one offset by ornate organ interludes and home-spun plainchant. Monteverdi is well represented, as one would expect, but by introducing resident composers (who were regularly employed by the great basilica) a strong Venetian sensibility prevails in all these works despite the many contrasting styles of the new baroque age. The little-known Rigatti is arguably the sensation of this release with his highly dramatic and richly extravagant sonorities. The settings of *Dixit Dominus* and *Magnificat* are almost operatic at times though they maintain the spatial elements inspired by St Mark's. The Gabrieli Consort and Players is a group with an extraordinary homogeneity of sound and focused energy: Monteverdi's *Laetatus sum* is one of the many examples where it reaches new heights in early 17th-century performance. The solo performances are deliciously executed too, particularly those involving the falsettists. This two-disc set is an achievement of the highest order.

The Harp Consort

Spanish Gypsies – Celtic and Spanish Music in Shakespeare's England P

Anonymous Rowallan Manuscript – The Gypsy Lilt; Gregory Walker: Quadran Pavan; Buffins; Hay de Gie. Irish Ho-Hoane. Trenchmore. Rownde Scottishe tune. Lady Louthians Lilt **Byrd** Gypsy's Round, BK80 **Farnaby** Spagnioletta. Mal Sims **Holborne** Muy linda **Hume** Captaine Humes Poeticall Musicke – A Spanish Humour **R Johnson II** Gypies Metamorphosed – The Gypsies Song **Playford** The English Dancing Master – Part 1: The Wherligig; The Spanish Jeepsie; Pakington's Pound; Part 2: The Punks Delight; Lulle me beyond thee; Scotch Cap; Appendix: A new Scotch Jig. Musick's Hande-Maide – An Ayre called Corke; Sarabande to Corke

Harp Consort / Andrew Lawrence-King *hp*

Deutsche Harmonia Mundi 05472 77516-2 (71 minutes: DDD). Recorded 1999 Ⓕ ●●

The subtitle of this album says more about its content than does the main one. There is much titular reference to Spain and to gypsies, but only in 'The Spanish Jeepsies' do the two come together. It seems that in Shakespeare's time Spanish popular tunes were perceived as being of gypsy origin. More to the point, the programme is skilfully devoted to showing the influence of Celtic and Spanish idioms on English popular music – a difficult, labyrinthine process that it's not particularly helpful to try to summarise here, but it is well covered in Lawrence-King's annotation.

Charles I's Consorte opened the way for courtly instruments to 'fraternise' with humbler ones, creating a variety of new sounds, and the Harp Consort take full advantage of this 'social' freedom. The eight players form a kaleidoscope of broken consorts drawn from the 18 instruments (plucked, bowed, blown and percussed) at their disposal, producing a remarkable spectrum of sound from the ethereal ('Lady Louthians Lilt') to the downright boisterous ('The Wherligig'). Only five of the 23 items last for more than four minutes but one never has the impression of a trayful of canapés deputising for a good meal.

When it comes to putting together a coherent and well-researched programme of assorted small-scale items, only Peter Holman springs to mind as Andrew Lawrence-King's peer. Excellent recording is the icing on this delectable cake, one that takes 71 minutes to enjoy.

Henry's Eight

The Virgin and Christ Child

Anonymous Alma redemptoris mater. Alleluia – Now well may we mirthes make. Ave Maria. Gregorian Chant for Advent – Ave Maria **Arcadelt** Missa Noe, Noe **Isaac** Virgo prudentissima **Mouton** Nesciens mater virgo virum. Noe, Noe **Traditional** There is no rose of such virtue

Henry's Eight (Declan Costello, William Towers *countertens* Duncan Byrne, Nicholas Todd, Toby Watkin *tens* Robert-Jan Temmink, Giles Underwood *basses*) **/ Jonathan Brown** *bass*

Etcetera KTC1213 (64 minutes: DDD) Ⓕ
Texts and translations included ●

The most substantial work is the Mass by Arcadelt based on a motet by Jean Mouton. Henry's Eight have often championed neglected or under-represented composers in the past, and Arcadelt is better known for his madrigals than for his sacred music. One is struck by the music's sheer quality, for which Henry's Eight are once again persuasive advocates. Their vocal style is closer in its use of vibrato to that of Pro Cantione Antiqua than to that of, say, The Hilliard Ensemble or Gothic Voices; at times, the subtly varying degrees of vibrato between singers tend to draw too much attention to this aspect of their technique, but there will be those who welcome a more relaxed approach. The disc is rounded off with English carols, and two Marian motets by Isaac and Mouton. Isaac's *Virgo prudentissima*, composed for the coronation of Isaac's patron Maximilian as Holy Roman Emperor, is festal in scoring and design. In relation to rival recordings (from David Munrow and Paul Hillier for Mouton, and from The Tallis Scholars for Isaac) Henry's Eight do more than hold their own (barring the odd fluffed entry, as at the start of the second half of *Virgo prudentissima*). Yet more might have been made of certain special moments: the rich suspensions of the eight-voice *Nesciens mater*, or the thrilling climax of *Virgo prudentissima*. Against the broad canvas provided by these expansive works, the English carols seem out of place, especially with the modern English pronunciation adopted here. That aside, this is first-rate music in performances of real commitment.

Hespèrion XX/XXI

Battaglie & Lamenti 1600-1660

Anonymous Sarabande italienne[g] **Chilese** Canzon in Echo[gi] **Falconiero** Battaglia de Barbaso, yerno de Satanás[g] **Fontei** Pianto d'Erinna[afhi] **G Gabrieli** Canzon III a 6[g] **Guami** Canzon sopra la Battaglia[g] **Monteverdi** Lamento d'Arianna[abdefj] **Peri** Uccidimi, dolore[afi] **Rossi** Fantasia, 'Les pleurs d'Orphée'[g] **Scheidt** Pavane[g]. Galliard Battaglia[g] Strozzi Sul Rodano severo[acfhi]

[a]**Montserrat Figueras** *sop* [b]**Rolf Lislevand,** [c]**Robert Clancy** *theorbos* [d]**Paolo Pandolfo** *viol* [e]**Lorenz Duftschmid** *violone* [f]**Ton Koopman** *hpd* [g]**Hespèrion XXI / Jordi Savall** *va da gamba/* [h]*viol*

Alia Vox AV9815 (76 minutes: [i]ADD/DDD) Ⓕ

Texts and translations included.

Recorded 1981, 1989, 1999

This release brings together laments and battle pieces from the 17th century. This might at first glance seem an odd thematic coupling, but it makes for a good sense of contrast (all battles, or all laments would be too much), and the two are in some ways linked: both were set pieces of the early baroque, genres with a clearly defined frame of reference for composer and listener alike.

The laments here were originally recorded for the most part in 1981, while the instrumental battle pieces and canzonas date from much more recently. It is good to have the chance to appreciate the singing of Montserrat Figueras from 20 years ago, when her voice was probably at its finest: still fresh, yet with the added depth of maturity and experience. Indeed, comparing the laments by Peri, Fontei and Strozzi she recorded in 1981 and the version of Monteverdi's famous *Lamento d'Arianna* which she made in 1989 is interesting. The Monteverdi is interpreted in a powerfully expressive way, of course, and the plangent quality inherent in her voice makes it in many ways ideally suited. Yet, for example, the Peri, a lament by Iole for Hercules, was more moving, largely because the voice has the bloom of a singer at the height of her powers: there is more warmth, more flexibility, and thus the intensity of the complaint is maintained with greater ease.

Not all the instrumental items are battle pieces; in fact, one of the most striking and original works is the *Fantasia on 'Les pleurs d'Orphée'* by Luigi Rossi. This is a shortish piece, but so full of chromaticism and dense string writing that it makes an immediate impact. Savall and his team play it beautifully, the performance as crafted and intimate as that of a great string quartet; you get the sense (quite rare on disc) that the players are all listening intently to each other, and this helps to draw the listener in too. The battle pieces, by Scheidt, Guami and Falconiero, offer all the virtuosity you could hope to hear from strings and wind alike. Strongly recommended.

Elizabethan Consort Music

Alberti Pavin of Albarti. Gallyard **Anonymous** In Nomine a 5. Desperada. Gallyard I-III. Allemande. Ronda. La represa I and II. Allemana d'amor. Dance I and II. Pavana I and II. Brandeberges **Daman** Di sei soprani **W Mundy** O mater mundi **Parsons** In Nomines a 7 – IV; V. The Songe called Trumpetts **Strogers** In Nomines – III a 5; IV a 6 **Taverner** Quemadmodum. **R White** In Nomine V **Woodcock** Browning my dere. In Nomines a 5 – II; III

Hespèrion XX / Jordi Savall *va da gamba*

Alia Vox AV9804 (66 minutes: DDD) Ⓕ

Recorded 1997

It is unusual to commit the contents of a rare manuscript collection to CD. This is what Jordi Savall and Hespèrion XX have done in this recording of Elizabethan consort music. The manuscript, from the 1570s and 1580s, containing dances, transcriptions of chansons and motets and fantasies, was intended for performance at court by the Queen's musicians, we are reliably informed by Peter Holman; it now resides in the British Library. These performances are highly sonorous and imaginatively realised. Savall orchestrates the repeats of the dances and chansons, usually beginning with a drum, a solo treble viol or lute and then building up the layers of sound with each restatement. Here, more than in any of their previous recordings, the tambour and tambourines are used to great effect, not merely to mark the beat, but, as in the anonymous Allemande in track 7 or the *Brandeberges*, to presage the mood of the piece. The manuscript contains a fascinating array of pieces: numerous *In Nomines* which climax in the astonishingly rich seven-part settings by Robert Parsons contrast with transcriptions of bawdy chansons, the evergreen *Browning my dere*, an ethereal fantasy by William Daman for six treble viols (surely a collectors' item), William Mundy's eponymous *O mater mundi* (intended as a pun?) and the sublimity of John Taverner's *Quemadmodum*. And, as listeners will discover, there is more. This is music fit for a courtly Sunday Elizabethan banquet, with a bit of dancing thrown in, should you wish to entertain in that style. For some tastes, the slower pieces may be performed rather too seamlessly, and the balance between solo instrument – such as the lute in the first and second tracks or the treble viol in track 21 – and the rest of the ensemble does not always seem natural. The recording does offer a wonderful glimpse of the variety of music enjoyed at the court of Elizabeth I; it is a one-off and should be treasured as such.

Maria Cristina Kiehr *sop*

Canta la Maddelena

Agneletti Gloria[ab] **Bernabei** Heu me miseram et infelicem[ab] **Ferrari** Queste pungenti spine[ab] **Frescobaldi** Arie musicali per cantarsi[ab] – primo libro: A pie della gran croce; secondo libro: Dove, dove sparir. Toccata[c]. Canzona[c] **Gratiani** Dominus illuminatio mea[ab] **Kapsberger** Toccata arpeggiata[c]

Mazzocchi Dialoghi, e sonetti[ab] – Lagrime amare; Dunque ove tu Signor; Homai le luci erranti
L Rossi Pender non prima vide sopra vil tronco[ab]
M Rossi Toccata settima[c]
[a]**Maria Cristina Kiehr** *sop*
[b]**Concerto Soave** (Matthias Spaeter *archlte/cittarrone* Sylvie Moquet *bass viol* Mara Galassi *hp*) **/**
Jean-Marc Aymes *org/[c]hpd*
Harmonia Mundi HMC90 1698 (72 minutes: DDD) Ⓕ
Texts and translations included. Recorded 1999 **OO**

Much skill has gone into this programme celebrating the popular 17th-century emblem of Mary Magdalene's lamentation and deploration at the foot of the Cross. Framed by two exquisite and largely unknown works, one by Agneletti and a fine cantata by Ferrari, Maria Cristina Kiehr spins a shapely, instinctive line, nuanced rather than overwhelmed by expressive ardour. (How often vapid over-indulgence by undernourished voices rips the heart out of this music.) Kiehr shows admirable judgement in how she sustains the intensity of the most sectional work, Rossi's *Pender non prima* (taking as its model Monteverdi's *Lamento d'Arianna*). A noble and graciously covered mezzo register is the conduit for Kiehr's profound sensuality, heard delightfully in the Gratiani work, where her gleaming and accurate upper register shuns the piping angel and portrays a 'faithful grieving Lover' in a state of extreme emotion. The high tessitura is not the prettiest nor the most controlled, and it underlines her limited tonal range in works such as Bernabei's *Heu me miseram* where excitement results in some shrillness. She often makes up for this in the subtlety of her accentuation and inflexion. The Frescobaldi works fit her like a glove – paragraphed declamatory songs, beautifully formed and succinctly expressed. In 'A pie della gran croce', she shows a feeling for the text which lifts superficial narrative into heart-felt supplication. With some evocative and breezy instrumental contributions, the disc which tackles this music with distinction. These are mature readings of works whose performance too often misses the mark. Thumbs up, nearly all round.

The King's Consort

Lo Sposalizio – The Wedding of Venice to the Sea
Anonymous Fanfares – Rotta; Imperiale prima; Imperiale seconda. Sursum corda. Variazoni sopra 'La Ciaccona' **A Gabrieli** Vieni, vieni Himeneo. Cantiam de Dio **Canzona** La Battaglia. Intonationi – Primo tono; Settimo tono. Gloria a 16 **G Gabrieli** Lieto godea sedendo. Udite, chiari et generosi figli. Kyrie a 12. Sanctus a 12. Sonata XX **Guami** Canzona XXIV
Gussago Canzon XIX, 'La Leona'
Kapsberger Kapsberger **Massaino** Canzon per otto tromboni **Monteverdi** Christe, adoramus te
Piccinini Variazoni sopra 'La Folia' **Viadana** Canzona, 'La Veneziana'
The King's Consort Choir; The King's Consort / Robert King
Hyperion ② CDA67048 (89 minutes: DDD) Ⓜ
Texts and translations included. Recorded 1998 **O**

This mouth-watering celebration of Venice is devised with considerable expertise in ritual, contextual aspects and the imaginative allocation of music to, in this particular instance, the processions and journey across the lagoon and the subsequent solemn Mass held in San Nicolò. Robert King explains in the note, with his inimitable enthusiasm and clarity, how, from the 11th century, mariners congregated annually to ask for St Nicholas's protection. The festival became, over the centuries, an important social event in the calendar as the symbolic 'fertility rite': the marriage between Venice and her blessed Adriatic, prayerfully celebrated on Ascension Day. The central act was when the Doge would toss a gold ring into the sea from his resplendently ornate galley (rowed by 400 hapless slaves). He would them move amongst the flotilla, with glorious music wafting over the calm ripples of the lagoon, his progress punctuated by various stop-offs for blessings and further ceremonial. The musical journey across to the Lido is principally a secular exercise and we are treated to some delectable madrigals by both Gabrielis. Although some listeners may find the ensemble a touch undernourished in the first madrigal, *Vieni, vieni Himeneo*, it soon transpires that sweetness and balance are the essential ingredients for King; the result in the exquisite instrumental numbers is a sensitivity to matching timbre which is an unusual delight both in the Guami *Canzona XXIV a 8* and the imploring counterpoint that acts as a foil to the fencing in Andrea Gabrieli's *Battaglia*.

Indeed, what shines through with great dignity is the sense of an unfolding procession with a seemingly effortless choreography, the musical highlight of which is Giovanni Gabrieli's eight-part madrigal *Lieto godea sedendo*, set here with two falsettists and strings, portraying 'the disturbance of spring' in all its poignant and fleeting glory. The intimate and affectionate duetting of James Bowman and Robin Blaze, so beautifully rendered on this disc, is something of a landmark as the inimitable mentor shares the reins with the pick of the younger generation of countertenors.

The depth of quality and the control within individual voices of the vocal consort is a match for anyone in the effervescent and magisterial 16-part Gabrieli piece *Udite, chiari et generosi*, though the acoustic of St Jude's, Hampstead – and the pragmatic recording techniques required for such an undertaking – demand that *tutti* work is clearly defined and that a strong interpretative angle is projected. This is where the Gabrieli Mass movements for San Nicolò, which constitute the second disc, are far more successfully realised than in *Cantiam de Dio*: this is the only multi-voiced work where the performance appears prosaic compared with the poised elegance that informs the vocal and instrumental dialogue of the *Kyrie* and *Sanctus a 12*. This is a small gripe in an otherwise exceptional recorded event. Running through the veins of nearly all the pieces are the ingredients of commitment, immediacy and spontaneous musicianship which allow one to view this ravishing music on its own terms, rather than losing sight of it – as can happen too easily – with endless speculative reconstruction for its own sake. A very fine achievement all round.

The King's Noyse

Pavaniglia – Dances and Madrigals from 17th-Century Italy P

Douglass Tarantella[b] **Corbetta** Follia[c]. Ciaconna[c] **Farina** Pavana Terza[b] **Gesualdo** Tall' or sano desio[b]. Moro, lasso, al mio duolo[b] **Monteverdi** Voglio di vita uscir[ab]. Ohimè ch'io cado[ab] **Pesenti** Quanto t'inganni Amor[ab] **Rossi** Orfeo – Lasciate Averno, o pene, e me seguite![ab]. Passacaille del seigneur Luigi[b] (arr Douglass). Prima Canzon 'Scipione Stella'[d] **Sances** Lagrimosa beltà[b] **Zanetti** Il scolaro[b] – Intrata e Baletto del Marchese di Caravazzo con la sua Gagliarda; Pas è mezzo sù Chiave Maestro; Saltarello della pas è mezzo; Saltarello detto il Genovesino; Pavaniglia; La Sartorella; Il Gabonano; La Balloria; La Montagnura; Saltarello della Battagli

The King's Noyse ([a]Ellen Hargis *sop* [b]David Douglass, [b]Robert Mealy *vns* [b]Scott Metcalfe, [b]Margriet Tindemans *vas* [b]Emily Walhout *vc*) [c]**Paul O'Dette** *gtr/chit* [d]**Andrew Lawrence-King** *hp*

Harmonia Mundi HMU90 7246 (74 minutes: DDD) Ⓕ

Texts and translations included. Recorded 1999

This is a very engaging and well-constructed programme, containing some better-known pieces, but concentrating for the most part on Italian dance music: a pavan, a tarantella, a chaconne, a follia, to name only four. Some of the most refreshing selections are to be found among the 12 minutes' worth of dances from Zanetti's *Il scolaro*: the sound of two violins playing the top line in a string consort is extraordinarily evocative, and on this recording one readily understands why such string bands caught on so rapidly. The ensemble conveys such spontaneity that even the arranged pieces – such as Sances's *Lagrimosa beltà* – sound as though they were written specially for it. Only the Gesualdo madrigals – performed, again, with just strings – seem to not quite fit the medium, despite the superb polish of the performances. The individual contributions are impressive as well: Andrew Lawrence-King and Paul O'Dette each boast very effective solos, and Ellen Hargis is persuasive as always, especially in the livelier pieces, where her richness and her flexibility of tone are most impressively combined.

The King's Noyse set great store by the improvisatory, spontaneous character of the early Italian baroque, and by the flexibility with which music could be adapted to suit given ensembles. This disc bears out such notions, and also feeds the hope that they might push them further still in future. Many would argue that the word 'authenticity' is now best left alone; but if one wishes to define it – one of many possible definitions – as facilitating the suspension of disbelief (the illusion of actually 'being there'), then the King's Noyse succeed brilliantly.

Andrew Lawrence-King *hp*

His Majesty's Harper

Anonymous Scott's Lament **Byrd** Alman in G. La coranto. Fantasia. A gigg. Praeludium to Ye Fancie Fantasia. Rowland (arr Dowland) **Dowland** Awake, sweet loue, thou art return'd. Can she excuse. A fancy. Farwell. Fine knacks for Ladies. Frogg galliard. Go cristall teares. Mrs Winter's Jump. My dear Adieu, my sweet love farewell. My Lady Hunsdons Puffe. My thoughts are wingd with hopes. Pavana lacrima. Robin. Semper Dowland semper dolens. Suzanna Galliard. Tarleton's Jigge. Tarletones Riserrectione **le Flelle** The Queens Maske **Macdermott** Allmane. Cormacke. Mr Cormake Allman. Schoc.a.torum Cormacke

Andrew Lawrence-King *hp*

Deutsche Harmonia Mundi 05472 77504-2 Ⓕ

(65 minutes: DDD). Recorded 1998 ⭘

Andrew Lawrence-King's resourceful plundering of the harpsichord and lute books in search of an elusive early harp repertoire takes him here to music from 16th-century England. With some of the best instrumental music of the time on offer, much of it displaying that irresistible folk-like charm and melancholy peculiar to English melody, he cannot go far wrong. Here, making delightful appearances, are Dowland's *Pavana lacrima* and *Semper Dowland semper dolens*, some of his shorter catchy dance-songs, and more dances and contrapuntal pieces by Byrd. All transfer to the harp superbly in Lawrence-King's hands, which once again manage to find in his instrument the subtleties of the lute together with the power and agility of the harpsichord. More importantly, it is hard to imagine this music being played with a greater or more honest expressiveness. Most of the pieces here are played on a gut-string Italian triple harp – gentle and mellow of tone but powerful and macho when it needs to be – but there are also some intriguing contributions from the brass-strung Irish *cláirseach*, which Lawrence-King uses in the anonymous *Scott's Lament* and four pieces by Cormack Macdermott, harpist at the court of James I. It is an instrument which, if you have not come across it before, is almost certain to confound your expectations with its rippling, metallic sound. This is a thoroughly enjoyable disc, the kind which touches you with its sound alone; the music seems as if it could have been intended for the harp all along, a simple effectiveness which makes it all the more strange that so little real harp music from this time survives.

Gérard Lesne *counterten*

Dans un bois solitaire

Bernier Aminte et Lucrine **Clérambault** Pirame et Tisbé **Courbois** L'Amant timide **Du Buisson** Plainte sur la mort de Monsieur Lambert **Stuck** Les Festes bolonnoises

Gérard Lesne *counterten* **Il Seminario Musicale**

Virgin Classics Veritas VC5 45303-2 Ⓕ

(63 minutes: DDD). Texts and translation included. Recorded 1997 ⭘

A fascinating and still largely untapped corner of the repertoire, the *cantate française* was a popular form of home music-making in the early years of the 18th century, offering amateurs a chance, as the lexicographer Brossard put it, 'to soften the sorrows of solitude, without all the trouble expense and paraphernalia of an opera.' The reference to opera is significant, because these pieces – usually about a quarter-of-an-hour in length – really are like miniaturised operatic episodes, serving up a variety of moods and, in the best cases, capable of conveying considerable emotional power. The best works in this selection are *Aminte et Lucrine* by the French cantata's most prolific exponent, Nicolas Bernier, and *Pirame et Tisbé* by perhaps its most skilled master, Louis-Nicolas Clérambault. Hearing the impressively sonorous pronouncements of the Oracle of Diana in the former, or the roaring of the (continuo) lion in the latter, you begin to wonder why these two did not compose any operas themselves, unless it be that they were justifiably quite happy with what they had already achieved here. All the works on the disc, however, have something to offer both dramatically and lyrically, and the lack of familiarity of the composers' names should not be allowed to put anyone off. Gérard Lesne's singing is a constant pleasure. His distinctively rich and manly alto voice is a reliable and even-toned instrument, while his musical intelligence and excellent projection of words is insurance against the slightest hint of blandness. His continuo group is a little heavy-handed in places, though it is good to hear them being unafraid to enter into the dramatic spirit.

Musica Antiqua of London

The Triumph of Maximilian – Songs and Instrumental Music from 16th-Century Germany

Anonymous Elslein **Aich** Ein frolyk wesen. Elslein à 3. Der Hundt **Barbireau** Ein frolyk wesen **Busnois** Fortuna disperata **Dietrich** Elslein à 3 **Finck** Ich stünd an einem Morgen **Ghiselin** Ein frolyk wesen **Isaac** Fortuna disperata. Der Hundt. Ich stünd an einem Morgen **Josquin Desprez** Fortuna à 3. Missa pange lingua – Pleni sunt coeli (Quis seperabit) **Othmayr** Entlaubet ist der Walde **Rhau** Elslein à 2. Ich stünd an einem Morgen **Senfl** Es taget vor dem Walde. Es taget à 4. Es taget: Elslein à 4. Exemplum. Es taget. Entlaubet ist der Walde à 4. Entlaubet ist der Walde. Ich stünd an einem Morgen à 3. Ich stünd an einem Morgen à 5. Ich stünd an einem Morgen à 4. Ich stünd an einem Morgen ... Es taget ... Kein Adler. Pacientia muss ich han. Quattour. Will niemand singen **Senfl/Gerle** Elslein à 4 **Stolzer** Entlaubet ist der Waldea

Musica Antiqua of London / Philip Thorby with **John Potter** *ten*

Signum Records SIGCD004 (69 minutes: DDD) Ⓕ
Recorded 1993

Ludwig Senfl has not yet received the recognition that he deserves; and as this issue demonstrates, he is one of the most fascinating composers of the early 16th century. He combines an astonishing contrapuntal skill with a range of moods and formal control that make his German song settings among the finest of their century. One reason why he is little heard is that the music is hard to sing: for most of it you need a tenor with an extreme lightness of touch. But in John Potter they seem to have the perfect singer, perhaps the best ever heard in this repertory. He floats the lines with effortless grace and with an uncannily sensitive projection of the texts. Just listen to his control in the longest and most serious song on the disc, Senfl's *Pacientia muss ich han*. But he is also superbly supported by the viols and recorders of Musica Antiqua of London. Its playing, too, is apparently effortless. Some listeners may feel that the recorders are occasionally allowed to run too fast, giving less than full measure to the real substance of the music; but the playing is undeniably wonderful, and superbly recorded. For the viol playing, no praise is too high: they do everything with a pleasingly light touch and always with a real sensitivity to the music. There is another reason why we hear less Senfl than we should: that his best work needs to be understood within the broader context of the German *Tenorlied* repertory. To cope with this, the disc puts Senfl alongside settings of the same material by other composers of the time. This works nicely enough here, but it would have been so good to hear more of Senfl's own work, given the quality of these performances.

The Newberry Consort

A Candle in the Dark

Anonymous Doctor Faustus[a] **Byrd** Praeludium and Ground. Come woeful Orpheus[a]. An Aged Dame[b] **Campion** Move now with measured sound[ab] (arr Rosseter). Thrice tosse these oaken ashes in the ayre[b] **Dowland** In darknesse let mee dwell[a]. His golden locks time hath to silver turnd[b]. Sorrow, stay![b] **Ferrabosco I** So beautie on the waters stood[b] **Johnson** Johnson's Grounde **W Mundy** In nomine **Picforth** In nomine **Traditional** Devil's Dream **Tye** Trust. Passamezzo Pavan. Sit fast **R White** Fantasia II
[a]**Ellen Hargis** *sop* [b]**Drew Minter** *counterten*
Newberry Consort (David Douglass *vn/va da gamba* John Mark Rozendaal, Margriet Tindemans, Craig Trompeter *va da gambas* Jacob Heringman *lte*) / **Mary Springfels** *va da gamba*

Harmonia Mundi HMU90 7140 (66 minutes: DDD) Ⓕ
Recorded 1998

The subtitle of the booklet's accompanying essay, 'The Musical World of John Dee', gives a truer description of this programme's aims than does the rather equivocal title. John Dee was the Elizabethan age's foremost proponent of the occult, a magus whose connections extended into the same circles that patronised many of the musicians whose works are heard here. Accordingly, a bizarre streak runs through either the texts of the vocal pieces (famously Dowland's *In darknesse* or Byrd's *An Aged Dame*, and most explicitly Campion's *Thrice tosse these oaken ashes in the ayre*) or the instrumental pieces. The two pieces by Tye have already a certain notoriety in this respect, but the *In nomine* by the virtually unknown Picforth has a rather discombobulated eloquence which, no doubt, would look completely inarticulate on paper. The centrepiece of the recital is perhaps the contemporary ballad *Doctor Faustus*, a 16th-century version of the tale in 16 stanzas (all sung to the same tune). At 10 minutes, it is the most extended track here, at least in terms of length. The banality of the music is notably at odds with the subject matter; that would be of little consequence, but for the explicit contrivance of so much of the rest of the music here. That aside, the programme is admirably constructed: a fitting observation considering that the alchemist's art is an apt metaphor for that of devising good programmes.

The programme's strength is sufficient to recommend the disc, and to withstand the occasional solecism. The consort-playing, though fine, is not quite on a par with that of other exponents of this repertory (or with other discs from this group). For example, the faster divisions in the Byrd *Praeludium and Ground* seem to stretch the top part, and there is a certain unevenness in intonation and tone production. Of the instrumentalists, Jacob Heringman acquits himself best, his duets with either of the two singers providing some of the disc's finest moments (Ferrabosco's *So beautie on the waters stood* has an elegiac quality, reminiscent of the best *airs de cour* across the Channel, is very moving and memorable). Nor do the singers quite sparkle in the way they frequently have done elsewhere; having said which, Drew Minter shows off his low countertenor register to great effect in the Ferrabosco just mentioned, and his 'native' bass voice in the final duet with Hargis on the final track, Campion's *Move now with measured sound*. But the level of musicianship more than compensates for any reservations: lovers of this period need not hesitate, and less seasoned listeners will be similarly rewarded.

Nigel North *Ite*

A Varietie of Lute Lessons

Anonymous Fantasie No 2. Volt **Ballard** Coranto No 1. Volt No 2 **Bacheler** Monsieur's Almaine. Pavan No 4 **Cato** Fantasie No 1 **Dowland** Sir John Smith's Almain, P47. The King of Denmark's Galliard, P40. The Earl of Essex's Galliard, P42a. My Ladie Riches Galyerd, P43a. The Right Hon Ferdinando Earle of Darby's Galliard, P44. Lady Clifton's Spirit. Queen Elizabeth's Galliard. Sir Henry Guilforde's Almaine
A Ferrabosco II Fantasia No 5. Pavan No 6
Huwet Fantasie No 6 **Holborne** Pavan No 2.
Laurencini di Roma Fantasie No 4 **Moritz** Pavan
Morley Pavan No 3 **Perrichon** Coranto No 2
Saman Coranto No 4
Nigel North *lte*
Linn Records CKD097 (78 minutes: DDD) Ⓕ

A Varietie of Lute Lessons, compiled by Robert Dowland, was the last book of lute tablature to be published (1610) in England, and it is important both for the internationality and high quality of the music it contains. Six genres are represented, each by seven pieces: fantasies, pavans, galliards, almaines, corantos and voltes. Several items lack attribution in the original book, but the authors of *Sir John Smith's Almain* and *Volt* No 2 have been identified, and the named composer of *Fantasie* No 4, 'The Knight of the Lute', is revealed as Laurencini di Roma. Those naive enough to believe that early manuscripts were fault-free would be sorely mistaken in this instance. The first note and last chord in the first item, *Fantasie* No 1, by Diomedes Cato, are wrong; North has, of course, corrected them but has not corrected what is widely recognised as an error in *Sir John Smith's Almain* (track 12, 07'27"), confirmed in the division of the same strain (17'33"). The few others elsewhere are duly amended. In making his selection North has wisely passed over some of the 'pops' in favour of less well-known pieces, including: the magnificent *Pavan* No 1 dedicated to John Dowland and quoting from *Lachrymae*; the beautiful *Fantasie* No 4 of Laurencini with its joyous chain of suspensions at the climax; and Bacheler's unusually structured variations on *Monsieur's Almaine* – long, but worth every minute. Robert Dowland's *Lady Clifton's Spirit* edges interestingly away from the Renaissance and toward the Baroque. North's performances are full of warmth, unfailingly musical and stylish, and are recorded with clarity.

Paul O'Dette *Ite*

Alla Venetiana

Anonymous Laudate Dio **Capirola** Spagna seconda. Non ti spiaqua l'ascoltar. Padoana belissima. Ricercare I, II, V and XIII. Tientalora. La Villanella
Cara O mia cieca de dura sorte **Dalza** Calata ala Spagnola. Pavana alla ferrarese. Pavana alla venetiana. Piva I-III. Recercar. Recercar dietro. Saltarello **Ghizeghem** De tous bien playne (arr O'Dette). De tu biens plaene (arr Capirola)
Josquin Desprez Adieu mes amours. Et in terra pax. Qui tolis pechata mondi **Martini** Malor mi bat
Pesenti Che farala, che dirala **Spinacino** Recercare I and II
Paul O'Dette *lte*
Harmonia Mundi HMU90 7215 (73 minutes: DDD) Ⓕ
Recorded 1997 ●

When lutenists began to use the fingers of their right hands to pluck the strings, the instrument made a quantum leap forward. Three- and four-part counterpoint was suddenly on the agenda and the expanded range of the repertory made the lute popular even in Italian court circles. O'Dette focuses on two of the earliest printed books of tablature by Spinacino (1507), Dalza (1508), and the handwritten book of music by Capirola (*c*1520). Whoever it was who wrote the last of these, his student 'Vidal' or Capriola himself, touchingly showed his human fallibility; in a book written with much tender loving care and lavishly adorned with paintings, he had to insert the missing 'a' in 'Pado(a)na' with a caret! The selected items cover the basic genres of *tastar de corde*, *recercare*, dances and intabulations of vocal music by non-lutenist composers. In the last of these a lutenist demonstrated his skill in adapting and embellishing the original, as O'Dette does in his own intabulation of van Ghizegem's *De tous bien playne*. What comes through clearly is the joyous freshness of this music and the quickly acquired ingenuity in bringing more complex counterpoint to the fingerboard, as though the right-hand fingers had uncorked a bottle and released an inspirational genie. O'Dette has many talents, and an unusual ability to bring this music to life is one of them; another is shown in his superb annotation. A disc to lift the spirits and first-class recording too.

Orchestra of the Renaissance

The Marriage of England and Spain

Anonymous Introit: Benedicta sit Sancta Trinitas[a]. Gradual: Benedicta es[a]. Sequence: Alma chorus Domini[a]. Communion: Benedicamus Deum caeli[a]. Preface: Per Omnia saecula saeculorum[ae]. Postcommunion: Dominus vobiscum[a]
Bendinelli Fanfare, 'Levet'[g] **Cabezón** Diferencias sobre 'La dama le demanda'[b] **Gombert** Jouissance vous donnerai[g] **Morales** Jubilate Deo omnis terra[g]. O sacrum convivium[cdef]. Pater noster[dg] **Rhys** Missa in die Sanctae Trinitas[ab] – Kyrie **Sermisy** Tant que vivray[b] **Taverner** Missa Gloria tibi Trinitas[cdefg]
[a]**Josep Cabré** *bar* [b]**Silas Standage** *org* [c]**Carys Lane** *sop* [d]**William Missin** *counterten* [e]**Simon Berridge,** [e]**Tom Phillips** *tens* [f]**Jonathan Arnold,** [f]**Charles Gibbs basses** [g]**Orchestra of the Renaissance / Richard Cheetham** *sackbut*
Glossa GCD921401 (78 minutes: DDD) Ⓕ
Texts and translations included. Recorded 1998

Richard Cheetham's musical reconstruction of the marriage of Mary Tudor and Philip of Spain in 1554 is an imaginative attempt to recreate the meeting of the Castilian and English royal chapels on that auspicious occasion in Winchester Cathedral. The event was, according to contemporary descriptions, truly magnificent. Philip travelled to England with 21 singers, two organists (including Antonio de Cabezón) and 11 minstrels as well as the usual corps of trumpets and drums; these musicians joined forces with those of the Chapel Royal and the cathedral. Unfortunately, although the music is mentioned in the accounts of the wedding, no specific pieces are identified, and the choices made for this recording, however logical, must remain hypothetical. The selection of Taverner's *Missa Gloria tibi Trinitas* makes sense in the light of the English tradition to celebrate royal weddings with a Mass for the Holy Trinity, and the pieces by Morales, Cabezón and Gombert reflect the repertory of the Spanish chapel. Most of the decisions as to performing forces and scorings, though also hypothetical, are convincing. The addition of shawms and sackbuts to parts of Taverner's Mass, for example, works well in the more sustained passages (as at the opening of the *Credo*) but perhaps less so where the writing is more florid or intricate (although many of these sections are taken by voices or voices and organ alone). The shawms and sackbuts undoubtedly participated in the proceedings, but did they really accompany the Mass? Aside from this historical reservation, this is a thoroughly enjoyable mix of Sarum chant (superbly sung by Josep Cabré), English and Spanish polyphony (especially beguiling is the account of Morales's *Pater noster* arranged for solo voice and minstrels) and mid-16th-century organ music and trumpet fanfares, which add an appropriately ceremonial touch. The performances are of the high standard typical of the Orchestra of the Renaissance, and the recorded sound is excellent, with the single voices exceptionally well blended and sonorous. The organ (the instrument is unspecified) makes a fine noise, too.

Oxford Camerata

Let Voices Resound

Anonymous Songs from Piae Cantiones (1582) – Cedit hiems eminus. Aetas Carmen. Jesu dulcis memoria. Puer natus in Bethlehem. Ave maris stella. Tempus adest floridum. Parce Christus spes reorum. Resonet in laudibus. Personent hodie. Psallat fidelis concio. In dulci jubilo. Florens juventus virginis. Jeremiae prophetae
Women's voices of **Oxford Camerata / Jeremy Summerly**
Naxos 8 553578 (60 minutes: DDD) Ⓢ
Texts and translations included. Recorded 1995

This is the second collection from Naxos to focus on the *Piae Cantiones* of 1582. In contrast to the Retrover Ensemble's offering for mixed voices and instruments, Jeremy Summerly's survey has only voices, and only four female ones at that. This is a sensible decision, in that much of the collection's contents would have been sung by choirboys. (Obviously, a recording with choirboys would be even more 'authentic', and the quality of these two discs ought to convince an enterprising choral director to take up the challenge.) It is a fascinating, indeed unique collection, since much of the music is monophonic and may be traced back to the beginning of the millennium. In Summerly's selection, polyphony plays a greater role (though it is still in the minority), but this is hardly a problem: the opening *Aetas Carmen* sets a confident, almost brash tone, quite a contrast to the devotional *Jesu dulcis memoria*, one of only two four-voice pieces in the collection. Another outstanding piece is the simply but subtly constructed two-voice *Parce Christus spes reorum*. The tunes *Resonet in laudibus*, *In dulci jubilo* and *Tempus adest floridum* add a definite Christmassy feel, and give this super-budget-price issue a real stocking-stuffer potential. The singers (Carys-Anne Lane, Rebecca Outram, Helen Groves and Caroline Trevor) are deserving of individual mention for a fine achievement.

Palladian Ensemble

A Choice Collection

Anonymous Old Simon the King **Baltzar** John come kiss me now **J Banister** Divisions on a Ground **Blow** Ground in G minor **Butler** Variations on Callino Casturame **Locke** Broken Consorts – D; C **Matteis** Setts of Ayres – Book 2: No 10, Preludio in ostinatione; No 12, Andamento malincolico; Book 3: No 7, Preludio-Prestissimo; No 8, Sarabanda-Adagio; No 9, Gavotta con divisioni; Book 4: No 27, Bizzararrie sopra un basso malinconico; No 28, Aria amorosa-Adagio **Weldon** Sett of Ayres in D
Palladian Ensemble (Pamela Thorby *rec* Rachel Podger *vn* Susanne Heinrich *va da gamba* William Carter *gtr/theorbo*)
Linn Records CKD041 (66 minutes: DDD) Ⓕ
Recorded 1995 ○

The 'choice collection' of 'music of Purcell's London' is of items such as might have been heard at the concerts of then contemporary music held on the premises of Thomas Britton, the 'small coal man', surely one of the most unlikely patrons in the history of music. It is in effect complementary to the Palladian Ensemble's earlier disc ('An Excess of Pleasure', also on Linn Records, CKD010), with another liberal helping of Matteis's various and sometimes agreeably bizarre *Ayres* and two more of Locke's *Broken Consorts*, which we find absorbing rather than confusing – as Charles II did.

With this release John Weldon and Henry Butler are newcomers to the catalogue, the former with what amounts to an irregularly ordered suite, and the latter with splendid variations on *Callino Casturame* in which Susanne Heinrich plays most expressively – and proves that chords played on the viola da gamba do not have to sound like teeth being pulled. *Old Simon the King* could not have been heard in Purcell's own time in this anonymous setting from *The division flute* of 1706, but the tune was printed as early as 1652. If you are not already aware of the high quality of the instrumental playing, stylish musicality and imaginative approach of the Palladian Ensemble, then this disc provides a good opportunity to find out what you have been missing.

Held by the Ears

Anonymous Straloch Lute Book – Canaries; A Scots Tune; Gallus Tom; Whip my Toudie; Hench Me Mallie Gray. Rowallan manuscript – Gypsies Lilt. Divisions on a Ground in G. Roger of Coverly Divisions in D minor Matteis Sett of Ayres. Sett of Ayres in D. Sett of Ayres in D minor. Sett of Ayres in G. Sett of Ayres for the Guitar. Aria ad Imitatione della Trombetta Traditional The lass of Peatie's Mill. Dumbarton's Drums. Bonny Christie. When she came Ben she bobed. Gilliam Callum. A new Tune
Palladian Ensemble (Pamela Thorby *rec* Rachel Podger *vn* Susanne Heinrich *va da gamba* William Carter *gtr/lte/theorbo*)
Linn Records CKD126 (73 minutes: DDD) Ⓕ
Recorded 1999-2000 ○

A bit of an oddity. The Palladian Ensemble's very first recording featured a number of pieces by Nicola Matteis – the Italian violinist and guitarist who walked to London in the 1670s and caused a stir with his playing – and for a while they used one of them almost as a signature tune. Now they have drawn more items from his huge ragbag of short pieces for two melody instruments and continuo – Ayres with a whole range of titles, from 'Adagio' and 'Jigg' to 'Aria Burlesca con molto bizzarie' and 'Giga Al Genio Turchescho' – and made them the main subject of their latest disc, borrowing its title from Roger North's description of Matteis's playing: 'flaming as I have seen him, in a good humour he hath held the company by the ears ... for more than an hour together'.

Acknowledging, however, that Matteis's inspiration is a little hit-and-miss for a whole disc, they have mixed them with a few anonymous instrumental solos of the time and, most intriguingly, their own arrangements of Scottish folk tunes. In his insert-note, Palladian lutenist William Carter admits that the connection between Matteis and musical matters Caledonian is 'indefinable', but the ear picks it up all right, and the combination works well.

Not the least enjoyable feature is the convincingly folkish accent with which the Scottish tunes are performed; Pamela Thorby's soulful bends and grace notes are like an echo of the glens, while Rachel Podger's violin playing is as lithe as a fly-fisher's rod. As for Matteis, well, he is no genius, but his music can be fun, and besides, it does not seem to take much to get these players' imaginations going. After all, the Palladian Ensemble are a group whose quick-witted inventiveness and almost supernatural internal rapport never fail to delight, whatever the music.

Paolo Pandolfo *viol/va da gamba*

A Solo

Abel Arpeggiata. Adagio. Allegro **Anonymous** Aria della Monicha (arr Pandolfo) **Bach** Solo Cello Suite No 4 in E flat BWV1010 **Corkine** The Punckes delight. Come live with me **Hume** Captaine Humes Musicall Humors – A Pavane **Machy** Prélude **Marais** Pièces de viole – Les voix humaines; Le badinage **Ortiz** Trattado de glosas – Pass'emezzo antico; Pass'emezzo moderno **Pandolfo** A Solo
Sainte-Colombe le fils Aire en rondeau
Sumarte Daphne. Whoope doe me no harm
Paolo Pandolfo *viol/va da gamba*
Glossa GCD920403 (77 minutes: DDD) Ⓕ
Recorded 1997 ○○

Seventy-seven minutes of music for unaccompanied viola da gamba? Well yes, and every second of it is a pleasure in the company of one of the most brilliant of the instrument's current exponents. Using three different instruments Paolo Pandolfo takes us on a well-planned journey through gamba-playing Europe, starting with Italy and proceeding through early 17th-century England, mid-baroque France, 18th-century Germany and the brink of the classical style, and finally back to Italy for a composition of his own. Throughout, not a single accompanying instrument is heard, a feat Pandolfo makes light of by the simple expedient of dispensing with continuo parts where they exist and by exploiting to the full the gamba's ability to play chords. Surely few listeners will be prepared, however, for the variety of rich sonorities and colourings to be encountered in this recital, or for Pandolfo's expressive versatility; the Italian pieces are virtuosic and vigorous, the French ones refined and deeply personal, and the bold transcription of Bach's Fourth Solo Cello Suite, though it loses out in cleanness to cello performances, full of strength and energy. Most striking of all, however, is the English group: the soldier-musician, Tobias Hume has never sounded so touching as in the spread *pizzicatos* which open his Pavan, while Richard Sumarte's *Daphne* has a hauntingly wistful folk quality which comes as an almost eerie surprise. Pandolfo has put a lot of himself into this recording, not least in his own piece, which carries a touching personal dedication. The result is a beautiful and moving recital.

Parley of Instruments

A High-Priz'd Noise – Violin Music for Charles I P

A Ferrabosco II Pavan and Alman
R Johnson II The Prince's Alman and Coranto. Air in G minor. The Temporiser a 4. The Witty Wanton. Fantasia in G minor **W Lawes** Alman in D 'for the Violins of Two Trebles'. Airs for consort **Nau** Suite in F. Ballet in F. Pavan and Galliard in D minor
Notari Variations on the 'Ruggiero' **Webster** Four Consort pieces
Parley of Instruments Renaissance Violin Band / Peter Holman
Hyperion CDA66806 (67 minutes: DDD) Ⓕ
Recorded 1995 ●

This recording is less concerned with musical monuments, such as Lawes's large consorts, than in rejuvenating a repertoire which might have accompanied the King's recreation, or been the actual means for it. Most of the works are written in dance forms, though we can be reasonably certain that the majority would not have been conceived for accompanying dance. The violin's specific association with active dance music – except of a more base and popular kind – goes only so far, as the 17th century progresses. Of the courtly violin bands it is the more expansive one in the Presence Chamber (performing for public rather than private space at court) which has the most instantly appealing repertory – the opening set of works by Robert Johnson and the wonderful *Pavan and Alman* by Alphonso Ferrabosco II; the latter composition, although timeless in its exquisite part-writing, is given new life with a period violin band. Both pieces gleam with an engaging transparency, a compelling sound for those who have yet to hear this ensemble. The *Pavan* is magically forthcoming in its gracious lines with just a hint of melancholy, a poignant fragility which gives way to the noble rapture of the *Alman*. The Parley's 14-strong group of four violins, six violas and four bass violins is marshalled with a degree of characterisation that gleefully extricates this music from dusty library shelves. A high priz'd noise indeed, with further insights into our rich instrumental heritage, performed here with fragrance and deep affection.

Hille Perl *va da gamba*

Doulce Memoire – Glosas, Passeggiati and Diminutions around 1600 P

Bonnizzi Jouissance **Dalla Casa** Doulce memoire
Monteverdi Sinfonia **Notari** Ben qui si mostra il ciel
Ortiz Passamezzo antico. Recercada de canto llano. Recercada sobre tenore. Recercada quarta sobre Doulce memoire. Doulce memoire **Rogniono** Susanne ung jour. Anchor che c'ol partire **Rore** Ben qui si mostra il ciel **Selma** Vestiva hi colli **Terzi** Jouissance Trabaci Ancidetemi pur **Willaert** Jouissance vous donneray
Hille Perl *va da gamba* with **Robert Sagasser, Martina Rothbauer, Paulina van Laarhoven** *va da gambas* **Matthias Müller** *va da gamba/violone*
Andrew Lawrence-King *double hp* **Lee Santana** *lte/gtr/chittarone*
Deutsche Harmonia Mundi 05472 77502-2 Ⓕ
(63 minutes: DDD). Recorded 1998 ●

Viol watchers will know what to expect from a disc with this subtitle. In particular, they will be anticipating a selection of Diego Ortiz's *recercadas* from his *Trattado de glosas*, in which he demonstrated the many and various ways in which an instrumental player can improvise on existing dance tunes and contrapuntal vocal compositions. Less predictable is the rest of this beautifully planned and executed CD, on which Hille Perl and her friends from two of the groups in which she plays – The Harp Consort and Sirius Viols – play instrumental arrangements and derivations from works by some of the great names of late renaissance vocal music. The practices employed range from simply playing a madrigal on viols (as in Rore's *Ben qui si mostra*) to one viol playing an elaborate, newly composed part while a lute plays the rest straight (Selma's version of Palestrina's *Vestiva hi colli*), to the 'alla bastarda' method in which the viol plays florid decorations on as many parts as it can as it leaps from one to the other (Notari's version of the Rore).

If this sounds like it might be a vehicle for empty instrumental virtuosity, think again. Perl and co perform all these pieces from the heart, feeling every note and never losing touch with the music's origins. Helped by a warm and lovingly nurtured tone, Perl's playing is wonderfully expressive without ever losing its poise or subtlety, while her accompanists are impeccably sensitive and supportive. For good measure, Andrew Lawrence-King's solo, a Trabaci madrigal arrangement, is a perfect demonstration of the unique eloquence of the baroque harp.

As is her wont, Perl provides her own quirky

booklet-notes which, while not terrifically informative, are guaranteed to raise a smile and add to the disc's glow of amity. A richly civilising release – exquisitely played, handsomely recorded and elegantly presented – but then that is no more than you would expect from someone who shares her family home with music, cats and chickens, now is it?

Renaissance Camerata of Carcas

Baroque Music of Latin America
Anonymous El día de corpus. Esta noche yo baila **Araujo** Recordad jilguerillos. A recoger pasiones inhumanas **Bocanegra** Hanapachap cussicuinin **Cascante** Villancico al nascimiento **Castellanos** Ausente del alma mía. Si de rosa el nombre **Araujo Ceruti** A cantar un villancico **Fernandes** Tleycantimo choquilya. Dame albricia Mano Anton. Mano Fasiquiyo **J Herrera** A la fuente de bienes **J Mathias** Quien sale aqueste día disfraçado **De la Mota** Dios y Josef apuestan **Torrejón y Velasco** Cuando el bien que adoro. A este sol peregrino. Desvelado dueño mío **Velásquez** Niño mío
The Renaissance Camerata of Caracas / Isabel Palacios
Dorian DOR93199 (65 minutes: DDD) Ⓕ
Texts and translations included. Recorded 1992

This disc is a reissue of a recording made in 1992, but previously only available on a very limited basis: Dorian has performed a sterling service in making it available to a wider public. Most of the music recorded is barely known, even among specialists, and it certainly cannot be described as over-recorded. The Camerata is a group which reinforces the stereotypical idea that Latin American musicians are more successful when working with lively, rhythmical music, and less so when they are required to sing sustained melodic lines. A number of the pieces recorded here come across as somewhat bland because of this limitation, as one may hear in the somewhat under-characterised *Ausente del alma* by Rafael Antonio Castellanos, but in general the group has the measure of the style. Mathias's sarabande-like *Quien sale aqueste* and Castellanos's *Si de rosa el nombre* prove this amply, and the performance of Torrejón y Velasco's justly renowned *A este sol peregrino* is quite lovely.

The rather oddly baroque performance of the Quechua hymn *Hanapachap cussicuinin* heralds a change in a section balanced in favour of earlier repertoire, specifically villancicos by Gaspar Fernandes, an extraordinarily original composer of Portuguese origin who worked in Guatemala and Mexico. The Camerata give us three works by him, all done utterly idiomatically (especially the slinky rendition of *Mano Fasiquiyo*), though *Dame albricia Mano Anton* really is just a little too fast, however expert the singers are in getting their tongues round the text at that speed. The programme finishes with a brilliant rendition of the anonymous *Esta noche yo baila*, which reminds one of nothing so much as mambo. Recommended, but don't forget your dancing shoes.

Jordi Savall *va da gamba/viol*

La Folia, 1490-1701
Anonymous Folia: Rodrigo Martínez **Cabezón** Folia: Para quien crié cabellos **Corelli** Violin Sonata in D minor, Op 5 No 12, 'La folia' **Enzina** Folia: Hoy comamos y bebamos **Marais** Deuxième Livre de Pièces de viole – Couplets de folies
Martín y Coll Diferencias sobre las folias
Ortiz Ricercadas sobre la Folia – IV; VIII
Jordi Savall *va da gamba/viol* **Rolf Lislevand** *gtr/theorbo/vilhuela* **Michael Behringer** *org/hpd* **Arianna Savall** *triple hp* **Bruno Cocset** *vc* **Pedro Estevan** *perc* **Adela Gonzalez-Campa** *castanets*
Alia Vox AV9805 (55 minutes: DDD) Ⓕ
Recorded 1998

This release charts two centuries of musical madness in the shape of the *folia* (which can mean anything from 'wild amusement' to 'insanity'). The earliest references to the *folia* are to a Portuguese dance of popular origin that by the end of the 15th century had become still more popular in court circles. Its distinctively minimalist harmonic patterns, but on only four different chords, make it a perfect vehicle for instrumental jam sessions in the renaissance and it is this improvisatory tradition that is explored by Savall and his team. Virtuosity is a *sine qua non* in the *folia* business and Savall, of course, is an established virtuoso. Allied to this, is his ability to make the music seem as spontaneous and full of fantasy as the improvisatory practice from which the endless chameleon-like variations by Corelli and Marais sprang.

These works are well known to all aficionados of baroque music; less familiar is the set of *diferencias* by the Spanish composer Antonio Martín y Coll, although he is almost equally inventive. Here Savall chooses to emphasise the Iberian origin of the *folia* with an accompaniment of triple harp, baroque guitar and castanets which he describes as being 'in keeping with the characteristic Iberian sound of the period.' Such a sound world may well have more to do with late 20th-century preconceptions than historical fact and the castanets seem lost and uncertain in these elaborate, sophisticated variations.

Savall's re-creations of the early *folia* are much freer still; and, his version of *Rodrigo Martínez*, a dance-song from the *Cancionero Musical de Palacio*, is almost outrageously exuberant in its percussionisation. Still, Savall's attempt to trace an important improvisatory tradition is fascinating and it is a tribute to his musical imagination that the ear never tires of those four chords in almost an hour's music. Recommended – despite Savall's improvised humming!

Andreas Scholl *counterten*

English Folksongs and Lute Songs
Anonymous King Henry. Kemp's jig. Go from my window **Campion** I care not for these ladies. My love hath vow'd. My sweetest Lesbia **Dowland** The First Booke of Songs or Ayres – Can she excuse my

wrongs?; All ye, whom love or fortune.
The Second Booke of Songs or Ayres – I saw my Lady weepe; Flow my teares fall from your springs; Sorrow sorrow stay, lend true repentant tears.
The Third and Last Booke of Songs or Ayres – Behold a wonder heere; Me, me and none but me; Say, loue, if euer thou did'st find. The Lady Russell's pavan. Go from my window **Traditional** The three ravens. O waly, waly. I will give my love an apple. Barbara Allen. Lord Rendall
Andreas Scholl *counterten* **Andreas Martin** *lte*
Harmonia Mundi HMC90 1603 (69 minutes: DDD) Ⓕ
Texts included. Recorded 1996

'Interval' is not a word that has ever been inserted into a song recital on CD, but it would be quite a good idea if it were. In this instance the stopping-point hardly needs to be marked, as it is so natural and obvious; and that is one of the many attractions of this well-designed programme. A group of songs by Dowland, followed by a piece for lute, makes a substantial first section; then come two folk-songs, another couple by 'Anon.' and a lively, well-contrasted selection of songs by Campion. The second half starts with more Dowland, a satisfyingly representative sequence constituting the heart of the programme, with more folk-songs to conclude. The mixture is a charming one and delightfully well ordered.

The performances are equally pleasing. Perhaps it is inevitable that an English listener should still think of Alfred Deller in this repertoire, but here the name comes to mind also because of a distinct similarity of timbre. At the resonant centre of Scholl's voice is a passage of lower middle notes where the vibrancy is strong and rich in a way very comparable to Deller's. Stylistically, on the other hand, Scholl has developed an art that is quite independent of his great original: his manner is more forthright, less responsive to the spiritual intensity of *Sorrow sorrow stay*, though still capable of introducing that 'poisoned' intonation which Deller and his successors would bring to *All ye, whom love or fortune hath betrayed*. As regards balance, the lute is placed as the accompanying instrument rather than as one of an equal, intimate partnership; still, all is clear, and the lute solos are played with fine technical skill and sensitive feeling for the essential rhythmic flexibility.

Christopher Stembridge *hpd/org*

Consonanze stravaganti Ⓟ
Neapolitan music for organ, harpsichord and chromatic harpsichord
Christopher Stembridge *hpd/org*
Ars Musici AM1207-2 (68 minutes: DDD) Ⓕ
Recorded 1987 **OO**

This magnificent recital charts a relatively unexplored corner of Italian music, played on rare and beautiful Italian instruments (including exotic plucked keyboards with 'split' chromatic keys). The opening *Capriccio* by Giovanni de Macque is alone worth the price of admission. Christopher Stembridge draws more than other interpreters from this weird and wonderful repertory.

Taverner Consort

Una Stravaganza dei Medici – The 1589 Florentine Intermedii
Intermedio I – The Harmony of the Spheres (music by Archilei or de'Cavalieri, Malvezzi). Intermedio II – The Singing Contest between the Pierides and the Muses (Marenzio). Intermedio III – Apollo Slays the Monster at Delphi (Marenzio). Intermedio IV – The Golden Age is Foretold (Caccini, Malvezzi, de'Bardi). Intermedio V – Arion and the Dolphins (Malvezzi, Fantini, Peri). Intermedio VI – Jove's Gift to Mortals of Rhythm and Harmony (Malvezzi, de'Cavalieri)
Tessa Bonner, Emily van Evera, Emma Kirkby *sops* **Nigel Rogers** *ten* **Taverner Consort; Taverner Choir; Taverner Players / Andrew Parrott**
HMV Classics HMV5 73863-2 (70 minutes: DDD) Ⓑ
Recorded 1988 **OO**

These *Intermedii* of 1589 are the only complete examples of this genre of courtly entertainment to have found their way into print. They are not opera, and are closer in some ways to the modern-day musical: this staged music was designed for performance between the acts of a play, and to be at best incidental to its action. Of the three recordings made in the last 20 years, this one (first issued in 1988 and deleted shortly after) is the best. Compared with the Huelgas Ensemble's version a couple of years ago, Parrott scores higher on just about every count. More so than van Nevel, he captures the sense of festivity that is the music's *raison d'être* (it was part of a lavish wedding celebration). The word 'lavish' well describes his instrumental ensemble, by far the richer and more powerful of the two. Van Nevel's trademark shuffling of voices and instruments hardly succeeds in redressing the balance. And to a more conspicuous degree than van Nevel's, Parrott's cast of singers seems to relish the vocal pyrotechnics demanded of it by composer-singers such as Caccini and Peri.

There is another reason to prefer this reissue, which may have been prompted by the appearance of the Sony set: for value-for-money, it wins hands down – a single well-filled, budget-price CD against two full-price ones. The only drawback is the loss of the hugely informative insert-notes included in the original issue, but that is a small price to pay. This is one of the Taverner Consort's most memorable recordings.

Les Voix Humaines

'The Spirite of Musicke'
Coprario Songs of Mourning – 'Tis now dead night; To the World **A Ferrabosco II** Like hermit poore. So Beautie on the waters stood (all arr Little/Napper)
Hume Captaine Humes Poeticall Musicke – What greater grief; Sweet ayre; Cease leaden slumber. The First Part of Ayres – Touch me sweetly; The Spirite of Musicke **Jenkins** Suite in A minor
C Simpson Divisions on a Ground – F; G
Suzie Le Blanc *sop* **Les Voix Humaines** (Susie Napper, Margaret Little *vas da gamba*)
ATMA ACD22136 (63 minutes: DDD) Ⓕ
Texts included. Recorded 1997

Over the years they have been playing together as Les Voix Humaines, the bass viol players Susie Napper and Margaret Little have developed a command of their repertory and a rapport that few other ensembles have approached. They express themselves very clearly as individuals but play together with perfect precision. In Tobias Hume's flirtatious *Touch me sweetly* they banter playfully, their control of articulation and dynamics superb; so too in Hume's evocation of a bandora by two bass viols in *The Spirite of Musicke*. To Simpson's divisions for two bass viols they bring a depth of expression not often heard, but they seem especially in their element in John Jenkins's sublimely crafted Suite in A minor. Not content with the existing music for their instruments, they have taken inspiration from Hume, who composed the deeply affecting *Cease leaden slumber* and *What greater grief* for voice and two bass viols, and arranged the lute accompaniment of songs by the Jacobean violists Giovanni Coprario and Alfonso Ferrabosco II for two viols. The result is most often ravishing – the viol has after all been called a 'bowed lute' – although the melancholic simplicity of the vocal line of Coprario's *'Tis now dead night* is overpowered by busy viols. Elsewhere, in Coprario's *To the World* and Ferrabosco's *So Beautie on the waters stood*, their arrangements are more successful. They are joined on this recording by Suzie Le Blanc whose clear, bell-like upper register, excellent diction and formidable breath control suit the music ideally. She seems completely at one with the texts and their settings, investing just the right emotional weight to her readings. The viol players rely perhaps too much for this repertory on a swelled bow stroke which can add too much colour to a delicate accompaniment or unsteady a dance. All in all, though this is an appealing recording which you will want to listen to again and again.

Westminster Cathedral Choir

Exultate Deo – Masterpieces of Sacred Polyphony

Allegri Miserere mei[a] **Byrd** Ave verum corpus. Civitas sancti tui. Haec dies **G Gabrieli** Jubilate Deo I[b] **Lotti** Crucifixus[b] **Monteverdi** Cantate Domino[b] **Palestrina** Exsultate Deo. Sicut cervus desiderat **Parsons** Ave Maria **Philips** Ascendit Deus. Ave verum corpus Christi **Tallis** Salvator mundi, salva nos I. O nata lux de lumine. In manus tuas **Tye** Omnes gentes, plaudite **Viadana** Exultate justi[b] **Victoria** O quam gloriosum

[a]**Alexander Semprini,** [a]**Francis Faux,** [a]**Raymond Winterflood** *trebs* [a]**Adrian Peacock** *bass* **Westminster Cathedral Choir / James O'Donnell** with [b]**Joseph Cullen** *org*

Hyperion CDA66850 (72 minutes: DDD) Ⓕ
Texts and translations included. Recorded 1995

This anthology lives up to its billing: even those with only a nodding acquaintance with renaissance polyphony will probably have heard a fair proportion of these pieces. Most of them are mainstays, not just of the Catholic liturgical repertory, but of most major Anglican choral establishments. The selection of pieces here is wide-ranging and varied. More importantly, where pieces are especially famous, the standard of performance gives the competition a fair run for its money. There *is* the thrill in Allegri's *Miserere* of a boy treble (here, Alexander Semprini) hitting that high C – and no quibbles about the phrasing of the adjoining notes, either. The choir sound very well focused, and the unanimity of the trebles is admirable (though at times a slightly more veiled tone might have better suited the text). Where required, it sounds very bright and forward, despite a recording that could have been a bit withdrawn with a more timid choir.

Sophie Yates *hpd*

Romanesca – Italian Harpsichord Works Ⓟ

Frescobaldi Partite – XIV, sopra l'aria della Romanesca; VI, sopra l'aria di Follia; Cento Partite, sopra Passacagli. Toccata in A minor
Gesualdo Canzon francese del Principe
Macque Seconde stravaganze **Merulo** Susanne un jour **Picchi** Toccata. Intavolatura di Balli d'Arpicordo – Ballo ongaro; Ballo alla polacha; Todesca; Ballo ditto il Picchi **Rossi** Toccata settima **Valente** Tenore del passo e mezzo con sei mutanze

Sophie Yates *hpd*

Chandos Chaconne CHAN0601 (64 minutes: DDD) Ⓕ
Recorded 1996

Fleetness of finger, on which these early Italians set much store, is a requisite for performing this repertoire; and in this Sophie Yates is eminently accomplished. Another requisite is to convey a sense that the music is being improvised on the spur of the moment. This is especially so in toccatas but it also applies in the outwardly stricter form of partitas or variations, the commonest structural basis for keyboard music of the time. Yates provides a firm framework for Frescobaldi's variations on the *Folia* ground bass, but while neatly pointing its rhythmic quirks allows herself greater freedom in the set on the Romanesca; and she clearly relishes the harmonic twists in the variations on passacaglias. Valente's variations on the *Passamezzo antico* are different in kind, more overtly dance-like and lively, with a strongly marked rhythmic accompaniment. There are two canzonas – keyboard versions of songs – here: a highly elaborate working by Merulo of Lasso's famous Susanne un jour, and an extraordinary piece by Gesualdo which contains some weird and wonderful chromatic trills.

The most developed of the toccatas here is that by Frescobaldi, which inserts a formal contrapuntal section into its otherwise free style. Not the least of the pleasures on this disc is Yates's vigorous playing of four tuneful dances by Frescobaldi's contemporary, Picchi, of whom little more is known other than that he was an organist in Venice: how this dazzling Toccata of his found its way into the Fitzwilliam Virginal Book is a minor mystery.

DVD & Video

Orchestral

Mendelssohn

Symphony No 3 in A minor, 'Scottish', Op 56. Violin Concerto in E minor, Op 64[a]. A Midsummer Night's Dream – Overture; Wedding March
[a]**Frank-Michael Erben** *vn* **Leipzig Gewandhaus Orchestra / Kurt Masur**
Video director **Bob Coles**
Arthaus Musik **DVD** 100 030 Ⓕ
(82 minutes: Region 0). Recorded live in 1998

To merit repeated viewing, a conventional con cert needs a special element, visual or otherwise, or an unusually electric sense of occasion. This one, commemorating the composer who was once the orchestra's music director, has only the airy but anodyne modern Gewandhaus auditorium for a setting, and no extra immediacy, so its visual interest rests squarely on the players and conductor. Fortunately, the director does not resort to Karajanesque gimmickry to compensate.

Masur is a pleasure to watch as he shapes his interpretations, underpinned by the orchestra's clear, airy textures, which come over with proper clarity in the Dolby Digital Stereo soundtrack. His *Dream* Overture has plenty of fleet-footed magic, and needs only more of a smile. Erben, the orchestra's leader, is a fluent, committed but unspectacular soloist in the concerto, and is none the worse for that; it's refreshing to hear Mendelssohn speaking for himself, without overly stellar personalities intruding.

The notes memorably describe the *Scottish* Symphony as 'the composer's emotionally many-layered artistic selfliberation [*sic*]' and claim it was inspired by a visit to England! Despite this, it is a fine performance, capturing the first movement's melancholy with great grace, and there's plenty of energy in the *Scherzo* and final movement. Only the concluding Wedding March seems rather short of vitality. Visually natural if not especially exciting, it is an engaging programme, and represents a quite substantial body of music for the money.

Sir Thomas Beecham *cond*

Beecham in Chicago 1
Haydn Symphony No 102 in B flat **Mozart** Symphony No 38 in D, 'Prague', K504
Chicago Symphony Orchestra / Sir Thomas Beecham
NVC Arts VHS 8573-84095-3 (49 minutes: ADD) Ⓕ
Recorded live in 1960

Beecham in Chicago 2
Delius Florida Suite – By the River **Handel** Love in Bath – Suite **Mendelssohn** The Hebrides, Op 26 **Saint-Saëns** Le rouet d'Omphale, Op 31
Chicago Symphony Orchestra / Sir Thomas Beecham
NVC Arts VHS 8573-84096-3 (48 minutes: ADD) Ⓕ
Recorded live in 1960

Here is a rare quarry of film footage which can hardly fail to delight anyone who is interested in Beecham, the Chicago Symphony, or even the music itself. The concerts were specially staged for television in the Grand Ballroom of the Sheraton Towers in Chicago in March 1960. It was Beecham's last visit to the United States (he died the following March). He was in his 80th year, not in the best of health but seemingly in fine fettle. He conducts without a score, mostly standing, though after an electrifying performance of the first movement of Mozart's *Prague* Symphony, he draws up a chair from where he presides as only he could preside over an exquisite account of the slow movement.

The videos are billed as being the only extant footage of Beecham 'in colour'. This seems a sceptical selling-point until you see the videos. The fact is, black-and-white is fine for film, but TV concerts aren't films, they're reportage; and black-and-white reportage has a nasty habit of making relatively recent events seem strangely distant in time. This colour footage makes Beecham seem like our contemporary.

The actual picture quality is no more than fair. The original two-inch Kinescope tapes disappeared after someone dubbed them on to one-inch analogue tape in the 1980s. But it is perfectly watchable; expertly re-engineered, with good colour rendition and excellent sound. The non-concert hall staging also means that we have some tolerably enterprising camera-work, with Beecham himself, the Chicago strings, and two of the principal wind players, oboist Ray Still and flautist Donald Peck, getting the lion's share of the director's attention.

What a phenomenal ensemble the Chicago Symphony was in 1960! It is fascinating to watch the players at work here, connoisseurs of their craft in the presence of a Connoisseur-in-Chief. As the first violins bow their repeated Ds at the start of the *Prague* Symphony's *Allegro*, the camera catches a Humphrey Bogart look-alike on the second desk eyeing Beecham and gazing across the assembled banks of fiddles with a look that says 'Hey guys, listen to us!'. Later, as the coda kicks in with a typically Beechamesque blend of elegance and drive, the same

Region, Picture format & Sound coding

DVDs are encoded so that certain discs will play only on players in specific areas. Regions: 1=USA; 2=Europe, Japan; 3=South East Asia; 4=Latin America, Australia, New Zealand; 5=Russia, the rest of Asia (excluding China), Africa; Region 0=discs will play in any region. Most Region 2 players can be modified to play Region 1 discs, and multi-region machines are available. Most can translate the US NTSC signal for European PAL TV sets. A few cannot, only playing on common multi-standard TVs. Picture format: usually either 4:3 (standard TV screen ratio) or 16:9 (widescreen 'letterbox' format). Sound: 2.0=stereo sound; 5.1=surround (five-channel) sound. Readers are advised to check with their dealers and instruction manuals. For more information visit **www.dvdbuyingguide.com**

player shoots a huge grin across to his neighbour.

Fritz Reiner was Chicago's principal conductor at the time, he of the bull-frog gaze and minuscule beat. Beecham has a rather larger beat, unerringly precise, almost never *legato*, and with a habit of galvanising the rhythm with a movement of the stick which is often a millisecond quicker than expected. The left hand is sparingly used, though the left fist, raised and briefly brandished, is always impressive. Even in his 80th year, Beecham's stance is erect, almost bandmasterish, his hands and body moving in a way that is delicate and exact. His other principal weapon is his eyes: dark eyes emitting a gaze that is sometimes roguish, occasionally Mephistophelean, always penetrating and intent.

Both programmes are more or less equally enjoyable. The 'fun' programme is just that. The readings will be familiar to seasoned collectors of 78s and LPs but the performances are new-minted: the *Hebrides* Overture clear, alert and full of fantasy, the Saint-Saëns incisive and exquisitely polished, *Love in Bath*, as always, outrageously enjoyable. (What leading conductor nowadays would dare conduct *Le rouet d'Omphale* in public or draw up his own arrangement of the music of some much-revered baroque master?) Merely to watch Beecham's eyes while listening to his unfolding of music from Delius's *Florida* Suite is to understand why (and in what ways) this music was so precious to him.

Beecham usually travelled with his own meticulously annotated orchestral parts. *Love in Bath* would certainly have been played from his parts. And by the look of pleasure on the wind players' faces during these superlative performances of Haydn's Symphony No 102 and Mozart's *Prague*, these might have been, too.

A joyous discovery, then, which goes some way beyond the 'unique concerts in colour' tag. It is doubtful if there are better images anywhere of the old sorcerer at work than the ones here.

Various Artists

'The Art of Violin'

A film by Bruno Monsaingeon

Includes excerpts from performances by **Ivry Gitlis, Mischa Elman, Zino Francescatti, George Enescu, Boris Goldstein, Ida Haendel, Josef Hassid, Jascha Heifetz, Fritz Kreisler, Leonid Kogan, Laurent Korcia, Alexander Markov, Yehudi Menuhin, Nathan Milstein, Ginette Neveu, David Oistrakh, Michael Rabin, Ruggiero Ricci, Isaac Stern, Henryk Szeryng, Joseph Szigeti, Jacques Thibaud,** and **Eugène Ysaÿe**

NVC **DVD** 8573-85801-2 (113 minutes: Region 0) Ⓕ

▪▪ 8573-85801-3 (PAL) **oo**

The best of Bruno Monsaingeon's video productions marry a film maker's technical expertise with a musician's instinct, and in the context of *The Art of Violin* both qualities register more or less from the start. Within minutes, Itzhak Perlman is telling us that most of the 'old-world' violinists 'sounded different' from each other. No sooner has he spoken than Monsaingeon provides the evidence. He splices us from a 1958 David Oistrakh film of Mendelssohn's Concerto to Isaac Stern in 1957, Christian Ferras in 1963, Fritz Kreisler in 1927 (a charming shot of silent film with the 1935 commercial recording as its soundtrack) and Nathan Milstein in 1966. Then there's Yehudi Menuhin in 1979 and 1947 (under Dorati), Arthur Grumiaux in 1961, Jascha Heifetz in 1959 (the RCA recording with overlaid film footage) and, perhaps most interesting of all, Mischa Elman in London in 1962. And yes, they do all sound different – very different.

But what is the technical mechanism that turns these interpretative differences into sound? The interview evidence is as detailed as one could wish given the breadth of Monsaingeon's targeted audience. The principal commentators are Perlman, Ivry Gitlis, Ida Haendel, Menuhin and Hilary Hahn, all of them inspired to frequent eloquence and unflagging enthusiasm.

There are in effect two films. The first, 'The Devil's Instrument', contains some of the most interesting archive footage; the second, 'Transcending the Violin', veers more in the direction of specific instruments and overall musicianship. Menuhin stresses the self-destructive properties of soulless virtuosity and it's appropriate that the closing footage should give us the last section of Bach's *Chaconne* as played by Menuhin at Gstaad in 1972 – quite marvellously too. Earlier on, he offers an extraordinarily beautiful account of 'Erbarme dich' from Bach's *St Matthew Passion*, recorded in Hollywood in 1947.

Prior to Menuhin's Bach, we experience the piercing gaze and musical intensity of Ginette Neveu as she burns the closing pages of Chausson's *Poème* onto our memories. We see Szigeti dispatch Schubert's *The Bee* framed by apposite commentary from Haendel, Perlman and Gitlis. Elman's preoccupation with sound for sound's sake comes in for some stick, though the evidence is ravishing and his own claims that the new generation owes a certain debt to the old, is both honest and justified.

A brief prodigy section gives us the 12-year-old Ruggiero Ricci playing part of Vieuxtemps' Fifth Concerto – amazing stuff – and the long-forgotten Boris Goldstein performing Kreisler, beautiful in terms of tone but a trifle rigid in its delivery. The tragic case of Michael Rabin, who died from a drug overdose in 1972, comes freshly to life via a scintillating live *Tambourin chinois*. An Electrecord recording of Enescu's Third Violin Sonata with Enescu himself as soloist (and Dinu Lipatti at the piano) accompanies silent footage of the composer-violinist and Zino Francescatti, praised by Gitlis for his Mediterranean warmth, throws off Bazzini's *La ronde des lutins* with the aplomb of Heifetz.

We see rare silent film of Ysaÿe and valuable sound film of Jacques Thibaud, Leonid Kogan and Henryk Szeryng. And there are the surprises. For example, Perlman's attitude to Szeryng (and to a lesser extent Hilary Hahn's), which is guardedly negative. Both view Szeryng as a beautiful player who's lacking in character. Perlman puts it on the line. 'He sounds like everybody,' he says. 'If I'm listening, and I don't know who it is...I think, oh, it must be Szeryng'. Still, it's doubtful there's a better stereo version of Schumann's Violin Concerto than Szeryng's.

Nathan Milstein is seen and heard, cool as ever, in Bach and Paganini. An English interviewer asks him why so many Jewish executive musicians are exceptional, and Milstein replies that he knows quite a few who aren't. It's not race, he says, it's conditioning. Good point. Gitlis challenges the myth of Heifetz's coldness by asking us to close our eyes as we listen, while Perlman compares Heifetz's beautiful sound in concert with his more aggressive, close-up recordings. We see snippets of a 'staged' Heifetz recital, which has long circulated in private hands and where a bunch of college kids race through the campus shouting 'Hey guys, Heifetz is giving a free concert!' It was the bargain of a lifetime, especially Wieniawski's simply fantastic D major *Polonaise*.

Monsaingeon's Trinity consists of Heifetz, Menuhin and Oistrakh, with Isaac Stern a nearby fourth contender. Perlman compares 'Heifetz the god' with Menuhin, 'an angel come down to earth', a befitting image. Oistrakh and Menuhin are seen embracing and playing Bach in Bucharest, and Oistrakh plays Khachaturian's Violin Concerto under both Kyrill Kondrashin and the composer. We also see him tackle the huge transitional cadenza from Shostakovich's First Violin Concerto, calmly at first, then with slowly mounting intensity.

You'll already have gathered the tremendous pleasure these films give. Their appeal lies not only in the footage, which varies in quality yet never in value, but also in the well-edited commentary (so much wisdom and good humour) and the range of topics covered. It's a pity that Monsaingeon couldn't find any film of Adolf Busch or Bronislaw Huberman, though he had a good try. Violin lovers will be in seventh heaven, but what's perhaps more important is that non-specialists should enjoy the experience almost as much. *The Art of Violin* is utterly unmissable.

Instrumental

Sviatoslav Richter *pf*

Richter – The Enigma
A documentary film by Bruno Monsaingeon
Warner Music Vision/NVC Arts **DVD** 3984-23029-2 Ⓕ
(154 minutes: Regions 2-6)

Is Richter really an enigma? This epic documentary was originally titled 'Richter l'insoumis', meaning anything from 'irrepressible' to 'indomitable'. Constructed around interviews with Richter, his wife, and fellow luminaries such as Glenn Gould and Rubinstein, it reveals him as both – the precocious genius who never practised scales and chords, but instead launched into Chopin Etudes, and who lists his three masters as his father, his mentor Neuhaus and Wagner. And in his last years Monsaingeon's camera captures, not the grim scowl and prognathous jaw, but an urbane egotist whose deceptively naive charm must have helped him sail through life under the Soviet regime he despised, surviving to shed gentle vitriol on contemporaries. Prokofiev patronised him as 'fit for Rachmaninov'; Richter played at his funeral – 'Rachmaninov!' he adds, with a lethal twinkle. Among other victims are Oistrakh and Karajan.

Against this anecdotal ambience, though, are set some 50 performance extracts which capture the electrifying reality of Richter's playing – his vast repertoire, including Berg's *Kammerkonzert*, and the penetrating, expressive intensity which offsets his virtuoso eloquence and massive dynamics. It is not too fanciful to see him possessed and shaped by the score, especially in his native repertoire. Even those who are not primarily piano aficionados can hardly fail to respond. We even glimpse him happily playing Liszt – man and music – in a cameo film role.

Unlike videotape, DVD allows each excerpt to be accessed swiftly via its 'chapter', and its image quality enhances even elderly material. The worst flaw of this fascinating montage is that, although skilfully edited, it leaves one dangling, desperate to hear every single piece complete.

Vocal

Berlioz

La damnation de Faust, Op 24
Vesselina Kasarova *mez* **Paul Groves** *ten* **Willard White** *bass* **Andreas Macco** *bass* **San Sebastian People's Choral Society; Tölz Boys' Choir; Staatskapelle Berlin / Sylvain Cambreling**
Stage directors **Alex Olle, Carlos Pedrissa**
Video director **Alexandre Tarta**
ArtHaus Musik **DVD** 100 003 (146 minutes: DDD) Ⓕ
Recorded live in 1999

This production was the sensation of the 1999 Salzburg Festival, and this riveting DVD captures most of the excitement that must have been felt at the time in the evocative Felsenreitschule. The staging is a joint venture. The spectacular scenic realisation of Berlioz's 'Légende dramatique' originated with the Spanish theatre troupe La Fura dels Baus; the staging itself is the work of Olle and Pedrissa. The sets and costumes were conceived by the Spanish sculptor Jaume Piensa.

The results were described in the press as 'extreme theatre' – and one can see why when viewing the virtuoso treatment of the vast stage area. It is dominated by a transparent cylinder which serves all sorts of purposes, depicting in particular the soul-searching struggles of Faust and Méphistophélès; while the complex choral movements and an elaborate lighting plot are all carried out without a hint of a hitch. The interpretation, on first viewing, seems to be quasi-Jungian, exploring the meaning of Faust's soul and his relationship with his alter ego

Méphistophélès and his ideal, unattainable woman, Marguerite. The Ride to the Abyss is the zenith of the venture's appreciable accomplishments. The whole enterprise is extremely daring and could have gone disastrously wrong, but in the event seems to have been triumphant. Alexandre Tarta, the video director, catches as much as is possible of the inventive action.

It certainly inspired all the participants to heights of interpretative skill. Cambreling and the Berlin Staatskapelle perform with discipline and fire, wanting only that extra dedicated vision evinced by Colin Davis and the LSO on CD. Kasarova and Willard White, stage beings to their fingertips, sing and act with total conviction. Kasarova is the vulnerable, insecure, beautiful Marguerite to the life, every gesture and facial expression supporting her intense reading of the glorious music Berlioz wrote for her. Her vision of the great Romance is idiosyncratic to say the least, but a triumph of erotic communication on its own account, a cross between Callas and Ewing at their most individual.

White is commanding throughout – at once demonic, cynical, relaxed and satirical, his huge voice absolutely in command of the role. Groves is not quite on his colleagues' level of accomplishment, but acts and sings with the awe and sense of identity-seeking which this production requires of its Faust. The sound, as on most DVDs, is exemplary. Highly recommended.

Haydn

Die Schöpfung, HobXXI/2
Edith Mathis *sop* **Christoph Prégardien** *ten*
René Pape *bass* **Lucerne Festival Chorus; Scottish Chamber Orchestra / Peter Schreier**
Video Director **Elisabeth Birke-Malzer**
ArtHaus Musik **DVD** 100 040 (109 minutes: Region 0). Recorded live in 1992 Ⓕ

This enjoyable performance of Haydn's supreme choral masterpiece was recorded at the Lucerne Festival of 1992. It takes place in the appropriate setting of an evocative baroque church, which is not identified either on screen or in the (inadequate) supporting booklet. The small choir sings with attentive enthusiasm, and is weak only in the tenor department. The Scottish Chamber Orchestra players cover themselves in glory both as an ensemble and individually, and they are adept at imposing period practice on modern instruments. Schreier's direction is relaxed and benevolent, yet his keen ear for rhythmic precision and flexibility in phrasing is constantly felt.

The soloists are all Swiss. The veteran Mathis remains a paragon of classical style, phrasing her arias and contributions to the ensembles with firm tone and finely honed phrasing. Prégardien's liquid, silvery tenor and sensitive way with words is just what the tenor part calls for. The young Pape's sonorous bass and confident, long-breathed delivery are ideal; he and Mathis make an appealing Adam and Eve in Part 3.

The video direction is discreet, and prompt in homing in on the right performer at the right time. The sound picture is as spacious and well defined as one expects from the new medium, which – of course – allows us to hear the whole, long work without a break.

Schubert

Winterreise, D911
Ian Bostridge *ten* **Julius Drake** *pf*
Stage director **David Alden**
Video director **Peter West**
NVC Arts **DVD** 8573-83780-2 Ⓕ
(124 minutes: Regions 2-6); 📼 8573-83780-3 (124 minutes: PAL). Includes documentary on the making of the film. Recorded 1997 ●

Winterreise lives on its own without any staging. The initially dubious Bostridge and Drake make that point at the start of the feature, their faces filling with dismay as Alden describes his seemingly hare-brained ideas to turn it into a melodrama about a crazed protagonist. It is implied in what follows that singer and pianist gained confidence in what Alden had in mind, while the director came to respect Bostridge's intelligence and dramatic gifts. Indeed, the project would have collapsed had not the tenor the ability to sear the soul as much visually as aurally. His piercing eyes, striking looks and age make him an ideal candidate for such an experiment.

Inspired by a disused mental asylum in north London, Alden and his designer, Ian MacNeil, create a huge, empty space, as desolate as the abandoned asylum itself, in which the beginning and end of the cycle are enacted. In-between, Bostridge is projected on to a white background, arrestingly so in the case of 'Die Krähe', where the singer is viewed from above by the crow with Bostridge spread-eagled on the floor below, an astonishing image, mirroring the bird's menace. Among the unforgettable shots are the picture of the forlorn shattered figure in 'Die Nebensonnen', which Alden and Bostridge agree has a mystic, religious aura to it, the lone protagonist seen at a distance in 'Das Wirtshaus', the singer seated back to back with the pianist in 'Mut'. Doubts arise only with the introduction during two songs of the unfaithful girl and her family, disturbing the vision of the lonely sufferer.

At the heart of the video lies Bostridge's silvery tone, special, highly individual intensity of utterance and identification with the man's desperate plight. Drake supports him with playing of equal insight. The sound, fairly closely miked, is excellent; the camerawork highly imaginative.

Tavener

Fall and Resurrection
Patricia Rozario *sop* **Michael Chance** *counterten*
Martyn Hill *ten* **Stephen Richardson** *bass* **BBC Singers; St Paul's Cathedral Choir; City of London Sinfonia / Richard Hickox**
Video Director **David Kremer**
Etcetera **DVD** KTCD102 (96 minutes: Region 0, in PAL and NTSC versions). Recorded live in 2000 Ⓕ ●

This could be called Tavener's *Creation*, an oratorio-like account of the Biblical tale beginning with a representation of primordial Chaos. It takes the story much further than Haydn, through Adam's fall to the Incarnation, ending in a 'Cosmic Dance of the Resurrection'. But, like Haydn's, this too is a warmly mature work, epitomising its composer's style and personality.

The première at St Paul's Cathedral in January 2000, recorded here, was broadcast on TV and radio and released on CD by Chandos soon after. The disc was hailed in *Gramophone* as 'a wonderful document of an extraordinary evening of music'. There is little cause to disagree. Tavener's richly exotic textures, all founded on variations of an austere Byzantine chant and leavened with arcane instruments such as the shofar, or ram's horn, Tibetan temple bowls and Arabic kaval flutes, are beautifully evoked by Hickox and his forces, especially the vocal soloists.

The main question is whether DVD adds anything; and we believe it does. Visually, St Paul's, with its muted Byzantine influences, makes a splendid backdrop for this piece, which is infused with dramatic instrumental conflicts and clashes. Director David Kremer exploits the cathedral's spectacular aspects and perspectives, with discreet *chiaroscuro* lighting to underline these, and the Dolby 5.1 surround soundtrack accordingly strengthens the sense of spaciousness without seeming unduly unnatural. Even if you videoed the broadcast, this is far superior. And the disc includes brief but useful introductions from Stephanie Hughes and Sir John himself, plus a half-hour interview. If you like Tavener, you need not hesitate.

Maria Callas *sop*

Maria Callas: A Documentary by John Ardoin
Franco Zefirelli *narr*
Bel Canto ▣ BCS0194 (117 minutes: ADD) Ⓜ
Recorded 1978. Includes bonus documentary, featuring Ardoin, Gobbi, Rescigno and Scotto, also recorded 1978 ●

The film begins with a newsreel of Callas's funeral in Paris, and it is not immediately apparent that it is to be more than an anthology of pious platitudes, oral and visual, assembled and marketed in the emotional floodtide following her then-recent death. Zefirelli is stationed in the auditorium of La Scala, where he can look toward the stage which 'still seems to reverberate with the sound of her voice'. Then we see Callas herself – but not herself, for this is her persona as gracious and glamorous purveyor of artistic truth. Then the witnesses arrive, starting with Menotti, who recalls an association with fear and, in her voice, 'something bitter'. This is more interesting, but instead of pursuing it the film moves on. From Rescigno comes 'a supremely dedicated performer', from Caballé 'Thank you, Maria, for coming to us,' and from Zefirelli 'She literally changed the face of opera.'

Yet in spite of the patchwork method and flaccid generalisations, the film does succeed in what were presumably its primary aims – to show the fascination of the woman and the artist, the interaction of the one with the other, and, in doing so, to move its audience with the strange mixture of glorious public achievement and deep personal unfulfilment. Stranger still, perhaps, is the stirring of so many conflicting reactions. In the midst of such insistent testimony, the film-footage of Callas 'in action' inevitably tests the claims. Does it truly support them? Is that filmed 'Vissi d'arte', for instance, really the work of a great operatic actress? Often it rather strengthens the view that with Callas, as with all great opera singers, most of the acting is done with the voice. And yet at the end we are left with her singing 'Ah, non credea mirarti' from *La sonnambula*, where the voice becomes frail and unsteady while the face is transfigured, infinitely touching. No: it's not a film to be missed, and the bonus footage sheds interesting light on its making, especially from the late John Ardoin, clearly one of its prime movers.

Opera

Beethoven

Fidelio
Gabriela Beňačková *sop* Leonore; **Josef Protschka** *ten* Florestan; **Monte Pederson** *bar* Don Pizarro; **Robert Lloyd** *bass* Rocco; **Marie McLaughlin** *sop* Marzelline; **Neill Archer** *ten* Jaquino; **Hans Tschammer** *bass-bar* Don Fernando; **Lynton Atkinson** *ten* First Prisoner; **Mark Beesley** *bar* Second Prisoner; **Royal Opera House Chorus and Orchestra, Covent Garden / Christoph von Dohnányi**
Video director **Derek Bailey.** *Stage director* **Adolf Dresen**
ArtHaus Musik **DVD** 100 074 Ⓕ
(129 minutes: Regions 2 and 5). ●

'Triumph! Triumph! Triumph!' as nasty Pizarro exultantly cries. He, of course, is in for a disappointment. Not so the listener and viewer of this performance, which is caught in fine sound and skilfully filmed. Pizarro will, for instance, have no place in the great festival of light that is the finale. Here the rejoicing is so powerful that we close down the video, turn off the television and go to bed with the surge and sequence of inspired creation fully in possession, convinced that in the whole of opera there is nothing to match it. That is the sign of a great *Fidelio*, and it means that, throughout, the proportions, structure and balance of the work have been rendered with clarity and conviction. That in turn means that the opening scene – the Marzelline-Jaquino duet and the solos which might seem to be from some other opera – has been integrated, so that the work is a journey from light into the blackest tunnel and out again into an infinitely greater light.

A prime contribution to the success of this process in the present performance is made by the portrayal of Rocco, the gaoler. Instead of the bumbling, coarse-grained character of convention, Robert Lloyd presents a full human being, a man with a rueful-realistic twinkle, and above all a loving father. This of itself guards against the alien introduction of comic opera, and helps to fashion the role so that even here our concern is with real humanity. Also, Rocco's scenes with Leonore and Pizarro carry a conviction in which Lloyd's warmth and natural dignity make a notable difference. Pizarro is here a fine, handsome presence whose inward ugliness is evident in the ruthlessness of expression. Florestan, by contrast, is a fat man of no romantic presence, his goodness and nobility matching his suffering.

Leonore is the radiant Beňačková, and she presents a problem. The camera reveals unsparingly a disguise which just possibly might pass in the theatre. It says much for her singing, and for something in the spirit of her performance, that the willing suspension of disbelief can prevail as well as it does. In all other respects (except perhaps in the pointless speculation as to why the date of these events should have been advanced by about a century) the visual element satisfies well; and musically, under Dohnányi's direction, this is a memorable and moving *Fidelio*.

Debussy

Pelléas et Mélisande

François Le Roux *bar* Pelléas; **Colette Alliot-Lugaz** *sop* Mélisande; **José Van Dam** *bar* Golaud; **Roger Soyer** *bass* Arkel; **Jocelyne Taillon** *mez* Geneviève; **Françoise Golfier** *sop* Yniold; **René Schirrer** *bar* Doctor; **Frank Morazanni** *bar* Shepherd; **Chorus and Orchestra of the Lyon Opera / Sir John Eliot Gardiner** *Stage director* **Pierre Strosser.** *Video director* **Jean-François Jung**

ArtHaus Musik **DVD** 100 100 (147 minutes: Regions 2/5). Recorded 1987 Ⓕ **OO**

This staging, first presented at the Lyon Opera in the mid-1980s, is Pierre Strosser's original concept of setting the whole action in a large drawing-room of a French château. Thus none of the intended settings materialise, Mélisande doesn't hang her hair from a balcony, there is no fountain and so on. Yet such is the magnetism of the performance and the conviction of the singers that these absent props to the action are hardly missed. A particular coup of the staging concerns the windows that open on to some brightly lit other world, into which Mélisande eventually departs. As the work is already part of a dream-like world, another layer of dreaming seems in order. On DVD, with superb lighting and camera work, the results are even more convincing than they were in the theatre.

Gardiner, who worked hard on the score to cleanse it of mistakes, conducts a translucent, firmly shaped account. His interpretation brings the piece even more clearly into a post-Wagnerian world of sound, and the Orchestra of the Lyon Opera play up to the hilt for their music director at that time. The cast, entirely Francophone, is one of the best assembled for recording the work, challenging the hegemony of the audio-only versions conducted by Desormière (EMI) and the earlier Ansermet set (Decca – nla).

The staging can be seen as being all Golaud's dream or nightmare, and José van Dam, in possibly his greatest role, is very much centrestage. He sings with all the sense of a tormented soul that it demands. His voice, in pristine form in 1987, is ideal for the part, as is his carefully crafted control of dynamics and text, and his concentrated acting. Le Roux, who was very much the Pelléas of the day, gives the role all the eager palpitation it calls for, and his tone has just the right texture. He, too, acts with gratifying discernment, as indeed does Alliot-Lugaz as Mélisande. She captures in voice and mien the character's beauty, fey charm and, above all, mystery. Soyer is a properly wise, world-weary Arkel, Taillon reads Geneviève's letter as to the manner born, Golfier finds the right boyish timbre for little Yniold, and Frank Morazanni's kindly, down-to-earth presence as the sane, supportive servant acts as an antidote to all the hangups of the principals.

Jung's video direction is positive, and the sound is well balanced. An experience not to be missed.

Handel

Ariodante

Ann Murray *mez* Ariodante; **Joan Rodgers** *sop* Ginevra; **Lesley Garrett** *sop* Dalinda; **Christopher Robson** *counterten* Polinesso; **Paul Nilon** *ten* Lurcanio; **Gwynne Howell** *bass* King of Scotland; **Mark Le Brocq** *ten* Odoardo; **English National Opera Chorus and Orchestra / Ivor Bolton** *Stage director* **David Alden.** *Video director* **Kriss Rusmanis**

Arthaus Musik **DVD** 100 064 (178 minutes: Regions 2, 3, 5). Recorded live in 1996 Ⓕ **O**

David Alden's staging of *Ariodante* was generally praised when it was first staged by WNO, a joint venture with ENO. This DVD is a recording of the much-admired revival at the ENO in 1996. Its appearance confirms the extraordinary perspicacity of Alden's production, which explains, from an almost Freudian viewpoint, the loves, hates, fears and fantasies of the principal characters so unerringly and deeply delineated in Handel's masterly score, in which aria after aria exposes new layers of emotional thrust and instability. At its heart is the unswerving, almost hysterical love of Ariodante for his royal bride Ginevra, herself bowled over by first love, then distraught when accused – wrongly – even by her father, of being a harlot. What that does to her psyche is arrestingly uncovered in Alden's treatment of her behaviour.

That Alden had willing accomplices in his devastating exposé of interior feelings is proved in Ann Murray's committed performance of the unhinged Ariodante. Murray displays a physical and vocal virtuosity only occasionally vitiated by a harsh tone. The great arias, 'Scherza infida' and 'Dopo notte' are just the climactic moments they should be. Joan Rodgers as Ginevra is hardly less impressive in her portrayal of the myriad feelings suggested by Handel and Alden.

Christopher Robson, as the villain Polinesso, is the very incarnation of evil lasciviousness, for which his edgy countertenor is not inappropriate. Lesley Garrett gives Dalinda just the right touch of vulnerability as she submits to Polinesso's wiles while being sexually captivated by him. Gwynne Howell is the upright King to the life. Ivor Bolton conducts a vital, well-played account of the score with modern strings sounding very much like their period counterparts. The BBC's Kriss Rusmanis catches the claustrophobia of Alden's enclosed world, capturing the agony and ecstasies of the plot as they happen. Almost three hours of gripping music-drama pass in a trice, helped by the unbroken sequence of DVD. The sound is commendable, the picture superb.

Janáček

Kát'a Kabanová

Nancy Gustafson *sop* Kát'a Kabanová; **Barry McCauley** *ten* Boris; **Felicity Palmer** *mez* Kabanicha; **Donald Adams** *bass* Dikoj; **Ryland Davies** *ten* Tichon; **John Graham-Hall** *ten* Kudrjáš; **Louise Winter** *mez* Varvara; **Robert Poulton** *bar* Kuligin; **Christine Bunning** *mez* Glaša; **Linda Ormiston** *mez* Fekluša; **Rachael Hallawell** *mez* Woman; **Christopher Ventris** *ten* Bystander

Stage director **Nikolaus Lehnhoff**. *Video director* **Derek Bailey**

Glyndebourne Festival Chorus and Orchestra / Sir Andrew Davis

ArtHaus Musik **DVD** 100 158 Ⓕ

(99 minutes: Regions 2 and 5). Recorded live in 1988

This is a transfer to DVD of a 1988 Virgin VHS. It houses an entirely recommendable staging by Lehnhoff for Glyndebourne with sets by Tobias Hoheisel derived from Russian art from the period of the story's genesis. The resulting brightly lit primary colours with no shadows provide an appropriate setting for Lehnhoff's stark, expressionist staging, although he misses the needed claustrophobia in the Act 3 scene where Káta reveals her adultery.

Lehnhoff directs his excellent cast with an astonishing ability to delineate their inner feelings, receiving the most positive response from Nancy Gustafson in the title-role. She presents, from her initial entry, an overwrought, highly impressionable girl frustrated beyond endurance by the casual attentions of her husband Tichon and longing for the erotic charge offered by the attractive Boris. When she finally capitulates to his advances, she mirrors the sense of release tinged with guilt evinced in the music. Her singing is firm, soaring, vibrant.

Palmer is the very picture of buttoned-up severity as Kabanicha. Her command over Káta and Tichon is terrible to behold. Davies suggests Tichon's lack of backbone. McCauley's Boris conveys the man's ability to infatuate the repressed Káta. His tenor is keen, though under strain in the upper register. The supporting roles are all faithfully taken. Andrew Davis brings out all the passion and anguish in the wonderful score. Picture and sound are an improvement on the VHS counterpart.

Mozart

Don Giovanni

Sir Thomas Allen *bar* Don Giovanni; **Carolyn James** *sop* Donna Anna; **Carol Vaness** *sop* Donna Elvira; **Kjell Magnus Sandve** *ten* Don Ottavio; **Ferruccio Furlanetto** *bass* Leporello; **Andrea Rost** *sop* Zerlina; **Reinhard Dorn** *bass* Masetto; **Matthias Hölle** *bass* Commendatore; **Cologne Opera Chorus; Cologne Gürzenich Orchestra / James Conlon**

Stage director **Michael Hampe.** *Video director* **José Montes-Bequer**

ArtHaus Musik **DVD** 100 020 (173 minutes: Ⓕ

Region 0). Recorded live in 1991 ●

For all those tired of and/or irritated by modern, psychological stagings of *Don Giovanni*, this traditional yet highly intelligent Cologne production will come as a blessed relief. The staging, by Michael Hampe, derives from the Cologne Opera in 1991, at a time when he was intendant at the house.

In Hampe's own dark-hued, spare and consistent sets, the drama moves swiftly to its appointed end, and the only disappointment is his failure to make Giovanni's descent into Hell at all threatening. Hampe is adept at giving his characters just enough to do, in terms of *Personenregie*, without taking them beyond the bounds of the feasible in terms of acting while singing. In the title-role, Allen probably needed no coaching at all, as by 1991 he was acknowledged as the leading Giovanni of his day, perhaps any day. He confirms that reputation here in an interpretation that blends magnetism, single-minded purpose (seduction) and cruelty in about equal measures. His murderous intents towards the Commendatore and in Act 2 towards Masetto, and his beating and threatening of Leporello all exhibit the idea of the Don as near-psychopath.

Allen sings the role with total command of every nuance in aria, ensemble and recitative. It is an absolutely riveting performance, finely seconded by Furlanetto's Leporello, also alive to every aspect of his part's text and movement. As a Giovanni himself elsewhere, he knows exactly how to be his master's alter ego, and his command of his native language is, of course, exemplary.

Nobody else in the cast achieves quite that level of distinction, although Carol Vaness, hitherto an Anna, sings Elvira with spirit and acts convincingly within a given convention. Her warm, firm soprano is equal to all the demands Mozart places on it. Carolyn James is a properly distraught Anna and sings with some flair, but her largish voice hardens uncomfortably under pressure. The Ottavio is adequate, no more, as is true of the Masetto and Commendatore, but Rost's youthful, appealing Zerlina is worth watching and hearing, especially in her encounter with Giovanni, where she exactly evinces the girl's uncertain, vulnerable reactions.

Conlon conducts a direct, unfussy reading at

sensible speeds, very much in agreement with the action taking place above him, and his orchestra plays with grace and drive as required. The picture and sound are exemplary.

Offenbach

La belle Hélène

Vesselina Kasarova *mez* Hélène; **Steve Davislim** *ten* Achille; **Deon van der Walt** *ten* Paris; **Oliver Widmer** *bar* Agamemnon; **Ruben Amoretti** *ten* Ajax I; **Cheyne Davidson** *bar* Ajax II; **Ruth Rohner** *sop* Bacchis; **Carlos Chausson** *bar* Calchas; **Volker Vogel** *ten* Ménélas; **Liliana Nichiteanu** *mez* Oreste; **Jakob Baumann** *bar* Slave; **Zurich Opera House Chorus and Orchestra / Nikolaus Harnoncourt**
Stage director **Helmut Lohner.** *Video director* **Hartmut Schottler**
Arthaus Musik **DVD** 100 086 (124 minutes: Region 0) Recorded live in 1997 Ⓕ

This Zurich production from 1997 fully enters into the spirit of Offenbach's satirical romp, hardly ever stepping over into farce. Everything is at once disciplined, contained and at the same time appropriately zany under the observant stage direction of Helmut Lohner. He engaged Jean-Charles de Castellbajac to design the fantastic, multi-coloured costumes, which add greatly to the viewer's pleasure. Certain liberties are taken with the original scenario but the spoken and sung text is very little altered.

Then there is Harnoncourt in the pit to ensure that the musical values are as exemplary as the visual ones. His Zurich band is of a suitably small enough size to allow for all the instrumental detail to be clearly delineated. Strings use little vibrato. Rhythms, as always with this conductor, are precise and taut, tempos measured but never too slow. The composer's innate wit is to the fore. In sum, the score sounds fresh-minted.

The polyglot cast, speaking and singing excellent French, enjoys its collective self, headed by Kasarova's languidly erotic Helen. She sings her music in a suitably suggestive manner, flaunting her vocal as much as her physical attributes. Deon van der Walt, a lively Paris, sings with the sweetness and sensitivity of the best French tenors of the past in this genre. The comic roles are all enthusiastically taken, but among the lesser parts Liliana Nichiteanu steals the honours with her cheeky Oreste, sung in a firmly projected, attractive mezzo and with a glint in her eye – surely a star in the making.

Add perceptive video direction by Hartmut Schottler and superb sound and you have what amounts to an outright winner.

Poulenc

Les dialogues des Carmélites

Didier Henry *bar* Marquis de la Force; **Anne Sophie Schmidt** *sop* Blanche de la Force; **Laurence Dale** *ten* Chevalier de la Force; **Léonard Pezzino** *ten* L'Aumônier; **Christophe Fel** *bass* Le geôlier; **Nadine Denize** *mez* Madame de Croissy; **Valérie Millot** *sop* Madame Lidoine; **Hedwig Fassbender** *mez* Mère Marie; **Patricia Petibon** *sop* Soeur Constance; **Michèle Besse** *contr* Mère Jeanne; **Allison Elaine Cook** *mez* Soeur Mathilde; **Ivan Ludlow** *ten* L'Officier; **Vincent de Rooster** *ten* First Commissaire; **Merih Kazbek** *bass* Second Commissaire; **Yves Ernst** *bar* Thierry; **Jenz Kiertzner** *bar* Javelinot; **Rhine National Opera Chorus; Strasbourg Philharmonic Orchestra / Jan Latham-König**
Stage director **Marthe Keller.** *Video director* **Don Kent**
ArtHaus Musik **DVD** 100 004 (149 minutes: Region 0). Recorded live in 1999 Ⓕ

Marthe Keller's staging of Poulenc's austere, deeply eloquent opera about the martyrdom of a group of nuns during the French Revolution was produced at the Opéra du Rhin early in 1999. It came to the Proms later that year in a semi-staged form, and was much liked. Keller's simple ideas march precisely with the intentions of the original, the plain sets and economy of movement mirroring the direct simplicity of Poulenc's beautifully wrought score.

This approach places the responsibility on the singers to create the mood of dedication, the fears, the uncertainties of the nuns and finally their implacable courage as they go to their deaths. Every artist here performs in a wholly dedicated fashion as part of a well-tutored ensemble, no one more so than Anne Sophie Schmidt in depicting the psychological struggle and vulnerability of the central character, Blanche de la Force. With her greatly expressive features and her refined voice, Schmidt's portrayal is starkly moving. In complete contrast is the bright, radiant, perfectly sung Constance of Petibon. Among the older members of the Convent community, Nadine Denize plays her two scenes as the Old Prioress with the authority and concentration they call for, going to her death as she loses her faith in an agonising bout of self-understanding. Hedwig Fassbender is all stern authority as Mother Marie, although one senses sympathy behind the harsh exterior, which is how it should be in this part. Valérie Millot is outwardly more sympathetic and warm as the new Prioress, Madame Lidoine, who instils courage in her charges when it comes to the crunch and, one by one, they go to the guillotine.

Latham-König conducts a clear, unfussy account of the score, which is finely played. Video direction, sound and picture quality are admirable. This is one of the most worthwhile opera performances yet to appear in the new format.

Puccini

La bohème

Mirella Freni *sop* Mimì; **Luciano Pavarotti** *ten* Rodolfo; **Sandra Pacetti** *sop* Musetta; **Gino Quilico** *bar* Marcello; **Nicolai Ghiaurov** *bass* Colline; **Stephen Dickson** *bar* Schaunard; **Italo Tajo** *bass* Benoit; Alcindoro; **Chorus and Orchestra of the San Francisco Opera / Tiziano Severini**
Stage Director **Francesca Zambello.** *Video Director* **Brian Large**
ArtHaus Musik **DVD** 100 046 (116 minutes: Region 0). Recorded live in 1988 Ⓕ

This recording received a complimentary review from John Steane when it appeared in LaserDisc format back in May 1993. One can share his enthusiasm for the restraint and experience of Freni and Pavarotti, who (even in 1988, when the performance took place) didn't look like the young lovers predicated by the libretto, but who made up for it with the 'rich humanity' (JBS's words) of their portrayals, although both evinced the occasional moment of strain that confirms they were no longer in the full flush of vocal youth. Ghiaurov, at 59, remains a tower of strength as Colline, although his voice sounds a shade rusty. These veterans tend to show up the relatively casual, upfront performances of the remaining singers. The conductor is sympathetic to the needs of singers and score.

The staging is traditional in the best sense, even if it cannot rival the great Zeffirelli/La Scala production, also with Freni, which is still available on VHS conducted by Karajan. Brian Large has his cameras in the right place at the right time, with a fine balance of distant and close-up shots. The sound has plenty of atmosphere, but, as with many LaserDiscs and DVDs, the voices aren't given enough prominence.

Rossini

L'italiana in Algeri
Nuccia Focile *sop* Elvira; **Rudolf Hartmann** *bass* Haly; **Doris Soffel** *mez* Isabella; **Robert Gambill** *ten* Lindoro; **Günter von Kannen** *bass* Mustafà; **Enric Serra** *bar* Taddeo; **Susan McLean** *mez* Zulma; **Bulgarian Male Chorus, Sofia; Stuttgart Radio Symphony Orchestra / Ralf Weikert**
Stage director **Michael Hampe.** *Video director* **Claus Viller**
Arthaus Musik **DVD** 100 120 (117 minutes: Region 0). Recorded live in 1987 Ⓕ ⭘

Bravi tutti! For a start, the house and stage: just the right size. And then, comprehensively, the whole team, with every aspect of the production delightfully cared for. Ralf Weikert conducts with zestful elegance, and the excellent players respond. The chorus is alert and precise, the camera catching never a lifeless face and several very funny ones. Each of the soloists fits the part, working both as individuals and as an ensemble. The comic roles are played amusingly without clowning. Doris Soffel as Isabella has charm and dignity. The range and runs are well managed, though she is probably best in the lyrical phrases of the cavatina 'Per lui che adoro' and the aristocracy of her bearing in 'Pensa alla patria'. The Mustafà, Günter von Kannen, specialises in comic roles but probably not in rapid passage-work, of which there is much here; nevertheless, his weighty, sonorous voice establishes character, and his expressive mouth and eyes do the rest. And a great asset is the American tenor, Robert Gambill, a real Rossini singer, a lively actor and an appropriately good-looking young man.

But for once the producer deserves top billing: he does his rightful job extremely well and doesn't exceed it. All the staging is effective, graceful and confident. With sets and costumes that are a distinct pleasure to look at, Michael Hampe's production is never short of good ideas and never imposes 'concepts'. It puts faith in Rossini, the performers and the audience, and provides delightful entertainment whether in the theatre or with excellent sound on the DVD.

Shostakovich

Lady Macbeth of the Mtsensk district
Galina Vishnevskaya *sop* **Katerina** Izmailova; **Nicolai Gedda** *ten* Sergei; **Dimiter Petkov** *bass* Boris Izmailov; **Werner Krenn** *ten* Zinovi Izmailov; **Robert Tear** *ten* Shabby Peasant; **Taru Valjakka** *sop* Aksinya; **Martyn Hill** *ten* Teacher; **Leonard Andrzej Mróz** *bass* Priest; **Aage Haugland** *bass* Police Sergeant; **Birgit Finnilä** *mez* Sonyetka; **Alexander Malta** *bass* Old Convict; **Leslie Fyson** *ten* Millhand; Officer; **Scott Emerson** *ten* Porter; **John Noble** *bar* Steward; **Colin Appleton** *ten* Coachman; Foreman I; **Alan Byers** *ten* Foreman II; **James Lewington** *ten* Foreman III; **Oliver Broome** *bass* Policeman; **Edgar Fleet** *ten* Drunken Guest; **David Beavan** *bass* Sentry; **Linda Richardson** *mez* Woman Convict; **Ambrosian Opera Chorus; London Philharmonic Orchestra / Mstislav Rostropovich**
Film director **Petr Weigl**
Carlton Entertainment **DVD** ID5655CLDVD (100 minutes: Region 1). Ⓕ ⭘

Petr Weigl returns to form with this remarkable realisation of Shostakovich's scarifying drama. Filming in his native Czech Republic, as usual with actors lip-synching singers, he nevertheless brings its nasty and brutish setting to vivid life. Only the Siberian trek looks a little milder than traditional depictions, but it is accurate enough. The atmospheric photography of the Izmailov farm's barren, lamplit rooms and bathhouse adds a *verismo* dimension to the music's quasi-expressionist force. You really feel a place like this would breed adultery and impulsive murder. Nonetheless, it's noticeable that not even the athletically explicit sexual episodes have anything like the queasily pornographic impact of Shostakovich's whooping trombones; no wonder Stalin's bourgeois soul was shocked. The soundtrack is the classic Rostropovich recording, generally preferable to Myung-Whun Chung's more recent version with Maria Ewing (DG).

Its splendid pace and vivid playing suit the film, as do its lively effects, though it is substantially cut. The generally excellent actors do their best with the limitations of lip-synch, no doubt assisted by Czech's kinship with Russian. The Katerina is youngish, nervy and intense, tragically ripe pickings for Sergei's – and indeed her own – passion, but Vishnevskaya's maturely resonant dramatic soprano sits uneasily on her. The Sergei melds better with Gedda's bright tones to suggest the ruthless predator beneath the boyish charm, and Aksinya, old Izmailov and the Old Convict are splendidly portrayed. The studio acoustic is too evident, especially with the clarity of DVD mastering, to make the outdoor scenes convincing. But they achieve their effect through the music nonetheless. Highly recommended.

J Strauss II

Die Fledermaus

Pamela Coburn *sop* Rosalinde; **Janet Perry** *sop* Adele; **Eberhard Waechter** *bar* Eisenstein; **Josef Hopferwieser** *ten* Alfred; **Wolfgang Brendel** *bar* Doctor Falke; **Brigitte Fassbaender** *mez* Prince Orlofsky; **Benno Kusche** *bar* Frank; **Ferry Gruber** *ten* Doctor Blind; **Irene Steinbeisser** *sop* Ida; **Franz Muxeneder** *spkr* Frosch; **Ivan Unger** *spkr* Ivan

Bavarian State Orchestra and Opera Chorus / Carlos Kleiber

Stage director **Otto Schenk**. *Video director* **Brian Large**

DG **DVD** 073 007-9GH (155 minutes: Picture format 4:3: Sound 2.0: Region 0). Recorded live in 1987 Ⓕ

Carlos Kleiber is for many the outstanding Johann Strauss conductor of our time, finding grace and subtlety in the music that evades all others. His audio recording of *Die Fledermaus* (DG) is acknowledged as nigh perfect, spoilt only by its bizarre casting of Ivan Rebroff as Orlofsky.

Happily there's no such drawback here, and indeed there could scarcely be anyone better than Brigitte Fassbaender to portray the youthful Russian prince. The only real concern is with veteran baritone Eberhard Waechter as Eisenstein, giving the suggestion of an elderly roué rather than more youthful high spirits. Reviewing the LaserDisc issue (DG), reservations were expressed about the two leading ladies; but here it is hard not to be won over by both their singing and their looks.

Günther Schneider-Siemssen's lavish sets are magnificent, and Otto Schenk's staging quite superb, with every movement apt to both music and situation. The riotous ballet sequence (Strauss's *Unter Donner und Blitz*) justly stops the show. Brian Large's film direction is perfectly judged, and the Act 2 finale, with Kleiber joyfully sharing the expressions of fraternity, is a particular moment to cherish. In Act 3, Franz Muxeneder's comic Frosch completes the feeling of Viennese *Gemütlichkeit*. One really cannot imagine a more winning performance.

Die Fledermaus[a].

Bishop Home, sweet home[b]. **Cilea** L'arlesiana[c] – E la solita storia. **Rossini** Semiramide[d] – Serbami ognor sì fido. **Saint-Saëns** Samson et Dalila[e] – Mon coeur s'ouvre à ta voix **Verdi** La traviata[f] – Parigi, o cara

[a]**Nancy Gustafson** *sop* Rosalinde; [a]**Judith Howarth** *sop* Adele; [a]**Louis Otey** *bar* Eisenstein; [a]**Bonaventura Bottone** *ten* Alfred; [a]**Anthony Michaels-Moore** *bar* Doctor Falke; [a]**Jochen Kowalski** *counterten* Prince Orlofsky; [a]**Eric Garrett** *bar* Frank; [a]**John Dobson** *ten* Doctor Blind; [a]**Glenys Groves** *sop* Ida; [a]**John Sessions** *spkr* Frosch; [a]**Peter Archer** *spkr* Ivan; [bdf]**Dame Joan Sutherland** *sop* [cf]**Luciano Pavarotti** *ten* [de]**Marilyn Horne** *mez*

Royal Opera House Chorus and Orchestra, Covent Garden / Richard Bonynge

Stage director **John Cox**. *Video director* **Humphrey Burton**

ArtHaus Musik ② **DVD** 100 134 (197 minutes: Region 2 and 5). Recorded live in 1990 Ⓕ

'Oh, what a night!' sings everybody on stage as Prince Orlofsky's ballroom takes leave of its earthly confines and sails for the happy isles borne on a tide of waltzes and a sea of champagne. It's always a good moment in *Die Fledermaus*, and this particular night was special. Most of those present at Covent Garden had seen a few New Year's Eves in their time, but never a one like this on December 31, 1990. And never, surely, has a prima donna been treated to such a stage party for her farewell. Dame Joan Sutherland sang that night for the last time in the house where she had made her début in 1952. Somebody had a brainwave when they thought of this as the occasion for what might otherwise have been a rather tearful event: Joan and two of her most illustrious partners of many performances would themselves be guests at Orlofsky's party in Act 2. Husband Richard Bonynge would conduct, so the party would therefore be complete. The production did not have to be built round them as it existed already, a brilliant item in the house repertoire. The guests slot in nicely at the moment when the revels are at their height. And there was New Year's Eve to celebrate.

If the plan had a drawback it was one that concerned the opera itself. Act 3 of *Fledermaus* is always something of an anticlimax, and, with a celebrity recital thrown in, the middle act could seem to end with chords that cried 'Follow that!'. Happily, the production has a good move in store when, for the Finale, the backdrop for the prison scene goes up to reveal Orlofsky's ballroom aglow and once more ready to receive its guests. As for Act 1, it is extremely probable that the audiences at home will spend at least a part of it marvelling at the quality of sound and sight offered by the new medium of DVD.

Without in the least dominating, the orchestra here are present with a quite remarkable immediacy and naturalness. The singers, too, are caught very faithfully. What so often has not been reflected accurately in recorded sound is the distinction between voices that are pure and those in which the purity is compromised. Here, as on that occasion in the opera house, the outstanding voices among the cast were (in respect of pure tone) those of Judith Howarth and Anthony Michaels-Moore. Among the three celebrities, gallantly as both ladies sang, it was (and is on the film) Pavarotti whose voice had retained its quality. The film also brought back memories of the great beauty, refinement and, in the climax, real Italian passion of Pavarotti's solo on that occasion, the 'solita storia' from *L'arlesiana*.

There is also plenty to watch, and with enjoyment. All on stage, including the chorus, act well, and Julia Trevelyan Oman's sets are the kind that rejoice in inspection by the cameras. Humphrey Burton has supervised the filming so that the home viewer has the most privileged seat of all. Still, no after-viewing can quite catch the passing moment on such an occasion, and when, at the end, a shower of gold rained down from the dome, it might magically have been Zeus's very own.

R Strauss

Elektra
Eva Marton *sop* Elektra; **Brigitte Fassbaender** *mez* Klytemnestra; **Cheryl Studer** *sop* Chrysothemis; **Franz Grundheber** *bar* Orestes; **James King** *ten* Aegisthus; **Goran Simic** *bass* Tutor; **Waltraud Winsauer** *mez* Confidante; **Noriko Sasaki** *sop* Trainbearer; **Wilfried Gahmlich** *ten* Young Servant; **Claudio Otelli** *bass-bar* Old Servant; **Gabriele Lechner** *sop* Overseer; **Margarita Lilowa** *mez* First Maidservant; **Gabriele Sima** *mez* Second Maidservant; **Margareta Hintermeier** *contr* Third Maidservant; **Brigitte Poschner-Klebel** *sop* Fourth Maidservant; **Joanna Borowska** *sop* Fifth Maidservant; **Vienna State Opera Chorus and Orchestra / Claudio Abbado**
Stage director **Harry Kupfer.** *Video director* **Brian Large**
ArtHaus Musik **DVD** 100 048 (109 minutes: DDD) Ⓕ
Recorded live in 1989 ●●

This is an enjoyable performance, if that is the right word for *Elektra*'s gruesome drama, of Strauss's opera (taken from the first night of a new production at the Vienna State Opera in 1989), still one of the most sensational scores of the last century, even more than its laserdisc incarnation, not least because of Harry Kupfer's superlative direction. He may have conceived the work in even more lurid terms than its creators Hofmannsthal and Strauss intended, but the principals' psychotic behaviour is so convincingly enacted that we are carried into the soul of all their personal tortures of the mind. Elektra herself is a determined, raddled, single-minded harridan, lording it over sister and mother, a portrayal Eva Marton carries out with a deal of conviction, once one accepts the judder in her voice. Chrysothemis becomes a writhing, overwrought, frustrated figure, at one stage seeming to fake an orgasm, all of which Studer conveys with much emphasis on physical contact with her sister. She sings the taxing role with opulent tone and soaring phraseology.

Physicality is also of the essence in Fassbaender's study of guilt and inner disintegration as a Klytemnestra of intriguing complexity, yet she still somehow manages to suggest the character's feminine attraction. This portrayal alone makes this DVD essential viewing. Grundheber is the avenging Orestes to the life, with savagely piercing eyes and implacable tone. King is a properly futile paramour. In the activity of the extras, and such episodes as the butchering of Aegisthus and Chrysothemis wallowing in his blood-stained cloak, very little is left to the imagination. This is an enclosed world where licence and human sacrifices, unbridled in their ferocity, have taken over from order and humanity, and that was surely Kupfer's intention, so that Orestes' arrival has even more of a cleansing effect than usual.

In the pit, Abbado conducts with a single-minded intensity, constantly aware of the score's brutal and tragic aspects, and he procures playing of tremendous concentration from the Vienna Philharmonic. Although the staging takes place in Stygian gloom, you can discern more of its detail in this reincarnation on DVD, which has the added advantage of containing the whole opera on a single disc.

The booklet is exemplary in giving the necessary information on work and performance, but, unfortunately, the numbering of the tracks is throughout one step behind what is offered on screen. But, unless and until the Decca Friedrich/Böhm version reaches DVD, this is a version to buy for its absorbing, fully integrated view of Strauss's masterpiece.

Der Rosenkavalier
Dame Felicity Lott *sop* Die Feldmarschallin; **Anne Sofie von Otter** *mez* Octavian; **Kurt Moll** *bass* Baron Ochs; **Barbara Bonney** *sop* Sophie; **Gottfried Hornik** *bar* Faninal; **Anna Gonda** *mez* Annina; **Heinz Zednik** *ten* Valzacchi; **Olivera Miljakovic** *sop* Leitmetzerin; **Wolfgang Bankl** *bass* Notary; **Peter Wimberger** *bass-bar* Police Commissioner; **Waldemar Kmentt** *ten* Marschallin's Majordomo; **Franz Kasemann** *ten* Faninal's Majordomo; **Keith Ikaia-Purdy** *ten* Singer; **Vienna State Opera Chorus and Orchestra / Carlos Kleiber**
Stage director **Otto Schenk.** *Film director* **Horant H Hohlfield**
DG ② **DVD** 073 008-9GH2 Ⓕ
(193 minutes: Region 0). ●

That unpredictable spark of brilliance, Kleiber, rarely records, but he has made two video *Rosenkavalier*s, both excellent. If this is marginally less successful than his earlier, Munich version (DG), it still has much in its favour, in particular two of the three pivotal roles. Felicity Lott does not have the refulgent vocal power of Gwyneth Jones in Munich, but she commands the Straussian style, 'float' and all, and is much the finer actress. She creates a livelier, more humorous but also more convincingly vulnerable Marschallin, her fears and final renunciation deeply felt. Despite his mellow characterisation Manfred Jungwirth's raspingly inadequate voice handicaps the Munich set. Moll is cavernously secure from high F to low E and every bit as idiomatic, an aristocratic ox whose boorishness springs more from sublime narcissism than rustic ill-breeding. Von Otter is a convincingly boyish Octavian, valiant but gawky, and a hilariously toothy Mariandel. Her Mozartian voice is fresher than Munich's Brigitte Fassbaender, but she lacks the power to deliver the Rose with quite the right soaring beauty. Bonney's pretty young Sophie displays the finest voice on stage. The Valzacchi, Faninal and Commissioner are excellent; Annina, the Tenor and the Leitmetzerin less so.

Kleiber's conducting is the most constant element: lively, swift, careful in dynamics, incisive in detail – especially effective with Lott in Act 1's soliloquies. He never pours on lush sentiment, yielding champagne rather than whipped cream, and superbly so; the orchestra is superior.

Otto Schenk handles both stagings well, although this Marschallin's bedchamber looks rather drab. The video direction is less sure, especially in cutting away distractingly to highlight Kleiber's freeform conducting. As well as visual clarity and optional subtitles, DVD greatly improves the originally disappointing sound. Strongly recommended.

Verdi

Aida

Maria Chiara *sop* Aida; **Ghena Dimitrova** *sop* Amneris; **Luciano Pavarotti** *ten* Radames; **Juan Pons** *bar* Amonasro; **Nicolai Ghiaurov** *bass* Ramfis; **Paata Burchuladze** *bass* King; **Ernesto Gavazzi** *ten* Messenger; **Francesca Garbi** *mez* Priestess; **Chorus and Orchestra of La Scala, Milan / Lorin Maazel**

Stage director **Luca Ronconi**

Video director **Derek Bailey**

Arthaus Musik ② **DVD** 100 058 (160 minutes: Regions 2/5/6). Recorded in 1985 Ⓕ

Aida returned to La Scala in 1985 after a long break with this imaginative production by Luca Ronconi. Decadence is the theme of the interiors, in a mode portrayed by turn-of-the-century orientalist painters such as Alma-Tadema. The Triumphal scene, by contrast, shows a mobile, flexible Egypt arising from the bowels of the earth as if it had just been brought to light by archaeologists, though its full impact is hard to discern when the video director seldom allows us time to see the scene as a whole. Act 3 by the Nile successfully evokes night-time heat against an azure background and features a reed boat.

Maazel's conducting is efficient, somewhat inflexible, but gains enormously in conviction in Acts 3 and 4 when the work itself really catches fire. By 1985 Chiara's exemplary style and refined phraseology were beginning to be undermined by wear on her tone – she is heard to better advantage on an NVC video (A/97) recorded four years earlier at Verona – but she remains an exemplary Verdian even when her acting looks a shade old-fashioned. Dimitrova is a grand, vocally imposing Amneris (at a later performance she became the Aida) of the old school – and that's enough to convince me of her worth.

Pavarotti's dignified ardour and pathos as Radames is rather moving in its simplicity. Though his basically lyric voice was always stretched by the role, he is here in sovereign voice throughout and rightly acclaimed by the audience. His duets with Chiara and Dimitrova in Acts 3 and 4 are the performance highlights. Those wanting this souvenir of him on stage will not be disappointed. Pons sings with power and excellent definition as Amonasro, but his acting is rudimentary. Ghiaurov is a rusty Ramphis.

Derek Bailey's video direction isn't quite as fluent as it ought to be. The sound is superb, catching the grateful acoustics of the theatre. Although we await the even better-sung Verona performance's transfer to DVD, this one boasts a cast that could not be matched today.

Don Carlos

Roberto Alagna *ten* Don Carlos; **Karita Mattila** *sop* Elisabeth de Valois; **Waltraud Meier** *mez* Eboli; **Thomas Hampson** *bar* Rodrigue; **José van Dam** *bass-bar* Philippe II; **Eric Halfvarson** *bass-bar* Grand Inquisitor; **Csaba Airizer** *bass* Monk; **Anat Efraty** *sop* Thibault; **Scot Weir** *ten* Comte de Lerme; Herald; **Donna Brown** *sop* Voice from Heaven; **Chorus of the Théâtre du Châtelet, Paris; Orchestre de Paris / Antonio Pappano**

Stage director **Luc Bondy**

Video director **Yves André Hubert**

NVC Arts **DVD** 0630-16318-2 (211 minutes: Regions 2-6). Recorded live in 1996 Ⓕ

This performance appeared on VHS back in March 1997. On a new, wide-screen television, it makes a far more arresting effect (on VHS the top and bottom of the picture were cut off because of the wide-screen format). The action seems to be happening in the room with you. That is due not only to the format but also to director Luc Bondy's wish to portray the personal relationships, the characters' trials and tribulations in the most intimate manner. In contrast to most stagings of Verdi's epic, this one turns all but the outdoor scenes, mainly the Inquisition, into almost a domestic drama.

For better or worse, the principals seem very modern. With the exception of Thomas Hampson as Rodrigue, sporting a huge Charles II-like wig, the singers appear with their own hair or lack of it. José van Dam, a magnificent and moving Philippe II, does sometimes remind one of an out-of-sorts bank manager rather than a ruler of an empire, with his troubled wife, in the attractive person and voice of Mattila, as workaday Queen. Charisma is excluded by this interpretation. The relationship of Carlos and Rodrigue, obviously a very close one, is a touchy-feely affair, one that Alagna, in a sincere, beautifully sung assumption, and a palpitating Thomas Hampson, execute with flair. The Grand Inquisitor, in Halvarson's superbly toad-like form stalks his prey, the King, with relentless menace, a truly formidable fellow. As ever, Meier is not content with conventional acting: her Eboli is a scheming and seductive presence, consoling us with the intensity of her singing with a voice a shade light for her part. Indeed, on re-appraising the musical side of the performance, which was recorded live at the Châtelet in Paris, it strikes you that all the voices are a degree lighter than we are used to in the piece, but that suits the French text, giving an ease and fluidity to the vocal line that is, in truth, its own justification.

Even more impressive on re-hearing is Pappano's conducting, alive to every nuance of the long work yet aware of its overall structure. In the new medium the clarity and immediacy of the picture is arresting. The sound, though a shade soft in focus, is a great improvement on its 'ordinary' video counterpart. Owners of DVD players who want to add this unforgettable work to their collection need not hesitate – provided they can see it on a wide screen.

La traviata
Angela Gheorghiu *sop* Violetta; **Frank Lopardo** *ten* Alfredo; **Leo Nucci** *bar* Germont; **Leah-Marian Jones** *mez* Flora; **Gillian Knight** *mez* Annina; **Robin Leggate** *ten* Gastone; **Richard Van Allan** *bass* Baron; **Roderick Earle** *bass* Marquis; **Mark Beesley** *bar* Doctor; **Neil Griffiths** *ten* Giuseppe; **Bryan Secombe** *bass* Messenger; **Rodney Gibson** *ten* Servant; **Chorus and Orchestra of the Royal Opera House, Covent Garden / Sir Georg Solti**
Stage director **Richard Eyre**
Video directors **Humphrey Burton and Peter Maniura**
Decca **DVD** 071 431-9DH (135 minutes: Region O) Ⓕ
Recorded live in 1994

This is the classic performance that cleared TV schedules and launched Gheorghiu to superstardom. Now the glamour of the occasion has receded a little, the performance can be assessed as a whole. It still stands up extremely well. The 29-year-old remains a gripping heroine, remarkably beautiful personally and vocally, characterised with an appropriately febrile, nervy intensity. Recording emphasises the beat in her voice, and some unsteadiness under pressure, as at the end of 'Sempre libera', but her sheer beauty of tone overrides such nitpicking. The other star is Solti, in his first *Traviata*, underpinning her passion with his own, combining tautly propulsive rhythmic control with a clarity and melting tenderness, brought out in excellent orchestral playing.

Other performers don't quite reach this level. Alfredo in these pre-Alagna days is Frank Lopardo, also a handsome presence with a fine but rather nasal tone and stiff delivery, his manner occasionally a touch arrogant. Nucci is a vocally unsteady and rather lacklustre Germont, but the lesser roles could use his Italianate authority. The chorus is in good voice. The superb DVD picture captures the shadowy richness of Richard Eyre's straightforward production but can't disguise the functional stage set. The surround soundtrack is disappointingly boomy; the stereo track much crisper.

This knocks spots off its only DVD rival, the tacky La Fenice staging under Carlo Rizzi with Edita Gruberová's uncharismatic Violetta. The Glyndebourne video (Universal) not yet on DVD, offers a deeper production, but it still can't match this for excitement.

La traviata
Edita Gruberová *sop* Violetta; **Neil Shicoff** *ten* Alfredo; **Giorgio Zancanaro** *bar* Germont; **Mariana Pentcheva** *mez* Flora; **Antonella Trevisan** *mez* Annina; **Max-René Cosotti** *ten* Gastone; **Orazio Mori** *bass* Baron; **Paolo Orecchia** *bass* Marquis; **Francesco Musini** *bass* Doctor; **Paolo Zizich** *ten* Giuseppe; **Giovanni Antonini** *bass* Messenger; **Adriano Tomaello** *ten* Servant; **Chorus and Orchestra of La Fenice, Venice / Carlo Rizzi**
Stage director **Pier Luigi Pizzi**
Video director **Derek Bailey**
NVC Arts **DVD** 4509 92409-2 (130 minutes: Regions 2-6). Recorded live in 1992 Ⓕ

A moving and memorable *Traviata*, more so than the sound recording on Teldec with the same principals and conductor, who is a relatively weak element in both. Rizzi favours slow speeds, but that is not the trouble. There is something nerveless, unresponsive, about his handling of this score which is itself continually changing in mood and impulse. The great ensemble ending Act 2, for instance, finely sung and well acted, is almost lifeless in musical direction. The playing itself is of a good standard and well-recorded, but the great merits of the performance lie elsewhere.

One of these is that it has a real Alfredo: that is, an Alfredo who is an individual, and an interesting one – not at all a stock operatic hero, but a bespectacled young man, rather naive and vulnerable, utterly sincere, with a gift for happiness and an unpreparedness for loss. Schicoff is perhaps strangely matched with this Violetta, who is clearly older than him and too sharp of feature and homely of manner for her role of beautiful and brilliant courtesan. What she is inwardly, though, Gruberová catches to the life: and the further into the opera we go, the clearer it becomes that she knows this woman as from the inside. Her scene with Germont *père* is touchingly and painfully convincing as, stage by stage, she sees her way ahead, the sacrifice becoming steadily more absolute. In the last scene, acting and singing are so powerfully fused that at the end it is quite difficult to shake off the tragedy and join in the curtain-calls.

As in the CD recording, Gruberová sings a brilliant 'Sempre libera' and an 'Addio del passato' of rare beauty. In the entire role no phrase is given without some evidence of imagination and intelligence. Schicoff certainly matches her well in this respect, and his solo (shorn of its cabaletta) is a scrupulously observant piece of singing. In Zancanaro as the father we have the best Italian baritone of the post-Bruson generation: less remarkable, perhaps, for new insights than for old virtues such as a fine voice and steady production.

For other kinds of production – those for stage and television – much gratitude is due, in that all appropriate skills are put to the service of Verdi. The opera has an intimacy that takes well to the small screen and the tragedy is made affectingly real. A different tragedy, no less affecting, is the sight of La Fenice, so beautifully viewed at the end of the opera, so shortly to be reduced to ashes and a shell.

Wagner

Die Meistersinger von Nürnberg
Wolfgang Brendel *bass-bar* Hans Sachs; **Gösta Winbergh** *ten* Walther; **Eva Johansson** *sop* Eva; **Victor von Halem** *bass* Pogner; **Elke Wilm Schulte** *bar* Beckmesser; **Uwe Peper** *ten* David; **Ute Walther** *mez* Magdalene; **Lenus Carlson** *bass* Kothner; **David Griffith** *ten* Vogelgesang; **Barry McDaniel** *bar* Nachtigall; **Volker Horn** *ten* Zorn; **Peter Maus** *ten* Eisslinger; **Otto Heuer** *ten* Moser; **Ivan Sardi** *bass* Schwarz; **Friedrich Molsberger** *bass* Foltz;

Peter Edelmann *bass* Nightwatchman; **Berlin Opera Orchestra and Chorus / Rafael Frühbeck de Burgos**
Stage director **Götz Friedrich**
Video director **Brian Large**
Arthaus Musik ② **DVD** 100 152 (266 minutes: Region 0). Recorded live in 1995 Ⓕ **oo**

This has to be one of the most engrossing and satisfactory performances of *Die Meistersinger* in memory. Pleasure derives as much as anything from the sense of a complete intregration of music and action in a staging that has been scrupulously rehearsed on all sides. This is a 1995 revival with the same cast as the 1993 original, and it is clear how keen the response of the singers to each other is. The credit for one's profound enjoyment undoubtably goes to the late, lamented Götz Friedrich. Renowned for his handling of characters and their interaction on stage, his skills in that sphere have seldom if ever been more fruitfully displayed. The action and reaction of the masters in their Act 1 disputations, the subtle relationship between Sachs and Eva, the ebb and flow of the arguments between Sachs and Beckmesser, and the friendly interplay between Walther and Sachs, the disciple eagerly learning from the teacher in Act 1 scene 3, are all revelatory. In these and other scenes, more of the characters' humanity is expressed than has ever been shown before. This is operatic acting on the highest level of achievement.

Frühbeck de Burgos enhances the director's approach with his chamber-like treatment of the orchestra, allowing the singers' clear enunciation to be heard at all times. He is also to be commended for the discerning ebb and flow of his reading as a whole, which is at once lively and unforced. Wolfgang Brendel presents an affectionate, sympathetic, somewhat laid-back, ruminative Sachs, his voice lacking in warmth only at the bottom of his register, the sound more baritone than bass-orientated. As we know from Covent Garden, Winbergh is a well-nigh ideal Walther, singing his role with unwonted ease and lyrical breadth, responsive always to the text's meaning. Johansson is a knowing, flirtatious Eva, forthcoming in voice and mien; her earthbound start of the Quintet comes as a disappointment after her gloriously outgoing 'O Sachs, mein Freund'. Schulte sings and acts Beckmesser to perfection, never resorting to caricature in depicting the self-important, didactic town clerk and giving the role a wealth of nuance, always keeping to the notes. Peper is a well-routined, likeable David, Von Halem an imposing, properly fatherly Pogner.

An attractive scale model of Nuremberg's medieval skyline graces the first and last scene so that a jarring touch, the momentary vision of the bombed city, can be excused. Interiors look lived-in. The costumes straddle the centuries yet manage some kind of consistency. Act 2, after a magical, lilac-laden start, looked a shade cramped. As a whole, this is a performance to treasure. It has admirably balanced sound and perceptive video direction by the ultra-experienced Brian Large. Highly recommended.

Die Walküre
Gary Lakes *ten* Siegmund; **Jessye Norman** *sop* Sieglinde; **Hildegard Behrens** *sop* Brünnhilde; **James Morris** *bass* Wotan; **Christa Ludwig** *mez* Fricka; **Kurt Moll** *bass* Hunding; **Pyramid Sellers** *sop* Gerhilde; **Katarina Ikonomu** *sop* Helmwige; **Martha Thigpen** *sop* Ortlinde; **Joyce Castle** *mez* Waltraute; **Jacalyn Bower** *mez* Rossweisse; **Diane Kesling** *mez* Siegrune; **Wendy Hillhouse** *mez* Grimgerde; **Sondra Kelly** *contr* Schwertleite
Metropolitan Opera Chorus and Orchestra, New York / James Levine
Stage director **Otto Schenk.** *Video director* **Brian Large**
DG **DVD** ② 073 011-9GH2 Ⓕ
(241 minutes: Region 0). Recorded live in 1989

The *Ring* comes to DVD at last. Or at least one part of it, although determined collectors may well have already tracked down the whole of Levine's Metropolitan Opera set or EMI's Sawallisch-Munich version which are both currently available on DVD in Japan and obtainable over the Internet for about £200. The Met's celebrated live recording has been available for years on video and LaserDisc, so the immediate question is whether this first instalment gains from the new medium. DVD's unforgiving digital clarity reveals some graininess in the original master. Nonetheless, with purer colours increasing detail and contrast, and digitally remastered sound far clearer even than LaserDisc, it considerably enhances the performance.

The Met production is the only one of the four *Rings* on video which Wagner would remotely have recognised. Unfortunately, Otto Schenk's stodgy staging and some unhappy casting undermine its virtues. Why did the Met choose two such heavyweights as Gary Lakes *and* Jessye Norman for video? He is a stolid but decent Heldentenor, his voice better served by the remastering. She sings with characteristic fervour, but sails about the stage with prima donna poise and gesture, snubbing Kurt Moll's sonorously oafish Hunding. Physical contact is minimal, the love scenes lifeless.

In the later acts, though, the quality picks up. Hildegard Behrens is a marvellously engaging Brünnhilde, unusually fresh-voiced, feminine and vulnerable. Morris's Wotan, early in his career, has been called dull, especially compared with John Tomlinson's hyperactive bully-boy on Barenboim's Bayreuth video (Teldec). Morris, though, has the finer and fuller voice, and many subtler ideas – some, like his *pianissimo*s, adopted from his mentor Hotter. Ludwig's once magnificent Fricka now sounds sadly worn, but Lakes gains intensity in the 'Todesverkündigung', and the Valkyries are a mixed but spirited bunch. Levine's conducting resembles his studio version, rich and expansive, with the orchestra in fine form, although his occasional abrupt gearshifts trip up several singers at times. His presence in the preludes is distracting – oh, for a hooded pit!

As a whole, though, an impressive performance, its very straightforwardness possibly less ephemeral than formerly 'modern' rivals, and definitely revitalised on DVD.

The Indexes

Index to Couplings

Index to Artists